P9-EAN-978

How to use the dictionary

c'mon [kə'man] (*fam*) *see* **come on** **CO** [ˌsi·'oʊ] *n* ❶ GEOG *abbrev of* **Colorado** ... **Co.** [koʊ] *n abbrev of* **company** **c/o** [ˌsi·'oʊ] *abbrev of* **care of** c/o, bei **coach** [koʊtʃ] **I.** *n* ❶ SPORTS Trainer(in) *m(f)*; ...	All **entries** (including words, abbreviations, compounds, variant spellings and cross-references) appear in alphabetical order and are printed in bold type.
bring <brought, brought> [brɪŋ] *vt* ... ◆**bring about** *vt* verursachen	English phrasal verbs come directly after the base verb and are marked with a diamond (◆).
incense[1] ['ɪn·sens] *n* (*substance*) Räuchermittel *nt*; ... **incense**[2] [ɪn·'sens] *vt* empören	Superscript or raised numbers indicate identically spelled words with different meanings (so-called **homographs**).
flexibility [ˌflek·sə·'bɪl·ɪ·ṭi] *n* ... **flexible** ['flek·sə·bəl] *adj* ... **flextime** ['fleks·taɪm] *n* ...	The International Phonetic Alphabet is used for all **phonetic transcriptions.** Centered dots are used for syllable division. Please note that this does not always correspond with the orthographic division into syllables.
'tie tack *n* Krawattennadel *f* **'tie-up** *n* Stillstand *m*	Where no phonetic code is given, the main spoken emphasis of the headword is indicated by a stress mark.
'daughter-in-law <*pl* daughters-> *n* ... **begin** <-nn-, began, begun> ... **unruly** <-ier, -iest *or* more ~, most ~> ...	Angle brackets are used to show **irregular plural forms** and, **forms of irregular verbs and adjectives**.
	A vertical line shows where a **separable verb** can be separated.
	Old spellings are marked with a superscript ALT symbol. New spellings are marked with a superscript RR symbol.
mute [mjut] **I.** *n* ❶ (*person*) Stumme(r) *f(m)* ❷ MUS (*quieting device*) Dämpfer *m* **II.** *vt sound, noise* dämpfen **III.** *adj* stumm	**Roman numerals** are used for the parts of speech of a word, and **Arabic numerals** for sense divisions.
sky [skaɪ] *n* ❶ (*the sky*) Himmel *m*; **in the ~** im Himmel ❷ (*area above earth*) ■**skies** *pl* Himmel *m*; **cloudy skies** bewölkter Himmel ▶ PHRASES: **the ~'s the <u>limit</u>** alles ist möglich	The **swung dash** represents the entry word in examples and idioms. The ▶ sign introduces **a block of set expressions, idioms and proverbs**. Key words are <u>underlined</u> as a guide.
◆**win back** *vt* ❶ SPORTS **to ~ back ⊂ the trophy** den Pokal zurückholen ❷ *customers* zurückgewinnen	The symbol ⊂ in **phrasal verb** entries and the label *sep* in translations show that the sequence of object and complement can be reversed.
	Various kinds of **meaning indicators** are used to guide users to the required translation:
horn [hɔrn] **I.** *n* ❶ ZOOL Horn *nt* ❷ MUS Horn *nt*	• **Subject labels** (which indicate areas of specialization)
wild [waɪld] **I.** *adj* ❶ *inv* (*undomesticated*) wild; *cat, duck, goose* Wild- ❷ (*uncultivated*) *country, landscape* rau, wild; ...	• **Definitions** or **synonyms,** typical **context partners, subjects** or **objects** of the entry
dinner ['dɪn·ər] *n* ❶ (*evening meal*) Abendessen *nt*; DIAL (*warm lunch*) Mittagessen *nt*; **to go out for ~** essen gehen; ...	• **Regional vocabulary and variants** are shown both as headwords and translations
jumble ['dʒʌm·bəl] **I.** *n* (*a. fig: chaos*) Durcheinander *nt a. fig*; ...	• **Usage Labels** (which indicate restriction to a particular level or style of usage)
downsizing *n* ECON Entlassung *f* (*aus Arbeitsmangel oder Rationalisierungsgründen*) **hash 'browns** *npl* Kartoffelpuffer *pl*, ≈ Rösti *pl* SÜDD, SCHWEIZ	When a word or expression has no direct translation, an **explanation** or **approximate equivalent**, marked with the symbol ≈, is given. Where a translation may be ambiguous, it is followed by an explanation in brackets.
March <*pl* -es> [martʃ] *n* März *m*; *see also* **February**	*see also* and *s. a.* (*siehe auch*) invite the reader to consult a **model entry** for further information.

GERMAN–ENGLISH Dictionary

Wörterbuch
DEUTSCH–ENGLISCH

SECOND EDITION

BARRON'S

FOREIGN LANGUAGE GUIDES

GERMAN-ENGLISH Dictionary

Wörterbuch DEUTSCH–ENGLISCH

SECOND EDITION

Barron's Foreign Language Guides
German-English Dictionary
Wörterbuch Deutsch-Englisch

Second edition for the United States and Canada published in 2016 by Kaplan, Inc. First edition for the United States and Canada published in 2007 by Kaplan, Inc.

© Copyright 2016, 2007 by Ernst Klett Sprachen GmbH, Stuttgart, Germany and Kaplan, Inc., NY, USA

Editorial Management: Ursula Martini
Contributor: Dr. Christiane Wirth
Typesetting: Dörr + Schiller, Stuttgart, Germany
Data Processing: Andreas Lang, conTEXT AG für Informatik und Kommunikation, Zürich, Switzerland

All rights reserved.
No part of this publication may be reproduced or distributed in any form or by any means without the written permission of the copyright owner.

Published by Barron's Educational Series, Inc.
750 Third Avenue
New York, NY 10017
www.barronseduc.com

ISBN: 978-1-4380-0709-0
Library of Congress Control No.: 2014953319

9 8 7 6 5 4

Barron's Educational Series, Inc. print books are available at special quantity discounts to use for sales promotions, employee premiums, or educational purposes. For more information or to purchase books, please call the Simon & Schuster special sales department at 866-506-1949.

Inhalt
Contents

Introduction
Vorwort

This is a new bilingual dictionary designed to meet the needs of people in a time of ever-expanding communication among English and German speakers. It has been written and edited by a large team of native speakers of both languages so that it constitutes an updated, comprehensive, and most useful linguistic tool.

This dictionary provides accurate coverage of current vocabulary in English and German, as well as abundant examples of words used in context to illustrate idiomatic usage. To facilitate self-expression, pronunciation is provided in both languages, so that the users may express themselves correctly and idiomatically — both orally and in writing.

A unique characteristic is the possibility of downloading this dictionary into your home computer, laptop, and nearly all PDAs and smartphones. In addition, attention is given to small but meaningful features that include alphabet tabs for ease of use, maps and cultural boxes to enrich the process of language acquisition, and useful explanatory sections.

Dieses neue zweisprachige Wörterbuch wurde für das steigende Bedürfnis einer modernen Kommunikation zwischen Sprechern des Englischen und des Deutschen konzipiert. Es wurde von einem großen Team deutscher und englischer Muttersprachler neu entwickelt und bearbeitet und ist somit ein aktuelles, umfassendes und hilfreiches linguistisches Nachschlagewerk.

Dieses Wörterbuch deckt den aktuellen englischen und deutschen Wortschatz ab und illustriert anhand zahlreicher Anwendungsbeispiele den idiomatischen Gebrauch. Um die mündliche Kommunikation zu erleichtern, wird sowohl für die englischen als auch für die deutschen Stichwörter die phonetische Umschrift angegeben. Auf diese Weise ist dem Benutzer eine korrekte und idiomatische Ausdrucksweise im schriftlichen wie im mündlichen Gebrauch der Fremdsprache gewährleist.

Ein Alleinstellungsmerkmal dieses Wörterbuches ist die Möglichkeit die Inhalte auf PC, Laptop, fast alle PDAs und Smartphones herunterzuladen. Zusätzlich enthält das Wörterbuch praktische Extras wie das Daumenregister für schnelleres Nachschlagen, Landkarten und Informationsfenster mit Erklärungen zu landeskundlichen Phänomenen, die den Sprachenlernprozess abrunden sowie ausführliches und vielfältiges Zusatzmaterial im Anhang.

Lautschriftzeichen für Deutsch

German phonetic symbols

Vokale
Vowels

[a]	matt
[ɐ]	bitter
[ɐ̯]	Uhr
[ã]	Arangement
[ã:]	Gourmand
[e]	Etage
[e:]	Beet, Mehl
[ɛ]	Nest, Wäsche
[ɛ:]	wählen
[ɛ̃]	Cousin
[ɛ̃:]	Teint
[ə]	halte
[ɪ]	Bitte
[i]	Vitamin
[i:]	Bier
[i̯]	Studie
[j]	ja
[o]	Oase

[o:]	Boot, drohen
[o̯]	loyal
[ɔ]	Post
[õ]	Fondue
[õ:]	Fonds
[ø]	Ökonomie
[ø:]	Öl
[œ]	Götter
[œ:]	Server
[u]	zunächst
[u:]	Hut
[u̯]	aktuell
[ʊ]	Mutter
[y]	Aerodynamik
[y:]	Typ
[y̆]	Etui
[ʏ]	füllen

Diphthonge
Diphthongs

[ai]	heiß
[au]	Haus
[ɔy]	Mäuse

Konsonanten
Consonants

[b]	Ball
[ç]	ich
[d]	dicht
[dʒ]	Budget, Job
[f]	Fett, viel
[g]	Geld
[h]	Hut
[k]	Kohl, Computer
[kv]	Quadrat
[l]	Last
[l̩]	Nebel
[m]	Meister
[n]	nett
[n̩]	sprechen

[ŋ]	Ring, blinken
[p]	Papst
[pf]	Pfeffer
[r]	Rad
[s]	Rast, besser, heiß
[ʃ]	Schaum, sprechen, Chef
[t]	Test
[ts]	Zaun
[tʃ]	Matsch, Tschüs
[v]	wann
[x]	Schlauch
[ks]	Fix, Axt, Lachs
[z]	Hase, sauer
[ʒ]	Genie

Zeichen
Signs

ʔ	glottal stop
ˈ	primary stress
ˌ	secondary stress

:	length symbol
.	syllable division

English phonetic symbols

Lautschriftzeichen für Englisch

Vowels

Vokale

[a]	farm, not
[æ]	cat, man, sad
[e]	best, get, hair, dare
[ə]	Africa, better, actor, potato, anonymous, virus
[ɜ]	bird, berth, curb
[i]	read, meet, belief, hobby

[ɪ]	sit, wish, near
[ɔ]	caught, all, law, sauce, floor
[u]	moose, lose, you
[ʊ]	book, put, sure, tour
[ʌ]	bust, multi
[ɑ̃]	genre

Diphthongs

Diphthonge

[aɪ]	ride, my, buy
[aʊ]	house, now
[eɪ]	rate, lame

[ɔɪ]	boy, noise
[oʊ]	rope, piano, road, toe, show, plateau
[ju]	accuse, beauty

Consonants

Konsonanten

[b]	big, blind
[d]	dad, had
[ð]	father, bathe
[dʒ]	edge, juice, object
[f]	fast, wolf
[g]	beg, gold
[h]	hello
[j]	yellow
[ʒ]	pleasure
[k]	cat, king, milk
[l]	little, ill, oil
[m]	man, am
[n]	nice, manner

[ŋ]	long, sing, prank
[p]	paper, happy
[r]	right, dry, current, player, part
[s]	soft, yes, cent, capacity
[ʃ]	shift, station, fish
[t]	take, fat
[t̬]	butter, interstate
[θ]	think, bath
[tʃ]	chip, patch
[v]	vitamin, live
[w]	wish, why, wore
[z]	zebra, jazz, gaze

Signs

Zeichen

ˈ	primary stress
ˌ	secondary stress
·	syllable division

Aa

A, a <-, - *o fam* -s, -s> [aː] *nt* ❶ (*Buchstabe*) A, a; **~ wie Anton** A as in Alpha ❷ MUS A, a; **A-Dur/a-Moll** A major/A minor ► WENDUNGEN: **das ~ und [das] O** the be all and end all; **von ~ bis Z** from beginning to end

à [a] *präp* at; **20 Flaschen ~ 8 Euro** 20 bottles at 8 euros each

Aachen <-s> [ˈaːxn̩] *nt* Aachen

Aal <-[e]s, -e> [aːl] *m* eel

aalen [ˈaːlən] *vr* (*fam*) ■ **sich** *akk* **auf dem Sofa ~** to stretch out on the sofa; ■ **sich** *akk* **in der Sonne ~** to bask in the sun

aalglatt [ˈaːl·ˈglat] **I.** *adj* slippery **II.** *adv* artfully

Aas[1] <-es, -e> [aːs] *nt* (*Tierleiche*) carrion

Aas[2] <-es, Äser> [aːs, *pl* ˈɛːzɐ] *nt* (*fam*) jerk; (*männliche Person*) bastard; (*weibliche Person*) bitch

Aasfresser <-s, -> *m* carrion-eating animal

Aasgeier *m* vulture *a. pej*

ab [ap] **I.** *adv* ❶ (*weg, entfernt*) off; **links ~** off to the left; **weit ~ liegen** to be far away ❷ (*abgetrennt*) off; **~ sein** to be broken [off]; **mein Knopf ist ~** I've lost a button; **erst muss die alte Farbe ~** first you have to remove the old paint ► WENDUNGEN: **~ und zu** now and then **II.** *präp* + *dat* ❶ (*räumlich*) from; **~ Köln** from Cologne ❷ (*zeitlich*) from; **~ heute** starting today ❸ (*von ... aufwärts*) from; **Kinder ~ 14 Jahren** children age 14 and older ❹ SCHWEIZ (*bei der Uhrzeit*) after; **Viertel ~ 8** quarter after eight, eight fifteen ❺ SCHWEIZ (*von*) on; **~ Kassette** on cassette

ạb|ändern *vt* to amend (**in** + *akk* to); *Programm* to change

Ạbänderung *f* amendment

ạb|arbeiten I. *vt* ❶ (*durch Arbeit tilgen*) to work off *sep* ❷ (*erledigen*) to work through **II.** *vr* (*fam*) ■ **sich** *akk* **~** to work like a dog, to slave away

ạbartig I. *adj* ❶ (*abnorm*) abnormal; (*fam*) gross; (*pervers a.*) perverted ❷ (*sl: verrückt*) crazy **II.** *adv* abnormally

Ạbbau <-s> *m kein pl* ❶ (*Förderung*) *von Bodenschätzen* mining ❷ (*Verringerung*) revocation; **der ~ von Vorurteilen** the breaking down of prejudices

ạbbaubar *adj* CHEM, MED degradable; **biologisch ~** biodegradable

ạb|bauen I. *vt* ❶ *Bodenschätze* to mine ❷ (*demontieren*) to dismantle, to take apart *sep* ❸ (*verringern*) to reduce ❹ CHEM, MED to break down *sep* **II.** *vi* ■ **jd baut ab** sb is wilting; (*geistig*) sb is deteriorating

ạb|beißen *irreg* **I.** *vt* to bite off *sep* **II.** *vi* to take a bite

ạb|bekommen* *vt irreg* ❶ (*Anteil erhalten*) to get one's share; **die Hälfte von etw** *dat* **~** to receive half of sth ❷ (*beschädigt werden*) to get damaged ❸ (*verletzt werden*) to be injured ❹ (*entfernen können*) to get off *sep*

ạb|bestellen* *vt Zeitung, Reservierung* to cancel; **den Klempner ~** to tell the plumber he doesn't need to come anymore

ạb|bezahlen* *vt* to pay off *sep*

ạb|biegen *irreg* **I.** *vi sein* **[nach] links/rechts ~** to turn left/right; *Straße* to curve **II.** *vt haben* (*fam*) ■ **etw ~** to get out of sth; *Plan* to prevent

Ạbbiegespur *f* turning lane

Ạbbild *nt* image; (*im Spiegel*) reflection

ạb|bilden *vt* to copy; *Person* to portray; *Landschaft* to depict; **auf dem Foto war ... abgebildet** the photo showed ...

Ạbbildung <-, -en> *f* (*Illustration*) illustration

ạb|binden *irreg vt* to untie

ạb|blasen *vt irreg* (*fam: absagen*) to call off *sep*

ạb|blättern *vi sein* to peel [off [of]]

ạb|blenden *vi* AUTO to dim the lights

Ạbblendlicht *nt* AUTO low beam headlights

ạb|blitzen *vi sein* (*fam*) ■ **bei jdm ~** to not get anywhere with sb; **jdn ~ lassen** to turn down *sep* sb

ạb|blocken I. *vt* to block **II.** *vi* to refuse to talk; POL to stonewall

ạb|brechen *irreg* **I.** *vt haben* ❶ (*lösen*) to break off *sep* ❷ *Zelt* to take down; **ein Lager ~** to break camp ❸ *Gebäude* to tear down *sep* ❹ (*beenden*) to stop; *Beziehung* to break off; *Streik* to call off; **das Studium ~** to drop out of college; **den Urlaub ~** to cut short *sep* one's vacation **II.** *vi sein* ❶ (*sich lösen*) to break off ❷ (*aufhören*) to stop; *Beziehung* to end; **etw ~ lassen** to break off sth *sep*

ạb|bremsen *vt, vi* to slow down *sep*

ạb|brennen *irreg vi sein* to burn down

ạb|bringen *vt irreg* ■ **jdn von etw** *dat* **~** to get sb to give up sth; (*abraten*) to change sb's mind about sth; ■ **jdn davon ~, etw zu tun** to prevent sb from doing sth; **jdn vom Thema ~** to get sb off the subject

ạb|bröckeln *vi sein* to crumble (**von** + *dat* away from)

Ạbbruch *m* ❶ *eines Gebäudes* demolition ❷ (*Beendigung*) breaking off

ạbbruchreif *adj* ❶ (*baufällig*) dilapidated ❷ SCHWEIZ (*schrottreif*) ready for the junk yard *pred*

ạb|buchen *vt Bank* to debit; **etw [vom Konto] ~** to deduct sth [from a/one's bank account]

ạb|bürsten *vt* ❶ (*entfernen*) to brush off *sep* ❷ **einen Anzug ~** to brush down a suit

ạb|büßen *vt* to serve

ạb|checken [-tʃɛ·kn] *vt* (*fam*) to check out *sep*; ■ **etw mit jdm ~** to confirm sth with sb

Abc-Schütze, -Schützin [aːbeːˈtseː-] *m, f* child attending school for the first time

ABC-Waffen [aːbeːˈtseː-] *pl* nuclear, biological

A

and chemical [*or* NBC] weapons *pl*
ab|danken *vi* to resign; *König* to abdicate
Abdankung <-, -en> *f* ❶ (*Rücktritt*) resignation; *König* abdication ❷ SCHWEIZ (*Trauerfeier*) funeral service
ab|decken *vt* ❶ (*bedecken*) to cover [over *sep*] ❷ *Gebäude* to lift the roof off ❸ (*berücksichtigen*) to cover ❹ *Tisch* to clear
Abdeckung <-, -en> *f* cover
ab|dichten *vt* ❶ *Leitung* to seal; *Leck* to stop, to plug ❷ (*gegen Feuchtigkeit*) to seal
Abdichtung *f kein pl* (*das Abdichten*) sealing; *eines Lecks* plugging
ab|drängen *vt* to push
ab|drehen I. *vt* ❶ (*abstellen*) to turn off *sep* ❷ (*entfernen*) to twist [off *sep*] II. *vi* (*fam*) to go crazy
ab|driften *vi sein* (*sl: abgleiten*) to drift
Abdruck[1] <-drücke> *m* ❶ (*Spur*) print ❷ (*Umriss*) impression
Abdruck[2] <-drucke> *m* ❶ (*Veröffentlichung*) printing ❷ *kein pl* (*das Nachdrucken*) reprint
ab|drucken *vt* to print
ab|drücken *vi* (*feuern*) to shoot
ab|dunkeln *vt* ❶ (*abschirmen*) to dim ❷ (*dunkler machen*) to darken; *Fenster* to black out *sep* ❸ (*dunkler werden lassen*) to tone down *sep*
ab|ebben *vi sein* to subside; *Lärm* to die down
abend[ALT] *adv s.* **Abend**
Abend <-s, -e> ['a:bn̩t] *m* evening; **gestern/morgen** ~ yesterday/tomorrow evening; **heute** ~ tonight, this evening; **jdm guten** ~ **sagen** [*o* **wünschen**] to wish sb a good evening, to say "good evening" to sb; **zu** ~ **essen** to eat dinner; **am** ~ in the evening; ~ **für** [*o* **um**] ~ every night, night after night; **gegen** ~ toward evening; **den ganzen** ~ **über** the whole evening, all evening [long]
Abendandacht *f* evening service
Abendbrot *nt* supper
Abenddämmerung *f* dusk
Abendessen *nt* dinner
abendfüllend *adj* all-night *attr,* lasting all [*or* the whole] evening *pred*
Abendkasse *f* evening box office
Abendkleid *nt* evening dress
Abendkurs *m* evening [*or* night] class
Abendland *nt kein pl* (*geh*) ■ **das** ~ the Occident
abendländisch *adj* (*geh*) occidental
abendlich ['a:bn̩tlɪç] *adj* evening
Abendmahl *nt* [Holy] Communion; **das Letzte** ~ the Last Supper
Abendrot <-s> ['a:bn̩t·ro:t] *nt kein pl* [red] sunset; **im** ~ in the evening glow
abends ['a:bn̩ts] *adv* in the evening
Abendschule *f* evening [*or* night] school
Abendsonne *f kein pl* sunset
Abendstunde *f meist pl* evening [hour]
Abendvorstellung *f* FILM evening showing; THEAT evening performance
Abenteuer <-s, -> ['a:bn̩·tɔyɐ] *nt* ❶ (*aufregendes Erlebnis*) adventure ❷ (*Liebesabenteuer*) fling; **auf** [**ein**] ~ **aus sein** to be looking for a one-night stand *fam* ❸ (*risikoreiches Unternehmen*) venture
Abenteuerferien *pl* adventure [*or* extreme] vacation
abenteuerlich ['a:bn̩·tɔyɐ·lɪç] *adj* ❶ (*abenteuerlustig*) adventurous ❷ *Geschichte* fantastic ❸ (*riskant*) *Vorhaben* risky, hazardous
Abenteuerlust *f* thirst for adventure
abenteuerlustig *adj* adventurous
Abenteuerroman *m* adventure novel
Abenteuerspielplatz *m* adventure playground
Abenteurer, Abenteu(r)erin <-s, -> ['a:bn̩·tɔy·rɐ, 'a:bn̩·tɔy·(r)ə·rɪn] *m, f* adventurer
Abenteurertum <-s> ['a:bn̩·tɔy·rə·tu:m] *nt kein pl* (*pej*) [reckless] adventurism
aber ['a:bɐ] *konj* but; ~ **dennoch ...** but in spite of this ...; **oder** ~ or else
Aber <-s, - *o fam* -s> ['a:bɐ] *nt* but *fam;* **kein** ~**!** no buts [about it]!
Aberglaube *m* ❶ (*falscher Glaube*) superstition ❷ (*fam: Unsinn*) nonsense
abergläubisch ['a:bɐ·glɔy·bɪʃ] *adj* superstitious
aberhundert, Aberhundert[RR] *adj* (*geh*) hundreds upon hundreds of
ab|erkennen* ['ap·ʔɛɐ̯·kɛnən] *vt irreg* ■ **jdm etw** ~ to divest sb of sth *form*
abermals ['a:bɐ·ma:ls] *adv* once again
ab|ernten *vt* to harvest
abertausend, Abertausend[RR] *adj* (*geh*) thousands upon thousands of
aberwitzig *adj* (*geh*) ludicrous
abfahrbereit *adj s.* **abfahrtbereit**
ab|fahren *irreg* I. *vi sein* ❶ (*losfahren*) to depart ❷ ■ **jdn** ~ **lassen** (*abweisen*) to turn down *sep* sb ❸ ■ **auf jdn/etw** ~ (*sl*) to be crazy about sb/sth II. *vt* ❶ *sein o haben* (*suchend*) *Strecke* to [drive along and] check ❷ *haben* (*abnutzen*) *Reifen* to wear down *sep*
Abfahrt *f* ❶ (*Wegfahren*) departure ❷ (*Autobahnabfahrt*) exit ❸ (*beim Skifahren, Rodeln*) run; (*Abfahrtsstrecke*) slope
abfahrtbereit *adj* ready to depart *pred*
Abfahrtszeit *f* departure time
Abfall *m* garbage, trash
Abfallaufbereitung <-, -en> *f* waste processing
Abfallbehälter *m* garbage container; (*kleiner*) garbage can
Abfallbeseitigung *f* garbage [*or* trash] removal, waste disposal
Abfalleimer *m* garbage [*or* trash] can
ab|fallen *vi irreg sein* ❶ (*herunterfallen*) to fall off ❷ (*schlechter werden*) to fall behind ❸ (*übrig bleiben*) to be left over ❹ *Gelände* to slope [downward]
Abfallentsorgung *f* trash collection, waste disposal; *industriell* waste management
Abfallhaufen *m* garbage [*or* trash] pile
abfällig I. *adj* derogatory; *Lächeln* derisive II. *adv* disparagingly; **sich** ~ **über jdn/etw**

äußern to make derogatory remarks about sb/sth
Abfallprodukt *nt* ❶ CHEM waste product ❷ (*Nebenprodukt*) by-product
Abfallsortierung *f kein pl* waste sorting (*for recycling purposes*)
Abfallstoff *m meist pl* waste product
Abfalltonne *f* garbage [*or* trash] can
Abfallvermeidung *f* waste reduction
Abfallverwertung *f* recycling, waste utilization
ab|färben *vi* to run (**auf** +*akk* onto); ■ **auf jdn ~** (*fig*) to rub off (**auf** +*akk* on)
ab|fassen *vt* to write
ab|faulen *vi sein Blätter* to rot away
ab|federn *vt Stoß* to cushion
ab|fegen *vt* ❶ *Schmutz, Schnee* to sweep away *sep* ❷ *Treppe, Terrasse* to brush off *sep*
ab|feiern *vt* (*fam*) **Überstunden ~** to take comp time
ab|feuern *vt* to fire; *Flugkörper, Granate* to launch
ab|finden *irreg* **I.** *vt* (*entschädigen*) to compensate (**mit** +*dat* with) **II.** *vr* (*fam*) ■ **sich** *akk* **mit etw** *dat* **~** to put up with sth
Abfindung <-, -en> *f* compensation; (*bei Entlassung*) severance pay
ab|flauen *vi sein Wind, Sturm* to subside, to abate; *Nachfrage* to decrease; *Lärm* to drop; *Interesse* to wane
ab|fliegen *vi irreg sein* to take off
ab|fließen *vi irreg sein Wasser* to flow away
Abflug *m* departure, takeoff
abflugbereit *adj* ready for departure *pred*
Abflughalle *f* departure[s] lounge
Abflugzeit *f* flight departure time
Abfluss[RR] *m* (*Rohr*) drain pipe
Abflussrinne[RR] *f* drainage channel
Abflussrohr[RR] *nt* drain pipe
Abfolge *f* sequence
Abfrage *f von Daten* query
ab|fragen *vt* ❶ (*prüfen*) to test; ■ **jdn etw ~** *Vokabeln, Chemie, etc.* to test sb on sth ❷ *Daten* to call up *sep*
Abfuhr <-, -en> *f* (*Zurückweisung*) snub; **jdm eine ~ erteilen** to snub sb
ab|führen **I.** *vt* ❶ *Person* to lead away ❷ *Geld* to pay **II.** *vi* MED to loosen the bowels
Abführmittel *nt* laxative
ab|füllen *vt* ❶ *Flüssigkeit* to fill (**in** +*akk* into); (*in Flaschen*) to bottle ❷ (*sl: betrunken machen*) to get drunk
Abgabe *f* ❶ (*Gebühr*) [additional] charge ❷ (*Steuer*) tax
abgabenfrei **I.** *adj* nontaxable **II.** *adv* tax-free
abgabenpflichtig *adj* taxable
Abgabetermin *m* submission deadline
Abgang *m* ❶ *kein pl* (*Schulabgang*) leaving ❷ ÖSTERR (*Fehlbetrag*) deficit
Abgangszeugnis *nt* diploma
Abgas *nt* exhaust
abgasarm *adj* low-emission
ab|geben *irreg* **I.** *vt* ❶ (*übergeben*) to give (**an** +*akk* to); (*einreichen*) to submit, to hand in *sep* (**an** +*akk* to) ❷ (*hinterlassen*) to leave; *Gepäck* to check in *sep*; **den Mantel an der Garderobe ~** to check one's coat ❸ (*verschenken*) to give away *sep* ❹ (*überlassen*) ■ **jdm etw ~** to give sb sth [*or* sth to sb]; ■ **etw [an jdn] ~** to hand over *sep* sth [to sb] ❺ (*teilen*) **jdm die Hälfte [von etw** *dat*] **~** to go halves [on sth] with sb; **jdm nichts ~** to not share with sb ❻ *Erklärung, Urteil* to make; *Gutachten* to submit; *Stimme* to cast ❼ (*darstellen*) to be; **die perfekte Hausfrau ~** to be the perfect wife **II.** *vr* ❶ (*sich beschäftigen*) ■ **sich** *akk* **mit jdm ~** to look after sb; ■ **sich** *akk* **mit etw** *dat* **~** to spend [one's] time on sth ❷ (*fam: sich einlassen*) ■ **sich** *akk* **mit jdm ~** to associate with sb
abgebrannt **I.** *adj* (*fam*) broke **II.** *pp von* **abbrennen**
abgebrüht *adj* (*fam*) unscrupulous
abgedroschen *adj* (*pej fam*) hackneyed
abgefahren **I.** *adj* (*sl*) ❶ (*außergewöhnlich, schräg*) far-out ❷ (*begeisternd*) cool, sweet **II.** *pp von* **abfahren**
abgefuckt ['ap·gə·fakt] *adj* (*sl*) fucked-up *attr*, fucked up *pred*
abgehackt **I.** *adj* broken; **~e Worte** clipped words **II.** *adv* **~ sprechen** to clip one's words **III.** *pp von* **abhacken**
ab|gehen *irreg vi sein* ❶ (*sich lösen*) to come off ❷ **von der Schule ~** to drop out of school ❸ (*abzweigen*) to branch off (**von** +*dat* from) ❹ (*fam: sich abspielen*) to go; **was geht hier ab?!** what's going on here!? ❺ (*fam: fehlen*) ■ **jdm ~** to be lacking in sb
abgehoben **I.** *adj* (*weltfremd*) far from reality *pred* **II.** *pp von* **abheben**
abgekartet *adj* (*fam*) rigged; **ein ~es Spiel treiben** to play a double game
abgeklärt **I.** *adj* prudent **II.** *adv* prudently **III.** *pp von* **abklären**
abgelegen *adj* remote
abgeneigt *adj* ■ **nicht ~ sein etw zu tun** to not be averse to doing sth
Abgeordnete(r) ['ap·gə·ʔɔrd·nə·tə, -tɐ] *f(m) dekl wie adj* member of Congress, representative
Abgeordnetenhaus *nt* ≈ House of Representatives
Abgeordnetensitz *m* seat in Congress
abgerissen **I.** *adj* ❶ (*zerlumpt*) tattered ❷ (*heruntergekommen*) scruffy ❸ (*unzusammenhängend*) incoherent **II.** *pp von* **abreißen**
Abgesandte(r) *f(m) dekl wie adj* envoy
abgeschieden (*geh*) **I.** *adj* isolated **II.** *adv* in isolation
Abgeschiedenheit <-> *f kein pl* isolation
abgeschmackt ['ap·gə·ʃmakt] **I.** *adj* tasteless **II.** *adv* tastelessly
abgesehen **I.** *adj* **es auf jdn ~ haben** (*schikanieren wollen*) to have it in for sb; (*interessiert sein*) to have a thing for sb; **es auf etw ~ haben** to have one's eye on sth; **du hast es**

A

nur darauf ~, mich zu ärgern you're just out to annoy me **II.** *adv* ■ **~ von jdm/etw** except for sb/sth; ■ **~ davon, dass ...** apart [*or* aside] from the fact that ... **III.** *pp von* **absehen**

ạbgespannt *adj, adv* tired out, exhausted

ạbgestanden I. *adj* stale; *Limonade* flat **II.** *adv* **~ schmecken** to taste flat **III.** *pp von* **abstehen**

ạbgetragen *adj* worn *attr,* worn out *pred*

ạbgetreten I. *adj* worn *attr,* worn down *pred* **II.** *pp von* **abtreten**

ạbgewetzt *adj* worn

ạb|gewinnen* *vt irreg* ■ **einer S.** *dat* **etwas/nichts ~** to get something/not get anything out of sth

ạbgewogen I. *adj* well-considered **II.** *pp von* **abwägen, abwiegen**

ạb|gewöhnen* *vt* ■ **jdm etw ~** to get sb to stop doing sth; ■ **sich** *dat* **etw ~** to give up sth

ạbgezehrt *adj* emaciated

ạb|gießen *vt irreg Flüssigkeit* to pour off *sep; Nudeln, Kartoffeln* to drain, to strain

ạb|gleiten *vi irreg sein* (*geh*) ❶ (*abrutschen*) to slip (**von** +*dat* off) ❷ (*abprallen*) ■ **an jdm ~** to bounce off sb

ạbgöttisch I. *adj* inordinate **II.** *adv* **jdn ~ lieben** to idolize sb

ạb|grasen *vt* ❶ (*abfressen*) to graze on ❷ (*fam: absuchen*) to comb

ạb|grenzen *vt* ❶ (*mit einem Zaun, einer Hecke*) to enclose; ■ **etw** [**von etw** *dat*] **~** to close off *sep* sth [from sth] ❷ **zwei Begriffe gegeneinander ~** to differentiate between two terms

Ạbgrund *m* ❶ (*steiler Hang*) precipice; (*Schlucht*) abyss ❷ (*Verderben*) abyss; **am Rande des ~s stehen** to be on the brink of disaster

ạbgrundhässlich[RR] *adj* ugly as sin *pred*

abgrundtief ['apgrʊnt·'tiːf] *adj* ❶ (*äußerst groß*) profound ❷ (*äußerst tief*) bottomless

ạb|gucken *vt, vi* to copy (**bei** +*dat* from)

ạb|hacken *vt* to chop down *sep; Finger* to chop off *sep*

ạb|haken *vt* ❶ (*in einer Liste*) to check off *sep* ❷ (*vergessen*) to forget; **die Affäre ist abgehakt** the affair is over and done with

ạb|halten *vt irreg* ❶ (*hindern*) ■ **jdn von etw** *dat* **~** to keep sb from sth; ■ **sich ~ lassen** to be deterred ❷ (*fernhalten*) *Hitze* to protect from; *Insekten* to repel ❸ (*veranstalten*) to hold; *Demonstration* to stage

abhanden|kommen[RR] [ap·'handn̩-] *vi irreg sein* to get lost

Ạbhang *m* inclination

ạb|hängen¹ *vt* ❶ (*abnehmen*) to take down *sep* ❷ (*abkoppeln*) to uncouple ❸ (*fam: hinter sich lassen*) ■ **jdn ~** to lose sb

ạb|hängen² *vi irreg* ❶ (*bedingt sein*) to depend (**von** +*dat* on); **das hängt davon ab** that [all] depends ❷ (*angewiesen sein*) to be dependent (**von** +*dat* on) ❸ (*meist pej sl: nichts tun*) to hang out

ạbhängig *adj* ❶ (*bedingt*) ■ **von etw** *dat* **~ sein** to depend on sth ❷ (*angewiesen*) ■ **von jdm ~ sein** to be dependent on sb ❸ (*süchtig*) addicted; ■ [**von etw** *dat*] **~ sein** to be addicted [to sth]

Ạbhängigkeit <-, -en> *f* ❶ (*Bedingtheit, Angewiesensein*) dependence ❷ (*Sucht*) addiction

ạb|härten *vt, vi* to harden (**gegen** +*akk* to)

ạb|hauen <haute ab, ạbgehauen> *vi sein* (*fam: sich davonmachen*) to disappear; (*weggehen*) to skip [out of] town; **hau ab!** get lost!

ạb|heben *irreg* **I.** *vi* ❶ *Flugzeug* to take off ❷ (*den Hörer abnehmen*) to answer [the phone] **II.** *vt Geld* to withdraw **III.** *vr* ■ **sich** *akk* **von jdm/etw ~** to stand out from sb/sth

ạb|heften *vt* to file [away *sep*]

ạb|heilen *vi sein Wunde* to heal [up]

ạb|helfen *vi irreg* ■ **etw** *dat* **~** to remedy sth

ạb|hetzen *vr* ■ **sich** *akk* **~** to stress oneself out

Ạbhilfe *f kein pl* remedy; **~ schaffen** to do something about it

ạbholbereit *adj* ready to be picked up *pred*

ạb|holen *vt* ■ **jdn/etw ~** to pick up *sep* sb/sth

Ạbholmarkt *m* furniture superstore (*that does not offer a delivery service*)

Ạbholpreis *m* price without delivery, cash-and-carry price

ạb|holzen *vt Bäume* to fell; *Wald* to clear-cut

Ạbholzung <-, -en> *f* deforestation

Abi <-s, -s> ['abi] *nt pl selten* (*fam*), **Abitur** <-s, -e> [abi·'tuːɐ̯] *nt pl selten* Abitur (*written and oral final examination usually taken at the end of the 13th year of school*)

> The **Abitur** is an examination that students take in order to graduate from high school. Most students take the **Abitur**, or **Abi** as it is commonly known, at the end of their final year of high school, when they are in the thirteenth grade. However, at some schools it is possible for students to take the **Abitur** at the end of the twelfth grade. In both Austria and Switzerland, the **Abitur**, known as the *Matura* and *eidgenössische Matura*, respectively, can be taken as early as the end of the ninth grade.

Abiturient(in) <-en, -en> [abi·tu·'ri̯ɛnt] *m(f)* Abitur student (*student who is taking or has passed the Abitur*)

Abiturzeugnis *nt* Abitur certificate [*or* diploma]

Abk. *f Abk von* **Abkürzung** abbr.

ạb|kapseln *vr* ■ **sich** *akk* **~** to cut oneself off

ạb|kassieren* **I.** *vt* **das Essen ~** to ask a customer to pay for their meal **II.** *vi* ❶ (*fam: finanziell profitieren*) to clean up (**bei** +*dat* with); **kräftig ~** to make quite a profit ❷ (*abrechnen*) ■ **bei jdm ~** to hand sb the bill; **darf ich bei Ihnen ~?** would you mind paying now, please?

A

ab|kauen *vt* **sich** *dat* **die Fingernägel ~** to bite one's nails
ab|kaufen *vt* ■ **jdm etw ~** (*a. fam: glauben*) to buy sth off [of] sb; **das kaufe ich dir nicht ab!** I don't buy that!
ab|kehren *vt s.* **abfegen**
ab|kippen *vt* to dump
ab|klappern *vt* (*fam*) ■ **etw** [**nach jdm/etw**] **~** to look everywhere [for sb/sth]
ab|klären *vt* ■ **etw** [**mit jdm**] **~** to clear up *sep* sth [with sb]; [**mit jdm**] **~, ob ...** to check [with sb] whether ...
Abklatsch <-[e]s, -e> *m* (*pej*) poor imitation
ab|klemmen *vt* ❶ (*abquetschen*) to crush ❷ *Kabel* to disconnect
ab|klingen *vi irreg sein* ❶ (*leiser werden*) to fade away ❷ (*schwinden*) to subside
ab|klopfen *vt* ❶ (*abschlagen*) to knock off *sep* ❷ (*reinigen*) ■ **etw ~** to beat the dust out of sth
ab|knallen *vt* (*sl*) to blast
ab|knöpfen *vt* ■ **jdm etw ~** (*fam*) to get sth off [of] sb
ab|knutschen *vt* (*fam*) to make out
ab|kochen *vt* to boil
ab|kommen *vi irreg sein* ❶ *von der Straße* to veer off; *vom Weg* to stray from ❷ (*aufgeben*) to give up; **von einer Meinung ~** to change one's mind ❸ **vom Thema ~** to digress from the topic
Abkommen <-s, -> *nt* agreement; **ein ~ abschließen** to sign a treaty
ab|können *vt irreg* (*fam*) ❶ (*leiden können*) ■ **jdn/etw nicht ~** to not be able to stand sb/sth ❷ (*vertragen*) **nicht viel ~** to not [be able to] take very much
ab|koppeln *vt* to uncouple; RAUM to undock
ab|kratzen I. *vt haben* to scratch [*or* scrape] off *sep* **II.** *vi sein* (*sl*) to kick the bucket
ab|kriegen *vt* (*fam*) *s.* **abbekommen**
ab|kühlen I. *vi sein* ❶ (*kühler werden*) to cool [down]; **das Wetter hat stark abgekühlt** the weather has gotten a lot cooler ❷ (*an Intensität verlieren*) to cool [off]; *Begeisterung* to wane **II.** *vr haben* ■ **sich** *akk* **~** *Person* to cool off; *Wetter* to get cooler
ab|kürzen *vt* ❶ *Wort* to abbreviate ❷ *Weg, Gespräch* to cut short *sep*
Abkürzung *f* ❶ (*Wort*) abbreviation ❷ (*Weg*) shortcut; **eine ~ nehmen** to take a shortcut
Abkürzungsverzeichnis *nt* list of abbreviations
ab|küssen *vt* to smother in kisses
ab|laden *vt irreg* ❶ (*deponieren*) to dump ❷ (*entladen*) to unload ❸ (*fam: absetzen*) ■ **jdn ~** to drop off *sep* sb ❹ (*abreagieren*) **seinen Ärger bei jdm ~** to take out one's anger on sb ❺ (*abwälzen*) ■ **etw auf jdn ~** to shift sth onto sb
Ablage *f* ❶ (*Möglichkeit zum Deponieren*) storage place ❷ (*Aktenablage*) filing cabinet ❸ SCHWEIZ (*Annahmestelle*) delivery point; (*Zweigstelle*) branch [office]
ab|lagern *vr* ■ **sich ~** to be deposited
ab|lassen *irreg vt Wasser, Öl* to drain; *Dampf* to let off (**aus** +*dat* from)
Ablauf <-es, -läufe> *m* ❶ (*Verlauf*) course; *von Verbrechen, Unfall* sequence of events ❷ *kein pl* **nach/vor ~ der Frist** after/before a deadline ❸ (*Abflussrohr*) outlet pipe
ab|laufen *irreg* **I.** *vi sein* ❶ (*verlaufen*) to proceed ❷ (*abfließen*) to run (**aus** +*dat* out of); **das Badewasser ~ lassen** to drain the bathtub ❸ (*sich leeren*) to empty ❹ (*ungültig werden*) to expire ❺ (*zu Ende gehen*) to run out **II.** *vt haben Schuhe* to wear down *sep*
Ableben *nt kein pl* (*geh*) demise
ab|lecken *vt* ❶ *Blut, Marmelade* to lick off *sep* ❷ *Finger, Teller* to lick [clean]
ab|legen I. *vt* ❶ (*deponieren*) to put ❷ *Eid* to swear; *Prüfung* to pass; **ein Geständnis ~** to confess, to make a confession **II.** *vi* NAUT to set sail
Ableger <-s, -> *m* BOT shoot
ab|lehnen I. *vt* ❶ (*zurückweisen*) to turn down *sep; Antrag* to reject; ■ **jdn ~** to reject sb ❷ (*sich weigern*) ■ **es ~, etw zu tun** to refuse to do sth ❸ (*missbilligen*) to disapprove of **II.** *vi* (*nein sagen*) to refuse
ablehnend I. *adj* negative **II.** *adv* negatively; ■ **jdm/etw ~ gegenüberstehen** to disapprove of sb/sth
Ablehnung <-, -en> *f* ❶ (*Zurückweisung*) rejection ❷ (*Missbilligung*) disapproval; **auf ~ stoßen** to meet with disapproval
ab|leisten *vt* **seinen Wehrdienst ~** to do one's [compulsory] military service
ab|leiten I. *vt* ❶ (*umleiten*) to divert; *Blitz* to conduct ❷ LING to derive ❸ (*logisch folgern*) to deduce **II.** *vr* ■ **sich ~** ❶ LING to stem (**von, aus** +*dat* from) ❷ (*logisch folgen*) to be derived (**aus** +*dat* from)
ab|lenken I. *vt* ❶ (*zerstreuen*) to divert; **Gartenarbeit lenkt ihn ab** working in the garden helps him to relax ❷ (*abbringen*) to distract (**von** +*dat* from) ❸ (*eine andere Richtung geben*) to divert **II.** *vi* ❶ (*ausweichen*) to change the subject ❷ (*stören*) to distract
Ablenkung *f* ❶ (*Zerstreuung*) diversion; **zur ~** in order to relax ❷ (*Störung*) distraction
Ablenkungsmanöver *nt* diversionary tactic
ab|lesen *irreg vt, vi* ❶ *Messgeräte, Strom* to read ❷ [**etw**] **von etw ~** to read [sth] from sth ❸ (*folgern*) to construe (**aus** +*dat* from)
ab|lichten *vt* (*fam: fotografieren*) to take a picture of
ab|liefern *vt* ❶ (*abgeben*) to turn [*or* hand] in *sep* ❷ (*liefern*) to deliver (**bei** +*dat* to) ❸ (*fam: nach Hause bringen*) ■ **jdn ~** to hand over *sep* sb
ab|lösen I. *vt* ❶ (*abmachen*) to remove; *Pflaster* to peel off *sep* ❷ **einen Kollegen ~** to take over for a colleague; **die Wache ~** to change the guard ❸ (*fig: ersetzen*) to replace **II.** *vr* ■ **sich ~** ❶ (*abgehen*) to peel off ❷ (*abwechseln*) to take turns (**bei** +*dat* at); **sich bei der**

Arbeit ~ to work in shifts

Ạblösesumme *f* transfer fee

ạb|luchsen [-lʊk·sn] *vt* (*fam*) ■ **jdm etw** ~ to coax sth out of sb

ạb|machen *vt* ① (*entfernen*) to take off *sep* ② (*vereinbaren*) ■ **etw** [**mit jdm**] ~ to arrange sth [with sb] ③ (*klären*) to sort out *sep;* **wir sollten das lieber unter uns** ~ it would be better if we handled this by ourselves

Ạbmachung <-, -en> *f* agreement; **sich** *akk* [**nicht**] **an eine** ~ **halten** to [not] keep an agreement

ạb|magern *vi sein* to get thin; ■ **abgemagert** very thin; **völlig abgemagert** emaciated

Ạbmagerungskur *f* diet

Ạbmahnung *f* warning

ạb|malen *vt* to paint

ạb|melden I. *vt* ① **jdn bei einem Verein** ~ to cancel sb's membership [with an association]; **jdn von einer Schule** ~ to withdraw sb from a school ② **ein Auto** ~ to cancel one's car registration; **das Telefon** ~ to have one's phone disconnected; **ein Fernsehgerät/Radio** ~ to cancel a reception license for TV/radio ③ (*fam*) ■ **bei jdm abgemeldet sein** no longer be of interest to sb; **er ist endgültig bei mir abgemeldet** I've had it with him **II.** *vr* ■ **sich** *akk* ~ (*bei einem Umzug*) to notify the authorities of a change of address

ạb|messen *vt irreg* ① (*ausmessen*) to measure ② (*abschätzen*) **etw** ~ **können** to be able to assess sth

Ạbmessung *f meist pl* measurements; (*von dreidimensionalen Objekten a.*) dimensions

ạb|montieren* *vt* (*entfernen*) to remove; (*auseinanderbauen*) to disassemble

ạb|mühen *vr* ■ **sich** *akk* ~ to work hard (**mit** +*dat* at); ■ **sich** *akk* ~ **etw zu tun** to try hard to do sth

ạb|nabeln *vr* ■ **sich** *akk* [**von jdm/etw**] ~ to become independent [of sb/sth]

ab|nagen *vt Knochen* to gnaw clean

Abnahme <-, -n> ['ap·naː·mə] *f* ① (*Verringerung*) reduction [in] ② (*das Nachlassen*) loss; *der Kräfte* weakening

ạb|nehmen *irreg* **I.** *vi* ① (*Gewicht verlieren*) to lose weight ② (*sich verringern*) to decrease ③ (*nachlassen*) to diminish; *Nachfrage* to drop ④ (*den Hörer abheben*) to answer [the phone] **II.** *vt* ① (*wegnehmen*) ■ **jdm etw** ~ to take sth [away *sep*] from sb ② (*herunternehmen*) to take down *sep; Hut* take off *sep* ③ *Telefonhörer* to pick up *sep* ④ (*tragen helfen*) ■ **jdm etw** ~ to take sth [from sb] ⑤ (*a. fig: abkaufen*) ■ **jdm etw** ~ to buy sth [from [*or* off] sb] ⑥ (*übernehmen*) ■ **jdm etw** ~ to take over *sep* sth for sb; **deine Arbeit kann ich dir nicht** ~ I can't do your work for you

Ạbnehmer(in) <-s, -> *m(f)* (*Käufer*) customer

Ạbneigung *f* dislike (**gegen** +*akk* of)

ạb|nicken *vt* (*fam*) ■ **etw** ~ to give sth the nod

abnorm [ap·'nɔrm], **abnormal** ['ap·nɔr·maːl] *adj bes* ÖSTERR, SCHWEIZ abnormal

ạb|nutzen, **ạb|nützen** SÜDD, ÖSTERR **I.** *vt* to wear out *sep;* ■ **abgenutzt** worn **II.** *vr* ■ **sich** ~ ① (*verschleißen*) to wear ② (*an Wirksamkeit verlieren*) to lose effect

Ạbnutzungserscheinungen *pl* signs of wear

Abo <-s, -s> ['abo] *nt* MEDIA (*fam*), **Abonnement** <-s, -s> [abɔ·nə·'mãː] *nt* subscription; (*Theaterabonnement*) season tickets

Abonnent(in) <-en, -en> [abɔ·'nɛnt] *m(f)* subscriber

abonnieren* [abɔ·'niː·rən] *vt* to subscribe to

Ạbordnung *f* delegation

ạb|passen *vt* ① (*abwarten*) to wait for; **die richtige Gelegenheit** ~ to bide one's time ② (*timen*) **etw gut** ~ to time sth well ③ (*abfangen*) to waylay

ạb|plagen *vr* ■ **sich** *akk* [**mit etw** *dat*] ~ to struggle [with sth]

ạb|prallen *vi sein* ① (*zurückprallen*) to rebound (**von** +*dat* off [of]) ② (*nicht treffen*) ■ **an jdm** ~ to bounce off sb

ạb|pumpen *vt* to pump (**aus** +*dat* out of)

ạb|putzen *vt* to clean; ■ **jdm etw** ~ to clean sb's sth; ■ **sich** *dat* **etw** ~ to clean sth; **putz dir die Schuhe ab!** wipe your shoes!

ạb|quälen *vr* ① ■ **sich** *akk* [**mit etw** *dat*] ~ to struggle [with sth] ② ■ **sich** *dat* **etw** ~ to force sth

ạb|rackern *vr* (*fam*) ■ **sich** *akk* [**mit etw** *dat*] ~ to slave [over [*or* away at] sth]; ■ **sich** *akk* **für jdn/etw** ~ to work one's fingers to the bone for sb/sth

ạb|rasieren* *vt* to shave [off *sep*]

ạb|raten *vi irreg* ■ **jdm von etw** *dat* ~ to advise sb against sth

ạb|räumen *vt Tisch* to clear

ab|reagieren* ['ap·rea·giː·rən] **I.** *vt Wut, Frust* to work off *sep* **II.** *vr* ■ **sich** *akk* ~ to calm down

ạb|rechnen I. *vt* (*abziehen*) to deduct (**von** +*dat* from) **II.** *vt, vi* to settle up; **die Kasse** ~ to count out the register **III.** *vi* (*zur Rechenschaft ziehen*) ■ **mit jdm** ~ to call sb to account

Ạbrechnung *f* ① (*Erstellung der Rechnung*) preparation of a bill; **die** ~ **machen** to add up the bill ② (*Aufstellung*) itemized bill ③ (*Rache*) payoff; **der Tag der** ~ the day of reckoning

Ạbrede *f* (*geh*) **etw in** ~ **stellen** to deny sth

ạb|regen *vr* (*fam*) ■ **sich** *akk* ~ to calm down; **reg dich ab!** calm down!, relax!

Ạbreibung <-, -en> *f* (*fam*) ① (*Prügel*) a good beating *fam* ② (*Tadel*) criticism

Ạbreise *f kein pl* departure

ạb|reisen *vi sein* to depart

ạb|reißen *irreg* **I.** *vt haben* ① (*abtrennen*) to tear (**von** +*dat* off); *Blumen* to pull up, to rip out; ■ **sich** *dat* **etw** ~ to tear off *sep* sth ② *Gebäude* to tear down **II.** *vi sein* ① (*sich lösen*) to tear off ② (*aufhören*) to break off; ■ **nicht** ~ to go on and on; **den Kontakt nicht** ~ **lassen** to not lose contact

ạb|richten *vt* (*dressieren*) to train

A

ạb|riegeln *vt* ① *Straße, Gebiet* to cordon off *sep* ② *Tür, Fenster* to bolt
ạb|ringen *irreg* **I.** *vt* ■**jdm etw ~** to force sth out of sb **II.** *vr* **sich ein Lächeln ~** to force a smile
Ạbriss[RR] *m eines Gebäudes* demolition
Ạbruf *m von Daten* recall
ạb|rufen *vt irreg Daten* to retrieve (**aus** *+dat* from)
ạb|runden *vt* ① *Zahl, Betrag* to round (**auf** *+akk* to); **einen Betrag nach oben/unten ~** to round a sum up/down ② (*perfektionieren*) to round off
abrupt [a'brʊpt] **I.** *adj* abrupt **II.** *adv* abruptly
ạb|rüsten *vi* MIL to disarm
Ạbrüstung *f kein pl* MIL disarmament
ạb|rutschen *vi sein* ① (*abgleiten*) to slip (**an** *+dat* on, **von** *+dat* from) ② (*sich verschlechtern*) to drop (**auf** *+akk* to)
ABS <-> [a:be:'ɛs] *nt Abk von* **Antiblockiersystem** ABS
ạb|sacken *vi sein* (*fam*) ① *Boden, Fundament* to sink ② *Flugzeug* to drop ③ *Leistung* to drop (**auf** *+akk* to); **sie ist in ihren Leistungen sehr abgesackt** her performance has deteriorated considerably ④ *Blutdruck* to sink
Ạbsage <-, -n> *f* ① (*negativer Bescheid*) refusal; *auf eine Bewerbung* rejection ② (*Ablehnung*) ■**eine ~ an etw** a rejection of sth
ạb|sagen I. *vt* (*rückgängig machen*) to cancel **II.** *vi* ■**jdm ~** to decline sb's invitation; **ich muss leider ~** I'm afraid I have to cancel *fam;* **hast du ihr schon abgesagt?** have you already told her you're not going?
ạb|sägen *vt* ① (*abtrennen*) *Ast* to saw off *sep; Baum* to cut down *sep* ② (*um seine Stellung bringen*) ■**jdn ~** (*fam*) to give sb the ax
ạb|sahnen *vt, vi* (*fam*) to cream off *sep;* **100 Euro ~** to pocket 100 euros
Ạbsatz *m* ① (*Schuhabsatz*) heel ② (*Abschnitt*) paragraph ③ (*Treppenabsatz*) landing ④ (*Verkauf*) sales *pl;* **~ finden** to find a market
ạb|saugen *vt* ① *Flüssigkeit* to draw off *sep; Fett* to siphon off *sep* ② *Teppich, Sofa* to vacuum
ạb|schaben *vt* (*entfernen*) to scrape (**von** *+dat* off [of])
ạb|schaffen *vt* ① (*außer Kraft setzen*) to do away with; *Gesetz* to repeal; *Todesstrafe* to abolish ② (*weggeben*) to get rid of
Ạbschaffung <-, -en> *f pl selten einer Regel* suspension; *eines Gesetzes* repeal; *der Todesstrafe* abolition
ạb|schalten I. *vt* (*abstellen*) to turn off *sep* **II.** *vi* (*fam: unaufmerksam werden*) to switch off
ạb|schätzen *vt* ① (*einschätzen*) to assess; **ich kann ihre Reaktion schlecht ~** I can't even guess what her reaction will be ② (*ungefähr schätzen*) to estimate
abschätzig ['ap·ʃɛ·tsɪç] **I.** *adj* disparaging **II.** *adv* disparagingly; **sich** *akk* **~ über jdn/etw äußern** to make disparaging remarks about sb/sth
ạb|schauen *vt, vi* SÜDD, ÖSTERR, SCHWEIZ *s.* **abgucken**
Ạbschaum *m kein pl* (*pej*) scum
Abscheu <-[e]s> ['ap·ʃɔy] *m kein pl* (*Ekel*) revulsion (**vor** *+dat* against)
abscheulich [ap·'ʃɔy·lɪç] **I.** *adj* ① (*entsetzlich*) revolting; *Verbrechen* horrifying ② (*fam: unerträglich*) dreadful **II.** *adv* **~ wehtun** to hurt like hell *fam;* **~ kalt/warm** awfully cold/hot
Absch<u>eu</u>lichkeit <-, -en> *f* ① *kein pl* (*Scheußlichkeit*) atrociousness ② (*schreckliche Sache*) atrocity
ạb|schicken *vt E-Mail* to send [off *sep*]; *Brief, Paket* to mail
ạb|schieben *irreg vt* ① (*ausweisen*) to deport ② (*abwälzen*) ■**etw auf jdn ~** to pass sth on to sb; **die Schuld auf jdn ~** to shift the blame onto sb
Ạbschiebestopp *m* halt on deportation
Ạbschiebung <-, -en> *f* deportation
Ạbschied <-[e]s, -e> ['ap·ʃi:t] *m* farewell; **der ~ fiel ihr nicht leicht** she found it difficult to say goodbye; **von jdm ~ nehmen** to say goodbye to sb; **zum ~** as a farewell token *liter;* **sie gab ihm zum ~ einen Kuss** she gave him a goodbye kiss
Ạbschiedsbrief *m* farewell letter
Ạbschiedsfeier *f* goodbye party
Ạbschiedsgruß *m* goodbye
Ạbschiedskuss[RR] *m* goodbye kiss
ạb|schlachten *vt* to slaughter
ạb|schlaffen *vi sein* (*fam*) to droop; ■**abgeschlafft** dog-tired; **sie wirkt in letzter Zeit ziemlich abgeschlafft** she's been looking pretty frazzled lately
Ạbschlag *m* ① (*Preisnachlass*) discount ② (*Vorschuss*) ■**ein ~ auf etw** an advance payment on sth
ạb|schlagen *irreg vt* ① (*durch Schlagen abtrennen*) to knock (**von** *+dat* off); *Ast* to knock down; **jdm den Kopf ~** to chop off *sep* sb's head ② *Bitte, Wunsch* to turn down; **er kann keinem etwas ~** he can't refuse anybody anything
abschlägig ['ap·ʃlɛ:·gɪç] *adj* negative
Ạbschlag(s)zahlung *f* partial payment
ạb|schleifen *irreg vt* to sand [down *sep*]
Ạbschleppdienst *m* towing service
ạb|schleppen I. *vt* ① *Fahrzeug, Schiff* to tow [away *sep*] ② (*fam*) *Person* to pick up *sep;* **jede Woche schleppt er eine andere ab** he comes home with a different girl every week **II.** *vr* (*fam*) ■**sich** *akk* **~** to struggle (**mit** *+dat* with)
Ạbschleppseil *nt* tow rope
Ạbschleppwagen *m* tow truck
ạb|schließen *irreg* **I.** *vt* ① (*verschließen*) to lock ② (*beenden*) to finish; *Diskussion* to end ③ (*vereinbaren*) *Geschäft* to close; *Versicherung* to take out *sep; Vertrag* to sign; *Wette* to place **II.** *vi* (*zuschließen*) to lock up
ạbschließend I. *adj* closing; **einige ~e**

A

Bemerkungen machen to make a few closing remarks **II.** *adv* finally
Ạbschluss[RR] *m* ❶ *kein pl* (*Ende*) conclusion; **zum ~ kommen** to draw to a conclusion; **kurz vor dem ~ stehen** to be nearly over ❷ (*abschließendes Zeugnis*) diploma, degree; **welchen ~ haben Sie?** what degree do you have? ❸ (*das Vereinbaren*) settlement; *einer Versicherung* taking out; *eines Vertrags* signing ❹ (*Jahresabrechnung*) accounts, books
Ạbschlussprüfung[RR] *f* SCH final [exam]
Ạbschlusszeugnis[RR] *nt* SCH diploma
ạb|schmecken *vt* ❶ (*probieren*) to taste ❷ (*würzen*) to season
ạb|schminken I. *vr, vt* ■**sich** *akk* ~ to take off one's makeup **II.** *vt* (*fam: aufgeben*) ■**sich** *dat* **etw** ~ to give up *sep* sth; **das können Sie sich ~!** you can forget about that!
ạb|schnallen I. *vt* (*losschnallen*) to unbuckle **II.** *vi* (*sl*) ❶ (*nicht verstehen können*) to be lost ❷ (*fassungslos sein*) to be thunderstruck; **da schnallst du ab!** that's amazing! **III.** *vr* ■**sich** *akk* ~ to unfasten one's seat belt
ạb|schneiden *irreg* **I.** *vt* ❶ (*abtrennen*) to cut [off *sep*] ❷ (*unterbrechen, absperren*) **jdm den Weg ~** to intercept sb; **jdm das Wort ~** to cut sb off [*or* short] ❸ (*isolieren*) **jdn von der Außenwelt ~** to cut sb off from the outside world **II.** *vi* (*fam*) **bei etw** *dat* **gut/schlecht ~** to do well/poorly on sth
Ạbschnitt *m* ❶ (*Textabschnitt*) passage ❷ (*Zeitabschnitt*) phase, period; **ein neuer ~ der Geschichte** a new era in history; **ein neuer ~ in seinem Leben** a new chapter of his life ❸ (*Unterteilung*) part; *einer Autobahn* section
ab|schotten ['ap·ʃɔ·tn̩] **I.** *vt* (*isolieren*) to cut off *sep* **II.** *vr* ■**sich** *akk* ~ to isolate oneself
ạb|schrauben *vt* to unscrew
ạb|schrecken I. *vt* ❶ (*abhalten*) ■**jdn** [**von etw** *dat*] ~ to deter sb [from doing sth] ❷ KOCHK to shock **II.** *vi* (*abschreckend sein*) to deter
ạbschreckend I. *adj* deterrent; **ein ~es Beispiel** a warning **II.** *adv* **~ wirken** to act as a deterrent
Ạbschreckung <-, -en> *f* deterrent; **als ~ dienen** to act as a deterrent
ạb|schreiben *irreg vt* ❶ *Text* to copy ❷ (*verloren geben*) to write off *sep*
Ạbschrift *f* duplicate
ạb|schürfen *vt Haut* to scrape
Ạbschürfung <-, -en> *f* (*Wunde*) scrape
abschüssig ['ap·ʃʏ·sɪç] *adj* steep
Ạbschussliste[RR] *f* hit list
ạb|schütteln *vt* to shake off *sep*
ạb|schütten *vt s.* **abgießen**
ạb|schwächen *vt* to tone down *sep*
ạb|schwatzen, ạb|schwätzen *vt* SÜDD (*fam*) ■**jdm etw ~** to talk sb into parting with sth
ạb|schweifen *vi sein Gedanken* to deviate (**von** +*dat* from); **vom Thema ~** to digress [from a topic]; **bitte schweifen Sie nicht ab!** please stick to the point
ạb|schwellen *vi irreg sein* ❶ *Körperteil* to go down; **sein Knöchel ist abgeschwollen** the swelling in his ankle has gone down ❷ *Lärm* to fade away
ạb|schwören *vi irreg* ■**einer S.** *dat* ~ to give up *sep* sth
ạb|segnen *vt* (*fam: genehmigen*) to bless; ■**etw von jdm ~ lassen** to get sb's blessing on sth
absehbar ['ap·zeː·baːɐ̯] *adj* foreseeable; **das Ende ist nicht ~** the end is not in sight; **in ~er Zeit** in the foreseeable future
ạb|sehen *irreg* **I.** *vt* (*voraussehen*) to predict **II.** *vi* (*verzichten auf*) ■**von etw** *dat* ~ to refrain from sth; ■**davon ~, etw zu tun** to refrain from doing sth
ạb|seilen *vr* (*fam: verschwinden*) ■**sich** *akk* ~ to beat it *sl*
ạb|sein[ALT] *vi irreg s.* **ab I 2**
abseits ['ap·zaits] *präp* +*gen* **ein wenig ~ der Straße** not far from the road
abseits|halten[RR] *vr irreg* **sich** *akk* ~ to be aloof
abseits|stehen[RR] *vi irreg* to stand on the sidelines
ạb|senden *vt reg o irreg s.* **abschicken**
Ạbsender(in) <-s, -> *m(f)* sender
ab|servieren* [-zɛr·'viː·rən] *vt* (*fam*) ■**jdn ~** to get rid of sb; (*sl: umbringen*) to bump off *sep* sb; **sich** *akk* **von jdm ~ lassen** to let oneself be pushed around
ạb|setzen I. *vt* ❶ (*des Amtes entheben*) to remove [from office]; *Herrscher* to depose; *König, Königin* to dethrone ❷ *Hut, Brille* to take off *sep* ❸ (*hinstellen*) to put down *sep* ❹ (*aussteigen lassen*) ■**jdn ~** to drop off *sep* sb ❺ **etw von der Steuer ~** to deduct sth from one's taxes ❻ *Medikament* to stop taking **II.** *vr* ■**sich** *akk* ~ ❶ *Dreck, Staub* to settle ❷ (*fam: verschwinden*) to clear out; **sich ins Ausland ~** to leave the country
ạb|sichern *vr* ■**sich** *akk* ~ to cover oneself (**gegen** +*akk* against); **sich** *akk* **vertraglich ~** to protect oneself by signing a contract
Ạbsicht <-, -en> *f* intention; **~ sein** to be intentional; **das war nicht meine ~!** I didn't mean to do it!; **die ~ haben, etw zu tun** to intend to do sth; **mit/ohne ~** intentionally/unintentionally
absichtlich ['ap·zɪçt·lɪç] **I.** *adj* deliberate, intentional **II.** *adv* on purpose, deliberately
ạb|sitzen *irreg vt Zeit* to sit out; *Haftstrafe* to serve
absolut [ap·zo·'luːt] **I.** *adj* absolute; **~e Ruhe** complete calm **II.** *adv* (*fam*) absolutely; **~ nicht/nichts** absolutely not/nothing
Absolvent(in) <-en, -en> [ap·zɔl·'vɛnt] *m(f)* graduate
absolvieren* [ap·zɔl·'viː·rən] *vt* ❶ (*bestehen*) to [successfully] complete; *Prüfung* to pass ❷ (*ableisten*) to do
absonderlich [ap·'zɔn·dɐ·lɪç] **I.** *adj* peculiar

II. *adv* peculiarly

ạb|sondern **I.** *vt* ① (*ausscheiden*) to secrete ② (*isolieren*) to isolate; ■ **jdn von jdm ~** to separate sb from sb **II.** *vr* ■ **sich** *akk* **~** to keep oneself apart

absorbieren* [ap·zɔr·ˈbiː·rən] *vt* to absorb

ạb|spalten *vr* ■ **sich ~** to split away/off

Ạbspann <-[e]s, -e> *m* FILM, TV credits *pl*

ab|specken [ˈap·ʃpɛ·kn̩] (*fam*) **I.** *vi* (*abnehmen*) to slim down **II.** *vt* (*reduzieren*) ■ **etw ~** to reduce the size of sth

ạb|speichern *vt* to store; COMPUT to save

ạb|speisen *vt* ■ **jdn mit etw ~** to palm off *sep* sth on sb

abspenstig [ˈap·ʃpɛns·tɪç] *adj* **jdm etw ~ machen** to take away *sep* sth from sb

ạb|sperren **I.** *vt* ① (*versperren*) to cordon off *sep* ② (*abstellen*) *Strom, Wasser* to cut off *sep* ③ SÜDD (*zuschließen*) to lock **II.** *vi* SÜDD (*die Tür verschließen*) to lock up

Ạbsperrung *f* (*Sperre*) cordon; *durch Polizei* police cordon

ạb|spielen **I.** *vr* (*ablaufen*) ■ **sich ~** to happen; **was hat sich hier abgespielt?** what happened here? **II.** *vt* ① (*laufen lassen*) to play ② *Ball* to pass

Ạbsprache *f* agreement; **eine ~ treffen** to come to an agreement

ạb|sprechen *irreg* **I.** *vt* ① (*vereinbaren*) to agree on ② (*aberkennen*) ■ **jdm etw ~** to deny sb sth **II.** *vr* ■ **sich** *akk* **mit jdm ~** to come to an agreement with sb (**wegen** *+gen* on)

ạb|springen *vi irreg sein* ① (*fam: sich zurückziehen*) to bale out (**von** *+dat* of) ② (*hinunterspringen*) to jump (**von** *+dat* from); *mit dem Fallschirm* to parachute ③ (*sich lösen*) to come off

Ạbsprung *m* ① (*Sprung*) jump ② (*fam: Ausstieg*) getting out; **den ~ schaffen** to make a getaway; **den ~ verpassen** to miss the boat

ạb|spülen **I.** *vt* ① (*reinigen*) to rinse ② (*entfernen*) to wash off *sep* **II.** *vi* to do the dishes

ạb|stammen *vi* ■ **~ von** to descend from; LING to stem from

Ạbstammung <-, -en> *f* origins *pl;* **adeliger ~ sein** to be of noble birth

Ạbstand *m* ① (*räumlich*) distance; **ein ~ von 20 Metern** a distance of 65 feet; **in einigem ~** at some distance; **~ halten** to maintain a distance; **fahr nicht so dicht auf, halt ~!** don't tailgate! ② (*zeitlich*) interval; **in kurzen/regelmäßigen Abständen** at short/regular intervals ③ (*emotional*) aloofness

ab|statten [ˈap·ʃta·tn̩] *vt* (*geh*) **jdm einen Besuch ~** to pay sb a visit

ạb|stauben *vt* ① (*fam: ergattern*) to rip off *sep* ② (*vom Staub befreien*) to dust

ạb|stechen *irreg* **I.** *vt* to stab to death; ■ **ein Tier ~** to slit an animal's throat **II.** *vi* (*sich abheben*) to stand out (**von** *+dat* from)

Ạbstecher <-s, -> *m* ① (*Ausflug*) trip ② (*Umweg*) detour

ạb|stehen *vi irreg* to stick out; **er hat ~de Ohren** his ears stick out

Ạbsteige <-, -n> *f* (*schäbiges Hotel*) dive, flophouse

ạb|steigen *vi irreg sein* ① (*heruntersteigen*) to dismount; **von einer Leiter ~** to get down off a ladder ② (*fam*) **in einem Hotel ~** to stay in a hotel ③ **beruflich/gesellschaftlich ~** to slide down the job/social ladder

ạb|stellen *vt* ① *Gerät* to turn off *sep* ② *Wasser, Strom* to cut off *sep;* **den Haupthahn ~** to turn off the main shutoff valve ③ (*absetzen*) to put down *sep* ④ (*parken*) to park

Ạbstellgleis *nt* siding

Ạbstellkammer *f* broom closet

Ạbstellraum *m* storeroom

ạb|stempeln *vt* ① (*mit einem Stempel versehen*) to stamp ② (*pej*) ■ **jdn [als etw] ~** to brand sb [as sth]

ạb|sterben *vi irreg sein* ① *Zellen, Blätter* to die ② *Finger, Zehen* to go numb

Ạbstieg <-[e]s, -e> *m* ① (*das Hinabklettern*) descent ② (*Niedergang*) decline; **der berufliche/gesellschaftliche ~** descent down the job/social ladder

ạb|stillen *vt, vi Baby* to stop breastfeeding

ạb|stimmen **I.** *vi* (*die Stimme abgeben*) to vote; **[über etw] ~ lassen** to [have a] vote [on sth] **II.** *vt* (*anpassen*) ■ **aufeinander ~** to coordinate [with each other]; *Farben, Kleidung* to match

Ạbstimmung *f* (*Stimmabgabe*) vote (**über** *+akk* on)

abstinent [ap·sti·ˈnɛnt] **I.** *adj* ① (*enthaltsam*) abstinent; ■ **~ sein** to be a teetotaler ② (*sexuell enthaltsam*) celibate **II.** *adv* abstinently; (*sexuell*) in celibacy

Abstinenz <-> [ap·sti·ˈnɛnts] *f kein pl* abstinence; (*sexuell*) celibacy

Abstinẹnzler(in) <-s, -> *m(f)* (*pej*) teetotaler

ạb|stoßen *irreg vt* ① MED to reject ② (*anwidern*) to repel ③ (*durch einen Stoß abschlagen*) to chip off *sep;* (*durch Stöße abnutzen*) to damage ④ (*verkaufen*) to get rid of

ạbstoßend **I.** *adj* repulsive **II.** *adv* in a repulsive way; **~ aussehen** to look repulsive; **~ riechen** to smell disgusting

ạb|stottern *vt* (*fam*) to pay in installments

abstrahieren* [ap·stra·ˈhiː·rən] *vi* to abstract

abstrakt [ap·ˈstrakt] **I.** *adj* abstract **II.** *adv* in the abstract

ạb|streifen *vt* ① (*abziehen*) to take off *sep* ② (*säubern*) *Füße* to wipe

ạb|streiten *vt irreg* to deny; **er stritt ab, sie zu kennen** he denied knowing her

ạb|stumpfen *vi sein* to blunt; (*fig*) to become inured, accustomed (**gegen** *+akk* to), to dull

Ạbsturz *m* ① (*Sturz in die Tiefe*) fall; *von Flugzeug* crash ② *von Computer* crash

ạb|stürzen *vi sein* ① *Person* to fall; *Flugzeug* to crash ② *Computer* to crash ③ (*fam: sich betrinken*) to get hammered *sl*

ạb|stützen *vt* to support

A

ab|suchen *vt* ① (*durchstreifen*) to search (**nach** +*dat* for) ② (*untersuchen*) to examine (**nach** +*dat* for)

absurd [ap·'zʊrt] *adj* absurd

Absurdität <-, -en> *f* absurdity

Abszess^RR <-es, -e>, **Abszeß**^ALT <-sses, -sse> [aps·'tsɛs] *m* MED abscess

Abt, **Äbtissin** <-[e]s, Äbte> [apt, ɛp·'tɪsɪn, *pl* 'ɛp·tə] *m, f* abbot *masc,* abbess *fem*

Abt. *f Abk von* **Abteilung** dept.

ab|tanzen *vi* (*sl*) to boogie *fam,* to get down [on the dance floor]

ab|tasten *vt* ① (*medizinisch*) ■**jdn ~** to examine sb ② **jdn nach Waffen ~** to frisk sb for weapons ③ COMPUT to scan

ab|tauen I. *vi sein Eis* to thaw **II.** *vt haben Kühlschrank* to defrost

Abtei <-, -en> *f* abbey

Abteil *nt* compartment

ab|teilen *vt* to partition off *sep*

Abteilung *f* department; *eines Krankenhauses* ward

Abteilungsleiter(in) *m(f) einer Verkaufsabteilung* department manager; *einer Firma* department head

ab|tippen *vt* (*fam*) to type [up *sep*]

ab|töten *vt* ① *Keime* to destroy ② *Gefühl* to deaden

abträglich ['ap·trɛːk·lɪç] *adj* (*geh*), **abträgig** *adj* SCHWEIZ ■**etw** *dat* **~ sein** to be detrimental to sth

ab|transportieren* *vt* to transport [away *sep*]

ab|treiben *irreg vi, vt* [**ein Kind**] **~ lassen** to have an abortion

Abtreibung <-, -en> *f* abortion

Abtreibungspille *f* morning-after pill

ab|trennen *vt* ① (*ablösen*) to detach ② (*abteilen*) to divide off *sep* ③ *Körperteil* to cut off *sep*

ab|treten *irreg vt* ① (*übertragen*) *Rechte* to transfer; *Land* to cede ② (*fam: überlassen*) ■**jdm etw ~** to give sth to sb; **er hat ihr seinen Platz abgetreten** he gave up his seat to her ③ **seine Schuhe ~** (*säubern*) to wipe off *sep* one's shoes ④ (*durch Treten entfernen*) to stomp off *sep*

Abtreter <-s, -> *m* (*fam*) doormat

ab|trocknen I. *vt haben* to dry **II.** *vt, vi haben* [**das Geschirr**] **~** to dry the dishes **III.** *vi sein* to dry

ab|tropfen *vi sein* to drain; ■**etw ~ lassen** to leave sth to drain

abtrünnig ['ap·trʏ·nɪç] *adj* renegade; *Provinz, Staat* rogue

ab|tun *vt irreg* to dismiss; **etw mit einem Achselzucken/Lächeln ~** to shrug/laugh sth off

abturnen [-tøːɐ·nən] (*sl*) **I.** *vi* to be a turnoff **II.** *vt* ■**jdn ~** to turn sb off

abturnend ['ap·tøːɐ̯·nənt] *adj* (*sl*) repulsive; **das finde ich super ~** I think that's a major turnoff

ab|verlangen* *vt* to demand

ab|wägen *vt irreg* ■**etw** [**gegeneinander**] **~** to weigh sth [against sth else]; **die Vor- und Nachteile ~** to weigh the advantages and disadvantages

ab|wählen *vt Schulfach* to drop; ■**jdn ~** to vote sb out [of office]

ab|wälzen *vt* ■**etw** [**auf jdn**] **~** to unload sth [on[to] sb]; *Kosten* to pass on *sep; Verantwortung* to shift

ab|wandeln *vt* to adapt; *Vertrag* to modify

ab|wandern *vi sein* to migrate (**aus** +*dat* from, **in** +*akk* to); (*in ein anderes Land*) to emigrate (**aus** +*dat* from, **in** +*akk* to)

Abwanderung *f* migration

ab|warten *vt, vi* to wait [for]; **das bleibt abzuwarten** that remains to be seen

abwärts ['ap·vɛrts] *adv* ① (*nach unten*) down, downward[s]; **den Fluss ~** downstream ② (*bergab*) downhill

abwärts|gehen *vi irreg sein* ■**es geht mit jdm/etw abwärts** sb/sth is going downhill

abwärtskompatibel *adj* COMPUT backward [*or* downward] compatible

Abwärtstrend *m* downward trend

Abwasch[1] <-[e]s> *m kein pl* ① (*Spülgut*) dirty dishes *pl* ② (*das Spülen*) **den ~ machen** to do the dishes

Abwasch[2] <-, -en> *f* ÖSTERR (*Spülbecken*) sink

abwaschbar *adj* washable

ab|waschen *irreg* **I.** *vt* ① (*reinigen*) to wash up *sep* ② (*entfernen*) to wash off **II.** *vi* to do the dishes

Abwasser <-wässer> *nt* waste water; *von Industrieanlagen* effluent

Abwasseraufbereitung *f* sewage treatment

Abwasserkanal *m* sewer

Abwasserleitung *f* sewage pipe

ab|wechseln [-vɛk·sl̩n] *vi, vr* ■[**sich**] **~** ① (*im Wechsel handeln*) to take turns ② (*im Wechsel erfolgen*) to alternate; **Sonne und Regen wechselten** [**sich**] **ab** the weather was a mix of sun and rain

abwechselnd [-vɛk·sl̩nd] *adv* alternately

Abwechselung [-vɛk·sə·lʊŋ], **Abwechslung** <-, -en> [-vɛks·lʊŋ] *f* change; **die ~ lieben** to like variety; **zur ~** for a change

abwechslungshalber [-vɛks-] *adv* for the sake of change

abwechslungslos *adj* unchanging

abwechslungsreich *adj* varied

Abweg *m meist pl* **jdn auf ~e führen** to lead sb astray; **auf ~e geraten** to go astray; (*moralisch*) to stray from the straight and narrow

abwegig ['ap·veː·gɪç] *adj* ① (*unsinnig*) absurd; *Idee* far-fetched; *Verdacht* unfounded ② (*merkwürdig*) strange

Abwehr <-> *f kein pl* ① (*inneres Widerstreben*) resistance ② SPORT (*Verteidigung*) defense; (*die Abwehrspieler*) defenders

ab|wehren I. *vt* ① MIL to repel ② SPORT to fend off *sep; Ball* to clear ③ (*abwenden*) to turn away *sep; Gefahr, Unheil, Verdacht* to avert; *Vorwurf* to fend off *sep* **II.** *vi* (*ablehnen*) to refuse

A

Abwehrkräfte *pl* the body's defenses
Abwehrmechanismus *m* PSYCH, MED defense mechanism
Abwehrspieler(in) *m(f)* SPORT defender
ab|weichen *vi irreg sein* ① (*abkommen*) to deviate (**von** +*dat* from) ② (*sich unterscheiden*) ■ **von jdm/etw ~** to differ from sb/sth
abweichend *adj* different
Abweichung <-, -en> *f* ① (*Unterschiedlichkeit*) difference; *einer Auffassung* deviation ② (*das Abkommen*) deviation ③ TECH **zulässige ~** tolerance
ab|weisen *vt irreg* ① (*wegschicken*) to turn away *sep;* **sich** *akk* [**von jdm**] **nicht ~ lassen** to not take no for an answer [from sb] ② (*ablehnen*) to turn down *sep; Antrag, Bitte* to deny
abweisend *adj* cold
ab|wenden I. *vr reg o irreg* ■ **sich** *akk* **~** to turn away **II.** *vt* ① *reg* **eine Katastrophe ~** to avert a catastrophe ② *reg o irreg* **die Augen ~** to look away
ab|werben *vt irreg* to entice away *sep*
ab|werfen *irreg vt* to drop; *Blätter, Nadeln* to lose
ab|werten *vt* ① *Währung* to devalue (**um** +*akk* by) ② (*Bedeutung mindern*) to debase
abwertend I. *adj* derogatory **II.** *adv* derogatorily
Abwertung *f* ① *einer Währung* devaluation ② (*Bedeutungsminderung*) debasement
abwesend ['ap·veː·zn̩t] *adj* ① (*nicht da*) absent ② (*geistesabwesend*) absent-minded
Abwesenheit <-, -en> *f pl selten* ① (*Fehlen*) absence ② (*Geistesabwesenheit*) absent-mindedness
ab|wickeln *vt* ① (*von etw wickeln*) to unwind ② (*erledigen*) to deal with; *Auftrag* to process; *Geschäft* to carry out
ab|wiegen *vt irreg* to weigh [out]
ab|wimmeln *vt* (*fam*) ■ **jdn ~** to get rid of sb; ■ **etw ~** to get out of [doing] sth
ab|winken *vi* to signal one's refusal
ab|wischen *vt* to wipe; **sich** *dat* **die Tränen ~** to dry one's tears; **sich** *dat* **den Schweiß von der Stirn ~** to wipe the sweat from one's brow
ab|würgen *vt* (*fam*) ① *Motor* to stall ② (*im Keim ersticken*) to nip in the bud; ■ **jdn ~** (*unterbrechen*) to cut sb off [*or* short]
ab|zahlen *vt* to pay off; (*in Raten*) to pay in installments
ab|zählen I. *vt* to count out *sep;* **bitte das Fahrgeld abgezählt bereithalten** please have exact change ready **II.** *vi* to count
Abzeichen *nt* ① (*Anstecknadel*) badge ② MIL rank insignia
ab|zeichnen I. *vt* ① (*abmalen*) to copy ② (*signieren*) to initial **II.** *vr* ■ **sich ~** ① (*erkennbar werden*) to become apparent ② (*Umrisse erkennen lassen*) to show
ab|ziehen *irreg* **I.** *vi sein* ① *Truppen* to withdraw (**aus** +*dat* from) ② *Rauch* to clear (**aus** +*dat* from) ③ (*fam: weggehen*) to go away; **zieh ab!** beat it! *sl* **II.** *vt haben* ① (*einbehalten*) to deduct (**von** +*dat* from) ② MATH to subtract (**von** +*dat* from) ③ *Truppen* to withdraw (**aus** +*dat* from) ④ *Bett* to strip ⑤ *Schlüssel* to take out *sep* ⑥ SCHWEIZ (*ausziehen*) to take off *sep* **III.** *vr* SCHWEIZ (*sich ausziehen*) ■ **sich** *akk* **~** to get undressed, to undress
ab|zielen *vi* ■ **auf jdn/etw ~** to aim at sb/sth
Abzocke <-> *f kein pl* (*pej fam*) price gouging
ab|zocken *vt* (*sl*) ■ **jdn ~** to swindle sb
Abzug *m* ① (*das Einbehalten*) deduction ② *von Fotos* print ③ *von Truppen* withdrawal ④ (*Dunstabzug*) exhaust fan
abzüglich ['ap·tsyːk·lɪç] *präp* +*gen* minus sth
Abzugshaube *f* exhaust hood
ab|zweigen I. *vi sein* to branch off; **nach links ~** to turn off to the left **II.** *vt* (*fam*) **Geld ~** to put aside money (**für** +*akk* for)
Abzweigung <-, -en> *f* turnoff
Accessoire <-s, -s> [ak·sɛ·'so̯·aːɐ̯] *nt meist pl* accessory
Ach [ax] *nt* ▶ WENDUNGEN: **mit ~ und Krach** (*fam*) by the skin of one's teeth
Achse <-, -n> ['ak·sə] *f* ① AUTO axle ② (*Linie*) axis ▶ WENDUNGEN: **auf ~ sein** (*fam*) to be on the move [*or* go]
Achsel <-, -n> ['ak·sl] *f* ① ANAT armpit ② **mit den ~n zucken** to shrug one's shoulders
Achselhaare ['ak·sl-] *pl* armpit hair
Achselhöhle *f* armpit
Achselzucken <-> *nt kein pl* shrug [of the shoulders]
Achsenbruch ['ak·sn-] *m* broken axle
acht[1] [axt] *adj* eight; **das kostet ~ Euro** that costs eight euros; **die Linie ~ fährt zum Bahnhof** the No. 8 [bus/streetcar/etc.] goes to the train station; **es steht ~ zu drei** the score is [*or* it's] eight to three; **~ [Jahre alt] sein/werden** to be/turn eight [years old]; **mit ~ [Jahren]** at the age of eight; **~ Uhr sein** to be eight o'clock; **gegen ~ [Uhr]** [at] about eight [o'clock]; **um ~** at eight [o'clock]; **... [Minuten] nach/vor ~** ... [minutes] after/to eight [o'clock]; **alle ~ Tage** every eight days; **heute/Freitag in ~ Tagen** a week from today/Friday; **heute/Freitag vor ~ Tagen** a week ago today/Friday
acht[2] [axt] *adv* **wir waren zu ~** there were eight of us
Acht[1] <-, -en> [axt] *f* ① (*Zahl*) eight ② (*etw von der Form einer 8*) **ich habe eine ~ im Vorderrad** my front wheel is buckled; **auf dem Eis eine ~ laufen** to skate a figure eight on the ice ③ KARTEN **die Kreuz~** the eight of clubs ④ (*Verkehrslinie*) ■ **die ~** the [number] eight
Acht[RR2] [axt] *f* **~ geben** to be careful; **sie gab genau Acht, was der Professor sagte** she paid careful attention to what the professor said; **auf jdn/etw ~ geben** to look after sb/sth; **etw außer ~ lassen** to not take sth into account; **sich** *akk* [**vor jdm/etw**] **in ~ nehmen** to be wary [of sb/sth]
achtbar *adj* (*geh*) respectable

achte(**r, s**) ['ax·tə, -tɐ, -təs] *adj* ❶ (*an achter Stelle*) eighth; **an ~r Stelle** [in] eighth [place]; **die ~ Klasse** eighth grade ❷ (*Datum*) eighth; **am ~n August** on August eighth

Achte(**r**) ['ax·tə, -tɐ] *f(m) dekl wie adj* ❶ (*Person*) ■ **der/die/das ~** the eighth; **du bist jetzt der ~, der fragt** you're the eighth person to ask; **als ~ an der Reihe** [*o* **dran**] **sein** to be the eighth [in line]; **~**[**r**] **sein/werden** to be/finish [in] eighth [place]; **als ~r durchs Ziel gehen** to finish eighth, to cross the line in eighth place; **jeder ~** every eighth person, one in eight [people] ❷ (*bei Datumsangabe*) ■ **der ~** [*o geschrieben* **der 8.**] the eighth *spoken,* the 8th *written;* **heute ist der ~** it's the eighth today; ■ **am ~n** on the eighth ❸ (*Namenszusatz*) **Karl der ~** [*o geschrieben* **Karl VIII.**] Karl the Eighth *spoken* [*or written* Karl VIII]

Achteck <-[e]s, -e> ['axt·ʔɛk] *nt* octagon

ạchteckig *adj* octagonal, eight-sided *attr*

achtel ['ax·tl̩] *adj* eighth

Achtel <-s, -> ['ax·tl̩] *nt* eighth

Ạchtelfinale *nt* round of the last sixteen; (*Basketball*) Sweet Sixteen

achten ['ax·tn̩] **I.** *vt* (*schätzen*) to respect **II.** *vi* ❶ (*aufpassen*) ■ **auf jdn/etw ~** to look after [*or* watch] sb/sth ❷ (*beachten*) ■ **auf jdn/etw ~** to pay attention to sb/sth; ■ **darauf ~, etw zu tun** to make sure to do sth; **achtet darauf, dass ihr nichts umwerft!** be careful not to knock anything over!

ächten ['ɛç·tn̩] *vt* (*verdammen*) to ostracize

achtens ['ax·tn̩s] *adv* eighthly

Ạchterbahn *f* roller coaster

achtfach, 8fach ['axt·fax] **I.** *adj* eightfold; **die ~e Menge** eight times the amount **II.** *adv* eightfold, eight times over

ạcht|geben *vi irreg s.* **Acht²**

achthundert ['axt·'hʊndɐt] *adj* eight hundred

achtjährig, 8-jährigRR ['axt·jɛː·rɪç] *adj* ❶ (*Alter*) eight-year-old *attr,* eight years old *pred;* **das ~e Jubiläum einer S.** *gen* the eighth anniversary of sth ❷ (*Zeitspanne*) eight-year *attr;* **eine ~e Amtszeit** an eight-year term of office

ạchtlos I. *adj* careless **II.** *adv* without noticing

Ạchtlosigkeit <-> *f kein pl* ❶ (*Unachtsamkeit*) carelessness ❷ (*unachtsames Verhalten*) thoughtlessness

achtmal, 8-malRR ['axt·maːl] *adv* eight times; **~ so viel/so viele** eight times as much/as many

achtsam ['axt·zaːm] (*geh*) **I.** *adj* careful **II.** *adv* carefully

Achtstundentag [axt·'ʃtʊn·dn̩·taːk] *m* eight-hour day

achtstündig, 8-stündigRR ['axt·ʃtʏn·dɪç] *adj* eight-hour *attr,* lasting eight hours *pred*

achttägig, 8-tägigRR ['axt·tɛː·gɪç] *adj* eight-day *attr,* lasting eight days *pred*

achttausend ['axt·'tau·zn̩t] *adj* ❶ (*Zahl*) eight thousand ❷ (*fam:* €*8.000*) eight grand

Achtundsẹchziger(**in**) <-s, -> *m(f) sb who took an active part in the demonstrations and student revolts of 1968*

Achtung <-> ['ax·tʊŋ] *f kein pl* respect (**vor** *+dat* for); **~!** attention!

Ạchtungserfolg *m* reasonable success

achtzehn ['axt·seːn] *adj* eighteen; **ab ~ frei**[**gegeben**] **sein** *Film* ≈ NC-17; ■ **~ Uhr** 6 p.m.; MIL 1800 hrs *written,* eighteen hundred hours *spoken; s. a.* **acht ¹**

ạchtzehnte(**r, s**) *adj* ❶ (*an achtzehnter Stelle*) eighteenth; *s. a.* **achte**(**r, s**) **1** ❷ (*Datum*) eighteenth, 18th; *s. a.* **achte**(**r, s**) **2**

achtzig ['axt·sɪç] *adj* ❶ (*Zahl*) eighty; **die Linie ~ fährt zum Bahnhof** the No. 80 [bus/streetcar/etc.] goes to the train station; **~** [**Jahre alt**] **sein** to be eighty [years old]; **mit ~** [**Jahren**] at the age of eighty, at eighty [years old], as an eighty-year-old ❷ (*fam: Stundenkilometer*) eighty [kilometers an hour]; [**mit**] **~ fahren** to do eighty [kilometers an hour] ▶ WENDUNGEN: **jdn auf ~ bringen** (*fam*) to make sb's blood boil

achtziger, 80er ['axt·sɪgɐ] *adj attr* (*das Jahrzehnt von 80 bis 90*) **die ~ Jahre** the eighties, the '80s

achtzigste(**r, s**) ['axt·sɪç·stə, -tɐ, -təs] *adj* eightieth; *s. a.* **achte**(**r, s**) **1**

ächzen ['ɛç·tsn̩] *vi* ❶ (*stöhnen*) to groan ❷ (*knarren*) to creak

Acker <-s, Äcker> ['akɐ, *pl* 'ɛkɐ] *m* field

Ạckerbau *m kein pl* [arable] farming; **~ betreiben** to farm [the land]

Ạckerland *nt kein pl* arable [farm]land

ackern ['akɐn] *vi* (*fam: hart arbeiten*) to slave away

Acryl <-s> [a'kryːl] *nt kein pl* acrylic

Ạctionfilm *m* action film

Ạctionheld(**in**) ['ɛk·ʃən-] *m(f)* action hero

Adamsapfel *m* Adam's apple

Adamskostüm *nt* ▶ WENDUNGEN: **im ~** (*hum fam*) in one's birthday suit

Adapter <-s, -> [a'dap·tɐ] *m* adapter

adaptieren* [adap·'tiː·rən] *vt* ❶ (*umarbeiten*) to adapt (**für** *+akk* for) ❷ ÖSTERR (*herrichten*) to renovate

adäquat [adɛ·'kvaːt] *adj* adequate; *Position, Stellung* suitable

addieren* [a'diː·rən] *vt* to add up *sep;* ■ **etw zu etw** *dat* **~** to add sth to sth

Addition <-, -en> [adi·'tsi̯oːn] *f* addition

Additiv <-s, -e> [adi·'tiːf, *pl* adi·'tiː·və] *nt* additive

ade [a'deː] *interj* SÜDD goodbye

Adel <-s> ['aːdl̩] *m kein pl* nobility, aristocracy

adelig ['aːdə·lɪç] *adj s.* **adlig**

Adelige(**r**) ['aːdə·lɪ·gə, -gɐ] *f(m) dekl wie adj s.* **Adlige**(**r**)

adeln ['aːdl̩n] *vt* ❶ (*den Adel verleihen*) to bestow a title [up]on ❷ (*geh: auszeichnen*) to ennoble

Adelstitel *m* title [of nobility]

Ader <-, -n> ['aːdɐ] *f* ❶ (*Vene*) vein; (*Schlagader*) artery ❷ (*Begabung*) **eine ~ für etw haben** to have a talent for sth; **eine künstle-**

rische ~ **haben** to have an artistic bent
ad hoc [at·'hɔk] *adv* (*geh*) ad hoc
Adjektiv <-s, -e> ['at·jɛk·tiːf, *pl* -tiːvə] *nt* adjective
Adler <-s, -> ['aːdlɐ] *m* eagle
Adlernase *f* aquiline nose
adlig ['aːdlɪç] *adj* aristocratic, noble; ■ ~ **sein** to have a title
Adlige(r) ['aːdl·ɪgə, -gɐ] *f(m) dekl wie adj* aristocrat, nobleman *masc*, noblewoman *fem*
Administration <-, -en> [at·mi·nɪs·tra·'tsi̯oːn] *f* administration
administrativ [at·minɪs·tra·'tiːf] **I.** *adj* administrative **II.** *adv* administratively
adoptieren* [adɔp·'tiː·rən] *vt* to adopt
Adoption <-, -en> [adɔp·'tsi̯oːn] *f* adoption; **ein Kind zur ~ freigeben** to put a child up for adoption
Adoptiveltern [adɔp·'tiːf-] *pl* adoptive parents
Adoptivkind *nt* adopted child
Adrenalin <-s> [adre·na·'liːn] *nt kein pl* adrenalin
Adrenalinspiegel *m* adrenalin level
Adrenalinstoß *m* adrenalin rush
Adressat(in) <-en, -en> [adrɛ·'saːt] *m(f)* addressee
Adressatenkreis *m* target group
Adrẹssbuch^RR^ *nt* address book
Adresse <-, -n> [a'drɛ·sə] *f* address
adressieren* [adrɛ·'siː·r·ən] *vt* to address (**an** +*akk* to)
adrett [ad'rɛt] **I.** *adj* smart **II.** *adv* smartly; **sie ist immer ~ gekleidet** she's always elegantly dressed
Adria <-> ['aːdria] *f* Adriatic [Sea]
Advent <-s, -e> [at·'vɛnt] *m* Advent [season]; ■**im** ~ during [the] Advent [season]; **erster ~** first Sunday of/in Advent
Advẹntskalender *m* Advent calendar
Advẹntskranz *m* Advent wreath
Advẹntszeit *f* Advent [season]
Adverb <-s, -ien> [at·'vɛrp, *pl* -'vɛrbi̯ən] *nt* adverb
Advokat(in) <-en, -en> [at·vo·'kaːt] *m(f)* ❶ ÖSTERR, SCHWEIZ (*Rechtsanwalt*) lawyer, attorney ❷ (*geh: Fürsprecher*) advocate
Advokatur <-, -en> [at·vo·ka·'tuːɐ̯] *f* SCHWEIZ ❶ (*Amt eines Advokaten*) legal profession ❷ (*Kanzlei*) lawyer's [*or* law] office
Aerobic <-s> [ɛ·'roː·bɪk] *nt kein pl* aerobics + *sing/pl vb*
Aerodynamik [ae·ro·dy·'naː·mɪk] *f* aerodynamics + *sing/pl vb*
aerodynamisch [ae·ro·dy·'naː·mɪʃ] **I.** *adj* aerodynamic **II.** *adv* aerodynamically
Affäre <-, -n> [a'fɛː·rə] *f* ❶ (*Angelegenheit*) business ❷ (*Liebesabenteuer*) [love] affair ❸ (*unangenehmer Vorfall*) affair; (*Skandal*) scandal ▶ WENDUNGEN: **sich** *akk* **aus der ~ ziehen** (*fam*) to wriggle one's way out of a sticky situation
Affe <-n, -n> ['afə] *m* ❶ (*Tier*) ape, monkey ❷ (*sl: blöder Kerl*) dope; **ein eingebildeter ~** (*fam*) a conceited jackass
Affekt <-[e]s, -e> [a'fɛkt] *m* affect; **im ~ handeln** to act in the heat of the moment
Affẹkthandlung *f* act committed in the heat of the moment
affektiert [afɛk·'tiːɐ̯t] (*geh*) **I.** *adj* affected **II.** *adv* affectedly
affengeil ['afn̩·'gail] *adj* (*sl*) sweet, awesome
Affenhitze ['afn̩·'hɪtsə] *f* (*fam*) scorching heat
Ạffenschande *f* (*fam*) **es ist eine ~** it's a sin
Ạffentempo *nt* (*fam*) breakneck speed; **in einem ~** at breakneck speed
Ạffentheater *nt* (*pej fam*) [**wegen etw** *gen*] **ein ~ machen** to make a real fuss [about sth]
Affiche <-, -n> [a'fiʃə] *f* SCHWEIZ (*Plakat*) poster
affig ['afɪç] (*fam*) **I.** *adj* (*pej*) affected **II.** *adv* (*pej*) affectedly
Affront <-s, -s> [a'frõː] *m* (*geh*) affront
Afghane, **Afghanin** <-n, -n> [af·'gaː·nə, af·'gaː·nɪn] *m*, *f* Afghan; *s. a.* **Deutsche(r)**
afghanisch [af·'gaː·nɪʃ] *adj* Afghan; *s. a.* **deutsch**
Afghanistan <-s> [af·'gaː·nɪ·staːn] *nt* Afghanistan; *s. a.* **Deutschland**
Afrika <-s> ['aːfri·ka] *nt* Africa
Afrikaner(in) <-s, -> [afri·'kaː·nɐ] *m(f)* African
afrikanisch [afri·'kaː·nɪʃ] *adj* African
Afroamerikaner(in) ['aːfro-] *m(f)* African-American
ạfroamerikanisch *adj* African-American
After <-s, -> ['af·tɐ] *m* (*geh*) anus
Aftershave^RR^ <-[s], -s> ['aːf·tɐ·ʃeːf] *nt* aftershave
AG <-, -s> [aː'geː] *f Abk von* **Aktiengesellschaft** corporation, joint stock company
Ägäis <-> [ɛ'gɛː·ɪs] *f* the Aegean [Sea]
Agave <-, -n> [a'gaː·və] *f* agave
Agent(in) <-en, -en> [a'gɛnt] *m(f)* ❶ (*Spion*) spy ❷ (*Generalvertreter*) agent
Agentur <-, -en> [agɛn·'tuːɐ̯] *f* agency
Agenturbericht *m*, **Agenturmeldung** *f* [news] agency report
Agglomeration <-, -en> [aglo·me·ra·'tsi̯oːn] *f* SCHWEIZ (*Ballungsraum*) metropolitan area
Aggregat <-[e]s, -e> [agre·'gaːt] *nt* unit; (*Stromaggregat*) power unit
Aggression <-, -en> [agrɛ·'si̯oːn] *f* aggression; **~en gegen jdn/etw empfinden** to feel aggressive toward sb/sth
aggressiv [agrɛ·'siːf] **I.** *adj* aggressive **II.** *adv* aggressively
Aggressivität <-> [agrɛ·sivi·'tɛːt] *f kein pl* aggressiveness
agieren* [a'giː·rən] *vi* (*geh*) to act
agil [a'giːl] *adj* (*geh*) agile
Agrarfläche *f* agrarian land
Agrarmarkt *m* agricultural market
Agrarpolitik *f* agricultural policy
Agrarwirtschaft *f* agricultural economy
Ägypten <-s> [ɛ'gʏp·tn̩] *nt* Egypt; *s. a.* **Deutschland**
Ägypter(in) <-s, -> [ɛ'gʏp·tɐ] *m(f)* Egyptian;

A

s. a. **Deutsche(r)**

ägyptisch [ɛ'gʏp·tɪʃ] *adj* Egyptian; *s. a.* **deutsch**

Aha-Erlebnis [a'haː-] *nt* PSYCH "aha[!]" experience

ahnden ['aːn·dn̩] *vt* (*geh*) to punish

ähneln ['ɛːnl̩n] *vt* to resemble, to look like; **du ähnelst meiner Frau** you remind me of my wife

ahnen ['aːnən] *vt* ❶ (*vermuten*) to suspect ❷ (*voraussehen*) to have a premonition of; **das kann/konnte ich doch nicht ~!** how can/could I know that?

Ahnenforschung *f* genealogy

ähnlich ['ɛːn·lɪç] **I.** *adj* similar **II.** *adv* similarly; ■**jdm ~ sehen** to look like sb

Ähnlichkeit <-, -en> *f* ❶ (*ähnliches Aussehen*) resemblance; ■**mit jdm/etw ~ haben** to resemble sb/sth ❷ (*Vergleichbarkeit*) similarity

ähnlich|sehenRR *vi irreg* (*fam: typisch sein für*) **das sieht ihm/ihr [ganz] ähnlich!** that's just like him/her *fam*

Ahnung <-, -en> *f* ❶ (*Vorgefühl*) premonition; **~en haben** to have premonitions ❷ (*Vermutung*) suspicion; **es ist eher so eine ~** it's more of a hunch *fam* ❸ (*Idee*) idea; **keine ~ haben** to have no idea; **keine blasse ~ haben** to not have the slightest idea; **hast du eine ~!** (*iron fam*) that's what you think!; **keine ~!** (*fam*) [I have] no idea!

ahnungslos **I.** *adj* ❶ (*nichts ahnend*) unsuspecting ❷ (*unwissend*) ignorant **II.** *adv* unsuspectingly

Ahorn <-s, -e> ['aːhɔrn] *m* maple [tree]

Ähre <-, -n> ['ɛːrə] *f* ❶ (*Samenstand*) ear ❷ (*Blütenstand*) spike

Aids <-> [eːts] *nt Akr von* **acquired immune deficiency syndrome** AIDS

Aidserreger *m* AIDS virus

aidsinfiziert *adj* infected with AIDS *pred*

aidskrank *adj* suffering from AIDS *pred*

Aidstest *m* AIDS test

Aidsvirus *nt* AIDS virus

Airbag <-s, -s> ['ɛːɐ̯·bɛk] *m* airbag

Airbus ['ɛːɐ̯·bʊs] *m* airbus

Ajatollah <-s, -s> [aja·'tɔ·la] *m* Ayatollah

Akademie <-, -n> [aka·de·'miː, *pl* -'miː·ən] *f* ❶ (*Fachhochschule*) college ❷ (*wissenschaftliche Vereinigung*) academy

Akademiker(in) <-s, -> [aka·'deː·mi·kɐ] *m(f)* (*Absolvent einer Universität*) college [*or* university] graduate; (*Gelehrte(r)*) academic

akademisch [aka·'deː·mɪʃ] **I.** *adj* academic **II.** *adv* **~ gebildet sein** to be college educated

akklimatisieren* [akli·ma·ti·'ziː·rən] *vr* ■**sich** *akk* **~** ❶ (*klimatisch*) to become acclimated ❷ (*sich einleben*) to get used to sth

Akklimatisierung <-, -en> *f* acclimatization

Akkord <-[e]s, -e> [a'kɔrt, *pl* a'kɔrdə] *m* piecework; ■**im ~ arbeiten** to be doing piecework

Akkordarbeit *f* piecework

Akkordeon <-s, -s> [a'kɔr·de·ɔn] *nt* accordion

Akku <-s, -s> ['aku] *m* (*fam*) *kurz für* **Akkumulator** rechargeable battery

akkurat [aku·'raːt] **I.** *adj* ❶ (*sorgfältig*) meticulous ❷ (*exakt*) accurate **II.** *adv* ❶ (*sorgfältig*) meticulously ❷ (*exakt*) accurately

Akkusativ <-s, -e> ['aku·za·tiːf] *m* accusative [case]

Akne <-, -n> ['aknə] *f* acne

akribisch [a'kriː·bɪʃ] (*geh*) **I.** *adj* meticulous **II.** *adv* meticulously

Akrobat(in) <-en, -en> [akro·'baːt] *m(f)* acrobat

akrobatisch *adj* acrobatic

Akronym <-s, -e> [akro·'nyːm] *nt* acronym

Akt¹ <-[e]s, -e> [akt] *m* ❶ (*Gemälde*) nude [painting] ❷ (*Handlung*) act; **ein ~ der Rache** an act of revenge ❸ (*Zeremonie*) ceremony ❹ *eines Theaterstücks* act

Akt² <-[e]s, -en> [akt] *m* ÖSTERR (*Akte*) file

Akte <-, -n> ['aktə] *f* file; **die ~ Borgfeld** the Borgfeld file ▶ WENDUNGEN: **etw zu den ~n legen** to lay sth to rest

Aktenkoffer *m* briefcase

Aktenordner *m* file

Aktenschrank *m* filing cabinet

Aktentasche *f* briefcase

Aktenzeichen *nt* file reference [number]

Aktfoto *nt* nude photograph

Aktie <-, -n> ['ak·tsi̯ə] *f* BÖRSE share, stock; **die ~n stehen gut/schlecht** (*einen guten/schlechten Kurs haben*) the stock is doing well/badly; (*fig: die Umstände sind vorteilhaft*) things are/aren't looking good

Aktienfonds *m* stock fund

Aktiengesellschaft *f* corporation, joint stock company

Aktienkurs *m* stock price

Aktienmarkt *m* stock market

Aktion <-, -en> [ak·'tsi̯oːn] *f* ❶ (*Handlung*) action; **in ~ sein** to be [constantly] in action; **in ~ treten** to come into action ❷ (*Sonderverkauf*) sale ❸ (*Militär-, Werbeaktion*) campaign

Aktionär(in) <-s, -e> [ak·tsi̯o·'nɛːɐ̯] *m(f)* FIN stockholder, shareholder

Aktionspreis *m* special offer

Aktionsradius *m* ❶ (*Reichweite*) radius of action ❷ (*Wirkungsbereich*) sphere of activity

aktiv [ak·'tiːf] **I.** *adj* active **II.** *adv* actively

Aktiv <-s, -e> ['ak·tiːf, *pl* 'ak·tiː·və] *nt pl selten* LING active [voice]

aktivieren* [ak·ti·'viː·rən] *vt* ❶ (*anspornen*) ■**jdn ~** to get sb moving ❷ (*aktiver gestalten*) to intensify ❸ (*anregen*) to stimulate ❹ (*in Gang setzen*) to activate

Aktivierung <-, -en> *f* activation

Aktivist(in) <-en, -en> [ak·ti·'vɪst] *m(f)* activist

Aktivität <-, -en> [ak·ti·vi·'tɛːt] *f* activity

Aktmalerei *f* nude painting

Aktmodell *nt* nude model

aktualisieren* *vt* to update

Aktualisierung <-, -en> [ak·tu̯a·li·ˈziː·rʊŋ] *f* update

Aktualität <-> [ak·tu̯a·li·ˈtɛːt] *f kein pl* up-to-dateness

aktuell [ak·ˈtu̯ɛl] *adj* ❶ (*gegenwärtig*) current; **~e Vorgänge** current events ❷ (*modern*) fashionable, in fashion *pred*

Ạktzeichnung *f* nude drawing

Akupressur <-, -en> [aku·prɛ·ˈsuːɐ̯] *f* acupressure

akupunktieren* [aku·pʊŋk·ˈtiː·rən] *vt, vi* to perform acupuncture [on sb]

Akupunktur <-, -en> [aku·pʊŋk·tuːɐ̯] *f* acupuncture

Akustik <-> [aˈkʊs·tɪk] *f kein pl* acoustics + *pl vb;* **der Raum hat eine gute ~** the room has good acoustics

akustisch [aˈkʊs·tɪʃ] **I.** *adj* acoustic **II.** *adv* acoustically; **ich habe dich rein ~ nicht verstanden** I just didn't hear what you said

akut [aˈkuːt] *adj* ❶ (*plötzlich auftretend*) acute ❷ (*dringend*) urgent

AKW <-s, -s> [aːkaːˈveː] *nt Abk von* **Atomkraftwerk**

Akzent <-[e]s, -e> [ak·ˈtsɛnt] *m* ❶ (*Aussprache*) accent ❷ LING (*Zeichen*) accent ❸ (*Betonung*) stress ❹ (*Schwerpunkt*) emphasis; **den ~ auf etw legen** to emphasize sth

akzẹntfrei *adj, adv* without an accent

akzentuieren* [ak·tsɛn·tu·ˈiː·rən] *vt* (*geh*) ❶ (*betonen*) to emphasize ❷ (*hervorheben*) to accentuate

akzeptabel [ak·tsɛp·ˈtaː·bl̩] *adj* acceptable (**für** +*akk* to)

Akzeptanz <-> [ak·tsɛp·ˈtants] *f* acceptance

akzeptieren* [ak·tsɛp·ˈtiː·rən] *vt* to accept

Alarm <-[e]s, -e> [aˈlarm] *m* ❶ (*Warnsignal*) alarm; ■ **~ schlagen** to sound the alarm ❷ (*Alarmzustand*) alert

Alạrmanlage *f* alarm [system]

Alạrmbereitschaft *f* standby; ■ **in ~ sein** to be on standby

alarmieren* [alar·ˈmiː·rən] *vt* ❶ (*zum Einsatz rufen*) to call ❷ (*aufschrecken*) to alarm

Alạrmsignal *nt* alarm signal

Alaska <-s> [aˈlas·ka] *nt* Alaska

Albaner(in) <-s, -> [al·ˈbaː·nɐ] *m(f)* Albanian; *s. a.* **Deutsche(r)**

Albanien <-s> [alˈbaːni̯ən] *nt* Albania; *s. a.* **Deutschland**

albanisch [al·ˈbaː·nɪʃ] *adj* Albanian; *s. a.* **deutsch**

Albatros <-, -se> [ˈalba·trɔs] *m* albatross

Alben *pl von* **Album**

albern[1] [ˈal·bɐn] **I.** *adj* ❶ (*kindisch*) childish; (*dumm*) silly ❷ (*unbedeutend*) trivial **II.** *adv* childishly

albern[2] [ˈal·bɐn] *vi* to fool around

Ạlbernheit <-, -en> *f* ❶ *kein pl* (*kindisches Wesen*) childishness ❷ (*Belanglosigkeit*) triviality ❸ (*kindische Handlung*) silliness

Albino <-s, -s> [al·ˈbiː·no] *m* albino

Ạlbtraum[RR] *m* nightmare

Album <-s, Alben> [ˈal·bʊm, *pl* ˈal·bən] *nt* album

Alchemie <-> [al·ça·ˈmiː], **Alchimie** <-> [al·çi·ˈmiː] *f kein pl bes* ÖSTERR alchemy

Alge <-, -n> [ˈal·gə] *f* alga

Ạlgenpest *f* ÖKOL plague of algae

Algerien <-s> [al·ˈgeː·ri̯·ən] *nt* Algeria; *s. a.* **Deutschland**

Alge̲rier(in) <-s, -> *m(f)* Algerian; *s. a.* **Deutsche(r)**

algerisch [al·ˈgeː·rɪʃ] *adj* Algerian; *s. a.* **deutsch**

alias [ˈaːli̯as] *adv* alias

Alibi <-s, -s> [ˈaːli·bi] *nt* ❶ (*bei Tatverdacht*) alibi ❷ (*Vorwand*) excuse

A̲libifunktion *f* use as an alibi; ■ [**nur**] **~ haben** to [only] serve as an alibi

Alien <-, -s> [ˈeɪː·lɪən] *m* alien

Alimente [ali·ˈmɛn·tə] *pl* alimony

Alkohol <-s, -e> [ˈal·ko·hoːl] *m* alcohol

Ạlkoholeinfluss[RR] *m* influence of alcohol

Ạlkoholfahne *f* (*fam*) boozy breath; ■ **eine ~ haben** to smell of alcohol

ạlkoholfrei *adj* nonalcoholic

Ạlkoholgehalt *m* alcohol[ic] content

Ạlkoholgenuss[RR] *m* alcohol consumption

ạlkoholhaltig *adj* alcoholic

Alkoholiker(in) <-s, -> [al·ko·ˈhoː·li·kɐ] *m(f)* alcoholic; **~ sein** to be an alcoholic

alkoholisch [al·ko·ˈhoː·lɪʃ] *adj* alcoholic

alkoholisiert [al·ko·ho·li·ˈziːɐ̯t] *adj* inebriated

Alkoholismus <-> [al·ko·ho·ˈlɪs·mʊs] *m kein pl* alcoholism

ạlkoholkrank *adj* alcoholic

Ạlkoholmissbrauch[RR] *m kein pl* alcohol abuse

Ạlkoholpegel *m* (*hum*), **Ạlkoholspiegel** *m* alcohol level in one's blood

ạlkoholsüchtig *adj* alcoholic

Ạlkoholsünder(in) *m(f)* (*fam*) [convicted] drunk driver *fam*

Ạlkoholtest *m* breath test *fam*

Ạlkoholverbot *nt* ban on alcohol

Ạlkoholvergiftung *f* alcohol poisoning

Ạlkoholwirkung *f* effect of alcohol

all [al] *pron indef* all; **~ ihr Geld** all her money

All <-s> [al] *nt kein pl* space

allabendlich [al·ˈʔaːbn̩t·lɪç] **I.** *adj* regular evening *attr;* **der ~e Spaziergang** the regular evening walk **II.** *adv* every evening

Allah <-s> [aˈlaː] *m kein pl* REL Allah

alldem [al·ˈdeːm] *pron* all that; **trotz ~** in spite of that

alle [ˈalə] *adj pred* (*fam*) ❶ (*aufgebraucht*) ■ **~ sein** to be all gone; **etw ~ machen** to finish sth off *sep* ❷ (*erschöpft*) ■ **~ sein** to be finished

alle(r, s) [ˈalə, -lɐ, -ləs] *pron indef* ❶ *attr* (*mit Singular*) all; **er hat ~s Geld verloren** he's lost all his money; [**ich wünsche dir**] **~s Gute** [I wish you] all the best ❷ (*mit Plural*) all, all the; **~e Anwesenden** all those present; **~ auf einmal** all at once ❸ *substantivisch* (*jeder*)

A

■ ~ all of you, everyone, all of them; **und damit sind ~ gemeint** and that means everyone; **ihr seid ~ beide Schlitzohren!** you're both a couple of sly little weasels!; **wir haben ~ kein Geld mehr** none of us have any money left; ■ **~ die[jenigen], die ...** everyone, who ... ④ *substantivisch* (*aller Dinge*) ■ **~s** everything; **das ist ~s** that's everything; **ist das schon ~s?** is that it? ⑤ *substantivisch* (*insgesamt*) ■ **~s** all [that]; **das ist doch ~s Unsinn** that's all nonsense ⑥ (*bei Zeit- und Maßangaben*) every; **~ fünf Minuten/Meter** every five minutes/meters ▶ WENDUNGEN: **~s in ~m** all in all; **[wohl] nicht mehr ~ haben** (*fam*) to have a screw loose; **vor ~m** above all, especially

Allee <-, -n> [a'le:, *pl* a'le:·ən] *f* avenue

allein [a'lain], **alleine** [a'lai·nə] (*fam*) **I.** *adj pred* ① (*ohne andere*) alone; **jdn ~ lassen** to leave sb alone; **sind Sie ~ oder in Begleitung?** are you by yourself or with someone? ② (*einsam*) lonely ③ (*ohne Hilfe*) on one's own **II.** *adv* ① (*bereits*) just; **~ der Schaden war schon schlimm genug** the damage alone was bad enough; **~ der Gedanke daran** the mere thought of it ② (*ausschließlich*) exclusively; **das ist ~ deine Entscheidung** it's your decision [and yours alone] ③ (*ohne Hilfe*) by oneself; **er kann sich schon ~ anziehen** he can already get himself dressed; **~ erziehend sein** to be a single parent; **von ~** by itself/oneself; **ich wäre auch von ~ darauf gekommen** I would have thought of it [by] myself ④ (*unbegleitet*) unaccompanied; (*isoliert*) alone

Alleinerbe, -erbin *m, f* sole heir *masc* [*or fem* heiress]

Alleinerziehende(r) *f(m) dekl wie adj* single parent

Alleingang <-gänge> *m* (*fam*) solo effort; **etw im ~ machen** to do sth on one's own

Alleinherrschaft *f* absolute power

Alleinherrscher(in) *m(f)* absolute ruler

alleinig [a'lai·nɪç] *adj attr* sole

allein|lassen[RR] *vt irreg* (*im Stich lassen*) **sich alleingelassen fühlen** to feel abandoned

Alleinsein <-s> *nt kein pl* solitariness; (*Einsamkeit*) loneliness

alleinstehend *adj* single

Alleinstehende(r) *f(m) dekl wie adj* unmarried person, single

Alleinunterhalter(in) <-s, -> *m(f)* solo entertainer

allemal ['alə·'ma:l] *adv* without any trouble; **was er kann, kann ich ~** whatever he can do, I can do too ▶ WENDUNGEN: **ein für ~** once and for all

allenfalls ['alən·'fals] *adv* at [the] most, at best

allerbeste(r, s) ['alɐ·'bɛstə, -tɐ, -təs] *adj* very best; **ich wünsche dir das A~** I wish you all the best

allerdings ['alɐ·'dɪŋs] *adv* ① (*jedoch*) although; **ich rufe dich an, ~ erst morgen** I'll call you, though not until tomorrow ② (*in der Tat*) definitely; **~!** indeed!, you bet! *fam;* **hast du mit ihm gesprochen? – ~!** did you speak to him? — I certainly did!

allererste(r, s) ['alɐ·'ʔe:ɐ̯stə, -tɐ, -təs] *adj* the [very] first; ■ **als A~r** the first; ■ **als A~s** first of all

allerfrühestens *adv* at the [very] earliest

Allergie <-, -n> [alɛr·'gi:, *pl* -'gi:·ən] *f* allergy (**gegen** +*akk* to); **~ auslösend** allergenic

Allergietest *m* allergy test

Allergiker(in) <-s, -> *m(f)* person with allergies

allergisch [a'lɛr·gɪʃ] **I.** *adj* allergic (**gegen** +*akk* to) **II.** *adv* **~ auf etw reagieren** MED to have an allergic reaction to sth; (*fig*) to get steamed up about sth

allerhand ['alɐ·'hant] *adj* (*fam*) all sorts of; (*ziemlich viel*) a great deal of; **ich habe noch ~ zu tun** I still have so much to do ▶ WENDUNGEN: **das ist ja ~!** that's a bit much!

Allerheiligen <-> ['alɐ·'hai·lɪ·gn̩] *nt* All Saints' Day

allerlei ['alɐ·'lai] *adj* ① *substantivisch* (*viel*) a lot; **ich muss noch ~ erledigen** I still have a lot to do ② *attr* (*viele Sorten*) all sorts of

allerletzte(r, s) ['alɐ·'lɛts·tə, -tɐ, -təs] *adj* [very] last ▶ WENDUNGEN: **das A~ sein** (*fam*) to be beyond the pale, to be the pits *fam;* **er ist das A~!** he's the worst [*or* such a loser]!

allerliebste(r, s) ['alɐ·'li:ps·tə, -tɐ, -təs] *adj* favorite; ■ **am ~n** most [of all]; **mir wäre es am ~n, wenn ...** I would prefer it if ...

allermeiste(r, s) ['alɐ·'mais·tə, -tɐ, -təs] *adj* most *generalization,* the most *comparison;* ■ **am ~n** most of all; **die ~n Leute** the vast majority of the people

allerneueste(r, s), allerneuste(r, s) *adj* latest; **auf dem ~n Stand** state-of-the-art; ■ **das A~** the latest

Allerseelen <-> ['alɐ·'ze:·lən] *nt* All Souls' Day

allerspätestens *adv* at the latest

allerwenigste(r, s) *adj* (*zählbar*) fewest; (*unzählbar*) least; **in den ~n Fällen** in only very few cases; **das ~ Geld** the least money; ■ **am ~n** the least

Allerwerteste ['alɐ·'ve:ɐ̯·təs·tə] *m dekl wie adj* (*hum*) behind

allesamt ['alə·'zamt] *adv* all [of them/you/us]; **die Politiker sind doch ~ korrupt** all politicians are corrupt

Allesfresser <-s, -> *m* BIOL omnivore

Alleskleber *m* all-purpose glue

allg. *adj Abk von* **allgemein**

Allgäu <-s> ['al·gɔy] *nt* ■ **das ~** the Allgäu (*German Alpine region*)

allgegenwärtig *adj* ubiquitous; REL omnipresent

allgemein ['al·gə·'main] **I.** *adj* general; **von ~em Interesse sein** to be of general interest; **zur ~en Überraschung** to everyone's surprise; **~e Vorschriften** universal regulations;

das ~e Wohl the common good ▶ WENDUNGEN: **im A~en** (*normalerweise*) generally speaking; (*insgesamt*) on the whole **II.** *adv* generally; **~ bekannt sein** to be common knowledge; **~ gültig** general; **~ verständlich** intelligible to everybody

Allgemeinbefinden <-s> ['al·gə·'main·bə·fɪn·dn̩] *nt kein pl* general health

Allgemeinbildung *f kein pl* general education

allgemeingültig *adj attr s.* **allgemein II**

Allgemeingültigkeit *f* [universal] validity

Allgemeinheit <-> ['al·gə·'main·hait] *f kein pl* ① (*Öffentlichkeit*) general public ② (*Undifferenziertheit*) generality

Allgemeinmedizin *f* general medicine

allgemeinverständlich *adj s.* **allgemein II**

Allgemeinwissen *nt* general knowledge

Allgemeinwohl *nt* welfare of the general public

Allgemeinzustand *m* general health

Allheilmittel *nt* cure-all

Allianz <-, -en> [a'li̯·ants] *f* alliance

Alligator <-s, -en> [ali·'ga:·to:ɐ̯, *pl* -'to:·rən] *m* alligator

Alliierte(r) [ali·'i:ɐ̯·tə -tɐ] *f(m) dekl wie adj* ally; ■**die ~n** the Allies

alljährlich ['al·'jɛ:ɐ̯·lɪç] **I.** *adj attr* annual **II.** *adv* annually

Allmacht ['al·maxt] *f kein pl* unlimited power; REL omnipotence

allmächtig [al·'mɛç·tɪç] *adj* all-powerful; REL omnipotent

allmählich [al·'mɛ:·lɪç] **I.** *adj attr* gradual **II.** *adv* ① (*langsam*) gradually; **~ geht er mir auf die Nerven** he's beginning to get on my nerves ② (*endlich*) **wir sollten jetzt ~ gehen** it's time we left

Allradantrieb *m* four-wheel drive

allseits ['al·zaits] *adv* everywhere

Alltag ['al·ta:k] *m* ① (*Werktag*) workday ② *kein pl* (*Realität*) everyday life

alltäglich ['al·tɛ:k·lɪç] *adj* ① *attr* (*tagtäglich*) daily, everyday ② (*gang und gäbe*) usual; **diese Probleme sind bei uns ~** these problems are part of everyday life here ③ (*gewöhnlich*) ordinary

alltags ['al·ta:ks] *adv* on workdays

Allüren [a'ly:·rən] *pl* ① (*geziertes Verhalten*) affectation ② (*Starallüren*) airs and graces

allwissend ['al·'vɪ·sn̩t] *adj* knowing it all; REL omniscient

allzu ['al·tsu:] *adv* **~ oft** only too often; **nicht ~ oft** not [all] too often; **~ sehr** too much; **~ viel** too much

Allzweckhalle *f* multipurpose hall

Allzweckreiniger *m* general-purpose cleaner

Alm <-, -en> [alm] *f* mountain pasture

Almosen <-s, -> ['al·mo:·zn̩] *nt* ① (*pej: geringer Betrag*) pittance ② (*geh: Spende*) alms

Alpen ['al·pn̩] *pl* ■**die ~** the Alps

AlpenpassRR *m* alpine pass

Alpenvorland [al·pn̩·'fo:ɐ̯·lant] *nt kein pl* foothills *pl* of the Alps

Alphabet <-[e]s, -e> [al·fa·'be:t] *nt* alphabet

alphabetisch [al·fa·'be:·tɪʃ] **I.** *adj* alphabetical **II.** *adv* alphabetically

alphabetisieren* [al·fa·beti·'zi:·rən] *vt* ① (*ordnen*) to put into alphabetical order ② ■**jdn ~** to teach sb to read and write

alphanumerisch [alfa·nu·'me:·rɪʃ] *adj* COMPUT alphanumeric

alpin [al·'pi:n] *adj* alpine

Alptraum ['alp·traum] *m* nightmare

als [als] *konj* ① (*zeitlich*) when, as; **ich kam, ~ er ging** I came as he was leaving; **gleich, ~ ...** as soon as ...; **damals, ~ ...** back in the days when ...; **gerade ~ ...** just when ... ② *nach Komparativ* than; **der Bericht ist interessanter ~ erwartet** the report is more interesting than would have been expected ③ (*wie*) as; **alles andere ~ ...** everything but ...; **anders ~ jd sein** to be different from sb; **niemand anders ~ ...** (*a. hum, iron*) none other than ... ④ ■**..., ~ habe/könne/sei/würde ...** as if; **..., als habe er es schon geahnt ...,** as if he had already known; **es sieht aus, ~ würde es bald schneien** it looks like snow ⑤ (*in der Eigenschaft*) as; **schon ~ Kind hatte er immer Albträume** even as a child, he had nightmares; **sich ~ wahr/falsch erweisen** to prove to be true/false

also ['alzo] *adv* (*folglich*) so, therefore *form*

Alsterwasser *nt* NORDD (*Bier mit Limonade*) *beer mixed with lemon-lime soda or ginger ale*

alt <älter, älteste> [alt] *adj* ① (*betagt*) old; ■**älter sein/werden** to be/get older; **ältere Mitbürger** senior citizens; **A~ und Jung** young and old alike ② (*ein bestimmtes Alter habend*) old; **wie ~ ist er? – er ist 18 Monate/21 Jahre ~** how old is he? — he's 18 months [old]/ 21 [years old] ③ (*aus früheren Zeiten*) ancient ▶ WENDUNGEN: **~ aussehen** (*fam: dumm dastehen*) to look like a complete fool

Altar <-s, Altäre> [al·'ta:ɐ̯, *pl* al·'tɛ:·rə] *m* altar

altbacken *adj* ① (*nicht mehr frisch*) stale ② (*altmodisch*) old-fashioned

Altbau <-bauten> *m* old building

Altbauwohnung *f* apartment in an old building

altbekannt ['alt·bə·'kant] *adj* well-known

altbewährt ['alt·bə·'vɛ:ɐ̯t] *adj* ① (*seit langem bewährt*) tried-and-true ② (*lange gepflegt*) well-established; **eine ~e Freundschaft** a long-standing friendship

Altbier *nt top-fermented dark beer*

Alte(r) ['altə, -tɐ] *f(m) dekl wie adj* (*fam*) ① (*alter Mann*) old geezer *sl;* (*alte Frau*) old lady ② (*Ehemann, Vater*) old man *sl;* (*Ehefrau, Mutter*) old lady; ■**meine ~n** (*Eltern*) my folks ③ (*Vorgesetzte(r)*) ■**der/die ~** the boss

alteingesessen *adj* long-established, old-established

Altenheim *nt s.* **Altersheim**

Altenhilfe *f* geriatric [*or* elderly] care

Altenpflege *f* geriatric [*or* elderly] care

A

Altenpfleger(in) *m(f)* geriatric nurse
Altenwohnheim *nt* nursing home, retirement home
Alter <-s, -> ['altɐ] *nt* ① (*Lebensalter*) age; **in jds** *dat* ~ at sb's age; **in jds ~ sein** to be the same age as sb; **er ist in meinem ~** he's my age; **mittleren ~s** middle-aged ② (*Bejahrtheit*) old age; **er hat keinen Respekt vor dem ~** he doesn't respect his elders; **im ~** in old age ▶ WENDUNGEN: **~ schützt vor Torheit nicht** (*prov*) there's no fool like an old fool *prov*
älter ['ɛltɐ] *adj komp von* **alt**
altern ['al·tɐn] *vi sein Mensch* to age
alternativ [al·tɛr·na·'ti:f] **I.** *adj* alternative **II.** *adv* **~ leben** to live an alternative lifestyle
Alternative <-, -n> [al·tɛr·na·'ti:·və] *f* alternative
Alternativreisende(r) *f(m) dekl wie adj* TOURIST alternative traveler
Altersarmut *f* poverty in old age
altersbedingt *adj* due to old age; **~e Kurzsichtigkeit** myopia caused by old age
Altersbeschwerden *pl* complaints *pl* of old age
Altersbezüge *pl* pension
Alterserscheinung *f* symptom of old age
Altersgenosse, -genossin *m, f* person of the same age, contemporary
Altersgrenze *f* age limit; (*für den Rentenbeginn*) retirement age
Altersgründe *pl* ■ **aus ~n** because of one's age
Altersgruppe *f* age group
Altersheim *nt* nursing [*or* retirement] home
Altersrente *f* social security
altersschwach *adj* ① (*gebrechlich*) frail ② (*fam: abgenutzt*) decrepit
Altersschwäche *f kein pl* (*Gebrechlichkeit*) infirmity
altersspezifisch *adj* age-related
Altersunterschied *m* age difference
Altersversorgung *f* pension; (*betrieblich*) retirement plan
altertümlich ['al·tɐ·ty:m·lɪç] *adj* ① (*veraltet*) dated ② (*archaisch*) ancient; LING archaic
Alterung <-, -en> *f* aging
älteste(r, s) ['ɛl·təs·tə, -tɐ, -təs] *adj superl von* **alt** oldest
Altgerät *nt* secondhand equipment
Altglas *nt* glass for recycling
Altglascontainer *m* glass recycling container [*or* bin]
altgriechisch *adj* classical Greek
althergebracht ['alt·'he:ɐ̯·gə·braxt] *adj* traditional
Altkleidersammlung *f* collection of used clothing
altklug ['alt·'klu:k] *adj* precocious
ältlich ['ɛlt·lɪç] *adj* oldish
Altmaterial *nt* waste material
Altmetall *nt* scrap metal
altmodisch I. *adj* old-fashioned; (*rückständig*) old-fangled **II.** *adv* **~ gekleidet** dressed in old-fashioned clothes; **~ eingerichtet** furnished in an old-fashioned style
Altöl *nt* used oil
Altpapier *nt* waste paper
Altpapiersammlung *f* paper recycling
Altschulden *pl* POL, ÖKON *public debt left behind by the former GDR*
Altstadt *f* old town center
Altstoff *m* waste material
Altstoffcontainer *m* waste container; (*für wiederverwertbare Stoffe*) recycling bin
Altwarenhändler(in) *m(f)* secondhand dealer
Altweiberfas(t)nacht *f* DIAL *part of the carnival celebrations: the last Thursday before Ash Wednesday when women assume control*
Altweibersommer [alt·'vaibɐ·zɔ·mɐ] *m* Indian summer
Alu ['a:lu] *nt kurz für* **Aluminium**
Alufelge *f* aluminum [wheel] rim
Alufolie *f* aluminum [*or* tin] foil
Aluminium <-s> [alu·'mi:·ni̯·ʊm] *nt kein pl* aluminum
Alzheimer <-s> ['alts·hai·mɐ] *m kein pl* (*fam*), **AlzheimerkrankheitRR** *f kein pl* Alzheimer's [disease]
am [am] ① = **an dem** *s.* **an** ② + *Superlativ* **ich fände es ~ besten, wenn ...** I think it would be best if ...; **es wäre mir ~ liebsten, wenn ...** I would prefer it if ...; **~ schnellsten/schönsten sein** to be [the] fastest/most beautiful ③ (*fam: beim*) **ich bin ~ Schreiben!** I'm writing!
Amateur(in) <-s, -e> [ama·'tø:ɐ̯] *m(f)* amateur
Amateurliga *f* amateur league
Amazonas <-> [ama·'tso:·nas] *m* Amazon
Ambiente <-> [am·'bi̯ɛn·tə] *nt kein pl* (*geh*) ambience
Ambition <-, -en> [am·bi·'tsi̯o:n] *f meist pl* ambition; **~en haben** to be ambitious
ambitioniert [am·bi·tsi̯o·'ni:rt] *adj* (*geh*) ambitious
ambulant [am·bu·'lant] **I.** *adj* **ein ~er Patient** an outpatient **II.** *adv* **jdn ~ behandeln** to treat sb as an outpatient
Ambulanz <-, -en> [am·bu·'lants] *f* ① (*im Krankenhaus*) outpatient department ② (*Unfallwagen*) ambulance
Ameise <-, -n> ['a:mai·zə] *f* ant
Ameisenbär *m* anteater
Ameisenhaufen *m* anthill
Amen <-s, -> ['a:mɛn] *nt* Amen
Amerika <-s> [a'me:·ri·ka] *nt* ① (*Kontinent*) America ② (*USA*) the USA, the United States, the States *fam*
Amerikaner(in) <-s, -> [ame·ri·'ka:·nɐ] *m(f)* American; *s. a.* **Deutsche(r)**
amerikanisch [ameri·'ka:·nɪʃ] *adj* American
amerikanisieren* [ameri·ka·ni·'zi:·rən] *vt* to Americanize
Amerikanismus <-, -men> [ameri·ka·'nɪs·mʊs] *m* LING Americanism
Ami <-s, -s> ['ami] *m* ① (*fam: US-Bürger*)

A

American, Yankee *fam* ② (*sl: US-Soldat*) GI
Amiland *nt kein pl* (*sl: USA*) America
Amme <-, -n> ['amə] *f* wet nurse
Ammenmärchen *nt* (*fam*) old wives' tale
Amnesie <-, -n> [am·ne·'ziː, *pl* -'ziː·ən] *f* amnesia
Amnestie <-, -n> [am·nɛs·'tiː, *pl* -'tiː·ən] *f* amnesty; **eine ~ verkünden** to declare amnesty
amnestieren* [am·nɛs·'tiː·rən] *vt* to grant amnesty to
Amok ['aːmɔk] *m* **~ laufen** to run amok
Amokläufer(in) *m(f)* madman *masc*, madwoman *fem*
amortisieren* [amɔr·ti·'ziː·rən] **I.** *vt* **eine Investition ~** to amortize an investment **II.** *vr* ■ **sich ~** to pay for itself
amourös [amu·'røːs] *adj* (*geh*) amorous
Ampel <-, -n> ['am·pl̩] *f* traffic light; **die ~ ist auf Rot gesprungen** the light turned red; **du hast eine rote ~ überfahren** you just ran a red light
Amphetamin <-s, -e> [am·fe·ta·'miːn] *nt* amphetamine
Amphibie <-, -n> [am·'fiː·bi̯ə, *pl* -bi·ən] *f* amphibian
Amphitheater [am·'fiː·teaː·tɐ] *nt* amphitheater
Ampulle <-, -n> [am·'pʊ·lə] *f* ampoule
Amputation <-, -en> [am·pu·ta·'tsi̯oːn] *f* amputation
amputieren* [am·pu·'tiː·rən] *vt, vi* to amputate
Amsel <-, -n> ['amzl̩] *f* blackbird
Amt <-[e]s, Ämter> [amt, *pl* 'ɛm·tɐ] *nt* ① (*Behörde*) office, department; **aufs ~ gehen** (*fam*) to go to the authorities; **Auswärtiges ~** State Department ② (*öffentliche Stellung*) post, position; (*ehrenamtliche Stellung*) office; **im ~ sein** to be in office; **ein ~ antreten** to take up one's post; **ein ~ innehaben** to hold an office
Ämterhäufung *f* holding of multiple positions
amtieren* [am'tiːrən] *vi* ① (*ein Amt innehaben*) to hold office (**als** as); ■ **~d** official ② (*fungieren*) ■ **als etw ~** to act as sth
amtlich I. *adj* official **II.** *adv* officially
Amtsantritt *m* assumption of office
Amtsdeutsch *nt* (*pej*) officialese *pej*
Amtseid *m* oath of office
Amtsenthebung <-, -en> *f*, **Amtsentsetzung** <-, -en> *f* SCHWEIZ dismissal, removal from office
Amtsgericht *nt* ≈ local [*or* district] court
Amtshandlung *f* official duty
Amtsmissbrauch[RR] *m* abuse of authority
Amtsperiode *f* term of office
Amtsrichter(in) *m(f)* ≈ local [*or* district] court judge
Amtssprache *f* official language
Amtszeit *f* term of office
Amulett <-[e]s, -e> [amu·'lɛt] *nt* amulet
amüsant [amy·'zant] *adj* amusing
amüsieren* [amy·'ziː·rən] **I.** *vr* ■ **sich** *akk* **~** to enjoy oneself; **amüsiert euch gut!** have a good time!; ■ **sich** *akk* **mit jdm ~** to have a good time with sb; ■ **sich** *akk* **über jdn/etw ~** to laugh at sb/sth **II.** *vt* ■ **jdn ~** to amuse sb
Amüsierviertel *nt* red light district
an [an] **I.** *präp* ① + *akk o dat* (*räumlich*) ■ **etw hängt ~ der Wand** sth is hanging on the wall; **sich** *akk* **~ den Tisch setzen** to sit down at the table; **am Tisch sitzen** to sit at the table; **~s Telefon gehen** to answer the telephone; **am Telefon sein** to be on the phone; **etw ~ die Tafel schreiben** to write sth on the board; **jdn ~ die Hand nehmen** to take sb by the hand; **Tür ~ Tür wohnen** to be next-door neighbors ② + *dat* (*zeitlich*) **am Freitag** on Friday; **am Morgen** in the morning; **~ jenem Morgen** that morning; **~ Weihnachten** at Christmas; (*25. Dezember*) on Christmas Day ③ + *dat* (*Eigenschaft*) **das Angenehme ~ etw** *dat* the pleasant thing about sth; **was ist ~ ihm so besonders?** what's so special about him? ④ + *dat* (*mit Hilfe von*) **jdn ~ der Stimme erkennen** to recognize sb by his/her voice; **~ Krücken gehen** to walk on crutches ⑤ SCHWEIZ (*auf*) on; (*bei*) at; (*in*) in; (*zu*) to; **das kam gestern am Fernsehen** it was on television yesterday ▶ WENDUNGEN: **~ [und für] sich** actually **II.** *adv* ① (*ungefähr*) ■ **~ die ...** approximately ... ② (*fam: angeschaltet*) on; *Licht a.* burning
Anabolikum <-s, -ka> [ana·'boː·li·kʊm] *nt* anabolic steroid
anachronistisch [ana·kro·'nɪs·tɪʃ] *adj* (*geh*) anachronistic
analog [ana·'loːk] *adj* ① (*entsprechend*) analogous ② COMPUT analog
Analogie <-, -n> [ana·lo·'giː, *pl* -'giː·ən] *f* analogy
Analphabet(in) <-en, -en> ['an·ʔal·fa·beːt] *m(f)* illiterate
Analphabetentum <-s> *nt kein pl*, **Analphabetismus** <-> [an·ʔal·fa·be·'tɪs·mʊs] *m kein pl* illiteracy
Analverkehr *m* anal sex
Analyse <-, -n> [ana·'lyː·zə] *f* analysis
analysieren* [ana·ly·'ziː·rən] *vt* to analyze
Ananas <-, - *o* -se> ['ana·nas] *f* pineapple
Anarchie <-, -n> [anar·'çiː, *pl* -'çiː·ən] *f* anarchy
Anarchismus <-> [anar·'çɪs·mʊs] *m kein pl* anarchism
Anarchist(in) <-en, -en> [anar·'çɪst] *m(f)* anarchist
anarchistisch *adj* anarchic
Anatomie <-, -n> [ana·to·'miː, *pl* -'miː·ən] *f* anatomy
anatomisch [ana·'toː·mɪʃ] **I.** *adj* anatomic **II.** *adv* anatomically
an|baggern *vt* (*sl*) to hit on
an|bahnen *vr* ■ **sich ~** to be in the making; **zwischen ihnen bahnt sich etwas an** there's sth going on there

A

an|bändeln ['an·bɛn·dl̩n] *vi* ■**mit jdm ~** to flirt with sb
Anbau¹ *m kein pl* AGR cultivation
Anbau² <-bauten> *m* (*Nebengebäude*) annex, addition
an|bauen *vt* ❶ *Gemüse* to grow ❷ *Gebäude* to build an extension [*or* addition] to
Anbaufläche *f* AGR ❶ (*zum Anbau geeignet*) land suitable for cultivation ❷ (*bebaut*) acreage
Anbaugebiet *nt* AGR arable land
an|beißen *irreg* **I.** *vi* to take the bait **II.** *vt* ■**etw ~** to take a bite of sth ▶WENDUNGEN: **zum A~** (*fam*) hot *sl*
an|bellen *vt* to bark at
an|beten *vt* ❶ REL to worship ❷ (*verehren*) to adore
Anbetracht *m* ■**in ~ einer S.** *gen* in view of
an|biedern ['an·biː·dɐn] *vr* (*pej*) ■**sich** *akk* **bei jdm ~** to curry favor with sb
an|bieten *irreg* **I.** *vt* to offer **II.** *vr* ■**sich** *akk* **~** ❶ (*sich zur Verfügung stellen*) to offer one's services; ■**sich ~ etw zu tun** to offer to do sth ❷ (*naheliegen*) to be just the right thing
Anbieter(in) <-s, -> *m(f)* supplier
an|binden *vt irreg* (*festbinden*) to tie (**an** +*akk* to)
Anblick *m* sight; **beim ersten ~** at first sight
an|blicken *vt* to look at
an|brechen *irreg* **I.** *vi sein* to begin; *Tag* to dawn; *Winter, Abend* to set in; *Dunkelheit, Nacht* to fall **II.** *vt haben* ❶ (*zu verbrauchen beginnen*) to open; **die Vorräte ~** to break into supplies ❷ (*teilweise brechen*) to chip
an|brennen *irreg vi sein* to burn; ■**etw ~ lassen** to let sth burn; **es riecht hier so angebrannt** something smells burned in here ▶WENDUNGEN: **nichts ~ lassen** (*fam*) to not hesitate
an|bringen *vt irreg* ❶ (*befestigen*) to affix, to stick to ❷ (*vorbringen*) to introduce
Anbruch *m kein pl* (*geh*) **bei ~ des Tages** at the break of day; **bei ~ der Dunkelheit** at dusk
an|brüllen *vt* to shout at
Andacht <-, -en> ['an·daxt] *f* prayer service
andächtig ['an·dɛç·tɪç] **I.** *adj* ❶ REL devout ❷ (*ehrfürchtig*) reverent; (*in Gedanken versunken*) rapt **II.** *adv* ❶ REL devoutly ❷ (*hum: ehrfürchtig*) reverently; (*inbrünstig*) raptly
an|dauern *vi* to continue; *Gespräche* to go on
andauernd **I.** *adj* continuous **II.** *adv* continuously
Anden ['an·dn̩] *pl* Andes *npl*
Andenken <-s, -> *nt* ❶ (*Souvenir*) souvenir ❷ (*Erinnerungsstück*) keepsake ❸ *kein pl* (*Erinnerung*) memory; **zum ~ an jdn** in memory of sb
andere(r, s) ['an·də·rə, -rɐ, -rəs] *pron indef* ❶ (*abweichend*) different, other; **das ist eine ~ Frage** that's another question; **das ~ Geschlecht** the opposite sex; **ein ~s Mal** another time ❷ (*weitere*) other; **haben Sie noch ~ Fragen?** do you have any more questions? ❸ *substantivisch* **es gibt noch ~, die warten!** there are others waiting!; ■**ein ~r/eine ~** someone else; **alle ~n** all [the] others; **wir ~n** the rest of us; **das T-Shirt ist schmutzig – hast du noch ein ~s** this T-shirt is dirty — do you have another one?; **das ist etwas ganz ~s!** that's something entirely different; **es bleibt uns nichts ~s übrig** there's nothing else we can do; **unter ~m ...** ... among other things
anderenfalls ['an·də·rən·fals] *adv* otherwise
anderenorts ['an·də·rən·ʔɔrts] *adv* (*geh*) elsewhere
andererseits ['an·də·rɐ·zaits] *adv* on the other hand
andermal ['an·dɐ·maːl] *adv* ■**ein ~** another time
ändern ['ɛn·dɐn] *vt, vr* ■[**sich** *akk*] **~** to change; **ich kann es nicht ~** I can't do anything about it; **daran kann man nichts ~** there's nothing you can do about it; **seine Meinung ~** to change one's mind; **es hat sich nichts geändert** nothing's changed
andernfalls ['an·dɐn·fals] *adv* otherwise
andernorts ['an·dɐn·ʔɔrts] *adv* (*geh*) elsewhere
anders ['an·dɐs] *adv* ❶ (*verschieden*) differently; ■**~ als ...** different from [*or* than] ...; **~ als sonst** different than usual; **es sich** *dat* **~ überlegen** to change one's mind; **~ denkend** dissenting ❷ (*sonst*) otherwise; **~ kann ich es mir nicht erklären** I can't think of another explanation; **jemand ~** somebody else; **niemand ~** nobody else; **es ging leider nicht ~** I'm afraid I couldn't do anything about it ▶WENDUNGEN: **nicht ~ können** (*fam*) to be unable to help it; **jdm wird ganz ~** sb feels dizzy
andersartig ['an·dɐs·ʔaː̯ɐ·tɪç] *adj* different
andersdenkend *adj attr* dissenting
Andersdenkende(r) *f(m) dekl wie adj* dissident
andersfarbig **I.** *adj* of a different color **II.** *adv* a different color; **~ lackiert** painted a different color
andersgläubig *adj* of a different faith
anders(he)rum ['an·dɐs·(hɛ)rʊm] **I.** *adv* the other way around **II.** *adj pred* (*fam: homosexuell*) gay
anderswo ['an·dɐs·voː] *adv* ❶ (*an einer anderen Stelle*) somewhere else ❷ (*an anderen Orten*) elsewhere
anderthalb ['an·dɐt·'halp] *adj* one and a half; **~ Stunden** an hour and a half
Änderung <-, -en> *f* change; **eine ~ an etw** *dat* **vornehmen** to change sth; **geringfügige ~en** slight alterations
Änderungsschneider(in) *m(f)* ≈ tailor *masc*, ≈ seamstress *fem*
Änderungsvorschlag *m* proposed change
Änderungswunsch *m* change request
anderweitig ['an·dɐ·vai·tɪç] **I.** *adj attr* other

II. *adv* ① (*mit anderen Dingen*) ~ **beschäftigt sein** to be otherwise busy ② (*bei anderen Leuten*) ~ **verpflichtet sein** to have other commitments ③ (*an einen anderen*) to somebody else ④ (*anders*) **etw ~ verwenden** to use sth in a different way

ạn|deuten *vt* ① (*erwähnen*) to indicate ② (*zu verstehen geben*) to imply

Ạndeutung *f* hint; **eine versteckte ~** an insinuation; **eine ~ machen** to imply

ạndeutungsweise *adv* ① (*indirekt*) as an indication of ② (*rudimentär*) as an intimation

Andorra <-s> [an·'dɔ·ra] *nt* Andorra; *s. a.* **Deutschland**

Andorraner(in) <-s, -> [an·dɔ·'raː·nɐ] *m(f)* Andorran; *s. a.* **Deutsche(r)**

andorranisch *adj* Andorran; *s. a.* **deutsch**

Ạndrang *m kein pl* rush

andre(r, s) ['an·drə, -drɐ, -drəs] *pron indef s.* **andere(r, s)**

ạn|drehen *vt* ① (*anstellen*) to turn on ② (*fam: verkaufen*) ■**jdm etw ~** to sell sb sth; ■**sich** *dat* **etw ~ lassen** to be sold sth

andrerseits ['an·drɐ·zaits] *adv s.* **andererseits**

ạn|drohen *vt* ■**jdm etw ~** to threaten sb with sth

ạn|ecken *vi sein* (*fam*) to shock

ạn|eignen *vr* ■**sich** *dat* **etw ~** ① (*an sich nehmen*) to take sth ② *Wissen* to learn sth

aneinander [an·ʔai·'nan·dɐ] *adv* to one another; **etw ~ finden** to see sth in each other; **~ vorbeireden** to be working at cross-purposes

aneinạnder|fügen *vt* ■**etw ~** to put sth together

aneinạnder|geraten* *vi irreg sein* to have a fight

aneinạnder|reihen *vt* ■**etw ~** to string sth together

aneinạnder|schmiegen *vr* ■**sich ~** to cuddle

aneinạnder|stellen *vt* ■**etw ~** to put sth next to each other, to put sth together

Anekdote <-, -n> [anɛk·'doː·tə] *f* anecdote

ạn|ekeln *vt* ■**jdn ~** to make sb sick; ■**von etw** *dat* **angeekelt sein** to be disgusted by sth

Anemone <-, -n> [ane·'moː·nə] *f* BOT anemone

ạnerkannt *adj* recognized

an|erkennen* ['an·ʔɛɐ̯·kɛ·nən] *vt irreg* ① (*offiziell akzeptieren*) to recognize (**als** *+akk* as); *Kind* to acknowledge; *Forderung* to accept ② (*würdigen*) to appreciate ③ (*gelten lassen*) to accept; *Meinung* to respect

ạnerkennend I. *adj* acknowledging; **ein ~er Blick** a look of acknowledg[e]ment **II.** *adv* in acknowledg[e]ment

ạnerkennenswert *adj* commendable

Ạnerkennung <-, -en> *f* ① (*offizielle Bestätigung*) recognition ② (*lobende Zustimmung*) praise; **~ finden** to gain recognition

ạn|erziehen* *vt irreg* ■**jdm etw ~** to teach sb sth; ■**anerzogen sein** to be acquired

ạn|fachen *vt* (*fig geh*) to arouse

ạn|fahren *irreg* **I.** *vi sein* to drive off; *Zug* to pull in **II.** *vt haben* ① (*beim Fahren streifen*) to hit ② (*schelten*) ■**jdn ~** to snap at sb ③ TRANSP to stop at; **einen Hafen ~** to pull in at a port

Ạnfahrt *f* trip [to]

Ạnfall *m* ① MED attack; **epileptischer ~** epileptic seizure ② (*Wutanfall*) fit [of rage]; **einen ~ kriegen** to throw a fit ③ (*Anwandlung*) ■**in einem ~ von etw** *dat* in a fit of sth

ạn|fallen *irreg* **I.** *vi sein* ① (*entstehen*) to arise ② *Kosten* to incur ③ (*sich anhäufen*) to accumulate; *Arbeit a.* to pile up **II.** *vt haben* (*angreifen*) to attack

ạnfällig *adj* to be prone (**für** *+akk* to); AUTO, TECH temperamental

Ạnfang <-[e]s, -fänge> *m* ① (*Beginn*) beginning, start; **den ~ machen** to start; **einen neuen ~ machen** to make a fresh start; **~ September/der Woche** at the beginning of September/the week; **der Täter war ca. ~ 40** the perpetrator was in his early 40s; **von ~ bis Ende** from start to finish; **am ~** (*zu Beginn*) in the beginning; (*anfänglich*) to begin with; **von ~ an** from the [very] start ② (*Ursprung*) origin[s] *usu pl* ▶ WENDUNGEN: **der ~ vom Ende** the beginning of the end; **aller ~ ist schwer** (*prov*) the first step is always the hardest

ạn|fangen *irreg* **I.** *vi, vt* to begin, to start **II.** *vt* (*machen*) **etw anders ~** to do sth differently; **jd kann mit etw** *dat/***jdm nichts ~** (*fam*) sth/sb is [of] no use to sb; **was soll ich damit ~?** what am I supposed to do with that?; **mit jdm ist nichts anzufangen** nothing can be done with sb; **nichts mit sich** *dat* **anzufangen wissen** to not know what to do with oneself

Ạnfänger(in) <-s, -> *m(f)* beginner; (*im Straßenverkehr*) student driver; **~ sein** to be a novice

Ạnfängerkurs *m* beginners' course

ạnfänglich I. *adj attr* initial *attr* **II.** *adv* initially

ạnfangs I. *adv* at first **II.** *präp* SCHWEIZ at the start of

Ạnfangsbuchstabe *m* initial, first letter

Ạnfangsschwierigkeiten *pl* initial difficulties *pl*

Ạnfangsstadium *nt* initial stage[s] *usu pl*

Ạnfangszeit *f* early stages *pl*

ạn|fassen I. *vt* ① (*berühren*) to touch ② (*behandeln*) to treat **II.** *vi* ■**mit ~** to lend a hand

ạn|fauchen *vt* ① *Katze* to spit [*or* hiss] at ② (*fig fam*) to snap at

ạn|fechten *vt irreg* to dispute; JUR to contest

ạn|fertigen *vt* to make

ạn|feuchten *vt* to moisten

ạn|feuern *vt* ① (*ermutigen*) to cheer on ② (*anzünden*) to light

ạn|flehen *vt* to beg (**um** *+akk* for)

ạn|fliegen *irreg vt* to fly to

Ạnflug *m* ① LUFT approach ② (*fig: Andeutung*) hint; (*Anfall*) fit

ạn|fordern *vt* (*die Zusendung erbitten*) to re-

A

quest; *Katalog* to order

Ạnforderung *f* ① *kein pl* (*das Anfordern*) request; *Katalog* ordering; ■**auf ~** [up]on request ② *meist pl* (*Anspruch*) demands; **~en [an jdn] stellen** to place demands [on sb]; **du stellst zu hohe ~en** you're too demanding

Ạnfrage *f* inquiry; ■**auf ~** [up]on request

ạn|fragen *vi* to ask

an|freunden ['an·frɔyn·dn̩] *vr* ① (*Freunde werden*) ■**sich ~** to become friends; ■**sich** *akk* **mit jdm ~** to make friends with sb ② (*sich gewöhnen*) ■**sich** *akk* **mit etw** *dat* **~** to get to like sth

ạn|fügen *vt* to add

ạn|fühlen *vr* **sich weich ~** to feel soft

ạn|führen *vt* ① (*vorangehen*) to lead ② (*zitieren*) to quote; *Beispiel, Grund* to give ③ (*benennen*) to name

Ạnführer(in) *m(f)* leader

Ạnführungsstrich *m,* **Ạnführungszeichen** *nt meist pl* quotation mark[s]

Ạngabe <-, -n> *f* ① *meist pl* (*Mitteilung*) details *pl;* **genauere ~n** further details; **~n zur Person** personal details; **~n machen** to give details (**über** +*akk* about, **zu** +*dat* about) ② *kein pl* (*Prahlerei*) bragging, boasting

ạn|gaffen *vt* (*pej*) to gape [*or* gawk] at

ạn|geben *irreg* **I.** *vt* ① (*nennen*) to give; **seinen Namen ~** to give one's name; **jdn als Zeugen ~** to cite sb as a witness ② (*behaupten*) to claim ③ (*anzeigen*) to indicate ④ (*bestimmen*) to set; *Takt* to give; **das Tempo ~** to set the pace **II.** *vi* (*prahlen*) to brag [*or* boast] (**mit** +*dat* about)

Ạngeber(in) <-s, -> *m(f)* showoff, poser

Angeberei <-, -en> [an·geː·bə·'rai] *f* (*fam*) boasting, bragging

ạngeberisch **I.** *adj* pretentious **II.** *adv* pretentiously

Ạngebetete(r) *f(m) dekl wie adj* (*hum*) beloved

angeblich ['an·geːp·lɪç] **I.** *adj attr* alleged **II.** *adv* allegedly; **er hat ~ nichts gewusst** supposedly, he didn't know anything about it

ạngeboren *adj* innate; MED congenital

Ạngebot *nt* ① (*das Anbieten*) offer ② *kein pl* (*Warenangebot*) variety of goods; **~ und Nachfrage** supply and demand ③ (*Sonderangebot*) special offer; **im ~** on sale

ạngebracht **I.** *adj* ① (*sinnvoll*) sensible ② (*angemessen*) suitable **II.** *pp von* **anbringen**

ạngegossen *adj* ►WENDUNGEN: **wie ~ sitzen** (*fam*) to fit like a glove

ạngegriffen **I.** *adj* frail; *Nerven* raw **II.** *adv* **~ aussehen** to look exhausted **III.** *pp von* **angreifen**

angeheitert ['an·gə·hai·tɐt] *adj* (*fam*) tipsy

ạn|gehen *irreg* **I.** *vi sein* ① (*sich einschalten, entzünden*) *Licht, Radio* to come on; *Feuer* to start ② (*bekämpfen*) ■**gegen etw ~** to fight against sth **II.** *vt* ① *haben o* SÜDD, ÖSTERR *sein* (*in Angriff nehmen*) to tackle ② *haben* (*betreffen*) to concern; **was geht mich das an?** what's that got to do with me?; **das geht dich nichts an!** (*fam*) that's none of your business!; **was mich angeht, ...** as far as I am concerned, ...

ạngehend *adj* prospective

ạn|gehören* *vi* to belong to

Ạngehörige(r) *f(m) dekl wie adj* ① (*Familienangehörige*) relative; **die nächsten ~n** the next of kin ② (*Mitglied*) member

Ạngeklagte(r) *f(m) dekl wie adj* accused

Angel <-, -n> ['aŋl̩] *f* rod and reel, fishing pole

Ạngelegenheit <-, -en> *f* matter; **sich** *akk* **um seine eigenen ~en kümmern** to mind one's own business

Ạngelhaken *m* fishhook

angeln ['aŋ|n] **I.** *vi* ① (*Fische fangen*) to fish ② (*zu greifen versuchen*) to fish [around] (**nach** +*dat* for) **II.** *vt* to catch; **sich** *dat* **einen Mann ~** (*fam*) to catch oneself a man

Ạngelpunkt *m* crucial point

Ạngelrute *f* fishing rod

Angelsachse, -sächsin <-n, -n> ['aŋl̩·zak·sə] *m, f* Anglo-Saxon

ạngemessen **I.** *adj* ① (*entsprechend*) fair; ■**einer S.** *dat* **~ sein** to be proportionate to sth ② (*passend*) appropriate **II.** *adv* ① (*entsprechend*) proportionately ② (*passend*) appropriately

ạngenehm **I.** *adj* pleasant; *Nachricht* good; *Wetter* agreeable ►WENDUNGEN: **das A~e mit dem <u>Nützlichen</u> verbinden** to mix business with pleasure **II.** *adv* pleasantly

ạngepasst^RR^, **ạngepaßt**^ALT^ **I.** *adj, adv* conformist **II.** *pp von* **annehmen**

ạngeregt **I.** *adj* animated **II.** *adv* animatedly; **sie diskutierten ~** they had an animated discussion **III.** *pp von* **anregen**

ạngesagt **I.** *adj* (*fam*) ■**~ sein** (*in Mode*) to be in; (*geplant*) to be scheduled **II.** *pp von* **ansagen**

ạngeschlagen **I.** *adj* weak[ened]; *Gesundheit* poor **II.** *pp von* **anschlagen**

ạngesehen **I.** *adj* respected; *Firma* of good standing **II.** *pp von* **ansehen**

Ạngesicht *nt* (*geh*) **von ~ zu ~** face to face

ạngesichts *präp* +*gen* in the face of

ạngespannt **I.** *adj* tense; *Situation* critical **II.** *adv* **~ wirken** to seem tense; **etw ~ verfolgen** to follow sth closely **III.** *pp von* **anspannen**

ạngestammt *adj* (*geerbt*) hereditary; (*überkommen*) traditional

ạngestaubt *adj* outdated; **~e Ansichten** antiquated views

Ạngestellte(r) *f(m) dekl wie adj* employee

ạngestrengt **I.** *adj* ① *Gesicht* strained ② (*intensiv*) hard **II.** *adv* (*konzentriert*) intently; **~ diskutieren** to discuss intensively **III.** *pp von* **anstrengen**

ạngetan **I.** *adj* ■**von jdm/etw ~ sein** to be taken with sb/sth; ■**es jdm ~ haben** to appeal to sb **II.** *pp von* **antun**

ạngetrunken **I.** *adj* tipsy, buzzed *fam* **II.** *pp von* **antrinken**

A

angewandt I. *adj attr* applied II. *pp von* **anwenden**
angewiesen I. *adj* dependent (**auf** +*akk* [up]-on) II. *pp von* **anweisen**
an|gewöhnen* *vt* ■ **sich** *dat* **etw** ~ to get into the habit of [doing] sth
Angewohnheit *f* habit
angewurzelt *adj* ▶ WENDUNGEN: **wie ~ dastehen** to stand rooted to the spot
an|gleichen *irreg* I. *vt* to bring into line II. *vr* ■ **sich** *akk* ~ to adapt oneself (+*dat* to)
Angleichung *f* adaptation
Angler(in) <-s, -> ['aŋ·lɐ] *m(f)* angler
an|gliedern *vt* to incorporate (+*dat* into)
anglikanisch [aŋ·gli·'kaː·nɪʃ] *adj* Anglican; **die ~e Kirche** the Church of England
Anglizismus <-, -men> [aŋ·gli·'tsɪs·mʊs] *m* LING Anglicism
an|glotzen *vt* (*fam*) to stare at
an|graben *irreg vt* ■ **jdn** ~ (*sl*) to come on to sb
angreifbar *adj* contestable
an|greifen *irreg* I. *vt, vi* (*attackieren*) to attack II. *vt* ❶ (*schädigen*) to damage ❷ (*zersetzen*) to corrode
Angreifer(in) <-s, -> *m(f)* ❶ MIL attacker ❷ *meist pl* SPORT attacking player
an|grenzen *vi* to border (**an** +*akk* on)
angrenzend *adj attr* bordering; **die ~en Bauplätze** the adjoining building sites
Angriff *m* ❶ MIL attack; **zum ~ übergehen** to go on the offensive ❷ SPORT (*Vorgehen*) attack; (*die Angriffsspieler*) forwards *pl*; **im ~ spielen** to play on offense ▶ WENDUNGEN: **etw in ~ nehmen** to tackle sth
Angriffsfläche *f* target
Angriffslust *f kein pl* aggressiveness
angriffslustig *adj* aggressive
Angriffspunkt *m* target
an|grinsen *vt* to grin at
angst [aŋst] *adj* ■ **jdm ist/wird ~ [und bange]** sb is/becomes afraid
Angst <-, Ängste> [aŋst, *pl* 'ɛŋs·tə] *f* fear (**vor** +*dat* of); **~ bekommen** (*fam*) to get scared; **~ [vor etw** *dat*] **haben** to be afraid [of sth]; **~ um etw haben** to be worried about sth; **jdm ~ machen** to frighten sb
Angsthase *m* (*fam*) scaredy-cat
ängstigen ['ɛŋs·tɪ·gn̩] I. *vt* ❶ (*in Furcht versetzen*) to frighten ❷ (*beunruhigen*) to worry II. *vr* ■ **sich** *akk* ~ ❶ (*Furcht haben*) to be afraid ❷ (*sich sorgen*) to worry
ängstlich ['ɛŋst·lɪç] *adj* ❶ (*verängstigt*) frightened, timid ❷ (*besorgt*) worried
Ängstlichkeit <-> *f kein pl* ❶ (*Furchtsamkeit*) fear ❷ (*Besorgtheit*) anxiety
Angstmacher(in) *m(f)* (*pej*) scaremonger
Angstmacherei <-> ['aŋst·ma·xə·rai] *f kein pl* (*pej*) scaremongering
Angstschweiß *m* cold sweat
an|gucken *vt* (*fam*) to look at
an|gurten *vr* ■ **sich** *akk* ~ to fasten one's seat belt, to buckle up
an|haben *vt irreg* ❶ *Kleidung* to have on ❷ (*Schaden zufügen*) **jdm nichts ~ können** to be unable to harm sb
an|halten *irreg* I. *vi* ❶ (*stoppen*) to stop ❷ (*fortdauern*) to continue II. *vt* ❶ (*stoppen*) to bring to a stop ❷ (*anleiten*) ■ **jdn [zu etw** *dat*] ~ to teach sb [to do sth]
anhaltend *adj* continuous; *Lärm* incessant; *Schmerz* persistent; **die ~e Hitzewelle** the continuing heat wave
Anhalter(in) <-s, -> ['an·hal·tɐ] *m(f)* hitchhiker; **per ~ fahren** to hitchhike
Anhaltspunkt *m* clue
anhand [an·'hant] *präp* +*gen* on the basis of
Anhang <-[e]s, -hänge> *m* ❶ (*Nachtrag*) appendix ❷ *kein pl* (*Angehörige*) [close] family, dependants ❸ *kein pl* (*Gefolgschaft*) followers ❹ COMPUT attachment
an|hängen *vt* ❶ (*ankuppeln*) to couple (**an** +*akk* to) ❷ (*hinzufügen*) to add ❸ (*fam: anlasten*) ■ **jdm etw** ~ to blame sth on sb ❹ COMPUT to attach
Anhänger <-s, -> *m* ❶ AUTO trailer ❷ (*Schmuckstück*) pendant ❸ (*Gepäckanhänger*) label
Anhänger(in) <-s, -> *m(f)* ❶ SPORT fan ❷ (*Gefolgsmann*) follower, supporter
Anhängerschaft <-> *f kein pl* ❶ (*Gefolgsleute*) followers *pl*, supporters *pl* ❷ SPORT fans *pl*
anhänglich ['an·hɛŋ·lɪç] *adj* (*sehr an jdm hängend*) devoted; (*sehr zutraulich*) friendly; **die Kinder sind sehr anhänglich** the children won't leave their mother's side
Anhänglichkeit <-> *f kein pl* ❶ (*anhängliche Art*) devotion ❷ (*Zutraulichkeit*) trusting nature
an|hauchen *vt* to breathe on
an|hauen *vt irreg* (*sl*) to accost; **jdn um 5 Euro ~** to hit sb up for 5 euros
an|häufen *vt, vr* ■ **[sich]** ~ ❶ (*aufhäufen*) to pile up ❷ (*fig: ansammeln*) to accumulate
Anhäufung <-, -en> *f* ❶ (*das Aufhäufen*) piling up ❷ (*fig: das Ansammeln*) accumulation
an|heben *irreg vt* ❶ (*hochheben*) to lift [up *sep*] ❷ (*erhöhen*) to increase
Anhebung <-, -en> *f* increase; **die ~ der Preise** the increase in prices
an|heften *vt* ❶ (*daran heften*) to attach ❷ (*anstecken*) to pin on *sep*
Anhieb *m* **auf ~** (*fam*) right away; **das kann ich nicht auf ~ sagen** I can't say off the top of my head
an|himmeln *vt* (*fam*) to idolize
Anhöhe *f* high ground
an|hören I. *vt* ❶ (*zuhören*) ■ **[sich** *dat*] **etw** ~ to listen to sth ❷ (*mithören*) **ein Geheimnis [mit] ~** to overhear a secret ❸ (*anmerken*) ■ **jdm etw** ~ to hear sth in sb['s voice]; **dass er Däne ist, hört man ihm nicht an** you can't tell from his accent that he's Danish II. *vr* (*klingen*) ■ **sich** ~ to sound
Animateur(in) <-s, -e> [anima·'tøːɐ̯] *m(f)*

host *masc*, hostess *fem*
animieren* [ani·ˈmiː·rən] *vt* to encourage
Anis <-[es], -e> [aˈniːs] *m* ① (*Pflanze*) anise ② (*Gewürz*) aniseed
an|kämpfen *vi* to fight (**gegen** +*akk* against); **sie kämpfte gegen ihre Tränen an** she fought back her tears
Ankauf *m* buy
an|kaufen *vt* to buy
an|keksen [ˈan·keːk·sən] *vt* ■**jdn** ~ (*sl*) to get on sb's nerves
Anker <-s, -> [ˈaŋ·kɐ] *m* anchor; **vor ~ gehen** to drop anchor [somewhere]; **den ~ lichten** to weigh anchor; **vor ~ liegen** to lie at anchor
ankern [ˈaŋ·kɐn] *vi* ① (*Anker werfen*) to drop anchor ② (*vor Anker liegen*) to lie at anchor
Ankerplatz *m* anchorage
an|ketten *vt* to chain up (**an** +*akk* to)
Anklage <-, -n> *f* ① (*Beschuldigung*) accusation ② *kein pl* JUR charge; **gegen jdn ~ [wegen etw** *gen*] **erheben** to charge sb [with sth]; **unter ~ stehen** to be charged
Anklagebank <-bänke> *f pl selten* JUR dock; **auf der ~ sitzen** to be in the dock
an|klagen *vt* ① JUR to charge ② (*beschuldigen*) to accuse ③ (*anprangern*) to denounce
Anklang *m* ▶ WENDUNGEN: **~ finden** to meet with approval
an|kleben *vt* to stick on
Ankleideraum *m* dressing room
an|klicken *vt* COMPUT to click on
an|klopfen *vi* to knock
an|knabbern *vt* (*fam*) to gnaw [away] at
an|knipsen *vt* (*fam*) to flick on *fam*
an|knüpfen I. *vt* to tie (**an** +*akk* to) **II.** *vi* (*wieder aufnehmen*) ■**an etw ~** to resume sth; **an ein altes Argument ~** to take up an old argument
an|kommen *irreg* **I.** *vi sein* ① (*eintreffen*) to arrive; **seid ihr gut angekommen?** did you arrive safely? ② (*gelangen zu*) ■**bei etw** *dat* ~ to reach sth ③ (*fam: Anklang finden*) ■**[bei jdm] ~** *Sache* to go over well [with sb]; *Person* to make an impression [on sb] ④ (*sich durchsetzen*) ■**gegen jdn/etw ~** to get the better of sb/sth **II.** *vi impers sein* ① (*wichtig sein*) ■**auf etw ~** sth matters; ■**es kommt darauf an, dass ...** what matters is that ... ② (*abhängen von*) ■**auf jdn/etw ~** to be dependent on sb/sth; **das kommt darauf an** it depends
Ankömmling <-s, -e> *m* newcomer
an|kotzen *vt* (*derb: anwidern*) to make sick
an|kreiden *vt* ■**jdm etw ~** to hold sth against sb
an|kreuzen *vt* to mark with a cross
an|kündigen *vt* to announce
Ankündigung *f* announcement
Ankunft <-, -künfte> [ˈan·kʊnft, *pl* -kʏnf·tə] *f* arrival
Ankunftshalle *f* arrival[s] lounge
an|kurbeln *vt* ÖKON to boost
an|lächeln *vt* to smile at
an|lachen *vr* (*fam*) ■**sich** *dat* **jdn ~** to flirt with sb
Anlage <-, -n> *f* ① (*Fabrikanlage*) plant ② (*Grünanlage*) park ③ (*Sportanlage*) facility ④ (*Stereoanlage*) sound system ⑤ **sanitäre ~n** sanitary facilities ⑥ (*Kapitalanlage*) investment ⑦ *meist pl* (*Veranlagung*) disposition
an|langen *vt* SÜDD (*anfassen*) to touch
Anlass[RR] <-es, -lässe>, **Anlaß**[ALT] <-sses, -lässe> [ˈan·las, *pl* ˈan·lɛsə] *m* ① (*Grund*) reason; **es besteht kein ~ zu etw** *dat*/, **etw zu tun** there are no grounds for sth/to do sth; **[jdm] ~ zu etw** *dat* **geben** to give [sb] grounds for sth; **keinen ~ haben, etw zu tun** to have no grounds to do sth; **etw zum ~ nehmen, etw zu tun** to use sth as an opportunity to do sth ② (*Gelegenheit*) occasion; **dem ~ entsprechend** to fit the occasion
an|lassen *irreg vt* ① AUTO to start [up *sep*] ② (*fam: anbehalten*) to keep on *sep* ③ (*fam: in Betrieb lassen*) to leave on *sep*
Anlasser <-s, -> *m* AUTO starter [motor]
anlässlich[RR], **anläßlich**[ALT] [ˈan·lɛs·lɪç] *präp* +*gen* on the occasion of
an|lasten *vt* ■**jdm etw ~** to blame sb for sth
Anlauf <-[e]s, -läufe> *m* ① SPORT running start; **~ nehmen** to take a running start; **mit ~** with a running start ② (*fig: Versuch*) attempt
an|laufen *irreg* **I.** *vi sein* ① (*beginnen*) to begin ② *Brillengläser, Glasscheibe* to steam [*or* fog] up; *Metall* to tarnish ③ **vor Wut rot ~** to turn purple with rage **II.** *vt haben* **den Hafen ~** to put into port
Anlaufschwierigkeit *f meist pl* initial difficulty
Anlaufstelle *f* refuge
an|legen I. *vt* ① (*erstellen*) to compile; *Liste* to draw up ② *Garten, Park* to lay out ③ *Vorrat* to stock up ④ *Geld* to invest **II.** *vi Schiff* to berth **III.** *vr* ■**sich** *akk* **mit jdm ~** to pick a fight with sb
Anlegeplatz *m* dock
an|lehnen I. *vt* ① (*daran lehnen*) to lean [against] ② *Tür* to leave ajar **II.** *vr* ■**sich ~ an** to lean against; *Text* to follow
Anlehnung *f* **in ~ an jdn/etw** following sb/sth
anlehnungsbedürftig *adj* in need of affection *pred*
an|leiern *vt* (*fam*) to get going
an|leiten *vt* to instruct
Anleitung *f* ① (*Gebrauchsanleitung*) instructions *pl* ② (*das Anleiten*) instruction; **unter jds** *dat* ~ under sb's guidance
an|lernen *vt* to train
an|lesen *irreg* **I.** *vt* (*den Anfang von etw lesen*) to start to read **II.** *vr* (*sich durch Lesen aneignen*) ■**sich** *dat* **etw ~** to learn sth by reading
an|liefern *vt* to deliver
an|liegen *vi irreg* (*fam: zu erledigen sein*) to be on the agenda; ■**was liegt an?** (*fam*) what's up?
Anliegen <-s, -> *nt* request
Anlieger <-s, -> *m* ① (*Anwohner*) resident;

~ **frei** residents only ❷ (*Anrainer*) neighbor

ạn|locken *vt* to attract; *Tier* to lure

ạn|lügen *vt irreg* to lie to

Ạnmache <-> *f kein pl* (*sl: Annäherungsversuch*) come-on

ạn|machen *vt* ❶ (*einschalten*) to turn on ❷ (*anzünden*) to light ❸ *Salat* to dress ❹ (*sl: aufreizen*) to turn on *sep* ❺ (*sl: aufreißen wollen*) to pick up *sep* ❻ (*sl: rüde ansprechen*) to go off on sb

an|mailen ['an·meɪ·lən] *vt* to e-mail

ạn|malen **I.** *vt* to paint; **mit Buntstiften** ~ to color in with pencils **II.** *vr* (*fam: sich schminken*) ■ **sich** *akk* ~ to paint one's face

ạn|maßen *vr* ■ **sich** *dat* **etw** ~ to claim sth [unduly] for oneself; **was maßen Sie sich an!** what right do you [think you] have!

anmaßend ['an·maː·sn̩t] *adj* arrogant

Ạnmaßung <-, -en> *f* arrogance

Ạnmeldegebühr *f* registration fee

ạn|melden **I.** *vt* ❶ **jdn zu einem Kurs** ~ to enroll sb in a course [*or* class]; **ein Kind in der Schule** ~ to enroll a child at a school ❷ (*ankündigen*) to announce ❸ **ein Fernsehgerät/Radio** ~ to get a TV/radio reception license; **ein Auto** ~ to register a car; **das Telefon** ~ to get phone service ❹ (*geltend machen*) to assert; **Bedenken** ~ to make [one's] misgivings known **II.** *vr* ■ **sich** *akk* ~ ❶ (*sich ankündigen*) to give notice of a visit (**bei** +*dat* to) ❷ (*sich eintragen lassen*) to apply (**zu** +*dat* for) ❸ (*bei einem Umzug*) to register one's change of address with the authorities

Ạnmeldung <-, -en> *f* ❶ (*Ankündigung*) [advance] notice [of a visit]; **ohne** ~ without an appointment ❷ SCH enrollment ❸ (*Registrierung*) registration ❹ (*Anmelderaum*) reception

ạn|merken *vt* ❶ (*bemerken*) to notice; **er ließ sich nichts** ~ he didn't let it show ❷ (*eine Bemerkung machen*) to add ❸ (*notieren*) to make a note of

Ạnmerkung <-, -en> *f* ❶ (*Erläuterung*) note ❷ (*Fußnote*) footnote ❸ (*Kommentar*) comment

ạn|motzen *vt* (*fam*) ■ **jdn** ~ to bite sb's head off

Anmut <-> ['an·muːt] *f kein pl* (*geh*) ❶ (*Grazie*) grace[fulness] ❷ (*liebliche Schönheit*) beauty

ạnmutig *adj* (*geh*) ❶ (*graziös*) graceful ❷ (*hübsch anzusehen*) beautiful

ạn|nähen *vt* to sew on

ạn|nähern **I.** *vr* ■ **sich** [**einander**] ~ to come closer [to one another] **II.** *vt* ■ **aneinander** ~ to bring into line with each other

ạnnähernd **I.** *adj* approximate **II.** *adv* approximately

Ạnnäherung <-, -en> *f* convergence

Ạnnäherungsversuch *m* advance[s] *esp pl;* ~**e machen** to make advances

ạnnäherungsweise *adv* approximately; ■ **nicht** ~ nowhere near

Annahme <-, -n> ['an·naː·mə] *f* ❶ (*Vermutung*) assumption; **von einer ~ ausgehen** to proceed on the assumption; **in der ~, dass ...** on the assumption that ... ❷ (*das Annehmen*) acceptance

ạnnehmbar **I.** *adj* ❶ (*akzeptabel*) acceptable ❷ (*nicht übel*) reasonable **II.** *adv* reasonably

ạn|nehmen *irreg* **I.** *vt* ❶ (*entgegennehmen, akzeptieren*) to accept ❷ (*übernehmen*) *Job, Auftrag* to take [on] ❸ (*vermuten, voraussetzen*) to assume; ■ **angenommen, das stimmt ...** assuming that's right ... ❹ (*sich zulegen*) to adopt ❺ (*zulassen*) *Patienten, Schüler* to take on ❻ (*fam: adoptieren*) to adopt **II.** *vr* ❶ (*sich kümmern*) ■ **sich jds** *gen* ~ to look after sb ❷ (*erledigen*) ■ **sich einer S.** *gen* ~ to take care of sth

Ạnnehmlichkeit <-, -en> *f meist pl* convenience

annektieren* [anɛk·'tiː·rən] *vt* to annex

Anno, **anno** ['ano] *adv* ÖSTERR in the year ▶ WENDUNGEN: **von** ~ **dazumal** (*fam*) from long ago

Annonce <-, -n> [a'nõː·sə] *f* advertisement, [want] ad

annoncieren* [anõ·'siː·rən] *vi* to advertise

annullieren* [anʊ·'liː·rən] *vt* JUR to annul

an|öden ['an·'øːdn̩] *vt* (*fam*) to bore stiff

anomal [ano·'maːl] *adj* abnormal

Anomalie <-, -n> [ano·ma·'liː, *pl* -'liːən] *f* ❶ (*Missbildung*) abnormality ❷ (*Unregelmäßigkeit*) anomaly

anonym [ano·'nyːm] **I.** *adj* anonymous; ~ **bleiben** to remain anonymous **II.** *adv* anonymously

anonymisieren* [ano·ny·mi·'ziː·rən] *vt* to make anonymous

Anonymität <-> [ano·ny·mi·'tɛːt] *f kein pl* anonymity

Anorak <-s, -s> ['ano·rak] *m* anorak, parka

ạn|ordnen *vt* ❶ (*festsetzen*) to order ❷ (*ordnen*) to arrange (**nach** +*dat* according to)

Ạnordnung <-, -en> *f* ❶ (*Verfügung*) order; **auf ~ seines Arztes** on [his] doctor's orders ❷ (*systematische Ordnung*) order

anormal ['anɔr·maːl] *adj* abnormal

ạn|packen **I.** *vt* ❶ (*anfassen*) to touch ❷ (*beginnen*) to tackle; **packen wir's an!** let's get started! **II.** *vi* (*mithelfen*) ■ [**mit**] ~ to lend a hand

ạn|passen **I.** *vt* ❶ (*adaptieren*) to adapt (**an** +*akk* to) ❷ (*entsprechend verändern*) ■ **etw einer S.** *dat* ~ to adjust sth to sth **II.** *vr* ❶ (*sich darauf einstellen*) ■ **sich** ~ to adjust ❷ (*sich angleichen*) ■ **sich jdm/etw** ~ to fit in with sb/sth; (*gesellschaftlich*) to conform to sth

Ạnpassung <-, -en> *f* ❶ (*Abstimmung*) adaptation (**an** +*akk* to); **mangelnde** ~ maladaptation ❷ (*Angleichung*) conformity *no art* (**an** +*akk* to)

ạnpassungsfähig *adj* adaptable

Ạnpassungsfähigkeit *f* adaptability

Ạnpassungsschwierigkeiten *pl* difficulty in

adapting

ạn|peilen *vt* (*fam*) ① (*ansteuern wollen*) to head for ② (*anvisieren*) to set one's sights on

ạn|pfeifen *irreg vt* **das Spiel** ~ to blow the whistle [to start the game]

Ạnpfiff *m* ① SPORT ~ **[des Spiels]** whistle [to start the game]; FBALL *a.* kickoff ② (*fam: Rüffel*) chewing-out

ạn|pflanzen *vt* (*setzen*) to plant; (*anbauen*) to grow

ạn|pflaumen *vt* (*fam*) ■ **jdn** ~ to make fun of sb

ạn|pirschen *vr* ■ **sich** *akk* **[an ein Tier]** ~ to stalk [an animal]; ■ **sich** *fam* **[an jdn]** ~ *akk* to creep up [on sb]

ạn|pöbeln *vt* (*fam*) ■ **jdn** ~ to get snotty with sb

an|prangern ['an·praŋɐn] *vt* to denounce

ạn|preisen *vt irreg* to extol

Ạnprobe *f* fitting

ạn|probieren* *vt* to try on *sep*

ạn|pumpen *vt* (*fam*) ■ **jdn** ~ to pump sb for cash *sl;* **jdn um 100 Euro** ~ to hit sb up for 100 euros *sl*

ạn|quatschen *vt* (*fam*) to speak to; (*anbaggern*) to hit on

Ạnrainerstaat *m* neighboring country

ạn|rechnen *vt* ① (*gutschreiben*) to take into consideration; **die 2000 Euro werden auf die Gesamtsumme angerechnet** the 2000 euros will be deducted from the total ② (*in Rechnung stellen*) ■ **jdm etw** ~ to charge sb with sth ③ (*bewerten*) ■ **jdm etw als Fehler** ~ to count sth as a mistake; (*fig*) to consider sth as a fault on sb's part; **dass er ihr geholfen hat, rechne ich ihm hoch an** I think very highly of him for having helped her

Ạnrecht *nt* ■ **ein** ~ **auf etw haben** to have a right to sth

Ạnrede *f* form of address

ạn|reden I. *vt* **jdn** ~ to address sb **II.** *vi* ■ **gegen jdn** ~ to argue against sb

ạn|regen I. *vt* ① (*ermuntern*) ■ **jdn [zu etw** *dat*] ~ to encourage sb [to do sth] ② (*vorschlagen*) to suggest ③ (*stimulieren*) to stimulate; **den Appetit** ~ to whet the appetite **II.** *vi* (*beleben*) to be a stimulant

ạnregend *adj* ① (*stimulierend*) stimulating ② (*sexuell stimulierend*) sexually arousing

Ạnregung *f* ① (*Vorschlag*) idea; **auf jds** ~ at sb's suggestion ② (*Impuls*) stimulus ③ *kein pl* (*Stimulierung*) stimulation

Ạnreise *f* ① (*Anfahrt*) trip [here/there] ② (*Ankunft*) arrival

ạn|reisen *vi sein* ① (*ein Ziel anfahren*) to travel [to a destination] ② (*eintreffen*) to arrive

Ạnreiz *m* incentive

ạn|rempeln *vt* to bump into

ạn|rennen *vi irreg sein* ■ **gegen etw** ~ to storm sth

Ạnrichte <-, -n> *f* sideboard

ạn|richten *vt* ① (*zubereiten*) to prepare ② (*fam: anstellen*) **Unfug** ~ to be up to no good *fam;* **was hast du da wieder angerichtet!** what have you done now! ③ *Schaden, Unheil* to cause

anrüchig ['an·rʏ·çɪç] *adj* indecent

Ạnruf *m* [phone] call

Ạnrufbeantworter <-s, -> *m* answering machine

ạn|rufen *irreg vt, vi* to call [on the telephone], to phone; ■ **angerufen werden** to get a [phone] call

Ạnrufer(in) <-s, -> *m(f)* caller

Ạnrufweiterschaltung *f* call forwarding

ạn|rühren *vt* ① (*anfassen*) to touch; **rühr mich ja nicht an!** don't you touch me! ② *meist verneint* (*konsumieren*) ■ **etw nicht** ~ to not touch sth ③ (*zubereiten*) to mix; *Soße* to blend

ans [ans] = **an das** *s.* **an**

Ạnsage *f* announcement

ạn|sagen I. *vt* to announce **II.** *vr* ■ **sich** *akk* ~ to announce a visit

Ansager(in) <-s, -> ['an·zaː·gɐ] *m(f)* RADIO announcer

ạn|sammeln I. *vt* to accumulate; *Vorräte* to build up **II.** *vr* ■ **sich** ~ *Staub* to collect; *Krimskrams, Müll* to accumulate

Ạnsammlung *f* ① *von Menschen* crowd ② *von Dingen* accumulation

ansässig ['an·zɛ·sɪç] *adj* resident; **in einer Stadt** ~ **sein** to reside in a city

Ạnsatzpunkt *m* starting point

ạnsatzweise *adv* basically

ạn|saufen *vr irreg* (*sl*) ■ **sich** *dat* **einen [Rausch]** ~ to get plastered [*or* hammered]

ạn|schaffen I. *vt* (*kaufen*) to buy; ■ **sich** *dat* **etw** ~ to buy oneself sth **II.** *vi* (*sl*) ~ **[gehen]** to hook *pej fam*

Ạnschaffung <-, -en> *f* purchase; **eine** ~ **machen** to make a purchase

ạn|schalten *vt* to switch on

ạn|schauen I. *vt* to look at; *Film* to watch **II.** *vr* **sich** *dat* **etw [genauer]** ~ to take a [closer] look at sth

ạnschaulich I. *adj* illustrative **II.** *adv* vividly

Ạnschauung <-, -en> *f* view; **eine** ~ **teilen** to share a view

Ạnschauungsmaterial *nt* visual aids *pl*

Ạnschein *m* appearance; **den** ~ **erwecken, als [ob]** ... to give the impression that ...; **den** ~ **haben, als [ob]** ... to seem that ...; **allem** ~ **nach** to all appearances

ạnscheinend *adv* apparently

ạn|scheißen *vt irreg* (*sl*) ① (*zurechtweisen*) to chew out ② (*betrügen*) to screw [over]

ạn|schieben *vt irreg Fahrzeug* to push

ạn|schießen *irreg* **I.** *vt* (*durch Schuss verletzen*) to shoot and wound **II.** *vi* ■ **angeschossen kommen** (*fam*) to come shooting along

Ạnschiss[RR] <-es, -e>, **Ạnschiß**[ALT] <-sses, -sse> *m* (*sl*) chewing out

Ạnschlag *m* ① (*Attentat*) attempted assassination; **einen** ~ **auf jdn/etw verüben** to make an attack on sb/sth; **einen** ~ **auf jdn vorha-**

ben (*hum fam*) to have a request for sb ❷ (*Plakat*) placard

Anschlagbrett *nt* bulletin board

an|schlagen *irreg* **I.** *vt haben* ❶ *Aushang, Plakat* to put up *sep* ❷ (*Splitter abschlagen*) to chip; (*Sprung, Riss verursachen*) to crack ❸ ÖSTERR (*anzapfen*) **ein Fass ~** to tap a barrel **II.** *vi* ❶ *sein* (*anprallen*) ■ **mit etw** *dat* **~** to knock sth *sep* (**an** +*dat* on) ❷ *haben Hund* to bark ❸ *haben* (*wirken*) to have an effect

an|schleichen *vr irreg* ■ **sich an jdn/etw ~** to creep up on sb/up to sth

an|schleppen *vt* to drag along

an|schließen *irreg* **I.** *vt* ❶ TECH to connect (**an** +*akk* to) ❷ (*befestigen*) *Fahrrad* to lock [up] ❸ (*hinzufügen*) to add **II.** *vr* ❶ (*sich zugesellen*) ■ **sich** *akk* **jdm ~** to join sb ❷ (*beipflichten*) ■ **sich** *akk* **jdm/etw ~** to fall in with sb/sth; **dem schließe ich mich an** I think I'd go along with that

anschließend **I.** *adj* following; **die ~e Diskussion** the ensuing discussion **II.** *adv* afterward

Anschluss^RR^ *m* ❶ TELEK connection; **der ~ ist gestört** there's a disturbance in the line ❷ TECH connecting ❸ **im ~ an etw** after sth ❹ *kein pl* (*Kontakt*) contact; **~ finden** to make friends; **~ suchen** to try to make friends ❺ BAHN, LUFT (*Verbindung*) connection; **den ~ verpassen** to miss one's connecting train/flight

an|schmiegen *vr* ■ **sich** *akk* [**an jdn/etw**] **~** to cuddle up [to sb/sth]; *Katze, Hund* to nestle [up to sb/into sth]

anschmiegsam *adj* ❶ (*anlehnungsbedürftig*) affectionate ❷ (*weich*) soft

an|schnallen *vr* ■ **sich** *akk* **~** to fasten one's seat belt, to buckle up

Anschnallpflicht *f kein pl* mandatory seat belt law

an|schnauzen *vt* (*fam*) to yell at

an|schneiden *vt irreg* ❶ *Brot, Fleisch* to cut ❷ *Thema* to touch on

an|schrauben *vt* to screw (**an** +*akk* to)

an|schreiben *irreg* **I.** *vt* ❶ (*an eine Tafel*) to write (**an** +*akk* on) ❷ ■ **jdn ~** to write to sb **II.** *vi* (*fam*) ■ **~ lassen** to buy on credit

an|schreien *vt irreg* to shout at

Anschrift *f* address

an|schuldigen *vt* ■ **jdn** [**einer S.** *gen*] **~** to accuse sb [of sth]

Anschuldigung <-, -en> *f* accusation

an|schwärzen *vt* (*fam*) ■ **jdn ~** ❶ (*schlechtmachen*) to blacken sb's name ❷ (*denunzieren*) to denounce sb

an|schweigen *vr irreg* ■ **sich ~** to say nothing to each other

an|schwellen *vi irreg sein* ❶ *Körperteil* to swell [up] ❷ *Lärm, Beifall* to rise; *Fluss a.* to swell

an|schwemmen *vt* to wash up

an|schwindeln *vt* (*fam*) to tell lies

an|sehen *irreg vt* ❶ (*ins Gesicht sehen*) to look at; **jdn böse ~** to give sb an angry look ❷ *Film* to watch; *Theaterstück, Fußballspiel* to see ❸ (*betrachten*) to take a look at; **etw genauer ~** to take a closer look at sth; **hübsch anzusehen sein** to be pretty to look at ❹ (*ablesen können*) **jdm sein Alter nicht ~** sb doesn't look his/her age; **ihre Erleichterung war ihr deutlich anzusehen** her relief was obvious ❺ (*hinnehmen*) ■ **etw** [**mit**] **~** to stand by and watch sth; **das kann ich nicht länger mit ~** I can't stand it anymore

Ansehen <-s> *nt kein pl* reputation; **an ~ verlieren** to lose standing

ansehnlich *adj* ❶ (*beträchtlich*) considerable; **eine ~e Leistung** an impressive performance ❷ (*stattlich*) good-looking

an|setzen **I.** *vt* ❶ (*anfügen*) to attach (**an** +*akk* to) ❷ (*daran setzen*) to place in position; *Trinkgefäß* to raise to one's lips; **wo muss ich den Wagenheber ~?** where should I put the jack? ❸ (*veranschlagen*) to estimate ❹ (*auf jdn hetzen*) ■ **jdn auf jdn/etw ~** to sic [*or* set] sb on sb/sth **II.** *vi* ❶ (*beginnen*) to start; **zum Überholen ~** to begin to pass ❷ (*dick werden*) to put on weight

Ansicht <-, -en> *f* view, opinion; **in etw** *dat* **geteilter ~ sein** to have a different view of sth; **ich bin ganz Ihrer ~** I agree with you completely; **der ~ sein, dass ...** to be of the opinion that ...; **meiner ~ nach** in my opinion

Ansichtskarte *f* [picture] postcard

Ansichtssache *f* [**reine**] **~ sein** to be [purely] a matter of opinion

an|siedeln **I.** *vt* (*ansässig machen*) to settle; *Tierart* to introduce **II.** *vr* ■ **sich ~** (*sich niederlassen*) to settle

Ansiedlung *f* ❶ (*Siedlung*) settlement ❷ (*das Ansiedeln*) introduction ❸ (*Etablierung*) establishment

ansonsten [an·ˈzɔns·tn̩] *adv* otherwise

an|spannen *vt* ❶ (*zusammenziehen*) to tighten; *Muskeln* to tense [up] ❷ (*überanstrengen*) to strain; **jdn** [**zu sehr**] **~** to [over]tax sb

Anspannung *f* strain; (*körperlich*) effort

an|spielen *vi* (*andeuten*) to allude (**auf** +*akk* to); (*böse*) to insinuate; **worauf willst du ~?** what are you driving at?

Anspielung <-, -en> *f* allusion (**auf** +*akk* to); (*böse*) insinuation

an|spitzen *vt* ❶ (*spitz machen*) to sharpen ❷ (*fam: antreiben*) to egg on

Ansporn <-[e]s> *m kein pl* incentive; **innerer ~** motivation

an|spornen *vt* to spur on (**zu** +*dat* to); *Spieler* to cheer on

Ansprache *f* speech; **eine ~ halten** to make a speech

ansprechbar *adj pred* ❶ (*zur Verfügung stehend*) available ❷ (*bei Bewusstsein*) responsive

an|sprechen *irreg* **I.** *vt* ❶ (*anreden*) to speak to ❷ **jdn** [**mit Peter/mit seinem Namen**] **~** to address sb [as Peter/by his name] ❸ (*meinen*) to concern ❹ (*erwähnen*) to mention ❺ (*gefal-

A

len) ■ **jdn ~** to appeal to sb **II.** *vi* (*reagieren*) to respond (**auf** +*akk* to)

ansprechend *adj* appealing; *Umgebung* pleasant

Ansprechpartner(in) *m(f)* contact [person]

an|springen *irreg vi sein* ❶ *Motor* to start ❷ (*fam: reagieren*) ■ **auf etw ~** to jump at sth

Anspruch *m* ❶ (*Recht*) claim (**auf** +*akk* to); **~ auf etw erheben** to make a claim for sth; **~ auf etw haben** *akk* to be entitled to sth ❷ (*Anforderung*) demand; **den Ansprüchen [voll] gerecht werden** to [fully] meet the requirements; **Ansprüche stellen** to be very demanding ▸ WENDUNGEN: **etw in ~ nehmen** to claim sth; **jds Hilfe in ~ nehmen** to accept help from sb

anspruchslos *adj* ❶ (*keine Ansprüche habend*) modest ❷ (*trivial*) trivial ❸ (*pflegeleicht*) undemanding

Anspruchslosigkeit <-> *f kein pl* ❶ (*anspruchsloses Wesen*) modesty ❷ (*Trivialität*) triviality ❸ (*Pflegeleichtigkeit*) undemanding nature

anspruchsvoll *adj* ❶ (*besondere Anforderungen habend*) demanding ❷ (*geistige Ansprüche stellend*) demanding; *Lesestoff, Film a.* highbrow; *Geschmack* discriminating ❸ (*qualitativ hochwertig*) high-quality

an|spucken *vt* to spit at

an|stacheln *vt* to drive (**zu** +*dat* to)

Anstalt <-, -en> ['an·ʃtalt] *f* institute; **öffentliche ~** public institution

Anstand *m kein pl* decency; **keinen ~ haben** to have no sense of decency

anständig I. *adj* ❶ (*gesittet*) decent ❷ (*ehrbar*) respectable ❸ (*fam: ordentlich*) proper **II.** *adv* ❶ (*gesittet*) decently; **sich** *akk* **~ benehmen** to behave oneself ❷ (*fam: ausgiebig*) properly; **~ essen/ausschlafen** to get a decent meal/a good night's sleep

anständigerweise *adv* out of decency

Anständigkeit <-> *f kein pl* ❶ (*Ehrbarkeit*) respectability ❷ (*Sittsamkeit*) decency

Anstandsbesuch *m* courtesy call

anstandshalber *adv* out of politeness

anstandslos *adv* without difficulty

an|starren *vt* to stare at

anstatt [an·'ʃtat] **I.** *präp* +*gen* instead of **II.** *konj* ■ **~ etw zu tun** instead of doing sth

an|stauen I. *vt* to dam up *sep* **II.** *vr* ■ **sich ~** to accumulate; *Blut* to congest

an|stechen *vt irreg* ❶ KOCHK to pierce ❷ *Fass* to tap

an|stecken I. *vt* ❶ (*befestigen*) to pin on *sep* ❷ *Zigarette, Kerze* to light [up] ❸ *Gebäude* to set on fire ❹ (*infizieren*) to infect (**mit** +*dat* with); **ich möchte dich nicht ~** I don't want to give you my cold **II.** *vr* (*sich infizieren*) ■ **sich** *akk* **[bei jdm] ~** to catch sth [from sb]; **sich** +*akk* **leicht/schnell ~** to get sick easily **III.** *vi* (*fig: sich übertragen*) to be contagious

ansteckend *adj* ❶ MED infectious; (*durch Berührung*) contagious ❷ (*fig: sich leicht übertragend*) contagious

Ansteckung <-, -en> *f pl selten* infection

Ansteckungsgefahr *f* risk of infection

an|stehen *vi irreg haben o* SÜDD *sein* ❶ (*Schlange stehen*) to line up (**nach** +*dat* for) ❷ (*zu erledigen sein*) **steht bei dir heute etwas an?** are you planning on doing anything today?; **~de Fragen** questions on the agenda

an|steigen *vi irreg sein* ❶ (*sich erhöhen*) to go up (**auf** +*akk* to, **um** +*akk* by) ❷ (*steiler werden*) to ascend; **stark/steil ~** to ascend steeply

anstelle [an·'ʃtɛ·lə] *präp* +*gen* instead of

an|stellen I. *vt* ❶ (*einschalten*) to turn on ❷ (*beschäftigen*) to employ ❸ (*durchführen*) **Betrachtungen/Vermutungen [über etw] ~** to make observations/assumptions [about sth]; **Nachforschungen [über etw] ~** to conduct inquiries [into sth] ❹ (*fam: bewerkstelligen*) to manage; **etw geschickt ~** to pull sth off ❺ (*fam: anrichten*) **Blödsinn ~** to be up to no good; **was hast du da wieder angestellt?** what have you done now? *fam* **II.** *vr* ■ **sich** *akk* **~** ❶ (*Schlange stehen*) to line up; **sich hinten ~** to get in the back of a line ❷ (*fam: sich verhalten*) to act; **sich dumm ~** to play the fool ❸ (*wehleidig sein*) to make a fuss; **stell dich nicht [so] an!** don't make such a fuss!

Anstellung *f* job, position

Anstieg <-[e]s> ['an·ʃtiːk] *m kein pl* (*Zunahme*) rise

an|stiften *vt* ❶ (*anzetteln*) to instigate ❷ (*veranlassen*) **jdn zu einem Verbrechen ~** to incite sb to commit a crime; ■ **jdn [dazu] ~, etw zu tun** to incite sb to do sth

Anstifter(in) <-s, -> *m(f)* instigator

an|stimmen *vt* ❶ *Lied* to begin singing ❷ **ein Geschrei ~** to start screaming; **ein Gelächter ~** to burst out laughing

Anstoß *m* ❶ (*Ansporn*) impetus (**zu** +*dat* for); **den ~ zu etw** *dat* **bekommen** to be encouraged to do sth; **jdm den ~ geben, etw zu tun** to encourage sb to do sth ❷ (*geh: Ärgernis*) **~ erregen** to be annoying; **an etw** *dat* **~ nehmen** to take offense at sth ❸ SPORT start of the game; (*Billard*) break; ([*am.*] *Fußball*) kickoff; (*Eishockey*) face-off ❹ SCHWEIZ (*Angrenzung*) ■ **~ an etw** border to sth

an|stoßen *irreg* **I.** *vi* ❶ *sein* **mit dem Kopf an etw** *akk o dat* **~** to bump one's head on sth ❷ *haben* **auf jdn/etw ~** to drink to sb/sth; **lasst uns ~!** let's drink to it/that! **II.** *vt haben* ❶ (*leicht stoßen*) to bump ❷ (*in Gang setzen*) to set in motion **III.** *vr haben* **sich** *dat* **den Kopf/Arm ~** to bang one's head/arm

anstößig I. *adj* offensive **II.** *adv* offensively

an|strahlen *vt* (*strahlend ansehen*) to beam at

an|streben *vt* to strive for; SCH, UNI to work towards

an|streichen *vt irreg* ❶ (*mit Farbe bestreichen*) to paint; **etw neu/frisch ~** to give sth a new/fresh coat of paint ❷ (*markieren*) to mark; **etw rot ~** to mark sth [in] red

A

Anstreicher(in) <-s, -> *m(f)* [house] painter
an|strengen I. *vr* ■ **sich** *akk* ~ ❶ (*sich intensiv einsetzen*) to work hard (**bei** +*dat* at, **für** +*akk* for); **sich mehr** ~ to make a greater effort ❷ (*sich besondere Mühe geben*) to try hard **II.** *vt* ❶ (*strapazieren*) ■ **jdn** ~ to tire sb out ❷ (*intensiv beanspruchen*) to strain; *Geist, Muskeln* to exert
anstrengend *adj* strenuous; (*geistig*) taxing; (*körperlich*) exhausting; **das ist ~ für die Augen** it's a strain on the eyes
Anstrengung <-, -en> *f* ❶ (*Kraftaufwand*) exertion ❷ (*Bemühung*) effort; **mit letzter** ~ with one last effort
Anstrich *m* ❶ *kein pl* (*das Anstreichen*) painting ❷ (*Farbüberzug*) coat [of paint]
Ansturm *m* (*Andrang*) rush (**auf** +*akk* on)
Antarktis <-> [ant·ˈʔark·tɪs] *f* Antarctic
antarktisch [ant·ˈʔark·tɪʃ] *adj* Antarctic *attr*
an|tasten *vt* ❶ **jds Ehre/Würde** ~ to offend sb's honor/dignity; **jds Privileg/Recht** ~ to encroach [up]on sb's privilege/right ❷ **Vorräte/Ersparnisse** ~ to dip into supplies/savings
Anteil [ˈan·tail] *m* ❶ (*Teil*) share (**an** +*dat* of); ~ **an einem Werk** contribution to a work; **der ~ an Asbest** the proportion of asbestos ❷ (*geh: Mitgefühl*) sympathy (**an** +*dat* for) ❸ (*Beteiligung*) interest (**an** +*dat* in); ~ **an etw** *dat* **haben** to take part in sth; ~ **an etw** *dat* **nehmen** to show an interest in sth
anteilig, anteilmäßig *adj* proportionate
Anteilnahme <-> [ˈan·tail·naː·mə] *f kein pl* (*Beileid*) sympathy
Antenne <-, -n> [an·ˈtɛ·nə] *f* antenna
antiautoritär [an·ti·ʔau·to·ri·ˈtɛːɐ̯] *adj* anti[-]authoritarian
Antibabypille [an·ti·ˈbeː·bi·pɪ·lə] *f* (*fam*) the [contraceptive] pill
antibakteriell I. *adj* antibacterial **II.** *adv* antibacterially; ~ **wirken** to kill germs
Antibiotikum <-s, -biotika> [an·ti·ˈbi̯oː·ti·kʊm, *pl* -ˈbi̯oː·tika] *nt* antibiotic
Antiblockiersystem [an·ti·blɔ·ˈkiːɐ̯-] *nt* antilock [braking] system, ABS
Antidepressivum <-s, -va> [an·ti·de·prɛ·ˈsiː·vʊm, *pl* -va] *nt* antidepressant
Antifaltencreme *f* anti-wrinkle cream
Antifaschismus [an·ti·fa·ˈʃɪs·mʊs] *m* antifascism
Antifaschist(in) [an·ti·fa·ˈʃɪst] *m(f)* antifascist
antik [an·ˈtiːk] *adj* ❶ *Möbel* antique ❷ (*aus der Antike*) ancient; ~**e Kunst** ancient art forms *pl*
Antike <-> [an·ˈtiː·kə] *f kein pl* antiquity; **die Kunst der** ~ the art of the ancient world
Antikörper *m* MED antibody
Antilope <-, -n> [an·ti·ˈloː·pə] *f* antelope
Antipathie <-, -n> [an·ti·pa·ˈtiː, *pl* -ˈtiː·ən] *f* antipathy (**gegen** +*akk* towards)
an|tippen *vt* ■ **jdn** ~ to give sb a tap; ■ **etw** ~ to touch sth
Antiquariat <-[e]s, -e> [an·ti·kva·ˈri̯aːt] *nt* secondhand bookstore
antiquiert [an·ti·ˈkviːrt] *adj* (*pej*) antiquated
Antiquität <-, -en> [an·ti·kvi·ˈtɛːt] *f* antique
Antiquitätengeschäft *nt* antique shop
Antisemit(in) <-en, -en> [an·ti·ze·ˈmiːt] *m(f)* anti-Semite; ~[**in**] **sein** to be anti-Semitic
antisemitisch [an·ti·ze·ˈmiː·tɪʃ] *adj* anti-Semitic
Antisemitismus <-> [an·ti·ze·mi·ˈtɪs·mʊs] *m kein pl* anti-Semitism
antiseptisch [an·ti·ˈzɛp·tɪʃ] *adj* antiseptic
Antiterroreinheit *f* antiterrorist squad
Antivirenprogramm *nt* COMPUT antivirus [program]
antizipieren* [an·ti·tsi·ˈpiː·rən] *vt* (*geh*) to anticipate
an|törnen *vt* (*sl*) to give a kick
Antrag <-[e]s, -träge> [ˈan·traːk, *pl* ˈan·trɛː·gə] *m* ❶ (*Beantragung*) application (**auf** +*akk* for); **einen ~ stellen** to put in an application ❷ (*Formular*) application form (**auf** +*akk* for) ❸ (*Heiratsantrag*) [marriage] proposal; **jdm einen ~ machen** to propose to sb
Antragsformular *nt* application form
Antragsteller(in) <-s, -> *m(f)* applicant
an|treffen *vt irreg* ❶ (*treffen*) to catch ❷ (*vorfinden*) to come across
an|treiben *irreg vt* ❶ (*vorwärtstreiben*) to drive [on *sep*] ❷ (*drängen*) to urge; (*aufdringlicher*) to push ❸ TECH to drive
an|treten *irreg vt* ❶ (*beginnen*) to begin ❷ (*übernehmen*) to take up; **seine Amtszeit** ~ to take office; **ein Erbe** ~ to come into an inheritance; **eine Stellung** ~ to take on a position ❸ *Motorrad* to kick-start
Antrieb *m* ❶ AUTO, LUFT drive ❷ (*Impuls*) energy *no indef art*; **aus eigenem** ~ on one's own initiative
Antriebskraft *f* TECH [driving] power
Antriebswelle *f* TECH drive shaft
an|trinken *irreg* **I.** *vt* (*fam*) **eine Flasche** ~ to drink a little from a bottle; **eine angetrunkene Flasche** an opened bottle **II.** *vr* (*fam*) **sich** *dat* **einen** [**Schwips**] ~ to get tipsy *fam*
Antritt *m kein pl* ❶ (*Beginn*) start ❷ (*Übernahme*) **nach ~ seines Amtes/der Erbschaft** after assuming office/coming into the inheritance
Antrittsbesuch *m* first courtesy call
Antrittsrede *f* maiden speech
an|tun *vt irreg* ■ **jdm etwas/nichts** ~ to do something/not to do anything to sb; **tu mir das nicht an!** (*hum fam*) spare me, please! ▶ WENDUNGEN: **sich** *dat* **etwas** ~ to kill oneself
Antwort <-, -en> [ˈant·vɔrt] *f* ❶ (*Beantwortung*) answer (**auf** +*akk* to); **jdm** [**eine**] ~ **geben** to give sb an answer ❷ (*Reaktion*) response (**auf** +*akk* to); **als ~ auf etw** in response to sth
antworten [ˈant·vɔr·tn̩] *vi* ❶ (*als Antwort geben*) [**jdm/auf etw**] ~ to answer [sb/sth], to reply [to sb/sth]; **mit Ja/Nein** ~ to answer yes/no; **schriftlich** ~ to answer in writing

❷ (*reagieren*) to respond (**mit** +*dat* with)

Ạntwortschreiben *nt* reply

an|vertrauen* [ˈan·fɛɐ̯·trau·ən] **I.** *vt* ■**jdm etw ~** (*übergeben*) to entrust sb with sth; (*erzählen*) to confide sth to sb **II.** *vr* ■**sich** *akk* **jdm ~** to confide in sb

ạn|wachsen [-ks-] *vi irreg sein* ❶ (*festwachsen*) to grow ❷ (*zunehmen*) to increase (**auf** +*akk* to)

Anwalt, **Anwältin** <-[e]s, -wälte> [ˈan·valt, ˈan·vɛl·tɪn, *pl* ˈan·vɛl·tə] *m, f* ❶ (*Rechtsanwalt*) lawyer, attorney; **sich** *dat* **einen ~ nehmen** to hire a lawyer ❷ (*geh: Fürsprecher*) advocate

Ạnwaltsbüro *nt* ❶ *s.* **Anwaltskanzlei** ❷ (*Anwaltsfirma*) law firm

Ạnwaltskanzlei *f* lawyer's [*or* law] office, law firm

Ạnwaltskosten *pl* legal expenses

Ạnwandlung <-, -en> *f* mood; **aus einer ~ heraus** on an impulse; **in einer ~ von Großzügigkeit** in a burst of generosity; **~en bekommen** (*fam*) to go into a fit

Ạnwärter(in) *m(f)* candidate (**auf** +*akk* for); SPORT contender (**auf** +*akk* for)

ạn|weisen *vt irreg* ❶ (*beauftragen*) ■**jdn ~ etw zu tun** to order sb to do sth ❷ (*anleiten*) to instruct

Ạnweisung <-, -en> *f* ❶ (*Anordnung*) order ❷ (*Anleitung*) instruction ❸ (*Gebrauchsanweisung*) instructions *pl*

ạnwendbar *adj* applicable (**auf** +*akk* to); **in der Praxis ~** practicable

ạn|wenden *vt reg o irreg* ❶ (*gebrauchen*) to use (**bei** +*dat* on) ❷ (*übertragen*) to apply (**auf** +*akk* to)

Ạnwender(in) <-s, -> *m(f)* COMPUT user

ạnwenderfreundlich *adj* COMPUT user-friendly

ạnwenderorientiert *adj* COMPUT user-oriented

Ạnwenderprogramm *nt* COMPUT application program

Ạnwendersoftware *f* application software

Ạnwendung *f* ❶ (*Gebrauch*) use ❷ (*Übertragung*) application (**auf** +*akk* to) ❸ (*therapeutische Maßnahme*) administration

Ạnwendungsbereich *m* area of application

ạn|werben *vt irreg* to recruit (**für** +*akk* for)

Ạnwesen <-s, -> *nt* (*geh*) estate

ạnwesend *adj* present *pred;* ■**~ sein** to be present (**bei** +*dat* at); **nicht ganz ~ sein** (*hum fam*) to be a million miles away

Ạnwesende(r) *f(m) dekl wie adj* person present; ■**die ~n** those present

Ạnwesenheit <-> *f kein pl* presence; *von Studenten* attendance; **in jds ~** in sb's presence

an|widern [ˈan·viː·dɐn] *vt* to disgust

Ạnwohner(in) <-s, -> *m(f)* [local] resident

Anwohnerparkplatz *m* resident parking

Ạnzahl *f kein pl* number

ạn|zahlen *vt* **500 Euro ~** to make a 500 euro down payment; **ein Auto ~** to make a down payment on a car

Ạnzahlung *f* down payment

ạn|zapfen *vt* (*a. fam*) to tap

Ạnzeichen *nt* sign; MED symptom

Ạnzeige <-, -n> *f* ❶ (*Strafanzeige*) charge (**wegen** +*gen* of) ❷ (*Inserat*) ad[vertisement] ❸ (*Bekanntgabe*) announcement ❹ TECH (*Instrument*) gauge; (*ablesbarer Wert*) display

ạn|zeigen *vt* ❶ ■**jdn** [**wegen etw** *gen*] **~** to report sb [for sth] ❷ (*angeben*) to indicate; (*digital*) to display

Ạnzeigenblatt *nt* advertising paper

Ạnzeigenteil *m* classified section

Ạnzeigetafel *f* LUFT, BAHN departures and arrivals board; SPORT scoreboard

ạn|zetteln *vt Schlägerei, Streit* to provoke; *Aufstand, Krieg* to instigate

ạn|ziehen *irreg* **I.** *vt* ❶ *Kleidungsstück* to put on *sep; Person* to get dressed ❷ (*festziehen*) *Schraube* to tighten; *Handbremse* to apply, to put on ❸ *Arm, Bein* to draw up ❹ (*anlocken*) to attract; **sich** *akk* **von jdm/etw angezogen fühlen** to be attracted to sb/sth ❺ SCHWEIZ **das Bett frisch ~** to change the bed **II.** *vi Preise* to rise, to go up **III.** *vr* ■**sich** *akk* **~** to get dressed; **sich warm ~** to dress warm[ly]; **sich schick ~** to dress up

ạnziehend *adj* attractive

Ạnziehung <-, -en> *f* ❶ (*Reiz*) attraction ❷ *kein pl s.* **Anziehungskraft 2**

Ạnziehungskraft *f* ❶ PHYS [force of] attraction; **~ der Erde** [force of] gravitation ❷ *kein pl* (*Verlockung*) appeal; **auf jdn eine ~ ausüben** to appeal to sb

Ạnzug *m* ❶ (*Herrenanzug*) suit ❷ SCHWEIZ (*Bezug*) duvet cover

anzüglich [ˈan·tsyːk·lɪç] *adj* ❶ (*schlüpfrig*) insinuating ❷ (*zudringlich*) personal; ■**~ werden** to get personal

Ạnzüglichkeit <-, -en> *f* ❶ *kein pl* (*Schlüpfrigkeit*) suggestiveness ❷ *kein pl* (*Zudringlichkeit*) advances *pl* ❸ (*zudringliche Handlung*) pushiness

ạn|zünden *vt* ❶ *Feuer, Zigarette* to light ❷ *Haus* to set on fire

ạn|zweifeln *vt* to question

apart [aˈpart] *adj* striking

Apartheid <-> [aˈpaːɐ̯t·hait] *f kein pl* POL (*hist*) apartheid

Apartment <-s, -s> [aˈpart·mənt] *nt* apartment

Apathie <-, -n> [apa·ˈtiː, *pl* -ˈtiːən] *f* apathy; MED listlessness

apathisch [aˈpaː·tɪʃ] **I.** *adj* apathetic; MED listless **II.** *adv* apathetically; MED listlessly

Aperitif <-s, -s *o* -e> [ape·ri·ˈtiːf] *m* aperitif

Apfel <-s, Äpfel> [ˈap·fl̩, *pl* ˈɛp·fl̩] *m* apple ▶ WENDUNGEN: **in den sauren ~ beißen** (*fam*) to bite the bullet; **der ~ fällt nicht weit vom Stamm** (*prov*) like father, like son

Apfelbaum *m* apple tree

Apfelkuchen *m* apple pie

Apfelmus *nt* apple sauce

Apfelsaft *m* apple juice

Apfelsine <-, -n> [ap·fl̩·ˈziː·nə] *f* orange

Apfelwein *m* hard cider
Apostel <-s, -> [a'pɔs·tl̩] *m* apostle
Apostroph <-s, -e> [apo·'stroːf] *m* apostrophe
Apotheke <-, -n> [apo·'teː·kə] *f* pharmacy
Apotheker(in) <-s, -> [apo·'teː·kɐ] *m(f)* pharmacist
App. *Abk von* **Appartement** apt.
Apparat <-[e]s, -e> [apa·'raːt] *m* ❶ TECH apparatus *form;* (*kleineres Gerät*) gadget ❷ (*Telefon*) telephone; **am ~ bleiben** to hold on; **am ~!** speaking! ❸ (*sl: großer Gegenstand*) whopper
Appartement <-s, -s> [apartə·'mãː] *nt s.* **Apartment**
Appell <-s, -e> [a'pɛl] *m* appeal; **einen ~ an jdn richten** to make an appeal to sb
appellieren* [apɛ·'liː·rən] *vi* ❶ ■ **an jdn ~** to appeal to sb ❷ **an jds Vernunft ~** to appeal to sb's common sense ❸ SCHWEIZ (*Berufung einlegen*) ■ **gegen etw ~** to appeal against sth
Appenzell <-s> [apn̩·'tsɛl] *nt* Appenzell [cheese]
Appetit <-[e]s> [ape·'tiːt] *m kein pl* appetite; **~ auf etw haben** to feel like [having] sth; **[jdm] ~ machen** to whet sb's appetite; **jdm den ~ verderben** to spoil sb's appetite; **guten ~!** enjoy your meal!
appetitanregend *adj* ❶ (*appetitlich*) appetizing ❷ (*appetitfördernd*) **ein ~es Mittel** an appetite stimulant
Appetithappen *m* canapé
appetitlich **I.** *adj* ❶ (*Appetit anregend*) appetizing ❷ (*fam: Lust anregend*) tempting **II.** *adv* appetizingly, temptingly
Appetitlosigkeit <-> *f kein pl* lack of appetite
Appetitzügler <-s, -> *m* appetite suppressant
applaudieren* [aplau·'diː·rən] *vi* (*geh*) to applaud
Applaus <-es, -e> [a'plaus, *pl* a'plauzə] *m pl selten* (*geh*) applause
Apr. *Abk von* **April** Apr.
Aprikose <-, -n> [apri·'koː·zə] *f* apricot
April <-s, -e> [a'prɪl] *m pl selten* April; *s. a.* **Februar** ▶ WENDUNGEN: **~! ~!** April fool!; **jdn in den ~ schicken** to make an April fool of sb
Aprilscherz *m* April fools' joke
apropos [apro·'poː] *adv* ❶ (*übrigens*) by the way ❷ (*was ... angeht*) **~ Männer, ...** speaking of men, ...
Aquaplaning <-s> [akva·'plaː·nɪŋ] *nt kein pl* aquaplaning
Aquarell <-s, -e> [akva·'rɛl] *nt* watercolor [painting]
Aquarium <-s, -rien> [a'kvaː·ri̯ʊm, *pl* -ri̯ən] *nt* aquarium
Äquator <-s> [ɛ'kvaː·toːɐ̯] *m kein pl* equator
Äquivalent <-s, -e> [ɛkvi·va·'lɛnt] *nt* equivalent
Araber(in) <-s, -> ['ara·bɐ] *m(f)* Arab
Arabien <-s> [a'raː·bi̯ən] *nt* Arabia
arabisch [a'raː·bɪʃ] *adj* ❶ GEOG Arabian; **A~es Meer** Arabian Sea ❷ LING Arabic; **auf ~** in Arabic
Arbeit <-, -en> ['ar·bait] *f* ❶ (*Tätigkeit*) work; **gute/schlechte ~ leisten** to do a good/bad job; **sich** *akk* **an die ~ machen** to get down to work ❷ (*Arbeitsplatz*) job; **er fand ~ als Kranfahrer** he got a job as a crane operator ❸ (*handwerkliches Produkt*) handiwork ❹ (*schriftliches Werk*) work ❺ SCH test; **eine ~ schreiben** to take a test; **eine schriftliche ~** a [term] paper ❻ *kein pl* (*Mühe*) effort; **sich** *dat* **~ machen** to take the trouble ▶ WENDUNGEN: **erst die ~, dann das Vergnügen** (*prov*) business before pleasure *prov*
arbeiten ['ar·bai·tn̩] *vi* ❶ (*tätig sein*) to work; ■ **an etw** *dat* **~** to be working on sth ❷ (*berufstätig sein*) to have a job ❸ (*funktionieren*) *Maschine* to work; *Körperorgan* to function
Arbeiter(in) <-s, -> *m(f)* (*Industrie*) [blue-collar] worker; (*Landwirtschaft*) laborer
Arbeiterbewegung *f* POL labor movement
Arbeiterfamilie *f* working-class family
Arbeiterschaft <-> *f kein pl* work force + *sing/pl vb*
Arbeiterviertel *nt* working-class area
Arbeiterwohlfahrt *f kein pl* workers' rights organization
Arbeitgeber(in) <-s, -> *m(f)* employer
Arbeitgeberverband *m* employers' association
Arbeitnehmer(in) <-s, -> *m(f)* employee
Arbeitsablauf *m* work routine
Arbeitsamt *nt* unemployment office
Arbeitsaufwand *m* expenditure of energy; **was für ein ~!** what a lot of work!
arbeitsaufwändig[RR] *adj* labor-intensive
Arbeitsbedingungen *pl* working conditions *pl*
Arbeitsbeschaffungsmaßnahme *f* job creation plan
Arbeitseifer *m* enthusiasm for one's work
Arbeitseinstellung *f* ❶ (*Streik*) walkout ❷ (*Arbeitsauffassung*) attitude toward work
Arbeitseinteilung *f* work allocation
Arbeitserlaubnis *f* work permit
Arbeitserleichterung *f* labor saving; **zur ~** to facilitate work
Arbeitsessen *nt* business lunch/dinner
arbeitsfähig *adj* able to work
Arbeitsgemeinschaft *f* work[ing] group; SCH study group
Arbeitsgericht *nt a court that handles labor disputes*
Arbeitsgruppe *f* team
arbeitsintensiv *adj* labor-intensive
Arbeitskampf *m* labor dispute
Arbeitskleidung *f* work clothes *pl*
Arbeitsklima *nt* work climate, atmosphere
Arbeitskollege, -kollegin *m, f* colleague
Arbeitskraft *f* ❶ *kein pl* (*Leistungskraft*) work capacity; **die menschliche ~** human labor ❷ (*Mitarbeiter*) worker
Arbeitslager *nt* labor camp
Arbeitslohn *m* wages *pl*

A

arbeitslos *adj* unemployed
Arbeitslose(r) *f(m) dekl wie adj* unemployed person; ■ **die ~n** the unemployed
Arbeitslosengeld *nt* unemployment benefit
Arbeitslosenhilfe *f* unemployment aid
Arbeitslosenquote *f* unemployment figures *pl*
Arbeitslosenzahlen *pl* unemployment figures *pl*
Arbeitslosigkeit <-> *f kein pl* unemployment *no indef art, + sing vb*
Arbeitsmangel *m* lack of work
Arbeitsmarkt *m* job market
Arbeitsmittel *nt* material required for work
Arbeitsmoral *f* work morale
Arbeitsniederlegung *f* walkout
Arbeitsoberfläche *f* COMPUT user interface
Arbeitspensum *nt* work quota
Arbeitsplatz *m* ❶ (*Arbeitsstätte*) workplace; **am ~** at work ❷ (*Stelle*) job; **freier ~** vacancy
Arbeitsplatzsicherung *f kein pl* safeguarding of jobs
Arbeitsplatzwechsel *m* change of employment
arbeitsreich *adj* busy
arbeitsscheu *adj* (*pej*) work-shy
Arbeitsspeicher *m* COMPUT main memory
Arbeitsstelle *f* job
Arbeitssuche *f* search for employment; **auf ~ sein** to be [out] job-hunting
Arbeitstag *m* work day
Arbeitsteilung *f* job-sharing
Arbeitsuchende(r) *f(m) dekl wie adj* jobseeker
arbeitsunfähig *adj* unable to work; **jdn ~ schreiben** to put sb on sick leave
Arbeitsunfähigkeit *f* inability to work
Arbeitsunfall *m* work-related accident
Arbeitsvertrag *m* employment contract
Arbeitsverweigerung *f* refusal to work
arbeitswillig *adj* willing to work
Arbeitswoche *f* work week
Arbeitswut *f* (*fam*) work mania
arbeitswütig *adj* (*fam*) ■ **~ sein** to be a workaholic
Arbeitszeit *f* ❶ (*tägliche betriebliche Arbeit*) working hours *pl;* **gleitende ~** flexitime, flextime ❷ (*benötigte Zeit*) required [working] time
Arbeitszeugnis *nt* reference
Arbeitszimmer *nt* study
Archäologe, Archäologin <-n, -n> [ar·çɛo·ˈloː·gə, arçɛo·ˈloː·gɪn] *m, f* archaeologist
Archäologie <-> [arçɛo·lo·ˈgiː] *f kein pl* archaeology
Arche <-, -n> [ˈar·çə] *f* ark; **die ~ Noah** REL Noah's Ark
Architekt(in) <-en, -en> [ar·çi·ˈtɛkt] *m(f)* architect
Architektur <-, -en> [ar·çi·tɛk·ˈtuːɐ̯] *f* architecture
Archiv <-s, -e> [ar·ˈçiːf, *pl* -və] *nt* archives *pl*
archivieren* [ar·çi·ˈviː·rən] *vt* to archive
Areal <-s, -e> [are·ˈaːl] *nt* ❶ (*Gebiet*) area ❷ (*Grundstück*) grounds *pl*

Ären *pl von* **Ära**
Arena <-, Arenen> [aˈreː·na, *pl* aˈreː·nən] *f* ❶ (*Manege*) [circus] ring ❷ SPORT [sports] arena ❸ (*Stierkampfarena*) [bull]ring
arg <ärger, ärgste> [ark] *bes* SÜDD **I.** *adj* ❶ (*schlimm*) bad ❷ *attr* (*groß*) *Enttäuschung* big **II.** *adv* (*sehr*) badly; **tut es ~ weh?** does it hurt badly?; **er hat dazu ~ lang gebraucht** it took him forever to do it
Argentinien <-s> [ar·gɛn·ˈtiː·ni̯·ən] *nt* Argentina; *s. a.* **Deutschland**
Argentinier(in) <-s, -> [ar·gɛn·ˈtiː·ni̯ɐ] *m(f)* Argentinian; *s. a.* **Deutsche(r)**
argentinisch [ar·gɛn·ˈtiː·nɪʃ] *adj* Argentinian; *s. a.* **deutsch**
ärger [ˈɛrgɐ] *adj komp von* **arg**
Ärger <-s> [ˈɛrgɐ] *m kein pl* ❶ (*Wut*) anger ❷ (*Unannehmlichkeiten*) trouble; **~ bekommen** to get into trouble; **~ haben** to have problems; **[jdm] ~ machen** to cause [sb] trouble
ärgerlich I. *adj* ❶ (*verärgert*) annoyed (**über** *+akk* about); **jdn ~ machen** to annoy sb ❷ (*unangenehm*) unpleasant, annoying **II.** *adv* (*verärgert*) annoyed, angrily
ärgern [ˈɛr·gɐn] **I.** *vt* ❶ (*ungehalten machen*) to annoy ❷ (*reizen*) to tease (**wegen** *+gen* about) **II.** *vr* ■ **sich** *akk* **~** to be annoyed (**über** *+akk* about); **ich ärgere mich, dass ich nicht hingegangen bin** I'm upset with myself for not going
Arglist <-> *f kein pl* (*geh*) cunning
arglistig I. *adj* cunning **II.** *adv* cunningly
arglos *adj* innocent
ärgste(r, s) [ˈɛrks·tə, -tɐ, -təs] *adj superl von* **arg**
Argument <-[e]s, -e> [argu·ˈmɛnt] *nt* argument; **das ist kein ~** (*unsinnig*) that's a poor argument; (*keine Entschuldigung*) that's no excuse
Argumentation <-, -en> [argu·mɛn·ta·ˈtsi̯oːn] *f* argumentation
argumentieren* *vi* to argue; ■ **mit etw** *dat* **~** to use sth as an argument
Argwohn <-s> [ˈark·voːn] *m kein pl* suspicion; **jds ~ erregen** to arouse sb's suspicion[s]
argwöhnen [ˈark·vøː·nən] *vt* (*geh*) to suspect
argwöhnisch [ˈark·vøː·nɪʃ] **I.** *adj* suspicious **II.** *adv* suspiciously
Aristokrat(in) <-en, -en> [arɪs·to·ˈkraːt] *m(f)* aristocrat
Aristokratie <-, -n> [arɪs·to·kra·ˈtiː, *pl* -ˈtiːən] *f* aristocracy
aristokratisch *adj* aristocratic
Arktis <-> [ˈark·tɪs] *f* Arctic
arktisch [ˈark·tɪʃ] *adj* arctic
arm <ärmer, ärmste> [arm] *adj* ❶ (*besitzlos, bedauernswert*) poor ❷ **~ dran sein** (*fam*) to have a hard time
Arm <-[e]s, -e> [arm] *m* arm; **jdn im ~ halten** to hold sb in one's arms; **ein Kind auf den ~ nehmen** to pick up a child ▶ WENDUNGEN: **jdm [mit etw** *dat*] **unter die ~e greifen** to help sb

out [with sth]; **jdn auf den ~ nehmen** to pull sb's leg

Armaturenbrett *nt* AUTO dashboard

Armband <-bänder> *nt* ❶ (*Uhrarmband*) [watch] strap ❷ (*Schmuckarmband*) bracelet

Armbanduhr *f* [wrist]watch

Armee <-, -n> [ar·'meː, *pl* -'meː·ən] *f* army

Ärmel <-s, -> ['ɛr·ml̩] *m* sleeve; **sich** *dat* **die ~ hochkrempeln** to roll up one's sleeves ▶ WENDUNGEN: **etw aus dem ~ schütteln** (*fam*) to produce/do sth just like that

Ärmelkanal *m* ■ **der ~** the [English] Channel

ärmellos *adj* sleeveless

Armenien <-s> [ar·'meː·ni̯·ən] *nt* Armenia; *s. a.* **Deutschland**

Armenier(in) <-s, -> [ar·'meː·ni̯·ɐ] *m(f)* Armenian; *s. a.* **Deutsche(r)**

armenisch [ar·'meː·nɪʃ] *adj* Armenian; *s. a.* **deutsch**

Armenviertel *nt* poor district

ärmer ['ɛr·mɐ] *adj komp von* **arm**

Armlehne *f* armrest

Armleuchter *m* (*pej fam: Dummkopf*) dummy

ärmlich ['ɛrm·lɪç] **I.** *adj* ❶ (*von Armut zeugend*) poor; (*Kleidung*) shabby ❷ (*dürftig*) meager **II.** *adv* poorly; **~ gekleidet sein** to be shabbily dressed

armselig *adj* ❶ (*primitiv*) shabby ❷ (*dürftig*) miserable ❸ (*meist pej: unzulänglich*) pathetic

ärmste(r, s) ['ɛrms·tə, -tɐ, -təs] *adj superl von* **arm**

Armut <-> ['ar·muːt] *f kein pl* poverty

Armutsflüchtling *m* economic refugee

Armutsgrenze *f* poverty line

Armutszeugnis *nt* ▶ WENDUNGEN: **ein ~ für jdn sein** to be the proof of sb's inadequacy

Aroma <-s, Aromen *o* -s *o* -ta> [a'roː·ma] *nt* ❶ (*Geruch*) aroma; (*Geschmack*) taste, flavor ❷ (*Aromastoff*) flavor[ing]

Aromastoff *m* flavoring

Aromata *pl von* **Aroma**

aromatisch [aro·'maː·tɪʃ] **I.** *adj* aromatic; (*wohlschmeckend*) flavorful **II.** *adv* **~ schmecken** to have a distinctive taste

aromatisieren* [aro·ma·ti·'ziː·rən] *vt* to aromatize

Aromen *pl von* **Aroma**

Arrangement <-s, -s> [arãʒə·'mãː] *nt* (*geh*) arrangement

arrangieren* [arã·'ʒiː·rən] **I.** *vt* to arrange; ■ **~, dass ...** to arrange so that ... **II.** *vr* ❶ (*übereinkommen*) ■ **sich** +*akk* **[mit jdm] ~** to come to an arrangement [with sb] ❷ (*sich abfinden*) ■ **sich** +*akk* **[mit etw** *dat***] ~** to come to terms [with sth]

Arrest <-[e]s, -e> [a'rɛst] *m* JUR (*Freiheitsentzug*) detention

arretieren* [are·'tiː·rən] *vt* (*feststellen*) to lock

arrogant [aro·'gant] **I.** *adj* arrogant **II.** *adv* arrogantly

Arroganz <-> [aro·'gants] *f kein pl* arrogance

Arsch <-[e]s, Ärsche> [arʃ, *pl* 'ɛr·ʃə] *m* (*derb*) ❶ (*Hintern*) ass ❷ (*blöder Kerl*) dumb ass, asshole ▶ WENDUNGEN: **am ~ der Welt** (*sl*) out in the boonies; **jdm in den ~ kriechen** to kiss sb's ass *sl;* **jdn [mal] am ~ lecken können** sb can shove it *sl* [*or vulg* fuck off]; **im ~ sein** (*sl*) to be screwed

Arschbacke *f* (*derb*) [butt] cheek

Arschkriecher(in) <-s, -> *m(f)* (*pej derb*) ass kisser

Arschloch *nt* (*derb*) asshole

Arschtritt *m* (*derb*) kick in the ass

Arsen <-s> [ar·'zeːn] *nt kein pl* CHEM arsenic

Arsenal <-s, -e> [ar·ze·'naːl] *nt* arsenal

Art <-, -en> [aːɐ̯t, *pl* 'aːɐ̯·tn̩] *f* ❶ (*Sorte*) sort, kind ❷ (*Methode*) way; **auf diese ~ und Weise** [in] this way ❸ (*Wesensart*) nature ❹ (*Verhaltensweise*) behavior; **das ist doch keine ~!** (*fam*) that's no way to behave! ❺ BIOL species ❻ (*Stil*) style ▶ WENDUNGEN: **nach ~ des Hauses** à la maison

Artenreichtum *m kein pl* BIOL abundance of species

Artenschutz *m* protection of species

Artensterben *nt kein pl* extinction of the species

Artenvielfalt <-> *f kein pl* BIOL abundance of species

Arterie <-, -n> [ar·'teː·ri̯ə] *f* artery

Artgenosse, -genossin *m, f* BIOL plant/animal of the same species

artgerecht *adj, adv* appropriate to a species

artig ['aːɐ̯·tɪç] *adj* well-behaved

Artikel <-s, -> [ar·'tiː·kl̩] *m* ❶ (*Zeitungsartikel*) article ❷ (*Lexikoneintrag*) entry ❸ (*Ware*) item ❹ LING article

Artischocke <-, -n> [ar·ti·'ʃɔ·kə] *f* artichoke

Artist(in) <-en, -en> [ar·'tɪst] *m(f)* (*Zirkuskunst etc.*) performer

artistisch *adj* ❶ (*Zirkuskunst betreffend*) spectacular ❷ (*sehr geschickt*) skillful

Arznei <-, -en> [aːɐ̯ts·'nai] *f* medicine

Arzneiflasche *f* medicine bottle

Arzneimittel *nt* drug

Arzneimittelabhängigkeit *f* drug addiction

Arzneimittelallergie *f* drug allergy

Arzneimittelvergiftung *f* prescription drug overdose

Arzneipflanze *f* medicinal plant

Arzt, Ärztin <-es, Ärzte> [aːɐ̯tst, 'ɛːɐ̯ts·tɪn, *pl* 'ɛɐ̯ts·tə] *m, f* doctor; **~ für Allgemeinmedizin** family physician, GP

Arztbesuch *m* ❶ (*Besuch des Arztes*) visit by a doctor ❷ (*Aufsuchen eines Arztes*) visit to a doctor

Arzthelfer(in) *m(f)* doctor's assistant

Arztkosten *pl* medical costs *pl*

ärztlich ['ɛːɐ̯tst·lɪç] **I.** *adj* medical **II.** *adv* medically; **sich** *akk* **~ behandeln lassen** to get medical advice

Arztpraxis *f* doctor's office

As[ALT] <-ses, -se> [as] *nt s.* **Ass**

Asbest <-[e]s> [as·'bɛst] *nt kein pl* asbestos

aschblond *adj* ash-blond

Asche <-, -n> ['aʃə] *f* ash

A

Aschenbecher *m,* **Ascher** <-s, -> ['aʃɐ] *m* (*fam*) ashtray
Aschermittwoch [aʃɐ·'mɪt·vɔx] *m* REL Ash Wednesday
aschgrau *adj* ash-gray
Äser *pl von* **Aas²**
asexuell ['azɛ·ksu̯·ɛl] *adj* asexual
Asiat(in) <-en, -en> *m(f)* Asian
asiatisch [a'zi̯a:·tɪʃ] *adj* Asiatic; *Sprache, Kultur* Asian
Asien <-s> ['a:zi̯ən] *nt* Asia
asketisch *adj* ascetic
asozial ['azo·tsi̯a:l] **I.** *adj* antisocial **II.** *adv* antisocially
Asoziale(r) *f(m) dekl wie adj* (*pej*) social misfit
Aspekt <-[e]s, -e> [as·'pɛkt] *m* aspect
Asphalt <-[e]s, -e> [as·'falt] *m* asphalt
asphaltieren* [as·fal·'ti:·rən] *vt* to asphalt, to tar
Aspirin® <-s> [as·pi·'ri:n] *nt kein pl* aspirin
Ass^RR <-es, -e> *nt* ace ▶ WENDUNGEN: **[noch] ein ~ im Ärmel haben** to have an ace up one's sleeve
aß [a:s] *imp von* **essen**
Assistent(in) <-en, -en> [asɪs·'tɛnt] *m(f)* assistant
Assistenzarzt, -ärztin *m, f* [hospital] intern
assistieren* [asɪs·'ti:·rən] *vi* to assist (**bei** +*dat* with)
Assoziation <-, -en> [aso·tsi̯a·'tsi̯o:n] *f* (*geh*) association
assoziieren* [aso·tsi·'i:·rən] *vt* (*geh*) to associate
Ast <-[e]s, Äste> [ast, *pl* 'ɛs·tə] *m* branch ▶ WENDUNGEN: **auf dem absteigenden ~ sein** (*fam*) sb/sth is going downhill; **sich** *dat* **einen ~ lachen** (*sl*) to double up with laughter
Aster <-, -n> ['as·tɐ] *f* aster
Astgabel *f* fork of a tree
Ästhetik <-> [ɛs·'te:·tɪk] *f kein pl* aesthetics *pl*
ästhetisch [ɛs·'te:·tɪʃ] *adj* aesthetic
Asthma <-s> ['ast·ma] *nt kein pl* asthma
Asthmatiker(in) <-s, -> [ast·'ma:·ti·kɐ] *m(f)* asthmatic
asthmatisch [ast·'ma:·tɪʃ] **I.** *adj* asthmatic **II.** *adv* asthmatically
astrein *adj* ❶ (*fam: moralisch einwandfrei*) aboveboard ❷ (*sl: spitze*) fantastic
Astrologe, Astrologin <-n, -n> [as·tro·'lo:·gə, as·tro·'lo:·gɪn] *m, f* astrologer
Astrologie <-> [as·tro·lo·'gi:] *f kein pl* astrology
astrologisch [as·tro·'lo:·gɪʃ] **I.** *adj* astrological **II.** *adv* astrologically
Astronaut(in) <-en, -en> [as·tro·'naut] *m(f)* astronaut
Astronom(in) <-en, -en> [as·tro·'no:m] *m(f)* astronomer
Astronomie <-> [as·tro·no·'mi:] *f kein pl* astronomy
astronomisch [as·tro·'no:·mɪʃ] *adj* (*a. fig*) astronomical
Asyl <-s, -e> [a'zy:l] *nt* asylum; **um ~ bitten** to apply for [political] asylum; **jdm ~ gewähren** to grant sb [political] asylum
Asylant(in) <-en, -en> [azy·'lant] *m(f) s.* **Asylbewerber**
Asylantenwohnheim *nt* home for asylum seekers
Asylantrag *m* application for political asylum
Asylbewerber(in) *m(f)* asylum seeker
Asylsuchende(r) *f(m) dekl wie adj* asylum seeker
asymmetrisch ['azʏ·me:·trɪʃ] *adj* asymmetric
Atelier <-s, -s> [atə·'li̯e:] *nt* KUNST studio
Atem <-s> ['a:təm] *m kein pl* breath; **den ~ anhalten** to hold one's breath; **~ holen** to take a breath; **wieder zu ~ kommen** to catch one's breath; **außer** ~ out of breath ▶ WENDUNGEN: **den längeren ~ haben** to have the upper hand; **jdn in ~ halten** to keep sb on their toes; **jdm den ~ verschlagen** to take sb's breath away
atemberaubend *adj* breathtaking
Atembeschwerden *pl* breathing difficulties *pl*
Atemgerät *nt* respirator; (*von Taucher*) breathing apparatus
atemlos **I.** *adj* ❶ (*außer Atem*) breathless ❷ (*perplex*) speechless **II.** *adv* breathlessly
Atemnot *f kein pl* shortness of breath
Atempause *f* breather
Atemstillstand *m* respiratory arrest
Atemwege *pl* respiratory tracts *pl*
Atemwegserkrankung *f* respiratory disease
Atemzug *m* breath
Atheismus <-> [ate·'ɪs·mʊs] *m kein pl* atheism
Atheist(in) <-en, -en> [ate·'ɪst] *m(f)* atheist
atheistisch *adj* atheist
Athen <-s> [a'te:n] *nt* Athens
ätherisch [ɛ'te:·rɪʃ] *adj* ethereal
Äthiopien <-s> [ɛ'ti̯o:·pi̯·ən] *nt* Ethiopia; *s. a.* **Deutschland**
Äthiopier(in) <-s, -> [ɛ'ti̯o:·pi̯·ɐ] *m(f)* Ethiopian; *s. a.* **Deutsche(r)**
äthiopisch [ɛ'ti̯o:·pɪʃ] *adj* Ethiopian; *s. a.* **deutsch**
Athlet(in) <-en, -en> [at·'le:t] *m(f)* athlete
athletisch [at·'le:·tɪʃ] *adj* athletic
Atlanten *pl von* **Atlas**
Atlantik <-s> [at·'lan·tɪk] *m* Atlantic
atlantisch [at·'lan·tɪʃ] *adj* Atlantic
Atlas <- *o* -ses, Atlanten *o* -se> ['at·las, *pl* 'at·lasə, at·'lan·tn̩] *m* atlas
atmen ['a:t·mən] *vi, vt* to breathe
Atmosphäre <-, -n> [at·mo·'sfɛ:·rə] *f* atmosphere
Atmung <-> *f kein pl* breathing
atmungsaktiv *adj* MODE breathable
Atoll <-s, -e> [a'tɔl] *nt* atoll
Atom <-s, -e> [a'to:m] *nt* atom
Atomangriff *m* nuclear attack
Atomausstieg *m* denuclearization, nuclear [power] phase-out
Atombombe *f* nuclear bomb
Atombombenexplosion *f* nuclear explosion

Atombombenversuch *m* nuclear [weapons] test
Atombunker *m* nuclear fallout shelter
Atomenergie *f* nuclear energy
Atomgegner(in) *m(f)* person who is against nuclear power
Atomindustrie *f* nuclear industry
atomisieren* [ato·mi·ˈziː·rən] *vt* to atomize
Atomkraft *f kein pl* nuclear power
Atomkraftwerk *nt* nuclear power plant
Atomkrieg *m* nuclear war
Atommacht *f* nuclear power
Atommüll *m* nuclear waste
Atomrakete *f* nuclear missile
Atomreaktor *m* nuclear reactor
Atomsprengkopf *m* nuclear warhead
Atomtest *m* nuclear [weapons] test
Atomuhr *f* atomic clock
Atomwaffe *f* nuclear weapon
Attacke <-, -n> [aˈta·kə] *f* ❶ (*Angriff*) attack (**gegen** +*akk* against) ❷ (*Anfall*) attack
attackieren* [ata·ˈkiː·rən] *vt* to attack
Attentat <-[e]s, -e> [ˈatn̩·taːt] *nt* attempt on sb's life; **ein ~ auf jdn verüben** to make an attempt on sb's life
Attentäter(in) [ˈatn̩·tɛː·tɐ] *m(f)* assassin
Attest <-[e]s, -e> [aˈtɛst] *nt* certificate; **jdm ein ~ ausstellen** to certify sth
attestieren* [atɛs·ˈtiː·rən] *vt* to confirm; (*ärztlich*) to certify
Attraktion <-, -en> [atrak·ˈtsi̯oːn] *f* attraction
attraktiv [atrakˈtiːf] *adj* attractive
Attraktivität <-> [atrak·ti·vi·ˈtɛːt] *f kein pl* attractiveness
Attrappe <-, -n> [aˈtrapə] *f* fake, dummy
atypisch [ˈatyː·pɪʃ] *adj* atypical
ätzend *adj* ❶ *Substanz* corrosive ❷ *Geruch* pungent ❸ (*sl: sehr übel*) lousy
Aubergine <-, -n> [obɛr·ˈʒiː·nə] *f* eggplant
auch [aux] *adv* ❶ (*ebenfalls*) too, also, as well; **ich ~** me too; **~ nicht** not ... either, ... [n]either; **ich ~ nicht** me [n]either; **ich gehe nicht mit! – ich ~ nicht!** I'm not going [along]! — neither am I!; **wenn du nicht hingehst, gehe ich ~ nicht** if you don't go, I won't either ❷ (*sogar*) even; **~ wenn** even if ❸ (*tatsächlich*) too ❹ (*einräumend*) **wie dem ~ sei** whatever
Audienz <-, -en> [au·ˈdi̯·ɛnts] *f* audience
Audioführung *f* audio tour
Audiokassette *f* audio cassette
audiovisuell [audi̯o·vi·zu̯·ˈɛl] *adj* audio-visual
auf [auf] **I.** *präp* ❶ +*dat* on, upon *form;* **~ dem Stuhl** on the chair ❷ +*akk* on, onto; **sie fiel ~ den Rücken** she fell on[to] her back ❸ +*akk* (*zu*) to; **~ die Post/das Fest** to the post office/party ❹ +*dat* (*in, bei*) at; **sie ist** [*o* **arbeitet**] **~ der Post** she works at the post office ❺ +*akk* (*bei Zeitangaben*) on; **etw** +*akk* **~ morgen verlegen** to postpone sth until tomorrow ❻ +*dat* (*während*) on; **~ der Busfahrt wurde es einigen schlecht** some people felt sick on the bus ride **II.** *adv* **~ sein** (*fam: geöffnet*) to be open; (*nicht mehr im Bett*) to be up ▶WENDUNGEN: **~ und ab** up and down; **~ und davon** (*fort*) up and away
auf|arbeiten *vt* ❶ *Akten, Korrespondenz* to get through ❷ *Vergangenheit* to reappraise
auf|atmen *vi* [**erleichtert**] **~** to heave a sigh of relief
auf|bahren [ˈauf·baː·rən] *vt* to lay out in state
Aufbau *m kein pl* ❶ (*das Zusammenbauen*) assembling ❷ (*Schaffung*) *eines Landes* the building ❸ (*Wiedererrichtung*) reconstruction ❹ (*Struktur*) structure
auf|bauen I. *vt* ❶ (*zusammenbauen*) to assemble, to put together ❷ (*errichten*) *Zelt* to put up *sep; Haus, Stadt* to build; **ein Haus neu ~** to rebuild a house ❸ (*aufmuntern*) **jdn** [**wieder**] **~** to cheer up *sep* sb ❹ (*schaffen*) *Partei, Existenz* to build; ■ **sich** *dat* **etw ~** to build up *sep* sth ❺ (*basieren*) to base (**auf** +*dat* on) ❻ (*gliedern*) to structure **II.** *vr* ❶ (*sich bilden*) ■ **sich** *akk* **~** to build up ❷ (*fam*) ■ **sich** *akk* **vor jdm ~** to stand up in front of sb
Aufbaukurs *m* continuation course
auf|bäumen *vr* ■ **sich** *akk* **~** to revolt (**gegen** +*akk* against)
auf|bauschen *vt* ❶ (*übertreiben*) to blow up *sep* (**zu** +*dat* into) ❷ (*blähen*) to fill
auf|bekommen* *vt irreg* (*fam*) ❶ (*öffnen*) to get open *sep* ❷ *Hausaufgaben* to get as homework
auf|bereiten* *vt* ❶ (*verwendungsfähig machen*) to process; *Trinkwasser* to purify ❷ *Text* to edit
Aufbereitung <-, -en> *f* ❶ (*das Aufbereiten*) processing; *von Trinkwasser* purification ❷ *eines Texts* editing
auf|bessern *vt* to improve; *Gehalt* to increase
auf|bewahren* *vt* ❶ (*aufheben*) to keep ❷ (*lagern*) to store
Aufbewahrung <-> *f kein pl* [safe]keeping
auf|bieten *vt irreg* to muster
auf|binden *vt irreg* ❶ (*öffnen, lösen*) to untie ❷ **jdm eine Lüge ~** (*fam*) to tell sb a lie
auf|blähen *vr* ■ **sich** *akk* **~** (*pej: sich wichtigmachen*) to puff oneself up
auf|blasen *irreg* **I.** *vt* to inflate; *Luftballon* to blow up *sep* **II.** *vr* ■ **sich** *akk* **~** (*pej: sich wichtigmachen*) to puff oneself up
auf|bleiben *vi irreg sein* ❶ (*nicht zu Bett gehen*) to stay up ❷ (*geöffnet bleiben*) to stay open
auf|blenden *vi* ❶ AUTO to put the high beams on ❷ FOTO to increase the aperture
auf|blicken *vi* ■ **zu jdm ~** to look up at sb; (*verehrend*) to look up to sb
auf|blitzen *vi* to flash
auf|blühen *vi sein* ❶ *Blume* to bloom ❷ (*aufleben*) to blossom out
auf|brauchen *vt* to use up *sep*
auf|brausen *vi sein* (*wütend werden*) to flare up
aufbrausend *adj* quick-tempered
auf|brechen *irreg* **I.** *vt haben* to break open

A

sep; **ein Auto ~** to break into a car **II.** *vi sein* ❶ (*aufplatzen*) to break up; *Wunde* to open ❷ (*sich auf den Weg machen*) to start off; **ich glaube, wir müssen ~** I think we have to go

auf|bringen *vt irreg* ❶ *Geld* to raise; *Mut, Kraft, Geduld* to summon [up *sep*] ❷ (*wütend machen*) to irritate ❸ (*aufwiegeln*) ■ **jdn gegen jdn ~** to set sb against sb

Aufbruch *m kein pl* departure

Aufbruchsstimmung *f kein pl* ❶ (*vor dem Aufbrechen*) atmosphere of departure; **in ~ sein** to be ready to go; **hier herrscht schon ~** things are already winding down here ❷ (*Stimmung der Erneuerung*) atmosphere of awakening

auf|brühen *vt* to brew up *sep*

auf|brummen *vt* (*fam*) ■ **jdm etw ~** to land sb with sth

auf|bürden *vt* (*geh*) *Verantwortung, Arbeit* to burden with

auf|decken *vt* ❶ (*enthüllen*) to uncover ❷ (*bloßlegen*) to expose; *Fehler* to discover; *Verbrechen, Skandal* to reveal

auf|donnern *vr* ■ **sich** *akk* ~ (*pej fam*) to doll oneself up

auf|drängen I. *vt* ■ **jdm etw ~** to force sth on sb **II.** *vr* ■ **sich** *akk* **jdm ~** to impose oneself on sb

auf|drehen I. *vt* ❶ (*durch Drehen öffnen*) to turn on *sep; Flasche, Ventil* to open; *Schraubverschluss* to unscrew ❷ (*fam: lauter stellen*) to turn up *sep* **II.** *vi* (*fam: loslegen*) to get going; ■ **aufgedreht sein** to be full of go

aufdringlich *adj* ❶ *Benehmen* obtrusive, importunate; *Person* insistent ❷ *Geruch* pungent

auf|drücken *vt* ❶ *Tür* to push open *sep* ❷ (*fam: aufzwingen*) ■ **jdm etw ~** to impose sth on sb

aufeinander [auf·ʔai·ˈnan·dɐ] *adv* ❶ (*räumlich*) on top of each other ❷ (*zeitlich*) after each other; **dicht ~ folgen** to come hard and fast *a. hum;* **~ folgend** successive ❸ (*gegeneinander*) **~ losgehen** to hit away at each other ❹ (*wechselseitig*) **~ angewiesen sein** to be dependent [up]on each other; **~ zugehen** to approach each other

aufeinander|folgen *vi sein s.* **aufeinander 2**

aufeinanderfolgend *adj s.* **aufeinander 2**

aufeinander|stoßen *vi irreg sein* to clash

Aufenthalt <-[e]s, -e> [ˈauf·ʔɛnt·halt] *m* ❶ (*das Verweilen*) stay ❷ (*das Wohnen*) residence ❸ (*Aufenthaltsort*) place of residence ❹ BAHN stop[over]; **wie lange haben wir in Köln ~?** how long are we stopping in Cologne?

Aufenthaltserlaubnis *f,* **Aufenthaltsgenehmigung** *f* residence permit

Aufenthaltsort *m* whereabouts *+ sing/pl vb*

Aufenthaltsraum *m* day room; (*in Firma*) employee lounge

auf|erlegen* [ˈauf·ʔɛɐ̯·leː·gn̩] *vt* (*geh*) ■ **jdm etw ~** to impose sth on sb

auf|erstehen* *vi irreg sein* REL to rise from the dead; *Christus* to rise again

Auferstehung <-, -en> *f* REL resurrection; **Christi ~** the Resurrection [of Christ]

auf|essen *irreg vt, vi* to eat up *sep*

auf|fahren *irreg vi sein* ❶ (*aufprallen*) ■ **auf jdn/etw ~** to run into sb/sth ❷ (*näher heranfahren*) to drive up (**auf** *+akk* to); **zu dicht ~** to tailgate ❸ (*hochschrecken*) to startle ❹ (*aufbrausen*) to fly into a rage

Auffahrt *f* ❶ (*Autobahnauffahrt*) [freeway] on-ramp ❷ (*vor einem Haus*) drive[way] ❸ SCHWEIZ *s.* **Himmelfahrt**

Auffahrunfall *m* collision; (*von mehreren Fahrzeugen*) pile-up

auf|fallen *vi irreg sein* ❶ ■ **jdm fällt etw auf** sb notices sth; **ist Ihnen etwas Ungewöhnliches aufgefallen?** did you notice anything unusual?; **jdm positiv ~** to make a positive impression on sb ❷ ■ **etw/jd fällt auf** to attract attention, to stand out, to be noticeable; **unangenehm ~** to make a bad impression

auffallend I. *adj* conspicuous, striking **II.** *adv* conspicuously; **~ schön** strikingly beautiful

auffällig I. *adj* conspicuous; ■ **an jdm ~ sein** to be noticeable about sb; ■ **etwas A~es** something conspicuous **II.** *adv* conspicuously

auf|fangen *vt irreg* ❶ (*einfangen, mitbekommen*) to catch ❷ (*kompensieren*) to offset ❸ (*sammeln*) to collect

Auffanglager *nt* reception camp

auf|fassen *vt* to interpret (**als** as); **etw falsch ~** to misinterpret sth

Auffassung *f* opinion; **ich bin der ~, dass ...** I think [that] ...; **nach jds ~** in sb's opinion

Auffassungsgabe *f kein pl* perception

auffindbar *adj* detectable; ■ **etw ist nicht ~** sth cannot be found

auf|finden *vt irreg* to find

auf|fliegen *vi irreg sein* ❶ *Vogel* to fly up ❷ *Tür* to fly open ❸ (*fam: öffentlich bekannt werden*) to leak out; *Betrug, Machenschaften* to be exposed; ■ **jdn/etw ~ lassen** to blow the whistle on sb/sth

auf|fordern *vt* ■ **jdn ~, etw zu tun** to ask sb to do sth; **jdn zum Tanz ~** to ask sb to dance

Aufforderung *f* request; (*stärker*) demand; **~ zum Tanz** invitation to dance

auf|fressen *irreg vt* to eat up *sep; Beute* to devour

auf|frischen I. *vt haben* ❶ *Beziehung* to renew; *Erinnerung* to refresh; *Kenntnisse* to polish up *sep;* **sein Englisch ~** to brush up on one's English ❷ *Anstrich* to brighten up *sep; Make-up* to touch up **II.** *vi sein o haben Wind* to freshen, to pick up

Auffrischungskurs *m* refresher course

auf|führen I. *vt* ❶ *Theaterstück* to perform ❷ (*auflisten*) to list; *Beispiele, Zeugen* to cite **II.** *vr* ■ **sich** *akk* ~ to behave; **sich ~, als ob ...** to act as if ...; **Hans hat sich richtig aufgeführt!** Hans made a real fuss!

Aufführung *f* THEAT performance

auf|füllen *vt* ❶ (*befüllen*) to fill up *sep*

❷ (*nachfüllen*) to top up *sep*

Aufgabe <-, -n> *f* ❶ (*Pflicht*) job, task ❷ *meist pl* (*Übungsaufgabe*) exercise; (*Hausaufgabe*) homework ❸ (*zu lösendes Problem*) question; **eine schwierige ~ lösen** to solve a difficult problem ❹ (*Zweck*) purpose ❺ *kein pl* (*Verzicht auf weiteren Kampf*) surrender

auf|gabeln *vt* (*fam: kennen lernen*) to pick up sb *sep*

Aufgabenbereich *m,* **Aufgabengebiet** *nt* area of responsibility

Aufgang *m* ❶ *der Sonne, des Mondes* rising ❷ (*Treppenaufgang*) staircase

auf|geben *irreg* **I.** *vt* ❶ *Brief, Päckchen* to mail ❷ *Gepäck* to register; LUFT to check in ❸ *Anzeige* to place ❹ (*mit etw aufhören*) to give up *sep;* **eine Gewohnheit ~** to break [with] a habit ❺ (*verloren geben*) ■**jdn ~** to give up on sb **II.** *vi* (*sich geschlagen geben*) to give up; MIL to surrender

aufgeblasen I. *adj* (*pej: arrogant*) self-important **II.** *pp von* **aufblasen**

aufgebracht I. *adj* outraged (**über** +*akk* with) **II.** *pp von* **aufbringen**

aufgedunsen *adj* bloated; *Gesicht* puffy

auf|gehen *vi irreg sein* ❶ (*sich öffnen*) to open; *Vorhang* to rise; *Knoten, Reißverschluss etc.* to come undone ❷ *Sonne, Mond* to rise ❸ *Samen* to sprout ❹ *Teig* to rise ❺ (*klar werden*) ■**jdm ~** to dawn on sb ❻ (*seine Erfüllung finden*) ■**in etw** *dat* **~** to be wrapped up in sth

aufgehoben I. *adj* [**bei jdm**] **gut/schlecht ~ sein** to be/not be in good hands [with sb] **II.** *pp von* **aufheben**

auf|geilen (*sl*) **I.** *vt* to turn on *sep,* to get worked up *sep* **II.** *vr* ■**sich** *akk* [**an jdm/etw**] **~** to be turned on [by sb/sth], to get off [on sb/sth]

aufgekratzt I. *adj* (*fam*) full of vim and vigor **II.** *pp von* **aufkratzen**

aufgelegt I. *adj* **gut/schlecht ~ sein** to be in a good/bad mood; ■**dazu ~ sein, etw zu tun** to feel like doing sth **II.** *pp von* **auflegen**

aufgelöst I. *adj* ■**~ sein** to be beside oneself **II.** *pp von* **auflösen**

aufgeregt I. *adj* ❶ (*gespannt*) excited ❷ (*nervös*) nervous; (*durcheinander*) flustered **II.** *adv* ❶ (*gespannt*) excitedly ❷ (*nervös*) nervously **III.** *pp von* **aufregen**

aufgeschlossen I. *adj* open-minded **II.** *adv* **neuen Ideen ~ gegenüberstehen** to be open to new ideas **III.** *pp von* **aufschließen**

Aufgeschlossenheit <-> *f kein pl* open-mindedness

aufgeschmissen *adj* (*fam*) ■**~ sein** to be in a jam

aufgesetzt I. *adj Lächeln* false **II.** *pp von* **aufsetzen**

aufgeweckt I. *adj* bright **II.** *pp von* **aufwecken**

auf|gießen *vt irreg* ❶ *Kaffee, Tee* to make ❷ (*nachfüllen*) *Kaffee, Tee* to warm; *kaltes Getränk* to refresh

auf|gliedern *vt* to subdivide (**in** +*akk* into)

auf|greifen *vt irreg* ❶ (*festnehmen*) to pick up *sep* ❷ (*weiterverfolgen*) to take up *sep*

aufgrund, auf Grund [aufˈgrʊnt] *präp* +*gen* because of

auf|haben *irreg* (*fam*) **I.** *vt* ❶ (*geöffnet haben*) *Knopf* to have undone; *Tür, Fenster* to have open ❷ *Hut, Mütze* to wear **II.** *vi Geschäft, Museum* to be open

auf|halsen *vt* (*fam*) ■**jdm etw ~** to saddle sb with sth

auf|halten *irreg* **I.** *vt* ❶ (*am Weiterkommen hindern*) to hold up *sep* ❷ (*zum Halten bringen*) to stop ❸ (*abhalten*) to keep back (**bei** +*dat* from) ❹ **jdm die Tür ~** to hold open *sep* the door for sb; **die Hand ~** to hold out *sep* one's hand **II.** *vr* ❶ (*verweilen*) ■**sich** *akk* **~** to stay ❷ (*sich weiterhin befassen*) ■**sich** *akk* **mit jdm/etw ~** to spend time [dealing] with sb/sth

auf|hängen I. *vt* ❶ (*daran hängen*) to hang up *sep* ❷ (*durch Erhängen töten*) to hang **II.** *vr* ■**sich** *akk* **~** to hang oneself

Aufhänger <-s, -> *m* ❶ (*Schlaufe*) loop ❷ (*Anknüpfungspunkt*) peg

auf|heben *irreg* **I.** *vt* ❶ (*vom Boden nehmen*) to pick up *sep* ❷ (*nicht wegwerfen*) to keep ❸ (*aufbewahren*) to keep, to preserve ❹ *Gesetz* to abolish; *Urteil* to reverse; *Verbot* to lift **II.** *vr* (*sich ausgleichen*) ■**sich ~** to offset each other

Aufhebung <-, -en> *f* abolition; *eines Urteils* reversal; *eines Verbots* lifting

auf|heitern I. *vt* to cheer up *sep* **II.** *vr, vi impers* ■[**sich**] **~** *Wetter* to brighten up

Aufheiterung <-, -en> *f* METEO bright period

auf|hellen I. *vt* ❶ (*blonder, heller machen*) to lighten ❷ (*klarer machen*) to throw light upon **II.** *vr* ■**sich ~** (*sonniger werden*) to brighten [up]

auf|hetzen *vt* (*pej*) to incite (**gegen** +*akk* against)

auf|holen I. *vt* to make up *sep* **II.** *vi* to catch up; *Läufer, Rennfahrer* to make up ground

auf|horchen *vi* to prick up one's ears

auf|hören *vi* to stop

auf|kaufen *vt* to buy up *sep*

aufklappbar *adj* hinged; **~es Verdeck** fold[-]down top

auf|klappen *vt* ❶ *Buch* to open [up *sep*]; *Liegestuhl* to unfold; *Messer* to unclasp; *Verdeck* to fold back *sep* ❷ *Kragen* to turn up *sep*

auf|klären I. *vt* ❶ (*erklären*) to clarify; *Irrtum, Missverständnis* to resolve ❷ (*aufdecken*) to solve; *Verbrechen* to clear up ❸ (*informieren*) to inform (**über** +*akk* about) ❹ (*sexuell informieren*) to explain the facts of life; ■**aufgeklärt sein** to know the facts of life **II.** *vr* ■**sich ~** ❶ *Geheimnis, Irrtum* to resolve itself ❷ (*sonniger werden*) to brighten [up]

Aufklärung *f* ❶ (*Erklärung*) clarification; *von Irrtum, Missverständnis* resolution ❷ (*Aufdeckung*) solution (+*gen* of, **von** +*dat* to); *von*

A

Verbrechen clearing up ❸ (*Information*) information (**über** +*akk* about) ❹ (*sexuelle Information*) sex education ❺ PHIL, LIT ■ **die** ~ the Enlightenment

Aufklärungsbedarf *m kein pl* need for information

Aufklärungskampagne *f* information campaign

auf|kleben *vt* to stick (**auf** +*akk* on); *Briefmarke* to put on *sep*

Aufkleber *m* sticker

auf|knöpfen *vt* to unbutton; *Knopf* to undo

auf|kochen I. *vt haben* to bring to a boil II. *vi sein* to come to a boil

auf|kommen *vi irreg sein* ❶ (*finanziell*) ■ **für etw** ~ to pay for sth; ■ **für jdn** ~ to pay for sb's upkeep ❷ (*entstehen*) to arise; *Nebel, Regen* to set in; *Wind* to pick up; ■ **etw** ~ **lassen** to give rise to sth

auf|kratzen *vt Wunde* to scratch open *sep*

auf|kreischen *vi* to shriek

auf|krempeln *vt* to roll up *sep*

auf|kreuzen *vi sein* (*fam*) to turn up

auf|kriegen *vt* (*fam*) *s.* **aufbekommen**

auf|lachen *vi* to [give a] laugh

auf|laden *irreg vt* ❶ **etw auf den Wagen** ~ to load on[to] a vehicle ❷ ■ **jdm etw** ~ to burden sb with sth ❸ *Batterie* to charge

Auflage <-, -n> *f* ❶ *eines Buchs* edition; **verbesserte** ~ revised edition ❷ (*Auflagenhöhe*) *eines Buchs* number of copies; *einer Zeitung* circulation ❸ (*Bedingung*) condition; **die** ~ **haben, etw zu tun** to be obliged to do sth ❹ (*Polster*) pad

auf|lassen *vt irreg* (*fam*) ❶ (*offen lassen*) to leave open *sep* ❷ (*aufbehalten*) to leave on *sep*

auf|lauern *vi* ■ **jdm** ~ to lie in wait for sb

Auflauf *m* ❶ KOCHK casserole ❷ (*Menschenauflauf*) crowd

auf|laufen *vi irreg sein* ❶ (*sich ansammeln*) to accumulate ❷ (*auf Grund laufen*) to run aground ❸ ■ **jdn** ~ **lassen** (*fam*) to show sb up

auf|leben *vi sein* ❶ (*munter werden*) to liven up ❷ (*neuen Lebensmut bekommen*) to find a new lease on life ❸ (*wieder belebt werden*) to revive

auf|legen *vt* ❶ (*herausgeben*) to publish; **ein Buch neu** ~ to reprint a book; (*neue Bearbeitung*) to bring out a new edition of a book ❷ **eine CD** ~ to put on *sep* a CD ❸ **den Hörer** ~ to hang up ❹ **Holz/Kohle** ~ to put on *sep* more wood/coal

auf|lehnen *vr* ■ **sich** *akk* ~ to revolt (**gegen** +*akk* against)

auf|lesen *vt irreg* (*fam*) ❶ (*aufsammeln*) to pick up *sep* ❷ **jdn [von der Straße]** ~ (*fam*) to pick sb up [off the street]

auf|leuchten *vi sein o haben* to light up

auf|listen *vt* to list

auf|lockern I. *vt* ❶ (*abwechslungsreicher machen*) to liven up *sep* ❷ (*zwangloser machen*) to loosen up ❸ (*weniger streng machen*) to soften ❹ **die Erde** ~ to break up *sep* the earth II. *vr* ■ **sich** ~ (*sich zerstreuen*) to break up; **aufgelockerte Bewölkung** thinning cloud cover

auf|lösen I. *vt* ❶ (*in Flüssigkeit lösen*) to dissolve ❷ (*aufklären*) to clear up *sep* ❸ (*das Bestehen beenden*) *Partei, Verein* to disband; *Parlament* to dissolve; *Konto, Geschäft* to close; *Haushalt* to break up *sep* II. *vr* ■ **sich** ~ ❶ (*in Flüssigkeit zergehen*) to dissolve ❷ (*sich klären*) to resolve itself ❸ *Bewölkung* to break up; *Nebel a.* to lift

Auflösung *f* ❶ (*Beendigung des Bestehens*) *einer Partei, eines Vereins* disbanding; *des Parlaments* dissolution; *eines Kontos, Geschäfts* closing; *eines Haushalts* breaking up ❷ (*Lösung*) *eines Rätsels* solution ❸ (*Bildqualität*) resolution

auf|machen I. *vt* ❶ (*fam: öffnen*) to open; *Knopf* to undo ❷ (*gestalten*) to make up *sep* II. *vi* (*fam*) ❶ (*die Tür öffnen*) to open the door ❷ (*ein Geschäft eröffnen*) to open up III. *vr* ■ **sich** *akk* ~ to set out (**in** +*akk* for)

Aufmachung <-, -en> *f* ❶ (*Kleidung*) outfit ❷ (*Gestaltung*) *eines Buchs* presentation; *einer Seite, Zeitschrift* layout

aufmerksam I. *adj* attentive; ■ **auf etw** ~ **werden** to take notice of sth; **jdn auf etw** ~ **machen** to draw sb's attention to sth; **das ist sehr** ~ **[von Ihnen]**! that's most kind [of you] II. *adv* attentively

Aufmerksamkeit <-, -en> *f* ❶ *kein pl* (*aufmerksames Verhalten*) attention ❷ *kein pl* (*Zuvorkommenheit*) attentiveness ❸ (*Geschenk*) token [gift]

auf|möbeln *vt* (*fam*) ❶ (*restaurieren*) to do up *sep* ❷ (*aufmuntern*) to cheer up *sep*

auf|mucken, auf|mucksen *vi* (*fam*) ■ **gegen etw** ~ to protest against sth

auf|muntern *vt* ❶ (*aufheitern*) to cheer up *sep* ❷ (*beleben*) to liven up *sep* ❸ (*Mut machen*) to encourage

aufmunternd I. *adj* encouraging II. *adv* encouragingly

Aufmunterung <-, -en> *f* ❶ (*Aufheiterung*) cheering up ❷ (*Ermutigung*) encouragement ❸ (*Belebung*) livening up

aufmüpfig *adj* (*fam*) rebellious

Aufnahme <-, -n> *f* ❶ (*Fotografie*) photo[graph]; **eine** ~ **machen** to take a photo[graph] ❷ (*Tonbandaufnahme*) [tape] recording ❸ (*Beginn*) start; *von Tätigkeit a.* taking up; *von Beziehung, Verbindung a.* establishment ❹ (*Verleihung der Mitgliedschaft*) admission (**in** +*akk* into)

aufnahmefähig *adj* ■ **[für etw]** ~ **sein** to be able to grasp *sep*

Aufnahmegebühr *f* membership fee

Aufnahmelager *nt* POL, SOZIOL refugee camp

Aufnahmeprüfung *f* entrance exam[ination]

auf|nehmen *vt irreg* ❶ (*fotografieren*) to photograph ❷ (*filmen*) to film ❸ (*aufzeichnen*) to record (**auf** +*akk* on) ❹ (*unterbringen*) ■ **jdn** [**bei sich** *dat*] ~ to take in *sep* sb ❺ (*beitreten lassen*) to admit (**in** +*akk* [in]to) ❻ (*geistig registrieren*) to grasp ❼ (*auflisten*) to include ❽ (*beginnen*) to begin; *Tätigkeit* to take up *sep;* **Kontakt mit jdm** ~ to contact sb ❾ (*absorbieren*) to absorb ❿ (*auf etw reagieren*) to receive; **wie hat sie es aufgenommen?** how did she take it? ⓫ NORDD (*aufwischen*) to wipe up *sep*

auf|nötigen *vt* ■ **jdm etw** ~ to force sth on sb

auf|opfern *vr* ■ **sich** *akk* ~ to sacrifice oneself

aufopfernd, aufopferungsvoll I. *adj* devoted **II.** *adv* with devotion

auf|passen *vi* ❶ (*aufmerksam sein*) to pay attention; **genau** ~ to pay close attention; ■ **pass auf!** (*sei aufmerksam*) [be] careful!; (*Vorsicht*) watch out! ❷ (*beaufsichtigen*) to keep an eye (**auf** +*akk* on); **auf die Kinder** ~ to watch the children

Aufpasser(in) <-s, -> *m(f)* (*pej*) watchdog

auf|peitschen *vt* (*aufhetzen*) to inflame; (*stärker*) to whip up *sep* into a frenzy

auf|peppen ['auf·pɛpn̩] *vt* (*sl*) to jazz up *sep*

auf|platzen *vi sein* to burst open; *Wunde* to open up

auf|plustern *vr* ■ **sich** *akk* ~ ❶ *Vogel* to ruffle [up *sep*] its feathers ❷ (*pej fam*) *Mensch* to puff oneself up

Aufprall <-[e]s, -e> *m* impact

auf|prallen *vi sein* ■ **auf etw** ~ to hit sth; *Mensch, Fahrzeug a.* to run into sth

Aufpreis *m* surcharge; **gegen** ~ for an additional charge

auf|probieren* *vt* to try [on *sep*]

auf|pumpen *vt* to pump up *sep*

auf|putschen I. *vt* ❶ (*aufwiegeln*) to stir up *sep* (**gegen** +*akk* against) ❷ (*Leistungsfähigkeit steigern*) to stimulate **II.** *vr* ■ **sich** *akk* [**mit etw** *dat*] ~ to pump oneself up [with sth]

Aufputschmittel *nt* stimulant

auf|quellen *vi irreg sein* to swell [up]

auf|raffen *vr* ❶ ■ **sich** *akk* [**vom Stuhl**] ~ to pull oneself up [from a chair] ❷ (*überwinden*) ■ **sich** *akk* **zu etw** *dat* ~ to bring oneself to do sth

auf|ragen *vi* to rise; (*sehr hoch*) to tower [up]

auf|rappeln *vr* (*fam*) ■ **sich** *akk* ~ ❶ (*sich erholen*) to recover ❷ *s.* **aufraffen**

auf|räumen I. *vt Zimmer* to clean [up *sep*]; *Schrank* to clear out; *Schreibtisch* to clear [off *sep*]; *Spielsachen* to put away *sep* **II.** *vi* ❶ (*Ordnung machen*) to clean up ❷ (*beseitigen*) ■ **mit etw** *dat* ~ to do away with sth

Aufräumungsarbeiten *pl* cleanup operation

aufrecht ['auf·rɛçt] *adj, adv* upright

aufrecht|erhalten* ['auf·rɛçt·ʔɛɐ̯·hal·tn̩] *vt irreg* to maintain; *Freundschaft* to keep up *sep;* **seine Behauptung** ~ to stick to one's claim; **seine Entscheidung** ~ to abide by one's decision

auf|regen I. *vt* (*erregen*) to excite; (*verärgern*) to annoy; (*nervös machen*) to make nervous **II.** *vr* ■ **sich** *akk* ~ to get worked up (**über** +*akk* about); **reg dich nicht so auf!** don't get [yourself] so worked up!

aufregend *adj* exciting

Aufregung *f* ❶ (*aufgeregte Erwartung*) excitement ❷ (*Beunruhigung*) agitation; **nur keine ~!** don't get flustered; **in heller** ~ in utter confusion; **jdn in ~ versetzen** to make sb lose their composure *fam*

aufreibend *adj* trying

auf|reißen *irreg vt haben* ❶ *Tüte, Geschenk* to tear open *sep* ❷ *Fenster, Tür* to fling open *sep* ❸ *Augen, Mund* to open wide *sep* ❹ ■ **jdn** ~ (*sl: aufgabeln*) to pick up *sep* sb

auf|reizen *vt* ❶ (*erregen*) to excite; (*stärker*) to inflame ❷ (*provozieren*) to provoke

aufreizend I. *adj* exciting; (*sexuell*) provocative; *Unterwäsche a.* sexy *fam* **II.** *adv* provocatively

auf|richten I. *vt* ❶ (*in aufrechte Lage bringen*) to set upright ❷ (*Mut machen*) ■ **jdn** [**wieder**] ~ to encourage sb **II.** *vr* ■ **sich** *akk* ~ to straighten up

aufrichtig I. *adj* honest; *Gefühl* sincere; *Liebe* true **II.** *adv* sincerely

Aufrichtigkeit <-> *f kein pl* sincerity

auf|rollen *vt* ❶ (*zusammenrollen*) to roll up *sep; Kabel* to coil [up *sep*], to wind [up *sep*] ❷ (*entrollen*) to unroll ❸ (*erneut aufgreifen*) to reopen

auf|rücken *vi sein* ❶ (*weiterrücken*) to move up; (*auf einer Bank a.*) to scoot over ❷ (*avancieren*) to be promoted (**zu** +*dat* to)

Aufruf *m* ❶ (*Appell*) appeal ❷ COMPUT call; *von Daten a.* retrieval

auf|rufen *irreg* **I.** *vt* ❶ *Zeuge, Schüler* to call [out *sep*] ❷ (*auffordern*) ■ **jdn ~, etw zu tun** to request that sb do sth ❸ COMPUT to call up *sep; Daten* to retrieve **II.** *vi* ■ **zu etw** *dat* ~ to call for sth

Aufruhr <-[e]s, -e> ['auf·ruːɐ̯] *m* ❶ *kein pl* (*Erregung*) turmoil; (*in der Stadt/im Volk*) unrest ❷ (*Aufstand*) revolt

aufrührerisch *adj* ❶ *attr* (*rebellisch*) rebellious ❷ (*aufwiegelnd*) inflammatory

auf|runden *vt* to round up *sep* (**auf** +*akk* to)

auf|rüsten I. *vi, vt* MIL to [re]arm **II.** *vt* (*hochwertiger machen*) to upgrade

Aufrüstung *f kein pl* MIL arming, armament

auf|rütteln *vt* ❶ **jdn** [**aus dem Schlaf**] ~ to rouse sb [from sleep] ❷ (*fig*) **jds Gewissen** ~ to stir sb's conscience

aufs [aufs] ❶ = **auf das** *s.* **auf** ❷ + *Superlativ* ~ **entschiedenste/grausamste** most decisively/cruelly

auf|sagen *vt* to recite

auf|sammeln *vt* to gather [up *sep*]; (*Fallengelassenes*) to pick up *sep*

aufsässig ['auf·zɛ·sɪç] *adj* ❶ (*widerspenstig*) unruly ❷ (*widersetzlich*) rebellious

Aufsatz *m* ❶ (*Text*) essay ❷ (*oberer Teil*) top part

auf|saugen *vt reg o irreg* ❶ *Flüssigkeit* to soak

up *sep* ❷ (*mit dem Staubsauger*) to vacuum up *sep* ❸ (*fig: in sich aufnehmen*) to absorb

auf|schauen *vi s.* **aufblicken**

auf|scheuchen *vt* ❶ *Tiere* to frighten away *sep* ❷ (*fam*) *Person* to disturb

auf|schichten *vt* to stack

auf|schieben *vt irreg* ❶ *Fenster, Tür* to slide open *sep; Riegel* to push back *sep* ❷ (*verschieben*) to postpone ▶ WENDUNGEN: **aufgeschoben ist nicht aufgehoben** (*prov*) there'll be another opportunity

Aufschlag *m* ❶ (*Aufprall*) impact ❷ (*Aufpreis*) surcharge

auf|schlagen *irreg* **I.** *vi* ❶ *sein* (*auftreffen*) to strike; **mit dem Kopf [auf etw** *akk o dat*] ~ to hit one's head [on sth] ❷ *haben* (*sich verteuern*) to go up (**um** +*akk* by) **II.** *vt haben* ❶ (*aufklappen*) to open; **Seite 35** ~ to turn to page 35 ❷ (*durch Schläge aufbrechen*) to break open *sep* ❸ (*aufbauen*) to put up *sep* ❹ (*verteuern*) to raise (**um** +*akk* by)

auf|schließen *irreg* **I.** *vt Tür* to unlock **II.** *vi* ■ [**jdm**] ~ to unlock the door [for sb]

auf|schlitzen *vt* to slash [open *sep*]

AufschlussRR *m* ~ **über jdn/etw geben** to give information about sb/sth

auf|schlüsseln *vt* to classify (**nach** +*dat* according to)

aufschlussreichRR *adj* informative; (*enthüllend*) revealing

auf|schnappen *vt* (*fam: mitbekommen*) to pick up *sep,* to pick up on

auf|schneiden *irreg* **I.** *vt* ❶ (*in Scheiben schneiden*) to slice ❷ (*öffnen*) to cut open *sep* **II.** *vi* (*fam: angeben*) to brag

Aufschneider(in) *m(f)* (*fam*) bragger, braggart

Aufschnitt *m kein pl* (*Wurstaufschnitt*) cold cuts *npl;* (*Käseaufschnitt*) assorted sliced cheese[s *pl*]

auf|schnüren *vt* to untie; *Paket* to unwrap; *Schuh* to unlace

auf|schrauben *vt* to unscrew; *Flasche* to take the cap off

auf|schrecken I. *vt* <schreckte auf, aufgeschreckt> *haben* to startle (**aus** +*dat* from) **II.** *vi* <schreckte *o* schrak auf, aufgeschreckt> *sein* to start [up] (**aus** +*dat* from)

Aufschrei *m* ❶ (*schriller Schrei*) scream ❷ (*Lamento*) outcry

auf|schreiben *vt irreg* to write down *sep;* ■ **sich** *dat* **etw** ~ to make a note of sth

auf|schreien *vi irreg* to shriek

Aufschrift *f* inscription

Aufschub *m* ❶ (*Verzögerung*) delay (+*gen* in); (*das Hinauszögern*) postponement ❷ (*Stundung*) respite; **jdm ~ gewähren** to grant sb an extension

auf|schütten *vt* (*aufhäufen*) to heap up *sep*

auf|schwatzen *vt* DIAL (*fam*) ■ **jdm etw** ~ to palm off *sep* sth on sb; ■ **sich** *dat* **etw ~ lassen** to get talked into buying sth

Aufschwung *m* ❶ (*Auftrieb*) impetus; **jdm neuen ~ geben** to give sb a boost ❷ (*Aufwärtstrend*) upswing

auf|sehen *vi irreg s.* **aufblicken**

Aufsehen <-s> *nt kein pl* sensation; **ohne [großes]** ~ without any [real] fuss; **etw erregt [großes]** ~ sth causes a [great] sensation; ~ **erregend** sensational

aufsehenerregend *adj* sensational

Aufseher(in) <-s, -> *m(f)* (*Gefängnisaufseher*) [prison] guard; (*Museumsaufseher*) attendant

auf|seinALT *vi irreg sein* (*fam*) *s.* **auf II**

aufseiten [auf-'zai-tn̩] *präp* +*gen* on the part of

auf|setzen I. *vt* ❶ *Hut, Brille* to put on *sep* ❷ *Essen, Wasser* to put on *sep* ❸ (*zur Schau tragen*) to put on *sep* **II.** *vr* ■ **sich** *akk* ~ to sit up **III.** *vi* to land (**auf** +*dat* on)

Aufsicht <-, -en> *f* ❶ *kein pl* (*Überwachung*) supervision (**über** +*akk* of) ❷ (*Person*) person in charge

Aufsichtspflicht *f kein pl* supervisory responsibility [*or* duty] (*legal responsibility to look after sb, esp. children*); **die elterliche** ~ parental responsibility

Aufsichtsrat *m* supervisory board

auf|spannen *vt Schirm* to open

auf|sparen *vt* to save

auf|sperren *vt* ❶ (*fam: weit öffnen*) to open wide *sep* ❷ SÜDD, ÖSTERR (*aufschließen*) to unlock

auf|spielen *vr* (*fam*) ■ **sich** *akk* ~ to show off

auf|spießen *vt* **ein Stück Fleisch** ~ to skewer a piece of meat; **etw mit der Gabel** ~ to stab one's fork into sth

auf|springen *vi irreg sein* ❶ (*hochspringen*) to jump up ❷ **auf ein Fahrzeug** ~ to jump on[to] a vehicle ❸ (*sich abrupt öffnen*) to burst open

auf|spüren *vt* to track down *sep*

auf|stacheln *vt* ■ **jdn [zu etw** *dat*] ~ to incite sb [to do sth]; ■ **jdn gegen jdn** ~ to turn sb against sb

Aufstand *m* rebellion

Aufständische(r) *f(m) dekl wie adj* rebel; (*einer politischen Gruppe a.*) insurgent

auf|stapeln *vt* to stack [up *sep*]

auf|stauen *vr* ■ **sich** ~ *Ärger, Wut* to be bottled up

auf|stehen *vi irreg* ❶ *sein* (*sich erheben*) to stand up ❷ *sein* (*das Bett verlassen*) to get up ❸ *haben* (*fam: offen sein*) to be open

auf|steigen *vi irreg sein* ❶ (*sich in die Luft erheben*) to soar [up]; *Flugzeug* to climb; *Ballon* to ascend ❷ (*besteigen*) ■ [**auf etw**] ~ to climb [*or* get] on[to] [sth] ❸ (*befördert werden*) to be promoted (**zu** +*dat* to) ❹ (*entstehen*) ■ **in jdm** ~ *Gefühl* to well up in sb

auf|stellen I. *vt* ❶ (*aufbauen*) to put up *sep; Maschine* to install; *Denkmal* to erect; *Falle* to set ❷ *Rekord* to set ❸ *Kandidat* to nominate ❹ *Wache* to post ❺ (*aufrichten*) to prick up *sep* ❻ SCHWEIZ (*aufmuntern*) to perk up *sep* **II.** *vr* ■ **sich** ~ to stand; **sich hintereinander** ~ to line up; **sich im Kreis** ~ to form a circle

Aufstieg <-[e]s, -e> ['auf·ʃtiːk] *m* ① (*Verbesserung*) rise; **sozialer ~** social advancement; **den ~ ins Management schaffen** to work one's way up into management ② (*Weg zum Gipfel*) climb (**auf** +*akk* up)

Aufstiegschance [-ʃãː·sə] *f*, **Aufstiegsmöglichkeit** *f* chance of promotion

auf|stöbern *vt* ■**jdn ~** to track down *sep* sb; ■**etw ~** to discover sth

auf|stocken *vt* to increase (**um** +*akk* by); **ein Team ~** to add players to a team

auf|stoßen *irreg* **I.** *vi* ① *haben* (*rülpsen*) to burp; **das Essen stößt mir immer noch auf** that food is still repeating on me ② *sein* (*fam*) **jdm sauer/übel ~** to stick in sb's throat **II.** *vt haben* (*öffnen*) to push open *sep* **III.** *vr haben* **sich** *dat* **den Kopf/das Knie ~** to hit one's head/knee

auf|stützen *vr* ■**sich** *akk* [**auf etw**] **~** to support oneself [on sth]; *Gebrechliche a.* to prop oneself up [on sth]

auf|suchen *vt* (*geh*) ① ■**jdn ~** to go to [see] sb ② ■**etw ~** to go to sth

Auftakt *m* prelude (**zu** +*dat* to); **den ~ zu etw** *dat* **bilden** to mark the beginning of sth

auf|tanken *vt, vi* to fill up *sep; Flugzeug* to refuel

auf|tauchen *vi sein* ① (*an die Oberfläche kommen*) to surface; *Taucher a.* to come up ② (*zum Vorschein kommen*) to turn up; *verlorener Gegenstand a.* to be found ③ (*plötzlich da sein*) to suddenly appear ④ (*sichtbar werden*) to appear (**aus** +*dat* out of)

auf|tauen **I.** *vi sein* ① *Eis* to thaw ② (*fig*) to open up **II.** *vt haben* to thaw [out *sep*]

auf|teilen *vt* ① (*aufgliedern*) to divide [up *sep*] (**in** +*akk* into) ② (*verteilen*) to share *sep* (**unter** +*dat* among)

Aufteilung *f* division (**in** +*akk* into)

auf|tischen *vt* (*fam: erzählen*) to tell; **jdm Lügen ~** to tell sb a pack of lies

Auftrag <-[e]s, Aufträge> ['auf·traːk, *pl* 'auf·trɛː·gə] *m* ① (*Beauftragung*) contract; (*an Freiberufler*) commission ② (*Bestellung*) [sales] order (**über** +*akk* for) ③ (*Anweisung*) orders *pl*; **jdm den ~ geben, etw zu tun** to instruct sb to do sth ④ *pl selten* (*Mission*) mission; **„~ erledigt!"** "mission accomplished!"

auf|tragen *irreg vt* ① (*aufstreichen*) to apply (**auf** +*akk* to) ② (*in Auftrag geben*) ■**jdm etw ~** to instruct sb to do sth ③ *Kleidung* to wear out *sep*

Auftraggeber(in) <-s, -> *m(f)* client

Auftragslage *f* order status

auf|treiben *vt irreg* (*fam*) ■**jdn/etw ~** to get [a] hold of sb/sth

auf|trennen *vt* to undo

auf|treten *irreg* **I.** *vi sein* ① (*eintreten*) to occur; *Schwierigkeiten* to arise ② (*erscheinen*) to appear [on the scene *a. pej*] (**als** as) ③ (*in einem Stück spielen*) to appear [on the stage] (**als** as) ④ (*sich benehmen*) to behave; **selbstbewusst ~** to exhibit self-confidence **II.** *vt haben Tür* to kick open *sep*

Auftreten <-s> *nt kein pl* (*Benehmen*) behavior

Auftrieb *m kein pl* (*Schwung*) impetus; **jdm neuen ~ geben** to give sb a [new] boost

Auftritt *m* (*Erscheinen auf der Bühne*) entrance

auf|trumpfen *vi* to show one's superiority

auf|tun *irreg* **I.** *vr* ■**sich ~** *Möglichkeit* to open [up] **II.** *vt* (*sl: ausfindig machen*) to find

auf|wachen *vi sein* to wake [up]

auf|wachsen [-ks-] *vi irreg sein* to grow up

Aufwand <-[e]s> ['auf·vant] *m kein pl* ① (*Einsatz*) expenditure; **der ~ war umsonst** it was a waste of energy/money/time ② (*großer Luxus*) extravagance; [**großen**] **~ treiben** to be [very] extravagant

aufwändigRR **I.** *adj* ① (*teuer und luxuriös*) lavish; **~es Material** costly material[s *pl*] ② (*umfangreich*) costly, expensive **II.** *adv* lavishly

Aufwandsentschädigung *f* expense allowance

auf|wärmen **I.** *vt* ① *Essen* to heat up *sep* ② (*fam*) *Thema* to drag up *sep* **II.** *vr* ■**sich** *akk* **~** ① (*bei Kälte*) to warm oneself [up] ② (*Muskulatur auflockern*) to warm up

aufwärts ['auf·vɛrts] *adv* ① (*nach oben*) up, upward[s]; **den Fluss ~** upstream ② (*bergauf*) uphill

Aufwärtsentwicklung *f* upward trend (+*gen* in)

aufwärts|gehen *vi irreg sein* ■**es geht** [**mit jdm/etw**] **aufwärts** things are looking up [for sb/sth]

Aufwärtstrend *m*, **Aufwärtstendenz** *f* upward trend

auf|wecken *vt* to wake [up *sep*]

auf|weichen **I.** *vt haben Boden* to soak **II.** *vi sein Boden* to become soft

auf|weisen *vt irreg* to show; **zahlreiche Fehler ~** to be full of mistakes

auf|wenden *vt irreg o reg* to use; *Zeit, Mühe* to expend; *Geld* to spend; **viel Energie ~, etw zu tun** to put a lot of energy into doing sth

aufwendig *adj, adv s.* **aufwändig**

auf|werfen *irreg vt Frage* to raise

auf|werten *vt* ① *Währung* to revalue (**um** +*akk* by) ② (*fig*) to increase the value of

Aufwertung <-, -en> *f* ① *einer Währung* revaluation (**um** +*akk* by) ② (*fig*) enhancement

auf|wickeln *vt* ① (*aufrollen*) to roll up *sep* ② (*auseinanderwickeln*) to unwind

auf|wiegen *vt irreg* to compensate for

Aufwind *m* ① *kein pl* (*Aufschwung*) impetus; [**neuen**] **~ bekommen** to be given a boost ② LUFT upcurrent, updraft

auf|wirbeln *vi, vt* to swirl up

auf|wischen *vt, vi* to wipe [up *sep*]

auf|wühlen *vt* ■**jdn** [**innerlich**] **~** to stir up *sep* sb

auf|zählen *vt* to list

Aufzählung <-, -en> *f* list; *von Gründen, Namen a.* enumeration

A

auf|zeichnen *vt* ❶ (*aufnehmen*) to record (**auf** +*akk* on); *mit dem Videorekorder* to videotape ❷ (*als Zeichnung erstellen*) to draw (**auf** +*akk* on) ❸ (*notieren*) to note [down *sep*]
Aufzeichnung *f* ❶ (*Aufnahme*) recording; (*auf Band a.*) taping; (*auf Videoband a.*) videotaping ❷ *meist pl* (*Notizen*) notes
auf|zeigen *vt* to show, to demonstrate
auf|ziehen *irreg* **I.** *vt haben* ❶ (*durch Ziehen öffnen*) to open; *Reißverschluss* to unzip; *Vorhänge* to draw [*or* pull] back *sep* ❷ **die Uhr ~** to wind up *sep* the clock ❸ (*großziehen*) to raise ❹ (*fam: verspotten*) to tease (**mit** +*dat* about) **II.** *vi sein* (*sich nähern*) to gather
Aufzucht *f* raising
Aufzug *m* ❶ (*Fahrstuhl*) elevator; [**mit dem**] **~ fahren** to take the elevator ❷ (*pej fam: Kleidung*) getup
auf|zwingen *irreg vt* ■ **jdm etw ~** to force sth on sb
Aug. *Abk von* **August** Aug.
Augapfel ['auk·ʔapfl̩] *m* eyeball
Auge <-s, -n> ['au·gə] *nt* ❶ (*Sehorgan*) eye; **gute/schlechte ~n haben** to have good/poor eyesight *sing* ❷ (*Punkt beim Würfeln*) point ▶ WENDUNGEN: **mit einem blauen ~ davonkommen** (*fam*) to get off lightly; **mit offenen ~n schlafen** (*fam*) to daydream; **unter vier ~n** in private; **jdm etw aufs ~ drücken** (*fam*) to force sth on sb; **ins ~ gehen** (*fam*) to backfire; **ein ~ auf jdn/etw werfen** to have one's eye on sb/sth; **jdn nicht aus den ~n lassen** to not let sb out of one's sight; **ins ~ springen** to catch sb's eye; **etw aus den ~n verlieren** to lose track of sth; **sich aus den ~n verlieren** to lose touch with; **die ~n vor etw** *dat* **verschließen** to close one's eyes to sth; **ein ~/beide ~n zudrücken** (*fam*) to turn a blind eye to; **kein ~ zutun** (*fam*) to not sleep a wink; **~n zu und durch** (*fam*) take a deep breath and do it
Augenarzt, -ärztin *m, f* optometrist; (*Augenchirurg*) ophthalmologist
Augenaufschlag *m* look
Augenblick ['au·gn̩·blɪk] *m* moment; **im ersten ~** for a moment; **im letzten ~** at the [very] last moment; **~ mal!** just a minute!
augenblicklich ['au·gn̩·blɪk·lɪç] **I.** *adj* ❶ (*sofortig*) immediate ❷ (*derzeitig*) present **II.** *adv* ❶ (*sofort*) immediately; (*herausfordernd*) at once, this minute ❷ (*zurzeit*) at present
Augenbraue *f* eyebrow; **die ~n hochziehen** to raise one's eyebrows
augenfällig *adj* obvious
Augenfarbe *f* eye color
Augenhöhe *f* ■ **in ~** at eye level
Augenlicht *nt kein pl* (*geh*) [eye]sight
Augenlid *nt* eyelid
Augenmerk <-s> *nt kein pl* attention; **sein ~ auf jdn/etw richten** to give one's attention to sb/sth
Augenoptiker(in) *m(f)* optician
Augenringe *pl* rings under one's eyes *pl*
Augenschein *m kein pl* (*Anschein*) appearance; **dem ~ nach** by all appearances ▶ WENDUNGEN: **jdn/etw in ~ nehmen** to look closely at sb/sth
augenscheinlich ['au·gn̩·ʃain·lɪç] **I.** *adj* apparent **II.** *adv* apparently
Augentropfen *pl* eye drops *npl*
Augenweide *f* feast for one's eyes; **nicht gerade eine ~** something of an eyesore
Augenwinkel *m* corner of the eye
Augenwischerei <-, -en> *f* (*pej*) eyewash
Augenzeuge, -zeugin *m, f* eyewitness (**bei** +*dat* to)
augenzwinkernd *adv* with a wink
August <-[e]s, -e> [au·'gʊst] *m* August; *s. a.* **Februar**
Auktion <-, -en> *f* auction
Auktionshaus *nt* auction house, auctioneers *pl*
Aula <-, Aulen> ['au·la, *pl* 'au·lən] *f* [assembly] hall
Au-pair-Mädchen [o'pɛːɐ̯-] *nt* au pair [girl]
Aura <-> ['au·ra] *f kein pl* (*geh*) aura
aus [aus] **I.** *präp* +*dat* ❶ (*von innen nach außen*) out of; **~ dem Fenster/der Tür** out of the window/door; **das Öl tropfte ~ dem Fass** the oil was dripping from the barrel ❷ (*Herkunft*) from; **~ Stuttgart kommen** to be from Stuttgart; **~ dem 17. Jahrhundert stammen** to be [from the] 17th century; **Zigaretten ~ dem Automaten** cigarettes from a vending machine ❸ (*Ursache*) **~ Dummheit/Angst/Verzweiflung** out of stupidity/fear/desperation; **~ Unachtsamkeit** due to carelessness; **~ einer Laune heraus** on a whim ❹ (*Material*) **~ Glas/Holz** [made] of glass/wood **II.** *adv* (*fam*) ❶ (*gelöscht*) out ❷ (*ausgeschaltet*) off ❸ (*zu Ende*) ■ **~ sein** to have finished; *Krieg* to have ended; *Schule* to be out; **mit etw** *dat* **ist es ~** sth is over; **es ist ~** [**zwischen jdm**] (*fam*) it's over [between sb] ▶ WENDUNGEN: **~ und vorbei sein** to be over and done with; **auf jdn/etw ~ sein** to be after sb/sth
aus|arten *vi sein* ❶ (*außer Kontrolle geraten*) to get out of hand ❷ (*zu etw werden*) to degenerate (**in** +*akk*/**zu** +*dat* into)
aus|atmen *vi, vt* to exhale
aus|baden *vt* (*fam*) to pay for
Ausbau *m kein pl* ❶ *eines Gebäudes* extension (**zu** +*dat* into); (*innen*) conversion (**zu** +*dat* [in]to) ❷ (*das Herausmontieren*) removal (**aus** +*dat* from)
aus|bauen *vt* ❶ *Gebäude* to extend (**zu** +*dat* into); (*innen*) to remodel ❷ (*herausmontieren*) to remove (**aus** +*dat* from)
aus|bessern *vt* to repair
Ausbesserung <-, -en> *f* repairing
aus|beuten *vt* to exploit
Ausbeuter(in) <-s, -> *m(f)* (*pej*) exploiter
Ausbeutung <-, -en> *f* exploitation
aus|bezahlen* *vt Betrag* to pay out *sep; Person* to pay off *sep*

A

aus|bilden *vt* ① (*beruflich qualifizieren*) to train; (*unterrichten a.*) to instruct; (*akademisch*) to educate; **jdn zum Arzt ~** to train sb to be a doctor ② (*entwickeln*) to develop
Ausbilder(in) <-s, -> *m(f),* **Ausbildner(in)** <-s, -> *m(f)* ÖSTERR, SCHWEIZ trainer; MIL instructor
Ausbildung <-, -en> *f* ① (*Schulung*) training; (*Unterricht*) instruction; (*akademisch*) education; **in der ~ sein** to be in training; (*akademisch*) to still be in school [*or* college] ② (*Entwicklung*) development
Ausbildungsplatz *m* internship
aus|blasen *vt irreg* to blow out *sep*
aus|bleiben *vi irreg sein* to fail to appear; *Regen, Schnee* to hold off
aus|blenden *vt* (*fam*) *Problem* to forget
Ausblick *m* ① (*Aussicht*) view; **ein Zimmer mit ~ aufs Meer** a room overlooking the sea ② (*Zukunftsvision*) prospect
aus|borgen *vt* (*fam*) *s.* **ausleihen**
aus|brechen *irreg vi sein* ① (*entkommen*) to escape (**aus** +*dat* from) ② (*sich befreien*) to break away (**aus** +*dat* from) ③ *Vulkan* to erupt ④ *Feuer, Seuche, Panik* to break out ⑤ **in Gelächter/Tränen ~** to burst into laughter/tears
Ausbrecher(in) <-s, -> *m(f)* escapee
aus|breiten I. *vt* ① *Decke, Landkarte* to spread [out *sep*] ② *einzelne Gegenstände* to lay out *sep* ③ *Arme, Flügel* to spread [out *sep*] **II.** *vr* ■ **sich** *akk* **~** ① (*sich erstrecken*) to spread [out] ② (*übergreifen*) to spread (**auf** +*akk* to) ③ (*fam: sich breitmachen*) to spread oneself out
Ausbreitung <-, -en> *f* spread (**auf** +*akk* to)
Ausbruch *m* ① (*Gefängnisausbruch*) escape (**aus** +*dat* from) ② (*Beginn*) outbreak ③ *eines Vulkans* eruption ④ (*Gefühlsausbruch*) outburst
aus|brüten *vt* ① *Eier* to hatch ② (*fam*) *Erkältung* to become sick; **er brütet irgendetwas aus** he's feeling a cold coming on
aus|büchsen *vi sein* (*fam: abhauen*) to run away
aus|bürgern ['aus·bʏr·gɐn] *vt* to expatriate
Ausbürgerung <-, -en> *f* expatriation
aus|bürsten *vt* to brush [out *sep*]
Ausdauer *f kein pl* ① (*Beharrlichkeit*) perseverance ② (*körperlich*) endurance
aus|dehnen I. *vr* ■ **sich ~** ① (*größer werden*) to expand ② (*sich ausbreiten*) to spread (**auf** +*akk* to) **II.** *vt* ① (*verlängern*) to extend ② (*erweitern, vergrößern*) to expand (**auf** +*akk* to)
Ausdehnung <-, -en> *f* ① (*Verlängerung*) extension ② (*Ausbreitung*) spread[ing] (**auf** +*akk* to) ③ (*Erweiterung, Vergrößerung*) expansion ④ (*Fläche*) area; **eine ~ von 10.000 km²** **haben** to cover an area of about 4,000 mi²
aus|denken *vr irreg* ■ **sich** *dat* **etw ~** to think up *sep* sth; **sich eine Überraschung ~** to plan a surprise
aus|diskutieren* *vt* to finish discussing
aus|drehen *vt* (*fam*) to turn off *sep*
Ausdruck¹ <-drücke> *m* ① (*Bezeichnung*) expression ② (*Gesichtsausdruck*) [facial] expression ③ **als ~ der Dankbarkeit** as an expression of one's gratitude; **etw zum ~ bringen** to express sth
Ausdruck² <-drucke> *m* [computer] printout; **einen ~ [von etw** *dat*] **machen** to run off *sep* a copy [of sth]
aus|drucken *vt* to print [out *sep*]
aus|drücken I. *vt* ① (*bekunden*) to express ② (*formulieren*) to put into words; **anders ausgedrückt** in other words; **einfach ausgedrückt** put simply ③ (*zeigen*) to show ④ (*auspressen*) to squeeze ⑤ *Zigarette* to snuff out *sep* **II.** *vr* ■ **sich** *akk* **~** to express oneself; **sich falsch ~** to use the wrong word
ausdrücklich ['aus·drʏk·lɪç] **I.** *adj attr* explicit **II.** *adv* explicitly; (*besonders*) particularly
ausdruckslos *adj* inexpressive; *Gesicht* expressionless; (*ungerührt*) impassive; *Blick* vacant
ausdrucksvoll *adj* expressive
Ausdrucksweise *f* way one expresses oneself
auseinander [aus·ʔai·'nan·dɐ] *adv* apart
auseinander|biegen *vt* to bend apart *sep*
auseinander|fallen *vi irreg sein* to fall apart
auseinander|falten *vt* to unfold
auseinander|gehen *vi irreg sein* ① *Menschen* to part ② *Beziehung* to break up; *Ehe a.* to fall apart ③ *Meinungen* to differ ④ (*fam: dick werden*) to [start to] fill out *a. hum*
auseinander|nehmen *vt irreg* (*demontieren*) to take apart *sep* sth; (*zerstören*) to tear apart *sep* sth
auseinander|setzen I. *vt* ■ **jdm etw ~** to explain sth to sb **II.** *vt* ■ **sich** *akk* **mit etw** *dat* **~** to tackle sth
Auseinandersetzung <-, -en> [aus·ʔai·'nan·dɐ·zɛtsʊŋ] *f* ① (*Streit*) argument ② (*Beschäftigung*) ■ **die ~ mit etw** *dat* the examination of sth
aus|erwählen* *vt* (*geh*) to choose (**zu** +*dat* for)
aus|fahren *irreg vt* ① (*spazieren fahren*) to take [out *sep*] for a drive ② (*ausliefern*) to deliver
Ausfahrt *f* ① (*Spazierfahrt*) drive; **eine ~ machen** to go for a drive ② (*Hof-, Garagenausfahrt*) exit; (*mit Tor*) gateway ③ (*Autobahnausfahrt*) exit [ramp]
Ausfall *m* ① (*Verlust*) loss ② (*das Versagen*) failure; AUTO breakdown; (*Produktionsausfall*) stoppage; MED failure ③ *kein pl* (*das Nichtstattfinden*) cancellation; (*das Fehlen*) absence
aus|fallen *vi irreg sein* ① (*herausfallen*) to fall out ② (*nicht stattfinden*) to be canceled; ■ **etw ~ lassen** to cancel sth ③ (*nicht funktionieren*) *Niere* to fail; *Motor* to break down ④ (*entfallen*) to be lost ⑤ (*nicht zur Verfügung stehen*) to be absent
ausfallend, ausfällig *adj* abusive; ■ **~ werden** to become abusive (**gegen** +*akk* toward)

A

Ausfallstraße *f* arterial road

ausfindig *adj* ■ **jdn/etw ~ machen** to locate sb/sth

aus|fließen *vi irreg sein* to leak out

aus|flippen ['aus·flɪpn̩] *vi sein* (*fam*) ① (*wütend werden*) to freak out ② (*sich wahnsinnig freuen*) to jump for joy ③ (*überschnappen*) to lose it [completely]

Ausflucht <-, Ausflüchte> *f* excuse; **Ausflüchte machen** to make excuses

Ausflug *m* outing; SCH field trip

Ausflügler(in) <-s, -> ['aus·fly:k·lɐ] *m(f)* excursionist; (*für einen Tag*) day-tripper, sb taking a day trip

Ausflugslokal *nt* tourist café

Ausflugsort *m* day trip destination

aus|fragen *vt* to question

aus|fransen *vi sein* to fray

aus|fressen *vt irreg* (*fam*) ■ **etwas/nichts ausgefressen haben** to have done something/nothing wrong

Ausfuhr <-> *f kein pl* export[ation]

Ausfuhrbestimmungen *pl* export regulations *pl*

aus|führen *vt* ① (*durchführen*) to carry out *sep; Befehl* to execute ② (*spazieren führen*) to take out *sep;* **jdn zum Essen ~** to take sb out *sep* for dinner ③ (*exportieren*) to export (**in** +*akk* to) ④ (*erläutern*) to explain; (*darlegen*) to elaborate on *sep*

ausführlich ['aus·fy:ɐ̯·lɪç] **I.** *adj* detailed **II.** *adv* in detail; **sehr ~** in great detail

Ausführlichkeit <-> *f kein pl* detail[edness]; **in aller ~** in [great] detail

Ausführung *f* ① *kein pl* (*Durchführung*) carrying out; *von Befehl* execution ② (*Qualität*) quality; *von Möbel a.* workmanship ③ (*Modell*) model ④ *meist pl* (*Darlegung, Erklärung*) explanation

Ausfuhrzoll *m* export duty

aus|füllen *vt* ① *Formular* to fill in [*or* out] *sep* ② (*befriedigen*) to satisfy ③ **seine Zeit mit etw** *dat* **~** to fill one's time with sth ④ (*füllen*) to fill

Ausgabe *f* ① *kein pl* (*Austeilung*) distribution; (*Aushändigung a.*) handing out ② MEDIA, LIT edition; *von Zeitschrift a.* issue; (*Version*) version ③ *pl* (*Kosten*) expenses

Ausgabenbeleg *m* FIN receipt [for an expenditure]

Ausgang *m* ① (*Weg nach draußen*) exit (+*gen* from) ② (*Erlaubnis zum Ausgehen*) permission to go out; MIL pass; **~ haben** to have permission to go out; MIL to be on leave ③ *kein pl* (*Ende*) end; *einer Epoche a.* close; *von Film, Roman a.* ending; (*Ergebnis*) outcome

Ausgangsbasis *f* basis

Ausgangsposition *f* starting position

Ausgangspunkt *m* starting point; *einer Reise a.* departure

Ausgangssperre *f* MIL (*für die Bevölkerung*) curfew; (*für Soldaten*) confinement to barracks

aus|geben *irreg* **I.** *vt* ① *Geld* to spend (**für** +*akk* on) ② (*austeilen*) to distribute (**an** +*akk* to); (*aushändigen a.*) to hand out *sep* ③ (*fam: spendieren*) ■ **jdm etw ~** to treat sb to sth; **eine Runde ~** to buy a round; [**jdm**] **einen ~** (*fam*) to buy sb a drink **II.** *vr* ■ **sich** *akk* **als jd/etw ~** to pass oneself off as sb/sth

ausgebrannt *adj* drained *fam;* (*geistig erschöpft a.*) burned-out

ausgebucht *adj* booked up

ausgedehnt **I.** *adj* ① (*lang*) long ② (*umfangreich*) extensive **II.** *pp von* **ausdehnen**

ausgedient *adj* (*fam*) worn-out; ■ **~ haben** to have had its day

ausgefallen **I.** *adj* unusual; (*sonderbar*) weird **II.** *pp von* **ausfallen**

ausgeflippt **I.** *adj* freaky **II.** *pp von* **ausflippen**

ausgeglichen **I.** *adj* even; *Mensch* easy-going **II.** *pp von* **ausgleichen**

Ausgeglichenheit <-> *f kein pl* evenness; *Mensch* level-headedness

aus|gehen *vi irreg sein* ① (*abends weggehen*) to go out ② *Feuer, Licht* to go out ③ *Haare* to fall out ④ (*herrühren*) ■ **von jdm ~** to come from sb ⑤ (*als Basis nehmen*) ■ **von etw** *dat* **~** to take sth as a basis; ■ **davon ~, dass ...** to assume that ...; **davon kann man nicht ~** you can't go by that ⑥ (*enden*) to end; ■ **gut/schlecht ~** to turn out well/badly; *Buch, Film* to have a happy/sad ending

ausgehungert *adj* ① (*sehr hungrig*) starved ② (*ausgezehrt*) emaciated

ausgeklügelt *adj* ingenious, cleverly thought-out

ausgekocht *adj* (*pej fam*) cunning

ausgelassen **I.** *adj* wild; *Kinder* boisterous **II.** *adv* **es wurde ~ gefeiert** there was a lively party going on **III.** *pp von* **auslassen**

Ausgelassenheit <-> *f kein pl* wildness; *von Kindern* boisterousness

ausgelutscht ['aus·gə·lʊtʃt] *adj* (*sl*) worn-out *fam*

ausgemacht **I.** *adj attr* (*komplett*) complete; **~er Unsinn** complete [*or* utter] nonsense **II.** *pp von* **ausmachen**

ausgemergelt *adj* emaciated; *Gesicht* gaunt

ausgenommen **I.** *konj* except; **wir kommen, ~ es regnet** we'll come, but only if it doesn't rain **II.** *pp von* **ausnehmen**

ausgepowert [-pauɐt] *adj* (*fam*) beat

ausgeprägt *adj* distinctive; *Interesse* pronounced; *Stolz* deep-seated

ausgerechnet ['aus·gə·rɛç·nət] **I.** *adv* ① *personenbezogen* ■ **~ jd/jdn/jdm** sb of all people ② *zeitbezogen* ■ **~ jetzt** now of all times; ■ **~ gestern/heute** yesterday/today of all days **II.** *pp von* **ausrechnen**

ausgeschlossen **I.** *adj pred* **es ist nicht ~, dass ...** it is still possible that ...; ■ [**völlig**] **~!** [that's] [completely] out of the question **II.** *pp von* **ausschließen**

ausgeschnitten *adj* **tief ~** *Kleid, Bluse* low-cut

ausgesorgt *adv* ■ **~ haben** to be set up for life *fam*
ausgesprochen **I.** *adv* really **II.** *pp von* **aussprechen**
ausgestorben **I.** *adj* ❶ *Tier-, Pflanzenart* extinct ❷ *Straßen, Dorf* deserted **II.** *pp von* **aussterben**
ausgesucht **I.** *adj* ❶ (*erlesen*) choice ❷ (*gewählt*) well-chosen **II.** *adv* extremely **III.** *pp von* **aussuchen**
ausgewachsen [-vaks-] *adj* ❶ (*voll entwickelt*) fully grown ❷ (*fam: komplett*) utter
ausgewogen *adj* balanced
ausgezeichnet ['aus·gə·tsaiç·nət] **I.** *adj* excellent, great **II.** *adv* extremely well **III.** *pp von* **auszeichnen**
ausgiebig ['aus·giː·bɪç] **I.** *adj* extensive; *Mahlzeit* substantial; *Mittagsschlaf* long **II.** *adv* extensively; **~ schlafen** to have a good [long] sleep
aus|gießen *vt irreg* ❶ *Gefäß* to empty [out *sep*]; *Inhalt* to pour away *sep* ❷ (*füllen*) to fill [in *sep*] (**mit** +*dat* with)
Ausgleich <-[e]s, -e> *m pl selten* evening out, balancing
aus|gleichen *irreg* **I.** *vt* *Unterschied* to even out; *Mangel* to compensate for; *Meinungsverschiedenheit* to reconcile; *Konto* to balance **II.** *vr* ■ **sich ~** to balance out
aus|graben *vt irreg* ❶ (*aus der Erde graben*) to dig up *sep; Altertümer* to excavate ❷ (*hervorholen*) to dig out *sep; alte Geschichten* to bring up *sep*
Ausgrabung <-, -en> *f* (*Grabungsarbeiten*) excavation[s *pl*]; (*Grabungsort*) excavation site; (*Grabungsfund*) [archaeological] find
aus|grenzen *vt* to exclude (**aus** +*dat* from)
Ausgrenzung <-> *f kein pl* exclusion (**aus** +*dat* from)
Ausguss[RR] *m* ❶ (*Spüle*) sink ❷ (*Tülle*) spout
aus|haben *irreg vt* (*fam: ausgezogen haben*) to have taken off *sep*
aus|halten *irreg vt* ❶ (*ertragen können*) to bear; **hältst du es noch eine Stunde aus?** can you hold out [for] another hour?; **die Kälte ~** to endure the cold; **es ist nicht [länger] auszuhalten** it's [getting to be] unbearable; **es lässt sich hier ~** it's not a bad place ❷ (*standhalten*) to be resistant to; **eine hohe Temperatur ~** to withstand a high temperature; **den Druck ~** to [with]stand the pressure; **viel ~** to take a lot ❸ (*fam: finanziell*) ■ **jdn ~** to support sb
aus|handeln *vt* to negotiate
aus|händigen ['aus·hɛn·dɪ·gn̩] *vt* to hand over *sep*
Aushang *m* notice
aus|hängen **I.** *vt* (*aufhängen*) to put up *sep; Plakat* to post **II.** *vi irreg* to be/have been put up; **am schwarzen Brett ~** to be on the bulletin board
Aushängeschild *nt* ❶ (*Reklametafel*) sign[board] ❷ (*Renommierstück*) showpiece
aus|harren *vi* to wait [patiently]
aus|heben *vt irreg Graben, Grab* to dig
aus|hecken *vt* (*fam*) to hatch; **neue Streiche ~** to think up new tricks
aus|helfen *vi irreg* to help out *sep* (**mit** +*dat* with)
aus|heulen *vr* (*fam*) ■ **sich** *akk* **bei jdm ~** to have a good cry on sb's shoulder
Aushilfe *f* temporary worker; [**bei jdm**] **als ~ arbeiten** to temp [for sb] *fam*
aus|höhlen *vt* ❶ (*Inneres herausmachen*) to hollow out *sep* ❷ (*fig: untergraben*) to undermine
aus|holen *vi* ❶ (*Schwung nehmen*) ■ [**mit etw** *dat*] **~** to swing back *sep* [sth]; [**mit der Hand**] **~** to take a swing ❷ (*ausschweifen*) to beat around the bush
aus|horchen *vt* (*fam*) to sound out *sep* (**über** +*akk* about)
aus|kehren *vt* **das Haus ~** to sweep [out *sep*] the house
aus|kennen *vr irreg* ❶ ■ **sich irgendwo ~** to know one's way around somewhere ❷ ■ **sich** [**in etw** *dat*] **~** to know a lot [about sth]
aus|kippen *vt Gefäß* to empty [out *sep*]; *Inhalt* to pour out *sep*
aus|klammern *vt* to ignore
Ausklang *m kein pl* conclusion; **zum ~ des Abends** to conclude the evening
aus|klappen *vt* to open out *sep*
aus|klingen *vi irreg sein* (*geh*) to conclude (**mit** +*dat* with); *Abend, Feier a.* to finish off
aus|klopfen *vt* to beat the dust out of; *Teppich* to beat; *Pfeife* to knock out *sep*
aus|knipsen *vt* (*fam*) to switch off *sep*
aus|knobeln *vt* to work out *sep*
aus|kommen *vi irreg sein* ❶ (*ausreichend haben*) ■ **mit etw** *dat* **~** to get by on sth; ■ **ohne jdn/etw ~** to manage without sb/sth; (*nicht benötigen*) to go without sb/sth ❷ (*sich mit jdm vertragen*) ■ **mit jdm** [**gut**] **~** to get along [well] with sb ❸ ÖSTERR (*entkommen*) to escape
Auskommen <-s> *nt kein pl* livelihood; **sein ~ haben** to get by
aus|kosten *vt* to make the most of; **das Leben ~** to enjoy life to the fullest; **den Moment/seine Rache ~** to savor the moment/one's revenge
aus|kotzen (*derb*) **I.** *vt* to puke [up *sep*] **II.** *vr* (*fam*) ■ **sich** *akk* **bei jdm ~** to complain like crazy to sb
aus|kramen *vt* (*hervorholen*) to unearth; (*alte Geschichten*) to bring up *sep*
aus|kratzen *vt* to scrape out *sep*
aus|kriegen *vt* (*fam: ausziehen können*) to get off *sep*
aus|kugeln *vt* to dislocate
Auskunft <-, Auskünfte> ['aus·kʊnft, *pl* 'aus·kʏnf·tə] *f* ❶ (*Information*) information (**über** +*akk* about); **nähere ~** more information ❷ (*Auskunftsschalter*) information counter/desk ❸ (*Fernsprechschalter*) the operator, in-

formation

aus|kurieren* (*fam*) **I.** *vt* to cure [completely] **II.** *vr* ■ **sich** *akk* ~ to get better

aus|lachen *vt* to laugh at; (*höhnisch*) to jeer at

aus|laden *irreg vt* ① (*entladen*) to unload; NAUT *a.* to discharge ② (*Einladung widerrufen*) ■ **jdn** ~ to tell sb not to come; (*förmlich*) to cancel sb's invitation

Auslage <-, -n> *f* ① (*ausgestellte Ware*) display ② (*Schaufenster*) store window; (*Schaukasten*) showcase ③ *meist pl* (*finanziell*) expenses *npl*

Ausland ['aus·lant] *nt kein pl* ■ [**das**] ~ foreign countries *pl;* ■ **aus dem** ~ from abroad; ■ **ins/im** ~ abroad

Ausländer(in) <-s, -> ['aus·lɛn·dɐ] *m(f)* foreigner; JUR alien

Ausländerbeauftragte(r) *f(m) dekl wie adj* Commissioner for Foreigners' Affairs

ausländerfeindlich *adj* racist

Ausländerfeindlichkeit <-> *f kein pl* racism

Ausländerpolitik *f* policy regarding foreigners

Ausländerwohnheim *nt* home for immigrants

ausländisch ['aus·lɛn·dɪʃ] *adj attr* foreign

Auslandsbeziehungen *pl* POL foreign relations

Auslandseinsatz *m* MIL foreign [military] deployment

Auslandsgespräch *nt* TELEK international call

Auslandskorrespondent(in) *m(f)* foreign correspondent

aus|lassen *irreg* **I.** *vt* ① (*weglassen*) to omit; (*überspringen*) to skip ② (*verpassen*) to miss ③ (*abreagieren*) ■ **etw an jdm** ~ to vent sth on sb ④ (*fam: ausgeschaltet lassen*) to keep turned off ⑤ ÖSTERR (*loslassen*) to let go of; (*aus einem Käfig etc. freilassen*) to let out *sep* **II.** *vr* ■ **sich** *akk* **über jdn/etw** ~ to go on about sb/sth *pej* **III.** *vi* ÖSTERR to let go

Auslassung <-, -en> ['aus·la·sʊŋ] *f kein pl* omission

aus|lasten *vt* ① *Maschine, Betrieb* to use to capacity; ■ **voll ausgelastet sein** to be running to capacity *pred;* **teilweise ausgelastet** running at partial capacity *pred* ② *Person* to occupy fully

aus|laufen *irreg vi sein* ① (*herauslaufen*) to run out (**aus** +*dat* of); (*wegen Undichtheit*) to leak out ② (*undicht sein*) to leak ③ (*Hafen verlassen*) to [set] sail (**nach** +*dat* for) ④ (*enden*) to end; *Vertrag* to expire

Auslaufmodell *nt* discontinued model

aus|laugen *vt* to exhaust

aus|leben *vr* ■ **sich** *akk* ~ to live it up

aus|leeren *vt Gefäß* to empty [out *sep*]; *Inhalt* to pour away *sep*

aus|legen *vt* ① (*ausbreiten*) to lay out *sep* ② (*deuten*) to interpret; **etw falsch** ~ to misinterpret sth ③ **jdm Geld** ~ to lend sb money ④ (*konzipieren*) to design (**für** +*akk* for)

Auslegung <-, -en> *f* interpretation

Auslegungssache *f* matter of interpretation

aus|leiern I. *vt haben* to wear out *sep* **II.** *vi sein* to wear out

aus|leihen *irreg vt* ■ **jdm etw** *akk* ~ to lend sb sth; ■ [**sich** *dat*] **etw** *akk* **von jdm** ~ to borrow sth from sb

Auslese <-> *f kein pl* (*Auswahl*) selection; **die natürliche** ~ natural selection

aus|lesen *irreg* **I.** *vt, vi* to finish reading **II.** *vt* (*auswählen*) to pick out *sep* (**aus** +*dat* from)

aus|liefern *vt* ① *Waren* to deliver (**an** +*akk* to) ② *Menschen* to hand over *sep* (**an** +*akk* to) ③ (*fig*) ■ **jdm/etw ausgeliefert sein** to be at the mercy of sb/sth

Auslieferung *f* ① *von Waren* delivery ② *von Menschen* handing over (**an** +*akk* to); *an ein anderes Land* extradition (**an** +*akk* to)

aus|liegen *vi irreg* to be [made] available (**für** +*akk* to/for); (*im Schaufenster*) to be displayed

aus|löffeln *vt* ▶WENDUNGEN: **etw** ~ **müssen** (*fam*) to take the consequences

aus|loggen *vr* ■ **sich** *akk* ~ COMPUT to log off

aus|löschen *vt* (*löschen*) to extinguish

aus|losen I. *vt* ■ **jdn/etw** ~ to draw sb/sth **II.** *vi* to draw lots

aus|lösen *vt* ① (*in Gang setzen*) to set off *sep; Bombe* to trigger ② (*bewirken*) *Aufstand* to unleash; *Begeisterung* to arouse; *Beifall* to elicit; *Erleichterung, allergische Reaktion* to cause ③ (*einlösen*) to redeem; *Gefangene* to release; (*durch Lösegeld*) to ransom

Auslöser <-s, -> *m* ① FOTO [shutter] release ② PSYCH trigger mechanism ③ (*fam: Anlass*) trigger

Auslosung <-, -en> *f* draw

aus|machen *vt* ① (*löschen*) to extinguish ② (*ausschalten*) to turn off *sep; Motor a.* to switch off *sep* ③ (*vereinbaren*) to agree [up]on ④ (*betragen*) to amount to ⑤ (*bewirken*) ■ **kaum etwas** ~ to hardly make any difference; ■ **nichts** ~ to not make any difference; ■ **viel** ~ to make a big difference ⑥ (*stören*) ■ **es macht jdm nichts/viel aus, etw zu tun** sb doesn't mind/really does mind doing sth; **macht es Ihnen etwas aus, wenn ...?** do you mind if ...?

aus|malen *vr* ■ **sich** *dat* **etw** ~ to imagine sth

Ausmaß *nt* ① (*Größe*) size; (*Fläche*) area; **das** ~ **von etw** *dat* **haben** to cover the area of sth ② (*fig: Tragweite*) extent

aus|merzen *vt* to exterminate; *Unkraut* to eradicate

aus|messen *vt irreg* to measure [out]

aus|misten *vt* ① *Stall* to muck out *sep* ② (*fam*) *Zimmer* to clean up *sep; alte Sachen* to throw out *sep*

aus|mustern *vt* (*aussortieren*) to take out *sep* of service; *Möbel* to discard

Ausnahme <-, -n> ['aus·na:mə] *f* exception ▶WENDUNGEN: ~**n bestätigen die Regel** (*prov*) the exception proves the rule *prov*

Ausnahmefall *m* exception[al case]

Ausnahmegenehmigung *f* special license

Ausnahmezustand *m* POL state of emergency;

den ~ verhängen to declare a state of emergency (**über** +*akk* in)
ausnahmslos *adv* without exception
ausnahmsweise *adv* for a change
aus|nehmen *irreg vt* ❶ (*ausweiden*) to gut; *Geflügel* to draw ❷ (*ausschließen*) to exempt (**von** +*dat* from); **ich nicht ausgenommen** myself not excepted ❸ (*fam: viel Geld abnehmen*) ■**jdn ~** to fleece sb *fam;* (*beim Glücksspiel*) to clean out *sep* sb *fam* ❹ ÖSTERR (*erkennen*) ■**jdn/etw ~** to make out *sep* sb/sth
ausnehmend *adv* exceptionally; **das gefällt mir ~ gut** I really like it a lot
aus|nüchtern *vi* to sober up
aus|nutzen *vt* ❶ (*ausbeuten*) to exploit ❷ (*sich zunutze machen*) to make the most of; **jds Leichtgläubigkeit ~** to take advantage of sb's gullibility
aus|packen I. *vt* to unpack; *Geschenk* to unwrap **II.** *vi* (*fam: gestehen*) to talk
aus|peitschen *vt* to whip
aus|pfeifen *vt irreg* to boo off the stage/to boo at
aus|plaudern *vt* to let out *sep*
aus|plündern *vt Menschen* to plunder; *Laden* to loot
aus|posaunen* *vt* (*fam*) to broadcast
aus|pressen *vt* **eine Zitrone/Orange ~** to squeeze a lemon/an orange; **den Saft ~** to press the juice
aus|probieren* **I.** *vt* to try [out *sep*] **II.** *vi* ■**~, ob/wie ...** to see whether/how ...
Auspuff <-[e]s, -e> *m* exhaust [pipe], tailpipe
Auspuffrohr *nt* exhaust [pipe], tailpipe
aus|pumpen *vt* ❶ (*leer pumpen*) to pump out *sep* ❷ (*fam: völlig erschöpfen*) to drain; ■**ausgepumpt sein** to be completely drained
aus|quartieren* *vt* to move out *sep*
aus|quetschen *vt* ❶ **Orangen ~** to squeeze oranges; **den Saft ~** to squeeze out *sep* the juice ❷ (*fam: ausfragen*) ■**jdn ~** to pump sb [for information]; *Polizei* to grill sb
aus|radieren* *vt* ❶ (*mit Radiergummi entfernen*) to erase *sep* ❷ (*vernichten*) to wipe out *sep*
aus|rangieren* [-raŋ·ʒiː·rən] *vt* to throw out *sep*
aus|rasten *vi sein* ❶ (*herausspringen*) to come out ❷ (*fam: wild werden*) to lose one's temper, to freak out *fam*
aus|rauben *vt* to rob
aus|räumen *vt* ❶ *Möbel* to move out *sep; Zimmer* to clear out *sep* ❷ (*beseitigen*) to clear up *sep; Zweifel, Missverständnis* to dispel
aus|rechnen *vt* to calculate
Ausrede *f* excuse
aus|reden I. *vi* to finish speaking **II.** *vt* ■**jdm etw ~** to talk sb out of sth
aus|reichen *vi* to be sufficient [*or* enough] (**für** +*akk* for)
ausreichend I. *adj* sufficient; *Kenntnisse, Leistungen* adequate; ■**nicht ~** insufficient/inadequate **II.** *adv* sufficiently
Ausreise *f* departure [from a country]; **jdm die ~ verweigern** to prohibit sb from leaving the country
Ausreiseerlaubnis *f,* **Ausreisegenehmigung** *f* exit permit
aus|reisen *vi sein* to leave the country
Ausreisevisum [-viː-] *nt* exit visa
aus|reißen *irreg* **I.** *vt haben* to pull out *sep; Haare* to tear out *sep; Blätter* to rip out *sep* **II.** *vi sein* (*fam: davonlaufen*) to run away
Ausreißer(in) <-s, -> *m(f)* (*fam*) runaway
aus|reiten *irreg* **I.** *vi sein* to ride out **II.** *vt haben* ■**ein Pferd ~** to take out *sep* a horse
aus|renken *vt* to dislocate
aus|richten *vt* ❶ (*übermitteln*) ■**jdm etw ~** to tell sb sth; **kann ich etwas ~?** can I give him/her a message?; **richten Sie ihr einen Gruß [von mir] aus** give her my regards ❷ (*veranstalten*) to organize; *Fest* to arrange ❸ (*erreichen*) ■**bei jdm etwas/nichts ~** to achieve something/nothing with sb ❹ ÖSTERR (*schlechtmachen*) ■**jdn ~** to badmouth sb ❺ SCHWEIZ (*zahlen*) ■**jdm etw ~** to pay sb sth
aus|rollen *vt* to roll out
aus|rotten *vt* to exterminate; *Termiten* to destroy; *Unkraut* to wipe out *sep; Ideen, Religion* to eradicate
aus|rücken *vi sein Truppen, Polizei* to turn out; *Feuerwehr* to go out on a call
Ausruf *m* cry
aus|rufen *vt irreg* to call out *sep; Streik* to call; *Krieg* to declare; ■**jdn ~** to put out a call for sb
Ausrufezeichen *nt,* **Ausrufungszeichen** *nt,* **Ausrufzeichen** *nt* ÖSTERR, SCHWEIZ exclamation point
aus|ruhen *vi, vr* ■**[sich** *akk*] **~** to rest, to relax; ■**ausgeruht [sein]** [to be] well rested
aus|rüsten *vt* to equip; *Fahrzeug, Schiff* to outfit
Ausrüstung <-> *f* ❶ *kein pl* (*das Ausrüsten*) equipping; *Fahrzeug, Schiff* outfitting ❷ (*Ausrüstungsgegenstände*) equipment; *Expedition a.* tackle; (*Kleidung*) outfit
aus|rutschen *vi sein* ❶ (*ausgleiten*) to slip (**auf** +*dat* on); **sie ist ausgerutscht** she slipped ❷ (*entgleiten*) ■**jdm ~** to slip [out of sb's hand]; **mir ist die Hand ausgerutscht** I lost my temper and slapped him/her
Ausrutscher <-s, -> *m* (*fam*) slip-up
aus|säen *vt* to sow
Aussage *f* ❶ *a.* JUR (*Darstellung*) statement; (*Zeugenaussage*) evidence; **eine ~ machen** to make a statement ❷ *eines Texts* message
aussagekräftig *adj* convincing
aus|sagen *vt* ■**etw [über jdn/etw] ~** to say sth [about sb/sth]
aus|schalten *vt* ❶ (*abstellen*) to turn off *sep* ❷ (*eliminieren*) to eliminate
Ausschau *f* ■**~ halten** to keep an eye out (**nach** +*dat* for)
aus|schauen *vi* DIAL, SÜDD, ÖSTERR *s.* **aussehen**
aus|scheiden *irreg* **I.** *vi sein* ❶ (*nicht weitermachen*) to retire (**aus** +*dat* from); *aus Verein*

to leave ❷ SPORT to drop out ❸ (*nicht in Betracht kommen*) to be ruled out **II.** *vt haben* (*absondern*) to excrete

Ausscheidungen *pl* (*Exkremente*) excrement

aus|schenken *vt* (*servieren*) to serve; *Bier* to pour

aus|scheren *vi sein* to pull out; (*ausschwenken*) to swing out

Ausschilderung *f* putting up of signs

aus|schimpfen *vt* ■ **jdn** ~ to tell sb off, to give sb hell

aus|schlachten *vt* ❶ (*Verwertbares ausbauen*) to cannibalize ❷ (*fam: ausnutzen*) to exploit

aus|schlafen *irreg* **I.** *vt* ■ **etw** ~ to sleep off *sep* sth **II.** *vi, vr* ■ [**sich** *akk*] ~ to sleep in

Ausschlag *m* MED rash ▶ WENDUNGEN: [**bei etw** *dat*] **den** ~ **geben** to be the decisive factor [for/in sth]

aus|schlagen *irreg vt* ❶ (*ablehnen*) to turn down *sep;* (*höflicher*) to decline; *Erbschaft a.* to disclaim; ■ **jdm etw** ~ to refuse sb sth ❷ **jdm einen Zahn** ~ to knock out *sep* one of sb's teeth

ausschlaggebend *adj* decisive; **von** ~**er Bedeutung sein** to be of primary importance

aus|schließen *irreg* **I.** *vt* ❶ (*entfernen*) to exclude (**aus** +*dat* from); (*als Strafe a.*) to bar; *Mitglied* to expel; (*vorübergehend*) to suspend ❷ (*für unmöglich halten*) to rule out *sep* ❸ (*aussperren*) ■ **jdn** ~ to lock out *sep* sb **II.** *vr* ■ **sich** *akk* ~ to lock oneself out

ausschließlich ['aus·ʃliːs·lɪç] **I.** *adj attr* exclusive **II.** *adv* exclusively; **darüber habe ~ ich zu bestimmen** I'm the one to decide on this matter **III.** *präp* excluding; (*geschrieben a.*) excl.

aus|schlüpfen *vi sein* to hatch out (**aus** +*dat* of)

AusschlussRR *m* exclusion; *von Mitglied* expulsion; (*vorübergehend*) suspension; **unter ~ der Öffentlichkeit stattfinden** to be closed to the public

aus|schmücken *vt* ❶ (*dekorieren*) to decorate ❷ (*ausgestalten*) to embellish

aus|schneiden *vt irreg* to cut out *sep* (**aus** +*dat* of)

Ausschnitt *m* ❶ (*Zeitungsausschnitt*) clipping ❷ (*an Kleidung*) neckline; **ein tiefer** ~ a low neckline ❸ (*Teil*) part (**aus** +*dat* of); *aus einem Gemälde, Foto* detail; *aus einem Roman* excerpt; *aus einem Film* clip

aus|schöpfen *vt Möglichkeiten, Reserven* to exhaust

aus|schreiben *vt irreg* ❶ (*ungekürzt schreiben*) to write out *sep* ❷ (*bekannt machen*) to announce; (*um Angebote zu erhalten*) to invite bids for; *Stelle* to advertise

Ausschreitung <-, -en> *f meist pl* riot[s *pl*]

AusschussRR *m* ❶ (*Gremium*) committee ❷ *kein pl* (*fehlerhaftes Teil*) rejects *pl*

aus|schütteln *vt* to shake out *sep*

aus|schütten *vt Gefäß* to empty; *Inhalt* to pour out ▶ WENDUNGEN: **sich** *akk* **vor Lachen** ~ to laugh until one cries

ausschweifend *adj Leben* hedonistic; *Fantasie* wild

Ausschweifung <-, -en> *f meist pl* excess

aus|schweigen *vr irreg* ■ **sich** *akk* ~ to remain silent; **sich eisern** ~ to maintain a stony silence

aus|schwenken *vt* ❶ (*ausspülen*) to rinse out *sep* ❷ (*zur Seite schwenken*) to swing out

aus|schwitzen *vt* to sweat out *sep*

aus|sehen *vi irreg* to look; ■ ~ **wie ...** to look like ...; **es sieht gut/schlecht aus** things are looking good/not looking too good; **nach Schnee/Regen** ~ to look like it's going to snow/rain; **seh' ich so aus?** what do you take me for?; **wie sieht's aus?** (*fam*) how's [*or* how're] things?

Aussehen <-s> *nt kein pl* appearance; ■ **dem ~ nach** judging by appearances

außen ['ausn̩] *adv* on the outside; **links/rechts** ~ on the outside left/right; ■ **von** ~ from the outside ▶ WENDUNGEN: **jdn/etw ~ vor lassen** to leave sb/sth out; ~ **vor sein** to be left out

Außenbeleuchtung *f* exterior lighting

Außenbezirk *m* outer district

Außenhandel *m* foreign trade

Außenminister(in) *m(f)* Secretary of State

Außenministerium *nt* State Department

Außenpolitik ['ausn̩·po·li·tiːk] *f* foreign policy

außenpolitisch ['ausn̩·po·liː·tɪʃ] **I.** *adj* foreign policy *attr;* ~**er Sprecher** foreign policy spokesman **II.** *adv* as regards foreign policy

Außenseite *f* outside; *eines Gebäudes* exterior

Außenseiter(in) <-s, -> *m(f)* (*a. fig*) outsider

Außenspiegel *m* AUTO [out]side mirror

Außenstehende(r) *f(m) dekl wie adj* outsider

Außenstelle *f* branch

Außenwelt *f* outside world

Außenwirtschaft *f* ÖKON foreign trade

außer ['ausɐ] **I.** *präp* +*dat* ❶ (*abgesehen von*) apart from ❷ (*zusätzlich zu*) in addition to ❸ ~ **Betrieb/Sicht/Gefahr sein** to be out of order/sight/danger ▶ WENDUNGEN: [**über jdn/etw**] ~ **sich** *dat* **sein** to be beside oneself [about sb/sth] **II.** *konj* ■ ~ **dass** except that; ■ ~ [**wenn**] except [when]

außerdem ['ausɐ·deːm] *adv* besides

äußere(r, s) ['ɔy·sə·rə, -rɐ, -rəs] *adj* ❶ (*außen gelegen*) outer; *Verletzung* external ❷ (*von außen wahrnehmbar*) exterior ❸ (*außenpolitisch*) external

Äußere(s) ['ɔy·sə·rə, -rəs] *nt dekl wie adj* outward appearance

außerehelich *adj* extramarital; *Kind* illegitimate

außereuropäisch *adj attr* non-European

außergerichtlich *adj, adv* out of court *attr*

außergewöhnlich ['au·sɐ·gə·'vøːn·lɪç] **I.** *adj* unusual; *Leistung* extraordinary; *Mensch* remarkable **II.** *adv* extremely

außerhalb ['au·sɐ·halp] **I.** *adv* outside; **von** ~ from out of town **II.** *präp* +*gen* outside

außerirdisch *adj* extraterrestrial
äußerlich ['ɔy·se·lɪç] *adj* ❶ (*außen befindlich*) external ❷ (*oberflächlich*) superficial
Äußerlichkeit <-, -en> *f* ❶ (*Oberflächlichkeit*) superficiality; (*Formalität*) formality ❷ *pl* (*oberflächliche Details*) trivialities *pl*
äußern ['ɔy·sen] **I.** *vr* ■ **sich** *akk* ~ ❶ (*Stellung nehmen*) to say something (**zu** +*dat* about); **sich über jdn/etw** ~ to make comments about sb/sth ❷ (*sich manifestieren*) to manifest itself **II.** *vt* (*sagen*) to say; (*zum Ausdruck bringen*) to utter; *Kritik* to voice; *Wunsch* to express
außerordentlich ['au·se·'ʔɔr·dn̩t·lɪç] **I.** *adj* extraordinary **II.** *adv* extraordinarily
außerorts *adv* SCHWEIZ, ÖSTERR out of town
außerplanmäßig ['au·se·plaːn·mɛː·sɪç] *adj* unscheduled; *Ausgaben, Kosten* nonbudgetary
äußerst ['ɔy·sest] *adv* extremely
außerstande [au·se·'ʃtan·də] *adj* ■ ~, **etw zu tun** unable to do sth
äußerste(**r, s**) *adj* ❶ (*entfernteste*) outermost; **am ~n Ende der Welt** at the farthest point of the globe; **der ~ Norden/Süden** the extreme north/south ❷ (*höchste*) utmost; **von ~r Wichtigkeit** of supreme importance; **der ~ Preis** the ultimate price
Äußerste *nt* **bis zum ~n gehen** to go to any extreme
äußerstenfalls ['ɔy·sestn̩·'fals] *adv* at the most
Äußerung <-, -en> *f* ❶ (*Bemerkung*) comment ❷ (*Zeichen*) expression
aus|setzen **I.** *vt* ❶ *Kind, Haustier* to abandon ❷ **eine Belohnung** ~ to offer a reward ❸ (*preisgeben*) ■ **jdn/etw einer S.** *dat* ~ to expose sb/sth to sth ❹ (*bemängeln*) **an etw** *dat* **etwas auszusetzen haben** to find fault with sth; **was hast du an ihr auszusetzen?** what don't you like about her?; **daran ist nichts auszusetzen** there's nothing wrong with that **II.** *vi* ❶ (*versagen*) to stop; *Motor* to fail ❷ (*unterbrechen*) ■ **mit etw** *dat* ~ to interrupt sth; **ohne auszusetzen** nonstop
Aussicht *f* ❶ (*Blick*) view; ■ **die ~ auf etw** the view overlooking sth ❷ (*Chance*) prospect; ■ **die ~ auf etw** the chance of sth; **etw in ~ haben** to have good prospects of sth; **jdm etw in ~ stellen** to promise sb sth
aussichtslos *adj* hopeless
Aussichtslosigkeit <-> *f kein pl* hopelessness
Aussichtsplattform *f* observation platform
Aussichtspunkt *m* viewpoint
aussichtsreich *adj* promising
Aussichtsturm *m* lookout tower
aus|siedeln *vt* to resettle
Aussiedler(**in**) *m(f)* emigrant
aus|sitzen *vt* to sit out
aus|söhnen ['aus·zøː·nən] *vr* ■ **sich** *akk* ~ to make [it] up; ■ **sich** *akk* **mit jdm/etw** ~ to reconcile with sb/to become reconciled with sth
Aussöhnung <-, -en> *f* reconciliation
aus|sondern *vt* to sort out
aus|sortieren* *vt* to sort out
aus|spannen **I.** *vi* to relax **II.** *vt* **jdm die Freundin/den Freund** ~ (*fam*) to steal sb's girlfriend/boyfriend
aus|sperren **I.** *vt* ■ **jdn** ~ to lock sb out **II.** *vr* ■ **sich** *akk* ~ to lock oneself out
aus|spielen *vt* ■ **jdn gegen jdn** ~ to play sb off against sb
aus|spionieren* *vt* to spy out
Aussprache *f* ❶ (*Akzent*) pronunciation; (*Art des Artikulierens*) articulation ❷ (*Unterredung*) talk
aus|sprechen *irreg* **I.** *vt* ❶ (*artikulieren*) to pronounce ❷ (*äußern*) to express; *Warnung* to issue; **ein Lob** ~ to give a word of praise ❸ (*ausdrücken*) ■ **jdm etw** ~ to express sth to sb **II.** *vr* ■ **sich** *akk* ~ ❶ (*sein Herz ausschütten*) to talk things over ❷ ■ **sich** *akk* **für/gegen jdn/etw** ~ to voice one's support for/opposition against sb/sth **III.** *vi* to finish [speaking]
Ausspruch *m* remark; (*geflügeltes Wort*) saying
aus|spucken **I.** *vt* to spit out *sep* **II.** *vi* to spit
aus|spülen *vt* to wash out *sep*
aus|staffieren* *vt* (*fam*) ❶ (*ausstatten*) to equip (**mit** +*dat* with) ❷ (*einkleiden*) to deck out *sep* (**mit** +*dat* in)
Ausstand *m* ❶ (*Streik*) **im ~ sein** to be on strike; **in den ~ treten** to go on strike ❷ SCHWEIZ, ÖSTERR, SÜDD (*Ausscheiden aus Stelle o Schule*) going away; **seinen ~ geben** to hold a going-away party
aus|statten ['aus·ʃtatn̩] *vt* ❶ (*versorgen*) to provide (**mit** +*dat* with) ❷ (*einrichten*) to furnish (**mit** +*dat* with) ❸ (*versehen*) to equip (**mit** +*dat* with)
Ausstattung <-, -en> *f* ❶ *kein pl* (*Ausrüstung*) equipment; (*das Ausrüsten*) equipping ❷ (*Einrichtung*) furnishings *pl* ❸ (*Aufmachung*) features *pl*
aus|stehen *irreg* **I.** *vt* ❶ (*ertragen*) to endure; **jdn/etw nicht ~ können** to not be able to stand sb/sth ❷ (*durchmachen*) to go through; **ausgestanden sein** (*vorbei sein*) to be all over [and done with] **II.** *vi* (*noch nicht da sein*) to be due; **die Antwort steht seit 5 Wochen aus** the reply has been due for 5 weeks
aus|steigen *vi irreg sein* ❶ (*aus einem Bus, Zug, Flugzeug*) to get off; (*aus einem Auto*) to get out of; **du kannst mich dort ~ lassen** you can drop me off over there ❷ (*aufgeben*) to drop out (**aus** +*dat* of)
aus|stellen **I.** *vt* ❶ (*zur Schau stellen*) to display; (*auf Messe, in Museum*) to exhibit ❷ [**jdm**] **eine Rechnung** ~ to issue [sb] an invoice; **sie ließ sich die Bescheinigung** ~ she had the certificate made out in her name ❸ (*ausschalten*) to switch off *sep* **II.** *vi* (*als Aussteller*) to exhibit
Aussteller(**in**) <-s, -> *m(f)* (*Messeaussteller*) exhibitor
Ausstellung *f* (*Kunstausstellung, Messe*) exhibition

A

Ausstellungsgelände *nt* exhibition site

Ausstellungshalle *f* exhibition hall

aus|sterben *vi irreg sein* to die out; *Geschlecht, Spezies* to become extinct

Aussteuer <-, -n> *f* dowry

Ausstieg <-[e]s, -e> *m* ❶ (*Öffnung*) exit ❷ (*das Aufgeben*) ■**der ~ aus etw** *dat* abandoning sth; **der ~ aus der Kernenergie** abandoning [of] nuclear energy

aus|stopfen *vt* to stuff

aus|stoßen *vt irreg* ❶ (*hinausblasen*) to eject; *Gase* to emit ❷ *Seufzer* to utter; *Schrei* to give [out]; *Laute* to make ❸ (*ausschließen*) to expel (**aus** +*dat* from)

aus|strahlen I. *vt* ❶ (*abstrahlen, verbreiten*) to radiate; *Licht, Wärme* to give off; *Radioaktivität* to emit ❷ RADIO, TV to transmit **II.** *vi* ■**in etw ~** *Schmerz* to extend to sth

Ausstrahlung *f* ❶ (*besondere Wirkung*) radiance; **eine besondere ~ haben** to have a special charisma ❷ RADIO, TV broadcast[ing]

aus|strecken I. *vt Hände, Beine* to stretch out **II.** *vr* ■**sich** *akk* **[auf dem Sofa] ~** to stretch oneself out [on the sofa]

aus|streichen *vt irreg* (*durchstreichen*) to cross out *sep*

aus|streuen *vt* to scatter

aus|strömen I. *vi sein Gas, Dampf* to escape (**aus** +*dat* from); *Flüssigkeit* to stream, to pour (**aus** +*dat* out of) **II.** *vt haben Hitze* to radiate; *Duft* to give off

aus|suchen *vt* to choose; ■**[sich** *dat*] **etw ~** to choose sth; ■**[sich** *dat*] **jdn ~** to pick sb

Austausch *m* exchange

austauschbar *adj* interchangeable; *defekte Teile, Mensch* replaceable

aus|tauschen I. *vt* ❶ (*ersetzen*) to replace (**gegen** +*akk* with) ❷ (*miteinander wechseln*) to exchange **II.** *vr* ■**sich** *akk* **über jdn/etw ~** to exchange stories about sb/sth

Austauschschüler(in) *m(f)* [high-school] exchange student

Austauschstudent(in) *m(f)* [college/university] exchange student

aus|teilen *vt* to distribute (**an** +*akk* to)

Auster <-, -n> ['aus·tɐ] *f* oyster

Austernpilz *m* oyster mushroom

aus|toben *vr* ■**sich** *akk* **~** to romp [*or* run] around

aus|tragen *vt irreg* ❶ *Post, Zeitung* to deliver ❷ *Baby* to carry to [full] term ❸ **einen Streit mit jdm ~** to have it out with sb ❹ SPORT *Wettkampf* to hold

Australien <-s> [aus·'traː·li̯·ən] *nt* Australia; *s. a.* **Deutschland**

Australier(in) <-s, -> [aus·'traː·li̯·ɐ] *m(f)* Australian; *s. a.* **Deutsche(r)**

australisch [aus·'traː·lɪʃ] *adj* Australian; *s. a.* **deutsch**

aus|treiben *irreg* **I.** *vt* ❶ ■**jdm etw ~** to knock sth out of sb ❷ *Teufel* to exorcise **II.** *vi* BOT to sprout

aus|treten *irreg* **I.** *vi sein* ❶ (*herausdringen*) to come out (**aus** +*dat* of); *Öl* to leak (**aus** +*dat* from); *Gas* to escape (**aus** +*dat* from) ❷ (*fam: zur Toilette gehen*) to go to the bathroom ❸ (*ausscheiden*) to leave (**aus** +*dat* from) **II.** *vt haben* ❶ (*auslöschen*) to stamp out ❷ *Schuhe* to wear out

aus|tricksen *vt* (*fam*) to trick

aus|trinken *irreg* **I.** *vt* to finish **II.** *vi* to drink up

Austritt *m* (*das Ausscheiden*) departure (**aus** +*dat* from)

aus|trocknen *vi sein* to dry out; *Fluss* to dry up; *Haut* to dehydrate; *Kehle* to become parched

aus|tüfteln *vt* (*fam: geschickt ausarbeiten*) to work out; (*sich ausdenken*) to think up

aus|üben *vt* ❶ *Beruf* to practice; *Amt* to hold; *Aufgabe, Funktion* to perform ❷ *Macht, Recht* to exercise; *Druck, Einfluss* to exert (**auf** +*akk* on); *Wirkung* to have (**auf** +*akk* on)

aus|ufern ['aus·ʔuː·fɐn] *vi sein* to escalate (**zu** +*dat* into)

Ausverkauf *m von Waren* clearance sale

ausverkauft *adj* sold out

Auswahl *f* ❶ (*Warenangebot*) selection (**an** +*dat* of) ❷ *kein pl* (*das Aussuchen*) **eine ~ treffen** to make one's choice (**unter** +*dat* from) ❸ SPORT all-star team

aus|wählen *vt, vi* to choose (**unter** +*dat* from)

Auswanderer, -wanderin *m, f* emigrant

aus|wandern *vi sein* to emigrate (**nach** +*dat* to)

Auswanderung *f* emigration

auswärtig ['aus·vɛr·tɪç] *adj attr* ❶ (*nicht vom Ort*) from out of town ❷ POL foreign

auswärts ['aus·vɛrts] *adv* ❶ (*außerhalb des Ortes*) out of town; **von ~ kommen** to be from another town ❷ **~ essen** to eat out

aus|waschen *vt irreg* ❶ (*entfernen*) to wash out (**aus** +*dat* from) ❷ (*säubern*) to rinse

auswechselbar *adj* (*untereinander auswechselbar*) interchangeable; (*ersetzbar*) replaceable

aus|wechseln [-ks-] *vt* to replace (**gegen** +*akk* with); *Spieler* to substitute (**gegen** +*akk* for)

Auswechselung, Auswechslung <-, -en> *f* replacement; SPORT substitution

Ausweg *m* way out (**aus** +*dat* of); **der letzte ~** the last resort

ausweglos *adj* hopeless

aus|weichen *vi irreg sein* ❶ (*vermeiden*) ■**[etw** *dat*] **~** to get out of the way [of sth] ❷ (*zu entgehen versuchen*) to evade ❸ (*als Alternative*) ■**auf etw ~** to fall back on sth

aus|weichend I. *adj* evasive **II.** *adv* **~ antworten** to be evasive

Ausweichmanöver *nt* ❶ AUTO, LUFT evasive maneuver ❷ (*Ausflucht*) evasion

Ausweichmöglichkeit *f* alternative

aus|weinen *vr* ■**sich** *akk* **bei jdm ~** to have a good cry on sb's shoulder

Ausweis <-es, -e> ['aus·vais] *m* ID; (*Personal-, Firmenausweis a.*) identity card; (*Mit-

glieds-, Leserausweis a.) card; (*Behindertenausweis*) identification card
aus|weisen *irreg* **I.** *vt* (*abschieben*) to deport **II.** *vr* ❶ (*sich identifizieren*) ■**sich** *akk* ~ to identify oneself; **können Sie sich ~?** do you have any [means of] identification? ❷ SCHWEIZ (*nachweisen*) ■**sich** *akk* **über etw** ~ to have proof of sth
Ausweiskontrolle *f* ID check
Ausweispapiere *pl* identification [*or* ID] papers *pl*
Ausweisung *f* ADMIN deportation
aus|weiten **I.** *vt* ❶ (*weiter machen*) to stretch ❷ (*umfangreicher machen*) to expand **II.** *vr* ■**sich** ~ ❶ (*weiter werden*) to stretch [out] ❷ (*sich ausdehnen*) to extend ❸ (*eskalieren*) to escalate
auswendig *adv* by heart; **etw ~ können** to know sth by heart
aus|werfen *vt irreg Netz, Leine* to cast out
aus|werten *vt Statistiken, Daten* to analyze
aus|wickeln *vt* to unwrap (**aus** +*dat* from)
aus|wirken *vr* ■**sich** ~ to have an effect (**auf** +*akk* on)
Auswirkung *f* (*Wirkung*) effect; (*Folge*) consequence
aus|wischen *vt* ❶ (*wegwischen*) to wipe ❷ (*sauber wischen*) to wipe clean *sep* ▶ WENDUNGEN: **jdm eins** ~ (*fam*) to put one over on sb
aus|wringen *vt irreg* to wring out *sep*
Auswuchs <-es, -wüchse> *m* (*Missstand*) excess
aus|zahlen **I.** *vt* ❶ *Lohn, Betrag* to pay out ❷ (*abfinden*) to pay off *sep; Kompagnon, Miterben* to buy out *sep* **II.** *vr* (*sich lohnen*) ■**sich** [**für jdn**] ~ to pay [off] [for sb]
aus|zählen *vt* to count
aus|zeichnen **I.** *vt* ❶ *Ware* to price ❷ (*ehren*) to honor; **jdn mit einem Preis** ~ to give sb an award ❸ (*positiv hervorheben*) ■**jdn** ~ to distinguish sb [from all others] **II.** *vr* ■**sich** *akk* ~ to stand out
Auszeichnung *f* (*Medaille*) medal; (*Orden*) decoration; (*Preis*) award
Auszeit *f* time out
aus|ziehen *irreg* **I.** *vt haben* ❶ (*ablegen*) ■[**sich** *dat*] **etw** ~ to take off *sep* sth ❷ (*entkleiden*) to get undressed ❸ (*herausziehen*) to pull out *sep* ❹ (*verlängern*) to extend **II.** *vi sein* [**aus einem Haus**] ~ to move out [of a house]
Auszubildende(r) *f(m) dekl wie adj* trainee
Auszug *m* ❶ (*aus einer Wohnung*) move ❷ (*Ausschnitt*) excerpt; *Buch a.* extract ❸ (*Kontoauszug*) statement ❹ PHARM extract (**aus** +*dat* of)
auszugsweise *adv* in excerpts [*or* extracts]
authentisch [au·ˈtɛn·tɪʃ] *adj* authentic
Auto <-s, -s> [ˈau·to] *nt* car; **~ fahren** to drive [a car]; (*als Mitfahrer*) to drive [by car]; **mit dem ~ fahren** to take the car
Autoatlas *m* road atlas
Autobahn *f* highway, freeway; (*in Deutschland a.*) autobahn

> The **Autobahn** is the German equivalent of a freeway. There is no speed limit on the **Autobahn** in Germany but in Austria, the speed limit for cars is 130 km/h and in Switzerland the speed limit for cars is 120 km/h.

Autobahnauffahrt *f* highway on-ramp
Autobahnausfahrt *f* highway exit
Autobahndreieck *nt* highway junction
Autobahngebühr *f* highway toll
Autobahnkreuz *nt* highway intersection
Autobahnraststätte *f* service area, rest stop
Autobatterie *f* car battery
AutobiografieRR, **Autobiographie** [au·to·bio·gra·ˈfiː] *f* autobiography
autobiografischRR, **autobiographisch** *adj* autobiographical
Autobombe *f* car bomb
Autobus [ˈau·to·bʊs] *m*, **Autocar** [ˈau·to·kaːɐ̯] *m* SCHWEIZ bus
Autodidakt(in) <-en, -en> [au·to·di·ˈdakt] *m(f)* self-educated person
Autofahrer(in) *m(f)* [car] driver
Autofahrt *f* car trip
Autofriedhof *m* (*fam*) junkyard
autogen [au·to·ˈgeːn] *adj* **~es Training** relaxation through self-hypnosis
Autogramm <-s, -e> [au·to·ˈgram] *nt* autograph
Autohändler(in) *m(f)* car dealer
Autokennzeichen *nt* license plate; (*Länderkennzeichen*) international license plate code
Autokino [ˈau·to·kiː·no] *nt* drive-in [movie theater]
Automat <-en, -en> [au·to·ˈmaːt] *m* (*Geldautomat*) ATM; (*Musikautomat*) jukebox; (*Spielautomat*) slot machine; (*Verkaufsautomat*) vending machine
Automatik <-, -en> [au·to·ˈmaː·tɪk] *f* ❶ (*Steuerungsautomatik*) automatic system ❷ (*Automatikgetriebe*) automatic transmission
automatisch [au·to·ˈmaː·tɪʃ] **I.** *adj* automatic **II.** *adv* automatically
automatisieren* [au·to·ma·ti·ˈziː·rən] *vt* to automate
Automatisierung <-, -en> *f* automation
Automobilindustrie *f* auto industry
autonom [au·to·ˈnoːm] *adj* POL autonomous
Autonome(r) *f(m) dekl wie adj* POL independent
Autonomie <-, -n> [au·to·no·ˈmiː, *pl* -ˈmiː·ən] *f* POL autonomy
Autonummer *f* license plate number
Autopilot [ˈau·to·pi·loːt] *m* LUFT autopilot
Autopsie <-, -n> [au·tɔ·ˈpsiː, *pl* -ˈpsiː·ən] *f* MED autopsy
Autor, **Autorin** <-s, Autoren> [ˈau·tɔɐ̯, au·ˈtoː·rɪn, *pl* au·ˈtoː·rən] *m, f* author

Autoradio *nt* car radio
Autoreifen *m* car tire
Autorennen *nt* motor race; (*Rennsport*) motor racing
autorisieren* [au·to·ri·'ziː·rən] *vt* to authorize; **ich habe ihn dazu autorisiert** I gave him authorization for it
autoritär [au·to·ri·'tɛːɐ̯] *adj* authoritarian
Autorität <-, -en> [au·to·ri·'tɛːt] *f* authority
Autoschlange *f* line of cars
Autoschlosser(in) *m(f)* auto mechanic
Autoschlüssel *f* car key
Autoskooter <-s, -> [-skuː·te] *m* bumper car
Autostopp ['au·to·ʃtɔp] *m* hitchhiking
Autotelefon *nt* car phone
Autounfall *m* car accident
Autoverleih <-[e]s, -e> *m*, **Autovermietung** <-, -en> *f* car rental company
Autowerkstatt *f* garage, car repair shop
avancieren* [avã·'siː·rən] *vi sein* (*geh*) to advance (**zu** +*dat* to)
Aversion <-, -en> [avɛr·'zi̯oːn] *f* aversion (**gegen** +*akk* to)
Avocado <-, -s> [avo·'kaː·do] *f* avocado
Axt <-, Äxte> [akst, *pl* 'ɛks·tə] *f* ax
Azoren [a'tsoː·rən] *pl* ■ **die** ~ the Azores *npl*
Azubi [a·'tsuː·bi] *m* <-s, -s>, *f* <-, -s> *kurz für* **Auszubildende(r)**

Bb

B, b <-, - *o fam* -s, -s> [beː] *nt* ❶ (*Buchstabe*) B, b; ~ **wie Berta** B as in Bravo ❷ MUS (*Note*) B flat; (*Erniedrigungszeichen*) flat
babbeln ['ba·bl̩n] *vi, vt* (*fam*) to babble; (*viel reden a.*) to chatter
Baby <-s, -s> ['beː·bi] *nt* baby
Babyklappe ['beː·bi-] *f hatch or container in which unwanted babies can be left anonymously*
Babypause ['beː·bi-] *f* (*fam*) parental leave
babysitten ['beː·bi·zɪ·tn̩] *vi meist infin* to babysit
Babysitter(in) <-s, -> ['beː·bi·zɪ·tɐ] *m(f)* babysitter
Babyspeck *m* (*hum fam*) baby fat
Babystrich *m* (*fam*) child prostitution
Bach <-[e]s, Bäche> [bax, *pl* 'bɛ·çə] *m* brook, creek; (*kleiner a.*) stream ▶ WENDUNGEN: **den ~ runtergehen** (*fam*) to go down the drain
Backblech *nt* baking sheet
Backbord <-[e]s> ['bak·bɔrt] *nt kein pl* NAUT port [side]
backbord(s) *adv* NAUT on the port side
Backe <-, -n> ['ba·kə] *f* (*Wange*) cheek; (*fam: Pobacke a.*) buttock
backen <backt *o* bäckt, backte, gebacken> ['ba·kn̩] *vt, vi* (*im Ofen*) to bake; (*in Fett*) to fry (**in** +*dat* in)
Backenknochen *m* cheekbone
Backenzahn *m* molar
Bäcker(in) <-s, -> ['bɛ·kɐ] *m(f)* ❶ (*Mensch*) baker ❷ (*Bäckerei*) bakery
Bäckerei <-, -en> [bɛ·kə·'rai] *f* ❶ (*Betrieb, Laden*) bakery ❷ ÖSTERR (*Gebäck*) small pastries and cookies
Backfisch ['bak·fɪʃ] *m* batter-fried fish
Backform *f* baking pan; (*Kuchenform a.*) cake pan
Backmischung *f* cake mix
Backofen ['bak·ʔoː·fn̩] *m* oven
Backpulver *nt* baking powder
Backröhre *f*, **Backrohr** *nt* ÖSTERR oven
Backstein *m* BAU brick
Backstube *f* bakery
bäckt *3. pers sing pres von* **backen**
Backup <-s, -s> ['bæk·ʌp] *nt o m* COMPUT backup [copy]
Backwaren *pl* baked goods *npl*
Bad <-[e]s, Bäder> [baːt, *pl* 'bɛː·dɐ] *nt* ❶ (*Wannenbad*) bath; **jdm/sich** *dat* **ein ~ einlassen** to run sb/oneself a bath ❷ (*Badezimmer*) bathroom ❸ (*Schwimmbad*) swimming pool ❹ (*Heilbad*) spa; (*Seebad*) seaside resort
Badeanzug *m* swimsuit, bathing suit
Badehose *f* swim[ming] trunks *npl*
Badekappe *f* swim[ming] cap
Bademantel *m* bathrobe
Bademeister(in) *m(f)* lifeguard
baden ['baː·dn̩] **I.** *vi* ❶ (*ein Wannenbad nehmen*) to take a bath ❷ (*schwimmen*) to swim (**in** +*dat* in); ~ **gehen** to go for a swim **II.** *vt* ■ **jdn** ~ to bathe sb **III.** *vr* ■ **sich** *akk* ~ to take a bath
Baden-Württemberg <-s> ['baː·dn̩·vʏr·təm·bɛrk] *nt* Baden-Württemberg
Badeort *m* ocean resort; (*Kurort*) spa resort
Badeschuh *m* flip-flop
Badetuch *nt* bath towel
Badewanne *f* bathtub
Badezimmer *nt* bathroom
baff [baf] *adj* (*fam*) ■ ~ **sein** to be flabbergasted
BAföG, Bafög <-> ['baː·fœk] *nt kein pl Akr von* **Bundesausbildungsförderungsgesetz** [student] grant; ~ **bekommen** to receive a grant
Bagatelle <-, -n> [ba·ga·'tɛ·lə] *f* trifle
bagatellisieren* [ba·ga·tɛ·li·'ziː·rən] *vt, vi* to trivialize
Bagger <-s, -> ['bagɐ] *m* digger; BAU excavator
baggern ['bagɐn] *vi* ❶ BAU to dig ❷ (*sl*) to flirt
Baggersee *m* manmade lake
Baguette <-s, -s> [ba·'gɛt] *nt* baguette,

French bread

Bahamas [ba·ˈhaː·mas] *pl* ■ **die** ~ the Bahamas *pl*

Bahn <-, -en> [baːn] *f* ❶ (*Eisenbahn*) train; (*Straßenbahn*) streetcar; **mit der ~ fahren** to take the train/streetcar ❷ *kein pl* (*Eisenbahngesellschaft*) railroad ❸ SPORT track; *eines Schwimmbeckens* lane ❹ (*Fahrbahn*) lane ▶ WENDUNGEN: **freie ~ haben** to have the go-ahead; **auf die schiefe ~ kommen** to get off the straight and narrow; **jdn aus der ~ werfen** to get sb off course

Bahnbeamte(r) *f(m)*, **-beamtin** *f* railroad official

bahnbrechend *adj* groundbreaking

Bahncard <-, -s> [-kaːd] *f a German discount rail pass*

bahnen *vt* **sich** *dat* **einen Weg durch etw** *akk* ~ to fight one's way through sth

Bahnfahrt *f* train trip

Bahngleis *nt* train track

Bahnhof *m* train station ▶ WENDUNGEN: **nur [noch] ~ verstehen** (*hum fam*) to not have the foggiest [idea]

Bahnhofshalle *f* [train] station concourse

Bahnhofsvorsteher(in) *m(f)*, **Bahnhofsvorstand** *m* ÖSTERR, SCHWEIZ station agent

Bahnlinie *f* train line

Bahnpolizei *f* railroad police

Bahnschranke *f*, **Bahnschranken** *m* ÖSTERR grade crossing gate

Bahnsteig <-[e]s, -e> *m* [train] platform

Bahnübergang *m* grade [*or fam* train] crossing

Bahnunterführung *f* [railroad] underpass

Bahnverbindung *f* [train] connection

Bahnwärter(in) *m(f)* grade crossing attendant

Bahre <-, -n> [ˈbaː·rə] *f* stretcher; (*Totenbahre*) bier

Bakterie <-, -n> [bak·ˈteː·ri̯ə] *f meist pl* bacterium

bakteriell [bak·te·ˈri̯ɛl] *adj* MED bacterial, bacteria *attr*

bakteriologisch [bak·te·ri̯o·ˈloː·gɪʃ] *adj* bacteriological

Balance <-, -n> [ba·ˈlãːsə] *f* balance

balancieren* [ba·lã·ˈsiː·rən] *vi, vt* to balance (**auf** +*dat* on)

bald [balt] *adv* soon; **wird's ~?** (*fam*) move it!; **bis ~!** see you later!; **nicht so ~** not as soon

Bälde [ˈbɛl·də] *f* **in ~** in the near future

baldmöglichst *adv* as soon as possible

Baldrian <-s, -e> *m* BOT valerian

Balearen [ba·le·ˈaː·rən] *pl* ■ **die** ~ the Balearic Islands *pl*

Balg¹ <-[e]s, Bälge> [balk, *pl* ˈbɛl·gə] *m* (*Blasebalg*) bellows *npl*

Balg² <-[e]s, Bälger> [balk, *pl* ˈbɛl·gɐ] *m o nt* (*pej fam: Kind*) brat

balgen [ˈbal·gn̩] *vr* ■ **sich** *akk* **[um etw]** ~ to scrap [over sth]

Balgerei <-, -en> [bal·gə·ˈrai] *f* scrap

Balkan <-s> [ˈbal·kaːn] *m* ❶ (*Halbinsel, Länder*) ■ **der ~** the Balkans *pl*; **auf dem ~** on the Balkans ❷ (*Balkangebirge*) Balkan Mountains *pl*

Balkanländer *pl* Balkan States

Balken <-s, -> [ˈbal·kn̩] *m a.* SPORT beam ▶ WENDUNGEN: **lügen, dass sich die ~ biegen** (*fam*) to lie through one's teeth

Balkon <-s, -s *o* -e> [bal·ˈkɔŋ, bal·ˈkõː] *m* ❶ ARCHIT balcony ❷ THEAT dress circle

Balkontür *f* French window[s]

Ball¹ <-[e]s, Bälle> [bal, *pl* ˈbɛ·lə] *m* ball ▶ WENDUNGEN: **am ~ bleiben/sein** to stay/be on the ball

Ball² <-[e]s, Bälle> [bal, *pl* ˈbɛ·lə] *m* (*Tanzfest*) ball; (*mit Mahl a.*) dinner-dance

Ballade <-, -n> [ba·ˈlaː·də] *f* ballad

Ballast <-[e]s, -e> [ˈba·last, ba·ˈlast] *m pl selten* NAUT, LUFT ballast; (*fig*) burden

Ballaststoffe *pl* fiber

ballen [ˈba·lən] **I.** *vt* to press together [into a ball]; *Papier* to crumple [into a ball]; *Faust* to clench **II.** *vr* ■ **sich** *akk* ~ to crowd [together]; *Wolken* to gather

Ballen <-s, -> [ˈba·lən] *m* ❶ (*rundlicher Packen*) bale ❷ (*an Hand o Fuß*) ball; (*bei Tieren*) pad

Ballerina¹ <-, Ballerinen> [ba·lə·ˈriː·na, *pl* ba·lə·ˈriː·nən] *f* (*Tänzerin*) ballerina

Ballerina² <-s, -s> [ba·lə·ˈriː·na] *m* (*Schuh*) pump *usu pl*

ballern [ˈba·lɐn] (*fam*) **I.** *vi* ❶ (*schießen*) to shoot; **zu Silvester wird viel geballert** there are lots of fireworks on New Year's Eve ❷ (*knallen, poltern*) to bang; **gegen die Tür ~** to bang on the door **II.** *vt* **jdm eine ~** to punch sb

Ballett <-[e]s, -e> [ba·ˈlɛt] *nt* ❶ (*Tanz*) ballet ❷ (*Tanzgruppe*) ballet [company]; **zum ~ gehen** to become a ballet dancer

Ballettänzer(in)ALT, **Balletttänzer(in)**RR *m(f)* ballet dancer

Balljunge *m* TENNIS ball boy

Ballkleid *nt* ball gown

Ballmädchen *nt* TENNIS ball girl

Ballon <-s, -s *o* -e> [ba·ˈlɔŋ, ba·ˈlõː] *m* balloon

Ballsaal *m* ballroom

Ballungsgebiet *nt*, **Ballungsraum** *m* metropolitan area

Ballungszentrum *nt* population center; **industrielles ~** center of industry

Balsam <-s, -e> [ˈbal·zaːm] *m* ❶ (*Salbe*) balsam ❷ (*fig*) balm

Balte, Baltin <-n, -n> [ˈbal·tə] *m, f* Balt, person from the Baltic; *s. a.* **Deutsche(r)**

Baltikum <-s> [ˈbal·ti·kʊm] *nt* ■ **das ~** the Baltic states

baltisch [ˈbal·tɪʃ] *adj* Baltic; *s. a.* **deutsch**

balzen [ˈbal·tsn̩] *vi* ORN to perform a courtship display

Bambus <-ses *o* -, -se> [ˈbam·bʊs] *m* bamboo

Bambussprossen *pl* bamboo shoots *pl*

Bammel <-s> [ˈba·ml̩] *m* (*fam*) ■ **~ vor jdm/**

B

etw haben to be afraid of sb/sth
banal [ba·ˈnaːl] *adj* banal; *Angelegenheit, Ausrede* trivial; *Bemerkung* trite; *Thema* commonplace
banalisieren* [ban·ali·ˈziː·rən] *vt* (*geh*) to trivialize
Banalität <-, -en> [ban·ali·ˈtɛːt] *f* ❶ *kein pl* (*Beschaffenheit*) banality; *eines Themas, einer Angelegenheit* triviality ❷ *meist pl* (*Äußerung*) platitude
Banane <-, -n> [ba·ˈnaː·nə] *f* banana
Bananenschale *f* banana peel
Banause <-n, -n> [ba·ˈnau·zə] *m* (*pej*) philistine
band [bant] *imp von* **binden**
Band[1] <-[e]s, Bänder> [bant, *pl* ˈbɛn·dɐ] *nt* ❶ (*Stoffstreifen*) ribbon; (*Hutband*) hatband; (*Schürzenband*) apron string ❷ (*Tonband*) [recording] tape; **etw auf ~ aufnehmen** to tape[-record] sth ❸ (*Fließband*) conveyor belt; **am ~ arbeiten** to work on an assembly line ❹ *meist pl* ANAT ligament ▶WENDUNGEN: **am laufenden ~** (*fam*) nonstop
Band[2] <-[e]s, Bände> [bant, *pl* bɛn·də] *m* (*Buch*) volume ▶WENDUNGEN: **Bände sprechen** (*fam*) to speak volumes
Band[3] <-, -s> [bɛnt] *f* MUS band
Bandage <-, -n> [ban·ˈdaː·ʒə] *f* bandage ▶WENDUNGEN: **mit harten ~n kämpfen** (*fam*) to fight with no holds barred
bandagieren* [ban·da·ˈʒiː·rən] *vt* to bandage
Bạndaufnahme *f* tape recording
Bạndbreite *f* ❶ (*geh*) range ❷ RADIO, INET bandwidth
Bande[1] <-, -n> [ˈban·də] *f* (*Gruppe*) gang
Bande[2] <-, -n> [ˈban·də] *f* SPORT barrier; *eines Billardtisches* cushion; *einer Reitbahn* boards
Bänderriss[RR] [ˈbɛn·dɐ-] *m* torn ligament
bändigen [ˈbɛn·dɪ·gn̩] *vt* ❶ (*zähmen*) to tame ❷ (*zügeln*) to bring under control; *Haare* to control; *Naturgewalten* to harness
Bandit(in) <-en, -en> [ban·ˈdiːt] *m(f)* bandit
Bạndmaß *nt* tape measure
Bạndnudel *f* tagliatelle
Bạndscheibe *f* ANAT [intervertebral] disc; **es an den ~n haben** to have a slipped disc
Bạndwurm *m* tapeworm
bạng <-er *o* bạnger, -ste *o* bạngste> [baŋ] *adj* scared; *Schweigen* uneasy; **es ist/wird jdm ~ [zumute]** sb is/becomes uneasy
Bange [ˈbaŋə] *f* **jdm ~ machen** to scare sb; **[nur] keine ~!** (*fam*) don't be afraid!; (*keine Sorge*) don't worry!
bangen [ˈbaŋən] *vi* ■ **um jdn/etw ~** to worry about sb/sth; **um jds Leben ~** to fear for sb's life
bạnger, bạ̈nger *adj komp von* **bang**
bạngste(r, s), bạ̈ngste(r, s) *adj superl von* **bang**
Bank[1] <-, Bänke> [baŋk, *pl* ˈbɛŋ·kə] *f* bench ▶WENDUNGEN: **etw auf die lange ~ schieben** (*fam*) to put sth off; **[alle] durch die ~** (*fam*) every single one [of them]
Bank[2] <-, -en> [baŋk] *f* FIN bank; **ein Konto bei einer ~ haben** to have a bank account
Bạnkangestellte(r) *f(m)* bank employee
Bạnkautomat *m* automated teller machine, ATM
Bankett <-[e]s, -e> [baŋ·ˈkɛt] *nt* banquet
Bạnkgeheimnis *nt kein pl* [a bank's duty to maintain] confidentiality
Bạnkgeschäfte *pl* banking transactions *pl*
Bankier <-s, -s> [baŋ·ˈki̯eː] *m* banker
Bạnkkaufmann, -frau *m, f* banker, bank employee
Bạnkkonto *nt* bank account
Bạnkkredit *m* bank loan
Bạnkleitzahl *f* [bank] routing number
Bạnknote *f* bill, banknote
Bạnkraub *m* bank robbery
Bạnkräuber(in) *m(f)* bank robber
bankrott [baŋk·ˈrɔt] *adj* bankrupt; **jdn ~ machen** to bankrupt sb
Bankrott <-[e]s, -e> [baŋk·ˈrɔt] *m* bankruptcy
bankrọtt|gehen[RR] *vi irreg sein* to go bankrupt
Bạnkschließfach *nt* safe-deposit box
Bạnküberfall *m* bank robbery
Bạnküberweisung *f* bank transfer
Bạnkverbindung *f* bank account
Bann <-[e]s> [ban] *m kein pl* (*geh*) spell; **in jds ~** *akk* **geraten** to fall under sb's spell; **jdn in seinen ~ ziehen** to cast one's spell over sb
bannen [ˈba·nən] *vt* ❶ (*geh: faszinieren*) to entrance ❷ *Gefahr* to avert
Banner <-s, -> [ˈba·nɐ] *nt* banner
bar [baːɐ̯] *adj* ❶ FIN cash; **[in] ~ bezahlen** to pay [in] cash ❷ *attr* (*rein*) pure; *Unsinn* utter
Bar <-, -s> [baːɐ̯] *f* bar
Bär <-en, -en> [bɛːɐ̯] *m* bear; **wie ein ~ schlafen** (*fam*) to sleep like a log ▶WENDUNGEN: **jdm einen ~en aufbinden** (*fam*) to put sb on
Baracke <-, -n> [ba·ˈra·kə] *f* shack
Barbar(in) <-en, -en> [bar·ˈbaːɐ̯] *m(f)* (*pej*) barbarian
Barbarei <-, -en> [bar·ba·ˈrai] *f* ❶ (*Unmenschlichkeit*) barbarity ❷ *kein pl* (*Kulturlosigkeit*) barbarism
barbarisch [bar·ˈbaː·rɪʃ] **I.** *adj* ❶ (*grausam*) barbarous, barbaric; *Folter* brutal; *Strafe* cruel ❷ (*unkultiviert*) barbaric **II.** *adv* ❶ (*grausam*) barbarously ❷ (*unkultiviert*) barbarically
bärbeißig [ˈbɛːɐ̯·bai·sɪç] *adj* (*fam*) grumpy
Barcode <-s, -s> [ˈbaː·koːt] *m* COMPUT bar code
Bardame *f* barmaid
Bärendienst *m* ▶WENDUNGEN: **jdm einen ~ erweisen** to do sb a disservice
Bärenhunger *m* (*fam*) a massive appetite; **einen ~ haben** to be starved
Bärenkräfte *pl* the strength of an ox
bärenstark *adj* ❶ (*fam: sehr stark*) as strong as an ox *pred* ❷ (*sl: toll*) cool
barfuß [ˈbaːɐ̯·fuːs] *adj pred* barefoot[ed]
barg [bark] *imp von* **bergen**
Bargeld *nt* cash

bargeldlos **I.** *adj* cashless **II.** *adv* without using cash
Barhocker *m* bar stool
Barkasse <-, -n> [bar·'ka·sə] *f* launch
Barkauf *m* cash purchase
Barke <-, -n> ['bar·kə] *f* skiff
Barkeeper(in) <-s, -> ['baːɐ·kiːpɐ] *m(f)*, **Barmann** *m* bartender
barmherzig [barm·'hɛr·tsɪç] *adj* compassionate; ■ **~ sein** to show compassion
Barmherzigkeit <-> *f kein pl* mercy
Barmixer(in) <-s, -> *m(f)* bartender
Barock <-[s]> [ba·'rɔk] *nt o m kein pl* baroque
Barometer <-s, -> [baro·'meː·tɐ] *nt* barometer
Baron(in) <-s, -e> [ba·'roːn] *m(f)* baron *masc*, baroness *fem*
Barren <-s, -> ['ba·rən] *m* ❶ SPORT parallel bars *pl* ❷ (*Goldbarren*) bar, ingot
Barriere <-, -n> [ba·'ri̯eː·rə] *f* (*a. fig*) barrier
Barrikade <-, -n> [ba·ri·'kaː·də] *f* barricade
barsch [barʃ] **I.** *adj* curt **II.** *adv* curtly
Barsch <-[e]s, -e> [barʃ] *m* perch
barst [barst] *imp von* **bersten**
Bart <-[e]s, Bärte> [baːɐ̯t, *pl* 'bɛːɐ̯·tə] *m* ❶ (*Vollbart*) beard; **sich** *dat* **einen ~ wachsen lassen** to grow a beard ❷ (*Schnurrbart*) moustache ❸ ZOOL whiskers
bärtig ['bɛːɐ̯·tɪç] *adj* bearded
bartlos *adj* beardless
Bartstoppeln *pl* stubble *sing*
Bartwuchs *m* beard growth; (*Frau*) facial hair
Barvermögen *nt* cash assets
Barzahlung *f* cash payment
Basar <-s, -e> [ba·'zaːɐ̯] *m* bazaar
Base <-, -n> ['baː·zə] *f* ❶ (*veraltet: Cousine*) cousin ❷ SCHWEIZ *s.* **Tante** aunt
Basel <-s> ['baː·zl̩] *nt* Basel
Basen *pl von* **Base, Basis**
basieren* [ba·'ziː·rən] *vi* to be based (**auf** +*dat* on)
Basilika <-, Basiliken> [ba·'ziː·li·ka, *pl* ba·'ziː·li·kən] *f* basilica
Basilikum <-s> [ba·'ziː·li·kʊm] *nt kein pl* basil
Basis <-, Basen> ['baː·zɪs, *pl* 'baː·zn̩] *f* ❶ (*Grundlage*) basis ❷ POL (*die Parteimitglieder/die Bürger*) ■ **die ~** the grass roots ❸ MIL base
Basiswissen *nt* basic knowledge
Baske, Baskin <-n, -n> ['bas·kə, 'bas·kɪn] *m, f* Basque; *s. a.* **Deutsche(r)**
Baskenland *nt* ■ **das ~** the Basque region
Baskenmütze *f* beret
baskisch ['bas·kɪʃ] *adj* Basque; *s. a.* **deutsch**
Bass[RR] <-es, Bässe>, **Baß**[ALT] <-sses, Bässe> [bas, *pl* 'bɛsə] *m* bass
Bastard <-[e]s, -e> ['bas·tart] *m* (*fam*) ❶ (*mieser Kerl*) bastard ❷ (*pej: uneheliches Kind*) bastard
basteln ['bas·tl̩n] **I.** *vi* ❶ (*als Hobby*) to do arts and crafts ❷ ■ **an etw** *dat* **~** to work on sth **II.** *vt* (*fertigen*) to make; *Gerät* to build
Bastler(in) <-s, -> *m(f)* handicraft enthusiast; **ein guter ~ sein** to be good with one's hands
bat [baːt] *imp von* **bitten**
Batik <-, -en> ['baː·tɪk] *f* batik
Batterie <-, -n> [ba·tə·'riː, *pl* -'riː·ən] *f* ELEK, MIL battery
batteriebetrieben *adj* battery-powered
Batzen <-s, -> ['ba·tsn̩] *m* ❶ (*Klumpen*) lump; *Erde* clump ❷ **ein schöner ~ [Geld]** (*fam*) a pile [of money]
Bau[1] <-[e]s, -ten> [bau, *pl* 'bautn̩] *m* ❶ *kein pl* (*das Bauen*) building; **im ~ sein** to be under construction ❷ (*Gebäude*) building; (*Bauwerk*) construction ❸ *kein pl* (*fam: Baustelle*) construction site
Bau[2] <-[e]s, -e> [bau] *m* (*Erdhöhle*) burrow; (*Biberbau*) [beaver] lodge; (*Fuchsbau*) den
Bauamt *nt* building inspector's office
Bauarbeiten *pl* construction [work] *sing*; **wegen ~ gesperrt** closed for repairs
Bauarbeiter(in) *m(f)* construction worker
Bauch <-[e]s, Bäuche> [baux, *pl* 'bɔy·çə] *m* stomach, tummy *fam*; (*Fettbauch*) belly; **sich** *dat* **den ~ vollschlagen** (*fam*) to stuff oneself ▶ WENDUNGEN: **aus dem ~** (*fam*) from the heart; **aus dem hohlen ~ [heraus]** (*fam*) off the top of one's head
Bauchentscheidung *f* (*fam*) gut decision *fam*
Bauchfell *nt* ANAT peritoneum
Bauchfellentzündung *f* peritonitis
Bauchfleisch *nt* belly
Bauchgefühl *nt kein pl* (*fam*) gut feeling *fam*
Bauchhöhle *f* abdominal cavity
bauchig ['baux·ɪç] *adj* bulbous
Bauchlandung *f* (*fam*) belly flop
Bauchnabel *m* navel, belly button *fam*
Bauchredner(in) *m(f)* ventriloquist
Bauchschmerzen *pl* stomachache
Bauchspeck *m* ❶ (*Fleischstück*) bacon [streaked with fat] ❷ (*Fettansatz*) spare tire
Bauchspeicheldrüse *f* ANAT pancreas
Bauchtanz *m* belly dance
Bauchtänzerin *f* belly dancer
Bauchweh *nt s.* **Bauchschmerzen**
Baudenkmal *nt* architectural monument
bauen ['bau·ən] **I.** *vt* ❶ (*errichten, herstellen*) to build ❷ (*zusammenbauen*) to construct; *Auto, Flugzeug* to build ❸ (*fam: verursachen*) to cause; **Mist ~** to mess things up **II.** *vi* ❶ (*eigenes Haus*) to build a house ❷ (*vertrauen*) ■ **auf jdn/etw ~** to rely on sb/sth
Bauer, Bäuerin[1] <-n, -n> ['bau·ɐ, 'bɔyə·rɪn] *m, f* ❶ (*Landwirt*) farmer ❷ (*pej: ungehobelter Mensch*) yokel ❸ (*Schachfigur*) pawn
Bauer[2] <-s, -> ['bauɐ] *nt o selten m* (*Vogelkäfig*) [bird] cage
Bäuerchen <-s, -> *nt* (*Kindersprache*) burp; **~ machen** to burp
Bauernfänger <-s, -> *m* (*pej fam*) con man
Bauernhaus *nt* farmhouse
Bauernhof *m* farm
Bauernregel *f* country saying
bauernschlau *adj* crafty
Bauernverband *m* farmers' association

B

baufällig *adj* dilapidated
Baufirma *f* construction company
Baugelände *nt* construction site
Baugenehmigung *f* building permit
Baugerüst *nt* scaffolding
Baugesellschaft *f* construction company
Baugewerbe *nt kein pl* construction business
Baugrube *f* [building] excavation
Baugrundstück *nt* plot of land
Bauholz *nt* lumber
Bauingenieur(in) *m(f)* civil engineer
Baujahr *nt* ❶ (*Jahr der Errichtung*) year of construction ❷ (*Produktionsjahr*) year of manufacture
Baukasten *m* construction set
Bauklotz *m* building block
Baulärm *m* construction noise
Bauleiter(in) *m(f)* [construction] site manager
baulich I. *adj* structural **II.** *adv* structurally
Baum <-[e]s, Bäume> [baum, *pl* 'bɔy·mə] *m* tree ▸ WENDUNGEN: **jd könnte Bäume ausreißen** (*fam*) sb is full of energy
Baumarkt *m* building supplies store, hardware store
Baumaterial *nt* building material
Baumbestand *m* tree population
baumeln ['bau·mḷn] *vi* to dangle (**an** +*dat* from)
Baumgrenze *f* tree line
Baumkrone *f* treetop
Baumrinde *f* [tree] bark
Baumschule *f* tree nursery
Baumstamm *m* tree trunk
Baumsterben *nt* dying[-off] of trees
Baumwipfel *m* treetop
Baumwolle *f* cotton
Bauplan *m* building plans *pl*
Bauplatz *m* [construction] site
Bauruine *f* (*fam*) abandoned unfinished building
bauschig *adj* full; *Hose* baggy
Bauschutt *m* construction rubble [*or* waste]
bausparen *vi nur Infinitiv* to have an account with a mortgage lender
Bausparkasse *f* mortgage lender
Bausparvertrag *m* savings account for home construction
Baustein *m* ❶ (*Material zum Bauen*) building stone ❷ (*Bestandteil*) element ❸ COMPUT chip
Baustelle *f* construction site
Baustil *m* architectural style
Baustoff *m* building material
Bauteil *nt einer Maschine* component; **fertiges** ~ prefabricated element
Bauten *pl von* **Bau**[1]
Bauunternehmen *nt* builder, building contractor
Bauunternehmer(in) *m(f)* builder
Bauvorhaben *nt* construction project
Bauweise *f* ❶ (*Art des Bauens*) construction method ❷ (*Baustil*) style
Bauwerk *nt* (*Gebäude*) building; (*Brücke etc.*) construction

Bayer(in) <-n, -n> ['bai·ɐ] *m(f)* Bavarian; *s. a.* **Deutsche(r)**
bayerisch ['baiə·rɪʃ] *adj* Bavarian; *s. a.* **deutsch**
Bayern <-s> ['bai·ɐn] *nt* Bavaria; *s. a.* **Deutschland**
bayrisch ['bai·rɪʃ] *adj s.* **bayerisch**
Bazillus <-, Bazillen> [ba·'tsɪ·lʊs, *pl* ba·'tsɪ·lən] *m* MED bacillus
beabsichtigen* [bə·'ʔap·zɪç·tɪ·gṇ] *vt* to intend; **das hatte ich nicht beabsichtigt!** I didn't mean to do that!
beachten* [bə·'ʔax·tṇ] *vt* ❶ (*befolgen*) to observe; *Anweisung, Rat* to follow; **die Vorfahrt** ~ to yield [the right of way] ❷ (*Aufmerksamkeit schenken*) to pay attention, to take notice ❸ (*berücksichtigen*) to take into account
beachtenswert *adj* remarkable
beachtlich *adj* considerable; *Erfolg, Leistung* notable; *Verbesserung* marked
Beachtung *f* ❶ (*Befolgung*) observance; *der Vorschriften* compliance ❷ (*Aufmerksamkeit*) ~ **finden** to receive attention; **keine** ~ **finden** to be ignored; **jdm/etw** ~ **schenken** to pay attention to sb/sth
Beamte(r) [bə·'ʔam·tə, bə·'ʔam·tɐ] *f(m) dekl wie adj,* **Beamtin** <-, -nen> [bə·'ʔam·tɪn] *f* public official, civil servant
beängstigen* *vt* (*geh*) to alarm
beängstigend I. *adj* alarming **II.** *adv* alarmingly
beanspruchen* [bə·'ʔan·ʃprʊ·xṇ] *vt* ❶ (*fordern*) to claim ❷ (*brauchen*) to require; *Zeit, Platz* to take up ❸ (*Anforderungen stellen*) ■**jdn** ~ to make demands on sb; **ich will Sie nicht länger** ~ I don't want to take up any more of your time; ■**etw** ~ to demand sth; **jds Zeit** ~ to make demands on sb's time; **jds Geduld** ~ to try sb's patience ❹ (*belasten*) to put under stress
beanstanden* [bə·'ʔan·ʃtan·dṇ] *vt* ■**etw** ~ to complain about sth; **das ist beanstandet worden** there have been complaints about that
Beanstandung <-, -en> *f* complaint
beantragen* *vt* to apply for; POL to propose
beantworten* *vt* ❶ (*Antwort geben*) to answer ❷ (*reagieren*) ■**etw mit etw** *dat* ~ to respond to sth with sth
Beantwortung <-, -en> *f* answer
bearbeiten* *vt* ❶ (*behandeln*) to work on; **Holz** ~ to work wood ❷ (*sich befassen mit*) to deal with ❸ (*redigieren*) to revise ❹ (*fam: auf jdn einwirken*) ■**jdn** ~ to work on sb; **wir haben ihn so lange bearbeitet, bis er zusagte** we pressed him until he agreed ❺ *Feld* to cultivate ❻ (*adaptieren*) *Musikstück* to arrange (**für** +*akk* for)
beargwöhnen* *vt* to regard with suspicion
beatmen* *vt* to give artificial respiration to
beaufsichtigen* [bə·'ʔauf·zɪç·tɪ·gṇ] *vt* to supervise; *Kinder* to look after; (*bei Prüfung*) to

proctor
beauftragen* *vt Architekt, Künstler* to commission; *Firma* to hire; ■ **jdn mit etw** *dat* ~ to give sb the job of doing sth; ■ **jdn ~, etw zu tun** to ask sb to do sth
Beauftragte(r) *f(m) dekl wie adj* representative
beäugen* *vt* (*fam*) to eyeball
bebauen* *vt* ❶ *Baugrundstück* to build on; **dicht bebaut sein** to be heavily built-up ❷ *Acker, Feld* to cultivate
beben ['beː·bn̩] *vi* to tremble; **vor Zorn** ~ to shake with anger
Beben <-s, -> ['beː·bn̩] *nt* (*Erdbeben*) earthquake
bebildern* [bə·'bɪl·dɐn] *vt* to illustrate
Becher <-s, -> ['bɛ·çɐ] *m* ❶ (*Trinkgefäß*) glass; (*aus Plastik*) cup; (*für Tee/Kaffee*) mug ❷ (*Verpackung*) carton ❸ SCHWEIZ (*Bierglas*) mug
bechern ['bɛ·çɐn] *vi* (*hum fam*) to booze [away]
becircen* *vt s.* **bezirzen**
Becken <-s, -> ['bɛ·kn̩] *nt* ❶ (*Bassin*) basin; (*Spülbecken*) sink; (*von Toilette*) bowl; (*Schwimmbecken*) pool ❷ ANAT pelvis ❸ MUS cymbals *pl*
bedacht [bə·'daxt] **I.** *pp von* **bedenken II.** *adj* ❶ (*überlegt*) cautious ❷ ■ **auf etw** *akk* ~ **sein** to be concerned about sth **III.** *adv* carefully
bedächtig [bə·'dɛç·tɪç] **I.** *adj* ❶ (*ohne Hast*) deliberate ❷ (*besonnen*) thoughtful **II.** *adv* ❶ (*ohne Hast*) deliberately; ~ **sprechen** to speak in measured tones ❷ (*besonnen*) carefully
bedanken* *vr* ■ **sich** *akk* ~ to express one's thanks; ■ **sich** *akk* **bei jdm** ~ to thank sb (**für** +*akk* for); **ich bedanke mich!** thank you!
Bedarf <-[e]s> [bə·'darf] *m kein pl* need (**an** +*dat* for); **der tägliche ~ an Vitaminen** the daily requirement of vitamins; **Dinge des täglichen ~s** everyday necessities; **bei** ~ if required; [**je**] **nach** ~ as required
Bedarfsfall *m* **im** ~ if necessary
bedauerlich *adj* regrettable; **sehr ~!** how unfortunate!; ■ **~ sein, dass ...** to be unfortunate that ...
bedauerlicherweise *adv* unfortunately
bedauern* *vt* ❶ (*schade finden*) to regret ❷ (*bemitleiden*) to feel sorry [for]
Bedauern <-s> *nt kein pl* regret
bedauernswert *adj* pitiful, unfortunate
bedecken* **I.** *vt* to cover **II.** *vr* ■ **sich** *akk* ~ *Himmel* to cloud over
bedeckt *adj pred* (*bewölkt*) overcast ► WENDUNGEN: **sich** *akk* ~ **halten** to keep a low profile
bedenken* *irreg vt* to consider; [**jdm**] **etw zu ~ geben** to ask [sb] to consider sth; [**jdm**] **zu ~ geben, dass ...** to ask [sb] to keep in mind that ...
Bedenken <-s, -> *nt meist pl* doubt; **~ haben** to have doubts; **moralische** ~ moral scruples; **jdm kommen** ~ sb has second thoughts; **ohne** ~ without hesitation
bedenkenlos *adv* ❶ (*ohne Überlegung/Zögern*) without hesitation ❷ (*rücksichtslos*) unscrupulously
bedenkenswert *adj* worthy of consideration
bedenklich *adj* ❶ (*fragwürdig*) questionable ❷ (*Besorgnis erregend*) disturbing; *Gesundheitszustand* serious; **jdn ~ stimmen** to give sb cause for concern
Bedenkzeit *f* time to think about sth
bedeuten* *vt* ❶ (*bezeichnen, meinen*) to mean, to signify; **das hat nichts zu** ~ that doesn't mean a thing ❷ (*wichtig sein*) [**jdm**] **etw** ~ to mean something [to sb]
bedeutend I. *adj* ❶ (*wichtig*) important; *Politiker* leading; **eine ~e Rolle spielen** to play a significant role ❷ (*beachtlich*) considerable **II.** *adv* considerably
bedeutsam *adj* ❶ (*wichtig*) important; *Entscheidung, Verbesserung* significant ❷ (*vielsagend*) meaningful
Bedeutung <-, -en> *f* ❶ (*Sinn*) meaning, significance; **in wörtlicher/übertragener** ~ in the literal/figurative sense ❷ (*Wichtigkeit*) importance; [**für jdn/etw**] **von ~ sein** to be of importance [to sb/sth]; **nichts von** ~ nothing important
bedeutungslos *adj* ❶ (*ohne große Wirkung*) insignificant ❷ (*nichts besagend*) meaningless
Bedeutungslosigkeit <-> *f kein pl* insignificance
bedeutungsvoll *adj s.* **bedeutsam**
Bedeutungswandel *m* change in meaning
bedienen* **I.** *vt* ❶ *Kunde, Gast* to serve ❷ *Maschine* to operate ► WENDUNGEN: **bedient sein** (*fam*) to have had enough **II.** *vi* to serve; **wird hier nicht bedient?** isn't anyone working here? **III.** *vr* ❶ (*sich Essen nehmen*) ■ **sich** *akk* [**mit etw** *akk*] ~ to help oneself [to sth]; **~ Sie sich!** help yourself! ❷ (*geh: gebrauchen*) ■ **sich einer S.** *gen* ~ to make use of sth
bedienerfreundlich *adj* user-friendly
Bedienstete(r) *f(m) dekl wie adj* employee
Bedienung <-, -en> *f* ❶ (*Kellner*) waiter *masc,* waitress *fem* ❷ *kein pl* (*Handhabung*) operation ❸ *kein pl* (*das Bedienen*) service; **~ inbegriffen** service included
Bedienungsanleitung *f* [operating] instructions *pl*
Bedienungsfehler *m* operator['s] error
bedingen* [bə·'dɪ·ŋən] *vt* ❶ (*verursachen*) to cause; ■ **durch etw** *akk* **bedingt sein** to be a result of sth ❷ (*verlangen*) to require
bedingt I. *adj* ❶ (*eingeschränkt*) qualified ❷ JUR conditional **II.** *adv* ❶ (*eingeschränkt*) to some extent; **~ gültig** of limited validity ❷ JUR SCHWEIZ, ÖSTERR (*mit Bewährungsfrist*) conditionally
Bedingung <-, -en> *f* ❶ (*Voraussetzung*) condition; **unter der ~, dass ...** on the condition that ... ❷ (*Forderung*) [**jdm**] **eine ~ stellen** to place a condition [on sb] ❸ *pl* (*Umstände*) conditions
bedingungslos I. *adj* unconditional; *Gehor-*

B

sam, Treue unquestioning **II.** *adv* unconditionally; *gehorchen* unquestioningly
bedrängen* *vt* to pester (**mit** +*dat* with); ■ **jdn ~, etw zu tun** to pressure sb into doing sth
Bedrängnis <-ses, -se> [bə·'drɛŋ·nɪs] *f* (*geh*) difficulties *pl;* **jdn in ~ bringen** to get sb into trouble
bedrohen* *vt* ① (*drohen*) to threaten (**mit** +*dat* with) ② (*gefährden*) to endanger
bedrohlich **I.** *adj* threatening **II.** *adv* alarmingly
Bedrohung *f* threat
bedrucken* *vt* to print on
bedrücken* *vt* to depress; **was bedrückt dich?** what's troubling you?
bedrückend *adj* depressing; *Stimmung* oppressive
bedrückt *adj* depressed; **~es Schweigen** oppressive silence
Beduine, **Beduinin** <-n, -n> [bedu·'iː·nə, bedu·'iː·nɪn] *m, f* Bed[o]uin
Bedürfnis <-ses, -se> [bə·'dʏrf·nɪs] *nt* need; **die ~se des täglichen Lebens** everyday needs; **das ~ haben, etw zu tun** to feel the need to do sth
bedürftig *adj* needy *attr,* in need *pred;* ■ **die B~en** the needy + *pl vb*
Bedürftigkeit <-> *f kein pl* need, neediness
Beefsteak <-s, -s> ['biːf·steːk, -ʃteːk] *nt bes* NORDD steak; **deutsches ~** hamburger
beehren* *vt* (*geh*) to honor (**mit** +*dat* with)
beeilen* *vr* ■ **sich** *akk* **~** to hurry [up]; ■ **sich** *akk* **~, etw zu tun** to hurry to do sth
beeindrucken* [bə·'ʔain·drʊ·kn̩] *vt* to impress; **sich** *akk* [**von etw** *dat*] **nicht ~ lassen** to not be impressed [by sth]
beeindruckend *adj* impressive
beeinflussbarRR, **beeinflußbar**ALT *adj* easily influenced *pred*
beeinflussen* [bə·'ʔain·flʊ·sn̩] *vt* to influence
Beeinflussung <-, -en> *f* influence
beeinträchtigen* [bə·'ʔain·trɛç·tɪ·gn̩] *vt* to disturb; *Reaktionsvermögen, Leistungsfähigkeit* to impair; *Verhältnis* to damage; **jdn in seiner Freiheit ~** to restrict sb's freedom
beenden* *vt* to end
Beendigung <-> *f kein pl* ending
Beendung <-> *f kein pl* completion
beerben* *vt* to be heir to
beerdigen* [bə·'ʔeːɐ̯·dɪ·gn̩] *vt* to bury
Beerdigung <-, -en> *f* funeral
Beerdigungsfeier *f* funeral service
Beerdigungsinstitut *nt* funeral home
Beere <-, -n> ['beːrə] *f* berry
Beet <-[e]s, -e> [beːt] *nt* bed; (*Blumenbeet*) flower bed; (*Gemüsebeet*) vegetable patch
befähigen* [bə·'fɛː·ɪ·gn̩] *vt* ■ **jdn dazu ~, etw zu tun** to enable sb to do sth
befähigt [bə·'fɛː·ɪçt] *adj* qualified; ■ **für etw ~ sein** to be competent at sth
Befähigung <-> *f kein pl* qualification[s]
befahl [bə·'faːl] *imp von* **befehlen**
befahrbar *adj* passable; NAUT navigable; **nicht ~** impassable; NAUT unnavigable
befahren* **I.** *vt irreg Straße, Weg* to drive along; **diese Straße darf nur in einer Richtung ~ werden** this road is only open in one direction; **eine Strecke ~** to use a route **II.** *adj Straße* used; **kaum/stark ~ sein** to be little/heavily used; **eine viel ~e Kreuzung** a busy intersection
befangen [bə·'fa·ŋən] *adj* ① (*gehemmt*) inhibited ② (*voreingenommen*) biased; **jdn als ~ ablehnen** to disqualify sb on grounds of bias
Befangenheit <-> *f kein pl* ① (*Gehemmtheit*) inhibition ② (*Voreingenommenheit*) bias
befassen* *vr* ■ **sich** *akk* **mit etw** *dat* **~** to concern oneself with sth; *mit einer Angelegenheit* to look into; *mit einem Problem* to tackle; ■ **sich** *akk* **mit jdm ~** to spend time with sb
Befehl <-[e]s, -e> [bə·'feːl] *m* ① (*Anweisung*) order; **jdm den ~ geben, etw zu tun** to order sb to do sth ② COMPUT command
befehlen <befiehlt, befahl, befohlen> [bə·'feː·lən] *vt* to order; **von dir lasse ich mir nichts ~!** I won't take orders from you!
Befehlsform *f* LING imperative
Befehlshaber(in) <-s, -> [bə·'feːls·haː·bɐ] *m(f)* MIL commander
Befehlszeile *f* COMPUT command line
befestigen* *vt* ① (*anbringen*) to fasten (**an** +*dat* to); *Boot* to tie ② BAU *Fahrbahn, Straße* to pave; *Böschung* to stabilize; *Damm, Deich* to reinforce
befeuchten* *vt* to moisten
befiehlt [bə·'fiːlt] *pp von* **befehlen**
befinden* *irreg* **I.** *vr* ■ **sich** *akk* **irgendwo ~** to be somewhere; **unter den Geiseln ~ sich zwei Deutsche** the hostages include two Germans **II.** *vi* ■ **über etw** *akk* **~** to decide [on] sth
befingern* *vt* (*fam*) to finger
beflecken* *vt* ① (*schmutzig machen*) to stain (**mit** +*dat* with); **etw mit Farbe ~** to get paint [stains] on sth ② **jds Ehre ~** to tarnish sb's honor
beflissen [bə·'flɪ·sn̩] **I.** *adj* diligent **II.** *adv* diligently
beflügeln* *vt* (*geh*) to inspire; **Hoffnung beflügelte seine Schritte** hope spurred him on; **die Fantasie ~** to fire the imagination
befohlen [bə·'foː·lən] *pp von* **befehlen**
befolgen* *vt Rat* to follow; *Vorschrift, Befehl* to obey
befördern* *vt* ① (*transportieren*) to transport ② (*beruflich*) to promote (**zu** +*dat* to)
Beförderung *f* ① (*Transport*) transportation ② (*beruflich*) promotion (**zu** +*dat* to)
Beförderungsmittel *nt* means of transportation
befrachten* *vt* ① (*beladen*) to load ② (*fig geh*) to overload
befragen* *vt* to question (**zu** +*dat* about); **jdn nach seiner Meinung ~** to ask sb for his/her opinion
Befragung <-, -en> *f* ① (*das Befragen*) questioning ② (*Umfrage*) survey, [opinion] poll

befreien* **I.** *vt* ❶ *Gefangene* to free (**aus** +*dat* from) ❷ *Volk, Land* to liberate (**von** +*dat* from) ❸ (*freistellen*) to excuse (**von** +*dat* from); *vom Wehrdienst* to exempt ❹ (*Störendes entfernen*) to clear (**von** +*dat* of); **seine Schuhe vom Dreck ~** to remove the dirt from one's shoes ❺ (*von Schmerzen, Sorgen*) to free (**von** +*dat* from) **II.** *vr* ❶ (*freikommen*) ■ **sich** *akk* ~ *Gefangene* to escape (**aus** +*dat* from) ❷ (*etw überwinden*) ■ **sich** *akk* **von etw** *dat* ~ to rid oneself of sth

Befreier(in) <-s, -> *m(f)* liberator

Befreiung <-, -en> *f pl selten* ❶ *von Gefangenen* release ❷ *eines Volkes, Landes* liberation ❸ (*Freistellung*) exemption (**von** +*dat* from)

Befreiungsbewegung *f* liberation movement

Befreiungskampf *m* struggle for freedom

befremden* **I.** *vt* to disconcert **II.** *vi* to be disconcerting

Befremden <-s> *nt kein pl* disconcertment

befremdend, befremdlich [bə·ˈfrɛmt·lɪç] *adj* (*geh*) disconcerting

befreunden* [bə·ˈfrɔyn·dn̩] *vr* ■ **sich** *akk* **mit jdm ~** to make friends with sb; **mit jdm befreundet sein** to be friends with sb

befrieden* [bə·ˈfriː·dn̩] *vt* **ein Land ~** to bring peace to a country

befriedigen* [bə·ˈfriː·dɪ·gn̩] **I.** *vt* to satisfy; *Ansprüche, Wünsche* to fulfill; **leicht/schwer zu ~ sein** to be easily/not easily satisfied **II.** *vi* (*zufrieden stellend sein*) to be satisfactory **III.** *vr* ■ **sich** *akk* [**selbst**] ~ to masturbate

befriedigend *adj* satisfactory; ■ **~ sein** to be satisfying

Befriedigung <-> *f kein pl* satisfaction

befristen* *vt* to limit (**auf** +*akk* to)

befruchten* *vt* ❶ BIOL to fertilize; *Blüte* to pollinate; **künstlich ~** to artificially inseminate ❷ (*fig: anregen*) to stimulate

Befruchtung <-, -en> *f* fertilization; *Blüte* pollination; **künstliche ~** *Mensch* in vitro fertilization, IVF; *Tier* artificial insemination, AI

Befugnis <-ses, -se> [bə·ˈfuːk·nɪs] *f* authorization; **zu etw** *dat* **keine ~ haben** to not be authorized to do sth

befugt [bə·ˈfuːkt] *adj* authorized

befühlen* *vt* to feel

Befund <-[e]s, -e> *m* MED result[s *pl*]; **ohne ~** negative

befunden [bə·ˈfʊn·dn̩] *pp von* **befinden**

befürchten* *vt* to fear; ■ **~, dass ...** to be afraid that ...

Befürchtung <-, -en> *f meist pl* fear; **die ~ haben, dass ...** to fear that ...

befürworten* [bə·ˈfyːɐ̯·vɔr·tn̩] *vt* to be in favor of

Befürworter(in) <-s, -> *m(f)* supporter

begabt [bə·ˈgaːpt] *adj* gifted, talented; ■ **für etw** *akk* **~ sein** to have a gift for sth; **künstlerisch sehr ~ sein** to be very artistic

Begabung <-, -en> *f* gift, talent

begangen *pp von* **begehen**

begann [bə·ˈgan] *imp von* **beginnen**

begatten* *vt* ZOOL ■ **ein Weibchen ~** to mate with a female

begeben* *vr irreg* (*geh*) ❶ (*gehen*) ■ **sich** *akk* **irgendwohin ~** to proceed somewhere; **sich** *akk* **nach Hause ~** to set off for home; **sich** *akk* **zur Ruhe ~** to retire ❷ (*beginnen*) ■ **sich** *akk* **an etw ~** to commence sth ❸ **sich** *akk* **in Gefahr ~** to expose oneself to danger ❹ **sich** *akk* **in ärztliche Behandlung ~** to undergo medical treatment

Begebenheit <-, -en> *f* (*geh*) event

begegnen* [bə·ˈgeːg·nən] *vi sein* ❶ (*treffen*) ■ **jdm ~** to meet sb; ■ **sich** *dat* **~** to meet ❷ (*antreffen*) ■ **etw ~** to encounter sth ❸ (*entgegentreten*) *Person* to treat; *Sache* to face; *Vorschlag a.* to respond to

Begegnung <-, -en> *f* meeting, encounter

Begegnungsstätte *f* meeting place

begehbar *adj* accessible [by foot]; **~er Kleiderschrank** walk-in closet

begehen* *vt irreg* ❶ (*verüben*) to commit; *Fehler* to make; **eine Dummheit ~** to do something stupid ❷ (*betreten*) to walk across/along/into ❸ *Feiertag, Jubiläum* to celebrate

begehren* [bə·ˈgeː·ɐ̯n] *vt* (*geh*) ■ **jdn ~** to desire sb

begehrenswert *adj* desirable

begehrlich *adj* (*geh*) longing

begehrt *adj* ❶ (*sehr umworben*) [much] sought-after; *Frau, Mann* desirable; *Junggeselle* eligible; *Preis* [much-]coveted ❷ (*beliebt, gefragt*) popular

begeistern* **I.** *vt* to fill with enthusiasm (**für** +*akk* for) **II.** *vr* ■ **sich** *akk* **für jdn/etw ~** to be enthusiastic about sb/sth

begeistert **I.** *adj* enthusiastic (**von** +*dat* about) **II.** *adv* enthusiastically

Begeisterung <-> *f kein pl* enthusiasm (**für** +*akk* for)

begeisterungsfähig *adj* able to get enthusiastic *pred; Publikum* appreciative

Begeisterungssturm *m* storm of enthusiasm

Begierde <-, -n> [bə·ˈgiːɐ̯·də] *f* desire (**nach** +*dat* for)

begierig **I.** *adj* ❶ (*gespannt*) eager (**auf** +*akk* for) ❷ (*verlangend*) longing **II.** *adv* ❶ (*gespannt*) eagerly ❷ (*verlangend*) longingly

begießen* *vt irreg* (*fam: feiern*) to celebrate [with a drink]; **das muss begossen werden!** that calls for a drink!

Beginn <-[e]s> [bə·ˈgɪn] *m kein pl* beginning, start; **zu ~** at the beginning

beginnen <begann, begonnen> [bə·ˈgɪ·nən] *vi, vt* ❶ (*anfangen*) to begin (**mit** +*dat* with) ❷ (*eine Arbeit aufnehmen*) ■ **als etw ~** to start out as sth

beginnend *adj attr* beginning; **im ~en 20. Jahrhundert** in the early 20th century

beglaubigen* [bə·ˈglau·bɪ·gn̩] *vt* to authenticate; **eine beglaubigte Kopie** a certified [*or* notarized] copy

Beglaubigung <-, -en> *f* certification, notarization

begleichen* *vt irreg Schulden* to pay; *Rechnung* to settle

Begleitbrief *m* cover letter

begleiten* *vt* (*a. fig*) to accompany; **jdn zur Tür ~** to show sb to the door

Begleiter(in) <-s, -> *m(f)* companion

Begleiterscheinung *f* concomitant *form;* MED [accompanying] symptom

Begleitperson *f* escort

Begleitumstände *pl* attendant circumstances *pl*

Begleitung <-, -en> *f* ❶ (*das Begleiten*) company; **kommst du allein oder in ~?** are you coming by yourself or with someone?; **in** [**jds** *gen*] **~** accompanied by sb; **ohne ~** unaccompanied ❷ (*Begleiter*[*in*]) companion ❸ MUS accompaniment; **ohne ~ spielen** to play unaccompanied

beglücken* *vt* (*geh*) ❶ (*glücklich stimmen*) to make happy ❷ (*hum: sexuell befriedigen*) to bestow favors on *hum fam*

beglückt I. *adj* happy **II.** *adv* happily

beglückwünschen* *vt* to congratulate (**zu** +*dat* on)

begnadet [bə·ˈgnaː·dət] *adj* (*geh*) gifted

begnadigen* [bə·ˈgnaː·dɪ·gn̩] *vt* to pardon

begnügen* [bə·ˈgnyː·gn̩] *vr* ■**sich** *akk* **mit etw** *dat* **~** to be satisfied with sth

begonnen [bə·ˈgɔ·nən] *pp von* **beginnen**

begossen [bə·ˈgɔ·sn̩] *pp von* **begießen**

begraben* *vt irreg* ❶ (*beerdigen*) to bury ❷ (*aufgeben*) *Hoffnung, Plan* to abandon; **einen Streit ~** to bury the hatchet

Begräbnis <-ses, -se> [bə·ˈgrɛp·nɪs] *nt* burial

begradigen* [bə·ˈgraː·dɪ·gn̩] *vt* BAU to straighten [out]

begreifbar *adj* comprehensible; **leicht/schwer ~** easy/difficult to understand

begreifen* *irreg* **I.** *vt* ❶ (*verstehen*) to understand; (*erfassen*) to comprehend; ■**~, dass ...** to realize that ...; **kaum zu ~ sein** to be incomprehensible ❷ (*für etw halten*) to regard (**als** +*akk* as) **II.** *vi* **langsam/schnell ~** to be slow/quick on the uptake **III.** *vr* ■**sich** *akk* **als etw ~** to consider oneself to be sth

begreiflich *adj* understandable; **jdm etw ~ machen** to make sth clear to sb

begreiflicherweise *adv* understandably

begrenzen* *vt* ❶ (*räumlich*) to mark the border of ❷ (*beschränken*) to limit (**auf** +*akk* to); **die Geschwindigkeit auf ... km/h ~** to impose a speed limit of ... kmph

begrenzt I. *adj* limited; **in einem zeitlich ~en Rahmen** in a limited time frame **II.** *adv* with limits; **nur ~ möglich sein** to be only somewhat possible

Begrenztheit <-> *f kein pl* limitedness

Begrenzung <-, -en> *f* ❶ (*räumliches Begrenzen*) limiting ❷ (*das Beschränken*) restriction ❸ (*Grenze*) boundary

Begriff <-[e]s, -e> *m* ❶ (*Ausdruck*) term; **ein ~ aus der Philosophie** a philosophical term ❷ (*Vorstellung*) idea; **jdm ein/kein ~ sein** to mean sth/nothing to sb; **für jds ~e** in sb's opinion ▶WENDUNGEN: **schwer von ~ sein** (*fam*) to be quick/slow on the uptake; **im ~ sein, etw zu tun** to be about to do sth

begrifflich *adj attr* conceptual

begriffsstutzig *adj* slow on the uptake

Begriffsstutzigkeit <-> *f kein pl* slow-wittedness

begründen* *vt* ❶ (*Gründe angeben*) to give reasons for; *Ablehnung, Forderung* to justify; *Behauptung, Verdacht* to substantiate ❷ (*gründen*) to found

Begründer(in) *m(f)* founder

begründet *adj* well-founded; **in etw** *dat* **~ liegen** to be the result of sth

Begründung <-, -en> *f* ❶ (*Grund*) reason ❷ (*das Gründen*) foundation

begrünen* *vt* to cover with greenery

begrüßen* *vt* ❶ (*willkommen heißen*) to greet ❷ (*gutheißen*) to welcome; **es ist zu ~, dass ...** it is a good thing that ...

begrüßenswert *adj* welcome

Begrüßung <-, -en> *f* greeting; **offizielle ~** official welcome

Begrüßungsansprache *f* welcome speech

begucken* *vt* (*fam*) to [have [*or* take] a] look at

begünstigen* [bə·ˈgʏn·stɪ·gn̩] *vt* ❶ *Export, Wachstum* to favor, to encourage; **von etw** *dat* **begünstigt werden** to be helped by sth ❷ (*bevorzugen*) to favor

Begünstigung <-, -en> *f* (*Bevorzugung*) preferential treatment

begutachten* *vt* ❶ (*fachlich prüfen*) to examine ❷ (*fam*) ■**jdn/etw ~** to take a look at sb/sth

Begutachtung <-, -en> *f* assessment; *eines Gebäudes* survey

begütert [bə·ˈgyː·tɐt] *adj* (*geh*) affluent

behaart [bə·ˈhaːɐ̯t] *adj* hairy; **stark/schwach ~ sein** to be very/not very hairy

Behaarung <-, -en> *f* hair

behäbig [bə·ˈhɛː·bɪç] *adj* ❶ (*gemütlich, geruhsam*) placid; (*langsam, schwerfällig*) ponderous ❷ (*dicklich*) portly ❸ SCHWEIZ (*stattlich*) imposing

behaftet *adj* ■**mit etw** *dat* **~ sein** to be marked with sth; (*mit Makel*) to be flawed with sth; **mit Problemen ~ sein** to be fraught with problems

behagen* [bə·ˈhaː·gn̩] *vi* ■**etw behagt jdm** sth pleases sb, sb likes sth

behaglich [bə·ˈhaːk·lɪç] **I.** *adj* ❶ (*gemütlich*) cozy; **es sich** *dat* **~ machen** to make oneself comfortable ❷ (*genussvoll*) **ein ~es Schnurren** a contented purring **II.** *adv* ❶ (*gemütlich*) cozily ❷ (*genussvoll*) contentedly

Behaglichkeit <-> *f kein pl* coziness

behalten* *vt irreg* ❶ (*nicht wegwerfen*) to keep ❷ (*nicht preisgeben*) **etw für sich** *akk* **~** to keep sth to oneself ❸ (*bewahren*) to maintain; **die Nerven ~** to keep one's composure ❹ (*sich merken*) to remember; **etw im**

Kopf ~ to keep sth in one's head
Behälter <-s, -> *m* container
behạmmert *adj* (*fam*) *s.* **bescheuert**
behänd[RR] [bə·ˈhɛnt], **behände**[RR] [bə·ˈhɛn·də] **I.** *adj* nimble **II.** *adv* nimbly
behạndeln* *vt* ❶ (*damit umgehen, bearbeiten*) to treat (**mit** +*dat* with); **jdn gut/schlecht ~** to treat sb well/badly ❷ (*abhandeln*) *Antrag, Punkt* to deal with
Behạndlung <-, -en> *f* treatment
Behạndlungsmethode *f* treatment method
Behạndlungsraum *m,* **Behạndlungszimmer** *nt* treatment room
behạngen* **I.** *vt* to hang (**mit** +*dat* with); *Weihnachtsbaum* to decorate **II.** *vr* (*pej fam*) ■ **sich** *akk* ~ *mit Schmuck* to load on
behạrren* *vi* to insist (**auf** +*akk* on); **auf seiner Meinung ~** to stick to one's opinion
behạrrlich I. *adj* insistent; (*ausdauernd*) persistent **II.** *adv* persistently; **~ schweigen** to persist in remaining silent
Behạrrlichkeit <-> *f kein pl* insistence
behaupten* [bə·ˈhaup·tn̩] **I.** *vt* ❶ (*äußern*) to claim; ■ **von jdm ~, dass ...** to say of sb that ...; ■ **es wird behauptet, dass ...** it is said that ... ❷ (*aufrechterhalten*) to maintain; **seinen Vorsprung gegen jdn ~** to maintain one's lead over sb **II.** *vr* ■ **sich** *akk* ~ to assert oneself (**gegen** +*akk* against/over); **sich gegen die Konkurrenz ~ können** to hold one's own against the competition
Behauptung <-, -en> *f* assertion; **eine ~ aufstellen** to make an assertion
Behausung <-, -en> *f* (*hum*) accommodation
beheben* *vt irreg* to remove; *Fehler, Mangel* to rectify; *Missstände* to remedy; *Schaden, Störung* to repair
Behebung <-, -en> *f* removal; *eines Fehlers, Mangels* rectification; *eines Schadens, einer Störung* repair
beheimatet [bə·ˈhai·maː·tət] *adj* ❶ (*ansässig*) ■ **~ sein** to be resident ❷ BOT, ZOOL native; **in Kalifornien ~ sein** to be native to California
beheizen* *vt* to heat (**mit** +*dat* with)
Behelf <-[e]s, -e> [bə·ˈhɛlf] *m* [temporary] replacement
behẹlfen* *vr irreg* **sich** *dat* **mit etw** *dat* ~ [**müssen**] to [have to] make do with sth; ■ **sich** *dat* ~ [**können**] to [be able to] manage
behẹlfsmäßig I. *adj* temporary **II.** *adv* temporarily
behelligen* [bə·ˈhɛ·lɪ·gn̩] *vt* to bother
behẹnd(e)[ALT] *adj, adv s.* **behänd(e)**
behẹrbergen* *vt* to accommodate
behẹrrschen* **I.** *vt* ❶ (*als Herrscher regieren*) to rule ❷ (*im Griff haben*) to control; **ein Fahrzeug ~** to have control over a vehicle ❸ (*gut können*) to have mastered; **ein Instrument ~** to play an instrument well; **eine Sprache ~** to have good command of a language; **alle Tricks ~** to know all the tricks ❹ (*prägen, dominieren*) to dominate **II.** *vr* ■ **sich** *akk* ~ to control oneself
behẹrrscht I. *adj* [self-]controlled **II.** *adv* with self-control
Behẹrrschung <-> *f kein pl* ❶ (*das Gutkönnen*) mastery ❷ (*Selbstbeherrschung*) self-control
beherzigen* [bə·ˈhɛr·tsɪ·gn̩] *vt* to take to heart; *Rat* to follow
behẹrzt I. *adj* intrepid **II.** *adv* intrepidly
behilflich [bə·ˈhɪlf·lɪç] *adj* ■ **jdm ~ sein** to help sb
behịndern* *vt* ■ **jdn ~** to obstruct [*or* hinder] sb; ■ **etw ~** to hinder sth
behịndert *adj* disabled; **geistig/körperlich ~** mentally/physically disabled
Behịnderte(r) *f(m) dekl wie adj* disabled person; ■ **die B~n** the disabled
behịndertengerecht *adj* handicapped-accessible
Behịndertenparkplatz *m* handicapped parking spot
Behịnderung <-, -en> *f* ❶ (*das Behindern*) obstruction; **es muss mit ~en gerechnet werden** delays should be expected ❷ MED disability; **geistige/körperliche ~** mental/physical disability
Behörde <-, -n> [bə·ˈhøːɐ̯·də] *f* ❶ (*Amt*) department; ■ **die ~n** the authorities ❷ (*Amtsgebäude*) government offices
behördlich [bə·ˈhøːɐ̯t·lɪç] **I.** *adj* official **II.** *adv* officially; **~ genehmigt** authorized by the authorities
behüten* *vt* ❶ (*schützend bewachen*) to watch over ❷ (*bewahren*) to protect (**vor** +*dat* from)
behutsam [bə·ˈhuːt·zaːm] **I.** *adj* gentle **II.** *adv* gently
Behutsamkeit <-> *f kein pl* care
bei [bai] *präp* +*dat* ❶ (*in der Nähe von*) near; **eine Stadt ~ Stuttgart** a town near Stuttgart ❷ ■ **~ jdm** [**zu Hause**] at sb's place; **~ uns zu Hause** at our house [*or* place]; **ich war ~ meinen Eltern** I was at my parents' [house] ❸ (*berufliche/geschäftliche Verbindung*) **er ist ~ der Bahn** he works for the railroad; **~m Bäcker/Friseur** at the bakery/hairdresser's; **~ wem nimmst du Klavierstunden?** who's your piano teacher? ❹ **etw ~ sich** *dat* **haben** to have sth on [*or* with] one; **ich habe gerade kein Geld ~ mir** I don't have any money on me at the moment ❺ (*Ereignis*) **~ dem Zugunglück starben viele Menschen** many people died in the train crash ❻ (*zeitlich*) **~ Tag/Nacht** by day/night; **~m Lesen kann ich nicht Radio hören** I cannot read and listen to the radio at the same time; **störe mich bitte nicht ~ der Arbeit!** please stop disturbing me while I'm working! ❼ (*Begleitumstände*) by; **wir können das ja ~ einer Flasche Wein besprechen** let's talk about it over a bottle of wine; **~ dieser Hitze/Kälte** in such heat/cold; **~ Nebel/Regen** when it is foggy/raining; **~ Wind und Wetter** come rain or shine; **~ 45° unter null** at 45° below zero

[Celsius] ⑧ (*ungefähr*) around; **der Preis liegt ~ 1.000 Euro** the price is around 1,000 euros ⑨ (*wegen, mit*) with; **~ deinen Fähigkeiten** with your talents

bei|behalten* *vt irreg* to maintain; *Tradition, Brauch* to uphold; *Meinung* to stick to

Beiboot *nt* NAUT tender

bei|bringen *vt irreg* (*fam*) ① (*übermitteln*) **jdm etw [schonend] ~** to break sth [gently] to sb ② (*lehren*) to teach

Beichte <-, -n> ['baiç·tə] *f* confession; **die ~ ablegen** to make one's confession; **jdm die ~ abnehmen** to hear sb's confession

beichten ['baiç·tn̩] **I.** *vt* ■ **[jdm] etw ~** to confess sth [to sb] **II.** *vi* to confess; **~ gehen** to go to confession

Beichtgeheimnis *nt kein pl* seal of confession [*or* the confessional]

Beichtstuhl *m* confessional

beide ['bai·də] *pron* both; **meine ~n Töchter** my two daughters; **alle ~** both of them; **~ Mal[e]** both times; **keiner von ~n** neither of them; ■ **ihr ~** the two of you; **ihr habt ~ Recht** both of you are right; ■ **wir ~** the two of us; ■ **die ~n** both [of them]; **die ersten/letzten ~n** the first/last two; **einer von ~n** one of the two; ■ **~s** both; **~s ist möglich** both are possible

beiderlei ['bai·dɐ·'lai] *adj attr* both

beiderseitig ['bai·dɐ·zai·tɪç] *adj* on both sides; *Abkommen* bilateral; *Vertrauen, Einverständnis, Zufriedenheit* mutual

beiderseits ['bai·dɐ·'zaits] *adv* on both sides

beidseitig ['baid·zai·tɪç] *adj, adv* on both sides; *Beschichtung* double-sided

beieinander [bai·ʔai·'nan·dɐ] *adv* together ▶ WENDUNGEN: **gut/schlecht ~ sein** (*fam: körperlich*) to be in good/bad shape; (*geistig*) to be with it/not all there

beieinander|haben *vt* (*fam*) ■ **etw [wieder] ~** to have [got] sth together [again] ▶ WENDUNGEN: **jd hat sie nicht [mehr] alle beieinander** sb has a screw loose

beieinander|liegen *vi irreg* to lie together

beieinander|sitzen *vi irreg* to sit together

beieinander|stehen *vi irreg* to stand together

Beifahrer(in) *m(f)* front-seat passenger; (*zusätzlicher Fahrer*) additional driver

Beifahrerairbag [-ɛːɐ·bɛk] *m* passenger airbag

Beifahrersitz *m* [front] passenger seat

Beifall <-[e]s> *m kein pl* ① (*Applaus*) applause; **~ klatschen** to applaud ② (*Zustimmung*) approval; **[jds** *akk*] **~ finden** to meet with [sb's] approval

beifällig I. *adj* approving **II.** *adv* approvingly

bei|fügen *vt* ① (*mitsenden*) to enclose ② (*hinzufügen*) to add

beige [beːʃ, 'beː·ʒə] *adj* beige

bei|geben *vt irreg* to add ▶ WENDUNGEN: **klein ~** to give in

Beigeschmack *m* [after]taste; (*fig*) overtone[s]

Beihilfe *f* (*finanzielle Unterstützung*) financial aid

Beil <-[e]s, -e> [bail] *nt* [short-handled] ax

Beilage *f* ① (*beigelegte Speise*) side order [*or* dish] ② (*Beiheft*) supplement, addition ③ (*beigelegte Werbung*) insert ④ ÖSTERR (*Anlage*) enclosure

beiläufig I. *adj* passing **II.** *adv* ① (*nebenbei*) in passing; **etw ~ erwähnen** to mention sth in passing ② ÖSTERR (*ungefähr*) about

bei|legen *vt* ① (*dazulegen*) to insert in; **einem Brief einen Rückumschlag ~** to enclose a return envelope in a letter ② (*schlichten*) to settle

Beilegung <-, -en> *f pl selten* (*Schlichtung*) settlement

beileibe [bai·'lai·bə] *adv* on no account; **~ nicht!** certainly not

Beileid *nt* condolence[s *pl*]; **[mein] herzliches ~** [you have] my heartfelt sympathy; **jdm [zu etw** *dat*] **sein ~ aussprechen** to offer sb one's condolences [on sth]

Beileidskarte *f* condolence card

bei|liegen *vi irreg* (*einem Brief, Paket*) to be enclosed [in]

beiliegend *adj* enclosed

beim [baim] = **bei dem** *s.* **bei**

bei|mengen *vt* to add

bei|messen *vt irreg* **etw** *dat* **Bedeutung/Wert ~** to attach importance/value to sth

bei|mischen *vt* to add

Bein <-[e]s, -e> [bain] *nt* ① (*Körperteil*) leg; **jdm auf die ~e helfen** to help sb back on his/her feet; **jdm ein ~ stellen** to trip sb; **die ~e übereinanderschlagen** to cross one's legs; **unsicher auf den ~en sein** to be unsteady on one's feet ② (*Hosenbein*) leg ▶ WENDUNGEN: **sich** *dat* **die ~e in den Bauch stehen** (*fam*) to be standing around for ages; **mit dem linken ~ zuerst aufgestanden sein** to have gotten up on the wrong side of the bed; **sich** *dat* **[bei etw** *dat*] **kein ~ ausreißen** (*fam*) to not [exactly] bust one's ass [doing sth] *vulg;* **wieder auf die ~e kommen** (*gesundheitlich*) to be up on one's feet again; (*finanziell*) to regain one's financial standing; **jdm ~e machen** (*fam*) to give sb a kick in the ass *vulg;* **auf den ~en sein** (*in Bewegung sein*) to be on one's feet; (*auf sein*) to be up and about; **etw auf die ~e stellen** to get sth going

beinah ['bai·naː, 'bai·'naː, bai·'naː], **beinahe** ['bai·naːə, 'bai·'naːə, bai·'naːə] *adv* almost

Beiname *m* epithet

Beinbruch *m* leg fracture ▶ WENDUNGEN: **das ist kein ~!** (*fam*) it's not as bad as all that!

beinhalten* [bə·'ʔɪn·hal·tn̩] *vt* to contain

Beinprothese *f* prosthetic leg

Beipackzettel *m* instruction sheet

bei|pflichten *vi* ■ **jdm ~** to agree with sb

beirren* *vt* ■ **sich** *akk* **[nicht] ~ lassen** to [not] let oneself be put off

Beirut <-s> [bai·'ruːt, '--] *nt* Beirut

beisammen [bai·'za·mən] *adv* ① (*zusammen*) together; **~ sein** to be [all] together ② (*fam: geistig rege*) **[nicht] gut ~ sein** to [not] be with it

Beisammensein *nt* get-together

Beischlaf *m* sexual intercourse

Beisein *nt* ■**in jds ~** in sb's presence

beiseite [bai·ˈzai·tə] *adv* to one side

beiseite|gehen[RR] *vi irreg sein* to step aside

beiseite|lassen[RR] *vt irreg* ■**etw ~** to leave aside *sep* sth

beiseite|legen[RR] *vi irreg* ■**etw ~** (*weglegen*) to put sth to one side; (*sparen*) to put aside *sep* sth

bei|setzen *vt* (*geh*) to inter; *Urne* to install

Beisetzung <-, -en> *f* (*geh*) interment; *einer Urne* installing [in its resting place]

Beispiel <-[e]s, -e> [ˈbai·ʃpiːl] *nt* example; **anschauliches ~** illustration; **praktisches ~** demonstration; **zum ~** for example; **wie zum ~** such as ▶WENDUNGEN: **mit gutem ~ vorangehen** to set a good example

beispielhaft *adj* ❶ (*vorbildlich*) exemplary ❷ (*typisch*) typical (**für** +*akk* of)

beispiellos *adj* ❶ (*unerhört*) outrageous ❷ (*einzigartig*) unprecedented

Beispielsatz *m* example [sentence]

beispielsweise *adv* for example

beißen <biss, gebissen> [ˈbai·sn̩] **I.** *vt* to bite ▶WENDUNGEN: **etw/nichts zu ~ haben** (*fam*) to have something/nothing to eat **II.** *vi* ❶ (*mit den Zähnen*) ■**auf/in etw** *akk* **~** to bite into sth ❷ (*brennend sein*) to sting; *Säure* to burn; **in den Augen ~** to make one's eyes sting ▶WENDUNGEN: **an etw** *dat* **zu ~ haben** to have sth to chew on **III.** *vr* ❶ **sich** *akk o dat* **auf die Zunge ~** to bite one's tongue ❷ (*nicht harmonieren*) *Farben* ■**sich** *akk* [**mit etw** *dat*] **~** to clash [with sth]

beißend *adj* **~er Geruch** acrid [*or* pungent] smell; **~e Kälte** bitter cold; **~e Kritik** sharp criticism; **~er Witz** caustic humor

Beißzange *f* DIAL *s.* **Kneifzange**

Beistand *m kein pl* (*Unterstützung*) support; (*Hilfe*) assistance; *eines Priesters* attendance; **ärztlicher ~** medical aid; **jdm ~ leisten** to give sb one's support

bei|stehen *vi irreg* ■**jdm ~** to stand by sb

bei|steuern *vt* to contribute (**zu** +*dat* to)

bei|stimmen *vi s.* **zustimmen**

Beistrich *m bes* ÖSTERR comma

Beitrag <-[e]s, -träge> [ˈbai·traːk, *pl* ˈbai·trɛː·gə] *m* ❶ (*Mitgliedsbeitrag*) fee; (*Versicherungsbeitrag*) premium ❷ (*Artikel*) article ❸ (*Mitwirkung*) contribution; **einen ~ zu etw** *dat* **leisten** to make a contribution to sth ❹ SCHWEIZ (*Subvention*) subsidy

bei|tragen *vt, vi irreg* to contribute (**zu** +*dat* to); **seinen Teil zur Rettung der Hungernden ~** to do one's part to help the starving

beitragspflichtig *adj* liable to pay contributions

Beitragssatz *m* membership rate

bei|treten *vi irreg sein* to join [as a member]; **der EU ~** to join the EU

Beitritt *m* entry (**zu** +*dat* into); **der ~ zur EU** the accession to the EU

Beitrittserklärung *f* confirmation of membership

Beitrittsgespräch *nt meist pl* POL [EU] accession discussion

Beiwagen *m* sidecar

Beize[1] <-, -n> [ˈbai·tsə] *f* ❶ (*Beizmittel*) stain[ing agent] ❷ (*Marinade*) marinade

Beize[2] <-, -n> [ˈbai·tsə] *f* DIAL (*fam: Kneipe*) bar, pub

beizeiten [bai·ˈtsai·tn̩] *adv* in good time

beizen [ˈbai·tsn̩] *vt* ❶ (*mit einem Beizmittel behandeln*) to stain ❷ (*marinieren*) to marinade

bejahen* [bə·ˈjaː·ən] *vt* ❶ (*mit Ja beantworten*) to answer in the affirmative, to say yes to ❷ (*gutheißen*) to approve [of]

bejahend I. *adj* affirmative **II.** *adv* affirmatively

bejammern* *vt* to lament

bejammernswert *adj* lamentable

bejubeln* *vt* to cheer; ■**bejubelt werden** to be met with cheering

bekämpfen* **I.** *vt* to fight; **Schädlinge ~** to control pests **II.** *vr* ■**sich** *akk* [**gegenseitig**] **~** to fight one another

bekannt [bə·ˈkant] *adj* ❶ (*allgemein gekannt*) well-known; **etw ist allgemein ~** sth is common knowledge; **etw ~ geben** to announce sth; *Presse* to publish sth; **etw ~ machen** (*öffentlich*) to make sth known to the public ❷ (*berühmt*) **jdn ~ machen** to make sb famous; **~ werden** to become famous; **für etw** *akk* **~ sein** to be well-known for sth ❸ (*nicht fremd, vertraut*) familiar; **ist dir dieser Name ~?** are you familiar with this name?; **mit jdm ~ sein** to be acquainted with sb

Bekannte(r) *f(m) dekl wie adj* acquaintance; **ein guter ~r** a friend

Bekanntenkreis *m* circle of friends

bekanntermaßen *adv s.* **bekanntlich**

Bekanntgabe *f pl selten* announcement; *Presse* publication

bekannt|geben *vt irreg s.* **bekannt 1**

Bekanntheit <-> *f kein pl* fame

Bekanntheitsgrad *m* degree of fame

bekanntlich *adv* as is [generally] known

bekannt|machen *vt s.* **bekannt 1, 2**

Bekanntmachung <-, -en> *f* announcement; **öffentliche ~** public announcement

Bekanntschaft <-, -en> *f* ❶ *pl selten* (*das Bekanntsein*) acquaintance; **eine nette ~ machen** to meet a nice person; **mit etw** *dat* **~ machen** (*iron*) to get to know sth ❷ (*Bekannte[r]*) acquaintance; (*Bekanntenkreis*) acquaintances *pl*

bekehren* *vt* to convert (**zu** +*dat* to)

Bekehrung <-, -en> *f* conversion

bekennen* *irreg* **I.** *vt* to confess **II.** *vr* ❶ (*eintreten für*) ■**sich** *akk* **zu jdm/etw ~** to declare one's support for sb/sth; **sich zu einem Glauben ~** to profess a faith ❷ (*zugeben*) **sich** *akk* **zu einem Irrtum/einer Tat ~** to admit [to] a mistake/doing sth

bekieken *vt* NORDD (*fam*) to look at

bekifft [bə·ˈkɪft] *adj* (*fam*) stoned, high

beklagen* I. *vt* to lament; **bei dem Unglück waren 23 Tote zu ~** the accident claimed 23 lives II. *vr* ■ **sich** *akk* [**bei jdm**] **~** to complain [to sb] (**über** +*akk* about)

beklagenswert *adj* lamentable; *Irrtum, Versehen* unfortunate

beklauen* *vt* (*fam*) to rob

bekleckern* (*fam*) I. *vt* to stain II. *vr* (*fam*) **sich** *akk* **mit Soße ~** to spill sauce all over oneself

beklecksen* *vt* to splatter

bekleidet *adj* ■ **mit etw** *dat* **~ sein** to be wearing sth

Bekleidung *f* clothing

beklemmend I. *adj* ❶ *Raum* claustrophobic ❷ (*drückend*) *Gefühl, Schweigen* oppressive; *Gedanke* depressing II. *adv* oppressively

Beklemmung <-, -en> *f* constriction

beklommen [bə·ˈklɔ·mən] I. *adj* anxious; (*von Mensch a.*) uneasy II. *adv* anxiously

Beklommenheit <-> *f kein pl* anxiety; (*von Mensch a.*) uneasiness

bekloppt [bə·ˈklɔpt] *adj* (*fam*) *s.* **bescheuert**

Bekloppte(r) *f(m) dekl wie adj* (*fam*) idiot

beknackt [bə·ˈknakt] *adj* (*fam*) *s.* **bescheuert**

bekochen* *vt* to cook for

bekommen* *irreg* I. *vt haben* ❶ (*erhalten*) to receive; *Genehmigung* to obtain; *Massage, Spritze* to be given; *Ohrfeige, Ermäßigung, Geschenk* to get; **sie bekommt 21 Euro die Stunde** she earns 21 euros an hour; **was ~ Sie dafür?** how much is it?; **ich bekomme noch 4.000 Euro von dir** you still owe me 4,000 euros; **Ärger/Schwierigkeiten ~** to get into trouble/difficulties; **etw in die Hände ~** (*fam*) to get [a] hold of sth ❷ (*erreichen*) **den Bus ~** to catch the bus ❸ (*serviert erhalten*) ■ **etw ~** to be served with sth; **ich bekomme ein Bier** I'd like a beer ❹ (*entwickeln*) **eine Erkältung ~** to catch a cold; **eine Glatze/graue Haare ~** to go bald/gray; **Heimweh ~** to get homesick; **Lust ~, etw zu tun** to feel like doing sth ❺ + *Infinitiv* **etw zu essen/trinken ~** to get sth to eat/drink; **etw zu hören/sehen ~** to get to hear/see sth; **der wird von mir etwas zu hören ~!** (*fam*) I'll give him a piece of my mind! ❻ + *pp o adj* **etw bezahlt ~** to get paid for sth; **etw gemacht ~** to get sth done; **etw geschenkt ~** to be given sth [as a present] II. *vi* **jdm** [**gut**]**/schlecht ~** to do sb good/to not do sb any good; *Essen* to agree/to disagree with sb

bekömmlich [bə·ˈkœm·lɪç] *adj* [easily] digestible

bekräftigen* *vt* to confirm (**durch** +*akk* by, **mit** +*dat* by); **etw noch einmal ~** to reaffirm sth; ■ **jdn in etw** *dat* **~** to strengthen sb's sth

bekreuzigen* *vr* ■ **sich** *akk* [**vor jdm/etw**] **~** to cross oneself [upon seeing sb/sth]

bekriegen* I. *vt* ■ **jdn/etw ~** to wage war on sb/sth II. *vr* ■ **sich** *akk* [**gegenseitig**] **~** to be warring [with one another]

bekümmern* *vt* to worry

bekümmert *adj* worried (**über** +*akk* about)

bekunden* [bə·ˈkʊn·dn̩] *vt* to express

belächeln* *vt* to smile at; ■ **belächelt werden** to be a target of ridicule

beladen* *irreg vt* to load [up *sep*]

Belag <-[e]s, Beläge> [bə·ˈlaːk, *pl* bə·ˈlɛː·gə] *m* ❶ (*Schicht*) coating ❷ (*Pizza-, Brotbelag*) topping; (*Sandwich*) filling ❸ (*Zahnbelag*) film; (*Zungenbelag*) fur ❹ (*Fußbodenbelag*) covering, flooring; (*Straßenbelag*) surface

belagern* *vt* to besiege

Belagerung <-, -en> *f* siege

belämmertRR [bə·ˈlɛ·mɐt] *adj* (*fam*) sheepish

Belang <-[e]s, -e> [bə·ˈlaŋ] *m* ❶ *kein pl* ■ **ohne/von ~ sein** to be of/of no importance ❷ *pl* (*Interessen*) interests; **jds ~e vertreten** to represent sb's interests

belangen* *vt* JUR to prosecute (**wegen** +*gen* for)

belanglos *adj* (*unwichtig*) unimportant; (*nebensächlich*) irrelevant

belassen* *vt irreg* ❶ ■ **es bei etw** *dat* **~** to leave it at sth; **~ wir es dabei!** let's leave it at that ❷ **etw an seinem Platz ~** to leave sth in its place

belastbar *adj* ❶ (*zu belasten*) loadable; ■ **bis zu etw** *dat* **~ sein** to have a maximum load of sth ❷ (*fig: beanspruchbar*) **kein Mensch ist unbegrenzt ~** nobody can take work/abuse indefinitely; **unter Stress ist ein Mitarbeiter weniger ~** stress reduces an employee's working capacity; **Training macht das Herz ~er** conditioning strengthens the heart

Belastbarkeit <-, -en> *f* ❶ (*durch Gewicht*) load-bearing capacity ❷ (*Beanspruchbarkeit*) ability to withstand stress; *von Organen, Körper* maximum resilience

belasten* *vt* ❶ (*mit Gewicht*) to load (**mit** +*akk* with) ❷ (*seelisch/geistig*) to burden; **jdn mit Problemen ~** to burden sb with problems; **jdn** [**schwer**] **~** to weigh [heavily] on one's mind; ■ **~d** crippling ❸ (*leistungsmäßig beanspruchen*) to strain; **jdn/etw zu sehr ~** to overstrain sb/sth; MED **etw belastet das Herz** sth puts a strain on the heart ❹ JUR to incriminate; **~des Material** incriminating evidence ❺ *Umwelt* to pollute ❻ FIN *Konto* to debit; **etw mit einer Hypothek ~** to mortgage sth

belästigen* [bə·ˈlɛs·tɪ·gn̩] *vt* (*lästig werden*) to bother; (*zudringlich werden*) to pester; **jdn sexuell ~** to harass sb sexually

Belästigung <-, -en> *f* annoyance; **sexuelle ~** sexual harassment

Belastung <-, -en> *f* ❶ (*das Belasten*) loading ❷ (*Gewicht*) load; **die maximale ~ des Aufzugs** the maximum load for the elevator ❸ (*Anstrengung*) burden ❹ (*leistungsmäßige Beanspruchung*) strain (**für** +*akk* on) ❺ ÖKOL pollution

belauern* *vt* (*lauernd*) to observe unseen;

(*argwöhnisch*) to watch secretly
belaufen* *vr irreg* ■**sich** *akk* **auf etw ~** to amount to sth
belauschen* *vt* to eavesdrop on
beleben* **I.** *vt* ❶ (*anregen*) *Konjunktur* to stimulate; *Party, Unterhaltung* to liven up ❷ (*erfrischen*) to make feel better ❸ (*zum Leben erwecken*) to bring [back] to life **II.** *vr* ■**sich** *akk* **~** to liven up; *Konjunktur* to be stimulated
belebend *adj* ❶ (*anregend*) invigorating ❷ (*erfrischend*) refreshing
belebt [bə·ˈleːpt] *adj* ❶ (*bevölkert*) busy ❷ (*lebendig*) animated
Belebung <-, -en> *f* stimulation
Beleg <-[e]s, -e> [bə·ˈleːk, *pl* bə·ˈleː·gə] *m* ❶ (*Quittung*) receipt ❷ (*Beweis*) proof
belegen* *vt* ❶ (*mit Belag versehen*) **ein Brot mit etw** *dat* **~** to put sth on a slice of bread; **belegte Brote** [open-faced] sandwiches ❷ (*beweisen*) to verify; *Behauptung* to substantiate; *Zitat* to give a reference for ❸ (*auferlegen*) ■**jdn mit etw** *dat* **~** to impose sth on sb ❹ *Kurs* to enroll [*or* register] for ❺ (*okkupieren*) to occupy; ■**belegt sein** to be occupied; **ist der Stuhl hier schon belegt?** is this chair free? ❻ SPORT **den vierten Platz ~** to take fourth place
Belegexemplar *nt* specimen copy
Belegschaft <-, -en> *f* (*Beschäftigte*) staff; (*Arbeiter*) workforce
belegt *adj Stimme* hoarse
belehren* *vt* (*informieren*) to inform; **sich** *akk* **von jdm ~ lassen** to listen to sb
belehrend I. *adj* didactic **II.** *adv* didactically
Belehrung <-, -en> *f* (*belehrender Rat*) explanation; **deine ~en kannst du dir sparen!** there's no need to lecture [to] me *fam*
beleibt [bə·ˈlaipt] *adj* corpulent
beleidigen* [bə·ˈlai·dɪ·gn̩] *vt* to insult
beleidigend I. *adj* insulting **II.** *adv* insultingly
Beleidigung <-, -en> *f* insult
beleihen* *vt irreg* to lend money on
belemmertALT *adj* (*fam*) *s.* **belämmert**
belesen [bə·ˈleː·zn̩] *adj* well-read
beleuchten* *vt* ❶ (*durch Licht erhellen*) to light [up *sep*] ❷ (*anstrahlen*) to light up *sep* ❸ (*fig: betrachten*) to throw light on
Beleuchtung <-, -en> *f* ❶ *pl selten* (*das Beleuchten*) lighting ❷ (*künstliches Licht*) light; (*Lichter*) lights *pl;* **die ~ der Straßen** street lighting
Belgien <-s> [ˈbɛl·gi̯ən] *nt* Belgium; *s. a.* **Deutschland**
Belgier(in) <-s, -> [ˈbɛl·gi̯ɐ] *m(f)* Belgian; *s. a.* **Deutsche(r)**
belgisch [ˈbɛl·gɪʃ] *adj* Belgian; *s. a.* **deutsch**
belichten* *vt* FOTO to expose
Belichtung *f* FOTO exposure
Belieben *nt* [**ganz**] **nach ~** just as you/they etc. like
beliebig [bɛ·ˈliː·bɪç] **I.** *adj* any; **eine ~ Zahl** any number at all; ■**jeder B~e** anyone at all **II.** *adv* **~ lange/viele** as long/many as you like; **etw ~ verändern** to change sth at will
beliebt [bə·ˈliːpt] *adj* popular (**bei** *+dat* with); **sich** *akk* [**bei jdm**] **~ machen** to make oneself popular [with sb]
Beliebtheit <-> *f kein pl* popularity
beliefern* *vt* to supply
Belieferung *f* delivery
bellen [ˈbɛ·lən] *vi* to bark
belohnen* *vt* to reward
Belohnung <-, -en> *f* ❶ (*das Belohnen*) rewarding ❷ (*Lohn*) reward; **eine ~ aussetzen** to offer a reward
belüften* *vt* to ventilate
Belüftung *f* ❶ *kein pl* (*das Belüften*) ventilating ❷ ELEK ventilation *no indef art*
Belüftungsanlage *f* ventilation system
belügen* *irreg* **I.** *vt* ■**jdn ~** to lie to sb **II.** *vr* ■**sich** *akk* **selbst ~** to deceive oneself
belustigen* [bə·ˈlʊs·tɪ·gn̩] *vt* to amuse; **was belustigt dich?** what's so funny?
Belustigung <-, -en> *f* amusement; **zu jds ~** for sb's amusement
bemalen* *vt* ■**etw** [**mit etw** *dat*] **~** to paint [sth on] sth
bemängeln* [bə·ˈmɛ·ŋl̩n] *vt* to find fault with
bemannt [bə·ˈmant] *adj* manned, occupied; **~e Raumfahrt** manned space flight
bemerkbar *adj* (*wahrnehmbar*) noticeable; **sich** *akk* [**bei jdm**] **~ machen** to attract [sb's] attention; **ich werde mich schon ~ machen, wenn ich Sie benötige** I'll let you know when I need you
bemerken* *vt* ❶ (*wahrnehmen*) to notice ❷ (*äußern*) to say
bemerkenswert I. *adj* remarkable **II.** *adv* remarkably
Bemerkung <-, -en> *f* remark; **eine ~ über etw machen** to remark on sth; **eine ~ fallen lassen** to drop a remark
bemitleiden* [bə·ˈmɪt·lai·dn̩] **I.** *vt* to pity **II.** *vr* ■**sich** *akk* [**selbst**] **~** to feel sorry for oneself
bemitleidenswert *adj* pitiful
bemühen* *vr* ■**sich** *akk* **~** to try hard; **sich vergebens ~** to try in vain; **sich um eine Stelle ~** to try hard to get a job
Bemühen <-s> *nt kein pl* (*geh*) efforts *pl* (**um** *+akk* for)
bemüht *adj* keen; ■**um etw ~ sein** to try hard to do sth
Bemühung <-, -en> *f* effort; **danke für Ihre ~en** thank you for your trouble
bemuttern* [bə·ˈmʊ·tɐn] *vt* to mother
benachbart [bə·ˈnax·baːɐ̯t] *adj* ❶ (*in der Nachbarschaft gelegen*) nearby; (*nebenan*) neighboring *attr;* **das ~e Haus** the house next door ❷ (*angrenzend*) adjoining
benachrichtigen* [bə·ˈnaːx·rɪç·tɪgn̩] *vt* to inform; (*amtlich*) to notify
Benachrichtigung <-, -en> *f* notification
benachteiligen* [bə·ˈnaːx·tai·lɪ·gn̩] *vt* to put at a disadvantage; (*wegen Rasse, Geschlecht, Glaube*) to discriminate against

Benachteiligung <-, -en> *f* discrimination; ■**die ~ einer Person** discrimination against sb

Benefizkonzert *nt* benefit concert

benehmen* *vr irreg* ■**sich** *akk* **~** to behave [oneself]; **benimm dich!** behave yourself!; **sich** *akk* **gut/schlecht ~** to behave well/badly

Benehmen <-s> *nt kein pl* manners *pl*

beneiden* *vt* ■**jdn** [**um etw**] **~** to envy sb [sth]

beneidenswert **I.** *adj* enviable **II.** *adv* amazingly

Beneluxländer, **Beneluxstaaten** ['be:·ne·lʊks-] *pl* Benelux countries *pl*

benennen* *vt irreg* to name (**nach** *+dat* after); **Gegenstände ~** to denote objects

Benennung <-, -en> *f* ❶ (*das Benennen*) naming ❷ (*Bezeichnung*) name

Bengel <-s, -[s]> ['bɛ·ŋl̩] *m* rascal

benommen [bə·'nɔ·mən] *adj* dazed; **jdn ~ machen** to throw sb

Benommenheit <-> *f kein pl* daze[d state]; **ein Gefühl von ~** a dazed feeling

benoten* [bə·'no:·tn̩] *vt* to grade; **ihr Aufsatz wurde mit „sehr gut" benotet** she got an "A" on her essay

benötigen* *vt* to need

benutzen* *vt*, **benützen*** *vt* DIAL, ÖSTERR ❶ (*gebrauchen*) to use; **den Aufzug ~** to take the elevator ❷ (*ausnutzen*) ■**jdn ~** to take advantage of sb; **sich** *akk* **benutzt fühlen** to feel [that one has been] used

Benutzer(in) <-s, -> *m(f)*, **Benützer(in)** <-s, -> *m(f)* DIAL, ÖSTERR COMPUT user

benutzerdefiniert *adj* COMPUT user-defined

Benutzerebene *f* COMPUT user interface

benutzerfreundlich *adj* user-friendly

Benutzerhandbuch *nt* user manual

Benutzername *m* COMPUT user name

Benutzeroberfläche *f* COMPUT user interface

Benutzung *f*, **Benützung** *f* DIAL, ÖSTERR use; **jdm etw zur ~ überlassen** to put sth at sb's disposal

Benutzungsgebühr *f* rental fee

Benzin <-s, -e> [bɛn·'tsi:n] *nt* gas[oline]

Benzinkanister *m* gasoline can[ister]

Benzinpumpe *f* gas[oline] [*or* fuel] pump

Benzintank *m* gas[oline] [*or* fuel] tank

Benzinverbrauch *m* gas[oline] [*or* fuel] consumption

beobachten* [bə·'ʔo:b·ax·tn̩] *vt* ❶ (*betrachten*) to observe; ■**jdn** [**bei etw** *dat*] **~** to watch sb [doing sth]; **gut beobachtet!** good observation! ❷ (*überwachen*) ■**beobachtet werden** to be kept under surveillance; ■**jdn ~ lassen** to put sb under surveillance ❸ (*bemerken*) ■**etw an jdm ~** to notice sth in sb

Beobachter(in) <-s, -> *m(f)* observer

Beobachtung <-, -en> *f* ❶ (*das Betrachten*) observation ❷ (*Überwachung*) surveillance ❸ *meist pl* (*Ergebnis des Beobachtens*) observations *pl*

bepacken* *vt* to load up *sep*

bepflanzen* *vt* to plant

bequatschen* *vt* (*fam*) ❶ (*bereden*) ■**etw** [**mit jdm**] **~** to talk over sth *sep* [with sb] ❷ (*überreden*) ■**jdn ~** [**etw zu tun**] to talk sb into doing sth

bequem [bə·'kve:m] **I.** *adj* ❶ (*angenehm*) comfortable; **es sich** *dat* **~ machen** to make oneself comfortable ❷ (*leicht zu bewältigen*) easy; **ein ~es Leben haben** to have an easy life ❸ (*pej: träge*) idle **II.** *adv* ❶ (*leicht*) easily ❷ (*angenehm*) comfortably

Bequemlichkeit <-, -en> *f* ❶ (*Behaglichkeit*) comfort ❷ (*Trägheit*) idleness; **aus** [**reiner**] **~** out of [sheer] laziness

berappen* [bə·'rapn̩] *vt* (*fam*) to fork out *sep*

beraten* *irreg* **I.** *vt* ❶ (*Rat geben*) to advise; **jdn finanziell ~** to give sb financial advice; ■**sich** *akk* [**von jdm**] **~ lassen** to ask sb's advice ❷ (*besprechen*) to discuss; POL to debate **II.** *vi* ■**über etw** *akk* **~** to discuss sth

beratend *adj* advisory

Berater(in) <-s, -> *m(f)* advisor; (*in politischen Sachen a.*) counselor; (*Fachberater*) consultant

beratschlagen* [bə·'ra:t·ʃla:·gn̩] *vt, vi* to discuss

Beratung <-, -en> *f* ❶ *kein pl* (*das Beraten*) advice ❷ (*Besprechung*) discussion; POL debate ❸ (*beratendes Gespräch*) consultation

Beratungsstelle *f* advice center

berauben* *vt* to rob

berauschen* (*geh*) **I.** *vt* to intoxicate; *Alkohol a.* to inebriate; *Geschwindigkeit* to exhilarate **II.** *vr* ■**sich** *akk* **an etw** *dat* **~** to become intoxicated by sth

berauschend *adj* intoxicating

berechenbar [bə·'rɛ·çn̩·ba:g̯] *adj* ❶ (*voraussehbar*) predictable ❷ (*auszurechnen*) calculable

Berechenbarkeit <-> *f kein pl* (*Einschätzbarkeit*) predictability

berechnen* *vt* ❶ (*ausrechnen*) to calculate ❷ (*in Rechnung stellen*) to charge

berechnend *adj* (*pej*) scheming

Berechnung *f* ❶ (*Ausrechnung*) calculation; **nach meiner ~** according to my calculations ❷ (*pej: Eigennutz*) scheming; **aus ~** in cold deliberation

berechtigen* [bə·'rɛç·tɪ·gn̩] *vt* ■**zu etw** *dat* **~** ❶ (*bevollmächtigen*) to entitle to [do] sth; **sich** *akk* **zu etw** *dat* **berechtigt fühlen** to feel justified in doing sth ❷ (*Anlass geben*) to give grounds for sth

berechtigt [bə·'rɛç·tɪçt] *adj* justifiable; *Frage, Hoffnung, Anspruch* legitimate; *Vorwurf* just

berechtigterweise *adv* legitimately

Berechtigung <-, -en> *f pl selten* ❶ (*Befugnis*) authority; **die/keine ~ haben, etw zu tun** to have the/no authorization to do sth ❷ (*Rechtmäßigkeit*) justifiability

bereden* **I.** *vt* to discuss **II.** *vr* ■**sich** *akk* [**über etw** *akk*] **~** to discuss [sth]; **wir ~ uns noch** we are still discussing it

Beredsamkeit <-> *f kein pl* eloquence
beredt [bə·ˈreːt] *adj* eloquent
Bereich <-[e]s, -e> *m* ❶ (*Gebiet*) area; **im ~ des Möglichen liegen** to be within the realm of possibility ❷ (*Fachgebiet*) field
bereichern* [bə·ˈrai·çɐn] *vr* ■**sich** *akk* [**an etw** *dat*] ~ to grow rich [on sth]
bereinigen* *vt* to resolve; **eine Meinungsverschiedenheit ~** to settle differences
bereisen* *vt* ■**etw ~** to travel around sth; **die Welt ~** to travel the world
bereit [bə·ˈrait] *adj meist pred* ❶ (*fertig*) ready; (*vorbereitet*) prepared ❷ (*willens*) ■**zu etw** *dat* **~ sein** to be prepared to do sth; **sich** *akk* **~ erklären, etw zu tun** to agree to do sth
bereiten* *vt* ❶ (*verursachen*) to cause; *Freude, Überraschung* to give; **jdm Kopfschmerzen ~** to give sb a headache ❷ (*zubereiten*) to prepare
bereit|finden[RR] *vr irreg* ■**sich** *akk* **zu etw** *dat* ~ to be willing to do sth
bereit|halten *vt irreg* ❶ (*griffbereit haben*) to have readily available ❷ (*in petto haben*) to have in store
bereit|legen *vt* to lay out *sep* (*so that it is ready to be used*)
bereit|liegen *vi irreg* ❶ (*abholbereit liegen*) to be ready [to be picked up] ❷ (*griffbereit liegen*) to be within reach
bereit|machen *vr* ■**sich** *akk* ~ to get ready
bereits [bə·ˈraits] *adv* already; **~ damals** even then
Bereitschaft <-, -en> [bə·ˈrait·ʃaft] *f* ❶ *kein pl* willingness; **seine ~ zu etw** *dat* **erklären** to express one's willingness to do sth ❷ *kein pl* (*Bereitschaftsdienst*) emergency service; **~ haben** *Apotheke* to provide emergency services; *Arzt, Feuerwehr* to be on call; (*im Krankenhaus*) to be on duty; *Polizei, Soldaten* to be on standby; *Beamter* to be on duty ❸ (*Einheit der Bereitschaftspolizei*) [police] squad
Bereitschaftsdienst *m* emergency service; *von Apotheker a.* after-hours service
bereit|stehen *vi irreg* to be ready; *Truppen* to stand by
bereit|stellen *vt* ❶ (*zur Verfügung stellen*) to provide; *Truppen* to put on standby ❷ (*vorbereitend hinstellen*) to make ready
bereitwillig **I.** *adj Auskunft* given willingly; *Helfer* willing; *Verkäufer* obliging; **~e Hilfe** eager hands **II.** *adv* readily
Bereitwilligkeit <-> *f kein pl* willingness
bereuen* *vt* to regret; **das wirst du noch ~!** you'll be sorry [for that]!
Berg <-[e]s, -e> [bɛrk] *m* ❶ GEOG mountain; (*kleiner*) hill; **am ~ liegen** to lie at the foot of the hill ❷ (*große Menge*) ■**~e von etw** *dat* piles of sth; **~e von Papier** mountains of paper ▶ WENDUNGEN: **über alle ~e sein** (*fam*) to be miles away; **mit etw** *dat* **hinterm ~ halten** to keep quiet about sth; **über den ~ sein** to be out of the woods; **die Patientin ist noch nicht über den ~** the [female] patient is still in critical condition
bergab [bɛrk·ˈʔap] *adv* (*a. fig*) downhill; **mit seinem Geschäft geht es ~** his business is going downhill
Bẹrgabhang *m* mountainside
Bẹrgarbeiter(in) *m(f)* miner
bergauf [bɛrk·ˈʔauf] *adv* uphill; **es geht wieder ~** (*fig*) things are looking up
Bẹrgbahn *f* mountain railroad; (*Seilbahn*) funicular railroad
Bẹrgbau *m kein pl* mining
Bẹrgdorf *nt* mountain village
bergen <birgt, barg, geborgen> [ˈbɛr·gn̩] *vt* ❶ (*retten*) to rescue (**aus** *+dat* from); *Giftstoffe, Tote* to recover; *Schiff* to salvage ❷ (*geh: enthalten*) to hold ❸ (*geh: mit sich bringen*) to involve
Bẹrgführer(in) *m(f)* mountain guide
Bẹrggipfel *m* mountain top
Bẹrghütte *f* mountain cabin [*or* hut]
bergig [ˈbɛr·gɪç] *adj* hilly; (*gebirgig*) mountainous
Bẹrgkette *f* mountain range
Bẹrgrücken *m* mountain ridge
Bẹrgrutsch *m* landslide
Bẹrgsteigen <-s> *nt kein pl* mountain climbing
Bẹrgsteiger(in) <-s, -> *m(f)* mountain climber
Bẹrgtour *f* [mountain] climb
Bẹrg-und-Tal-Fahrt *f* (*fig*) roller coaster ride
Bẹrgung <-, -en> *f* rescuing; *eines Schiffs* salvaging; *von Toten, Giftstoffen* recovering
Bẹrgungsarbeiten *pl* rescue work; *von Schiff[sladung]* salvage work
Bẹrgungsmannschaft *f* rescue team; *von Schiff[sladung]* salvage team
Bẹrgwacht <-, -en> *f* mountain rescue service
Bẹrgwand *f* mountain face
Bẹrgwerk *nt* mine
Bericht <-[e]s, -e> [bə·ˈrɪçt] *m* report; (*Zeitungsbericht a.*) article
berịchten* **I.** *vt* ❶ (*mitteilen*) to tell ❷ SCHWEIZ **falsch/recht berichtet** wrong/right; **bin ich falsch/recht berichtet, wenn ich annehme ...?** am I wrong/right in assuming ...? **II.** *vi* ❶ ■**über etw** *akk* ~ to report on sth; **wie unser Korrespondent berichtet** according to our correspondent; **wie soeben berichtet wird, ...** we are just receiving reports that ... ❷ (*Bericht erstatten*) ■**jdm ~** to tell sb (**über** *+akk* about) ❸ SCHWEIZ (*erzählen*) to talk
Berịchterstatter(in) <-s, -> *m(f)* reporter; (*Korrespondent*) correspondent
Berịchterstattung <-, -en> *f* reporting (**über** *+akk* on)
berichtigen* [bə·ˈrɪç·tɪ·gn̩] *vt* to correct
Berịchtigung <-, -en> *f* correction
berieseln* *vt* ❶ (*bewässern*) to spray ❷ (*fig fam*) ■**von etw** *dat* **berieselt werden** to be exposed to a constant stream of sth
Berieselung <-, -en> *f* (*Bewässerung*) spraying
Berlin <-s> [bɛr·ˈliːn] *nt* Berlin

Berliner[1] <-s, -> [bɛr·ˈliː·nɐ] *m* (*Gebäck*) ≈ jelly donut
Berliner[2] [bɛr·ˈliː·nɐ] *adj attr* Berlin

The **Berliner Filmfestspiele** (Berlin Film Festival), also called the "Berlinale," has been held since 1951. Among those who have received acclaim in Berlin for their work are Ingmar Bergman, Roman Polanski, Jean-Luc Godard, and Claude Chabrol. Two special aspects of the **Berliner Filmfestspiele** are the youth film competition and the forum for young international filmmakers. The main awards are the Golden and Silver Bears and, since 1986, the Berlinale Camera.

Bermudas[1] [bɛr·ˈmuːdas] *pl* ■ **die** ~ Bermuda *no art, + sing vb;* **auf den** ~ in Bermuda
Bermudas[2] [bɛr·ˈmuːdas], **Bermudashorts** [bɛr·ˈmuː·da·ʃɔrts, -ʃɔːɐts] *pl* Bermuda shorts
Bern <-s> [bɛrn] *nt* Bern[e]
Berner [ˈbɛr·nɐ] *adj attr* Berne[se]
Bernhardiner <-s, -> [bɛrn·har·ˈdiː·nɐ] *m* Saint Bernard [dog]
Bernstein [ˈbɛrn·ʃtain] *m kein pl* amber
bersten <birst, barst, geborsten> [ˈbɛrs·tn̩] *vi sein* ❶ (*platzen*) to explode; *Ballon* to burst; *Glas, Eis* to break; *Erde* to burst open ❷ (*fig*) ■ **vor etw** *dat* ~ to burst with sth
berüchtigt [bə·ˈrʏç·tɪçt] *adj* notorious (**für** +*akk* for)
berücksichtigen* [bə·ˈrʏk·zɪç·tɪ·gn̩] *vt* ❶ (*beachten*) to take into consideration ❷ (*positiv bedenken*) to consider
Berücksichtigung <-> *f kein pl* consideration; **unter ~ einer S.** *gen* in consideration of sth
Beruf <-[e]s, -e> [bə·ˈruːf] *m* occupation; (*Stellung*) job; **sie ist Ärztin von** ~ she's a doctor; **was sind Sie von ~?** what do you do [for a living]?; **ein akademischer** ~ an academic profession; **ein handwerklicher** ~ a trade
berufen[1] *adj* ■ **zu etw** *dat* **~ sein** to have a vocation for sth; **sich** *akk* **~ fühlen, etw zu tun** to feel a calling to do sth
berufen*[2] *irreg* **I.** *vt* ■ **jdn zu etw** *dat* ~ to appoint sb to sth **II.** *vr* ■ **sich** *akk* **auf jdn/etw** ~ to refer to sb/sth **III.** *vi* JUR ÖSTERR (*Berufung einlegen*) to [file an] appeal
beruflich **I.** *adj* professional; **~e Aussichten** career prospects; **~e Laufbahn** career **II.** *adv* as far as work is concerned; **was macht sie ~?** what does she do for a living?; **sich** *akk* **~ weiterbilden** to attend professional seminars/workshops; **~ unterwegs sein** to be away on business; **~ verhindert sein** to be detained by work

The **Berufsakademie** (University of Cooperative Education) combines three years of college-level academics with on-the-job training.

Berufsarmee *f* regular army
Berufsausbildung *f* [professional] training; (*zum Handwerker*) apprenticeship
Berufsaussichten *pl* career prospects *pl*
berufsbedingt *adj* occupational
Berufsberater(in) *m(f)* career advisor
Berufsberatung *f* ❶ (*Beratungsstelle*) career advisory service ❷ (*das Beraten*) career advice
Berufsbezeichnung *f* [official] job title
berufserfahren *adj* [professionally] experienced
Berufserfahrung *f* work experience
berufsfremd *adj* with no experience in a field
Berufsgeheimnis *nt kein pl* secret of a profession
Berufskleidung *f* work[ing] clothes *npl*
Berufskrankheit *f* occupational disease
Berufsleben *nt* professional life
Berufspendler(in) *m(f)* commuter
Berufspraxis *f kein pl* professional practice
Berufsrisiko *nt* occupational hazard
Berufsschule *f* vocational school, technical college
Berufssoldat(in) *m(f)* regular soldier
berufstätig *adj* working; ■ **~ sein** to be employed; **sie ist nicht mehr** ~ she's no longer working
Berufstätige(r) *f(m) dekl wie adj* working person; ■ **die ~n** the working people
berufsunfähig *adj* disabled; **zu 10 % ~ sein** to have a 10% occupational disability
Berufsunfähigkeit *f* occupational disability
Berufsunfall *m* occupational accident
Berufsverband *m* professional organization
Berufsverbot *nt official debarment from one's profession;* **~ haben** to be banned from one's profession
Berufsverkehr *m* rush-hour traffic
Berufswahl *f kein pl* career choice
Berufswechsel *m* career change
Berufung <-, -en> *f* ❶ JUR appeal; **in die ~ gehen** to file an appeal ❷ (*in ein Amt*) appointment ❸ (*innerer Auftrag*) vocation (**zu** +*dat* for) ❹ (*das Sichbeziehen*) **unter ~ auf jdn/etw** with reference to sb/sth
beruhen* *vi* ■ **auf etw** *dat* ~ to be based on sth
▶ WENDUNGEN: **etw auf sich** *akk* **~ lassen** to drop sth
beruhigen* [bə·ˈruːɪ·gn̩] **I.** *vt* ❶ (*beschwichtigen*) ■ **jdn** ~ to comfort sb; **jds Gewissen** ~ to ease sb's conscience ❷ (*ruhig machen*) to calm down *sep*; *Nerven* to soothe; *Schmerzen* to ease; **dieses Getränk wird deinen Magen** ~ this drink will settle your stomach; **den Verkehr** ~ to introduce traffic-calming measures **II.** *vr* ■ **sich** *akk* ~ ❶ (*ruhig werden*) to calm down; *politische Lage* to stabilize; *Meer* to grow calm ❷ (*abflauen*) *Unwetter, Nachfrage* to die down; *Krise* to ease off

B

beruhigend **I.** *adj* ① (*ruhig machend*) reassuring; *Musik, Bad, Massage* soothing ② MED (*ruhigstellend*) sedative **II.** *adv* reassuringly; *Spritze, Medikament* with a sedative effect

beruhigt [bə·ˈruːɪçt] **I.** *adj* relieved; **dann bin ich ~!** what [*or* that's] a relief! **II.** *adv* with an easy mind

Beruhigung <-, -en> *f* ① (*das Beschwichtigen*) reassurance ② (*das Beruhigen*) soothing; **geben Sie der Patientin etwas zur ~** give the patient something to calm her [down]; **ein Mittel zur ~** a sedative ③ (*Erleichterung*) **zu jds ~** to sb's relief; **sehr zu meiner ~** much to my relief

Beruhigungsmittel *nt* sedative

Beruhigungspille *f* tranquilizer

berühmt [bə·ˈryːmt] *adj* famous (**für** +*akk* for)

Berühmtheit <-, -en> *f* ① *kein pl* (*Ruf*) fame; **~ erlangen** to rise to fame ② (*berühmter Mensch*) celebrity

berühren* *vt* ① (*Kontakt haben*) to touch ② (*seelisch bewegen*) to move; **das berührt mich überhaupt nicht!** I couldn't care less! ③ (*kurz erwähnen*) to allude to

Berührung <-, -en> *f* contact, touch; **jdn mit etw** *dat* **in ~ bringen** to bring sb into contact with sth; **mit jdm/etw in ~ kommen** (*physisch*) to brush up against sb/sth; (*in Kontakt kommen*) to come into contact with sb/sth

Berührungsangst *f meist pl* fear of contact

Berührungsbildschirm *m* touchscreen

Berührungsfläche *f* area of contact

Berührungspunkt *m* point of contact

besänftigen* [bə·ˈzɛnf·tɪ·gn̩] **I.** *vt* to soothe **II.** *vr* ■ **sich** *akk* **~** to calm down; *Sturm, Unwetter* to die down

besänftigend *adj* soothing

Besänftigung <-, -en> *f* soothing

Besatz <-es, Besätze> [bə·ˈzats, *pl* bə·ˈzɛ·tsə] *m* (*Borte*) trimming

Besatzung <-, -en> [bə·ˈza·tsʊŋ] *f* ① (*Mannschaft*) crew ② MIL occupation

Besatzungsgebiet *nt* occupied territory

Besatzungsmacht *f* occupying power

Besatzungszone *f* occupation zone

besaufen* *vr irreg* (*fam*) ■ **sich** *akk* **~** to get sloshed

Besäufnis <-ses, -se> *nt* (*fam*) drinking party

beschädigen* *vt* to damage

Beschädigung <-, -en> *f* damage

beschaffen*[1] **I.** *vt* ■ **[jdm] etw ~** to get sth [for sb] **II.** *vr* ■ **sich** *dat* **etw ~** to get sth; **du musst dir Arbeit ~** you've got to find yourself a job

beschaffen[2] *adj* ■ **so ~ sein, dass ...** to be made in such a way that ...

beschäftigen* [bə·ˈʃɛf·tɪ·gn̩] **I.** *vt* ① (*einstellen*) to employ ② (*eine Tätigkeit geben*) to keep busy ③ (*gedanklich*) ■ **jdn ~** to be on sb's mind; **mit einer Frage/einem Problem beschäftigt sein** to be preoccupied with a question/problem **II.** *vr* ■ **sich** *akk* **[mit etw** *dat***] ~** to occupy oneself [with sth]; **hast du genug, womit du dich ~ kannst?** do you have enough to do?; ■ **sich** *akk* **mit jdm ~** to pay attention to sb; **du musst dich mehr mit den Kindern ~** you should spend more time with the children

beschäftigt [bə·ˈʃɛf·tɪçt] *adj* ① (*befasst*) busy (**mit** +*dat* with) ② (*angestellt*) employed (**als** as); **wo bist du ~?** where do you work?

Beschäftigte(r) *f(m) dekl wie adj* employee

Beschäftigung <-, -en> *f* ① (*Anstellung*) employment, job ② (*Tätigkeit*) occupation ③ (*geistige Auseinandersetzung*) consideration (**mit** +*dat* of)

Beschäftigungslage *f* job market [situation]

beschäftigungslos *adj* (*arbeitslos*) unemployed

Beschäftigungsmaßnahme *f* ÖKON job creation plan

Beschäftigungspolitik *f* employment policy

Beschäftigungstherapie *f* occupational therapy

beschämen* *vt* ■ **jdn ~** to shame sb; **es beschämt mich, zuzugeben ...** I'm ashamed to admit ...

beschämend *adj* ① (*schändlich*) shameful ② (*demütigend*) humiliating; **ein ~es Gefühl** a feeling of shame

beschämt *adj* ashamed; (*verlegen*) shamefaced; ■ **von etw** *dat* **~ sein** to be embarrassed by sth

beschatten* *vt* to shadow

beschauen* *vt* ① *Fleisch* to inspect ② DIAL (*betrachten*) to look at

beschaulich **I.** *adj* peaceful; **ein ~es Leben führen** to lead a contemplative life **II.** *adv* peacefully

Bescheid <-[e]s, -e> [bə·ˈʃait] *m* information; ADMIN answer; **~ erhalten** to be informed; **jdm ~ geben** to inform sb; **jdm ~ sagen, dass ...** to let sb know that ...; **ich habe noch keinen ~** I still haven't heard anything; **[über etw** *akk***] ~ wissen** to know [about sth] ▸ WENDUNGEN: **jdm ordentlich ~ sagen** (*fam*) to give sb a piece of one's mind

bescheiden [bə·ˈʃai·dn̩] **I.** *adj* ① (*genügsam, einfach*) modest; **ein ~es Leben führen** to lead a humble life ② (*gering*) meager ③ (*euph fam: beschissen*) lousy; **seine Leistung war eher ~** his performance was pretty lousy **II.** *adv* ① (*selbstgenügsam*) modestly ② (*einfach*) plainly

Bescheidenheit <-> *f kein pl* modesty

bescheinigen* [bə·ˈʃai·nɪ·gn̩] *vt* ■ **jdm etw ~** to certify sth for sb *form;* (*quittieren*) to provide sb with a receipt; ■ **[jdm] ~, dass ...** to confirm [to sb] in writing that ...; ■ **sich** *dat* **etw ~ lassen** to have sth certified

Bescheinigung <-, -en> *f* certification

bescheißen* *irreg* (*derb*) **I.** *vt* ■ **jdn ~** to rip off *sep* sb **II.** *vi* ■ **[bei etw** *dat***] ~** to cheat [at sth]

beschenken* *vt* ■ **jdn ~** to give sb a present; **reich beschenkt werden** to be showered with presents; ■ **sich** *akk* **[gegenseitig] ~** to

give each other presents
Bescherung <-, -en> *f* giving of Christmas presents ▶ WENDUNGEN: [**das ist ja**] **eine schöne ~!** (*iron*) what a fine mess!

> On Christmas Eve (December 24), presents are placed under the Christmas tree in preparation for the **Bescherung**, when they are passed out. Many parents allow their children to unwrap their presents after Christmas dinner, following a visit by the *Christkind* (baby Jesus).

bescheuert (*fam*) **I.** *adj* ❶ (*blöd*) screwy; **dieser ~e Kerl** that stupid idiot; **der ist etwas ~** he's got a screw loose *fam* ❷ (*unangenehm*) stupid; **so was B~es!** how stupid! **II.** *adv* stupidly; **du siehst total ~ aus** you look totally ridiculous; **sich** *akk* **~ anstellen** to act like an idiot
beschichten* *vt* to coat (**mit** +*dat* with)
Beschichtung <-, -en> *f* coating
beschießen* *vt irreg* to shoot at
beschildern* *vt* (*im Straßenverkehr*) to put up [traffic] signs; **gut/schlecht beschildert** [**sein**] [to be] well/poorly marked with signs
Beschilderung <-, -en> *f* ❶ (*das Beschildern*) putting up of signs ❷ (*Verkehrsschild*) [traffic] sign
beschimpfen* *vt* to insult, to curse sb out; ■**sich** *akk* [**gegenseitig**] ~ to insult each other
Beschimpfung <-, -en> *f* insult
BeschissRR <-es> *m kein pl* (*derb*) rip-off
beschissen (*sl*) **I.** *adj* lousy **II.** *adv* in a lousy fashion; **es geht ihr wirklich ~** she's miserable; **~ behandelt werden/aussehen** to be treated/to look like shit *vulg*
beschlagen* *irreg vi sein Spiegel, Scheibe* to fog up
beschlagnahmen* [bə·ˈʃlaːk·naː·mən] *vt* to seize, to confiscate
Beschlagnahmung <-, -en> *f* JUR confiscation
beschleichen* *vt irreg* ■**jdn ~** to come over sb
beschleunigen* [bə·ˈʃlɔy·nɪ·gn̩] **I.** *vt* to accelerate; *Tempo* to increase; *Schritte* to quicken; *Vorgang* to speed up **II.** *vi* to accelerate
Beschleunigung <-, -en> *f* acceleration
beschließen* *irreg* **I.** *vt* ❶ (*entscheiden über*) to decide; **ein Gesetz ~** to pass a motion ❷ (*beenden*) to conclude **II.** *vi* ■**über etw ~** to decide on sth
beschlossen *adj* decided; **das ist ~e Sache** the matter is settled
BeschlussRR <-es, Beschlüsse> *m* decision
beschmieren* **I.** *vt* ❶ (*bestreichen*) ■**etw mit etw** *akk* **~** to spread sth on sth ❷ (*besudeln*) **du bist da am Kinn ja ganz beschmiert** you've got something smeared on your chin; **etw mit Gekritzel ~** to scribble all over sth **II.** *vr* ■**sich** *akk* **~** to get oneself dirty
beschmutzen* **I.** *vt* ❶ (*schmutzig machen*) to dirty up ❷ (*fig: in den Schmutz ziehen*) to tarnish **II.** *vr* ■**sich** *akk* ~ to get oneself dirty
beschneiden* *vt irreg* ❶ (*zurechtschneiden*) to cut; (*stutzen*) to clip; HORT to prune ❷ MED, REL to circumcise
Beschneidung <-, -en> *f* ❶ (*das Zurechtschneiden*) cutting; (*das Stutzen*) clipping; HORT pruning ❷ MED, REL circumcision
beschnitten *adj* circumcised
beschnüffeln* *vt* ❶ (*riechen an*) to sniff at ❷ (*pej fam: bespitzeln*) to check out
beschnuppern* *vt* ❶ (*riechen an*) to sniff at ❷ (*fam: prüfend kennen lernen*) to size up
beschönigen* [bə·ˈʃøː·nɪ·gn̩] *vt* to gloss over
beschränken* **I.** *vt* ❶ (*begrenzen*) to limit (**auf** +*akk* to) ❷ (*einschränken*) to curtail; **jdn in seinen Rechten ~** to limit sb's rights **II.** *vr* ■**sich** *akk* [**auf etw**] ~ to restrict oneself [to sth]; **sich** *akk* **auf das Wesentliche ~** to keep to the essential points
beschränkt *adj* restricted; *Sicht* low; *Intelligenz* limited; *Sichtweise* narrow-minded; **finanziell/räumlich/zeitlich ~ sein** to have a limited amount of cash/space/time; **Gesellschaft mit ~er Haftung** corporation
Beschränkung <-, -en> *f* restriction
beschreiben* *vt irreg* ❶ (*darstellen*) to describe ❷ (*vollschreiben*) to cover with writing
Beschreibung <-, -en> *f* ❶ (*Darstellung*) description ❷ (*fam: Beipackzettel*) description; (*Gebrauchsanweisung*) instructions *pl*
beschriften* [bə·ˈʃrɪf·tn̩] *vt* to inscribe; (*mit Etikett*) to label
Beschriftung <-, -en> *f* inscription
beschuldigen* [bə·ˈʃʊl·dɪ·gn̩] *vt* to accuse (+*gen* of)
Beschuldigung <-, -en> *f* accusation
beschützen* *vt* to protect (**vor** +*dat* from)
Beschützer(in) <-s, -> *m(f)* protector
beschwatzen* *vt* (*fam*) ❶ (*überreden*) to talk into [doing]; (*schmeichelnd*) to wheedle ❷ (*bereden*) to chat about
Beschwerde <-, -n> [bə·ˈʃveːɐ̯·də] *f* ❶ (*Beanstandung, Klage*) complaint; **Grund zur ~ haben** to have grounds for complaint ❷ *pl* MED complaint *form;* **~n mit etw** *dat* **haben** to have problems with sth; **mein Magen macht mir ~n** my stomach is giving me trouble
beschweren* [bə·ˈʃveː·rən] **I.** *vr* ■**sich** *akk* ~ to complain (**über** +*akk* about) **II.** *vt* to weight [down]
beschwerlich *adj* difficult, exhausting; **das Laufen ist für ihn sehr ~** walking is hard for him
beschwichtigen* [bə·ˈʃvɪç·tɪ·gn̩] *vt* to soothe
beschwichtigend I. *adj* soothing **II.** *adv* soothingly
Beschwichtigung <-, -en> *f* soothing
beschwindeln* *vt* (*fam*) ❶ (*belügen*) to tell lies ❷ (*betrügen*) to con
beschwingt I. *adj* lively; *Mensch a.* vivacious **II.** *adv* **sich** *akk* **~ fühlen** to feel elated
beschwipsen *vt* (*fam*) to make tipsy

beschwipst [bə·ˈʃvɪpst] *adj* (*fam*) tipsy

beschwören* *vt irreg* ❶ (*beeiden*) to swear [to]; **~ kann ich das nicht** I wouldn't like to swear to it ❷ (*anflehen*) ■**jdn ~** to beg sb

besehen* *irreg vt* to look at; **etw näher ~** to inspect sth closely

beseitigen* [bə·ˈzai·tɪ·gn̩] *vt* ❶ (*entfernen*) to dispose of; *Missverständnis, Zweifel* to clear up; *Hindernis* to clear away; *Fehler* to eliminate; *Ungerechtigkeiten* to abolish ❷ (*euph: umbringen*) to eliminate

Besen <-s, -> [ˈbeː·zn̩] *m* ❶ (*Kehrbesen*) broom; (*kleiner*) brush; *einer Hexe* broomstick ❷ (*pej fam: kratzbürstige Frau*) old bag ❸ SÜDD (*fam*) *Swabian vineyard's wine bar, indicated by a broom hanging outside the door* ▶ WENDUNGEN: **ich fresse einen ~, wenn ...** (*fam*) I'll eat my hat if ...

besessen [bə·ˈzɛ·sn̩] *adj* obsessed (**von** +*dat* with); **wie ~** like crazy

Besessenheit <-> *f kein pl* obsession

besetzen* *vt* ❶ (*belegen*) to reserve; *Stühle, Plätze* to occupy; **die Leitung ist besetzt** the line is busy ❷ *Land* to occupy; *Haus* to squat ❸ *Posten* to fill

Besetztzeichen *nt* busy signal

Besetzung <-, -en> *f Land* occupation; *Haus* squatting

besichtigen* [bə·ˈzɪç·tɪ·gn̩] *vt* to visit; *Sehenswürdigkeit a.* to see; *Betrieb* to take a tour of; *Haus, Wohnung* to look at, to view

Besichtigung <-, -en> *f* visiting; *Wohnung, Haus etc.* viewing; **eine ~ der Sehenswürdigkeiten** a sightseeing tour; **die ~ einer Stadt** a tour of a town

besiedeln* *vt* to settle; (*kolonisieren*) to colonize; **dicht/dünn besiedelt** densely/thinly populated

besiegeln* *vt* to seal

besiegen* *vt* ❶ (*schlagen*) to beat; *Land* to conquer ❷ (*überwinden*) to overcome

besinnen* *irreg vr* ■**sich** *akk* **~** ❶ (*überlegen*) to think [for a moment]; **sich anders ~** to change one's mind [about sth] ❷ (*sich erinnern*) to remember; **wenn ich mich recht besinne** if I remember correctly

Besinnung <-> *f kein pl* (*Bewusstsein*) consciousness; **die ~ verlieren** to faint; [**wieder**] **zur ~ kommen** to come around

besinnungslos *adj* ❶ (*ohnmächtig*) unconscious; ■**~ werden** to pass out ❷ (*blind*) insensate; *Wut* blind; **~ vor Angst** blind with fear

Besinnungslosigkeit <-> *f kein pl* unconsciousness

Besitz <-es> [bə·ˈzɪts] *m kein pl* ❶ (*Eigentum*) property; (*Vermögen*) possessions *pl* ❷ AGR land; (*Landsitz, Gut*) estate ❸ (*das Besitzen*) possession; **von etw** *dat* **~ ergreifen** (*geh*) to take possession of sth; **in den ~ einer S.** *gen* **gelangen** to come into possession of sth; **in staatlichem/privatem ~** state-owned/privately-owned

besitzen* *vt irreg* ❶ (*Eigentümer sein*) to own ❷ (*haben, aufweisen*) to have [got]; **die Frechheit ~, etw zu tun** to have the nerve to do sth; **jds Vertrauen ~** to have sb's confidence

Besitzer(in) <-s, -> *m(f)* owner; *eines Geschäfts etc.* proprietor; **den ~ wechseln** to change hands

besitzergreifend *adj* possessive

besitzlos *adj* poor

Besitztum <-s, -tümer> *nt* property; *Land* estate

besoffen [bə·ˈzɔfn̩] *adj* (*fam*) sloshed; **total ~** hammered *sl*

Besoffene(r) *f(m) dekl wie adj* (*fam*) drunk

besohlen* *vt* to sole

besolden* [bə·ˈzɔl·dn̩] *vt* to pay

Besoldung <-, -en> *f* salary

besondere(r, s) [bə·ˈzɔn·də·rə, -ərɐ, -ərəs] *adj* ❶ (*ungewöhnlich*) unusual; (*eigentümlich*) peculiar; (*außergewöhnlich*) particular ❷ (*speziell*) special; **ein ~s Interesse an etw** *dat* **haben** to be especially interested in sth; **von ~r Bedeutung** of great significance; **~n Wert auf etw legen** to attach great importance to sth

Besonderheit <-, -en> *f* (*Merkmal*) feature; (*Außergewöhnlichkeit*) special quality; (*Eigentümlichkeit*) peculiarity

besonders [bəˈzɔn·dɐs] *adv* ❶ (*außergewöhnlich*) particularly; [**nicht**] **~ klug/fröhlich** [not] especially bright/happy; **~ viel** a great deal ❷ (*vor allem*) in particular, above all ❸ (*fam*) **nicht ~ sein** to be nothing out of the ordinary; **jd fühlt sich** *akk* **nicht ~** sb does not feel too good

besonnen [bə·ˈzɔ·nən] **I.** *adj* sensible; **~ bleiben** to stay calm **II.** *adv* sensibly, calmly

Besonnenheit <-> *f kein pl* calmness

besorgen* *vt* ❶ (*beschaffen*) to get; **sich** *dat* **einen Job ~** to find oneself a job ❷ (*kaufen*) to buy ❸ (*erledigen*) to see to; *Angelegenheiten* to take care of ▶ WENDUNGEN: **es jdm ~** (*fam: verprügeln*) to beat up *sep* sb; (*derb: sexuell befriedigen*) to do sb

Besorgnis <-, -se> [bə·ˈzɔrk·nɪs] *f pl selten* ❶ (*Sorge*) concern; **jds** *akk* **~ erregen** to cause sb concern; **~ erregend** worrying; **kein Grund zur ~!** no need to worry! ❷ (*Befürchtung*) misgivings *pl*, fears *pl*

besorgniserregend *adj* worrying

besorgt [bə·ˈzɔrkt] *adj* worried (**wegen** +*gen* about); **ein ~es Gesicht machen** to look troubled; ■**um jdn/etw ~ sein** to be concerned about sb/sth

Besorgungen *pl* **~ machen** to run some errands

bespannen* *vt* to cover (**mit** +*dat* with); **einen Schläger neu ~** to restring a racket

bespielbar *adj* ❶ *Kassette* capable of being recorded on ❷ *Platz* in playing shape

bespielen* *vt* ❶ *Kassette* to record ❷ *Platz* to play on

B

bespitzeln* *vt* to spy on
besprechen* *irreg vt* ❶ (*erörtern*) to discuss; **wie besprochen** as agreed ❷ *Buch, Film* to review ❸ *Kassette* to make a recording on
Besprechung <-, -en> *f* ❶ (*Konferenz*) meeting; (*Unterredung*) discussion ❷ (*Rezension*) review
bespritzen* *vt* to splash (**mit** +*dat* with)
besser ['bɛ·sɐ] **I.** *adj komp von* **gut** better; *Qualität* superior; **etwas/nichts B~es** something/nothing better ▶ WENDUNGEN: **jdn eines B~en belehren** to enlighten sb; **ich lasse mich gerne eines B~en belehren** I'm willing to admit [it when] I'm wrong **II.** *adv* ❶ (*nicht mehr schlecht*) **es geht jdm ~** sb feels better ❷ (*fam: lieber*) better; **dem solltest du ~ aus dem Wege gehen!** it would be better if you avoided him! ▶ WENDUNGEN: **es ~ haben** to be better off
besser|gehen *vi impers, irreg sein s.* **besser II. 1**
Bessergestellte(r) *f(m) dekl wie adj* better-off person
bessern ['bɛ·sɐn] *vr* ■ **sich** *akk* ~ to improve; *Person* to better oneself
Besserung <-> *f kein pl* improvement; **gute ~!** get well soon!; **auf dem Weg der ~ sein** to be on one's way to recovery
Besserverdienende(r) *f(m) dekl wie adj* high earner
Besserwisser(in) <-s, -> *m(f)* (*pej*) know-it-all
Besserwisserei <-> *f kein pl* (*pej*) know-it-all manner; **verschone uns mit deiner ständigen ~!** spare us this Mr./little Miss Know-it-all attitude of yours!
besserwisserisch (*pej*) **I.** *adj* know-it-all **II.** *adv* like a know-it-all
Bestand <-[e]s, Bestände> *m* ❶ *kein pl* (*Fortdauer*) survival; **~ haben** to be long-lasting ❷ (*vorhandene Menge*) supply (**an** +*dat* of); *Bäume* stand [of trees]
bestanden *adj* SCHWEIZ (*alt, bejahrt*) advanced in years *pred*
beständig *adj* ❶ *attr* (*ständig*) constant ❷ (*gleich bleibend*) consistent; *Wetter* steady ❸ (*widerstandsfähig*) resistant (**gegen** +*akk* to)
Beständigkeit <-> *f kein pl* ❶ (*das Anhalten*) persistence; METEO continuation ❷ (*gleich bleibende Eigenschaft*) consistency ❸ (*Widerstandsfähigkeit*) resistance (**gegen** +*akk* to)
Bestandsaufnahme *f* ❶ ÖKON inventory; **eine ~ machen** to take inventory; (*in der Gastronomie, im Haushalt*) to make an inventory ❷ (*fig: Bilanz*) taking stock; **eine ~ machen** to review
Bestandteil *m* part; SCI component; **notwendiger ~** essential part; **etw in seine ~e zerlegen** to dismantle
bestärken* *vt* ■ **jdn [in etw** *dat*] ~ to encourage sb['s sth]; **jdn in einem Verdacht ~** to reinforce sb's suspicion
bestätigen* [bə·'ʃtɛː·tɪ·gn̩] **I.** *vt* ❶ (*für zutreffend erklären*) to confirm; *Alibi* to corroborate; **die Richtigkeit einer S.** *gen* ~ to verify sth; **ein ~des Kopfnicken** a nod of confirmation ❷ (*bestärken*) ■ **jdn [in etw** *dat*] ~ to support sb [in sth] ❸ (*quittieren*) to certify; *Empfang* to confirm ❹ **jdn im Amt ~** to confirm sb in office **II.** *vr* ■ **sich** *akk* ~ to prove to be true
Bestätigung <-, -en> *f* confirmation; (*Schriftstück*) written confirmation, certification
bestatten* [bə·'ʃta·tn̩] *vt* (*geh*) to bury, to lay to rest
Bestattung <-, -en> *f* (*geh*) funeral
Bestattungsinstitut *nt,* **Bestattungsunternehmen** *nt* (*geh*) funeral home
bestäuben* *vt* ❶ KOCHK to dust (**mit** +*dat* with) ❷ BOT to pollinate
Bestäubung <-, -en> *f* BOT pollination
bestaunen* *vt* to admire
bestbezahlte(r, s) *adj attr* highest paid
beste(r, s) ['bɛs·tə, 'bɛs·tɐ, 'bɛs·təs] *adj superl von* **gut** *attr* best; **„mit den ~n Wünschen"** "best wishes"; **in ~r Laune** in a great mood [*or* the best of spirits]; ■ **am ~n ...** it would be best if ...; **es wäre am ~n, wenn Sie jetzt gingen** you had better leave now
bestechen* *irreg* **I.** *vt Beamte* to bribe **II.** *vi* (*Eindruck machen*) to be impressive; ■ **durch etw ~** to impress with sth
bestechend I. *adj* captivating; *Angebot* tempting; *Gedanke* fascinating; *Lächeln* winning; *Geist* brilliant **II.** *adv* winningly
bestechlich [bə·'ʃtɛç·lɪç] *adj* corrupt
Bestechlichkeit <-> *f kein pl* corruptibility
Bestechung <-, -en> *f* bribery
Bestechungsgeld *nt meist pl* bribe
Bestechungsversuch *m* bribery attempt
Besteck <-[e]s, -e> [bə·'ʃtɛk] *nt* ❶ (*Essbesteck*) cutlery *n sing* [*or* silverware] *n sing* ❷ (*Instrumentensatz*) set of instruments; *eines Heroinsüchtigen* needles *pl*
bestehen* *irreg* **I.** *vt Prüfung* to pass; **einen Kampf ~** to win a battle; ■ **etw nicht ~** to fail sth; **die Prüfer ließen ihn nicht ~** the inspectors failed him **II.** *vi* ❶ (*existieren*) to be; + *Zeitangabe* to exist; **es ~ gute Aussichten, dass ...** the prospects are good that ...; **es besteht die Gefahr, dass ...** there is a danger of ...; **es besteht kein Zweifel** there is no doubt; **~ bleiben** (*weiterhin existieren*) to last; (*weiterhin gelten*) *Versprechen, Wort* to remain; **etw ~ lassen** to retain sth ❷ (*sich zusammensetzen*) to consist (**aus** +*dat* of); *Material* to be made (**aus** +*dat* [out] of) ❸ (*beinhalten*) ■ **in etw** *dat* ~ to consist of sth; **das Problem/der Unterschied besteht darin, dass ...** the problem/difference is that ... ❹ (*beharren*) ■ **auf etw** *dat* ~ to insist on sth; **auf einer Meinung ~** to stick to an opinion; ■ **darauf ~, dass ...** to insist that ...; **wenn Sie darauf ~!** if you insist!
bestehend *adj* existing
bestehlen* *vt irreg* to rob

besteigen* *vt irreg* ❶ (*auf etw klettern*) to climb [[up] onto]; *Podest* to get up onto ❷ *Thron* to ascend ❸ *Pferd, Fahrrad, Motorrad* to mount, to get on ❹ *Bus* to get on; *Taxi, Auto* to get into; *Flugzeug* to board; *Schiff* to go on board

bestellen* *vt* ❶ (*in Auftrag geben*) to order (**bei** +*dat* from); *Zeitung* to subscribe to ❷ (*reservieren*) to reserve ❸ (*ausrichten*) to tell; [**jdm**] **Grüße** ~ to send [sb] one's regards; **können Sie ihr etwas ~?** may I leave a message for her? ❹ (*kommen lassen*) to ask to come; *Taxi* to call ❺ *Acker* to cultivate ▶ WENDUNGEN: **mit etw** *dat* **ist es schlecht bestellt** things look bad for sth; **wie bestellt und nicht abgeholt** (*hum fam*) standing around looking like a lost sheep

Bestellnummer *f* order number

Bestellschein *m* order form

Bestellung <-, -en> *f* order

bestenfalls ['bɛs·tn̩·'fals] *adv* at best

bestens ['bɛs·tn̩s] *adv* very well

besteuern* *vt* to tax

Besteuerung <-, -en> *f* taxation

Bestform *f* top form

bestialisch [bɛs·'ti̯a:·lɪʃ] **I.** *adj* atrocious; *Gestank* revolting; *Schmerz* excruciating; ~ **stinken** to stink to high heaven **II.** *adv* (*fam*) dreadfully

besticken* *vt* to embroider

Bestie <-, -n> ['bɛs·ti̯ə] *f* ❶ (*Tier*) beast *form* ❷ (*Mensch*) brute

bestimmen* **I.** *vt* ❶ (*festsetzen*) to decide on; *Preis* to set, to fix; *Ort, Zeit* to set, to specify; *Grenze* to set ❷ (*prägen*) to set the tone for; **Wälder ~ das Landschaftsbild** forests dominate the scenery ❸ (*vorsehen*) **für jdn/etw bestimmt sein** to be for sb/sth; **füreinander bestimmt** meant for each other **II.** *vi* ❶ (*befehlen*) to be in charge ❷ (*verfügen*) ■ **über jdn/etw** ~ to control sb/sth

bestimmt [bə·'ʃtɪmt] **I.** *adj* ❶ (*speziell*) particular; **ganz ~e Vorstellungen** very particular ideas ❷ (*festgelegt*) *Tag, Termin* set, appointed, specified ❸ LING **ein ~er Artikel** a definite article ❹ (*entschieden*) *Auftreten* firm ❺ (*genau*) *Anweisung* precise **II.** *adv* ❶ (*sicher*) definitely; **ganz ~ kommt er noch** he'll be here [sooner or later]; **Sie sind ~ derjenige, der ...** you must be the person who ...; **das ist ~ für dich** *Anruf, Besuch* it must be for you; **etw ganz ~ wissen** to be positive about sth; ~ **nicht** certainly not ❷ (*entschieden*) determinedly, firmly

Bestimmtheit <-> *f kein pl* determination; **etw in aller ~ ablehnen** to categorically refuse sth; **etw mit ~ sagen können** to be able to state sth definitely

Bestimmung <-, -en> *f* ❶ (*Vorschrift*) regulation ❷ (*Schicksal*) destiny

Bestimmungsort *m* destination

Bestleistung *f* best performance; **jds persönliche ~** sb's personal best

bestmöglich ['bɛst·'mø:k·lɪç] *adj* best possible

bestrafen* *vt* to punish (**mit** +*dat* by/with, **für** +*akk* for); **etw wird mit Gefängnis bestraft** sth is punishable by imprisonment

Bestrafung <-, -en> *f* punishment; **zur ~** as a punishment

bestrahlen* *vt* ❶ MED to treat with radiotherapy ❷ (*beleuchten*) to illuminate

Bestrahlung <-, -en> *f* MED radiotherapy

Bestreben <-s> *nt kein pl* endeavor[s]

bestrebt *adj* ■ **~ sein, etw zu tun** to be eager to do sth

bestreichen* *vt irreg* ❶ (*beschmieren*) ■ **etw mit etw** *dat* ~ to spread sth on sth; **eine Scheibe Brot mit Butter ~** to butter a slice of bread ❷ (*einpinseln*) to coat (**mit** +*dat* with); *mit Farbe* to paint

bestreiken* *vt* to go on strike against; **dieser Betrieb wird bestreikt** there is a strike in progress at this company

bestreiten* *vt irreg* ❶ (*leugnen*) to deny; *Behauptung* to reject; **es lässt sich nicht ~, dass ...** it cannot be denied that ... ❷ (*finanzieren*) to finance; *Kosten* to cover; **seinen Unterhalt ~** to earn a living

bestreuen* *vt* to strew; *mit Puderzucker* to dust; *mit Zucker* to sprinkle

Bestseller <-s, -> ['bɛst·zɛ·lɐ] *m* bestseller

Bestsellerautor(in) *m(f)* bestselling author

Bestsellerliste *f* bestseller list

bestürmen* *vt* to bombard

bestürzen* *vt* to upset

bestürzt **I.** *adj* upset (**über** +*akk* about/by); **zutiefst ~** deeply dismayed **II.** *adv* in a dismayed [*or* distraught] manner

Bestürzung <-> *f kein pl* consternation

Besuch <-[e]s, -e> [bə·'zu:x] *m* ❶ (*das Besuchen*) visit (**bei** +*dat* to, **in** +*dat* to); **jdm einen ~ abstatten** to pay sb a visit; (*kurz*) to drop in on sb; [**bei jdm**] **auf ~ sein** to be visiting [sb]; **ich bin hier nur zu ~** I'm just visiting ❷ (*Besucher*) visitor[s]; (*eingeladen*) guest[s], company

besuchen* *vt* ❶ (*als Besuch kommen*) to visit; **besuch mich bald mal wieder!** come again soon! ❷ (*aufsuchen*) *Ausstellung, Museum* to visit; *Konzert* to attend ❸ (*teilnehmen*) **die Schule ~** to go to school; **einen Kurs ~** to take a class

Besucher(in) <-s, -> *m(f)* visitor, guest; *Kino* moviegoer; *Theater* theatergoer; *Sportveranstaltung* spectator; **ein regelmäßiger ~** a frequenter

Besuchszeit *f* visiting hours *pl*

besudeln* (*geh*) **I.** *vt* ❶ (*beschmieren*) to besmear; **jetzt habe ich meine Bluse mit Kaffee besudelt** now I've got coffee all over my blouse ❷ (*herabwürdigen*) *Name, Ruf* to besmirch **II.** *vr* ■ **sich** *akk* ~ to soil oneself

betasten* *vt* to feel; MED to palpate

betätigen* **I.** *vt Schalter* to press; *Hebel* to operate; *Bremse* to apply **II.** *vr* ■ **sich** *akk* ~ to busy oneself; **sich** *akk* **politisch ~** to be politically active; **sich** *akk* **sportlich ~** to exercise

Betätigung <-, -en> [bəˈtɛː·tɪ·gʊŋ] *f* (*Aktivität*) activity; (*berufliche Tätigkeit*) work

Betätigungsfeld *nt* field of activity

betatschen* *vt* (*pej fam*) to paw

betäuben* [bə·ˈtɔy·bn̩] *vt* ① (*narkotisieren*) to anesthetize; **die Entführer betäubten ihr Opfer** the kidnappers drugged their victim ② (*unempfindlich machen*) to deaden; *Schmerz* to kill ③ (*ruhigstellen*) to silence; *Emotionen* to suppress; *Gewissen* to ease; **seinen Kummer mit Alkohol ~** to drown one's sorrows in alcohol

Betäubung <-, -en> *f* ① (*das Narkotisieren*) anesthetization ② (*das Betäuben*) deadening; *von Schmerz* killing ③ (*Narkose*) anesthetic; **örtliche ~** local anesthetic

Betäubungsmittel *nt* anesthetic

beteiligen* [bə·ˈtai·lɪ·gn̩] **I.** *vt* to give a share (**an** +*dat* of/in) **II.** *vr* ■ **sich** *akk* [**an etw** *dat*] **~** to participate [in sth]; *an einem Unternehmen* to have a stake in

beteiligt [bə·ˈtai·lɪçt] *adj* ■ **an etw** *dat* **~ sein** ① (*mit dabei*) to be involved in sth ② FIN, ÖKON to hold a stake in sth

Beteiligte(r) *f(m) dekl wie adj* person involved

beten [ˈbeːtn̩] **I.** *vi* to pray (**zu** +*dat* to) **II.** *vt* to recite

beteuern* [bə·ˈtɔy·ɐn] *vt* ■ **jdm ~, dass ...** to protest to sb that ...; **seine Unschuld ~** to protest one's innocence

Beteuerung <-, -en> *f* protestation

Beton <-s, *selten* -s> [be·ˈtɔŋ, be·ˈtõː] *m* concrete

betonen* *vt* ① (*hervorheben*) to stress; *die Figur* to accentuate ② LING *Wort* to stress

betonieren* [be·to·ˈniː·rən] *vt* to concrete

Betonklotz *m* ① (*Klotz aus Beton*) concrete block ② (*pej: grässlicher Betonbau*) concrete monstrosity

betont **I.** *adj* emphatic; **~e Höflichkeit** studied politeness **II.** *adv* markedly

Betonung <-, -en> *f* ① *kein pl* (*das Hervorheben*) accent[uation] ② LING stress ③ (*Gewicht*) emphasis

betören* [bə·ˈtøː·rən] *vt* to bewitch

betörend *adj* bewitching

Betracht [bə·ˈtraxt] *m* **in ~ kommen** to be considered; **etw außer ~ lassen** to disregard sth; **jdn/etw in ~ ziehen** to consider sb/sth

betrachten* *vt* ① (*anschauen*) to look at; **bei näherem B~** [up]on closer examination ② (*halten für*) to regard [*or* see] (**als** +*akk* as)

Betrachter(in) <-s, -> *m(f)* observer

beträchtlich [bə·ˈtrɛçt·lɪç] **I.** *adj* considerable; *Schaden* extensive **II.** *adv* considerably

Betrachtung *f kein pl* contemplation; **bei näherer ~** [up]on closer examination

Betrachtungsweise *f* way of looking at things

Betrag <-[e]s, Beträge> [bə·ˈtraːk, *pl* bə·ˈtrɛː·gə] *m* amount

betragen* *irreg* **I.** *vi* to be; **die Rechnung beträgt 10 Euro** the bill comes to 10 euros **II.** *vr* ■ **sich** *akk* **~** to behave

Betragen <-s> *nt kein pl* behavior; SCH conduct

betrauen* *vt* to entrust (**mit** +*dat* with)

betrauern* *vt* to mourn

betreffen* *vt irreg* ① (*angehen*) ■ **jdn ~** to concern sb; ■ **etw ~** to affect sth; **was das betrifft, ...** as far as that is concerned ② (*bestürzen*) to affect

betreffend *adj attr* ① (*erwähnt*) in question *pred*; **die ~e Person** the person in question ② (*in Bezug auf*) concerning

betreiben* *vt irreg* ① *Laden, Firma* to run ② (*antreiben*) to power (**mit** +*dat* with); **das U-Boot wird atomar betrieben** the submarine is nuclear-powered

Betreiber(in) <-s, -> *m(f)* (*Firma, Träger*) operator

betreten*[1] *vt irreg* (*hineingehen*) to enter; (*auf etw treten*) to walk on; (*steigen auf*) to step on[to]

betreten[2] **I.** *adj* embarrassed **II.** *adv* embarrassedly

betreuen* [bə·ˈtrɔy·ən] *vt* ① (*sich kümmern um*) to look after ② (*verantwortlich sein für*) to be responsible for

Betreuer(in) <-s, -> *m(f)* caregiver; (*auf Ausflügen*) chaperone

Betreuung <-, -en> *f* ① (*das Betreuen*) looking after; *von Patienten* care ② (*Betreuer*) nurse

Betrieb <-[e]s, -e> [bə·ˈtriːp] *m* ① (*Firma*) company ② (*die Belegschaft*) workforce ③ *kein pl* (*Betriebsamkeit*) activity; **heute war nur wenig/herrschte großer ~** it was very quiet/busy today ④ (*Tätigkeit*) operation; **etw in ~ nehmen** to put sth into operation; **außer ~** out of order; **in ~** in operation

betrieblich [bə·ˈtriːp·lɪç] *adj attr* (*den Betrieb betreffend*) operational; (*vom Betrieb geleistet*) company; **das ist eine rein ~e Angelegenheit** that is purely an internal matter

betriebsam [bə·ˈtriːp·zaːm] **I.** *adj* busy **II.** *adv* busily

Betriebsamkeit <-> *f kein pl* business

Betriebsangehörige(r) *f(m) dekl wie adj* employee

Betriebsanleitung *f* [operating] instructions *pl*

Betriebsarzt, -ärztin *m, f* company doctor

Betriebsausflug *m* staff outing

betriebsbedingt *adj* operational; **~e Kündigung** layoff

betriebsbereit *adj* ready for operation

betriebseigen *adj* company[-owned]

Betriebsferien *pl* vacation close-down

Betriebsfest *nt* company party

Betriebsgeheimnis *nt* trade secret

Betriebsgelände *nt* company grounds *pl*

Betriebsklima *nt* work atmosphere

Betriebskosten *pl* operating costs; *einer Maschine* running costs

Betriebsleitung *f* management

Betriebsrat *m* employee representative com-

mittee
Betriebsschließung *f* company closure
Betriebsschluss^RR *m* end of business hours; **nach ~** after work
Betriebsstilllegung^RR *f s.* **Betriebsschließung**
Betriebsstörung *f* interruption of service
Betriebssystem *nt* COMPUT operating system
Betriebsunfall *m* ≈ occupational accident (*accident at or on the way to or from work*)
Betriebsversammlung *f* company [*or* staff] meeting
Betriebswirtschaft *f* business management
betrinken* *vr irreg* ■ **sich** *akk* [**mit etw** *dat*] **~** to get drunk [on sth]
betroffen **I.** *pp von* **betreffen** **II.** *adj* shocked; **~es Schweigen** stunned silence **III.** *adv* **jdn ~ anschauen** to look at sb with dismay; **~ schweigen** to be too upset to say anything
Betroffene(r) *f(m) dekl wie adj* person affected
Betroffenheit <-> *f kein pl* shock
betrüben* *vt* to sadden
betrübt **I.** *adj* sad (**über** *+akk* about) **II.** *adv* sadly
Betrug <-[e]s, SCHWEIZ Betrüge> [bə·'truːk, *pl* bə·'tryː·gə] *m* fraud
betrügen* *irreg* **I.** *vt* ❶ (*vorsätzlich täuschen*) to cheat (**um** *+akk* out of); **ich fühle mich betrogen!** I feel betrayed! ❷ (*durch Seitensprung*) to be unfaithful to **II.** *vr* ■ **sich** *akk* **~** to deceive oneself
Betrüger(in) <-s, -> [bə·'tryː·gɐ] *m(f)* con man
betrunken [bə·'trʊn·kn̩] **I.** *adj* drunken *attr,* drunk *pred* **II.** *adv* drunkenly
Betrunkene(r) *f(m) dekl wie adj* drunk
Bett <-[e]s, -en> [bɛt] *nt* ❶ (*Schlafstätte*) bed; **jdn ins ~ bringen** to put sb to bed; **ins ~ gehen** to go to bed; **jdn aus dem ~ holen** to get sb out of bed; **das ~ hüten müssen** to be confined to [one's] bed ❷ (*Oberbett*) comforter ❸ (*Flussbett*) [river] bed
Bettbezug *m* duvet cover
Bettcouch *f* sofa bed
Bettdecke *f* blanket; (*Steppdecke*) duvet, comforter
Bettelei <-, -en> [bɛ·tə·'lai] *f* (*pej*) begging
betteln ['bɛ·tl̩n] *vi* to beg (**um** *+akk* for)
bettlägerig *adj* bedridden, confined to bed *pred*
Bettlaken *nt s.* **Betttuch**
Bettler(in) <-s, -> ['bɛt·lɐ] *m(f)* beggar
bettreif *adj* (*fam*) ready for bed *pred*
Bettruhe *f* bed rest
Betttuch^RR, **Bettuch**^ALT ['bɛt·tuːx] *nt* sheet
Bettwäsche *f* bed linens *pl,* sheets *pl*
Bettzeug *nt* bedding
betucht [bə·'tuːxt] *adj* (*fam*) well off
betüddeln [bə·'tyː·dl̩n] *vt* (*fam*) to coddle
betulich [bə·'tuː·lɪç] **I.** *adj* ❶ (*übertrieben besorgt*) fussing ❷ (*gemächlich*) leisurely **II.** *adv* in a leisurely manner
beugen ['bɔy·gn̩] **I.** *vt* ❶ (*neigen*) to bend; *Kopf* to bow ❷ LING (*konjugieren*) to conjugate; (*deklinieren*) to decline **II.** *vr* ❶ (*sich neigen*) ■ **sich** *akk* **nach vorn/hinten ~** to bend forward/backward; **sich** *akk* **aus dem Fenster ~** to lean out [of] the window ❷ (*sich unterwerfen*) ■ **sich** *akk* [**jdm/etw**] **~** to submit [to sb/sth]; **ich werde mich der Mehrheit ~** I will bow to the majority
Beugung <-, -en> *f* LING *von Adjektiv, Substantiv* declension; *von Verb* conjugation
Beule <-, -n> ['bɔy·lə] *f* ❶ (*Delle*) dent ❷ (*Schwellung*) bump
beunruhigen* [bə·'ʔʊn·ruːɪ·gn̩] *vt* to worry
beunruhigend *adj* disturbing
Beunruhigung <-, -en> *f pl selten* concern
beurkunden* [bə·'ʔuːɐ̯·kʊn·dn̩] *vt* to certify
beurlauben* [bə·'ʔuːɐ̯·lau·bn̩] *vt* ❶ (*Urlaub geben*) to give time off; **können Sie mich für eine Woche ~?** can you give me a week off? ❷ (*suspendieren*) to suspend; **Sie sind bis auf weiteres beurlaubt** you are suspended until further notice
beurteilen* *vt* ❶ (*einschätzen*) to judge ❷ (*abschätzen*) to assess
Beurteilung <-, -en> *f* assessment
Beute <-> ['bɔy·tə] *f kein pl* ❶ (*Jagdbeute*) prey ❷ (*erbeutete Dinge*) loot; [**fette**] **~ machen** to make a [big] haul
Beutel <-s, -> ['bɔy·tl̩] *m* ❶ (*Tasche*) bag ❷ (*fam: Geldbeutel*) wallet, change purse ❸ ZOOL pouch
beuteln ['bɔy·tl̩n] *vt* (*fam*) to shake
bevölkern* [bə·'fœl·kɐn] *vt* ❶ (*beleben*) to fill ❷ (*besiedeln*) to inhabit; **dicht bevölkert** densely populated
Bevölkerung <-, -en> *f* population
Bevölkerungsdichte *f* population density
Bevölkerungsexplosion *f* population explosion
Bevölkerungsgruppe *f* population group
bevölkerungsreich *adj* populous
Bevölkerungsschicht *f* class [of society]
Bevölkerungszahl *f* population
bevollmächtigen* *vt* to authorize (**zu** *+dat* to)
Bevollmächtigte(r) *f(m) dekl wie adj* authorized representative; POL plenipotentiary
Bevollmächtigung <-, -en> *f pl selten* authorization
bevor [bə·'foːɐ̯] *konj* before; ■ **nicht ~** not until
bevormunden* [bə·'foːɐ̯·mʊn·dn̩] *vt* to treat like a child
Bevormundung <-, -en> *f* being treated like a child
bevor|stehen *vi irreg* ❶ (*zu erwarten haben*) ■ **jdm ~** to await sb; **der schwierigste Teil steht dir erst noch bevor!** the most difficult part is yet to come! ❷ (*in Kürze eintreten*) to be approaching
bevorzugen* [bə·'foːɐ̯·tsuː·gn̩] *vt* ❶ (*begünstigen*) to favor [*or* prefer] (**vor** *+dat* over); **keines unserer Kinder wird bevorzugt** none of our children receive preferential treatment;

hier wird niemand bevorzugt! there's no favoritism around here! ❷ (*den Vorzug geben*) to prefer

bevorzugt [bə·ˈfoːɐ̯·tsuːkt] **I.** *adj* ❶ (*privilegiert*) privileged; *Behandlung* preferential ❷ (*beliebteste*) favorite **II.** *adv* **etw ~ abfertigen** to give sth priority; **jdn ~ behandeln** to give sb preferential treatment

bewachen* *vt* to guard

bewachsen [bə·ˈvak·sn̩] *adj* overgrown; **mit Gras ~ sein** to be overgrown with grass

Bewachung <-, -en> *f* ❶ (*das Bewachen*) guarding; **unter** [**strenger**] **~** under [close] guard ❷ (*Wachmannschaft*) guard

bewaffnen* *vt* to arm (**mit** +*dat* with)

Bewaffnung <-, -en> *f* ❶ *kein pl* (*das Bewaffnen*) arming ❷ (*Gesamtheit der Waffen*) weapons *pl*

bewahren* *vt* ❶ (*schützen*) to save (**vor** +*dat* from); **vor etw** *dat* **bewahrt bleiben** to be spared sth ❷ (*geh: aufheben*) to keep ❸ (*erhalten, behalten*) ■[**sich** *dat*] **etw ~** to keep sth

bewähren* *vr* ■**sich** *akk* **~** ❶ *Gerät, Methode, Medikament* to prove itself ❷ *Mensch* to prove oneself; **sich** *akk* **als Freund ~** to prove to be a friend

bewahrheiten* [bə·ˈvaːɐ̯·hai·tn̩] *vr* ■**sich** *akk* **~** to come true

bewährt *adj* proven; *Mitarbeiter* reliable

Bewährung <-, -en> *f* JUR probation; **eine Strafe zur ~ aussetzen** to suspend a sentence

Bewährungshelfer(in) *m(f)* JUR probation officer

Bewährungsprobe *f* [acid] test; **jdn/etw einer ~ unterziehen** to put sb/sth to the test

bewältigen* [bə·ˈvɛl·tɪ·gn̩] *vt* ❶ (*meistern*) to cope with, to handle; *Schwierigkeiten* to overcome ❷ (*überwinden*) to get over; *Vergangenheit* to come to terms with

Bewältigung <-, -en> *f* ❶ (*das Meistern*) coping with; *von Schwierigkeiten* overcoming; *einer Strecke* covering ❷ (*das Überwinden*) getting over; *der Vergangenheit* coming to terms with

bewandert [bə·ˈvan·dɐt] *adj* well-versed (**in** +*dat* in)

Bewandtnis [bə·ˈvant·nɪs] *f* **mit etw** *dat* **hat es eine besondere ~** there is a particular reason for sth

bewässern* *vt Feld* to irrigate; *Garten* to water

Bewässerung <-, -en> *f Feld* irrigation; *Garten* watering

bewegen*¹ [bə·ˈveː·gn̩] **I.** *vt* ❶ (*regen*) *Gegenstand, Körperteil* to move ❷ (*beschäftigen*) ■**etw bewegt jdn** sth concerns sb, sth in on sb's mind ❸ (*innerlich aufwühlen*) ■**etw bewegt jdn** sth moves sb ❹ (*bewirken*) to achieve; **etw/nichts/viel/wenig ~** to achieve something/nothing/a lot/little **II.** *vr* ■**sich** *akk* **~** ❶ (*sich regen/rühren*) to move ❷ (*sich körperlich betätigen*) to [get some] exercise ❸ (*variieren, schwanken*) to range; **der Preis bewegt sich um 3.000 Euro** the price is around 3,000 euros

bewegen*² <bewog, bewogen> [bə·ˈveː·gn̩] *vt* (*veranlassen*) ■**jdn dazu ~, etw zu tun** to move sb to do sth

Beweggrund *m* motive (+*gen* for)

beweglich [bə·ˈveːk·lɪç] *adj* ❶ (*bewegbar*) movable; *Glieder* supple; *Feiertag* movable ❷ (*leicht manövrierbar*) maneuverable ❸ (*körperlich mobil*) mobile; (*geistig wendig*) agile-minded

Beweglichkeit <-> *f kein pl* ❶ (*Mobilität*) mobility ❷ (*geistige Wendigkeit*) mental agility ❸ (*bewegliche Beschaffenheit*) suppleness

bewegt *adj* ❶ (*innerlich gerührt*) moved; **mit ~er Stimme** in an emotional voice ❷ *Leben, Vergangenheit* eventful

Bewegung <-, -en> *f* ❶ (*körperliche Aktion*) movement; **jdn in ~ halten** to keep sb moving ❷ *kein pl* (*körperliche Betätigung*) exercise ❸ (*Ergriffenheit*) emotion ❹ KUNST, POL movement

Bewegungsablauf *m* sequence of movements

Bewegungsfreiheit *f* freedom to move

bewegungslos *adj* motionless

Bewegungsmangel *m kein pl* lack of exercise

Bewegungsmelder <-s, -> *m* motion detector

bewegungsunfähig **I.** *adj* unable to move **II.** *adv* paralyzed

beweinen* *vt* to weep over

Beweis <-es, -e> [bə·ˈvais] *m* proof (**für** +*akk* of)

beweisen* *irreg vt* ❶ (*nachweisen*) to prove ❷ (*erkennen lassen*) to show

Beweislage *f* JUR evidence

Beweismaterial *nt* JUR [body of] evidence

Beweisstück *nt* JUR exhibit

bewerben* *irreg vr* ■**sich** *akk* **~** to apply (**bei** +*dat* to, **um** +*akk* for)

Bewerber(in) <-s, -> *m(f)* applicant

Bewerbung <-, -en> *f* application

Bewerbungsgespräch *nt* [job] interview

Bewerbungsschreiben *nt* application [letter]

Bewerbungsunterlagen *pl* documents in support of an application

bewerfen* *vt irreg* to throw at

bewerkstelligen* [bə·ˈvɛrk·ʃtɛ·lɪ·gn̩] *vt* to manage

bewerten* *vt* to assess; ■**jdn/etw nach etw** *dat* **~** to judge sb/sth according to sth; **etw zu hoch/niedrig ~** to overvalue/undervalue sth

Bewertung *f* assessment

Bewertungsmaßstab *m* assessment criterion

bewilligen* [bə·ˈvɪ·lɪ·gn̩] *vt* to approve; FIN to grant; *Stipendium* to award

bewirken* *vt* ❶ (*verursachen*) to cause ❷ (*erreichen*) ■**etwas ~** to achieve something

bewirten* *vt* to entertain (**mit** +*dat* with)

bewirtschaften* *vt* ❶ (*betreiben*) to run ❷ AGR to work

bewog [bə·ˈvoːk] *imp von* **bewegen²**

bewogen *pp von* **bewegen²**

bewohnbar *adj* habitable

bewohnen* *vt* ① *Haus* to live in ② *Gegend, Insel* to inhabit

Bewohner(in) <-s, -> *m(f)* ① (*Einwohner*) inhabitant ② *eines Hauses, Zimmers* occupant

bewölken* *vr* ■ **sich** *akk* ~ to cloud over

bewölkt *adj* cloudy; **leicht** ~ partly cloudy

Bewölkung <-, -en> *f* cloud cover; **wechselnde** ~ variably cloudy

Bewunderer, Bewunderin <-s, -> [bə·ˈvʊnd·rɐ, bə·ˈvʊn·də·rɪn] *m, f* admirer

bewundern* *vt* to admire (**wegen** +*gen* for)

bewundernswert I. *adj* admirable **II.** *adv* admirably

Bewunderung <-, -en> *f pl selten* admiration

bewusst[RR], **bewußt**[ALT] [bə·ˈvʊst] **I.** *adj* ① (*vorsätzlich*) **~es Nichtbefolgen von Anordnungen** willful disobedience of orders ② (*überlegt*) considered; **eine ~e Entscheidung** a deliberate decision; **~e Lebensführung** socially and environmentally aware lifestyle ③ **jdm etw ~ machen** to make sb realize sth; **sich** *dat* **etw ~ machen** to realize sth; ■ **sich** *dat* **etw** *gen* **~ sein** to be aware of sth; ■ **jdm ~ sein** to be clear to sb **II.** *adv* ① (*vorsätzlich*) deliberately ② (*überlegt*) **~ leben** to practice social and environmental awareness

bewusstlos[RR], **bewußtlos**[ALT] [bə·wʊst·loːs] **I.** *adj* unconscious; **~ werden** to faint **II.** *adv* unconsciously

Bewusstlosigkeit[RR], **Bewußtlosigkeit**[ALT] <-> *f kein pl* unconsciousness

Bewusstsein[RR], **Bewußtsein**[ALT] <-s> *nt kein pl* consciousness; **bei [vollem] ~ sein** to be [fully] conscious; **etw aus dem ~ verdrängen** to banish sth from one's mind; **jdm etw ins ~ rufen** to remind sb of sth

Bewusstseinsstörung[RR] *f* reduced consciousness

bezahlbar *adj* affordable

bezahlen* **I.** *vt* to pay; *Rechnung* to settle; *Getränke, Speisen* to pay for **II.** *vi* to pay; **~, bitte!** [the] check, please!

Bezahlung *f* (*Lohn*) pay; **gegen ~** for a fee, in exchange for payment

bezaubern* *vt, vi* to enchant

bezeichnen* **I.** *vt* ① (*benennen*) to call ② (*bedeuten*) to denote **II.** *vr* ■ **sich** *akk* **als etw** *akk* ~ to call oneself sth

bezeichnend *adj* typical (**für** +*akk* of)

bezeichnenderweise *adv* typically

Bezeichnung *f* term

bezeugen* *vt* to testify to

bezichtigen* [bə·ˈtsɪç·tɪ·gn̩] *vt* to accuse (+*gen* of)

beziehen* *irreg* **I.** *vt* ① (*überziehen*) to cover; **das Bett neu ~** to change the bed [*or* sheets] ② *Wohnung, Haus* to move into ③ (*bekommen*) to receive ④ *Standpunkt* to adopt; **zu etw** *dat* **Stellung ~** to take a stand on sth ⑤ (*kaufen*) to obtain ⑥ SCHWEIZ (*einziehen*) to collect ⑦ (*in Beziehung setzen*) to apply (**auf** +*akk* to); **warum bezieht er immer alles gleich auf sich?** why does he always take everything personally? **II.** *vr* ① *Himmel* ■ **sich** *akk* ~ to cloud over ② (*betreffen, sich berufen*) ■ **sich** *akk* **auf jdn/etw ~** to refer to sb/sth

Beziehung <-, -en> [bə·ˈtsiː·ʊŋ] *f* ① (*Verhältnis*) relationship (**zu** +*dat* with); (*sexuell*) [romantic] relationship; **menschliche ~en** human relations ② (*Verbindung*) connection; **etw zu etw** *dat* **in ~ setzen** to connect sth to [*or* with] sth ③ *meist pl* (*fördernde Bekanntschaften*) **~en haben** to have connections; **seine ~en spielen lassen** to pull [some] strings ④ (*Hinsicht*) **in jeder ~** in every respect; **in mancher ~** in many respects

Beziehungskiste *f* (*sl*) relationship

beziehungslos I. *adj* unconnected **II.** *adv* without any connection

beziehungsweise *konj* or rather

beziffern* [bə·ˈtsɪfɐn] *vt* to estimate (**auf** +*akk* at)

Bezirk <-[e]s, -e> [bə·ˈtsɪrk] *m* district

bezirzen* [bə·ˈtsɪr·tsn̩] *vt* (*fam*) to bewitch

bezug[ALT] [bə·ˈtsuːk] *s.* **Bezug 8**

Bezug <-[e]s, Bezüge> [bə·ˈtsuːk, *pl* bə·ˈtsyː·gə] *m* ① (*Kissenbezug*) pillowcase; (*Bettbezug*) duvet cover ② (*Bezugsstoff*) covering ③ *kein pl* (*das Kaufen*) purchasing ④ *pl* (*Einkünfte*) income *sing* ⑤ (*Verbindung*) connection; **etw zu etw** *dat* **in ~ setzen** to connect sth to [*or* with] sth ⑥ SCHWEIZ (*das Einziehen*) collection ⑦ SCHWEIZ (*das Beziehen*) moving in[to] ⑧ **~ auf etw** *akk* **nehmen** to refer to sth; ■ **in ~ auf etw** *akk* with regard to sth

bezüglich [bə·ˈtsyːk·lɪç] *präp* +*gen* regarding

bezugsfertig *adj* ready to be moved into

Bezugsperson *f* [personal] role model

bezuschussen* [bə·ˈtsuː·ʃʊ·sn̩] *vt* to subsidize

bezwecken* [bə·ˈtsvɛ·kn̩] *vt* to aim to achieve; **was willst du damit ~?** what do you hope to achieve by doing that?

bezweifeln* *vt* to question, to doubt

bezwingen* *irreg vt* ① (*besiegen*) to defeat; *Berg* to conquer ② (*bezähmen*) to keep under control; *Durst, Hunger, Schmerz* to master; *Emotionen* to overcome; *Neugierde* to restrain

BH <-[s], -[s]> [beː·ˈhaː] *m Abk von* **Büstenhalter** bra

Bhf. *Abk von* **Bahnhof** stn.

bibbern [ˈbɪ·bɐn] *vi* (*fam*) to tremble (**vor** +*dat* with); (*vor Kälte*) to shiver; ■ **um etw** *akk* ~ to fear for sth

Bibel <-, -n> [ˈbiː·bl̩] *f* Bible

bibelfest *adj* well-versed in the Bible *pred*

Biber <-s, -> [ˈbiː·bɐ] *m* beaver

Bibliografie[RR], **Bibliographie** <-, -n> [bib·lio·gra·ˈfi, *pl* -ˈfiː·ən] *f* bibliography

Bibliothek <-, -en> [bib·lio·ˈteːk] *f* library

Bibliothekar(in) <-s, -e> [bib·lio·te·ˈkaːɐ̯] *m(f)* librarian

biblisch [ˈbiː·blɪʃ] *adj* biblical

bieder [ˈbiː·dɐ] *adj* (*pej: spießig*) conventional, narrow-minded; *Geschmack* conservative

biegen <bog, gebogen> [ˈbiː·gn̩] **I.** *vt haben*

❶ (*krümmen*) to bend ❷ LING ÖSTERR (*flektieren*) to inflect **II.** *vi sein* (*abbiegen*) to turn **III.** *vr haben* ■ **sich** *akk* ~ to bend
biegsam ['bi:k·za:m] *adj Material* flexible
Biegung <-, -en> *f* ❶ (*Kurve*) bend; **eine ~ machen** to turn ❷ LING ÖSTERR (*Flexion*) inflection
Biene <-, -n> ['bi:·nə] *f* bee
Bienenhonig *m* [bee] honey
Bienenkönigin *f* queen bee
Bienenschwarm *m* swarm of bees
Bienenstich *m* ❶ (*Stich einer Biene*) bee sting ❷ (*Kuchen*) *sheet cake with an almond and sugar coating and a custard cream filling*
Bienenwabe *f* honeycomb
Bier <-[e]s, -e> [bi:ɐ̯] *nt* beer; **~ vom Fass** draft beer ▶ WENDUNGEN: **das ist dein ~** (*fam*) that's your business; **das ist nicht mein ~** (*fam*) that has nothing to do with me
Bierbauch *m* (*fam*) beer belly
Bierbrauerei *f* brewery
Bierdeckel *m* beer mat
Bierdose *f* beer can
bierernst ['bi:ɐ̯·ʔɛrnst] *adj* (*fam*) dead[ly] serious
Bierfass[RR] *nt* beer keg
Bierflasche *f* beer bottle
Biergarten *m* beer garden
Bierlaune *f* (*fam*) ▶ WENDUNGEN: **aus einer ~ heraus** in a cheery mood [after a few beers]
Bierschinken *m* KOCHK ≈ ham sausage (*type of sausage containing large pieces of ham*)
Biest <-[e]s, -er> [bi:st] *nt* (*pej fam*) ❶ (*lästiges Insekt*) [damn] bug; (*bösartiges Tier*) creature ❷ (*bösartiger Mensch*) beast
biestig (*pej*) **I.** *adj* (*fam*) beastly **II.** *adv* (*fam*) nastily
bieten <bot, geboten> ['bi:·tn̩] **I.** *vt* ❶ (*anbieten*) to offer ❷ (*geben*) to give; *Gewähr, Sicherheit, Schutz* to provide ❸ (*zumuten*) **sich** *dat* **etw nicht ~ lassen** to not stand for sth **II.** *vr* ■ **sich** *akk* [**jdm**] ~ *Möglichkeit, Gelegenheit* to present itself [to sb]
Bigamie <-, -n> [bi·ga·'mi:, *pl* -'mi:·ən] *f* bigamy
Bigamist(in) <-en, -en> [bi·ga·'mɪst] *m(f)* bigamist
bigott [bi·'gɔt] *adj* (*frömmelnd*) sanctimonious; (*scheinheilig*) hypocritical
Bikini <-s, -s> [bi·'ki:·ni] *m* bikini
Bilanz <-, -en> [bi·'lants] *f* ❶ ÖKON balance sheet ❷ (*Ergebnis*) end result ▶ WENDUNGEN: **~ ziehen** to take stock
bilateral ['bi:·la·te·ra:l] *adj* bilateral
Bild <-[e]s, -er> [bɪlt, *pl* 'bɪl·dɐ] *nt* picture ▶ WENDUNGEN: **ein ~ für die Götter** (*fam*) a sight for sore eyes; **sich** *dat* **von jdm/etw ein ~ machen** to form an opinion about sb/sth; **im ~e sein** to be in the picture
bilden ['bɪl·dn̩] **I.** *vt* ❶ (*hervorbringen, formen*) to form ❷ *Ausschuss* to set up *sep* ❸ (*darstellen*) to make up; *Gefahr, Problem* to constitute ❹ (*mit Bildung versehen*) to educate **II.** *vr* ❶ (*entstehen*) ■ **sich** *akk* ~ to develop; CHEM to form; BOT to grow ❷ (*sich Bildung verschaffen*) ■ **sich** *akk* ~ to educate oneself ❸ (*sich formen*) ■ **sich** *dat* **eine Meinung ~** to form an opinion **III.** *vi* ■ **etw bildet** sth broadens the mind
Bilderbuch *nt* picture book
Bildergalerie *f* art gallery
Bilderrahmen *m* picture frame
Bildfläche *f* FILM, FOTO projection surface ▶ WENDUNGEN: **auf der ~ erscheinen** (*fam*) to appear on the scene; **von der ~ verschwinden** (*fam*) to disappear from the scene
bildhaft **I.** *adj* vivid; *Beschreibung* graphic **II.** *adv* vividly
Bildhauer(in) <-s, -> ['bɪlt·hauɐ] *m(f)* sculptor
bildhübsch ['bɪlt·'hʏpʃ] *adj* as pretty as a picture
bildlich **I.** *adj* figurative **II.** *adv* figuratively; **~ gesprochen** metaphorically speaking; **sich** *dat* **etw ~ vorstellen** to picture sth
Bildnis <-ses, -se> ['bɪlt·nɪs, *pl* -nɪsə] *nt* (*geh*) portrait
Bildqualität *f* TV, FILM picture quality; FOTO print quality
Bildröhre *f* TV picture tube
Bildschirm *m* TV, COMPUT screen
Bildschirmschoner *m* screen saver
bildschön ['bɪlt·'ʃø:n] *adj s.* **bildhübsch**
Bildstörung *f* TV interference
Bildtelefon *nt* videophone
Bildung <-> *f kein pl* education; **keine ~ haben** to be uneducated
Bildungsbürger(in) *m(f)* member of the educated classes
Bildungseinrichtung *f* educational institution
Bildungslücke *f* gap in one's education
Bildungsniveau *nt* level of education
Bildungspolitik *f* education policy
Bildungsreform *f* reform of the education system
Bildungsstand *m s.* **Bildungsniveau**
Bildungssystem *nt* education system
bilingual [bi·lɪŋ·'gu̯a:l] *adj* bilingual
Billard <-s, -e *o* ÖSTERR -s> ['bɪl·jart] *nt* billiards + *sing vb*, pool
Billardkugel ['bɪl·jart-] *f* billiard ball
Billardstock *m* billiard [*or* pool] cue
Billardtisch *m* billiard [*or* pool] table
Billett <-[e]s, -s *o* -e> [bɪl·'jɛ(t)] *nt* ❶ SCHWEIZ (*Fahrkarte*) ticket ❷ SCHWEIZ (*Eintrittskarte*) admission ticket ❸ ÖSTERR (*Glückwunschkarte*) greeting card
Billiarde <-, -n> [bɪ·'li̯ar·də] *f* thousand trillion, quadrillion
billig ['bɪ·lɪç] **I.** *adj* cheap **II.** *adv* cheaply; **~ abzugeben** going cheap ▶ WENDUNGEN: **~ davonkommen** (*fam*) to get off lightly
Billiganbieter *m* supplier of cheap products
Billigarbeiter(in) *m(f)* cheap laborer
billigen ['bɪ·lɪgn̩] *vt* to approve of
Billigflieger *m* (*fam*) budget airline, no-frills airline

Billigflug *m* cheap flight
Billiglinie *f* low-cost airline
Billigprodukt *nt* cheap product
Billigung <-, -en> *f pl selten* approval
Billigware *f* cheap goods *pl*
Billion <-, -en> [bɪ·ˈli̯o:n] *f* trillion
bimmeln [ˈbɪ·ml̩n] *vi* (*fam*) to ring
bin [bɪn] *1. pers sing pres von* **sein**
binär [bi·ˈnɛ:ɐ̯] *adj* binary
Binde <-, -n> [ˈbɪn·də] *f* ❶ MED bandage; (*Schlinge*) sling ❷ (*Monatsbinde*) sanitary napkin
Bindegewebe *nt* ANAT connective tissue
Bindehaut *f* ANAT conjunctiva
Bindehautentzündung *f* conjunctivitis
Bindemittel *nt* binder; KOCHK *a.* thickener
binden <band, gebunden> [ˈbɪn·dn̩] **I.** *vt* ❶ (*befestigen*) to tie [up *sep*] (**an** +*akk* to) ❷ (*zusammenbinden*) *Schnürsenkel* to tie; *Krawatte* to knot; *Kranz, Blumenstrauß, Buch* to bind ▶ WENDUNGEN: **mir sind die Hände gebunden** my hands are tied **II.** *vr* ❶ (*sich verpflichten*) ■ **sich** *akk* **an jdn/etw ~** to commit oneself to sb/sth ❷ (*feste Partnerschaft eingehen*) **ich will mich momentan nicht ~** I don't want to tie myself down right now
bindend *adj* binding
Bindestrich *m* hyphen
Bindfaden *m* string
Bindung <-, -en> *f* ❶ (*Verbundenheit*) bond (**an** +*dat* to) ❷ (*Verpflichtung*) commitment; **eine vertragliche ~ eingehen** to enter into a binding contract ❸ (*am Ski*) binding
binnen [ˈbɪ·nən] *präp* +*dat o gen* (*geh*) within; **~ kurzem** shortly
Binnengewässer *nt* inland water *no indef art*
Binnenhafen *m* inland port
Binnenland [ˈbɪ·nən·lant] *nt* landlocked country
Binnenmarkt *m* domestic market; **der [Europäische] ~** the Single [European] Market
Binnenmeer *nt* inland sea
Binnensee *m* lake
Binse <-, -n> [ˈbɪn·zə] *f* BOT rush ▶ WENDUNGEN: **in die ~n gehen** (*fam*) *Vorhaben* to fall through; *Veranstaltung* to be a washout *fam*
Binsenwahrheit *f*, **Binsenweisheit** *f* truism
Bioabfall *m* ÖKOL organic waste [matter]
Biobrennstoff *m* biofuel
biochemisch [bio·ˈçe:·mɪʃ] *adj* biochemical
Bioenergie *f kein pl* bioenergy
Biogas *nt* biogas
Biografie[RR] <-, -n> [bio·gra·ˈfi:, *pl* -ˈfi:·ən] *f* ❶ (*Buch*) biography ❷ (*Lebenslauf*) life [history]
biografisch[RR] [bio·ˈgra:·fɪʃ] *adj* biographical
Biographie <-, -n> [bio·gra·ˈfi:, *pl* -ˈfi:·ən] *f s.* **Biografie**
biographisch [bio·ˈgra:·fɪʃ] *adj s.* **biografisch**
Biokost *f* organic food
Bioladen *m* health food store
Biolandbau *m kein pl* organic farming
Biologe, Biologin <-n, -n> [bio·ˈlo:·gə, bio·ˈlo:·gɪn] *m, f* biologist
Biologie <-> [bio·lo·ˈgi:] *f kein pl* biology
biologisch I. *adj* biological; (*natürlich*) natural **II.** *adv* biologically; **~ abbaubar** biodegradable
Biomüll *m* organic waste [matter]
Biorhythmus *m* biorhythm
Biosphäre [bio·ˈsfɛ:·rə] *f* ÖKOL biosphere
Biosprit *m* biofuel, ethanol gas blend
Biotechnik [bio·ˈtɛç·nɪk] *f* bioengineering
Biotonne *f bin for compostable waste*
Biotop <-s, -e> [bio·ˈto:p] *nt* ÖKOL biotope
Biotreibstoff *m* biofuel
Biowaffe *f* biological weapon
Biowaschmittel *nt* organic detergent
birgt [bɪrkt] *3. pers sing pres von* **bergen**
Birke <-, -n> [ˈbɪr·kə] *f* birch [tree]
Birma <-s> [ˈbɪr·ma] *nt* Burma; *s. a.* **Deutschland**
Birnbaum *m* pear [tree]
Birne <-, -n> [ˈbɪr·nə] *f* ❶ (*Frucht*) pear ❷ ELEK [light] bulb ❸ (*fam: Kopf*) noggin *fam*
birst *3. pers sing pres von* **bersten**
bis [bɪs] **I.** *präp* +*akk* ❶ *zeitlich* until, till; (*nicht später als*) by; **~ jetzt** up to now; **~ morgen!** see you tomorrow!; **~ bald!** see you soon!; **~ anhin** SCHWEIZ (*bis jetzt*) up to now ❷ *räumlich* as far as; **~ dort/dorthin/dahin** [up] to there; **~ hierher** up to this point ❸ (*erreichend*) up to; **ich zähle ~ drei** I'll count [up] to three; **die Tagestemperaturen steigen ~ [zu] 30°C** daytime temperatures will reach 30°C; **Kinder ~ sechs Jahre** children up to the age of six ❹ (*mit Ausnahme von*) ■ **~ auf** [*o* SCHWEIZ **~ an**] except [for] **II.** *konj* ❶ (*ungefähre Angabe*) to; **400 ~ 500 Gramm Schinken** 400 to 500 grams of ham ❷ *zeitlich* **~ es dunkel wird, möchte ich zu Hause sein** I want to be home by the time it gets dark; **ich warte noch, ~ es dunkel wird** I'll wait until it gets dark
Biscaya *f s.* **Biskaya**
Bischof, Bischöfin <-s, Bischöfe> [ˈbɪ·ʃɔf, ˈbɪ·ʃœ·fɪn, *pl* ˈbɪ·ʃœ·fə] *m, f* bishop
bischöflich [ˈbɪ·ʃœf·lɪç, ˈbɪ·ʃø:f·lɪç] *adj* episcopal
bisexuell [bi·zɛ·ˈksu̯·ɛl, ˈbi:-] *adj* bisexual
bisher [bɪs·ˈhe:ɐ̯] *adv* until now
Biskaya <-> [bɪs·ˈka:ja] *f* ■ **die ~** [the Bay of] Biscay
Biskuit <-[e]s, -s *o* -e> [bɪs·ˈkvi:t, bɪs·ˈku̯i:t] *nt o m* sponge cake
bislang [bɪs·ˈlaŋ] *adv s.* **bisher**
Bison <-s, -e> [ˈbi:·zɔn] *m* bison
biss[RR], **biß**[ALT] [bɪs] *imp von* **beißen**
Biss[RR] <-es, -e>, **Biß**[ALT] <-sses, -sse> [bɪs] *m* ❶ (*das Zubeißen, Bisswunde*) bite ❷ (*fam: engagierter Einsatz*) drive; **~ haben** to have drive
bisschen[RR], **bißchen**[ALT] [ˈbɪs·çən] *pron indef* ❶ + *Substantiv* ■ **ein ~ ...** a little ...; ■ **kein ~ ...** not one [little] bit of ...; ■ **das ~ ...** the little bit of ... ❷ + *Adjektiv/Adverb/Verb* ■ **ein ~ ...** a bit ...; **das war ein ~ dumm von** ▸

B

ihr! that was a little stupid of her!; ■**kein ~ ...** not the slightest bit ...
Bissen <-s, -> ['bɪ·sn̩] *m* morsel; **kann ich einen ~ von deinem Brötchen haben?** can I have a bite of your roll?; **er brachte keinen ~ herunter** he couldn't eat a thing
bissig ['bɪ·sɪç] *adj* ❶ **ein ~er Hund** a dog that bites ❷ (*sarkastisch*) sarcastic; *Kritik* scathing
BisswundeRR *f* bite
bist [bɪst] *2. pers sing pres von* **sein**
Bistum <-s, Bistümer> ['bɪs·tuːm, *pl* 'bɪs·tyː·mɐ] *nt* bishopric
bisweilen [bɪs·'vai·lən] *adv* (*geh*) at times
Bit <-[s], -[s]> [bɪt] *nt* COMPUT bit
bitte ['bɪ·tə] *interj* ❶ (*auffordernd*) please; **~ nicht!** please don't! [*or* no, thank you!]; **ja, ~?** (*am Telefon*) hello?; **tun Sie [doch] ~ ...** won't you please ... ❷ (*Dank erwidernd*) **danke für die Auskunft! – ~[, gern geschehen]** thanks for the information — you're [very] welcome!; **danke, dass du mir geholfen hast! – ~[, gern geschehen]!** thanks for helping me — not at all!; **danke schön! – ~ schön, war mir ein Vergnügen!** thank you! — don't mention it, my pleasure!; **Entschuldigung! – ~!** Excuse me! — go right ahead! ❸ (*anbietend*) **~ schön** here you are ❹ (*um Wiederholung bittend*) **~? könnten Sie die Nummer noch einmal wiederholen?** I'm sorry, can you [please] repeat the number?
Bitte <-, -n> ['bɪ·tə] *f* request (**um** *+akk* for)
bitten <bat, gebeten> ['bɪ·tn̩] *vt, vi* to ask (**um** *+akk* for); **könnte ich dich um einen Gefallen ~?** could I ask you a favor? ▶ WENDUNGEN: **wenn ich ~ darf!** if you wouldn't mind!
bitter ['bɪ·tɐ] **I.** *adj* ❶ (*herb*) bitter; *Schokolade* dark ❷ (*schmerzlich*) *Verlust, Wahrheit* bitter; *Reue* deep **II.** *adv* (*sehr*) bitterly
bitterböse ['bɪ·tɐ·'bøː·zə] *adj* furious
bitterernst ['bɪ·tɐ·'ʔɛrnst] *adj* extremely serious; ■**jdm ist es mit etw** *dat* **~** sb is dead[ly] serious about sth
bitterkalt ['bɪ·tɐ·'kalt] *adj attr* bitterly cold
Bitterkeit <-> *f kein pl* bitterness
bitterlich **I.** *adj* slightly bitter **II.** *adv* bitterly
bittersüß ['bɪ·tɐ·'zyːs] *adj* bittersweet *a. fig*
Bittsteller(in) <-s, -> *m(f)* petitioner
bizarr [bi·'tsar] *adj* bizarre
Bizeps <-es, -e> ['biː·tsɛps] *m* biceps
BKA <-> [beː·kaː·'ʔaː] *nt kein pl Abk von* **Bundeskriminalamt**
Blabla <-s> [bla·'blaː] *nt kein pl* (*pej fam*) blah
Blackout, Black-outRR <-s, -s> ['blɛk·ʔaut, 'blɛk·ʔaut, blɛk·'ʔaut] *m* ❶ (*Gedächtnislücke*) memory lapse ❷ (*Bewusstseinsverlust, Stromausfall*) blackout
blähen ['blɛː·ən] **I.** *vt* ❶ (*mit Luft füllen*) to fill [out *sep*] ❷ ANAT to distend **II.** *vr* ■**sich** *akk* **~** to billow; ANAT to dilate **III.** *vi* (*blähend wirken*) to cause flatulence, to give gas
Blähung <-, -en> *f meist pl* flatulence; **~en haben** to have flatulence [*or* gas]
Blamage <-, -n> [bla·'maː·ʒə] *f* (*geh*) disgrace
blamieren* [bla·'miː·rən] **I.** *vt* to disgrace **II.** *vr* ■**sich** *akk* **~** to make a fool of oneself
blanchieren* [blã·'ʃiː·rən] *vt* KOCHK to blanch
blank [blaŋk] **I.** *adj* ❶ (*glänzend, sauber*) shining ❷ (*abgescheuert*) shiny ❸ (*total*) *Chaos, Unsinn* utter ❹ (*fam: pleite*) ■**~ sein** to be broke **II.** *adv* **~ gewetzt** shiny; **~ poliert** brightly polished
Blankoscheck *m* blank check
Blankovollmacht *f* carte blanche
Blase <-, -n> ['blaː·zə] *f* ❶ ANAT bladder ❷ MED blister; **sich** *dat* **~n laufen** to get blisters on one's feet ❸ (*Hohlraum*) bubble
Blasebalg <-[e]s, -bälge> *m* bellows *npl*
blasen <bläst, blies, geblasen> ['blaː·zn̩] *vt, vi* to blow
Blasenentzündung *f* bladder infection
Blasenschwäche *f* bladder weakness
Blasentee *m herbal tea that helps to relieve bladder problems*
Blasinstrument *nt* wind instrument
Blaskapelle *f* brass band
Blasmusik *f* brass-band music
Blasphemie <-, -n> [blas·fe·'miː, *pl* -'miː·ən] *f* (*geh*) blasphemy
Blasrohr *nt* blowpipe
blassRR, **blaß**ALT [blas] *adj* ❶ (*bleich*) pale; **~ um die Nase sein** to be green about the gills *hum* ❷ (*hell, matt*) pale; *Schrift* faint ❸ (*schwach*) vague; *Erinnerung* dim
Blässe <-> ['blɛ·sə] *f* paleness
bläst [blɛːst] *3. pers sing pres von* **blasen**
Blatt <-[e]s, Blätter> [blat, *pl* 'blɛ·tɐ] *nt* ❶ BOT leaf ❷ (*Papierseite*) sheet ❸ (*Zeitung*) paper ▶ WENDUNGEN: **kein ~ vor den Mund nehmen** to not mince one's words; **das ~ hat sich gewendet** things have changed
blättern ['blɛ·tɐn] *vi* **in einem Buch ~** to flip [*or* leaf] through a book
Blätterteig *m* puff pastry
Blattgold *nt* gold leaf
Blattgrün *nt* chlorophyll
Blattlaus *f* aphid
Blattsalat *m* lettuce
blau [blau] *adj* ❶ (*Farbe*) blue ❷ (*blutunterlaufen*) bruised; **ein ~er Fleck** a bruise; **ein ~es Auge** a black eye ❸ *meist pred* (*fam: betrunken*) plastered *sl*
blauäugig *adj* ❶ (*blaue Augen habend*) blue-eyed ❷ (*naiv*) naïve
Blaubeere *f s.* **Heidelbeere**
Blaue *nt* ▶ WENDUNGEN: **jdm das ~ vom Himmel versprechen** (*fam*) to promise sb the world; **ins ~ hinein** (*fam*) at random; **eine Fahrt ins ~** a mystery tour
blaugrau *adj* blue-gray
blaugrün *adj* blue-green
Blauhelm *m* (*sl*) blue beret
Blaukraut *nt* SÜDD, ÖSTERR red cabbage
bläulich *adj* bluish
Blaulicht *nt* flashing blue light
blau|machen *vi* (*fam: krankfeiern*) to call in

sick; SCH to play hooky
Blaumann <-männer> *m* (*fam*) blue [workers'] overalls
Blausäure *f* hydrocyanic acid
Blauschimmelkäse *m* blue cheese
blauschwarz *adj* blue-black
Blazer <-s, -> ['ble:·zɐ] *m* blazer
Blech <-[e]s, -e> [blɛç] *nt* ❶ *kein pl* (*Material*) sheet metal ❷ (*Blechstück*) metal plate ❸ (*Backblech*) [baking] tray
Blechdose *f* tin
blechen ['blɛç·n̩] *vt, vi* (*fam*) to fork out (**für** +*akk* for)
Blechlawine *f* (*fig fam*) river of metal *fig*
Blechschaden *m* AUTO damage to the bodywork
Blechtrommel *f* tin drum
Blei <-[e]s> [blai] *nt kein pl* lead
Bleibe <-, -n> ['blai·bə] *f* place to stay
bleiben <blieb, geblieben> ['blai·bn̩] *vi sein* ❶ (*verweilen*) to stay; **wo bleibst du so lange?** what's taking you so long [to get here]?; **wo sie nur so lange bleibt?** where the heck is she? ❷ (*weiterhin sein*) to remain; **unbeachtet ~** to go unnoticed; **wach ~** to stay awake; **das bleibt unter uns** that's [just] between you and me ❸ (*übrig bleiben*) **eine Möglichkeit bleibt uns noch** we still have one possibility left; **es blieb mir keine andere Wahl** I was left with no other choice
bleibend *adj* lasting
Bleiberecht *nt kein pl* POL right of residence
bleich [blaiç] *adj* pale
bleichen ['blai·çn̩] *vt* to bleach
Bleichmittel *nt* bleach
bleifrei *adj* lead-free
bleihaltig *adj* containing lead
Bleistift *m* pencil
Blende <-, -n> ['blɛn·də] *f* ❶ (*Lichtschutz*) blind ❷ FOTO aperture
blenden ['blɛn·dn̩] **I.** *vt* ❶ (*quasi blind machen*) to dazzle ❷ (*täuschen*) to deceive (**durch** +*akk* with) **II.** *vi* to be dazzling
blendend I. *adj* brilliant; **~er Laune sein** to be in a fantastic mood **II.** *adv* wonderfully; **sich** *akk* **~ amüsieren** to have a great time
Blender(in) <-s, -> *m(f)* fraud
Blick <-[e]s, -e> [blɪk] *m* ❶ (*das Blicken*) look; **er warf einen ~ aus dem Fenster** he glanced out the window; **auf einen ~** at a glance; **auf den ersten ~** at first sight; **auf den zweiten ~** upon closer inspection; **jds ~ ausweichen** to avoid sb's gaze; **einen ~ auf jdn/etw werfen** to glance at sb/sth ❷ (*Augenausdruck*) look in one's eye ❸ (*Ausblick*) view; **ein Zimmer mit ~ auf den Strand** a room overlooking the beach
blicken ['blɪ·kn̩] **I.** *vi* ❶ (*schauen*) to look (**auf** +*akk* at), to take a look (**auf** +*akk* at) ❷ **sich** *akk* **~ lassen** to put in an appearance; **sie hat sich hier nicht wieder ~ lassen** she hasn't shown up here again **II.** *vt* (*sl: verstehen*) to understand
Blickfang *m* eye-grabber
Blickfeld *nt* field of vision
Blickkontakt *m* visual contact; **~ haben** to have eye contact
Blickpunkt *m* ❶ (*Standpunkt*) point of view ❷ (*Fokus*) **im ~ [der Öffentlichkeit] stehen** to be the focus of [public] attention
Blickrichtung *f* line of sight
Blickwinkel *m* perspective; (*Gesichtspunkt a.*) point of view
blies *imp von* **blasen**
Blimp <-s, -s> [blɪmp] *m* LUFT blimp
blind [blɪnt] **I.** *adj* blind; ■ **~ werden** to go blind; **~ vor Hass/Eifersucht sein** to be blinded by hatred/jealousy **II.** *adv* blindly
Blindbewerbung *f* unsolicited application
Blinddarm *m* appendix
Blinddarmentzündung *f* appendicitis
Blinde(r) *f(m) dekl wie adj* blind person, blind man *masc,* blind woman *fem*
Blindenhund *m* guide dog
Blindenschrift *f* Braille *no art*
Blindflug *m* ❶ LUFT blind flight ❷ (*fig*) process of trial and error
blindgläubig I. *adj* credulous **II.** *adv* blindly
Blindheit <-> *f kein pl* blindness
blindlings ['blɪnt·lɪŋs] *adv* blindly
blinken ['blɪŋ·kn̩] *vi* ❶ (*funkeln*) to gleam ❷ (*Blinkzeichen geben*) to flash; (*zum Abbiegen*) to put one's turn signal on; **mit der Lichthupe ~** to flash one's [head]lights
Blinker <-s, -> ['blɪŋ·kɐ] *m* AUTO turn signal
Blinklicht *nt* ❶ TRANSP flashing light ❷ (*fam*) *s.* **Blinker**
Blinkzeichen *nt* flashing signal; **~ geben** to flash a signal
blinzeln ['blɪn·tsl̩n] *vi* to blink; (*geblendet*) to squint
Blitz <-es, -e> [blɪts] *m* ❶ (*Blitzstrahl*) lightning; **vom ~ getroffen werden** to be struck by lightning ❷ FOTO flash ► WENDUNGEN: **wie vom ~ getroffen** thunderstruck; **wie ein ~ einschlagen** to come as a bombshell; **wie der ~** (*fam*) like lightning
Blitzableiter <-, -> *m* lightning rod
Blitzaktion *f* lightning operation
blitzartig I. *adj* lightning *attr* **II.** *adv* like lightning; **er ist ~ verschwunden** he disappeared as quickly as a flash
blitzblank *adj* squeaky clean
blitzen ['blɪ·tsn̩] **I.** *vi impers* ■ **es blitzt** there is [a flash of] lightning **II.** *vi* ❶ (*strahlen*) to sparkle ❷ (*funkeln*) to flash (**vor** +*dat* with) ❸ FOTO (*fam*) to use [a] flash **III.** *vt* (*fam: in Radarfalle*) ■ **geblitzt werden** to be photographed [*or fam* zapped] by a traffic camera
Blitzgerät *nt* FOTO flash [unit]
Blitzlicht *nt* FOTO flash[light]
blitzsauber ['blɪts·'zaubɐ] *adj* (*fam*) sparkling clean
Blitzschlag *m* lightning strike
blitzschnell ['blɪts·'ʃnɛl] *adj s.* **blitzartig**
Blizzard <-s, -s> ['blɪzɐt] *m* blizzard

Block[1] <-[e]s, Blöcke> [blɔk, *pl* blœ·kə] *m* (*Form*) block

Block[2] <-[e]s, Blöcke *o* -s> [blɔk, *pl* blœ·kə] *m* ❶ (*Häuserblock*) block; (*großes Mietshaus*) apartment building ❷ (*Papierstapel*) pad of paper; **ein ~ Briefpapier** a stationery pad

Blockade <-, -n> [blɔ·ˈkaː·də] *f* ❶ (*Wirtschaftsblockade*) blockade ❷ MED block ❸ (*Denkhemmung*) mental block

blocken [ˈblɔ·kn̩] *vt* ❶ (*verhindern*) to block, to stall ❷ SÜDD (*bohnern*) to polish

Blockflöte *f* recorder

Blockhütte *f* log cabin

blockieren* [blɔ·ˈkiː·rən] **I.** *vt* to block; *Stromzufuhr* to interrupt; *Verkehr* to stop **II.** *vi* *Bremse, Räder* to lock

Blocksatz *m* TYPO justification

Blockschrift *f* block capitals *pl*

blöd [bløːt], **blöde** [ˈbløː·də] **I.** *adj* (*fam*) ❶ (*dumm*) silly; (*stärker*) stupid ❷ (*unangenehm*) disagreeable; *Situation* awkward; **ein ~es Gefühl** a funny feeling; **zu ~!** how annoying! **II.** *adv* (*fam*) idiotically; **frag doch nicht so ~!** don't ask such stupid questions!; **sich** *akk* **~ anstellen** to act stupid

Blödelei <-, -en> *f* (*fam*) ❶ (*das Blödeln*) messing around; **lass endlich diese ~!** quit messing around [already]! ❷ (*Albernheit*) silly prank

blödeln [ˈbløː·dl̩n] *vi* (*fam*) to tell silly jokes

blöderweise *adv* (*fam*) stupidly

Blödheit <-, -en> *f* (*fam*) ❶ *kein pl* (*Dummheit*) stupidity ❷ (*dumme Bemerkung*) stupid remark

Blödian <-[e]s, -e> [ˈbløː·di̯aːn] *m*, **Blödmann** *m* (*fam*) idiot

Blödsinn *m kein pl* (*pej fam*) nonsense; **machen Sie keinen ~!** don't mess around!

blödsinnig [ˈbløːt·zɪnɪç] *adj* (*pej fam*) idiotic

blöken [ˈbløː·kn̩] *vi* to bleat

blond [blɔnt] *adj* blond[e]; (*hellgelb*) light blond[e]

blondieren* [blɔn·ˈdiː·rən] *vt* to bleach

Blondine <-, -n> [blɔn·ˈdiː·nə] *f* blonde

bloß [bloːs] **I.** *adj* ❶ (*unbedeckt*) bare; **mit ~em Oberkörper** stripped to the waist ❷ *attr* (*nichts als*) mere; (*allein schon*) very; **mit ~em Auge** with the naked eye **II.** *adv* (*nur*) only **III.** *part* (*verstärkend*) **lass mich ~ in Ruhe!** just leave me alone!; **was er ~ hat?** what's his problem?

Blöße [ˈbløː·sə] *f* ▶WENDUNGEN: **sich** *dat* **keine ~ geben** to not show any weakness

bloß|legen *vt* ❶ (*ausgraben*) to uncover ❷ (*enthüllen*) to bring to light

bloß|stellen *vt* ❶ (*verraten*) to expose ❷ (*blamieren*) to show up *sep*

blubbern [ˈblʊ·bɐn] *vi* (*fam*) to bubble

Bluff <-[e]s, -s> [blʊf, blaf, blœf] *m* bluff

bluffen [ˈblʊfn̩, ˈblafn̩, ˈblœfn̩] *vi* to bluff

blühen [ˈblyː·ən] *vi* ❶ (*Blüten haben*) to bloom ❷ (*florieren*) to flourish ❸ (*fam*) ■**jdm ~** to be in store for sb; **dann blüht dir aber was!** then you'll be in for it!

blühend *adj* ❶ (*in Blüte sein*) blossoming ❷ (*strahlend*) radiant ❸ (*prosperierend*) flourishing ❹ (*fam*) **eine ~e Fantasie haben** to have a fertile imagination

Blume <-, -n> [ˈbluː·mə] *f* flower; (*Topfblume*) potted plant ▶WENDUNGEN: **jdm etw durch die ~ sagen** to say sth in a roundabout way to sb

Blumenbeet *nt* flower bed

Blumenerde *f* potting soil

Blumenkasten *m* flower box

Blumenkohl *m kein pl* cauliflower

Blumenladen *m* flower shop

Blumenstrauß <-sträuße> *m* bouquet of flowers

Blumentopf *m* flowerpot

Blumenvase *f* flower vase

Blumenzwiebel *f* bulb

blumig *adj* flowery

Bluse <-, -n> [ˈbluː·zə] *f* blouse

Blut <-[e]s> [bluːt] *nt kein pl* blood; **jdm ~ abnehmen** to take a blood sample from sb ▶WENDUNGEN: **~ und Wasser schwitzen** (*fam*) to sweat blood [and tears]; **[nur] ruhig ~!** [just] calm down!; **~ geleckt haben** to have developed a liking for sth; **jdm im ~ liegen** to be in sb's blood

Blutabnahme *f* **eine ~ machen** to take a blood sample

Blutalkoholspiegel *m* blood alcohol level

Blutbad *nt* bloodbath

Blutbahn *f* bloodstream

Blutbank <-banken> *f* blood bank

Blutdruck *m kein pl* blood pressure

Blüte <-, -n> [ˈblyː·tə] *f* ❶ (*Pflanzenteil*) bloom; *Baum* blossom; **in voller ~ stehen** to be in full bloom; **~n treiben** to [be in] bloom; *Baum* to [be in] blossom ❷ (*Blütezeit*) blooming ❸ (*fam: falsche Banknote*) fake [*or* counterfeit] [bill] ▶WENDUNGEN: **merkwürdige ~n treiben** to take on strange forms

Blutegel *m* leech

bluten [ˈbluː·tn̩] *vi* to bleed (**an/aus** +*dat* from)

Blütenblatt *nt* petal

Blütenstaub *m* pollen

blütenweiß *adj* snow white

Bluter(in) <-s, -> [ˈbluː·tɐ] *m(f)* MED hemophiliac

Bluterguss[RR] <-es, -ergüsse>, **Bluterguß**[ALT] <-sses, -ergüsse> *m* bruise

Blütezeit *f* ❶ (*Zeit des Blühens*) blossoming ❷ (*fig*) heyday

Blutfleck *m* bloodstain

Blutgefäß *nt* blood vessel

Blutgerinnsel *nt* blood clot

Blutgerinnung *f* blood clotting

Blutgruppe *f* blood group

Bluthochdruck *m* high blood pressure

Bluthund *m* bloodhound

blutig [ˈbluː·tɪç] **I.** *adj* ❶ (*blutend*) bloody;

(*blutbefleckt*) bloodstained ❷ KOCHK underdone; **sehr** ~ rare ❸ (*mit Blutvergießen verbunden*) bloody **II.** *adv* bloodily

blutjung ['blu:t·'jʊŋ] *adj* very young

Blutkonserve [-kɔn·sɛr·və] *f* unit of stored blood

Blutkrebs *m* MED leukemia

Blutkreislauf *m* [blood] circulation

Blutlache *f* pool of blood

Blutorange *f* blood orange

Blutplasma *nt* blood plasma

Blutprobe *f* ❶ (*Entnahme*) blood sample ❷ (*Untersuchung*) blood test

Blutrache *f* blood vendetta

blutrot *adj* blood-red

blutrünstig ['blu:t·rʏns·tɪç] *adj* bloodthirsty

Blutsauger *m* ZOOL bloodsucker

Blutsbruder *m* blood brother

Blutsbrüderschaft *f* blood brotherhood

Blutschande *f* incest

Blutspende *f* blood donation

Blutspender(in) *m(f)* blood donor

Blutspur *f* trail of blood; **~en** traces of blood

blutsverwandt *adj* related by blood *pred*

Blutsverwandte(r) *f(m)* blood relation

Blutsverwandtschaft *f* blood relationship

Bluttat *f* (*geh*) bloody act

Bluttransfusion *f* blood transfusion

blutüberströmt *adj* streaming with blood *pred*

Blutung <-, -en> *f* ❶ (*das Bluten*) bleeding; **innere ~en** internal bleeding ❷ **[monatliche]** ~ menstruation

blutunterlaufen *adj Augen* bloodshot

Bluntersuchung *f* blood test

Blutvergießen <-s> *nt kein pl* bloodshed

Blutvergiftung *f* blood poisoning *no indef art*

Blutverlust *m* blood loss

Blutwäsche *f* MED hemodialysis

Blutwurst *f* blood sausage

Blutzuckerspiegel *m* MED blood sugar level

Blutzuckerwert *m* MED blood sugar count

BLZ <-> [be:·ʔɛl·'tsɛt] *f Abk von* **Bankleitzahl**

Bö <-, -en> [bø:] *f* gust [of wind]

Boa <-, -s> ['bo:a] *f* ZOOL, MODE boa

Bob <-s, -s> [bɔp] *m* bob[sled]

Bock <-[e]s, Böcke> [bɔk, *pl* 'bœkə] *m* ❶ ZOOL buck; (*Schafsbock*) ram; (*Ziegenbock*) billy goat ❷ (*pej*) **ein alter** ~ an old goat; **ein sturer** ~ a stubborn bastard ▶ WENDUNGEN: ~ **[auf etw] haben** (*sl*) to feel like [doing sth]; **einen ~ schießen** (*fam*) to screw up

bocken ['bɔ·kn̩] *vi* ❶ *Esel, Pferd* to refuse to move ❷ (*fam: trotzig sein*) to act up

bockig ['bɔ·kɪç] *adj* (*fam*) stubborn

Bockshorn ['bɔks·hɔrn] *nt* ▶ WENDUNGEN: **sich** *akk* **[von jdm] ins ~ jagen lassen** (*fam*) to be intimidated [by sb]

Bockwurst *f* bockwurst (*type of sausage*)

Boden <-s, Böden> ['bo:·dn̩, *pl* bø:·dn̩] *m* ❶ (*Erdreich, Acker*) soil; **magerer** ~ barren soil ❷ (*Erdboden*) ground; (*Fußboden*) floor ❸ *kein pl* (*Territorium*) land; **auf amerikanischem** ~ on American soil ❹ (*Dachboden*) attic ❺ (*Grund*) bottom; *eines Gefäßes a.* base ▶ WENDUNGEN: **am ~ zerstört sein** (*fam*) to be devastated; **etw [mit jdm] zu ~ reden** SCHWEIZ to chew over sth *sep* [with sb]

Bodenbelag *m* floor covering

Bodenbelastung *f* ÖKOL ground pollution

Bodenfrost *m* light frost

bodenlos I. *adj* ❶ (*fam: unerhört*) outrageous; **das ist eine ~e Frechheit!** that's absolutely outrageous! ❷ (*sehr tief*) bottomless **II.** *adv* extremely

Bodennebel *m* ground fog

Bodenpersonal *nt* LUFT ground crew

Bodenprobe *f* soil sample

Bodensatz *m* sediment; *von Kaffee* grounds *npl*

Bodenschätze *pl* mineral resources *pl*

Bodensee ['bɔ·dn̩·ze:] *m* ■ **der** ~ Lake Constance

bodenständig *adj* ❶ (*lange ansässig*) long-established ❷ (*unkompliziert*) uncomplicated

Bodenstation *f* RAUM ground station

Bodenstreitkräfte *pl* MIL ground forces *pl*

Body <-s, -s> ['bɔdi] *m* bodysuit

Bodybuilding <-s> [-bɪl·dɪŋ] *nt kein pl* bodybuilding

Böe <-, -n> ['bø:·ə] *f s.* **Bö**

bog [bo:g] *imp von* **biegen**

Bogen <-s, - *o* ÖSTERR, SCHWEIZ, SÜDD Bögen> ['bo:·gn̩, *pl* 'bø:·gn̩] *m* ❶ (*Kurve*) curve; *eines großen Flusses a.* sweep; **einen ~ machen** to curve [around] ❷ (*Blatt Papier*) sheet [of paper] ❸ (*Schusswaffe*) bow; **Pfeil und ~** bow and arrow[s *pl*] ❹ ARCHIT arch ▶ WENDUNGEN: **in hohem ~ hinausfliegen** (*fam*) to be thrown out; **den ~ heraushaben** (*fam*) to have got the hang of it; **einen [großen] ~ um jdn/etw machen** (*fam*) to steer clear of sb/sth

bogenförmig *adj* arched

Bogenschießen *nt kein pl* SPORT archery

Böhmen <-s> ['bø:·mən] *nt* Bohemia

böhmisch ['bø:·mɪʃ] *adj* Bohemian

Bohne <-, -n> ['bo:·nə] *f* bean; **dicke/grüne/rote/weiße ~n** broad/green/kidney/navy beans

Bohnenkaffee *m* ❶ (*gemahlen*) ground coffee ❷ (*ungemahlen*) unground coffee [beans *pl*]

Bohnenstange *f* (*a. hum*) beanpole *a. hum*

bohnern ['bo:·nɐn] *vt* to polish

Bohnerwachs [-vaks] *nt* floor polish

bohren ['bo:·rən] **I.** *vt* ❶ *Loch* to bore; (*mit Bohrmaschine*) to drill; *Brunnen* to sink ❷ (*hineinstoßen*) to sink (**in** +*akk* into); **sie bohrte ihm das Messer in den Bauch** she plunged the knife into his stomach **II.** *vi* ❶ (*mit dem Bohrer arbeiten*) to drill ❷ (*stochern*) **in der Nase ~** to pick one's nose ❸ (*fam: drängen*) ■ **so lange ~, bis ...** to keep on asking until ...

bohrend *adj* gnawing; *Blick* piercing; *Fragen* probing

Bohrer <-s, -> *m* drill

Bohrinsel *f* drilling rig; (*Öl a.*) oil rig

Bohrmaschine *f* drill

Bohrturm *m* derrick
böig ['bøː·ɪç] *adj* gusty; *Wetter* windy
Boiler <-s, -> ['bɔy·lɐ] *m* hot-water tank
Boje <-, -n> ['boː·jə] *f* buoy
Bolivianer(in) <-s, -> [boli·'vi̯aː·nɐ] *m(f)* Bolivian; *s. a.* **Deutsche(r)**
bolivianisch [boli·'vi̯a·nɪʃ] *adj* Bolivian; *s. a.* **deutsch**
Bolivien <-s> [bo·'liː·vi̯·ən] *nt* Bolivia; *s. a.* **Deutschland**
Böller <-s, -> ['bœ·lɐ] *m* (*fam: Feuerwerkskörper*) firecracker, fireworks *pl*
bombardieren* [bɔm·bar·'diː·rən] *vt* ❶ MIL to bomb ❷ (*fam: überschütten*) to bombard
Bombardierung <-, -en> *f* MIL bombing
bombastisch *adj* (*pej*) ❶ (*schwülstig*) bombastic ❷ (*pompös*) pompous
Bombe <-, -n> ['bɔm·bə] *f* ❶ (*Sprengkörper*) bomb; **wie eine ~ einschlagen** to come as a bombshell ❷ (*Geldbombe*) strongbox
Bombenangriff *m* bomb attack
Bombenanschlag *m* bomb strike
Bombendrohung *f* bomb scare
Bombenerfolg *m* (*fam*) smash hit
Bombengeschäft *nt* (*fam*) booming business
bombensicher ['bɔm·bn̩·zɪçɐ] *adj* ❶ MIL bombproof ❷ (*fam*) sure
Bombenstimmung *f kein pl* (*fam*) ■ **in ~ sein** to be in a great mood; **auf der Party herrschte eine ~** that was one happening party *sl*
Bomber <-s, -> ['bɔm·bɐ] *m* (*fam*) bomber
bombig ['bɔm·bɪç] *adj* (*fam*) fantastic
Bon <-s, -s> [bɔŋ, bõː] *m* ❶ (*Kassenzettel*) receipt ❷ (*Gutschein*) coupon, gift certificate
Bonbon <-s, -s> [bɔŋ·'bɔŋ, bõ·'bõː] *m o* ÖSTERR *nt* ❶ (*Süßigkeit*) piece of candy ❷ (*etwas Besonderes*) treat
Bonus <- *o* -ses, - *o* -se *o* Boni> ['boː·nʊs, *pl* 'boː·ni] *m* FIN bonus
Bonze <-n, -n> ['bɔn·tsə] *m* (*pej*) bigwig
Boom <-s, -s> [buːm] *m* ÖKON boom
boomen ['buː·mən] *vi* ÖKON to [be on the] boom
Boot <-[e]s, -e> [boːt] *nt* boat; (*Segelboot*) yacht; **~ fahren** to go boating
Bootsfahrt *f* boat trip
Bootsflüchtlinge *pl* boat people
Bootshaus *nt* boathouse
Bootsverleih *m* boat rental
Bord[1] [bɔrt] *m* **an ~** aboard; **an ~ gehen** to board; **über ~ gehen** to go overboard; **Mann über ~!** man overboard!; **von ~ gehen** *Lotse* to leave the plane/ship; *Passagier a.* to disembark
Bord[2] <-[e]s, -e> [bɔrt] *nt* shelf
Bordbuch *nt* logbook
Bordcomputer *m* RAUM, LUFT onboard computer; AUTO trip computer
Bordell <-s, -e> [bɔr·'dɛl] *nt* brothel
Bordkarte *f* boarding pass
Bordpersonal *nt kein pl* crew
Bordstein *m*, **Bordsteinkante** *f* curb
Bordüre <-, -n> [bɔr·'dyː·rə] *f* border
borgen ['bɔr·gn̩] *vt* ❶ (*sich leihen*) to borrow ❷ (*verleihen*) to lend
Borke <-, -n> ['bɔr·kə] *f* BOT bark
Borkenkäfer *m* bark beetle
borniert [bɔr·'niːɐ̯t] *adj* (*pej*) bigoted
Börse <-, -n> ['bœr·zə] *f* (*Wertpapierhandel*) stock market; (*Gebäude*) stock exchange; **an die ~ gehen** to go public; **an der ~ [gehandelt]** [traded] on the exchange
Börsenmakler(in) *m(f)* stockbroker
Borste <-, -n> ['bɔrs·tə] *f* bristle
borstig ['bɔrs·tɪç] *adj* bristly
Borte <-, -n> ['bɔr·tə] *f* border
bösartig *adj* ❶ (*tückisch*) malicious; *Tier* vicious ❷ MED malignant; *Krankheit* virulent
Böschung <-, -en> ['bœ·ʃʊŋ] *f* embankment; *eines Flusses, einer Straße a.* bank
böse ['bøː·zə] **I.** *adj* ❶ (*sittlich schlecht*) bad; (*stärker*) evil; **~ Absicht** malice; **das war keine ~ Absicht!** no harm intended!; **jdm B~s tun** to cause sb harm ❷ *attr* (*unangenehm, übel*) bad; **ein ~s Ende nehmen** to end in disaster; **~ Folgen haben** to have dire consequences; **eine ~ Geschichte** a nasty affair [*or* bad situation]; **eine ~ Überraschung erleben** to have an unpleasant surprise; **ein ~r Zufall** a terrible coincidence; **nichts B~s ahnen** to not suspect anything is wrong ❸ (*verärgert*) angry; (*stärker*) furious; **ein ~s Gesicht machen** to scowl ❹ (*fam: unartig*) bad, naughty **II.** *adv* ❶ (*übelwollend*) evilly; **das habe ich nicht ~ gemeint** I meant no harm; **~ lächeln** to give an evil smile ❷ (*fam: sehr, schlimm*) badly; **sich** *akk* **~ irren** to make a serious mistake; **~ ausgehen** to end in disaster; **~ [für jdn] aussehen** to look bad [for sb]
Bösewicht <-[e]s, -er *o* -e> ['bøː·zə·vɪçt] *m* ❶ (*hum fam*) little rascal ❷ (*veraltend: Schurke*) villain
boshaft ['boːs·haft] **I.** *adj* malicious **II.** *adv* **~ grinsen** to give an evil grin
Bosheit <-, -en> *f* malice; (*Bemerkung*) nasty remark
Bosnien <-s> ['bɔs·niən] *nt* Bosnia; *s. a.* **Deutschland**
Bosnien-Herzegowina, Bosnien und Herzegowina <-s> *nt* ÖSTERR Bosnia-Herzegovina; *s. a.* **Deutschland**
Bosnier(in) <-s, -> ['bɔs·niɐ] *m(f)* Bosnian; *s. a.* **Deutsche(r)**
Boss[RR] <-es, -e>, **Boß**[ALT] <-sses, -sse> [bɔs] *m* boss
böswillig **I.** *adj* malevolent; JUR willful **II.** *adv* malevolently
Böswilligkeit <-> *f kein pl* malevolence
bot [bɔt] *imp von* **bieten**
Botanik <-> [bo·'taː·nɪk] *f kein pl* botany
botanisch [bo·'taː·nɪʃ] *adj* botanical
Bote, Botin <-n, -n> ['boː·tə, 'boː·tɪn] *m, f* ❶ (*Kurier*) courier; (*mit Nachricht*) messenger ❷ *bes* SÜDD (*Postbote*) mailman

Botengang <-gänge> *m* errand; **einen ~ machen** to run an errand

Botschaft <-, -en> ['bo:t·ʃaft] *f* ❶ (*Nachricht*) message; **hast du schon die freudige ~ gehört?** have you heard the good news yet? ❷ (*Botschaftsgebäude*) embassy

Botschafter(in) <-s, -> *m(f)* ambassador

Bottich <-[e]s, -e> ['bɔ·tɪç] *m* tub; (*für Wäsche*) washtub

Bouillon <-, -s> [bʊl·'jɔŋ, bʊl·'jõ:] *f* [beef] bouillon; (*im Restaurant*) consommé

Boulevard <-s, -s> [bu·lə·'vaːɐ̯] *m* boulevard

Boulevardpresse *f* (*fam*) yellow press

Boulevardzeitung *f* tabloid

Boutique <-, -n> [bʊ·'ti:k] *f* boutique

Bowle <-, -n> ['bo:·lə] *f* ❶ (*Getränk*) punch ❷ (*Schüssel*) punch bowl

Bowling <-s, -s> ['bo:·lɪŋ] *nt* [tenpin] bowling

Box <-, -en> [bɔks] *f* ❶ (*Behälter*) box ❷ (*fam: Lautsprecher*) loudspeaker

boxen ['bɔ·ksn̩] **I.** *vi* to box; ■**gegen jdn ~** to fight sb **II.** *vt* (*schlagen*) to punch **III.** *vr* (*fam*) ■**sich** *akk* **[mit jdm] ~** to have a fist fight [with sb]

Boxen <-s> ['bɔ·ksn̩] *nt kein pl* boxing *no art*

Boxer(in) <-s, -> ['bɔ·ksɐ] *m(f)* boxer

Boxershorts, Boxer-Shorts [-ʃo:ɐts, -ʃɔrts] *pl* boxer shorts *npl*

Boxhandschuh *m* boxing glove

Boxkampf *m* boxing match

Boykott <-[e]s, -e *o* -s> [bɔɪ·'kɔt] *m* boycott

boykottieren* [bɔɪ·kɔ·'ti:·rən] *vt* to boycott

brabbeln ['bra·bl̩n] *vi, vt* (*fam*) to babble; *Säugling* to gurgle

brach [bra:x] *imp von* **brechen**

brachial [bra·'xi̯a:l] *adj* **mit ~er Gewalt vorgehen** to use brute force

Brachland *nt* fallow [land]

brach|liegen *vi irreg Land* to lie fallow; (*fig*) to be left unexploited

brachte ['brax·tə] *imp von* **bringen**

Brainstorming <-s> ['brəɪn·stɔ:·mɪŋ] *nt kein pl* brainstorming session

Branche <-, -n> ['brã:·ʃə] *f* ❶ (*Wirtschaftszweig*) line of business ❷ (*Tätigkeitsbereich*) field

Branchenbuch *nt* ≈ Yellow Pages

Branchenverzeichnis *nt* ≈ Yellow Pages

Brand <-[e]s, Brände> [brant, *pl* 'brɛn·də] *m* fire; **in ~ geraten** to catch fire; **etw in ~ stecken** to set sth on fire

brandaktuell *adj* (*fam*) latest; *Buch, CD, Schallplatte* hot-off-the-press; *Thema, Frage* red-hot

Brandanschlag *m* arson attack

brandeilig *adj* (*fam*) extremely urgent

branden ['bran·dn̩] *vi* to break (**an/gegen** +*akk* against)

Brandherd *m* source of the fire

Brandkatastrophe *f* conflagration

Brandmal <-s, -e> *nt* brand

brandmarken *vt* to brand (**als** as)

brandneu ['brant·'nɔy] *adj* (*fam*) brand-new

Brandsatz *m* incendiary mixture

Brandschaden *m* fire damage

Brandschutz *m kein pl* fire safety, fire protection

Brandstifter(in) <-s, -> *m(f)* arsonist

Brandstiftung *f* arson

Brandung <-, -en> *f* surf

Brandwunde *f* burn

Brandy <-s, -s> ['brɛn·di] *m* brandy

brannte ['bran·tə] *imp von* **brennen**

Branntwein ['brant·vain] *m* spirits *pl*

Brasilianer(in) <-s, -> [bra·zi·'li̯a:·nɐ] *m(f)* Brazilian; *s. a.* **Deutsche(r)**

brasilianisch [bra·zi·'li̯a:·nɪʃ] *adj* Brazilian; *s. a.* **deutsch**

Brasilien <-s> [bra·'zi:·li̯·ən] *nt* Brazil; *s. a.* **Deutschland**

brät *3. pers sing pres von* **braten**

Bratapfel *m* baked apple

braten <brät, briet, gebraten> ['bra:·tn̩] *vt, vi* (*in der Pfanne*) to fry; (*am Spieß*) to roast

Braten <-s, -> ['bra:·tn̩] *m* roast [meat]; **kalter ~** cold meat ▶ WENDUNGEN: **ein fetter ~** (*fam*) a good catch; **den ~ riechen** (*fam*) to smell a rat *fam*

Bratensaft *m* drippings

Bratensoße *f* gravy

Brathähnchen *nt*, **Brathendl** <-s, -[n]> *nt* ÖSTERR, SÜDD grilled chicken

Bratkartoffeln *pl* fried potatoes *pl*

Bratpfanne *f* frying pan

Bratrost *m* grill

Bratsche <-, -n> ['bra:·tʃə] *f* viola

Bratwurst *f* bratwurst, [fried] sausage; (*vor dem Braten*) [frying] sausage

Brauch <-[e]s, Bräuche> [braux, *pl* 'brɔy·çə] *m* custom; **[bei jdm so] ~ sein** to be customary [with sb]

brauchbar *adj* useful; **nicht ~ sein** to be of no use

brauchen ['brau·xn̩] **I.** *vt* ❶ (*benötigen*) to need; **wozu brauchst du das?** what do you need that for?; **ich brauche bis zum Bahnhof eine Stunde** it takes me an hour to get to the train station ❷ DIAL (*fam: gebrauchen*) to use; **kannst du die Dinge ~?** can you find a use for these things? ❸ (*fam: verbrauchen*) to use **II.** *modal vb* (*müssen*) to need; ■**etw nicht [zu] tun ~** to not need to do sth; **du hättest doch nur etwas [zu] sagen ~** you should have just said something **III.** *vt impers* SCHWEIZ, SÜDD ■**es braucht etw** sth is needed

Brauchtum <-[e]s, -tümer> *nt pl selten* customs *pl*; **ein altes ~** a tradition

Braue <-, -n> ['brauə] *f* [eye]brow

brauen ['brau·ən] *vt* ❶ *Bier* to brew ❷ (*fam: zubereiten*) to make; *Zaubertrank* to concoct

Brauer(in) <-s, -> ['brau·ɐ] *m(f)* brewer

Brauerei <-, -en> [brau·ə·'rai] *f* brewery

Brauhaus *nt* [privately-owned] brewery

braun [braun] *adj* ❶ (*Farbe*) brown ❷ (*sonnengebräunt*) *Haut* [sun]tanned, brown ❸ (*pej: nationalsozialistisch*) Nazi *attr*; ■**die**

B

B~en *pl* the Brown Shirts *pl*
Braunbär *m* brown bear
Bräune <-> ['brɔy·nə] *f kein pl* (*Sonnenbräune*) [sun]tan
bräunen ['brɔy·nən] **I.** *vt Haut* to tan **II.** *vr* ■ **sich** *akk* ~ (*sich sonnen*) to get a tan; (*braun werden*) to turn brown
Braunkohle *f* lignite
Brause <-, -n> ['brau·zə] *f* ❶ DIAL (*Dusche*) shower ❷ (*Aufsatz von Gießkannen*) spray [attachment], sprinkler ❸ (*Limonade*) carbonated drink; (*Brausepulver*) effervescent powder
brausen ['brau·zn̩] *vi* ❶ *haben* (*tosen*) to roar; *Wind, Sturm* to howl ❷ *sein* (*fam: rasen*) to storm; *Wagen* to race
Brausetablette *f* effervescent tablet
Braut <-, Bräute> [braut, *pl* 'brɔy·tə] *f* ❶ (*bei Hochzeit*) bride ❷ (*veraltend: Verlobte*) fiancée
Brautführer *m* bride's male attendant
Bräutigam <-s, -e> ['brɔy·tɪ·gam, 'brɔy·ti-] *m* ❶ (*bei Hochzeit*) [bride]groom ❷ (*veraltend: Verlobter*) fiancé
Brautjungfer *f* bridesmaid
Brautkleid *nt* wedding dress
Brautleute *pl*, **Brautpaar** *nt* ❶ (*bei Hochzeit*) bride and groom + *pl vb* ❷ (*veraltend: Verlobte*) engaged couple
Brautschau *f* **auf ~ gehen** (*hum*) to go looking for a wife
brav [bra:f] **I.** *adj* ❶ (*artig*) good; **sei schön ~!** be a good boy/girl ❷ (*bieder*) plain ❸ (*rechtschaffen*) worthy **II.** *adv* ❶ (*folgsam*) **geh ~ spielen!** be a good boy/girl and go play ❷ (*rechtschaffen*) worthily
bravo ['bra:·vo] *interj* well done
Bravour, Bravur^RR <-> [bra·'vu:ɐ̯] *f kein pl* (*geh*) brilliance; ■ **mit ~** with style
BRD <-> [be:·ʔɛr·'de:] *f Abk von* **Bundesrepublik Deutschland** FRG
Brechdurchfall *m* vomiting and diarrhea *no art*
Brecheisen *nt* crowbar; **etw mit einem ~ aufbrechen** to crowbar sth [open]
brechen <bricht, brach, gebrochen> ['brɛ·çn̩] **I.** *vt haben* ❶ (*zerbrechen*) to break ❷ *Abmachung, Vertrag* to break; *Eid a.* to violate; **sein Schweigen ~** to break one's silence **II.** *vi* ❶ *sein* (*auseinander*) to break [apart] ❷ *haben* ■ **mit jdm ~** to break with sb ❸ (*sich erbrechen*) to throw up
Brechmittel *nt* emetic [agent]
Brechreiz *m kein pl* nausea
Brei <-[e]s, -e> [brai] *m* ❶ (*Nahrungsmittel*) porridge, mash ❷ (*zähe Masse*) paste ► WENDUNGEN: **um den [heißen] ~ herumreden** to beat around the bush *fam*
breiig ['brai·ɪç] *adj* pulpy
breit [brait] **I.** *adj* ❶ (*flächig ausgedehnt*) wide; *Schultern* broad; **etw ~er machen** to widen sth ❷ (*ausgedehnt*) wide; **die ~e Öffentlichkeit** the general public; **~e Zustimmung** wide[-ranging] approval ❸ *Dialekt* broad ❹ DIAL (*sl: betrunken*) hammered **II.** *adv* **~ gebaut** strongly built; **sich** *akk* **~ hinsetzen** to plump down
breitbeinig *adj* with one's legs apart
Breite <-, -n> ['brai·tə] *f* ❶ (*bei Maßen*) width; **von 4 cm ~** 4 cm in width ❷ (*Vielfalt*) **die ~ des Angebots** the wide range of offers
Breitengrad *m* [degree of] latitude
breit|machen *vr* (*fam*) ■ **sich** *akk* ~ to spread oneself [out]
breit|schlagen *vt irreg* (*fam*) to talk sb into sth
breitschult(e)rig *adj* broad-shouldered *attr*
breit|treten *vt irreg* (*fam*) *Thema* to go on [and on] about
Bremen <-s> ['bre:·mən] *nt* Bremen
Bremer(in) <-s, -> ['bre:·mɐ] *m(f)* native of Bremen
Bremse[1] <-, -n> ['brɛm·zə] *f* (*Bremsvorrichtung*) brake
Bremse[2] <-, -n> ['brɛm·zə] *f* (*Stechfliege*) horsefly
bremsen ['brɛm·zn̩] **I.** *vi Fahrzeug* to brake **II.** *vt* ❶ *Fahrzeug* to brake ❷ (*verzögern*) to slow down *sep* ❸ (*zurückhalten*) to check; **sie ist nicht zu ~** there's no holding her back
Bremsflüssigkeit *f* brake fluid
Bremsklotz *m* brake pad
Bremslicht *nt* brake light
Bremsspur *f* skid mark
Bremsweg *m* braking distance
brennbar *adj* combustible
brennen <brannte, gebrannt> ['brɛ·nən] **I.** *vi* ❶ (*in Flammen stehen*) to be on fire; **es brennt!** fire! fire!; **in der Fabrik brennt es** there's a fire in the factory; **lichterloh ~** to be ablaze ❷ (*angezündet sein*) to burn, to be on fire ❸ ELEK (*fam: an sein*) to be on; *Licht a.* to be burning; ■ **etw ~ lassen** to leave sth on ❹ (*schmerzen*) to be sore; **auf der Haut ~** to burn the skin ❺ ■ **darauf ~, etw zu tun** to be dying to do sth **II.** *vt* ❶ *Schnaps* to distill ❷ *CD* to burn
brennend **I.** *adj* burning; *Frage* urgent; *Wunsch* fervent **II.** *adv* ► WENDUNGEN: **etw interessiert jdn ~** sb is dying to know sth
Brenner <-s, -> ['brɛ·nɐ] *m* TECH burner
Brennerei <-, -en> [brɛ·nə·'rai] *f* distillery
Brennessel^ALT ['brɛn·nɛ·sl̩] *f s.* **Brennnessel**
Brennholz *nt* firewood
Brennmaterial *nt* [heating] fuel
Brennnessel^RR ['brɛn·nɛ·sl̩] *f* stinging nettle
Brennpunkt *m* ❶ PHYS focal point ❷ (*Zentrum*) focus
Brennspiritus *m* methylated spirit
Brennstab *m* (*Kernphysik*) fuel rod
Brennstoff *m* fuel
brenzlig ['brɛnts·lɪç] *adj* (*fam*) dicey; **die Situation wird mir zu ~** things are getting too hot for me
Bresche <-, -n> ['brɛ·ʃə] *f* breach ► WENDUNGEN: **[für jdn] in die ~ springen** to step in [for sb]
Bretagne <-> [bre·'tan·jə, brə·'tan·jə] *f*

■ **die ~** Brittany

Brett <-[e]s, -er> [brɛt] *nt* ❶ (*Holzplatte*) [wooden] board; (*Planke*) plank; (*Sprungbrett*) [diving] board; (*Regalbrett*) shelf; **schwarzes ~** bulletin board ❷ (*Spielbrett*) [game] board ▶ WENDUNGEN: **ein ~ vorm Kopf haben** (*fam*) to be slow on the uptake

brettern ['brɛ·tɐn] *vi sein* (*fam*) to hammer

Bretterzaun *m* wooden fence

Brettspiel *nt* board game

Brezel <-, -n> ['bre:·tsl̩] *f* pretzel

> **Brezeln** (pretzels) are a southern German specialty. Before they are baked, **Brezeln** are dipped in a salt solution, a process that turns the light-colored pretzel dough brown. The pretzels are then sprinkled with coarse salt and sold in bakeries and at pretzel stands. Pretzels that are served with butter are called *Butterbrezeln*.

bricht [brɪçt] *3. pers sing pres von* **brechen**

Brief <-[e]s, -e> [bri:f] *m* letter

Briefbeschwerer <-s, -> *m* paperweight

Briefbogen *m* [sheet of] writing paper

Briefbombe *f* letter bomb

Brieffreund(in) *m(f)* pen pal

Briefgeheimnis *nt kein pl* privacy of correspondence

Briefkasten *m* mailbox

Briefkopf *m* letterhead

Briefmarke *f* [postage] stamp

Briefmarkenautomat *m* stamp machine

Briefmarkensammlung *f* stamp collection

Brieföffner *m* letter opener

Briefpapier *nt* stationery

Brieftasche *f* wallet, billfold

Brieftaube *f* carrier pigeon

Briefträger(in) *m(f)* mail carrier, mailman *masc*, mailwoman *fem*

Briefumschlag *m* envelope

Briefwaage *f* letter scale

Briefwahl *f* absentee ballot

Briefwechsel *m* correspondence

briet [bri:t] *imp von* **braten**

Brikett <-s, -s> [bri·'kɛt] *nt* briquette

brillant [brɪl·'jant] **I.** *adj* brilliant **II.** *adv* brilliantly

Brillant <-en, -en> [brɪl·'jant] *m* brilliant

Brille <-, -n> ['brɪ·lə] *f* ❶ (*Sehhilfe*) [eye]glasses *npl*; ■ **eine ~** a pair of glasses; **eine ~ tragen** to wear glasses ❷ (*Toilettenbrille*) [toilet] seat

Brillenetui *nt* eyeglass case

Brillengestell *nt* [eyeglass] frames

Brillenglas *nt* lens

Brillenschlange *f* ❶ ZOOL [spectacled] cobra ❷ (*pej fam*) four eyes

Brillenträger(in) *m(f)* person who wears glasses

bringen <brachte, gebracht> ['brɪ·ŋən] *vt* ❶ (*hinbringen*) to bring ❷ (*befördern, begleiten*) **jdn nach Hause ~** to take sb home; **den Müll nach draußen ~** to take out the garbage; **die Kinder ins Bett ~** to put the children to bed ❸ (*senden*) to broadcast; TV to show ❹ (*versetzen*) **jdn in Bedrängnis ~** to get sb in[to] trouble; **jdn ins Gefängnis ~** to put sb in prison; **jdn ins Grab ~** to be the death of sb; **jdn in Schwierigkeiten ~** to put sb into a difficult position ❺ (*rauben*) ■ **jdn um etw** *akk* **~** to rob sb of sth; **jdn um den Verstand ~** to drive sb crazy ❻ (*einbringen*) to bring in; **das bringt nicht viel Geld** that won't bring in much money [for us] ❼ (*bewegen*) ■ **jdn dazu ~, etw zu tun** to get sb to do sth ❽ + *substantiviertem Verb* (*bewerkstelligen*) **jdn zum Laufen/Singen/Sprechen ~** to make sb run/sing/talk; **jdn zum Schweigen ~** to silence sb ❾ (*sl: machen*) **das kannst du doch nicht ~!** you can't [go and] do that! ❿ (*fam: gut sein*) **sie bringt's** she's got what it takes; **das bringt er nicht** he's not up to it; **das bringt nichts** it's pointless; **das bringt's nicht** that's useless ▶ WENDUNGEN: **etw hinter sich** *akk* **~** to get sth over [and done] with; **etw bringt etw mit sich** sth involves sth; **es nicht über sich** *akk* **~, etw zu tun** to not be able to bring oneself to do sth

brisant [bri·'zant] *adj* explosive

Brisanz <-> [bri·'zants] *f kein pl* explosive nature

Brise <-, -n> ['bri:·zə] *f* breeze

Britannien <-s> [bri·'ta·ni̯ən] *nt* HIST Britannia; (*Großbritannien*) Britain; *s. a.* **Deutschland**

Brite, Britin <-n, -n> ['brɪ·tə, 'bri:·tə, 'brɪ·tɪn, 'bri:·tɪn] *m, f* Briton, Brit *fam; s. a.* **Deutsche(r)**

britisch ['brɪ·tɪʃ, 'bri:·tɪʃ] *adj* British, Brit *attr fam; s. a.* **deutsch**

bröckelig ['brœ·kə·lɪç] *adj* ❶ (*zerbröckelnd*) crumbling *attr* ❷ (*leicht bröckelnd*) crumbly

bröckeln ['brœ·kl̩n] *vi* to crumble

Brocken <-s, -> ['brɔ·kn̩] *m* ❶ (*Bruchstück*) chunk ❷ *pl* LING **ein paar ~ Russisch** a smattering of Russian ❸ (*fam: massiger Mensch*) hefty guy ▶ WENDUNGEN: **ein harter ~ sein** (*fam*) to be a tough one

brodeln ['bro:·dl̩n] *vi* to bubble; *Lava a.* to seethe

Broker(in) <-s, -> ['bro:·kɐ] *m(f)* FIN broker

Brokkoli ['brɔ·ko·li] *pl* broccoli

Brombeere ['brɔm·be:·rə] *f* ❶ (*Strauch*) blackberry bush ❷ (*Frucht*) blackberry

Bronchie <-, -n> ['brɔn·çi̯ə, *pl* -çi̯·ən] *f meist pl* bronchial tube

Bronchitis <-, Bronchitiden> [brɔn·'çi:·tɪs, *pl* brɔn·çi·'ti:·dn̩] *f* bronchitis *no art*

Bronze <-, -n> ['brõ:·sə] *f* bronze

bronzefarben *adj* bronze-colored

Bronzemedaille [-me·dal·jə] *f* bronze medal

Brosche <-, -n> ['brɔ·ʃə] *f* brooch

Broschüre <-, -n> [brɔ·'ʃy:·rə] *f* brochure

Brösel <-s, -> ['brø:·zl̩] *m* DIAL crumb

B

Brot <-[e]s, -e> [bro:t] *nt* bread; (*Laib*) loaf [of bread]; **ein ~ mit Käse** a slice of bread with cheese; **belegtes ~** [open-faced] sandwich; **sich** *dat* **sein ~ verdienen** to earn [*or* make] one's living

Brotaufstrich *m* [sandwich] spread

Brotbelag *m* topping

Brötchen <-s, -> ['brø:t·çən] *nt* [bread] roll ▶ WENDUNGEN: **sich** *dat* **seine ~ verdienen** (*fam*) to earn [*or* make] one's living

Brötchengeber <-s, -> *m* (*hum fam*) provider, breadwinner

Broteinheit *f* MED carbohydrate unit

Broterwerb *m* [way to earn a] living

Brotkasten *m* bread box

Brotkorb *m* bread basket

Brotkrume *f*, **Brotkrümel** *m* breadcrumb

Brotmesser *nt* bread knife

Brotrinde *f* [bread] crust

Brotschneidemaschine *f* bread slicer

Brotzeit *f* DIAL ① (*Pause*) coffee break ② (*Essen*) snack

browsen ['braʊ·zn̩] *vi* INET to browse

Browser <-s, -> ['braʊ·zɐ] *m* INET browser

Bruch <-[e]s, Brüche> [brʊx, *pl* 'brʏ:·çə] *m* ① (*das Brechen*) violation, infringement; *eines Vertrags* infringement; *von Vertrauen* breach ② (*in Beziehung, Freundschaft*) rift; **in die Brüche gehen** to go to pieces ③ (*Knochenbruch*) fracture; **ein komplizierter ~** a compound fracture ④ (*Eingeweidebruch*) hernia; **sich** *dat* **einen ~ heben** to give oneself a hernia

Bruchbude *f* (*pej fam*) dump

bruchfest *adj* unbreakable

brüchig ['brʏ·çɪç] *adj* ① (*bröckelig*) crumbly; *Leder* cracked ② *Stimme* cracked

Bruchlandung *f* crash landing

Bruchstück *nt* fragment

bruchstückhaft I. *adj* fragmentary II. *adv* in fragments

Bruchteil *m* fraction; **im ~ einer Sekunde** in a split second

Brücke <-, -n> ['brʏ·kə] *f* ① (*Bauwerk*) bridge ② NAUT [captain's] bridge ③ (*Zahnbrücke*) [dental] bridge ④ (*Teppich*) rug

Brückenbau *m kein pl* bridge building *no art*

Brückenpfeiler *m* [bridge] pier

Brückentag *m an extra day off, such as a Monday or a Friday, to make for a long weekend when a holiday falls on a Tuesday or Thursday*

Bruder <-s, Brüder> ['bru:·dɐ, *pl* 'bry:·dɐ] *m* ① (*Verwandter*) brother; ■ **die Brüder Schmitz/Grimm** the Schmitz brothers/the Brothers Grimm ② (*Mönch*) brother ③ (*pej sl: Kerl*) guy, pal

Bruderkrieg *m* war between brothers

brüderlich I. *adj* fraternal II. *adv* like brothers; **~ teilen** to share and share alike

Brüderlichkeit <-> *f kein pl* fraternity

Brudermord *m* fratricide

Bruderschaft <-, -en> *f* REL fraternity

Brüderschaft <-> *f kein pl* intimate friendship; **mit jdm ~ schließen** to make close friends with sb; **mit jdm ~ trinken** to mutually agree to use the informal "du" [over a drink]

Brühe <-, -n> ['bry:·ə] *f* ① (*Suppe*) [clear] soup ② (*pej fam: schmutziges Wasser*) sludge ③ (*pej fam: Getränk*) slop

brühen ['bry:·ən] *vt* **einen Kaffee/Tee ~** to make coffee/tea

brühwarm ['bry:·'varm] (*fam*) I. *adj Neuigkeiten* hot II. *adv* **etw ~ weitererzählen** to immediately start spreading sth around

Brühwürfel *m* bouillon cube

brüllen ['brʏ·lən] I. *vi* ① (*schreien*) to roar, to shout; (*weinen*) to bawl; **vor Lachen/Schmerzen ~** to roar with laughter/pain ② *Löwe* to roar; *Stier* to bellow; *Affe* to howl II. *vt* ■ **jdm etw ins Ohr ~** to shout sth in sb's ear

Brummbär ['brʊm-] *m* (*fam*) grouch

brummeln ['brʊ·mļn] *vi, vt* (*fam*) to mumble

brummen ['brʊ·mən] I. *vi* ① *Insekt, Klingel* to buzz; *Bär* to growl; *Wagen, Motor* to drone; *Bass* to rumble ② (*fam: in Haft sein*) to be doing time ③ (*murren*) to grumble II. *vt* to mumble

Brummer <-s, -> *m* (*fam: Fliege*) bluebottle; (*Hummel*) bumblebee; (*Lastwagen*) heavy truck

Brummschädel *m* (*fam*) headache; (*durch Alkohol a.*) hangover

Brunch <-[e]s, -[e]s *o* -e> [brantʃ] *nt* brunch

brunchen [bran·tʃn̩] *vi* to brunch

brünett [bry·'nɛt] *adj* brunet[te]

Brunnen <-s, -> ['brʊ·nən] *m* ① (*Wasserbrunnen*) well ② (*Springbrunnen*) fountain

Brunnenschacht *m* well shaft

Brunst <-, Brünste> [brʊnst, *pl* 'brʏns·tə] *f* (*Brunstzeit*) rutting season

brünstig ['brʏns·tɪç] *adj männliches Tier* rutting; *weibliches Tier* in heat *pred*

brüsk [brʏsk] I. *adj* brusque II. *adv* brusquely

brüskieren* [brʏs·'ki:·rən] *vt* to snub

Brüssel <-s> ['brʏ·sl̩] *nt* Brussels

Brust <-, Brüste> [brʊst, *pl* 'brʏs·tə] *f* ① (*Brustkasten*) chest; **es auf der ~ haben** (*fam*) to have chest trouble ② (*weibliche Brust*) breast; **einem Kind die ~ geben** to breastfeed a baby ③ KOCHK breast; (*von Rind*) brisket ▶ WENDUNGEN: **schwach auf der ~ sein** (*hum fam: eine schlechte Kondition haben*) to have weak lungs; (*an Geldmangel leiden*) to be a bit short on cash

Brustbein *nt* ANAT breastbone

Brustbeutel *m* [neck] travel pouch [*or* wallet]

brüsten ['brʏs·tn̩] *vr* ■ **sich** *akk* **~** to boast (**mit** *+dat* about)

Brustfell *nt* ANAT pleura

Brustkasten *m* ANAT chest

Brustkorb *m* ANAT chest

Brustkrebs *m* breast cancer

Brustmuskel *m* pectoral muscle

Brustschwimmen *nt* breaststroke

Brustumfang *m* chest measurement; *Frau* bust

measurement

Brüstung <-, -en> ['brʏs·tʊŋ] *f* parapet; (*Fensterbrüstung*) breast

Brustwarze *f* nipple

Brut <-, -en> [bruːt] *f* ❶ *kein pl* (*das Brüten*) brooding ❷ (*die Jungen*) brood; (*von Hühnern*) clutch; (*von Bienen*) nest ❸ *kein pl* (*pej: Gesindel*) mob

brutal [bru·'taːl] **I.** *adj* ❶ (*roh*) brutal; **ein ~er Kerl** a brute ❷ (*fam: besonders groß, stark*) terrible; **~e Kopfschmerzen haben** (*fam*) to have a pounding headache; **eine ~e Niederlage** a crushing defeat **II.** *adv* ❶ (*roh*) brutally ❷ (*fam: sehr*) **das tut ~ weh** it hurts like hell; **das war ~ knapp!** that was damn close!; **~ viel[e]** a hell of a lot

Brutalität <-, -en> [bru·ta·li·'tɛːt] *f* ❶ *kein pl* (*Rohheit*) brutality ❷ (*Gewalttat*) brutal act

brüten ['bryː·tn̩] *vi* ❶ (*über den Eiern sitzen*) to brood; *Hühner a.* to sit ❷ (*grübeln*) to brood (**über** +*dat* over)

Brüter <-s, -> *m* (*Kernphysik*) [nuclear] breeder [reactor]; **schneller ~** fast breeder

Brutkasten *m* MED incubator

Brutplatz *m* breeding place; (*von Hühnern*) hatchery

Brutstätte <-, -n> *f* (*a. fig*) breeding ground *a. fig* (+*gen* for)

brutto ['brʊ·to] *adv* gross; **3.800 Euro ~ verdienen** to have a gross income of 3,800 euros

Bruttoeinkommen *nt* gross income

Bruttolohn *m* gross wages *pl*

brutzeln ['brʊ·tsl̩n] **I.** *vi* (*braten*) to sizzle **II.** *vt* to fry

BSE <-> [beː·ʔɛs·'ʔeː] *f* MED *Abk von* **Bovine Spongiforme Enzephalopathie** BSE

Bub <-en, -en> [buːp, *pl* buː·bn̩] *m* SÜDD, ÖSTERR, SCHWEIZ boy

Bube <-n, -n> ['buː·bə] *m* (*Spielkarte*) jack

Bubenstreich *m* childish prank

Buch <-[e]s, Bücher> [buːx, *pl* 'byː·çɐ] *nt* ❶ LIT book ❷ *meist pl* ÖKON (*Geschäftsbuch*) books *pl;* [**jdm**] **die Bücher führen** to keep sb's books ▸ WENDUNGEN: **ein ~ mit sieben Siegeln** a closed book; **über etw** *akk* **~ führen** to keep a record of sth

Buchbinder(in) <-s, -> *m(f)* bookbinder

Buchbinderei <-, -en> *f* bookbindery

Buchdruck *m kein pl* letterpress printing *no art*

Buchdrucker(in) *m(f)* [letterpress] printer

Buche <-, -n> ['buː·xə] *f* beech

Buchecker <-, -n> *f* beechnut

buchen ['buː·xn̩] *vt* ❶ (*vorbestellen*) to book, to reserve ❷ ÖKON (*verbuchen*) to enter (**als** as)

Bücherbord <-e> *nt,* **Bücherbrett** *nt* bookshelf

Bücherei <-, -en> [byː·çə·'rai] *f* [lending] library

Bücherregal *nt* bookshelf

Bücherschrank *m* bookcase

Bücherwurm *m* (*hum*) bookworm

Buchführung *f* bookkeeping

Buchhalter(in) *m(f)* bookkeeper

Buchhaltung *f* ❶ (*Abteilung*) accounts department ❷ *s.* **Buchführung**

Buchhandel *m* book trade; **im ~ erhältlich** available in bookstores

Buchhändler(in) *m(f)* bookseller

Buchhandlung *f* bookstore

Buchmesse *f* book fair

Buchsbaum ['bʊks-] *m* box [tree]

Büchse <-, -n> ['bʏk·sə] *f* ❶ (*Dose*) can ❷ (*Sammelbüchse*) collection box ❸ (*Jagdgewehr*) rifle

Büchsenmilch *f* evaporated milk

Büchsenöffner *m* can opener

Buchstabe <-n[s], -n> ['buːx·ʃtaː·bə] *m* character, letter

buchstabieren* [buːx·ʃta·'biː·rən] *vt* to spell

buchstäblich ['buːx·ʃtɛːb·lɪç] *adv* literally

Buchstütze *f* bookend

Bucht <-, -en> [bʊxt] *f* bay

Buchung <-, -en> *f* ❶ (*Reservierung*) booking, reservation ❷ FIN (*Verbuchung*) book entry

Buchweizen *m* buckwheat

Buckel <-s, -> ['bʊ·kl̩] *m* ❶ (*fam: Rücken*) back; **einen [krummen] ~ machen** to arch one's back ❷ ANAT hunchback, humpback ❸ (*kleine Wölbung*) bump ▸ WENDUNGEN: **etw auf dem ~ haben** (*fam*) to have been through sth; **rutsch mir [doch] den ~ runter!** (*fam*) get off my back!

buckeln ['bʊ·kl̩n] *vi* (*pej: sich unterwürfig verhalten*) to crawl (**vor** +*dat* up to)

bücken ['bʏ·kn̩] *vr* ■**sich** *akk* [**nach etw** *dat*] **~** to bend down [to pick sth up]

Bückling <-s, -e> ['bʏk·lɪŋ] *m* ❶ (*Fisch*) smoked herring ❷ (*hum fam: Verbeugung*) bow

buddeln ['bʊ·dl̩n] (*fam*) **I.** *vi* to dig [up] **II.** *vt* to dig [out *sep*]

Buddhismus <-> [bʊ·'dɪs·mʊs] *m kein pl* Buddhism

Buddhist(in) <-en, -en> [bʊ·'dɪst] *m(f)* Buddhist

buddhistisch *adj* Buddhist

Bude <-, -n> ['buː·də] *f* ❶ (*Hütte*) [wood] cabin; (*Baubude*) trailer [on a construction site] ❷ (*fam: Wohnung*) pad; **sturmfreie ~ haben** (*fam*) to have the place [all] to oneself

Budget <-s, -s> [bʏ·'dʒeː] *nt* budget

budgetieren* [bʏ·dʒe·'tiː·rən] *vt* to draw up a budget for

Büfett <-[e]s, -s *o* -e> [bʏ·'fɛt, bʏ·'feː] *nt,* **Buffet** <-s, -s> [bʏ·'feː] *nt bes* ÖSTERR, SCHWEIZ ❶ (*Essen*) buffet ❷ (*Anrichte*) sideboard ❸ SCHWEIZ (*Bahnhofsgaststätte*) train station restaurant

Büffel <-s, -> ['bʏ·fl̩] *m* buffalo

Bug <-[e]s, Büge *o* -e> [buːk, *pl* 'byː·gə] *m* NAUT bow; LUFT nose

Bügel <-s, -> ['byː·gl̩] *m* ❶ (*Kleiderbügel*) coat hanger ❷ (*Brillenbügel*) earpiece, temple ❸ (*Steigbügel*) stirrup ❹ (*beim Schlepplift*) handle

Bügelbrett *nt* ironing board

Bügeleisen <-s, -> *nt* iron
Bügelfalte *f* crease
bügelfrei *adj* wrinkle-free
bügeln ['byː·gl̩n] *vt, vi* to iron
bugsieren* [bʊ'ksiː·rən] *vt* (*fam*) ① (*mühselig bewegen*) to shift ② (*drängen*) to shove
buhen ['buː·ən] *vi* (*fam*) to boo
Buhmann *m* (*fam*) scapegoat, fall guy
Bühne <-, -n> ['byː·nə] *f* stage; **auf der ~ stehen** to be on [the] stage; **hinter der ~** behind the scenes ▶WENDUNGEN: **etw über die ~ bringen** (*fam*) to get sth over with; **über die ~ gehen** (*fam*) to take place
Bühnenbild *nt* scenery
Bühnenbildner(in) <-s, -> *m(f)* scene painter
bühnenreif *adj* ① THEAT fit for the stage ② (*iron: theatralisch*) dramatic
Bühnenstück *nt* [stage] play
Buhruf *m* [cry of] boo
Bulette <-, -n> [bu·'lɛ·tə] *f* DIAL (*Frikadelle*) hamburger
Bulgare, Bulgarin <-n, -n> [bʊl·'gaː·rə, bʊl·'gaː·rɪn] *m, f* Bulgarian; *s. a.* **Deutsche(r)**
Bulgarien <-s> [bʊl·'gaː·ri̯·ən] *nt* Bulgaria; *s. a.* **Deutschland**
bulgarisch [bʊl·'gaː·rɪʃ] *adj* Bulgarian; *s. a.* **deutsch**
Bullauge ['bʊl-] *nt* porthole
Bulldogge *f* bulldog
Bulldozer <-s, -> ['bʊl·doː·zɐ] *m* bulldozer
Bulle <-n, -n> ['bʊ·lə] *m* ① (*männliches Tier*) bull ② (*sl: Polizist*) cop *fam;* ■**die ~n** *pl* the cops *pl sl* ③ (*fam: starker Mann*) hulk
Bullenhitze *f kein pl* (*fam*) stifling heat
Bullette <-, -n> ['bʊ·lɛ·tə] *f* (*hum sl: Polizistin*) policewoman
bullig ['bʊ·lɪç] *adj* (*fam*) hulking
Bumerang <-s, -s *o* -e> ['buː·mə·raŋ] *m* boomerang
Bummel <-s, -> ['bʊ·ml̩] *m* stroll
Bummelei <-> [bʊ·mə·'lai] *f kein pl* (*pej fam*) dilly-dallying
bummeln ['bʊ·ml̩n] *vi* ① *sein* (*spazieren gehen*) to stroll; **~ gehen** to take [*or* go for] a stroll ② *haben* (*fam: trödeln*) to dilly-dally
Bummelzug *m* (*fam*) local [passenger] train
bumsen ['bʊm·zn̩] **I.** *vi* ① *haben* (*fam: schlagen*) to bang (**an/gegen** *+akk* against) ② *sein* (*fam: prallen, stoßen*) to bang (**gegen** *+akk* against) **II.** *vi, vt haben* (*derb: Sex haben*) ■**[jdn/mit jdm]** ~ to screw [sb]
Bund[1] <-[e]s, Bünde> [bʊnt, *pl* 'bʏn·də] *m* ① (*Vereinigung, Gemeinschaft*) association ② (*die Bundesrepublik Deutschland*) ■**der ~** the Federal Republic of Germany; **~ und Länder** the Federation and the [German] States ③ SCHWEIZ (*Eidgenossenschaft*) confederation ④ (*fam: Bundeswehr*) ■**der ~** the [German] army; **beim ~ sein** to be serving in the military ⑤ *eines Kleidungsstücks* waistband
Bund[2] <-[e]s, -e> [bʊnt, *pl* 'bʊn·də] *nt* bundle, bunch
Bündel <-s, -> ['bʏn·dl̩] *nt* bundle
bündeln *vt* to tie in[to] bundles; *Karotten* to tie in[to] bunches
Bundesanstalt *f* federal institute; **~ für Arbeit** German Federal Department of Labor
Bundesbahn *f* **die [Deutsche] ~** German Federal Railroad
Bundesbank *f kein pl* **die** [**Deutsche**] ~ [German] Federal [Reserve] Bank
Bundesbehörde *f* federal agency
Bundesbürger(in) *m(f)* German citizen
Bundesgebiet *nt* BRD, ÖSTERR federal territory
Bundesgericht *nt* SCHWEIZ [Swiss] Federal Court
Bundesgerichtshof *m* BRD [German] Federal Supreme Court
Bundesgesetzblatt *nt* JUR BRD, ÖSTERR Federal Law Gazette, ≈ [United States] Statutes at Large
Bundesgrenzschutz *m* BRD [German] Border Police
Bundeshauptstadt *f* federal capital
Bundesinnenminister(in) *m(f)* [German] Secretary of the Interior
Bundeskanzler(in) *m(f)* BRD German Chancellor; ÖSTERR Austrian Chancellor; SCHWEIZ Head of the Federal Chancellery

> In Germany, the **Bundeskanzler** (Federal Chancellor) is nominated by the Head of State, the Federal President, and elected by the *Bundestag* (Lower House of the Federal Parliament) by majority vote. In Austria, the **Bundeskanzler** is nominated by the largest party in the *Nationalrat* (National Assembly) and appointed by the President. As the leader of the government, the **Bundeskanzler** heads the *Bundeskanzleramt* (Federal Chancellor's Office), which in Switzerland is called the *Bundeskanzlei*.

Bundeskanzleramt *nt* POL Federal Chancellor's Office
Bundeskriminalamt *nt* [German] Federal Criminal Police Office, ≈ Federal Bureau of Investigation
Bundesland *nt* federal state; **die alten/neuen Bundesländer** the federal states of the former West/East Germany

> Since the reunification, the Federal Republic of Germany has consisted of 16 **Bundesländer** (Federal States). Austria is divided into nine Federal States. As in the United States, each state has a capital where the seat of state government is located.

Bundesliga *f kein pl the highest level sports league, often divided into two sub-leagues, the 1st and 2nd Bundesliga*
Bundesminister(in) *m(f)* BRD, ÖSTERR federal secretary

Bụndesministerium *nt* BRD, ÖSTERR federal department
Bụndespost *f kein pl* [German] Federal Post Office
Bụndespräsident(in) *m(f)* BRD, ÖSTERR President of the Federal Republic of Germany/Austria; SCHWEIZ President of the Confederation

> The **Bundespräsident(in)** (Federal President) in Germany and Austria is a separate Head of State who performs mainly ceremonial functions. In Switzerland, however, the **Bundespräsident(in)** has a more active role in government and is one of the seven members of the *Bundesrat* (Federal Council) that elects one of its own to be Federal President every year, albeit as *Primus inter Pares* (first among equals).

Bụndesrat *m* ❶ BRD, ÖSTERR Bundesrat, ≈ Senate ❷ SCHWEIZ [Swiss] Federal Council (*executive body*)

> The **Bundesrat** (Upper House of the German Parliament) is composed of members of the individual state governments. The number of representatives from each state depends on the size of the state. The **Bundesrat** has a legislative function. In Austria, the **Bundesrat** is the part of parliament where the *Länder* (states) are represented according to their population. The exact number of representatives from each state is stipulated by the Federal President after each national census. In Switzerland, the **Bundesrat**, chaired by the Federal President, has an executive function. The seven members of the **Bundesrat**, each elected to a four-year term, collectively constitute the government and assume the functions of Head of State.

Bụndesregierung *f* federal government
Bụndesrepublik *f* federal republic; **die ~ Deutschland** the Federal Republic of Germany
Bụndesstaat *m* ❶ (*Staatenbund*) confederation ❷ (*Gliedstaat*) federal state; **im ~ Kalifornien** in the state of California
Bụndesstraße *f* BRD, ÖSTERR highway
Bụndestag *m kein pl* BRD Bundestag, ≈ House of Representatives

> **Der Bundestag** (the Lower House of the German Parliament) is the representative body of the people and is elected every four years. The **Bundestag** elects the *Bundeskanzler* (Federal Chancellor) and debates on and passes bills.

Bụndestagsabgeọrdnete(r) *f(m)* member of the Bundestag, representative
Bụndestagsausschuss[RR] *m* congressional committee
Bụndestagsbeschluss[RR] *m* congressional decision [*or* vote]
Bụndestagswahl *f* Bundestag election
Bụndestrainer(in) *m(f)* BRD national team coach
Bụndesverfassungsgericht *nt kein pl* BRD [German] Federal Constitutional Court (*supreme legal body that settles issues relating to the basic constitution*)
Bụndesversammlung *f* POL ❶ BRD Federal Assembly, ≈ U.S. Congress ❷ SCHWEIZ Parliament
Bụndeswehr *f* [Federal] Armed Forces
bụndesweit *adj, adv* throughout Germany *pred*
Bündnis <-ses, -se> ['bʏnt·nɪs] *nt* alliance
Bungalow <-s, -s> ['bʊŋ·ga·loː] *m* bungalow
Bungeespringen <-s> ['ban·dʒi·ʃprɪ·ŋən] *nt kein pl* bungee jumping
Bunker <-s, -> ['bʊŋ·kɐ] *m* ❶ (*Schutzraum*) bunker; (*Luftschutzbunker*) air-raid shelter ❷ (*beim Golf*) bunker ❸ (*sl: Gefängnis*) slammer
bunkern ['bʊŋ·kɐn] *vt* to hoard
bunt [bʊnt] **I.** *adj* ❶ (*farbig*) colorful ❷ (*ungeordnet*) jumbled; (*vielfältig*) varied **II.** *adv* ❶ (*farbig*) colorfully; **~ gestreift** with colorful stripes *pl*; **~ kariert** with a colored check pattern ❷ (*ungeordnet*) **~ gemischt** (*abwechslungsreich*) diverse; (*vielfältig*) varied ▶ WENDUNGEN: **es zu ~ treiben** (*fam*) to go too far; **jdm wird es zu ~** (*fam*) sb has had enough
bụntgemischt *adj attr s.* **bunt II 2**
Bụntstift *m* colored pencil
Bụntwäsche *f* coloreds, colored laundry
Bürde <-, -n> ['bʏr·də] *f* (*geh*) ❶ (*Last*) load ❷ (*Beschwernis*) burden
Burg <-, -en> [bʊrk] *f* castle
Bürge, **Bürgin** <-n, -n> ['bʏr·gə, 'bʏr·gɪn] *m, f* guarantor, sponsor
bü̦rgen *vi* ❶ ■ **für jdn ~** to vouch for sb ❷ (*fig: garantieren*) ■ **für etw** *akk* **~** to be a guarantee of sth
Bü̦rger(in) <-s, -> ['bʏr·gɐ] *m(f)* citizen
Bü̦rgerbegehren *nt* BRD public petition for a referendum
Bü̦rgerbewegung *f* citizens' movement
bü̦rgerfern *adj* unresponsive to the concerns of the people, out of touch with the people *pred*
Bü̦rgerinitiative *f* citizens' group
Bü̦rgerkrieg *m* civil war
bü̦rgerlich ['bʏr·gɐ·lɪç] *adj* ❶ *attr* (*den Staatsbürger betreffend*) civil; **~e Pflicht** civic duty ❷ (*dem Bürgerstand angehörend*) bourgeois *pej*
Bü̦rgermeister(in) ['bʏr·gɐ·mais·tɐ] *m(f)* mayor
bü̦rgernah *adj* responsive to the public, in touch with the people *pred*
Bü̦rgernähe *f kein pl* responsiveness [*or* open-

ness] to the [needs of the] public
Bürgerpflicht *f* civic duty
Bürgerrecht *nt meist pl* civil right
Bürgerrechtler(in) <-s, -> *m(f)* civil rights activist
Bürgerrechtsbewegung *f* civil rights movement
Bürgersteig <-[e]s, -e> *m* sidewalk
Bürgertum <-s> *nt kein pl* bourgeoisie + *sing/pl vb*
Bürgerversammlung *f* public meeting
Burgruine *f* castle ruin
Bürgschaft <-, -en> *f* JUR ❶ (*gegenüber Gläubigern*) guaranty; **die ~ für jdn übernehmen** to act as sb's guarantor ❷ (*Haftungssumme*) security
Burgund <-[s]> [bʊr·ˈgʊnt] *nt* Burgundy
Büro <-s, -s> [by·ˈroː] *nt* office
Büroangestellte(r) *f(m)* office worker
Büroarbeit *f* office work
Bürobedarf *m* office supplies *pl*
Bürogebäude *nt* office building
Bürokaufmann, -kauffrau *m, f* [male] office administrator [with business training]
Büroklammer *f* paper clip
Bürokram *m kein pl* (*pej fam*) [bureaucratic] paperwork
Bürokrat(in) <-en, -en> [by·ro·ˈkraːt] *m(f)* (*pej*) bureaucrat
Bürokratie <-, -n> [by·ro·kra·ˈtiː, *pl* -ˈtiː·ən] *f* bureaucracy
bürokratisch I. *adj* ❶ *attr* bureaucratic ❷ (*pej*) involving a lot of red tape **II.** *adv* bureaucratically
Büroraum *m* office
Bürostunden *pl*, **Bürozeit** *f* office hours *pl*
Bursche <-n, -n> [ˈbʊr·ʃə] *m* ❶ (*Halbwüchsiger*) adolescent ❷ (*fam: Kerl*) guy
burschikos [bʊr·ʃi·ˈkoːs] **I.** *adj* (*salopp*) casual; (*Mensch*) laid-back; **~es Mädchen** tomboy **II.** *adv* casually
Bürste <-, -n> [ˈbʏrs·tə] *f* brush
bürsten [ˈbʏrs·tn̩] *vt* to brush
Bus <-ses, -se> [bʊs, *pl* ˈbʊ·sə] *m* bus; (*Reisebus*) tour bus
Busbahnhof *m* bus station
Busch <-[e]s, Büsche> [bʊʃ, *pl* ˈbʏ·ʃə] *m* ❶ (*Strauch*) shrub ❷ (*Buschwald*) bush ▶ WENDUNGEN: **mit etw** *dat* **hinter dem ~ halten** (*fam*) to keep sth to oneself; **da ist etw im ~** (*fam*) sth is up; **bei jdm auf den ~ klopfen** (*fam*) to sound sb out
Buschbohne *f* bush bean
Büschel <-s, -> [ˈbʏ·ʃl̩] *nt* tuft
büschelweise *adv* in tufts
buschig *adj* bushy
Buschmesser *nt* machete
Busen <-s, -> [ˈbuː·zn̩] *m* bust
Busenfreund(in) *m(f)* buddy
Busfahrer(in) *m(f)* bus driver
Bushaltestelle *f* bus stop
Buslinie *f* bus route
Bussard <-s, -e> [ˈbʊ·sart, *pl* ˈbʊ·sar·də] *m* buzzard
Buße <-, -n> [ˈbuː·sə] *f* (*Geldbuße*) fine
Bussel <-s, -(n)> [ˈbʊ·səl] *nt s.* **Busserl**
büßen [ˈbyː·sn̩] **I.** *vt* ❶ (*bezahlen*) to pay for; **das wirst du mir ~!** I'll make you pay for that! ❷ SCHWEIZ (*mit einer Geldbuße belegen*) to fine **II.** *vi* (*leiden*) to suffer (**für** +*akk* because of); **dafür wird er mir ~!** I'll make him suffer for that!
Busserl <-s, -[n]> [ˈbʊ·sɐl] *nt* SÜDD, ÖSTERR (*fam*) kiss
Bußgeld *nt* fine (*for traffic or tax offenses*)
Bußgeldbescheid *m* notice of a fine
Bussi <-s, -s> [ˈbʊ·si] *nt* SÜDD, ÖSTERR kiss
Bußtag *m* day of repentance; **Buß- und Bettag** day of prayer and repentance (*on the Wednesday before Advent*)
Büste <-, -n> [ˈbʏs·tə] *f* bust
Büstenhalter *m* bra[ssiere]
Busverbindung *f* bus service
Butangas *nt* butane gas
Butter <-> [ˈbʊ·tɐ] *f kein pl* butter ▶ WENDUNGEN: **weich wie ~** as soft as can be
Butterblume *f* buttercup
Butterbrot *nt* slice of buttered bread
Butterbrotpapier *nt* wax paper
Buttermilch *f* buttermilk
Butterschmalz *nt* clarified butter
butterweich [ˈbʊ·tɐ·ˈvaiç] **I.** *adj* really soft **II.** *adv* softly
Button <-s, -s> [ˈba·tn̩] *m* badge
b. w. *Abk von* **bitte wenden** PTO
Byte <-s, -s> [bait] *nt* byte
bzw. *adv Abk von* **beziehungsweise**

Cc

C, c <-, - *o fam* -s, -s> [tseː] *nt* ❶ C, c; **~ wie Cäsar** C as in Charlie ❷ MUS C, c; **das hohe ~** high C
C *Abk von* **Celsius** C
ca. *Abk von* **circa** approx., ca
Cabrio <-s, -s> [ˈkaː·brio] *nt s.* **Kabriolett**
Café <-s, -s> [ka·ˈfeː] *nt* café
Cafetẹria <-, -s> [ka·fe·tə·ˈriːa] *f* cafeteria
Calcium <-s> [ˈkal·tsi̯·ʊm] *nt kein pl s.* **Kalzium**
Camion <-s, -s> [ka·ˈmjõ] *m* SCHWEIZ truck
campen [ˈkɛm·pn̩] *vi* to camp
campieren* [kam·ˈpiː·rən] *vi* ❶ *s.* **kampieren** ❷ ÖSTERR, SCHWEIZ to camp
Camping <-s> [ˈkɛm·pɪŋ] *nt kein pl* camping
Campingplatz *m* campsite
Car <-s, -s> [ˈkaːɐ̯] *m* SCHWEIZ *kurz für* **Autocar** bus
Car-Sharing, **Carsharing** <-s> [ˈkaːɐ̯·ʃɛː·ɐ̯rɪŋ] *nt kein pl* car sharing
Cartoon <-s, -s> [kar·ˈtuːn] *m* cartoon
Casino <-s, -s> [ka·ˈziː·no] *nt s.* **Kasino**
CD <-, -s> [tseː·ˈdeː] *f Abk von* **Compactdisc** CD
CD-Brenner *m* CD burner
CD-ROM <-, -s> [tseː·deː·ˈrɔm] *f* CD-ROM
CD-Spieler *m s.* **CD-Player**
CDU <-> [tseː·deː·ˈʔuː] *f Abk von* **Christlich-Demokratische Union** CDU
Cellist(in) <-en, -en> [tʃɛ·ˈlɪst] *m(f)* cellist
Cello <-s, -s *o* Celli> [ˈtʃɛ·lo, *pl* ˈtʃ·ɛli] *nt* cello
Cellophan® <-s> [tsɛ·lo·ˈfaːn] *nt kein pl* cellophane
Celsius [ˈtsɛl·zi̯·ʊs] *no art, inv* Celsius
Cembalo <-s, -s *o* Cembali> [ˈtʃɛm·ba·lo, *pl* -li] *nt* harpsichord
Cent <-(s), -(s)> [ˈsɛnt] *m* cent
Champagner <-s, -> [ʃam·ˈpan·jɐ] *m* champagne
Champignon <-s, -s> [ˈʃam·pɪn·jɔŋ] *m* mushroom
Chance <-, -n> [ˈʃãː·sə, a. ʃãːs, ʃaŋ·s(ə), *pl* -sn̩] *f* chance; **die ~n** *pl* **stehen gut/schlecht** there's a good chance/there's little chance
Chancengleichheit *f kein pl* equal opportunity
chancenlos *adj* no chance
Chaos <-> [ˈkaː·ɔs] *nt kein pl* chaos
Chaot(in) <-en, -en> [ka·ˈoːt] *m(f)* chaotic person
chaotisch [ka·ˈoː·tɪʃ] **I.** *adj* chaotic **II.** *adv* chaotically
Charakter <-s, -e> [ka·ˈrak·tɐ, *pl* -ˈteː·rə] *m* character; *eines Gesprächs* nature *no indef art*
Charạktereigenschaft *f* characteristic
charạkterfest *adj* with strength of character *pred*
charakterisieren* [ka·rak·te·ri·ˈziː·rən] *vt* to characterize
charakteristisch [ka·rak·te·ˈrɪs·tɪʃ] *adj* characteristic (**für** +*akk* of)
charạkterlich **I.** *adj* of sb's character *pred* **II.** *adv* in character, as far as sb's character is concerned *pred*
Charạkterstärke *f* strength of character
Charạkterzug *m* characteristic
charmant [ʃar·ˈmant] **I.** *adj* charming **II.** *adv* charmingly
Charme <-s> [ˈʃarm] *m kein pl* charm
chartern [ˈtʃar·tɐn] *vt* to charter
Chauffeur(in) <-s, -e> [ʃɔ·ˈføːɐ̯] *m(f)* chauffeur
Chauvinismus <-> [ʃo·vi·ˈnɪs·mʊs] *m kein pl* chauvinism
Chauvinist(in) <-en, -en> [ʃo·vi·ˈnɪst] *m(f)* chauvinist
chauvinistisch [ʃo·vi·ˈnɪs·tɪʃ] **I.** *adj* chauvinistic **II.** *adv* chauvinistically
checken [ˈtʃɛ·kn̩] *vt* ❶ (*überprüfen*) to check ❷ (*sl: begreifen*) ■**etw ~** to get sth
Check-in <-s, -s> [ˈtʃɛk·ʔɪn] *m o nt* check-in
Chef(in) <-s, -s> [ˈʃɛf] *m(f)* head; (*einer Firma*) manager, boss *fam*
Chẹfarzt, -ärztin *m, f* head doctor
Chẹfkoch, -köchin *m, f* head cook
Chẹfredakteur(in) *m(f)* editor in chief
Chẹfsekretär(in) *m(f)* executive secretary
Chemie <-> [çe·ˈmiː] *f kein pl* chemistry
Chemiefaser *f* man-made fiber
Chemiekonzern *nt* chemical manufacturer
Chemikalie <-, -n> [çe·mi·ˈkaː·li̯ə] *f meist pl* chemical
Chemiker(in) <-s, -> [ˈçeː·mi·kɐ] *m(f)* chemist
chemisch [ˈçeː·mɪʃ] **I.** *adj* chemical **II.** *adv* chemically
Chemotherapie *f* chemotherapy
chic [ˈʃɪk] *adj s.* **schick**
Chiffre <-, -n> [ˈʃɪf·rə] *f* ❶ (*Kennziffer*) box number ❷ (*Zeichen*) cipher
Chile <-s> [ˈtʃiː·le] *nt* Chile; *s. a.* **Deutschland**
Chilene, Chilenin <-n, -n> [tʃi·ˈleː·nə] *m, f* Chilean; *s. a.* **Deutsche(r)**
chilenisch [tʃi·ˈleː·nɪʃ] *adj* Chilean; *s. a.* **deutsch**
Chili <-s> [ˈtʃiː·li] *m kein pl* chili
China <-s> [ˈçiː·na] *nt* China; *s. a.* **Deutschland**
Chịnakohl *m* Chinese cabbage
Chinese, Chinesin <-n, -n> [çi·ˈneː·zə, çi·ˈneː·zɪn] *m, f* Chinese [person]; *s. a.* **Deutsche(r)**
chinesisch [çi·ˈneː·zɪʃ] *adj* Chinese ▶ WENDUNGEN: **~ für jdn sein** (*fam*) to be all Greek to sb; *s. a.* **deutsch**
Chip <-s, -s> [tʃɪp] *m* ❶ COMPUT [micro]chip ❷ (*Jeton*) chip ❸ *meist pl* KOCHK chip *usu pl*
Chịpkarte *f* smart card

Chirurg(in) <-en, -en> [çi·'rʊrk, *pl* -'rʊr·gn̩] *m(f)* surgeon
Chirurgie <-, -n> [çi·rʊr·'gi:] *f kein pl* surgery
chirurgisch [çi·'rʊr·gɪʃ] **I.** *adj* surgical **II.** *adv* surgically
Chlor <-s> [klo:ɐ̯] *nt kein pl* chlorine
Chloroform <-s> [klo·ro·'fɔrm] *nt kein pl* chloroform
Chlorophyll <-s> [klo·ro·'fʏl] *nt kein pl* chlorophyll
Cholera <-> ['ko:·le·ra] *f kein pl* cholera
Choleriker(in) <-s, -> [ko·'le:·ri·kɐ] *m(f)* choleric person
cholerisch [ko·'le:·rɪʃ] *adj* choleric
Cholesterin <-s> [kol·ɛs·te·'ri:n, a. ço...] *nt kein pl* cholesterol
Cholesterinspiegel *m* cholesterol level
Chor <-[e]s, Chöre> [ko:ɐ̯, *pl* 'kø:·rə] *m* chorus; REL choir
Choral <-s, Choräle> [ko·'ra:l, *pl* ko·'rɛ:·lə] *m* choral[e]
Choreograf(in)RR <-en, -en> [ko·reo·'gra:f] *m(f)* choreographer
ChoreografieRR <-, -n> [ko·reo·gra·'fi:] *f* choreography
choreografischRR [ko·reo·'gra:·fɪʃ] *adj* choreographic
Choreograph(in) <-en, -en> *m(f) s.* **Choreograf**
Choreographie <-, -n> *f s.* **Choreografie**
choreographisch *adj s.* **choreografisch**
Chose <-, -n> ['ʃo:·zə] *f* (*fam*) ❶ (*Angelegenheit*) thing, affair ❷ (*Zeug*) stuff; ■ **die [ganze]** ~ everything, the whole shebang *sl*
Chr. *Abk von* **Christus, Christi** Christ
Christ(in) <-en, -en> ['krɪst] *m(f)* Christian
Christbaum *m* DIAL Christmas tree
Christentum <-s> *nt kein pl* Christianity
Christi ['krɪsti] *gen von* **Christus**
Christkind *nt* ❶ (*Jesus*) Christ child ❷ (*weihnachtliche Gestalt*) Santa Claus; **ans ~ glauben** to believe in Santa Claus
christlich **I.** *adj* Christian **II.** *adv* in a Christian manner
Christmesse *f,* **Christmette** *f* Christmas mass
Christus <Christi, *dat - o geh* Christo, *akk - o geh* Christum> ['krɪs·tʊs] *m* Christ; **nach/vor** ~ A.D./B.C.; **Christi Himmelfahrt** Ascension
Chrom <-s> ['kro:m] *nt kein pl* chrome
chromatisch [kro·'ma:·tɪʃ] *adj* MUS, ORN chromatic
Chromosom <-s, -en> [kro·mo·'zo:m] *nt* chromosome
Chronik <-, -en> ['kro:·nɪk] *f* chronicle
chronisch ['kro:·nɪʃ] *adj* chronic; ■ **etw ist bei jdm** ~ sb has [a] chronic [case of] sth
Chronist(in) <-en, -en> [kro·'nɪst] *m(f)* chronicler
Chronologie <-> [kro·no·lo·'gi:] *f kein pl* ❶ (*zeitliche Abfolge*) sequence ❷ (*Zeitrechnung*) chronology
chronologisch [kro·no·'lo:·gɪʃ] **I.** *adj* chronological **II.** *adv* chronologically, in chronological order
circa ['tsɪr·ka] *adv s.* **zirka**
Cis, cis <-, -> ['tsɪs] *nt* MUS C sharp
cl *Abk von* **Zentiliter** cl
Clan <-s, -s> ['kla:n] *m* ❶ (*Stamm*) clan ❷ (*Clique*) clique
clean ['kli:n] *adj pred* (*sl*) ■ **~ sein** to be clean
clever ['klɛ·vɐ] **I.** *adj* ❶ (*aufgeweckt*) smart, bright ❷ (*raffiniert*) cunning **II.** *adv* ❶ (*geschickt*) artfully ❷ (*pej*) cunningly
Clinch <-[e]s> ['klɪntʃ] *m kein pl* clinch; **[mit jdm] im ~ liegen** (*fig*) to be [involved] in a dispute [with sb]
Clip <-s, -s> ['klɪp] *m* ❶ (*Klemme*) clip ❷ (*Ohrschmuck*) clip-on [earring] ❸ (*Videoclip*) video
Clique <-, -n> ['klɪ·kə] *f* circle of friends; (*pej*) clique
Clou <-s, -s> ['klu:] *m* ❶ (*Glanzpunkt*) highlight ❷ (*Kernpunkt*) crux ❸ (*Pointe*) punch line
Clown(in) <-s, -s> [klaun] *m(f)* clown ▶ WENDUNGEN: **sich** *akk* **zum ~ machen** to make a fool of oneself
Club <-s, -s> ['klʊp] *m s.* **Klub**
cm *Abk von* **Zentimeter** cm
c-Moll <-s> ['tse:·mɔl] *nt kein pl* MUS C flat minor
Coach <-[s], -s> [koʊtʃ] *m* coach
Cockpit <-s, -s> ['kɔk·pɪt] *nt* cockpit
Cocktail <-s, -s> ['kɔk·te:l] *m* cocktail
CO_2-Fußabdruck [tse·ʔo·'tsvɛɪ-] *m* carbon footprint
Code <-s, -s> ['ko:t] *m s.* **Kode**
codieren* [ko·'di:·rən] *vt* to code, to encode
Codierung <-, -en> *f s.* **Kodierung**
Cognac® <-s, -s> ['kɔn·jak] *m* cognac
Coiffeuse <-, -n> [ko̯a·'føzə] *f* SCHWEIZ hairdresser
Come-backRR, **Comeback** <-[s], -s> [kam·'bɛk] *nt* comeback
Comic <-s, -s> ['kɔ·mɪk] *m meist pl* comic
Compact Disc, Compact DiskRR <-, -s> [kɔm·'pakt 'dɪsk] *f* compact disc
Computer <-s, -> [kɔm·'pju:·tɐ] *m* computer; **[etw] auf ~ umstellen** to computerize [sth]
computergesteuert **I.** *adj* computer-controlled **II.** *adv* under computer control
computerlesbar *adj* machine-readable
Computerprogramm *nt* [computer] program
Computerspiel *nt* computer game
Computersystem *nt* computer system
computerunterstützt *adj* computer-aided
Computervirus *nt o m* computer virus
Comtesse <-, -n> [kɔm·'tɛs, a. kõ·'tɛs, *pl* -'tɛ·sn̩] *f* countess
Conférencier <-s, -s> [kõ·fe·rã·'si̯e:] *m* master of ceremonies
Consultingfirma [kɔn·'zal·tɪŋ-] *f* consulting firm
Container <-s, -> [kɔn·'te:·nɐ] *m* container
Cookie <-s, -s> ['kʊ·kɪ] *nt* INET cookie

cool ['kuːl] *adj* (*sl*) ❶ (*gefasst*) calm and collected ❷ (*sehr zusagend*) cool
Copilot(in) ['koː·pi·loːt] *m(f)* copilot
Copyright <-s, -s> ['kɔ·pi·rait] *nt* copyright
Cord <-s> ['kɔrt] *m kein pl* corduroy
Corner <-s, -> ['kɔːg̊·nɐ] *m* ÖSTERR, SCHWEIZ (*Eckball*) corner [kick]
Cornflakes® ['koːg̊n·fleːks] *pl* cornflakes *pl*
Cornichon <-s, -s> [kɔr·ni·'ʃõː] *nt* cornichon
Costa Rica <-s> ['kɔs·ta 'riː·ka] *nt* Costa Rica; *s. a.* **Deutschland**
Couch <-, -s *o* -en> [kautʃ] *f o* SCHWEIZ *m* couch
Couchgarnitur *f* couch set
Couchtisch *m* coffee table
Count-downRR, **Countdown** <-s, -s> ['kaunt·'daun] *m o nt* countdown
Coup <-s, -s> ['kuː] *m* coup
Coupé <-s, -s> [ku·'peː] *nt* ❶ (*Sportlimousine*) coupé, coupe ❷ ÖSTERR (*Zugabteil*) train compartment
couragiert [ku·ra·'ʒiːg̊t] **I.** *adj* bold **II.** *adv* boldly
Cousin, **Cousine** <-s, -s> [ku·'zɛ̃ː, ku·'ziː·nə] *m, f* cousin
Cover <-s, -s> ['kavɐ] *nt* ❶ (*Titelseite*) [front] cover ❷ (*Plattenhülle*) [record] sleeve
Cowboy <-s, -s> ['kau·bɔy] *m* cowboy
Crack1 <-s, -s> ['krɛk] *m* (*ausgezeichneter Spieler*) ace
Crack2 <-s> ['krɛk] *nt kein pl* (*Rauschgift*) crack
Crashkurs ['krɛʃ-] *m* crash course
Creme <-, -s> ['kreːm, 'krɛːm] *f* ❶ (*Salbe*) cream ❷ (*Sahnespeise*) mousse
cremefarben *adj* cream-colored, cream
cremig *adj* creamy
Crêpe <-, -s> ['krɛp] *m s.* **Krepp**1
Creutzfeldt-Jakob-Krankheit ['krɔyts·fɛlt-] *f* MED Creutzfeldt-Jakob disease
Crew <-, -s> ['kruː] *f* crew
C-Schlüssel *m* C clef
CSU <-> [tseː·ʔɛs·'ʔuː] *f Abk von* **Christlich-Soziale Union** CSU
Curry <-s, -s> ['kœri] *m o nt* curry
CVP <-> *f kein pl* SCHWEIZ *Abk von* **Christlichdemokratische Volkspartei** Christian Democratic People's Party

D

Dd

D, d <-, - *o fam* -s, -s> [deː] *nt* ❶ (*Buchstabe*) D, d; ~ **wie Dora** D as in Delta ❷ MUS D, d
da ['daː] **I.** *adv* ❶ (*dort*) there; (*hier*) here; ~ **sein** to be there/here; ~ **bist du ja!** there you are!; ~ **drüben/vorne** over there; ~ **hinten** back there; ~ **draußen/drinnen** out/in there; **der/die/das ...** ~ this ... [over] here [*or* that ... [over] there] ❷ (*dann*) then; **von ~ an herrschte endlich Ruhe** after that it was finally quiet ❸ (*in diesem Fall*) in this case; ~ **bin ich ganz deiner Meinung** I completely agree with you **II.** *konj* (*weil*) since, as
da|behalten* ['daː·bə·hal·tn̩] *vt irreg* to keep here/there
dabei [da·'bai] *adv* ❶ (*örtlich*) with [it/them]; **die Rechnung war nicht** ~ the bill was not enclosed; **direkt/nahe** ~ right next to/near it ❷ (*zeitlich*) at the same time; (*dadurch*) as a result; (*währenddessen*) while doing it ❸ (*anwesend, beteiligt*) there; ~ **sein** to be there; **bist du ~?** are you with us? ❹ (*damit verbunden*) through it/them; **was hast du dir denn ~ gedacht?** what [on earth] were you thinking?; **ich habe mir nichts ~ gedacht** I didn't mean anything by it; **da ist [doch] nichts ~** there's nothing to it; **das Dumme/Schöne ~ ist, ...** the stupid/good thing about it is ...
dabei|bleiben *vi irreg sein* ■**bei jdm** ~ to stay with sb; ■**bei etw** *dat* ~ to continue doing [*or* stick with] sth
dabei|haben *vt irreg* ■**etw** ~ to have sth on oneself; ■**jdn** ~ to have sb with oneself
dabei|seinALT *vi irreg sein s.* **dabei 3, 4**
dabei|stehen *vi irreg* ■**[mit]** ~ to be there; (*untätig a.*) to stand there
da|bleiben *vi irreg sein* to stay [*or* wait] there
Dach <-[e]s, Dächer> ['dax, *pl* 'dɛ·çɐ] *nt* (*Gebäudeteil, a. vom Auto*) roof ▶WENDUNGEN: [**von jdm**] **eins aufs ~ kriegen** (*fam: geohrfeigt werden*) to get a slap upside the head [from sb]; (*getadelt werden*) to be given a talking-to [by sb]; **jdm aufs ~ steigen** (*fam*) to jump down sb's throat
Dachbalken *m* roof beam
Dachboden *m* attic
Dachdecker(in) <-s, -> *m(f)* roofer
Dachfenster *nt* skylight
Dachgepäckträger *m* roof rack
DachgeschossRR *nt* attic
Dachkammer *f* attic room
Dachlawine *f mass of snow sliding from a roof*
Dachrinne *f* gutter
Dachs <-es, -e> ['daks] *m* badger
Dachschaden *m* **einen ~ haben** (*fam*) to have a screw loose
Dachstuhl *m* roof truss
dachte ['dax·tə] *imp von* **denken**
Dachverband *m* umbrella organization
Dachwohnung *f* attic apartment
Dachziegel *m* [roofing] tile
Dackel <-s, -> ['da·kl̩] *m* dachshund
Daddler <-s, -> ['dɛd·lɐ] *m* COMPUT (*fam*) gamer
dadurch [da·'dʊrç] *adv* ❶ *örtlich* through [it/

them]; (*emph.*) through there ❷ (*aus diesem Grund*) so; (*auf diese Weise*) this is how; ■ **~, dass ...** because ...

dafür [da·ˈfyːɐ̯] *adv* ❶ (*für das*) for it/this/that; **warum ist er böse? er hat doch keinen Grund ~** why's he angry? he has no reason to be; **es ist ein Beweis ~, dass ...** it's proof that ...; **~ bin ich ja da** that's what I'm here for ❷ (*als Gegenleistung*) in return ❸ (*andererseits*) **in Mathematik ist er schlecht, ~ kann er gut Fußball spielen** he's bad at math, but he makes up for it with soccer; **er ist zwar nicht kräftig, ~ aber intelligent** he may not be strong, but [at least] he's smart ❹ (*im Hinblick darauf*) ■ **~, dass ...** seeing [that] ... ❺ ■ **~ sein** (*zustimmen*) to be for it/that

dafür|können *vt irreg* **er kann nichts dafür** it's not his fault, he can't help it

dagegen [da·ˈgeː·gn̩] **I.** *adv* ❶ (*räumlich*) against it ❷ (*als Einwand, Ablehnung*) against it/that; **~ müsst ihr was tun** you have to do something about it; **etwas/nichts ~ haben** to mind/not mind sth; **ich habe nichts ~ [einzuwenden]** that's fine by me ❸ (*als Gegenmaßnahme*) **das hilft/ist gut ~** this will help; **~ lässt sich nichts machen** you can't do anything about it ❹ (*verglichen damit*) compared with it/that/them ❺ ■ **~ sein** (*nicht zustimmen*) to be against it **II.** *konj* (*jedoch*) whereas

da|haben *vt irreg* ❶ ■ **etw ~** (*vorrätig*) to have sth in stock; (*zur Hand*) to have sth ❷ (*zu Besuch*) ■ **jdn ~** to have sb over

daheim [da·ˈhaim] *adv* SÜDD, ÖSTERR, SCHWEIZ at home

daher [ˈdaː·heːɐ̯] *adv* ❶ (*von dort*) from there ❷ (*aus diesem Grunde*) [and] that's why ❸ (*aus dieser Quelle, dadurch begründet*) **~ hat er das** that's where he got it [from]; **~ weißt du es also** so that's how you know [that]; **das kommt ~, dass ...** that is because ... ❹ DIAL (*hierher*) here/there

daher|reden (*pej*) **I.** *vi* to talk [*or* rattle] away; **dumm ~** to talk nonsense **II.** *vt* to say sth without thinking; **das war nur so dahergeredet!** that was just talk!

dahin [da·ˈhɪn] *adv* ❶ (*an diesen Ort*) there; **kommst du mit ~?** are you coming along?; **ist es noch weit bis ~?** is there still a ways to go? *fam,* are we there yet? ❷ (*zeitlich*) ■ **bis ~** until then ❸ (*in dem Sinne*) **er äußerte sich ~ gehend, dass ...** he said something to the effect that ...

dahingestellt [da·ˈhɪn·gə·ʃtɛlt] *adj* ■ **~ sein/bleiben** to be/remain an open question

dahin|sagen *vt* ■ **etw [nur so] ~** to say sth without [really] thinking

dahin|schleppen *vr* ■ **sich** *akk* **~** to drag on

dahin|schmelzen *vi irreg sein* (*hum*) to melt, to get [all] gooey *fam*

dahinten [da·ˈhɪn·tn̩] *adv* back there

dahinter [da·ˈhɪn·tɐ] *adv* behind it/that/them etc.

dahinter|klemmen *vr* (*fam*) **sich** *akk* **~ klemmen** to buckle down

dahinter|kommen *vi irreg sein* (*fam: erfahren*) to find out; (*begreifen*) to figure out

dahinter|stecken *vi* (*fam*) **wer steckt ~?** who's behind it?

Dahlie <-, -n> [ˈdaː·li̯ə] *f* dahlia

da|lassen *vt irreg* ■ **jdn ~** to leave sb here/there; ■ **jdm etw ~** to leave sb sth

damalig [ˈdaː·maː·lɪç] *adj attr* at that time *pred*

damals [ˈdaː·maːls] *adv* [back] then, at that time, back in the day *fam*

Dame <-, -n> [ˈdaː·mə, *pl* ˈdaː·mən] *f* ❶ (*geh*) lady; **meine ~n und Herren!** ladies and gentlemen! ❷ (*Damespiel*) checkers + *sing vb* ❸ (*bei Schach, Karten*) queen

Damebrett [ˈdaː·mə·brɛt] *nt* checkerboard

Damenbegleitung *f* female company

Damenbekanntschaft *f* lady friend

Damenbinde *f* sanitary napkin [*or* pad]

Damenfahrrad *nt* women's bicycle

Damenfriseur *m* [women's] hairdresser

damenhaft I. *adj* ladylike **II.** *adv* like a lady

Damenmannschaft *f* women's team

Damenmode *f* women's fashion[s]

Damentoilette *f* ladies' room

Damenwahl *f* ladies' choice

Damespiel *nt* [game of] checkers + *sing vb*

damisch [ˈdaː·mɪʃ] *adj* SÜDD, ÖSTERR (*fam: dämlich*) stupid

damit [da·ˈmɪt] **I.** *adv* with it/that; **was soll ich ~?** what am I supposed to do with this/that?; **weißt du, was sie ~ meint?** do you know what she means by that?; **ist Ihre Frage ~ beantwortet?** has that answered your question?; **ich habe nichts ~ zu tun** I have nothing to do with this; **hör auf ~!** knock it off!; **sind Sie ~ einverstanden?** do you agree [to/with it/that]? **II.** *konj* so that

dämlich [ˈdɛːm·lɪç] (*fam*) **I.** *adj* stupid **II.** *adv* **sich** *akk* **~ anstellen** to be awkward

Dämlichkeit <-, -en> *f* (*fam*) ❶ *kein pl* (*Verhalten*) stupidity ❷ (*Bemerkung*) stupid [*or* dumb] remark

Damm <-[e]s, Dämme> [ˈdam, *pl* ˈdɛmə] *m* (*Staudamm*) dam; (*Deich*) dike ▶ WENDUNGEN: **wieder auf dem ~ sein** to be on one's feet again

dämmen [ˈdɛ·mən] *vt* to insulate

dämmerig [ˈdɛ·mərɪç] *adj s.* **dämmrig**

dämmern [ˈdɛ·mɐn] **I.** *vi* ❶ *Tag, Morgen* to dawn; *Abend* to approach ❷ (*fig*) ■ **jdm ~** to [gradually] dawn on sb **II.** *vi impers* ■ **es dämmert** (*morgens*) dawn is breaking; (*abends*) night is falling

Dämmerung <-, -en> *f* twilight; (*Abenddämmerung*) dusk; (*Morgendämmerung*) dawn

dämmrig [ˈdɛm·rɪç] *adj Beleuchtung* dim

Dämon <-s, Dämonen> [ˈdɛː·mɔn, *pl* dɛ·ˈmoː·nən] *m* demon

dämonisch [dɛ·ˈmoː·nɪʃ] *adj* demonic

Dampf <-[e]s, Dämpfe> [ˈdampf, *pl* ˈdɛm·pfə] *m* steam; **~ ablassen** (*a. fig*) to let off steam

Dạmpfbad *nt* steam bath

Dạmpfbügeleisen *nt* steam iron

Dạmpfdruck *m* steam pressure

dampfen ['dam·pfn̩] *vi* to steam

dämpfen ['dɛm·pfn̩] *vt* ① *Gemüse* to steam ② *Stimme* to lower ③ *Stoß, Begeisterung* to dampen

Dampfer <-s, -> ['dam·pfɐ] *m* steamship ▶WENDUNGEN: **auf dem falschen ~ sein** (*fam*) to be barking up the wrong tree

Dämpfer <-s, -> ['dɛm·pfɐ] *m* MUS, TECH damper ▶WENDUNGEN: **jdm einen ~ aufsetzen** to dampen sb's spirits

Dạmpfkochtopf *m* pressure cooker

Dạmpfkraftwerk *nt* steam[-driven] power plant

Dạmpflok *f* steam engine

Dạmpfmaschine *f* steam engine

Dạmpfschiff *nt s.* **Dampfer**

Dạmpfwalze *f* steamroller

danach [da·'naːx] *adv* ① *zeitlich* after it/that; (*nachher a.*) afterwards; **ein paar Minuten ~** a few minutes later ② *örtlich* behind [her/him/it/them etc.] ③ (*dementsprechend*) **~ gekleidet** appropriately dressed ④ (*laut dem*) according to that ⑤ (*nach dieser Sache*) **~ greifen** to [make a] grab for it; **sich** *akk* **~ sehnen** to long for it/that; ■**jdm ist ~/nicht ~** (*fam*) sb feels/doesn't feel like it

Däne, Dänin <-n, -n> ['dɛː·nə, 'dɛː·nɪn] *m, f* Dane; *s. a.* **Deutsche(r)**

daneben [da·'neː·bn̩] *adv* ① (*räumlich*) next to her/him/it/that etc.; **links/rechts ~** (*bei Gegenständen*) to the left/right of it/them; (*bei Menschen*) to her/his left/right ② (*verglichen damit*) compared with her/him/it/that etc. ③ (*außerdem*) in addition [to that] ▶WENDUNGEN: **~ sein** (*unangemessen*) to be inappropriate

danebenǀbenehmen* *vr irreg* (*fam*) ■**sich** *akk* **~** to make a fool of oneself

danebenǀgehen *vi irreg sein* ① (*Ziel verfehlen*) to miss; *Pfeil, Schuss a.* to miss its/their mark ② (*scheitern*) to go wrong

danebenǀgießen *vt irreg* ■**etw ~** to spill sth

danebenǀliegen *vi irreg* (*fam*) ■**jd liegt daneben** sb is wide of the mark; **er liegt mit seiner Vermutung völlig daneben** his suspicion is way off base

Dänemark <-s> ['dɛː·nə·mark] *nt* Denmark; *s. a.* **Deutschland**

dänisch ['dɛː·nɪʃ] *adj* Danish; *s. a.* **deutsch**

dank ['daŋk] *präp +gen* (*a. iron*) thanks to

Dank <-[e]s> ['daŋk] *m kein pl* gratitude; **besten/vielen ~!** thank you very much!, thanks a lot! *fam;* **das ist der [ganze] ~ dafür!** that is/was all the thanks one gets/got!; **als ~ für etw** *akk* in grateful recognition of sth

dankbar ['daŋk·baːɐ̯] *adj* grateful; ■**jdm ~ sein** to be grateful to sb

Dạnkbarkeit <-> *f kein pl* gratitude

dạnke *interj* thank you, thanks *fam*

danken ['daŋ·kn̩] **I.** *vi* ■**jdm ~** to thank sb, to express one's thanks to sb; **nichts zu ~** you're welcome **II.** *vt* ■**jdm etw ~** to repay sb for sth; **wie kann ich Ihnen das jemals ~?** how can I ever thank you?

dankenswert ['daŋ·kn̩s·veːɐ̯t] *adj* commendable

Dạnksagung <-, -en> *f* note of thanks

dann ['dan] *adv* ① (*danach*) then; **noch eine Woche, ~ ist Weihnachten** one more week until Christmas ② (*zu dem Zeitpunkt*) ■**immer ~, wenn ...** whenever ... ③ (*unter diesen Umständen*) then; ■**wenn ..., ~ ...** if ..., [then] ...; **etw nur ~ tun, wenn ...** to only do sth when/if ...; ■**selbst ~** even then ④ (*außerdem*) ■**und ~ auch noch ...** on top of that ... ▶WENDUNGEN: **~ und wann** now and then

daran [da·'ran] *adv* ① (*räumlich*) **halt deine Hand ~!** put your hand [up] against it; **etw ~ kleben/befestigen** to stick/fasten sth to it; **~ riechen** to smell it; **~ vorbei** past it ② (*zeitlich*) **im Anschluss ~** following that/this ③ (*an dieser Sache*) **es ändert sich nichts ~** it won't change; **denk ~!** don't forget!; **das Gute ~ ist, dass ...** the good thing about it is that ...; **kein Interesse ~** no interest in it/that; **~ arbeiten** to work on it/that; **sich** *akk* **~ beteiligen** to take part in it/that; **sich** *akk* **~ erinnern** to remember it/that

ˌdarạnǀgehen *vi irreg sein* to get started

darạnǀmachen *vr* (*fam*) ■**sich** *akk* **~** to get started

daranǀsetzen [da·'ran·zɛt·sn̩] *vt* **alles ~, etw zu tun** to make every effort to do sth

darauf [da·'rauf] *adv* ① (*räumlich*) on it/that/them etc. ② (*zeitlich*) after that; **bald ~** shortly afterwards; **am Abend ~** the next evening; **im Jahr ~** [in] the following year ③ (*auf das*) **wir müssen ~ Rücksicht nehmen** we must take that into consideration; **~ antworten/reagieren** to reply/react to it/that; **etw ~ sagen** to say sth to it/this/that; **ein Recht ~** a right to it/that; **sich** *akk* **~ verlassen** to rely on it/that; **sich** *akk* **~ vorbereiten** to prepare for it/that

daraufﬁolgend *adj attr* following

daraufhin [da·rauf·'hɪn] *adv* (*infolgedessen*) as a result [of this/that]

daraufǀlegen[RR] *vt* ■**etw ~** to place sth on top

daraus [da·'raus] *adv* ① (*aus Gefäß o Raum*) out of it/that/them; **etw ~ entfernen** to remove sth from it ② (*aus diesem Material*) out of it/that/them ③ (*aus dieser Tatsache*) **~ ergibt sich/folgt, dass ...** the result of which is that ...

Darbietung <-, -en> ['daːɐ̯·biː·tʊŋ] *f* performance

darin [da·'rɪn] *adv* ① (*in dem/der*) in there; (*in vorher Erwähntem*) in it/them; **was steht ~ [geschrieben]?** what does it say? ② (*in dem Punkt*) in that respect; **~ übereinstimmen, dass** *akk* to agree that ...

darǀlegen ['daːɐ̯·leː·gn̩] *vt* to explain

Darlehen <-s, -> ['daːɐ̯·leː·ən] *nt* loan

D

Darm <-[e]s, Därme> ['darm, *pl* 'dɛr·mə] *m* intestine

Darmgrippe *f* stomach flu

Darmverschluss[RR] *m* intestinal obstruction

dar|stellen ['daːɐ̯·ʃtɛ·lən] **I.** *vt* ❶ (*wiedergeben*) *a.* THEAT to portray ❷ (*beschreiben*) to describe; **etw knapp ~** to give a brief description of sth ❸ (*bedeuten*) to represent **II.** *vr* ■ **sich** *akk* [**jdm**] ~ to appear [to sb]

Darsteller(in) <-s, -> ['daːɐ̯·ʃtɛ·lɐ] *m(f)* actor *masc*, actress *fem*

Darstellung <-, -en> *f* ❶ (*bildlich*) portrayal ❷ THEAT performance ❸ (*das Schildern*) representation

darüber [da·'ryː·bɐ] *adv* ❶ (*räumlich*) over it/that/them; (*direkt auf etw*) on top [of it/that]; (*oberhalb von etw*) above [it/that/them]; (*über etw hinweg*) over [it/that/them] ❷ (*hinsichtlich einer Sache*) about it/that/them; **~ spricht er nicht gern** he doesn't like to talk about it/that ❸ (*dabei und deswegen*) in the process ❹ (*über dieser Grenze*) above [that]; **Kinder im Alter von 12 Jahren und ~** children 12 [years] and older/over; **10 Stunden oder ~** 10 hours and/or longer ▶ WENDUNGEN: **~ hinaus** what is more; **~ hinweg sein** to have gotten over it

darüber|stehen *vi irreg* (*a. fig*) to be above it [all]

darum [da·'rʊm] *adv* ❶ (*deshalb*) that's why ❷ (*um das*) **~ bitten** to ask for it/that; **es geht nicht ~, wer zuerst kommt** it's not a question of who comes first; **~ geht es ja gerade!** that's just it!, that's exactly what I'm/we're talking about! ❸ (*räumlich*) ■ **~ [herum]** around it

darunter [da·'rʊn·tɐ] *adv* ❶ (*räumlich*) under it/that; (*unterhalb von etw*) below [it/that]; **~ hervorgucken** to look out [from underneath] ❷ (*unter dieser Sache*) **was verstehst du ~?** what do you understand it/that to mean?; **~ kann ich mir nichts vorstellen** it doesn't mean anything to me ❸ (*dazwischen*) among[st] them ❹ (*unter dieser Grenze*) lower; **Kinder im Alter von 12 Jahren und ~** children 12 [years] and younger/under

darunter|liegen *vi irreg* to be less

das[1] <*gen:* dęs, *dat:* dem, *akk:* dąs, *pl:* die> ['das] *art def, sing nt* the; **~ Kind/Tier/Schiff** the child/animal/ship; *s. a.* **der**[1], **die**[1]

das[2] <*gen:* dęssen, *dat:* dem, *akk:* dąs, *pl:* die> ['das] *pron dem, sing nt* that; **~ Kind/Haus [da]** that child/house [there]; **was ist denn ~?** (*fam*) what on earth is that/this?; *s. a.* **der**[2], **die**[3]

das[3] <*gen:* dęssen, *dat:* dem, *akk:* dąs, *pl:* die> ['das] *pron rel, sing nt* that; (*Person a.*) who, whom *form;* (*Gegenstand, Tier a.*) which; **ich sah ein Auto, ~ um die Ecke fuhr** I saw a car driving around the corner; **ein Mädchen, ~ gut singen kann** a girl who can sing well; *s. a.* **der**[3], **die**[5]

da|sein[ALT] ['daː·zain] *vi irreg sein s.* **da I. 1**

Dasein <-s> ['daː·zain] *nt kein pl* (*Existenz*) existence; (*Anwesenheit*) presence

Daseinsberechtigung *f* right to exist

da|sitzen ['daː·zɪtsn̩] *vi irreg* to sit there

dasjenige <*gen:* dęsjenigen, *dat:* demjenigen, *akk:* dąsjenige, *pl:* diejenigen> ['das·jeː·nɪ·gə] *pron dem* ❶ *substantivisch* ■ **~, was ...** that which ... ❷ *adjektivisch* **~ Kind, das ...** the child that ...; *s. a.* **diejenige, derjenige**

dass[RR], **daß**[ALT] ['das] *konj* that; **ich habe gehört, ~ du Vater geworden bist** I heard [that] you became a father; **die Tatsache, ~ ...** the fact that ...

dasselbe <*gen:* dessęlben, *dat:* demsęlben, *akk:* dassęlbe, *pl:* dieselben> *pron dem* **~ Kleid** the same dress; *s. a.* **derselbe, dieselbe**

da|stehen ['daː·ʃteː·ən] *vi irreg* to stand there; **dumm ~** to stand there like an idiot ▶ WENDUNGEN: **besser/schlechter ~** to be in a better/worse position

Datei <-, -en> [da·'tai] *f* [data] file

Dateiname *m* filename

Daten ['daː·tn̩] *pl* ❶ (*Angaben*) data ❷ *pl von* **Datum**

Datenabruf *m* data retrieval

Datenaufbereitung *f* data processing

Datenbank <-banken> *f* database

Dateneingabe *f* data entry

Datenerfassung *f* data collection

Datenflut *f* flood of data

Datenformat *nt* data format

Datenhandschuh *m* data glove

Datenklau <-s> *m kein pl* (*fam*) data theft

Datennetz *nt* data network

Datenschutz *m* data [privacy] protection

Datenschutzbeauftragte(r) *f(m) dekl wie adj* controller for data protection

Datenschützer(in) <-s, -> *m(f)* (*fam*) data watchdog

Datensicherheit *f kein pl* data protection

Datensicherung *f* [data] backup

Datenträger *m* data medium

Datenübertragung *f* data transmission

Datenverarbeitung *f* data processing

datieren* [da·'tiː·rən] *vt, vi* to date

Dativ <-s, -e> ['daː·tiːf, *pl* 'daː·tiː·və] *m* dative [case]

Dattel <-, -n> ['da·tl̩, *pl* 'da·tl̩n] *f* date

Datum <-s, Daten> ['daː·tʊm, *pl* 'daː·tn̩] *nt* date; **welches ~ haben wir heute?** what's today's date?

Dauer <-> ['dau·ɐ] *f kein pl* duration; *eines Aufenthalts* length ▶ WENDUNGEN: **von kurzer ~ sein** to be short-lived; **auf die ~** in the long run; **diesen Lärm kann auf die ~ keiner ertragen** nobody can stand this noise for any length of time

Dauerarbeitslosigkeit *f* long-term unemployment

Dauerbeschäftigung *f* permanent employment

Dauerbetrieb *m kein pl* continuous operation

Dauererfolg *m* continuous success
Dauerfrost *m* long period of frost
dauerhaft **I.** *adj Beziehung* permanent; *Frieden, Wirkung* durable, lasting; **~er Schaden** lasting [*or* permanent] damage **II.** *adv* permanently
Dauerkarte *f* season ticket [*or* pass]
dauern ['dau·ɐn] *vi* ① (*anhalten*) to last; **der Film dauert 3 Stunden** the film is 3 hours long ② *impers* (*Zeit erfordern*) to take; **vier Stunden? das dauert mir zu lange** four hours? that's too long for me; **einen Augenblick, es wird nicht lange ~** just a moment, it won't take long
dauernd ['dau·ɐnt] **I.** *adj* constant **II.** *adv* constantly; **etw ~ tun** to keep [on] doing sth
Dauerstress^RR *m* continuous stress
Dauerthema *nt* permanent topic
Dauerwelle *f* perm
Dauerzustand *m* permanent state of affairs
Däumchen ['dɔym·çən] *nt* ▶WENDUNGEN: **~ drehen** (*fam*) to twiddle one's thumbs
Daumen <-s, -> ['dau·mən] *m* thumb; **am ~ lutschen** to suck one's thumb ▶WENDUNGEN: **jdm die ~ drücken** to keep one's fingers crossed [for sb]
Daune <-, -n> ['dau·nə] *f* down
Daunendecke *f* duvet
davon [da·'fɔn] *adv* ① (*räumlich*) **links/rechts ~** to the left/right of it/that/them; **etw ~ lösen** to loosen sth from it/that ② (*von dieser Sache*) **was hältst du ~?** what do you think of it/that/them?; **~ weiß ich nichts** I don't know anything about that; **das Gegenteil ~** the opposite of it/that; **die Hälfte ~** half of it/that/them; **~ essen/trinken** to eat/drink some of it/that; **etwas/nichts ~ haben** to have some/not have any of it
davon|fliegen *vi irreg sein* to fly away; *Vögel a.* to fly off
davon|gehen *vi irreg sein* to go [away]
davon|jagen **I.** *vt haben* (*verscheuchen*) ■**jdn ~** to drive sb away *sep; Kinder, Tiere* to chase sb away *sep* **II.** *vi sein* (*schnell wegfahren*) to speed off
davon|kommen *vi irreg sein* **mit dem Leben ~** to escape with one's life; **mit einem Schock ~** to come away with no more than a shock
davon|laufen *vi irreg sein* ■**jdm ~** ① (*weglaufen*) to run away from sb ② (*jdn abhängen*) to run ahead of sb ③ (*überraschend verlassen*) to run out on sb
davon|machen *vr* (*fam*) ■**sich** *akk* **~** to slip away
davon|schleichen *irreg* **I.** *vi sein* to slink away **II.** *vr haben* ■**sich** *akk* **~** to steal away
davon|stehlen *irreg vr* ■**sich** *akk* **~** to steal away
davon|tragen *vt irreg* ① (*wegtragen*) ■**jdn/etw ~** to take sb/sth away ② (*geh*) *Preis* to carry off; *Ruhm* to achieve; *Sieg* to score ③ **Verletzungen/Knochenbrüche ~** to suffer injury/broken bones
davor [da·'foːɐ̯, 'daː·foːɐ̯] *adv* ① (*räumlich*) in front [of it/that/them]; **~ musst du links abbiegen** you have to turn left before [you get to] it ② (*zeitlich*) before [it/that/them/etc.] ③ *mit Verben* **er hat Angst ~** he's afraid of it/that; **er hatte mich ~ gewarnt** he warned me about it/that
dazu [da·'tsuː, 'daː·tsuː] *adv* ① (*zu dem gehörend*) with it ② (*außerdem*) at the same time ③ (*zu diesem Ergebnis*) **wie konnte es nur ~ kommen?** how could that happen?; **~ reicht das Geld nicht** we/I don't have enough money for that ④ **im Gegensatz ~** in contrast to that; **im Vergleich ~** compared to that ⑤ (*zu dieser Sache*) **ich würde dir ~ raten** I would advise you to do that; **ich bin noch nicht ~ gekommen** I haven't gotten around to it/that yet; **es gehört viel Mut ~** that takes a lot of courage ⑥ (*dafür*) **ich bin ~ nicht bereit** I'm not prepared to do that; **~ ist es da** that's what it's there for ⑦ (*darüber*) **er hat sich noch nicht ~ geäußert** he hasn't commented on it/that yet; **was meinst du ~?** what do you think about it/that?
dazu|geben *vt irreg* to add
dazu|gehören* *vi* ① (*zu der Sache gehören*) to belong [to it/etc.] ② (*nicht wegzudenken sein*) be a part of it
dazugehörig [da·'tsuː·gə·høː·rɪç] *adj attr* to go with it/them *pred,* which goes/go with it/them *pred*
dazu|gesellen* *vr* ■**sich** *akk* **~** to join them/her/him/you/us/etc.
dazu|kommen *vi irreg sein* ① (*hinzukommen*) to arrive; (*zufällig*) to happen to arrive ② (*hinzugefügt werden*) to be added
dazu|lernen *vt* **einiges ~** to learn a few [new] things
dazu|rechnen *vt* to add on
dazu|setzen *vr* ■**sich** *akk* [**zu jdm**] **~** to sit down [at sb's table]; **kann ich mich ~?** do you mind if I join you?
dazu|tun *vt irreg* (*fam*) to add
Dazutun *nt* **ohne jds ~** without sb's intervention
dazwischen [da·'tsvɪ·ʃn̩] *adv* ① (*zwischen zwei Dingen*) [in] between; (*darunter*) among[st] them ② (*zeitlich*) in between
dazwischen|funken *vi* (*fam*) ■[**jdm**] **~** to mess sth up *sep* [for sb]
dazwischen|kommen *vi irreg sein* **wenn nichts dazwischenkommt!** if everything goes according to plan!; **leider ist** [**mir**] **etwas dazwischengekommen** I'm afraid something has come up
dazwischen|reden *vi* ■[**jdm**] **~** to interrupt [sb]
dazwischen|treten *vi irreg sein* to intervene
DDR <-> [deː·deː·'ʔɛr] *f* HIST *Abk von* **Deutsche Demokratische Republik:** ■**die ~** the GDR
Deal <-s, -s> [diːl] *m* deal

dealen ['diː·lən] *vi* (*sl*) [**mit Drogen** *dat*] ~ to deal [drugs]
Dealer(**in**) <-s, -> ['diː·lɐ] *m(f)* (*sl*) drug dealer
Debakel <-s, -> [de·'baː·kl̩] *nt* (*geh*) debacle; (*Sport*) shutout
Debatte <-, -n> [de·'ba·tə] *f* debate; (*schwächer*) discussion; **zur ~ stehen** to be under discussion; **das steht hier nicht zur ~** that's beside the point
debattieren* [de·ba·'tiː·rən] *vt* to debate; (*schwächer*) to discuss
Debüt <-s, -s> [de·'byː] *nt* debut
Deck <-[e]s, -s> ['dɛk] *nt* deck
Decke <-, -n> ['dɛ·kə] *f* ❶ (*Zimmerdecke*) ceiling ❷ (*Tischdecke*) tablecloth ❸ (*Wolldecke*) blanket; (*Bettdecke*) covers *pl* ▶ WENDUNGEN: **jdm fällt die ~ auf den Kopf** sb feels really cooped up; **an die ~ gehen** to go through the roof
Deckel <-s, -> ['dɛ·kl̩] *m* ❶ (*Verschluss*) lid; *von Glas, Schachtel a.* top ❷ (*Buchdeckel*) cover ▶ WENDUNGEN: **jdm eins auf den ~ geben** to slap sb upside the head
deckeln ['dɛ·kl̩n] *vt* ■**jdn ~** to take [*or* knock] sb down a peg [or two]
decken ['dɛ·kn̩] **I.** *vt* ❶ *Tisch* to set ❷ *Dach* to shingle ❸ (*etw verheimlichen*) ■**jdn ~** to cover up for sb; ■**etw ~** to cover up *sep* sth ❹ *Nachfrage* to meet; *Kosten* to cover **II.** *vi* **diese Farbe deckt besser** this paint covers better **III.** *vr* ■**sich** *akk* **~** *Aussagen* to correspond
Deckenbeleuchtung *f* ceiling lights *pl*
Deckmantel *m* ■**unter dem ~ einer S.** *gen* under the guise of sth
Deckname *m* code name
Deckung <-, -en> *f* ❶ (*Schutz*) cover; **jdm ~ geben** to give sb cover ❷ ÖKON **die ~ der Kosten** to cover the costs; **die ~ der Nachfrage** to meet the demand
Decoder <-s, -> [de·'koː·dɐ] *m* decoder
defekt [de·'fɛkt] *adj* faulty
Defekt <-[e]s, -e> [de·'fɛkt] *m* defect
defensiv [de·fɛn·'ziːf] **I.** *adj* defensive **II.** *adv* defensively
Defensive [de·fɛn·'ziː·və] *f* **in die ~ gehen** to go on the defensive
definieren* [de·fi·'niː·rən] *vt* to define
Definition <-, -en> [de·fi·ni·'tsi̯oːn] *f* definition
definitiv [de·fi·ni·'tiːf] **I.** *adj* (*genau*) definite; (*endgültig a.*) definitive **II.** *adv* (*genau*) definitely; (*endgültig a.*) definitively
Defizit <-s, -e> ['deː·fi·tsɪt] *nt* deficit
deformieren* [de·fɔr·'miː·rən] *vt* to deform
deftig ['dɛf·tɪç] *adj Mahlzeit* hearty; *Witz* crude
degenerieren* [de·ge·ne·'riː·rən] *vi* to degenerate
degradieren* [de·gra·'diː·rən] *vt* MIL to demote
dehnbar *adj* ❶ *Material* elastic ❷ *Begriff* flexible
dehnen ['deː·nən] *vt, vr* ■[**sich** *akk*] **~** to stretch
Deich <-[e]s, -e> ['daiç] *m* dike
deichseln ['daik·sl̩n] *vt* (*fam*) to wangle
dein ['dain] *pron poss, adjektivisch* your; **herzliche Grüße, ~e Anita/~ Paul** best wishes, love Anita/Paul
deine(**r, s**) ['dai·nə] *pron poss, substantivisch* yours; **diese Tasche ist ~** this bag is yours
deiner ['dainɐ] *pron pers gen von* **du**: **wir werden uns ~ erinnern** (*geh*) we will remember you
deinerseits ['dai·nɐ·'zaits] *adv* (*von dir aus*) on your part; (*auf deiner Seite*) for your part
deinesgleichen ['dai·nəs·'glai·çn̩] *pron inv* people like you; (*pej*) the likes of you; ■**du und ~** you and your kind
deinetwegen ['dai·nət·veː·gn̩] *adv* ❶ (*wegen dir*) because of you ❷ (*dir zuliebe*) for your sake
deinetwillen ['dai·nət·vɪ·lən] *adv* ■**um ~** for your sake
deins ['dains] *pron poss, substantivisch* yours; **welches Auto ist ~?** which car is yours?
Déjà-vu-Erlebnis [de·ʒa·'vyː-] *nt* déjà vu
Dekade <-, -n> [de·'kaː·də] *f* decade
dekadent [de·ka·'dɛnt] *adj* decadent
Dekadenz <-> [de·ka·'dɛnts] *f kein pl* decadence
Dekan(**in**) <-s, -e> [de·'kaːn] *m(f)* UNIV dean; REL deacon
deklarieren* [de·kla·'riː·rən] *vt* to declare
Deklination <-, -en> [de·kli·na·'tsi̯oːn] *f* LING declension
deklinieren* [de·kli·'niː·rən] *vt* to decline
dekodieren* [de·ko·'diː·rən] *vt* to decode
Dekolleté, Dekolletee[RR] <-s, -s> [de·kɔl·'teː] *nt* ❶ (*Körperpartie*) cleavage ❷ MODE low-cut neckline
Dekor <-s, -s *o* -e> [de·'koːɐ̯] *m o nt* pattern
Dekorateur(**in**) <-s, -e> [de·ko·ra·'tøːɐ̯] *m(f)* (*Schaufensterdekorateur*) window dresser
Dekoration <-, -en> [de·ko·ra·'tsi̯oːn] *f* decoration
dekorativ [de·ko·ra·'tiːf] **I.** *adj* decorative **II.** *adv* decoratively
dekorieren* [de·ko·'riː·rən] *vt* to decorate
Dekret <-[e]s, -e> [de·'kreːt] *nt* decree *form*
Delegation <-, -en> [de·le·ga·'tsi̯oːn] *f* delegation
delegieren* [de·le·'giː·rən] *vt* to delegate (**an** +*akk* to)
Delegierte(**r**) *f(m) dekl wie adj* delegate
Delfin[RR] <-s, -e> [dɛl·'fiːn] *m s.* **Delphin**
delikat [de·li·'kaːt] *adj* ❶ (*wohlschmeckend*) delicious ❷ (*heikel*) sensitive
Delikatesse <-, -n> [de·li·ka·'tɛ·sə] *f* delicacy
Delikatessengeschäft *nt* gourmet shop
Delikt <-[e]s, -e> [de·'lɪkt] *nt* (*Vergehen*) offense; (*Straftat*) crime
Delinquent(**in**) <-en, -en> [de·lɪŋ·'kvɛnt] *m(f)* (*geh*) offender
Delirium <-s, -rien> [de·'liː·ri̯·ʊm, *pl* de·'liː·ri̯·ən] *nt* delirium

Delle <-, -n> ['dɛ·lə] *f* dent
Delphin <-s, -e> [dɛl·'fiːn] *m* dolphin
dem ['deːm] **I.** *art def dat sing von* **der**[1], **das**[1]: **er gab ~ Kind das Geld** he gave the child the money [*or* the money to the child]; **ich werde es ~ Klaus sagen** (*fam*) I'll tell Klaus **II.** *pron dem dat sing von* **der**[2], **das**[2]: **das Fahrrad gehört ~ Mann/Kind** [**da**] the bike belongs to that man/child [[over] there] **III.** *pron rel dat sing von* **der**[3]: **der Freund, mit ~ ich mich gut verstehe** the [male] friend that I get along so well with; **der Hund, ~ er zu fressen gibt** the dog that he is feeding
Demagoge, **Demagogin** <-n, -n> [de·ma·'goː·gə, de·ma·'goː·gɪn] *m, f* demagogue
demagogisch [de·ma·'goː·gɪʃ] *adj* demagogic
demaskieren* [de·mas·'kiː·rən] *vt* to expose
Dementi <-s, -s> [de·'mɛn·ti] *nt* [official] denial
dementieren* [de·mɛn·'tiː·rən] *vt* to deny
dementsprechend ['deːm·ʔɛnt·'ʃprɛ·çn̩t] **I.** *adj* appropriate **II.** *adv* correspondingly; (*demnach*) accordingly; **sich** *akk* **~ äußern** to utter words to that effect; **~ bezahlt werden** to be paid commensurately *form*
demgegenüber ['deːm·geː·gn̩·ʔyːbɐ] *adv* in contrast
Demission <-, -en> [de·mɪ·'si̯oːn] *f* resignation
demnach ['deːm·naːx] *adv* therefore
demnächst [deːm·'nɛːçst] *adv* soon
Demo <-, -s> ['deː·mo] *f* (*fam*) demo
Demokrat(**in**) <-en, -en> [de·mo·'kraːt] *m(f)* democrat
Demokratie <-, -n> [de·mo·kra·'tiː, *pl* de·mo·kra·'tiː·ən] *f* democracy
demokratisch [de·mo·'kraː·tɪʃ] **I.** *adj* democratic **II.** *adv* democratically
demokratisieren* [de·mo·kra·ti·'ziː·rən] *vt* to democratize
Demokratisierung <-, -en> *f* democratization
demolieren* [de·mo·'liː·rən] *vt* *Auto* to wreck; *Gebäude* to demolish
Demonstrant(**in**) <-en, -en> [de·mɔn·'strant] *m(f)* demonstrator
Demonstration <-, -en> [de·mɔn·stra·'tsi̯oːn] *f* demonstration (**für** *+akk* in support of, **gegen** *+akk* against)
demonstrativ [de·mɔn·stra·'tiːf] **I.** *adj* demonstrative **II.** *adv* demonstratively
Demonstrativpronomen *nt* demonstrative pronoun
demonstrieren* [de·mɔn·'striː·rən] *vi, vt* to demonstrate (**für** *+akk* in support of, **gegen** *+akk* against)
demontieren* [de·mɔn·'tiː·rən] *vt* to dismantle; *Reifen* to take off *sep*
demoralisieren* [de·mo·ra·li·'ziː·rən] *vt* to demoralize
demotiviert ['deː·mo·ti·viːrt] *adj* demotivated
Demut <-> ['deː·muːt] *f kein pl* humility (**gegenüber** *+dat* before)
demütig ['deː·myː·tɪç] **I.** *adj* humble **II.** *adv* humbly
demütigen ['deː·myː·tɪ·gn̩] *vt* to humiliate
Demütigung <-, -en> *f* humiliation
den ['deːn] **I.** *art def* ❶ *akk sing von* **der**[1]: **er kennt ~ Mann** he knows the man; **grüße bitte ~ Klaus von mir** (*fam*) please say hi to Klaus for me [*or* give Klaus my regards] ❷ *dat pl von* **die**[2]: **sie hilft ~ Armen** she helps the poor **II.** *pron dem akk sing von* **der**[2]: **~ Mann da** [**drüben**] that man [over] there **III.** *pron rel akk sing von* **der**[3]: **der Mann, ~ ich gesehen habe** the man [that] I saw; **der Hund, ~ er füttert** the dog [that] he is feeding
denen ['deː·nən] *pron rel dat pl von* **die**[4]: **Menschen, ~ ich vertraue** people [whom] I trust; **Menschen, ~ ich Geld gegeben habe** people [that] I gave money to; **Geschichten, ~ sie zuhören** stories [that] they listen to
Den Haag <-s> [den 'haːk] *nt* The Hague
Denkanstoß *m* **jdm einen ~ geben** to give sb food for thought
Denkaufgabe *f* [brain]teaser
denkbar **I.** *adj* imaginable, conceivable **II.** *adv* **das ~ beste/schlechteste Wetter** the best/worst possible weather
Denkblockade *f* PSYCH mental block
denken <dachte, gedacht> ['dɛŋ·kn̩] *vi, vt* ❶ (*überlegen*) to think (**an** *+akk* of); **langsam/schnell ~** to think slowly/quickly ❷ (*meinen, glauben*) to think; **ich denke nicht** I don't think so; **wer hätte das** [**von ihr**] **gedacht!** who'd have expected that/it [from her]? ❸ (*urteilen*) to think (**über** *+akk* about); **wie ~ Sie darüber?** what's your view [on it/that]?; **ich denke genauso darüber** that's exactly what I think ❹ (*sich erinnern*) **solange ich ~ kann** [for] as long as I can remember; **die wird noch an mich ~!** she won't forget me in a hurry! ❺ ■ **für jdn/etw gedacht sein** to be meant for sb/sth ❻ (*beabsichtigen*) **ich habe mir nichts Böses dabei gedacht**[**, als ...**] I meant no harm [when ...] ▶ WENDUNGEN: **jdm zu ~ geben** to give sb food for thought; **das gab mir zu ~** that made me think
Denker(**in**) <-s, -> *m(f)* thinker
denkfaul *adj* [mentally] lazy
Denkfehler *m* error in one's/the logic
Denkmal <-s, Denkmäler> ['dɛŋk·maːl, *pl* 'dɛŋk·mɛː·lɐ] *nt* monument (**für** *+akk* to); **jdm ein ~ setzen** to erect a memorial/statue for sb
Denkmalschutz *m* protection of historical monuments; **unter ~ stehen** to be designated as a historical landmark
Denkpause *f* pause for thought
Denkweise *f* way of thinking
denkwürdig *adj* memorable
Denkzettel *m* (*fam*) **jdm einen ~ verpassen** to give sb a warning [he/she/etc. won't forget in a hurry]
denn ['dɛn] *konj* ❶ (*weil*) because; **~ sonst** otherwise ❷ ■ **es sei ~, [dass]** ... unless ... ❸ **kräftiger/schöner ~ je** stronger/more

beautiful than ever

dennoch ['dɛ·nɔx] *adv* still, nonetheless *form*

Denunziant(in) <-en, -en> [de·nʊn·'tsi̯·ant] *m(f)* informer

denunzieren* [de·nʊn·'tsiː·rən] *vt* to denounce

Deo <-s, -s> ['deːo] *nt* (*fam*), **Deodorant** <-s, -s *o* -e> [deʔo·do·'rant] *nt* deodorant

Deoroller *m* roll-on [deodorant]

Deospray *nt o m* deodorant spray

deplatziert[RR], **deplaziert**[ALT] [de·pla·'tsiːɐ̯t] *adj* misplaced

Deponie <-, -n> [de·po·'niː, *pl* de·po·'niː·ən] *f* disposal site

deponieren* [de·po·'niː·rən] *vt* to deposit

deportieren* [de·pɔr·'tiː·rən] *vt* to deport

Depot <-s, -s> [de·'poː] *nt* ① (*Lager*) depot ② (*für Straßenbahnen, Omnibusse*) [streetcar/bus] depot ③ SCHWEIZ (*Flaschenpfand*) deposit

Depp <-en *o* -s, -e[n]> ['dɛp] *m* SÜDD, ÖSTERR, SCHWEIZ (*fam*) idiot

Depression <-, -en> [de·prɛ·'si̯oːn] *f* PSYCH, ÖKON depression

depressiv [de·prɛ·'siːf] **I.** *adj* depressive; (*deprimiert*) depressed **II.** *adv* ~ **gestimmt/veranlagt** depressed/prone to depression

deprimieren* [de·pri·'miː·rən] *vt* to depress, to be depressing

der[1] <*gen:* des, *dat:* dem, *akk:* den, *pl:* die> ['deːɐ̯] *art def, sing m* the; ~ **Nachbar/Hengst/Käse** the neighbor/stallion/cheese; ~ **Papa hat's mir erzählt** (*fam*) dad told me; ~ **Andreas lässt dich grüßen** (*fam*) Andreas says hi [*or* sends his love]; *s. a.* **das**[1], **die**[1]

der[2] <*gen:* dessen, *dat:* dem, *akk:* den, *pl:* die> ['deːɐ̯] *pron dem, sing m* that; ~ **Mann/Hengst/Stuhl** [**da**] that man/stallion/chair [[over] there]; ~ **mit den roten Haaren** the guy/man/one with the red hair; **wo ist dein Bruder? – ~ kommt gleich** (*fam*) where's your brother? — he'll be here soon; *s. a.* **das**[2], **die**[3]

der[3] <*gen:* dessen, *dat:* dem, *akk:* den, *pl:* die> ['deːɐ̯] *pron rel, sing m* that; (*Person a.*) who, whom *form;* (*Gegenstand, Tier a.*) which; **der Mann, ~ es eilig hatte** the man who [*or* that] was in a hurry; **ein Film, ~ gut ankommt** a highly-acclaimed film; **ein Zahn, ~ wackelt** a tooth that is loose; *s. a.* **das**[3], **die**[5]

der[4] ['deːɐ̯] **I.** *art def* ① *gen sing von* **die**[1]: **die Augen ~ Katze** the eyes of the cat, the cat's eyes ② *dat sing von* **die**[1]: **er half ~ Frau** he helped the woman; **an ~ Decke hängen** to hang from the ceiling; **ich werde es ~ Anne sagen** (*fam*) I'll tell Anne ③ *gen pl von* **die**[2]: **die Wünsche ~ Männer/Frauen/Kinder** the men's/women's/children's wishes; **das Ende ~ Ferien** the end of vacation **II.** *pron dem dat sing von* **die**[3]: **das Fahrrad gehört ~ Frau** [**da**] the bike belongs to that woman [over there] **III.** *pron rel dat sing von* **die**[5]: **die Freundin, mit ~ ich mich gut verstehe** my [girl]friend that I get along so well with; **die Katze, ~ er zu fressen gibt** the cat [that] he is feeding; **die Hitze, unter ~ sie leiden** the heat [that] they're suffering from

derart ['deːɐ̯·ʔaːɐ̯t] *adv* so, such; ~ **ekelhaft/heiß sein, dass ...** to be so disgusting/hot that ...; **sie ist eine ~ unzuverlässige Frau, dass ...** she is such an unreliable woman that ...

derartig ['deːɐ̯·ʔaːɐ̯·tɪç] **I.** *adj* such; [**etwas**] **D~es habe ich noch nie gesehen** I've never seen anything like it **II.** *adv* such; ~ **schreien, dass ...** to scream so much [*or* loudly] that ...

derb ['dɛrp] **I.** *adj* ① (*grob*) coarse; *Manieren* rough; *Ausdrucksweise, Witz* crude ② (*fest*) *Material, Schuhe* strong **II.** *adv* **jdn ~ anfassen** to handle sb roughly; **sich** *akk* **~ ausdrücken** to be crude

deren ['deː·rən] **I.** *pron dem* ① *gen sing von* **die**[3]: **die Tochter und ~ Freundin** my daughter and her [girl]friend ② *gen pl von* **die**[4]: **meine Schwestern und ~ Kinder** my sisters and their children **II.** *pron rel* ① *gen sing von* **die**[3] whose; *auf eine Sache bezogen a.* of which; **eine Frau, ~ Namen ich nicht weiß** a woman whose name I do not know; **die Überschwemmung, ~ Folgen schrecklich waren** the flooding, the consequences of which were horrible ② *gen pl von* **die**[6] whose; *auf Sachen bezogen a.* of which; **Freunde, ~ Eltern ich nicht mag** friends whose parents I do not like; **Autos, ~ Reifen abgefahren sind** cars that have worn tires

derer ['deː·rɐ] *pron dem gen pl von* **die**[4]: **die Zahl ~, die einsam sind ...** the number of those who are lonely ...

dergleichen [deːɐ̯·'glai·çn̩] *pron dem* ① *adjektivisch* such, like that *pred,* of that kind *pred* ② *substantivisch* that sort of thing; **nichts ~** nothing like it; **ich will nichts ~ hören!** I'm not interested in hearing any of that/it

derjenige <*gen:* desjenigen, *dat:* demjenigen, *akk:* denjenigen, *pl:* diejenigen> ['deːɐ̯·jeː·nɪ·gə] *pron dem* ① *substantivisch* ■ **~, der ...** *auf eine Person bezogen* the person who ..., whoever ...; *auf eine Sache bezogen* the one that ... ② *adjektivisch* that; **~ Mann, der ...** the [*or* that] man who ...; *s. a.* **dasjenige, diejenige**

derlei ['deːɐ̯·lai] *pron* such, like that *pred*

dermaßen ['deːɐ̯·maːsn̩] *adv* **eine ~ lächerliche Frage** such a ridiculous question; **jdn ~ unter Druck setzen, dass ...** to put sb under so much pressure that ...

derselbe <*gen:* desselben, *dat:* demselben, *akk:* denselben, *pl:* dieselben> [deːɐ̯·'zɛlbə] *pron dem* ~ **Pulli** the same sweater; *s. a.* **dasselbe, dieselbe**

derweil [deːɐ̯·'vail] *adv* meanwhile

derzeit ['deːɐ̯·tsait] *adv* at present

derzeitig ['deːɐ̯·tsai·tɪç] *adj attr* present; (*aktu-*

ell a.) current

des ['dɛs] *art def gen sing von* **der**[1], **das**[1]: **das Aussehen ~ Kindes/Mannes** the child's/man's appearance; **ein Zeichen ~ Unbehagens** a sign of uneasiness

Desaster <-s, -> [de·'zas·tɐ] *nt* disaster

Deserteur(in) <-s, -e> [de·zɛr·'tøːɐ] *m(f)* deserter

desertieren* [de·zɛr·'tiː·rən] *vi sein* ■[**von etw** *dat*] ~ to desert [sth]

desgleichen [dɛs·'glai·çn̩] *adv* likewise

deshalb ['dɛs·'halp] *adv* ❶ (*daher*) therefore ❷ (*aus dem Grunde*) because of it; ~ **frage ich ja** that's why I'm asking; **also ~!** [so] that's why!

Design <-s, -s> [di·'zain] *nt* design

Designer(in) <-s, -> [di·'zai·nɐ] *m(f)* designer

Designerdroge *f* designer drug

Designermode *f* designer fashion

Desinfektion <-, -en> [dɛs·ʔɪn·fɛk·'tsi̯oːn] *f* disinfection

Desinfektionsmittel *nt* disinfectant; (*für Wunden a.*) antiseptic

desinfizieren* [dɛs·ʔɪn·fi·'tsiː·rən] *vt* to disinfect

Desinteresse ['dɛs·ʔɪn·tə·rɛsə] *nt kein pl* indifference

desinteressiert ['dɛs·ʔɪn·tə·rɛ·siːɐ̯t] *adj* indifferent

desorientiert [dɛs·ʔɔri̯·ɛn·'tiːɐ̯t, dezɔ-] *adj* disoriented

Desorientierung [dɛs·ʔɔ-, dez·ɔ-] *f* disorientation

Despot(in) <-en, -en> [dɛs·'poːt] *m(f)* despot

despotisch [dɛs·'poː·tɪʃ] **I.** *adj* despotic **II.** *adv* despotically

dessen ['dɛ·sn̩] **I.** *pron dem gen sing von* **der**[2], **das**[2]: **ein Freund und ~ Schwester** a [male] friend and his sister; **ein Buch und ~ Inhalt** a book and its contents **II.** *pron rel gen von* **der**[3], **das**[3] whose; (*von Sachen a.*) of which; **ein Junge, ~ Name ich nicht weiß** a boy whose name I do not know; **ein Buch, ~ Seiten verkleckst sind** a book that has stained pages

Dessert <-s, -s> [dɛ·'seːɐ, dɛ·'sɛːɐ] *nt* dessert

Dessous <-, -> [dɛ·'suː, *pl* dɛ·'suːs] *nt meist pl* undergarments, underwear

destabilisieren [de·sta·bi·li·'ziː·rən] *vt* to destabilize

destillieren* [dɛs·tɪ·'liː·rən] *vt* to distill

desto ['dɛsto] *konj* **je einfacher ~ besser** the simpler the better; **~ eher** the earlier; **~ schlimmer** so much the worse

destruktiv [des·trʊk·'tiːf] *adj* destructive

deswegen ['dɛs·'veː·gn̩] *adv s.* **deshalb**

Detail <-s, -s> [de·'tai, de·'taːj] *nt* detail; **im ~** in detail

detailliert [de·ta·'jiːɐt] **I.** *adj* detailed **II.** *adv* in detail

Detektei <-, -en> [de·tɛk·'tai] *f* [private] detective agency

Detektiv(in) <-s, -e> [de·tɛk·'tiːf, *pl* de·tɛk·'tiː·və] *m(f)* (*Privatdetektiv*) private investigator

Detektivroman *m* detective novel

Detonation <-, -en> [de·to·na·'tsi̯oːn] *f* explosion

detonieren* [de·to·'niː·rən] *vi sein* to detonate

Deut ['dɔyt] *m* [**um**] **keinen ~ besser sein** to be not the least bit better

deuten ['dɔy·tn̩] **I.** *vt* to interpret; **die Zukunft ~** to read the future; **etw falsch ~** to misinterpret sth **II.** *vi* [**mit dem Finger**] **auf jdn/etw ~** to point [one's finger] at sb/sth

deutlich ['dɔyt·lɪç] **I.** *adj* clear; *Umrisse* distinct; **das war ~!** that was very clear! **II.** *adv* ❶ (*klar*) clearly; **sich** *akk* **~ ausdrücken** to make oneself clear; **~ fühlen, dass ...** to have the distinct feeling that ... ❷ (*spürbar*) **~ besser/wärmer** clearly better/warmer

Deutlichkeit <-> *f kein pl* clarity; [**jdm**] **etw in aller ~ sagen** to make sth perfectly clear [to sb]

deutsch ['dɔytʃ] *adj* ❶ (*Deutschland betreffend*) German; **~er Abstammung sein** to be of German origin; **die ~e Sprache** German, the German language; **die ~e Staatsbürgerschaft besitzen** [*o* **haben**] to have German citizenship, to be a German citizen; **das ~e Volk** [the] Germans, [the] German people; **die ~e Wiedervereinigung** ZIEL...: [the] **German Reunification** the reunification of Germany; **typisch ~ sein** to be typically German ❷ LING German; **die ~e Schweiz** German-speaking Switzerland, the German-speaking part of Switzerland; **~ sprechen** [**können**] to speak German; **etw ~ aussprechen** to pronounce sth with a German accent ▶ WENDUNGEN: **mit jdm ~ reden** (*fam*) to be blunt with sb

Deutsch ['dɔytʃ] *nt dekl wie adj* ❶ LING German; **können Sie ~?** do you speak/understand German?; **er spricht akzentfrei ~** he speaks German without an accent; **sie spricht fließend ~** she speaks German fluently [*or* fluent German]; **~ lernen/sprechen** to learn/speak German; **~ verstehen/kein ~ verstehen** to understand/not understand [a word of [*or* any]] German; ■**auf ~** in German; **etw auf ~ sagen** to say sth in German; ■**in ~** in German; **in ~ abgefasst sein** (*geh*) to be written in German; **etw in ~ schreiben** to write sth in German; ■**zu ~** in German ❷ (*Fach*) German; **~ unterrichten** to teach German ▶ WENDUNGEN: **auf gut ~** [**gesagt**] (*fam*) in plain English

Deutsche(r) *f(m) dekl wie adj* German; **er hat eine ~ geheiratet** he married a German [woman]; ■**die ~n** the Germans; **~ sein** to be German, to be from Germany

Deutschland <-s> ['dɔytʃ·lant] *nt* Germany; **aus ~ kommen** to come from Germany; **in ~ leben** to live in Germany

deutschsprachig ['dɔytʃ·ʃpraː·xɪç] *adj* ❶ (*Deutsch sprechend*) German-speaking *attr*

D

❷ (*in deutscher Sprache*) German[-language] *attr*
deutschstämmig *adj* of German origin *pred*
Deutung <-, -en> ['dɔy·tʊŋ] *f* interpretation
Devise <-, -n> [de·'viː·zə] *f* motto
Dez. *Abk von* **Dezember** Dec.
Dezember <-s, -> [de·'tsɛm·bɐ] *m* December; *s. a.* **Februar**

D

dezent [de·'tsɛnt] **I.** *adj* discreet; *Farbe* modest, subdued **II.** *adv* discreetly
dezentral [de·tsɛn·'traːl] *adj* decentralized
dezentralisieren* [de·tsɛn·tra·li·'ziː·rən] *vt* to decentralize
dezimieren* [de·tsi·'miː·rən] *vt* to decimate
d. h. *Abk von* **das heißt** i.e.
Dia <-s, -s> ['diːa] *nt* slide
Diabetes <-> [dia·'beː·tɛs] *m kein pl* diabetes
Diabetiker(in) <-s, -> [dia·'beː·ti·kɐ] *m(f)* diabetic
diabolisch [dia·'boː·lɪʃ] (*geh*) **I.** *adj* diabolical **II.** *adv* diabolically
Diagnose <-, -n> [dia·'gnoː·zə] *f* diagnosis
diagnostizieren* [dia·gnɔs·ti·'tsiː·rən] *vt* to diagnose
diagonal [dia·go·'naːl] *adj* diagonal
Diagonale <-, -n> [dia·go·'naː·lə] *f* diagonal [line]
Diagramm <-s, -e> [dia·'gram] *nt* diagram
Diakon(in) <-s *o* -en, -e[n]> [dia·'koːn] *m(f)* deacon
Dialekt <-[e]s, -e> [dia·'lɛkt] *m* dialect
dialektal [dia·lɛk·'taːl] *adj* dialectal
Dialog <-[e]s, -e> [dia·'loːk, *pl* dia·'loː·gə] *m* dialogue
Diamant <-en, -en> [dia·'mant] *f* diamond
Diaprojektor *m* slide projector
Diät <-, -en> [di·'ɛːt] *f* diet; **~ halten** to keep to a diet; **auf ~ sein** (*fam*) to be on a diet; **jdn auf ~ setzen** (*fam*) to put sb on a diet
diätetisch [diɛ·'teː·tɪʃ] *adj* dietetic
Diätkur *f* diet therapy
Diavortrag *nt* slide show
dich ['dɪç] **I.** *pron pers akk von* **du** you **II.** *pron refl* yourself; **du solltest ~ da raushalten** you should keep out of that/this; **wie fühlst du ~?** how do you feel?
dicht ['dɪçt] **I.** *adj* ❶ (*eng beieinander*) dense; *Haar* thick ❷ (*undurchdringlich*) dense; *Verkehr* heavy ❸ (*wasserdicht*) watertight; **die Fenster sind wieder ~** [now] the windows are sealed again ▶WENDUNGEN: **nicht ganz ~ sein** (*pej fam*) to be out of one's mind *pej fam* **II.** *adv* ❶ (*örtlich*) closely; **~ vor jdm** just [*or* directly] in front of sb; **~ beieinander/hintereinander** close together; **~ gedrängt** squeezed together ❷ (*zeitlich*) **~ bevorstehen** to be coming up soon ❸ (*sehr stark*) densely
Dichte <-, -n> ['dɪç·tə] *f* density
dichten¹ ['dɪç·tn̩] **I.** *vt* **ein Sonett ~** to write a sonnet **II.** *vi* (*Gedichte verfassen*) to write poetry
dichten² ['dɪç·tn̩] *vt* (*dicht machen*) to seal
Dichter(in) <-s, -> ['dɪç·tɐ] *m(f)* poet
dichterisch ['dɪç·tə·rɪʃ] **I.** *adj* poetic[al] **II.** *adv* poetically
dichtgedrängt *adj attr s.* **dicht II 1**
dicht|halten ['dɪçt·haltn̩] *vi irreg* (*sl*) to keep one's mouth shut
dicht|machen *vt, vi* (*fam*) to close [up shop], to go out of business
Dichtung <-, -en> ['dɪç·tʊŋ] *f* ❶ *kein pl* (*Dichtkunst*) poetry ❷ TECH seal[ing]
dick ['dɪk] **I.** *adj* ❶ (*von großem Umfang*) fat; *Backen* chubby; *Stamm, Buch, Kleidung* thick; **etwa fünf Meter ~** about fifteen feet thick ❷ (*geschwollen*) swollen; *Beule* big ❸ (*dickflüssig*) thick ❹ (*fam*) *Freunde* close **II.** *adv* ❶ (*warm*) **sich** *akk* **~ anziehen** to dress warmly ❷ (*reichlich*) thickly; **etw 10 cm ~ auftragen** *Farbe* to apply a 4-inch coat of sth; *Butter* to spread sth 4-inches thick ❸ (*fam*) **mit jdm ~ befreundet sein** to be good friends with sb ▶WENDUNGEN: **~ auftragen** (*pej fam*) to lay it on thick *sl;* **jdn/etw ~ [e] haben** (*fam*) to be sick of sb/sth
dickbäuchig *adj* potbellied
Dickdarm *m* large intestine
Dicke <-, -n> ['dɪ·kə] *f* thickness
dickfellig *adj* (*pej fam*) thick-skinned
dickflüssig *adj* thick, viscous
Dickhäuter <-s, -> *m* ❶ (*Tier*) pachyderm ❷ (*fig*) **ein ~ sein** to have a thick skin
Dickicht <-[e]s, -e> ['dɪ·kɪçt] *nt* thicket
Dickkopf *m* (*fam*) **ein ~ sein/einen ~ haben** to be stubborn; **seinen ~ durchsetzen** to get one's way
dickköpfig *adj* stubborn, obstinate
dicklich *adj* (*etwas dick*) chubby
Dickschädel *m* (*fam*) *s.* **Dickkopf**
Dickwanst <-es, -wänste> *m* (*pej fam*) fatso, butterball
didaktisch [di·'dak·tɪʃ] **I.** *adj* didactic **II.** *adv* didactically
die¹ <*gen:* der, *dat:* der, *akk:* die, *pl:* die> ['diː] *art def, sing fem* the; **~ Tochter/Stute/Theorie** the daughter/mare/theory; **~ Mama hat's mir erzählt** (*fam*) mom told me; **ich bin ~ Susi** (*fam*) I'm Susi; *s. a.* **das¹, der¹**
die² <*gen:* der, *dat:* den, *akk:* die> ['diː] *art def, pl* **~ Männer/Mütter/Pferde** the men/mothers/horses; *s. a.* **das¹, der¹**
die³ <*gen:* deren, *dat:* der, *akk:* die, *pl:* die> ['diː] *pron dem, sing fem* that; **~ Frau/Stute/Tasche** [**da**] that woman/mare/bag [[over] there]; **~ mit den roten Haaren** the girl/woman/one with the red hair; **wo ist deine Schwester? – ~ kommt gleich** (*fam*) where's your sister? — she'll be here soon; *s. a.* **das², der²**
die⁴ <*gen:* deren/derer, *dat:* denen, *akk:* die> ['diː] *pron dem, pl* **~ Männer/Frauen/Stühle** [**da**] the [*or* those] men/women/chairs [over there]; **~ mit den roten Haaren** the girls/women/ones with the red hair; **~ waren es!** it was them!; **welche Bücher? ~ da? oder ~ hier?** which books? those [over there]?

or these [over here]?; *s. a.* **das[2], der[2]**

die[5] <*gen:* deren, *dat:* der, *akk:* die> ['diː] *pron rel, sing fem* that; (*Person a.*) who, whom *form;* (*Gegenstand, Tier a.*) which; **die Frau, ~ da drüben läuft** the woman walking along over there; **die Katze, ~ nicht fressen mag** the cat that doesn't want to eat; **eine Geschichte, ~ Millionen gelesen haben** a story [that has been] read by millions; *s. a.* **das[3], der[3]**

die[6] <*gen:* deren, *dat:* denen, *akk:* die> ['diː] *pron rel, pl* that; (*Person a.*) who, whom *form;* (*Gegenstand, Tier a.*) which; **ich sah zwei Autos, ~ um die Ecke fuhren** I saw two cars driving around the corner; **die Abgeordneten, ~ dagegenstimmten** the members of Congress who voted against it; *s. a.* **das[3], der[3]**

Dieb(in) <-[e]s, -e> ['diːp, *pl* 'diː·bə] *m(f)* thief

diebisch ['diː·bɪʃ] **I.** *adj* thieving **II.** *adv* ▶ WENDUNGEN: **sich** *akk* **~ [über etw** *akk*] **freuen** to take malicious pleasure [in sth]

Diebstahl <-[e]s, -stähle> ['diːp·ʃtaːl, *pl* -ʃtɛːlə] *m* theft

Diebstahlsicherung *f* antitheft device

diejenige <*gen:* derjenigen, *dat:* derjenigen, *akk:* diejenige, *pl:* diejenigen> ['diː·jeː·nɪ·gə] *pron dem* ❶ *substantivisch* ■ **~, die ...** *auf eine Person bezogen* the person who ...; *auf eine Sache bezogen* the one that ...; ■ **~n, die ...** *auf Personen bezogen* the people who ..., whoever ...; *auf Gegenstände bezogen* the ones that ... ❷ *adjektivisch* that; **~ Frau, die ...** the [*or* that] woman who ...; *s. a.* **dasjenige, derjenige**

Diele <-, -n> ['diː·lə] *f* ❶ (*Vorraum*) foyer, hall ❷ (*Bodenbrett*) floorboard

dienen ['diː·nən] *vi* ❶ (*nützlich sein*) ■ **etw** *dat* **~** to be [important] for sth; **einem guten Zweck ~** to be for a good cause ❷ (*behilflich sein*) **womit kann ich Ihnen ~?** how can I help you?; **jdm ist mit etw** *dat* **nicht/kaum gedient** sth is of no/little use to sb ❸ (*verwendet werden*) ■ **[jdm] als etw ~** to serve [sb] as sth

Diener[1] <-s, -> ['diː·nɐ] *m* (*fam: Verbeugung*) bow

Diener(in)[2] <-s, -> ['diː·nɐ] *m(f)* servant

dienlich *adj* useful

Dienst <-[e]s, -e> ['diːnst] *m* ❶ *kein pl* (*berufliche Tätigkeit*) work; **~ haben** to be on duty; **im ~** at work ❷ *kein pl* (*Arbeitszeit*) **während/nach dem ~** during/outside working hours ❸ *kein pl* (*Amt*) **diplomatischer/öffentlicher ~** diplomatic/civil service ❹ *kein pl* (*Bereitschaftsdienst*) **~ haben** to be on call; **der ~ habende Arzt** the doctor on duty ❺ (*Service*) service; **~ am Kunden** customer service ▶ WENDUNGEN: **jdm einen guten/schlechten ~ erweisen** to do sb a service/disservice

Dienstag ['diːns·taːk] *m* Tuesday; **wir haben heute ~** today's Tuesday; **treffen wir uns ~?** would you like to get together on Tuesday?; **in der Nacht [von Montag] auf [*o* zu] ~** [on] Monday night, in the early hours of Tuesday morning; **~ in acht Tagen** a week from Tuesday; **~ vor acht Tagen** a week ago Tuesday, the Tuesday before last; **diesen [*o* an diesem] ~** this Tuesday; **eines ~s** one Tuesday; **den ganzen ~ über** all day Tuesday; **jeden ~** every Tuesday; **letzten [*o* vorigen] ~** last Tuesday; **seit letzten [*o* letztem] ~** since last Tuesday; **[am] nächsten ~** next Tuesday; **ab nächsten [*o* nächstem] ~** starting next Tuesday, from next Tuesday on; **am ~** on Tuesday; **[am] ~ früh** early Tuesday [morning]; **an ~en** on Tuesdays; **an einem ~** one [*or* on a] Tuesday; **am ~, den 4. März** on Tuesday, March 4th [*or* the 4th of March]

dienstagabends[RR] *adv* [on] Tuesday evenings

dienstags ['diːns·taːks] *adv* [on] Tuesdays; **~ abends/nachmittags/vormittags** [on] Tuesday evenings/afternoons/mornings

Dienstausweis *m* official identity card

Dienstbote, -botin *m, f* (*veraltend*) [domestic] servant

Diensteifer *m* diligence

dienstfrei *adj* **~er Tag** day off

Dienstgeheimnis *nt* official secret

diensthabend *adj attr s.* **Dienst 4**

Dienstleistung *f meist pl* services *npl*

Dienstleistungsberuf *m* job in the service industry

Dienstleistungsgesellschaft *f* ÖKON service economy

Dienstleistungsgewerbe *nt,* **Dienstleistungsindustrie** *f* service industry sector

dienstlich **I.** *adj* official **II.** *adv* **~ unterwegs sein** to be away on business

Dienstmädchen *nt* (*veraltend*) maid

Dienstplan *m* [work] schedule

Dienstreise *f* business trip

Dienstschluss[RR] *m* closing time, time to go home *fam*

Dienststelle *f* office

Dienststunden *pl* office hours *npl*

Dienstwagen *m* company car

Dienstzeit *f* ❶ ADMIN tenure ❷ (*Arbeitszeit*) working hours *pl*

dies ['diːs] *pron dem* **~ ist mein kleiner Bruder** this is my younger brother; **~ sind meine Eltern** these are my parents; **~ und das** this and that

diesbezüglich ['diːs·bə·tsyːk·lɪç] **I.** *adj* relating to this **II.** *adv* with respect to this

diese(r, s) ['diː·zə] *pron dem* ❶ *adjektivisch* this *sing,* these *pl* ❷ this one *sing,* these *pl;* **~ und jenes** this and that

Diesel[1] <-s> ['diː·zl̩] *nt kein pl* (*fam*) diesel

Diesel[2] <-s, -> ['diː·zl̩] *m* (*fam*) ❶ (*Wagen mit Dieselmotor*) diesel ❷ *s.* **Dieselmotor**

dieselbe <*gen:* derselben, *dat:* derselben, *akk:* dieselbe, *pl:* dieselben> *pron dem* **~ Frau** the same woman; **~n Männer** the same men; *s. a.* **dasselbe, derselbe**

Dieselmotor *m* diesel engine

D

Dieselöl *nt* diesel

dieser ['diː·zɐ], **dieses** ['diː·zəs] *pron dem s.* **diese(r, s)**

diesig ['diː·zɪç] *adj* misty

diesjährig ['diːs·jɛːrɪç] *adj attr* this year's

diesmal ['diːs·maːl] *adv* this time

diesseits ['diːs·zaits] *präp +gen* this side of

Dietrich <-s, -e> ['diːt·rɪç] *m* picklock

Differenz <-, -en> [dɪfə·'rɛnts] *f* ① (*Unterschied*) difference ② *meist pl* (*Meinungsverschiedenheit*) difference of opinion

differenzieren* [dɪfə·rɛn·'tsiː·rən] *vi* ■ **[bei etw** *dat***]** ~ to discriminate [in doing sth]

differenziert **I.** *adj* discriminating **II.** *adv* **etw ~ beurteilen** to differentiate in making judgments

digital [di·gi·'taːl] **I.** *adj* digital **II.** *adv* digitally

digitalisieren* [di·gi·ta·li·'ziː·rən] *vt* to digitize

Digitalkamera *f* digital camera

Diktator, **Diktatorin** <-s, -toren> [dɪk·'taː·toːɐ̯, dɪk·ta·'toː·rɪn, *pl* -'toː·rən] *m, f* despot, dictator

diktatorisch [dɪk·ta·'toː·rɪʃ] **I.** *adj* dictatorial **II.** *adv* like a dictator

Diktatur <-, -en> [dɪk·ta·'tuːɐ̯] *f* dictatorship

diktieren* [dɪk·'tiː·rən] *vt* to dictate

Diktiergerät *nt* Dictaphone®

Dilettant(in) <-en, -en> [di·lɛ·'tant] *m(f)* dilettante

dilettantisch [di·lɛ·'tan·tɪʃ] **I.** *adj* amateurish **II.** *adv* amateurishly

Dill <-s, -e> ['dɪl] *m* dill

Dimension <-, -en> [di·mɛn·'zi̯oːn] *f* dimension

Ding <-[e]s, -e *o fam* -er> ['dɪŋ] *nt* ① (*Gegenstand*) thing ② (*fam: Mädchen*) **ein junges ~/junge ~er** a young thing/young things ③ (*Angelegenheit*) matters *pl;* **so wie die ~e liegen** as things stand [at the moment] ▶ WENDUNGEN: **krumme ~er drehen** (*fam*) to pull a fast one *sl;* **das ist nicht so ganz mein ~** (*fam*) that's not really my thing; **das ist [ja] ein ~!** (*fam*) wow!, get a load of that! *sl;* **über den ~en stehen** to be above it all

dingfest *adj* **jdn ~ machen** to put sb behind bars

Dings <-> ['dɪŋs] *nt kein pl* (*fam*), **Dingsbums** <-> ['dɪŋs·bʊms] *nt kein pl* (*fam*), **Dingsda** <-> ['dɪŋs·daː] *nt kein pl* (*Sache*) whatchamacallit, thingamajig

Dinosaurier <-s, -> [di·no·'zau·ri̯·ɐ] *m* dinosaur

Diphtherie <-, -n> [dɪf·te·'riː, *pl* -'riː·ən] *f* diphtheria

Diphthong <-s, -e> [dɪf·'tɔŋ] *m* diphthong

Diplom <-s, -e> [di·'ploːm] *nt* (*Hochschulzeugnis*) degree; (*Zeugnis, Urkunde*) diploma

> A **Diplom** is a degree that is awarded to graduates in economics, engineering, and the social and natural sciences. Students who are pursuing a **Diplom** concentrate on a major (sometimes combined with a minor) and its practical application. Holders of a **Diplom** are fully qualified academically and professionally and are entitled to work independently in their professional field.

Diplomat(in) <-en, -en> [di·plo·'maːt] *m(f)* diplomat

Diplomatie <-> [di·plo·ma·'tiː] *f kein pl* diplomacy

diplomatisch [di·plo·'maː·tɪʃ] **I.** *adj* diplomatic **II.** *adv* diplomatically

Diplomingenieur(in) [-ɪn·ʒe·ni̯øːɐ̯] *m(f) sb with a Master of Science in engineering*

dir ['diːɐ̯] *pron* ① *pers dat von* **du** you; **ich hoffe, es geht ~ wieder besser** I hope you're feeling better; **Freunde von ~** friends of yours ② *refl dat von* **sich** yourself, you; **was wünscht du ~ zum Geburtstag?** what would you like for your birthday?; **du solltest ~ die Haare waschen** you should wash your hair

direkt [di·'rɛkt] **I.** *adj* direct; *Übertragung* live **II.** *adv* (*fam*) ① (*fam: geradezu*) almost; **das war ja ~ lustig** that was actually funny for a change ② (*unverblümt*) directly; **etw ~ zugeben** to admit sth outright ③ (*mit Ortsangabe*) direct[ly]; **~ am Bahnhof** right by the train station ④ (*unverzüglich*) immediately

Direktbank <-banken> *f telephone and Internet based commercial bank*

Direktflug *m* nonstop flight

Direktion <-, -en> [di·rɛk·'tsi̯oːn] *f* ① (*Leitung*) management; (*Vorstand*) board of directors ② SCHWEIZ (*Ressort*) department

Direktor, **Direktorin** <-s, -toren> [di·'rɛk·toːɐ̯, di·rɛk·'toː·rɪn, *pl* -'toː·rən] *m, f eines Unternehmens* manager; *einer öffentlichen Einrichtung* director; *einer Schule* principal

Direktübertragung *f* live broadcast

Direktverbindung *f* direct flight/train

Dirigent(in) <-en, -en> [di·ri·'gɛnt] *m(f)* conductor

dirigieren* [di·ri·'giː·rən] *vt, vi* MUS to conduct

Dirndl <-s, -> ['dɪrn·dl̩] *nt* ① (*Kleid*) dirndl ② SÜDD, ÖSTERR (*Mädchen*) gal

Dirne <-, -n> ['dɪr·nə] *f* (*veraltend*) prostitute

Disco <-, -s> ['dɪs·ko] *f s.* **Disko**

Diskette <-, -n> [dɪs·'kɛ·tə] *f* disk

Diskettenlaufwerk *nt* disk drive

Diskjockey <-s, -s> ['dɪsk·dʒɔ·ke, -dʒɔ·ki] *m* disc jockey

Disko <-, -s> ['dɪs·ko] *f* disco

Diskothek <-, -en> [dɪs·ko·'teːk] *f* discotheque

Diskrepanz <-, -en> [dɪs·kre·'pants] *f* (*geh*) discrepancy

diskret [dɪs·'kreːt] **I.** *adj* ① (*vertraulich*) confidential ② (*unauffällig*) discreet **II.** *adv* **etw ~ behandeln** to treat sth confidentially; **sich** *akk*

~ **verhalten** to behave discreetly
Diskretion <-> [dɪs·kre·ˈtsi̯oːn] *f kein pl* discretion
diskriminieren* [dɪs·kri·mi·ˈniː·rən] *vt* ■**jdn** ~ to discriminate against sb
diskriminierend *adj* discriminatory
Diskriminierung <-, -en> *f* discrimination
Diskussion <-, -en> [dɪs·kʊ·ˈsi̯oːn] *f* discussion
diskutieren* [dɪs·ku·ˈtiː·rən] *vt, vi* to discuss
Display <-s, -s> [dɪs·ˈpleː] *nt* display
Dispokredit [ˈdɪs·po-] *m* (*fam*) *s.* **Dispositionskredit**
Disposition <-, -en> [dɪs·pozi·ˈtsi̯oːn] *f* disposal; **zur ~ stehen** to be available
Dispositionskredit *m* overdraft allowance
Disput <-[e]s, -e> [dɪs·ˈpuːt] *m* (*geh*) dispute
disqualifizieren* [dɪs·kva·li·fi·ˈtsiː·rən] *vt* to disqualify (**wegen** +*gen* for)
Dissident(in) <-en, -en> [dɪ·si·ˈdɛnt] *m(f)* dissident
Dissonanz <-, -en> [dɪ·so·ˈnants] *f* disharmony
Distanz <-, -en> [dɪs·ˈtants] *f* distance
distanzieren* [dɪs·tan·ˈtsiː·rən] *vr* ■**sich** *akk* ~ to distance oneself (**von** +*dat* from)
distanziert **I.** *adj* distant **II.** *adv* distantly; **sich** *akk* ~ **verhalten** to be aloof
Distel <-, -n> [ˈdɪs·tl̩] *f* thistle
Disziplin <-, -en> [dɪs·tsi·ˈpliːn] *f* discipline
diszipliniert [dɪs·tsi·pli·ˈniːɐ̯t] **I.** *adj* disciplined **II.** *adv* in a disciplined way
disziplinlos **I.** *adj* undisciplined **II.** *adv* in an undisciplined way
Divergenz <-, -en> [di·vɛr·ˈgɛnts] *f* divergence
divergieren* [di·vɛr·ˈgiː·rən] *vi* to diverge (**von** +*dat* from)
divers [di·ˈvɛrs] *adj attr* diverse
Dividende <-, -n> [di·vi·ˈdɛn·də] *f* dividend
dividieren* [di·vi·ˈdiː·rən] *vt* to divide (**durch** +*akk* by)
Division <-, -en> [di·vi·ˈzi̯oːn] *f* division
DNS <-> [deː·ʔɛn·ˈɛs] *f Abk von* **Desoxyribonukleinsäure** DNA
doch [dɔx] **I.** *konj* (*jedoch*) but, however **II.** *adv* (*emph*) ❶ (*dennoch*) even so; **zum Glück ist aber ~ nichts passiert** fortunately, nothing happened ❷ (*einräumend*) **du hattest ~ Recht** you were right after all ❸ (*Widerspruch ausdrückend*) **du gehst jetzt ins Bett – nein! – ~!** you need to go to bed now — no! — oh yes you do! ❹ (*ja*) yes; **hat es dir nicht gefallen? – ~[, ~]!** didn't you enjoy it? — yes, I did!
Docht <-[e]s, -e> [ˈdɔxt] *m* wick
Dock <-s, -s> [ˈdɔk] *nt* dock
döfer *adj komp von* **doof**
döfste(r, s) *adj superl von* **doof**
Dogge <-, -n> [ˈdɔgə] *f* mastiff
Dogma <-s, -men> [ˈdɔg·ma, *pl* ˈdɔg·mən] *nt* dogma
doktern [ˈdɔk·tɐn] *vi* (*fam*) ■**an etw** *dat* ~ to tinker [around] with sth
Doktor, Doktorin <-s, -toren> [ˈdɔk·toːɐ̯, dɔk·ˈtoː·rɪn, *pl* -ˈtoː·rən] *m, f a.* MED doctor; **er ist ~ der Physik** he's got a PhD in physics
Doktortitel *m* doctorate
Doktrin <-, -en> [dɔk·ˈtriːn] *f* doctrine
Doku <-, -s> [ˈdo·ku] *f kurz für* **Dokumentarfilm, -bericht** documentary
Dokument <-[e]s, -e> [do·ku·ˈmɛnt] *nt* document
Dokumentarfilm *m* documentary [film]
Dokumentation <-, -en> [do·ku·mɛn·ta·ˈtsi̯oːn] *f* documentation
dokumentieren* [do·ku·mɛn·ˈtiː·rən] *vt* to document
Dolch <-[e]s, -e> [ˈdɔlç] *m* dagger
Dollar <-[s], -s> [ˈdɔ·lar] *m* dollar
dolmetschen [ˈdɔl·mɛt·ʃn̩] *vi, vt* to interpret
Dolmetscher(in) <-s, -> [ˈdɔl·mɛt·ʃɐ] *m(f)* interpreter
Dolomiten [do·lo·ˈmiː·tn̩] *pl* ■**die ~** the Dolomites
Dom <-[e]s, -e> [ˈdoːm] *m* (*Kirche*) cathedral
Domäne <-, -n> [do·ˈmɛː·nə] *f* domain
dominant [do·mi·ˈnant] *adj* dominant; *Mensch* domineering
Dominanz <-, -en> [do·mi·ˈnants] *f* dominance
dominieren* [do·mi·ˈniː·rən] *vi, vt* to dominate
Dominikanische Republik *f* Dominican Republic
Domino <-s, -s> [ˈdoː·mi·no] *nt* dominoes + *sing vb*
Domizil <-s, -e> [do·mi·ˈtsiːl] *nt* residence
Dompteur(in) <-s, -e> [dɔmp·ˈtøːɐ̯] *m(f)*, **Dompteuse** <-, -n> [dɔmp·ˈtøː·zə] *f* animal trainer
Domstadt *f kein pl* Cathedral City (*nickname for the city of Cologne*)
Donau <-> [ˈdoː·nau] *f* ■**die ~** the Danube
Donner <-s, -> [ˈdɔ·nɐ] *m pl selten* thunder
donnern [ˈdɔ·nɐn] **I.** *vi impers haben* **hörst du, wie es donnert?** can you hear the thunder?; **es hat geblitzt und gedonnert** there was thunder and lightning **II.** *vi sein* (*krachen*) to crash (**gegen/in** +*akk* into) **III.** *vt haben* ■**etw irgendwohin ~** to fling sth somewhere; **er hat die Tür zugedonnert** he slammed the door shut
Donnerstag [ˈdɔ·nɐs·taːk] *m* Thursday; *s. a.* **Dienstag**
donnerstagabends[RR] *adv* [on] Thursday evenings
donnerstags *adv* [on] Thursdays; *s. a.* **dienstags**
Donnerwetter [ˈdɔ·nɐ·vɛ·tɐ] *nt* (*fam: Schelte*) a tongue-lashing; **zum ~!** [god]damn it!
doof <doofer *o* döfer, doofste *o* döfste> [ˈdoːf] *adj* (*fam*) stupid
Doofheit <-, -en> *f* (*fam*) stupidity
Doofkopp <-s, -köppe> [-kɔp, *pl* -kœpə] *m*, **Doofmann** <-s, -männer> *m* (*fam*) jerk

Dope <-s, -s> [doːp] *nt* (*sl*) pot
dopen ['doː·pn̩, 'dɔ·pn̩] *vt* to smoke pot
Doping <-s, -s> ['doː·pɪŋ, 'dɔ·pɪŋ] *nt* doping
Dopingkontrolle ['doː·pɪŋ-] *f*, **Dopingtest** ['doː·pɪŋ-] *m* drug test
Dopingsperre ['doː·pɪŋ-, 'dɔ·pɪŋ-] *f* SPORT doping ban
Doppel <-s, -> ['dɔpl̩] *nt* ❶ (*Duplikat*) duplicate ❷ SPORT doubles; **gemischtes ~** mixed doubles
Dọppelbelastung *f* double burden
Dọppelbett *nt* double bed
Dọppeldecker <-s, -> *m* ❶ (*Flugzeug*) biplane ❷ (*fam: Omnibus*) double-decker [bus]
doppeldeutig ['dɔpl̩·dɔy·tɪç] *adj* ambiguous
Dọppelgänger(in) <-s, -> [-gɛŋɐ] *m(f)* lookalike
Dọppelhaus *nt* duplex
dọppel|klicken *vi* to double-click
Dọppelleben *nt* double life
Dọppelmoral *f* double standards *pl*
Dọppelpunkt *m* colon
doppelt ['dɔpl̩t] **I.** *adj* ❶ (*zweifach*) double; *Staatsangehörigkeit* dual; **die ~e Menge** double the amount; **aus ~em Grunde** for two reasons ❷ (*verdoppelt*) doubled; **mit ~em Einsatz arbeiten** to redouble one's efforts **II.** *adv* ❶ (*zweimal*) twice; **~ so groß/klein** twice as big/small; **~ so viel/viele** twice as much/many ❷ (*umso mehr*) doubly; **~ vorsichtig sein** to be doubly careful ▸ WENDUNGEN: **~ sehen** (*fam*) to see double
Dọppelverdiener(in) <-s, -> *m(f)* ❶ (*Person mit zwei Einkünften*) double wage earner ❷ *pl* (*Paar mit zwei Gehältern*) double-income couple
Dọppelzentner *m* ≈ 2.2 [short] hundredweights (*220 pounds*)
Dọppelzimmer *nt* double [room]
Dorf <-[e]s, Dörfer> ['dɔrf, *pl* 'dœr·fɐ] *nt* [small] town, village
Dọrfgemeinschaft *f* SOZIOL small-town [*or* village] society
Dọrfschaft <-, -en> *f* SCHWEIZ [small] town, village
Dọrftrottel *m* (*fam*) village idiot
Dorn <-[e]s, -en> ['dɔrn] *m* thorn ▸ WENDUNGEN: **jdm ein ~ im Auge sein** to be a thorn in sb's side
dornig ['dɔr·nɪç] *adj* thorny
Dornröschen <-> [-'røːs·çən] *nt kein pl* Sleeping Beauty
dörren ['dœ·rən] **I.** *vt haben* to dry [out *sep*] **II.** *vi sein* to wither
Dọ̈rrobst *nt* dried fruit
dort ['dɔrt] *adv* there; **~ drüben** over there
dorther ['dɔrt·'heːɐ̯] *adv* from [over] there
dorthin ['dɔrt·'hɪn] *adv* [over] there
dorthinaus ['dɔrt·hɪ·'naʊs] *adv* ▸ WENDUNGEN: **bis ~** (*fam*) awfully; **das ärgert mich bis ~!** that drives me up the wall!
dortig ['dɔr·tɪç] *adj attr* local
Dose <-, -n> ['doː·zə, *pl* 'doː·zn̩] *f* ❶ (*Blechdose*) can; (*Büchse*) box ❷ (*Steckdose*) socket
Dosen *pl von* **Dose, Dosis**
dösen ['døː·zn̩] *vi* (*fam*) to doze
Dosenbier *nt* canned beer
Dosenmilch *f* condensed milk
Dosenmusik *f* (*hum fam*) canned music, Muzak®
Dosenöffner *m* can opener
Dosenpfand *nt kein pl* deposit
dosieren* [do·'ziː·rən] *vt* to measure out *sep*
Dosierung <-, -en> *f* dosage
Dosis <-, Dosen> ['doː·zɪs, *pl* 'doː·zn̩] *f* dose
dotieren* [do·'tiː·rən] *vt* **eine gut dotierte Stelle** a well-paid position; **die Stelle wird mit 10.000 Dollar dotiert** this position pays 10,000 dollars
Dotter <-s, -> ['dɔ·tɐ] *m o nt* yolk
doubeln ['duː·bln] *vt* ■ **jdn ~** to double for sb
Double <-s, -s> ['duː·bl] *nt* double
Download <-s, -s> ['daʊn·loʊd] *m* INET download
downloaden ['daʊn·loʊ·dn̩] *vt* INET to download
Downsyndrom *nt kein pl* Down's syndrome
Dozent(in) <-en, -en> [do·'tsɛnt] *m(f)* lecturer
dozieren* [do·'tsiː·rən] *vi* to lecture
Dr. *Abk von* **Doktor** Dr.
Drache <-n, -n> ['dra·xə] *m* dragon
Drachen <-s, -> ['dra·xn̩] *m* ❶ (*Spielzeug*) kite; **einen ~ steigen lassen** to fly a kite ❷ (*Fluggerät*) hang glider ❸ (*fam: zänkisches Weib*) witch
Drạchenflieger(in) <-s, -> *m(f)* hang glider
Draht <-[e]s, Drähte> ['draːt, *pl* 'drɛː·tə] *m* wire ▸ WENDUNGEN: **zu jdm einen guten ~ haben** to be on good terms with sb
Drahtbürste *f* wire brush
Drahtesel *nt* (*fam*) bike
Drahtgitter *nt* wire grating
drahtig *adj* wiry
drahtlos *adj* wireless
Drahtseil *nt* wire cable
Drahtseilbahn *f* gondola
Drahtzaun *m* wire fence
Drahtzieher(in) <-s, -> *m(f)* ringleader
drakonisch [dra·'koː·nɪʃ] **I.** *adj* draconian **II.** *adv* harshly
drall ['dral] *adj* well-rounded; *Mädchen* shapely
Drama <-s, -men> ['draː·ma, *pl* 'draː·mən] *nt* drama
dramatisch [dra·'maː·tɪʃ] **I.** *adj* dramatic **II.** *adv* dramatically
dramatisieren* [dra·ma·ti·'ziː·rən] *vt* ❶ LIT to dramatize ❷ (*fig: übertreiben*) to express in a dramatic way, to be dramatic about
Dramen *pl von* **Drama**
dran ['dran] *adv* (*fam*) ❶ (*fertig*) **[zu] früh/spät ~ sein** to be [too] early/late ❷ (*an der Reihe*) **jetzt bist du ~!** now it's your turn!; **wer ist als Nächster ~?** who's next? ❸ (*zutreffen*) **an dem Gerücht ist etw/nichts ~**

there is something/nothing to the rumor ▶ WENDUNGEN: **besser ~ sein als ...** to be better off than ...; **schlecht ~ sein** (*gesundheitlich*) to be in bad shape; (*schlechte Möglichkeiten haben*) to be having a hard time [of it]

dran|bleiben *vi irreg sein* (*fam*) ❶ ■ **an jdm/etw ~** to stay close to sb/sth ❷ (*am Telefon*) to hold on

drang ['draŋ] *imp von* **dringen**

Drang <-[e]s, Dränge> ['draŋ, *pl* 'drɛŋə] *m* longing; **ein starker ~** a strong desire

dran|gehen *vi irreg sein* (*fam*) ❶ (*ans Telefon*) to answer [the phone], to pick up *fam*, to get it *fam* ❷ *s.* **darangehen**

Drängelei <-, -en> [drɛŋə·'lai] *f* (*pej fam*) ❶ (*in Menschenmenge*) jostling ❷ (*Bedrängen*) pestering

drängeln ['drɛŋ·əln] (*fam*) **I.** *vi* to push **II.** *vt, vi* (*bedrängen*) ■ **[jdn] ~** to pester [sb]

drängen ['drɛŋ·ən] **I.** *vi* ❶ (*schiebend drücken*) to push ❷ (*fordern*) ■ **auf etw** *akk* **~** to insist [up]on sth; **warum drängst du so zur Eile?** why are you in such a hurry? ❸ (*pressieren*) **die Zeit drängt** time is running out; **es drängt nicht** there's no hurry **II.** *vt* ❶ (*schiebend drücken*) to push ❷ (*antreiben*) ■ **jdn ~, etw zu tun** to pressure sb into doing sth; ■ **jdn [zu etw** *dat*] **~** to force sb [to do sth] **III.** *vr* ■ **sich** *akk* **~** to crowd; **sich** *akk* **nach vorne ~** to push forward; **sich** *akk* **durch die Menge ~** to force one's way through the crowd

drangsalieren* [draŋ·za·'liː·rən] *vt* to plague

dran|halten *irreg* (*fam*) **I.** *vt* ■ **etw [an etw** *akk*] **~** hold sth up [to sth] **II.** *vr* ■ **sich** *akk* **~** to keep at it

dran|hängen *vt* (*fam*) ❶ (*aufhängen*) to hang (**an** +*akk* on) ❷ ■ **etw ~** to add on sth

dran|kommen *vi irreg sein* (*fam: an die Reihe kommen*) **Sie kommen noch nicht dran** it's not your turn yet; **warte, bis du drankommst** wait your turn

dran|lassen *vt irreg* (*fam: nicht entfernen*) to leave (**an** +*dat* on)

dran|nehmen *vt irreg* (*fam: zur Behandlung*) to take

drapieren* [dra·'piː·rən] *vt* to drape (**um** +*akk* around, **mit** +*dat* with)

drastisch ['dras·tɪʃ] **I.** *adj* drastic **II.** *adv* drastically

drauf ['drauf] *adv* (*fam*) ❶ (*darauf*) on it/them ❷ **gut/schlecht ~ sein** (*fam*) to be in a good/bad mood ▶ WENDUNGEN: **~ und dran sein, etw zu tun** to be on the verge of doing sth; **etw ~ haben** (*fam: etw beherrschen*) to have mastered sth

drauf|bekommen* *vt irreg* (*fam*) ▶ WENDUNGEN: **eins ~** to get it [good]

Draufgänger(in) <-s, -> ['drauf·gɛŋɐ] *m(f)* go-getter *fam*

draufgängerisch ['drauf·gɛŋə·rɪʃ] *adj* go-getting *fam*

drauf|gehen ['drauf·geː·ən] *vi irreg sein* (*fam*) ❶ (*sterben*) to kick the bucket ❷ (*verbraucht werden*) to be spent ❸ (*kaputtgehen*) to break

drauf|haben *vt irreg* (*fam*) ■ **nichts/viel ~** to know nothing/a lot

drauf|hauen *vi irreg* (*fam*) **jdm eins ~** to hit sb

drauf|kommen *vi irreg sein* (*fam*) ❶ (*herausbekommen*) to figure [it] out ❷ (*sich erinnern*) to remember

drauf|kriegen *vt* (*fam*) *s.* **draufbekommen**

drauf|lassen *vt irreg* (*fam*) to leave on

drauf|legen *vt* (*fam*) ❶ (*zusätzlich geben*) **wenn Sie noch 5.000 ~, können Sie das Auto haben!** for another 5,000 the car is yours! ❷ (*legen*) ■ **etw auf etw** *akk* **~** to put sth on sth

drauflos|arbeiten *vi* (*fam*) to get right down to work

drauflos|gehen *vi irreg sein* (*fam*) to set off

drauflos|reden *vi* (*fam*) to start talking

drauflos|schlagen *vi irreg* (*fam*) ■ **auf jdn ~** to take a swing at sb, to go after sb

drauf|machen *vt* (*fam*) to put on ▶ WENDUNGEN: **einen ~** (*fam*) to paint the town red

drauf|seinALT *vi irreg sein* (*fam*) *s.* **drauf 2**

Drauf|sicht *f* top view

drauf|stehen *vi irreg* (*fam*) **ich kann nicht lesen, was da auf dem Etikett draufsteht** I can't read what the label says

drauf|stoßen *irreg* (*fam*) **I.** *vi sein* to come to it **II.** *vt haben* (*fam*) ■ **jdn ~** to point it out to sb

drauf|zahlen *vi* (*fam*) **500 Euro ~** to pay an extra 500 euros; **~ müssen** to lose money

draus ['draus] *adv* (*fam*) *s.* **daraus**

draußen ['drau·sn̩] *adv* outside; **nach ~** outside

Dreck <-[e]s> ['drɛk] *m kein pl* (*Schmutz, Erde*) dirt; (*Schlamm*) mud; (*Müll*) trash ▶ WENDUNGEN: **jdn wie den letzten ~ behandeln** (*fam*) to treat sb like dirt *fam*

Dreckarbeit *f* (*fam*) menial work

Dreckfinger *pl* (*fam*) dirty hands *pl*

Dreckfink *m* (*fam*) ❶ (*Kind*) filthy kid ❷ (*unmoralischer Mensch*) scumbag

dreckig **I.** *adj* dirty **II.** *adv* ▶ WENDUNGEN: **jdm geht es ~** sb feels terrible; (*finanziell*) sb is not doing [too] well

Dreckloch *nt* (*fam*) dump

Drecknest *nt* (*fam*) hole

Dreckpfoten *pl* (*fam*) grubby paws *pl*

Drecksack *m* (*fam*) bastard

Drecksau *m* (*fam*), **Dreckschwein** *nt* (*fam*) [filthy] pig

Dreckskerl *m* (*fam*) bastard

Dreckspatz *m* (*fam*) filthy kid

Dreh <-s, -s *o* -e> ['dreː] *m* (*fam*) trick; **den [richtigen] ~ heraushaben** to get the hang of it

Dreharbeit *f meist pl* shooting

drehbar *adj, adv* revolving

Drehbuch *nt* screenplay

Drehbuchautor(in) *m(f)* screenplay writer

drehen ['dreː·ən] **I.** *vt* ❶ (*herumdrehen*) to turn ❷ *Zigarette* to roll ❸ FILM to shoot ❹ **das**

D

Radio lauter/leiser ~ to turn the radio up/down ▶ WENDUNGEN: **wie man es auch dreht und wendet** no matter how you look at it **II.** *vi* ① FILM to shoot ② ■ **an etw** *dat* ~ to turn sth ③ *Wind* to change **III.** *vr* ① (*rotieren*) ■ **sich** *akk* ~ to turn ② (*wenden*) *zur Seite, auf den Bauch* to turn ③ (*betreffen*) ■ **sich** *akk* **um jdn/etw** ~ to be about sb/sth; **das Gespräch dreht sich um Sport** the conversation revolves around sports ▶ WENDUNGEN: **jdm dreht sich alles** sb's head is spinning

Drehorgel *f* barrel organ

Drehtür *f* revolving door

Drehung <-, -en> *f* revolution; **eine ~ machen** to turn

Drehzahl *f* [number of] revolutions *pl; eines Motors* revolutions *pl* per minute

drei ['drai] *adj* three

Drei <-, -en> ['drai] *f* ① (*Zahl*) three ② (*Zeugnisnote*) C

dreidimensional *adj* three-dimensional

Dreieck <-s, -e> ['drai·ʔɛk] *nt* triangle

dreieckig, 3-eckigRR ['drai·ʔɛ·kɪç] *adj* triangular

Dreiecksverhältnis *nt* love triangle

dreieinhalb ['drai·ʔain·'halp] *adj* three and a half

dreifach, 3fach ['drai·fax] **I.** *adj* threefold; **die ~e Arbeit** triple the work **II.** *adv* threefold, three times over

dreihundert ['drai·'hʊn·dɐt] *adj* three hundred

dreijährig, 3-jährigRR *adj* ① (*Alter*) three-year-old *attr,* three years old *pred; s. a.* **achtjährig 1** ② (*Zeitspanne*) three-year *attr; s. a.* **achtjährig 2**

Dreikäsehoch <-s, -s> [drai·'kɛː·zə·hoːx] *m* (*hum fam*) little guy

Dreiländereck <-s, -e> *nt region where three countries meet*

dreimal, 3-malRR ['drai·maːl] *adv* three times; *s. a.* **achtmal** ▶ WENDUNGEN: **~ darfst du raten!** (*fam*) I'll give you three guesses

drein|blicken ['drain·blɪ·kn̩] *vi* to look

drein|schauen *vi* to look

Dreirad *nt* tricycle

dreißig ['drai·sɪç] *adj* thirty; *s. a.* **achtzig 1, 2**

dreißigjährig, 30-jährigRR ['drai·sɪç·jɛː·rɪç] *adj attr* ① (*Alter*) thirty-year-old *attr,* thirty years old *pred* ② (*Zeitspanne*) thirty-year *attr*

dreißigste(r, s) *adj* ① (*an dreißigster Stelle*) thirtieth; *s. a.* **achte(r, s) 1** ② (*Datum*) thirtieth, 30th; *s. a.* **achte(r, s) 2**

dreist ['draist] **I.** *adj* brazen **II.** *adv* **~ sein/werden** to be/become bold [*or* brazen]

dreistellig, 3-stelligRR *adj* three-figure *attr*

Dreistigkeit <-, -en> *f* audacity

Dreitagebart *m* designer stubble

dreitausend ['drai·'tau·zn̩t] *adj* three thousand

dreiteilig, 3-teiligRR *adj* three-part; *Besteck* three-piece

Dreiviertelstunde ['drai·fɪr·tl̩·'ʃtʊn·də] *f* 45 minutes

dreizehn ['drai·tseːn] *adj* thirteen; **~ Uhr** 1 p.m.; *s. a.* **acht**1 ▶ WENDUNGEN: **jetzt schlägt's aber ~** (*fam*) enough is enough

dreizehnte(r, s) *adj* ① (*an dreizehnter Stelle*) thirteenth; *s. a.* **achte(r, s) 1** ② (*Datum*) thirteenth, 13th; *s. a.* **achte(r, s) 2**

Dresche <-> ['drɛ·ʃə] *f kein pl* (*fam*) licking, thrashing; **~ kriegen** to get a beating

dreschen <drịscht, drọsch, gedrọschen> ['drɛ·ʃn̩] *vt* ① AGR to thresh ② (*fam: prügeln*) to beat

dressieren* [drɛ·'siː·rən] *vt* to train [an animal]

Dressing <-s, -s> ['drɛ·sɪŋ] *nt* dressing

Dressman <-s, -men> ['drɛs·mən] *m* male model

Dressur <-, -en> [drɛ·'suːɐ̯] *f* training [of animals]

driften ['drɪf·tn̩] *vi sein* (*a. fig*) to drift

Drill <-[e]s> ['drɪl] *m kein pl* drill

drillen ['drɪ·lən] *vt* to drill

Drilling <-s, -e> ['drɪ·lɪŋ] *m* triplet

drin ['drɪn] *adv* (*fam*) ① (*darin*) in it ② (*drinnen*) inside ▶ WENDUNGEN: **bei jdm ist alles ~** anything is possible with sb; **für jdn ist noch alles ~** anything is still possible for sb

dringen <drạng, gedrụngen> ['drɪŋ·ən] *vi* ① *sein* (*stoßen*) ■ **durch/in etw** *akk* ~ to penetrate sth; **durch die Bewölkung/den Nebel ~** to pierce the clouds/fog ② *sein* (*vordringen*) ■ **an etw** *akk*/**zu jdm** ~ to get through to sth/sb; **an die Öffentlichkeit ~** to leak to the public ③ *haben* (*fordern*) ■ **auf etw** *akk* ~ to insist [up]on sth

dringend ['drɪŋ·ənt] **I.** *adj* urgent, pressing; **eine ~e Bitte** an urgent request **II.** *adv* urgently; **ich muss dich ~ sehen** I really need to see you

dringlich ['drɪŋ·lɪç] *adj* urgent, pressing

Drịnglichkeit <-> *f kein pl* urgency

drịnhängen *vi irreg* (*fam*) to be mixed up (**in** +*dat* in)

drinnen ['drɪ·nən] *adv* inside

drịn|stecken *vi* (*fam*) ■ **in etw** *dat* ~ ① (*sich befinden*) to be in sth ② (*investiert sein*) to go into sth ③ (*verwickelt sein*) to be mixed up in sth

drịn|stehen *vi* (*fam*) to be in it

drịscht *3. pers sing pres von* **dreschen**

dritt ['drɪt] *adv* **wir waren zu ~** there were three of us

dritte(r, s) ['drɪ·tə] *adj* ① (*an dritter Stelle*) third; *s. a.* **achte(r, s) 1** ② (*Datum*) third, 3rd; *s. a.* **achte(r, s) 2**

drittel ['drɪ·tl̩] *adj* third

Drittel <-s, -> ['drɪ·tl̩] *nt* third

drittens ['drɪ·tn̩s] *adv* thirdly, in the third place; *s. a.* **achtens**

Drịtte-Wẹlt-Laden *m* Third World import store

Drịtte-Wẹlt-Land *nt* Third World country

drịttklassig *adj* (*pej*) third-rate

Drịttländer, Drịttstaaten *pl* non-member [*or*

third-party] countries *pl*

DRK <-> [deː·ɛr·ˈkaː] *nt Abk von* **Deutsches Rotes Kreuz** German Red Cross

droben [ˈdroː·bn̩] *adv* (*geh*) up there

Droge <-, -n> [ˈdroː·gə] *f* drug

drogenabhängig *adj* addicted to drugs *pred*

Drogenabhängige(r) *f(m) dekl wie adj* drug addict

Drogenabhängigkeit *f* drug addiction

Drogenbekämpfung *f kein pl* war on drugs

Drogenhandel *m* drug trade

Drogenkonsument(in) *m(f)* drug user

Drogenmissbrauch[RR] *f kein pl* drug abuse

Drogensucht *f s.* **Drogenabhängigkeit**

drogensüchtig *adj s.* **drogenabhängig**

Drogensüchtige(r) *f(m) dekl wie adj s.* **Drogenabhängige(r)**

Drogenszene *f* drug scene

Drogentote(r) *f(m) sb who died of a drug overdose*

Drogerie <-, -n> [dro·gə·ˈriː, *pl* dro·gə·ˈriː·ən] *f* drugstore

Drogist(in) <-en, -en> [dro·ˈgɪst] *m(f)* pharmacist

Drohbrief *m* threatening letter

drohen [ˈdroː·ən] *vi* ① (*bedrohen*) to threaten (**mit** +*dat* with) ② (*bevorstehen*) to threaten; **ein neuer Krieg droht** there is the threat of renewed war; **die Mauer drohte einzustürzen** the wall threatened to collapse

drohend **I.** *adj* ① (*einschüchternd*) threatening ② (*bevorstehend*) impending **II.** *adv* threateningly

dröhnen [ˈdrøː·nən] *vi* ① (*dumpf klingen*) to roar; *Donner* to rumble; *Lautsprecher, Musik, Stimme* to boom ② **jdm dröhnt der Kopf/~ die Ohren** sb's head is/ears are ringing

Drohung <-, -en> [ˈdroː·ʊŋ] *f* threat

drollig [ˈdrɔ·lɪç] *adj* ① (*belustigend*) amusing ② (*niedlich*) cute

Dromedar <-s, -e> [dro·me·ˈdaːɐ̯] *nt* dromedary

drosch [ˈdrɔʃ] *imp von* **dreschen**

Drossel <-, -n> [ˈdrɔ·sl̩] *f* thrush

drosseln [ˈdrɔ·sl̩n] *vt* **die Heizung ~** to turn the heat down; **die Produktion ~** to decrease [*or* cut] production; **das Tempo ~** to reduce speed

drüben [ˈdryː·bn̩] *adv* over there

drüber [ˈdryː·bɐ] *adv* (*fam*) *s.* **darüber**

Druck[1] <-[e]s, Drücke> [ˈdrʊk, *pl* ˈdrʏ·kə] *m* pressure; **unter ~ stehen** to be under pressure; **jdn unter ~ setzen** to put pressure on sb

Druck[2] <-[e]s, -e> [ˈdrʊk] *m* TYPO printing

Druckbuchstabe *m* **in ~n** in print

Drückeberger <-s, -> *m* (*pej fam*) shirker

drucken [ˈdrʊ·kn̩] *vt, vi* to print

drücken [ˈdrʏ·kn̩] **I.** *vi* ① (*pressen*) ■ **[auf etw** *akk*] **~** to push [sth]; **auf einen Knopf ~** to push a button ② *Kleidung* to pinch; **die Schuhe ~** the shoes are pinching my feet **II.** *vt* ① (*pressen*) ■ **etw ~** to press sth; **einen Knopf ~** to press a button; ■ **etw aus etw** *dat* **~** to squeeze sth from sth ② (*Kleidung*) ■ **jdn ~** to be too tight for sb ③ (*umarmen*) ■ **jdn ~** to hug sb ④ (*herabsetzen*) **den Preis ~** to force down the price **III.** *vr* (*fam*) ■ **sich** *akk* [**vor etw** *dat*/**um etw** *akk*] **~** to dodge [sth]

drückend *adj* heavy; *Armut* extreme; *Sorgen* serious; *Stimmung, Hitze* oppressive

Drucker <-s, -> *m* COMPUT printer

Drucker(in) <-s, -> *m(f)* printer

Drücker *m* ► WENDUNGEN: **auf den letzten ~** at the last minute

Druckerei <-, -en> [drʊ·kə·ˈrai] *f* printer's, print shop

Druckerschwärze *f* printer's ink

Druckertreiber *m* printer driver

Druckfehler *m* typographical error

druckfrisch *adj* hot off the press *pred*

Druckknopf *m* snap

Druckluft *f kein pl* compressed air

Druckmaschine *f* printing press

Druckmesser *m* pressure gauge

Druckmittel *nt* **jdn/etw als ~ benutzen** to use sb/sth as a means of exerting pressure

druckreif *adj* ready for publication *pred*

Drucksache *f* printed matter

Druckschrift *f* **in ~ schreiben** to write in print

drucksen [ˈdrʊk·sn̩] *vi* (*fam*) to be indecisive

Druckstelle *f* mark [where pressure has been applied]

Druckverband *m* tourniquet

Druckwelle *f* shock wave

drum [ˈdrʊm] *adv* (*fam*) *s.* **darum** ► WENDUNGEN: **das D~ und Dran** the whole works, the whole shebang *fam*

Drumherum <-s> [ˈdrʊm·hɛ·ˈrʊm] *nt kein pl* (*fam*) ■ **das [ganze] ~** all the trappings

drunten [ˈdrʊn·tn̩] *adv* DIAL down there

drunter [ˈdrʊn·tɐ] *adv* (*fam*) *s.* **darunter** ► WENDUNGEN: **alles geht ~ und drüber** it's all chaos

Drüse <-, -n> [ˈdryː·zə] *f* gland

Dschungel <-s, -> [ˈdʒʊŋ·əl] *m* jungle

du <*gen:* deiner, *dat:* dir, *akk:* dich> [ˈduː] *pron pers* you; **bist ~ das, Peter?** is that [*or* it] you, Peter?

Du <-[s], -[s]> [ˈduː] *nt* you, "du" (*familiar form of address*); **jdm das ~ anbieten** to suggest that sb use the familiar form of address

Dübel <-s, -> [ˈdyː·bl̩] *m* drywall anchor

dubios [du·ˈbi̯·oːs] *adj* dubious

ducken [ˈdʊ·kn̩] *vr* ■ **sich** *akk* **~** to duck one's head

Duckmäuser(in) <-s, -> [ˈdʊk·mɔy·zɐ] *m(f)* (*pej*) yes man

dudeln [ˈduː·dl̩n] *vi* (*pej fam*) to drone [on]; *Lautsprecher* to blare

Dudelsack [ˈduː·dl̩·zak] *m* bagpipes *pl*

Duell <-s, -e> [du·ˈɛl] *nt* duel

duellieren* [duɛ·ˈliː·rən] *vr* ■ **sich** *akk* **~** to [fight a] duel

Duft <-[e]s, Düfte> [ˈdʊft, *pl* ˈdʏf·tə] *m* [pleas-

ant] smell; *einer Blume, eines Parfüms* scent; *von Essen, Kaffee* aroma
dufte ['dʊf·tə] *adj* (*fam*) great
duften ['dʊf·tn̩] *vi* ■ [**nach etw** *dat*] ~ to smell [of sth]
duftend *adj attr* fragrant
Dụftstoff *m* aromatic substance; BIOL scent
dulden ['dʊl·dn̩] *vt* to tolerate
duldsam ['dʊlt·zaːm] *adj* tolerant (**gegenüber** +*dat* of/toward)
Dụldung <-, -en> *f pl selten* toleration
dumm <dụmmer, dụmmste> ['dʊm] **I.** *adj* ❶ (*geistig beschränkt*) stupid ❷ (*unklug*) foolish; **kein ~er Vorschlag!** not a bad idea!; **so etwas D~es!** how stupid! ❸ (*albern*) silly; ■ **etw wird jdm zu ~** sb has had enough of sth ❹ (*fam: ärgerlich*) *Geschichte, Sache* unpleasant **II.** *adv* stupidly; **frag nicht so ~** don't ask such stupid questions ▶ WENDUNGEN: **~ dastehen** to look stupid; **jdn für ~ verkaufen** (*fam*) to take sb for a ride
Dụmme(r) *f(m) dekl wie adj* idiot; **einen ~n finden** to find some idiot ▶ WENDUNGEN: **der ~ sein** to be left holding the bag
Dummejungenstreich [dʊ·mə·'jʊŋən·ʃtraiç] *m* (*fam*) silly prank
dụmmer *adj komp von* **dumm**
dụmmerweise *adv* ❶ (*leider*) unfortunately ❷ (*unklugerweise*) stupidly
Dụmmheit <-, -en> *f* ❶ *kein pl* (*geringe Intelligenz*) stupidity ❷ (*unkluge Handlung*) foolish action
Dụmmkopf *m* (*pej fam*) idiot
dụmmste(r, s) *adj superl von* **dumm**
dumpf ['dʊmpf] *adj* ❶ (*hohl klingend*) dull; *Geräusch, Ton* muffled ❷ (*unbestimmt*) vague; *Gefühl* sneaking; *Schmerz* dull ❸ (*feucht-muffig*) musty; *Atmosphäre, Luft* oppressive
Dumpingpreis ['dam·pɪŋ-] *m* dumping price
Düne <-, -n> ['dyː·nə] *f* dune
Dung <-[e]s> ['dʊŋ] *m kein pl* dung
Dụ̈ngemittel *nt* fertilizer
düngen ['dʏŋən] *vt* to fertilize
Dụ̈nger <-s, -> *m* fertilizer
dunkel ['dʊŋ·kl̩] **I.** *adj* ❶ (*nicht hell*) dark; *Ton* deep ❷ (*unklar*) *Erinnerung* vague; **ein dunkles Kapitel** a dark chapter ❸ (*pej: zwielichtig*) dubious, shady ▶ WENDUNGEN: **im D~n tappen** to be groping around in the dark **II.** *adv* **sich** *akk* **~ an etw** *akk* **erinnern** to remember sth vaguely
dụnkelblond *adj* dirty blond
dụnkelhaarig *adj* dark-haired
dụnkelhäutig *adj* dark-skinned
Dụnkelheit <-> *f kein pl* darkness
Dụnkelziffer *f* number of unreported cases
dünn ['dʏn] **I.** *adj* ❶ (*von geringer Stärke*) thin ❷ *Kleidung* light; *Strümpfe* fine **II.** *adv* thinly; **~ besiedelt** sparsely populated; **~ gesät** thinly scattered
Dụ̈nndarm *m* small intestine
dụ̈nnflüssig *adj* runny
dụ̈nn|machen *vr* (*fam*) ■ **sich** *akk* ~ to make oneself scarce
Dụ̈nnpfiff <-[e]s> *m kein pl* (*fam*) the runs *npl*
Dụ̈nnschiss[RR] *m kein pl* (*derb*) the shits *npl*
Dunst <-[e]s, Dünste> ['dʊnst, *pl* 'dʏns·tə] *m* ❶ (*leichter Nebel*) haze; (*durch Abgase*) smog *npl* ❷ (*Dampf*) steam
dünsten ['dʏns·tn̩] *vt* to steam; *Fleisch* to braise
Dụnstglocke *f* blanket of smog
dunstig ['dʊns·tɪç] *adj* METEO hazy
Dụnstkreis *m* (*geh*) entourage
Dụnstschleier *m* [thin] layer of haze
Dụnstwolke *f* cloud of smog
Duo <-s, -s> ['duːo] *nt* ❶ (*Paar*) duo ❷ MUS duet
Duplikat <-[e]s, -e> [du·pli·'kaːt] *nt* duplicate
durch ['dʊrç] **I.** *präp* ❶ (*räumlich*) through; **~ den Fluss waten** to wade across the river; **mitten ~ etw** *akk* through the middle of sth ❷ (*vermittels*) by [means of]; **~ [einen] Zufall** by chance ❸ (*zeitlich*) throughout; **die ganze Nacht ~** all night long ❹ MATH [**dividiert**] ~ divided by **II.** *adj pred* ❶ (*durchgetrennt*) through ❷ (*fam: vorbei*) **es ist schon 12 Uhr ~** it's already past 12 [o'clock]; **der Zug ist vor zwei Minuten ~** the train left two minutes ago ❸ (*gar, reif*) ■ **~ sein** *Steak* to be well-done; *Käse* to be ripe ❹ (*kaputt*) ■ **~ sein** *Kleidung* to be worn out ❺ (*fertig*) ■ **mit etw/jdm ~ sein** to be through with sth/sb
durch|ackern ['dʊrç·ʔakɐn] (*fam*) **I.** *vt* to plow through **II.** *vr* ■ **sich** *akk* [**durch etw** *akk*] ~ to plow one's way [through sth]
durch|arbeiten ['dʊrç·ʔar·bai·tn̩] **I.** *vt* to go through **II.** *vi* to keep working [until the end]
durch|atmen ['dʊrç·ʔaːt·mən] *vi* to breathe deeply
durchaus ['dʊrç·ʔaus, dʊrç·'ʔaus] *adv* **~ kein schlechtes Angebot** not a bad offer [at all]; **ich bin ~ deiner Meinung, aber ...** I completely agree with you, but ...; **~ möglich sein** to be quite possible; **~ nicht schlecht sein** to be by no means bad
durch|beißen ['dʊrç·baisn̩] *irreg* **I.** *vt* to bite through **II.** *vr* (*fam*) ■ **sich** *akk* [**durch etw** *akk*] ~ to fight through [sth]
durch|bekommen* ['dʊrç·bə·kɔ·mən] *vt irreg* (*fam*) ❶ (*durchtrennen können*) to cut through ❷ (*durch eine Öffnung*) to get through ❸ *einen Kranken* to pull through
durch|biegen ['dʊrç·biː·gn̩] *irreg* **I.** *vt* to bend **II.** *vr* ■ **sich** *akk* ~ to sag
durch|blättern ['dʊrç·blɛ·tɐn], **durchblättern*** [dʊrç·'blɛ·tɐn] *vt* to leaf through
Durchblick ['dʊrç·blɪk] *m* (*fam*) overall view; **den ~ [bei etw** *dat*] **haben** to know what's going on [in/with sth]
durch|blicken ['dʊrç·blɪ·kn̩] *vi* ❶ ■ [**durch etw** *akk*] ~ to look through [sth] ❷ (*fam: den Überblick haben*) to know what's going on ❸ **etw ~ lassen** to hint at sth
durchbluten* [dʊrç·'bluː·tn̩] *vt* ANAT to sup-

ply with blood; **gut/schlecht durchblutet** having good/poor circulation
Durchblutung [dʊrç·'bluː·tʊŋ] *f* circulation
Durchblutungsstörung *f* circulatory problem
durchbohren*¹ [dʊrç·'boː·rən] *vt* ■**etw** [**mit etw** *dat*] ~ to pierce sth [with sth]
durch|bohren² ['dʊrç·boː·rən] *vt* ■**etw durch etw** *akk* ~ to drill sth through sth
durch|boxen ['dʊrç·bɔ·ksn̩] (*fam*) **I.** *vt* to push through **II.** *vr* **sich** *akk* **nach oben** ~ to fight one's way up [*or* to the top]
durch|braten ['dʊrç·braː·tn̩] *irreg vt* ■**etw** ~ to cook sth until it is well-done
durch|brechen¹ ['dʊrç·brɛ·çn̩] *irreg* **I.** *vt haben* to break in two **II.** *vi sein* (*zerfallen*) to break in two
durchbrechen*² [dʊrç·'brɛ·çn̩] *vt irreg Absperrung, Blockade* to burst [*or* break] through
durch|brennen ['dʊrç·brɛ·nən] *irreg vi sein* ❶ ELEK to burn out; *Sicherung* to blow ❷ (*fam*) ■[**jdm**] ~ to run away [from sb]
durch|bringen ['dʊrç·brɪŋən] *vt irreg* ❶ (*durch eine Öffnung*) to get passed ❷ (*für Unterhalt sorgen*) to support ❸ *einen Kranken* to pull through
Durchbruch ['dʊrç·brʊx] *m* ❶ *a.* MIL breakthrough ❷ (*Öffnung*) opening
durch|checken ['dʊrç·tʃɛ·kn̩] *vt* (*fam*) *Patienten* to check up on; **sich** *akk* ~ **lassen** to have a checkup
durch|denken ['dʊrç·dɛŋ·kn̩], **durchdenken*** [dʊrç·'dɛŋ·kn̩] *vt irreg* to think through; ■**durchdacht** thought-out
durch|drängeln ['dʊrç·drɛŋln̩] *vr* (*fam*), **durch|drängen** ['dʊrç·drɛŋən] *vr* ■**sich** *akk* **durch etw** *akk* ~ to push one's way through sth
durch|drehen ['dʊrç·dreː·ən] *vi* (*fam*) to crack up
durch|dringen¹ ['dʊrç·drɪŋən] *irreg vi sein* ❶ (*durch etw dringen*) to come through ❷ (*erreichen*) ■**zu jdm** ~ to make one's way up to sb
durchdringen*² [dʊrç·'drɪŋən] *irreg vt* to penetrate
durchdringend *adj* piercing; *Geruch* pungent; *Gestank* penetrating; *Kälte, Wind* biting; *Schmerz* excruciating
durch|drücken ['dʊrç·drʏ·kn̩] *vt* (*erzwingen*) to push through
durch|dürfen ['dʊrç·dʏr·fn̩] *vi irreg* (*fam*) to be allowed through
durcheinander [dʊrç·ʔai·'nan·dɐ] *adj pred* ■~ **sein** (*in Unordnung*) to be in a mess; (*verwirrt*) to be confused
Durcheinander <-s> [dʊrç·ʔai·'nan·dɐ] *nt kein pl* ❶ (*Unordnung*) mess ❷ (*Wirrwarr*) confusion
durcheinander|bringen *vt irreg* ■**etw** ~ (*in Unordnung bringen*) to mess up *sep* sth; (*verwechseln*) to mix up *sep* sth; ■**jdn** [**mit etw** *dat*] ~ to confuse sb [with sth]
durcheinander|reden *vi* to all talk at once
durch|fahren¹ ['dʊrç·faː·rən] *vi irreg sein* ❶ (*hindurch*) **durch eine Stadt** ~ to drive through a city ❷ (*nicht anhalten*) **bei Rot** ~ to run a red light; **die Nacht** ~ to drive all night long; **der Zug fährt bis Berlin durch** the train travels nonstop all the way to Berlin
durchfahren*² [dʊrç·'faː·rən] *vt irreg* ■**jdn** ~ *Gedanke* to flash through sb's mind; *Gefühl* to go through sb
Durchfahrt ['dʊrç·faːɐ̯t] *f* ❶ (*Öffnung*) entrance; ~ **bitte freihalten** please do not block the entrance/exit ❷ (*das Durchfahren*) ~ **verboten** do not enter; **auf der ~ sein** to be passing through
Durchfahrtsstraße *f* through road
Durchfall ['dʊrç·fal] *m* diarrhea
durch|fallen ['dʊrç·fa·lən] *vi irreg sein* ❶ ■[**durch etw** *akk*] ~ to fall through [sth] ❷ (*fam*) **bei einer Prüfung** ~ to fail an exam
durch|feiern ['dʊrç·fai·ɐn] *vi* (*fam*) to celebrate nonstop
durch|finden ['dʊrç·fɪn·dn̩] *irreg vi, vr* ■[**sich** *akk*] ~ to find one's way
durch|fliegen¹ ['dʊrç·fliː·gn̩] *vi irreg sein* ❶ LUFT to fly nonstop ❷ (*fam*) **durch ein Prüfung** ~ to fail an exam
durchfliegen*² [dʊrç·'fliː·gn̩] *vt irreg* to fly through
durch|fließen¹ ['dʊrç·fliː·sn̩] *vi irreg sein* to flow through
durchfließen*² [dʊrç·'fliː·sn̩] *vt irreg* to flow through
durchforschen* [dʊrç·'fɔr·ʃn̩] *vt* ❶ (*durchstreifen*) to explore ❷ (*durchsuchen*) to search through (**nach** +*dat* for)
durchforsten* [dʊrç·'fɔrs·tn̩] *vt* (*fam*) to sift through (**nach** +*dat* for)
durch|fragen ['dʊrç·fraː·gn̩] *vr* ■**sich** *akk* ~ to find one's way by asking
durch|fressen ['dʊrç·frɛ·sn̩] *irreg vr* ❶ *Tier* ■**sich** *akk* [**durch etw** *akk*] ~ to eat [its way] through [sth] ❷ (*pej*) ■**sich** *akk* [**bei jdm**] ~ to live off of sb's hospitality
durchführbar *adj* feasible
durch|führen ['dʊrç·fyː·rən] **I.** *vt* (*verwirklichen*) to carry out **II.** *vi* ■**durch etw** *akk* ~ to run through sth
Durchführung *f* carrying out
durch|füttern ['dʊrç·fʏ·tɐn] *vt* (*fam*) to support
Durchgang ['dʊrç·gaŋ] *m* ❶ (*Passage*) path[way] ❷ (*das Durchgehen*) entry; **kein ~!** no pedestrians allowed!; (*an Türen*) no admittance!
durchgängig ['dʊrç·gɛŋɪç] **I.** *adj* universal **II.** *adv* universally
Durchgangslager *nt* transit camp
Durchgangsstraße *f* through road
Durchgangsverkehr *m* through traffic
durch|geben ['dʊrç·geː·bn̩] *vt irreg Lottozahlen* to read; **eine Meldung** ~ to make an announcement

D

durchgefroren *adj* frozen solid *pred*
durch|gehen ['dʊrç·geː·ən] *irreg vi sein* ❶ (*hindurchgehen*) to go through ❷ (*fam: weglaufen*) to run off ❸ (*angenommen werden*) to go through; *Antrag, Gesetz* to pass ❹ (*gehalten werden*) ■**für etw ~** to pass [*or* be mistaken] for sth ❺ *Pferd* to bolt ▶WENDUNGEN: **jdm etw ~ lassen** to let sb get away with sth
durchgehend ['dʊrç·geː·ənt] **I.** *adj* ❶ (*nicht unterbrochen*) continuous ❷ BAHN direct **II.** *adv* **„wir haben von 9 - 18 Uhr ~ geöffnet"** "we're open from 9 a.m. - 6 p.m." (*not closed for lunch*)
durchgeknallt *adj* (*sl*) ■**~ sein** to have gone crazy
durch|greifen ['dʊrç·grai·fn̩] *vi irreg* ❶ (*wirksam vorgehen*) to take drastic action ❷ (*hindurchfassen*) to reach through
durchgreifend **I.** *adj* drastic **II.** *adv* drastically
durch|gucken ['dʊrç·gʊ·kn̩] *vi* (*fam*) to look through
durch|haben ['dʊrç·haː·bn̩] *vt irreg* (*fam*) ❶ (*durchgelesen haben*) to be through [reading] ❷ (*durchgearbeitet haben*) to have finished
durch|halten ['dʊrç·hal·tn̩] *irreg* **I.** *vt* ❶ *Belastung* to withstand ❷ (*beibehalten*) to keep up *sep* **II.** *vi* to hold out
Durchhaltevermögen *nt kein pl* stamina, perseverance
durch|hängen ['dʊrç·hɛŋən] *vi irreg* ❶ (*nach unten hängen*) to sag ❷ (*fam: erschöpft sein*) to be drained; (*deprimiert sein*) to be down
Durchhänger <-s, -> *m* **einen** [**totalen**] **~ haben** (*fam*) to be on a [real] downer
durch|hauen ['dʊrç·hau·ən] *irreg vt* (*spalten*) to split [in two]
durch|helfen ['dʊrç·hɛl·fn̩] *irreg vi* ■**jdm** [**durch etw** *akk*] **~** to help sb through [sth]
durch|kämmen¹ ['dʊrç·kɛ·mən] *vt Haar* to comb through *sep*
durchkämmen*² [dʊrç·'kɛ·mən] *vt* ■**etw** [**nach jdm/etw**] **~** to comb sth [for sb/sth]
durch|kämpfen ['dʊrç·kɛmp·fn̩] **I.** *vt* (*durchsetzen*) to force through *sep* **II.** *vr* ■**sich** *akk* **~** to battle one's way through
durch|kauen ['dʊrç·kau·ən] *vt* ❶ (*gründlich kauen*) to chew thoroughly ❷ (*fam*) to discuss thoroughly
durch|kommen ['dʊrç·kɔ·mən] *vi irreg sein* ❶ (*durchfahren*) ■[**durch etw** *akk*] **~** to come through [sth] ❷ *Sonne* to come through ❸ *Charakterzug* to become noticeable ❹ (*Erfolg haben*) ■**mit etw** *dat* **~** to get away with sth ❺ (*durch eine Öffnung*) to get through *sep* ❻ (*überleben*) to pull through
durch|können ['dʊrç·kœ·nən] *vi irreg* (*fam*) to be able to get through
durchkreuzen*¹ [dʊrç·'krɔy·tsn̩] *vt* (*vereiteln*) to foil
durch|kreuzen² ['dʊrç·krɔy·tsn̩] *vt* to cross out *sep*
durch|kriechen ['dʊrç·kriː·çn̩] *vi irreg sein* to crawl through
durch|kriegen *vt* (*fam*) *s.* **durchbekommen**
durch|lassen ['dʊrç·la·sn̩] *vt irreg* ❶ (*vorbei lassen*) ■**jdn/etw ~** to let sb/sth through ❷ (*durchlässig sein*) ■**etw ~** to let through *sep* sth ❸ (*fam: durchgehen lassen*) ■**jdm etw ~** to let sb get away with sth
durchlässig ['dʊrç·lɛ·sɪç] *adj* porous (**für** +*akk* to)
durch|laufen¹ ['dʊrç·lau·fn̩] *irreg* **I.** *vi sein* to run through **II.** *vt haben Schuhe* to wear through *sep*
durchlaufen*² [dʊrç·'lau·fn̩] *vt irreg* ❶ (*im Lauf durchqueren*) to run through ❷ (*zurücklegen*) to cover
durchleben* [dʊrç·'leː·bn̩] *vt* **schwere Zeiten ~** to go through hard times
durchleiden* [dʊrç·'lai·dn̩] *vt irreg* to endure
durch|lesen ['dʊrç·leː·zn̩] *vt irreg* to read through *sep*
durchleuchten*¹ [dʊrç·'lɔyç·tn̩] *vt* ❶ (*röntgen*) to x-ray ❷ (*kritisch prüfen*) to investigate
durch|leuchten² ['dʊrç·lɔyç·tn̩] *vi* to shine through
durch|lüften ['dʊrç·lʏf·tn̩] *vt Raum* to air out
durch|machen ['dʊrç·ma·xn̩] **I.** *vt Phase* to go through; *Krankheit* to suffer **II.** *vi* (*fam*) ❶ (*feiern*) **die ganze Nacht ~** to stay up all night ❷ (*durcharbeiten*) to keep working [until the end]
Durchmesser <-s, -> ['dʊrç·me·sɐ] *m* diameter
durch|mogeln *vr* (*fam*) ■**sich** *akk* **~** to fake one's way through
durch|müssen ['dʊrç·mʏ·sn̩] *vi irreg* (*fam*) to have to go through
durchnässen* [dʊrç·'nɛ·sn̩] *vt* to drench
durch|nehmen ['dʊrç·neː·mən] *vt irreg* to do
durch|probieren* *vt* to try one after the other
durchqueren* [dʊrç·'kveː·rən] *vt* to cross
durch|rasseln *vi sein* (*fam*) to fail
durch|rechnen ['dʊrç·rɛç·nən] *vt* to calculate; (*überprüfen*) to check thoroughly
durch|regnen ['dʊrç·reːg·nən] *vi impers* to rain continuously
Durchreise ['dʊrç·rai·zə] *f* journey through; **auf der ~ sein** to be passing through
durch|reisen¹ ['dʊrç·rai·zn̩] *vi sein* to pass through
durchreisen*² [dʊrç·'rai·zn̩] *vt* **die ganze Welt ~** to travel all over the world
durch|reißen ['dʊrç·rai·sn̩] *irreg* **I.** *vt haben* ■**etw ~** to tear sth in two **II.** *vi sein* to rip, to tear [in half]
durch|ringen ['dʊrç·rɪŋən] *vr irreg* ■**sich** *akk* **zu etw** *dat* **~** to finally manage to do sth; **sich** *akk* **zu einer Entscheidung ~** to force oneself to make a decision
durch|rosten ['dʊrç·rɔs·tn̩] *vi sein* to rust through
durch|rufen *vi irreg* (*fam*) to give sb a call
durch|rühren *vt* to stir well

durchs ['dʊrçs] (*fam*) = **durch das** *s.* **durch**

Durchsage <-, -n> ['dʊrç·za:gə] *f* announcement

durch|sagen ['dʊrç·za:·gn̩] *vt* to announce

durch|sägen *vt* to saw through *sep*

durchschaubar [dʊrç·'ʃau·ba:ɐ̯] *adj* obvious; **leicht ~** easy to see through; **schwer ~** enigmatic

durchschauen*[1] [dʊrç·'ʃau·ən] *vt* ■**jdn ~** to see through sb

durch|schauen[2] ['dʊrç·ʃau·ən] *vt* to look through

durch|scheinen ['dʊrç·ʃai·nən] *vi irreg* ❶ *Licht, Sonne* to shine through ❷ *Farbe, Muster* to show [through]

durch|schieben *vt irreg* to push through *sep*

durch|schlafen ['dʊrç·ʃla:·fn̩] *vi irreg* to sleep through [it]

durch|schlagen[1] ['dʊrç·ʃla:·gn̩] *irreg* **I.** *vt haben* ❶ (*durchbrechen*) to split [in two] ❷ **einen Nagel durch etw** *akk* **~** to hammer a nail through sth **II.** *vi sein* (*durchdringen*) ■**[durch etw** *akk*] ~ to come through [sth] **III.** *vr haben* ■**sich** *akk* **~** ❶ (*seine Existenz behaupten*) to struggle along ❷ (*ans Ziel gelangen*) to make one's way through

durchschlagen*[2] [dʊrç·'ʃla:·gn̩] *vt irreg* to chop through

durchschlagend ['dʊrç·ʃla:·gn̩t] *adj* ❶ (*überwältigend*) sweeping; *Erfolg* huge; **eine ~e Wirkung haben** to be extremely effective ❷ (*überzeugend*) convincing; *Beweis* conclusive

Durchschlagskraft *f kein pl* ❶ (*Wucht*) penetration ❷ (*fig*) effectiveness

durch|schlängeln *vr* ■**sich** *akk* **~** to thread one's way through

durch|schleusen ['dʊrç·ʃlɔy·zn̩] *vt* (*fam*) to smuggle through *sep*

durch|schneiden ['dʊrç·ʃnai·dn̩] *vt irreg* to cut through

Durchschnitt ['dʊrç·ʃnɪt] *m* average; **im ~** on average; **über/unter dem ~ liegen** to be above/below average

durchschnittlich ['dʊrç·ʃnɪt·lɪç] **I.** *adj* ❶ (*Mittelwert betreffend*) average *attr* ❷ (*mittelmäßig*) ordinary **II.** *adv* ❶ (*im Schnitt*) on average ❷ (*mäßig*) moderately; **~ intelligent** of average intelligence

Durchschnittsalter *nt* average age

Durchschnittsgeschwindigkeit *f* average speed

Durchschnittsmensch *m* average person

Durchschnittstemperatur *f* average temperature

durch|schütteln ['dʊrç·ʃʏ·tl̩n] *vt* ■**etw ~** to shake sth thoroughly; ■**jdn ~** to give sb a good shake

durch|schwitzen ['dʊrç·ʃvɪ·tsn̩] *vt* to soak in sweat

durch|sehen ['dʊrç·ze:·ən] *irreg* **I.** *vt* ■**etw ~** to go over sth **II.** *vi* ■**durch etw** *akk* **~** to look through sth

durch|seinALT *vi irreg sein s.* **durch II.**

durch|setzen ['dʊrç·zɛ·tsn̩] **I.** *vt Maßnahmen* to impose; *Reformen* to carry out; *Ziel* to achieve; ■**etw bei jdm ~** to get sb to agree to sth; **seinen Willen [gegen jdn] ~** to get one's own way [with sb] **II.** *vr* ❶ (*sich Geltung verschaffen*) ■**sich** *akk* **~** to assert oneself (**gegen** +*akk* against); ■**sich** *akk* **mit etw** *dat* **~** to be successful with sth ❷ (*Gültigkeit erreichen*) ■**sich** *akk* **~** to gain acceptance; *Trend* to catch on

Durchsetzungsvermögen *nt kein pl* assertiveness

Durchsicht ['dʊrç·zɪçt] *f* inspection; **zur ~** for inspection

durchsichtig ['dʊrç·zɪç·tɪç] *adj* transparent *a. fig; Bluse, Kleid* see-through

durch|sickern ['dʊrç·zɪ·kɐn] *vi sein* ❶ *Flüssigkeit* to seep through ❷ *Nachricht, Neuigkeit* to leak out

durch|spielen *vt* (*durchdenken*) to go through

durch|sprechen ['dʊrç·ʃprɛ·çn̩] *vt irreg* to discuss thoroughly

durch|stechen ['dʊrç·ʃtɛ·çn̩] *vt irreg* to pierce

durch|stehen ['dʊrç·ʃte:·ən] *vt irreg* to get through; *Qualen* to endure; *Schwierigkeiten* to cope

durch|steigen ['dʊrç·ʃtai·gn̩] *vi irreg sein* ❶ (*durch etw steigen*) to climb through ❷ (*fam: verstehen*) ■**bei etw** *dat* **~** to get sth; **da soll mal einer ~!** just let someone try and figure this one out!

durch|stellen *vt* **ein Gespräch ~** to put a call through

durchstöbern* [dʊrç·'ʃtø:·bɐn], **durch|stöbern** ['dʊrç·ʃtø:·bɐn] *vt* to rummage through (**nach** +*dat* for)

durchstoßen*[1] [dʊrç·'ʃto:·sn̩] *vt irreg* to go through

durch|stoßen[2] ['dʊrç·ʃto:·sn̩] *irreg vt* **einen Pfahl durch etw ~** to drive a stake through sth

durch|streichen ['dʊrç·ʃtrai·çn̩] *vt irreg Fehler* to cross out

durchstreifen* [dʊrç·'ʃtrai·fn̩] *vt* to roam through

durch|strömen[1] ['dʊrç·ʃtrø:·mən] *vi sein* to stream through

durchströmen*[2] [dʊrç·'ʃtrø:·mən] *vt* (*a. fig*) to flow through

durchsuchen* [dʊrç·'zu:·xn̩] *vt* to search (**nach** +*dat* for)

Durchsuchung <-, -en> [dʊrç·'zu:·xʊŋ] *f* search

durchtrainiert *adj* thoroughly fit

durch|treten ['dʊrç·tre:·tn̩] *irreg vt* **die Bremse ~** to step on the brakes

durchtrieben [dʊrç·'tri:·bn̩] *adj* crafty

durchwachsen [dʊrç·'vak·sn̩] *adj* ❶ *Speck* marbled ❷ *pred* (*mittelmäßig*) so-so

Durchwahl *f* ❶ (*Durchwahlnummer*) extension [number] ❷ *kein pl* (*das Durchwählen*) direct dialing

D

durch|wählen ['dʊrç·vɛː·lən] *vi* to dial direct

durchweg ['dʊrç·vɛk] *adv,* **durchwegs** ['dʊrç·veːks] *adv* ÖSTERR without exception

durch|winken *vt irreg* to wave through

durch|wühlen[1] ['dʊrç·vyː·lən] *vr* ■**sich** *akk* [**durch etw** *akk*] ~ to plow through [sth]

durchwühlen*[2] [dʊrç·'vyː·lən] *vt* (*durchstöbern*) to comb (**nach** + *dat* for)

durch|zählen ['dʊrç·tsɛː·lən] *vt, vi* to count out *sep*

durch|ziehen ['dʊrç·tsiː·ən] *irreg* **I.** *vt haben* ❶ (*durch eine Öffnung*) ■**etw** [**durch etw** *akk*] ~ to pull sth through [sth] ❷ (*fam: vollenden*) to see through **II.** *vi sein* to come through **III.** *vr haben* ■**sich** *akk* **durch etw** *akk* ~ to occur throughout sth

durchzucken* [dʊrç·'tsʊ·kn̩] *vt* ❶ **den Himmel** ~ to flash across the sky ❷ ■**jdn** ~ to flash through sb's mind

Durchzug ['dʊrç·tsuːk] *m kein pl* (*Luftzug*) draft

dürfen ['dʏr·fn̩] **I.** *modal vb* <darf, durfte, dürfen> ❶ (*Erlaubnis haben*) ■**etw** [**nicht**] **tun** ~ to [not] be allowed to do sth ❷ *verneint* **wir** ~ **den Zug nicht verpassen** we can't miss the train; **du darfst ihm das nicht übel nehmen** you shouldn't hold that against him ❸ *im Konjunktiv* (*sollen*) ■**das/es dürfte ...** that/it should [*or* ought to] ...; **es dürfte wohl das Beste sein, wenn ...** it would probably be best if ... **II.** *vi* <darf, durfte, gedurft> **darf ich nach draußen?** may I go outside?; **sie hat nicht gedurft** she wasn't allowed to **III.** *vt* <darf, durfte, gedurft> ■**etw** ~ to be allowed to do sth; **darfst du das?** are you allowed to [do that]?

dürftig ['dʏrf·tɪç] **I.** *adj* ❶ (*karg*) paltry; *Unterkunft* poor ❷ (*schwach*) poor; *Ausrede* feeble; *Kenntnisse* little ❸ (*spärlich*) *Informationen* sparse **II.** *adv* scantily

dürr ['dʏr] *adj* ❶ (*trocken*) dry; ~**es Laub** withered leaves ❷ (*mager*) [painfully] thin

Dürre <-, -n> ['dʏ·rə] *f* drought

Durst <-[e]s> ['dʊrst] *m kein pl* thirst; ■~ **haben** to be thirsty

dursten ['dʊrs·tn̩] *vi* (*geh*) to be thirsty

dürsten ['dʏrs·tn̩] *vi* (*geh*) ■**mich dürstet** [**es**] I am thirsty

durstig ['dʊrs·tɪç] *adj* thirsty

durstlöschend *adj* thirst-quenching

Durststrecke *f* lean period

Dusche <-, -n> ['duː·ʃə] *f* shower; **unter die ~ gehen** to take a shower

duschen ['duː·ʃn̩] **I.** *vi* to shower **II.** *vr* ■**sich** *akk* ~ to take a shower **III.** *vt* ■**jdn** ~ to give sb a shower

Duschgel *nt* body wash

Duschkabine *f* shower stall

Düse <-, -n> ['dyː·zə] *f* ❶ TECH nozzle ❷ LUFT jet

Dusel <-s> ['duː·zl̩] *m kein pl* (*fam*) ❶ (*Glück*) ~ **haben** to be lucky ❷ SCHWEIZ, SÜDD ■**im** ~ (*benommen*) in a daze; (*angetrunken*) tipsy

düsen ['dyː·zn̩] *vi sein* (*fam: fahren*) to race; (*schnell gehen*) to dash

Düsenantrieb *m* jet propulsion

Düsenflugzeug *nt* jet plane

dusselig ['dʊ·sə·lɪç], **dusslig**[RR] ['dʊs·lɪç], **dußlig**[ALT] ['dʊs·lɪç] (*fam*) **I.** *adj* daft **II.** *adv* ❶ (*dämlich*) **sich** *akk* ~ **anstellen** to act stupidly ❷ (*enorm viel*) **sich** *akk* ~ **arbeiten** to work oneself silly

düster ['dyːs·tɐ] *adj Himmel, Wetter* gloomy; **eine** ~**e Ahnung** a dark foreboding; ~**e Gedanken** black thoughts; **eine** ~**e Miene** a gloomy face; ~ **Prognosen** grim predictions

Dutzend <-s, -e> ['dʊ·tsn̩t, *pl* 'dʊ·tsn̩·də] *nt* dozen

dutzendmal *adv* dozens of times; *s. a.* **Mal**[1] **1**

dutzendweise ['dʊ·tsn̩t·vai·zə] *adv* by the dozen

duzen ['duː·tsn̩] *vt* ■**jdn** ~ to use "du" when addressing sb

DVD-Player <-s, -> [-pleːɐ] *m* DVD player

Dynamik <-> [dy·'naː·mɪk] *f kein pl* ❶ PHYS dynamics + *sing vb, no art* ❷ (*Triebkraft*) dynamism

dynamisch [dy·'naː·mɪʃ] **I.** *adj* dynamic **II.** *adv* dynamically

Dynamit <-s> [dy·na·'miːt] *nt kein pl* dynamite

Dynamo <-s, -s> [dy·'naː·mo] *m* generator

Dynastie <-, -n> [dyn·as·'tiː, *pl* dy·nas·'tiː·ən] *f* dynasty

Ee

E, e <-, - *o fam* -s, -s> [eː] *nt* ❶ (*Buchstabe*) E, e; ~ **wie Emil** E as in Echo ❷ MUS E, e
Ebbe <-, -n> [ˈɛbə] *f* ebb [*or* low] tide; (*Wasserstand*) low water; ~ **und Flut** the tides *pl;* **bei** ~ at low tide
eben[1] [ˈeːbn̩] **I.** *adj* ❶ (*flach*) flat ❷ (*glatt*) level **II.** *adv* evenly
eben[2] [ˈeːbn̩] **I.** *adv* ❶ *zeitlich* just ❷ (*nun einmal*) just; **das ist** ~ **so** that's [just] the way it is ❸ (*gerade noch*) just [about] ❹ (*kurz*) **mal** ~ for a minute **II.** *part* ❶ (*genau das*) precisely ❷ (*Abschwächung von Verneinung*) **das ist nicht** ~ **billig** that's/it's not exactly cheap
Ebenbild *nt* image
ebenbürtig [ˈeːbn̩·bʏr·tɪç] *adj* equal (**an** +*dat* in); **einander** [**nicht**] ~ **sein** to be [un]evenly matched
ebenda [ˈeːbn̩·ˈdaː] *adv* ❶ (*genau dort*) exactly there ❷ (*bei Zitat*) ibidem; (*geschrieben a.*) ibid.
ebender [eːbn̩·ˈdeːɐ̯], **ebendie** [eːbn̩·ˈdiː], **ebendas** [ˈeːbn̩·ˈdas] *pron* he/she/it
Ebene <-, -n> [ˈeːbə·nə] *f* ❶ (*Tiefebene*) plain; (*Hochebene*) plateau ❷ MATH, PHYS plane ❸ (*fig*) **auf wissenschaftlicher** ~ at the scientific level
ebenfalls [ˈeːbn̩·fals] *adv* as well; **danke,** ~**!** thanks, [and the] same to you
Ebenmaß *nt kein pl* (*geh*) regularity
ebenmäßig **I.** *adj* evenly proportioned **II.** *adv* symmetrically
ebenso [ˈeːbn̩·zoː] *adv* ❶ (*genauso*) just as; **er schwimmt** ~ **gern wie ich** he likes to swim just as well [*or* much] as I do; ~ **gut/oft/lang**(**e**) just as well/often/long; ~ **sehr/viel** just as much; ~ **wenig** just as little ❷ (*auch*) as well
ebensogern[ALT] *adv s.* **ebenso 1**
ebensogut[ALT] *adv s.* **ebenso 1**
ebensolang(**e**)[ALT] *adv s.* **ebenso 1**
ebensooft[ALT] [-zo·ʔɔft] *adv s.* **ebenso 1**
ebensosehr[ALT] *adv s.* **ebenso 1**
ebensoviel[ALT] *adv s.* **ebenso 1**
ebensowenig[ALT] *adv s.* **ebenso 1**
Eber <-s, -> [ˈeːbɐ] *m* boar
ebnen [ˈeːb·nən] *vt* to level [off] ▶ WENDUNGEN: **jdm/etw den Weg** ~ to pave the way for sb/sth
EC[1] <-s, -s> [eːˈtseː] *m Abk von* **Eurocity** Eurocity train
EC[2] <-s, -s> [eːˈtseː] *m* FIN *Abk von* **Electronic Cash** electronic cash (*a debit card system*)
Echo <-s, -s> [ˈɛço] *nt* ❶ (*Effekt*) echo ❷ (*Reaktion*) response (**auf** +*akk* to)
Echolot *nt* sonar
Echse <-, -n> [ˈɛk·sə] *f* lizard, saurian *spec*
echt [ˈɛçt] **I.** *adj* ❶ (*nicht künstlich, wirklich*) real; (*nicht gefälscht*) genuine; *Haarfarbe* natural; *Silber, Gold* pure ❷ *Freundschaft, Schmerz* sincere ❸ (*typisch*) typical ❹ *Farben* fast **II.** *adv* ❶ (*typisch*) typically ❷ (*fam: wirklich*) really
Echtheit <-> *f kein pl* ❶ (*das Echtsein*) authenticity ❷ (*Aufrichtigkeit*) sincerity
Eck <-[e]s, -e> [ˈɛk] *nt* ❶ ÖSTERR, SÜDD (*Ecke*) corner ❷ SPORT corner [of the goal]
EC-Karte [eːˈtseː-] *f* debit card
Eckball *m* SPORT corner [kick]
Ecke <-, -n> [ˈɛkə] *f* ❶ (*spitze Kante*) corner; (*Tischkante*) edge ❷ (*Straßen-, Zimmerecke*) corner ❸ (*fam: Gegend*) area ❹ SPORT corner [kick]
eckig [ˈɛk·ɪç] *adj* ❶ (*nicht rund*) square; *Gesicht* angular ❷ (*ungelenk*) jerky
Eckpfeiler *m* ❶ (*liter*) corner pillar ❷ (*fig*) cornerstone
Eckstein [ˈɛk·ʃtain] *m* cornerstone
Eckzahn *m* canine [tooth]
Ecuador, Ekuador <-s> [ekua̯·ˈdoːɐ̯] *nt* Ecuador; *s. a.* **Deutschland**
Ecuadorianer(**in**) <-s, -> [ekua̯·do·ˈri̯aː·nɐ] *m(f)* Ecuadorean; *s. a.* **Deutsche**(**r**)
ecuadorianisch [ekua̯·do·ˈri̯aː·nɪʃ] *adj* Ecuadorean; *s. a.* **deutsch**
edel [ˈeːdl̩] **I.** *adj* ❶ (*großherzig*) generous ❷ (*hochwertig*) fine ❸ (*aristokratisch*) noble **II.** *adv* nobly
Edelfrau *f* noblewoman
Edelgas *nt* inert gas
Edelkastanie *f* sweet chestnut
Edelmann <-leute> *m* nobleman
Edelmetall *nt* precious metal
Edelmut *m kein pl* (*geh*) magnanimity
edelmütig [ˈeːdl̩·myː·tɪç] **I.** *adj* (*geh*) magnanimous **II.** *adv* magnanimously
Edelstahl *m* stainless steel
Edelstein *m* precious stone
Edeltanne *f* silver fir
Edelweiß <-[es], -e> [ˈeːdl̩·vais] *nt* BOT edelweiss
Edikt <-[e]s, -e> [eˈdɪkt] *nt* edict
editieren* [edi·ˈtiː·rən] *vt* COMPUT to edit
Edition <-, -en> [edi·ˈtsi̯oːn] *f* (*die Ausgabe*) edition
EDV <-> [eː·deː·ˈfau] *f* COMPUT *Abk von* **elektronische Datenverarbeitung** EDP
Efeu <-s> [ˈeːfɔy] *m kein pl* ivy
Effeff [ˈɛf·ˈʔɛf] *nt kein pl* **etw aus dem** ~ **beherrschen** to know sth backwards and forwards
Effekt <-[e]s, -e> [ɛˈfɛkt] *m* effect
Effekten [ɛˈfɛk·tn̩] *pl* securities *pl*
effektiv [ɛfɛk·ˈtiːf] **I.** *adj* ❶ (*wirksam*) effective ❷ *attr* (*tatsächlich*) actual *attr* **II.** *adv* ❶ (*wirksam*) effectively ❷ (*tatsächlich*) actually
Effektivität <-> [ɛfɛk·ti·vi·ˈtɛːt] *f kein pl* effectiveness
effektvoll *adj* effective

E

effizient [ɛfi·ˈtsi̯ɛnt] (*geh*) **I.** *adj* efficient **II.** *adv* efficiently

EG <-> [eːˈgeː] *f* (*hist*) *Abk von* **Europäische Gemeinschaft** EC

e.G., E.G. <-> [eːˈgeː] *f* ÖKON *Abk von* **eingetragene Genossenschaft** registered cooperative society

egal [eˈgaːl] (*fam*) **I.** *adj* ■**jdm ~ sein** to be all the same to sb; **das ist mir ~** I don't care; (*unhöflicher*) I couldn't care less ▶WENDUNGEN: **~, was/wie/wo/warum ...** no matter what/how/where/why ... **II.** *adv* DIAL (*gleich*) identically; **~ lang** identical in length

Egoismus <-, Egoismen> [ego·ˈɪs·mʊs] *m* ego[t]ism

Egoist(in) <-en, -en> [ego·ˈɪst] *m(f)* ego[t]ist

egoistisch [ego·ˈɪs·tɪʃ] **I.** *adj* ego[t]istical **II.** *adv* ego[t]istically

Egotrip <-s, -s> [ˈeːgo·trɪp] *m* **auf dem ~ sein** (*fam*) to be on an ego trip

Egozentriker(in) <-s, -> [ego·ˈtsɛn·tri·kɐ] *m(f)* (*geh*) egocentric

egozentrisch [ego·ˈtsɛn·trɪʃ] *adj* (*geh*) egocentric

eh[1] [ˈeː] *interj* (*sl*) ❶ (*Anrede*) hey ❷ (*was?*) eh?

eh[2] [eː] **I.** *adv bes* ÖSTERR, SÜDD (*sowieso*) anyway ▶WENDUNGEN: **wie ~ und je** as always **II.** *konj s.* **ehe**

ehe [ˈeːə] *konj* before; **~ das Wetter nicht besser wird ...** until the weather changes for the better ...

Ehe <-, -n> [ˈeːə] *f* marriage

eheähnlich *adj* **in einer ~en Gemeinschaft leben** to cohabit

Ehebett *nt* double bed

Ehebrecher(in) <-s, -> *m(f)* adulterer *masc*, adulteress *fem*

Ehebruch *m* adultery; **~ begehen** to commit adultery

Ehefrau *f fem form von* **Ehemann** wife

Ehegatte *m* (*geh*) ❶ *s.* **Ehemann** ❷ *pl* (*Ehepartner*) ■**die ~n** [married] partners *pl*

Ehegattensplitting [-splɪtɪŋ] *nt* separate taxation for married couples, ≈ married, filing separately

Ehegattin *f* (*geh*) *fem form von* **Ehegatte** wife

Ehekrach *m* (*fam*) marital fight

Eheleben *nt kein pl* married life

Eheleute *pl* (*geh*) married couple + *sing/pl vb*

ehelich [ˈeːə·lɪç] **I.** *adj* marital; *Kind* legitimate **II.** *adv* legitimately

ehemalig [ˈeːə·maː·lɪç] *adj attr* former

ehemals [ˈeːə·maːls] *adv* (*geh*) formerly

Ehemann <-männer> *m* husband

Ehepaar *nt* [married] couple + *sing/pl vb*

eher [ˈeːɐ] *adv* ❶ (*früher*) sooner ❷ (*wahrscheinlicher*) more likely ❸ (*mehr*) more ❹ (*lieber*) rather

Ehering *m* wedding ring

Ehescheidung *f* divorce

Eheschließung *f* (*geh*) wedding

ehest [ˈeːəst] *adv* ÖSTERR (*baldigst*) as soon as possible

eheste(r, s) I. *adj attr* earliest **II.** *adv* ■**am ~n** ❶ (*am wahrscheinlichsten*) [the] most likely ❷ (*zuerst*) the first

ehestens [ˈeːəs·tn̩s] *adv* ❶ (*frühestens*) at the earliest ❷ ÖSTERR (*baldigst*) *s.* **ehest**

Ehevermittlung *f kein pl* matchmaking

Ehevertrag *m* prenuptial contract

ehrbar [ˈeːɐ̯·baːɐ̯] *adj* respectable

Ehrbegriff *m kein pl* sense of honor

Ehre <-, -n> [ˈeːrə] *f* honor; **jdm eine ~ sein** to be an honor for sb; **jdm wird die ~ zuteil, etw zu tun** sb is given the honor of doing sth ▶WENDUNGEN: **habe die ~!** ÖSTERR, SÜDD (*ich grüße Sie!*) [I'm] pleased to meet you

ehren [ˈeːr·ən] *vt* to honor (**mit** +*dat* with)

Ehrenamt *nt* honorary position

ehrenamtlich I. *adj* **~e Tätigkeiten** volunteer work **II.** *adv* on a voluntary basis

Ehrenbürger(in) *m(f)* honorary citizen

Ehrendoktor, -doktorin *m, f* honorary doctor

Ehrengast *m* guest of honor

ehrenhaft [ˈeːrən·haft] **I.** *adj* honorable **II.** *adv* honorably

Ehrenkodex *m* code of honor

Ehrenmann *m* man of honor

Ehrenplatz *m* place of honor

Ehrenrettung *f* vindication of one's honor; **zu jds ~** in sb's defense

Ehrenrunde *f* ❶ SPORT victory lap ❷ SCH (*fam: Wiederholung einer Klasse*) repetition of a grade

Ehrensache *f* matter of honor

Ehrenurkunde *f* certificate of honor

ehrenvoll *adj* honorable

ehrenwert *adj s.* **ehrbar**

Ehrenwort <-worte> *nt* word of honor

Ehrfurcht *f kein pl* respect; (*fromme Scheu*) reverence; **vor jdm/etw ~ haben** to have [great] respect for sb/sth

ehrfürchtig [ˈeːɐ̯·fʏrç·tɪç], **ehrfurchtsvoll I.** *adj* reverent **II.** *adv* reverentially

Ehrgefühl *nt kein pl* sense of honor

Ehrgeiz [ˈeːɐ̯·gaits] *m kein pl* ambition

ehrgeizig [ˈeːɐ̯·gai·tsɪç] *adj* ambitious

ehrlich [ˈeːɐ̯·lɪç] **I.** *adj* honest; **~e Zuneigung** genuine affection **II.** *adv* ❶ (*legal, vorschriftsmäßig*) **~ verdientes Geld** honestly earned money ❷ (*fam: wirklich*) honestly ▶WENDUNGEN: **~ gesagt ...** to be [quite] honest ...

Ehrlichkeit *f kein pl* ❶ (*Aufrichtigkeit*) sincerity ❷ (*Zuverlässigkeit*) honesty

ehrlos I. *adj* dishonorable **II.** *adv* dishonorably

Ehrlosigkeit <-> *f kein pl* dishonorableness

Ehrung <-, -en> *f* honor

Ehrwürden <*bei Voranstellung* -[s] *o bei Nachstellung* -> [ˈeːɐ̯·vʏr·dn̩] *m kein pl, ohne art* REL Reverend

ehrwürdig [ˈeːɐ̯·vʏr·dɪç] *adj* venerable

Ei <-[e]s, -er> [ˈai] *nt* ❶ (*Vogel-, Schlangenei*) egg; **ein hart/weich gekochtes ~** a hard-boiled/soft-boiled egg ❷ (*Eizelle*) ovum ❸ *pl* (*sl: Hoden*) balls *pl* ❹ *pl* (*sl: Geld*) ≈ bucks *pl fam*

Eiche <-, -n> ['ai·çə] *f* (*a. Holz*) oak
Eichel <-, -n> ['ai·çl̩] *f* ❶ BOT acorn ❷ ANAT glans
eichen ['ai·çn̩] *vt* to gauge; *Instrument, Messgerät* to calibrate
Eichhörnchen ['aiç·hœrn·çən] *nt* squirrel
Eid <-[e]s, -e> ['ait, *pl* 'ai·də] *m* oath; **einen ~ ablegen** to swear an oath
Eidechse ['ai·dɛk·sə] *f* lizard
eidesstattlich JUR **I.** *adj* in lieu of [an] oath **II.** *adv* **etw ~ erklären** to declare sth under oath
Eidgenosse, **-genossin** ['ait·gə·nɔ·sə, -gə·nɔ·sɪn] *m, f* Swiss [citizen]
Eidgenossenschaft *f* **Schweizerische ~** the Swiss Confederation
eidgenössisch ['ait·gə·nœ·sɪʃ] *adj* Swiss
eidlich ['ait·lɪç] **I.** *adj* [made] under oath **II.** *adv* under oath
Eidotter *m o nt* egg yolk
Eierbecher *m* egg cup
Eierkuchen *m* pancake
Eierlikör *m* egg liqueur
eiern ['ai·ɐn] *vi* (*fam*) to wobble
Eierschale *f* eggshell
Eierstock *m* ANAT ovary
Eiertanz *m* (*fam*) careful treading *fig*
Eieruhr *f* egg timer
Eifer <-s> ['ai·fɐ] *m kein pl* enthusiasm ► WENDUNGEN: **im ~ des Gefechts** (*fam*) in the heat of the moment
eifern ['ai·fɐn] *vi* (*geh*) ❶ (*wettern*) ■ **gegen etw** *akk* **~** to rail against sth ❷ (*veraltend: streben*) ■ **nach etw** *dat* **~** to strive for sth
Eifersucht ['ai·fɐ·zʊxt] *f kein pl* jealousy
eifersüchtig ['ai·fɐ·zʏç·tɪç] *adj* jealous
Eifersuchtsszene *f* **jdm eine ~ machen** to make a scene [in a fit of jealousy]
eifrig ['ai·frɪç] **I.** *adj* eager; *Leser, Sammler* avid **II.** *adv* eagerly; **~ lernen** to study hard [*or* diligently]
Eigelb <-s, -e *o bei Zahlenangaben* -> *nt* egg yolk
eigen ['ai·gn̩] *adj* ❶ (*jdm gehörig*) own; **seine ~e Meinung/Wohnung haben** to have one's own opinion/apartment ❷ (*separat*) **mit ~em Eingang** with a separate entrance ❸ (*typisch*) **mit dem ihr ~en Optimismus ...** with her characteristic optimism ... ❹ (*eigenartig*) peculiar
Eigenart ['ai·gn̩·ʔaːɐ̯t] *f* ❶ (*besonderer Wesenszug*) characteristic ❷ (*Flair*) individuality
eigenartig ['ai·gn̩·ʔaːɐ̯·tɪç] **I.** *adj* strange **II.** *adv* strangely
Eigenbedarf *m* **zum ~** for one's [own] personal use
Eigenbrötler(in) <-s, -> ['aign̩·brøːt·lɐ] *m(f)* loner
eigenbrötlerisch ['aign̩·brøːt·lə·rɪʃ] *adj* reclusive
eigenhändig ['aign̩·hɛn·dɪç] **I.** *adj* personal; *Brief* handwritten; *Testament* holographic **II.** *adv* personally
Eigenheim *nt* home of one's own
Eigenheit <-, -en> *f s.* **Eigenart**
Eigeninitiative *f* **in ~** on one's own initiative
Eigenkapital *nt* (*einer Firma*) equity capital
eigenmächtig ['aign̩·mɛç·tɪç] **I.** *adj* highhanded **II.** *adv* highhandedly
Eigenname *m* LING proper noun
Eigennutz <-es> *m kein pl* self-interest
eigennützig ['aign̩·nʏ·tsɪç] **I.** *adj* selfish **II.** *adv* selfishly
eigens ['ai·gn̩s] *adv* [e]specially
Eigenschaft <-, -en> ['ai·gn̩·ʃaft] *f* ❶ (*Charakteristik*) quality, trait ❷ (*Funktion*) capacity
Eigenschaftswort <-wörter> *nt* LING adjective
eigensinnig ['ai·gn̩·zɪ·nɪç] **I.** *adj* stubborn **II.** *adv* stubbornly
eigenständig ['ai·gn̩·ʃtɛn·dɪç] **I.** *adj* independent **II.** *adv* independently
eigentlich ['ai·gn̩t·lɪç] **I.** *adj* ❶ (*wirklich*) real; *Wesen* true ❷ (*ursprünglich*) original **II.** *adv* ❶ (*normalerweise*) really; **da hast du ~ Recht** you may be right there ❷ (*wirklich*) actually **III.** *part* (*überhaupt*) **was ist ~ mit dir los?** what [on earth] is wrong with you?; **wie alt bist du ~?** how old are you anyway?
Eigentor *nt* own goal
Eigentum <-s, *selten* -e> ['ai·gn̩·tuːm] *nt* property
Eigentümer(in) <-s, -> ['ai·gn̩·tyː·mɐ] *m(f)* owner
eigentümlich ['ai·gn̩·tyːm·lɪç] **I.** *adj* ❶ (*merkwürdig*) strange ❷ (*geh: typisch*) ■ **jdm/einer S. ~** characteristic of sb/sth **II.** *adv* strangely
Eigentümlichkeit <-, -en> *f* ❶ (*Besonderheit*) characteristic ❷ (*Eigenheit*) peculiarity
Eigentumswohnung *f* condominium
eigenverantwortlich **I.** *adj* with sole responsibility *pred* **II.** *adv* on one's own authority
Eigenverantwortung *f* personal responsibility
eigenwillig ['ai·gn̩·vɪ·lɪç] *adj* ❶ (*eigensinnig*) stubborn ❷ (*unkonventionell*) unconventional
eignen ['aig·nən] *vr* ■ **sich** *akk* **für etw** *akk* **~** to be suited to sth
Eignung <-, -en> ['aig·nʊŋ] *f* suitability
Eignungsprüfung *f*, **Eignungstest** *m* aptitude test
Eilbeschluss[RR] *m* JUR quick decision
Eilbote, **-botin** *m, f* express messenger; **per ~n** [by] express [delivery]
Eilbrief *m* express letter
Eile <-> ['ai·lə] *f kein pl* haste; **etw hat ~** sth is urgent; **in ~ sein** to be in a hurry
Eileiter <-s, -> *m* ANAT fallopian tube
eilen ['ai·lən] **I.** *vi* ❶ *sein* (*schnell gehen*) ■ **irgendwohin ~** to hurry somewhere ❷ *haben* (*dringlich sein*) ■ **etw eilt** sth is urgent **II.** *vi impers haben* ■ **es eilt** it's urgent
Eilgut *nt kein pl* express freight
eilig ['ai·lɪç] **I.** *adj* ❶ (*schnell*) hurried ❷ (*dringend*) urgent; **es ~ haben** to be in a hurry **II.** *adv* quickly
Eiltempo *nt* **im ~** (*fam*) as quickly as possible

Eilzug *m* BAHN *a type of express train*
Eimer <-s, -> ['ai·mɐ] *m* bucket
ein[1] ['ain] *adv* (*eingeschaltet*) on; **E~ / Aus** on/off
ein[2] ['ain], **eine** ['ai·nə], **ein** ['ain] **I.** *adj* one; **mir fehlt noch ~ Cent** I need one more cent ▶ WENDUNGEN: **~ für alle Mal** once and for all **II.** *art indef* ❶ (*einzeln*) a/an; **was für ~ Lärm!** what a noise! ❷ (*jeder*) a/an
Einakter <-s, -> ['ain·ʔaktɐ] *m* THEAT one-act play
einander [ai·'nan·dɐ] *pron* each other
ein|arbeiten **I.** *vr* ■ **sich** *akk* [**in etw** *akk*] ~ to get used to [sth] **II.** *vt* ❶ (*praktisch vertraut machen*) ■ **jdn** [**in etw** *akk*] ~ to train sb [for sth] ❷ (*einfügen*) ■ **etw** [**in etw** *akk*] ~ to add sth in[to sth] ❸ ÖSTERR (*nachholen*) *Zeitverlust* to make up [for] sth
Einarbeitungszeit *f* training period
ein|äschern ['ain·ʔɛʃɐn] *vt Leiche* to cremate
ein|atmen *vt, vi* to breathe in *sep*
einäugig ['ain·ʔɔy·gɪç] *adj* one-eyed
Einbahnstraße *f* one-way street
ein|balsamieren* *vt Leiche* to embalm
Einband <-bände> ['ain·bant, *pl* -bɛn·də] *m* [book] cover
einbändig ['ain·bɛn·dɪç] *adj* VERLAG one-volume *attr*
Einbau <-bauten> *m* ❶ *kein pl* installation ❷ *meist pl* (*eingebautes Teil*) built-in part *usu pl*
ein|bauen *vt* ■ **etw** [**in etw** *akk*] ~ ❶ (*installieren*) to build sth in[to] sth; *Batterie, Motor* to install sth in[to] sth ❷ (*fam: einfügen*) to incorporate sth [into sth]
Einbauküche *f* fitted kitchen
Einbauschrank *m* built-in cupboard; (*im Schlafzimmer*) built-in closet
ein|behalten* *vt irreg Abgaben, Steuern* to withhold
ein|berufen* *vt irreg* ❶ (*zusammentreten lassen*) to convene ❷ MIL to draft, to conscript
Einberufung *f* ❶ (*das Einberufen*) convention ❷ MIL draft card
ein|betten *vt* to embed (**in** + *akk* in)
Einbettzimmer *nt* single room
ein|beziehen* *vt irreg* to include (**in** + *akk* in)
ein|biegen *vi irreg sein* to turn (**in** + *akk* into)
ein|bilden *vr* ❶ (*fälschlicherweise glauben*) ■ **sich** *dat* **etw** ~ to imagine sth; ■ **sich** *dat* **~, dass ...** to think that ...; **was bildest du dir eigentlich ein?** (*fam*) what has gotten into your head? ❷ (*stolz sein*) ■ **sich** *dat* **etw auf etw** *akk* ~ to be proud of sth
Einbildung *f* ❶ *kein pl* (*Fantasie*) imagination ❷ *kein pl* (*Arroganz*) conceitedness
Einbildungskraft *f kein pl* [powers of] imagination
ein|binden *vt irreg* ❶ VERLAG ■ **etw** ~ to bind sth (**in** + *akk* in) ❷ (*einbeziehen*) ■ **jdn/etw** ~ to integrate sb/sth (**in** + *akk* into)
ein|blenden *vt* to insert; *Geräusche, Musik* to dub in
Einblick *m* insight; **~ in etw** *akk* **haben** to be able to see into sth; (*informiert sein*) to have insight into sth
ein|brechen *irreg* **I.** *vi* ❶ *sein o haben* (*Einbruch verüben*) to break in ❷ *sein Dämmerung, Nacht* to fall ❸ *sein* (*nach unten durchbrechen*) to fall through ❹ *sein* (*einstürzen*) to cave in **II.** *vt haben* to break down *sep*
Einbrecher(in) <-s, -> *m(f)* burglar
ein|bringen *irreg* **I.** *vt* ❶ (*eintragen*) to bring; **Zinsen ~** to earn interest ❷ (*einfließen lassen*) **seine Erfahrung ~** to bring one's experience to sth ❸ *Ernte* to bring in ❹ (*vorschlagen*) **einen Antrag ~** to table a motion **II.** *vr* ■ **sich** *akk* ~ to contribute
ein|brocken *vt* (*fam*) ■ **jdm etw ~** to land sb in trouble
Einbruch <-[e]s, -brüche> ['ain·brʊx, *pl* -brʏ·çə] *m* ❶ JUR break-in ❷ (*das Eindringen*) penetration ❸ *Mauer* collapse ❹ (*plötzlicher Beginn*) onset; **bei ~ der Dunkelheit** at nightfall
ein|bürgern ['ain·bʏr·gɐn] **I.** *vt* ❶ ADMIN ■ **jdn** ~ to naturalize sb ❷ (*heimisch werden*) ■ **eingebürgert werden** to become established **II.** *vr* (*übernommen werden*) ■ **sich** ~ to become established
Einbürgerung <-, -en> *f* ADMIN naturalization
ein|büßen **I.** *vt* to lose **II.** *vi* ■ **an etw** *dat* ~ to lose sth
ein|checken [-tʃɛkn̩] **I.** *vi* to check in **II.** *vt* ■ **etw/jdn** ~ to check in *sep* sth/sb
ein|cremen ['ain·kre:·mən] *vt* ■ **sich** *dat* **etw** ~ to put cream [*or* lotion] on sth
ein|dämmen *vt* to dam, to contain
ein|decken **I.** *vr* ■ **sich** *akk* [**mit etw** *dat*] ~ to stock up [on sth] **II.** *vt* (*fam: überhäufen*) ■ **jdn mit etw** *dat* ~ to swamp sb with sth
eindeutig ['ain·dɔy·tɪç] **I.** *adj* ❶ (*unmissverständlich*) unambiguous ❷ (*unzweifelhaft*) clear **II.** *adv* ❶ (*unmissverständlich*) unambiguously ❷ (*klar*) clearly
ein|dicken ['ain·dɪkn̩] **I.** *vt haben* KOCHK to thicken **II.** *vi sein* to thicken
eindimensional *adj* one-dimensional
ein|dringen *vi irreg sein* ❶ (*einbrechen*) ■ **in etw** *akk* ~ to force one's way into sth ❷ (*vordringen*) ■ **in etw** *akk* ~ to force one's way into sth; MIL to penetrate [into] sth ❸ (*hineindringen*) ■ **in etw** *akk* ~ to penetrate [into] sth ❹ (*bestürmen*) ■ **auf jdn** ~ to besiege sb
eindringlich **I.** *adj* (*nachdrücklich*) powerful **II.** *adv* strongly
Eindringling <-s, -e> ['ain·drɪŋ·lɪŋ] *m* intruder
Eindruck <-[e]s, -drücke> ['ain·drʊk, *pl* -drʏ·kə] *m* (*Vorstellung*) impression; **den ~ erwecken/haben, dass ...** to give/have the impression that ...
ein|drücken **I.** *vt* (*nach innen drücken*) to push in *sep; Kotflügel* to dent; *Fenster* to break **II.** *vr* (*einen Abdruck hinterlassen*) ■ **sich in etw** *akk* ~ to make an imprint in sth

eindrücklich ['ain·drʏk·lɪç] *adj* SCHWEIZ (*eindrucksvoll*) impressive

eindrucksvoll **I.** *adj* impressive **II.** *adv* impressively

eine(r, s) ['ai·nə] *pron indef* ① (*jemand*) someone, somebody; **~s von den Kindern** one of the children ② (*fam: man*) one; **und das soll noch ~r glauben?** and I'm expected to swallow that? ③ (*ein Punkt*) ■ **~s** one thing

eineiig ['ain·ʔai·ɪç] *adj* BIOL identical

eineinhalb ['ain·ʔain·'halp] *adj* one and a half

ein|engen ['ain·ɛŋ·ən] *vt* ① (*beschränken*) ■ **jdn in etw** *dat* **~** to restrict sb in sth ② (*drücken*) ■ **jdn ~** to restrict sb's movement[s] ③ (*begrenzen*) ■ **etw ~** to restrict sth

einer ['ai·nɐ] *pron s.* **eine(r, s)**

einerlei ['ai·nɐ·'lai] *adj pred* (*egal*) **das ist mir ganz ~** it's all the same to me

einerseits ['ai·nɐ·zaits] *adv* **~ ... andererseits ...** on the one hand ..., on the other hand ...

einfach ['ain·fax] **I.** *adj* ① (*leicht*) easy, simple ② (*gewöhnlich*) simple ③ (*nur einmal gemacht*) single; **eine ~e Fahrkarte** a one-way ticket **II.** *adv* (*leicht*) easily; **~ zu verstehen** easy to understand **III.** *part* ① (*ohne weiteres*) simply, just ② + *Verneinung* (*zur Verstärkung*) simply, just; **das geht ~ nicht!** we/you just can't do that!

Einfachheit <-> *f kein pl* ① (*Unkompliziertheit*) straightforwardness ② (*Schlichtheit*) plainness ▶ WENDUNGEN: **der ~ halber** for the sake of simplicity

ein|fädeln ['ain·fɛː·dl̩n] **I.** *vt* ① (*Faden*) to thread ② (*fam: anbahnen*) to engineer *fig* **II.** *vr* AUTO ■ **sich** *akk* **~** to merge

ein|fahren *irreg* **I.** *vi sein* (*hineinfahren*) ■ **in etw** *akk* **~** to pull in to sth; **auf einem Gleis ~** to arrive on a platform **II.** *vt haben* ① (*kaputtfahren*) ■ **etw ~** to drive [*or* crash] *sep* into sth ② *Antenne, Objektiv* to retract ③ *Gewinne* to make ④ *Heu, Korn* to harvest

Einfahrt <-, -en> *f* ① *kein pl* (*das Einfahren*) entry; **die ~ eines Zuges** the arrival of a train ② (*Zufahrt*) entrance; (*Auffahrt*) driveway

Einfall ['ain·fal] *m* ① (*Idee*) idea ② MIL (*das Eindringen*) ■ **~ in etw** *akk* invasion of sth ③ (*das Eindringen*) incidence

ein|fallen *vi irreg sein* ① (*in den Sinn kommen*) ■ **etw fällt jdm ein** sth occurs to sb ② (*in Erinnerung kommen*) ■ **etw fällt jdm ein** sb remembers sth ③ (*einstürzen*) to collapse ④ (*eindringen*) **in ein Land ~** to invade a country ⑤ (*einsetzen*) ■ **[in etw** *akk*] **~** *Chor, Instrument* to join in [on] [sth]; (*dazwischenreden*) to interrupt [sth] ⑥ (*Wangen*) to become hollow

einfallslos **I.** *adj* unimaginative **II.** *adv* unimaginatively

einfallsreich **I.** *adj* imaginative **II.** *adv* imaginatively

Einfallsreichtum *m kein pl* imaginativeness

Einfalt <-> ['ain·falt] *f kein pl* naivety

einfältig ['ain·fɛl·tɪç] **I.** *adj* naive **II.** *adv* naively

Einfaltspinsel *m* (*pej fam*) simpleton

Einfamilienhaus *nt* single-family house

ein|fangen *irreg* **I.** *vt* ■ **jdn/ein Tier [wieder]** **~** to [re]capture sb/an animal **II.** *vr* (*fam*) ■ **sich** *dat* **etw ~** to catch sth

einfarbig *adj* in one color

ein|fassen *vt* ■ **etw ~** ① (*umgeben*) to border sth; *Garten* to enclose sth ② (*umsäumen*) to hem sth ③ *Diamant* to set sth

ein|fetten *vt* to grease

ein|finden *vr irreg* (*geh*) ■ **sich** *akk* **[irgendwo]** **~** to arrive [somewhere]

ein|fließen *vi irreg sein* ① FIN (*als Zuschuss gewährt werden*) ■ **[in etw** *akk*] **~** to pour in[to sth] ② (*anmerken*) **~ lassen, dass ...** to let [it] slip that ... ③ METEO ■ **in etw** *akk* **~** to move into sth

ein|flößen *vt* ① (*langsam eingeben*) ■ **jdm etw ~** to give sb sth ② (*erwecken*) **jdm Angst/Vertrauen ~** to instill fear/confidence in sb

Einflugschneise *f* approach [path]

Einfluss[RR], **Einfluß**[ALT] <-flusses, -flüsse> ['ain·flʊs, *pl* -flʏ·sə] *m* ① (*Einwirkung*) influence; **auf etw/jdn ~ haben** to have an influence on sth/sb ② (*Beziehungen*) influence

einflussreich[RR] *adj* influential

ein|fordern *vt* (*geh*) ■ **etw [von jdm] ~** to demand payment of sth [from sb]

einförmig ['ain·fœr·mɪç] **I.** *adj* monotonous; *Landschaft* uniform **II.** *adv* monotonously

ein|frieren *irreg* **I.** *vi sein* ① (*zufrieren*) to freeze up ② (*von Eis eingeschlossen werden*) ■ **in etw** *dat* **~** to become icebound in sth **II.** *vt haben* ① (*konservieren*) to [deep-]freeze ② (*suspendieren*) to suspend; *Projekt* to shelve ③ ÖKON to freeze

ein|fügen **I.** *vt* ■ **etw [in etw** *akk*] **~** ① (*einpassen*) to fit sth in[to sth] ② (*einfließen lassen*) to add sth [to sth] **II.** *vr* ■ **sich** *akk* **[in etw** *akk*] **~** ① (*sich anpassen*) to adapt [oneself] [to sth] ② (*hineinpassen*) to fit in [with sth]

ein|fühlen *vr* ■ **sich** *akk* **in jdn ~** to empathize with sb

einfühlsam **I.** *adj* sensitive; *Worte* understanding; *Mensch* empathetic **II.** *adv* sensitively

Einfühlungsvermögen *nt* empathy

Einfuhr <-, -en> ['ain·fuːɐ̯] *f* importation

Einfuhrbestimmungen *pl* import regulations *pl*

ein|führen **I.** *vt* ① (*importieren*) to import ② (*bekannt machen*) ■ **etw ~** to introduce sth; *Artikel, Firma* to establish ③ (*vertraut machen*) ■ **jdn ~** to introduce sb (**in** +*akk* to) ④ (*hineinschieben*) ■ **etw ~** to insert sth (**in** +*akk* into) **II.** *vi* ■ **in etw** *akk* **~** to serve as an introduction to sth

Einführung *f* introduction

Einführungspreis *m* introductory price

Einfuhrzoll *m* import tax [*or* duty]

Eingabe <-, -en> *f* ① (*Petition*) petition (**bei** +*dat* to) ② *kein pl Arznei* administration ③ *kein pl Daten, Informationen* entry

Eingabedaten *pl* COMPUT input data *usu + sing vb*

Eingabetaste *f* COMPUT enter [*or* return] key

Eingang <-[e]s, -gänge> ['ain·gaŋ, *pl* -gɛŋə] *m* ① (*Tür, Tor, Zugang*) entrance; *eines Waldes* opening; **„kein ~!“** “no entry” ② *pl* (*eingetroffene Sendungen*) incoming mail ③ *kein pl* (*Erhalt*) receipt ④ *kein pl* (*Beginn*) start

eingängig **I.** *adj* ① (*einprägsam*) catchy ② (*verständlich*) comprehensible **II.** *adv* clearly

eingangs ['ain·gaŋs] **I.** *adv* at the start **II.** *präp* at the start of

Eingangshalle *f* entrance hall

Eingangskontrolle *f* HANDEL incoming inspection

ein|geben *irreg vt* ① (*verabreichen*) ■**jdm etw ~** to administer sth to sb ② COMPUT ■**etw ~** to input sth (**in** +*akk* into) ③ (*geh: inspirieren*) ■**jdm etw ~** to put sth into sb's head

eingebildet *adj* ① (*pej: hochmütig*) conceited (**auf** +*akk* about) ② (*imaginär*) imaginary

eingeboren ['ain·gə·bo:·rən] *adj* native

Eingeborene(r) *f(m)* native

Eingebung <-, -en> *f* (*Inspiration*) inspiration

eingefahren *adj* well-worn

eingefallen *adj* hollow; *Gesicht* gaunt

ein|gehen *irreg* **I.** *vi sein* ① (*Aufnahme finden*) **in die Geschichte ~** to go down in history ② (*ankommen*) to arrive [somewhere] ③ ([*ab*]*sterben*) to die (**an** +*dat* of); *Laden* to go bust *fam* ④ (*aufgenommen werden*) ■**jdm ~** to be grasped by sb ⑤ (*einlaufen*) to shrink ⑥ (*sich beschäftigen mit*) ■**auf etw~** to deal with sth; ■**auf jdn ~** to pay attention to sb ⑦ (*zustimmen*) ■**auf etw** *akk* **~** to agree to sth; (*sich einlassen*) to accept sth **II.** *vt sein* ■**etw ~** to enter into sth; **ein Risiko ~** to take a risk; **ich gehe jede Wette ein, dass ...** I'll bet you anything that ...

eingehend ['ain·ge:·ənt] **I.** *adj* detailed; *Prüfung* extensive **II.** *adv* in detail

Eingemachte(s) *nt dekl wie adj* KOCHK preserved fruit

eingeschnappt *adj* (*fam*) ■**~ sein** to be miffed

eingeschrieben **I.** *adj* registered **II.** *adv* **~ schicken** to send by registered mail

eingespannt *adj pred* ■[**sehr**] **~ sein** to be [very] busy

eingespielt *adj* working well together

Eingeständnis ['ain·gə·ʃtɛnt·nɪs] *nt* admission

ein|gestehen* *irreg* **I.** *vt* ■[**jdm**] **etw ~** to admit sth [to sb] **II.** *vr* ■**sich** *dat* **~, dass ...** to admit to oneself that ...

eingestellt *adj* ① (*gesinnt*) **fortschrittlich/ökologisch ~** progressively/environmentally minded; ■**jd ist gegen jdn ~** sb is set against sb ② (*vorbereitet*) ■**auf etw** *akk* **~ sein** to be prepared for sth

eingetragen *adj Mitglied, Verein, Warenzeichen* registered

Eingeweide <-s, -> ['ain·gə·vai·də] *nt meist pl* entrails *npl*

Eingeweihte(r) *f(m)* initiate

ein|gewöhnen* *vr* ■**sich** *akk* **~** to settle in, to acclimatize

Eingewöhnung *f* settling in, acclimatization

ein|gießen *vt irreg* ■[**jdm**] **etw ~** to pour [sb] sth (**in** +*akk* into)

eingleisig ['ain·glai·zɪç] *adj* single-track

ein|gliedern **I.** *vt* ① (*integrieren*) ■**jdn ~** to integrate sb (**in** +*akk* into) ② ADMIN, POL (*einbeziehen*) ■**etw ~** to incorporate sth (**in** +*akk* into) **II.** *vr* ■**sich** *akk* **~** to integrate oneself (**in** +*akk* into)

Eingliederung *f* ① (*Integration*) integration ② ADMIN, POL incorporation

ein|graben *irreg* **I.** *vt* ■**etw ~** to bury sth **II.** *vr* ① (*sich verschanzen*) ■**sich** *akk* **~** to dig [oneself] in ② (*sich einprägen*) **sich in jds Gedächtnis ~** to burn itself into sb's memory ③ (*eindringen*) ■**sich in etw** *akk* **~** to dig into sth

ein|gravieren* *vt* to engrave (**in** +*akk* in/on)

ein|greifen *vi irreg* ① (*einschreiten*) to intervene (**in** +*akk* in) ② TECH (*sich hineinschieben*) ■**in etw** *akk* **~** to mesh with sth

Eingreiftruppe *f* intervention force

ein|grenzen *vt* ■**etw ~** to limit sth (**auf** +*akk* to)

Eingriff *m* ① (*Einschreiten*) intervention (**in** +*akk* in) ② MED operation

ein|haken **I.** *vt* ■**etw** [**in etw** *akk*] **~** to hook sth in[to sth] **II.** *vi* (*fam*) ■[**bei etw** *dat*] **~** to butt in [on sth] **III.** *vr* ■**sich** *akk* [**bei jdm**] **~** to link arms [with sb]

Einhalt ['ain·halt] *m kein pl* **jdm/einer S. ~ gebieten** (*geh*) to put a stop to sb/sth

ein|halten *irreg vt* **eine Diät ~** to stick to a diet; **einen Vertrag ~** to honor [the terms of] a contract; **die Spielregeln/Vorschriften ~** to obey the rules

Einhaltung <-, -en> *f* adherence; *von Spielregeln, Vorschriften* compliance

ein|handeln **I.** *vt* ■**etw gegen etw** *akk* **~** to trade sth for sth **II.** *vr* (*fam*) **sich** *dat* **eine Krankheit ~** to catch a disease

einhändig ['ain·hɛn·dɪç] **I.** *adj* one-handed **II.** *adv* with one hand

ein|hängen **I.** *vt* ① (*einsetzen*) ■**etw ~** to hang sth; *Fenster* to install ② *Hörer* to hang up **II.** *vr* ■**sich** *akk* [**bei jdm**] **~** to link arms [with sb]

einheimisch ['ain·hai·mɪʃ] *adj* ① (*ortsansässig*) local ② BOT, ZOOL indigenous

Einheimische(r) *f(m)* (*Ortsansässige*[*r*]) local; (*Inländer*) native [citizen]

Einheit <-, -en> ['ain·hait] *f* unity

The Treaty on the Final Settlement with Respect to Germany was signed by the

Federal Republic of Germany (the FRG or West Germany), the German Democratic Republic (the GDR or East Germany), and the four victorious powers of the Second World War in Moscow on September 12, 1990. The treaty led to the reunification of Germany with the GDR becoming part of the FRG on October 3, 1990. Since then, October 3 has been celebrated as the **Tag der deutschen Einheit** (Day of German Unity).

einheitlich ['ain·hait·lɪç] **I.** *adj* ❶ (*gleich*) uniform ❷ (*in sich geschlossen*) integrated; *Front* united **II.** *adv* ~ **gekleidet** dressed the same

Einheitswährung *f* single currency

ein|heizen *vi* (*gründlich heizen*) to turn the heat on

einhellig ['ain·hɛ·lɪç] **I.** *adj* unanimous **II.** *adv* unanimously

ein|holen **I.** *vt* ❶ (*einziehen*) to pull in *sep; Fahne, Segel* to lower ❷ *Genehmigung* to ask for ❸ (*erreichen, nachholen*) ■**jdn/etw** ~ to catch up with [*or* to] sb/sth ❹ (*wettmachen*) ■**etw** ~ to make up for sth **II.** *vt, vi* DIAL (*einkaufen*) to go shopping

Einhorn ['ain·hɔrn] *nt* unicorn

ein|hüllen *vt* (*geh*) ■**jdn/etw** ~ to wrap [up *sep*] sb/sth (**in** +*akk* in)

einhundert ['ain·'hʊn·dɐt] *adj* (*geh*) one hundred

einig ['ai·nɪç] *adj* ❶ (*geeint*) united ❷ *pred* (*einer Meinung*) ■**sich** *dat* [**über etw** *akk*] ~ **sein** to agree [*or* be in agreement] [on sth]

einige(r, s) ['ai·nɪ·gə] *pron indef* ❶ *sing, adjektivisch* (*ziemlich*) some; (*etwas*) a little; **nach ~r Zeit** after some time ❷ *sing, substantivisch* (*viel*) ■**~s** quite a lot ❸ *pl, adjektivisch* (*mehrere*) several; **vor ~n Tagen** a few days ago ❹ *pl, substantivisch* (*Dinge*) some; (*Menschen*) some; ~ **von euch** some of you; ~ **wenige** a few

einigen ['ai·nɪgn̩] **I.** *vt* (*einen*) to unite **II.** *vr* (*sich einig werden*) ■**sich** ~ to agree (**auf** +*akk* on)

einigermaßen ['ai·nɪ·gɐ·'maː·sn̩] *adv* ❶ (*ziemlich*) fairly ❷ (*leidlich*) all right

Einigkeit <-> ['ai·nɪç·kait] *f kein pl* ❶ (*Eintracht*) unity ❷ (*Übereinstimmung*) agreement

Einigung <-, -en> *f* ❶ POL unification ❷ (*Übereinstimmung*) agreement (**über** +*akk* on)

ein|impfen *vt* ■**jdm etw** ~ to drum sth into sb

ein|jagen *vt* **jdm Angst/Furcht/Schrecken** ~ to scare/frighten/terrify sb

einjährig, 1-jährig^RR ['ain·jɛː·rɪç] *adj* ❶ (*Alter*) one-year-old *attr,* one year old *pred; s. a.* **achtjährig 1** ❷ BOT annual ❸ (*Zeitspanne*) one-year *attr,* [of] one year *pred; s. a.* **achtjährig 2**

ein|kalkulieren* *vt* ■**etw** [**mit**] ~ to take sth into account

ein|kassieren* *vt* ■**etw** ~ ❶ (*kassieren*) to collect sth ❷ (*fam: wegnehmen*) to confiscate sth

Einkauf *m* ❶ (*das Einkaufen*) shopping; **beim ~ von Lebensmitteln ...** when buying food ... ❷ (*eingekaufter Artikel*) purchase

ein|kaufen **I.** *vt* (*käuflich erwerben*) to buy **II.** *vi* to shop **III.** *vr* (*einen Anteil erwerben*) ■**sich** *akk* **in etw** *akk* ~ to buy [one's way] into sth

Einkäufer(in) *m(f)* buyer

Einkaufsbummel *m* shopping trip

Einkaufspassage [-pa·saː·ʒə] *f* galleria

Einkaufspreis *m* purchase price

Einkaufswagen *m* shopping cart

Einkaufszentrum *nt* shopping center [*or* mall]

Einkaufszettel *m* shopping list

ein|kehren *vi sein* ❶ (*veraltend: besuchen*) ■[**in etw** *dat*] ~ to stop off [at sth] ❷ (*geh: kommen*) to set in

ein|klagen *vt* JUR ■**etw** ~ to sue for sth

ein|klammern *vt* ■**etw** ~ to put sth in parentheses

Einklang *m* (*geh*) harmony

ein|kleben *vt* ■**etw** [**in etw** *akk*] ~ to stick sth [into sth]; (*mit Klebstoff*) to glue sth [into sth]

ein|kleiden *vt* ■**sich** *akk* [**neu**] ~ to buy oneself a new wardrobe

ein|klemmen *vt* ■**etw** ~ ❶ (*quetschen*) to catch [*or* trap] sth ❷ (*festdrücken*) to clamp sth

ein|kochen KOCHK **I.** *vt haben* to preserve **II.** *vi sein* to thicken

Einkommen <-s, -> *nt* income

einkommensschwach *adj* low-income *attr*

einkommensstark *adj* high-income *attr*

Einkommensteuer *f* income tax

ein|kreisen *vt* ❶ (*einkringeln*) to circle ❷ (*umschließen*) ■**jdn/ein Tier** ~ to surround sb/an animal

ein|kriegen *vr* (*fam*) **sich** *akk* **nicht** [**mehr**] ~ [**können**] to not be able to contain oneself [anymore]

Einkünfte ['ain·kʏnf·tə] *pl* income

ein|laden *irreg vt* ❶ (*Hochzeit, Party*) to invite (**zu** +*dat* to) ❷ (*Gegenstände*) to load (**in** +*akk* in[to])

einladend **I.** *adj* ❶ (*auffordernd*) inviting *attr* ❷ (*appetitlich*) appetizing **II.** *adv* invitingly

Einladung *f* invitation

Einlage <-, -n> *f* ❶ (*eingezahltes Geld*) deposit ❷ FIN investment ❸ *Schuhe* insole ❹ THEAT interlude ❺ (*Beilage*) enclosure; (*in Zeitung*) supplement ❻ (*provisorische Zahnfüllung*) temporary filling

ein|lagern *vt* to store

Einlass^RR, **Einlaß**^ALT <-lasses, -lässe> ['ain·las, *pl* 'ain·lɛ·sə] *m* admission

ein|lassen *irreg* **I.** *vt* ❶ (*eintreten lassen*) ■**jdn** ~ to let sb in ❷ (*einlaufen lassen*) **jdm ein Bad** ~ to run sb a bath ❸ (*einfügen*) ■**etw** ~ to set sth (**in** +*akk* in) **II.** *vr* ❶ (*auf etw eingehen*) ■**sich** *akk* **auf etw** *akk* ~ to get involved in sth; *Abenteuer* to embark on sth;

Kompromiss to accept sth ② (*bes pej: Kontakt aufnehmen*) ■**sich** *akk* **mit jdm** ~ to get involved with sb

ein|laufen *irreg* **I.** *vi sein* ① (*schrumpfen*) to shrink ② (*Badewasser*) to run ③ SPORT **als Erster** ~ to come in first ④ (*einfahren*) ■**[in etw** *akk*] ~ to arrive **II.** *vt haben* **Schuhe** ~ to wear shoes in

ein|leben *vr* ■**sich** *akk* ~ to settle in

ein|legen *vt* ① (*hineintun*) ■**etw [in etw** *akk*] ~ to put sth in [sth] ② AUTO **den zweiten Gang** ~ to shift into second [gear] ③ KOCHK ■**etw [in etw** *dat o akk*] ~ to pickle sth [in sth] ④ (*zwischendurch machen*) **eine Pause** ~ to take a break ⑤ (*einreichen*) **einen Protest** ~ to lodge a protest; JUR to file a protest ⑥ *Geld* to deposit ⑦ (*intarsieren*) to inlay

ein|leiten *vt* ① (*in die Wege leiten*) **Schritte [gegen jdn]** ~ to take steps [against sb] ② MED to induce ③ (*eröffnen*) ■**etw** ~ to open sth ④ (*hineinfließen lassen*) ■**etw in etw** *akk* ~ to empty sth into sth

einleitend **I.** *adj* introductory **II.** *adv* as an introduction

Einleitung *f* (*a. Vorwort*) introduction; *eines Verfahrens* institution; *einer Untersuchung* opening

ein|lenken *vi* ① (*nachgeben*) to give in (**in** +*akk* to), to make concessions (**in** +*akk* in) ② (*einbiegen*) *Straße* to turn (**in** +*akk* into)

ein|leuchten *vi* ■**[jdm]** ~ to make sense [to sb]

einleuchtend **I.** *adj* evident; *Argument* convincing; *Erklärung* plausible **II.** *adv* clearly

ein|liefern *vt* ① (*stationär aufnehmen lassen*) ■**jdn** ~ to admit sb ② (*aufgeben*) ■**etw** ~ to hand in *sep* sth

Einlieferung *f* ① MED admission ② *Brief, Paket* handing-in

ein|lochen *vt* ① (*fam: inhaftieren*) ■**jdn** ~ to lock sb up ② (*Golf*) to hole out

ein|loggen ['ain·lɔ·gn̩] *vi* ■**[sich** *akk*] ~ to log in

ein|lösen *vt* ① *Scheck* to cash ② *Pfand* to redeem (**bei** +*dat* at) ③ *Versprechen* to honor

ein|machen **I.** *vt* to preserve; (*in Essig*) to pickle sth **II.** *vi* to preserve [sth]

Einmachglas *nt* [preserving] jar

einmal[1], **1-mal**[RR] ['ain·maːl] *adv* ① (*ein Mal*) once ② (*ein einziges Mal*) once; ~ **am Tag/in der Woche/im Monat** once a day/week/month; **auf** ~ all of a sudden; (*an einem Stück*) all at once ③ (*mal*) first ④ (*früher*) once; **es war** ~ once upon a time ⑤ (*später*) sometime ▶ WENDUNGEN: ~ **ist keinmal** (*prov*) just once doesn't count

einmal[2] ['ain·maːl] *part* ① (*eben*) **so liegen die Dinge nun** ~ that's [just] the way things are ② (*einschränkend*) **nicht** ~ not even

Einmaleins <-> [ain·maːl·'ʔains] *nt kein pl* ■**das** ~ multiplication tables *pl*

einmalig ['ain·maː·lɪç] **I.** *adj* ① (*nicht wiederkehrend*) unique ② (*fam: ausgezeichnet*) outstanding **II.** *adv* (*besonders*) really

Einmalspritze *f* disposable syringe

Einmannbetrieb *m* ① (*Einzelunternehmen*) one-man business ② TRANSP one-man operation

Einmarsch *m* invasion (**in** +*akk* of)

ein|marschieren* *vi sein* **in ein Land** ~ to invade a country

ein|mischen *vr* ■**sich** *akk* ~ to interfere (**bei** +*dat* with/in, **in** +*akk* with/in)

Einmischung *f* interference

einmotorig *adj* single-engine

ein|münden *vi sein* ■**in etw** *akk* ~ ① (*auf etw führen*) to lead into sth ② (*in etw münden*) to flow into sth

Einmündung *f eines Flusses* confluence

einmütig ['ain·myː·tɪç] **I.** *adj* unanimous **II.** *adv* unanimously

Einnahme <-, -n> ['ain·naː·mə] *f* ① FIN earnings *npl; bei einem Geschäft* receipts *npl* ② *kein pl Arzneimittel, Mahlzeiten* taking ③ (*Eroberung*) capture

Einnahmequelle *f* source of income

ein|nehmen *vt irreg* ① *Geld* to take; *Steuern* to collect ② (*zu sich nehmen*) to take; *Mahlzeit* to have ③ (*geh*) *Platz* to take ④ *Standpunkt* to hold ⑤ SPORT to hold ⑥ (*erobern*) to take ⑦ (*beeinflussen*) ■**jdn für sich** *akk* ~ to win favor with sb ⑧ *Raum* to take up

einnehmend ['ain·neː·mənt] *adj* engaging

ein|nicken *vi sein* (*fam*) to doze off

ein|nisten *vr* ① (*sich niederlassen*) ■**sich** *akk* **bei jdm** ~ to ensconce oneself [with sb] ② *Ungeziefer* ■**sich** ~ to nest

Einöde ['ain·ʔøː·də] *f* wasteland

ein|ordnen **I.** *vt* ① (*einsortieren*) ■**etw** ~ to organize sth ② (*klassifizieren*) ■**jdn/etw** ~ to classify sb/sth **II.** *vr* ① (*sich einfügen*) ■**sich** *akk* ~ to integrate (**in** +*akk* into) ② (*Fahrspur wechseln*) ■**sich** *akk* **links/rechts** ~ to merge [to the] left/right

ein|packen **I.** *vt* ① (*verpacken*) ■**etw** ~ to wrap sth; (*um zu verschicken*) to pack sth ② (*einstecken*) ■**[jdm] etw** ~ to pack sth [for sb] ③ (*fam: einmummeln*) ■**jdn** ~ to wrap sb up **II.** *vi* (*Koffer etc. füllen*) to pack [one's things] [up]

ein|parken *vi, vt* to park; (*am Strassenrand*) to parallel park

ein|passen **I.** *vt* ■**etw** ~ to fit sth (**in** +*akk* into) **II.** *vr* ■**sich** *akk* ~ to integrate (**in** +*akk* into)

ein|pendeln *vr* ■**sich** ~ *Währung, Preise* to level off

Einpersonenhaushalt *m* (*geh*) single-person household

ein|pferchen *vt* to cram in; *Tiere* to pen (**in** +*akk* in)

ein|pflanzen *vt* ① (*Pflanze*) to plant (**in** +*akk* in) ② MED ■**[jdm] etw** ~ to implant sth [in sb]

ein|planen *vt* to plan; ■**etw [mit]** ~ to take sth into consideration

ein|prägen **I.** *vr* ① (*sich etw einschärfen*) ■**sich** *dat* **etw** ~ to make a mental note of sth ② (*im Gedächtnis haften*) ■**sich jdm** ~ *Bil-*

der, Eindrücke, Worte to be imprinted on [*or* in] sb's memory **II.** *vt* ■ **jdm etw ~** to drum sth into sb's head

einprägsam ['ain·prɛːk·zaːm] *adj* easy to remember *pred; Melodie* catchy

ein|quartieren* ['ain·kvar·tiː·rən] **I.** *vt* ① (*unterbringen*) ■ **jdn ~** to put up *sep* sb ② MIL ■ **jdn irgendwo ~** to billet sb somewhere **II.** *vr* ■ **sich** *akk* **bei jdm ~** to move in with sb

ein|rahmen *vt* to frame

ein|rasten *vi sein* to click into place

ein|räumen *vt* ① (*in etw räumen*) to put sth away (**in** +*akk* in) ② (*mit Möbeln füllen*) *Zimmer* to arrange ③ (*zugestehen*) ■ [**jdm gegenüber**] **etw ~** to concede [*or* admit] sth [to sb] ④ (*gewähren*) ■ **jdm etw ~** *Frist, Kredit* to give sb sth

ein|rechnen *vt* ① (*mit einbeziehen*) ■ **jdn** [**mit**] **~** to include sb ② (*als inklusiv rechnen*) ■ **etw** [**mit**] **~** to include sth

ein|reden **I.** *vt* ■ **jdm etw ~** to talk sb into thinking sth **II.** *vi* (*bedrängen*) ■ **auf jdn ~** to pester sb *fam* **III.** *vr* ■ **sich** *dat* **etw ~** to talk oneself into thinking sth

ein|reiben *vt irreg* **jdn mit Sonnenöl ~** to put suntan oil on sb

ein|reichen *vt a.* JUR ■ **etw** [**bei jdm**] **~** to submit sth [to sb]

ein|reihen **I.** *vt* (*zuordnen*) ■ **jdn/etw unter etw** *akk* **~** to classify sb/sth under sth **II.** *vr* (*sich einfügen*) ■ **sich** *akk* **in etw** *akk* **~** to join sth

Einreise *f* entry [into a country]

Einreisegenehmigung *f* entry permit

ein|reisen *vi sein* (*geh*) to enter

Einreiseverbot *nt* refusal of entry

Einreisevisum *nt* [entry] visa

ein|reißen *irreg* **I.** *vi sein* ① (*einen Riss bekommen*) to tear; *Haut* to crack ② (*fam: zur Gewohnheit werden*) to become a habit **II.** *vt haben* ① (*niederreißen*) to tear down *sep* ② (*mit Riss versehen*) to tear

ein|renken ['ain·rɛŋ·kn̩] **I.** *vt* ① MED ■ [**jdm**] **etw ~** to pop sth back in [place] [for sb] ② (*fam: bereinigen*) ■ **etw** [**wieder**] **~** to straighten out *sep* sth [again] **II.** *vr* (*fam: ins Lot kommen*) ■ **sich wieder ~** to sort itself out

ein|rennen *irreg* **I.** *vr* (*fam: sich anstoßen*) **sich** *dat* **den Kopf an der Wand ~** to bang one's head against the wall **II.** *vt* (*fam: einstoßen*) ■ **etw ~** to break down *sep* sth

ein|richten **I.** *vt* ① (*möblieren*) to furnish; *Praxis* to equip ② (*gründen*) to set up *sep* ③ *Konto* to open ④ (*arrangieren*) ■ **es ~, dass ...** arrange it so that ... ⑤ MED **einen gebrochenen Arm ~** to set a broken arm ⑥ (*vorbereitet sein*) ■ **auf etw** *akk* **eingerichtet sein** to be prepared for sth **II.** *vr* ① (*sich möblieren*) **ich richte mich völlig neu ein** I'm completely refurnishing my home ② (*sich einbauen*) ■ **sich** *dat* **etw ~** to install sth ③ (*sich der Lage anpassen*) ■ **sich** *akk* **~** to adapt [to a situation] ④ (*sich einstellen*) ■ **sich** *akk* **auf etw** *akk* **~** to be prepared for sth

Einrichtung <-, -en> *f* ① (*Möbel*) furnishings *npl;* (*Ausstattung*) decorations *npl* ② (*das Möblieren*) furnishing; (*das Ausstatten*) decorating ③ (*das Installieren*) installation ④ (*Eröffnung*) opening; *eines Lehrstuhles* establishment ⑤ FIN opening ⑥ TRANSP establishment ⑦ (*Institution*) organization

Einrichtungsgegenstand *m* piece of furniture, decoration

ein|rollen **I.** *vr haben* ■ **sich** *akk* **~** to curl up **II.** *vi sein* (*einfahren*) to pull in

ein|rosten *vi sein* ① (*rostig werden*) to rust ② (*ungelenkig werden*) to get stiff

ein|rücken **I.** *vi sein* ① MIL ■ [**in etw** *akk*] **~** to march [into sth] ② MIL (*eingezogen werden*) ■ [**zu etw** *dat*] **~** to enlist [in sth] **II.** *vt haben* ① (*vom Rand entfernen*) to indent ② VERLAG ■ [**jdm**] **etw ~** to print sth [for sb]

eins ['ains] **I.** *adj* one; *s. a.* **acht**[1] ▶ WENDUNGEN: **~ A** (*fam*) first-class **II.** *adj pred* ① (*eine Ganzheit*) [all] one ② (*egal*) ■ **etw ist jdm ~** sth is all the same to sb ③ (*einig*) ■ **~ mit jdm/sich/etw sein** to be [at] one with sb/oneself/sth

einsam ['ain·zaːm] **I.** *adj* ① (*verlassen*) lonely, lonesome ② (*vereinzelt*) solitary ③ (*abgelegen*) isolated ④ (*menschenleer*) deserted ⑤ (*fam: absolut*) absolute **II.** *adv* (*abgelegen*) **~ liegen** to be situated in a remote place

Einsamkeit <-, *selten* -en> *f* ① (*Verlassenheit*) loneliness ② (*Abgeschiedenheit*) remoteness

ein|sammeln *vt* ■ **etw ~** ① (*sich aushändigen lassen*) to collect sth ② (*aufsammeln*) to pick up *sep* sth

Einsatz <-es, Einsätze> *m* ① (*eingesetzte Leistung*) effort; **unter ~ ihres Lebens** by putting her own life at risk ② *beim Glücksspiel* bet ③ FIN deposit ④ (*Verwendung*) use; *von Truppen* deployment ⑤ (*Aktion*) assignment; **im ~ sein** to be on duty ⑥ MUS entry; **den ~ geben** to cue in *sep* sth ⑦ (*eingesetztes Teil*) inset ⑧ (*eingelassenes Stück*) insert

einsatzbereit *adj* ready for use *pred; Menschen* ready for action; MIL ready for combat *pred*

Einsatzbereitschaft *f* readiness for action; *von Maschinen* readiness for use; **in ~ sein** to be on standby

Einsatzfreude *f* enthusiasm

Einsatzwagen *m* (*Polizeifahrzeug*) squad car

ein|saugen *vt* to suck; *Luft* to inhale

ein|schalten **I.** *vt* ① (*in Betrieb setzen*) to switch on *sep* ② (*hinzuziehen*) ■ **jdn ~** to call in *sep* sb **II.** *vr* ■ **sich** *akk* [**in etw** *akk*] **~** ① RADIO, TV to tune in[to sth] ② (*sich einmischen*) to intervene [in sth]

Einschaltquote *f* [audience] ratings *npl*

ein|schärfen **I.** *vt* (*zu etw ermahnen*) ■ **jdm etw ~** to impress on sb the importance of sth **II.** *vr* ■ **sich** *dat* **etw ~** to remember sth

ein|schätzen *vt* to assess, to judge; **Sie haben ihn richtig eingeschätzt** your opinion of him was right

Einschätzung *f* assessment; *einer Person* opinion

ein|schenken *vt* ■**jdm etw ~** to pour sb sth

ein|schieben *vt irreg* ❶ (*in etw schieben*) ■**etw ~** to insert sth (**in** +*akk* into) ❷ (*zwischendurch einfügen*) ■**etw ~** to fit sth in

ein|schiffen I. *vt* ■**jdn/etw ~** to take sb/sth on board II. *vr* (*an Bord gehen*) ■**sich** *akk* **~** to embark

einschl. *Abk von* **einschließlich** incl.

ein|schlafen *vi irreg sein* ❶ (*in Schlaf fallen*) ■[**bei etw** *dat*] **~** to fall asleep [during sth] ❷ (*taub werden*) to fall asleep ❸ (*nachlassen*) to peter out

ein|schläfern ['ain·ʃlɛː·fɐn] *vt* ❶ (*jds Schlaf herbeiführen*) ■**jdn ~** to lull sb to sleep ❷ (*schläfrig machen*) ■**jdn ~** to put sb to sleep ❸ ([*schmerzlos*] *töten*) ■**ein Tier ~** to put an animal to sleep

einschläfernd ['ain·ʃlɛː·fɐnt] *adj* ❶ MED **ein ~es Mittel** a sleep-inducing drug ❷ (*langweilig*) ■**~ sein** to put sb to sleep

Einschlag *m* ❶ METEO *eines Blitzes* strike ❷ MIL shot; *einer Granate* burst of shellfire; *einer Kugel* bullet hole ❸ (*Anteil*) strain

ein|schlagen *irreg* I. *vt haben* ❶ (*in etw schlagen*) ■**etw ~** to hammer in *sep* sth ❷ (*durch Schläge öffnen*) **eine Tür ~** to break down *sep* a door ❸ (*zerschmettern*) **jdm die Zähne ~** to knock sb's teeth out ❹ (*einwickeln*) ■**etw ~** to wrap sth ❺ *Laufbahn, Weg* to choose ❻ AUTO to turn ❼ MODE to take in II. *vi* ❶ *sein o haben* ■[**in etw** *akk*] **~** *Blitz* to strike [sth] ❷ *sein Granaten* to fall ❸ *sein o haben* (*durchschlagende Wirkung*) to have an impact ❹ *haben* (*einprügeln*) ■**auf jdn ~** to hit sb ❺ *haben* (*Anklang finden*) to catch on

einschlägig ['ain·ʃlɛː·gɪç] I. *adj* (*entsprechend*) relevant II. *adv* JUR in this connection

ein|schleichen *vr irreg* ■**sich** *akk* [**in etw** *akk*] **~** ❶ (*in etw schleichen*) to sneak in[to sth] ❷ (*unbemerkt auftreten*) to creep in[to sth]

ein|schließen *vt irreg* ❶ (*in einen Raum schließen*) ■**jdn ~** to lock up *sep* sb ❷ (*wegschließen*) ■**etw ~** to lock away *sep* sth ❸ (*einbegreifen*) ■**jdn ~** to include sb ❹ (*einkesseln*) ■**jdn/etw ~** to surround sb/sth

einschließlich ['ain·ʃliːs·lɪç] I. *präp* (*inklusive*) ■**~ einer S.** *gen* including sth II. *adv* (*inbegriffen*) inclusive

ein|schmeicheln *vr* ■**sich** *akk* [**bei jdm**] **~** to ingratiate oneself [with sb]

ein|schmieren *vt* ❶ (*einölen*) to lubricate ❷ (*einreiben*) **etw mit Salbe ~** to rub cream into sth ❸ (*beschmutzen*) **sich** *akk* **mit Dreck ~** to cover oneself with dirt

einschnappen *vi sein* ❶ (*ins Schloss fallen*) to click shut ❷ (*fam: beleidigt sein*) to get in a huff

ein|schneiden *irreg* I. *vt* ■**etw ~** *Papier, Stoff* to make a cut in sth II. *vi* (*schmerzhaft eindringen*) ■[**in etw** *akk*] **~** to cut [into sth]

einschneidend ['ain·ʃnai·dn̩t] *adj* **eine ~e Veränderung** a drastic change

Einschnitt *m* ❶ MED incision ❷ (*eingeschnittene Stelle*) cut ❸ (*Zäsur*) turning point

ein|schränken ['ain·ʃrɛŋ·kn̩] I. *vt* ■**etw ~** ❶ (*reduzieren*) to cut [back on] sth ❷ (*beschränken*) to curb sth II. *vr* ■**sich** *akk* **~** to cut back (**in** +*dat* on)

Einschränkung <-, -en> *f* ❶ (*Beschränkung*) restriction ❷ (*Vorbehalt*) reservation ❸ (*das Reduzieren*) reduction

ein|schreiben *irreg* I. *vt* to register II. *vr* ❶ (*sich eintragen*) ■**sich** *akk* **~** to put one's name down ❷ SCH, UNI ■**sich** *akk* **~** to register

Einschreiben *nt* registered letter

ein|schreiten *vi irreg sein* to take action (**gegen** +*akk* against)

Einschub *m* insertion

ein|schüchtern ['ain·ʃʏç·tɐn] *vt* ■**jdn ~** to intimidate sb

ein|schulen *vt* to enroll in [elementary] school

Einschuss[RR], **Einschuß**[ALT] <-schusses, *pl* -schüsse> *m* (*Schussloch*) bullet hole; (*Einschussstelle*) entry point of a bullet

ein|schweißen *vt Nahrungsmittel, Bücher* to seal, to shrink-wrap

ein|sehen *vt irreg* ❶ (*begreifen*) to see ❷ (*in etw hineinsehen*) ■**etw ~** to look into sth [from outside]

einseitig ['ain·zai·tɪç] I. *adj* ❶ (*eine Person betreffend*) one-sided ❷ MED one-sided ❸ (*beschränkt*) one-sided; **eine ~e Ernährung** an unbalanced diet ❹ (*voreingenommen*) bias[s]ed II. *adv* ❶ (*auf einer Seite*) on one side ❷ (*beschränkt*) in a one-sided way ❸ (*parteiisch*) from a one-sided point of view

Einseitigkeit <-, *selten* -en> *f* ❶ (*Voreingenommenheit*) bias ❷ (*Beschränktheit*) one-sidedness; *Ernährung* imbalance

ein|senden *vt irreg* ■**etw ~** to send sth (**an** +*akk* to)

Einsender(in) *m(f)* sender

Einsendeschluss[RR] *m* deadline [for entries]

einsetzbar *adj* applicable

ein|setzen I. *vt* ❶ (*einfügen*) to insert ❷ (*einnähen*) ■**etw** [**in etw** *akk*] **~** to sew sth in[to sth] ❸ *Kommission* to set up ❹ (*ernennen*) ■**jdn** [**als etw** *akk*] **~** to appoint sb [as sth] ❺ (*zum Einsatz bringen*) ■**jdn/etw** [**gegen jdn**] **~** to use sb/sth [against sb]; SPORT to put in *sep* ❻ (*aufbieten*) to use ❼ (*wetten*) to bet, to wager II. *vi* ❶ (*anheben*) to start [up] ❷ MUS to begin to play III. *vr* ❶ (*sich engagieren*) ■**sich** *akk* **~** to make an effort ❷ (*sich verwenden für*) ■**sich** *akk* **für jdn/etw ~** to support sb/sth

Einsicht *f* ❶ (*Vernunft*) sense; (*Erkenntnis*) insight; **jdn zur ~ bringen** to make sb see reason ❷ (*prüfende Durchsicht*) **~ in etw** *akk* **nehmen** to have access to sth

einsichtig ['ain·zɪç·tɪç] *adj* ❶ (*verständlich*) understandable ❷ (*vernünftig*) reasonable

einsilbig ['ain·zɪl·bɪç] *adj a.* LING monosyllabic

ein|sinken *vi irreg sein Morast, Schnee etc.* to sink in; *Boden* to cave in

ein|sortieren* *vt* to sort [out]; *Dokumente* to file away

ein|spannen *vt* ① (*heranziehen*) ■ **jdn [für etw** *akk*] ~ to call sb in [for [*or* to do] sth] ② (*in etw spannen*) to insert; (*in einen Schraubstock*) to clamp ③ *Tiere* to harness ④ (*viel zu tun haben*) ■ **sehr eingespannt sein** to be very busy

ein|sparen *vt* ① (*ersparen*) to save ② (*kürzen*) ■ **etw** ~ to save on sth

Einsparung <-, -en> *f* ① (*das Einsparen*) saving ② (*Kürzung*) cutting down

ein|sperren *vt* ① (*in etw sperren*) ■ **jdn/ein Tier** ~ to lock sb/an animal up ② (*inhaftieren*) ■ **jdn** ~ to lock sb up

ein|spielen **I.** *vr* ① (*einstellen*) ■ **sich** ~ *Methode, Regelung* to get going ② (*sich aneinander gewöhnen*) ■ **sich aufeinander** ~ to get used to each other ③ SPORT ■ **sich** *akk* ~ to warm up **II.** *vt* FILM ■ **etw** ~ to bring in sth; *Produktionskosten* to cover sth

einsprachig *adj* monolingual

ein|springen *vi irreg sein* (*fam*) ① (*vertreten*) ■ [**für jdn**] ~ to cover [for sb] ② (*aushelfen*) ■ [**mit etw** *dat*] ~ to help out [with sth]

Einspruch *m* (*Protest*) *a.* JUR objection

einspurig ['ain·ʃpuː·rɪç] **I.** *adj* ① TRANSP one-lane ② (*pej*) ~**es Denken** one-track mind **II.** *adv* TRANSP **die Straße ist nur ~ befahrbar** only one lane of the road is open [to traffic]

einst ['ainst] *adv* ① (*früher*) once ② (*geh: in Zukunft*) one day

Einstand *m* ① *bes* SÜDD, ÖSTERR (*Arbeitsanfang*) start of a new job ② TENNIS deuce

ein|stecken *vt* ① (*in die Tasche stecken*) *Geld, Schlüssel* to pocket, to put in one's pocket ② *Brief* to mail ③ (*fam: hinnehmen*) ■ **etw** ~ to put up with sth ④ (*verkraften*) ■ **etw** ~ to take sth ⑤ ELEK ■ **etw** ~ to plug in *sep* sth

ein|stehen *vi irreg sein* ① (*sich verbürgen*) ■ **für jdn/etw** ~ to vouch for sb/sth ② (*aufkommen*) ■ **für etw** *akk* ~ to take responsibility for sth

ein|steigen *vi irreg sein* ■ [**in etw** *akk*] ~ ① (*besteigen*) *Auto* to get in [sth]; *Bus, Flugzeug* to get on [*or* board] [sth] ② (*fam: hineinklettern*) to climb in[to sth] ③ ÖKON to buy into sth ④ (*sich engagieren*) to get involved [in sth]

ein|stellen **I.** *vt* ① (*anstellen*) to employ ② (*beenden*) to stop; *Suche* to call off; *Projekt* to shelve ③ MIL to stop; **das Feuer** ~ to cease fire ④ JUR to abandon ⑤ FOTO, TECH to adjust ⑥ ELEK to set ⑦ TV, RADIO to tune ⑧ (*hineinstellen*) **das Auto in die Garage** ~ to put the car in the garage ⑨ SPORT **den Rekord** ~ to tie the record **II.** *vr* ① (*auftreten*) ■ **sich** ~ *Bedenken* to begin; MED *Fieber, Symptome* to develop ② (*sich anpassen*) ■ **sich** *akk* **auf jdn/etw** ~ to adapt to sb/sth ③ (*sich vorbereiten*) ■ **sich** *akk* **auf etw** *akk* ~ to prepare oneself for sth ④ (*geh: sich einfinden*) ■ **sich** *akk* ~ to arrive **III.** *vi* (*beschäftigen*) to hire

einstellig *adj* single-digit *attr*

Einstellung *f* ① (*Gesinnung*) attitude ② (*Anstellung*) employment ③ (*Beendigung*) stopping ④ FOTO adjustment ⑤ FILM take ⑥ ELEK setting ⑦ TV, RADIO tuning

Einstieg <-[e]s, -e> ['ain·ʃtiːk, *pl* 'ain·ʃtiː·gə] *m* ① *kein pl* (*das Einsteigen*) boarding ② (*Tür zum Einsteigen*) *Bahn* door; *Bus a.* entrance; *Panzer* hatch ③ (*Aufnahme*) start

ein|stimmen **I.** *vi* ■ [**in etw** *akk*] ~ to join in [sth] **II.** *vt* (*innerlich einstellen*) ■ **jdn auf etw** *akk* ~ to get sb in the right frame of mind for sth

einstimmig[1] ['ain·ʃtɪ·mɪç] **I.** *adj* MUS **ein ~es Lied** a song for one voice **II.** *adv* MUS in unison

einstimmig[2] ['ain·ʃtɪ·mɪç] **I.** *adj* unanimous **II.** *adv* unanimously

einstöckig ['ain·ʃtœ·kɪç] *adj* one-story *attr*

ein|streuen *vt* ■ **etw** ~ ① (*einflechten*) to work sth in ② (*ganz bestreuen*) to scatter sth

ein|studieren* *vt* to rehearse

ein|stufen ['ain·ʃtuː·fn̩] *vt* ① (*eingruppieren*) ■ **jdn in etw** *akk* ~ to place sb in sth ② (*zuordnen*) ■ **etw in etw** *akk* ~ to categorize sth as sth

einstündig, **1-stündig**[RR] *adj* one-hour *attr*, lasting one hour *pred*

Einsturz *m* collapse; *Decke a.* cave-in; *Mauer* falling-down

ein|stürzen *vi sein* ① (*zusammenbrechen*) to collapse; *Decke a.* to cave in ② (*heftig eindringen*) ■ **auf jdn** ~ to overwhelm sb

Einsturzgefahr *f kein pl* danger of collapsing

einstweilen ['ainst·'vai·lən] *adv* ① (*vorläufig*) for the time being ② (*in der Zwischenzeit*) in the meantime

einstweilig ['ainst·'vai·lɪç] *adj attr* temporary

eintägig, **1-tägig**[RR] *adj* one-day *attr*, lasting one day *pred*

Eintagsfliege *f* ① ZOOL mayfly ② (*von kurzer Dauer*) **eine ~ sein** to be here today gone tomorrow

ein|tauchen **I.** *vt haben* ■ **etw** ~ to dip sth in **II.** *vi sein* ■ [**in etw** *akk*] ~ to dive in[to sth]

ein|tauschen *vt* ■ **etw** ~ ① (*tauschen*) to exchange sth (**gegen** +*akk* for) ② (*umtauschen*) to [ex]change sth (**gegen** +*akk* for)

eintausend ['ain·'tau·zn̩t] *adj* one thousand

ein|teilen **I.** *vt* ① (*unterteilen*) ■ **etw in etw** *akk* ~ to divide sth up into sth ② (*sinnvoll aufteilen*) ■ **etw** ~ to plan sth [out]; ■ [**sich** *dat*] **etw** ~ *Geld, Vorräte, Zeit* to be careful with sth ③ (*für etw verpflichten*) ■ **jdn zu etw** *dat* ~ to assign sb to sth **II.** *vi* (*fam: haushalten*) to budget

Einteilung *f* ① (*Aufteilung*) management ② (*Verpflichtung*) ■ **jds ~ zu etw** *dat* sb's assignment to sth

eintönig ['ain·tøː·nɪç] **I.** *adj* monotonous **II.** *adv* monotonously; ~ **klingen** to sound monotonous

Eintönigkeit <-> *f kein pl* monotony

E

Eintopf *m*, **Eintopfgericht** *nt* stew
Eintracht <-> ['ain·traxt] *f kein pl* harmony
einträchtig ['ain·trɛç·tɪç] **I.** *adj* harmonious **II.** *adv* harmoniously
Eintrag <-[e]s, Einträge> ['ain·traːk, *pl* -trɛː·gə] *m* ❶ (*Vermerk*) note ❷ (*im Nachschlagewerk*) entry ❸ ADMIN record
ein|tragen *vt irreg* ❶ (*einschreiben*) ■**jdn** ~ to record sb's name (**in** +*akk* in) ❷ (*amtlich registrieren*) to register ❸ (*einzeichnen*) ■**etw** ~ to note sth [down]
Eintragung <-, -en> *f* JUR (*form*) entry, registration
ein|treffen *vi irreg sein* ❶ (*ankommen*) to arrive ❷ (*in Erfüllung gehen*) to come true; *Ereignis, Katastrophe* to happen
ein|treiben *vt irreg* ■**etw** [**von jdm**] ~ to collect sth [from sb]
ein|treten *irreg* **I.** *vi* ❶ *sein* (*betreten*) to enter ❷ *sein* (*beitreten*) *Partei, Verein* to join ❸ *sein* (*sich ereignen*) to occur; **sollte der Fall ~, dass ...** if it should happen that ... ❹ *sein* (*sich einsetzen*) ■**für jdn/etw** ~ to stand up for sb/sth ❺ *haben* (*wiederholt treten*) ■**auf jdn/ein Tier** ~ to kick sb/an animal [repeatedly] **II.** *vt haben* ■**etw** ~ to kick sth in
Eintritt *m* ❶ (*geh: das Betreten*) ~ **verboten** do not enter ❷ (*Beitritt*) ■**jds ~ in etw** *akk* sb's joining sth ❸ (*Eintrittsgeld*) admission ❹ (*Beginn*) onset
Eintrittskarte *f* [admission] ticket
Eintrittspreis *m* admission charge
ein|üben *vt* to practice; *Rolle, Stück* to rehearse
ein|verleiben* ['ain·fɛɐ̯·lai·bn̩] **I.** *vt* ■**etw einer S.** *dat* ~ *Gebiet, Land* to incorporate sth into sth **II.** *vr* ■**sich** *dat* **etw** ~ ❶ ÖKON to incorporate sth ❷ (*hum fam: verzehren*) to put sth away
Einvernehmen <-s> *nt kein pl* agreement
einverstanden ['ain·fɛɐ̯·ʃtan·dn̩] *adj pred* ■~ **sein** to agree (**mit** +*dat* with)
Einverständnis ['ain·fɛɐ̯·ʃtɛnt·nɪs] *nt* ❶ (*Zustimmung*) consent ❷ (*Übereinstimmung*) agreement
Einwand <-[e]s, Einwände> ['ain·vant, *pl* -vɛn·də] *m* objection (**gegen** +*akk* to)
Einwanderer, -wand[r]erin *m, f* immigrant
ein|wandern *vi sein* to immigrate
Einwanderung *f* immigration (**nach** to, **in** into); **kontrollierte** ~ selective [*or* controlled] immigration
Einwanderungsgesetz *nt* immigration laws *usu pl*
Einwanderungspolitik *f kein pl* immigration policy
einwandfrei ['ain·vant·frai] *adj* ❶ (*tadellos*) flawless; *Obst* perfect; *Qualität* excellent; *Benehmen* impeccable ❷ (*unzweifelhaft*) irrefutable
ein|wechseln *vt* ❶ *Währung* to change (**in** +*akk* into) ❷ SPORT ■**jdn** [**für jdn**] ~ to substitute sb [for sb]
Einwegflasche *f* nonreturnable bottle
ein|weichen *vt* ■**etw** [**in etw** *dat*] ~ to soak sth [in sth]
ein|weihen *vt* ❶ (*offiziell eröffnen*) ■**etw** ~ to open sth [officially], to have a grand opening ❷ (*vertraut machen*) ■**jdn** ~ to initiate sb (**in** +*akk* into)
Einweihung <-, -en> *f* ❶ (*das Eröffnen*) inauguration ❷ (*das Vertrautmachen*) initiation
ein|weisen *vt irreg* ❶ (*unterweisen*) ■**jdn** ~ to brief sb (**in** +*akk* about) ❷ MED to refer
ein|wenden *vt irreg* ■**etw** [**gegen etw** *akk*] ~ to object [to sth]
ein|werfen *irreg* **I.** *vt* ■**etw** ~ ❶ *Brief* to mail sth ❷ (*durch Wurf zerschlagen*) to break sth ❸ SPORT to throw in *sep* sth ❹ (*etw zwischendurch bemerken*) to throw in *sep* sth **II.** *vi* ❶ SPORT to throw in ❷ (*zwischendurch bemerken*) ■**~, dass ...** to throw in that ...
ein|wickeln *vt* ❶ (*in etw wickeln*) ■**etw** ~ to wrap [up *sep*] sth ❷ (*fam: überlisten*) ■**jdn** ~ to take sb in
ein|willigen ['ain·vɪ·lɪ·gn̩] *vi* ■[**in etw** *akk*] ~ to consent [to sth]
Einwilligung <-, -en> *f* consent
ein|wirken *vi* ❶ (*beeinflussen*) ■**auf jdn/etw** ~ to have an effect on sb/sth ❷ PHYS, CHEM (*Wirkung entfalten*) ■**auf etw** *akk* ~ to react to sth
Einwirkung *f* ❶ (*Beeinflussung*) influence (**auf** +*akk* on) ❷ PHYS, CHEM **nach ~ der Salbe** once the ointment takes effect
Einwohner(in) <-s, -> ['ain·voː·nɐ] *m(f)* inhabitant
Einwohnermeldeamt *nt* ≈ Town Clerk['s Office]
Einwohnerzahl *f* population
Einwurf *m* ❶ (*geh: das Hineinstecken*) *Münzen* insertion; *Briefe, Pakete* mailing ❷ (*beim Fußball*) throw-in ❸ (*Zwischenbemerkung*) interjection ❹ (*schlitzartige Öffnung*) slit
Einzahl ['ain·tsaːl] *f* LING singular
ein|zahlen *vt* to pay [in]
Einzahlung *f* FIN deposit
ein|zäunen ['ain·tsɔy·nən] *vt* ■**etw** ~ to fence in *sep* sth
ein|zeichnen *vt* ■**etw** ~ to draw in *sep* sth (**auf** +*akk* on)
Einzel <-s, -> ['ain·tsl̩] *nt* TENNIS singles + *sing vb*
Einzelfahrschein *m* one-way ticket
Einzelfall *m* individual case; **im** ~ in each case
Einzelgänger(in) <-s, -> *m(f)* (*Mensch, Tier*) loner
Einzelhaft *f* solitary confinement
Einzelhandel *m* retail trade
Einzelhändler(in) *m(f)* retailer
Einzelheit <-, -en> *f* detail
Einzelkind *nt* only child
einzeln ['ain·tsl̩n] **I.** *adj* ❶ (*für sich allein*) individual ❷ (*Detail*) ■**im E~en** in detail ❸ (*individuell*) individual; **jede(r, s) E~e** each [and every] individual ❹ (*alleinstehend*) single ❺ *pl* (*einige wenige*) a few ❻ *pl* METEO **~e Schauer**

scattered showers **II.** *adv* (*separat*) separately

Einzelstück *nt* unique piece

Einzelteil *nt* (*einzelnes Teil*) separate part; (*Ersatzteil*) spare part

Einzelzimmer *nt* single room

ein|ziehen *irreg* **I.** *vt haben* ❶ *Beiträge, Gelder* to collect ❷ (*aus dem Verkehr ziehen*) to withdraw ❸ (*beschlagnahmen*) ■**etw** ~ to take away *sep* sth ❹ MIL **jdn** [**zum Militär**] ~ to draft sb [into the army] ❺ (*nach innen ziehen*) ■**etw** ~ to take in *sep* sth ❻ (*entgegengesetzt bewegen*) ■**etw** ~ to draw in *sep* sth; **den Kopf** ~ to duck one's head ❼ *Antenne, Periskop* to retract ❽ BAU **eine Wand** ~ to put in *sep* a wall ❾ (*einsaugen*) ■**etw** ~ to draw up *sep* sth; **Luft** ~ to breathe in **II.** *vi sein* ❶ (*in etw ziehen*) ■**bei jdm** ~ to move in with sb ❷ SPORT, MIL (*einmarschieren*) ■**in etw** *akk* ~ to march into sth ❸ (*Flüssigkeit*) ■[**in etw** *akk*] ~ to soak [into sth]

einzig ['ain·tsɪç] **I.** *adj* ❶ *attr* only ❷ (*alleinige*) ■**der/die E~e** the only one; ■**das E~e** the only thing ❸ (*fam: unglaublich*) total; **ein ~er Idiot** a complete idiot **II.** *adv* (*ausschließlich*) only

einzigartig ['ain·tsɪç·ʔaːɐ̯·tɪç] **I.** *adj* unique **II.** *adv* astoundingly

Einzigartigkeit <-> *f kein pl* uniqueness

Einzug *m* ❶ (*das Einziehen*) move (**in** +*akk* into) ❷ (*Einmarsch*) entry ❸ FIN collection

Eis <-es> ['ais] *nt kein pl* ❶ (*gefrorenes Wasser*) ice ❷ (*Eisdecke*) ice ❸ (*Eiswürfel*) ice cube; (*Nachtisch*) ice cream

Eisbahn *f* SPORT skating rink

Eisbär *m* polar bear

Eisbecher *m* ❶ (*Pappbecher*) [ice-cream] carton; (*Metallschale*) sundae dish ❷ (*Eiscreme*) sundae

Eisberg *m* GEOG iceberg

Eisbrecher *m* NAUT icebreaker

Eischnee *m* whipped egg white

Eiscreme [-kreːm], **Eiskrem** *f* ice cream

Eisdiele *f* ice cream parlor

Eisen <-s, -> ['aizn̩] *nt kein pl* iron

Eisenbahn ['ai·zn̩·baːn] *f* train

Eisenbahner(in) <-s, -> *m(f)* (*fam*) railroad employee

Eisenbahnnetz *nt* rail[road] network

Eisenbahnwagen *m* (*Personenwagen*) passenger car; (*Güterwaggon*) freight car

eisenhaltig ['ai·zn̩·hal·tɪç] *adj*, **eisenhältig** ['ai·zn̩·hɛl·tɪç] *adj* ÖSTERR iron-bearing; ■~ **sein** to contain iron

Eisenmangel *m* MED iron deficiency

Eisenwaren *pl* hardware

eisern ['ai·zɐn] **I.** *adj* ❶ *attr* CHEM iron ❷ (*unnachgiebig*) iron **II.** *adv* resolutely

Eisfach *nt* freezer [compartment]

Eisfläche *f* [surface of the] ice

eisfrei *adj* METEO, GEOG free of ice

eisgekühlt *adj* ice-cold

Eisglätte *f* black ice

Eishockey *nt* ice hockey

eisig ['ai·zɪç] **I.** *adj* ❶ (*bitterkalt*) icy ❷ (*abweisend*) icy; *Schweigen* frosty ❸ (*jäh*) chilling; **ein ~er Schreck durchfuhr sie** a cold shiver ran through her [body] **II.** *adv* coolly

eiskalt ['ais·'kalt] **I.** *adj* ❶ (*bitterkalt*) ice-cold ❷ (*kalt und berechnend*) cold-blooded ❸ (*dreist*) cool **II.** *adv* (*kalt und berechnend*) coolly

Eiskunstlauf *m* figure skating

eis|laufen *vi irreg sein* to ice-skate

Eislaufen <-s> *nt kein pl* ice skating

Eismeer ['ais·meːɐ̯] *nt* polar sea

Eisprung *m* ovulation

Eisregen *m* sleet

Eisschnellauf[ALT], **Eisschnelllauf**[RR] *m* speed skating

Eisscholle *f* ice floe

Eiswürfel *m* ice cube

Eiszapfen *m* icicle

Eiszeit *f* Ice Age

eitel ['ai·tl̩] *adj* vain; (*eingebildet*) conceited

Eitelkeit <-, -en> ['ai·tl̩·kait] *f* vanity

Eiter <-s> ['ai·tɐ] *m kein pl* pus

eiterig ['ai·tə·rɪç] *adj Ausfluss* purulent; *Geschwür, Pickel, Wunde* festering; ■~ **sein** to fester

eitern ['ai·tɐn] *vi* to fester

eitrig ['ai·trɪç] *adj s.* **eiterig**

Eiweiß ['ai·vais] *nt* ❶ CHEM protein ❷ KOCHK egg white

Eizelle *f* ovum

Ekel[1] <-s> ['eːkl̩] *m kein pl* disgust; ~ **erregend** revolting

Ekel[2] <-s, -> ['eːkl̩] *nt* (*fam*) disgusting person

ekelerregend *adj s.* **Ekel**[1]

ekelhaft **I.** *adj* ❶ (*widerlich*) disgusting ❷ (*fam: fies*) nasty **II.** *adv* ❶ (*widerlich*) disgusting ❷ (*fam: fies*) horribly

ekelig <-er, -ste> ['eːkəl·ɪç] *adj s.* **ekelhaft**

ekeln ['eːkl̩n] **I.** *vt* ■**jdn** ~ to disgust sb **II.** *vt impers* **es ekelt mich vor diesem Geruch** this smell is disgusting **III.** *vr* ■**sich** *akk* **vor etw** *dat* ~ to find sth disgusting

EKG <-s, -s> [eː·kaː·'geː] *nt* MED *Abk von* **Elektrokardiogramm** EKG, ECG

Eklat <-s, -s> [e'klaː] *m* (*geh*) sensation

eklatant <-er, -este> [ekla·'tant] *adj* (*geh*) *Beispiel* striking; *Fall* spectacular; *Fehler* glaring

eklig <-er, -ste> ['eːk·lɪç] *adj s.* **ekelhaft**

Ekstase <-, -n> [ɛk·'staː·zə] *f* ecstasy

Ekzem <-s, -e> [ɛk·'tseːm] *nt* eczema

Elan <-s> [e'laːn] *m kein pl* vigor

elastisch [e'las·tɪʃ] **I.** *adj* ❶ (*flexibel*) elastic; *Federkern* springy; *Stoff, Binde* stretchy ❷ (*spannkräftig*) *Gelenk, Muskel, Mensch* supple; *Gang* springy **II.** *adv* supplely

Elastizität <-, -en> [elas·ti·tsi·'tɛːt] *meist sing f* ❶ (*elastische Beschaffenheit*) elasticity ❷ *eines Muskel* suppleness

Elbe <-> ['ɛl·bə] *f* Elbe River

Elch <-[e]s, -e> ['ɛlç] *m* elk

Electronic Cash [ɪlɛk·'trɔ·nɪk 'kæʃ] *nt kein pl*

electronic cash (*a debit card system*)
Elefant <-en, -en> [ele·'fant] *m* elephant
elegant [ele·'gant] **I.** *adj* elegant **II.** *adv* ❶ MODE elegantly ❷ (*geschickt*) nimbly
Eleganz <-> [ele·'gants] *f kein pl* ❶ (*geschmackvolle Beschaffenheit*) elegance ❷ (*Gewandtheit*) deftness
Elektrik <-, -en> [e'lɛk·trɪk] *f* electrical system
Elektriker(in) <-s, -> [e'lɛk·tri·kɐ] *m(f)* electrician

E

elektrisch [e'lɛk·trɪʃ] *adj* electric; **~e Geräte** electrical appliances
elektrisieren* [elɛk·tri·'ziː·rən] *vt* ❶ (*fig*) to electrify ❷ (*aufladen*) to charge with electricity
Elektrizität <-> [elɛk·tri·tsi·'tɛːt] *f kein pl* electricity
Elektrizitätswerk *nt* [electric] power plant
Elektrode <-, -n> [elɛk·'troː·də] *f* electrode
Elektrofahrrad *nt* electric bicycle, e-bike
Elektrogerät *nt* electrical appliance
Elektrogeschäft *nt* appliance and electronics store
Elektroherd [e'lɛk·tro·heːɐ̯t] *m* electric stove
Elektroingenieur(in) [-ɪn·ʒe·ni̯øːɐ̯] *m(f)* electrical engineer
Elektroinstallateur(in) *m(f)* electrician
Elektrokardiogramm [elɛk·tro·kar·di̯o·'gram] *nt* MED electrocardiogram, EKG, ECG
Elektromagnet [e'lɛk·tro·ma·gneːt] *m* electromagnet
elektromagnetisch **I.** *adj* electromagnetic **II.** *adv* electromagnetically
Elektromotor [e'lɛk·tro·moː·toːɐ̯] *m* electric motor
Elektron <-s, -tronen> ['eːlɛk·trɔn, e'lɛk·trɔn, elɛk·'troːn] *nt* electron
Elektronenmikroskop *nt* electron microscope
Elektronik <-, -en> [elɛk·'troː·nɪk] *f kein pl* electronics + *sing vb*
elektronisch [elɛk·'troː·nɪʃ] **I.** *adj* electronic **II.** *adv* electronically
Elektrorasierer *m* electric razor
Elektroschock [e'lɛk·tro·ʃɔk] *m* electroshock
Elektrosmog [-smɔk] *m* electrosmog
Elektrotechnik [elɛk·tro·'tɛç·nɪk] *f* electrical engineering
Elektrotechniker(in) *m(f)* ❶ (*mit Hochschulabschluss*) electrical engineer ❷ (*Elektriker*) electrician
Elektrozaun *m* electric fence
Element <-[e]s, -e> [ele·'mɛnt] *nt* element
elementar [ele·mɛn·'taːɐ̯] *adj* ❶ (*wesentlich*) elementary ❷ (*urwüchsig*) elemental
elend ['eːlɛnt] **I.** *adj* ❶ (*beklagenswert*) miserable ❷ (*krank*) wretched ❸ (*erbärmlich*) dreadful ❹ (*gemein*) miserable **II.** *adv* (*fam*) awfully
Elend <-[e]s> ['eːlɛnt] *nt kein pl* misery
Elendsviertel *nt* slum
elf ['ɛlf] *adj* eleven; *s. a.* **acht**[1]
Elf[1] <-, -en> ['ɛlf] *f* ❶ (*Zahl*) eleven ❷ FBALL team, eleven
Elf[2] <-en, -en> ['ɛlf] *m*, **Elfe** <-, -n> ['ɛl·fə] *f* elf
Elfenbein ['ɛl·fn̩·bain] *nt* ivory
Elfenbeinküste *f* Ivory Coast
Elfmeter [ɛlf·'meː·tɐ] *m* penalty kick; **einen ~ schießen** to take a penalty kick
Elfmeterschießen *nt* penalty shootout
elfte(r, s) ['ɛlf·tə] *adj* ❶ (*Zahl*) eleventh; *s. a.* **achte(r, s) 1** ❷ (*Datum*) eleventh, 11th; *s. a.* **achte(r, s) 2**
eliminieren* [eli·mi·'niː·rən] *vt* to eliminate
elitär [eli·'tɛːɐ̯] *adj* elitist
Elite <-, -n> [e'liː·tə] *f* elite
Eliteeinheit *f*, **Elitetruppe** *f* MIL elite troops *pl*
Elixier <-s, -e> [elɪ·'ksiːɐ̯] *nt* elixir
Ellbogengesellschaft *f* dog-eat-dog society
Elle <-, -n> ['ɛlə] *f* ❶ ANAT ulna ❷ HIST (*altes Längenmaß*) cubit
Ellenbogen ['ɛlən·boːgn̩] *m* elbow
Ellenbogenmensch *m* ruthless person
ellenlang *adj* (*fam*) incredibly long; **ein ~er Kerl** an incredibly tall guy
Ellipse <-, -n> [ɛ'lɪp·sə] *f* MATH ellipse; LING ellipsis
elliptisch [ɛ'lɪp·tɪʃ] *adj* MATH, LING elliptic[al]
El Salvador <-s> [ɛl zal·va·'doːɐ̯] *nt* El Salvador; *s. a.* **Deutschland**
Elsass[RR], **Elsaß**[ALT] <- *o* Elsasses> ['ɛl·zas] *nt* ■ **das ~** Alsace
Elsässer(in) <-s, -> ['ɛlzɛ·sɐ] *m(f)* inhabitant of Alsace
elsässisch ['ɛl·zɛ·sɪʃ] *adj* ❶ GEOG Alsatian ❷ LING Alsatian
Elsass-Lothringen[RR] *nt* Alsace-Lorraine
Elster <-, -n> ['ɛl·stɐ] *f* magpie
Eltern ['ɛl·tɐn] *pl* parents *pl*
Elternhaus *nt* ❶ (*Familie*) family ❷ (*Haus*) [parental] home
Elternteil *m* parent
Email <-s, -s> [e'mai, e'maːj] *nt* enamel
E-Mail <-, -s> ['iːmeːl] *f* e-mail, email
E-Mail-Adresse ['iːmeːl-] *f* e-mail address
Emaille <-, -n> [e'maljə, e'mai, e'maːj] *f s.* **Email**
Emanze <-, -n> [e'man·tsə] *f* (*fam*) women's libber
Emanzipation <-, -en> [eman·tsi·pa·'tsi̯oːn] *f* ❶ (*Gleichstellung der Frau*) emancipation ❷ (*Befreiung aus Abhängigkeit*) liberation
emanzipieren* [emaṇ·tsi·'piː·rən] *vr* ■ **sich** *akk* **~** to emancipate oneself
emanzipiert *adj* emancipated
Embargo <-s, -s> [ɛm·'bar·go] *nt* embargo
Emblem <-[e]s, -e> [ɛm·'bleːm, ã'bleːm] *nt* ❶ (*Zeichen*) emblem ❷ (*Sinnbild*) symbol
Embolie <-, -n> [ɛm·bo·'liː, *pl* ɛm·bo·'liː·ən] *f* embolism
Embryo <-s, -s *o* Embryonen> ['ɛm·bryo, *pl* ɛm·bry'oː·nən] *m o* ÖSTERR *nt* embryo
Emigrant(in) <-en, -en> [emi·'grant] *m(f)* ❶ (*Auswanderer*) emigrant ❷ (*politischer Flüchtling*) émigré

Emigration <-, -en> [emi·gra·ˈtsi̯oːn] *f* emigration
emigrieren* [emi·ˈgriː·rən] *vi sein* to emigrate
Emirat <-[e]s, -e> [emi·ˈraːt] *nt* emirate; **die Vereinigten Arabischen ~e** the United Arab Emirates, U.A.E.
Emission <-, -en> [emɪ·ˈsi̯oːn] *f* emission
emittieren [emɪ·ˈtiː·rən] *vt* ① *Wertpapiere* to issue ② *Abgase* to emit
Emmentaler <-s, -> [ˈɛmən·taːlɐ] *m* Emmental [cheese], Swiss cheese
e-Moll <-s> [ˈeːmɔl] *nt kein pl* MUS E flat minor
Emotion <-, -en> [emo·ˈtsi̯oːn] *f* emotion
emotional [emo·tsi̯o·ˈnaːl] **I.** *adj* emotional **II.** *adv* emotionally
emotionsgeladen *adj* emotionally charged
empathisch [ɛm·ˈpaː·tɪʃ] *adj* (*geh*) empathic
empfahl [ɛm·ˈpfaːl] *imp von* **empfehlen**
empfand [ɛm·ˈpfant] *imp von* **empfinden**
Empfang <-[e]s, Empfänge> [ɛm·ˈpfaŋ, *pl* -ˈpfɛŋə] *m* ① *kein pl* (*das Entgegennehmen*) receipt ② (*Begrüßung*) reception ③ *kein pl* TV, RADIO reception ④ (*Hotelrezeption*) reception [desk]
empfangen <empfing, empfangen> [ɛm·ˈpfaŋən] *vt* ① RADIO, TV to receive ② (*begrüßen*) ■ **jdn mit etw** *dat* ~ to receive sb with sth
Empfänger(in) <-s, -> [ɛm·ˈpfɛŋɐ] *m(f)* ① (*Adressat*) addressee ② FIN payee
Empfänger <-s, -> [ɛm·ˈpfɛŋɐ] *m* RADIO, TV (*geh*) receiver
empfänglich [ɛm·ˈpfɛŋ·lɪç] *adj* ■ **für etw** *akk* **~ sein** ① (*zugänglich*) to be receptive to sth ② (*beeinflussbar, anfällig*) to be susceptible to sth
Empfängnis <-, -se> [ɛm·ˈpfɛŋ·nɪs, *pl* -ˈpfɛŋ·nɪsə] *f pl selten* conception
Empfängnisverhütung *f* contraception
Empfangsbescheinigung *f,* **Empfangsbestätigung** *f* [confirmation of] receipt
Empfangsdame *f* receptionist
empfehlen <empfahl, empfohlen> [ɛm·ˈpfeː·lən] **I.** *vt* ■ **[jdm] etw ~** to recommend sth [to sb] **II.** *vr impers* ■ **es empfiehlt sich, etw zu tun** it is advisable to do sth
empfehlenswert *adj* ① (*wert, empfohlen zu werden*) recommendable ② (*ratsam*) ■ **es ist ~, etw zu tun** it is advisable to do sth
Empfehlung <-, -en> *f* ① (*Vorschlag*) recommendation ② (*Referenz*) reference; **auf ~ von jdm** on the recommendation of sb ③ (*geh*) **mit den besten ~en** with best regards
Empfehlungsschreiben *nt* letter of recommendation
empfiehl [ɛm·ˈpfiːl] *imp sing von* **empfehlen**
empfinden <empfand, empfunden> [ɛm·ˈpfɪn·dn̩] *vt* ① (*fühlen*) to feel ② (*auffassen*) ■ **jdn/etw als etw** *akk* ~ to feel like sb/sth is sth
empfindlich [ɛm·ˈpfɪnt·lɪç] **I.** *adj* ① (*auf Reize leicht reagierend*) sensitive (**gegen** +*akk* to) ② (*leicht verletzbar*) sensitive; (*reizbar*) touchy ③ (*anfällig*) *Gesundheit* delicate; **~ gegen Kälte** sensitive to cold **II.** *adv* ① (*sensibel*) **auf etw** *akk* **~ reagieren** to be very sensitive to sth ② (*spürbar*) severely; **es ist ~ kalt** it's bitterly cold
Empfindlichkeit <-, *selten* -en> *f* ① (*Feinfühligkeit*) sensitiveness ② (*Verletzbarkeit*) sensitivity; (*Reizbarkeit*) touchiness ③ *kein pl* (*Anfälligkeit*) delicateness
empfindsam [ɛm·ˈpfɪnt·zaːm] *adj* ① (*von feinem Empfinden*) sensitive; (*einfühlsam*) empathetic ② (*sentimental*) *Geschichte* sentimental
Empfindsamkeit <-> *f kein pl* (*Feinfühligkeit*) sensitivity
Empfindung <-, -en> *f* ① (*Wahrnehmung*) perception ② (*Gefühl*) emotion
empfing [ɛm·ˈpfɪŋ] *imp von* **empfangen**
empfohlen [ɛm·ˈpfoː·lən] **I.** *pp von* **empfehlen** **II.** *adj* **sehr ~** highly recommended
empfunden [ɛm·ˈpfʊn·dn̩] *pp von* **empfinden**
empor|arbeiten *vr* (*geh*) ■ **sich** *akk* ~ to work one's way up (**zu** +*dat* to)
Empore <-, -n> [ɛm·ˈpoː·rə] *f* gallery
empören* [ɛm·ˈpøː·rən] **I.** *vt* ■ **jdn ~** to fill sb with indignation **II.** *vr* ■ **sich** *akk* ~ to be outraged
empörend *adj* outrageous
empor|steigen *irreg* **I.** *vi sein* (*geh*) to rise; **Zweifel stiegen in ihm empor** doubt arose in his mind **II.** *vt sein* (*geh*) ■ **etw ~** to climb [up] sth
empört **I.** *adj* scandalized (**über** +*akk* by) **II.** *adv* indignantly
Empörung <-, -en> *f kein pl* ■ **~ über jdn/etw** indignation about sb/sth
emsig [ˈɛm·zɪç] **I.** *adj* busy **II.** *adv* industriously; **überall wird ~ gebaut** they are busy building everywhere
Emu <-s, -s> [ˈeːmu] *m* ORN emu
Endabrechnung *f* final invoice
Endbetrag *m* final amount
Ende <-s, -n> [ˈɛn·də] *nt* ① (*Schluss*) end; **~ August/des Monats/~ 2007** the end of August/the month/2007; **~ 20 sein** to be in one's late 20s; **damit muss es jetzt ein ~ haben** this must stop now; **einer S.** *dat* **ein ~ machen** to put an end to sth; **das nimmt gar kein ~** there's no end to it; **am ~** (*fam*) finally; **etw zu ~ bringen** to complete sth; **zu ~ sein** to be finished ② FILM, LIT ending ③ (*räumliches Ende*) end ▶ WENDUNGEN: **~ gut, alles gut** (*prov*) all's well that ends well
Endeffekt [ˈɛnt·ʔɛfɛkt] *m* **im ~** (*fam*) in the end
enden [ˈɛn·dn̩] *vi* ① *haben* (*nicht mehr weiterführen*) to end ② *haben* (*auslaufen*) to expire ③ *haben* LING ■ **auf etw** *akk* ~ to end with sth ④ *sein* (*fam: landen*) to end up
Endergebnis *nt* final result
endgültig **I.** *adj* final; *Antwort* definitive **II.** *adv* finally
Endgültigkeit <-> *f kein pl* finality

E

Ẹndhaltestelle *f* terminal stop
Endiviensalat *m* endive
Ẹndkampf *m* SPORT final
Ẹndlager *nt* ÖKOL permanent disposal site
ẹndlagern *vt* ÖKOL ■**etw** [**irgendwo**] ~ to permanently store sth [somewhere]
Ẹndlagerung *f* permanent disposal
endlich ['ɛnt·lɪç] **I.** *adv* ❶ (*nunmehr*) at last; **lass mich ~ in Ruhe!** just leave me alone already! ❷ (*schließlich*) finally; **na ~!** (*fam*) at last! **II.** *adj* ASTRON, MATH finite
ẹndlos I. *adj* endless **II.** *adv* interminably
Ẹndlosigkeit *f kein pl* infinity
Ẹndphase *f* final stage
Ẹndprodukt *nt* end product
Ẹndrunde *f* SPORT final round; *einer Meisterschaft* finals *pl; eines Autorennens* final lap
Ẹndsilbe *f* final syllable
Ẹndspiel *nt* SPORT final
Ẹndspurt *m* final spurt
Ẹndstadium *nt* final stage; MED terminal stage
Ẹndstation *f* terminus, end of the line, last [*or* final] stop
Ẹndsumme *f* [sum] total
Ẹndung <-, -en> *f* ending
Ẹndverbraucher(in) *m(f)* end-user
Energie <-, -n> [enɛr·'giː, *pl* -'giː·ən] *f* ❶ PHYS energy ❷ (*Tatkraft*) energy
Energiebedarf *m* energy requirement[s]
Energiegewinnung *f kein pl* energy generation
Energiequelle *f* energy source
Energiesparen *nt* energy saving
Energiesparmaßnahme *f* energy-saving measure
Energieverbrauch *m* energy consumption
Energieverschwendung *f kein pl* waste of energy
Energieversorgung *f* energy supply
energisch [e'nɛr·gɪʃ] **I.** *adj* ❶ (*Tatkraft ausdrückend*) energetic ❷ (*entschlossen*) firm **II.** *adv* vigorously
eng ['ɛŋ] **I.** *adj* ❶ (*schmal*) narrow ❷ (*knapp sitzend*) tight ❸ (*beengt*) cramped ❹ (*wenig Zwischenraum habend*) close together *pred* ❺ (*intim*) close ❻ (*eingeschränkt*) limited; **im ~eren Sinn** in the stricter sense **II.** *adv* ❶ (*knapp*) **ein ~ anliegendes Kleid** a close-fitting dress ❷ (*dicht*) densely; **~ nebeneinanderstehen** to stand close to each other ❸ (*intim*) closely; **~ befreundet sein** to be close friends ❹ (*akribisch*) **etw zu ~ sehen** to take too narrow a view of sth
Engagement <-s, -s> [ãga·ʒə·'mãː] *nt* ❶ (*Eintreten*) commitment (**für** +*akk* to) ❷ THEAT engagement
engagieren* [ãga·'ʒiːr·ən] **I.** *vt* ■**jdn ~** to engage sb **II.** *vr* ■**sich** *akk* [**für jdn/etw**] **~** to be committed [to sb/sth]
engagiert [ãga·'ʒiːɐt] *adj* (*geh*) **politisch/sozial ~** politically/socially committed
ẹnganliegend *adj attr s.* **eng II 1**
ẹngbefreundet *adj attr s.* **eng II 3**

Enge <-, -n> ['ɛŋə] *f* ❶ (*schmale Beschaffenheit*) narrowness ❷ *kein pl* (*Beschränktheit*) confinement
Engel <-s, -> ['ɛŋl̩] *m* angel
Ẹngel(s)geduld *f* **eine** [**wahre**] **~ haben** to have the patience of a saint
England <-s> ['ɛŋ·lant] *nt* ❶ (*Teil Großbritanniens*) England ❷ (*falsch für Großbritannien*) Great Britain; *s. a.* **Deutschland**
Engländer(in) <-s, -> ['ɛŋ·lɛn·dɐ] *m(f)* Englishman *masc*, Englishwoman *fem*; ■**die ~** the English
englisch ['ɛŋ·lɪʃ] *adj* English; *s. a.* **deutsch**
Englisch ['ɛŋ·lɪʃ] *nt dekl wie adj* English; *s. a.* **Deutsch**
ẸngpassRR *m* ❶ GEOG [narrow] pass ❷ (*Fahrbahnverengung*) bottleneck ❸ (*Verknappung*) bottleneck
engstirnig ['ɛŋ·ʃtɪr·nɪç] **I.** *adj* narrow-minded **II.** *adv* narrow-mindedly
Enkel(in) <-s, -> ['ɛŋ·kl̩] *m(f)* grandchild
Ẹnkelsohn *m* (*geh*) grandson
Ẹnkeltochter *f* (*geh*) granddaughter
enorm [e'nɔrm] **I.** *adj* enormous; *Summe* vast **II.** *adv* (*fam*) tremendously; **~ viel/viele** an enormous amount/number
Ensemble <-s, -s> [ã·'sãː·bl̩] *nt* ensemble
ent|behren* [ɛnt·'beː·rən] **I.** *vt* ❶ (*ohne auskommen*) ■**jdn/etw ~ können** to be able to do without sb/sth ❷ (*geh: vermissen*) ■**jdn/etw ~** to miss sb/sth **II.** *vi* (*geh*) to go without
Entbehrung <-, -en> *f meist pl* privation
ent|bịnden* *irreg* **I.** *vt* ❶ MED to deliver; ■[**von einem Kind**] **entbunden werden** to give birth to a baby ❷ (*dispensieren, befreien*) ■**jdn von etw** *dat* **~** to release sb from sth **II.** *vi* to give birth
Entbịndung *f* delivery
Entbịndungsstation *f* maternity ward
ent|blößen* [ɛnt·'bløː·sn̩] *vt* (*geh*) ■**sich** *akk* **~** to take one's clothes off
ent|dẹcken* *vt* ❶ (*zum ersten Mal finden*) to discover; *ein fremdes Land* to explore ❷ (*ausfindig machen*) ■**jdn/etw ~** to find sb/sth; *Fehler* to spot
Entdecker(in) <-s, -> [ɛnt·'dɛ·kɐ] *m(f)* discoverer; **der berühmte ~ Captain Cook** the famous explorer Captain Cook
Entdẹckung *f* discovery
Entdẹckungsreise *f* voyage of discovery
Ente <-, -n> ['ɛn·tə] *f* ❶ ORN duck ❷ (*fam: Zeitungsente*) canard ▶WENDUNGEN: **lahme ~** (*fam*) slowpoke
ent|eignen* *vt* ■**jdn ~** to dispossess sb
Enteignung <-, -en> *f* dispossession
ent|ẹrben* *vt* ■**jdn ~** to disinherit sb
Enterich <-s, -e> ['ɛn·tə·rɪç] *m* ORN drake
entern ['ɛn·tɐn] *vt haben* to board
Entertainer(in) <-s, -> [ɛn·tɐ·'teː·nɐ] *m(f)* entertainer
ent|fachen* [ɛnt·'fa·çn̩] *vt* (*geh*) ❶ (*zum Brennen bringen*) to kindle; *Brand* to start ❷ (*entfesseln*) to provoke; *Leidenschaft* to arouse

ent|fahren* *vi irreg sein* ■ **etw entfährt jdm** sth escapes sb's lips

ent|fallen* *vi irreg sein* ❶ (*dem Gedächtnis entschwinden*) ■ **jdm ~** to slip sb's mind ❷ (*wegfallen*) to be dropped ❸ (*als Anteil zustehen*) ■ **auf jdn ~** to be allotted to sb

ent|falten* **I.** *vt* ❶ (*auseinanderfalten*) *Landkarte, Brief* to unfold ❷ (*beginnen, entwickeln*) *Fähigkeiten, Kräfte* to develop ❸ (*darlegen*) ■ **etw ~** to set sth forth ❹ (*zur Geltung bringen*) to display **II.** *vr* ❶ (*sich öffnen*) ■ **sich [zu etw** *dat*] ~ *Blüte, Fallschirm* to open [into sth] ❷ (*sich voll entwickeln*) ■ **sich** *akk* ~ to fully develop

Entfaltung <-, -en> *f* ❶ (*das Entfalten*) unfolding ❷ (*Entwicklung*) development

ent|färben* **I.** *vt* ■ **etw ~** to remove the color from sth **II.** *vr* ■ **sich ~** to lose its color

ent|fernen* [ɛnt·ˈfɛr·nən] **I.** *vt* ❶ (*beseitigen*) ■ **etw ~** to remove sth (**aus/von** +*dat* from) ❷ MED **jdm den Blinddarm ~** to take out *sep* sb's appendix ❸ (*weit abbringen*) ■ **jdn von etw** *dat* ~ to take sb away from sth **II.** *vr* ❶ (*weggehen*) ■ **sich** *akk* ~ to go away (**von/aus** +*dat* from); **sich vom Weg ~** to go off the path ❷ (*nicht bei etw bleiben*) ■ **sich** *akk* **von etw** *dat* ~ to depart from sth

entfernt I. *adj* ❶ (*weitläufig*) distant ❷ (*gering*) *Ähnlichkeit* slight; *Ahnung* vague ❸ (*abgelegen*) remote **II.** *adv* vaguely; **weit davon ~ sein, etw zu tun** to not have the slightest intention of doing sth

Entfernung <-, -en> *f* ❶ (*Distanz*) distance ❷ ADMIN (*geh: Ausschluss*) removal

ent|fesseln* *vt* (*auslösen*) to unleash

ent|flammen* [ɛnt·ˈflamən] **I.** *vt haben* ❶ (*anzünden*) to light ❷ *Leidenschaft* to [a]rouse **II.** *vr haben* ❶ (*sich entzünden*) ■ **sich ~** to ignite ❷ (*sich begeistern*) **sie entflammte sich für seine Idee** she was filled with enthusiasm for his idea **III.** *vi sein* (*geh: plötzlich entstehen*) **ein Kampf um die Macht ist entflammt** a power struggle has erupted

ent|fremden* [ɛnt·ˈfrɛm·dn̩] **I.** *vt* to estrange; ■ **etw seinem Zweck ~** to use sth for a different purpose; (*falscher Zweck*) to use sth for the wrong purpose **II.** *vr* ■ **sich** *akk* **jdm ~** to become estranged from sb

Entfremdung <-, -en> *f* estrangement

ent|führen* *vt* ■ **jdn ~** to abduct sb; *Fahrzeug, Flugzeug* to hijack

Entführer(in) *m(f)* kidnapper; *eines Fahrzeugs/Flugzeugs* hijacker

Entführung *f* kidnapping; *eines Fahrzeugs/Flugzeugs* hijacking

entgegen [ɛnt·ˈgeː·gn̩] **I.** *adv* (*geh*) toward **II.** *präp* against

entgegen|bringen *vt irreg* (*bezeigen*) ■ **jdm etw ~** to display sth toward sb

entgegen|fahren *vi irreg sein* ■ **jdm ~** to go to meet sb

entgegen|fiebern* *vi* ■ **einer S.** *dat* ~ to feverishly look forward to sth

entgegen|gehen *vi irreg sein* ■ **jdm ~** to go to meet sb

entgegengesetzt [ɛnt·ˈgeː·gn̩·gə·zɛtst] **I.** *adj* ❶ (*gegenüberliegend*) opposite ❷ (*einander widersprechend*) opposing; *Auffassungen* conflicting **II.** *adv* ~ **denken/handeln** to think/do the exact opposite

entgegen|halten *vt irreg* ❶ (*in eine bestimmte Richtung halten*) ■ **jdm etw ~** to hold sth out toward sb ❷ (*einwenden*) **jdm einen Einwand ~** to express an objection to sb

entgegen|kommen [ɛnt·ˈgeː·gn̩·kɔ·mən] *vi irreg sein* ❶ (*in jds Richtung kommen*) ■ **jdm ~** to come [over] to meet sb ❷ (*Zugeständnisse machen*) ■ **jdm/einer S. ~** to accommodate sb/sth ❸ (*entsprechen*) ■ **jdm/einer S. ~** to fit in with sb/sth

Entgegenkommen <-s, -> [ɛnt·ˈgeː·gn̩·kɔ·mən] *nt kein pl* ❶ (*gefällige Haltung*) cooperation ❷ (*Zugeständnis*) concession

entgegenkommend *adj* obliging

entgegen|laufen *vi irreg sein* ❶ (*in jds Richtung laufen*) ■ **jdm ~** to run to meet sb ❷ (*im Gegensatz stehen*) ■ **einer S.** *dat* ~ to run counter to sth

entgegen|nehmen *vt irreg* ■ **etw ~** *Lieferung* to receive sth; **nehmen Sie meinen Dank entgegen** (*form*) please accept my gratitude

entgegen|schlagen *vi irreg sein* ■ **jdm ~** to confront sb

entgegen|sehen *vi irreg* ❶ (*geh: erwarten*) ■ **einer S.** *dat* ~ to await sth ❷ (*in jds Richtung sehen*) ■ **jdm/etw ~** to watch sb/sth

entgegen|setzen I. *vt* ■ **einer S.** *dat* **etw ~** to oppose sth with sth **II.** *vr* ■ **sich** *akk* **einer S.** *dat* ~ to resist sth

entgegen|stehen *vi irreg* ■ **einer S.** *dat* ~ to stand in the way of sth

entgegen|stellen *vr* ■ **sich** *akk* **jdm/einer S.** ~ to resist sb/sth

entgegen|steuern *vi* to act against; *Entwicklung, Trend* to counter

entgegen|treten *vi irreg sein* ❶ (*in den Weg treten*) ■ **jdm ~** to walk up to sb ❷ (*sich zur Wehr setzen*) ■ **einer S.** *dat* ~ to counter sth

entgegen|wirken *vi* ■ **einer S.** *dat* ~ to oppose sth

ent|gegnen* [ɛnt·ˈgeːg·nən] *vt* to reply

Entgegnung <-, -en> *f* reply

ent|gehen* *vi irreg sein* ❶ (*entkommen*) ■ **jdm/einer S. ~** to escape sb/sth ❷ (*nicht bemerkt werden*) ■ **etw entgeht jdm** sth escapes sb['s notice] ❸ (*versäumen*) ■ **sich** *dat* **etw ~ lassen** to miss sth

entgeistert [ɛnt·ˈgais·tɐt] **I.** *adj* dumbfounded **II.** *adv* in amazement

Entgelt <-[e]s, -e> [ɛnt·ˈgɛlt] *nt* ❶ (*Bezahlung*) payment; (*Entschädigung*) compensation ❷ (*Gebühr*) **gegen ~** for a fee

ent|gleisen* [ɛnt·ˈglaizn̩] *vi sein* ❶ (*aus den Gleisen springen*) to derail ❷ (*geh: ausfallend werden*) to make a gaffe

Entgleisung <-, -en> *f* ❶ (*das Entgleisen*) de-

E

railment ❷ (*Taktlosigkeit*) gaffe

ent|gleiten* *vi irreg sein* ❶ (*geh: aus den Händen gleiten*) ■ **etw entgleitet jdm** sb loses his/her grip on sth ❷ (*verloren gehen*) ■ **jdm** ~ to slip away from sb

ent|haaren* *vt* to depilate

Enthaarung <-, -en> *f* depilation

ent|halten* *irreg* **I.** *vt* ❶ (*in sich haben*) to contain ❷ (*umfassen*) to include (**in** +*dat* in) **II.** *vr* (*verzichten*) to refrain

enthaltsam [ɛnt·ˈhalt·zaːm] *adj* [self-]restrained; (*genügsam*) abstinent; (*keusch*) chaste; (*sexuell*) celibate

Enthaltsamkeit <-> *f kein pl* abstinence; (*sexuelle Abstinenz*) chastity

Enthaltung *f* POL abstention

ent|haupten* [ɛnt·ˈhaup·tn̩] *vt* ■ **jdn** ~ (*durch Scharfrichter*) to behead sb; (*durch Unfall*) to decapitate sb

ent|heben* *vt irreg* ■ **jdn einer S.** *gen* ~ ❶ (*suspendieren*) to relieve sb of sth ❷ (*geh: entbinden*) to release sb from sth

enthemmt **I.** *adj* uninhibited **II.** *adv* uninhibitedly

ent|hüllen* *vt* ■ [**jdm**] **etw** ~ ❶ (*aufdecken*) to reveal sth [to sb] ❷ (*von einer Bedeckung befreien*) to unveil sth [to sb]

Enthüllung <-, -en> *f* ❶ (*die Aufdeckung*) disclosure; *von Skandal, Lüge* exposure ❷ (*das Enthüllen*) *von Denkmal, Gesicht* unveiling

Enthusiasmus <-> [ɛn·tu·ˈzi̯as·mʊs] *m kein pl* enthusiasm

enthusiastisch **I.** *adj* enthusiastic **II.** *adv* enthusiastically

ent|jungfern* [ɛnt·ˈjʊŋ·fɐn] *vt* ■ **jdn** ~ to deflower sb

ent|kernen* [ɛnt·ˈkɛr·nən] *vt* ■ **etw** ~ ❶ (*von Kernen befreien*) to stone sth; *Apfel* to core sth ❷ ARCHIT to remove the core of sth

ent|knoten* *vt* to untie

entkoffeiniert [ɛnt·kɔ·fei·ˈniːɐ̯t] *adj* decaffeinated

ent|kommen* *vi irreg sein* to escape

Entkommen <-s> *nt kein pl* escape

ent|kräften* [ɛnt·ˈkrɛf·tn̩] *vt* ❶ (*kraftlos machen*) ■ **jdn** ~ (*durch Anstrengung*) to weaken sb; (*durch Krankheit*) to debilitate sb *form* ❷ (*widerlegen*) ■ **etw** ~ to refute sth

ent|laden* *irreg* **I.** *vt* ❶ (*Ladung herausnehmen*) to unload ❷ ELEK to drain **II.** *vr* ■ **sich** ~ ❶ (*zum Ausbruch kommen*) *Gewitter, Sturm* to break ❷ ELEK *Akku, Batterie* to run down ❸ (*fig: plötzlich ausbrechen*) *Begeisterung, Zorn etc.* to be vented

entlang [ɛnt·ˈlaŋ] **I.** *präp* (*längs*) along; **den Fluss** ~ along the river **II.** *adv* ■ **an etw** *dat* ~ along sth

entlang|fahren *vt irreg sein* ❶ *Straße* to drive [*or* go] along ❷ (*eine Linie nachziehen*) to trace

entlang|gehen *irreg* **I.** *vt sein* (*zu Fuß folgen*) ■ **etw** ~ to walk [*or* go] along sth **II.** *vi sein* ■ **an etw** *dat* ~ ❶ (*parallel zu etw gehen*) to walk [*or* go] along the side of sth ❷ (*parallel zu etw verlaufen*) to run alongside sth

ent|larven* [ɛnt·ˈlar·fn̩] *vt* ■ **jdn/etw** [**als etw** *akk*] ~ *Dieb, Spion* to expose sb/sth [as sth]

ent|lassen* *vt irreg* ❶ (*kündigen*) ■ **jdn** ~ (*Stellen abbauen*) to lay off *sep* sb; (*gehen lassen*) to dismiss sb ❷ MED, MIL to discharge sb ❸ (*entbinden*) ■ **jdn aus etw** *dat* ~ to release sb from sth

Entlassung <-, -en> *f* (*Kündigung*) pink slip *fam*

ent|lasten* *vt* ❶ JUR ■ **jdn** [**von etw** *dat*] ~ to clear sb [of sth] ❷ (*von einer Belastung befreien*) ■ **jdn** ~ to relieve sb

Entlastung <-, -en> *f* ❶ JUR exoneration ❷ (*das Entlasten*) relief

ent|laufen*[1] *vi irreg sein* ■ **jdm** ~ to run away from sb

entlaufen[2] *adj* (*entflohen*) escaped; (*weggelaufen*) on the run *pred*

ent|ledigen* [ɛnt·ˈleː·dɪ·gn̩] *vr* ■ **sich** *akk* **einer S.** *gen* ~ ❶ (*geh: ablegen*) to put down *sep* sth; *Kleidungsstück* to remove sth ❷ (*loswerden*) to get rid of sth

ent|leeren* *vt* to empty

entlegen [ɛnt·ˈleː·gn̩] *adj* remote

ent|locken* *vt* ■ **jdm etw** ~ to elicit sth from sb

ent|lohnen* *vt* ■ **jdn** [**für etw** *akk*] ~ ❶ (*bezahlen*) to pay sb [for sth] ❷ (*entgelten*) to reward sb [for sth]

Entlohnung <-, -en> *f* payment

ent|machten* [ɛnt·ˈmax·tn̩] *vt* ■ **jdn/etw** ~ to disempower sb/sth

ent|militarisieren* [ɛnt·mi·li·ta·ri·ˈziː·rən] *vt* to demilitarize

ent|mündigen* [ɛnt·ˈmʏn·dɪ·gn̩] *vt* ■ **jdn** ~ **lassen** to have sb declared legally incompetent

Entmündigung <-, -en> *f* JUR legal incompetency

ent|mutigen* [ɛnt·ˈmuː·tɪ·gn̩] *vt* ■ **jdn** ~ to discourage sb

Entnahme <-, -n> [ɛnt·ˈnaː·mə] *f* removal; *von Blut* extraction

ent|nehmen* *vt irreg* ❶ (*herausnehmen*) ■ **etw** ~ to take sth (+*dat* from) ❷ MED ■ **jdm etw** ~ to take sth from sb ❸ (*fig: aus etw schließen*) ■ **aus etw** *dat* ~, **dass ...** to gather from sth that ...

entnervt **I.** *adj* (*der Nerven beraubt*) nerve-[w]racked; (*der Kraft beraubt*) enervated **II.** *adv* out of nervous exhaustion

ent|puppen* [ɛnt·ˈpʊ·pn̩] *vr* (*fig: sich enthüllen*) ■ **sich** *akk* [**als etw** *akk*] ~ to turn out to be sth

ent|reißen* *vt irreg* ❶ (*wegreißen*) ■ **jdm etw** ~ to snatch sth [away] from sb ❷ (*geh: retten*) ■ **jdn einer S.** *dat* ~ to rescue sb from sth

ent|richten* *vt* (*geh*) *Gebühren, Steuern* to pay

ent|rinnen *vi irreg sein* (*geh: entkommen*) ■ **jdm/einer S.** ~ to escape from sb/sth

Entrinnen *nt* **es gab kein ~ mehr** there was

no escape
ent|rümpeln* *vt* ■**etw** ~ to clear out *sep* sth
ent|rüsten* **I.** *vt* (*empören*) ■**jdn** ~ to make sb indignant; (*stärker*) to outrage sb **II.** *vr* (*sich empören*) ■**sich** *akk* **über jdn/etw** ~ to be indignant about sb/sth; (*stärker*) to be outraged by sb/sth
entrüstet **I.** *adj* indignant (**über** +*akk* about/at) **II.** *adv* indignantly
Entrüstung *f* indignation (**über** +*akk* about/at)
ent|sagen* *vi* (*geh*) ■**einer S.** *dat* ~ to renounce sth
ent|schädigen* *vt* ■**jdn** [**für etw** *akk*] ~ ❶ (*Schadensersatz leisten*) to compensate sb [for sth] ❷ (*ein lohnender Ausgleich sein*) to make up to sb [for sth]
Entschädigung *f* compensation
ent|schärfen* *vt* (*a. fig*) ■**etw** ~ to defuse sth
ent|scheiden* *irreg* **I.** *vt* ❶ (*beschließen*) to decide; (*gerichtlich*) to rule ❷ (*endgültig klären*) to settle **II.** *vi* (*beschließen*) to decide (**über** +*akk* on); ■**für/gegen jdn/etw** ~ to decide in favor/against sb/sth; (*gerichtlich*) to rule in favor/against sb/sth **III.** *vr* ■**sich** *akk* [**dazu**] ~ to decide
entscheidend [ɛnt·ˈʃai·dn̩t] **I.** *adj* ❶ (*ausschlaggebend*) decisive ❷ (*gewichtig*) crucial **II.** *adv* (*in entschiedenem Maße*) decisively
Entscheidung *f* ❶ (*Beschluss*) decision; **eine ~ treffen** to make a decision ❷ JUR ruling
entschieden [ɛnt·ˈʃiː·dn̩] **I.** *pp von* **entscheiden** **II.** *adj* ❶ (*entschlossen*) resolute ❷ (*eindeutig*) definite **III.** *adv* ❶ (*entschlossen*) **etw ~ ablehnen** to categorically reject sth ❷ (*eindeutig*) **diesmal bist du ~ zu weit gegangen** this time you've definitely gone too far
Entschiedenheit <-, *selten* -en> *f* determination; **etw mit [aller] ~ ablehnen** to flatly refuse sth; **mit ~ dementieren** to categorically deny
ent|schließen* *vr irreg* (*sich entscheiden*) ■**sich** *akk* ~ to decide (**für/zu** +*akk/dat* on)
Entschließung *f* (*geh*) decision
entschlossen [ənt·ˈʃlɔ·sn̩] **I.** *pp von* **entschließen** **II.** *adj* (*zielbewusst*) determined **III.** *adv* resolutely
Entschlossenheit <-> *f kein pl* determination
Entschluss[RR], **Entschluß**[ALT] <-schlusses, -schlüsse> [ɛnt·ˈʃlʊs, *pl* ɛnt·ˈʃlʏ·sə] *m* decision
ent|schlüsseln* [ɛnt·ˈʃlʏ·sl̩n] *vt* to decode
entschlussfreudig[RR] *adj* decisive
entschuldbar [ɛnt·ˈʃʊlt·baːɐ̯] *adj* excusable
ent|schuldigen* [ɛnt·ˈʃʊl·dɪ·gn̩] **I.** *vi* (*als Höflichkeitsformel*) ~ **Sie** excuse me **II.** *vr* ■**sich** *akk* ~ ❶ (*um Verzeihung bitten*) to apologize ❷ (*eine Abwesenheit begründen*) to ask to be excused **III.** *vt* ❶ (*als verzeihlich begründen*) ■**etw mit etw** *dat* ~ to use sth as an excuse for sth ❷ (*eine Abwesenheit begründen*) ■**jdn bei jdm** ~ to ask sb to excuse sb ❸ (*als verständlich erscheinen lassen*) ■**etw** ~ to excuse sth
Entschuldigung <-, -en> *f* ❶ (*Bitte um Verzeihung*) apology ❷ (*Begründung, Rechtfertigung*) **als ~ für etw** *akk* as an excuse for sth ❸ (*als Höflichkeitsformel*) **~!** sorry! ❹ SCH note
ent|schwinden* *vi irreg sein* (*geh*) ❶ (*verschwinden*) to vanish ❷ (*rasch vergehen*) to pass quickly
ent|senden* *vt irreg o reg* ■**jdn** ~ to send sb; *Boten* to dispatch sb
Entsendung *f* (*von Abgeordneten*) dispatch
ent|setzen* **I.** *vt* (*in Grauen versetzen*) ■**jdn** ~ to horrify sb **II.** *vr* (*die Fassung verlieren*) ■**sich** *akk* ~ to be horrified (**über** +*akk* at/about)
Entsetzen <-s> *nt kein pl* horror; **voller ~** filled with horror; **mit ~** horrified
entsetzlich [ɛnt·ˈzɛts·lɪç] **I.** *adj* ❶ (*schrecklich*) horrible ❷ (*fam: sehr stark*) terrible **II.** *adv* ❶ (*in furchtbarer Weise*) terribly ❷ (*fam*) awfully
entsetzt **I.** *adj* horrified **II.** *adv* (*großes Entsetzen zeigend*) **sie schrie ~ auf** she let out a horrified scream
ent|sorgen* *vt* ÖKOL ■**etw** ~ to dispose of sth
ent|spannen* **I.** *vr* ■**sich** *akk* ~ ❶ (*relaxen*) to unwind ❷ (*sich glätten*) to relax ❸ POL *a.* (*sich beruhigen*) to ease **II.** *vt* ■**etw** ~ ❶ (*lockern*) to relax sth ❷ (*Spannung beseitigen*) to ease sth
Entspannung *f* ❶ (*innerliche Ruhe*) relaxation ❷ POL easing of tension
ent|sprechen* *vi irreg* ■**einer S.** *dat* ~ ❶ (*übereinstimmen*) to correspond to sth ❷ (*genügen*) to fulfill sth ❸ (*geh: nachkommen*) to comply with sth
entsprechend [ɛnt·ˈʃprɛ·çn̩t] **I.** *adj* ❶ (*angemessen*) appropriate ❷ (*zuständig*) relevant **II.** *präp* in accordance with
Entsprechung <-, -en> *f* equivalence
ent|springen* *vi irreg sein* ■**einer S.** *dat* ~ ❶ GEOG to rise from sth ❷ (*seinen Ursprung haben*) to spring from sth
ent|stammen* *vi sein* ■**einer S.** *dat* ~ ❶ (*aus etw stammen*) to come from sth ❷ (*aus einer bestimmten Zeit stammen*) to originate from sth; (*abgeleitet sein*) to be derived from sth
ent|stehen* *vi irreg sein* ■[**aus etw** *dat/* **durch etw** *akk*] ~ ❶ (*zu existieren beginnen*) to come into being [from sth] ❷ (*verursacht werden*) to arise [from sth] ❸ CHEM (*sich bilden*) to be produced [from/through sth] ❹ (*sich ergeben*) to arise [from sth]
Entstehung <-, -en> *f* ❶ (*das Werden*) creation; *des Lebens* origin; *eines Gebäudes* construction ❷ CHEM formation
ent|stellen* *vt* ❶ (*verunstalten*) to disfigure ❷ (*verzerren*) **der Schmerz entstellte ihre Züge** her features were contorted with pain ❸ (*verzerrt wiedergeben*) **etw entstellt wiedergeben** to distort sth
Entstellung *f* ❶ (*entstellende Narbe*) disfig-

urement ② (*Verzerrung*) *der Tatsachen, Wahrheit* distortion

ent|strömen* *vi sein* (*geh*) ■ **einer S.** *dat* ~ to pour out of sth; *Gas, Luft* to escape from sth

ent|täuschen* **I.** *vt* ① (*Erwartungen nicht erfüllen*) ■ **jdn** ~ to disappoint sb ② (*nicht entsprechen*) **jds Hoffnungen** ~ to dash sb's hopes **II.** *vi* (*enttäuschend sein*) to be disappointing

enttäuschend *adj* disappointing

enttäuscht **I.** *adj* disappointed (**über** +*akk* about, **von** +*dat* by) **II.** *adv* disappointedly

Enttäuschung *f* disappointment

ent|waffnen* [ɛnt·'vaf·nən] *vt* (*a. fig*) ■ **jdn** ~ to disarm sb

entwaffnend **I.** *adj* disarming **II.** *adv* disarmingly

Entwarnung *f* all clear

ent|wässern* *vt* ① AGR, BAU to drain ② MED to dehydrate

Entwässerung, Entwässrung <-, -en> *f* ① (*von Moor, Gelände*) drainage ② (*Kanalisation*) drainage [system] ③ CHEM dehydration

entweder [ɛnt·'veː·dɐ] *konj* ~ **... oder ...** either...or

ent|weichen* *vi irreg sein* ■ [**aus etw** *dat*] ~ ① (*sich verflüchtigen*) to leak [from sth] ② (*geh: fliehen*) to escape [from sth]

ent|wenden* *vt* (*hum geh*) ■ [**jdm**] **etw** ~ to purloin [*or hum* liberate] sth [from sb]

ent|werfen* *vt irreg* ① (*zeichnerisch gestalten*) to sketch ② (*designen*) to design ③ (*im Entwurf erstellen*) to draft

ent|werten* *vt* ① (*ungültig machen*) to invalidate; *Fahrkarte* to stamp; *Banknoten* to demonetize ② (*weniger wert machen*) *Preise* to devalue

Entwertung *f* invalidation; (*Wertminderung*) devaluation

ent|wickeln* **I.** *vt* ① (*erfinden, entwerfen*) *a.* FOTO to develop ② CHEM (*entstehen lassen*) to produce **II.** *vr* ① (*zur Entfaltung kommen*) ■ **sich** *akk* [**zu etw** *dat*] ~ to develop [into sth] ② (*vorankommen*) **na, wie entwickelt sich euer Projekt?** well, how is your project coming along? ③ CHEM (*entstehen*) ■ **sich** ~ to be produced

Entwicklung <-, -en> *f* ① (*das Entwickeln, das Entwerfen*) *a.* FOTO development ② (*das Vorankommen*) progression ③ ÖKON, POL trend

Entwicklungshelfer(in) *m(f)* development aid worker

Entwicklungshilfe *f* development aid

Entwicklungsland *nt* developing country

entwürdigend **I.** *adj* degrading **II.** *adv* degradingly

Entwurf *m* ① (*Skizze*) sketch ② (*Design*) design ③ (*Konzept*) draft

ent|wurzeln* *vt* ■ **etw** ~ to uproot sth

ent|ziehen* *irreg* **I.** *vt* ■ **jdm etw** ~ to withdraw sth from sb **II.** *vr* ① (*sich losmachen*) to evade ② (*nicht berühren*) **das entzieht sich meiner Kenntnis** that's beyond my knowledge

Entziehungskur *f* treatment for an addiction

ent|ziffern* [ɛnt·'tsɪ·fɐn] *vt* to decipher

ent|zücken* *vt* (*begeistern*) ■ **jdn** ~ to delight sb

Entzücken <-s> *nt kein pl* delight; [**über etw** *akk*] **in** ~ **geraten** to be ecstatic [about sth]

entzückend [ɛnt·'tsʏ·kn̩t] *adj* delightful

Entzug <-[e]s> *m kein pl* ① ADMIN revocation ② MED withdrawal; (*Entziehungskur*) withdrawal treatment

Entzugserscheinung *f* withdrawal symptom *usu pl*

ent|zünden* **I.** *vt* (*geh: anzünden*) to light **II.** *vr* ① MED ■ **sich** ~ to become infected ② (*in Brand geraten*) ■ **sich** ~ to catch fire ③ (*fig: aufflackern*) ■ **sich an etw** *dat* ~ to be sparked off by sth

entzündet *adj* MED infected

entzündlich [ɛnt·'tsʏnt·lɪç] *adj* ① MED inflammatory ② *Substanz* inflammable; **leicht** ~ highly inflammable

Entzündung *f* MED *eines Gelenks* inflammation; *durch Bakterien* infection

entzwei [ɛnt·'tsvai] *adj pred* in two [pieces]; (*zersprungen*) broken

entzwei|gehen *vi irreg sein* to break [in two]

Enzian <-s, -e> ['ɛn·tsi̯·aːn] *m* ① BOT gentian ② (*Schnaps*) *spirit distilled from the roots of gentian*

Enzyklopädie <-, -n> [ɛn·tsy·klo·pɛ·'diː, *pl* -'diː·ən] *f* encyclopedia

enzyklopädisch [ɛn·tsy·klo·'pɛː·dɪʃ] **I.** *adj* encyclopedic **II.** *adv* encyclopedically

Enzym <-s, -e> [ɛn·'tsyːm] *nt* enzyme

Epen *pl von* **Epos**

Epidemie <-, -n> [epi·de·'miː, *pl* -'miː·ən] *f* epidemic

Epilepsie <-, -n> [epi·lɛ·'psiː, *pl* -'psiː·ən] *f* epilepsy

Epileptiker(in) <-s, -> [epi'lɛp·ti·kɐ] *m(f)* epileptic

epileptisch [epi'lɛp·tɪʃ] **I.** *adj* epileptic **II.** *adv* tending to have epileptic seizures

Epilog <-s, -e> [epi'loːk, *pl* epi'loː·gə] *m* epilog(ue)

episch ['eːpɪʃ] *adj* epic

Episode <-, -n> [epi'zoː·də] *f* episode

Epoche <-, -n> [e'pɔ·xə] *f* epoch

Epos <-, Epen> ['eːpɔs, *pl* 'eːp·ən] *nt* epic

er <*gen* seiner, *dat* ihm, *akk* ihn> ['eːɐ̯] *pron pers* he; **sie ist ein Jahr jünger als** ~ she is a year younger than him

Erachten <-s> [ɛɐ̯·'ʔax·tn̩] *nt kein pl* **meines** ~**s** in my opinion

er|ahnen* *vt* (*geh*) to guess; ■ **etw** ~ **lassen** to give an idea of sth

er|arbeiten* *vt* ① (*durch Arbeit erwerben*) ■ [**sich** *dat*] **etw** ~ *Vermögen* to work for sth ② (*erstellen*) ■ **etw** ~ *Entwurf* to work out sth

Erbanlage *f meist pl* hereditary factor

er|barmen* [ɛɐ̯·'bar·mən] **I.** *vt* (*leidtun*) ■ **jdn** ~ to arouse sb's pity **II.** *vr* ■ **sich** *akk*

jds/einer S. ~ to take pity on sb/sth
Erbarmen <-s> [ɛɐ̯ˈbar·mən] *nt kein pl* pity; ■~ **mit jdm** [**haben**] [to have] pity for sb; **ohne** ~ merciless[ly]
erbärmlich [ɛɐ̯ˈbɛrm·lɪç] **I.** *adj* (*pej*) ❶ (*fam: gemein*) miserable ❷ (*furchtbar*) terrible ❸ (*jämmerlich*) *Zustand* wretched **II.** *adv* (*pej*) ❶ (*gemein*) abominably ❷ (*fam: furchtbar*) terribly
erbarmungslos [ɛɐ̯ˈbar·mʊŋs·loːs] **I.** *adj* merciless **II.** *adv* mercilessly
er|bauen* **I.** *vt* ❶ (*errichten*) to build ❷ (*seelisch bereichern*) ■**jdn** ~ to uplift sb ❸ (*fam: begeistert sein*) ■[**von etw** *dat*] **erbaut sein** to be enthusiastic [about sth] **II.** *vr* (*sich innerlich erfreuen*) ■**sich** *akk* **an etw** *dat* ~ to be uplifted by sth
Erbauer(in) <-s, -> *m(f)* architect
Erbauung <-, -en> *f* ❶ (*Errichtung*) building ❷ (*seelische Bereicherung*) edification
Erbe <-s> [ˈɛr·bə] *nt kein pl* ❶ (*Erbschaft*) inheritance ❷ (*fig: Hinterlassenschaft*) legacy
Erbe, Erbin <-n, -n> [ˈɛr·bə, *pl* ˈɛr·bn̩] *m, f* heir *masc*, heiress *fem*
erben [ˈɛr·bn̩] **I.** *vt* ■**etw** [**von jdm**] ~ to inherit sth [from sb] **II.** *vi* (*Erbe sein*) to receive an inheritance
er|beuten* [ɛɐ̯ˈbɔy·tn̩] *vt* ■**etw** ~ ❶ (*als Beute erhalten*) to get away with sth ❷ (*als Kriegsbeute bekommen*) to capture sth ❸ (*als Beute fangen*) to carry off *sep* sth
Erbfaktor *m* hereditary factor
Erbfehler *m* BIOL hereditary defect
Erbfolge *f* [line of] succession
Erbgut *nt kein pl* genetic makeup
Erbin <-, -nen> [ˈɛr·bɪn] *f fem form von* **Erbe** heiress
erbittert **I.** *adj* bitter **II.** *adv* bitterly
Erbitterung <-> *f kein pl* bitterness
Erbkrankheit *f* hereditary disease
er|blassen* [ɛɐ̯ˈbla·sn̩] *vi sein* ■[**vor etw** *dat*] ~ to turn pale [with sth]
er|bleichen* *vi sein* (*geh*) ■[**vor etw** *dat*] ~ to turn pale [with sth]
erblich [ˈɛrp·lɪç] **I.** *adj* hereditary **II.** *adv* by inheritance
er|blicken* *vt* (*geh*) ■**jdn/etw** ~ to catch sight of sb/sth
er|blinden* [ɛɐ̯ˈblɪn·dn̩] *vi sein* ■[**durch etw** *akk*] ~ to go blind [as a result of sth]
Erblindung <-, -en> *f* loss of sight
Erbonkel *m* (*hum fam*) rich uncle
er|brechen*[1] *irreg* **I.** *vt* (*ausspucken*) ■**etw** ~ to bring up *sep* sth **II.** *vi* (*den Mageninhalt erbrechen*) to throw up *sl* **III.** *vr* (*sich übergeben*) ■**sich** *akk* ~ to be sick
er|brechen*[2] *irreg vt* (*geh o veraltet*) ■**etw** ~ to break open *sep* sth
Erbrecht *nt* law of inheritance
er|bringen* *vt irreg* ❶ (*aufbringen*) *a.* FIN to raise ❷ (*als Resultat zeitigen*) to produce ❸ JUR *Proof* to produce
Erbschaft <-, -en> [ˈɛrp·ʃaft] *f* inheritance
Erbse <-, -n> [ˈɛrp·sə] *f* pea
Erbsünde *f* original sin
Erbtante *f* (*hum fam*) rich aunt
Erdachse [ˈeːɐ̯d·aksə] *f* earth's axis
erdacht [ɛɐ̯ˈdaxt] *adj* invented
Erdanziehung *f kein pl* earth's gravitational pull
Erdapfel *m* SÜDD, ÖSTERR (*Kartoffel*) potato
Erdatmosphäre *f* Earth's atmosphere
Erdball *m* (*geh*) globe
Erdbeben *nt* earthquake
Erdbeere [ˈeːɐ̯t·beː·rə] *f* strawberry
Erdbevölkerung *f* world population
Erdboden *m* ground
Erde <-, -n> [ˈeːɐ̯·də] *f* ❶ *kein pl* (*Welt*) earth; **auf der ganzen** ~ in the whole world ❷ (*Erdreich*) earth ❸ (*Boden*) ground; **zu ebener** ~ at street level
er|denken* *vt irreg* to devise
erdenklich *adj attr* conceivable
Erdgas *nt* natural gas
ErdgeschossRR *nt* ground [*or* first] floor
er|dichten* *vt* (*geh*) to fabricate
erdig [ˈeːɐ̯·dɪç] **I.** *adj* ❶ (*nach Erde riechend/schmeckend*) earthy ❷ (*mit Erde beschmutzt*) muddy **II.** *adv* ~ **schmecken** to have an earthy taste
Erdkugel *f* globe
Erdkunde *f* geography
ErdnussRR *f* peanut
Erdoberfläche *f* Earth's surface
Erdöl *nt* oil
Erdölvorkommen *nt* oil deposit
er|dreisten* [ɛɐ̯ˈdrai·stn̩] *vr* ■**sich** *akk* ~ to take liberties; ■**sich** *akk* **~, etw zu tun** to have the audacity to do sth
er|drosseln* *vt* ■**jdn** ~ to strangle sb
er|drücken* *vt* ❶ (*zu Tode drücken*) ■**jdn/ein Tier** ~ to crush sb/an animal to death ❷ (*fam: Eigenständigkeit nehmen*) ■**jdn** [**mit etw** *dat*] ~ to stifle sb [with sth] ❸ (*sehr stark belasten*) ■**jdn** ~ to overwhelm sb
Erdrutsch *m* (*a. fig*) landslide
Erdstoß *m* seismic shock
Erdteil *m* continent
er|dulden* *vt* ■**etw** ~ *Kränkungen, Leid* to endure sth
Erdumdrehung *f* Earth's rotation
Erdumkreisung *f* orbit around the Earth
Erdumlaufbahn *f* [Earth] orbit
er|eifern* *vr* ■**sich** *akk* [**über etw** *akk*] ~ to get worked up [about sth]
er|eignen* [ɛɐ̯ˈʔaig·nən] *vr* ■**sich** ~ to occur
Ereignis <-ses, -se> [ɛɐ̯ˈʔaig·nɪs, *pl* -nɪ·sə] *nt* event; (*etw Besonderes*) occasion
ereignislos **I.** *adj* uneventful **II.** *adv* uneventfully
ereignisreich *adj* eventful
Erektion <-, -en> [erɛk·ˈtsi̯oːn] *f* erection
Eremit(in) <-en, -en> [ere·ˈmiːt] *m(f)* hermit
er|fahren[1] [ɛɐ̯ˈfaː·rən] *irreg* **I.** *vt* ❶ (*zu hören bekommen*) ■**etw** [**über jdn/etw**] ~ to hear sth [about sb/sth] ❷ (*erleben*) to experience

II. *vi* (*Kenntnis erhalten*) ■**von etw** *dat*/**über etw** *akk* ~ to learn of sth
erfahren² [ɛɐ̯ˈfaː·rən] *adj* (*versiert*) experienced; ■~ **sein** to be experienced (**in** +*dat* in)
Erfahrung <-, -en> *f* ① (*prägendes Erlebnis*) experience (**mit** +*dat* with); **nach meiner ~** in my experience ② (*Übung*) experience ③ (*Kenntnis*) **etw in ~ bringen** to find out *sep* sth
Erfahrungsaustausch *m* exchange of experiences
erfahrungsgemäß *adv* in sb's experience; ~ **ist ...** experience shows ...
Erfahrungswert *m meist pl* empirical value *spec*
er|fassen* *vt* ① (*mitreißen*) ■**etw/jdn** ~ *Auto, Strömung* to catch sth/sb ② (*befallen*) ■**jdn** ~ to seize sb ③ (*begreifen*) to understand ④ (*registrieren*) to record ⑤ (*eingeben*) *Daten, Text* to enter
Erfassung *f* ① (*Registrierung*) recording ② *Daten, Text* entering
er|finden* [ɛɐ̯ˈfɪn·dn̩] *vt irreg* to invent
Erfinder(in) [ɛɐ̯ˈfɪn·dɐ] *m(f)* inventor
erfinderisch [ɛɐ̯ˈfɪn·də·rɪʃ] *adj* inventive
Erfindung <-, -en> *f* invention
Erfolg <-[e]s, -e> [ɛɐ̯ˈfɔlk, *pl* -fɔl·gə] *m* ① (*positives Ergebnis*) success; ~ **versprechend** promising; **viel ~!** good luck! ② (*Folge*) result, outcome
er|folgen* *vi sein* (*geh*) to occur
erfolglos [ɛɐ̯ˈfɔlk·loːs] *adj* ① (*ohne Erfolg*) unsuccessful ② (*vergeblich*) futile
Erfolglosigkeit <-> *f kein pl* ① (*mangelnder Erfolg*) lack of success ② (*Vergeblichkeit*) futility
erfolgreich *adj* successful
Erfolgsaussichten *pl* prospects *pl* of success
Erfolgsautor(in) *m(f)* bestselling author
Erfolgsdruck *m kein pl* performance pressure
Erfolgserlebnis *nt* sense of achievement
erforderlich [ɛɐ̯ˈfɔr·dɐ·lɪç] *adj* necessary
er|fordern* *vt* to require
Erfordernis <-ses, -se> [ɛɐ̯ˈfɔr·dɐ·nɪs] *nt* requirement (**für** +*akk* for)
er|forschen* *vt* ① (*durchstreifen und untersuchen*) to explore ② (*prüfen*) to investigate; *Gewissen* to examine
Erforschung *f* ① (*das Erforschen*) exploration ② (*das Prüfen*) investigation
er|fragen* *vt* ■**etw** [**von jdm**] ~ to ask [sb] about sth; *Einzelheiten* to obtain
er|freuen* **I.** *vt* (*freudig stimmen*) ■**jdn** ~ to please sb **II.** *vr* ① (*Freude haben*) ■**sich** *akk* **an etw** *dat* ~ to take pleasure in sth ② (*geh: genießen*) ■**sich** *akk* **einer S.** *gen* ~ to enjoy sth
erfreulich [ɛɐ̯ˈfrɔy·lɪç] **I.** *adj Anblick* pleasant; *Nachricht* welcome **II.** *adv* happily
erfreulicherweise *adv* happily
er|frieren* *vi irreg sein* ① (*durch Frost eingehen*) to be killed by frost ② *Gliedmaßen* to get frostbitten ③ (*an Kälte sterben*) to freeze to death
er|frischen* [ɛɐ̯ˈfrɪ·ʃən] **I.** *vt* ■**jdn** ~ to refresh sb **II.** *vi* (*abkühlen*) to be refreshing **III.** *vr* (*sich abkühlen*) ■**sich** *akk* ~ to refresh oneself
erfrischend *adj* refreshing
Erfrischung <-, -en> *f* ① (*Abkühlung, Belebung*) refreshment ② (*erfrischendes Getränk*) refreshment
Erfrischungsgetränk *nt* refreshment
er|füllen* **I.** *vt* ① (*ausführen*) to fulfill ② (*durchdringen*) **von Ekel/Angst erfüllt sein** to be filled with disgust/fear ③ (*anfüllen*) to fill **II.** *vr* (*sich bewahrheiten*) ■**sich** ~ to come true
Erfüllung *f* ① (*die Ausführung*) realization; *von Traum, Verpflichtung* fulfillment; *von Amtspflichten* execution ② (*innere Befriedigung*) fulfillment; **etw geht in ~** sth comes true
erfunden [ɛɐ̯ˈfʊn·dn̩] *pp von* **erfinden**
er|gänzen* [ɛɐ̯ˈgɛn·tsn̩] *vt* ■**etw** ~ to supplement sth; *Vorräte* to replenish sth; (*vollenden*) to complete sth
ergänzend **I.** *adj* additional **II.** *adv* additionally
Ergänzung <-, -en> *f* ① (*das Auffüllen*) replenishment; *einer Sammlung* completion ② (*das Hinzufügen*) supplementing ③ (*Zusatz*) addition
er|gattern* [ɛɐ̯ˈga·tɐn] *vt* (*fam*) ■**etw** ~ to get [a] hold of sth
er|gaunern* [ɛɐ̯ˈgau·nɐn] *vt* (*fam*) ■[**sich** *dat*] **etw** ~ to hustle sth
er|geben*¹ *irreg* **I.** *vt* ① MATH ■**etw** ~ to amount to sth ② (*als Resultat haben*) ■**etw ergibt etw** sth produces sth **II.** *vr* ① (*kapitulieren*) ■**sich** *akk* [**jdm**] ~ to surrender [to sb] ② (*sich fügen*) **sich** *akk* **in sein Schicksal** ~ to resign oneself to one's fate ③ (*sich hingeben*) **sich** *akk* **dem Glücksspiel** ~ to take to gambling ④ (*daraus folgen*) ■**sich aus etw** *dat* ~ to result from sth
ergeben² *adj* ① (*demütig*) humble ② (*treu*) devoted
Ergebenheit <-> *f kein pl* ① (*Demut*) humility ② (*Treue*) devotion
Ergebnis <-ses, -se> [ɛɐ̯ˈgeːp·nɪs, *pl* -nɪ·sə] *nt* result; SPORT score
ergebnislos *adj* without result
er|gehen* *irreg* **I.** *vi sein* ① (*offiziell erlassen*) ■**etw ~ lassen** to issue sth ② (*geduldig hinnehmen*) **etw über sich** *akk* **~ lassen** to endure sth ③ (*geh: abgesandt werden*) ■[**an jdn**] ~ to be sent [to sb] **II.** *vi impers sein* (*widerfahren*) **es ergeht jdm schlecht** it's not going well for sb
ergiebig [ɛɐ̯ˈgiː·bɪç] *adj* ① (*sparsam im Verbrauch*) economical ② (*nützlich*) productive
er|gießen *irreg* **I.** *vt* (*verströmen*) to pour over; (*geh*) to pour forth *liter* **II.** *vr* (*in großer Menge fließen*) to pour [out]
er|götzen* [ɛɐ̯ˈgœ·tsn̩] **I.** *vt* (*geh: vergnügen*) ■**jdn** ~ to amuse sb **II.** *vr* (*sich vergnügen*) ■**sich** *akk* [**an etw** *dat*] ~ to derive pleasure [from sth]

er|gre̲i̲fen* *vt irreg* ① *(fassen)* to seize ② *(dingfest machen)* ■**jdn** ~ to apprehend sb ③ *(übergreifen) Feuer* to engulf ④ *(fig: wahrnehmen)* ■**etw** ~ to seize sth ⑤ *(in die Wege leiten) Maßnahmen* to take ⑥ *(gefühlsmäßig bewegen)* ■**jdn** ~ to seize sb; *(Angst)* to grip sb

ergre̲ifend *adj* moving

Ergre̲ifung <-, -en> *f* ① *(Festnahme)* capture ② *(Übernahme)* seizure

ergriffen [ɛɐ̯·ˈgrɪ·fn̩] *adj* moved

er|grụnden* *vt* to discover

erhaben [ɛɐ̯·ˈhaː·bn̩] *adj* ① *(feierlich stimmend) Gedanken* lofty; *Anblick* awe-inspiring; *Augenblick* solemn; *Schönheit* sublime ② *(über etw stehend)* ■**über etw** *akk* ~ **sein** to be above sth

Erha̲benheit <-> *f kein pl* grandeur; *eines Augenblicks* solemnity; *von Schönheit* sublimity

Erhạlt <-[e]s> *m kein pl (geh)* ① *(geh: das Bekommen)* receipt; **den ~ einer S.** *gen* **bestätigen** to confirm receipt of sth ② *(das Aufrechterhalten)* maintenance

er|hạlten* *irreg* **I.** *vt* ① *(bekommen)* to receive; *Befehl* to be given ② *(erteilt bekommen)* ■**etw** ~ to receive sth ③ *(eine Vorstellung gewinnen)* **einen Eindruck [von jdm/etw]** ~ to get an impression [of sb/sth] ④ *(bewahren)* to maintain ⑤ BAU to preserve **II.** *vr* ① *(sich halten)* **sich** *akk* **gesund** ~ to keep [oneself] healthy ② *(bewahrt bleiben)* ■**sich** ~ to remain preserved

erhältlich [ɛɐ̯·ˈhɛlt·lɪç] *adj* obtainable

Erhạltung *f kein pl* ① *(das Erhalten)* preservation ② *(Aufrechterhaltung)* maintenance

er|hạ̈ngen* **I.** *vt* ■**jdn** ~ to hang sb **II.** *vr* ■**sich** *akk* ~ to hang oneself

er|hạ̈rten* **I.** *vt* ■**etw** ~ to support sth **II.** *vr* ■**sich** ~ to be reinforced

er|he̲ben* *irreg* **I.** *vt* ① *(hochheben)* to raise ② *(einfordern)* ■**etw** ~ to levy sth ③ *Daten, Informationen* to gather ④ *(zum Ausdruck bringen)* **ein Geschrei/Gejammer** ~ to kick up a fuss/to start whining; *Protest* to voice; *Einspruch* to raise **II.** *vr* ■**sich** *akk* ~ ① *(aufstehen)* to stand up (**von** +*dat* from) ② *(sich auflehnen)* to rise up [*or* revolt] (**gegen** +*akk* against) ③ *(aufragen)* to rise up (**über** +*dat* above) ④ *(entstehen, aufkommen)* to start; *Wind* to pick up; *Sturm* to blow up

erheblich [ɛɐ̯·ˈheːp·lɪç] **I.** *adj* ① *(beträchtlich)* considerable; *Nachteil, Vorteil a.* great; *Störung, Verspätung a.* major; *Verletzung* serious ② *(relevant)* relevant **II.** *adv* considerably

Erhe̲bung *f* ① *(Aufstand)* uprising ② *von Abgaben, Steuern* levying ③ *(amtliche Ermittlung)* gathering

er|heitern* [ɛɐ̯·ˈhai·tɐn] *vt* ■**jdn** ~ to amuse sb

Erhe̲iterung <-, *selten* -en> *f* amusement

er|hellen* [ɛɐ̯·ˈhɛ·lən] **I.** *vt* ■**etw** ~ ① *(hell machen)* to light up sth ② *(klären)* to throw light on sth **II.** *vr* ■**sich** ~ to clear

er|hitzen* [ɛɐ̯·ˈhɪ·tsn̩] **I.** *vt* ① *(heiß machen)* ■**etw** ~ to heat sth ② *(zum Schwitzen bringen)* ■**jdn** ~ to make sb sweat **II.** *vr (sich erregen)* ■**sich** *akk* ~ to get excited (**an** +*dat* about)

er|họffen* *vt* ■**[sich** *dat*] **etw** ~ to hope for sth

er|höhen* [ɛɐ̯·ˈhøː·ən] **I.** *vt* ■**etw** ~ ① *(höher machen)* to raise sth (**um** +*akk* by) ② *(anheben)* to increase sth (**auf** +*akk* to, **um** +*akk* by) ③ *(verstärken)* to heighten sth ④ MUS to raise [*or* sharpen] **II.** *vr* ■**sich** ~ ① *(steigen)* to increase (**auf** +*akk* to, **um** +*akk* by) ② *(sich verstärken)* to increase

erhö̲ht *adj* ① *(verstärkt)* high; *Herzschlag, Puls* rapid ② *(gesteigert)* increased

Erhö̲hung <-, -en> *f* ① *(Steigerung)* increase ② *(Anhebung)* raising ③ *(Verstärkung)* heightening

er|ho̲len* *vr* ■**sich** *akk* ~ ① *(wieder zu Kräften kommen)* to recover (**von** +*dat* from) ② *(ausspannen)* to take a break (**von** +*dat* from) ③ BÖRSE to rally

erholsam [ɛɐ̯·ˈhoːl·zaːm] *adj* relaxing

Erho̲lung <-> *f kein pl* relaxation

er|hö̲ren* *vt (geh) Bitte* to grant; *Flehen, Gebete* to answer

er|innern* [ɛɐ̯·ˈʔɪn·ɐn] **I.** *vt* ① *(zu denken veranlassen)* ■**jdn an etw** *akk* ~ to remind sb about sth ② *(denken lassen)* ■**jdn an jdn/etw** ~ to remind sb of sb/sth **II.** *vr (sich entsinnen)* ■**sich** *akk* **an jdn/etw** ~ to remember sb/sth **III.** *vi* ① *(in Erinnerung bringen)* ■**an jdn/etw** ~ to be reminiscent of sb/sth *form* ② *(ins Gedächtnis rufen)* ■**daran ~, dass ...** to point out that ...

Erịnnerung <-, -en> *f* ① *(Gedächtnis)* memory ② *pl (Eindrücke von Erlebnissen)* memories *pl* ③ *(geh: Mahnung)* reminder

er|kälten* [ɛɐ̯·ˈkɛl·tn̩] *vr* ■**sich** *akk* ~ to catch a cold

erkạ̈ltet **I.** *adj* ~ **sein** to have a cold *pred* **II.** *adv* **du hörst dich ~ an** you sound as if you've got a cold

Erkạ̈ltung <-, -en> *f* cold; **eine ~ bekommen** to catch a cold

er|kạ̈mpfen* *vt* ■**[sich** *dat*] **etw** ~ to fight to get sth

er|ka̲u̲fen* *vt* ① *(durch Bezahlung erhalten)* to buy ② *(durch Opfer erlangen)* **etw teuer** ~ to pay dearly for sth

erkẹnnbar *adj* ① *(sichtbar)* discernible ② *(wahrnehmbar)* ■**für jdn/etw ~ sein** to be perceptible to sb/sth (**an** +*dat* from)

er|kẹnnen* *irreg* **I.** *vt* ① *(wahrnehmen)* ■**jdn/etw** ~ to see sb/sth ② *(identifizieren)* ■**jdn/etw** ~ to recognize sb/sth (**an** +*dat* by) ③ *(einsehen)* **einen Irrtum** ~ to realize one's mistake ④ *(feststellen)* to detect **II.** *vi* ① *(wahrnehmen)* ■~ **ob/um was/wen ...** to see whether/what/who ... ② *(einsehen)* ■~**, dass/wie ...** to realize that/how ...

erkenntlich [ɛɐ̯·ˈkɛnt·lɪç] *adj* grateful; ■**sich**

E

akk ~ **zeigen** to show one's appreciation (**für** +*akk* for)

Erkenntnis <-, -se> [ɛɐ̯·ˈkɛnt·nɪs, *pl* -nɪ·sə] *f* ❶ (*Einsicht*) insight; **zu der ~ kommen, dass ...** to realize that ... ❷ *ohne pl* (*das Erkennen*) understanding

Erkennungszeichen *nt* identification mark

Erker <-s, -> [ˈɛr·kɐ] *m* oriel

er|klären* **I.** *vt* ❶ (*erläutern*) ■ [**jdm**] **etw** ~ to explain sth [to sb] ❷ (*interpretieren*) ■ [**jdm**] **etw** ~ to interpret sth [for sb] ❸ (*bekannt geben*) to announce ❹ (*offiziell bezeichnen*) ■ **jdn für etw** *akk* ~ to pronounce sb sth **II.** *vr* ❶ (*sich deuten*) **wie ~ Sie sich, dass ...** how do you explain that ... ❷ (*sich aufklären*) ■ **sich** ~ to become clear ❸ (*sich bezeichnen*) **sich zufrieden** ~ to voice one's satisfaction; **sich bereit ~, etwas zu tun** to volunteer to do sth

erklärt *adj attr* declared

Erklärung *f* ❶ (*Darlegung*) explanation ❷ (*Mitteilung*) statement

Erkrankung <-, -en> *f* illness

er|kunden* [ɛɐ̯·ˈkʊn·dn̩] *vt* ■ **etw** ~ ❶ (*auskundschaften*) to scout out *sep* sth ❷ (*in Erfahrung bringen*) to discover sth

er|kundigen* [ɛɐ̯·ˈkʊn·dɪ·gn̩] *vr* ■ **sich** *akk* [**nach jdm/etw**] ~ to ask [about sb/sth]

Erkundigung <-, -en> *f* inquiry

Erkundung <-, -en> *f* MIL reconnaissance

er|langen* [ɛɐ̯·ˈlaŋən] *vt* (*geh*) to obtain

Erlass[RR], **Erlaß**[ALT] <Erlasses, Erlasse *o* ÖSTERR Erlässe> [ɛɐ̯·ˈlas, *pl* ɛɐ̯·ˈlɛ·sə] *m* ❶ (*Verfügung*) decree ❷ (*das Erlassen*) remission

er|lassen* *vt irreg* ❶ (*verfügen*) to issue ❷ (*von etw befreien*) ■ **jdm etw** ~ to remit sb's sth

er|lauben* [ɛɐ̯·ˈlau·bn̩] **I.** *vt* ❶ (*gestatten*) ■ **jdm etw** ~ to allow sb to do sth ❷ (*geh: zulassen*) **ich komme, soweit es meine Zeit erlaubt** if time permits, I'll come ▸ WENDUNGEN: ~ **Sie mal!** what do you think you're doing? **II.** *vr* ❶ (*sich gönnen*) ■ **sich** *dat* **etw** ~ to allow oneself sth ❷ (*sich herausnehmen*) ■ **sich** *dat* **~, etw zu tun** to take the liberty of doing sth

Erlaubnis <-, *selten* -se> *f* ❶ (*Genehmigung*) permission ❷ (*genehmigendes Schriftstück*) permit

er|läutern* *vt* ■ [**jdm**] **etw** ~ to explain sth [to sb]

Erläuterung <-, -en> *f* explanation

Erle <-, -n> [ˈɛr·lə] *f* alder

er|leben* *vt* ❶ (*im Leben mitmachen*) ■ **etw** ~ to live to see sth ❷ (*erfahren*) to experience ❸ (*durchmachen*) ■ **etw** ~ to go through sth ❹ (*mit ansehen*) ■ **es ~, dass/wie ...** to see that/how ...; **so wütend habe ich ihn noch nie erlebt** I've never seen him so furious

Erlebnis <-ses, -se> [ɛɐ̯·ˈleːp·nɪs, *pl* -nɪ·sə] *nt* experience

er|ledigen* [ɛɐ̯·ˈleː·dɪ·gn̩] **I.** *vt* ❶ (*ausführen*) ■ **etw** ~ to take care of sth ❷ (*fam: erschöpfen*) ■ **jdn** ~ to wear out *sep* sb ❸ (*sl: umbringen*) ■ **jdn** ~ to bump off *sep* sb **II.** *vr* ■ **etw erledigt sich** [**von selbst**] sth sorts itself out [on its own]

erledigt [ɛɐ̯·ˈleː·dɪçt] *adj pred* ❶ (*fam: erschöpft*) exhausted, beat *fam* ❷ (*fam: am Ende*) ■ ~ **sein** to have had it ❸ (*abgehakt*) ■ **etw ist** [**für jdn**] ~ sth is over and done with [as far as sb is concerned]; (*schon vergessen*) sth is forgotten [as far as sb is concerned]

Erledigung <-, -en> *f* ❶ (*Ausführung*) dealing with ❷ (*Besorgung*) errand

er|legen* *vt* ❶ (*zur Strecke bringen*) ■ **ein Tier** ~ to shoot [*or spec* bag] an animal ❷ ÖSTERR (*bezahlen*) to pay

er|leichtern* [ɛɐ̯·ˈlaiç·tɐn] *vt* ❶ (*ertragbarer machen*) ■ **etw** ~ to make sth easier ❷ (*innerlich beruhigen*) ■ **jdn** ~ to be a relief to sb ❸ (*fam: beklauen*) ■ **jdn um etw** *akk* ~ to relieve sb of sth

Erleichterung <-, -en> *f* ❶ (*Linderung*) relief ❷ *kein pl* (*Beruhigung*) relief; **zu jds** ~ to sb's relief ❸ (*Vereinfachung*) simplification

er|leiden* *vt irreg* ■ **etw** ~ to suffer sth

erlesen *adj* exquisite

er|liegen* *vi irreg sein* ■ **einer S.** *dat* ~ ❶ (*verfallen*) to fall prey to sth ❷ (*geh: zum Opfer fallen*) to fall victim to sth ▸ WENDUNGEN: **zum E~ kommen** to come to a standstill

er|lischt [ɛɐ̯·ˈlɪʃt] *3. pers sing pres von* **erlöschen**

Erlös <-es, -e> [ɛɐ̯·ˈløːs, *pl* -ˈløː·zə] *m* proceeds *npl*

er|löschen <erlischt, erlosch, erloschen> *vi sein* ❶ (*zu brennen aufhören*) to stop burning ❷ (*vergehen*) to fizzle out ❸ (*seine Gültigkeit verlieren*) to expire; *Ansprüche* to become invalid

er|lösen* *vt* ■ **jdn** ~ ❶ (*befreien*) to release sb (**aus/von** +*dat* from) ❷ REL to redeem sb (**aus/von** +*dat* from)

erlösend **I.** *adj* relieving **II.** *adv* in a relieving manner *pred*

Erlösung *f* ❶ (*Erleichterung*) relief ❷ REL redemption

er|mächtigen* [ɛɐ̯·ˈmɛç·tɪ·gn̩] *vt* ■ **jdn** [**zu etw** *dat*] ~ to authorize sb [to do sth]

Ermächtigung <-, -en> *f* authorization

er|mahnen* *vt* ❶ (*warnend mahnen*) ■ **jdn** ~ to warn sb ❷ (*anhalten*) ■ **jdn zu etw** *dat* ~ to admonish sb to do sth

Ermahnung *f* warning

Ermäßigung <-, -en> *f* reduction

ermattet *adj* (*geh*) exhausted

er|messen* *vt irreg* ■ **etw** ~ to comprehend sth

Ermessen <-s> *nt kein pl* discretion

er|mitteln* **I.** *vt* ■ **etw** ~ ❶ (*herausfinden*) to find out *sep* sth ❷ (*errechnen*) to determine sth **II.** *vi* (*eine Untersuchung durchführen*) ■ [**gegen jdn**] ~ to investigate [sb]

Ermittlung <-, -en> *f* ❶ *kein pl* (*das Ausfindigmachen*) determining ❷ (*Untersuchung*) investigation

Ermittlungsverfahren *nt* preliminary proceedings

er|möglichen* [ɛɐ̯·ˈmøːk·lɪ·çn̩] *vt* ■**jdm etw ~** to enable sb to do sth

er|morden* *vt* ■**jdn ~** to murder sb

Ermordung <-, -en> *f* murder

er|müden* [ɛɐ̯·ˈmyː·dn̩] **I.** *vt haben* ■**jdn ~** to tire [out *sep*] sb **II.** *vi sein* ① (*müde werden*) to become tired ② TECH to wear

ermüdend *adj* tiring

Ermüdung <-, *selten* -en> *f* ① (*das Ermüden*) tiredness ② TECH wear

er|muntern* [ɛɐ̯·ˈmʊn·tɐn] *vt* ① (*ermutigen*) ■**jdn [zu etw** *dat*] **~** to encourage sb [to do sth] ② (*beleben*) ■**jdn ~** to perk up *sep* sb

Ermunterung <-, -en> *f* encouragement

er|mutigen* [ɛɐ̯·ˈmuː·tɪ·gn̩] *vt* ■**jdn [zu etw** *dat*] **~** to encourage sb [to do sth]

ermutigend *adj* encouraging

Ermutigung <-, -en> *f* encouragement

er|nähren* **I.** *vt* ① (*mit Nahrung versorgen*) ■**jdn/ein Tier ~** to feed sb/an animal ② (*unterhalten*) ■**jdn ~** to support sb **II.** *vr* ① (*sich speisen*) ■**sich** *akk* **von etw** *dat* **~** to live on sth ② (*sich unterhalten*) ■**sich** *akk* [**von etw** *dat*] ~ to support oneself [by doing sth]

Ernährer(in) <-s, -> [ɛɐ̯·ˈnɛː·rɐ] *m(f)* breadwinner

Ernährung <-> *f kein pl* ① (*das Ernähren*) feeding ② (*Nahrung*) diet ③ (*Unterhalt*) support

Ernährungsberater, -beraterin *m, f* nutritionist

Ernährungsgewohnheiten *pl* eating habits *npl*

Ernährungswissenschaft *f* nutritional science

Ernährungswissenschaftler(in) *m(f)* nutritionist

er|nennen* *vt irreg* ■**jdn [zu etw** *dat*] ~ to appoint sb [[as] sth]

Ernennung *f* appointment (**zu** +*dat* as)

erneuerbar *adj* renewable

er|neuern* [ɛɐ̯·ˈnɔy·ɐn] *vt* ① (*auswechseln*) to replace ② (*renovieren*) to renovate; *Fenster, Leitungen* to repair ③ (*verlängern*) to renew ④ (*restaurieren*) to restore

Erneuerung *f* ① (*das Auswechseln*) changing ② (*Renovierung*) renovation ③ (*Verlängerung*) renewal ④ (*Restaurierung*) restoration

erneut [ɛɐ̯·ˈnɔyt] **I.** *adj attr* repeated **II.** *adv* again

er|niedrigen* [ɛɐ̯·ˈniː·drɪ·gn̩] *vt* ■**jdn/sich ~** to demean sb/oneself

Erniedrigung <-, -en> *f* humiliation

ernst [ˈɛrnst] *adj* ① (*gravierend*) serious ② (*aufrichtig*) genuine; **es ~ meinen [mit jdm/etw]** to be serious [about sb/sth]; **jdn/etw ~ nehmen** to take sb/sth seriously ③ *Anlass* solemn

Ernstfall *m* emergency

ernstgemeint *adj attr s.* **ernst 2**

ernsthaft **I.** *adj* ① (*gravierend*) serious ② (*aufrichtig*) sincere **II.** *adv* seriously

Ernsthaftigkeit <-> *f kein pl* seriousness

ernstlich **I.** *adj attr* serious **II.** *adv* seriously

Ernte <-, -n> [ˈɛrn·tə] *f* harvest

Ernte(dank)fest *nt* Thanksgiving, harvest festival

ernten [ˈɛrn·tn̩] *vt* ① (*einbringen*) to harvest ② (*erzielen*) *Lob, Spott* to earn; *Anerkennung* to gain; *Applaus* to win

er|nüchtern* [ɛɐ̯·ˈnʏç·tɐn] *vt* ■**jdn ~** ① (*wieder nüchtern machen*) to sober up *sep* sb ② (*in die Realität zurückholen*) to bring sb back to reality

Ernüchterung <-, -en> *f* disillusionment

Eroberer, Erob(r)erin <-s, -> *m, f* conqueror

er|obern* [ɛɐ̯·ˈʔoː·bɐn] *vt* ① (*mit Waffengewalt besetzen*) to conquer ② (*durch Bemühung erlangen*) ■**etw ~** to win sth [with effort]

Eroberung <-, -en> *f* ① (*das Erobern*) conquest ② (*erobertes Gebiet*) conquered territory

er|öffnen* **I.** *vt* ① (*zugänglich machen*) to open ② (*beginnen*) to commence; *Sitzung, Ball* to open; **das Feuer [auf jdn] ~** to open fire [on sb] ③ (*hum: mitteilen*) ■**jdm etw ~** to reveal sth to sb **II.** *vr* (*sich bieten*) ■**sich jdm ~** to open up to sb

Eröffnung *f* ① (*das Eröffnen*) opening ② (*das Einleiten*) opening ③ (*Beginn*) commencing ④ (*geh: Mitteilung*) revelation

er|örtern* [ɛɐ̯·ˈœr·tɐn] *vt* ■**etw ~** to discuss sth [in detail]

Erörterung <-, -en> *f* discussion

Erotik <-> [eˈroː·tɪk] *f kein pl* eroticism

erotisch [eˈroː·tɪʃ] *adj* erotic

Erpel <-s, -> [ˈɛr·pl̩] *m* drake

erpicht [ɛɐ̯·ˈpɪçt] *adj* ■**auf etw** *akk* **~ sein** to be after sth

er|pressen* *vt* ① (*durch Drohung nötigen*) ■**jdn ~** to blackmail sb ② (*abpressen*) ■**etw [von jdm] ~** to extort sth [from sb]

Erpresser(in) <-s, -> *m(f)* blackmailer

Erpressung <-, -en> *f* blackmail

Erpressungsversuch *m* attempted blackmail

er|proben* *vt* to test

erprobt *adj* ① (*erfahren*) experienced ② (*zuverlässig*) reliable

Erprobung <-, -en> *f* trial

er|raten* *vt irreg* to guess

er|rechnen* *vt* to calculate

erregbar *adj* ① (*leicht aufzuregen*) excitable ② (*sexuell zu erregen*) easily aroused

er|regen* **I.** *vt* ① (*aufregen*) ■**jdn ~** to irritate sb ② (*sexuell anregen*) ■**jdn ~** to arouse sb ③ (*hervorrufen*) ■**etw ~** to cause **II.** *vr* ■**sich** *akk* **über jdn/etw ~** to get annoyed about sb/sth

Erreger <-s, -> *m* pathogen

Erregung *f* ① (*erregter Zustand*) irritation ② (*sexuell erregter Zustand*) arousal

erreichbar *adj* ■**[für jdn] ~ sein** to be able to be reached [by sb]

er|reichen* *vt* ① (*rechtzeitig hinkommen*) to

catch ② (*antreffen*) ■ **jdn** ~ to reach sb ③ (*eintreffen*) ■ **etw** ~ to reach sth ④ (*erzielen*) to reach ⑤ (*einholen*) ■ **jdn** ~ to catch up with sb ⑥ (*bewirken*) ■ **etw** [**bei jdm**] ~ to get somewhere [with sb] ⑦ (*an etw reichen*) ■ **etw** ~ to reach sth

er|richten* *vt* ■ **etw** ~ ① (*aufstellen*) to erect sth *form* ② (*erbauen*) to erect sth *form* ③ (*begründen*) to found sth

er|röten* *vi sein* to blush

E

Errungenschaft <-, -en> [ɛɐ̯·ˈrʊŋən·ʃaft] *f* achievement

Ersatz <-es> [ɛɐ̯·ˈzats] *m kein pl* ① (*ersetzender Mensch*) substitute; (*ersetzender Gegenstand*) replacement ② (*Entschädigung*) compensation

Ersatzbank *f* bench

Ersatzdienst *m nonmilitary service for conscientious objectors*

Ersatzlösung *f* alternative solution

Ersatzmann <-männer *o* -leute> *m* substitute

Ersatzmittel *nt* substitute

Ersatzreifen *m* spare tire

Ersatzteil *nt* spare part

ersatzweise *adv* as an alternative

er|schaffen *vt irreg* (*geh*) ■ **jdn/etw** ~ to create sb/sth

Erschaffung *f* creation

er|schaudern* *vi sein* (*geh*) to shudder

er|scheinen* *vi irreg sein* ① (*auftreten*) to appear ② (*sichtbar werden*) to be able to be seen ③ (*veröffentlicht werden*) to come out ④ (*sich verkörpern*) ■ **jdm** ~ *Geist* to appear to sb ⑤ (*scheinen*) to seem; **das erscheint mir recht weit hergeholt** that seems pretty farfetched to me

Erscheinen <-s> *nt kein pl* ① (*das Auftreten*) appearance ② (*die Verkörperung*) appearance ③ (*die Veröffentlichung*) publication

Erscheinung <-, -en> *f* ① (*Phänomen*) phenomenon ② (*Persönlichkeit*) ■ **eine bestimmte** ~ a certain figure ③ (*Vision*) vision ▶ WENDUNGEN: **in ~ treten** to appear

Erscheinungsbild *nt* appearance

er|schießen* *irreg vt* ■ **jdn** ~ to shoot sb dead

Erschießung <-, -en> *f* shooting

er|schlaffen* [ɛɐ̯·ˈʃlafn̩] *vi sein* ① (*schlaff werden*) to become limp ② (*die Straffheit verlieren*) to become loose ③ (*welk werden*) to wither

er|schlagen*[1] *vt* ■ **jdn** ~ *irreg* ① (*totschlagen*) to beat sb to death ② (*durch Darauffallen töten*) to strike dead ③ (*überwältigen*) to overwhelm sb

erschlagen[2] *adj* (*fam*) ■ ~ **sein** to be pooped *sl*

er|schließen* *irreg vt* ① *Land* to develop ② (*nutzbar machen*) ■ [**jdm**] **etw** ~ to make accessible [to sb]

Erschließung *f* ① (*das Zugänglichmachen*) development ② (*das Nutzbarmachen*) tapping

er|schöpfen* *vt* ① (*ermüden*) ■ **jdn** ~ to exhaust sb ② (*aufbrauchen*) ■ **etw** ~ to exhaust sth

erschöpfend **I.** *adj* ① (*zur Erschöpfung führend*) exhausting ② (*ausführlich*) exhaustive **II.** *adv* exhaustively

Erschöpfung <-, *selten* -en> *f* exhaustion

erschossen [ɛɐ̯·ˈʃɔ·sn̩] *adj* (*fam*) pooped *sl*

er|schrak *imp von* **erschrecken II**

er|schrecken **I.** *vt* <erschreckte, erschreckt> *haben* ■ **jdn** ~ ① (*in Schrecken versetzen*) to give sb a scare ② (*bestürzen*) to shock sb **II.** *vi* <erschrickt, erschreckte *o* erschrak, erschreckt *o* erschrocken> *sein* ■ [**vor jdm/etw**] ~ to be scared [by sb/sth] **III.** *vr* <erschrickt, erschreckte, erschreckt *o* erschrocken> *haben* (*fam*) ■ **sich** *akk* [**über etw** *akk*] ~ to be shocked [by sth]

erschreckend **I.** *adj* alarming **II.** *adv* ① (*schrecklich*) terrible ② (*fam: unglaublich*) incredibly

erschrickt *3. pers sing pres von* **erschrecken**

erschrocken **I.** *pp von* **erschrecken II, III** **II.** *adj* alarmed **III.** *adv* with a start *pred*

er|schüttern* [ɛɐ̯·ˈʃʏ·tɐn] *vt* ① (*zum Beben bringen*) to shake ② (*in Frage stellen*) to shake; *Ansehen* to damage; *Glaubwürdigkeit* to undermine ③ (*tief bewegen*) ■ **jdn** ~ to shake sb

erschütternd *adj* distressing

erschüttert *adj* shaken (**über** +*akk* by)

Erschütterung <-, -en> *f* ① (*erschütternde Bewegung*) shake ② (*das Erschüttern*) shaking ③ (*seelische Ergriffenheit*) distress

er|schweren* [ɛɐ̯·ˈʃveː·rən] *vt* ■ [**jdm**] **etw** ~ to make sth more difficult [for sb]

erschwerend **I.** *adj* complicating **II.** *adv* ~ **kommt noch hinzu ...** to make matters worse ...

erschwinglich [ɛɐ̯·ˈʃvɪŋ·lɪç] *adj* affordable

er|sehen* *vt irreg* (*geh*) ■ **etw aus etw** *dat* ~ to see sth from sth

er|sehnen* *vt* (*geh*) ■ **etw** ~ to long for sth

ersetzbar [ɛɐ̯·ˈzɛts·baːɐ̯] *adj* replaceable

er|setzen* *vt* ① (*austauschen*) ■ **etw** [**durch etw** *akk*] ~ to replace sth [with sth] ② (*vertreten*) ■ **jdn/etw** ~ to replace sb/sth ③ (*erstatten*) ■ **jdm etw** ~ to reimburse sb for sth

ersichtlich *adj* apparent; ■ **aus etw** *dat* ~ **sein, dass ...** to be apparent from sth that ...

er|sparen* *vt* ① (*von Ärger verschonen*) ■ **jdm etw** ~ to spare sb sth ② (*durch Sparen erwerben*) ■ [**sich** *dat*] **etw** ~ to save up [to buy] sth

Ersparnis <-, -se> [ɛɐ̯·ˈʃpaːɐ̯·nɪs, *pl* -nɪ·sə] *f* ① *kein pl* (*Einsparung*) ■ **eine ~ an etw** *dat* savings *npl* on sth ② *meist pl* (*erspartes Geld*) savings *npl*

Erspartes *nt* savings *npl*

erst [ˈeːɐ̯st] **I.** *adv* ① (*zuerst*) [at] first ② (*nicht früher als*) only; **wecken Sie mich bitte ~ um 8 Uhr!** please don't wake me up until 8 o'clock! ③ (*bloß*) only **II.** *part* (*verstärkend*) **an deiner Stelle würde ich ~ gar nicht anfangen zu ...** if I were in your shoes I

wouldn't even start to ... ▶WENDUNGEN: ~ **recht** all the more
er|starren* *vi sein* ① (*fest werden*) to solidify ② (*starr werden*) to freeze
er|statten* [ɛɐ̯·ˈʃta·tn̩] *vt* ① (*ersetzen*) ■**[jdm] etw** ~ to reimburse [sb] for sth ② (*geh: mitteilen*) **Anzeige** ~ to report a crime
Erstattung <-, -en> *f von Auslagen, Unkosten* reimbursement
Erstaufführung *f* première
er|staunen* I. *vt haben* ■**jdn** ~ to amaze sb II. *vi sein* ■**über etw** *akk* ~ to be amazed by sth
Erstaunen *nt* amazement; **jdn in ~ versetzen** to amaze sb
erstaunlich [ɛɐ̯·ˈʃtaun·lɪç] I. *adj* amazing II. *adv* amazingly
erstaunlicherweise *adv* amazingly
erstaunt I. *adj* amazed II. *adv* in amazement
erstbeste(r, s) *adj attr* first; ■**der/die/das E~** the next best
erste(r, s) [ˈeːɐ̯s·tə] *adj* ① (*an erster Stelle*) first; **das E~, was ...** the first thing that ...; *s. a.* **achte(r, s) 1** ② (*Datum*) first, 1st; *s. a.* **achte(r, s) 2** ③ (*führend*) leading ▶WENDUNGEN: **fürs E~** to begin with
Erste(r) [ˈeːɐ̯s·tə] *f(m)* ① (*an erster Stelle kommend*) first; *s. a.* **Achte(r) 1** ② (*bei Datumsangabe*) ■**der ~** [*o geschrieben* **der 1.**] the first *spoken,* the 1st *written; s. a.* **Achte(r) 2** ③ (*Namenszusatz*) **Ludwig der ~** *geschrieben* Louis the First; **Ludwig I.** *geschrieben* Louis I; *s. a.* **Achte(r) 3** ④ (*beste*) the best
er|stechen* *vt irreg* ■**jdn** ~ to stab sb to death
er|stehen* [ɛɐ̯·ˈʃteː·ən] *irreg vt haben* (*fam*) ■**etw** ~ to pick up *sep* sth
Erste-Hilfe-Kasten [eːɐ̯s·tə·ˈhɪl·fə·kas·tn̩] *m* first-aid kit
er|steigern *vt* to buy [at an auction]
er|stellen* *vt* ① (*geh: errichten*) to build ② *Plan* to draw up; *Liste* to put together
erstemalALT *adv s.* **Mal**
erstenmalALT *adv s.* **Mal**
erstens [ˈeːɐ̯s·tn̩s] *adv* firstly
erstere(r, s) *adj* ■**der/die/das E~** the former
er|sticken* I. *vt haben* ① (*durch Erstickung töten*) ■**jdn** ~ to suffocate sb ② (*erlöschen lassen*) to extinguish ③ (*dämpfen*) to deaden ④ (*unterdrücken*) to crush II. *vi sein* ① (*durch Erstickung sterben*) ■**an etw** *dat* ~ to choke to death on sth ② (*erlöschen*) to go out ③ (*übermäßig viel haben*) ■**in etw** *dat* ~ to drown in sth
Erstickung <-> *f kein pl* suffocation
erstklassig [ˈeːɐ̯st·klasɪç] *adj* first-class
erstmalig [ˈeːɐ̯st·maː·lɪç] I. *adj* first II. *adv* (*geh*) *s.* **erstmals**
erstmals [ˈeːɐ̯st·maːls] *adv* for the first time
erstrangig [ˈeːɐ̯st·raŋɪç] *adj* ① (*sehr wichtig*) major ② (*erstklassig*) first-class
er|streben* *vt* (*geh*) ■**etw** ~ to strive for sth
erstrebenswert [ɛɐ̯·ˈʃtreː·bn̩s·veːɐ̯t] *adj* worth striving for *pred*
er|strecken* I. *vr* ① (*sich ausdehnen*) ■**sich [über etw** *akk*] ~ to extend [over sth] ② (*betreffen*) ■**sich auf etw** *akk* ~ to include sth II. *vt* SCHWEIZ (*verlängern*) ■**etw** ~ to extend sth
er|tappen* I. *vt* ■**jdn [bei etw** *dat*] ~ to catch sb [doing sth] II. *vr* ■**sich** *akk* **bei etw** *dat* ~ to catch oneself doing sth
er|tönen* *vi sein* (*geh*) ① (*zu hören sein*) to sound ② (*widerhallen*) ■**von etw** *dat* ~ to resound with sth
Ertrag <-[e]s, Erträge> [ɛɐ̯·ˈtraːk, *pl* ɛɐ̯·ˈtrɛː·gə] *m* ① (*Ernte*) yield; ~ **bringen** to bring yields ② *meist pl* (*Einnahmen*) revenue
er|tragen* *vt irreg* to bear
erträglich [ɛɐ̯·ˈtrɛː·k·lɪç] *adj* bearable
ertragreich *adv* productive; *Land* fertile
er|tränken* *vt* ■**jdn/ein Tier** ~ to drown sb/an animal
er|träumen* *vt* ■**[sich** *dat*] **etw** ~ to dream about sth
er|trinken* *vi irreg sein* to drown
er|übrigen* [ɛɐ̯·ˈʔyːbrɪ·gn̩] I. *vr* ■**sich** ~ to be superfluous II. *vt* (*aufbringen*) **etw ~ können** *Geld, Zeit* to spare sth
er|wachen* *vi sein* (*geh*) to wake up
erwachsen [ɛɐ̯·ˈvak·sn̩] *adj* adult
Erwachsene(r) *f(m)* adult
Erwachsenenbildung [ɛɐ̯·ˈvak·se·nən-] *f* adult education
erwägen* *vt irreg* to consider
Erwägung <-, -en> *f* consideration
er|wähnen* *vt* to mention
erwähnenswert *adj* worth mentioning *pred*
Erwähnung <-, -en> *f* comment
er|wärmen* I. *vt* to warm [up] II. *vr* ① (*warm werden*) ■**sich** ~ to warm up ② (*sich begeistern*) ■**sich** *akk* **für jdn/etw** ~ to work up enthusiasm for sb/sth
Erwärmung <-, -en> *f* warming [up]; **globale** ~ global warming
er|warten* I. *vt* ① (*entgegensehen*) to expect ② (*auf etw warten*) ■**etw** ~ to wait for sth ③ (*voraussetzen*) ■**von jdm ~, dass ...** to expect sb to do sth ④ (*mit etw rechnen*) **etw war zu** ~ sth was to be expected II. *vr* (*sich versprechen*) ■**sich** *dat* **etw von jdm/etw** ~ to expect sth from [*or* of] sb/sth
Erwartung <-, -en> *f* ① *kein pl* (*Ungeduld*) anticipation ② *pl* (*Hoffnung*) expectations *pl;* **den ~en entsprechen** to fulfill expectations
Erwartungsdruck <-[e]s> *m kein pl* **unter ~ stehen** to be under pressure to perform
erwartungsgemäß *adv* as expected
Erwartungshaltung *f* expectation
erwartungsvoll I. *adj* expectant, full of expectation *pred* II. *adv* expectantly
er|wecken* *vt* ① (*hervorrufen*) ■**etw** ~ to arouse sth; **den Eindruck ~, ...** to give the impression ... ② (*geh: aufwecken*) ■**jdn** ~ to wake sb
er|weisen* *irreg* I. *vt* ① (*nachweisen*) to prove ② (*zeigen*) ■**etw wird ~, dass/ob ...** sth will

show that/whether ... ③ (*geh: entgegenbringen*) **jdm einen Dienst/Gefallen** ~ to do somebody a service/favor **II.** *vr* ① (*sich herausstellen*) ■**sich als etw** ~ to prove to be sth ② (*sich zeigen*) **sie sollte sich dankbar [ihm gegenüber]** ~ she should be grateful [to him]

er|weitern* **I.** *vt* ■**etw** ~ ① *Straße, Kleidung* to widen sth (**um** +*akk* by) ② (*vergrößern*) to expand sth (**um** +*akk* by) ③ (*umfangreicher machen*) to increase sth (**um** +*akk* by) **II.** *vr* ① (*sich verbreitern*) ■**sich** *akk* ~ to widen (**um** +*akk* by) ② MED, ANAT ■**sich** ~ to dilate

Erweiterung <-, -en> *f* ① (*Verbreiterung*) *Anlagen, Fahrbahn* widening ② (*Vergrößerung*) expansion ③ (*Ausweitung*) increase ④ MED, ANAT dilation

Erwerb <-[e]s, -e> [ɛɐ̯ˈvɛrp, *pl* ɛɐ̯ˈvɛr·bə] *m* ① *kein pl* (*geh: Kauf*) purchase ② (*berufliche Tätigkeit*) occupation

er|werben* *vt irreg* ① (*kaufen*) ■**etw** ~ to purchase sth ② (*an sich bringen*) ■**etw [durch etw** *akk*] ~ to acquire sth [through sth] ③ (*gewinnen*) ■**[sich** *dat*] **etw** ~ to earn sth

erwerbsfähig *adj* (*geh*) fit for gainful employment *pred*

erwerbslos *adj* (*geh*) unemployed

erwerbstätig *adj* working

Erwerbstätigkeit <-> *f kein pl* employment

erwerbsunfähig *adj* (*geh*) unfit for gainful employment

er|widern* [ɛɐ̯ˈviː·dɐn] *vt* ① (*antworten*) ■**[jdm] etw [auf etw** *akk*] ~ to give [sb] a reply [to sth] ② (*zurückgeben*) ■**etw** ~ to return sth

Erwiderung <-, -en> *f* ① (*Antwort*) reply ② (*das Erwidern*) returning

erwiesenermaßen [ɛɐ̯·viː·zə·nɐ·ˈmaː·sn̩] *adv* as has been proved

er|wischen* [ɛɐ̯ˈvɪ·ʃn̩] *vt* (*fam*) ① (*ertappen*) ■**jdn [bei etw** *dat*] ~ to catch sb [doing sth] ② (*ergreifen, erreichen*) ■**jdn/etw** ~ to catch sb/sth

erworben *adj* acquired

erwünscht [ɛɐ̯ˈvʏnʃt] *adj* ① (*gewünscht*) desired ② (*willkommen*) welcome; *Anwesenheit* desirable

er|würgen* *vt* to strangle

Erz <-es, -e> [ˈeːɐ̯ts] *nt* ore

er|zählen* **I.** *vt* ① (*anschaulich berichten*) to explain ② (*sagen*) to tell **II.** *vi* to tell a story/stories

Erzähler(in) <-s, -> [ɛɐ̯ˈtsɛː·lɐ] *m(f)* storyteller; (*Schriftsteller(in)*) author; (*Romanperson*) narrator

Erzählung *f* ① (*Geschichte*) story ② *kein pl* (*das Erzählen*) telling

Erzbischof, -bischöfin [ˈɛrts·bɪ·ʃɔf, -bɪ·ʃœ·fɪn] *m, f* archbishop

Erzengel [ˈɛrts·ʔɛŋl̩] *m* archangel

er|zeugen* *vt* ① *bes* ÖSTERR (*produzieren*) to produce ② ELEK, SCI to generate ③ (*hervorrufen*) to create

Erzeuger(in) <-s, -> *m(f)* ① *bes* ÖSTERR (*geh: Produzent*) producer ② (*hum fam: Vater*) father

Erzeugnis <-ses, -se> [ɛɐ̯ˈtsɔyk·nɪs, *pl* -nɪ·sə] *nt* product

Erzeugung <-, -en> *f* ① *kein pl* ELEK, SCI generation ② (*Produktion*) production

Erzfeind(in) *m(f)* archenemy

Erzherzog(in) [ˈɛrts·hɛr·tsoːk] *m(f)* archduke *masc*, archduchess *fem*

erziehbar *adj* educable; **schwer** ~ **sein** to have behavioral problems

er|ziehen* *vt irreg* ① (*aufziehen*) ■**jdn** ~ to raise sb ② (*anleiten*) ■**jdn zu etw** *dat* ~ to teach sb to be sth

Erzieher(in) <-s, -> [ɛɐ̯ˈtsiː·ɐ] *m(f)* teacher

Erziehung *f kein pl* ① (*das Erziehen*) education ② (*Aufzucht*) upbringing

erziehungsberechtigt *adj* acting as legal guardian *pred*

Erziehungsberechtigte(r) *f(m)* legal guardian

Erziehungsgeld *nt* child benefit (*paid for at least 6 months after the child's birth to compensate the parent on parental leave*)

Erziehungsjahr *nt* maternity [*or* paternity] leave (*for 1 year*)

Erziehungsmethode *f* method of education

Erziehungsurlaub *m* maternity [*or* paternity] leave (*for up to 3 years*)

Erziehungswissenschaft *f kein pl* childhood education

Erziehungswissenschaftler(in) *m(f)* specialist in childhood education

er|zielen* *vt* ① (*erreichen*) to achieve; *Einigung* to reach ② SPORT ■**etw** ~ to score sth (**gegen** +*akk* against)

erzkonservativ *adj* ultraconservative

er|zwingen* *vt irreg* ■**etw [von jdm]** ~ to force sth [out of [*or* from] sb]; **ein Geständnis [von jdm]** ~ to make sb confess

es <*gen* seiner, *dat* ihm, *akk* es> [ˈɛs] *pron pers, unbestimmt* ① *auf Dinge bezogen* (*das, diese*) it; **wer ist da? – ich bin** ~ who's there? — it's me ② *auf vorangehenden Satzinhalt bezogen* it; **kommt er auch? – ich hoffe** ~ is he coming too? — I hope so ③ *rein formales Subjekt* it; **hier stinkt** ~ something smells bad in here; ~ **gefällt mir** I like it ④ *rein formales Objekt* **er hat** ~ **gut** he's got it made ⑤ *Subjekt bei unpers Ausdrücken* ~ **klopft** there's a knock at the door; ~ **regnet** it's raining ⑥ *Einleitewort mit folgendem Subjekt* ~ **waren Tausende** there were thousands

Esche <-, -n> [ˈɛʃə] *f* ash

Esel(in) <-s, -> [ˈeːzl̩] *m(f)* ① (*Tier*) donkey ② *nur m* (*fam: Dummkopf*) idiot

Eselsbrücke *f* (*fam*) mnemonic [device]

Eselsohr *nt* dog-ear

Eskalation <-, -en> [ɛs·ka·la·ˈtsi̯oːn] *f* escalation

eskalieren* [ɛs·ka·ˈliː·rən] *vi, vt* to escalate (**zu** +*dat* into)

Eskapade <-, -n> [ɛs·ka·ˈpaː·də] *f* escapade

Eskimo, -frau <-s, -s> [ˈɛs·ki·mo] *m, f* Eskimo

Eskorte <-, -n> [ɛs·ˈkɔr·tə] *f* escort

Esoterik <-> [ezo·ˈteː·rɪk] *f kein pl* esotericism
esoterisch [ezo·ˈteː·rɪʃ] *adj* esoteric
Espe <-, -n> [ˈɛs·pə] *f* aspen
Espenlaub *nt* ▶ WENDUNGEN: **zittern wie** ~ to be shaking like a leaf
Esperanto <-s> [ɛs·pe·ˈran·to] *nt kein pl* Esperanto
Espresso <-[s], -s *o* Espressi> [ɛs·ˈprɛ·so, *pl* ɛs·ˈprɛ·si] *m* espresso
Esprit <-s> [ɛs·ˈpriː] *m kein pl* (*geh*) wit
Essay <-s, -s> [ˈɛse, ɛˈseː] *m o nt* essay
essbarRR, **eßbar**ALT *adj* edible
essen <isst, aß, gegessen> [ˈɛsn̩] **I.** *vt* to eat; ~ **Sie gern Äpfel?** do you like apples?; **etw zum Nachtisch** ~ to have sth for dessert **II.** *vi* to eat; **griechisch/italienisch** ~ to eat Greek/Italian food
Essen <-s, -> [ˈɛsn̩] *nt* ❶ (*Mahlzeit*) meal ❷ (*Nahrung*) food
Essen(s)marke *f* meal voucher [*or* ticket]
Essenszeit *f* mealtime
essentiell *adj, adv s.* **essenziell**
Essenz <-, -en> [ɛˈsɛnts] *f* essence
essenziellRR [ɛsɛn·ˈtsi̯ɛl] **I.** *adj* essential **II.** *adv* essentially
EssgewohnheitenRR *pl* eating habits *pl*
Essig <-s, -e> [ˈɛsɪç, *pl* ˈɛsɪ·gə] *m* vinegar
Essiggurke *f* pickle
Essigsäure *f* acetic acid
EsskastanieRR *f* sweet chestnut
EsslöffelRR *m* ❶ (*Essbesteck*) soup spoon ❷ (*Maßeinheit beim Kochen*) tablespoon
EssstörungRR *f meist pl* eating disorder
EsssuchtRR *f kein pl* compulsive eating
EsszimmerRR *nt* dining room
Este, Estin <-n, -n> [ˈeːstə, ˈeːs·tɪn] *m, f* Estonian; *s. a.* **Deutsche(r)**
Estland <-s> [ˈeːst·lant] *nt* Estonia; *s. a.* **Deutschland**
estnisch [ˈeːst·nɪʃ] *adj* Estonian; *s. a.* **deutsch**
Estragon <-s> [ˈɛs·tra·gɔn] *m kein pl* tarragon
etablieren* [eta·ˈbliː·rən] (*geh*) **I.** *vt* to establish **II.** *vr* ■ **sich** *akk* ~ to establish oneself
etabliert *adj* (*geh*) established
Etablissement <-s, -s> [eta·blɪsə·ˈmãː] *nt* (*geh*) establishment
Etage <-, -n> [eˈtaː·ʒə] *f* floor; **auf der 5.** ~ on the 6th floor
Etagenbett [eˈtaː·ʒən-] *nt* bunk bed
Etagenwohnung [eˈtaː·ʒən-] *f* apartment (*occupying a whole floor*)
Etappe <-, -n> [eˈtapə] *f* ❶ (*Abschnitt*) **in ~n arbeiten** to work in stages ❷ (*Teilstrecke*) leg ❸ MIL communications zone
Etat <-s, -s> [eˈtaː] *m* budget
etc. [ɛt·ˈtseː·tera] *Abk von* **et cetera** etc.
etepetete [ˈeːtə·pe·ˈteː·tə] *adj pred* (*fam*) finicky
Ethik <-> [ˈeːtɪk] *f kein pl* ❶ (*Wissenschaft*) ethics + *sing vb* ❷ (*moralische Haltung*) ethics *npl* ❸ (*bestimmte Werte*) ethic
ethisch [ˈeːtɪʃ] *adj* ethical
ethnisch [ˈɛt·nɪʃ] *adj* ethnic
Ethnologe, Ethnologin [ɛt·no·ˈloː·gə] *m, f* ethnologist
Ethnologie <-, -n> [ɛt·no·lo·ˈgiː, *pl* -ˈgiː·ən] *f* ethnology
Etikett <-[e]s, -e> [eti·ˈkɛt] *nt* ❶ (*Preisschild*) price tag ❷ (*Aufnäher*) label
Etikette <-, -n> [eti·ˈkɛ·tə] *f* (*geh*) etiquette
etikettieren* [eti·kɛ·ˈtiː·rən] *vt* ■ **etw** ~ to label sth; *Preis* to put a price tag on sth
etliche(r, s) [ˈɛt·lɪ·çə] *pron indef* ❶ *adjektivisch, sing o pl* quite a lot of ❷ *substantivisch, pl* quite a few ❸ *substantivisch, sing* ■ **~s** quite a lot
Etui <-s, -s> [ɛt·ˈviː, eˈtÿiː] *nt* case; (*verziert a.*) etui
etwa [ˈɛt·va] **I.** *adv* ❶ (*ungefähr, annähernd*) about; **in** ~ more or less ❷ (*zum Beispiel*) **wie** ~ **mein Bruder** like my brother for instance **II.** *part* ❶ (*womöglich*) **soll das ~ heißen, dass ...?** is that supposed to mean [that] ...?; **willst du ~ schon gehen?** you don't want to go already, do you? ❷ (*Verstärkung der Verneinung*) **ist das ~ nicht wahr?** do you mean to say it's not true?
etwaig [ɛt·ˈvaː·ɪç] *adj attr* any
etwas [ˈɛt·vas] *pron indef* ❶ *substantivisch* (*eine unbestimmte Sache*) something; (*bei Fragen*) anything ❷ *adjektivisch* (*nicht näher bestimmt*) something; (*bei Fragen*) anything; ~ **anderes** something else; [**noch**] ~ **Geld/Kaffee** some [more] money/coffee ❸ *adverbial* (*ein wenig*) a little
Etwas <-> [ˈɛt·vas] *nt kein pl* **ein hartes/spitzes** ~ something hard/sharp; **das gewisse** ~ that certain something
Etymologie <-, -n> [ety·mo·lo·ˈgiː, *pl* -ˈgiː·ən] *f* etymology
etymologisch [ety·mo·ˈloː·gɪʃ] *adj* etymological
EU [eːˈuː] *f Abk von* **Europäische Union** EU
EU-Beitritt *m* accession to the EU
EU-Bürger(in) *m(f)* EU citizen, citizen of the EU
euch [ˈɔyç] **I.** *pron pers akk o dat von* **ihr** you[-all], you guys *sl;* **ein Freund/eine Freundin von** ~ a friend of yours **II.** *pron refl* **beeilt ~!** hurry up!; **macht ~ fertig!** get [*fam* yourselves] ready!
euer [ˈɔye] **I.** *pron poss, adjektivisch* your; **es ist ~/eu[e]re/~[e]s** it's yours; **viele Grüße, ~ Martin!** love, Martin **II.** *pron pers gen von* **ihr: wir werden ~ gedenken** (*geh*) we will think of you
euere(r, s) [ˈɔyə·rə] *pron poss, substantivisch s.* **eure(r, s)**
EU-Gipfel *m* EU summit
Eukalyptus <-, -lypten> [ɔy·ka·ˈlʏp·tʊs] *m* ❶ (*Baum*) eucalyptus [tree] ❷ (*Öl*) eucalyptus [oil]
EU-Kommission *f* EU Commission
EU-Land *nt* EU country
Eule <-, -n> [ˈɔy·lə] *f* owl
EU-Mitgliedsland *nt* EU member state

Eunuch <-en, -en> [ɔy·'nuːx] *m* eunuch
Euphorie <-, -n> [ɔy·fo·'riː, *pl* -'riː·ən] *f* euphoria
euphorisch [ɔy·'foː·rɪʃ] *adj* euphoric
Euratom <-> [ɔy·ra·'toːm] *f Akr von* **Europäische Atomgemeinschaft** Euratom
eure(r, s) ['ɔy·rə] *pron poss* (*geh*) ■**[der/die/das] E~** yours; **tut ihr das E~** you do your part
eurerseits ['ɔy·rɐ·'zaits] *adv* (*soweit es euch angeht*) for your part; (*von eurer Seite aus*) on your part
euresgleichen ['ɔy·rəs·'glai·çn̩] *pron inv* people like you; (*pej: Leute eures Standes*) [people of] your [own] kind
euretwegen ['ɔy·rət·'veː·gn̩] *adv* (*wegen euch*) because of you; (*euch zuliebe*) for your sake[s]
euretwillen ['ɔy·rət·vɪ·lən] *adv* for your sake[s]
Euro ['ɔy·ro] *m* (*Währungseinheit*) euro; **hundert ~ spenden** to donate a hundred euros
Eurobanknote *f* euro bill
Eurocent *m* euro cent
Eurocity, EurocityzugRR ['ɔy·ro·sɪti-] *m* Eurocity train (*connecting major European cities*)
Eurogeld *nt* eurocurrency
Eurokratie *f* POL eurocracy
Eurokrise *f* eurozone [*or* euro] crisis
Euromünze *f* euro coin
Europa <-s> [ɔy·'roː·pa] *nt* Europe
Europaabgeordnete(r) *f(m)* Member of the European Parliament
Europäer(in) <-s, -> [ɔy·ro·'pɛː·ɐ] *m(f)* European
Europafrage *f* POL European question
europäisch [ɔy·ro·'pɛː·ɪʃ] *adj* European; **E~e Einheitswährung** single European currency, euro; **E~e Gemeinschaft** [*o* **EG**] European Community, EC; **E~er Gerichtshof** European Court of Justice; **das E~e Parlament** the European Parliament; **E~er Rat** European Council; **die ~en Staaten** the European countries; **E~e Union** European Union, EU; **E~es Währungssystem** [*o* **EWS**] European Monetary System, EMS; **E~e Währungsunion** [*o* **EWU**] European Monetary Union, EMU; **E~e Wirtschaftsgemeinschaft** [*o* **EWG**] [European] Common Market; **E~e Zentralbank** [*o* **EZB**] European Central Bank, ECB
Europameister(in) *m(f)* (*als Einzelner*) European champion; (*als Team, Land*) European champions *pl*
Europameisterschaft *f* European championship
Europaparlament *nt* the European Parliament
Europapokal *m* European cup tournament
Europarat *m kein pl* Council of Europe
Europawahl *f* European elections *pl*
Europol ['ɔy·ro·poːl] *f* Europol
Euro-Rettungsschirm, Eurorettungsschirm *m kein pl* FIN (*organization*) European Financial Stability Facility, EFSF; (*fund*) euro bailout fund
Eurotunnel *m* Channel tunnel, Chunnel
Eurozone <-> *f kein pl* Eurozone
Euter <-s, -> ['ɔy·tɐ] *nt o m* udder
EU-Vertrag *m* JUR Treaty of Rome
ev. *adj Abk von* **evangelisch**
e.V., E.V. [eː'fau] *m Abk von* **eingetragener Verein** membership corporation
evakuieren* [eva·ku·'iː·rən] *vt* ❶ (*an sicheren Ort bringen*) ■**jdn/etw ~** to evacuate sb/move sth (**aus** +*dat* from, **in/auf** +*akk* to) ❷ (*auslagern*) to move (**in** +*akk* to)
Evakuierung <-, -en> *f* evacuation
evangelisch [evaŋ·'geː·lɪʃ] *adj* Protestant
Evangelium <-s, -lien> [evaŋ·'geː·li·ʊm, *pl* -li·ən] *nt* Gospel; (*fig*) gospel
Eventualität <-, -en> [evɛn·tu̯a·li·'tɛːt] *f* eventuality
eventuell [evɛn·'tu̯·ɛl] **I.** *adj attr* possible; **bei ~en Rückfragen wenden Sie sich bitte an ...** if you have any questions, please contact ... **II.** *adv* possibly
Evolution <-, -en> [evo·lu·'tsi̯oːn] *f* evolution
evtl. *adj, adv Abk von* **eventuell**
E-Werk ['eː·v·ɛrk] *nt s.* **Elektrizitätswerk**
EWI <-[s]> *nt kein pl Abk von* **Europäisches Währungsinstitut** EMI
ewig ['eːvɪç] **I.** *adj* ❶ (*immer während*) eternal ❷ (*pej fam: ständig*) **~es Gejammer** never-ending moaning and groaning **II.** *adv* ❶ (*dauernd*) eternally; (*seit jeher*) always ❷ (*fam: ständig*) always ❸ (*fam: lange Zeitspanne*) for ages
Ewigkeit <-, -en> ['eːvɪç·kait] *f* eternity; **eine [halbe] ~ dauern** (*hum fam*) to last forever
EWS <-> [eː·veː·'ɛs] *nt kein pl Abk von* **Europäisches Währungssystem** EMS
EWU <-> [eː·veː·'uː] *f Abk von* **Europäische Währungsunion** EMU
ex ['ɛks] *adv* **etw [auf] ~ trinken** to down sth [in one gulp] ▶ WENDUNGEN: **~ und hopp** (*fam*) here today, gone tomorrow
exakt [ɛ'ksakt] **I.** *adj* exact **II.** *adv* exactly; **~ arbeiten** to be accurate in one's work
Examen <-s, - *o* Examina> [ɛ'ksaː·mən, *pl* ɛ'ksaː·mi·na] *nt* **mündliches/schriftliches ~** oral/written exam; **das ~ bestehen** to pass one's final [exam]; **durch das ~ fallen** to fail one's final [exam]
Exekution <-, -en> [ɛkse·ku·'tsi̯oːn] *f* (*geh*) execution
Exekutive <-, -n> [ɛkse·ku·'tiː·və] *f* JUR executive authority
Exempel <-s, -> [ɛ'ks·ɛm·pl] *nt* (*geh*) example that serves as a warning
Exemplar <-s, -e> [ɛks·ɛm·'plaːɐ̯] *nt* specimen; (*Ausgabe*) *Buch, Heft* copy; *Zeitung* issue
exemplarisch [ɛks·ɛm·'plaː·rɪʃ] **I.** *adj* exemplary **II.** *adv* as an example
exerzieren* [ɛks·ɛr·'tsiː·rən] *vi* MIL to drill
Exhibitionismus <-> [ɛks·hi·bi·tsi̯o·'nɪs·mʊs] *m kein pl* exhibitionism
Exhibitionist(in) <-en, -en> [ɛks·hi·bi·tsi̯o·

ˈnɪst] *m(f)* exhibitionist

exhumieren* [ɛks·hu·ˈmiː·rən] *vt* (*geh*) to exhume

Exil <-s, -e> [ɛˈksiːl] *nt* exile

Existenz <-, -en> [ɛksɪs·ˈtɛnts] *f* ❶ *kein pl* (*das Vorhandensein*) existence ❷ (*Lebensgrundlage, Auskommen*) livelihood ❸ (*Dasein, Leben*) life

Existenzberechtigung *f kein pl* right to exist

Existenzgründer(in) *m(f)* founder of a new business

Existenzgrundlage *f* basis of one's livelihood

Existenzkampf *m* struggle for survival

Existenzminimum *nt* subsistence level

Existenzrecht *nt kein pl* right to existence

Existenzsicherung *f kein pl* guarantee of a continued existence

existieren* [ɛksɪs·ˈtiː·rən] *vi* ❶ (*vorhanden sein*) to exist ❷ (*sein Auskommen haben*) ■ [**von etw** *dat*] ~ to live [on [*or* off of] sth]

exklusiv [ɛks·klu·ˈziːf] *adj* exclusive

exkommunizieren* [ɛks·kɔ·mu·ni·ˈtsiː·rən] *vt* to excommunicate

Exkrement <-[e]s, -e> [ɛks·kre·ˈmɛnt] *nt meist pl* (*geh*) excrement

Exkurs <-es, -e> [ɛks·ˈkʊrs, *pl* -ˈkʊr·zə] *m* digression

Exkursion <-, -en> [ɛks·kʊr·ˈzi̯oːn] *f* (*geh*) UNIV study trip; SCH field trip

Exmatrikulation <-, -en> [ɛks·ma·tri·ku·la·ˈtsi̯oːn] *f withdrawal from a university*

exmatrikulieren* [ɛks·ma·tri·ku·ˈliː·rən] **I.** *vt* ■ **jdn** ~ to withdraw sb from a university **II.** *vr* ■ **sich** *akk* ~ to withdraw from a university

Exot(in) <-en, -en> [ɛˈksoːt] *m(f)* ❶ (*Person*) exotic foreigner; (*Pflanze oder Tier*) exotic [plant/animal] ❷ (*fam: Rarität, ausgefallenes Exemplar*) rarity; (*Person*) eccentric

exotisch [ɛˈksoː·tɪʃ] *adj* ❶ (*aus fernem Land*) exotic ❷ (*fam: ausgefallen*) unusual

expandieren* [ɛks·pan·ˈdiː·rən] *vi* to expand

Expansion <-, -en> [ɛks·pan·ˈzi̯oːn] *f* expansion

Expedition <-, -en> [ɛks·pe·di·ˈtsi̯oːn] *f* expedition

Experiment <-[e]s, -e> [ɛks·pe·ri·ˈmɛnt] *nt* experiment

experimentell [ɛks·pe·ri·mɛn·ˈtɛl] **I.** *adj* experimental **II.** *adv* by [way of] experiment

experimentieren* [ɛks·pe·ri·mɛn·ˈtiː·rən] *vi* ■ [**an/mit etw** *dat*] ~ to experiment [on/with sth]

Experte, Expertin <-n, -n> [ɛks·ˈpɛr·tə] *m, f* expert

Expertenausschuss[RR] *m,* **Expertengruppe** *f* panel of experts

Experteneinschätzung *f* expert opinion

Expertise <-, -n> [ɛks·pɛr·ˈtiː·zə] *f* expert's report

explodieren* [ɛks·plo·ˈdiː·rən] *vi sein* to explode *a. fig*

Explosion <-, -en> [ɛks·plo·ˈzi̯oːn] *f* explosion *a. fig;* **etw zur ~ bringen** to detonate sth

explosionsartig *adv* explosively

Explosionsgefahr *f* danger of explosion

explosiv [ɛks·plo·ˈziːf] *adj* explosive

Exponat <-[e]s, -e> [ɛks·po·ˈnaːt] *nt* exhibit

Exponent <-en, -en> [ɛks·po·ˈnɛnt] *m* MATH exponent

Export <-[e]s, -e> [ɛks·ˈpɔrt] *m kein pl* export

Exportartikel *m* exported article; *pl* exports

Exporteur(in) <-s, -e> [ɛkspɔr·ˈtøːɐ̯] *m(f)* exporter

Exportfirma *f* export company

exportieren* [ɛks·pɔr·ˈtiː·rən] *vt* to export

Express[RR], **Expreß**[ALT] <Expresses> [ɛks·ˈprɛs] *m kein pl* ❶ (*Eilzug*) express [train] ❷ (*schnell*) **etw per ~ senden** to send sth express [*or* by express delivery]

Expressionismus <-> [ɛks·prɛ·si̯o·ˈnɪs·mʊs] *m kein pl* expressionism

expressionistisch *adj* expressionist[ic]

exquisit [ɛks·kvi·ˈziːt] (*geh*) **I.** *adj* exquisite **II.** *adv* exquisitely

Extension <-, -en> [ɛks·tɛn·ˈzi̯oːn] *f* (*geh*) extension

extern [ɛks·ˈtɛrn] *adj* external

extra [ˈɛks·tra] *adv* ❶ (*besonders*) extra ❷ (*zusätzlich*) extra ❸ (*eigens*) just ❹ (*fam: absichtlich*) on purpose ❺ (*gesondert*) separately; KOCHK on the side

Extrablatt *nt* special supplement

Extrakt <-[e]s, -e> [ɛks·ˈtrakt] *m o fachspr a. nt* extract

extravagant [ɛks·tra·va·ˈgant] **I.** *adj* extravagant **II.** *adv* extravagantly

Extravaganz <-, -en> [ɛks·tra·va·ˈgants] *f* extravagance; *von Kleidung a.* flamboyance

extravertiert [ɛks·tra·vɛr·ˈtiːɐ̯t] *adj* extroverted

Extrawurst *f* (*fam: Sonderwunsch*) **jdm eine ~ braten** to make an exception for sb

extrem [ɛks·ˈtreːm] **I.** *adj* extreme; **~e Anforderungen** excessive demands **II.** *adv* (*sehr*) extremely; **~ links/rechts** POL ultra-left/right

Extremfall *m* extreme [case]

Extremismus <-, *selten* -men> [ɛks·tre·ˈmɪs·mʊs] *m* extremism

Extremist(in) <-en, -en> [ɛks·tre·ˈmɪst] *m(f)* extremist

extremistisch *adj* extremist

Extremitäten [ɛks·tre·mi·ˈtɛː·tn̩] *pl* extremities *npl*

Extremsport *m* extreme sport

Extremsportart *f* adventure sport

extrovertiert [ɛks·tro·vɛr·ˈtiːɐ̯t] *adj s.* **extravertiert**

Extrovertiertheit *f kein pl* PSYCH extrovertedness

exzellent [ɛks·tsɛ·ˈlɛnt] (*geh*) **I.** *adj* excellent **II.** *adv* excellently; **sich** *akk* **~ fühlen** to feel great; **~ schmecken** to taste delicious

Exzellenz <-, -en> [ɛks·tsɛ·ˈlɛnts] *f* Excellency

exzentrisch [ɛks·ˈtsɛn·trɪʃ] *adj* (*geh*) eccentric

Exzess[RR], **Exzeß**[ALT] <Exzesses, Exzesse> [ɛks·ˈtsɛs] *m meist pl* excess; **etw bis zum ~ treiben** to take sth to extremes

exzessiv [ɛks·tsɛ·ˈsiːf] *adj* (*geh*) excessive
Eyeliner <-s, -> [ˈai·lai·nɐ] *m* eyeliner
EZB <-> [eː·tsɛt·ˈbeː] *f kein pl* FIN *Abk von* **Europäische Zentralbank** ECB
E-Zug [ˈeː·tsuːk] *m kurz für* **Eilzug** express train

Ff

F, f <-, - *o fam* -s, -s> [ɛf] *nt* ❶ (*Buchstabe*) F, f; ~ **wie Friedrich** F as in Foxtrot ❷ MUS F, f
f. ❶ *Abk von* **folgende** [**Seite**] [the] following [page] ❷ *Abk von* **für**
Fabel <-, -n> [ˈfaː·bl̩] *f* LIT fable
Fabrik <-, -en> [fa·ˈbriːk] *f* factory
Fabrikarbeiter(**in**) *m(f)* factory worker
Fabrikationsfehler *m* manufacturing defect
Fabrikgelände *nt* factory site
fabrikneu *adj* brand-new
Fach <-[e]s, Fächer> [fax, *pl* ˈfɛ·çɐ] *nt* ❶ (*im Schrank*) shelf; (*Ablegefach*) box ❷ (*Sachgebiet*) subject; **vom ~ sein** to be a specialist
Facharbeiter(**in**) *m(f)* skilled worker
Facharzt, -ärztin *m, f* specialist (**für** +*akk* in)
Fachausdruck *m* technical term; **juristischer ~** legal term
Fächer <-s, -> [ˈfɛ·çɐ] *m* fan
Fachgebiet *nt* field of expertise
Fachhandel *m* retail trade
Fachhändler(**in**) *m(f)* retail dealer
Fachhochschule *f* ≈ University of Applied Sciences

> Most of the classes that are offered at a **Fachhochschule** (University of Applied Sciences) are in the field of engineering, but classes in such subjects as architecture, computer science, business administration, and graphic design are not uncommon. Students who graduate from a **Fachhochschule** (or FH) receive a *Diplom* (diploma) with the abbreviation "FH" included in their title. Engineering graduates, for instance, have the title *Diplom Ingenieur (FH)*, which is generally abbreviated to *Dipl.Ing. (FH)*. In Austria, students can also take courses at a **Fachhochschule** that lead to a Master's degree. A **Fachhochschule** focuses on giving students practical knowledge, rather than the more theoretical or scholarly training that universities stress.

Fachkenntnis *f meist pl* specialized knowledge
Fachkraft *f* specialist
Fachleute *pl* experts *pl*
fachlich **I.** *adj* ❶ (*fachbezogen*) specialist ❷ (*kompetent*) informed **II.** *adv* professionally; **sich** *akk* **~ qualifizieren** to gain expertise in one's field
Fachliteratur *f* technical literature
Fachmann, -frau <-leute> *m, f* expert, specialist
Fachpresse *f* technical publications *pl*
Fachrichtung *f* subject area
Fachsprache *f* [technical] jargon
Fachwerkhaus *nt* half-timbered house
Fachwissen *nt* specialized knowledge
Fachwort *nt* technical term
Fachwörterbuch *nt* technical dictionary; **ein medizinisches ~** a dictionary of medical terms
Fachzeitschrift *f* technical journal; (*für bestimmte Berufe*) trade journal
Fackel <-, -n> [ˈfa·kl̩] *f* torch
fade [ˈfaː·də] *adj*, **fad** [faːt] *adj* SÜDD, ÖSTERR ❶ *Essen, Geschmack.* bland ❷ (*langweilig*) dull
Faden <-s, Fäden> [ˈfaː·dn̩, *pl* ˈfɛ·dn̩] *m* ❶ (*Woll-, Zwirnfaden*) thread ❷ MED stitch; **die Fäden ziehen** to remove sb's stitches ▶ WENDUNGEN: **der rote ~** the central theme; **den ~ verlieren** to lose one's train of thought
Fagott <-[e]s, -e> [fa·ˈgɔt] *nt* bassoon
fähig [ˈfɛ·ɪç] *adj* able, competent; (*imstande*) capable; ■**zu etw** *dat* [**nicht**] **~ sein** to be [in]capable of sth
Fähigkeit <-, -en> *f* ability
fahnden [ˈfaːn·dn̩] *vi* to search (**nach** +*dat* for)
Fahndung <-, -en> *f* search (**nach** +*dat* for); **eine ~ nach jdm einleiten** to conduct a search for sb, to put out an APB for sb
Fahndungsfoto *nt* mug shot *fam*
Fahne <-, -n> [ˈfaː·nə] *f* ❶ (*Banner*) flag ❷ (*fig fam: Alkoholgeruch*) smell of alcohol *no indef art* ▶ WENDUNGEN: **mit fliegenden ~n zu jdm** [**über**]**wechseln** to rush to join sb
Fahnenmast *m* flagpole
Fahrausweis *m* ❶ (*Fahrkarte*) ticket ❷ SCHWEIZ (*Führerschein*) driver's license
Fahrbahn *f* road; **von der ~ abkommen** to leave the road
Fähre <-, -n> [ˈfɛː·rə] *f* ferry
fahren <fährt, fuhr, gefahren> [ˈfaː·rən] **I.** *vi* ❶ *sein* (*sich fortbewegen*) to go; (*als Fahrer*) to drive; **mit dem Bus/Zug ~** to take [*or* ride] the bus/train; **mit dem Auto ~** to drive, to take the car; **gegen etw** *akk* **~** to drive into sth; **wie lange fährt man von hier nach Basel?** how long does it take to get to Basel from here? ❷ *sein* (*losfahren*) to go, to leave ❸ *sein* (*verkehren*) to run; **die Bahn fährt alle 20 Minuten** the train runs every 20 min-

utes ❹ *sein* (*reisen*) to go; **in Urlaub ~** to go on vacation ❺ *sein* (*blitzschnell bewegen*) **aus dem Schlaf ~** to wake with a start; **was ist denn in dich ge~?** what's gotten into you? ❻ *sein o haben* (*streichen*) **sich** *dat* **mit der Hand über die Stirn ~** to rub one's forehead ❼ *sein* (*zurechtkommen*) **gut/schlecht ~** to do/not do well **II.** *vt* ❶ *haben* (*lenken*) to drive; *Fahrrad, Motorrad* to ride ❷ *sein* **Fahrrad/Motorrad ~** to ride a bicycle/motorcycle; **Schlittschuh ~** to ice-skate ❸ *haben* (*verwenden*) **Sommerreifen ~** to use normal tires ❹ *haben* (*befördern*) to take; **ich fahr dich nach Hause** I'll take you home ❺ *sein* (*eine bestimmte Geschwindigkeit haben*) **90 [km/h] ~** to be doing 90 kmph **III.** *vr haben* **der Wagen fährt sich gut** the car handles well

Fahrer(in) <-s, -> ['faː·rɐ] *m(f)* ❶ (*Autofahrer*) driver; (*Motorradfahrer*) motorcycle rider, biker *fam* ❷ (*Chauffeur*) driver

Fahrerflucht *f* hit-and-run

Fahrgast *m* passenger

Fahrgemeinschaft *f* carpool; **eine ~ bilden** to carpool

Fahrkarte *f* ticket (**nach** +*dat* to)

Fahrkartenautomat *m* ticket machine

Fahrkartenschalter *m* ticket office

fahrlässig ['faːɐ̯·lɛ·sɪç] **I.** *adj* negligent; **grob ~** reckless **II.** *adv* negligently; **~ handeln** to act with negligence

Fahrlässigkeit <-, -en> *f* negligence; **grobe ~** recklessness

Fahrlehrer(in) *m(f)* driving instructor

Fahrplan *m* timetable, schedule

Fahrpreis *m* fare

Fahrprüfung *f* driving test

Fahrrad ['faːɐ̯·raːt] *nt* bicycle, bike *fam;* **~ fahren** to ride a bicycle [*or fam* bike]

Fahrradfahrer(in) *m(f)* cyclist

Fahrradweg *m* bicycle [*or fam* bike] path

Fahrschein *m* ticket

Fahrschule *f* ❶ (*Firma*) driving school ❷ (*Unterricht*) driving lessons *pl*

Fahrschüler(in) *m(f)* student driver

Fahrspur *f* [traffic] lane

Fahrstuhl *m* elevator

Fahrstunde *f* driving lesson

Fahrt <-, -en> [faːɐ̯t] *f* ❶ (*das Fahren*) trip ❷ (*Fahrgeschwindigkeit*) speed; AUTO, BAHN **mit voller ~** at full speed ❸ (*Reise*) trip; **gute ~!** [have a] safe trip!; **eine einfache ~** a one-way [ticket]; **eine ~ ins Blaue** a Sunday drive ▶WENDUNGEN: **in ~ kommen/sein** (*fam: wütend werden/sein*) to get/be all riled up *fam;* (*in Schwung kommen*) to get going

fährt [fɛːɐ̯t] *3. pers sing pres von* **fahren**

Fährte <-, -n> ['fɛɐ̯·tə] *f* trail, tracks *pl;* **jdn auf eine falsche ~ locken** (*fig*) to throw sb off the track; **auf der falschen/richtigen ~ sein** (*fig*) to be on the wrong/right track

fahrtüchtig *adj Fahrzeug* roadworthy; *Mensch* fit to drive *pred*

Fahrzeug <-s, -e> *nt* vehicle

Fahrzeugbrief *m* title

Fahrzeughalter(in) *m(f)* vehicle owner

Fahrzeugpapiere *pl* vehicle registration papers *npl*

Fahrzeugschein *m* [motor vehicle] registration

fair [fɛːɐ̯] *adj* fair; ■**[jdm gegenüber] ~ sein** to be fair [to sb]

FairnessRR, **Fairneß**ALT <-> ['fɛːɐ̯·nɛs] *f kein pl* fairness

Fakten ['faktn̩] *pl* facts *pl*

Faktor <-s, -toren> ['fak·toːɐ̯, *pl* -'toː·rən] *m* factor

Fakultät <-, -en> [fa·kʊl·'tɛt] *f* department

Falke <-n, -n> ['fal·kə] *m* falcon, hawk

Fall <-[e]s, Fälle> [fal, *pl* 'fɛ·lə] *m* ❶ *kein pl* (*Sturz*) fall ❷ (*Untergang*) downfall ❸ (*Umstand, Angelegenheit*) case, circumstance; **klarer ~!** (*fam*) you bet!; **auf alle Fälle** in any case; (*unbedingt*) absolutely; **auf keinen ~** never, under no circumstances; **für alle Fälle** just in case; **im günstigsten/schlimmsten ~[e]** at best/worst; **in diesem ~** in this case; **von ~ zu ~** from case to case ❹ JUR, MED case ▶WENDUNGEN: **[nicht] jds ~ sein** (*fam*) to [not] be sb's cup of tea [*or* thing]

Fallbeil *nt* guillotine

Falle <-, -n> ['fa·lə] *f* trap; **~n stellen** to set traps; **jdm in die ~ gehen** to fall into sb's trap; **jdn in eine ~ locken** to lure sb into a trap; **in der ~ sitzen** to be trapped

fallen <fällt, fiel, gefallen> ['fa·lən] *vi sein* ❶ (*nach unten*) *Person* to fall; *Gegenstand* to drop; *Beil* to fall; *Klappe, Vorhang* to drop ❷ (*stolpern*) ■**über etw** *akk* **~** to trip over sth ❸ (*fam: nicht bestehen*) ■**durch etw** *akk* **~** to fail [*or fam* flunk] sth ❹ *Preise* to fall; *Temperatur* to drop; *Fieber, Wasserstand* to go down ❺ (*im Krieg*) to be killed ❻ (*stattfinden*) ■**auf etw** *akk* **~** to fall on sth; **der 1. April fällt auf einen Montag** April 1st falls on a Monday ❼ SPORT *Tor* to be scored ❽ *Schuss* to be fired ❾ (*verlauten*) to be spoken; **eine Bemerkung ~ lassen** to drop a remark ❿ (*aufgeben*) **jdn/etw ~ lassen** to abandon sb/sth

fällen ['fɛ·lən] *vt* ❶ (*umhauen*) to fell ❷ (*entscheiden*) *Urteil* to reach

fallen|lassen* *vt irreg s.* **fallen 9, 10**

fällig ['fɛ·lɪç] *adj* ❶ (*anstehend*) due *usu pred* ❷ (*fam: dran sein*) ■**~ sein** to be in for it

Fälligkeit <-, -en> *f* FIN due date

falls [fals] *konj* if

Fallschirm *m* parachute

Fallschirmspringen *nt* parachuting

Fallschirmspringer(in) *m(f)* parachutist

fällt [fɛlt] *3. pers sing pres von* **fallen**

Falltür *f* trapdoor

falsch [falʃ] **I.** *adj* ❶ (*verkehrt*) wrong; **~e Anschuldigung** false accusation; **einen ~en Namen angeben** to give a false name; **~e Vorstellung** wrong idea ❷ (*unecht*) fake; **~es Geld** counterfeit money ❸ (*hinterhältig*) two-faced ❹ (*unangebracht*) false; ~**e Scham** false shame **II.** *adv* wrongly; **etw ~ aussprechen** to mispronounce sth; **jdn ~ informieren** to misinform sb; **~ singen** to sing out of tune

Fạlschaussage *f* JUR false testimony

fälschen ['fɛl·ʃn̩] *vt* to forge; ÖKON to falsify; *Geld* to counterfeit

Fälscher(in) <-s, -> *m(f)* forger; *Geld* counterfeiter

Fạlschgeld *nt kein pl* counterfeit money

fạlsch|liegen *vi irreg* ■ [**mit etw** *dat*] ~ to be wrong [in sth]

Fạlschmeldung *f* false report

Fạlschmünzer(in) <-s, -> *m(f)* counterfeiter

fạlsch|spielen *vi* to cheat

Fälschung <-, -en> *f* forgery

fälschungssicher *adj* counterfeit-proof

Fạltblatt *nt* leaflet

Fạlte <-, -n> ['fal·tə] *f* ❶ (*in Kleidung*) crease; **~n bekommen** to get wrinkled ❷ (*in Stoff*) fold; **~n werfen** to fall in folds ❸ (*Hautfalte*) wrinkle; **die Stirn in ~n legen** to furrow one's brow

falten ['fal·tn̩] *vt* to fold; **die Stirn ~** to furrow one's brow

Falter <-s, -> ['fal·tɐ] *m* (*Tagfalter*) butterfly; (*Nachtfalter*) moth

faltig ['fal·tɪç] *adj* ❶ *Kleidung* creased, wrinkled ❷ *Haut* wrinkled

falzen ['fal·tsn̩] *vt* to fold

familiär [fa·mi·'li̯ɛɐ̯] *adj* ❶ (*die Familie betreffend*) family *attr;* **aus ~en Gründen** for family reasons ❷ (*zwanglos*) familiar; **in ~er Atmosphäre** in an informal atmosphere

Familie <-, -n> [fa·'miː·li̯ə] *f* family; **„~ Lang"** "The Lang Family"; **das liegt in der ~** it runs in the family; **eine vierköpfige ~** a family of four; **~ haben** to have a family

Familienangehörige(r) *f(m) dekl wie adj* relative

Familienfeier *f* family get-together

Familienmitglied *nt* member of the family

Familienname *m* last name, surname

Familienplanung *f* family planning *no art*

Familienstand *m* marital status

Familienzuwachs *m* addition to the family

Fan <-s, -s> [fɛn] *m* fan; (*Fußballfan a.*) supporter

Fanatiker(in) <-s, -> [fa·'naː·ti·kɐ] *m(f)* fanatic; **ein politischer ~** an extremist

fanatisch [fa·'naː·tɪʃ] **I.** *adj* fanatical **II.** *adv* fanatically

Fanatismus <-> [fa·na·'tɪs·mʊs] *m kein pl* fanaticism

fand ['fant] *imp von* **finden**

Fang <-[e]s, Fänge> [faŋ, *pl* 'fɛŋə] *m* ❶ SPORTS catch ❷ *kein pl* (*Beute*) catch; *Fisch* haul ▶ WENDUNGEN: **einen guten ~ machen** to make a good catch

Fänge ['fɛŋə] *pl von* **Fang**

fangen <fängt, fing, gefangen> ['faŋən] **I.** *vt* to catch **II.** *vi* **F~ spielen** to play catch **III.** *vr* ■ **sich** *akk* ~ to steady oneself

Fạngfrage *f* trick question

fängt [fɛŋt] *3. pers sing pres von* **fangen**

Fantasie <-, -n> [fan·ta·'ziː, *pl* -'ziː·ən] *f* ❶ *kein pl* (*Einbildungsvermögen*) imagination ❷ *meist pl* (*Fantasterei*) fantasy

fantasieren* [fan·ta·'ziː·rən] **I.** *vi* to fantasize (**von** + *dat* about) **II.** *vt* to imagine

fantasievoll *adj* [highly] imaginative

fantạstisch **I.** *adj* fantastic, incredible; **das klingt ~** that sounds incredible **II.** *adv* fantastically, incredibly

FAQ [ɛf·ʔeɪ·ʔkjuː] *pl* COMPUT *Abk von* **Frequently Asked Questions** FAQ

Fạrbabzug *m* FOTO color print

Fạrbbildschirm *m* color screen [*or* monitor]

Fạrbdruck *m* (*Druckverfahren*) color printing; (*Bild*) color print

Farbe <-, -n> ['far·bə] *f* ❶ (*Farbton*) color; **sanfte ~n** soft hues ❷ (*Anstreichmittel*) paint; (*Färbemittel*) dye ▶ WENDUNGEN: **~ bekennen** to come clean

Fạ̈rbemittel *nt* dye

färben ['fɛr·bn̩] **I.** *vt* to dye; **rassistisch gefärbt sein** (*fig*) to have racist overtones **II.** *vi* (*abfärben*) to run **III.** *vr* ■ **sich** *akk* ~ to change color; **die Blätter ~ sich gelb** the leaves are turning yellow

fạrbenblind *adj* color blind

Färber(in) <-s, -> ['fɛr·bɐ] *m(f)* dyer

Färberei <-, -en> [fɛr·bə·'rai] *f* dye works

Fạrbfernsehen *nt* color television

Fạrbfilm *m* color film

Fạrbfoto *nt* color photo[graph]

farbig ['far·bɪç] **I.** *adj* ❶ (*bunt*) colored ❷ (*anschaulich*) colorful ❸ *attr* (*Hautfarbe betreffend*) of color; **die ~e Bevölkerung** people of color **II.** *adv* ❶ (*bunt*) in color ❷ (*anschaulich*) colorfully

Fạrbige(r) *f(m) dekl wie adj* person of color; (*Schwarzamerikaner*) African-American

Fạrbkasten *m* paint box

Fạrbkopierer *m* color copier

farblich ['farp·lɪç] **I.** *adj* color **II.** *adv* in color

farblos ['farp·loːs] *adj* ❶ (*ohne Farbe*) colorless; *Lippenstift* clear ❷ (*langweilig*) dull

Fạrbskala *f* color scale

Fạrbstift *m* colored pencil

Fạrbstoff *m* ❶ (*Färbemittel*) dye; (*in Nahrungsmitteln*) artificial coloring ❷ (*Pigment*) pigment

Fạrbton *m* shade

Färbung <-, -en> *f* ❶ *kein pl* (*das Färben*) coloring ❷ (*Tönung*) shade; (*von Blättern*) hue

Farm <-, -en> [farm] *f* farm

Farmer(in) <-s, -> ['farmɐ] *m(f)* farmer

Farn <-[e]s, -e> [farn] *m*, **Fạrnkraut** *nt* fern

Fasan <-s, -e[n]> [fa·'zaːn] *m* pheasant

Fasching <-s, -e *o* -s> ['fa·ʃɪŋ] *m* SÜDD, ÖSTERR (*Fastnacht*) carnival

Faschismus <-> [fa·'ʃɪs·mʊs] *m kein pl* fascism

Faschist(in) <-en, -en> [fa·'ʃɪst] *m(f)* fascist

faschistisch [fa·'ʃɪs·tɪʃ] *adj* fascist

Faser <-, -n> ['fa:·zɐ] *f* fiber
faserig ['fa:·zə·rɪç] *adj* fibrous
Fass[RR] <-es, Fässer>, **Faß**[ALT] <-sses, Fässer> [fas, *pl* 'fɛ·sɐ] *nt* barrel; **Bier vom ~** draft beer ▶WENDUNGEN: **das ~ zum Überlaufen bringen** to be the final straw
Fassade <-, -n> [fa·'sa:·də] *f* façade, front; **nur ~ sein** (*fig*) to be just [a] show
fassbar[RR], **faßbar**[ALT] *adj* tangible
fassen ['fasn̩] **I.** *vt* ① (*ergreifen*) to grasp; **jdn am Arm ~** to grab sb's arm; **jdn bei der Hand ~** to take sb by the hand ② *Täter* to apprehend ③ (*zu etw gelangen*) to reach; *Entschluss, Vorsatz* to make; **keinen klaren Gedanken ~ können** to not be able to think clearly ④ (*begreifen*) to comprehend; **er konnte sein Glück kaum fassen** he could hardly believe his luck ⑤ (*etw enthalten*) to contain ⑥ (*einfassen*) to mount (**in** +*akk* in) **II.** *vi* ① (*greifen*) to grip; *Schraube, Zahnrad* to bite ② (*berühren*) to touch; **sie fasste in das Loch** she felt inside the hole ③ *Hund* **fass!** sic [*or* get] [him/her]! **III.** *vr* ■ **sich** *akk* **~** to pull oneself together
Fassung <-, -en> *f* ① (*Rahmen*) mounting ② (*Brillengestell*) frame ③ (*für Lampen*) socket ④ (*Bearbeitung*) version, draft ⑤ *kein pl* (*Selbstbeherrschung*) composure; **die ~ bewahren** to maintain one's composure; **jdn aus der ~ bringen** to rattle sb; **die ~ verlieren** to lose one's self-control
fassungslos I. *adj* stunned **II.** *adv* in bewilderment; **~ zusehen, wie ...** to watch in disbelief as ...
Fassungslosigkeit <-> *f kein pl* complete bewilderment
Fassungsvermögen *nt* capacity
fast [fast] *adv* almost, nearly; **~ nie** hardly ever
fasten ['fas·tn̩] *vi* to fast
Fastenzeit *f* REL Lent, period of fasting
Fast Food[RR], **Fastfood**[RR], **Fast food**[ALT] <-> ['fa:st·fu:t] *nt kein pl* fast food
Fastnacht ['fast·naxt] *f kein pl* DIAL carnival

> The Swabian-Alemannic carnival known as **Fastnacht** or *Fasnet* begins on January 6, *Heilige Dreikönige* (Epiphany), and takes place in Baden-Württemberg, parts of Bavaria, northern Switzerland, and Alsace, France. **Fastnacht** is characterized by a reversal of the social order, which includes people dressing up in costumes and wearing masks. The real celebrating starts on the Thursday before Ash Wednesday, which is known in the south as *Schmutziger Donnerstag* or *Fettdonnerstag* and in other areas as *Weiberfastnacht* (Women's Carnival). On that day, women traditionally take over town halls and are allowed to cut in half the tie of any male who happens to come along, in exchange for a kiss.

Faszination <-> [fas·tsi·na·'tsi̯o:n] *f kein pl* fascination
faszinieren* [fas·tsi·'ni:·rən] *vt, vi* to fascinate; **was fasziniert dich so an ihm?** what do you find so fascinating about him?
faszinierend *adj* fascinating
fatal [fa·'ta:l] *adj* (*geh*) ① (*verhängnisvoll*) fatal ② (*peinlich*) *Lage* awkward
Fatalismus <-> [fa·ta·'lɪs·mʊs] *m kein pl* (*geh*) fatalism
Fata Morgana <- -, - Morganen *o* -s> ['fa:·ta mɔr·'ga:·na, *pl* -'ga:·nən] *f* ① (*Luftspiegelung*) mirage ② (*Wahnvorstellung*) Fata Morgana
fauchen ['fau·xn̩] *vi* ① (*Tierlaut*) to hiss ② (*wütend zischen*) to spit
faul [faul] *adj* ① (*nicht fleißig*) lazy ② (*verfault*) rotten ③ (*fam: nicht einwandfrei*) bad; ■ **an etw** *dat* **ist etw ~** something is fishy about sth
Fäule <-> ['fɔy·lə] *f kein pl* (*geh: Fäulnis*) rot; (*Zahnfäule*) [tooth] decay
faulen ['fau·lən] *vi sein o haben* to rot; *Wasser* to stagnate
faulenzen ['fau·lɛn·tsn̩] *vi* to laze around, to vegetate
Faulenzer(in) <-s, -> ['fau·lɛn·tsɐ] *m(f)* (*pej*) loafer *pej,* slacker *pej*
Faulenzerei <-, *selten* -en> [fau·lɛn·tsə·'rai] *f* (*pej*) idleness, laziness
Faulheit <-> *f kein pl* laziness
faulig ['fau·lɪç] *adj* rotten; *Geruch, Geschmack* foul; *Wasser* stagnant
Fäulnis <-> ['fɔy·lnɪs] *f kein pl* decay, rot
Faulpelz *m* (*pej fam*) lazybones, lazy bum *pej*
Faultier *nt* ① (*Tier*) sloth ② (*fam*) *s.* **Faulpelz**
Fauna <-, Faunen> ['fau·na, *pl* 'fau·nən] *f* fauna
Faust <-, Fäuste> [faust, *pl* fɔys·tə] *f* fist; **die ~ ballen** to clench one's fist ▶WENDUNGEN: **wie die ~ aufs Auge passen** (*nicht passen*) to clash horribly; (*perfekt passen*) to be a perfect fit; **auf eigene ~** on one's own initiative
Fäustchen <-s, -> ['fɔyst·çən] *nt dim von* **Faust** little fist ▶WENDUNGEN: **sich** *dat* **ins ~ lachen** (*fam*) to laugh up one's sleeve
Fausthandschuh *m* mitten
Faustregel *f* rule of thumb
favorisieren* [fa·vo·ri·'zi:·rən] *vt* (*geh*) to favor
Favorit(in) <-en, -en> [fa·vo·'ri:t, *pl* -'ri:·tn̩] *m(f)* favorite
Fax <-, -e> [faks] *nt* ① (*Schriftstück*) fax ② (*Gerät*) fax [machine]
faxen ['faksn̩] *vi, vt* to fax
Faxen ['faksn̩] *pl* ① (*Albereien*) clowning around; **lass die ~!** stop clowning around! ② (*fam: Grimassen*) grimaces *pl;* **~ machen** to make faces
Faxmodem *nt* fax modem
Fazit <-s, -s *o* -e> ['fa:·tsɪt] *nt* result; **das ~ aus etw** *dat* **ziehen** to sum up *sep* sth; (*Bilanz ziehen*) to take stock of sth
FCKW <-s, -s> [ɛf·tse:·ka:·'ve:] *m Abk von*

F

Fluorchlorkohlenwasserstoff CFC
FCKW-frei *adj* CFC-free
FDP <-> [ɛf·deː·ˈpeː] *f Abk von* **Freie Demokratische Partei** FDP
Febr. *Abk von* **Februar** Feb.
Februar <-[s], *selten* -e> [ˈfeː·bru·aːɐ̯] *m* February; **Anfang/Ende ~** at the beginning/end of February; **Mitte ~** in the middle of February, mid-February; **jetzt haben wir schon ~, und ...** it's already February and ...; **im ~** in February; **im Laufe des ~s** [*o* **des Monats ~**] during February, in February; **im Monat ~** in [the month of] February; **diesen/jeden ~** this/every February; **bis in den ~** [**hinein**] until some time in [*or* well into] February; **den ganzen ~ über** throughout February; **am 14. ~** (*geschrieben*) on February 14th; (*gesprochen*) on the 14th of February [*or* February [the] 14th]; **am Freitag, dem** [*o* **den**] **14. Februar** on Friday, February [the] 14th; **Hamburg, den 14. ~ 2005** Hamburg, February 14, 2005; **auf den 14. ~ fallen/legen** to fall on/to schedule for February 14th
fechten <fechtet *o* ficht, focht, gefochten> [ˈfɛç·tn̩] *vi* to fence (**mit** *+dat* with, **gegen** *+akk* against)
Fechten <-s> [ˈfɛç·tn̩] *nt kein pl* fencing
Fechter(in) <-s, -> [ˈfɛç·tɐ] *m(f)* fencer
Feder <-, -n> [ˈfɛ·dɐ] *f* ❶ (*Teil des Gefieders*) feather ❷ (*Schreibfeder*) quill ❸ (*elastisches Metallteil*) spring ❹ (*Bett*) **noch in den ~n liegen** (*fam*) to still be in bed; **raus aus den ~n!** (*fam*) rise and shine! ▶ WENDUNGEN: **sich** *akk* **mit fremden ~n schmücken** to take the credit for sb else's work

Federball *m* ❶ *kein pl* (*Spiel*) badminton ❷ (*Ball*) birdie
Federbett *nt* comforter, duvet
Federgewicht *nt kein pl* SPORT featherweight
federleicht [ˈfeː·dɐ·ˈlai·çt] *adj* [as] light as a feather *pred*
federn [ˈfeː·dɐn] **I.** *vi* ❶ (*nachgeben*) to be springy ❷ SPORT to flex **II.** *vt* ■**etw ~** to spring-load
federnd *adj* springy
Federung <-, -en> *f* springing; (*für Auto a.*) suspension
Federvieh *nt* (*fam*) poultry
Fee <-, -n> [feː, *pl* ˈfeː·ən] *f* fairy
Feed-back[RR], **Feedback** <-s, -s> [ˈfiːt·bɛk] *nt* feedback
Feeling <-s> [ˈfiː·lɪŋ] *nt kein pl* ❶ (*Gefühl*) feeling ❷ (*Gefühl für etw*) feel; **ein ~ für etw** *akk* **haben** to have a feel for sth
Fegefeuer [ˈfeː·gə-] *nt* purgatory
fegen [ˈfeː·gn̩] **I.** *vt haben* ❶ (*kehren*) to sweep ❷ SCHWEIZ (*feucht wischen*) to wipe **II.** *vi* ❶ *haben* (*ausfegen*) to sweep up ❷ *sein* (*fam: schnell fahren*) to tear
Fehde <-, -n> [ˈfeː·də] *f* feud; **mit jdm in ~ liegen** (*geh*) to be feuding with sb
fehl [feːl] *adj* **~ am Platz** out of place
Fehlalarm *m* false alarm
Fehlanzeige *f* (*fam*) negative report; ■**~!** wrong!, nope! *fam*
Fehlbetrag *m* ÖKON deficit
Fehldiagnose *f* misdiagnosis
Fehleinschätzung *f* misjudgment
fehlen [ˈfeː·lən] **I.** *vi* ❶ (*nicht vorhanden sein*) ■**etw fehlt** sth is missing ❷ (*abhandengekommen sein*) ■**jdm fehlt etw** sb is missing sth ❸ (*abwesend sein*) to be missing (**in** *+dat* from); **unentschuldigt ~** to be absent without an excuse ❹ (*schmerzlich vermissen*) ■**jd fehlt jdm** sb misses sb ❺ (*an etw leiden*) **fehlt Ihnen etwas?** is there something wrong [with you]? **II.** *vi impers* ❶ (*abhandengekommen sein*) to be missing ❷ (*mangeln*) ■**jdm fehlt es an etw** *dat* sb is lacking sth; **jdm fehlt es an nichts** (*geh*) sb wants for nothing
Fehlentscheidung *f* wrong [*or* bad] decision
Fehler <-s, -> [ˈfeː·lɐ] *m* ❶ (*Irrtum*) error, mistake; **einen ~ machen** [*o* **begehen**] to make a mistake; **jds ~ sein** to be sb's fault ❷ (*Mangel*) defect ❸ (*schlechte Eigenschaft*) fault; **jeder hat** [**seine**] **~** everyone has [their] faults
fehlerfrei *adj s.* **fehlerlos**
fehlerhaft *adj* ❶ (*mangelhaft*) poor; (*bei Waren*) defective ❷ (*falsch*) incorrect
fehlerlos *adj* faultless, perfect
Fehlermeldung *f* COMPUT error message
Fehlerquelle *f* source of error
Fehlersuche *f* COMPUT troubleshooting
Fehlfunktion *f* defective function
Fehlgeburt *f* miscarriage
Fehlgriff *m* mistake
Fehlinformation *f* misinformation
Fehlkonstruktion *f* (*pej*) flawed product; **eine totale ~ sein** to be poorly designed
fehl|schlagen *vi irreg sein* to fail
Fehlstart *m* ❶ LUFT faulty launch ❷ SPORT false start
Fehltritt *m* (*geh*) ❶ (*Fauxpas*) lapse ❷ (*Ehebruch*) indiscretion
Fehlverhalten *nt* inappropriate behavior
Feier <-, -n> [ˈfaiɐ] *f* celebration; **zur ~ des Tages** in honor of the occasion
Feierabend [ˈfai·ɐ·ʔaː·bn̩t] *m* ❶ (*Arbeitsschluss*) end of work; **hoffentlich ist bald ~** I hope it's time to go home soon; **für mich ist jetzt ~!** I'm calling it a day!; ■**~!** that's it for today!; **~ machen** to finish work for the day ❷ (*Zeit nach Arbeitsschluss*) evening; **schönen ~!** have a nice evening!
feierlich [ˈfai·ɐ·lɪç] **I.** *adj* ❶ (*erhebend*) *Akt* ceremonial; **ein ~er Anlass** a formal occasion ❷ (*nachdrücklich*) solemn **II.** *adv* ❶ (*würdig*) formally; **etw ~ begehen** to celebrate sth ❷ (*nachdrücklich*) solemnly
Feierlichkeit <-, -en> *f* ❶ *kein pl* (*würdevolle Beschaffenheit*) solemnity ❷ *meist pl* (*Feier*) celebrations
feiern [ˈfai·ɐn] *vt, vi* ❶ (*festlich begehen*) to celebrate; **eine Party ~** to have a party ❷ (*umjubeln*) ■**jdn ~** to acclaim [*or* celebrate] sb
Feiertag [ˈfai·ɐ·taːk] *m* holiday

feiertags ['fai·ɐ·ta:ks] *adv* on holidays
feig(e) *adj* cowardly; **los, sei nicht ~!** come on, don't be a chicken! *fam*
Feige <-, -n> ['fai·gə] *f* fig
Feigheit <-, -en> *f kein pl* cowardice
Feigling <-s, -e> ['faik·lɪŋ] *m (pej)* coward
Feile <-, -n> ['fai·lə] *f* file
feilen ['fai·lən] **I.** *vt* to file **II.** *vi* ■**an etw** *dat* ~ ❶ *(mit einer Feile bearbeiten)* to file sth ❷ *(verbessern)* to polish sth
feilschen ['fail·ʃn̩] *vi (pej)* to haggle (**um** +*akk* over)
fein [fain] **I.** *adj* ❶ *(nicht grob)* fine; *(zart)* delicate ❷ *(vornehm)* distinguished; **jd ist sich** *dat* **für etw** *akk* **zu ~** sth is beneath sb; **sich** *akk* **~ machen** to get dressed up ❸ *(von hoher Qualität)* exquisite; **vom F~sten** of the highest quality ❹ *(rein)* pure; **aus ~em Gold** made out of pure gold ❺ *(fam: anständig)* decent; *(iron)* fine ❻ *(feinsinnig)* keen; **eine ~e Nase haben** to have a very keen sense of smell ❼ *Humor* delicate; *Ironie* subtle ❽ *(fam: erfreulich)* fine, great ▶WENDUNGEN: **~ raus sein** to be in a nice position **II.** *adv* ❶ *(genau)* precise; **~ säuberlich** accurate ❷ *(zart, klein)* finely; **~ gemahlen** fine-ground
Feind(in) <-[e]s, -e> [faint, *pl* 'fain·də] *m(f)* ❶ *(Gegner)* enemy; **sich** *dat* **jdn zum ~ machen** to make an enemy of sb ❷ *(Opponent)* opponent; ■**ein ~ einer S.** *gen* an opponent of sth
Feindbild *nt* concept of an/the enemy
feindlich *adj* ❶ *(gegnerisch)* enemy *attr* ❷ *(feindselig)* hostile; ■**jdm ~ gegenüberstehen** to be hostile to sb
Feindschaft <-, -en> *f kein pl* animosity, hostility
feindselig ['faint·ze:·lɪç] **I.** *adj* hostile **II.** *adv* hostilely
Feindseligkeit <-, -en> *f* ❶ *kein pl (feindselige Haltung)* hostility ❷ *pl (Kampfhandlungen)* hostilities *npl*
feinfühlig ['fain·fy:·lɪç] *adj* sensitive
Feingefühl *nt kein pl* sensitivity; **etw verlangt viel ~** sth requires a great deal of tact
Feinheit <-, -en> *f* ❶ *(Feinkörnigkeit)* fineness; *(Zartheit)* delicacy ❷ *pl (Nuancen)* subtleties *pl*
feinkörnig *adj* ❶ *(aus kleinen Teilen)* fine-grained ❷ FOTO fine-grain
Feinkostgeschäft *nt* gourmet shop
Feinmechanik *f* precision engineering
Feinschmecker(in) <-s, -> *m(f)* gourmet
feinsinnig *adj* sensitive
Feld <-[e]s, -er> [felt, *pl* 'fɛl·dɐ] *nt* ❶ *(offenes Gelände, Acker)* field; **auf freiem ~** in the open country ❷ *(abgeteilte Fläche)* section, field; *(auf Spielbrett)* square ❸ *kein pl (Schlachtfeld)* [battle]field ❹ *(Bereich)* area; **ein weites ~ sein** to be a broad subject ▶WENDUNGEN: **das ~ räumen** to clear the way; **jdm das ~ überlassen** to leave the field open to sb; **gegen etw** *akk* **zu ~e ziehen** *(geh)* to campaign against sth
Feldarbeit *f* work in the fields
Feldforschung *f* field research
Feldfrucht <-, -früchte> *f meist pl* agricultural crop
Feldherr(in) *m(f)* MIL, HIST general, strategist
Feldlager *nt (Heerlager)* encampment
Feldlazarett *nt* MIL field hospital
Feldpost *f* MIL armed forces postal service
Feldsalat *m* mâche, corn salad
Feldstecher <-s, -> *m* binoculars *npl*
Feldwebel(in) <-s, -> ['felt·ve:·bl̩] *m(f)* sergeant major
Feldweg *m* field path
Feldzug *m* campaign
Felge <-, -n> ['fɛl·gə] *f* rim
Fell <-[e]s, -e> [fɛl] *nt* fur ▶WENDUNGEN: **jdm das ~ über die Ohren ziehen** *(fam)* to take sb to the cleaners; **ein dickes ~ haben** *(fam)* to be thick-skinned
Fels <-en, -en> [fɛls] *m* ❶ *(geh)* cliff ❷ *(Gestein)* rock
Felsblock <-blöcke> *m* boulder
Felsen <-s, -> ['fɛl·zn̩] *m* cliff
felsenfest ['fɛl·zn̩'fɛst] **I.** *adj* rock solid, steadfast **II.** *adv* steadfastly; **~ von etw** *dat* **überzeugt sein** to be firmly convinced of sth
felsig ['fɛl·zɪç] *adj* rocky
Felsvorsprung *m* ledge
Felswand *f* rock face
feminin [fe·mi·'ni:n] *adj* feminine
Feminismus <-> [fe·mi·'nɪs·mʊs] *m kein pl* feminism
Feminist(in) <-en, -en> [fe·mi·'nɪst] *m(f)* feminist
feministisch *adj* feminist
Fenchel <-s> ['fɛn·çl̩] *m kein pl* BOT fennel
Fenster <-s, -> ['fɛn·stɐ] *nt* window ▶WENDUNGEN: **weg vom ~ sein** *(fam)* to be out of the running
Fensterbank <-bänke> *f* windowsill
Fensterglas *nt* window glass
Fensterladen *m* shutter
Fensterplatz *m* window seat
Fensterputzer(in) <-s, -> *m(f)* window cleaner
Fensterrahmen *m* window frame
Fensterscheibe *f* window pane
Ferien ['fe:·ri̯·ən] *pl* ❶ *(Schulferien)* [school] vacation; **die großen ~** summer vacation; **~ haben** to be on vacation ❷ *(Urlaub)* vacation; **in die ~ fahren** to go on vacation
Ferienhaus *nt* vacation home
Ferienkurs *m* summer school
Ferienlager *nt* vacation camp
Ferienort *m* vacation resort
Ferienwohnung *f* vacation apartment
Ferienzeit *f* vacation
Ferkel <-s, -> ['fɛr·kl̩] *nt* ❶ *(junges Schwein)* piglet ❷ *(pej fam: unsauberer Mensch)* pig ❸ *(pej fam: obszöner Mensch)* filthy pig
Ferkelei <-, -en> *f (pej fam)* ❶ *(Unsauberkeit)* mess ❷ *meist pl (obszöner Witz)* dirty joke

F

fern [fɛrn] **I.** *adj* ❶ (*räumlich entfernt*) faraway, far off; *Länder* distant; **von ~ betrachtet** viewed from a distance ❷ (*zeitlich entfernt*) distant; **in nicht allzu ~er Zeit** in the not too distant future **II.** *präp +dat* far [away] from
Fẹrnbedienung *f* remote control
fẹrn|bleiben *vi irreg sein* (*geh*) to stay away
Ferne <-, *selten* -n> ['fɛr·nə] *f* ❶ (*Entfernung*) distance; **aus der ~** from a distance; **in der ~** in the distance ❷ (*geh: ferne Länder*) distant lands *pl;* **in der ~** abroad ❸ (*längst vergangen*) **etw liegt [schon] in weiter ~** sth already happened such a long time ago ❹ (*in ferner Zukunft*) **das liegt [noch] in weiter ~** there is still a long way to go
ferner ['fɛr·nɐ] **I.** *adj* ❶ *komp von* **fern** more distant ❷ (*künftig, weiter*) in [the] future; **in der ~en Zukunft** in the distant future ▶ WENDUNGEN: **unter ~ liefen** (*fam*) to be a runner-up **II.** *konj* furthermore
Fẹrnfahrer(in) *m(f)* long-distance truck driver
Fẹrnflug *m* long-distance flight
Fẹrngespräch *nt* long-distance call
fẹrngesteuert *adj* remote-controlled
Fẹrnglas *nt* [pair of] binoculars
fẹrn|gucken *vi* (*fam: fernsehen*) to watch TV
fẹrn|halten *irreg vr* ■ **sich** *akk* **von jdm/etw ~** to keep away from sb/sth
Fẹrnkurs *m* correspondence course
Fẹrnlicht *nt* AUTO high beams
fẹrn|liegen *vi irreg* ■ **etw liegt jdm fern** sth is far from sb's mind; **es liegt mir fern, jemanden zu beschuldigen** far be it from me to blame someone
Fẹrnmeldetechnik *f kein pl* telecommunications engineering
Fẹrnmeldewesen *nt kein pl* telecommunications + *sing vb*
Fernost ['fɛrn·'ʔɔst] *kein art* **aus/in/nach ~** from/in/to the Far East
fernöstlich ['fɛrn·'ʔœst·lɪç] *adj* Far Eastern
Fẹrnrohr *nt* telescope
Fẹrnsehansager(in) *m(f)* television announcer
Fẹrnsehanstalt *f* television company
Fẹrnsehantenne *f* television antenna
Fernsehen <-s> ['fɛrn·zeːən] *nt kein pl* television; **das ~ bringt nur Wiederholungen** they're only showing reruns on TV; **im ~ kommen** to be on television
fern|sehen ['fɛrn·zeːən] *vi irreg* to watch television
Fẹrnseher <-s, -> *m* television [set]
Fẹrnsehfilm *m* television movie
Fẹrnsehgebühr *f meist pl* television license fee
Fẹrnsehinterview *nt* televised interview
Fẹrnsehjournalist(in) *m(f)* television reporter
Fẹrnsehnachrichten *pl* television news + *sing vb*
Fẹrnsehprogramm *nt* ❶ (*Programm im Fernsehen*) television program ❷ (*Kanal*) [television] channel
Fẹrnsehsender *m* television station
Fẹrnsehsendung *f* television program
Fẹrnsehturm *m* television tower
Fẹrnsehübertragung *f* television broadcast
Fẹrnsehzeitschrift *f* TV guide
Fẹrnsicht *f* view; **bei guter ~** with good visibility
fẹrn|steuern *vt* to operate by remote control
Fẹrnsteuerung *f* remote control
Fẹrnstraße *f* highway, freeway, interstate
Fẹrnstudium *nt* correspondence course
Fẹrnuniversität *f* distance learning campus
Fẹrnverkehr *m* long-distance traffic
Fẹrnweh <-[e]s> *nt kein pl* (*geh*) wanderlust
Fẹrnziel *nt* long-term objective
Ferse <-, -n> ['fɛr·zə] *f* heel ▶ WENDUNGEN: **sich** *akk* **jdm an die ~n hängen** to stick close to sb; **jdm [dicht] auf den ~n sein** to be [hot] on sb's tail
fertig ['fɛr·tɪç] **I.** *adj* ❶ (*abgeschlossen*) finished; **etw ~ haben** to have finished sth; **mit etw** *dat* **~ sein** to be finished with sth; **mit etw** *dat* **~ werden** to finish sth ❷ (*bereit*) ready ❸ (*fam: erschöpft*) exhausted ❹ (*fam: Beziehung beendet*) ■ **mit jdm ~ sein** to be through with sb ❺ (*fam: im Griff haben*) **mit jdm/etw ~ werden** to cope with sb/sth **II.** *adv* ❶ (*zu Ende*) **etw ~ bekommen** to complete sth; **etw ~ machen [*o* stellen]** to finish [*or* complete] sth ❷ (*bereit*) **sich** *akk* **~ machen** to get ready [for sth] ▶ WENDUNGEN: **auf die Plätze, ~, los!** on your marks, get set, go!
Fẹrtigbau <-bauten> *m* ❶ *kein pl* (*Bauweise*) prefabricated construction ❷ (*Gebäude*) prefab
Fẹrtigbauweise *f kein pl* prefabricated construction
fẹrtig|bekommen* *vt irreg* (*fam*) ❶ (*zu Ende bringen*) *s.* **fertig II 1** ❷ (*hinkriegen*) ■ **es ~, etw zu tun** to manage to do sth
fertigen ['fɛr·tɪ·gn̩] *vt* (*geh*) to manufacture
Fẹrtiggericht *nt* instant meal
Fẹrtighaus *nt* prefabricated house
Fẹrtigkeit <-, -en> *f* ❶ *kein pl* (*Geschicklichkeit*) skill ❷ *pl* (*Fähigkeiten*) competence
fẹrtig|machen I. *vt, vr s.* **fertig II 1, II 2 II.** *vt* (*fam*) ❶ ■ **etw macht jdn fertig** (*zermürben*) sth wears out *sep* sb ❷ **jdn ~** (*schikanieren*) to wear sb down *sep;* (*sl: zusammenschlagen*) to beat sb up *sep*
Fẹrtigprodukt *nt* finished product
fẹrtig|stellen *vt s.* **fertig II 1**
Fẹrtigstellung *f* completion
Fẹrtigteil *nt* prefabricated component
Fẹrtigung <-, -en> *f* manufacture
fesch [fɛʃ] *adj* SÜDD, ÖSTERR (*fam: flott*) chic
Fessel <-, -n> ['fɛsl̩] *f* ❶ (*Schnur*) bond; (*Kette*) shackles *npl;* **jdm ~n anlegen** to tie sb up ❷ ANAT (*von Mensch*) ankle; (*von Huftier*) pastern
fesseln ['fɛ·sl̩n] *vt* ❶ (*Fesseln anlegen*) to tie [up] (**an** +*akk* to) ❷ (*faszinieren*) to captivate

fesselnd *adj* captivating

fest [fɛst] **I.** *adj* ❶ (*hart, stabil*) strong, tough; *Schuhe* sturdy ❷ (*nicht flüssig*) solid; (*erstarrt*) solidified ❸ (*sicher, entschlossen*) firm; *Zusage* definite ❹ (*kräftig*) firm; *Händedruck* sturdy ❺ (*nicht locker*) tight ❻ (*konstant*) permanent; (*festgesetzt*) fixed; (*dauerhaft*) lasting; *Freund, Freundin* steady **II.** *adv* ❶ (*kräftig*) firmly; **jdn ~ an sich** *akk* **drücken** to give someone a big hug ❷ (*nicht locker*) tightly; **~ anziehen** to screw in tightly; **~ treten** to trample ❸ (*mit Nachdruck*) definitely; **jdm etw ~ versprechen** to make sb a firm promise ❹ (*dauernd*) permanently; **Geld ~ anlegen** to invest in a certificate of deposit; **~ angestellt sein** to have a permanent job

Fest <-[e]s, -e> [fɛst] *nt* ❶ (*Feier*) celebration; **ein ~ geben** to throw a party ❷ (*Feiertag*) feast; **frohes ~!** Merry Christmas/Happy Easter, etc. ▸WENDUNGEN: **man soll die ~e feiern, wie sie fallen** (*prov*) one should make hay while the sun shines *prov*

Festakt *m* ceremony

festangestellt *adj s.* **fest II 4**

Festangestellte(r) *f(m) dekl wie adj* permanent employee

Festanstellung *f* steady employment

fest|beißen *vr irreg* ■**sich** *akk* **~** ❶ (*sich verbeißen*) to bite down hard ❷ (*nicht weiterkommen*) to get stuck (**an** *+dat* on)

fest|binden *vt irreg* to tie tight (**an** *+akk* to)

feste ['fɛs·tə] *adv* (*fam*) like mad

Festessen *nt* banquet

fest|fahren *vr irreg* ■**sich** *akk* **~** to get stuck

Festgeld *nt* FIN certificate of deposit

Festgeldkonto *nt* FIN certificate of deposit account

fest|haken **I.** *vt* (*mit einem Haken befestigen*) to hook (**an** *+dat* to) **II.** *vr* (*hängen bleiben*) ■**sich** *akk* **an/in etw** *dat* **~** to get caught on/in sth

fest|halten *irreg* **I.** *vt* ❶ (*fest ergreifen*) to grab (**an** *+dat* by) ❷ (*gefangen halten*) to detain ❸ (*konstatieren*) to record **II.** *vi* ■**an etw** *dat* **~** to adhere to sth **III.** *vr* ■**sich** *akk* **~** to hold on (**an** *+dat* to)

festigen ['fɛs·tɪ·gn̩] **I.** *vt* to strengthen; *Freundschaft* to establish; *Stellung* to secure **II.** *vr* ■**sich** *akk* **~** to become more firmly established

Festiger <-s, -> *m* setting lotion

Festigkeit <-> ['fɛs·tɪç·kait] *f kein pl* strength

Festival <-s, -s> ['fɛs·ti·vl] *nt* festival

fest|klammern **I.** *vt* to clip (**an** *+dat* to) **II.** *vr* ■**sich** *akk* **~** to cling (**an** *+dat* to)

fest|kleben **I.** *vt haben* to stick [on]; **auf etw** *dat* **festgeklebt sein** to be stuck on sth **II.** *vi sein* to stick (**an** *+dat* to)

Festland ['fɛst·lant] *nt kein pl* mainland

fest|legen **I.** *vt* ❶ (*bestimmen*) to determine; ■**~, dass ...** to stipulate that ... ❷ (*bindend verpflichten*) ■**jdn** [**auf etw** *akk*] **~** to oblige sb [to do sth] **II.** *vr* (*sich verpflichten*) ■**sich** *akk* **~** to commit [oneself] (**auf** *+akk* to)

festlich **I.** *adj* festive **II.** *adv* festively; **~ gekleidet sein** to be dressed up

Festlichkeit <-, -en> *f* festivity

fest|liegen *vi irreg* ❶ (*festgesetzt sein*) to be determined; **die Termine liegen jetzt fest** the schedules have now been set ❷ (*nicht weiterkönnen*) to be stranded

fest|machen **I.** *vt* ❶ (*befestigen*) to fasten (**an** *+dat* to) ❷ (*vereinbaren*) to arrange ❸ (*herleiten*) ■**etw an etw** *akk* **~** to link sth to sth **II.** *vi* NAUT to tie up

fest|nageln *vt* ❶ (*mit Nägeln befestigen*) to nail (**an** *+akk* to) ❷ (*fam: festlegen*) ■**jdn ~** to nail sb down (**auf** *+akk* to)

Festnahme <-, -n> ['fɛst·na:·mə] *f* arrest

fest|nehmen *vt irreg* to take into custody; **Sie sind festgenommen** you're under arrest

Festnetz *nt* landline; **jdn vom** [*o* **aus dem**] **~ anrufen** to call sb on the landline

Festplatte *f* COMPUT hard disk

Festplattenlaufwerk *nt* COMPUT hard disk drive

Festrede *f* official speech; **eine ~ halten** to give a formal address

Festsaal *m* banquet hall

fest|schnallen **I.** *vt* to strap in *sep* **II.** *vr* ■**sich** *akk* **~** to fasten one's seat belt, to buckle up

fest|schrauben *vt* to screw tight *sep*

fest|setzen **I.** *vt* (*bestimmen*) to determine **II.** *vr* (*fest anhaften*) ■**sich** *akk* **~** to collect

fest|sitzen *vi irreg* to be stuck

fest|stehen *vi irreg* ❶ (*festgelegt sein*) to be certain; **steht das Datum schon fest?** has the date been set yet? ❷ (*sicher sein*) to be firm; ■**es steht fest, dass ...** it is certain that ...

fest|stellen *vt* ❶ (*ermitteln*) to identify; **den Täter ~** to identify the guilty party ❷ (*bemerken*) to detect; **zu meinem Erstaunen muss ich ~, dass ...** I am astounded to see that ...

Feststellung *f* ❶ (*Bemerkung*) remark ❷ (*Beobachtung*) observation; **die ~ machen, dass ...** to see that ... ❸ (*Ergebnis*) **zu der ~ kommen, dass ...** to come to the conclusion that ... ❹ JUR ascertainment

Festtag *m* ❶ (*Ehrentag*) special day ❷ (*Feiertag*) holiday

Festung <-, -en> ['fɛs·tʊŋ] *f* fortress

fest|ziehen *vt irreg* to tighten

fett [fɛt] *adj* ❶ (*fetthaltig*) fatty ❷ (*pej: dick*) fat ❸ TYPO bold; **~ gedruckt** in bold [type] *pred* ❹ (*üppig*) *Ackerboden* fertile; (*fam*) *Beute* rich

Fett <-[e]s, -e> [fɛt] *nt* ❶ (*Fettgewebe*) fat; **~ ansetzen** *Mensch* to gain weight; *Tier* to put on fat ❷ (*zum Schmieren*) grease; **pflanzliches/tierisches ~** vegetable/animal fat ▸WENDUNGEN: **sein ~ abbekommen** (*fam*) to get one's comeuppance

fettarm *adj* low-fat

Fettdruck *m* bold [type]

fetten ['fɛtn̩] **I.** *vt* (*einfetten*) to grease **II.** *vi* (*Fett absondern*) to become greasy

Fettfleck, **Fettflecken** *m* grease mark
fettgedruckt *adj attr s.* **fett 3**
Fettgehalt *m* fat content
fettig [ˈfɛ·tɪç] *adj* greasy
fettlöslich *adj* fat-soluble
Fettnäpfchen *nt* ► WENDUNGEN: **ins ~ treten** to put one's foot in one's mouth
Fettpolster *nt* (*fam*) spare tire *fam*
Fettschicht *f* layer of fat
fetzen [ˈfɛtsn̩] *vt haben* (*fam: prügeln*) ■**sich** *akk* ~ to tear each other apart
Fetzen <-s, -> [ˈfɛtsn̩] *m* ❶ (*Stück*) scrap; *Haut* patch; **etw in ~ reißen** to tear sth to pieces ❷ *einer Unterhaltung* fragments *pl* ❸ (*sl: billiges Kleid*) rag ► WENDUNGEN: **... dass die ~ fliegen** (*fam*) ... like crazy
fetzig [ˈfɛtsiç] *adj* (*sl: mitreißend*) fantastic; *Musik* hot; (*schick, flott*) trendy; *Typ* cool
feucht [fɔyçt] *adj* ❶ (*leicht nass*) damp; *Hände, Stirn* clammy; *Augen* misty ❷ *Klima, Luft* humid
Feuchtigkeit <-> [ˈfɔyç·tɪç·kait] *f kein pl* ❶ (*leichte Nässe*) dampness ❷ (*Wassergehalt*) moisture; *Luft* humidity
Feuchtigkeitscreme [-kreːm] *f* moisturizer, moisturizing cream
Feuchtigkeitsgehalt *m* moisture content; **der ~ der Luft** the humidity level
feudal [fɔy·ˈdaːl] *adj* ❶ HIST feudal ❷ (*fam*) magnificent; *Essen* sumptuous
Feudalherrschaft *f*, **Feudalismus** <-> [fɔy·da·ˈlɪs·mʊs] *m kein pl* feudalism
Feuer <-s, -> [ˈfɔy·ɐ] *nt* ❶ (*Flamme*) fire; **das olympische ~** the Olympic flame; **~ speien** to spit fire; *Vulkan* to spew out fire; *Drachen* to breathe fire; **~ machen** to make a fire; **am ~** by the fire ❷ (*für Zigarette*) **jdm ~ geben** to give sb a light; **~ haben** to have a light ❸ (*Kochstelle*) **etw vom ~ nehmen** to take sth off the heat ❹ (*Brand*) fire; **~ fangen** to catch [on] fire ❺ MIL (*Beschuss*) fire; **~ frei!** open fire!; **das ~ eröffnen/einstellen** to open/cease fire ► WENDUNGEN: **~ und Flamme [für etw] sein** (*fam*) to be enthusiastic [about sth]; **wie ~ brennen** to sting like mad; **mit dem ~ spielen** to play with fire
Feueralarm *m* fire alarm
Feuerbestattung *f* cremation
feuerfest *adj* fireproof; *Geschirr* ovenproof
Feuergefahr *f* fire hazard
feuergefährlich *adj* [in]flammable
Feuergefecht *nt* MIL gunfight
Feuerleiter *f* ❶ (*Fluchtweg*) fire escape ❷ (*auf einem Feuerwehrauto*) [fire engine] ladder
Feuerlöscher *m* fire extinguisher
Feuermelder <-s, -> *m* fire alarm
feuern I. *vi* to fire (**auf** +*akk* at) II. *vt* (*fam*) ❶ (*werfen*) to fire, to hurl ❷ (*fam: entlassen*) to fire; ■**gefeuert werden** to get the ax
feuersicher [ˈfɔy·ɐ·zɪ·çɐ] *adj* fireproof
Feuerstelle *f* fireplace; (*draußen*) campfire site
Feuerung <-, -en> *f* ❶ *kein pl* (*Brennstoff*) fuel ❷ (*Heizung*) heating system, heater
Feuerversicherung *f* fire insurance
Feuerwache *f* fire station
Feuerwaffe *f* firearm
Feuerwehr <-, -en> *f* fire department
Feuerwehrauto *nt* fire engine
Feuerwehrmann, **-frau** <-leute *o* -männer> *m, f* firefighter, fireman *masc*, firewoman *fem*
Feuerwerk *nt* fireworks *npl*
Feuerwerkskörper *m* firework
Feuerzeug *nt* lighter
Feuilleton <-s, -s> [fœ·jə·ˈtõː] *nt* (*Zeitungsteil*) culture section
ff. [ɛf·ˈʔɛf] *Abk von* **folgende Seiten**: **[auf] Seite 200 ~** pages [*or* pp.] 200 ff.
FH [ɛf·ˈhaː] *f Abk von* **Fachhochschule**
ficht [fɪçt] *3. pers sing pres von* **fechten**
Fichte <-, -n> [fɪç·tə] *f* spruce
ficken [ˈfɪ·kn̩] (*vulg*) I. *vi* to fuck; ■**das F~** fucking II. *vt* ■**jdn ~** to fuck sb
Fidschiinseln *pl* Fiji Islands *pl*
Fieber <-s, -> [ˈfiːbɐ] *nt* fever; **~ haben** to have a temperature [*or* fever]
fieberhaft I. *adj* feverish II. *adv* feverishly
fiebern [ˈfiː·bɐn] *vi* ❶ (*Fieber haben*) to have a temperature [*or* fever] ❷ (*aufgeregt sein*) to be in a fever
Fieberthermometer *nt* [clinical] thermometer
fiebrig [ˈfiː·brɪç] *adj* feverish
fiel [ˈfiːl] *imp von* **fallen**
fies [fiːs] *adj* (*pej fam*) ❶ (*abstoßend*) horrible, disgusting ❷ (*gemein*) mean
Fiesling <-s, -e> *m* (*fam*) [mean] bastard
Figur <-, -en> [fi·ˈguːɐ̯] *f* ❶ (*Gestalt*) figure; **auf seine ~ achten** to watch one's figure ❷ FILM, LIT character
Filet <-s, -s> [fi·ˈleː] *nt* fillet
Filetsteak [fi·ˈleː·steːk] *nt* fillet steak
Filiale <-, -n> [fi·ˈli̯aː·lə] *f* branch
Filialleiter(in) *m(f)* branch manager
Film <-[e]s, -e> [fɪlm] *m* ❶ (*Spielfilm*) movie, film ❷ FOTO film ❸ (*Filmbranche*) movie industry; **beim ~ arbeiten** to work in the movie industry ❹ (*dünne Schicht*) film
filmen [ˈfɪl·mən] *vt, vi* to film
Filmfestspiele *nt pl* film festival
Filmgeschäft *nt kein pl* movie business
Filmkamera *f* movie camera
Filmmusik *f* soundtrack
Filmregisseur(in) *m(f)* movie [*or* film] director
Filmstar *m* movie star
Filmvorschau *f* [movie] preview
Filter <-s, -> [ˈfɪl·tɐ] *nt o m* filter
Filteranlage *f* filter
Filterkaffee *m* filter [*or* drip] coffee
filtern [ˈfɪl·tɐn] *vt* to filter
Filterpapier *nt* filter paper
Filterzigarette *f* filter cigarette
Filz <-es, -e> [fɪlts] *m* felt
Filzstift *m* felt-tip pen
Finale <-s, -s *o* -> [fi·ˈnaː·lə] *nt* final
Finanzamt *nt* ■**das ~** Department of the Treasury

Finanzbeamte(r), **-beamtin** *m, f* tax official
Finanzen [fi·'nan·tsn̩] *pl* ❶ (*Einkünfte*) finances *npl* ❷ (*Geldmittel*) means *npl;* **jds ~ übersteigen** to be beyond sb's means
finanziell [fi·nan·'tsi̯ɛl] **I.** *adj* financial **II.** *adv* financially
finanzieren* [fi·nan·'tsiː·rən] *vt* to finance; **etw [nicht] ~ können** to [not] be able to afford sth
Finanzierung <-, -en> *f* financing
finanzkräftig *adj* financially strong
Finanzminister(in) *m(f)* finance minister, Secretary of the Treasury, Treasury Secretary
Finanzministerium *nt* Department of the Treasury, Treasury [Department]
Finanzpolitik *f kein pl* financial policy/policies
finden <fand, gefunden> ['fɪn·dn̩] **I.** *vt* ❶ (*entdecken*) to find; **es muss doch irgendwo zu ~ sein!** it must [*or* it's gotta] be somewhere!; **einen Vorwand [für etw** *akk*] **~** to find an excuse [for sth] ❷ (*erhalten*) to find; **Unterstützung ~** to receive support; **Zustimmung [bei jdm] ~** to meet with approval [from sb] ❸ (*empfinden*) to find; **ich finde, die Ferien sind zu kurz** I think the vacation is too short; **jdn blöd/nett ~** to think [that] sb is stupid/nice; **es kalt/warm ~** to find it cold/warm ▶ WENDUNGEN: **etwas an jdm/etw ~** to see sth in sb/sth; **nichts an jdm/etw ~** to not think much of sb/sth **II.** *vi* ❶ (*den Weg finden*) ■ **zu jdm/etw ~** to find one's way to sb/sth; **zu sich** *dat* **selbst ~** to find oneself ❷ (*meinen*) to think; **~ Sie?** [do] you think so? **III.** *vr* ■ **sich** *akk* **~** ❶ (*wieder auftauchen*) to turn up ❷ (*zu verzeichnen sein*) to be found; **es fand sich niemand, der ...** there was nobody to be found who... ❸ (*in Ordnung kommen*) to sort itself out
Finder(in) <-s, -> *m(f)* finder
Finderlohn *m* reward [for the finder]
fing ['fɪŋ] *imp von* **fangen**
Finger <-s, -> ['fɪŋɐ] *m* finger; **der kleine ~** the little finger, the pinkie *fam;* **~ weg!** hands off!; **jdm auf die ~ klopfen** (*fig fam*) to give sb a rap across the knuckles; **mit dem ~ auf jdn/etw zeigen** to point [one's finger] at sb/sth ▶ WENDUNGEN: **etw in die ~ bekommen** (*fam*) to get one's hands on sth; **überall seine ~ im Spiel haben** (*fam*) to have a finger in every pie; **jdn juckt es in den ~n[, etw zu tun]** (*fam*) sb is itching to do sth; **keinen ~ krumm machen** (*fam*) to not lift a finger; **lange ~ machen** (*hum fam*) to be light-fingered; **die ~ von jdm/etw lassen** (*fam*) to keep away from sb/sth; **sich** *dat* **etw aus den ~n saugen** (*fam*) to conjure up *sep* sth; **sich** *dat* **nicht die ~ schmutzig machen** to not get one's hands dirty; **jdm auf die ~ sehen** (*fam*) to keep a watchful eye on sb
Fingerabdruck *m* fingerprint
fingerfertig *adj* nimble-fingered
Fingerfertigkeit *f* dexterity
Fingerhut *m* ❶ (*fürs Nähen*) thimble ❷ BOT foxglove
Fingerkuppe *f* fingertip
fingern ['fɪŋɐn] **I.** *vi* to fiddle (**mit/an** +*dat* with) **II.** *vt* (*fam: tricksen*) ■ **etw ~** *dat* to fiddle sth
Fingernagel *m* fingernail; **an den Fingernägeln kauen** to bite one's nails
Fingerspitze *f* fingertip
Fingerspitzengefühl *nt kein pl* tact [and sensitivity]; **~/kein ~ haben** to be tactful/tactless
Fink <-en, -en> [fɪŋk] *m* finch
Finne, **Finnin** <-n, -n> ['fɪnə, 'fɪnɪn] *m, f* Finn, Finnish man/woman/boy/girl; ■ **~ sein** to be Finnish
finnisch ['fɪ·nɪʃ] *adj* Finnish
Finnland <-s> ['fɪn·lant] *nt* Finland
finster ['fɪns·tɐ] *adj* ❶ (*düster*) dark ❷ (*mürrisch*) grim ❸ (*unheimlich*) sinister
Finsternis <-, -se> ['fɪns·tɐ·nɪs] *f* darkness
Firma <-, Firmen> ['fɪr·ma, *pl* 'fɪr·mən] *f* company
Firmament <-s> [fɪr·ma·'mɛnt] *nt kein pl* ■ **das ~** the firmament
firmen ['fɪr·mən] *vt* to confirm
Firmen ['fɪr·mən] *pl von* **Firma**
Firmengründung *f* establishment of a business [*or* company]
Firmeninhaber(in) *m(f)* company owner
Firmenleitung *f* company management
Firmenwagen *m* company car
Firmenzeichen *nt* company logo, trademark
Firmung <-, -en> *f* confirmation
First <-[e]s, -e> [fɪrst] *m* roof ridge
Fis <-, -> [fɪs] *nt* MUS F sharp
Fisch <-[e]s, -e> [fɪʃ] *m* ❶ (*Tier*) fish ❷ *kein pl* ASTROL Pisces ▶ WENDUNGEN: **weder ~ noch Fleisch sein** to be neither fish nor fowl; **ein großer ~** a big fish; **ein kleiner ~** a small fry
fischen ['fɪʃn̩] *vi* to fish; ■ **das F~** fishing
Fischer(in) <-s, -> ['fɪ·ʃɐ] *m(f)* fisher, fisherman *masc,* fisherwoman *fem*
Fischerboot *nt* fishing boat
Fischerdorf *nt* fishing village
Fischerei <-> [fɪ·ʃə·'rai] *f kein pl* fishing
Fischernetz *nt* fishing net
Fischfang *m kein pl* fishing
Fischfilet [-fileː] *nt* fillet of fish
Fischhändler(in) *m(f)* ÖKON fish distributor
Fischkonserve *f* canned fish
Fischkutter *m* fishing cutter
Fischotter *m* otter
Fischstäbchen *nt* fish stick
Fischsterben *nt* fish mortality
Fischzucht *f* fish farming
fiskalisch [fɪs·'kaː·lɪʃ] *adj* fiscal
Fiskus <-, -se *o* Fisken> ['fɪs·kʊs, *pl* 'fɪs·kən] *m* ■ **der ~** the Treasury
Fisole <-, -n> [fi·'zoː·lə] *f* ÖSTERR green bean
fit [fɪt] *adj pred* fit; **sich** *akk* **~ halten** to keep fit, to stay in shape
Fitness[RR], **Fitneß**[ALT] <-> ['fɪ·tnɛs] *f kein pl* fitness
Fitnesscenter[RR] [-sɛn·tɐ] *nt* gym

Fitnessgerät[RR] [ˈfɪt·nɛs-] *nt* SPORT fitness [*or* gym] equipment
Fitnessstudio[RR] *m s.* **Fitnesscenter**
fix [fɪks] **I.** *adj* ① (*feststehend*) fixed ② (*fam: flink*) quick; ~ **gehen** to not take long; ~ **machen** to hurry up ▶ WENDUNGEN: ~ **und fertig sein** (*erschöpft*) to be exhausted; (*am Ende*) to be at the end of one's rope; **jdn ~ und fertig machen** (*fam*) to wear out sb *sep* **II.** *adv* quickly
Fixa [ˈfɪksa] *pl von* **Fixum**
fixen [ˈfɪk·sn̩] *vi* (*sl*) to fix
Fixer(in) <-s, -> [ˈfɪk·sɐ] *m(f)* (*sl*) junkie
fixieren* [fɪk·ˈsiː·rən] *vt* ① (*anstarren*) to fix one's eyes on ② PSYCH ■ **auf etw** *akk* **fixiert sein** to be fixated on sth ③ FOTO to fix ④ (*geh: festlegen*) to fix ⑤ SCHWEIZ (*befestigen*) to fix
Fixierung <-, -en> *f* ① (*Festlegung*) specification ② PSYCH (*Ausrichtung*) fixation
Fixkosten *pl* fixed costs *pl*
Fixum <-s, Fixa> [ˈfɪk·sʊm, *pl* ˈfɪk·sa] *nt* basic salary; (*Zuschuss*) fixed allowance
Fjord <-[e]s, -e> [fjɔrt] *m* fjord
FKK [ɛf·kaː·ˈkaː] *kein art Abk von* **Freikörperkultur**
FKK-Strand *m* nude beach
flach [flax] **I.** *adj* flat; (*nicht hoch*) low; (*nicht steil*) gentle **II.** *adv* ~ **abfallen** to slope down gently; ~ **atmen** to take shallow breaths
Flachbildschirm *m* flat screen [*or* panel]
Flachdach *nt* flat roof
Fläche <-, -n> [ˈflɛ·çə] *f* ① (*flache Außenseite*) surface; (*Würfelfläche*) face ② (*Gebiet*) expanse; (*mit Maßangaben*) area
Flächenausdehnung *f* surface area
flächendeckend *adj* comprehensive *pred*
Flächeninhalt *m* [surface] area
Flächenmaß *nt* [unit of] square measure
flach|fallen *vi sep irreg sein* (*fam*) to fall flat
flächig [ˈflɛ·çɪç] *adj* ① (*breit*) flat ② (*ausgedehnt*) extensive
Flachland *nt* lowland
flach|legen (*fam*) **I.** *vt* to knock out *sep* **II.** *vr* ■ **sich** *akk* ~ to lie down; (*flach hinfallen*) to fall flat [on one's face]
flach|liegen *vi irreg* (*fam*) to be laid up [in bed]
Flachmann *m* (*fam*) hip flask
Flachs <-es> [flaks] *m kein pl* ① (*Pflanze*) flax ② (*fam: Witzelei*) kidding *fam;* **ohne** ~ [all] joking aside
flackern [ˈflakɐn] *vi* to flicker
Fladenbrot *nt* KOCHK fladen bread, ≈ [thick] pita bread
Flagge <-, -n> [ˈfla·gə] *f* flag; **die amerikanische ~ führen** to fly the United States flag ▶ WENDUNGEN: ~ **zeigen** to nail one's colors to the mast
Flair <-s> [flɛːɐ̯] *nt o selten m kein pl* (*geh*) flair, aura
Flame, Flamin *o* **Flämin** <-n, -n> [ˈfla·mə, flaː·mɪn, flɛː·mɪn] *m, f* Fleming, Flemish man/woman/boy/girl
Flamingo <-s, -s> [fla·ˈmɪŋ·go] *m* flamingo
flämisch [ˈflɛ·mɪʃ] *adj* Flemish
Flamme <-, -n> [ˈfla·mə] *f* flame; **in ~n aufgehen** to go up in flames; **etw auf großer/kleiner ~ kochen** to cook sth on high/low heat
Flammenwerfer <-s, -> *m* flamethrower
Flandern <-s> [ˈflan·dɐn] *nt* Flanders + *sing vb*
Flanke <-, -n> [ˈflaŋ·kə] *f* ① ANAT flank ② (*im Fußball*) cross
flankieren* [flaŋ·ˈkiː·rən] *vt* to flank
Flasche <-, -n> [ˈfla·ʃə] *f* ① (*Behälter*) bottle; **einem Kind die ~ geben** to bottle-feed a child ② (*fam: Versager*) loser; (*einfältiger Mensch*) dork
Flaschenbier *nt* bottled beer
Flaschengärung *f* fermentation in the bottle
Flaschengestell *nt* bottle rack
Flaschenhals *m* bottleneck
Flaschenöffner *m* bottle opener
Flaschenpfand *m* bottle deposit
Flaschenpost *f* message in a bottle
Flaschenzug *m* TECH pulley
Flaschner(in) <-s, -> *m(f)* SÜDD, SCHWEIZ (*Klempner*) plumber
flattern [ˈfla·tɐn] *vi* ① *haben* (*mit den Flügeln*) to flap ② *haben* (*vom Wind bewegt*) to flutter; *lange Haare* to stream
flau [flau] *adj* ① (*leicht unwohl*) queasy ② (*träge*) *Geschäft* slack
Flaum <-[e]s> [flaum] *m kein pl* down
flauschig *adj* fleecy
Flaute <-, -n> [ˈflau·tə] *f* ① (*Windstille*) calm ② (*mangelnde Nachfrage*) lull
Flechte <-, -n> [ˈflɛç·tə] *f* BOT, MED lichen
flechten <flocht, geflochten> [ˈflɛç·tn̩] *vt Haare* to braid (**zu** + *dat* into); *Korb, Kranz* to weave (**zu** + *dat* into)
Fleck <-[e]s, -e *o* -en> [flɛk] *m* ① (*Schmutzfleck*) stain; **~en machen** to stain ② (*dunkle Stelle*) mark; **ein blauer ~** a bruise ③ (*Stelle*) spot, place; **sich** *akk* **nicht vom ~ rühren** to not move [an inch]
Fleckchen <-s, -> *nt* ① *dim von* **Fleck** mark ② (*Gegend*) **ein schönes ~ Erde** a nice little spot
fleckig [ˈflɛ·kɪç] *adj* ① (*befleckt*) marked, stained ② (*voller dunkler Stellen*) blemished; *Haut* blotchy
Fledermaus [ˈfleː·dɐ·maus] *f* bat
Fleece <-> [fliːs] *nt kein pl* fleece
Flegel <-s, -> [ˈfleː·gl̩] *m* (*pej: Lümmel*) lout
Flegeljahre *pl* awkward age
flehen [ˈfleː·ən] *vi* (*geh*) to beg (**um** + *akk* for)
Fleisch <-[e]s> [ˈflaiʃ] *nt kein pl* ① (*Nahrungsmittel*) meat; ~ **fressend** carnivorous ② (*Gewebe*) flesh ▶ WENDUNGEN: **jdm in ~ und Blut übergehen** to become sb's second nature; **sich** *dat o akk* **ins eigene ~ schneiden** to cut off one's nose to spite one's face
Fleischbrühe *f* ① (*Bouillon*) bouillon ② (*Fond*) meat stock
Fleischer(in) <-s, -> [ˈflai·ʃɐ] *m(f)* butcher

Fleischerei <-, -en> [flai·ʃə·'rai] *f* butcher shop, butcher's
fleischfarben *adj* flesh-colored
fleischig ['flai·ʃɪç] *adj* fleshy
Fleischkäse *m fine-textured pork loaf served warm*
Fleischklößchen *nt* [small] meatball
fleischlich *adj attr* **~e Genüsse** meat delicacies; **~ Begierden** (*fig*) carnal desires, desires of the flesh
Fleischpastete *f* meat vol-au-vent
Fleischwolf *m* meat grinder
Fleischwunde *f* flesh wound
Fleischwurst *f* ≈ pork sausage (*similar to bologna*)
Fleiß <-[e]s> [flais] *m kein pl* industriousness, hard work ▶WENDUNGEN: **ohne ~ kein Preis** (*prov*) success doesn't come easily
fleißig ['flai·sɪç] **I.** *adj* industrious, hard-working **II.** *adv* industriously, diligently; **~ arbeiten** to work hard
fletschen ['flɛt·ʃn̩] *vt* **die Zähne ~** to bare one's/its teeth
flexibel [flɛ'k·siː·bl̩] *adj* ① (*anpassungsfähig*) flexible ② (*elastisch*) pliable
flexibilisieren *vt* to adapt; **die Arbeitszeit ~** to introduce flexible working hours [*or* flextime]
Flexibilität <-> [flɛk·si·bi·li·'tɛːt] *f kein pl* ① (*Anpassungsfähigkeit*) flexibility ② (*Elastizität*) pliability
Flexion <-, -en> [flɛ'k·si̯oːn] *f* (*Deklinieren*) inflection; (*Konjugieren*) conjugation
flicht *imp sing und 3. pers sing pres von* **flechten**
flicken ['flɪ·kn̩] *vt* to mend; *Fahrradschlauch* to patch [up *sep*]
Flicken <-s, -> ['flɪ·kn̩] *m* patch
Flickzeug *nt kein pl* ① (*für Fahrräder*) [flat] repair kit ② (*Nähzeug*) sewing kit
Flieder <-s, -> ['fliː·dɐ] *m* lilac
Fliege <-, -n> ['fliː·gə] *f* ① (*Insekt*) fly ② MODE bow tie ▶WENDUNGEN: **die ~ machen** (*fam*) to beat it
fliegen <flog, geflogen> ['fliː·gn̩] *vi sein* ① (*durch die Luft*) to fly ② (*sl: hinausgeworfen werden*) to get kicked out ③ (*fam: fallen*) to fall
fliegend *adj attr* mobile
Fliegenfänger *m* flypaper
Fliegengewicht *nt kein pl* flyweight
Fliegengitter *nt* [window] screen
Fliegenklatsche *f* fly swatter
Fliegenpilz *m* fly agaric
Flieger <-s, -> *m* (*fam*) plane
Flieger(in) <-s, -> *m(f)* (*Pilot*) pilot
fliehen <floh, geflohen> ['fliː·ən] *vi sein* to flee; *aus dem Gefängnis* to escape
Fliehkraft *f kein pl* centrifugal force
Fliese <-, -n> [fliː·zə] *f* tile
fliesen ['fliː·zn̩] *vt* to tile
Fliesenleger(in) <-s, -> *m(f)* tiler
Fließband <-bänder> *nt* assembly line; (*Förderband*) conveyer [belt]; **am ~ arbeiten** to work on the production line
fließen <floss, geflossen> ['fliː·sn̩] *vi sein* to flow
fließend I. *adj* ① (*flüssig*) fluent ② (*übergangslos*) fluid **II.** *adv* ① (*bei Wasser*) **~ warmes und kaltes Wasser** running hot and cold water ② (*ohne zu stocken*) fluently; **~ Französisch sprechen** to speak French fluently
flimmern ['flɪ·mɐn] *vi* to flicker
flink [flɪŋk] *adj* quick
Flinte <-, -n> ['flɪn·tə] *f* shotgun ▶WENDUNGEN: **die ~ ins Korn werfen** (*fam*) to throw in the towel
Flipper <-s, -> ['flɪ·pɐ] *m* pinball machine
flippern ['flɪ·pɐn] *vi* to play pinball
flippig *adj* (*fam*) hip
Flirt <-s, -s> [fløːɐ̯t] *m* flirt[ation]
flirten ['fløɐ̯·tn̩] *vi* to flirt
Flitterwochen *pl* honeymoon *nsing*
flitzen ['flɪ·tsn̩] *vi sein* to dash
flocht ['flɔxt] *imp von* **flechten**
Flocke <-, -n> ['flɔ·kə] *f* ① (*Schneeflocke*) snowflake ② (*Staubflocke*) ball of fluff
flog ['floːk] *imp von* **fliegen**
Floh <-[e]s, Flöhe> [floː, *pl* 'fløː·ə] *m* flea ▶WENDUNGEN: **jdm einen ~ ins Ohr setzen** to put an idea into sb's head
floh ['floː] *imp von* **fliehen**
Flohmarkt *m* flea market
Flora <-, Floren> ['floː·ra, *pl* 'floː·rən] *f* flora *npl*
Florist(in) <-en, -en> [flo·'rɪst] *m(f)* florist
Floskel <-, -n> ['flɔs·kl̩] *f* set phrase
Floß <-es, Flöße> [floːs, *pl* 'fløː·sə] *nt* raft
floss^RR^, **floß**^ALT^ ['flɔs] *imp von* **fließen**
Flosse <-, -n> ['flɔ·sə] *f* ① (*Fischflosse*) fin ② (*Schwimmflosse*) flipper
Flöte <-, -n> ['fløː·tə] *f* ① (*Musikinstrument*) pipe; (*Querflöte*) flute; (*Blockflöte*) recorder ② (*Kelchglas*) flute [glass]
flöten ['fløː·tn̩] *vi, vt* ① (*Flöte spielen*) to play the flute ② (*hum fam: süß sprechen*) to warble ▶WENDUNGEN: **etw geht jdm ~** sb loses sth
Flötenspieler(in) *m(f)* piper; (*Querflötenspieler*) flute player; (*Blockflötenspieler*) recorder player
Flötist(in) <-en, -en> [flø·'tɪst] *m(f)* flutist
flott [flɔt] **I.** *adj* ① (*zügig*) quick; **aber ein bisschen ~!** (*fam*) make it snappy!; **ein ~es Tempo** [a] high speed ② (*schwungvoll*) lively ③ (*schick*) smart **II.** *adv* ① (*zügig*) fast ② (*schick*) smartly
Flotte <-, -n> ['flɔ·tə] *f* fleet
flottlmachen *vt* to get back in working order; **ein Auto ~** to get a car back on the road
Fluch <-[e]s, Flüche> [fluːx, *pl* 'flyː·çə] *m* curse
fluchen ['fluː·xn̩] *vi* to curse (**auf/über** *+akk* at)
Flucht <-, -en> [flʊxt] *f* escape (**vor** *+dat* from); ■ **die ~ in etw** *akk* refuge in sth; **die ~ ergreifen** (*geh*) to take flight; **auf der ~ sein**

to be on the run ▶WENDUNGEN: **die ~ nach vorn antreten** to take the bull by the horns
fluchtartig **I.** *adj* hasty **II.** *adv* hastily, in a hurry
flüchten ['flʏç·tn̩] **I.** *vi sein* to flee; (*aus der Gefangenschaft, einer Gefahr*) to escape **II.** *vr haben* ■ **sich** *akk* **irgendwohin** ~ to seek refuge somewhere; ■ **sich** *akk* **in etw** *akk* ~ (*fig*) to take refuge in sth; **sich** *akk* **in Ausreden** ~ to resort to excuses
Fluchtfahrzeug *nt* getaway car
flüchtig ['flʏç·tɪç] **I.** *adj* ① (*geflüchtet*) fugitive *attr;* ■ ~ **sein** to be a fugitive ② (*kurz*) fleeting, brief ③ (*oberflächlich*) cursory; **eine ~e Bekanntschaft** a passing acquaintance **II.** *adv* ① (*kurz*) briefly ② (*oberflächlich*) cursorily; **jdn ~ kennen** to have met sb briefly
Flüchtigkeit <-> *f kein pl* ① (*Kürze*) briefness ② (*Oberflächlichkeit*) cursoriness
Flüchtigkeitsfehler *m* careless mistake
Flüchtling <-s, -> ['flʏçt·lɪŋ] *m* refugee
Flüchtlingslager *nt* refugee camp
Flüchtlingsstrom *m* flood of refugees
Fluchtweg *m* escape route
Flug <-[e]s, Flüge> [fluːk, *pl* 'flyː·gə] *m* flight ▶WENDUNGEN: **wie im ~[e]** in a flash
Flugabwehr *f* air defense
Flugabwehrrakete *f* antiaircraft missile
Flugangst *f* fear of flying
Flugbahn *f* flight path; (*Kreisbahn*) orbit; *einer Kugel, Rakete* trajectory
Flugbegleiter(in) *m(f)* flight attendant, steward *masc*, stewardess *fem*
Flugblatt *nt* leaflet, flyer
Flügel <-s, -> ['flyː·gl̩] *m* ① (*zum Fliegen*) wing; (*Hubschrauberflügel*) rotor ② *einer Windmühle* sail ③ ARCHIT, POL, SPORT wing; *eines Altars* sidepiece; *eines Fensters* casement ④ (*Konzertflügel*) grand piano ▶WENDUNGEN: **die ~ hängen lassen** (*fam*) to lose heart
Flügeltür *f* double door
Fluggast *m* passenger
Fluggeschwindigkeit *f* (*von Flugzeug*) flying speed; (*von Rakete, Geschoss*) velocity; (*von Vögeln*) speed of flight
Fluggesellschaft *f* airline
Flughafen *m* airport
Flughöhe *f* altitude
Flugkapitän(in) *m(f)* captain
Flugleitung *f* air traffic control
Fluglinie *f* ① (*Strecke*) flight route ② (*Fluggesellschaft*) airline
Fluglotse, -lotsin *m, f* air traffic controller
Flugobjekt *nt* **unbekanntes ~** unidentified flying object, UFO
Flugplatz *m* airfield
Flugreise *f* flight
Flugschein *m* ① (*Pilotenschein*) pilot's license ② (*Ticket*) [plane] ticket
Flugschreiber *m* flight recorder, black box *fam*
Flugsicherheit *f kein pl* air safety
Flugstrecke *f* ① (*Distanz*) flight route ② (*Etappe*) leg ③ (*Route*) route
Flugticket *nt* [plane] ticket
Flugverbindung *f* [flight] connection
Flugverbot *nt* LUFT (*Menschen*) flying ban; (*Flugzeug*) aircraft grounding
Flugverkehr *m* air traffic
Flugwaffe *f* SCHWEIZ Swiss Air Force
Flugzeit *f* flight time
Flugzeug <-[e]s, -e> *nt* [air]plane; **mit dem ~** by [air]plane
Flugzeugabsturz *m* plane crash
Flugzeugbesatzung *f* flight crew
Flugzeugentführer(in) *m(f)* [aircraft] hijacker
Flugzeugentführung *f* [aircraft] hijacking
Flugzeughalle *f* hangar
Flugzeugträger *m* aircraft carrier
Flunder <-, -n> ['flʊn·dɐ] *f* flounder
flunkern ['flʊŋ·kɐn] *vi* (*fam*) to fib
Fluor <-s> ['fluː·oːɐ̯] *nt kein pl* fluorine
Fluorchlorkohlenwasserstoff *m* chlorofluorocarbon, CFC
Fluorkohlenwasserstoff *m* fluorocarbon
Flur[1] <-[e]s, -e> [fluːɐ̯] *m* corridor, hall[way]; (*Hausflur*) entrance hall
Flur[2] <-, -en> [fluːɐ̯] *f* ① (*Gebiet*) plot ② (*geh: freies Land*) open fields *pl* ▶WENDUNGEN: **allein auf weiter ~ sein** to be [all] alone
Fluss[RR] <-es, Flüsse>, **Fluß**[ALT] <-sses, Flüsse> [flʊs, *pl* 'flʏ·sə] *m* ① (*Wasserlauf*) river; **am ~** next to the river ② (*Verlauf*) flow; **sich** *akk* **im ~ befinden** to be in a state of flux
flussab[RR] [flʊs·'ʔap], **flussabwärts**[RR] [flʊs·'ʔap·vɛrts] *adv* downriver
flussaufwärts[RR] [flʊs·'ʔauf·vɛrts] *adv* upriver
Flussbett[RR] *nt* riverbed
Flussdiagramm[RR] *nt* flow chart
flüssig ['flʏ·sɪç] **I.** *adj* ① (*nicht fest*) liquid; *Glas, Stahl* molten; **etw ~ machen** to melt sth; **~ werden** to melt ② (*fließend*) flowing; *Verkehr* moving ③ FIN (*fam*) liquid; **[nicht] ~ sein** to [not] have a lot of money **II.** *adv* flowingly; **~ lesen** to read effortlessly; **~ sprechen** to speak fluently
Flüssiggas *nt* liquid gas
Flüssigkeit <-, -en> *f* ① (*flüssiger Stoff*) liquid, fluid ② *kein pl* (*fließende Beschaffenheit*) liquidity; *einer Rede* fluency
Flüssigseife *f* liquid soap
Flusskrebs[RR] *m* crayfish, crawfish
Flusslauf[RR] *m* course of a river
Flussmündung[RR] *f* river mouth
Flusspferd[RR] *nt* hippopotamus
Flussschifffahrt[RR] *f* river navigation
Flussufer[RR] *nt* river bank
flüstern ['flʏs·tɐn] *vi, vt* to whisper; ■ **man flüstert, dass ...** rumor has it that ...
Flüsterton *m* whisper; **im ~** in a whisper
Flut <-, -en> [fluːt] *f* ① (*angestiegener Wasserstand*) high tide; **die ~ geht zurück** the tide is going out; **es ist ~** the tide's in; **die ~ kommt** the tide is coming in; **bei ~** at high tide ② *meist pl* (*Wassermassen*) torrent ③ (*große Menge*) ■ **eine ~ von etw** *dat* a flood of sth
fluten ['fluː·tn̩] *vi, vt* to flood
Fluthilfe *f* flood relief

Flutkatastrophe *f* flood disaster
Flutlicht *nt kein pl* floodlight
flutschen ['flʊt·ʃn̩] **I.** *vi sein* (*fam: rutschen*) to slip **II.** *vi impers sein o haben* (*fam: gut verlaufen*) to go smoothly
Flutwelle *f* tidal wave
f-Moll <-s, -> ['ɛf·mɔl] *nt kein pl* MUS F flat minor
focht ['fɔxt] *imp von* **fechten**
Föderalismus <-> [fø·de·raː·'lɪs·mʊs] *m kein pl* federalism
föderalistisch [fø·de·raː·'lɪs·tɪʃ] *adj* federalist
Föderation <-, -en> [fø·de·ra·'tsi̯oːn] *f* federation
Fohlen <-s, -> ['foː·lən] *nt* foal
Föhn^RR <-[e]s, -e> [føːn] *m* ① (*Wind*) foehn [*or* föhn] [wind] ② (*Haartrockner*) hair dryer
föhnen^RR *vt* to blow-dry
Fokus <-, -se> ['foː·kʊs] *m* focus
Folge <-, -n> ['fɔl·gə] *f* ① (*Auswirkung*) consequence; **etw zur ~ haben** to result in sth; **als ~ von etw** *dat* as a consequence/result of sth ② (*Abfolge*) series; *von Bildern, Tönen a.* sequence; **in rascher ~** in quick succession ③ (*Teil einer TV-Serie*) episode ▶ WENDUNGEN: **einem Befehl ~ leisten** to comply with an order
Folgeerscheinung *f* consequence
folgen ['fɔl·gn̩] *vi* ① *sein* (*nachgehen, als Nächstes kommen*) ■ **jdm ~** to follow sb; **es folgt die Ziehung der Lottozahlen** the lotto drawing is [*or* will be] next; **wie folgt** as follows; ■ **auf etw** *akk* **~** to come after sth ② *haben* (*gehorchen*) to be obedient; *einem Befehl* to follow ③ *sein* (*verstehen*) **jdm/etw ~ können** to be able to follow sb/sth ④ *sein* (*sich richten nach*) **einer Politik ~** to pursue a policy; **einem Vorschlag ~** to act on a suggestion ⑤ *sein* (*hervorgehen*) ■ **aus etw** *dat* **~** to follow from sth; ■ **es folgt, dass ...** it follows that ...
folgend ['fɔl·gn̩t] *adj* following; ■ **F~es** the following; ■ **im F~en** in the following
folgendermaßen ['fɔl·gn̩·dɐ·'maː·sn̩] *adv* as follows
folgenlos *adj pred* without consequence
folgenschwer *adj* serious; *Entscheidung* momentous
folgerichtig *adj* logical
folgern ['fɔl·gɐn] **I.** *vt* to conclude (**aus** +*dat* from) **II.** *vi* to draw a conclusion; **vorschnell ~** to jump to conclusions
Folgerung <-, -en> *f* conclusion; **eine ~ aus etw** *dat* **ziehen** to draw a conclusion from sth
Folgeschaden *m* consequential loss
Folgezeit *f* aftermath
folglich ['fɔlk·lɪç] *adv* therefore
folgsam ['fɔlk·zaːm] *adj* obedient
Folie <-, -n> ['foː·li̯ə] *f* ① (*Plastikfolie*) [plastic] film; KOCHK plastic wrap; (*Metallfolie*) foil ② (*Projektorfolie*) transparency, slide
Folter <-, -n> ['fɔl·tɐ] *f* torture ▶ WENDUNGEN: **jdn auf die ~ spannen** to keep sb on tenterhooks
Folterkammer *f* torture chamber
foltern ['fɔl·tɐn] *vt* to torture
Folterung <-, -en> *f* torture
Fon [foːn] *nt* (*fam*) *kurz für* **Telefon** phone
Fön®, **Föhn**^RR <-[e]s, -e> [føːn] *m* hair dryer
Fonds <-, -> [fõː, *pl* fõːs] *m* FIN (*Geldreserve*) fund; (*Kapital*) funds *pl*
Fondsmanager(in) *m(f)* BÖRSE fund manager
Fondue <-s, -s> [fõ·'dyː] *nt* fondue
fönen^ALT ['føː·nən] *vt s.* **föhnen**
Fontäne <-, -n> [fɔn·'tɛː·nə] *f* fountain
Fora ['foː·ra] *pl von* **Forum**
forcieren* [fɔr·'siː·rən] *vt* (*geh*) to push ahead with; *Export, Produktion* to boost
Förderband <-bänder> *nt* conveyor belt
Förderer, Förderin <-s, -> *m, f* sponsor
Fördergelder *pl* ADMIN development funds
förderlich *adj* useful
Fördermittel *nt* means of conveyance
fordern ['fɔr·dɐn] **I.** *vt* ① (*verlangen*) to demand ② (*erfordern*) to require (**von** +*dat* of/from) ③ (*kosten*) to claim; **der Flugzeugabsturz forderte 123 Menschenleben** the plane crash claimed 123 lives ④ (*Leistung abverlangen*) ■ **jdn ~** to make demands on sb ⑤ (*herausfordern*) *zum Duell, Kampf* to challenge **II.** *vi* (*verlangen*) to make demands; ■ **[von jdm] ~, dass ...** to demand [of sb] that ...
fördern ['fœr·dɐn] *vt* ① (*unterstützen*) to support; *Karriere, Talent* to further; ■ **jdn ~** *Gönner, Förderer* to sponsor; **die Verdauung ~** to aid digestion ② (*steigern*) to promote; *Konjunktur, Umsatz* to boost ③ (*abbauen*) to mine for; *Erdöl* to drill for
fordernd I. *adj* overbearing **II.** *adv* in a domineering manner *pred*
Forderung <-, -en> *f* ① (*nachdrücklicher Wunsch*) demand; **jds ~en erfüllen** to meet sb's demands; **~en [an jdn] stellen** to make demands [on sb] ② ÖKON debt claim
Förderung <-, -en> *f* ① (*Unterstützung*) support ② (*das Fördern*) promotion ③ MED (*Anregung*) stimulation ④ BERGB mining; **die ~ von Erdöl** drilling for oil
Forelle <-, -n> [fo·'rɛ·lə] *f* trout
Foren ['fo·rən] *pl von* **Forum**
Form <-, -en> [fɔrm] *f* ① (*äußere Gestalt*) shape; **seine ~ verlieren** to lose shape ② (*Kunstform*) form ③ (*Substanz, Ausmaße*) **~ annehmen** to take shape; **in ~ von etw** *dat* in the form of sth ④ (*Art und Weise*) form; **in mündlicher/schriftlicher ~** verbally/in writing ⑤ (*fixierte Verhaltensweise*) conventions *pl;* **die ~ wahren** (*geh*) to remain polite ⑥ (*Kondition*) form, shape *fam;* **in ~ bleiben** to stay in shape; **nicht in ~ sein** to be out of shape ⑦ (*Gussform*) mold
formal [fɔr·'maːl] **I.** *adj* formal **II.** *adv* formally
Formalität <-, -en> [fɔr·ma·li·'tɛt] *f* formality
Format <-[e]s, -e> [fɔr·'maːt] *nt* ① (*Größenverhältnis*) format ② (*Niveau*) quality; **inter-**

nationales ~ international standing; **[kein] ~ haben** to have [no] class
formatieren* [fɔr·ma·ˈtiː·rən] *vt* to format
Formatierung *f* formatting
Formation <-, -en> [fɔr·ma·ˈtsi̯oːn] *f* formation
fọrmbar *adj* malleable
Formel <-, -n> [ˈfɔr·ml̩] *f* ❶ CHEM, MATH formula ❷ *in Brief, Eid* wording
formell [fɔr·ˈmɛl] **I.** *adj* official, formal **II.** *adv* officially, formally
formen [ˈfɔr·mən] *vt* ❶ (*modellieren, prägen*) to mold (**aus** *+dat* from); **wohl geformt** well formed ❷ (*bilden*) to form

Fọrmfehler *m* ❶ (*gegen Vorschriften*) irregularity ❷ (*gegen Etikette*) breach of etiquette
formieren* [fɔr·ˈmiː·rən] **I.** *vr* ■ **sich** *akk* ~ ❶ (*sich ordnen*) to form up ❷ (*sich bilden*) to form **II.** *vt* ■ **etw ~** to form sth
Formierung <-, -en> *f* formation
förmlich [ˈfœrm·lɪç] **I.** *adj Bitte, Entschuldigung* official, formal **II.** *adv* ❶ (*unpersönlich*) formally ❷ (*geradezu*) really
Förmlichkeit <-, -en> *f kein pl* formality
fọrmlos *adj* ❶ (*gestaltlos*) formless; (*die äußere Gestalt betreffend*) shapeless ❷ (*zwanglos*) informal
Fọrmsache *f* formality; **eine [reine] ~ sein** to be a [mere] formality
fọrmschön *adj* well-shaped
Formular <-s, -e> [fɔr·mu·ˈlaːɐ̯] *nt* form
formulieren* [fɔr·mu·ˈliː·rən] *vt* to formulate; **... wenn ich es mal so ~ darf ...** if I might put it that way
Formulierung <-, -en> *f* wording
fọrmvollendet **I.** *adj* perfect[ly shaped] **II.** *adv* perfectly
forsch [fɔrʃ] **I.** *adj* bold **II.** *adv* boldly
forschen [ˈfɔr·ʃn̩] *vi* to research; ■ **nach jdm/etw ~** to search for sb/sth
fọrschend **I.** *adj* inquiring **II.** *adv* inquiringly
Fọrscher(in) <-s, -> *m(f)* ❶ (*Wissenschaftler*) researcher ❷ (*Forschungsreisender*) explorer
Fọrschung <-, -en> *f* research; **~ und Lehre** research and teaching
Fọrschungsarbeit *f* ❶ (*Tätigkeit*) research [work] ❷ (*Veröffentlichung*) research paper
Fọrschungsergebnis *nt* result of the research
Fọrschungsreise *f* expedition
Fọrschungszentrum *nt* research center
Forst <-[e]s, -e[n]> [fɔrst] *m* [commercial] forest
Fọrstamt *nt* Forest Service
Förster(in) <-s, -> [ˈfœr·stɐ] *m(f)* forester
Fọrstwirtschaft *f kein pl* forestry
fort [fɔrt] *adv* ❶ (*weg*) away; **nur ~ von hier!** (*geh*) let's leave!, let's get out of here ❷ (*weiter*) **und so ~** and so on; **in einem ~** constantly
Fort <-s, -s> [foːɐ̯] *nt* fort
Fọrtbestand *m kein pl* continued existence
fọrt|bestehen* *vi irreg* to survive
fọrt|bewegen* *vt, vr* ■ **[sich** *akk*] ~ to move
Fọrtbewegung *f kein pl* movement
Fọrtbewegungsmittel *nt* means of locomotion
fọrt|bilden **I.** *vt* ■ **jdn ~** to provide sb with further training **II.** *vr* ■ **sich** *akk* ~ to further one's training [*or* education]
Fọrtbildung *f kein pl* supplementary [*or* additional] training
Fọrtbildungskurs *m*, **Fọrtbildungskursus** *m* training seminar
fọrt|bleiben *vi irreg sein* to stay away (**von** *+dat* from)
fort|bringen [ˈfɔrt·brɪŋən] *vt irreg* to take away *sep; Brief, Packet* to mail
fọrt|dauern *vi* to continue
fọrt|entwickeln* *vt, vr* to develop [further]
Fọrtentwicklung *f kein pl* development
fọrt|fahren *vi* ❶ *sein* (*wegfahren*) to drive [away/off] ❷ *sein o haben* (*weiterreden, -machen*) to continue
fọrt|führen *vt* ❶ (*fortsetzen*) to continue ❷ (*wegführen*) to lead away
Fọrtgang *m kein pl* ❶ (*weiterer Verlauf*) continuation ❷ (*Weggang*) departure
fọrt|gehen *vi sein* to go away
fọrtgeschritten *adj* advanced; **im ~en Alter** at an advanced age
Fọrtgeschrittene(r) *f(m) dekl wie adj* advanced student
Fọrtgeschrittenenkurs *m*, **Fọrtgeschrittenenkursus** *m* advanced course
fọrtgesetzt *adj* constant
fọrt|jagen *vt haben* to chase away
fọrt|kommen *vi sein* ❶ (*fam: wegkommen*) to leave, to get away (**aus/von** *+dat* from); **mach, dass du fortkommst!** (*fam*) get lost!, get out of here! ❷ (*abhandenkommen*) to go missing
Fọrtkommen *nt* progress
fọrt|können *vi irreg* to be able to go
fọrt|lassen *vt irreg* ❶ (*weggehen lassen*) ■ **jdn ~** to let sb go ❷ (*auslassen*) ■ **etw ~** to leave out *sep* sth
fọrt|laufen *vi irreg sein* to run away; **uns ist unsere Katze fortgelaufen** our cat has disappeared
fọrtlaufend **I.** *adj* (*ständig wiederholt*) continual; (*ohne Unterbrechung*) continuous **II.** *adv* (*ständig*) constantly; (*in Serie*) consecutively
fọrt|müssen *vi irreg* to have to go
fọrt|pflanzen *vr* ■ **sich** *akk* ~ to reproduce
Fọrtpflanzung *f kein pl* reproduction
fọrtpflanzungsfähig *adj* able to reproduce *pred*
Fọrtpflanzungsklinik *f* MED fertility [*or* IVF] clinic
fọrt|räumen *vt* to clear away *sep*
fọrt|reißen *vt irreg* ■ **etw mit sich** *dat* ~ to sweep away *sep* sth
fọrt|rennen *vi irreg sein* (*fam*) to run away
fọrt|schaffen *vt* to get rid of
fọrt|schicken *vt* to send away
fọrt|schreiten *vi irreg sein* to progress

Fortschritt ['fɔrt·ʃrɪt] *m* ❶ (*Schritt nach vorn*) step forward; [**gute**] **~e machen** to make progress ❷ (*Verbesserung*) improvement
fortschrittlich **I.** *adj* progressive **II.** *adv* progressively
Fortschrittlichkeit <-> *f kein pl* progressiveness
fort|setzen *vt, vi* to continue
Fortsetzung <-, -en> ['fɔrt·zɛ·tsʊŋ] *f* ❶ *kein pl* (*das Fortsetzen*) continuation ❷ *eines Buches, Films* sequel; *einer Fernsehserie, eines Hörspiels* episode; **„~ folgt"** "to be continued"
Fortsetzungsroman *m* serialized novel
fort|stehlen *vr irreg* ■ **sich** *akk* **~** to steal away *sep*
fort|tragen *vt irreg* to carry away *sep*
fort|treiben *irreg* **I.** *vt haben* ❶ (*verjagen*) to chase away ❷ (*an einen anderen Ort treiben*) to sweep away **II.** *vi sein* to drift away
fortwährend ['fɔrt·vɛː·rənt] **I.** *adj attr* constant **II.** *adv* constantly
fort|ziehen *irreg* **I.** *vt haben* to pull away **II.** *vi sein* to move [away]
Forum <-s, Foren *o* Fora> ['foː·rʊm, *pl* 'foː·rən, 'foː·ra] *nt* ❶ (*Personenkreis*) audience ❷ *pl* (*öffentliche Diskussion*) public discussion ❸ (*Ort für öffentliche Diskussion*) forum ❹ INET [discussion] forum
Fossil <-s, -ien> [fɔ·'siːl, *pl* -i̯ən] *nt* fossil
Föten ['føː·tən] *pl von* **Fötus**
Foto <-s, -s> ['foː·to] *nt* photograph, photo *fam,* picture; **ein ~** [**von jdm/etw**] **machen** to take a photo [of sb/sth]
Fotoalbum *nt* photo album
Fotoapparat *m* camera
Fotograf(in) <-en, -en> [fo·to·'graːf] *m(f)* photographer
Fotografie <-, -n> [fo·to·gra·'fiː, *pl* fo·to·gra·'fiː·ən] *f* ❶ *kein pl* (*Verfahren*) photography ❷ (*Bild*) photograph
fotografieren* [fo·to·gra·'fiː·rən] **I.** *vt* ■ **jdn/etw ~** to take a photograph [*or* picture] of sb/sth **II.** *vi* to take photographs [*or* pictures]
fotografisch [fo·to·'graː·fɪʃ] **I.** *adj* photographic **II.** *adv* photographically
Fotokopie [fo·to·ko·'piː] *f* photocopy
fotokopieren* [fo·to·ko·'piː·rən] *vt* to photocopy
Fotokopierer *m* photocopier
Fotolabor *nt* photo lab
Fotomodell ['foː·to·mo·dɛl] *nt* photo[graphic] model
Fotomontage *f* photo montage
Fötus <-[ses], Föten *o* -se> ['føː·tʊs, *pl* 'føː·tən, 'føː·tʊ·sə] *m* fetus
Foul <-s, -s> [faul] *nt* foul
foulen ['fau·lən] *vt, vi* to foul
Fr. *Abk von* **Frau** Mrs., Ms.
Fracht <-, -en> ['fraxt] *f* ❶ (*Ladung*) cargo ❷ (*Beförderungspreis*) freight, shipping
Frachter <-s, -> ['frax·tɐ] *m* freighter
Frachtgut *nt* freight
Frachtkosten *pl* shipping [costs *pl*], freight
Frachtraum *m Schiff* cargo hold; *Flugzeug* cargo compartment
Frachtschiff *nt* cargo boat; (*groß*) cargo ship, freighter
Frack <-[e]s, Fräcke *o* -s> [frak, *pl* 'frɛ·kə] *m* tails *npl;* **einen ~ tragen** to wear tails; **im ~** in tails
Frage <-, -n> ['fraː·gə] *f* ❶ (*zu beantwortende Äußerung*) question; **eine ~ zu etw** *dat* **haben** to have a question about sth; **jdm eine ~ stellen** to ask sb a question ❷ (*Problem*) question, problem, issue; **keine ~** no problem; **ohne ~** without [a] doubt; **eine strittige ~** a controversial issue; **ungelöste ~en** unresolved issues; **~en aufwerfen** to raise questions ❸ (*Betracht*) **in ~ kommen** to be worthy of consideration; **für diese Aufgabe kommt nur ein Spezialist in ~** this task requires an expert; **nicht in ~ kommen** to be out of the question
Fragebogen *m* questionnaire
fragen ['fraː·gn̩] **I.** *vi* to ask; **man wird ja wohl noch ~ dürfen** (*fam*) I was only asking; **ohne** [**lange**] **zu ~** without asking [a lot of] questions; ■ **nach jdm ~** to ask for sb; **nach der Uhrzeit ~** to ask [for] the time; **nach dem Weg ~** to ask for directions; **nach jds Gesundheit ~** to inquire about sb's health **II.** *vr* ■ **sich** *akk* **~, ob/wann/wie ...** to wonder whether/when/how ...; ■ **es fragt sich, ob ...** it is doubtful whether ... **III.** *vt* ■ [**jdn**] **etw ~** to ask [sb] sth
Fragesatz *m* LING interrogative clause
Fragestellung *f* ❶ (*Formulierung*) formulation of a question ❷ (*Problem*) problem
Fragezeichen *nt* question mark
fraglich ['fraːk·lɪç] *adj* ❶ (*fragwürdig*) suspect; **eine ~e Angelegenheit** a suspicious matter ❷ (*unsicher*) doubtful; ■ **es ist ~, ob ...** it's doubtful whether ... ❸ *attr* (*betreffend*) in question *pred;* **zur ~en Zeit** at the time in question
Fragment <-[e]s, -e> [fra·'gmɛnt] *nt* fragment
fragmentarisch [frag·mɛn·'taː·rɪʃ] **I.** *adj* fragmentary **II.** *adv* in fragments
fragwürdig ['fraːk·vʏr·dɪç] *adj* (*pej*) dubious
Fraktion <-, -en> [frak·'tsi̯oːn] *f* faction
Fraktionsvorsitzende(r) *f(m) dekl wie adj* chairman of a political party
frankieren* [fraŋ·'kiː·rən] *vt* to stamp, to put postage on; (*mit Frankiermaschine*) to meter
Frankierung <-, -en> *f* ❶ (*das Frankieren*) stamping ❷ (*Porto*) postage
Frankreich <-s> ['fraŋk·raiç] *nt* France; *s. a.* **Deutschland**
Franse <-, -n> ['fran·zə] *f* fringe
Franzose <-n, -n> [fran·'tsoː·zə] *m* adjustable wrench
Franzose, Französin <-n, -n> [fran·'tsoː·zə, fran·'tsøː·zɪn] *m, f* Frenchman *masc,* Frenchwoman *fem;* **~ sein** to be French; ■ **die ~n** the French; *s. a.* **Deutsche(r)**
französisch [fran·'tsøː·zɪʃ] *adj* French; **~es**

Bett double bed; *s. a.* **deutsch**
Französisch [fran·'tsøː·zɪʃ] *nt dekl wie adj* French; **auf ~** in French; *s. a.* **Deutsch**
fräsen ['frɛː·zn̩] *vt* to mill
Fräsmaschine *f* router
Fraß <-es, *selten* -e> [fraːs] *m* (*pej fam: schlechtes Essen*) slop
fraß ['fraːs] *imp von* **fressen**
Fratze <-, -n> ['fra·tsə] *f* ❶ (*hässliches Gesicht*) grotesque face ❷ (*Grimasse*) grimace; [**jdm**] **eine ~ schneiden** to make a face [at sb]
Frau <-, -en> [frau] *f* ❶ (*weiblicher Mensch*) woman ❷ (*Ehefrau*) wife ❸ (*Anrede*) Mrs., Ms.; **~ Doktor** Doctor; **gnädige ~** (*geh*) my dear lady
Frauenarzt, -ärztin *m, f* gynecologist
Frauenbewegung *f kein pl* women's rights movement
frauenfeindlich *adj* misogynous
Frauenhaus *nt* women's shelter
Frauenheilkunde *f* gynecology
Frauenheld *m* ladies' man
Frauenklinik *f* gynecological clinic
Fräulein <-s, - *o* -s> ['frɔy·lain] *nt* (*fam*) ❶ (*veraltend: unverheiratete Frau*) young [unmarried] woman ❷ (*veraltend: Anrede*) Miss

> Unmarried women used to be addressed as **Fräulein** (Miss). However, since the 1970s, the women's liberation movement has been campaigning against this form of address since the male equivalent *Herrlein* – literally *little man* – does not exist. Today, the normal form of address for both married and unmarried women is *Frau* (Mrs. or Ms.).

frech [frɛç] **I.** *adj* ❶ (*dreist*) brazen; **~ sein** to be rude; *Kind* to backtalk ❷ (*kess*) daring; *Frisur* sassy **II.** *adv* ❶ (*dreist*) brazenly ❷ (*kess*) daringly; **~ angezogen sein** to be provocatively dressed
Frechdachs *m* (*fam*) little rascal
Frechheit <-, -en> *f* ❶ *kein pl* (*Dreistigkeit*) impudence; (*Unverfrorenheit*) shamelessness; **die ~ haben, etw zu tun** to have the nerve to do sth ❷ (*freche Äußerung*) rude remark; (*freche Handlung*) insolent behavior
frei [frai] **I.** *adj* ❶ (*nicht gefangen, unabhängig*) free; **~e Meinungsäußerung** freedom of speech; **~e(r) Mitarbeiter(in)** freelance[r]; **aus ~en Stücken** of one's own free will ❷ (*freie Zeit*) **~ haben/nehmen** to have/take time off; **er hat heute ~** he's off today; **eine Woche ~ haben** to have a week off ❸ (*verfügbar*) available; ■**sich** *akk* [**für jdn/etw**] **~ machen** to make oneself available [for sb/sth] ❹ (*nicht besetzt*) free; *Stelle, Zimmer* vacant; **ist dieser Platz ~?** is this seat taken?; **eine Zeile ~ lassen** to skip a line ❺ (*kostenlos*) free; **„Eintritt ~"** "admission free"; **„Lieferung ~ Haus"** "free [home] delivery" ❻ (*ohne etw*) ■**~ von etw** *dat* **sein** to be free of sth ❼ (*ohne Hilfsmittel*) off-the-cuff; *Rede* impromptu ❽ (*offen*) *Gelände* open ❾ (*ungezwungen*) free and easy ❿ (*unbekleidet*) bare; **sich** *akk* **~ machen** to get undressed ⓫ (*ungefähr*) **~ nach ...** roughly quoting... **II.** *adv* ❶ (*unbeeinträchtigt*) freely; **er läuft immer noch ~ herum!** he is still on the loose!; **~ atmen** to breathe easy ❷ (*uneingeschränkt*) casually; **sich** *akk* **~ bewegen können** to be able to move [around] freely ❸ (*nach eigenem Belieben*) **~ erfunden** to be completely made up ❹ (*ohne Hilfsmittel*) **~ sprechen** to speak off the cuff; **~ in der Luft schweben** to hover in the air ❺ (*nicht gefangen*) **~ laufend** *Tiere* free-range; **~ lebend** living in the wild
Freibad *nt* outdoor swimming pool
frei|bekommen* *vt irreg* ❶ (*fam: nicht arbeiten müssen*) **einen Tag ~** to be given a day off ❷ (*befreien*) ■**jdn ~** to have sb released
Freiberufler(in) <-s, -> *m(f)* freelance[r]
freiberuflich *adj* freelance
Freibetrag *m* allowance
Freibier *nt* free beer
Freibrief *m* charter
Freie(r) *f(m) dekl wie adj* freeman
Freier <-s, -> *m* ❶ (*Kunde einer Hure*) John ❷ (*veraltet: Bewerber*) suitor
Freiexemplar *nt* free copy
frei|geben *irreg vt* ❶ (*nicht mehr zurückhalten*) to unblock; (*zur Verfügung stellen*) to make accessible ❷ (*Urlaub geben*) to give time off
frei|haben *vi irreg* to have time off; **ich habe heute frei** I have the day off today
frei|halten *vt irreg* ❶ (*nicht versperren*) to keep clear ❷ (*reservieren*) to save
Freihandelszone *f* free trade zone
freihändig ['frai·hɛn·dɪç] *adv* **~ zeichnen** to draw freehand; **~ Rad fahren** to ride a bike with no hands
Freiheit <-, -en> ['frai·hait] *f* ❶ *kein pl* (*das Nichtgefangensein*) freedom; **in ~ sein** to have escaped ❷ ([*Vor*]*recht*) liberty; **sich** *dat* **die ~ nehmen, etw zu tun** to take the liberty of doing sth; **dichterische ~** poetic license
freiheitlich *adj* liberal
Freiheitsberaubung *f* unlawful detention
Freiheitskampf *m* struggle for freedom
Freiheitsstatue *f* ■**die ~** the Statue of Liberty
Freiheitsstrafe *f* prison sentence
Freikarte *f* free [*or* complimentary] ticket
frei|kaufen I. *vt* ■**jdn ~** to pay for sb's release **II.** *vr* ■**sich** *akk* **~** to buy one's freedom; ■**sich** *akk* **von etw** *dat* **~** to buy one's way out of sth
frei|kommen *vi irreg sein* to be freed (**aus** +*dat* from)
Freikörperkultur *f kein pl* nudism
Freilandei *nt* cage-free egg
Freilandgemüse *nt* vegetables grown outdoors
frei|lassen *vt irreg* to free

Freilassung <-, -en> *f* release
freilaufend *adj s.* **frei II 5**
freilllegen *vt* to uncover
freilich ['frai·lɪç] *adv* ❶ (*allerdings*) though, however ❷ *bes* SÜDD (*natürlich*) of course
Freilichtbühne *f* open-air theater
freilmachen I. *vt* (*frankieren*) to stamp **II.** *vi* (*fam: nicht arbeiten*) to take time off
Freimaurer ['frai·mau·rɐ] *m* Freemason
freimütig ['frai·myː·tɪç] *adj* frank
Freimütigkeit <-> *f kein pl* frankness
Freiraum *m* freedom
freischaffend *adj attr* freelance
freilsetzen *vt* to release
Freisetzung <-, -en> *f* release
freilsprechen *vt irreg* JUR to acquit
Freisprechmikrofon *nt* wireless headset
Freispruch *m* acquittal; **auf ~ plädieren** to plead for an acquittal
Freistaat *m* free state
freilstehen *vi irreg* ■ **jdm steht es frei, etw zu tun** sb is free to do sth
freilstellen *vt* ❶ (*selbst entscheiden lassen*) ■ **jdm etw ~** to leave sth up to sb ❷ (*befreien*) to release; *vom Wehrdienst* to exempt ❸ (*euph: entlassen*) ■ **jdn ~** to lay sb off *sep*
Freistoß *m* free kick
Freitag <- [e]s, -e> ['frai·taːk, *pl* -taː·gə] *m* Friday; *s. a.* **Dienstag**
freitags ['frai·taːks] *adv* [on] Fridays
Freitod *m* (*euph*) suicide
Freitreppe *f* flight of stairs
freiwillig ['frai·vɪ·lɪç] **I.** *adj* voluntary **II.** *adv* voluntarily; **sich** *akk* **~ versichern** to take out a voluntary insurance policy
Freiwillige(r) ['frai·vɪ·lɪ·gə, 'frai·vɪ·lɪ·gɐ] *f(m) dekl wie adj* volunteer
Freiwilligkeit <-> *f kein pl* voluntary nature
Freizeichen *nt* dial tone
Freizeit *f* free time
Freizeitaktivitäten *pl* leisure activities *pl*
Freizeitkleidung *f* leisurewear
Freizeitpark *m* amusement park
freizügig *adj* ❶ (*großzügig*) generous ❷ (*liberal*) liberal ❸ (*offenherzig*) revealing *a. hum*
Freizügigkeit <-> *f kein pl* ❶ (*Großzügigkeit*) generosity ❷ (*lockere Einstellung*) liberalness ❸ (*Freiheit in der Wahl des Wohnortes*) freedom of movement
fremd [frɛmt] *adj* ❶ (*anderen gehörig*) somebody else's ❷ (*fremdländisch*) *Länder, Sitten* foreign; *bes* ADMIN alien ❸ (*unbekannt*) strange, unfamiliar; **ich bin hier ~** I'm not from around here
fremdartig ['frɛmt·ʔaːɐ̯·tɪç] *adj* (*ungewöhnlich*) strange; (*exotisch*) exotic
Fremdartigkeit <-> *f kein pl* (*Ungewöhnlichkeit*) strangeness; (*exotische Art*) exoticism
fremdbestimmt *adj* heteronomous
Fremdbestimmung *f* SOZIOL, POL foreign control
Fremde <-> ['frɛm·də] *f kein pl* (*geh*) ■ **die ~** foreign territory *npl;* **in der ~ sein** to be abroad
fremdenfeindlich *adj* hostile to strangers *pred,* xenophobic
Fremdenfeindlichkeit *f* hostility to strangers, xenophobia
Fremdenführer(in) *m(f)* [tour] guide
Fremdenlegion *f kein pl* [French] Foreign Legion
Fremdenverkehr *m* tourism
Fremdenverkehrsamt *nt* tourist office
fremdlgehen *vi irreg sein* (*fam*) to be unfaithful
Fremdheit <-, *selten* -en> *f* strangeness
Fremdherrschaft *f kein pl* foreign rule
Fremdkörper *m* ❶ MED foreign body ❷ (*fig*) alien element
fremdländisch ['frɛmt·lɛn·dɪʃ] *adj* foreign, exotic
Fremdsprache *f* foreign language
Fremdsprachenkorrespondent(in) *m(f)* bilingual [*or* multilingual] secretary
Fremdsprachensekretär(in) *m(f)* bilingual [*or* multilingual] secretary
fremdsprachig *adj* foreign-language *attr*
fremdsprachlich *adj* foreign-language *attr*
Fremdverschulden *nt* JUR third-party responsibility
Fremdwort *nt* borrowed word
Fremdwörterbuch *nt* dictionary of borrowed words
Frequenz [fre·'kvɛnts] *f* frequency
Fresko <-s, Fresken> ['frɛs·ko, *pl* 'frɛs·kən] *nt* fresco
Fressalien [frɛ·'saː·li̯·ən] *pl* (*fam*) grub
Fresse <-, -n> ['frɛsə] *f* (*derb*) ❶ (*Mund*) trap ❷ (*Gesicht*) mug ▶ WENDUNGEN: **die ~ halten** to shut up, to shut one's face; **jdm die ~ polieren** to smash sb's face in
fressen <fraß, gefressen> ['frɛ·sn̩] **I.** *vi* ❶ (*von Tieren*) to eat ❷ (*pej derb: von Menschen*) to gobble ❸ (*fig: langsam zerstören*) to eat away (**an** + *dat* at) **II.** *vt* ❶ *Tiere* to eat; (*sich ernähren*) to feed on; **etw leer ~** to lick sth clean ❷ (*fig: verbrauchen*) to gobble up *sep* sth ▶ WENDUNGEN: **jdn zum F~ gernhaben** (*fam*) sb is good enough to eat
Fressen <-s> ['frɛ·sn̩] *nt kein pl* ❶ (*Tierfutter*) food, feed ❷ (*pej sl: Fraß*) slop; (*Festessen*) blowout ▶ WENDUNGEN: **ein gefundenes ~ für jdn sein** (*fam*) to be handed to sb on a plate
Fresskorb[RR] *m* (*fam*) food basket
Fressnapf[RR] *m* [feeding] bowl
Frettchen <-s, -> ['frɛt·çən] *nt* ferret
Freude <-, -n> ['frɔy·də] *f* pleasure, joy, delight; **was für eine ~, dich wiederzusehen!** what a pleasure to see you again!; **~ an etw** *dat* **haben** to get pleasure from sth; **jdm eine ~ machen** to make sb happy; **etw macht jdm ~** sb enjoys sth; **zu unserer großen ~** to our great delight
Freudenfest *nt* [joyful] celebration
Freudengeschrei *nt* cries of joy
Freudenhaus *nt* brothel

Freudenmädchen *nt* (*veraltend*) prostitute
Freudentanz *m* dance of joy; **einen ~ aufführen** to dance with joy
freudestrahlend **I.** *adj nicht pred* beaming [with delight] **II.** *adv* joyfully
freudig ['frɔy·dɪç] **I.** *adj* ① (*voller Freude*) joyful ② (*erfreulich*) pleasant **II.** *adv* with joy; **~ überrascht** pleasantly surprised
freudlos ['frɔyt·loːs] *adj* cheerless
freuen ['frɔy·ən] **I.** *vr* ① (*voller Freude sein*) ■**sich** *akk* **~** to be happy (**über** +*akk* about); ■**sich** *akk* **für jdn ~** to be happy for sb; ■**sich** *akk* **mit jdm ~** to share sb's happiness ② (*freudig erwarten*) ■**sich** *akk* **auf etw** *akk* **~** to look forward to sth ▶ WENDUNGEN: **sich** *akk* **zu früh ~** to get one's hopes up too soon, to count one's chickens before they're hatched **II.** *vt impers* ■**es freut mich, dass ...** I'm pleased [*or* happy] that ...
Freund(in) <-[e]s, -e> ['frɔynt, 'frɔyn·dɪn, *pl* 'frɔyn·də] *m(f)* ① (*Kamerad*) friend ② (*intimer Bekannter*) boyfriend; (*intime Bekannte*) girlfriend; **jdn zum ~ haben** to be going [out] with sb ③ (*fig: Anhänger*) lover; **ein ~ der Natur** a nature lover
Freundeskreis *m* circle of friends; **im engsten ~** with one's closest friends
freundlich ['frɔynt·lɪç] **I.** *adj* ① (*liebenswürdig*) kind; **das ist sehr ~ von Ihnen** that's very kind of you ② (*hell, heiter*) pleasant; *Himmel* beckoning; *Ambiente* friendly; *Farben* cheerful; **bitte recht ~!** smile please! ③ (*wohlwollend*) friendly; **eine ~e Einstellung** a friendly attitude (**gegenüber** +*dat* toward) **II.** *adv* in a friendly way, kindly
freundlicherweise *adv* kindly; **er trug uns ~ die Koffer** he was kind enough to carry our suitcases
Freundlichkeit <-, -en> *f* ① *kein pl* (*Art*) friendliness ② (*Handlung*) kindness ③ *meist pl* (*Bemerkung*) kind word
Freundschaft <-, -en> *f kein pl* friendship; **~ schließen** to make friends
freundschaftlich **I.** *adj* friendly **II.** *adv* **jdm ~ auf die Schulter klopfen** to give sb a friendly slap on the back; **jdm ~ gesinnt sein** to be well-disposed toward sb
Freundschaftspreis *m* [special] price for friends
Frevel <-s, -> ['freː·fl̩] *m* (*geh*) ① (*Verstoß*) heinous crime ② REL sacrilege
Frevler(in) <-s, -> ['freːf·lɐ] *m(f)* REL (*geh*) sinner
Friede <-ns, -n> ['friː·də] *m* peace; **~ seiner Asche** God rest his soul
Frieden <-s, -> ['friː·dn̩] *m* ① (*Gegenteil von Krieg*) peace; **~ schließen** to make peace; **im ~** in peacetime ② (*Friedensschluss*) peace treaty ③ (*Harmonie*) peace, tranquillity; **ich traue dem ~ nicht** there's something fishy going on; **der häusliche ~** domestic harmony; **jdn in ~ lassen** to leave sb in peace; **~ stiften** to bring about peace
Friedensbewegung *f* peace movement
Friedenseinsatz *m* MIL peacekeeping troops [*or* forces] *pl*
Friedensmarsch *m* peace march
Friedensnobelpreis *m* Nobel peace prize
Friedenspfeife *f* peace pipe
Friedensrichter(in) *m(f)* justice of the peace
Friedenstaube *f* peace dove
Friedensverhandlungen *pl* peace negotiations
Friedensvertrag *m* peace treaty
friedfertig *adj* peaceable
Friedhof *m* graveyard; (*in Städten*) cemetery
friedlich ['friːt·lɪç] **I.** *adj* ① (*gewaltlos*) peaceful ② (*friedfertig*) peaceable; *Tier* placid ③ *Gegend* peaceful **II.** *adv* peacefully
frieren <fror, gefroren> ['friː·rən] **I.** *vi* ① *haben* (*sich kalt fühlen*) ■**jd friert** sb is freezing ② *sein* (*gefrieren*) to freeze **II.** *vi impers haben* ■**es friert** it's freezing
Friese, Friesin <-n, -n> ['friː·zə, 'friː·zɪn] *m, f* Fri[e]sian; *s. a.* **Deutsche(r)**
friesisch ['friː·zɪʃ] *adj* Fri[e]sian; *s. a.* **deutsch**
Frikadelle <-, -n> [fri·ka·'dɛ·lə] *f* hamburger
frisch [frɪʃ] **I.** *adj* ① (*noch nicht alt*) fresh ② (*neu, rein*) fresh, clean; **sich** *akk* **~ machen** to freshen up ③ *Farbe* wet ④ (*gesund*) *Hautfarbe* fresh, healthy; **~ und munter sein** (*fam*) to be [as] fresh as a daisy ⑤ (*kühl*) *Wind* fresh, cool **II.** *adv* (*gerade erst, neu*) freshly; **die Betten ~ beziehen** to change the sheets; **~ gebacken** freshly baked; **~ gestrichen** newly painted
Frische <-> ['frɪ·ʃə] *f kein pl* ① *von Backwaren, Obst, etc.* freshness ② (*Kühle*) freshness, coolness ③ (*Sauberkeit*) freshness, cleanness ④ (*Fitness*) health; **in alter ~** (*fam*) as always
Frischfleisch *nt* fresh meat
frischgebacken *adj s.* **frisch II**
Frischhaltebox *f* airtight container
Frischhaltefolie *f* plastic wrap
Frischkäse *m* cream cheese
Friseur <-s, -e> [fri·'zøːɐ̯] *m* hairdresser's; (*Herrensalon*) barbershop; **zum ~ gehen** to go to the hairdresser's/barbershop
Friseur(in) <-s, -e> [fri·'zøːɐ̯] *m(f)*, **Friseuse** <-, -n> [fri·'zøː·zə] *f* hairdresser; (*Herrenfriseur*) barber
frisieren* [fri·'ziː·rən] *vt* ① *Haare* ■**jdn ~** to do sb's hair ② (*fam: fälschen*) *Bericht, Beweis* to doctor ③ (*fam*) *Auto, Mofa* to soup up *sep*
Frisiersalon *m* hair stylist['s]; (*für Damen*) hairdresser's; (*für Herren*) barbershop
Frisör <-s, -e> [fri·'zøːɐ̯] *m*, **Frisöse** <-, -n> [fri·'zøː·zə] *f s.* **Friseur(in)**
friss[RR], **friß**[ALT] *imp sing von* **fressen**
Frist <-, -en> [frɪst] *f* ① (*Zeitspanne*) period; **festgesetzte ~** fixed time; **gesetzliche ~** statutory period; **innerhalb einer ~ von zwei Wochen** within two week deadline ② (*Aufschub*) respite; (*bei Zahlung*) extension
fristlos **I.** *adj* instant **II.** *adv* without notice; **jdn ~ entlassen** to fire sb on the spot

Frisur <-, -en> [fri·'zu:ɐ̯] *f* hairstyle
frittieren*RR, **fritieren***ALT [frɪ·'ti:·rən] *vt* to [deep-]fry
frivol [fri·'vo:l] *adj* ❶ (*anzüglich*) suggestive ❷ (*leichtfertig*) frivolous
Frl. *nt* (*veraltend*) *Abk von* **Fräulein** Miss
froh [fro:] *adj* ❶ (*erfreut*) happy; ■ ~ **sein** to be pleased (**über** +*akk* with/about); ~ **gelaunt** cheerful ❷ (*erfreulich*) pleasing; **die F~e Botschaft** the Gospel; **eine ~e Nachricht** good news ❸ (*glücklich*) **~e Feiertage!** have a nice holiday!; **~e Ostern!** Happy Easter!; **~e Weihnachten!** Merry Christmas!
fröhlich ['frø:·lɪç] **I.** *adj* ❶ (*heiter*) cheerful ❷ (*glücklich*) *s.* **froh 3 II.** *adv* cheerfully
Fröhlichkeit <-> *f kein pl* cheerfulness
fromm <frömmer *o* -er, frömmste *o* -ste> [frɔm] *adj* devout
Frömmigkeit <-> ['frœ·mɪç·kait] *f kein pl* devoutness
Fronleichnam <-[e]s> [fro:n·'laiç·na:m] *m kein pl, meist ohne art* [the Feast of] Corpus Christi
Front <-, -en> [frɔnt] *f* ❶ (*Vorderseite*) face, front, frontage ❷ MIL front; **in vorderster ~ stehen** to be on the front lines ❸ (*Opposition*) **~ gegen jdn/etw machen** to make a stand against sb/sth ▸ WENDUNGEN: **klare ~en schaffen** to clarify one's position
frontal [frɔn·'ta:l] **I.** *adj attr* frontal; *Zusammenstoß* head-on **II.** *adv* frontally; **~ zusammenstoßen** to collide head-on
Frontalzusammenstoß *m* head-on collision
Frontantrieb *m* front-wheel drive
Frontscheibe *f* AUTO windshield
fror ['fro:ɐ̯] *imp von* **frieren**
Frosch <-[e]s, Frösche> [frɔʃ, *pl* 'frœ·ʃə] *m* frog ▸ WENDUNGEN: **einen ~ im Hals haben** (*fam*) to have a frog in one's throat
Froschperspektive *f* worm's-eye view
Froschschenkel *m* frog's leg
Frost <-[e]s, Fröste> [frɔst, *pl* 'frœs·tə] *m* frost; **~ abbekommen** to get frostbitten
frösteln ['frœs·tl̩n] *vi* to shiver
frostig ['frɔs·tɪç] *adj* frosty
Frostschaden *m* frost damage
Frostschutzmittel *nt* antifreeze
Frottee <-s, -s> [frɔ·'te:] *nt o m* terrycloth
frotzeln ['frɔ·tsl̩n] *vi* (*fam*) to tease
Frucht <-, Früchte> [frʊxt, *pl* 'frʏç·tə] *f* fruit; **kandierte Früchte** candied fruit; **Früchte tragen** to bear fruit
fruchtbar ['frʊxt·ba:ɐ̯] *adj* fertile
Fruchtbarkeit <-> *f kein pl* fertility
Fruchtblase *f* ANAT amniotic sac
fruchten ['frʊx·tn̩] *vi meist verneint* ■ **nichts/wenig ~** to be of no/little use
Fruchtfleisch *nt* [fruit] pulp
fruchtig *adj* fruity
fruchtlos *adj* (*fig*) fruitless
Fruchtsaft *m* fruit juice
Fruchtwasser *nt* MED amniotic fluid
Fruchtzucker *m* fructose
früh [fry:] **I.** *adj* early; **~ am Morgen** early in the morning; **der ~e Goethe** the young Goethe; **ein ~er Picasso** an early Picasso **II.** *adv* early; **Montag ~** Monday morning; **~ genug** early [*or* soon] enough; **von ~ bis spät** from morning until night
Frühaufsteher(in) <-s, -> *m(f)* early riser
Frühdienst *m* early duty
Frühe <-> ['fry:·ə] *f kein pl* **in aller ~** at the crack of dawn; SÜDD, ÖSTERR **in der ~** early in the morning
früher ['fry:·ɐ] **I.** *adj* ❶ (*vergangen*) earlier; **in ~en Zeiten** in the past ❷ (*ehemalig*) former; *Adresse* previous; **~e Freundin** ex[-girlfriend] **II.** *adv* ❶ (*eher*) earlier; **~ geht's nicht** it can't be done any earlier; **~ oder später** sooner or later ❷ (*ehemals*) **ich habe ihn ~ [mal] gekannt** I used to know him; **~ war das alles anders** things were different in the [good] old days; **von ~** from the past
Früherkennung *f* early diagnosis
frühestens *adv* at the earliest
frühestmöglich *adj attr* earliest possible
Frühgeburt *f* ❶ (*zu frühe Geburt*) premature birth ❷ (*zu früh geborenes Kind*) premature baby
Frühjahr ['fry:·ja:ɐ̯] *nt* spring
Frühjahrsmüdigkeit *f* springtime lethargy
Frühling <-s, -e> ['fry:·lɪŋ] *m* spring[time]; **es wird ~** spring is coming
Frühlingsanfang *m* first day of spring
frühlingshaft *adj* spring-like
Frühlingsrolle *f* spring roll
frühmorgens [fry:·'mɔr·gn̩s] *adv* early in the morning
Frühnebel *m* early morning fog
Frühpensionierung *f* early retirement
frühreif *adj* precocious
Frührentner(in) *m(f) person who has retired early*
Frühschicht *f* morning shift; **~ haben** to be on the morning shift
Frühschoppen *m* eye-opener
Frühsport *m* [early] morning workout
Frühstadium *nt* early stage
Frühstart *m* SPORT false start
Frühstück <-s, -e> ['fry:·ʃtʏk] *nt* breakfast; **zum ~** for breakfast; **zweites ~** midmorning snack
frühstücken ['fry:·ʃtʏ·kn̩] **I.** *vi* to have [one's] breakfast **II.** *vt* ■ **etw ~** to have sth for breakfast
Frühstückspause *f* morning break
Frühwerk *nt kein pl eines Künstlers* early work
frühzeitig ['fry:·tsai·tɪç] **I.** *adj* early **II.** *adv* early; **möglichst ~** as soon as possible
Frust <-[e]s> [frʊst] *m kein pl* (*fam*) frustration; **einen ~ haben** to be frustrated
Frustration <-, -en> [frʊs·tra·'tsi̯o:n] *f* frustration
frustrieren* [frʊs·'tri:·rən] *vt* (*fam*) ■ **jdn frustriert etw** sth is frustrating sb
frustrierend *adj* frustrating

F

F-Schlüssel ['ɛf-] *m* MUS F clef

Fuchs, Füchsin <-es, Füchse> [fʊks, 'fʏk·sɪn, *pl* 'fʏk·sə] *m, f* ❶ (*Tier*) fox; (*weibliches Tier*) vixen ❷ (*fam: schlauer Mensch*) sly fox

Fụchsbau *m* [fox's] den

Fụchsschwanz *m* ❶ (*Schwanz des Fuchses*) [fox's] tail ❷ (*Säge*) [straight back] hand saw

fuchsteufelswild ['fʊks·'tɔy·fl̩s·'vɪlt] *adj* (*fam*) mad as hell

Fuchtel <-, -n> ['fʊx·tl̩] *f* ÖSTERR, SÜDD (*fam*) shrew; **unter jds ~ stehen** to be [well] under sb's control

fuchteln ['fʊx·tl̩n] *vi* (*fam*) ■ **mit etw** *dat* ~ to wave sth about [wildly]; (*drohend*) to brandish sth

fuffzig ['fʊf·tsɪç] (*fam*) *s.* **fünfzig**

Fuffziger <-s, -> ['fʊf·tsɪ·gɐ] *m* DIAL fifty-cent piece

Fuge <-, -n> ['fuː·gə] *f* joint; **aus den ~n geraten** (*fig*) to be turned upside down

fügen ['fyː·gn̩] **I.** *vt* ❶ (*anfügen*) to add; **Wort an Wort ~** to string words together ❷ (*geh: bewirken*) ■ **etw fügt etw** sth brings about sth **II.** *vr* ❶ (*sich unterordnen*) ■ **sich** *akk* ~ to toe the line; ■ **sich** *akk* **jdm ~** to bow to sb; **sich** *akk* **den Anordnungen ~** to obey instructions ❷ (*akzeptieren*) ■ **sich** *akk* **in etw** *akk* ~ to submit to sth ❸ ([*hinein*]*passen*) ■ **sich** *akk* **in etw** *akk* ~ to fit into sth ❹ *impers* (*geh: geschehen*) **es wird sich schon alles ~** it'll all work out in the end

fügsam ['fyːk·zaːm] *adj* (*geh*) obedient

Fü̲gung <-, -en> *f* stroke of fate; **eine ~ des Schicksals** an act of fate; **eine glückliche ~** a stroke of luck; **eine göttliche ~** divine providence

fühlbar *adj* noticeable

fühlen ['fyː·lən] **I.** *vt* to feel (**nach** +*dat* for) **II.** *vr* ❶ (*das Empfinden haben*) **wie ~ Sie sich?** how do you feel?; **sich** *akk* **besser ~** to feel better ❷ (*sich einschätzen*) ■ **sich** *akk* **als jd ~** to regard oneself as sb

Fü̲hler <-s, -> *m* ❶ (*Tastorgan*) antenna; (*von Schnecke*) horn ❷ (*Messfühler*) sensor ▶ WENDUNGEN: **die ~ [nach etw** *dat*] **ausstrecken** (*fam*) to put out [one's] feelers [for sth]

fuhr ['fuːɐ̯] *imp von* **fahren**

Fuhre <-, -n> ['fuː·rə] *f* [cart]load

führen ['fyː·rən] **I.** *vt* ❶ (*geleiten*) to take (**zu** +*dat* to, **durch** +*akk* through, **über** +*akk* across); (*vorangehen*) to lead; **was führt Sie zu mir?** (*geh*) what brings you to me?; **jdn durch ein Museum ~** to show sb around a museum ❷ (*leiten*) *Geschäft* to run; *Armee* to command; *Gruppe* to lead ❸ (*lenken*) ■ **jdn ~** to lead sb (**auf** +*akk* to); **jdn auf Abwege ~** to lead sb astray ❹ (*registriert haben*) **jdn auf einer Liste ~** to have a record of sb on a list ❺ (*handhaben*) *Bogen, Pinsel* to wield; *Kamera* to pan; **etw zum Mund**[**e**] ~ to raise sth to one's mouth ❻ (*geh*) *Titel, Namen* to bear ❼ (*geh: haben*) ■ **etw mit sich** *dat* ~ to carry sth ❽ (*im Angebot haben*) to stock **II.** *vi* ❶ (*in Führung liegen*) **mit drei Punkten ~** to lead by three points ❷ (*verlaufen*) *Weg, etc.* to lead; *Kabel* to run ❸ (*als Ergebnis haben*) ■ **zu etw** *dat* ~ to lead to sth

fü̲hrend *adj* leading *attr*

Führer <-s, -> ['fyː·rɐ] *m* (*Buch*) guide[book]

Führer(**in**) <-s, -> ['fyː·rɐ] *m(f)* ❶ (*Leiter*) leader; ■ **der ~** HIST (*Hitler*) the Führer ❷ (*Fremdenführer*) [tour] guide

Fü̲hrerhaus *nt* AUTO [driver's] cab

Fü̲hrerschein *m* driver's license; **den ~ machen** (*das Fahren lernen*) to learn to drive; (*die Fahrprüfung ablegen*) to take one's driving test

Fü̲hrerscheinentzug *m* driver's license revocation

Fu̲hrpark *m* fleet [of vehicles]

Fü̲hrung <-, -en> *f* ❶ *kein pl* (*Leitung*) leadership; MIL command ❷ *kein pl* (*die Direktion*) management ❸ (*Besichtigung*) guided tour (**durch** +*akk* of) ❹ *kein pl* (*Vorsprung*) lead; (*in einer Liga o. Tabelle*) first place; **in ~ liegen/gehen** to be in/take the lead ❺ *kein pl* (*Betragen*) conduct; **bei guter ~** for good conduct ❻ *kein pl* (*das fortlaufende Eintragen*) **die ~ der Akten** keeping the files

Fü̲hrungselite *f* POL leadership elite

Fü̲hrungsetage *f* management level

Fü̲hrungskraft *f* executive [officer]

Fü̲hrungsqualitäten *pl* leadership qualities *pl*

Fü̲hrungszeugnis *nt* **polizeiliches ~** [criminal] background check

Fu̲hrunternehmen [fuːɐ̯-] *nt* trucking company

Fu̲hrwerk [fuːɐ̯-] *nt* wagon; (*mit Pferden*) horse and cart

Fülle <-> ['fʏ·lə] *f kein pl* ❶ (*Körperfülle*) portliness ❷ (*Intensität*) richness; (*Volumen*) *Haar* volume ❸ (*Menge*) wealth; **in** [**Hülle und**] **~** in abundance

füllen ['fʏ·lən] **I.** *vt* ❶ (*vollmachen*) to fill ❷ KOCHK to stuff ❸ (*einfüllen*) ■ **etw in etw** *akk* ~ to put sth into sth; **etw in Flaschen ~** to bottle sth **II.** *vr* ■ **sich** *akk* ~ to fill [up]

Füller <-s, -> ['fʏ·lɐ] *m* fountain pen; (*mit Tintenpatrone*) cartridge pen

Fụ̈llgewicht *nt* ❶ ÖKON net weight ❷ (*Fassungsvermögen*) maximum load

Fụ̈llung <-, -en> *f* stuffing

fummeln ['fʊ·ml̩n] *vi* (*fam*) ❶ (*hantieren*) to fumble [around] ❷ (*Petting betreiben*) to pet

Fund <-[e]s, -e> [fʊnt, *pl* 'fʊn·də] *m* ❶ *kein pl* (*geh: das Entdecken*) discovery ❷ (*das Gefundene*) find

Fundament <-[e]s, -e> [fʊn·da·'mɛnt] *nt* foundation[s *npl*]; **das ~ für etw** *akk* **sein** to form a basis for sth

fundamental [fʊn·da·mɛn·'taːl] **I.** *adj* fundamental **II.** *adv* fundamentally

Fundamentalismus <-> [fʊn·da·mɛn·ta·'lɪs·mʊs] *m kein pl* fundamentalism

fundamentalịstisch *adj* fundamentalist

Fụndbüro *nt* lost-and-found [office]

fundiert *adj* sound; **gut ~** well-founded; **schlecht ~** unsound
fündig ['fʏn·dɪç] *adj* **~ werden** to discover what one is looking for
Fundsache *f* found object; (*in Fundbüro*) lost and found item; ■ **~n** lost and found items
fünf [fʏnf] *adj* five; *s. a.* **acht**[1]
Fünf <-, -en> [fʏnf] *f* ❶ (*Zahl*) five; *s. a.* **Acht**[1] ❷ (*Note: mangelhaft*) "unsatisfactory", ≈ "F"
Fünfer <-s, -> ['fʏn·fɐ] *m* SCH (*fam: Note: mangelhaft*) "unsatisfactory", ≈ "F"
fünffach, 5fach ['fʏnf·fax] **I.** *adj* fivefold; **die ~e Menge** five times the amount **II.** *adv* fivefold, five times over
fünfhundert ['fʏnf·'hʊn·dɐt] *adj* five hundred
Fünfling <-s, -e> *m* quintuplet
fünfmal, 5-mal[RR] *adv* five times; *s. a.* **achtmal**
Fünfprozenthürde *f* POL five-percent hurdle
Fünftagewoche *f* five-day week
fünftausend ['fʏnf·'tau·zn̩t] *adj* five thousand
fünfte(r, s) ['fʏnf·tə, 'fʏnf·tɐ, 'fʏnf·təs] *adj* ❶ (*an fünfter Stelle*) fifth; *s. a.* **achte(r, s) 1** ❷ (*Datum*) fifth, 5th; *s. a.* **achte(r, s) 2**
fünftel ['fʏnf·tl̩] *adj* fifth
Fünftel <-s, -> ['fʏnf·tl̩] *nt* fifth
fünftens ['fʏnf·tn̩s] *adv* fifth[ly], in [the] fifth place
Fünfunddreißigstundenwoche, 35-Stunden-Woche *f* thirty-five-hour work week
fünfzehn ['fʏnf·tseːn] *adj* fifteen; **~ Uhr** 3 p.m.; *s. a.* **acht**[1]
fünfzehnte(r, s) *adj* ❶ (*an fünfzehnter Stelle*) fifteenth; *s. a.* **achte(r, s) 1** ❷ (*Datum*) fifteenth, 15th; *s. a.* **achte(r, s) 2**
fünfzig ['fʏnf·tsɪç] *adj* fifty; *s. a.* **achtzig 1, 2**
Fünfziger <-s, -> ['fʏnf·tsɪ·gɐ] *m* (*Fünfzigcentstück*) fifty-cent piece
fünfzigste(r, s) *adj* fiftieth; *s. a.* **achte(r, s) 1**
Funk <-s> [fʊŋk] *m kein pl* radio; **etw über ~ durchgeben** to announce sth on the radio
Funkausstellung *f* radio and television exhibition
Funke <-ns, -n> ['fʊŋ·kə], **Funken** <-s, -> ['fʊŋ·kn̩] *m* ❶ (*glimmendes Teilchen*) spark; **~n sprühen** to emit sparks; **der zündende ~** (*fig*) the vital spark ❷ (*geringes Maß*) scrap; **ein ~ [von] Anstand** a shred of decency; **ein ~ Hoffnung** a gleam of hope
funkeln ['fʊŋ·kl̩n] *vi* to sparkle; *Edelsteine, Gold* to glitter
funken ['fʊŋ·kn̩] **I.** *vt* to radio; **SOS ~** to send out *sep* an SOS **II.** *vi* ❶ (*senden*) to radio ❷ (*Funken sprühen*) to spark **III.** *vi impers* (*fam*) ❶ (*verstehen*) to click; **endlich hat es [bei ihm] gefunkt!** it finally clicked [with him] ❷ (*sich verlieben*) **zwischen den beiden hat's gefunkt** those two have really clicked
Funker(in) <-s, -> *m(f)* radio operator
Funkgerät *nt* ❶ (*Sende- und Empfangsgerät*) radiotelephone unit ❷ (*Sprechfunkgerät*) walkie-talkie
Funksignal *nt* radio signal
Funkspruch *m* radio message
Funkstille *f* radio silence; **bei jdm herrscht ~** (*fig*) sb is [completely] incommunicado
Funktelefon *nt* cordless phone
Funktion <-, -en> [fʊŋk·'tsi̯oːn] *f* ❶ *kein pl* (*Zweck*) function ❷ (*Stellung*) position; **in jds ~ als etw** in sb's capacity as sth ❸ MATH function ❹ (*Benutzbarkeit*) function; **in/außer ~ sein** to [not] be working
funktional [fʊŋk·tsi̯o·'naːl] *adj s.* **funktionell**
Funktionär(in) <-s, -e> [fʊŋk·tsi̯o·'nɛːɐ̯] *m(f)* official; **ein hoher ~** a high-ranking official
funktionell [fʊŋk·tsi̯o·'nɛl] *adj* ❶ MED functional; **eine ~e Störung** a dysfunction ❷ (*funktionsgerecht*) practical
funktionieren* [fʊŋk·tsi̯o·'niː·rən] *vi* ❶ (*betrieben werden, aufgebaut sein*) to work; *Maschine a.* to operate ❷ (*reibungslos ablaufen, intakt sein*) to work [out]; *Organisation* to run smoothly
funktionsfähig *adj* in working order *pred; Anlage* operative; **voll ~** fully operative, in full working order
Funktionsweise *f* functioning
Funkverbindung *f* radio contact
Funkverkehr *m* radio communication *no art*
für [fyːɐ̯] *präp +akk* ❶ (*Zweck betreffend*) ■ **~ jdn/etw** for sb/sth; **sind Sie ~ den Gemeinsamen Markt?** do you support the Common Market?; **~ was ist denn dieses Werkzeug?** DIAL what's this tool [used] for?; **~ ganz** SCHWEIZ (*für immer*) for good, forever; **~ sich** *akk* **bleiben** to remain by oneself ❷ (*was ... angeht*) for; **~ ihr Alter ist sie noch rüstig** she's in great shape for someone her age; **~ diese Jahreszeit ist es ziemlich kalt** it's pretty cold for this time of year ❸ MED (*gegen*) for; **gut ~ Migräne** good for migraines ❹ (*zugunsten*) for, in favor of; **was Sie da sagen, hat manches ~ sich** there's something to what you're saying ❺ (*in Austausch mit*) for; **er hat es ~ 45 Euro bekommen** he got it for 45 euros ❻ (*statt*) for, instead of ❼ (*als etw*) **ich halte sie ~ intelligent** I think she is intelligent ❽ + *was* **was ~ ein Blödsinn!** what nonsense!; **was ~ ein Pilz ist das?** what kind of mushroom is that?
Für <-> [fyːɐ̯] *nt* **das ~ und Wider** the pros and cons
Fürbitte ['fyːɐ̯·bɪ·tə] *f* intercession
Furche <-, -n> ['fʊr·çə] *f* ❶ (*Ackerfurche*) furrow ❷ (*Wagenspur*) rut
Furcht <-> ['fʊrçt] *f kein pl* fear; **~ [vor jdm/etw] haben** to fear sb/sth; **hab' keine ~!** don't be afraid!; **~ erregend** terrifying
furchtbar **I.** *adj* terrible **II.** *adv* terribly
fürchten ['fʏrç·tn̩] **I.** *vt* to fear; ■ **zum F~** (*furchtbar*) frightful; ■ **~, dass ...** to be afraid that ... **II.** *vr* ■ **sich** *akk* **~** to be afraid (**vor** +*dat* of); **sich** *akk* **im Dunkeln ~** to be afraid of the dark
fürchterlich *adj s.* **furchtbar**
furchterregend *adj s.* **Furcht**
furchtlos **I.** *adj* fearless **II.** *adv* fearlessly, without fear

F

Furchtlosigkeit <-> *f kein pl* fearlessness
füreinander [fy:ɐ̯·ʔai·ˈnan·dɐ] *adv* for each other; ~ **einspringen** to help each other out
Furie <-, -n> [ˈfu:·ri̯ə] *f* ① (*pej: wütende Frau*) hellcat ② (*mythisches Wesen*) fury
Furnier <-s, -e> [fʊr·ˈni:ɐ̯] *nt* veneer
furnieren* [fʊr·ˈni:·rən] *vt* to veneer
Fürsorge [ˈfyɐ̯·zɔr·gə] *f kein pl* ① (*Betreuung*) care ② (*fam: Sozialamt*) Department of Social [*or* Human] Services *npl* ③ (*fam: Sozialhilfe*) social security *no art,* welfare; **von der ~ leben** to live on welfare
Fürsorgepflicht *f employer's obligation to provide welfare benefits*
fürsorglich [ˈfy:ɐ̯·zɔrk·lɪç] **I.** *adj* considerate (**zu** +*dat* toward) **II.** *adv* with care
Fürsorglichkeit <-> *f kein pl* care
Fürsprache [ˈfy:ɐ̯·ʃpra:·xə] *f* recommendation
Fürsprecher(in) [ˈfyɐ̯·ʃprɛ·çɐ] *m(f)* ① (*Interessenvertreter*) advocate ② JUR SCHWEIZ (*Anwalt*) attorney
Fürst(in) <-en, -en> [fʏrst] *m(f)* prince *masc,* princess *fem*
Fürstentum *nt* principality; **das ~ Monaco** the principality of Monaco
fürstlich [ˈfʏrst·lɪç] **I.** *adj* ① (*den Fürsten betreffend*) princely ② (*fig: prächtig*) lavish **II.** *adv* lavishly; ~ **speisen** to eat like a king
Furt <-, -en> [ˈfʊrt] *f* ford
Furz <-[e]s, Fürze> [fʊrts, *pl* ˈfʏr·tsə] *m* (*derb*) fart
furzen [ˈfʊr·tsn̩] *vi* (*derb*) to fart
Fusion <-, -en> [fu·ˈzi̯o:n] *f* ① ÖKON merger ② PHYS fusion
fusionieren* [fu·zi̯o·ˈni:·rən] *vi* ÖKON to merge (**zu** +*dat* into, **mit** +*dat* with)
Fuß <-es, Füße> [fu:s, *pl* ˈfy:·sə] *m* ① (*Körperteil*) foot; **gut/schlecht zu ~ sein** to be steady/not so steady on one's feet; **etw ist zu ~ zu erreichen** sth is within walking distance; **zu ~ gehen** to walk; **jdm auf die Füße treten** to step on sb's feet; (*fig: jdn beleidigen*) to step on sb's toes; **bei ~!** (*Befehl für Hunde*) heel! ② SÜDD, ÖSTERR (*Bein*) leg ③ (*Sockel*) base; (*vom Schrank, Berg*) foot ④ *kein pl* (*Längenmaß*) foot; **sie ist sechs ~ groß** she's six feet tall ► WENDUNGEN: **keinen ~ vor die Tür setzen** to not set foot outside; **auf eigenen Füßen stehen** to stand on one's own two feet; **jdn auf dem falschen ~ erwischen** to catch sb by surprise; **sich** *akk* **auf freiem ~[e] befinden** to be free; *Ausbrecher* to be at large; **auf großem ~[e] leben** to live the high life; **kalte Füße bekommen** to get cold feet; **auf wackligen Füßen stehen** to rest on shaky ground; **jdm zu Füßen fallen** to get down on one's knees in front of sb; **[festen] ~ fassen** to gain a [solid] foothold; **jdm zu Füßen liegen** to lie at sb's feet; **sich** *dat* **die Füße vertreten** to stretch one's legs
Fußball [ˈfu:s·bal] *m* ① *kein pl* (*Spiel*) soccer ② (*Ball*) soccer ball
Fußballer(in) <-s, -> [ˈfu:s·ba·lɐ] *m(f)* (*fam*) soccer player
Fußballfan *m* soccer fan
Fußballmannschaft *f* soccer team
Fußballplatz *m* soccer field
Fußballspiel *nt* soccer game
Fußballspieler(in) *m(f)* soccer player
Fußballstadion *nt* soccer stadium
Fußballverein *m* soccer club
Fußballweltmeisterschaft *f* soccer world championship[s]
Fußbank <-bänke> *f* footrest
Fußboden *m* floor
Fußbodenbelag *m* floor covering
Fußbremse *f* [foot] brake
Fussel <-s, -> [ˈfʊ·sl̩] *m* lint; **ein(e) ~** a piece of lint
fusselig [ˈfʊ·sə·lɪç] *adj* fluffy, lint-covered *attr,* full of lint *pred*
fusseln [ˈfʊ·sl̩n] *vi* to pill
Fußgänger(in) <-s, -> *m(f)* pedestrian
Fußgängerbrücke *f* footbridge
Fußgängerüberweg *m,* **Fußgängerstreifen** *m* SCHWEIZ pedestrian crossing
Fußgängerzone *f* pedestrian zone
Fußgelenk *nt* ankle
fusslig[RR], **fußlig**[ALT] [ˈfʊs·lɪç] *adj s.* **fusselig**
Fußmarsch *m* ① MIL march ② (*anstrengender Marsch*) long hike
Fußmatte *f* doormat
Fußnagel *m* toenail
Fußnote *f* LIT footnote
Fußpilz *m kein pl* athlete's foot
Fußsohle *f* sole
Fußspitze *f* toes *pl*
Fußspur *f meist pl* footprints *pl*
Fußstapfen <-s, -> *m* footprint; **in jds ~ treten** (*fig*) to follow in sb's footsteps
Fußtritt *m* kick
Fußvolk *nt kein pl* ① MIL (*veraltet*) infantry ② (*pej: bedeutungslose Masse*) ■**das ~** the rank and file
Fußweg *m* ① (*Pfad*) footpath ② (*beanspruchte Zeit zu Fuß*) **es sind nur 15 Minuten ~** it's only a 15 minute walk
Fußzeile *f* COMPUT footer
Futter[1] <-s, -> [ˈfʊ·tɐ] *nt* ([*tierische*] *Nahrung*) [animal] feed; *von Pferd, Vieh a.* fodder
Futter[2] <-s> [ˈfʊ·tɐ] *nt kein pl* (*Innenstoff*) lining
Futteral <-s, -e> [fʊ·tə·ˈra:l] *nt* case
füttern[1] [ˈfʏ·tɐn] *vt* to feed
füttern[2] [ˈfʏ·tɐn] *vt* (*mit Stofffutter versehen*) to line
futtern [ˈfʊ·tɐn] **I.** *vi* (*hum fam*) to stuff oneself **II.** *vt* (*hum fam*) ■**etw ~** to scarf sth down *sep sl*
Futternapf *m* [feeding] bowl
Fütterung <-, -en> *f* feeding
Futur <-s, -e> [fu·ˈtu:ɐ̯] *nt* LING future [tense]
Futurismus <-> [fu·tu·ˈrɪs·mʊs] *m kein pl* futurism
futuristisch [fu·tu·ˈrɪs·tɪʃ] *adj* futurist[ic]

Gg

G, **g** <-, - *o fam* -s, -s> [geː] *nt* ① (*Buchstabe*) G, g; ~ **wie Gustav** G as in Golf ② MUS G, g

g *Abk von* **Gramm** g

gab ['gaːp] *imp von* **geben**

Gabe <-, -n> ['gaː·bə] *f* ① (*geh: Geschenk*) gift; **eine milde ~** alms *pl* ② (*Begabung*) gift ③ SCHWEIZ (*Preis, Gewinn*) prize

Gabel <-, -n> ['gaː·bl̩] *f* ① (*Essensgabel*) fork ② (*Heu-, Mistgabel*) pitchfork ③ (*Radgabel*) fork ④ TELEK cradle

gabeln ['gaː·bl̩n] *vr* ■ **sich ~** *Straße, Ast* to fork

Gabelstapler <-s, -> [-ʃtaː·p·lɐ] *m* forklift

Gabelung <-, -en> ['gaː·bə·lʊŋ] *f* fork

gackern ['ga·kɐn] *vi* ① *Huhn* to cluck ② (*fig fam*) to cackle

Gag <-s, -s> [gɛk] *m* (*fam*) gag

Gage <-, -n> ['gaː·ʒə] *f* THEAT fee

gähnen ['gɛː·nən] *vi* to yawn

Gala <-, -s> ['gaː·la] *f* ① *kein pl* formal dress ② (*Vorstellung*) gala performance

galant [ga·'lant] *adj* (*veraltend*) chivalrous

Galaxie <-, -n> [ga·la·'ksiː, *pl* ga·la·'ksiː·ən] *f* galaxy

Galeere <-, -n> [ga·'leː·rə] *f* galley

Galerie <-, -n> [ga·lə·'riː, *pl* -'riː·ən] *f* ① ARCHIT gallery ② (*Gemäldegalerie*) art gallery; (*Kunsthandlung*) art dealership ③ ÖSTERR, SCHWEIZ (*Tunnel mit fensterartigen Öffnungen*) gallery

Galgen <-s, -> ['gal·gn̩] *m* gallows + *sing vb*

Galgenfrist *f* (*fam*) stay of execution

Galle <-, -n> ['ga·lə] *f* ① (*Gallenblase*) gall bladder ② (*Gallenflüssigkeit*) bile

Gallien <-s> ['ga·li̯·ən] *nt* HIST Gaul

gallisch ['ga·lɪʃ] *adj* Gallic; *s. a.* **deutsch**

Galopp <-s, -s *o* -e> [ga·'lɔp] *m* gallop

galoppieren* [ga·lɔ·'piː·rən] *vi sein o haben* to gallop

galt ['galt] *imp von* **gelten**

galvanisieren* [gal·va·ni·'ziː·rən] *vt* to galvanize

gammelig ['ga·mə·lɪç] *adj* (*pej fam*) ① (*ungenießbar*) bad ② (*unordentlich*) scruffy

gammeln ['ga·ml̩n] *vi* ① (*ungenießbar werden*) to go bad ② (*herumhängen*) to hang around

GämseRR <-, -n> ['gɛm·zə] *f* chamois

Gang[1] <-[e]s, Gänge> ['gaŋ, *pl* 'gɛŋə] *m* ① *kein pl* (*Gangart*) gait ② (*Weg*) walk; (*Besorgung*) errand ③ *kein pl* TECH **den Motor in ~ halten** to keep the engine running; (*a. fig*) **etw in ~ bringen** to get sth going; (*a. fig*) **in ~ kommen** *Mensch* to get going; *Geschäft* to get off the ground ④ (*Ablauf*) course; **alles geht wieder seinen gewohnten ~** everything is back to normal ⑤ (*in einer Speisenfolge*) course ⑥ AUTO gear; (*Fahrrad a.*) speed ⑦ (*eingefriedeter Weg*) passageway; (*Korridor*) corridor; *Theater, Flugzeug, Laden* aisle

Gang[2] <-, -s> [gɛŋ] *f* (*Bande*) gang

Gangart *f* walk; (*bei Pferden*) pace

gangbar *adj* ① (*begehbar*) passable ② (*fig*) practicable

gängig ['gɛŋɪç] *adj* ① (*üblich*) common ② (*gut verkäuflich*) in demand ③ (*im Umlauf befindlich*) current

Gangschaltung *f* gearshift

Ganove <-n, -n> [ga·'noː·və] *m* (*pej fam*) crook

Gans <-, Gänse> ['gans, *pl* 'gɛn·zə] *f* goose

Gänseblümchen *nt* daisy

Gänsefüßchen *pl* (*fam*) quotation marks *pl*

Gänsehaut *f kein pl* goose bumps *pl*

Gänsemarsch *m kein pl* **im ~** in single file

Gänserich <-s, -e> ['gɛn·zə·rɪç] *m* gander

ganz ['gants] **I.** *adj* ① (*vollständig*) all; **die ~e Wahrheit** the whole truth; **den ~en Tag** all [*or* the whole] day ② (*unbestimmtes Zahlwort*) **eine ~e Drehung** a complete turn; **eine ~e Menge** quite a lot; **eine ~e Note** a whole note ③ (*fam: unbeschädigt*) intact; **etw wieder ~ machen** to fix sth ④ (*fam: nicht mehr als*) no more than **II.** *adv* ① (*sehr, wirklich*) really; **das war ~ lieb von dir** that was really kind of you; **~ besonders** particularly ② (*ziemlich*) quite ③ (*vollkommen*) completely; **~ und gar** completely; **~ und gar nicht** not at all ④ (*räumliche Position ausdrückend*) **~ hinten/vorne** all the way in [the] back/up front

Ganze(s) *nt* ① (*alles zusammen*) whole; **im ~n** on the whole ② (*die ganze Angelegenheit*) the whole business

Ganzheit <-, *selten* -en> *f* (*Einheit*) unity; (*Vollständigkeit*) entirety

ganzheitlich **I.** *adj* integral *attr* **II.** *adv* all in all

gänzlich ['gɛnts·lɪç] **I.** *adj* (*selten*) complete **II.** *adv* completely

ganztägig **I.** *adj* all-day **II.** *adv* all day

Ganztagsschule *f* all-day school

gar[1] ['gaːɐ̯] *adj* KOCHK done

gar[2] ['gaːɐ̯] *adv* ① (*überhaupt*) at all, whatsoever; **~ keine[r]** no one at all; **hattest du denn ~ keine Angst?** weren't you even the least bit scared?; **~ nichts** nothing at all [*or* whatsoever] ② ÖSTERR, SCHWEIZ, SÜDD (*sehr*) really

Garage <-, -n> [ga·'raː·ʒə] *f* garage

Garantie <-, -n> [ga·ran·'tiː, *pl* -'tiː·ən] *f* guarantee

garantieren* [ga·ran·'tiː·rən] *vt, vi* to guarantee

Garde <-, -n> ['gar·də] *f* guard

Garderobe <-, -n> [gar·də·'roː·bə] *f* ① (*Kleiderablage*) coat rack; (*Aufbewahrungsraum*) cloakroom ② *kein pl* (*geh: Kleidung*) wardrobe ③ THEAT (*Ankleideraum*) dressing room

Gardine <-, -n> [gar·'diː·nə] *f* curtain

garen ['gaː·rən] *vt, vi* to cook

gären ['gɛː·rən] *vi sein o haben* ① (*sich in Gärung befinden*) to ferment ② (*fig*) to seethe

G

Garn <-[e]s, -e> ['garn] *nt* thread
Garnele <-, -n> [gar·'neː·lə] *f* prawn
garnieren* [gar·'niː·rən] *vt* ■**etw ~** ① KOCHK to garnish sth (**mit** *+dat* with) ② (*fig*) to embellish sth (**mit** *+dat* with)
Garnitur <-, -en> [gar·ni·'tuːɐ̯] *f* set
Garten <-s, Gärten> ['gar·tn̩, *pl* 'gɛr·tn̩] *m* garden
Gartenarbeit *f* gardening
Gartenarchitekt(in) *m(f)* landscape gardener
Gartenbau *m kein pl* horticulture
Gartenlokal *nt* open-air restaurant
Gartenzwerg *m* garden gnome
Gärtner(in) <-s, -> ['gɛrt·nɐ] *m(f)* gardener
Gärtnerei <-, -en> [gɛrt·nə·'rai] *f* nursery
Gärung <-, -en> ['gɛː·rʊŋ] *f* fermentation
Gas <-es, -e> ['gaːs, *pl* 'gaː·zə] *nt* ① (*luftförmiger Stoff*) gas ② (*fam*) **~ geben** to accelerate; (*fig*) to speed up on it
Gasflasche *f* gas canister
gasförmig *adj* gaseous
Gasheizung *f* gas heating [system]
Gasherd *m* gas stove
Gaskammer *f* HIST gas chamber
Gaskocher *m* camping stove
Gasleitung *f* gas pipe
Gasmaske *f* gas mask
Gaspedal *nt* gas [pedal], accelerator
Gasse <-, -n> ['ga·sə] *f* ① (*schmale Straße*) alley[way] ② ÖSTERR (*Straße*) street
Gast <-es, Gäste> ['gast, *pl* 'gɛs·tə] *m* ① (*eingeladene Person*) guest ② (*Besucher einer fremden Umgebung*) **~ in einer Stadt/einem Land sein** to be visiting a city/country ③ (*Besucher eines Lokals, Hotels*) customer
Gastarbeiter(in) *m(f)* guest worker

> **Gastarbeiter** are foreign workers who live and work in Germany on a temporary basis. During the economic boom of the 1950s and 1960s, workers from southern European countries and Turkey were invited to work in the FRG. Many of them have made Germany their home.

Gästebuch *nt* guest book
Gästezimmer *nt* guestroom
gastfreundlich *adj* hospitable
Gastfreundschaft *f* hospitality
Gastgeber(in) <-s, -> *m(f)* host *masc,* hostess *fem*
Gasthaus, **Gasthof** *m* inn
Gastland *nt* host country
gastlich ['gast·lɪç] (*geh*) **I.** *adj* hospitable **II.** *adv* hospitably
Gastritis <-, Gastritiden> [gas·'triː·tɪs, *pl* gas·tri·'tiː·dn̩] *f* gastritis
Gastronomie <-,-n> [gas·tro·no·'miː, *pl* -'miː·ən] *f* ① (*geh: Gaststättengewerbe*) catering trade ② (*geh: Kochkunst*) gastronomy
gastronomisch *adj* gastronomic
Gastspiel *nt* THEAT guest performance
Gaststätte *f* restaurant
Gastwirt(in) *m(f)* restaurant manager; *einer Kneipe* barkeeper
Gastwirtschaft *f s.* **Gaststätte**
Gaswerk *nt* gasworks + *sing vb*
Gaszähler *m* gas meter
Gatte, **Gattin** <-n, -n> ['ga·tə, 'ga·tɪn] *m, f* (*geh*) spouse
Gatter <-s, -> ['ga·tɐ] *nt* fence
Gattung <-, -en> ['ga·tʊŋ] *f* ① BIOL genus ② KUNST, LIT genre
GAU <-s, -s> ['gau] *m Akr von* **größter anzunehmender Unfall** MCA
Gaudi <-> ['gau·di] *f o nt kein pl* ÖSTERR, SÜDD (*fam: Spaß*) fun
Gaukler(in) <-s, -> ['gauk·lɐ] *m(f)* (*veraltet*) traveling performer
Gaul <-[e]s, Gäule> ['gaul, *pl* 'gɔy·lə] *m* (*pej*) nag
Gaumen <-s, -> ['gau·mən] *m* palate
Gauner(in) <-s, -> ['gau·nɐ] *m(f)* ① (*Betrüger*) crook ② (*Schelm*) rogue
Gaunerei <-, -en> [gau·nə·'rai] *f* cheating
Gazelle <-, -n> [ga·'tsɛ·lə] *f* gazelle
geartet [gə·'ʔaːɐ̯·tət] *adj* ① (*veranlagt*) natured ② (*beschaffen*) constituted
Geäst <-[e]s> [gə·'ʔɛst] *nt kein pl* branches *pl*
geb. *Abk von* **geboren** née, born
Gebäck <-[e]s, -e> [gə·'bɛk] *nt pl selten* (*Plätzchen*) cookies *pl;* (*Teilchen*) pastries *pl*
gebacken *pp von* **backen**
Gebälk <-[e]s, -e> [gə·'bɛlk] *nt pl selten* timberwork
geballt **I.** *adj* ① (*konzentriert*) concentrated ② (*zur Faust gemacht*) **~e Fäuste** clenched fists **II.** *adv* in clusters
gebannt *adj* fascinated; (*stärker*) spellbound
gebar [gə·'baːɐ̯] *imp von* **gebären**
Gebärde <-, -n> [gə·'bɛːɐ̯·də] *f* gesture
gebärden* [gə·'bɛːɐ̯·dn̩] *vr haben* ■**sich** *akk* ~ to behave
gebären <gebiert, gebar, geboren> [gə·'bɛː·rən] **I.** *vt* ① (*zur Welt bringen*) ■**geboren werden** to be born ② (*eine natürliche Begabung haben*) ■**zu etw** *dat* **geboren sein** to be born to sth **II.** *vi* (*ein Kind zur Welt bringen*) to give birth
Gebärmutter *f* womb
Gebäude <-s, -> [gə·'bɔy·də] *nt* ① (*Bauwerk*) building ② (*Gefüge*) structure
gebaut *adj* built; ■**gut/stark ~ sein** to be well-built
Gebein <-[e]s, -e> [gə·'bain] *nt* ■**~e** *pl* bones *pl; eines Heiligen* relics *pl*
geben <gibt, gab, gegeben> ['geː·bn̩] **I.** *vt* ① (*reichen*) ■**jdm etw** *akk* ~ to give sb sth [*or* sth to sb]; (*beim Kartenspiel*) to deal sb sth ② (*schenken*) to give [as a present] ③ (*mitteilen*) **jdm seine Telefonnummer ~** to give sb one's telephone number ④ (*verkaufen*) ■**jdm etw** *akk* ~ to get sb sth; **~ Sie mir bitte fünf Brötchen** I'd like five rolls please ⑤ (*spenden*) ■**etw gibt jdm etw** *akk* sth gives [sb] sth;

Schutz, Schatten to provide ⑥ TELEK ■**jdm jdn ~** to put sb through to sb; **~ Sie mir bitte Frau Schmidt** can I please speak to Mrs. Schmidt? ⑦ (*stellen*) **eine Aufgabe/ein Problem/ein Thema ~** to assign a task/problem/topic; **jdm etw zu tun ~** to give sb sth to do ⑧ *Pressekonferenz* to hold ⑨ (*zukommen lassen*) **jdm einen Namen ~** to name sb ⑩ (*veranstalten*) **ein Fest ~** to give a party ⑪ KOCHK to add ⑫ (*ergeben*) **7 mal 7 gibt 49** 7 times 7 equals 49; **keinen Sinn ~** to make no sense ⑬ (*äußern*) ■**etw von sich** *dat* **~** to utter sth **II.** *vi* ① KARTEN to deal ② SPORT to serve; **du gibst!** it's your serve **III.** *vt impers* ① (*gereicht werden*) **was gibt es zum Frühstück?** what's for breakfast?; **freitags gibt es bei uns immer Fisch** we always have fish on Fridays ② (*eintreten*) **heute gibt es noch Regen** it's going to rain [later] today ③ (*existieren, passieren*) **das gibt's doch nicht!** (*fam*) that's unbelievable!, I can't believe it!; **was gibt's?** (*fam*) what's up? **IV.** *vr* ① (*nachlassen*) ■**etw gibt sich** sth is letting up; (*sich erledigen*) sth sorts itself out ② (*sich benehmen, aufführen*) **sie gab sich sehr überrascht** she acted very surprised; **nach außen gab er sich heiter** outwardly, he acted cheerful

Gebet <-[e]s, -e> [gə·ˈbeːt] *nt* prayer

gebeten [gə·ˈbeː·tn̩] *pp von* **bitten**

gebiert [gə·ˈbiːɐ̯t] *3. pers sing pres von* **gebären**

Gebiet <-[e]s, -e> [gə·ˈbiːt] *nt* ① (*Fläche*) area; (*Region a.*) region; (*Staatsgebiet*) territory ② (*Fach*) field

ge|bieten* [gə·ˈbiː·tn̩] *irreg* (*geh*) **I.** *vt* ① (*befehlen*) ■**[jdm] etw** *akk* **~** to command [sb] to do sth; **Einhalt ~** to put an end to sth ② (*verlangen, erfordern*) ■**etw ~** to demand sth **II.** *vi* ① (*herrschen*) ■**über jdn/etw ~** to have control over sb/sth ② (*verfügen*) ■**über etw** *akk* **~** to have sth at one's disposal

Gebilde <-s, -> [gə·ˈbɪl·də] *nt* ① (*Ding*) thing ② (*Form*) shape; (*Struktur*) structure

gebildet *adj* educated

Gebirge <-s, -> [gə·ˈbɪr·gə] *nt* mountain range

gebirgig [gə·ˈbɪr·gɪç] *adj* mountainous

Gebiss[RR] <-es, -e>, **Gebiß**[ALT] <-sses, -sse> [gə·ˈbɪs] *nt* ① (*Zähne*) [set of] teeth ② (*Zahnprothese*) dentures *npl*

gebissen [gə·ˈbɪ·sn̩] *pp von* **beißen**

geblasen *pp von* **blasen**

geblieben [gə·ˈbliː·bn̩] *pp von* **bleiben**

gebogen [gə·ˈboː·gn̩] **I.** *pp von* **biegen II.** *adj* bent

geboren [gə·ˈboː·rən] **I.** *pp von* **gebären II.** *adj* **der ~e Koch sein** to be a born cook

geborgen [gə·ˈbɔr·gn̩] **I.** *pp von* **bergen II.** *adj* safe

Geborgenheit <-> *f kein pl* safety, security

geborsten [gə·ˈbɔr·stn̩] *pp von* **bersten**

Gebot <-[e]s, -e> [gə·ˈboːt] *nt* ① (*Gesetz*) law; (*Verordnung*) decree ② REL **die zehn ~e** the Ten Commandments ③ (*geh: Erfordernis*) requirement ④ ÖKON bid

geboten [gə·ˈboː·tn̩] **I.** ① *pp von* **gebieten** ② *pp von* **bieten II.** *adj* (*geh: notwendig*) necessary; (*angebracht*) advisable

gebracht [gə·ˈbraxt] *pp von* **bringen**

gebrannt [gə·ˈbrant] **I.** *pp von* **brennen II.** *adj* burned, burnt; **~e Mandeln** roasted almonds

gebraten *pp von* **braten**

Gebrauch <-[e]s, Gebräuche> [gə·ˈbraux, *pl* gə·ˈbrɔy·çə] *m* ① *kein pl* (*Verwendung*) use; (*Anwendung*) application ② *usu pl* **Sitten und Gebräuche** manners and customs

ge|brauchen* *vt* (*verwenden*) to use

gebräuchlich [gə·ˈbrɔyç·lɪç] *adj* ① (*allgemein üblich*) customary; (*in Gebrauch*) in use ② (*herkömmlich*) conventional

Gebrauchsanweisung *f* operating instructions *pl*, directions *pl*

gebraucht *adj* secondhand

Gebrauchtwagen *m* used car

gebrechlich [gə·ˈbrɛç·lɪç] *adj* frail

gebrochen [gə·ˈbrɔ·xn̩] **I.** *pp von* **brechen II.** *adj* (*völlig entmutigt*) broken **III.** *adv* imperfectly; **sie sprach nur ~ Deutsch** she only spoke broken German

Gebrüder [gə·ˈbryː·dɐ] *pl* (*veraltet*) brothers

Gebrüll <-[e]s> [gə·ˈbrʏl] *nt kein pl Löwe* roaring; (*pej*) *Kind* bawling; *Mensch* screaming

Gebühr <-, -en> [gə·ˈbyːɐ̯] *f* charge; (*Honorar, Beitrag*) fee

ge|bühren* [gə·ˈbyː·rən] (*geh*) **I.** *vi* (*zukommen*) ■**jdm/etw gebührt etw** *akk* sb/sth deserves sth **II.** *vr* ■**sich ~** to be fitting

gebührend I. *adj* (*zustehend*) due; (*angemessen*) appropriate **II.** *adv* appropriately

gebührenfrei *adj, adv* free [of charge]

gebührenpflichtig I. *adj* subject to a charge **II.** *adv* **jdn ~ verwarnen** to fine sb

gebunden [gə·ˈbʊn·dn̩] **I.** *pp von* **binden II.** *adj* **~es Buch** hardcover; **vertraglich ~ sein** to be bound by contract

Geburt <-, -en> [gə·ˈbuːɐ̯t] *f* birth

Geburtenkontrolle *f kein pl* birth control

Geburtenrückgang *m* decline in the birth rate

Geburtenzahl *f* birth rate

gebürtig [gə·ˈbʏr·tɪç] *adj* by birth; **er ist ~er Neu Engländer** he is a native New Englander

Geburtsdatum *nt* date of birth

Geburtshilfe *f kein pl* obstetrics

Geburtsjahr *nt* year of birth

Geburtsort *m* place of birth

Geburtstag *m* birthday; (*Geburtsdatum*) date of birth; **„herzlichen Glückwunsch zum ~"** "Happy Birthday [to you]"

Geburtstagskind *nt* (*hum*) birthday boy/girl

Geburtstermin *m* due date

Geburtsurkunde *f* birth certificate

Gebüsch <-[e]s, -e> [gə·ˈbʏʃ] *nt* bushes *pl*; (*Unterholz*) undergrowth

gedacht [gə·ˈdaxt] ① *pp von* **denken** ② *pp von* **gedenken**

G

Gedächtnis <-ses, -se> [gə·ˈdɛçt·nɪs, *pl* -nɪ·sə] *nt* memory
Gedächtnisverlust *m kein pl* memory loss
gedämpft *adj* **~er Schall/~e Stimme** muffled echo/voice
Gedanke <-ns, -n> [gə·ˈdaŋ·kə] *m* ① (*das Gedachte, Überlegung*) thought; **jdn auf andere ~n bringen** to take sb's mind off [of] sth; **sich** *dat* **über etw** *akk* **~n machen** to be worried about sth ② (*Einfall*) idea
Gedankenaustausch *m* exchange of ideas
gedankenlos **I.** *adj* thoughtless **II.** *adv* thoughtlessly
Gedankenstrich *m* dash
gedanklich [gə·ˈdaŋk·lɪç] *adj* intellectual
Gedärm <-[e]s, -e> [gə·ˈdɛrm] *nt*, **Gedärme** <-s, -> [gə·ˈdɛr·mə] *nt* (*selten*) entrails *pl old liter*
Gedeck <-[e]s, -e> [gə·ˈdɛk] *nt* place setting
gedeckt **I.** *pp von* **decken** **II.** *adj* muted
ge|deihen <gedieh, gediehen> [gə·ˈdai·ən] *vi sein* ① (*sich gut entwickeln*) to flourish ② (*vorankommen*) to make headway
ge|denken* *vi irreg* (*geh*) ① (*ehrend zurückdenken*) ■ **jds/einer S. ~** to remember sb/sth ② (*beabsichtigen*) ■ **~, etw zu tun** to intend to do sth
Gedenken <-s> [gə·ˈdɛŋ·kn̩] *nt kein pl* memory
Gedenkfeier *f* commemoration
Gedenkminute *f* moment of silence
Gedenkstätte *f* memorial
Gedenktag *m* day of remembrance
Gedicht <-[e]s, -e> [gə·ˈdɪçt] *nt* poem
gediegen [gə·ˈdiː·gn̩] *adj* ① (*rein*) pure ② (*solide gearbeitet*) high quality ③ (*geschmackvoll*) tasteful ④ (*gründlich*) **~e Kenntnisse haben** to have sound knowledge
gedieh [gə·ˈdiː] *imp von* **gedeihen**
gediehen [gə·ˈdiː·ən] *pp von* **gedeihen**
Gedränge <-s> [gə·ˈdrɛŋə] *nt kein pl* ① (*drängende Menschenmenge*) crowd ② (*das Drängen*) jostling
gedroschen [gə·ˈdrɔ·ʃn̩] *pp von* **dreschen**
gedrungen [gə·ˈdrʊŋən] **I.** *pp von* **dringen** **II.** *adj* stocky
Geduld <-> [gə·ˈdʊlt] *f kein pl* patience
ge|dulden* *vr* ■ **sich** *akk* **~** to be patient
geduldig [gə·ˈdʊl·dɪç] *adj* patient
gedurft [gə·ˈdʊrft] *pp von* **dürfen**
geehrt *adj* honored; **sehr ~e Damen, sehr ~e Herren!** ladies and gentlemen!; (*Anrede in Briefen*) **sehr ~e Damen und Herren!** Dear Sir or Madam
geeignet [gə·ˈʔaig·nət] *adj* suitable
Gefahr <-, -en> [gə·ˈfaːɐ̯] *f* danger; **jdn in ~ bringen** to endanger sb; **auf eigene ~** at one's own risk
ge|fährden* [gə·ˈfɛːɐ̯·dn̩] *vt* ■ **sich/jdn/etw ~** to endanger oneself/sb/sth; **den Erfolg einer S.** *gen* **~** to jeopardize the success of sth
Gefährdung <-, -en> *f* threat
gefahren *pp von* **fahren**

gefährlich [gə·ˈfɛːɐ̯·lɪç] **I.** *adj* dangerous; (*risikoreich*) risky **II.** *adv* dangerously
gefahrlos [gə·ˈfaːɐ̯·loːs] *adj* safe
Gefährte, Gefährtin <-n, -n> [gə·ˈfɛːɐ̯·tə, gə·ˈfɛːɐ̯·tɪn] *m, f* (*geh*) companion
Gefälle <-s, -> [gə·ˈfɛ·lə] *nt* ① (*Neigungsgrad*) gradient; (*Land*) slope; (*Fluss*) drop ② (*fig: Unterschied*) difference
ge|fallen <gefiel, gefallen> **I.** *vi* ■ **etw gefällt jdm** sth pleases sb, sb likes sth **II.** *vr* (*fam*) ■ **sich** *dat* **etw ~ lassen** to put up with sth
Gefallen[1] <-s, -> *m* favor; **jdn um einen ~ bitten** to ask sb for a favor; **jdm einen ~ tun** to do sb a favor
Gefallen[2] <-s> *nt kein pl* (*geh*) pleasure
Gefallene(r) *f(m)* soldier killed in action
gefällig [gə·ˈfɛ·lɪç] *adj* ① (*hilfsbereit*) helpful ② (*ansprechend*) pleasant ③ (*a. iron form: gewünscht*) **Kaffee ~?** would you care for [some] coffee? *form*
Gefälligkeit <-, -en> *f* ① (*Gefallen*) favor ② *kein pl* (*Hilfsbereitschaft*) helpfulness
gefangen [gə·ˈfaŋən] **I.** *pp von* **fangen** **II.** *adj* ① (*in Gefangenschaft*) **jdn ~ halten** to hold sb captive; **jdn ~ nehmen** MIL to take sb prisoner; (*verhaften*) to arrest sb ② (*beeindruckt*) **jdn ~ halten** to captivate sb
Gefangene(r) *f(m)* captive; (*im Gefängnis*) prisoner; (*im Krieg*) prisoner of war
gefangen|halten[ALT] *vt irreg s.* **gefangen II 2**
Gefangennahme <-, -n> *f* ① MIL capture ② (*Verhaftung*) arrest
gefangen|nehmen[ALT] *vt irreg s.* **gefangen II 1**
Gefangenschaft <-, *selten* -en> *f* captivity
Gefängnis <-ses, -se> [gə·ˈfɛŋ·nɪs, *pl* -nɪ·sə] *nt* ① (*Haftanstalt*) prison, jail; **ins ~ kommen** to be sent to prison ② *kein pl* (*Haftstrafe*) imprisonment
Gefängnisstrafe *f* prison sentence
Gefäß <-es, -e> [gə·ˈfɛːs] *nt* ① (*Behälter*) container ② (*Ader*) vessel
gefasst[RR], **gefaßt**[ALT] **I.** *adj* ① (*beherrscht*) composed ② (*eingestellt*) ■ **auf etw** *akk* **~ sein** to be prepared for sth **II.** *adv* calmly
Gefecht <-[e]s, -e> [gə·ˈfɛçt] *nt* (*a. fig*) battle
Gefieder <-s, -> [gə·ˈfiː·dɐ] *nt* plumage
Geflecht <-[e]s, -e> [gə·ˈflɛçt] *nt* ① (*Flechtwerk*) wickerwork ② (*Gewirr*) tangle
geflochten [gə·ˈflɔx·tn̩] *pp von* **flechten**
geflogen [gə·ˈfloː·gn̩] *pp von* **fliegen**
geflohen [gə·ˈfloː·ən] *pp von* **fliehen**
geflossen [gə·ˈflɔ·sn̩] *pp von* **fließen**
Geflügel <-s> [gə·ˈflyː·gl̩] *nt kein pl* poultry
geflügelt [gə·ˈflyː·gl̩t] *adj* winged
Geflüster <-s> [gə·ˈflʏs·tɐ] *nt kein pl* whispering
gefochten [gə·ˈfɔx·tn̩] *pp von* **fechten**
Gefolge <-s, -> [gə·ˈfɔl·gə] *nt* retinue
Gefolgschaft <-, -en> *f* ① (*Anhängerschaft*) following ② HIST retinue ③ *kein pl* (*veraltend: Treue*) allegiance (**gegenüber** *+dat* to)
gefragt *adj* in demand *pred*

gefräßig [gə·ˈfrɛː·sɪç] *adj* ❶ (*fressgierig*) voracious ❷ (*pej: unersättlich*) greedy
gefressen [gə·ˈfrɛ·sn̩] *pp von* **fressen**
ge|frieren* *vi irreg sein* to freeze
Gefrierfach *nt* freezer [compartment]
Gefrierpunkt *m* freezing point
gefroren [gə·ˈfroː·rən] *pp von* **frieren, gefrieren**
gefügig [gə·ˈfyː·gɪç] *adj* compliant
Gefühl <-[e]s, -e> [gə·ˈfyːl] *nt* ❶ (*Sinneswahrnehmung*) feeling ❷ (*seelische Empfindung, Instinkt*) feeling ❸ (*Sinn*) sense; **ein ~ für etw** *akk* [**haben**] [to have] a feeling for sth
gefühllos I. *adj* ❶ (*ohne Sinneswahrnehmung*) numb ❷ (*herzlos*) insensitive II. *adv* insensitively
Gefühlsausbruch *m* emotional outburst
gefühlsbetont *adj* emotional
gefühlskalt *adj* cold
gefühlsmäßig *adv* instinctively
gefühlvoll I. *adj* (*empfindsam*) sensitive II. *adv* with feeling
gefunden [gə·ˈfʊn·dn̩] *pp von* **finden**
gegangen [gə·ˈgaŋən] *pp von* **gehen**
gegeben [gə·ˈgeː·bn̩] I. *pp von* **geben** II. *adj* ❶ (*vorhanden*) given ❷ (*geeignet*) right
gegebenenfalls [gə·ˈgeː·bə·nən·ˈfals] *adv* if necessary
Gegebenheit <-, -en> *f meist pl* fact
gegen [ˈgeː·gn̩] I. *präp +akk* ❶ (*wider*) against; **etwas ~ eine Erkältung** sth for a cold ❷ (*ablehnend*) ■ **~ jdn/etw sein** to be against sb/sth ❸ (*entgegen*) contrary to ❹ JUR, SPORT versus ❺ (*an*) against ❻ (*gegenüber*) toward, to ❼ (*für*) for; **~ Kaution/Quittung** with a deposit/receipt ❽ (*verglichen mit*) compared with ❾ (*ungefähr*) **~ Morgen/Abend** toward morning/evening II. *adv* **er kommt ~ drei Uhr an** he's arriving around three o'clock
Gegenangriff *m* counterattack
Gegenargument *nt* counterargument
Gegenbeispiel *nt* counterexample
Gegend <-, -en> [ˈgeː·gn̩t, *pl* ˈgeː·gn̩·dən] *f* ❶ (*Gebiet*) region; **durch die ~ fahren/laufen** (*fam*) to drive/walk around ❷ (*Wohngegend*) neighborhood ❸ (*Nähe*) area
Gegendarstellung *f* ❶ MEDIA reply ❷ (*gegensätzliche Darstellung*) the other side of the story
gegeneinander [geː·gn̩·ʔai·ˈnan·dɐ] *adv* against each other
gegeneinander|halten *vt irreg* ■ **etw ~** to hold up side by side
gegeneinander|prallen *vi sein* to collide
Gegengift *nt* antidote
Gegenleistung *f* **eine/keine ~ erwarten** to expect something/nothing in return
Gegenmaßnahme *f* countermeasure
Gegenmittel *nt* (*gegen Gift*) antidote; (*gegen Krankheit*) remedy
Gegenrichtung *f* opposite direction
Gegensatz *m* ❶ (*Gegenteil*) opposite; **im ~ zu jdm/etw** unlike sb/sth ❷ *pl* differences; **unüberbrückbare Gegensätze** irreconcilable differences
gegensätzlich [ˈgeː·gn̩·zɛts·lɪç] I. *adj* conflicting; *Menschen, Temperamente* different II. *adv* differently
Gegensätzlichkeit <-, -en> *f* difference[s *pl*]
Gegenseite *f* other side
gegenseitig [ˈgeː·gn̩·zai·tɪç] I. *adj* mutual II. *adv* mutually
Gegenseitigkeit <-> *f kein pl* mutuality
Gegenspieler(in) *m(f)* opponent
Gegenstand <-[e]s, Gegenstände> *m* ❶ (*Ding*) object ❷ (*Thema*) subject
gegenständlich [ˈgeː·gn̩·ʃtɛnt·lɪç] KUNST I. *adj* representational II. *adv* representationally
gegenstandslos *adj* ❶ (*unbegründet*) unfounded ❷ (*hinfällig*) invalid
Gegenteil [ˈgeː·gn̩·tail] *nt* opposite
gegenteilig [ˈgeː·gn̩·tai·lɪç] I. *adj* opposite II. *adv* to the contrary
gegenüber [geː·gn̩·ˈʔyː·bɐ] I. *präp +dat* ❶ (*örtlich*) ■ **jdm/einer S. ~** opposite sb/sth ❷ (*in Bezug auf*) ■ **jdm/einer S. ~** toward sb/sth ❸ (*vor*) ■ **jdm ~** in front of sb ❹ (*im Vergleich zu*) ■ **jdm ~** in comparison with sb II. *adv* opposite
Gegenüber <-s, -> [geː·gn̩·ˈʔyː·bɐ] *nt* ❶ (*Mensch*) person on the opposite side; (*beim Sport*) opponent ❷ (*Terrain*) land on the opposite side
gegenüberliegend *adj attr* opposite
gegenüber|stehen *irreg* I. *vi* ❶ (*zugewandt stehen*) ■ **jdm ~** to stand opposite sb ❷ (*eingestellt sein*) ■ **jdm/einer S. [...] ~** to have a [...] attitude toward sb/sth II. *vr* ■ **sich** *dat* **als etw ~** to face each other as sth
gegenüber|stellen *vt* ❶ (*konfrontieren*) ■ **jdm jdn ~** to confront sb with sb ❷ (*vergleichen*) ■ **einer S.** *dat* **etw ~** to compare sth with sth
Gegenüberstellung *f* ❶ (*Konfrontation*) confrontation ❷ (*Vergleich*) comparison
Gegenverkehr *m* oncoming traffic
Gegenwart <-> [ˈgeː·gn̩·vart] *f kein pl* ❶ (*jetziger Augenblick*) present ❷ (*heutiges Zeitalter*) present [day]; **die Literatur/Musik der ~** contemporary literature/music ❸ LING present [tense] ❹ (*Anwesenheit*) presence
gegenwärtig [ˈgeː·gn̩·vɛr·tɪç] I. *adj* ❶ *attr* (*derzeitig*) present ❷ (*heutig*) present[-day] II. *adv* currently
Gegenwert *m* equivalent; **im ~ von etw** *dat* in the value of sth
Gegenwind *m* headwind
Gegenzug *m* counter[move]
gegessen [gə·ˈgɛ·sn̩] *pp von* **essen**
geglichen [gə·ˈglɪ·çn̩] *pp von* **gleichen**
geglitten [gə·ˈglɪ·tn̩] *pp von* **gleiten**
geglommen [gə·ˈglɔ·mən] *pp von* **glimmen**
Gegner(in) <-s, -> [ˈgeːg·nɐ] *m(f)* ❶ (*Feind*) enemy ❷ (*Gegenspieler*) *a.* SPORT opponent
gegnerisch *adj attr* opposing

G

G

Gegnerschaft <-, -en> *f* opposition
gegolten [gə·ˈgɔl·tn̩] *pp von* **gelten**
gegoren [gə·ˈgoː·rən] *pp von* **gären**
gegossen [gə·ˈgɔ·sn̩] *pp von* **gießen**
gegraben *pp von* **graben**
gegriffen [gə·ˈgrɪ·fn̩] *pp von* **greifen**
Gehackte(s) *nt* ground meat
Gehalt¹ <-[e]s, Gehälter> [gə·ˈhalt, *pl* gə·ˈhɛl·tɐ] *nt o* ÖSTERR *m* salary
Gehalt² <-[e]s, -e> [gə·ˈhalt] *m* ❶ (*Anteil*) content ❷ (*geistiger Wert*) meaning
gehalten *pp von* **halten**
gehaltlos *adj* ❶ (*nährstoffarm*) without nutritional value ❷ (*oberflächlich*) insubstantial
Gehaltserhöhung *f* pay raise
gehaltvoll *adj* ❶ (*nahrhaft*) nutritious, nourishing ❷ (*gedankliche Tiefe aufweisend*) stimulating
gehangen [gə·ˈhaŋən] *pp von* **hängen**
gehässig [gə·ˈhɛ·sɪç] **I.** *adj* spiteful **II.** *adv* spitefully
Gehässigkeit <-, -en> *f* ❶ *kein pl* (*Boshaftigkeit*) spite[fulness] ❷ (*gehässige Bemerkung*) spiteful remark
gehauen *pp von* **hauen**
gehäuft **I.** *adj* ❶ (*hoch gefüllt*) heaped ❷ (*wiederholt*) repeated **II.** *adv* in large numbers
Gehäuse <-s, -> [gə·ˈhɔy·zə] *nt* ❶ (*Schale*) casing; (*Kamera a.*) body ❷ (*Schneckengehäuse*) shell ❸ (*Kerngehäuse*) core
gehbehindert *adj* **leicht/stark ~ sein** to have a slight/severe mobility handicap
Gehege <-s, -> [gə·ˈheː·gə] *nt* enclosure, cage
geheim [gə·ˈhaim] **I.** *adj* secret **II.** *adv* secretly; **etw [vor jdm] ~ halten** to keep sth secret [from sb]
Geheimagent(in) *m(f)* secret agent
Geheimdienst *m* secret service
geheim|haltenALT *vt irreg s.* **geheim II**
Geheimnis <-ses, -se> [gə·ˈhaim·nɪs, *pl* -nɪ·sə] *nt* secret
geheimnisvoll **I.** *adj* mysterious **II.** *adv* mysteriously
Geheimnummer *f* ❶ TELEK unlisted number ❷ (*Geheimzahl*) PIN
GeheimtippRR *m* inside tip
Geheimzahl *f* FIN PIN
geheißen *pp von* **heißen**
gehemmt **I.** *adj* inhibited **II.** *adv* **sich** *akk* **~ benehmen** to act self-conscious
gehen <ging, gegangen> [ˈgeː·ən] **I.** *vi sein* ❶ (*sich fortbewegen*) to go; (*zu Fuß*) to walk ❷ (*besuchen*) ■ **zu jdm ~** to go [and] visit sb; **in die Kirche/Schule/ins Theater ~** to go to church/school/the theater ❸ (*weggehen*) to go; (*abfahren a.*) to leave; **ich muss jetzt ~** I have to go; **wann geht der Zug nach Hamburg?** when does the train to Hamburg leave? ❹ (*führen*) to go; **die Brücke geht über den Fluss** the bridge crosses the river; **wohin geht dieser Weg?** where does this path lead [to]? ❺ (*funktionieren*) to work; **meine Uhr geht nicht mehr** my watch [has] stopped ❻ (*gelingen*) **versuch's einfach, es geht ganz leicht** just try it — it's really easy; **kannst du mir bitte erklären, wie das Spiel geht?** can you please explain how the game goes? ❼ ÖKON **das Geschäft geht vor Weihnachten immer gut** business is always good before Christmas ❽ (*hineinpassen*) **es ~ über 450 Besucher in das neue Theater** the new theater holds over 450 people; **wie viele Leute ~ in deinen Wagen?** how many people [can] fit in your car? ❾ (*dauern*) **dieser Film geht drei Stunden** this movie lasts three hours ❿ (*reichen*) **der Rock geht ihr bis zum Knie** the skirt goes down to her knee; **in die Tausende ~** to run into the thousands ⓫ KOCHK *Teig* to rise ⓬ (*verkleidet sein*) ■ **als etw ~** to go as sth ⓭ (*möglich sein*) **haben Sie am nächsten Mittwoch Zeit? – nein, das geht [bei mir] nicht** are you free next Wednesday? — no, that's no good [for me]; **ich muss mal telefonieren – geht das?** I have to make a phone call — would that be alright? ⓮ (*beeinträchtigen*) **zu viel Alkohol geht auf die Leber** too much alcohol is bad for your liver; **das geht [mir] ganz schön an die Nerven** that really wears on my nerves ⓯ (*gerichtet sein*) ■ **an jdn ~** to be addressed to sb ⓰ (*fam: liiert sein*) ■ **mit jdm ~** to be going out with sb ⓱ (*überschreiten*) **zu weit ~** to go too far ⓲ (*fam: akzeptabel sein*) **er geht gerade noch, aber seine Frau ist furchtbar** he's not that bad, but his wife is awful; **wie ist das Hotel? – es geht [so]** how's the hotel? — it's ok ▶ WENDUNGEN: **es geht nichts über jdn/etw** *akk* there's nothing like sb/sth; **[ach] geh, ...!** (*fam*) [oh] come on, ...!; ÖSTERR, SÜDD **geh, was du nicht sagst!** come on, you're kidding! **II.** *vi impers sein* ❶ + *adv* (*sich befinden*) **wie geht es Ihnen? – danke, mir geht es gut!** how are you? — fine, thank you!; **nachher ging es ihr wieder besser** afterwards she felt better again ❷ + *adv* (*verlaufen*) **wie war denn die Prüfung? – ach, es ging ganz gut** how was the exam? — oh, it went quite well ❸ (*sich handeln um*) **worum geht es in diesem Film?** what is this movie about? ❹ (*wichtig sein*) **worum geht es dir eigentlich?** what are you trying to say?; **es geht mir ums Prinzip** it's a matter of principle ❺ (*ergehen*) **mir ist es ähnlich/genauso/nicht anders gegangen** it was the same/just the same/no different with me; **lass es dir/lasst es euch gut ~!** take care of yourself/yourselves! ❻ (*sich machen lassen*) **ich werde arbeiten, solange es geht** I will continue working as long as possible; **geht es, oder soll ich dir tragen helfen?** can you manage, or should I help you carry it/them? ❼ (*nach jds Kopf gehen*) **wenn es nach mir ginge** if it were up to me ▶ WENDUNGEN: **geht's noch!?** SCHWEIZ (*iron*) are you crazy?! **III.** *vt sein* **ich gehe immer diese Straße/diesen Weg** I always take this road/walk this way **IV.** *vr haben*

❶ *impers* **in diesen Schuhen geht es sich bequem** these shoes are very comfortable for walking ❷ (*sich nicht beherrschen*) **sich** *akk* **~ lassen** to lose one's self-control; (*nachlässig sein*) to let oneself go

gehen|lassen* *vr irreg s.* **gehen IV 2**

geheuer [gə·ˈhɔy·ɐ] *adj* [**jdm**] **nicht** [**ganz**] **~ sein** to seem [a bit] suspicious [to sb]

Gehilfe, Gehilfin <-n, -n> [gə·ˈhɪl·fə, gə·ˈhɪl·fɪn] *m, f* assistant

Gehirn <-[e]s, -e> [gə·ˈhɪrn] *nt* brain

Gehirnerschütterung *f* concussion

Gehirnschlag *m* stroke

gehoben [gə·ˈhoː·bn̩] **I.** *pp von* **heben II.** *adj* ❶ LING formal ❷ *Stimmung* festive

geholfen [gə·ˈhɔl·fn̩] *pp von* **helfen**

Gehör <-[e]s, *selten* -e> [gə·ˈhøːɐ̯] *nt* hearing; **sich** *dat* **~ verschaffen** to make oneself heard

gehorchen* *vi* ❶ (*gefügig sein*) to obey ❷ (*reagieren*) ■ **jdm ~** to respond to sb

ge|hören* **I.** *vi* ❶ (*jds Eigentum sein*) ■ **jdm ~** to belong to sb; **ihm ~ mehrere Häuser** he owns several houses ❷ (*jdm zugewandt sein*) ■ **jdm/einer S. ~** to belong to sb/sth; **ihre ganze Liebe gehört ihrem Sohn** she gives all her love to her son ❸ (*den richtigen Platz haben*) **die Kinder ~ ins Bett** the children belong in bed ❹ (*angebracht sein*) **nicht zum Thema ~** to be beside the point, irrelevant ❺ (*Mitglied sein*) ■ **zu jdm/einer S. ~** to belong to sb/sth; **zur Familie ~** to be one of the family ❻ (*Teil sein von*) ■ **zu etw** *dat* **~** to be [a] part of sth ❼ (*Voraussetzung, nötig sein*) to require; **es gehört viel Mut dazu, ...** it takes a lot of courage to ... **II.** *vr* ■ **sich ~** to be fitting; **wie es sich gehört** as it should be; **sich** [**einfach/eben**] **nicht ~** to be [simply/just] not good manners

gehörig [gə·ˈhøː·rɪç] **I.** *adj* ❶ *attr* (*fam: beträchtlich*) good *attr;* **eine ~e Achtung vor jdm haben** to have a healthy respect for sb ❷ *attr* (*entsprechend*) proper ❸ (*geh: gehörend*) ■ **zu etw** *dat* **~** belonging to sth; **nicht zur Sache ~ sein** to not be relevant **II.** *adv* (*fam*) **jdn ~ ausschimpfen** to really tell sb off

Gehörlose(**r**) *f(m)* (*geh*) deaf person

gehorsam [gə·ˈhoːɐ̯·zaːm] **I.** *adj* obedient **II.** *adv* obediently

Gehorsam <-s> [gə·ˈhoːɐ̯·zaːm] *m kein pl* obedience

Gehsteig *m s.* **Bürgersteig**

Gehweg *m* ❶ *s.* **Bürgersteig** ❷ (*Fußweg*) walk

Geier <-s, -> [ˈgai·ɐ] *m* vulture

Geige <-, -n> [ˈgai·gə] *f* violin, fiddle *fam*

geigen [ˈgai·gn̩] **I.** *vi* to play the violin **II.** *vt* ■ **etw ~** to play sth on the violin

Geiger(**in**) <-s, -> [ˈgai·gɐ] *m(f)* violinist

geil [ˈgail] **I.** *adj* ❶ (*lüstern*) lecherous; ■ **~ auf jdn sein** to have the hots for sb ❷ (*sl: toll*) cool, awesome **II.** *adv* ❶ (*lüstern*) lecherously ❷ (*sl*) cool

Geisel <-, -n> [ˈgai·zl̩] *f* hostage

Geiselnehmer(**in**) <-s, -> *m(f)* kidnapper, abductor

Geiß <-, -en> [ˈgais] *f* SÜDD, ÖSTERR, SCHWEIZ [nanny] goat

Geißbock *m* SÜDD, ÖSTERR, SCHWEIZ billy goat

geißeln [ˈgai·sl̩n] *vt* ❶ (*mit der Geißel schlagen*) ■ **jdn/sich ~** to flagellate sb/oneself ❷ (*anprangern*) ■ **etw ~** to castigate sth

Geist <-[e]s, -er> [ˈgaist] *m* ❶ *kein pl* (*Vernunft*) mind ❷ *kein pl* (*Esprit*) wit ❸ *kein pl* (*Wesen, Sinn, Gesinnung*) spirit ❹ (*körperloses Wesen*) ghost; **böse/gute ~er** evil/good spirits; **der Heilige ~** the Holy Ghost ▶ WENDUNGEN: **von allen guten ~ern verlassen sein** (*fam*) to have taken leave of one's senses; **den ~ aufgeben** (*fig fam*) to give up the ghost

geisterhaft I. *adj* ghostly **II.** *adv* eerily

Geisterhand *f* ▶ WENDUNGEN: **wie von ~** as if by magic

geistern [ˈgais·tɐn] *vi sein* ■ **durch etw** *akk* **~** ❶ (*herumgehen*) to wander around sth like a ghost ❷ (*spuken*) to haunt sth

geistesabwesend I. *adj* absent-minded **II.** *adv* absent-mindedly

Geistesgegenwart *f* presence of mind

geistesgegenwärtig I. *adj* quick-witted **II.** *adv* with great presence of mind

geistesgestört *adj* mentally disturbed

Geisteskrankheit *f* mental illness

Geisteswissenschaften *pl* humanities

Geisteswissenschaftler(**in**) *m(f)* ❶ (*Wissenschaftler*) humanities scholar ❷ (*Student*) humanities student

geistig [ˈgais·tɪç] **I.** *adj* ❶ (*verstandesmäßig*) mental ❷ (*spirituell*) spiritual **II.** *adv* mentally

geistlich [ˈgaist·lɪç] **I.** *adj* ❶ (*religiös*) religious ❷ (*kirchlich*) ecclesiastical; *Amt* religious **II.** *adv* spiritually

Geistliche(**r**) *f(m)* clergyman *masc,* clergywoman *fem*

geistlos *adj* ❶ (*dumm*) witless ❷ (*einfallslos*) inane

geistreich *adj Mensch* witty

Geiz <-es> [ˈgaits] *m kein pl* stinginess

geizen [ˈgai·tsn̩] *vi* ■ **mit etw** *dat* **~** ❶ (*knauserig sein*) to be stingy with sth ❷ (*zurückhaltend sein*) to be sparing with sth

Geizhals *m* cheapskate

geizig [ˈgai·tsɪç] *adj* stingy, cheap *fam*

Gejammer <-s> [gə·ˈja·mɐ] *nt kein pl* (*pej fam*) whining

gekannt [gə·ˈkant] *pp von* **kennen**

Geklimper <-s> [gə·ˈklɪm·pɐ] *nt kein pl* (*pej fam*) ❶ (*auf dem Klavier*) plunking ❷ (*mit Saiteninstrument*) twanging

geklommen [gə·ˈklɔ·mən] *pp von* **klimmen**

geklungen [gə·ˈklʊŋən] *pp von* **klingen**

geknickt *adj* (*fam*) glum

gekniffen [gə·ˈknɪ·fn̩] *pp von* **kneifen**

gekommen *pp von* **kommen**

gekonnt [gə·ˈkɔnt] **I.** *pp von* **können II.** *adj* accomplished

Gekritzel <-s> [gə·ˈkrɪtsl̩] *nt kein pl* (*pej*) scrawl

gekrochen [gə·ˈkrɔ·xn̩] *pp von* **kriechen**
gekünstelt *adj* (*pej*) artificial; **~es Lächeln** forced smile; *Sprache, Benehmen* affected
Gel <-s, -e> [ˈgeːl] *nt* gel
Gelächter <-s, *selten* -> [gə·ˈlɛç·tɐ] *nt* laughter
geladen **I.** *pp von* **laden** **II.** *adj* (*fam*) ■ **~ sein** to be furious
gelähmt **I.** *pp von* **lähmen** **II.** *adj* paralyzed
Gelände <-s, -> [gə·ˈlɛn·də] *nt* ① (*Land*) terrain ② (*bestimmtes Stück Land*) site
Geländer <-s, -> [gə·ˈlɛn·dɐ] *nt* handrail; (*Treppengeländer*) banister
Geländewagen *m* all-terrain vehicle, ATV
gelang [gə·ˈlaŋ] *imp von* **gelingen**
ge|langen* *vi sein* ① (*hinkommen*) **ans Ziel ~** to reach one's destination ② (*erwerben*) ■ **zu etw** *dat* **~** to achieve sth; *Ruhm, Reichtum* to gain ③ SCHWEIZ ■ **an jdn ~** to turn to sb (**mit** +*dat* about)
gelangweilt *adj, adv* bored
gelassen [gə·ˈla·sn̩] **I.** *pp von* **lassen** **II.** *adj* calm **III.** *adv* calmly
Gelassenheit <-> *f kein pl* calmness
Gelatine <-> [ʒe·la·ˈtiː·nə] *f kein pl* gelatin[e]
gelaufen *pp von* **laufen**
geläufig [gə·ˈlɔy·fɪç] *adj* familiar
gelaunt [gə·ˈlaunt] *adj pred* ■ **gut/schlecht ~ sein** to be in a good/bad mood
gelb [ˈgɛlp] *adj* yellow
Gelb <-s, - *o* -s> [ˈgɛlp] *nt* yellow
Geld <-[e]s, -er> [ˈgɛlt, *pl* ˈgɛl·dɐ] *nt kein pl* (*Zahlungsmittel*) money; **bares ~** cash ▶ WENDUNGEN: **jdm das ~ aus der Tasche ziehen** to squeeze money out of sb
Geldanlage *f* [financial] investment
Geldautomat *m* automated teller machine, ATM
Geldbetrag *m* sum
Geldbeutel *m* SÜDD, **Geldbörse** *f* ÖSTERR (*sonst geh: Portmonee*) wallet
Geldbuße *f* fine
Geldgeber(in) <-s, -> *m(f)* [financial] backer
Geldinstitut *nt* financial institution
Geldschein *m* bill
Geldschrank *m* safe
Geldstrafe *f* fine
Geldwechsel *m* foreign exchange
Gelee <-s, -s> [ʒe·ˈleː, ʒə·ˈleː] *m o nt* jelly
gelegen [gə·ˈleː·gn̩] **I.** *pp von* **liegen** **II.** *adj* (*passend*) convenient; **jdm ~ kommen** to come at the right time for sb
Gelegenheit <-, -en> [gə·ˈleː·gn̩·hait] *f* ① (*günstiger Moment*) opportunity ② (*Anlass*) occasion
Gelegenheitsarbeit *f* casual labor
Gelegenheitsarbeiter(in) *m(f)* casual laborer
gelegentlich [gə·ˈleː·gn̩t·lɪç] **I.** *adj attr* occasional **II.** *adv* ① (*manchmal*) occasionally ② (*bei Gelegenheit*) **wenn Sie ~ in der Nachbarschaft sind ...** if you happen to be in the neighborhood ...
gelehrig [gə·ˈleː·rɪç] **I.** *adj* quick to learn **II.** *adv* **sich** *akk* **~ anstellen** to be quick to learn
gelehrt *adj* ① (*gebildet*) learned ② (*wissenschaftlich*) scholarly
ge|leiten* *vt* (*geh*) to escort
Geleitschutz *m* escort; **jdm/einer S. ~ geben** to escort sb/sth
Gelenk <-[e]s, -e> [gə·ˈlɛŋk] *nt* ANAT, TECH joint
Gelenkentzündung *f* arthritis
gelenkig [gə·ˈlɛŋ·kɪç] *adj* supple
gelernt *adj* skilled *attr;* (*qualifiziert*) trained *attr*
gelesen *pp von* **lesen**
Geliebte(r) *f(m)* lover
geliehen [gə·ˈliː·ən] *pp von* **leihen**
ge|lingen <gelang, gelungen> [gə·ˈlɪŋən] *vi sein* ■ **jdm gelingt es, etw zu tun** sb manages to do sth; ■ **jdm gelingt es nicht, etw zu tun** sb fails to do sth
gelitten [gə·ˈlɪ·tn̩] *pp von* **leiden**
gell [ˈgɛl], **gelle** [ˈgɛl(ə)] *interj* SÜDD, SCHWEIZ right?
ge|loben* *vt* (*geh*) ■ **[jdm] etw ~** to vow sth [to sb]
Gelöbnis <-ses, -se> [gə·ˈløː·p·nɪs, *pl* -nɪ·sə] *nt* (*geh*) vow
gelogen [gə·ˈloː·gn̩] *pp von* **lügen**
gelöst *adj* relaxed
gelten <gilt, galt, gegolten> [ˈgɛl·tn̩] **I.** *vi* ① (*gültig sein*) ■ **[für jdn] ~** *Regelung* to be valid [for sb]; *Bestimmungen* to apply [to sb]; *Gesetz* to be in force ② (*bestimmt sein für*) ■ **jdm/einer S. ~** to be meant for sb/sth; *Buhrufe* to be aimed at sb/sth; *Frage* to be directed at sb ③ (*gehalten werden*) ■ **als etw ~** to be regarded as sth ▶ WENDUNGEN: **etw ~ lassen** to accept sth **II.** *vi impers* (*geh*) ■ **es gilt, etw zu tun** it is necessary to do sth; **das gilt nicht!** that's not allowed!
geltend *adj attr* (*gültig*) current; (*vorherrschend*) prevailing; **Ansprüche/Forderungen ~ machen** to make claims/demands
Geltung <-> *f kein pl* ① (*Gültigkeit*) validity ② (*Ansehen*) prestige; **etw zur ~ bringen** to show off *sep* sth to its advantage
Gelübde <-s, -> [gə·ˈlʏp·də] *nt* (*geh*) vow
gelungen [gə·ˈlʊŋən] **I.** *pp von* **gelingen** **II.** *adj attr* successful
gemächlich [gə·ˈmɛːç·lɪç] **I.** *adj* leisurely; *Leben* quiet **II.** *adv* leisurely
Gemälde <-s, -> [gə·ˈmɛːl·də] *nt* painting
gemäß [gə·ˈmɛːs] **I.** *präp* +*dat* in accordance with; **~ § 198** according to § 198 **II.** *adj* ■ **jdm/einer S. ~** appropriate for sb/sth
gemäßigt *adj* ① METEO temperate ② (*moderat*) moderate
gemein [gə·ˈmain] **I.** *adj* ① (*niederträchtig*) mean; (*böse*) nasty ② *attr, kein komp/superl* BOT, ZOOL common ③ *pred* (*geh: gemeinsam*) **etw mit jdm/etw ~ haben** to have sth in common with sb/sth **II.** *adv* (*fam*) horribly
Gemeinde <-, -n> [gə·ˈmain·də] *f* ① (*Kommune*) community; (*politische Einheit*) mu-

nicipality ② (*Pfarrgemeinde*) parish; (*Gläubige a.*) parishioners *pl*
Gemeindehaus *nt* REL parish house
Gemeinderat[1] *m* town council
Gemeinderat, -rätin[2] *m, f* (*Gemeinderatsmitglied*) councilman *masc,* councilwoman *fem*
Gemeindeverwaltung *f* town council
gemeingefährlich *adj* constituting a public danger *pred*
Gemeinheit <-, -en> *f* ① *kein pl* (*Niedertracht*) meanness ② (*niederträchtiges Handeln*) **so eine ~!** that was a mean thing to do/say!; (*Bemerkung*) mean remark
gemeinhin *adv* generally
gemeinnützig [gə·ˈmain·nʏ·tsɪç] *adj* charitable
gemeinsam [gə·ˈmain·zaːm] **I.** *adj* ① (*mehreren gehörend*) common; *Konto* joint; *Freund* mutual ② (*von mehreren unternommen*) joint *attr;* **etw ~ haben** to have sth in common **II.** *adv* jointly
Gemeinsamkeit <-, -en> *f* common ground
Gemeinschaft <-, -en> *f* ① POL community; **die Europäische ~** the European Community ② *kein pl* (*gegenseitige Verbundenheit*) sense of community
gemeinschaftlich *adj s.* **gemeinsam**
Gemeinschaftsarbeit *f* teamwork
Gemeinschaftspraxis *f* joint practice
Gemeinschaftsproduktion *f* ① *kein pl* joint production ② MEDIA, FILM co-production *spec*
Gemeinschaftssinn *m kein pl* community spirit
Gemeinwohl *nt* ■ **das ~** the public welfare
Gemenge <-s, -> [gə·ˈmɛŋə] *nt* ① (*Mischung*) mixture (**aus** *+dat* of) ② (*Gewühl*) crowd ③ (*Durcheinander*) jumble
gemessen [gə·ˈmɛ·sn̩] **I.** *pp von* **messen** **II.** *adj* (*geh*) proper; (*würdig langsam*) measured
Gemetzel <-s, -> [gə·ˈmɛ·tsl̩] *nt* bloodbath
gemieden [gə·ˈmiː·dn̩] *pp von* **meiden**
Gemisch <-[e]s, -e> [gə·ˈmɪʃ] *nt* mixture (**aus** *+dat* of)
gemischt *adj* mixed
gemocht [gə·ˈmɔxt] *pp von* **mögen**
gemolken [gə·ˈmɔl·kn̩] *pp von* **melken**
Gemse[ALT] <-, -n> *f s.* **Gämse**
Gemurmel <-s> [gə·ˈmʊr·ml̩] *nt kein pl* murmuring
Gemüse <-s, *selten* -> [gə·ˈmyː·zə] *nt* vegetables *pl;* ■ **ein ~** a vegetable
Gemüsehändler(in) *m(f)* produce market
Gemüseschäler *m* vegetable peeler
gemusst[RR], **gemußt**[ALT] [gə·ˈmʊst] *pp von* **müssen**
gemustert *adj* patterned
Gemüt <-[e]s, -er> [gə·ˈmyːt] *nt* ① (*Mensch, Seele*) soul ② (*Emotionen*) feelings *pl*
gemütlich I. *adj* ① (*bequem*) cozy, comfy *fam;* **es sich/jdm** *dat* **~ machen** to make oneself/sb comfortable ② (*gesellig*) pleasant; (*ungezwungen*) informal **II.** *adv* ① (*gemächlich*) leisurely ② (*behaglich*) comfortably
Gemütlichkeit <-> *f kein pl* coziness; (*Ungezwungenheit*) informality
Gemütsbewegung *f* [signs *pl* of] emotion
gemütskrank *adj* emotionally disturbed
Gemütsmensch *m* (*fam*) good-natured person
Gemütsruhe *f* calmness; **in aller ~** (*fam*) at one's own pace
Gemütsverfassung *f,* **Gemütszustand** *m* mood
Gen <-s, -e> [ˈgeːn] *nt* gene
genannt [gə·ˈnant] *pp von* **nennen**
genas [gə·ˈnaːs] *imp von* **genesen**
genau [gə·ˈnau] **I.** *adj* ① (*exakt*) exact; **man weiß noch nichts G~es** nobody knows any details yet ② (*gewissenhaft*) meticulous **II.** *adv* exactly; **~ in der Mitte** right in the middle; **~ genommen** strictly speaking
genaugenommen *adv s.* **genau II**
Genauigkeit <-> [gə·ˈnau·ɪç·kait] *f kein pl* exactness; *Daten* accuracy; (*Sorgfalt*) meticulousness
genauso [gə·ˈnau·zoː] *adv* just the same; **~ gut/viel/wenig** just as well/much/little
Gendarm <-en, -en> [ʒan·ˈdarm, ʒã·ˈdarm] *m* ÖSTERR (*Polizist*) policeman
Gendarmerie <-, -n> [ʒan·dar·mə·ˈriː, ʒã·dar·mə·ˈriː, *pl* -ˈriː·ən] *f* ÖSTERR (*Polizeistation*) police station
Gendefekt *m* BIOL, MED genetic defect
genehm [gə·ˈneːm] *adj* (*geh*) acceptable; ■ **jdm [nicht] ~ sein** to [not] be agreeable to sb
ge|nehmigen* [gə·ˈneː·mɪ·gn̩] **I.** *vt* ■ **[jdm] etw ~** to grant [sb] permission to do sth **II.** *vr* ■ **sich** *dat* **etw ~** to indulge in sth
Genehmigung <-, -en> *f* ① (*das Genehmigen*) approval ② (*Berechtigungsschein*) permit
geneigt *adj* (*geh*) ■ **~ sein, etw zu tun** to be inclined to do sth
Genera [ˈgɛ·ne·ra] *pl von* **Genus**
General(in) <-[e]s, -e *o* Generäle> [ge·nə·ˈraːl, *pl* ge·nə·ˈrɛː·lə] *m(f)* general
Generaldirektor(in) *m(f)* general manager
Generalprobe *f* THEAT dress rehearsal; MUS final rehearsal
Generalsekretär(in) *m(f)* secretary general
Generalstreik *m* general strike
Generaluntersuchung *f* complete checkup
Generation <-, -en> [ge·nə·ra·ˈtsi̯oːn] *f* generation
Generationskonflikt *m* generation gap
Generationswechsel *m* ① SOZIOL generation change ② BIOL alternation of generations
Generator <-s, -toren> [ge·nə·ˈraː·toːɐ̯, *pl* -ˈtoː·rən] *m* generator
generell [ge·nə·ˈrɛl] **I.** *adj* general **II.** *adv* generally
genervt [gə·ˈnɛrft] *adj* annoyed; (*stärker*) at the end of one's rope
ge|nesen <genas, genesen> [gə·ˈneː·zn̩] *vi sein* (*geh*) to recover (**von** *+dat* from)
Genesung <-, *selten* -en> [gə·ˈneː·zʊŋ] *f*

(*geh*) convalescence
Genetik <-> [ge·ˈneː·tɪk] *f kein pl* genetics + *sing vb*
genetisch [ge·ˈneː·tɪʃ] *adj* genetic
Genforscher(in) *m(f)* genetic researcher
Genforschung *f* genetic research
genial [ge·ˈni̯aːl] *adj* ❶ (*überragend*) brilliant; (*erfinderisch*) ingenious ❷ *Idee* inspired
Genialität <-> [ge·ni̯a·li·ˈtɛːt] *f kein pl* ❶ (*überragende Art*) genius ❷ (*Erfindungsreichtum*) ingenuity
Genick <-[e]s, -e> [gə·ˈnɪk] *nt* neck ▶ WENDUNGEN: **jdm das ~ brechen** (*fig*) to finish [off *sep*] sb
Genie <-s, -s> [ʒe·ˈniː] *nt* genius
genieren* [ʒe·ˈniː·rən] *vr* ■ **sich** *akk* ~ to be embarrassed
genießbar *adj* (*essbar*) edible; (*trinkbar*) drinkable
ge|nießen <genoss, genossen> [gə·ˈniː·sn̩] *vt* ■ **etw** ~ ❶ (*auskosten*) to enjoy sth; (*bewusst kosten*) to savor sth ❷ (*essen*) to eat sth
Genießer(in) <-s, -> *m(f)* gourmet
genießerisch **I.** *adj* appreciative **II.** *adv* with pleasure
genital [ge·ni·ˈtaːl] *adj* genital
Genitalbereich *m* genital area
Genitalien [ge·ni·ˈtaː·li̯·ən] *pl* genitals *npl*
Genitiv <-s, -e> [ˈgeː·ni·tiːf, *pl* ˈgeː·ni·tiː·və] *m* genitive [case]
Genmanipulation *f* gene[tic] manipulation
genommen [gə·ˈnɔ·mən] *pp von* **nehmen**
genormt *adj* standardized
genoss[RR], **genoß**[ALT] [gə·ˈnɔs] *imp von* **genießen**
Genosse, Genossin <-n, -n> [gə·ˈnɔ·sə, gə·ˈnɔ·sɪn] *m, f* comrade
genossen [gə·ˈnɔ·sn̩] *pp von* **genießen**
Genossenschaft <-, -en> [gə·ˈnɔ·sn̩·ʃaft] *f* cooperative
genossenschaftlich **I.** *adj* cooperative **II.** *adv* ~ **organisiert** organized as a cooperative
genötigt *adj* forced
Genre <-s, -s> [ˈʒã·rə] *nt* genre
Gentechnik *f* genetic engineering
Gentechniker(in) *m(f)* genetic engineer
gentechnisch **I.** *adj* ~**e Methoden** genetic engineering methods **II.** *adv* **etw ~ manipulieren** to genetically manipulate sth
Gentechnologie *f* genetic engineering
genug [gə·ˈnuːk] *adv* enough
Genüge [gə·ˈnyː·gə] *f kein pl* **zur ~** [quite] enough; (*oft genug*) often enough
ge|nügen* [gə·ˈnyː·gn̩] *vi* ❶ (*ausreichen*) ■ [**jdm**] ~ to be enough [for sb] ❷ (*gerecht werden*) ■ **einer S.** *dat* ~ to fulfill sth
genügend [gə·ˈnyː·gn̩t] *adv* enough
genügsam [gə·ˈnyːk·zaːm] **I.** *adj* (*bescheiden*) modest; (*pflegeleicht*) undemanding **II.** *adv* modestly
Genugtuung <-, *selten* -en> [gə·ˈnuːk·tuː·ʊŋ] *f* satisfaction

Genus <-, Genera> [ˈgɛ·nʊs, *pl* ˈgɛ·nera] *nt* gender
Genuss[RR] <-es, Genüsse>, **Genuß**[ALT] <-sses, Genüsse> [gə·ˈnʊs, *pl* gə·ˈnʏ·sə] *m* ❶ (*Köstlichkeit*) [culinary] delight ❷ *kein pl* (*geh: das Zusichnehmen*) consumption ❸ (*das Genießen*) enjoyment; **in den ~ einer S.** *gen* **kommen** to [come to] enjoy sth; (*aus etw Nutzen ziehen a.*) to benefit from sth
genüsslich[RR], **genüßlich**[ALT] **I.** *adj* pleasurable **II.** *adv* with [great] pleasure
Genussmittel[RR] *nt* luxury foods, alcohol and tobacco
genussvoll[RR], **genußvoll**[ALT] **I.** *adv essen, trinken* with [great] pleasure **II.** *adj* (*genüsslich*) appreciative; (*erfreulich*) highly enjoyable
Geograf(in)[RR] <-en, -en> *m(f) s.* **Geograph**
Geografie[RR] <-> *f kein pl s.* **Geographie**
geografisch[RR] *adj s.* **geographisch**
Geograph(in) <-en, -en> [geo·ˈgraːf] *m(f)* geographer
Geographie <-> [geo·gra·ˈfiː] *f kein pl* geography
geographisch [geo·ˈgraː·fɪʃ] *adj* geographic[al]
Geologe, Geologin <-n, -n> [geo·ˈloː·gə, geo·ˈloː·gɪn] *m, f* geologist
Geologie <-> [geo·lo·ˈgiː] *f kein pl* geology
geologisch [geo·ˈloː·gɪʃ] *adj* geological
Geometrie <-> [geo·me·ˈtriː] *f kein pl* geometry
geometrisch [geo·ˈmeː·trɪʃ] *adj* geometric
Geoökologie [geo·ʔøko·lo·ˈgiː] *f* geoecology
Geophysik [geo·fy·ˈziːk] *f* geophysics *no art,* + *sing vb*
Gepäck <-[e]s> [gə·ˈpɛk] *nt kein pl* baggage, luggage
Gepäckabfertigung *f* baggage [*or* luggage] check-in
Gepäckablage *f* baggage [*or* luggage] rack
Gepäckannahme *f* baggage [*or* luggage] check-in
Gepäckausgabe *f* baggage [*or* luggage] claim
Gepäckkontrolle *f* baggage [*or* luggage] inspection
Gepäckstück *nt* piece of baggage [*or* luggage]
Gepäckträger *m* (*am Fahrrad*) rear rack
Gepäckträger(in) *m(f)* porter
Gepäckwagen *m* baggage cart
Gepard <-s, -e> [ˈgeː·part, *pl* ˈgeː·par·də] *m* cheetah
gepfeffert **I.** *pp von* **pfeffern** **II.** *adj* (*fam*) *Preis, Miete* steep
gepfiffen [gə·ˈpfɪ·fn̩] *pp von* **pfeifen**
gepflegt **I.** *adj* ❶ (*nicht vernachlässigt*) well looked after; *Aussehen* well-groomed; *Garten* well-tended; *Park* well-kept ❷ (*fam: kultiviert*) civilized; *Ausdrucksweise* sophisticated ❸ (*erstklassig*) first-rate **II.** *adv* ❶ (*kultiviert*) **sich** *akk* **~ ausdrücken** to speak in a sophisticated manner ❷ (*erstklassig*) **~ essen gehen** to go to a fine restaurant

Geplärr <-[e]s> [gə·ˈplɛr], **Geplärre** <-s> [gə·ˈplɛ·rə] *nt kein pl* (*pej fam*) bawling

Geplauder <-s> [gə·ˈplau·dɐ] *nt kein pl* small talk

gepriesen [gə·ˈpriː·zn̩] *pp von* **preisen**

gepụnktet *adj* ❶ *Linie* dotted ❷ *Stoff* spotted

gequält **I.** *adj* forced **II.** *adv* ~ **lachen/seufzen** to give a forced smile/sigh

Gequatsche <-s> [gə·ˈkva·tʃə] *nt kein pl* (*pej sl*) gabbing

gequollen [gə·ˈkvɔ·lən] *pp von* **quellen**

gerade [gə·ˈraː·də] **I.** *adj* ❶ (*nicht krumm*) straight; (*aufrecht*) upright; **etw ~ biegen** to straighten out *sep* sth; **etw ~ halten** to hold sth straight; **~ sitzen/stehen** to sit/stand up straight ❷ (*opp: ungerade*) even **II.** *adv* (*fam*) ❶ (*im Augenblick, soeben*) just; **haben Sie ~ einen Moment Zeit?** do you have a minute?; **da du ~ da bist, ...** while you're here, ...; **ich wollte mich ~ ins Bad begeben, da ...** I was just about to take a bath when ...; **da wir ~ von Geld sprechen, ...** speaking of money, ... ❷ (*knapp*) just; **sie hat die Prüfung ~ so bestanden** she [just] barely passed the exam ❸ (*genau*) just; **~ heute hab' ich an dich gedacht** I was just thinking of you today **III.** *part* (*ausgerechnet*) **warum ~ er/ich?** why him/me of all people?; **warum ~ jetzt?** why now of all times?; **~ deswegen** that's exactly why ▶ WENDUNGEN: **das hat ~ noch gefehlt!** (*iron*) that's all I need!; **~, weil ...** especially because ...

Gerade <-n, -n> [gə·ˈraː·də] *f* ❶ MATH straight line ❷ SPORT stretch, straightaway

geradeaus [gə·raː·də·ˈʔaus] *adv* straight ahead

gerade|biegen *vt irreg* ■ **etw ~** (*fam: in Ordnung bringen*) to straighten out *sep* sth

geradeheraus [gə·raː·də·hɛ·ˈraus] **I.** *adj pred* (*fam*) straightforward **II.** *adv* (*fam*) frankly

gerade|stehenALT1 *vi irreg* (*aufrecht stehen*) *s.* **gerade I 1**

gerade|stehen² *vi irreg* (*einstehen*) ■ **für jdn/etw ~** to answer for sb/sth

geradewegs [gə·ˈraː·də·veːks] *adv* straight; **~ nach Hause** straight home

geradezu [gə·ˈraː·də·tsuː] *adv* really

geradlinig *adj, adv* straight

gerạmmelt *adv* **~ voll** (*fam*) jam-packed

Gerangel <-s> [gə·ˈraŋl̩] *nt kein pl* ❶ (*Balgerei*) scrap; (*Geschubse*) scuffle ❷ (*Auseinandersetzung*) fight, skirmish

Geranie <-, -n> [ge·ˈraː·ni̯ə] *f* geranium

gerann [gə·ˈran] *imp von* **gerinnen**

gerannt [gə·ˈrant] *pp von* **rennen**

Gerät <-[e]s, -e> [gə·ˈrɛːt] *nt* ❶ (*Vorrichtung*) device, gadget; (*Gartengerät*) tool ❷ ELEK, TECH appliance ❸ SPORT (*Turngerät*) apparatus ❹ *kein pl* (*Ausrüstung*) equipment; *eines Handwerkers* tools *pl*

ge|raten¹ <gerät, geriet, geraten> *vi sein* ❶ (*zufällig gelangen*) **in eine Schlägerei/einen Stau ~** to get into a fight/get stuck in a traffic jam ❷ (*unbeabsichtigt kommen*) to fall; **in einen Sturm ~** to get caught in a storm ❸ (*sich konfrontiert sehen mit*) ■ **in etw** *akk* **~** to get into sth; **in Armut ~** to end up in poverty; **in eine Falle ~** to fall into a trap; **in Gefangenschaft ~** to be taken prisoner; **in Schwierigkeiten/eine Situation ~** to get into difficulties/a situation ❹ (*erfüllt werden von*) **in Panik ~** to start to panic; **in Verlegenheit/Wut ~** to get embarrassed/angry ❺ (*beginnen, etw zu tun*) **in Brand ~** to catch fire; **ins Schleudern ~** to go into a skid; **ins Schwärmen/Träumen ~** to fall into a rapture/dream; **ins Stocken ~** to come to a halt; **in Vergessenheit ~** to fall into oblivion ❻ (*ausfallen*) **zu groß/klein ~** to turn out too big/short ❼ (*gelingen*) to turn out; **das Soufflé ist mir ~/mir nicht ~** my soufflé turned out/didn't turn out well ❽ (*fam: kennen lernen*) ■ **an jdn ~** to come across sb ❾ (*arten*) ■ **nach jdm ~** to take after sb

geraten² **I.** *pp von* **raten** **II.** *adj* (*geh*) advisable

Geratewohl [gə·raː·tə·ˈvoːl, gə·ˈraː·tə·voːl] *nt* ▶ WENDUNGEN: **aufs ~** (*fam: auf gut Glück*) on the off chance; (*willkürlich*) randomly

geraum [gə·ˈraum] *adj attr* (*geh*) some *attr;* **seit ~er Zeit** for some time; **vor ~er Zeit** some time ago

geräumig [gə·ˈrɔy·mɪç] *adj* spacious

Geräusch <-[e]s, -e> [gə·ˈrɔyʃ] *nt* sound; (*unerwartet, unangenehm a.*) noise

geräuschempfindlich *adj* sensitive to noise *pred*

Geräuschkulisse *f* background noise

geräuschlos **I.** *adj* silent **II.** *adv* silently

geräuschvoll **I.** *adj* loud **II.** *adv* loudly

gerben [ˈgɛr·bn̩] *vt* to tan

Gerber(in) <-s, -> [ˈgɛr·bɐ] *m(f)* tanner

Gerberei <-, -en> [gɛr·bə·ˈrai] *f* tannery

gerecht [gə·ˈrɛçt] **I.** *adj* ❶ (*rechtgemäß*) just; ■ **~ sein** to be fair [*or* just] ❷ (*verdient*) just; **einen ~en Lohn** (*Geld*) a fair wage; (*Anerkennung*) a just reward ❸ (*berechtigt*) **eine ~e Sache** a just cause ❹ (*angemessen beurteilen*) ■ **jdm/einer S. ~ werden** to do justice to sb/sth ❺ (*eine Aufgabe erfüllen*) ■ **einer S.** *dat* **~ werden** to fulfill sth; **Erwartungen ~ werden** to meet expectations **II.** *adv* justly

gerẹchtfertigt *adj* justified

Gerechtigkeit <-> [gə·ˈrɛç·tɪç·kait] *f kein pl* ❶ (*das Gerechtsein*) justice ❷ (*Unparteilichkeit*) fairness

Gerẹchtigkeitsgefühl *nt,* **Gerẹchtigkeitssinn** *m kein pl* sense of justice

Gerede <-s> [gə·ˈreː·də] *nt kein pl* gossip; (*Geschwätz*) talk; **kümmere dich nicht um das ~ der Leute** don't worry about what [other] people are saying

geregelt *adj* regular

gereizt **I.** *adj* (*verärgert*) irritated; (*nervös*) edgy **II.** *adv* irritably

Gericht¹ <-[e]s, -e> [gə·ˈrɪçt] *nt* (*Speise*) dish

Gericht² <-[e]s, -e> [gə·ˈrɪçt] *nt* ❶ JUR court [of

justice]; (*Gebäude*) law courts *pl* ② (*die Richter*) court ► WENDUNGEN: **mit jdm ins ~ gehen** to sharply criticize sb
gerichtlich I. *adj attr* judicial II. *adv* legally; **~ gegen jdn vorgehen** to take sb to court
Gerichtsakten *pl* court records *pl*
Gerichtsbarkeit <-, -en> *f* jurisdiction
Gerichtshof *m* court of law
Gerichtsmedizin *f* forensic medicine
Gerichtssaal *m* courtroom
Gerichtsstand *m* court of jurisdiction
Gerichtsverfahren *nt* legal proceedings *pl*; **ein ~ gegen jdn einleiten** to take legal action against sb
Gerichtsverhandlung *f* trial; (*zivil*) hearing
Gerichtsvollzieher(in) <-s, -> *m(f)* U.S. Marshal
gerieben [gə·ˈriː·bn̩] *pp von* **reiben**
geriet [gə·ˈriːt] *imp von* **geraten**[1]
gering [gə·ˈrɪŋ] I. *adj* ① (*niedrig*) low; *Anzahl, Menge* small; **von ~em Wert** of little value; **nicht das G~ste** nothing at all; **das stört mich nicht im G~sten** it doesn't bother me in the slightest ② (*unerheblich*) slight; *Bedeutung* minor; *Chance* slim II. *adv* **jdn/etw ~ schätzen** to have a low opinion of sb/sth
geringfügig [gə·ˈrɪŋ·fyː·gɪç] I. *adj* insignificant; *Betrag, Einkommen* small; *Unterschied* slight; *Vergehen, Verletzung* minor II. *adv* slightly
Geringfügigkeit <-, -en> *f* insignificance
gering|schätzen *vt s.* **gering II**
geringschätzig [gə·ˈrɪŋ·ʃɛ·tsɪç] I. *adj* contemptuous II. *adv* disparagingly
Geringschätzung *f kein pl* contempt
ge|rinnen <gerann, geronnen> *vi sein* to coagulate; *Blut a.* to clot; *Milch a.* to curdle
Gerinnsel <-s, -> [gə·ˈrɪn·zl̩] *nt* [blood] clot
Gerinnung <-, *selten* -en> *f* coagulation; *von Blut a.* clotting; *von Milch a.* curdling
Gerippe <-s, -> [gə·ˈrɪ·pə] *nt* skeleton
gerissen [gə·ˈrɪ·sn̩] I. *pp von* **reißen** II. *adj* (*fam*) crafty; *Plan* cunning
Gerissenheit <-> *f kein pl* (*fam*) cunning
geritten [gə·ˈrɪ·tn̩] *pp von* **reiten**
Germane, Germanin <-n, -n> [gɛr·ˈmaː·nə, gɛr·ˈmaː·nɪn] *m, f* Teuton
germanisch [gɛr·ˈmaː·nɪʃ] *adj* ① HIST Teutonic ② LING Germanic
Germanistik <-> [gɛr·ma·ˈnɪs·tɪk] *f kein pl* German [studies *npl*]
gern(e) <lieber, am liebsten> [ˈgɛr·n(ə)] *adv* ① (*freudig*) with pleasure; **ich mag ihn sehr ~** I like him a lot; **etw ~ tun** to like doing/to do sth; **seine Arbeit ~ machen** to enjoy one's work; **ich hätte ~ gewusst, ...** I would like to know ... ② (*ohne weiteres*) **das kannst du ~ haben** you're welcome to [have] it; **das glaube ich ~!** I [really] believe it! ► WENDUNGEN: **~ geschehen!** don't mention it!
gerochen [gə·ˈrɔ·xn̩] *pp von* **riechen**
Geröll <-[e]s, -e> [gə·ˈrœl] *nt* scree *spec*, talus; (*größer*) boulders *pl*

geronnen [gə·ˈrɔ·nən] *pp von* **rinnen, gerinnen**
Gerste <-, -n> [ˈgɛrs·tə] *f* barley
Gerte <-, -n> [ˈgɛr·tə] *f* switch
Geruch <-[e]s, Gerüche> [gə·ˈrʊx, *pl* gə·ˈrʏ·çə] *m* smell; *einer Blume, eines Parfüms* scent; (*Gestank*) stench
geruchlos *adj* odorless
Geruch(s)sinn *m kein pl* sense of smell
Gerücht <-[e]s, -e> [gə·ˈrʏçt] *nt* rumor; **ein ~ in die Welt setzen** to start a rumor
gerufen *pp von* **rufen**
geruhsam I. *adj* peaceful II. *adv* leisurely
Gerümpel <-s> [gə·ˈrʏm·pl̩] *nt kein pl* junk
Gerundium <-s, -ien> [ge·ˈrʊn·di̯·ʊm, *pl* ge·ˈrʊn·di̯·ən] *nt* gerund *spec*
gerungen [gə·ˈrʊŋən] *pp von* **ringen**
Gerüst <-[e]s, -e> [gə·ˈrʏst] *nt* ① BAU scaffold[ing] ② (*Grundplan*) framework
ges, Ges <-, -> [gɛs] *nt* MUS G flat
gesalzen [gə·ˈzal·tsn̩] I. *pp von* **salzen** II. *adj* (*fam: überteuert*) steep
gesamt [gə·ˈzamt] *adj attr* whole, entire; *Kosten* total
Gesamtausgabe *f* complete edition
Gesamtbetrag *m* total [amount]
Gesamteindruck *m* overall impression
Gesamtgewicht *nt* AUTO gross [vehicle] weight
Gesamtheit <-> *f kein pl* totality; **in seiner ~** in its entirety
Gesamtkosten *pl* total cost[s *pl*]
Gesamtschule *f* ≈ integrated school
Gesamtwerk *nt* complete works *pl*
Gesamtwert *m* total value
gesandt [gə·ˈzant] *pp von* **senden**[2]
Gesandte(r) [gə·ˈzan·tə] *f(m)*, **Gesandtin** [gə·ˈzan·tɪn] *f* envoy
Gesang <-[e]s, Gesänge> [gə·ˈzaŋ, *pl* gə·ˈzɛŋə] *m* ① *kein pl* (*das Singen*) singing ② (*Lied*) song; **ein Gregorianischer ~** a Gregorian chant
Gesangbuch *nt* hymn book
Gesangverein *m* glee club
Gesäß <-es, -e> [gə·ˈzɛːs] *nt* rear end *fam*
geschaffen *pp von* **schaffen**[2]
Geschäft <-[e]s, -e> [gə·ˈʃɛft] *nt* ① (*Laden*) store, shop ② (*Gewerbe, Handel*) business; **mit jdm ins ~ kommen** (*einmalig*) to make a deal with sb; (*dauerhaft*) to do business with sb; **wie gehen die ~e?** how's business? ③ (*Geschäftsabschluss*) deal; **ein gutes ~ machen** to get a good deal ④ DIAL (*Firma*) work; **ich gehe um 8 Uhr ins ~** I go to work at 8 o'clock ⑤ DIAL (*große, mühsame Arbeit*) job *fam* ⑥ (*Angelegenheit*) business ► WENDUNGEN: **kleines/großes ~** (*fam*) number one/number two
geschäftig [gə·ˈʃɛf·tɪç] I. *adj* busy II. *adv* busily
geschäftlich [gə·ˈʃɛft·lɪç] I. *adj* business *attr* II. *adv* on business; **~ verreist** away on business
Geschäftsbedingungen *pl* terms and condi-

tions [of sale] *pl*
Geschäftsbeziehung *f* business connection; **gute ~en** good business relationships
Geschäftsbrief *m* business letter
Geschäftsessen *nt* business lunch/dinner
geschäftsfähig *adj* legally competent
Geschäftsfrau *f fem form von* **Geschäftsmann** businesswoman *fem*
Geschäftsfreund(in) *m(f)* business associate
geschäftsführend *adj attr* acting
Geschäftsführer(in) *m(f)* ❶ ADMIN manager ❷ (*in einem Verein*) secretary
Geschäftsführung *f s.* **Geschäftsleitung**
Geschäftsleitung *f* management
Geschäftsmann *m* businessman
Geschäftsreise *f* business trip
geschäftsschädigend *adj* bad for business
GeschäftsschlussRR *m* ❶ (*Ladenschluss*) closing time ❷ (*Büroschluss*) **nach ~** after work
Geschäftsstelle *f* (*Büro*) office; *einer Bank, Firma* branch
geschäftstüchtig *adj* business-minded
Geschäftswagen *m* company car
Geschäftszeit *f* business hours
geschah [gə·'ʃaː] *imp von* **geschehen**
ge|schehen <geschah, geschehen> [gə·'ʃeː·ən] *vi sein* ❶ (*stattfinden*) to happen; **es muss etwas ~** something has to be done ❷ (*ausgeführt werden*) to be carried out ❸ (*widerfahren*) ■**jdm geschieht etw** sth happens to sb; **das geschieht dir recht!** [it] serves you right! ❹ (*verfahren werden*) **es ist um etw** *akk* **~** sth is ruined; **nicht wissen, wie einem geschieht** to not know whether one is coming or going
Geschehen <-s, -> [gə·'ʃeː·ən] *nt* events *pl*
gescheit [gə·'ʃait] *adj* clever; **du bist wohl nicht [recht] ~?** (*fam*) are you out of your mind?; **sei ~!** be sensible!; **aus etw** *dat* **nicht ~ werden** to be unable to make heads or tails of sth
Geschenk <-[e]s, -e> [gə·'ʃɛŋk] *nt* present
Geschenkgutschein *m* gift certificate
Geschenkpapier *nt*, **Geschenkspapier** *nt* ÖSTERR gift wrap, wrapping paper
Geschichte <-, -n> [gə·'ʃɪçtə] *f* ❶ *kein pl* (*Historie*) history; **Alte/Neue ~** ancient/modern history ❷ (*Erzählung*) story ❸ (*fam: Angelegenheit, Sache*) business; **die ganze ~** everything; **das sind ja schöne ~n!** (*iron*) that's a fine state of affairs!
geschichtlich [gə·'ʃɪçt·lɪç] **I.** *adj* ❶ (*die Geschichte betreffend*) historical ❷ (*bedeutend*) historic **II.** *adv* historically
Geschichtsbuch *nt* history book
Geschick[1] <-[e]s> [gə·'ʃɪk] *nt kein pl* skill
Geschick[2] <-[e]s, -e> [gə·'ʃɪk] *nt* (*Schicksal*) fate
Geschicklichkeit <-> *f kein pl* skill
geschickt **I.** *adj* skillful; *Verhalten* diplomatic; **mit den Händen ~ sein** to be clever with one's hands **II.** *adv* skillfully
geschieden [gə·'ʃiː·dn̩] **I.** *pp von* **scheiden** **II.** *adj* divorced
geschienen [gə·'ʃiː·nən] *pp von* **scheinen**
Geschirr <-[e]s, -e> [gə·'ʃɪr] *nt* ❶ *kein pl* (*Haushaltsgefäße*) dishes *pl* ❷ (*Service*) [tea/dinner] service ❸ (*Riemenzeug*) harness
Geschirrspülmaschine *f* dishwasher
Geschirrspülmittel *nt* dish soap
Geschirrtuch *nt* dishcloth
geschissen [gə·'ʃɪ·sn̩] *pp von* **scheißen**
geschlafen *pp von* **schlafen**
geschlagen *pp von* **schlagen**
Geschlecht <-[e]s, -er> [gə·'ʃlɛçt] *nt* ❶ *kein pl* BIOL gender; **das andere ~** the opposite sex; **männlichen/weiblichen ~s** (*geh*) male/female ❷ (*Sippe*) family ❸ LING gender
geschlechtlich [gə·'ʃlɛçt·lɪç] **I.** *adj* sexual **II.** *adv* sexually
Geschlechtskrankheit *f* sexually transmitted disease
Geschlechtsorgan *nt* sexual organ
Geschlechtsteil *nt* genitals *npl*
Geschlechtstrieb *m* sex drive
Geschlechtsumwandlung *f* sex change
Geschlechtsverkehr *m* sexual intercourse
geschlichen [gə·'ʃlɪ·çn̩] *pp von* **schleichen**
geschliffen [gə·'ʃlɪ·fn̩] **I.** *pp von* **schleifen**[2] **II.** *adj* polished
geschlossen [gə·'ʃlɔ·sn̩] **I.** *pp von* **schließen** **II.** *adj* ❶ (*gemeinsam*) united; *Ablehnung* unanimous ❷ (*nicht geöffnet*) closed **III.** *adv* (*einheitlich*) unanimously
geschlungen [gə·'ʃlʊŋən] *pp von* **schlingen**
Geschmack <-[e]s, Geschmäcke> [gə·'ʃmak, *pl* gə·'ʃmɛ·kə] *m* ❶ *kein pl* (*Aroma*) taste ❷ *kein pl* (*Geschmackssinn*) sense of taste ❸ (*ästhetisches Empfinden*) taste; **einen guten/keinen guten ~ haben** to have good/bad taste; **auf den ~ kommen** to acquire a taste for sth ▶ WENDUNGEN: **über ~ lässt sich [nicht] streiten** (*prov*) there's no accounting for taste
geschmacklich *adj, adv* in terms of taste
geschmacklos *adj* ❶ KOCHK bland ❷ (*taktlos*) tasteless
Geschmacklosigkeit <-, -en> *f* ❶ *kein pl* (*Taktlosigkeit*) *a.* KOCHK tastelessness ❷ (*taktlose Bemerkung*) tasteless remark
Geschmackssache *f* **~ sein** to be a matter of taste
geschmackvoll **I.** *adj* tasteful **II.** *adv* tastefully
geschmeidig [gə·'ʃmai·dɪç] **I.** *adj* ❶ (*schmiegsam*) sleek; *Haar, Fell* silky; *Haut* soft; **~es Leder** supple leather; *Masse, Teig* smooth ❷ (*biegsam*) supple **II.** *adv* (*biegsam*) supplely
geschmissen [gə·'ʃmɪ·sn̩] *pp von* **schmeißen**
geschmolzen [gə·'ʃmɔl·tsn̩] *pp von* **schmelzen**
geschniegelt [gə·'ʃniː·gl̩t] *adj* **~ und gebügelt** (*fam*) dressed to the nines *pred*
geschnitten [gə·'ʃnɪ·tn̩] *pp von* **schneiden**

G

geschoben [gə·ˈʃoː·bn̩] *pp von* **schieben**
gescholten [gə·ˈʃɔl·tn̩] *pp von* **schelten**
Geschöpf <-[e]s, -e> [gə·ˈʃœpf] *nt* ❶ (*Lebewesen*) creature ❷ (*Fantasiefigur*) creation
geschoren [gə·ˈʃoː·rən] *pp von* **scheren**[1]
GeschossRR <-es, -e>, **Geschoß**ALT <-sses, -sse> [gə·ˈʃɔs] *nt* ❶ MIL projectile ❷ (*Wurfgeschoss*) missile ❸ (*Stockwerk*) floor, story
geschossen [gə·ˈʃɔ·sn̩] *pp von* **schießen**
geschraubt **I.** *adj* (*pej*) affected **II.** *adv* affectedly
Geschrei <-s> [gə·ˈʃrai] *nt kein pl* ❶ (*Schreien*) shouting; (*schrill*) shrieking ❷ (*fam: Lamentieren*) fuss
geschrieben [gə·ˈʃriː·bn̩] *pp von* **schreiben**
geschrie(e)n [gə·ˈʃriː(·ə)n] *pp von* **schreien**
geschritten [gə·ˈʃrɪ·tn̩] *pp von* **schreiten**
geschunden [gə·ˈʃʊn·dn̩] *pp von* **schinden**
Geschütz <-es, -e> [gə·ˈʃʏts] *nt* gun
Geschwätz <-es> [gə·ˈʃvɛts] *nt kein pl* (*pej fam*) ❶ (*dummes Gerede*) hot air *pej fam* ❷ (*Klatsch*) gossip
geschwätzig [gə·ˈʃvɛ·tsɪç] *adj* (*pej*) talkative
Geschwätzigkeit <-> *f kein pl* (*pej*) talkativeness
geschweige [gə·ˈʃvai·gə] *konj* ■ ~ [**denn**] never mind, let alone
geschwiegen [gə·ˈʃviː·gn̩] *pp von* **schweigen**
geschwind [gə·ˈʃvɪnt] **I.** *adj* SÜDD (*veraltet: rasch*) swift **II.** *adv* quickly
Geschwindigkeit <-, -en> [gə·ˈʃvɪn·dɪç·kait] *f* speed
Geschwindigkeitsbegrenzung *f*, **Geschwindigkeitsbeschränkung** *f* speed limit
Geschwindigkeitsüberschreitung *f* speeding
Geschwister [gə·ˈʃvɪs·tɐ] *pl* siblings *pl*
geschwollen [gə·ˈʃvɔ·lən] **I.** *pp von* **schwellen** **II.** *adj* (*pej*) pompous **III.** *adv* in a pompous way
geschwommen [gə·ˈʃvɔ·mən] *pp von* **schwimmen**
geschworen [gə·ˈʃvoː·rən] **I.** *pp von* **schwören** **II.** *adj attr* sworn *attr*
Geschworene(r) *f(m)* juror; **die ~n** the jury
Geschwulst <-, Geschwülste> [gə·ˈʃvʊlst, *pl* gə·ˈʃvʏls·tə] *f* tumor
geschwunden [gə·ˈʃvʊn·dn̩] *pp von* **schwinden**
geschwungen [gə·ˈʃvʊŋən] **I.** *pp von* **schwingen** **II.** *adj* curved
Geschwür <-s, -e> [gə·ˈʃvyːɐ̯] *nt* abscess; **Magengeschwür** [stomach] ulcer
gesehen *pp von* **sehen**
Geselle, Gesellin <-n, -n> [gə·ˈzɛ·lə, gə·ˈzɛ·lɪn] *m, f* ❶ (*Handwerksgeselle*) journeyman ❷ (*Kerl*) guy
ge|sellen* [gə·ˈzɛ·lən] *vr* (*geh*) ❶ (*sich anschließen*) ■ **sich** *akk* **zu jdm ~** to join sb ❷ (*hinzukommen*) ■ **sich** *akk* **zu etw** *dat* **~** to add to sth
gesellig [gə·ˈzɛ·lɪç] **I.** *adj* sociable; *Abend* convivial; **ein ~es Beisammensein** a friendly get-together **II.** *adv* **~ zusammensitzen** to sit together and chat
Geselligkeit <-, -en> *f* gregariousness
Gesellschaft <-, -en> [gə·ˈzɛl·ʃaft] *f* ❶ (*Gemeinschaft*) society ❷ ÖKON corporation ❸ (*Fest*) party ❹ (*Kreis von Menschen*) group of people; **in schlechte ~ geraten** to get in with the wrong crowd; **jdm ~ leisten** to join sb ❺ (*Umgang*) company
Gesellschafter(in) <-s, -> *m(f)* (*Teilhaber*) shareholder
gesellschaftlich *adj* social
gesellschaftsfähig *adj* socially acceptable
Gesellschaftsschicht *f* social class
Gesellschaftsvertrag *m* ÖKON partnership agreement
gesessen [gə·ˈzɛ·sn̩] *pp von* **sitzen**
Gesetz <-es, -e> [gə·ˈzɛts] *nt* law
Gesetzbuch *nt* statute book; **Bürgerliches ~** Civil Code
Gesetzentwurf *m* draft legislation
gesetzestreu *adj* law-abiding
gesetzgebend *adj attr* legislative
Gesetzgeber <-s, -> *m* legislature
Gesetzgebung <-, -en> *f* legislation
gesetzlich [gə·ˈzɛts·lɪç] **I.** *adj* legal; *Verpflichtung* statutory **II.** *adv* legally
gesetzmäßig **I.** *adj* ❶ (*gesetzlich*) lawful ❷ (*regelmäßig*) regular **II.** *adv* (*einem Naturgesetz folgend*) according to the law of nature; (*rechtmäßig*) lawfully
Gesetzmäßigkeit <-, -en> *f* ❶ (*Gesetzlichkeit*) legality ❷ (*Rechtmäßigkeit*) legitimacy ❸ (*Regelmäßigkeit*) regularity
gesetzt **I.** *adj* dignified **II.** *konj* (*angenommen, ...*) ■ **~, ...** assuming that ...; (*vorausgesetzt, dass ...*) providing that ...
gesetzwidrig **I.** *adj* unlawful *form* **II.** *adv* illegally
gesichert **I.** *pp von* **sichern** **II.** *adj* secure[d]; *Erkenntnisse* solid; **~es Einkommen** fixed income; **~e Existenz** secure livelihood
Gesicht[1] <-[e]s, -er> [gə·ˈzɪçt] *nt* (*Antlitz*) face; **jdn/etw zu ~ bekommen** to set eyes on sb/sth; **jdm etw** *akk* **vom ~ ablesen** to see sth from sb's expression; **ein böses/trauriges ~ machen** to look angry/sad ▶WENDUNGEN: **sein wahres ~ zeigen** to show one's true colors; **jdm wie aus dem ~ geschnitten sein** to be the spitting image of sb
Gesicht[2] <-[e]s, -e> [gə·ˈzɪçt] *nt* (*Anblick*) sight
Gesichtsfarbe *f* complexion
Gesichtspunkt *m* point of view
Gesichtszug *m meist pl* facial feature
Gesindel <-s> [gə·ˈzɪn·dl̩] *nt kein pl* (*pej*) riffraff
gesinnt [gə·ˈzɪnt] *adj meist pred* minded; **jdm gut/übel ~ sein** to be well-disposed/ill-disposed toward sb
Gesinnung <-, -en> *f* conviction
Gesinnungswandel *m* change in attitude
gesittet [gə·ˈzɪ·tət] **I.** *adj* well-brought up

II. *adv* **sich** *akk* **~ aufführen** to be well-behaved
gesoffen [gə·ˈzɔ·fn̩] *pp von* **saufen**
gesogen [gə·ˈzoː·gn̩] *pp von* **saugen**
gesondert [gə·ˈzɔn·dɐt] **I.** *adj* separate; (*für sich*) individual **II.** *adv* separately; (*für sich*) individually
gesonnen [gə·ˈzɔ·nən] **I.** *pp von* **sinnen** **II.** *adj* (*geh*) ■ **~ sein, etw zu tun** to feel inclined to do sth
gespalten [gə·ˈʃpal·tn̩] *pp von* **spalten**
gespạnnt *adj* ❶ (*sehr erwartungsvoll*) expectant; ■ **~ sein, ob/was ...** to be anxious to see [*or* know] whether/what ...; **ich bin auf seine Reaktion ~** I wonder what his reaction will be *a. iron* ❷ (*konfliktträchtig*) tense
Gespenst <-[e]s, -er> [gə·ˈʃpɛnst] *nt* ghost
gespenstisch [gə·ˈʃpɛns·tɪʃ] *adj* eerie
gespielt *adj* feigned
gesponnen [gə·ˈʃpɔ·nən] *pp von* **spinnen**
Gespött <-[e]s> [gə·ˈʃpœt] *nt kein pl* mockery; **jdn/sich zum ~ [der Leute] machen** to make a laughing stock of sb/oneself
Gespräch <-[e]s, -e> [gə·ˈʃprɛːç] *nt* ❶ (*Unterredung*) conversation; **mit jdm ins ~ kommen** to get into a conversation with sb; **im ~ sein** to be under consideration ❷ (*Anruf*) [tele]phone call
gesprächig [gə·ˈʃprɛː·çɪç] *adj* talkative
gesprächsbereit *adj* ready to talk; (*bereit zu verhandeln*) ready to begin talks
Gesprächspartner(in) *m(f)* **ein angenehmer ~** a pleasant person to talk to
Gesprächsstoff *m* conversation topics
Gesprächsthema *nt* topic of conversation
gesprochen [gə·ˈʃprɔ·xn̩] *pp von* **sprechen**
gesprossen [gə·ˈʃprɔ·sn̩] *pp von* **sprießen**
gesprungen [gə·ˈʃprʊŋən] *pp von* **springen**
Gespür <-s> [gə·ˈʃpyːɐ̯] *nt kein pl* instinct; **ein gutes ~ für Farben** a good feel for colors
Gestalt <-, -en> [gə·ˈʃtalt] *f* ❶ (*Mensch*) figure; **eine verdächtige ~** a suspicious character ❷ (*Wuchs*) build ❸ (*Person, Persönlichkeit*) character; **in ~ jds** in the form of sb ▶ WENDUNGEN: **~ annehmen** to take shape
gestalten* [gə·ˈʃtal·tn̩] **I.** *vt* ■ **etw irgendwie ~** ❶ (*einrichten*) to design sth; *Garten* to lay out; *Schaufenster* to dress; **etw anders/neu ~** to redesign sth ❷ (*organisieren*) to organize sth ❸ ARCHIT to build sth **II.** *vr* (*geh*) ■ **sich irgendwie ~** to turn out to be somehow
gestalterisch [gə·ˈʃtal·tə·rɪʃ] **I.** *adj* (*Design betreffend*) **eine ~e Frage** a question of design; *Talent* creative **II.** *adv* **~ gelungen** well-designed; (*schöpferisch*) creatively
Gestạltung <-, -en> *f* ❶ (*das Einrichten*) design; *eines Gartens* laying out; *eines Schaufensters* window dressing ❷ (*das Organisieren*) organization ❸ ARCHIT building
gestạnd *imp von* **gestehen**
gestanden [gə·ˈʃtan·dn̩] **I.** *pp von* **stehen, gestehen** **II.** *adj attr* experienced
geständig [gə·ˈʃtɛn·dɪç] *adj* ■ **~ sein** to have confessed
Geständnis <-ses, -se> [gə·ˈʃtɛnt·nɪs, *pl* gə·ˈʃtɛnt·nɪ·sə] *nt* admission; *eines Verbrechens* confession
Gestank <-[e]s> [gə·ˈʃtaŋk] *m kein pl* stench
ge|statten* [gə·ˈʃta·tn̩] (*geh*) **I.** *vt* ❶ (*erlauben*) to permit ❷ (*als Höflichkeitsformel*) ■ **jdm ~, etw zu tun** to allow sb to do sth **II.** *vi* **wenn Sie ~, das war mein Platz!** if you don't mind, that was my seat! **III.** *vr* (*sich erlauben*) ■ **sich** *dat* **etw ~** to allow oneself sth
Geste <-, -n> [ˈgeːs·tə, ˈgɛs·tə] *f* gesture
ge|stehen <gestạnd, gestạnden> *vi, vt* to confess
Gestein <-[e]s, -e> [gə·ˈʃtain] *nt* rock
Gestell <-[e]s, -e> [gə·ˈʃtɛl] *nt* ❶ (*Bretterregal*) shelves *pl* ❷ (*Brillengestell*) frame ❸ (*Fahrgestell*) chassis
gestẹllt *adj* arranged
gestern [gɛs·tɐn] *adv* (*der Tag vor heute*) yesterday; **~ vor einer Woche** a week ago yesterday ❷ (*von früher*) **nicht von ~ sein** (*fig fam*) to not be born yesterday
gestiegen [gə·ˈʃtiː·gn̩] *pp von* **steigen**
Gestik <-> [ˈgeːs·tɪk, ˈgɛs·tɪk] *f kein pl* gestures *pl*
gestikulieren* [gɛs·ti·ku·ˈliː·rən] *vi* to gesticulate
Gestirn <-[e]s, -e> [gə·ˈʃtɪrn] *nt* (*geh: Stern*) star
gestochen [gə·ˈʃtɔ·xn̩] **I.** *pp von* **stechen** **II.** *adj* (*sehr exakt*) exact **III.** *adv* **~ scharf** crystal clear
gestohlen [gə·ˈʃtoː·lən] *pp von* **stehlen**
gestorben [gə·ˈʃtɔr·bn̩] *pp von* **sterben**
gestört *adj* PSYCH ❶ (*beeinträchtigt*) disturbed ❷ (*fam: verrückt*) insane
gestoßen [gə·ˈʃtoː·sn̩] *pp von* **stoßen**
Gestotter <-s> [gə·ˈʃtɔ·tɐ] *nt kein pl* stammering
gestreift **I.** *pp von* **streifen** **II.** *adj* striped
gestrẹsst[RR], **gestrẹßt**[ALT] *adj* stressed [out]
gestrichen [gə·ˈʃtrɪ·çn̩] **I.** *pp von* **streichen** **II.** *adj* level **III.** *adv* **~ voll** full to the brim
gestrig [ˈgɛst·rɪç] *adj attr* yesterday's *attr,* [of] yesterday *pred*
gestritten [gə·ˈʃtrɪ·tn̩] *pp von* **streiten**
Gestrüpp <-[e]s, -e> [gə·ˈʃtrʏp] *nt* undergrowth
gestunken [gə·ˈʃtʊŋ·kn̩] *pp von* **stinken**
Gesuch <-[e]s, -e> [gə·ˈzuːx] *nt* (*veraltend*) request; (*Antrag*) application
gesucht *adj* (*gefragt*) in demand *pred,* much sought-after
gesund <gesụnder, gesụndeste> [gə·ˈzʊnt] *adj* healthy; **geistig und körperlich ~** of sound mind and body; **~ und munter** in good shape; **Rauchen ist nicht ~** smoking is bad for you
Gesụndheit <-> *f kein pl* health; **~!** gesundheit!, bless you!

G

gesundheitlich I. *adj* health; **aus ~en Gründen** for health reasons **II.** *adv* (*hinsichtlich der Gesundheit*) with regard to health; **wie geht es Ihnen ~?** how are you doing, healthwise?
Gesundheitsamt *nt* local public health department
gesundheitsbewusst[RR] *adj* health conscious
gesundheitsschädlich *adj* bad for one's health
Gesundheitsversorgung *f kein pl* healthcare
gesungen [gə·'zʊŋən] *pp von* **singen**
gesunken [gə·'zʊŋ·kn̩] *pp von* **sinken**
getan [gə·'taːn] *pp von* **tun**
getragen [gə·'traː·gn̩] **I.** *pp von* **tragen II.** *adj* ❶ (*feierlich*) solemn ❷ (*gebraucht*) second-hand

Getränk <-[e]s, -e> [gə·'trɛŋk] *nt* drink
Getränkeautomat *m* drink dispenser
ge|trauen* *vr* (*wagen*) ■**sich** *akk* **~, etw zu tun** to dare to do sth
Getreide <-s, -> [gə·'trai·də] *nt* cereal; (*geerntet*) grain
getrennt I. *adj* separate **II.** *adv* separately
getreten *pp von* **treten**
getreu[1] [gə·'trɔy] *adj* ❶ (*genau*) exact; *Wiedergabe* faithful ❷ (*geh: treu*) loyal
getreu[2] [gə·'trɔy] *präp +dat* (*gemäß*) ■**~ einer S.** *dat* in accordance with sth
Getriebe <-s, -> [gə·'triː·bə] *nt* TECH transmission
getrieben [gə·'triː·bn̩] *pp von* **treiben**
getroffen [gə·'trɔ·fn̩] *pp von* **treffen, triefen**
getrogen [gə·'troː·gn̩] *pp von* **trügen**
getrost [gə·'troːst] *adv* (*ohne weiteres*) safely
getrunken [gə·'trʊŋ·kn̩] *pp von* **trinken**
Getto <-s, -s> ['gɛ·to] *nt* ghetto
gettoisieren [gɛ·toi·'ziː·rən] *vt* to ghettoize
Getue <-s> [gə·'tuː·ə] *nt kein pl* (*pej*) fuss
getüpfelt [gə·'tʏp·fəlt] *adj* spotted; *Ei, Fell* speckled
Getuschel <-s> [gə·'tʊ·ʃl̩] *nt kein pl* whispering
geübt *adj* experienced; *Auge, Ohr, Griff* trained
Gewächs <-es, -e> [gə·'vɛks] *nt* ❶ (*Pflanze*) plant ❷ (*Geschwulst*) growth
gewachsen I. *pp von* **wachsen**[1] **II.** *adj* (*ebenbürtig*) equal; **einem Gegner ~ sein** to be a match for an opponent; **sie ist der Aufgabe ~** she is certainly up to the task
Gewächshaus *nt* greenhouse
gewagt *adj* ❶ (*kühn*) audacious; (*gefährlich*) risky ❷ (*freizügig*) risqué
gewählt I. *adj* refined **II.** *adv* in an elegant way
Gewähr <-> [gə·'vɛːɐ̯] *f kein pl* guarantee; **ohne ~** subject to change
ge|währen* [gə·'vɛː·rən] *vt* ❶ (*einräumen*) ■**[jdm] etw ~** to grant [sb] sth; **jdm einen Rabatt ~** to give sb a discount; **jdn ~ lassen** (*geh*) to give sb free rein ❷ (*zuteilwerden lassen*) *Trost* to afford; *Sicherheit* to provide
gewährleisten* [gə·'vɛːɐ̯·lais·tn̩] *vt* to guarantee
Gewährleistung *f* guarantee
Gewahrsam <-s> [gə·'vaːɐ̯·zaːm] *m kein pl* ❶ (*Verwahrung*) place; **etw in ~ nehmen** to put sth into safekeeping ❷ (*Haft*) custody
Gewalt <-, -en> [gə·'valt] *f* ❶ (*Machtbefugnis, Macht*) power; **elterliche ~** parental authority; **höhere ~** act of God, circumstances beyond sb's control; **ein Gebiet/ein Land in seine ~ bringen** to bring a region/a country under one's control; **~ über jdn haben** to exercise [complete] control over sb; **sich** *akk* **in der ~ haben** to have oneself under control; **in jds ~ sein** to be in sb's hands ❷ *kein pl* (*gewaltsames Vorgehen*) force; (*Gewalttätigkeit*) violence; **nackte ~** brute force; **sich** *dat* **~ antun** to force oneself ❸ *kein pl* (*Heftigkeit*) force
gewaltbereit *adj* violent
Gewaltbereitschaft *f* willingness to use violence
gewaltfrei *adj* nonviolent, peaceful *attr*
Gewaltherrschaft *f kein pl* tyranny
gewaltig [gə·'val·tɪç] **I.** *adj* ❶ (*heftig*) enormous ❷ (*wuchtig*) powerful; *Last* heavy; (*riesig*) huge ❸ (*fam: sehr groß*) tremendous **II.** *adv* (*fam: sehr*) considerably; **sich** *akk* **~ irren** to be very much mistaken
gewaltlos I. *adj* nonviolent, peaceful, without violence *pred* **II.** *adv* without violence
Gewaltlosigkeit <-> *f kein pl* nonviolence
gewaltsam [gə·'valt·zaːm] **I.** *adj* violent; **~es Aufbrechen** forced opening **II.** *adv* by force
Gewalttat *f* act of violence
Gewalttäter(in) *m(f)* violent criminal
gewalttätig *adj* violent
Gewalttätigkeit *f* violence
Gewaltverbrechen *nt* violent crime
Gewaltverbrecher(in) *m(f)* violent criminal
gewandt [gə·'vant] **I.** *pp von* **wenden II.** *adj* skillful; *Auftreten* confident; *Bewegung* deft; *Redner* good **III.** *adv* skillfully
gewann [gə·'van] *imp von* **gewinnen**
gewaschen *pp von* **waschen**
Gewässer <-s, -> [gə·'vɛ·sɐ] *nt* body of water
Gewebe <-s, -> [gə·'veː·bə] *nt* ❶ (*Stoff*) fabric ❷ ANAT, BIOL tissue
Gewehr <-[e]s, -e> [gə·'veːɐ̯] *nt* rifle; (*Schrotflinte*) shotgun
Gewehrlauf *m* rifle [*or* shotgun] barrel
Geweih <-[e]s, -e> [gə·'vai] *nt* antlers *pl*
Gewerbe <-s, -> [gə·'vɛr·bə] *nt* ❶ (*Betrieb*) [commercial] business ❷ (*Handwerk, Handel*) trade
Gewerbegebiet *nt* industrial park
Gewerbeschein *m* business license
Gewerbesteuer *f* business tax
Gewerbetreibende(r) *f(m)* business person; (*Handwerker*) tradesperson
gewerblich [gə·'vɛrp·lɪç] **I.** *adj* (*handwerklich*) trade; (*kaufmännisch*) commercial; (*industriell*) industrial **II.** *adv* **Räume ~ nutzen** to use rooms for commercial purposes
Gewerkschaft <-, -en> [gə·'vɛrk·ʃaft] *f* [trade] union

Gewerkschaft(l)er(in) <-s, -> [gə·ˈvɛrk·ʃaft(l)ɐ] *m(f)* trade unionist
gewerkschaftlich **I.** *adj* [trade] union **II.** *adv* **~ organisiert sein** to belong to a [trade] union
Gewerkschaftsbund *m* federation of trade unions
Gewerkschaftsführer(in) *m(f)* [trade] union leader
Gewerkschaftsmitglied *nt* [trade] union member
gewesen [gə·ˈveː·zn̩] **I.** *pp von* **sein**[1] **II.** *adj attr* (*ehemalig*) former *attr*
gewichen [gə·ˈvɪ·çn̩] *pp von* **weichen**
Gewicht <-[e]s, -e> [gə·ˈvɪçt] *nt* ① *kein pl* (*Schwere eines Körpers*) weight + *sing vb;* **ein großes/geringes ~ haben** to be very heavy/light ② *kein pl* (*fig: Wichtigkeit*) weight; **ins ~ fallen** to count; **auf etw** *akk* **[großes] ~ legen** to attach importance to sth ③ (*Metallstück zum Beschweren*) weight
• **ge|wichten*** [gə·ˈvɪç·tn̩] *vt* to weight
Gewichtheben <-s> *nt kein pl* weightlifting
gewichtig [gə·ˈvɪç·tɪç] *adj* significant
Gewichtsverlust *m* weight loss
Gewichtszunahme *f* weight gain
gewieft [gə·ˈviːft] (*fam*) **I.** *adj* crafty **II.** *adv* with cunning
gewiesen [gə·ˈviː·zn̩] *pp von* **weisen**
gewillt [gə·ˈvɪlt] *adj* ■ **~ sein, etw zu tun** to be inclined to do sth
Gewimmel <-s> [gə·ˈvɪ·ml̩] *nt kein pl* (*Insekten*) swarm; (*Menschen*) throng
Gewinde <-s, -> [gə·ˈvɪn·də] *nt* TECH thread
Gewinn <-[e]s, -e> [gə·ˈvɪn] *m* ① ÖKON profit; **~ bringen** to make a profit ② (*Preis*) prize; (*beim Lotto, Wetten*) winnings *npl* ③ *kein pl* ([*innere*] *Bereicherung*) gain
Gewinnbeteiligung *f* profit sharing
gewinnbringend *adj* profitable
ge|winnen <gewann, gewonnen> [gə·ˈvɪ·nən] **I.** *vt* ① (*als Gewinn erhalten*) to win ② (*überzeugen*) ■ **jdn ~** to win sb over; **jdn als Freund ~** to win sb as a friend; **jdn als Kunden ~** to gain sb as a customer ③ (*erzeugen*) to obtain; *Kohle, Metall* to extract (**aus** +*dat* from) ④ *Einfluss, Selbstsicherheit* to gain **II.** *vi* ① (*Gewinner sein*) to win (**bei/in** +*dat* at) ② (*profitieren*) to profit (**bei** +*dat* from)
gewinnend *adj* charming, winning *attr*
Gewinner(in) <-s, -> *m(f)* winner; MIL *a.* victor
Gewinnlos *nt* winning ticket
Gewinnmarge <-, -n> [-mar·ʒə] *f* ÖKON profit margin
Gewinnspanne *f* profit margin
Gewinnung <-> *f kein pl* extraction
Gewinnzahl *f* winning number
Gewirr <-[e]s> [gə·ˈvɪr] *nt kein pl* (*Drähte, Fäden*) tangle; (*Gedanken*) confusion; *Stimmen* babble; *Straßen* maze
gewiss[RR], **gewiß**[ALT] [gə·ˈvɪs] **I.** *adj* ① *attr* (*nicht näher bezeichnet*) certain; **eine ~e Frau Schmidt** a [certain] Ms. Schmidt ② (*geh: sicher*) ■ **sich** *dat* **einer S.** *gen* **~ sein** to be certain of sth **II.** *adv* (*geh*) certainly; **aber ~!** sure!, of course!
Gewissen <-s> [gə·ˈvɪ·sn̩] *nt kein pl* conscience; **jdn/etw auf dem ~ haben** to have sb/sth on one's conscience; **jdm ins ~ reden** to appeal to sb's conscience
gewissenhaft *adj* conscientious
gewissenlos **I.** *adj* unscrupulous **II.** *adv* without scruple[s *pl*]
Gewissenlosigkeit <-, -en> *f* unscrupulousness
Gewissensbisse *pl* **~ haben** to have a bad [*or* guilty] conscience
Gewissensentscheidung *f* question of conscience
Gewissensgründe *pl* conscientious reasons
Gewissenskonflikt *m* moral conflict
gewissermaßen *adv* so to speak
Gewissheit[RR], **Gewißheit**[ALT] <-, -en> *f selten pl* certainty; **~ haben** to be certain; **sich** *dat* **~ [über etw** *akk*] **verschaffen** to find out for certain [about sth]
Gewitter <-s, -> [gə·ˈvɪ·tɐ] *nt* thunderstorm
ge|wittern* *vi impers* ■ **es gewittert** it's thundering
Gewitterstimmung *f* **es herrscht ~** there is thunder in the air *fig*
gewittrig [gə·ˈvɪt·rɪç] *adj* thundery; **~e Schwüle** oppressive heat
gewitzt [gə·ˈvɪtst] *adj* wily
gewoben [gə·ˈvoː·bn̩] *pp von* **weben**
gewogen [gə·ˈvoː·gn̩] **I.** *pp von* **wiegen**[1] **II.** *adj* (*geh*) well-disposed
ge|wöhnen* [gə·ˈvøː·nən] **I.** *vt* ■ **jdn an etw** *akk* **~** to accustom sb to sth **II.** *vr* ■ **sich** *akk* **an jdn/etw ~** to get used to sb/sth; ■ **sich** *akk* **daran ~, etw zu tun** to get used to doing sth
Gewohnheit <-, -en> *f* habit
Gewohnheitsmensch *m* creature of habit
Gewohnheitsrecht *nt* (*als Rechtssystem*) common law *no art*
Gewohnheitstrinker(in) *m(f)* habitual drinker
gewöhnlich [gə·ˈvøːn·lɪç] **I.** *adj* ① *attr* (*üblich*) usual ② (*normal*) normal ③ (*pej: ordinär*) common **II.** *adv* ① (*üblicherweise*) usually; **für ~** normally; **wie ~** as usual ② (*pej*) **sich** *akk* **~ ausdrücken** to use common language
gewohnt [gə·ˈvoːnt] *adj* usual; *Umgebung* familiar; ■ **etw ~ sein** to be used to sth; ■ **es ~ sein, etw zu tun** to be used to doing sth
Gewöhnung <-> *f kein pl* habituation *form;* **das ist [alles] ~** it's [all] a question of habit
gewöhnungsbedürftig *adj* requiring getting used to
Gewöhnungssache *f* matter of getting used to [it]
Gewölbe <-s, -> [gə·ˈvœl·bə] *nt* vault
gewölbt *adj Dach, Decke* vaulted; *Stirn* domed; *Rücken* rounded
gewonnen [gə·ˈvɔ·nən] *pp von* **gewinnen**
geworben [gə·ˈvɔr·bn̩] *pp von* **werben**
geworden [gə·ˈvɔr·dn̩] *pp von* **werden**
geworfen [gə·ˈvɔr·fn̩] *pp von* **werfen**

G

Gewühl <-[e]s> [gə·ˈvyːl] *nt kein pl* ① (*Gedränge*) throng ② (*pej: andauerndes Kramen*) rummaging around

gewunden [gə·ˈvʊn·dn̩] **I.** *pp von* **winden**[1] **II.** *adj* ① (*in Windungen verlaufend*) winding ② (*umständlich*) tortuous

gewunken [gə·ˈvʊŋ·kn̩] DIAL *pp von* **winken**

Gewürz <-es, -e> [gə·ˈvʏrts] *nt* spice

Gewürzgurke *f* gherkin

Gewürzpflanze *f* spice plant; (*Kräutersorte*) herb

gewusst[RR], **gewußt**[ALT] [gə·ˈvʊst] *pp von* **wissen**

gez. *Abk von* **gezeichnet** sgd

gezackt *adj* jagged; *Hahnenkamm* toothed; *Blatt* serrated

Gezänk <-s> [gə·ˈtsɛŋk], **Gezanke** <-s> [gə·ˈtsaŋ·kə] *nt kein pl* (*pej fam*) squabbling

gezeichnet *adj* marked

Gezeiten [gə·ˈtsai·tn̩] *pl* tide[s *pl*]

Gezeitenwechsel *m* turn of the tide

Gezeter <-s> [gə·ˈtseː·tɐ] *nt kein pl* (*pej fam*) racket

gezielt **I.** *adj* well-directed; *Fragen* specific **II.** *adv* specifically; ~ **fragen** to ask questions with sth mind

ge|ziemen* *vr impers* (*veraltend*) ■ **es geziemt sich** it is proper; **wie es sich für ein artiges Kind geziemt** as befits a well-behaved child *form*

geziert (*pej*) **I.** *adj* affected **II.** *adv* affectedly

gezogen [gə·ˈtsoː·gn̩] *pp von* **ziehen**

Gezwitscher <-s> [gə·ˈtsvɪ·tʃɐ] *nt kein pl* chirping

gezwungen [gə·ˈtsvʊŋən] **I.** *pp von* **zwingen** **II.** *adj* (*gekünstelt*) forced; *Benehmen* stiff **III.** *adv* (*gekünstelt*) stiffly; ~ **lachen** to give a forced laugh

gezwungenermaßen *adv* of necessity

ggf. *adv Abk von* **gegebenenfalls**

Ghetto <-s, -s> *nt s.* **Getto**

ghettoisieren* *vt s.* **gettoisieren**

Gicht <-> [ˈgɪçt] *f kein pl* gout

Giebel <-s, -> [ˈgiː·bl̩] *m* gable [end]

Gier <-> [ˈgiːɐ̯] *f kein pl* greed (**nach** +*dat* for); (*nach etw Ungewöhnlichem*) craving (**nach** +*dat* for)

gieren [ˈgiː·rən] *vi* ■ **nach etw** *dat* ~ to crave sth

gierig [ˈgiː·rɪç] **I.** *adj* greedy; ~ **nach Macht/Reichtum sein** to crave power/riches **II.** *adv* greedily; **etw ~ trinken** to gulp down *sep* sth

gießen <goss, gegossen> [ˈgiː·sn̩] **I.** *vt* ① (*bewässern*) to water ② (*schütten*) to pour (**auf** +*akk* on, **über** +*akk* over) ③ TECH **etw [in Barren/Bronze] ~** to cast sth [into bars/in bronze] **II.** *vi impers* (*stark regnen*) **es gießt in Strömen** it's pouring

Gießerei <-, -en> [giː·sə·ˈrai] *f* foundry

Gießkanne *f* watering can

Gift <-[e]s, -e> [ˈgɪft] *nt* ① (*giftige Substanz*) poison; (*Schlangengift*) venom; **jdm ~ geben** to poison sb; **darauf kannst du ~ nehmen** (*fig fam*) you can bet your life on that ② (*fig: Bosheit*) venom; ~ **und Galle spucken** (*fam*) to vent one's spleen

Giftgas *nt* poison gas

giftgrün *adj* garish green

giftig [ˈgɪf·tɪç] **I.** *adj* ① (*Gift enthaltend*) poisonous ② (*boshaft*) venomous ③ (*grell*) garish **II.** *adv* (*pej*) ~ **antworten** to give a nasty reply

Giftmüll *m* toxic waste

Giftschlange *f* poisonous snake

Giftstoff *m* toxic substance

Giftwolke *f* cloud of toxins

Gigant(in) <-en, -en> [gi·ˈgant] *m(f)* giant; (*fig a.*) colossus

gigantisch [gi·ˈgan·tɪʃ] *adj* gigantic

gilt [ˈgɪlt] *3. pers sing pres von* **gelten**

ging [ˈgɪŋ] *imp von* **gehen**

Ginster <-s, -> [ˈgɪns·tɐ] *m* broom

Gipfel <-s, -> [ˈgɪp·fl̩] *m* ① (*Bergspitze*) peak; (*höchster Punkt*) summit; DIAL (*Wipfel*) treetop ② (*fig: Zenit*) peak; (*Höhepunkt*) height ③ POL summit

Gipfelkonferenz *f* summit conference

gipfeln [ˈgɪp·fl̩n] *vi* ■ **in etw** *dat* ~ to culminate in sth

Gipfelpunkt *m* high point

Gipfeltreffen *nt* summit [meeting]

Gips <-es, -e> [ˈgɪps] *m* ① (*Baumaterial*) plaster; (*in Mineralform*) gypsum; (*zum Modellieren*) plaster of Paris ② (*Kurzform für Gipsverband*) [plaster] cast; **den Arm/Fuß in ~ haben** to have one's arm/foot in a cast

Gipsabdruck <-abdrücke> *m*, **Gipsabguss**[RR] *m* plaster cast

Gipsbein *nt* (*fam*) leg in a cast

gipsen [ˈgɪp·sn̩] *vt* ■ **etw ~** ① (*mit Gips reparieren*) to plaster sth ② MED to put sth in a cast

Gipsverband *m* plaster cast

Giraffe <-, -n> [gi·ˈra·fə] *f* giraffe

Girlande <-, -n> [gɪr·ˈlan·də] *f* garland (**aus** +*dat* of)

Giro <-s, -s *o* Giri> [ˈʒiː·ro, *pl* ˈʒiː·ri] *nt* FIN ÖSTERR [bank] transfer

Girokonto [ˈʒiː·ro-] *nt* ≈ checking account

Gischt <-[e]s, -e (m) o -, -en (f)> [ˈgɪʃt] *m o f pl selten* [sea] spray

Gitarre <-, -n> [gi·ˈta·rə] *f* guitar

Gitarrist(in) <-en, -en> [gi·ta·ˈrɪst] *m(f)* guitarist

Gitter <-s, -> [ˈgɪtɐ] *nt* ① (*Absperrung*) fencing; (*vor Türen, Fenstern: engmaschig*) screen; (*grobmaschig*) grate; (*parallel laufende Stäbe*) bars *pl;* (*für Gewächse*) trellis ② (*fig fam*) **jdn hinter ~ bringen** to put sb behind bars

Gitterfenster *nt* barred window

Gitterrost *m* grate

Glace <-, -n> [ˈglasə] *f* SCHWEIZ ice cream

glamourös [gla·mu·ˈrøːs] *adj* glamorous

Glanz <-es> [ˈglants] *m kein pl* ① (*das Glänzen*) shine; *Augen* sparkle; *Lack* gloss; *Perlen, Seide* sheen ② (*herrliche Pracht*) splendor

glänzen [ˈglɛn·tsn̩] *vi* ① (*widerscheinen*) to

shine; (*von polierter Oberfläche*) to gleam; *Augen* to sparkle; *Haut, Stoff* to be shiny; *Wasseroberfläche* to glisten; *Sterne* to twinkle ❷ (*sich hervortun*) to shine

glänzend ['glɛn·tsn̩t] **I.** *adj* ❶ (*widerscheinend*) shining; *Oberfläche* gleaming; *Augen* sparkling; *Haar* shiny; *Papier* glossy ❷ (*hervorragend*) brilliant **II.** *adv* (*hervorragenderweise*) splendidly; **sich** *akk* **~ amüsieren** to have a great time

Glanzleistung *f* brilliant achievement

glanzvoll *adj* brilliant

Glas <-es, Gläser> ['gla:s, *pl* 'glɛ:·zɐ] *nt* ❶ (*Werkstoff*) glass *no indef art, + sing vb;* **„Vorsicht ~!"** "glass — handle with care" ❷ (*Trinkgefäß*) glass ❸ (*Brillenglas*) lens; (*Fernglas*) binoculars *npl*

Glasbläser(in) *m(f)* glassblower

Glascontainer [-kɔn·te:·nɐ] *m* recycling container for glass

Glaser(in) <-s, -> ['gla:·zɐ] *m(f)* glazier

Glaserei [gla:·zə·'rai] *f* glazier's workshop

gläsern ['glɛ:·zɐn] *adj* ❶ (*aus Glas*) glass *attr,* [made] of glass *pred* ❷ (*fig*) **~e Augen/~er Blick** glassy eyes/gaze

Glasfaser *f meist pl* fiber glass

Glasfaserkabel *nt* fiber optic cable

Glashaus *nt* greenhouse; (*in botanischen Gärten*) glass house

glasieren* [gla·'zi:·rən] *vt* to glaze

glasig ['gla:·zɪç] *adj* ❶ (*ausdruckslos*) glassy ❷ KOCHK *Zwiebeln* transparent

glasklar **I.** *adj* ❶ (*durchsichtig*) transparent ❷ (*fig: klar und deutlich*) crystal clear **II.** *adv* (*klar und deutlich*) in no uncertain terms

Glasscheibe *f* ❶ (*dünne Glasplatte*) sheet of glass ❷ (*Fensterscheibe*) pane of glass

Glasscherbe *f* glass shard

Glasur [gla·'zu:ɐ̯] *f* ❶ (*Keramikglasur*) glaze ❷ KOCHK icing

glatt <-er *o fam* glätter, -este *o fam* glätteste> ['glat] **I.** *adj* ❶ *Fläche, Haut* smooth; *Gesicht* unlined; *Haar* straight; **~ rasiert** clean-shaven; **etw ~ hobeln/schmirgeln** to plane down/sand down sth; **etw ~ streichen** to smooth out *sep* sth ❷ *Straße* slippery ❸ (*problemlos*) smooth ❹ *attr* (*fam: eindeutig*) outright; *Lüge* downright **II.** *adv* (*fam: rundweg*) plainly; (*ohne Umschweife*) straight up; *leugnen* flatly

Glätte <-> ['glɛ·tə] *f kein pl* ❶ (*Ebenheit*) smoothness ❷ (*Rutschigkeit*) slipperiness

Glatteis *nt* [thin sheet of] ice; **„Vorsicht ~!"** "danger — black ice" ▶ WENDUNGEN: **sich** *akk* **auf ~ begeben** to skate on thin ice

Glatteisgefahr <-> *f kein pl* danger of black ice

glätten ['glɛ·tn̩] **I.** *vt* ❶ (*glatt streichen*) to smooth out *sep;* **sich** *dat* **die Haare ~** to smooth down *sep* one's hair ❷ (*besänftigen*) **jds Zorn ~** to calm sb's anger **II.** *vr* ■**sich ~** ❶ *Meer, Wellen* to subside ❷ (*fig*) *Wut, Erregung* to die down

glattrasiert *adj s.* **glatt I 1**

glatt|streichen *vt irreg s.* **glatt I 1**

glattweg ['glat·vɛk] *adv* (*fam*) just like that; **etw ~ ablehnen** to turn sth down flat out; **etw ~ abstreiten** to flatly deny sth

Glatze <-, -n> ['glatsə] *f* bald head; **eine ~ bekommen/haben** to go/be bald

Glatzkopf *m* (*fam*) ❶ (*Kopf*) bald head ❷ (*Mann*) baldy

glatzköpfig ['glats·kœp·fɪç] *adj* bald[-headed]

Glaube <-ns> ['glau·bə] *m kein pl* ❶ (*Überzeugung*) belief (**an** +*akk* in); (*gefühlsmäßige Gewissheit*) faith (**an** +*akk* in); **den festen ~n haben, dass ...** to firmly believe that ...; **in gutem ~n** in good faith; **jdm/einer S. [keinen] ~n schenken** to [not] believe sb/sth; **den ~n an jdn/etw verlieren** to lose faith in sb/sth ❷ REL [religious] faith

glauben ['glau·bn̩] **I.** *vt* ❶ (*für wahr halten*) ■**etw ~** to believe sth; **kaum zu ~** unbelievable, incredible ❷ (*wähnen*) **sich** *akk* **allein/unbeobachtet ~** to think [that] one is alone/nobody is watching **II.** *vi* ❶ (*vertrauen*) ■**jdm ~** to believe sb; **jdm aufs Wort ~** to take sb's word for it; ■**an jdn/etw ~** to believe in sb/sth ❷ (*für wirklich halten*) ■**an etw** *akk* **~** to believe in sth ▶ WENDUNGEN: **dran ~ müssen** (*sl: sterben müssen*) to kick the bucket; (*weggeworfen werden müssen*) to get tossed out; (*etw tun müssen*) to be stuck with it

Glauben <-s> ['glau·bn̩] *m kein pl s.* **Glaube**

Glaubensbekenntnis *nt* (*Religionszugehörigkeit*) profession [of faith]

Glaubensfreiheit *f* religious freedom

Glaubensgemeinschaft *f* denomination

glaubhaft **I.** *adj* believable **II.** *adv* convincingly

Glaubhaftigkeit <-> *f kein pl* credibility

gläubig ['glɔy·bɪç] *adj* ❶ (*religiös*) religious ❷ (*vertrauensvoll*) trusting

Gläubige(r) ['glɔy·bɪ·gə] *f(m)* believer

Gläubiger(in) <-s, -> ['glɔy·bɪ·gɐ] *m(f)* ÖKON creditor

glaubwürdig *adj* credible

Glaubwürdigkeit <-> *f kein pl* credibility

gleich ['glaiç] **I.** *adj* ❶ (*übereinstimmend*) same; **2 mal 2 [ist] ~ 4** 2 times 2 is 4; **~ alt** the same age; **~ groß/lang** equal in size/length; **~ schwer** equally heavy; **~ gesinnt** like-minded ❷ (*unverändert*) **es ist immer das [ewig] G~e** it's always the same [old thing]; **~ bleibend gut** consistently good ❸ (*gleichgültig*) ■**jdm ~ sein** to be all the same to sb; ■**ganz ~ wer/was [...]** no matter who/what [...] **II.** *adv* ❶ (*sofort, bald*) right away; **bis ~!** see you soon!; (*sofort*) see you in a minute!; **ich komme ~!** I'll be right there!; **~ darauf** soon afterward; (*sofort*) right away; **~ heute/morgen** [first thing] today/tomorrow; **~ nach dem Frühstück** right after breakfast ❷ (*unmittelbar daneben/danach*) immediately; ■**~ als ...** as soon as ...; **~ daneben** right beside it ❸ (*zugleich*) at once **III.** *part* ❶ *in Aussagesätzen* (*emph*) just as well ❷ *in Fragesätzen* (*noch*) again; **wie war doch ~ Ihr**

G

Name? what was your name again? **IV.** *präp +dat* (*geh: wie*) like

gleichalt(e)rig ['glaiç·ʔalt(ə)·rɪç] *adj* [of] the same age *pred*

gleichartig *adj* of the same kind *pred;* (*ähnlich*) similar

Gleichbehandlung *f* equal treatment

gleichberechtigt *adj* ■ **~ sein** to have equal rights

Gleichberechtigung *f kein pl* equal rights *+ sing/pl vb*

gleichbleibend *adj, adv s.* **gleich I 2**

gleichen <glịch, geglịchen> ['glai·çn̩] *vt* ■ **jdm/einer S. ~** to be [just] like sb/sth; ■ **sich** *dat* **~** to be alike

gleichermaßen *adv* equally

gleichfalls *adv* likewise; **danke ~!** thanks, [and the] same to you *a. iron*

gleichförmig **I.** *adj* uniform **II.** *adv* uniformly

gleichgeschlechtlich *adj* (*homosexuell*) homosexual; **~e Ehe** same-sex [*or* gay] marriage

gleichgesinnt *adj s.* **gleich I 1**

Gleichgewicht *nt kein pl* balance; **im ~ sein** to be balanced; **aus dem ~ kommen** to lose one's balance

Gleichgewichtsstörung *f* problem with one's equilibrium

gleichgültig **I.** *adj* ① (*uninteressiert*) indifferent (**gegenüber** *+dat* to[ward]); (*apathisch*) apathetic (**gegenüber** *+dat* toward) ② (*unwichtig*) immaterial; ■ **etw ist jdm ~** sb couldn't care less about sth **II.** *adv* (*uninteressiert*) with indifference; (*apathisch*) with apathy

Gleichgültigkeit ['glaiç·gʏl·tɪç·kait] *f kein pl* (*Desinteresse*) indifference; (*Apathie*) apathy

Gleichheit <-, -en> *f* ① (*Übereinstimmung*) similarity ② *kein pl* (*gleiche Stellung*) equality

Gleichheitszeichen *nt* equal[s] sign

gleich|kommen *vi irreg sein* ① (*Gleiches erreichen*) ■ **jdm/einer S. ~** to equal sb/sth (**an** *+dat* in) ② (*gleichbedeutend sein*) ■ **einer S.** *dat* **~** to be tantamount to sth

gleich|machen *vt* ■ **etw/alles ~** to make sth/everything the same

gleichmäßig **I.** *adj* even; *Bewegungen* regular; *Puls, Tempo* steady **II.** *adv* ① (*in gleicher Stärke/Menge*) equally; **~ schlagen** *Herz, Puls* to beat steadily; **~ atmen** to breathe regularly ② (*ohne Veränderungen*) consistently

Gleichmäßigkeit ['glaiç·mɛː·sɪç·kait] *f* regularity; *von Puls, Tempo a.* steadiness

Gleichnis <-ses, -se> ['glaiç·nɪs, *pl* -nɪ·sə] *nt* allegory; (*aus der Bibel*) parable

gleichrangig *adj* equal in rank *pred,* at the same level *pred*

Gleichschritt *m kein pl* **im ~ marschieren** to march in step

gleichseitig ['glaiç·zai·tɪç] *adj* equilateral

gleich|setzen *vt* to equate (**mit** *+dat* with)

Gleichstand *m kein pl* tie

gleich|stellen *vt* ■ **jdn jdm ~** to give sb the same rights as sb

Gleichstellung *f kein pl* equality (*+gen* of/for)

Gleichstrom *m* ELEK direct current

gleich|tun *vt impers, irreg* ① (*imitieren*) ■ **es jdm ~** to follow sb['s example] ② (*gleichkommen*) ■ **es jdm ~** to match sb (**in** *+dat* in)

Gleichung <-, -en> ['glai·çʊŋ] *f* equation

gleichwertig *adj* equal; ■ **~ sein** to be equally matched

gleichzeitig **I.** *adj* simultaneous **II.** *adv* ① (*zur gleichen Zeit*) simultaneously ② (*ebenso, zugleich*) at the same time

gleich|ziehen *vi irreg* (*fam*) ■ [**mit jdm**] **~** to catch up [to [*or* with] sb]

Gleis <-es, -e> ['glais, *pl* 'glai·zə] *nt* track; (*einzelne Schiene*) rail; (*Bahnsteig*) platform; **~ 2 ...** platform [*or* track] 2 ...

gleiten <glịtt, geglịtten> ['glai·tn̩] *vi* ① *sein* (*schweben*) to glide; *Wolke* to sail ② *sein* (*streichen, huschen*) ■ **über etw** *akk* **~** *Augen* to wander over sth; *Blick* to pass over sth; *Finger* to explore sth; *Hand* to slide over sth ③ *sein* (*rutschen*) to slide; **zu Boden/ins Wasser ~** to slip to the ground/into the water

Gleitmittel *nt* lubricant

Gleitzeit *f* (*fam*) flextime

Gletscher <-s, -> ['glɛ·tʃɐ] *m* glacier

Gletscherspalte *f* crevasse

glich ['glɪç] *imp von* **gleichen**

Glied <-[e]s, -er> ['gliːt, *pl* 'gliː·dɐ] *nt* ① (*Körperteil*) limb; (*Fingerspitze*) fingertip; **an allen ~ern zittern** to be shivering all over ② (*Penis*) [male] member *form* ③ (*Kettenglied*) link *a. fig* ④ (*Teil*) part

gliedern ['gliː·dɐn] **I.** *vt* ■ **etw ~** (*unterteilen*) to [sub]divide sth (**in** *+akk* into); (*ordnen*) to organize sth (**in** *+akk* into); (*einordnen*) to classify sth (**in** *+akk* under) **II.** *vr* ■ **sich in etw** *akk* **~** to be [sub]divided into sth

Gliederschmerz *m meist pl* rheumatic pains *pl*

Gliederung <-, -en> *f* ① *kein pl* (*das Gliedern*) structuring (**in** *+akk* into); (*das Unterteilen*) subdivision (**in** *+akk* into); (*nach Eigenschaften a.*) classification ② (*Aufbau*) structure

Gliedmaßen *pl* limbs

glimmen <glọmm, geglọmmen> ['glɪ·mən] *vi* to glow; *Feuer, Asche a.* to smolder

Glimmstängel[RR], **Glimmstengel**[ALT] *m* (*hum fam*) smoke

glimpflich ['glɪmpf·lɪç] **I.** *adj* ① (*ohne schlimmere Folgen*) without serious consequences *pred* ② (*mild*) mild **II.** *adv* ① (*ohne schlimmere Folgen*) **~ abgehen** to pass [by] without serious consequences; **~ davonkommen** to get off lightly ② (*mild*) **mit jdm ~ umgehen** to treat sb leniently

glitschig ['glɪt·ʃɪç] *adj* (*fam*) slippery

glitt ['glɪt] *imp von* **gleiten**

glitzerig ['glɪ·tsə·rɪç], **glitzrig** ['glɪts·rɪç] *adj* (*fam*) sparkly

glitzern ['glɪ·tsɐn] *vi* to glitter; *Stern* to twinkle

global [glo·'baːl] **I.** *adj* ① (*weltweit*) global ② (*umfassend*) general **II.** *adv* ① (*weltweit*)

globally ❷ (*ungefähr*) generally
Globalisierung <-> *f* globalization
Globus <- *o* -ses, Globen *o* -se> ['glo:·bʊs, *pl* 'glo:·bn̩] *m* globe
Glocke <-, -n> ['glɔ·kə] *f* ❶ (*Läutewerk*) bell ❷ (*glockenförmiger Deckel*) [glass] cover ▶ WENDUNGEN: **etw an die große ~ hängen** (*fam*) to shout sth from the rooftops
Glockenblume *f* bellflower
glockenförmig *adj* bell-shaped
Glockengeläut(e) *nt kein pl* peal of bells
Glockenspiel *nt* ❶ (*in Kirch- oder Stadttürmen*) carillon ❷ (*Musikinstrument*) glockenspiel
Glockenturm *m* belfry
glomm ['glɔm] *imp von* **glimmen**
glorifizieren* [glo·ri·fi·'tsi:·rən] *vt* to glorify (**als** +*akk* as)
glorreich *adj* ❶ (*meist iron*) magnificent ❷ (*großartig*) glorious
Glossar <-s, -e> [glɔ·'sa:ɐ̯] *nt* glossary
Glosse <-, -n> ['glɔ·sə] *f* commentary; (*polemisch*) ironic comment[ary]
Glotze <-, -n> ['glɔ·tsə] *f* (*fam*) boob tube
glotzen ['glɔ·tsn̩] *vi* (*pej fam*) to gape [*or* stare] (**auf** +*akk* at)
Glück <-[e]s> ['glʏk] *nt kein pl* ❶ (*günstige Fügung*) luck; (*Fortuna*) fortune; **ein ~, dass ...** it is/was lucky that ...; **jdm zum Geburtstag ~ wünschen** to wish sb [a] happy birthday; **mehr ~ als Verstand haben** (*fam*) to have more luck than brains; **viel ~ [bei etw** *dat*]! good luck [with sth]!; **~/kein ~ haben** to be lucky/unlucky; **zum ~** luckily ❷ (*Freude*) happiness ▶ WENDUNGEN: **etw auf gut ~ tun** to do sth on the off chance; **~ im Unglück haben** it could have been much worse [for sb]
glücken ['glʏ·kn̩] *vi sein* ❶ (*gelingen*) to be successful; ■**jdm glückt etw** sb succeeds in sth ❷ (*vorteilhaft werden*) to turn out well
gluckern ['glʊ·kɐn] *vi* to gurgle
glücklich ['glʏk·lɪç] **I.** *adj* ❶ (*vom Glück begünstigt*) lucky ❷ (*vorteilhaft, erfreulich*) happy; **~er Ausgang** a happy ending; **eine ~e Nachricht** [some] good news +*sing vb;* *Umstand* fortunate ❸ (*froh*) happy (**mit** +*dat* with, **über** +*akk* about) **II.** *adv* ❶ (*vorteilhaft, erfreulich*) happily ❷ (*froh und zufrieden*) **~ [mit jdm] verheiratet sein** to be happily married [to sb] ❸ (*fam: zu guter Letzt*) after all
glücklicherweise *adv* luckily
Glücksbringer <-s, -> *m* lucky charm
Glücksfall *m* stroke of luck
Glückskind *nt* (*fam*) a lucky person
Glückspilz *m* (*fam*) lucky devil
Glückssache *f* ■**etw ist [reine] ~** sth's a matter of [sheer] luck
Glücksspiel *nt* game of chance
Glückssträhne *f* lucky streak
Glückstag *m* lucky day
Glückstreffer *m* stroke of luck; (*beim Schießen*) lucky shot
Glückwunsch *m* congratulations *npl* (**zu** +*dat* on)
Glückwunschkarte *f* greeting card
Glühbirne *f* light bulb
glühen ['gly:·ən] *vi* ❶ (*rot vor Hitze sein*) to glow ❷ (*geh*) ■**vor etw** *dat* **~** to burn with sth
glühend **I.** *adj* ❶ (*rot vor Hitze*) glowing; *Metall* [red-]hot ❷ (*brennend, sehr heiß*) burning; *Hitze* blazing **II.** *adv* **~ heiß** burning hot
Glühlampe *f* (*geh*) light bulb
Glühwein *m* [hot] mulled wine

Glühwein (hot red wine, spiced with cinnamon, sugar, aniseed, and cloves) is traditionally sold in winter, especially at the Christmas markets.

Glühwürmchen <-s, -> *nt* glowworm; (*fliegend*) firefly
Glut <-, -en> ['glu:t] *f* embers *npl;* (*Tabak*) burning ash
glutrot *adj* fiery red
GmbH <-, -s> [ge:·ʔɛm·be:·ha:] *f Abk von* **Gesellschaft mit beschränkter Haftung** ≈ Inc.
g-Moll <-> ['ge:·mɔl] *nt kein pl* MUS G flat minor
Gnade <-, -n> ['gna:·də] *f* ❶ (*Gunst*) favor ❷ (*Nachsicht*) mercy; **~ vor Recht ergehen lassen** to temper justice with mercy
Gnadenfrist *f* [temporary] reprieve
gnadenlos **I.** *adj* merciless **II.** *adv* mercilessly
gnädig ['gnɛ:·dɪç] **I.** *adj* ❶ (*herablassend*) gracious *a. iron* ❷ (*Nachsicht zeigend*) merciful ❸ (*veraltend: verehrt*) **~e Frau** madam; **~es Fräulein** madam; (*jünger*) miss; **~er Herr** (*veraltet*) sir **II.** *adv* ❶ (*herablassend*) graciously ❷ (*milde*) leniently
Gnom <-en, -en> ['gno:m] *m* (*pej*) gnome
Gnu <-s, -s> ['gnu:] *nt* gnu
Goal <-s, -s> [go:l] *nt* FBALL ÖSTERR, SCHWEIZ goal
Gockel <-s, -> ['gɔ·kl̩] *m bes* SÜDD rooster
Gold <-[e]s> ['gɔlt] *nt kein pl* gold; **nicht mit ~ zu bezahlen sein** to be worth one's/its weight in gold; **aus ~** gold ▶ WENDUNGEN: **es ist nicht alles ~, was glänzt** (*prov*) all that glitters is not gold
Goldader *f* vein of gold
Goldbarren *m* gold ingot
golden ['gɔl·dn̩] **I.** *adj attr* gold[en *liter*] **II.** *adv* like gold
Goldfisch *m* goldfish
goldgelb *adj* golden yellow; KOCHK golden brown
Goldgräber(in) <-s, -> *m(f)* gold digger
Goldgrube *f* (*fig*) goldmine
Goldhamster *m* [golden] hamster
goldig ['gɔl·dɪç] *adj* ❶ (*fam: allerliebst*) cute ❷ *pred* DIAL (*fam: rührend nett*) sweet *a. iron* ❸ DIAL (*iron fam*) **du bist aber ~!** very [*or* you're] funny!

G

Goldmedaille [-me·dal·jə] *f* gold [medal]
goldrichtig *adj* (*fam*) ❶ (*völlig richtig*) absolutely right ❷ *pred* (*in Ordnung*) all right
Goldschatz *m* ❶ (*Schatz*) golden treasure ❷ (*Kosewort*) treasure *fam*
Goldschmied(in) *m(f)* goldsmith
Goldschnitt *m kein pl* gilt edging
Goldstück *nt* ❶ (*veraltet*) piece of gold ❷ (*Kosewort*) treasure *fam*
Goldwaage *f* gold scales; **bei ihm muss man jedes Wort auf die ~ legen** one really has to weigh one's words with him
Golf[1] <-[e]s, -e> ['gɔlf] *m* GEOL gulf
Golf[2] <-s> ['gɔlf] *nt kein pl* SPORT golf
Golfkrieg *m* ■ **der ~** the Gulf War
Golfplatz *m* golf course + *sing/pl vb*
Golfspieler(in) *m(f)* golfer
Golfstaat *m* ■ **die ~en** the Gulf States
Golfstrom *m* GEOL ■ **der ~** the Gulf Stream
Gondel <-, -n> ['gɔn·dl̩] *f* ❶ (*Boot in Venedig*) gondola ❷ (*Seilbahngondel*) cable car ❸ (*Ballongondel*) basket
Gong <-s, -s> ['gɔŋ] *m* gong; SPORT bell
gönnen ['gœ·nən] **I.** *vt* ❶ (*gern zugestehen*) ■ **jdm etw ~** to not begrudge sb sth; **ich gönne ihm diesen Erfolg von ganzem Herzen!** I'm absolutely delighted that he succeeded! ❷ (*iron: es gern sehen*) ■ **es jdm ~, dass ...** to be pleased [to see] that sb ... **II.** *vr* ■ **sich** *dat* **etw ~** to allow oneself sth; **sich ein Glas Wein ~** to treat oneself to a glass of wine
Gönner(in) <-s, -> ['gœ·nɐ] *m(f)* patron *masc*, patroness *fem*
gönnerhaft **I.** *adj* (*pej*) patronizing **II.** *adv* patronizingly
gor ['go:ɐ̯] *imp von* **gären**
Göre <-, -n> ['gø:·rə] *f* (*fam*) brat
Gorilla <-s, -s> [go'·rɪ·la] *m* gorilla
Gospel <-s, -s> ['gɔs·pl̩] *nt o m* gospel
goss[RR], **goß**[ALT] ['gɔs] *imp von* **gießen**
Gosse <-, -n> ['gɔ·sə] *f* (*veraltend: Rinnstein*) gutter
Gotik <-> ['go:·tɪk] *f kein pl* Gothic period
gotisch ['go:·tɪʃ] *adj* Gothic
Gott, Göttin <-es, Götter> ['gɔt, *pl* 'gœ·tɐ] *m, f* ❶ (*ein Gott*) god *masc*, goddess *fem* ❷ *kein pl* (*das höchste Wesen*) God; **~ sei Dank!** (*a. fig fam*) thank God!; **bei ~ schwören** to swear to Almighty God ▶ WENDUNGEN: **wie ~ in Frankreich leben** (*fam*) to live in the lap of luxury; **über ~ und die Welt reden** to talk about everything under the sun; **ach du lieber ~!** good heavens!, oh Lord!; **~ bewahre!** God forbid!; **grüß ~!** *bes* SÜDD, ÖSTERR hello!; **~ weiß was/wann ...** (*fam*) God [only] knows what/when ...; **das wissen die Götter** (*fam*) heaven [*or* God] only knows; **ach ~** (*resignierend*) oh God!; (*tröstend*) oh dear; **um ~es willen!** (*emph: o je!*) [oh] my God!; (*bitte*) for God's sake!
Gottesdienst *m* [church] service
Gotteshaus *nt* place of worship
Gotteslästerung *f* blasphemy
Gottheit <-, -en> *f* deity
Göttin <-, -nen> ['gœ·tɪn] *f fem form von* **Gott** goddess
göttlich ['gœt·lɪç] *adj* divine
gottlos *adj* godless
gottverdammt *adj attr* (*emph sl*) [god]-damn[ed]
gottverlassen *adj* (*emph fam*) godforsaken *pej*
Götze <-n, -n> ['gœ·tsə] *m* (*pej*) ❶ (*heidnischer Gott*) false god ❷ *s.* **Götzenbild**
Götzenbild *nt* (*pej*) idol, graven image
Gouverneur(in) <-s, -e> [gu·vɛr·'nø:ɐ̯] *m(f)* governor
Grab <-[e]s, Gräber> ['gra:p, *pl* 'grɛ:·bɐ] *nt* grave ▶ WENDUNGEN: **sich** *dat* **sein eigenes ~ schaufeln** to dig one's own grave; **schweigen können wie ein ~** to be [as] silent as the grave; **jd würde sich** *akk* **im ~[e] umdrehen, wenn ...** (*fam*) sb would turn in their grave if ...
graben <grub, gegraben> ['gra:·bn̩] **I.** *vi* to dig (**nach** +*dat* for) **II.** *vt Loch* to dig **III.** *vr* ■ **sich** *akk* **in etw** *akk* **~** to sink into sth
Graben <-s, Gräben> ['gra:·bn̩, *pl* 'grɛ:·bn̩] *m* ❶ (*Vertiefung in der Erde*) ditch ❷ MIL trench ❸ (*Festungsgraben*) moat
Grabkammer *f* burial chamber
Grabmal *nt* ❶ (*Grabstätte*) mausoleum ❷ (*Gedenkstätte*) memorial
Grabrede *f* funeral speech, eulogy
Grabschändung *f* desecration of a grave
Grabstein *m* gravestone
Grad <-[e]s, -e> ['gra:t, *pl* 'gra:·də] *m* ❶ SCI, MATH degree; **2 ~ unter/über null** 2 degrees below/above [zero] ❷ (*Maß, Stufe*) level; **im höchsten/in hohem ~[e]** extremely/to a great extent ▶ WENDUNGEN: **um [ein]hundertachtzig ~** (*fam*) complete[ly]
grade ['gra:·də] *adj, adv* (*fam*) *s.* **gerade**
Graf, Gräfin[1] <-en, -en> ['gra:f, *pl* 'gra:·fən] *m, f* count *masc*, countess *fem*
Graf[RR2] <-en, -en> *m* LING, SCI *s.* **Graph**
Grafik ['gra:·fɪk] *f* ❶ *kein pl* (*grafische Technik*) graphic arts *pl* ❷ (*grafische Darstellung*) graphic ❸ (*Schaubild*) diagram
Grafiker(in) <-s, -> ['gra:·fi·kɐ] *m(f)* graphic artist
Grafikkarte *f* COMPUT graphics card
Gräfin <-, -nen> ['grɛ:·fɪn] *f fem form von* **Graf** countess *fem*
grafisch ['gra:·fɪʃ] **I.** *adj* ❶ KUNST graphic ❷ (*schematisch*) diagrammatic **II.** *adv* diagrammatically
Grafit[RR] <-s, -e> [gra·'fi:t] *m s.* **Graphit**
Grafschaft <-, -en> *f* HIST count's land
grämen ['grɛ:·mən] *vr* (*geh*) ■ **sich** *akk* **~** to grieve (**über** +*akk* over)
Gramm <-s, -e *o bei Zahlenangaben* -> ['gram] *nt* gram
Grammatik <-, -en> [gra·'ma·tɪk] *f* grammar
grammatikalisch [gra·ma·ti·'ka:·lɪʃ] *adj s.* **grammatisch**

grammatisch [gra·ˈma·tɪʃ] *adj* grammatical
Grammofon[RR], **Grammophon**® <-s, -e> [gra·mo·ˈfoːn] *nt* gramophone
Granat <-[e]s, -e o ÖSTERR -en> [gra·ˈnaːt] *m* garnet
Granate <-, -n> [gra·ˈnaː·tə] *f* shell, grenade
grandios [gran·ˈdi̯·oːs] *adj* magnificent
Granit <-s, -e> [gra·ˈniːt] *m* granite
Grapefruit <-, -s> [ˈgreːp·fruːt] *f* grapefruit
Graph <-en, -en> [graːf] *m* SCI graph
Graphik <-, -en> *f s.* **Grafik**
Graphiker(in) <-s, -> *m(f) s.* **Grafiker(in)**
graphisch *adj, adv s.* **grafisch**
Graphit <-s, -e> [gra·ˈfiːt] *m* graphite
grapschen [ˈgrapʃn̩] **I.** *vr* (*fam*) ① (*an sich raffen*) ■ **sich** *dat* **etw ~** to grab sth [for oneself] ② (*packen*) ■ **sich** *dat* **jdn ~** to grab hold of sb **II.** *vi* (*fam*) ■ **nach etw** *dat* **~** to make a grab for sth
Gras <-es, Gräser> [ˈgraːs, *pl* ˈgrɛː·zɐ] *nt* BOT grass ▶ WENDUNGEN: **ins ~ beißen** (*sl*) to bite the dust; **das ~ wachsen hören** to have a sixth sense; **über etw** *akk* **wächst ~** (*fam*) [the] dust settles on sth
grasen [ˈgraː·zn̩] *vi* to graze
Grashalm *m* blade of grass
Grashüpfer <-s, -> *m* (*fam*) grasshopper
grassieren* [gra·ˈsiː·rən] *vi* ① (*sich verbreiten*) to be rampant ② (*um sich greifen*) to be rife
grässlich[RR], **gräßlich**[ALT] [ˈgrɛs·lɪç] **I.** *adj* ① (*furchtbar*) horrible; **~e Kopfschmerzen haben** to have a splitting headache ② (*fam: widerlich*) horrible; **was für ein ~es Wetter!** what lousy weather! **II.** *adv* (*fam*) terribly
Grat <-[e]s, -e> [ˈgraːt] *m* ① (*oberste Kante*) ridge ② ARCHIT hip
Gräte <-, -n> [ˈgrɛː·tə] *f* [fish]bone
gratinieren* [gra·ti·ˈniː·r·ən] *vt* KOCHK ■ **etw ~** to brown [the top of] sth
gratis [ˈgraː·tɪs] *adv* free [of charge]
Gratisprobe *f* free sample
Gratulant(in) <-en, -en> [gra·tu·ˈlant] *m(f)* well-wisher
Gratulation <-, -en> [gra·tu·la·ˈtsi̯oːn] *f* ① (*das Gratulieren*) congratulating ② (*Glückwunsch*) congratulations *npl*
gratulieren* [gra·tu·ˈliː·rən] *vi* ■ **[jdm] ~** to congratulate [sb] (**zu** +*dat* on); **jdm zum Geburtstag ~** to wish sb a happy birthday; **[ich] gratuliere** [my] congratulations!
grau [ˈgrau] *adj* ① (*Farbe*) gray; **~ meliert** (*leicht ergraut*) graying; MODE flecked with gray *pred* ② (*trostlos*) drab; **der ~e Alltag** the dullness of everyday life
Graubrot *nt* DIAL (*Mischbrot*) *bread made from rye and wheat flour*
Gräueltat[RR] *f* atrocity
grauen[1] [ˈgrau·ən] *vi* (*geh: dämmern*) to dawn; **der Tag graut** day is breaking
grauen[2] [ˈgrau·ən] *vi impers* ■ **es graut jdm vor jdm/etw** sb is terrified of sb/sth
Grauen <-s> [ˈgrau·ən] *nt kein pl* horror; **~ erregend** terrible
grauenerregend *adj s.* **Grauen**
grauenhaft, **grauenvoll** *adj* ① (*furchtbar*) terrible ② (*fam: schlimm*) dreadful
grauhaarig *adj* gray-haired
gräulich[1] [ˈgrɔy·lɪç] *adj* grayish
gräulich[RR2] *adj s.* **grässlich**
Graupelschauer *m* sleet shower
grausam [ˈgrau·zaːm] **I.** *adj* ① (*brutal*) cruel ② (*furchtbar*) terrible **II.** *adv* cruelly
Grausamkeit <-, -en> *f* ① *kein pl* (*Brutalität*) cruelty ② (*grausame Tat*) act of cruelty
grausen [ˈgrau·zn̩] *vi impers s.* **grauen**[2]
Grausen <-s> [ˈgrau·zn̩] *nt kein pl* horror
Grauzone *f* gray area
gravieren* [gra·ˈviː·rən] *vt* to engrave (**in** +*akk* on)
gravierend [gra·ˈviː·rənt] *adj* serious; *Unterschiede* considerable
Gravierung <-, -en> *f* engraving
Gravitation <-> [gra·vi·ta·ˈtsi̯oːn] *f kein pl* gravitation[al pull]
Gravur <-, -en> [gra·ˈvuːɐ̯] *f* engraving
Grazie <-, -n> [ˈgraː·tsi̯ə] *f* ① *kein pl* (*Anmut*) grace ② (*hum veraltet: schöne junge Frau*) lovely
gregorianisch [gre·go·ˈri̯aː·nɪʃ] *adj* Gregorian
greifbar *adj* ① *pred* (*verfügbar*) **etw ~ haben/halten** to have/keep sth handy ② (*konkret*) tangible
greifen <griff, gegriffen> [ˈgrai·fn̩] **I.** *vt* ■ **[sich** *dat*] **etw ~** to take hold of sth **II.** *vi* ① (*fassen*) ■ **in etw** *akk* **~** to reach into sth; **sie griff mich bei der Hand** she took my hand; ■ **nach etw** *dat* **~** to reach for sth ② (*einsetzen*) **zu Drogen/zur Zigarette ~** to turn to drugs/reach for a cigarette ③ TECH *Reifen, Zahnrad* ■ **etw greift** sth grips ④ (*wirksam werden*) *Methoden* to take effect ▶ WENDUNGEN: **um sich ~** (*sich ausbreiten*) to spread
Greis(in) <-es, -e> [ˈgrais, *pl* ˈgrai·zə] *m(f)* very old man/woman
grell [ˈgrɛl] **I.** *adj* ① (*hell*) *Licht, Sonne* glaring, bright ② (*schrill*) *Stimme, Schrei* piercing ③ (*auffallend*) *Muster* loud **II.** *adv* ① (*sehr hell*) dazzlingly ② (*schrill*) **~ klingen** to sound shrill
Gremium <-s, -ien> [ˈgreː·mi̯·ʊm, *pl* ˈgreː·mi̯·ən] *nt* committee
Grenze <-, -n> [ˈgrɛn·tsə] *f* ① (*Landesgrenze*) border; **an der ~** on the border; **über die ~ fahren/gehen** to cross the border ② (*Trennlinie*) boundary ③ (*äußerstes Maß*) limit; **alles hat seine ~n** there is a limit to everything; **seine ~n kennen** to know one's limitations; **sich in ~n halten** to be limited
grenzen [ˈgrɛn·tsn̩] *vi* ■ **an etw** *akk* **~** to border on sth
grenzenlos **I.** *adj* ① (*unbegrenzt*) endless ② (*maßlos*) extreme; *Vertrauen* blind **II.** *adv* extremely
Grenzfall *m* borderline case

G

Grenzgebiet *nt* POL border area
Grenzkontrolle *f* border control
Grenzlinie *f* SPORT line [marking the boundary of a playing surface]
Grenzstein *m* boundary stone
Grenzstreitigkeit *f meist pl* border dispute
Grenzübergang *m* border crossing point
grenzüberschreitend *adj attr* JUR, ÖKON **~er Handel** international trade; **~er Verkehr** cross-border traffic
Grenzwert *m* limiting value
Grieche, Griechin <-n, -n> ['griː·çə] *m, f* Greek; *s. a.* **Deutsche(r)**
Griechenland <-s> ['griː·çn̩·lant] *nt* Greece; *s. a.* **Deutschland**

G

griechisch ['griː·çɪʃ] *adj* Greek; *s. a.* **deutsch**
Griesgram <-[e]s, -e> ['griːs·graːm] *m* (*pej*) grouch
griesgrämig ['griːs·grɛː·mɪç] *adj* grumpy
Grieß <-es, -e> ['griːs] *m* semolina
Grießbrei *m* semolina
griff ['grɪf] *imp von* **greifen**
Griff <-[e]s, -e> ['grɪf] *m* ❶ (*Zugriff*) grip ❷ (*Handgriff*) movement; **mit einem ~** in a flash ❸ SPORT hold ❹ (*Öffnungsmechanismus*) *Tür, Revolver* handle; *Messer* hilt ▶ WENDUNGEN: **etw in den ~ bekommen** (*fam*) to get the hang of sth; **jdn/etw im ~ haben** to have sb/sth under control
griffbereit *adj* **etw ~ haben** to have sth handy; **~ liegen** to be readily accessible
griffig ['grɪ·fɪç] *adj* ❶ (*festen Griff ermöglichend*) easy to grip *pred* ❷ (*Widerstand bietend*) nonslip; *Fußboden, Profil* antiskid ❸ (*eingängig*) **ein ~er Slogan** a catchy slogan
Grill <-s, -s> ['grɪl] *m* ❶ (*Gerät*) grill ❷ (*Grillrost*) barbecue; **vom ~** grilled
Grille <-, -n> ['grɪ·lə] *f* cricket
grillen ['grɪ·lən] **I.** *vi* to have a barbecue **II.** *vt* to barbecue, to grill
Grimasse <-, -n> [gri·'ma·sə] *f* grimace; **~n schneiden** to make faces
grimmig ['grɪ·mɪç] **I.** *adj* ❶ (*zornig*) furious; *Gesicht* angry ❷ (*sehr groß, heftig*) severe; *Hunger* ravenous **II.** *adv* angrily; **~ lächeln** to smile grimly
grinsen ['grɪn·zn̩] *vi* to grin; **frech ~** to smirk; **höhnisch ~** to sneer
Grinsen <-s> ['grɪn·zn̩] *nt kein pl* grin; **freches ~** smirk; **höhnisches ~** sneer
Grippe <-, -n> ['grɪ·pə] *f* influenza, flu
Grippemittel *nt* flu medicine *fam*
Grippevirus *nt o m* influenza [*or* flu] virus
Grips <-es, *selten* -e> ['grɪps] *m* (*fam*) brains *pl*; **~ haben** to have plenty up top
grob <gröber, gröbste> ['groːp] **I.** *adj* ❶ (*nicht fein*) coarse ❷ (*ungefähr*) rough; **in ~en Umrissen** roughly ❸ (*unhöflich*) rude; ■ **~ werden** to get rude ❹ (*unsanft, unsensibel*) rough ▶ WENDUNGEN: **aus dem Gröbsten heraus sein** the worst is over **II.** *adv* ❶ (*nicht fein*) coarsely; **~ gemahlen** coarsely ground ❷ (*in etwa*) roughly; **~ geschätzt** at a rough estimate; **etw ~ erklären/wiedergeben** to give a rough explanation/account of sth ❸ (*unhöflich*) rudely ❹ (*unsanft, unsensibel*) roughly ❺ (*schlimm*) **sich** *akk* **~ täuschen** to be badly mistaken
grobgemahlen *adj attr s.* **grob II 1**
Grobheit <-, -en> *f* ❶ *kein pl* (*gefühllose Art*) rudeness ❷ (*grobe Äußerung*) rude remark ❸ (*unsanfte Art, Behandlung*) roughness
Grobian <-[e]s, -e> ['groː·bi̯·aːn] *m* (*pej*) boor
grobkörnig *adj* coarse-grained
groggy ['grɔgi] *adj pred* ❶ (*schwer angeschlagen*) groggy ❷ (*fam: erschöpft*) exhausted
grölen ['grøː·lən] **I.** *vi* (*pej fam*) to shout [loudly] **II.** *vt* (*pej fam*) to bellow
Groll <-[e]s> ['grɔl] *m kein pl* (*geh*) resentment; **[einen] ~ gegen jdn hegen** to harbor a grudge against sb
grollen ['grɔ·lən] *vi* (*geh*) ❶ (*zürnen*) ■ **[jdm] ~** to be resentful [of sb] ❷ (*dumpf hallen*) to rumble
Grönland ['grøːn·lant] *nt* Greenland; *s. a.* **Deutschland**
Grönländer(in) <-s, -> ['grøːn·lɛn·dɐ] *m(f)* Greenlander; *s. a.* **Deutsche(r)**
grönländisch ['grøːn·lɛn·dɪʃ] *adj* Greenlandic; *s. a.* **deutsch**
Gros <-, -> [groː] *nt* ■ **das ~** the majority
Groschen <-s, -> ['grɔ·ʃn̩] *m* ÖSTERR groschen ▶ WENDUNGEN: **der ~ fällt** (*hum fam*) a big light went on
groß <größer, größte> ['groːs] **I.** *adj* ❶ (*flächenmäßig*) large, big ❷ (*lang*) long; **ein ~er Turm** a high tower ❸ (*das Maß oder Ausmaß betreffend*) great; **in ~en/größeren Formaten/Größen** in large/larger formats/sizes; **mit ~er Geschwindigkeit** at high speed ❹ (*hoch gewachsen*) tall; **du bist ~ geworden** you've grown; **er ist 1,78 m ~** he is 1.78 m [*or* 5 feet 10 inches] [tall] ❺ (*älter*) big, elder ❻ (*zeitlich ausgedehnt*) lengthy; **auf große[r] Fahrt** on a long journey ❼ (*bevölkerungsreich*) large; **die ~e Masse** the majority of [the] people ❽ (*erheblich*) great; *Durchbruch, Reinfall* major; *Misserfolg* abject ❾ (*hoch*) large ❿ (*beträchtlich*) great; *Nachfrage* big; *Schrecken* nasty; *Schwierigkeiten* serious; **~e Angst haben** to be terribly afraid; **eine ~e Dummheit** sheer stupidity ⓫ (*bedeutend*) great; *Unternehmen, Supermarkt* leading ⓬ (*in Eigennamen*) **Friedrich der G~e** Frederick the Great ⓭ (*besonders [gut]*) **im Meckern ist sie ganz ~** she's moans about everything; **ich bin kein ~er Redner** I'm no great speaker ▶ WENDUNGEN: **im G~en und Ganzen [gesehen]** on the whole **II.** *adv* ❶ (*fam: besonders*) **was soll man da schon ~ sagen?** there's really not much to say; **ich habe mich nie ~ für Politik interessiert** I've never been particularly interested in politics ❷ MODE **etw größer machen** to let out *sep* sth ❸ (*von weitem Ausmaß*) **~ angelegt**

large-scale

Großalarm *m* red alert

großartig ['groːs·ʔaːɐ̯·tɪç] **I.** *adj* ① (*prächtig*) magnificent ② (*hervorragend*) brilliant ③ (*wundervoll*) wonderful **II.** *adv* magnificently

Großaufnahme *f* close-up

Großbetrieb *m* large business; AGR large farm

Großbritannien <-s> [groːs·bri·'tanɪ̯ən] *nt* Great Britain; *s. a.* **Deutschland**

Großbuchstabe *m* capital [letter]

Größe <-, -n> ['grøːsə] *f* ① (*räumliche Ausdehnung*) *a.* ÖKON, MODE size ② (*Höhe, Länge*) height ③ MATH, PHYS quantity ④ *kein pl* (*Erheblichkeit*) magnitude; *eines Problems* seriousness; *eines Erfolgs* extent ⑤ *kein pl* (*Bedeutsamkeit*) significance

Großeinkauf *m* bulk purchase

Großeinsatz *m* large-scale operation

Großeltern *pl* grandparents *pl*

Großenkel(in) *m(f)* great-grandchild, great-grandson *masc,* great-granddaughter *fem*

Größenordnung *f* order of magnitude

großenteils *adv* largely

Größenwahn(sinn) *m* megalomania

größenwahnsinnig *adj* megalomanic

größer ['grøːsɐ] *adj komp von* **groß**

Großfahndung *f* large-scale search

Großfamilie *f* extended family

Großhandel *m* wholesale trade; **etw im ~ kaufen** to buy sth wholesale

Großhändler(in) *m(f)* wholesaler

großherzig *adj* (*geh*) magnanimous

Großherzigkeit <-> *f kein pl* (*geh*) magnanimity

Großherzog(in) ['groːs·hɛr·tsoːk] *m(f)* grand duke *masc,* grand duchess *fem*

Großherzogtum *nt* grand duchy

Großhirn *nt* cerebrum

Großkind *nt* SCHWEIZ (*Enkelkind*) grandchild

großkotzig *adj* (*pej sl*) swanky

Großmacht *f* great power

Großmaul *nt* (*pej fam*) big mouth

Großmut *f s.* **Großherzigkeit**

großmütig ['groːs·myːtɪç] *adj s.* **großherzig**

Großmutter *f* grandmother, grandma *fam,* granny *fam*

Großraum *m* metropolitan area; **im ~ Berlin** in Greater Berlin

Großraumabteil *nt* BAHN open-plan car

Großraumbüro *nt* open-plan office, office with an open floor plan

großräumig *adj* ① (*geräumig*) spacious ② (*große Flächen betreffend*) extensive

groß|schreiben *vt irreg* ① (*mit großem Anfangsbuchstaben*) ■**etw ~** to capitalize sth ② (*fam: wichtig nehmen*) ■**etw wird bei jdm großgeschrieben** to be high on sb's list of priorities

Großschreibung *f* capitalization

großspurig *adj* (*pej*) boastful

Großstadt ['groːs·ʃtat] *f* [big] city

großstädtisch ['groːs·ʃtɛːtɪʃ] *adj* big-city *attr*

größte(r, s) ['grøːstə] *adj superl von* **groß**

Großteil *m* ① (*ein großer Teil*) ■**ein ~** a large part ② (*der überwiegende Teil*) ■**der ~** the majority; **zum ~** for the most part

größtenteils *adv* for the most part

größtmöglich ['grøːst·'møːk·lɪç] *adj attr* greatest possible

groß|tun *irreg* **I.** *vi* (*pej*) to boast **II.** *vr* ■**sich** *akk* **mit etw** *dat* **~** to boast about sth

Großunternehmen *nt s.* **Großbetrieb**

Großunternehmer(in) *m(f)* entrepreneur

Großvater *m* grandfather, grandpa *fam*

Großverdiener(in) *m(f)* high-income earner

groß|ziehen ['groːs·tsiːən] *vt irreg* **ein Kind ~** to raise a child; **ein Tier ~** to rear an animal

großzügig **I.** *adj* ① (*generös*) generous ② (*nachsichtig*) lenient ③ (*in großem Stil*) grand; **ein ~er Plan** a large-scale plan **II.** *adv* ① (*generös*) generously ② (*nachsichtig*) leniently ③ (*weiträumig*) spaciously

Großzügigkeit <-> *f kein pl* ① (*Generosität*) generosity ② (*Toleranz*) leniency ③ (*Weiträumigkeit*) spaciousness

grotesk [gro·'tɛsk] *adj* grotesque

Grotte <-, -n> ['grɔ·tə] *f* grotto

grub ['gruːp] *imp von* **graben**

Grübchen <-s, -> ['gryːp·çən] *nt* dimple

Grube <-, -n> ['gruː·bə] *f* ① (*größeres Erdloch*) [large] hole ② (*Bergwerk*) pit ▶ WENDUNGEN: **wer andern eine ~ gräbt, fällt selbst hinein** (*prov*) you can easily fall into your own trap

Grübelei <-, -en> [gryː·bə·'lai] *f* brooding

grübeln ['gryː·bl̩n] *vi* to brood (**über** *+akk* over)

Grubenarbeiter *m* miner

Grubenunglück *nt* mine [*or* mining] disaster

grüblerisch ['gryːb·lə·rɪʃ] *adj* broody

grüezi ['gryːɛ·tsi] *interj* SCHWEIZ (*fam*) hi

Gruft <-, Grüfte> ['grʊft, *pl* 'grʏf·tə] *f* (*Grabgewölbe*) vault; (*Kirche*) crypt

grummeln ['grʊ·ml̩n] *vi* (*fam*) ① (*brummeln*) to mumble ② (*leise rollen*) to rumble

grün ['gryːn] *adj* (*Farbe*) *a.* POL green ▶ WENDUNGEN: **sich ~ und blau ärgern** to be furious; **jdn ~ und blau schlagen** (*fam*) to beat sb black and blue

Grün <-s, - *o fam* -s> ['gryːn] *nt* ① (*Farbe*) green ② (*Grünflächen*) green spaces; *am Golfplatz* green ③ (*grüne Pflanzen*) greenery; **das erste ~ nach dem Winter** the first green shoots of spring ▶ WENDUNGEN: **das ist dasselbe in ~** (*fam*) it's one and the same [thing]

Grünanlage *f* green space

Grund <-[e]s, Gründe> ['grʊnt, *pl* 'grʏn·də] *m* ① (*Ursache, Veranlassung*) reason, cause; **keinen/nicht den geringsten ~** no/not the slightest reason; **jdm ~ [zu etw** *dat*] **geben** to give sb reason [to do sth]; ■**ein/kein ~ zu etw** *dat* [no] reason for sth ② (*Motiv*) grounds *pl;* **~ zu der Annahme haben, dass ...** to have reason to believe that ...; **aus finanziellen/gesundheitlichen Gründen**

for financial/health reasons; **aus gutem ~** with good reason; **aus unerfindlichen Gründen** for some obscure reason; **aus diesem/welchem ~[e]** for this/what reason ❸ *kein pl* (*Erdboden*) ground ❹ DIAL (*Land, Acker*) land; **~ und Boden** land ❺ (*Boden eines Gewässers*) bed; **am ~e des Meeres** at the bottom of the sea ❻ *kein pl* (*Untergrund*) background ▶ WENDUNGEN: **jdn in ~ und Boden reden** to shoot sb's arguments to pieces; **im ~e jds Herzens** (*geh*) in one's heart of hearts; **auf ~ einer S.** *gen* on the basis of sth; **im ~e [genommen]** basically; **von ~ auf** [*o* **aus**] completely; (*von Anfang an*) from scratch

Grụndausbildung *f* basic training

Grụndbedeutung *f* fundamental meaning; LING original meaning

Grụndbegriff *m meist pl* ❶ (*elementarer Begriff*) basic notion ❷ SCH rudiments *npl*

Grụndbesitz *m* real estate, property

Grụndbesitzer(in) *m(f)* landowner

Grụndbuch *nt* real property register

grundehrlich ['grʊnt·'ʔeːɐ̯·lɪç] *adj* (*emph*) thoroughly honest

gründen ['grʏn·dn̩] **I.** *vt* ❶ (*neu schaffen*) to found; *Firma* to set up; *Partei* to form ❷ (*fußen lassen*) ■ **etw auf etw** *akk* **~** to base sth on sth **II.** *vr* ■ **sich auf etw** *akk* **~** to be based on sth

Gründer(in) <-s, -> *m(f)* founder

grundfalsch ['grʊnt·'falʃ] *adj* (*emph*) completely wrong

Grụndfarbe *f* ❶ (*Primärfarbe*) primary color ❷ (*als Untergrund aufgetragene Farbe*) primer

Grụndfläche *f* area

Grụndgebühr *f* basic charge [*or* fee]

Grụndgedanke *m* basic idea

Grụndgesetz *nt* basic [*or* fundamental] law

> The **Grundgesetz** is the constitution of the Federal Republic of Germany. It outlines Germany's legal and political system, and defines, among other things, the basic rights of people living in Germany and the relationship between the *Länder* (Federal States) and the federal government.

grundieren* [grʊn·'diː·rən] *vt* to prime

Grundierung <-, -en> *f* primary coat

Grụndkenntnis *f meist pl* basic knowledge

Grụndkurs *m* SCH basic course [*or* class]; (*Einführungskurs*) introductory course

Grụndlage *f* basis

grụndlegend I. *adj* fundamental **II.** *adv* fundamentally

gründlich ['grʏnt·lɪç] **I.** *adj* thorough; **eine ~e Bildung** a broad education **II.** *adv* ❶ (*fam: total*) completely ❷ (*gewissenhaft*) thoroughly

Gründlichkeit <-> *f kein pl* thoroughness

Grụndlinie *f* ❶ MATH ground line ❷ SPORT baseline

grụndlos I. *adj* ❶ (*unbegründet*) unfounded ❷ (*ohne festen Boden*) bottomless **II.** *adv* groundlessly

Grụndmauer *f* foundation wall

Grụndnahrungsmittel *nt* basic food[stuff]

Gründonnerstag [gryːn·'dɔnɐs·taːk] *m* Maundy Thursday

Grụndpfeiler *m* ❶ (*tragender Pfeiler*) supporting pillar; *Brücke* supporting pier ❷ (*fig: wesentliches Element*) cornerstone

Grụndrecht *nt* basic right

Grụndregel *f* basic rule

Grụndriss[RR] *m* ❶ BAU floor plan ❷ (*Abriss*) outline

Grundsatz ['grʊnt·zats] *m* principle

grundsätzlich ['grʊnt·zɛts·lɪç] **I.** *adj* ❶ (*grundlegend*) fundamental; *Bedenken, Zweifel* serious ❷ (*prinzipiell*) in principle *pred* **II.** *adv* ❶ (*völlig*) completely ❷ (*prinzipiell*) in principle ❸ (*kategorisch*) absolutely

Grụndschule *f* elementary school

Grụndstein *m* foundation stone; **den ~ zu etw** *dat* **legen** to lay the foundation for sth

Grụndstoff *m* ❶ (*Rohstoff*) raw material ❷ CHEM element

Grụndstück *nt* [piece of] property

Grụndstücksmakler(in) *m(f)* real estate agent

Grụndton *m* ❶ (*eines Akkords*) root; (*einer Tonleiter*) keynote ❷ (*Grundfarbe*) primer

Gründung <-, -en> *f* ❶ (*das Gründen*) foundation; *eines Betriebs* establishment ❷ BAU foundation

grundverschieden ['grʊnt·fɛɐ̯·'ʃiː·dn̩] *adj* (*emph*) completely different

Grụndwasser *nt* ground water

Grụndwasserspiegel *m* groundwater level

Grụndwortschatz *m* basic vocabulary

Grüne(r) ['gryː·nə] *f(m)* POL [member of the] Green [Party]; **die ~n** the Green Party

Grüne(s) ['gryː·nə(s)] *nt* ❶ (*Schmuckreisig*) ■ **~s** greenery *sing* ❷ (*Gemüse*) ■ **~s** greens ▶ WENDUNGEN: **ins ~ fahren** (*fam*) to drive into the country

> Many bottles, cans, cartons, and other packages and containers are marked with a special **Grüner Punkt** (green dot) which indicates that they can be recycled according to the *Duales System* (recycling system). The recycling leads to the elimination of mountains of garbage.

Grünfläche *f* green space

Grünkohl *m* [curly] kale

grünlich ['gryːn·lɪç] *adj* greenish

Grünschnabel *m* (*fam*) greenhorn

Grünspan ['gryːn·ʃpaːn] *m kein pl* verdigris

Grünstreifen *m* median [strip]; (*am Straßenrand*) grassy shoulder

grunzen ['grʊn·tsn̩] *vi, vt* to grunt

Grünzeug *nt* (*fam*) ❶ (*Kräuter*) herbs *pl* ❷ (*Salat*) green salad; (*Gemüse*) greens *pl*

Gruppe <-, -n> ['grʊ·pə] *f* group
Grụppenarbeit *f kein pl* teamwork
Grụppenaufnahme, **Grụppenbild** *nt* group photograph
Grụppendynamik *f* group dynamics + *sing/pl vb, no art*
Grụppenleiter(in) *m(f)* team leader
Grụppenreise *f* group travel
grụppenweise *adv* in groups
gruppieren* [grʊ'·piː·rən] **I.** *vt* ■**etw** ~ to group sth **II.** *vr* ■**sich** ~ to be grouped
Gruppierung <-, -en> *f* ① (*Gruppe*) group ② (*Aufstellung*) grouping
Gruselfilm *m* horror film
Gruselgeschichte *f* horror story
gruselig ['gruː·zə·lɪç], **gruslig** ['gruːz·lɪç] *adj* gruesome, creepy
gruseln ['gruː·zl̩n] **I.** *vt, vi impers* ■**jdn gruselt es** sb gets the creeps **II.** *vr* ■**sich** *akk* [**vor jdm**] ~ to shudder [at the sight of sb]
Gruß <-es, Grüße> ['gruːs, *pl* 'gryː·sə] *m* ① (*Begrüßung*) greeting; MIL salute; **einen** [**schönen**] ~ **an Ihre Gattin** [please] give my regards to your wife, say hi to your wife for me *fam* ② (*am Briefschluss*) regards; **mit freundlichen Grüßen** sincerely; **herzliche Grüße** best wishes
grüßen ['gryː·sn̩] **I.** *vt* ① (*begrüßen*) ■**jdn** ~ to greet sb; MIL to salute sb; **grüß dich!** (*fam*) hello [there]! ② (*Grüße übermitteln*) ■**jdn von jdm** ~ to send sb sb's regards; **jdn** ~ **lassen** to say hello to sb **II.** *vi* to say hello **III.** *vr* ■**sich** ~ to say hello to one another
Grußwort *nt* welcome speech
gucken ['gʊ·kn̩] *vi* ① (*sehen*) to look; (*heimlich*) to peek; **was guckst du so dumm!** wipe that silly look off your face! ② (*ragen*) ■**aus etw** *dat* ~ to stick out of sth
Gụckloch *nt* peephole
Guerillakämpfer(in) [ge·'rɪ·lja-] *m(f)* guerrilla
Guerillakrieg [ge·'rɪ·lja-] *m* guerrilla war[fare]
Guillotine <-, -n> [gɪl·jo·'tiː·nə, gi·jo·'tiː·nə] *f* guillotine
Gulasch <-[e]s, -e *o* -s> ['gʊ·laʃ] *nt o m* goulash, stew
Gulden <-s, -> ['gʊl·dn̩] *m* guilder
Gully <-s, -s> ['gʊ·li] *m o nt* drain
gültig ['gʏl·tɪç] *adj* ① (*Geltung besitzend*) valid; **der Sommerfahrplan ist ab dem 1.4.** ~ the summer schedule takes effect April 1st ② (*allgemein anerkannt*) universal
Gụltigkeit <-> *f kein pl* ① (*Geltung*) validity ② (*gesetzliche Wirksamkeit*) legal force
Gummi <-s, -s> ['gʊmi] *nt o m* ① (*Material*) rubber ② (*fam: Radiergummi*) eraser ③ (*fam: Gummiband*) rubber band ④ (*Gummizug*) elastic ⑤ (*fam: Kondom*) rubber *sl*
Gụmmiband *nt* rubber band
Gụmmibaum *m* ① (*Kautschukbaum*) rubber tree ② (*Zimmerpflanze*) rubber plant
Gụmmihandschuh *m* rubber glove
Gụmmistiefel *m* rubber boot
Gụmmizelle *f* padded cell
Gụmmizug *m* elastic
Gunst <-> ['gʊnst] *f kein pl* ① (*Wohlwollen*) goodwill; **in jds ~ stehen** to be in sb's favor ② (*Vergünstigung*) **zu jds ~en** in sb's favor
günstig ['gʏns·tɪç] **I.** *adj* ① (*zeitlich gut gelegen*) convenient ② (*begünstigend*) favorable ③ (*preisgünstig*) reasonable **II.** *adv* ① (*preisgünstig*) reasonably ② (*passend, geeignet*) favorably
Gurgel <-, -n> ['gʊr·gl̩] *f* throat
gurgeln ['gʊr·gl̩n] *vi* ① (*den Rachen spülen*) to gargle ② (*von ablaufender Flüssigkeit*) to gurgle
Gurke <-, -n> ['gʊr·kə] *f* cucumber; (*Essiggurke*) pickle
gurren ['gʊ·rən] *vi Tauben* to coo; (*fam*) *Mensch* to purr
Gurt <-[e]s, -e> ['gʊrt] *m* ① (*Riemen*) strap ② (*Sicherheitsgurt*) seat belt ③ (*breiter Gürtel*) belt
Gürtel <-s, -> ['gʏr·tl̩] *m* belt
Gürtellinie *f* waist[line]
Gụrtelschnalle *f* belt buckle
Gụrteltasche *f* fanny pack
Gụrteltier *nt* armadillo
Gurtpflicht *f* seatbelt law
Guru <-s, -s> ['guːru] *m* guru
Guss[RR] <-es, Güsse>, **Guß**[ALT] <-sses, Güsse> ['gʊs, *pl* 'gʏ·sə] *m* ① (*fam: Regenguss*) downpour ② (*Zuckerguss*) icing
Gụsseisen[RR] *nt* cast iron
Gụssform[RR] *f* mold
gut <bẹsser, bẹste> ['guːt] **I.** *adj* ① (*ausgezeichnet, hervorragend*) good; **jdm geht es ~/nicht ~** sb is fine/not well ② (*fachlich qualifiziert*) good ③ *attr* (*lieb*) good; (*intim*) close ④ *meist attr* (*untadelig*) good ⑤ (*nicht übel, vorteilhaft*) good; **das kann nicht ~ gehen!** there's no way that'll work!, this won't be good! ⑥ (*in Wünschen*) good; **~en Appetit!** enjoy your meal!; **~e Besserung/Erholung!** get well soon!; **~e Fahrt/Reise!** have a good [*or* nice] trip!; **ein ~es neues Jahr!** Happy New Year! ▶ WENDUNGEN: ~ **beieinander sein** SÜDD to be a bit chubby; ~ **drauf sein** (*fam*) to be in a good mood; ~ **gegen etw** *akk* **sein** (*fam*) to be good for sth; ~ **in etw** *dat* **sein** to be good at sth; **lass mal ~ sein!** (*fam*) let's drop the subject!; **wer weiß, wozu es ~ ist** perhaps it's for the best; ~ **werden** to turn out all right; **wieder ~ werden** to be all right; **also ~!** well, all right then!; **schon ~!** (*fam*) all right!; ~ **so!** that's great! [*or* perfect!]; **und das ist auch ~ so** and it's/that's a good thing, too; **sei so ~ und ...** would you be kind enough to ...; **wozu ist das ~?** (*fam*) what's the use of that?; [**wie**] **~, dass ...** it's a good thing that ...; **~!** (*in Ordnung!*) OK!; **~, ~!** okay, okay! **II.** *adv* ① (*nicht schlecht*) well; **~ aussehend** *attr* good-looking; **~ bezahlt** *attr* well-paid; **~ gehend** *attr* flourishing; **~ gelaunt** in a good mood; **~ gemeint** *attr* well-meant; **du sprichst aber ~ Englisch!**

G

your English is really good, you speak English really well; ~ **verdienend** *attr* high-income *attr* ② (*geschickt*) well ③ (*reichlich*) **es dauert noch ~ eine Stunde, bis Sie an der Reihe sind** it'll be a good hour before it's your turn ④ (*einfach, recht*) **ich kann ihn jetzt nicht ~ im Stich lassen** I can't just leave him like that [now] ⑤ (*leicht, mühelos*) **hast du die Prüfung ~ hinter dich gebracht?** did you make it through the exam all right?; ~ **leserlich** very legible ⑥ (*angenehm*) **hm, wonach riecht das denn so ~ in der Küche?** hmm, what's that great smell coming from the kitchen?; **schmeckt es dir auch ~?** do you like it, too? ▶ WENDUNGEN: ~ **und gern** easily; **so ~ es geht** as best one can; **[das hast du] ~ gemacht!** good job!; **es ~ haben** to be lucky, to have it good; **das kann ~ sein** that's quite possible; **mach's ~!** (*fam*) bye!; **pass ~ auf!** be [very] careful!; **sich** *akk* ~ **mit jdm stellen** to get in good with sb

Gut <-[e]s, Güter> ['gu:t, *pl* 'gy:·tɐ] *nt* ① (*Landgut*) estate ② (*Ware*) commodity ③ *kein pl* (*das Gute*) good; ~ **und Böse** good and evil

Gutachten <-s, -> ['gu:t·ʔax·tn̩] *nt* [expert's] report

Gutachter(in) <-s, -> *m(f)* expert

gutartig *adj* ① MED benign ② (*nicht widerspenstig*) good-natured

gutbürgerlich ['gu:t·'bʏr·gɐ·lɪç] *adj* middle-class; KOCHK homemade; ~**e Küche** home-style cooking

Gutdünken <-s> *nt kein pl* discretion

Gute(s) *nt* ① (*Positives*) ■ ~**s** good; **man hört viel ~s über ihn** you hear a lot of good things about him; ■ **etwas ~s** something good; **er tat in seinem Leben viel ~s** he did a lot of good [things] in his life; **[auch] sein ~s haben** to have its good points [too]; **ein ~s hat die Sache** there is one good thing about it; **jdm schwant nichts ~s** sb has a bad feeling about sth; **nichts ~s versprechen** to not sound very promising; **jdm ~s tun** to be good to sb; **was kann ich dir denn ~s tun?** how can I spoil you?; **sich zum ~n wenden** to take a turn for the better; **alles ~!** all the best!; **das ~ daran** the good thing about it ② (*friedlich*) **im ~n** amicably; **lass dir's im ~n gesagt sein, dass ich das nicht dulde** take a bit of friendly advice — I won't put up with it/that!; **sich** *akk* **im ~n trennen** to part on friendly terms ③ (*gute Charakterzüge*) **das ~ im Menschen** the good in man; ~**s tun** to do good ▶ WENDUNGEN: ~**s mit Bösem/~m vergelten** (*geh*) to return evil/good for good; **des ~n zu viel sein** to be too much [of a good thing]; **das ist wirklich des ~n zu viel!** that's really overdoing it/things!; **alles hat sein ~s** (*prov*) every cloud has a silver lining *prov;* **im ~n wie im Bösen** (*mit Güte wie mit Strenge*) every way possible; (*in guten und schlechten Zeiten*) through good [times] and bad

Güte <-> ['gy:·tə] *f kein pl* ① (*milde Einstellung*) kindness; **die ~ haben, zu ...** to be so kind as to ... ② (*Qualität*) [good] quality ▶ WENDUNGEN: **erster ~** (*fam*) of the first order; **ach du liebe ~!** (*fam*) oh my goodness! *fam;* **in ~** amicably

Gutenachtgeschichte [gu:·tə·'naxt-] *f* bedtime story

Güterbahnhof *m* freight depot

Gütergemeinschaft *f* JUR community property; **in ~ leben** to have community property

Gütertrennung *f* JUR separate [*or* separation of] property; **in ~ leben** to have separate property

Güterzug *m* freight train

Gütezeichen *nt* mark of quality

gutgläubig *adj* trusting, gullible

Gutgläubigkeit *f* gullibility

gut|haben *vt irreg* ■ **etw bei jdm ~** to be owed sth by sb

Guthaben <-s, -> *nt* credit balance

gut|heißen *vt irreg* ■ **etw ~** to approve of sth

gütig ['gy:·tɪç] *adj* kind; **würden Sie so ~ sein, zu ...** (*geh*) would you be so kind as to ...; **[danke,] zu ~!** (*iron*) [thank you,] you're too kind!

gütlich ['gy:t·lɪç] **I.** *adj* amicable **II.** *adv* amicably ▶ WENDUNGEN: **sich** *akk* **an etw** *dat* ~ **tun** to help oneself freely to sth

gut|machen *vt* ① (*in Ordnung bringen*) ■ **etw ~** to make sth right; **etw an jdm gutzumachen haben** to owe sb sth ② (*entgelten*) ■ **etw ~** to repay sth ③ (*wettmachen*) ■ **etw mit etw** *dat* ~ to make up for sth by doing sth

gutmütig ['gu:t·my:·tɪç] *adj* good-natured

Gutmütigkeit <-> *f kein pl* good nature

Gutsbesitzer(in) *m(f)* landowner

Gutschein *m* coupon, gift certificate

gut|schreiben *vt irreg* ■ **jdm etw** *akk* ~ to credit sb with sth

Gutschrift *f* ① *kein pl* (*Vorgang*) crediting ② (*Bescheinigung*) voucher

Gutsherr(in) *m(f)* lord/lady of the manor

Gutshof *m* estate, manor

gut|tun *vi irreg* ■ **es tut jdm gut, etw zu tun** it does sb good to do sth

gutwillig **I.** *adj* (*entgegenkommend*) willing, obliging **II.** *adv* (*freiwillig*) voluntarily

Gymnasiallehrer(in) *m(f),* **Gymnasialprofessor(in)** *m(f)* ÖSTERR ≈ high-school teacher

Gymnasiast(in) <-en, -en> [gʏm·na·'zi̯·ast] *m(f)* ≈ high-school student

Gymnasium <-s, -ien> [gʏm·'na:·zi̯·ʊm, *pl* gʏm·'na:·zi̯·ən] *nt* ≈ high school

After finishing elementary school, Germans who plan to study at a university attend a **Gymnasium** for grades 5–13. In Austria, students attend a Gymnasium for eight years. In Switzerland, students may attend a Gymnasium starting at the age of 13. Traditionally, secondary schools specialize in one of four categories: the classical languages (Latin and Greek); modern languages (including Latin sometimes); math and either science or economics; and music and art.

Gymnastik <-> [gʏm·ˈnas·tɪk] *f kein pl* gymnastics + *sing vb*

Gynäkologe, **Gynäkologin** <-n, -n> [gy·nɛ·ko·ˈloː·gə] *m, f* gynecologist

Gynäkologie <-> [gy·nɛ·ko·lo·ˈgiː] *f kein pl* gynecology

gynäkologisch [gy·nɛ·ko·ˈloː·gɪʃ] *adj* gynecological

Hh

H, h <-, - *o fam* -s, -s> [haː] *nt* ❶ (*Buchstabe*) H, h; ~ **wie Heinrich** H as in Hotel ❷ MUS B, b

h *Abk. von* **hora**[e] hr. ❶ *gesprochen: Uhr* (*Stunde der Uhrzeit*) **22** ~ 2200 hrs.; **Abfahrt des Zuges: 9 h 17** train departure: 9:17 a.m. ❷ *gesprochen: Stunde* (*Stunde*) h

ha [haː] *Abk von* **Hektar** ha

Haar <-[e]s, -e> [haːɐ̯] *nt* ❶ (*einzelnes Haar*) hair ❷ *sing o pl* (*gesamtes Kopfhaar*) hair; **graue ~e bekommen** to go gray; **sich** *dat* **die ~e schneiden lassen** to have one's hair cut ► WENDUNGEN: **jdm stehen die ~e zu Berge** (*fam*) sb's hair is standing on end; **sich** *dat* **in die ~e geraten** to argue; **etw ist an den ~en herbeigezogen** sth is far-fetched; **um ein** ~ within a hair's breadth

Haarausfall *m* hair loss

Haarbürste *f* hairbrush

Haarbüschel *nt* tuft of hair

haaren [ˈhaː·rən] *vi* to molt

Haarfarbe *f* color of one's hair

haargenau *adj* exact

haarig [ˈhaː·rɪç] *adj* ❶ (*behaart*) hairy ❷ (*fig: heikel*) hairy; *Angelegenheit* tricky

haarklein [ˈhaːɐ̯·ˈklain] *adv* in minute detail

Haarnadel *f* hairpin

haarscharf *adv* ❶ (*ganz knapp*) by a hair's breadth ❷ (*sehr exakt*) exactly

Haarschnitt *m* haircut

Haarspalterei <-, -en> [haːɐ̯·ʃpal·te·ˈrai] *f* (*pej*) splitting hairs

Haarspange *f* barrette

haarsträubend [ˈhaːɐ̯·ʃtrɔy·bn̩t] *adj* hair-raising

Haartrockner *m* hair dryer

Hab [haːp] *nt* ~ **und Gut** (*geh*) belongings *npl*, possessions *pl*

Habe <-> [ˈhaː·bə] *f kein pl* (*geh*) belongings *npl*, possessions *pl*

haben <hatte, gehabt> [ˈhaː·bn̩] **I.** *vt* ❶ (*besitzen, aufweisen*) to have ❷ (*erhalten*) to have; **ich hätte gern ein Bier** I'd like a beer, please ❸ *in Maßangaben* **ein Meter hat 100 Zentimeter** there are 100 centimeters in a meter ❹ (*von etw erfüllt sein*) **Durst/Hunger/Angst/Sorgen** ~ to be thirsty/hungry/afraid/worried; **gute/schlechte Laune** ~ to be in a good/bad mood ❺ (*herrschen*) **wir ~ heute den 13.** it's the 13th today, today is the 13th ❻ + *adj* **es bei jdm gut** ~ to have got it made with sb ❼ (*tun müssen*) ■**etw zu tun** ~ to have sth to do; **ich habe noch zu arbeiten** I still have work to do ❽ DIAL (*geben*) ■**es hat ...** there is/are ... ❾ + *prep* ■**etw an sich** *dat* ~ to be sth about one; **jetzt weiß ich, was ich an ihr habe** now I know how lucky I am to have her; **das hast du jetzt davon!** now look where it's gotten you!; **nichts davon** ~ to not gain a thing from it; ■**jdn vor sich** *dat* **haben** to deal with sb; **wissen Sie überhaupt, wen Sie vor sich haben?** do you have any idea who you are dealing with? ► WENDUNGEN: **noch/nicht mehr zu ~ sein** (*fam*) to still/no longer be available; **da hast du's** [*o* ~ **wir's**]! (*fam*) there you are [*or* go]!; **was hat es damit auf sich?** what's all this about?; **wie gehabt** as usual **II.** *aux vb* ■**etw getan** ~ to have done sth; **also, ich hätte das nicht gemacht** well, I wouldn't have done that

Haben <-s> [ˈhaː·bn̩] *nt kein pl* credit; **mit etw** *dat* **im ~ sein** to be in the black by sth

Habenichts <-[es], -e> [ˈhaː·bə·nɪçts] *m* (*fam*) have-not *usu pl*

Habgier [ˈhaːp·giːɐ̯] *f* (*pej*) greed

habgierig [ˈhaːp·giː·rɪç] *adj* (*pej*) greedy

Habicht <-s, -e> [ˈhaː·bɪçt] *m* hawk

Habsburger(in) <-s, -> [ˈhaːps·bʊr·gɐ] *m(f)* Hapsburg

Habseligkeiten [ˈhaːp·zeː·lɪç·kaitn̩] *pl* [meager] belongings *npl*

Habsucht *f s.* **Habgier**

habsüchtig [ˈhaːp·zʏç·tɪç] *adj s.* **habgierig**

Hackbraten *m* meat loaf

Hacke <-, -n> [ˈha·kə] *f* ❶ (*Gartengerät*) hoe ❷ ÖSTERR (*Axt*) ax ❸ DIAL (*Ferse*) heel

hacken[1] [ˈha·kn̩] **I.** *vt* ❶ *Gemüse, Nüsse* to chop [up *sep*] ❷ *Boden* to hoe ❸ *Stücke* to hack (**in** +*akk* into) **II.** *vi* ❶ (*mit dem Schnabel*) to peck ❷ (*mit der Hacke*) to hoe

hacken[2] [ˈhɛ·kn̩] *vi* COMPUT (*sl*) ■**das H~** hacking

Hacker(in) <-s, -> [ˈhɛ·kə] *m(f)* (*sl: Computerpirat*) hacker

Hackfleisch *nt* ground meat

hadern [ˈhaː·dɐn] *vi* (*geh*) to argue (**mit** +*dat* with); **mit seinem Schicksal** ~ to rail against one's fate

Hafen¹ <-s, Häfen> ['haː·fn̩, *pl* 'hɛː·fn̩] *m* ❶ (*Ankerplatz*) harbor, port ❷ (*geh: Zufluchtsort*) [safe] haven

Hafen² <-s, Häfen *o* -> ['haː·fn̩, *pl* 'hɛː·fn̩] *m o nt* DIAL, BES ÖSTERR ❶ (*größerer Topf*) pot ❷ (*Nachttopf*) chamber pot

Hafenarbeiter(in) *m(f)* docker

Hafenbehörde *f* port authority

Hafenstadt *f* port [city]

Hafer <-s, -> ['haː·fɐ] *m* oats *pl*

Haferflocken *pl* oatmeal

Haft <-> [haft] *f kein pl* (*Haftstrafe*) imprisonment; (*Haftzeit*) prison sentence; **in ~ sein** to be in custody

Haftanstalt *f* detention center, prison

haftbar ['haft·baːɐ̯] *adj* ■ **für etw** *akk* **~ sein** to be liable for sth; **jdn für etw** *akk* **~ machen** to hold sb responsible for sth

Haftbefehl *m* [arrest] warrant

haften¹ ['haf·tn̩] *vi* ❶ ÖKON to be liable (**mit** +*dat* for) ❷ (*die Haftung übernehmen*) to be responsible (**für** +*akk* for)

haften² ['haf·tn̩] *vi* ❶ (*festkleben*) ■ **auf etw** *dat* **~** to adhere to sth ❷ (*sich festsetzen*) ■ **an etw** *dat* **~** to cling to sth ❸ (*hängen bleiben*) ■ **an jdm ~** to stick to sb

Haftentlassung *f* release from custody

Häftling <-s, -e> ['hɛft·lɪŋ] *m* prisoner

Haftnotiz *f* sticky note, Post-it®

Haftpflicht *f* ❶ (*Schadenersatzpflicht*) liability ❷ (*fam: Haftpflichtversicherung*) personal liability insurance; AUTO third-party insurance

Haftpflichtversicherung *f* personal liability insurance; AUTO third-party insurance

Haftrichter(in) *m(f)* magistrate

Haftstrafe *f* (*veraltend*) *s.* **Freiheitsstrafe**

Haftung¹ <-, -en> ['haf·tʊŋ] *f* JUR liability

Haftung² <-> ['haf·tʊŋ] *f kein pl* AUTO road handling

Hafturlaub *m* parole

Hagebutte <-, -n> ['haː·gə·bu·tə] *f* rose hip

Hagel <-s> ['haː·gl̩] *m kein pl* ❶ METEO hail ❷ (*Kanonade*) torrent

Hagelkorn <-körner> *nt* hailstone

hageln ['haː·gl̩n] **I.** *vi impers* to hail **II.** *vt impers* (*fam*) ■ **es hagelt etw** there is a hail of sth

hager ['haː·gɐ] *adj* gaunt

haha [ha·'haː], **hahaha** [ha·ha·'haː] *interj* haha, ha, ha, ha

Hahn¹ <-[e]s, Hähne> [haːn, *pl* 'hɛ·nə] *m* rooster

Hahn² <-[e]s, Hähne *o* -en> [haːn, *pl* 'hɛ·nə] *m* ❶ (*Wasserhahn*) faucet ❷ (*an Schusswaffen*) hammer

Hähnchen <-s, -> ['hɛn·çən] *nt* chicken

Hai <-[e]s, -e> ['hai] *m*, **Haifisch** ['hai·fɪʃ] *m* shark

Hain <-[e]s, -e> [hain] *m* (*poet, geh*) grove

Haiti <-s> [ha·'iːti] *nt* Haiti; *s. a.* **Deutschland**

häkeln ['hɛ·kl̩n] *vi, vt* to crochet

Häkelnadel *f* crochet hook

Haken <-s, -> ['haː·kn̩] *m* ❶ (*gebogene Halterung*) hook ❷ (*beim Boxen*) hook ❸ (*hakenförmiges Zeichen*) check [mark] ❹ (*fam: hindernde Schwierigkeit*) **einen ~ haben** (*fam*) to have a catch

Hakenkreuz *nt* swastika

Hakennase *f* hooked nose

halb [halp] **I.** *adj* ❶ (*die Hälfte von*) half ❷ (*halbe Stunde der Uhrzeit*) **es ist genau ~ sieben** it is exactly six[-]thirty ❸ *kein art* (*ein Großteil*) **~ Deutschland verfolgt die Fußballweltmeisterschaft** half of Germany is following the World Cup ▶ WENDUNGEN: **nichts H~es und nichts Ganzes** neither this nor that **II.** *adv* ❶ *vor vb* (*zur Hälfte*) half; **etw nur ~ machen** to only half do sth; **~ so ... sein** to be half as ...; **~ ..., ~ ...** half ..., half ... ❷ *vor adj, adv* (*halbwegs*) half; **~ nackt/offen/voll** half-naked/half-open/half-full ▶ WENDUNGEN: **[mit jdm] ~e-~e machen** to go halves with sb; **das ist ~ so schlimm** it's not as bad as all that

Halbbruder *m* half brother

Halbdunkel ['halp·dʊn·kl̩] *nt* semidarkness

Halbedelstein *m* semiprecious stone

halber ['hal·bɐ] *präp* +*gen nachgestellt* (*geh*) ■ **der ... ~** for the sake of ...

halbfertig *adj attr* half-finished

Halbfinale *nt* semifinal[s]

Halbgott, -göttin *m, f* demigod *masc*, demigoddess *fem*

halbherzig *adj* half-hearted

halbieren* [hal·'biː·rən] *vt* ❶ (*teilen*) to divide in half ❷ (*um die Hälfte vermindern*) to halve

Halbinsel ['halp·ʔɪn·zl̩] *f* peninsula

Halbjahr *nt* half year

halbjährig ['halp·jɛː·rɪç] *adj attr* ❶ (*ein halbes Jahr dauernd*) six-month *attr* ❷ (*ein halbes Jahr alt*) six-month-old *attr*

halbjährlich ['halp·jɛːɐ̯·lɪç] **I.** *adj* half-yearly **II.** *adv* every six months, twice a year

Halbkreis *m* semicircle

Halbkugel *f* hemisphere

halblang *adj* MODE mid-calf length; *Haar* medium-length ▶ WENDUNGEN: [**nun**] **mach mal ~!** (*fam*) cut it out!

halblaut **I.** *adj* quiet **II.** *adv* quietly

Halbleiter *m* ELEK semiconductor

halbmast ['halp·mast] *adv* at half mast

Halbmond *m* ❶ ASTRON half moon ❷ (*Figur*) crescent

Halbpension *f* breakfast and dinner

halbrund *adj* semicircular

Halbschlaf *m* light sleep; **im ~ sein** to be half asleep

Halbschuh *m* shoe

Halbschwester *f* half sister

Halbstarke(r) *f(m) dekl wie adj* (*veraltend fam*) [young] hooligan

halbstündig ['halp·ʃtʏn·dɪç] *adj attr* half-hour *attr*

halbstündlich ['halp·ʃtʏnt·lɪç] **I.** *adj* half-hourly **II.** *adv* every half hour

halbtags *adv* on a part-time basis; ~ **arbeiten** to work half-time
Halbtagsbeschäftigung *f* half-time [*or* part-time] job
Halbtagskraft *f* part-time worker
Halbton *m* MUS semitone
Halbwaise *f* child without a father/mother; ~ **sein** to be fatherless/motherless
halbwegs ['halp·'ve:ks] *adv* ① (*einigermaßen*) partly ② (*nahezu*) almost ③ (*veraltend: auf halbem Wege*) halfway
Halbwert(s)zeit *f* PHYS half-life
Halbwüchsige(r) *f(m) dekl wie adj* adolescent
Halbzeit *f* halftime
Halde <-, -n> ['hal·də] *f* ① (*Müllhalde*) landfill ② BERGB slag heap ③ (*unverkaufte Ware*) stockpile
half ['half] *imp von* **helfen**
Hälfte <-, -n> ['hɛlf·tə] *f* half; **um die** ~ by half
Halfter¹ <-s, -> ['half·tɐ] *m o nt* (*Zaum*) halter
Halfter² <-s, - *o* -, -n> ['half·tɐ] *nt o f* (*Tasche für Pistolen*) holster
Hall <-[e]s, -e> [hal] *m* ① (*dumpfer Schall*) reverberation ② (*Widerhall*) echo
Halle <-, -n> ['halə] *f* ① (*großer Raum*) hall ② (*Werkshalle*) workshop ③ (*Sporthalle*) gymnasium; **in der** ~ indoors ④ (*Hangar*) hangar
hallen ['ha·lən] *vi* to echo
Hallenbad *nt* indoor swimming pool
Halligalli <-s> ['ha·li·ga·li] *nt kein pl* (*meist pej fam*) hubbub
hallo [ha·'lo:] *interj* hello
Hallo <-s, -s> [ha·'lo:] *nt* hello
Halluzination <-, -en> [ha·lu·tsi·na·'tsi̯o:n] *f* hallucination
Halm <-[e]s, -e> [halm] *m* ① (*Stängel*) stalk ② (*Trinkhalm*) straw
Halogenscheinwerfer *f* AUTO halogen headlamp
Hals <-es, Hälse> [hals, *pl* 'hɛl·zə] *m* ① ANAT neck; **den ~ recken** to crane one's neck ② (*Kehle*) throat ③ (*Flaschenhals*) neck ▶ WENDUNGEN: ~ **über Kopf** in a hurry; **aus vollem** ~[**e**] at the top of one's voice
Halsabschneider(in) *m(f)* (*pej fam*) shark
Halsband *nt* ① (*für Haustiere*) collar ② (*Samtband*) choker
halsbrecherisch ['hals·brɛ·ça·rɪʃ] *adj* breakneck *attr*
Halsentzündung *f* sore throat
Halskette *f* necklace
Hals-Nasen-Ohren-Arzt, **-Ärztin** *m, f* ear, nose, and throat specialist
Halsschlagader *f* carotid [artery]
Halsschmerzen *pl* sore throat
Halstuch *nt* scarf, neckerchief
halt¹ [halt] *interj* halt!
halt² [halt] *adv* DIAL (*eben*) just; **du musst es ~ noch mal machen** you'll just have to do it again
Halt <-[e]s, -e> [halt] *m* ① (*Stütze*) hold; ~ **geben** to support; **den ~ verlieren** to lose one's grip [*or* footing] ② (*inneres Gleichgewicht*) stability ③ (*Stopp*) stop; ~ **machen** to stop
haltbar ['halt·ba:ɐ̯] *adj* ① (*nicht leicht verderblich*) nonperishable; ■~ **sein** to keep; ~ **machen** to preserve ② (*widerstandsfähig*) durable
Haltbarkeit <-> *f kein pl* ① (*Lagerfähigkeit*) shelf life ② (*Widerstandsfähigkeit*) durability
Haltbarkeitsdatum *nt* sell-by date
halten <hielt, gehalten> ['hal·tn̩] **I.** *vt* ① (*festhalten, stützen*) to hold ② (*zum Bleiben veranlassen*) to stop, to keep ③ (*in Position bringen*) to put; **er hielt die Hand in die Höhe** he put his hand up ④ (*besitzen*) to keep ⑤ (*weiter innehaben*) to hold on to ⑥ (*in einem Zustand erhalten*) to keep ⑦ (*abhalten*) *Rede, Vortrag* to give ⑧ (*erfüllen*) **der Film hält nicht, was der Titel verspricht** the film doesn't live up to its title ▶ WENDUNGEN: **das kannst du ~, wie du willst** that's completely up to you; **viel/nichts davon ~, etw zu tun** to consider/not consider it important to do sth; **jdn/etw für jdn/etw** ~ to take sb/sth for sb/sth; **etw von jdm/etw** ~ to think sth of sb/sth **II.** *vi* ① (*festhalten*) to hold ② (*haltbar sein*) to keep ③ (*anhalten*) to stop ▶ WENDUNGEN: **an sich** *akk* ~ to control oneself; **zu jdm** ~ to stand by sb **III.** *vr* ① (*sich festhalten*) ■**sich** *akk* **an etw** *dat* ~ to hold on to sth ② METEO (*konstant bleiben*) ■**sich** *akk* ~ to last ③ (*eine Richtung beibehalten*) ■**sich** *akk* **irgendwohin/nach ...** ~ to keep to somewhere/heading toward ... ④ (*sich richten nach*) ■**sich** *akk* **an etw** *akk* ~ to stick to sth ⑤ (*eine bestimmte Haltung haben*) ■**sich** *akk* **irgendwie** ~ to carry oneself in a certain manner ▶ WENDUNGEN: **sich** *akk* **gut gehalten haben** (*fam*) to have worn well
Halter <-s, -> *m* holder
Halterung <-, -en> *f* mounting, support
Haltestelle *f* stop
Halteverbot *nt kein pl* no stopping [any time]; **eingeschränktes** ~ ≈ loading/unloading zone
haltlos *adj* ① (*labil*) weak; *Mensch* unsteady ② (*unbegründet*) groundless, unfounded
Haltung¹ <-, -en> ['hal·tʊŋ] *f* ① (*Körperhaltung*) posture; (*typische Stellung*) stance ② (*Einstellung*) attitude ③ *kein pl* (*Verhalten*) manner ▶ WENDUNGEN: ~ **bewahren** to keep one's composure
Haltung² <-> ['hal·tʊŋ] *f kein pl von Tieren* keeping
Haltungsfehler *m* bad posture
Halunke <-n, -n> [ha·'lʊŋ·kə] *m* ① (*pej: Gauner*) scoundrel ② (*hum: Schlingel*) rascal
hämisch ['hɛ:·mɪʃ] **I.** *adj* malicious **II.** *adv* maliciously
Hammel <-s, -> ['ha·ml̩] *m* ① (*Tier*) wether ② *kein pl* (*Fleisch*) mutton
Hammelfleisch *nt* mutton
Hammer <-s, Hämmer> ['ha·mɐ, *pl* 'hɛ·mɐ] *m* ① (*Werkzeug*) hammer ② SPORT (*Wurfgerät*) hammer ③ (*sl: schwerer Fehler*) ma-

jor mistake ❹ (*Unverschämtheit*) outrageous thing

hämmern ['hɛ·mɐn] *vi, vt* ❶ (*mit dem Hammer arbeiten*) to hammer ❷ (*wie Hammerschläge ertönen*) to make a hammering noise ❸ (*fam: auf dem Klavier spielen*) to hammer away on the piano ❹ (*rasch pulsieren*) to pound

Hämorrhoide, Hämorride <-, -n> [hɛ·mɔ·'riː·də] *f meist pl* hemorrhoids *pl*

Hampelmann <-männer> ['ham·pl̩·man, *pl* -mɛ·nɐ] *m* ❶ (*Spielzeug*) jumping jack ❷ (*pej fam: labiler Mensch*) puppet

hampeln ['ham·pl̩n] *vi* (*fam*) to fidget

Hamster <-s, -> ['ham·stɐ] *m* hamster

Hạmsterbacken *pl* (*fam*) chubby cheeks

Hạmsterkauf *m* panic buying

hamstern ['ham·stɐn] *vt, vi* to hoard

Hand <-, Hände> [hant, *pl* 'hɛn·də] *f* ❶ ANAT hand; **Hände hoch!** hands up!; **linker/rechter ~** on the left/right; **jdm etw in die ~ drücken** to slip sth into sb's hand; **jdm die ~ geben** to shake sb's hand; **etw in die ~ nehmen** to pick up *sep* sth; **Hände weg!** [get your] hands off! ❷ *kein pl* SPORT (*Handspiel*) handball ❸ (*Besitz*) hands; **der Besitz gelangte in fremde Hände** the property passed into foreign hands ▶ WENDUNGEN: **~ und Fuß haben** to be well thought-out; **die Hände in den Schoß legen** to sit back and do nothing; [**bei etw** *dat*] **die Hände im Spiel haben** to have a hand in sth; **mit der bloßen ~** with one's bare hand[s]; **aus erster/zweiter ~** firsthand/secondhand; **in festen Händen sein** (*fam*) to be spoken for; **jds rechte ~ sein** to be sb's right-hand man; **eine starke ~** a firm hand; **alle Hände voll zu tun haben** to have one's hands full; **etw gegen jdn in der ~ haben** to have sth on sb; **zur ~ sein** to be on hand; [**klar**] **auf der ~ liegen** (*fam*) to be [perfectly] obvious; **an ~ einer S.** *gen* with the aid of sth; [**bar**] **auf die ~** (*fam*) cash in hand; **~ in ~** hand in hand; **von ~** by hand; **zu Händen von jdm** attn: sb, for sb's attention

Hạndarbeit *f* ❶ (*Gegenstand*) handicraft; **~ sein** to be handmade; **in ~** by hand ❷ *kein pl* (*körperliche Arbeit*) manual labor ❸ (*Nähen, Stricken etc.*) needlework; (*Gegenstand*) needlework

Hạndball *m o fam nt* SPORT handball

Hạndbewegung *f* movement of the hand, gesture

Handbreit <-, -> ['hant·brait] *f* a couple inches

Hạndbremse *f* hand brake

Hạndbuch *nt* manual

Händchen <-s, -> ['hɛnt·çən] *nt dim von* **Hand** small hand; **für etw** *akk* **ein ~ haben** (*fam*) to have a knack for sth; **~ halten** (*fam*) to hold hands

Hạndcreme [-kreːm] *f* hand cream [*or* lotion]

Hạ̈ndedruck *m kein pl* handshake

Handel <-s> ['han·dl̩] *m kein pl* ❶ (*Wirtschaftszweig der Händler*) commerce ❷ (*Warenverkehr*) trade ❸ (*fam: Abmachung, Geschäft*) deal ❹ (*das Handeln*) dealing, trading (**mit** *+dat* in) ❺ (*Laden*) business; **im ~ sein** to be on the market

handeln ['han·dl̩n] **I.** *vi* ❶ (*kaufen und verkaufen*) to trade (**mit** *+dat* in); **mit Drogen ~** to deal drugs ❷ (*feilschen*) to haggle (**um** *+akk* about/over) ❸ (*agieren*) to act ❹ (*befassen*) ■**von etw** *dat* **~** to be about [*or* deal with] sth **II.** *vr impers* ■**sich** *akk* **um jdn/etw ~** to concern [*or* be about] sb/sth **III.** *vt* (*angeboten und verkauft werden*) ■[**für etw** *akk*] **gehandelt werden** to be traded [at/for sth]

Hạndelsabkommen *nt* trade agreement

Hạndelsbank *f* merchant bank

Hạndelsbeziehungen *pl* trade relations

Hạndelsbilanz *f* **aktive/passive ~** balance of trade surplus/deficit

handelseinig ['han·dl̩s·ʔai·nɪç], **handelseins** ['han·dl̩s·ʔains] *adj pred* ■ **~ sein/werden** to come to an agreement

Hạndelskammer *f* chamber of commerce

Hạndelsmarke *f* trademark, brand

Hạndelsrecht *nt* commercial law

Hạndelsregister *nt* register of business names

Hạndelsschiff *nt* trading vessel

Hạndelsschule *f* business school

hạndelsüblich *adj* in accordance with standard commercial practice; **eine ~e Größe** a standard size

Hạndelsvertrag *m* JUR trade agreement

Hạndelsvertreter(in) *m(f)* commercial agent

Hạndelsware *f* commodity

Hạndeltreibende(r) *f(m) dekl wie adj* trader

Hạndfeger <-s, -> *m* hand brush

Hạndfertigkeit *f* dexterity

hạndfest *adj* ❶ (*deftig*) substantial ❷ (*robust*) sturdy; **ein ~er Skandal** a full-blown scandal ❸ (*hieb- und stichfest*) well-founded; **~e Beweise** solid proof

Hạndfeuerwaffe *f* handgun

Hạndfläche *f* palm of one's hand

hạndgearbeitet *adj* handmade

Hạndgelenk *nt* wrist ▶ WENDUNGEN: **etw aus dem ~ schütteln** (*fam*) to do sth effortlessly

Hạndgemenge *nt* scuffle

Hạndgepäck *nt* carry-on luggage

hạndgeschrieben *adj* handwritten

Hạndgranate *f* hand grenade

handgreiflich ['hant·graif·lɪç] *adj* violent (**gegen** *+akk* toward)

Hạndgreiflichkeit <-, -en> *f kein pl* (*Tätlichkeit*) fight; **bei dem Streit kam es zu ~en** the argument became violent

Hạndgriff *m* ❶ (*Aktion*) movement; **mit einem ~** with a flick of the wrist ❷ (*Griff*) handle

handhaben ['hant·haː·bn̩] *vt* ❶ (*bedienen*) to handle; *Maschine a.* to operate ❷ (*anwenden*) to apply ❸ (*verfahren*) to manage

Hạndhabung <-> *f kein pl* ① (*Bedienung*) operation ② (*Anwendung*) application
Handicap, Handikap <-s, -s> ['hɛn·di·kɛp] *nt* handicap
Hạndkoffer *m* small suitcase
Hạndkuss^RR *m* kiss on the hand
Handlanger(in) <-s, -> ['hant·laŋɐ] *m(f)* ① (*Helfer*) laborer ② (*pej: Erfüllungsgehilfe*) stooge
Händler(in) <-s, -> ['hɛnd·lɐ] *m(f)* dealer; **fliegender ~** hawker
handlich ['hant·lɪç] *adj* ① (*bequem zu handhaben*) easy to handle, manageable ② (*leicht lenkbar*) maneuverable
Handlung <-, -en> ['hand·lʊŋ] *f* ① (*Tat*) act ② (*im Buch, Film*) action, plot, story
Hạndlungsbevollmächtigte(r) *f(m)* authorized agent
hạndlungsfähig *adj* capable of acting
Hạndlungsfreiheit *f kein pl* freedom of action
Hạndlungsspielraum *m* room for maneuvering
hạndlungsunfähig *adj* incapable of acting
Hạndlungsweise *f* conduct
Hạndrücken *m* back of the hand
Hạndschelle *f meist pl* handcuffs *pl*
Hạndschlag *m* handshake
Handschrift ['hant·ʃrɪft] *f* ① (*Schrift*) handwriting ② (*Text*) manuscript
hạndschriftlich **I.** *adj* ① (*von Hand geschrieben*) handwritten ② (*als Handschrift überliefert*) in manuscript form **II.** *adv* (*von Hand*) by hand
Hạndschuh *m* glove
Hạndschuhfach *nt* glove compartment
Hạndtasche *f* handbag, purse
Hạndtuch <-tücher> *nt* towel
Handumdrehen ['hant·ʔʊm·dreː·ən] *nt* ▶ WENDUNGEN: **im** ~ in a jiffy
Hạndvoll <-, -> *f* handful
Hạndwäsche *f* ① (*Vorgang*) hand wash ② *kein pl* (*Wäschestücke*) laundry to be hand-washed
Hạndwerk *nt* trade ▶ WENDUNGEN: **jdm das ~ legen** to put an end to sb's game; **sein ~ verstehen** to know one's job
Hạndwerker(in) <-s, -> *m(f)* tradesman
hạndwerklich **I.** *adj* relating to a trade; **~es Können** craftsmanship **II.** *adv* concerning craftsmanship
Hạndwerkszeug *nt kein pl* tools of the trade, equipment
Handy <-s, -s> ['hɛn·di] *nt* TELEK cell[ular] [tele]phone
Hạndzeichen *nt* gesture, sign
Hạndzettel *m* leaflet
Hanf <-[e]s> [hanf] *m kein pl* hemp
Hang <-[e]s, Hänge> [haŋ, *pl* 'hɛŋə] *m* ① (*Abhang*) slope ② *kein pl* (*Neigung*) tendency; **sie hat einen ~ zu Übertreibungen** she tends to exaggerate; **den ~ haben, etw zu tun** to be inclined to do sth
Hạ̈ngebrücke *f* suspension bridge
Hạ̈ngematte *f* hammock
hängen ['hɛŋ·ən] **I.** *vi* <hịng, gehạngen> ① (*angebracht sein*) *Gegenstand, Verbrecher* to hang (**an** +*dat* on, **über** +*dat* over, **von** +*dat* from) ② (*sich neigen*) to lean ③ (*befestigt sein*) ■**an etw** *dat* ~ *Anhänger, Wohnwagen* to be attached to sth ④ (*fam: angeschlossen sein*) ■**an etw** *dat* ~ *Patient* to be connected to sth ⑤ (*fam: emotional*) ■**an etw/jdm** ~ to be attached to sth/sb ⑥ (*festhängen*) [**mit etw** *dat*] **an etw** *dat* ~ **bleiben** to get [sth] caught on sth ⑦ (*fam: sich aufhalten*) **er hängt den ganzen Tag vorm Fernseher** he spends all day in front of the television ⑧ (*fam: zu erledigen sein*) **etw bleibt an jdm** ~ sth is up to sb ⑨ (*fam: in der Erinnerung bleiben*) ■[**bei jdm**] ~ **bleiben** to stick [in sb's mind] ⑩ (*nach unten*) **etw ~ lassen** to dangle sth **II.** *vt* <hạ̈ngte *o* DIAL hịng, gehạ̈ngt *o* DIAL gehạngen> ① (*anbringen*) ■**etw an/auf etw** *akk* ~ to hang sth on sth ② (*henken*) to hang ③ (*anschließen*) ■**etw an etw** *akk* ~ to attach sth to sth ④ (*im Stich lassen*) ■**jdn ~ lassen** to let sb down **III.** *vr* <hạ̈ngte *o* DIAL hịng, gehạ̈ngt *o* DIAL gehạngen> ① (*sich festhalten*) ■**sich** *akk* **an jdn/etw** ~ to hang on to sb/sth ② (*sich gehen lassen*) ■**sich** *akk* **~ lassen** to let oneself go
Hanse <-> ['hanzə] *f kein pl* HIST Hanseatic League

> The **Hanse** (Hanseatic League) was originally an association of towns lying on important trade routes. The aim of these *Hansestädte* was to protect and control trade. The German Hanse had a trade monopoly on the Baltic for 200 years. Today, seven cities in northern Germany still call themselves *Hansestädte*: Hamburg, Bremen, Lübeck, Greifswald, Rostock, Stralsund, and Wismar.

Hänselei <-, -en> *f* teasing
hänseln ['hɛn·zl̩n] *vt* to tease (**wegen** +*gen* about)
Hạnsestadt *f* ① (*eine der sieben nordd. Städte*) Hanseatic city ② HIST city of [*or* in] the Hanseatic League
Hantel <-, -n> ['han·tl̩] *f* SPORT dumbbell
hantieren* [han·'tiː·rən] *vi* ① (*sich beschäftigen*) to be busy (**mit** +*dat* with) ② (*herumwerkeln*) to work (**an** +*dat* on)
hapern ['haː·pɐn] *vi impers* (*fam*) ① (*fehlen*) ■**an etw** *dat* ~ to be lacking sth ② (*schlecht bestellt sein*) ■**es hapert** [**bei jdm**] **mit etw** *dat* sb has a problem with sth
hạppchenweise *adv* (*fam*) in small mouthfuls; (*nach und nach*) bit by bit
Happen <-s, -> ['hapn̩] *m* (*fam: kleine Mahlzeit*) snack
happig ['ha·pɪç] *adj* (*fam: hoch*) *Preis* steep
happy ['hɛ·pi] *adj* (*fam*) happy
Harem <-s, -s> ['haː·rɛm] *m* harem

Harfe <-, -n> ['har·fə] *f* harp
Harke <-, -n> ['har·kə] *f bes* NORDD rake
Harlekin <-s, -e> ['har·le·ki:n] *m* Harlequin
harmlos I. *adj* ❶ (*ungefährlich*) harmless ❷ (*arglos*) innocent II. *adv* ❶ (*ungefährlich*) harmlessly ❷ (*arglos*) innocently
Harmonie <-, -n> [har·mo·'ni:, *pl* -'ni:·ən] *f* harmony
harmonieren* [har·mo·'ni:·rən] *vi* ❶ (*zusammenklingen*) to harmonize ❷ (*zueinander passen*) to go with ❸ (*gut zusammenpassen*) to get along well [with each other]
Harmonika <-, -s *o* Harmoniken> [har·'mo:·ni·ka] *f* accordion
harmonisch [har·'mo:·nɪʃ] I. *adj* harmonious II. *adv* harmoniously
harmonisieren* [har·mo·ni·'zi:·rən] *vt* to harmonize
Harmonium <-s, -ien> [har·'mo:·ni̯·ʊm, *pl* -'mo:·ni·ən] *nt* harmonium
Harn <-[e]s, -e> [harn] *m* urine
Harnblase *f* bladder
Harnsäure *f* uric acid
harntreibend I. *adj* (*geh*) diuretic II. *adv* (*geh*) having a diuretic effect
Harpune <-, -n> [har·'pu:·nə] *f* harpoon
harren ['ha·rən] *vi* (*geh*) ■ **einer S.** *gen* ~ to await sth
hart <härter, härteste> [hart] I. *adj* ❶ (*nicht weich*) hard; (*straff*) firm ❷ (*heftig*) *Aufprall, Ruck, Winter* severe ❸ *Akzent* harsh ❹ *Schnaps* strong; *Drogen* hard; *Pornografie* hard-core ❺ (*brutal*) *Film, Konflikt* violent ❻ (*abgehärtet*) *Kerl* tough ❼ (*streng, unerbittlich*) *Regime, Gesetze, Worte* harsh; *Mensch* hard; *Strafe* severe; ■ ~ **mit jdm sein** to be hard on sb ❽ (*schwer zu ertragen*) cruel; *Zeiten* hard; *Realität, Wahrheit* harsh; **der Tod ihres Mannes war für sie ein ~er Schlag** the death of her husband was a cruel blow for her ❾ (*mühevoll*) tough; *Arbeit* hard ▸ WENDUNGEN: [**in etw** *dat*] ~ **bleiben** to remain firm [about sth]; ~ **im Nehmen sein** to be resilient II. *adv* ❶ (*nicht weich*) hard; ~ **gefroren** frozen hard *pred;* ~ **gekocht** hard-boiled ❷ (*heftig*) **bei dem Sturz ist er ~ gefallen** he had a severe fall ❸ (*rau*) harshly; **die Sprache klingt ziemlich ~** the language sounds quite harsh ❹ (*mühevoll*) hard; ~ **arbeiten** to work hard ▸ WENDUNGEN: **jdn ~ treffen** to hit sb hard
Härte <-, -n> ['hɛr·tə] *f* ❶ (*Härtegrad*) hardness ❷ *kein pl* (*Wucht*) force ❸ *kein pl* (*Robustheit*) robustness ❹ *kein pl* (*Stabilität*) stability ❺ *kein pl* (*Strenge*) severity; (*Unerbittlichkeit*) relentlessness ❻ (*schwere Erträglichkeit*) cruelty
Härtefall *m* hardship case
Härtetest *m* endurance test
hartherzig *adj* hard-hearted
hartnäckig I. *adj* ❶ (*beharrlich*) persistent ❷ (*langwierig*) stubborn II. *adv* (*beharrlich*) persistently
Hartnäckigkeit <-> *f kein pl* ❶ (*Beharrlichkeit*) persistence ❷ (*Langwierigkeit*) stubbornness
Hartz IV [haɐ̯ts·'fiɐ̯] Hartz IV (*German labor market reform of 2005 that regulates and brings together unemployment and social security benefits*)
Harz[1] <-es, -e> [ha:ɐ̯ts] *nt* resin
Harz[2] <-es> [ha:ɐ̯ts] *m* ■ **der** ~ the Harz Mountains
harzig ['ha:ɐ̯·tsɪç] *adj* resinous
Haschisch <-[s]> ['ha·ʃɪʃ] *nt o m kein pl* hashish
Hase <-n, -n> ['ha:·zə] *m* ❶ (*wild lebendes Nagetier*) hare ❷ (*Kaninchen*) rabbit
Haselnuss[RR] ['ha:·zl̩·nʊs] *f* ❶ (*Nuss*) hazelnut ❷ (*Hasel*) hazel
Hass[RR] <-es>, **Haß**[ALT] <-sses> [has] *m kein pl* hate, hatred, loathing; **einen ~ auf jdn haben** to hate sb; **aus ~** out of hatred
hassen ['ha·sn̩] *vt* to hate; ■ **es ~, etw zu tun** to hate doing sth
hasserfüllt[RR] *adj, adv* full of hate
hässlich[RR], **häßlich**[ALT] ['hɛs·lɪç] I. *adj* ❶ (*unschön*) ugly ❷ (*gemein*) nasty ❸ (*unerfreulich*) unpleasant II. *adv* (*gemein*) nastily
Hässlichkeit[RR], **Häßlichkeit**[ALT] <-, -en> *f* ugliness, nastiness
hasten ['has·tn̩] *vi sein* (*geh*) to hurry
hastig ['has·tɪç] I. *adj* hurried, rushed; **nicht so ~!** not so fast! II. *adv* hastily, hurriedly
hat *3. pers sing pres von* **haben**
hätscheln ['hɛ:·tʃl̩n] *vt* ❶ (*liebkosen*) to cuddle ❷ (*gut behandeln*) to pamper ❸ (*gerne pflegen*) to cherish
hatschi [ha·'tʃi:] *interj* atchoo
hatte ['ha·tə] *imp von* **haben**
Haube <-, -n> ['hau·bə] *f* ❶ (*weibliche Kopfbedeckung*) bonnet ❷ (*Trockenhaube*) hair dryer ❸ (*Motorhaube*) hood ❹ ÖSTERR, SÜDD (*Mütze*) cap
Hauch <-[e]s, -e> [haux] *m* (*geh, poet*) ❶ (*Atemhauch*) breath ❷ (*Luftzug*) breath of air ❸ (*leichter Duft*) whiff, waft ❹ (*Flair*) aura
hauchdünn ['haux·'dʏn] *adj* ❶ (*äußerst dünn*) wafer-thin; *Stoff* airy, gauzy ❷ (*äußerst knapp*) **eine ~e Mehrheit** a narrow majority
hauchen ['hau·xn̩] I. *vi* (*sanft blasen*) to breathe II. *vt* (*flüstern*) to whisper
Haue <-, -n> ['hauə] *f* ❶ SÜDD, SCHWEIZ, ÖSTERR (*Hacke*) hoe ❷ *kein pl* (*fam: Prügel*) thrashing
hauen <haute, gehauen *o* DIAL gehaut> ['hau·ən,] I. *vt* ❶ <haute, gehauen> (*fam: schlagen*) to hit ❷ <haute, gehauen> (*fam: verprügeln*) to hit; ■ **sie ~ sich** they're beating each other up ❸ <haute, gehauen> (*meißeln*) to carve II. *vr* (*fam: sich setzen, legen*) ■ **sich** *akk* **auf/in etw** *akk* ~ to throw oneself onto/into sth
Häufchen <-s, -> ['hɔyf·çən] *nt dim von* **Haufen** small pile ▸ WENDUNGEN: **ein ~ Elend** (*fam*) a picture of misery
Haufen <-s, -> ['hau·fn̩] *m* ❶ (*Anhäufung*) heap, pile ❷ (*fam: große Menge*) ton; **du**

erzählst da einen ~ Quatsch! what a bunch of nonsense! ③ (*Schar*) crowd ④ (*Gruppe, Gemeinschaft*) bunch ▶ WENDUNGEN: **jdn über den ~ rennen/fahren** (*fam*) to run over *sep* sb; **etw über den ~ werfen** (*fam*) to mess up *sep* sth; **auf einem ~** (*fam*) in one place

häufen [ˈhɔy·fn̩] **I.** *vt* (*aufhäufen*) to pile on **II.** *vr* ■ **sich** *akk* **~** ① (*zahlreicher werden*) to accumulate, to become more frequent, to multiply ② (*türmen*) to pile up

haufenweise *adv* ① (*in Haufen*) in piles ② (*fam*) in great quantities; **etw ~ haben** to have tons of sth

häufig [ˈhɔy·fɪç] **I.** *adj* frequent **II.** *adv* frequently, often

Häufigkeit <-, -en> *f* frequency

Haupt <-[e]s, Häupter> [haupt, *pl* ˈhɔyp·tɐ] *nt* (*geh*) head; **gesenkten/erhobenen ~es** with one's head bowed/raised

hauptamtlich I. *adj* full-time **II.** *adv* on a full-time basis

Hauptaspekt *m eines Experiments* central focus; *eines Romans* main theme

Hauptaufgabe *f* main duty

Hauptausgang *m* main exit

Hauptbahnhof *m* main [train] station

hauptberuflich I. *adj* full-time **II.** *adv* on a full-time basis

Hauptdarsteller(in) *m(f)* leading man [*or* actor]

Haupteingang *m* main entrance

Hauptfach *nt* SCH major

Hauptfigur *f* LIT main character

Hauptgang *m* ① (*Hauptgericht*) main course ② (*zentraler Gang*) main corridor ③ (*Waschgang*) main [wash] cycle

Hauptgericht *nt* main course

Hauptgeschäftszeit *f* peak shopping hours *pl*, main business hours *pl*

Hauptgewinn *m* first prize

Hauptleute *pl von* **Hauptmann**

Häuptling <-s, -e> [ˈhɔypt·lɪŋ] *m* chief

Hauptmann <-leute> [ˈhaupt·man] *m* captain

Hauptmenü *nt* COMPUT main menu

Hauptperson *f* ① (*wichtigste Person*) central figure ② (*die tonangebende Person*) center of attention, main person

Hauptquartier *nt* headquarters *npl*

Hauptrolle *f* leading role ▶ WENDUNGEN: **[bei etw** *dat*] **die ~ spielen** to play a leading part [in sth]

Hauptsache [ˈhaupt·za·xə] *f* main thing; **~, du bist glücklich!** the main thing is that you're happy!

hauptsächlich [ˈhaupt·zɛç·lɪç] **I.** *adj* main, chief **II.** *adv* mainly, especially, above all

Hauptsaison [-zɛ·zɔŋ] *f* peak season

Hauptsatz *m* LING main clause

Hauptschlagader *f* aorta

Hauptschule *f* ≈ junior high school (*a school for grades 5 to 10 in Germany or grades 5 to 8 in Austria*)

> A **Hauptschule** is a type of junior high school that caters to students whose grade point average at the end of elementary school does not satisfy the entrance requirements of the *Realschule* or the *Gymnasium*. Students who graduate from a *Hauptschule* often have trouble obtaining the additional training required for most kinds of employment. In Austria, students who meet the necessary standards can transfer to a *Gymnasium* after completing four years in a *Hauptschule*.

Hauptschüler(in) *m(f)* a student at a Hauptschule

Hauptsitz *m* headquarters *npl*, main office

Hauptspeise *f* main course

Hauptstadt *f* capital [city]

Hauptverkehrsstraße *f* main road [*or* thoroughfare]

Hauptverkehrszeit *f* rush hour

Hauptversammlung *f* general meeting

Hauptverwaltung *f* ADMIN main office, headquarters *npl*

Hauptwohnsitz *m* permanent residence

Hauptwort *nt* noun

Haus <-es, Häuser> [haus, *pl* ˈhɔy·zɐ] *nt* ① (*Gebäude*) house; **jdn nach ~e bringen** to take [*or* bring] sb home; **sich** *akk* **wie zu ~e fühlen** to feel at home; **außer ~ essen** to eat out; **[etw] ins ~ liefern** to deliver [sth] to the door; **frei ~ liefern** to deliver free of charge; **nach ~e** [*o* ÖSTERR, SCHWEIZ *a.* **nachhause**[RR]] home; **zu ~e** [*o* ÖSTERR, SCHWEIZ *a.* **zuhause**[RR]] at home; **bei jdm zu ~e** [*o* ÖSTERR, SCHWEIZ *a.* **zuhause**] at sb's house ② (*Familie*) household; **er ist ein alter Freund des ~es** he's an old friend of the family; **aus gutem ~e** from a good family ③ (*geh: Unternehmen*) company; **das erste ~ am Platze** the best company in the area; **im ~e sein** to be in ④ POL (*Kammer*) House ▶ WENDUNGEN: **~ halten** to be economical; **von ~e aus** originally

Hausangestellte(r) *f(m)* domestic servant

Hausarbeit *f* ① (*Arbeit im Haushalt*) housework ② SCH (*Schulaufgaben*) homework; (*wissenschaftliche Arbeit*) assignment

Hausarrest *m* ① (*elterliche Strafe*) **~ haben** to be grounded ② JUR house arrest

Hausarzt, -ärztin *m, f* family physician

Hausaufgabe *f* homework assignment; ■ **~n** homework

Hausbesitzer(in) *m(f)* homeowner; (*Vermieter*) landlord

Hausbewohner(in) *m(f)* tenant

Hausboot *nt* houseboat

Häuschen <-s, -> [ˈhɔys·çən] *nt* ① *dim von* **Haus** small house ② SCHWEIZ (*Kästchen auf kariertem Papier*) square

Hausdurchsuchung *f* JUR house search

Hauseingang *m* entrance [to a house]

H

hausen ['hau·zn̩] *vi* ❶ (*pej fam: erbärmlich wohnen*) to live [in poor conditions] ❷ (*wüten*) to wreak havoc
Hausflur *m* entrance hall
Hausfrau *f* ❶ (*nicht berufstätige Frau*) housewife ❷ ÖSTERR, SÜDD (*Zimmerwirtin*) landlady
Hausfreund(in) *m(f)* ❶ (*Freund der Familie*) friend of the family ❷ *nur m* (*euph fam: Liebhaber der Ehefrau*) man friend
Hausfriedensbruch *m* trespassing
Hausgebrauch *m* **für den ~** for domestic use; (*für durchschnittliche Ansprüche*) for average requirements
Haushalt <-[e]s, -e> *m* ❶ (*Hausgemeinschaft*) household ❷ (*Haushaltsführung*) housekeeping; [**jdm**] **den ~ führen** to keep house [for sb] ❸ MED, BIOL balance ❹ ÖKON budget
haus|halten *vi irreg* to be economical (**mit** + *dat* with)
Haushaltsgeld *nt* money for household expenses
Haushaltshilfe *f* household help
Haushaltsplan *m* budget
Hausherr(in) <-en, -en> *m(f)* head of the household; (*Gastgeber*) host
haushoch ['haus·hoːx] **I.** *adj* ❶ (*euph: sehr hoch*) huge, as high as a house; *Flammen, Wellen* gigantic ❷ SPORT (*eindeutig*) clear; *Niederlage* crushing; *Sieg* overwhelming; *Favorit* obvious **II.** *adv* (*eindeutig*) clearly
hausieren* [hau·'ziː·rən] *vi* to hawk; **H~ verboten!** no soliciting!
Hausierer(in) <-s, -> *m(f)* solicitor
Hauslehrer(in) *m(f)* private tutor
häuslich ['hɔys·lɪç] **I.** *adj* ❶ (*die Hausgemeinschaft betreffend*) domestic ❷ (*das Zuhause liebend*) home-loving **II.** *adv* **sich** *akk* **~ einrichten** to make oneself at home; **sich** *akk* **~ niederlassen** to settle down
Hausmädchen *nt* maid
Hausmann ['haus·man] *m* house husband
Hausmannskost *f kein pl* KOCHK home cooking
Hausmeister(in) *m(f)* janitor, custodian
Hausmittel *nt* household remedy
Hausordnung *f* house rules *pl*
Hausrat *m kein pl* household contents *pl*
Hausratversicherung *f* home owner's insurance
Hausschlüssel *m* house key
Hausschuh *m* slipper
Hausse <-, -n> ['hoː·sə] *f* BÖRSE bull market
Haustier *nt* pet
Haustür *f* front door
Hausverbot *nt* **jdm ~ erteilen** to ban sb from entering sb's/one's premises
Hauswirt(in) *m(f)* landlord *masc*, landlady *fem*
Hauswirtschaft *f kein pl* home economics + *sing vb*
Haut <-, Häute> [haut, *pl* 'hɔy·tə] *f* skin; **nass bis auf die ~** soaked to the skin [*or* bone] ▶ WENDUNGEN: **mit ~ und Haar[en]** (*fam*) completely; **auf der faulen ~ liegen** (*fam*) to take it easy; **mit heiler ~ davonkommen** (*fam*) to escape unscathed; **sich** *akk* **nicht wohl in seiner ~ fühlen** (*fam*) to not feel too good; **aus der ~ fahren** (*fam*) to hit the roof; **jd möchte nicht in jds ~ stecken** sb would not like to be in sb's shoes
Hautabschürfung *f* graze
Hautarzt, -ärztin *m, f* dermatologist
Hautausschlag *m* [skin] rash
Hautcreme *f* skin cream [*or* lotion]
häuten ['hɔy·tn̩] **I.** *vt* to skin **II.** *vr* ■ **sich** *akk* ~ *Schlange* to shed one's skin
hauteng *adj, adv* skin-tight
Hautfarbe *f* skin color
hautnah **I.** *adj* ❶ (*sehr eng*) very close ❷ (*fam: wirklichkeitsnah*) vivid **II.** *adv* ❶ (*sehr eng*) very closely ❷ (*fam: wirklichkeitsnah*) vividly
Häutung <-, -en> *f* ❶ (*das Häuten*) skinning ❷ (*das Sichhäuten*) shedding of the skin
Hbf. *Abk von* **Hauptbahnhof**
h.c. [haː·'ʔtseː] *Abk von* **honoris causa** h.c.
he [heː] *interj* hey!
Hebamme <-, -n> ['heːp·ʔamə] *f* midwife
Hebebühne *f* hydraulic lift
Hebel <-s, -> ['heː·bl̩] *m* lever ▶ WENDUNGEN: **am längeren ~ sitzen** (*fam*) to hold the upper hand
heben <hob, gehoben> ['heː·bn̩] **I.** *vt* ❶ (*nach oben bewegen*) to lift; **den Kopf ~** to raise one's head ❷ (*ans Tageslicht befördern*) to dig up; *Wrack* to raise ❸ (*verbessern*) *Stimmung, Niveau* to improve ❹ SÜDD (*halten*) to hold **II.** *vr* ■ **sich** *akk* ~ *Vorhang* to rise **III.** *vi* ❶ (*Lasten hochhieven*) to lift loads; **er musste den ganzen Tag schwer ~** he had to do a lot of heavy lifting all day ❷ SÜDD (*haltbar sein*) *Lebensmittel* to keep
Hebräer(in) <-s, -> [he·'brɛː·ɐ] *m(f)* Hebrew
hebräisch [he·'brɛː·ɪʃ] *adj* Hebrew
Hebung <-, -en> *f* ❶ (*das Hinaufbefördern*) raising ❷ GEOL elevation ❸ (*Verbesserung*) improvement
hecheln ['hɛ·çl̩n] *vi* to pant
Hecht <-[e]s, -e> [hɛçt] *m* pike ▶ WENDUNGEN: **ein toller ~** (*fam*) an incredible guy
Heck <-[e]s, -e *o* -s> [hɛk] *nt* AUTO rear, back; NAUT stern; LUFT tail
Hecke <-, -n> ['hɛ·kə] *f* hedge
Heckenschere *f* hedge clippers *npl*
Heckenschütze, -schützin *m, f* sniper
Heckklappe *f* AUTO tailgate
Heckscheibe *f* AUTO rear window
Heer <-[e]s, -e> [heːɐ̯] *nt* ❶ (*Armee*) armed forces *npl* ❷ (*fig: große Anzahl*) ■ **ein ~ von ...** an army of ...
Heerschar *f meist pl* ❶ (*veraltet: Truppe*) troop[s] ❷ (*fig: Horde*) horde ❸ REL **die himmlischen ~en** the heavenly host
Hefe <-, -n> ['heː·fə] *f* yeast
Hefeteig *m* yeast dough
Heft <-[e]s, -e> [hɛft] *nt* ❶ (*Schreibheft*) notebook ❷ (*Zeitschrift*) magazine; (*Ausgabe*) issue ❸ (*geheftetes Büchlein*) booklet
heften ['hɛf·tn̩] *vt* ❶ (*befestigen*) to stick (**an**

+*akk* to) ❷ (*nähen*) *Naht, Saum* to baste ❸ (*mit Heftklammer*) to staple (**an** +*akk* to)
Hefter <-s, -> *m* ❶ (*Mappe*) [loose-leaf] folder ❷ (*Heftmaschine*) stapler
heftig ['hɛf·tɪç] **I.** *adj* ❶ (*stark*) *Aufprall, Schlag* violent; *Kopfschmerzen* splitting; *Schneefälle* heavy; *Kämpfe* fierce ❷ (*intensiv*) *Leidenschaft, Sehnsucht* intense ❸ (*scharf*) *Reaktion* vehement; *Kritik* fierce **II.** *adv* violently; **es schneite ~** it snowed heavily; **etw ~ dementieren** to vehemently deny sth
Heftigkeit <-> *f kein pl* ❶ (*Stärke*) violence ❷ (*Intensität*) intensity; *Diskussion* ferocity; *Widerstand* severity ❸ (*Schärfe*) *Reaktion* vehemence
Heftklammer *f* staple
Heftpflaster *nt* Band-Aid®
Heftzwecke *f* thumbtack
hegen ['he:·gn̩] *vt* ❶ *Wild* to preserve ❷ (*sorgsam bewahren*) to look after; **jdn ~ und pflegen** to lavish care and attention on sb
Heide <-, -n> ['hai·də] *f* ❶ (*Heideland*) heath, moor ❷ (*Heidekraut*) heather
Heide, Heidin <-n, -n> ['hai·də, 'hai·dɪn] *m, f* heathen, pagan
Heidekraut *nt* heather
Heidelbeere ['hai·dl̩·be:·rə] *f* blueberry
Heidenangst *f* mortal fear; ■ **eine ~ vor etw** *dat* **haben** to be scared stiff of sth
Heidenlärm *m* awful racket
Heidenspaß *m* (*fam*) great fun
Heidentum *nt kein pl* ■ **das ~** paganism; (*die Heiden*) pagans *pl*
heikel ['hai·kl̩] *adj* ❶ (*schwierig, gefährlich*) delicate; *Frage, Situation a.* tricky ❷ DIAL ■ **in etw** *dat* **~ sein** to be fussy about sth
heil [hail] *adj, adv* ❶ (*unverletzt*) uninjured ❷ (*unbeschädigt*) intact
Heil [hail] **I.** *nt* <-s> *kein pl* well-being; **sein ~ in etw** *dat* **suchen** to seek one's salvation in sth **II.** *interj* **~ dem Kaiser!** hail to the emperor!
Heiland <-[e]s, -e> ['hai·lant] *m* Savior
Heilanstalt *f* (*veraltet*) ❶ (*Trinkerheilanstalt*) rehab[ilitation center] ❷ (*Irrenanstalt*) psychiatric hospital
heilbar *adj* curable
Heilbutt <-s, -e> ['hail·bʊt] *m* halibut
heilen ['hai·lən] **I.** *vi sein* (*gesund werden*) to heal [up] **II.** *vt* ❶ (*gesund machen*) to cure (**von** +*dat* of) ❷ (*kurieren*) ■ **von jdm/etw geheilt sein** to have gotten over sb/sth
Heilfasten *nt kein pl* therapeutic fasting
heilfroh ['hail·'fro:] *adj pred* (*fam*) really glad
heilig ['hai·lɪç] *adj* ❶ (*geweiht*) holy; **die ~e Kommunion** Holy Communion ❷ (*bei Namen von Heiligen*) Saint; **die H~e Jungfrau** the Blessed Virgin
Heiligabend [hai·lɪç·'ʔa:bn̩t] *m* Christmas Eve
Heilige(r) ['hai·lɪ·gə, -gɐ] *f(m) dekl wie adj* saint
heiligen ['hai·lɪ·gn̩] *vt* ❶ (*weihen*) to hallow; ■ **geheiligt** hallowed ❷ (*heilighalten*) to keep holy
Heiligenschein *m* halo
heilig|sprechen *vt irreg* ■ **jdn ~** to canonize sb
Heiligtum <-[e]s, -tümer> ['hai·lɪç·tu:m, *pl* -ty:·mɐ] *nt* shrine; **jds ~ sein** (*fam*) to be sb's sanctuary
Heilkraft *f* healing power
Heilkraut *nt meist pl* medicinal herb
Heilkunde *f kein pl* medicine
heillos ['hail·lo:s] **I.** *adj* terrible **II.** *adv* hopelessly
Heilmittel *nt* remedy (**gegen** +*akk* for); (*Präparat*) medicine
Heilpflanze *f* medicinal plant
Heilpraktiker(in) *m(f)* nonmedical practitioner
Heilquelle *f* medicinal spring
heilsam ['hail·za:m] *adj* salutary
Heilung <-, -en> ['hai·lʊŋ] *f* ❶ (*Genesungsprozess*) recovery ❷ (*Krankenbehandlung*) curing ❸ (*Abheilen einer Wunde*) healing
heim [haim] *adv* DIAL home
Heim <-[e]s, -e> [haim] *nt* ❶ (*Zuhause*) home ❷ (*Seniorenheim, Jugendanstalt*) home ❸ (*Stätte eines Clubs*) club[house] ❹ (*Erholungsheim*) convalescent home
Heimat <-, -en> ['hai·ma:t] *f* ❶ (*Gegend, Ort*) hometown; (*Heimatland*) homeland ❷ BOT, ZOOL (*Herkunftsland*) natural habitat
Heimatland *nt* native country
heimatlich *adj* native; *Brauchtum, Lieder* local
heimatlos *adj* homeless; POL stateless
Heimatlose(r) *f(m) dekl wie adj* stateless person; (*durch den Krieg*) displaced person
Heimatstadt *f* hometown
heim|bringen *vt irreg* DIAL to take home
heim|fahren *irreg* DIAL **I.** *vi sein* to drive home **II.** *vt haben* ■ **jdn ~** to drive sb home
Heimfahrt *f* trip [*or* ride] home
heim|gehen *vi irreg sein* DIAL to go home
heimisch ['hai·mɪʃ] *adj* ❶ (*einheimisch*) indigenous, native; **sich** *akk* **~ fühlen** to feel at home ❷ (*bewandert*) ■ **in etw** *dat* **~ sein** to be at home with sth
Heimkehr <-> *f kein pl* return home, homecoming
heim|kehren ['haim·ke:·rən] *vi sein* (*geh*) to return home (**aus/von** +*dat* from)
heim|kommen *vi irreg sein* DIAL to come home
heimlich ['haim·lɪç] **I.** *adj* ❶ (*geheim*) secret ❷ (*verstohlen*) furtive **II.** *adv* ❶ (*unbemerkt*) secretly ❷ (*verstohlen*) furtively
Heimlichkeit <-, -en> *f* ❶ *kein pl* (*heimliche Art*) secrecy ❷ (*Geheimnis*) secret
Heimlichtuerei <-, -en> [haim·lɪç·tu:ə·'rai] *f* (*pej*) secrecy, secretiveness
heim|müssen *vi irreg* DIAL to have to go home
Heimreise *f* trip home
heim|schicken *vt* DIAL to send home
Heimspiel *nt* SPORT home game
heim|suchen ['haim·zu:·xn̩] *vt* ❶ (*überfallen*) to strike; **von Armut/Dürre heimgesucht** poverty-/drought-stricken ❷ (*bedrängen*) to haunt; **von Albträumen heimgesucht wer-**

den to be haunted by nightmares

heimtückisch ['haim·tʏ·kɪʃ] **I.** *adj* ① (*tückisch*) malicious ② (*gefährlich*) insidious **II.** *adv* maliciously

Heimweg *m* way home; **sich** *akk* **auf den ~ machen** to head home

Heimweh <-[e]s> *nt kein pl* homesickness; *kein art, kein pl;* **~ haben** to be homesick (**nach** *+dat* for)

Heimwerker(in) *m(f)* handyman

heim|zahlen *vt* ■**jdm etw ~** to pay sb back for sth, to get sb for sth

Heirat <-, -en> ['hai·ra:t] *f* marriage

heiraten ['hai·ra:·tn̩] **I.** *vt* to marry **II.** *vi* to get married; **sie hat reich geheiratet** she married into money

Heiratsantrag *m* [marriage] proposal; **jdm einen ~ machen** to propose to sb

H

Heiratsanzeige *f* ① (*Briefkarte*) wedding announcement ② (*Annonce für Partnersuche*) ad for a marriage partner

Heiratsurkunde *f* marriage license

heiser ['hai·zɐ] **I.** *adj Stimme* hoarse; (*rauchig*) husky **II.** *adv* hoarsely, in a hoarse voice

Heiserkeit <-, *selten* -en> *f* hoarseness

heiß [hais] **I.** *adj* ① (*sehr warm*) hot; **etw ~ machen** to heat up *sep* sth; ■**jdm ist/wird es ~** sb is/is getting hot ② *Debatte* heated; *Kampf* fierce ③ *Liebe* burning; *Wunsch* fervent ④ (*fam: aufreizend*) hot; *Kleid* sexy ⑤ (*fam: gestohlen*) hot ⑥ (*brisant*) **ein ~es Thema** an explosive issue ⑦ (*aufregend*) *Musik, Party* hot ⑧ *attr* (*fam: aussichtsreich*) hot; **die Polizei ist auf einer ~en Fährte** the police are on a hot trail ⑨ (*sl: großartig*) fantastic; **echt ~** really cool ⑩ (*fam: brünstig*) in heat ⑪ (*fam: neugierig*) ■**auf etw** *akk* **~ sein** to be dying to know [about] sth **II.** *adv* ① (*sehr warm*) hot; **~ laufen** (*Maschinenteil*) to overheat ② (*innig*) ardently, fervently; **~ ersehnt** greatly longed for; **~ geliebt** dearly beloved ③ (*erbittert*) fiercely; **~ umstritten** hotly disputed

heißblütig ['hais·bly:·tɪç] *adj* ① (*impulsiv*) hot-tempered ② (*leidenschaftlich*) passionate

heißen <hieß, geheißen> ['hai·sn̩] **I.** *vi* ① (*den Namen haben*) to be called; **wie ~ Sie?** what's your name? ② (*bedeuten*) to mean; **„ja" heißt auf Japanisch „hai"** "hai" is Japanese for "yes"; **was heißt eigentlich „Liebe" auf Russisch?** how do you say "love" in Russian?; **was soll das [denn] ~?** what's that supposed to mean?; **das heißt, ...** that is to say ...; (*vorausgesetzt*) that is, ...; (*sich verbessernd*) or should I say, ... ③ (*lauten*) **das Sprichwort heißt anders** that's not how the proverb goes **II.** *vi impers* ① (*zu lesen sein*) **Auge um Auge, wie es im Alten Testament heißt** an eye for an eye, as it says in the Old Testament ② (*als Gerücht kursieren*) ■**es heißt, dass ...** there is a rumor [going around] that ...

Heißhunger *m* craving; **mit ~** ravenously

heiß|laufenALT1 *vi irreg sein* (*Maschinenteil*) *s.* **heiß II 1**

heiß|laufen² *vi irreg sein* (*Debatte, Gespräch*) to become heated

Heißluft *f kein pl* hot air

heiter ['hai·tɐ] *adj* ① (*fröhlich*) cheerful ② (*fröhlich stimmend*) amusing ③ METEO bright

Heiterkeit <-> *f kein pl* ① (*heitere Stimmung*) cheerfulness ② (*Belustigung*) amusement

Heizanlage *f* heater

Heizdecke *f* electric blanket

heizen ['hai·tsn̩] **I.** *vi* ① (*die Heizung betreiben*) **mit Gas/Öl ~** to heat with natural gas/oil ② (*Wärme abgeben*) to give off heat **II.** *vt* ① (*beheizen*) to heat ② (*anheizen*) to stoke

Heizkessel *m* boiler

Heizkissen *nt* heating pad

Heizkörper *m* radiator

Heizlüfter *m* fan heater

Heizöl *nt* fuel oil

Heizstrahler *m* radiant heater

Heizung <-, -en> *f* ① (*Zentralheizung*) heating ② (*Heizkörper*) radiator

Heizungskeller *m* boiler room

Heizungsrohr *nt* heating pipe

Hektar <-s, -e *o bei Maßangaben* -> [hɛkt·'a:ɐ̯] *nt o m* hectare

Hektare <-, -n> ['hɛk·ta:·rə] *f* SCHWEIZ hectare

Hektik <-> ['hɛk·tɪk] *f kein pl* hectic pace; **nur keine ~!** take it easy!

hektisch ['hɛk·tɪʃ] **I.** *adj* hectic **II.** *adv* frantically

Held(in) <-en, -en> [hɛlt] *m(f)* hero *masc*, heroine *fem*

heldenhaft *adj* heroic

Heldenmut *m* heroic courage

Heldensage *f* heroic saga

Heldentat *f* heroic deed

Heldentod *m* (*euph geh*) death in battle; **den ~ sterben** to die in battle

Heldentum <-s> *nt kein pl* heroism

Heldin <-, -nen> *f fem form von* **Held** heroine

helfen <half, geholfen> ['hɛl·fn̩] *vi* ① (*unterstützen*) to help (**bei** *+dat* with); **warte mal, ich helfe dir** wait, I'll help you ② (*dienen, nützen*) ■**jdm ist mit etw** *dat* **geholfen/nicht geholfen** sth is of help/no help to sb; **Knoblauch soll gegen Arteriosklerose ~** garlic is supposed to help prevent arteriosclerosis ▶ WENDUNGEN: **ich kann mir nicht ~, [aber]** ... I'm sorry, but ...; **man muss sich** *dat* **nur zu ~ wissen** you just have to be resourceful

Helfer(in) <-s, -> ['hɛl·fɐ] *m(f)* ① (*unterstützende Person*) helper; (*Komplize*) accomplice ② (*fam: nützliches Gerät*) aid

Helikopter <-s, -> [he·li·'kɔp·tɐ] *m* helicopter

Helium <-s> ['he:·li̯·ʊm] *nt kein pl* helium

hell [hɛl] **I.** *adj* ① (*nicht dunkel*) light; **es wird ~** it's getting light [out] ② (*kräftig leuchtend*) bright ③ (*gering gefärbt*) light-colored; *Haar, Haut* fair ④ *Stimme, Ton* clear ⑤ (*fam: aufgeweckt*) bright; **du bist ein ~es Köpf-**

chen you've got brains ③ *attr* (*rein, pur*) *Freude* sheer, pure **II.** *adv* ① (*licht*) brightly ② (*hoch*) high and clear

hellhäutig *adj* fair-skinned

hellhörig ['hɛl·høː·rɪç] *adj* badly soundproofed ▶ WENDUNGEN: ~ **werden** to prick up one's ears

Helligkeit <-, -en> *f* ① *kein pl* (*Lichtfülle*) lightness; (*helles Licht*) [bright] light ② (*Lichtstärke*) brightness ③ ASTRON (*Leuchtkraft*) luminosity

hellsehen *vi nur Infinitiv* ~ **können** to be clairvoyant

Hellseher(in) ['hɛl·zeːɐ] *m(f)* clairvoyant

hellwach ['hɛl·'vax] *adj* wide-awake

Helm <-[e]s, -e> ['hɛlm] *m* helmet

Hemd <-[e]s, -en> [hɛmt, *pl* 'hɛm·dən] *nt* shirt; (*Unterhemd*) undershirt

hemmen [hɛ·mən] *vt* ① (*ein Hemmnis sein*) to hinder ② (*bremsen*) to stop ③ PSYCH to inhibit

Hemmschwelle *f* inhibition level

Hemmung <-, -en> *f* ① *kein pl* (*das Hemmen*) obstruction ② *pl* PSYCH inhibitions *pl* ③ (*Bedenken, Skrupel*) ~**en haben** to feel inhibited; **nur keine ~en!** don't hold back!

hemmungslos **I.** *adj* ① (*zügellos*) unrestrained, uncontrolled ② (*skrupellos*) unscrupulous **II.** *adv* ① (*zügellos*) unrestrainedly, without restraint ② (*skrupellos*) unscrupulously

Hengst <-[e]s, -e> [hɛŋst] *m* stallion; (*Esel, Kamel*) male

Henkel <-s, -> ['hɛŋ·kl̩] *m* handle

Henker <-s, -> *m* executioner

Henne <-, -n> ['hɛ·nə] *f* hen

Hepatitis <-, Hepatitiden> [he·pa·'tiː·tɪs, *pl* he·pa·ti·'tiː·dn̩] *f* hepatitis

her [heːɐ̯] *adv* ① (*raus*) here, to me; ~ **damit!** (*fam*) give it here! ② (*herum*) ■ **um jdn** ~ all around sb ③ (*von einem Punkt aus*) ■ **von etw** *dat* ~ *räumlich* from sth; **von weit** ~ from a long way away; ■ **von ...** ~ *zeitlich* from ...; **ich kenne ihn von meiner Studienzeit** ~ I know him from my college days; **lang ~ sein, dass ...** to have been a long time since ... ④ (*verfolgen*) ■ **hinter etw** *dat* ~ **sein** to be after sth

herab [hɛ·'rap] *adv* (*geh*) down

herab|blicken *vi* (*geh*) *s.* **herabsehen**

herab|fallen *vi irreg* (*geh*) to fall down (**von** +*dat* from)

herab|lassen *irreg* **I.** *vt* (*geh: herunterlassen*) to let down *sep,* to lower **II.** *vr* ■ **sich** *akk* [**zu etw** *dat*] ~ to lower oneself [to [do] sth]; ■ **sich** *akk* [**dazu**] **~, etw zu tun** to condescend to doing sth

herablassend **I.** *adj* condescending, patronizing **II.** *adv* condescendingly, patronizingly

herab|sehen *vi irreg* to look down (**auf** +*akk* [up]on)

herab|setzen *vt* ① (*reduzieren*) *Geschwindigkeit, Preise* to reduce ② (*schlechtmachen*) to belittle

heran [hɛ·'ran] *adv verstärkend* close up, near

heran|bringen *vt irreg* ① (*räumlich*) to bring [up] to ② (*vertraut machen*) to introduce to

heran|fahren *vi irreg sein* to drive up (**an** +*akk* to)

heran|führen **I.** *vt* ① (*hinbringen*) ■ **jdn** [**an etw** *akk*] ~ to bring sb [to sth] ② (*einweihen in*) ■ **jdn** ~ to introduce sb (**an** +*akk* to) **II.** *vi* ■ **an etw** *akk* ~ to lead [up] to sth

heran|gehen *vi irreg sein* ① (*zu etw hingehen*) to go up to ② (*in Angriff nehmen*) to tackle

Herangehensweise *f* approach

heran|kommen *vi irreg sein* ① (*herbeikommen*) to approach; (*bis an etw kommen*) to get to ② (*herangelangen können*) to reach ③ (*sich beschaffen können*) to get [a] hold of ④ (*in persönlichen Kontakt kommen*) ■ **an jdn** ~ to get a hold of sb ⑤ (*gleichwertig sein*) to be up to the standard of

heran|machen *vr* (*fam*) ■ **sich** *akk* **an jdn** ~ to approach sb

heran|reichen *vi* ① (*gleichkommen*) to measure up to [the standard of] ② (*bis an etw reichen*) to reach [as far as]

heran|tasten *vr* ■ **sich** *akk* **an jdn/etw** ~ ① (*sich tastend nähern*) to feel one's way toward sb/sth ② (*sich vorsichtig heranarbeiten*) to approach sb/sth cautiously

heran|wachsen [-'vak·sn̩] *vi irreg sein* (*geh*) to grow up (**zu** +*dat* into)

Heranwachsende [-vak·sn̩·də] *pl* adolescents *pl*

heran|wagen *vr* ■ **sich** *akk* **an etw** *akk* ~ ① (*heranzukommen wagen*) to dare to go near sth ② (*sich zu beschäftigen wagen*) to dare to attempt sth

heran|ziehen *irreg* **I.** *vt* ① (*näher holen*) to pull (**an** +*akk* to/toward) ② (*einsetzen*) ■ **jdn** [**zu etw** *dat*] ~ to use sb [for [*or* as] sth] ③ (*aufziehen*) *Pflanze* to grow; **ein Tier** [**zu etw** *dat*] ~ to rear an animal [to be sth] **II.** *vi sein* MIL (*näher ziehen*) to advance

herauf [hɛ·'rauf] **I.** *adv* ■ **von ... ~: von da unten bis oben** ~ from down there all the way up here **II.** *präp* +*akk* up; **sie ging die Treppe** ~ she went up the stairs

herauf|beschwören* *vt irreg* ① (*wachrufen*) to evoke ② (*herbeiführen*) to cause

herauf|kommen *vi irreg sein* to come up (**zu** +*dat* to)

herauf|ziehen *irreg* **I.** *vt haben* to pull up *sep* **II.** *vi sein Gewitter* to approach

heraus [hɛ·'raus] *adv* ① (*nach draußen*) out; ■ **aus etw** *dat* ~ out of sth ② (*entfernt sein*) ■ ~ **sein** to have been taken out [*or* removed] ③ MEDIA (*veröffentlicht sein*) ■ ~ **sein** to be out ④ (*entschieden sein*) ■ ~ **sein** to have been decided ⑤ (*hinter sich haben*) ■ **aus etw** *dat* ~ **sein** to leave behind *sep* sth; **aus dem Alter bin ich** ~ that's all behind me ⑥ (*gesagt worden sein*) ■ ~ **sein** to have been said

heraus|bekommen* *vt irreg* ① (*entfernen*) to get out (**aus** +*dat* of) ② (*herausfinden*) to find out *sep* ③ (*ausgezahlt bekommen*) to get back

heraus|bilden *vr* ■ **sich** *akk* [**aus etw** *dat*] ~ to develop [out of sth]

heraus|bringen *vt irreg* ① (*nach draußen bringen*) to bring sth out[side] ② (*auf den Markt bringen*) to launch ③ (*der Öffentlichkeit vorstellen*) to publish ④ (*sagen*) to utter

heraus|finden *irreg* **I.** *vt* ① (*dahinterkommen*) to find out, to discover ② (*herauslesen*) to find (**aus** +*dat* from amongst) **II.** *vi* (*den Weg finden*) to find one's way out (**aus** +*dat* of)

Herausforderer, -forderin <-s, -> *m, f* challenger

heraus|fordern **I.** *vt* ① (*auffordern*) to challenge (**zu** +*dat* to) ② (*provozieren*) to provoke ③ (*heraufbeschwören*) to invite; *Gefahr* to court; **das Schicksal ~** to tempt fate **II.** *vi* ■ **etw fordert zu etw** *dat* **heraus** sth invites sth

H

herausfordernd **I.** *adj* provocative, challenging **II.** *adv* provocatively

Herausforderung *f* ① (*Aufforderung*) challenge ② (*Provokation*) provocation ③ (*Bewährungsprobe*) **die ~ annehmen** to accept the challenge

Herausgabe <-, -n> *f* ① MEDIA (*Veröffentlichung*) publication ② (*Rückgabe*) return ③ ADMIN *Banknoten, Briefmarken* issue

heraus|geben *irreg* **I.** *vt* ① (*veröffentlichen*) to publish ② (*zurückgeben*) to return ③ (*herausreichen*) to pass **II.** *vi* to give change; **falsch ~** to give [back] the wrong change

Herausgeber(in) <-s, -> *m(f)* MEDIA (*Verleger*) publisher; (*editierender Lektor*) editor

heraus|gehen *vi irreg sein* ① (*herauskommen*) to go out (**aus/von** +*dat* of) ② (*entfernt werden können*) to come out (**aus** +*dat* of) ③ (*lebhaft werden*) ■ **aus sich** *dat* ~ to come out of one's shell

heraus|greifen *vt irreg* to pick out *sep* (**aus** +*dat* from)

heraus|haben *vt irreg* (*fam*) ① (*entfernt haben*) ■ **etw** [**aus etw** *dat*] ~ to have gotten sth out [of sth] ② (*begriffen haben*) to get the knack of ③ (*herausgefunden haben*) to have solved; *Geheimnis, Namen, Ursache* to have found out

heraus|halten *irreg* **I.** *vt* ① (*nach draußen halten*) to hold out (**aus** +*dat* of) ② (*nicht verwickeln*) to keep out (**aus** +*dat* of) **II.** *vr* ■ **sich** *akk* [**aus etw** *dat*] ~ to keep out [of sth]

heraus|hängen **I.** *vi* to hang out (**aus** +*dat* of) **II.** *vt* ① (*nach außen hängen*) to hang out ② (*herauskehren, zeigen*) to show off

heraus|heben *vr irreg* ■ **sich** *akk* **aus etw** *dat* ~ *Masse, Hintergrund* to stand out from sth

heraus|holen *vt* to get out (**aus** +*dat* of)

heraus|hören *vt* ■ **etw** [**aus etw** *dat*] ~ ① (*durch Hinhören wahrnehmen*) to hear sth [in sth] ② (*abwägend erkennen*) to detect sth [in sth]

heraus|kommen [hɛraus·kɔ·mən] *vi irreg sein* ① (*nach draußen kommen*) to come out (**aus** +*dat* of) ② (*etw verlassen können*) ■ **aus etw** *dat* ~ to get out of sth ③ (*aufhören können*) ■ **aus etw** *dat* **kaum/nicht** ~ to hardly/not be able to stop doing sth ④ (*fam: überwinden können*) **aus Schwierigkeiten/Sorgen** ~ to get over one's difficulties/worries ⑤ (*auf den Markt kommen*) to be launched; (*erscheinen*) to come out ⑥ (*bekannt gegeben werden*) to be published; *Gesetz, Verordnung* to be enacted ⑦ (*bekannt werden*) ■ **es kam heraus, dass ...** it came out that ... ⑧ (*zur Sprache bringen*) ■ **mit etw** *dat* ~ to come out with sth ⑨ (*als Resultat haben*) ■ **bei etw** *dat* ~ to come of sth; **und was soll dabei ~?** and what good will that do?; **auf dasselbe ~** to amount to the same thing ▶ WENDUNGEN: **groß** ~ (*fam*) to be a great success

heraus|nehmen *irreg* **I.** *vt* ① (*entnehmen*) to take out (**aus** +*dat* of); *Zahn* to pull, to extract ② (*aus einer Umgebung entfernen*) ■ **jdn aus etw** *dat* ~ to take sb away from sth **II.** *vr* ① (*pej: frech für sich reklamieren*) ■ **sich** *dat* **etw** ~ to take liberties; **sich** *dat* **zu viel** ~ to go too far ② (*sich erlauben*) ■ **sich** *dat* **~, etw zu tun** to have the nerve to do sth

heraus|putzen *vt* ■ **jdn** ~ to smarten up *sep* sb; ■ **etw** ~ to deck out *sep* sth; ■ **sich** *akk* ~ to dress oneself up

heraus|ragen *vi s.* **hervorragen**

heraus|reden *vr* ■ **sich** *akk* ~ to talk one's way out of it

heraus|reißen *vt irreg* ① (*aus etw reißen*) to tear out (**aus** +*dat* of); *Baum, Wurzel* to pull out ② (*ablenken*) **jdn aus seiner Arbeit** ~ to interrupt sb in their work ③ (*fam: wettmachen*) to save

heraus|rücken **I.** *vt haben* (*fam*) to hand over *sep* **II.** *vi sein* (*fam*) ■ **mit etw** *dat* ~ to come out with sth

heraus|rutschen *vi sein* ① (*aus etw rutschen*) to slip out [of sth] ② (*fam: ungewollt entschlüpfen*) ■ **etw rutscht jdm heraus** sb lets sth slip out

heraus|schauen *vi* DIAL ① (*zu sehen sein*) to be showing ② (*nach draußen schauen*) to look out

heraus|schneiden *vt irreg* to cut out *sep* (**aus** +*dat* of)

heraußen *adv* SÜDD, ÖSTERR (*hier draußen*) out here

heraus|springen *vi irreg sein* ① (*aus etw springen*) to jump out (**aus** +*dat* of) ② (*abbrechen*) to chip off ③ ELEK (*den Kontakt unterbrechen*) to blow

heraus|spritzen *vi* to squirt out

heraus|stellen **I.** *vt* ① (*nach draußen stellen*) to put outside ② (*hervorheben*) to emphasize **II.** *vr* ■ **sich** *akk* ~ to come to light; ■ **sich als etw** *akk* ~ to be shown to be sth; **es stellte sich heraus, dass ...** it turned out that ...

heraus|streichen *vt irreg* ① (*aus etw tilgen*) to cross out *sep* ② (*betonen*) to stress

heraus|suchen *vt* to pick out *sep* (**aus** +*dat*

from)

heraus|wagen *vr* ■ **sich** ~ to venture out

heraus|ziehen **I.** *vt irreg haben* ❶ *Schublade* to pull out; *Stecker* to unplug ❷ *Truppen* to pull out (**aus** +*dat* of) ❸ *Zahn* to extract (**aus** +*dat* from) **II.** *vi irreg sein* (*wegziehen*) to move away

herb [hɛrp] **I.** *adj* ❶ (*bitter-würzig*) sharp, astringent; *Duft, Parfüm* tangy; *Wein* dry ❷ (*schmerzlich*) bitter; *Erkenntnis* sobering ❸ (*etwas streng*) severe; *Schönheit* austere ❹ (*scharf*) *Kritik* harsh **II.** *adv* ~ **schmecken** to taste sharp; ~ **duften/riechen** to smell tangy

herbei [hɛɐ̯·ˈbai] *adv* (*geh*) ~ **zu mir!** come here [*or old* hither]!

herbei|eilen *vi sein* to rush over

herbei|führen [hɛɐ̯·ˈbai·fyː·rən] *vt* ❶ (*bewirken*) to bring about *sep* ❷ MED (*verursachen*) to cause, to lead to

herbei|rufen *vt irreg* (*geh*) ■ **jdn** ~ to call sb

herbei|sehnen *vt* (*geh*) to long for

Herberge <-, -n> [ˈhɛr·bɛr·gə] *f* hostel

her|bestellen* *vt* to ask to come, to summon

her|bringen *vt irreg* to bring [over] here

Herbst <-[e]s, -e> [hɛrpst] *m pl selten* fall, autumn

herbstlich [ˈhɛrpst·lɪç] *adj* fall *attr,* autumnal

Herd <-[e]s, -e> [heːɐ̯t, *pl* ˈheːɐ̯·də] *m* ❶ (*Küchenherd*) stove ❷ (*Krankheitsherd*) focus ❸ GEOL (*Zentrum*) epicenter

Herde <-, -n> [ˈheːɐ̯·də] *f* herd; *Schafe* flock

Herdentier *nt* ❶ (*Tier*) gregarious animal ❷ (*pej: unselbstständiger Mensch*) sb who follows the crowd

Herdplatte *f* burner

herein [hɛ·ˈrain] *adv* in [here]; ~**!** come in!

herein|bitten *vt irreg* to ask [to come] in[to one's office]

herein|brechen [hɛ·ˈrain·brɛ·çn̩] *vi irreg sein* ❶ (*zusammenstürzen*) to collapse (**über** +*dat* on top of) ❷ (*hart treffen*) *Katastrophe, Unglück* ■ [**über jdn/etw**] ~ to befall [sb/sth] ❸ (*geh: anbrechen*) to fall; *Winter* to set in

herein|bringen *vt irreg* to bring in *sep*

herein|dürfen *vi irreg* (*fam*) to be allowed [to come] in

herein|fallen *vi irreg sein* ❶ (*nach innen fallen*) ■ [**in etw** *akk*] ~ to fall in[to sth] ❷ (*fam: betrogen werden*) to be taken in (**auf** +*akk* by)

herein|holen *vt* to bring in *sep*

herein|kommen *vi irreg sein* to come in; **wie bist du hier hereingekommen?** how did you get in here?

herein|lassen *vt irreg* to let in

herein|legen *vt* ❶ (*fam: betrügen*) to cheat, to take sb for a ride (**mit** +*dat* with) ❷ (*nach drinnen legen*) to put in

herein|platzen *vi sein* (*fam*) ■ [**bei jdm**] ~ to burst in [on sb]; ■ **bei etw** *dat* ~ to burst into sth

her|fahren *irreg vi sein* to drive [over] here; ■ **hinter jdm/etw** ~ to drive behind sb/sth, to follow sb/sth [in a vehicle]; ■ **vor jdm/etw** ~ to drive [along] in front of sb/sth

Herfahrt *f* trip [*or* ride] [over] here; **auf der** ~ on the way here

her|fallen *vi irreg sein* ❶ (*überfallen*) ■ **über jdn** ~ to attack sb; (*kritisieren*) to tear sb to pieces; (*mit Fragen*) to besiege sb (**mit** +*dat* with) ❷ (*sich stürzen*) ■ **über jdn/etw** ~ to fall upon sth

her|finden *vi irreg* to find one's way [over] here

Hergang <-[e]s> *m kein pl* course of events

her|geben *irreg* **I.** *vt* ❶ (*weggeben*) to give away *sep* ❷ (*aushändigen*) to hand over *sep* [to] ❸ (*fam: erbringen*) to say; **der Artikel gibt eine Fülle an Information her** the article contains a lot of information ❹ (*leihen*) **seinen guten Namen für etw** *akk* ~ to lend one's name to sth **II.** *vr* ■ **sich** *akk* **für etw** *akk* ~ to have something to do with sth

her|gehen *irreg* **I.** *vi sein* ❶ (*entlanggehen*) ■ **hinter/neben/vor jdm** ~ to walk behind/beside/in front of sb ❷ (*sich erdreisten*) ■ ~ **und ...** to just go [ahead] and ... ❸ SÜDD, ÖSTERR (*herkommen*) to come [[over] here] **II.** *vi impers sein* (*fam: zugehen*) **bei der Diskussion ging es heiß her** it was a heated discussion

her|haben *vt irreg* (*fam*) **wo haben Sie das her?** where did you get that [from]?

her|halten *irreg* **I.** *vt* to hold out **II.** *vi* ■ **als etw** ~ **müssen** to be used as sth

her|hören *vi* (*fam*) to listen; **alle mal** ~**!** listen [up], everybody!

Hering <-s, -e> [ˈheː·rɪŋ] *m* ❶ (*Fisch*) herring ❷ (*Zeltpflock*) [tent] peg

herinnen [hɛ·ˈrɪ·nən] *adv* SÜDD, ÖSTERR (*drinnen*) in here

her|kommen *vi irreg sein* ❶ (*herbeikommen*) to come [over] here ❷ (*herstammen*) to come from

herkömmlich *adj* traditional, conventional

Herkunft <-, *selten* Herkünfte> [ˈheːɐ̯·kʊnft, *pl* ˈheːr·kʏnf·tə] *f* ❶ (*Abstammung*) origins *pl,* descent ❷ (*Ursprung*) origin; **von ...** ~ **sein** to have a/an ... origin

Herkunftsland *nt* country of origin

her|laufen *vi irreg sein* ❶ (*gelaufen kommen*) to run over here (**zu** +*dat* to) ❷ (*begleiten*) ■ **hinter/neben/vor jdm** ~ to run [along] behind/beside/in front of sb

her|leiten **I.** *vt* ■ **etw aus etw** *dat* ~ ❶ (*ableiten*) to derive sth from sth ❷ (*folgern*) to deduce sth from sth **II.** *vr* ■ **sich** *akk* **von etw** *dat* ~ to derive from sth

her|machen **I.** *vr* (*fam*) ❶ (*beschäftigen*) ■ **sich** *akk* **über etw** *akk* ~ to dive into sth ❷ (*Besitz ergreifen*) ■ **sich** *akk* **über etw** *akk* ~ to pounce on sth ❸ (*herfallen*) ■ **sich** *akk* **über jdn** ~ to attack sb **II.** *vt* (*fam*) **das macht doch nicht viel her!** that's not very impressive!

Hermelin <-s, -e> [hɛr·mə·ˈliːn] *nt* ZOOL (*braun*) stoat; (*weiß*) ermine

hermetisch [hɛr·ˈmeː·tɪʃ] **I.** *adj* hermetic **II.** *adv* hermetically, airtight

her|nehmen *vt irreg* ❶ (*beschaffen*) ■**etw irgendwo ~** to get sth [from] somewhere ❷ DIAL (*fam: stark fordern*) ■**jdn ~** to overwork sb

Heroin <-s> [he·ro·ˈiːn] *nt kein pl* heroin

Herpes <-> [ˈhɛr·pɛs] *m kein pl* herpes

Herr(in) <-n, -en> [hɛr] *m(f)* ❶ *nur m* (*männliche Anrede*) Mr.; **die ~en Schmidt und Müller** Mr. Schmidt and Mr. Müller; **sehr geehrter ~ ...** Dear Mr. ...; **sehr geehrte ~en!** Dear Sirs! ❷ *nur m* (*Tanzpartner, Begleiter*) [male] companion, partner ❸ *nur m* (*geh: Mann*) gentleman ❹ (*Herrscher*) ruler; ■**~/~in über jdn/etw sein** to be [the] ruler of sb/sth; (*Gebieter*) master *masc*, mistress *fem*; **~ der Lage sein** to be master of the situation; **sein eigener ~ sein** to be one's own boss ❺ REL (*Gott*) Lord ▶ WENDUNGEN: **aus aller ~en Länder** from all over the world

Herrenbekanntschaft *f* male acquaintance

Herrenbekleidung *f* menswear

Herren(fahr)rad *nt* men's bicycle

Herrenfriseur, -friseuse *m, f* barber

Herrenhaus *nt* manor house

herrenlos *adj* abandoned; *Hund, Katze* stray

Herrenmode *f* men's fashion

Herrentoilette *f* men's restroom

Herrgott [ˈhɛr·gɔt] *m* SÜDD, ÖSTERR (*fam*) ■**der/unser ~** God, the Lord [God]; **~!** (*fam*) for God's sake!

her|richten I. *vt* ❶ (*vorbereiten*) to prepare, to arrange ❷ (*in Stand setzen, ausbessern*) to repair, to fix **II.** *vr* DIAL (*sich zurechtmachen*) ■**sich** *akk* **~** to get [oneself] ready

Herrin <-, -nen> *f fem form von* **Herr** mistress, lady

herrisch [ˈhɛ·rɪʃ] **I.** *adj* domineering, overbearing; *Ton* commanding **II.** *adv* imperiously

herrje(h) [hɛr·ˈjeː], **herrjemine** [hɛr·ˈjeː·mi·ne] *interj* goodness gracious!

herrlich I. *adj* ❶ (*prächtig*) marvelous; *Aussicht* magnificent; *Sonnenschein* glorious; *Urlaub* delightful; **das Wetter ist ~ heute!** the weather is great today! ❷ (*köstlich*) delicious, exquisite **II.** *adv* ❶ (*prächtig*) **sich** *akk* **~ amüsieren** to have a wonderful time ❷ (*köstlich*) **~ schmecken** to taste delicious

Herrlichkeit <-, -en> *f kein pl* magnificence; **die ~ Gottes** REL the glory of God

Herrschaft <-, -en> [ˈhɛr·ʃaft] *f* ❶ *kein pl* (*Macht, Kontrolle*) rule, reign ❷ *pl* (*Damen und Herren*) ■**die ~en** ladies and gentlemen; **darf ich den ~en sonst noch etwas bringen?** would any of you ladies or gentlemen care for anything else?

herrschaftlich *adj* grand

herrschen [ˈhɛrʃn̩] **I.** *vi* to rule (**über** *+akk* over); *Meinung* to prevail; *Ruhe, Stille* to reign; *Hunger, Krankheit, Not* to be rampant **II.** *vi impers* **es herrscht Stille** silence reigns; **es herrscht Zweifel, ob ...** there is doubt whether ...

herrschend *adj* ruling, dominant; *Meinung* prevailing; *Mode* current; ■**die H~en** those in power

Herrscher(in) <-s, -> *m(f)* ruler, sovereign; ■**~ über jdn/etw** *akk* ruler of sb/sth

Herrschergeschlecht *nt*, **Herrscherhaus** *nt* [ruling] dynasty

Herrschsucht *f* thirst for power; PSYCH domineering nature

herrschsüchtig *adj* domineering

her|rufen *vt irreg* ❶ (*zu jdm rufen*) to call [over sep] ❷ (*nachrufen*) ■**etw hinter jdm ~** to yell sth to sb (*after the person has just left*)

her|rühren *vi* (*geh*) ■**von etw** *dat* **~** to come from sth

her|schicken *vt* ❶ (*zu jdm schicken*) to send over [here] ❷ (*nachschicken*) ■**etw hinter jdm ~** to send sth on to sb

her|schieben *irreg* **I.** *vt* (*schieben*) to pull toward oneself **II.** *vr* ■**etw vor sich** *dat* **~** ❶ (*schieben*) to push sth ❷ (*fig: verschieben*) to put off

her|stammen *vi* to originate from

her|stellen *vt* ❶ (*erzeugen*) to produce, to manufacture ❷ (*gesundheitlich*) ■**jdn wieder ~** to restore sb back to health ❸ (*irgendwohin stellen*) to put [over] here

Hersteller(in) <-s, -> *m(f)* manufacturer, producer

Herstellung *f kein pl* production, manufacturing, making

her|trauen *vr* ■**sich** *akk* **~** to dare to come over [here]

Hertz <-, -> [hɛrts] *nt* hertz

herüben *adv* SÜDD, ÖSTERR (*auf dieser Seite*) over here

herüber [hɛ·ˈryː·bɐ] *adv* over here

herum [hɛ·ˈrʊm] *adv* ❶ (*um etw im Kreis*) ■**um etw** *akk* **~** around sth ❷ (*überall in jds Nähe*) ■**um jdn ~** [all] around sb ❸ (*gegen*) ■**um ... ~** around ...

herum|albern *vi* (*fam*) to fool around

herum|ärgern *vr* (*fam*) ■**sich** *akk* **mit jdm/etw ~** to keep getting worked up about sb/sth

herum|bekommen* *vt irreg* ■**jdn [zu etw** *dat*] **~** to talk sb around [to [doing] sth]

herum|bummeln *vi* (*fam*) ❶ *haben* (*trödeln*) to dawdle ❷ *sein* (*herumspazieren*) to stroll around

herum|doktern *vi* (*fam*) ■**an jdm/etw ~** ❶ (*zu kurieren versuchen*) to try treating sb ❷ (*zu reparieren versuchen*) to tinker around with sth

herum|drehen I. *vt* ❶ (*um die Achse drehen*) to turn ❷ (*wenden*) to turn over **II.** *vr* ■**sich** *akk* **~** to turn around

herum|fahren *irreg vi, vt* ❶ *sein* (*umherfahren*) to drive around ❷ *sein* (*im Kreis darum fahren*) ■**um jdn/etw ~** to drive around sb/sth ❸ *sein* (*sich rasch umdrehen*) to spin around quickly

herum|fuchteln *vi* (*fam*) ■**[mit etw** *dat*] **~** to

wave sth around, to fidget with sth
herụm|führen I. *vt* ■ **jdn** ~ to show sb around **II.** *vi* ■ **um etw** *akk* ~ to go around sth
herụm|fummeln *vi* (*fam*) ① (*hantieren*) to fiddle around (**an** +*dat* with) ② (*mit sexueller Absicht*) to grope
herụm|geben *vt irreg* to pass around, to circulate
herụm|gehen *vi irreg sein* ① (*einen Kreis gehen*) to walk around (*in a circular pattern*) ② (*ziellos umhergehen*) to wander around ③ (*herumgereicht werden*) to be passed around ④ (*weitererzählt werden*) to go around ⑤ (*vorübergehen*) to go by, to pass
herụm|hängen *vi irreg sein* (*sl*) ① (*an einem Ort*) to hang around ② (*untätig sein*) to lounge [*or* bum] around
herụm|irren *vi sein* to wander around
herụm|kommandieren* **I.** *vt* (*fam*) to boss around **II.** *vi* (*fam*) to give orders
herụm|kommen *vi irreg sein* (*fam*) ① (*herumfahren können*) to get around ② (*vermeiden können*) to get out of ③ (*reisen*) to get around; **viel** ~ to do a lot of traveling
herụm|kriegen *vt* (*fam*) *s.* **herumbekommen**
herụm|laufen *vi irreg sein* ① (*um etw laufen*) to run around ② (*fam: umherlaufen*) to go around; **[noch] frei** ~ to be [still] at large
herụm|liegen *vi irreg* (*fam*) to lie around; ■ **etw** ~ **lassen** to leave sth lying around
herụm|lungern *vi* (*fam*) to hang around; JUR to loiter
herụm|quälen *vr* (*fam*) ① (*sich befassen*) ■ **sich** *akk* **mit jdm/etw** ~ to struggle with sb/sth ② (*leiden*) ■ **sich** *akk* **[mit etw** *dat*] ~ to be plagued [by sth]
herụm|reden *vi* (*fam*) to beat around the bush; ■ **um etw** *akk* ~ to talk around sth
herụm|schlagen *irreg* **I.** *vt* (*geh*) ■ **etw um etw** *akk* ~ to wrap sth around sth **II.** *vr* (*fam*) ■ **sich mit jdm/etw** ~ to struggle with sb/sth
herụm|schnüffeln *vi* (*pej fam: spionieren*) to snoop around (**in** +*dat* in)
herụm|sitzen *vi irreg sein* ① (*fam: untätig dasitzen*) to sit around ② (*sitzend gruppiert sein*) ■ **um jdn/etw** ~ to sit around sb/sth
herụm|sprechen *vr irreg* ■ **sich** *akk* ~ to get around
herụm|stehen *vi irreg sein* ① (*fam: in der Gegend stehen*) to stand around ② (*stehend gruppiert sein*) ■ **um jdn/etw** ~ to stand around sb/sth
herụm|toben *vi* (*fam*) ① *sein o haben* (*ausgelassen umherlaufen*) to run around ② *haben* (*wüst schimpfen*) to rant and rave
herụm|treiben *vr irreg* ■ **sich** *akk* **irgendwo** ~ to hang around somewhere
Herụmtreiber(in) <-s, -> *m(f)* (*pej*) ① (*Mensch ohne feste Arbeit, Wohnsitz*) down-and-out, tramp ② (*fam: Streuner*) lazybones, good-for-nothing
herụm|ziehen *irreg vi sein* ■ **mit jdm** ~ to move around with sb
herunten [hɛ·ˈrʊn·tn̩] *adv* SÜDD, ÖSTERR (*hier unten*) down here
herunter [hɛ·ˈrʊn·tɐ] **I.** *adv* down; ~ **vom Sofa!** [get] off the sofa!; ~ **mit der Mütze!** take off that hat! **II.** *präp nachgestellt* **den Berg** ~ **geht es leichter als hinauf** it's easier to go down the hill than up it
herụnter|fallen *vi irreg sein* to fall off; **mir ist der Hammer heruntergefallen** I dropped the hammer
herụnter|gehen *vi irreg sein* ① (*nach unten gehen*) to go down; ■ **von etw** *dat* ~ to get off [of] sth ② (*fig: sinken*) *Preise* to drop, to go down ③ (*Flughöhe verringern*) to descend ④ (*reduzieren*) to reduce, to lower; **mit der Geschwindigkeit** ~ to slow down
herụntergekommen *adj* (*pej*) ① (*abgewohnt*) rundown, dilapidated ② (*verwahrlost*) down-and-out
herụnter|handeln *vt* (*fam*) to talk down *sep*
herụnter|hängen *vi irreg* to hang down (**von** +*dat* from, **auf** +*akk* over)
herụnter|hauen *vt irreg* (*fam*) ■ **jdm eine** ~ to slap sb
herụnter|kippen *vt* (*fam*) ■ **etw** ~ *Schnaps, Bier* to chug [down *sep*] sth
herụnter|klappen *vt* to put down *sep; Kragen* to turn down; *Deckel* to close
herụnter|kommen *vi irreg sein* to come down
herụnter|laden *vt* COMPUT to download
herụnter|machen *vt* (*fam*) ① (*schlechtmachen*) to tear to pieces ② (*zurechtweisen*) to tell off
herụnter|purzeln *vt Treppe* to tumble down; (*vom Baum*) to fall out of
herụnter|reißen *vt irreg* ① (*abreißen*) to pull off *sep;* (*von der Wand*) to tear down ② (*sl: absitzen*) to get through
herụnter|spielen *vt* ■ **etw** ~ (*verharmlosen*) to play down *sep* sth
herụnter|springen *vi irreg* to jump down
herụnter|werfen *vt irreg* to throw down *sep*
herụnter|wirtschaften *vt* (*pej fam*) to ruin
hervor [hɛɐ̯·ˈfoːɐ̯] *interj* ■ ~ **mit dir/euch!** (*geh*) out you come!, come on out!
hervo̲r|bringen *vt irreg* to produce
hervo̲r|gehen *vi irreg sein* ① (*geh: entstammen*) ■ **aus etw** *dat* ~ to come from sth ② (*sich ergeben*) **aus etw** *dat* **geht hervor ...** it follows from sth ..., sth proves ...
hervo̲r|gucken *vi* (*fam*) to peek out (**unter** +*dat* from under)
hervo̲r|heben *vt irreg* ① (*betonen*) to emphasize, to stress ② (*besonders kennzeichnen*) to make stand out
hervo̲r|holen *vt* to take out *sep* (**aus** +*dat* from)
hervo̲r|kommen *vi irreg sein* to come out (**aus** +*dat* of, **hinter** +*dat* from behind), to emerge (**aus** +*dat* from)
hervo̲r|ragen [hɛɐ̯·ˈfoːɐ̯·raː·gn̩] *vi* ① (*sich auszeichnen*) to stand out ② (*vorstehen*) to jut

H

out (**aus** +*dat* from)

hervorragend **I.** *adj* excellent, outstanding **II.** *adv* excellently

hervor|rufen *vt irreg* to evoke; *Bestürzung, Entsetzen* to cause

hervor|treten *vi irreg sein* ❶ (*heraustreten*) to step out (**hinter** +*dat* from behind) ❷ *Wangenknochen, Kinn* to protrude ❸ (*erkennbar werden*) to become evident ❹ (*in Erscheinung treten*) to distinguish oneself

hervor|tun *vr irreg* (*fam*) ■**sich** *akk* ~ ❶ (*sich auszeichnen*) to distinguish oneself (**mit** +*dat* with) ❷ (*sich wichtigtun*) to show off

hervor|wagen *vr* ■**sich** *akk* ~ to dare to come out, to venture forth

Herz <-ens, -en> [hɛrts] *nt* ❶ ANAT heart ❷ (*Gemüt, Gefühl*) heart; **mit ganzem ~en** wholeheartedly; **von ganzem ~en** sincerely; **im Grunde seines ~ens** in his heart of hearts; **leichten ~ens** lightheartedly; **schweren ~ens** with a heavy heart; **jds ~ erweichen** to soften up *sep* sb ❸ (*Zentrum*) heart ❹ (*Schatz, Liebling*) dear, love ❺ KARTEN hearts *pl* ▶ WENDUNGEN: **ein ~ und eine Seele sein** to be the best of friends; **seinem ~en einen Stoß geben** to pluck up the courage; **jds ~ höherschlagen lassen** to make sb's heart beat faster; **jdm das ~ brechen** to break sb's heart; **etw nicht übers ~ bringen** to not have the heart to do sth; **etw auf dem ~en haben** to have sth on one's mind; **jds ~ hängt an etw** *dat* sb is attached to sth; **jdm etw ans ~ legen** to entrust sb with sth; **jdm liegt etw am ~en** sb is concerned about sth; **jdn in sein ~ schließen** to take sb into one's heart; **jd wächst jdm ans ~** sb is growing fond of sb

Hẹrzanfall *m* heart attack

her|zeigen *vt* to show; **zeig mal her!** let me see!

Hẹrzensangelegenheit *f* ❶ (*wichtiges Anliegen*) matter close to one's heart ❷ (*Liebe betreffende Angelegenheit*) affair of the heart

Hẹrzensbrecher(in) *m(f)* heartbreaker, ladykiller *dated*

herzensgut ['hɛr·tsn̩s·gu:t] *adj* good-hearted, kind-hearted

Hẹrzenslust *f kein pl* **nach ~** to one's heart's content

Hẹrzenswunsch *m* dearest wish, heart's desire

hẹrzergreifend *adj* heart-rending

hẹrzerweichend **I.** *adj* heart-rending **II.** *adv* heart-rendingly

Hẹrzfehler *m* heart defect

hẹrzhaft **I.** *adj* ❶ (*würzig-kräftig*) tasty, savory; *Essen, Eintopf* hearty ❷ (*kräftig*) hearty, substantial **II.** *adv* ❶ (*würzig-kräftig*) **~ schmecken** to be tasty ❷ (*kräftig*) heartily; **~ gähnen** to yawn loudly

her|ziehen *irreg* **I.** *vt haben* ❶ (*heranziehen*) to pull closer ❷ (*mitschleppen*) ■**etw hinter/neben sich** *dat* ~ to pull sth [along] behind/beside oneself **II.** *vi* ❶ *sein* (*hierhin ziehen*) to move [over] here ❷ *haben* (*fam: sich auslassen*) ■**über jdn/etw ~** to tear sb/sth to pieces

herzig ['hɛr·tsɪç] *adj* cute

Hẹrzinfarkt *m* heart attack

Hẹrzklopfen *nt kein pl* pounding of the heart, palpitations *pl*

hẹrzkrank *adj* suffering from a heart condition *pred;* ■**~ sein** to have a heart condition

Herz-Kreislauf-Erkrankung *f* MED cardiovascular disease

hẹrzlich **I.** *adj* ❶ (*warmherzig*) warm, friendly, cordial; *Lachen* hearty ❷ (*in Grußformeln*) kind **II.** *adv* ❶ (*aufrichtig*) warmly, with pleasure; **sich** *akk* **bei jdm ~ bedanken** to thank sb very much; **jdn ~ gratulieren** to congratulate sb warmly ❷ (*recht*) thoroughly, really; **~ wenig** precious little

Hẹrzlichkeit <-> *f kein pl* ❶ (*herzliches Wesen*) warmth ❷ (*Aufrichtigkeit*) sincerity, cordiality

hẹrzlos *adj* heartless

Hẹrzlosigkeit <-, -en> *f* heartlessness

Herzog(in) <-s, Herzöge> ['hɛr·tso:k, *pl* 'hɛr·tsø:·gə] *m(f)* duke *masc,* duchess *fem*

Hẹrzogtum <-s, -tümer> *nt* duchy, dukedom

Hẹrzschlag *m* ❶ (*Kontraktion des Herzmuskels*) heartbeat ❷ (*Herzstillstand*) heart failure, cardiac arrest

Hẹrzschrittmacher *m* pacemaker

Hẹrzstillstand *m* cardiac arrest

hẹrzzerreißend *adj s.* **herzerweichend**

Hesse, Hessin <-n, -n> ['hɛ·sə, 'hɛ·sɪn] *m, f* Hessian

Hessen <-s> ['hɛ·sn̩] *nt* Hesse

hessisch ['hɛ·sɪʃ] *adj* Hessian

heterogen [he·te·ro·'ge:n] *adj* (*geh*) heterogeneous

Heterosexualität <-> [he·te·ro·zɛ·ksu̯a·li·'tɛ:t] *f kein pl* heterosexuality

heterosexuell [he·te·ro·zɛ·'ksu̯·ɛl] *adj* heterosexual

Hetze <-, -n> ['hɛtsə] *f* ❶ *kein pl* (*übertriebene Hast*) mad rush ❷ *pl selten* (*pej: Aufhetzung*) smear campaign; (*gegen Minderheiten*) hate campaign

hetzen ['hɛtsn̩] **I.** *vi* ❶ *haben* (*sich abhetzen*) to rush around ❷ *sein* (*eilen*) to rush ❸ *haben* (*pej: Hass schüren*) to stir up hatred (**gegen** +*akk* against) **II.** *vt haben* ❶ (*jagen*) to hunt ❷ (*losgehen lassen*) ■**jdn/einen Hund auf jdn ~** to set sb/a dog on sb ❸ (*fam: antreiben*) to rush ❹ (*vertreiben*) to chase (**von** +*dat* off)

Hetzerei <-, -en> *f* ❶ *kein pl* (*ständige Hetze*) mad rush, rushing around ❷ (*ständiges Hetzen*) rabble-rousing, malicious agitation

Hẹtzkampagne *f* (*pej*) smear campaign

Hẹtzparole *f meist pl* (*pej*) inflammatory slogan

Heu <-[e]s> [hɔy] *nt kein pl* hay ▶ WENDUNGEN: **Geld wie ~ haben** to have heaps of money

Heuchelei <-, -en> [hɔy·çə·'lai] *f* (*pej*) ❶ (*Heucheln*) hypocrisy ❷ (*heuchlerische

Äußerung) hypocritical remark

heucheln ['hɔy·çl̩n] **I.** *vi* to be hypocritical **II.** *vt* ■ **etw ~** to feign sth

Heuchler(in) <-s, -> ['hɔy·çlɐ] *m(f)* (*pej*) hypocrite

heuchlerisch **I.** *adj* hypocritical **II.** *adv* hypocritically

heuer ['hɔy·ɐ] *adv* SÜDD, ÖSTERR, SCHWEIZ (*in diesem Jahr*) this year

Heuhaufen *m* haystack

heulen ['hɔy·lən] *vi* ❶ (*fam: weinen*) to cry; **es ist zum H~** (*fam*) it's enough to make you cry ❷ *Wolf, Sturm* to howl; *Motor* to wail; *Motorrad, Flugzeug* to roar

Heulsuse <-, -n> *f* (*pej fam*) crybaby

Heuschnupfen *m* hay fever

Heuschrecke <-, -n> *f* grasshopper; (*Wanderheuschrecke*) locust

heute ['hɔy·tə] *adv* ❶ (*an diesem Tag*) today; **~ Abend** this evening; **~ Nacht** tonight; **~ früh** [early] this morning; **ab ~** as of today; **~ in/vor acht Tagen** a week from today/ago today ❷ (*der Gegenwart*) today; **von ~ auf morgen** all of a sudden, overnight ❸ (*heutzutage*) nowadays, today

heutig ['hɔy·tɪç] *adj attr* ❶ (*heute stattfindend*) today's ❷ (*von heute*) *Zeitung, Nachrichten* today's; **der ~e Anlass** this occasion ❸ (*gegenwärtig*) **die ~e Zeit** nowadays; **der ~e Stand der Technik** today's technology

heutzutage ['hɔyt·tsu·taː·gə] *adv* nowadays, these days

Hexe <-, -n> ['hɛ·ksə] *f* ❶ (*böses Fabelwesen*) witch ❷ (*pej fam: zeternde Frau*) shrew; **eine alte ~** an old hag

hexen ['hɛ·ksn̩] *vi* to cast spells, to do magic; **ich kann doch nicht ~** (*fig*) I can't work miracles

HexenschussRR *m kein pl* (*fam*) lumbago

Hexer <-s, -> *m* sorcerer

Hexerei <-, -en> [hɛ·ksə·'rai] *f* magic, sorcery *pej,* witchcraft *pej*

hg. *Abk von* **herausgegeben** ed.

hieb ['hiːp] *imp von* **hauen**

Hieb <-[e]s, -e> [hiːp *pl* 'hiː·bə] *m* ❶ (*Schlag*) blow; (*Peitschenhieb*) lash [of a whip] ❷ *pl* (*Prügel*) beating *sing,* thrashing *sing*

hieb- und stichfest *adj* conclusive, irrefutable; *Alibi* iron

hielt ['hiːlt] *imp von* **halten**

hier [hiːɐ̯] *adv* ❶ here; **er müsste doch schon längst wieder ~ sein!** he should have been back a long time ago!; **~ ist/spricht Dr. Günther** [this is] Dr. Günther [speaking]; **~ draußen/drinnen** out/in here; **~ entlang** this way; **~ oben/unten** up/down here; **~ vorn/hinten** here at the front/at the back; **von ~ aus** from here; **von ~ sein** to be from here ❷ (*in diesem Moment*) at this point; **von ~ an** from now on ▶ WENDUNGEN: **~ und da** (*stellenweise*) here and there; (*gelegentlich*) now and then

hieran ['hiː·'ran] *adv* here; **sich** *akk* **~ erinnern** to remember this

Hierarchie <-, -n> [hie·rar·'çiː, *pl* -'çiː·ən] *f* hierarchy

hierarchisch [hie·'rar·çɪʃ] **I.** *adj* hierarchical **II.** *adv* hierarchically

hierauf ['hiːɐ̯·'auf] *adv* ❶ (*obendrauf*) here, on this ❷ (*daraufhin*) as a result of this/that

hieraus ['hiːɐ̯·'aus] *adv* ❶ (*aus diesem Gegenstand*) from [*or* out of] here ❷ (*aus diesem Material*) out of this ❸ (*aus dem Genannten*) from this ❹ (*aus diesem Werk*) from this

hierbei ['hiːɐ̯·'bai] *adv* ❶ (*währenddessen*) while doing this ❷ (*nahe bei etw*) in the same place ❸ (*dabei*) here; **~ sind gewisse Punkte zu beachten** you need to pay attention to certain things here

hier|bleiben *vi irreg sein* to stay here; **hiergeblieben!** [you] stay here!

hierdurch ['hiːɐ̯·'dʊrç] *adv* ❶ (*hier hindurch*) through here ❷ (*dadurch*) in this way

hierfür ['hiːɐ̯·'fyːɐ̯] *adv* for this

hierher ['hiːɐ̯·'heːɐ̯] *adv* here; **~ kommen** to come [over] here; **bis ~** up to here; **bis ~ und nicht weiter** this far and no farther

hierherum ['hiːɐ̯·hɛ·'rʊm] *adv* ❶ (*in diese Richtung*) around [*or* over] this way ❷ (*fam: in dieser Gegend*) around here

hierhin ['hiːɐ̯·'hɪn] *adv* here; **~ und dorthin** here and there; **bis ~** up to here

hierin ['hiːɐ̯·'ɪn] *adv* ❶ (*in diesem Raum*) in here ❷ (*was das angeht*) in this

hiermit ['hiːɐ̯·'mɪt] *adv* (*geh*) with this; **~ erkläre ich, dass ...** I hereby declare that ...; **~ wird bescheinigt, dass ...** this is to certify that ...; **~ ist die Angelegenheit erledigt** that is the end of the matter

hierüber ['hiːɐ̯·'yːbɐ] *adv* ❶ (*über diese Stelle*) over here ❷ (*geh: über diese Angelegenheit*) about this

hierunter ['hiːɐ̯·'ʊntɐ] *adv* ❶ (*unter diesem Gegenstand*) under here ❷ (*in dieser Gruppe*) among it/them; **~ fallen** to fall in[to] this category

hiervon ['hiːɐ̯·'fɔn] *adv* ❶ (*von diesem Gegenstand*) of this/these ❷ (*über dieses Thema*) about this [*or* it]

hierzu ['hiːɐ̯·'tsuː] *adv* ❶ (*dazu*) with it ❷ (*zu dieser Kategorie*) **~ gehört ...** this includes ... ❸ (*zu diesem Punkt*) to this; **sich** *akk* **~ äußern** to say something about this

hierzulande, hier zu Lande ['hiːɐ̯·tsu·'lan·də] *adv* [here] in these parts, around here *fam*

hieß ['hiːs] *imp von* **heißen**

Hi-Fi-Anlage ['hai·fi-] *f* stereo system, hi-fi

hihi [hi·'hiː] *interj* hee hee

Hilfe <-, -n> ['hɪl·fə] *f* ❶ *kein pl* (*Beistand, Unterstützung*) help, assistance; **jdn um ~ bitten** to ask sb for help; **jdm zu ~ kommen** to come to sb's assistance; **um ~ rufen** to call for help; **[zu] ~!** help!; **ohne fremde ~** without outside help; **erste ~** first aid ❷ (*Zuschuss*) **finanzielle ~** financial aid; (*für Notleidende*) relief; **wirtschaftliche ~** economic aid

H

❸ (*Hilfsmittel*) aid ❹ (*Haushaltshilfe*) help

Hilferuf *m*, **Hilfeschrei** *m* cry for help

Hilfestellung *f* **jdm ~ geben** to give sb a hand

hilflos ['hɪlf·loːs] **I.** *adj* ❶ (*auf Hilfe angewiesen*) helpless ❷ (*ratlos*) at a loss *pred* **II.** *adv* ❶ (*schutzlos*) helplessly; **jdm/etw ~ ausgeliefert sein** to be at the mercy of sb/sth ❷ (*ratlos*) at a loss

Hilflosigkeit <-> *f kein pl* ❶ (*Hilfsbedürftigkeit*) helplessness ❷ (*Ratlosigkeit*) bafflement, perplexity

hilfreich *adj* helpful; (*nützlich a.*) useful

Hilfsaktion *f* aid [*or* relief] program

hilfsbedürftig *adj* ❶ (*auf Hilfe angewiesen*) in need of help *pred* ❷ FIN (*bedürftig*) needy, in need *pred*

hilfsbereit *adj* helpful

Hilfsbereitschaft *f* helpfulness, willingness to help

Hilfsmittel *nt* ❶ MED [health] aid [product] ❷ *pl* (*Geldmittel*) [financial] aid

Hilfsverb *nt* auxiliary verb

Himbeere ['hɪm·beː·rə] *f* raspberry

Himmel <-s, *poet* -> ['hɪ·ml̩] *m* ❶ (*Firmament*) sky; **unter freiem ~** outdoors ❷ (*Himmelreich*) heaven; **in den ~ kommen** to go to heaven ❸ (*Baldachin*) canopy ❹ AUTO [interior] roof ▸ WENDUNGEN: **aus heiterem ~** out of the blue; **um ~s willen** (*fam*) for heaven's sake

himmelblau ['hɪ·ml̩·blau] *adj* sky-blue

Himmelfahrt *f* ❶ (*Feiertag*) [**Christi**] **~** Ascension Day ❷ (*Auffahrt*) ascension into heaven

Himmelreich *nt kein pl* REL heaven, paradise

Himmelskörper *m* celestial [*or* heavenly] body

Himmelsrichtung *f* direction; **die vier ~en** the four points of the compass

himmelweit **I.** *adj* (*fam*) enormous; *Unterschied* considerable **II.** *adv* **sich** *akk* **~ unterscheiden** to be completely different

himmlisch ['hɪm·lɪʃ] **I.** *adj attr* heavenly, divine **II.** *adv* divinely, wonderfully

hin [hɪn] *adv* ❶ *räumlich* (*dahin*) there; **~ und her laufen** to run back and forth; **der Balkon liegt zur Straße ~** the balcony faces the street; **~ und zurück** there and back ❷ *zeitlich* (*sich hinziehend*) **über die Jahre ~** over the years ❸ (*fig*) **auf jds Bitte/Vorschlag ~** at sb's request/suggestion; **auf jds Rat ~** on sb's advice; **auf die Gefahr ~, dass ich mich wiederhole** at the risk of repeating myself ▸ WENDUNGEN: **nach langem H~ und Her** after careful consideration; **~ und wieder** from time to time

hinab [hɪ·'nap] *adv* (*geh*) *s.* **hinunter**

hin|arbeiten *vi* ■ **auf etw** *akk* **~** to work [one's way] toward sth

hinauf [hɪ·'nauf] *adv* up; [**die Treppe**] **~gehen** to go up[stairs]; **den Fluss ~** upstream; **bis ~ zu etw** *dat* up to sth

hinauf|fahren *irreg vi sein* to go [*or* drive] up

hinauf|führen *vi* to lead up (**auf** +*akk* to)

hinauf|gehen *vi irreg sein* ❶ (*nach oben gehen*) to go [*or* walk] up (**auf** +*akk* to) ❷ (*steigen*) *Preise* to go up, to increase ❸ (*hochgehen*) **mit dem Preis ~** to raise the price

hinauf|steigen *vi irreg sein* to climb up (**auf** +*akk* onto)

hinaus [hɪ·'naus] **I.** *interj* (*nach draußen*) get out [of here]! **II.** *adv* ❶ (*von hier nach draußen*) out; **hier/da/dort ~ bitte!** this/that way out, please!; ■ **aus etw** *dat* **~** out of sth; **nach hinten/vorne ~ liegen** to be [situated] at the back/front [of a house] ❷ (*fig*) ■ **über etw** *akk* **~ sein** to be past sth; **über etw** *akk* **~ reichen** to include sth ❸ (*zeitlich*) **auf Jahre ~** for years to come; ■ **über etw** *akk* **~** more than [*or* well over] sth

hinaus|bringen *vt irreg* ❶ (*nach draußen begleiten*) ■ **jdn ~** to see sb out ❷ (*nach draußen bringen*) to take out

hinaus|finden *vi irreg* to find one's way out (**aus** +*dat* of)

hinaus|fliegen *vi irreg sein* ❶ (*nach draußen fliegen*) to fly out ❷ (*fam: rausfallen*) to fall out ❸ (*fam: entlassen werden*) to be kicked out

hinaus|gehen [hɪ·'naus·geː·ən] *irreg* **I.** *vi sein* ❶ (*nach draußen gehen*) to go out (**aus** +*dat* of); **auf die Straße ~** to go out to the street ❷ (*abgeschickt werden*) to be sent off ❸ (*gerichtet sein*) ■ **auf etw** *akk* **~** to look out onto sth; **nach Osten ~** to face east ❹ (*überschreiten*) ■ [**weit**] **über etw** *akk* **~** to go [far] beyond sth **II.** *vi impers sein* **es geht dort hinaus!** that's the way out!, the door is right there!

hinaus|kommen *vi irreg sein* ❶ (*nach draußen kommen*) to get out/outside ❷ (*gelangen*) ■ **über etw** *akk* **~** to get beyond sth ❸ (*gleichbedeutend mit etw sein*) **das kommt auf dasselbe hinaus** it's all the same

hinaus|lassen *vt irreg* to let out (**aus** +*dat* of)

hinaus|laufen *vi irreg sein* ❶ (*nach draußen laufen*) to run out ❷ (*gleichbedeutend mit etw sein*) ■ **auf etw** *akk* **~** to be [*or* mean] the same as sth; **auf was soll das ~?** what's that supposed to mean?; **auf dasselbe ~** to come to the same thing

hinaus|lehnen *vr* ■ **sich** *akk* **~** to lean out

hinaus|schicken *vt* to send out

hinaus|schieben *vt irreg* ❶ (*nach draußen schieben*) to push out ❷ (*auf später verschieben*) to put off, to postpone (**bis** until)

hinaus|schmeißen *vt irreg* (*fam*) to throw out (**aus** +*dat* of)

hinaus|wachsen [-vak·sn̩] *vi irreg sein* ❶ (*durch Leistung übertreffen*) ■ **über jdn ~** to surpass sb ❷ (*überwinden*) ■ **über etw** *akk* **~** to rise above sth

hinaus|werfen *vt irreg* ❶ (*nach draußen werfen*) to throw out (**aus** +*dat* of) ❷ (*fam: entlassen*) to fire

hinaus|wollen *vi* ❶ (*nach draußen wollen*) **auf den Hof/in den Garten ~** to want to go out into the courtyard/garden ❷ (*etw anstreben*) ■ **auf etw** *akk* **~** to get at sth; **worauf**

wollen Sie hinaus? what are you getting at?, what is your point?

hinaus|zögern I. *vt* to put off *sep,* to delay **II.** *vr* ■ **sich** *akk* ~ to be delayed

hin|bekommen* *vt irreg s.* **hinkriegen**

hin|biegen *vt irreg* (*fam*) ❶ (*bereinigen*) to sort out *sep; Problem a.* to iron out ❷ (*pej: drehen*) ■ **es so ~, dass ...** to manage it so that ... ❸ (*beeinflussen*) ■ **jdn ~** to lick sb into shape

Hinblick *m* **im ~ auf etw** *akk* (*angesichts*) in view of sth; (*in Bezug auf*) with regard to sth

hin|bringen *vt irreg* ❶ (*bringen*) ■ **[jdm] etw ~** to bring [*or* take] sth [to sb] ❷ (*begleiten*) ■ **jdn ~** to take sb

hinderlich ['hɪn·dɐ·lɪç] *adj* (*geh*) ❶ (*behindernd*) ■ **~ sein** to be a hindrance, to get in the way ❷ (*ein Hindernis darstellend*) ■ **jdm/für etw** *akk* **~ sein** to be an obstacle for sb/sth

hindern ['hɪn·dɐn] *vt* ❶ (*abhalten*) ■ **jdn daran ~, etw zu tun** to stop [*or* prevent] sb from doing sth ❷ (*hemmen*) ■ **jdn bei etw** *akk* ~ to hamper sb in [doing] sth

Hindernis <-ses, -se> ['hɪn·dɐ·nɪs] *nt* obstacle; **jdm ~se in den Weg legen** to put obstacles in sb's way; (*bei Leichtathletik*) hurdle

Hindernislauf *m* hurdle race

hin|deuten *vi* ■ **auf etw** *akk* ~ to suggest sth

hin|drehen I. *vt* (*fam: ausbügeln*) to sort out *sep* **II.** *vr* ■ **sich** *akk* **[zu jdm/etw]** ~ to turn [to sb/sth]

Hindu <-[s], -[s]> ['hɪn·du] *m* Hindu

Hinduismus <-> [hɪn·du·'ɪs·mʊs] *m kein pl* Hinduism *no art*

hinduistisch [hɪn·du·'ɪs·tɪʃ] *adj, adv* Hindu

hindurch [hɪn·'dʊrç] *adv* ❶ *räumlich* through ❷ *zeitlich* through, throughout; **die ganze Zeit ~** all the time

hinein [hɪ·'nain] *adv* in; **~ mit dir!** (*fam*) in with you!, get in there!

hinein|denken *vr irreg* ■ **sich** *akk* **in jdn ~** to put oneself in sb's position; ■ **sich** *akk* **in etw** *akk* ~ to think one's way into sth

hinein|fressen *vt irreg* ■ **etw in sich** *akk* ~ ❶ (*fam: verschlingen*) to gobble sth [up], to wolf sth down ❷ (*unterdrücken*) to bottle up [*or* suppress] sth

hinein|gehen *vi irreg sein* ❶ (*betreten*) to go in[to], to enter ❷ (*fam: hineinpassen*) ■ **in etw** *akk* ~ to fit in[to] sth

hinein|geraten* *vi irreg sein* to be drawn in; **in eine Schlägerei/Unannehmlichkeit ~** to get into a fight/difficulties

hinein|lassen *vt irreg* to let in[to]

hinein|legen I. *vt* ❶ (*in etw legen*) to put in[to] ❷ (*hineindeuten*) to read into **II.** *vr* ■ **sich** *akk* **[in etw** *akk***]** ~ to lie down [in sth]

hinein|passen *vi* to fit in[to]

hinein|pfuschen *vi* (*fam*) ■ **jdm in seine Arbeit ~** to interfere with sb's work

hinein|reden *vi* ■ **jdm in seine Angelegenheiten ~** to meddle in sb's affairs

hinein|schlingen *vt irreg* to scarf down *sep* sth *fam*

hinein|spazieren* *vi sein* (*fam*) to walk in[to]

hinein|stecken *vt* ❶ (*in etw stecken*) to put in[to]; *Nadel* to stick in[to] ❷ (*investieren*) to put in[to]

hinein|steigern *vr* ■ **sich** *akk* **in etw** *akk* ~ to get in[to] sth

hinein|versetzen* *vr* ■ **sich in jdn ~** to put oneself in sb's place; ■ **sich** *akk* **in etw** *akk* ~ to acquaint oneself with sth

hinein|wachsen [-vak·sn̩] *vi irreg sein* ❶ (*durch Wachstum*) to grow into ❷ (*mit etw vertraut werden*) to get used to

hin|fahren *irreg* **I.** *vi sein* ■ **irgendwo ~** to go [*or* drive] somewhere **II.** *vt haben* ■ **jdn ~** to take [*or* drive] sb; **jdn zum Flughafen ~** to drive sb to the airport

Hinfahrt *f* drive, trip; **auf der ~** on the way there

hin|fallen *vi irreg sein* to fall [down]

hinfällig *adj* ❶ (*gebrechlich*) frail ❷ (*ungültig*) invalid

hin|finden *vi irreg* (*fam*) to find one's way

Hinflug *m* flight

hin|führen I. *vt* (*irgendwohin geleiten*) ■ **jdn [irgendwo] ~** to take sb [somewhere] **II.** *vi* (*in Richtung auf etw verlaufen*) to lead [to]

hing ['hɪŋ] *imp von* **hängen**

Hingabe *f kein pl* (*rückhaltlose Widmung*) dedication; (*zu einem Mensch*) devotion; **sie spielt die Flöte mit ~** she plays the flute with passion

hin|geben *irreg* **I.** *vt* (*geh*) to give **II.** *vr* ■ **sich** *akk* **etw** *dat* ~ to abandon oneself to sth

Hingebung <-> *f kein pl s.* **Hingabe**

hingebungsvoll I. *adj* dedicated; *Blick, Pflege* devoted **II.** *adv* with dedication

hingegen [hɪn·'ge:·gn̩] *konj* (*geh*) but, however

hin|gehen *vi irreg sein* ❶ (*dorthin gehen*) to go ❷ (*geh: vergehen*) to pass, to go by

hin|gehören* *vi* (*fam*) to belong

hin|geraten* *vi irreg sein* ■ **irgendwo ~** to land somewhere; **wo bin ich denn hier ~?** what am I doing here?

hingerissen I. *adj* spellbound **II.** *adv* raptly, with rapt attention

hin|gucken *vi* (*fam*) to look

hin|halten *vt irreg* ❶ (*entgegenhalten*) ■ **jdm etw ~** to hold sth out to sb ❷ (*aufhalten*) to keep waiting

Hinhaltetaktik *f* stall tactics

hin|hauen *irreg* **I.** *vi* (*fam*) ❶ (*klappen*) to work ❷ (*ausreichen*) to be enough ❸ (*zuschlagen*) to take a swing **II.** *vr* (*sl*) ■ **sich** *akk* ~ ❶ (*schlafen*) to turn in ❷ (*sich hinflegeln*) to plunk [oneself] down **III.** *vt* (*fam: schlampig erledigen*) to rush through; (*Schriftstück*) to dash off

hin|hören *vi* to listen; **genau ~** to listen carefully

hinken ['hɪŋ·kn̩] *vi* ❶ *haben* (*das Bein nachziehen*) to limp ❷ *haben* (*nicht ganz zutreffen*) **der Vergleich hinkt** that's not a good com-

parison
hịn|knien *vi, vr vi: sein* to kneel down
hịn|kommen *vi irreg sein* ❶ *(irgendwohin gelangen)* ■ **irgendwo ~** to get somewhere ❷ *(an bestimmten Platz gehören)* ■ **etw kommt irgendwohin** sth belongs somewhere ❸ *(fam: auskommen)* to manage (**mit** *+dat* with) ❹ *(fam: stimmen)* to be [about] right
hịn|kriegen *vt (fam)* ❶ *(reparieren)* to fix ❷ *(fertigbringen)* to manage
hịnlänglich I. *adj* sufficient, adequate II. *adv* sufficiently, adequately
hịn|laufen *vi irreg sein* ■ **[irgendwo] ~** ❶ *(an eine bestimmte Stelle eilen)* to run [somewhere] ❷ DIAL *(fam: zu Fuß gehen)* to walk somewhere
hịn|legen I. *vt* ❶ *(niederlegen)* to put down ❷ *(flach lagern)* to lay down ❸ *(ins Bett bringen)* to put to bed ❹ *(fam: bezahlen)* to fork out ❺ *(fam: eindrucksvoll darbieten)* to do; **eine brillante Rede ~** to give a brilliant speech II. *vr* ■ **sich** *akk* ~ ❶ *(schlafen gehen)* to go sleep ❷ *(fam: hinfallen)* to fall [over]
hịn|nehmen *vt irreg* to accept; **eine Niederlage/einen Verlust ~ [müssen]** to [have to] suffer a defeat/a loss
hịnreichend I. *adj* sufficient; *Gehalt, Einkommen* adequate II. *adv* sufficiently, adequately; **~ lange/oft** long/often enough
Hịnreise *f* trip [somewhere]; *(mit dem Auto)* drive
hịn|reißen *vt irreg* ❶ *(begeistern)* to enchant ❷ *(spontan verleiten)* **sich** *akk* **zu etw** *dat* **~ lassen** to allow oneself to be provoked into doing sth
hịnreißend I. *adj* enchanting, captivating; *Schönheit* striking II. *adv* enchantingly
hịn|rennen *vi irreg sein s.* **hinlaufen 1**
hịn|richten *vt* to execute
Hịnrichtung *f* execution
hịn|schauen *vi* DIAL to look
hịn|scheiden *vi irreg (geh)* to pass away
hịn|schicken *vt* to send [to]
hịn|schmeißen *vt irreg (fam) s.* **hinwerfen**
hịn|sehen *vi irreg* to look
hịn|setzen I. *vr* ■ **sich** *akk* ~ to sit down II. *vt* to put down
Hịnsicht *f kein pl* **in gewisser ~** in certain respects
hịnsichtlich *präp +gen (geh)* with regard to
hịn|stellen I. *vt* ❶ *(an einen Platz stellen)* to put ❷ *(fam: bauen)* to put up ❸ *Fahrzeug* to park ❹ *(charakterisieren)* ■ **jdn als etw** *akk* ~ to make sb out to be sth II. *vr* ❶ *(sich aufrichten)* ■ **sich** *akk* ~ to stand up straight ❷ *(an eine bestimmte Stelle)* ■ **sich** *akk* **vor jdn ~** to plant oneself in front of sb
hinten ['hɪn·tn̩] *adv* ❶ *(entfernt)* at the end; **~ im Buch** at the back of the book; **sich** *akk* **~ anstellen** to get in line [at the back]; **das wird weiter ~ erklärt** that's explained further toward the end ❷ *(auf der abgewandten Seite)* at/in the back
hintendrauf ['hɪn·tn̩·'drauf] *adv (fam)* at/in the back; **jdm eins ~ geben** to slap sb on the butt
hintenherum ['hɪn·tn̩·hɛ·'rʊm] *adv (fam: auf Umwegen)* indirectly; **ich habe es ~ erfahren** a little bird told me *prov*
hinter ['hɪn·tɐ] I. *präp +dat* ❶ *(dahinter)* behind; **~ dem Baum** behind the tree ❷ *(jenseits von etw)* behind; **~ der Grenze** on the other side of the border ❸ *(fig)* **~ etw kommen** to find out about sth; **sich** *akk* **~ jdn stellen** to back sb up II. *präp +akk* ❶ *(auf die Rückseite von etw)* behind ❷ *zeitlich* after; **etw ~ sich** *akk* **bringen** to get sth over with III. *part (fam) s.* **dahinter**
Hịnterachse [-ak·sə] *f* rear axle
Hịnterausgang *m* rear exit; *(zu einem privaten Haus)* back door
Hịnterbacke *f meist pl (fam)* buttock
Hịnterbein *nt* hind leg
Hinterbliebene(r) [hɪn·tɐ·'bliː·bə·nə, -nɐ] *f(m) dekl wie adj* bereaved [family]; ■ **die ~n** the surviving dependants
hintere(r, s) ['hɪn·tə·rə, -rɐ, -rəs] *adj* ■ **der/die/das ~ ...** the rear ...
hintereinander [hɪn·tɐ·ʔain·'an·dɐ] *adv* ❶ *räumlich (einer hinter dem anderen)* one behind the other ❷ *zeitlich (aufeinander folgend)* one after the other; **mehrere Tage ~** several days in a row
Hịntereingang *m* the rear entrance; *(zu einem privaten Haus)* back door
hinterfotzig ['hɪn·tɐ·fɔ·tsɪç] *adj* DIAL *(derb)* underhand, devious
hinterfragen* [hɪn·tɐ·'fraː·gn̩] *vt (geh)* to question, to analyze
Hịntergedanke *m* ulterior motive
hintergehen* [hɪn·tɐ·'geː·ən] *vt irreg (betrügen)* to deceive; *(sexuell)* to be unfaithful, to two-time; *(um Profit zu machen)* to cheat, to double-cross
Hịntergrund *m* ❶ *(hinterer Teil des Blickfeldes)* background; **der ~ eines Raums** the back of a room ❷ *(Umstände)* ■ **der ~ einer S.** *gen* the background to sth; **der ~ einer Geschichte** the setting of a story ❸ *pl (Zusammenhänge)* ■ **die Hintergründe einer S.** *gen* the [true] facts about sth
hịntergründig I. *adj* enigmatic, mysterious II. *adv* mysteriously
Hịnterhalt *m (pej)* ambush
hinterhältig ['hɪn·tɐ·hɛl·tɪç] I. *adj (pej)* underhanded, devious II. *adv (pej)* in an underhanded manner
Hịnterhältigkeit <-, -en> *f (pej)* ❶ *kein pl (Heimtücke)* underhandedness, deviousness ❷ *(heimtückische Tat)* underhanded act
hinterher [hɪn·tɐ·'heːɐ̯] *adv* ❶ *räumlich* behind; ■ **jdm ~ sein** to be after sb ❷ *zeitlich* after that, afterwards
hinterhe̲r|fahren *vi irreg sein* to follow, to drive behind
hinterhe̲r|hecheln *vi (pej fam)* to try to catch

up with

hinterher|laufen [hɪn·tɐ·ˈheːɐ̯·lau·fn̩] *vi irreg sein* to run after

Hi̱nterhof *m* courtyard; (*Garten*) backyard

Hi̱nterkopf *m* back of the head ▶ WENDUNGEN: **etw im ~ behalten** to keep sth in mind

Hi̱nterland *nt kein pl* hinterland

hinterlassen* [hɪn·tɐ·ˈla·sn̩] *vt irreg* to leave; **bei jdm einen Eindruck ~** to leave an impression on sb

Hinterla̱ssenschaft <-, -en> *f* ① (*literarisches Vermächtnis*) posthumous works ② (*fam: übrig gelassene Dinge*) leftovers *pl*

hinterlegen* [hɪn·tɐ·ˈleː·gn̩] *vt* ■ **etw [bei jdm] ~** to leave sth [with sb]; *Sicherheitsleistung, Betrag* to supply [sb with] sth

Hi̱nterlist *f kein pl* ① (*Heimtücke*) deceit, deception ② (*Trick, List*) trick, ploy

hi̱nterlistig I. *adj* deceptive, shifty II. *adv* deceitfully, deceptively

hinterm [ˈhɪn·tɐm] = **hinter dem** *s.* **hinter**

Hi̱ntermann <-männer> *m* ① (*räumlich*) the person behind ② *meist pl* (*Drahtzieher*) ringleader, brains [behind the operation]

hintern [ˈhɪn·tɐn] = **hinter den** *s.* **hinter**

Hintern <-s, -> [ˈhɪn·tɐn] *m* (*fam: Gesäß*) butt, rear end

Hi̱nterrad *nt* rear wheel

Hi̱nterradantrieb *m* rear-wheel drive

hinterrücks [ˈhɪn·tɐ·rʏks] *adv* ① (*von hinten*) from behind ② (*im Verborgenen*) behind sb's back

hinters [ˈhɪn·tɐs] = **hinter das** *s.* **hinter**

hi̱ntersinnig *adj* with a deeper meaning; *Bemerkung a.* subtle, profound

Hi̱ntersitz *m* (*Rücksitz*) back seat

hinterste(r, s) [ˈhɪn·tɐs·tə, stɐ, -stəs] *adj superl von* **hintere(r, s)** last; (*entlegenste*) farthest

Hi̱nterteil *nt* (*fam*) *s.* **Hintern**

Hi̱ntertreffen *nt kein pl* **im ~ sein** to be at a disadvantage

Hi̱ntertür *f*, **Hi̱ntertürl** <-s, -[n]> *nt* ÖSTERR ① (*hintere Eingangstür*) back entrance; (*zu einem privaten Haus*) back door ② (*fam: Ausweg*) back door, loophole

Hinterwäldler(in) <-s, -> [ˈhɪn·tɐ·vɛlt·lɐ] *m(f)* (*pej fam*) country bumpkin

hi̱nterwäldlerisch *adj* (*pej fam*) country bumpkin

hinterziehen* [hɪn·tɐ·ˈtsiː·ən] *vt irreg* **Steuern ~** to evade tax[es]

hi̱n|tun *vt irreg* (*fam: hinlegen*) ■ **etw irgendwohin ~** to put sth somewhere

hinüber [hɪ·ˈnyː·bɐ] *adv* ① (*nach drüben*) across, over ② (*fam: verdorben*) bad ③ (*fam: kaputt, erschöpft*) ■ **etw/jd ist ~** sth has had it

hinunter [hɪ·ˈnʊn·tɐ] *adv* down

hinu̱nter|fahren *irreg* I. *vi sein* to go [*or* drive] down II. *vt* to go [*or* drive] down

hinu̱nter|fallen *irreg sein* I. *vi* to fall down/off II. *vt* ■ **etw ~** to fall down sth

hinunter|gehen [hɪ·ˈnʊn·tɐ·geː·ən] *irreg sein* I. *vi* ① (*nach unten gehen*) to go down ② (*die Flughöhe verringern*) to descend (**auf** + *akk* to) II. *vt* ■ **etw ~** to go down sth

hinu̱nter|schlucken *vt* ① (*schlucken*) to swallow [down *sep*] ② (*fam: sich verkneifen*) to suppress; **eine Antwort ~** to stifle a reply

hinu̱nter|spülen *vt* ① (*wegspülen*) to flush down *sep* ② (*mit einem Getränk*) to wash down *sep* (**mit** + *dat* with)

hinu̱nter|werfen *vt irreg* to throw down

hinu̱nter|würgen *vt* to choke down *sep*

hi̱n|wagen *vr* ■ **sich** *akk* **~** to dare [to] approach

hinweg [hɪn·ˈvɛk] *adv* (*geh*) ■ **~!** (*veraltend*) begone!; **über jdn/etw ~ sein** to have gotten over sb/sth; **über lange Jahre ~** for many [long] years

Hinweg [ˈhɪn·veːk] *m* way there

hinweg|gehen [hɪn·ˈvɛk·geː·ən] *vi irreg sein* ■ **über etw** *akk* **~** to disregard sth

hinwe̱g|helfen *vi irreg* ■ **jdm über etw** *akk* **~** to help sb [to] get over sth

hinwe̱g|kommen *vi irreg sein* ■ **über etw** *akk* **~** to get over sth

hinwe̱g|sehen *vi irreg* ■ **über jdn/etw ~** ① (*darüber sehen*) to see over sb['s head]/sth ② (*nicht wichtig nehmen*) to overlook sb/sth

hinwe̱g|setzen *vr* ■ **sich** *akk* **über etw** *akk* **~** to disregard sth

Hinweis <-es, -e> [ˈhɪn·vais, *pl* -vai·zə] *m* ① (*Rat*) advice, tip ② (*Anhaltspunkt*) clue, indication

hi̱n|weisen *irreg* I. *vt* ■ **jdn darauf ~, dass ...** to point out [to sb] that ... II. *vi* ■ **auf jdn/etw ~** to point to sb/sth

Hi̱nweisschild *nt* sign

hi̱n|werfen *irreg vt* ① (*zuwerfen*) ■ **jdm etw ~** to throw sth to sb ② (*auf den Boden werfen*) to throw down *sep* ③ (*fam: aufgeben*) to give up *sep* ④ *Bemerkung* to drop ⑤ (*flüchtig zu Papier bringen*) to dash off

hi̱n|wollen *vi* (*fam*) to want to go

hi̱n|ziehen *irreg* I. *vt haben* ① (*zu sich ziehen*) ■ **jdn/etw zu sich** *dat* **~** to pull sb/sth toward oneself ② (*anziehen*) ■ **es zieht jdn zu etw/jdm hin** *dat* sb is attracted to sth/sb ③ (*hinauszögern*) to delay II. *vi sein* (*an einen Ort*) to move III. *vr* ■ **sich** *akk* **~** ① (*sich verzögern*) to drag on ② (*sich erstrecken*) to extend along

hi̱n|zielen *vi* ■ **auf etw** *akk* **~** (*zum Ziel haben*) to aim at sth; (*auf etw gerichtet sein*) to be aimed at sth

hinzu [hɪn·ˈtsuː] *adv* in addition, besides

hinzu̲|fügen *vt* ① (*beilegen*) to enclose ② (*zusätzlich bemerken*) to add ③ (*nachträglich hineingeben*) to add

hinzu|kommen [hɪn·ˈtsuː·kɔ·mən] *vi irreg sein* ① (*eintreffen*) to arrive; **die anderen Gäste kommen dann später hinzu** the other guests will come along later ② (*sich noch ereignen*) ■ **es kommt [noch] hinzu, dass ...** there is also the fact that ... ③ (*dazukommen*)

kommt sonst noch etwas hinzu? can I get you anything else?
hinzu|ziehen *vt irreg* to consult
Hiobsbotschaft ['hiː·ɔps-] *f* bad news
Hippie <-s, -s> ['hɪ·pi] *m* hippie
Hirn <-[e]s, -e> [hɪrn] *nt* ❶ (*Gehirn*) brain ❷ (*Hirnmasse*) brains *pl*
Hirngespinst *nt* fantasy
Hirnhaut *f* meninx *spec*
Hirnhautentzündung *f* meningitis
hirnrissig *adj* (*pej fam*) harebrained
Hirnschlag *m* MED stroke
Hirnstrom *m meist pl* BIOL, MED brain wave activity
Hirntod *m* brain death
hirnverbrannt *adj* (*fam*) *s.* **hirnrissig**
Hirsch <-es, -e> [hɪrʃ] *m* ❶ (*Rothirsch*) deer ❷ (*Hirschfleisch*) venison
Hirschgeweih *nt* antlers *pl*
Hirschkäfer *m* stag beetle
Hirschkuh *f* hind
Hirse <-, -n> ['hɪr·zə] *f* millet
Hirt(in) <-en, -en> ['hɪrt] *m(f)* herdsman *masc;* (*Schafhirt*) shepherd *masc,* shepherdess *fem*
Hirtenbrief *m* REL pastoral letter
his, His <-, -> [hɪs] *nt* MUS B sharp
hissen ['hɪ·sn̩] *vt* to hoist
Histamin <-s> [hɪs·ta·'miːn] *nt kein pl* histamine
Historiker(in) <-s, -> [hɪs·'toː·ri·kɐ] *m(f)* historian
historisch [hɪs·'toː·rɪʃ] **I.** *adj* ❶ (*die Geschichte betreffend*) historical ❷ (*geschichtlich bedeutsam*) historic **II.** *adv* historically
Hit <-s, -s> [hɪt] *m* (*fam*) ❶ (*erfolgreicher Schlager*) hit ❷ (*Umsatzrenner*) huge success
Hitliste *f* charts *npl*
Hitparade *f* ❶ (*Musiksendung*) ≈ weekly top 40 [countdown] ❷ *s.* **Hitliste**
Hitze <-, *fachspr* -n> ['hɪ·tsə] *f* heat; **bei mittlerer ~ backen** to bake at medium heat
hitzebeständig *adj* heat-resistant
Hitzewallung *f meist pl* hot flash
Hitzewelle *f* heat wave
hitzig ['hɪ·tsɪç] **I.** *adj* ❶ (*leicht aufbrausend*) *Mensch* hotheaded, quick-tempered; *Reaktion* heated; *Temperament* fiery ❷ (*leidenschaftlich*) passionate; *Debatte* heated **II.** *adv* passionately
Hitzkopf *m* (*fam*) hothead
hitzköpfig *adj* (*fam*) hotheaded
Hitzschlag *m* heatstroke; (*von der Sonne a.*) sunstroke
HIV <-[s]> [haː·ʔiː·'fau] *nt Abk von* **human immunodeficiency virus** HIV
HIV-infiziert [haː·ʔiː·'fau-] *adj* HIV-positive
HIV-negativ [haː·ʔiː·'fau-] *adj* HIV-negative
HIV-positiv [haː·ʔiː·'fau-·'poː·zi·tiːf] *adj* HIV-positive
Hiwi <-s, -s> ['hiː·vi] *m* (*sl*) assistant
Hl. *Abk von* **Heilige(r)** St.
hm *interj* ❶ (*anerkennendes Brummen*) hm ❷ (*fragendes Brummen*) er[m]
H-Milch ['haː] *f* UHT milk
h-Moll ['haː·'mɔl] *nt* MUS B minor
HNO-Arzt, -Ärztin [haː·ʔɛn·'ʔoː-] *m, f* ENT specialist
hob ['hoːp] *imp von* **heben**
Hobby <-s, -s> ['hɔ·bi] *nt* hobby
Hobel <-s, -> ['hoː·bl̩] *m* ❶ (*Werkzeug*) plane ❷ (*Küchengerät*) slicer
Hobelbank <-bänke> *f* carpenter's bench
hobeln ['hoː·bl̩n] *vt, vi* ❶ (*mit dem Hobel glätten*) to plane ❷ (*mit dem Hobel schneiden*) to slice
hoch [hoːx] **I.** *adj* <*attr* hohe(r, s), höher, *attr* höchste(r, s)> ❶ (*räumlich*) high, tall; *Baum* tall ❷ (*beträchtlich, groß*) large; *Kosten* high; *Druck, Geschwindigkeit, Lebensstandard* high; *Verlust* severe; *Sachschaden* extensive ❸ (*bedeutend*) great, high; *Position* senior ▶ WENDUNGEN: **etw ist jdm zu hoch** sth is above sb's head **II.** *adv* <höher, am höchsten> ❶ (*nach oben*) **etw ~ halten** to hold up *sep* sth ❷ (*in einiger Höhe*) **~ gelegen** high-lying *attr;* **~ oben** high up ❸ (*sehr*) highly; **~ konzentriert arbeiten** to be completely focused on one's work; **jdm etw ~ anrechnen** to give sb a lot of credit for sth; **etw/jdn ~ schätzen** to appreciate sth/sb very much ❹ (*eine hohe Summe umfassend*) highly; **~ gewinnen** to win big *fam;* **~ verschuldet** deep in debt *pred* ❺ MATH (*Bezeichnung der Potenz*) **2 ~ 4** 2 to the power of 4 ▶ WENDUNGEN: **etw ~ und heilig versprechen** to promise sth faithfully; **wenn es ~ kommt** (*fam*) at the most
Hoch[1] <-s, -s> [hoːx] *nt* cheer
Hoch[2] <-s, -s> [hoːx] *nt* METEO high
Hochachtung *f* deep respect
hochachtungsvoll *adv* (*geh*) your obedient servant *dated form*
hochaktuell *adj* ❶ (*äußerst aktuell*) [most] up-to-date ❷ MODE highly fashionable, all the rage *pred*
hochanständig *adj* very decent
hoch|arbeiten *vr* ■ **sich** *akk* ~ to work one's way up
Hochbahn *f* elevated railroad
Hochbau *m kein pl* structural engineering
hoch|bekommen* *vt irreg* to [manage to] lift up
hochberühmt *adj* very famous
hochbetagt *adj* (*geh*) aged
Hochbetrieb *m* intense activity; **~ haben** to be very busy
Hochburg *f* stronghold
hochdeutsch ['hoːx·dɔytʃ] *adj* High [*or* Standard] German

> The term **Hochdeutsch** describes German that is free of regional accents or dialects. Although **Hochdeutsch** is spoken in most public institutions throughout Germany,

> the German that is spoken in and around the city of Hanover, in northern Germany, is considered the best example of **Hochdeutsch**.

Hochdruck *m kein pl* high pressure
Hochebene *f* plateau
hocherfreut *adj* overjoyed
hoch|fahren *irreg* **I.** *vi sein* ❶ (*nach oben fahren*) to go up ❷ (*sich plötzlich aufrichten*) **aus dem Schlaf ~** to wake up with a start ❸ (*aufbrausen*) to flare up **II.** *vt haben* ❶ (*nach oben fahren*) **können Sie uns nach Hamburg ~?** can you drive us up to Hamburg? ❷ (*auf volle Leistung bringen*) *Produktion* to raise; *Computer* to boot
Hochformat *nt* portrait format
Hochfrequenz *f* high frequency
Hochgarage *f* multistory parking lot
Hochgebirge *nt* high mountains *pl*
Hochgefühl *nt* elation
hoch|gehen *irreg sein* **I.** *vi* ❶ (*hinaufgehen*) to go up ❷ (*fam: detonieren*) to go off *sep* ❸ (*fam: wütend werden*) to blow one's top ❹ (*fam*) *Preise* to go up ❺ (*fam: enttarnt werden*) to get caught **II.** *vt* ■ **etw ~** to go up sth
Hochgenuss^RR *m* real delight
Hochgeschwindigkeitszug *m* high-speed train
Hochglanz *m* FOTO high gloss
Hochglanzmagazin *nt* glossy magazine
hochgradig **I.** *adj* extreme **II.** *adv* extremely
hochhackig *adj* high-heeled
hoch|halten *vt irreg* ❶ (*in die Höhe halten*) to hold up *sep* ❷ (*ehren*) to uphold
Hochhaus *nt* high-rise building
hoch|heben *vt irreg* ❶ *Last* to lift up *sep* ❷ *Arm, Hand, Kind* to put up *sep*
hochinteressant *adj* most interesting
hoch|jubeln *vt* to hype
hochkant ['hoːx·kant] *adv* **etw ~ stellen** to stand sth on end
hochkantig ['hox·kan·tɪç] *adv* on end
Hochkonjunktur *f* [economic] boom
hoch|krempeln *vt* to roll up *sep*
hoch|kriegen *vt* (*fam*) *s.* **hochbekommen**
Hochkultur *f* [very] advanced civilization
hoch|laden *vt irreg* INET to upload
Hochland ['hoːx·lant] *nt* highland *usu pl*
Hochleistung *f* first-rate performance
Hochleistungssport *m* demanding sport
hochmodern **I.** *adj* ultramodern **II.** *adv* in the latest fashion[s]
Hochmut ['hoːx·muːt] *m* (*pej*) arrogance
hochmütig ['hoːx·myː·tɪç] *adj* (*pej*) arrogant
hochnäsig ['hoːx·nɛː·zɪç] **I.** *adj* (*pej fam*) conceited **II.** *adv* (*pej fam*) conceitedly
Hochnebel *m* METEO [low] stratus *spec*
hoch|nehmen *vt irreg* ❶ (*nach oben heben*) to lift up *sep* ❷ (*fam: auf den Arm nehmen*) ■ **jdn ~** to put sb on
hochnotpeinlich *adj* cringe-worthy
Hochofen *m* blast furnace
hochprozentig *adj* ❶ (*Alkohol enthaltend*) high-proof ❷ (*konzentriert*) highly concentrated
hochrangig *adj attr* high-ranking
hoch|rechnen *vt* to project
Hochrechnung *f* projection
hochrot ['hoːx·'roːt] *adj* bright red
Hochsaison *f* ❶ (*Zeit stärksten Betriebes*) busy season ❷ (*Hauptsaison*) high season
Hochschulabschluss^RR *m* college [*or* university] degree
Hochschulabsolvent(in) <-en, -en> *m(f)* college [*or* university] graduate
Hochschule ['hoːx·ʃuː·lə] *f* ❶ (*Universität*) university ❷ (*Fachhochschule*) college
Hochschüler(in) *m(f)* student
Hochschullehrer(in) *m(f)* college [*or* university] professor
Hochschulreife *f entrance requirement for higher education*
hochschwanger *adj* in an advanced stage of pregnancy *pred*
Hochsee *f kein pl* high sea[s *npl*]
Hochseefischerei *f* deep-sea fishing
Hochsitz *m* (*Jagdwesen*) raised blind
Hochsommer *m* midsummer, height of summer
Hochspannung *f* ❶ ELEK high voltage ❷ *kein pl* (*Belastung*) enormous tension
Hochsprache *f* standard language
Hochsprung *m* high jump
höchst [høːçst] **I.** *adj s.* **höchste(r, s)** **II.** *adv* most, extremely
Höchstalter *nt* maximum age
Hochstapler(in) <-s, -> ['hoːx·ʃtaːp·lɐ] *m(f)* (*pej*) con man
höchste(r, s) *attr* **I.** *adj superl von* **hoch** ❶ (*räumlich*) *Baum* tallest; *Berg* highest ❷ (*bedeutendste*) highest; *Profit* largest; **aufs H~** extremely, most; **von ~r Bedeutung sein** to be of the utmost importance **II.** *adv* ❶ (*räumlich*) the highest ❷ (*in größtem Ausmaß*) the most, most of all ❸ (*die größte Summe umfassend*) the most
hoch|steigen *vi irreg Angst, Freude, Wut* to well up
höchstens ['høːç·stn̩s] *adv* ❶ (*bestenfalls*) at [the] most, at best ❷ (*nicht mehr als*) not more than
Höchstfall *m* **im ~** at [the] most, at best
Höchstgebot *nt* highest bid
Höchstgeschwindigkeit *f* ❶ (*mögliche Geschwindigkeit*) maximum speed ❷ (*zulässige Geschwindigkeit*) speed limit
Hochstimmung *f kein pl* **in ~** in high spirits
Höchstmaß *nt* maximum amount
höchstpersönlich *adv* in person, personally
Höchststand *m* highest level
Höchststrafe *f* maximum penalty
höchstwahrscheinlich ['høːçst·vaːɐ̯·'ʃain·lɪç] *adv* most likely
höchstzulässig *adj attr* maximum [permis-

H

sible]

Hochtechnologie *f* high technology

Hochtour *f* ❶ SPORT (*Hochgebirgstour*) high-altitude mountain climbing trip ❷ *pl* TECH (*größte Leistungsfähigkeit*) **auf ~en laufen** to operate [*or* work] at full speed; (*fig*) to be in full swing

hochtrabend (*pej*) **I.** *adj* pompous **II.** *adv* pompously

hoch|treiben *vt irreg* to drive up *sep; Kosten, Löhne, Preise a.* to force up *sep*

hochverehrt *adj attr* highly respected

Hochverrat *m* high treason

Hochwasser *nt* ❶ (*Flut*) high tide ❷ (*überhoher Wasserstand*) high [level of] water ❸ (*Überschwemmung*) flood

hochwertig ['ho:x·ve:ɐ̯·tɪç] *adj* ❶ (*von hoher Qualität*) [of *pred*] high quality ❷ (*von hohem Nährwert*) highly nutritious

Hochzeit[1] <-, -en> ['hɔx·tsait] *f* (*Heirat*) wedding

Hochzeit[2] <-, -en> ['ho:x·tsait] *f* (*geh: Blütezeit*) golden age

Hochzeitsfeier *f* wedding reception

Hochzeitskleid *nt* wedding dress

Hochzeitsreise *f* honeymoon

Hochzeitstag *m* ❶ (*Tag der Hochzeit*) wedding day ❷ (*Jahrestag*) wedding anniversary

hoch|ziehen *irreg vt* ❶ (*nach oben ziehen*) to pull up *sep* ❷ (*fam: rasch bauen*) to build [rapidly]

Hocke <-, -n> ['hɔ·kə] *f* ❶ (*Körperhaltung*) crouching position; **in die ~ gehen** to squat [down] ❷ (*Turnübung*) squat vault

hocken ['hɔ·kn̩] *vi* ❶ *haben* (*kauern*) to crouch, to squat ❷ *haben* (*fam: sitzen*) to sit ❸ *sein* SPORT (*in der Hocke springen*) to squat-vault (**über** +*akk* over)

Hocker <-s, -> *m* stool

Höcker <-s, -> ['hœ·kɐ] *m* ❶ (*Wulst*) hump ❷ (*kleine Wölbung*) bump

Hockey <-s> ['hɔ·ki] *nt kein pl* hockey, field hockey

Hoden <-s, -> ['ho:·dn̩] *m* testicle

Hodensack *m* scrotum

Hof <-[e]s, Höfe> [ho:f, *pl* 'hø:·fə] *m* ❶ (*Innenhof*) courtyard; (*Schulhof*) schoolyard, playground ❷ (*Bauernhof*) farm ❸ HIST (*Fürstensitz, Hofstaat*) court

hoffen ['hɔ·fn̩] **I.** *vi* to hope (**auf** +*akk* for) **II.** *vt* **das will ich ~** I hope so

hoffentlich ['hɔ·fn̩t·lɪç] *adv* hopefully; ■ **~ nicht** I hope not

Hoffnung <-, -en> ['hɔf·nʊŋ] *f* hope (**auf** +*akk* for/of); **jds letzte ~ sein** to be sb's last hope; **sich** *dat* **~en machen** to have hope

hoffnungslos **I.** *adj* hopeless **II.** *adv* ❶ (*ohne Hoffnung*) without hope ❷ (*völlig*) hopelessly; **sich** *akk* **~ in jdn verlieben** to fall head over heels in love with sb

Hoffnungslosigkeit <-> *f kein pl* hopelessness; (*Verzweiflung*) despair

Hoffnungsschimmer *m* (*geh*) glimmer of hope

hoffnungsvoll **I.** *adj* hopeful; *Karriere* promising **II.** *adv* full of hope

höfisch ['hø:·fɪʃ] *adj* courtly

höflich ['hø:f·lɪç] **I.** *adj* polite, courteous **II.** *adv* politely, courteously

Höflichkeit <-, -en> *f* ❶ *kein pl* (*höfliche Art*) courtesy, politeness ❷ (*höfliche Bemerkung*) compliment

Höflichkeitsfloskel *f* polite phrase

Höfling <-s, -e> ['hø:f·lɪŋ] *m* HIST courtier

Hofnarr *m* HIST court jester

hohe(r, s) ['ho:·ə, 'ho:·ɐ, 'ho:·əs] *adj s.* **hoch**

Höhe <-, -n> ['hø:·hə] *f* ❶ (*Ausdehnung nach oben*) height; **aus der ~** from above; **auf halber ~** halfway up; **in einer ~ von** at a height of ❷ (*Gipfel*) summit, top ❸ (*Ausmaß*) amount, level; **ein Betrag in ~ von ...** an amount totaling ...; **die ~ des Schadens** the extent of the damage; **in die ~ gehen** *Preise* to rise ▶ WENDUNGEN: **das ist doch die ~!** (*fam*) enough is enough [already]!

Hoheit <-, -en> ['ho:·hait] *f* ❶ (*Mitglied einer fürstlichen Familie*) member of the royal family; **Ihre Königliche ~** Your Royal Highness ❷ *kein pl* (*oberste Staatsgewalt*) sovereignty

Hoheitsgebiet *nt* sovereign territory

Hoheitsgewässer *pl* territorial waters *npl*

Hoheitsrecht *nt meist pl* POL sovereign right

Höhenangst *f* fear of heights, acrophobia

Höhenmesser *m* LUFT altimeter

Höhenunterschied *m* difference in altitude

höhenverstellbar *adj* height-adjustable

Höhepunkt *m* ❶ (*bedeutendster Teil*) high point; *einer Veranstaltung* highlight ❷ (*Gipfel*) height, peak; **die Krise hatte ihren ~ erreicht** the crisis had reached its climax ❸ (*Orgasmus*) climax

höher ['hø:·ɐ] **I.** *adj komp von* **hoch** ❶ (*räumlich*) higher, taller ❷ (*bedeutender, größer*) *Forderungen, Druck, Verlust* greater; *Gewinn, Preis, Temperatur* higher; *Strafe* more severe **II.** *adv komp von* **hoch** ❶ (*weiter nach oben*) higher, taller ❷ (*mit gesteigertem Wert*) higher; **sich** *akk* **~ versichern** to increase one's insurance

höher|schrauben *vt* **seine Anforderungen ~** to increase one's demands

höher|stufen *vt* ■ **jdn ~** to upgrade sb

hohl [ho:l] *adj, adv* ❶ (*leer*) hollow; **mit der ~en Hand** with cupped hands; **~e Wangen** sunken cheeks ❷ (*pej: nichts sagend*) empty

Höhle <-, -n> ['hø:·lə] *f* ❶ (*Felshöhle*) cave ❷ (*Tierbehausung*) cave, den ❸ (*Höhlung*) hollow

Höhlenmalerei *f* cave painting

Höhlenmensch *m* cave dweller, caveman *masc,* cavewoman *fem*

Hohlkopf *m* (*pej fam*) blockhead, airhead

Hohlkreuz *nt* hollow back

Hohlmaß *nt* ❶ (*Maßeinheit*) measure of capacity, cubic measure *spec* ❷ (*Messgefäß*) dry measure

Hohlraum *m* cavity, hollow space
Hohlspiegel *m* concave mirror
Hohn <-[e]s> [hoːn] *m kein pl* scorn, mockery
höhnen *vi* to sneer
höhnisch [ˈhøː·nɪʃ] **I.** *adj* scornful, sneering **II.** *adv* scornfully, sneeringly
hoi [hɔɪ] *interj* SCHWEIZ hello, hi
Hokuspokus <-> [hoː·kʊs·ˈpoː·kʊs] *m kein pl* ① (*Zauberformel*) **~ Fidibus!** abracadabra ② (*fam: fauler Zauber*) hocus-pocus ③ (*fam: Brimborium*) fuss
Holding <-, -s> [ˈhoːl·dɪŋ] *f,* **Holdinggesellschaft** *f* holding company
holen [ˈhoː·lən] **I.** *vt* ① (*hervorholen*) to get (**aus** *+dat* out of, **von** *+dat* from) ② (*herholen*) **Sie können den Patienten jetzt ~** you can send for the patient now; ■**jdn ~ lassen** to go get sb; **Hilfe ~** to get help **II.** *vr* (*fam*) ■**sich** *dat* **etw ~** ① (*sich nehmen*) to get oneself sth (**aus** *+dat* out of, **von** *+dat* from) ② (*sich zuziehen*) to catch sth (**an** *+dat* from, **bei** *+dat* in); **bei dem kalten Wetter holst du dir eine Erkältung** you'll catch a cold in this chilly weather ③ (*sich einhandeln*) *Abfuhr, Rüge* to get
Holland <-s> [ˈhɔ·lant] *nt* ① (*fam: Niederlande*) the Netherlands *npl,* Holland; *s. a.* **Deutschland** ② (*Provinz der Niederlande*) Holland
Holländer <-s> [ˈhɔ·lɛn·dɐ] *m kein pl* Dutch cheese
Holländer(in) <-s, -> [ˈhɔ·lɛn·dɐ] *m(f)* (*fam*) Dutchman *masc,* Dutchwoman *fem;* ■**die ~** the Dutch *+ pl vb*
holländisch [ˈhɔ·lɛn·dɪʃ] *adj* (*fam*) Dutch; *s. a.* **deutsch**
Hölle <-, -n> [ˈhœ·lə] *f* (*pl selten*) hell ▶WENDUNGEN: **jdm die ~ heißmachen** (*fam*) to give sb hell; **die ~ ist los** (*fam*) all hell has broken loose
Höllenangst [ˈhœ·lən·ˈʔaŋst] *f* (*fam*) awful fear
Höllenlärm [ˈhœ·lən·ˈlɛrm] *m* racket
Höllenqual [ˈhœ·lən·ˈkvaːl] *f* (*fam*) agony
höllisch [ˈhœ·lɪʃ] **I.** *adj* ① *attr* infernal ② (*fam: fürchterlich*) terrible, dreadful, hell *pred;* **ein ~er Lärm** an awful noise **II.** *adv* (*fam*) dreadfully, terribly
Holocaust <-s> [ˈhoː·lo·kaust] *m kein pl* holocaust
Hologramm <-e> [ho·lo·ˈgram] *nt* hologram
holperig [ˈhɔl·pə·rɪç] *adj* ① *Straße* bumpy, uneven ② *Sprache, Stil* clumsy
holprig [ˈhɔl·prɪç] *adj s.* **holperig**
Holunder <-s, -> [ho·ˈlʊn·dɐ] *m* elder
Holz <-es, Hölzer> [hɔlts, *pl* ˈhœl·tsɐ] *nt* ① *kein pl* (*Material*) wood; **~ fällen** to cut down *sep* trees; **tropische Hölzer** tropical wood; **aus ~** wood[en]; **massives ~** solid wood ② *pl* (*Bauhölzer*) timber ③ SPORT *Golf* wood
Holzbein *nt* wooden leg, peg leg *dated fam*
Holzblasinstrument *nt* woodwind instrument
hölzern [ˈhœl·tsɐn] **I.** *adj* wooden **II.** *adv* woodenly
Holzfäller(in) <-s, -> *m(f)* lumberjack
holzgetäfelt [ˈhɔlts·gə·tɛː·flt] *adj Raum, Wand* wood-paneled
Holzhammer *m* mallet
Holzhammermethode *f* (*fam*) sledgehammer approach
holzig [ˈhɔl·tsɪç] *adj Spargel, Radieschen* stringy
Holzklotz *m* wooden block
Holzkohle *f* charcoal
Holzschuh *m* clog, wooden shoe
Holzweg *m* ▶WENDUNGEN: **auf dem ~ sein** (*fam*) to be barking up the wrong tree
Holzwurm *m* woodworm
Homecomputer [ˈhoːm-] *m* home computer
Homepage <-, -s> [ˈhoːm·peːtʃ] *f* COMPUT home page
Homo <-s, -s> [ˈhoː·mo] *m* (*veraltend fam*) homo
Homo-Ehe *f* (*fam*) gay marriage
homogen [ho·mo·ˈgeːn] *adj* (*geh*) homogeneous
homogenisieren* [ho·mo·ge·ni·ˈziː·rən] *vt* to homogenize
Homöopath(in) <-en, -en> [ho·møo·ˈpaːt] *m(f)* homeopath
Homöopathie <-> [ho·møo·pa·ˈtiː] *f kein pl* homeopathy
homöopathisch [ho·møo·ˈpaː·tɪʃ] *adj* homeopathic
Homosexualität [ho·mo·zɛ·ksu̯a·li·ˈtɛːt] *f* homosexuality
homosexuell [ho·mo·zɛ·ˈksu̯·ɛl] *adj* homosexual
Homosexuelle(r) *f(m) dekl wie adj* homosexual
Honig <-s, -e> [ˈhoː·nɪç] *m* honey; **türkischer ~** halva[h] ▶WENDUNGEN: **jdm ~ ums Maul schmieren** (*fam*) to butter up *sep* sb
Honigbiene *f* honeybee
Honigkuchen *m* honey cake
Honigkuchenpferd *nt* simpleton ▶WENDUNGEN: **wie ein ~ grinsen** (*hum fam*) to grin like a Cheshire cat
Honiglecken *nt* ▶WENDUNGEN: **kein ~ sein** (*fam*) to be no picnic
Honigmelone *f* honeydew melon
Honigwabe *f* honeycomb
Honorar <-s, -e> [ho·no·ˈraːɐ̯] *nt* fee; *eines Autors* royalties *npl;* **gegen ~** for a fee
honorieren* [ho·no·ˈriː·rən] *vt* ① (*würdigen*) to appreciate ② (*bezahlen*) to pay ③ ÖKON (*akzeptieren*) to honor
Hooligan <-s, -s> [ˈhuː·li·gn̩] *m* hooligan
Hopfen <-s, -> [ˈhɔp·fn̩] *m* hops *pl* ▶WENDUNGEN: **bei jdm ist ~ und Malz verloren** (*fam*) sb is a hopeless case
hopp [hɔp] (*fam*) **I.** *interj* hop to it! **II.** *adv* ▶WENDUNGEN: **~, ~!** look alive!
hoppeln [ˈhɔ·pl̩n] *vi sein* to lollop [along]
hoppla [ˈhɔp·la] *interj* ① (*o je!*) [wh]oops!

❷ (*Moment!*) hang on!; **~, wer kommt denn da?** hello, who's that [coming over this way]?

hopsen ['hɔp·sn̩] *vi sein* (*fam*) to skip; (*auf einem Bein*) to hop

hops|gehen *vi irreg sein* (*sl*) ❶ (*umkommen*) to kick the bucket ❷ (*verloren gehen*) to go missing

hörbar *adj* audible

Hörbuch *nt* audio book

horchen ['hɔr·çn̩] *vi* ❶ (*lauschen*) to listen in (**an** +*dat* on); (*heimlich a.*) to eavesdrop ❷ DIAL (*hinhören*) ■ **horch!** listen!; ■ **auf etw** *akk* ~ to listen [out] for sth

Horde <-, -n> ['hɔr·də] *f* ❶ (*wilde Schar*) horde ❷ HORT rack

hören ['hø:·rən] **I.** *vt* ❶ (*mit dem Gehör vernehmen*) to hear; **..., wie ich höre** I hear ...; **wie man hört, ...** word has it ...; **nie gehört!** never heard of him/her/it!; **das will ich nicht gehört haben** I'll ignore that comment; **sich** *akk* **gern reden ~** to like the sound of one's own voice ❷ (*anhören*) to listen ► WENDUNGEN: **etwas [von jdm] zu ~ bekommen** to get chewed out [by sb]; **ich kann das nicht mehr ~!** enough [of that] already!; **etw/nichts von sich** *dat* **~ lassen** to keep/not keep in touch **II.** *vi* ❶ (*zuhören*) to listen; **hör mal!/~ Sie mal!** listen! ❷ (*vernehmen*) ■ **~, was/wie ...** to hear what/how ...; **gut/schlecht ~** to have good/poor hearing ❸ (*erfahren*) ■ **~, dass ...** to hear [that] ...; ■ **von jdm/etw ~** to hear of [*or* about] sb/sth ❹ (*gehorchen*) to listen (**auf** +*akk* to); **auf dich hört er!** he listens to you! ► WENDUNGEN: **na hör/~ Sie mal!** (*euph*) [now] look here!; **lass von dir/lassen Sie von sich ~!** keep in touch!; **man höre und staune!** would you believe it!?

Hörensagen ['hø·rən·za:·gn̩] *nt* **vom ~** from hearsay

Hörer <-s, -> *m* (*Telefonhörer*) receiver; **den ~ auflegen** to hang up [on sb]

Hörer(in) <-s, -> *m(f)* listener

Hörerschaft <-, -en> *f meist sing* audience; (*Radiohörerschaft*) listeners *pl*

Hörfunk *m* radio

Hörgerät *nt* hearing aid

hörig ['hø:·rɪç] *adj* ❶ (*sexuell abhängig*) sexually dependent ❷ HIST (*an die Scholle gebunden*) in serfdom *pred*

Horizont <-[e]s, -e> [ho·ri·'tsɔnt] *m* horizon; **am ~** on the horizon; **über jds ~ gehen** to be beyond sb

horizontal [ho·ri·tsɔn·'ta:l] *adj* horizontal

Horizontale [ho·ri·tsɔn·'ta:·lə] *f dekl wie adj* horizontal [line]

Hormon <-s, -e> [hɔr·'mo:n] *nt* hormone

hormonal [hɔr·mo·'na:l], **hormonell** [hɔr·mo·'nɛl] **I.** *adj* hormone *attr,* hormonal **II.** *adv* hormonally; **~ gesteuert** controlled by hormones

Hörmuschel *f* TELEK earpiece

Horn <-[e]s, Hörner> [hɔrn, *pl* 'hœr·nɐ] *nt* ❶ (*Auswuchs*) horn; **das ~ von Afrika** the Horn of Africa ❷ (*Material*) horn ❸ MUS horn ❹ AUTO (*Hupe*) horn; (*Martinshorn*) siren

Hornbrille *f* horn-rimmed glasses *npl*

Hörnchen <-s, -> ['hœrn·çən] *nt* ❶ *dim von* **Horn 1** small horn ❷ (*Gebäck*) crescent roll; (*aus Blätterteig*) croissant

Hornhaut *f* ❶ (*des Auges*) cornea ❷ (*der Haut*) callus

Hornisse <-, -n> [hɔr·'nɪ·sə] *f* hornet

Hornist(in) <-en, -en> [hɔr·'nɪst] *m(f)* horn player

Hornochs(e) *m* (*fam*) stupid idiot

Horoskop <-s, -e> [ho·ro·'sko:p] *nt* horoscope

horrend [hɔ·'rɛnt] *adj Preise* horrendous

Horror <-s> ['hɔ·ro:ɐ̯] *m kein pl* horror; **einen ~ vor etw** *dat* **haben** to have a fear of sth

Horrorfilm *m* horror movie

Horrortrip *m* ❶ (*grässliches Erlebnis*) nightmare ❷ (*negativer Drogenrausch*) bad trip

Hörsaal *m* ❶ (*Räumlichkeit*) lecture hall ❷ *kein pl* (*Zuhörerschaft*) audience

Hörspiel *nt* ❶ *kein pl* (*Gattung*) radio drama ❷ (*Stück*) radio play

Horst <-[e]s, -e> [hɔrst] *m* ❶ (*Nest*) nest, aerie ❷ MIL (*Fliegerhorst*) military airbase

Hörsturz *m* sudden hearing loss

Hort <-[e]s, -e> [hɔrt] *m* ❶ (*Kinderhort*) after-school care center ❷ (*geh: Zufluchtsort*) shelter, refuge

horten ['hɔr·tn̩] *vt* to hoard; *Rohstoffe* to stockpile

Hortensie <-, -n> [hɔr·'tɛn·zi̯ə] *f* hydrangea

Hörweite *f* hearing range, earshot; **in/außer ~** within/out of earshot

Hose <-, -n> ['ho:·zə] *f* pants *npl,* trousers *npl;* **kurze ~[n]** shorts *npl* ► WENDUNGEN: **jdm ist das Herz in die ~ gerutscht** (*fam*) sb's heart was in their mouth; **die ~n [gestrichen] voll haben** (*sl*) to be scared shitless; **tote ~** (*sl*) boring as hell; **in die ~ gehen** to be a failure; **[sich** *dat*] **in die ~[n] machen** to wet oneself

Hosenanzug *m* pantsuit

Hosenbein *nt* pants leg

Hosenboden *m* (*Gesäßteil der Hose*) seat [of pants] ► WENDUNGEN: **sich** *akk* **auf den ~ setzen** (*fam*) to buckle down

Hosenscheißer *m* (*sl*) ❶ (*hum: kleines Kind*) ankle-biter ❷ (*pej: Feigling*) chicken, scaredy-cat

Hosenschlitz *m* fly; **dein ~ ist offen!** your fly is down!

Hosenstall *m* (*hum fam*) *s.* **Hosenschlitz**

Hosentasche *f* pants pocket

Hosenträger *pl* suspenders *npl*

Hospital <-s, -e *o* Hospitäler> [hɔs·pi·'ta:l, *pl* hɔs·pi·'tɛ:·lɐ] *nt* ❶ DIAL hospital ❷ (*veraltet: Pflegeheim*) home for the elderly

Hostess <-, -en> ['hɔs·tɛs] *f* ❶ (*im Flugzeug*) stewardess, flight attendant ❷ (*auf Reisen, Messen o.ä.*) [female] tour guide ❸ (*euph: Prostituierte*) escort

Hostie <-, -n> ['hɔs·ti̯ə] *f* REL host

HotdogRR <-s, -s>, **Hot Dog**RR <-s, -s>, **Hot dog**ALT <-s, -s> ['hɔt·'dɔk] *nt o m* hot dog
Hotel <-s, -s> [ho·'tɛl] *nt* hotel
Hotelboy *f* bellboy
Hotelfachschule *f* school of hotel management
Hotelgewerbe *nt* hotel trade
Hotelier <-s, -s> [ho·tə·'li̯eː] *m* hotelier
Hotellerie <-> [ho·tɛ·lə·'riː] *f kein pl* hospitality
Hotelzimmer *nt* hotel room
Hotline <-, -s> ['hɔt·laɪn] *f* hotline
Hr. *Abk von* **Herr**
Hrsg. *Abk von* **Herausgeber** ed.
HTML <-, -> [haː·teː·ʔɛm·'ʔɛl] *nt o f kein pl* COMPUT *Abk von* **hypertext markup language** HTML
HTTP <-, -> [haː·teː·teː·'peː] *nt* COMPUT *Abk von* **Hypertext Transfer Protokoll** HTTP
Hubraum *m* cubic capacity
hübsch [hʏpʃ] *adj* ❶ (*Aussehen*) pretty; **na, ihr zwei H~en?** (*fam*) well, my two lovelies?; **sich** *akk* **~ machen** to get all dressed up ❷ (*fam: beträchtlich*) real, pretty; **ein ~es Sümmchen** a pretty penny ❸ (*fam: sehr angenehm*) nice and ...; **das wirst du ~ bleiben lassen** you'll do no such thing
Hubschrauber <-s, -> *m* helicopter
huch [hʊx] *interj* (*Ausruf der Überraschung*) oh!; (*Ausruf bei unangenehmen Empfindungen*) ugh!
Hucke <-, -n> ['hʊ·kə] *f* ▸ WENDUNGEN: **jdm die ~ vollhauen** to beat up *sep* sb; **sich** *dat* **die ~ vollsaufen** to get hammered
huckepack ['hʊ·kə·pak] *adv* piggyback; **jdn ~ nehmen** to give sb a piggyback ride
Huf <-[e]s, -e> [huːf] *m* hoof
Hufeisen *nt* horseshoe
Hufnagel *m* horseshoe nail
Hufschmied(in) *m(f)* blacksmith
Hüfte <-, -n> ['hʏf·tə] *f* ❶ (*Körperpartie*) hip ❷ *kein pl* KOCHK (*Fleischstück*) inside round; (*vom Rind*) top sirloin
Hüftgelenk *nt* hip joint
Hüfthalter *m* girdle
Hüftsteak *nt* rump steak
Hügel <-s, -> ['hyː·gl̩] *m* hill; (*Erdhaufen*) mound
hügelig ['hyː·gə·lɪç], **hüglig** ['hyːg·lɪç] *adj* hilly; **eine ~e Landschaft** rolling countryside
Huhn <-[e]s, Hühner> [huːn, *pl* 'hyː·nɐ] *nt* ❶ (*Haushuhn*) hen, chicken; **frei laufende Hühner** free-range chickens ❷ (*Hühnerfleisch*) chicken ❸ (*Person*) **dummes ~!** (*pej fam*) stupid idiot!; **ein verrücktes ~** a nutcase ▸ WENDUNGEN: **da lachen ja die Hühner** (*fam*) you must be joking
Hühnchen <-s, -> ['hyːn·çən] *nt dim von* **Huhn** spring chicken ▸ WENDUNGEN: **mit jdm ein ~ zu rupfen haben** (*fam*) to have a bone to pick with sb
Hühnerauge *nt* corn
Hühnerbrühe *f* chicken broth
Hühnerbrust *f* ❶ (*Fleisch*) chicken breast ❷ (*fig*) **eine ~ haben** to be pigeon-breasted
Hühnerei *nt* chicken egg
Hühnerstall *m* hencoop
Hühnerstange *f* chicken roost
huldigen ['hʊl·dɪgn̩] *vi* (*geh*) ❶ (*anhängen*) ■**etw** *dat* **~** to subscribe to sth ❷ (*veraltend: seine Reverenz erweisen*) ■**jdm ~** to pay homage to sb
Huldigung <-, -en> *f* (*veraltet*) homage, tribute
Hülle <-, -n> ['hʏ·lə] *f* cover ▸ WENDUNGEN: **in ~ und Fülle** (*geh*) in abundance
hüllen ['hʏ·lən] *vt* (*geh*) to wrap (**in** +*akk* in); **in Dunkelheit gehüllt** shrouded in darkness; **sich** *akk* **in Schweigen ~** to maintain one's silence
hüllenlos *adj* naked, in one's birthday suit *hum*
Hülse <-, -n> ['hʏl·zə] *f* ❶ BOT (*Schote*) pod ❷ (*röhrenförmige Hülle*) capsule
Hülsenfrucht ['hʏl·zn̩-] *f meist pl* legume
human [hu·'maːn] *adj* ❶ (*menschenwürdig*) humane; *Strafe* lenient ❷ *Chef, Lehrer* considerate (**gegenüber** +*dat* toward) ❸ (*Menschen betreffend*) human
Humanismus <-> [hu·ma·'nɪs·mʊs] *m kein pl* humanism
humanistisch *adj* ❶ (*im Sinne des Humanismus*) humanistic; **der ~e Geist** the spirit of humanism ❷ HIST (*dem Humanismus angehörend*) humanist ❸ (*altsprachlich*) humanistic, classical; **eine ~e Bildung** a classical education
humanitär [hu·ma·ni·'tɛːɐ̯] *adj* humanitarian
Humanität [hu·ma·ni·'tɛːt] *f kein pl* (*geh*) humanity
Humbug <-s> ['hʊm·bʊk] *m kein pl* (*pej fam*) ❶ (*Unfug*) trash ❷ (*Schwindel*) humbug
Hummel <-, -n> ['hʊ·ml̩] *f* bumblebee ▸ WENDUNGEN: **~n im Hintern haben** (*fam*) to have ants in one's pants
Hummer <-s, -> ['hʊ·mɐ] *m* lobster
Humor <-s, -e> [hu·'moːɐ̯] *m* (*pl selten*) ❶ (*Laune*) good humor, cheerfulness ❷ (*Witz, Wesensart*) [sense of] humor; **etw mit ~ nehmen** to take sth good-humoredly; **[einen Sinn für] ~ haben** to have a sense of humor
humoristisch *adj* humorous, amusing
humorlos *adj* humorless
humorvoll *adj* humorous
humpeln ['hʊm·pl̩n] *vi sein o haben* to limp
Humus ['huː·mʊs] *m kein pl* humus
Hund <-[e]s, -e> [hʊnt, *pl* 'hʊn·də] *m* ❶ (*Tier*) dog; (*Jagdhund*) hound; **„[Vorsicht,] bissiger ~!"** "beware of dog!" ❷ (*Mensch*) swine; **ein armer ~ sein** (*fam*) to be a poor soul; **[du] gemeiner ~** [you] dirty dog ▸ WENDUNGEN: **bekannt sein wie ein bunter ~** (*fam*) to be known far and wide; **das ist ja ein dicker ~** (*sl*) that is absolutely outrageous; **da liegt der ~ begraben** (*fam*) that's the crux of the matter; **~e, die bellen, beißen nicht** (*prov*) sb's bark is worse than their bite
hundeelend ['hʊn·də·ʔeː·lɛnt] *adj* (*fam*) **jd**

H

fühlt sich *akk* ~ sb feels awful
Hụndefutter *nt* dog food
Hụndehütte *f* doghouse
Hụndekuchen *m* dog biscuit
Hụndeleine *f* dog leash
hundemüde ['hʊn·də·'myː·də] *adj pred* (*fam*) dog-tired
Hụnderasse *f* breed of dog
hundert ['hʊn·dɐt] *adj* ❶ (*Zahl*) [a [*or* one]] hundred ❷ (*fam: sehr viele*) a hundred, hundreds ❸ *pl, auch großgeschrieben* (*viele hundert*) hundreds *pl; s. a.* **Hundert[1] 2**
Hundert[1] <-s, -e> ['hʊn·dɐt] *nt* ❶ (*Einheit von 100*) hundred; **mehrere ~** several hundred ❷ *pl, auch kleingeschrieben* (*viele hundert*) hundreds *pl;* **einige/viele ~e ...** a few/several hundred ...; **~e von ...** hundreds of ...; **in die ~e gehen** (*fam*) *Kosten, Schaden* to run into the hundreds; **~e und aber ~e** hundreds upon hundreds
Hundert[2] <-, -en> ['hʊn·dɐt] *f* [one [*or* a]] hundred
Hunderter <-s, -> ['hʊn·dɐtɐ] *m* ❶ (*fam: Banknote zu 100 Euro*) hundred-euro [*or* hundred-dollar] bill; **es hat mich einen ~ gekostet** it cost me a hundred euros [*or* dollars] ❷ (*100 als Zahlenbestandteil*) hundred
Hunderteuroschein *m* hundred-euro bill
Hundertjahrfeier [hʊn·dɐt·'jaːɐ̯·fai·ɐ] *f* centenary [celebration]
hundertjährig, 100-jährig[RR] ['hʊn·dɐt·jɛː·rɪç] *adj* ❶ (*Alter*) hundred-year-old *attr,* one hundred years old *pred; s. a.* **achtjährig 1** ❷ (*Zeitspanne*) hundred-year *attr; s. a.* **achtjährig 2**
Hụndertjährige(r), 100-Jährige(r)[RR] *f(m)* *dekl wie adj* hundred-year-old [person], centenarian
hundertmal, 100-mal[RR] ['hʊn·dɐt·maːl] *adv* a hundred times
hundertprozentig ['hʊn·dɐt·pro·tsɛn·tɪç] **I.** *adj* ❶ (*100 % umfassend*) one hundred percent; (*Alkohol*) pure ❷ (*fam: typisch*) through and through; **er ist ein ~er Bayer** he's a Bavarian through and through **II.** *adv* (*fam*) absolutely, completely; **das weiß ich ~** I know that for certain; **sich** *dat* **~ sicher sein** to be absolutely sure
Hundertstel <-s, -> ['hʊn·dɐts·tl̩] *nt o* SCHWEIZ *m* hundredth
hunderttausend ['hʊn·dɐt·'tau·zn̩t] *adj* ❶ (*Zahl*) a [*or* one] hundred thousand ❷ *auch großgeschrieben* (*ungezählte Mengen*) hundreds of thousands
Hụndescheiße *f* (*derb*) dog shit
Hụndeschlitten *m* dog sled
Hụndewetter *nt* (*fam*) *s.* **Sauwetter**
Hündin ['hʏn·dɪn] *f* bitch
hundsgemein ['hʊnts·gə·'main] *adj* (*fam*) lowdown, rotten *fam;* **er kann ~ sein** he can be really nasty
hundsmiserabel ['hʊnts·mi·zə·'raː·bl̩] *adj* (*fam*) ❶ (*niederträchtig*) lowdown ❷ (*äußerst schlecht*) awful; **sich** *akk* **~ fühlen** to feel really lousy
Hüne <-n, -n> ['hyː·nə] *m* giant
hünenhaft *adj* gigantic, colossal
Hunger <-s> ['hʊŋɐ] *m kein pl* ❶ (*Hungergefühl*) hunger; **~ bekommen/haben** to get/be hungry; **~ auf etw** *akk* **haben** to feel like [eating] sth; **~ leiden** (*geh*) to starve, to go hungry; **~ wie ein Bär haben** to be [as] hungry as a bear ❷ (*Hungersnot*) famine ❸ (*geh: großes Verlangen*) ■**jds ~ nach etw** *dat* sb's thirst for sth ▶ WENDUNGEN: **~ ist der beste Koch** (*prov*) hunger is the best sauce *prov*
Hụngerhilfe *f kein pl* famine relief
Hụngerkur *f* starvation diet
Hụngerlohn *m* (*pej*) pittance; **für einen ~ arbeiten** to work for peanuts
hụngern *vi* ❶ (*Hunger leiden*) to go hungry, to starve; (*fam: fasten*) to fast ❷ (*geh: verlangen*) to hunger [*or* thirst] *fig* (**nach** +*dat* for)
Hụngersnot *f* famine
Hụngerstreik *m* hunger strike; **in den ~ treten** to go on a hunger strike
Hụngertuch *nt* ▶ WENDUNGEN: **am ~ nagen** (*hum fam*) to be starving
hungrig ['hʊŋ·rɪç] *adj* hungry; **etw macht ~** sth works up an appetite
Hupe <-, -n> ['huː·pə] *f* horn; **auf die ~ drücken** to honk the horn
hupen ['huː·pn̩] *vi* to honk [the [*or* one's] horn]
hüpfen ['hʏp·fn̩] *vi sein* to hop; *Lamm, Zicklein* to frolic; *Ball* to bounce; **vor Freude ~** to jump for joy
Hürde <-, -n> ['hʏr·də] *f* ❶ SPORT hurdle; **110 Meter ~n laufen** to run the 110-meter hurdles ❷ (*tragbare Einzäunung für Tiere*) fold, pen ▶ WENDUNGEN: **eine ~ nehmen** to overcome an obstacle
Hụ̈rdenlauf *m* hurdling, hurdles *npl*
Hure <-, -n> ['huː·rə] *f* whore
Hurenbock *m* (*pej vulg*) horny bastard
Hurensohn *m* (*pej vulg*) son of a bitch
hurra [hʊ·'raː] *interj* hurray
Hurrikan <-s, -e> ['hʊ·ri·kan] *m* hurricane
huschen ['hʊ·ʃn̩] *vi sein* to dart, to flit; *Maus* to scurry; *Licht* to flash; **ein Lächeln huschte über ihr Gesicht** a smile flitted across her face
hüsteln ['hyːs·tl̩n] *vi* to cough [slightly]; **nervös ~** to clear one's throat
husten ['huːs·tn̩] **I.** *vi* to cough **II.** *vt* (*auswerfen*) **Schleim/Blut ~** to cough up mucus/blood
Husten <-s> ['huːs·tn̩] *m kein pl* cough
Hustenanfall *m* coughing fit
Hustenbonbon *m o nt* cough drop
Hustenreiz *m* tickly throat
Hustensaft *m* cough syrup
Hut[1] <-[e]s, Hüte> [huːt, *pl* 'hyː·tə] *m* ❶ (*Kopfbedeckung*) hat; **den ~ aufsetzen/abnehmen** to put on/take off one's hat ❷ BOT (*von Pilzen*) cap ▶ WENDUNGEN: **vor jdm/etw den ~ ziehen** to take one's hat off to sb/sth; **~ ab [vor jdm]!** (*fam*) hats off to sb!; **etw unter**

einen ~ bringen to reconcile sth; (*Termine*) to fit in *sep* sth; **mit etw** *dat* **nichts am ~ haben** (*fam*) to not really have anything in common with sth

Hut² <-> [huːt] *f* (*geh*) protection; **auf der ~ [vor etw** *dat*] **sein** to be on one's guard [against sth]

hüten ['hyː·tn̩] **I.** *vt* ❶ (*beaufsichtigen*) to look after; *Schafe* to tend ❷ (*geh: bewahren*) to keep **II.** *vr* (*sich in Acht nehmen*) ■ **sich** *akk* **vor etw** *dat* **~** to be on one's guard against sth; ■ **sich** *akk* **~, etw zu tun** to take care not to do sth

Hüter(in) <-s, -> *m(f)* (*geh*) guardian

Hutkrempe *f* brim

Hutmacher(in) *m(f)* hatter; *für Damen* milliner

Hütte <-, -n> ['hʏ·tə] *f* ❶ (*kleines Haus*) hut; (*ärmlich*) shack ❷ (*Berghütte*) [mountain] hut [*or* shelter]; (*Holzhütte*) cabin

Hüttenindustrie *f* iron and steel industry

Hüttenkäse *m* cottage cheese

Hyäne <-, -n> ['hy̆ɛː·nə] *f* hyena

Hyazinthe <-, -n> [hy̆a·'tsɪn·tə] *f* hyacinth

Hydrant <-en, -en> [hy·'drant] *m* hydrant

Hydraulik <-> [hy·'drau·lɪk] *f kein pl* hydraulics *npl*

hydraulisch [hy·'drau·lɪʃ] *adj* hydraulic

Hydrodynamik <-> [hy·dro·dy·'naː·mɪk] *f* hydrodynamics + *sing vb, no art*

Hydrokultur *f* hydroponics + *sing vb spec*

Hydrotherapie [hy·dro·tɛ·ra·'piː] *f* hydrotherapy

Hygiene <-> [hy·'gi̯eː·nə] *f kein pl* hygiene

hygienisch [hy·'gi̯eː·nɪʃ] *adj* hygienic

Hymne <-, -n> ['hʏm·nə] *f* hymn

hyperaktiv *adj* hyperactive

Hyperaktivität [hypɐ·ak·ti·vi·'tɛt] *f* hyperactivity

Hyperbel <-, -n> [hy·'pɛr·bl̩] *f* ❶ MATH hyperbola ❷ LING hyperbole

hyperkorrekt [hypɐ·kɔ·'rɛkt] *adj* hypercorrect

Hyperlink <-s, -s> ['hai·pɐ·lɪŋk] *m* COMPUT hyperlink

Hypermedia [hai·pɐ·'meːdi̯a] *nt* COMPUT hypermedia

hypermodern *adj* (*fam*) ultramodern

hypersensibel *adj* hypersensitive

Hypertext ['hai·pɐ·tɛkst] *m* COMPUT hypertext

Hypnose <-, -n> [hʏp·'noː·zə] *f* hypnosis; **jdn in ~ versetzen** to hypnotize sb

hypnotisch [hʏp·'noː·tɪʃ] *adj* hypnotic

hypnotisieren* *vt* to hypnotize

Hypochonder <-s, -> [hy·po·'xɔn·dɐ] *m* hypochondriac

Hypothek <-, -en> [hy·po·'teːk] *f* mortgage

Hypothekenbank <-banken> *f* mortgage bank

Hypothese <-, -n> [hy·po·'teː·zə] *f* hypothesis; **eine ~ aufstellen/widerlegen** to advance/refute a hypothesis

hypothetisch [hy·po·'teː·tɪʃ] *adj* hypothetical

Hysterie <-, -n> [hʏs·te·'riː] *f* hysteria

hysterisch [hʏs·'teː·rɪʃ] *adj* hysterical

Hz *Abk von* **Hertz** Hz

I i

I, i <-, - *o fam* -s, -s> [iː] *nt* I, i; **~ wie Ida** I as in India

i [iː] *interj* ❶ (*fam: Ausdruck von Ablehnung, Ekel*) ugh; **~, wie ekelig** yuck, how disgusting ❷ (*abwertend*) **~ wo!** no way! *fam*

i.A. *Abk von* **im Auftrag** p.p.

iberisch [iˈbeːrɪʃ] *adj* Iberian

IC <-s, -s> [iːˈtseː] *m Abk von* **Intercity**

ICE <-s, -s> [iːtseːˈʔeː] *m Abk von* **Intercity Express** *a high-speed train*

ich <*gen* meiner, *dat* mir, *akk* mich> [ɪç] *pron pers* I, me; **~ bin/war es** it's/it was me; **~ nicht!** not me!; **~ selbst** I myself

Ich <-[s], -s> [ɪç] *nt* ❶ (*das Selbst*) self ❷ PSYCH (*Ego*) ego; **jds anderes ~** sb's alter ego; **jds besseres ~** sb's better self

I

Ichform *f* first person form; **in der ~** in the first person

ideal [ideˈaːl] **I.** *adj* ideal **II.** *adv* ideally

Ideal <-s, -e> [ideˈaːl] *nt* ideal

Idealismus <-> [ideaˈlɪsmʊs] *m kein pl* idealism

Idealist(in) <-en, -en> [ideaˈlɪst] *m(f)* idealist

Ideallösung *f* ideal solution

Idee <-, -n> [iˈdeː, *pl* iˈdeːən] *f* ❶ (*Einfall, Vorstellung*) idea; **eine fixe ~** an obsession; **keine ~ haben** to have no idea; **jdn auf eine ~ bringen** to give sb an idea; **jdn auf andere ~n bringen** to take sb's mind off of sth/it; **auf eine ~ kommen** to get an idea ❷ (*Leitbild*) ideal ❸ (*fam: ein wenig*) **keine ~ besser sein** to be not one bit better; **eine ~ ...** a little bit ...

Ideenreichtum *m kein pl* inventiveness

Identifikation <-, -en> [idɛntifikaˈtsi̯oːn] *f* identification

identifizieren* [idɛntifiˈtsiːrən] **I.** *vt* to identify (**als** +*akk* as, **mit** +*dat* with) **II.** *vr* ■ **sich** *akk* **mit jdm/etw ~** to identify with sb/sth

Identifizierung <-, -en> *f* identification

identisch [iˈdɛntɪʃ] *adj* identical (**mit** +*dat* to)

Identität <-> [idɛntiˈtɛːt] *f kein pl* ❶ (*Echtheit*) identity ❷ (*Übereinstimmung*) identicalness

Identitätskarte *f bes* SCHWEIZ identity card

Ideologie <-, -n> [ideoloˈgiː, *pl* -ˈgiːən] *f* ideology

ideologisch [ideoˈloːgɪʃ] **I.** *adj* ideologic[al] **II.** *adv* ideologically

idiomatisch [idi̯oˈmaːtɪʃ] **I.** *adj* idiomatic **II.** *adv* idiomatically

Idiot(in) <-en, -en> [iˈdi̯oːt] *m(f)* (*pej fam*) idiot

idiotensicher **I.** *adj* (*hum fam*) foolproof **II.** *adv* (*fam*) effortlessly

idiotisch [iˈdi̯oːtɪʃ] *adj* (*fam*) idiotic

Idol <-s, -e> [iˈdoːl] *nt* idol

Idylle <-, -n> [iˈdʏlə] *f* idyll

idyllisch [iˈdʏlɪʃ] **I.** *adj* idyllic **II.** *adv* idyllically

Igel <-s, -> [ˈiːgl̩] *m* hedgehog

igitt(igitt) [iˈgɪt(igɪt)] *interj* ugh, yuck

Iglu <-s, -s> [ˈiːglu] *m o nt* igloo

Ignoranz <-> [ɪgnoˈrants] *f kein pl* (*pej geh*) ignorance

ignorieren* [ɪgnoˈriːrən] *vt* to ignore

IHK <-, -s> [iːhaːˈkaː] *f Abk von* **Industrie- und Handelskammer**

ihm [iːm] *pron pers dat von* **er, es** ❶ (*dem Genannten*) him; **es geht ~ nicht gut** he's not feeling very well; *nach Präpositionen* him; **ich war gestern bei ~** I was at his place yesterday; **das ist ein Freund von ~** that's a friend of his ❷ *bei Tieren und Dingen* (*dem genannten Tier oder Ding*) it; (*bei Haustieren*) him

ihn [iːn] *pron pers akk von* **er** ❶ (*den Genannten*) him ❷ *bei Tieren und Dingen* (*das genannte Tier oder Ding*) it; (*bei Haustieren*) him

ihnen [ˈiːnən] *pron pers dat pl von* **sie** them; *nach Präpositionen* them; **ich war die ganze Zeit bei ~** I was at their place the whole time

Ihnen [ˈiːnən] *pron pers dat sing o pl von* **Sie** you; *nach Präpositionen* you

ihr¹ <*gen* euer, *dat* euch, *akk* euch> [iːɐ̯] *pron pers 2. pers pl nomin von* **sie** you [all]

ihr² [iːɐ̯] *pron pers dat sing von* **sie** (*der Genannten*) her

ihr³ [iːɐ̯] *pron poss, adjektivisch* ❶ *sing* her ❷ *pl* their

ihre(r, s) *pron poss, substantivisch* ❶ *sing* (*dieser weiblichen Person*) her; **das ist nicht seine Aufgabe, sondern ~** he's not responsible for doing that, she is; ■ **der/die/das ~** hers ❷ *pl* theirs

Ihre(r, s)¹ *pron poss, substantivisch, auf „Sie" bezüglich* ❶ *sing* your; ■ **der/die/das ~** yours ❷ *pl* your; ■ **der/die/das ~** yours ❸ *sing und pl* (*Angehörige*) ■ **die ~n** your loved ones ❹ *sing und pl* (*Eigentum*) ■ **das ~** yours; **Sie haben alle das ~ getan** you have all done your part

Ihre(r, s)² *pron poss, substantivisch, auf „sie" sing bezüglich* ❶ (*Angehörige*) ■ **der/[die] ~[n]** her loved one[s] ❷ (*Eigentum*) ■ **das ~** hers

Ihre(r, s)³ *pron poss, substantivisch, auf „sie" pl bezüglich* ❶ (*Angehörige*) ■ **der/[die] ~[n]** their loved ones ❷ (*Eigentum*) ■ **das ~** their things

ihrer *pron pers gen von* **sie** ❶ *sing* (*geh*) her ❷ *pl* them; **es waren ~ sechs** (*geh*) there were six of them

Ihrer *pron pers* (*geh*) *gen von* **Sie** ❶ *sing* [of] you ❷ *pl* you

ihrerseits [ˈiːrɐˈzaits] *adv* ❶ *sing* for her [*or* its] part ❷ *pl* for their part

Ihrerseits [ˈiːrɐˈzaits] *adv sing o pl* (*von Ihrer Seite aus*) for your part

ihresgleichen ['iːrəs·'glai·çn̩] *pron inv* ❶ *sing* people *npl* like her; (*pej: Leute wie sie*) her [own] kind ❷ *pl* people like them; (*pej: Leute wie sie*) their [own] kind

Ihresgleichen ['iːrəs·'glai·çn̩] *pron inv* ❶ *sing* people like you ❷ *pl* (*pej: Leute wie Sie*) your [own] kind; **ich kenne** [**Sie und**] **~** I know your kind!

ihretwegen ['iːrət·'veː·gn̩] *adv* ❶ *fem sing* (*wegen ihr*) as far as she is/was concerned; **~ brauchen wir uns keine Sorgen zu machen** we don't need to worry about her ❷ *pl* (*wegen ihnen*) as far as they are/were concerned; **ich mache mir ~ schon Sorgen** I'm starting to worry about them

Ihretwegen ['iːrət·'veː·gn̩] *adv sing/pl* because of you, for you; **ich bin nur ~ geblieben** I've only stayed for you

Ikone <-, -n> [i'koː·nə] *f* icon

illegal ['ɪle·gaːl] *adj* illegal

Illegalität <-, -en> ['ɪle·ga·li·tɛːt, ɪle·ga·li·'tɛːt] *f* ❶ *kein pl* (*Gesetzwidrigkeit*) illegality ❷ (*illegale Tätigkeit*) something illegal

Illusion <-, -en> [ɪlu·'zi̯oːn] *f* illusion; **sich** *akk* **der ~ hingeben,** [**dass**] to be under the illusion [that]; **sich** *dat* **keine ~en machen** to not have any illusions

illusorisch [ɪlu·'zoː·rɪʃ] *adj* ❶ (*trügerisch*) illusory ❷ (*zwecklos*) futile

Illustration <-, -en> [ɪlʊs·tra·'tsi̯oːn] *f* illustration

illustrieren* [ɪlʊs·'triː·rən] *vt* to illustrate

Illustrierte <-n, -n> *f* magazine

Iltis <-ses, -se> ['ɪl·tɪs] *m* polecat

im ['ɪm] = **in dem** ❶ (*sich dort befindend*) in the; **~ Bett/Haus** in bed/the house; **~ Januar** in January; **~ Begriff sein, etw zu tun** to be about to do sth; **~ Bau sein** to be under construction ❷ (*dabei seiend, etw zu tun*) while; **etw ist ~ Kommen** sth is coming; **er ist noch ~ Wachsen** he is still growing

Image <-[s], -s> ['ɪm·ɪtʃ] *nt* image

Imbiss[RR] <-es, -e> ['ɪm·bɪs], **Imbiß**[ALT] <-sses, -sse> *m* ❶ (*kleine Mahlzeit*) snack ❷ (*fam*) *s.* **Imbissstand**

Imbissstand[RR] *m* food stand

Imbissstube[RR] *f* snack bar

Imitat <-[e]s, -e> [imi·'taːt] *nt* imitation, fake

Imitation <-, -en> [imi·ta·'tsi̯oːn] *f* imitation

imitieren* [imi·'tiː·rən] *vt* to imitate sth; (*im Kabarett*) to impersonate

Imker(in) <-s, -> ['ɪm·kɐ] *m(f)* beekeeper

Immatrikulation <-, -en> [ɪma·tri·ku·la·'tsi̯oːn] *f* matriculation; (*an der Universität*) registration

immatrikulieren* [ɪma·tri·ku·'liː·rən] **I.** *vt* ❶ (*einschreiben*) to matriculate, to register ❷ SCHWEIZ (*zulassen*) *Fahrzeug* to register **II.** *vr* (*sich einschreiben*) ■ **sich** *akk* **~** to matriculate, to register

immer ['ɪmɐ] **I.** *adv* ❶ (*ständig, jedes Mal*) always, all the time; **für ~** forever; **~ und ewig** for ever and ever; **wie ~** as usual [*or* always]; **~ weiter** keep going [*or* it up]; **~ mit der Ruhe** take it easy; **~ wenn** every time; **etw ~ wieder tun** to keep on doing sth ❷ (*zunehmend*) increasingly; **~ häufiger** more and more frequently; **~ mehr** more and more ❸ (*fam: jeweils*) each; **~ am vierten Tag** every fourth day **II.** *part* [**nur**] **~ her damit!** (*fam*) hand it/them over!; **~ mal** (*fam*) now and again; **~ noch** still; **~ noch nicht** still not; **wann/was/wer/wie/wo** [**auch**] **~** whenever/whatever/whoever/however/wherever

immerhin ['ɪmɐ·'hɪn] *adv* ❶ (*wenigstens*) at least ❷ (*schließlich*) after all ❸ (*allerdings, trotz allem*) all the same

Immigrant(in) <-en, -en> [ɪmi·'grant] *m(f)* immigrant

Immigration <-, -en> [ɪmi·gra·'tsi̯oːn] *f* immigration

immigrieren* [ɪmi·'griː·rən] *vi sein* to immigrate

Immobilie <-, -n> [ɪmo·'biː·li̯ə] *f meist pl* real estate; ■ **~n** property

Immobilienmakler(in) *m(f)* real estate agent

immun [ɪ'muːn] *adj* (*a. fig*) ■ **~ sein** to be immune (**gegen** *+akk* to)

Immunität <-, *selten* -en> [ɪmu·ni·'tɛːt] *f* immunity (**gegen** *+akk* to)

Immunsystem *nt* immune system

Imperativ <-s, -e> ['ɪm·pe·ra·tiːf, *pl* -tiː·ve] *m* LING imperative [form] *spec*

Imperfekt <-s, -e> ['ɪm·pɛr·fɛkt] *nt* imperfect [tense] *spec*

Imperialismus <-, *selten* -lismen> [ɪm·pe·ri̯a·'lɪs·mʊs] *m* imperialism

imperialistisch [ɪm·pe·ri̯a·'lɪs·tɪʃ] *adj* (*pej*) imperialist[ic]

Imperium <-s, -rien> [ɪm·'peː·ri̯·ʊm, *pl* -ri̯·ən] *nt* ❶ HIST (*Weltreich, Kaiserreich*) empire ❷ (*geh: Machtbereich*) imperium *fig*

impfen ['ɪm·pfn̩] *vt* to vaccinate (**gegen** *+akk* against)

Impfpass[RR] *m* vaccination card

Impfstoff *m* vaccine

Impfung <-, -en> *f* vaccination

Implantat <-[e]s, -e> [ɪm·plan·'taːt] *nt* implant

implantieren [ɪm·plan·'tiː·rən] *vt* ■ [**jdm**] **etw ~** to implant sth [into sb]

imponieren* [ɪm·po·'niː·rən] *vi* to impress

imponierend *adj* impressive

Import <-[e]s, -e> [ɪm·'pɔrt] *m* import

importieren* [ɪm·pɔr·'tiː·rən] *vt* to import

imprägnieren* [ɪm·prɛg·'niː·rən] *vt* ❶ (*wasserabweisend machen*) to waterproof ❷ (*behandeln*) to impregnate

Impressionismus <-> [ɪm·prɛ·si̯o·'nɪs·mʊs] *m* Impressionism

impressionistisch *adj* Impressionist

Impressum <-s, Impressen> [ɪm·'prɛ·sʊm] *nt* imprint

improvisieren* [ɪm·pro·vi·'ziː·rən] *vi, vt* to improvise

Impuls <-es, -e> [ɪm·'pʊls] *m* ❶ (*Anstoß, Auf-*

trieb) impetus; **etw** *akk* **aus einem ~ heraus tun** to do sth on impulse ❷ ELEK pulse ❸ PHYS impulse
impulsiv [ɪm·pʊl·ˈziːf] *adj* impulsive
imstande, im Stande [ɪm·ˈʃtan·də] *adj pred* ■ **zu etw** *dat* **~ sein** to be capable of doing sth; **~ sein, etw zu tun** to be able to do sth; **zu allem ~ sein** (*fam*) to be capable of anything; **zu nichts mehr ~ sein** (*fam*) to be exhausted
in[1] [ˈɪn] *präp* ❶ *+dat* (*darin befindlich*) in; **bist du schon mal in New York gewesen?** have you ever been to New York?; **ich arbeite seit einem Jahr ~ dieser Firma** I've been working for this company for a year ❷ *+akk* (*hin zu einem Ziel*) into; **~ die Kirche/Schule gehen** to go to church/school ❸ *+dat* (*innerhalb von*) in; **~ diesem Augenblick** at the moment; **~ diesem Jahr/Monat/Sommer** this year/month/summer; **~ einem Jahr bin ich 18** in a year I'll be 18 ❹ *+akk* (*bis zu einer Zeit*) until ❺ *+dat o akk* (*Verweis auf ein Objekt*) at; **sich** *akk* **~ jdm täuschen** to be wrong about sb; **er ist Fachmann ~ seinem Beruf** he is an expert in his field ❻ *+dat* (*auf eine Art und Weise*) in; **~ Wirklichkeit** in reality
in[2] [ˈɪn] *adj* (*fam*) in *fam;* ■ **~ sein** to be in
Inbegriff [ˈɪn·bə·grɪf] *m kein pl* epitome (of)
inbegriffen [ˈɪn·bə·grɪ·fn̩] *adj pred* inclusive; ■ **in etw** *dat* **~ sein** to be included in sth
indem [ɪn·ˈdeːm] *konj* ❶ (*dadurch, dass*) by ❷ (*während*) while
Inder(in) <-s, -> [ˈɪn·dɐ] *m(f)* Indian; *s. a.* **Deutsche(r)**
indes [ɪn·ˈdɛs], **indessen** [ɪn·ˈdɛ·sn̩] **I.** *adv* ❶ (*inzwischen*) in the meantime, meanwhile ❷ (*jedoch*) however **II.** *konj* (*geh*) while
Index <-[es], -e *o* Indizes> [ˈɪn·dɛks, *pl* ˈɪn·di·tseːs] *m* index
Indianer(in) <-s, -> [ɪn·ˈdi̯aː·nɐ] *m(f)* Indian *esp pej,* Native American
indianisch [ɪn·ˈdi̯aː·nɪʃ] *adj* Native American, Indian *esp pej*
Indien <-s> [ˈɪn·di̯ən] *nt* India; *s. a.* **Deutschland**
Indikativ <-s, -e> [ˈɪn·di·ka·tiːf, *pl* -tiː·və] *m* indicative [mood] *spec*
Indio <-s, -s> [ˈɪn·di̯o] *m* Indian (*from Central or Latin America*)
indirekt [ˈɪn·di·rɛkt, ɪn·di·ˈrɛkt] *adj* indirect
indisch [ˈɪn·dɪʃ] *adj* ❶ (*Indien betreffend*) Indian; *s. a.* **deutsch 1** ❷ LING Indian; *s. a.* **deutsch 2**
indiskret [ˈɪn·dɪs·kreːt, ɪn·dɪs·ˈkreːt] *adj* indiscreet
Indiskretion <-, -en> [ɪn·dɪs·kre·ˈtsi̯oːn, ˈɪn·dɪs·kre·tsi̯oːn] *f* ❶ (*Mangel an Verschwiegenheit*) indiscretion ❷ (*Taktlosigkeit*) tactlessness
Individualität <-, en> [ɪn·di·vi·du̯·a·li·ˈtɛːt] *f* ❶ (*Besonderheit eines Menschen*) individuality ❷ (*Persönlichkeit*) personality
individuell [ɪn·di·vi·ˈdu̯·ɛl] *adj* individual
Individuum <-s, -duen> [ɪn·di·ˈviː·du·ʊm, *pl* -du̯·ən] *nt* (*a. pej geh*) individual
Indiz <-es, -ien> [ɪn·ˈdiːts, *pl* ɪn·ˈdiː·tsi̯·ən] *nt* ❶ JUR piece of circumstantial evidence ❷ (*Anzeichen*) ■ **ein ~ für etw** *akk* **sein** to be a sign of sth
Indizes *pl von* **Index**
Indonesien <-s> [ɪn·do·ˈneː·zi̯·ən] *nt* Indonesia; *s. a.* **Deutschland**
Indonesier(in) <-s, -> [ɪn·do·ˈneː·zi̯·ɐ] *m(f)* Indonesian; *s. a.* **Deutsche(r)**
indonesisch [ɪn·do·ˈneː·zɪʃ] *adj* Indonesian; *s. a.* **deutsch**
Industrie <-, -n> [ɪn·dʊs·ˈtriː] *f* industry *no art*
Industriebetrieb *m* industrial plant
Industriegebiet *nt* industrial area
Industrie- und Handelskammer *f* Chamber of Commerce
Industriezweig *m* branch of industry
ineinander [ɪn·ʔai·ˈnan·dɐ] *adv* in each other; **~ verliebt sein** to be in love with each other; **~ übergehen** to merge
ineinander|greifen *vi irreg* to mesh
ineinander|schieben *vt irreg* ■ **etw ~** to telescope sth
Infanterie <-, -n> [ɪn·fan·tə·ˈriː] *f* infantry
Infanterist(in) <-en, -en> [ɪn·fan·tə·ˈrɪst] *m(f)* infantryman
Infarkt <-[e]s, -e> [ɪn·ˈfarkt] *m* ❶ MED infarction *spec* ❷ (*Herzinfarkt*) coronary
Infekt <-[e]s, -e> [ɪn·ˈfɛkt] *m* infection; **grippaler ~** influenza
Infektion <-, -en> [ɪn·fɛk·ˈtsi̯oːn] *f* ❶ (*Ansteckung*) infection ❷ (*fam: Entzündung*) inflammation
Infinitiv <-s, -e> [ˈɪn·fi·ni·tiːf, *pl* -tiː·və] *m* infinitive *spec*
infizieren* [ɪn·fi·ˈtsiː·rən] **I.** *vt* to infect **II.** *vr* ■ **sich** *akk* **[an etw** *dat***/bei jdm] ~** to be infected [by sth/sb]
Inflation <-, -en> [ɪn·fla·ˈtsi̯oːn] *f* ❶ ÖKON inflation ❷ (*übermäßig häufiges Auftreten*) proliferation
infolge [ɪn·ˈfɔl·gə] **I.** *präp +gen* owing to **II.** *adv* ■ **~ von etw** *dat* as a result of sth
infolgedessen [ɪn·fɔl·gə·ˈdɛ·sn̩] *adv* consequently
Informatik <-> [ɪn·fɔr·ˈmaː·tɪk] *f kein pl* computer science
Informatiker(in) <-s, -> [ɪn·fɔr·ˈmaː·ti·kɐ] *m(f)* computer specialist
Information <-, -en> [ɪn·fɔr·ma·ˈtsi̯oːn] *f* ❶ (*Mitteilung, Hinweis*) [a piece of] information ❷ (*das Informieren*) informing; **zu Ihrer ~** for your information ❸ (*Informationsstand*) information desk
Informationsmaterial *nt* informative material
informativ [ɪn·fɔr·ma·ˈtiːf] (*geh*) **I.** *adj* informative **II.** *adv* in an informative manner *pred*
informieren* [ɪn·fɔr·ˈmiː·rən] **I.** *vt* to inform (**über** *+akk* about); **jd ist gut informiert** sb is well-informed **II.** *vr* ■ **sich** *akk* [**über etw**

akk] ~ to find out [about sth]

infrageRR [ɪn·ˈfraː·gə] **~ kommen** to be possible; **nicht ~ kommen** to be out of the question

infrarot [ˈɪn·fra·roːt] *adj* infrared

Infusion <-, -en> [ɪn·fu·ˈzi̯oːn] *f* infusion; **eine ~ bekommen** to receive a transfusion

Ing. *Abk von* **Ingenieur**

Ingenieur(in) <-s, -e> [ɪn·ʒe·ˈni̯øːɐ̯] *m(f)* engineer

Ingwer <-s> [ˈɪŋ·vɐ] *m kein pl* ginger

Inhaber(in) <-s, -> [ˈɪn·haː·bɐ] *m(f)* ❶ (*Besitzer*) owner ❷ (*Halter*) holder; *Scheck* bearer

Inhalt <-[e]s, -e> [ˈɪn·halt] *m* ❶ (*enthaltene Gegenstände*) contents *pl* ❷ (*Sinngehalt*) content ❸ (*wesentliche Bedeutung*) meaning ❹ MATH (*Flächeninhalt*) area; (*Volumen*) volume

inhaltlich **I.** *adj* in terms of content **II.** *adv* with regard to content

Inhaltsangabe *f* summary; *Buch, Film, Theaterstück* synopsis

Inhaltsstoff *m* ingredient

Inhaltsverzeichnis *nt* table of contents *npl*

Initiative <-, -n> [in·its i̯a·ˈtiː·və] *f* ❶ (*erster Anstoß*) initiative; **aus eigener ~** on one's own initiative; [**in etw** *dat*] **die ~ ergreifen** to take the initiative [in sth] ❷ *kein pl* (*Unternehmungsgeist*) drive ❸ (*Bürgerinitiative*) pressure group ❹ SCHWEIZ (*Volksbegehren*) demand for a referendum

Injektion <-, -en> [ɪn·jɛk·ˈtsi̯oːn] *f* injection

Inka <-[s], -s> [ˈɪŋ·ka] *m* Inca

inkl. *Abk von* **inklusive** incl.

inklusive [ɪn·klu·ˈziː·və] **I.** *präp +gen* including **II.** *adv* including; **bis ~** up to and including

Inkrafttreten <-s> *nt kein pl* coming into effect

Inland [ˈɪn·lant] *nt kein pl* ❶ (*das eigene Land*) home ❷ (*Binnenland*) inland

Inlandflug *m* domestic flight

Inlandsmarkt *m* domestic market

inmitten [ɪn·ˈmɪ·tn̩] **I.** *präp +gen* (*geh*) in the middle of **II.** *adv* (*geh*) in the midst of

innen [ˈɪnən] *adv* ❶ (*im Inneren*) on the inside; **~ und außen** [on the] inside and outside; **nach ~** inside; **die Tür geht nach ~ auf** the door opens inwards; **von ~** from the inside ❷ (*auf der Innenseite*) on the inside ❸ *bes* ÖSTERR (*drinnen*) inside

Innenarchitektur *f* interior design

Innendienst *m* office work

Inneneinrichtung *f* ❶ (*das Einrichten*) interior design ❷ (*die Einrichtung*) interior furnishings *pl*

Innenhof *m* inner courtyard

Innenminister(in) *m(f)* Secretary of the Interior, Interior Secretary

Innenministerium *nt* Department of the Interior

Innenpolitik *f* domestic policy

Innenraum *m a.* AUTO interior

Innenspiegel *m* AUTO rearview mirror

Innenstadt *f* downtown

innere(r, s) [ˈɪnə·rə] *adj* ❶ *Tasche* inside ❷ *a.* MED, ANAT inner, internal

Innere(s) [ˈɪnə·rə] *nt* ❶ (*innerer Teil*) inside ❷ GEOL center ❸ PSYCH heart; **in jds ~n** in sb's soul; **tief in seinem ~n war ihm klar, dass ...** deep down, he knew that ...

Innereien [ɪnə·ˈrai·ən] *pl* KOCHK innards *npl*

innerhalb [ˈɪnɐ·halp] **I.** *präp +gen* ❶ (*in einem begrenzten Bereich*) inside ❷ (*binnen eines Zeitraums*) within **II.** *adv* ■ **~ von etw** within sth

innerlich [ˈɪnɐ·lɪç] **I.** *adj* ❶ MED internal ❷ PSYCH inner **II.** *adv* ❶ (*im Inneren des Körpers*) internally ❷ PSYCH inwardly; **~ war er sehr aufgewühlt** he was in inner turmoil

innerorts *adv* SCHWEIZ in a built-up area

innerste(r, s) [ˈɪnɐs·tə] *adj superl von* **innere(r, s)** ❶ GEOL *Stadtbezirk, Landesteil, etc.* innermost ❷ PSYCH (*jds tiefes Inneres betreffend*) innermost

Innerste(s) [ˈɪnɐs·tə(s)] *nt* core being; **tief in ihrem ~n wusste sie ...** deep down, she knew ...

innelwohnen *vi* ■ **jdm/einer S. ~** to be inherent in sb/a thing

innig [ˈɪnɪç] **I.** *adj* ❶ (*tief empfunden*) deep; *Dank* heartfelt ❷ *Beziehung* intimate **II.** *adv* deeply

Innovation <-, -en> [ɪno·va·ˈtsi̯oːn] *f* innovation

innovativ [ɪno·va·ˈtiːf] **I.** *adj* innovative **II.** *adv* innovatively

Innung <-, -en> [ˈɪn·ʊŋ] *f* guild

inoffiziell *adj* unofficial

in puncto [ɪn ˈpʊŋk·to] *adv* (*fam*) concerning

Input <-s, -s> [ˈɪn·pʊt] *m* ❶ COMPUT input ❷ (*Anregung*) stimulus; (*Einsatz*) commitment

Inquisition <-> [ɪn·kvi·zi·ˈtsi̯oːn] *f kein pl* Inquisition

ins [ˈɪns] = **in das** *s.* **in**

Insasse, Insassin <-n, -n> [ˈɪn·za·sə] *m, f* ❶ (*Fahrgast*) passenger ❷ (*Heimbewohner*) resident ❸ (*Bewohner einer Heilanstalt*) patient ❹ (*Gefängnis- o Lager~*) inmate

insbesondere [ɪns·bə·ˈzɔn·də·rə] *adv* especially

Inschrift [ˈɪn·ʃrɪft] *f* inscription

Insekt <-[e]s, -en> [ɪn·ˈzɛkt] *nt* insect

Insektenstich *m* insect sting [*or* bite]

Insektenvernichtungsmittel *nt* insecticide

Insel <-, -n> [ˈɪn·zl̩] *f* island

Inselgruppe *f* archipelago

Inserat <-[e]s, -e> [ɪn·ze·ˈraːt] *nt* advertisement

inserieren* [ɪn·ze·ˈriː·rən] *vi, vt* to advertise

insgeheim [ɪns·gə·ˈhaim] *adv* secretly

insgesamt [ɪns·gə·ˈzamt] *adv* ❶ (*alles zusammen*) altogether ❷ (*im Großen und Ganzen*) on the whole

Insider(in) <-s, -> [ˈɪn·zaɪ·dɐ] *m(f)* insider

insistieren* [ɪn·zɪs·ˈtiː·rən] *vi* (*geh*) to insist (**auf** *+dat* on)

I

inskünftig ['ɪns·kʏnf·tɪç] *adv* SCHWEIZ *s.* **zukünftig**
insofern [ɪn·zo·'fɛrn, ɪn·'zo:·fɛrn] **I.** *adv* in this respect; ~ **..., als** in that **II.** *konj* ÖSTERR (*vorausgesetzt, dass*) if; ~ **als** insofar as
insoweit [ɪn·zo·'vait, 'ɪn·zo·vait, ɪn·'zo·vait] **I.** *adv* in this respect **II.** *konj bes* ÖSTERR ~ **als** if
Inspektion <-, -en> [ɪn·spɛk·'tsi̯o:n] *f* ❶ (*technische Wartung*) service ❷ (*Überprüfung*) inspection
Inspektor, Inspektorin <-s, -en> [ɪn·'spɛk·to:ɐ̯, *pl* -'to:·rən] *m, f* ❶ ADMIN executive officer; (*Kriminalpolizei*) inspector ❷ (*Prüfer*) supervisor
Inspiration <-, -en> [ɪn·spi·ra·'tsi̯o:n] *f* (*geh*) inspiration
inspirieren* [ɪn·spi·'ri:·rən] *vt* ■**jdn** [**zu etw** *dat*] ~ to inspire sb [to do sth]; ■**sich** *akk* **von etw** *dat* [**zu etw** *dat*] ~ **lassen** to get one's inspiration from sth [to do sth]
inspizieren* [ɪn·spi·'tsi:·rən] *vt* (*geh*) to inspect
instabil ['ɪn·sta·bi:l] *adj* (*geh*) unstable
Installateur(in) <-s, -e> [ɪn·sta·la·'tø:ɐ̯] *m(f)* (*Elektroinstallateur*) electrician; (*Klempner*) plumber
Installation <-, -en> [ɪn·sta·la·'tsi̯o:n] *f* ❶ *kein pl* (*das Installieren*) installation; (*installierte Leitungen od. Anlage*) installations *pl* ❷ SCHWEIZ (*Amtseinsetzung*) installation
installieren* [ɪn·sta·'li:·rən] *vt* ❶ TECH (*einbauen*) ■[**jdm**] **etw** ~ to install sth [for sb] ❷ COMPUT (*einprogrammieren*) ■[**jdm**] **etw** [**auf etw** *akk*] ~ to install sth [for sb] [on sth]
instand, in Stand [ɪn·'ʃtant] *adj* in working order; **etw** ~ **halten** to keep sth in good condition; **etw** ~ **setzen** to repair sth
Instandhaltung *f* (*geh*) maintenance
inständig ['ɪn·ʃtɛn·dɪç] **I.** *adj Bitte etc.* urgent **II.** *adv* urgently; ~ **um etw** *akk* **bitten** to beg for sth
Instanz <-, -en> [ɪn·'stants] *f* ❶ ADMIN authority ❷ (*Stufe eines Gerichtsverfahrens*) **in erster/zweiter/oberster** ~ trial court/appellate court/supreme court
Instinkt <-[e]s, -e> [ɪn·'stiŋkt] *m* instinct
instinktiv [ɪn·stɪŋk·'ti:f] *adj* instinctive
Institut <-[e]s, -e> [in·sti·'tu:t] *nt* institute
Institution <-, -en> [ɪn·sti·tu·'tsi̯o:n] *f* institution
Instruktion <-, -en> [ɪn·strʊk·'tsi̯o:n] *f* (*Anweisung*) instruction; (*Anleitung*) instruction[s] *usu pl;* **laut** ~ according to [the] instructions
Instrument <-[e]s, -e> [ɪn·stru·'mɛnt] *nt* ❶ MUS instrument; (*Gerät für wissenschaftliche Zwecke*) instrument ❷ (*a. fig geh: Werkzeug*) tool
Insulaner(in) <-s, -> [ɪn·zu·'la:·nɐ] *m(f)* islander
Insulin <-s> [ɪn·zu·'li:n] *nt kein pl* insulin
inszenieren* [ɪns·tse·'ni:·rən] *vt* ❶ (*dramaturgisch gestalten*) to stage ❷ (*pej*) to stage-manage
Inszenierung <-, -en> *f* ❶ FILM, MUS, THEAT production ❷ (*pej: Bewerkstelligung*) engineering
intakt [ɪn·'takt] *adj* ❶ (*unversehrt*) intact ❷ (*voll funktionsfähig*) in working order
Integration <-, -en> [ɪn·te·gra·'tsi̯o:n] *f* integration
integrieren* [ɪn·te·'gri:·rən] **I.** *vt* (*eingliedern*) to integrate (**in** +*akk* into) **II.** *vr* (*sich einfügen*) ■**sich** *akk* [**in etw** *akk*] ~ to become integrated [into sth]
Integrität <-> [ɪn·te·gri·'tɛ:t] *f kein pl* (*geh*) integrity
Intellekt <-[e]s> [ɪn·tɛ·'lɛkt] *m kein pl* intellect
intellektuell [ɪn·tɛ·lɛk·'tu̯·ɛl] *adj* intellectual
Intellektuelle(r) *f(m)* intellectual
intelligent [ɪn·tɛ·li·'gɛnt] *adj* intelligent, smart
Intelligenz <-, -en> [ɪn·tɛ·li·'gɛnts] *f* ❶ *kein pl* (*Verstand*) intelligence ❷ *kein pl* (*Gesamtheit der Intellektuellen*) intelligentsia ❸ (*vernunftbegabtes Lebewesen*) intelligence ❹ COMPUT **künstliche** ~ artificial intelligence
Intensität <-, *selten* -en> [ɪn·tɛn·zi·'tɛ:t] *f* intensity
intensiv [ɪn·tɛn·'zi:f] **I.** *adj* ❶ (*gründlich*) intensive ❷ (*eindringlich, durchdringend*) *Duft, Schmerz* intense **II.** *adv* ❶ (*gründlich*) intensively; ~ **bemüht sein, etw zu tun** to make intense efforts to do sth ❷ (*eindringlich, durchdringend*) strongly
intensivieren* [ɪn·tɛn·zi·'vi:·rən] *vt* to intensify
Intensivierung <-, *selten* -en> *f* intensification
Intensivkurs *m* intensive course
Intensivstation *f* intensive care unit
Intention <-, -en> [ɪn·tɛn·'tsi̯o:n] *f* (*geh*) intention
interaktiv [ɪn·te·ʔak·'ti:f] *adj* interactive
Intercity <-s, -s> [ɪn·te·'sɪ·ti], **Intercityzug**RR *m* intercity [train]
IntercityexpressRR, **Intercity-Expreß**ALT *m* intercity express
interessant [ɪn·tə·rɛ·'sant] **I.** *adj* ❶ (*Interesse erweckend*) interesting; **sich** *akk* [**bei jdm**] ~ **machen** to attract [sb's] attention ❷ *Angebot, Gehalt* attractive **II.** *adv* interestingly; **der Vorschlag hört sich ~ an** the proposal sounds interesting
interessanterweise *adv* interestingly enough
Interesse <-s, -n> [ɪn·tə·'rɛ·sə] *nt* ❶ *kein pl* (*Aufmerksamkeit*) interest; ~ [**an jdm/etw**] **haben** to have an interest [*or* be interested] [in sb/sth]; **hätten Sie ~ daran, für uns tätig zu werden?** would you be interested in working for us? ❷ *pl* (*Neigungen*) interests *pl;* **aus** ~ out of interest ❸ *pl* (*Belange*) interests *pl* ❹ (*Nutzen*) interest; [**für jdn**] **von ~ sein** to be of interest [to sb]; **in jds ~ liegen** to be in sb's interest
Interessengemeinschaft *f* community of interests
Interessenskonflikt *m* conflict of interest

Interessent(in) <-en, -en> [ɪn·tə·rɛ·ˈsɛnt] *m(f)* ❶ (*an einer Teilnahme Interessierter*) interested party ❷ (*an einem Kauf Interessierter*) potential buyer

interessieren* [ɪn·tə·rɛ·ˈsiː·rən] **I.** *vt* ❶ (*jds Interesse hervorrufen*) to interest ❷ (*jds Interesse auf etw lenken*) ■**jdn für etw ~** *akk* to interest sb in sth **II.** *vr* (*mit Interesse verfolgen*) ■**sich** *akk* **für jdn/etw ~** to be interested in sb/sth

interessiert **I.** *adj* ❶ (*Interesse zeigend*) interested; **sie ist politisch ~** she is interested in politics ❷ (*mit ernsthaften Absichten*) ■**an jdm/etw ~ sein** to be interested in sb/sth; ■**daran ~ sein, etw zu tun** to be interested in doing sth **II.** *adv* with interest

Interieur <-s, -s *o* -e> [ɛ̃·te·ˈri̯øːɐ̯] *nt* (*geh*) interior

Interimslösung *f* interim solution

Interimsregierung *f* interim government

interkontinental [ɪn·tɐ·kɔn·ti·nɛn·ˈtaːl] *adj* intercontinental

Internat <-[e]s, -e> [ɪn·tɐ·ˈnaːt] *nt* boarding school

international [ɪn·tɐ·na·tsi̯o·ˈnaːl] **I.** *adj* international **II.** *adv* internationally

Internet <-s> [ˈɪntɐ·nɛt] *nt kein pl* Internet; **im ~ surfen** to surf the Internet

Internetadresse *f* COMPUT Internet address, URL

Internetportal *nt* INET web [*or* Internet] portal

internieren* [ɪn·tɐ·ˈniː·rən] *vt* ❶ (*in staatlichen Gewahrsam nehmen*) to intern ❷ MED to isolate

Internierung <-, -en> *f* ❶ (*Einsperrung*) internment ❷ MED isolation

Internierungslager *nt* internment camp

Internist(in) <-en, -en> [ɪn·tɐ·ˈnɪst] *m(f)* internist

Interpretation <-, -en> [ɪn·tɐ·pre·ta·ˈtsi̯oːn] *f* interpretation

interpretieren* [ɪn·tɐ·pre·ˈtiː·rən] *vt* to interpret

Interpunktion <-> [ɪn·tɐ·pʊŋk·ˈtsi̯oːn] *f kein pl* punctuation

Interrailkarte [ˈɪn·tɐ·reːl-] *f* BAHN inter-rail ticket

Interregio <-s, -s> [ɪn·tɐ·ˈreː·gi̯o] *m* interregional train

Intervention <-, -en> [ɪn·tɐ·vɛn·ˈtsi̯oːn] *f* (*geh*) *a.* POL intervention

Interview <-s, -s> [ˈɪn·tɐ·vjuː, ɪn·tɐ·ˈvjuː] *nt* interview

interviewen* [ɪn·tɐ·ˈvjuː·ən, ˈɪn·tɐ·vjuː·ən] *vt* ❶ (*durch ein Interview befragen*) ■**jdn [zu etw** *dat*] **~** to interview sb [about sth]; ■**sich** *akk* **[von jdm] ~ lassen** to give [sb] an interview ❷ (*hum fam: befragen*) ■**jdn ~ [ob/wann/wo etc.]** to consult sb about [whether/when/where, etc.]

intim [ɪn·ˈtiːm] *adj* ❶ (*innig, persönlich*) intimate; *Freund, Bekannter* close ❷ (*sexuell liiert*) ■**mit jdm ~ sein/werden** to be/become intimate with sb

Intimität <-, -en> [ɪn·ti·mi·ˈtɛːt] *f* (*geh*) ❶ *kein pl* (*Vertrautheit*) intimacy ❷ *pl* (*private Angelegenheit*) intimate affairs *pl* ❸ *usu pl* (*sexuelle Handlung o Äußerung*) intimacy ❹ *kein pl einer Kneipe* intimacy

Intimsphäre *f* (*geh*) private life

Intimverkehr *m kein pl* (*euph*) intimate relations *pl*

intolerant [ˈɪn·to·le·rant, ɪn·to·le·ˈrant] **I.** *adj* (*geh*) intolerant **II.** *adv* intolerantly

Intoleranz [ˈɪn·to·le·rants, ɪn·to·le·ˈrants] *f* (*geh*) intolerance

intransitiv [ˈɪn·tran·zi·tiːf] *adj* intransitive

intrigant [ɪn·tri·ˈgant] *adj* (*geh*) scheming

Intrigant(in) <-en, -en> [ɪn·tri·ˈgant] *m(f)* (*geh*) schemer

Intrige <-, -n> [ɪn·ˈtriː·gə] *f* (*geh*) conspiracy

intrigieren* [ɪn·tri·ˈgiː·rən] *vi* (*geh*) to scheme (**gegen** +*akk* against)

introvertiert [ɪn·tro·vɛr·ˈtiːɐ̯t] *adj* introverted

Intuition <-, -en> [ɪn·tui·ˈtsi̯oːn] *f* intuition

invalid [ɪn·va·ˈliːt], **invalide** [ɪn·va·ˈliː·də] *adj* invalid

Invalide, Invalidin <-n, -n> [ɪn·va·ˈliː·də] *m, f* invalid

Invalidität <-> [ɪn·va·li·di·ˈtɛːt] *f kein pl* disability

Invasion <-, -en> [ɪn·va·ˈzi̯oːn] *f* invasion

Inventar <-s, -e> [ɪn·vɛn·ˈtaːɐ̯] *nt* inventory

Inventur <-, -en> [ɪn·vɛn·ˈtuːɐ̯] *f* inventory; **~ machen** to take inventory

investieren* [ɪn·vɛs·ˈtiː·rən] *vt* to invest

Investition <-, -en> [ɪn·vɛs·ti·ˈtsi̯oːn] *f* investment

Investor(in) <-s, -en> [ɪn·ˈvɛs·toːɐ̯, *pl* -ˈtoː·rən] *m(f)* investor

involvieren* [ɪn·vɔl·ˈviː·rən] *vt* (*geh*) to involve

inwiefern [ɪn·vi·ˈfɛrn] *adv* in what way

Inzucht [ˈɪn·tsʊxt] *f* inbreeding

inzwischen [ɪn·ˈtsvɪ·ʃn̩] *adv* in the meantime

Irak <-s> [iˈraːk] *m* ■**[der] ~** Iraq; *s. a.* **Deutschland**

Iraker(in) <-s, -> [iˈraː·kɐ] *m(f)* Iraqi; *s. a.* **Deutsche(r)**

irakisch [iˈraː·kɪʃ] *adj* Iraqi; *s. a.* **deutsch**

Iran <-s> [iˈraːn] *m* ■**der ~** Iran; *s. a.* **Deutschland**

Iraner(in) <-s, -> [iˈraː·nɐ] *m(f)* Iranian; *s. a.* **Deutsche(r)**

iranisch [iˈraː·nɪʃ] *adj* ❶ (*den Iran betreffend*) Iranian; *s. a.* **deutsch 1** ❷ LING Iranian; *s. a.* **deutsch 2**

Ire, Irin <-n, -n> [ˈiːrə] *m, f* Irishman *masc,* Irishwoman *fem;* ■**die ~n** the Irish; **[ein] ~ sein** to be Irish

irgend [ˈɪr·gn̩t] *adv* at all; **wenn ~ möglich** if at all possible; **„wer war am Apparat?" – „ach, wieder ~ so ein Spinner!"** "who was that on the phone?" — "oh, some lunatic again"

irgendein [ˈɪr·gn̩t·ˀain], **irgendeine(r, s)** [ˈɪr·

gn̩t·ʔainə], **irgendeins** [ˈɪr·gn̩t·ʔains] *pron indef* ❶ *adjektivisch* (*was auch immer für ein*) some; **haben Sie noch irgendeinen Wunsch?** would you like anything else?; **nicht irgendein/e ...** *adjektivisch* not any [old] ... ❷ *substantivisch* (*ein Beliebiger*) any [old] one; **ich werde doch nicht irgendeinen einstellen** I'm not going to hire just anybody

irgendetwasRR [ˈɪr·gn̩t·ˈʔɛt·vas] *pron indef* something; (*bei Fragen*) anything; ~ **anderes** sth else; **nicht [einfach]** ~ not just anything

irgendjemandRR [ˈɪr·gn̩t·ˈʔjeː·mant] *pron indef pron* someone, somebody; (*fragend, verneinend*) anyone, anybody; ~ **anderer** sb else; **nicht [einfach]** ~ not just anybody

irgendwann [ˈɪr·gn̩t·ˈvan] *adv* some time or other

irgendwas [ˈɪr·gn̩t·ˈvas] *pron indef* (*fam*) *s.* **irgendetwas**

irgendwer [ˈɪr·gn̩t·ˈveːɐ̯] *pron indef* (*fam*) somebody; **nicht [einfach]** ~ not just anybody

irgendwie [ˈɪr·gn̩t·ˈviː] *adv* somehow [or other]; **Sie kommen mir ~ bekannt vor** you seem familiar somehow

irgendwo [ˈɪr·gn̩t·ˈvoː] *adv* ❶ (*wo auch immer*) somewhere [or other] ❷ (*in irgendeiner Weise*) somehow [or other]; ~ **versteh ich das nicht** somehow I don't understand [that]

irisch [ˈiːrɪʃ] *adj* ❶ (*Irland betreffend*) Irish; *s. a.* **deutsch 1** ❷ LING Irish; *s. a.* **deutsch 2**

Irland [ˈɪr·lant] *nt* Ireland, Eire; *s. a.* **Deutschland**

Ironie <-, *selten* -n> [iro·ˈniː, *pl* -ˈniː·ən] *f* irony

ironisch [iˈroː·nɪʃ] **I.** *adj* ironic **II.** *adv* ironically; ~ **lächeln** to give an ironic smile

irrational [ˈɪra·tsi̯o·naːl, ɪra·tsi̯o·ˈnaːl] *adj* (*geh*) irrational

Irre[1] <-> [ˈɪrə] *f* **jdn in die ~ führen** to mislead sb

Irre[2] [ˈɪrə] *f(m)* lunatic

irre [ɪrə] **I.** *adj* ❶ (*verrückt*) crazy; **jdn für ~[e] halten** (*fam*) to think sb is crazy ❷ (*verstört*) crazy; **so ein Blödsinn! du redest ~s Zeug!** such nonsense! what kind of crazy talk is that!; **jdn [noch] ganz ~ machen** (*fam*) to drive sb crazy *fam* ❸ (*sl: toll*) fantastic **II.** *adv* ❶ (*verrückt, verstört*) insanely; **wie ~** (*fam*) like mad ❷ (*sl: ausgeflippt*) wacky; (*toll*) fantastically *fam* ❸ (*sl: äußerst*) incredibly

irre|führen *vt* to mislead; ■ **sich** *akk* **von jdm/etw ~ lassen** to be misled by sb/sth

irreführend *adj* misleading

Irreführung *f* deception

irre|machen *vt* to confuse; ■ **sich** *akk* **[durch jdn/etw] nicht ~ lassen** to not let oneself be thrown [by sb/sth]

irren[1] [ˈɪrən] *vi sein* ■ **durch/über etw** *akk* ~ to wander through/across sth

irren[2] [ˈɪrən] **I.** *vi* (*geh*) (*sich täuschen*) to be wrong ▶WENDUNGEN: **I~ ist menschlich** (*prov*) to err is human **II.** *vr* (*sich täuschen*) ■ **sich** *akk* ~ to be wrong (**in** +*dat* about); **da irrst du dich** you're wrong there; **wenn ich mich nicht irre, ...** if I am not mistaken ...

Irrenhaus *nt* (*veraltet o pej*) insane asylum; **wie im ~** (*fam*) like [in] a loony bin

Irrfahrt *f* odyssey

Irrgarten *m* maze

Irrglaube(n) *m* ❶ (*irrige Ansicht*) mistaken belief ❷ (*veraltend: falscher religiöser Glaube*) heretical belief

Irritation <-, -en> [ɪri·ta·ˈtsi̯oːn] *f* (*geh*) *a.* MED irritation

irritieren* [ɪri·ˈtiː·rən] *vt* ❶ (*verwirren*) to confuse ❷ (*stören*) to annoy

Irrläufer *m* misdirected item

Irrlicht [ˈɪr·lɪçt] *nt* jack-o'-lantern

Irrsinn [ˈɪr·zɪn] *m kein pl* ❶ (*veraltet: psychische Krankheit*) insanity ❷ (*fam: Unsinn*) [sheer] madness

irrsinnig [ˈɪr·zɪ·nɪç] **I.** *adj* ❶ (*veraltet: psychisch krank*) insane ❷ (*fam: völlig wirr, absurd*) crazy ❸ (*fam: stark, intensiv*) tremendous; *Hitze, Kälte, Verkehr* incredible; *Kopfschmerzen* terrible **II.** *adv* (*fam: äußerst*) terribly; **das schmerzt wie ~!** it hurts like crazy!

Irrtum <-[e]s, Irrtümer> [ˈɪr·tuːm, *pl* ˈɪr·tyː·mɐ] *m* ❶ (*irrige Annahme*) error; **[schwer] im ~ sein** to be [badly] mistaken ❷ (*fehlerhafte Handlung*) mistake

irrtümlich [ˈɪr·tyːm·lɪç] **I.** *adj attr* mistaken **II.** *adv* mistakenly

Irrweg *m* wrong path

Ischias <-> [ˈɪʃi̯as] *m o nt kein pl* sciatica

Islam <-s> [ɪs·ˈlaːm, ˈɪs·lam] *m kein pl* Islam; ■ **der ~** Islam

islamisch [ɪs·ˈlaː·mɪʃ] *adj* Islamic

Islamist(in) <-en, -en> [ɪs·la·ˈmɪst] *m(f)* Islamist

islamistisch [ɪs·la·ˈmɪs·tɪʃ] *adj* Islamist *attr*

Island [ˈiːs·lant] *nt* Iceland; *s. a.* **Deutschland**

Isländer(in) <-s, -> [ˈiːs·lɛn·dɐ] *m(f)* Icelander; ~ **sein** to be an Icelander; *s. a.* **Deutsche(r)**

isländisch [ˈiːs·lɛn·dɪʃ] *adj* ❶ (*Island betreffend*) Icelandic; *s. a.* **deutsch 1** ❷ LING Icelandic; *s. a.* **deutsch 2**

Isolation <-, -en> [iz·o·la·ˈtsi̯oːn] *f* ❶ (*das Abdichten*) insulation ❷ (*das Isolieren*) *von Patienten, Häftlingen, etc.* isolation ❸ (*Abgeschlossenheit*) isolation (**von** +*dat* from)

isolieren* [izo·ˈliː·rən] **I.** *vt* ❶ TECH to insulate (**gegen** +*akk* against) ❷ JUR, MED to isolate (**von** +*dat* from) **II.** *vr* (*sich absondern*) ■ **sich** *akk* **[von jdm/etw]** ~ to isolate oneself [from sb/sth]

Isolierkanne *f* thermos [flask]

isoliert **I.** *adj* (*aus dem Zusammenhang gegriffen*) isolated **II.** *adv* ❶ (*abgeschlossen, abgesondert*) isolated ❷ (*aus dem Zusammenhang gegriffen*) in an isolated way

Isolierung <-, -en> *f s.* **Isolation**

Israel <-s> [ˈɪs·ra·eːl, ˈɪs·ra·ɛl] *nt* Israel; *s. a.* **Deutschland**

Israeli [ɪs·ra·ˈeː·li] *m* <-[s], -[s]>, *f* <-, -[s]> Is-

raeli; *s. a.* **Deutsche(r)**
israelisch [ɪs·ra·ˈeːlɪʃ] *adj* Israeli; *s. a.* **deutsch**
isst[RR] [ˈɪst], **ißt**[ALT] *3. pers sing pres von* **essen**
ist [ˈɪst] *3. pers sing pres von* **sein**[1]
Italien <-s> [iˈtaː·li̯·ən] *nt* Italy; *s. a.* **Deutschland**
Italiener(in) <-s, -> [ita·ˈli̯eː·nɐ] *m(f)* Italian; **~ sein** to be [an] Italian; *s. a.* **Deutsche(r)**
italienisch [ita·ˈli̯eː·nɪʃ] *adj* ① (*Italien betreffend*) Italian; *s. a.* **deutsch 1** ② LING Italian; *s. a.* **deutsch 2**
I-Tüpfelchen <-s, -> *nt* finishing touch
i.V. *Abk von* **in Vertretung** p.p.
IWF <-> [iː·veː·ˈʔɛf] *m kein pl Abk von* **Internationaler Währungsfonds** IMF

J j

J, j <-, - *o fam* -s, -s> [jɔt] *nt* J, j; **~ wie Julius** J as in Juliet
ja [ˈjaː] *part* ① (*bestätigend: so ist es*) yes; **~, bitte?** yes, [how] may I help you?; **das sag' ich ~!** (*fam*) that's exactly what I'm talking about!; **aber ~!** [yes,] of course! ② (*fragend: so? tatsächlich?*) really?; **ach ~?** [oh] really? ③ (*warnend: bloß*) make sure; **sei ~ vorsichtig mit dem Messer!** be sure to be careful with the knife! ④ (*abschwächend, einschränkend: schließlich*) after all; **ich kann es ~ mal versuchen** I can certainly give it a try ⑤ (*revidierend, steigernd: und zwar*) in fact ⑥ (*anerkennend, triumphierend: doch*) **siehst du, ich habe es ~ immer gesagt!** see — what did I tell you?; **es musste ~ mal so kommen!** it was bound to happen; **wo steckt nur der verfluchte Schlüssel? ach, da ist er ~!** where's the damn key? oh, there it is! ⑦ (*bekräftigend: allerdings*) **das ist ~ kaum zu glauben!** that is really hard to believe!; **ich verstehe das ~, aber trotzdem finde ich's nicht gut** I do understand what you're saying, but I still don't think it's okay; **das ist ~ die Höhe!** that is [absolutely] outrageous!; **es ist ~ immer dasselbe** some things will never change ⑧ (*na*) well ⑨ (*als Satzabschluss: nicht wahr?*) isn't it?; **es bleibt doch bei unserer Abmachung, ~?** we're sticking to what we agreed to, right? ⑩ (*ratlos: nur*) **ich weiß ~ nicht, wie ich es ihm beibringen soll** I have no idea how [I'm going] to teach him that ⑪ (*beschwichtigend*) **ich komm ~ schon!** okay! okay! I'm coming! ▶ WENDUNGEN: **~ und amen zu etw sagen** (*fam*) to give sth one's blessing; **wenn ~** if so
Ja <-s, -[s]> [ˈjaː] *nt* yes
Jacke <-, -n> [ˈja·kə] *f* (*Stoffjacke*) jacket; (*Strickjacke*) cardigan
Jackentasche *f* jacket pocket
Jackett <-s, -s> [ʒa·ˈkɛt] *nt* jacket
Jackpot <-s, -s> [ˈdʒɛk·pɔt] *m* ① KARTEN stake [money] ② (*Lottogewinn*) jackpot
Jagd <-, -en> [ˈjaːkt] *f* ① (*das Jagen*) hunting; **auf der ~ sein** to be [out] hunting; **~ auf jdn/etw machen** (*pej*) to hunt for sb/sth ② (*Revier*) *s.* **Jagdrevier** ③ (*Verfolgung*) hunt (**auf** +*akk* for) ④ (*pej: wildes Streben*) pursuit (**nach** +*dat* of)
Jagdbeute *f* kill
Jagdbomber *m* fighter-bomber
Jagdgewehr *nt* hunting rifle
Jagdhund *m* hound
Jagdrevier *nt* preserve
Jagdschein *m* hunting license
jagen [ˈjaː·gn̩] **I.** *vt haben* ① (*auf der Jagd verfolgen*) to hunt ② (*hetzen*) to pursue ③ (*fam: antreiben, vertreiben*) ■ **jdn aus etw** *dat* **~** to drive sb out of sth; **eine Sache jagt die andere** one thing comes after another ④ (*fam*) **jeden Tag kriege ich eine Spritze in den Hintern gejagt** they stick a needle in my rear end every day *fam* ▶ WENDUNGEN: **jdn mit etw** *dat* **~ können** (*fam*) to not be able to stand sth **II.** *vi* ① *haben* (*auf die Jagd gehen*) to hunt ② *sein* (*rasen*) to race (**aus** +*dat* out of, **durch, in** +*akk* through, into); **er kam plötzlich aus dem Haus gejagt** he suddenly came racing out of the house
Jäger(in) <-s, -> [ˈjɛː·gɐ] *m(f)* hunter
Jaguar <-s, -e> [ˈjaː·gu̯·aːɐ̯] *m* jaguar
jäh [ˈjɛː] **I.** *adj* (*geh*) ① (*abrupt, unvorhergesehen*) abrupt; *Bewegung* sudden ② (*steil*) steep **II.** *adv* (*geh*) ① (*abrupt, unvorhergesehen*) abruptly ② (*steil*) steeply
Jahr <-[e]s, -e> [ˈjaːɐ̯] *nt* ① (*Zeitraum von 12 Monaten*) year; **die 20er-/30er-~e** the twenties/thirties + *sing/pl vb;* **anderthalb ~e** a year and a half; **ein dreiviertel ~** nine months; **das ganze ~ über** throughout the whole year, all year long; **das neue ~** the New Year; **~ für ~** year after year; **zweimal im ~** twice a year; **letztes/nächstes ~** last/next year; **in diesem/im nächsten ~** this/next year; **vor einem ~** a year ago; **alle ~e wieder** every year; **Buch des ~es** book of the year ② (*Lebensjahre*) **er ist 10 ~e alt** he's 10 years old ▶ WENDUNGEN: **in den besten ~en [sein]** [to be] in one's prime; **in die ~e kommen** (*euph fam*) to be getting on in years
jahrelang [ˈjaː·rə·laŋ] **I.** *adj attr* lasting for years; **die Frucht ~er Forschungen** the fruits of years of research **II.** *adv* for years
Jahresanfang, Jahresbeginn *m* beginning of the year; **bei/nach/vor ~** at/after/before the beginning of the year

Jahresdurchschnitt *m* annual average
Jahreseinkommen *nt* annual income
Jahresende *nt* end of the year; **bis zum/vor ~** by/before the end of the year
Jahresfrist *f* **nach ~** after a period of one year; **vor ~** within a period of one year
Jahresgehalt *nt* annual salary
Jahrestag *m* anniversary
Jahresurlaub *m* annual vacation
Jahreswechsel *m* turn of the year; **zum ~** at the turn of the year
Jahreszahl *f* year
Jahreszeit *f* season
Jahrgang *m* ❶ (*Personen eines Geburtsjahrs*) *people born in the same year;* (*Gesamtheit der Schüler eines Schuljahres*) class of [a year] ❷ (*Erntejahr*) vintage; (*Herstellungsjahr*) year
Jahrhundert <-s, -e> [jaːɐ̯ˈhʊn·dɐt] *nt* century
jahrhundertelang **I.** *adj* [lasting] for centuries *pred;* **es hat einer ~en Entwicklung bedurft** it required centuries of development **II.** *adv* for centuries
Jahrhundertwende *f* turn of the century
jährlich [ˈjɛːɐ̯·lɪç] *adj* annual
Jahrmarkt *m* fair
Jahrtausend <-s, -e> [jaːɐ̯·ˈtau·zn̩t] *nt* millennium
Jahrzehnt <-[e]s, -e> [jaːɐ̯·ˈtseːnt] *nt* decade
jahrzehntelang **I.** *adj* decades of *attr* **II.** *adv* for decades
Jähzorn [ˈjɛː·tsɔrn] *m* violent outburst
jähzornig *adj* irascible
Jalousie <-, -n> [ʒa·lu·ˈziː, *pl* -ˈziː·ən] *f* venetian blind
Jamaika <-s> [ja·ˈmai·ka] *nt* Jamaica
Jammer <-s> [ˈja·mɐ] *m kein pl* ❶ (*Kummer*) sorrow; **es ist ein ~, wie wenig Zeit wir haben** (*fig fam*) it's a real shame how little time we have ❷ (*das Wehklagen*) wailing
jämmerlich [ˈjɛ·mɐ·lɪç] **I.** *adj attr* ❶ (*beklagenswert*) wretched ❷ (*kummervoll*) sorrowful ❸ (*fam*) *Ausrede* pathetic ❹ (*pej fam: verächtlich*) miserable **II.** *adv* ❶ (*elend*) miserably ❷ (*fam: erbärmlich*) awfully
jammern [ˈjam·ɐn] *vi* ❶ (*a. pej: lamentieren*) to whine (**über** *+akk* about, **wegen** *+dat* about); **lass das J~** stop [your] moaning ❷ (*wimmernd verlangen*) to beg (**nach** *+dat* for)
Jan. *Abk von* **Januar** Jan.
Jänner <-s, -> [ˈjɛ·nɐ] *m* ÖSTERR January
Januar <-[s], *selten* -e> [ˈja·nu̯·aːɐ̯] *m* January; *s. a.* **Februar**
Japan <-s> [ˈjaː·pan] *nt* Japan; *s. a.* **Deutschland**
Japaner(in) <-s, -> [ja·ˈpaː·nɐ] *m(f)* Japanese; ■ **die ~** the Japanese; *s. a.* **Deutsche(r)**
japanisch [ja·ˈpaː·nɪʃ] *adj* ❶ (*Japan betreffend*) Japanese; *s. a.* **deutsch 1** ❷ LING Japanese; *s. a.* **deutsch 2**
Jasmin <-s, -e> [jas·ˈmiːn] *m* jasmine
Jastimme *f* "yes" vote
jäten [ˈjɛː·tn̩] **I.** *vt* ❶ (*aushacken*) to hoe ❷ (*von Unkraut befreien*) to weed **II.** *vi* to weed
jauchzen [ˈjau·xtsn̩] *vi* (*geh*) to shout with joy
jaulen [ˈjau·lən] *vi* to howl
jawohl [ja·ˈvoːl] *adv* yes
Jawort *nt* **jdm das ~ geben** to agree to marry sb; (*bei Trauung*) to say "I do"
Jazz <-> [ˈdʒɛs, ˈjats] *m kein pl* jazz
je [ˈjeː] **I.** *adv* ❶ (*jemals*) ever ❷ (*jeweils*) each **II.** *präp +akk* (*pro*) per **III.** *konj* **~ öfter du übst, desto besser kannst du dann spielen** the more you practice, the better you will be able to play; **~ nachdem!** it [all] depends!; **~ nachdem, ob/wann/wie ...** depending on whether/when/how ...
Jeans <-, -> [ˈdʒiːnz] *f meist pl* jeans *npl*
Jeansjacke [ˈdʒiːnz-] *f* denim jacket
jede(r, s) [ˈjeː·də] *pron indef* ❶ *attr* (*alle einzelnen*) each, every ❷ *attr* (*jegliche*) any ❸ *attr* (*in einem/einer beliebigen*) any; **zu ~r Zeit** at any time ❹ *substantivisch* everyone; (*stärker*) each and every one; **das weiß doch ein ~r!** everybody knows that!; DIAL (*jeweils der/die einzelne*) each [one]; **~e[r, s] zweite/dritte ...** one in two/three ...
jedenfalls [ˈjeː·dn̩·ˈfals] *adv* ❶ (*immerhin*) in any case ❷ (*auf jeden Fall*) anyhow, anyway
jederzeit [ˈjeː·dɐ·ˈtsait] *adv* ❶ (*zu jeder beliebigen Zeit*) at any time ❷ (*jeden Augenblick*) at any moment
jedesmal[ALT] *adv s.* **Mal**[1] **1**
jedoch [je·ˈdɔx] *konj, adv* however
Jeep® <-s, -s> [ˈdʒiːp] *m* jeep
jemals [ˈjeː·maːls] *adv* ever
jemand [ˈjeː·mant] *pron indef* somebody; (*bei Fragen, Negation, etc.*) anyone
Jemen <-s> [ˈjeː·mən] *m* Yemen; *s. a.* **Deutschland**
jene(r, s) [ˈjeː·nə] *pron dem* (*geh*) ❶ (*der/die/das Bewusste*) that *sing,* those *pl* ❷ (*der/die/das dort*) that *sing,* those *pl*
jenseits [ˈjeːn·zaits] **I.** *präp +gen* (*auf der anderen Seite*) on the other side **II.** *adv* (*über ... hinaus*) ■ **~ von etw** *dat* beyond sth
Jenseits <-> [ˈjeːn·zaits] *nt kein pl* hereafter
Jerusalem <-s> [je·ˈruː·za·lɛm] *nt* Jerusalem
Jesuit <-en, -en> [je·zu·ˈiːt] *m* Jesuit
Jesus *<gen o dat* Jesu, *akk* Jesum> [ˈjeː·zʊs] *m* Jesus; **~ Christus** Jesus Christ
Jetlag <-s, -s> [ˈdʒɛt·lɛg] *m* jet lag
Jetset[RR], **Jet-set**[ALT] <-s, *selten* -s> [ˈdʒɛt·sɛt] *m* (*fam*) jet set
jetzig [ˈjɛt·sɪç] *adj attr* current
jetzt [ˈjɛtst] *adv* ❶ (*zurzeit*) now; **~ gleich** right now; **~ oder nie!** [it's] now or never!; **~ schon?** already?; **bis ~** so far ❷ (*verstärkend: nun*) now; **habe ich ~ den Brief eingeworfen oder nicht?** did I just mail the letter or not?; **wer ist das ~ schon wieder?** now who is it? ❸ (*heute*) now[adays]
jeweilig [ˈjeː·ˈvai·lɪç] *adj attr* prevailing
jeweils [ˈjeː·ˈvails] *adv* ❶ (*jedes Mal*) each time; **die Miete ist ~ monatlich im Voraus**

fällig the rent is due each month in advance; **die ~ Betroffenen können gegen die Bescheide Einspruch einlegen** everyone affected by the decisions has the right to file a complaint ② (*immer zusammengenommen*) each; **~ drei Pfadfinder mussten sich einen Teller Eintopf teilen** there was only one plate of stew for every three scouts ③ (*zur entsprechenden Zeit*) at the time

Jh. *Abk von* **Jahrhundert** century

JH *Abk von* **Jugendherberge** YH

Job <-s, -s> [dʒɔp] *m* (*fam*) job

jobben ['dʒɔ·bn̩] *vi* (*fam*) to work odd jobs

Jobsuche ['dʒɔb-] *f kein pl* (*fam*) job hunting

Jockei, Jockey <-s, -s> ['dʒɔ·ke, 'dʒɔ·ki] *m* jockey

jodeln ['joː·dl̩n] *vi* to yodel

Jodsalz ['joːt-] *nt kein pl* iodate; KOCHK, MED, PHARM iodized salt

Joga <-[s]> ['joː·ga] *m o nt kein pl* yoga

joggen ['dʒɔ·gn̩] *vi* ① *haben* (*als Jogger laufen*) to jog ② *sein* ■ **irgendwohin ~** to jog somewhere

Jogger(in) <-s, -> ['dʒɔ·gɐ] *m(f)* jogger

Jogging <-s> ['dʒɔ·gɪŋ] *nt kein pl* jogging

Jogginganzug ['dʒɔ·gɪŋ-] *m* tracksuit

Joghurt, Jogurt[RR] <-[s], -[s]> ['joː·gʊrt] *m o nt* yog[h]urt

Johannisbeere [jo·'ha·nɪs-] *f* currant; **rote/schwarze ~** red/black currant

johlen ['joː·lən] *vi* to yell

Joint <-s, -s> [dʒɔynt] *m* (*sl*) joint

Jo-Jo <-s, -s> [jo'joː] *nt* yo-yo

Joker <-s, -> ['joː·kɐ, 'dʒoː·kɐ] *m* joker

Jongleur(in) <-s, -e> [ʒõ·'gløːɐ̯, *a.* ʒɔŋ·'(g)løːɐ̯] *m(f)* juggler

jonglieren* [ʒɔŋ·'liː·rən] *vi* to juggle

Jordan <-s> ['jɔr·dan] *m* Jordan

Jordanien <-s> [jɔr·'daː·ni̯·ən] *nt* Jordan; *s. a.* **Deutschland**

Jordanier(in) <-s, -> [jɔr·'daː·ni̯·ɐ] *m(f)* Jordanian; *s. a.* **Deutsche(r)**

jordanisch [jɔr·'daː·nɪʃ] *adj* Jordanian; *s. a.* **deutsch**

Joule <-[s], -> ['ʒuːl] *nt* joule

Journal <-s, -e> [ʒʊr·'naːl] *nt* journal

Journalismus <-> [ʒʊr·na·'lɪs·mʊs] *m kein pl* ① (*Pressewesen*) press ② (*journalistische Berichterstattung*) journalism

Journalist(in) <-en, -en> [ʒʊr·na·'lɪst] *m(f)* journalist

journalistisch [ʒʊr·na·'lɪs·tɪʃ] **I.** *adj* journalistic **II.** *adv* journalistically

jr. *adj Abk von* **junior** jr.

Jubel <-s> ['juːbl̩] *m kein pl* cheering

jubeln ['juː·bl̩n] *vi* ■ **[über etw** *akk*] **~** to celebrate [sth]

Jubelruf *m* cheer

Jubilar(in) <-s, -e> [ju·bi·'laːɐ̯] *m(f) person celebrating an anniversary*

Jubiläum <-s, Jubiläen> [ju·bi·'lɛː·ʊm, *pl* ju·bi·'lɛː·ən] *nt* anniversary

juchzen ['jʊx·tsn̩] *vi* (*fam*) to shout with joy

jucken ['jʊ·kn̩] **I.** *vi* (*Juckreiz erzeugen*) to itch **II.** *vi impers* to itch **III.** *vt impers* ① (*zum Kratzen reizen*) **mich juckt's am Rücken** my back's itching ② (*fam: reizen*) ■ **jdn juckt es, etw zu tun** sb's itching to do sth **IV.** *vt* ① (*kratzen*) **das Unterhemd juckt mich** my undershirt is itchy ② *meist verneint* (*fam: kümmern*) **das juckt mich doch nicht** I couldn't care less **V.** *vr* (*fam: sich kratzen*) ■ **sich** *akk* **[an etw** *dat*] **~** to scratch [one's sth]

Juckreiz *m* itch[ing]

Jude, Jüdin <-n, -n> ['juː·də] *m, f* Jew *masc*, Jewess *fem*; **~ sein** to be Jewish

Judentum <-s> *nt kein pl* Jewry, Jews *pl*

Judenverfolgung *f* persecution of [the] Jews

Judenvernichtung *f kein pl* extermination of the Jews; (*im 3. Reich*) Holocaust

Jüdin <-, -nen> ['jyː·dɪn] *f fem form von* **Jude**

jüdisch ['jyː·dɪʃ] *adj* Jewish

Judo <-s> ['juː·do] *nt kein pl* judo

Jugend <-> ['juː·gn̩t] *f kein pl* ① (*Jugendzeit*) youth; **frühe/früheste ~** early/earliest youth; **in jds ~** in sb's youth; **in meiner ~ ...** when I was young, ... ② (*Jungsein*) youthfulness ③ (*junge Menschen*) **die heutige ~** young people today

Jugendamt *nt* ≈ *office of youth services*

Jugendarbeit *f* youth development [work]

Jugendbuch *nt* young adult book

jugendfrei *adj* (*veraltend*) *Film* [rated] G

Jugendfreund(in) *m(f)* childhood friend

jugendgefährdend *adj* morally damaging to minors

Jugendgruppe *f* youth group

Jugendherberge *f* youth hostel

Jugendkriminalität *f kein pl* juvenile delinquency

jugendlich ['juː·gn̩t·lɪç] **I.** *adj* ① (*jung*) young ② (*durch jds Jugend bedingt*) youthful ③ (*jung wirkend*) youthful **II.** *adv* youthfully

Jugendliche(r) *f(m)* young person

Jugendliebe *f* childhood sweetheart

Jugendschutz *m kein pl* legal protection of minors

Jugendstil *m* Art Nouveau

Jugendstrafe *f* sentence for juvenile offenders

Jugendtraum *m* childhood dream

Jugendzeit *f kein pl* youth

Jugendzentrum *nt* youth center

Jugoslawe, Jugoslawin <-n, -n> [ju·go·'slaː·və] *m, f* (*hist*) Yugoslav; *s. a.* **Deutsche(r)**

Jugoslawien <-s> [ju·go·'slaː·vi̯·ən] *nt* (*hist*) Yugoslavia; *s. a.* **Deutschland**

Jugoslawin <-, -nen> [ju·go·'slaː·vɪn] *f* (*hist*) *fem form von* **Jugoslawe**

jugoslawisch [ju·go·'slaː·vɪʃ] *adj* (*hist*) Yugoslav[ian]; *s. a.* **deutsch**

Juli <-[s], -s> ['juː·li] *m* July; *s. a.* **Februar**

jun. *adj Abk von* **junior**

jung <jünger, jüngste> [jʊŋ] **I.** *adj* ① (*noch nicht älter*) young; ■ **jünger [als jd] sein** to be younger [than sb] ② (*jung wirkend*) youthful; **das hält ~!** it keeps you young! ③ (*später* *geboren*) young; ■**der/die Jüngere/der/die Jüngste** the younger/the youngest ❹ (*erst kurz existierend*) new **II.** *adv* (*in jungen Jahren*) young; ~ **heiraten/sterben** to marry/die young

Junge <-n, -n> ['jʊŋə] *m* ❶ (*männliches Kind*) boy ❷ (*fam*) ■**Jungs** *pl* (*veraltend fam: Leute*) guys *pl* ▶ WENDUNGEN: **alter** ~ (*fam*) old buddy, dude *sl;* **mein** ~ (*fam*) my boy, son; ~, ~**!** (*fam*) boy, oh boy!

Junge(s) ['jʊŋə(s)] *nt* ORN, ZOOL young

jünger ['jʏŋɐ] *adj* ❶ *komp von* **jung** younger ❷ (*noch nicht allzu alt*) youngish ❸ (*wenig zurückliegend*) recent

Jünger(in) <-s, -> ['jʏŋɐ] *m(f)* disciple

Jungfernfahrt ['jʊŋ·fɐn-] *f* maiden voyage

Jungfernhäutchen *nt* hymen

Jungfrau ['jʊŋ·frau] *f* ❶ (*Frau vor ihrem ersten Koitus*) virgin; **die ~ Maria** the Virgin Mary; **die ~ von Orléans** Joan of Arc ❷ ASTROL Virgo

jungfräulich ['jʊŋ·frɔy·lɪç] *adj* (*geh*) ❶ (*Zustand*) virgin ❷ (*noch unberührt*) virgin; **~er Schnee** virgin snow

Junggeselle, -gesellin ['jʊŋ·gə·zɛ·lə] *m, f* bachelor

Jüngling <-s, -e> ['jʏŋ·lɪŋ] *m* (*geh: junger Mann*) young man

jüngste(r, s) *adj* ❶ *superl von* **jung** youngest; [**auch**] **nicht mehr der/die Jüngste sein** (*hum*) to be no spring chicken anymore [either] ❷ (*nicht lange zurückliegend*) [most] recent ❸ (*neueste*) latest

Jungtier *nt* young animal

jungverheiratet *adj inv* newlywed

Juni <-[s], -s> ['juː·ni] *m* June; *s. a.* **Februar**

junior ['juː·ni̯oːɐ̯] *adj* (*geh*) junior

Junior, Juniorin <-s, -en> ['juː·ni̯oːɐ̯, *pl* ju·'ni̯oː·rən] *m, f* ❶ (*Juniorchef*) boss' [*or* owner's] son *masc*/daughter *fem* ❷ (*fam: Sohn*) junior ❸ *pl* (*junge Sportler zwischen 18 und 23*) [*members of the*] *junior team npl*

Juniorchef, -chefin *m, f* boss' [*or* owner's] son *masc*/daughter *fem*

Juniorin <-, -nen> [ju·'ni̯oː·rɪn] *f fem form von* **Junior**

Junkie <-s, -s> ['dʒaŋ·ki] *m* (*sl*) junkie

Jupiter <-s> ['juː·pi·tɐ] *m* Jupiter

Jura¹ ['juː·ra] *kein art* SCH law

Jura² <-s> ['juː·ra] *m* GEOL Jurassic [period/system]

Jura³ <-s> ['juː·ra] *m kein pl* GEOG ❶ (*Gebirge in der Ostschweiz*) Jura Mountains *pl* ❷ (*Schweizer Kanton*) Jura

Jurist(in) <-en, -en> [ju·'rɪst] *m(f)* ❶ (*Akademiker*) jurist ❷ (*fam: Jurastudent*) law student

Juristerei <-> [ju·rɪs·tə·'rai] *f kein pl* law

Juristin <-, -nen> [ju·'rɪs·tɪn] *f fem form von* **Jurist**

juristisch [ju·'rɪs·tɪʃ] **I.** *adj* ❶ (*Jura betreffend*) legal; **~es Studium** legal studies ❷ (*die Rechtsprechung betreffend*) law *attr;* **ein ~es Problem** a juridical problem **II.** *adv* **~ argumentiert/betrachtet** argued/seen from a legal point of view

Juror, Jurorin <-s, -en> ['juː·roːɐ̯, *pl* ju·'roː·rən] *m, f meist pl* juror

Jury <-, -s> [ʒy·'riː, 'ʒyː·ri, 'dʒuː·ri] *f* jury

Justiz <-> [jʊs·'tiːts] *f kein pl* JUR ❶ (*Gerichtsbarkeit*) justice ❷ (*Justizbehörden*) legal authorities *pl*

Justizbeamte(r) *f(m)* judicial officer

Justizbehörde *f* legal authority

Justizgebäude *nt* courthouse

Justizirrtum *m* miscarriage of justice

Justizminister, -ministerin *m, f* Attorney General

Justizministerium *nt* Justice Department, Department of Justice

Justizvollzugsanstalt *f* (*geh*) place of detention

Juwel¹ <-s, -en> [ju·'veːl] *m o nt* ❶ (*Schmuckstein*) gem[stone], jewel ❷ *pl* (*Schmuck*) jewelry

Juwel² <-s, -e> [ju·'veːl] *nt* ❶ (*geschätzte Person oder Sache*) gem; **ein ~ von einer Köchin sein** to be a great cook *sl* ❷ (*kostbares Exemplar*) gem, jewel; **der Schwarzwald ist ein ~ unter den deutschen Landschaften** the Black Forest is one of the jewels of the German countryside; **das ~ der Sammlung** the jewel of the collection

Juwelier(in) <-s, -e> [ju·ve·'liːɐ̯] *m(f)* ❶ (*Besitzer eines Juweliergeschäftes*) jeweler ❷ (*Juweliergeschäft*) jeweler's

Jux <-es, *selten* -e> ['jʊks] *m* (*fam: Scherz*) joke; **aus** [**lauter**] **~ und Tollerei** (*fam*) out of sheer fun; **aus ~** as a joke

Kk

K, k <-, - *o fam* -s, -s> [kaː] *nt* K, k; ~ **wie Kaufmann** K as in Kilo

Kabarett <-s, -e *o* -s> [ka·ba·ˈrɛt] *nt* cabaret

Kabarettist(in) <-en, -en> [ka·ba·rɛ·ˈtɪst] *m(f)* cabaret artist

Kabel <-s, -> [ˈkaː·bl̩] *nt* ❶ ELEK wire; (*größer*) cable ❷ TELEK, TV cable

KabelanschlussRR *m* cable connection

Kabelfernsehen *nt* cable TV

Kabeljau <-s, -e *o* -s> [ˈkaː·bl̩·jau] *m* cod

Kabine <-, -n> [ka·ˈbiː·nə] *f* ❶ (*Umkleidekabine*) changing room ❷ NAUT cabin

Kabinett <-s, -e> [ka·bi·ˈnɛt] *nt* POL cabinet

Kabrio <-[s], -s> [ˈkaː·brio] *nt,* **Kabriolett** <-s, -s> [ka·brio·ˈlɛt] *nt* convertible

Kachel <-, -n> [ˈka·xl̩] *f* tile

kacheln [ˈka·xl̩n] *vt* to tile

Kachelofen [ˈka·xl̩·ʔoː·fn̩] *m* tiled masonry heater

Kacke <-> [ˈka·kə] *f kein pl* (*derb*) shit

kacken [ˈka·kn̩] *vi* (*derb*) to shit

Kadaver <-s, -> [ka·ˈdaː·vɐ] *m* carcass

Kader <-s, -> [ˈkaː·dɐ] *m* ❶ MIL cadre ❷ SPORT squad

Käfer <-s, -> [ˈkɛ·fɐ] *m* ❶ ZOOL beetle ❷ (*fam: Volkswagen*) [VW] bug [*or* beetle]

Kaff <-s, -s *o* -e> [ˈkaf] *nt* (*pej fam*) hole

Kaffee <-s, -s> [ˈka·fe] *m* coffee

Kaffeeautomat *m* coffeemaker; (*coin-operated*) coffee vending machine

Kaffeefilter *m* coffee filter; (*Filterpapier a.*) filter paper

Kaffeehaus *nt* ÖSTERR coffee house

Kaffeekanne *f* coffeepot

Kaffeemaschine *f* coffeemaker

Kaffeepad <-s, -s> [-pɛd] *nt* K-cup®, coffee pod

Kaffeepause *f* coffee break

Käfig <-s, -e> [ˈkɛː·fɪç] *m* cage

kahl [kaːl] **I.** *adj* ❶ (*ohne Kopfhaar*) bald; ~ **geschoren** shaved ❷ *Baum, Wand* bare; *Landschaft* barren **II.** *adv* **etw ~ fressen** to strip sth bare; **jdn ~ scheren** to shave sb's head

Kahlkopf *m* bald head

kahlköpfig *adj* bald-headed

Kahlschlag *m* ❶ (*abgeholzte Fläche*) clearing ❷ *kein pl* (*das Abholzen*) deforestation

Kahn <-[e]s, Kähne> [kaːn, *pl* ˈkɛː·nə] *m* (*flaches Boot*) small boat; (*Schleppkahn*) barge

Kai <-s, -e *o* -s> [kai] *m* quay

Kaiser(in) <-s, -> [ˈkai·zɐ] *m(f)* emperor *masc,* empress *fem*

kaiserlich [ˈkai·zɐ·lɪç] *adj* imperial

Kaiserschmarr(e)n *m* KOCHK ÖSTERR, SÜDD *a warm dessert of sliced crepes and raisins, topped with powdered sugar, often served with apple sauce or plum jam*

> **Kaiserschmarrn** is a type of thick pancake, common in Austria, southern Germany, and Switzerland. The pancake, usually filled with raisins, is split into bite-size pieces, topped with powdered sugar, and traditionally served with apple sauce or plum jam. Its origins can be traced back to Empress Elisabeth of Austria.

Kaiserschnitt *m* Caesarean [section]

Kajak <-s, -s> [ˈkaː·jak] *m o nt* kayak

Kajüte <-, -n> [ka·ˈjyː·tə] *f* cabin

Kakao <-s, -s> [ka·ˈkau] *m* cocoa; (*heiß*) hot chocolate; (*Pulver*) cocoa [powder]

Kakaobutter [ka·ˈkau-] *f kein pl* cocoa butter

Kakaopulver *nt* cocoa powder

Kakerlake <-, -n> [ˈkaː·kɐ·la·kə] *f* cockroach

Kaktee <-, -n> [kak·ˈteː·ə] *f,* **Kaktus** <-, Kakteen *o fam* -se> [ˈkak·tʊs, *pl* kak·ˈteː·ən, -ʊ·sə] *m* cactus

Kalb <-[e]s, Kälber> [kalp, *pl* ˈkɛl·bɐ] *nt* calf

kalben [ˈkal·bn̩] *vi* to calve

Kalbfleisch *nt* veal

Kalbsbraten *m* roast veal

Kalbskotelett *nt* veal chop

Kalbsschnitzel *nt* veal cutlet

Kaldaune <-, -n> [kal·ˈdau·nə] *f meist pl* entrails *npl*

Kaleidoskop <-s, -e> [ka·lai·do·ˈskoːp] *nt* kaleidoscope

Kalender <-s, -> [ka·ˈlɛn·dɐ] *m* calendar

Kalenderjahr *nt* calendar year

Kalifornien <-s> [ka·li·ˈfɔr·ni̯·ən] *nt* California

Kalium <-s> [ˈkaː·li̯·ʊm] *nt kein pl* potassium

Kalk <-[e]s, -e> [kalk] *m* ❶ (*Kalziumkarbonat*) lime ❷ BAU whitewash ❸ (*Kalzium*) calcium

kalkhaltig *adj* chalky; *Wasser* hard

Kalkulation <-, -en> [kal·ku·la·ˈtsi̯oːn] *f* calculation

kalkulierbar *adj* calculable

kalkulieren* [kal·ku·ˈliː·rən] *vi, vt* to calculate (**mit** +*dat* with)

Kalorie <-, -n> [ka·lo·ˈriː, *pl* -ˈriː·ən] *f* calorie

kalorienarm I. *adj* low-calorie **II.** *adv* ~ **essen** to eat diet food

Kalorienbombe *f* (*fam*) **eine echte ~ sein** to be loaded with calories

kalorienreich *adj* high-calorie

kalt <kälter, kälteste> [kalt] **I.** *adj* cold; **mir ist ~** I'm cold **II.** *adv* ❶ (*mit kaltem Wasser*) ~ **duschen** to take a cold shower ❷ (*ohne Aufwärmen*) **etw ~ essen** to eat sth cold ❸ (*an einen kühlen Ort*) **etw ~ stellen** to chill sth ► WENDUNGEN: **jdn überläuft es ~** cold shivers run down sb's back

kaltblütig [ˈkalt·blyː·tɪç] **I.** *adj* cold-blooded

K

II. *adv* in cold blood, unscrupulously

Kaltblütigkeit <-> *f kein pl* ① (*Emotionslosigkeit*) coolness ② (*Skrupellosigkeit*) unscrupulousness; *Mörder* cold-bloodedness

Kälte <-> ['kɛl·tə] *f kein pl* cold; **vor ~** with cold; **zehn Grad ~** ten below zero

kältebeständig *adj* resistant to cold *pred*

Kälteeinbruch *m* cold snap

kälteempfindlich *adj* sensitive to cold *pred*

kälter *adj komp von* **kalt**

Kälteschutzmittel *nt* antifreeze

Kältewelle *f* cold spell

Kaltfront *f* cold front

kalt|lassen *vi irreg* ■**etw lässt jdn kalt** sth leaves sb cold

Kaltluft *f* cold air

kalt|machen *vt* ■**jdn ~** to do sb in

Kaltmiete *f* rent not including utilities

kaltschnäuzig (*fam*) **I.** *adj* callous **II.** *adv* callously

Kalzium <-s> ['kal·tsi̯·ʊm] *nt kein pl* calcium

kam *imp von* **kommen**

Kambodscha <-s> [kam·'bɔ·dʒa] *nt* Cambodia; *s. a.* **Deutschland**

Kamel <-[e]s, -e> [ka·'meːl] *nt* camel

Kamelle <-, -n> [ka·'mɛ·lə] *f* DIAL candy ► WENDUNGEN: **das sind alte ~** (*fam*) that's old hat

Kamera <-, -s> ['ka·mə·ra] *f* camera

Kamerad(in) <-en, -en> [ka·mə·'raːt, *pl* -'raː·dn̩] *m(f)* comrade

Kameradschaft <-, -en> [ka·mə·'raːt·ʃaft] *f* camaraderie

kameradschaftlich **I.** *adj* friendly **II.** *adv* on a friendly basis

Kamerun <-s> ['ka·mə·ruːn] *nt* Cameroon; *s. a.* **Deutschland**

Kamille <-, -n> [ka·'mɪ·lə] *f* camomile

Kamin <-s, -e> [ka·'miːn] *m o* DIAL *nt* ① (*offene Feuerstelle*) fireplace ② (*Schornstein*) chimney

Kaminfeger(in) <-s, -> *m(f)* DIAL, **Kaminkehrer(in)** <-s, -> *m(f)* DIAL (*Schornsteinfeger*) chimney sweep

Kamm <-[e]s, Kämme> [kam, *pl* 'kɛ·mə] *m* ① (*Frisierkamm*) comb ② *eines Vogels* comb ③ (*Bergrücken*) ridge

kämmen ['kɛ·mən] *vt* to comb

Kammer <-, -n> ['kamɐ] *f* ① (*kleiner Raum*) small room ② POL, JUR chamber ③ (*Berufsvertretung*) professional association

Kammerjäger(in) *m(f)* pest controller

Kampagne <-, -n> [kam·'pan·jə] *f* campaign

Kampf <-[e]s, Kämpfe> [kampf, *pl* 'kɛm·pfə] *m* ① (*a. fig: Auseinandersetzung*) fight (**gegen** +*akk* against) ② (*innerlich*) struggle; **innere Kämpfe** inner struggles ③ (*das Ringen*) struggle (**um** +*akk* for) ④ MIL battle; **im ~ fallen** to be killed in action; **in den ~ [gegen jdn/etw] ziehen** to take up arms [against sb/sth] ⑤ SPORT fight (**um** +*akk* for) ► WENDUNGEN: **jdm/etw den ~ ansagen** to declare war on sb/sth

Kampfansage *f* declaration of war

kämpfen ['kɛmp·fn̩] **I.** *vi* ① *a.* MIL, SPORT to fight ② (*ringen*) ■**mit sich** *dat*/**etw** *dat* **~** to struggle with oneself/sth **II.** *vr* ■**sich** *akk* **durch etw** *akk* **~** to struggle through sth

Kämpfer(in) <-s, -> ['kɛmp·fɐ] *m(f)* ① (*engagierter Streiter*) *a.* MIL fighter ② SPORT contender

kämpferisch **I.** *adj* ① SPORT attacking ② (*Kampfgeist aufweisend*) aggressive ③ MIL fighting **II.** *adv* aggressively; **~ gestimmt** in a fighting mood

Kämpfernatur *f* fighter

Kampfflugzeug *nt* combat aircraft

Kampfgeist *m kein pl* fighting spirit

Kampfhandlung *f meist pl* MIL hostilities *pl*

Kampfhund *m* fighting dog

kampflos **I.** *adj* peaceful **II.** *adv* peacefully

Kampfsport *m kein pl* martial arts *pl*

kampfunfähig *adj* unable to fight; MIL unfit for battle

kampieren* [kam·'piː·rən] *vi* to camp [out]

Kanada <-s> ['ka·na·da] *nt* Canada; *s. a.* **Deutschland**

Kanadier(in) <-s, -> [ka·'naː·di̯ɐ] *m(f)* Canadian; *s. a.* **Deutsche(r)**

kanadisch [ka·'naː·dɪʃ] *adj* Canadian; *s. a.* **deutsch**

Kanaille <-, -n> [ka·'nal·jə] *f* (*pej*) scoundrel

Kanake <-n, -n> [ka·'naː·kə] *m* ① (*Südseeinsulaner*) *a South Sea Islander* ② (*pej sl: exotischer Asylant*) dago *pej* ③ (*pej sl: türkischer Arbeitnehmer*) Turkish immigrant worker

Kanal <-s, Kanäle> [ka·'naːl, *pl* ka·'nɛ·lə] *m* ① NAUT, TRANSP canal ② (*Abwasserkanal*) sewer ③ *kein pl* (*Ärmelkanal*) ■**der ~** the [English] Channel ④ RADIO, TV channel

Kanalinseln *pl* ■**die ~** the Channel Islands *pl*

Kanalisation <-, -en> [ka·na·li·za·'tsi̯oːn] *f* (*Abwassernetz*) sewage system, sewer [system]

kanalisieren* [ka·na·li·'ziː·rən] *vt* ① (*mit einer Kanalisation versehen*) to install a sewage system ② (*geh: in Bahnen lenken*) to channel

Kanaltunnel *m* ■**der ~** the Channel Tunnel, the Chunnel *fam*

kanarisch [ka·'naː·rɪʃ] *adj* Canary; **die K~en Inseln** the Canary Islands

Kandidat(in) <-en, -en> [kan·di·'daːt] *m(f)* candidate; **jdn als ~en [für etw] aufstellen** POL to nominate sb [for sth]

Kandidatur <-, -en> [kan·di·da·'tuːɐ̯] *f* candidature

kandidieren* [kan·di·'diː·rən] *vi* POL ■**[für etw] ~** to run [for sth]

kandiert *adj* candied

Kandis <-> *m*, **Kandiszucker** ['kan·dɪs-] *m kein pl* rock candy

Känguru[RR], **Känguruh**[ALT] <-s, -s> ['kɛŋ·gu·ru] *nt* kangaroo

Kaninchen <-s, -> [ka·'niːn·çən] *nt* rabbit

Kanister <-s, -> [ka·'nɪs·tɐ] *m* canister

kann *3. pers sing pres von* **können**

Kanne <-, -n> ['kanə] *f* (*Wasserkanne*) pitcher; (*Kaffee-, Teekanne*) pot; (*Gießkanne*) watering can
Kannibale <-n, -n> [ka·ni·'ba:·lə] *m* cannibal
kannte ['kan·tə] *imp von* **kennen**
Kanone <-, -n> [ka·'no:·nə] *f* ❶ (*Geschütz*) cannon ❷ (*sl: Pistole*) pistol ▶ WENDUNGEN: **unter aller ~ sein** (*fam*) to be lousy
Kanonenkugel *f* cannonball
Kante <-, -n> ['kan·tə] *f* (*Rand*) edge ▶ WENDUNGEN: **etw auf die hohe ~ legen** (*fam*) to put sth away [for a rainy day]
kantig ['kan·tɪç] *adj* ❶ (*Kanten besitzend*) squared ❷ (*markant*) angular
Kantine <-, -n> [kan·'ti:·nə] *f* cafeteria
Kanton <-s, -e> [kan·'tɔ:n] *m* canton

Switzerland is a confederation of 23 **Kantone** (cantons), three of which (Unterwalden, Basel, and Appenzell) are divided into *Halbkantone* (half-cantons), for a total of 26 cantons. The cantons elect a total of 46 representatives to the *Ständerat*, one of the two chambers of the Swiss legislature. The three largest cantons in terms of area are Graubünden, Bern, and Valais.

kantonal [kan·to·'na:l] *adj* cantonal
Kanu <-s, -s> ['ka:·nu] *nt* canoe
Kanzlei <-, -en> [kants·'lai] *f* office
Kanzler(in) <-s, -> ['kants·lɐ] *m(f)* chancellor
Kanzleramt *nt* POL ❶ (*Büro*) chancellor's office ❷ *kein pl* (*Amt*) chancellorship
Kanzlerin <-, -nen> *f fem form von* **Kanzler**
Kanzlerkandidat(in) *m(f)* POL candidate for chancellor
Kap <-s, -s> [kap] *nt* cape; **~ der Guten Hoffnung** Cape of Good Hope
Kap. *Abk von* **Kapitel** chap.
Kapazität <-, -en> [ka·pa·tsi·'tɛt] *f* ❶ *pl selten* (*Fassungsvermögen*) capacity ❷ (*Leistungsvermögen*) capacity
Kapelle[1] <-, -n> [ka·'pɛ·lə] *f* REL chapel
Kapelle[2] <-, -n> [ka·'pɛ·lə] *f* MUS orchestra
Kaper <-, -n> ['ka:·pɐ] *f* caper
kapieren* [ka·'pi:·rən] *vt* (*fam*) to get; ■**~, dass/was/wie/wo ...** to understand that/what/how/where ...
Kapital <-s, -e *o* -ien> [ka·pi·'ta:l, *pl* -'ta:·li·ən] *nt* FIN, ÖKON capital ▶ WENDUNGEN: **~ aus etw** *dat* **schlagen** to cash in on sth
Kapitalgesellschaft *f* corporation
Kapitalismus <-> [ka·pi·ta·'lɪs·mʊs] *m kein pl* capitalism
Kapitalist(in) <-en, -en> [ka·pi·ta·'lɪst] *m(f)* capitalist
kapitalistisch *adj* capitalist[ic]
kapitalkräftig *adj* financially strong
Kapitalverbrechen *nt* capital offense
Kapitän(in) <-s, -e> [ka·pi·'tɛ:n] *m(f)* captain
Kapitel <-s, -> [ka·'pɪ·tl̩] *nt* chapter
Kapitulation <-, -en> [ka·pi·tu·la·'tsi̯o:n] *f* capitulation
kapitulieren* [ka·pi·tu·'li:·rən] *vi* ❶ (*sich ergeben*) to capitulate ❷ (*fam: aufgeben*) ■**vor etw** *dat* **~** to give up in the face of sth
Kaplan <-s, Kapläne> [ka·'pla:n, *pl* ka·'plɛ:·nə] *m* chaplain
Kappe <-, -n> ['ka·pə] *f* ❶ (*Mütze*) cap, hat ❷ (*Verschluss*) top
kappen ['ka·pn̩] *vt* ❶ (*durchtrennen*) to cut ❷ (*fam: beschneiden*) *Zuschüsse* to cut back [on]
kapriziös [ka·pri·'tsi̯ø:s] *adj* capricious
Kapsel <-, -n> ['kap·sl̩] *f* ❶ PHARM, RAUM capsule ❷ (*kleiner Behälter*) small container
kaputt [ka·'pʊt] *adj* (*fam*) ❶ (*zerbrochen*) broken ❷ (*beschädigt*) damaged; (*Kleidung: zerrissen*) torn ❸ (*erschöpft*) shattered ❹ (*ruiniert*) ruined
kaputt|gehen *vi irreg sein* (*fam*) ❶ (*zerstört werden*) to break; *Gerät* to break down ❷ (*beschädigt werden*) to become damaged ❸ (*ruiniert werden*) ■[**an etw** *dat*] **~** to be ruined [because of sth]; (*Ehe, Partnerschaft*) to break up [because of sth]
kaputt|lachen *vr* (*fam*) ■**sich** *akk* **~** to die laughing
kaputt|machen (*fam*) **I.** *vt* ❶ (*zerstören*) to break ❷ (*ruinieren*) to ruin ❸ (*erschöpfen*) ■**jdn ~** to wear sb out **II.** *vr* ■**sich** *akk* **~** to wear oneself out
Kapuze <-, -n> [ka·'pu:·tsə] *f* hood
Kapuziner <-s, -> [ka·pu·'tsi:·nɐ] *m* ÖSTERR (*Milchkaffee*) café latté
Karacho [ka·'ra·xo] *nt* **mit ~** (*fam*) full tilt
Karaffe <-, -n> [ka·'ra·fə] *f* carafe
Karambolage <-, -n> [ka·ram·bo·'la:·ʒə] *f* pile-up
KaramelALT, **Karamell**RR <-s> [ka·ra·'mɛl] *m kein pl* caramel
Karate <-[s]> [ka·'ra:·tə] *nt kein pl* karate
Karawane <-, -n> [ka·ra·'va:·nə] *f* caravan
Kardamom <-s> [kar·da·'mo:m] *m o nt kein pl* cardamom
Kardinal <-s, Kardinäle> [kar·di·'na:l, *pl* -'nɛ:·lə] *m* REL, ORN cardinal
Kardinalfrage *f* essential question
Kardinalzahl *f* cardinal number
Kardiologe, Kardiologin <-n, -n> [kar·di̯o·'lo:·gə] *m, f* cardiologist
Karenzzeit *f* ❶ (*Wartezeit*) waiting period ❷ ÖSTERR (*Mutterschaftsurlaub*) maternity leave
Karfiol <-s> [kar·'fi̯o:l] *m kein pl* SÜDD, ÖSTERR (*Blumenkohl*) cauliflower
Karfreitag [ka:ɐ̯·'frai·ta:k] *m* Good Friday
karg [kark] **I.** *adj* ❶ (*unfruchtbar*) barren ❷ (*dürftig*) sparse; *Einkommen, Mahl* meager **II.** *adv* sparsely; **die Portionen sind ~ bemessen** they're stingy with the portions
kärglich ['kɛrk·lɪç] *adj* ❶ (*ärmlich*) shabby; **ein ~es Leben führen** to live a life of poverty ❷ (*sehr dürftig*) meager; **ein ~er Lohn** a pittance, peanuts *fam*

K

Karibik <-> [ka·ˈriː·bɪk] *f* ■**die** ~ the Caribbean

karibisch [ka·ˈriː·bɪʃ] *adj* Caribbean

kariert [ka·ˈriːrt] *adj* ❶ *Stoff* plaid ❷ *Papier* squared

Karies <-> [ˈka·ri̯·ɛːs] *f kein pl* tooth decay; **er hat** ~ he has a cavity

Karikatur <-, -en> [ka·ri·ka·ˈtuːɐ̯] *f* (*a. pej*) caricature

Karikaturist(in) <-en, -en> [ka·ri·ka·tu·ˈrɪst] *m(f)* cartoonist

karikieren* [ka·ri·ˈkiː·rən] *vt* to caricature

kariös [ka·ˈri̯·øːs] *adj* decayed

karitativ [ka·ri·ta·ˈtiːf] **I.** *adj* charitable **II.** *adv* charitably

Karneval <-s, -e *o* -s> [ˈkar·nə·val] *m* carnival

Karnickel <-s, -> [kar·ˈnɪ·kl̩] *nt* (*fam*) bunny [rabbit]

Kärnten <-s> [ˈkɛrn·tn̩] *nt* Carinthia

Karo <-s, -s> [ˈkaː·ro] *nt* ❶ (*Raute*) rhombus ❷ *kein pl* KARTEN diamonds *pl*

Karomuster *nt* checked pattern

Karosse <-, -n> [ka·ˈrɔ·sə] *f* ❶ (*Prunkkutsche*) state carriage ❷ (*fam*) *s.* **Karosserie**

Karosserie <-, -n> [ka·rɔ·sə·ˈriː, *pl* -ˈriː·ən] *f* bodywork

Karotte <-, -n> [ka·ˈrɔ·tə] *f* carrot

Karpfen <-s, -> [ˈkar·pfn̩] *m* carp

Karre <-, -n> [ˈka·rə] *f s.* **Karren**

Karree <-s, -s> [ka·ˈreː] *nt* ❶ (*Quadrat*) square ❷ (*Häuserblock*) block; **ums** ~ around the block ❸ ÖSTERR (*Rippenstück*) loin

Karren <-s, -> [ˈka·rən] *m* ❶ (*fam: Auto*) old clunker ❷ (*Schubkarre*) wheelbarrow ❸ (*offener Pferdewagen*) cart ▶WENDUNGEN: **den ~ [für jdn] aus dem Dreck ziehen** to get [sb] out of a mess

Karriere <-, -n> [ka·ˈri̯eː·rə] *f* career

Karrierefrau *f* career woman

Karsamstag [kaːɐ̯·ˈzams·taːk] *m* Easter Saturday

Karte <-, -n> [ˈkar·tə] *f* ❶ (*Ansichtskarte*) [post]card ❷ (*Eintritts-, Fahrkarte*) ticket ❸ (*Visitenkarte*) [business] card ❹ FBALL **die gelbe/rote** ~ the yellow/red card ❺ (*Auto-, Landkarte*) map ❻ (*Speisekarte*) menu ❼ (*Spielkarte*) card ▶WENDUNGEN: **alles auf eine ~ setzen** to risk everything [*or* it all] on one card

Kartei <-, -en> [kar·ˈtai] *f* card index

Karteikarte *f* index card

Kartenspiel *nt* ❶ (*Spiel*) game of cards ❷ (*Satz Karten*) deck [*or* pack] of cards

Kartentelefon *nt a public telephone that accepts phone cards*

Kartenvorverkauf *m* advance ticket sales

Kartoffel <-, -n> [kar·ˈtɔ·fl̩] *f* potato

Kartoffelbrei *m* mashed potatoes *pl*

Kartoffelchips *pl* [potato] chips *pl*

Kartoffelklöße *pl* potato dumplings *pl*

Kartoffelpuffer <-s, -> *m* potato pancake, latke

Kartoffelpüree *nt s.* **Kartoffelbrei**

Kartoffelsalat *m* potato salad

Karton <-s, -s> [kar·ˈtɔŋ] *m* ❶ (*Schachtel*) cardboard box ❷ (*Pappe*) cardboard

Karussell <-s, -s *o* -e> [ka·rʊ·ˈsɛl] *nt* merry-go-round

Karwoche [ˈkaːɐ̯·vɔ·xə] *f* Holy Week

Karzinom <-s, -e> [kar·tsi·ˈnoːm] *nt* carcinoma, malignant growth

kaschieren* [ka·ˈʃiː·rən] *vt* to conceal

Kaschmir¹ <-s> [ˈkaʃ·miːɐ̯] *nt* GEOG Kashmir

Kaschmir² <-s, -e> [ˈkaʃ·miːɐ̯] *m* cashmere

Käse <-s, -> [ˈkɛː·zə] *m* ❶ (*Lebensmittel*) cheese; **weißer** ~ DIAL quark (*low-fat curd cheese*) ❷ (*pej fam: Quatsch*) nonsense

Käseblatt *nt* (*pej fam*) local rag

Käsekuchen *m* cheesecake

Käserei <-, -en> *f* cheese dairy

Kaserne <-, -n> [ka·ˈzɛr·nə] *f* barracks *pl*

käseweiß, käsig [ˈkɛ·sɪç] *adj* (*fam*) pasty

kaspern [ˈkas·pɐn] *vi* (*fam*) to fool around

Kassa <-, Kassen> [ˈka·sa, *pl* ˈka·sən] *f* ÖSTERR (*Kasse*) [cash] register

Kasse <-, -n> [ˈka·sə] *f* ❶ (*Zahlstelle*) [cash] register; (*im Supermarkt*) checkout counter ❷ (*Kartenverkauf*) ticket office ❸ (*Registrierkasse*) cash register ▶WENDUNGEN: **gut/schlecht bei ~ sein** (*fam*) to be well-off/not well-off; **jdn zur ~ bitten** to ask sb to pay

Kasseler <-s> [ˈka·sə·lɐ] *nt kein pl s.* **Kassler**

Kassen *pl von* **Kassa, Kassen**

Kassenarzt, -ärztin *m, f* ≈ HMO doctor

Kassenautomat *m* pay station

Kassenbon *m* [sales] receipt

Kassenpatient(in) *m(f)* ≈ HMO patient

Kassenschlager *m* (*fam*) ❶ (*erfolgreicher Film*) box-office smash ❷ (*Verkaufsschlager*) bestseller

Kassenzettel *m s.* **Kassenbon**

Kassette <-, -n> [ka·ˈsɛ·tə] *f* ❶ (*Videokassette*) videotape; (*Musikkassette*) [cassette] tape ❷ (*Kästchen*) case ❸ (*Schutzkarton*) box

Kassettenrekorder *m* cassette recorder

kassieren* [ka·ˈsiː·rən] **I.** *vt* ❶ (*einziehen*) ■**etw [bei jdm]** ~ *Miete* to collect sth [from sb] ❷ (*fam: einstreichen*) *Zinsen, Abfindung* to pick up ❸ (*fam: einbehalten*) to confiscate **II.** *vi* to settle the bill; **darf ich schon [bei Ihnen] ~?** would you mind paying the check now?

Kassierer(in) <-s, -> [ka·ˈsiː·rɐ] *m(f) Geschäft* cashier; *Bank* teller

Kassler^RR^, **Kaßler**^ALT^ <-s> [ˈkas·lɐ] *nt kein pl lightly smoked loin of pork*

Kastanie <-, -n> [kas·ˈtaː·ni̯ə] *f* (*Rosskastanie*) [horse] chestnut; (*Esskastanie*) chestnut

Kaste <-, -n> [ˈkas·tə] *f* caste

Kasten <-s, Kästen> [ˈkas·tn̩, *pl* ˈkɛs·tn̩] *m* ❶ (*kantiger Behälter*) box ❷ (*offene Kiste*) crate ❸ ÖSTERR, SCHWEIZ (*Schrank*) cupboard

kastrieren* [kas·ˈtriː·rən] *vt* to castrate

Kasus <-, -> [ˈkaː·zʊs] *m* LING case

Kat <-s, -s> [kat] *m kurz für* **Katalysator** cat *fam*

Katalog <-[e]s, -e> [ka·ta·ˈloːk, *pl* -ˈloː·gə] *m*

catalog

katalogisieren* [ka·ta·lo·gi·ˈziː·rən] *vt* to catalog

Katalysator <-s, -toren> [ka·ta·ly·ˈzaː·toːɐ̯, *pl* -ˈtoː·rən] *m* ① AUTO catalytic converter; **geregelter ~** regulated catalytic converter ② CHEM catalyst

Katarr[RR], **Katarrh** <-s, -e> [ka·ˈtar] *m* catarrh

katastrophal [ka·tas·tro·ˈfaːl] **I.** *adj* catastrophic **II.** *adv* catastrophically

Katastrophe <-, -n> [ka·ta·ˈstroː·fə] *f* catastrophe

Katastrophenalarm *m* red alert

Katastrophengebiet *nt* disaster area

Katastrophenhilfe *f kein pl* disaster aid

Katastrophenopfer *nt* disaster victim

Katastrophenschutz *m* disaster control

Katastrophenstimmung *f* hysteria

Kategorie <-, -n> [ka·te·go·ˈriː, *pl* -ˈriː·ən] *f* category

kategorisch [ka·te·ˈgoː·rɪʃ] (*emph*) **I.** *adj* categorical **II.** *adv* categorically

Kater[1] <-s, -> [ˈkaː·tɐ] *m* tomcat

Kater[2] <-s, -> [ˈkaː·tɐ] *m* (*fam*) hangover

Katerfrühstück *nt* hangover breakfast

kath. *adj Abk von* **katholisch**

Kathedrale <-, -n> [ka·te·ˈdraː·lə] *f* cathedral

Katholik(in) <-en, -en> [ka·to·ˈliːk] *m(f)* [Roman] Catholic

katholisch [ka·ˈtoː·lɪʃ] **I.** *adj* Roman Catholic **II.** *adv* Catholic

Katholizismus <-> [ka·to·liː·ˈtsɪs·mʊs] *m kein pl* Catholicism

Katz <-, -e> [kats] *f* SÜDD cat ▶WENDUNGEN: **~ und Maus mit jdm spielen** (*fam*) to play cat and mouse with sb

katzbuckeln [ˈkats·bʊ·kl̩n] *vi* (*pej fam*) ■**[vor jdm] ~** to grovel [before sb]

Katze <-, -n> [ˈka·tsə] *f* cat ▶WENDUNGEN: **die ~ aus dem Sack lassen** (*fam*) to let the cat out of the bag; **die ~ im Sack kaufen** (*fam*) to buy a pig in a poke

Katzenjammer *m* (*fam*) the blues + *sing vb*

Katzensprung *m* (*fam*) **[nur] einen ~ entfernt sein** to be [only] a stone's throw away

Katzenwäsche *f* (*hum fam*) ≈ quick shower

Kauderwelsch <-[s]> [ˈkau·dɐ·vɛlʃ] *nt kein pl* (*pej*) ① (*Sprachgemisch*) gibberish ② (*Fachsprache*) jargon

kauen [ˈkau·ən] *vt, vi* to chew (**an** + *dat* on)

kauern [ˈkau·ɐn] **I.** *vi* to be huddled [up] **II.** *vr* ■**sich** *akk* **hinter etw** *akk* **~** to crouch behind sth; **sich** *akk* **in eine Ecke ~** to cower in a corner

Kauf <-[e]s, Käufe> [kauf, *pl* ˈkɔy·fə] *m* ① (*das Kaufen*) buying; **etw zum ~ anbieten** to offer sth for sale ② (*Ware*) buy ▶WENDUNGEN: **etw in ~ nehmen** to accept sth

kaufen [ˈkau·fn̩] *vt* ① (*einkaufen*) to buy ② (*fam: bestechen*) ■**jdn ~** to buy sb [off *sep*], to bribe sb

Käufer(in) <-s, -> [ˈkɔy·fɐ] *m(f)* buyer

Kauffrau *f* businesswoman

Kaufhaus *nt* department store

Kaufkraft *f* ① (*Geldwert*) purchasing power ② (*Finanzkraft*) spending power

Kaufleute *pl s.* **Kaufmann**

käuflich **I.** *adj* ① (*zu kaufen*) for sale *pred* ② (*bestechlich*) bribable **II.** *adv* **~ erwerben** to purchase

Kaufmann <-leute> [ˈkauf·man] *m* businessman

kaufmännisch **I.** *adj* commercial **II.** *adv* commercially

Kaufpreis *m* purchase price

Kaufrausch *m kein pl* spending spree

Kaufvertrag *m* bill of sale

Kaugummi *m* chewing gum

Kaukasus <-> [ˈkau·ka·zʊs] *m* Caucasus

kaum [kaum] *adv* hardly; **wir haben ~ noch Zeit** we hardly have any time left; **~ eine[r]** hardly anyone

kausal [kau·ˈzaːl] **I.** *adj* causal **II.** *adv* causally

Kaution <-, -en> [kau·ˈtsi̯oːn] *f* ① JUR bail ② (*Mietkaution*) deposit

Kauz <-es, Käuze> [kauts, *pl* ˈkɔy·tsə] *m* ① (*Eulenvogel*) [tawny] owl ② (*Sonderling*) oddball *fam*

kauzig [ˈkau·tsɪç] *adj* odd

Kavalier <-s, -e> [ka·va·ˈliːɐ̯] *m* gentleman

Kavaliersdelikt *nt* petty offense

Kaviar <-s, -e> [ˈkaː·vi̯·ar] *m* caviar[e]

KB [ˈkaː·ˈbeː] *nt Abk von* **Kilobyte** KB, kbyte

keck [kɛk] **I.** *adj* cheeky **II.** *adv* cheekily

Kegel <-s, -> [ˈkeː·gl̩] *m* ① (*Spielfigur*) pin ② MATH, GEOG cone

Kegelbahn *f* ① (*Anlage*) bowling alley ② (*einzelne Bahn*) [bowling] lane

kegeln [ˈkeː·gl̩n] *vi* to go bowling

Kehle <-, -n> [ˈkeː·lə] *f* throat

Kehlkopf *m* larynx

Kehrbesen *m* SÜDD broom

Kehrblech *nt* SÜDD *s.* **Kehrschaufel**

kehren[1] [ˈkeː·rən] *vt* (*wenden*) ■**etw ~** to turn sth; **jdm/etw den Rücken ~** to turn one's back on sb/sth

kehren[2] [ˈkeː·rən] *vt, vi* DIAL (*fegen*) to sweep

Kehricht <-s> [ˈkeː·rɪçt] *m o nt kein pl* ① (*zusammengefegter Dreck*) sweepings *npl* ② SCHWEIZ (*Müll*) garbage ▶WENDUNGEN: **jdn einen feuchten ~ angehen** (*fam*) to not be any of sb's [damned] business

Kehrschaufel *f* dustpan

Kehrseite *f* ① (*veraltend: Rückseite*) back ② (*Schattenseite*) downside ③ (*hum: Rücken, Gesäß*) back

kehrt|machen *vi* to turn [around and go] back

Kehrtwendung *f* (*fig*) about-face, U-turn *fam*

Kehrwoche *f* SÜDD *a week in which it is a resident's turn to clean the common areas in and around an apartment building*

The **Kehrwoche** (literally: sweeping week) is a Swabian invention. Residents of apartment buildings take turns cleaning the communal areas in and around their building, such as the stairwell and the sidewalks.

keifen ['kai·fn̩] *vi* (*pej*) to nag
Keil <-[e]s, -e> [kail] *m* TECH wedge
Keilerei <-, -en> [kai·lə·'rai] *f* (*fam*) scuffle
Keilriemen *m* AUTO fan belt
Keim <-[e]s, -e> [kaim] *m* ❶ BOT shoot ❷ (*befruchtete Eizelle*) embryo ❸ (*Erreger*) germ ▶ WENDUNGEN: **etw im ~ ersticken** to nip sth in the bud
keimen ['kai·mən] *vi* ❶ BOT to germinate ❷ (*fig*) to stir
keimfrei *adj* sterile; **etw ~ machen** to sterilize sth
Keimling <-s, -e> *m* BOT shoot
kein [kain] **I.** *pron indef, attr* ❶ (*verneint ein Substantiv*) no, not any; **ich habe ~ Geld/~e Freunde** I don't have any money/friends, I have no money/friends; **ich habe jetzt wirklich ~e Zeit** I really don't have any time now; **er sagte ~ Wort** he didn't say a word ❷ (*verneint ein Adjektiv*) not; **das ist ~ dummer Gedanke** that's not a bad idea; **das ist ~ großer Unterschied** that's not much of a difference ❸ (*vor Zahlwörtern*) less than, not; **er wartete ~e 3 Minuten** he waited less than 3 minutes; **die Reparatur dauert ~e 5 Minuten** it won't even take 5 minutes to repair it **II.** *pron indef, substantivisch* ❶ (*von Menschen*) nobody, no one; **~er von uns** none of us; **ich habe ~en gesehen** I didn't see anyone; **~e/~er von beiden** neither [of them] ❷ (*von Gegenständen*) none, any; **ist Saft da? – nein, ich habe ~en gekauft** is there any juice? — no, I didn't buy any; **~s von beiden** neither [of them]; **~s von beiden gefällt mir** I don't like either of them ❸ (*nachgestellt*) **Lust habe ich schon, aber Zeit habe ich ~e** I'd like to, it's just that I don't have time; **ich gehe zu der Verabredung, aber Lust hab ich ~e** I'm going to keep the appointment, but I don't feel like going
keinerlei ['kai·nɐ·'lai] *adj attr* no ... at all
keinesfalls ['kai·nəs·'fals] *adv* under no circumstances
keineswegs ['kai·nəs·'veːks] *adv* not at all, by no means
keinmal ['kain·maːl] *adv* not [even] once, never
Keks <-es, -e> [keːks] *m* cookie ▶ WENDUNGEN: **jdm auf den ~ gehen** (*fam*) to get on someone's nerves
Keller <-s, -> ['kɛ·lɐ] *m* cellar
Kellerei <-, -en> [kɛ·lə·'rai] *f* winery
Kellergeschoss[RR] *nt* basement
Kellner(in) <-s, -> ['kɛl·nɐ] *m(f)* waiter *masc*, waitress *fem*
kellnern ['kɛl·nɐn] *vi* (*fam*) to work as a waiter/waitress
Kelte, Keltin <-n, -n> ['kɛl·tə, 'kɛl·tɪn] *m, f* Celt
keltern ['kɛl·tɐn] *vt* to press
Keltin <-, -nen> *f fem form von* **Kelte**
keltisch ['kɛl·tɪʃ] *adj* Celtic
Kenia <-s> ['keː·ni̯a] *nt* Kenya; *s. a.* **Deutschland**
Kenianer(in) <-s, -> [ke·'ni̯aː·nɐ] *m(f)* Kenyan; *s. a.* **Deutsche(r)**
kenianisch [ke·'ni̯aː·nɪʃ] *adj* Kenyan; *s. a.* **deutsch**
kennen <kannte, gekannt> ['kɛ·nən] *vt* ❶ (*jdm bekannt sein*) ■ **jdn/etw ~** to know sb/sth; **du kennst dich doch!** you know what you're like; **kennst du mich noch?** do you remember me?; **so kenne ich dich gar nicht** I've never seen you like this; **jdn ~ lernen** to get to know sb; **sich** *akk* **~ lernen** (*erstmals begegnen*) to meet ❷ (*jdm vertraut sein*) ■ **etw ~** to be familiar with sth; **kennst du das Buch/diesen Film?** have you read this book/seen this movie?; **das ~ wir [schon]** (*iron*) we've heard all that before ▶ WENDUNGEN: **jdn noch ~ lernen** (*fam*) to still have sb to deal with
Kenner(in) <-s, -> ['kɛ·nɐ] *m(f)* expert, authority
kenntlich ['kɛnt·lɪç] *adj* ■ **~ sein** to be recognizable (**an** + *dat* by); **etw [als etw] ~ machen** to label sth [[as] sth]
Kenntnis <-, -se> ['kɛnt·nɪs] *f* ❶ *kein pl* (*Vertrautheit*) knowledge; **etw zur ~ nehmen** to make [a] note of sth; **zur ~ nehmen, dass ...** to note that ...; **jdn von etw** *dat* **in ~ setzen** (*geh*) to inform sb of sth ❷ *pl* (*Wissen*) knowledge
Kenntnisnahme <-> *f kein pl* (*geh*) **zur ~** for sb's attention
Kennwort <-wörter> *nt* ❶ (*Codewort*) code word ❷ (*Losungswort*) password
Kennzeichen *nt* ❶ (*Autokennzeichen*) license plate ❷ (*Merkmal*) mark
kennzeichnen ['kɛn·tsaiç·nən] *vt* ❶ (*markieren*) to mark ❷ (*charakterisieren*) to characterize
kennzeichnend *adj* typical, characteristic
kentern ['kɛn·tɐn] *vi sein* to capsize
Keramik <-, -en> [ke·'raː·mɪk] *f* ❶ *kein pl* (*Töpferwaren*) pottery *no indef art* ❷ (*einzelner Gegenstand*) piece of pottery
Kerbe <-, -n> ['kɛr·bə] *f* notch ▶ WENDUNGEN: **in die gleiche ~ hauen** (*fam*) to take the same line
Kerker <-s, -> ['kɛr·kɐ] *m* ❶ HIST (*Verlies*) dungeon ❷ ÖSTERR (*Zuchthaus*) prison
Kerl <-s, -e *o* -s> [kɛrl] *m* ❶ (*fam: Bursche*) guy ❷ (*Mensch*) person
Kern <-[e]s, -e> [kɛrn] *m* ❶ *Kernobst* pip; *Steinobst* pit ❷ (*Atom-, Zellkern*) nucleus ❸ (*wichtigster Teil*) core ▶ WENDUNGEN: **in ihr steckt ein guter ~** she's good at heart; **einen wahren ~ haben** to contain a core of truth
Kernenergie *f* nuclear energy
Kernforschung *f* nuclear research
Kernfrage *f* central issue

K

Kẹrngedanke *m* central idea
Kẹrngehäuse *nt* BOT, HORT core
kẹrngesund *adj* fit as a fiddle *pred*
kernig ['kɛr·nɪç] *adj* ① (*voller Obstkerne*) pithy ② (*urwüchsig*) earthy
Kẹrnkraft *f* nuclear power
Kẹrnkraftbefürworter(in) *m(f)* supporter of nuclear power
Kẹrnkraftgegner(in) *m(f)* opponent of nuclear power
Kẹrnkraftwerk *nt* nuclear power plant
Kẹrnproblem *nt* central problem
Kẹrnseife *f* tallow soap
Kẹrnstück *nt* crucial part
Kẹrnwaffe *f meist pl* nuclear weapon
Kerosin <-s, -e> [ke·ro·'ziːn] *nt* kerosene
Kerze <-, -n> ['kɛr·tsə] *f* ① (*Wachskerze*) candle ② AUTO spark plug
kẹrzengerade **I.** *adj* erect **II.** *adv* [as] straight as an arrow
Kẹrzenleuchter *m* candlestick
Kẹrzenlicht *nt kein pl* candlelight
Kẹrzenständer *m* candlestick
kess[RR], **keß**[ALT] [kɛs] **I.** *adj* ① (*frech und pfiffig*) cheeky ② (*flott*) jaunty **II.** *adv* cheekily
Kessel <-s, -> ['kɛ·səl] *m* ① (*Wasserkessel*) kettle ② (*großer Kochtopf*) pot
Ketchup, Ketschup[RR] <-[s], -s> ['kɛt·ʃap] *m o nt* ketchup
Kette <-, -n> ['kɛ·tə] *f* ① (*Gliederkette*) chain; (*Fahrradkette*) [bicycle] chain; (*Schmuckkette*) necklace ② (*Serie*) line; **eine ~ von Ereignissen** a chain of events; **eine ~ von Unglücksfällen** a series of accidents
ketten ['kɛ·tn̩] *vt* ■**jdn/ein Tier an etw ~** to chain sb/an animal to sth; ■**jdn an sich** *akk* **~** (*fig*) to tie sb to oneself
Kẹttenraucher(in) *m(f)* chain smoker
Kẹttenreaktion *f* chain reaction
Ketzer(in) <-s, -> ['kɛ·tsɐ] *m(f)* heretic
kẹtzerisch *adj* heretical
keuchen ['kɔy·çn̩] *vi* to pant
Keuchhusten *m* whooping cough *no art*
Keule <-, -n> ['kɔy·lə] *f* ① (*Waffe*) club ② KOCHK leg
keusch [kɔyʃ] **I.** *adj* chaste **II.** *adv* **~ leben** to lead a chaste life
Keuschheit <-> *f kein pl* chastity
Kfz <-[s], -[s]> [kaː·ɛf·'tsɛt] *nt Abk von* **Kraftfahrzeug**
kg *Abk von* **Kilogramm** kg
Kichererbse ['kɪçe·ʔɛrp·sə] *f* chickpea
kichern ['kɪ·çɐn] *vi* to giggle
kicken ['kɪ·kn̩] (*fam*) **I.** *vi* to play soccer **II.** *vt* to kick
Kicker(in) <-s, -> ['kɪ·kɐ] *m(f)* (*fam*) soccer player
kidnappen ['kɪt·nɛ·pn̩] *vt* to kidnap
Kidnapper(in) <-s, -> ['kɪt·nɛ·pɐ] *m(f)* kidnapper
Kidnapping <-s, -s> ['kɪt·nɛ·pɪŋ] *nt* kidnapping
Kiefer[1] <-, -n> ['kiː·fɐ] *f* BOT pine
Kiefer[2] <-s, -> ['kiː·fɐ] *m* ANAT jaw [bone]
Kiefernnadel *f* pine needle
Kiefernwald *m* pine forest
Kieferorthopäde, -orthopädin <-n, -n> *m, f* orthodontist
kieken ['kiː·kn̩] *vi* NORDD (*gucken*) to look
Kieme <-, -n> ['kiː·mə] *f* gill
Kies <-es, -e> [kiːs] *m* ① (*kleines Geröll*) gravel ② *kein pl* (*fam: Geld*) dough *no indef art*
Kieselstein *m* pebble
Kiesgrube *f* gravel pit
Kiesweg *m* gravel path
kiffen ['kɪ·fn̩] *vi* (*sl*) to smoke weed
killen ['kɪ·lən] *vt* (*sl*) to bump off *sep*
Killer(in) <-s, -> ['kɪ·lɐ] *m(f)* (*sl*) hit man
Kilo <-s, -[s]> ['kiː·lo] *nt* kilo
Kilobyte ['kiː·lo·bait] *nt* kilobyte
Kilogrạmm *nt* kilogram
Kilojoule ['kiː·lo·dʒaul] *nt* kilojoule
Kilokalorie ['kiː·lo·ka·lo·riː] *f* kilocalorie
Kilometer [ki·lo·'meː·tɐ] *m* kilometer
kilometerlang **I.** *adj* stretching for miles *pred* **II.** *adv* for miles on end
Kilometerstand *m* mileage [reading]
kilometerweit *adv* for miles [and miles]
Kilometerzähler *m* mileage counter
Kind <-[e]s, -er> [kɪnt, *pl* kɪn·dɐ] *nt* child; **ein ~ [von jdm] bekommen** to be expecting a baby [from sb]; **von ~ auf** from an early age; **ein großes ~ sein** to be a big baby ▶ WENDUNGEN: **mit ~ und Kegel** (*hum fam*) with the whole family; **kein ~ von Traurigkeit sein** (*hum*) to be sb who enjoys life; **wir werden das ~ schon schaukeln** (*fam*) we'll manage to sort it out
Kịnderarbeit *f* child labor
Kịnderarzt, -ärztin *m, f* pediatrician
Kịnderbuch *nt* children's book
Kinderei <-, -en> [kɪn·də·'rai] *f* childishness
Kịndererziehung *f* bringing up children
kịnderfeindlich **I.** *adj* not child-friendly **II.** *adv* with little regard for children
kịnderfreundlich **I.** *adj* child-friendly **II.** *adv* with children in mind
Kịndergarten *m* kindergarten

> In Germany, a **Kindergarten** is a public institution that is usually run by the local authorities. Children of pre-school age are supervised by specially trained teachers for 4–6 hours a day. Every German 3-year-old has the right to attend **Kindergarten**.

Kịndergärtner(in) *m(f)* kindergarten teacher
Kịndergeburtstag *m* child's birthday
Kịndergeld *nt a monthly government subsidy paid to parents or guardians for each child under 18*
Kịnderheim *nt* children's home
Kịnderhort *m* daycare [facility]
Kịnderklinik *f* children's clinic
Kịnderkrankheit *f* ① (*Krankheit*) childhood

disease ❷ *meist pl* (*Anfangsproblem*) teething troubles *pl*

Kinderkriegen <-s> *nt kein pl* (*fam*) giving birth *no art*

Kinderkrippe *f* daycare [facility]

Kinderlähmung *f* polio

kinderleicht ['kɪn·dɐ·'laiçt] (*fam*) **I.** *adj* very easy; ■**~ sein** to be child's play **II.** *adv* very easily; **etw ist ~ zu bedienen** sth is easy to operate

kinderlieb ['kɪn·dɐ·li:p] *adj* fond of children *pred*

Kinderlied *nt* nursery rhyme

kinderlos *adj* childless

Kindermädchen *f* nanny

Kindermärchen *nt* (*fam*) fairy tale

Kinderpornografie^RR^ *f* child pornography

kinderreich *adj* with many children *pred;* **eine ~e Familie** a large family

Kinderschänder(in) <-s, -> *m(f)* child molester

Kinderschreck *m kein pl* bo[o]geyman

Kinderschuh *m* child's shoe ▶WENDUNGEN: **etw steckt noch in den ~en** sth is still in its infancy

Kindersicherung *f* child[proof] safety lock

Kindersitz *m Auto* child safety seat; *Fahrrad* child carrier [seat]

Kinderspiel *nt* children's game ▶WENDUNGEN: [**für jdn**] **ein ~ sein** to be child's play [for sb]

Kinderspielplatz *m* playground

Kinderstube *f* ▶WENDUNGEN: **eine/keine gute ~ gehabt haben** to have been well/poorly raised

Kindertagesstätte *f s.* **Kinderhort**

Kinderteller *m* child's portion

Kinderwagen *m* baby carriage

Kindesbeine *pl* **von ~n an** from childhood [*or* an early age]

Kindesentführung *f* child abduction [*or* kidnapping]

Kindesmissbrauch^RR^ *m* child abuse

Kindesmisshandlung^RR^ *f* child abuse

kindgemäß I. *adj* suitable for children *pred* **II.** *adv* suitably for children

Kindheit <-> *f kein pl* childhood; **von ~ an** from childhood [*or* an early age]

Kindheitserinnerung *f* childhood memory *usu pl*

Kindheitserlebnis *nt* childhood experience

Kindheitstraum *m* childhood dream

kindisch ['kɪn·dɪʃ] **I.** *adj* childish **II.** *adv* childishly

kindlich ['kɪnt·lɪç] **I.** *adj* childlike **II.** *adv* **~ scheinen/wirken** to appear/seem childlike

Kindskopf ['kɪnts·kɔpf] *m* (*fam*) big kid, kid at heart

King <-s> [kɪŋ] *m* **der ~ sein** (*sl*) to be [the] top dog *fam*

Kinn <-[e]s, -e> [kɪn] *nt* chin

Kinnhaken *m* hook to the chin

Kino <-s, -s> ['ki:·no] *nt* [movie] theater; **im ~ kommen** to be playing at the movies [*or* [movie] theater]

Kinobesucher(in) *m(f)* moviegoer

Kinofilm *m* movie

Kinogänger(in) <-s, -> *m(f)* moviegoer

Kinoprogramm *nt* movie listings

Kinovorstellung *f* showing [of a film]

Kiosk <-[e]s, -e> ['ki:·ɔsk] *m* kiosk

Kipfe(r)l <-s, -[n]> *nt* ÖSTERR (*Hörnchen*) croissant

Kippe <-, -n> ['kɪ·pə] *f* (*fam*) ❶ (*Deponie*) dump ❷ (*Zigarettenstummel*) cigarette butt; (*Zigarette*) cigarette ▶WENDUNGEN: **es steht auf der ~, ob ...** it's touch and go whether ...

kippen ['kɪ·pn̩] **I.** *vt haben* ❶ (*schütten*) to tip ❷ (*schräg stellen*) to tilt ❸ (*fam: scheitern lassen*) ■**jdn/etw ~** to topple sb/to halt sth; *Gesetzesvorlage* to vote down *sep; Urteil* to overturn ▶WENDUNGEN: [**gerne**] **einen/ein paar ~** (*fam*) to like a drink [or two] **II.** *vi sein* ❶ (*umfallen*) to topple over ❷ (*fallen*) ■**von etw** *dat* **~** to fall off [of] sth ❸ (*scheitern*) *System* to collapse

Kirche <-, -n> ['kɪr·çə] *f* ❶ (*Gebäude, Gottesdienst*) church ❷ (*Glaubensgemeinschaft*) Church, religion ❸ (*Institution*) Church

Kirchenasyl *nt* religious asylum

Kirchenbesuch *m* church attendance

Kirchenchor *m* church choir

Kirchenfest *nt* religious festival

Kirchengemeinde *f* ❶ (*Bezirk*) parish ❷ (*Angehörige*) church members *pl*

Kirchenglocke *f* church bell

Kirchenlied *nt* hymn

Kirchensteuer *f taxes taken out of one's paycheck which are allotted to the state church one belongs to*

> Everyone who belongs to a Protestant or Catholic church has to pay a **Kirchensteuer** (church tax) equivalent to about 8% of their earnings, in addition to income tax. The tax is usually paid directly to the church by the German equivalent of the IRS. In Austria, the churches themselves collect the contributions. In Switzerland, church tax is regulated by cantonal law.

kirchlich ['kɪrç·lɪç] **I.** *adj* church *attr,* ecclesiastical; **ein ~er Feiertag** a religious holiday **II.** *adv* **~ bestattet werden** to have a church funeral; **sich** *akk* **~ trauen lassen** to get married in church

Kirchplatz *m* church square

Kirchturm *m* [church] steeple

kirre ['kɪ·rə] *adj pred* (*fam*) **jdn ~ machen** to bring sb to heel; **~ werden** to get confused

Kirschbaum ['kɪrʃ·baum] *m* cherry tree

Kirsche <-, -n> ['kɪr·ʃə] *f* cherry

Kissen <-s, -> ['kɪ·sn̩] *nt* (*Kopfkissen*) pillow; (*Zierkissen*) cushion

Kissenbezug *m* (*für Kopfkissen*) pillowcase;

(*für Zierkissen*) cushion cover

Kiste <-, -n> ['kɪs·tə] *f* ❶ (*Behälter*) box, crate ❷ (*fam: Auto*) [old] clunker ❸ (*fam: Fernseher*) tube ❹ (*fam: Bett*) sack; **ab in die ~!** hit the sack!

Kitsch <-es> [kɪtʃ] *m kein pl* kitsch

kitschig ['kɪt·ʃɪç] *adj* kitschy

Kittchen <-s, -> ['kɪt·çən] *nt* (*fam*) slammer *sl*

Kittel <-s, -> ['kɪ·tl̩] *m* (*Arbeitskittel*) smock; *eines Arztes/Laboranten* lab coat

kitten ['kɪ·tn̩] *vt* ❶ (*verspachteln*) to putty ❷ (*fig: in Ordnung bringen*) to patch up *sep*

Kitzel <-s, -> ['kɪ·tsl̩] *m* ❶ (*Juckreiz*) tickling feeling ❷ (*Lust auf Verbotenes*) thrill

kitzelig ['kɪ·tsə·lɪç] *adj* ticklish

kitzeln ['kɪ·tsl̩n] **I.** *vt* ❶ ■ **jdn irgendwo ~** to tickle sb somewhere ❷ (*reizen*) to titillate; **den Gaumen ~** to titillate the palate ❸ (*anregen*) to arouse **II.** *vi* to tickle **III.** *vt impers* ❶ (*jucken*) **es kitzelt mich** it tickles ❷ (*reizen*) **es kitzelt mich sehr, da mitzumachen** I'm really itching to join in

Kịtzler <-s, -> *m* ANAT clitoris

kitzlig [kɪts·lɪç] *adj s.* **kitzelig**

Kiwi <-, -s> ['kiː·vi] *f* kiwi [fruit]

kJ *Abk von* **Kilojoule** kJ

KKW <-s, -s> [kaː·kaː·'veː] *nt Abk von* **Kernkraftwerk**

Klacks <-es, -e> [klaks] *m* (*fam*) dab ▶ WENDUNGEN: [**für jdn**] **ein ~ sein** (*einfach*) to be a piece of cake [for sb]; (*wenig*) to be nothing [to sb]

klaffen ['kla·fn̩] *vi* to yawn; *Schnitt, Wunde* to gape

kläffen ['klɛ·fn̩] *vi* (*pej fam*) to yap

Kläffer <-s, -> *m* (*pej fam*) yapper

Klage <-, -n> ['klaː·gə] *f* ❶ (*geh: Wehklage*) lament[ation] ❷ (*Beschwerde*) complaint (**über** +*akk* about) ❸ JUR [legal] action; **eine ~ abweisen** to dismiss a suit; **eine ~** [**gegen jdn**] **einreichen** to take legal action [against sb]; **eine ~ auf Schadenersatz** a claim for compensation [*or* damages]

klagen ['klaː·gn̩] **I.** *vi* ❶ (*jammern*) to moan (**über** +*akk* about) ❷ (*sich beklagen*) to complain (**über** +*akk* about); **ich kann nicht ~** I can't complain; **ohne zu ~** without complaining ❸ JUR ■ [**gegen jdn**] **~** to take legal action [against sb]; **auf Schadenersatz ~** to sue for damages **II.** *vt* ❶ (*Bedrückendes erzählen*) ■ **jdm etw ~** to pour out one's sth to sb ❷ ÖSTERR (*verklagen*) ■ **jdn ~** to take legal action against sb

klagend *adj* (*jammernd*) moaning

Kläger(in) <-s, -> *m(f)* JUR plaintiff

kläglich ['klɛːk·lɪç] **I.** *adj* pathetic; *Anblick* pitiful **II.** *adv* pitifully; **~ scheitern** to fail miserably

klaglos ['klaːk·loːs] *adv* without complaint [*or* complaining]

klamm [klam] *adj* ❶ (*steif vor Kälte*) numb ❷ (*nass und kalt*) dank ❸ (*sl: knapp bei Kasse*) ■ **~ sein** to be [a little] strapped for cash *fam*

Klammer <-, -n> ['kla·mɐ] *f* ❶ (*Wäscheklammer*) clothespin; (*Heftklammer*) staple; (*Haarklammer*) [hair] clip; MED clip ❷ (*Zahnklammer*) braces *pl*, retainer ❸ (*grafisches Zeichen: rund*) parentheses; (*eckig*) square bracket; (*spitz*) angle bracket; **in ~n** (*rund*) in parentheses; (*eckig o spitz*) in brackets

Klạmmeraffe *m* ❶ ZOOL spider monkey ❷ INET "at" symbol

klammern ['kla·mɐn] **I.** *vt* ❶ (*zusammenheften*) to staple (**an** +*akk* to) ❷ MED to close with clips **II.** *vr* ■ **sich** *akk* **~** (*a. fig*) to cling (**an** +*akk* to)

klammheimlich ['klam·'haim·lɪç] (*fam*) **I.** *adj* clandestine **II.** *adv* clandestinely; **sich** *akk* **~ fortstehlen** to slip away [unseen]

Klamotten [kla·'mɔ·tn̩] *pl* (*fam*) ❶ (*Kleidung*) clothes *npl* ❷ (*alte Sachen*) stuff

klang [klaŋ] *imp von* **klingen**

Klang <-[e]s, Klänge> [klaŋ, *pl* 'klɛŋə] *m* sound

klạngvoll *adj* sonorous; *Melodie* tuneful; *Stimme* melodious

Klappe <-, -n> ['kla·pə] *f* ❶ (*Deckel*) flap ❷ (*sl: Mund*) trap; **halt die ~!** shut up!; **eine große ~ haben** to have a big mouth

klappen ['kla·pn̩] **I.** *vt* to fold **II.** *vi* (*fam: funktionieren*) to work out; **alles hat geklappt** everything went as planned [*or* worked out]

klapperdürr ['kla·pɐ·'dʏr] *adj* (*fam*) [as] thin as a rake *pred*

klapperig ['kla·pə·rɪç] *adj* (*fam*) ❶ (*gebrechlich*) frail ❷ (*instabil und wacklig*) rickety

Klạpperkiste *f* (*fam: Auto*) rattletrap

klappern ['kla·pɐn] *vi* to rattle

Klạpperschlange *f* rattlesnake

Klạppfahrrad *nt* folding bicycle

Klạppmesser *nt* switchblade

Klạpprad *nt* folding bicycle

klapprig ['klap·rɪç] *adj s.* **klapperig**

Klạppstuhl *m* folding chair

Klạpptisch *m* folding table

Klaps <-es, -e> [klaps] *m* (*fam*) smack

Klapse <-, -n> ['klap·sə] *f* (*sl*), **Klạpsmühle** *f* (*sl*) loony bin *pej*, funny farm *pej*

klar [klaːɐ̯] **I.** *adj* ❶ (*ungetrübt*) clear ❷ (*unmissverständlich*) clear; *Antwort* straight; *Frage* direct ❸ (*eindeutig*) clear; *Ergebnis* clear-cut; **alles ~?** (*fam*) is everything okay?; **na ~!** (*fam*) of course! ❹ (*bewusst*) ■ **jdm ~ sein** to be clear to sb; ■ **sich** *dat* **über etw ~ werden** to get sth clear in one's mind ❺ (*bereit*) ready **II.** *adv* ❶ (*deutlich*) clearly; **~ im Nachteil/Vorteil sein** to be at a clear disadvantage/advantage; **jdm etw ~ sagen/zu verstehen geben** to make sth clear to sb; **~ und deutlich** clearly and unambiguously ❷ (*eindeutig*) **jdn ~ besiegen** to defeat sb soundly; **etw ~ erkennen** to see sth clearly ❸ (*ungetrübt*) **~ denkend** clear-thinking

Kläranlage *f* sewage plant

Klare(r) *m* (*fam*) colorless schnapps

K

klären ['klɛ·rən] **I.** *vt* ❶ (*aufklären*) to clear up *sep; Frage* to settle; *Problem* to resolve ❷ *Abwässer* to treat **II.** *vr* (*sich aufklären*) ■ **sich** *akk* ~ to be cleared up
klar|gehen *vi irreg sein* (*fam*) to go okay
Klarheit <-> *f kein pl* ❶ (*Deutlichkeit*) clarity; **sich** *dat* ~ **[über etw** *akk*] **verschaffen** to get to the bottom [of sth] *fam;* **jdm etw in aller ~ sagen** to make sth perfectly clear to sb ❷ (*Reinheit*) clearness
klar|kommen *vi irreg sein* (*fam*) ❶ (*bewältigen*) ■ **[mit etw** *dat*] ~ to manage [sth] ❷ (*zurechtkommen*) ■ **mit jdm** ~ to cope with sb
klar|machen *vt* ■ **jdm etw** ~ to make sth clear to sb; ■ **sich** *dat* **etw** ~ to realize sth
klar|stellen *vt* to clear up *sep;* ■ **~, dass ...** to make it clear that ...
Klarstellung *f* clarification
Klartext *m* ▶ WENDUNGEN: **mit jdm ~ reden** (*fam*) to be frank with sb
Klärung <-, -en> *f* ❶ (*Aufklärung*) clarification; *Frage* settling; *Problem* resolving ❷ *von Abwässern* treatment
klasse ['kla·sə] (*fam*) **I.** *adj* fantastic, great **II.** *adv* fantastically, very well
Klasse <-, -n> ['kla·sə] *f* ❶ (*Schulklasse*) class, grade; **eine ~ wiederholen/überspringen** to repeat/skip a grade ❷ (*Klassenraum*) classroom ❸ (*Gesellschaftsgruppe*) class ❹ (*Güteklasse*) class; **wir fahren immer erster ~** we always travel first class
Klassenkamerad(in) *m(f)* classmate
Klassenlehrer(in) *m(f)* teacher
Klassenzimmer *nt* classroom
klassifizieren* [kla·si·fi·'tsiː·rən] *vt* to classify (**als** +*akk* as)
Klassik <-> ['kla·sɪk] *f kein pl* (*fam: klassische Musik*) classical music
Klassiker <-s, -> ['kla·si·kɐ] *m* (*zeitloses Werk*) classic
klassisch ['kla·sɪʃ] *adj* ❶ KUNST, LIT, MUS classical ❷ (*typisch*) classic
Klatsch <-[e]s> [klatʃ] *m kein pl* (*pej fam*) ~ **[und Tratsch]** gossip
Klatschbase *f* (*pej fam*) gossip[monger]
klatschen ['klat·ʃn̩] **I.** *vi* ❶ (*mit den Händen*) to clap; **in die Hände ~** to clap one's hands ❷ (*Klaps geben*) ■ **jdm irgendwohin ~** to smack sb somewhere ❸ (*platschen*) ■ **auf/in etw** *akk* ~ to land with a splat on/in sth ❹ (*applaudieren*) to applaud ❺ (*fam: tratschen*) to gossip (**über** +*akk* about) **II.** *vt* ❶ (*fam: werfen*) ■ **etw irgendwohin ~** to chuck sth somewhere ❷ (*applaudieren*) **jdm Beifall ~** to applaud sb
Klatschmaul *nt* (*pej fam*) gossip[monger]; (*bösartig a.*) scandalmonger *pej*
klatschnassRR *adj* (*fam*) soaking wet; ■ **~ sein/werden** to be/get soaked
Klatschspalte *f* (*pej fam*) gossip column
Klatschtante *f,* **Klatschweib** *nt s.* **Klatschbase**
klauben ['klau·bn̩] *vt* SÜDD, ÖSTERR, SCHWEIZ ❶ (*pflücken*) to pick ❷ (*sammeln*) to collect; *Holz, Pilze* to gather; *Kartoffeln* to dig ❸ (*auslesen*) ■ **etw aus/von etw** *dat* ~ to pick sth out *sep* of/from sth
Klaue <-, -n> ['klau·ə] *f* ❶ (*Krallen*) claw; *Vogel a.* talon ❷ (*pej sl: Hand*) paw *hum fam* ❸ (*pej sl: Handschrift*) scrawl
klauen ['klau·ən] (*fam*) **I.** *vt* ■ **[jdm] etw ~** to steal sth [from sb] **II.** *vi* to steal [things]
Klausel <-, -n> ['klau·zl̩] *f eines Vertrags* clause
Klaustrophobie <-, -n> [klau·stro·fo·'biː, *pl* -'biː·ən] *f* claustrophobia *spec*
Klavier <-s, -e> [kla·'viːɐ̯] *nt* piano
Klavierlehrer(in) *m(f)* piano teacher
Klavierspieler(in) *m(f)* pianist
Klebeband <-bänder> ['kleː·bə-] *nt* [adhesive] tape
kleben ['kleː·bn̩] **I.** *vi* ❶ (*klebrig sein*) to be sticky ❷ (*haften*) to stick (**an** +*dat* to); **[an jdm/etw] ~ bleiben** to stick [to sb/sth] ❸ (*fig: festhalten*) to cling (**an** +*dat* to) **II.** *vt* ❶ (*reparieren*) to glue ❷ (*befestigen*) to stick (**an** +*akk* to) ▶ WENDUNGEN: **jdm eine ~** (*fam*) to clock sb
Kleber <-s, -> ['kleː·bɐ] *m* ❶ (*fam*) glue ❷ SÜDD, SCHWEIZ (*Aufkleber*) sticker
Klebestift *m* glue stick
Klebestreifen *m s.* **Klebstreifen**
klebrig ['kleː·brɪç] *adj* sticky
Klebstoff *m* adhesive; (*Leim*) glue
Klebstreifen *m* [adhesive] tape
Kleckerbetrag *m meist pl* peanuts *pl fam*
kleckern ['klɛ·kɐn] (*fam*) **I.** *vt* ■ **etw irgendwohin ~** to spill sth somewhere **II.** *vi* (*beim Essen*) to make a mess; ■ **mit etw** *dat* ~ to spill sth ▶ WENDUNGEN: **nicht ~, sondern klotzen!** think big!
kleckerweise *adv* in dribs and drabs
Klecks <-es, -e> ['klɛks] *m* ❶ (*Fleck*) stain ❷ (*kleine Menge*) blob; **ein ~ Senf** a dab of mustard
klecksen ['klɛk·sn̩] **I.** *vi* ❶ *haben* (*Kleckse verursachen*) ■ **[mit etw** *dat*] ~ to make a mess [with sth] ❷ *haben* (*tropfen*) to blot; *Farbe* to drip ❸ *sein* (*tropfen*) ■ **etw kleckst irgendwohin** sth is spilling on[to] sth **II.** *vt haben* ■ **etw auf etw ~** to splatter sth on sth
Klee <-s> [kleː] *m kein pl* clover
Kleeblatt *nt* cloverleaf; **vierblättriges ~** four-leaf clover
Kleid <-[e]s, -er> [klait, *pl* 'klai·dɐ] *nt* ❶ (*Damenkleid*) dress ❷ *pl* (*Bekleidungsstücke*) clothes *npl*
kleiden ['klai·dn̩] **I.** *vt, vr* ■ **[sich** *akk*] ~ to dress **II.** *vt* (*geh*) **etw in schöne Worte ~** to couch sth in fancy rhetoric [*or* language]
Kleiderbügel *m* coat hanger
Kleiderbürste *f* clothes brush
Kleiderhaken *m* coat hook
Kleiderschrank *m* clothes closet
Kleidung <-, -en> *f pl selten* clothing
Kleidungsstück *nt* garment
klein [klain] **I.** *adj* small, little **II.** *adv*

K

~ **gedruckt** *attr* in small print *pred;* **etw ~ hacken** to chop up *sep* sth ▶WENDUNGEN: **~ anfangen** (*fam: ganz unten beginnen*) to start at the bottom; (*mit ganz wenig beginnen*) to start [off] small; **~ beigeben** to give in [quietly]; **von ~ auf** from childhood

Kleinasien [klain·ˈʔaːzi̯·ən] *nt* Asia Minor

Kleinbuchstabe *m* small [*or* lower-case] letter

Kleingedruckte(s) *nt* fine print

kleingeistig *adj* (*pej*) small-minded

Kleingeld *nt* [small [*or* loose]] change

Kleinholz *nt kein pl* chopped wood ▶WENDUNGEN: **aus jdm/etw ~ machen** (*fam*) to make mincemeat [out] of sb/sth

Kleinigkeit <-, -en> [ˈklai·nɪç·kait] *f* ❶ (*Bagatelle*) small matter; **wegen jeder ~** for the slightest reason, at every opportunity ❷ (*Einzelheit*) minor detail; **muss ich mich um jede ~ kümmern?** do I have to do every little thing myself? ❸ (*ein wenig*) **eine ~ zu hoch/tief** a little too high/low ❹ (*Sache*) little something; **ich habe dir eine ~ mitgebracht** I brought you a little something; **eine ~ essen** to have a bite to eat ▶WENDUNGEN: **[jdn] eine ~ kosten** (*iron*) to cost [sb] a pretty penny

kleinkariert I. *adj* ❶ (*mit kleinen Karos*) finely checkered ❷ (*fam: engstirnig*) narrow-minded II. *adv* in a narrow-minded way

Kleinkind *nt* toddler

Kleinkram *m* (*fam*) ❶ (*Zeug*) odds and ends ❷ (*Trivialitäten*) trivialities *pl*

Kleinkrämerei <-> [klain·krɛː·mə·ˈrai] *f kein pl* (*pej*) tinkering around [at] the edges

Kleinkrieg *m* running battle

klein|kriegen *vt* (*fam*) ❶ (*kaputtmachen*) to smash ❷ (*gefügig machen*) ■**jdn ~** to bring sb into line

Kleinkriminelle(r) *f(m)* petty criminal

kleinlaut I. *adj* sheepish; (*gefügig*) subdued II. *adv* sheepishly; **~ fragen** to ask meekly; **etw ~ gestehen** to shamefacedly admit sth

kleinlich [ˈklain·lɪç] *adj* (*pej*) ❶ (*knauserig*) mean ❷ (*engstirnig*) petty

Kleinlichkeit <-> *f kein pl* (*pej*) ❶ (*Knauserigkeit*) meanness ❷ (*Engstirnigkeit*) pettiness

klein|schreibenRR *irreg vt* ■**ein Wort ~** to begin a word with a lower-case letter

Kleinstadt *f* small town

kleinstädtisch *adj* small-town *attr;* (*pej*) provincial

Kleinwagen *m* small [*or* compact] car

kleinwüchsig *adj* short, of small stature *pred*

Klemme <-, -n> [ˈklɛ·mə] *f* ❶ (*Haarklammer*) [hair] clip ❷ (*fam: schwierige Lage*) jam; **in der ~ sitzen** to be in a jam

klemmen [ˈklɛ·mən] I. *vt* to stick II. *vr* **sich** *dat* **den Finger in der Tür ~** to get one's finger caught in the door ▶WENDUNGEN: **sich** *akk* **hinter etw ~** to get on sth; **ich werde mich mal hinter die Sache ~** I'll get on it III. *vi* ❶ (*blockieren*) to jam ❷ (*angeheftet sein*) to be stuck

Klempner(in) <-s, -> [ˈklɛmp·nɐ] *m(f)* plumber

Klempnerei <-, -en> [ˈklɛmp·nə·ˈrai] *f* plumbery

Klempnerin <-, -nen> *f fem form von* **Klempner**

Klerus <-> [ˈkleː·rʊs] *m kein pl* clergy

Klette <-, -n> [ˈklɛ·tə] *f* ❶ (*Pflanze*) burdock ❷ (*pej fam: anhänglicher Mensch*) nuisance; **an jdm wie eine ~ hängen** (*fam*) to stick to sb like glue

klettern [ˈklɛ·tɐn] *vi sein* to climb; **auf einen Baum ~** to climb a tree; **aus einem/in ein Auto ~** to climb out of/into a car

KlettverschlussRR *m* Velcro® fastener

klicken [klɪ·kn̩] *vi* to click

Klient(in) <-en, -en> [kli·ˈɛnt] *m(f)* client

Klientel <-, -en> [kli·ɛn·ˈteːl] *f* clientele + *sing/pl vb*

Klientin <-, -nen> *f fem form von* **Klient**

Klima <-s, Klimata> [ˈkliː·ma] *nt* climate

Klimaanlage *f* air-conditioning

Klimakatastrophe *f kein pl* climate[-related] disaster

Klimaschutz *m* climate protection

klimatisch [kli·ˈmaː·tɪʃ] I. *adj attr* climatic II. *adv* climatically

klimatisiert *adj* air-conditioned

Klimaveränderung *f*, **Klimawechsel** *m* climate change

Klimazone *f* climatic zone

klimpern [ˈklɪm·pɐn] *vi Münzen* to jingle; *Schlüssel* to jangle; ■**auf etw** *dat* **~** to pluck away on sth *fam*

Klinge <-, -n> [ˈklɪŋə] *f* blade; (*Rasierklinge*) [razor] blade

Klingel <-, -n> [ˈklɪŋl̩] *f* bell

klingeln [ˈklɪŋl̩n] *vi* to ring; **an der Tür ~** to ring the doorbell; ■**[nach] jdm ~** to ring for sb ▶WENDUNGEN: **hat es jetzt endlich geklingelt?** do you get it, finally?

Klingelzeichen *nt* ring

klingen <klang, geklungen> [ˈklɪŋən] *vi* ❶ (*erklingen*) *Glas* to clink; *Glocke* to ring ❷ (*sich anhören*) to sound; **das klingt gut/interessant** that sounds good/interesting

Klinik <-, -en> [ˈkliː·nɪk] *f* clinic

klinisch [ˈkliː·nɪʃ] I. *adj* clinical II. *adv* clinically

Klinke <-, -n> [ˈklɪn·kə] *f* [door] handle

Klippe <-, -n> [ˈklɪ·pə] *f* (*Felsklippe*) cliff; (*im Meer*) [coastal] rock

klirren [ˈklɪ·rən] *vi* ❶ *Gläser* to tinkle; *Fensterscheiben* to rattle ❷ *Lautsprecher, Mikrophon* to crackle ❸ *Ketten, Sporen* to jangle; *Waffen* to clash

Klischee <-s, -s> [kli·ˈʃeː] *nt* stereotype, cliché

Klitoris <-, - *o* Klitorides> [ˈkliː·to·rɪs, *pl* kli·ˈtoː·ri·deːs] *f* clitoris

klitschnassRR [ˈklɪtʃ·ˈnas] *adj* (*fam*) *s.* **klatschnass**

klitzeklein [ˈklɪtsə·ˈklain] *adj* (*fam*) teeny-weeny, itsy-bitsy

Klo <-s, -s> [kloː] *nt* (*fam*) john

Kloake <-, -n> [klo·ˈaː·kə] *f* (*a. fig*) cesspool
klobig [ˈkloː·bɪç] *adj* bulky; *Hände* massive
Klobrille *f* (*fam*) toilet seat
Klobürste *f* (*fam*) toilet brush
Klodeckel *m* (*fam*) toilet lid
Klon <-s, -e> [kloːn] *m* clone
klonen [ˈkloː·nən] *vt* to clone
klönen [ˈkløː·nən] *vi* (*fam*) ■[**mit jdm**] ~ to chat [with sb]
Klopapier *nt* (*fam*) toilet paper
klopfen [ˈklɔp·fn̩] **I.** *vi* to knock (**auf** +*akk* on, **gegen** +*akk* against); ■**jdm auf etw** ~ (*mit der flachen Hand*) to pat sb on sth; (*mit dem Finger*) to tap sb on sth **II.** *vt Teppich, Fleisch* to beat
Klopfzeichen *nt* knock
Kloppe [ˈklɔ·pə] *f* DIAL (*fam*) ►WENDUNGEN: [**von jdm**] ~ **kriegen** NORDD to get a walloping [from sb]
kloppen [ˈklɔ·pn̩] *vr* DIAL (*fam*) ■**sich** *akk* [**mit jdm**] ~ to fight [with sb]
Klopperei <-, -en> [klɔ·pə·ˈrai] *f* NORDD (*fam*) fight; (*mit mehreren Personen a.*) brawl
Klops <-es, -e> [klɔps] *m* ❶ (*Fleischkloß*) meatball ❷ (*fam: Schnitzer*) blunder
Klosett <-s, -e *o* -s> [klo·ˈzɛt] *nt* (*veraltend*) privy *old*
Kloß <-es, Klöße> [kloːs, *pl* ˈkløː·sə] *m* dumpling ►WENDUNGEN: **einen ~ im Hals haben** (*fam*) to have a lump in one's throat
Kloster <-s, Klöster> [ˈkloːs·tɐ, *pl* ˈkløːs·tɐ] *nt* (*Mönchskloster*) monastery; (*Nonnenkloster*) convent
Klotz <-es, Klötze> [klɔts, *pl* ˈklœtsə] *m* ❶ (*Holzklotz*) block [of wood] ❷ (*pej fam: hässliches Gebäude*) monstrosity ►WENDUNGEN: [**jdm**] **ein ~ am Bein sein** (*fam*) to be a heavy burden for sb
klotzen [ˈklɔ·tsən] *vi* (*fam*) ❶ (*hart arbeiten*) to slave away; (*schnell arbeiten*) to work like hell ❷ (*Mittel massiv einsetzen*) ■[**bei etw** *dat*] ~ to splurge [on sth]
Klub <-s, -s> [klʊp] *m* club
Kluft[1] <-, Klüfte> [klʊft, *pl* ˈklʏf·tə] *f* ❶ GEOG [deep] fissure ❷ (*scharfer Gegensatz*) gulf; **tiefe** ~ deep rift
Kluft[2] <-, -en> [klʊft] *f* DIAL (*hum*) uniform
klug <klüger, klügste> [kluːk] **I.** *adj* smart, clever; (*vernünftig*) wise; *Entscheidung* prudent; *Rat* sound; **es wäre klüger, ...** it would be more sensible ...; **da soll einer draus ~ werden** I can't make heads or tails of it; **genauso ~ wie zuvor sein** to be none the wiser **II.** *adv* (*a. iron*) cleverly
klugerweise *adv* [very] cleverly
Klugheit <-, -en> [ˈkluːk·hait] *f kein pl* intelligence, cleverness; (*Vernunft*) wisdom
Klugscheißer(in) <-s, -> *m(f)* (*sl*) smart-ass
klügste(r, s) *adj superl von* **klug**
klumpen [ˈklʊm·pn̩] *vi* to get lumpy; *Salz* to cake
Klumpen <-s, -> [ˈklʊm·pn̩] *m* lump; ~ **bilden** to get lumpy
klumpig [ˈklʊm·pɪç] *adj* lumpy
Klüngel <-s, -> [ˈklʏŋ|] *m* (*pej fam*) clique
km [kaː·ˈɛm] *m Abk von* **Kilometer** km
km/h [kaː·ɛm·ˈhaː] *m Abk von* **Kilometer pro Stunde** kmph
knabbern [ˈkna·bɐn] **I.** *vi* ■**an etw** *dat* ~ ❶ (*knabbernd verzehren*) to nibble on sth ❷ (*geistig/emotional verarbeiten*) to chew on sth **II.** *vt* to nibble; **etwas zum K~** something to nibble on
Knabe <-n, -n> [ˈknaː·bə] *m* (*veraltend geh*) boy; **na, alter ~!** (*fam*) hey, dude! *sl*
Knäckebrot *nt* crispbread
knacken [kna·kn̩] **I.** *vt* to crack **II.** *vi* ❶ (*Knacklaut von sich geben*) to crack; *Diele* to creak; *Zweige* to snap ❷ (*fam: schlafen*) **eine Runde ~** to catch forty winks
Knacker <-s, -> *m* DIAL (*fam*) guy; **ein alter ~** an old geezer
Knacki <-s, -s> [ˈkna·ki] *m* (*sl*) ex-con
knackig [ˈkna·kɪç] **I.** *adj* ❶ *Gemüse, Obst* crisp ❷ (*fam: drall*) well-formed ❸ (*fam: zünftig*) real; *Typ* natural **II.** *adv* (*fam*) really; **sie kam ~ braun aus dem Urlaub wieder** she came back from vacation really tan
Knackpunkt *m* (*fam*) crucial point
Knacks <-es, -e> [knaks] *m* ❶ (*Laut*) crack ❷ (*Schaden*) problem; **einen ~ haben** *Ehe* to be in trouble; *Freundschaft* to be suffering; *Mensch* to have a screw loose
Knackwurst *f* knockwurst *spec*
Knall <-[e]s, -e> [knal] *m* bang; *vom Korken* pop; *einer Tür* bang ►WENDUNGEN: **~ auf Fall** (*fam*) all of a sudden; **einen ~ haben** (*fam*) to be off one's rocker
knallen [ˈknalən] **I.** *vi* ❶ *haben* (*ertönen*) to bang; *Auspuff* to backfire; *Feuerwerkskörper* to [go] bang; *Korken* to [go] pop; *Schuss* to ring out; **mit der Peitsche ~** to crack the whip; **mit der Tür ~** to slam the door [shut] ❷ *sein* (*fam: stoßen*) ■**auf/gegen etw ~** to bang on/against sth **II.** *vi impers haben* ■**es knallt** there's a bang; **..., sonst knallt's!** (*fam: oder/und es gibt eine Ohrfeige!*) ... or/and I'll slap you!; (*oder/und ich schieße!*) ... or/and I'll shoot! **III.** *vt* (*werfen*) to slam ►WENDUNGEN: **jdm eine ~** (*fam*) to whack sb
knallhart [ˈknal·ˈhart] (*fam*) **I.** *adj* ❶ (*rücksichtslos*) really tough, [as] tough as nails *pred* ❷ *Schuss* fierce; *Schlag* crushing **II.** *adv* brutally; **~ verhandeln** to drive a hard bargain
knallig [ˈkna·lɪç] *adj* (*fam*) gaudy
Knallkopf *m*, **Knallkopp** *m* (*fam*) idiot
knallrot [ˈknal·ˈroːt] *adj* bright red
knapp [knap] **I.** *adj* ❶ (*gering*) meager; *Geld* tight; ■[**mit etw** *dat*] **~ sein** to be short [on sth] ❷ (*eng* [*sitzend*]) tight[-fitting]; ■[**jdm**] **zu ~ sein** to be too tight [for sb] ❸ (*noch genügend*) just enough; *Mehrheit, Sieg* narrow; *Ergebnis* close ❹ (*nicht ganz*) almost; **in einer ~en Stunde** in just under an hour ❺ (*gerafft*) succinct; **in wenigen ~en Worten** in a few brief words; **er gab ihr nur eine**

~e Antwort he replied rather tersely **II.** *adv* ① (*mäßig*) sparingly; **~ bemessen sein** to not be very generous; **seine Zeit ist ~ bemessen** he only has a limited amount of time ② (*nicht ganz*) almost; **~ eine Stunde** just under an hour ③ (*haarscharf*) narrowly

knạpp|halten *vt irreg* ■ **jdn** [**mit etw** *dat*] **~** to keep sb on a tight leash [with sth]

Knạppheit <-> *f kein pl* shortage (**an** + *dat* of)

Knarre <-, -n> ['kna·rə] *f* (*sl*) gun

knarren ['kna·rən] *vi* to creak

Knast <-[e]s, Knäste> [knast, *pl* 'knɛs·tə] *m* (*sl*) prison; ■ **im ~** in the slammer; **im ~ sitzen** to do time

Knatsch <-es> [kna:tʃ] *m kein pl* (*fam*) trouble

knatschig ['kna:·tʃɪç] *adj* (*fam: quengelig*) whiny *pej;* (*brummig*) grumpy

knattern ['kna·tɐn] *vi* to clatter; *Motorrad* to roar

Knäuel <-s, -> ['knɔ·yəl] *m o nt* ball

Knauf <-[e]s, Knäufe> [knauf, *pl* 'knɔy·fə] *m* knob

knauserig ['knau·zə·rɪç] *adj* (*pej fam*) stingy

knausern ['knau·zɐn] *vi* (*pej fam*) ■ [**mit etw** *dat*] **~** to be stingy [with sth]

knautschen ['knau·tʃn̩] **I.** *vi* to crease **II.** *vt* to crumple

Knebel <-s, -> ['kne:·bl̩] *m* gag

knebeln ['kne:·bl̩n] *vt* (*a. fig*) to gag

kneifen <kniff, gekniffen> ['knai·fn̩] **I.** *vt* to pinch; ■ **jdn in etw ~** to pinch sb's sth **II.** *vi* ① (*zwicken*) to pinch ② (*fam: zurückscheuen*) ■ [**vor etw** *dat*] **~** to chicken out [of sth]; ■ **vor jdm ~** to shy away from sb

Kneifzange *f* tweezers *npl*

Kneipe <-, -n> ['knai·pə] *f* (*fam*) bar

Kneipenbummel *m,* **Kneipentour** *f* bar hop

Kneipenwirt(in) *m(f)* barkeeper

Knete <-> ['kne:·tə] *f kein pl* ① (*sl: Geld*) bread ② (*fam*) *s.* **Knetgummi**

kneten ['kne:·tn̩] *vt* ① (*durchwalken*) to knead ② (*formen*) to model

Knetgummi *m o nt,* **Knetmasse** *f* Play-Doh®

Knick <-[e]s, -e *o* -s> [knɪk] *m* [sharp] bend; (*im Schlauch/Draht*) kink; **einen ~ machen** *Straße* to bend [sharply]

knicken ['knɪ·kn̩] *vt* ① (*falten*) to fold; **„nicht ~!"** "[please] do not bend!" ② (*brechen*) to snap

knickerig ['knɪ·kə·rɪç], **knickrig** ['knɪk·rɪç] *adj* DIAL (*knauserig*) penny-pinching, stingy

Knie <-s, -> [kni:, *pl* 'kni:ə] *nt* knee; [**vor jdm**] **auf die ~ fallen** (*geh*) to fall to one's knees [before sb]; **jdm zittern die ~** sb's knees are shaking; (*aus Angst*) sb's knees are knocking ▶ WENDUNGEN: **weiche ~ bekommen** (*fam*) to go weak at the knees; **etw übers ~ brechen** (*fam*) to rush into sth; **in die ~ gehen** to give in

Kniebeuge *f* knee bend

Kniegelenk *nt* knee joint

Kniekehle *f* back of the knee

knien [kni:n] **I.** *vi* to kneel **II.** *vr* ■ **sich** *akk* **~** ① (*auf die Knie gehen*) to kneel [down] (**auf** + *akk* on) ② (*fam: sich intensiv beschäftigen*) ■ **sich** *akk* **in etw** *akk* **~** to get down to sth

Knies <-> [kni:s] *m kein pl* DIAL (*Knatsch*) fight, argument; (*schwächer*) spat *fam*

Kniescheibe *f* kneecap

Knieschützer *m* kneepad

Kniestrumpf *m* knee sock

kniff [knɪf] *imp von* **kneifen**

Kniff <-[e]s, -e> [knɪf] *m* ① (*Kunstgriff*) trick ② (*Falte*) fold; (*unabsichtlich a.*) crease

kniffelig ['knɪ·fə·lɪç], **knifflig** ['knɪf·lɪç] *adj* (*fam*) tricky

Knilch <-s, -e> [knɪlç] *m* (*pej sl: Scheißkerl*) bastard *vulg;* (*Niete*) loser *fam*

knipsen ['knɪp·sn̩] **I.** *vt* ① (*fam: fotografieren*) ■ **jdn/etw ~** to take a picture of sb/sth ② (*lochen*) to punch **II.** *vi* (*fam*) to take pictures; (*wild drauflos*) to snap away

Knirps <-es, -e> [knɪrps] *m* ① (*fam: kleiner Junge*) little guy ② (*Faltschirm*) folding umbrella

knirschen ['knɪ·rʃn̩] *vi* to crunch; *Getriebe* to grind

knistern ['knɪs·tɐn] *vi Feuer* to crackle; *Papier* to rustle; ■ **mit etw** *dat* **~** to rustle sth

knittern ['knɪ·tɐn] *vi, vt* to crease

knobeln ['kno:·bl̩n] *vi* ① (*würfeln*) to play dice ② (*nachgrübeln*) ■ [**an etw** *dat*] **~** to puzzle [over sth]

Knoblauch <-[e]s> *m kein pl* garlic

Knoblauchzehe *f* clove of garlic

Knöchel <-s, -> ['knœ·çl̩] *m* ① (*Fußknöchel*) ankle ② (*Fingerknöchel*) knuckle

Knochen <-s, -> ['knɔ·xn̩] *m* bone ▶ WENDUNGEN: **bis auf die ~ abgemagert sein** to be all skin and bone[s]; **bis auf die ~ nass werden** to get soaked to the bone

Knọchenarbeit *f* (*fam*) backbreaking work

Knọchenbruch *m* fracture

Knọchengerüst *nt* skeleton

Knọchenmark *nt* bone marrow

knochentrocken ['knɔ·xn̩·'trɔ·kn̩] *adj* (*fam*) bone dry; *Humor, Bemerkung* wry

knochig ['knɔ·xɪç] *adj* bony

Knödel <-s, -> ['knø:·dl̩] *m* SÜDD, ÖSTERR dumpling

> The **Knödel**, a southern German and Austrian specialty, is a small dumpling made with a variety of ingredients. They are cooked in hot water and served with meat dishes. *Kartoffelknödel* (potato dumplings) and *Semmelknödel* (bread dumplings) are particularly common in the south.

Knöllchen <-s, -> ['knœl·çən] *nt* (*fam*) [parking] ticket

Knolle <-, -n> ['knɔ·lə] *f* ① BOT nodule; *der Kartoffel* tuber ② (*fam: dicke Nase*) bulbous nose

Knollengemüse *nt kein pl* root vegetables
Knopf <-[e]s, Knöpfe> [knɔpf, *pl* knœp·fə] *m* ❶ (*an Kleidung*) button ❷ (*an Geräten*) [push]button
knöpfen ['knœp·fn̩] *vt* to button
Knopfloch *nt* buttonhole
Knorpel <-s, -> ['knɔr·pl̩] *m* ANAT cartilage; KOCHK gristle
knorpelig ['knɔr·pə·lɪç], **knorplig** ['knɔrp·lɪç] *adj* ANAT cartilaginous *spec;* KOCHK gristly
knorrig ['knɔ·rɪç] *adj* gnarled
Knospe <-, -n> ['knɔs·pə] *f* bud; **~n treiben** to bud
knospen *vi* to bud
knoten ['kno:·tn̩] *vt* to knot
Knoten <-s, -> ['kno:·tn̩] *m* ❶ (*Verschlingung*) knot ❷ MED lump ❸ (*Haarknoten*) bun
Knotenpunkt *m* AUTO, BAHN junction
knotig ['kno:·tɪç] *adj* ❶ (*Knoten aufweisend*) knotty; ■**~ sein** *Haar* to be full of knots ❷ (*knorrig*) *Baum, Holz, Finger* knotty, gnarled ❸ MED nodular
Know-how <-s> [no:·'hau] *nt kein pl* expertise, know-how
knuddeln ['knʊ·dl̩n] *vt* (*fam*) ■**jdn ~** to hug and kiss sb
knülle ['knʏ·lə] *adj* NORDD (*fam*) ■**~ sein** to be pie-eyed
knüllen ['knʏ·lən] **I.** *vt* to crumple [up *sep*] **II.** *vi* to crumple
Knüller <-s, -> ['knʏ·lɐ] *m* (*fam*) sensation; (*Nachricht*) scoop
knüpfen ['knʏp·fn̩] **I.** *vt* ❶ (*verknoten*) to tie; *Netz* to mesh; *Teppich* to knot ❷ (*gedanklich verbinden*) **eine Bedingung an etw ~** to attach a condition to sth; **Hoffnungen an etw ~** to pin hopes on sth **II.** *vr* ■**sich** *akk* **an etw** *akk* **~** to be linked with sth
Knüppel <-s, -> ['knʏ·pl̩] *m* cudgel, club; (*Polizeiknüppel*) nightstick
knüppeldick ['knʏ·pl̩·'dɪk] *adv* (*fam*) excessively; **~ auftragen** to lay it on thick
knurren ['knʊ·rən] *vi, vt* to growl; (*wütend*) to snarl
knurrig ['knʊ·rɪç] *adj* grumpy
knusperig ['knʊs·pə·rɪç], **knusprig** ['knʊs·prɪç] *adj Brot, Braten* crisp[y]; *Brot a.* crusty; *Gebäck, Nüsse* crunchy
knutschen ['knu:·tʃn̩] (*fam*) **I.** *vt* to kiss **II.** *vi* ■**[mit jdm] ~** to smooch [with sb]
Knutschfleck *m* (*fam*) love bite, hickey
Koala <-s, -s> [ko·'a:la] *m,* **Koalabär** [ko·'a:·la-] *m* koala [bear]
koalieren* [ko·ʔa'li:·rən] *vi* ■**[mit jdm] ~** to form a coalition [with sb]
Koalition <-, -en> [ko·ʔali·'tsi̯o:n] *f* coalition
Kobold <-[e]s, -e> ['ko:·bɔlt, *pl* 'ko:·bɔl·də] *m* imp, goblin
Koch, Köchin <-s, Köche> [kɔx, 'kœ·çɪn, *pl* 'kœ·çə] *m, f* cook; (*Küchenchef*) chef
Kochbuch *nt* cookbook
kochen ['kɔ·xn̩] **I.** *vi* ❶ (*Speisen zubereiten*) to cook ❷ (*brodeln*) to boil; **etw zum K~ bringen** to bring sth to a boil; **~d heiß** boiling hot ❸ (*in Aufruhr sein*) to seethe; **vor Wut ~** to seethe with rage **II.** *vt* ❶ (*zubereiten*) to cook; **Kaffee/Suppe ~** to make coffee/soup ❷ *Wäsche* to wash hot
Kocher <-s, -> ['kɔ·xɐ] *m* cooker
Köchin <-, -nen> ['kœ·çɪn] *f fem form von* **Koch**
Kochkunst *f kein pl* art of cooking
Kochlöffel *m* wooden spoon
Kochnische *f* kitchenette
Kochplatte *f* ❶ (*Herdplatte*) hotplate ❷ (*transportabler Kocher*) small [electric] stove
Kochrezept *nt* recipe
Kochtopf *m* [cooking] pot; (*mit Stiel*) saucepan
Kochwäsche *f* laundry that can be washed in boiling-hot water
Kode <-s, -s> [ko:t] *m* code
Köder <-s, -> ['kø:·dɐ] *m* bait
ködern ['kø:·dɐn] *vt* to lure; **sich** *akk* **von jdm/etw ~ lassen** to be tempted by sb/sth
Kodierung <-, -en> *f* coding
Koexistenz ['ko·ʔɛksɪs·tɛnts] *f kein pl* coexistence
Koffein <-s> [kɔ·fe·'i:n] *nt kein pl* caffeine
koffeinfrei *adj* decaffeinated
koffeinhaltig *adj* containing caffeine *pred*
Koffer <-s, -> ['kɔ·fɐ] *m* suitcase
Kofferradio *nt* portable radio
Kofferraum *m* trunk
Kognak <-s, -s *o* -e> ['kɔn·jak] *m* brandy
kohärent [ko·hɛ·'rɛnt] *adj* coherent
Kohl <-[e]s, -e> [ko:l] *m* cabbage
Kohldampf *m* (*fam*) ■**~ haben** to be starving
Kohle <-, -n> ['ko:·lə] *f* ❶ (*Brennstoff*) coal ❷ (*sl: Geld*) dough *no indef art* ▶ WENDUNGEN: **wie auf [glühenden] ~n sitzen** to be on tenterhooks
Kohlehydrat <-[e]s, -e> *nt s.* **Kohlenhydrat**
Kohlekraftwerk *nt* coal-fired power plant
Kohlendioxid *nt kein pl* carbon dioxide
Kohlengrube *f* coal mine
Kohlenhydrat <-[e]s, -e> *nt* carbohydrate
Kohlenmonoxid *nt kein pl* carbon monoxide
Kohlenpott *m* (*fam*) ■**der ~** the Ruhr [area]
Kohlensäure *f* carbonic acid; **mit ~** carbonated; **ohne ~** noncarbonated
kohlensäurehaltig *adj* carbonated
Kohleofen *m* [coal-burning] stove
Kohlkopf *m* [head of] cabbage
kohlrabenschwarz ['ko:l·'ra:·bn̩·'ʃvarts] *adj* jet-black
Kohlrabi <-[s], -[s]> [ko:l·'ra:·bi] *m* kohlrabi
Kohlroulade [-ru·la:·də] *f* stuffed cabbage
Koitus <-, - *o* -se> ['ko:i·tʊs] *m* coitus
Koje <-, -n> ['ko:·jə] *f* ❶ NAUT bunk ❷ (*fam: Bett*) bed; **sich** *akk* **in die ~ hauen** to hit the sack
Kojote <-n, -n> [ko·'jo:·tə] *m* coyote
Kokain <-s> [ko·ka·'i:n] *nt kein pl* cocaine
kokainsüchtig *adj* addicted to cocaine *pred*
kokeln ['ko:·kl̩n] *vi* (*fam*) to play with fire
kokett [ko·'kɛt] **I.** *adj* flirtatious **II.** *adv* flirta-

tiously
kokettieren* [ko·kɛ·'ti:·rən] *vi* ① (*flirten*) to flirt ② (*geh: liebäugeln*) **mit einem Gedanken ~** to toy with an idea
Kokolores <-> [ko·ko·'lo:·rɛs] *m kein pl* (*fam*) nonsense
Kokosmilch *f* coconut milk
KokosnussRR *f* coconut
Koks[1] <-es, -e> [ko:ks] *m* ① (*Brennstoff*) coke ② *kein pl* (*sl: Geld*) dough *no indef art*
Koks[2] <-es> [ko:ks] *m o nt kein pl* (*sl: Kokain*) coke *fam*
koksen ['ko:k·sn̩] *vi* (*sl*) to snort [*or* do] coke
Kolben <-s, -> ['kɔl·bn̩] *m* ① AUTO piston ② (*Gewehrkolben*) butt ③ CHEM retort ④ (*Maiskolben*) cob
Kolbenstange *f* piston rod
Kolibakterien ['ko:·li·bak·te:·ri̯·ən] *pl* coliform bacteria *pl spec*
Kolik <-, -en> ['ko:·lɪk] *f* colic
kollabieren* [kɔ·la·'bi:·rən] *vi sein* to collapse
Kollaborateur(in) <-s, -e> [kɔ·la·bo·ra·'tø:ɐ] *m(f)* collaborator
kollaborieren* [kɔ·la·bo·'ri:·rən] *vi* to collaborate
Kollaps <-es, -e> ['kɔ·laps] *m* collapse
Kollege, Kollegin <-n, -n> [kɔ·'le:·gə] *m, f* colleague
kollegial [kɔ·le·'gi̯a:l] **I.** *adj* considerate and friendly (*towards one's colleagues*) **II.** *adv* in a considerate and friendly way
Kollegialität <-> [kɔ·le·gi̯a·li·'tɛ:t] *f kein pl* friendly cooperation
Kollegin <-, -nen> *f fem form von* **Kollege**
Kollektion <-, -en> [kɔ·lɛk·'tsi̯o:n] *f* collection
Kollektiv <-s, -e> [kɔ·lɛk·'ti:f, *pl* -'ti:·və] *nt* collective
Koller <-s, -> ['kɔ·lɐ] *m* (*fam*) rage; **einen ~ bekommen** to fly into a rage
kollidieren* [kɔ·li·'di:·rən] *vi* ① *sein* (*zusammenstoßen*) to collide ② *sein o haben* (*unvereinbar sein*) to clash
Kollier <-s, -s> [kɔ·'li̯e:] *nt* necklace
Kollision <-, -en> [kɔ·li·'zi̯o:n] *f* collision
Kolloquium <-s, -ien> [kɔ·'lo:·kvi·ʊm, *pl* -kvi·ən] *nt* ÖSTERR (*kleinere Prüfung*) test
Köln <-s> [kœln] *nt* Cologne
Kölnischwasser, Kölnisch Wasser ['kœl·nɪʃ·va·sɐ] *nt* [eau de] cologne
kolonial [ko·lo·'ni̯a:l] *adj* colonial
Kolonie <-, -n> [ko·lo·'ni:, *pl* -'ni:·ən] *f* colony
Kolonisation <-, -en> [ko·lo·ni·za·'tsi̯o:n] *f* colonization
kolonisieren* [ko·lo·ni·'zi:·rən] *vt* ① (*zur Kolonie machen*) to colonize ② (*bevölkern*) ■**etw ~** to settle sth
Kolonne <-, -n> [ko·'lɔ·nə] *f* ① AUTO line [of traffic]; (*von Polizei*) convoy ② (*lange Reihe von Menschen*) column ③ (*eingeteilte Arbeitsgruppe*) gang
KolossRR <-es, -e>, **Koloß**ALT <-sses, -sse> [ko·'lɔs] *m* ① (*fam: riesiger Mensch*) colossus ② (*gewaltiges Gebilde*) colossal thing
kolossal [ko·lɔ·'sa:l] **I.** *adj* colossal; **eine ~e Dummheit begehen** to do sth incredibly stupid **II.** *adv* tremendously; **sich** *akk* **~ verschätzen** to make a huge miscalculation
Kolumbianer(in) <-s, -> [ko·lʊm·'bi̯a·nɐ] *m(f)* Colombian; *s. a.* **Deutsche(r)**
kolumbianisch [ko·lʊm·'bi̯a·nɪʃ] *adj* Colombian; *s. a.* **deutsch**
Kolumbien <-s> [ko·'lʊm·bi̯·ən] *nt* Colombia; *s. a.* **Deutschland**
Kolumne <-, -n> [ko·'lʊm·nə] *f* column
Kolumnist(in) <-en, -en> [ko·lʊm·'nɪst] *m(f)* columnist
Koma <-s, -s *o* -ta> ['ko:·ma] *nt* coma
Kombi <-s, -s> ['kɔm·bi] *m* (*fam*) station wagon
Kombination <-, -en> [kɔm·bi·na·'tsi̯o:n] *f* ① (*Zusammenstellung, Zahlenkombination*) combination ② (*Schlussfolgerung*) conclusion ③ MODE outfit; (*Overall*) jumpsuit
Kombinationsgabe *f kein pl* powers *pl* of deduction
kombinieren* [kɔm·bi·'ni:·rən] **I.** *vt* to combine **II.** *vi* to deduce; **gut ~ können** to be good at deducing; **falsch/richtig ~** to come to the wrong/right conclusion
Komet <-en, -en> [ko·'me:t] *m* comet
Komfort <-s> [kɔm·'fo:ɐ̯] *m kein pl* comfort
komfortabel [kɔm·fɔr·'ta:·bl̩] *adj* ① (*großzügig ausgestattet*) luxurious ② (*bequem*) comfortable
Komik <-> ['ko:·mɪk] *f kein pl* comic
Komiker(in) <-s, -> ['ko:·mɪ·kɐ] *m(f)* comedian
komisch ['ko:·mɪʃ] **I.** *adj* ① (*zum Lachen reizend*) funny ② (*sonderbar*) strange; **etw kommt jdm ~ vor** (*eigenartig*) sth seems funny/strange to sb; (*suspekt*) sth seems fishy to sb; **sich** *akk* **~ fühlen** to feel funny **II.** *adv* (*eigenartig*) strangely
komischerweise *adv* (*fam*) strangely enough
Komitee <-s, -s> [ko·mi·'te:] *nt* committee
Komma <-s, -s *o* -ta> ['kɔ·ma, *pl* -ta] *nt* ① (*Satzzeichen*) comma ② MATH [decimal] point
kommandieren* [kɔ·man·'di:·rən] **I.** *vt* ① (*befehligen*) to command ② (*befehlen*) ■**jdn irgendwohin ~** to order sb somewhere **II.** *vi* ① (*befehlen*) to be in command ② (*fam: Anweisungen erteilen*) ■**[gern] ~** [to like] to give [the] orders
Kommando <-s, -s> [kɔ·'man·do] *nt* ① (*Befehl, Befehlsgewalt*) command; **auf ~** on command; **das ~ haben** to be in command ② (*abkommandierte Gruppe*) commando
Kommata *pl von* **Komma**
kommen <kam, gekommen> ['kɔ·mən] **I.** *vi sein* ① (*eintreffen, hinkommen*) to come; **ich komme schon!** I'm coming!; **der Zug kommt aus Paris** the train is coming from Paris; **da kommt Anne/der Bus** there's Anne/the bus; **ist Post für mich gekom-**

K

men? was there any mail for me?; **wann soll das Baby ~?** when's the baby due?; **das Schlimmste kommt noch** the worst is yet to come; **als Erster/Letzter** ~ to be the first/last to arrive; **mit dem Auto/Fahrrad** ~ to come by car/bike; **zu Fuß** ~ to come on foot ❷ (*besuchen*) ■ **zu jdm** ~ to visit sb, to come and see sb ❸ (*gelangen*) ■ **irgendwohin** ~ to get somewhere; **wie komme ich von hier zum Bahnhof?** how do I get to the train station from here?; **zu Fuß kommt man am schnellsten dahin** the quickest way [to get] there is to walk; **ans Ziel** ~ to reach the finish line; **zu der Erkenntnis ~, dass ...** to realize that ...; **zu Geld** ~ to come into money; **zu Kräften** ~ to gain strength; **zu sich** *dat* ~ to regain consciousness ❹ (*gehen, fahren*) to come; **kommst du mit uns ins Kino?** are you coming to the movies with us?; **durch einen Ort/Tunnel** ~ to pass through a place/tunnel ❺ (*stammen*) ■ **irgendwoher** ~ to come from somewhere; **woher kommst du?** where are you from?; **ich komme aus Germersheim** I'm from Germersheim ❻ (*an der Reihe sein*) **jd kommt an die Reihe** it's sb's turn; **ich komme zuerst an die Reihe** I'm first; **wer kommt [jetzt]?** whose turn is it [now]? ❼ (*Aufenthalt beginnen*) **ins Gefängnis/Krankenhaus** ~ to go to prison/to be admitted to a hospital; **in die Schule/Lehre** ~ to start school/an apprenticeship ❽ **den Arzt/ein Taxi ~ lassen** to send for the doctor/a taxi ❾ (*herannahen*) to approach; (*eintreten, geschehen*) to come about; **das kam doch anders als erwartet** it/that turned out differently than expected; **es kam eins zum anderen** one thing led to another; **und so kam es, dass ...** and that's how it came about that ...; **wie kommt es, dass ...?** how come ...?; **es musste ja so** ~ it/that was bound to happen; **es hätte viel schlimmer ~ können** it could have been much worse; **was auch immer ~ mag** whatever happens; **so weit ~, dass ...** to get to the point where ... ❿ (*erfassen*) ■ **über jdn** ~ *Gefühl* to come over sb; **jdm ~ die Tränen** sb is starting to cry; **jdm ~ Zweifel, ob ...** sb doubts whether ... ⓫ (*geraten*) **wir kamen plötzlich ins Schleudern** we suddenly started to skid; **in Gefahr/Not** ~ to get into danger/difficulty; **in Verlegenheit** ~ to get embarrassed ⓬ (*Grund haben*) **das kommt davon, dass ...** that's because ...; **das kommt davon, wenn ...** that's what happens when ... ⓭ (*sich erinnern*) ■ **auf etw** *akk* ~ to remember sth ⓮ (*Idee haben*) ■ **auf etw** *akk* ~: **wie kommst du darauf?** what makes you think that? ⓯ ■ **hinter etw** *akk* ~ *Pläne* to find out *sep* sth; **hinter ein Geheimnis** ~ to uncover a secret ⓰ RADIO, TV (*gesendet werden*) to be on ⓱ (*Zeit finden*) ■ **zu etw** *dat* ~ to get around to doing sth ⓲ (*ansprechen*) **auf etw** *akk* **zu sprechen** ~ to get around to [talking about] sth; **ich werde gleich darauf** ~ I'll come to that in a second; **auf einen Punkt/eine Angelegenheit** ~ to broach a point/matter ⓳ (*sl: Orgasmus haben*) to come **II.** *vt sein* (*fam*) **die Reparatur kam mich sehr teuer** the repairs cost a lot [of money]

kommend *adj* ❶ (*nächste*) coming, next ❷ (*künftig*) future; **in den ~en Jahren** in the years to come

Kommentar <-s, -e> [kɔ·mɛn·ˈtaːɐ̯] *m* ❶ (*Stellungnahme*) statement; (*Meinung*) opinion; **einen ~ [zu etw** *dat*] **abgeben** to comment [on] sth; **kein ~!** no comment! ❷ (*kommentierendes Werk*) commentary

kommentarlos *adj* without comment *pred*

Kommentator(in) <-s, -toren> [kɔ·mɛn·ˈtaː·toːɐ̯, kɔ·mɛn·ta·ˈtoː·rɪn, *pl* -taˈtoːrən] *m(f)* commentator

kommentieren* [kɔ·mɛn·ˈtiː·rən] *vt* ❶ (*Stellung nehmen*) ■ **etw** ~ to comment on sth ❷ (*erläutern*) to annotate

kommerzialisieren [kɔ·mɛr·tsi̯a·li·ˈziː·rən] *vt* to commercialize

kommerziell [kɔ·mɛr·ˈtsi̯ɛl] **I.** *adj* commercial **II.** *adv* commercially

Kommissar(in) <-s, -e> [kɔ·mɪ·ˈsaːɐ̯] *m(f)* commissioner

Kommissär(in) <-s, -e> [kɔ·mɪ·ˈsɛɐ̯] *m(f)* ÖSTERR, SCHWEIZ inspector

Kommissariat <-[e]s, -e> [kɔ·mɪ·ˈsaː·ri̯aːt] *nt* ❶ (*Amtszimmer des Polizeikommissars*) commissioner's office ❷ ÖSTERR (*Polizeidienststelle*) police station

Kommissarin <-, -nen> *f fem form von* **Kommissar**

Kommissärin <-, -nen> *f fem form von* **Kommissär**

kommissarisch [kɔ·mɪ·ˈsaː·rɪʃ] **I.** *adj* temporary **II.** *adv* temporarily

Kommission <-, -en> [kɔ·mɪ·ˈsi̯oːn] *f* ❶ (*Gremium, Ausschuss*) committee ❷ (*EU-Kommission*) Commission ❸ (*Auftrag*) commission; **etw in ~ geben** to commission sb to sell sth

Kommode <-, -n> [kɔ·ˈmoː·də] *f* bureau, dresser

kommunal [kɔ·mu·ˈnaːl] *adj* municipal

Kommunalpolitik *f* local politics *pl*

Kommunalwahl *f* local [government] elections *pl*

Kommune <-, -n> [kɔ·ˈmuː·nə] *f* ❶ (*Gemeinde*) local authority ❷ (*Wohngemeinschaft*) commune

Kommunikation <-, -en> [kɔ·mu·ni·ka·ˈtsi̯oːn] *f* communication

Kommunikationsmittel *nt* means of communication + *sing vb*

Kommunikationsweg *m* channel of communication

Kommunion <-, -en> [kɔ·mu·ˈni̯oːn] *f* (*Sakrament der katholischen Kirche*) Holy Communion; (*Erstkommunion*) First Communion

Kommunismus <-> [kɔ·mu·ˈnɪs·mʊs] *m kein pl* communism

K

Kommunist(in) <-en, -en> [kɔ·mu·ˈnɪst] *m(f)* communist
kommunistisch [kɔ·mu·ˈnɪs·tɪʃ] *adj* communist
kommunizieren* [kɔ·mu·ni·ˈtsiː·rən] *vi* ❶ (*sich verständigen*) to communicate ❷ REL to receive/take Holy Communion
Komödie <-, -n> [ko·ˈmøː·di̯ə] *f* ❶ (*Bühnenstück*) comedy ❷ (*pej: Verstellung*) play-acting
Kompagnon <-s, -s> [ˈkɔm·pa·njɔŋ] *m* partner
kompakt [kɔm·ˈpakt] *adj* compact
Komparativ <-s, -e> [ˈkɔm·pa·ra·tiːf] *m* comparative
KompassRR <-es, -e>, **Kompaß**ALT <-sses, -sse> [ˈkɔm·pas] *m* compass
kompatibel [kɔm·pa·ˈtiː·bl̩] *adj* compatible
Kompatibilität <-, -en> [kɔm·pa·ti·bi·li·ˈtɛt] *f* compatibility
Kompensation <-, -en> [kɔm·pɛn·za·ˈtsi̯oːn] *f* compensation
kompensieren* [kɔm·pɛn·ˈziː·rən] *vt* to compensate
kompetent [kɔm·pe·ˈtɛnt] **I.** *adj* ❶ (*sachverständig*) competent ❷ (*zuständig*) responsible **II.** *adv* competently
Kompetenz <-, -en> [kɔm·pe·ˈtɛnts] *f* ❶ (*Befähigung*) competence ❷ (*Befugnis*) responsibility
komplett [kɔm·ˈplɛt] **I.** *adj* complete **II.** *adv* completely
komplex [kɔm·ˈplɛks] **I.** *adj* complex **II.** *adv* complexly, in a complicated manner *pred;* **~ aufgebaut sein** to have a complex structure
Komplex <-es, -e> [kɔm·ˈplɛks] *m* complex
Komplexität <-> [kɔm·plɛ·ksi·ˈtɛt] *f kein pl* (*geh*) complexity
Komplikation <-, -en> [kɔm·pli·ka·ˈtsi̯oːn] *f* complication
Kompliment <-[e]s, -e> [kɔm·pli·ˈmɛnt] *nt* compliment; **jdm ein ~ machen** to pay sb a compliment
Komplize, Komplizin <-n, -n> [kɔm·ˈpliː·tsə] *m, f* accomplice
komplizieren* [kɔm·pli·ˈtsiː·rən] **I.** *vt* to complicate **II.** *vr* ■ **sich** *akk* ~ to become complicated
kompliziert **I.** *adj* complicated **II.** *adv* in a complicated manner *pred*
Komplizin <-, -nen> *f fem form von* **Komplize**
Komplott <-[e]s, -e> [kɔm·ˈplɔt] *nt* plot
Komponente <-, -n> [kɔm·po·ˈnɛn·tə] *f* component
komponieren* [kɔm·po·ˈniː·rən] *vt, vi* to compose
Komponist(in) <-en, -en> [kɔm·po·ˈnɪst] *m(f)* composer
Kompositum <-s, Komposita> [kɔm·ˈpoː·zi·tʊm, *pl* kɔm·ˈpoː·zi·ta] *nt* compound
Kompost <-[e]s, -e> [kɔm·ˈpɔst] *m* compost
Komposthaufen *m* compost pile
kompostieren* [kɔm·pɔs·ˈtiː·rən] *vt* to compost
Kompott <-[e]s, -e> [kɔm·ˈpɔt] *nt* compote
komprimieren* [kɔm·pri·ˈmiː·rən] *vt* to compress
KompromissRR <-es, -e>, **Kompromiß**ALT <-sses, -sse> [kɔm·pro·ˈmɪs] *m* compromise; **fauler ~** false compromise
kompromissbereitRR *adj* willing to compromise *pred;* **eine ~e Haltung** a willingness to compromise
KompromissbereitschaftRR *f* willingness to compromise
kompromisslosRR *adj* ❶ (*zu keinem Kompromiss bereit*) uncompromising ❷ (*uneingeschränkt*) unqualified
KompromisslösungRR *f* compromise
kompromittieren* [kɔm·pro·mɪ·ˈtiː·rən] *vt* ■ **jdn ~** to compromise sb; ■ **sich** *akk* ~ to compromise oneself
kondensieren* [kɔn·dɛn·ˈziː·rən] *vi, vt sein o haben* to condense
Kondensmilch *f* condensed milk
Kondenswasser *nt kein pl* condensation
Kondition <-, -en> [kɔn·di·ˈtsi̯oːn] *f* ❶ (*Leistungsfähigkeit*) [physical] fitness; **[keine] ~ haben** to [not] be fit ❷ (*Bedingung*) condition
Konditionstraining *nt* fitness training
Konditor(in) <-s, -toren> [kɔn·ˈdiː·toːɐ̯, kɔn·di·ˈtoː·rɪn, *pl* -di·ˈtoː·rən] *m(f)* pastry chef, confectioner
Konditorei <-, -en> [kɔn·di·to·ˈrai] *f* pastry shop
Konditorin <-, -nen> *f fem form von* **Konditor**
Kondolenzschreiben *nt* letter of condolence
kondolieren* [kɔn·do·ˈliː·rən] *vi* (*geh*) ■ **[jdm]** ~ to pay one's condolences [to sb]
Kondom <-s, -e> [kɔn·ˈdoːm] *m o nt* condom
Kondor <-s, -e> [ˈkɔn·doːɐ̯] *m* condor
Konfekt <-[e]s, -e> [kɔn·ˈfɛkt] *nt* confections *pl*
Konfektion <-, -en> [kɔn·fɛk·ˈtsi̯oːn] *f pl selten* ready-made clothing
Konfektionsgröße *f* size
Konferenz <-, -en> [kɔn·fe·ˈrɛnts] *f* ❶ (*Besprechung*) conference ❷ (*Komitee*) committee
Konferenzsaal *m* conference hall
Konferenzschaltung *f* conference call function
Konfession <-, -en> [kɔn·fɛ·ˈsi̯oːn] *f* denomination
konfessionell [kɔn·fɛ·si̯o·ˈnɛl] **I.** *adj* denominational **II.** *adv* denominationally
konfessionslos *adj* not belonging to any denomination
Konfiguration <-, -en> [kɔn·fi·gu·ra·ˈtsi̯oːn] *f* COMPUT configuration
konfigurieren [kɔn·fi·gu·ˈriː·rən] *vt* COMPUT to configure
Konfirmand(in) <-en, -en> [kɔn·fɪr·ˈmant, *pl* -ˈman·dn̩] *m(f)* confirmand
Konfirmation <-, -en> [kɔn·fɪr·ma·ˈtsi̯oːn] *f* confirmation

konfirmieren* [kɔn·fɪr·ˈmiː·rən] *vt* to confirm
konfiszieren* [kɔn·fɪs·ˈtsiː·rən] *vt* to confiscate
Konfitüre <-, -n> [kɔn·fi·ˈtyː·rə] *f* jam, preserves *pl*
Konflikt <-s, -e> [kɔn·ˈflɪkt] *m* conflict
Konflịktherd *m* area of conflict
Konflịktlösung *f* solution to a conflict
Konflịktstoff *m* cause of conflict
Konföderation <-, -en> [kɔn·fø·de·ra·ˈtsi̯oːn] *f* confederation
konform [kɔn·ˈfɔrm] *adj* concurrent; **mit jdm [in etw** *dat*] **~ gehen** to agree with sb [on sth]
konformịstisch *adj* conformist
Konfrontation <-, -en> [kɔn·frɔn·ta·ˈtsi̯oːn] *f* confrontation
Konfrontationskurs *m* confrontational course
konfrontieren* [kɔn·frɔn·ˈtiː·rən] *vt* to confront
konfus [kɔn·ˈfuːs] **I.** *adj* confused **II.** *adv* confusedly
Konfusion <-, -en> [kɔn·fu·ˈzi̯oːn] *f* confusion
KongressRR <-es, -e>, **Kongreß**ALT <-sses, -sse> [kɔn·ˈgrɛs] *m* ❶ (*Fachtagung*) congress ❷ (*Parlament der USA*) ■ **der ~** Congress
KongrẹsshalleRR *f* conference hall

K

König <-s, -e> [ˈkøː·nɪç] *m* king
Königin <-, -nen> [ˈkøː·nɪ·gɪn] *f fem form von* **König** queen
königlich [ˈkøː·nɪk·lɪç] **I.** *adj* ❶ (*dem König gehörend*) royal ❷ (*großzügig*) handsome **II.** *adv* ❶ (*fam: köstlich*) ■ **sich** *akk* **~ amüsieren** to have a whale of a time ❷ (*großzügig*) handsomely
Königreich [ˈkøː·nɪk·raiç] *nt* kingdom
königstreu *adj* loyal to the king *pred*
Königtum <-, -tümer> [ˈkøː·nɪç·tuːm] *nt* ❶ *kein pl* (*Monarchie*) monarchy ❷ (*veraltend*) *s.* **Königreich**
Konjugation <-, -en> [kɔn·ju·ga·ˈtsi̯oːn] *f* conjugation
konjugieren* [kɔn·ju·ˈgiː·rən] *vt* to conjugate
Konjunktur <-, -en> [kɔn·jʊnk·ˈtuːɐ̯] *f* state of the economy; **steigende/rückläufige ~** [economic] boom/slump
konjunkturell [kɔn·jʊŋk·tu·ˈrɛl] *adj* economic
Konjunkturlage *f* state of the economy
Konjunkturpolitik *f* economic policy
konkret [kɔn·ˈkreːt] **I.** *adj* concrete **II.** *adv* specifically; **das kann ich Ihnen noch nicht ~ sagen** I can't tell you for sure yet
konkretisieren* [kɔn·kre·ti·ˈziː·rən] *vt* to clearly define
Konkurrent(in) <-en, -en> [kɔn·kʊ·ˈrɛnt] *m(f)* competitor
Konkurrenz <-, -en> [kɔn·kʊ·ˈrɛnts] *f* ❶ (*Konkurrent*) competitor; **keine ~ [für jdn] sein** to be no competition [for sb] ❷ *kein pl* (*Wettbewerb*) competition; **mit jdm in ~ stehen** to be in competition with sb; **außer ~** unofficially
konkurrẹnzfähig *adj* competitive
Konkurrẹnzkampf *m* competition; (*zwischen Menschen*) rivalry
konkurrẹnzlos **I.** *adj* ■ **~ sein** to have no competition **II.** *adv* incomparably; **mit unseren Preisen sind wir ~ billig** nobody can match our low prices
konkurrieren* [kɔn·kʊ·ˈriː·rən] *vi* to compete
Konkurs <-es, -e> [kɔn·ˈkʊrs] *m* bankruptcy; **~ machen** (*fam*) to go bankrupt; **~ anmelden** to declare oneself bankrupt
Konkụrsverfahren *nt* bankruptcy proceedings *pl*
können [ˈkœ·nən] **I.** *vt* <kạnn, kọnnte, gekọnnt> ❶ (*beherrschen*) ■ **etw ~** to know sth; **eine Sprache ~** to speak a language ❷ (*verantwortlich sein*) **etwas/nichts für etw** *akk* **~** to be able/to not be able to do anything about sth ▶ WENDUNGEN: **du kannst mich mal** (*euph sl*) kiss my ass! *vulg*, fuck off! *vulg* **II.** *vi* <kạnn, kọnnte, gekọnnt> to be able; **nicht mehr ~** (*erschöpft sein*) to not be able to go on; (*überfordert sein*) to have had enough; (*satt sein*) to be full; **noch ~** (*weitermachen können*) to be able to continue; (*weiteressen können*) to be able to eat more; **wie konntest du nur!** how could you?! **III.** *modal vb* <kạnn, kọnnte, kọnnen> ❶ (*fähig sein*) ■ **etw tun ~** to be able to do sth ❷ (*dürfen*) **kann ich das Foto sehen?** can I see the picture? ❸ (*möglicherweise sein*) **solche Dinge ~ eben manchmal passieren** these things [can] happen sometimes; **[ja,] kann sein** [yes,] that's possible; **könnte es nicht sein, dass ...?** could it be that ...?
Können <-s> [ˈkœ·nən] *nt kein pl* ability
konnte [ˈkɔn·tə] *imp von* **können**
Konsens <-es, -e> [kɔn·ˈzɛns] *m* (*geh*) consensus
konsequent [kɔn·ze·ˈkvɛnt] **I.** *adj* consistent; ■ **~ sein** to be consistent (**bei/in** +*dat* in) **II.** *adv* consistently
Konsequenz <-, -en> [kɔn·ze·ˈkvɛnts] *f* ❶ (*Folge*) consequence; **~en [für jdn] haben** to have consequences [for sb]; **die ~en tragen** to take the consequences ❷ *kein pl* (*Unbeirrbarkeit*) consistency
konservativ [kɔn·zɛr·va·ˈtiːf] **I.** *adj* conservative **II.** *adv* **~ eingestellt sein** to have a conservative attitude
Konserve <-, -n> [kɔn·ˈzɛr·və] *f* preserved food
Konservenbüchse [kɔn·ˈzɛr·vən-] *f*, **Konservendose** *f* can
konservieren* [kɔn·zɛr·ˈviː·rən] *vt* to preserve
Konservierung <-, -en> [kɔn·zɛr·ˈviː·rʊŋ] *f* preservation
Konservierungsmittel *nt* preservative
Konsistenz <-> [kɔn·zɪs·ˈtɛnts] *f kein pl* (*geh*) consistency
Konsole <-, -n> [kɔn·ˈzoː·lə] *f* ❶ (*Bord*) shelf ❷ (*Bedienerkonsole*) console
Konsonant <-en, -en> [kɔn·zo·ˈnant] *m* consonant
Konsorten [kɔn·ˈzɔr·tn̩] *pl* (*pej*) **Miller und ~**

Miller and his gang
Konsortium <-s, -ien> [kɔn·ˈzɔr·tsi·ʊm, *pl* -ˈzɔr·tsi·ən] *nt* consortium
konspirativ [kɔn·spi·ra·ˈtiːf] *adj* (*geh*) conspiratorial
konstant [kɔn·ˈstant] **I.** *adj* constant **II.** *adv* constantly
Konstante <-[n], -n> [kɔn·ˈstan·tə] *f* constant
Konstellation <-, -en> [kɔn·stɛ·la·ˈtsi̯oːn] *f* constellation
konsternieren* [kɔn·stɛr·ˈniː·rən] *vt* (*geh*) to consternate
Konstitution <-, -en> [kɔn·sti·tu·ˈtsi̯oːn] *f* constitution
konstitutionell [kɔn·sti·tu·tsi̯o·ˈnɛl] *adj* constitutional; **~e Monarchie** constitutional monarchy
konstruieren* [kɔn·stru·ˈiː·rən] *vt* ❶ (*aufbauen*) to construct ❷ (*entwerfen*) to design
Konstrukteur(in) <-s, -e> [kɔn·strʊk·ˈtøːɐ̯] *m(f)* designer
Konstruktion <-, -en> [kɔn·strʊk·ˈtsi̯oːn] *f* ❶ (*Bauweise*) construction ❷ (*Entwurf*) design
Konstruktionsfehler *m* ❶ (*Fehler im Entwurf*) design fault ❷ (*herstellungsbedingter Fehler*) construction fault
konstruktiv [kɔn·strʊk·ˈtiːf] **I.** *adj* constructive **II.** *adv* constructively
Konsul(in) <-s, -n> [ˈkɔn·zʊl] *m(f)* consul
Konsulat <-[e]s, -e> [kɔn·zu·ˈlaːt] *nt* consulate
Konsulin <-, -nen> *f fem form von* **Konsul**
konsultieren* [kɔn·zʊl·ˈtiː·rən] *vt* ■**jdn ~** to consult sb (**wegen** +*gen* about); ■**etw ~** to consult sth
Konsum <-s> [kɔn·ˈzuːm] *m kein pl* consumption
Konsument(in) <-en, -en> [kɔn·zu·ˈmɛnt] *m(f)* consumer
Konsumgesellschaft *f* consumer society
Konsumgüter *pl* consumer goods
konsumieren* [kɔn·zu·ˈmiː·rən] *vt* to consume
konsumorientiert *adj* consumer-orientated
Konsumverhalten *nt* consumer behavior
Kontakt <-[e]s, -e> [kɔn·ˈtakt] *m a.* ELEK contact; **mit jdm ~ aufnehmen** to get in touch with sb; [**mit jdm**] **in ~ bleiben** to keep in touch [with sb]; **keinen ~ mehr** [**zu jdm**] **haben** to have lost touch [with sb]; **mit jdm in ~ kommen** to come into contact with sb
Kontaktanzeige *f* personal [ad]
kontaktarm *adj* ■**~ sein** to have little contact with other people
kontaktfreudig *adj* ■**~ sein** to be sociable
Kontaktlinse *f* contact lens
Kontaktperson *f* contact [person]
Kontamination <-, -en> [kɔn·ta·mi·na·ˈtsi̯oːn] *f* contamination
kontaminieren* [kɔn·ta·mi·ˈniː·rən] *vt* to contaminate
Konten [ˈkɔn·tn̩] *pl von* **Konto**
Konter <-s, -> [ˈkɔn·tɐ] *m* SPORT counterattack
kontern [ˈkɔn·tɐn] *vt, vi* to counter
Kontext <-[e]s, -e> [ˈkɔn·tɛkst] *m* context
Kontinent <-[e]s, -e> [ˈkɔn·ti·nɛnt] *m* continent
kontinental [kɔn·ti·nɛn·ˈtaːl] *adj* continental
Kontingent <-[e]s, -e> [kɔn·tɪŋ·ˈgɛnt] *nt* ❶ MIL contingent ❷ (*Teil einer Menge*) quota
kontinuierlich [kɔn·ti·nu·ˈiːɐ̯·lɪç] **I.** *adj* continuous **II.** *adv* continuously
Kontinuität <-> [kɔn·ti·nui·ˈtɛt] *f kein pl* (*geh*) continuity
Konto <-s, Konten> [ˈkɔnto, *pl* ˈkɔn·tn̩] *nt* account ▶ WENDUNGEN: **auf jds ~ gehen** (*fam: verantworten*) to be sb's fault; (*bezahlen*) to be on sb
Kontoauszug *m* bank statement
Kontoinhaber(in) *m(f)* account holder
Kontonummer *f* account number
Kontostand *m* account balance
kontra [ˈkɔn·tra] *adv* against
Kontrahent(in) <-en, -en> [kɔn·tra·ˈhɛnt] *m(f)* (*geh*) adversary
kontrahieren* [kɔn·tra·ˈhiː·rən] *vi, vr* ■[**sich** *akk*] **~** to contract
Kontraktion <-, -en> [kɔn·trak·ˈtsi̯oːn] *f* contraction
kontraproduktiv [ˈkɔn·tra·pro·dʊk·tiːf] *adj* counterproductive
Kontrapunkt [ˈkɔn·tra·pʊŋkt] *m* counterpoint
konträr [kɔn·ˈtrɛːɐ̯] *adj* (*geh*) contrary
Kontrast <-[e]s, -e> [kɔn·ˈtrast] *m* contrast; **im ~ zu etw** *dat* **stehen** to contrast with sth
kontrastieren* [kɔn·tras·ˈtiː·rən] *vi* (*geh*) to contrast
Kontrastprogramm *nt* alternative program
kontrastreich *adj* rich in contrast
Kontrollampe[ALT] *f s.* **Kontrolllampe**
Kontrolle <-, -n> [kɔn·ˈtrɔ·lə] *f* ❶ (*Überprüfung*) check; **eine ~ durchführen** to conduct an inspection ❷ (*Überwachung*) monitoring ❸ (*Herrschaft*) control (**über** +*akk* of); **etw unter ~ bringen** to bring sth under control; **jdn/etw unter ~ haben** to have sb/sth under control; **die ~ über etw/sich** *akk* **verlieren** to lose control of sth/oneself
Kontrolleur(in) <-s, -e> [kɔn·trɔ·ˈløːɐ̯] *m(f)* inspector
Kontrollfunktion *f* supervisory function
kontrollierbar *adj* ❶ (*beherrschbar*) controllable ❷ (*überprüfbar*) verifiable
kontrollieren* [kɔn·trɔ·ˈliː·rən] *vt* ❶ (*überprüfen*) to check; ■**etw auf etw ~** to check sth for sth ❷ (*überwachen*) to monitor ❸ (*beherrschen*) to control
Kontrolllampe[RR] *f* indicator light
Kontrollturm *m* control tower
kontrovers [kɔn·tro·ˈvɛrs] **I.** *adj* ❶ (*gegensätzlich*) *Meinungen* conflicting ❷ (*umstritten*) *Thema* controversial **II.** *adv* in an argumentative manner *pred*
Kontroverse <-, -n> [kɔn·tro·ˈvɛr·zə] *f* conflict

Kontur <-, -en> [kɔn·ˈtuːɐ̯] *f meist pl* contour; **~ gewinnen** to take shape; **an ~ verlieren** to become less clear
Konvention <-, -en> [kɔn·vɛn·ˈtsi̯oːn] *f* convention
Konventionalstrafe *f* fixed penalty
konventionell [kɔn·vɛn·tsi̯o·ˈnɛl] **I.** *adj* conventional **II.** *adv* conventionally
Konversation <-, -en> [kɔn·vɛr·za·ˈtsi̯oːn] *f* conversation
Konversion <-, -en> [kɔn·vɛr·ˈzi̯oːn] *f* conversion
konvertieren* [kɔn·vɛr·ˈtiː·rən] *vi sein o haben* to convert (**zu** + *dat* to)
Konvoi <-s, -s> [ˈkɔn·vɔy] *m* convoy
Konzentrat <-[e]s, -e> [kɔn·tsɛn·ˈtraːt] *nt* concentrate
Konzentration <-, -en> [kɔn·tsɛn·tra·ˈtsi̯oːn] *f* concentration (**auf** + *akk* on)
Konzentrationsfähigkeit *f kein pl* ability to concentrate
Konzentrationslager *nt* concentration camp
Konzentrationsschwäche *f* short attention span, weak concentration
konzentrieren* [kɔn·tsɛn·ˈtriː·rən] **I.** *vr* ■ **sich** *akk* ~ to concentrate (**auf** + *akk* on) **II.** *vt* to concentrate
konzentriert **I.** *adj* ❶ *Aufmerksamkeit* focused ❷ CHEM concentrated **II.** *adv* with focus; **sie haben ~ gespielt** they played with focus; **~ zuhören** to listen intently
Konzept <-[e]s, -e> [kɔn·ˈtsɛpt] *nt* ❶ (*Entwurf*) draft; **als ~** in draft form ❷ (*Plan*) plan, concept; **jdn aus dem ~ bringen** to throw sb for a loop *fam;* **aus dem ~ geraten** to lose one's train of thought; **jdm nicht ins ~ passen** to not fit in with sb's plans
Konzeption <-, -en> [kɔn·tsɛp·ˈtsi̯oːn] *f* (*geh*) concept
Konzern <-s, -e> [kɔn·ˈtsɛrn] *m* group
Konzert <-[e]s, -e> [kɔn·ˈtsɛrt] *nt* concert
Konzertflügel *m* concert grand
Konzertsaal *m* concert hall
Konzession <-, -en> [kɔn·tsɛ·ˈsi̯oːn] *f* concession (**an** + *akk* to)
konzipieren* [kɔn·tsi·ˈpiː·rən] *vt* to plan
Kooperation <-, -en> [ko·ʔope·ra·ˈtsi̯oːn] *f* cooperation
kooperativ [ko·ʔope·ra·ˈtiːf] *adj* cooperative
kooperieren* [ko·ʔope·ˈriː·rən] *vi* to cooperate
Koordinate <-, -n> [ko·ʔɔr·di·ˈnaː·tə] *f* coordinate
Koordination <-, -en> [ko·ʔɔr·di·na·ˈtsi̯oːn] *f* coordination
Koordinator(in) <-s, -toren> [ko·ʔɔr·di·ˈnaː·toɐ̯, -na·ˈtoː·rɪn, *pl* -ˈtoː·rən] *m(f)* coordinator
koordinieren* [ko·ʔɔr·di·ˈniː·rən] *vt* to coordinate
Kopf <-[e]s, Köpfe> [kɔpf, *pl* ˈkœp·fə] *m* ❶ (*Haupt*) head; **von ~ bis Fuß** from head to toe; **einen roten ~ bekommen** to go red [in the face] ❷ (*oberer Teil*) head; (*Briefkopf*) letterhead; **~ oder Zahl?** (*bei Münzen*) heads or tails? ❸ (*Gedanken*) head; **etw will jdm nicht aus dem ~** sb can't get sth out of one's head; **sich** *dat* **etw durch den ~ gehen lassen** to mull sth over; **nichts als Sport/Arbeit im ~ haben** to think of nothing but sports/work; **sich** *dat* [**über etw**] **den ~ zerbrechen** (*fam*) to rack one's brain [over sth] ❹ (*Verstand, Intellekt*) mind; **nicht ganz richtig im ~ sein** (*fam*) to be not quite right in the head ❺ (*Wille*) mind; **seinen eigenen ~ haben** (*fam*) to have a mind of one's own; **seinen ~ durchsetzen** to get one's way ❻ (*Person*) head; ■ **der ~ einer S.** *gen* the person behind sth; **pro ~** per person ▶ WENDUNGEN: [**bei etw** *dat*] **~ und Kragen riskieren** (*fam*) to risk life and limb [doing sth]; **mit dem ~ durch die Wand** [**rennen**] **wollen** (*fam*) to be determined to get one's way; **~ hoch!** [keep your] chin up!; **jdn einen ~ kürzer machen** (*sl*) to chop sb's head off; **nicht auf den ~ gefallen sein** (*fam*) to not have been born yesterday; **etw auf den ~ hauen** (*fam*) to spend all of sth; **etw auf den ~ stellen** (*gründlich durchsuchen*) to turn sth upside down; (*ins Gegenteil verkehren*) to turn sth on its head; **jdn vor den ~ stoßen** to offend sb
Kopf-an-Kopf-Rennen *nt* (*a. fig*) neck-and-neck race
Kopfarbeit *f* brain work
Kopfball *m* header
Kopfbedeckung *f* headgear
Kopfbewegung *f* movement of the head
Köpfchen [ˈkœpf·çən] *nt* ▶ WENDUNGEN: **~ haben** (*fam*) to have brains
köpfen [ˈkœp·fn̩] **I.** *vt* (*fam: enthaupten*) to behead **II.** *vi* SPORT to head the ball
Kopfende *nt* head
Kopfhaut *f* scalp
Kopfhörer *m* headphones *pl*
Kopfkissen *nt* pillow
kopflos **I.** *adj* ❶ (*ganz verwirrt*) confused ❷ (*enthauptet*) headless **II.** *adv* in a bewildered manner
Kopfmensch *m* (*fam*) cerebral person
Kopfrechnen *nt* mental arithmetic
Kopfsalat *m* lettuce
kopfscheu *adj* ▶ WENDUNGEN: **jdn ~ machen** (*fam*) to confuse sb; **~ werden** (*fam*) to get confused
Kopfschmerz *m meist pl* headache; **jdm ~en machen** (*fam*) to give sb a headache
Kopfschmerztablette *f* pain reliever
kopfschüttelnd **I.** *adj* shaking one's head *pred* **II.** *adv* with a shake of the head
Kopfstand *m* headstand
Kopfsteinpflaster *nt* cobblestones *pl*
Kopfstütze *f* headrest
Kopftuch *nt* headscarf
kopfüber [kɔpf·ˈʔyːbɐ] *adv* head first
Kopfweh *nt s.* **Kopfschmerz**
Kopfzeile *f* header
Kopfzerbrechen *nt* ▶ WENDUNGEN: **jdm ~**

K

bereiten to make sb's head hurt; **sich** *dat* **über jdn/etw ~ machen** to worry about sb/sth

Kopie <-, -n> [ko·ˈpiː, *pl* ko·ˈpiː·ən] *f* copy

kopieren* [ko·ˈpiː·rən] *vt* to copy

Kopierer <-s, -> *m* (*fam*), **Kopiergerät** *nt* [photo]copier

Kopierschutz *m* copy protection

Kopiersperre *f* copy protection [device]

Kopilot(in) [ˈkoː·pi·loːt] *m(f)* copilot

Koppel <-, -n> [ˈkɔ·pl̩] *f* pasture

koppeln [ˈkɔ·pl̩n] *vt* ❶ (*anschließen*) to connect (**an** +*akk* to) ❷ (*miteinander verbinden*) to couple (**an** +*akk* to)

Kopp(e)lung <-, -en> *f* connection

kopulieren* [ko·pu·ˈliː·rən] *vi* to copulate

Koralle <-, -n> [ko·ˈra·lə] *f* coral

Korallenriff *nt* coral reef

Koran <-s> [ko·ˈraːn] *m kein pl* Koran

Koranvers *m* REL Koranic verse, sura

Korb <-[e]s, Körbe> [kɔrp, *pl* ˈkœr·bə] *m* ❶ *a.* SPORT basket; **einen ~ erzielen** to score a basket ❷ *kein pl* (*Weidengeflecht*) wicker ❸ (*fam: Abfuhr*) rejection; **[von jdm] einen ~ bekommen** to be rejected [by sb]; (*bei einem Date*) to get stood up [by sb]; **jdm einen ~ geben** to turn sb down; (*bei einem Date*) to stand sb up

Korbball *m* netball (*a game that resembles basketball without the backboards*)

Kord <-[e]s, -e> [kɔrt] *m s.* **Cord**

Kordel <-, -n> [ˈkɔr·dl̩] *f* cord

Korea <-s> [ko·ˈreːa] *nt* Korea; *s. a.* **Deutschland**

Koreaner(in) [ko·re·ˈaː·nɐ] *m(f)* Korean; *s. a.* **Deutsche(r)**

koreanisch [ko·re·ˈaː·nɪʃ] *adj* Korean; *s. a.* **deutsch**

Koriander <-s, -> [ko·ˈri̯an·dɐ] *m* coriander

Korinthe <-, -n> [ko·ˈrɪn·tə] *f* current

Korinthenkacker(in) <-s, -> *m(f)* (*pej fam*) nitpicker

Kork <-[e]s, -e> [kɔrk] *m* cork

Korken <-s, -> [ˈkɔr·kn̩] *m* cork

Korkenzieher <-s, -> *m* corkscrew

Korn¹ <-[e]s, Körner> [kɔrn, *pl* ˈkœr·nɐ] *nt* ❶ (*Samenkorn*) grain ❷ (*Getreide*) corn, grain

Korn² <-[e]s, -> [kɔrn] *m* (*Kornbranntwein*) schnapps

Körnchen <-s, -> [ˈkœrn·çən] *nt dim von* **Korn¹** grain; **ein ~ Wahrheit** a grain of truth

Kornfeld [ˈkɔrn·fɛlt] *nt* cornfield

körnig [ˈkœr·nɪç] *adj* granular

Körper <-s, -> [ˈkœr·pɐ] *m* body; **am ganzen ~** all over

Körperbau *m kein pl* physique

Körperbeherrschung *f kein pl* body control

Körperbehinderte(r) *f(m)* physically disabled person

Körperfülle *f* corpulence

Körpergeruch *m* body odor

Körpergewicht *nt* weight

Körpergröße *f* size

Körperhaltung *f* posture

Körperkontakt *m* body contact

körperlich I. *adj* physical II. *adv* physically; **~ arbeiten** to do physical labor

Körperpflege *f* personal hygiene

Körpersprache *f* body language

Körperteil *m* part of the body, body part

Körperverletzung *f* bodily harm; **fahrlässige ~** bodily injury caused by negligence; **schwere ~** aggravated assault

korpulent [kɔr·pu·ˈlɛnt] *adj* (*geh*) corpulent

korrekt [kɔ·ˈrɛkt] I. *adj* correct II. *adv* correctly

Korrektheit <-> *f kein pl* correctness

Korrektur <-, -en> [kɔ·rɛk·ˈtuːɐ̯] *f* correction; *von Schularbeiten* grading; **[etw] ~ lesen** to proofread [sth]

Korrespondent(in) <-en, -en> [kɔ·rɛs·pɔn·ˈdɛnt] *m(f)* correspondent

Korrespondenz <-, -en> [kɔ·rɛs·pɔn·ˈdɛnts] *f* correspondence

korrespondieren* *vi* ❶ (*in Briefwechsel stehen*) to correspond (**mit** +*dat* with) ❷ (*geh: entsprechen*) ■ **mit etw** *dat* **~** to correspond to sth

Korridor <-s, -e> [ˈkɔ·ri·doːɐ̯] *m* corridor

korrigierbar *adj* correctable

korrigieren* [kɔ·ri·ˈgiː·rən] *vt* to correct; *Klassenarbeit, Aufsatz* to grade; *Manuskript* to proofread

korrupt [kɔ·ˈrʊpt] *adj* corrupt

Korruption <-, -en> [kɔ·rʊp·ˈtsi̯oːn] *f* corruption

Korse, Korsin <-n, -n> [ˈkɔr·zə] *m, f* Corsican; *s. a.* **Deutsche(r)**

Korsika <-s> [ˈkɔr·zi·ka] *nt kein pl* Corsica

Korsin <-, -nen> *f fem form von* **Korse**

korsisch [ˈkɔr·sɪʃ] *adj* Corsican; *s. a.* **deutsch**

Kosak(in) <-en, -en> [ko·ˈzak] *m(f)* Cossack

koscher [ˈkoː·ʃɐ] I. *adj* kosher ▶ WENDUNGEN: **nicht [ganz] ~ sein** to not be [entirely] on the level II. *adv* according to kosher requirements

Kosename *m* pet name

Kosewort *nt* term of endearment

Kosmetik <-> [kɔs·ˈmeː·tɪk] *f kein pl* cosmetics *pl*

Kosmetiker(in) <-s, -> [kɔs·ˈmeː·ti·kɐ] *m(f)* beautician

kosmetisch [kɔs·ˈmeː·tɪʃ] I. *adj* cosmetic II. *adv* cosmetically

kosmisch [ˈkɔs·mɪʃ] *adj* cosmic

Kosmonaut(in) <-en, -en> [kɔs·mo·ˈnaut] *m(f)* cosmonaut

Kosmopolit(in) <-en, -en> [kɔs·mo·po·ˈliːt] *m(f)* (*geh*) cosmopolitan

Kosmos <-> [ˈkɔs·mɔs] *m kein pl* cosmos

Kosovo <-s> [ˈkɔ·sɔ·vɔ] *m* Kosovo

Kost <-> [kɔst] *f kein pl* food; **[freie] ~ und Logis** [free] room and board; **geistige ~** intellectual fare

kostbar [ˈkɔst·baːɐ̯] *adj* valuable, precious; **jdm ~ sein** to mean a lot to sb

Kostbarkeit <-, -en> *f* ❶ (*wertvoller Gegenstand*) precious object ❷ *kein pl* (*Erlesenheit*)

preciousness

kosten¹ ['kɔs·tn̩] *vt* ① (*als Preis haben*) to cost ② (*erfordern*) to take [up]

kosten² ['kɔs·tn̩] *vt, vi* (*probieren*) to taste; ■ **von etw** *dat* ~ to have a taste of sth

Kosten ['kɔs·tn̩] *pl* costs *pl*, expenses *pl*; ~ **sparend** economical; **die ~ tragen** to bear the cost[s] ▶ WENDUNGEN: **auf seine ~ kommen** to get one's money's worth; **auf ~ von jdm/etw** *dat* at the expense of sb/sth

Kostenbeteiligung *f* cost sharing

kostendeckend I. *adj* cost-effective II. *adv* cost-effectively

Kostenerstattung *f* reimbursement of expenses

Kostenfrage *f* question of cost

kostengünstig *adj* economical

kostenintensiv *adj* cost-intensive

kostenlos I. *adj* ■ ~ **sein** to be free [of charge] II. *adv* free [of charge]

Kostenvoranschlag *m* quotation; **sich** *dat* **einen ~ machen lassen** to get an estimate

Kostgeld *nt* board

köstlich ['kœst·lɪç] I. *adj* ① (*herrlich*) delicious ② (*fam: amüsant*) priceless II. *adv* (*herrlich*) delicious; **sich** *akk* ~ **amüsieren** to have a wonderful time

Kostprobe *f* ① (*etwas zum Probieren*) taste ② (*Vorgeschmack, Beispiel*) sample

kostspielig *adj* expensive

Kostüm <-s, -e> [kɔs·'tyːm] *nt* ① MODE suit ② HIST, THEAT costume

Kostümball *m* costume ball

kostümieren* [kɔs·ty·'miː·rən] *vt* ■ **sich** *akk* [**als etw**] ~ to dress up [as sth]

Kot <-[e]s> [koːt] *m kein pl* excrement

Kotelett <-s, -s> [kɔt·'lɛt] *nt* chop

Köter <-s, -> ['køː·tɐ] *m* (*pej*) mutt

Kotflügel *m* wing

Kotzbrocken *m* (*pej sl*) slimeball

Kotze <-> ['kɔ·tsə] *f kein pl* (*fam*) puke *sl*

kotzen ['kɔ·tsn̩] *vi* (*fam*) to puke; **das ist zum K~** that makes me want to puke *sl*

kotzübel ['kɔts·'ʔyː·bl̩] *adj* (*fam*) **mir ist/wird** ~ I feel like I'm going to puke *sl*

Krabbe <-, -n> ['kra·bə] *f* ① ZOOL (*Taschenkrebs*) crab ② KOCHK (*Garnele*) prawn

krabbeln ['kra·bl̩n] *vi sein* to crawl

Krach <-[e]s, Kräche> [krax, *pl* 'krɛ·çə] *m* ① *kein pl* (*Lärm*) noise ② (*fam: Streit*) quarrel; ~ [**mit jdm**] **haben** to have an argument [with sb]; **sie haben ~** they're not on speaking terms; **mit jdm ~ kriegen** to get into trouble with sb ▶ WENDUNGEN: ~ **schlagen** (*fam*) to make a fuss

krachen ['kra·xn̩] I. *vi* ① *haben* (*laut hallen*) to crash; *Ast* to creak; *Schuss* to ring out ② *sein* (*fam: prallen*) to crash II. *vr* (*fam*) ■ **sich** *akk* ~ to have an argument

krächzen ['krɛç·tsn̩] *vi, vt* ① ORN to caw ② (*fam: heiser sprechen*) to croak

Kraft <-, Kräfte> [kraft, *pl* 'krɛf·tə] *f* ① ([*körperliche*] *Stärke*) strength; **mit frischer ~** with renewed energy; **mit letzter ~** with one's last ounce of strength; **mit vereinten Kräften** with combined efforts; **aus eigener ~** by oneself; **die treibende ~** the driving force; **wieder zu Kräften kommen** to regain one's strength; **über jds Kräfte gehen** to be more than sb can cope with; **seine Kräfte sammeln** to gather one's strength ② (*Geltung*) power; **in ~ sein** to be in effect; **in ~ treten** to take effect; **außer ~ sein** to be no longer in effect; **etw außer ~ setzen** to cancel sth ③ PHYS (*Energie*) power ④ *meist pl* (*Einfluss ausübende Gruppe*) force

Kraftakt *m* act of strength

Kraftanstrengung *f* exertion

Kraftaufwand *m* effort

Kraftausdruck *m* swear word

Kraftfahrer(in) *m(f)* driver

Kraftfahrzeug *nt* motor vehicle

Kraftfahrzeugbrief *m* title

Kraftfahrzeugpapiere *pl* vehicle registration papers *npl*

Kraftfahrzeugschein *m* [motor vehicle] registration

Kraftfahrzeugsteuer *f* motor vehicle tax

Kraftfahrzeugversicherung *f* auto insurance

Kraftfeld *nt* force field

kräftig ['krɛf·tɪç] I. *adj* ① (*physisch stark*) strong ② (*kraftvoll*) powerful; *Händedruck* firm; *Haarwuchs* healthy; *Stimme* powerful ③ (*intensiv*) strong; *Farbe* rich ④ KOCHK (*nahrhaft*) hearty II. *adv* ① (*angestrengt*) vigorously; **etw ~ rühren** to give sth a good stir; ~ **niesen** to sneeze violently ② METEO (*stark*) heavily ③ (*deutlich*) substantially; **jdm ~ die Meinung sagen** to strongly express one's opinion

kraftlos I. *adj* weak II. *adv* feebly

Kraftlosigkeit <-> *f kein pl* weakness

Kraftprobe *f* test of strength

Kraftprotz <-es, -e> *m* (*fam*) muscle man

Kraftrad *nt* motorcycle

Kraftreserven *pl* strength reserves *pl*

Kraftstoff *m* fuel

kraftvoll I. *adj* strong; *Stimme* powerful II. *adv* forcefully; ~ **zubeißen** to take a hearty bite

Kraftwagen *m* motor vehicle

Kraftwerk *nt* power plant

Kragen <-s, - *o* Krägen> ['kraː·gən, *pl* 'krɛː·gn̩] *m* collar ▶ WENDUNGEN: **jdm geht es an den ~** (*derb*) sb is in for it; **etw kostet jdn den ~** (*derb*) sth is sb's downfall; **jdm platzt der ~** (*fam*) sb is blowing his/her top

Kragenweite *f* collar size ▶ WENDUNGEN: **genau/nicht jds ~ sein** (*fam*) to be just/not sb's cup of tea

Krähe <-, -n> ['krɛː·ə] *f* crow

krähen ['krɛː·ən] *vi* ① ORN to crow ② (*fam*) to squeal

Krakauer <-, -> *f Polish garlic sausage*

Krake <-n, -n> ['kraː·kə] *m* octopus

krakeelen* [kra·'keː·lən] *vi* (*pej fam*) to make a racket

Krakelei <-, -en> *f* (*pej fam*) scribble

krakelig ['kraː·kə·lɪç] *adj, adv* (*pej fam*) scrawly
Kralle <-, -n> ['kra·lə] *f* ORN, ZOOL claw ▶ WENDUNGEN: **jdn in seine ~n bekommen** to get one's claws into sb
krallen ['kra·lən] **I.** *vr* ■ **sich** *akk* **an jdn/etw ~** to cling onto sb/sth **II.** *vt* ❶ (*fest bohren*) ■ **etw in etw ~** to dig sth into sth ❷ (*sl: klauen*) ■ [**sich** *dat*] **etw ~** to pilfer sth *fam*
Kram <-[e]s> [kraːm] *m kein pl* (*fam*) ❶ (*Krempel*) junk ❷ (*Angelegenheit*) affairs *pl;* **den ganzen ~ hinschmeißen** to pack it all in; **jdm in den ~ passen** to suit sb fine; **jdm nicht in den ~ passen** to be a real nuisance to sb
kramen ['kraː·mən] **I.** *vi* ❶ (*fam*) ■ [**in etw** *dat*] **~** to rummage around [in sth] (**nach** +*dat* for) ❷ SCHWEIZ (*Kleinhandel betreiben*) to hawk **II.** *vt* (*fam*) ■ **etw aus etw** *dat* **~** to fish sth out of sth
Krampf <-[e]s, Krämpfe> [krampf, *pl* 'krɛmp·fə] *m* cramp
krampfen ['kramp·fn̩] *vt* to clench (**um** +*akk* around)
krampfhaft **I.** *adj* ❶ (*angestrengt*) desperate ❷ MED convulsive **II.** *adv* desperately
Kran <-[e]s, Kräne> [kraːn, *pl* 'krɛː·nə] *m* TECH crane
krank <kränker, kränkste> [kraŋk] *adj* sick, ill ▶ WENDUNGEN: **du bist wohl ~!** (*iron*) are you out of your mind?; **jdn** [**mit etw** *dat*] **~ machen** to get on sb's nerves [with sth]
Kranke(r) *f(m) dekl wie adj* sick person
kränkeln ['krɛŋ·kl̩n] *vi* to be in poor health
kranken ['kraŋ·kn̩] *vi* ■ **an etw** *dat* **~** to suffer from sth
kränken ['krɛŋ·kn̩] *vt* ■ **jdn ~** to hurt sb's feelings; ■ **gekränkt sein** to feel hurt; ■ **es kränkt jdn, dass ...** it hurts sb['s feelings], that ...; ■ **~d** hurtful
Krankenbesuch *m* sick call
Krankengeld *nt* sick pay
Krankengymnastik *f* physical therapy
Krankenhaus *nt* hospital, clinic; **ins ~ kommen/müssen** to go/have to go to the hospital; **im ~ liegen** to be in a hospital
Krankenkasse *f* health insurance company
Krankenpflege *f* nursing
Krankenpfleger(in) *m(f)* male nurse
Krankenschwester *f* nurse
Krankenversicherung *f* health insurance

> In Germany and Austria, everyone who is gainfully employed and not self-employed is entitled to **Krankenversicherung** (health insurance). In Switzerland, health insurance is voluntary. Nevertheless, over 95% of the Swiss have health insurance.

Krankenwagen *m* ambulance
kränker *adj komp von* **krank**
krank|feiern *vi* (*fam*) to call in sick
krankhaft **I.** *adj* morbid **II.** *adv* morbidly
Krankheit <-, -en> *f* disease; MED *a.* illness
Krankheitserreger *m* pathogen
krank|lachen *vr* (*fam*) ■ **sich** *akk* **~** to almost die laughing (**über** +*akk* about)
kränklich ['krɛŋk·lɪç] *adj* sickly
krank|machen *vi* (*fam*) *s.* **krankfeiern**
krank|meldenRR *vr* ■ **sich** *akk* **~** to call in sick
Krankmeldung *f* notification of illness
krank|schreibenRR *vt* ■ **jdn ~** *to excuse sb from* [*going to*] *work because he/she is sick*
kränkste(r, s) *adj superl von* **krank**
Kränkung <-, -en> *f* insult
Kranz <-es, Kränze> [krants, *pl* 'krɛn·tsə] *m* ❶ (*Ring aus Pflanzen*) wreath ❷ DIAL (*Hefekranz*) Danish ring
krassRR, **kraß**ALT [kras] **I.** *adj* **~es Beispiel** glaring example; **~e Bemerkung** crass remark; **ein ~er Fall/Unterschied** an extreme case/difference; **~er Gegensatz** stark contrast **II.** *adv* (*sl*) crassly; **sich** *akk* **~ benehmen** to behave crassly; **~ gesagt** to put it bluntly
kratzbürstig ['krats·byrs·tɪç] *adj* (*pej fam*) prickly
Krätze <-> ['krɛ·tsə] *f kein pl* scabies
kratzen ['kra·tsn̩] **I.** *vt* ❶ (*mit den Nägeln ritzen*) to scratch; ■ **etw von etw** *dat* **~** to scratch sth off [of] sth ❷ (*fam: kümmern*) **das kratzt mich nicht** I couldn't care less about that **II.** *vi* ❶ (*jucken, scharren*) to scratch; **das Unterhemd kratzt** the undershirt itches ❷ (*beeinträchtigen*) ■ **an etw** *dat* **~** to scratch away at sth; **an jds Stellung ~** to undermine sb's position
Kratzer <-s, -> ['kra·tsɐ] *m* scratch
kraulen1 ['krau·lən] *vi sein o haben* (*schwimmen*) to do [*or* swim] the crawl
kraulen2 ['krau·lən] *vt* (*streicheln*) to fondle; **einen Hund zwischen den Ohren ~** to scratch a dog between its ears
kraus [kraus] *adj Haare* frizzy; *Stirn* wrinkled
kräuseln ['krɔy·zl̩n] **I.** *vt Haare* to crimp; *Stoff* to ruffle; **die starke Bö kräuselte die Oberfläche des Wassers** the strong gust ruffled the surface of the water **II.** *vr* ■ **sich** *akk* **~** *Haare* to frizz; *Wasseroberfläche* to ruffle
kraus|ziehen *vt irreg* **die Stirn ~** to frown
Kraut <-[e]s, Kräuter> [kraut, *pl* krɔy·tɐ] *nt* ❶ BOT herb ❷ *kein pl* (*grüne Teile von Pflanzen*) foliage ❸ *kein pl* DIAL (*Kohl*) cabbage; (*Sauerkraut*) sauerkraut ❹ *kein pl* DIAL (*Sirup*) syrup ▶ WENDUNGEN: **wie ~ und Rüben durcheinanderliegen** (*fam*) to lie around all over the place
Kräutermischung *f* herb mixture
Kräutertee *m* herbal tea
Krautkopf *m* SÜDD, ÖSTERR (*Kohlkopf*) head of cabbage
Krautsalat *m* coleslaw (*without carrots*)
Krawall <-s, -e> [kra·'val] *m* ❶ (*Tumult*) riot; **~ schlagen** to make a fuss ❷ *kein pl* (*fam: Lärm*) racket; **~ machen** to make a racket
Krawallmacher(in) <-s, -> *m(f)* (*pej fam*)

K

hooligan
Krawatte <-, -n> [kra·'va·tə] *f* tie
Kreation <-, -en> [krea·'tsi̯o:n] *f* creation
kreativ [krea·'ti:f] **I.** *adj* creative **II.** *adv* creatively
Kreativität <-> [krea·ti·vi·'tɛt] *f kein pl* creativity
Kreatur <-, -en> [krea·'tu:ɐ̯] *f* creature
Krebs <-es, -e> [kre:ps] *m* ❶ ZOOL crayfish ❷ *kein pl* KOCHK (*Krebsfleisch*) crab ❸ MED cancer ❹ *kein pl* ASTROL Cancer
krebserregend *adj* carcinogenic
Krebserreger *m* carcinogen
Krebsforschung *f kein pl* cancer research
Krebsfrüherkennung *f kein pl* early cancer diagnosis
Krebsgeschwür *nt* cancerous ulcer
krebskrank *adj* ■ **~ sein** to suffer from cancer
Krebskranke(r) *f(m)* cancer victim
Krebsoperation *f operation conducted on cancer patient*
krebsrot ['kre:ps·ro:t] *adj* red as a lobster
Krebsvorsorge *f kein pl* cancer prevention
Krebsvorsorgeuntersuchung *f* cancer checkup
Krebszelle *f* cancer cell
Kredit <-[e]s, -e> [kre·'di:t] *m* credit; (*Darlehen*) loan; [**bei jdm**] **~ haben** to have a credit account with sb; **einen ~ [bei jdm] aufnehmen** to take out a loan [with sb]; **auf ~** on credit
Kredithai *m* (*fam*) loan shark
Kreditinstitut *nt* bank
Kreditkarte *f* credit card
kreditwürdig *adj* creditworthy
Kreide <-, -n> ['krai·də] *f* chalk ▶ WENDUNGEN: **bei jdm [tief] in der ~ stehen** (*fam*) to owe sb [a lot of] money
kreidebleich, **kreideweiß** *adj* as white as a sheet
Kreidezeichnung *f* chalk drawing
kreieren* [kre·'i:·rən] *vt* to create
Kreis <-es, -e> [krais, *pl* 'krai·zə] *m* ❶ MATH circle; **einen ~ um jdn bilden** to form a circle around sb; **sich** *akk* **im ~[e] drehen** to turn around in a circle ❷ (*Personengruppe*) circle; **die Hochzeit fand im engsten ~ statt** only close friends and family were invited to the wedding ❸ ADMIN district
Kreisbewegung *f* circular movement
kreischen ['krai·ʃn̩] *vi* ❶ ORN to squawk ❷ (*hysterisch schreien*) to shriek ❸ *Bremsen, Reifen* to screech
Kreisel <-s, -> ['krai·zl̩] *m* ❶ (*Spielzeug*) top ❷ TRANSP (*fam*) traffic circle
kreisen ['krai·zn̩] *vi sein o haben* ❶ ASTRON, RAUM ■ **um etw** *akk* **~** to orbit sth ❷ LUFT, ORN ■ [**über etw** *dat*] **~** to circle [above sth] ❸ (*in einem Kreislauf sein*) ■ [**in etw** *dat*] **~** to circulate [through sth] ❹ (*sich ständig drehen*) ■ **um jdn/etw ~** to revolve around sb/sth
kreisförmig I. *adj* circular **II.** *adv* in a circle
Kreislauf *m* ❶ MED circulation ❷ (*Zirkulation*) cycle
Kreislaufstörungen *pl* circulatory disorder
Kreisstadt *f* county seat
Kreisumfang *m* circumference
Kreisverkehr *m* traffic circle
Krematorium <-s, -rien> [krema'to:·ri̯·ʊm, *pl* -'to:·ri·ən] *nt* crematorium
kremig ['kre:·mɪç] **I.** *adj* creamy **II.** *adv* **etw ~ schlagen/rühren** to whip/stir sth until it's creamy
Kreml <-s> ['krɛ:·ml̩] *m* Kremlin
Krempe <-, -n> ['krɛm·pə] *f* brim
Krempel <-s> ['krɛm·pl̩] *m kein pl* (*pej fam*) ❶ (*ungeordnete Sachen*) stuff ❷ (*Ramsch*) junk ▶ WENDUNGEN: **den ganzen ~ hinwerfen** to throw in the towel *fam*
Kreolen [kre·'o:·lən] *pl* hoop earrings *pl*
krepieren* [kre·'pi:·rən] *vi sein* (*sl: zugrunde gehen*) to croak; ■ **jdm ~** to die on sb *fam*
Krepp[1] <-s, -e *o* -s> [krɛp] *m* (*Gewebe*) crêpe
Krepp[RR2] <-s, -s> [krɛp] *m* KOCHK crêpe
Kresse <-, -n> ['krɛ·sə] *f* cress
Kreta <-s> ['kre:·ta] *nt* Crete
Kreter(in) <-s, -> ['kre:·tɐ] *m(f)* Cretan; *s. a.* **Deutsche(r)**
kretisch ['kre:·tɪʃ] *adj* Cretan; *s. a.* **deutsch**
kreuz [krɔyts] ▶ WENDUNGEN: **~ und quer** all over the place *fam,* all over
Kreuz <-es, -e> [krɔyts] *nt* ❶ (*Zeichen in Form eines X*) cross; **über ~** crosswise ❷ REL cross; (*Kruzifix*) crucifix; **jdn ans ~ schlagen** to crucify sb ❸ (*Teil des Rückens*) lower back; **es im ~ haben** (*fam*) to have back trouble ❹ (*Autobahnkreuz*) intersection ❺ *kein pl* KARTEN clubs *pl* ▶ WENDUNGEN: **das Rote ~** the Red Cross; **zu ~e kriechen** to eat humble pie *fam;* **jdn aufs ~ legen** (*fam*) to fool sb; **drei ~e machen** (*fam*) to be so relieved
kreuzen ['krɔy·tsn̩] **I.** *vt haben a.* BIOL to cross **II.** *vr haben* ■ **sich** *akk* **~** to cross **III.** *vi sein o haben* NAUT ❶ *Flugzeug, Schiff* to cruise ❷ NAUT (*wenden*) to tack
Kreuzer <-s, -> ['krɔy·tsɐ] *m* NAUT cruiser
Kreuzfahrt *f* cruise
Kreuzfeuer *nt* crossfire ▶ WENDUNGEN: [**von allen Seiten**] **ins ~ [der Kritik] geraten** to come under fire [from all sides]
kreuzigen ['krɔy·tsɪ·gn̩] *vt* to crucify
Kreuzigung <-, -en> *f* crucifixion
Kreuzotter *f* adder
Kreuzschlüssel *m* 4-way lug wrench
Kreuzspinne *f* cross [*or* garden] spider
Kreuzung <-, -en> *f* ❶ (*Straßenkreuzung*) crossroad *meist pl* ❷ *kein pl* BIOL (*das Kreuzen*) crossbreeding ❸ ZOOL, BIOL (*Bastard*) mongrel
Kreuzweg ['krɔyts·ve:k] *m* ▶ WENDUNGEN: **am ~ stehen** to be at a/the crossroads
kreuzweise *adv* crosswise ▶ WENDUNGEN: **du kannst mich ~!** (*derb*) fuck off! *vulg*
Kreuzworträtsel *nt* crossword [puzzle]
Kreuzzug *m* crusade
kribbelig ['krɪ·bə·lɪç] *adj* ❶ (*unruhig*) edgy

K

❷ (*prickelnd*) tingly

kribbeln ['krɪ·bl̩n] **I.** *vi* ❶ *haben* (*prickeln*) **das kribbelt so schön auf der Haut** it's so nice and tingly on the skin ❷ *sein* (*krabbeln*) **~ und krabbeln** to swarm around **II.** *vi impers haben* **mir kribbelt es im Rücken** my back is itching

kribblig ['krɪb·lɪç] *adj s.* **kribbelig**

Kricket <-s, -s> ['krɪ·kət] *nt* SPORT cricket

kriechen <kroch, gekrochen> ['kriː·çn̩] *vi* ❶ *sein* (*sich auf dem Bauch bewegen*) to crawl ❷ *sein* (*langsam vergehen*) to creep by ❸ *sein o haben* (*pej: unterwürfig sein*) ■**[vor jdm] ~** to grovel [before sb]

Kriecher(in) <-s, -> *m(f)* (*pej fam*) ass-kisser

kriecherisch *adj* (*pej fam*) ass-kissing

Kriechtier *nt* reptile

Krieg <-[e]s, -e> [kriːk, *pl* 'kriː·gə] *m* war; **jdm/einem Land den ~ erklären** to declare war on sb/a country; **~ [gegen jdn/mit jdm] führen** to wage war [on sb]; **in den ~ ziehen** to go to war

kriegen ['kriː·gn̩] *vt* (*fam*) ❶ (*bekommen*) to get; **den Schrank in den Aufzug ~** to get the cupboard into the elevator; **ich kriege noch 20 Euro von dir** you still owe me 20 euros; **hast du die Arbeit auch bezahlt gekriegt?** did you get paid for the work?; **etw zu sehen ~** to get to see sth; **ein Kind ~** to have a baby; **eine Krankheit ~** to get a disease; **Prügel ~** to get a beating ❷ (*erwischen*) ■**jdn ~** to catch sb; **den Zug ~** to catch the train ❸ (*es schaffen*) ■**jdn dazu ~, etw zu tun** to get sb to do sth; **ich kriege das schon geregelt** I'll take care of it ▶WENDUNGEN: **es mit jdm zu tun ~** to be in trouble with sb

Krieger(in) <-s, -> ['kriː·gɐ] *m(f)* warrior

kriegerisch **I.** *adj* ❶ (*kämpferisch*) warlike ❷ (*militärisch*) military **II.** *adv* belligerently

Kriegsausbruch *m* outbreak of war

Kriegsbeil *nt* tomahawk ▶WENDUNGEN: **das ~ begraben** to bury the hatchet

Kriegsberichterstatter(in) *m(f)* war correspondent

Kriegsbeschädigte(r) *f(m) dekl wie adj* sb wounded in action, disabled vet[eran]

Kriegsdienstverweigerer <-s, -> *m* conscientious objector

Kriegserklärung *f* declaration of war

Kriegsfilm *m* war movie

Kriegsflüchtling *m* war refugee

Kriegsfuß *m* ▶WENDUNGEN: **mit jdm auf ~ stehen** (*fam*) to be at loggerheads with sb; **mit etw** *dat* **auf ~ stehen** to be no good with sth

Kriegsgefangene(r) *f(m)* prisoner of war

Kriegsgefangenschaft *f* captivity; **in ~ geraten** to become a prisoner of war

Kriegsgericht *nt* court martial

Kriegsindustrie *f* weapons industry

Kriegsopfer *nt* victim of war

Kriegsschauplatz *m* theater of war

Kriegsschiff *nt* warship

Kriegsverbrechen *nt* war crime

Kriegsverbrecher(in) *m(f)* war criminal

Kriegsverletzung *f* war wound

Krimi <-s, -s> ['krɪ·mi] *m* (*fam*) ❶ (*Buch*) detective novel ❷ (*Film*) [crime] thriller

Kriminalbeamte(r) *f(m)*, **-beamtin** *f* detective

Kriminalfilm *m* thriller

Kriminalität <-> [kri·mi·na·li·'tɛt] *f kein pl* ❶ (*Straffälligkeit*) criminality ❷ (*Rate der Straffälligkeit*) crime rate

Kriminalpolizei *f* criminal investigation department

Kriminalroman *m* detective novel

kriminell [kri·mi·'nɛl] *adj* criminal

Kriminelle(r) [kri·mi·'nɛ·lə, -lɐ] *f(m) dekl wie adj* criminal

Krimskrams <-es> ['krɪms·krams] *m kein pl* (*fam*) junk

Kringel <-s, -> ['krɪŋl̩] *m* ❶ KOCHK ring-shaped cookie ❷ (*Schnörkel*) squiggle

kringeln ['krɪŋl̩n] *vr* ❶ (*sich umbiegen*) ■**sich** *akk* **~** to curl [up] ❷ (*fam*) ■**sich** *akk* **[vor Lachen] ~** to die [laughing]

Kripo <-, -s> ['kriː·po] *f* (*fam*) *kurz für* **Kriminalpolizei**

Krippe <-, -n> ['krɪ·pə] *f* ❶ (*Futterkrippe*) *a.* REL manger ❷ (*Kinderkrippe*) daycare [center]

Krise <-, -n> ['kriː·zə] *f* crisis

kriseln ['kriː·zl̩n] *vi impers* (*fam*) **es kriselt** a crisis is looming

krisenanfällig *adj* crisis-prone

krisenfest *adj* crisis-proof

Krisengebiet *nt* crisis zone

Krisenherd *m* trouble spot

Krisenmanagement *nt* crisis management

Krisenstab *m kein pl* action committee

Kristall <-s, -e> [krɪs·'tal] *m* crystal

kristallklar *adj* crystal-clear

Kriterium <-s, -rien> [kri·'teː·ri·ʊm, *pl* -'teː·ri·ən] *nt* criterion

Kritik <-, -en> [kri·'tiːk] *f* ❶ *kein pl* (*Tadel*) criticism; **an jdm/etw ~ üben** to criticize sb/sth; **ohne jede ~** uncritically ❷ (*Beurteilung*) critique ❸ MEDIA (*Rezension*) review; **gute/schlechte ~en bekommen** to receive good/bad reviews ▶WENDUNGEN: **unter aller ~ sein** (*pej fam*) to be beneath contempt

Kritiker(in) <-s, -> ['kriː·ti·kɐ] *m(f)* critic

kritiklos **I.** *adj* uncritical **II.** *adv* uncritically

kritisch ['kriː·tɪʃ] **I.** *adj* critical **II.** *adv* critically

kritisieren* [kri·ti·'ziː·rən] *vt* to criticize

Kritzelei <-, -en> [krɪ·tsə·'lai] *f* (*pej fam*) ❶ *kein pl* (*das Kritzeln*) scribbling ❷ (*Gekritzel*) scribble

kritzeln ['krɪ·tsl̩n] *vi, vt* to scribble

Kroate, Kroatin <-n, -n> [kro·'aː·tə, kro·'aː·tɪn] *m, f* Croat; *s. a.* **Deutsche(r)**

Kroatien <-s> [kro·'aː·tsi̯·ən] *nt* Croatia; *s. a.* **Deutschland**

kroatisch [kro·'aː·tɪʃ] *adj* Croatian; *s. a.* **deutsch**

kroch [krɔx] *imp von* **kriechen**

Krokette <-, -n> [kro·'kɛ·tə] *f* croquette

Krokodil <-s, -e> [kro·ko·'diːl] *nt* crocodile

K

Krokodilstränen *pl* (*fam*) crocodile tears *pl*
Krone <-, -n> ['kroː·nə] *f* ❶ (*Kopfschmuck, Zahnkrone*) crown ❷ (*Baumkrone*) top ❸ (*Währungseinheit: in Skandinavien*) krone; (*in der Tschechei*) crown ▶WENDUNGEN: **einen in der ~ haben** (*fam*) to have had one too many; **die ~ sein** (*fam*) to beat everything
krönen ['krøː·nən] *vt* to crown
Kronenkorken *m* bottle cap
Kronprinz, -prinzessin *m, f* crown prince *masc*, crown princess *fem*
Krönung <-, -en> *f* ❶ (*Höhepunkt*) high point ❷ (*das Krönen*) coronation
Kropf <-[e]s, Kröpfe> [krɔpf, *pl* 'krœp·fə] *m* ORN crop
kross[RR], **kroß**[ALT] [krɔs] **I.** *adj* crusty **II.** *adv* crustily
Kröte <-, -n> ['krøː·tə] *f* ❶ ZOOL toad ❷ *pl* (*sl: Geld*) pennies *pl* ❸ (*pej: Kind*) brat
Krücke <-, -n> ['krʏ·kə] *f* ❶ (*Stock*) crutch; **an ~n gehen** to walk on crutches ❷ (*sl: Nichtskönner*) loser *pej fam*
Krückstock *m* walking stick
Krug <-[e]s, Krüge> [kruːk, *pl* 'kryː·gə] *m* (*Gefäß*) jug; (*Trinkgefäß*) tankard
Krümel <-s, -> ['kryː·ml̩] *m* crumb
krümelig ['kryː·mə·lɪç] *adj* crumbly
krümeln ['kryːm·l̩n] *vi* ❶ (*Krümel machen*) to make crumbs ❷ (*leicht zerbröseln*) to crumble
krumm [krʊm] **I.** *adj* ❶ (*verbogen*) crooked; **~ und schief** askew ❷ (*gebogen*) *Nase* hooked; *Rücken* hunched; *Beine* bowed; **etw ~ biegen** to bend sth ❸ (*pej fam: unehrlich*) crooked; **ein ~es Ding drehen** to pull a fast one *sl*; **es auf die ~e Tour versuchen** to try to pull some monkey business with sth *sl* **II.** *adv* **~ gehen** to walk with a stoop; **~ sitzen/stehen** to slouch ▶WENDUNGEN: **sich** *akk* **~ und schief lachen** (*fam*) to bust a gut laughing
krümmen ['krʏ·mən] **I.** *vt* to bend; **den Rücken ~** to arch one's back; **die Schultern ~** to slouch one's shoulders **II.** *vr* ❶ (*eine Biegung machen*) ■**sich** *akk* ~ *Fluss* to wind; *Straße* to bend ❷ (*sich beugen*) ■**sich** *akk* ~ to bend; **sich** *akk* **vor Schmerzen/Lachen ~** to double up in pain/with laughter
krummlachen *vr* (*fam*) ■**sich** *akk* ~ to laugh one's head off (**über** +*akk* at)
krummnehmen *vt irreg* (*fam*) ■[**jdm**] **etw ~** to take offense at sth [sb said or did]
Krüppel <-s, -> ['kryː·pl̩] *m* cripple
Kruste <-, -n> ['krʊs·tə] *f* crust; *Braten* cracklings *pl*; *Wunde* scab
Kruzifix <-es, -e> ['kruː·tsi·fɪks] *nt* crucifix
Krypta <-, Krypten> ['krʏp·ta, *pl* 'krʏp·tən] *f* crypt
Kto. *Abk von* **Konto** acct., a/c
Kuba <-s> ['kuː·ba] *nt* Cuba; *s. a.* **Deutschland**
Kubaner(in) <-s, -> [ku·'baː·nɐ] *m(f)* Cuban; *s. a.* **Deutsche(r)**
kubanisch [ku·'baː·nɪʃ] *adj* Cuban; *s. a.* **deutsch**
Kübel <-s, -> ['kyː·bl̩] *m* ❶ (*großer Eimer*) bucket ❷ (*Pflanzkübel*) container
Kubikmeter [ku·'biːk-] *m o nt* cubic meter
Küche <-, -n> ['kʏ·çə] *f* kitchen
Kuchen <-s, -> ['kuː·xn̩] *m* cake
Kuchenblech *nt* cake pan
Küchenchef(in) *m(f)* chef
Kuchenform *f* cake pan
Küchenherd *m* stove
Küchenmaschine *f* food processor
Küchenmesser *nt* kitchen knife
Küchenschabe *f* cockroach
Kuchenteig *m* [cake] batter
Kücken <-s, -> ['kʏ·kn̩] *nt* ÖSTERR (*Küken*) chick
kucken ['kʊ·kn̩] *vi* NORDD (*fam*) *s.* **gucken**
Kuckuck <-s, -e> ['kʊ·kʊk] *m* ORN cuckoo ▶WENDUNGEN: **[das] weiß der ~!** (*fam*) God only knows!; **zum ~ [noch mal]!** (*fam*) [god]damn it!
Kuddelmuddel <-s> *m o nt kein pl* (*fam*) muddle; (*Unordnung*) mess; (*Verwirrung*) confusion
Kugel <-, -n> ['kuː·gl̩] *f* ❶ MATH sphere ❷ SPORT ball; (*Kegelkugel*) bowling ball ❸ (*Geschoss*) bullet ▶WENDUNGEN: **eine ruhige ~ schieben** (*fam*) to have it pretty easy
kugelförmig *adj* spherical
kugeln ['kuː·gl̩n] *vi sein* to roll ▶WENDUNGEN: **zum K~ sein** (*fam*) to be hilarious
kugelrund ['kuː·gl̩·'rʊnt] *adj* ❶ (*kugelförmig*) ■**~ sein** to be round as a ball ❷ (*fam: feist und rundlich*) tubby
Kugelschreiber *m* ballpoint pen
kugelsicher *adj* bulletproof
Kuh <-, Kühe> [kuː, *pl* 'kyː·ə] *f* ❶ ZOOL cow ❷ (*pej fam: Frau*) bitch; **blöde ~** stupid chick
Kuhdorf *nt* (*pej fam*) one-horse town
Kuhfladen *m* cow patty
Kuhhandel *m* (*pej fam*) horse trade
Kuhhaut *f* cowhide ▶WENDUNGEN: **das geht auf keine ~** (*sl*) that's going too far *fam*
Kuhhirt(e), -hirtin *m, f* cowherd, cowboy *masc*, cowgirl *fem*
kühl [kyːl] **I.** *adj* ❶ (*recht kalt*) cool; **draußen wird es ~** it's getting chilly outside ❷ (*reserviert*) cool **II.** *adv* ❶ (*recht kalt*) **etw ~ lagern** to store sth in a cool place ❷ (*reserviert*) coolly
Kühlanlage *f* cold-storage facility
Kühlbox *f* cooler
Kuhle <-, -n> ['kuː·lə] *f* hollow
Kühle <-> ['kyː·lə] *f kein pl* (*geh*) ❶ (*kühle Beschaffenheit*) cool ❷ (*Reserviertheit*) coolness
kühlen ['kyː·lən] **I.** *vt* to chill **II.** *vi* to cool
Kühler <-s, -> ['kyː·lɐ] *m* AUTO radiator
Kühlerhaube *f* hood
Kühlflüssigkeit *f* coolant
Kühlhaus *nt* refrigerated warehouse
Kühlraum *m* cold [*or* refrigerated] storage room
Kühlschrank *m* refrigerator, fridge *fam*
Kühltasche *f* cooler bag

Kühltruhe *f* freezer [chest]
Kühlturm *m* cooling tower
Kühlung <-, -en> ['ky:·lʊŋ] *f* cooling; **zur ~** to cool down
Kühlwagen *m* (*Lkw*) refrigerated truck
Kühlwasser *nt kein pl* coolant
Kuhmilch *f* cow's milk
kühn [ky:n] *adj* ❶ (*wagemutig*) brave ❷ (*gewagt*) bold
Kühnheit <-, -en> *f* ❶ *kein pl* (*Wagemut*) bravery ❷ *kein pl* (*Gewagtheit*) boldness ❸ (*Dreistigkeit*) audacity
Kuhstall *m* cowshed
Küken <-s, -> ['ky:·kn̩] *nt* chick
kulant [ku·'lant] *adj* obliging
Kulanz <-> [ku·'lants] *f kein pl* willingness to oblige
Kuli <-s, -s> ['ku:·li] *m* (*fam*) pen
kulinarisch [ku·li·'na:·rɪʃ] *adj* culinary
Kulisse <-, -n> [ku·'lɪ·sə] *f* THEAT scenery ▶WENDUNGEN: **hinter die ~n blicken** to look behind the scenes; **nur ~ sein** (*pej fam*) to be merely a facade
Kulleraugen *pl* (*fam*) big wide eyes *pl*
kullern ['kʊ·lɐn] *vi sein* (*fam*) to roll
Kult <-[e]s, -e> [kʊlt] *m* cult
Kultfigur *f* cult figure
Kultfilm *m* cult film
kultisch *adj* ritual
kultivieren* [kʊl·ti·'vi:·rən] *vt* to cultivate
kultiviert [kʊl·ti·'vi:·ɐt] **I.** *adj* ❶ (*gepflegt*) refined ❷ (*von feiner Bildung*) ■**~ sein** to be cultured **II.** *adv* ❶ (*gepflegt*) sophisticatedly ❷ (*zivilisiert*) in a refined manner
Kultivierung <-, -en> [kʊl·ti·'vi:·rʊŋ] *f* cultivation
Kultstätte *f* place of ritual worship
Kultur <-, -en> [kʊl·'tu:ɐ̯] *f* ❶ (*Zivilisation*) civilization ❷ *kein pl* (*Zivilisationsniveau*) culture
Kulturaustausch *m* cultural exchange
Kulturbanause *m* (*pej fam*) philistine
Kulturbeutel *m* toiletries bag
Kulturdenkmal *nt* cultural monument
kulturell [kʊl·tu·'rɛl] **I.** *adj* cultural **II.** *adv* culturally
Kulturgut *nt* cultural asset
Kulturkreis *m* cultural environment
Kulturschock *m* culture shock
Kulturzentrum *nt* ❶ (*Ort des kulturellen Lebens*) cultural center ❷ (*Anlage mit kulturellen Einrichtungen*) arts center
Kultusminister(in) *m(f)* Secretary of Education and Cultural Affairs
Kümmel <-s, -> ['kʏ·ml̩] *m* caraway
Kummer <-s> ['kʊ·mɐ] *m kein pl* ❶ (*Gefühl*) grief; **jdm ~ machen** to cause sb grief ❷ (*Anlass*) worry, trouble; **wenn das dein einziger ~ ist** if that's your only problem; **~ haben** to have worries
kümmerlich ['kʏ·mɐ·lɪç] **I.** *adj* ❶ (*pej: armselig*) miserable; *Mahlzeit* measly ❷ (*miserabel*) pitiful ❸ (*unterentwickelt*) puny **II.** *adv* (*notdürftig*) in a miserable way
kümmern ['kʏ·mɐn] **I.** *vt* ■**etw/jd kümmert jdn** sth/sb concerns sb; **was kümmert mich das?** what concern is that of mine? **II.** *vr* ■**sich** *akk* **um jdn ~** to look after sb; ■**sich** *akk* **um etw ~** to take care of sth; ■**sich** *akk* **darum ~, dass ...** to see to it that ...; **kümmere dich um deine eigenen Angelegenheiten** mind your own business
Kummerspeck *m* (*hum fam*) excess weight due to emotional problems
kummervoll **I.** *adj* sorrowful **II.** *adv* sorrowfully
Kumpan(in) <-s, -e> [kʊm·'pa:n] *m(f)* (*pej fam*) pal
Kumpel <-s, -> *m* ❶ (*Bergmann*) miner ❷ (*fam: Kamerad*) buddy
kündbar ['kʏnt·ba:ɐ̯] *adj* terminable
Kunde, Kundin <-n,-n> ['kʊn·də, 'kʊn·dɪn] *m, f* customer
Kundenberatung *f* customer service
Kundendienst *m* ❶ *kein pl* (*Service*) customer service ❷ (*Servicestelle*) customer service [office]
Kundenkarte *f* customer card
Kundennummer *f* customer account number
Kundenstamm *m* regular clientele
Kundgebung <-, -en> *f* rally
kündigen ['kʏn·dɪ·gn̩] **I.** *vi* ❶ (*Arbeitsverhältnis beenden*) ■**jdm ~** to give sb notice, to lay off *sep* sb; **jdm fristlos ~** to lay off *sep* sb without notice ❷ (*Mietverhältnis beenden*) **dem Mieter/Vermieter ~** to give a tenant/landlord notice **II.** *vt* ❶ (*Arbeitsverhältnis beenden*) ■**jdn ~** to give sb notice, to lay off *sep* sb; **jdn fristlos ~** to lay off *sep* sb without notice; **[bei jdm] seine Stelle ~** to give one's notice [to sb] ❷ (*Mietverhältnis beenden*) **jdm eine Wohnung ~** to give notice ❸ *Kredit, Vertrag* to terminate; *Abonnement* to cancel
Kündigung <-, -en> *f* ❶ (*durch den Arbeitnehmer*) handing in one's notice; (*durch den Arbeitgeber*) dismissal, layoff; **fristlose ~** dismissal without notice ❷ *eines Kredits, eines Abonnements* cancellation; *eines Vertrags* termination
Kündigungsfrist *f* period of notice
Kündigungsgrund *m* reason for giving notice, grounds for dismissal
Kundin <-, -nen> *f fem form von* **Kunde**
Kundschaft <-, -en> ['kʊnt·ʃaft] *f* customers *pl;* (*bei Dienstleistungen*) clientele
künftig ['kʏnf·tɪç] **I.** *adj* future **II.** *adv* in the future
Kunst <-, Künste> [kʊnst, *pl* 'kʏn·stə] *f* art ▶WENDUNGEN: **das ist die ganze ~** that's all there is to it; **keine ~ sein** (*fam*) to be easy
Kunstausstellung *f* art exhibit[ion]
Kunstfaser *f* synthetic fiber
Kunstfehler *m* professional error
kunstfertig **I.** *adj* skillful **II.** *adv* skillfully
Kunstgattung *f* genre
Kunstgegenstand *m* objet d'art, piece of art

Kunstgriff *m* trick
Kunstleder *nt* imitation leather
Künstler(in) <-s, -> ['kʏns·tlɐ] *m(f)* [visual] artist
künstlerisch ['kʏnst·lə·rɪʃ] **I.** *adj* artistic **II.** *adv* artistically
Künstlername *m* pseudonym; *Schauspieler* stage name
Künstlerpech *nt kein pl* (*hum fam*) hard luck
künstlich ['kʏnst·lɪç] **I.** *adj* artificial **II.** *adv* artificially
Kunstsammlung *f* art collection
Kunstseide *f* imitation silk
Kunststoff *m* synthetic material
Kunststück *nt* ❶ (*artistische Leistung*) trick ❷ (*schwierige Leistung*) feat; **das ist doch kein ~!** (*fam*) there's nothing to it!
kunstvoll **I.** *adj* elaborate **II.** *adv* ornately
Kunstwerk *nt* work of art
kunterbunt ['kʊn·tɐ·bʊnt] **I.** *adj* ❶ (*vielfältig*) varied ❷ (*sehr bunt*) colorful ❸ (*wahllos gemischt*) motley; **ein ~es Durcheinander** a jumble **II.** *adv* (*ungeordnet*) **~ durcheinander** completely jumbled up
Kupfer <-s, -> ['kʊ·pfɐ] *nt* copper
Kuppe <-, -n> ['kʊ·pə] *f* ❶ (*Bergkuppe*) [rounded] hilltop ❷ (*Fingerkuppe*) tip
Kuppel <-, -n> ['kʊ·pl̩] *f* dome
Kuppelei <-, -en> [kʊ·pə·'lai] *f* (*pej veraltend*) matchmaking
kuppeln ['kʊ·pl̩n] **I.** *vi* AUTO to work the clutch **II.** *vt* ■**etw an etw ~** to couple sth to sth
Kuppler(in) <-s, -> ['kʊp·lɐ] *m(f)* (*pej*) matchmaker
Kupplung <-, -en> ['kʊp·lʊŋ] *f* ❶ AUTO clutch ❷ (*Anhängevorrichtung*) coupling
Kur <-, -en> [kuːɐ̯] *f* treatment [at a health resort]; **in ~ fahren** to go to a spa
Kuraufenthalt *m* stay at a spa
Kurbel <-, -n> ['kʊr·bl̩] *f* crank
kurbeln ['kʊr·bl̩n] *vi, vt* to crank, to wind
Kurbelwelle *f* crankshaft
Kürbis <-ses, -se> ['kʏr·bɪs] *m* pumpkin
Kürbiskern *m* pumpkin seed
Kurde, Kurdin <-n, -n> ['kʊr·də] *m, f* Kurd; *s. a.* **Deutsche(r)**
kurdisch ['kʊr·dɪʃ] *adj* Kurdish; *s. a.* **deutsch**
Kurdistan <-s> ['kʊr·dɪs·taːn] *nt* Kurdistan; *s. a.* **Deutschland**
Kurgast *m* sb staying at a spa
Kurhaus *nt* main facility at a spa
Kurier <-s, -e> [ku·'riːɐ̯] *m* courier
Kurierdienst *m* ❶ (*Dienstleistung*) courier service ❷ (*Firma*) courier [service]
kurieren* [ku·'riː·rən] *vt* to cure (**von** + *dat* of)
kurios [ku·'ri̯·oːs] (*geh*) **I.** *adj* curious **II.** *adv* curiously
Kuriosität <-, -en> [ku·ri̯o·zi·'tɛːt] *f* (*geh*) ❶ *kein pl* (*kuriose Art*) oddity ❷ (*kurioser Gegenstand*) curiosity
Kurort *m* spa, health resort
Kurpfuscher(in) <-s, -> *m(f)* (*pej fam*) quack
Kurs <-es, -e> [kʊrs, *pl* 'kʊr·zə] *m* ❶ (*Richtung*) course; **vom ~ abkommen** to deviate from one's/its course ❷ (*Lehrgang*) course ❸ (*Wechselkurs*) exchange rate
Kurse ['kʊr·zə] *pl von* **Kursus**
kursieren* [kʊr·'ziː·rən] *vi Falschgeld* to be in circulation; *Gerücht* to circulate
kursiv [kʊr·'ziːf] **I.** *adj* italic **II.** *adv* in italics
Kursivschrift *f* italics
kursorisch [kʊr·'zoː·rɪʃ] (*geh*) **I.** *adj* cursory **II.** *adv* cursorily
Kursus <-, Kurse> ['kʊr·zʊs, *pl* 'kʊr·zə] *m* course
Kurswechsel *m* change of course
Kurve <-, -n> ['kʊr·və] *f* ❶ TRANSP curve; **aus der ~ fliegen** (*fam*) to wipe out on a curve; **sich** *akk* **in die ~ legen** to lean into the curve; **eine ~ machen** to curve ❷ (*gekrümmte Linie*) curve ❸ *pl* (*fam: Körperrundung*) curves *pl* ▶ WENDUNGEN: **die ~ kratzen** (*fam*) to scram *sl*, to beat it *sl*
kurvenreich ['kʊr·vən-], **kurvig** ['kʊr·vɪç] *adj* curvy
kurz <kürzer, kürzeste> [kʊrts] **I.** *adj* ❶ (*räumlich*) short ❷ (*zeitlich*) brief, short ❸ (*knapp*) brief ▶ WENDUNGEN: **den Kürzeren ziehen** (*fam*) to draw the short straw **II.** *adv* ❶ (*räumlich*) short; **[jdm] etw kürzer machen** MODE to shorten sth [for sb] ❷ (*zeitlich*) for a short time; **etw ~ braten** to flash-fry sth; **~ gesagt** in a word; **jdn ~ sprechen** to have a quick word with sb; **~ bevor** just before; **~ nachdem** shortly after; **vor ~em** just a little while ago; **bis vor ~em** up until recently ▶ WENDUNGEN: **~ entschlossen** without a moment's hesitation; **~ und gut** in a word; **über ~ oder lang** sooner or later; **~ und schmerzlos** (*fam*) quick[ly] and painless[ly]; **[bei etw** *dat*] **zu ~ kommen** to lose out [on sth]
Kurzarbeit *f kein pl* reduced working hours
kurz|arbeiten *vi* to work reduced hours
kurzärm(e)lig *adj* short-sleeved
kurzatmig *adj* short-winded
Kürze <-> ['kʏr·tsə] *f kein pl* shortness; **in aller ~** very briefly
Kürzel <-s, -> ['kʏr·tsl̩] *nt* shorthand symbol
kürzen ['kʏr·tsn̩] *vt* ❶ (*Länge/Umfang verringern*) to shorten (**um** + *akk* by); **die gekürzte Fassung eines Buches** the abridged edition of a book ❷ (*verringern*) to cut, to reduce
kürzer *adj komp von* **kurz**
kurzerhand ['kʊr·tsɐ·'hant] *adv* there and then
kürzeste(r, s) *adj superl von* **kurz**
kurz|fassenRR *vr* **sich** *akk* **~** to be brief
Kurzfassung *f* abridged version
Kurzfilm *m* short film
Kurzform *f* shortened form
kurzfristig ['kʊrts·frɪs·tɪç] **I.** *adj* ❶ (*innerhalb kurzer Zeit erfolgend*) on short notice ❷ (*für kurze Zeit geltend*) short-term **II.** *adv* ❶ (*innerhalb kurzer Zeit*) within a short [period of] time ❷ (*für kurze Zeit*) briefly
Kurzgeschichte *f* short story

kurzhaarig *adj* short-haired
kurzlebig ['kʊrts·le:·bɪç] *adj* ① (*nicht lange lebend*) *a.* MODE short-lived ② (*nicht lange haltend*) nondurable
kürzlich ['kʏrts·lɪç] *adv* not long ago
Kurznachrichten *pl* news in brief + *sing vb*
Kurzreise *f* short trip
kurz|schließen *irreg* **I.** *vt* to short-circuit **II.** *vr* ■ **sich** *akk* **mit jdm** ~ to get in touch with sb
KurzschlussRR *m* ① ELEK short circuit ② (*Affekthandlung*) moment of madness
KurzschlusshandlungRR *f*, **Kurzschlussreaktion**RR *f* knee-jerk reaction
Kurzschrift *f* shorthand
kurzsichtig **I.** *adj* (*a. fig*) shortsighted **II.** *adv* (*beschränkt*) in a shortsighted manner
Kurzsichtigkeit <-> *f kein pl* shortsightedness
Kurzstreckenflug *m* short-haul flight
kurzum [kʊrts·'ʔʊm] *adv* in short
Kürzung <-, -en> *f* ① *Text* abridgement ② FIN cut
Kurzurlaub *m* short vacation [*or* trip]
Kurzwaren *pl* dry goods *npl*
Kurzwarengeschäft *nt* dry goods store
kurzweilig ['kʊrts·vai·lɪç] *adj* entertaining
Kurzwelle *f* short wave
Kurzzeitgedächtnis *m* short-term memory
kurzzeitig **I.** *adj* short-term, brief **II.** *adv* brief, briefly, for a short time
kuschelig ['kʊʃ·əl·ɪç] **I.** *adj* cozy **II.** *adv* cozily
kuscheln ['kʊ·ʃl̩n] **I.** *vr* ■ **sich** *akk* **an jdn** ~ to cuddle up to sb; ■ **sich** *akk* **in etw** ~ to snuggle up in sth **II.** *vi* ■ [**mit jdm**] ~ to cuddle [with [*or* up to] sb]
Kuschelrock <-s, -> *m kein pl* MUS soft rock
Kuscheltier *nt* stuffed animal
kuschen ['kʊ·ʃn̩] *vi* ■ [**vor jdm**] ~ to obey [sb]
Kusine <-, -n> [ku·'zi:·nə] *f fem form von* **Cousin** cousin
KussRR <-es, Küsse>, **Kuß**ALT <-sses, Küsse> [kʊs, *pl* 'kʏ·sə] *m* kiss
küssen ['kʏ·sn̩] *vt, vi* to kiss
Küste <-, -n> ['kʏs·tə] *f* coast
Küstengebiet *nt* coastal area
Küstengewässer *pl* coastal waters *pl*
KüstenschifffahrtRR *f kein pl* coastal shipping
Küstenschutz *m* coastal protection
Kutsche <-, -n> ['kʊt·ʃə] *f* carriage
Kutscher(in) <-s, -> ['kʊt·ʃɐ] *m(f)* coachman
kutschieren* [kʊt·'ʃi:·rən] **I.** *vi sein* (*fam*) ■ **irgendwohin** ~ to go for a drive somewhere **II.** *vt haben* (*fam*) ■ **jdn irgendwohin** ~ to give sb a lift [*or* ride] somewhere
Kutte <-, -n> ['kʊ·tə] *f* habit
Kuttel <-, -n> ['kʊ·tl̩] *f meist pl* tripe *sing*
Kutter <-s, -> ['kʊ·tɐ] *m* cutter
Kuvert <-s, -s> [ku·'ve:ɐ̯] *nt* envelope
Kuwait <-s> ['ku:·vait] *nt* Kuwait; *s. a.* **Deutschland**
Kuwaiter(in) *m(f)* Kuwaiti; *s. a.* **Deutsche(r)**
kuwaitisch [ku·'vai·tɪʃ] *adj* Kuwaiti; *s. a.* **deutsch**
KZ <-s, -s> [ka:·'tsɛt] *nt Abk von* **Konzentrationslager**

K

L

L, l <-, - *o fam* -s, -s> [ɛl] *nt* L, l; ~ **wie Ludwig** L as in Lima
l [ɛl] *Abk von* **Liter** l
labil [la·ˈbiːl] *adj* ❶ MED *Gesundheit, Kreislauf etc.* poor ❷ (*geh: instabil*) *a.* PSYCH unstable
Labilität <-, *selten* -en> [la·bi·li·ˈtɛːt] *f* ❶ MED frailty ❷ (*geh: Instabilität*) *a.* PSYCH instability
Labor <-s, -s *o* -e> [la·ˈboːɐ̯] *nt* laboratory, lab *fam*
Laborant(in) <-en, -en> [la·bo·ˈrant] *m(f)* laboratory technician
Labyrinth <-[e]s, -e> [la·by·ˈrɪnt] *nt* maze
Lache¹ <-, -n> [ˈla·xə] *f* puddle
Lache² <-, -n> [ˈla·xə] *f* (*pej fam*) laugh
lächeln [ˈlɛ·çl̩n] *vi* ❶ (*freundlich lächeln*) to smile ❷ (*sich lustig machen*) to smirk (**über** +*akk* at)
Lächeln <-s> [ˈlɛ·çl̩n] *nt kein pl* smile
lachen [ˈla·xn̩] *vi* ❶ (*auflachen*) to laugh (**über** +*akk* at) ❷ (*auslachen*) to laugh (**über** +*akk* at) ▶ WENDUNGEN: **gut ~ haben** to be all right for sb to laugh
Lachen <-s> [ˈla·xn̩] *nt kein pl* ❶ (*Gelächter*) laughter ❷ (*Lache*) laugh
lächerlich [ˈlɛ·çɐ·lɪç] **I.** *adj* ❶ (*albern*) ridiculous; **jdn/sich ~ machen** to make a fool of sb/oneself ❷ (*geringfügig*) trivial; **ein ~er Preis** a ridiculously low price **II.** *adv* (*sehr*) ridiculously
Lächerlichkeit <-, -en> *f* ❶ *kein pl* (*Albernheit*) ridiculousness ❷ (*Geringfügigkeit*) triviality
lachhaft *adj* laughable
Lachkrampf *m* (*fig*) **einen ~ bekommen** to be in stitches, to be dying of laughter
Lachs <-es, -e> [laks] *m* salmon
lachsfarben *adj* salmon pink
Lack <-[e]s, -e> [lak] *m* ❶ (*Lackierung*) paint [job] ❷ (*Lackfarbe*) glossy paint; (*transparent*) varnish
lackieren* [la·ˈkiː·rən] *vt a. Fingernägel* to paint; *Holz* to varnish
Lackierung <-, -en> *f* ❶ (*das Lackieren*) painting ❷ (*aufgetragener Lack*) paint job
Lackleder <-s> *nt inv* patent leather
Ladefläche *f* AUTO cargo area
laden¹ <lädt, lud, geladen> [ˈlaː·dn̩] **I.** *vt* ❶ (*packen*) *a.* COMPUT to load (**auf, in** +*akk* on[to], in[to]), to unload (**aus** +*dat* from, out of) ❷ (*sich aufbürden*) ■**etw auf sich** *akk* ~ to saddle oneself with sth ❸ (*mit Munition versehen*) to load (**mit** +*dat* with) ❹ ELEK to charge **II.** *vi* ▶ WENDUNGEN: **geladen sein** (*fam*) to be hopping mad
laden² <lädt, lud, geladen> [ˈlaː·dn̩] *vt* ❶ (*geh: einladen*) to invite (**zu** +*dat* to) ❷ JUR (*geh*) to summon
Laden¹ <-s, Läden> [ˈlaː·dn̩, *pl* ˈlɛː·dn̩] *m* ❶ (*Geschäft*) store, shop ❷ (*fam: Betrieb*) business
Laden² <-s, Läden *o* -> [ˈlaː·dn̩, *pl* ˈlɛː·dn̩] *m* shutter
Ladenbesitzer(in) *m(f)* storeowner
Ladendieb(in) *m(f)* shoplifter
Ladenhüter *m* (*pej*) slow seller
Ladenpreis *m* retail price
LadenschlussRR *m kein pl* closing time
Ladentisch *m* store [*or* shop] counter
Laderampe *f* loading ramp
Laderaum *m* LUFT, NAUT cargo space
lädieren* [lɛ·ˈdiː·rən] *vt* to damage; **lädiert sein** (*hum*) to be the worse for wear
Ladung¹ <-, -en> *f* ❶ (*Fracht*) load; *Schiff, Flugzeug* cargo ❷ (*fam: größere Menge*) load ❸ (*Munition, Sprengstoff*) charge
Ladung² <-, -en> *f* JUR summons + *sing vb*
lag [laːk] *imp von* **liegen**
Lage <-, -n> [ˈlaː·gə] *f* ❶ (*geographisch*) location ❷ (*Liegeposition*) position ❸ (*Situation*) situation; **zu etw** +*dat* **in der ~ sein** to be in a position to do sth; **sich** *akk* **in jds ~ versetzen** to put oneself in sb's position ❹ (*Schicht*) layer
Lagebericht *m* status report
Lager <-s, -> [ˈlaː·gɐ] *nt* ❶ (*Warenlager*) warehouse; **etw auf ~ haben** to have sth in stock ❷ (*vorübergehende Unterkunft*) camp ❸ (*ideologische Gruppierung*) camp ❹ TECH bearing
Lagerfeuer *nt* campfire
Lagerhalle *f* warehouse
lagern [ˈlaː·gɐn] **I.** *vt* ❶ (*aufbewahren*) to store ❷ MED to lay; **die Beine hoch ~** to lie with one's legs up **II.** *vi* ❶ (*aufbewahrt werden*) **dunkel/kühl ~** to be stored in the dark/a cold place ❷ (*liegen*) to lie (**auf** +*dat* on) ❸ (*sich niederlassen*) to camp
Lagerraum *m* ❶ (*Raum*) storeroom ❷ (*Fläche*) storage space
Lagerung <-, -en> *f* storage, warehousing
lahm [laːm] *adj* ❶ (*gelähmt*) *Arm, Bein* lame ❷ (*fam: steif*) stiff ❸ (*fam: ohne Schwung arbeitend*) sluggish ❹ (*fam: schwach*) lame; *Erklärung* feeble
lähmen [ˈlɛː·mən] *vt* to paralyze
lahm|legen *vt* ■**etw ~** *Verkehr* to bring sth to a standstill
Lähmung <-, -en> *f* paralysis
Laib <-[e]s, -e> [laip, *pl* ˈlai·bə] *m bes* SÜDD loaf; (*Käse*) block
Laich <-[e]s, -e> [laiç] *m* spawn
laichen [ˈlai·çn̩] *vi* to spawn
Laie, Laiin <-n, -n> [ˈlaiə, ˈlai·ɪn] *m, f* layman, layperson
Laiendarsteller(in) *m(f)* amateur actor [*or fem* actress]
laienhaft *adj* amateurish
Lake <-, -n> [ˈlaː·kə] *f* brine
Laken <-s, -> [ˈlaː·kn̩] *nt* sheet

Lakritze <-, -n> [la·ˈkrɪt·sə] *f*, **Lakritz** <-es, -e> [la·ˈkrɪts] *m* DIAL licorice

lallen [ˈla·lən] *vi, vt* to slur

Lama <-s, -s> [ˈlaː·ma] *nt* ZOOL llama

Lamelle <-, -n> [la·ˈmɛ·lə] *f* ① (*dünne Platte*) slat ② (*Segment*) rib ③ BOT lamella

lamentieren* [la·mɛn·ˈtiː·rən] *vi* (*geh*) to complain (**über** +*akk* about)

Lametta <-s> [la·ˈmɛ·ta] *nt kein pl* tinsel

Lamm <-[e]s, Lämmer> [lam, *pl* ˈlɛmɐ] *nt* (*a. Fleisch*) lamb

Lạmmfell *nt* lambskin

Lạmmfleisch *nt* lamb

Lampe <-, -n> [ˈlam·pə] *f* lamp

Lạmpenfieber *nt* stage fright

Lạmpenschirm *m* lampshade

lancieren* [lã·ˈsiː·rən] *vt* (*geh*) ① (*publik werden lassen*) *Nachricht* to leak ② ÖKON, MEDIA to launch

Land <-[e]s, Länder> [lant, *pl* ˈlɛn·dɐ] *nt* ① (*Staat*) country; **andere Länder, andere Sitten** every country has its own customs ② (*Bundesland*) [federal] state ③ NAUT land; **~ in Sicht!** land ahoy!; **an ~ gehen** to go ashore; **jdn/etw an ~ ziehen** to pull sb/sth ashore ④ *kein pl* (*Gelände*) land ⑤ *kein pl* (*ländliche Gegend*) country; **auf dem ~[e]** in the country

> The representative bodies in nearly all the **Länder** in Germany and Austria are called *Landtage* (State Parliaments). In Hamburg and Bremen, however, they are called *Bürgerschaften* (City Parliaments), and in Berlin the representative body is called the *Abgeordnetenhaus* (House of Representatives). In Vienna, Austria, the representative body is called the *Gemeinderat* (City Council). In Switzerland, depending on the canton, the representative bodies are either called *Kantonsrat* or *Landsrat* (Cantonal Council) or *Großer Rat* (Great Council).

Lạndarbeit *f kein pl* agricultural work

Lạndarbeiter(in) *m(f)* farm hand

Lạndebahn *f* runway

landẹinwärts *adv* inland

landen [ˈlandn̩] **I.** *vi sein* ① (*niedergehen*) *Flugzeug, Raumschiff, Vogel* to land (**auf** +*dat* on, in) ② (*fam: hingelangen o enden*) to end up ③ (*fam: Eindruck machen*) **mit deinen Schmeicheleien kannst du bei mir nicht ~** your flattery won't get you very far with me **II.** *vt haben* LUFT, RAUM, MIL to land

Lạndeplatz *m* ① (*kleiner Flugplatz*) airstrip ② (*Landungsplatz*) landing spot

Ländereien [lɛn·də·ˈrai·ən] *pl* estates *pl*

Lạndesebene *f* [federal] state level (**auf** +*dat* at/on)

Lạndesgrenze *f* ① (*Staatsgrenze*) border ② (*Grenze eines Bundeslandes*) state border [*or* line]

Lạndeshauptstadt *f* state capital

Lạndesinnere(s) *nt* interior

Lạndeskunde *f kein pl* regional studies *pl*

Lạndesrat, -rätin *m, f* ÖSTERR member of state government

Lạndesregierung *f* state government

Lạndessprache *f* national language

Lạndesteil *m* region

lạndesüblich *adj* customary

Lạndesverrat *m* treason

Lạndeswährung *f* national currency

Lạndfriedensbruch *m* disturbing the peace

Lạndgericht *nt* district court

Lạndhaus *nt* country manor

Lạndkarte *f* map

Lạndkreis *m* administrative district

lạndläufig *adj* generally accepted; *Ansicht* popular

Lạndleben *nt* country life

ländlich [ˈlɛnt·lɪç] *adj* rural; *Idylle* pastoral

Lạndrat, -rätin *m, f* ① BRD *administrative head of a county* ② SCHWEIZ parliament of a canton

Lạndratsamt *nt* district administration

Lạndschaft <-, -en> [ˈlant·ʃaft] *f* ① (*Gegend*) landscape; (*ländlich*) countryside ② (*Gemälde*) landscape

lạndschaftlich **I.** *adj* scenic **II.** *adv* scenically

Lạndschaftsschutzgebiet *nt* conservation area

Lạndsitz *m* country estate

Lạndsmann, -männin <-leute> *m, f* compatriot

Lạndstraße *f* country road

Lạndstreicher(in) <-s, -> *m(f)* tramp

Lạndstrich *m* area

Lạndtag *m* state parliament

Lạndung <-, -en> *f a.* MIL landing

Lạndungsbrücke *f* pier

Lạndurlaub *m* shore leave

Lạndvermessung *f* [land] surveying

Lạndweg *m* overland route (**auf** +*dat* by)

Lạndwirt(in) *m(f)* farmer

Lạndwirtschaft *f* ① *kein pl* (*Tätigkeit*) agriculture ② (*landwirtschaftlicher Betrieb*) farm

lạndwirtschaftlich **I.** *adj* agricultural; *Bẹtrieb* farm **II.** *adv* agriculturally

lang <lạ̈nger, lạ̈ngste> [laŋ] **I.** *adj* ① (*räumlich ausgedehnt*) long ② (*zeitlich ausgedehnt*) long; **noch/schon ~** for a long time ③ (*fam: groß gewachsen*) tall **II.** *adv* ① (*eine lange Dauer*) long; **die Verhandlungen ziehen sich schon ~e hin** the negotiations have been dragging on for a long time; **wo bist du denn so ~e geblieben?** where have you been all this time? ② (*für die Dauer von etw*) **sie hielt einen Moment ~ inne** she paused for a moment ③ (*der Länge nach*) **~ gestreckt** long; **~ gezogen** prolonged

lạngärm(e)lig *adj* long-sleeved

lạngatmig *adj* (*pej*) long-winded

lange [ˈlaŋə] *adv s.* **lang II 1**

Länge <-, -n> ['lɛŋə] *f* ❶ (*räumliche Ausdehnung*) length; **der ~ nach** lengthwise; **Pfähle von drei Metern ~** ten-foot-long poles ❷ (*zeitliche Ausdehnung*) length, duration; **in voller ~** in its entirety; **sich** *akk* **in die ~ ziehen** to drag on ❸ (*fam: Größe*) height ❹ SPORT length ❺ (*Abstand vom Nullmeridian*) longitude

langen ['laŋən] **I.** *vi* (*fam*) ❶ (*ausreichen*) ■[**jdm**] **~** to be enough [for sb] ❷ (*sich erstrecken*) to reach ❸ (*fassen*) to reach; **lange bloß nicht mit der Hand an die Herdplatte** make sure you don't touch the hot plate with your hand ❹ DIAL (*auskommen*) **mit dem Brot ~ wir bis morgen** the bread will last us until tomorrow ❺ *impers* (*fam*) **jetzt langt's aber!** I've just about had enough! **II.** *vt* (*fam*) (*reichen*) ■**jdm etw ~** to hand sb sth ► WENDUNGEN: **jdm eine ~** (*fam*) to smack sb in the mouth

Lạngengrad *m* degree of longitude

länger ['lɛŋɐ] *adj, adv s.* **lang**

lạngerfristig I. *adj* fairly long-term **II.** *adv* on a fairly long-term basis

Langeweile <*gen* - *o* Langerweile, *dat* Langenweile> ['laŋə·vai·lə] *f kein pl* boredom

lạngfristig I. *adj* long-term **II.** *adv* on a long-term basis

lạnghaarig *adj* long-haired

lạngjährig *adj* of many years' standing; *Freundschaft* long-standing

Lạnglauf *m kein pl* cross-country skiing

lạnglebig *adj* ❶ (*lange lebend*) long-lived ❷ (*lange Zeit zu gebrauchen*) long-lasting ❸ (*hartnäckig*) persistent

länglich ['lɛŋ·lɪç] *adj* longish

längs [lɛŋs] **I.** *präp +gen* ■**~ einer S.** *gen* along sth **II.** *adv* (*der Länge nach*) lengthwise; **~ gestreift** with vertical stripes

langsam ['laŋ·zaːm] **I.** *adj* ❶ (*nicht schnell*) slow ❷ (*allmählich*) gradual **II.** *adv* ❶ (*nicht schnell*) slowly ❷ (*fam: allmählich*) gradually

Lạngsamkeit <-> *f kein pl* slowness

Lạngschläfer(in) *m(f)* late riser

Lạngspielplatte *f* long-playing record, LP

längst [lɛŋst] *adv* ❶ (*lange*) long since, for a long time ❷ (*bei weitem*) **~ nicht** by no means

längste(r, s) *adj, adv superl von* **lang**

längstens ['lɛŋ·stn̩s] *adv* ❶ (*höchstens*) at the most ❷ (*spätestens*) at the latest

Lạngstreckenflug *m* long-haul flight

Lạngstreckenlauf *m* long-distance race

Languste <-, -n> [laŋ·'gʊs·tə] *f* crayfish

langweilen ['laŋ·vai·lən] **I.** *vt* to bore **II.** *vi* (*pej*) to be boring **III.** *vr* ■**sich** *akk* **~** to be bored

langweilig ['laŋ·vai·lɪç] **I.** *adj* boring **II.** *adv* boringly

Lạngwelle *f* long wave

langwierig ['laŋ·viː·rɪç] *adj* long-drawn-out

Lạngzeitarbeitslose(r) *f(m) dekl wie adj* long-term unemployed person

Lạngzeitarbeitslosigkeit *f* long-term unemployment

Lạngzeitgedächtnis *nt* long-term memory

Lanze <-, -n> ['lan·tsə] *f* lance

Lappalie <-, -n> [la·'paː·li̯ə] *f* trifle

Lappe, Lappin <-n, -n> ['lapə] *m, f* Laplander; *s. a.* **Deutsche(r)**

Lappen <-s, -> ['lapn̩] *m* rag ► WENDUNGEN: **jdm durch die ~ gehen** (*fam*) to slip through sb's fingers

läppisch ['lɛpɪʃ] **I.** *adj* ❶ (*fam: lächerlich*) *Betrag* ridiculous ❷ (*pej: albern*) silly **II.** *adv* (*pej*) in a silly manner

Lappland <-[e]s> ['lap·lant] *nt* Lapland; *s. a.* **Deutschland**

Lapsus <-, -> ['lap·sʊs] *m* (*geh*) slip

Laptop <-s, -s> ['lɛp·tɔp] *m* laptop

Lärche <-, -n> ['lɛr·çə] *f* larch

Lärm <-[e]s> [lɛrm] *m kein pl* noise

Lärmbelästigung *f* noise pollution

lạ̈rmempfindlich *adj* sensitive to noise

lärmen ['lɛr·mən] *vi* to be noisy

lạ̈rmend I. *adj* noisy; *Menge* raucous **II.** *adv* noisily

Lạ̈rmpegel *m* noise level

Lạ̈rmschutz *m* noise protection

Larve <-, -n> ['lar·fə] *f* larva, grub

las [laːs] *imp von* **lesen**

lasch [laʃ] **I.** *adj* (*fam*) ❶ (*schlaff*) feeble; *Händedruck* limp ❷ (*nachsichtig*) lax **II.** *adv* (*fam: schlaff*) limply

Lasche <-, -n> ['la·ʃə] *f* flap; (*Kleidung*) loop

Laser <-s, -> ['leː·zɐ, 'leɪ·zə] *m* laser

Laserdrucker *m* laser printer

Laserstrahl *m* laser beam

lassen <lạ̈sst, ließ, gelạssen> ['la·sn̩] **I.** *vt* ❶ (*unterlassen*) to stop; **wenn du keine Lust dazu hast, dann lass es doch** if you don't feel like it, [then] don't do it; **er kann es nicht ~** he can't help [*or* stop] it ❷ (*zurücklassen*) ■**jdn/etw irgendwo ~** to leave sb/sth somewhere ❸ (*überlassen, behalten lassen*) ■**jdm etw ~** to let sb have sth; **ich lasse dir das Auto** you can have the car ❹ (*gehen lassen*) to let; **lass den Hund nicht nach draußen** don't let the dog out [*or* go outside] ❺ (*in einem Zustand lassen*) **jdn ohne Aufsicht ~** to leave sb unsupervised ❻ (*fam: loslassen*) ■**jdn/etw ~** to let sb/sth go ❼ (*in Ruhe lassen*) ■**jdn ~** to leave sb alone ❽ (*gewähren lassen*) **ich möchte so gerne mit, lässt du mich?** I really want to go along — will you let me? ❾ (*hineinlassen*) **frische Luft ins Zimmer ~** to let some fresh air into the room ❿ (*hinauslassen*) **sie haben mir die Luft aus den Reifen gelassen!** they let the air out of my tires! ⓫ (*zugestehen*) **eines muss man ihm ~, er versteht sein Handwerk** you have to give him one thing: he knows his job ► WENDUNGEN: **einen ~** (*fam*) to let one rip **II.** *aux vb* <lạ̈sst, ließ, lạssen> *modal* ❶ (*veranlassen*) ■**jdn etw tun ~** to have sb do sth; **jdn kommen ~** to send for sb; **~ Sie Herrn Braun hereinkommen** send Mr. Braun in;

der Chef hat es nicht gerne, wenn man ihn warten lässt the boss doesn't like to be kept waiting; ■**etw machen ~** to have sth done; **ich lasse mir die Haare schneiden** I'm going to get a haircut [*or* having my hair cut] ❷ (*zulassen*) ■**jdn etw tun ~** to let sb do sth; **lass sie gehen!** let her go!; **er lässt sich nicht so leicht betrügen** it won't be that easy to trick him; **das lasse ich nicht mit mir machen** I won't stand for it!; **viel mit sich machen ~** to put up with a lot ❸ (*belassen*) **das Wasser sollte man eine Minute kochen ~** the water should be allowed to boil for one minute ❹ (*Möglichkeit ausdrückend*) **das lässt sich machen!** that can be done! ❺ *als Imperativ* **lass uns jetzt lieber gehen** let's go now **III.** *vi* <lässt, ließ, gelassen> (*ablassen*) **sie kann einfach nicht von ihm ~** she simply can't part from him; **vom Alkohol ~** to give up alcohol; **lass nur!** that's all right!

lässig ['lɛsɪç] **I.** *adj* ❶ (*ungezwungen*) casual ❷ (*fam: leicht*) **die Fragen waren total ~!** the questions were really easy! **II.** *adv* ❶ (*ungezwungen*) casually ❷ (*fam: mit Leichtigkeit*) no problem

Lässigkeit <-> *f kein pl* casualness

Lasso <-s, -s> ['laso] *m o nt* lasso

Last <-, -en> [last] *f* ❶ (*zu tragender Gegenstand*) load ❷ (*schweres Gewicht*) weight ❸ (*Bürde*) burden ❹ *pl* (*finanzielle Belastung*) burden; **zu jds ~en gehen** to be charged to sb ▶WENDUNGEN: **jdm zur ~ fallen** to become a burden on sb

lasten ['las·tn̩] *vi* ❶ (*als Last liegen auf*) ■**auf etw** *dat* **~** to rest on sth ❷ (*eine Bürde sein*) ■**auf jdm ~** *Verantwortung* to rest with sb ❸ (*stark belasten*) ■**auf etw** *dat* **~** to weigh heavily on sth

Lastenaufzug *m* freight elevator

Laster[1] <-s, -> ['las·tɐ] *m* (*fam: Lastwagen*) truck

Laster[2] <-s, -> ['las·tɐ] *nt* (*schlechte Gewohnheit*) vice

Lästerer, Lästerin <-s, -> ['lɛs·tə·rɐ] *m, f* detractor *form,* unfair critic

lästern ['lɛstɐn] *vi* to make disparaging remarks (**über** +*akk* about)

lästig ['lɛs·tɪç] *adj* ❶ (*unangenehm*) *Husten, Kopfschmerzen etc.* irritating ❷ (*störend, nervend*) annoying; *Person a.* tiresome

Lasttier *nt* pack animal

Lastwagen *m* truck

Lastzug *m* tractor-trailer

Lasur <-, -en> [la'zu:ɐ̯] *f* [clear] varnish

lasziv [las·'tsi:f] **I.** *adj* (*geh*) lascivious **II.** *adv* (*geh*) lasciviously

Latein <-s> [la·'tain] *nt* Latin ▶WENDUNGEN: **mit seinem ~ am Ende sein** to be at one's wits' end

Lateinamerika *nt* Latin America

Lateinamerikaner(in) <-s, -> *m(f)* Latin American; *s. a.* **Deutsche(r)**

lateinamerikanisch *adj* Latin American

lateinisch *adj* Latin; **auf L~** in Latin

latent [la·'tɛnt] **I.** *adj* (*geh*) latent **II.** *adv* (*geh*) latently

Laterne <-, -n> [la·'tɛr·nə] *f* ❶ (*Straßenlaterne*) street lamp ❷ (*Lichtquelle mit Schutzgehäuse*) lantern ❸ (*Lampion*) Chinese lantern

Laternenpfahl *m* lamppost

Latex <-, Latizes> ['la:·tɛks, *pl* 'la:·ti·tse:s] *m* latex

latschen ['la:t·ʃn̩] *vi sein* (*fam*) ❶ (*schwerfällig gehen*) to trudge; (*lässig gehen*) to wander ❷ DIAL (*eine Ohrfeige geben*) ■**jdm eine ~** to slap sb in the face

Latschen <-s, -> ['la:t·ʃn̩] *m* (*fam*) ❶ (*Hausschuh*) slipper ❷ (*pej: ausgetretener Schuh*) worn-out shoe ▶WENDUNGEN: **aus den ~ kippen** (*fam*) to keel over; (*sehr überrascht sein*) to be bowled over

Latschenkiefer *f* mountain pine

Latte <-, -n> ['latə] *f* ❶ (*kantiges Brett*) slat ❷ SPORT bar ❸ (*Torlatte*) crossbar ▶WENDUNGEN: **eine ganze ~ von etw** *dat* (*fam*) a slew of sth

Lattenzaun *m* picket fence

Latz <-es, Lätze *o* ÖSTERR -e> [lats, *pl* 'lɛtsə] *m* bib

Latzhose *f* overalls *npl*

lau [lau] *adj* ❶ (*mild*) mild ❷ (*lauwarm*) lukewarm; (*mäßig*) moderate ❸ (*halbherzig*) halfhearted

Laub <-[e]s> [laup] *nt kein pl* foliage

Laubbaum *m* deciduous tree

Laube <-, -n> ['lau·bə] *f* arbor

Laubfrosch *m* tree frog

Laubsäge *f* jigsaw

Laubwald *m* deciduous forest

Lauch <-[e]s, -e> [laux] *m* leek

Lauer <-> ['lauɐ] *f* **auf der ~ liegen** to lie in wait

lauern ['lau·ɐn] *vi* ❶ (*in einem Versteck warten*) to lie in wait (**auf** +*akk* for) ❷ (*fam*) **die anderen lauerten nur darauf, dass sie einen Fehler machte** the others were just waiting for her to make a mistake

Lauf <-[e]s, Läufe> [lauf, *pl* 'lɔy·fə] *m* ❶ *kein pl* (*das Laufen*) run ❷ SPORT (*Durchgang*) round; (*Rennen*) heat ❸ *kein pl eines Flusses* course; *eines Sterns* path ❹ (*Verlauf, Entwicklung*) course; **das ist der ~ der Dinge** that's the way things go; **seinen ~ nehmen** to take its course; **im ~e der Jahrhunderte** over the centuries ❺ (*Gewehrlauf*) barrel ▶WENDUNGEN: **einer S.** *dat* **freien ~ lassen** to give sth free rein

Laufbahn *f* career

Laufbursche *m* (*veraltend: Bote*) errand boy

laufen <läuft, lief, gelaufen> ['lau·fn̩] **I.** *vi sein* ❶ (*rennen*) SPORT to run ❷ (*fam: gehen*) to go ❸ (*zu Fuß gehen*) to walk ❹ (*fließen*) to run; **jdm eiskalt über den Rücken ~** (*fig*) a chill runs down sb's spine ❺ (*funktionieren*) to work; *Getriebe, Maschine, Motor* to run; (*eingeschaltet sein*) to be on ⑥ FILM, THEAT (*gezeigt werden*) **was läuft [im Kino]?** what's playing [at the movies]? ⑦ (*gültig sein*) *Vertrag* to run ⑧ (*seinen Gang gehen*) to go; **wie läuft es?** how's it going? ⑨ (*geführt werden*) **auf jds Namen ~** to be issued in sb's name ⑩ (*gut verkäuflich sein*) **das neue Produkt läuft gut** the new product is selling well ► WENDUNGEN: **die Sache ist gelaufen** it's too late now **II.** *vt haben o sein* ① SPORT to run; **einen Rekord ~** to set a record ② (*zurücklegen*) to run ③ (*fahren*) **Rollschuh/Schlittschuh/Ski ~** to roller-skate/ice-skate/ski **III.** *vr impers haben* **mit diesen Schuhen wird es sich besser ~** it will be easier to walk in these shoes

laufend I. *adj attr* ① (*geh: derzeitig*) current ② (*ständig*) constant ► WENDUNGEN: **jdn [über etw** *akk*] **auf dem L~en halten** to keep sb up-to-date [on sth] **II.** *adv* (*fam*) constantly

Läufer[1] <-s, -> ['lɔy·fɐ] *m* ① (*Schachfigur*) bishop ② (*Teppich*) runner

Läufer(in)[2] <-s, -; -nen> ['lɔy·fɐ] *m(f)* runner

läufig ['lɔy·fɪç] *adj* in heat

Laufkundschaft *f kein pl* window-shoppers

Laufmasche *f* run

Laufschritt *m* **im ~** at a quick pace; MIL double time

Laufstall *m* playpen

Laufsteg *m* catwalk

Laufwerk *nt einer Maschine* drive mechanism; *einer Uhr* clockwork; *eines Computers* disk drive

Laufzeit *f* duration

Lauge <-, -n> ['lau·gə] *f* ① (*Seifenlauge*) soapy water, suds ② (*wässrige Lösung einer Base*) lye; (*von Salz*) salt solution

Laune <-, -n> ['lau·nə] *f* ① (*Stimmung*) mood; **schlechte ~ haben** to be in a bad mood; **seine ~n an jdm auslassen** to take it out on sb *fig fam* ② (*abwegige Idee*) whim

launenhaft *adj* (*kapriziös*) moody; *Wetter* unsettled

Laus <-, Läuse> [laus, *pl* 'lɔy·zə] *f* ① (*Blut saugendes Insekt*) louse ② (*Blattlaus*) aphid

Lausbub *m* SÜDD (*fam*) rascal

lauschen ['lau·ʃn̩] *vi* (*heimlich zuhören*) to eavesdrop

lauschig ['lau·ʃɪç] *adj* (*veraltend: gemütlich*) snug

lausen ['lau·zn̩] *vt* to delouse

lausig ['lau·zɪç] **I.** *adj* (*pej fam*) ① (*entsetzlich*) *Arbeit, Zeiten etc.* awful, lousy ② (*geringfügig*) measly **II.** *adv* (*pej fam*) ① (*entsetzlich*) terribly ② (*geringfügig*) **~ bezahlt** paid badly

laut[1] [laut] **I.** *adj* ① (*weithin hörbar*) loud; **etw ~er stellen** to turn up *sep* sth; **musst du immer gleich ~ werden?** do you always have to get so upset right away? ② (*voller Lärm*) noisy **II.** *adv* (*weithin hörbar*) loudly; **kannst du ~er sprechen?** can you speak up?; **~ denken** to think out loud

laut[2] [laut] *präp +gen o dat* **~ Zeitungsberichten ...** according to newspaper reports ...

Laut <-[e]s, -e> [laut] *m* noise; **keinen ~ von sich geben** to not make a sound

Laute <-, -n> ['lau·tə] *f* lute

lauten ['lau·tn̩] *vi* ① (*zum Inhalt haben*) to read; **wie lautet die Frage?** what is the question?; **wie lautet der letzte Absatz?** how does the final paragraph go?; **die Anklage lautete auf Erpressung** the charge is blackmail ② (*ausgestellt sein*) **die Papiere ~ auf seinen Namen** the papers are in his name

läuten ['lɔy·tn̩] **I.** *vi* ① *Klingel, Telefon* to ring; *Glocke a.* to chime; (*feierlich*) to toll ② ■ **nach jdm ~** to call for sb ► WENDUNGEN: **ich habe davon ~ gehört, dass ...** I've heard rumors that ... **II.** *vi impers* **es hat geläutet** there was a ring at the door; **es läutet sechs Uhr** the clock is striking six

lauter ['lau·tɐ] *adj inv* just; **das sind ~ Lügen** that's nothing but lies; **vor ~ Arbeit** because of all the work I have

Läuterung <-, -en> *f* (*geh*) reformation

lauthals ['lau·thals] *adv* at the top of one's lungs *pred*

Lautlehre *f kein pl* phonetics + *sing vb*

lautlos ['lau·tlo:s] **I.** *adj* noiseless, silent **II.** *adv* noiselessly, silently

Lautschrift *f* phonetic alphabet

Lautsprecher *m* loudspeaker

Lautsprecherbox *f* speaker

lautstark I. *adj* loud; *Protest* strong **II.** *adv* loudly, strongly

Lautstärke *f* volume

lauwarm ['lau·varm] *adj* lukewarm

Lava <-, Laven> ['la:·va, *pl* 'la:·vən] *f* lava

Lavendel <-s, -> [la·'vɛn·dl̩] *m* lavender

Lawine <-, -n> [la·'vi:·nə] *f* (*a. fig*) avalanche

lax [laks] *adj* lax

Lay-out[RR], Layout <-s, -s> [leɪ·'aʊt] *nt* layout

layouten* [le:·'aʊ·tn̩] *vt* TYPO, COMPUT to layout

Lazarett <-[e]s, -e> [la·tsa·'rɛt] *nt* military hospital

leasen ['li:·zn] *vt* to lease

Leasing <-s, -s> ['li:·zɪŋ] *nt* leasing

leben ['le:·bn̩] **I.** *vi* ① (*lebendig sein*) to live; **Gott sei Dank, er lebt [noch]** thank God, he's [still] alive ② (*ein bestimmtes Leben führen, wohnen*) to live; **vegetarisch ~** to be [a] vegetarian; **getrennt ~** to live apart ③ (*seinen Lebensunterhalt bestreiten*) **vom Schreiben ~** to make a living as a writer ► WENDUNGEN: **leb[e] wohl!** farewell! **II.** *vt* ① (*verbringen*) **ich lebe mein eigenes Leben!** I'm leading my own life! ② (*verwirklichen*) to live; **seinen Glauben ~** to live according to one's beliefs **III.** *vi impers* **wie lebt es sich denn als Millionär?** what's life as a millionaire like?

Leben <-s, -> ['le:·bn̩] *nt* (*das Lebendigsein*) life; **am ~ sein** to be alive; **[bei etw** *dat*] **ums ~ kommen** to die [doing sth]; **sich** *dat* **das ~ nehmen** (*euph*) to take one's life; **das tägli-**

che ~ everyday life; **so ist das ~ [eben]** that's life ▶ WENDUNGEN: **nie im ~** (*fam*) never; **etw ins ~ rufen** to establish sth; **[bei etw** *dat*] **sein ~ aufs Spiel setzen** to risk one's life [doing sth]; **es geht um ~ und Tod** it's a matter of life and death

lebend I. *adj* living **II.** *adv* alive

lebendig [le·ˈbɛn·dɪç] **I.** *adj* ① (*lebend*) living; ■**~ sein** to be alive ② (*anschaulich, lebhaft*) vivid; *Kind* lively **II.** *adv* ① (*lebend*) alive ② (*lebhaft*) **etw ~ schildern** to give a lively description of sth

Lebendigkeit <-> *f kein pl* vividness

Lebensabend *m* (*geh*) twilight years *pl*

Lebensabschnitt *m* chapter in one's life

Lebensalter *nt* age

Lebensbedingungen *pl* living conditions

lebensbedrohend *adj inv* life-threatening

Lebensdauer *f* ① (*Dauer des Lebens*) life span ② (*Dauer der Funktionsfähigkeit*) [working] life

Lebensende *nt kein pl* death; **bis ans/an jds ~** until one's/sb's death

Lebenserfahrung *f* life experience

Lebenserinnerungen *pl* memoirs

Lebenserwartung *f* life expectancy

lebensfähig *adj* capable of surviving

Lebensform *f* ① (*Lebensweise*) way of life ② (*Organisation von biol. Leben*) life form

Lebensfreude *f kein pl* joie de vivre, love of life

lebensfroh *adj* full of life *pred*

Lebensgefahr *f* mortal danger; **jd ist in/außer ~** sb's life is in/no longer in danger

lebensgefährlich I. *adj* extremely dangerous; (*Krankheiten*) life-threatening **II.** *adv* ① (*mit Lebensgefahr verbunden*) **~ verletzt** seriously injured ② (*fam: sehr gefährlich*) dangerously

Lebensgefährte, -gefährtin *m, f* (*geh*) partner

Lebensgemeinschaft *f* long-term relationship

Lebensgewohnheiten *pl* habits

lebensgroß *adj* life-size[d]

Lebenshaltungskosten *pl* cost of living

Lebensjahr *nt* year [of one's life]; **im 14. ~** at 14

Lebenslage *f* situation [in life]

lebenslang I. *adj* ① (*das ganze Leben dauernd*) lifelong ② JUR *s.* **lebenslänglich I** **II.** *adv* (*das ganze Leben*) all one's life

lebenslänglich [ˈleː·bn̩s·lɛŋ·lɪç] **I.** *adj* JUR life *attr*, for life *pred*; **„~" bekommen** (*fam*) to get life [in prison] **II.** *adv* all one's life

Lebenslauf *m* résumé

Lebensmittel *nt meist pl* food

Lebensmittelallergie *f* food allergy

Lebensmittelgeschäft *nt* grocery store

Lebensmittelvergiftung *f* food poisoning

lebensmüde *adj* weary of life *pred*; **bist du ~?** (*hum fam*) are you tired of living?

Lebensmut *m kein pl* courage to face life

lebensnah *adj* true-to-life

Lebenspartnerschaft *f* domestic partnership; **eingetragene ~** civil union

Lebensqualität *f kein pl* quality of life

Lebensraum *m* ① *kein pl* (*Entfaltungsmöglichkeiten*) living space ② (*Biotop*) habitat

Lebensretter(in) *m(f)* lifesaver

Lebensstandard *m kein pl* standard of living

Lebensstil *m* lifestyle

Lebensunterhalt *m kein pl* living; **das deckt noch nicht einmal meinen ~** that doesn't even cover my basic needs

Lebensversicherung *f* life insurance

Lebenswandel *m kein pl* way of life; **einen einwandfreien/lockeren ~ führen** to live a clean/loose life

Lebensweise *f* lifestyle

Lebensweisheit *f* ① (*weise Lebenserfahrung*) worldly wisdom ② (*Wahlspruch*) maxim

Lebenswerk *nt* life['s] work

lebenswert *adj* worth living *pred*

lebenswichtig *adj* vital, essential

Lebenswille *m kein pl* will to live

Lebenszeichen *nt* (*a. fig*) sign of life

Lebenszeit *f* lifetime; **auf ~** for life

Lebensziel *nt* goal in life

Leber <-, -n> [ˈleː·bɐ] *f* (*Organ*) *a.* KOCHK liver

Leberfleck *m* liver spot; (*Muttermal*) mole

Leberkäs(e) *m kein pl fine-textured meatloaf made of liver and pork*

Leberknödel *m* liver dumpling

Leberpastete *f* liver pâté

Lebertran *m* cod-liver oil

Leberwert *m meist pl* liver function reading

Leberwurst *f* liver sausage

Lebewesen *nt* living thing; **menschliches ~** human being

Lebewohl <-[e]s, -s *o geh* -e> [leː·bə·ˈvoːl] *nt* (*geh*) farewell

lebhaft [ˈleːp·haft] **I.** *adj* ① (*temperamentvoll*) lively ② (*angeregt*) lively; *Beifall* thunderous ③ (*belebt*) lively; *Verkehr* brisk ④ (*anschaulich*) *Darstellung* vivid **II.** *adv* ① (*anschaulich*) vividly ② (*sehr stark*) intensely

Lebhaftigkeit <-> *f kein pl* ① (*temperamentvolle Art*) liveliness ② (*Anschaulichkeit*) vividness

Lebkuchen [ˈleːp·kuː·xn̩] *m* gingerbread

leblos [ˈleːp·loːs] *adj* (*geh*) lifeless

Lebtag [ˈleːp·taːk] *m* (*fam*) **ihr ~ lang** for the rest of her days; **das hätte ich mein ~ nicht gedacht** never in all my life would I have thought that

Lebzeiten *pl* **zu jds ~** (*Zeit*) in sb's day; (*Leben*) in sb's lifetime

lechzen [ˈlɛ·çtsn̩] *vi* (*geh*) ■**nach etw** *dat* **~** to long for sth

leck [lɛk] *adj* leaky

Leck <-[e]s, -s> [lɛk] *nt* leak

lecken¹ [ˈlɛ·kn̩] *vi* to leak

lecken² [ˈlɛ·kn̩] *vi* to lick

lecker [ˈlɛ·kɐ] **I.** *adj* delicious **II.** *adv* deliciously

Leckerbissen *m* delicacy

Leckerei <-, -en> [lɛ·kə·ˈrai] *f* ① KOCHK *s.* **Leckerbissen** ② *kein pl* (*pej fam: das*

Lecken) licking

Leckermaul *nt* (*fam*) ■**ein ~ sein** to have a sweet tooth

Leder <-s, -> ['leːdɐ] *nt* leather; **zäh wie ~** (*fam*) tough as nails

Lederhose *f* ① (*lederne Trachtenhose*) lederhosen *npl* ② (*Hose aus Leder*) leather pants *npl*

Lederjacke *f* leather jacket

Lederwaren *pl* leather goods

ledig ['leː·dɪç] *adj* single

lediglich ['leː·dɪk·lɪç] *adv* (*geh*) merely

leer [leːɐ̯] **I.** *adj* ① (*ohne Inhalt*) empty; **etw ~ machen** to empty sth ② (*menschenleer*) empty ③ (*nicht bedruckt*) blank ④ (*ausdruckslos*) vacant; *Versprechungen, Worte* empty **II.** *adv* **wie ~ gefegt sein** to be deserted ► WENDUNGEN: [**bei etw** *dat*] **~ ausgehen** to go away empty-handed

Leere <-> ['leː·rə] *f kein pl* emptiness

leeren ['leː·rən] **I.** *vt* ① (*entleeren*) to empty; **sie leerte ihre Tasse nur halb** she only drank half of her cup ② DIAL, ÖSTERR (*ausleeren*) ■**etw in etw** *akk* **~** to empty sth into sth **II.** *vr* ■**sich** *akk* **~** to empty

Leergut *nt kein pl* empties *pl fam*

Leerlauf *m* ① (*Gangeinstellung*) neutral [gear] ② (*unproduktive Phase*) unproductiveness

Leertaste *f* space bar

Leerung <-, -en> *f* emptying; *von Post* collection

legal [le·'gaːl] **I.** *adj* legal **II.** *adv* legally

legalisieren* [le·ga·li·'ziː·rən] *vt* to legalize

Legalität <-> [le·ga·li·'tɛːt] *f kein pl* legality

Legastheniker(in) <-s, -> [le·gas·'teː·ni·kɐ] *m(f)* dyslexic

legen ['leː·gn̩] **I.** *vt* ① ■**jdn/etw irgendwohin ~** to put sb/sth somewhere; **seinen Arm um jdn ~** to put one's arm around sb; **~ Sie ihn auf den Rücken** lay him on his back ② **die Stirn in Falten ~** to frown ③ *Teppich, Kabel, Eier* to lay **II.** *vr* ① (*hinlegen*) ■**sich** *akk* **~** to lie down; **sich** *akk* **ins Bett/in die Sonne/auf den Rücken ~** to go to bed/lie down in the sun/lie on one's back ② (*sich niederlassen*) ■**sich** *akk* **auf etw** *akk* **~** to settle on sth; (*schädigen*) **sich auf die Bronchien ~** to settle in one's bronchial tubes ③ (*nachlassen*) ■**sich** *akk* **~** *Aufregung, Empörung, Sturm, Begeisterung* to subside; *Nebel* to lift

legendär [le·gɛn·'dɛːɐ̯] *adj* legendary

Legende <-, -n> [le·'gɛn·də] *f* ① (*fromme Sage*) legend ② (*Lügenmärchen*) myth

leger [le·'ʒeːɐ, le·'ʒɛːɐ] **I.** *adj* ① (*bequem*) loose-fitting ② (*ungezwungen*) casual **II.** *adv* casually

Leggings ['lɛg·ɪŋs] *pl* leggings

Legierung <-, -en> *f* alloy

Legion <-, -en> [le·'gi̯oːn] *f* legion

Legionär <-s, -e> [le·gi̯o·'nɛːɐ̯] *m* legionary

Legislative <-n, -n> [le·gɪs·la·'tiː·və] *f* legislative power

Legislaturperiode [le·gɪs·la·'tuːɐ̯-] *f* legislative period

Legitimation <-, -en> [le·gi·ti·ma·'tsi̯oːn] *f* (*geh*) authorization

legitimieren* [le·gi·ti·'miː·rən] **I.** *vt* (*geh*) ① (*berechtigen*) to authorize (**zu** +*dat* to) ② (*für gesetzmäßig erklären*) to legitimize (**durch** +*akk* by) **II.** *vr* (*geh: ausweisen*) ■**sich** *akk* **~** to identify oneself

Legitimität <-> [le·gi·ti·mi·'tɛːt] *f kein pl* (*geh*) legitimacy

Leguan <-s, -e> [le·'gu̯aːn, 'leː·gu̯aːn] *m* iguana

Lehm <-[e]s, -e> [leːm] *m* clay

lehmig ['leː·mɪç] *adj* (*aus Lehm bestehend*) clay; (*voller Lehm*) clayey; *Weg* muddy

Lehne <-, -n> ['leː·nə] *f* (*Armlehne*) armrest; (*Rückenlehne*) back

lehnen ['leː·nən] **I.** *vt* (*anlehnen*) to lean (**an/gegen** +*akk* against) **II.** *vi* (*schräg angelehnt sein*) ■**an etw** *dat* **~** to lean against sth **III.** *vr* (*sich beugen*) ■**sich** *akk* **an jdn/etw ~** to lean on sb/sth; ■**sich** *akk* **über etw** *akk* **~** to lean over sth

Lehnstuhl *m* armchair

Lehramt ['leːɐ̯-] *nt* (*geh*) ■**das ~** the position of teacher; (*Studiengang*) teacher training [program]

Lehrbeauftragte(r) *f(m)* visiting [*or* adjunct] lecturer

Lehrberuf *m* teaching profession

Lehrbuch *nt* textbook

Lehre <-, -n> ['le·rə] *f* ① ([*handwerkliche*] *Ausbildung*) apprenticeship; **eine ~ [als etw] machen** to serve an apprenticeship [as sth] ② (*Erfahrung, aus der man lernt*) lesson; **jdm eine ~ erteilen** to teach sb a lesson ③ (*ideologisches System*) doctrine ④ (*Theorie*) theory

lehren ['leː·rən] *vt* (*unterrichten*) to teach; **die Erfahrung hat uns gelehrt, dass ...** experience has taught us that ...

Lehrer(in) <-s, -> ['leː·rɐ] *m(f)* teacher

Lehrfach *nt* subject

Lehrgang <-gänge> *m* course; **auf einem ~ sein** to be at a seminar

Lehrgeld *nt* **~ zahlen** [**müssen**] *akk* to [have to] learn the hard way

Lehrjahr *nt* year spent as an apprentice

Lehrkörper *m* teaching staff + *sing/pl vb*

Lehrling <-s, -e> ['leːɐ̯·lɪŋ] *m* (*veraltend*) *s.* **Auszubildende(r)**

Lehrmittel *nt* (*fachspr*) teaching aid

Lehrplan *m* syllabus

lehrreich *adj* instructive

Lehrsatz *m* theorem

Lehrstelle *f* apprenticeship

Lehrstuhl *m* chair, professorship

Lehrzeit *f* (*veraltend*) *s.* **Lehre 1**

Leib <-[e]s, -er> [laip] *m* (*Körper*) body; **etw** *akk* **am eigenen ~ erfahren** to experience sth firsthand; **bei lebendigem ~** alive ► WENDUNGEN: **mit ~ und Seele** wholeheartedly

Leibarzt, -ärztin *m, f* personal physician *form*

Leibeskraft *f* **aus Leibeskräften** with all

one's might
Leibgarde *f* bodyguard
Leibgericht *nt* favorite meal
leibhaftig [laip·'haf·tɪç] **I.** *adj* real; **sie ist die ~e Sanftmut** she is gentleness personified ▶WENDUNGEN: **der L~e** (*euph*) the devil incarnate **II.** *adv* in person *pred*
leiblich ['laip·lɪç] *adj* ❶ (*körperlich*) physical ❷ (*blutsverwandt*) natural; **~e Verwandte** blood relations
Leibwache *f* bodyguard
Leibwächter(in) *m(f)* bodyguard
Leiche <-, -n> ['lai·çə] *f* corpse, body ▶WENDUNGEN: **über ~n gehen** (*pej fam*) to stop at nothing
Leichenbeschauer(in) <-s, -> *m(f) doctor conducting a postmortem;* (*amtlich*) coroner
leichenblass[RR] *adj* deathly pale
Leichenhalle *f* mortuary
Leichenschauhaus *nt* morgue
Leichenschmaus *m* wake
Leichenverbrennung *f* cremation
Leichenwagen *m* hearse
Leichenzug *m* (*geh*) funeral procession
Leichnam <-s, -e> ['laiç·naːm] *m* (*geh*) corpse, body
leicht [laiçt] **I.** *adj* ❶ (*geringes Gewicht habend*) light ❷ (*eine dünne Konsistenz habend*) light ❸ (*einfach*) easy; **nichts ~er als das!** no problem!; **~e Lektüre** light reading ❹ METEO (*schwach*) *Regen* light; *Donner* distant ❺ (*sacht*) light; *Akzent* slight; *Schlag* gentle ❻ *Eingriff, Verbrennung* minor ❼ (*nicht belastend*) *Mahlzeit* light; *Zigarette* mild ❽ (*unbeschwert*) ■**jdm ist ~er** sb is relieved ❾ (*nicht massiv*) lightweight **II.** *adv* ❶ **~ bekleidet** dressed in light clothing ❷ (*einfach*) easily; **etw geht [ganz] ~** sth is [quite] easy; **es jdm ~ machen** to make it easy for sb ❸ METEO (*schwach*) lightly ❹ (*nur wenig, etwas*) lightly; **~ verärgert sein** to be slightly annoyed ❺ (*schnell*) easily; **das sagst du so ~!** that's easy for you to say!; **~ zerbrechlich** fragile ❻ (*problemlos*) easily
Leichtathlet(in) *m(f)* track and field athlete
Leichtathletik *f* track and field *+ sing vb, no art*
leichtfertig **I.** *adj* thoughtless **II.** *adv* thoughtlessly
Leichtgewicht *nt* ❶ *kein pl* (*Gewichtsklasse*) lightweight category ❷ (*fig: Sportler*) lightweight *a. fig*
leichtgläubig *adj* gullible
Leichtgläubigkeit *f kein pl* gullibility
leichthin ['laiçt·'hɪn] *adv* ❶ (*ohne langes Nachdenken*) unthinkingly; **etw ~ versprechen** to make a promise lightly; **das kannst du heute so ~ sagen, aber ...** you might say that today, but ... ❷ (*nebenbei*) easily; **etw ~ sagen** to say sth in passing
Leichtigkeit <-> *f* ❶ *kein pl* (*Einfachheit*) simplicity; **mit ~** effortlessly ❷ (*Leichtheit*) lightness
Leichtmetall *nt* light metal
leicht|nehmen *vt irreg* ■**etw ~** to take sth lightly
Leichtsinn ['laiçt·zɪn] *m kein pl* carelessness
leichtsinnig ['laiçt·zɪnɪç] **I.** *adj* careless **II.** *adv* carelessly
leid [lait] *adj pred* (*überdrüssig*) **ich bin es ~, das immer tun zu müssen** I'm sick of having to do this all the time
Leid <-[e]s> [lait] *nt kein pl* sorrow; **jdm sein ~ klagen** to tell sb one's troubles
leiden <litt, gelitten> ['laidn̩] **I.** *vi* ❶ (*Schmerzen ertragen*) to suffer ❷ (*an einem Leiden erkrankt sein*) ■**an etw** *dat* **~** to suffer from sth ❸ (*seelischen Schmerz empfinden*) to suffer; ■**unter jdm ~** to suffer because of sb; ■**unter etw** *dat* **~** to suffer from sth ❹ (*in Mitleidenschaft gezogen werden*) *Beziehung, Gesundheit* to suffer; *Möbelstück, Stoff* to get damaged **II.** *vt* (*erdulden*) ■**etw ~** to suffer sth ▶WENDUNGEN: **jdn/etw ~ können** to like sb/sth; **ich kann das nicht ~** I can't stand that
Leiden <-s, -> ['laidn̩] *nt* ❶ (*chronische Krankheit*) ailment ❷ *pl* (*leidvolle Erlebnisse*) suffering
leidend *adj* ❶ (*geplagt*) mournful ❷ (*geh: chronisch krank*) ■**~ sein** to be sick
Leidenschaft <-, -en> ['lai·dn̩·ʃaft] *f* passion; **mit [großer/wahrer] ~** passionately; **er ist Maler aus ~** he is passionate about painting
leidenschaftlich **I.** *adj* passionate **II.** *adv* passionately; ■**etw ~ gern tun** to love doing sth; **ich esse ~ gern Himbeereis** I [absolutely] love raspberry ice cream
leidenschaftslos **I.** *adj* dispassionate **II.** *adv* dispassionately
Leidensgefährte, -gefährtin *m, f,* **Leidensgenosse, -genossin** *m, f* fellow sufferer
Leidensmiene *f* dejected expression
leider ['lai·dɐ] *adv* unfortunately; **ich habe das ~ vergessen** I'm sorry, I forgot about that; **das ist ~ so** that's just the way it is
leidig ['lai·dɪç] *adj attr* (*pej*) tedious; **immer das ~e Geld!** it always comes down to money!
Leidtragende(r) *f(m)* ■**der/die ~** the one to suffer
leid|tun[RR] *vi irreg* **es tut mir leid** I'm sorry; **es tut mir [so] leid, dass ...** I'm [so] sorry that ...; **er tut mir leid** I feel sorry for him
leidvoll *adj* (*geh*) sorrowful *liter*
Leidwesen *nt kein pl* ■**zu jds ~** much to sb's regret
Leier <-, -n> ['laiɐ] *f* MUS lyre
Leierkasten *m* (*fam*) *s.* **Drehorgel**
leiern ['lai·ɐn] *vt* (*fam*) ❶ (*lustlos aufsagen*) *Gedicht* to drone [out *sep*] ❷ (*kurbeln*) to wind sth
Leihbücherei *f* lending library
leihen <lieh, geliehen> ['lai·ən] *vt* ❶ (*ausleihen*) to lend; ■**geliehen** borrowed ❷ (*borgen*) ■**sich** *dat* **etw** *akk* **[von jdm] ~** to bor-

L

row sth [from sb]
Leihfrist *f* lending [*or* borrowing] period
Leihgabe *f* loan
Leihgebühr *f* rental fee; (*für Buch*) lending [*or* borrowing] fee
Leihhaus *nt* pawn shop
Leihmutter *f* surrogate mother
Leihwagen *m* rental car
leihweise *adv* (*geh*) on loan
Leim <-[e]s, -e> [laim] *m* glue ▶WENDUNGEN: **jdm auf den ~ gehen** (*fam*) to fall for sb's tricks; **aus dem ~ gehen** (*fam*) to fall apart
leimen ['lai·mən] *vt* ❶ (*mit Leim zusammenfügen*) to glue together ❷ (*fam: hereinlegen*) ■**jdn ~** to take sb for a ride
Leine <-, -n> ['lai·nə] *f* ❶ (*dünnes Seil*) rope ❷ (*Wäscheleine*) [clothes]line ❸ (*Hundeleine*) leash ❹ **zieh ~!** (*sl*) beat it!
leinen ['lai·nən] *adj* linen
Leinen <-s, -> ['lai·nən] *nt* linen; **aus ~** made of linen
Leinsamen *m* linseed
Leintuch <-tücher> *nt* SÜDD, ÖSTERR, SCHWEIZ (*Laken*) sheet
Leinwand *f* ❶ (*Projektionswand*) screen ❷ *kein pl* (*Gewebe aus Flachsfasern*) *a.* KUNST canvas
leise ['lai·zə] **I.** *adj* ❶ (*nicht laut*) quiet; **etw ~ stellen** to turn down *sep* sth ❷ (*gering*) slight; *Ahnung, Verdacht* vague; **es fiel ~r Regen** it was drizzling **II.** *adv* ❶ (*nicht laut*) quietly ❷ (*kaum merklich*) slightly
Leiste <-, -n> ['lais·tə] *f* ❶ (*schmale Latte*) strip ❷ (*Übergang zum Oberschenkel*) groin
leisten ['lais·tn̩] **I.** *vt* ❶ (*an Arbeitsleistung erbringen*) **ganze Arbeit ~** to do a good job; **viel ~** to get a lot done ❷ TECH, PHYS to generate ❸ *Funktionsverb* **Hilfe ~** to help; **eine Anzahlung ~** to make a down payment; **gute Dienste ~** to serve sb well **II.** *vr* ❶ (*sich gönnen*) ■**sich** *dat* **etw ~** to treat oneself to sth ❷ (*sich herausnehmen*) **da hast du dir ja was geleistet!** you've really outdone yourself!; **er hat sich eine Dummheit geleistet** he behaved stupidly; (*tragen können*) **tolles Kleid – sie kann es sich ~, bei der Figur!** great dress — she can certainly get away with it with a figure like that! ❸ (*finanziell in der Lage sein*) **sich etw ~ können** to be able to afford sth; **es sich** *dat* **~ können, etw zu tun** to be able to afford to do sth
Leistenbruch *m* hernia
Leistung <-, -en> *f* ❶ *kein pl* (*das Leisten*) performance ❷ (*geleistetes Ergebnis*) accomplishment; **eine sportliche/hervorragende ~** an athletic achievement/outstanding piece of work; **schulische ~en** performance at school; **ihre ~en lassen zu wünschen übrig** her work leaves a lot to be desired ❸ TECH, PHYS power; *einer Fabrik* output ❹ FIN (*Entrichtung*) payment
Leistungsdruck *m kein pl* pressure to perform
leistungsfähig *adj* ❶ (*zu hoher Arbeitsleistung fähig*) efficient ❷ (*zu hoher Produktionsleistung fähig*) productive ❸ (*zur Abgabe großer Energie fähig*) powerful ❹ FIN competitive
Leistungsfähigkeit *f kein pl* ❶ (*Arbeitsleistung*) performance ❷ (*Produktionsleistung*) productivity ❸ (*Abgabe von Energie*) power ❹ FIN competitiveness
Leistungsgesellschaft *f* meritocracy
Leistungskurs *m* SCH ≈ advanced placement [*or* AP] class
Leistungsnachweis *m* SCH evidence of academic achievement
leistungsschwach *adj* weak; *Maschine, Motor* low-performance
Leistungssport *m* competitive sports *no art*
leistungsstark *adj* ❶ (*große Produktionskapazität besitzend*) [highly-]efficient ❷ AUTO, ELEK, TECH [very] powerful; *Motor* high-performance
Leistungsträger(in) *m(f)* SPORT, ÖKON go-to guy *fam*
Leistungsvermögen *nt kein pl* capability *usu pl*
Leitartikel *m* editorial [article]
Leitbild *nt* [role] model
leiten ['lai·tn̩] **I.** *vt* ❶ (*verantwortlich sein*) *Firma* to run; **eine Abteilung/Schule ~** to be head of a department/school ❷ (*den Vorsitz führen*) to lead; *Sitzung, Debatte* to chair ❸ TECH (*transportieren*) to conduct; *Erdöl* to pipe ❹ TRANSP *Zug* to divert ❺ (*führen*) to lead, to guide; ■**sich** *akk* **durch etw** *akk* **~ lassen** to [let oneself] be guided by sth; ■**sich** *akk* **von etw** *dat* **~ lassen** to [let oneself] be governed by sth **II.** *vi* PHYS to conduct; **gut/schlecht ~** to be a good/bad conductor
leitend I. *adj* ❶ (*führend*) leading ❷ (*in hoher Position*) managerial; **~er Angestellter** executive; **~er Redakteur** editor in chief ❸ PHYS conductive **II.** *adv* **~ tätig sein** to hold a managerial position
Leiter[1] <-, -n> ['lai·tɐ] *f* (*Sprossenleiter*) ladder; (*Stehleiter*) stepladder
Leiter[2] <-s, -> ['lai·tɐ] *m* PHYS conductor
Leiter(in) <-s, -> ['lai·tɐ] *m(f)* ❶ (*leitend Tätiger*) head; *einer Firma, eines Geschäfts* manager; *einer Schule* principal ❷ (*Sprecher*) leader; *einer Delegation* head; **~ einer Diskussion** person chairing a discussion
Leitfaden *m* MEDIA compendium
Leitfähigkeit *f* PHYS conductivity
Leitgedanke *m* central idea
Leitlinie *f* ❶ (*Grundsatz*) guideline ❷ (*Fahrbahnmarkierung*) lane marker
Leitmotiv *nt* central theme; (*in der Musik, Literatur*) leitmotiv
Leitplanke *f* guardrail
Leitsatz *m* guiding principle
Leitung <-, -en> *f* ❶ *kein pl* (*Führung*) management; **die ~ einer Sitzung haben** to chair a meeting; ■**unter der ~ von jdm** MUS conducted by sb ❷ (*leitendes Gremium*) management ❸ (*Rohr*) pipe ❹ (*Kabel*) cable ❺ TELEK line; **die ~ ist gestört** it's a bad connection

▶ WENDUNGEN: **eine lange ~ haben** (*hum fam*) to be slow on the uptake
Leitungsrohr *nt* pipe
Leitungswasser *nt* tap water
Leitwährung *f* leading currency
Leitzins *m* prime rate
Lektion <-, -en> [lɛk·ˈtsi̯oːn] *f* ❶ SCH (*Kapitel*) chapter; (*Stunde*) lesson ❷ (*geh: Lehre*) lesson; **jdm eine ~ erteilen** to teach sb a lesson
Lektor(in) <-s, -toren> [ˈlɛk·toːɐ̯, lɛk·ˈtoː·rɪn, *pl* lɛk·ˈtoː·rən] *m(f)* ❶ (*in einem Verlag*) editor ❷ (*an der Universität*) *lecturer who teaches in his/her native language at a university in a foreign country*
Lektorat <-[e]s, -e> [lɛk·to·ˈraːt] *nt* ❶ (*Verlagsabteilung*) editorial office ❷ (*Lehrauftrag*) *teaching assignment as a lecturer who teaches in his/her native language at a university in a foreign country*
Lektüre <-, -n> [lɛk·ˈtyː·rə] *f* ❶ *kein pl* (*das Lesen*) reading ❷ (*Lesestoff*) reading material
Lende <-, -n> [ˈlɛn·də] *f* ANAT, KOCHK loin
Lẹndenschurz *m* loincloth
Lẹndenstück *nt* KOCHK tenderloin
lenkbar [ˈlɛŋk·baːɐ̯] *adj* steerable; **gut ~ sein** to be easy to steer
lenken [ˈlɛŋ·kn̩] **I.** *vt* ❶ (*steuern*) to steer ❷ (*dirigieren*) to direct ❸ (*beeinflussen*) to control ❹ (*geh*) **seinen Blick auf jdn/etw ~** to turn one's gaze to [*or* toward] sb/sth ❺ (*richten*) ■ **etw auf etw** *akk* **~** to direct sth to sth; **jds Aufmerksamkeit auf etw ~** to draw sb's attention to sth; *Gespräch, Unterhaltung* to steer **II.** *vi* to drive
Lẹnker <-s, -> *m* handlebar *usu pl*
Lẹnkrad *nt* steering wheel
Lẹnkung <-, -en> *f* ❶ AUTO steering ❷ *kein pl* (*Beeinflussung*) controlling
Lenz <-es, -e> [lɛnts] *m* (*liter: Frühling*) springtide
Leopard <-en, -en> [leo·ˈpart] *m* leopard
Lepra <-> [ˈleː·p·ra] *f kein pl* leprosy
Lerche <-, -n> [ˈlɛr·çə] *f* ORN lark
lẹrnbegierig *adj* eager to learn *pred*
lẹrnbehindert *adj* with learning difficulties *pred*; ■ **~ sein** to have learning difficulties
Lẹrneifer *m* eagerness to learn
lernen [ˈlɛr·nən] **I.** *vt* ❶ (*sich als Kenntnis aneignen*) to learn; **er lernt's nie** he'll never learn ❷ (*fam: eine Ausbildung machen*) ■ **etw ~** to train to be sth ▶ WENDUNGEN: **gelernt ist [eben] gelernt** once learned, never forgotten; **etw will gelernt sein** sth takes [a lot of] practice **II.** *vi* ❶ (*für die Schule*) to study, to [do school]work ❷ (*beim Lernen unterstützen*) ■ **mit jdm ~** to tutor sb ❸ (*eine Ausbildung machen*) ■ **[bei jdm] ~** to apprentice [with sb]; **er hat bei verschiedenen Firmen gelernt** he has apprenticed with several companies; **sie lernt noch** she is still an apprentice
lẹrnfähig *adj* ■ **~ sein** to be capable of learning
Lẹrnfähigkeit *f kein pl* ability to learn
LẹrnprozessRR *m* learning process
Lẹrnsoftware *f* educational software
Lẹrnziel *nt* [educational] goal
Lesart [ˈleːs·aːɐ̯t] *f* version
lesbar [ˈleːs·baːɐ̯] *adj* ❶ *Handschrift* legible ❷ (*verständlich*) clear
Lesbe <-, -n> [ˈlɛs·bə] *f* (*fam*), **Lesbierin** <-, -nen> [ˈlɛs·bi̯ə·rɪn] *f* lesbian
lesbisch [ˈlɛs·bɪʃ] *adj* lesbian; ■ **~ sein** to be [a] lesbian
Lese <-, -n> [ˈleː·zə] *f* AGR harvest
Lesebrille *f* reading glasses *npl*
Lesebuch *nt* reader
Lesegerät *nt* COMPUT reader
Leselampe *f* reading lamp
lesen[1] <liest, las, gelesen> [ˈleː·zn̩] **I.** *vt* to read **II.** *vi* ❶ (*als Lektüre*) to read ❷ (*Hochschulwesen*) to lecture (**über** +*akk* on, about) **III.** *vr* **etw liest sich leicht** sth is easy to read
lesen[2] <liest, las, gelesen> [ˈleː·zn̩] *vt* ❶ (*sammeln*) to pick; *Ähren* to glean ❷ (*auflesen*) **etw vom Boden ~** to pick sth off the floor
lesenswert *adj* worth reading *pred*
Leser(in) <-s, -> [ˈleː·zɐ] *m(f)* reader
Leseratte *f* (*hum fam*) bookworm
Leserbrief *m* letter to the editor
leserlich *adj* legible; **gut ~ sein** to be easy to read
Leserschaft <-, *selten* -en> *f* (*geh*) readership
Lesesaal *m* reading room
Lesestoff *m* reading material
Lesezeichen *nt* bookmark
Lesezirkel *m* magazine subscription service (*company which loans magazines to readers*)
Lesung <-, -en> *f a.* POL reading
Lette, Lettin <-n, -n> [ˈlɛ·tə] *m, f* Latvian
lettisch [ˈlɛ·tɪʃ] *adj* Latvian; *s. a.* **deutsch**
Lettland [ˈlɛt·lant] *nt* Latvia; *s. a.* **Deutschland**
Letzt [lɛtst] *f* ▶ WENDUNGEN: **zu guter ~** finally
lẹtzte(r, s) *adj* ❶ (*den Schluss bezeichnend*) last; **sie saß in der ~n Reihe** she sat in the back row; **der L~ des Monats** the last [day] of the month ❷ (*das zuletzt Mögliche bezeichnend*) last; *Versuch, Angebot* final; *Zug* last; **das ist das L~, was ...** this is the last thing that ...; **in ~r Minute** at the last minute ❸ SPORT **sie ging als ~ Läuferin durchs Ziel** she was the last runner to cross the finish line; ■ **L~ werden** to finish last [*or* in last place] ❹ (*restlich*) last; **das ~ Brot** the last of the bread ❺ **es ist das ~ Mal, dass ...** this is the last time that ...; **beim ~n Mal** last time; **zum ~n Mal** the last time; **im ~n Jahr** last year ❻ (*an letzter Stelle erwähnt*) last ❼ (*neueste*) *Nachricht, Mode* latest ❽ (*fam: schlechteste*) **das ist doch der ~ Kerl!** what a total loser!
Lẹtzte(s) *nt* (*letzte Bemerkung*) ■ **ein ~s** one last thing ▶ WENDUNGEN: **sein ~s [her]geben** to give [it] one's all; **das ist ja wohl das ~!** (*fam*) enough is enough!

letztendlich ['lɛtst·ʔɛnt·lɪç] *adv* at the end of the day

letztens ['lɛts·tn̩s] *adv* recently; **erst ~** just the other day

letztlich ['lɛtst·lɪç] *adv* in the end

letztmalig [-maː·lɪç] *adj attr* final

Leuchtboje *f* light buoy

Leuchtdiode *f* light-emitting diode

Leuchte <-, -n> ['lɔyç·tə] *f* (*Stehlampe*) floor lamp ▶ WENDUNGEN: **nicht gerade eine ~ sein** (*fam*) to not be all that bright

leuchten ['lɔyç·tn̩] *vi* ❶ (*Licht ausstrahlen*) to shine; *Abendsonne* to glow; **leuchte mit der Lampe mal hier in die Ecke** shine the light over here in the corner [please] ❷ (*Licht reflektieren*) to glow; **die Kinder hatten vor Freude ~de Augen** the children's eyes were sparkling with joy

leuchtend *adj* ❶ (*strahlend*) bright ❷ (*herrlich*) shining *fig; Farben* glowing, bright

Leuchter <-s, -> *m* candlestick; (*mehrarmig*) candelabra

Leuchtfarbe *f* fluorescent paint

Leuchtfeuer *nt* beacon; (*auf der Landebahn*) runway lights

Leuchtkäfer *m* glowworm

Leuchtkraft *f kein pl* luminosity

Leuchtrakete *f* [rocket] flare

Leuchtreklame *f* neon sign

Leuchtschrift *f* neon lettering *pl*

Leuchtsignal *nt* signal flare

Leuchtturm *m* lighthouse

Leuchtzifferblatt *nt* luminous dial

leugnen ['lɔyg·nən] **I.** *vt* to deny; **es ist nicht zu ~, dass ...** there is no denying the fact that ... **II.** *vi* to deny it

Leugnung <-, -en> *f* denial

Leukämie <-, -n> [lɔy·kɛ·'miː, *pl* lɔy·kɛ·'miː·ən] *f* leukemia

Leute ['lɔy·tə] *pl* ❶ (*Menschen*) people *npl;* **alle/keine/kaum ~** everybody/nobody/hardly anybody; **unter ~ gehen** to get out and about ❷ (*fam: Kameraden, Verwandte*) folks *npl* ❸ MIL, NAUT (*Mitarbeiter*) men *pl;* **meine ~** my men ▶ WENDUNGEN: **etw unter die ~ bringen** (*fam*) to make sth known

Leutnant <-s, -s> ['lɔyt·nant] *m* second lieutenant; **~ zur See** ensign

Level <-s, -s> ['lɛ·vl] *m* (*geh*) level

Leviten [le·'viː·tən] *pl* ▶ WENDUNGEN: **jdm die ~ lesen** (*fam*) to read sb the riot act

Lexikon <-s, Lexika> ['lɛk·si·kɔn, *pl* 'lɛk·si·ka] *nt* encyclopedia

lfd. *Abk von* **laufend** regular; (*jetzig*) current

Liaison <-, -s> [liɛ·'zõː] *f* (*geh*) liaison

Libanese, **Libanesin** <-n, -n> [li·ba·'neː·zə] *m, f* Lebanese; *s. a.* **Deutsche(r)**

libanesisch [li·ba·'neː·zɪʃ] *adj* Lebanese; *s. a.* **deutsch**

Libanon <-[s]> ['liː·ba·nɔn] *m* ■ **der ~** Lebanon; *s. a.* **Deutschland**

Libelle <-, -n> [li·'bɛ·lə] *f* dragonfly

liberal [li·be·'raːl] **I.** *adj a.* POL liberal **II.** *adv* liberally

liberalisieren* [li·be·ra·li·'ziː·rən] *vt* to liberalize

Liberalisierung <-, -en> *f* liberalization

Liberalismus <-> [li·be·ra·'lɪs·mʊs] *m kein pl* liberalism

Liberia <-s> [li·'beː·ri̯a] *nt* Liberia; *s. a.* **Deutschland**

Liberianer(in) <-s, -> [li·be·'ri̯aː·nɐ] *m(f)* Liberian; *s. a.* **Deutsche(r)**

liberianisch [li·be·'ri̯aː·nɪʃ] *adj* Liberian; *s. a.* **deutsch**

Libero <-s, -s> ['liː·be·ro] *m* sweeper

Libido <-> ['liː·bi·do, li·'biː·do] *f kein pl* libido

Libyen <-s> ['liː·by̆·ən] *nt* Libya; *s. a.* **Deutschland**

Libyer(in) <-s, -> ['liː·by̆·ɐ] *m(f)* Libyan; *s. a.* **Deutsche(r)**

libysch ['liː·bʏʃ] *adj* Libyan; *s. a.* **deutsch**

licht [lɪçt] *adj* ❶ (*hell*) light ❷ (*nicht dicht bewachsen*) **~es Haar haben** to have a receding hairline ❸ ARCHIT, BAU **~e Höhe/Weite** vertical [*or* height]/horizontal [*or* width] clearance

Licht <-[e]s, -er> [lɪçt] *nt* ❶ *kein pl* (*Helligkeit*) light ❷ ELEK light; **das ~ brennt** the light is on; **das ~ ausschalten** to turn out the light[s]; **etw gegen das ~ halten** to hold sth up to the light ▶ WENDUNGEN: **etw erscheint in einem anderen ~** sth appears in a different light; **etw ans ~ bringen** to bring sth to light; **~ in etw** *akk* **bringen** to shed [some] light on sth; **jdn hinters ~ führen** to hoodwink sb; **mir geht ein ~ auf** (*fam*) now I see, it has suddenly dawned on me; **kein großes ~ sein** (*fam*) to be no great genius; **grünes ~ [für etw** *akk*] **geben** to give [sth] the go-ahead; **etw ins rechte ~ rücken** to show sth in its correct light; **das ~ der Welt erblicken** (*geh*) to [first] see the light of day

Lichtbild *nt* (*veraltend*) ❶ (*geh: Passbild*) passport photograph ❷ (*Dia*) slide

Lichtblick *m* ray of hope

lichtdurchlässig *adj* translucent

Lichteffekt *m* lighting effect

Lichteinwirkung *f* effects *pl* of the light

lichtempfindlich *adj* sensitive to light *pred;* FOTO photosensitive

lichten ['lɪç·tn̩] **I.** *vt* FORST, HORT to thin out *sep* **II.** *vr* ■ **sich** *akk* **~** ❶ (*dünner werden*) to [grow] thin ❷ (*spärlicher werden*) to go down ❸ (*klarer werden*) to be cleared up

Lichterkette *f* chain of lights

lichterloh ['lɪç·tɐ·'loː] *adv* **~ brennen** to be ablaze

Lichtermeer *nt* (*geh*) sea of lights

Lichtgeschwindigkeit *f kein pl* **mit ~** at the speed of light

Lichthupe *f* **die ~ betätigen** to flash one's high beams

Lichtjahr *nt* light year

Lichtmaschine *f* generator

Lichtquelle *f* light source

Lichtreklame *f s.* **Leuchtreklame**
Lichtschacht *m* light well
Lichtschalter *m* light switch
lichtscheu *adj* ❶ BOT, ZOOL *Pflanze* shade-loving; **ein ~es Tier** an animal that avoids the light ❷ (*fig*) **~es Gesindel** shady characters *pl*
Lichtschranke *f* light barrier
Lichtschutzfaktor *m* [sun] protection factor
Lichtstärke *f* ❶ PHYS light intensity ❷ FOTO *von Objektiv* speed
Lichtstrahl *m* light beam
lichtundurchlässig *adj* opaque
Lichtung <-, -en> *f* clearing
Lichtverhältnisse *pl* lighting conditions *pl*
Lid <-[e]s, -er> [liːt] *nt* [eye]lid
Lidschatten *m* eye shadow
Lidstrich *m* eyeliner
lieb [liːp] *adj* ❶ (*liebenswürdig*) kind, nice; **sei/seien Sie so ~ und ...** would you be so kind as to ... ❷ (*artig*) good; **sei ein ~es Mädchen!** be a good girl! ❸ (*niedlich*) cute ❹ (*geschätzt*) dear; **L~er Karl, L~e Amelie!** (*als Anrede in Briefen*) Dear Karl and Amelie,; **[mein] L~es** [my] love; **[ach] du ~e Güte** (*fam*) good heavens!; **jdn ~ haben** to love sb; **man muss ihn einfach ~ haben** it's impossible not to like him ❺ (*angenehm*) welcome; **das wäre mir weniger ~** I'd rather you didn't [do it]; **ich mag Vollmilchschokolade am ~sten** milk chocolate is my favorite; **am ~sten hätte ich ja abgelehnt** I would have rather said no
liebäugeln [ˈliːp·ʔɔy·gl̩n] *vi* ■ **mit etw** *dat* **~** to have one's eye on sth; ■ **damit ~, etw** *akk* **zu tun** to toy with the idea of doing sth
Liebe <-, -n> [ˈliː·bə] *f* ❶ *kein pl* (*Gefühl starker Zuneigung*) love; **aus ~ zu jdm** out of love for sb; **aus ~ zu etw** *dat* for the love of sth; **aus ~ heiraten** to marry for love; **käufliche ~** (*geh*) prostitution ❷ (*Mensch*) love; **die ~ meines Lebens** the love of my life ▶ WENDUNGEN: **~ auf den ersten Blick** love at first sight; **~ macht blind** (*prov*) love is blind
Liebelei <-, -en> [liː·bə·ˈlai] *f* (*fam*) flirtation
lieben [ˈliː·bn̩] **I.** *vt* ❶ (*Liebe entgegenbringen*) to love; ■ **sich** *akk* **~** to love each other ❷ (*gerne mögen*) to love ❸ (*euph: Geschlechtsverkehr miteinander haben*) ■ **jdn ~** to make love to sb; ■ **sich** *akk* **~** to make love **II.** *vi* to be in love
Liebende(r) *f(m)* lover
liebenswert *adj* lovable
liebenswürdig *adj* kind
liebenswürdigerweise *adv* kindly
Liebenswürdigkeit <-, -en> *f* kindness; **würden Sie die ~ haben, ...?** (*geh*) would you be so kind as to ...?
lieber [ˈliː·bɐ] **I.** *adj komp von* **lieb: mir wäre es ~, wenn ...** I would prefer it if ...; **was ist Ihnen ~, das Theater oder das Kino?** would you prefer to go to the theater or the movies? **II.** *adv* ❶ *komp von* **gern** rather; **etw ~ mögen** to prefer sth; **ich würde ~ in der Karibik als an der Ostsee Urlaub machen** I would rather take a vacation in the Caribbean than on the Baltic ❷ (*besser*) better; **darüber schweige ich ~** I think it's better to remain silent; **wir sollten ~ gehen** we [really] should get going; **das hätten Sie ~ nicht gesagt** you shouldn't have said that; **das möchte ich dir ~ nicht sagen** I'd rather not tell you that
Liebesabenteuer *nt* romance
Liebesaffäre *f* love affair
Liebesbeziehung *f* love affair
Liebesbrief *m* love letter
Liebeserklärung *f* declaration of love; **jdm eine ~ machen** to declare one's love to sb
Liebesfilm *m* love story
Liebesgeschichte *f* ❶ (*Lektüre*) love story ❷ (*fam: Liebesaffäre*) love affair
Liebeskummer *m* lovesickness; **~ haben** to be lovesick
Liebesleben *nt* love life
Liebeslied *nt* love song
Liebesmüh(e) *f* ▶ WENDUNGEN: **vergebliche ~ sein** to be a waste of time
Liebespaar *nt* lovers *pl*
Liebesroman *m* romance novel
liebestoll *adj* love-crazed
liebevoll I. *adj* loving; *Kuss* affectionate **II.** *adv* ❶ (*zärtlich*) affectionately ❷ (*mit besonderer Sorgfalt*) lovingly
Liebhaber(in) <-s, -> [ˈliːp·haː·bɐ] *m(f)* ❶ (*Partner*) lover ❷ (*Freund (der Künste)*) enthusiast
Liebhaberei <-, -en> [liːp·haː·bə·ˈrai] *f* hobby
Liebhaberwert *m kein pl* collector's value
liebkosen* [liːp·ˈkoː·zn̩] *vt* (*geh*) to caress
Liebkosung <-, -en> *f* (*geh*) caress
lieblich [ˈliːp·lɪç] **I.** *adj* ❶ (*angenehm süß*) sweet; *Wein* medium sweet ❷ (*erhebend*) lovely; *Töne* melodious **II.** *adv* **~ duften/schmecken** to smell/taste sweet
Liebling <-s, -e> [ˈliːp·lɪŋ] *m* ❶ (*Geliebte(r)*) darling ❷ (*Favorit*) favorite
Lieblingsbeschäftigung *f* favorite hobby
Lieblingsgericht *nt* favorite food
lieblos [ˈliːp·loːs] **I.** *adj* ❶ (*keine liebevolle Zuwendung gebend*) unloving ❷ (*Nachlässigkeit zeigend*) unfeeling **II.** *adv* (*nachlässig*) carelessly
Lieblosigkeit <-, -en> *f* ❶ *kein pl* (*Mangel an liebevoller Zuwendung*) lack of feeling ❷ (*Verhalten*) unkind act
liebste(r, s) [ˈliːps·tə, ˈliːps·tɐ, ˈliːps·təs] *adj superl von* **lieb** dearest; **das mag ich am ~n** I like that the best; **am ~n möchte ich schlafen** I'd really just like to sleep
Liebste(r) [ˈliːps·tə, ˈliːps·tɐ] *f(m)* sweetheart
Lied <-[e]s, -er> [liːt] *nt* song ▶ WENDUNGEN: **es ist immer das alte ~** (*fam*) it's always the same old story; **ein ~ von etw** *dat* **singen können** to be able to tell sb a thing or two about sth
Liederbuch *nt* songbook
Liedermacher(in) *m(f)* singer-songwriter
lief [liːf] *imp von* **laufen**

Lieferant(in) <-en, -en> [li·fə·'rant] *m(f)* ❶ (*Firma*) supplier ❷ (*Auslieferer*) deliveryman *masc*, deliverywoman *fem*
lieferbar *adj* ❶ (*erhältlich*) available, in stock ❷ (*zustellbar*) **Ihre Bestellung ist leider erst später ~** unfortunately, we won't be able to ship your order until a later date
Lieferbedingungen *pl* terms of delivery
Lieferfrist *f* delivery deadline
liefern ['li:·fɐn] **I.** *vt* ❶ (*ausliefern*) ■**[jdm] etw** *akk* **~** to deliver sth [to sb] ❷ *Beweis* to provide ❸ (*erzeugen*) to yield ❹ SPORT **einen spannendes Spiel ~** to put on an exciting game **II.** *vi* to deliver
Lieferschein *m* packing slip
Lieferstopp *m* suspension of deliveries
Liefertermin *m* delivery date
Lieferung <-, -en> *f* ❶ (*das Liefern*) delivery; **bei ~** on delivery ❷ (*gelieferte Ware*) consignment
Lieferwagen *m* delivery van; (*offen*) pickup truck
Lieferzeit *f s.* **Lieferfrist**
Liege <-, -n> ['li:·gə] *f* ❶ (*Bett ohne Fuß-/Kopfteil*) day bed ❷ (*Liegestuhl*) lounge chair, chaise lounge
liegen <lag, gelegen> ['li:·gn̩] *vi haben o* SÜDD *sein* ❶ (*sich in horizontaler Lage befinden*) to lie; **ich liege noch im Bett** I'm still [lying] in bed; **deine Brille müsste eigentlich auf dem Schreibtisch ~** your glasses must be on the desk; **in diesem Liegestuhl liegt man am bequemsten** this is the most comfortable lounge chair [to lie in]; **~ bleiben** (*nicht aufstehen*) to stay in bed; (*nicht mehr aufstehen*) to remain lying down; **etw ~ lassen** to leave sth [where it is] ❷ (*sich abgesetzt haben*) **hier liegt oft bis Mitte April noch Schnee** there will often be snow on the ground until mid-April here; **über allen Möbeln lag eine dicke Staubschicht** a thick layer of dust covered all the furniture ❸ (*lagern*) **Hände weg, das Buch bleibt [da] ~!** hands off — that book's not going anywhere!; **~ bleiben** (*nicht verkauft werden*) to remain unsold ❹ (*vergessen werden*) **irgendwo ~ bleiben** to be left behind somewhere ❺ (*geografisch gelegen sein*) to lie; **Cannes liegt in Frankreich** Cannes is in France ❻ (*eine bestimmte Lage haben*) to be situated; **ihr Haus liegt an einem See** they have a house on a lake; **diese Wohnung liegt zur Straße** this apartment faces [out onto] the street ❼ (*begraben sein*) ■**irgendwo ~** to be buried somewhere ❽ NAUT to be moored ❾ AUTO **~ bleiben** to break down ❿ SPORT to be; **wie ~ unsere Schwimmer im Wettbewerb?** how are our swimmers doing in the competition? ⓫ (*angesiedelt sein*) **der Preis dürfte bei 4.500 Euro ~** the price is probably around 4,500 euros ⓬ (*verursacht sein*) **das liegt nur an dir** it's all your fault; **woran mag es nur ~, dass ...** why is it that ... ⓭ (*wichtig sein*) **du weißt doch, wie sehr mir daran liegt** you know how important it is to me; **mir ist viel daran gelegen** this means a lot to me ⓮ *meist verneint* (*zusagen*) **Sport liegt mir nicht** I don't like sports; **körperliche Arbeit liegt ihr nicht** she's not really cut out for physical work ⓯ (*lasten*) ■**auf jdm ~** *Schuld* to weigh down on sb ⓰ (*abhängig sein*) **das liegt ganz bei Ihnen** it's entirely up to you ⓱ (*nicht ausgeführt werden*) **~ bleiben** *Arbeit* to be left undone ▶ WENDUNGEN: **an mir soll es nicht ~!** don't let me stop you!
Liegenschaft <-, -en> *f meist pl* real estate
Liegesitz *m* recliner
Liegestuhl *m* (*Liege*) chaise longue; (*Stuhl*) deck chair
Liegestütz <-es, -e> *m* pushup
Liegewagen *m* couchette car
Liegewiese *f* lawn for sunbathing
lieh [li:] *imp von* **leihen**
ließ [li:s] *imp von* **lassen**
liest *3. pers sing pres von* **lesen**
Lift <-[e]s, -e *o* -s> [lɪft] *m* elevator
Liftboy <-s, -s> ['lɪf·tbɔy] *m* elevator operator
liften ['lɪf·tn̩] *vt* MED to lift; **sich** *dat* **das Gesicht ~ lassen** to have a facelift
Liga <-, Ligen> ['li:·ga, *pl* 'li:·gn̩] *f* league
light [laɪt] *adj Nahrungsmittel* low-calorie
liieren* [li·'i:·rən] *vr* (*geh*) ■**sich** *akk* **~** to become close friends *euph;* ■**[mit jdm] liiert sein** to have a relationship [with sb]
Likör <-s, -e> [li·'kø:ɐ̯] *m* liqueur
lila ['li:·la] *adj inv* purple
Lilie <-, -n> ['li:·liə] *f* lily
Liliputaner(in) <-s, -> [li·li·pu·'ta:·nɐ] *m(f)* dwarf
Limit <-s, -s *o* -e> ['lɪ·mɪt] *nt* limit
limitieren* [li·mi·'ti:·rən] *vt* to limit
Limo <-, -s> ['lɪ·mo, 'li:·mo] *f* (*fam*) lemon-lime soda
Limonade <-, -n> [li·mo·'na:·də] *f* lemon-lime soda
Limousine <-, -n> [li·mu·'zi:·nə] *f* sedan; (*größerer Luxuswagen*) limousine
Linde <-, -n> ['lɪn·də] *f* linden [tree]
Lindenblütentee *m* linden blossom tea

> **Lindenstraße**, which celebrated its thousandth episode in January 2005, is the longest-running TV soap opera in Germany. The popular series is broadcast on Sunday evenings on the television station *ARD*.

lindern ['lɪn·dɐn] *vt a.* MED to alleviate; *Husten, Sonnenbrand* to soothe
Linderung <-> *f kein pl a.* MED relief
Lineal <-s, -e> [li·ne·'a:l] *nt* ruler
linear [li·ne·'a:ɐ̯] *adj* linear
Linguist(in) <-en, -en> [lɪŋ·'gu̯·ɪst] *m(f)* linguist
Linguistik <-> [lɪŋ·'gu̯·ɪs·tɪk] *f kein pl* linguistics + *sing vb, no art*

linguistisch *adj* linguistic
Linie <-, -n> ['liːni̯ə] *f* ❶ (*längerer Strich*) line; **eine geschlängelte/gestrichelte ~** a wavy/broken line; **eine ~ ziehen** to draw a line ❷ (*Verkehrsverbindung*) **eine Bus~** a bus line; **nehmen Sie am besten die ~ 19** it's best if you take the [number] 19 ❸ POL *a.* (*allgemeine Richtung*) line ▶ WENDUNGEN: **die schlanke ~** (*fam*) one's figure; **in vorderster ~ stehen** to be on the front lines *pl*
Linienbus *m* regular [service] bus
Linienflug *m* scheduled flight
Linienrichter *m* (*beim Fußball*) linesman; (*beim Tennis*) line judge
liniert *adj inv* lined
link [lɪŋk] *adj* (*fam*) shady
Link <-s, -s> [lɪŋk] *nt* COMPUT link
Linke <-n, -n> ['lɪŋ·kə] *f* ❶ (*linke Hand*) left hand ❷ (*im Boxen*) left ❸ POL ■ **die ~** the left ▶ WENDUNGEN: **zur ~n von jdm** (*geh*) to sb's left
linke(r, s) *adj attr* ❶ (*zur Seite des Herzens*) left; *Fahrbahn, Spur* left-hand ❷ POL left-wing
Linke(r) *f(m)* POL left-winger
linken ['lɪŋ·kn̩] *vt* (*sl*) to take for a ride *fam*
linkisch ['lɪŋ·kɪʃ] *adj* clumsy
links [lɪŋks] **I.** *adv* ❶ (*auf der linken Seite*) on the left; **sich ~ halten** to keep [to the] left; ■ **~ neben/von ...** to the left of ...; **~ oben/unten** in the top [*or* upper]/bottom [*or* lower] left-hand corner; **nach ~** [to the] left; **von ~** from the left ❷ TRANSP **~ abbiegen** to turn [to the] left; **sich ~ einordnen** to go into the left lane; **sich ~ halten** to keep [to the] left ❸ MODE **~ stricken** to purl ❹ **etw auf ~ waschen** to wash sth inside out ❺ POL left-wing; **~ stehen** to be left-wing ❻ MIL **~ um!** left face! ▶ WENDUNGEN: **jdn ~ liegen lassen** (*fam*) to ignore sb; **mit ~** (*fam*) easily **II.** *präp +gen* ■ **~ einer S.** to the left of sth
Linksaußen <-, -> [lɪŋks·'ʔau·sn̩] *m* ❶ SPORTS left winger ❷ POL (*fam*) extreme left-winger
linksextrem *adj inv* extreme left-wing *attr*
Linksextremismus *m* left-wing extremism
Linksextremist(in) *m(f)* left-wing extremist
linksextremistisch *adj inv* left-wing extremist
linksgerichtet *adj* POL left-wing oriented
Linkshänder(in) <-s, -> ['lɪŋks·hɛn·dɐ] *m(f)* left-hander
linkshändig ['lɪŋks·hɛn·dɪç] **I.** *adj* left-handed **II.** *adv* with one's left hand
linksherum ['lɪŋks·hɛ·rʊm] *adv* [around] to the left; **etw ~ drehen** to turn sth counterclockwise
Linkskurve *f* left-hand curve
linksradikal **I.** *adj* radical left-wing *attr* **II.** *adv* radically left-wing
linksrum *adv* (*fam*) *s.* **linksherum**
Linoleum <-s> [li·'noː·le·ʊm, li·no·'leː·ʊm] *nt kein pl* linoleum
Linse <-, -n> ['lɪn·zə] *f* ❶ *meist pl* BOT, KOCHK lentil ❷ ANAT, PHYS lens
Lipgloss[RR], **Lipgloß**[ALT] <-, -> ['lɪp·glɔs] *nt* lip gloss
Lippe <-, -n> ['lɪpə] *f* ANAT lip ▶ WENDUNGEN: **etw nicht über die ~n bringen** to not be able to bring oneself to say sth; **an jds ~n hängen** to hang on sb's every word
Lippenbekenntnis *nt* **ein ~ ablegen** to pay lip service
Lippenstift *m* lipstick
liquid [li·'kviːt], **liquide** [li·'kviː·də] *adj* FIN ❶ (*geh: solvent*) solvent ❷ (*verfügbar*) **~es Vermögen** liquid assets *pl*
liquidieren* [li·kvi·'diː·rən] *vt* (*euph*) *a.* ÖKON to liquidate
Liquidität <-> [li·kvi·di·'tɛːt] *f kein pl* ÖKON [financial] solvency
lispeln ['lɪs·pl̩n] *vi* to lisp
Lissabon <-s> ['lɪsa·bɔn, lɪsa·'bɔn] *nt* Lisbon
List <-, -en> [lɪst] *f* trick; **eine ~ anwenden** to use a little cunning ▶ WENDUNGEN: **mit ~ und Tücke** (*fam*) with cunning and trickery
Liste <-, -n> ['lɪs·tə] *f* list ▶ WENDUNGEN: **auf der schwarzen ~ stehen** to be blacklisted
listig ['lɪs·tɪç] *adj* cunning
Litauen <-s> ['liː·tau·ən] *nt* Lithuania; *s. a.* **Deutschland**
Litauer(in) <-s, -> ['liː·tau·ɐ] *m(f)* Lithuanian; *s. a.* **Deutsche(r)**
litauisch ['liː·tau·ɪʃ, 'lɪ·tau·ɪʃ] *adj* ❶ (*Litauen betreffend*) Lithuanian; *s. a.* **deutsch 1** ❷ LING Lithuanian; *s. a.* **deutsch 2**
Liter <-s, -> ['liː·tɐ] *m o nt* liter
literarisch [lɪ·tə·'raː·rɪʃ] *adj* literary
Literatur <-, -en> [lɪ·tə·ra·'tuːɐ̯] *f* literature
Literaturangabe *f* bibliographical reference
Literaturkritik *f* literary criticism
Literaturpreis *m* literary prize
Literaturwissenschaft *f* literary studies *pl*
Literaturwissenschaftler(in) *m(f)* literary specialist
literweise *adv* by the liter
Litfaßsäule ['lɪt·fas·zɔy·lə] *f* advertising column
Lithographie, **Lithografie**[RR] <-, -n> [li·to·gra·'fiː, *pl* -gra·'fiː·ən] *f* ❶ *kein pl* (*Technik*) lithography ❷ (*Druck*) lithograph
litt [lɪt] *imp von* **leiden**
Liturgie <-, -n> [li·tʊr·'giː, *pl* -'giː·ən] *f* liturgy
liturgisch [li·'tʊr·gɪʃ] *adj* liturgical
live [laif] *adj pred* live
Livesendung[RR], **Live-Sendung** *f* live broadcast
Lizentiat <-[e]s, -e> [li·tsɛn·'tsi̯aːt] *nt s.* **Lizenziat**
Lizenz <-, -en> [li·'tsɛnts] *f* license; **in ~** under license
Lizenzausgabe *f* licensed edition
Lizenzgebühr *f* licensing fee; VERLAG royalty
Lizenziat[RR] <-[e]s, -e> [li·tsɛn·'tsi̯aːt] *m* SCHWEIZ (*akademischer Grad*) licentiate

The **Lizenziat** (licentiate) is the first academic degree attainable at a Swiss university. A **Lizenziat** is equivalent to a Master's degree, and, as such, qualifies the holder to carry on with postgraduate studies to work toward a doctorate.

Lkw, LKW <-[s], -[s]> [ɛl·kaː·veː] *m Abk von* **Lastkraftwagen** truck

Lkw-Maut [ɛl·ka·'ve-] *f* truck toll

Lob <-[e]s, *selten* -e> [loːp] *nt* praise; **~ für etw** *akk* **bekommen** to be praised for sth; **des ~es voll sein** to be full of praise

Lobby <-, -s *o* Lobbies> ['lɔbi] *f* lobby

loben ['loː·bn̩] **I.** *vt* to praise; **solches Engagement lob' ich mir** that's the sort of commitment I like [to see] **II.** *vi* to praise

lobenswert *adj* commendable

löblich ['løːp·lɪç] *adj* (*geh*) laudable

Loblied *nt* ►WENDUNGEN: **ein ~ auf jdn/etw singen** to sing sb's praises/the praises of sth

Lobrede *f* eulogy; **eine ~ auf jdn halten** to eulogize sb

Loch <-[e]s, Löcher> [lɔx, *pl* 'lœ·çɐ] *nt* ① (*offene Stelle*) hole; **ein ~ im Reifen** a puncture; **schwarzes ~** ASTRON black hole ② (*fam: elende Wohnung*) hole ►WENDUNGEN: **jdm ein ~ in den Bauch fragen** (*fam*) to flood sb with questions; **Löcher in die Luft starren** (*fam*) to stare into space; **auf dem letzten ~ pfeifen** (*fam: finanziell am Ende sein*) to be broke; (*völlig erschöpft sein*) to be on one's last legs; **saufen wie ein ~** (*fam*) to drink like a fish

lochen ['lɔ·xn̩] *vt* ① (*mit dem Locher stanzen*) ■**etw ~** to punch holes in sth ② (*veraltend: mit der Lochzange entwerten*) to punch

Locher <-s, -> ['lɔ·xɐ] *m* hole punch[er]

löcherig ['lœ·çərɪç] *adj* full of holes *pred,* holey

löchern ['lœçɐn] *vt* (*fam*) to pester

Lochkarte *f* punch card

Locke <-, -n> ['lɔkə] *f* curl; **~n haben** to have curly hair

locken¹ ['lɔ·kn̩] **I.** *vt* to curl **II.** *vr* ■**sich** *akk* **~** to curl

locken² ['lɔ·kn̩] *vt* ① (*anlocken*) to lure; **mich lockt es jedes Jahr in die Karibik** every year I feel the lure of the Caribbean ② (*verlocken*) to tempt; **Ihr Vorschlag könnte mich schon ~** I'm [very] tempted by your offer

lockend *adj* tempting

Lockenstab *m* curling iron

Lockenwickler <-s, -> *m* roller

locker ['lɔ·kɐ] **I.** *adj* ① (*nicht stramm*) loose ② (*nicht fest*) loose, loosely-packed *attr,* loosely packed *pred* ③ KOCHK light ④ (*nicht gespannt*) slack; **~e Muskeln** relaxed muscles; **ein ~es Mundwerk haben** (*fig fam*) to have a big mouth ⑤ (*leger, unverkrampft*) relaxed, laid-back *attr fam,* laid back *pred fam* ⑥ (*oberflächlich*) casual **II.** *adv* ① (*nicht stramm*) loosely; **~ sitzen** *Kleidungsstück* to be loose ② (*oberflächlich*) casually; **ich kenne ihn nur ~** I only know him in passing ③ (*sl: ohne Schwierigkeiten*) **das mache ich ganz ~** I can do it no problem *fam*

Lockerheit <-> *f kein pl* ① (*lockere Beschaffenheit*) looseness ② (*bei einem Seil*) slackness ③ KOCHK lightness

locker|lassen *vi irreg* (*fam*) **lass nicht ~** don't give up

locker|machen *vt* (*fam*) to shell out

lockern ['lɔ·kɐn] **I.** *vt* ① (*locker machen*) to loosen ② (*entspannen*) *Muskeln* to loosen up *sep* ③ (*weniger streng gestalten*) *Regeln* to relax **II.** *vr* ■**sich** *akk* **~** ① (*locker werden*) *Backstein, Schraube, Zahn* to work loose; *Bremsen* to come loose; *Bewölkung, Nebel* to lift ② SPORT (*die Muskulatur entspannen*) to loosen up ③ (*sich entkrampfen*) **die Verkrampfung lockerte sich zusehends** the tension eased visibly

lockig ['lɔ·kɪç] *adj* ① (*gelockt*) curly ② (*lockiges Haar besitzend*) curly-headed

Lockmittel *nt* lure

Lockung <-, -en> *f* temptation

Lockvogel *m* (*a. pej*) decoy

lodern ['loː·dɐn] *vi* ① *haben* (*emporschlagen*) to blaze ② *sein* (*schlagen*) **die Flammen sind zum Himmel gelodert** the flames reached up [in]to the sky

Löffel <-s, -> ['lœ·fl̩] *m* ① (*als Besteck*) spoon ② (*Maßeinheit*) a spoonful [of] ►WENDUNGEN: **den ~ abgeben** (*sl*) to kick the bucket; **sich** *dat* **etw hinter die ~ schreiben** to get sth into one's head

löffeln ['lœ·fl̩n] *vt* ■**etw ~** to eat sth with a spoon

löffelweise *adv* by the spoonful

log¹ [lɔk] *m Abk von* **Logarithmus** log

log² [loːk] *imp von* **lügen**

Logarithmus <-, -rithmen> [lo·ga·'rɪt·mʊs, *pl* -'rɪt·mən] *m* logarithm

Logbuch ['lɔk·buːx] *nt* log[book]

Loge <-, -n> ['loː·ʒə] *f* ① FILM, THEAT box ② (*Pförtnerloge*) lodge ③ (*Geheimgesellschaft von Freimaurern*) lodge

logieren* [lo·'ʒiː·rən] *vi* to stay

Logik <-> ['loː·gɪk] *f kein pl* logic

logisch ['loː·gɪʃ] *adj* ① (*in sich stimmig*) logical ② (*fam: selbstverständlich*) [**na,**] **~!** of course!

logischerweise *adv* naturally [enough]

Logistik <-> [lo·'gɪs·tɪk] *f kein pl* logistics *npl*

logistisch [lo·'gɪs·tɪʃ] *adj inv, attr* logistic[al]

Logo <-s, -s> ['loː·go] *nt* logo

Logopäde, Logopädin <-n, -n> [lo·go·'pɛː·də] *m, f* speech therapist

Lohn <-[e]s, Löhne> [loːn, *pl* 'løː·nə] *m* ① (*Arbeitsentgelt*) wage[s *pl*], pay ② *kein pl* (*Belohnung*) reward

Lohnabrechnung *f* payroll [accounting]

Lohnausfall *m* loss of earnings

Lohnempfänger(in) *m(f)* (*geh*) wage earner

lohnen ['loː·nən] **I.** *vr* ① (*sich bezahlt machen*) ■**sich** *akk* [**für jdn**] **~** to be worthwhile [for sb]; **unsere Mühe hat sich gelohnt** our efforts were worth it ② (*es wert sein*) ■**sich** *akk*

~, etw zu tun to be worth doing sth **II.** *vt* ❶ (*rechtfertigen*) **das lohnt den Aufwand kaum** it is hardly worth the effort ❷ (*belohnen*) **sie hat mir meine Hilfe mit Undank gelohnt** she repaid my help with ingratitude

lohnend *adj* (*einträglich*) lucrative; (*nutzbringend*) worthwhile

Lohnerhöhung *f* pay raise

Lohnforderung *f* wage demand

Lohnfortzahlung *f* continued payment of wages

Lohnkosten *pl* wage costs *pl*

Lohnkürzung *f* wage cut

Lohnsteuer *f* income tax

Lohnsteuerjahresausgleich *m* ≈ tax return

Lohnsteuerkarte *f* ≈ W-2 [form]

lokal [lo·'ka:l] *adj* local

Lokal <-s, -e> [lo·'ka:l] *nt* bar, pub; (*Restaurant*) restaurant

lokalisieren* [lo·ka·li·'zi:·rən] *vt* ❶ (*örtlich bestimmen*) to locate ❷ (*eingrenzen*) to localize (**auf** +*akk* in)

Lokalität <-, -en> [lo·ka·li·'tɛ:t] *f* locality

Lokalverbot *nt* ~ **bekommen/haben** to get/be banned from a bar

Lokomotive <-, -n> [lo·ko·mo·'ti:·və, -fə] *f* locomotive

Lokomotivführer(in) *m(f)* engineer

Lolli <-s, -s> ['lɔ·li] *m* (*fam*) lollipop

Longdrink ['lɔŋ·drɪŋk] *m* long drink

Look <-s, -s> [lʊk] *m* MODE look

Looping <-s, -s> ['lu:·pɪŋ] *m o nt* LUFT loop; **einen ~ machen** to loop the loop

Lorbeer <-s, -en> ['lɔr·be:ɐ] *m* ❶ (*Baum*) laurel [tree] ❷ (*Gewürz*) bay leaf ▶ WENDUNGEN: **sich** *akk* **auf seinen ~en ausruhen** (*fam*) to rest on one's laurels

Lorbeerblatt *nt* bay leaf

Lord <-s, -s> [lɔrt] *m* ❶ (*Adelstitel*) Lord ❷ (*Titelträger*) lord

los [lo:s] **I.** *adj pred* ❶ (*von etwas getrennt*) ■ **~ sein** to have come off ❷ (*fam: losgeworden*) ■ **jdn/etw ~ sein** to be rid of sb/sth; **er ist sein ganzes Geld ~** he's lost all his money ▶ WENDUNGEN: **mit jdm ist etwas ~** (*fam*) sth's up with sb; **dort ist nichts ~** (*fam*) nothing is going on there; **da ist immer viel ~** (*fam*) that's where the action always is; **mit jdm ist nichts ~** (*fam: jd ist langweilig*) sb is really boring; **was ist ~?** (*fam*) what's up?; **was ist denn hier/da ~?** (*fam*) what's going on here/there? **II.** *adv* ❶ (*fortgegangen*) **Ihre Frau ist schon vor fünf Minuten ~** your wife left five minutes ago ❷ (*gelöst*) ■ **etw ist ~** sth is loose; **noch ein paar Umdrehungen, dann ist die Schraube ~!** just a couple more turns and the screw is out! ▶ WENDUNGEN: **~!** (*mach!*) come on!

Los <-es, -e> [lo:s] *nt* ❶ (*Lotterielos*) [lottery] ticket; (*Kirmeslos*) [raffle] ticket ❷ (*für Zufallsentscheidung*) lot; **das ~ entscheidet** to be decided by drawing lots ❸ *kein pl* (*geh: Schicksal*) fate ▶ WENDUNGEN: **jd hat mit jdm/etw das große ~ gezogen** sb has hit the jackpot with sb/sth

lösbar ['lø:s·ba:ɐ̯] *adj inv* ❶ *Problem* solvable ❷ (*löslich*) soluble

los|binden *vt irreg* to untie (**von** +*dat* from)

los|brechen *irreg* **I.** *vt haben* to break off **II.** *vi sein* ❶ (*abbrechen*) to break off ❷ (*plötzlich beginnen*) to break out

löschen ['lœ·ʃn̩] **I.** *vt* ❶ (*auslöschen*) *Feuer, Flammen* to extinguish; *Licht* to turn off ❷ (*tilgen*) *a.* COMPUT to delete ❸ (*eine Aufzeichnung entfernen*) to erase **II.** *vi* to extinguish a fire

Löschfahrzeug *nt* fire engine

Löschmannschaft *f* firefighting team

Löschpapier *nt* blotting paper

Löschung <-, -en> *f* cancellation; *von Schulden* repayment; *von Eintragungen* deletion; *von Computerdaten* erasing; *von Bankkonto* closing

lose ['lo:·zə] *adj* ❶ (*locker, einzeln*) loose ❷ (*hum: frech*) **ein ~s Mundwerk haben** to have a big mouth

Lösegeld ['lø:·sə-] *nt* ransom

Lösegeldforderung *f* ransom demand

losen ['lo:·zn̩] *vi* to draw lots (**um** +*akk* for)

lösen ['lø:·zn̩] **I.** *vt* ❶ (*ablösen*) to remove (**von** +*dat* from) ❷ (*aufbinden*) to untie; *Fesseln, Knoten* to undo ❸ *Bremse* to release ❹ *Schraube, Verband* to loosen ❺ (*klären*) to solve; *Konflikt, Schwierigkeit* to resolve ❻ (*aufheben, annullieren*) to break off; *Verbindung* to sever; *Vertrag* to cancel ❼ (*zergehen lassen*) to dissolve **II.** *vr* ❶ (*sich ablösen*) ■ **sich** *akk* [**von etw** *dat*] **~** to come off [of sth] ❷ (*sich freimachen, trennen*) ■ **sich** *akk* **von jdm ~** to free oneself of sb ❸ (*sich aufklären*) ■ **sich** *akk* **~** to be solved ❹ (*sich auflösen*) ■ **sich** *akk* [**in etw** *dat*] **~** to dissolve [in sth] ❺ (*sich lockern*) to loosen; **langsam löste sich die Spannung** (*fig*) the tension [slowly] faded away

los|fahren *vi irreg sein* to drive off; to leave

los|gehen *irreg* **I.** *vi sein* ❶ (*weggehen*) to leave [on foot] ❷ (*auf ein Ziel losgehen*) ■ **auf etw ~** to set off for/toward sth; **wir gingen früh los** we set off early ❸ (*fam: beginnen*) to start; **das Konzert geht erst in einer Stunde los** the concert doesn't start for another hour ❹ (*angreifen*) ■ [**mit etw** *dat*] **auf jdn ~** to lay into sb [with sth] ❺ *Schusswaffen* to go off **II.** *vi impers sein* (*fam: beginnen*) to start; **jetzt geht's los** (*fam*) here we go

los|kaufen *vt* to ransom

los|kommen *vi irreg sein* (*fam*) ❶ (*wegkommen*) to get away ❷ (*sich befreien*) ■ **von jdm ~** to free oneself of sb; **von einem Gedanken ~** to get sth out of one's head; **von einer Sucht ~** to overcome an addiction

los|kriegen *vt* (*fam*) ❶ (*lösen können*) to get sth off (**von** +*dat* of) ❷ (*loswerden*) ■ **jdn/etw ~** to get rid of sb/sth ❸ (*verkaufen können*) to sell [off], to move

los|lassen *vt irreg* ❶ (*nicht mehr festhalten*) to let go ❷ (*beschäftigt halten*) **der Gedanke lässt mich nicht mehr los** I can't get the thought out of my head [*or* mind] ❸ (*fam: auf den Hals hetzen*) **die Hunde auf jdn ~** to sic dogs on sb ❹ (*fam: von sich geben*) **einen Witz ~** to crack a joke
los|laufen *vi irreg sein* to start running
los|legen *vi* (*fam*) ■[**mit etw** *dat*] ~ to start [doing sth]; **leg los!** go ahead!
löslich ['løːs·lɪç] *adj* soluble
los|lösen I. *vt* (*ablösen*) to remove (**von** +*dat* from) **II.** *vr* ❶ (*sich ablösen*) ■**sich** *akk* [**von etw** *dat*] ~ to come off [of sth] ❷ (*sich freimachen*) ■**sich** *akk* **von jdm** ~ to free oneself of sb
Lösung <-, -en> ['løː·zʊŋ] *f* ❶ (*das Lösen*) *a.* CHEM solution ❷ (*Aufhebung*) cancellation; *einer Beziehung/Verlobung* breaking off ❸ (*das Sichlösen*) breaking away (**von** +*dat* from)
Lösungsmittel *nt* solvent
los|werden *vt irreg sein* ❶ (*sich entledigen*) to get rid of ❷ (*aussprechen*) to tell ❸ (*fam: ausgeben*) to shell out ❹ (*fam: verkaufen*) to sell [off], to move
Lot <-[e]s, -e> [loːt] *nt* ❶ (*Senkblei*) plumb bob; **etw ins** [**rechte**] **~ bringen** to sort sth out; **aus dem/nicht im ~ sein** (*fig*) to be in poor health; **im ~ sein** (*fig*) to be all right ❷ MATH perpendicular; **das ~ auf eine Gerade fällen** to drop a perpendicular
löten ['løː·tn̩] *vt* to solder (**an** +*akk* to)
Lothringen <-s> ['loː·trɪŋən] *nt* Lorraine
Lotion <-, -en> [lo·'tsi̯oːn] *f* lotion
Lötkolben ['løːt-] *m* soldering iron
Lotse, Lotsin <-n, -n> ['loː·tsə] *m, f* pilot
lotsen ['loː·tsn̩] *vt* ❶ (*als Lotse dirigieren*) to pilot ❷ (*fam: führen*) ■**jdn irgendwohin ~** to take sb somewhere
Lotterie <-, -n> [lɔ·tə·'riː, *pl* -'riː·ən] *f* lottery; **in der ~ spielen** to play the lottery [*or* lotto]
Lotterielos *nt* lottery ticket
Lotto <-s, -s> ['lɔto] *nt* ❶ (*Zahlenlotto*) lottery; **~ spielen** to play the lottery ❷ (*Spiel*) lotto
Lottozahlen *pl* winning lottery numbers
Löwe ['løː·və] *m* ❶ (*Raubtierart*) lion ❷ ASTROL Leo
Löwenzahn *m kein pl* dandelion
loyal [lo̯a·'jaːl] *adj* (*geh*) loyal
Loyalität <-, *selten* -en> [lo̯a·ja·li·'tɛːt] *f* loyalty (**gegenüber** +*dat* to)
LP <-, -s> [ɛl·'peː, ɛl·'piː] *f Abk von* **Langspielplatte** LP
lt. *präp kurz für* **laut**[2] according to
Luchs <-es, -e> [lʊks] *m* lynx
Lücke <-, -n> ['lʏ·kə] *f* ❶ (*Zwischenraum*) gap ❷ (*Unvollständigkeit*) gap; (*Gesetzeslücke*) loophole
lückenhaft *adj* ❶ (*leere Stellen aufweisend*) full of gaps ❷ (*unvollständig*) fragmentary; *Wissen, Sammlung* incomplete; *Bericht, Erinnerung* sketchy
lückenlos *adj* ❶ (*ohne Lücke*) comprehensive ❷ (*vollständig*) complete; *Alibi* solid; *Kenntnisse* thorough; **etw ~ beweisen/nachweisen** to prove sth conclusively
lud [luːt] *imp von* **laden**[1, 2]
Luft <-, *liter* Lüfte> [lʊft, *pl* 'lʏf·tə] *f* ❶ *kein pl* (*Atemluft*) air; **die ~ anhalten** to hold one's breath; **an die** [**frische**] **~ gehen** to get some fresh air; [**tief**] **~ holen** to take a deep breath; **nach ~ schnappen** to gasp for breath ❷ *pl geh* (*Raum über dem Erdboden*) air; **in die ~ gehen** (*a. fig fam*) to explode; **etw ist aus der ~ gegriffen** (*fig*) sth is completely made up ❸ *kein pl* (*Platz, Spielraum*) space ▶ WENDUNGEN: **sich in ~ auflösen** to vanish into thin air; **jdm bleibt** [**vor Erstaunen**] **die ~ weg** (*fam*) sb is flabbergasted; **da ist dicke ~** (*fam*) the mood is tense; **die ~ ist rein** (*fam*) the coast is clear; **jdn/etw in der ~ zerreißen** (*sehr wütend auf jdn sein*) to [want to] make mincemeat of sb/sth; (*jdn scharf kritisieren*) to tear sb to pieces
Luftabwehr *f* air defense
Luftangriff *m* air raid
Luftballon *m* balloon
Luftblase *f* bubble
luftdicht *adj* airtight
Luftdruck *m kein pl* air pressure
lüften ['lʏf·tn̩] **I.** *vt* ❶ (*mit Frischluft versorgen*) to air ❷ (*preisgeben*) to reveal; *Geheimnis* to disclose **II.** *vi* (*Luft hereinlassen*) to let some air in
Luftfahrt *f kein pl* (*geh*) aviation
Luftfeuchtigkeit *f* humidity
Luftfracht *f* ❶ (*Frachtgut*) air freight ❷ (*Frachtgebühr*) air freight charge
Luftgewehr *nt* air gun
luftig ['lʊf·tɪç] *adj* ❶ (*gut belüftet*) well ventilated ❷ (*dünn und luftdurchlässig*) airy; *Kleid* light ❸ (*hoch gelegen*) dizzy
Luftkissenboot *nt* air-cushion vehicle
Luftkühlung *f* air-cooling
Luftkurort *m health resort area with particularly good air*
luftleer *adj pred* vacuous
Luftlinie *f* as the crow flies
Luftmatratze *f* inflatable mattress
Luftpost *f* airmail (**per** +*dat* by)
Luftpumpe *f* pump; *für Fahrrad* bicycle pump
Luftraum *m* airspace
Luftröhre *f* windpipe
Luftschlange *f* [paper] streamer
Luftschutzbunker *m* air raid bunker
Lüftung <-, -en> *f* ❶ (*das Lüften*) ventilation ❷ (*Ventilationsanlage*) ventilation system
Luftverschmutzung *f* air pollution
Luftwaffe *f* air force + *sing vb*
Luftzufuhr *f kein pl* air supply
Luftzug *m* breeze; (*durch das Fenster*) draft
Lüge <-, -n> ['lyː·gə] *f* lie; **jdm ~n auftischen** (*fam*) to tell sb lies ▶ WENDUNGEN: **~n haben kurze Beine** (*prov*) the truth will come out

lügen <log, gelogen> ['ly:·gn̩] **I.** *vt* (*selten*) to make up *sep* **II.** *vi* to lie; **das ist gelogen!** that's a lie! ► WENDUNGEN: **~ wie gedruckt** (*fam*) to lie one's head off

Lügengeschichte *f* made-up story

Lügner(in) <-s, -> ['ly:g·nɐ] *m(f)* (*pej*) liar

Luke <-, -n> ['lu:·kə] *f* ❶ *bes* NAUT (*verschließbarer Einstieg*) hatch ❷ (*Dachluke*) skylight; (*Kellerluke*) trapdoor

lukrativ [lu·kra·'ti:f] *adj* (*geh*) lucrative

Lumpen <-s, -> ['lʊm·pn̩] *m* ❶ *pl* (*pej: zerschlissene Kleidung, Stofffetzen*) rags *pl* ❷ DIAL (*Putzlappen*) rag

lumpig ['lʊm·pɪç] *adj* (*pej*) ❶ *attr* (*pej fam: kümmerlich*) miserable ❷ (*pej: gemein*) mean

Lunch <-[e]s *o* -, -[e]s *o* -e> [lanʃ] *m* lunch

Lunge <-, -n> ['lʊŋə] *f* lung

Lungenentzündung *f* pneumonia

lungern ['lʊŋɐn] *vi haben* (*selten fam*) to hang around

Lunte <-, -n> ['lʊn·tə] *f* (*Zündschnur*) fuse ► WENDUNGEN: **~ riechen** (*fam*) to smell a rat

Lupe <-, -n> ['lu:·pə] *f* magnifying glass ► WENDUNGEN: **jdn/etw unter die ~ nehmen** (*fam*) to examine sb/sth with a fine-tooth[ed] comb

Lust <-, Lüste> [lʊst, *pl* 'lʏs·tə] *f* ❶ *kein pl* (*freudiger Drang*) desire; **~/keine ~ zu etw** *dat* **haben** to feel like/not feel like doing sth; **~ an etw** *dat* **empfinden** to enjoy doing sth; **die ~ an etw** *dat* **verlieren** to lose interest in sth ❷ (*Freude*) joy, pleasure ❸ (*sexuelle Begierde*) desire

lüstern ['lʏs·tɐn] *adj* (*geh*) lustful

Lustgefühl *nt* feeling of pleasure

lustig ['lʊs·tɪç] *adj* ❶ (*fröhlich*) cheerful; *Abend* fun; **sich über jdn/etw ~ machen** to make fun of sb/sth; **er kam und ging wie er ~ war** he came and went as he pleased ❷ (*fam: unbekümmert*) happily

lustlos *adj* listless

LustschlossRR *nt* summer residence

Lustspiel *nt* comedy

lustvoll *adj* (*geh: mit Lust*) pleasurable; *Schrei* passionate

lutschen ['lʊ·tʃn̩] *vt, vi* to suck

Lutscher <-s, -> *m* lollipop

Luxemburg <-s> ['lʊ·ksm·bʊrk] *nt* Luxembourg; *s. a.* **Deutschland**

Luxemburger(in) <-s, -> ['lʊ·ksm·bʊr·gɐ] *m(f)* Luxembourger; *s. a.* **Deutsche(r)**

luxemburgisch ['lʊ·ksm·bʊr·gɪʃ] *adj* Luxembourgian; *s. a.* **deutsch**

luxuriös [lʊ·ksu·'ri̯øːs] *adj* luxurious

Luxus <-> ['lʊ·ksʊs] *m kein pl* luxury

Luxusartikel *m* luxury item

Luxushotel *nt* luxury hotel

Luzifer <-s> ['lu:·tsi·fɛr] *m* Lucifer

Lymphknoten *m* lymph node

lynchen ['lʏn·çn̩] *vt* (*a hum*) to lynch

Lynchjustiz *f* lynch law

Lyrik <-> ['ly:·rɪk] *f kein pl* lyric [poetry]

lyrisch ['ly:·rɪʃ] *adj* ❶ (*zur Lyrik gehörend*) lyric ❷ (*dichterisch, stimmungsvoll*) poetic

Mm

M, m <-, - *o fam* -s, -s> [ɛm] *nt* M, m; ~ **wie Martha** M as in Mike

m *m kurz für* **Meter** m

Maastricht <-(e)s> ['maːst·rɪçt] *nt* Maastricht; ~**er Vertrag** Maastricht Treaty

Machart *f* style

machbar *adj* feasible

Mache ['ma·xə] *f* ▶ WENDUNGEN: **etw/jdn in der ~ haben** (*sl*) to be working on sth/sb

machen ['ma·xn̩] **I.** *vt* ① (*tun, unternehmen*) to do; **~, was man will** to do as one pleases [*or* what one wants]; **eine Reise/einen Spaziergang ~** to go on a trip/for a walk ② (*erzeugen, verursachen*) to make; *Fotos* to take; **einen Fleck in etw ~** to stain sth; **jdm Angst ~** to frighten sb; **sich** *dat* **Sorgen ~** to worry; **jdm Hoffnung/Mut ~** to give sb hope/courage ③ (*zubereiten*) *Tee, Kaffee* to make ④ (*absolvieren*) to do; **einen Kurs ~** to take a course; **eine Ausbildung ~** to train to be sth ⑤ (*kosten*) **das macht zehn Euro** that's ten euros [please]; **was macht das zusammen?** what does that come to? ⑥ (*ausmachen*) **macht nichts!** no problem!; **macht das was?** does it matter?; **das macht [doch] nichts!** never mind! ▶ WENDUNGEN: **mach's gut** (*fam*) take care [*or* it easy] **II.** *vi* ① (*werden lassen*) **Liebe macht blind** love is blind ② (*aussehen lassen*) **Querstreifen ~ dick** horizontal stripes make you look fat **III.** *vr* ① (*viel leisten*) **die neue Sekretärin macht sich** *akk* **gut** the new secretary is doing a good job ② (*passen*) **das Bild macht sich gut an der Wand** the picture looks good on the wall ③ (*sich begeben*) ■ **sich an etw** *akk* **~** to get on with sth; **sich an die Arbeit ~** to get down to work ④ (*gewinnen*) **sich** *dat* **Feinde ~** to make enemies ⑤ + *adj* (*werden*) **sich** *akk* **verständlich ~** to make oneself understood ⑥ (*gelegen sein*) **sich** *dat* **etwas/viel/wenig aus jdm/etw ~** to care/care a lot/not care much for sb/sth

Machenschaft <-, -en> *pl* (*pej*) machinations *npl*

Macher(in) <-s, -> *m(f)* (*fam*) doer

Macho <-s, -s> ['ma·tʃo] *m* (*fam*) macho

Macht <-, Mächte> ['maxt, *pl* 'mɛç·tə] *f* power; **etw liegt in jds ~** sth is within sb's power; **an die ~ kommen** to come [in]to power

Machtergreifung *f* seizure of power

Machtfrage *f* question of power

Machthaber(in) <-s, -> [-haː·bɐ] *m(f)* ruler

mächtig **I.** *adj* ① (*einflussreich*) powerful ② (*gewaltig, beeindruckend*) mighty **II.** *adv* (*fam: sehr*) extremely; **sich** *akk* **~ beeilen** to move it

Machtkampf *m* power struggle

machtlos *adj* powerless

Machtlosigkeit <-> *f kein pl* powerlessness

MachtmissbrauchRR *m* abuse of power

Machtpolitik *f* power politics *npl*

Machtprobe *f* test of strength

Machtstellung *f* position of power

Machtübernahme *f s.* **Machtergreifung**

machtvoll *adj* powerful, mighty

Machtwechsel *m* change of government

Machwerk *nt* **ein übles ~** a poor piece of workmanship

Macke <-, -n> ['ma·kə] *f* (*fam*) ① (*Schadstelle*) defect ② (*fam: Tick, Eigenart*) quirk; **eine ~ haben** to have a screw loose

Mädchen <-s, -> ['mɛːt·çən] *nt* girl ▶ WENDUNGEN: **~ für alles** (*fam*) jack-of-all-trades

mädchenhaft *adj* girlish

Mädchenname *m* ① (*Vorname*) girl's name ② (*Geburtsname einer Ehefrau*) maiden name

Made <-, -n> ['maː·də] *f* maggot ▶ WENDUNGEN: **wie die ~[n] im Speck leben** (*fam*) to live the life of Riley

Mädel <-s, -[s]> ['mɛː·dl̩] *nt*, **Madel** <-s, -n> ['maː·dl̩] *nt* SÜDD, ÖSTERR girl

madig ['maː·dɪç] *adj* worm-eaten

madig|machenRR *vt* ■ **jdm etw ~** (*fam*) to spoil sth for sb

Mafia <-, s> ['ma·fi̯a] *f* ■ **die ~** the Mafia

mag *3. pers sing pres von* **mögen**

Magazin <-s, -e> [ma·ga·'tsiːn] *nt* (*Zeitschrift*) magazine

Magen <-s, Mägen *o* -> ['maː·gn̩, *pl* 'mɛː·gn̩] *m* stomach; **auf nüchternen ~** on an empty stomach ▶ WENDUNGEN: **jdm dreht sich der ~ um** sb's stomach is turning; **etw schlägt jdm auf den ~** (*fam*) sth gets to sb

Magenbitter <-s, -> *m* bitters *npl*

Magengeschwür *nt* stomach ulcer

Magengrube *f* pit of the stomach

Magenkrampf *m meist pl* stomach cramps *pl*

Magenleiden *nt* stomach trouble

Magensäure *f* stomach acid

Magenschmerzen *pl* stomachache

Magenverstimmung *f* upset stomach

mager ['maː·gɐ] *adj* ① (*dünn*) thin ② (*fettarm*) low-fat; *Fleisch* lean ③ (*dürftig*) feeble; *Ernte* poor

Magermilch *f* skim milk

Magersucht *f kein pl* anorexia

magersüchtig *adj* anorexic

Magie <-> [ma·'giː] *f kein pl* magic

Magier(in) <-s, -> ['maː·gi̯·ɐ] *m(f)* magician

magisch ['maː·gɪʃ] **I.** *adj* magic **II.** *adv* magically; **wie ~** as if by magic

Magister, Magistra <-s, -> [ma·'gɪs·tɐ, ma·'gɪs·tra] *m, f* ① *kein pl* (*Universitätsgrad*) [Master's] degree ② ÖSTERR (*Apotheker*) pharmacist

> The **Magister Artium** is the most commonly awarded degree in the humanities

M

and social sciences. Only certain combinations of major and minor subjects are permitted in a **Magister** course of study. Generally, either two majors or one major and two minors may be combined.
The introduction of the Bachelor's and Master's degrees a few years ago started a small revolution at German universities. The new programs give students the opportunity to complete their education faster so they can move on to the working world in a relatively short time.

Magistrat[1] <-[e]s, -e> [ma·gɪs·ˈtraːt] *m* (*Stadtverwaltung*) city/town council
Magistrat[2] <-en, -en> [ma·gɪs·ˈtraːt] *m* SCHWEIZ Federal Councilor
Magma <-s, Magmen> [ˈmag·ma, *pl* ˈmag·mən] *nt* magma
Magnesium <-s> [ma·ˈgneː·zi̯·ʊm] *nt kein pl* magnesium
Magnet <-[e]s *o* -en, -e[n]> [ma·ˈgneːt] *m* magnet
Magnetband *nt* magnetic tape
Magnetfeld *nt* magnetic field
magnetisch [ma·ˈgneː·tɪʃ] *adj* magnetic
Magnetschwebebahn *f* magnetic levitation train, maglev [train] *fam*
Magnetstreifen *m* magnetic strip
Mahagoni <-s> [ma·ha·ˈgoː·ni] *nt kein pl* mahogany
Mähdrescher <-s, -> *m* combine harvester
mähen [ˈmɛː·ən] *vt Gras* to mow; *Feld* to harvest
Mahl <-[e]s, -e *o* Mähler> [ˈmaːl, *pl* ˈmɛː·lɐ] *nt pl selten* (*geh*) meal
mahlen <mahlte, gemahlen> [ˈmaː·lən] *vt* to grind
Mahlzeit [ˈmaːl·tsait] *f* meal; **~!** DIAL (*fam*) ≈ [good] afternoon! (*greeting used during the lunch break in parts of Germany and Austria*)
Mähne <-, -n> [ˈmɛː·nə] *f* mane
mahnen [ˈmaː·nən] *vt* ❶ (*nachdrücklich erinnern*) to warn ❷ (*an eine Rechnung erinnern*) to remind
Mahngebühr *f* late fee
Mahnmal <-[e]s, -e> [ˈmaːn·maːl] *nt* memorial
Mahnung <-, -en> *f* ❶ (*mahnende Äußerung*) warning ❷ (*Mahnbrief*) reminder
Mahnwache *f* vigil
Mai <-[e]s *o* -, -e> [ˈmai] *m* May; *s. a.* **Februar**
Maiglöckchen *nt* lily of the valley
Mailand <-s> [ˈmai·lant] *nt* Milan
Mailbox <-, -en> [ˈmeːl·bɔks] *f* INET mailbox
mailen [ˈmeː·lən] *vt, vi* INET to e-mail
Mais <-es, -e> [ˈmais, *pl* ˈmai·zə] *m* ❶ (*Anbaupflanze*) corn ❷ (*Maisfrucht*) sweet corn
Maiskolben *m* corncob
majestätisch [ma·jɛs·ˈtɛː·tɪʃ] **I.** *adj* majestic **II.** *adv* majestically
Majonäse <-, -n> [ma·jo·ˈnɛː·zə] *f* mayonnaise
Majoran <-s, -e> [ˈmaː·jo·ran] *m* marjoram
makaber [ma·ˈkaː·bɐ] *adj* macabre
Makel <-s, -> [ˈmaː·kl̩] *m* flaw
makellos *adj* ❶ (*untadelig*) *Ruf* untarnished ❷ (*fehlerlos*) perfect
mäkeln [ˈmɛː·kl̩n] *vi* to whine [about sth]
Make-up <-s, -s> [meːk·ˈʔap] *nt* makeup
Makkaroni [ma·ka·ˈroː·ni] *pl* macaroni
Makler(in) <-s, -> [ˈmaːk·lɐ] *m(f)* broker; (*Immobilienmakler*) realtor
Maklergebühr *f* brokerage fee, commission
Makrele <-, -n> [ma·ˈkreː·lə] *f* mackerel
mal[1] [ˈmaːl] *adv* ❶ MATH times; **drei ~ drei ergibt neun** three times three is nine ❷ (*eben so*) **gerade ~** (*fam*) only
mal[2] [maːl] *adv* (*fam*) *kurz für* **einmal**
Mal[1] <-[e]s, -e *o* nach Zahlwörtern: -> [maːl] *nt* (*Zeitpunkt*) time; **einige/etliche ~e** sometimes/very often; **ein/kein einziges ~** once/not once; **jedes ~** every time; **zum ersten/letzten ~** for the first/last time; **bis zum nächsten ~!** see you [around]!; **das x-te ~** (*fam*) the millionth time; **das eine oder andere ~** [every] now and again ▶ WENDUNGEN: **ein für alle ~** once and for all; **mit einem ~[e]** all of a sudden
Mal[2] <-[e]s, -e *o* Mäler> [ˈmaːl, *pl* ˈmɛː·lɐ] *nt* mark; (*Muttermal*) birthmark
Malaria <-> [ma·ˈlaː·ri̯a] *f kein pl* malaria
Malaysia <-s> [ma·ˈlai·zi̯a] *nt* Malaysia; *s. a.* **Deutschland**
Malaysier(in) <-s, -> [ma·ˈlai·zi̯·ɐ] *m(f)* Malaysian; *s. a.* **Deutsche(r)**
malaysisch [ma·ˈlai·zɪʃ] *adj* Malayan; *s. a.* **deutsch**
malen [ˈmaː·lən] *vt, vi* ❶ (*ein Bild herstellen*) to paint ❷ DIAL (*anstreichen*) to paint
Maler(in) <-s, -> [ˈmaː·lɐ] *m(f)* painter
Malerei <-, -en> [ma·lə·ˈrai] *f* ❶ *kein pl* (*Malkunst*) painting ❷ *meist pl* (*Gemälde*) picture, painting
malerisch *adj* picturesque
Malheur <-s, -s *o* -e> [ma·ˈløːɐ̯] *nt* mishap
Mallorca <-s> [ma·ˈjɔr·ka] *nt* Mallorca
mal|nehmen [ˈmaːl·neː·mən] *vt irreg* (*fam*) to multiply (**mit** +*dat* by)
Malstift *m* crayon
Malta <-s> [ˈmal·ta] *nt* Malta; *s. a.* **Deutschland**
Malteser(in) <-s, -> [mal·ˈteː·zɐ] *m(f)* Maltese; *s. a.* **Deutsche(r)**
maltesisch [mal·ˈteː·zɪʃ] *adj* Maltese; *s. a.* **deutsch**
Malz <-es> [ˈmalts] *nt kein pl* malt
Malzkaffee *m* malted coffee
Mama <-, -s> [ˈma·ma] *f*, **Mami** <-, -s> [ˈma·mi] *f* (*fam*) mommy
Mammut <-s, -s *o* -e> [ˈma·mʊt, ˈma·muːt] *nt* mammoth
mampfen [ˈmam·pfn̩] *vt, vi* (*sl*) to munch
man[1] <*dat* einem, *akk* einen> [ˈman] *pron indef* ❶ (*irgendjemand*) one *form*, you; **das**

hat ~ mir gesagt that's what I was told ❷ (*die Leute*) people; **so etwas tut ~ nicht** that's not the way things work [around here] ❸ (*ich*) **~ versteht sein eigenes Wort nicht** I can't hear myself think

man² ['man] *adv* NORDD (*fam: nur [als Bekräftigung]*) just; **lass' ~ gut sein** just leave it alone

Management <-s, -s> ['mɛn·ɪtʃ·mənt] *nt* management + *sing/pl vb*

managen ['mɛ·nɪ·dʒn̩] *vt* to manage

Manager(in) <-s, -> ['mɛ·nɪ·dʒɐ] *m(f)* manager

mạnche(r, s) *pron indef* ❶ + *pl* (*einige*) some ❷ + *sing* **~r Mann/~ Frau** many a man/woman

mancherlei ['man·çɐ·'lai] *pron indef, adjektivisch* various

manchmal ['manç·ma:l] *adv* ❶ (*gelegentlich*) sometimes ❷ SCHWEIZ (*oft*) often

Mandarine <-, -n> [man·da·'ri:·nə] *f* mandarin

Mandel <-, -n> ['man·dl̩] *f* ❶ (*Frucht*) almond ❷ *meist pl* ANAT tonsils *pl*

Mạndelentzündung *f* tonsillitis

Manege <-, -n> [ma·'ne:·ʒə] *f* ring

Mangel¹ <-s, Mängel> ['ma·ŋl̩, *pl* 'mɛ·ŋl̩] *m* ❶ (*Fehler*) flaw ❷ *kein pl* (*Knappheit*) lack (**an** + *dat* of); **ein ~ an Vitamin C** vitamin C deficiency

M

Mangel² ['ma·ŋl̩] *f* ▶ WENDUNGEN: **jdn in die ~ nehmen** (*fam*) to grill sb

Mạngelerscheinung *f* deficiency symptom

mạngelhaft *adj* ❶ (*unzureichend*) inadequate ❷ (*Mängel aufweisend*) faulty

mangeln ['ma·ŋl̩n] *vi* ■ **es mangelt an etw** *dat* there is a shortage of sth; **es mangelt jdm an Ernst** sb is not serious enough

mạngelnd *adj* inadequate; **~es Selbstvertrauen** lack of self-confidence

Mạngelware *f* scarce commodity

Mango <-, -gonen *o* -s> ['maŋ·go, *pl* maŋ·'go:·nən] *f* mango

Mangold <-[e]s, -e> ['maŋ·gɔlt, *pl* 'maŋ·gɔl·də] *m* Swiss chard

Manie <-, -n> [ma·'ni:, *pl* ma·'ni:·ən] *f* (*geh*) obsession

Manier <-, -en> [ma·'ni:ɐ̯] *f* ❶ *kein pl* (*geh: Art und Weise*) manner; **nach bewährter ~** following a tried and true method ❷ *pl* (*Umgangsformen*) manners

Manifest <-[e]s, -e> [ma·ni·'fɛst] *nt* manifesto

Maniküre <-> [ma·ni·'ky:·rə] *f kein pl* manicure

maniküren* [ma·ni·'ky:·rən] *vt* ■ **jdn ~** to give sb a manicure

Manipulation <-, -en> [ma·ni·pu·la·'tsi̯o:n] *f* manipulation

manipul<u>ie</u>rbar *adj* manipulable; **leicht ~ sein** to be easily manipulated; **schwer ~ sein** to be difficult to manipulate

manipulieren* [ma·ni·pu·'li:·rən] **I.** *vt* to manipulate **II.** *vi* ■ **an etw** *dat* **~** to tamper with sth

manisch ['ma:·nɪʃ] *adj* manic

m<u>a</u>nisch-depress<u>i</u>v *adj* manic-depressive

Manko <-s, -s> ['maŋ·ko] *nt* (*Nachteil*) shortcoming

Mann <-[e]s, Männer> ['man, *pl* 'mɛ·nɐ] *m* ❶ (*männlicher Mensch*) man; ■ **Männer** men; (*im Gegensatz zu den Frauen a.*) males ❷ (*Ehemann*) husband ▶ WENDUNGEN: **der ~ auf der <u>Straße</u>** the man in the street, John Doe; **jd ist ein <u>gemachter</u> ~** sb has got it made

Männchen <-s, -> ['mɛn·çən] *nt* (*männliches Tier*) male

Mannequin <-s, -s> ['ma·nə·kɛ̃, ma·nə·'kɛ̃:] *nt* model

Männer ['mɛ·nɐ] *pl von* **Mann**

Mạ̈nnersache *f* man's job, sth for men

männlich ['mɛn·lɪç] *adj* ❶ ANAT male ❷ (*für den Mann typisch*) male; **ein ~er Duft** a masculine scent ❸ LING masculine

Mạ̈nnlichkeit <-> *f kein pl* masculinity

Mạnnsbild *nt* SÜDD, ÖSTERR (*fam*) he-man

Mạnnschaft <-, -en> *f* ❶ SPORT team ❷ (*Schiffs- o Flugzeugbesatzung*) crew ❸ (*Gruppe von Mitarbeitern*) staff + *sing/pl vb*

Manöver <-s, -> [ma·'nø:·vɐ] *nt* ❶ MIL maneuver ❷ (*Manövrieren eines Fahrzeugs*) maneuver ❸ (*pej: Winkelzug*) trick

manövrieren* [ma·nø·'vri:·rən] *vi, vt* to maneuver

Mantel <-s, Mäntel> ['man·tl̩, *pl* 'mɛn·tl̩] *m* coat

manuell [ma·'nu̯·ɛl] **I.** *adj* manual **II.** *adv* manually

Mappe <-, -n> ['ma·pə] *f* ❶ (*Schnellhefter*) folder ❷ (*Aktenmappe*) briefcase

Maracuja <-, -s> [ma·ra·'ku:·ja] *f* passion fruit

Marathon <-s, -s> ['ma:·ra·tɔn] *m* (*a. fig*) marathon

Märchen <-s, -> ['mɛ:ɐ̯·çən] *nt* fairy tale

m<u>ä</u>rchenhaft **I.** *adj* fabulous **II.** *adv* fabulously

Marder <-s, -> ['mar·dɐ] *m* marten

Margarine <-, -n> [mar·ga·'ri:·nə] *f* margarine

Mar<u>i</u>enkäfer *m* ladybug

Marille <-, -n> [ma·'rɪ·lə] *f* ÖSTERR apricot

Marinade <-, -n> [ma·ri·'na:·də] *f* marinade

Marine <-, -n> [ma·'ri:·nə] *f* NAUT, MIL navy; ■ **bei der ~** in the navy

mar<u>i</u>neblau *adj* navy blue

marinieren* [ma·ri·'ni:·rən] *vt* to marinate

Marionette <-, -n> [ma·ri̯o·'nɛ·tə] *f* puppet *a. fig*

Mark¹ <-, - *o hum* Märker> ['mark] *f* (*hist*) mark; **Deutsche ~** German mark

Mark² <-[e]s> ['mark] *nt kein pl* marrow ▶ WENDUNGEN: **etw geht jdm durch ~ und <u>Bein</u>** sth sets sb's teeth on edge

markant [mar·'kant] *adj* ❶ (*ausgeprägt*) bold ❷ (*auffallend*) striking

Marke <-, -n> ['mar·kə, *pl* 'mar·kn̩] *f* ❶ (*fam: Briefmarke*) stamp; **eine ~ zu 55 Cent** a 55-cent stamp ❷ (*Warensorte*) brand; **das ist**

~ **Eigenbau** (*hum*) I made it myself

Markenartikel *m* brand-name product

Markenname *m* brand name

Markenzeichen *nt* trademark *a. fig*

markerschütternd *adj* heart-rending

markieren* [mar·ˈkiː·rən] *vt* ① (*kennzeichnen*) to mark ② (*fam*) to play

Markierung <-, -en> *f* marking

Markise <-, -n> [mar·ˈkiː·zə] *f* awning

Markt <-[e]s, Märkte> [ˈmarkt, *pl* ˈmɛrk·tə] *m* ① (*Wochenmarkt*) market ② (*Marktplatz*) marketplace ③ ÖKON, FIN market; **etw auf den ~ bringen** to put sth on the market

Marktbude *f* [market] stand

Marktfrau *f* [female] market vendor

Marktführer *m* market leader

Markthalle *f* indoor market

Marktlage *f* state of the market

Marktlücke *f* niche in the market

Marktplatz *m* marketplace

Marktpreis *m* ÖKON market price

Marktwert *m* market value

Marmelade <-, -n> [mar·mə·ˈlaː·də] *f* jam; (*aus Zitrusfrüchten*) marmalade

Marmor <-s, -e> [ˈmar·moːɐ̯] *m* marble

marmorieren* [mar·mo·ˈriː·rən] *vt* to marble

Marmorkuchen *m* marble cake

Marokkaner(in) <-s, -> [ma·rɔ·ˈkaː·nɐ] *m(f)* Moroccan; *s. a.* **Deutsche(r)**

marokkanisch [ma·rɔ·ˈkaː·nɪʃ] *adj* Moroccan; *s. a.* **deutsch**

Marokko <-s> [ma·ˈrɔ·ko] *nt* Morocco; *s. a.* **Deutschland**

Marone <-, -n> [ma·ˈroː·nə] *f*, **Maroni** <-, -> [ma·ˈroː·ni] *f* SÜDD, ÖSTERR [edible] chestnut

Mars <-> [ˈmars] *m* ■ **der** ~ Mars

Marsch <-[e]s, Märsche> [ˈmarʃ, *pl* ˈmɛr·ʃə] *m a.* MUS march

marschieren* [mar·ˈʃiː·rən] *vi sein* ① MIL to march ② (*zu Fuß gehen*) to walk quickly

Marsmensch *m* Martian

martern [ˈmar·tɐn] *vt* (*geh*) to torture

Märtyrer(in) <-s, -> [ˈmɛr·ty·rɐ, ˈmɛr·ty·rə·rɪn] *m(f)* (*a. fig*) martyr

Martyrium <-, -rien> [mar·ˈtyː·ri̯·ʊm, *pl* mar·ˈtyː·ri̯·ən] *nt* martyrdom

Marxismus <-> [mar·ˈksɪs·mʊs] *m kein pl* Marxism

Marxist(in) <-en, -en> [mar·ˈksɪst] *m(f)* Marxist

März <-[es], -e> [ˈmɛrts] *m* March; *s. a.* **Februar**

Marzipan <-s, -e> [mar·tsi·ˈpaːn] *nt o m* marzipan

Masche <-, -n> [ˈma·ʃə] *f* ① (*Strickmasche*) stitch ② SÜDD, ÖSTERR, SCHWEIZ (*Schleife*) bow ③ (*fam: Trick*) trick

Maschendraht *m* wire mesh

Maschinbau *m kein pl* ÖSTERR *s.* **Maschinenbau**

Maschine <-, -n> [ma·ˈʃiː·nə] *f* ① (*Automat*) machine ② (*Motorrad*) bike ③ (*Schreibmaschine*) typewriter; ~ **schreiben** to type

maschinell [ma·ʃi·ˈnɛl] **I.** *adj* machine *attr* **II.** *adv* by machine

Maschinenbau *m kein pl* ① (*das Bau*) machine construction ② (*Fachgebiet*) mechanical engineering

Maschinenpistole *f* submachine gun

Maschinenschrift *f* type[script]

Maschinschrift *f* ÖSTERR *s.* **Maschinenschrift**

Masern [ˈmaː·zɐn] *pl* measles

Maske <-, -n> [ˈmas·kə] *f* (*a. fig*) mask

Maskenball *m* masquerade [ball]

maskieren* [mas·ˈkiː·rən] **I.** *vt* to disguise **II.** *vr* ■ **sich** *akk* ~ ① (*sich verkleiden*) to dress up ② (*sich vermummen*) to put on a mask

Maskottchen <-s, -> [mas·ˈkɔt·çən] *nt* [lucky] mascot

maskulin [mas·ku·ˈliːn] *adj* masculine

Masochismus <-> [ma·zɔ·ˈxɪs·mʊs] *m kein pl* masochism

Masochist(in) <-en, -en> [ma·zɔ·ˈxɪst] *m(f)* masochist

masochistisch *adj* masochistic

maß [ˈmaːs] *imp von* **messen**

Maß[1] <-es, -e> [ˈmaːs] *nt* ① (*Maßeinheit*) measure ② *pl* (*gemessene Größe*) measurements; (*Raum*) dimensions; **jds ~e nehmen** to measure sb ③ (*Ausmaß*) extent; **in besonderem ~[e]** especially; **in zunehmendem ~e** increasingly ▶ WENDUNGEN: **das ~ ist voll** enough is enough; **in ~en** in moderation

Maß[2] <-, -> [ˈmaːs] *f* SÜDD liter [mug] of beer

Massage <-, -n> [ma·ˈsaː·ʒə] *f* massage

Massaker <-s, -> [ma·ˈsaː·kɐ] *nt* massacre

massakrieren* [ma·sa·ˈkriː·rən] *vt* to massacre

Maßangabe *f* measurement

Maßband *nt* tape measure

Masse <-, -n> [ˈma·sə] *f* ① (*breiiges Material*) mass ② (*Menschenmasse*) crowd; **in ~n** in droves ③ (*große Anzahl*) mass; **eine [ganze] ~** a lot [of] ④ PHYS mass

Maßeinheit *f* unit of measurement

Massenandrang *m* crush [of people]

Massenarbeitslosigkeit *f* mass unemployment *no art*

Massenartikel *m* mass-produced product

Massenentlassung *f meist pl* mass layoffs *pl*

Massengrab *nt* mass grave

massenhaft I. *adj* on a huge scale **II.** *adv* (*fam*) in droves

Massenkarambolage [-ka·ram·bo·laː·ʒə] *f* pile-up

Massenmedien *pl* mass media + *sing/pl vb*

Massenmord *m* mass murder

Massenmörder(in) *m(f)* mass murderer

Massenproduktion *f* mass production

Massentierhaltung *f* factory farming

Massentourismus *m kein pl* mass tourism

massenweise *adv* in droves

Masseur(in) <-s, -e> [ma·ˈsøːɐ̯] *m(f)* masseur *masc*, masseuse *fem*

Masseuse <-, -n> [ma·ˈsøː·zə] *f* ① (*euph: Prostituierte*) masseuse ② (*veraltend*) *fem*

M

form von **Masseur**
maßgebend, maßgeblich ['maːs·geːp·lɪç] **I.** *adj* ❶ (*ausschlaggebend*) decisive ❷ (*bedeutend*) significant **II.** *adv* decisively; **an etw** *dat* **~ beteiligt sein** to play a leading role in sth
maßgeschneidert *adj* tailored
massieren* [ma·'siː·rən] *vt* to massage
massig ['ma·sɪç] *adj* massive
mäßig ['mɛː·sɪç] **I.** *adj* ❶ (*maßvoll, gering*) moderate ❷ (*mittelmäßig*) mediocre, indifferent **II.** *adv* ❶ (*in Maßen*) with moderation ❷ (*nicht besonders*) indifferently
mäßigen ['mɛː·sɪ·gn̩] **I.** *vt* to curb **II.** *vr* ■ **sich** *akk* ~ to restrain oneself
Mäßigung <-> *f kein pl* restraint
massiv [ma·'siːf] *adj* ❶ (*solide*) solid *attr* ❷ (*wuchtig*) solid, massive ❸ (*drastisch, heftig*) serious; *Kritik* heavy
Massiv <-s, -e> [ma·'siːf, *pl* ma·'siː·və] *nt* massif
Maßkrug *m* one-liter beer mug
maßlos I. *adj* extreme; ■ **~ sein** to be immoderate **II.** *adv* ❶ (*äußerst*) extremely ❷ (*unerhört*) hugely
Maßlosigkeit <-> *f kein pl* excess; ■ **~ in etw** *dat* lack of moderation in sth
Maßnahme <-, -n> ['maːs·naː·mə] *f* measure
Maßregel *f meist pl* rule
maßregeln *vt* to reprimand
Maßstab ['maːs·ʃtaːp] *m* ❶ (*Größenverhältnis*) scale; **im ~ 1:250.000** on a scale of 1:250,000 ❷ (*Kriterium*) criterion; **Maßstäbe setzen** to set standards
maßstab(s)gerecht, maßstab(s)getreu *adj* true to scale
maßvoll I. *adj* moderate; **~es Verhalten** moderation **II.** *adv* moderately
Mast¹ <-[e]s, -en *o* -e> ['mast] *m* ❶ NAUT mast ❷ (*Stange*) pole
Mast² <-, -en> ['mast] *f pl selten* (*das Mästen*) fattening
mästen ['mɛs·tn̩] *vt* to fatten
masturbieren* [mas·tʊr·'biː·rən] *vi* to masturbate
Material <-s, -ien> [ma·te·'ri̯aːl, *pl* ma·te·'ri̯aː·li̯·ən] *nt* material
Materialismus <-> [ma·te·ri̯a·'lɪs·mʊs] *m kein pl* materialism
Materialist(in) <-en, -en> [ma·te·ri̯a·'lɪst] *m(f)* materialist
materialistisch [ma·te·ri̯a·'lɪs·tɪʃ] *adj* materialist[ic]
Materie <-, -n> [ma·'teː·ri̯ə] *f* ❶ *kein pl* PHYS, CHEM matter ❷ (*Thema*) subject
materiell [ma·te·'ri̯ɛl] *adj* ❶ (*stofflich*) material ❷ (*finanziell*) financial
Mathematik <-> [ma·te·ma·'tiːk] *f kein pl* mathematics + *sing vb,* math *fam*
mathematisch [ma·te·'maː·tɪʃ] *adj* mathematical
Matjes <-, -> ['mat·jəs] *m,* **Matjeshering** *m* matjes herring
Matratze <-, -n> [ma·'tra·tsə] *f* mattress
Mätresse <-, -n> [mɛ·'trɛ·sə] *f* mistress
Matrikel <-, -n> [ma·'triː·kl̩] *f* ❶ SCH matriculation register ❷ ADMIN ÖSTERR register
Matrose <-n, -n> [ma·'troː·zə] *m* sailor
Matsch <-[e]s> ['matʃ] *m kein pl* ❶ (*schlammige Erde*) mud; (*Schneematsch*) slush ❷ (*breiige Masse*) mush
matschig ['mat·ʃɪç] *adj* (*fam*) ❶ *Erde* muddy; *Schnee* slushy ❷ (*breiig*) mushy
matt ['mat] **I.** *adj* ❶ (*erschöpft, schwach*) weak; *Händedruck* limp; *Lächeln, Stimme* faint; *Licht* dim ❷ (*glanzlos*) mat[te]; *Augen* dull; *Farben* pale **II.** *adv* ❶ (*schwach*) dimly ❷ (*ohne Nachdruck*) feebly
Matte¹ <-, -n> ['ma·tə] *f* mat
Matte² <-, -n> ['ma·tə] *f* SCHWEIZ, ÖSTERR (*Bergwiese*) alpine meadow
Mattscheibe *f* (*fam: Bildschirm*) screen; (*Fernseher*) tube ▶ WENDUNGEN: **~ haben** (*fam*) to draw a [mental] blank
Matura <-> [ma·'tuː·ra] *f kein pl* SCHWEIZ, ÖSTERR (*Abitur*) ≈ high-school diploma
Mauer <-, -n> ['mau·ɐ] *f* (*a. fig*) wall
mauern ['mau·ɐn] *vt* to build
Maueröffnung *f kein pl* POL fall of the [Berlin] Wall
Maul <-[e]s, Mäuler> ['maul, *pl* 'mɔy·lɐ] *nt* ❶ (*bei Tieren*) mouth; *Raubtier* jaws *pl* ❷ (*derb: Mund*) trap ▶ WENDUNGEN: **halt's ~!** (*vulg*) shut up!; **jdm das ~ stopfen** (*vulg*) to shut sb up
maulen ['mau·lən] *vi* (*fam*) to grumble [*or* gripe]
Maulesel ['maul·ʔeːzl̩] *m* mule
maulfaul *adj* (*fam*) uncommunicative
Maulheld(in) *m(f)* big mouth
Maulkorb *m* muzzle
Maultaschen *pl* SÜDD KOCHK *large pasta squares filled with meat, cheese, spinach, etc.*
Maultier ['maul·tiːɐ̯] *nt s.* **Maulesel**
Maulwurf <-[e]s, -würfe> ['maul·vʊrf, *pl* -vʏr·fə] *m* (*a. fig*) mole
Maurer(in) <-s, -> ['mau·rɐ] *m(f)* bricklayer
maurisch ['mau·rɪʃ] *adj* Moorish
Maus <-, Mäuse> ['maus, *pl* 'mɔy·zə] *f* ❶ *a.* COMPUT mouse ❷ *pl* (*sl: Geld*) dough *sing*
mauscheln ['mau·ʃl̩n] *vi* (*pej fam*) to fiddle
Mausefalle *f* mousetrap
Mauseloch *nt* mouse hole
mausen ['mau·zn̩] *vt* (*hum: stehlen*) to pilfer *fam*
mausern ['mau·zɐn] *vr* ■ **sich** *akk* ~ to molt; (*fig*) to blossom
mausetot ['mau·zə·'toːt] *adj* (*fam o hum*) deader than dead
Maut <-, -en> ['maut] *f,* **Mautgebühr** *f* toll [charge]
Mautstelle *f* tollbooth
Maxima ['ma·ksi·ma] *pl von* **Maximum**
maximal [ma·ksi·'maːl] **I.** *adj* maximum *attr;* (*höchste a.*) highest *attr* **II.** *adv* at maximum; **das ~ zulässige Gesamtgewicht** the maximum weight; **~ 25.000 Euro** 25,000 euros at

most

maximieren* [ma·ksi·ˈmiː·rən] *vt* to maximize

Maximum <-s, Maxima> [ˈma·ksi·mʊm, *pl* ˈma·ksi·ma] *nt* maximum (**an** +*dat* of)

Mayonnaise <-, -n> [ma·jɔ·ˈnɛː·zə] *f s.* **Majonäse**

Mazedonien <-s> [ma·tse·ˈdoː·ni̯·ən] *nt* Macedonia; *s. a.* **Deutschland**

m.E. *Abk von* **meines Erachtens** in my opinion

Mechanik <-, -en> [me·ˈçaː·nɪk] *f* mechanics + *sing vb*

Mechaniker(in) <-s, -> [me·ˈçaː·nɪ·kɐ] *m(f)* mechanic

mechanisch [me·ˈçaː·nɪʃ] (*a. fig*) **I.** *adj* mechanical **II.** *adv* mechanically

Mechanisierung <-, -en> *f* mechanization

Mechanismus <-, -nismen> [me·ça·ˈnɪs·mʊs, *pl* -ˈnɪs·mən] *m* mechanism

Meckerei <-, -en> *f* (*pej fam*) moaning and groaning

meckern [ˈmɛ·kɐn] *vi* ❶ (*der Ziege*) to bleat ❷ (*fig fam*) to complain, to bellyache *fam* (**über** +*akk* about)

Mecklenburg <-s> [ˈmɛk·lən·bʊrk] *nt* Mecklenburg

mecklenburgisch [ˈmɛk·lən·bʊr·gɪʃ] *adj* Mecklenburg *attr*

Mecklenburg-Vorpommern <-s> [ˈmɛk·lən·bʊrk·ʔfoːɐ̯·pɔ·mɐn] *nt* Mecklenburg-West Pomerania

Medaille <-, -n> [me·ˈdal·jə] *f* medal

Medaillon <-s, -s> [me·dal·ˈjõː] *nt* locket

Medien [ˈmeː·di̯·ən] *pl* ❶ *pl von* **Medium** ❷ (*Informationsträger*) ■**die** ~ the media + *sing/pl vb;* **die digitalen** ~ digital media

Medienereignis *nt* media event

mediengerecht *adj* suitable for the media

Medienlandschaft *f* media landscape

Medienrummel *m* (*fam*) media excitement

Medikament <-[e]s, -e> [me·di·ka·ˈmɛnt] *nt* medicine

Medikamentenmissbrauch[RR] *m* drug abuse

Medikamentensucht *f* drug addiction

medikamentös [me·di·ka·mɛn·ˈtøːs] *adj* medicinal

Meditation <-, -en> [me·di·ta·ˈtsi̯oːn] *f* meditation (**über** +*akk* about/on)

mediterran [me·di·tɛ·ˈraːn] *adj* Mediterranean

meditieren* [me·di·ˈtiː·rən] *vi* to meditate

Medium <-s, Medien> [ˈmeː·di̯·ʊm, *pl* ˈmeː·di̯·ən] *nt* medium

Medizin <-, -en> [me·di·ˈtsiːn] *f* ❶ *kein pl* (*Heilkunde*) medicine ❷ (*fam: Medikament*) medicine

Mediziner(in) <-s, -> [me·di·ˈtsiː·nɐ] *m(f)* doctor

medizinisch [me·di·ˈtsiː·nɪʃ] **I.** *adj* ❶ (*ärztlich*) medical ❷ (*heilend*) medicinal **II.** *adv* medically; **jdn ~ behandeln** to give sb medical treatment

Medizinmann <-männer> [-man, *pl* -mɛnɐ] *m* (*indianisch*) medicine man; (*afrikanisch*) witch doctor

Meer <-[e]s, -e> [ˈmeːɐ̯] *nt* sea; (*Weltmeer*) ocean; **das Schwarze/Tote** ~ the Black/Dead Sea; **ans ~ fahren** to go to the ocean; **am** ~ by the water

Meerenge *f* strait

Meeresalge *f* seaweed + *sing vb*

Meeresforschung *f* oceanography

Meeresfrüchte *pl* seafood + *sing vb*

Meeresgrund *m kein pl* seabed

Meeresspiegel *m* sea level

Meerrettich *m* horseradish

Meerschweinchen *nt* guinea pig

Meerwasser *nt* sea [*or* salt] water

Megabyte [me·ga·ˈbait, ˈmeː·ga·bait] *nt* COMPUT megabyte

Megafon[RR], **Megaphon** <-s, -e> [me·ga·ˈfoːn] *nt* megaphone

Mehl <-[e]s, -e> [ˈmeːl] *nt* flour

mehlig [ˈmeː·lɪç] *adj Kartoffeln* floury

mehr [ˈmeːɐ̯] **I.** *pron indef komp von* **viel** more; **immer** ~ more and more; **~ oder weniger** more or less **II.** *adv* more; **nicht** ~ no longer; **es war keiner ~ da** there was nobody left; **ich kann nicht** ~ I can't take it any longer; **nie** ~ never again; **niemand** ~ nobody else

Mehr <-[s]> [ˈmeːɐ̯] *nt kein pl* ❶ (*zusätzlicher Aufwand*) **mit einem [kleinen] ~ an Mühe** with a [little] bit more effort ❷ POL SCHWEIZ majority

Mehraufwand *m* additional expenditure

mehrbändig *adj* multivolume *attr form,* in several volumes *pred*

Mehrbetrag *m* ❶ (*zusätzliche Kosten*) additional amount ❷ (*Überschuss*) surplus

mehrdeutig *adj* ambiguous

Mehrdeutigkeit <-> *f kein pl* ambiguity

mehrdimensional *adj* multidimensional

mehrere [ˈmeː·rə·rə] *pron indef* ❶ *adjektivisch* (*einige*) several *attr;* (*verschiedene*) various ❷ *substantivisch* (*einige*) several; **~ davon** several [of them]

mehrfach [ˈmeːɐ̯·fax] **I.** *adj* numerous, multiple; **eine ~e Medaillengewinnerin** a winner of numerous medals; **ein ~er Meister im Hochsprung** several-time champion pole vaulter **II.** *adv* several times

Mehrfachsteckdose *f* multiple outlet power strip (*without cable*)

Mehrfamilienhaus [-liən-] *nt* multi-family house

mehrfarbig *adj* multicolored

Mehrheit <-, -en> *f a.* POL majority

mehrheitlich *adv* **~ entscheiden** to reach a majority decision; **wir sind ~ dafür** the majority of us are for it

Mehrheitsbeschluss[RR] *m* POL majority decision

mehrjährig *adj attr* several years of *attr,* of several years *pred*

Mehrkosten *pl* additional costs *pl*

M

mehrmalig ['meːɐ̯·maː·lɪç] *adj attr* repeated
mehrmals ['meːɐ̯·maːls] *adv* repeatedly
mehrsprachig *adj* multilingual
mehrstöckig *adj* multistory
mehrstündig *adj* lasting several hours *pred*
mehrtägig *adj* lasting several days *pred*
Mehrverbrauch *m kein pl* additional consumption
Mehrwegflasche *f* deposit [*or* returnable] bottle
Mehrwegverpackung *f* reusable packaging
Mehrwertsteuer *f* ≈ sales tax
mehrwöchig *adj* lasting several weeks *pred*
Mehrzahl *f kein pl* ❶ (*Mehrheit*) majority; **die ~ aller Leute** most people ❷ LING plural [form]
meiden <mied, gemieden> ['mai·dn̩] *vt* to avoid
Meile <-, -n> ['mai·lə] *f* mile
Meilenstein *m* (*a. fig*) milestone
meilenweit ['mai·lən·vait] *adv* for miles
mein ['main] *pron poss, adjektivisch* my
meine(r, s) ['mai·nə] *pron poss, substantivisch* mine
Meineid ['main·ʔait] *m* JUR perjury; **einen ~ leisten** to commit perjury
meinen ['mai·nən] *vt, vi* ❶ (*denken, annehmen*) to think; **und was ~ Sie dazu?** and what do you think about that?; **~ Sie?** [do] you think so? ❷ (*sagen wollen*) **was ~ Sie [damit]?** what do you mean [by that]? ❸ (*ansprechen*) **damit bist du gemeint** that means you ❹ (*beabsichtigen*) to mean, to intend; **ich meine es ernst** I'm serious [about it]; **es gut ~** to mean well; **es gut mit jdm ~** to do one's best for sb; **so war das nicht gemeint** I didn't mean it like that
meiner ['mai·nɐ] *pron pers gen von* **ich**: **gedenke ~** (*geh*) remember me
meinerseits ['mai·nɐ·'zaits] *adv* for my part; **ganz ~** the pleasure was [all] mine
meinesgleichen ['mai·nəs·'glai·çn̩] *pron inv* people like me; (*pej: Leute meines Standes*) my [own] kind
meinetwegen ['mai·nət·'veː·gn̩] *adv* ❶ (*wegen mir*) because of me ❷ (*mir zuliebe*) for my sake ❸ (*von mir aus*) as far as I'm concerned; **darf ich? – ~!** may I? — sure! [*or* go right ahead!]
meinetwillen ['mai·nət·'vɪ·lən] *adv* ■ **um ~** for my sake
meins ['mains] *pron poss, substantivisch* mine
Meinung <-, -en> ['mai·nʊŋ] *f* opinion; (*Anschauung a.*) view; **geteilter ~ sein** to have differing opinions; **ähnlicher/anderer ~ sein** to have a similar/different opinion; **eine eigene ~ haben** to have one's own opinion; **die öffentliche ~** public opinion; **nach meiner ~** in my opinion; **jdm die ~ sagen** to give sb a piece of one's mind
Meinungsäußerung *f* expression of an opinion
Meinungsaustausch *m* exchange of views
Meinungsforschung *f kein pl* opinion polling
Meinungsfreiheit *f kein pl* free[dom of] speech
Meinungsumfrage *f* opinion poll
Meinungsverschiedenheit *f* ❶ (*unterschiedliche Ansichten*) difference of opinion ❷ (*Auseinandersetzung*) argument
Meise <-, -n> ['mai·zə] *f* ORN tit ▶WENDUNGEN: **eine ~ haben** (*fam*) to have a screw loose
meist ['maist] *adv s.* **meistens**
meiste(r, s) *pron indef superl von* **viel** ❶ *adjektivisch* most; **das ~ Geld** the most money; (*als Anteil*) most of the money; **die ~ Zeit** the most time; (*meistens*) most of the time ❷ *substantivisch* ■ **die ~n** most people; **die ~n von uns** most of us; ■ **das ~** most of it; (*als Anteil*) the most; ■ **das ~ von dem, was ...** most of what ...; ■ **am ~n** [the] most
meistens ['mais·tn̩s] *adv* mostly, more often than not; (*zum größten Teil*) for the most part
Meister(in) <-s, -> ['mais·tɐ] *m(f)* ❶ (*Handwerksmeister*) master [craftsman]; **seinen ~ machen** to take one's master craftsman's exam ❷ SPORT champion ▶WENDUNGEN: **es ist noch kein ~ vom Himmel gefallen** (*prov*) practice makes perfect
Meisterbrief *m* master craftsman's diploma
meisterhaft **I.** *adj* masterly; (*geschickt*) masterful **II.** *adv* in a masterly manner; (*geschickt*) masterfully
Meisterleistung *f* [real] achievement; **nicht gerade eine ~** nothing to write home about
meistern ['mais·tɐn] *vt* to master; **Schwierigkeiten ~** to overcome difficulties
Meisterschaft <-, -en> *f* ❶ (*Wettkampf*) championship; (*Veranstaltung*) championships *pl* ❷ *kein pl* (*Können*) mastery
Meisterwerk *nt* masterpiece
Melancholie <-, -n> [me·laŋ·ko·'liː, *pl* -'liː·ən] *f* melancholy
melancholisch [me·laŋ·'koː·lɪʃ] *adj* melancholy
Meldeamt *nt* (*fam*) ≈ city/town clerk['s office]
Meldefrist *f* registration period
melden ['mɛl·dn̩] **I.** *vt* ❶ (*anzeigen*) to report ❷ RADIO, TV to report; **für morgen ist Schneefall gemeldet** snow is in the forecast for tomorrow; **das Wahlergebnis wurde soeben gemeldet** the results of the election have just been announced ▶WENDUNGEN: **nichts zu ~ haben** (*fam*) to have no say **II.** *vr* ❶ (*sich zur Verfügung stellen*) **sich** *akk* **zur Arbeit ~** to report for [*or* to] work; **sich** *akk* **zu etw** *dat* **freiwillig ~** to volunteer for sth ❷ **sich** *akk* **[am Telefon] ~** to answer the telephone; **es meldet sich keiner** there's no answer ❸ (*in Kontakt bleiben*) ■ **sich** *akk* **[bei jdm] ~** to get in touch [with sb]
Meldepflicht *f kein pl* obligation to report sth; **polizeiliche ~** *legal obligation in Germany to register one's residence with the local authorities*
meldepflichtig *adj* **~e Krankheit** disease doctors are required to report
Meldung <-, -en> *f* ❶ (*Nachricht*) piece of

news; **kurze ~en vom Tage** the day's news headlines ② (*offizielle Mitteilung*) report

meliert [me·ˈliːɐ̯t] *adj* ① (*Haar*) graying ② (*Gewebe*) flecked, mottled

Melisse <-, -n> [me·ˈlɪ·sə] *f* [lemon] balm

melken <mẹlkte, gemọlken *o* gemẹlkt> [ˈmɛl·kn̩] *vt* ① *Kuh* to milk ② (*fam*) *Person* to fleece

Melodie <-, -n> [me·lo·ˈdiː, *pl* -ˈdiː·ən] *f* melody, tune

melodisch [me·ˈloː·dɪʃ] **I.** *adj* melodic **II.** *adv* melodically

Melone <-, -n> [me·ˈloː·nə] *f* ① (*Frucht*) melon ② (*fam: Hut*) bowler [hat], derby

Memoiren [me·ˈmo̯a·ːrən] *pl* memoirs

Menge <-, -n> [ˈmɛ·ŋə] *f* ① (*bestimmte Anzahl*) amount, quantity ② (*große Anzahl*) **eine ~ Geld** a lot of money; **eine ~ zu sehen** a lot to see; **jede ~ Arbeit** a ton of work ③ (*Menschenmenge*) crowd ▸WENDUNGEN: **in rauen ~n** (*fam*) in vast quantities

mẹngenmäßig *adv* quantitatively

Mẹngenrabatt *m* bulk discount

Mensa <-, Mensen> [ˈmɛn·za, *pl* ˈmɛn·zn̩] *f* university cafeteria

Mensch <-en, -en> [ˈmɛnʃ] *m* ① (*menschliches Lebewesen*) man; ■**die ~en** man *sing, no art,* human beings *pl;* **auch nur ein ~ sein** to be only human ② (*Person, Persönlichkeit*) person; ■**~en** people; **kein ~** no one; **sie sollte mehr unter ~en gehen** she should get out more ▸WENDUNGEN: **wie der erste ~** (*fam*) very clumsily

Mẹnschenaffe *m* [anthropoid] ape

Mẹnschenauflauf *m* crowd [of people]

Mẹnschenfeind(in) *m(f)* misanthropist

Mẹnschenfresser(in) <-s, -> *m(f)* cannibal

Mẹnschenfreund(in) *m(f)* philanthropist

Menschengedenken [ˈmɛn·ʃn̩·gə·dɛŋ·kn̩] *nt* **seit ~** as long as anyone can remember

Mẹnschenhandel *m kein pl* human trafficking

Mẹnschenkenner(in) <-s, -> *m(f)* judge of character

Mẹnschenkenntnis *f kein pl* ability to judge character

Mẹnschenkette *f* human chain

Mẹnschenleben *nt* ① (*Todesopfer*) life ② (*Lebenszeit*) lifetime

mẹnschenleer *adj* ① (*unbesiedelt*) uninhabited ② (*unbelebt*) deserted

Mẹnschenliebe *f* **aus reiner ~** out of the sheer goodness of one's heart

Mẹnschenmasse *f* (*pej*), **Mẹnschenmenge** *f* crowd [of people]

menschenmöglich [ˈmɛn·ʃn̩·ˈmøːk·lɪç] *adj* **ich werde alles M~e tun** I'll do everything [that is] humanly possible

Mẹnschenrecht *nt meist pl* human right *usu pl*

Mẹnschenrechtsverletzung *f* human rights violation

mẹnschenscheu *adj* afraid of people

Menschenseele [ˈmɛn·ʃn̩·ˈzeː·lə] *f* human soul; **keine ~** not a [living] soul

mẹnschenunwürdig I. *adj* inhumane; (*Behausung*) unfit for human habitation **II.** *adv* in an inhumane way, inhumanely

mẹnschenverachtend *adj* inhuman

Mẹnschenverachtung *f* misanthropy, disregard for humankind

Mẹnschenverstand *m* **gesunder ~** common sense

Mẹnschenwürde *f kein pl* human dignity

mẹnschenwürdig I. *adj* humane **II.** *adv* humanely; **~ leben/wohnen** to live in conditions fit for human beings

Mẹnschheit <-> *f kein pl* ■**die ~** mankind, humanity

menschlich [ˈmɛnʃ·lɪç] **I.** *adj* ① (*des Menschen*) human ② (*human*) humane; *Vorgesetzter* sympathetic **II.** *adv* ① (*human*) humanely ② (*fam*) **wieder ~ aussehen** to look presentable again

Mẹnschlichkeit <-> *f kein pl* humanity

Mẹnsen *pl von* **Mensa**

Menstruation <-, -en> [mɛns·trua·ˈtsi̯oːn] *f* menstruation

menstruieren* [mɛns·tru·ˈiːrən] *vi* to menstruate

mental [mɛn·ˈtaːl] **I.** *adj* mental **II.** *adv* mentally

Mentalität <-, -en> [mɛn·ta·li·ˈtɛːt] *f* mentality

Menthol <-s, -e> [mɛn·ˈtoːl] *nt* menthol

Menu <-s, -s> *nt* (*geh*), **Menü** <-s, -s> [me·ˈnyː] *nt a.* COMPUT menu

Mẹrkblatt *nt* leaflet

merken [ˈmɛr·kn̩] **I.** *vt, vi* ① (*spüren*) to feel; **es war kaum zu ~** it was barely noticeable ② (*wahrnehmen*) to notice; **ich habe nichts davon gemerkt** I didn't notice a thing ③ (*behalten*) ■**leicht zu ~ sein** to be easy to remember **II.** *vr* ① (*im Gedächtnis behalten*) ■**sich** *dat* **etw ~** to remember sth ② (*im Auge behalten*) ■**sich** *dat* **jdn/etw ~** to make a mental note of sb/sth

merklich [ˈmɛrk·lɪç] **I.** *adj* noticeable **II.** *adv* noticeably

Merkmal <-s, -e> [ˈmɛrk·maːl] *nt* feature

mẹrkwürdig I. *adj* strange **II.** *adv* strangely

mẹrkwürdigerweise *adv* strangely enough

mẹssbar[RR], **mẹßbar**[ALT] *adj* measurable; ■**schwer ~ sein** to be difficult to measure

Messe[1] <-, -n> [ˈmɛ·sə] *f* (*Gottesdienst*) mass

Messe[2] <-, -n> [ˈmɛ·sə] *f* (*Ausstellung*) trade show, convention

Mẹssegelände *nt* convention center

Mẹssehalle *f* exhibit hall

messen <mịsst, maß, gemẹssen> [ˈmɛ·sn̩] **I.** *vt* ① (*Ausmaß oder Größe ermitteln*) to measure; *Blutdruck, Temperatur* to take ② (*beurteilen nach*) to judge (**an** +*dat* by) **II.** *vr* (*geh*) **sich** *akk* **mit jdm ~ können** to be able to compete with sb

Messer <-s, -> [ˈmɛ·sɐ] *nt* knife ▸WENDUNGEN: **bis aufs ~** (*fam*) to the bitter end; **jdn ans ~ liefern** (*fam*) to betray sb

messerscharf [ˈmɛ·sɐ·ˈʃarf] **I.** *adj* razor-sharp

M

a. fig **II.** *adv* very astutely
Messerspitze *f* tip of a knife; **eine ~ Muskat** a pinch of nutmeg
Messerstecherei <-, -en> *f* knife fight
Messias <-> [mɛ·ˈsiːas] *m* REL Messiah
Messing <-s> [ˈmɛ·sɪŋ] *nt kein pl* brass
Messinstrument[RR] *nt* measuring instrument
Messung <-, -en> *f* ❶ (*das Messen*) measuring ❷ (*Messwert*) reading
Metall <-s, -e> [me·ˈtal] *nt* metal
Metallarbeiter(in) *m(f)* metalworker
metallisch [me·ˈta·lɪʃ] **I.** *adj* ❶ (*aus Metall*) metal ❷ (*metallartig*) metallic **II.** *adv* like metal
Metapher <-, -n> [me·ˈta·fɐ] *f* metaphor
Metastase <-, -n> [me·ta·ˈstaː·zə] *f* MED metastasis
Meteorit <-en, -en> [me·teo·ˈriːt] *m* meteorite
Meteorologe, Meteorologin <-n, -n> [me·teo·ro·ˈloː·gə, me·teo·ro·ˈloː·gɪn] *m, f* meteorologist
Meter <-s, -> [ˈmeː·tɐ] *m o nt* meter
Metermaß *nt* ❶ (*Bandmaß*) tape measure ❷ (*Zollstock*) measuring stick, ≈ yardstick
meterweise *adv* by the meter
Methode <-, -n> [me·ˈtoː·də] *f* method
Methodik <-, -en> [me·ˈtoː·dɪk] *f* methodology
methodisch [me·ˈtoː·dɪʃ] **I.** *adj* methodical **II.** *adv* methodically
M
Metier <-s, -s> [me·ˈti̯eː] *nt* forte; **sein ~ beherrschen** to know one's job
Metro <-, -s> [ˈmeː·tro] *f* subway
Metropole <-, -n> [me·tro·ˈpoː·lə] *f* metropolis
Mettwurst *f* smoked beef/pork sausage
Metzger(in) <-s, -> [ˈmɛts·gɐ] *m(f)* butcher
Metzgerei <-, -en> [mɛts·gə·ˈrai] *f* butcher shop
Meute <-, -n> [ˈmɔy·tə] *f* ❶ (*pej: Gruppe*) mob ❷ (*Jägersprache*) pack [of hounds]
Meuterei <-, -en> [mɔy·tə·ˈrai] *f* mutiny
Meuterer <-s, -> *m* mutineer
meutern [ˈmɔy·tɐn] *vi* ❶ (*sich auflehnen*) to mutiny ❷ (*fam: meckern*) to grumble, complain
Mexikaner(in) <-s, -> [mɛ·ksi·ˈkaː·nɐ] *m(f)* Mexican; *s. a.* **Deutsche(r)**
mexikanisch [mɛ·ksi·ˈkaː·nɪʃ] *adj* Mexican; *s. a.* **deutsch**
Mexiko <-s> [ˈmɛ·ksi·ko] *nt* Mexico; *s. a.* **Deutschland**
miauen* [mi·ˈau·ən] *vi* to meow
mich [ˈmɪç] **I.** *pron pers akk von* **ich** me **II.** *pron refl* myself; **ich fühle ~ nicht so gut** I don't feel very well
mickerig [ˈmɪ·kə·rɪç], **mickrig** [ˈmɪk·rɪç] *adj* ❶ (*sehr gering*) measly ❷ (*schwächlich*) puny ❸ (*zurückgeblieben*) stunted
mied [ˈmiːt] *imp von* **meiden**
Mief <-s> [ˈmiːf] *m kein pl* (*fam*) stench
miefen [ˈmiː·fn̩] *vi* (*fam*) to stink
Miene <-, -n> [ˈmiː·nə] *f* expression ▶ WENDUNGEN: **ohne eine ~ zu verziehen** without turning a hair
mies [ˈmiːs] *adj* (*fam*) lousy, rotten
Miesepeter <-s, -> [ˈmiː·zə·peː·tɐ] *m* (*fam*) sourpuss
mies|machen *vt* (*fam*) ■ **etw/jdn ~** to belittle sth/sb
Miesmuschel [ˈmiːs·mʊ·ʃl] *f* [blue] mussel
Mietauto *nt* rental car
Miete <-, -n> [ˈmiː·tə] *f* rent; **zur ~ wohnen** to rent
mieten [ˈmiː·tn̩] *vt Boot, Wagen* to rent; *Haus, Wohnung, Büro a.* to lease
Mieter(in) <-s, -> *m(f)* tenant
Mieterschutz *m* legal protection of tenants
mietfrei *adj, adv* rent-free
Mietshaus *nt* apartment building
Mietvertrag *m* rental agreement
Mietwagen *m* rental car
Mietwohnung *f* rented apartment
Miezekatze *f* (*Kindersprache*) kitty cat
Migräne <-, -n> [mi·ˈgrɛː·nə] *f* migraine
Migration <-, -en> [mi·gra·ˈtsi̯oːn] *f* migration
Mikro <-s, -s> [ˈmiː·kro] *nt* (*fam*) *kurz für* **Mikrofon** mike
Mikrobe <-, -n> [mi·ˈkroː·bə] *f* microbe
Mikrochip [-tʃɪp] *m* microchip
Mikrofaser *f* microfiber
Mikrofon <-s, -e> [mi·kro·ˈfoːn] *nt* microphone
Mikrokosmos <-> [-kɔs·mɔs] *m kein pl* microcosm
Mikroorganismus [ˈmiː·kro·ʔɔr·ga·nɪs·mʊs] *m* microorganism
Mikrophon <-s, -e> [mi·kro·ˈfoːn] *nt s.* **Mikrofon**
Mikroprozessor [ˈmiː·kro·pro·tsɛ·soːɐ̯] *m* microprocessor
Mikroskop <-s, -e> [mi·kro·ˈskoːp] *nt* microscope
mikroskopisch **I.** *adj* microscopic **II.** *adv* microscopically; **etw ~ untersuchen** to examine sth under the microscope
Mikrowelle [ˈmiː·kro·vɛ·lə] *f* microwave
Milbe <-, -n> [ˈmɪl·bə] *f* mite
Milch <-> [ˈmɪlç] *f kein pl* milk
Milchflasche *f* milk bottle; (*für Babys*) baby's bottle
Milchglas *nt* milk glass
milchig [ˈmɪl·çɪç] *adj* milky
Milchkaffee *m* [caffe] latte
Milchkuh *f* dairy cow
Milchprodukt *nt* milk product
Milchpulver *nt* powdered milk
Milchreis *m* ❶ (*Gericht*) rice pudding ❷ (*Reis*) arborio rice
Milchschokolade *f* milk chocolate
Milchstraße *f* ■ **die ~** the Milky Way
Milchtüte *f* milk carton
Milchzahn *m* milk tooth
mild [ˈmɪlt] **I.** *adj* ❶ *a.* METEO, KOCHK mild ❷ (*nachsichtig*) lenient **II.** *adv* ❶ (*nicht wür-*

zig) mild ❷ (*nachsichtig*) leniently

Milde <-> ['mɪl·də] *f kein pl* mildness; (*Nachsichtigkeit*) leniency

mildern ['mɪl·dɐn] *vt* ❶ (*abschwächen*) to moderate; **das Strafmaß ~** to reduce the sentence; **~de Umstände** mitigating circumstances ❷ (*weniger schlimm machen*) to alleviate

Milieu <-s, -s> [mi·'li̯øː] *nt* environment

Militär <-s> [mi·li·'tɛːɐ̯] *nt kein pl* armed forces *pl*, military; **beim ~ sein** to be in the military *pl*

Militärdienst *m kein pl* military service

Militärdiktatur *f* military dictatorship

militärisch [mi·li·'tɛː·rɪʃ] *adj* military

Militärpolizei *f* military police

Miliz <-, -en> [mi·'liːts] *f* ❶ (*Bürgerwehr*) militia ❷ (*in sozialistischen Staaten: Polizei*) police

Mille <-, -> ['mɪlə] *f* (*sl*) grand

Milliardär(in) <-s, -e> [mɪ·li̯ar·'dɛːɐ̯] *m(f)* billionaire

Milliarde <-, -n> [mɪ·'li̯ar·də] *f* billion

Milliliter ['mɪ·li·liː·tɐ, 'mɪ·li·lɪ·tɐ, mɪ·li·'liː·tɐ] *m o nt* milliliter

Millimeter <-s, -> ['mɪ·li·meː·tə, mɪ·li·'meː·tɐ] *m o nt* millimeter

Million <-, -en> [mɪ·'li̯oːn] *f* million

Millionär(in) <-s, -e> [mɪ·li̯o·'nɛːɐ̯] *m(f)* millionaire *masc*, millionairess *fem*

Millionengeschäft *nt* deal worth millions

Millionenstadt *f* city with a million inhabitants or more

Milz <-, -en> ['mɪlts] *f* spleen

Mimik <-> ['miː·mɪk] *f kein pl* [gestures and] facial expression[s]

Mimose <-, -n> [mi·'moː·zə] *f* ❶ BOT mimosa ❷ (*fig: sehr empfindlicher Mensch*) sensitive person

minder ['mɪn·dɐ] *adv* less; **nicht ~** no less

mindere(r, s) *adj attr* lesser; **von ~r Qualität sein** to be of inferior quality

Minderheit <-, -en> *f* minority

Minderheitenschutz *m* protection of minorities

minderjährig ['mɪn·dɐ·jɛː·rɪç] *adj* underage

Minderjährige(r) *f(m) dekl wie adj* minor

mindern ['mɪn·dɐn] *vt* to reduce (**um** +*akk* by)

Minderung <-, -en> *f* reduction

minderwertig *adj* inferior

Minderwertigkeit <-> *f kein pl* inferiority

Minderwertigkeitsgefühl *nt* feeling of inferiority

Minderwertigkeitskomplex *m* inferiority complex

Minderzahl *f kein pl* minority

Mindestabstand *m* minimum distance

Mindestalter *nt* minimum age

Mindestanforderung *f* minimum requirement

mindeste(r, s) *adj attr* slightest; **das wäre das M~ gewesen** that's the least he/she/you etc. could have done

Mindesteinkommen *nt* minimum income

mindestens ['mɪn·dəs·tn̩s] *adv* at least

Mindesthaltbarkeitsdatum *nt* best-before date

Mindestmaß *nt* minimum (**an** +*dat* of)

Mindeststrafe *f* minimum sentence

Mine <-, -n> ['miː·nə] *f* ❶ *eines Bleistifts* lead; *eines Filz-, Kugelschreibers* refill ❷ (*Sprengkörper*) mine ❸ (*Bergwerk*) mine

Minenfeld *nt* MIL minefield

Mineral <-s, -e *o* -ien> [mi·ne·'raːl, *pl* mi·ne·'raː·li̯·ən] *nt* mineral

mineralisch [mi·ne·'raː·lɪʃ] *adj* mineral

Mineralöl *nt* mineral oil

Mineralölsteuer *f* tax on oil

Mineralstoff *m meist pl* minerals

Mineralwasser *nt* mineral water

Mini <-s, -s> ['mɪ·ni] *m* MODE (*fam*) mini[skirt]

Miniatur <-, -en> [mi·ni̯a·'tuːɐ̯] *f* miniature

Minikleid *nt* minidress

Minima ['miː·ni·ma] *pl von* **Minimum**

minimal [mi·ni·'maːl] **I.** *adj* minimal **II.** *adv* minimally

minimieren* [mi·ni·'miː·rən] *vt* to minimize

Minimum <-s, Minima> ['miː·ni·mʊm, *pl* 'miː·ni·ma] *nt* minimum (**an** +*dat* of); **ein ~ an Respekt** a modicum of respect

Minirock *m* miniskirt

Minister(in) <-s, -> [mi·'nɪs·tɐ] *m(f)* POL Secretary

Ministerium <-s, -rien> [mi·nɪs·'teː·ri̯·ʊm, *pl* -'teː·ri̯·ən] *nt* POL department

Ministerpräsident(in) *m(f)* (*eines Landes*) prime minister; (*eines Bundeslandes*) minister-president (*leader of a German state*)

> The leader of a *Bundesland* (federal state) is called the **Ministerpräsident/-in**. In Austria, the **Ministerpräsident/-in** is called the *Landeshauptmann/-frau* (State Prime Minister). The head of the government of a Swiss canton is called the *Kantonalpräsident/-in* (Cantonal President).

Minorität <-, -en> [mi·no·ri·'tɛːt] *f* (*geh*) *s.* **Minderheit**

minus ['miː·nʊs] *präp, konj, adv* minus; **~ 15°C** minus 15°C

Minus <-, -> ['miː·nʊs] *nt* ❶ (*Minuszeichen*) minus ❷ ÖKON (*Fehlbetrag*) deficit; **~ machen** to lose money; [**mit etw** *dat*] **im ~ sein** to be in the red [with sth]

Minuspol *m* negative pole

Minuspunkt *m* minus point

Minuszeichen *nt* minus sign

Minute <-, -n> [mi·'nuː·tə] *f* minute; **in letzter ~** at the last minute; **auf die ~** on the dot

minutenlang I. *adj attr* lasting [for] several minutes *pred* **II.** *adv* for several minutes

Minutenzeiger *m* minute hand

Minze <-, -n> ['mɪn·tsə] *f* mint

mir ['miːɐ̯] *pron* ❶ *pers dat von* **ich** me; **eine alte Bekannte von ~** an old acquaintance of mine; **komm mit zu** ~ come back to my place ❷ *refl dat von* **sich** one's; **ich wasche** ~ **die Haare morgen** I'll wash my hair tomorrow ▶ WENDUNGEN: ~ **nichts, dir nichts** (*fam*) just like that

Mirabelle <-, -n> [mi·ra·'bɛlə] *f* Mirabelle [plum]

Mischbrot *nt* bread made from rye and wheat flour

Mischehe *f* mixed marriage

mischen ['mɪ·ʃn̩] **I.** *vt* to mix; KARTEN to shuffle **II.** *vr* ❶ (*sich vermengen*) ■ **sich** ~ to mix (**mit** +*dat* with) ❷ **sich** *akk* **unter die Zuschauer** ~ to mingle with the crowd ❸ ■ **sich** *akk* **in etw** ~ to interfere in sth; **sich in ein Gespräch** ~ to butt in on a conversation

Mischgewebe *nt* mixed fibers *pl*

Mischling <-s, -e> ['mɪʃ·lɪŋ] *m* ❶ (*Mensch*) person of mixed parentage ❷ ZOOL half-breed; (*Hund*) mongrel

Mischlingskind *nt* child of mixed parentage

Mischung <-, -en> *f* mixture; (*Kaffee, Tee, Tabak*) blend

Mischungsverhältnis *nt* ratio

Mischwald *m* mixed forest

miserabel [mi·zə·'ra:·bl̩] **I.** *adj* miserable, terrible **II.** *adv* miserably, terribly; ~ **schlafen** to sleep really badly

Misere <-, -n> [mi·'ze:·rə] *f* (*geh*) misery

missachten*RR, **mißachten***ALT [mɪs·'ʔax·tn̩] *vt* ❶ (*ignorieren*) to disregard ❷ (*gering schätzen*) ■ **jdn** ~ to be disdainful of sb; ■ **etw** ~ to disdain sth

MissachtungRR, **Mißachtung**ALT ['mɪs·ʔax·tʊŋ] *f* ❶ (*Ignorierung*) disregard ❷ (*Geringschätzung*) disdain

missbehagen*RR, **mißbehagen***ALT ['mɪs·bə·ha:·gn̩] *vi* (*geh*) to displease

MissbehagenRR, **Mißbehagen**ALT <-s> ['mɪs·bə·ha:·gn̩] *nt kein pl* (*geh*) ❶ (*Unbehagen*) uneasiness ❷ (*Missfallen*) displeasure

MissbildungRR, **Mißbildung**ALT <-, -en> *f* deformity

missbilligen*RR, **mißbilligen***ALT [mɪs·'bɪ·lɪ·gn̩] *vt* to disapprove of

missbilligendRR, **mißbilligend**ALT [mɪs·'bɪ·lɪ·gn̩t] **I.** *adj* disapproving **II.** *adv* disapprovingly

MissbilligungRR, **Mißbilligung**ALT <-, -en> [mɪs·'bɪ·lɪ·gʊŋ] *f pl selten* disapproval

MissbrauchRR, **Mißbrauch**ALT ['mɪs·braux] *m* abuse

missbrauchen*RR, **mißbrauchen***ALT [mɪs·'brau·çn̩] *vt* to abuse

missdeuten*RR, **mißdeuten***ALT [mɪs·'dɔy·tn̩] *vt* to misinterpret

MissdeutungRR, **Mißdeutung**ALT ['mɪs·dɔy·tʊŋ] *f* misinterpretation

missen ['mɪ·sn̩] *vt* ■ **jdn/etw nicht** ~ **möchten/wollen** (*geh*) not to like/want to do without sb/sth; **mein Telefon möchte ich nicht** ~ I wouldn't want to have to do without my [tele]phone

MisserfolgRR, **Mißerfolg**ALT *m* failure

MissernteRR, **Mißernte**ALT *f* crop failure

missfallen*RR, **mißfallen***ALT [mɪs·'fa·lən] *vi irreg* **jdm missfällt etw** [**an jdm**] sb dislikes sth [about sb]

MissfallenRR, **Mißfallen**ALT <-s> ['mɪs·fa·lən] *nt kein pl* displeasure

missgebildetRR, **mißgebildet**ALT *adj* deformed

MissgeburtRR, **Mißgeburt**ALT ['mɪs·gə·bu:ɐ̯t] *f* (*pej*) monster

MissgeschickRR, **Mißgeschick**ALT <-[e]s, -e> ['mɪs·gə·ʃɪk] *nt* mishap

missglücken*RR, **mißglücken***ALT [mɪs·'glʏ·kn̩] *vi sein* to fail

missgönnen*RR, **mißgönnen***ALT [mɪs·'gœ·nən] *vt* **jdm seinen Erfolg** ~ to resent sb's success

MissgriffRR, **Mißgriff**ALT *m* mistake

MissgunstRR, **Mißgunst**ALT ['mɪs·gʊnst] *f* envy

missgünstigRR, **mißgünstig**ALT **I.** *adj* envious **II.** *adv* enviously

misshandeln*RR, **mißhandeln***ALT [mɪs·'han·dl̩n] *vt* to mistreat

MisshandlungRR, **Mißhandlung**ALT [mɪs·'han·dlʊŋ] *f* mistreatment

missinterpretieren*RR, **mißinterpretieren***ALT ['mɪs·in·te·pre·ti:·rən] *vt* to misinterpret

Mission <-, -en> [mɪ·'si̯o:n] *f* mission

Missionar(in) <-s, -e> [mɪ·si̯o·'na:ɐ̯] *m(f)*, **Missionär(in)** <-s, -e> [mɪ·si̯o·'nɛ:ɐ̯] *m(f)* ÖSTERR missionary

misslangRR, **mißlang**ALT [mɪs·'laŋ] *imp von* **misslingen**

missliebigRR, **mißliebig**ALT ['mɪs·li:·bɪç] *adj* unpopular

misslingenRR, **mißlingen**ALT <misslang, misslungen> [mɪs·'lɪŋ·ən] *vi sein* to fail

MisslingenRR, **Mißlingen**ALT <-s> [mɪs·'lɪŋ·ən] *nt kein pl* failure

misslungenRR, **mißlungen**ALT *pp von* **misslingen**

MissmutRR, **Mißmut**ALT ['mɪs·mu:t] *m* moroseness

missmutigRR, **mißmutig**ALT *adj* morose, sullen

missraten*RR, **mißraten***ALT [mɪs·'ra:·tn̩] *vi irreg sein* to go wrong; **ein** ~**es Kind** a child who has turned out badly

MissstandRR, **Mißstand**ALT *m* sorry state of affairs; **soziale Missstände** social evils

MissstimmungRR, **Mißstimmung**ALT ['mɪs·ʃtɪ·mʊŋ] *f kein pl* discord

misstRR, **mißt**ALT ['mɪst] *3. pers sing pres von* **messen**

misstrauen*RR, **mißtrauen***ALT [mɪs·'trau·ən] *vi* to mistrust

MisstrauenRR, **Mißtrauen**ALT <-s> ['mɪs·trau·ən] *nt kein pl* mistrust

misstrauischRR, **mißtrauisch**ALT ['mɪs·trau·

M

ɪʃ] **I.** *adj* mistrustful; (*argwöhnisch*) suspicious **II.** *adv* mistrustfully; (*argwöhnisch*) suspiciously

Mịssverhältnis[RR], **Mịßverhältnis**[ALT] [ˈmɪs·fɛɐ̯·hɛlt·nɪs] *nt* disproportion; **im ~ zu etw** *dat* **stehen** to be disproportionate to sth

mịssverständlich[RR], **mịßverständlich**[ALT] **I.** *adj* unclear; ■**[zu] ~ sein** to be [too] easily misunderstood **II.** *adv* unclearly

Mịssverständnis[RR], **Mịßverständnis**[ALT] <-ses, -se> [ˈmɪs·fɛɐ̯·ʃtɛnt·nɪs] *nt* misunderstanding

mịssverstehen*[RR], **mịßverstehen***[ALT] [ˈmɪs·fɛɐ̯·ʃteː·ən] *vt irreg* to misunderstand

Mịsswirtschaft[RR], **Mịßwirtschaft**[ALT] *f* mismanagement

Mist <-es> [ˈmɪst] *m kein pl* ❶ (*Stalldünger*) dung; **~!** shit! *vulg* ❷ (*fam: Quatsch*) nonsense ❸ (*fam: Schund*) junk ▶WENDUNGEN: **~ bauen** (*fam*) to screw up; **so ein ~!** (*fam*) damn [it]!

Mistel <-, -n> [ˈmɪs·tl̩] *f* mistletoe

Mịstgabel *f* pitchfork

Mịsthaufen *m* dunghill

Mịstkerl *m* (*fam*) bastard *vulg*

Mịststück *nt* (*fam*) bastard *masc vulg,* bitch *vulg*

Mịstvieh *nt* (*fam*) [god]damned animal *pej*

mit [ˈmɪt] **I.** *präp +dat* ❶ with; ■**~ jdm [zusammen]** [together] with sb ❷ (*per*) by; **~ der Bahn/dem Fahrrad/der Post** by train/bicycle/mail ❸ **~ 18 [Jahren]** at [the age of] 18 **II.** *adv* too, as well; **~ dabei sein** to be there [too]

Mịtarbeit *f kein pl* ❶ (*Arbeit an etw*) collaboration; **unter ~ von jdm** in collaboration with sb ❷ SCH participation

mịt|arbeiten [ˈmɪt·ʔar·bai·tn̩] *vi* ❶ (*als Mitarbeiter*) ■**an etw** *dat* **~** to collaborate on sth ❷ SCH to participate (**in** *+dat* in)

Mịtarbeiter(in) *m(f)* ❶ (*Mitglied der Belegschaft*) employee; **neue ~ einstellen** to hire new staff; **freier ~** freelance employee ❷ (*Kollege*) colleague

mịt|bekommen* *vt irreg* ❶ (*mitgegeben bekommen*) ■**etw [von jdm] ~** to be given sth [by sb] ❷ (*wahrnehmen*) ■**etw ~** to be aware of sth ❸ (*verstehen*) **hast du etwas davon ~?** did you catch any of that? ❹ (*fam: vererbt bekommen*) ■**etw von jdm ~** to get sth from sb

mịt|benutzen* *vt,* **mịt|benützen*** *vt* SÜDD to share

mịt|bestimmen* **I.** *vi* to have a say (**bei** *+dat* in) **II.** *vt* to have an influence on

Mịtbestimmung *f kein pl* participation; **das Recht zur ~ bei ...** the right to participate in ...

Mịtbewerber(in) *m(f)* ❶ (*ein weiterer Bewerber*) fellow applicant ❷ (*Konkurrent*) competitor

Mịtbewohner(in) *m(f)* housemate; (*in einem Zimmer*) roommate

mịt|bringen [ˈmɪt·ʔbrɪŋən] *vt irreg* ❶ *Gegenstand* to bring ❷ *Begleitung* **hast du denn niemanden mitgebracht?** didn't you bring anyone along [*or* with you]? ❸ *Vorraussetzungen* to meet

Mịtbürger(in) *m(f)* fellow citizen

mịt|denken *vi irreg* ■**bei etw** *dat* **~** to follow sth; (*bemerken*) to pick up on sth

mịt|dürfen *vi irreg* (*fam*) **darf ich mit dir mit?** can I come [*or* go] [along] with you?

Mịteigentümer(in) *m(f)* co-owner

miteinander [mɪt·ʔai·ˈnan·dɐ] *adv* ❶ (*jeder mit dem anderen*) with each other; **~ reden** to talk to each other; **~ verfeindet sein** to be enemies ❷ (*zusammen*) together; **alle ~** all together

Miteinander <-s> [mɪt·ʔai·ˈnan·dɐ] *nt kein pl* cooperation

mịt|erleben* *vt Ereignisse* to live through; *eine Zeit* to witness; *im Fernsehen* to follow

mịt|essen *irreg* **I.** *vt* **die Schale ~** to eat the skin as well; **setz dich doch, iss einen Teller Suppe mit!** sit down and have a bowl of soup with us! **II.** *vi irreg* ■**[bei jdm] ~** to eat along with sb, to join sb for a meal

Mịtesser <-s, -> *m* blackhead

mịt|fahren *vi irreg sein* ❶ (*begleiten*) **bei jdm [im Auto] ~** to go [*or* ride along] with sb [in his/her car] ❷ (*Mitfahrgelegenheit haben*) **darf ich [bei Ihnen] ~?** can you give me a lift [*or* ride]?

Mịtfahrer(in) *m(f)* fellow passenger

Mịtfahrgelegenheit *f* ride, lift

Mịtfahrzentrale *f* ride-sharing agency

mịt|fühlen **I.** *vt* **etw ~** to feel sth **II.** *vi* ■**mit jdm ~** to sympathize with sb; **ich kann ~, wie dir zu Mute sein muss** I can imagine how you must feel

mitfühlend *adj* sympathetic

mịt|geben *vt irreg* ■**jdm etw ~** to give sb sth to take with him/her

Mịtgefühl *nt kein pl* sympathy

mịt|gehen *vi irreg sein* ❶ (*begleiten*) ■**mit jdm ~** to come [*or* go] [along] with sb ❷ (*stehlen*) **etw ~ lassen** to walk off with sth

mịtgenommen **I.** *adj* (*fam*) worn-out **II.** *pp von* **mitnehmen**

Mịtglied [ˈmɪt·gliːt] *nt* member

Mịtgliedsausweis *m* membership card

Mịtgliedsbeitrag *m* membership fee

Mịtgliedschaft <-, -en> *f* membership

Mịtgliedsland *nt* member country

Mịtgliedsstaat *m* member state

mịt|halten *vi irreg* (*fam*) to keep up (**bei** *+dat* with)

mịt|helfen *vi irreg* to help (**bei** *+dat* with)

Mithilfe [ˈmɪt·hɪl·fə] *f kein pl* assistance

mịt|hören *vt, vi* to listen in; **ein Gespräch ~** to listen in on a conversation; (*zufällig*) to overhear a conversation

Mịtinhaber(in) *m(f)* co-owner

mịt|kommen *vi irreg sein* ❶ (*begleiten*) to come along ❷ (*Schritt halten können*) to keep up ❸ (*fam: verstehen*) **da komme ich nicht**

M

mit that's [*or* it's] beyond me

mit|kriegen *vt* (*fam*) *s.* **mitbekommen**

Mitleid ['mɪt·lait] *nt kein pl* sympathy (**mit** +*dat* for), pity; **ein ~ erregender Anblick** a sorry sight

Mitleidenschaft *f* **jdn in ~ ziehen** to affect sb

mitleiderregend *adj Anblick* pitiful

mitleidig ['mɪt·lai·dɪç] **I.** *adj* ❶ (*mitfühlend*) sympathetic ❷ (*verächtlich*) pitying **II.** *adv* ❶ (*voller Mitgefühl*) sympathetically ❷ (*verächtlich*) pityingly

mit|machen I. *vi* ❶ (*teilnehmen*) to take part (**bei** +*dat* in) ❷ (*fam: gut funktionieren*) **wenn das Wetter mitmacht** if the weather cooperates; **solange meine Beine ~** as long as my legs hold out **II.** *vt* (*fam*) ❶ (*hinnehmen*) to go along with ❷ (*erleiden*) **viel ~** to go through a lot

Mitmensch *m* fellow man

mit|mischen *vi* (*fam*) to be involved (**bei** +*dat* in)

mit|müssen *vi irreg* to have to come [*or* go] along

Mitnahmemarkt *m* cash-and-carry

mit|nehmen *vt irreg* ❶ (*mit sich nehmen*) to take [along] ❷ (*transportieren*) to take [along]; **könnten Sie mich ~?** (*im Auto*) could you give me a lift? [*or* ride] ❸ (*erschöpfen*) to take it out of sb

mit|rechnen *vt* to include [in a calculation]

mit|reden *vi* ❶ (*mitbestimmen*) to have a say (**bei** +*dat* in) ❷ (*sich beteiligen*) **bei einer Diskussion ~ können** to be able to join in [on] a discussion; **da kann ich nicht ~** I wouldn't know anything about that

Mitreisende(r) *f(m)* fellow passenger

mit|reißen *vt irreg* ❶ (*mit sich reißen*) to sweep away ❷ (*begeistern*) to get going

mitsamt [mɪt·'zamt] *präp* +*dat* complete with

mit|schicken *vt* (*im Brief*) to enclose, to include, to send along

mit|schleppen *vt* (*fam*) to schlep [along]

mit|schreiben *irreg* **I.** *vt* to write [*or* take] down **II.** *vi* to take notes

Mitschuld *f* **eine ~ tragen** to be partly to blame (**an** +*dat* for)

mitschuldig *adj* ■**an etw** *dat* **~ sein** to be partly to blame for sth

Mitschüler(in) *m(f)* classmate

mit|singen *irreg vi* to sing along

mit|spielen *vi* ❶ SPORT to play (**bei** +*dat* in); **in einer Mannschaft ~** to play on a team ❷ FILM, THEAT to act (**bei/in** +*dat* in) ❸ (*bei Kinderspielen*) to play ❹ (*fam: mitmachen*) to go [along] with it; **das Wetter spielte nicht mit** the weather didn't cooperate ❺ (*wichtig sein*) ■[**bei etw** *dat*] **~** to play a [big] part [in sth] ❻ **jdm übel ~** to play a nasty trick on sb

Mitspracherecht *nt kein pl* right to have a say; **ein ~ bei etw** *dat* **haben** to have a say in sth

Mittag <-[e]s, -e> ['mɪ·taːk, *pl* 'mɪ·taː·gə] *m* ❶ (*zwölf Uhr*) noon, midday; (*Essenszeit*) lunchtime; ■**gegen ~** around noon; **zu ~ essen** to have lunch; **etw zu ~ essen** to have sth for lunch ❷ (*fam: Mittagspause*) **~ machen** to take one's lunch break

Mittagessen *nt* lunch

mittags ['mɪ·taːks] *adv* in the middle of the day, at lunchtime

Mittagspause *f* lunch break

Mittagsruhe *f kein pl* ≈ siesta; **~ halten** to rest after lunch

Mittagsschlaf *m* [afternoon] nap; **einen ~ machen** to take a nap

Mittagstisch *m* lunch table

Mittagszeit *f kein pl* lunchtime; ■**in der ~** at lunchtime

Mittäter(in) *m(f)* accomplice

Mitte <-, -n> ['mɪ·tə] *f* ❶ (*räumlich*) middle; **in der ~ zwischen ...** halfway between ... ❷ (*Mittelpunkt*) center ❸ (*zur Hälfte*) **~ Januar** mid-January; **~ des Jahres** in the middle of the year; **sie ist ~ dreißig** she's in her mid-thirties ▶ WENDUNGEN: **die goldene ~** a happy medium

mit|teilen ['mɪt·tai·lən] **I.** *vt* to tell **II.** *vr* ■**sich** *akk* [**jdm**] **~** to communicate [with sb]

mitteilsam *adj* talkative

Mitteilung *f* notification; **eine amtliche ~** an official communication

Mittel <-s, -> ['mɪ·tl̩] *nt* ❶ (*Hilfsmittel*) means *sing*; **es gibt ein ~, das herauszufinden** there is a way to find that out ❷ (*Heilmittel*) drug; **ein ~ gegen etw** a remedy for sth ❸ *pl* (*Geldmittel*) funds ❹ (*Mittelwert*) average; **im ~** on average ▶ WENDUNGEN: **ein ~ zum Zweck** a means to an end

Mittelalter ['mɪ·tl̩·ʔal·tɐ] *nt kein pl* ■**das ~** the Middle Ages *npl*

mittelalterlich ['mɪ·tl̩·ʔal·tɐ·lɪç] *adj* medieval

Mittelamerika ['mɪ·tl̩·ʔa'meː·ri·ka] *nt* Central America

mittelamerikanisch *adj* Central American

mittelbar ['mɪ·tl̩·baːɐ̯] **I.** *adj* indirect **II.** *adv* indirectly

Mittelding *nt* (*fam*) ■**ein ~** something in between; **ein ~ zwischen ... und ...** something between ... and ...

Mitteleuropa ['mɪ·tl̩·ʔɔy·'roː·pa] *nt* Central Europe

Mitteleuropäer(in) *m(f)* Central European

mitteleuropäisch ['mɪ·tl̩·ʔɔy·ro·'pɛː·ɪʃ] *adj* Central European

Mittelfinger *m* middle finger

mittelfristig I. *adj* medium-term *attr* **II.** *adv* **~ planen** to plan for the medium term

Mittelgebirge *nt* low mountain range

mittelgroß ['mɪ·tl̩·groːs] *adj* medium-sized; *Person* of medium height *pred*

Mittellinie *f* ❶ (*Straße*) center line ❷ (*Spielfeld*) center line; (*American Football*) 50-yard line; (*Basketball*) half-court line; (*Eishockey*) red line; (*Fußball*) midfield line

mittellos *adj* destitute

Mittellosigkeit <-> *f kein pl* poverty

Mittelmaß *nt kein pl* average

mittelmäßig I. *adj* average; (*pej*) mediocre II. *adv* **er spielte nur ~** his performance was just mediocre
Mittelmäßigkeit <-> *f kein pl* mediocrity
Mittelmeer ['mɪ·tl̩·meːɐ̯] *nt* ■ **das ~** the Mediterranean [Sea]
Mittelmeerraum *m* ■ **der ~** the Mediterranean [region]
Mittelpunkt *m* ① (*Zentrum*) center ② (*zentrale Figur*) **~ sein/im ~ stehen** to be the center of attention
mittels ['mɪ·tl̩s] *präp +gen* (*geh*) by means of
Mittelschicht *f* SOZIOL middle class
Mittelsmann <-männer *o* -leute> *m* middleman
Mittelstand *m* ① SOZIOL middle class ② (*Unternehmen*) medium-sized business
mittelständisch *adj* medium-sized
Mittelweg *m* middle course ▶ WENDUNGEN: **der goldene ~** a happy medium
Mittelwert *m* mean [value]
mitten ['mɪ·tn̩] *adv* ■ **~ auf/in** *dat* in the middle of; **~ unter Menschen** in the midst of people
mittendrin [mɪ·tn̩·'drɪn] *adv* right in the middle (**in** *+dat* of)
mittendurch [mɪ·tn̩·'dʊrç] *adv* right through the middle
Mitternacht ['mɪ·tɐ·naxt] *f kein pl* midnight *no art*
mittlere(r, s) ['mɪ·tlə·rə] *adj attr* ① (*in der Mitte zwischen zweien*) middle; **mein ~r Bruder** my second oldest/youngest [*or* middle] brother ② (*durchschnittlich*) average *attr or pred* ③ (*mittelgroß*) medium-sized
mittlerweile ['mɪ·tlɐ·'vai·lə] *adv* (*unterdessen*) in the meantime; (*seit dem*) since then; (*bis zu diesem Zeitpunkt*) by now
Mittwoch <-s, -e> ['mɪt·vɔx] *m* Wednesday; *s. a.* **Dienstag**
mittwochabendsRR *adv* [on] Wednesday evenings
mittwochs ['mɪt·vɔxs] *adv* [on] Wednesdays; *s. a.* **dienstags**
mitunter [mɪt·'ʔʊn·tɐ] *adv* now and then
mitverantwortlich *adj* jointly responsible *pred*
mit|verdienen* *vi* to go out and work as well
mit|versichern* *vt* ■ **jdn/etw ~** to include sb/sth in one's insurance [coverage]
mit|wirken *vi* ① (*beteiligt sein*) to collaborate (**bei/an** *+dat* on) ② (*wichtig sein*) to play a part ③ FILM, THEAT **in einem Stück ~** to appear in a play
mit|wollen ['mɪt·vɔ·lən] *vi* to want to go [*or* come], too
mit|zählen I. *vi* to count II. *vt* to include
Mix <-, -e> ['mɪks] *m* mix (**aus** *+dat* of)
mixen ['mɪ·ksn̩] *vt* to mix
Mixer <-s, -> ['mɪ·ksɐ] *m* blender
Mixgetränk *nt* mixed drink
mobben *vt* (*sl*) to bully
Mobbing <-s> ['mɔ·bɪŋ] *nt kein pl* (*sl*) bullying in the workplace
Möbel <-s, -> ['møː·bl̩] *nt* ① *sing* piece of furniture ② *pl* furniture
Möbelspedition *f* moving company
mobil [mo·'biːl] *adj* ① (*beweglich*) mobile ② (*fam: munter*) lively
Mobilfunk *m* mobile communications *pl*
Mobilfunkanbieter *m* wireless carrier, cell phone provider
mobilisieren* [mo·bi·li·'ziː·rən] *vt* ① (*aktivieren*) to mobilize; *Kraft* to summon up ② (*verfügbar machen*) to make available
Mobilität <-> [mo·bi·li·'tɛːt] *f kein pl* mobility
Mobiltelefon *nt* cell phone
möblieren* [mø·'bliː·rən] *vt* to furnish
mochte *imp von* **mögen**
Mode <-, -n> ['moː·də] *f* fashion, style; **aus der/in ~ kommen** to go out of/come into fashion
modebewusstRR *adj* fashion-conscious
Modedesigner(in) <-s, -> [-di·zai·nɐ] *m(f)* fashion designer
Modegeschäft *nt* fashion store [*or* boutique]
Model <-s, -s> ['mɔ·dl̩] *nt* (*Mannequin*) model
Modell <-s, -e> [mo·'dɛl] *nt* model
modellieren* [mo·dɛ·'liː·rən] *vt* to model
Modem <-s, -s> ['moː·dɛm] *nt o m* TELEK modem
Modenschau *f* fashion show
Moderation <-, -en> [mo·de·ra·'tsi̯oːn] *f* RADIO, TV presentation
Moderator, Moderatorin <-s, -toren> [mo·de·'raː·toɐ̯, mo·de·ra·'toː·rɪn, *pl* -'toː·rən] *m, f* RADIO, TV host, presenter
moderieren* [mo·de·'riː·rən] *vt* RADIO, TV to host, to present
moderig ['moː·də·rɪç], **modrig** ['moː·drɪç] *adj* musty
modern1 ['moː·dɐn] *vi sein o haben* to decay, to get moldy
modern2 [mo·'dɛrn] I. *adj* ① (*zeitgemäß*) modern; **~ste Technik** state-of-the-art technology ② (*modisch*) fashionable II. *adv* ① (*modisch*) fashionably ② (*fortschrittlich*) progressively; **~ eingestellte Eltern/Lehrer** parents/teachers with progressive ideas
modernisieren* [mo·dɛr·ni·'ziː·rən] *vt* to modernize
Modernisierung <-, -en> *f* modernization
Modeschmuck *m* costume jewelry
Modeschöpfer(in) *m(f)* fashion designer
Modewort *nt* buzzword
Modezeitschrift *f* fashion magazine
Modi ['mɔ·di] *pl von* **Modus**
modisch ['moː·dɪʃ] I. *adj* fashionable, trendy II. *adv* fashionably, trendily
modrig ['moː·drɪç] *adj* musty
Modul <-s, -e> [mo·'duːl] *nt* module
Modus <-, Modi> ['mɔ·dʊs, *pl* 'mɔ·di] *m* COMPUT mode
Mofa <-s, -s> ['moː·fa] *nt* moped
mogeln ['moː·gl̩n] *vi* (*fam*) to cheat (**bei** *+dat* at/on)

M

mögen ['mø:·gn̩] **I.** *modal vb* <mag, mochte, mögen> ❶ (*wollen*) **etw tun ~** to want to do sth; **ich möchte gerne kommen** I'd like to come ❷ (*Vermutung*) **sie mag Recht haben** she may be right; **das mag schon stimmen** that might [well] be true; **was mag das wohl bedeuten?** what's that supposed to mean? **II.** *vt* <mag, mochte, gemocht> ❶ (*gernhaben*) to like; (*lieben*) to love ❷ (*Gefallen finden*) **~ Sie Fisch?** do you like fish?; **ich mag lieber Bier** I prefer beer; **am liebsten mag ich Eintopf** stew is my favorite [meal] ❸ (*haben wollen*) to want; **möchtest du ein Bier?** would you like a beer?; **ich möchte ein Stück Kuchen** I'd like a piece of cake

möglich ['mø:k·lɪç] *adj* possible; **alle ~en ...** all kinds [*or* sorts] of ...; **es für ~ halten, dass ...** to consider it possible that ...; **sein M~stes tun** to do everything in one's power; **schon ~** (*fam*) maybe

möglicherweise *adv* possibly

Möglichkeit <-, -en> *f* ❶ (*Gelegenheit*) opportunity ❷ (*Möglichsein*) possibility; **nach ~** if possible

möglichst *adv* **~ bald** as soon as possible

Mohn <-[e]s, -e> ['mo:n] *m* poppy; (*Mohnsamen*) poppy seed

Möhre <-, -n> ['mø:·rə] *f*, **Mohrrübe** *f* NORDD carrot

Mokka <-s, -s> ['mɔ·ka] *m* mocha

Mole <-, -n> ['mo:·lə] *f* NAUT mole

Molke <-> ['mɔl·kə] *f kein pl* whey

Molkerei <-, -en> [mɔl·kə·'rai] *f* dairy

mollig ['mɔ·lɪç] *adj* (*fam*) ❶ (*rundlich*) plump ❷ (*behaglich*) cozy ❸ (*angenehm warm*) snug

Moment <-[e]s, -e> [mo·'mɛnt] *m* moment; ■ **im ~** at the moment; **im ersten ~** at first; **im falschen/letzten ~** at the wrong/last moment; **einen [kleinen] ~!** just a minute!

momentan [mo·mɛn·'ta:n] **I.** *adj* ❶ (*derzeitig*) present *attr*, current *attr* ❷ (*vorübergehend*) momentary **II.** *adv* ❶ (*derzeit*) at present ❷ (*vorübergehend*) momentarily

Momentaufnahme *f* snapshot

Monarch(in) <-en, -en> [mo·'narç, mo·'nar·çɪn] *m(f)* monarch

Monarchie <-, -n> [mo·nar·'çi:, *pl* -'çi:·ən] *f* monarchy

monarchistisch *adj* monarchist

Monat <-[e]s, -e> ['mo:·nat] *m* month; **im vierten ~ sein** to be four months pregnant

monatelang ['mo:·na·tə·laŋ] **I.** *adj attr* lasting for months *pred* **II.** *adv* for months

monatlich ['mo:·nat·lɪç] *adj, adv* monthly

Monatsanfang *m* beginning of the month; **am/zum ~** at the beginning of the month

Monatsbinde *f* sanitary napkin

Monatsblutung *f s.* **Menstruation**

Monatsende *nt* end of the month; **am/zum ~** at the end of the month

Monatsgehalt *nt* monthly salary

Monatsrate *f* monthly installment

Mönch <-[e]s, -e> ['mœnç] *m* monk

Mond <-[e]s, -e> ['mo:nt, *pl* 'mo:n·də] *m* moon; **der ~ nimmt ab/zu** the moon is waning/waxing ▶ WENDUNGEN: **hinter dem ~ leben** to be out of touch [with the world]

Mondfinsternis *f* eclipse of the moon

Mondschein *m* moonlight

Mongole, **Mongolin** <-n, -n> [mɔŋ·'go:·lə] *m, f* Mongol, Mongolian; *s. a.* **Deutsche(r)**

Mongolei <-> [mɔŋ·go·'lai] *f* ■ **die ~** Mongolia; *s. a.* **Deutschland**

mongolisch [mɔŋ·'go:·lɪʃ] *adj* Mongolian; *s. a.* **deutsch**

Mongolismus <-> [mɔŋ·go·'lɪs·mʊs] *m kein pl* MED mongolism

Monitor <-s, -toren *o* -e> ['mo:·ni·to:ɐ̯, *pl* -'to:·rən] *m* monitor

monogam [mo·no·'ga:m] *adj* monogamous

Monogamie <-> [mo·no·ga·'mi:] *f kein pl* monogamy

Monokultur ['mɔ·no·kʊl·tu:ɐ̯] *f* AGR monoculture

Monolog <-[e]s, -e> [mo·no·'lo:k, *pl* -'lo:·gə] *m* monolog[ue]

Monopol <-s, -e> [mo·no·'po:l] *nt* monopoly (**auf** +*akk* on)

monoton [mo·no·'to:n] **I.** *adj* monotonous **II.** *adv* monotonously

Monotonie <-, -n> [mo·no·to·'ni:, *pl* -'ni:·ən] *f* monotony

Monster <-s, -> ['mɔns·tɐ] *nt* monster

Monstren ['mɔns·trən] *pl von* **Monstrum**

monströs [mɔn·'strø:s] *adj* (*geh*) monstrous

Monstrum <-s, Monstren> ['mɔns·trʊm, *pl* 'mɔns·trən] *nt* monster

Monsun <-s, -e> [mɔn·'zu:n] *m* monsoon

Montag <-s, -e> ['mo:n·ta:k, *pl* 'mo:n·ta:·gə] *m* Monday; *s. a.* **Dienstag**

montagabends[RR] *adv* [on] Monday evenings

Montage <-, -n> [mɔn·'ta:·ʒə] *f* ❶ (*Zusammenbau*) assembly ❷ (*fam*) **auf ~ sein** to be away on a job

montags ['mo:n·ta:ks] *adv* [on] Mondays; *s. a.* **dienstags**

Monteur(in) <-s, -e> [mɔn·'tø:ɐ] *m(f)* mechanic, fitter

montieren* [mɔn·'ti:·rən] *vt* ❶ (*zusammenbauen*) to assemble ❷ (*installieren*) to install (**an/auf** +*akk* to)

Montur <-, -en> [mɔn·'tu:ɐ̯] *f* work clothes *npl*

Monument <-[e]s, -e> [mo·nu·'mɛnt] *nt* monument

Moor <-[e]s, -e> ['mo:ɐ̯] *nt* swamp

moorig ['mo:·rɪç] *adj* swampy

Moos <-es, -e> ['mo:s, *pl* 'mø:·zə] *nt* ❶ (*Pflanze*) moss ❷ *kein pl* (*fam: Geld*) dough

Moped <-s, -s> ['mo:·pɛt] *nt* moped

Mops <-es, Möpse> ['mɔps, *pl* 'mœp·sə] *m* ❶ (*Hund*) pug [dog] ❷ (*fam: dicke Person*) pudge ❸ *pl* (*fam: Brüste*) boobs *pl sl*, tits *pl vulg*

Moral <-> [mo·'ra:l] *f kein pl* ❶ (*ethische Grundsätze*) morals *pl*; **eine doppelte ~**

haben to have double standards ❷ (*einer Geschichte*) moral
Moralapostel *m s.* **Moralprediger**
moralisch [mo·ˈraː·lɪʃ] **I.** *adj* moral **II.** *adv* morally
Moralprediger(in) *m(f)* (*pej*) moralizer
Moralpredigt *f* homily
Moralvorstellung *f* ideas on [*or* concept of] morality
Morast <-[e]s> [mo·ˈrast] *pl m kein pl* mud
Mord <-[e]s, -e> [ˈmɔrt, *pl* ˈmɔr·də] *m* murder ▶ WENDUNGEN: **dann gibt es ~ und Totschlag** there'll be hell to pay
Mordanschlag *m* attempt on sb's life; POL *a.* assassination attempt
Morddrohung *f* death threat
morden [ˈmɔr·dn̩] *vi* to murder, to kill
Mörder(in) <-s, -> [ˈmœr·dɐ] *m(f)* murderer, killer
mörderisch [ˈmœr·də·rɪʃ] (*fam*) **I.** *adj* murderous; *Hitze* awful **II.** *adv* dreadfully; **~ weh tun** to hurt like hell
Mordfall *m* murder case
Mordkommission *f* homicide [division]
Mordsglück *nt* (*fam*) incredibly good luck; **ein ~ haben** to be incredibly lucky
Mordshunger *m* (*fam*) ravenous hunger; **einen ~ haben** to be starving *fig*
Mordskerl [ˈmɔrts·ˈkɛrl] *m* (*fam*) great guy
Mordskrach *m* (*fam*) ❶ *kein pl* (*Lärm*) terrible racket, a real commotion ❷ (*Streit*) big argument
Mordslärm [ˈmɔrts·lɛrm] *m* (*fam*) terrible racket, a real commotion
mordsmäßig [ˈmɔrts·mɛː·sɪç] (*fam*) **I.** *adj* terrible; **ich habe einen ~en Hunger** I'm starving *fig* **II.** *adv* terribly
Mordsschrecken *m* (*fam*) one hell of a scare
Mordsspaß *m* (*fam*) **einen ~ haben** to have a whale of a [*or* great] time
Mordswut *f* (*fam*) terrible rage
Mordverdacht *m* suspicion of murder; **unter ~ stehen** to be suspected of murder
Mordversuch *m* attempted murder
Mordwaffe *f* murder weapon
morgen [ˈmɔr·gn̩] *adv* tomorrow; **~ Früh/Mittag** tomorrow morning/at lunchtime; **bis ~!** see you tomorrow!
Morgen <-s, -> [ˈmɔr·gn̩] *m* morning; **am ~** in the morning; **eines ~s** one morning; **den ganzen ~ [über]** all morning [long]; **guten ~!** good morning!; **zu ~ essen** SCHWEIZ (*frühstücken*) to have breakfast
Morgendämmerung *f s.* **Morgengrauen**
morgendlich [ˈmɔr·gn̩·tlɪç] *adj* ❶ (*morgens üblich*) morning *attr* ❷ (*morgens stattfindend*) in the morning *pred*
Morgenessen *nt* SCHWEIZ (*Frühstück*) breakfast
Morgengrauen <-s, -> *nt* daybreak
Morgenmantel *m s.* **Morgenrock**
Morgenmuffel <-s, -> *m* (*fam*) **ein [großer] ~ sein** to always be [very] grumpy in the morning
Morgenrock *m* [bath]robe
Morgenrot *nt kein pl* red sky [in the morning]
morgens [ˈmɔr·gn̩s] *adv* in the morning
morgig [ˈmɔr·gɪç] *adj attr* tomorrow's; **der ~e Termin** tomorrow's appointment
Morphium <-s> [ˈmɔr·fi̯·ʊm] *nt kein pl* morphine
morsch [ˈmɔrʃ] *adj* rotten; **~es Holz** rotting wood
morsen [ˈmɔr·zn̩] **I.** *vi* to signal in Morse [code] **II.** *vt* to send in Morse [code]
Mosaik <-s, -e[n]> [mo·za·ˈiːk] *nt* mosaic
Moschee <-, -n> [mo·ˈʃeː, *pl* mo·ˈʃeː·ən] *f* mosque
Möse <-, -n> [ˈmøː·zə] *f* (*vulg*) cunt *vulg*
Mosel <-> [ˈmoː·zl̩] *f* ■ **die ~** the Moselle
mosern [ˈmoː·zɐn] *vi* (*fam*) to gripe (**über** +*akk* about)
Moskito <-s, -s> [mos·ˈkiː·to] *m* mosquito
Moslem, Moslemin <-s, -s> [ˈmɔs·lɛm, mɔs·ˈleː·mɪn] *m, f* Muslim
moslemisch [mɔs·ˈleː·mɪʃ] *adj attr* Muslim
Most <-[e]s> [ˈmɔst] *m kein pl* ❶ (*Fruchtsaft*) fruit juice ❷ SÜDD, SCHWEIZ, ÖSTERR (*Obstwein*) hard cider
Motel <-s, -s> [mo·ˈtɛl] *nt* motel
Motiv <-s, -e> [mo·ˈtiːf, *pl* mo·ˈtiː·və] *nt* motive
Motivation <-, -en> [mo·ti·va·ˈtsi̯oːn] *f* motivation
motivieren* [mo·ti·ˈviː·rən] *vt* to motivate
Motor <-s, Motoren> [ˈmoː·toːɐ̯, *pl* mo·ˈtoː·rən] *m* (*Verbrennungsmotor*) engine; (*Elektromotor*) motor
Motorboot *nt* motor boat
Motorhaube *f* hood
motorisieren* [mo·to·ri·ˈziː·rən] *vt* to motorize
Motoröl *nt* motor oil
Motorrad [ˈmo·to·rat, mo·ˈtoː·rat] *nt* motorcycle, motorbike *fam*
Motorradfahrer(in) *m(f)* motorcyclist
Motorroller *m* [motor] scooter
Motorschaden *m* engine damage
Motte <-, -n> [ˈmɔ·tə] *f* moth
Motto <-s, -s> [ˈmɔ·to] *nt* motto
motzen [ˈmɔ·tsn̩] *vi* (*fam*) to complain (**über** +*akk* about)
Möwe <-, -n> [ˈmøː·və] *f* [sea]gull
Mücke <-, -n> [ˈmʏ·kə] *f* mosquito ▶ WENDUNGEN: **aus einer ~ einen Elefanten machen** to make a mountain out of a molehill
Mückenstich *m* mosquito bite
Mucks [ˈmʊks] *m* (*fam*) **keinen ~ sagen** to not say a word; **ohne einen ~** without a murmur
mucksmäuschenstill [ˈmʊks·mɔys·çən·ˈʃtɪl] *adj* (*fam*) completely quiet; **~ sein** to not make a sound
müde [ˈmyː·də] *adj* ❶ (*schlafbedürftig*) tired ❷ (*überdrüssig*) ■ **einer S.** *gen* **~ sein/werden** to be/grow tired of sth; ■ **nicht ~ werden, etw zu tun** to never tire of doing sth

M

Müdigkeit <-> ['myː·dɪç·kait] *f kein pl* tiredness
Muffe <-, -n> ['mʊ·fə] *f* TECH sleeve ▶ WENDUNGEN: **jdm geht die ~** (*sl*) sb is scared stiff
Muffel <-s, -> ['mʊ·fl̩] *m* (*fam*) grouch
muffelig ['mʊ·fə·lɪç] *adj* (*fam*) grouchy
Muffensausen *nt* ▶ WENDUNGEN: **~ haben/kriegen** (*fam*) to be/get scared stiff
muffig ['mʊ·fɪç] **I.** *adj* ❶ (*dumpf*) musty ❷ (*schlecht gelaunt*) grumpy **II.** *adv* ❶ (*dumpf*) musty ❷ (*lustlos*) listlessly
mufflig ['mʊf·lɪç] *adj s.* **muffelig**
Mühe <-, -n> ['myːə] *f* trouble; **der ~ wert sein** to be worth the trouble; **sich** *dat* **[große] ~ geben[, etw zu tun]** to take [great] pains [to do sth]; **sich** *dat* **keine ~ geben[, etw zu tun]** to make no effort [to do sth]; **~ haben, etw zu tun** to have trouble doing sth; **[jdn] ~ kosten** to be hard work [for sb]; **machen Sie sich keine ~!** [please] don't go to any trouble! ▶ WENDUNGEN: **mit ~ und Not** [just] barely
mühelos I. *adj* effortless **II.** *adv* effortlessly
muhen ['muː·ən] *vi* to moo
Mühle <-, -n> ['myː·lə] *f* mill
Mühlrad *nt* mill wheel
Mühlstein *m* millstone
mühsam ['myː·zaːm] **I.** *adj* arduous **II.** *adv* laboriously; **~ verdientes Geld** hard-earned money
Mulde <-, -n> ['mʊl·də] *f* ❶ (*Bodenvertiefung*) hollow ❷ NORDD (*großer Trog*) big trough
Müll <-[e]s> ['mʏl] *m kein pl* garbage
Müllabfuhr <-, -en> *f* garbage [*or* trash] collection
Müllberg *m* mountain of garbage [*or* trash]
Müllbeseitigung *f kein pl* garbage [*or* trash] collection
Müllbeutel *m* garbage [*or* trash] bag
Müllbinde *f* MED gauze bandage
Mülldeponie *f* garbage [*or* trash] dump
Mülleimer *m* garbage [*or* trash] can
Müller(in) <-s, -> ['mʏ·lɐ] *m(f)* miller
Müllhalde *f* garbage [*or* trash] dump
Müllkippe *f* garbage [*or* trash] dump
Müllmann *m* (*fam*) garbage [*or* trash] man
Mülltonne *f* garbage [*or* trash] can
Mülltrennung *nt* garbage separation
Müllverwertung *f* recycling [of garbage]
mulmig ['mʊl·mɪç] *adj* (*fam*) ❶ (*unbehaglich*) uneasy; **jdm ist ~ zumute** sb has butterflies in their stomach ❷ (*brenzlig*) precarious; **es wird ~** it's getting dicey *fam*
Multi <-s, -s> ['mʊl·ti] *m* (*fam*) multinational [company]
multikulturell *adj* multicultural
multimedial ['mʊl·ti·me·di̯·aːl] *adj* multimedia *attr*
Multimillionär(in) [mʊl·ti·mɪ·li̯o·'nɛːɐ̯] *m(f)* multimillionaire
Multiplexkino ['mʊl·ti·plɛks-] *nt* multiplex [movie theater]
Multiplikation <-, -en> [mʊl·ti·pli·ka·'tsi̯oːn] *f* multiplication
multiplizieren* [mʊl·ti·pli·'tsiː·rən] *vt* to multiply (**mit** +*dat* by)
Multitalent *nt* all-around talent
Mumie <-, -n> ['muː·mi̯ə] *f* mummy
Mumm <-s> ['mʊm] *m kein pl* guts *npl*
Mumps <-> ['mʊmps] *m kein pl* MED [the] mumps + *sing/pl vb*
München <-s> ['mʏn·çn̩] *nt* Munich
Mund <-[e]s, Münder> ['mʊnt, *pl* 'mʏn·dɐ] *m* mouth; **etw in den ~ nehmen** to put sth in one's mouth; **mit vollem ~** with one's mouth full ▶ WENDUNGEN: **den ~ [zu] voll nehmen** to talk [too] big; **jdm über den ~ fahren** to cut sb off; **halt den ~!** shut up!
münden ['mʏn·dn̩] *vi sein o haben Fluss* to flow (**in** +*akk* into); *Weg* to lead (**in** +*akk* into)
Mundgeruch *m* bad breath *no indef art*, halitosis *no indef art*
Mundharmonika *f* harmonica
Mundhöhle *f* ANAT oral cavity
mündig ['mʏn·dɪç] *adj* ■**~ sein/werden** to be/come of age
mündlich ['mʏnt·lɪç] **I.** *adj* oral **II.** *adv* orally; **etw ~ abmachen** to agree to sth verbally
Mundpropaganda *f* word of mouth
mundtot *adj* **jdn ~ machen** (*fam*) to silence sb
Mündung <-, -en> ['mʏn·dʊŋ] *f* ❶ *eines Flusses* mouth ❷ *einer Schusswaffe* muzzle
Mundwasser *nt* mouthwash
Mundwerk *nt* **ein loses ~ haben** to be foul-mouthed
Mundwinkel *m* corner of one's mouth
Mund-zu-Mund-Beatmung *f* mouth-to-mouth resuscitation
Munition <-, -en> [mu·ni·'tsi̯oːn] *f* ammunition
munkeln ['mʊŋ·kl̩n] *vt* to rumor; **man munkelt, dass ...** there is a rumor [going around] that ...
Münster <-s, -> ['mʏns·tɐ] *nt* cathedral
munter ['mʊn·tɐ] *adj* ❶ (*aufgeweckt*) bright ❷ (*heiter*) lively ❸ (*wach*) ■**~ sein/werden** to be awake/to wake up
Muntermacher <-s, -> *m* stimulant; (*Getränk bes.*) pick-me-up
Münzautomat *m* vending machine
Münze <-, -n> ['mʏn·tsə] *f* coin ▶ WENDUNGEN: **etw für bare ~ nehmen** to take sth at face value
münzen ['mʏn·tsn̩] *vt* ■**auf jdn/etw gemünzt sein** to be aimed at sb/sth
mürb ['mʏrp], **mürbe** ['mʏr·bə] *adj* ❶ (*zart*) tender; *Gebäck* short ❷ (*brüchig*) worn-out
mürbe|machenRR *vt* ■**jdn ~** to wear sb down
Murks <-es> ['mʊrks] *m kein pl* (*fam*) screw-up; **~ machen** to botch up a job
murksen ['mʊrk·sn̩] *vi* (*fam*) to do a botched job
Murmel <-, -n> ['mʊr·ml̩] *f* marble
murmeln ['mʊr·ml̩n] **I.** *vi* to murmur **II.** *vt* to mutter
Murmeltier ['mʊr·ml̩·tiːɐ̯] *nt* marmot, woodchuck ▶ WENDUNGEN: **wie ein ~ schlafen** to

sleep like a log

murren ['mʊ·rən] *vi* to grumble

mürrisch ['mʏ·rɪʃ] **I.** *adj* grumpy **II.** *adv* grumpily

Mus <-es, -e> ['muːs, *pl* 'muː·zə] *nt* KOCHK purée

Muschel <-, -n> ['mʊ·ʃl̩] *f* ❶ *a.* KOCHK mussel ❷ (*Muschelschale*) [sea] shell

Muschi <-, -s> ['mʊ·ʃi] *f* (*sl*) pussy *vulg*

Museum <-s, Museen> [mu·'zeː·ʊm, *pl* mu·'zeː·ən] *nt* museum

Musik <-, -en> [mu·'ziːk] *f* music

musikalisch [mu·zi·'kaː·lɪʃ] **I.** *adj* musical **II.** *adv* musically

Musikant(in) <-en, -en> [mu·zi·'kant] *m(f)* musician

Musiker(in) <-s, -> ['muː·zi·kɐ] *m(f)* musician

Musi̲kinstrument *nt* [musical] instrument

Musi̲kkapelle *f* band

Musi̲kkassette *f* [cassette] tape

musizieren* [mu·zi·'tsiː·rən] *vi* to play a musical instrument

Muskat <-[e]s, -e> [mʊs·'kaːt] *m* nutmeg

Muskel <-s, -n> ['mʊs·kl̩] *m* muscle

Mụskelkater *m kein pl* sore muscles *pl*

Mụskelkraft *f* muscular strength

Mụskelprotz <-es, -e> *m* (*fam*) muscleman

Mụskelzerrung *f* pulled muscle

Muskulatur <-, -en> [mʊs·ku·la·'tuːɐ̯] *f* musculature

muskulös [mʊs·ku·'løːs] **I.** *adj* muscular **II.** *adv* **~ gebaut sein** to have a muscular build

Müsli <-[s], -s> ['myːs·li] *nt* muesli

Muslim, Muslimin <-, -e> ['mʊs·lɪm, mʊs·'liː·mɪn] *m, f* Muslim

muslimisch [mʊs·'liː·mɪʃ] *adj attr* Muslim

muss[RR], **muß**[ALT] ['mʊs] *3. pers sing pres von* **müssen**

Muss[RR], **Muß**[ALT] <-> ['mʊs] *nt kein pl* must *fam*

Muße <-> ['muː·sə] *f kein pl* leisure

müssen ['mʏ·sn̩] **I.** *modal vb* <mụss, mụsste, mụ̈ssen> ❶ (*gezwungen sein*) ■**etw tun ~** to have to do sth ❷ (*notwendig sein*) ■**etw [nicht] tun ~** to [not] need to do sth; **warum muss es heute regnen?** why does it have to rain today?; **muss das [denn] sein?** is that really necessary? ❸ (*eigentlich sollen*) ought to; ■**jd müsste etw tun** sb should do sth; **ich hätte es ahnen ~!** I should have known! ❹ (*Vermutung*) **es müsste jetzt acht Uhr sein** it must be eight o'clock [now]; **es müsste bald ein Gewitter geben** there's supposed to be a thunderstorm soon; **das muss wohl stimmen** that must be true **II.** *vi* <mụss, mụsste, gemụsst> ❶ (*gehen müssen*) to have to go; **ich muss zur Post** I have to go to the post office ❷ (*gebracht werden müssen*) ■**irgendwohin ~** to have to get somewhere; **dieser Brief muss heute noch zur Post** this letter has to be mailed today ❸ (*euph fam*) **[mal] ~** to have to go [to the bathroom]

müßig ['myː·sɪç] *adj* (*geh: zwecklos*) futile, pointless

musste[RR], **mußte**[ALT] ['mʊs·tə] *imp von* **müssen**

Muster <-s, -> ['mʊs·tɐ] *nt* ❶ (*Warenmuster*) sample ❷ MODE pattern

Mụsterbeispiel *nt* prime example

Mụsterbrief *m* sample letter

Mụsterexemplar *nt* ❶ (*vorbildlich*) fine specimen ❷ (*Warenmuster*) sample

mụstergültig, **mụsterhaft** **I.** *adj* exemplary; **ein ~es Beispiel** a perfect example **II.** *adv* exemplary

Mụsterknabe *m* (*iron*) paragon of virtue

mustern ['mʊs·tɐn] *vt* (*eingehẹnd betrachten*) to scrutinize

Mụsterschüler(in) *m(f)* model student

Mut <-[e]s> ['muːt] *m kein pl* courage

Mutation <-, -en> [mu·ta·'tsi̯oːn] *f* ❶ (*Missbildung*) mutation ❷ SCHWEIZ (*Änderungen im Personal*) change of personnel

mutieren* [mu·'tiː·rən] *vi* (*fam*) ■**zu etw** *dat* **~** to mutate into sth

mutig ['muː·tɪç] **I.** *adj* brave **II.** *adv* bravely

mu̲tlos *adj* discouraged; **jdn ~ machen** to discourage sb

Mu̲tlosigkeit <-> *f kein pl* discouragement

mutmaßen ['muːt·maː·sn̩] **I.** *vi* to conjecture, to guess **II.** *vt* to suspect

mu̲tmaßlich **I.** *adj attr* presumed, suspected **II.** *adv* presumably

Mu̲tmaßung <-, -en> *f* conjecture

Mu̲tprobe *f* test of courage

Mutter[1] <-, Mütter> ['mʊ·tɐ, *pl* 'mʏ·tɐ] *f* mother; **~ werden** to be having a baby

Mutter[2] <-, -n> ['mʊ·tɐ] *f* TECH nut

Mụtterinstinkt *m* maternal instinct

Mụtter-Kịnd-Pạss[RR] *m document held by pregnant women with details of the pregnancy*

Mụtterland *nt* mother country

Mụtterleib *m* womb

mütterlich ['mʏ·tɐ·lɪç] *adj* ❶ (*von der Mutter*) maternal ❷ (*umsorgend*) motherly; **ein ~er Typ sein** to be the maternal type

mụ̈tterlicherseits *adv* on one's mother's side; **meine Oma ~** my maternal grandmother

Mụtterliebe *f* motherly love

Mụttermal *nt* birthmark; (*kleiner*) mole

Mụttermilch *f* breast milk

Mụttermund *m* ANAT cervix

Mụtterschaftsurlaub *m* maternity leave

mutterseelenallein ['mʊ·tɐ·'zeː·lən·a'lain] **I.** *adj pred* all alone *pred* **II.** *adv* all on one's own

Mụttersöhnchen <-s, -> *nt* (*pej fam*) mama's boy *fam*

Mụttersprache *f* native language

Mụttersprachler(in) <-s, -> [-ʃpraː·xlɐ] *m(f)* native speaker

Mụttertag *m* Mother's Day

Mutti <-, -s> ['mʊ·ti] *f* (*fam*) mommy

mu̲twillig **I.** *adj* mischievous; (*böswillig*) mali-

M

cious **II.** *adv* deliberately
Mütze <-, -n> ['mʏ·tsə] *f* cap, hat ▶ WENDUNGEN: **[von jdm] was auf die ~ kriegen** (*fam*) to get smacked [by sb]
MwSt. *f Abk von* **Mehrwertsteuer** VAT, ≈ sales tax
Mysterien [mʏs·'teː·ri̯·ən] *pl von* **Mysterium**
mysteriös [mʏs·tə·'ri̯øːs] *adj* mysterious
Mysterium <-s, -ien> [mʏs·'teː·ri̯·ʊm, *pl* -'teː·ri̯·ən] *nt* (*geh*) mystery
Mythen *pl von* **Mythos**
mythisch ['myː·tɪʃ] *adj* (*geh*) mythical
Mythologie <-> [my·to·lo·'giː] *f kein pl* mythology
Mythos <-, Mythen> ['myː·tɔs] *m* myth

Nn

N, n <-, - *o fam* -s, -s> [ɛn] *nt* N, n; **~ wie Nordpol** N as in November
Nabel <-s, -> ['naː·bl̩] *m* navel
Nabelschnur *f* (*a. fig*) umbilical cord
nach [naːx] *präp* +*dat* ❶ (*räumlich: bis hin zu*) to; **der Weg führt ~ ...** this is the way to ... ❷ (*räumlich: hinter*) behind; **du stehst ~ mir auf der Liste** you're after me on the list ❸ (*zeitlich: im Anschluss an*) after ❹ (*gemäß*) according to; **~ allem, was ich gehört habe** from what I've heard ❺ (*in Anlehnung an*) after ▶ WENDUNGEN: **~ und ~** little by little; **~ wie vor** still
nach|ahmen *vt* ❶ (*imitieren*) to imitate ❷ (*kopieren*) to copy
nachahmenswert *adj* exemplary
Nachahmung <-, -en> *f* ❶ *kein pl* (*Imitation*) imitation ❷ (*Kopie*) copy
nach|arbeiten *vt* ❶ (*aufholen*) to make up [for] ❷ (*nachträglich bearbeiten*) to touch up *sep*
Nachbar(in) <-n *o* -s, -n> ['nax·baːɐ̯] *m(f)* neighbor; (*nebenan sitzend*) sb sitting next to one
Nachbarhaus *nt* house next door
Nachbarland *nt* neighboring country
nachbarlich *adj* ❶ (*benachbart*) neighboring *attr* ❷ (*unter Nachbarn üblich*) neighborly
Nachbarschaft <-, -en> *f* ❶ (*nähere Umgebung*) neighborhood ❷ (*die Nachbarn*) neighbors
Nachbeben *nt* aftershock
nach|bessern *vt* to retouch; *Produkt* to make improvements to; *Vertrag* to amend
nach|bestellen* *vt* to reorder
nach|bezahlen* *vt* to pay later
nach|bilden *vt* to reproduce (+*dat* from)
Nachbildung *f* reproduction; (*exakt*) copy
nachdem [naːx·'deːm] *konj* ❶ *zeitlich* after ❷ (*da*) since
nach|denken *vi irreg* to contemplate (**über** +*akk* about); **laut ~** to think out loud
nachdenklich ['naːx·dɛŋk·lɪç] *adj* pensive; **jdn ~ machen** to make sb think
Nachdenklichkeit <-> *f kein pl* pensiveness
Nachdruck[1] *m kein pl* emphasis; **~ auf etw** *akk* **legen** to stress sth; **etw mit ~ sagen** to say sth emphatically
Nachdruck[2] <-[e]s, -e> *m* VERLAG ❶ (*nachgedrucktes Werk*) reprint ❷ *kein pl* (*das Nachdrucken*) reprinting
nach|drucken *vt* VERLAG to reprint
nachdrücklich ['naːx·drʏk·lɪç] **I.** *adj* insistent; *Warnung* firm **II.** *adv* firmly
nach|eifern *vi* (*geh*) to emulate
nacheinander [naːx·ʔai·'nan·dɐ] *adv* one after another
nach|empfinden* *vt irreg* ■ **etw ~ können** to empathize with sth
nach|erzählen* *vt* to retell
Nachfahr(in) <-en, -en> ['naːx·faːɐ̯] *m(f)* (*geh*) *s.* **Nachkomme**
nach|fahren *vi irreg sein* ❶ (*hinterherfahren*) to follow ❷ (*später fahren*) to come [along] later
nach|feiern *vt* to celebrate later
nachfolgend *adj* following
Nachfolger(in) <-s, -> *m(f)* successor
nach|forschen *vi* to make [further] inquiries (**in** +*dat* about); ■ **~, wie/ob ...** to try to find out how/whether ...
Nachforschung *f* inquiry; (*polizeilich*) investigation
Nachfrage *f* ÖKON demand (**nach** +*dat* for)
nach|fragen *vi* to inquire
nach|fühlen *vt s.* **nachempfinden**
nachfüllbar *adj* refillable
nach|füllen *vt Behältnis* to refill; **Zucker ~** to fill back up with sugar
Nachfüllpack <-s, -s> *m*, **Nachfüllpackung** *f* refill [pack]
nach|geben *irreg vi* ❶ (*einlenken*) to give in (+*dat* to) ❷ (*nicht standhalten*) *Boden, Knie* to give way
Nachgebühr *f* surcharge
nach|gehen *vi irreg sein* ❶ (*hinterhergehen*) to follow ❷ *Uhr* to be slow ❸ (*fig: verfolgen*) **einem Problem ~** to look into a problem ❹ (*form: ausüben*) to practice; *Interessen* to pursue
Nachgeschmack *m* aftertaste
nachgiebig ['naːx·giː·bɪç] *adj* accommodating; **[jdm gegenüber] zu ~ sein** to be too soft [on sb]
Nachgiebigkeit <-> *f kein pl* softness
nach|gießen *irreg vi, vt* ■ **jdm ~** to top off *sep* sb [*or* sb's glass]; **jdm Wein ~** to give sb some

more wine; **darf ich ~?** would you like some more?

nach|grübeln *vi* to think (**über** *+akk* about)

nach|gucken *vi* (*fam*) to [take a] look (**in** *+dat* in)

nach|haken *vi* (*fam*) to dig deeper

Nachhall *m* echo

nachhaltig ['naːx·hal·tɪç] **I.** *adj* ❶ (*dauerhaft*) lasting ❷ ÖKOL sustainable **II.** *adv* **jdn ~ beeindrucken** to leave a lasting impression on sb

Nachhaltigkeit <-> *f kein pl* ÖKOL sustainability

nach|hängen *vi irreg* **seinen Gedanken ~** to lose oneself in one's thoughts

Nachhauseweg [naːx·'hau·zə·veːk] *m* way home

nach|helfen *vi irreg* ❶ (*zusätzlich beeinflussen*) to help along *sep* ❷ (*auf die Sprünge helfen*) ■ **jdm ~** to give sb a helping hand

nachher [naːx·'eːɐ, 'naːx·eːɐ] *adv* ❶ (*danach*) afterwards ❷ (*irgendwann später*) later; **bis ~!** see you later! ❸ (*fam: womöglich*) possibly

Nachhilfe *f* private tutoring

Nachhilfestunde *f* private lesson

Nachhinein im ~ in retrospect; (*nachträglich*) later

Nachholbedarf *m* **großen ~ haben** to have a lot to catch up on

nach|holen *vt* ❶ (*aufholen*) to make up for ❷ (*zu sich holen*) **seine Familie ~** to have one's family join one

nach|jagen *vi sein* ❶ (*zu erreichen trachten*) to pursue ❷ (*eilends hinterherlaufen*) to chase after

nach|kaufen *vt* to buy later

Nachkomme <-n, -n> ['naːx·kɔ·mə] *m* descendant

nach|kommen *vi irreg sein* ❶ (*folgen*) to come [along] later; ■ **jdn ~ lassen** to have sb join one later; **sein Gepäck ~ lassen** to have one's luggage sent on ❷ (*Schritt halten*) to keep up ❸ (*erfüllen*) to fulfill; *Anordnung, Pflicht* to carry out *sep; Forderung* to meet ❹ SCHWEIZ (*verstehen*) to follow

nach|kontrollieren* *vt* to check over *sep* (**auf** *+akk* for); ■ **~, ob ...** to check whether ...

Nachkriegszeit *f* postwar period

Nachlass^{RR} <-es, -e *o* -lässe> *m* ❶ (*hinterlassene Werke*) unpublished works *npl* ❷ (*hinterlassener Besitz*) estate ❸ (*Rabatt*) discount (**auf** *+akk* on)

nach|lassen *irreg* **I.** *vi* to diminish; *Druck, Schmerz* to ease off; *Gehör, Sehkraft* to deteriorate; *Nachfrage* to fall; *Sturm* to die down **II.** *vt* [**jdm**] **10 % vom Preis ~** to give [sb] a 10% discount

nachlässig ['naːx·lɛ·sɪç] **I.** *adj* careless; *Arbeit a.* slipshod *pej* **II.** *adv* carelessly

Nachlässigkeit <-, -en> *f* ❶ *kein pl* (*Art*) carelessness ❷ (*Handlung*) negligence

nach|laufen *vi irreg sein* (*a. fig*) to run after

nach|lesen *vt irreg* to look up

nach|liefern *vt* to deliver at a later date

nach|lösen *vt* **eine [Fahr]karte ~** to buy a ticket (*after boarding a train, bus etc.*)

nach|machen *vt* ❶ (*imitieren*) to imitate ❷ (*nachahmen*) ■ **jdm etw ~** to copy sth from sb ❸ (*fam: nachträglich anfertigen*) to make up *sep*

nach|messen *irreg vt* to measure again

Nachmieter(in) *m(f)* new tenant *no indef art*

nachmittag^{ALT} *adv s.* **Nachmittag**

Nachmittag ['naːx·mɪ·taːk] *m* afternoon; **am [frühen] ~** in the [early] afternoon; **im Laufe des ~s** during [the course of] the afternoon

nachmittags *adv* in the afternoon

Nachmittagsvorstellung *f* matinee [performance]

Nachnahme <-, -n> ['naːx·naː·mə] *f* cash [*or* collect] on delivery; **etw per ~ schicken** to send sth COD

Nachname *m* surname, last name

nach|plappern *vt* (*fam*) to parrot *pej*

nachprüfbar *adj* verifiable

nach|prüfen *vt, vi* to verify

nach|rechnen *vt, vi* to check again

Nachrede *f* **üble ~** slander, defamation [of character] *form*

nach|reichen *vt* to hand [*or* turn] in later

Nachricht <-, -en> ['naːx·rɪçt] *f* ❶ MEDIA news *no indef art, + sing vb;* ■ **eine ~** a news item; ■ **die ~en** the news *+ sing vb* ❷ (*Mitteilung*) message; ■ **eine gute ~** [a piece of] good news; **jdm ~ geben** to let sb know

Nachrichtenagentur *f* news agency

Nachrichtendienst *m* ❶ (*Geheimdienst*) intelligence service ❷ *s.* **Nachrichtenagentur**

Nachrichtenmagazin *nt* news magazine

Nachrichtensperre *f* news embargo

Nachrichtensprecher(in) *m(f)* newscaster

Nachruhm *m* posthumous fame *form*

nach|rüsten **I.** *vt* to update; *Computer* to upgrade **II.** *vi* MIL to deploy new arms

Nachrüstung *f kein pl* ❶ TECH modernization ❷ MIL deployment of new arms

nach|sagen *vt* ❶ (*von jdm behaupten*) **jdm Schlechtes ~** to say bad things about sb; **es wird ihr nachgesagt, dass ...** she is accused of ..., supposedly she ... ❷ (*nachsprechen*) ■ [**jdm**] **etw ~** to repeat sth [after sb]

Nachsaison [-zɛ·zõː, -zɛ·zɔŋ] *f* off-season

nach|schauen **I.** *vi* ❶ (*mit Blicken folgen*) to watch ❷ (*nachschlagen*) to look it up ❸ (*prüfen*) to check **II.** *vt* (*nachschlagen*) to look up *sep* (**in** *+dat* in)

nach|schenken *vi, vt* (*geh*) *s.* **nachgießen**

nach|schicken *vt* ❶ (*nachsenden*) to forward ❷ (*hinterher schicken*) ■ **jdm jdn ~** to send sb after sb

Nachschlag *m von Essen* second helping, seconds *pl*

nach|schlagen *irreg* **I.** *vt* to look up *sep* (**in** *+dat* in) **II.** *vi* ❶ *haben* **in einem Wörterbuch ~** to consult a dictionary ❷ *sein* (*geh: ähneln*) ■ **jdm ~** to take after sb

Nachschlagewerk *nt* reference book

Nachschlüssel *m* duplicate key

N

nach|sehen *irreg* **I.** *vi* ❶ (*nachschlagen*) to look it up ❷ (*prüfen*) to have a look **II.** *vt* ❶ (*mit Blicken folgen*) to watch ❷ (*nachschlagen*) to look up *sep* (**in** +*dat* in) ❸ (*verzeihen*) ■**jdm etw** ~ to forgive sb for sth

Nachsehen *nt* ►WENDUNGEN: [**bei/in etw** *dat*] **das** ~ **haben** to come off worse [in sth]; (*leer ausgehen*) to be left empty-handed [in sth]; (*keine Chance haben*) to not get anywhere [with sth]

Nachsendeantrag *f* application to have one's mail forwarded

nach|senden *vt irreg* to forward

Nachsicht <-> *f kein pl* leniency; ~ **üben** to be lenient

nachsichtig **I.** *adj* lenient; (*verzeihend*) merciful **II.** *adv* leniently

Nachsilbe *f* suffix

nach|sinnen *vi irreg* to ponder (**über** +*akk* over)

Nachspann <-s, -e> *m* FILM, TV credits *npl*

Nachspeise *f* dessert

Nachspiel *nt* (*unangenehme Folgen*) consequences *pl*

nach|spionieren* *vi* (*fam*) to spy on

nach|sprechen *irreg vt* ■[**jdm**] **etw** ~ to repeat sth [after sb]

nächstbeste(r, s) ['nɛːçst·'bɛs·tə] *adj attr* ■**der/die/das** ~ **...** the first ... one/sb sees; **die** ~ **Gelegenheit** the next possible occasion that comes along

nächste(r, s) ['nɛːçs·tə] *adj superl von* **nahe** ❶ *räumlich* (*zuerst folgend*) next; **im** ~**n Haus** next door; (*nächstgelegen*) nearest ❷ *Angehörige* close ❸ *temporal* (*darauf folgend*) next; **bis zum** ~**n Mal!** until next time!; **am** ~**n Tag** the next day; **in den** ~**n Tagen** in the next few days; **als N**~**s** next

nach|stehen *vi irreg* **jdm an Intelligenz nicht** ~ to be every bit as intelligent as sb; ■**jdm in nichts** ~ to be sb's equal in every way [possible]

nach|stellen **I.** *vt* ❶ LING ■[**etw** *dat*] **nachgestellt werden** to be put after [sth] ❷ TECH (*neu einstellen*) to adjust; (*wieder einstellen*) to readjust; (*korrigieren*) to correct; *Uhr* to turn back *sep* ❸ (*nachspielen*) to reconstruct **II.** *vi* ■**jdm** ~ ❶ (*geh: verfolgen*) to follow sb ❷ (*umwerben*) to pester sb

Nächstenliebe *f* compassion

nächstens ['nɛːçs·tn̩s] *adv* ❶ (*bald*) [some time] soon ❷ (*fam: womöglich*) next

nächstgelegen *adj attr* nearest

nächstliegend *adj attr* most plausible

nächstmöglich ['nɛːçst·'møːk·lɪç] *adj attr* next possible *attr; Termin a.* earliest possible; *Gelegenheit* next

nach|suchen *vi* (*nachsehen*) to look (**in** +*dat* in)

Nacht <-, Nächte> ['naxt, *pl* 'nɛç·tə] *f* night; ■~ **sein/werden** to be/get dark; **bis weit in die** ~ far into the night; **bei** ~ at night; **in der** ~ at night; **über** ~ overnight; **über** ~ **bleiben** to stay the night; **diese/letzte** ~ tonight/last night ►WENDUNGEN: **bei** ~ **und Nebel** (*fam*) in the dead of night; **die** ~ **zum Tage machen** to stay up all night; **zu** ~ **essen** SÜDD, ÖSTERR to have dinner

nachtblind *adj* night blind

Nachtdienst *m* night shift

Nachteil <-[e]s, -e> ['naːx·tail] *m* disadvantage; **jdm** ~**e bringen** to be disadvantageous to sb; **durch etw** ~**e haben** to be at a disadvantage because of sth; **sich** *akk* **zu seinem** ~ **verändern** to change for the worse

nachteilig ['naːx·tai·lɪç] **I.** *adj* disadvantageous (**für** +*akk* for) **II.** *adv* unfavorably

nächtelang ['nɛç·tə·laŋ] *adv* for nights on end

Nachtessen *nt* SÜDD, ÖSTERR, SCHWEIZ (*Abendessen*) dinner, supper

Nachtfalter *m* moth

Nachthemd *nt* nightgown

Nachtigall <-, -en> ['nax·tɪgal] *f* nightingale

nächtigen ['nɛç·tɪ·gn̩] *vi* (*geh*) to stay the night (**bei** +*dat* with)

Nachtisch *m s.* **Nachspeise**

Nachtleben *nt* nightlife

Nachtlokal *nt* nightclub

Nachtportier [-pɔr·ti̯eː] *m* night porter

Nachtquartier *nt* place to sleep [for the night]

Nachtrag <-[e]s, -träge> ['naːx·traːk, *pl* -trɛː·gə] *m* ❶ (*im Brief*) postscript ❷ *pl* (*Ergänzungen*) supplement

nach|tragen *vt irreg* ❶ (*hinterhertragen*) to carry after ❷ (*nachträglich ergänzen*) to add ❸ (*nicht verzeihen können*) ■**jdm etw** ~ to hold sth against sb; ■**jdm** ~**, dass ...** to hold it against sb that ...

nachtragend ['naːx·traː·gn̩t] *adj* unforgiving

nachträglich ['naːx·trɛːk·lɪç] **I.** *adj* later; (*verspätet*) belated **II.** *adv* later, belatedly

nach|trauern *vi* ■**jdm/etw** ~ to shed a tear for sb/sth

Nachtruhe *f* night's sleep

nachts ['naxts] *adv* at night; **montags** ~ [on] Monday nights

Nachtschicht *f* night shift

Nachtschwester *f* night nurse

nachtsüber ['naxts·ʔyːbɐ] *adv* at night

Nachttisch *m* bedside table

Nacht-und-Nebel-Aktion *f* cloak-and-dagger operation

Nachtwache *f* night duty

Nachtwächter(in) *m(f)* night watchman

Nachuntersuchung *f* follow-up examination

nachvollziehbar *adj* comprehensible; **es ist für mich nicht ganz** ~**, wie ...** I don't quite understand how ...

nach|vollziehen* *vt irreg* to understand

nach|wachsen *vi irreg sein* to grow back

Nachwehen *pl* (*geh: üble Folgen*) painful aftermath

nach|weinen *vi* ■**jdm/etw** ~ to shed a tear for sb/sth

Nachweis <-es, -e> ['naːx·vais, *pl* -vai·zə] *m* proof

nachweisbar I. *adj* provable; *Giftstoffe* detectable; **Fehler** demonstrable II. *adv* provably
nach|weisen *vt irreg* ❶ (*beweisen*) to establish proof of; **man kann mir nichts ~** nothing can be proved against me ❷ (*finden*) to detect (**in** +*dat* in)
nachweislich ['naːx·vais·lɪç] I. *adj* provable; **~e Fehler** mistakes that can be proven II. *adv* provably
Nachwelt *f kein pl* ■ **die ~** posterity
nach|werfen *vt irreg* ❶ (*hinterherwerfen*) ■ **jdm etw ~** to throw sth at sb ❷ (*fam: überlassen*) ■ **jdm etw ~** to [practically] give sth away to sb
nach|wirken *vi* to continue to have an effect
Nachwirkung *f* aftereffect; (*fig*) consequence
Nachwort <-worte> *nt* epilogue
Nachwuchs *m kein pl* ❶ (*fam: Kinder*) offspring ❷ (*junge Fachkräfte*) young professionals *pl*
nach|zahlen *vt* ❶ (*nachträglich*) to pay at a later date ❷ (*zusätzlich*) to pay extra
nach|zählen *vt, vi* to check
Nachzahlung *f* ❶ (*nachträglich*) back payment ❷ (*zusätzlich*) additional payment
nach|ziehen *irreg vt* ❶ *Schraube* to tighten [up *sep*] ❷ *Bein* to drag ❸ *Linie* to go over; **sich** *dat* **die Augenbrauen ~** to pencil in *sep* one's eyebrows
Nachzügler(in) <-s, -> ['naːx·tsyːk·lɐ] *m(f)* late arrival
Nackedei <-[e]s, -e *o* -s> ['na·kə·dai] *m* (*hum fam*) naked baby [*or* person]
Nacken <-s, -> ['na·kn̩] *m* neck ▶ WENDUNGEN: **jdm im ~ sitzen** to breathe down sb's neck
nackend ['na·kn̩t] *adj* (*fam*) naked, nude
Nackenhaar *nt meist pl* hair[s *pl*] on the back of one's neck
Nackenstütze *f* headrest
nackig ['na·kɪç] *adj* (*fam*) naked
nackt ['nakt] I. *adj* ❶ (*unbekleidet*) naked, nude; *Haut, Arme* bare ❷ (*kahl*) *Wand* bare ❸ (*unverblümt*) naked; *Tatsachen* bare; *Wahrheit* plain II. *adv* naked, in the nude
Nacktbadestrand *m* nude beach
Nacktheit <-> *f kein pl* nudity
Nadel <-, -n> ['naː·dl̩] *f* ❶ (*Nähnadel, Tannennadel*) needle ❷ (*Zeiger*) needle ▶ WENDUNGEN: **an der ~ hängen** (*sl*) to be hooked on heroin
Nadelbaum *m* conifer
Nagel <-s, Nägel> ['naː·gl̩, *pl* 'nɛː·gl̩] *m* (*Metallstift, Fingernagel*) nail ▶ WENDUNGEN: **jdm brennt es unter den Nägeln, etw zu tun** (*fam*) sb is dying to do sth; **etw an den ~ hängen** (*fam*) to give up *sep* sth; **sich** *dat* **etw unter den ~ reißen** (*sl*) to steal [*or* make off with] sth
Nagelfeile *f* nail file
Nagellack *m* nail polish
Nagellackentferner *m* nail polish remover
nageln ['naː·gl̩n] *vt* to nail (**an** +*akk* to)
nagelneu ['naː·gl̩·'nɔy] *adj* (*fam*) brand-new
Nagelschere *f* nail scissors *npl*
nagen ['naː·gn̩] I. *vi, vt* to gnaw (**an** +*dat* at, on) II. *vi* (*quälen*) ■ **an jdm ~** to nag [at] sb
nagend ['naː·gn̩t] *adj* nagging; *Hunger* gnawing
Nager <-s, -> *m*, **Nagetier** *nt* rodent
nah ['naː] *adj, adv s.* **nahe** ▶ WENDUNGEN: **von ~ und fern** from near and far
Nahaufnahme *f* close-up
nahe <näher, nächste> ['naː·ə] I. *adj* ❶ *räumlich* nearby, close [by] *pred;* **von ~m** from close up ❷ *zeitlich* near, approaching ❸ (*eng*) close; ■ **jdm ~ sein** to be close to sb II. *adv* ❶ *räumlich* nearby, close [by]; ■ **~ an/bei etw** *dat* close to sth ❷ *zeitlich* close ❸ (*fast*) **sie war ~ am Aufgeben** she almost gave up ❹ (*eng*) closely; **~ mit jdm verwandt sein** to be a close relative of sb ▶ WENDUNGEN: **jdm zu ~ treten** to offend sb III. *präp* +*dat* near to
Nähe <-> ['nɛː·ə] *f kein pl* ❶ (*geringe Entfernung*) proximity; **aus der ~** from close up; **in der ~** near ❷ (*Anwesenheit*) closeness; **in jds ~** close to sb ❸ (*naher Zeitpunkt*) closeness
nahebei ['naː·ə·'bai] *adv* nearby
nahe|gehen *vi irreg sein* ■ **jdm ~** to upset sb
nahe|kommen *vr irreg sein* ■ **sich** *dat* **~** to become close
nahe|legen *vt* ■ **jdm ~, etw zu tun** to advise sb to do sth
naheliegend *adj* **~ sein** to seem to suggest itself; **aus ~en Gründen** for obvious reasons
nahen ['naː·ən] *vi sein* (*geh*) to approach
nähen ['nɛː·ən] *vt* to sew; MED to stitch
näher ['nɛː·ɐ] I. *adj komp von* **nahe** ❶ (*in geringerer Entfernung*) nearer, closer ❷ (*kürzer bevorstehend*) closer, sooner *pred; Zukunft* near ❸ (*detaillierter*) further *attr;* **die ~en Umstände** the precise circumstances ❹ (*enger*) closer; *Verwandte* immediate II. *adv komp von* **nahe** ❶ (*in geringeren Abstand*) closer, nearer; **kommen Sie ~!** come closer! ❷ (*eingehender*) in more detail; **etw ~ ansehen** to have a closer look at sth; **sich** *akk* **~ mit etw** *dat* **befassen** to go into sth in greater detail ❸ (*enger*) closer; **jdn/etw ~ kennen** to know sb/sth well; **jdn/etw ~ kennen lernen** to get to know sb/sth better
näher|bringen *vt irreg* ■ **jdm etw ~** to bring sth home to sb
näher|kommen *vi irreg sein* ■ **etw** *dat* [**schon**] **~** to be closer to the mark
nähern ['nɛː·ɐn] *vr* ❶ (*näher herankommen*) ■ **sich** *akk* [**jdm/etw**] **~** to get closer [to sb/sth] ❷ (*einen Zeitpunkt erreichen*) ■ **sich** *akk* **etw** *dat* **~** to get close to sth; **unser Urlaub nähert sich seinem Ende** our vacation is drawing to a close
nahe|stehen *vr irreg* ■ **sich** *dat* **~** to be close
nahezu ['naː·ə·'tsuː] *adv* almost, virtually
Nähgarn *nt* cotton
Nähkästchen *nt* ▶ WENDUNGEN: **aus dem ~ plaudern** (*fam*) to gossip about private matters

Nähkasten *m* sewing box
nahm ['na:m] *imp von* **nehmen**
Nähmaschine *f* sewing machine
Nähnadel *f* [sewing] needle
Nahost [na:-'ʔɔst] *m kein art* the Middle East
nahrhaft *adj* nutritious
Nährstoff *m* nutrient
Nahrung <-> ['na:·rʊŋ] *f kein pl* food; **flüssige/feste ~** liquids/solids *pl*
Nahrungskette *f* food chain
Nahrungsmittel *nt* food
Nahrungsmittelallergie *f* food allergy
Nährwert *m* nutritional value
Naht <-, Nähte> ['na:t, *pl* 'nɛ:·tə] *f* ① (*bei Kleidung*) seam ② MED suture *spec* ③ TECH weld
nahtlos I. *adj* ① MODE seamless ② (*lückenlos*) smooth **II.** *adv* smoothly
Nahverkehr *m* local traffic; **der öffentliche ~** local public transportation
Nahverkehrsmittel *pl* means of local public transportation
Nahverkehrszug *m* local train
Nähzeug *nt* sewing kit
naiv [na·'i:f] *adj* naive
Naivität <-> [na·ivi·'tɛ:t] *f kein pl* naivety
Name <-ns, -n> ['na:·mə] *m* name; **in jds ~n** on behalf of sb; **er ist mir nur mit ~n bekannt** I only know him by name; **sich** *dat* **einen ~n als etw** *akk* **machen** to make a name for oneself as sth
namenlos *adj* nameless; *Helfer, Spender* anonymous
namens ['na:·məns] *adv* by the name of
Namensschild *nt* nameplate; (*an Kleidung*) name badge
Namenstag *m* Saint's day
Namensvetter *m* namesake
namhaft *adj* famous
nämlich ['nɛ:m·lɪç] *adv* namely
nannte ['nan·tə] *imp von* **nennen**
Napf <-[e]s, Näpfe> ['napf, *pl* 'nɛp·fə] *m* bowl
Narbe <-, -n> ['nar·bə] *f* scar
Narkose <-, -n> [nar·'ko:·zə] *f* anesthesia
Narr, Närrin <-en, -en> ['nar, 'nɛ·rɪn] *m, f* fool; **jdn zum ~en halten** to make a fool of sb; **sich** *akk* **zum ~en machen** to make a fool of oneself
Narrenfreiheit *f* ▶ WENDUNGEN: **~ haben** to have the freedom to do whatever one wants
narrensicher *adj* foolproof
närrisch ['nɛ·rɪʃ] *adj* (*verrückt*) crazy; (*unvernünftig*) foolish; ■ **[ganz] ~ auf jdn/etw sein** (*fam*) to be crazy about sb/sth
Narzisse <-, -n> [nar·'tsɪ·sə] *f* narcissus
naschen ['na·ʃn̩] **I.** *vi* to snack, to nosh *fam;* **etwas zum N~** something sweet [to snack on] **II.** *vt* (*essen*) ■ **etw ~** to snack on sth
Naschkatze *f* (*fam*) person with a sweet tooth
Nase <-, -n> ['na:·zə] *f* nose; **sich** *dat* **die ~ putzen** to blow one's nose ▶ WENDUNGEN: **jdm etw auf die ~ binden** (*fam*) to tell sb sth; **sich** *dat* **an seine eigene ~ fassen** (*fam*) to blame oneself; **auf die ~ fliegen** (*fam*) to fall flat on one's face; **sich** *dat* **eine goldene ~ verdienen** to earn a fortune; **die ~ vorn haben** to be one step ahead; **jdn an der ~ herumführen** (*fam*) to lead sb on; **jdm auf der ~ herumtanzen** (*fam*) to walk all over sb; **pro ~** (*hum fam*) per person; **die ~ von jdm/etw voll haben** (*fam*) to be fed up with sb/sth; **jdm etw aus der ~ ziehen** (*fam*) to get sth out of sb
näseln ['nɛ:·zl̩n] *vi* to talk through one's nose
Nasenbluten <-s> *nt kein pl* nosebleed
Nasenflügel *m* side of the nose
Nasenlänge *f* ▶ WENDUNGEN: **mit einer ~** (*Pferdesport*) by a nose
Nasenloch *nt* nostril
Nasenspitze *f* tip of the nose ▶ WENDUNGEN: **jdm etw an der ~ ansehen** to be able to tell sth from sb's face
Nasenspray *m o nt* nasal spray
Nasentropfen *pl* nose drops
Naseweis <-es, -e> ['na:·zə·vais] *m* (*Besserwisser*) know-it-all *fam,* wise guy *fam*
Nashorn *nt* rhino[ceros]
nass^{RR}, **naß**^{ALT} <nasser *o* nässer, nasseste *o* nässeste> ['nas] *adj* wet; **~ geschwitzt** soaked with sweat *pred*
Nässe <-> ['nɛ·sə] *f kein pl* wetness; **vor ~ triefen** to be soaking wet
nasser, nässer *adj komp von* **nass**
nasseste, nässeste *adj superl von* **nass**
nasskalt^{RR} *adj* cold and damp
Nassrasur^{RR} *f* wet shave
Nation <-, -en> [na·'tsi̯o:n] *f* nation; **die Vereinten ~en** the United Nations
national [na·tsi̯o·'na:l] **I.** *adj* ① national ② (*patriotisch*) nationalist **II.** *adv* nationalistic
Nationalfeiertag *m* national holiday
Nationalhymne *f* national hymn
Nationalismus <-> [na·tsi̯o·na·'lɪs·mʊs] *m kein pl* nationalism
Nationalist(in) <-en, -en> [na·tsi̯o·na·'lɪst] *m(f)* nationalist
nationalistisch *adj, adv* nationalist[ic]
Nationalität <-, -en> [na·tsi̯o·na·li·'tɛ:t] *f* ① (*Staatsangehörigkeit*) nationality ② (*Volkszugehörigkeit*) ethnic origin
Nationalmannschaft *f* national team
Nationalpark *m* national park
Nationalrat *m kein pl* SCHWEIZ National Council; ÖSTERR National Assembly
Nationalsozialismus [na·tsi̯o·'na:l·zo·tsi̯a·lɪs·mʊs] *m* National Socialism
nationalsozialistisch *adj* Nazi, National Socialist
Nationalversammlung *f* National Assembly
NATO, Nato <-> ['na:·to] *f kein pl Akr von* **North Atlantic Treaty Organization:** ■ **die ~** NATO
Natter <-, -n> ['na·tɐ] *f* adder
Natur <-, -en> [na·'tu:ɐ̯, *pl* na'tu:·rən] *f* ① *kein pl* BIOL nature ② *kein pl* (*Landschaft*) countryside; **in freier ~** in the wild ③ (*Wesensart*) nature; **von ~ aus** by nature

N

Naturalien [-liən] *pl* natural produce; **in ~** in kind
Naturdenkmal *nt* natural monument
Naturell <-s, -e> [na·tu·ˈrɛl] *nt* (*geh*) temperament
Naturereignis *nt* natural phenomenon
Naturfaser *f* natural fiber
Naturfreund(**in**) *m(f)* nature lover
naturgemäß I. *adj* natural **II.** *adv* ❶ (*natürlich*) naturally ❷ (*der Natur entsprechend*) in accordance with nature
Naturgesetz *nt* law of nature
naturgetreu *adj, adv* true to life
Naturheilmittel *nt* natural medicine
Naturkatastrophe *f* natural disaster
Naturkostladen *m* health food store
natürlich [na·ˈtyːɐ̯·lɪç] **I.** *adj* natural **II.** *adv* ❶ (*selbstverständlich*) naturally, of course ❷ (*in der Natur*) naturally
Natürlichkeit <-> *f kein pl* naturalness
Naturpark *m* nature park
Naturprodukt *nt* natural product
Naturschutz *m* [nature] conservation; **unter ~ stehen** to be protected
Naturschutzgebiet *nt* nature reserve
naturverträglich *adj* eco-friendly
Naturvolk *nt* primitive people
Naturwissenschaft *f* ❶ (*Wissenschaft*) natural sciences *pl* ❷ (*Fach*) natural science
Naturwissenschaftler(**in**) *m(f)* natural scientist
naturwissenschaftlich *adj* natural-scientific
Navi <-s, -s> [ˈnaː·vi, ˈna·vi] *nt* (*fam*) *Abk von* **Navigationsgerät** GPS
Navigation <-> [na·vi·gaː·ˈtsi̯oːn] *f kein pl* navigation
Navigationsgerät *nt,* **Navigationssystem** *nt* navigation system; (*tragbares Gerät*) GPS
Nazi <-s, -s> [ˈnaː·tsi] *m* Nazi
n. Chr. *Abk von* **nach Christus** AD
ne [ˈneː] *adv* (*fam*) no
'ne [nə] *art indef* (*fam*) *kurz für* **eine** a[n]
Neandertaler <-s, -> [ne·ˈan·dɐ·taː·lɐ] *m* Neanderthal man
Neapel <-s> *nt* Naples
Nebel <-s, -> [ˈneː·bl̩] *m* ❶ fog; **bei ~** in foggy conditions ❷ ASTRON nebula
nebelig [ˈneː·bə·lɪç] *adj* foggy
Nebelscheinwerfer *m* fog light
Nebelschwaden *pl* wafts of mist *pl*
neben [ˈneː·bn̩] *präp* ❶ *+akk, dat* (*an der Seite*) beside, next to ❷ *+dat* (*außer*) apart from ❸ *+dat* (*verglichen mit*) compared to
nebenan [neː·bn̩·ˈʔan] *adv* next door
nebenbei [neː·bn̩·ˈbai] *adv* ❶ (*neben der Arbeit*) on the side ❷ (*beiläufig*) incidentally; **~ [bemerkt]** by the way
Nebenbemerkung *f* side remark
nebenberuflich I. *adj* **eine ~e Tätigkeit** a side [*or* second] job **II.** *adv* as a side [*or* second] job
Nebenbeschäftigung *f* side job, sideline
Nebenbuhler(**in**) <-s, -> *m(f)* rival
nebeneinander [neː·bn̩·ʔai·ˈnan·dɐ] *adv* ❶ (*Seite an Seite*) side by side ❷ (*zugleich*) simultaneously, at the same time
nebeneinander|setzen *vr* ■ **sich** *akk* **~** to sit [down] next to each other
Nebenerscheinung *f* side effect
Nebenfluss^RR^ *m* tributary
Nebengebäude *nt* ❶ outbuilding ❷ (*benachbartes Gebäude*) neighboring building
nebenher [neː·bn̩·ˈheːɐ̯] *adv* in addition
Nebenhöhle *f* ANAT sinus
Nebenkosten *pl* additional costs *pl*
Nebenmann <-es, -männer *o* -leute> *m* neighbor; **mein ~** the person next to me
Nebenraum *m* next room [over]
Nebenrolle *f* FILM, THEAT supporting role
Nebensache *f* trivial matter; **~ sein** to be irrelevant
nebensächlich *adj* irrelevant
Nebensaison *f* off-season
Nebensatz *m* LING subordinate clause ▶ WENDUNGEN: **im ~** in passing
Nebenstraße *f* side street
Nebenverdienst *m* additional income
Nebenwirkung *f* side effect
Nebenzimmer *nt* next room [over]
neblig [ˈneː·blɪç] *adj* foggy
Necessaire <-s, -s> [ne·sɛ·ˈsɛːɐ̯] *nt* (*für Maniküre*) manicure set
necken [ˈnɛ·kn̩] *vt* to tease
nee [ˈneː] *adv* (*fam*) no
Neffe <-n, -n> [ˈnɛ·fə] *m* nephew
negativ [ˈneː·ga·tiːf] **I.** *adj* negative **II.** *adv* negatively
Negativ <-s, -e> [ˈneː·ga·tiːf, *pl* ˈneː·ga·tiː·və] *nt* negative
Neger(**in**) <-s, -> [ˈneː·gɐ] *m(f)* (*pej: Schwarzer*) Negro *pej,* nigger *pej*
nehmen <nimmt, nahm, genommen> [ˈneː·mən] *vt* ❶ (*ergreifen, aussuchen*) to take; **nimm dir noch Kuchen** help yourself to more cake ❷ (*wegnehmen*) ■ **jdm etw ~** to take sth [away] from sb; **jdm die Sicht ~** to block sb's view ❸ (*annehmen*) to accept; **jdn ~, wie er ist** to take sb as he is ❹ (*verlangen*) to ask (**für** *+akk* for); **was nimmst du dafür?** what do you want for it? ❺ (*benutzen*) *Zutaten* to take; **den Bus/die Bahn/ein Taxi ~** to take the bus/the train/a taxi ❻ (*einnehmen*) to take; **etw zu sich** *dat* **~** (*geh*) to have sth to eat ❼ (*überwinden*) to overcome ▶ WENDUNGEN: **es sich** *dat* **nicht ~ lassen, etw zu tun** to insist on doing sth
Neid <-[e]s> [ˈnaɪt] *m kein pl* jealousy, envy (**auf** *+akk* of)
neiden [ˈnai·dn̩] *vt* ■ **jdm etw ~** to envy sb [for] sth
Neider(**in**) <-s, -> *m(f)* jealous person
neiderfüllt [ˈnaid·ɛɐ̯·fʏlt] **I.** *adj* (*geh*) filled with envy **II.** *adv* enviously
Neidhammel *m* (*fam*) **du alter ~!** you're just jealous!

N

neidisch ['nai·dɪʃ], **neidig** ['nai·dɪç] SÜDD, ÖSTERR **I.** *adj* jealous, envious (**auf** *+akk* of) **II.** *adv* jealously, enviously

neidlos I. *adj* ungrudging, without envy **II.** *adv* without envy

neigen ['nai·gn̩] **I.** *vr* ■ **sich** *akk* ~ ❶ (*sich beugen*) ■ **sich** *akk* **zu jdm** ~ to lean over to sb; **sich** *akk* **nach vorne** ~ to lean forward ❷ (*schräg abfallen*) to slope ❸ (*sich biegen*) *Äste* to bow down ❹ (*kippen*) to tilt **II.** *vt* ❶ (*beugen*) to bend ❷ (*kippen*) to tilt **III.** *vi* ❶ (*anfällig sein für*) ■ **zu etw** *dat* ~ *Krankheiten* to be prone to sth ❷ (*tendieren*) ■ **zu etw** *dat* ~ to tend to [do] sth

Neigung <-, -en> *f* ❶ (*Vorliebe*) inclination ❷ (*Tendenz*) tendency ❸ (*Gefälle*) slope

nein ['nain] *adv* no

Nein <-s> ['nain] *nt kein pl* no

Neinsager(in) <-s, -> [-za:·gɐ] *m(f)* naysayer

Neinstimme *f* no, "no" vote

Nektar <-s, -e> ['nɛk·tar] *m* nectar

Nektarine <-, -n> [nɛk·ta·'ri:·nə] *f* nectarine

Nelke <-, -n> ['nɛl·kə] *f* ❶ BOT carnation ❷ KOCHK clove

'nen ['nən] *art indef* (*fam*) *kurz für* **einen** a[n]

nennen <nannte, genannt> ['nɛ·nən] *vt* ❶ (*benennen, anreden*) to call; **wie nennt man das?** what do you call that? ❷ (*sagen*) *Namen* to name; *Grund* to give; **können Sie mir einen guten Anwalt ~?** can you give me the name of a good lawyer?

nennenswert *adj* considerable; ■ **nichts N~es** nothing worth mentioning

N

Nennung <-, -en> *f* naming

Neofaschismus <-> ['ne:o·fa·ʃɪs·mʊs] *m kein pl* neofascism

Neon <-s> ['ne:·ɔn] *nt kein pl* neon

Neonazi <-s, -s> ['ne:o·na:·tsi] *m kurz für* **Neonazist** neo-Nazi

Neonlicht *nt* neon light

Neonreklame *f* neon sign

Neonröhre *f* strip light

Nepal <-s> ['ne:·pal, ne·'pa:l] *nt* Nepal; *s. a.* **Deutschland**

Nepalese, Nepalesin <-n, -n> [ne·pa·'le:·zə] *m, f* Nepalese; *s. a.* **Deutsche(r)**

nepalesisch [ne·pa·'le:·zɪʃ] *adj* Nepalese; *s. a.* **deutsch**

Nepp <-s> ['nɛp] *m kein pl* (*fam*) rip-off

neppen ['nɛ·pn̩] *vt* (*fam*) to rip off

Nerv <-s *o* -en, -en> ['nɛrf, *pl* 'nɛr·fn̩] *m* nerve ▶ WENDUNGEN: **die ~en behalten/verlieren** to keep calm/lose one's cool; **jdm auf die ~en gehen** (*fam*) to get on sb's nerves; **du hast vielleicht ~en!** (*fam*) you've got some nerve!

nerven ['nɛr·fn̩] *vt* (*fam*) ■ **jdn [mit etw** *dat*] ~ to bug sb [with sth]

Nervenarzt, -ärztin *m, f* neurologist

nervenaufreibend *adj* nerve-racking

Nervenbelastung *f* nervous strain

Nervenbündel *nt* (*fam*) bundle of nerves

Nervengas *nt* nerve gas

Nervenkitzel <-s, -> *m* (*fam*) thrill

Nervensache *f* [**eine/reine**] ~ **sein** (*fam*) to be just a question of nerves

Nervensäge *f* (*fam*) pain in the neck

Nervensystem *nt* nervous system

Nervenzentrum *nt* nerve center

Nervenzusammenbruch *m* nervous breakdown

nervig ['nɛr·fɪç] *adj* (*sl: nervenaufreibend*) irritating

nervlich I. *adj* nervous *attr* **II.** *adv* **jd ist ~ erschöpft** sb's nerves have reached the breaking point; **~ bedingt** nervous

nervös [nɛr·'vø:s] *adj* nervous

Nervosität <-> [nɛr·vo·zi·'tɛ:t] *f kein pl* nervousness

nervtötend ['nɛrf·tø:·tənt] *adj* (*fam*) nerve-racking

Nerz <-es, -e> ['nɛrts] *m* mink

Nessel <-, -n> ['nɛ·sl̩] *f* BOT nettle ▶ WENDUNGEN: **sich** *akk* **in die ~n setzen** (*fam*) to put one's foot in one's mouth

Nessessär <-s, -s> [nɛ·sɛ·'sɛ:ɐ̯] *nt s.* **Necessaire**

Nest <-[e]s, -er> ['nɛst] *nt* ❶ nest ❷ (*fam: Kaff*) hole ▶ WENDUNGEN: **sich** *akk* **ins gemachte ~ setzen** (*fam*) to have got it made

Nesthäkchen <-s, -> *nt* (*fam*) baby of the family

Nestwärme *f* warmth and security

Netiquette <-, -n> [nɛ·ti·'kɛ·tə] *f* netiquette

nett ['nɛt] *adj* nice; **sei so ~ und ...** would you mind ...

netterweise [nɛ·tɐ·'vai·zə] *adv* kindly

Nettigkeit <-, -en> ['nɛ·tɪç·kait] *f* ❶ *kein pl* (*Liebenswürdigkeit*) kindness ❷ (*liebenswürdige Bemerkung*) kind words *pl* ❸ *pl* (*iron fam: boshafte Bemerkung*) insult

netto ['nɛ·to] *adv* net

Nettoeinkommen *nt* net income

Nettogewicht *nt* net weight

Netz <-es, -e> ['nɛts] *nt* ❶ net ❷ (*Einkaufsnetz*) string bag; (*Gepäcknetz*) baggage net ❸ SPORT net; **ins ~ gehen** *Tennisball* to hit the net ❹ (*Spinnennetz*) web ❺ ELEK, TELEK network; (*Strom*) power grid ❻ *kein pl* COMPUT network; ■ **das ~** the Net ❼ TRANSP system, network

Netzgerät *nt* power supply unit

Netzhaut *f* retina

Netzstecker *m* power plug

Netzstrumpf *m* fishnet stocking

Netzwerk *nt a.* COMPUT network; **soziales ~** social network

neu ['nɔy] **I.** *adj* ❶ (*nicht alt*) new; **die ~este Mode** the latest fashion; **ein ~eres System** a more up-to-date system; ■ **der/die N~e** (*fam*) the newcomer; ■ **das N~e [an etw** *dat*] the new thing [about sth]; ■ **das N~este** the latest [thing]; **was gibt's N~es?** (*fam*) what's new? ❷ (*abermalig*) new; **einen ~en Anfang machen** to make a fresh start; **einen ~en Anlauf nehmen** to make another attempt

▶ WENDUNGEN: **auf ein N~es!** here's to a fresh start!; **seit ~[e]stem** [since] recently; **von ~em** all over again **II.** *adv* ❶ (*von vorn*) **~ bearbeitet** MEDIA revised; **~ anfangen** to start all over again; **~ gestalten** to redesign ❷ (*zusätzlich*) anew; **33 Mitarbeiter ~ einstellen** to hire 33 new employees ❸ (*erneut*) again ❹ (*seit kurzem da*) newly; **~ eröffnet** newly opened; (*erneut eröffnet*) reopened ▶ WENDUNGEN: **wie ~ geboren** like a new man/woman

Neuankömmling <-s, -e> *m* newcomer

neuartig ['nɔy·ʔaːɐ̯·tɪç] *adj* new, new type of

Neuauflage *f* ❶ (*unveränderter Nachdruck*) reprint ❷ (*veränderte Neuausgabe*) new edition

Neubau <-bauten> ['nɔy·bau, *pl* -bau·tn̩] *m* ❶ *kein pl* (*neue Errichtung*) [new] building ❷ (*neu erbautes Gebäude*) new building

Neubaugebiet *nt* development area; (*schon bebaut*) new development

Neubauwohnung *f* newly built apartment

Neubewertung *f* reassessment; ÖKON revaluation

Neu-Delhi <-s> [nɔy·'deː·li] *nt* New Delhi

neuerdings ['nɔy·ɐ·'dɪŋs] *adv* recently

Neueröffnung *f* ❶ new opening ❷ (*Wiedereröffnung*) reopening

Neuerscheinung *f* new publication

Neuerung <-, -en> ['nɔy·ə·rʊŋ] *f* reform

Neufassung *f* new version; *eines Films* remake

Neufundland <-s> [nɔy·'fʊnt·lant] *nt* Newfoundland

Neugeborene(s) *nt* newborn

Neugier(de) <-> ['nɔy·giːɐ̯(·də)] *f kein pl* curiosity

neugierig I. *adj* curious; **~ sein, ob ...** to be curious [to know] whether ...; **sei nicht so ~!** don't be so nosy! **II.** *adv* curiously, full of curiosity

Neuguinea <-s> [-gi·'neːa] *nt* New Guinea

Neuigkeit <-, -en> ['nɔy·ɪç·kait] *f* news

Neujahr *nt kein pl* New Year; **prost ~!** here's to the New Year!

Neukaledonien <-s> [nɔy·ka·le·'doː·ni̯·ən] *nt* New Caledonia

Neuland *nt* ▶ WENDUNGEN: **~ betreten** to enter unknown territory

neulich ['nɔy·lɪç] *adv* the other day

Neuling <-s, -e> ['nɔy·lɪŋ] *m* beginner

neumodisch I. *adj* ❶ (*sehr modern*) fashionable ❷ (*pej: unverständlich neu*) newfangled **II.** *adv* fashionably

Neumond *m kein pl* new moon

neun ['nɔyn] *adj* nine; *s. a.* **acht**[1]

neunfach, 9fach ['nɔyn·fax] **I.** *adj* **die ~e Menge nehmen** to take nine times the amount **II.** *adv* nine times

neunhundert ['nɔyn·'hʊn·dɐt] *adj* nine hundred; *s. a.* **hundert**

neunmal ['nɔyn·maːl] *adv* nine times; *s. a.* **achtmal**

neunmalklug ['nɔyn·maːl·kluːk] *adj* (*iron fam*) smart-aleck *attr*

neuntausend ['nɔyn·'tauː·zn̩t] *adj* nine thousand; *s. a.* **tausend**

neunte(r, s) ['nɔyn·tə(ɐ, s)] *adj* ❶ (*an neunter Stelle*) ninth; *s. a.* **achte(r, s) 1** ❷ (*Datum*) ninth, 9th; *s. a.* **achte(r, s) 2**

neuntel ['nɔn·tl̩] *nt* ninth

neunzehn ['nɔyn·tseːn] *adj* nineteen; *s. a.* **acht**[1]

neunzehnte(r, s) *adj* ❶ (*an neunzehnter Stelle*) nineteenth; *s. a.* **achte(r, s) 1** ❷ (*Datum*) nineteenth, 19th; *s. a.* **achte(r, s) 2**

neunzig ['nɔyn·tsɪç] *adj* ninety; *s. a.* **achtzig 1, 2**

neunzigste(r, s) ['nɔyn·tsɪg·stə] *adj* ninetieth; *s. a.* **achte(r, s) 1**

Neuorientierung *f* (*geh*) reorientation

Neuregelung, Neureglung *f* revision; *Verkehr* new measures *pl*

neureich *adj* nouveau riche

Neureiche(r) *f(m)* nouveau riche

Neurodermitis <-, -dermitiden> [nɔy·ro·dɛr·'miː·tɪs, *pl* -dɛr·mi·'tiː·dn̩] *f* neurodermatitis

Neurologe, Neurologin <-n, -n> [nɔy·ro·'loː·gə] *m, f* neurologist

Neurose <-, -n> [nɔy·'roː·zə] *f* neurosis

Neurotiker(in) <-s, -> [nɔy·'roː·ti·kɐ] *m(f)* neurotic

neurotisch [nɔy·'roː·tɪʃ] *adj* neurotic

Neuschnee *m* fresh snow

Neuseeland <-s> [nɔy·'zeː·lant] *nt* New Zealand; *s. a.* **Deutschland**

Neuseeländer(in) <-s, -> [nɔy·'zeː·lɛn·dɐ] *m(f)* New Zealander; *s. a.* **Deutsche(r)**

neuseeländisch [nɔy·'zeː·lɛn·dɪʃ] *adj* New Zealand *attr*, from New Zealand *pred*

neutral [nɔy·'traːl] *adj, adv* neutral

neutralisieren* [nɔy·tra·li·'ziː·rən] *vt* to neutralize

Neutralität <-> [nɔy·tra·li·'tɛːt] *f kein pl* neutrality

Neuverschuldung *f* new debt

Neuwahl *f* reelection

neuwertig *adj* as new

Neuzeit *f kein pl* ■ **die ~** modern times *pl*

Newsgroup <-, -s> ['njuːz·gruːp] *f* newsgroup

Nicaragua <-s> [ni·ka·'raː·gu̯a] *nt* Nicaragua; *s. a.* **Deutschland**

Nicaraguaner(in) <-s, -> [ni·ka·ra·'gu̯aː·nɐ] *m(f)* Nicaraguan; *s. a.* **Deutsche(r)**

nicaraguanisch [ni·ka·ra·'gu̯aː·nɪʃ] *adj* Nicaraguan; *s. a.* **deutsch**

nicht [nɪçt] *adv* not; **ich weiß ~** I don't know; **ich bin es ~ gewesen** it wasn't me; **~ öffentlich** *attr* not open to the public *pred*; **~ [ein]mal** not even; **~ mehr** not any more, no longer; **~ mehr als ...** no more than ...; **bitte ~!** please don't!

Nichtbeachtung *f*, **Nichtbefolgung** *f* noncompliance

Nichte <-, -n> ['nɪç·tə] *f* niece

N

nichtehelich *adj* illegitimate
Nichterscheinen <-s> *nt kein pl* failure to appear
Nichteuropäer(in) *m(f)* non-European
nichtig ['nɪç·tɪç] *adj* ❶ (*ungültig*) invalid ❷ (*geh: belanglos*) trivial
Nichtigkeit <-, -en> *f* ❶ *kein pl* (*Ungültigkeit*) invalidity ❷ *meist pl* (*geh*) triviality
Nichtraucher(in) *m(f)* nonsmoker
nichts ['nɪçts] *pron indef* ❶ (*nicht etwas*) not anything, nothing; **es ist ~** it's nothing; **~ als ...** (*nur*) nothing but ...; **~ mehr** nothing more [*or* else]; **~ wie raus!** let's get out of here!; **~ ahnend** unsuspecting; **~ sagend** meaningless; **damit will ich ~ zu tun haben** I don't want anything to do with it ❷ *vor substantiviertem adj* nothing; **~ anderes [als ...]** nothing other [than ...]; **hoffentlich ist es ~ Ernstes** I hope it's nothing serious ▶ WENDUNGEN: **~ da!** (*fam*) no chance!; **für ~** for nothing; **für ~ und wieder ~** (*fam*) [all] for nothing
Nichts <-, -e> ['nɪçts] *nt* ❶ *kein pl* (*leerer Raum*) void ❷ (*unbedeutender Mensch*) nonentity ▶ WENDUNGEN: **aus dem ~ auftauchen** to show up from out of nowhere; **vor dem ~ stehen** to be left with nothing
Nichtschwimmer(in) *m(f)* nonswimmer
nichtsdestotrotz [nɪçts·dɛs·to·'trɔts] *adv* nonetheless
nichtsdestoweniger [nɪçts·dɛs·to·'veː·nɪ·gɐ] *adv* nevertheless
Nichtsnutz <-es, -e> ['nɪçts·nʊts] *m* (*pej*) good-for-nothing
nichtsnutzig *adj* (*pej*) useless
Nichtstun *nt* ❶ (*das Faulenzen*) idleness ❷ (*Untätigkeit*) inactivity
Nichtzahlung *f* nonpayment
Nickel <-s> ['nɪ·kl̩] *nt kein pl* nickel
nicken ['nɪ·kn̩] *vi* to nod
Nickerchen <-s, -> ['nɪ·kɐ·çən] *nt* (*fam*) nap; **ein ~ machen** to take a nap
nie ['niː] *adv* never; **~ mehr** never again; **das hätte ich ~ im Leben gedacht** I never would have thought that ▶ WENDUNGEN: **~ und nimmer** never ever
nieder|beugen *vr* ■ **sich** *akk* **[zu jdm/etw]** ~ to bend down [to sb/sth]
nieder|brennen *irreg* **I.** *vi sein* to burn down **II.** *vt haben* to burn down
niederdeutsch ['niː·dɐ·dɔytʃ] *adj* Low German
Niederfrequenz *f* low frequency
Niedergang <-[e]s> *m kein pl* decline
niedergedrückt *adj* downcast
niedergelassen [-gə·la·sn̩] *adj* SCHWEIZ resident
niedergeschlagen [-gə·ʃlaː·gn̩] *adj* downcast
Niedergeschlagenheit <-> *f kein pl* despondency
nieder|knien **I.** *vi sein* to kneel [down] (**vor** +*dat* before) **II.** *vr haben* ■ **sich** *akk* ~ to kneel [down] (**vor** +*dat* before)
Niederlage *f* defeat
Niederlande ['niː·dɐ·lan·də] *pl* ■ **die** ~ the Netherlands; *s. a.* **Deutschland**
Niederländer(in) <-s, -> ['niː·dɐ·lɛn·dɐ] *m(f)* Dutchman *masc,* Dutchwoman *fem; s. a.* **Deutsche(r)**
niederländisch ['niː·dɐ·lɛn·dɪʃ] *adj* Dutch; *s. a.* **deutsch**
Niederländisch ['niː·dɐ·lɛn·dɪʃ] *nt dekl wie adj* Dutch
nieder|lassen *vr irreg* ❶ (*ansiedeln*) ■ **sich** *akk* ~ to settle down ❷ (*beruflich etablieren*) ■ **sich** *akk* **[als etw]** ~ to establish oneself [as sth]; **niedergelassener Arzt** *licensed doctor with his/her own practice* ❸ (*geh: hinsetzen*) ■ **sich** *akk* **[auf etw** *dat*] ~ to sit down [on sth]; *Vogel* to settle [on sth]
Niederlassung <-, -en> *f* (*Zweigstelle*) branch
nieder|legen *vt* ❶ (*hinlegen*) to put down *sep* ❷ (*aufgeben*) to give up; *Amt, Mandat* to resign; *Arbeit* to stop
nieder|machen *vt* (*fam*) ❶ (*kaltblütig töten*) to butcher ❷ (*heruntermachen*) to run down *fam*
Niederösterreich ['niː·dɐ·ʔøːs·tə·raiç] *nt* Lower Austria
nieder|reißen *vt irreg* to pull down *sep*
Niedersachsen <-s> ['niː·dɐ·zak·sn̩] *nt* Lower Saxony
nieder|schießen *irreg vt* to shoot down *sep*
Niederschlag *m* ❶ (*Regen*) rainfall; (*Schnee*) snowfall; (*Hagel*) hail ❷ (*Ausdruck*) **seinen ~ in etw** *dat* **finden** to find expression in sth
nieder|schlagen *irreg* **I.** *vt* ❶ (*zu Boden schlagen*) to floor ❷ (*unterdrücken*) to crush; *Streik* to break up; *Unruhen* to suppress ❸ *Augen* to lower **II.** *vr* ❶ (*kondensieren*) ■ **sich** *akk* **[an etw** *dat*] ~ to condense [on sth] ❷ (*zum Ausdruck kommen*) ■ **sich** *akk* **in etw** *dat* ~ to find expression in sth
nieder|schmettern *vt* ❶ (*niederschlagen*) to send crashing down ❷ (*fig: erschüttern*) to devastate
niederschmetternd ['niː·dɐ·ʃmɛ·tɐnt] *adj* deeply distressing; *Nachricht* devastating
nieder|schreiben *vt irreg* to write down *sep*
Niederspannung *f* low voltage
Niedertracht <-> *f kein pl* ❶ (*Gesinnung*) malice ❷ (*Tat*) despicable act
niederträchtig *adj* contemptible; *Einstellung, Lüge, Person a.* despicable
Niederträchtigkeit <-, -en> *f* ❶ (*Tat*) despicable act ❷ *kein pl* malice
Niederung <-, -en> ['niː·də·rʊŋ] *f* (*Senke*) lowland; (*Mündungsgebiet*) flats *pl*
niedlich ['niːt·lɪç] **I.** *adj* cute, sweet **II.** *adv* sweetly
niedrig ['niː·drɪç] **I.** *adj* ❶ (*nicht hoch*) low ❷ (*gering*) low; *Betrag* small **II.** *adv* low
niemals ['niː·maːls] *adv* never
niemand ['niː·mant] *pron indef* nobody, no one; (*bei Fragen und Verneinung*) anyone, anybody

Niemandsland ['ni:·mants·lant] *nt kein pl* no man's land
Niere <-, -n> ['ni:·rə] *f* kidney ▶ WENDUNGEN: **jdm an die ~n gehen** (*fam*) to get to sb
Nierenbecken *nt* renal pelvis
Nierengurt *m* kidney belt
Nierenstein *m* kidney stone
Nierenversagen *nt kein pl* kidney failure
nieseln ['ni:·zl̩n] *vi impers* ■ **es nieselt** it's drizzling
Nieselregen ['ni:·zl̩-] *m* drizzle
niesen ['ni:·zn̩] *vi* to sneeze
Niete[1] <-, -n> ['ni:·tə] *f* ❶ (*Nichttreffer*) blank ❷ (*fam: Versager*) loser
Niete[2] <-, -n> ['ni:·tə] *f* TECH rivet
nieten ['ni:·tn̩] *vt* to rivet
niet- und nagelfest ['ni:t·ʔʊnt·'na:·gl̩·fɛst] *adj* ▶ WENDUNGEN: **alles, was nicht ~ ist** (*fam*) everything that's not nailed down
Nigeria <-s> [ni·'ge:·ri̯a] *nt* Nigeria; *s. a.* **Deutschland**
Nigerianer(in) <-s, -> [ni·ge·'ri̯a:·nɐ] *m(f)* Nigerian; *s. a.* **Deutsche(r)**
nigerianisch [ni·ge·'ri̯a:·nɪʃ] *adj* Nigerian; *s. a.* **deutsch**
Nikolaus <-, -e *o* -läuse> ['nɪ·ko·laus, *pl* -lɔy·zə] *m* ❶ (*verkleidete Gestalt*) St. Nicholas (*figure who brings children presents on December 6*) ❷ *kein pl* (*6. Dezember*) St. Nicholas' Day
Nikotin <-s> [ni·ko·'ti:n] *nt kein pl* nicotine
nikotinfrei *adj* nicotine-free
Nil <-s> [ni:l] *m* ■ **der ~** the Nile
Nilpferd *nt* hippo[potamus]
nimmer ['nɪ·mɐ] *adv* ❶ (*veraltend geh: niemals*) never ❷ SÜDD, ÖSTERR (*nicht mehr*) no longer
Nimmerwiedersehen [nɪ·mɐ·'vi:·de·ze:·ən] *nt* **auf ~** (*fam*) never to be seen again
nimmt ['nɪmt] *3. pers sing pres von* **nehmen**
nippen ['nɪ·pn̩] *vi* to sip (**an** +*dat* on)
Nippes ['nɪ·pəs, 'nɪps, 'nɪp] *pl* knickknacks *pl*
nirgends ['nɪr·gn̩ts], **nirgendwo** ['nɪr·gn̩t·'vo:] *adv* nowhere; **ich konnte ihn ~ finden** I couldn't find him anywhere
nirgendwohin ['nɪr·gn̩t·vo·'hɪn] *adv* nowhere
Nische <-, -n> ['ni:·ʃə] *f* niche
nisten ['nɪs·tn̩] *vi* to nest
Nistkasten *m* nesting box
Nitrat <-[e]s, -e> [ni·'tra:t] *nt* nitrate
Niveau <-s, -s> [ni·'vo:] *nt* ❶ (*Anspruch*) caliber; **~ haben** to have class; **kein ~ haben** to be lowbrow; **das ist unter meinem ~** this is beneath me *fig* ❷ (*Höhe einer Fläche*) level
niveaulos [ni·'vo:-] *adj* primitive
niveauvoll *adj* intellectually stimulating
nivellieren* [ni·vɛ·'li:·rən] *vt* (*geh: einander angleichen*) to even out *sep*
nix ['nɪks] *pron indef* (*fam*) *s.* **nichts**
Nixe <-, -n> ['nɪk·sə] *f* mermaid
Nizza <-s> ['nɪ·tsa] *nt* Nice
nobel ['no:·bl̩] **I.** *adj* ❶ (*edel*) noble ❷ (*luxuriös*) luxurious ❸ (*großzügig*) generous **II.** *adv* ❶ (*edel*) honorably ❷ (*großzügig*) generously
Nobelpreis [no·'bɛl·prais] *m* Nobel Prize
Nobelpreisträger(in) *m(f)* Nobel Prize winner
noch ['nɔx] **I.** *adv* ❶ (*bis jetzt*) still; **ein ~ ungelöstes Problem** an as yet unsolved problem; ■ **~ immer [nicht]** still [not]; ■ **~ nicht** not yet; ■ **~ nichts** nothing yet; ■ **~ nie** never; **die Luft war klar wie ~ nie** the sky was clearer than ever before ❷ (*irgendwann*) some time; **er kommt schon ~** he will eventually come ❸ (*nicht später als*) by the end of; **~ gestern habe ich davon nichts gewusst** even yesterday I didn't know a thing about it; **~ heute** today ❹ (*bevor etw anderes geschieht*) **bleib ~ ein wenig** stay a little longer ❺ (*womöglich*) **wir kommen ~ zu spät** we're going to end up being late ❻ (*zusätzlich*) in addition; **möchtest du ~ etwas essen?** would you like something else to eat?; **möchten Sie ~ eine Tasse Kaffee?** would you like another cup of coffee?; ■ **~ eine(r, s)** another ❼ *vor komp* (*mehr als*) even [more] **II.** *konj* ■ **weder ... ~ ...** neither ... nor ...
nochmalig ['nɔx·ma:·lɪç] *adj attr* further
nochmals ['nɔx·ma:ls] *adv* again
Nomade, Nomadin <-n, -n> [no·'ma:·də] *m, f* nomad
Nomen <-s, Nomina> ['no:·mən, *pl* 'no:·mi·na] *nt* LING noun
Nominativ <-[e]s, -e> ['no:·mi·na·ti:f, *pl* 'no:·mi·na·ti:·və] *m* nominative
nominieren* [no·mi·'ni:·rən] *vt* to nominate
Nominierung <-, -en> *f* nomination
Noname-produkt[RR], **No-Name-Produkt**[RR] ['noʊ·ne:m-] *nt* no-name product
Nonne <-, -n> ['nɔ·nə] *f* nun
Nonplusultra <-> [nɔn·plʊs·'ʔʊl·tra] *nt kein pl* (*geh*) ■ **das ~** the ultimate
Nonsens <-[es]> ['nɔn·zɛns] *m kein pl* nonsense
nonstop [nɔn·'ʃtɔp, nɔn·'stɔp] *adv* nonstop
Nord <-[e]s, -e> ['nɔrt, *pl* 'nɔr·də] *m kein art, kein pl* north; **aus ~** from the north
Nordamerika ['nɔrt·ʔa'me:·ri·ka] *nt* North America
norddeutsch ['nɔrt·dɔytʃ] *adj* North German
Norddeutschland ['nɔrt·dɔytʃ·lant] *nt* North Germany
Norden <-s> ['nɔr·dn̩] *m kein pl, kein indef art* ❶ (*Himmelsrichtung*) north; **im/nach ~** in/to the north; **in Richtung ~** to[ward] the north ❷ (*nördliche Gegend*) north; **er wohnt im ~ der Stadt** he lives in the northern part of town
Nordeuropa ['nɔrt·ʔɔy·'ro:·pa] *nt* Northern Europe
Nordhalbkugel *f* Northern Hemisphere
Nordirland ['nɔrt·'ʔɪr·lant] *nt* Northern Ireland
Nordküste ['nɔrt·kʏs·tə] *f* north coast
nördlich ['nœrt·lɪç] **I.** *adj* ❶ (*Himmelsrichtung*) northern ❷ (*im Norden liegend*) northern; **weiter ~ liegen** to lie farther [to the] north ❸ (*von/nach Norden*) northerly; **in ~e Richtung** northward **II.** *adv* ■ **~ von ...** north

N

of ... **III.** *präp +gen* ~ **der Stadt** [to the] north of the town

Nordlicht *nt* ① (*Polarlicht*) northern lights *pl* ② (*hum, a. pej: Mensch aus Norddeutschland*) North German

Nordosten [nɔrt·ˈʔɔs·tn̩] *m kein indef art* northeast; *s. a.* **Norden**

nordöstlich [nɔrt·ˈʔœst·lɪç] **I.** *adj* ① (*Himmelsrichtung*) northeastern ② (*im Nordosten liegend*) northeastern ③ (*von/nach Nordosten*) northeastward **II.** *adv* ■ ~ **von ...** northeast of ... **III.** *präp +gen* northeast of; *s. a.* **nördlich**

Nordpol [ˈnɔrt·poːl] *m kein pl* ■ **der** ~ the North Pole

Nordrhein-Westfalen [ˈnɔrt·rain·vɛst·ˈfaː·lən] *nt* North Rhine-Westphalia

Nordsee [ˈnɔrt·zeː] *f* ■ **die** ~ the North Sea; **an der** ~ on the North Sea coast

Nord-Süd-Gefälle *nt* North-South divide

Nordwesten [nɔrt·ˈvɛs·tn̩] *m kein indef art* northwest; *s. a.* **Norden**

nordwestlich [nɔrt·ˈvɛst·lɪç] **I.** *adj* ① (*Himmelsrichtung*) northwestern ② (*im Nordwesten liegend*) northwestern ③ (*von/nach Nordwesten*) northwestward **II.** *adv* ■ ~ **von ...** northwest of ... **III.** *präp +gen* northwest of; *s. a.* **nördlich**

Nordwind *m* north wind

Nörgelei <-, -en> *f* ① (*Äußerung*) moaning [and groaning] ② *kein pl* (*das Nörgeln*) nagging

nörgeln [ˈnœr·gl̩n] *vi* to moan (**über** *+akk* about)

N

Nörgler(in) <-s, -> [ˈnœrg·lɐ] *m(f)* moaner

Norm <-, -en> [ˈnɔrm] *f* ① (*festgelegte Größe*) standard ② (*verbindliche Regel*) norm ③ (*Durchschnitt*) ■ **die** ~ the norm ④ (*festgesetzte Arbeitsleistung*) quota

normal [nɔr·ˈmaːl] **I.** *adj* ① (*üblich*) normal ② *meist verneint* (*fam: zurechnungsfähig*) right in the head; **du bist wohl nicht ~!** you are out of your mind! **II.** *adv* normally

Normalbenzin *nt* regular [unleaded] [gas]

normalerweise *adv* normally

Normalfall *m* normal case; **im** ~ usually

normalisieren* [nɔr·ma·li·ˈziː·rən] **I.** *vt* to normalize **II.** *vr* ■ **sich** *akk* ~ to normalize

Normalisierung <-, -en> *f* normalization

Normalität <-> [nɔr·ma·li·ˈtɛːt] *f kein pl* normality

Normalverbraucher(in) *m(f)* average consumer; **Otto** ~ (*fam*) the man in the street

Normalzustand *m kein pl* normality

Normandie <-> [nɔr·man·ˈdiː] *f* ■ **die** ~ Normandy

normen [ˈnɔr·mən] *vt* to standardize

normieren* [nɔr·ˈmiː·rən] *vt* (*geh*) to standardize

Normierung <-, -en> *f* (*geh*) standardization

Normung <-, -en> *f* standardization

Norwegen <-s> [ˈnɔr·veː·gn̩] *nt* Norway; *s. a.* **Deutschland**

Norweger(in) <-s, -> [ˈnɔr·veː·gɐ] *m(f)* Norwegian; *s. a.* **Deutsche(r)**

norwegisch [ˈnɔr·veː·gɪʃ] *adj* Norwegian; *s. a.* **deutsch**

Norwegisch [ˈnɔr·veː·gɪʃ] *nt dekl wie adj* ■ **das** ~**e** Norwegian

Nostalgie <-> [nɔs·tal·ˈgiː] *f kein pl* (*geh*) nostalgia

nostalgisch [nɔs·ˈtal·gɪʃ] *adj* (*geh*) nostalgic

Not <-, Nöte> [ˈnoːt, *pl* ˈnøː·tə] *f* ① *kein pl* (*Armut*) poverty ② (*Bedrängnis*) distress; **in ~ geraten** to be in dire straits; **jdm seine ~ klagen** to pour out one's troubles to sb ③ (*Mühe*) **seine [liebe] ~ haben mit jdm/etw** *dat* to have one's work cut out with sb/sth; **mit knapper ~** just ▶ WENDUNGEN: **~ macht erfinderisch** (*prov*) necessity is the mother of invention; **zur** ~ if need[s] be

Notar(in) <-s, -e> [no·ˈtaːɐ̯] *m(f)* notary [public]

Notariat <-[e]s, -e> [no·ta·ˈri̯aːt] *nt* (*Kanzlei*) notary's office

notariell [no·ta·ˈri̯ɛl] *adj* notarial; ~ **beglaubigt** notarized

Notarzt, -ärztin *m, f* ① (*bei Unfällen*) emergency doctor ② (*Arzt im Notdienst*) on-call physician

Notaufnahme *f* ① (*eines Kranken*) emergency admission ② (*Krankenhausstation*) emergency room

Notausgang *m* emergency exit

Notbehelf *m* stopgap [measure]

Notbremse *f* emergency brake

Notdienst *m* ~ **haben** to be on duty

notdürftig [ˈnoːt·dʏrf·tɪç] **I.** *adj* makeshift **II.** *adv* in a makeshift manner *pred*

Note <-, -n> [ˈnoː·tə] *f* ① MUS note; **ganze/halbe** ~ whole/half note; **~n lesen** to read music ② (*Zensur*) grade ③ (*Banknote*) [bank]note

Notebook <-s, -s> [ˈnoʊt·bʊk] *nt* COMPUT notebook

Notepad-Computer [ˈnoʊt·pæd-] *m* notepad [computer]

Notfall *m* emergency

notfalls [ˈnoːt·fals] *adv* if need be

notgedrungen *adv* willy-nilly

notieren* [no·ˈtiː·rən] *vt* to write down

nötig [ˈnøː·tɪç] *adj* necessary; ■ **alles N~e** everything necessary; ■ **das N~ste** the essentials; **etw [bitter] ~ haben** to be in [urgent] need of sth; **das haben wir nicht ~!** we don't have to put up with that!

nötigen [ˈnøː·tɪgn̩] *vt* to force

nötigenfalls [ˈnøː·tɪ·gn̩·ˈfals] *adv* (*form*) if necessary

Nötigung <-, -en> *f* (*Zwang*) coercion

Notiz <-, -en> [no·ˈtiːts] *f* ① (*Vermerk*) note ② (*Zeitungsmeldung*) short report ▶ WENDUNGEN: **[keine] ~ [von jdm/etw] nehmen** to take [no] notice [of sb/sth]

Notizblock <-blöcke> *m* notepad

Notizbuch *nt* notebook

Notlage *f* desperate situation

notlanden <notlandete, notgelandet> ['noːt·lan·dn̩] *vi sein* to make an emergency landing
Notlandung *f* emergency landing
Notlösung *f* stopgap [solution]
Notlüge *f* white lie
notorisch [no·'toː·rɪʃ] **I.** *adj* (*geh*) notorious **II.** *adv* (*geh*) notoriously
Notruf *m* ① (*Anruf*) emergency call ② *s.* **Notrufnummer**
Notrufnummer *f* emergency number
Notrufsäule *f* emergency telephone
Notsignal *nt* emergency signal
Notsitz *m a small folding seat used when there is lack of space*
Notstand *m* ① (*Notlage*) desperate situation ② JUR [state of] emergency
Notstandsgebiet *nt* disaster area
Notunterkunft *f* emergency accommodations *pl*
Notwehr <-> *f kein pl* self-defense
notwendig ['noːt·vɛn·dɪç] **I.** *adj* necessary **II.** *adv* necessarily; **etw ~ brauchen** to absolutely need sth
notwendigerweise ['noːt·vɛn·dɪ·ge·'vai·zə] *adv* necessarily
Notwendigkeit <-, -en> ['noːt·vɛn·dɪç·kait, not·'vɛn·dɪç·kait] *f* necessity
Nougat <-s, -s> ['nuː·gat] *m o nt* nougat
Nov. *Abk von* **November** Nov.
November <-s, -> [no·'vɛm·bɐ] *m* November; *s. a.* **Februar**
Nr. *Abk von* **Nummer** no.
NS [ɛn·'ɛs] *Abk von* **Nationalsozialismus** National Socialism
Nu ['nuː] *m* **im ~** in a flash
Nuance <-, -n> ['nỹ·ãːsə] *f* nuance
nüchtern ['nʏç·tɐn] *adj* ① (*mit leerem Magen*) with an empty stomach ② (*nicht betrunken*) sober ③ (*realitätsbewusst*) down-to-earth ④ *Tatsachen* plain; *Einrichtung* austere
Nüchternheit <-> *f kein pl* ① (*Realitätsbewusstsein*) rationality ② (*nicht alkoholisierter Zustand*) soberness
Nudel <-, -n> ['nuː·dl̩] *f meist pl* pasta + *sing vb, no indef art;* (*Suppennudel*) noodle *usu pl*
Nudist(in) <-en, -en> [nu·'dɪst] *m(f)* (*geh*) nudist
Nugat, Nougat <-s, -s> *m o nt* nougat
nuklear [nu·kle·'aːɐ̯] **I.** *adj attr* nuclear **II.** *adv* with nuclear weapons *pred*
Nuklearwaffe *f* nuclear weapon
null ['nʊl] *adj* zero ▶ WENDUNGEN: **gleich ~ sein** to be [practically] zero, to be extremely unrealistic; **in ~ Komma nichts** (*fam*) in a flash; **~ und nichtig sein** to be null and void
Null <-, -en> ['nʊl, *pl* 'nʊ·lṇ] *f* ① (*Zahl*) zero, null *liter* ② (*fam: Versager*) nothing
nullachtfuffzehn [nʊl·ʔaxt·'fʊf·tseːn], **nullachtfünfzehn** [nʊl·ʔaxt·'fʏnf·tseːn] *adj* (*fam*) run-of-the-mill
Nulldiät *f* starvation diet
Nulllösung^RR^, **Nullösung**^ALT^ *f* zero option
Nullpunkt *m kein pl* freezing point ▶ WENDUNGEN: **auf den ~ sinken** to reach rock bottom
Nullrunde *f round of wage negotiations in which the demand for a wage increase is dropped*
Nulltarif *m* ■ **zum ~** for free
Numeri ['nuː·me·ri] *pl von* **Numerus**
numerieren*^ALT^ [nu·mə·'riː·rən] *vt s.* **nummerieren**
numerisch [nu·'meː·rɪʃ] *adj* numeric[al]
Numerus <-, Numeri> ['nuː·me·rʊs, *pl* 'nuː·me·ri] *m* number; **~ clausus** enrollment limits, quota

> Universities regulate the number of students who are allowed to enroll in the most popular subjects by means of the quota-like **Numerus clausus** (N. C.), which means "closed number" in Latin. With successful completion of the *Gymnasium* (secondary school), a student passes the so-called *Abitur* and receives a document that confirms the passing of the exams and lists the grades. The sum of all *Abitur* passes is used to calculate the **N. C.** for each field of study and this then determines whether a student obtains permission to study at a particular university since the number of applicants usually far exceeds the number of available spots. The N. C. can vary from semester to semester.

Nummer <-, -n> ['nʊ·mɐ] *f* ① (*Zahl, Telefonnummer*) number ② MEDIA (*Ausgabe*) issue ③ (*Größe*) size ④ (*derb: Koitus*) fuck *vulg;* **eine ~ [mit jdm] schieben** (*sl*) to get it on [with sb] *sl* ▶ WENDUNGEN: **auf ~ Sicher gehen** (*fam*) to play it safe
nummerieren*^RR^ *vt* to number
Nummernschild *nt* license plate
nun ['nuːn] *adv* now; **es ist ~ [ein]mal so** that's [just] the way it is
nur ['nuːɐ̯] *adv* ① (*lediglich*) only; **sie fährt gut, ~ zu schnell** she drives well, but too fast ② (*bloß*) just; **wie konnte ich das ~ vergessen!** how on earth could I forget that! ③ (*ruhig*) just; **~ zu!** go [right] ahead!
Nürnberg <-s> ['nʏrn·bɛrk] *nt* Nuremberg
nuscheln ['nʊ·ʃl̩n] *vi, vt* (*fam*) to mumble
Nuss^RR^, **Nuß**^ALT^ <-, Nüsse> ['nʊs, *pl* 'nʏ·sə] *f* nut ▶ WENDUNGEN: **dumme ~** (*fam*) moron, idiot
Nussbaum^RR^ *m* nut tree
Nussknacker^RR^ <-s, -> *m* nutcracker
Nussschale^RR^ *f* nutshell
Nutte <-, -n> ['nʊ·tə] *f* (*sl*) whore
nutz ['nʊts] *adj pred* SÜDD, ÖSTERR *s.* **nütze**
nutzbar *adj* usable
nutzbringend **I.** *adj* gainful **II.** *adv* gainfully
nütze ['nʏ·tsə] *adj pred* ■ **zu etw** *dat* **~ sein** to be useful for sth; ■ **zu nichts ~ sein** to be good for nothing

N

nutzen ['nʊ·tsn̩], **nützen** ['nʏ·tsn̩] **I.** *vi* (*von Nutzen sein*) to be of use; ■ [**jdm**] **nichts** ~ to not do [sb] any good **II.** *vt* ❶ (*in Gebrauch nehmen*) to use ❷ (*ausnutzen*) to exploit; **eine Gelegenheit** ~ to take advantage of an opportunity

Nutzen <-s> ['nʊ·tsn̩] *m kein pl* benefit; **welchen ~ versprichst du dir davon?** what do you hope to gain from it?; [**jdm**] ~ **bringen** to be advantageous [to sb]; [**jdm**] **von ~ sein** to be of use [to sb]

Nutzfahrzeug *nt* utility vehicle

nützlich ['nʏts·lɪç] *adj* ❶ (*nutzbringend*) useful ❷ (*hilfreich*) helpful

nutzlos I. *adj* useless **II.** *adv* in vain *pred*

Nutzlosigkeit <-> *f kein pl* uselessness

Nutzpflanze *f* [economically] useful plant

Nutzung <-, -en> *f* use

Nylon® <-[s]> ['nai·lɔn] *nt kein pl* nylon

Nymphomanin <-, -nen> *f* nymphomaniac

Oo

O, o <-, - *o fam* -s, -s> [oː] *nt* O, o; ~ **wie Otto** O as in Oscar

Oase <-, -n> [o'aː·zə] *f* oasis

ob ['ɔp] *konj* whether; ~ **er morgen kommt?** I wonder if he's coming tomorrow?

Obdach <-[e]s> ['ɔp·dax] *nt kein pl* (*geh*) shelter

obdachlos *adj* homeless

Obdachlose(r) *f(m)* homeless person

Obdachlosenasyl *nt*, **Obdachlosenheim** *nt* homeless shelter

O-Beine *pl* bow legs *pl*

oben ['oːbn̩] *adv* ❶ (*in der Höhe*) top; **ich möchte die Flasche ~ links** I'd like the bottle [that's] on the top left; ■ ~ **auf etw** *dat o akk* on top of sth; **dort/hier** ~ up there/here; **ganz** ~ at the very top; **hoch** ~ high; **bis** ~ [**hin**] up to the top; **nach** ~ up; **nach ~ zu** further up; **von** ~ (*vom oberen Teil*) from above ❷ (*im oberen Stockwerk*) upstairs; **nach** ~ upstairs; **von** ~ from upstairs ❸ (*fam: auf höherer Ebene*) **sich** *akk* ~ **halten** to stay at the top; **der Befehl kommt von** ~ the order comes from the top; **solche Dinge werden ~ entschieden** these things are decided by the powers that be ❹ (*vorher*) above; **der/die/das ~ erwähnte** the above-mentioned ▶ WENDUNGEN: **dieser Job steht mir bis** [**hier**] ~ (*fam*) I'm fed up with this job *sl;* **ich weiß nicht mehr, wo ~ und unten ist** (*fam*) I don't know whether I'm coming or going *sl;* ~ **ohne** (*fam*) topless; **von ~ bis unten** from top to bottom

obenauf ['oːbn̩·'ʔauf] *adv* ❶ DIAL (*obendrauf*) on top ❷ ■ ~ **sein** (*guter Laune*) to be in a good mood; (*im Vorteil*) to be in a strong position

obendrauf ['oːbn̩·'drauf] *adv* (*fam*) on top

obendrein ['oːbn̩·'drain] *adv* on top

obenherum ['oːbn̩·hɛ·'rʊm] *adv* (*fam*) in the bust

obenhin ['oːbn̩·'hɪn] *adv* in passing

obenrum ['oːbn̩·'rʊm] *adv* (*fam*) *s.* **obenherum**

Ober <-s, -> ['oːbɐ] *m* waiter

Oberarm *m* upper arm

Oberarzt, -ärztin *m, f* assistant medical director

Oberbefehlshaber(in) *m(f)* commander in chief

Oberbegriff *m* generic term

Oberbekleidung *f* outer clothing

Oberbürgermeister(in) ['oːbɐ·bʏr·gɐ·mais·tɐ] *m(f)* mayor

obere(r, s) ['oːbə·rə, 'oːbə·rɐ, 'oːbə·rəs] *adj attr* ❶ (*oben befindlich*) top ❷ (*rangmäßig höher*) higher ❸ (*vorhergehend*) previous ❹ (*höher gelegen*) upper

Oberfläche ['oːbɐ·flɛ·çə] *f* surface; **an die ~ kommen** to surface

oberflächlich ['oːbɐ·flɛç·lɪç] **I.** *adj* superficial **II.** *adv* superficially; (*flüchtig*) in a slapdash manner *pred*

Oberflächlichkeit <-> *f kein pl* superficiality

ObergeschossRR *nt* top floor

Obergrenze *f* upper limit

oberhalb ['oːbɐ·halp] **I.** *präp* +*gen* above **II.** *adv* above

Oberhand ['oːbɐ·hant] *f* ▶ WENDUNGEN: **die ~** [**über jdn**] **gewinnen** to gain the upper hand [over sb]

Oberhaupt *nt* head

Oberhaus *nt* POL upper house, Senate

Oberhemd *nt* shirt

oberirdisch I. *adj* aboveground; *Leitung* overhead **II.** *adv* aboveground

Oberkellner(in) *m(f)* head waiter *masc,* head waitress *fem*

Oberkiefer *m* upper jaw

Oberkörper *m* torso

Oberlippe *f* upper lip

Oberösterreich ['oːbɐ·ʔøːstə·raiç] *nt* Upper Austria

Oberschenkel *m* thigh

Oberschicht *f* (*der Gesellschaft*) upper class

Oberschwester *f* head nurse

Oberseite *f* top

oberste(r, s) ['oːbɐ·stə, 'oːbɐ·stɐ, 'oːbɐ·stəs] *adj* ❶ (*räumlich*) top ❷ (*rangmäßig*) highest

Oberstübchen *nt* ▶ WENDUNGEN: **nicht ganz richtig im ~ sein** (*veraltend fam*) to have a screw loose *sl*

Oberstufe *f* ≈ sixth grade

Oberteil *nt o m* ❶ (*Aufsatz*) top part ❷ (*von Kleidung*) top
Obertrottel *m* (*fam*) prize idiot, total jerk *fam*
Oberweite *f* bust size
obgleich [ɔp·ˈglaiç] *konj* although
Obhut <-> [ˈɔp·huːt] *f kein pl* (*geh*) care; **unter jds ~ stehen** to be in sb's care
Objekt <-[e]s, -e> [ɔp·ˈjɛkt] *nt* ❶ (*Gegenstand, a. Grammatik*) object ❷ (*Immobilie*) [piece of] property ❸ (*Kunstgegenstand*) objet d'art, work of art
objektiv [ɔpjɛk·ˈtiːf] **I.** *adj* objective **II.** *adv* objectively
Objektiv <-s, -e> [ɔpjɛk·ˈtiːf, *pl* ɔpjɛk·ˈtiːvə] *nt* lens
Objektivität <-> [ɔpjɛk·tivi·ˈtɛːt] *f kein pl* objectivity
obligatorisch [obliga·ˈtoː·rɪʃ] *adj* (*geh*) mandatory
Oboe <-, -n> [o·ˈboːə] *f* oboe
Obrigkeit <-, -en> [ˈoːbrɪç·kait] *f* (*Verwaltung*) ■ **die ~** the authorities
obskur [ɔps·ˈkuːɐ̯] *adj* (*geh*) ❶ (*unbekannt*) obscure ❷ (*verdächtig*) suspicious
Obst <-[e]s> [ˈoːpst] *nt kein pl* fruit
Obstbaum *m* fruit tree
Obstgarten *m* orchard
Obstkuchen *m* fruit tart
Obstsaft *m* fruit juice
Obstsalat *m* fruit salad
obszön [ɔps·ˈtsøːn] *adj* obscene
Obszönität <-, -en> [ɔps·tsø·ni·ˈtɛːt] *f* obscenity
obwohl [ɔp·ˈvoːl] *konj* although
Ochse <-n, -n> [ˈɔksə] *m* ox
Ochsenschwanzsuppe *f* oxtail soup
öde [ˈøːdə] *adj* ❶ (*verlassen*) desolate ❷ (*fade*) *Landschaft* dull ❸ (*langweilig*) tedious, dull
oder [ˈoːdɐ] *konj* ❶ (*eines oder anderes*) or; **~ aber** or else; **~ auch** or [even]; **~ auch nicht** or [maybe] not ❷ (*stimmt's?*) **der Film hat dir auch gut gefallen, ~?** you liked the movie too, didn't you?; **er schuldet dir noch Geld, ~?** he still owes you money, doesn't he?
Ofen <-s, Öfen> [ˈoːfn̩, *pl* ˈøːfn̩] *m* ❶ (*Heizofen*) heater; (*Kohle-, Kachel-, Ölofen*) stove ❷ (*Backofen*) oven ❸ DIAL (*Herd*) stove ▶ WENDUNGEN: **jetzt ist der ~ aus** (*fam*) that does it
ofenfrisch *adj* oven-fresh
Ofenheizung *f* stove heating
offen [ˈɔfn̩] **I.** *adj* open; *Punkt* moot; *Problem, Rechnung* unsettled; *Frage* unanswered; **bei ~em Fenster** with the window open; **~er Wein** wine by the glass/carafe; **~ haben** *Laden, Geschäft* to be open **II.** *adv* openly; **~ gestanden** to be [perfectly] honest
offenbar [ɔfn̩·ˈbaːɐ̯] **I.** *adj* obvious **II.** *adv* obviously
offenbaren <*pp* offenbart *o* geoffenbart> [ɔfn̩·ˈbaː·rən] (*geh*) **I.** *vt* to reveal **II.** *vr* ❶ ■ **sich** *akk* **jdm ~** to confide in sb ❷ (*erweisen*) **es offenbarte sich als Reinfall** it proved to be a failure
Offenbarung <-, -en> [ɔfn̩·ˈbaː·rʊŋ] *f* revelation
Offenheit <-> *f kein pl* openness; **in aller ~** quite frankly
offenherzig *adj* ❶ (*freimütig*) open ❷ (*hum fam: tief ausgeschnitten*) revealing
offenkundig [ˈɔfn̩·kʊn·dɪç] *adj* obvious
offensichtlich [ˈɔfn̩·zɪçt·lɪç] **I.** *adj* obvious; *Irrtum, Lüge* blatant **II.** *adv* obviously
offensiv [ɔfɛn·ˈziːf] **I.** *adj* offensive; *Verhalten, Art* aggressive **II.** *adv* offensively, aggressively
Offensive <-, -n> [ɔfən·ˈziːvə] *f* offensive
öffentlich [ˈœfn̩·tlɪç] **I.** *adj* public **II.** *adv* publicly
Öffentlichkeit <-> *f kein pl* ■ **die ~** the [general] public + *sing/pl vb;* **in aller ~** in public; **etw an die ~ bringen** to make sth public
Öffentlichkeitsarbeit *f kein pl* public relations *npl*
öffentlichkeitswirksam *adj* ■ **~ sein** to be good publicity
öffentlich-rechtlich *adj attr* under public law *pred; Anstalt* public; **~e Rundfunkanstalt** public [service] broadcasting
offerieren* [ɔfe·ˈriː·rən] *vt* (*geh*) to offer
Offerte <-, -n> [ɔ·ˈfɛr·tə] *f* offer
offiziell [ɔfi·ˈtsi̯ɛl] **I.** *adj* ❶ (*amtlich*) official ❷ (*förmlich*) *Empfang, Feier* formal **II.** *adv* officially
Offizier(in) <-s, -e> [ɔfi·ˈtsiːɐ̯] *m(f)* officer
Offlinebetrieb^RR^, **Off-line-Betrieb**^ALT^ [ˈɔf·lain-] *m kein pl* offline operation
öffnen [ˈœf·nən] **I.** *vt* to open **II.** *vi* ■ [**jdm**] **~** to open the door [for sb] **III.** *vr* ❶ (*aufgehen*) ■ **sich** *akk* **~** *Tür* to open; *Blüte, Fallschirm* to open up ❷ (*sich zuwenden*) ■ **sich** *akk* [**jdm/etw**] **~** to open up [to sb/sth]
Öffner <-s, -> *m* ❶ (*Dosenöffner*) can opener; (*Flaschenöffner*) bottle opener ❷ (*Türöffner*) door opener
Öffnung <-, -en> *f* ❶ (*offene Stelle*) opening ❷ *kein pl* (*das Öffnen*) opening ❸ *kein pl* POL opening up
Öffnungszeiten *pl* hours of business *pl*
oft <öfter, am öftesten> [ˈɔft] *adv* often
öfter(s) [ˈœf·tɐ(s)] *adv* [every] once in a while; **ist dir das schon ~ passiert?** has that happened to you often?
öftesten [ˈœf·təs·tən] *superl von* **oft**
oftmals *adv* often
ohne [ˈoːnə] **I.** *präp +akk* ❶ (*nicht versehen mit*) without; **~ Geld** without any money; **~ Schutz** unprotected ❷ (*nicht eingerechnet*) excluding; **~ mich!** count me out! **II.** *konj* ■ **~ etw zu tun** without doing sth; ■ **~ dass etw geschieht** without sth happening; ■ **~ dass jd etw tut** without sb doing sth
ohnegleichen [oːnə·ˈglai·çn̩] *adj inv* ❶ (*unnachahmlich*) unparalleled ❷ (*außergewöhnlich*) [quite] exceptional
ohnehin [oːnə·ˈhɪn] *adv* anyhow, anyway[s *fam*]
Ohnmacht <-, -en> [ˈoːn·maxt] *f* ❶ (*Bewusst-*

O

seinszustand) faint; **in ~ fallen** to faint ❷ (*geh: Machtlosigkeit*) powerlessness

ohnmächtig ['oːn·mɛç·tɪç] **I.** *adj* ❶ (*bewusstlos*) unconscious; ~ **werden** to faint ❷ (*geh: machtlos*) powerless ❸ *attr Wut* helpless **II.** *adv* helplessly

Ohr <-[e]s, -en> ['oːɐ̯] *nt* ear ▶ WENDUNGEN: **es faustdick hinter den ~en haben** to be a sly one; **ganz ~ sein** (*hum fam*) to be all ears; **auf dem ~ taub sein** (*fam*) to be deaf to that sort of thing; **bis über beide ~en verliebt sein** to be head over heels in love; **jdm eins hinter die ~en geben** (*fam*) to whack sb on the back of the head; **viel um die ~en haben** (*fam*) to have a lot on one's plate; **jdn übers ~ hauen** (*fam*) to pull a fast one on sb; **jdm [mit etw** *dat*] **in den ~en liegen** to nag sb [about sth]; **die ~en spitzen** (*fam*) to prick up one's ears; **seinen ~en nicht trauen** to not believe one's ears

Ohrenarzt, -ärztin *m, f* ear specialist

ohrenbetäubend I. *adj* deafening **II.** *adv* deafeningly

Ohrenentzündung *f* ear infection

Ohrensausen <-s> *nt kein pl* buzzing in one's ears

Ohrenschmalz *nt kein pl* earwax

Ohrenschmaus <-es> *m kein pl* (*fam*) feast for the ear[s]

Ohrenschützer <-s, -> *m meist pl* earmuff *usu pl*

Ohrentropfen *pl* eardrops *pl*

Ohrenzeuge, -zeugin *m, f* witness (*to something heard*)

Ohrfeige <-, -n> *f* slap in the face

ohrfeigen *vt* ■ **jdn ~** to give sb a slap in the face

Ohrläppchen <-s, -> *nt* earlobe

Ohrmuschel *f* outer ear

Ohrring *m* earring

Ohrwurm *m* (*fam: Lied*) catchy tune

Ökobauer, -bäuerin *m, f* organic farmer

Ökoladen ['øːko·laːdn̩] *m* health food store

Ökologe, Ökologin <-n, -n> [øko·'loː·gə] *m, f* ecologist

Ökologie <-> [øko·lo·'giː] *f kein pl* ecology

Ökologiebewegung *f* environmental movement

ökologisch [øko·'loː·gɪʃ] **I.** *adj* ecological **II.** *adv* ecologically

Ökonom(in) <-en, -en> [øko·'noːm] *m(f)* (*geh*) economist

Ökonomie <-, -n> [øko·no·'miː, *pl* øko·no·'miːən] *f* ❶ *kein pl* (*Wirtschaftlichkeit*) economy ❷ (*Wirtschaft*) economy

ökonomisch [øko·'noː·mɪʃ] **I.** *adj* ❶ (*die Wirtschaft betreffend*) economic ❷ (*sparsam*) economical **II.** *adv* economically

Ökopartei *f* Green Party

Ökosteuer *f* environmental tax (*tax on products or processes which damage the environment*)

Ökosystem *nt* ecosystem

Ökotest *m test designed to measure the effect sth has on the environment*

Okt. *Abk von* **Oktober** Oct.

Oktober <-s, -> [ɔk·'toː·bɐ] *m* October; *s. a.* **Februar**

Okzident <-s> ['ɔktsid·ɛnt] *m kein pl* (*geh*) ■ **der ~** the Occident *form o poet*

Öl <-[e]s, -e> ['øːl] *nt* (*fette Flüssigkeit, a. Erdöl*) oil; (*Heizöl*) fuel oil; (*Schmieröl*) lubricating oil ▶ WENDUNGEN: **~ ins Feuer gießen** to add fuel to the fire

Oldie <-s, -s> ['oːl·di] *m* oldie

Oldtimer <-s, -> ['oːlt·taimɐ] *m* (*Auto*) vintage car; (*Flugzeug*) vintage airplane

Oleander <-s, -> [ole·'andɐ] *m* oleander

ölen ['øːlən] *vt* to oil

Ölfarbe *f* oil-based paint; KUNST oil [paint]

Ölfleck *m* oil spot

Ölgemälde *nt* oil painting

Ölgötze *m* (*pej sl*) **dastehen wie ein ~** to stand there like a zombie

Ölheizung *f* oil heater

ölig ['øːl·ɪç] *adj* oily; (*fettig*) greasy

Olive <-, -n> [o·'liː·və] *f* olive

Olivenbaum *m* olive tree

Olivenöl *nt* olive oil

olivgrün *adj* olive-green, olive *attr*

Öljacke *f* oilskin jacket

Ölkonzern *m* oil company

Ölkrise *f* oil crisis

Ölleitung *f* oil pipe; (*Pipeline*) oil pipeline

Ölpest *f* oil pollution

Ölplattform *f* oilrig

Ölpumpe *f* oil pump

Ölquelle *f* oil well

Ölsardine *f* sardine [in oil] ▶ WENDUNGEN: **wie die ~n** (*fam*) like sardines

Ölstand *m kein pl* oil level

Ölstandsmesser *m* oil pressure gauge

Öltanker *m* oil tanker

Ölteppich *m* oil slick

Ölverbrauch *m* oil consumption

Ölwechsel *m* oil change

Olympiade <-, -n> [olʏm·'pi̯aː·də] *f* Olympic Games *pl*

Olympiasieger(in) *m(f)* Olympic champion

Olympionike, Olympionikin <-n, -n> [olʏm·pi̯o·'niː·kə] *m, f* Olympic athlete

olympisch [o·'lʏm·pɪʃ] *adj* Olympic *attr*

Ölzweig *m* olive branch

Oma <-, -s> ['oːma] *f* (*fam*) granny *fam*, grandma *fam*

Omelett <-[e]s, -e *o* -s> *nt*, **Omelette** <-, -n> [ɔm(ə)·'lɛt, *pl* ɔm(ə)·'lɛtn̩] *f* SCHWEIZ, ÖSTERR omelette

Omen <-s, - *o* Omina> ['oːmən, *pl* 'oːmina] *nt* (*geh*) omen

Omnibus ['ɔmni·bʊs] *m* bus

Omnibushaltestelle *f* bus stop

onanieren* [ona·'niː·rən] *vi* to masturbate

Onkel <-s, -> ['ɔŋ·kl̩] *m* uncle

Onlinebanking <-[s]> ['ɔn·lain·bɛŋ·kɪŋ] *nt kein pl* online banking

Onlinebetrieb[RR], **On-line-Betrieb**[ALT] ['ɔn·

lain-] *m kein pl* online operation
Onlinechat ['ɔn·lain·tʃæt] *m* [online] chat
OnlinedienstRR ['ɔn·lain-] *m* online service
Onlinehandel ['ɔn·lain-] *m* INET ■**der** ~ e-commerce
Onlinelernen ['ɔn·lain-] *nt kein pl* e-learning
Onlineportal ['ɔn·lain-] *nt* INET web portal; ■**im** ~ on the web portal
Onlineshopping ['ɔn·lain·ʃɔ·pɪŋ] *nt* online shopping
OP <-s, -s> [oː·'peː] *m Abk von* **Operationssaal** OR *no art*
Opa <-s, -s> ['oːpa] *m* (*fam*) grandpa
Oper <-, -n> ['oːpɐ] *f* opera
Operation <-, -en> [opə·ra·'tsi̯oːn] *f* operation
Operationssaal *m* operating room
operativ [opə·ra·'tiːf] **I.** *adj* MED operative; **~er Eingriff** surgery **II.** *adv* MED surgically
operieren* [opə·'riː·rən] *vt* ■**jdn/etw** ~ to operate on sb/sth; **jdn am Bein** ~ to operate on sb's leg; ■**sich** *dat* **etw** ~ **lassen** to have sth operated on; ■**sich** *akk* ~ **lassen** to have an operation
Opernhaus *nt* opera house
Opernsänger(in) *m(f)* opera singer
Opfer <-s, -> ['ɔ·pfɐ] *nt* ❶ (*verzichtende Hingabe*) *a.* REL sacrifice; ~ **bringen** to make sacrifices ❷ (*geschädigte Person*) victim; *von Unfall, Krieg* casualty; **jdm/etw zum** ~ **fallen** to fall victim to sb/sth
opfern ['ɔ·pfɐn] *vt* to sacrifice; **sein Leben** ~ to offer up one's life
Opferung <-, -en> *f* sacrifice
Opiat <-[e]s, -e> [o·'pi̯aːt] *nt* opiate
Opium <-s> ['oː·pi̯ʊm] *nt kein pl* opium
Opponent(in) <-en, -en> [ɔpo·'nɛnt] *m(f)* (*geh*) opponent
opponieren* [ɔpo·'niː·rən] *vi* (*geh*) ■**gegen jdn/etw** ~ to oppose sb/sth
opportun [ɔ·pɔr·'tuːn] *adj* (*geh*) opportune
Opportunismus <-> [ɔpɔr·tu·'nɪs·mʊs] *m kein pl* (*geh*) opportunism
Opportunist(in) <-en, -en> [ɔp·ɔr·tu·'nɪst] *m(f)* opportunist
opportunistisch *adj* opportunistic
Opposition <-, -en> [ɔpo·zi·'tsi̯oːn] *f* POL ■**die** ~ the opposition
oppositionell [ɔpo·zi·tsi̯o·'nɛl] *adj* ❶ (*geh: gegnerisch*) opposed, opposing *attr* ❷ POL opposition *attr*
Oppositionsführer(in) *m(f)* opposition leader
Oppositionspartei *f* opposition party
OP-Schwester *f* operating room nurse
optieren* [ɔp·'tiː·rən] *vi* to opt (**für** *+akk* for)
Optik <-> ['ɔp·tɪk] *f kein pl* ❶ PHYS ■**die** ~ optics *+ sing vb* ❷ (*Eindruck*) appearance
Optiker(in) <-s, -> ['ɔp·ti·kɐ] *m(f)* optometrist
optimal [ɔp·ti·'maːl] **I.** *adj* optimal **II.** *adv* in the best possible way
optimieren* [ɔp·ti·'miː·rən] *vt* to optimize
Optimierung <-, -en> *f* optimization
Optimismus <-> [ɔp·ti·'mɪs·mʊs] *m kein pl* optimism
Optimist(in) <-en, -en> [ɔp·ti·'mɪst] *m(f)* optimist
optimistisch **I.** *adj* optimistic **II.** *adv* optimistically
Option <-, -en> [ɔp·'tsi̯oːn] *f* (*Möglichkeit*) option
optisch ['ɔp·tɪʃ] **I.** *adj Täuschung, Eindruck* optical; **aus ~en Gründen** for visual effect **II.** *adv* optically, visually
oral [o·'raːl] **I.** *adj* oral **II.** *adv* orally
orange [o·'rãːʒə, o·'raŋʒə] *adj inv* orange
Orange <-, -n> [o·'rãːʒə, o·'raŋʒə] *f* orange
orangenfarben, orangenfarbig *adj* orange[-colored]
Orangensaft *m* orange juice
Orangenschale *f* orange peel
Orang-Utan <-s, -s> ['oːraŋ·'ʔuːtan] *m* orangutan
Orchester <-s, -> [ɔr·'kɛs·tɐ, ɔr·'çɛs·tɐ] *nt* orchestra
Orchidee <-, -n> [ɔr·çi·'deː(ə)] *f* orchid
Orden <-s, -> ['ɔr·dn̩] *m* ❶ (*Ehrenzeichen*) decoration, medal; **jdm einen** ~ [**für etw** *akk*] **verleihen** to decorate sb [for sth] ❷ (*Gemeinschaft*) [holy] order
ordentlich ['ɔr·dn̩·tlɪç] **I.** *adj* ❶ (*aufgeräumt*) neat ❷ (*ordnungsliebend*) *Person* orderly, neat ❸ (*anständig*) *Leute* respectable; *Benehmen* proper ❹ (*fam: tüchtig*) proper; *Portion* decent **II.** *adv* ❶ (*säuberlich*) neatly ❷ (*anständig*) **sich** *akk* ~ **benehmen** to [really] behave oneself ❸ (*fam: tüchtig*) properly; ~ **essen** to eat well
Order <-, -s *o* -n> ['ɔr·dɐ] *f* order
ordern ['ɔr·dɐn] *vt* to order
Ordinalzahl [ɔr·di·'naːl-] *f* ordinal [number]
ordinär [ɔr·di·'nɛːɐ̯] **I.** *adj* ❶ (*vulgär*) vulgar ❷ (*alltäglich*) ordinary **II.** *adv* crudely
ordnen ['ɔrd·nən] *vt* to arrange; **neu** ~ to rearrange
Ordner <-s, -> *m* file; (*Hefter*) binder
Ordnung <-> ['ɔrd·nʊŋ] *f kein pl* order; **die öffentliche** ~ public order; ~ **schaffen** to straighten things up ▶WENDUNGEN: **etw in** ~ **bringen** (*aufräumen*) to clean sth up; (*klären*) to sort sth out; (*reparieren*) to fix sth; **es** [**ganz**] **in** ~ **finden, dass ...** to find it [perfectly] all right that ...; **geht in** ~**!** (*fam*) that's OK; **etw ist mit jdm/etw nicht in** ~ there's something wrong with sb/sth; **wieder in** ~ **kommen** to turn out all right; **in** ~ **sein** (*fam*) to be OK; **nicht in** ~ **sein** (*nicht funktionieren*) to not be working right; (*sich nicht gehören, nicht richtig sein*) to not be OK
Ordnungsamt *nt municipal authority responsible for registration, licensing, and regulating public events*
Ordnungsgeld *nt* fine
ordnungsgemäß **I.** *adj* according to the rules *pred* **II.** *adv* in accordance with the regulations
Ordnungshüter(in) *m(f)* (*hum*) person [engaged in] maintaining law and order

O

Ọrdnungsliebe *f kein pl* love of orderliness
Ọrdnungssinn *m kein pl* sense of order
Ọrdnungsstrafe *f* fine
ọrdnungswidrig **I.** *adj* improper **II.** *adv* improperly
Ọrdnungswidrigkeit *f* infringement [of the rules/law]
Ọrdnungszahl *f s.* **Ordinalzahl**
Oregano <-s> [o·'reː·gano] *m kein pl* oregano
Organ <-s, -e> [ɔr·'gaːn] *nt* ❶ ANAT organ ❷ (*fam: Stimme*) voice ❸ (*form: offizielle Zeitschrift/Einrichtung*) organ
Organhandel *m* organ trafficking
Organisation <-, -en> [ɔr·ga·ni·za·'tsi̯oːn] *f* organization
Organisationstalent *nt* ❶ *kein pl* (*Eigenschaft*) organizational ability ❷ (*Mensch*) skilled organizer
Organisator, **Organisatorin** <-s, -toren> [ɔr·ga·ni·'zaː·toːɐ̯, ɔr·ga·ni·za·'toː·rɪn, *pl* ɔr·ga·ni·za·'toː·rən] *m, f* organizer
organisatorisch [ɔr·ga·ni·za·'toː·rɪʃ] **I.** *adj* organizational **II.** *adv* organizationally
organisch [ɔr·'gaː·nɪʃ] **I.** *adj* organic **II.** *adv* organically
organisieren* [ɔr·ga·ni·'ziː·rən] **I.** *vt, vi* to organize; **er kann ausgezeichnet ~** he's an excellent organizer **II.** *vt* (*fam: beschaffen*) to get hold of; **wer organisiert einen CD-Spieler für die Party?** who is going to arrange for a CD player for the party? **III.** *vr* ■ **sich** *akk* ~ to get organized
Organismus <-, -nismen> [ɔr·ga·'nɪs·mʊs, *pl* ɔr·ga·'nɪs·mən] *m* organism
Organspende *f* organ donation
Organspender(in) *m(f)* organ donor
Organtransplantation *f,* **Organverpflanzung** *f* organ transplant
Orgasmus <-, Orgasmen> [ɔr·'gas·mʊs, *pl* ɔr·'gas·mən] *m* orgasm
orgastisch [ɔr·'gas·tɪʃ] *adj* orgasmic
Orgel <-, -n> ['ɔr·gl̩] *f* organ
Orgie <-, -n> ['ɔr·gi̯ə] *f* orgy
Orient <-s> ['oːri·ɛnt, o·'ri̯ɛnt] *m kein pl* ■ **der** ~ the Orient *form or dated;* **der Vordere** ~ the Middle East
Orientale, **Orientalin** <-n, -n> [o·ri̯ɛn·'taː·lə] *m, f* Oriental
orientalisch [o·ri̯ɛn·'taː·lɪʃ] *adj* oriental
orientieren* [o·ri̯ɛn·'tiː·rən] **I.** *vr* ■ **sich** *akk* ~ ❶ (*sich zurechtfinden*) to use as a point of reference; **sich an den Sternen ~** to get one's bearings by looking at the stars ❷ (*sich ausrichten*) **sich an etw** *dat* ~ *Bericht* to be based on; *Person* to adapt oneself to; **ich bin eher links orientiert** I tend more to the left ❸ (*sich informieren*) to familiarize oneself (**über** +*akk* with) **II.** *vt* to inform (**über** +*akk* about)
Orientierung <-, -en> [o·ri̯ɛn·'tiː·rʊŋ] *f* orientation; **die ~ verlieren** to lose one's sense of direction
Orientierungshilfe *f* orientation aid
Orientierungspunkt *m* reference point
Orientierungssinn *m kein pl* sense of direction
original [o·ri·gi·'naːl] **I.** *adj* ❶ (*echt*) genuine ❷ (*ursprünglich*) original **II.** *adv* in the original [condition]
Original <-s, -e> [o·ri·gi·'naːl] *nt* ❶ (*Urversion*) original ❷ (*Mensch*) character
Originalaufnahme *f* MUS original recording
originalgetreu **I.** *adj* true to the original *pred* **II.** *adv* in a manner true to the original
Originalität <-> [o·ri·gi·na·li·'tɛːt] *f kein pl* (*Einfallsreichtum*) originality
originell [o·ri·gi'nɛl] *adj* original
Orkan <-[e]s, -e> [ɔr·'kaːn] *m* hurricane
orkanartig *adj* hurricane-force *attr*
Ornament <-[e]s, -e> [ɔr·na·'mɛnt] *nt* ornament
Ornithologe, **Ornithologin** <-n, -n> [ɔr·ni·to'loː·gə] *m, f* ornithologist
Oropax® <-, -> ['oːro·paks] *nt* earplug *usu pl*
Ort[1] <-[e]s, -e> ['ɔrt] *m* ❶ (*Stelle*) place; **der ~ der Handlung** the scene of the action ❷ (*Ortschaft*) place; **am ~** in the place/[the] town ▶ WENDUNGEN: **an ~ und Stelle** on the spot, there and then
Ort[2] ['ɔrt] *nt* (*fam*) ▶ WENDUNGEN: **vor** ~ on site
Örtchen <-s, -> ['œrt·çən] *nt* ▶ WENDUNGEN: **das [stille] ~** (*euph fam*) the john; **ich muss mal schnell aufs ~** I just have to run to the bathroom
orten ['ɔr·tn̩] *vt* ❶ (*ausfindig machen*) to locate ❷ (*fam: sehen*) to spot
Orthografie[RR], **Orthographie** <-, -n> [ɔr·to·gra·'fiː, *pl* ɔr·to·gra·'fiː·ən] *f* orthography, spelling
orthografisch[RR], **orthographisch** [ɔr·to·'graː·fɪʃ] **I.** *adj* orthographic[al] *spec* **II.** *adv* orthographically *spec*
Orthopäde, **Orthopädin** <-n, -n> [ɔr·to·'pɛː·də] *m, f* orthopedist
orthopädisch [ɔr·to·'pɛː·dɪʃ] *adj* orthopedic
örtlich ['œrt·lɪç] **I.** *adj* ❶ (*lokal*) local ❷ METEO localized **II.** *adv* locally; **~ verschieden sein** to vary from place to place; **jdn ~ betäuben** to give sb a local anesthetic
Örtlichkeit <-, -en> *f* area
Ọrtsangabe *f* (*Standortangabe*) [name of] location; (*in Anschrift*) [name of the] city/town
ọrtsansässig *adj* local; ■ **~ sein** to live locally
Ọrtsausgang *m* village/town exit
Ọrtschaft <-, -en> *f* village/[small] town; **eine geschlossene ~** a built-up area
Ọrtseingang *m* village/town entrance
ọrtsfremd *adj* nonlocal; ■ **~ sein** to be a stranger
Ọrtsgespräch *nt* local call
Ọrtskenntnisse *pl* local knowledge; **[gute] ~ haben** to know the place [well]
ọrtskundig *adj* ■ **~ sein** to know one's way around
Ọrtsname *m* place name
Ọrtsnetz *nt* ❶ TELEK local exchange network ❷ ELEK local grid
Ọrtsschild *nt* sign for a town

O

Ortstarif *m* local [call] rate
Ortsteil *m* part of a town
Ortszeit *f* local time
Öse <-, -n> ['øː·zə] *f* eye[let]
Ossi <-, -s> ['ɔsi] *m o f* (*fam*) East German

> With the fall of the Berlin Wall as well as the rest of the border between East and West Germany, a new expression came into use in colloquial German: **Ossi**, a pejorative term for describing Germans from the former East Germany.

Ost <-[e]s, -e> [ɔst] *m kein pl, kein art* east; **aus ~** from the east
Ostasien *nt* East[ern] Asia
ostdeutsch ['ɔst·dɔytʃ] *adj* East German
Ostdeutschland ['ɔst·dɔytʃ·lant] *nt* East Germany
Osten <-s> ['ɔs·tn̩] *m kein pl, no indef art* ① (*Himmelsrichtung*) east; **der Ferne/Nahe ~** the Far/Middle East; *s. a.* **Norden¹** ② (*östliche Gegend*) east; *s. a.* **Norden²**
Osterei *nt* Easter egg
Osterglocke *f* BOT daffodil
Osterhase *m* Easter bunny
Osterinsel *f* ■ **die ~** Easter Island
österlich ['øːs·tɐ·lɪç] **I.** *adj* Easter *attr* **II.** *adv* like Easter
Ostermontag ['oːs·tɐ·'moːn·taːk] *m* Easter Monday
Ostern <-, -> ['oːs·tɐn] *nt* Easter; **frohe ~!** Happy Easter!
Österreich <-s> ['øːs·tə·raiç] *nt* Austria; *s. a.* **Deutschland**
Österreicher(in) <-s, -> ['øːs·tə·rai·çɐ] *m(f)* Austrian; *s. a.* **Deutsche(r)**
österreichisch ['øːs·tə·rai·çɪʃ] *adj* Austrian; ■ **das Ö~e** Austrian; *s. a.* **deutsch**
Ostersonntag ['oːs·tɐ·'zɔn·taːk] *m* Easter Sunday
Osterweiterung *f* eastward expansion
Osterwoche *f* Holy Week
Osteuropa ['ɔst·ʔɔy·'roː·pa] *nt* Eastern Europe
Ostfriese, -friesin <-n, -n> ['ɔst·'friː·zə] *m, f* East Frisian
ostfriesisch ['ɔst·'friː·zɪʃ] *adj* East Frisian
Ostfriesland ['ɔst·'friːs·lant] *nt* East Friesland
östlich ['œst·lɪç] **I.** *adj* ① (*Himmelsrichtung*) eastern; *s. a.* **nördlich I 1** ② (*im Osten liegend*) eastern; *s. a.* **nördlich I 2** ③ (*von/nach Osten*) eastward; *Richtung, Wind* easterly; *s. a.* **nördlich I 3 II.** *adv* ■ **~ von ...** east of ... **III.** *präp +gen* [to the] east of
Ostsee ['ɔst·zeː] *f* ■ **die ~** the Baltic [Sea]
Oststaaten *pl* (*in den USA*) Eastern states *pl*
Ost-West-Beziehungen ['ɔst·'vɛst-] *pl* East-West relations *pl*
Ostwind *m* east wind
Otter¹ <-, -n> ['ɔtɐ] *f* (*Schlangenart*) adder
Otter² <-s, -> ['ɔtɐ] *m* (*Fischotter*) otter
out [aut] *adj* (*fam*) ■ **~ sein** to be out
Outfit <-s, -s> ['aut·fɪt] *nt* (*sl*) outfit
Outing <-s, -s> ['au·tɪŋ] *nt* (*fam*) coming out
Output <-s, -s> ['aut·pʊt] *m o nt* output
oval [o·'vaːl] *adj* oval
Oval <-s, -e> [o·'vaːl] *nt* oval
Overall <-s, -s> ['oːvər·aːl, -roːl] *m* (*Schutzanzug*) overalls *npl*
Oxid <-[e]s, -e> [ɔ·'ksiːt, *pl* ɔ·'ksiː·də] *nt* oxide
Oxidation <-, -en> [ɔ·ksiː·da·'tsi̯oːn] *f* oxidation
oxidieren* [ɔ·ksi·'diː·rən] *vt, vi sein o haben* to oxidize
Ozean <-s, -e> ['oː·tseaːn] *m* ocean
Ozeandampfer *m* ocean liner
Ozon <-s> [o·'tsoːn] *nt o m kein pl* ozone
Ozonalarm *m* ozone warning
Ozongehalt *m* ozone concentration
Ozonloch *nt* ozone hole
Ozonschicht *f kein pl* ozone layer

O

Pp

P, p <-, - *o fam* -s, -s> [peː] *nt* P, p; **~ wie Paula** P as in Papa

paar [paːɐ̯] *adj inv* ■ **ein ~ ...** a few ...; **ein ~ Mal** a couple of times; **alle ~ Tage** every few days

Paar <-s, -e> [paːɐ̯] *nt* ❶ (*Menschen*) couple ❷ (*Dinge*) pair; **ein ~ Würstchen** a couple [of] sausages

paaren [paː·rən] *vr* ■ **sich** *akk* **~** ❶ (*kopulieren*) to mate ❷ (*sich verbinden*) to be coupled

Paarungszeit *f* mating season

paarweise *adv* in pairs

Pacht <-, -en> [paxt] *f* lease

pachten ['pax·tn̩] *vt* to lease

Pächter(in) <-s, -> ['pɛç·tɐ] *m(f)* tenant

Pack¹ <-[e]s, -e *o* Päcke> [pak, *pl* 'pa·kə, 'pɛ·kə] *m* (*Stapel*) stack; (*zusammengeschnürt*) pack

Pack² <-s> [pak] *nt kein pl* (*pej: Pöbel*) riffraff + *pl vb*

Packager(in) <-s, -> ['pɛ·kɪ·tʃə] *m(f)* sb [who goes] on a package tour

Päckchen <-s, -> ['pɛk·çən] *nt* ❶ (*Postsendung*) small package ❷ (*Packung*) pack, packet ❸ (*kleiner Packen*) small bundle

packen ['pa·kn̩] *vt* ❶ (*ergreifen*) to grab [hold of] (**bei, an** +*dat* by) ❷ (*vollpacken, verstauen*) to pack (**in** +*akk* in[to]); **ein Paket ~** to box up *sep* a package ❸ (*überkommen*) to seize; **von Ekel gepackt** utterly disgusted ❹ (*sl: bewältigen*) to manage; *Prüfung* to pass

Packen <-s, -> ['pakn̩] *m* stack; (*unordentlich a.*) pile; (*zusammengeschnürt*) bundle

packend *adj* absorbing; *Buch, Film* thrilling

Packesel *m* pack mule; (*fig*) packhorse

Packung <-, -en> *f* pack[age]; **eine ~ Pralinen** a box of chocolates

Pad <-s, -s> [pɛt] *nt* ❶ COMPUT [mouse] pad ❷ (*Wattebausch*) cotton ball ❸ (*Kaffeepad*) [coffee] pod

Pädagoge, Pädagogin <-n, -n> [pɛ·da·'goː·gə] *m, f* ❶ (*Lehrer*) teacher ❷ (*Erziehungswissenschaftler*) education[al] theorist

Pädagogik <-> [pɛ·da·'goː·gɪk] *f kein pl* pedagogy *spec*

pädagogisch [pɛ·da·'goː·gɪʃ] **I.** *adj* educational *attr;* **~e Fähigkeiten** teaching ability **II.** *adv* educationally

Paddel <-s, -> ['pa·dl̩] *nt* paddle

Paddelboot *nt* canoe

paddeln ['pa·dl̩n] *vi sein o haben* to paddle

paffen ['pa·fn̩] **I.** *vi* (*fam: rauchen*) to puff away; (*nicht inhalieren*) to puff **II.** *vt* (*fam*) ■ **etw ~** to puff away on sth

Page <-n, -n> ['paː·ʒə] *m* page

Paket <-[e]s, -e> [pa·'keːt] *nt* ❶ (*Postsendung*) package, parcel ❷ (*umhüllter Packen*) package ❸ (*Packung*) pack, packet ❹ (*Gesamtheit*) package ❺ (*Stapel*) stack

Paketbombe *f* parcel bomb

Paketschalter *m* package counter

Pakistan <-s> ['paː·kɪ·staːn] *nt* Pakistan; *s. a.* **Deutschland**

Pakistaner(in) <-s, -> [pa·kɪs·'taː·nɐ] *m(f),* **Pakistani** <-[s], -[s]> [pa·kɪs·'taː·ni] *m* Pakistani; *s. a.* **Deutsche(r)**

pakistanisch [pa·kɪs·'taː·nɪʃ] *adj* Pakistani; *s. a.* **deutsch**

Pakt <-[e]s, -e> [pakt] *m* pact

paktieren* [pak·'tiː·rən] *vi* ■ **mit jdm ~** to make a pact with sb

Palais <-, -> [pa·'lɛː, *pl* -'ɛːs] *nt* palace

Palast <-[e]s, Paläste> [pa·'last, *pl* pa·'lɛs·tə] *m* palace

Palästina <-s> [pa·lɛs·'tiː·na] *nt* Palestine; *s. a.* **Deutschland**

Palästinenser(in) <-s, -> [pa·lɛs·ti·'nɛn·zɐ] *m(f)* Palestinian; *s. a.* **Deutsche(r)**

palästinensisch [pa·lɛs·ti·'nɛn·zɪʃ] *adj* Palestinian

Palaver <-s, -> [pa·'laː·vɐ] *nt* (*fam*) palaver

palavern* [pa·'laː·vɐn] *vi* (*fam*) to palaver

Palette <-, -n> [pa·'lɛ·tə] *f* ❶ (*Stapelplatte*) pallet ❷ KUNST palette ❸ (*geh: reiche Vielfalt*) range

paletti [pa·'lɛ·ti] *adv* ▶ WENDUNGEN: **alles ~** (*sl*) everything's OK *fam*

Palme <-, -n> ['pal·mə] *f* palm [tree] ▶ WENDUNGEN: **jdn auf die ~ bringen** (*fam*) to drive sb up the wall

Palmsonntag [palm·'zɔn·taːk] *m* Palm Sunday

Palmtop <-s, -s> ['paːm·tɔp] *nt* COMPUT palmtop

Pampa <-, -s> ['pam·pa] *f* pampas + *sing/pl vb* ▶ WENDUNGEN: **[mitten] in der ~** (*fam*) in the middle of nowhere

Pampe <-> ['pam·pə] *f kein pl* DIAL (*pej fam*) mush; (*klebrig a.*) goo

Pampelmuse <-, -n> ['pam·pl̩·muː·zə, pam·pl̩·'muː·zə] *f* grapefruit

Pampers® <-, -> ['pɛm·pɐs] *f* Pampers®

pampig ['pam·pɪç] *adj* (*fam*) ❶ (*frech*) ill-tempered, snotty *fam* ❷ BES. NORDD, OSTD (*breiig*) mushy; (*klebrig a.*) gooey

Panama <-s> ['pa·na·ma] *nt* Panama; *s. a.* **Deutschland**

Panamaer(in) <-s, -> ['pa·na·ma·ɐ̯] *m(f)* Panamanian; *s. a.* **Deutsche(r)**

panamaisch [pa·na·'maː·ɪʃ] *adj* Panamanian; *s. a.* **deutsch**

Panda <-s, -s> ['pan·da] *m* [giant] panda

panieren* [pa·'niː·rən] *vt* to bread

Paniermehl *nt* breadcrumbs *pl*

Panik <-, -en> ['paː·nɪk] *f* panic; **in ~ geraten** to panic

panikartig *adj* panic-stricken

Panikmache <-> *f kein pl* (*pej fam*) scaremon-

P

gering

panisch ['paː·nɪʃ] **I.** *adj attr* panic-stricken **II.** *adv* in panic

Panne <-, -n> ['pa·nə] *f* ❶ AUTO, TECH breakdown ❷ (*Missgeschick*) mishap

Pannendienst <-es, -e> *m* tow[ing] service

Panorama <-s, Panoramen> [pa·no·'raː·ma, *pl* -'raː·mən] *nt* panorama

panschen ['pan·ʃn̩] **I.** *vt* to water down *sep* (*an alcoholic drink*) **II.** *vi* (*fam: planschen*) to splash around

PanterRR, **Panther** <-s, -> ['pan·tɐ] *m* panther

Pantoffel <-s, -n> [pan·'tɔ·fl̩] *m* [backless] slipper

Pantoffelheld *m* (*fam*) henpecked husband

Pantomime <-, -n> [pan·to·'miː·mə] *f* mime

Panzer <-s, -> ['pan·tsɐ] *m* ❶ MIL tank ❷ (*Schutzhülle*) shell; *eines Krokodils* bony plate; *eines Nashorns, Sauriers* armor

Panzerglas *nt* bulletproof glass

panzern ['pan·tsɐn] *vt* to armor-plate

Panzerschrank *m* safe

Panzerung <-, -en> *f* (*gepanzertes Gehäuse*) armor plating; *eines Reaktors* shield

Papa <-s, -s> ['pa·pa] *m* (*fam*) dad, daddy *esp childspeak*

Papagei <-s, -en> [pa·pa·'gai] *m* parrot

Paparazzo <-s, -zzi> [pa·pa·'ra·tso] *m* paparazzo

Papaya <-, -s> [pa·'paː·ja] *f* papaya

Paperback <-s, -s> ['peː·pɐ·bɛk] *nt* paperback

Papeterie <-, -n> [pa·pɛ·tə·'riː, *pl* -'riː·ən] *f* SCHWEIZ (*Schreibwarengeschäft*) stationary store

Papi <-s, -s> ['pa·pi] *m* (*fam*) *s.* **Papa**

Papier <-s, -e> [pa·'piːɐ̯] *nt* ❶ *kein pl* (*Material*) paper ❷ (*Schriftstück*) paper, document ❸ (*Ausweise*) ■ **~e** [identification] papers *pl*

Papierfabrik *f* paper mill

Papierhandtuch *nt* paper towel

Papierkorb *m* waste paper basket

Papierkram *m* (*fam*) paperwork

Papierkrieg *m* (*fam: Schreibtischarbeit*) paperwork, red tape

Papierstau *m* paper jam

Papiertaschentuch *nt* tissue

Pappbecher *m* paper cup

Pappdeckel *m* cardboard

Pappe <-, -n> ['pa·pə] *f* cardboard

Pappel <-, -n> ['pa·pl̩] *f* poplar

pappen ['pa·pn̩] *vt, vi* (*fam*) to stick (**an, auf** +*akk* on[to])

Pappenheimer ['pa·pn̩·hai·mɐ] *pl* ▶ WENDUNGEN: **seine ~ kennen** (*fam*) to know what to expect from them

pappig ['pa·pɪç] *adj* (*fam*) ❶ (*klebrig*) sticky ❷ (*breiig*) mushy

Pappkarton *m* ❶ (*Pappschachtel*) cardboard box ❷ (*Pappe*) cardboard

Pappteller *m* paper plate

Paprika <-s, -[s]> ['pa·pri·ka] *m* ❶ (*Strauch, Schote*) pepper ❷ *kein pl* (*Gewürz*) paprika

Paprikaschote *f* pepper

Papst <-[e]s, Päpste> [paːpst, *pl* 'pɛːps·tə] *m* ■ **der ~** the Pope

päpstlich ['pɛːpst·lɪç] *adj* papal *a. pej*

Parabolantenne [pa·ra·'boːl-] *f* satellite dish

Parade <-, -n> [pa·'raː·də] *f* ❶ MIL parade ❷ (*beim Ballspiel*) save

Paradebeispiel *nt* perfect example

Paradeiser <-s, -> [pa·ra·'dai·zɐ] *m* ÖSTERR tomato

Paradestück *nt* showpiece

Paradies <-es, -e> [pa·ra·'diːs, *pl* -'diː·zə] *nt* paradise *no def art* ▶ WENDUNGEN: **das ~ auf Erden** heaven on earth

paradiesisch [pa·ra·'diː·zɪʃ] **I.** *adj* heavenly **II.** *adv* **~ ruhig sein** to be blissfully quiet; **~ schön sein** to be [like] paradise

paradox [pa·ra·'dɔks] (*geh*) **I.** *adj* paradoxical **II.** *adv* paradoxically

paradoxerweise *adv* paradoxically

Paragliding <-s> ['paː·ra·glai·dɪŋ] *nt kein pl* paragliding

ParagrafRR, **Paragraph** <-en, -en> [pa·ra·'graːf] *m* paragraph

parallel [pa·ra·'leːl] *adj, adv* parallel

Parallele <-, -n> [pa·ra·'leː·lə] *f* ❶ MATH parallel [line] ❷ (*Entsprechung*) parallel; **eine ~ [zu etw** *dat*] **ziehen** to draw a parallel [to/with sth]

Parallelstraße *f* parallel street

Parameter <-s, -> [pa·'ra·me·tɐ] *m* parameter

paramilitärisch ['paː·ra·mi·li·tɛ·rɪʃ] *adj* paramilitary

paranoid [pa·ra·no·'iːt] *adj* paranoid

paranoisch [pa·ra·'noː·ɪʃ] *adj* paranoiac

paraphrasieren* [pa·ra·fra·'ziː·rən] *vt* to paraphrase

Parapsychologie ['paː·ra·psy·ço·lo·giː] *f* parapsychology

Parasit <-en, -en> [pa·ra·'ziːt] *m* parasite

parat [pa·'raːt] *adj* (*geh*) ready

Pärchen <-s, -> ['pɛːɐ̯·çən] *nt* ❶ (*Liebespaar*) couple ❷ (*zwei verbundene Teile*) pair

Pardon <-s> [par·'dõː] *m o nt kein pl* pardon; **kein ~ kennen** (*fam*) to know no mercy

Parfüm <-s, -e *o* -s> [par·'fyːm] *nt* perfume

Parfümerie <-, -n> [par·fy·mə·'riː, *pl* -'riː·ən] *f* perfumery

parfümieren* [par·fy·'miː·rən] *vt* to perfume; ■ **sich** *akk* **~** to put on *sep* perfume

parieren*1 [pa·'riː·rən] *vi* (*geh*) to obey

parieren*2 [pa·'riː·rən] *vt* (*geh*) to parry; (*beim Fußball*) to save [a goal]

Pariser1 [pa·'riː·zɐ] *adj attr* ❶ (*in Paris befindlich*) in Paris ❷ (*aus Paris stammend*) Parisian

Pariser2 <-s, -> [pa·'riː·zɐ] *m* (*sl*) condom

Park <-s, -s> [park] *m* park

Park-and-ride-System ['paːɐ̯k·ʔɛnt·'raɪt-] *nt* park-and-ride system

parken ['par·kn̩] *vi, vt* to park

Parkett <-s, -e> [par·'kɛt] *nt* ❶ (*Holzfußboden*) parquet [flooring] ❷ (*Tanzfläche*) dance

P

floor
Parkgebühr *f* parking fee
Parkhaus *nt* parking garage
parkinsonsche Krankheit^{RR} ['par·kɪn·zɔn-] *f* Parkinson's disease
Parkkralle *f* wheel clamp
Parklücke *f* parking space
Parkplatz *m* ① (*Parkbereich*) parking lot ② (*Parklücke*) parking space
Parkscheibe *f* parking disk (*for parking spaces with time limits to show what time the car was parked*)
Parkschein *m* parking lot ticket
Parkscheinautomat *m* ticket machine
Parksünder(in) *m(f)* parking offender
Parkuhr *f* parking meter
Parkverbot *nt* ① (*Verbot zu parken*) parking ban ② (*Parkverbotszone*) no-parking zone
Parkwächter(in) *m(f)* parking lot attendant
Parlament <-[e]s, -e> [par·la·'mɛnt] *nt* parliament; **das Europäische ~** the European Parliament
Parlamentarier(in) <-s, -> [par·la·mɛn·'taː·ri̯·ɐ] *m(f)* parliamentarian
parlamentarisch [par·la·mɛn·'taː·rɪʃ] *adj* parliamentary
Parlamentsausschuss^{RR} *m* parliamentary committee
Parlamentsbeschluss^{RR} *m* parliamentary decision [*or* vote]
Parmesan(käse) <-s> [par·me·'zaːn-] *m kein pl* Parmesan [cheese]
Parodie <-, -n> [pa·ro·'diː, *pl* -'diː·ən] *f* parody
parodieren* [pa·ro·'diː·rən] *vt* to parody
Parole <-, -n> [pa·'roː·lə] *f* ① MIL password ② (*Leitspruch*) slogan
Paroli [pa·'roː·li] *nt* ▶ WENDUNGEN: **jdm/etw ~ bieten** (*geh*) to defy sb/to counter sth
Part <-s, -s, o -e> [part] *m* ① (*Anteil*) share ② THEAT, MUS part
Partei <-, -en> [par·'tai] *f* ① POL, JUR party ② (*Mietpartei*) tenant ▶ WENDUNGEN: **für/gegen jdn ~ ergreifen** to side with/against sb
Parteibuch *nt* party membership book
Parteigenosse, -genossin <-n, -n> *m, f* party member
parteiisch [par·'tai·ɪʃ] **I.** *adj* biased **II.** *adv* in a biased way
parteilos *adj* independent
Parteimitglied *nt* party member
Parteinahme <-, -n> *f* partisanship
Parteipolitik *f* party politics + *sing vb*
Parteiprogramm *nt* party platform
Parteitag *m* ① (*Parteikonferenz*) party conference ② (*Beschlussorgan*) party executive
parteiübergreifend *adj* nonpartisan
Parteivorsitzende(r) *f(m)* party chairperson; party chairman *masc* [*or fem* -woman]
parterre [par·'tɛr] *adv* on the ground floor
Partie <-, -n> [par·'tiː, *pl* -'tiː·ən] *f* ① (*Köperbereich*) area ② SPORT game; **eine ~ Schach** a game of chess ▶ WENDUNGEN: **eine gute ~ machen** to marry well; **mit von der ~ sein** to be in on it
Partikelfilter *m* AUTO particulate filter
Partisan(in) <-s o -en, -en> [par·ti·'zaːn] *m(f)* partisan
Partizip <-s, -ien> [par·ti·'tsiːp, *pl* -'tsiː·pi̯·ən] *nt* participle
Partner(in) <-s, -> ['part·nɐ] *m(f)* partner
Partnerschaft <-, -en> *f* partnership; **in einer ~ leben** to live with somebody
partnerschaftlich I. *adj* based on partnership; **~es Zusammenleben** living together as partners **II.** *adv* as partners
Partnerstadt *f* sister city
Partnervermittlung *f* dating service
partout [par·'tuː] *adv* (*geh*) **etw ~ tun wollen** to insist on doing sth; **er wollte ~ nicht mitkommen** he did not want to come under any circumstances
Party <-, -s> ['paːɐ̯·ti] *f* party
Partyservice ['paːɐ·ti·zøːɐ̯·vɪs] *m* catering service
Parzelle <-, -n> [par·'tsɛ·lə] *f* plot [of land]
Pass^{RR}, **Paß**^{ALT} <Passes, Pässe> [pas, *pl* 'pɛ·sə] *m* ① (*Dokument*) passport ② GEOG pass
passabel [pa·'saː·bl̩] *adj* (*geh*) reasonable
Passage <-, -n> [pa·'saː·ʒə] *f* ① LIT, NAUT passage ② (*Ladenstraße*) [shopping] galleria
Passagier(in) <-s, -e> [pa·sa·'ʒiːɐ̯] *m(f)* passenger ▶ WENDUNGEN: **ein blinder ~** a stowaway
Passagierflugzeug *nt* passenger airplane
Passagierliste *f* passenger list
Passant(in) <-en, -en> [pa·'sant] *m(f)* passer-by
Passbild^{RR} *nt* passport photo[graph]
passé, passee^{RR} [pa·'seː] *adj* passé
passen ['pa·sn̩] *vi* ① (*von der Größe/Form her*) to fit ② (*harmonieren*) ■ **zu jdm ~** to suit sb; ■ **zu etw** *dat* **~** to go well with sth; **sie passt einfach nicht in unser Team** she simply doesn't fit in with our team ③ (*gelegen sein*) ■ **jdm ~** to suit sb; **der Termin passt mir zeitlich gar nicht** that day/time isn't convenient for me at all; **würde Ihnen der Dienstag besser ~?** would Tuesday be better for you?; **passt es Ihnen, wenn wir ...** is it okay with you if we ... ④ (*gefallen*) **ihr passt dieser Ton nicht** she doesn't like that tone of voice; ■ **jdm passt etw nicht [an jdm]** sb does not like sth [about sb] ⑤ (*fam*) ■ **[bei etw** *dat*] **~ müssen** (*überfragt sein*) to have to pass [on sth]
passend *adj* ① *Größe, Form* fitting; **ein ~er Anzug** a suit that fits ② *Farbe, Stil* matching ③ (*genehm*) convenient ④ (*richtig*) suitable; (*angemessen*) appropriate; *Bemerkung* fitting; **die ~en Worte finden** to find the right words ⑤ (*fam*) **es ~ haben** *Geldbetrag* to have exact change
Passfoto^{RR} *nt s.* **Passbild**
passierbar *adj Weg* negotiable; *Fluss* navigable
passieren* [pa·'siː·rən] **I.** *vi sein* to happen;

P

ist was passiert? has something happened?; **wie konnte das nur ~?** how could that happen?; **... sonst passiert was!** (*fam*) ... or else!; **so etwas passiert eben** shit happens *fam vulg* **II.** *vt haben* ① (*vorbeigehen, -fahren*) to pass ② (*überqueren*) to cross

Passierschein *m* permit

Passion <-, -en> [pa·ˈsi̯oːn] *f* (*geh: Leidenschaft*) passion

passioniert [pa·si̯o·ˈniːɐ̯t] *adj* (*geh*) passionate

Passionsfrucht *f* passion fruit

passiv [ˈpa·siːf] **I.** *adj* passive **II.** *adv* passively

Passiv <-s, -e> [ˈpa·siːf] *nt* passive

Passivität <-> [pa·si·vi·ˈtɛːt] *f kein pl* (*geh*) passivity

Passivrauchen *nt* passive smoking

Passkontrolle[RR] *f* ① (*das Kontrollieren*) passport check ② (*Kontrollstelle*) passport checkpoint

Passstelle[RR] *f* passport office

Passstraße[RR] *f* pass

Passwort[RR] <-es, -wörter> *nt* password

Paste <-, -n> [ˈpas·tə] *f* paste

Pastellfarbe *f* pastel color

Pastete <-, -n> [pas·ˈteː·tə] *f* pâté

Pastor, Pastorin <-s, -toren> [ˈpas·toːɐ̯, pas·ˈtoː·rɪn, *pl* -ˈtoː·rən] *m, f* NORDD *s.* **Pfarrer**

Pate, Patin <-n, -n> [ˈpaː·tə, ˈpaː·tɪn] *m, f* godfather *masc,* godmother *fem*

Patenkind *nt* godchild

Patenonkel *m* godfather

Patenschaft <-, -en> *f* ① REL godparenthood ② (*Fürsorgepflicht*) sponsorship

Patenstadt *f* sister city

patent [pa·ˈtɛnt] *adj* ① (*sehr brauchbar*) ingenious ② (*fam: tüchtig*) top-notch

Patent <-[e]s, -e> [pa·ˈtɛnt] *nt* ① (*amtlicher Schutz*) patent ② (*Ernennungsurkunde*) commission ③ SCHWEIZ (*staatliche Erlaubnis*) permit

Patentamt *nt* Patent Office

Patentante *f* godmother

patentieren* [pa·tɛn·ˈtiː·rən] *vt* ■ **[jdm] etw ~** to patent sth [for sb]

Patentlösung *f,* **Patentrezept** *nt* patent remedy, cure-all

pathetisch [pa·ˈteː·tɪʃ] (*geh*) **I.** *adj* impassioned **II.** *adv* [melo]dramatically

Pathologe, Pathologin <-n, -n> [pa·to·ˈloː·gə] *m, f* pathologist

Pathos <-> [ˈpaː·tɔs] *nt kein pl* emotiveness

Patient(in) <-en, -en> [pa·ˈtsi̯ɛnt] *m(f)* patient; **stationärer ~** inpatient

Patisserie <-, -n> [pa·tɪ·sə·ˈriː, *pl* -ˈriː·ən] *f* SCHWEIZ ① (*Konditorei*) patisserie ② (*Café*) café ③ (*Gebäck*) pastry

patriarchalisch [pa·tri·ar·ˈçaː·lɪʃ] *adj* patriarchal

Patriot(in) <-en, -en> [pa·tri·ˈoːt] *m(f)* patriot

patriotisch [pa·tri·ˈoː·tɪʃ] **I.** *adj* patriotic **II.** *adv* patriotically

Patriotismus <-> [pa·trio·ˈtɪs·mʊs] *m kein pl* patriotism

Patron(in) <-s, -e> [pa·ˈtroːn] *m(f)* ① REL patron saint ② (*Schirmherr*) patron ③ SCHWEIZ (*Arbeitgeber*) employer

Patrone <-, -n> [pa·ˈtroː·nə] *f* cartridge

Patrouille <-, -n> [pa·ˈtrʊl·jə] *f* patrol

patrouillieren* [pa·trʊl·ˈjiː·rən, pa·trʊ·ˈliː·rən] *vi* to patrol

Patsche [ˈpat·ʃə] *f* ▶ WENDUNGEN: **jdm aus der ~ helfen** (*fam*) to get sb out of a jam; **in der ~ sitzen** (*fam*) to be in a jam

patschnass[RR] [ˈpatʃ·ˈnas] *adj* (*fam*) soaking wet

Pattsituation *f* stalemate

Patzer <-s, -> *m* ① (*fam: Fehler*) slip-up ② ÖSTERR (*Klecks*) blob

patzig [ˈpa·tsɪç] *adj* (*fam*) snotty

Pauke <-, -n> [ˈpau·kə] *f* MUS kettledrum ▶ WENDUNGEN: **auf die ~ hauen** (*fam: angeben*) to toot one's [own] horn; (*ausgelassen feiern*) to paint the town red

pauken [ˈpau·kn̩] *vi, vt* (*fam*) to cram; **Vokabeln/Mathe ~** to cram for a vocabulary/math test

Pauker(in) <-s, -> [ˈpau·kɐ] *m(f)* (*fam*) teacher

Pausbacken [ˈpaus-] *pl* chubby cheeks *pl*

pauschal [pau·ˈʃaːl] **I.** *adj* ① (*undifferenziert*) sweeping ② FIN flat-rate *attr,* all-inclusive **II.** *adv* ① (*allgemein*) **etw ~ beurteilen** to make a wholesale judgment on sth ② FIN at a flat rate; **~ bezahlen** to pay in a lump sum

Pauschalbetrag *m* lump sum

Pauschale <-, -n> [pau·ˈʃaː·lə] *f* flat rate

pauschalisieren* [paʊ·ʃa·li·ˈziː·rən] *vt* to over-simplify

Pauschalpreis *m* all-inclusive price

Pauschalreise *f* package tour [*or* trip]

Pauschalurteil *nt* sweeping statement, overgeneralization

Pause <-, -n> [ˈpau·zə] *f* ① (*Unterbrechung*) break; SCH, POL recess; **[eine] ~ machen** to take a break ② (*Sprechpause*) pause ③ MUS rest

Pausenbrot *nt* snack

Pausenfüller *m* filler

Pausenhof *m* schoolyard

pausenlos **I.** *adj attr* continuous **II.** *adv* continuously

Pavillon <-s, -s> [ˈpa·vɪl·jõ, ˈpa·vɪl·jɔŋ] *m* pavilion

Pazifik <-s> [pa·ˈtsiː·fɪk] *m* ■ **der ~** the Pacific

pazifisch [pa·ˈtsiː·fɪʃ] *adj* Pacific; ■ **der P~e Ozean** the Pacific Ocean

Pazifist(in) <-en, -en> [pa·tsi·ˈfɪst] *m(f)* pacifist

pazifistisch *adj* pacifist

PC <-s, -s> [peː·ˈtseː] *m Abk von* **Personal Computer** PC

Pech <-[e]s> [pɛç] *nt kein pl* bad luck; **[bei etw** *dat***] ~ haben** to be unlucky [in/with sth]; **~ gehabt!** (*fam*) tough luck [*or fam vulg* shit]!

pechschwarz [ˈpɛç·ˈʃvarts] *adj* (*fam*) pitch-

P

black; *Haar* jet-black

Pechvogel *m* (*fam*) walking disaster *hum*

Pedal <-s, -e> [pe·ˈdaːl] *nt* pedal

Pedant(**in**) <-en, -en> [pe·ˈdant] *m(f)* pedant

pedantisch [pe·ˈdan·tɪʃ] **I.** *adj* pedantic **II.** *adv* pedantically

Pediküre <-, -n> [pe·di·ˈkyː·rə] *f* pedicure

Peeling <-s, -s> [ˈpiː·lɪŋ] *nt* exfoliation

Peepshow^RR <-, -s> [ˈpiːp·ʃoː] *f* peep show

Pegel <-s, -> [ˈpeː·gl̩] *m* ❶ (*Messlatte*) water level gauge ❷ *s.* **Pegelstand**

Pegelstand *m* water level

Peiniger(**in**) <-s, -> *m(f)* (*geh*) tormentor

peinlich [ˈpain·lɪç] **I.** *adj* ❶ (*unangenehm*) embarrassing; *Frage, Situation, Lage* awkward; **es war ihr sehr ~** she was really embarrassed [about it] ❷ (*äußerst*) painstaking; *Genauigkeit* meticulous; *Sauberkeit* scrupulous **II.** *adv* ❶ (*unangenehm*) **jdn ~ berühren** to be awkward for sb; **auf jdn ~ wirken** to be embarrassing for sb ❷ (*gewissenhaft*) painstakingly ❸ (*äußerst*) meticulously

Peitsche <-, -n> [ˈpai·tʃə] *f* whip

peitschen [ˈpai·tʃn̩] **I.** *vt haben* to whip **II.** *vi sein* to lash (**gegen** *+akk* against); **Regen peitscht gegen etw** rain is lashing against sth; **Wellen ~ an etw** waves are pounding sth

pejorativ [pe·jo·ra·ˈtiːf] **I.** *adj* pejorative **II.** *adv* pejoratively

Peking <-s> [ˈpeː·kɪŋ] *nt* Beijing

Pelikan <-s, -e> [ˈpeː·li·kaːn] *m* pelican

Pelle <-, -n> [ˈpɛ·lə] *f* (*fam: Haut*) skin ▶ WENDUNGEN: **jdm auf die ~ rücken** (*fam: sich dicht herandrängen*) to crowd sb; (*jdn bedrängen*) to badger sb

pellen [ˈpɛ·lən] *vt* (*fam*) to peel

Pellkartoffeln *pl* potatoes boiled in their skin

Pelz <-es, -e> [pɛlts] *m* fur

pelzig [ˈpɛl·tsɪç] *adj* furry

Pelzmantel *m* fur coat

Pendant <-s, -s> [pã·ˈdãː] *nt* (*geh*) counterpart (**zu** *+dat* to)

Pendel <-s, -> [ˈpɛn·dl̩] *nt* pendulum

pendeln [ˈpɛn·dl̩n] *vi* ❶ *haben* (*schwingen*) ■ [**hin und her**] **~** to swing [to and fro] ❷ *sein* TRANSP to commute

Pendelverkehr *m* ❶ (*Nahverkehrsdienst*) shuttle service ❷ (*Berufsverkehr*) commuter traffic

Pendler(**in**) <-s, -> [ˈpɛnd·lɐ] *m(f)* commuter

Penes [ˈpeː·neːs] *pl von* **Penis**

penetrant [pe·ne·ˈtrant] **I.** *adj* ❶ (*durchdringend*) penetrating; *Geruch* pungent ❷ (*aufdringlich*) overbearing **II.** *adv* penetratingly

penibel [pe·ˈniː·bl̩] *adj* (*geh*) *Ordnung* meticulous; *Mensch* fastidious (**in** *+dat* about)

Penicillin <-s, -e> [pe·ni·tsɪ·ˈliːn] *nt s.* **Penizillin**

Penis <-, -se *o* Penes> [ˈpeː·nɪs, *pl* ˈpeː·nɪ·sə, ˈpeː·neːs] *m* penis

Penizillin <-s, -e> [pe·ni·tsɪ·ˈliːn] *nt* penicillin

pennen [ˈpɛ·nən] *vi* (*fam o a. fig*) to sleep

Penner(**in**) <-s, -> *m(f)* (*pej fam: Stadtstreicher*) bum

Pensa [ˈpɛn·za], **Pensen** [ˈpɛn·zən] *pl von* **Pensum**

Pension <-, -en> [pã·ˈzi̯oːn, pɛn·ˈzi̯oːn] *f* ❶ TOURIST guesthouse ❷ (*Ruhegehalt*) pension; **in ~ gehen/sein** to retire/be retired

Pensionär(**in**) <-s, -e> [pã·zi̯o·ˈnɛːɐ, pɛn·zi̯o·ˈnɛːɐ] *m(f)* ❶ (*Ruheständler*) retiree ❷ SCHWEIZ boarding house guest

pensionieren* [pã·zi̯o·ˈniː·rən, pɛn·zi̯o·ˈniː·rən] *vt* ■ **pensioniert werden** to be retired off; ■ **sich** *akk* **~ lassen** to retire

Pensionierung <-, -en> *f* retirement

Pensionsalter *nt* retirement age

Pensum <-s, Pensa *o* Pensen> [ˈpɛn·zʊm, *pl* ˈpɛn·za, ˈpɛn·zən] *nt* (*geh*) work quota

Pentagon[1] <-s, -e> [pɛn·ta·ˈgoːn] *nt* (*Fünfeck*) pentagon

Pentagon[2] <-s> [ˈpɛn·ta·gɔn] *nt kein pl* (*US-Verteidigungsministerium*) ■ **das ~** the Pentagon

Penthaus, **Penthouse** <-, -s> [ˈpɛnt·haʊs, *pl* -haʊ·sɪz] *nt* penthouse

Pep <-[s]> [pɛp] *m kein pl* oomph

Peperoni [pe·pe·ˈroː·ni] *pl* ❶ (*scharfe Paprikas*) chili peppers *pl* ❷ SCHWEIZ (*Gemüsepaprikas*) bell peppers *pl*

peppig [ˈpɛ·pɪç] *adj* (*fam*) peppy

per [pɛr] *präp* ❶ (*durch*) by; **~ Post/Bahn** by mail/train ❷ **mit jdm ~ du/Sie sein** to address sb with "du"/"Sie"

perfekt [pɛr·ˈfɛkt] **I.** *adj* ❶ (*vollkommen*) perfect ❷ *pred* (*abgemacht*) ■ **~ sein** to be settled; **etw ~ machen** to settle sth **II.** *adv* perfectly

Perfekt <-s, -e> [ˈpɛr·fɛkt] *nt* perfect [tense]

Perfektion <-> [pɛr·fɛk·ˈtsi̯oːn] *f kein pl* perfection; **mit ~** to perfection

perfektionieren* [pɛr·fɛk·tsi̯o·ˈniː·rən] *vt* (*geh*) to perfect

Perfektionismus <-> [pɛr·fɛk·tsi̯o·ˈnɪs·mʊs] *m kein pl* perfectionism

Perfektionist(**in**) <-en, -en> [pɛr·fɛk·tsi̯o·ˈnɪst] *m(f)* perfectionist

Pergamentpapier *nt* wax paper

Periode <-, -n> [pe·ˈri̯oː·də] *f a.* BIOL period

periodisch [pe·ˈri̯oː·dɪʃ] **I.** *adj* periodic[al] **II.** *adv* periodically

Peripherie <-, -n> [pe·ri·fe·ˈriː, *pl* -ˈriː·ən] *f* periphery; COMPUT peripheral [device]

Perle <-, -n> [ˈpɛr·lə] *f* ❶ (*Schmuckperle*) pearl ❷ (*Kügelchen, Tropfen*) bead

Perlenkette *f* pearl necklace

Perlon® <-s> [ˈpɛr·lɔn] *nt kein pl* [type of] nylon

permanent [pɛr·ma·ˈnɛnt] (*geh*) **I.** *adj* permanent **II.** *adv* permanently

perplex [pɛr·ˈplɛks] *adj* dumbfounded

Perser(**in**) <-s, -> [ˈpɛr·zɐ] *m(f)* Persian

Perserteppich *m* Persian rug

Persien <-s> [ˈpɛr·zi̯·ən] *nt* Persia

persisch [ˈpɛr·zɪʃ] *adj* Persian

Person <-, -en> [pɛr·ˈzoːn] *f a.* LING person;

ich für meine ~ I myself
Personal <-s> [pɛr·zo·ˈnaːl] *nt kein pl* staff
Personalabbau *m* downsizing, staff cuts *pl*
Personalabteilung *f* personnel department, human resources
Personalausweis *m* identity card, ID
Personalchef(in) *m(f)* head of personnel [*or* human resources]
Personal Computer [ˈpəː·sə·nəl-] *m* personal computer
Personalien [pɛr·zo·ˈnaː·li̯·ən] *pl* particulars *npl*
Personalpronomen *nt* personal pronoun
personell [pɛr·zo·ˈnɛl] **I.** *adj* personnel *attr*, staff *attr* **II.** *adv* as regards personnel
Personenbeförderung *f* transportation of passengers
Personengedächtnis *nt* memory for faces
Personenkraftwagen *m* automobile
Personenkreis *m* group of people
Personennahverkehr *m* local passenger transportation
Personenschaden *m* personal injury
Personenschutz *m* personal security [*or* protection]
Personenverkehr *m* passenger transportation
persönlich [pɛr·ˈzøːn·lɪç] **I.** *adj* ❶ (*jdn selbst betreffend*) personal ❷ **~ werden** to get personal **II.** *adv* personally; **~ erscheinen** to appear in person; **~ befreundet sein** to be personal friends
Persönlichkeit <-, -en> *f* ❶ *kein pl* (*Eigenart*) personality ❷ (*markanter Mensch*) character ❸ (*Prominenter*) celebrity
Perspektive <-, -n> [pɛrs·pɛk·ˈtiː·və] *f* ❶ (*Blickwinkel*) perspective ❷ (*geh: Zukunftsaussicht*) prospect *usu pl*
perspektivlos *adj* without prospects
Perspektivlosigkeit <-> *f kein pl* hopelessness
Perücke <-, -n> [pe·ˈrʏ·kə] *f* wig
pervers [pɛr·ˈvɛrs] *adj* ❶ (*widernatürlich*) perverted ❷ (*fam: abartig*) perverse
Perversion <-, -en> [pɛr·vɛr·ˈzi̯oːn] *f* perversion
pervertieren* [pɛr·vɛr·ˈtiː·rən] (*geh*) **I.** *vt haben* to warp **II.** *vi sein* to become perverted (**zu** +*dat* into)
pesen [ˈpeː·zn̩] *vi sein* (*fam*) to dash
Pessar <-s, -e> [pɛ·ˈsaːɐ̯] *nt* MED diaphragm
Pessimismus <-> [pɛ·si·ˈmɪs·mʊs] *m kein pl* pessimism
Pessimist(in) <-en, -en> [pɛ·si·ˈmɪst] *m(f)* pessimist
pessimistisch [pɛ·si·ˈmɪs·tɪʃ] **I.** *adj* pessimistic **II.** *adv* pessimistically
Pest <-> [pɛst] *f kein pl* ■ **die ~** the plague ▶ WENDUNGEN: **jdn wie die ~ hassen** (*fam*) to hate sb's guts; **wie die ~ stinken** (*fam*) to stink to high heaven
Pestizid <-s, -e> [pɛs·ti·ˈtsiːt] *nt* pesticide
Petersilie <-, -n> [pe·tɐ·ˈziː·li̯·ə] *f* parsley
Petition <-, -en> [pe·ti·ˈtsi̯oːn] *f* petition
Petroleum <-s> [pe·ˈtroː·le·ʊm] *nt kein pl* kerosene
petto [ˈpɛto] *adv* ▶ WENDUNGEN: **etw in ~ haben** (*fam*) to have sth up one's sleeve
Petze <-, -n> [ˈpɛ·tsə] *f* (*pej fam*) tattletale
petzen [ˈpɛ·tsn̩] **I.** *vt* (*pej fam*) ■ **[jdm] etw ~** to tell [sb] about sth **II.** *vi* (*pej fam*) to tell
Pfad <-[e]s, -e> [pfaːt, *pl* ˈpfaː·də] *m* path
Pfadfinder(in) <-s, -> *m(f)* Boy Scout; (*Mädchen*) Girl Scout
Pfaffe <-n, -n> [ˈpfa·fə] *m* (*pej*) cleric
Pfahl <-[e]s, Pfähle> [pfaːl, *pl* ˈpfɛː·lə] *m* post, stake
Pfälzer(in) <-s, -> [ˈpfɛl·tsɐ] *m(f)* sb from the Palatinate
pfälzisch [ˈpfɛl·tsɪʃ] *adj* Palatine
Pfand <-[e]s, Pfänder> [pfant, *pl* ˈpfɛn·dɐ] *nt* deposit
pfänden [ˈpfɛn·dn̩] *vt* ❶ (*beschlagnahmen*) to impound ❷ (*Pfandsiegel anbringen*) ■ **jdn ~** to seize some of sb's possessions
Pfandflasche *f* deposit bottle
Pfandgeld *nt* deposit
Pfandhaus *nt* pawnshop
Pfandleihe <-, -n> *f* pawnshop
Pfandschein *m* pawn ticket
Pfändung <-, -en> *f* seizure
Pfanne <-, -n> [ˈpfa·nə] *f* ❶ (*Bratpfanne*) [frying] pan ❷ SCHWEIZ (*Topf*) pot ▶ WENDUNGEN: **jdn in die ~ hauen** (*sl*) to play a mean trick on sb
Pfannkuchen *m* pancake; (*dünner*) crepe
Pfarramt *nt* vicarage
Pfarrbezirk *m* parish
Pfarrei <-, -en> [pfa·ˈrai] *f* ❶ (*Gemeinde*) parish ❷ *s.* **Pfarramt**
Pfarrer(in) <-s, -> [ˈpfa·rɐ] *m(f)* (*katholisch*) priest; (*evangelisch*) minister
Pfarrgemeinde *f* parish
Pfau <-[e]s *o* -en, -en> [pfau] *m* peacock
Pfeffer <-s, -> [ˈpfɛ·fɐ] *m* pepper ▶ WENDUNGEN: **hingehen, wo der ~ wächst** (*fam*) to go to hell
Pfefferkorn [ˈpfɛ·fɐ·kɔrn] *nt* peppercorn
Pfefferminze *f kein pl* peppermint
Pfefferminztee *m* peppermint tea
Pfeffermühle *f* pepper mill
pfeffern [ˈpfɛ·fɐn] *vt* ❶ KOCHK to season with pepper ❷ (*fam: schleudern*) ■ **etw irgendwohin ~** to fling sth somewhere ▶ WENDUNGEN: **jdm eine ~** (*fam*) to smack sb in the face
Pfefferstreuer <-s, -> *m* pepper shaker
Pfeife <-, -n> [ˈpfai·fə] *f* ❶ (*Musikinstrument, Orgelpfeife*) pipe ❷ (*Trillerpfeife*) whistle ❸ (*Tabakpfeife*) pipe ❹ (*sl: Nichtskönner*) loser ▶ WENDUNGEN: **nach jds ~ tanzen** to dance to sb's tune
pfeifen <pfiff, gepfiffen> [ˈpfaifn̩] **I.** *vi, vt* to whistle **II.** *vi* ■ **auf etw ~** (*fam*) to not give a damn about sth
Pfeifkonzert *nt* chorus of boos
Pfeifton *m* whistle
Pfeil <-s, -e> [pfail] *m* (*a. Richtungspfeil*) ar-

P

row

Pfeiler <-s, -> ['pfai·lɐ] *m* pillar

Pfeilspitze *f* arrowhead

Pfennig <-s, -e *o meist nach Zahlenangaben* -> ['pfɛ·nɪç] *m* (*hist*) pfennig; **keinen ~ [Geld] haben** to be penniless ▶ WENDUNGEN: **keinen ~ wert sein** (*fam*) to be worthless; **jeden ~ umdrehen** (*fam*) to think twice about every penny one spends

Pfennigfuchser(in) <-s, -> [-fʊk·sɐ] *m(f)* (*fam*) stinge

pferchen ['pfɛr·çn̩] *vt* to cram (**in** +*akk* into)

Pferd <-[e]s, -e> [pfeːɐ̯t, *pl* -də] *nt* ❶ (*Tier*) horse ❷ (*Schachfigur*) knight ▶ WENDUNGEN: **das ~ beim Schwanz[e] aufzäumen** (*fam*) to put the cart before the horse; **die ~e scheu machen** (*fam*) to put people off; **ich glaub' mich tritt ein ~!** (*fam*) well I'll be damned!

Pferdeapfel *m meist pl* horse droppings *npl*

Pferderennen *nt* horse race

Pferdeschwanz *m* ❶ (*vom Pferd*) horse's tail ❷ (*Frisur*) ponytail

Pferdestall *m* stable

pfiff [pfɪf] *imp von* **pfeifen**

Pfiff <-s, -e> [pfɪf] *m* ❶ (*Pfeifton*) whistle ❷ (*fam: Reiz*) pizzazz

Pfifferling <-[e]s, -e> ['pfɪ·fɐ·lɪŋ] *m* chanterelle ▶ WENDUNGEN: **keinen ~ wert sein** to be worthless

pfiffig ['pfɪ·fɪç] **I.** *adj* smart **II.** *adv* smartly

Pfiffikus <-[ses], -se> ['pfɪ·fi·kʊs] *m* (*hum fam*) smart cookie *fig*

Pfingsten <-, -> ['pfɪŋs·tn̩] *nt meist ohne art* Whitsuntide

Pfingstmontag *m* Whitmonday

Pfingstsonntag *m* Pentecost, Whitsunday

Pfirsich <-s, -e> ['pfɪr·zɪç] *m* peach

Pflanze <-, -n> ['pflan·tsə] *f* plant

pflanzen ['pflan·tsn̩] **I.** *vt* to plant **II.** *vr* (*fam*) **sich** *akk* **auf das Sofa ~** to plunk oneself down on the sofa

Pflanzenöl *nt* vegetable oil

Pflanzenschutzmittel *nt* pesticide

pflanzlich *adj attr* ❶ (*vegetarisch*) vegetarian ❷ (*aus Pflanzen gewonnen*) plant-based

Pflaster <-s, -> ['pflas·tɐ] *nt* ❶ MED band-aid ❷ BAU pavement ▶ WENDUNGEN: **ein gefährliches ~** (*fam*) a dangerous place

pflastern ['pflas·tɐn] *vt* to surface; **etw mit Steinplatten ~** to pave sth with flagstones

Pflasterstein *m* paving stone

Pflaume <-, -n> ['pflau·mə] *f* ❶ (*Frucht*) plum ❷ (*fam: Pfeife*) twit *pej*

Pflaumenmus *nt* plum jam

Pflege <-> ['pfleː·gə] *f kein pl* ❶ *eines Kranken* [nursing] care ❷ *des Körpers* grooming ❸ *von Pflanzen, des Gartens* care ❹ (*Obhut*) **ein Kind in ~ nehmen** to foster a child

pflegebedürftig *adj* in need of care *pred*

Pflegeeltern *pl* foster parents *pl*

Pflegefall *m* sb who needs long-term care

Pflegeheim *nt* nursing home

Pflegekind *nt* foster child

pflegeleicht *adj* easy to care for *attr; Tier, Mensch* low-maintenance *attr*

pflegen ['pfleː·gn̩] **I.** *vt* ❶ *Kranke* to care for, to look after ❷ *Körper* to treat ❸ *Pflanzen, Garten* to tend ❹ (*gewöhnlich tun*) ■ **etw zu tun ~** to usually do sth **II.** *vr* ■ **sich** *akk* **~** to take care of one's appearance

Pflegepersonal *nt* nursing staff + *sing/pl vb*

Pfleger(in) <-s, -> *m(f)* [male] nurse *masc*, nurse *fem*

Pflegesatz *m* [daily] hospital charges *pl*

Pflegeversicherung *f* long-term care insurance

pfleglich ['pfleːk·lɪç] *adv* carefully, with care

Pflegschaft <-, -en> *f* guardianship

Pflicht <-, -en> [pflɪçt] *f* duty

pflichtbewusstRR *adj* conscientious

PflichtbewusstseinRR *nt* sense of duty

Pflichtgefühl *nt kein pl s.* **Pflichtbewusstsein**

pflichtgemäß **I.** *adj* dutiful **II.** *adv* dutifully

Pflichtverteidiger(in) *m(f)* court-appointed defense lawyer

Pflock <-[e]s, Pflöcke> [pflɔk, *pl* 'pflœ·kə] *m* stake; (*Zeltpflock*) peg

pflücken ['pflʏ·kn̩] *vt* to pick

Pflug <-es, Pflüge> [pfluːk, *pl* 'pflyː·gə] *m* plow

pflügen *vi, vt* to plow

Pflümli <-, -s> *nt* SCHWEIZ plum schnapps

Pforte <-, -n> ['pfɔr·tə] *f* gate

Pförtner(in) <-s, -> ['pfœrt·nɐ] *m(f)* doorman

Pfosten <-s, -> ['pfɔs·tn̩] *m a.* SPORT post

Pfote <-, -n> ['pfoː·tə] *f* ❶ (*von Tieren*) paw ❷ (*fam: Hand*) paw

Pfropfen <-s, -> ['pfrɔp·fn̩] *m* stopper

Pfund <-[e]s, -e *o nach Zahlenangaben* -> [pfʊnt, *pl* 'pfʊn·də] *nt* ❶ (*500 Gramm*) ≈ pound ❷ (*Währungseinheit*) pound; **in ~** in pounds

pfundig ['pfʊn·dɪç] *adj* (*fam*) great

Pfundskerl ['pfʊnts·'kɛrl] *m* DIAL (*fam*) great guy

Pfusch <-[e]s> [pfʊʃ] *m kein pl* (*fam*), **Pfuscharbeit** *f kein pl* (*fam*) lousy [*or* sloppy] job

pfuschen ['pfʊ·ʃn̩] *vi* ❶ (*schlampen*) to be sloppy ❷ DIAL (*mogeln*) to cheat (**bei** +*dat* at, in, on)

Pfuscherei <-, -en> [pfʊ·ʃɛ·'rai] *f* bungling

Pfütze <-, -n> ['pfʏ·tsə] *f* puddle

Phänomen <-s, -e> [fɛ·no·'meːn] *nt* phenomenon

phänomenal [fɛ·no·me·'naːl] *adj* phenomenal

Phantasie <-, -n> [fan·ta·'ziː, *pl* -'ziː·ən] *f s.* **Fantasie**

phantasieren* [fan·ta·'ziː·rən] *s.* **fantasieren**

Phantast(in) <-en, -en> [fan·'tast] *m(f) s.* **Fantast**

Phantasterei <-, -en> [fan·tas·tə·'rai] *f s.* **Fantasterei**

phantastisch [fan·'tas·tɪʃ] *adj, adv s.* **fantastisch**

P

Phantom <-s, -e> [fan·ˈtoːm] *nt* phantom
Phantombild *nt* composite sketch
Phantomschmerz *m* phantom limb pain
Pharmazie <-> [far·ma·ˈtsiː] *f kein pl* pharmacy
Phase <-, -n> [ˈfaː·zə] *f a.* ELEK phase
Philippinen [fi·lɪ·ˈpiː·nən] *pl* ■**die** ~ the Philippines *pl*
Philippiner(in) <-s, -> [fi·lɪ·ˈpiː·nɐ] *m(f)* Filipino; *s. a.* **Deutsche(r)**
philippinisch [fi·lɪ·ˈpiː·nɪʃ] *adj* Filipino; *s. a.* **deutsch**
Philologe, Philologin <-n, -n> [fi·lo·ˈloː·gə] *m, f* philologist
Philosoph(in) <-en, -en> [fi·lo·ˈzoːf] *m(f)* philosopher
Philosophie <-, -n> [fi·lo·zo·ˈfiː, *pl* -ˈfiː·ən] *f* philosophy
philosophieren* [fi·lo·zo·ˈfiː·rən] *vi* (*geh*) to philosophize (**über** +*akk* about)
philosophisch [fi·lo·ˈzoː·fɪʃ] *adj* philosophical
phlegmatisch [flɛg·ˈmaː·tɪʃ] *adj* (*geh*) phlegmatic
Phobie <-, -n> [fo·ˈbiː, *pl* -ˈbiː·ən] *f* phobia
Phosphat <-[e]s, -e> [fɔs·ˈfaːt] *nt* phosphate
Phosphor <-s> [ˈfɔs·foːɐ̯] *m kein pl* phosphorus
Photo <-s, -s> [ˈfoː·to] *nt s.* **Foto**
Phrase <-, -n> [ˈfraː·zə] *f* (*pej*) empty phrase
Physik <-> [fy·ˈziːk] *f kein pl* physics + *sing vb, no art*
physikalisch [fy·zi·ˈkaː·lɪʃ] *adj* physical
Physiker(in) <-s, -> [ˈfyː·zi·kɐ] *m(f)* physicist
Physiognomie <-, -n> [fy·zi̯o·gno·ˈmiː, *pl* -ˈmiː·ən] *f* (*geh*) physiognomy
Physiologie <-> [fy·zi̯o·lo·ˈgiː] *f kein pl* physiology
physiologisch [fy·zi̯o·ˈloː·gɪʃ] *adj* physiological
Physiotherapeut(in) <-en, -en> [fy·zi̯o·te·ra·ˈpɔyt] *m(f)* physical therapist
Physiotherapie [fy·zi̯o·te·ra·ˈpiː] *f kein pl* physical therapy
physisch [ˈfyː·zɪʃ] *adj* physical
Pianist(in) <-en, -en> [pi̯a·ˈnɪst] *m(f)* pianist
Piano <-s, -s> [ˈpi̯aː·no] *nt* (*geh*) piano
Pickel <-s, -> [ˈpɪ·kl̩] *m* ① (*Hautunreinheit*) pimple, zit *fam* ② (*Spitzhacke*) pickax; (*Eispickel*) ice pick
pickelig [ˈpɪ·kə·lɪç] *adj* pimply
picken [ˈpɪ·kn̩] **I.** *vi* ORN to peck (**nach** +*dat* at) **II.** *vt* ① (*fam*) *Person* to pick, to choose ② ÖSTERR (*kleben*) to stick
picklig [ˈpɪk·lɪç] *adj s.* **pickelig**
Picknick <-s, -s *o* -e> [ˈpɪk·nɪk] *nt* picnic
picknicken [ˈpɪk·nɪ·kn̩] *vi* to [have a] picnic
Piep [piːp] *m* (*fam*) ▶WENDUNGEN: **keinen ~ sagen** (*fam*) to not make a sound; **keinen ~ mehr sagen** (*fam*) to be a goner
piepe [ˈpiː·pə], **piepegal** [ˈpiːp·ʔe·ˈgaːl] *adj pred* (*fam*) ■**[jdm] ~ sein** to be all the same [to sb]
piepen [ˈpiː·pn̩] *vi* ① (*leise Pfeiftöne erzeugen*) to peep; (*Maus*) to squeak ② (*hohe Töne erzeugen*) *Gerät* to beep ③ **bei jdm piept es** (*fam*) sb is off their rocker *sl*
piepsen [ˈpiːp·sn̩] **I.** *vi* ① *s.* **piepen 1, 2** ② (*mit hoher Stimme sprechen/singen*) to pipe **II.** *vt* ■**etw ~** to say/sing sth in a squeaky voice
Piepser <-s, -> *m* (*fam*) beeper
piepsig [ˈpiːp·sɪç] *adj* (*fam*) *Stimme* squeaky
Pier <-s, -s *o* -e> [piːɐ̯] *m* pier
Piercing <-s, -s> [ˈpiːɐ̯·sɪŋ] *nt* piercing
piesacken [ˈpiː·za·kn̩] *vt* (*fam*) to pester
pieseln [ˈpiː·zl̩n] *vi* (*fam*) ① (*fein regnen*) to drizzle ② (*urinieren*) to pee
Pietät <-> [pi̯e·ˈtɛːt] *f kein pl* (*geh*) respect; (*Ehrfurcht*) reverence
pietätlos *adj* (*geh*) irreverent
pikant [pi·ˈkant] **I.** *adj* ① KOCHK spicy ② (*frivol*) racy **II.** *adv* piquantly
piken [ˈpiː·kn̩] *vt, vi* (*fam*) *s.* **piksen**
pikiert [pi·ˈkiːrt] (*geh*) **I.** *adj* peeved **II.** *adv* peevishly
piksen [ˈpiːk·sn̩] **I.** *vt* (*fam*) to prick (**mit** +*dat* with) **II.** *vi* (*fam*) to prickle
Pilger(in) <-s, -> [ˈpɪl·gɐ] *m(f)* pilgrim
Pilgerfahrt *f* pilgrimage
pilgern [ˈpɪl·gɐn] *vi sein* ① (*fam: gehen, marschieren*) to wend one's way ② (*wallfahren*) to make a pilgrimage (**nach** to)
Pille <-, -n> [ˈpɪ·lə] *f* pill; ■**die ~** (*Antibabypille*) the pill; **die ~ danach** the morning-after pill ▶WENDUNGEN: **eine bittere ~ schlucken müssen** (*fam*) to have a bitter pill to swallow
Pilot(in) <-en, -en> [pi·ˈloːt] *m(f)* pilot
Pilotprojekt *nt* pilot project
Pilotversuch *m* pilot project
Pils <-, -> [pɪls] *nt* pilsner
Pilz <-es, -e> [pɪlts] *m* ① BOT fungus; (*Speisepilz*) mushroom ② MED fungal skin infection ▶WENDUNGEN: **wie ~e aus dem Boden schießen** to shoot up
Pilzerkrankung *f* fungal disease
Pimmel <-s, -> [ˈpɪ·ml̩] *m* (*fam*) wiener *vulg sl,* weenie *vulg sl*
pingelig [ˈpɪŋə·lɪç] *adj* (*fam*) fussy
Pinguin <-s, -e> [ˈpɪŋ·guiːn] *m* penguin
pink [pɪŋk] *adj inv* pink
Pinkel[1] <-s, -> [ˈpɪŋ·kl̩] *m* **ein feiner ~** (*fam*) a dandy
Pinkel[2] <-, -n> [ˈpɪŋkl̩] *f* KOCHK NORDD *spicy smoked fatty pork/beef sausage (eaten with curly kale)*
pinkeln [ˈpɪŋ·kl̩n] *vi* (*fam*) to pee
Pinnwand *f* bulletin board
Pinsel <-s, -> [ˈpɪn·zl̩] *m* brush
Pinte <-, -n> [ˈpɪn·tə] *f* (*fam*) bar, pub
Pinzette <-, -n> [pɪn·ˈtsɛ·tə] *f* tweezers *npl*
Pionier(in) <-s, -e> [pi̯o·ˈniːɐ̯] *m(f)* (*geh: Wegbereiter*) pioneer
Pionierarbeit *f* pioneering work
Pipapo <-s> [pi·pa·ˈpoː] *nt kein pl* (*fam*) **mit allem ~** with all the frills; **das ganze ~** the whole shebang

P

Pipeline <-, -s> ['paip·lain] *f* pipeline
Pipi <-s> [pi·'piː] *nt kein pl* (*Kindersprache*) pee-pee, wee-wee; ~ **machen** to go pee-pee
Pipifax <-> ['pɪ·pi·faks] *nt kein pl* (*fam*) nonsense
Piranha <-[s], -s> [pi·'ran·ja] *m* piranha
Pirat(in) <-en, -en> [pi·'raːt] *m(f)* pirate
Pirsch [pɪrʃ] *f* **auf die ~ gehen** to go [deer] hunting
Pisse <-> ['pɪ·sə] *f kein pl* (*derb*) piss
pissen ['pɪ·sn̩] *vi* ❶ (*derb: urinieren*) to piss ❷ *impers* (*sl: stark regnen*) **es pisst** it's pouring
Pissoir <-s, -s *o* -e> [pɪ·'so̯aːɐ̯] *nt* urinal
Pistazie <-, -n> [pɪs·'taː·tsi̯ə] *f* pistachio
Piste <-, -n> ['pɪs·tə] *f* ❶ (*Skipiste*) ski slope [*or* run] ❷ (*unbefestigter Weg, Rennstrecke*) track ❸ (*Rollbahn*) runway
Pistole <-, -n> [pɪs·'toː·lə] *f* pistol ▶ WENDUNGEN: **jdm die ~ auf die Brust setzen** (*fam*) to hold a gun to sb's head
Pizza <-, -s> ['pɪ·tsa] *f* pizza
Pkw <-s, -s> ['peː·kaː·veː] *m Abk von* **Personenkraftwagen**
Plackerei <-, -en> [pla·kə·'rai] *f* (*fam*) grind
plädieren* [plɛ·'diː·rən] *vi* ❶ JUR ■ **auf etw ~** to plead sth; **auf schuldig ~** to plead guilty ❷ (*fig geh*) ■ **für etw ~** to plead for sth
Plädoyer <-s, -s> [plɛ·do̯a·'jeː] *nt* ❶ JUR summation ❷ (*fig geh*) plea
Plage <-, -n> ['plaː·gə] *f* nuisance
Plagegeist *m* (*pej fam*) nuisance
plagen ['plaː·gn̩] **I.** *vt* ❶ (*behelligen*) *mit Fragen, Bitten* to pester ❷ (*quälen*) to bother; **Zweifel plagten ihn** he was plagued with doubt **II.** *vr* ■ **sich** *akk* [**mit etw** *dat*] **~** ❶ (*sich abrackern*) to slave away [over sth] ❷ (*sich herumplagen*) to be bothered [by sth]
Plakat <-[e]s, -e> [pla·'kaːt] *nt* poster
Plakatwand *f* billboard
Plakette <-, -n> [pla·'kɛ·tə] *f* (*Anstecker*) badge; (*Aufkleber, TÜV-Plakette*) sticker
Plan <-[e]s, Pläne> [plaːn, *pl* 'plɛː·nə] *m* ❶ (*Vorhaben*) plan; **nach ~ laufen** to go according to plan; **jds Pläne durchkreuzen** to thwart sb's plans ❷ GEOG, TRANSP map ❸ (*zeichnerische Darstellung*) plan
Plane <-, -n> ['plaː·nə] *f* tarp *fam*
planen ['plaː·nən] *vt* to plan
Planer(in) <-s, -> *m(f)* planner
Planet <-en, -en> [pla·'neːt] *m* planet
Planetarium <-s, -tarien> [pla·ne·'taː·ri̯·ʊm, *pl* -'taː·ri̯·ən] *nt* planetarium
planieren* [pla·'niː·rən] *vt* to level [off]
Planierraupe *f* bulldozer
Planke <-, -n> ['plaŋ·kə] *f* plank
planlos *adj* ❶ (*ziellos*) aimless ❷ (*ohne System*) unsystematic
planmäßig **I.** *adj* ❶ TRANSP scheduled ❷ (*systematisch*) systematic **II.** *adv* ❶ TRANSP as scheduled, according to schedule ❷ (*systematisch*) systematically
Planschbecken *nt* kiddie pool
planschen ['plan·ʃn̩] *vi* to splash around
Plantage <-, -n> [plan·'taː·ʒə] *f* plantation
Planung <-, -en> *f* ❶ (*das Planen*) planning; **in der ~ befindlich** in the planning stage ❷ (*Plan*) plan
Plappermaul *nt* (*bes pej fam*) blabbermouth
plappern ['pla·pɐn] (*fam*) **I.** *vi* to chatter **II.** *vt* **Unsinn ~** to babble nonsense
plärren ['plɛ·rən] *vi* (*fam*) ❶ (*heulen*) to bawl ❷ (*blechern ertönen*) to blare [out]
Plastik¹ <-s> ['plas·tɪk] *nt kein pl* plastic
Plastik² <-, -en> ['plas·tɪk] *f* (*Kunstwerk*) sculpture
Plastikbecher *m* plastic cup
Plastikfolie *f* plastic wrap
Plastikgeld *nt* (*fam*) plastic [money]
Plastiktüte *f* plastic bag
plastisch ['plas·tɪʃ] **I.** *adj* (*anschaulich*) vivid **II.** *adv* (*anschaulich*) vividly
Platane <-, -n> [pla·'taː·nə] *f* plane tree
Plateau <-s, -s> [pla·'toː] *nt* plateau
Platin <-s> ['plaː·tiːn] *nt kein pl* platinum
Platine <-, -n> [pla·'tiː·nə] *f* ❶ TECH circuit board ❷ COMPUT card
platonisch [pla·'toː·nɪʃ] *adj* (*geh*) platonic
plätschern ['plɛ·tʃɐn] *vi* *Brunnen* to splash; *Bach* to babble; *Regen* to patter
platt [plat] **I.** *adj* ❶ (*flach*) flat ❷ (*geistlos*) dull ❸ (*fam: verblüfft*) ■ **~ sein** to be flabbergasted **II.** *adv* flat; **~ drücken/walzen** to flatten
Platt <-[s]> [plat] *nt kein pl*, **Plattdeutsch** ['plat·dɔytʃ] *nt* Low German
Platte <-, -n> ['pla·tə] *f* ❶ (*Steinplatte*) slab ❷ (*Metalltafel*) sheet ❸ (*Schallplatte*) record ❹ (*Servierteller, Gericht*) platter ❺ (*Kochplatte*) burner ❻ (*fam: Glatze*) **eine ~ haben** to be bald ▶ WENDUNGEN: **die ~ schon kennen** (*fam*) to have heard that one before
Plätteisen *nt* NORDD [smoothing] iron
Platten einen ~ haben to have a flat [tire]
plätten ['plɛ·tn̩] *vt* DIAL to iron
Plattenfirma *f* record company
Plattenlaufwerk *nt* disk drive
Plattenspieler *m* record player
Plattform *f a.* COMPUT platform
Plattfuß *m* ❶ MED flat foot ❷ (*fam: platter Reifen*) flat [tire]
Platz <-es, Plätze> [plats, *pl* 'plɛ·tsə] *m* ❶ (*Ort, Stelle*) place ❷ (*öffentlicher Platz*) square ❸ (*Sitzplatz*) seat; **~ nehmen** (*geh*) to take a seat ❹ (*freier Raum*) room ❺ (*Sportplatz*) playing field; **jdn vom ~ stellen** to throw [*or* kick] sb out ❻ (*Rang*) place; **er liegt jetzt auf ~ drei** he's now in third place ▶ WENDUNGEN: **fehl am ~[e] sein** to be out of place
Platzangst *f* ❶ (*fam*) claustrophobia ❷ (*Agoraphobie*) agoraphobia
Plätzchen <-s, -> ['plɛts·çən] *nt* ❶ *dim von* **Platz** spot ❷ (*Keks*) cookie
platzen ['pla·tsn̩] *vi sein* ❶ (*zerplatzen*) to burst; **vor Ärger/Neugier ~** (*fig*) to be bursting with anger/curiosity ❷ (*aufplatzen*) to split ❸ (*fam: scheitern*) to fall through; **das**

Fest ist geplatzt the party is off
platzieren*[RR] [pla·'tsiː·rən] *vt* to place
Platzierung[RR] <-, -en> *f* place; **eine ~ unter den ersten zehn** a place in the top ten
Platzkarte *f* seat reservation
Platzmangel *m* lack of room
Platzpatrone *f* blank [cartridge]
Platzregen *m* cloudburst
Platzwunde *f* laceration
Plauderei <-, -en> [plau·də·'rai] *f* chat
plaudern ['plau·dɐn] *vi* ❶ (*sich gemütlich unterhalten*) to [have a] chat ❷ (*fam: ausplaudern*) to gossip
Plauderstündchen *nt* [little] chat
Plausch <-[e]s, -e> [plauʃ] *m pl selten* (*fam*) chat
plauschen ['plau·ʃn̩] *vi* (*fam*) to [have a] chat
plausibel [plau·'ziː·bl̩] *adj* plausible; **jdm etw ~ machen** to explain sth to sb
Plausibilität <-> [plau·zi·bi·li·'tɛːt] *f kein pl* plausibility
Playboy <-s, -s> ['pleː·bɔy] *m* playboy
Plazenta <-, -s *o* Plazenten> [pla·'tsɛn·ta, *pl* pla·'tsɛn·tas, pla·'tsɛn·tən] *f* placenta
plazieren*[ALT] [pla·'tsiː·rən] *vt s.* **platzieren**
Plazierung[ALT] <-, -en> *f s.* **Platzierung**
pleite ['plai·tə] *adj* (*fam*) broke
Pleite <-, -n> ['plai·tə] *f* (*fam*) ❶ (*Bankrott*) bankruptcy; ~ **machen** to go bust ❷ (*Reinfall*) flop
pleite|gehen[RR] *vi irreg sein* to go bankrupt
Pleuelstange ['plɔy·əl-] *f* TECH connecting rod
Plexiglas® <-es> ['plɛksi·glaːs] *nt kein pl* Plexiglas®
Plombe <-, -n> ['plɔm·bə] *f* ❶ MED filling ❷ (*Bleisiegel*) lead seal
plombieren* [plɔm·'biː·rən] *vt* ❶ MED to fill ❷ (*amtlich versiegeln*) to seal
plötzlich ['plœts·lɪç] **I.** *adj* sudden **II.** *adv* suddenly, all of a sudden; **das kommt alles etwas/so ~** it's all happening rather/so suddenly; **aber etwas ~!** (*fam*) [and] hurry up!
plump [plʊmp] **I.** *adj* ❶ (*massig*) plump ❷ (*schwerfällig*) ungainly ❸ (*dummdreist*) obvious; *Lüge* blatant **II.** *adv* ❶ (*schwerfällig*) clumsily ❷ (*dummdreist*) crassly
plumpsen ['plʊmp·sn̩] *vi sein* (*fam*) to fall [with a thud]; **sich** *akk* **aufs Bett ~ lassen** to flop [oneself] down on the bed
Plumpsklo(sett) *nt* (*fam*) outhouse
Plunder <-s> ['plʊn·dɐ] *m kein pl* junk
plündern ['plʏn·dɐn] **I.** *vt* ❶ (*ausrauben*) to plunder ❷ (*fam: leeren*) to raid **II.** *vi* to plunder
Plünderung <-, -en> *f* looting
Plural <-s, -e> ['pluː·raːl] *m* plural
pluralistisch [plu·ra·'lɪs·tɪʃ] *adj* (*geh*) pluralistic
plus [plʊs] *konj, präp, adv* plus; **6 ~ 4 ist 10** 6 plus 4 is 10; **wir haben fünf Grad ~** it's five degrees above zero
Plus <-, -> [plʊs] *nt* ❶ (*Pluszeichen*) plus ❷ ÖKON surplus; **~ machen** to make a profit; [**mit etw** *dat*] **im ~ sein** to be in the black [with sth]
Plüsch <-[e]s, -e> [plʏʃ, *auch:* plyːʃ] *m* plush
Plüschtier *nt* stuffed animal
Pluspunkt *m* ❶ (*Vorteil*) bonus ❷ (*Wertungseinheit*) [plus] point
Plusquamperfekt <-s, -e> ['plʊs·kvam·pɛr·fɛkt] *nt* past perfect, pluperfect
Pluszeichen *nt* plus sign
Plutonium <-s> [plu·'toː·ni̯·ʊm] *nt kein pl* plutonium
PLZ <-> *f Abk von* **Postleitzahl**
pneumatisch [pnɔy·'maː·tɪʃ] *adj* pneumatic
Po <-s, -s> [poː] *m* (*fam*) butt
Pöbel <-s> ['pøː·bl̩] *m kein pl* (*pej*) mob
Pöbelei <-, -en> [pøː·bə·'lai] *f* (*fam*) swearing
pöbelhaft *adj* loutish
pöbeln ['pøː·bl̩n] *vi* (*ausfallend reden*) to swear; (*sich ausfallend benehmen*) to rile
pochen ['pɔ·xn̩] *vi* ❶ (*anklopfen*) to knock (**gegen/auf** +*akk* against/on) ❷ *Herz, Blut* to pound ❸ (*bestehen*) to insist (**auf** +*akk* on)
Pocken *pl* smallpox *no art*
Podest <-[e]s, -e> [po·'dɛst] *nt o m* podium, rostrum
Podium <-s, Podien> ['poː·di̯·ʊm, *pl* 'poː·di̯·ən] *nt* podium, rostrum
Podiumsdiskussion *f,* **Podiumsgespräch** *nt* panel discussion
Poesie <-> [poe·'ziː] *f kein pl* poetry
Poet(in) <-en, -en> [po·'eːt] *m(f)* poet
poetisch [po·'eː·tɪʃ] *adj* poetic[al]
pofen ['poː·fn̩] *vi* (*fam*) ❶ (*schlafen*) to sleep ❷ (*unaufmerksam sein*) to doze
Pointe <-, -n> ['po̯ɛ̃ː·tə] *f einer Erzählung* point; *eines Witzes* punch line
pointiert [poɛ̃·'tiː·ɐt] *adj* (*geh*) pointed
Pokal <-s, -e> [po·'kaːl] *m* ❶ (*Trinkbecher*) goblet ❷ SPORT trophy, cup
Pokalspiel *nt* cup [*or* tournament] game
Poker <-s> ['poː·kɐ] *nt kein pl* poker
Pokerface <-, -s> ['poː·kɐ·feːs] *nt,* **Pokergesicht** *nt* poker face
pokern ['poː·kɐn] *vi* ❶ KARTEN to play poker; ■ **um etw ~** to gamble for sth ❷ (*viel riskieren*) to stake a lot
Pol <-s, -e> [poːl] *m* GEOG, ELEK, PHYS pole ▶ WENDUNGEN: **der ruhende ~** the calming influence
Polarforscher(in) <-s, -> *m(f)* polar explorer
polarisieren* [po·la·ri·'ziː·rən] *vr* (*geh*) ■ **sich** *akk* **~** to polarize
Polarkreis *m* polar circle; **nördlicher/südlicher ~** Arctic/Antarctic circle
Polarlicht *nt* polar lights *pl*
Polarstern *m* Polaris
Pole, Polin <-n, -n> ['poː·lə] *m, f* Pole; *s. a.* **Deutsche(r)**
Polemik <-, -en> [po·'leː·mɪk] *f* (*geh*) ❶ *kein pl* (*polemischer Gehalt*) polemic ❷ (*scharfe Attacke*) polemics + *sing vb*
polemisch [po·'leː·mɪʃ] (*geh*) **I.** *adj* polemical **II.** *adv* **sich** *akk* **~ äußern** to voice a polemic

P

polemisieren* [po·le·mi·ˈziː·rən] *vi* (*geh*) to polemicize; ■**gegen jdn/etw ~** to inveigh against sb/sth
Polen <-s> [ˈpoː·lən] *nt* Poland; *s. a.* **Deutschland**
Police <-, -n> [po·ˈliː·sə] *f* policy
polieren* [po·ˈliː·rən] *vt* to polish
Politbüro [po·ˈlɪt-] *nt* politburo
Politesse <-, -n> [po·li·ˈtɛsə] *f* meter maid
Politik <-, -en> [po·li·ˈtiːk] *f* ① *kein pl* (*die politische Welt*) politics + *sing vb, no art* ② (*politischer Standpunkt*) politics + *sing vb, no art* ③ (*Strategie*) policy
Politika [po·ˈliː·ti·ka] *pl von* **Politikum**
Politiker(in) <-s, -> [po·ˈliː·ti·kɐ] *m(f)* politician
Politikum <-s, Politika> [po·ˈliː·ti·kʊm, *pl* po·ˈliː·ti·ka] *nt* (*geh: Sache*) political issue; (*Ereignis*) political event
politisch [po·ˈliː·tɪʃ] **I.** *adj* ① POL political ② (*klug*) politic **II.** *adv* ① POL politically ② (*klug*) judiciously
politisieren* [po·li·ti·ˈziː·rən] **I.** *vi* to talk politics **II.** *vt* ■**etw ~** to politicize sth; ■**jdn ~** to make sb politically aware
Politologe, Politologin <-n, -n> [po·li·to·ˈloː·gə] *m, f* political scientist
Politur <-, -en> [po·li·ˈtuːɐ̯] *f* polish
Polizei <-, -en> [po·li·ˈtsai] *f pl selten* ① (*Institution*) ■**die ~** the police + *sing/pl vb;* **bei der ~ sein** to be a police officer ② *kein pl* (*Dienstgebäude*) police station ▶ WENDUNGEN: **dümmer als die ~ erlaubt** (*fam*) [as] dumb as a rock
Polizeiaufgebot *nt* police presence
Polizeibeamte(r) *f(m)* *dekl wie adj* **-beamtin** *f* police officer
Polizeidienststelle *f* police station
Polizeifunk *m* police radio
polizeilich **I.** *adj attr* police *attr* **II.** *adv* by the police; **~ gemeldet sein** to be registered with the police
Polizeipräsident(in) *m(f)* chief of police
Polizeipräsidium *nt* police headquarters + *sing/pl vb*
Polizeirevier *nt* ① (*Dienststelle*) police station ② (*Bezirk*) [police] precinct
Polizeischutz *m* police protection
Polizeistreife *f* police patrol
Polizeiwache *f* police station
Polizist(in) <-en, -en> [po·li·ˈtsɪst] *m(f)* police officer, policeman *masc*, policewoman *fem*
Pollen <-s, -> [ˈpɔ·lən] *m* pollen
Pollenflug *m kein pl* pollen dispersal
Pollenflugvorhersage *f* pollen count forecast
polnisch [ˈpɔl·nɪʃ] *adj* Polish; *s. a.* **deutsch**
Polo <-s, -s> [ˈpoː·lo] *nt* polo
Polohemd *nt* polo shirt
Polster <-s, -> [ˈpɔls·tɐ] *nt o* ÖSTERR *m* ① *von Möbeln* upholstery ② *an Kleidung* pad ③ (*Rücklage*) cushion; **ein finanzielles ~** financial reserves *pl* ④ ÖSTERR (*Kissen*) cushion
polstern [ˈpɔls·tɐn] *vt* ① (*mit Polster versehen*) to upholster ② (*hum fam: ziemlich dick sein*) **gut gepolstert sein** to have padding; (*viel Geld haben*) to be well-off
Polterabend [ˈpɔl·tɐ-] *m party at the house of the bride's parents on the eve of a wedding, at which dishes are smashed to bring good luck*

Celebrated with friends and relatives, a **Polterabend** is held on the eve of a wedding. Traditionally, dishes and cups and other items made of earthenware are smashed to bring good luck and the bridal couple is left to sweep up the mess.

poltern [ˈpɔl·tɐn] *vi* ① *haben* (*rumpeln*) to bang ② *sein* (*krachend fallen*) **der Schrank polterte die Treppe hinunter** the cupboard went crashing down the stairs ③ *sein* (*lärmend gehen*) to stomp
Polyester <-s, -> [po·ly·ˈʔɛs·tɐ] *m* polyester
Polygamie <-> [po·ly·ga·ˈmiː] *f kein pl* polygamy
Pomade <-, -n> [po·ˈmaː·də] *f* pomade
Pommern <-s> [ˈpɔ·mɐn] *nt* Pomerania
Pommes [ˈpɔ·məs] *pl* (*fam*), **Pommes frites** [pɔm·ˈfrɪt] *pl* [French] fries *pl*
Pomp <-[e]s> [pɔmp] *m kein pl* pomp
pompös [pɔm·ˈpøːs] **I.** *adj* grandiose **II.** *adv* grandiosely
Poncho <-s, -s> [ˈpɔn·tʃo] *m* poncho
Pony[1] <-s, -s> [ˈpɔ·ni] *nt* (*Pferd*) pony
Pony[2] <-s, -s> [ˈpɔ·ni] *m* bangs *npl*
Pool <-s, -s> [puːl] *m* pool
Poolbillard [ˈpuːl·bɪl·jart] *nt* pool
Pop <-s> [pɔp] *m kein pl* pop
Popcorn <-s> [ˈpɔp·kɔrn] *nt kein pl* popcorn
Popel <-s, -> [ˈpoː·pl̩] *m* (*fam*) booger
popelig [ˈpoː·pə·lɪç] *adj* (*fam*) ① (*lausig*) lousy ② (*gewöhnlich*) crummy
popeln [ˈpoː·pl̩n] *vi* (*fam*) to pick one's nose
poplig [ˈpoːp·lɪç] *adj s.* **popelig**
Popmusik *f* pop music
Popo <-s, -s> [po·ˈpoː, *auch:* ˈpo·po] *m* (*fam*) butt
poppig [ˈpɔ·pɪç] *adj* (*fam*) trendy
populär [po·pu·ˈlɛːɐ̯] *adj* popular
popularisieren* [po·pu·la·ri·ˈziː·rən] *vt* to popularize
Popularität <-> [po·pu·la·ri·ˈtɛːt] *f kein pl* popularity
Population <-, -en> [po·pu·la·ˈtsi̯oːn] *f* population
Pore <-, -n> [ˈpoː·rə] *f* pore
Porno <-s, -s> [ˈpɔr·no] *m* (*fam*) porn
Pornografie[RR], **Pornographie** <-> [pɔr·no·gra·ˈfiː] *f kein pl* pornography
pornografisch[RR], **pornographisch** *adj* pornographic
porös [po·ˈrøːs] *adj* porous
Porree <-s, -s> [ˈpɔ·re] *m* leek
Portal <-s, -e> [pɔr·ˈtaːl] *nt* portal
Portemonnaie <-s, -s> [pɔrt·mɔ·ˈneː] *nt s.*

P

Portmonee
Porti ['pɔr·ti] *pl von* **Porto**
Portier <-s, -s> [pɔr·'ti̯eː] *m* doorman
Portion <-, -en> [pɔr·'tsi̯oːn] *f* ❶ (*beim Essen*) portion ❷ (*fam: Anteil*) amount ▶ WENDUNGEN: **eine halbe ~** (*fam*) a half-pint
Portmonee^RR <-s, -s> [pɔrt·mɔ·'neː] *nt* wallet, change purse
Porto <-s, -s *o* Porti> ['pɔr·to, *pl* 'pɔr·tos, 'pɔr·ti] *nt* postage
Porträt <-s, -s> [pɔr·'trɛː] *nt* portrait
porträtieren* [pɔr·trɛ·'tiː·rən] *vt* to portray
Portugal <-s> ['pɔr·tu·gal] *nt* Portugal; *s. a.* Deutschland
Portugiese, Portugiesin <-n, -n> [pɔr·tu·'giː·zə] *m, f* Portuguese; *s. a.* **Deutsche(r)**
portugiesisch [pɔr·tu·'giː·zɪʃ] *adj* Portuguese; *s. a.* **deutsch**
Portugiesisch [pɔr·tu·'giː·zɪʃ] *nt dekl wie adj* ❶ LING Portuguese; *s. a.* **Deutsch 1** ❷ (*Fach*) Portuguese; *s. a.* **Deutsch 2**
Portwein ['pɔrt·vain] *m* port [wine]
Porzellan <-s, -e> [pɔr·tsɛ·'laːn] *nt* ❶ (*Material*) porcelain ❷ *kein pl* (*Geschirr*) china
Porzellangeschirr *nt* china
Posaune <-, -n> [po·'zau·nə] *f* trombone
Pose <-, -n> ['poː·zə] *f* pose
posieren* [po·'ziː·rən] *vi* (*geh*) to pose
Position <-, -en> [po·zi·'tsi̯oːn] *f* position
positiv ['poː·zi·tiːf] **I.** *adj* positive; ■ **~ [für jdn] sein** to be good news [for sb] **II.** *adv* positively; **etw ~ beeinflussen** to have a positive influence on sth; **etw ~ bewerten** to judge sth favorably; **sich** *akk* **~ verändern** to change for the better
Posse <-, -n> ['pɔ·sə] *f* farce
Possessivpronomen [pɔ·sɛ·'siːf-] *nt* possessive pronoun
Post <-> [pɔst] *f kein pl* ❶ (*Institution*) Post Office; **etw per/mit der ~ schicken** to send sth in the mail, to mail sth; (*Dienststelle*) post office; **auf die/zur ~ gehen** to go to the post office ❷ (*Briefsendungen*) mail; **heute ist keine ~ für dich da** there's no mail for you today; **elektronische ~** electronic mail
Postamt *nt* post office
Postanweisung *f* money order
Postauto *nt* mail truck
Postbank *f* BRD *bank operated by the post office*
Postbeamte(r) *f(m) dekl wie adj* **-beamtin** *f* post office clerk
Postbote, -botin *m, f* mail carrier, postman *masc,* mailman *masc*
posten ['poʊs·tn̩] *vt* INET to post
Posten <-s, -> ['pɔs·tn̩] *m* ❶ (*zugewiesene Position*) post ❷ (*Anstellung*) position ❸ (*Wache*) guard; **~ beziehen** to take up position ❹ ÖKON (*Position*) item; (*Menge*) quantity ▶ WENDUNGEN: **auf verlorenem ~ kämpfen** to be fighting a losing battle; **nicht ganz auf dem ~ sein** (*fam*) to be a bit under the weather
Poster <-s, -[s]> ['poːs·tɐ] *nt* poster
Postfach *nt* ❶ (*Schließfach*) post office [*or* PO] box ❷ (*offenes Fach*) pigeonhole
Postgiroamt [-ʒiː·ro-] *nt bank operated by the post office*
Postgirokonto [-ʒiː·ro-] *nt* postal checking account
posthum [pɔst·'huːm] *adj* (*geh*) posthumous
Postkarte *f* postcard
Postleitzahl *f* Zip Code
postmodern ['pɔst·mo·dɛrn] *adj* postmodern
Postscheck *m* postal check
Postsendung *f* piece of mail
Postskript <-[e]s, -e> [pɔst·'skrɪpt] *nt,* **Postskriptum** <-s, -ta> [pɔst·'skrɪp·tʊm] *nt* (*geh*) postscript
Postsparkasse *f* ÖSTERR *bank operated by the post office*
Poststempel *m* ❶ (*Abdruck*) postmark ❷ (*Gerät*) canceling device
postulieren* [pɔs·tu·'liː·rən] *vt* (*geh*) to postulate
postum [pɔs·'tuːm] *adj* (*geh*) posthumous
Postweg *m* **etw auf dem ~ schicken** to send sth by mail
postwendend *adv* immediately
potent [po·'tɛnt] *adj* ❶ (*sexuell fähig*) potent ❷ (*zahlungskräftig*) affluent
Potential <-s, -e> [po·tɛn·'tsi̯aːl] *nt s.* **Potenzial**
potentiell [po·tɛn·'tsi̯ɛl] *adj* (*geh*) *s.* **potenziell**
Potenz <-, -en> [po·'tɛnts] *f* ❶ (*sexuell*) potency ❷ (*Leistungsfähigkeit*) strength
Potenzial^RR <-s, -e> *nt* potential
potenziell^RR *adj* (*geh*) potential
potenzieren* [po·tɛn·'tsiː·rən] *vt* (*geh*) to multiply
Potenzstörung *f* potency disorder
Potsdam <-s> ['pɔts·dam] *nt* Potsdam
Pott <-[e]s, Pötte> [pɔt, *pl* 'pœ·tə] *m* (*fam*) ❶ (*Topf*) pot ❷ (*a. pej: Schiff*) tub
potthässlich^RR ['pɔt·'hɛs·lɪç] *adj* (*fam*) butt-ugly *fam*
Pottwal ['pɔt·vaːl] *m* sperm whale
powern ['pau·ɐn] *vi* (*sl: sich voll einsetzen*) to give it one's all *fam*
PR-Abteilung [peː·'ɛr-] *f* PR department
Pracht <-> [praxt] *f kein pl* splendor ▶ WENDUNGEN: **eine wahre ~ sein** (*fam*) to be [really] great
Prachtexemplar *nt* fine specimen
prächtig ['prɛç·tɪç] *adj* ❶ (*prunkvoll*) magnificent ❷ (*großartig*) splendid
Prachtkerl *m* (*fam*) great guy
Prachtstück *nt s.* **Prachtexemplar**
prachtvoll *adj* (*geh*) *s.* **prächtig**
prädestinieren* [prɛ·dɛs·ti·'niː·rən] *vt* (*geh*) to predestine (**für** *+akk* for); **für etw prädestiniert sein** to be made for sth
Prädikat <-[e]s, -e> [prɛ·di·'kaːt] *nt* (*Auszeichnung*) rating
Präferenz <-, -en> [prɛ·fe·'rɛnts] *f* (*geh*) preference

Präfix <-es, -e> [prɛ·ˈfɪks, ˈprɛː·fɪks] *nt* prefix
Prag <-s> [praːk] *nt* Prague
prägen [ˈprɛː·gn̩] *vt* ❶ *Münzen* to mint ❷ *Wort* to coin ❸ (*fig: formen*) ■ **jdn ~** to leave its/their mark on sb
pragmatisch [prag·ˈmaː·tɪʃ] **I.** *adj* pragmatic **II.** *adv* pragmatically
prägnant [prɛ·ˈgnant] (*geh*) **I.** *adj* succinct; *Sätze* concise **II.** *adv* **sich** *akk* **~ ausdrücken** to be succinct; **etw ~ beschreiben** to give a succinct description of sth
Prägnanz <-> [prɛ·ˈgnants] *f kein pl* (*geh*) conciseness
prähistorisch [prɛ·hɪs·ˈtoː·rɪʃ] *adj* prehistoric
prahlen [ˈpraː·lən] *vi* to boast, to brag *pej fam* (**mit** +*dat* about)
Prahler(in) <-s, -> *m(f)* bragger
Prahlerei <-, -en> [praː·lə·ˈrai] *f* ❶ *kein pl* (*das Prahlen*) boasting, bragging *pej fam* ❷ (*Äußerung*) boast
prahlerisch *adj* boastful
Prahlhans <-es, -hänse> *m* (*fam*) showoff
Praktik <-, -en> [ˈprak·tɪk] *f meist pl* practice
Praktika [ˈprak·ti·ka] *pl von* **Praktikum**
praktikabel [prak·ti·ˈkaː·bl̩] *adj* practicable
Praktikant(in) <-en, -en> [prak·ti·ˈkant] *m(f)* intern
Praktiker(in) <-s, -> [ˈprak·ti·kɐ] *m(f)* practical person
Praktikum <-s, Praktika> [ˈprak·ti·kʊm, *pl* -ka] *nt* internship
praktisch [ˈprak·tɪʃ] **I.** *adj* practical; *Beispiel* concrete **II.** *adv* ❶ (*so gut wie*) practically ❷ (*in der Praxis*) in practice ❸ (*praxisbezogen*) **~ arbeiten** to do practical work
praktizieren* [prak·ti·ˈtsiː·rən] *vi, vt* to practice; **~der Arzt** practicing doctor; **seinen Glauben ~** to practice one's religion
Praline <-, -n> [pra·ˈliː·nə] *f*, **Praliné** <-s, -s> [pra·li·ˈneː] *nt* ÖSTERR, SCHWEIZ, **Pralinee** <-s, -s> [pra·li·ˈneː] *nt* ÖSTERR, SCHWEIZ praline, [piece of] chocolate
prall [pral] *adj* ❶ (*sehr voll*) *Brüste* well-rounded; *Schenkel, Waden* sturdy; *Euter* swollen; **eine ~ gefüllte Brieftasche** a bulging wallet; **etw ~ aufblasen/füllen** to inflate/fill sth to the bursting point ❷ *Sonne* blazing
prallen [ˈpra·lən] *vi sein* ❶ (*heftig auftreffen*) to crash; *Ball* to bounce; [**mit dem Wagen**] **gegen/vor etw** *akk* **~** to crash [one's car] into sth; **mit dem Kopf gegen etw** *akk* **~** to bang one's head on sth ❷ *Sonne* to blaze
prallvoll [ˈpral·ˈfɔl] *adj* (*fam*) bulging; *Kofferraum* tightly packed
Prämie <-, -n> [ˈprɛː·mi̯ə] *f* ❶ (*zusätzliche Vergütung*) bonus ❷ (*Versicherungsbeitrag*) [insurance] premium ❸ (*staatliche Prämie*) [government] premium
prämieren* [prɛ·ˈmiː·rən] *vt* **jdn/etw mit Euro 50.000 ~** to award sb/sth [a prize of] 50,000 euros; **ein prämierter Film** an award-winning film
Prämisse <-, -n> [prɛ·ˈmɪ·sə] *f* (*geh*) condition; **unter der ~, dass ...** on the condition that ...
pränatal [prɛ·na·ˈtaːl] *adj* prenatal
prangen [ˈpraŋ·ən] *vi* (*auffällig angebracht sein*) to be emblazoned
Pranger <-s, -> [ˈpraŋ·ɐ] *m* HIST pillory ▶ WENDUNGEN: **jdn/etw an den ~ stellen** to criticize sb/sth harshly
Pranke <-, -n> [ˈpraŋ·kə] *f* paw; (*hum a.*) mitt *sl*
Präparat <-[e]s, -e> [prɛ·pa·ˈraːt] *nt* (*Arzneimittel*) medication
präparieren* [prɛ·pa·ˈriː·rən] *vt* ❶ BIOL, MED (*konservieren*) to preserve ❷ (*vorbereiten*) to prepare
Präposition <-, -en> [prɛ·po·zi·ˈtsi̯oːn] *f* preposition
Prärie <-, -n> [prɛ·ˈriː, *pl* -ˈriː·ən] *f* prairie
Präsens <-, Präsentia *o* Präsenzien> [ˈprɛː·zɛns, *pl* prɛ·ˈzɛn·tsi̯a, prɛ·ˈzɛn·tsi̯ən] *nt* present tense
präsent [prɛ·ˈzɛnt] *adj* (*geh*) present ▶ WENDUNGEN: **etw ~ haben** to remember sth
Präsent <-[e]s, -e> [prɛ·ˈzɛnt] *nt* (*geh*) gift
Präsentation <-, -en> [prɛ·zɛn·ta·ˈtsi̯oːn] *f* presentation
Präsentia *pl von* **Präsens**
präsentieren* [prɛ·zɛn·ˈtiː·rən] *vt* ■ **jdm etw** *akk* **~** to present sb with sth
Präsentierteller *m* ▶ WENDUNGEN: **auf dem ~ sitzen** (*fam*) to be exposed to all
Präsenz <-> [prɛ·ˈzɛnts] *f kein pl* (*geh*) presence
Präsenzien *pl von* **Präsens**
Präser <-s, -> [ˈprɛː·zɐ] *m* (*sl*) *kurz für* **Präservativ** rubber
Präservativ <-s, -e> [prɛ·zɛr·va·ˈtiːf] *nt* condom
Präsident(in) <-en, -en> [prɛ·zi·ˈdɛnt] *m(f)* president
Präsidentschaft <-, -en> *f* presidency
Präsidentschaftskandidat(in) *m(f)* presidential candidate
Präsidien *pl von* **Präsidium**
präsidieren* [prɛ·zi·ˈdiː·rən] **I.** *vi* to preside (+*dat* over) **II.** *vt* SCHWEIZ **einen Verein ~** to be president of a society
Präsidium <-s, Präsidien> [prɛ·ˈziː·di̯·ʊm, *pl* -di̯·ən] *nt* ❶ (*Vorstand, Vorsitz*) chairmanship ❷ (*Führungsgruppe*) committee ❸ (*Polizeipräsidium*) [police] headquarters + *sing/pl vb*
prasseln [ˈpra·sl̩n] *vi* ❶ *sein Regen* to drum; (*stärker*) to beat ❷ *haben Feuer* to crackle
prassen [ˈpra·sn̩] *vi* to live it up; (*schlemmen*) to pig out *fam*
Präteritum <-s, -ta> [prɛ·ˈteː·ri·tʊm, *pl* -ta] *nt* preterite
Prävention <-, -en> [prɛ·vɛn·ˈtsi̯oːn] *f* prevention
präventiv [prɛ·vɛn·ˈtiːf] *adj* prevent[at]ive
Praxis <-, Praxen> [ˈprak·sɪs, *pl* ˈprak·sən] *f* ❶ (*Arztpraxis*) doctor's office; (*Anwaltspraxis*) law practice ❷ *kein pl* (*Erfahrung*) [practical]

experience; **langjährige ~** many years of experience ❸ *kein pl* (*Anwendung*) practice *no art;* **etw in die ~ umsetzen** to put sth into practice

Praxisbezug *m* practical orientation

praxisfern *adj* impractical

Praxisgebühr *f* ADMIN, MED ≈ co-pay

praxisnah I. *adj* practical **II.** *adv* practically

Präzedenzfall [prɛ·tse·'dɛnts-] *m* (*geh*) judicial precedent; **einen ~ schaffen** to set a precedent

präzis [prɛ·'tsiːs] *adj* (*geh*), **präzise** [prɛ·'tsiː·zə] *adj* (*geh*) precise; *Beschreibung* exact

präzisieren* [prɛ·tsi·'ziː·rən] *vt* (*geh*) to state more precisely

Präzision <-> [prɛ·tsi·'zi̯oːn] *f kein pl* (*geh*) precision

predigen ['preː·dɪ·gn̩] *vt, vi* to preach; ■ **jdm etw** *akk* **~** (*fam*) to lecture sb on/about sth

Prediger(in) <-s, -> *m(f)* preacher

Predigt <-, -en> ['preː·dɪçt] *f* (*a. fam*) sermon

Preis <-es, -e> [prais] *m* ❶ (*Kaufpreis*) price (**für** +*akk* of); **zum halben ~** at [*or* for] half-price ❷ (*Gewinn*) prize; **der erste ~** [the] first prize ▶ WENDUNGEN: **um jeden ~** at all costs

Preisanstieg *m* price increase

Preisaufschlag *m* surcharge

Preisausschreiben *nt* competition, contest

Preiselbeere ['prai·zl̩·beː·rə] *f* [mountain *spec*] cranberry

Preisempfehlung *f* recommended price

preisen <pries, gepriesen> ['prai·zn̩] *vt* (*geh*) to praise

Preisermäßigung *f* price reduction

Preisfrage *f* ❶ (*Quizfrage*) contest question ❷ (*vom Preis abhängende Entscheidung*) question of price

preis|geben ['prais·geː·bn̩] *vt irreg* (*geh*) ❶ *Geheimnis* to divulge; ■ **jdm etw** *akk* **~** to betray sth to sb ❷ **jdn der Lächerlichkeit ~** to expose sb to ridicule ❸ (*aufgeben*) to relinquish; *Gebiet* to surrender

preisgekrönt *adj* award-winning *attr*

Preisgeld <-[e]s, -er> *nt* prize money

preisgünstig *adj* inexpensive; *Angebot* very reasonable; **etw ~ bekommen** to get a good deal on sth

Preisklasse *f* price range

Preis-Leistungs-Verhältnis *nt kein pl* cost-effectiveness, cost-benefit ratio

preislich ['prais·lɪç] *adj attr* price, in price

PreisnachlassRR *m* discount

Preisrätsel *nt* puzzle competition

Preisrichter(in) *m(f)* judge [in a competition]

Preisschild *nt* price tag

Preissenkung *f* reduction in prices

Preissteigerung *f* price increase

Preisträger(in) *m(f)* prizewinner; (*Auszeichnung*) award winner

Preisverleihung *f* presentation of awards/prizes

preiswert *adj s.* **preisgünstig**

prekär [pre·'kɛːɐ̯] *adj* (*geh*) precarious

prellen ['prɛ·lən] *vt* ❶ (*betrügen*) ■ **jdn [um etw** *akk*] **~** to cheat sb [out of sth] ❷ (*verletzen*) **sich** *dat* **das Knie ~** to bruise one's knee

Prellung <-, -en> *f* contusion *spec* (**an** +*dat* to)

Premiere <-, -n> [prə·'mi̯eː·rə] *f* première

Premierminister(in) *m(f)* prime minister

Presse <-, -n> ['prɛ·sə] *f* ❶ (*Gerät*) press; (*Fruchtpresse*) juice extractor ❷ *kein pl* ■ **die ~** (*Zeitungen und Zeitschriften*) the press

Presseagentur *f* press agency

Presseamt *nt* press office

Presseausweis *m* press pass

Pressechef(in) *m(f)* publicity manager

Pressedienst *m* news agency service

Presseerklärung *f* press release

Pressefreiheit *f kein pl* freedom of the press

Pressekonferenz *f* press conference

Pressemeldung *f* press report

Pressemitteilung *f* press release

pressen ['prɛ·sn̩] *vt* ❶ (*drücken, glätten, herstellen*) to press ❷ *Obst* to press; *Saft* to squeeze (**aus** +*dat* out of)

Presseschau *f* news roundup

Pressesprecher(in) *m(f)* spokesman

Pressewesen <-s> *nt kein pl* press

Pressezensur *f kein pl* censorship of the press

pressieren* [prɛ·'siː·rən] **I.** *vi* SÜDD, ÖSTERR, SCHWEIZ (*dringlich sein*) to be pressing **II.** *vi impers* SÜDD, ÖSTERR, SCHWEIZ ■ **es pressiert** it's urgent; ■ **es pressiert jdm** sb is in a hurry; **es pressiert nicht** there's no hurry

Prestige <-s> [prɛs·'tiːʒə] *nt kein pl* (*geh*) prestige

Prestigeobjekt [prɛs·'tiːʒ-] *nt* object of prestige

Preuße, Preußin <-n, -n> ['prɔy·sə] *m, f* Prussian

Preußen <-s> ['prɔy·sn̩] *nt* Prussia

preußisch ['prɔy·sɪʃ] *adj* Prussian

prickeln ['prɪ·kl̩n] *vi* ❶ (*kribbeln*) to tingle; **ein P~ in den Beinen** pins and needles in one's legs ❷ (*erregen, reizen*) to thrill

prickelnd *adj Gefühl* tingling; *Humor* piquant; *Champagner* sparkling

pries [priːs] *imp von* **preisen**

Priester(in) <-s, -> ['priːs·tɐ] *m(f)* priest *masc*, priestess *fem*

Priestertum <-s> *nt kein pl* priesthood

prima ['priː·ma] *adj inv* (*fam*) great; **es läuft alles ~** everything is going really well

Primaballerina [pri·ma·ba·le·'riː·na] *f* prima ballerina

Primadonna <-, -donnen> [pri·ma·'dɔ·na] *f* prima donna *a. pej*

primär [pri·'mɛːɐ̯] (*geh*) **I.** *adj* (*vorrangig*) primary, prime *attr* **II.** *adv* primarily

Primarschule *f* SCHWEIZ (*Grundschule*) elementary school

primitiv [pri·mi·'tiːf] *adj* primitive; **ein ~er Kerl** a big ape

Primitivität <-> [pri·mi·ti·vi·'tɛːt] *f kein pl*

P

primitiveness

Primitivling <-s, -e> *m* (*pej fam*) peasant

Printmedien ['prɪnt-] *pl* [print] media

Prinz <-en, -en> [prɪnts] *m* prince

Prinzessin <-, -nen> ['prɪn·'tsɛ·sɪn] *f* princess

Prinzip <-s, -ien> [prɪn·'tsiːp, *pl* 'prɪn·'tsiː·pi̯·ən] *nt* principle; **aus/im ~** on/in principle

prinzipiell [prɪn·tsi·'pi̯·ɛl] **I.** *adj* fundamental **II.** *adv* (*aus Prinzip*) on principle; (*im Prinzip*) in principle

Prinzipienreiter(in) *m(f)* (*pej*) stickler for [one's] principles

Priorität <-, -en> [prio·ri·'tɛːt] *f* (*geh*) priority (**vor** + *dat* over)

Prise <-, -n> ['priː·zə] *f* pinch; **eine ~ Sarkasmus** (*fig*) a touch of sarcasm

Pritsche <-, -n> ['prɪt·ʃə] *f* ① (*Liege*) plank bed ② (*Ladefläche*) platform

privat [pri·'vaːt] **I.** *adj* private **II.** *adv* privately; **jdn ~ sprechen** to speak to sb in private; **sich** *akk* **~ versichern** to take out private insurance

Privatbesitz *m* private property

Privatdetektiv(in) *m(f)* private investigator

Privateigentum *nt* private property

Privatfernsehen *nt* (*fam*) privately-owned television *no art*

Privatgespräch *nt* private conversation; (*am Telefon*) personal call

Privatgrundstück *nt* private property *npl*

privatisieren* [pri·va·ti·'ziː·rən] *vt* to privatize

Privatisierung <-, -en> *f* privatization

Privatleben *nt kein pl* private life

Privatlehrer(in) *m(f)* tutor

Privatmann <-leute> *m* private citizen

Privatpatient(in) *m(f)* private patient

Privatperson *f* private person

Privatsache *f* private matter

Privatschule *f* private school

Privatsekretär(in) *m(f)* private secretary

Privatsphäre *f kein pl* privacy; **die ~ verletzen** to invade sb's privacy

Privatunterricht *m kein pl* private tutoring

Privatvermögen *nt* private property

Privatwirtschaft *f* ■ **die ~** the private sector

Privileg <-[e]s, -ien> [pri·vi·'leːk, *pl* -gi̯·ən] *nt* (*geh*) privilege

privilegieren* [pri·vi·le·'giː·rən] *vt* (*geh*) to grant privileges to

pro [proː] **I.** *präp* per; **~ Kopf** a head; **~ Person** per person; **~ Stück** each **II.** *adv* **sind Sie ~ oder kontra?** are you for or against [it]?

Pro <-> [proː] *nt kein pl* **[das] ~ und [das] Kontra** (*geh*) the pros and cons *pl*

Probe <-, -n> ['proː·bə] *f* ① (*Warenprobe, Testmenge*) sample ② MUS, THEAT rehearsal ③ (*Prüfung*) test ► WENDUNGEN: **jds Geduld auf eine harte ~ stellen** to try sb's patience; **jdn auf die ~ stellen** to put sb to the test; **auf ~** on probation; **zur ~** on a trial basis

Probealarm *m* fire drill

Probefahrt *f* test drive

Probelauf *m* trial run

proben ['proː·bn̩] *vt, vi* to rehearse

probeweise *adv* on a trial basis

Probezeit *f* probationary period

probieren* [pro·'biː·rən] *vt, vi* to try; ■ **von etw** *dat* **~** to try some of sth; ■ **~, ob ...** to try and see whether ...

Problem <-s, -e> [pro·'bleːm] *nt* problem; **vor einem ~ stehen** to be faced with a problem

Problematik <-> [pro·ble·'maː·tɪk] *f kein pl* (*geh*) problematic nature

problematisch [pro·ble·'maː·tɪʃ] *adj* problematic[al]; *Kind* difficult

Problemfall *m* problem; (*Mensch*) problem case

problemlos **I.** *adj* problem-free, unproblematic *attr* **II.** *adv* without any problems; **~ ablaufen** to run smoothly

Procedere <-, -> [pro·'tseː·də·rə] *nt* (*geh*) procedure

Produkt <-[e]s, -e> [pro·'dʊkt] *nt* product

Produktion <-, -en> [pro·dʊk·'tsi̯oːn] *f* production

Produktionsrückgang *m* decrease in production

Produktionssteigerung *f* increase in production

produktiv [pro·dʊk·'tiːf] *adj* (*geh*) productive; **~ zusammenarbeiten** to work together productively

Produktivität <-> [pro·dʊk·ti·vi·'tɛːt] *f kein pl* productivity

Produktpalette *f* product range

Produktpiraterie *f* [copyright] piracy

Produzent(in) <-en, -en> [pro·du·'tsɛnt] *m(f)* producer

produzieren* [pro·du·'tsiː·rən] **I.** *vt* to produce **II.** *vr* (*pej fam*) ■ **sich** *akk* **[vor jdm] ~** to show off [in front of sb]

profan [pro·'faːn] *adj* (*geh*) ① (*alltäglich*) prosaic; *Probleme* mundane ② (*weltlich*) profane; *Bauwerke, Kunst* secular

Professionalität <-> *f kein pl* professionalism

professionell [pro·fɛ·si̯o·'nɛl] *adj* professional

Professor, Professorin <-s, -soren> [pro·'fɛ·soːɐ̯, pro·fɛ·'soː·rɪn, *pl* -'soː·rən] *m, f* ① (*Universitätsprofessor*) professor ② ÖSTERR (*Gymnasiallehrer*) ≈ high-school teacher

Profi <-s, -s> ['proː·fi] *m* (*fam*) pro

Profil <-s, -e> [pro·'fiːl] *nt* ① *eines Reifens, einer Schuhsohle* tread ② (*Seitenansicht*) profile

profilieren* [pro·fi·'liː·rən] *vr* **sich** *akk* **politisch ~** to make one's mark as a politician; **sie hat sich als Künstlerin profiliert** she distinguished herself as an artist

Profilneurose *f* image complex

Profit <-[e]s, -e> [pro·'fiːt, pro·'fɪt] *m* profit; **etw mit ~ verkaufen** to sell sth for a profit

profitabel [pro·fi·'taː·bl̩] *adj* profitable; (*stärker*) lucrative

Profitgier *f* hunger for profit

profitieren* [pro·fi·'tiː·rən] *vi* (*geh*) to make a profit, to profit (**von, bei** + *dat* from, with)

P

pro forma [proː ˈfɔr·ma] *adv* pro forma, as a formality
Prognose <-, -n> [pro·ˈgnoː·zə] *f a.* MED prognosis; (*Wetter*) forecast
prognostizieren* [pro·gnɔs·ti·ˈtsiː·rən] *vt* to predict
Programm <-s, -e> [pro·ˈgram] *nt* ① (*geplanter Ablauf*) program; (*Tagesordnung*) agenda; (*Zeitplan*) schedule; **ein volles ~ haben** to have a full day/week etc. ahead [of oneself]; **was steht für heute auf dem ~?** what's the agenda/program/schedule for today? ② RADIO, TV (*Sender*) channel ③ (*Programmheft*) program ④ COMPUT [computer] program
Programmfehler *m* COMPUT program error, bug
programmgemäß I. *adj* [as *pred*] planned II. *adv* [according] to plan; **~ verlaufen** to run according to plan
programmieren* [pro·gra·ˈmiː·rən] *vt* COMPUT to program
Programmierer(in) <-s, -> *m(f)* programmer
Programmierung <-, -en> *f* COMPUT programming
Programmkino *nt* art cinema, repertory movie theater
Programmpunkt *m* item on the agenda; *einer Show* act
Programmsteuerung *f* COMPUT program control
Programmvorschau *f* preview, trailer
Programmzeitschrift *f* program guide; (*von Fernsehen a.*) TV guide
progressiv [pro·grɛ·ˈsiːf] *adj* (*geh*) progressive
Projekt <-[e]s, -e> [pro·ˈjɛkt] *nt* project
Projektion <-, -en> [pro·jɛk·ˈtsi̯oːn] *f* projection
Projektleiter(in) <-s, -> *m(f)* project manager
Projektor <-s, -toren> [pro·ˈjɛk·toːɐ̯, *pl* -ˈtoː·rən] *m* projector
projizieren* [pro·ji·ˈtsiː·rən] *vt* (*a. fig*) to project (**auf** +*akk* on[to])
proklamieren* [pro·kla·ˈmiː·rən] *vt* (*geh*) to proclaim
Pro-Kopf-Einkommen [pro·ˈkɔpf-] *nt* per capita income
Prolet <-en, -en> [pro·ˈleːt] *m* (*pej*) redneck *pej sl*
Proll <-s, -s> [ˈprɔl] *m* (*pej sl*) redneck
Prolo <-s, -s> [ˈproː·lo] *m* (*pej sl*) redneck *pej fam*
Prolog <-[e]s, -e> [pro·ˈloːk, *pl* -ˈloː·gə] *m* prolog[ue]
Promenade <-, -n> [pro·mə·ˈnaː·də] *f* promenade
Promenadenmischung *f* (*hum fam*) mongrel, mutt
Promi <-s, -s> [ˈprɔ·mɪ] *m* (*sl*) *kurz für* **Prominente(r)** VIP
Promille <-[s], -> [pro·ˈmɪ·lə] *nt* ① (*Tausendstel*) per mil[l]; **nach ~** in per mil[l] ② *pl* (*fam: Alkoholpegel*) [blood] alcohol level; **0,5 ~** blood alcohol level of 0.05 [percent]
Promillegrenze *f* legal [alcohol] limit
prominent [pro·mi·ˈnɛnt] *adj* prominent
Prominenz <-> [pro·mi·ˈnɛnts] *f kein pl* ① (*die Prominenten*) prominent figures *pl* ② (*geh: das Prominentsein*) fame
promoten* [pro·ˈmoː·tn̩] *vt* to promote
Promotion¹ <-, -en> [pro·mo·ˈtsi̯oːn] *f* ① (*Verleihung des Doktorgrads*) doctorate, PhD ② SCHWEIZ (*Versetzung*) promotion [to the next class] ③ ÖSTERR (*offizielle Feier mit Verleihung der Doktorwürde*) doctoral graduation ceremony
Promotion² <-> [pro·ˈmoː·ʃn̩] *f kein pl* promotion
prompt [prɔmpt] I. *adj* prompt II. *adv* ① (*sofort*) promptly ② (*meist iron fam: erwartungsgemäß*) sure enough; **er ist ~ auf den Trick hereingefallen** naturally, he fell for the trick
Pronomen <-s, - *o* Pronomina> [pro·ˈnoː·mən, *pl* -ˈnoː·mi·na] *nt* pronoun
Propaganda <-> [pro·pa·ˈgan·da] *f kein pl* ① (*a. pej: manipulierende Verbreitung von Ideen*) propaganda ② (*Werbung*) publicity
propagandistisch *adj* propagandist[ic] *a. pej*
propagieren* [pro·pa·ˈgiː·rən] *vt* (*geh*) to propagate
Propangas *nt kein pl* propane [gas]
Propeller <-s, -> [pro·ˈpɛ·lɐ] *m* propeller
Prophet(in) <-en, -en> [pro·ˈfeːt] *m(f)* prophet *masc*, prophetess *fem*
prophezeien* [pro·fe·ˈtsai·ən] *vt* to prophesy, to predict
Prophezeiung <-, -en> *f* prophecy
prophylaktisch [pro·fy·ˈlak·tɪʃ] *adj* ① MED prophylactic ② (*geh: zur Sicherheit*) preventative
Prophylaxe <-, -n> [pro·fy·ˈlak·sə] *f* MED prophylaxis *spec*
Proportion <-, -en> [pro·pɔr·ˈtsi̯oːn] *f* (*geh*) proportion
proportional [pro·pɔr·tsi̯o·ˈnaːl] *adj* (*geh*) proportional (**zu** +*dat* to)
proppenvoll [ˈprɔ·pn̩·ˈfɔl] *adj* (*fam*) jam-packed
Prosa <-> [ˈproː·za] *f kein pl* prose
prosit [ˈproː·zɪt] *interj s.* **prost**
Prospekt <-[e]s, -e> [pros·ˈpɛkt] *m* (*Werbebroschüre*) brochure; (*Werbezettel*) flier
prost [proːst] *interj* cheers
Prostata <-, Prostatae> [ˈprɔs·ta·ta, *pl* ˈprɔs·ta·tɛ] *f* prostate gland
prosten [ˈproːs·tn̩] *vi* ① (*prost rufen*) to say cheers ② (*ein Prost ausbringen*) ■ **auf jdn/etw ~** to toast sb/sth
prostituieren* [pros·ti·tu·ˈiː·rən] *vr* ■ **sich** *akk* **~** to prostitute oneself
Prostituierte(r) [pros·ti·tu·ˈiːɐ̯·tə, -tɐ] *f(m)* prostitute
Prostitution <-> [pros·ti·tu·ˈtsi̯oːn] *f kein pl* prostitution
Protagonist(in) <-en, -en> [pro·ta·go·ˈnɪst] *m(f)* (*geh*) protagonist
Protegé <-s, -s> [pro·te·ˈʒeː] *m* (*geh*) protégé
protegieren* [pro·te·ˈʒiː·rən] *vt* (*geh*) to pro-

P

mote
Protein <-s, -e> [pro·te·ˈiːn] *nt* protein
Protest <-[e]s, -e> [pro·ˈtɛst] *m* protest
Protestant(in) <-en, -en> [pro·tɛs·ˈtant] *m(f)* Protestant
protestantisch [pro·tɛs·ˈtan·tɪʃ] *adj* Protestant
Protestantismus <-> [pro·tɛs·tan·ˈtɪs·mʊs] *m kein pl* ■**der** ~ Protestantism
protestieren* [pro·tɛs·ˈtiː·rən] *vi* to protest
Protẹstkundgebung *f* [protest] rally
Protẹstwähler(in) *m(f)* protest voter
Prothese <-, -n> [pro·ˈteː·zə] *f* prosthesis *spec*
Protokoll <-s, -e> [pro·to·ˈkɔl] *nt* ❶ (*Niederschrift*) record[s *pl*]; (*einer Sitzung*) minutes *npl*; **etw zu ~ geben** (*bei der Polizei*) to make a statement ❷ DIAL (*Strafmandat*) ticket ❸ *kein pl* (*Zeremoniell*) **gegen das ~ verstoßen** to break with protocol
Prototyp [ˈproː·to·tyːp] *m* prototype; (*fig*) archetype
protzen [ˈprɔ·tsn̩] *vi* (*fam*) ■[**mit etw** *dat*] ~ to flaunt [sth]
protzig [ˈprɔ·tsɪç] *adj* (*fam*) showy; *Auto* fancy
Proviant <-s, -e> [pro·ˈvi̯·ant] *m pl selten* provisions; MIL supplies
Provider <-s, -> [pro·ˈvai·dɐ] *m* COMPUT provider
Provinz <-, -en> [pro·ˈvɪnts] *f* ❶ (*Verwaltungsgebiet*) province ❷ *kein pl* (*rückständige Gegend*) provinces *pl a. pej*; **in der ~ leben** to live [out] in the sticks *fam*
provinziell [pro·vɪn·ˈtsi̯ɛl] *adj* provincial *a. pej*
Provinzler(in) <-s, -> [pro·ˈvɪnts·lɐ] *m(f)* (*pej fam*) provincial
Provịnzstadt *f* provincial town
Provision <-, -en> [pro·vi·ˈzi̯oːn] *f* commission
Provisorien *pl von* **Provisorium**
provisorisch [pro·vi·ˈzoː·rɪʃ] **I.** *adj* provisional; *Unterkunft* temporary **II.** *adv* temporarily, for the time being
Provisorium <-s, -rien> [pro·vi·ˈzoː·ri̯·ʊm, *pl* -ri̯·ən] *nt* (*geh*) temporary solution
provokant [pro·vo·ˈkant] *adj* provocative
Provokation <-, -en> [pro·vo·ka·ˈtsi̯oːn] *f* provocation
provokativ [pro·vo·ka·ˈtiːf] *adj* provocative
provozieren* [pro·vo·ˈtsiː·rən] *vt* to provoke; *Streit* to cause; ■**jdn zu etw** *dat* ~ to provoke sb into [doing] sth
provozierend *adj* provocative
Prozedere <-, -> [pro·ˈtseː·də·rə] *nt* (*geh*) procedure
Prozedur <-, -en> [pro·tse·ˈduːɐ̯] *f* (*geh*) procedure
Prozent <-[e]s, -e> [pro·ˈtsɛnt] *nt* ❶ (*Hundertstel*) percent ❷ (*Alkoholgehalt*) alcohol content ❸ *pl* (*Rabatt*) discount
Prozẹntsatz *m* percentage
prozentual [pro·tsɛn·ˈtu̯aːl] *adj* (*geh*) **etw ~ ausdrücken** to express sth as a percentage
Prozess[RR] <-es, -e>, **Prozeß**[ALT] <-sses, -sse> [pro·ˈtsɛs] *m* ❶ (*Gerichtsverfahren*) [court] case; (*Strafverfahren*) trial; **einen ~ [gegen jdn] führen** to take legal action [against sb] ❷ (*geh: Vorgang*) process ❸ (*fig*) [**mit jdm/etw**] **kurzen ~ machen** (*fam*) to make short work of sb/sth
prozessieren* [pro·tsɛ·ˈsiː·rən] *vi* ■[**gegen jdn**] ~ to take [sb] to court
Prozession <-, -en> [pro·tsɛ·ˈsi̯oːn] *f* procession
Prozẹsskosten[RR] *pl* court costs
Prozessor <-s, -soren> [pro·ˈtsɛ·soːɐ̯, -ˈsoː·rən] *m* processor
prüde [ˈpryː·də] *adj* (*pej*) prudish
prüfen [ˈpryː·fn̩] *vt* ❶ (*überprüfen, untersuchen*) to check (**auf** +*akk* for); *Material* to test ❷ (*Kenntnisse abfragen*) to examine
Prüfung <-, -en> *f* ❶ (*Examen*) exam[ination]; (*für den Führerschein*) test; **mündliche ~ [in etw** *dat*] oral exam[ination] [in sth] ❷ (*Überprüfung*) checking; *von Material* test ❸ (*geh: Heimsuchung*) trial
Prüfungsangst *f* pre-exam jitters
Prüfverfahren *nt* test[ing] procedure
Prügel[1] [ˈpryː·gl̩] *pl* thrashing; **jdm eine Tracht ~ verabreichen** to give sb a [good] beating
Prügel[2] <-s, -> [ˈpryː·gl̩] *m* DIAL cudgel
Prügelei <-, -en> [pryː·gə·ˈlai] *f* (*fam*) [fist] fight
Prügelknabe *m* whipping boy
prügeln [ˈpryː·gl̩n] **I.** *vt, vi* to hit **II.** *vr* ■**sich** *akk* ~ to fight
Prügelstrafe *f* ■**die** ~ corporal punishment
Prunk <-s> [prʊnk] *m kein pl* magnificence
prụnkvoll *adj* splendid; *Kleidung* magnificent
prusten [ˈpruːs·tn̩] *vi* (*fam*) to snort; (*beim Trinken*) to splutter; **vor Lachen ~** to snort with laughter
PS <-, -> [pe·ˈʔɛs] *nt* ❶ *Abk von* **Pferdestärke** hp ❷ *Abk von* **Postskript(um)** PS
Pseudonym <-s, -e> [psɔy·do·ˈnyːm] *nt* pseudonym
Psyche <-, -n> [ˈpsyː·çə] *f* psyche
Psychiater(in) <-s, -> [psyˈçi̯aː·tɐ] *m(f)* psychiatrist
Psychiatrie <-, -n> [psyçi̯a·ˈtriː, *pl* -ˈtriː·ən] *f* ❶ *kein pl* (*Fachgebiet*) psychiatry *no art* ❷ (*fam: psychiatrische Abteilung*) psychiatric ward
psychiatrisch [psyˈçi̯aː·trɪʃ] *adj* psychiatric
psychisch [ˈpsyː·çɪʃ] *adj* psychological, mental
Psychoanalyse [psy·ço·ʔana·ˈlyː·zə] *f* psychoanalysis *no art*
Psychoanalytiker(in) [psy·ço·ʔana·ˈlyː·ti·kɐ] *m(f)* psychoanalyst
Psychologe, Psychologin <-n -n> [psy·ço·ˈloː·gə] *m, f* psychologist
Psychologie <-> [psy·ço·lo·ˈgiː] *f kein pl* psychology
psychologisch [psy·ço·ˈloː·gɪʃ] *adj* psychological
Psychopath(in) <-en, -en> [psy·ço·ˈpaːt] *m(f)* psychopath

Psychopharmakon <-s, -pharmaka> [psy·ço·'far·ma·kɔn, *pl* -'far·ma·ka] *nt meist pl* psychopharmaceutical [agent]
Psychose <-, -n> [psy·'ço:·zə] *f* psychosis
psychosomatisch [psy·ço·zo·'ma:·tɪʃ] **I.** *adj* psychosomatic **II.** *adv* psychosomatically
Psychoterror *m* (*fam*) psychological terror
Psychotherapeut(in) [psy·ço·te·ra·'pɔyt] *m(f)* psychotherapist
Psychotherapie [psy·ço·te·ra·'pi:] *f* psychotherapy
pubertär [pu·bɛr·'tɛ:ɐ̯] *adj* adolescent, of puberty *pred; Störungen* pubescent
Pubertät <-> [pu·bɛr·'tɛ:t] *f kein pl* puberty *no art*
pubertieren* [pu·bɛr·'ti:·rən] *vi* (*geh*) to reach puberty
Publicity <-> [pa·'blɪ·si·ti] *f kein pl* publicity
Public Relations ['pa·blɪk·ri·'le:·ʃns] *pl* public relations + *sing vb*
publik [pu·'bli:k] *adj pred* public; ■ **~ sein/werden** to be/become public knowledge; **etw ~ machen** to publicize sth
Publikation <-, -en> [pub·li·ka·'tsi̯o:n] *f* publication
Publikum <-s> ['pu:·bli·kʊm] *nt kein pl* audience; (*im Theater a.*) house; (*beim Sport*) crowd
Publikumsandrang *m* rush of spectators
Publikumserfolg *m* hit; (*Film*) box-office hit [*or* smash]
Publikumsliebling *m* fan favorite
Publikumsmagnet *m* crowd-pleaser
publikumswirksam *adj* appealing to the public
publizieren* [pu·bli·'tsi:·rən] *vt* to publish
Pudding <-s, -s> ['pʊ·dɪŋ] *m* pudding
Pudel <-s, -> ['pu:·dl̩] *m* poodle
Pudelmütze *f* pom-pom hat
pudelnassRR ['pu:·dl̩·'nas] *adj* (*fam*) ■ **~ sein/werden** to be/get soaking wet
pudelwohl ['pu:·dl̩·'vo:l] *adj* (*fam*) **sich** *akk* **~ fühlen** to feel like a million bucks
Puder <-s, -> ['pu:·dɐ] *m o fam nt* powder
pudern ['pu:·dɐn] *vt* to powder
Puderzucker *m* powdered [*or* confectioner's] sugar
Puerto Rico <-s> ['pu̯·ɛr·to 'ri:·ko] *nt* Puerto Rico
Puff1 <-[e]s, Püffe> [pʊf, *pl* 'pʏ·fə] *m* (*fam: Stoß*) thump; (*in die Seite*) prod
Puff2 <-[e]s, -s> [pʊf] *m* (*fam*) brothel, whorehouse
Puffer <-s, -> ['pʊ·fɐ] *m* ❶ BAHN bumper ❷ (*Reibekuchen*) potato pancake, ≈ latke
Pufferzone *f* buffer zone
pulen ['pu:·lən] **I.** *vt bes* NORDD (*fam*) *Krabben, Nüsse, Erbsen* to shell; ■ **etw aus etw** *dat* **~** to pick sth out of sth **II.** *vi bes* NORDD (*fam*) ■ **an etw** *dat* **~** to pick at sth; **in der Nase ~** to pick one's nose
Pulle <-, -n> ['pʊ·lə] *f* (*sl*) bottle ▶ WENDUNGEN: **volle ~ fahren** to drive flat out
Pulli <-s, -s> ['pʊli] *m* (*fam*) *kurz für* **Pullover** sweater
Pullover <-s, -s> [pʊ·'lo:·vɐ] *m* sweater
Pullunder <-s, -> [pʊ·'lʊn·dɐ] *m* sweater vest
Puls <-es, -e> [pʊls] *m* pulse
pulsieren* [pʊl·'zi:·rən] *vi* to pulsate
Pult <-[e]s, -e> [pʊlt] *nt* ❶ (*Rednerpult*) lectern ❷ (*Schaltpult*) control panel
Pulver <-s, -> ['pʊl·vɐ] *nt* powder; (*Schießpulver*) [gun]powder
Pulverkaffee *m* instant coffee
Pulverschnee *m* powder[y] snow
Puma <-s, -s> ['pu:·ma] *m* puma, mountain lion, cougar
pummelig ['pʊ·mə·lɪç], **pummlig** ['pʊm·lɪç] *adj* (*fam*) chubby
Pump [pʊmp] *m* ▶ WENDUNGEN: **auf ~** (*fam*) on credit
Pumpe <-, -n> ['pʊm·pə] *f* ❶ (*Gerät*) pump ❷ (*fam: Herz*) heart
pumpen ['pʊm·pn̩] *vt* ❶ (*mittels einer Pumpe*) to pump ❷ (*fam: investieren*) **Geld in etw** *akk* **~** to pump money in[to] sth ❸ (*fam: leihen*) ■ **jdm etw** *akk* **~** to lend sb sth; ■ **sich** *dat* **etw** *akk* [**bei/von jdm**] **~** to borrow sth [from sb]
Pumps <-, -> [pœmps] *m* pump
Punk <-s> [paŋk] *m kein pl* punk
Punker(in) <-s, -> ['paŋ·kɐ] *m(f)* punk [rocker]
Punkrock <-s> ['paŋk·rɔk] *m kein pl* punk [rock]
Punkt <-[e]s, -e> [pʊŋkt] *m* ❶ (*runder Fleck*) spot; (*in der Mathematik*) point ❷ (*Stelle*) spot; (*genauer*) point; **bis zu einem gewissen ~** up to a certain point ❸ (*Satzzeichen*) period; (*auf i, Auslassungszeichen*) dot ❹ (*Bewertungseinheit*) point ❺ (*Detailpunkt*) point; (*auf der Tagesordnung*) item ❻ **um ~ acht** [**Uhr**] at exactly eight [o'clock] ▶ WENDUNGEN: **ohne ~ und Komma reden** (*fam*) to rattle on and on; **ein dunkler ~** [**in jds Vergangenheit**] a dark chapter [in sb's past]; **der springende ~** the crucial point; **nun mach aber mal einen ~!** (*fam*) come off it!
pünktlich ['pʏŋkt·lɪç] **I.** *adj* punctual **II.** *adv* punctually
Pünktlichkeit <-> *f kein pl* punctuality
Punktzahl *f* SPORT score
Punsch <-es, -e> [pʊnʃ] *m* [hot] punch
Pupille <-, -n> [pu·'pɪ·lə] *f* pupil
Puppe <-, -n> ['pʊ·pə] *f* (*Spielzeug*) doll ▶ WENDUNGEN: **bis in die ~n** (*fam*) until the wee hours of the morning; **bis in die ~n schlafen** (*fam*) to sleep until all hours
Puppenhaus *nt* dollhouse
Puppentheater *nt* puppet theater
Puppenwagen *m* doll carriage
Pups <-es, -e> [pu:ps] *m* (*fam*) fart
pupsen ['pu:p·sn̩] *vi* (*fam*) to fart
pur [pu:ɐ̯] *adj* ❶ (*rein, unverdünnt*) pure; **etw ~ trinken** to drink sth straight ❷ (*fam: blank, bloß*) sheer, pure; *Wahnsinn* absolute

P

Püree <-s, -s> [py·'reː] *nt* ❶ (*passiertes Gemüse/Obst*) purée ❷ (*Kartoffelbrei*) mashed potatoes *pl*
pürieren [py·'riː·rən] *vt* to purée
Puritaner(in) <-s, -> [pu·ri·'taː·nɐ] *m(f)* (*fig*) puritan
puritanisch [pu·ri·'taː·nɪʃ] *adj* (*fig*) puritanical
purpurfarben, **purpurfarbig** *adj* purple
Purzelbaum ['pʊr·tsl̩-] *m* (*fam*) somersault
purzeln ['pʊr·tsl̩n̩] *vi sein a. Preise* to tumble
Puste <-> ['puːs·tə] *f kein pl* (*fam*) breath; **außer ~ sein** to be out of breath; **aus der ~ kommen** to get out of breath
Pusteblume *f* (*Kindersprache*) dandelion
Pustekuchen ['puːs·tə·kuː·xn̩] *m* **[ja] ~!** (*fam*) not a chance!
Pustel <-, -n> ['pʊs·tl̩] *f* pimple
pusten ['puːs·tn̩] *vt, vi* (*fam*) to blow
Pute <-, -n> ['puː·tə] *f* ❶ (*Tier*) turkey [hen] ❷ (*fam: Frau*) dumb broad *pej*
Putenfleisch <-[e]s> *nt kein pl* turkey [meat]
Puter <-s, -> ['puː·tɐ] *m* tom, gobbler
puterrot ['puː·tɐ·'roːt] *adj* scarlet
Putsch <-[e]s, -e> [pʊtʃ] *m* coup [d'état]
Putschist(in) <-en, -en> [pʊt·'ʃɪst] *m(f)* rebel
Putz <-es> [pʊts] *m kein pl* (*Wandverkleidung*) plaster; (*bei Außenmauern*) [soft lime] stucco; **etw mit ~ verkleiden** to plaster sth ▶WENDUNGEN: **auf den ~ hauen** (*fam: angeben*) to show off; (*übermütig sein*) to go wild [*or* to town]
putzen ['pʊ·tsn̩] **I.** *vt* to clean; *Gemüse* to prepare; *Spinat* to wash; **putz dir den Dreck von den Schuhen!** wipe the mud off your shoes!; **seine Schuhe/die Brille ~** to clean one's shoes/one's glasses; **sich** *dat* **die Nase ~** to blow one's nose; **sich** *dat* **die Zähne ~** to brush one's teeth **II.** *vi* **~ gehen** to work as a housekeeper
Putzfimmel *m* (*pej*) **einen ~ haben** to be an obsessive cleaner
Putzfrau *f* maid, cleaning lady
putzig ['pʊ·tsɪç] *adj* (*fam*) ❶ (*niedlich*) sweet; **ein ~es Tier** a cute animal ❷ (*merkwürdig*) odd, strange
Putzkolonne *f* cleaning crew
Putzlappen *m* rag
Putzmittel *nt* detergent
putzmunter *adj* (*fam*) chipper, wide awake *pred*
Putzteufel *m* (*fam*) cleaning maniac
Putztuch *nt* ❶ (*Poliertuch*) [polishing] cloth ❷ *s.* **Putzlappen**
putzwütig *adj* (*fam*) in a cleaning frenzy
Putzzeug *nt kein pl* (*fam*) cleaning supplies *pl*
Puzzle <-s, -s> ['pʊ·zl̩, 'pa·zl̩] *nt* jigsaw [puzzle]
PVC <-[s]> [peː·fau·'tseː] *nt kein pl Abk von* **Polyvinylchlorid** PVC
Pyjama <-s, -s> [py·'dʒaː·ma] *m* pajamas *npl*
Pyramide <-, -n> [py·ra·'miː·də] *f* pyramid
Pyrenäen [py·re·'nɛː·ən] *pl* ■**die ~** the Pyrenees *npl*
Pyromane, **Pyromanin** <-n, -n> [py·ro·'maː·nə] *m, f* pyromaniac
Python <-, -s> ['pyː·tɔn] *m*, **Pythonschlange** *f* python

P

Qq

Q, q <-, - *o fam* -s, -s> [ku:] *nt* Q, q; ~ **wie Quelle** Q as in Quebec
q [ku:] SCHWEIZ, ÖSTERR *Abk von* **Zentner** 100 kg
Quacksalber(in) <-s, -> ['kvak·zal·bɐ] *m(f)* (*pej*) quack [doctor]
Quadrat <-[e]s, -e> [kva·'dra:t] *nt* square
quadratisch *adj* square
Quadratkilometer *m* square kilometer
Quadratlatschen *pl* (*fam*) ❶ (*Schuhe*) clodhoppers ❷ (*Füße*) [really] big feet
Quadratmeter *m* square meter
Quadratzentimeter *m* square centimeter
Quai <-s, -s> [kɛ:, ke:] *m o nt* SCHWEIZ (*Kai*) quay
quaken ['kva:·kn̩] **I.** *vi* ❶ *Frosch* to croak; *Ente* to quack ❷ (*fam: reden*) to chat **II.** *vt* (*fam*) to waffle on *sep pej* (**über** *+akk* about)
Quäker(in) <-s, -> ['kvɛ:·kɐ] *m(f)* Quaker
Qual <-, -en> ['kva:l] *f* ❶ (*Quälerei*) struggle ❷ *meist pl* (*Pein*) agony ▶WENDUNGEN: **die ~ der Wahl haben** (*hum*) to be spoiled for choice
quälen ['kvɛ:·lən] **I.** *vt* ❶ (*misshandeln*) *Mensch, Tier* to be cruel to ❷ (*peinigen*) *Gedanken, Gefühle* to torment *fig; Schmerzen* to trouble ❸ (*belästigen*) to pester **II.** *vr* ❶ (*leiden*) ■**sich** *akk* ~ to suffer ❷ (*sich herumquälen*) ■**sich** *akk* **mit etw** *dat* ~ *Gedanken, Gefühle* to torment oneself with sth; *Hausaufgaben, Arbeit* to struggle [hard] with sth ❸ (*sich mühsam bewegen*) ■**sich** *akk* ~ to struggle
Quälerei <-, -en> [kvɛ:·lə·'rai] *f* ❶ (*körperlich, seelisch*) torture ❷ (*Belästigung*) pestering
Quälgeist *m* (*fam*) pest *fig*
Qualifikation <-, -en> [kva·li·fi·ka·'tsi̯o:n] *f* ❶ (*berufliche Befähigung*) qualifications *pl* ❷ SPORT qualifier
qualifizieren* [kva·li·fi·'tsi:·rən] **I.** *vr* ■**sich** *akk* [**für etw**] ~ to qualify [for sth] **II.** *vt* ■**jdn für etw** *akk* ~ to qualify sb for sth
Qualität <-, -en> [kva·li·'tɛ:t] *f* ❶ (*Güte, Beschaffenheit*) quality ❷ *pl* (*gute Eigenschafte2n*) qualities *pl*
qualitativ ['kva·li·ta·ti:f, kva·li·ta·'ti:f] **I.** *adj* qualitative **II.** *adv* qualitatively
Qualitätsarbeit *f* high-quality work[manship]
Qualitätsmerkmal *nt* sign of quality
Qualitätssicherung *f* quality assurance
Qualle <-, -n> ['kva·lə] *f* jellyfish
Qualm <-[e]s> ['kvalm] *m kein pl* [thick] smoke
qualmen ['kval·mən] **I.** *vi* (*a. fam: rauchen*) to smoke **II.** *vt* (*fam*) to puff away at
Qualmerei <-> *f kein pl* (*fam*) smoking
qualmig ['kval·mɪç] *adj* smoke-filled
qualvoll **I.** *adj* agonizing **II.** *adv* ~ **sterben** to die in agony
QuäntchenRR <-s, -> *nt* **ein ~ Glück** a little bit of luck; **ein ~ Hoffnung** a glimmer of hope
Quanten ['kvan·tən] *pl* ❶ *pl von* **Quantum** ❷ (*sl: Füße*) boats *fig*
Quantität <-, -en> [kvan·ti·'tɛ:t] *f* (*geh*) quantity
quantitativ ['kvan·ti·ta·ti:f, kvan·ti·ta·'ti:f] *adj* (*geh*) quantitative
Quantum <-s, Quanten> ['kvan·tʊm, *pl* 'kvan·tən] *nt* (*geh*) quantum
Quarantäne <-, -n> [ka·ran·'tɛ:·nə] *f* quarantine; **unter ~ stehen/stellen** to be in/place under quarantine
Quark <-s> ['kvark] *m kein pl* ❶ KOCHK quark, ≈ fromage frais ❷ (*fam: Quatsch*) nonsense
Quartal <-s, -e> [kvar·'ta:l] *nt* quarter
Quartalssäufer(in) *m(f)* (*fam*) periodic heavy drinker
Quartier <-s, -e> [kvar·'ti:ɐ̯] *nt* accommodation
Quarz <-es, -e> ['kva:ɐ̯ts] *m* quartz
quasi ['kva:·zi] *adv* almost, more or less *fam*
Quasselei <-, -en> [kva·sə·'lai] *f* (*fam*) babbling
quasseln ['kva·sl̩n] (*fam*) **I.** *vi* to babble **II.** *vt* **dummes Zeug** ~ to babble on about sth
Quasselstrippe <-, -n> *f* (*fam*) ❶ (*hum: Telefon*) **an der ~ hängen** to be on the phone ❷ (*pej: Person*) windbag
Quatsch <-es> ['kvatʃ] *m kein pl* (*fam*) ❶ (*dummes Gerede*) nonsense ❷ (*Unfug*) nonsense; ~ **machen** to mess [*or fam* screw] around
quatschen ['kva·tʃn̩] (*fam*) **I.** *vt* **dummes Zeug** ~ to talk nonsense **II.** *vi* (*fam*) ❶ (*viel und dumm reden*) to babble ❷ (*sich unterhalten*) to chat ❸ (*etw ausplaudern*) to blab
Quatschkopf *m* (*pej fam*) babbling idiot
Quecksilber ['kvɛk·zɪl·bɐ] *nt* mercury
Quelle <-, -n> ['kvɛ·lə] *f* source
quellen <quillt, quoll, gequollen> ['kvɛ·lən] *vi sein* ❶ (*herausfließen*) ■[**aus etw** *dat*] ~ to pour out [of sth] ❷ (*aufquellen*) to swell [up]
Quellgebiet *nt* GEOG head
Quellwasser *nt* spring water
Quengelei <-, -en> *f* whining
quengelig ['kvɛ·ŋə·lɪç] *adj* (*fam*) whining
quengeln ['kvɛ·ŋl̩n] *vi* (*fam*) ❶ (*weinerlich sein*) to whine ❷ (*nörgeln*) to moan
quenglig ['kvɛŋ·lɪç] *adj* (*fam*) *s.* **quengelig**
QuentchenALT <-s, -> ['kvɛnt·çən] *nt s.* **Quäntchen**
quer ['kve:ɐ̯] *adv* ❶ (*der Breite nach*) diagonally; ~ **gestreift** horizontally striped ❷ ~ **durch/über etw** *akk* straight through/across sth
Querachse *f* transverse axis
Querbalken *m* crossbeam
querbeet [kve:ɐ̯·'be:t] *adv* (*fam*) all over
Querdenker(in) *m(f)* nonconformist thinker

Q

querdurch [kveːɐ̯·ˈdʊrç] *adv* straight through
Quere [ˈkveː·rə] *f* ▶ WENDUNGEN: **jdm in die ~ kommen** to get in sb's way
Querele <-, -n> [kvɛ·ˈreː·lə] *f* (*geh*) argument
querfeldein [kveːɐ̯·fɛlt·ˈʔain] *adv* through the countryside
Querflöte *f* flute
Querformat *nt* landscape format
quer|gehen *vi irreg sein* (*fam*) ■**jdm ~** to go wrong for sb
Querkopf *m* (*fam*) *person with a different agenda from everyone else's*
quer|legen *vr* (*fam*) ■**sich** *akk* [**bei etw** *dat*] **~** to oppose sth actively
quer|schießen *vi irreg* (*sl*) to throw a wrench in the works
Querschläger *m* ricochet [shot]
Querschnitt *m* cross section
querschnitt(s)gelähmt *adj* paraplegic
Querschnitt(s)lähmung *f* paraplegia
Querstraße *f* crossroad
Querstrich *m* horizontal line
Querulant(in) <-en, -en> [kve·ru·ˈlant] *m(f)* (*geh*) querulous person
quetschen [ˈkvɛt·ʃn̩] **I.** *vt* **jdn an/gegen die Mauer ~** to crush sb against the wall; **Kleider in einen Koffer ~** to stuff clothes into a suitcase **II.** *vr; vt* (*verletzen*) ■**sich** *akk* **~** to bruise oneself; **sich** *dat* **den Fuß ~** to crush one's foot **III.** *vr* (*sich zwängen*) **sich** *akk* **in die U-Bahn ~** to squeeze into the subway train; **sich** *akk* **durch die Menge ~** to squeeze one's way through the crowd
Quetschung <-, -en> *f* MED (*verletzte Stelle*) bruise

Queue <-s, -s> [køː] *nt o m* cue
quieken [ˈkviː·kn̩] *vi* ❶ *Tier* to squeak ❷ **vor Vergnügen/Schreck ~** to squeal with joy/fright
quietschen [ˈkviːt·ʃn̩] *vi* ❶ *Tür, Bett* to squeak; **mit ~den Bremsen/Reifen** with screeching brakes/tires; **unter lautem Q~ kam das Fahrzeug zum Stehen** the vehicle came to a halt with a loud screech ❷ (*fam*) *s.* **quieken 2**
quietschfidel [ˈkviːtʃ·fi·ˈdeːl], **quietschvergnügt** [ˈkviːtʃ·fɛɐ̯·ˈgnyːkt] *adj* (*fam*) chipper *pred*
quillt *3. pers sing pres von* **quellen**
Quintessenz <-, -en> [ˈkvɪnt·ɛsɛnts] *f* (*geh*) quintessence *form*
quirlig [ˈkvɪr·lɪç] *adj* lively
quitt [kvɪt] *adj* ■[**mit jdm**] **~ sein** (*abgerechnet haben*) to be even [with sb] *fam;* (*sich getrennt haben*) to be finished [with sb]
Quitte <-, -n> [ˈkvɪ·tə] *f* quince
quittieren* [kvɪ·ˈtiː·rən] *vt* ❶ (*bestätigen*) ■**etw ~** to acknowledge [the] receipt of sth; ■**jdm etw ~** to give sb a receipt for sth; **sich** *dat* **etw ~ lassen** to obtain a receipt for sth ❷ (*reagieren auf*) ■**etw mit etw** *dat* **~** to meet sth with sth
Quittung <-, -en> [ˈkvɪ·tʊŋ] *f* ❶ (*Beleg*) receipt; **jdm eine ~** [**für etw** *akk*] **ausstellen** to give sb a receipt [for sth] ❷ (*Folgen*) **das ist die ~ für deine Faulheit** that's what you get for being so lazy
Quiz <-, -> [kvɪs] *nt* quiz
quoll [ˈkvɔl] *imp von* **quellen**
Quote <-, -n> [ˈkvoː·tə] *f* ❶ (*Anteil*) proportion ❷ (*Rate*) rate, quota; TV ratings *npl*

Rr

R, r <-, - *o fam* -s, -s> [ɛr] *nt* R, r; ~ **wie Richard** R as in Romeo; **das ~ rollen** to roll one's r's

Rabatt <-[e]s, -e> [ra·'bat] *m* discount (**auf** +*akk* on)

Rabauke <-n, -n> [ra·'bau·kə] *m* (*fam*) rowdy

Rabbi <-[s], -s *o* Rabbinen> ['ra·bi, *pl* ra·'biː·nən] *m,* **Rabbiner** <-s, -> [ra·'biː·nɐ] *m* rabbi

Rabe <-n, -n> ['raː·bə] *m* raven

Rabeneltern *pl* (*pej fam*) ≈ neglectful parents *pl*

Rabenmutter *f* (*pej fam*) ≈ bad mother

rabenschwarz ['raː·bn̩·'ʃvarts] *adj* jet-black

Rabenvater *m* (*pej fam*) ≈ distant father

rabiat [ra·'bi̯aːt] **I.** *adj* ① (*gewalttätig*) aggressive ② (*rigoros*) ruthless **II.** *adv* ruthlessly

Rache <-> ['ra·xə] *f kein pl* revenge

Racheakt *m* act of revenge

Rachen <-s, -> ['ra·xn̩] *m* ① (*von Mensch*) throat ② (*von Tier*) jaws *pl*

rächen ['rɛ·çn̩] **I.** *vt* ■ **etw** ~ to take revenge for sth; ■ **jdn** ~ to avenge sb **II.** *vr* ■ **sich** *akk* ~ to take [one's] revenge (**an** +*dat* on, **für** +*akk* for)

Rächer(in) <-s, -> *m(f)* (*geh*) avenger

Rachitis <-> [ra·'xiː·tɪs] *f kein pl* rickets

Rachsucht *f kein pl* vindictiveness

rachsüchtig *adj* vindictive

Rackerei <-> [ra·kə·'rai] *f kein pl* (*fam*) slog

rackern ['ra·kɐn] *vi* (*fam*) to slave away

Rad <-[e]s, Räder> [raːt, *pl* 'rɛː·dɐ] *nt* ① (*Fahrrad*) bicycle, bike *fam;* ~ **fahren** to ride a bicycle, to bike *fam* ② *eines Fahrzeugs* wheel ► WENDUNGEN: **ein ~ ab haben** (*sl*) to have a screw loose *hum fam*

Radar <-s> [ra·'daːɐ̯] *m o nt kein pl* radar

Radarkontrolle *f* radar speed enforcement

Radau <-s> [ra·'dau] *m kein pl* (*fam*) racket

radeln ['raː·dl̩n] *vi sein* (*fam*) to bike

Radfahrer(in) *m(f)* bicyclist

Radiator <-s, -toren> [ra·'di̯aː·toːɐ̯, *pl* -'toː·rən] *m* radiator

Radien *pl von* **Radius**

Radierer <-s, -> *m,* **Radiergummi** <-s, -s> *m* eraser

Radieschen <-s, -> [ra·'diːs·çən] *nt* radish

radikal [ra·di·'kaːl] **I.** *adj* ① POL radical ② (*völlig*) *Beseitigung, Bruch* complete ③ (*tief greifend*) *Veränderung* drastic **II.** *adv* ① POL radically ② (*völlig*) *brechen, entfernen* completely ③ (*tief greifend*) drastically

Radikale(r) *f(m) dekl wie adj* POL extremist

Radikalkur *f* ① MED drastic remedy ② (*Maßnahmen*) drastic measures *pl*

Radio <-s, -s> ['raː·di̯o] *nt o* SCHWEIZ, SÜDD *m* radio; **im ~** on the radio

radioaktiv [ra·di̯o·ʔak·'tiːf] **I.** *adj* radioactive **II.** *adv* ~ **verseucht/verstrahlt** contaminated by radioactivity

Radioaktivität <-> [ra·di̯o·ʔak·ti·vi·'tɛːt] *f kein pl* radioactivity

Radiologe, Radiologin <-n, -n> [ra·di̯o·'loː·gə] *m, f* radiologist

Radiosender *m* radio transmitter

Radiowecker *m* alarm clock radio

Radius <-, Radien> ['raː·di̯·ʊs, *pl* 'raː·di·ən] *m* radius

Radkappe *f* AUTO hub cap

Radlager *nt* wheel bearing

Radler(in) <-s, -> ['raːd·lɐ] *m(f)* (*fam*) biker

Radlerhose *f* bicycle shorts *npl*

Radrennen *nt* bike race

Radsport *m* cycling

Radtour [-tuːɐ] *f* bike ride

Radwandern *nt* bike riding

Radwanderung *f s.* **Radtour**

Radweg *m* bike path

raffen ['ra·fn̩] *vt* ① (*eilig greifen*) to grab ② (*in Falten legen*) to gather ③ (*fam: begreifen*) to get *fam*

Raffgier *f* greed

raffgierig *adj* greedy

Raffinerie <-, -n> [ra·fi·nə·'riː, *pl* -'riː·ən] *f* refinery

Raffinesse <-, -n> [ra·fi·'nɛ·sə] *f* ① *kein pl* (*Durchtriebenheit*) cunning ② (*Feinheit*) refinement

raffiniert **I.** *adj* ① *Öl, Zucker* refined ② (*gerissen*) *Person, Plan* cunning ③ (*ausgefallen*) *Kleidung* stylish **II.** *adv* ① (*durchtrieben*) cunningly ② (*ausgefallen*) stylishly

Rage <-> ['raː·ʒə] *f kein pl* rage; **in ~ sein** to be furious; **jdn in ~ bringen** to infuriate sb

ragen ['raː·gn̩] *vi* ① (*in die Höhe*) to rise up (**aus** +*dat* out of); *Gebirge* to tower up ② (*aus etw heraus*) to stick out

Ragout <-s, -s> [ra·'guː] *nt* ragout

Rahm <-[e]s> [raːm] *m kein pl* SÜDD, SCHWEIZ (*Sahne*) cream

rahmen ['raː·mən] *vt* to frame; *Dia* to mount

Rahmen <-s, -> ['raː·mən] *m* ① (*Einfassung*) frame ② (*Gestell*) *Fahrrad* frame; *Auto* chassis ③ (*begrenzter Umfang/Bereich*) framework; **sich** *akk* **im ~ halten** to stay within reasonable limits; [**mit etw** *dat*] **aus dem ~ fallen** to stand out [because of sth]

Rahmenbedingung *f meist pl* basic conditions *pl*

Rahmenhandlung *f* framework story

Rahmsoße *f* cream[y] sauce

räkeln ['rɛː·kl̩n] *vr s.* **rekeln**

Rakete <-, -n> [ra·'keː·tə] *f* rocket; MIL missile

Raketenstützpunkt *m* missile base

Rallye <-, -s> ['ra·li, 'rɛ·li] *f* rally

Rambazamba <-s> *nt kein pl* (*fam*) ~ **machen** to make a fuss

Rambo <-s, -s> ['ram·bo] *m* (*sl*) Rambo *fam*

rammeln ['ra·ml̩n] *vi* ① *Tiere* to mate ② (*derb*) *Menschen* to screw

R

rammen ['ra·mən] *vt* to ram (**in** +*akk* into)
Rampe <-, -n> ['ram·pə] *f* ramp; (*Laderampe*) loading ramp
Rampenlicht *nt* THEAT spotlight, footlight ▶ WENDUNGEN: **im ~ [der Öffentlichkeit] stehen** to be in the limelight
ramponieren* [ram·po·'niː·rən] *vt* (*fam*) to ruin
Ramsch <-[e]s> [ramʃ] *m kein pl* (*fam*) junk
ran [ran] *adv* (*fam*) *s.* **heran**
Rand <-es, Ränder> [rant, *pl* 'rɛn·dɐ] *m* ❶ (*obere Begrenzung*) *Glas, Tasse* brim; *Wanne* rim ❷ (*äußere Begrenzung*) edge; *Hut* brim ❸ *Blatt Papier* margin ❹ (*Schatten, Spur*) mark; **Ränder um die Augen haben** to have rings [*or* bags] around one's eyes ▶ WENDUNGEN: **außer ~ und Band geraten** (*fam*) to be beside oneself; **mit etw/jdm zu ~e kommen** to cope with sth/get along with sb; **am ~e** in passing
Randale <-> [ran·'daː·lə] *f kein pl* (*fam*) rioting; **~ machen** to riot
randalieren* [ran·da·'liː·rən] *vi* to riot
Randalierer(in) <-s, -> *m(f)* hooligan
Randerscheinung *f* peripheral phenomenon
Randfigur *f* minor figure
Randgebiet *nt* outlying area; (*einer Stadt*) outskirts *npl*
Randgruppe *f* fringe group
Randproblem *nt* secondary problem
Randstreifen *m* shoulder; *einer Autobahn* hard shoulder
rang [raŋ] *imp von* **ringen**
Rang <-[e]s, Ränge> [raŋ, *pl* 'rɛ·ŋə] *m* ❶ (*gesellschaftliche Position*) [social] standing ❷ *kein pl* (*Stellenwert*) status; *einer Entdeckung, Neuerung* importance ❸ MIL rank ▶ WENDUNGEN: **alles, was ~ und Namen hat** everybody who is anybody
Rangelei <-, -en> [raŋə·'lai] *f* (*fam*) scuffle
rangeln ['ra·ŋl̩n] *vi* (*fam*) to scuffle
Rangfolge *f* order of priority
rangieren* [rã·'ʒiː·rən] *vi* to rank, to be ranked
Rangliste *f* rankings, ranking list
Rangordnung *f* hierarchy
ran|halten *vr irreg* (*fam*) ■**sich** *akk* **~** to put one's back into it
rank [raŋk] *adj* (*hum*) **~ und schlank** slim and trim
Ranke <-, -n> ['raŋ·kə] *f* tendril
ranken ['raŋ·kn̩] *vr* ❶ *Pflanze* ■**sich** *akk* **um etw** *akk* **~** to wind itself around sth ❷ *Legende, Sage* ■**sich um jdn/etw ~** to have grown up around sb/developed around sth
ran|klotzen *vi* (*sl*) to get cracking *fam*
ran|kommen *vi irreg sein* (*fam*) ❶ (*erreichen*) ■**an etw** *akk* **~** to [be able to] reach sth ❷ (*vordringen*) **man kommt an ihn einfach nicht ran** it's impossible to reach him; **an diese Frau kommt keiner ran** nobody has a chance with her
ran|machen *vr* (*fam*) ■**sich** *akk* **an jdn ~** to make a pass at sb

R

rann [ran] *imp von* **rinnen**
rannte ['ran·tə] *imp von* **rennen**
ran|schmeißen *vr irreg* (*fam*) ■**sich** *akk* **an jdn ~** to throw oneself at sb
Ranzen <-s, -> ['ran·tsn̩] *m* ❶ SCH ≈ backpack ❷ (*fam: Bauch*) gut
ranzig ['ran·tsɪç] *adj* rancid
rapide [ra·'piː·də] **I.** *adj* rapid **II.** *adv* rapidly
Rappel <-s, -> ['ra·pl̩] *m* **einen ~ kriegen** (*fam*) to go completely crazy
rappeln ['ra·pl̩n] *vi* (*fam*) to rattle
rappelvoll *adj* (*fam*) jam-packed
rapplig ['rap·lɪç] *adj s.* **rappelig**
Raps <-es, -e> [raps] *m* rape[seed]
rar [raːɐ̯] *adj* rare; ■**~ sein/werden** to be/become hard to find
Rarität <-, -en> [ra·ri·'tɛːt] *f* rarity
rar|machen *vr* (*fam*) ■**sich** *akk* **~** to make oneself scarce
rasant [ra·'zant] **I.** *adj* fast, rapid; *Tempo* breakneck **II.** *adv* (*schnell*) rapidly; **~ fahren** to drive at breakneck speed
rasch [raʃ] **I.** *adj* quick **II.** *adv* quickly
rascheln ['ra·ʃl̩n] *vi* to rustle
rasen ['raː·zn̩] *vi* ❶ *sein* (*schnell fahren*) to speed; ■**gegen/in etw ~** to crash into sth ❷ *sein Zeit* to fly [by] ❸ *haben* **sie raste [vor Wut]** she was beside herself [with rage]
Rasen <-s, -> ['raː·zn̩] *m* lawn
rasend **I.** *adj* ❶ (*schnell*) breakneck ❷ (*wütend*) furious; **~ vor Wut sein** to be infuriated ❸ (*furchtbar*) terrible; *Durst* burning; *Schmerz* excruciating; *Wut* blind ❹ *Beifall* thunderous **II.** *adv* (*fam*) very; **ich würde das ~ gern tun** I'd love to do it
Rasenmäher <-s, -> *m* lawnmower
Rasensprenger <-s, -> *m* [lawn] sprinkler
Raser(in) <-s, -> ['raː·zɐ] *m(f)* (*fam*) speeder
Raserei <-, -en> [raː·zə·'rai] *f* ❶ (*fam: schnelles Fahren*) speeding ❷ *kein pl* (*Wutanfall*) rage
Rasierapparat *m* ❶ (*Elektrorasierer*) [electric] shaver ❷ (*Nassrasierer*) [safety] razor
rasieren* [ra·'ziː·rən] *vt, vr* ■**[sich** *akk*] **~** to shave; **sich** *akk* **trocken/nass ~** to dry-shave/wet-shave; **sich** *dat* **die Beine ~** to shave one's legs
Rasierer <-s, -> *m* (*fam*) *s.* **Rasierapparat**
Rasierklinge *f* razor blade
Rasiermesser *nt* straight razor
Rasierschaum *m* shaving cream
Rasierwasser *nt* aftershave
Raspel <-, -n> ['ras·pl̩] *f* KOCHK grater
raspeln ['ras·pl̩n] *vt* KOCHK to grate
Rasse <-, -n> ['ra·sə] *f Menschen* race; *Tiere* breed
rasseln ['ra·sl̩n] *vi* ❶ *haben* to rattle; ■**mit/an etw** *dat* **~** to rattle sth ❷ *sein* (*fam*) **durch eine Prüfung ~** to fail [*or* flunk] an exam
Rassendiskriminierung *f* racial discrimination
rassig ['ra·sɪç] *adj* spirited
rassisch ['ra·sɪʃ] *adj* racial

Rassismus <-> [ra·ˈsɪs·mʊs] *m kein pl* racism
Rassist(in) <-en, -en> [ra·ˈsɪst] *m(f)* racist
rassistisch *adj* racist
Rast <-, -en> [rast] *f* break
rasten [ˈras·tn̩] *vi* to take a break
Raster <-s, -> [ˈras·tɐ] *nt* (*Kategorie*) category
Rasthaus *nt* roadhouse; *Autobahn* rest [*or* truck] stop
rastlos *adj* ① (*unermüdlich*) tireless ② (*unruhig*) restless
Rastplatz *m* rest area [*or* stop]
Raststätte *f s.* **Autobahnraststätte**
Rasur <-, -en> [ra·ˈzuːɐ̯] *f* ① (*das Rasieren*) shaving ② (*Resultat des Rasierens*) shave
Rat[1] <-[e]s> [raːt] *m kein pl* advice; **jdm den ~ geben, etw zu tun** to advise sb to do sth; **sich** *dat* **keinen ~ [mehr] wissen** to be at one's wit's end; **jdn/etw zu ~e ziehen** to consult sb/sth
Rat[2] <-[e]s, Räte> [raːt, *pl* ˈrɛː·tə] *m* POL council; **der Europäische ~** the European Council; **Großer ~** SCHWEIZ [Swiss] cantonal parliament; **im ~ sitzen** (*fam*) ≈ to be a [Federal] Councilor (*to be a member of a* [*Swiss*] *cantonal parliament*)
rät *3. pers sing pres von* **raten**
Rate <-, -n> [ˈraː·tə] *f* installment
raten <rät, riet, geraten> [ˈraː·tn̩] **I.** *vi* ① (*Ratschläge geben*) ■ **[jdm] zu etw** *dat* **~** to advise [sb to do] sth ② (*schätzen*) to guess; **mal ~** to [take a] guess **II.** *vt* ① (*als Ratschlag geben*) ■ **jdm etw ~** to advise sb to do sth ② (*erraten*) to guess
Ratenkauf *m* installment plan
Ratenzahlung *f* ① *kein pl* (*Zahlung in Raten*) payment in installments ② (*einzelne Zahlung*) installment payment
Ratgeber <-s, -> *m* ① (*Werk*) manual, self-help book ② (*beratende Person*) advisor
Rathaus *nt* city [*or* town] hall
Ration <-, -en> [ra·ˈtsi̯oːn] *f* ration
rational [ra·tsi̯o·ˈnaːl] **I.** *adj* rational **II.** *adv* rationally
rationalisieren* [ra·tsi̯o·na·li·ˈziː·rən] *vt, vi* to streamline
Rationalisierung <-, -en> *f* streamlining
rationell [ra·tsi̯o·ˈnɛl] **I.** *adj* efficient **II.** *adv* efficiently
rationieren* [ra·tsi̯o·ˈniː·rən] *vt* to ration
Rationierung <-, -en> *f* rationing
ratlos **I.** *adj* helpless; **ich bin völlig ~** I'm completely at a loss **II.** *adv* helplessly
Ratlosigkeit <-> *f kein pl* helplessness
ratsam [ˈraːt·zaːm] *adj* advisable
Ratschlag <-s, Ratschläge> [ˈraːt·ʃlaːk, *pl* ˈraːt·ʃlɛː·gə] *m* advice; **jdm einen ~ geben** to give sb a piece of advice
Rätsel <-s, -> [ˈrɛː·tsl̩] *nt* ① (*Geheimnis*) mystery; **es ist [jdm] ein ~, warum/wie ...** it is a mystery [to sb] why/how ... ② (*Denkaufgabe*) riddle; **vor einem ~ stehen** to be baffled
rätselhaft *adj* mysterious; ■ **es ist jdm ~, warum ...** it's a mystery to sb why ...
rätseln [ˈrɛː·tsl̩n] *vi* to rack one's brains
Rätselraten <-s> *nt kein pl* ① (*das Lösen von Rätseln*) puzzle solving ② (*das Mutmaßen*) guessing game
Ratte <-, -n> [ˈra·tə] *f* (*a. fig*) rat
rattern [ˈra·tɐn] *vi* ① *haben* (*klappern*) to rattle ② *sein* (*sich fortbewegen*) to rattle along
ratzekahl [ˈra·tsə·ˈkaːl] *adv* (*fam*), **ratzeputz** *adv* DIAL (*fam*) **alles ~ aufessen** to polish off *sep* everything; **den Teller ~ leer essen** to clean one's plate
rau[RR] [rau] *adj* ① (*spröde*) *Hände, Haut* rough; *Lippen* chapped ② (*heiser*) *Stimme* hoarse; (*verführerisch*) husky ③ (*unwirtlich*) *Klima, Wetter* harsh; *Gegend* inhospitable ④ (*ungehobelt*) harsh; *Benehmen, Sitten* uncouth
Raub <-[e]s, -e> [raup] *m pl selten* ① (*das Rauben*) robbery ② (*das Geraubte*) loot
Raubdruck *m* pirate[d] edition
Raubein[RR] *nt* (*fam*) diamond in the rough
raubeinig[RR] *adj* (*fam*) rough-and-ready
rauben [ˈrau·bn̩] **I.** *vt* ① (*stehlen*) to rob; **das hat mir viel Zeit geraubt** this has cost me a lot of time ② (*entführen*) to abduct **II.** *vi* to rob
Räuber(in) <-s, -> [ˈrɔy·bɐ] *m(f)* robber
Raubkatze *f* big [predatory] cat
Raubkopie *f* pirate[d] copy
Raubmord *m* murder robbery
Raubmörder(in) *m(f)* robber and murderer
Raubtier *nt* predator
Raubüberfall *m* robbery; (*auf Geldtransport etc. a.*) holdup
Raubvogel *m* bird of prey
Rauch <-[e]s> [raux] *m kein pl* smoke ► WENDUNGEN: **sich in ~ auflösen** to go up in smoke
Rauchabzug *m* smoke vent
rauchen [ˈrau·xn̩] *vi, vt* to smoke
Raucher <-s, -> *m* BAHN (*fam*) *s.* **Raucherabteil**
Raucher(in) <-s, -> *m(f)* smoker
Raucherabteil *nt* BAHN smoking compartment [*or* car]
Raucherhusten *m* smoker's cough
Räucherlachs *m* smoked salmon
räuchern [ˈrɔy·çɐn] *vt, vi* to smoke
Räucherstäbchen *nt* [stick of] incense
Raucherzone *f* smoking area
Rauchfang *m* ① (*Abzugshaube*) range [*or* stove] hood ② ÖSTERR (*Schornstein*) chimney
rauchig [ˈrau·xɪç] *adj* smoky
Rauchmelder *m* smoke alarm
Rauchsignal *nt* smoke signal
Rauchverbot *nt* ban on smoking; **hier ist [o herrscht] ~** there's no smoking here, smoking isn't allowed here
Rauchwolke *f* cloud of smoke
rauf [rauf] *adv* (*fam*) *s.* **herauf, hinauf**
Raufbold <-[e]s, -e> [ˈrauf·bɔlt] *m* thug
raufen [ˈrau·fn̩] *vi, vr* ■ **[sich** *akk*] **~** to fight (**um** *+akk* over)
Rauferei <-, -en> [rau·fə·ˈrai] *f* fight
rauh[ALT] [rau] *adj s.* **rau**

R

Rauhbein[ALT] *nt s.* **Raubein**

rauhbeinig[ALT] *adj s.* **raubeinig**

Rauhreif[ALT] *m kein pl s.* **Raureif**

Raum <-[e]s, Räume> [raum, *pl* 'rɔy·mə] *m* ❶ (*Zimmer*) room ❷ *kein pl* (*Platz*) room *no art,* space *no art* ❸ GEOG (*Gebiet*) region, area; **im ~ Hamburg** in the Hamburg area ▶WENDUNGEN: **im ~ stehen** to be unresolved; **etw in den ~ stellen** to raise sth

räumen ['rɔy·mən] *vt* ❶ (*entfernen*) to remove (**aus/von** *+dat* from) ❷ (*einsortieren*) to put away *sep* (**in** *+akk* in/into) ❸ *Wohnung* to vacate; *Straße* to clear ❹ (*evakuieren*) to evacuate

Raumfähre *f* space shuttle

Raumfahrt *f kein pl* space travel *no art;* (*einzelner Raumflug*) space flight

Raumfahrtbehörde *f* space agency

Räumfahrzeug *nt* bulldozer; (*für Schnee*) snowplow

Raumflug *m* ❶ (*Flug in den Weltraum*) space flight ❷ *kein pl* (*Raumfahrt*) space travel

Raumgestaltung *f* interior design

räumlich ['rɔym·lɪç] **I.** *adj* ❶ (*den Raum betreffend*) spatial; **in großer ~er Entfernung** a long way[s *fam*] away ❷ (*dreidimensional*) three-dimensional **II.** *adv* ❶ (*platzmäßig*) spatially ❷ (*dreidimensional*) three-dimensionally

Räumlichkeiten *pl* premises *pl*

Raumpfleger(in) *m(f)* cleaner

Raumschiff *nt* spaceship

Raumstation *f* space station

Räumungsarbeiten *pl* work to clear an accident

Räumungsverkauf *m* clearance sale

Raupe <-, -n> ['rau·pə] *f* ❶ ZOOL caterpillar ❷ (*Planierraupe*) bulldozer

Raureif[RR] *m kein pl* hoarfrost

raus [raus] *adv* (*fam*) *s.* **heraus, hinaus**

raus|bringen *vt irreg* (*fam*) ❶ (*äußern*) **kein Wort ~** to not [be able to] utter a word ❷ *Müll* to take out *sep*

Rausch <-[e]s, Räusche> [rauʃ, *pl* 'rɔy·ʃə] *m* ❶ (*Trunkenheit*) intoxication; **einen ~ haben** to be drunk; **seinen ~ ausschlafen** to sleep it off ❷ (*Ekstase*) ecstasy

rauschen ['rau·ʃn̩] *vi* ❶ *haben* (*anhaltendes Geräusch erzeugen*) *Wasser, Verkehr* to roar; (*sanft*) to murmur; *Baum, Blätter* to rustle; *Lautsprecher* to hiss; *Rock, Vorhang* to swish ❷ *sein* (*sich geräuschvoll bewegen*) *Wasser* to rush; *Vogelschwarm* to swoosh ❸ *sein* (*fam: zügig gehen*) to sweep (**aus** *+dat* out of, **in** *+akk* into)

Rauschgift *nt* drug

Rauschgifthandel *m* drug trafficking

Rauschgifthändler(in) *m(f)* drug dealer; (*international*) drug trafficker

Rauschgiftsucht *f* drug addiction

rauschgiftsüchtig *adj* addicted to drugs *pred*

Rauschgiftsüchtige(r) *f(m)* drug addict

raus|ekeln ['raus·ʔeː·kl̩n] *vt* (*fam*) ■**jdn [aus etw** *dat*] **~** to drive sb [out of sth]

raus|fliegen *vi irreg sein* (*fam*) ❶ (*hinausgeworfen werden*) **aus der Schule ~** to be kicked out of school; **aus einem Betrieb ~** to be given the boot ❷ (*weggeworfen werden*) to get thrown out

raus|gehen *vi irreg sein* (*fam*) to go out; *Fleck, Korken* to come out

raus|kommen *vi irreg* (*fam*) *s.* **herauskommen, hinauskommen**

raus|kriegen *vt* (*fam*) ■**etw ~** to catch on to sth; *Rätsel* to figure out *sep;* ■**~, was/wer ...** to find out what/who ...

raus|nehmen *vt, vr irreg* (*fam*) *s.* **herausnehmen**

räuspern ['rɔys·pɐn] *vr* ■**sich** *akk* **~** to clear one's throat

raus|rücken *vt s.* **herausrücken**

raus|schmeißen *vt irreg* (*fam*) to throw out

Rausschmeißer <-s, -> *m* (*fam*) bouncer

Raute <-, -n> ['rau·tə] *f* rhombus

Razzia <-, Razzien> ['ra·tsi̯a, *pl* 'ra·tsi·ən] *f* raid

Reagenzglas *nt* test tube

reagieren* [rea·'giː·rən] *vi a.* CHEM to react (**auf** *+akk* to, **mit** *+dat* with)

Reaktion <-, -en> [reak·'tsi̯oːn] *f* reaction (**auf** *+dat* to)

reaktionär [reak·tsi̯o·'nɛːɐ̯] (*pej*) **I.** *adj* reactionary **II.** *adv* in a reactionary way

Reaktionszeit *f* reaction time

Reaktor <-s, -toren> [re·'ak·toːɐ̯, *pl* re·ak·'toː·rən] *m* reactor

real [re·'aːl] **I.** *adj* real **II.** *adv* **ein ~ denkender Mensch** a realistic thinker

Realeinkommen *nt* real income

realisierbar *adj* realizable; **schwer ~e Pläne/Projekte** plans/projects that are hard to accomplish

realisieren* [rea·li·'ziː·rən] *vt* to realize

Realisierung <-, -en> *f pl selten* realization; *Idee, Plan* implementation

Realismus <-> [rea·'lɪs·mʊs] *m kein pl* realism

Realist(in) <-en, -en> [rea·'lɪst] *m(f)* realist

realistisch [rea·'lɪs·tɪʃ] **I.** *adj* realistic **II.** *adv* realistically

Realität <-, -en> [rea·li·'tɛːt] *f* ❶ (*Wirklichkeit*) reality ❷ *pl* (*Gegebenheiten*) facts ❸ *pl* ÖSTERR (*Immobilien*) real estate

realitätsfern *adj* unrealistic; *Person* out of touch with reality

realitätsnah *adj* realistic; *Person* in touch with reality

Realitätssinn *m kein pl* sense of reality

Reallohn *m* actual earnings *pl*

Realschule *f* ≈ junior high school (*a school for grades 5–10 that prepares students either for the Gymnasium or for an apprenticeship in a trade or industry*)

In terms of academics, the **Realschule** lies somewhere between the *Hauptschule* and the *Gymnasium*. Students graduate after the tenth grade with a diploma called the *Mittlere Reife*. After graduation, most students complete three years of vocational training. However, students with very good grades have the chance to continue their education at a *Gymnasium*.

reanimieren* [re·ʔani·ˈmiː·rɛn] *vt* to resuscitate
Rebe <-, -n> [ˈreː·bə] *f* [grape]vine
Rebell(in) <-en, -en> [re·ˈbɛl] *m(f)* rebel
rebellieren* [re·bɛ·ˈliː·rən] *vi* to rebel (**gegen** *+akk* against)
Rebellion <-, -en> [re·bɛ·ˈli̯oːn] *f* rebellion; *Studenten* revolt
rebellisch [re·ˈbɛ·lɪʃ] *adj* rebellious
Rebstock *m* [grape]vine
Rechenaufgabe *f* math problem
Rechenfehler *m* calculation mistake
Rechenschaft <-> *f kein pl* account; **jdm [über etw** *akk*] **~ schulden** to be accountable to sb [for sth]; **jdn [für etw** *akk*] **zur ~ ziehen** to call sb to account [for sth]
Rechenzentrum *nt* computer center
Recherche <-, -n> [re·ˈʃɛr·ʃə] *meist pl f* research
recherchieren* [re·ʃɛr·ˈʃiː·rən] *vi, vt* to investigate, to research
rechnen [ˈrɛç·nən] **I.** *vt* ❶ (*mathematisch lösen*) to calculate ❷ (*zählen, messen*) to work out *sep;* **etw in Euro ~** to convert sth to euros ❸ (*veranschlagen*) to estimate; **wir müssen mindestens zehn Stunden ~** we have to count on at least ten hours; **zu hoch/niedrig gerechnet sein** to be an overestimate/underestimate ❹ (*einbeziehen, miteinrechnen*) to include ❺ (*berücksichtigen*) to take into account ❻ (*einstufen, gehören*) to count (**zu** *+dat* among); **ich rechne sie zu meinen besten Freundinnen** I consider her one of my best [girl]friends **II.** *vi* ❶ (*Rechenaufgaben lösen*) to do math; **ich konnte noch nie gut ~** I was never [any] good at math ❷ (*sich verlassen*) ■**auf jdn/etw ~** to count on sb/sth ❸ (*einkalkulieren*) ■**mit etw** *dat* **~** to count on sth; **wann ~ Sie mit einer Antwort?** when do you expect an answer?; **mit allem/dem Schlimmsten ~** to be prepared for anything/the worst ❹ (*fam: Haus halten*) to economize; **wir müssen mit jedem Cent ~** we have to watch every penny **III.** *vr* (*Gewinn einbringen*) ■**etw rechnet sich [nicht]** *akk* sth is [not] profitable
Rechner <-s, -> *m* ❶ (*Taschenrechner*) calculator ❷ COMPUT computer
rechnerisch I. *adj* arithmetic[al] **II.** *adv* ❶ (*kalkulatorisch*) arithmetically ❷ (*durch Rechnen*) by calculation
Rechnung <-, -en> *f* ❶ (*schriftliche Abrechnung*) bill; (*im Restaurant a.*) check; **das geht auf meine ~** I'll pay [for it], [you can] put that on my tab; **[jdm] etw in ~ stellen** to charge [sb] for sth ❷ (*Berechnung*) calculation; **die ~ stimmt nicht** the numbers don't add up ▶ WENDUNGEN: **er hatte die ~ ohne den Wirt gemacht** there was one thing he failed to take into consideration
recht [rɛçt] **I.** *adj* ❶ (*passend*) right ❷ (*richtig*) right; **ganz ~!** that's right [all right]! ❸ (*wirklich*) real ❹ (*angenehm*) ■**jdm ist etw ~** sth is all right with sb; **dieser Kompromiss ist mir durchaus nicht ~** I'm not at all happy with this compromise ❺ SCHWEIZ, SÜDD (*anständig*) decent; (*angemessen*) appropriate ▶ WENDUNGEN: **jdm ~ geschehen** to serve sb right; **nach dem R~en sehen** to make sure that everything's okay **II.** *adv* ❶ (*richtig*) correctly; **höre ich ~?** am I hearing things?; **ich sehe doch wohl nicht ~** I must be seeing things; **versteh mich bitte ~** please don't misunderstand me ❷ (*genau*) really; **nicht ~ wissen** to not really know ❸ (*ziemlich*) rather; (*gehörig*) properly ❹ (*fam: gelegen*) **jdm gerade ~ kommen** to come just in time for sb; (*iron*) to be all sb needs [right now]; **man kann es nicht allen ~ machen** you can't please everyone ▶ WENDUNGEN: **jetzt erst ~** now more than ever
Recht <-[e]s, -e> [rɛçt] *nt* ❶ *kein pl* (*Rechtsordnung*) law ❷ (*Anspruch*) right; **jds gutes ~ sein** to be sb's [legal] right; **jdm ~ geben** to agree with sb; **~ haben** to be [in the] right; **ein ~ auf jdn/etw haben** to have a right to sb/sth ❸ (*Befugnis*) right; **mit welchem ~?** by what right?; **mit ~** rightly; **und das mit ~!** and rightly so!
rechte(r, s) *adj attr* ❶ (*Gegenteil von linke*) right; **die ~ Seite** the right-hand side; **das ~ Fenster/Haus** the window/house on the right ❷ POL right[-wing] ❸ MATH **ein ~r Winkel** a right angle
Rechte <-n, -n> [ˈrɛç·tə] *f* ❶ (*rechte Hand*) right [hand] ❷ POL right; **ein Vertreter der radikalen ~n** a member of the extreme right
Rechteck <-[e]s, -e> *nt* rectangle
rechteckig *adj* rectangular
rechtfertigen I. *vt* to justify (**gegenüber** *+dat* to) **II.** *vr* ■**sich** *akk* **~** to justify oneself
Rechtfertigung *f* justification
rechthaberisch *adj* (*pej*) dogmatic
rechtlich I. *adj* legal **II.** *adv* legally
rechtlos *adj* without rights *pred*
rechtmäßig *adj* ❶ (*legitim*) lawful ❷ (*legal*) legal; **nicht ~** illegal
Rechtmäßigkeit <-> *f kein pl* ❶ (*Legitimität*) legitimacy ❷ (*Legalität*) legality
rechts [rɛçts] **I.** *adv* ❶ (*auf der rechten Seite*) on the right; **dein Schlüsselbund liegt ~ neben dir** your keys are just to your right; **~ oben/unten** on the top/bottom right; **nach/von ~** to/from the right ❷ TRANSP (*nach rechts*) [to the] right; **halte dich ganz ~** keep [to the] right; **~ abbiegen/ranfahren** to turn off/pull over to the right ❸ POL right; **~ einge-**

R

stellt sein to lean to the right ▶WENDUNGEN: **nicht mehr wissen, wo ~ und links ist** (*fam*) to not know whether one is coming or going **II.** *präp +gen* to [*or* on] the right of

Rẹchtsabteilung *f* legal department

Rẹchtsanwalt, -anwältin *m, f* lawyer, attorney; (*vor Gericht*) lawyer

rẹchtschaffen ['rɛçt·ʃa·fn̩] **I.** *adj* honest **II.** *adv* honestly

Rẹchtschreibfehler *m* spelling mistake

> The Vienna accord to reform German *Rechtschreibung* (orthography) was signed on July 1, 1996 and implemented on August 1, 1998. During the seven-year transitional phase until August 1, 2005, it was permissible to use spellings according to both the old and new rules. The *Rat für deutsche Rechtschreibung* (Commission for German Spelling) revised the **deutsche Rechtschreibreform** (German Spelling Reform) and the changes went into effect on August 1, 2006.
> The reform is an attempt to make German orthography easier to learn.

Rẹchtschreibung *f* spelling

Rẹchtsempfinden *nt* sense of right and wrong

rẹchtsextrem *adj* extreme right-wing

Rẹchtsextremismus *m kein pl* right-wing extremism

Rẹchtsextremist(in) *m(f)* right-wing extremist

rẹchtsextremistisch *adj* right-wing extremist

rẹchtsfähig *adj pred* **~ sein** to have legal capacity

Rẹchtsgrundlage *f* legal basis

rẹchtsgültig *adj* legally valid

Rẹchtshänder(in) <-s, -> ['rɛçts·hɛn·dɐ] *m(f)* right-hander; **~ sein** to be right-handed

rẹchtshändig ['rɛçts·hɛn·dɪç] **I.** *adj* right-handed **II.** *adv* right-handed, with one's right hand

rẹchtsherum *adv* [around] to the right; **etw ~ drehen** to turn sth clockwise

rẹchtskräftig I. *adj* legally valid; *Urteil* final **II.** *adv* with the force of law; **jdn ~ verurteilen** to pass final sentence on sb

Rẹchtskurve *f* right-hand curve

Rẹchtslage *f* legal position

Rẹchtsmittel *nt* legal means

Rẹchtsprechung <-, -en> *f pl selten* dispensation of justice

rẹchtsradikal I. *adj* ultra-right-wing **II.** *adv* with ultra right-wing tendencies

rechtsrum ['rɛçts·rʊm] *adv* (*fam*) *s.* **rechtsherum**

Rẹchtsschutzversicherung *f insurance that covers legal expenses*

Rẹchtssicherheit *f* guarantee of due process of law

Rẹchtsstaat *m* state founded on the rule of law

rẹchtsstaatlich *adj* under the rule of law *pred*

Rẹchtsstreit *m* lawsuit

Rẹchtsverdreher(in) <-s, -> *m(f)* (*hum fam: Anwalt*) legal eagle

Rẹchtsweg *m kein pl* judicial process; **den ~ beschreiten** (*geh*) to take legal action

rẹchtswidrig *adj* unlawful

Rẹchtswissenschaft *f kein pl* jurisprudence

rẹchtwink(e)lig *adj* right-angled

rẹchtzeitig I. *adj* punctual **II.** *adv* on time; **Sie hätten mich ~ informieren müssen** you should have given me enough [advance] notice

recken ['rɛ·kn̩] **I.** *vt* to stretch; **den Hals/Kopf [nach oben] ~** to crane one's neck [upward] **II.** *vr* ■ **sich** *akk* **~** to stretch

Recorder <-s, -> [re·'kɔr·dɐ] *m s.* **Rekorder**

recyceln* [ri·'sai·kl̩n] *vt* to recycle

recyclebar [ri·'sai·kl̩·baːɐ̯] *adj* recyclable

Recycling <-s> [ri·'sai·klɪŋ] *nt kein pl* recycling

Recyclingpapier [ri·'sai·klɪŋ-] *nt* recycled paper

Redakteur(in) <-s, -e> [re·dak·'tøːɐ] *m(f)* editor

Redaktion <-, -en> [re·dak·'tsi̯oːn] *f* ❶ (*redaktionelles Büro*) editorial department ❷ (*Redaktionsmitglieder*) editorial staff ❸ *kein pl* (*das Redigieren*) editing

redaktionell [re·dak·tsi̯o·'nɛl] **I.** *adj* editorial; **~e Bearbeitung** editing **II.** *adv* editorially; **etw ~ bearbeiten** to edit sth

Redaktionsschluss[RR] *m* press time

Redaktor(in) <-s, -en> [re·'dak·toːɐ] *m(f)* SCHWEIZ editor

Rede <-, -n> ['reː·də] *f* ❶ (*Ansprache*) speech ❷ (*das Reden, Gespräch*) talk; **wovon ist die ~?** what's it [all] about?; **es war gerade von dir die ~** we/they were just talking about you; **die ~ kam auf jdn/etw** the conversation turned to sb/sth ▶WENDUNGEN: **jdm ~ und Antwort stehen** to justify oneself to sb; **davon kann keine ~ sein** that's out of the question; **jdn zur ~ stellen** to take sb to task; **nicht der ~ wert sein** to be not worth mentioning

Redefluss[RR] *m kein pl* flow of words; **ich musste seinen ~ unterbrechen** I had to interrupt him in mid-sentence

Redefreiheit *f kein pl* freedom of speech

redegewandt *adj* eloquent

Redegewandtheit <-> *f kein pl* eloquence

reden ['reː·dn̩] **I.** *vi* ❶ (*sprechen*) to talk (**mit** *+dat* to/with, **über** *+akk* about); **mit jdm zu ~ haben** to need to speak to sb ❷ (*eine Rede halten*) to speak (**über** *+akk* about/on) ❸ (*diskutieren*) **darüber lässt sich ~** that's not out of the question; **mit sich** *dat* **[über etw** *akk*] **~ lassen** to be willing to discuss [sth] ▶WENDUNGEN: **du hast gut ~** that's easy for you to say **II.** *vt* ❶ (*sagen*) to say ❷ (*klatschen*) ■ **etw [über jdn/etw] ~** to say sth [about sb/sth]; **es wird über uns geredet** they're talking about

R

us **III.** *vr* **sich** *akk* **in Rage/Wut ~** to talk oneself into a rage/fury; **sich** *akk* **heiser ~** to talk oneself hoarse

Redensart *f* expression, figure of speech

Rederecht *nt kein pl* right to speak [out]

Redeschwall <-[e]s> *m kein pl* (*pej*) torrent of words

Redeverbot *nt* ban on speaking

Redeweise *f* manner of speaking

Redewendung *f* idiom

redigieren* [re·di·ˈgiː·rən] *vt* to edit

redlich [ˈreːt·lɪç] **I.** *adj* honest **II.** *adv* honestly

Redlichkeit <-> *f kein pl* honesty

Redner(in) <-s, -> [ˈreːd·nɐ] *m(f)* speaker

Rednerpult *nt* lectern

redselig [ˈreːt·zeː·lɪç] *adj* talkative

Redseligkeit <-> *f kein pl* talkativeness

Reduktion <-, -en> [re·dʊk·ˈtsi̯oːn] *f* (*form*) reduction

reduzierbar *adj* ■ **auf etw** *akk* **~ sein** to be reducible to sth

reduzieren* [re·du·ˈtsiː·rən] *vt* to reduce

Reduzierung <-, -en> *f* reduction; **eine ~ der Kosten** a reduction in cost[s]

Reederei <-, -en> [reː·də·ˈrai] *f* shipping company

reell [re·ˈɛl] *adj* ❶ (*tatsächlich*) real ❷ (*anständig*) straight; *Angebot, Preis* fair; *Geschäft* sound

Referat[1] <-[e]s, -e> [re·fe·ˈraːt] *nt* [seminar] paper; SCH project; **ein ~ [über jdn/etw] halten** to give a presentation [on sb/sth]

Referat[2] <-[e]s, -e> [re·fe·ˈraːt] *nt* ADMIN department

Referendum <-s, Referenden *o* Referenda> [re·fe·ˈrɛn·dʊm, *pl* re·fe·ˈrɛn·da] *nt* referendum

Referent(in) <-en, -en> [re·fe·ˈrɛnt] *m(f)* ❶ (*Berichterstatter*) speaker, presenter ❷ ADMIN head of an advisory department

Referenz <-, -en> [re·fe·ˈrɛnts] *f* ❶ *meist pl* (*Beurteilung*) **gute ~en aufzuweisen haben** to have good references ❷ (*Person*) referee

reflektieren* [re·flɛk·ˈtiː·rən] **I.** *vt* to reflect **II.** *vi* ❶ (*zurückstrahlen*) to reflect ❷ (*nachdenken*) to reflect (**über** +*akk* on/upon)

Reflektor <-s, -toren> [re·ˈflɛk·toːɐ̯, *pl* -ˈtoː·rən] *m* reflector

Reflex <-es, -e> [re·ˈflɛks] *m* ❶ (*Nervenreflex*) reflex ❷ (*Lichtreflex*) reflection

Reflexion <-, -en> [re·flɛ·ˈksi̯oːn] *f a.* PHYS reflection

Reform <-, -en> [re·ˈfɔrm] *f* reform

reformbedürftig *adj* in need of reform *pred*

Reformer(in) <-s, -> [re·ˈfɔr·mɐ] *m(f)* reformer

reformerisch [re·ˈfɔr·mə·rɪʃ] *adj* reforming

Reformhaus *nt* health food store

reformieren* [re·fɔr·ˈmiː·rən] *vt* to reform

Reformkost *f* health food

Refrain <-s, -s> [re·ˈfrɛ̃ː, rə-] *m* refrain

Regal <-s, -e> [re·ˈgaːl] *nt* shelf, shelving, rack; **etw aus dem ~ nehmen** to take sth off the shelf; **in/auf dem ~ stehen** to be on the shelf

Regatta <-, Regatten> [re·ˈga·ta, *pl* re·ˈga·tən] *f* regatta

rege [ˈreː·gə] **I.** *adj* ❶ (*lebhaft*) lively; *Anteilnahme, Beteiligung* active ❷ (*wach*) ■ **in jdm ~ werden** to be awakened in sb **II.** *adv* actively

Regel <-, -n> [ˈreː·gl̩] *f* ❶ (*Grundsatz*) rule; **sich** *dat* **etw zur ~ machen** to make a habit of sth; **in der ~** as a rule ❷ (*Menstruation*) period ▶ WENDUNGEN: **nach allen ~n der Kunst** with all the tricks of the trade

Regelblutung *f* menstruation

Regelfall *m kein pl* rule; **im ~** as a rule

regelmäßig **I.** *adj* regular **II.** *adv* ❶ (*immer wieder*) regularly ❷ (*ständig*) always; **sie kommt ~ zu spät** she is always late

Regelmäßigkeit <-> *f kein pl* regularity

regeln [ˈreː·gl̩n] **I.** *vt* ❶ (*in Ordnung bringen*) to settle; *Problem* to resolve ❷ (*regulieren*) to regulate **II.** *vr* ■ **sich** *akk* **[von selbst] ~** to sort itself out

regelrecht [ˈre·gl̩·rɛçt] **I.** *adj* real; *Frechheit* downright **II.** *adv* really; **~ betrunken sein** to be hammered *sl*

Regelung <-, -en> [ˈreː·gə·lʊŋ] *f* ❶ (*festgelegte Vereinbarung*) arrangement; (*Bestimmung*) ruling ❷ *kein pl* (*das Regulieren*) regulation

regelwidrig **I.** *adj* against the rules *pred* **II.** *adv* against the rules

regen [ˈreː·gn̩] *vr* ■ **sich** *akk* **~** ❶ (*sich bewegen*) to move ❷ (*geh*) *Zweifel, Gewissen, Hoffnung* to stir

Regen <-s, -> [ˈreː·gn̩] *m* rain; **saurer ~** acid rain; **bei/in strömendem ~** in [the] pouring rain ▶ WENDUNGEN: **vom ~ in die Traufe kommen** (*prov*) to jump out of the frying pan into the fire; **jdn im ~ stehen lassen** (*fam*) to leave sb in the lurch

Regenbogen *m* rainbow

Regenbogenpresse *f* gossip magazines *pl*

Regencape [ˈreː·gn̩·keːp] *nt* waterproof poncho

regenerieren* [re·ge·ne·ˈriː·rən] *vr* ■ **sich** *akk* **~** to regenerate; *Mensch* to recuperate

Regenfront *f* rain front

Regenmantel *m* raincoat

Regenrinne *f* gutter

Regenschauer *m* rain shower

Regenschirm *m* umbrella

Regent(in) <-en, -en> [re·ˈgɛnt] *m(f)* ruler; (*Vertreter des Herrschers*) regent

Regentschaft <-, -en> *f* ❶ (*Herrschaft*) reign ❷ (*Amtszeit*) regency

Regenwald *m* rainforest

Regenwetter *nt* rainy weather

Regenwurm *m* earthworm

Regie <-, -n> [re·ˈʒiː, *pl* re·ˈʒiː·ən] *f* FILM, THEAT direction; RADIO production; **[bei etw** *dat*] **die ~ haben** to direct [sth] ▶ WENDUNGEN: **in eigener ~** on one's own

R

regieren* [re·ˈgiː·rən] *vi, vt* to rule (**über** +*akk* over); *Monarch a.* to reign
Regierung <-, -en> [re·ˈgiː·rʊŋ] *f* POL ① (*Kabinett*) government ② (*Herrschaftsgewalt*) rule; **die ~ antreten** to take power [*or* office]; **an der ~ sein** to be in power
Regierungschef(in) *m(f)* head of a government
Regierungserklärung *f* government statement
Regierungspartei *f* ruling party
Regierungsrat *m kein pl* SCHWEIZ canton government
Regierungssprecher(in) *m(f)* government spokesperson
Regime <-s, -s> [re·ˈʒiːm] *nt* (*pej*) regime
Region <-, -en> [re·ˈgi̯oːn] *f* region
regional [re·gi̯o·ˈnaːl] **I.** *adj* regional **II.** *adv* regionally
Regionalteil [re·gi̯o·ˈnaːl-] *m* MEDIA local news section
Regisseur(in) <-s, -e> [re·ʒɪ·ˈsøːɐ̯] *m(f)* FILM, THEAT director; RADIO producer
Register <-s, -> [re·ˈgɪs·tɐ] *nt* ① (*alphabetischer Index*) index ② (*amtliches Verzeichnis*) register ▶ WENDUNGEN: **alle ~ ziehen** to pull out all the stops
registrieren* [re·gɪs·ˈtriː·rən] *vt* to register
Reglement <-s, -s> *nt* ① SPORT rules *pl* ② SCHWEIZ (*Vorschriften*) regulations *pl*
Regler <-s, -> [ˈreː·glɐ] *m* ELEK regulator; AUTO governor
reglos [ˈreːk·loːs] *adj s.* **regungslos**
regnen [ˈreːg·nən] **I.** *vi impers* to rain; ■ **es regnet** it's raining **II.** *vt* ■ **etw ~** to rain down sth; **es regnet Beschwerden** complaints are pouring in
regnerisch *adj* rainy
RegressRR <-es, -e>, **Regreß**ALT <-sses, -sse> [re·ˈgrɛs] *m* recourse
regulär [re·gu·ˈlɛːɐ̯] **I.** *adj* ① (*vorgeschrieben*) regular ② (*normal*) normal **II.** *adv* normally
regulierbar *adj* adjustable
regulieren* [re·gu·ˈliː·rən] **I.** *vt* ① (*einstellen*) to regulate ② *Bach, Fluss* to straighten **II.** *vr* ■ **sich** *akk* [**von selbst**] ~ to regulate itself
Regulierung <-, -en> *f* ① (*Einstellung*) regulation ② *eines Gewässers* straightening
Regung <-, -en> *f* ① (*Bewegung*) movement ② (*Empfindung*) feeling; **menschliche ~** human emotion
regungslos *adj* motionless; *Miene* impassive
Reh <-[e]s, -e> [reː] *nt* roe deer
Rehabilitation <-, -en> [re·ha·bi·li·ta·ˈtsi̯oːn] *f* rehabilitation
Rehabilitationszentrum *nt* rehab[ilitation center]
rehabilitieren* [re·ha·bi·li·ˈtiː·rən] *vt* to rehabilitate
Rehrücken *m* KOCHK saddle of venison
Reibe <-, -n> [ˈrai·bə] *f* grater
Reibekuchen *m* KOCHK DIAL (*Kartoffelpuffer*) potato pancake, ≈ latke

reiben <rieb, gerieben> [ˈrai·bn̩] **I.** *vt* ① (*zerkleinern*) to grate ② (*reibend verteilen*) ■ **etw auf/in etw** *akk* ~ to rub sth onto/into sth ③ (*reibend entfernen*) ■ **etw aus/von etw** *dat* ~ to rub sth out of/off sth **II.** *vr* **sich** *dat* **die Augen/Hände ~** to rub one's eyes/hands **III.** *vi* to rub (**an** +*dat* on); **die Schuhe ~ an den Zehen** my toes are rubbing [up] against the front of the shoes
Reibereien [rai·bə·ˈrai·ən] *pl* (*fam*) friction
Reibung <-, -en> *f* ① *kein pl* PHYS friction ② *pl s.* **Reibereien**
reibungslos **I.** *adj* smooth **II.** *adv* smoothly
reich [raiç] **I.** *adj* ① (*sehr wohlhabend*) rich, wealthy ② (*in Fülle habend*) rich (**an** +*dat* in); **~ an Erfahrung sein** to have a wealth of experience ③ (*ergiebig*) rich; *Ernte* abundant; *Ölquelle* productive; *Mahlzeit* lavish; *Erbschaft* substantial ④ (*vielfältig*) wide; *Möglichkeiten, Leben* rich; *Auswahl, Wahl* large; *Bestände* copious **II.** *adv* ① (*reichlich*) richly; **jdn ~ beschenken** to shower sb with presents ② (*mit viel Gelderwerb verbunden*) **~ heiraten/erben** to marry into/inherit money ③ (*reichhaltig*) richly
Reich <-[e]s, -e> [raiç] *nt* ① (*Imperium*) empire; **das ~ Gottes** the Kingdom of God; **das Dritte ~** HIST the Third Reich; **das Römische ~** HIST the Roman Empire ② (*fig: Bereich*) realm
Reiche(r) *f(m) dekl wie adj* rich man *masc*, rich woman *fem*
reichen [ˈrai·çn̩] **I.** *vi* ① (*ausreichen*) to be enough; **die Vorräte ~ noch Monate** there are enough supplies to last for months ② (*überdrüssig sein*) ■ **etw reicht jdm** sth is enough for sb; **mir reicht's!** I've had enough [of this]!; **jetzt reicht's** [**mir**] [**aber**]! enough is enough! ③ (*sich erstrecken*) ■ **bis zu etw** *dat* ~ to reach to sth; **von hier bis zum Horizont ~** to stretch from here to the horizon **II.** *vt* (*geh*) ① (*geben*) ■ **jdm etw ~** to give [*or* pass] sb sth ② (*zur Begrüßung*) ■ **jdm die Hand ~** to hold out one's hand to sb; **sich** [*o* **einander**] **die Hand ~** to shake hands
reichhaltig [ˈraiç·hal·tɪç] *adj* ① (*vielfältig*) wide; *Programm* varied ② *Bibliothek, Sammlung* well-stocked ③ (*üppig*) rich
reichlich [ˈraiç·lɪç] **I.** *adj* large; *Belohnung* ample; *Trinkgeld* generous; **~ Geld/Zeit haben** to have plenty of money/time **II.** *adv* (*ziemlich*) rather

During the years of the German Reich, the **Reichstag** (sovereign assembly) was composed of representatives who were elected to four-year terms according to the constitution of the Weimar Republic. After reunification, the parliament in Bonn decided to move the capital to Berlin, where, in 1994, the **Reichstag** building once again became the seat of the federal government in Germany.

Reichtum <-[e]s, Reichtümer> ['raiç·tu:m, *pl* -ty:·mɐ] *m* ① *kein pl* (*große Wohlhabenheit*) wealth; **zu ~ kommen** to get rich ② *pl* (*materieller Besitz*) riches *npl* ③ *kein pl* (*Reichhaltigkeit*) wealth (**an** +*dat* of)
Reichweite *f* range
reif [raif] *adj* ① AGR, HORT ripe ② (*ausgereift*) *a. Persönlichkeit* mature; **im ~en Alter von ...** at the ripe old age of ... ③ (*fam*) ■ **~ für etw** *akk* **sein** to be ready for sth
Reif <-[e]s> [raif] *m kein pl* METEO hoarfrost
Reife <-> ['rai·fə] *f kein pl* ① AGR, HORT (*das Reifen*) ripening; (*Reifezustand*) ripeness ② (*charakterlich*) maturity
reifen ['rai·fn̩] *vi sein* ① AGR, HORT to ripen; BIOL to mature ② (*sich entwickeln*) to mature (**zu** +*dat* into)
Reifen <-s, -> ['rai·fn̩] *m* tire
Reifendruck *m* tire pressure
Reifenpanne *f* flat [tire]
reiflich ['raif·lɪç] **I.** *adj* thorough; **nach ~er Überlegung** after [very] careful consideration **II.** *adv* thoroughly, carefully
Reihe <-, -n> ['raiə] *f* ① (*fortlaufende Folge*) row; **außer der ~** out of [the usual] order; **der ~ nach** in order ② (*das Drankommen*) ■ **jd ist an der ~** it's sb's turn; **ich war jetzt an der ~!** I was next!; **jeder kommt an die ~** everyone will get a turn ③ (*Menge*) **eine [ganze] ~ von** a [whole] lot of; **eine ganze ~ von Beschwerden** a slew of complaints ④ (*Linie von Menschen*) line; **sich** *akk* **in ~n aufstellen** to form lines ▶ WENDUNGEN: **etw auf die ~ kriegen** (*fam: kapieren*) to get sth into one's head; (*in Ordnung bringen*) to get sth together; **aus der ~ tanzen** to step out of line
reihen ['rai·ən] **I.** *vr* ■ **sich an etw ~** to follow [after] sth **II.** *vt* to string (**auf** +*akk* on)
Reihenfolge *f* order
Reihenhaus *nt* townhouse
reihenweise *adv* ① (*in großer Zahl*) by the dozen ② (*nach Reihen*) in rows
reihum [rai·'ʔʊm] *adv* in turn; **etw ~ gehen lassen** to pass sth around
Reim <-[e]s, -e> [raim] *m* ① (*Endreim*) rhyme ② *pl* (*Verse*) verse[s]
reimen ['rai·mən] **I.** *vr, vt* ■ **sich** *akk* **~** to rhyme (**auf** +*akk* with, **mit** +*dat* with) **II.** *vt* ■ **etw ~** to rhyme sth **III.** *vi* to make up rhymes
rein[1] [rain] *adv* (*fam*) *s.* **herein, hinein**
rein[2] [rain] **I.** *adj* ① (*unvermischt*) pure; *Wahrheit* plain ② (*fam: absolut*) *Zufall, Glück* pure; *Blödsinn* sheer; *Unsinn* utter; **das Kinderzimmer ist der ~ste Schweinestall!** the children's room is an absolute pigsty! ③ (*sauber*) clean; *Kleidung* fresh ④ (*makellos*) clear ▶ WENDUNGEN: **etw [für jdn] ins R~e bringen** to clear up sth *sep* [for sb]; **mit sich** *dat* **[selbst]/etw ins R~e kommen** to come to terms with oneself/sth; **etw ins R~e schreiben** to make a fair copy of sth **II.** *adv* ① (*ausschließlich*) purely; **eine ~ persönliche Meinung** a purely personal opinion ② (*fam: absolut*) absolutely; **~ zufällig** purely by chance
Reinemachefrau *f* cleaning lady
Reinerlös *m* net profit
Reinfall ['rain·fal] *m* (*fam*) disaster
rein|fallen *vi irreg sein* (*fam*) ① (*eine schwere Enttäuschung erleben*) to be taken in (**mit** +*dat* by) ② (*hineinfallen*) to fall in
Reingewinn *m* net profit
rein|hauen *vi* (*fig fam*) to stuff oneself; **hau rein!** dig in!
Reinheit <-> ['rain·hait] *f kein pl* ① (*frei von Beimengungen*) purity ② (*Sauberkeit*) cleanliness
Reinheitsgebot *nt* **Deutsches ~** *German beer purity regulation*

The German **Reinheitsgebot** is one of the oldest laws governing foodstuffs in Germany. Since 1516, the **Reinheitsgebot** has stipulated that only barley, hops, water, and, more recently, yeast, may be used in the production of beer.

reinigen ['rai·nɪ·gn̩] *vt* to clean
Reiniger <-s, -> ['rai·nɪ·gɐ] *m* cleaner
Reinigung <-, -en> *f* ① *kein pl* (*das Reinigen*) cleaning ② (*Reinigungsbetrieb*) cleaner's; **die chemische ~** the dry cleaner's
Reinigungskraft *f* (*form*) housekeeper, member of housekeeping staff
Reinigungsmittel *nt* cleaning agent
Reinkultur *f* monoculture; **in ~** unadulterated
rein|legen *vt* (*fam*) ① (*hineinlegen*) ■ **etw in etw** *akk* **~** to put sth in sth ② (*hintergehen*) ■ **jdn ~** to take sb for a ride
reinlich *adj* clean
Reinmachefrau *f s.* **Reinemachefrau**
reinrassig *adj* thoroughbred
rein|reiten *vt irreg* (*fam*) ■ **jdn ~** to get sb into a mess
rein|schneien *vi* (*fam*) ① *haben* (*schneien*) **es schneit rein** the snow's getting inside ② *sein* (*unangemeldet kommen*) to drop in
rein|würgen *vt* (*fam: widerwillig essen*) to force down ▶ WENDUNGEN: **jdm eine[n] ~** to teach sb a lesson
rein|ziehen *vr irreg* (*sl*) ① (*konsumieren*) **sich** *dat* **etw ~** to have something to drink/eat ② **sich** *dat* **einen Film ~** to watch a movie
Reis <-es, -e> [rais] *m* AGR, BOT rice
Reise <-, -n> ['rai·zə] *f* trip, journey; **gute ~!** have a good [*or* nice] trip!; **auf ~n gehen** to travel; **eine ~ machen** to take a trip
Reiseandenken *nt* souvenir
Reiseapotheke *f* first aid kit
Reisebüro *nt* travel agency
Reisebus *m* tour bus

R

reisefertig *adj* ready to go
Reisefieber *nt kein pl* ~ **haben** to be nervous and excited about traveling
Reiseführer *m* travel [*or* tour] guide
Reisegepäck *nt* luggage
Reisegesellschaft *f,* **Reisegruppe** *f* tour group
Reiseland *nt* popular travel destination
Reiseleiter(in) *m(f)* guide
reisen ['rai·zn̩] *vi sein* to travel (**nach** to)
Reisende(r) *f(m) dekl wie adj* traveler
ReisepassRR *m* passport
Reisescheck *m* traveler's check
Reisetasche *f* travel bag
Reiseveranstalter(in) *m(f)* tour operator
Reiseverkehr *m kein pl* holiday traffic
Reiseversicherung *f* travel insurance
Reisezeit *f* high [*or* tourist] season
Reiseziel *nt* destination
reißen <riss, gerissen> ['rai·sn̩] **I.** *vi* ❶ *sein* (*zerreißen*) *Seil, Faden* to break; *Papier, Stoff* to tear ❷ *haben* (*zerren*) to tug, to pull; **an seiner Leine ~** *Hund* to tug at its leash **II.** *vt haben* ❶ **etw in Fetzen/Stücke ~** to tear sth to shreds/pieces ❷ (*abreißen*) ■ **etw von etw** *dat* ~ *Ast, Bauteil* to break sth off [of] sth; *Papier, Stoff* to tear sth off [of] sth ❸ (*wegreißen*) **jdm etw aus der Hand ~** to snatch [*or* grab] sth from sb's hands ❹ (*stoßen*) **der Wind riss sie zu Boden** the wind threw her to the ground ❺ **jdn aus seinen Gedanken ~** to make sb lose their train of thought ❻ (*sich bemächtigen*) ■ **etw an sich** *akk* ~ to seize sth **III.** *vr haben* (*fam*) ■ **sich** *akk* **um jdn/etw ~** to scramble to get/see sb/sth; **um diese Arbeit reiße ich mich nicht** I'm not in any hurry to do this work
reißend *adj* (*Fluss*) raging
reißerisch **I.** *adj* sensational **II.** *adv* sensationally
ReißverschlussRR *m* zipper
Reißzwecke <-, -n> *f* thumbtack
reiten <ritt, geritten> ['rai·tn̩] **I.** *vi sein* to ride [a horse/pony]; **bist du schon mal geritten?** have you ever been horseback riding?; **im Galopp/Trab ~** to gallop/trot **II.** *vt haben* to ride
Reiter(in) <-s, -> ['rai·tɐ] *m(f)* [horseback] rider
Reiz <-es, -e> [raits] *m* ❶ (*Verlockung*) appeal, attraction; [**für jdn**] **den ~ verlieren** to lose its appeal [for sb] ❷ (*Stimulus*) stimulus ❸ *pl* (*sl: nackte Haut*) charms *npl*
reizbar *adj* irritable
Reizbarkeit <-> *f kein pl* irritability
reizen ['rai·tsn̩] **I.** *vt* ❶ (*verlocken*) ■ **jdn ~** to appeal to sb; ■ **es reizt jdn, etw zu tun** sb is tempted to do sth ❷ MED to irritate ❸ (*provozieren*) to provoke (**zu** + *dat* into) **II.** *vi* ❶ (*herausfordern*) ■ **zu etw** *dat* ~ to invite sth; **der Anblick reizte zum Lachen** what we saw made us laugh ❷ MED to irritate; **etw reizt jdn zum Husten** sth makes sb cough
reizend **I.** *adj* delightful, charming; **das ist ja ~!** (*iron*) that's charming! *iron* **II.** *adv* charmingly
reizlos *adj* dull
Reizthema *nt* emotional topic
Reizüberflutung *f* overstimulation
Reizung <-, -en> *f* irritation
reizvoll *adj* attractive
Reizwäsche *f kein pl* (*fam*) sexy underwear
Reizwort <-wörter> *nt* emotionally charged word
rekeln ['reː·kl̩n] *vr* ■ **sich** *akk* ~ to stretch out
Reklamation <-, -en> [re·kla·ma·'tsi̯oːn] *f* complaint
Reklame <-, -n> [re·'klaː·mə] *f* ❶ (*Werbeprospekt*) flyer ❷ (*Werbung*) commercials *pl*
Reklameschild *nt* advertising sign
Reklametafel *f* billboard
reklamieren* [re·kla·'miː·rən] *vt* ■ **etw ~** ❶ (*bemängeln*) to complain about sth ❷ (*beanspruchen*) to claim sth
rekonstruieren* [re·kɔn·stru·'iː·rən] *vt* to reconstruct
Rekord <-s, -e> [re·'kɔrt] *m* record
Rekorder <-s, -> [re·'kɔr·dɐ] *m* ❶ (*Kassettenrekorder*) cassette [*or* tape] recorder ❷ (*Videorekorder*) video recorder
Rekordhalter(in) <-s, -> *m(f)* record holder
Rekordzeit *f* record time
rekrutieren* [re·kru·'tiː·rən] **I.** *vt* to recruit **II.** *vr* ■ **sich** *akk* **aus etw** *dat* ~ to consist of sth
Relation <-, -en> [re·la·'tsi̯oːn] *f* ❶ (*Verhältnismäßigkeit*) proportion; **in ~ zu etw** *dat* **stehen** to be proportional to sth; **in keiner ~ zu etw** *dat* **stehen** to bear no relation to sth ❷ (*wechselseitige Beziehung*) relationship
relativ [re·la·'tiːf] **I.** *adj* relative **II.** *adv* relatively
relaxed [ri·'lɛkst] *adv* in a relaxed manner
relaxen* [ri·'lɛ·ksn̩] *vi* to relax
Religion <-, -en> [re·li·'gi̯oːn] *f* religion
Religionsfreiheit *f* freedom of religion
Religionszugehörigkeit <-, -en> *f meist sing* denomination
religiös [re·li·'gi̯øːs] **I.** *adj* religious **II.** *adv* in a religious manner
Religiosität <-> [re·li·gi̯o·zi·'tɛːt] *f kein pl* religiousness
Reling <-, -s *o* -e> ['reː·lɪŋ] *f* rail
Remoulade <-, -n> [re·mu·'laː·də] *f,* **Remouladensoße** *f* tartar sauce
rempeln ['rɛm·pl̩n] *vi* (*fam*) to jostle
Rendezvous <-, -> [rã·de·'vuː, 'rãː·de·vu] *nt* rendezvous *a. hum*
Rennbahn *f* racetrack
rennen <rannte, gerannt> ['rɛ·nən] *vi sein* ❶ (*laufen*) to run ❷ (*stoßen*) ■ **gegen etw** *akk* ~ to bump into sth
Rennen <-s, -> ['rɛ·nən] *nt* race; **gut/schlecht im ~ liegen** (*a. fig*) to be in a good/bad position
Renner <-s, -> ['rɛ·nɐ] *m* (*fam*) big seller
Rennfahrer(in) *m(f)* ❶ (*Autorennen*) racecar

driver ❷ (*Radrennen*) bicycle racer
Rennsport *m* ❶ (*Motorrennen*) motor racing ❷ (*Radrennsport*) bicycle racing ❸ (*Pferderennsport*) horse racing
Rennwagen *m* racecar
renovieren* [re·no·'viː·rən] *vt* to renovate
Renovierung <-, -en> *f* renovation
rentabel [rɛn·'taː·bl̩] **I.** *adj* profitable **II.** *adv* profitably
Rente <-, -n> ['rɛn·tə] *f* ❶ (*Ruhestand*) **in ~ gehen/sein** (*fam*) to retire/be retired ❷ (*Altersruhegeld*) pension; (*staatlich*) social security ❸ (*Zinseinkünfte*) annuity
Rentenalter *nt* retirement age
Rentenversicherung *f* Social Security
Rentier ['rɛn·tiːɐ̯] *nt* reindeer
rentieren* [rɛn·'tiː·rən] *vr* ■**sich** *akk* ~ to be worthwhile
Rentner(in) <-s, -> *m(f)* retiree
Reparatur <-, -en> [re·pa·ra·'tuːɐ̯] *f* repair
Reparaturwerkstatt *f* repair workshop; AUTO garage, mechanic's
reparieren* [re·pa·'riː·rən] *vt* to repair
Repertoire <-s, -s> [re·pɛr·'to̯aːɐ̯] *nt* repertoire
Reportage <-, -n> [re·pɔr·'taː·ʒə] *f* documentary
Reporter(in) <-s, -> [re·'pɔr·tɐ] *m(f)* reporter
Repräsentant(in) <-en, -en> [re·prɛ·zɛn·'tant] *m(f)* representative
Repräsentation <-, -en> [re·prɛ·zɛn·ta·'tsi̯oːn] *f* representation
repräsentativ [re·prɛ·zɛn·ta·'tiːf] **I.** *adj* ❶ (*aussagekräftig*) *Ergebnis, Querschnitt* representative ❷ (*vorzeigbar*) *Aufmachung, Auftreten* prestigious **II.** *adv* imposingly
repräsentieren* [re·prɛ·zɛn·'tiː·rən] **I.** *vt* to represent **II.** *vi* to perform official and social functions
reproduzieren* [re·pro·du·'tsiː·rən] *vt* to reproduce
Reptil <-s, -ien> [rɛp·'tiːl, *pl* -'tiː·li̯·ən] *nt* reptile
Republik <-, -en> [re·pu·'bliːk] *f* republic
Republikaner(in) <-s, -> [re·pu·bli·'kaː·nɐ] *m(f)* ❶ (*in den USA*) Republican ❷ (*in Deutschland*) member of the German Republican Party (*an ultra right-wing party*)
republikanisch [re·pu·bli·'kaː·nɪʃ] *adj* republican
Reservat <-[e]s, -e> [re·zɛr·'vaːt] *nt* reservation
Reserve <-, -n> [re·'zɛr·və] *f* ❶ (*Rücklage*) reserve ❷ (*Zurückhaltung*) reserve; **jdn aus der ~ locken** to bring sb out of his/her shell
Reservekanister *m* gas can
Reserverad *nt* spare tire
Reservereifen *m* spare tire
Reservespieler(in) *m(f)* substitute
reservieren* [re·zɛr·'viː·rən] *vt* to reserve
Reservierung <-, -en> *f* reservation
Reservoir <-s, -e> [re·zɛr·'vo̯aːɐ̯] *nt* reservoir
Residenz <-, -en> [re·zi·'dɛnts] *f* residence
resistent [re·zɪs·'tɛnt] *adj* resistant (**gegen** +*akk* to)
resolut [re·zo·'luːt] **I.** *adj* resolute **II.** *adv* resolutely
Resolution <-, -en> [re·zo·lu·'tsi̯oːn] *f* resolution
Resonanz <-, -en> [re·zo·'nants] *f* (*Entgegnung*) response (**auf** +*akk* to)
resozialisieren* [re·zo·tsi̯a·li·'ziː·rən] *vt* ■**jdn** ~ to reintegrate sb into society
Respekt <-s> [re·'spɛkt, rɛ-] *m kein pl* respect (**vor** +*dat* for); **bei allem ~!** with all due respect!; **sich** *dat* [**bei jdm**] ~ **verschaffen** to earn [sb's] respect
respektabel [re·spɛk·'taː·bl̩, rɛ-] **I.** *adj* ❶ (*beachtlich*) *Leistung* considerable ❷ (*ehrbar*) *Mensch* respectable **II.** *adv* ❶ (*beachtlich*) considerably ❷ (*ehrbar*) respectably
respektieren* [re·spɛk·'tiː·rən, rɛ-] *vt* to respect
respektlos **I.** *adj* disrespectful **II.** *adv* disrespectfully
Respektlosigkeit <-, -en> *f* ❶ *kein pl* (*Art*) disrespect ❷ (*Bemerkung*) disrespectful comment
Respektsperson *f* person commanding respect
respektvoll **I.** *adj* respectful **II.** *adv* respectfully
Ressentiment <-s, -s> [rɛ·sã·ti·'mãː] *nt* (*geh*) resentment
Ressort <-s, -s> [rɛ·'soːɐ̯] *nt* ❶ (*Zuständigkeitsbereich*) area of responsibility ❷ (*Abteilung*) department
Ressource <-, -n> [rɛ·'sʊr·sə] *f* ❶ (*Bestand an Geldmitteln*) resources *npl* ❷ (*natürlich vorhandener Bestand*) resource; *Energie* reserves *pl*
Rest <-[e]s, -e *o* SCHWEIZ *a.* -en> [rɛst] *m* rest; *Essen* leftovers *npl;* **der ~ ist für Sie!** (*beim Bezahlen*) keep the change!; **der letzte ~** the last bit; *Kuchen* the last crumb; *Wein* the last drop ▶ WENDUNGEN: **jdm den ~ geben** (*fam*) to be the final straw for sb
Restaurant <-s, -s> [rɛ·sto·'rãː] *nt* restaurant
Restauration[1] <-, -en> [re·stau·ra·'tsi̯oːn, rɛ-] *f a.* POL restoration
Restauration[2] <-, -en> [rɛ·sto·ra·'tsi̯oːn] *f* ÖSTERR (*veraltet: Gastwirtschaft*) restaurant
Restaurator, Restauratorin <-s, -toren> [re·stau·'raː·toːɐ̯, re·stau·raː·'toː·rɪn, *pl* re·stau·raː·'toː·rən] *m, f* restorer
restaurieren* [re·stau·'riː·rən, rɛ-] *vt* to restore
restlich *adj* remaining; **das ~e Geld** the rest of the money
restlos **I.** *adj* complete **II.** *adv* completely
Restmüll *m* trash (*garbage that cannot be recycled or composted*)
Restposten *m* surplus
Restrisiko *nt* residual risk
Resultat <-[e]s, -e> [re·zʊl·'taːt] *nt* result
resultieren* [re·zʊl·'tiː·rən] *vi* (*geh*) to result (**aus** +*dat* from, **in** +*dat* in)

R

Resümee <-s, -s> [re·zy·ˈmeː] *nt* (*geh*) ❶ (*Schlussfolgerung*) conclusion ❷ (*Zusammenfassung*) summary

resümieren* [re·zy·ˈmiː·rən] *vi, vt* (*geh*) to summarize

Retorte <-, -n> [re·ˈtɔr·tə] *f* retort ► WENDUNGEN: **aus der ~** (*fam*) artificially produced

retour [re·ˈtuːɐ̯] *adv* SCHWEIZ, ÖSTERR (*geh*) back; **eine Fahrkarte nach Wien und wieder ~** a round-trip ticket to Vienna, please

Retourbillett [ˈrə·tuːɐ̯·bɪl·jɛt] *nt* SCHWEIZ (*Rückfahrkarte*) round-trip ticket

Retourgeld *nt* SCHWEIZ (*Wechselgeld*) change

retten [ˈrɛ·tn̩] **I.** *vt* to save (**vor** +*dat* from); **das ist der ~de Einfall!** that's the idea that will save the day! ► WENDUNGEN: **bist du noch zu ~?** (*fam*) are you out of your mind? **II.** *vr* ■ **sich** *akk* **~** to save oneself (**vor** +*dat* from) ► WENDUNGEN: **rette sich, wer kann!** run for your lives!; **sich** *akk* **vor etw** *dat* **nicht mehr ~ können** to not have a chance against sth

Retter(in) <-s, -> *m(f)* rescuer, savior *liter*

Rettich <-s, -e> [ˈrɛ·tɪç] *m* radish

Rettung <-, -en> *f* ❶ (*das Retten*) rescue; **für jdn gibt es keine ~ mehr** there is no saving sb ❷ (*das Erhalten*) preservation ► WENDUNGEN: **jds letzte ~ sein** to be sb's last hope

Rettungsaktion *f* rescue operation

Rettungsboot *nt* lifeboat

Rettungshubschrauber *m* emergency rescue helicopter

rettungslos **I.** *adj* hopeless **II.** *adv* hopelessly

Rettungsring *m* ❶ NAUT life preserver ❷ (*hum fam: Fettpolster*) spare tire

Rettungsschwimmer(in) *m(f)* lifeguard

Rettungswagen *m* ambulance

Rettungsweste *f* life jacket

retuschieren* [re·tu·ˈʃiː·rən] *vt* to retouch, to touch up

Reue <-> [ˈrɔy·ə] *f kein pl* remorse

reuig [ˈrɔy·ɪç] *adj* remorseful

reumütig [ˈrɔy·myː·tɪç] **I.** *adj* remorseful; *Sünder* repentant **II.** *adv* remorsefully

Revanche <-, -n> [re·ˈvãː·ʃə, re·ˈvaŋ·ʃə] *f* ❶ (*Revanchespiel*) rematch ❷ (*Rache*) revenge

revanchieren* [re·vã·ˈʃiː·rən, re·vaŋ·ˈʃiː·rən] *vr* ■ **sich** *akk* **~** ❶ (*sich erkenntlich zeigen*) **sich bei jdm für eine Einladung ~** to return sb's invitation ❷ (*sich rächen*) to get one's revenge (**bei** +*dat* on)

revidieren* [re·vi·ˈdiː·rən] *vt* (*geh*) ❶ (*rückgängig machen*) to reverse ❷ (*abändern*) to revise

Revier <-s, -e> [re·ˈviːɐ̯] *nt* ❶ (*Polizeidienststelle*) police station ❷ (*Jagdrevier*) preserve ❸ (*Zuständigkeitsbereich*) area of responsibility

Revision <-, -en> [re·vi·ˈzi̯oːn] *f* ❶ FIN, ÖKON audit ❷ JUR appeal ❸ TYPO final proofreading

Revolte <-, -n> [re·ˈvɔl·tə] *f* revolt

Revolution <-, -en> [re·vo·lu·ˈtsi̯oːn] *f* revolution

revolutionär [re·vo·lu·tsi̯o·ˈnɛːɐ̯] *adj* revolutionary

Revolutionär(in) <-s, -e> [re·vo·lu·tsi̯o·ˈnɛːɐ̯] *m(f)* POL revolutionary

revolutionieren* [re·vo·lu·tsi̯o·ˈniː·rən] *vt* to revolutionize

Revolver <-s, -> [re·ˈvɔl·vɐ] *m* revolver

Revue <-, -n> [re·ˈvyː, rə·ˈvyː, *pl* -ˈvyː·ən] *f* THEAT revue

rezensieren* [re·tsɛn·ˈziː·rən] *vt* to review

Rezension <-, -en> [re·tsɛn·ˈzi̯oːn] *f* review

Rezept <-[e]s, -e> [re·ˈtsɛpt] *nt* ❶ KOCHK recipe ❷ MED prescription ❸ (*fig: Verfahren*) remedy (**gegen** +*akk* for)

rezeptfrei **I.** *adj* **~e Medikamente** over-the-counter medicine; ■ **~ sein** to be available without prescription **II.** *adv* over-the-counter; **~ zu bekommen sein** to be available without prescription

Rezeption <-, -en> [re·tsɛp·ˈtsi̯oːn] *f* reception

rezeptpflichtig *adj* requiring a prescription; ■ **~ sein** to be available only with a prescription

Rezession <-, -en> [re·tsɛ·ˈsi̯oːn] *f* recession

R-Gespräch [ˈɛr-] *nt* collect call

Rhabarber <-s, -> [ra·ˈbar·bɐ] *m* rhubarb

Rhein <-s> [rain] *m* Rhine

Rheinland <-[e]s> [ˈrain·lant] *nt* Rhineland

Rheinländer(in) <-s, -> [ˈrain·lɛn·dɐ] *m(f)* Rhinelander

Rheinland-Pfalz [ˈrain·lant-ˈpfalts] *nt* Rhineland-Palatinate

Rhetorik <-, -en> [re·ˈtoː·rɪk] *f* rhetoric

rhetorisch [re·ˈtoː·rɪʃ] **I.** *adj* rhetorical **II.** *adv* rhetorically

Rheuma <-s> [ˈrɔy·ma] *nt kein pl* (*fam*) rheumatism

rheumatisch [rɔy·ˈmaː·tɪʃ] *adj* rheumatic

Rheumatismus <-> [rɔy·ma·ˈtɪs·mʊs] *m kein pl* rheumatism

Rhinozeros <-[ses], -se> [ri·ˈnoː·tse·rɔs] *nt* ❶ (*Nashorn*) rhinoceros ❷ (*pej fam: Dummkopf*) blockhead

Rhythmen *pl von* **Rhythmus**

rhythmisch [ˈrʏt·mɪʃ] *adj* rhythmic[al]

Rhythmus <-, Rhythmen> [ˈrʏt·mʊs, *pl* ˈrʏt·mən] *m* rhythm

richten [ˈrɪç·tn̩] **I.** *vr* ❶ (*bestimmt sein*) ■ **sich** *akk* **an jdn ~** to be directed at sb; **dieser Vorwurf richtet sich an dich** you're the one being blamed ❷ (*herantreten*) ■ **sich** *akk* **an jdn/etw ~** to consult sb/sth ❸ (*sich orientieren*) ■ **sich** *akk* **nach jdm/etw ~** to comply with sb/sth; **wir richten uns ganz nach Ihnen** [we'll do] whatever is best for you ❹ (*abhängen von*) ■ **sich** *akk* **nach etw** *dat* **~** to be dependent [up]on sth; **das richtet sich danach, ob ...** that depends on whether ... **II.** *vt* ❶ (*lenken*) to direct (**auf** +*akk* toward/at); **seinen Blick auf etw** *akk* **~** to look at sth; **eine Schusswaffe auf jdn ~** to point a gun at sb ❷ (*adressieren*) to address (**an** +*akk* to)

R

❸ (*reparieren*) to fix ❹ (*bereiten*) to prepare **III.** *vi* (*geh*) to pass judgment (**über** +*akk* on)

Richter(in) <-s, -> ['rɪç·tɐ] *m(f)* judge

richterlich *adj attr* judicial

Richtgeschwindigkeit *f* recommended speed limit

richtig ['rɪç·tɪç] **I.** *adj* ❶ (*korrekt*) right; *Lösung* correct ❷ (*angebracht*) right; **es war ~, dass du gegangen bist** you were right to leave ❸ (*am richtigen Ort*) ■**irgendwo/bei jdm ~ sein** to be in the right place/at the right address ❹ (*echt*) real ❺ (*fam: regelrecht*) **du bist ein ~er Idiot!** you're a real idiot! ❻ (*passend*) right ❼ (*ordentlich*) real; **ein ~er Winter mit viel Schnee** a real winter with lots of snow ❽ (*fam: in Ordnung*) all right **II.** *adv* ❶ (*korrekt*) correctly; **Sie haben irgendwie nicht ~ gerechnet** you've miscalculated somehow; **ich höre doch wohl nicht ~?** you must be joking [*or* kidding]!; **eine ~ gehende Uhr** an accurate watch; **sehr ~!** that's correct! ❷ (*fam: regelrecht*) really; **das schmeckt ~ gut** this tastes really good

Richtigkeit <-> *f kein pl* correctness; **das wird schon seine ~ haben** I'm sure that's right

richtig|liegen *vi irreg* (*fam*) ■[**mit etw** *dat*] **~** to be right [about sth]; ■**bei jdm ~** to have come to the right person

richtig|stellen *vt* ■**etw ~** to correct sth

Richtlinie *f meist pl* guideline *usu pl*

Richtpreis *m* recommended price

Richtschnur *f kein pl* (*Grundsatz*) guiding principle

Richtung <-, -en> ['rɪç·tʊŋ] *f* ❶ (*Himmelsrichtung*) direction ❷ (*Tendenz*) trend; **sie vertritt politisch eine gemäßigte ~** she takes a politically moderate line; **irgendwas in der ~** something along those lines

richtungweisend *adj* pointing the way [ahead]

Richtwert *m* guideline

rieb [riːp] *imp von* **reiben**

riechen <rọch, gerọchen> ['riː·çn̩] **I.** *vi* ❶ (*duften*) to smell (**nach** +*dat* of); (*stinken a.*) to stink *pej* ❷ (*schnuppern*) ■**an jdm/etw ~** to smell sb/sth **II.** *vt* to smell; **riechst du nichts?** don't you smell anything? ▶WENDUNGEN: **das konnte ich nicht ~!** how was I supposed to know that!; **jdn nicht ~ können** to not be able to stand sb

Riecher <-s, -> ['riː·çɐ] *m* **einen guten ~ [für etw** *akk*] **haben** to have a good nose [*or* the right instinct] [for sth]

Riechkolben *m* (*hum fam*) schnoz *sl*

Ried <-(e)s, -e> ['riːt, *pl* 'riː·də] *nt* ❶ (*Schilf*) reeds *pl* ❷ SÜDD, SCHWEIZ (*Moor*) marsh

rief [riːf] *imp von* **rufen**

Riegel <-s, -> ['riː·gl̩] *m* ❶ (*Verschluss*) bolt; **vergiss nicht, den ~ vorzulegen** don't forget to bolt the door ❷ (*Schokoriegel*) bar ▶WENDUNGEN: **etw** *dat* **einen ~ vorschieben** to put a stop to sth

Riemen <-s, -> ['riː·mən] *m* (*schmaler Streifen*) strap ▶WENDUNGEN: **sich** *akk* **am ~ reißen** to pull oneself together

Riese, Riesin <-n, -n> ['riː·zə, 'riː·zɪn] *m, f* giant

rieseln ['riː·zl̩n] *vi sein* ❶ (*rinnen*) to trickle (**auf** +*akk* onto) ❷ (*bröckeln*) ■**von etw** *dat* **~** to flake off [of] sth

riesengroß ['riː·zn̩·'groːs] *adj* (*fam*) colossal, enormous; **eine ~e Dummheit** something really stupid; **eine ~e Enttäuschung/Überraschung** a huge disappointment/surprise

Riesenhunger *m* (*fam*) enormous appetite

Riesenrad *nt* Ferris wheel

Riesenschritt *m* giant stride; **der Termin für die Prüfung nähert sich mit ~en** the day of the exam is fast approaching

riesig ['riː·zɪç] **I.** *adj* ❶ (*ungeheuer groß*) gigantic ❷ (*gewaltig*) enormous; *Anstrengung, Enttäuschung* huge ❸ *pred* (*fam: gelungen*) great; **die Party war einfach ~** the party was really great **II.** *adv* (*fam*) enormously; **das war ~ nett von Ihnen** that was terribly nice of you

riet [riːt] *imp von* **raten**

Riff <-[e]s, -e> [rɪf] *nt* reef

Rille <-, -n> ['rɪ·lə] *f* groove

Rind <-[e]s, -er> [rɪnt] *nt* ❶ (*Kuh*) cow ❷ *kein pl* (*Rindfleisch*) beef

Rinde <-, -n> ['rɪn·də] *f* ❶ *Baum* bark ❷ *Brot* crust; *Käse* rind

Rinderbraten *m* roast beef

Rinderfilet *nt* fillet of beef

Rinderwahnsinn *m kein pl* mad cow disease *fam*

Rindfleisch *nt* beef

Rindvieh <-viecher> *nt* ❶ *kein pl* (*Rinder*) cattle *no art, + pl vb* ❷ (*sl: Dummkopf*) ass

Ring <-[e]s, -e> [rɪŋ] *m* ❶ (*Fingerring, Öse*) ring ❷ (*Ringstraße*) beltway ❸ (*Boxring*) ring

Ringbuch *nt* ring binder

ringeln ['rɪ·ŋl̩n] **I.** *vt* to wind (**um** +*akk* around) **II.** *vr* ■**sich** *akk* **~** to coil up

ringen <rạng, gerụngen> ['rɪ·ŋən] *vi* ❶ (*im Ringkampf kämpfen*) to wrestle ❷ (*kämpfen*) ■**mit sich** *dat* **~** to wrestle with oneself; **mit den Tränen ~** to fight back tears ❸ (*schnappen*) **nach Atem ~** to gasp for breath ❹ (*sich bemühen*) ■**um etw** *akk* **~** to struggle for sth

Ringen <-s> ['rɪ·ŋən] *nt kein pl* wrestling

Ringer(in) <-s, -> *m(f)* wrestler

Ringfahndung *f* manhunt [over an extensive area]

Ringfinger *m* ring finger

ringförmig **I.** *adj* ring-like; *Autobahn* circular **II.** *adv* in the shape of a ring; **die Umgehungsstraße führt ~ um die Ortschaft herum** the bypass circles around the town

Ringkampf *m* wrestling match

Ringkämpfer(in) *m(f) s.* **Ringer**

Ringrichter(in) *m(f)* referee

rings [rɪŋs] *adv* [all] around

ringsherum ['rɪŋs·hɛ·'rʊm] *adv s.* **ringsum**

Ringstraße *f* beltway

ringsum ['rɪŋs·'ʔʊm] *adv* [all] around

Rinne <-, -n> ['rɪ·nə] *f* ❶ (*Furche*) furrow

R

❷ (*Dachrinne, Regenrinne*) gutter
rinnen <rạnn, gerọnnen> ['rɪ·nən] *vi sein* ❶ (*fließen*) to run ❷ (*sickern*) *Tränen* to trickle
Rinnsal <-[e]s, -e> ['rɪn·za:l] *nt* ❶ (*winziger Wasserlauf*) rivulet *liter* ❷ (*rinnende Flüssigkeit*) trickle
Rịnnstein *m* ❶ (*Gosse*) gutter ❷ (*Bordstein*) curb
Rippchen <-s, -> ['rɪp·çən] *nt* smoked pork ribs *pl*, spare rib *usu pl*
Rippe <-, -n> ['rɪ·pə] *f* ANAT, KOCHK rib
Rịppenfell *nt* [costal] pleura
Rịppenfellentzündung *f* pleurisy
Rippli <-s, -> ['rɪp·li] *nt* KOCHK SCHWEIZ smoked pork ribs *pl*, spare rib *usu pl*
Risiko <-s, -s *o* Risiken *o* ÖSTERR Risken> ['ri:·zi·ko] *nt* risk
risikobereit *adj* prepared to take a risk *pred*
Risikobereitschaft *f* willingness to take [great] risks
risikofreudig *adj* prepared to take risks *pred*
Risikogruppe *f* [high-]risk group
riskant [rɪs·'kant] *adj* risky
riskieren* [rɪs·'ki:·rən] *vt* **ich riskiere es!** I'll chance it!; **seinen Job ~** to put one's job at risk; **sein Leben ~** to risk one's life; ■ **[es] ~, etw zu tun** to risk doing sth
riss[RR], **riß**[ALT] [rɪs] *imp von* **reißen**
Riss[RR] <-es, -e>, **Riß**[ALT] <Risses, Risse> [rɪs] *m* (*in Kleidung, Muskel, Wand*) tear
rissig ['rɪ·sɪç] *adj Leder, Wand* cracked; *Hände, Lippen* chapped
Riten *pl von* **Ritus**
ritt [rɪt] *imp von* **reiten**
Ritt <-[e]s, -e> [rɪt] *m* ride
Ritter <-s, -> ['rɪ·tɐ] *m* knight
rịtterlich *adj* ❶ (*höflich zu Damen*) chivalrous ❷ HIST knightly *liter*
rittlings ['rɪt·lɪŋs] *adv* astride
Ritual <-s, -e *o* -ien> [ri·'tu̯·a:l, *pl* ri·'tu̯a:·li̯·ən] *nt* ritual
rituell [ri·'tu̯·ɛl] *adj* ritual
Ritus <-, Riten> ['ri:·tʊs, *pl* 'ri:·tən] *m* rite
Ritze <-, -n> ['rɪ·tsə] *f* crack
ritzen ['rɪ·tsn̩] **I.** *vt* to carve **II.** *vr* ■ **sich** *akk* ~ to cut oneself
Rivale, Rivalin <-n, -n> [ri·'va:·lə, ri·'va:·lɪn] *m, f* rival
rivalisieren* [ri·va·li·'zi:·rən] *vi* (*geh*) ■ **mit jdm ~** to compete with sb; ■ **~d** rival *attr*
Rivalität <-, -en> [ri·va·li'tɛ:t] *f* (*geh*) rivalry
Roaminggebühr ['roʊ·mɪŋ-] *f meist pl* TELEC roaming charge
Roastbeef <-s, -s> ['ro:st·bi:f] *nt* roast beef
Robbe <-, -n> ['rɔ·bə] *f* seal
robben ['rɔ·bn̩] *vi sein* to crawl
Robe <-, -n> ['ro:·bə] *f* ❶ (*langes Abendkleid*) evening gown ❷ (*Talar*) robe[s *pl*]
Roboter <-s, -> ['rɔ·bɔ·tɐ] *m* robot
Robotik <-> ['rɔ·bɔ·tɪk] *f kein pl* robotics
robust [ro·'bʊst] *adj* robust
Robụstheit <-> *f kein pl* robustness
roch [rɔx] *imp von* **riechen**
röcheln ['rœ·çl̩n] *vi* to breath rattles; *Sterbender* to give the death rattle *liter*
Rock <-[e]s, Röcke> [rɔk, *pl* 'rœ·kə] *m* ❶ (*Damenrock*) skirt ❷ DIAL (*Jackett*) jacket ❸ SCHWEIZ (*Kleid*) dress
rocken ['rɔ·kn̩] *vi* to rock
Rocker(in) <-s, -> ['rɔ·kɐ] *m(f)* rocker
Rọckgruppe *f* rock group
Rodelbahn *f* toboggan run
rodeln ['ro:·dl̩n] *vi sein o haben* to sled, to toboggan
roden ['ro:·dn̩] *vt* to clear
Rogen <-s, -> ['ro:·gn̩] *m* roe
Roggen <-s> ['rɔ·gn̩] *m kein pl* rye
Rọggenbrot *nt* rye bread
roh [ro:] **I.** *adj* ❶ (*nicht zubereitet*) raw ❷ (*unbearbeitet*) crude; *Holzklotz* rough; *Marmorblock* unhewn ❸ (*grob*) rough; **mit ~er Gewalt** by brute force, with brute strength **II.** *adv* (*grob*) roughly
Rohbau <-bauten> *m* shell
Rohgewicht *nt* gross weight
Rohkost *f* raw vegetables *npl*
Rohling <-s, -e> ['ro:·lɪŋ] *m* (*brutaler Kerl*) brute
Rohmaterial *nt* raw material
Rohöl *nt* crude oil
Rohr <-[e]s, -e> [ro:ɐ̯] *nt* ❶ (*Röhre*) pipe; (*mit kleinerem Durchmesser, flexibel*) tube ❷ SÜDD, ÖSTERR (*Backofen*) oven
Rohrbruch *m* burst pipe
Röhre <-, -n> ['rø:·rə] *f* ❶ (*Hohlkörper*) tube ❷ (*Leuchtstoffröhre*) neon tube ❸ (*Backofen*) oven
röhren ['rø:·rən] *vi* ❶ *Hirsch* to bellow ❷ (*fam: heiser grölen*) to bawl ❸ (*laut dröhnen*) to roar
Rohrleitung *f* pipe
Rohrspatz *m* ▶ WENDUNGEN: **wie ein ~ schimpfen** (*fam*) to curse like a sailor
Rohrstock *m* cane
Rohrzange *f* pipe wrench
Rohrzucker *m* cane sugar
Rohstoff *m* raw material
Rohzustand *m* **im ~** in an unfinished state
Rolladen[ALT] <-s, Rolläden *o* -> *m s.* **Rollladen**
Rọllbahn *f* LUFT runway
Rọllbraten *m* rolled roast
Rolle <-, -n> ['rɔ·lə] *f* ❶ (*Gerolltes*) roll; **eine ~ Draht/Toilettenpapier** a roll of wire/toilet paper ❷ (*Garnrolle*) reel ❸ (*Laufrad*) roller; (*Möbelrolle*) caster ❹ (*Turnübung*) roll ❺ FILM, THEAT role, part; **eine ~ spielen** to play a part ❻ (*Beteiligung, Part*) role, part; **das spielt doch keine ~!** that doesn't matter! ❼ SOZIOL role ▶ WENDUNGEN: **aus der ~ fallen** to behave badly
rollen ['rɔ·lən] **I.** *vi sein* to roll ▶ WENDUNGEN: **etw ins R~ bringen** to set sth in motion **II.** *vt* ❶ (*zusammenrollen*) to roll [up *sep*] ❷ (*rollend fortbewegen*) to roll **III.** *vr* ■ **sich** *akk* ~

R

to curl up
Rollenspiel *nt* role play
Rollentausch *m kein pl* role reversal
Roller <-s, -> ['rɔ·lɐ] *m* ❶ (*Kinderfahrzeug*) scooter ❷ (*Motorroller*) [motor] scooter ❸ ÖSTERR (*Rollo*) [roller] blind [*or* shade]
Rolli <-s, -s> ['rɔ·lli] *m* MODE (*fam*) turtleneck
Rollkragen *m* turtleneck
Rollkragenpullover [-pʊl·o:vɐ] *m* turtleneck
Rollladen^RR <-s, Rollläden *o* -> *m* storm shutters *npl*
Rollmops ['rɔl·mɔps] *m* [rolled] pickled herring
Rollo <-s, -s> ['rɔ·lo, rɔ·'lo:] *nt* [roller] blind, shade
Rollschuh *m* roller skate; ~ **laufen** to roller-skate
Rollstuhl *m* wheelchair
Rollstuhlfahrer(in) *m(f)* wheelchair user
rollstuhlgerecht *adj* wheelchair-accessible
Rolltreppe *f* escalator
Rom <-s> [ro:m] *nt kein pl* Rome
Roman <-s, -e> [ro·'ma:n] *m* novel
romanisch [ro·'ma:·nɪʃ] *adj* ❶ LING, GEOG Romance ❷ HIST Romanesque *spec* ❸ SCHWEIZ (*rätoromanisch*) Rhaeto-Romanic
Romanistik <-> [ro·ma·'nɪs·tɪk] *f kein pl* Romance studies
Romanschriftsteller(in) *m(f)* novelist
Romantik <-> [ro·'man·tɪk] *f kein pl* ❶ (*Epoche*) ■ **die** ~ the Romantic period ❷ (*gefühlsbetonte Stimmung*) romanticism; [**einen**] **Sinn für ~ haben** to be a romantic
Romantiker(in) <-s, -> [ro·'man·ti·kɐ] *m(f)* ❶ (*Künstler*) Romantic writer/composer/poet ❷ (*gefühlsbetonter Mensch*) romantic
romantisch [ro·'man·tɪʃ] **I.** *adj* ❶ (*zur Romantik gehörend*) Romantic ❷ (*gefühlvoll*) romantic ❸ (*malerisch*) picturesque **II.** *adv* picturesquely
Romanze <-, -n> [ro·'man·tsə] *f* romantic affair
Römer(in) <-s, -> *m(f)* Roman
römisch ['rø:·mɪʃ] *adj* Roman
röntgen ['rœnt·gn̩] *vt* to X-ray; ■ **sich ~ lassen** to be X-rayed
Röntgenstrahlen *pl* X-rays *pl*
rosa ['ro:·za] *adj* pink
rosarot *adj* pink
Rose <-, -n> ['ro:·zə] *f* ❶ (*Strauch*) rose bush ❷ (*Blüte*) rose
Rosé <-s, -s> [ro·'ze:] *m* rosé
Rosenkohl *m* [Brussels] sprouts
Rosenmontag *m the Monday before Shrove Tuesday, the climax of the German carnival celebration*
rosig ['ro:·zɪç] *adj* rosy
Rosine <-, -n> [ro·'zi:·nə] *f* raisin
Rosmarin <-s> ['ro:s·ma·ri:n] *m kein pl* rosemary
Ross^RR <-es, -e *o* Rösser>, **Roß**^ALT <Rosses, Rosse *o* Rösser> [rɔs, *pl* 'rœ·sɐ] *nt* ❶ (*liter: Reitpferd*) steed ❷ SÜDD, ÖSTERR, SCHWEIZ (*Pferd*) horse
Rosskastanie^RR [-ka·sta:·ni̯ə] *f* [horse] chestnut
Rosskur^RR *f* (*hum*) drastic cure
Rost[1] <-[e]s> [rɔst] *m kein pl* (*auf Eisen, Stahl*) rust
Rost[2] <-[e]s, -e> [rɔst] *m* ❶ (*Gitter*) grating ❷ (*Grillrost*) grill ❸ (*Bettrost*) base
Rostbraten *m* roast beef
rostbraun *adj Haar* auburn; *Kleidungsstück, Fell* russet
rosten ['rɔs·tn̩] *vi sein o haben* to rust
rösten ['rø:s·tn̩, 'rœs·tn̩] *vt* to roast; *Brot* to toast
rostfrei *adj* stainless
Rösti ['rø:s·ti] *pl* SCHWEIZ ≈ hash browns *pl*
rostig ['rɔs·tɪç] *adj* rusty
rot <-er *o* röter, -este *o* röteste> [ro:t] **I.** *adj* red; ■ ~ **werden** to turn red; (*aus Scham a.*) to blush **II.** *adv* red; **etw ~ unterstreichen** to underline sth in red
Rotation <-, -en> [ro·ta·'tsi̯o:n] *f* rotation
rotblond *adj Frau* strawberry blond[e]; *Mann* sandy-haired
rotbraun *adj* reddish brown
Röte <-> ['rø:·tə] *f kein pl* (*geh*) red[ness]
Röteln ['rø:·tl̩n] *pl* rubella *spec*
röten ['rø:·tn̩] **I.** *vr* ■ **sich** *akk* ~ to turn red; *Wangen a.* to blush **II.** *vt* to redden
röter *adj komp von* **rot**
röteste(r, s) *adj superl von* **rot**
rothaarig *adj* red-haired; ■ ~ **sein** to have red hair
rotieren* [ro·'ti:·rən] *vi* ❶ (*sich drehen*) to rotate ❷ (*fam: hektisch agieren*) to run around like crazy
Rotkohl *m*, **Rotkraut** *nt* SÜDD, ÖSTERR red cabbage
rötlich ['rø:t·lɪç] *adj* reddish
Rotlichtmilieu *nt* demimonde *liter*
Rotlichtviertel *nt* red-light district
Rotschopf *m* redhead
rot|sehen *vi irreg* (*fam*) to see red
Rotstift *m* red pencil/pen ▶ WENDUNGEN: [**bei etw** *dat*] **den ~ ansetzen** to cut back [on sth]
Rötung <-, -en> *f* reddening
Rotwein *m* red wine
Rotz <-es> [rɔts] *m kein pl* snot ▶ WENDUNGEN: ~ **und Wasser heulen** (*fam*) to cry one's eyes out
Rotzfahne *f* (*sl*) snotrag *pej fam*
rotzfrech ['rɔts·'frɛç] (*fam*) **I.** *adj* cocky **II.** *adv* cockily
rotzig ['rɔ·tsɪç] *adj* ❶ *Nase, Taschentuch* snotty ❷ (*unverschämt*) shameless
Rotzjunge *m* (*pej fam*) snotty little brat
Rotznase *f* (*fam*) ❶ (*schleimige Nase*) snotty nose ❷ (*freches Kind*) snotty little brat
Roulade <-, -n> [ru·'la:·də] *f* roulade *spec*
Route <-, -n> ['ru:·tə] *f* route
Routine <-> [ru·'ti:·nə] *f kein pl* routine
routinemäßig **I.** *adj* routine **II.** *adv* as a matter of routine

R

Routinier <-s, -s> [ru·ti·ˈni̯eː] *m* experienced person
routiniert [ru·ti·ˈniːɐt] *adj* experienced
Rowdy <-s, -s> [ˈrau·di] *m* hooligan
rubbeln [ˈrʊ·bl̩n] *vi, vt* to rub hard
Rübe <-, -n> [ˈryː·bə] *f* ① KOCHK, BOT turnip; **Gelbe ~** SÜDD, SCHWEIZ carrot; **Rote ~** beet ② (*fam: Kopf*) nut; [**von jdm**] **eins auf die ~ kriegen** to get whacked in the head [by sb]
rüber [ˈryː·bɐ] *adv* (*fam*) *s.* **herüber, hinüber**
rüber|bringen *vt irreg* (*fam*) ■[**jdm**] **etw ~** to get across *sep* sth [to sb]
rüber|kommen *vi irreg sein* (*sl*) ■[**zu jdm**] **~** to come over [to sb]
Rubrik <-, -en> [ru·ˈbriːk] *f* ① (*Kategorie*) category ② (*Spalte*) column
Ruck <-[e]s, -e> [rʊk] *m* jolt ► WENDUNGEN: **sich** *dat* **einen ~ geben** (*fam*) to pull oneself together
ruckartig I. *adj* jerky, jolting *attr* II. *adv* with a jerk
Rückbesinnung *f* recollection (**auf** +*akk* of)
Rückblende *f* flashback
Rückblick *m* look back (**auf** +*akk* at); **im ~ auf etw** *akk* looking back at sth
rückblickend I. *adj* retrospective II. *adv* in retrospect
ruckeln [ˈrʊ·kl̩n] *vi* to tug (**an** +*dat* at/on)
rucken [ˈrʊ·kn̩] *vi* to jerk
rücken [ˈrʏ·kn̩] I. *vi sein* ① (*weiterrücken*) to move; **zur Seite ~** to move aside; (*auf einer Bank a.*) to scoot over *fam* ② (*gelangen*) **in den Mittelpunkt des Interesses ~** to become the center of interest II. *vt* ① (*schieben*) to move ② (*zurechtrücken*) **er rückte den Hut in die Stirn** he pulled his hat down over his forehead; **seine Krawatte gerade ~** to straighten one's tie
Rücken <-s, -> [ˈrʏ·kn̩] *m* ① ANAT back; **jdm den ~ zudrehen** to turn one's back on sb; **~ an ~** back to back; **auf dem ~** on one's back; **hinter jds ~** (*a. fig*) behind sb's back ② KOCHK saddle ③ (*Buchrücken*) spine ► WENDUNGEN: **jdm läuft es [eis]kalt über den ~** cold shivers run down sb's spine; **jdm in den ~ fallen** to stab sb in the back; **jdm den ~ stärken** to give sb moral support
Rückendeckung *f* backing; **finanzielle ~** financial backing
Rückenlehne *f* seat back
Rückenmark *nt* spinal cord
Rückenschmerzen *pl* back pain, backache
Rückenschwimmen *nt* backstroke
Rückenwind *m* tail wind
rückerstatten* *vt nur Infinitiv und pp* to refund; **jdm seine Verluste ~** to reimburse sb for his/her losses *form*
Rückerstattung *f* refund; *von Verlusten* reimbursement *form*
Rückfahrkarte *f* return ticket
Rückfahrt *f* return trip
Rückfall *m* ① MED relapse *form* ② JUR second offense ③ (*geh: erneutes Aufnehmen*) ■**ein ~ in etw** *akk* a relapse into sth
rückfällig *adj* ① JUR *Täter* recidivist *attr* ② *Alkoholiker, Raucher, Patient* relapsed; **~ werden** to suffer a relapse
Rückflug *m* return flight
Rückfrage *f* question (**zu** +*dat* regarding)
Rückgabe *f* return
Rückgang *m* drop, fall; **im ~ begriffen sein** to be dropping [*or* falling]
rückgängig *adj* **etw ~ machen** to cancel sth
Rückgewinnung *f* recovery
Rückgrat <-[e]s, -e> *nt* ① (*Wirbelsäule*) spine ② *kein pl* (*fig: Stehvermögen*) backbone
Rückhalt *m* support ► WENDUNGEN: **ohne ~** unreservedly
rückhaltlos I. *adj* ① (*bedingungslos*) *Unterstützung* unreserved ② (*schonungslos*) unsparing; *Kritik* ruthless; *Offenheit* complete II. *adv* unreservedly
Rückkehr <-> *f kein pl* return
Rücklage *f* ① (*Ersparnisse*) savings *npl* ② FIN (*Reserve*) reserve fund
rückläufig [ˈrʏk·lɔy·fɪç] *adj* declining, falling
Rücklicht *nt* tail light; *eines Fahrrads a.* rear light
Rücknahme <-, -n> *f pl selten* taking back
Rückporto *nt* return postage
Rückreise *f* return trip
Rückreiseverkehr *m kein pl* homebound traffic
Rückruf *m* ① (*Anruf als Antwort*) return call ② ÖKON (*das Einziehen*) recall
Rucksack [ˈrʊk·zak] *m* backpack
Rucksacktourist(in) [-tu·rɪst] *m(f)* backpacker
Rückschau <-> *f kein pl* ① (*Rückblick*) reflection; **~ auf etw halten** to look back on sth ② MEDIA review
Rückschlag *m* ① (*Verschlechterung*) setback; **einen ~ erleiden** to suffer a setback ② (*von Schusswaffe*) recoil
Rückschluss[RR] *m* conclusion (**aus** +*dat* from); [**aus etw** *dat*] **den ~ ziehen, dass ...** to conclude [from sth] that ...; [**aus etw** *dat*] **seine Rückschlüsse ziehen** to draw one's conclusions [from sth]
Rückschritt *m* step backwards
Rückseite *f* ① *Blatt, Buch, Münze* reverse [side] ② *Gebäude, Gerät* back, rear
Rücksicht <-, -en> [ˈrʏk·zɪçt] *f* consideration; **keine ~ kennen** to be ruthless; **~ [auf jdn] nehmen** to show consideration [for sb]; **~ auf etw** *akk* **nehmen** to take sth into consideration
Rücksichtnahme <-> *f kein pl* consideration
rücksichtslos I. *adj* inconsiderate; ■**jdm gegenüber ~ sein** to be inconsiderate toward sb; **mit ~er Offenheit** with ruthless candor II. *adv* inconsiderately, ruthlessly
Rücksichtslosigkeit <-> *f kein pl* thoughtlessness
rücksichtsvoll I. *adj* considerate (**zu** +*dat* toward) II. *adv* considerately

R

Rücksitz *m* rear seat
Rückspiegel *m* rearview mirror
Rückspiel *nt* rematch
Rücksprache *f* consultation; ~ **[mit jdm] halten** to consult [with sb]
Rückstand *m* ❶ (*Verzug*) arrears *npl;* **mit der Miete in ~ sein** to be behind on the rent ❷ *pl* (*fällige Zahlungen*) outstanding payments *pl* ❸ *von Chemikalien* residue *form*
rückständig ['rʏk·ʃtɛn·dɪç] *adj* ❶ (*überfällig*) overdue ❷ (*zurückgeblieben*) backward
Rückstrahler <-s, -> *m* reflector
Rücktritt *m* ❶ (*Amtsniederlegung*) resignation ❷ *von einem Vertrag* withdrawal (**von** *+dat* from)
Rücktrittsrecht *nt* right of withdrawal
rück|versichern* *vr nur Infinitiv und pp* ■**sich** *akk* **bei jdm/etw ~** to check back with sb/up on sth
Rückwand *f* ❶ (*rückwärtige Mauer*) back wall ❷ (*rückwärtige Platte*) back [panel]
rückwärtig ['rʏk·vɛr·tɪç] *adj* back *attr; Ausgang* rear *attr*
rückwärts ['rʏk·vɛrts] *adv* ❶ (*rücklings*) backwards; **~ einparken** to back into a parking space ❷ (*nach hinten*) backward; **Salto ~** backward somersault ❸ ÖSTERR (*hinten*) at the back; **von ~** SÜDD, ÖSTERR from behind
Rückwärtsgang *m* reverse [gear]
Rückweg *m* way back; **sich** *akk* **auf den ~ machen** to head back
ruckweise *adv* jerkily
rückwirkend I. *adj* retroactive **II.** *adv* retroactively
Rückwirkung *f* repercussion
Rückzahlung *f* repayment
Rückzieher <-s, -> *m* **einen ~ machen** (*fam: eine Zusage zurückziehen*) to back out [of a commitment]; (*nachgeben*) to back down
Rückzug *m* ❶ MIL retreat; **den ~ antreten** to retreat ❷ SCHWEIZ (*Abhebung von einem Konto*) withdrawal
Rüde <-n, -n> ['ry:·də] *m* [male] dog
Rudel <-s, -> ['ru:·dl̩] *nt* herd; *Wölfe* pack; *Menschen* swarm
Ruder <-s, -> ['ru:·dɐ] *nt* ❶ (*langes Paddel*) oar ❷ (*Steuerruder*) helm; *eines kleineren Bootes a.* rudder
Ruderboot *nt* rowboat
Ruderer, Ruderin <-s, -> *m, f* rower
rudern ['ru:·dɐn] *vi sein o haben* to row
Ruf <-[e]s, -e> [ru:f] *m* ❶ (*Ausruf*) shout; (*an jdn gerichtet*) call ❷ *kein pl* (*Ansehen*) reputation
rufen <rief, gerufen> ['ru:·fn̩] **I.** *vi* ❶ (*schreien*) to cry out ❷ (*a. fig: nach jdm/etw verlangen*) ■**[nach jdm] ~** to call [for sb]; **die Pflicht ruft** duty calls **II.** *vt* ❶ (*ausrufen*) to shout ❷ (*herbestellen*) to call; ■**jdn zu sich** *dat* **~** to summon sb; ■**jdn ~ lassen** to send for sb
Rüffel <-s, -> ['rʏ·fl̩] *m* (*fam*) scolding
Rufmord *m* slander, character assassination
Rufname *m* name that sb is called
Rufnummer *f* [tele]phone number
Rufschädigung *f* JUR defamation
Rufweite *f* **außer/in ~** out of/[with]in earshot
Rufzeichen *nt* ❶ TELEK ring ❷ ÖSTERR (*Ausrufungszeichen*) exclamation point
Ruhe <-> ['ru:·ə] *f kein pl* ❶ (*Stille*) quiet, silence; **~!** [be] quiet!, shhh! ❷ (*Frieden*) peace; **jdm keine ~ gönnen** to not let up [for a second]; **jdn [mit etw** *dat*] **in ~ lassen** to leave sb alone [about sth] ❸ (*Erholung*) rest; **sich** *dat* **keine ~ gönnen** to not allow oneself any rest; **jdm keine ~ lassen** to not give sb a moment's rest ❹ (*Gelassenheit*) calm[ness]; **[die] ~ bewahren** to keep calm; **jdn aus der ~ bringen** to throw sb [for a loop]; **sich** *akk* **[von jdm/etw] nicht aus der ~ bringen lassen** to not let oneself get rattled [by sb/sth]; **in [aller] ~** [really] calmly; **immer mit der ~!** (*fam*) take it easy!, easy does it! ▶ WENDUNGEN: **jdn zur letzten ~ betten** (*geh*) to lay sb to rest; **keine ~ geben, bis ...** to not rest until ...; **sich** *akk* **zur ~ setzen** to retire; **die ~ weghaben** (*fam*) to be unflappable
ruhelos I. *adj* restless **II.** *adv* restlessly
Ruhelosigkeit <-> *f kein pl* restlessness
ruhen ['ru:·ən] *vi* ❶ (*ausruhen*) to rest; **nicht eher ~, bis ...** to not rest until ... ❷ *Blick* to rest (**auf** *+dat* on) ❸ (*eingestellt sein*) to be suspended ❹ **ein Projekt ~ lassen** to drop a project; **die Vergangenheit ~ lassen** to forget the past
Ruhepause *f* break
Ruhestand *m kein pl* retirement; **in den ~ gehen** to retire; **im ~** retired
Ruheständler(in) <-s, -> ['ru:·əʃtɛnt·lɐ] *m(f)* retiree
Ruhestörung *f* disturbance of the peace
Ruhetag *m* (*arbeitsfreier Tag*) day off; (*Feiertag*) day of rest
ruhig ['ru:·ɪç] **I.** *adj* ❶ (*still*) quiet; **sei ~!** (*fam*) [be] quiet!, shhh! ❷ (*geruhsam*) *Abend* quiet ❸ (*unbewegt*) *Meer* calm; *Blick, Hand* steady ❹ (*gelassen*) *Person, Stimme* calm; *Gewissen* clear; **jd kann ganz ~ sein** sb does not have to worry **II.** *adv* ❶ (*untätig*) idly; **~ dastehen** to stand idly by ❷ (*gelassen*) calmly; **~ reagieren** to react calmly **III.** *part* (*fam*) **geh ~, ich komme schon alleine zurecht** it's okay if you leave; I can manage on my own; **du kannst ~ hierbleiben** you're welcome to stay here
Ruhm <-es> [ru:m] *m kein pl* fame
rühmen ['ry:·mən] **I.** *vt* to praise **II.** *vr* ■**sich** *akk* **einer S.** *gen* **~** to brag about sth
Ruhmesblatt *nt* glorious chapter
rühmlich *adj* praiseworthy
ruhmreich *adj* glorious
ruhmvoll *adj* glorious
Rührei ['ry:ɐ·ʔai] *nt* scrambled eggs *pl*
rühren ['ry:·rən] **I.** *vt* ❶ (*umrühren*) to stir ❷ (*innerlich*) *Herz* to touch; ■**jdn ~** to move sb; **das kann mich nicht ~** that doesn't both-

R

er me [at all] ❸ (*bewegen*) to move **II.** *vi* ❶ (*umrühren*) to stir ❷ (*die Rede auf etw bringen*) to touch (**an** +*akk* [up]on) **III.** *vr* (*sich bewegen*) ■ **sich** *akk* ~ to move

rührend I. *adj* touching, moving; **das war ~ von dir** that was sweet of you **II.** *adv* touchingly

Ruhrgebiet *nt kein pl* the Ruhr [region]

rührselig *adj* tear-jerking *fam;* **ein ~er Film/ein ~es Buch** a tearjerker *fam*

Rührteig *m* sponge cake batter

Rührung <-> *f kein pl* emotion

Ruin <-s> [ru·'iːn] *m kein pl* ruin

Ruine <-, -n> [ru·'iːnə] *f* ruin[s *pl*]

ruinieren* [rui·'niː·rən] *vt* to ruin

rülpsen ['rʏlp·sn̩] *vi* to burp

Rülpser <-s, -> *m* (*fam*) burp

Rum <-s, -s> [rʊm] *m* rum

rum [rʊm] *adv* (*fam*) *s.* **herum**

Rumäne, Rumänin <-n, -n> [ru·'mɛː·nə, ru·'mɛː·nɪn] *m, f* Romanian; *s. a.* **Deutsche(r)**

Rumänien <-s> [ru·'mɛː·ni̯·ən] *nt* Romania; *s. a.* **Deutschland**

rumänisch [ru·'mɛː·nɪʃ] *adj* Romanian; *s. a.* **deutsch**

rum|diskutieren *vi* (*fam*) to blather [on]

rum|kriegen *vt* (*sl*) ❶ (*zu etw bewegen*) ■ **jdn [zu etw** *dat*] ~ to talk sb into [doing] sth ❷ (*verbringen*) **einen Tag irgendwie ~** to get through a day somehow

rum|machen *vi* (*pej sl*) ■ **mit jdm ~** to play around with sb

Rummel <-s> ['rʊ·ml̩] *m kein pl* ❶ (*fam: Aufhebens*) [hustle and] bustle ❷ (*Betriebsamkeit*) commotion ❸ DIAL (*Rummelplatz*) fairground

Rummelplatz *m* fairground

rumoren* [ru·'moː·rən] *vi impers* **in meinem Magen rumort es** my stomach's rumbling

Rumpelkammer ['rʊm·pl̩-] *f* junk room

rumpeln ['rʊm·pl̩n] *vi* ❶ *haben* to rumble; *Geschirr* to clatter ❷ *sein* ■ **über etw** *akk* ~ *Fahrzeug* to rumble over sth

Rumpf <-[e]s, Rümpfe> [rʊmpf, *pl* 'rʏmp·fə] *m* ❶ (*Torso*) torso ❷ *eines Flugzeugs* fuselage; *eines Schiffes* hull

rümpfen ['rʏmp·fən] *vt* **die Nase [über etw] ~** to turn up *sep* one's nose [at sth]; (*sehr verächtlich*) to sneer [at sth]

Rumpsteak ['rʊmp·steːk, -ʃteːk] *nt* rump steak

Rumtopf *m a dessert of rum-soaked fruit aged in a crock pot*

rum|treiben *irreg vr* (*fam*) ■ **sich** *akk* ~ to hang out

Rumtreiber(in) <-s, -> *m(f)* goof-off *pej fam*

Run <-s, -s> [ran] *m* run (**auf** +*akk* on)

rund [rʊnt] **I.** *adj* ❶ (*kreisförmig*) round ❷ (*rundlich*) plump; *Hüften* well-rounded; *Wangen* chubby ❸ (*fam*) **eine ~e Summe** a round sum; **~e fünf Jahre** a good five years ❹ *Geschmack* full **II.** *adv* ❶ ■ **~ um ...** around ... ❷ (*etwa*) around; **~ 100 Euro** approximately 100 euros

Rundblick *m* panorama

Runde <-, -n> ['rʊn·də] *f* ❶ (*Gesellschaft*) company ❷ (*Rundgang*) rounds *pl; eines Polizisten* beat; *eines Briefträgers* route; **seine ~ machen** to make one's rounds; *Polizist* to patrol one's beat ❸ SPORT lap; (*im Boxen*) round ❹ *von [Tarif]gesprächen* round ❺ (*Bestellung*) round [of drinks]; **eine ~ spendieren** to buy a [*or* the next] round ► WENDUNGEN: **[mit etw** *dat*] **über die ~n kommen** to make ends meet [with sth]

Rundfahrt *f* [sightseeing] tour

Rundflug *m* sightseeing flight

Rundfunk *m* ❶ (*geh*) radio; **im ~** on the radio ❷ (*Sendeanstalt*) broadcasting

Rundgang *m* walk; (*zur Besichtigung*) tour

rund|gehen *irreg* **I.** *vi sein* ❶ (*herumgereicht werden*) to be passed around; ■ **etw ~ lassen** to pass around *sep* sth ❷ (*fam: herumerzählt werden*) to make the rounds **II.** *vi impers sein* (*fam*) **es geht rund im Büro** it's all happening at the office; **jetzt geht es rund!** (*es gibt Ärger*) now there'll be hell to pay!

rundheraus *adv* bluntly

rundherum *adv* ■ **~ [um etw** *akk*] all around [sth]

rundlich ['rʊnt·lɪç] *adj* plump; *Hüften* well-rounded; *Wangen* chubby

Rundreise *f* tour (**durch** +*akk* of)

rundum ['rʊnt·'ʔʊm] *adv* ❶ (*ringsum*) all around ❷ (*völlig*) completely

Rundung <-, -en> *f* ❶ (*Wölbung*) curve ❷ *pl* (*fam*) curves

Rundwanderweg *m* circular trail

rundweg ['rʊnt·'vɛk] *adv* flatly

Runkelrübe ['rʊn·kl̩-] *f,* **Runkel** <-, -n> *f* ÖSTERR, SCHWEIZ mangel-wurzel

runter ['rʊn·tɐ] *adv* (*fam*) *s.* **herunter, hinunter**

runter|hauen *vt* (*fam*) **jdm eine ~** to slap sb in the kisser

runter|holen *vt* ❶ (*herunternehmen*) to fetch (**von** +*dat* from) ❷ (*sl*) ■ **sich** *dat* **einen ~** to jerk off

Runzel <-, -n> ['rʊn·tsl̩] *f* wrinkle

runzelig ['rʊn·tsə·lɪç] *adj* wrinkled

runzeln ['rʊn·tsl̩n] **I.** *vt* to crease; *Brauen* to knit; *Stirn* to wrinkle **II.** *vr* ■ **sich** *akk* ~ to become wrinkled

runzlig ['rʊnts·lɪç] *adj s.* **runzelig**

Rüpel <-s, -> ['ryː·pl̩] *m* lout

rüpelhaft *adj* loutish; **~er Kerl** lout

rupfen ['rʊp·fn̩] *vt* ❶ (*Huhn*) to pluck ❷ (*zupfen*) to pull up *sep* (**aus** +*dat* out of)

ruppig ['rʊ·pɪç] **I.** *adj* gruff; *Antwort* abrupt **II.** *adv* gruffly; **sich** *akk* **~ verhalten** to be gruff

Rüsche <-, -n> ['ryː·ʃə] *f* frill

Ruß <-es> [ruːs] *m kein pl* soot; *Dieselmotor* particulate; *Kerze* smoke; *Lampe* lampblack

Russe, Russin <-n, -n> ['rʊ·sə] *m, f* Russian; *s. a.* **Deutsche(r)**

Rüssel <-s, -> ['rʏ·sl̩] *m* snout; *Elefant a.* trunk

rußen ['ruː·sn̩] **I.** *vi* to produce soot; *Fackel, Kerze* to smoke **II.** *vt* SCHWEIZ, SÜDD (*entrußen*) ■**etw ~** to clean the soot out of sth; **den Kamin ~** to sweep the chimney

rußig ['ruː·sɪç] *adj* blackened [with soot *pred*]; (*verschmutzt a.*) sooty

russisch ['rʊ·sɪʃ] *adj* Russian; *s. a.* **deutsch**

Russland[RR], **Rußland**[ALT] <-s> ['rʊs·lant] *nt* Russia; *s. a.* **Deutschland**

Rụsslanddeutsche(r)[RR] *f(m)* ethnic German from Russia; *s. a.* **Deutsche(r)**

rüsten ['rʏs·tn̩] **I.** *vi* to arm **II.** *vr* (*geh*) ■**sich** *akk* **zu etw** *dat* **~** to prepare for sth **III.** *vt* SCHWEIZ (*vorbereiten*) ■**etw ~** to get together *sep* sth

rüstig ['rʏs·tɪç] *adj* sprightly

rustikal [rʊs·ti·'kaːl] **I.** *adj* rustic **II.** *adv* in a rustic style

Rüstung <-, -en> ['rʏs·tʊŋ] *f* ① *kein pl* (*das Rüsten*) [re]armament ② (*Ritterrüstung*) armor

Rụ̈stungsindustrie *f* weapons industry

Rụ̈stungsunternehmen *nt* arms manufacturer

Rụ̈stzeug *nt kein pl* ① (*Werkzeug*) equipment ② (*Know-how*) skills *pl;* (*Qualifikationen*) qualifications *pl*

Rute <-, -n> ['ruː·tə] *f* ① (*Gerte*) switch ② (*Angelrute*) [fishing] rod

Rutsch <-es, -e> [rʊtʃ] *m* landslide ▶ WENDUNGEN: **in einem ~** (*fam*) in one go; **guten ~!** (*fam*) Happy New Year!

Rutsche <-, -n> ['rʊt·ʃə] *f* ① (*Rutschbahn*) slide ② TECH chute

rutschen ['rʊt·ʃn̩] *vi sein* ① (*ausrutschen*) to slip; *Auto* to skid ② (*fam: rücken*) to move; **auf dem Stuhl hin und her ~** to fidget in one's chair; **rutsch mal!** scoot over! ③ (*gleiten*) to slide; *Kleidung* to slip [down]

rụtschfest *adj* nonslip

Rụtschgefahr *f kein pl* danger of slipping; (*von Auto*) risk of skidding

rutschig ['rʊt·ʃɪç] *adj* slippery

rütteln ['rʏ·tl̩n] **I.** *vt* to shake **II.** *vi* ■**an etw** *dat* **~** to shake sth; **daran ist nicht zu ~** (*kein Zweifel*) there's no doubt about it

Ss

S, s <-, -> [ɛs] *nt* S, s; **~ wie Siegfried** S as in Sierra

s. *Abk von* **siehe**

S. *Abk von* **Seite** p[.]; (*Mehrzahl*) pp[.]

Saal <-[e]s, Säle> [zaːl, *pl* 'zɛː·lə] *m* hall

Saat <-, -en> [zaːt] *f* ① *kein pl* (*das Säen*) sowing ② (*Saatgut*) seed[s *pl*]

Sabbat <-s, -e> ['za·bat] *m* the Sabbath

Säbel <-s, -> ['zɛː·bl̩] *m* saber

Sabotage <-, -n> [za·bo·'taː·ʒə] *f* sabotage

Saboteur(in) <-s, -e> [za·bo·'tøːɐ] *m(f)* saboteur

sabotieren* [za·bo·'tiː·rən] **I.** *vt* to sabotage **II.** *vi* to practice sabotage

Saccharin, Sacharin <-s> [za·xa·'riːn] *nt kein pl* saccharin

Sạchbearbeiter(in) *m(f)* specialist; (*in einer Behörde*) official in charge

Sạchbeschädigung *f* vandalism

Sạchbuch *nt* nonfiction book

sạchdienlich *adj* relevant

Sache <-, -n> ['za·xə] *f* ① (*Ding*) thing ② (*Angelegenheit*) matter; **eine gute ~** a good cause; **das ist meine ~** that's my business ③ (*Aufgabe*) **mit jdm gemeinsame ~ machen** to collude with sb; **sie macht keine halben ~n** she finishes what she starts; **er macht seine ~ gut** he's doing well ④ (*Sachlage*) **sich** *dat* **seiner ~ sicher sein** to be confident about what one's doing; **zur ~ kommen** to get to the point; **bei der ~ sein** to concentrate, to pay attention; **nichts zur ~ tun** to be irrelevant

Sạchgebiet *nt* field

sạchgemäß I. *adj* proper; **bei ~er Verwendung** when properly used **II.** *adv* properly

Sạchkenntnis *f* expert knowledge

sạchkundig I. *adj* [well-]informed **II.** *adv* **~ antworten** to give an informed answer

Sạchlage *f kein pl* situation, state of affairs

Sạchleistung *f* payment in kind

sachlich ['zax·lɪç] **I.** *adj* ① (*objektiv*) objective ② (*inhaltlich*) *Fehler* factual ③ (*schmucklos*) *Stil* functional **II.** *adv* ① (*objektiv*) objectively ② (*inhaltlich*) factually

sächlich ['zɛç·lɪç] *adj* LING neuter

Sạchlichkeit <-> *f kein pl* objectivity

Sạchschaden *m* property damage

Sachsen <-s> ['zak·sn̩] *nt* Saxony

sächsisch ['zɛk·sɪʃ] *adj* Saxon, of Saxony *pred*

sacht [zaxt], **sachte** ['zax·tə] **I.** *adj* gentle **II.** *adv* gently

Sạchverhalt <-[e]s, -e> *m* facts *pl*

Sạchverständige(r) *f(m) dekl wie adj* expert

Sạchwert *m* real value

Sack <-[e]s, Säcke> [zak, *pl* 'zɛ·kə] *m* ① (*großer Beutel*) sack, bag ② SÜDD, ÖSTERR, SCHWEIZ (*Hosentasche*) [pants] pocket ▶ WENDUNGEN: **jdm auf den ~ gehen** (*derb*) to get on sb's nerves

sacken ['zakn̩] *vi sein* to subside; (*zur Seite*) to lean

Sạckgasse *f* (*a. fig*) dead end *a. fig*

Sadismus <-> [za·'dɪs·mʊs] *m kein pl* sadism

Sadist(in) <-en, -en> [za·'dɪst] *m(f)* sadist

sadịstisch I. *adj* sadistic **II.** *adv* sadistically

S

säen [ˈzɛː·ən] *vt, vi* to sow
Safari <-, -s> [za·ˈfaː·ri] *f* safari
Safran <-s, -e> [ˈzaf·raːn] *m* saffron
Saft <-[e]s, Säfte> [zaft, *pl* ˈzɛf·tə] *m* ❶ (*Fruchtsaft*) [fruit] juice ❷ (*Pflanzensaft*) sap ❸ (*fam: Strom*) juice
saftig [ˈzaf·tɪç] *adj* ❶ (*viel Saft enthaltend*) juicy, succulent ❷ (*üppig*) *Weide* lush ❸ *Rechnung* steep
Sạftpresse *f* fruit press
Sage <-, -n> [ˈzaː·gə] *f* legend
Säge <-, -n> [ˈzɛː·gə] *f* ❶ (*Werkzeug*) saw ❷ ÖSTERR (*Sägewerk*) sawmill
sagen [ˈzaː·gn̩] **I.** *vt* ❶ (*äußern*) to say; **warum haben Sie das nicht gleich gesagt?** why didn't you say so before?; **was ich noch ~ wollte, ...** [oh, and] one more thing ... ❷ (*mitteilen*) to tell; **wem ~ Sie das!** (*fam*) you don't need to tell me [that]!; **nichts zu ~ haben** to have nothing to say; **das ist nicht gesagt** that is by no means certain ❸ (*meinen*) **was ~ Sie dazu?** what do you think?; **das kann man wohl ~!** you can say that again! ❹ (*bedeuten*) ■**jdm etwas ~** to mean something to sb; **das hat nichts zu ~** it doesn't mean a thing **II.** *vi* ■**sag/~ Sie, ...** tell me, ...; **genauer gesagt** or to be more exact; **unter uns gesagt** between you and me; **sag bloß!** you don't say!
sägen [ˈzɛː·gn̩] *vt, vi* to saw
sa̲genhaft **I.** *adj* ❶ (*phänomenal*) incredible ❷ (*legendär*) legendary **II.** *adv* incredibly
Sä̲gespäne *pl* wood shavings *pl*
sah [zaː] *imp von* **sehen**
Sahara <-> [za·ˈhaː·ra, ˈzaː·ha·ra] *f kein pl* ■**die ~** the Sahara
Sahne <-> [ˈzaː·nə] *f kein pl* cream; (*Schlagsahne*) whipping cream
Sa̲hnetorte *f* layer cake
Saison <-, -s *o* SÜDD, ÖSTERR -en> [zɛ·ˈzõː, zɛ·ˈzɔŋ] *f* season; **außerhalb der ~** in the off-season
Saisonarbeit [zɛ·ˈzõː-, zɛ·ˈzɔŋ-] *f* seasonal work
Saisonarbeiter(in) *m(f)* seasonal worker
saisonbedingt *adj* seasonal
Saite <-, -n> [ˈzai·tə] *f* MUS string ▸ WENDUNGEN: **andere ~n aufziehen** to get tough
Sa̲iteninstrument *nt* string[ed] instrument
Sakko <-s, -s> [ˈzako] *m o nt* sports coat
Sakrament <-[e]s, -e> [za·kra·ˈmɛnt] *nt* sacrament
Salamander <-s, -> [za·la·ˈman·dɐ] *m* salamander
Salami <-, -s> [za·ˈlaː·mi] *f* salami
Salat <-[e]s, -e> [za·ˈlaːt] *m* ❶ (*Pflanze*) lettuce ❷ (*Gericht*) salad
Sala̲tbesteck *nt* salad servers *pl*
Sala̲tgurke *f* cucumber
Sala̲tsoße *f* salad dressing
Salbe <-, -n> [ˈzal·bə] *f* ointment, salve
Salbei <-s> [ˈzal·bai] *m kein pl* sage
Saldo <-s, -s *o* Saldi *o* Salden> [ˈzal·do, *pl* ˈzal·di, ˈzal·dn̩] *m* FIN balance
Sä̲le *pl von* **Saal**
Salmonẹllenvergiftung *f* salmonella poisoning
salopp [za·ˈlɔp] **I.** *adj* ❶ (*leger*) casual ❷ (*ungezwungen*) *Ausdrucksweise* slangy **II.** *adv* ❶ (*leger*) casually ❷ (*ungezwungen*) **sich** *akk* **~ ausdrücken** to use slang[y] expressions
Salto <-s, -s *o* Sạlti> [ˈzal·to, *pl* ˈzal·ti] *m* somersault; **einen ~ machen** to somersault
salü [za·ˈlyː, ˈza·ly] *interj* SCHWEIZ (*fam*) ❶ (*hallo*) hi ❷ (*tschüs*) bye
Salz <-es, -e> [zalts] *nt* salt

> The **Salzburger Festspiele** (Salzburg Festival) first took place in August 1920. In the early years, Max Reinhardt achieved great acclaim for his Shakespeare productions. The "Jedermann" ("Everyman") performances on the steps of the Salzburg cathedral have also become world famous.

salzen <sạlzte, gesạlzen> [ˈzal·tsn̩] **I.** *vt* to salt **II.** *vi* to add salt
sạlzhaltig *adj* salty
salzig [ˈzal·tsɪç] *adj* salty
Sạlzkartoffeln *pl* boiled potatoes
Sạlzsäure *f kein pl* hydrochloric acid
Sạlzstreuer <-s, -> *m* salt shaker
Sạlzwasser *nt kein pl* salt water
Samen <-s, -> [ˈzaː·mən] *m* ❶ (*Pflanzensamen*) seed ❷ *kein pl* (*Sperma*) sperm
Sa̲menbank *f* sperm bank
Sa̲menerguss^RR *m* ejaculation
Sa̲menspender *m* sperm donor
Sạmmelbegriff *m* collective term
Sạmmelbehälter *m* collection bin
sammeln [ˈza·mḷn] **I.** *vt* ❶ (*pflücken*) to pick ❷ (*aufsammeln*) to gather ❸ *Münzen, Unterschriften* to collect ❹ (*zusammentragen*) to gather; *Belege* to keep ❺ (*um sich scharen*) *Menschen* to gather **II.** *vr* ❶ (*zusammenkommen*) ■**sich** *akk* **~** to assemble ❷ (*sich anhäufen*) ■**sich** *akk* **~** to accumulate, to collect **III.** *vi* **für einen guten Zweck ~** to collect for a good cause
Sạmmeltaxi *nt* collective [*or* shared] taxi
Sạmmler(in) <-s, -> *m(f)* collector
Sạmmlung <-, -en> *f* collection
Samstag <-[e]s, -e> [ˈzams·taːk] *m* Saturday; *s. a.* **Dienstag**
Sạmstaga̲bend^RR *m* Saturday evening; *s. a.* **Dienstag**
sạmstaga̲bends^RR *adv* [on] Saturday evenings
sạmstags *adv* [on] Saturdays
Samt <-[e]s, -e> [zamt] *m* velvet
sạmtartig *adj* velvety, like velvet *pred*
samtig [ˈzam·tɪç] *adj* velvety
sämtlich [ˈzɛmt·lɪç] *adj* all; **~e Unterlagen wurden vernichtet** all the documents were destroyed; **seine ~en Unterlagen** all his documents
Sanatorium <-, -rien> [za·na·ˈtoː·ri̯ʊm, *pl* -ri̯·ən] *nt* sanatorium

Sand <-[e]s, -e> [zant] *m* sand ▶WENDUNGEN: **das gibt es wie ~ am Meer** there are tons of them; **im ~e verlaufen** to peter out
Sandale <-, -n> [zan̩ˈdaː·lə] *f* sandal
Sandalette <-, -n> [zan·da·ˈlɛ·tə] *f* high-heeled sandal
Sạndbank <-bänke> *f* sandbank
Sandelholz [ˈzan·dl̩·hɔlts] *nt* sandalwood
Sạndgrube *f* sandpit
Sạndhaufen *m* sand pile
sandig [ˈzan·dɪç] *adj* sandy, full of sand *pred*
Sạndkasten *m* sandbox
Sạndsack *m* ① (*zum Boxen*) punching bag ② (*zum Schutz*) sandbag
Sạndstein *m* sandstone
Sạndstrand *m* sandy beach
sandte [ˈzan·tə] *imp von* **senden²**
sanft [zanft] **I.** *adj* ① *Berührung, Stimme* gentle ② *Farben, Musik* soft **II.** *adv* gently
sạnftmütig *adj* gentle
sang [zaŋ] *imp von* **singen**
Sänger(in) <-s, -> [ˈzɛŋɐ] *m(f)* singer
sạng- und klạnglos *adv* (*fam*) unwept and unsung
sanieren* [za·ˈniː·rən] *vt* ① (*renovieren*) to clean up *sep* ② (*wieder rentabel machen*) to rehabilitate
Sanierung <-, -en> *f* ① (*Renovierung*) renovation ② (*von Firma, etc.*) rehabilitation
sanitär [zani·ˈtɛːɐ̯] *adj attr* sanitary; **~e Anlagen** sanitation
Sanitäter(in) <-s, -> [zani·ˈtɛː·tɐ] *m(f)* paramedic
sank [zaŋk] *imp von* **sinken**
Sanktion <-, -en> [zaŋk·ˈtsi̯oːn] *f* sanction
sanktionieren* [zaŋk·tsi̯o·ˈniː·rən] *vt* to sanction
sann [zan] *imp von* **sinnen**
Saphir <-s, -e> [ˈzaː·fɪr, ˈza·fiːɐ, za·ˈfiːɐ] *m* sapphire
Sardelle <-, -n> [zar·ˈdɛlə] *f* anchovy
Sardine <-, -n> [zar·ˈdiː·nə] *f* sardine
Sarg <-[e]s, Särge> [zark, *pl* ˈzɛr·gə] *m* coffin, casket
saß [zaːs] *imp von* **sitzen**
Satan <-s, -e> [ˈzaː·tan] *m kein pl* Satan
satanisch [za·ˈtaː·nɪʃ] **I.** *adj attr* satanic, diabolical **II.** *adv* diabolically
Satellit <-en, -en> [za·tɛ·ˈliːt] *m* satellite
Satellitenschüssel *f* satellite dish
Satellitenstadt *f* satellite town
Satin <-s, -s> [za·ˈtɛ̃ː] *m* satin
Satire <-, -n> [za·ˈtiː·rə] *f kein pl* satire (**auf** +*akk* about/on)
satirisch [za·ˈtiː·rɪʃ] *adj* satirical
satt [zat] *adj* ① (*gesättigt*) full *pred fam;* **ich bin ~** I'm full; **sich** *akk* **[an etw** *dat*] **~ essen** to eat one's fill [of sth]; **Nudeln machen ~** pasta is filling ② (*kräftig*) *Farben* rich, deep ③ (*fam: überdrüssig*) **etw ~ sein** to be fed up with sth
Sattel <-s, Sättel> [ˈza·tl̩, *pl* ˈzɛ·tl̩] *m* saddle
satteln [ˈza·tl̩n] *vt* to saddle
Sạttelschlepper <-s, -> *m* tractor-trailer
sạtt|habenRR *vi irreg* ■**etw ~** to be fed up with sth
sättigen [ˈzɛ·tɪ·gn̩] **I.** *vt* to satiate; ■**gesättigt sein** to be saturated **II.** *vi* to be filling
sạ̈ttigend *adj* filling
Sạ̈ttigung <-, *selten* -en> *f* saturation
Saturn <-s> [za·ˈtʊrn] *m kein pl* Saturn
Satz¹ <-es, Sätze> [zats, *pl* ˈzɛ·tsə] *m* ① LING sentence; **mitten im ~** in mid-sentence ② MUS movement ③ (*Set*) set; **ein ~ Weingläser** a set of wine glasses ④ (*Schriftsatz*) typesetting; (*das Gesetzte*) type[matter] ⑤ SPORT set
Satz² <-es, Sätze> [zats, *pl* ˈzɛ·tsə] *m* leap, jump; **einen ~ machen** to leap, to jump
Satz³ <-es> [zats] *m kein pl* dregs *npl;* (*Kaffeesatz*) grounds *npl*
Sạtzbau <-s> *m kein pl* sentence construction
Sạtzteil *m* LING part of a sentence
Satzung <-, -en> [ˈza·tsʊŋ] *f* constitution, statutes *npl*
Sạtzzeichen *nt* LING punctuation mark
Sau <-, Säue *o* Sauen> [zau, *pl* ˈzɔyə, ˈzau·ən] *f* ① *pl a.* (*weibliches Schwein*) sow ② (*sl: schmutziger Mensch*) filthy pig ▶WENDUNGEN: **jdn zur ~ machen** to chew sb out; **die ~ rauslassen** to let it all hang out; **das ist unter aller ~** it's enough to make you puke
sauber [ˈzau·bɐ] **I.** *adj* ① (*rein*) clean ② (*stubenrein*) ■**~ sein** *Tier* to be housebroken; *Kind* to be potty trained ③ (*sorgfältig*) neat ④ (*anständig*) honest **II.** *adv* ① (*rein*) **etw ~ halten** to keep sth clean ② (*perfekt*) neatly
Sauberkeit <-> *f kein pl* cleanliness
säuberlich [ˈzɔy·bɐ·lɪç] **I.** *adj* neat **II.** *adv* neatly
säubern [ˈzɔy·bɐn] *vt* ① (*reinigen*) to clean ② (*euph: befreien*) to purge (**von** +*dat* of)
Sauce <-, -n> [ˈzoː·sə] *f s.* **Soße**
saudụmm *adj* (*sl*) dumb as a rock
sauer [ˈzau·ɐ] **I.** *adj* ① (*nicht süß*) sour; (*sauer eingelegt*) pickled ② (*Säure enthaltend*) acid[ic] ③ (*übel gelaunt*) mad (**auf** +*akk* at), pissed off *pred* (**auf** +*akk* at/with) **II.** *adv* (*übel gelaunt*) **~ reagieren** to get pissed [off]
Sauerampfer <-, -n> *m* sorrel
Sauerbraten *m* sauerbraten (*beef roast marinated in vinegar and herbs*)
Sauerei <-, -en> [zauə·ˈrai] *f* (*sl*) ① (*schmutziger Zustand*) mess ② (*unmögliches Benehmen*) [downright] disgrace
Sauerkirsche *f* sour cherry
Sauerkraut *nt* DIAL sauerkraut
säuerlich [ˈzɔy·ɐ·lɪç] **I.** *adj* ① (*leicht sauer*) [slightly] sour ② (*übellaunig*) annoyed **II.** *adv* ① (*leicht sauer*) **~ schmecken** to taste sour [*or* tart] ② (*übellaunig*) sourly
Sauerrahm *m* sour cream
Sauerstoff [ˈzauɐ·ʃtɔf] *m kein pl* oxygen
Sauerstoffgerät *nt* (*Beatmungsgerät*) respirator
Sauerstoffmangel *m kein pl* lack of oxygen
Sauerteig *m* sourdough

S

saufen <säuft, soff, gesoffen> ['zau·fn̩] **I.** *vt* (*sl*) to drink; (*schneller*) to knock back *sep* **II.** *vi* ① (*sl: Alkoholiker sein*) to drink, to take to the bottle ② (*Tiere*) to drink

Säufer(in) <-s, -> ['zɔy·fɐ] *m(f)* (*sl*) drunk[ard], boozer

Sauferei <-, -en> [zau·fə·'rai] *f* (*sl: Besäufnis*) drinking party; (*übermäßiges Trinken*) boozing *fam*

säuft [zɔyft] *3. pers sing pres von* **saufen**

saugen <sog *o* saugte, gesogen *o* gesaugt> ['zau·gn̩] *vi, vt* to suck (**an** +*dat* on)

säugen ['zɔy·gn̩] *vt* ■ **sein Junges** ~ to suckle its young

Säugetier *nt* mammal

saugfähig *adj* absorbent

Säugling <-s, -e> ['zɔyk·lɪŋ] *m* baby

Säuglingsnahrung *f* baby food

saukalt ['zau·'kalt] *adj* (*sl*) freezing cold

Säule <-, -n> ['zɔy·lə] *f* ① ARCHIT column ② (*a. fig: Stütze*) pillar

Saum <-[e]s, Säume> [zaum, *pl* 'zɔy·mə] *m* hem

saumäßig **I.** *adj* (*sl*) ① (*unerhört*) outrageous *attr;* **du hattest ~es Glück** you were damn lucky ② (*miserabel*) lousy **II.** *adv* (*sl*) like hell; ~ **kalt/schwer** cold/heavy as hell

säumen ['zɔy·mən] *vt* ① (*Kleidung*) to hem ② (*fig geh: zu beiden Seiten stehen*) to line

Sauna <-, -s *o* Saunen> ['zau·na] *f* sauna

Säure <-, -n> ['zɔy·rə] *f* ① CHEM acid ② (*saure Beschaffenheit*) acidity, sourness

Saurier <-s, -> ['zau·ri̯ɐ] *m* dinosaur

sausen ['zau·zn̩] *vi* ① *sein* (*sich schnell bewegen*) to dash [off]; (*schnell fahren*) to roar ② *haben* (*von Wind*) to whistle; (*von Sturm*) to roar ③ (*sein lassen*) **etw ~ lassen** to forget sth; **lass deine Verabredung doch** ~ forget about your date

Saustall *m* pigsty

Sauwetter *nt* (*sl*) lousy weather *no indef art*

sauwohl *adj* **ich fühle mich** ~ (*sl*) I feel really good [*or* like a million bucks]

Savanne <-, -n> [za·'vanə] *f* savanna[h]

SaxofonRR, **Saxophon** <-[e]s, -e> [zak·so·'foːn] *nt* saxophone

SB [ɛs·'beː] *Abk von* **Selbstbedienung** self-service

S-Bahn ['ɛs-] *f* rapid transit train

S-Bahnhof *m* rapid transit [*or fam* train] station

SBB ['ɛs·beː·beː] *f Abk von* **schweizerische Bundesbahnen** Swiss Rail, ≈ Amtrak

scannen ['skɛ·nən] *vt* to scan

Scanner <-s, -> ['skɛ·nɐ] *m* scanner

Schabe <-, -n> ['ʃaː·bə] *f* [cock]roach

schaben ['ʃaː·bn̩] *vt* to scrape

schäbig ['ʃɛː·bɪç] *adj* ① (*unansehnlich*) shabby ② (*gemein*) mean ③ (*dürftig*) paltry

Schablone <-, -n> [ʃa·'bloː·nə] *f* stencil

Schach <-s> [ʃax] *nt kein pl* (*Spiel*) chess; (*Stellung*) check; **eine Partie** ~ a game of chess; ~ **und matt!** checkmate!

Schachbrett *nt* chessboard

Schachfigur *f* chess piece

schachmatt [ʃax·'mat] *adj* checkmate

Schachspiel *nt* ① (*Brett und Figuren*) chess set ② (*das Schachspielen*) chess

Schacht <-[e]s, Schächte> [ʃaxt, *pl* 'ʃɛç·tə] *m* shaft; *Brunnen* well

Schachtel <-, -n> ['ʃaxtl̩] *f* box; **eine ~ Zigaretten** a pack of cigarettes

Schachzug *m* move

schade ['ʃaː·də] *adj pred* ① (*bedauerlich*) **wie ~!** that's too bad, what a shame; **ich finde es ~, dass ...** it's too bad that ...; **es ist ~ um ihn** it's a shame about him ② (*zu gut*) ■ **für etw** *akk* **zu ~ sein** to be too good for sth

Schädel <-s, -> ['ʃɛː·dl̩] *m* skull; **einen dicken ~ haben** (*fam*) to have a hangover; **jdm brummt der** ~ (*fam*) sb's head is throbbing

Schädelbruch *m* fractured skull

schaden ['ʃaː·dn̩] *vi* ■ **jdm** ~ to [do] harm [to] sb; ■ **etw** *dat* ~ to damage sth

Schaden <-s, Schäden> ['ʃaː·dn̩, *pl* 'ʃɛː·dn̩] *m* damage (**durch** +*akk* caused by); **jdm ~ zufügen** to harm sb

Schadenersatz *m s.* **Schadensersatz**

Schadenfreude *f* schadenfreude

schadenfroh **I.** *adj* malicious, gloating; ■ ~ **sein** to delight in others' misfortunes **II.** *adv* ~ **grinsen** to grin maliciously

Schadensersatz *m kein pl* compensation; ~ **fordern** to claim damages

schadhaft ['ʃaːt·haft] *adj* faulty, defective

schädigen ['ʃɛː·dɪgn̩] *vt* to harm (**durch** +*akk* with)

Schädigung <-, -en> *f* harm (+*gen* to)

schädlich ['ʃɛːt·lɪç] *adj* harmful; (*giftig*) poisonous; ■ ~ **sein** to be damaging

Schädling <-s, -e> ['ʃɛːt·lɪŋ] *m* pest

Schädlingsbekämpfung *f* pest control

Schädlingsbekämpfungsmittel *nt* pesticide

Schadstoff *m* harmful substance; (*in der Umwelt*) pollutant

schadstoffarm *adj Motor* low-emission

Schadstoffausstoß *m* [pollution] emissions *pl*

Schadstoffbelastung *f* pollution

Schaf <-[e]s, -e> [ʃaːf] *nt* sheep

Schafbock *m* ram

Schäfer(in) <-s, -> ['ʃɛː·fɐ] *m(f)* shepherd *masc*, shepherdess *fem*

Schäferhund *m* German shepherd

Schaffell *nt* sheepskin

schaffen[1] <schaffte, geschafft> ['ʃafn̩] *vt* ① (*bewältigen*) to manage; *Examen* to pass; **einen Termin** ~ to make an appointment [*or* a deadline]; **es ist geschafft** it's done; ■ **es ~, etw zu tun** to manage to do sth ② (*gelangen*) **wir müssen es bis zur Grenze** ~ we have to get to the border ③ (*bringen*) *Ordnung* to bring

schaffen[2] <schuf, geschaffen> ['ʃafn̩] *vt* ① (*herstellen*) to create; **dafür bist du wie ge~** that's right up your alley *fam* ② (*verursachen*) to cause; **Frieden** ~ to make peace

schaffen[3] <schạffte, geschạfft> ['ʃafn̩] *vi* SÜDD, ÖSTERR, SCHWEIZ (*arbeiten*) to work; **nichts mit jdm/etw zu ~ haben** to have nothing to do with sb/sth; **jdm zu ~ machen** to give sb a hard time, to cause sb trouble

Schaffner(in) <-s, -> ['ʃaf·nɐ] *m(f)* conductor

Scha̱fherde *f* flock of sheep

Schafott <-[e]s, -e> [ʃa·'fɔt] *nt* scaffold

Scha̱fskäse *m* feta [cheese]

Schakal <-s, -e> [ʃa·'ka:l] *m* jackal

schal [ʃa:l] *adj* flat; *Wasser* stale

Schal <-s, -s *o* -e> [ʃa:l] *m* scarf

Schale[1] <-, -n> ['ʃa:·lə] *f* ❶ (*Nussschale*) shell ❷ (*Fruchtschale*) skin; (*abgeschält*) peel ▸ WENDUNGEN: **eine raue ~ haben** to be a rough diamond

Schale[2] <-, -n> ['ʃa:·lə] *f* bowl

schälen ['ʃɛ:·lən] **I.** *vt* to peel **II.** *vr* ■ **sich** *akk* ~ to peel

Scha̱lentier *nt* shellfish

Schall <-s, -e *o* Schälle> [ʃal, *pl* 'ʃɛ·lə] *m* sound

Schạlldämpfer <-s, -> *m einer Schusswaffe* silencer; *eines Auspuffs a.* muffler

schạlldicht *adj* soundproof

schallen ['ʃalən] *vi* to resound

Schạllgeschwindigkeit *f kein pl* PHYS speed of sound

Schạllisolierung *f* soundproofing

Schạllmauer *f* sound barrier; **die ~ durchbrechen** to break the sound barrier

Schạllplatte *f* record

Schạllwelle *f* sound wave

schalt [ʃalt] *imp von* **schelten**

Schaltanlage ['ʃalt-] *f* switchgear

schalten ['ʃaltn̩] **I.** *vi* ❶ AUTO to change gears, to shift ❷ (*fam: begreifen*) to get it; (*handeln*) to act ❸ (*sich einstellen*) **auf Rot ~** to switch to red **II.** *vt* (*einstellen*) to switch, to turn (**auf** +*akk* to)

Schalter <-s, -> ['ʃaltɐ] *m* ❶ ELEK switch ❷ ADMIN, BAHN counter

Schạlterbeamte(r), -beamtin *m, f dekl wie adj* clerk

Schạlterraum *m* BAHN ticket office

Schạlthebel *m* AUTO gearshift

Schạltjahr *nt* leap year

Schạltknüppel *m* gearshift

Schạlttafel *f* control panel

Schạltung <-, -en> *f* ❶ AUTO gearshift ❷ ELEK circuit

Scham <-> [ʃa:m] *f kein pl* ❶ (*Beschämung*) shame; **~ empfinden** to be [*or* feel] ashamed ❷ (*Verlegenheit*) embarrassment

Scha̱mbein *nt* pubic bone

schämen ['ʃɛ:·mən] *vr* ■ **sich** *akk* ~ to be ashamed (**wegen** +*dat* of); ■ **sich** *akk* **vor jdm ~** to be embarrassed in front of sb; **schäm dich!** shame on you!

Scha̱mhaar *nt* pubic hair

scha̱mhaft *adj* shy, bashful

Scha̱mlippen *pl* labia *pl*

scha̱mlos *adj* shameless, rude

Schande <-> ['ʃan·də] *f kein pl* disgrace, shame; **eine ~ sein** to be a disgrace

schänden ['ʃɛn·dn̩] *vt Grab, Denkmal* to desecrate

Schạndfleck *m* blemish [on the landscape]

schändlich ['ʃɛnt·lɪç] **I.** *adj* ❶ (*niederträchtig*) disgraceful, shameful; *Verbrechen* despicable ❷ (*schlecht*) appalling **II.** *adv* shamefully, disgracefully

Schạndtat *f* outrage; **zu jeder ~ bereit sein** (*hum*) to be ready for anything

Schạ̈ndung <-, -en> *f* desecration; (*Vergewaltigung*) molestation

Schanze <-, -n> ['ʃan·tsə] *f* ski jump

Schar <-, -en> [ʃa:ɐ̯] *f von Vögeln* flock; *von Menschen* crowd

scharen ['ʃa:·rən] **I.** *vt* **Dinge/Menschen um sich** *akk* ~ to gather things/people around oneself **II.** *vr* ■ **sich** *akk* **um jdn/etw ~** to gather around sb/sth

scha̱renweise *adv* in hordes

scharf <schạ̈rfer, schạ̈rfste> [ʃarf] **I.** *adj* ❶ (*gut geschliffen*) sharp ❷ (*spitz zulaufend*) sharp; **eine ~e Kurve** a hairpin turn ❸ KOCHK spicy; (*hochprozentig*) strong ❹ (*ätzend*) *Reinigungsmittel* aggressive ❺ (*schonungslos, heftig*) harsh, severe, tough; *Kontrolle* rigorous; *Konkurrenz* fierce; **eine ~e Zunge haben** to have a sharp tongue ❻ *Bombe* live ❼ (*konzentriert, präzise*) careful; *Beobachtung* astute; **einen ~en Verstand haben** to have a sharp mind ❽ *Foto, Umrisse* sharp; *Augen* keen ❾ (*sl: aufreizend*) spicy; ■ **auf jdn ~ sein** to have the hots for sb; ■ **auf etw** *akk* **~ sein** to be really interested in sth ❿ (*fam: toll*) fantastic, great **II.** *adv* ❶ (*intensiv gewürzt*) **ich esse gerne ~** I like [eating] spicy food; **etw ~ würzen** to highly season sth ❷ (*heftig*) sharply; *kritisieren* harshly; *verurteilen* strongly ❸ (*präzise*) **~ beobachten** to observe carefully; **~ sehen** to have good eyes ❹ (*abrupt*) abruptly; **~ links/rechts abbiegen** to take a sharp left/right; **~ bremsen** to slam on the brakes ❺ TECH, FOTO (*klar*) sharply; **das Bild ~ einstellen** to bring the picture into focus

Schạrfblick *m kein pl* astuteness

Schärfe <-, -n> ['ʃɛr·fə] *f* ❶ *von Messer, Degen* sharpness ❷ (*Heftigkeit*) severity; *von Kritik* sharpness; *von Worten* harshness; *der Augen* keenness ❸ *von Foto, Bild* sharpness; *einer Brille* strength

schärfen ['ʃɛr·fn̩] *vt* to sharpen

schạrfkantig *adj* sharp-edged

schạrf|machen *vt* (*sl: sexuell reizen*) ■ **jdn ~** to turn sb on

Schạrfschütze, -schützin *m, f* marksman *masc,* markswoman *fem*

schạrfsichtig *adj* sharp-sighted

Schạrfsinn *m kein pl* astuteness

schạrfsinnig **I.** *adj* astute, perceptive **II.** *adv* astutely, perceptively

Scharlach <-s> ['ʃar·lax] *m kein pl* MED scarlet fever

S

Scharlatan <-s, -e> [ˈʃar·la·tan] *m* (*Betrüger*) fraud
Scharnier <-s, -e> [ʃar·ˈniːɐ̯] *nt* hinge
Schärpe <-, -n> [ˈʃɛr·pə] *f* sash
scharren [ˈʃarən] *vi* to scratch; (*mit der Pfote*) to paw
Schaschlik <-s, -s> [ˈʃaʃ·lɪk] *nt* shish kebab
Schatten <-s, -> [ˈʃa·tn̩] *m* ① (*schattige Stelle*) shade; **30°C im ~** 30°C in the shade ② (*schemenhafte Gestalt, Umriss*) shadow; **einen ~ [auf etw** *akk*] **werfen** to cast a shadow [over sth] ▶WENDUNGEN: **in jds ~ stehen** to be overshadowed by sb; **jdn/etw in den ~ stellen** to outshine sb/sth
Schattenseite *f* dark side
schattig [ˈʃatɪç] *adj* shady
Schatulle <-, -n> [ʃa·ˈtʊlə] *f* casket
Schatz <-es, Schätze> [ʃats, *pl* ˈʃɛ·tsə] *m* ① (*kostbare Dinge*) treasure ② (*fam: Liebling*) sweetheart
schätzen [ˈʃɛtsn̩] **I.** *vt* ① (*einschätzen*) to guess; **meistens werde ich jünger geschätzt** people usually think I'm younger than I am; **grob geschätzt** roughly ② (*wertmäßig einschätzen*) to assess (**auf** +*akk* at) ③ (*würdigen*) to value (**als** +*akk* as); ■**jdn ~** to hold sb in high esteem; ■**etw ~** to appreciate sth **II.** *vi* to guess
Schatzkammer *f* treasure house
Schatzmeister(in) *m(f)* treasurer
Schätzung <-, -en> *f* ① *kein pl* (*wertmäßiges Einschätzen*) valuation ② (*Anschlag*) estimate
schätzungsweise *adv* approximately
Schau <-, -en> [ʃau] *f* show; **etw zur ~ stellen** to display sth
Schaubild *nt* diagram
Schauder <-s, -> [ˈʃau·dɐ] *m* shudder
schauderhaft *adj* (*grässlich*) ghastly, horrific; (*furchtbar*) awful
schaudern [ˈʃau·dɐn] **I.** *vt impers* **es schaudert mich bei dem Gedanken** the thought alone makes me shudder **II.** *vi* (*erschauern*) to shudder; *vor Kälte* to shiver
schauen [ˈʃau·ən] *vi* SÜDD, ÖSTERR, SCHWEIZ ① (*blicken*) to look (**auf** +*akk* at) ② (*darauf achten*) ■**auf etw** *akk* **~** to pay attention to sth ③ (*sich kümmern*) ■**nach jdm/etw ~** to look after sb/sth ④ (*suchen*) ■**[nach etw** *dat*] **~** to look [for sth] ▶WENDUNGEN: **da schaust du aber!** (*fam*) how about that!
Schauer <-s, -> [ˈʃau·ɐ] *m* ① (*Regenschauer*) shower ② *s.* **Schauder**
Schauergeschichte *f* (*fam*) horror story
schauerlich *adj* (*grässlich*) ghastly, horrific; (*furchtbar*) awful
Schaufel <-, -n> [ˈʃau·fl̩] *f* shovel; (*für Mehl o. Ä.*) scoop; (*für Kehricht*) dustpan
schaufeln [ˈʃau·fl̩n] *vi, vt* to shovel, to dig
Schaufenster *nt* store window
Schaufensterbummel *m* window-shopping; **einen ~ machen** to go window-shopping
Schaufensterpuppe *f* mannequin
Schaukampf *m* exhibition fight

S

Schaukel <-, -n> [ˈʃau·kl̩] *f* swing
schaukeln [ˈʃau·kl̩n] **I.** *vi* to swing; (*auf und ab wippen*) to rock **II.** *vt* to swing; *Baby* to rock
Schaukelpferd *nt* rocking horse
Schaukelstuhl *m* rocking chair
Schaum <-s, Schäume> [ʃaum, *pl* ˈʃɔy·mə] *m* foam; (*auf einer Flüssigkeit*) froth; (*Seifenschaum*) lather
Schaumbad *nt* bubble bath
schäumen [ˈʃɔy·mən] *vi* to foam; (*aufschäumen*) to froth; *Seife* to lather
Schaumfestiger *m* mousse
Schaumgummi *m* foam rubber
schaumig [ˈʃau·mɪç] *adj* frothy
Schaumwein *m* sparkling wine
Schauplatz *m* scene
schaurig [ˈʃau·rɪç] *adj* ① (*unheimlich*) eerie ② (*gruselig*) macabre, scary
Schauspiel [ˈʃau·ʃpiːl] *nt* ① THEAT play, drama *no indef art* ② (*geh: Anblick*) spectacle
Schauspieler(in) [ˈʃau·ʃpiː·lɐ] *m(f)* actor *masc*, actress *fem*
Schauspielhaus *nt* theater, playhouse
Schauspielschule *f* drama school
Schautafel *f* wall chart
Scheck <-s, -s> [ʃɛk] *m* check (**über** +*akk* for); **einen ~ ausstellen** to write a check; **einen ~ einlösen** to cash a check
scheckig [ˈʃɛ·kɪç] *adj* mottled
Scheckkarte *f* debit card
scheffeln [ˈʃɛ·fl̩n] *vt* to accumulate; **Geld ~** to rake in money
Scheibe <-, -n> [ˈʃai·bə] *f* ① (*dünnes Glasstück*) [piece of] glass; (*Fensterscheibe*) window [pane] ② KOCHK slice ③ (*kreisförmiger Gegenstand*) disk
Scheibenwaschanlage *f* windshield washer system
Scheibenwischer <-s, -> *m* windshield wiper
Scheich <-s, -e> [ʃaiç] *m* sheikh
Scheide <-, -n> [ˈʃai·də] *f* ① (*Schwert-/Dolchscheide*) scabbard ② (*Vagina*) vagina
scheiden <schied, geschieden> [ˈʃai·dn̩] **I.** *vt haben* to divorce; **die Ehe wurde 2002 geschieden** the marriage was dissolved in 2002; ■**sich** *akk* **~ lassen** to get divorced (**von** +*dat* from) **II.** *vi sein* ■**aus etw** *dat* **~** to leave sth; **aus einem Amt ~** to retire from a position
Scheidenzäpfchen *nt* MED vaginal suppository
Scheidung <-, -en> *f* divorce; **die ~ einreichen** to start divorce proceedings
Scheidungsgrund *m* grounds *npl* for divorce
Schein <-[e]s, -e> [ʃain] *m* ① *kein pl* (*Lichtschein*) light ② *kein pl* (*Anschein*) appearance; **den ~ wahren** to keep up appearances ③ (*Banknote*) bill, banknote ④ (*fam: Bescheinigung*) certificate

At German universities, students receive **Scheine** (certificates) when they pass a class. The **Scheine** allow them to progress from one year to the next. Only those students who have a certain number or type of **Scheine** will eventually qualify for the degree examination.

scheinbar *adj* apparent, seeming
scheinen <schien, geschienen> ['ʃai·nən] *vi* ❶ (*leuchten*) to shine ❷ (*den Anschein haben*) to appear, to seem
Scheinfirma *f* bogus company
scheinheilig ['ʃain·hai·lɪç] **I.** *adj* hypocritical; ~ **tun** to play the innocent **II.** *adv* hypocritically
Scheinschwangerschaft *f* false [*or* phantom] pregnancy
Scheinwerfer *m* ❶ (*Strahler*) spotlight ❷ AUTO headlight
Scheinwerferlicht *nt* spotlight ▶ WENDUNGEN: **im ~ stehen** to be in the public eye
Scheiß <-> [ʃais] *m kein pl* (*sl: Quatsch*) crap; **he, was soll der ~!** hey, what [the hell] are you doing?; **lass doch den ~** quit screwing around!; **mach keinen ~!** don't fuck around! *vulg;* **so ein ~!** shit! *vulg*
Scheißdreck *m* (*sl*) crap ▶ WENDUNGEN: **das geht dich einen ~ an** that's none of your [god]damn business; **wegen jedem ~** because of every little thing
Scheiße <-> ['ʃai·sə] *f kein pl* ❶ (*vulg: Darminhalt*) shit ❷ (*sl: Mist*) **~!** shit! *vulg;* **~ sein** to be a load of crap; **~ bauen** to make a complete mess [of sth] ▶ WENDUNGEN: **in der ~ sitzen** (*sl*) to be in deep shit *vulg*
scheißegal ['ʃais·ʔe'ga:l] *adj* (*sl*) **das ist mir ~** I don't give a damn *fam;* **es ist ~** who gives a shit? *vulg*
scheißen <schiss, geschissen> ['ʃai·sn̩] *vi* ❶ (*derb*) to shit ❷ (*vulg: verzichten können*) **ich scheiße auf deine Meinung** I don't give a shit about your opinion
scheißfreundlich ['ʃais·'frɔynt·lɪç] *adj* (*sl*) ■ **~ sein** to be as sweet as pie
Scheißkerl *m* (*sl*) bastard
Scheitel <-s, -> ['ʃai·tl̩] *m* part
scheitern ['ʃai·tɐn] *vi sein* to fail (**an** +*dat* because of); **kläglich ~** to fail miserably
Schellfisch *m* haddock
Schelm <-[e]s, -e> [ʃɛlm] *m* rascal
schelmisch *adj* mischievous
schelten <schilt, schalt, gescholten> ['ʃɛl·tn̩] *vt* to scold
Schema <-s, -ta *o* Schemen> ['ʃe:·ma, *pl* 'ʃe:·ma·ta, 'ʃe:·mən] *nt* ❶ (*Konzept*) concept; **nach einem ~** according to a concept ❷ (*Darstellung*) chart, diagram
schematisch [ʃe·'ma:·tɪʃ] **I.** *adj* schematic **II.** *adv* schematically; **etw ~ darstellen** to show sth with a chart
Schemel <-s, -> ['ʃe:·ml̩] *m* stool
Schemen *pl von* **Schema**
schemenhaft *adj* shadowy
Schenkel <-s, -> ['ʃɛŋ·kl̩] *m* thigh
schenken ['ʃɛŋ·kn̩] **I.** *vt* ❶ (*als Geschenk geben*) ■ **jdm etw ~** to give sb sth [as a present]; **er schenkte ihr ein Auto zum Geburtstag** he gave her a car for her birthday ❷ (*gewähren*) *Freiheit, Mut* to give; **jdm Aufmerksamkeit ~** to pay attention to sb; **jdm Vertrauen ~** to trust sb **II.** *vi* to give presents **III.** *vr* (*sich sparen*) ■ **sich** *dat* **etw ~** to spare oneself sth
Schenkung <-, -en> *f* gift
Scherbe <-, -n> ['ʃɛr·bə] *f* [sharp] piece; **von Glas** piece of glass
Schere <-, -n> ['ʃe:·rə] *f* ❶ (*Werkzeug*) scissors *npl* ❷ ZOOL claw
scheren[1] <schor, geschoren> ['ʃe:·rən] *vt Fell* to shear; *Bart* to crop; *Hecke* to prune
scheren[2] ['ʃe:·rən] *vr* ❶ (*sich kümmern*) ■ **sich** *akk* **um etw** *akk* **~** to care about sth ❷ (*fam: abhauen*) **scher dich weg!** get out of here!
Scherz <-es, -e> [ʃɛrts] *m* joke
Scherzartikel *m meist pl* gag toy
scherzen ['ʃɛr·tsn̩] *vi* (*geh*) to crack a joke/jokes; **mit ihm ist nicht zu ~** you shouldn't joke around with him
scherzhaft I. *adj* (*aus Spaß erfolgend*) jocular, joke *attr* **II.** *adv* jokingly, in a jocular fashion
scheu [ʃɔy] *adj* shy
Scheu <-> [ʃɔy] *f kein pl* shyness; **ohne jede ~** without holding back
scheuchen ['ʃɔy·çn̩] *vt* (*treiben*) to shoo; *Tiere* to drive
scheuen ['ʃɔy·ən] **I.** *vt* **Auseinandersetzungen ~** to avoid conflict **II.** *vi Pferd* to shy (**vor** +*dat* at)
Scheuerlappen *m* floor cloth
scheuern ['ʃɔy·ɐn] **I.** *vt* to scour ▶ WENDUNGEN: **jdm eine ~** (*sl*) to hit somebody **II.** *vi* to rub, to chafe **III.** *vr* ■ **sich** *akk* **an etw** *dat* **~** to rub on sth
Scheuklappe *f meist pl* blinders *pl*
Scheune <-, -n> ['ʃɔy·nə] *f* barn
Scheusal <-s, -e> ['ʃɔy·za:l] *nt* beast
scheußlich ['ʃɔys·lɪç] **I.** *adj* ❶ (*ekelhaft*) disgusting, revolting ❷ (*fam*) dreadful, awful, terrible **II.** *adv* ❶ (*widerlich*) in a disgusting manner ❷ (*fam*) terribly; **~ wehtun** to hurt like hell
Schi <-s, -er *o* -> [ʃi:, *pl* 'ʃi:ɐ] *m s.* **Ski**
Schicht <-, -en> [ʃɪçt] *f* ❶ (*Lage*) layer; *Farbe* coat ❷ (*Gesellschaftsschicht*) class ❸ (*Arbeitsschicht*) shift; **~ arbeiten** to do shift work
Schichtarbeit *f kein pl* shift work
Schichtarbeiter(in) *m(f)* shift worker
schichten ['ʃɪç·tn̩] *vt* to stack [up *sep*], to layer (**auf** +*akk* on/on top of)
Schichtwechsel [-vɛksl] *m* shift change
schichtweise *adv* in layers, layer upon layer
schick [ʃɪk] **I.** *adj* (*modisch elegant*) chic, fashionable; (*gepflegt*) smart **II.** *adv* (*modisch elegant*) fashionably, stylishly; (*gepflegt*) smartly
schicken ['ʃɪkn̩] **I.** *vt* to send; **etw mit der Post ~** to send sth by mail **II.** *vi* ■ **nach jdm ~**

to send for sb **III.** *vr* ■ **etw schickt sich** *akk* **nicht** [**für jdn**] sth is not suitable [for sb]
Schicksal <-s, -e> [ˈʃɪk·zaːl] *nt* destiny, fate; **ein hartes ~** a cruel fate; **etw dem ~ überlassen** to leave sth to fate
schicksalhaft *adj* fateful
Schicksalsschlag *m* stroke of fate
Schiebedach *nt* sunroof
schieben <schob, geschoben> [ˈʃiː·bn̩] *vt* ① (*vorwärtsbewegen*) to push ② (*stecken*) to put, to stick; **die Pizza in den Ofen ~** to stick the pizza in the oven ③ (*zuweisen*) **die Schuld auf jdn ~** to lay the blame on sb; ■ **etw auf etw/jdn ~** to blame sth/sb for sth ④ (*abweisen*) ■ **etw von sich** *dat* **~** to reject sth
Schiebetür *f* sliding door
Schiebung <-> *f kein pl* ① (*Begünstigung*) string-pulling ② SPORT fix
schied [ʃiːt] *imp von* **scheiden**
Schiedsgericht *nt* arbitration court
Schiedsrichter(in) *m(f)* SPORT referee; (*bei Tennis, Baseball*) umpire
schief [ʃiːf] **I.** *adj* ① (*schräg*) crooked, not straight *pred,* lopsided *fam* ② (*entstellt, falsch*) distorted **II.** *adv* (*schräg*) crooked, not straight, lopsided
schief|gehen *vi irreg sein* (*fam*) to go wrong
schief|lachen *vr* (*fam*) ■ **sich** *akk* **~** to crack up
schief|liegen *vi irreg* (*fam*) to miss the mark
schielen [ˈʃiː·lən] *vi* ① MED to squint, to be cross-eyed ② (*haben wollen*) ■ **nach etw** *dat* **~** to steal a glance at sth
schien [ʃiːn] *imp von* **scheinen**
Schienbein [ˈʃiːn·bain] *nt* shin; ANAT tibia
Schiene <-, -n> [ˈʃiː·nə] *f* ① (*Führungsschiene*) rail *usu pl* ② MED splint
schienen [ˈʃiː·nən] *vt* MED to splint
Schienenfahrzeug *nt* BAHN rail vehicle
Schienennetz *nt* BAHN rail network
Schienenverkehr *m kein pl* rail traffic
schier [ʃiːɐ̯] *adv* (*beinahe*) almost
Schießbude *f* shooting gallery
schießen <schoss, geschossen> [ˈʃiː·sn̩] *vi, vt* ① *haben* (*feuern*) to shoot (**auf** +*akk* at) ② *haben* FBALL to shoot; **ein Tor ~** to score [a goal] ③ *sein* (*schnell bewegen*) **das Auto kam um die Ecke geschossen** the car came flying around the corner; **jdm durch den Kopf ~** to flash through sb's mind
Schießerei <-, -en> [ʃiː·sə·ˈrai] *f* shooting
Schießplatz *m* firing range
Schießpulver *nt* gunpowder
Schiff <-[e]s, -e> [ʃɪf] *nt* ship
Schiffahrt^ALT *f s.* **Schifffahrt**
schiffbar *adj* navigable
Schiffbau *m kein pl* shipbuilding
Schiffbruch *m* shipwreck; **~ erleiden** to be shipwrecked
Schiffbrüchige(r) *f(m) dekl wie adj* shipwrecked person
Schiffer(in) <-s, -> [ˈʃɪfɐ] *m(f)* skipper
Schifffahrt^RR [ˈʃɪf·faːɐ̯t] *f* shipping
Schiffsschraube *f* ship propeller
Schikane <-, -n> [ʃi·ˈkaː·nə] *f* harassment *no indef art*
schikanieren* [ʃi·ka·ˈniː·rən] *vt* to harass
Schild¹ <-[e]s, -er> [ʃɪlt, *pl* ˈʃɪl·dɐ] *nt* (*Hinweisschild*) sign
Schild² <-[e]s, -e> [ʃɪlt, *pl* ˈʃɪl·də] *m* shield ▶ WENDUNGEN: **etw im ~e führen** to be up to sth
Schilddrüse *f* thyroid [gland]
schildern [ˈʃɪl·dɐn] *vt* to describe
Schilderung <-, -en> *f* description; *Ereignisse a.* account
Schildkröte [ˈʃɪlt·krøː·tə] *f* tortoise; (*Seeschildkröte*) turtle
Schilf <-[e]s, -e> [ʃɪlf] *nt* reeds *pl*
schillern [ˈʃɪlɐn] *vi* to shimmer
schillernd *adj* shimmering; *Persönlichkeit* flamboyant
schilt [ʃɪlt] *imp sing von* **schelten**
Schimmel¹ <-s> [ˈʃɪml̩] *m kein pl* mold
Schimmel² <-s, -> [ˈʃɪml̩] *m* (*Tier*) white horse
schimmelig [ˈʃɪmə·lɪç] *adj* moldy; *Leder, Buch* mildewed
schimmeln [ˈʃɪml̩n] *vi sein o haben* to get moldy
Schimmelpilz *m* mold
Schimmer <-s> [ˈʃɪmɐ] *m kein pl* shimmer; **ein ~ von Hoffnung** a glimmer of hope ▶ WENDUNGEN: **keinen blassen ~** [**von etw** *dat*] **haben** (*fam*) to not have the faintest idea [about sth]
schimmern [ˈʃɪmɐn] *vi* to shimmer
schimmlig [ˈʃɪm·lɪç] *adj s.* **schimmelig**
Schimpanse <-n, -n> [ʃɪm·ˈpan·zə] *m* chimpanzee
schimpfen [ˈʃɪm·pfn̩] *vi* ① (*sich ärgerlich äußern*) to grumble (**über/auf** +*akk* about) ② (*fluchen*) to swear ③ (*zurechtweisen*) ■ **mit jdm ~** to scold sb, to tell sb off
Schimpfwort *nt* swear word
schinden <schindete, geschunden> [ˈʃɪn·dn̩] **I.** *vr* ■ **sich** *akk* **~** to slave [away] **II.** *vt* ① (*grausam antreiben*) ■ **jdn ~** to work sb like a slave; *Tier* to mistreat ② (*fam*) **Eindruck ~** to play to the gallery; **Zeit ~** to play for time
Schinderei <-, -en> [ʃɪn·də·ˈrai] *f* grind
Schinken <-s, -> [ˈʃɪŋ·kn̩] *m* ham
Schippe <-, -n> [ˈʃɪpə] *f bes* NORDD shovel ▶ WENDUNGEN: **jdn auf die ~ nehmen** to pull sb's leg; **etw auf die ~ nehmen** to make fun of sth
Schirm <-[e]s, -e> [ʃɪrm] *m* (*Regenschirm*) umbrella; (*Sonnenschirm*) sunshade; (*tragbar*) parasol
Schirmherr(in) *m(f)* patron
Schirmherrschaft *f* patronage
Schirmmütze *f* baseball cap
Schirmständer *m* umbrella stand
schiss^RR, **schiß**^ALT [ʃɪs] *imp von* **scheißen**
Schiss^RR <-es>, **Schiß**^ALT <-sses> [ʃɪs] *m*

kein pl ~ [**vor jdm/etw**] **haben** (*sl*) to be scared shitless [of sb/sth]
schizophren [ʃi·tso·'fre:n, sçi·tso·'fre:n] *adj* schizophrenic
Schizophrenie <-, *selten* -n> [ʃi·tso·fre·'ni:, sçi·tso-, *pl* -'ni:·ən] *f* schizophrenia
Schlacht <-, -en> [ʃlaxt] *f* battle
schlachten ['ʃlax·tn̩] *vt, vi* to slaughter
Schlachter(in) <-s, -> *m(f)* ❶ (*Metzger*) butcher ❷ (*Schlachthofangestellter*) slaughterer
Schlachtfeld *nt* battlefield
Schlachtfest *nt* KOCHK slaughter festival (*celebration and feast following the slaughtering of a farm animal*)
Schlachthof *m* slaughterhouse
Schlacke <-, -n> ['ʃla·kə] *f* (*Verbrennungsrückstand*) slag
Schlaf <-[e]s> [ʃla:f] *m kein pl* sleep; **einen festen/leichten ~ haben** to be a deep [*or* sound]/light sleeper; **jdm den ~ rauben** to keep sb awake ▶WENDUNGEN: **nicht im ~ an etw** *akk* **denken** to not dream of [doing] sth; **etw im ~ können** (*fam*) to be able to do sth in one's sleep
Schlafanzug *m* pajamas *npl*
Schlafcouch *f* sofa bed
Schläfe <-, -n> ['ʃlɛ:·fə] *f* temple
schlafen <schlief, geschlafen> ['ʃla:·fn̩] *vi* to sleep; **er schläft noch** he is still asleep; **ein Kind ~ legen** to put a child to bed; **~ gehen** to go to bed; **fest/tief ~** to sleep deeply/soundly
schlaff [ʃlaf] **I.** *adj* ❶ (*locker fallend*) slack ❷ (*nicht straff*) sagging; *Händedruck* limp **II.** *adv* ❶ (*locker fallend*) slackly ❷ (*kraftlos*) feebly
Schlaffheit <-> *f kein pl* ❶ *der Haut* slackness; *der Muskulatur* flabbiness ❷ (*fig: Trägheit*) listlessness
Schlafgelegenheit *f* place to sleep
Schlaflied *nt* lullaby
schlaflos I. *adj* sleepless **II.** *adv* sleeplessly
Schlaflosigkeit <-> *f kein pl* insomnia
Schlafmittel *nt* sleeping pill
Schlafmütze *f* (*fam: verschlafene Person*) sleepy head
schläfrig ['ʃlɛ:f·rɪç] *adj* sleepy, drowsy
Schlafsaal *m* dormitory
Schlafsack *m* sleeping bag
Schlafstörungen *pl* insomnia
Schlaftablette *f* sleeping pill
schlaftrunken I. *adj* sleepy **II.** *adv* sleepily
Schlafwagen *m* sleeper
schlafwandeln *vi sein o haben* to sleepwalk
Schlafwandler(in) <-s, -> *m(f)* sleepwalker
Schlafzimmer *nt* bedroom
Schlag <-[e]s, Schläge> [ʃla:k, *pl* 'ʃlɛ:·gə] *m* ❶ (*Hieb*) blow, wallop *fam;* (*mit der Faust*) punch; (*mit der Hand*) slap; SPORT stroke, hit; (*Baseball*) hit; **Schläge bekommen** to get beaten up ❷ (*dumpfer Hall*) thud; **ein ~ an der Tür** a bang on the door ❸ (*rhythmisches Geräusch*) **die Schläge des Herzens** the heartbeats; **der ~ einer Uhr** the striking of a clock ❹ (*Schicksalsschlag*) blow ❺ ÖSTERR (*Schlagsahne*) whipped cream ❻ (*Stromstoß*) shock; **einen ~ kriegen** to get an electric shock ❼ (*Schlaganfall*) stroke; **einen ~ bekommen** to suffer a stroke ❽ MODE **eine Hose mit ~** flared pants ▶WENDUNGEN: **ein ~ ins Gesicht** a slap in the face; **jdn trifft der ~** (*fam*) sb is flabbergasted [*or* shocked]; **etw auf einen ~ tun** to get things done all at once; **~ auf ~** in rapid succession
Schlagabtausch *m* ❶ (*Rededuell*) exchange of words ❷ (*beim Boxen*) exchange of blows
Schlagader *f* artery
Schlaganfall *m* stroke
schlagartig I. *adj* sudden, abrupt **II.** *adv* suddenly, abruptly
Schlagbaum *m* barrier
Schlägel <-s, -> ['ʃlɛ:·gl̩] *m* MUS drumstick
schlagen <schlug, geschlagen> ['ʃla:·gn̩] **I.** *vt haben* ❶ (*hauen*) to hit; (*mit der Faust*) to punch; (*mit der Hand*) to slap; **die Hände vors Gesicht ~** to cover one's face with one's hands ❷ (*prügeln*) to beat; **jdn bewusstlos ~** to beat sb senseless ❸ (*besiegen*) to defeat; SPORT to beat (**in** + *dat* at); **jd ist nicht zu ~** sb is unbeatable; **sich ge~ geben** to admit defeat ❹ (*durch Schläge treiben*) **einen Nagel in die Wand ~** to hammer a nail into the wall; **den Ball ins Aus ~** to kick the ball out of play ❺ *Sahne* to whip; **Eier in die Pfanne ~** to crack eggs into the [frying] pan ❻ (*hinzufügen*) **die Unkosten auf den Verkaufspreis ~** to add the cost to the retail price ❼ (*legen*) **ein Bein über das andere ~** to cross one's legs; **die Decke zur Seite ~** to throw the blanket aside ❽ *Holz* to cut; *Bäume* to fell **II.** *vi* ❶ *haben* (*hauen*) to hit; ■[**mit etw** *dat*] **um sich** *akk* **~** to lash out [with sth]; ■**nach jdm ~** to lash out at sb ❷ *sein* (*auftreffen*) ■**gegen etw** *akk* **~** to strike against sth ❸ *haben* (*pochen*) to beat ❹ *haben* (*läuten*) *Uhr* to strike ❺ *sein* (*fam: jdm ähneln*) ■**nach jdm ~** to take after sb **III.** *vr haben* ■**sich** *akk* **~** to fight; ■**sich** *akk* **um etw** *akk* **~** to fight over sth
Schlager <-s, -> ['ʃla:·gɐ] *m* MUS ❶ (*Lied*) pop song ❷ (*Erfolg*) [big] hit, great success
Schläger <-s, -> ['ʃlɛ:·gɐ] *m* SPORT ❶ (*Tennisschläger*) racket; (*Tischtennisschläger*) paddle ❷ (*Stock*) stick, bat; (*Golfschläger*) golf club
Schlägerei <-, -en> [ʃlɛ:·gə·'rai] *f* fight, brawl
Schlagersänger(in) *m(f)* pop singer
schlagfertig I. *adj* quick-witted **II.** *adv* quick-wittedly
Schlaginstrument *nt* percussion instrument
schlagkräftig *adj* ❶ (*kampfkräftig*) powerful [in combat] ❷ *Argument* forceful; *Beweis* compelling
Schlagloch *nt* pothole
Schlagsahne *f* (*flüssig*) whipping cream; (*geschlagen*) whipped cream
Schlagstock *m* club; (*Gummiknüppel*) night

S

stick
Schlagwort *nt* ① <-worte> (*Parole*) slogan ② <-wörter> (*Stichwort*) keyword
Schlagzeile *f* headline
Schlagzeug <-[e]s, -e> *nt* drums *pl;* (*im Orchester*) percussion
Schlagzeuger(in) <-s, -> *m(f)* drummer; (*im Orchester*) percussionist
schlaksig ['ʃlaːk·sɪç] *adj* gangly, lanky
Schlamassel <-s, -> [ʃla·'ma·sl̩] *m o nt* mess
Schlamm <-[e]s, -e *o* Schlämme> [ʃlam, *pl* 'ʃlɛ·mə] *m* mud; (*breiige Rückstände*) sludge
schlammig ['ʃlamɪç] *adj* muddy
Schlammlawine *f* GEOG mudslide
Schlampe <-, -n> ['ʃlam·pə] *f* slut
Schlamperei <-, -en> [ʃlam·pə·'rai] *f* ① (*Nachlässigkeit*) sloppiness ② (*Unordnung*) mess, untidiness
schlampig ['ʃlam·pɪç] **I.** *adj* ① (*nachlässig*) sloppy; (*liederlich*) slovenly ② (*ungepflegt*) unkempt **II.** *adv* ① (*nachlässig*) sloppily ② (*ungepflegt*) in an unkempt way
schlang [ʃlaŋ] *imp von* **schlingen**
Schlange <-, -n> ['ʃlaŋə] *f* ① ZOOL snake ② (*lange Reihe*) line; ~ **stehen** to stand in line
schlängeln ['ʃlɛŋ·l̩n] *vr* ■ **sich** *akk* ~ (*sich winden*) to crawl; *Fluss, Straße* to meander
Schlangenleder *nt* snakeskin
schlank ['ʃlaŋk] *adj* thin, slim; *Handgelenk* slender; **du bist ~ geworden** you have lost weight
Schlankheit <-> *f kein pl* slimness
Schlankheitskur *f* diet
schlapp [ʃlap] *adj* ① *pred* (*erschöpft*) worn out ② (*ohne Antrieb*) feeble, listless
schlapp|machen *vi* ① (*aufgeben*) to give up ② (*umkippen*) to pass out
Schlappschwanz *m* (*pej*) wimp
schlau [ʃlau] *adj* ① (*gescheit*) clever; **ich werde nicht ~ aus der Bedienungsanleitung** I can't make heads or tails of the operating instructions ② (*gerissen*) crafty, wily; *Plan* ingenious
Schlauch <-[e]s, Schläuche> [ʃlaux, *pl* 'ʃlɔy·çə] *m* ① (*biegsame Leitung*) tube; (*für Wasser*) hose ② (*Reifenschlauch*) [inner] tube
Schlauchboot *nt* rubber boat
schlauchen ['ʃlau·xn̩] *vt, vi* to wear sb out; **das schlaucht ganz schön!** that really takes it out of you!
Schlaufe <-, -n> ['ʃlau·fə] *f* loop; (*aus Leder*) strap
Schlauheit <-> *f kein pl* shrewdness
schlecht [ʃlɛçt] **I.** *adj* ① (*nicht gut*) bad; *Leistung, Gehalt, Qualität* poor; *Zeiten* hard; *Augen* weak ② (*moralisch verkommen*) bad, wicked, evil; **ein ~es Gewissen haben** to have a bad conscience ③ (*übel*) **mir ist** ~ I feel sick ④ (*verdorben*) bad; **das Fleisch ist ~ geworden** the meat has spoiled ▶ WENDUNGEN: **es sieht ~ aus** things don't look good **II.** *adv* ① (*nicht gut*) badly, poorly; **so ~ habe ich selten gegessen** I've rarely had such bad food; **die Geschäfte gehen ~** business is bad; **~ gelaunt** in a bad mood *pred;* (*dauernd*) bad-tempered ② MED **jdm geht es ~** sb doesn't feel good; **~ hören** to be hard of hearing; **~ sehen** to have poor eyesight
schlecht|machen *vt* ■ **jdn ~** to badmouth sb
schlecken ['ʃlɛ·kn̩] **I.** *vt* to lick; (*aufschlecken*) to lap up *sep* **II.** *vi* ① SÜDD, ÖSTERR, SCHWEIZ (*naschen*) to nibble ② (*lecken*) ■ **an etw** *dat* ~ to lick sth
Schlegel <-s, -> ['ʃleː·gl̩] *m* ① MUS *s.* **Schlägel** ② KOCHK SÜDD, ÖSTERR, SCHWEIZ (*Hinterkeule*) drumstick
schleichen <schlich, geschlichen> ['ʃlai·çn̩] **I.** *vi sein* ① (*leise gehen*) to creep, to sneak ② (*langsam gehen/fahren*) to crawl along **II.** *vr haben* ■ **sich** *akk* **in das Zimmer ~** to sneak into the room; **sich aus dem Haus ~** to steal away softly
Schleier <-s, -> ['ʃlai·ɐ] *m* veil
schleierhaft *adj* ■ **~ sein** to be a mystery
Schleife <-, -n> ['ʃlai·fə] *f* ① MODE bow ② *Straße* loop
schleifen¹ ['ʃlai·fn̩] **I.** *vt haben* (*ziehen*) to drag **II.** *vi* ① *haben* (*reiben*) to rub (**an** + *dat* against) ② *sein o haben* (*gleiten*) to slide; *Schleppe* to trail
schleifen² <schliff, geschliffen> ['ʃlai·fn̩] *vt* ① (*schärfen*) to sharpen ② (*in Form polieren*) to polish; (*mit Sandpapier*) to sand; *Edelsteine* to cut
Schleifmaschine *f* sander
Schleifpapier *nt* sandpaper
Schleim <-[e]s, -e> [ʃlaim] *m* ① MED mucus; (*in Bronchien*) phlegm ② (*klebrige Masse*) slime
Schleimer(in) <-s, -> *m(f)* (*pej fam*) brown-noser
Schleimhaut *f* mucous membrane
schleimig ['ʃlai·mɪç] **I.** *adj* ① MED mucous ② (*glitschig*) slimy ③ (*pej: unterwürfig*) slimy, obsequious **II.** *adv* (*pej*) in a slimy way, obsequiously
schlemmen ['ʃlɛ·mən] *vi* to have a feast
Schlemmer(in) <-s, -> ['ʃlɛ·mɐ] *m(f)* gourmet
Schlemmerei <-, -en> [ʃlɛ·mə·'rai] *f* ① (*das Schlemmen*) feasting ② (*Schmaus*) feast
schlendern ['ʃlɛn·dɐn] *vi sein* to stroll along
schlenkern ['ʃlɛŋ·kɐn] *vi* to dangle
Schleppe <-, -n> ['ʃlɛ·pə] *f* MODE train
schleppen ['ʃlɛ·pn̩] **I.** *vt* ① (*tragen*) to carry, to lug *fam* ② (*zerren*) to drag ③ (*abschleppen*) to tow **II.** *vr* (*sich mühselig fortbewegen*) ■ **sich** *akk* ~ to drag oneself; *Verhandlungen* to drag on
schleppend **I.** *adj* ① (*zögerlich*) slow ② (*schwerfällig*) shuffling **II.** *adv* ① (*zögerlich*) slowly; **~ in Gang kommen** to be slow in getting started ② (*schwerfällig*) **~ gehen** to shuffle along
Schlepper¹ <-s, -> ['ʃlɛ·pɐ] *m* ① NAUT tug[boat] ② (*Zugmaschine*) tractor
Schlepper(in)² <-s, -> ['ʃlɛ·pɐ] *m(f)* people

S

smuggler, coyote *sl*

Schlẹppkahn *m* barge

Schlẹpplift *m* ski tow

Schlẹpptau *nt* towline; **im ~** in tow

schleudern ['ʃlɔy·dɐn] **I.** *vt haben* ❶ (*werfen*) to hurl ❷ *Wäsche* to spin **II.** *vi sein* to skid; **ins S~ geraten** to go into a skid; (*fig*) to be losing control of a situation

schleunigst *adv* right away, at once

Schleuse <-, -n> ['ʃlɔy·zə] *f* lock; (*Tor*) sluice [gate]

schleusen ['ʃlɔy·zn̩] *vt* (*fam*) ❶ (*schmuggeln*) to smuggle (**in** *+akk* into) ❷ (*geleiten*) ■**jdn durch etw** *akk* **~** to escort sb through sth ❸ NAUT to pass through a lock

Schleuserbande <-, -n> *f* people smugglers *pl*

schlich [ʃlɪç] *imp von* **schleichen**

schlicht [ʃlɪçt] **I.** *adj* ❶ (*einfach*) simple, plain ❷ (*wenig gebildet*) simple, unsophisticated ❸ *attr* (*bloß*) plain **II.** *part* (*ganz einfach*) simply

schlief [ʃli:f] *imp von* **schlafen**

schließen <schlọss, geschlọssen> ['ʃli:·sn̩] **I.** *vi* ❶ (*zugehen*) to close ❷ (*zumachen*) to close, to shut ❸ (*enden*) to close; **der Vorsitzende schloss mit den Worten ...** the chairman closed by saying ... ❹ (*schlussfolgern*) to conclude; **etw lässt auf etw** *akk* **~** sth indicates sth/that sth ... **II.** *vt* ❶ (*zumachen*) to close ❷ (*geh: beenden*) to close, to wind up ❸ (*eingehen*) **ein Bündnis ~** to enter into an alliance; **Freundschaft ~** to become friends; **Frieden ~** to make peace; **einen Kompromiss ~** to reach a compromise; **einen Pakt ~** to make a pact ❹ *Lücke* to fill ❺ (*schlussfolgern*) to conclude (**aus** *+dat* from) ❻ (*umfassen*) **jdn in die Arme ~** to take sb in one's arms

Schließfach *nt* (*Gepäckschließfach*) locker; (*Bankschließfach*) safe-deposit box; (*Postfach*) post office box

schließlich ['ʃli:s·lɪç] *adv* ❶ (*endlich*) at last, finally ❷ (*immerhin*) after all

Schließung <-, -en> *f* closure

schliff [ʃlɪf] *imp von* **schleifen²**

Schliff <-[e]s, -e> [ʃlɪf] *m* ❶ *kein pl* (*das Schleifen*) *von Edelsteinen* cutting; *von Glas* cutting and polishing ❷ (*geschliffener Zustand*) edge; *von Edelsteinen* cut; **einer S.** *dat* **den letzten ~ geben** to put the finishing touches on sth

schlimm [ʃlɪm] **I.** *adj* ❶ (*übel*) bad, terrible; ■**etwas S~es/S~eres** sth terrible/worse; **das ist nicht so ~** that's not so bad ❷ (*ernst*) serious ❸ (*moralisch schlecht*) bad; *Verbrechen* serious ▶ WENDUNGEN: **das ist halb so ~** it's not as bad as all that; **ist nicht ~!** no problem!, don't worry [about it]! **II.** *adv* ❶ (*gravierend*) seriously ❷ (*äußerst schlecht*) dreadfully; **jdn ~ zurichten** to beat sb to a pulp; **~ dran sein** (*fam*) to be hard up; **es hätte ~er kommen können** it could have been worse; **umso ~er** so much the worse

schlimmstenfalls ['ʃlɪm·stn̩·'fals] *adv* if worst comes to worst

Schlinge <-, -n> ['ʃlɪŋə] *f* ❶ (*Schlaufe*) loop; (*um jdn aufzuhängen*) noose ❷ (*Falle*) snare

schlingen¹ <schlạng, geschlụngen> ['ʃlɪŋən] **I.** *vt* to wind (**um** *+akk* around); **die Arme um jdn ~** to wrap one's arms around sb **II.** *vr* ■**sich** *akk* **um etw** *akk* **~** to wind itself around sth

schlingen² <schlạng, geschlụngen> ['ʃlɪŋən] *vi* (*fam*) to gobble one's food

schlingern ['ʃlɪŋɐn] *vi* NAUT to roll

Schlịngpflanze *f* creeper

Schlips <-es, -e> [ʃlɪps] *m* tie

Schlitten <-s, -> ['ʃlɪ·tn̩] *m* ❶ (*Rodel*) sledge, sled; (*Rodelschlitten*) toboggan; (*mit Pferden*) sleigh ❷ (*sl: Auto*) wheels *pl*

Schlịttenfahrt *f* sleigh ride

schlittern ['ʃlɪ·tɐn] *vi* ❶ *sein o haben* (*rutschen*) to slide; *Wagen* to skid ❷ *sein* (*fam: unversehens geraten*) ■**in etw** *akk* **~** to slide into sth

Schlittschuh ['ʃlɪt·ʃu:] *m* [ice] skate; **~ laufen** to [ice-]skate

Schlịttschuhbahn *f* ice rink

Schlịttschuhläufer(in) *m(f)* [ice] skater

Schlitz <-es, -e> [ʃlɪts] *m* ❶ (*Einsteckschlitz*) slot ❷ (*schmale Öffnung*) *a.* MODE slit

Schlịtzohr *nt* rogue

schloss^RR^, **schloß**^ALT^ [ʃlɔs] *imp von* **schließen**

Schloss^RR^ <-es, Schlösser>, **Schloß**^ALT^ <-sses, Schlösser> [ʃlɔs, *pl* 'ʃlœ·sɐ] *nt* ❶ (*Palast*) castle, palace ❷ (*Türschloss*) lock; **ins ~ fallen** to snap shut ❸ (*Verschluss*) catch ▶ WENDUNGEN: **jdn hinter ~ und Riegel bringen** to put sb behind bars

Schlosser(in) <-s, -> ['ʃlɔsɐ] *m(f)* locksmith

Schlosserei <-, -en> [ʃlɔ·sə·'rai] *f* locksmith's store

Schlọsspark^RR^ *m* castle grounds *npl*

schlottern ['ʃlɔ·tɐn] *vi* ❶ (*zittern*) to tremble (**vor** *+dat* with) ❷ (*schlaff herabhängen*) to flap (**um** *+akk* around)

Schlucht <-, -en> [ʃlʊxt] *f* ravine; (*tiefer*) gorge

schluchzen ['ʃlʊxtsn̩] *vi* to sob

Schluchzer <-s, -> ['ʃlʊx·tsɐ] *m* sob

Schluck <-[e]s, -e> [ʃlʊk] *m* mouthful; (*größer*) gulp; (*kleiner*) sip; **in einem ~** in one swallow

Schluckauf <-s> ['ʃlʊk·ʔauf] *m kein pl* hiccup

schlucken ['ʃlʊkn̩] *vt, vi* ❶ (*hinunterschlucken*) to swallow ❷ AUTO (*fam*) to guzzle sth; **der alte Wagen schluckt 14 Liter** the old car guzzles 14 liters for every 100 km ❸ (*fam: hinnehmen, glauben*) to swallow ❹ (*dämpfen*) to absorb

Schlụckimpfung *f* oral vaccination

schlụckweise *adv* in sips

schludern ['ʃlu:·dɐn] *vi* (*fam*) to do a sloppy job

schlug [ʃlu:k] *imp von* **schlagen**

S

Schlummer <-s> ['ʃlʊ·mɐ] *m kein pl* slumber
schlummern ['ʃlʊ·mɐn] *vi* to slumber
Schlund <-[e]s, Schlünde> [ʃlʊnt, *pl* 'ʃlʏn·də] *m* throat
schlüpfen ['ʃlʏp·fn̩] *vi sein* ① ORN, ZOOL to hatch (**aus** +*dat* out [of]) ② (*rasch kleiden*) to slip (**aus** +*dat* out of, **in** +*akk* into) ③ (*rasch bewegen*) to slip
Schlüpfer <-s, -> ['ʃlʏp·fɐ] *m* panties *npl*
Schlupfloch *nt* ① (*Öffnung*) opening, hole ② (*fig*) loophole
schlüpfrig ['ʃlʏpf·rɪç] *adj* ① (*unanständig*) lewd ② (*glitschig*) slippery
Schlupfwinkel *m* (*Versteck*) hiding place; (*von Gangstern*) hideout
schlurfen ['ʃlʊr·fn̩] *vi sein* to shuffle; (*absichtlich*) to scuff [one's feet]
schlürfen ['ʃlʏr·fn̩] *vt, vi* to slurp
Schluss^RR <-es, Schlüsse>, **Schluß**^ALT <Schlusses, Schlüsse> [ʃlʊs, *pl* 'ʃlʏ·sə] *m* ① *kein pl* (*zeitliches Ende*) end; **zum ~ kommen** to finish; [**mit etw** *dat*] **~ machen** (*fam*) to stop [sth]; [**mit jdm**] **~ machen** to break up [with sb]; **~ für heute!** that's enough for today!; **~ damit!** stop it!; **~ [jetzt]!** [that's] enough [already]!; **zum ~** at the end; (*schließlich*) in the end ② *kein pl* (*hinterster Teil*) end; **am ~ des Zuges** at the back of the train ③ (*abschließender Abschnitt*) end, last part ④ (*Folgerung*) conclusion
Schlussbemerkung^RR *f* final remark
Schlüssel <-s, -> ['ʃlʏ·sl̩] *m* key
Schlüsselbein *nt* clavicle
Schlüsseldienst *m* locksmith [service]
Schlüsselerlebnis *nt* crucial experience
schlüsselfertig *adj* ready for immediate occupancy
Schlüsselloch *nt* keyhole
Schlussfolgerung^RR, **Schlußfolgerung**^ALT <-, -en> *f* deduction, conclusion; **eine ~** [**aus etw** *dat*] **ziehen** to draw a conclusion [from sth]
schlüssig ['ʃlʏ·sɪç] *adj* ① (*folgerichtig*) logical; *Beweisführung* conclusive ② (*im Klaren*) ■**sich** *dat* **~ werden** to make up one's mind (**über** +*akk* about)
Schlusslicht^RR *nt* AUTO rear [*or* tail] light
Schlusspfiff^RR *m* final whistle
Schlussstrich^RR *m* **einen ~ unter etw** *akk* **ziehen** to put an end to sth
Schlussverkauf^RR *m* sale
schmachten ['ʃmax·tn̩] *vi* (*geh*) ① (*leiden*) to languish ② (*sich sehnen*) to crave
schmächtig ['ʃmɛç·tɪç] *adj* slight
schmackhaft *adj* tasty ▶ WENDUNGEN: **jdm etw ~ machen** to make sth tempting for sb
schmal <-er *o* schmäler, -ste *o* schmälste> [ʃma:l] *adj* narrow; *Mensch* slim
Schmalz <-es, -e> [ʃmalts] *nt* KOCHK drippings *npl;* (*vom Schwein*) lard
schmalzig ['ʃmal·tsɪç] *adj* (*pej fam*) schmaltzy, corny
schmarotzen* [ʃma·'rɔ·tsn̩] *vi* to sponge
Schmarotzer <-s, -> *m* parasite
Schmarren ['ʃma·rən], **Schmarrn** <-s, -> [ʃmarn̩] *m* SÜDD, ÖSTERR ① KOCHK *a warm dessert of sliced crepes and raisins, topped with powdered sugar, often served with apple sauce or plum jam* ② (*fam: Quatsch*) nonsense
schmatzen ['ʃma·tsn̩] *vi* to eat/drink noisily; (*mit Genuss*) to smack one's lips; **musst du immer so ~?** can't you eat quietly?
schmecken ['ʃmɛ·kn̩] **I.** *vi* ① (*munden*) **hat es geschmeckt?** did you enjoy it?; **das schmeckt aber gut** this tastes wonderful; **es sich** *dat* **~ lassen** to enjoy one's food; **lass es dir ~!** enjoy your meal! ② (*Geschmack haben*) to taste (**nach** +*dat* of) ③ SÜDD, ÖSTERR, SCHWEIZ (*riechen*) smell **II.** *vt* to taste
Schmeichelei <-, -en> [ʃmai·çə·'lai] *f* flattery
schmeichelhaft *adj* flattering
schmeicheln ['ʃmai·çl̩n] *vi* to flatter; ■**es schmeichelte ihm, dass ...** he was flattered that ...
Schmeichler(in) <-s, -> ['ʃmaiç·lɐ] *m(f)* flatterer
schmeichlerisch *adj* flattering
schmeißen <schmiss, geschmissen> ['ʃmai·sn̩] **I.** *vt, vi* (*fam*) ① (*werfen*) to throw; (*mit Kraft*) to hurl, to fling; **sie schmiss ihn aus dem Haus** she threw him out [of the house] ② (*sl: spendieren*) **eine Party ~** to throw a party; **eine Runde ~** to pay for a round of drinks ③ (*sl: managen*) to run ④ (*fam: abbrechen*) to quit **II.** *vr* (*sich fallen lassen*) ■**sich** *akk* **~** to throw oneself (**auf** +*akk* onto, **vor** +*akk* in front of)
Schmeißfliege *f* blowfly
schmelzen <schmolz, geschmolzen> ['ʃmɛl·tsn̩] **I.** *vi sein* to melt **II.** *vt haben* to melt; *Metall* to smelt
Schmelzkäse *m* KOCHK ① (*in Scheiben*) processed cheese ② (*streichfähig*) cheese spread
Schmelzofen *m* smelting furnace
Schmelzpunkt *m* melting point
Schmerz <-es, -en> [ʃmɛrts] *m* ① (*körperliche Empfindung*) pain; (*anhaltend und pochend*) ache; **~en haben** to be in pain ② *kein pl* (*Kummer*) [mental] anguish
schmerzempfindlich *adj* sensitive to pain *pred*
schmerzen ['ʃmɛr·tsn̩] *vi* to hurt; (*anhaltend und pochend*) to ache; ■**~d** painful, aching
Schmerzensgeld *nt* compensation
schmerzhaft *adj* painful
schmerzlich **I.** *adj* (*geh*) painful, distressing **II.** *adv* painfully
schmerzlindernd **I.** *adj* pain-relieving **II.** *adv* **~ wirken** to relieve pain
schmerzlos *adj* painless ▶ WENDUNGEN: **kurz und ~** short and sweet
Schmerzmittel *nt* painkiller; MED analgesic
schmerzstillend *adj* painkilling; ■**~ sein** to be a painkiller
Schmerztablette *f* painkiller

S

Schmetterling <-s, -e> ['ʃmɛ·tɐ·lɪŋ] *m* butterfly
schmettern ['ʃmɛ·tɐn] *vt* ❶ (*schleudern*) to fling ❷ SPORT to smash ❸ MUS to blare out; *Lied* to bawl out
Schmied(in) <-[e]s, -e> [ʃmiːt, *pl* 'ʃmiː·də] *m(f)* smith; (*Hufschmied*) blacksmith
Schmiede <-, -n> ['ʃmiː·də] *f* forge, smithy
schmiedeeisern *adj* wrought-iron
schmieden ['ʃmiː·dn̩] *vt* ❶ (*glühend hämmern*) to forge ❷ (*aushecken*) *Plan* to make
schmiegen ['ʃmiː·gn̩] *vr* to snuggle (**an** +*akk* up to); ■ **sich** *akk* [**an jdn**] ~ to cuddle up close [to sb]
Schmiere <-, -n> ['ʃmiː·rə] *f* (*schmierige Masse*) grease; (*schmieriger Schmutz*) ooze ▶ WENDUNGEN: ~ **stehen** to keep a lookout
schmieren ['ʃmiː·rən] **I.** *vt* ❶ (*streichen*) to spread; *Creme etc.* to rub, to smear; **Salbe auf eine Wunde** ~ to put cream on a wound ❷ (*fetten*) to lubricate, to grease ❸ (*pej: malen*) to scrawl ❹ (*fam: bestechen*) ■ **jdn** ~ to grease sb's palm ▶ WENDUNGEN: **jdm eine** ~ (*fam*) to whack sb; **wie geschmiert** (*fam*) like clockwork **II.** *vi* (*pej: unsauber schreiben*) to scribble; *Kuli* to smudge
Schmiererei <-, -en> [ʃmiː·rə·'rai] *f* (*pej fam*) [smudgy] mess
Schmiergeld *nt* (*fam*) bribe, kickback
schmierig ['ʃmiː·rɪç] *adj* ❶ (*nass und klebrig*) greasy ❷ (*pej: schleimig*) slimy
Schmieröl *nt* lubricating oil
Schmierseife *f* soft soap
Schmierstoff *m* lubricant
Schmierzettel *m* piece of scratch paper
Schminke <-, -n> ['ʃmɪŋ·kə] *f* makeup
schminken ['ʃmɪŋ·kn̩] *vt* to put makeup on; ■ **sich** *akk* ~ to put on makeup
schmirgeln ['ʃmɪr·gl̩n] *vt, vi* to sand down
Schmirgelpapier ['ʃmɪrgl̩-] *nt* sandpaper
schmiss[RR], **schmiß**[ALT] [ʃmɪs] *imp von* **schmeißen**
schmollen ['ʃmɔ·lən] *vi* to sulk
schmolz [ʃmɔlts] *imp von* **schmelzen**
Schmorbraten ['ʃmoːɐ̯-] *m* pot roast
schmoren ['ʃmoː·rən] *vt, vi* ❶ KOCHK to braise ❷ (*fam: schwitzen*) to swelter ▶ WENDUNGEN: **jdn ~ lassen** (*fam*) to let sb stew
Schmuck <-[e]s> [ʃmʊk] *m kein pl* ❶ (*Schmuckstücke*) jewelry ❷ (*Verzierung*) decoration, ornamentation
schmücken ['ʃmʏ·kn̩] **I.** *vt* (*dekorieren*) to decorate, to embellish **II.** *vr* ■ **sich** *akk* ~ to wear jewelry
schmucklos *adj* bare; *Fassade* plain
Schmuckstück *nt* ❶ (*Schmuckgegenstand*) piece of jewelry ❷ (*fam: Prachtstück*) jewel, masterpiece
schmuddelig ['ʃmʊdəlɪç], **schmuddlig** ['ʃmʊd·lɪç] *adj* grubby
Schmuggel <-s> ['ʃmʊgl̩] *m kein pl* smuggling
schmuggeln ['ʃmʊgl̩n] *vt* to smuggle
Schmuggelware *f* smuggled goods *pl,* contraband
Schmuggler(in) <-s, -> ['ʃmʊg·lɐ] *m(f)* smuggler
schmunzeln ['ʃmʊn·tsl̩n] *vi* to grin quietly to oneself (**über** +*akk* about)
Schmunzeln <-s> ['ʃmʊn·tsl̩n] *nt kein pl* grin
schmusen ['ʃmuː·zn̩] *vi* (*fam*) to cuddle, to neck
Schmutz <-es> [ʃmʊts] *m kein pl* dirt; **jdn/etw in den ~ ziehen** to ruin sb's name/sth's reputation
Schmutzfleck *m* dirt stain
schmutzig ['ʃmʊ·tsɪç] *adj* ❶ (*dreckig*) dirty; **sich** *akk* [**bei etw** *dat*] ~ **machen** to get dirty [doing sth] ❷ (*obszön*) smutty, lewd; *Witz* dirty ❸ (*pej: unlauter*) dubious, crooked; *Geld* dirty; *Geschäfte* shady
Schnabel <-s, Schnäbel> ['ʃnaː·bl̩, *pl* 'ʃnɛː·bl̩] *m* ❶ (*Vogelschnabel*) beak ❷ (*lange Tülle*) spout ❸ (*fam: Mund*) trap; **halt den ~!** shut up!
Schnake <-, -n> ['ʃnaː·kə] *f* ❶ (*Weberknecht*) daddy longlegs *fam* ❷ DIAL (*Stechmücke*) mosquito
Schnalle <-, -n> ['ʃnalə] *f* buckle
schnallen ['ʃna·lən] *vt* to buckle up *sep,* to fasten; **den Gürtel enger/weiter ~** to tighten/loosen one's belt
schnalzen ['ʃnal·tsn̩] *vi* **mit den Fingern ~** to snap one's fingers; **mit der Zunge ~** to click one's tongue
Schnäppchen <-s, -> ['ʃnɛp·çən] *nt* bargain
Schnäppchenjagd *f* bargain hunting
Schnäppchenmarkt *m* ÖKON (*fam*) bargain basement
schnappen ['ʃna·pn̩] **I.** *vi* ❶ *haben* (*greifen*) to grab (**nach** +*dat* for), to snatch (**nach** +*dat* at) ❷ *haben* (*mit den Zähnen*) to snap (**nach** +*dat* at) **II.** *vt haben* (*fam*) ❶ (*ergreifen*) ■ [**sich** *dat*] **etw ~** to grab sth; **etwas frische Luft ~** to get a breath of fresh air ❷ (*festnehmen*) to catch
Schnappschuss[RR] *m* snapshot
Schnaps <-es, Schnäpse> [ʃnaps, *pl* 'ʃnɛp·sə] *m* schnapps
Schnapsidee *f* harebrained idea *fam*
schnarchen ['ʃnar·çn̩] *vi* to snore
schnattern ['ʃna·tɐn] *vi* ❶ ORN to cackle ❷ (*fam: schwatzen*) to chatter
schnauben <schnaubte, geschnaubt> ['ʃnau·bn̩] *vi* to snort
schnaufen ['ʃnau·fn̩] *vi* ❶ *haben* (*angestrengt atmen*) to puff, to pant ❷ *haben bes* SÜDD (*atmen*) to breathe
Schnauzbart *m* walrus mustache
Schnauze <-, -n> ['ʃnau·tsə] *f* ❶ ZOOL snout ❷ (*sl: Mund*) trap; **eine große ~ haben** to have a big mouth; **die ~ halten** to shut up ▶ WENDUNGEN: **die ~ [von etw** *dat*] **voll haben** (*sl*) to be fed up [with sth]; [**mit etw** *dat*] **auf die ~ fallen** (*sl*) to fall flat on one's face [with sth]

S

schnauzen ['ʃnau·tsn̩] *vi* (*fam: barsch reden*) to bark

schnäuzen[RR] ['ʃnɔy·tsn̩] *vr* **sich** *akk* ~ to blow one's nose

Schnecke <-, -n> ['ʃnɛ·kə] *f* ❶ ZOOL snail; (*Nacktschnecke*) slug ❷ (*Gebäck*) ≈ cinnamon roll with raisins ▶ WENDUNGEN: **jdn zur ~ machen** to chew sb out

Schneckenhaus *nt* snail shell

Schneckentempo *nt* **im** ~ at a snail's pace

Schnee <-s> [ʃne:] *m kein pl* snow ▶ WENDUNGEN: ~ **von gestern** [ancient] history

Schneeball *m* snowball

schneebedeckt *adj* snow-covered

Schneebesen *m* whisk

Schneefall *m* snowfall

Schneeflocke *f* snowflake

Schneegestöber *nt* [snow] flurry

Schneeglöckchen <-s, -> *nt* snowdrop

Schneegrenze *f* snow line

Schneekette *f meist pl* snow chain[s *pl*]

Schneemann *m* snowman

Schneematsch *m* slush

Schneepflug *m* snowplow

Schneeregen *m* sleet

Schneeschaufel *f,* **Schneeschippe** *f* DIAL snow shovel

Schneesturm *m* snowstorm

schneeweiß ['ʃne:·'vais] *adj* as white as snow *pred,* snow-white

Schneewittchen <-s> [ʃne:·'vɪt·çən] *nt* Snow White

Schneide <-, -n> ['ʃnai·də] *f* edge, blade

schneiden <schnitt, geschnitten> ['ʃnai·dn̩] **I.** *vt* ❶ (*zerteilen*) to cut ❷ (*kürzen*) to cut, to trim; *Baum* to prune ❸ (*knapp einscheren*) *Auto* to cut ❹ FILM to edit ❺ (*meiden*) to snub **II.** *vr* ❶ (*sich verletzen*) to cut oneself; **sich** *akk* **in den Finger** ~ to cut one's finger ❷ (*sich kreuzen*) to intersect

schneidend *adj* ❶ (*durchdringend*) biting ❷ (*scharf*) sharp

Schneider(in) <-s, -> ['ʃnai·dɐ] *m(f)* tailor ▶ WENDUNGEN: **aus dem ~ sein** to be in the clear

S

Schneiderei <-, -en> [ʃnai·də·'rai] *f* tailor shop

schneidern ['ʃnai·dɐn] **I.** *vi* to work as a tailor; (*als Hobby*) to do dressmaking **II.** *vt* to make; *Anzug* to tailor; **selbst geschneidert** homemade

Schneidersitz *m* **im** ~ cross-legged

Schneidezahn *m* incisor

schneien ['ʃnai·ən] *vi impers* to snow

Schneise <-, -n> ['ʃnai·zə] *f* aisle

schnell [ʃnɛl] **I.** *adj* ❶ (*eine hohe Geschwindigkeit erreichend*) fast ❷ (*zügig*) prompt, rapid ❸ *attr* (*baldig*) swift, speedy **II.** *adv* ❶ (*mit hoher Geschwindigkeit*) fast ❷ (*zügig*) quickly; **es geht ganz** ~ it won't take long; ~ **machen** to hurry up

Schnellboot *nt* speedboat

schnellebig[ALT] *adj s.* **schnelllebig**

schnellen ['ʃnɛ·lən] *vi sein* **in die Höhe** ~ to shoot up

Schnellhefter *m* loose-leaf binder

Schnelligkeit <-, *selten* -en> *f* ❶ (*Geschwindigkeit*) speed ❷ (*Zügigkeit*) speediness; *Ausführung* promptness

Schnellimbiss[RR] *m* fast-food stand

Schnellkochtopf *m* pressure cooker

Schnellkurs *m* crash course

schnelllebig[RR] *adj* fast-moving

schnellstens *adv* as soon as possible

Schnellstraße *f* expressway

Schnellverfahren *nt* ❶ JUR summary trial ❷ (*fam*) **im** ~ in a hurry

Schnellzug *m* fast train

Schnepfe <-, -n> ['ʃnɛp·fə] *f* ❶ ORN snipe ❷ (*pej fam*) stupid chick

schneuzen[ALT] ['ʃnɔy·tsn̩] *vr s.* **schnäuzen**

schniefen ['ʃni:·fn̩] *vi* to sniffle

schnippeln ['ʃnɪ·pl̩n] *vi* to snip (**an** +*dat* at)

schnippen ['ʃnɪ·pn̩] **I.** *vi* **mit den Fingern** ~ to snap one's fingers **II.** *vt* ■**etw** [**von etw** *dat*] ~ to flick sth [off sth]

schnippisch ['ʃnɪ·pɪʃ] *adj* snippy, snotty

Schnipsel <-s, -> ['ʃnɪp·sl̩] *m o nt* shred

schnitt [ʃnɪt] *imp von* **schneiden**

Schnitt <-[e]s, -e> [ʃnɪt] *m* ❶ (*Schnittwunde*) cut ❷ (*Haarschnitt*) cut ❸ MODE cut ❹ FILM editing ❺ ARCHIT, MATH section; **im** ~ ARCHIT in section; (*durchschnittlich*) on average

Schnitte <-, -n> ['ʃnɪ·tə] *f* ❶ KOCHK slice ❷ (*belegtes Brot*) [open-faced] sandwich

Schnittfläche *f* cut surface

schnittig ['ʃnɪ·tɪç] *adj* stylish

Schnittlauch ['ʃnɪt·laux] *m kein pl* chives *npl*

Schnittpunkt *m* point of intersection

Schnittstelle *f* COMPUT interface

Schnittwunde *f* cut

Schnitzel[1] <-s, -> ['ʃnɪ·tsl̩] *nt* KOCHK veal cutlet; **Wiener** ~ Wiener schnitzel

Schnitzel[2] <-s, -> ['ʃnɪ·tsl̩] *nt o m* shred

schnitzen ['ʃnɪ·tsn̩] *vt, vi* to carve; ■**das S~** carving

Schnitzer(in) <-s, -> ['ʃnɪ·tsɐ] *m(f)* woodcarver

Schnitzer <-s, -> ['ʃnɪ·tsɐ] *m* (*fam*) blunder

Schnitzerei <-, -en> [ʃnɪ·tsə·'rai] *f* woodcarving

schnöde ['ʃnø:·də] **I.** *adj* despicable **II.** *adv* despicably

Schnorchel <-s, -> ['ʃnɔr·çl̩] *m* snorkel

schnorcheln ['ʃnɔr·çl̩n] *vi* to go snorkeling

Schnörkel <-s, -> ['ʃnœr·kl̩] *m* scroll

schnorren ['ʃnɔ·rən] *vi, vt* to sponge [*or* mooch]

Schnorrer(in) <-s, -> *m(f)* moocher, scrounger

schnüffeln ['ʃnʏ·fl̩n] *vi* ❶ (*schnuppern*) to sniff ❷ (*fam: spionieren*) to nose around

Schnüffler(in) <-s, -> *m(f)* ❶ (*Detektiv*) detective, snoop ❷ (*sl: Süchtiger*) glue sniffer

Schnuller <-s, -> ['ʃnʊ·lɐ] *m* pacifier, Binky® *fam*

Schnulze <-, -n> ['ʃnʊl·tsə] *f* corny love song

schnupfen ['ʃnʊpfn̩] **I.** *vi* to sniff **II.** *vt Tabak, Kokain* to snort
Schnupfen <-s, -> ['ʃnʊp·fn̩] *m* cold; **[einen] ~ haben** to have a cold
Schnupftabak *m* snuff
schnuppern ['ʃnʊ·pɐn] *vi, vt* to sniff (**an** *+dat* at)
Schnur <-, Schnüre> [ʃnuːɐ̯, *pl* 'ʃnyː·rə] *f* cord
Schnürchen <-s, -> ['ʃnyːɐ̯·çən] *nt dim von* **Schnur** thin cord ▶ WENDUNGEN: **wie am ~** like clockwork
schnüren ['ʃnyː·rən] *vt* to tie up *sep* (**zu** *+dat* into); *Schuhe* to tie
schnurgerade ['ʃnuːɐ̯·ge·'raː·də] **I.** *adj* [as] straight as an arrow **II.** *adv* in a straight line
schnurlos *adj* cordless
Schnurrbart ['ʃnʊr·baːɐ̯t] *m* mustache
schnurren ['ʃnʊ·rən] *vi* ❶ (*Katze*) to purr ❷ (*surren*) to whir
Schnurrhaare *pl* whiskers *pl*
Schnürschuh *m* shoe [with shoelaces]
Schnürsenkel *m* shoelace
Schnürstiefel *m* lace-up boot
schnurstracks ['ʃnuːɐ̯·'ʃtraks] *adv* straight; **~ nach Hause gehen** to go straight home
schob [ʃoːp] *imp von* **schieben**
Schock <-[e]s, -s> [ʃɔk] *m* shock; **unter ~ stehen** to be in [a state of] shock
schocken ['ʃɔ·kn̩] *vt* to shock
schockieren* [ʃɔ·'kiː·rən] *vt* to shock; ■ **schockiert sein** to be shocked (**über** *+akk* about)
Schöffe, Schöffin <-n, -n> ['ʃœfə, 'ʃœ·fɪn] *m, f* juror
Schokolade <-, -n> [ʃo·ko·'laː·də] *f* (*Kakaomasse*) chocolate; (*Kakaogetränk*) hot chocolate
Schokoriegel *m* chocolate bar
Scholle <-, -n> ['ʃɔ·lə] *f* ❶ ZOOL plaice ❷ (*flacher Erdklumpen*) clod [of earth] ❸ (*Eisbrocken*) [ice] floe
schon [ʃoːn] **I.** *adv* ❶ (*bereits*) already, yet; **sind wir ~ da?** are we there yet?; **du willst ~ gehen?** you want to leave already?; **~ damals** even at that time; **~ lange** for a long time; **~ mal** ever; **hast du ~ mal Austern gegessen?** have you ever eaten oysters?; **~ oft** several times [already] ❷ (*allein*) **~ aus dem Grund** for that reason alone; **~ die Tatsache, dass ...** the fact alone that ... ❸ (*irgendwann*) in the end, one day; **es wird ~ noch klappen** it will [all] work out in the end ❹ (*denn*) **was macht das ~?** what does it matter? ❺ (*irgendwie*) all right; **danke, es geht ~** thanks, I can manage ❻ (*ja*) **ich sehe ~, ...** I can see, ...; **~ immer** always; **~ längst** for ages, ages ago; **~ wieder** [once] again; **und wenn ~!** so what? **II.** *part* ❶ (*auffordernd*) **geh ~!** go on!; **gib ~ her!** come on, give it here!; **mach ~!** hurry up!; **[nun] sag ~!** come on, tell me! ❷ (*nur*) **wenn ich das ~ rieche/sehe!** I can't stand the smell/sight of that!; **wenn ich das ~ höre!** I'm sick of hearing that!
schön [ʃøːn] **I.** *adj* ❶ (*hübsch*) beautiful; (*ansprechend*) nice ❷ (*angenehm*) good, great, nice; *Tag* beautiful; **ich wünsche euch ~e Ferien** have a nice vacation; **[das ist ja alles] ~ und gut, aber ...** that's all very well, but ...; **na ~** all right then ❸ (*iron: unschön*) great; **das sind ja ~e Aussichten!** the future sure looks bright!; **das wird ja immer ~er!** things are getting worse and worse!; **das S~ste kommt erst noch** the best is yet to come ❹ (*beträchtlich*) great, good; **ein ~es Stück Arbeit** quite a lot of work **II.** *adv* ❶ (*ansprechend*) well; **~ singen** to sing well ❷ (*fam: genau*) thoroughly ❸ (*fam: besonders*) **~ groß** nice and big ❹ (*iron: ziemlich*) really; **das hat ganz ~ wehgetan!** that really hurt!
schonen ['ʃoː·nən] **I.** *vt* ❶ (*pfleglich behandeln*) to take care of ❷ (*nicht überbeanspruchen*) to go easy on; **das schont die Gelenke** it's easy on the joints ❸ (*verschonen*) to spare **II.** *vr* ■ **sich** *akk* **~** to take it easy
schonend **I.** *adj* ❶ (*nicht strapazierend*) gentle; (*pfleglich*) careful ❷ (*rücksichtsvoll*) considerate **II.** *adv* ❶ (*pfleglich*) carefully, with care ❷ (*rücksichtsvoll*) **jdm etw ~ beibringen** to break sth to sb gently
Schonfrist *f* grace period
schöngeistig *adj* aesthetic
Schönheit <-, -en> *f* beauty
Schönheitsfehler *m* ❶ (*kosmetische Beeinträchtigung*) blemish ❷ (*geringer Makel*) flaw
Schönheitsoperation *f* cosmetic surgery
Schonung <-> *f kein pl* ❶ (*das pflegliche Behandeln*) care ❷ (*Schutz*) protection ❸ (*Rücksichtnahme*) consideration
schonungslos **I.** *adj* blunt, merciless; *Kritik* savage; *Offenheit* unabashed **II.** *adv* bluntly, mercilessly
schöpfen[1] ['ʃœp·fn̩] *vt* ❶ (*mit einem Behältnis entnehmen*) to scoop; *Suppe* to ladle ❷ (*geh: gewinnen*) to draw; *Kraft* to summon [up]
schöpfen[2] ['ʃœp·fn̩] *vt* (*erschaffen*) to create; (*Ausdruck, Wort*) to coin
Schöpfer(in) <-s, -> *m(f)* creator; ■ **der ~** (*Gott*) the Creator
schöpferisch ['ʃœp·fə·rɪʃ] **I.** *adj* creative **II.** *adv* creatively
Schöpflöffel *m* ladle
Schöpfung <-, -en> *f* creation; ■ **die ~** REL the Creation
Schöpfungsgeschichte *f kein pl* ■ **die ~** the story of the Creation
schor [ʃoːɐ̯] *imp von* **scheren**[1]
Schorf <-[e]s, -e> [ʃɔrf] *m* scab
Schorle <-, -n> ['ʃɔr·lə] *f juice or wine mixed with seltzer water*
Schornstein ['ʃɔrn·ʃtain] *m* chimney
Schornsteinfeger(in) <-s, -> *m(f)* chimney sweep
schoss[RR], **schoß**[ALT] [ʃɔs] *imp von* **schießen**
Schoß <-es, Schöße> [ʃɔs, *pl* 'ʃøː·sə] *m* ❶ ANAT lap ❷ (*Mutterleib*) womb ▶ WENDUN-

S

GEN: **etw fällt jdm in den ~** sth falls into sb's lap

Schoßhund *m* lapdog

SchösslingRR, **Schößling**ALT <-s, -e> ['ʃœs·lɪŋ] *m* shoot

Schote <-, -n> ['ʃɔ·tə] *f* pod

Schotte, Schottin <-n, -n> ['ʃɔ·tə, 'ʃɔ·tɪn] *m, f* Scot, Scotsman *masc,* Scotswoman *fem; s. a.* **Deutsche(r)**

Schottenrock *m* ① (*Rock mit Schottenmuster*) plaid skirt ② (*Kilt*) kilt

Schotter <-s, -> ['ʃɔ·tɐ] *m* gravel

schottisch ['ʃɔ·tɪʃ] *adj* Scottish; *s. a.* **deutsch**

Schottland ['ʃɔt·lant] *nt* Scotland; *s. a.* **Deutschland**

schraffieren* [ʃra·'fiː·rən] *vt* to hatch

Schraffierung <-, -en> *f kein pl* hatching

schräg [ʃrɛːk] **I.** *adj* ① (*schief*) sloping; (*Linien*) diagonal, oblique ② (*von der Norm abweichend*) offbeat **II.** *adv* ① (*schief*) at an angle, askew; **das Bild hängt ~** that picture isn't hanging straight ② (*im schiefen Winkel*) **~ überqueren** to cross diagonally ▶ WENDUNGEN: **jdn ~ ansehen** to look at sb suspiciously

Schräge <-, -n> ['ʃrɛː·gə] *f* (*schräge Fläche*) slope, sloping surface

Schrägstrich *m* slash

Schramme <-, -n> ['ʃra·mə] *f* ① (*Schürfwunde*) scrape ② (*Kratzer*) scratch

schrammen ['ʃra·mən] *vi* to scrape (**über** +*akk* across)

Schrank <-[e]s, Schränke> [ʃraŋk, *pl* 'ʃrɛŋ·kə] *m* (*Geschirrschrank*) cupboard; (*Kleiderschrank*) closet

Schranke <-, -n> ['ʃraŋ·kə] *f* ① BAHN barrier, gate ② (*Grenze*) limit; **jdn in seine ~n weisen** to put sb in his/her place

Schranken <-s, -> ['ʃraŋ·kn̩] *m* BAHN ÖSTERR (*Schranke*) [railroad [crossing]] gate

schrankenlos *adj* unlimited, boundless

Schrankwand *f* wall unit

Schraubdeckel *m* screw cap [*or* lid]; *Flasche* screw top

Schraube <-, -n> ['ʃrau·bə] *f* ① TECH screw ② NAUT propeller ③ SPORT twist ▶ WENDUNGEN: **bei jdm ist eine ~ locker** (*fam*) sb has a screw loose

schrauben ['ʃrau·bn̩] *vt* ① (*mit Schrauben befestigen*) to screw (**an** +*akk* into, **auf** +*akk* onto) ② (*drehen*) **etw höher/niedriger ~** to raise/lower sth; **etw fester/loser ~** to tighten/loosen sth

Schraubenschlüssel *m* wrench

Schraubenzieher <-s, -> *m* screwdriver

Schraubstock *m* vice

SchraubverschlussRR *m* screw top

Schrebergarten ['ʃreː·bɐ-] *m small garden plot on a piece of land managed by a gardening club*

Schreck <-s> [ʃrɛk] *m kein pl* fright; **einen ~ bekommen** to get a fright; **jdm einen ~ einjagen** to give sb a scare

Schrecken <-s, -> ['ʃrɛ·kn̩] *m* fright, horror; **~ erregend** terrifying; **mit dem ~ davonkommen** to escape with no more than a scare

Schreckensherrschaft *f* reign of terror

Schreckgespenst *nt* bogey

schreckhaft *adj* jumpy

schrecklich ['ʃrɛk·lɪç] **I.** *adj* terrible, awful **II.** *adv* terribly, awfully

SchreckschussRR *m* warning shot

SchreckschusspistoleRR *f* blank pistol

Schrei <-[e]s, -e> [ʃrai] *m* scream, cry ▶ WENDUNGEN: **der letzte ~** (*fam*) the latest craze

Schreibblock <s, -blöcke> *m* writing pad

schreiben <schrieb, geschrieben> ['ʃrai·bn̩] **I.** *vt* ① (*verfassen*) to write ② (*schriftlich darstellen*) to spell; **etw falsch/richtig ~** to spell sth wrong/right **II.** *vi* ① (*Schrift erzeugen*) to write; ■**etwas zum S~** something to write with ② (*schreibend arbeiten*) **sie schreibt an einem Buch** she is writing a book ③ (*einen Brief schicken*) ■**jdm ~** to write to sb **III.** *vr* (*geschrieben werden*) **wie schreibt sich das Wort?** how do you spell that word?

Schreiben <-s, -> ['ʃrai·bn̩] *nt* (*geh*) letter

Schreiber <-s, -> ['ʃrai·bɐ] *m* (*fam*) pen

schreibfaul *adj* ■**~ sein** to be lazy when it comes to letter-writing

Schreibfehler *m* spelling mistake

Schreibheft *nt* exercise book

Schreibkraft *f* (*geh*) typist

Schreibmaschine *f* typewriter

Schreibpapier *nt* writing paper

Schreibpult *nt* [writing] desk

Schreibtisch *m* desk

Schreibtischlampe *f* desk lamp

Schreibung <-, -en> *f* spelling

Schreibwaren *pl* stationery

Schreibwarengeschäft *nt* stationery store

Schreibweise *f* ① (*Rechtschreibung*) spelling ② (*Stil*) [writing] style

Schreibzeug *nt* writing utensils *pl*

schreien <schrie, geschrie[e]n> ['ʃrai·ən] **I.** *vi* ① (*brüllen*) to yell ② ORN, ZOOL to cry ③ (*laut rufen*) to shout (**nach** +*dat* for) ④ (*heftig verlangen*) to cry out; **das Kind schreit nach der Mutter** the child is crying for his/her mother **II.** *vt* (*etw brüllen*) to shout [out]

schreiend *adj* ① (*grell*) *Farben* loud, garish ② (*flagrant*) *Ungerechtigkeit* flagrant, glaring

Schreierei <-, -en> [ʃrai·ə·'rai] *f* yelling

Schreihals *m* (*fam*) screamer

Schrein <-[e]s, -e> [ʃrain] *m* (*geh*) shrine

Schreiner(in) <-s, -> ['ʃrai·nɐ] *m(f)* carpenter

Schreinerei <-, -en> [ʃrai·nə·'rai] *f* ① (*Tischlerei*) carpenter's workshop ② (*das Tischlern*) carpentry

schreiten <schritt, geschritten> ['ʃrai·tn̩] *vi sein* ① (*gehen*) to stride ② (*etw in Angriff nehmen*) to proceed (**zu** +*dat* with)

schrie [ʃriː] *imp von* **schreien**

schrieb [ʃriːp] *imp von* **schreiben**

Schrift <-, -en> [ʃrɪft] *f* ① (*Handschrift*) [hand]writing ② (*Schriftsystem*) script ③ TYPO (*Druckschrift*) type; (*Computer*) font ④ (*Ab-*

S

handlung) paper; **die Heilige ~** the [Holy] Scriptures *pl*

Schriftart *f* type[face]

Schriftdeutsch *nt* standard German

Schriftführer(in) *m(f)* secretary

Schriftgröße *f* font size

schriftlich [ˈʃrɪft·lɪç] **I.** *adj* written; ■ **etwas S~es** something in writing **II.** *adv* in writing

Schriftsprache *f* standard language

Schriftsteller(in) <-s, -> [ˈʃrɪft·ʃtɛ·lɐ] *m(f)* author, writer

Schriftstück *nt* document

Schriftwechsel *m* correspondence

schrill [ʃrɪl] **I.** *adj* ❶ (*durchdringend hell*) shrill ❷ (*nicht moderat*) brash; (*Farbe*) garish **II.** *adv* shrilly

schritt [ʃrɪt] *imp von* **schreiten**

Schritt <-[e]s, -e> [ʃrɪt] *m* ❶ (*Tritt*) step; **~e machen** to take steps; **seinen ~ beschleunigen** to quicken one's pace; **[mit jdm/etw] ~ halten** to keep up [with sb/sth]; **~ für ~** step by step; **~e hören** to hear footsteps ❷ *kein pl* (*Gang*) walk, gait ❸ (*Maßnahme*) measure, step; **~e [gegen jdn/etw] unternehmen** to take steps [against sb/sth] ❹ MODE crotch

SchrittempoALT *nt s.* **Schritttempo**

Schrittgeschwindigkeit *f* walking speed

Schrittmacher <-s, -> *m* pacemaker

SchritttempoRR *nt* walking speed

schrittweise I. *adj* gradual **II.** *adv* gradually

schroff [ʃrɔf] **I.** *adj* ❶ (*barsch*) curt, brusque ❷ (*steil*) steep **II.** *adv* ❶ (*barsch*) curtly, brusquely ❷ (*steil*) steeply

schröpfen [ˈʃrœp·fn̩] *vt* (*fam: ausnehmen*) to cheat

Schrot <-[e]s, -e> [ʃroːt] *m o nt* ❶ *kein pl* AGR coarsely ground whole wheat ❷ (*aus Blei*) shot

Schrotflinte *f* shotgun

Schrott <-[e]s> [ʃrɔt] *m kein pl* ❶ (*Metallmüll*) scrap metal ❷ (*fam: wertloses Zeug*) junk; **ein Auto zu ~ fahren** (*fam*) to total a car

Schrotthändler(in) *m(f)* scrap dealer

Schrotthaufen *m* scrapheap

Schrottplatz *m* junkyard

schrubben [ˈʃrʊbn̩] *vt, vi* to scrub

Schrubber <-s, -> [ˈʃrʊ·bɐ] *m* scrubbing brush

schrumpelig [ˈʃrʊm·pə·lɪç] *adj* (*fam*) wrinkled

schrumpfen [ˈʃrʊmp·fn̩] *vi sein* to shrink; *Frucht* to shrivel; *Muskeln* to atrophy

schrumplig [ˈʃrʊmp·lɪç] *adj s.* **schrumpelig**

Schub <-[e]s, Schübe> [ʃuːp, *pl* ˈʃyː·bə] *m* ❶ PHYS (*Vortrieb*) thrust ❷ MED (*einzelner Anfall*) phase ❸ (*Antrieb*) drive

Schubkarre *f,* **Schubkarren** *m* wheelbarrow

Schublade <-, -n> [ˈʃuːp·laː·də] *f* drawer

Schubs <-es, -e> [ʃʊps] *m* (*fam*) shove

schubsen [ˈʃʊp·sn̩] *vt* (*fam*) to shove

schubweise *adv* ❶ MED in phases ❷ (*in Gruppen*) in batches

schüchtern [ˈʃʏç·tɐn] *adj* ❶ (*gehemmt*) shy ❷ (*zaghaft*) timid; *Versuch* half-hearted

Schüchternheit <-> *f kein pl* shyness

schuf [ʃuːf] *imp von* **schaffen²**

Schuft <-[e]s, -e> [ʃʊft] *m* villain

schuften [ˈʃʊf·tn̩] *vi* (*fam*) to slave away

Schufterei <-, -en> [ʃʊf·tə·ˈrai] *f* (*fam*) drudgery

Schuh <-[e]s, -e> [ʃuː] *m* shoe ▶ WENDUNGEN: **jdm etw in die ~e schieben** (*fam*) to put the blame for sth on sb

Schuhgeschäft *nt* shoe store

Schuhgröße *f* shoe size

Schuhlöffel *m* shoehorn

Schuhmacher(in) <-s, -> [ˈʃuː·ma·xɐ] *m(f)* ❶ (*Hersteller*) shoemaker ❷ (*für Reparaturen*) cobbler

Schuhputzer(in) <-s, -> *m(f)* shoeshine

Schuhputzmittel *nt* shoe polish

Schuhsohle *f* sole [of a/one's shoe]

Schuhwerk <-[e]s> *nt kein pl* footwear

Schulabbruch *m* dropout

Schularbeit *f,* **Schulaufgabe** *f* ❶ *meist pl* (*Hausaufgaben*) homework; **die/seine ~en machen** to do one's homework ❷ ÖSTERR (*Klassenarbeit*) [written] test

Schulbildung *f kein pl* school education

Schulbuch *nt* schoolbook, textbook

Schulbus *m* school bus

schuld [ʃʊlt] *adj* ■ **~ sein** to be to blame (**an** +*dat* for)

Schuld <-> [ʃʊlt] *f kein pl* ❶ (*Verschulden*) fault, blame; **jdm [die] ~ geben** to blame sb; **er hat ~** he did it; **es ist ihre ~, dass/wenn ...** it is their fault that/if ...; **die ~ auf sich nehmen** to take the blame ❷ (*verschuldete Missetat*) guilt; REL sin; **er ist sich keiner ~ bewusst** he's not aware of having done anything wrong ❸ *meist pl* FIN debt; **~en machen** to go into debt

schuldbewusstRR **I.** *adj* guilty **II.** *adv* guiltily

SchuldbewusstseinRR *nt* guilty conscience

schulden [ˈʃʊl·dn̩] *vt* to owe

SchuldenerlassRR *m* FIN release from debt

schuldenfrei *adj* free of debt

Schuldgefühl *nt* guilty feelings *pl*

schuldig [ˈʃʊl·dɪç] *adj* ❶ JUR guilty; **sich ~ bekennen** to plead guilty; **jdn ~ sprechen** to find sb guilty ❷ ■ **jdm etw ~ sein** *Geld, einen Gefallen etc.* to owe sb sth

Schuldige(r) *f(m) dekl wie adj* guilty party

Schuldigkeit <-> *f kein pl* duty; **seine ~ getan haben** to have met one's obligations

schuldlos I. *adj* blameless **II.** *adv* blamelessly

Schuldner(in) <-s, -> [ˈʃʊld·nɐ] *m(f)* debtor

Schule <-, -n> [ˈʃuː·lə] *f* school; **in die ~ gehen** to go to school; **in die ~ kommen** to start school; **in der ~** at school; **morgen ist keine ~** there is no school tomorrow ▶ WENDUNGEN: **~ machen** to catch on

schulen [ˈʃuː·lən] *vt* to train

Schüler(in) <-s, -> [ˈʃyː·lɐ] *m(f)* student; SCH *a.* schoolchild

Schüleraustausch *m* high school exchange program

S

Schülerausweis *m* student ID [card]
Schülerzeitung *f* school [news]paper
Schulfach *nt* [school] subject
Schulferien *pl* summer vacation
schulfrei *adj* ~ **haben** to not have school
Schulgeld *nt* tuition
Schulheft *nt* notebook
Schulhof *m* school playground
Schuljahr *nt* SCH ❶ (*Zeitraum*) school year ❷ (*Klasse*) grade
Schulklasse *f* [school] class
Schulleiter(in) *m(f)* principal
Schulmedizin *f* classical medicine
Schulpflicht *f kein pl* mandatory school attendance
schulpflichtig *adj* of school age; ~ **sein** to be required to attend school
Schulranzen *m* backpack (*for schoolchildren*)
Schulschwänzer(in) [ˈʃuːl·ʃvɛn·tsɐ] *m(f)* SCH (*fam*) truant
Schulsprecher(in) *m(f)* student body president
Schulstunde *f* period, lesson
Schultasche *f* backpack (*for schoolchildren*)
Schulter <-, -n> [ˈʃʊl·tɐ] *f* shoulder; **mit den ~n zucken** to shrug one's shoulders ▶ WENDUNGEN: **jdm die kalte ~ zeigen** to give sb the cold shoulder; **jd nimmt etw auf die leichte ~** sb takes sth very lightly, sb doesn't take sth very seriously
Schulterblatt *nt* shoulder blade
schulterfrei *adj* strapless
schulterlang *adj* shoulder-length
Schulterpolster *nt* shoulder pad
Schulung <-, -en> *f* training
Schulunterricht *m kein pl* [in-]class instruction
Schulverweis *m* SCH referral; (*befristet*) suspension
Schulweg *m* way to/from school
Schulzeit *f kein pl* school days *pl*
Schulzeugnis *nt* report card
schummeln [ˈʃʊ·mļn] *vi* (*fam*) to cheat
schummerig [ˈʃʊ·mə·rɪç], **schummrig** [ˈʃʊm·rɪç] *adj* dim
Schund <-[e]s> [ʃʊnt] *m kein pl* (*pej*) trash
Schuppe <-, -n> [ˈʃʊpə] *f* ❶ ZOOL scale ❷ *pl* MED dandruff
schuppen [ˈʃʊ·pņ] **I.** *vt* KOCHK to remove the scales **II.** *vr* **sich** *akk* ~ *Haut* to flake
Schuppen <-s, -> [ˈʃʊ·pņ] *m* ❶ (*Verschlag*) shed ❷ (*fam: Lokal*) joint
Schuppenflechte *f* psoriasis
schuppig [ˈʃʊ·pɪç] *adj Haut* flaky; ~**e Haare haben** to have dandruff
schüren [ˈʃyː·rən] *vt* ❶ (*anfachen*) to fan ❷ (*anstacheln*) **etw** ~ to stir up *sep* sth
schürfen [ˈʃʏr·fņ] **I.** *vi* ❶ (*graben*) to dig (**nach** +*dat* for) ❷ (*schleifen*) to scrape (**über** +*akk* across) **II.** *vt* **etw** ~ to mine sth
Schürfwunde *f* scrape
Schurke <-n, -n> [ˈʃʊr·kə] *m* (*veraltend*) scoundrel
Schurkenstaat *m* POL (*pej*) rogue state
Schurwolle *f* wool; **„reine ~"** "pure new wool"
Schürze <-, -n> [ˈʃʏr·tsə] *f* apron
SchussRR <-es, Schüsse>, **Schuß**ALT <-sses, Schüsse> [ʃʊs, *pl* ˈʃʏ·sə] *m* ❶ (*Ab- o Einschuss*) shot ❷ (*Patrone*) round ❸ (*Spritzer*) splash ❹ FBALL shot ❺ (*sl: Drogeninjektion*) shot; **sich** *dat* **einen ~ setzen** to shoot up ▶ WENDUNGEN: **weit vom ~ sein** (*fam*) to be miles away; **in** ~ in top shape; **mit** ~ with a shot (*of alcohol*)
Schüssel <-, -n> [ˈʃʏ·sļ] *f* bowl, dish
schusselig [ˈʃʊ·sə·lɪç], **schusslig**RR [ˈʃʊs·lɪç] *adj* (*fam*) scatterbrained
SchusslinieRR [-liː·niə] *f* line of fire
schusssicherRR *adj* bulletproof
SchussverletzungRR *f* gunshot wound
SchusswaffeRR *f* firearm
SchusswechselRR *m* exchange of fire
SchussweiteRR *f* range [of fire]; **sich** *akk* **in/außer ~ befinden** to be within/out of range
SchusswundeRR *f s.* **Schussverletzung**
Schuster(in) <-s, -> [ˈʃuː·stɐ] *m(f)* cobbler
Schutt <-[e]s> [ʃʊt] *m kein pl* rubble *no indef art* ▶ WENDUNGEN: **in ~ und Asche liegen** to be in ruins
Schüttelfrost *m* chills and fever
schütteln [ˈʃʏ·tļn] **I.** *vt* (*rütteln*) to shake **II.** *vr* **sich** *akk* **vor Kälte** ~ to shiver [with cold] **III.** *vi impers* **es schüttelte mich** I shuddered
schütten [ˈʃʏ·tņ] **I.** *vt* to pour **II.** *vi* ■ **es schüttet** *impers* (*fam*) it's pouring
schütter [ˈʃʏ·tɐ] *adj Haar, Stimme* thin
Schutthaufen *m* pile of rubble
Schutz <-es, -e> [ʃʊts] *m kein pl* (*Sicherheit*) protection (**vor** +*dat* from); ~ **suchen** to seek refuge; **im ~[e] der Dunkelheit** under cover of darkness; **zu Ihrem ~** for your own protection; **jdn [vor etw** *dat*] **in ~ nehmen** to protect sb [from sth]
Schutzanzug *m* protective clothing
Schutzbrief *m* [international] travel insurance
Schutzbrille *f* protective goggles *npl*
Schütze, Schützin <-n, -n> [ˈʃʏtsə, ˈʃʏtsɪn] *m, f* ❶ SPORT marksman *masc*, markswoman *fem*; (*beim Fußball, Eishockey*) scorer ❷ (*Jagdwesen*) hunter ❸ MIL private, rifleman ❹ *kein pl* ASTROL Sagittarius
schützen [ˈʃʏtsņ] **I.** *vt* to protect (**vor** +*dat* against/from); **vor Kälte ~!** keep away from cold!; **geschützte Pflanzen** protected plants; **urheberrechtlich geschützt** protected by copyright **II.** *vi* ■ [**vor etw** *dat*] ~ to give protection [from sth]
schützend *adj* protective
Schützenfest *nt rifle club festival featuring shooting matches*
Schutzengel *m* REL guardian angel
Schützengraben *m* trench
Schützenverein *m* rifle club
Schutzfaktor *m* safety factor; *Sonnenmilch* protection factor
Schutzgebiet *nt* ❶ POL protectorate ❷ (*Natur-*

schutzgebiet) [nature] preserve
Schutzgebühr *f* nominal fee
Schutzgeld *nt* protection money
Schutzhaft *f* ① POL preventive detention ② JUR protective custody
Schutzhelm *m* protective helmet, hard hat
Schutzhülle *f s.* **Schutzumschlag**
Schutzimpfung *f* vaccination
Schützling <-s, -e> ['ʃʏts·lɪŋ] *m* protégé
schutzlos I. *adj* defenseless **II.** *adv* **jdm ~ ausgeliefert sein** to be at sb's mercy
Schutzmarke *f* trademark
Schutzmaske *f* protective mask
Schutzmaßnahme *f* precaution, precautionary measure
Schutzpatron(in) <-s, -e> *m(f)* REL patron saint
Schutzraum *m* [fallout] shelter
Schutzschicht *f* protective layer
Schutzumschlag *m* dust jacket [*or* cover]
Schutzvorrichtung *f* safety device
Schutzweste *f* bulletproof vest
schwach <schwächer, schwächste> [ʃvax] **I.** *adj* ① (*nicht stark*) weak ② (*wenig leistend*) weak; *Sportler, Schüler* poor; *Batterie* low ③ (*gering*) weak; *Anzeichen* faint, slight; *Beteiligung* poor; **ein ~es Interesse/~er Trost** little interest/comfort ④ (*leicht*) *Atmung* faint; *Bewegung* slight; *Druck, Wind, Strömung* light; ■**schwächer werden** to become fainter ▸ WENDUNGEN: [**bei jdm/etw**] **~ werden** (*fam*) to be unable to refuse [sb/sth]; **nur nicht ~ werden!** (*standhaft bleiben!*) stay strong!; (*durchhalten!*) don't give in! **II.** *adv* ① (*leicht*) faintly ② (*spärlich*) sparsely; **die Ausstellung war nur ~ besucht** the exhibition was poorly attended ③ (*dürftig*) feebly; **~ spielen** to play poorly; **eine ~e Erinnerung an etw** *akk* **haben** to vaguely remember sth
Schwäche <-, -n> ['ʃvɛ·çə] *f* ① *kein pl* (*geringe Stärke*) weakness ② *kein pl* (*Unwohlsein*) [feeling of] faintness ③ (*Vorliebe*) weakness
schwächen ['ʃvɛ·çn̩] **I.** *vt* to weaken; ■**geschwächt** weakened **II.** *vi* to have a weakening effect
Schwachkopf *m* (*fam*) idiot, bonehead
schwächlich ['ʃvɛç·lɪç] *adj* weakly, feeble
Schwächling <-s, -e> ['ʃvɛç·lɪŋ] *m* weakling
Schwachpunkt *m* weak spot
Schwachsinn *m kein pl* (*fam: Quatsch*) nonsense
schwachsinnig *adj* (*fam: blödsinnig*) idiotic, ridiculous
Schwachstelle *f* weak spot
Schwächung <-, -en> *f* weakening
Schwaden <-s, -> ['ʃvaː·dn̩] *m* cloud
Schwager, Schwägerin <-s, Schwäger> ['ʃvaː·gɐ, 'ʃvɛː·gər·ɪn, *pl* 'ʃvɛː·gɐ] *m, f* brother-in-law *masc,* sister-in-law *fem*
Schwalbe <-, -n> ['ʃval·bə] *f* ORN swallow
Schwall <-[e]s, -e> [ʃval] *m* torrent
schwamm [ʃvam] *imp von* **schwimmen**
Schwamm <-[e]s, Schwämme> [ʃvam, *pl* 'ʃvɛ·mə] *m* ① (*zur Reinigung*) sponge ② SÜDD, ÖSTERR, SCHWEIZ (*essbarer Pilz*) mushroom ▸ WENDUNGEN: **~ drüber!** let's forget it!
schwammig ['ʃvamɪç] **I.** *adj* ① (*weich und porös*) spongy ② (*aufgedunsen*) puffy, bloated ③ (*vage*) vague, woolly **II.** *adv* vaguely
Schwan <-[e]s, Schwäne> [ʃvaːn, *pl* 'ʃvɛː·nə] *m* swan
schwand [ʃvant] *imp von* **schwinden**
schwang [ʃvaŋ] *imp von* **schwingen**
schwanger ['ʃvaŋɐ] *adj* pregnant (**von** *+dat* by)
Schwangere *f dekl wie adj* pregnant woman
schwängern ['ʃvɛŋɐn] *vt* to get pregnant
Schwangerschaft <-, -en> *f* pregnancy
Schwangerschaftsabbruch *m* abortion
Schwangerschaftsverhütung *f* contraception
schwanken ['ʃvaŋ·kn̩] *vi* ① *haben* (*schwingen*) to sway; **ins S~ geraten** to begin to sway ② *sein* (*wanken*) to stagger ③ *haben* (*nicht stabil sein*) to fluctuate ④ *haben* (*unentschlossen sein*) to be undecided; **zwischen zwei Dingen ~** to be torn between two things
schwankend *adj* ① *Baum* swaying ② *Boot* rocking; (*heftiger*) rolling ③ *Boden* shaking ④ *Charakter* wavering; (*zögernd*) hesitant ⑤ *Schritte* unsteady; *Gang* rolling ⑥ *Kurs, Preis* fluctuating; *Gesundheit* unstable
Schwankung <-, -en> *f* fluctuation, variation
Schwanz <-es, Schwänze> [ʃvants, *pl* 'ʃvɛn·tsə] *m* ① ZOOL tail ② ORN train, tail ③ (*sl: Penis*) dick, cock ▸ WENDUNGEN: **den ~ einziehen** (*fam*) to back down
schwänzen ['ʃvɛn·tsn̩] *vt, vi* SCH (*fam*) to play hooky
Schwanzflosse *f* tail fin
schwappen ['ʃva·pn̩] *vi* ① *sein* (*sich im Schwall ergießen*) to splash ② *haben* (*sich hin und her bewegen*) to slosh around
Schwarm¹ <-[e]s, Schwärme> [ʃvarm, *pl* 'ʃvɛr·mə] *m* swarm; *Fische* school; (*grösser*) shoal
Schwarm² <-[e]s> [ʃvarm] *m* (*fam: verehrter Mensch*) heartthrob
schwärmen¹ ['ʃvɛr·mən] *vi sein* to swarm
schwärmen² ['ʃvɛr·mən] *vi* ① *haben* (*begeistert reden*) to gush *fam* (**von** *+dat* about) ② (*begeistert verehren*) ■**für jdn ~** to be crazy about sb ③ (*sich begeistern*) ■**für etw** *akk* **~** to have a passion for sth
Schwärmer(in) <-s, -> *m(f)* dreamer
Schwärmerei <-, -en> [ʃvɛr·mə·'rai] *f* ① (*Wunschtraum*) [pipe] dream ② (*Passion*) passion
schwärmerisch *adj* enthusiastic, impassioned
Schwarte <-, -n> ['ʃvar·tə, 'ʃvaːɐ̯·tə] *f* KOCHK rind
schwarz <schwärzer, schwärzeste> [ʃvarts] **I.** *adj* ① (*Farbe*) black ② *attr* (*fam: illegal*) illicit; *Geld* untaxed ▸ WENDUNGEN: **~ auf weiß** in black and white **II.** *adv* ① (*mit schwarzer*

S

Farbe) black ② (*fam: auf illegale Weise*) illicitly

Schwarz <-[es]> [ʃvarts] *nt kein pl* black

Schwarzafrika *nt* sub-Saharan Africa

Schwarzafrikaner(in) *m(f)* sub-Saharan African

schwarzafrikanisch *adj* sub-Saharan African

Schwarzarbeit *f kein pl* work that pays cash

schwarz|arbeiten *vi* to work under the table [*or* for cash]

Schwarzarbeiter(in) *m(f)* worker who gets paid under the table [*or* in cash]

schwarz|ärgern *vr* (*fam*) ■ **sich** *akk* ~ to be hopping mad

schwarz|brennen *vt irreg Schnaps* to moonshine

Schwarzbrot *nt* brown [*or* pumpernickel] bread

Schwarze(r) *f(m) dekl wie adj* (*Mensch*) black

Schwärze <-, -n> [ˈʃvɛr·tsə] *f kein pl* ① (*Dunkelheit*) darkness ② (*Farbe*) black

schwarz|fahren *vi irreg sein to ride* [*public transportation*] *without paying the fare*

Schwarzfahrer(in) *m(f)* fare dodger

Schwarzhandel *m kein pl* black market (**mit** +*dat* for)

Schwarzmarkt *m* black market

schwarz|sehen *vi irreg* ■ **[für jdn/etw]** ~ to be pessimistic [about sb/sth]

Schwarztee *m* black tea

schwarz-weißRR, **schwarzweiß** [ʃvarts·ˈvais] *adj, adv* black-and-white *attr,* black and white *pred*

Schwarzweißfoto *nt* black-and-white photograph

Schwatz <-es, -e> [ʃvats] *m* (*fam*) chat

schwatzen [ˈʃvatsn̩] *vi,* **schwätzen** [ˈʃvɛtsn̩] *vi* SÜDD, ÖSTERR ① (*sich unterhalten*) to chat ② (*etw ausplaudern*) to blab *fam* ③ (*im Unterricht reden*) to talk during class

Schwätzer(in) <-s, -> *m(f)* (*pej: Schwafler*) windbag *fam;* (*Angeber*) bragger; (*Klatschmaul*) gossip

Schwebe <-> [ˈʃveːbə] *f kein pl* **in der ~ sein** to be in the balance; **etw in der ~ lassen** to leave sth undecided

Schwebebahn *f* ① (*an Schienen*) suspension railway ② *s.* **Seilbahn**

schweben [ˈʃveː·bn̩] *vi haben* to float; *Vogel* to hover; **in Lebensgefahr** ~ to be in danger of one's life; (*Patient*) to be in critical condition

Schwede, Schwedin <-n, -n> [ˈʃveː·də, ˈʃveː·dɪn] *m, f* Swede; *s. a.* **Deutsche(r)**

Schweden <-s> [ˈʃveː·dn̩] *nt* Sweden; *s. a.* **Deutschland**

schwedisch [ˈʃveː·dɪʃ] *adj* Swedish; *s. a.* **deutsch**

Schwedisch [ˈʃveː·dɪʃ] *nt dekl wie adj* Swedish; *s. a.* **Deutsch**

Schwefel <-s> [ˈʃveː·fl] *m kein pl* sulfur

Schwefeldioxid *nt* sulfur dioxide

schwefelhaltig *adj* sulfurous

Schwefelsäure *f* sulfuric acid

Schweif <-[e]s, -e> [ʃvaif] *m* tail

schweifen [ˈʃvai·fn̩] *vi sein* (*geh*) to roam, to wander; **seine Blicke ~ lassen** to let one's gaze wander

Schweigegeld *nt* hush money

Schweigemarsch *m* silent [protest] march

Schweigeminute *f* minute of silence

schweigen <schwieg, geschwiegen> [ˈʃvai·gn̩] *vi* to remain silent, to keep quiet ▶ WENDUNGEN: **ganz zu ~ von [etw]** *dat* let alone [sth]

Schweigen <-s> [ˈʃvai·gn̩] *nt kein pl* silence; **jdn zum ~ bringen** to silence sb

Schweigepflicht *f* obligation to [maintain] confidentiality; **der ~ unterliegen** to be bound to maintain confidentiality

schweigsam [ˈʃvaik·zaːm] *adj* ① (*wortkarg*) taciturn ② (*wenig gesprächig*) ■ **~ sein** to be quiet

Schweigsamkeit <-> *f kein pl* quietness, reticence

Schwein <-s, -e> [ʃvain] *nt* ① ZOOL pig ② *kein pl* (*Schweinefleisch*) pork ③ (*pej fam: gemeiner Kerl*) bastard ④ (*fam: unsauberer Mensch*) pig ⑤ (*fam: obszöner Mensch*) lewd person, pervert ⑥ (*fam: bedauernswerter Mensch*) **[ein] armes ~** [an] unlucky bastard ▶ WENDUNGEN: **[großes] ~ haben** (*fam*) to be [really] lucky; **kein ~** (*fam*) nobody

Schweinebraten *m* roast pork

Schweinefleisch *nt* pork

Schweinegrippe *f* MED swine flu, swine influenza

Schweinerei <-, -en> [ʃvai·nə·ˈrai] *f* (*fam*) ① (*Unordnung*) mess ② (*Gemeinheit*) dirty trick; **~!** bullshit! *vulg sl* ③ (*Skandal*) scandal

Schweinestall *m* [pig]sty, [pig]pen

schweinisch I. *adj* (*fam*) smutty, dirty **II.** *adv* (*fam*) **sich ~ aufführen** to act like a pig

Schweinshachse, Schweinshaxe *f* SÜDD knuckle of pork

Schweiß <-es> [ʃvais] *m kein pl* sweat; **jdm bricht der ~ aus** sb breaks out in a sweat

schweißen [ˈʃvai·sn̩] *vt, vi* to weld

Schweißen <-s> [ˈʃvai·sn̩] *nt kein pl* welding

Schweißfuß *m meist pl* sweaty foot

schweißgebadet *adj* bathed in sweat *pred*

Schweiz <-> [ʃvaits] *f* Switzerland; **die französische/italienische ~** French-speaking/Italian-speaking Switzerland; *s. a.* **Deutschland**

Schweizer *adj attr* Swiss

Schweizer(in) <-s, -> [ˈʃvai·tsɐ] *m(f)* Swiss; *s. a.* **Deutsche(r)**

schweizerdeutsch [ˈʃvai·tsɐ·dɔytʃ] *adj* LING Swiss-German; *s. a.* **deutsch**

Schweizerdeutsch <-[s]> [ˈʃvai·tsɐ·dɔytʃ] *nt dekl wie adj* LING Swiss German; *s. a.* **Deutsch**

schweizerisch [ˈʃvai·tsə·rɪʃ] *adj s.* **Schweizer**

schwelgen [ˈʃvɛl·gn̩] *vi* (*geh*) ① (*sich gütlich tun*) to indulge oneself ② (*übermäßig verwenden*) ■ **in etw** *dat* ~ to overindulge in sth; **in Erinnerungen** ~ to wallow in memories

Schwelle <-, -n> [ˈʃvɛ·lə] *f* ① (*Türschwelle*)

threshold ❷ (*Bahnschwelle*) [railroad] tie

schwellen <schwoll, geschwollen> [ˈʃvɛ·lən] *vi sein* ❶ MED to swell [up] ❷ (*sich verstärken*) to grow

Schwellung <-, -en> *f* swelling

Schwemme <-, -n> [ˈʃvɛ·mə] *f* (*Überangebot*) glut

schwemmen [ˈʃvɛ·mən] *vt* **an Land ~** to wash ashore

Schwenk <-[e]s, -s> [ʃvɛŋk] *m* ❶ TV, FILM (*Schwenkbewegung*) pan, panning movement ❷ (*Drehung*) twist, turn

schwenkbar *adj* swiveling; *Kamera* swivel-mounted

schwenken [ˈʃvɛŋ·kn̩] **I.** *vt haben* ❶ (*wedeln*) to wave ❷ (*die Richtung verändern*) to swivel; *Kamera* to pan ❸ KOCHK to toss **II.** *vi* ❶ *sein* (*zur Seite bewegen*) to wheel [around] ❷ *haben* TV, FILM (*sich richten*) to pan

schwer <schwerer, schwerste> [ʃveːɐ̯] **I.** *adj* ❶ (*nicht leicht*) heavy; ■**30 kg ~ sein** to weigh 30 kilos ❷ (*beträchtlich*) serious; *Verlust* bitter; **~e Mängel aufweisen** to be badly defective; **~e Verwüstung[en] anrichten** to cause utter devastation ❸ (*hart*) hard; *Schicksal* cruel; *Strafe* harsh ❹ (*körperlich belastend*) serious, grave; *Operation* difficult ❺ (*schwierig*) hard, difficult; *Lektüre* heavy ❻ *attr* (*heftig*) *Sturm, Gewitter, Kämpfe* heavy **II.** *adv* ❶ (*hart*) hard; **~ arbeiten** to work hard; **jdm ~ zu schaffen machen** to give sb a hard time, to cause sb trouble ❷ (*mit schweren Lasten*) heavily; **~ bepackt sein** to be heavily laden ❸ (*fam: sehr*) deeply; **~ betrunken** plastered *sl* ❹ (*mit Mühe*) with [great] difficulty; **ein ~ erziehbares Kind** a problem child; **~ verdaulich** indigestible ❺ (*ernstlich*) seriously; **sich** *akk* **~ erkälten** to catch a bad cold; **~ verunglückt sein** to have had a bad accident; **~ wiegend** serious ❻ (*schwierig*) difficult, not easy; **~ verständlich** (*kaum nachvollziehbar*) barely comprehensible; (*kaum zu verstehen*) hard to understand *pred;* **jdm das Leben ~ machen** to make life difficult for sb

Schwerarbeit *f kein pl* heavy labor

Schwerbehinderte(r) *f(m) dekl wie adj* severely disabled [*or dated* handicapped] person

Schwere <-> [ˈʃveː·rə] *f kein pl* ❶ (*ernste Art*) seriousness; *einer Krankheit, eines Schadens* severity ❷ (*Gewicht*) heaviness, weight

schwerelos *adj* weightless

Schwerelosigkeit <-> *f kein pl* weightlessness

schwer|fallen *vi irreg sein* ■**etw fällt jdm schwer** sth is difficult for sb [to do]

schwerfällig <-er, -ste> **I.** *adj* ❶ (*ungeschickt*) awkward, clumsy ❷ (*umständlich*) ponderous **II.** *adv* awkwardly, clumsily

Schwergewicht *nt* ❶ (*Gewichtsklasse*) heavyweight ❷ (*Schwerpunkt*) emphasis

schwergewichtig *adj* heavy

schwerhörig *adj* hard of hearing *pred*

Schwerhörigkeit *f kein pl* hardness of hearing

Schwerindustrie *f* heavy industry

Schwerkraft *f kein pl* gravity

Schwermetall *nt* heavy metal

Schwermut <-> *f kein pl* melancholy

schwermütig <-er, -ste> [ˈʃveːɐ̯·myː·tɪç] *adj* melancholy

schwer|nehmen *vt irreg* ■**etw ~** to take sth to heart

Schwerpunkt *m* ❶ (*Hauptgewicht*) main emphasis; **~e setzen** to set priorities ❷ PHYS center of gravity

schwerreich *adj attr* (*fam*) filthy rich

Schwert <-[e]s, -er> [ʃveːɐ̯t] *nt* sword

Schwertfisch *m* swordfish

Schwertlilie *f* iris

Schwertransport *m* HANDEL transportation of heavy loads

Schwertwal *m* killer whale

Schwerverbrecher(in) *m(f)* dangerous criminal, felon

Schwerverletzte(r) *f(m) dekl wie adj* critically injured person

Schwester <-, -n> [ˈʃvɛs·tɐ] *f* ❶ (*weibliches Geschwisterteil*) sister ❷ (*Krankenschwester*) nurse ❸ (*Nonne*) nun

schwieg [ʃviːk] *imp von* **schweigen**

Schwiegereltern [ˈʃviː·gɐ-] *pl* parents-in-law *pl,* in-laws *pl fam*

Schwiegermutter *f* mother-in-law

Schwiegersohn *m* son-in-law

Schwiegertochter *f* daughter-in-law

Schwiegervater *m* father-in-law

Schwiele <-, -n> [ˈʃviː·lə] *f* callus

schwierig [ˈʃviː·rɪç] **I.** *adj* ❶ (*nicht einfach*) difficult, hard ❷ (*verwickelt*) complicated; *Situation* tricky **II.** *adv* with difficulty

Schwierigkeit <-, -en> *f* ❶ *kein pl* (*Problematik*) difficulty; *einer Lage, eines Problems* complexity; *einer Situation* trickiness ❷ *pl* (*Probleme*) problems *pl;* **finanzielle ~en** financial difficulties *pl;* **jdn in ~en bringen** to get sb into trouble; **in ~en geraten** to get into trouble; **[jdm] ~en machen** to give sb trouble

Schwierigkeitsgrad *m* degree of difficulty; SCH level of difficulty

Schwimmbad *nt* swimming pool

Schwimmbecken *nt* [swimming] pool

schwimmen <schwamm, geschwommen> [ˈʃvɪ·mən] *vi* ❶ *sein* (*sich im Wasser fortbewegen*) to swim; **~ gehen** to go swimming ❷ *haben* (*fam: sich in Flüssigkeit bewegen*) to float

Schwimmer(in) <-s, -> [ˈʃvɪ·mɐ] *m(f)* swimmer

Schwimmflosse *f* flipper

Schwimmflügel *m* water wing

Schwimmhalle *f* indoor [swimming] pool

Schwimmweste *f* life jacket

Schwindel <-s> [ˈʃvɪn·dl̩] *m kein pl* ❶ (*Betrug*) swindle, fraud ❷ MED dizziness, vertigo; **~ erregend** (*fig*) astronomical

Schwindelanfall *m* MED dizzy spell

Schwindelei <-, -en> [ʃvɪn·də·ˈlai] *f* (*fam*) ❶ (*Lüge*) lying ❷ (*Betrügerei*) swindling

schwịndelfrei *adj* ■ **~ sein** to not suffer from vertigo
schwindelig ['ʃvɪn·də·lɪç] *adj pred* dizzy, giddy
schwindeln ['ʃvɪn·dl̩n] **I.** *vi* to lie **II.** *vi impers* ■ **mir schwindelt** [**es**] I feel dizzy
schwinden <schwạnd, geschwụnden> ['ʃvɪn·dn̩] *vi sein* (*geh*) to run out, to dwindle; *Wirkung* to be wearing off; *Interesse* to be waning; *Zuversicht* to be failing
Schwindler(in) <-s, -> ['ʃvɪnd·lɐ] *m(f)* ❶ (*Betrüger*) swindler ❷ (*Lügner*) liar
schwindlig ['ʃvɪnd·lɪç] *adj s.* **schwindelig**
schwingen <schwạng, geschwụngen> ['ʃvɪŋən] **I.** *vt haben* ❶ (*mit etw wedeln*) *Fahne* to wave ❷ (*mit etw ausholen*) *Axt* to brandish ❸ (*hin und her bewegen*) to swing **II.** *vi sein o haben* ❶ (*vibrieren*) to vibrate; *Brücke* to sway ❷ (*pendeln*) to swing ❸ SCHWEIZ (*ringen*) wrestle **III.** *vr haben* (*sich schwungvoll bewegen*) ■ **sich** *akk* **auf/in etw** *akk* **~** to jump onto/into sth; **sich** *akk* **aufs Fahrrad ~** to hop on one's bike
Schwịngung <-, -en> *f* oscillation; [**etw**] **in ~ versetzen** to set [sth] swinging
Schwips <-es, -e> [ʃvɪps] *m* (*fam*) **einen ~ haben** to be tipsy
schwirren ['ʃvɪ·rən] *vi sein Mücken* to buzz; *Vogel* to whir
schwitzen ['ʃvɪtsn̩] *vi* to sweat; **nass geschwitzt** drenched with sweat
schwoll [ʃvɔl] *imp von* **schwellen**
schwören <schwor, geschworen> ['ʃvøː·rən] **I.** *vi* to swear; **er schwört auf Vitamin C** he swears by vitamin C **II.** *vt* to promise
schwul [ʃvuːl] *adj* (*fam*) gay
schwül [ʃvyːl] *adj* humid, muggy
Schwule(r) *m dekl wie adj* (*fam*) gay
Schwüle <-> ['ʃvyː·lə] *f kein pl* humidity, mugginess
schwülstig ['ʃvʏls·tɪç] **I.** *adj* (*pej*) overly ornate, florid; *Stil* bombastic **II.** *adv* (*pej*) bombastically
Schwund <-[e]s> [ʃvʊnt] *m kein pl* decline, decrease; *Vorräte* dwindling; *der Muskulatur* atrophy
Schwung <-[e]s, Schwünge> [ʃvʊŋ, *pl* 'ʃvʏŋə] *m* ❶ (*schwingende Bewegung*) swing[ing movement]; **~ holen** to build up momentum ❷ *kein pl* (*Antriebskraft*) drive; **in ~ kommen** (*fam*) to get going; [**richtig**] **in ~ sein** (*fam*) to be in full swing ❸ (*Linienführung*) sweep, curve
schwụnghaft I. *adj* flourishing **II.** *adv* **sich** *akk* **~ entwickeln** to be booming
schwụngvoll I. *adj* ❶ (*weit ausholend*) sweeping ❷ (*mitreißend*) lively; *Rede* passionate **II.** *adv* lively
Schwur <-[e]s, Schwüre> [ʃvuːɐ̯, *pl* 'ʃvyː·rə] *m* ❶ (*Versprechen*) vow ❷ (*Eid*) oath
Schwurgericht *nt* jury court
Sciencefiction[RR], **Science-Fiction**[RR] <-, -s> ['saiəns·'fɪk·ʃn̩] *f* science fiction, sci-fi *fam*

sec *f Abk von* **Sekunde** sec.
sechs [zɛks] *adj* six; *s. a.* **acht**[1]
Sechs <-, -en> [zɛks] *f* ❶ (*Zahl*) six ❷ SCH (*schlechteste Zensur*) ≈ F ❸ SCHWEIZ (*beste Zensur*) ≈ A
Sẹchseck *nt* hexagon
sẹchseckig *adj* hexagonal
Sẹchserpack *m* six-pack
sechsfach, 6fach ['zɛks·fax] **I.** *adj* sixfold; **die ~e Menge** six times the amount **II.** *adv* sixfold, six times
sechshundert ['zɛks·'hʊn·dɐt] *adj* six hundred
sẹchsmal, 6-mal[RR] *adv* six times; *s. a.* **achtmal**
sechstausend ['zɛks·'tau·zn̩t] *adj* six thousand
sechste(r, s) ['zɛks·tə, 'zɛks·tɐ, 'zɛks·təs] *adj* ❶ (*an sechster Stelle*) sixth; *s. a.* **achte(r, s) 1** ❷ (*Datum*) sixth, 6th; *s. a.* **achte(r, s) 2**
sechstel ['zɛks·tl̩] *adj* sixth
Sechstel <-s, -> ['zɛks·tl̩] *nt* sixth
sechstens ['zɛks·tn̩s] *adv* sixthly, in sixth place
sechzehn ['zɛç·tseːn] *adj* sixteen; *s. a.* **acht**[1]
sẹchzehnte(r, s) *adj* ❶ (*an sechzehnter Stelle*) sixteenth; *s. a.* **achte(r, s) 1** ❷ (*Datum*) sixteenth, 16th; *s. a.* **achte(r, s) 2**
sechzig ['zɛç·tsɪç] *adj* sixty; *s. a.* **achtzig 1, 2**
Sẹchzigerjahre *pl* ■ **die ~** the sixties [*or* 60s] *npl*
sẹchzigste(r, s) *adj* sixtieth; *s. a.* **achte(r, s) 1**
Secondhandladen *m* secondhand store
See[1] <-s, -n> [zeː] *m* lake
See[2] <-, -n> [zeː] *f* ❶ (*Meer*) sea; **an der ~** by the sea; **auf ~** at sea; **auf hoher ~** on the high seas; **in ~ stechen** to put to sea ❷ (*Seegang*) heavy sea, swell
Seefahrer *m* seafarer
Seefahrt *f kein pl* sea travel, seafaring *no art*
Seefisch *m* saltwater fish
Seegang *m kein pl* swell; **schwerer ~** heavy seas
Seehund *m* seal
Seekarte *f* nautical chart
Seeklima *nt* maritime climate
seekrank *adj* seasick
Seekrankheit *f kein pl* seasickness
Seelachs *m* coalfish
Seele <-, -n> ['zeː·lə] *f* soul; **mit Leib und ~** wholeheartedly; **das tut mir in der ~ weh** it breaks my heart ► WENDUNGEN: **ein Herz und eine ~ sein** to be inseparable; **jdm aus der ~ sprechen** (*fam*) to have a heart-to-heart [talk] with sb
Seelenfriede(n) *m* peace of mind
Seelenruhe *f* **in aller ~** as calm as you like
seelenruhig ['zeː·lən·'ruːɪç] *adv* calmly
Seelenwanderung *f* REL transmigration of souls
Seeleute *pl von* **Seemann**
seelisch ['zeː·lɪʃ] **I.** *adj* psychological, emotional; **~es Gleichgewicht** mental balance **II.** *adv* **~ bedingt sein** to have psychological causes

S

Seelöwe, -löwin <-n, -n> *m, f* sea lion
Seelsorge *f kein pl* spiritual guidance
Seelsorger(in) <-s, -> ['ze:l·zɔr·gɐ] *m(f)* pastor
Seemacht *f* naval power
Seemann <-leute> ['ze:·man, *pl* -lɔy·tə] *m* sailor, seaman
Seemeile *f* nautical mile
Seenot *f kein pl* distress [at sea]; **in ~ geraten** to get into trouble
Seepferd(chen) *nt* sea horse
Seeräuber(in) *m(f)* pirate
Seereise *f* voyage; (*Kreuzfahrt*) cruise
Seerose *f* water lily
Seestern *m* starfish
Seetang *m* seaweed
seetüchtig *adj* seaworthy
Seeufer *nt* lakefront, lakeshore
Seeweg *m* sea route; **auf dem ~** by sea
Seezunge *f* sole
Segel <-s, -> ['ze:·gl̩] *nt* sail; **die ~ hissen** to hoist the sails
Segelboot *nt* sailboat
Segelflugzeug *nt* glider
segeln ['ze:·gl̩n] *vi sein* to sail
Segeln <-s> ['ze:·gl̩n] *nt kein pl* sailing
Segelschiff *nt* sailing ship
Segen <-s, -> ['ze:·gn̩] *m kein pl* blessing; **den ~ sprechen** to say the benediction; **ein ~ für die Menschheit** a benefit for mankind; **ein wahrer ~ sein** to be a real godsend
segensreich *adj* (*geh*) beneficial; *Erfindung* heaven-sent
Segler(in) <-s, -> ['ze:·glɐ] *m(f)* yachtsman *masc*, yachtswoman *fem*
Segment <-[e]s, -e> [zɛg·'mɛnt] *nt* segment
segnen ['ze:g·nən] *vt* to bless
Segnung <-, -en> *f* ❶ REL (*das Segnen*) blessing ❷ *meist pl* (*Vorzüge*) benefits, advantages
sehbehindert *adj* visually impaired
sehen <sah, gesehen> ['ze:·ən] **I.** *vt* ❶ (*erblicken, bemerken*) to see; **gut/schlecht zu ~ sein** to be easily/poorly visible; **etw kommen ~** to see sth coming; **ich kann kein Blut ~** I can't stand the sight of blood; **sich** *akk* **~ lassen können** to be something to be proud of; **das muss man ge~ haben** you have to see it to believe it; **das wollen wir [doch] erst mal ~!** (*fam*) [well,] we'll see about that!; **so ge~** from that point of view; **das sehe ich gar nicht gern!** I don't like that at all! ❷ (*ansehen, zusehen*) to watch ❸ (*treffen*) ■**jdn ~** to meet sb ❹ (*einschätzen*) **ich sehe das so: ...** the way I see it, ... **II.** *vi* ❶ (*ansehen*) to look; **lass mal ~** let me see ❷ (*Sehvermögen haben*) to see; **gut/schlecht ~** to have good/bad eyesight ❸ (*blicken*) to look; **aus dem Fenster ~** to look out [of] the window ❹ (*bemerken*) **~ Sie!/siehste!** (*fam*) [you] see? ❺ (*sich kümmern um*) ■**nach jdm/etw ~** to check on sb/sth; **ich werde ~, was ich für Sie tun kann** I'll see what I can do for you ❻ (*abwarten*) to wait and see **III.** *vr* **sich** *akk* **gezwungen ~, etw zu tun** to feel compelled to do sth
sehenswert *adj* worth seeing
Sehenswürdigkeit <-, -en> *f* sight; **~en besichtigen** to go sightseeing
Sehfehler *m* visual defect
Sehkraft *f kein pl* [eye]sight
Sehne <-, -n> ['ze:·nə] *f* ❶ ANAT tendon, sinew ❷ (*Bogensehne*) string
sehnen ['ze:·nən] *vr* ■**sich** *akk* **nach jdm/etw ~** to long for sb/sth
Sehnenscheidenentzündung *f* inflammation of a tendon, tenosynovitis *spec*
Sehnerv *m* optic nerve
sehnig ['ze:·nɪç] *adj* sinewy, stringy
Sehnsucht <-, -süchte> ['ze:n·zʊxt, *pl* -zʏç·tə] *f* longing, yearning (**nach** +*dat* for); **vor ~** with longing
sehnsüchtig ['ze:n·zʏç·tɪç] *adj attr* longing, yearning; *Blick* wistful; *Verlangen, Wunsch* ardent
sehr <[noch] mehr, am meisten> ['ze:ɐ̯] *adv* ❶ *vor vb* (*in hohem Maße*) very much, a lot; **danke ~!** thanks a lot; **bitte ~, bedienen Sie sich** go ahead and help yourself; **das will ich doch ~ hoffen** I very much hope so ❷ *vor adj, adv* (*besonders*) very; **jdm ~ dankbar sein** to be very grateful to sb; **das ist aber ~ schade** that's a real shame
Sehschärfe *f* visual acuity
Sehstörung *f* visual defect
Sehtest *m* eye test
Sehvermögen *nt kein pl* sight
Sehweise *f* way of seeing things
seicht [zaiçt] *adj* shallow
seid [zait] *2. pers pl pres von* **sein**
Seide <-, -n> ['zai·də] *f* silk
seiden ['zai·dn̩] *adj attr* silk
Seidenpapier *nt* tissue paper
Seidenraupe *f* silkworm
seidig ['zai·dɪç] *adj* silky
Seife <-, -n> ['zai·fə] *f* soap
Seifenblase *f* soap bubble
Seifenoper *f* TV soap opera
Seil <-[e]s, -e> [zail] *nt* rope; (*Drahtseil*) cable
Seilbahn *f* (*Standseilbahn*) funicular; (*Drahtseilbahn*) gondola
Seilschaft <-, -en> *f* ❶ (*Bergsteiger*) *group of mountain climbers who are roped together* ❷ (*in der Politik*) [good] old boy[s'] network *pej*
seil|springen *vi irreg, nur infin und pp sein* to skip rope
Seiltänzer(in) *m(f)* tightrope acrobat
sein[1] <bin, bist, ist, sind, seid, war, gewesen> [zain] **I.** *vi sein* ❶ (*existieren, sich befinden*) to be, to exist; ■**[irgendwo] ~** to be [somewhere]; **ich bin wieder da** I'm back [again]; **ist da jemand?** is anybody there? ❷ (*Eigenschaft haben*) **böse/klug ~** to be angry/clever; **freundlich/gemein zu jdm ~** to be friendly/mean to sb; **was ist mit dir?** what is the matter with you?; **er war so freundlich**

und hat das überprüft he was kind enough to check it out; **sei so lieb und ...** I would be grateful if ...; **sie ist Geschäftsführerin** she is an executive director; **Deutscher/Däne ~** to be German/Danish ③ (*gehören*) **das Buch ist meins** the book is mine; **er ist mein Cousin** he is my cousin ④ (*ergeben*) to be, to equal ⑤ (*sich ereignen*) to be, to take place; **was ist [denn schon wieder]?** what is it [now]?; **war was?** (*fam*) did anything happen?; **das wär's dann** that's it ⑥ (*hergestellt sein*) ■ **aus etw** *dat* **~** to be [made of] sth ⑦ (*sich fühlen*) **mir ist heiß/kalt** I'm hot/cold; **mir ist übel** I feel sick; **mir ist, als habe ich Stimmen gehört** I thought I heard voices ⑧ (*passieren*) **etw kann/darf/muss ~** sth can/might/must be; **das darf doch nicht wahr ~!** that can't be true!; **etw ~ lassen** (*fam*) to stop [doing sth]; **muss das ~?** do you [really] have to?; **was ~ muss, muss ~** (*fam*) what will be will be; **sie ist nicht zu sehen** she cannot be seen **II.** *vi impers* ① (*bei Zeitangaben*) **es ist Januar/hell/Nacht** it is January/light out/night[time]; **es ist jetzt 9 Uhr** it is now 9 o'clock ② (*der Fall sein*) **es sei denn, dass ...** unless ...; **wie wäre es mit jdm/etw?** how about sb/sth?; **es war einmal ...** once upon a time ...; **wie dem auch sei** be that as it may, in any case; **mit etw** *dat* **ist es nichts** (*fam*) sth doesn't amount to anything; **mir ist es zu kalt** I'm too cold **III.** *aux vb* ① *zur Bildung des Perfekts* **jd ist gefahren/gegangen/gerannt** sb drove/left/ran ② *zur Bildung des Zustandspassivs* **jd ist gebissen/verurteilt worden** sb has been bitten/convicted

sein² [zain] *pron poss, adjektivisch* ① (*einem Mann gehörend*) his; (*zu einem Gegenstand gehörend*) its; (*einer Frau gehörend*) her; (*zu einer Stadt, einem Land gehörend*) its ② *auf „man" bezüglich* one's; *auf „jeder" bezüglich* his, their *fam;* **jeder bekam ~ eigenes Zimmer** everyone got his/her own room

Sein <-s> [zain] *nt kein pl* existence

seine(r, s) ['zai·nə, 'zai·nɐ, 'zai·nəs] *pron poss, substantivisch* (*geh*) ■ **das S~** his [own]; **das S~ tun** (*geh*) to do one's part; **jedem das S~** to each his own; ■ **die S~n** his family

seiner ['zai·nɐ] *pron pers gen von* **er, es** him; **sich ~ erbarmen** to have pity on him

seinerseits ['sai·nɐ·'zaits] *adv* (*von ihm aus*) on his part, as far as he is concerned

seinesgleichen ['zai·nəs·'glai·çn̩] *pron* someone like him; (*pej: Leute seines Standes*) his equals

seinetwegen ['zai·nət·'ve:·gn̩] *adv* because of him

seinetwillen ['zai·nət·'vɪ·lən] *adv* **um ~** for his sake

seins *pron poss s.* **seine(r, s)**

seit [zait] **I.** *präp +dat* (*Anfangspunkt*) since; (*Zeitspanne*) for; **~ einiger Zeit** for a while; **~ damals** since then; **~ neuestem** recently; **~ wann?** since when? **II.** *konj* (*seitdem*) since

seitdem [zait·'de:m] **I.** *adv* since then; **~ hat sie kein Wort mehr mit ihr gesprochen** she hasn't said a word to her since [then] **II.** *konj* since

Seite <-, -n> ['zai·tə] *f* ① (*Fläche eines Körpers*) side; **die vordere/hintere/untere/obere ~** the front/back/bottom/top; **alles hat [seine] zwei ~n** there are two sides to everything ② (*rechts oder links der Mitte*) **zur ~ gehen** to step aside; **jdn zur ~ nehmen** to take sb aside ③ (*sparen*) **etw auf die ~ legen** to put sth aside ④ (*Papierblatt*) page; **gelbe ~n** Yellow Pages; **eine ~ aufschlagen** to open to a page; (*Seite eines Blattes*) side ⑤ (*Beistand*) **jdm zur ~ stehen** to stand by sb; **~ an ~** side by side ⑥ (*Aspekt*) **sich von seiner besten ~ zeigen** to be on one's best behavior; **auf der einen ~..., auf der anderen [~] ...** on the one hand, ..., on the other [hand], ...; **jds starke ~ sein** (*fam*) to be sb's forte ⑦ (*Partei, Gruppe*) side; **jdn auf seine ~ bringen** to get sb on one's side; **auf jds ~ stehen** to be on sb's side; **die ~n wechseln** to change sides

Seitenangabe *f* page reference

Seitenansicht *f* side view

Seitenaufbau *m* INET page construction; **die Seite hat einen extrem langsamen ~** the page takes forever to load

Seitenausgang *m* side exit

Seitenblick *m* sidelong glance

Seiteneingang *m* side entrance

Seitenflügel *m* ARCHIT side wing

Seitenhieb *m* sideswipe; **jdm einen ~ versetzen** to sideswipe sb

Seitenlage *f* lateral position; **in der ~** on one's side

seitenlang **I.** *adj* several pages long **II.** *adv* in several pages

seitens ['zai·tn̩s] *präp +gen* on the part of

Seitenscheitel *m* side part

Seitensprung *m* (*fam*) affair

Seitenstechen *nt kein pl* stitch [in one's side]; **~ haben** to have a stitch [in one's side]

Seitenstreifen *m* hard shoulder

seitenverkehrt *adj* the wrong way around

Seitenwind *m* crosswind

Seitenzahl *f* ① (*Anzahl der Seiten*) number of pages ② (*Ziffer*) page number

seither [zait·'he:ɐ̯] *adv* since then

seitlich ['zait·lɪç] **I.** *adj* side *attr* **II.** *adv* sideways; **~ gegen etw** *akk* **prallen** to crash sideways into sth **III.** *präp +gen* ■ **~ der Straße** at the side of the road

seitwärts ['zait·vɛrts] *adv* sideways

sek., Sek. *f Abk von* **Sekunde** sec.

Sekretär(in) <-s, -e> [zek·re·'tɛ:ɐ̯] *m(f)* secretary

Sekretariat <-[e]s, -e> [zek·re·ta·'ri̯a:t] *nt* administrative office

Sekt <-[e]s, -e> [zɛkt] *m* sparkling wine

Sekte <-, -n> ['zɛk·tə] *f* sect

Sektglas *nt* champagne flute [*or* glass]

S

Sektor <-s, -toren> ['zɛk·toːɐ̯, *pl* zɛk·'toː·rən] *m* sector
sekundär [ze·kʊn·'dɛːɐ̯] *adj* secondary
Sekundärliteratur *f* secondary literature
Sekundarstufe *f* ~ **I** *grades 5 through 10 at a Gymnasium;* ~ **II** *grades 11 through 13 at a Gymnasium*
Sekunde <-, -n> [ze·'kʊn·də] *f* second; **auf die ~ genau** to the second
Sekundenkleber *m* instant glue
Sekundenzeiger *m* second hand
selbe(r, s) ['zɛl·bə, 'zɛl·bɐ, 'zɛl·bəs] *pron* ■**der/die/das ~ ...** the same ...; **im ~n Haus** in the same house; **an der ~n Stelle** at/in the [very] same place; **zur ~n Zeit** at the same time
selber ['zɛl·bɐ] *pron dem* (*fam*) myself/yourself/himself etc.; **ich geh lieber ~** I'd better go myself
selbst [zɛlpst] **I.** *pron dem* ❶ (*persönlich*) myself/yourself/himself etc.; **mit jdm ~ sprechen** to speak to sb oneself ❷ (*ohne Hilfe, alleine*) by oneself; **etw ~ machen** to do sth by oneself; **von ~** automatically; **das versteht sich von ~** it goes without saying ❸ (*verkörpern*) **er ist die Ruhe ~** he is calmness itself **II.** *adv* ❶ (*eigen*) self; **~ ernannt** self-appointed; **~ gemacht** homemade; **~ gestrickt** hand-knit ❷ (*sogar*) even; **~ wenn** even if
Selbstachtung *f* self-respect
selbständig ['zɛlp·ʃtɛn·dɪç] *adj s.* **selbstständig**
Selbständigkeit <-> *f kein pl s.* **Selbstständigkeit**
Selbstauslöser *m* self-timer
Selbstbedienung *f* self-service
Selbstbedienungsladen *m* ≈ supermarket
Selbstbefriedigung *f* masturbation
Selbstbeherrschung *f* self-control
Selbstbestätigung *f* self-affirmation
Selbstbestimmungsrecht *nt kein pl* right to self-determination
selbstbewusst^RR *adj* self-confident
Selbstbewusstsein^RR *nt* self-confidence
Selbstbräunungscreme *f* self-tanning cream
Selbsterhaltungstrieb *m* survival instinct
Selbsterkenntnis *f kein pl* self-knowledge
selbstgefällig *adj* self-satisfied
selbstgerecht *adj* (*pej*) self-righteous
Selbstgespräch *nt* monologue; **Selbstgespräche führen** to talk to oneself
selbstherrlich *adj* (*pej*) highhanded
Selbsthilfegruppe *f* self-help group
Selbstjustiz *f* vigilantism
selbstklebend *adj* self-adhesive
Selbstkostenpreis *m* cost; **zum ~** at cost
Selbstkritik *f kein pl* self-criticism; **~ üben** to criticize oneself
selbstkritisch *adj* self-critical
selbstlos *adj* selfless, unselfish
Selbstmitleid *nt* self-pity
Selbstmord *m* suicide; **~ begehen** to commit suicide
Selbstmörder(in) *m(f)* suicidal person
selbstmörderisch *adj* suicidal
Selbstmordversuch *m* suicide attempt
Selbstschutz *m* self-protection
selbstsicher *adj* self-confident
Selbstsicherheit *f kein pl* self-confidence
selbstständig^RR ['zɛlpst·ʃtɛn·dɪç] *adj* ❶ (*eigenständig*) independent ❷ (*beruflich unabhängig*) self-employed; **sich** *akk* **~ machen** to start up *sep* one's own business
Selbstständige(r)^RR *f(m) dekl wie adj* self-employed person
Selbstständigkeit^RR <-> *f kein pl* ❶ (*Eigenständigkeit*) independence ❷ (*selbstständige Stellung*) self-employment
Selbsttäuschung *f* self-delusion
Selbstüberschätzung *f* overestimation of one's abilities
Selbstüberwindung *f* self-discipline
selbstverständlich **I.** *adj* natural; **das ist doch ~** don't mention it; **etw für** *akk* **~ halten** to take sth for granted **II.** *adv* naturally, of course; **wie ~** as if it were the most natural thing in the world; [**aber**] **~!** [but] of course!
Selbstverständlichkeit <-, -en> *f* naturalness; **eine ~ sein** to be the least that could be done
Selbstverteidigung *f* self-defense
Selbstvertrauen *nt* self-confidence
Selbstverwaltung *f* self-government
Selbstverwirklichung *f* self-realization
selbstzerstörerisch *adj* self-destructive
Selbstzweck *m kein pl* end in itself
Selen <-s> [ze'leːn] *nt* selenium
selig ['zeː·lɪç] *adj* (*überglücklich*) overjoyed ▸WENDUNGEN: **wer's glaubt, wird ~** (*iron fam*) that's a likely story
Seligkeit <-> *f kein pl* bliss
selig|sprechen *vt irreg* REL ■**jdn ~** to beatify sb
Sellerie <-s, -[s]> ['zɛ·ləri] *m* (*Knollensellerie*) celeriac; (*Stangensellerie*) celery
selten ['zɛl·tn̩] *adj* ❶ (*nicht häufig*) rare ❷ (*besonders*) exceptional
Seltenheit <-, -en> *f* ❶ *kein pl* (*seltenes Vorkommen*) rare occurrence ❷ (*seltene Sache*) rarity
Seltenheitswert *m kein pl* rarity value
seltsam ['zɛlt·zaːm] *adj* strange, weird, peculiar
seltsamerweise *adv* strangely enough
Semester <-s, -> [ze·'mɛs·tɐ] *nt* semester, term
Semesterferien *pl* semester break
Semifinale ['zeː·mi·fi·naː·lə] *nt* semifinal
Semikolon <-s, -s *o* -kola> [ze·mi·'koː·lɔn, *pl* -'koː·la] *nt* semicolon
Seminar <-s, -e *o* ÖSTERR -ien> [ze·mi·'naːɐ̯, *pl* ze·mi·'naː·ri̯ən] *nt* ❶ (*Lehrveranstaltung*) seminar ❷ (*Universitätsinstitut*) department; **das historische ~** the History Department
Semit(in) <-en, -en> [ze·'miːt] *m(f)* Semite
semitisch [ze·'miː·tɪʃ] *adj* Semitic

S

Semmel <-, -n> [ˈzɛml̩] *f* DIAL roll ▶ WENDUNGEN: **weggehen wie warme ~n** (*fam*) to go like hot cakes

sen. *adj Abk von* **senior**

Senat <-[e]s, -e> [zeˈnaːt] *m* senate

Senator, Senatorin <-s, -toren> [zeˈnaːtoːɐ̯, ze·na·ˈtoː·rɪn, *pl* -ˈtoː·rən] *m, f* senator

Sendeanstalt *f* broadcasting station

Sendegebiet *nt* broadcast area

senden[1] [ˈzɛn·dn̩] **I.** *vt* to broadcast; *Botschaft* to transmit **II.** *vi* to be on the air

senden[2] <sandte *o* sendete, gesandt *o* gesendet> [ˈzɛn·dn̩] *vt* to send; *Truppen* to dispatch

Sender <-s, -> [ˈzɛn·dɐ] *m* ❶ (*Sendeanstalt*) channel; *Radio* station ❷ (*Sendegerät*) transmitter

Sendereihe *f* series + *sing vb*

Sendeschluss[RR] *m* end of a broadcast

Sendezeit *f* airtime; **zur besten ~** at prime time

Sendung[1] <-, -en> *f* TV, RADIO ❶ (*Ausstrahlung*) broadcasting; *Signal* transmission; **auf ~ gehen/sein** to go/be on the air ❷ (*Rundfunk-, Fernsehsendung*) program

Sendung[2] <-, -en> *f* (*Briefsendung*) letter; (*Paketsendung*) package; (*Warensendung*) shipment

Senf <-[e]s, -e> [zɛnf] *m* mustard ▶ WENDUNGEN: **seinen ~ dazugeben** *dat* (*fam*) to have one's say

senil [zeˈniːl] *adj* senile

senior [ˈzeː·ni̯oːɐ̯] *adj* senior

Senior <-s, Senioren> [ˈzeː·ni̯oːɐ̯, *pl* ze·ˈni̯oː·rən] *m meist pl* (*ältere Menschen*) senior citizen

Seniorenheim *nt* nursing [*or* retirement] home

Senke <-, -n> [ˈzɛŋ·kə] *f* depression

senken [ˈzɛŋ·kn̩] **I.** *vt* ❶ (*niedriger machen*) to lower; *Fieber* to reduce ❷ (*abwärtsbewegen*) **den Kopf ~** to bow one's head; **die Stimme ~** (*fig*) to lower one's voice **II.** *vr* ❶ (*niedriger werden*) to sink; ■**sich** *akk* **~** to drop (**um** + *akk* by) ❷ (*sich niedersenken*) ■**sich** *akk* **~** to lower itself (**auf** + *akk* onto)

senkrecht [ˈzɛŋk·rɛçt] *adj* vertical

Senkrechte <-n, -n> *f dekl wie adj* (*senkrechte Linie*) vertical line

Senkung <-, -en> *f* ❶ *kein pl der Preise* reduction; *der Löhne* cut; *der Steuern* decrease ❷ (*das Senken*) drop, subsidence; *der Stimme* lowering

Sensation <-, -en> [zɛn·za·ˈtsi̯oːn] *f* sensation

sensationell [zɛn·za·tsi̯o·ˈnɛl] *adj* sensational

Sensationslust *f* craving for sensation

Sense <-, -n> [ˈzɛn·zə] *f* scythe

sensibel [zɛn·ˈziː·bl̩] *adj* sensitive

Sensibilität <-, -en> [zɛn·zi·bi·li·ˈtɛːt] *f* sensitivity

Sensor <-s, -soren> [ˈzɛn·zoːɐ̯, *pl* -ˈzoː·rən] *m* sensor

sentimental [zɛn·ti·mɛn·ˈtaːl] *adj* sentimental

Sentimentalität <-, -en> [zɛn·ti·mɛn·ta·li·ˈtɛːt] *f* sentimentality

separat [ze·pa·ˈraːt] *adj* separate

Separatismus <-> [ze·pa·ra·ˈtɪs·mʊs] *m kein pl* separatism

Separatist(in) <-en, -en> [ze·pa·ra·ˈtɪst] *m(f)* separatist

separatistisch *adj* separatist

Sept. *Abk von* **September** Sept.

September <-[s], -> [zɛp·ˈtɛm·bɐ] *m* September; *s. a.* **Februar**

Sequenz <-, -en> [zeˈkvɛnts] *f* sequence

Sera *pl von* **Serum**

Serbien <-s> [ˈzɛr·bi̯ən] *nt* Serbia; *s. a.* **Deutschland**

Seren *pl von* **Serum**

Serenade <-, -n> [ze·re·ˈnaː·də] *f* serenade

Serie [ˈzeː·ri̯ə] *f* ❶ (*Reihe*) MEDIA, TV series + *sing vb* ❷ ÖKON line; **in ~ gehen** to go into production

serienmäßig *adj* ❶ (*in Serienfertigung*) mass-produced ❷ (*bereits eingebaut sein*) standard

Serienmörder(in) *m(f)* serial killer

Seriennummer *f* serial number

Serienproduktion *f* mass production

Serientäter(in) *m(f)* repeat offender

seriös [zeˈri̯øːs] **I.** *adj* ❶ *Mensch* respectable; *Angebot* serious ❷ (*vertrauenswürdig*) respectable; *Unternehmen* reputable **II.** *adv* respectably

Serpentine <-, -n> [zɛr·pɛn·ˈtiː·nə] *f* winding road

Serum <-s, Seren *o* Sera> [ˈzeː·rʊm, *pl* ˈzeː·rən, ˈzeː·ra] *nt* serum

Server <-s, -> [ˈsœːr·vɐ] *m* COMPUT server

Service[1] <-, -s> [ˈzœr·vɪs] *m* ❶ *kein pl* (*Bedienung*) service ❷ TENNIS serve

Service[2] <-[s], -> [zɛr·ˈviːs] *nt* dinner/coffee service

servieren* [zɛr·ˈviː·rən] *vt* to serve

Serviette <-, -n> [zɛr·ˈvi̯ɛ·tə] *f* napkin

Servobremse [ˈzɛr·vo-] *f* power[-assisted] brake

Servolenkung *f* power[-assisted] steering

servus [ˈzɛr·vʊs] *interj* ÖSTERR, SÜDD (*hallo*) hi; (*tschüs*) [good]bye

Sesam <-s, -s> [ˈzeː·zam] *m* sesame

Sessel <-s, -> [ˈzɛ·sl̩] *m* armchair

Sessellift *m* chair lift

sesshaft[RR], **seßhaft**[ALT] [ˈzɛs·haft] *adj* ❶ (*bodenständig*) settled ❷ (*ansässig*) **er ist in Berlin ~** he lives in Berlin; **in Berlin ~ werden** to settle in Berlin

Set <-s, -s> [zɛt] *m o nt* set

setzen [ˈzɛ·tsn̩] **I.** *vt haben* ❶ (*platzieren*) to put, to place ❷ (*festlegen*) to set; **eine Frist/ein Ziel ~** to set a deadline/a goal ❸ (*bringen*) **etw in Betrieb ~** to set sth in motion; **jdn auf Diät ~** to put sb on a diet ❹ (*pflanzen*) to plant ❺ (*wetten*) **Geld auf jdn/etw ~** to bet money on sb/sth ❻ TYPO to set **II.** *vr haben* ■**sich** *akk* **~** ❶ (*sich niederlassen*) to sit [down]; **sich** *akk* **ins Auto ~** to get in the car; **bitte ~ Sie sich**

doch! please sit down!; ■ **sich** *akk* **zu jdm ~** to sit next to sb; **wollen Sie sich nicht zu uns ~?** won't you join us? ❷ (*sich senken*) *Kaffeesatz* to settle **III.** *vi* ❶ *haben* (*wetten*) ■ **auf jdn/etw ~** to bet on sb/sth ❷ *sein o haben* ■ **über etw** *akk* **~** (*springen*) to jump over sth; (*überschiffen*) to cross sth

Seuche <-, -n> ['zɔy·çə] *f* epidemic

Seuchenbekämpfung *f* epidemic control

Seuchengebiet *nt* epidemic zone

seufzen ['zɔyf·tsn̩] *vi* to sigh

Seufzer <-s, -> *m* sigh; **einen ~ ausstoßen** to heave a sigh

Sex <-[es]> [zɛks] *m kein pl* sex

Showgeschäft *nt kein pl* show business

Showmaster <-s, -> [-maːstɐ] *m* host, emcee

siamesisch [zi̯a·'meː·zɪʃ] *adj* Siamese

Sibirien <-s> [zi·'biː·ri̯ən] *nt* Siberia

sich [zɪç] *pron refl* ❶ *akk* oneself; ■ **er/sie/es ... ~** he/she/it ... himself/herself/itself; ■ **Sie ... ~** you ... yourself/yourselves; ■ **sie ... ~** they ... themselves; **man fragt ~, was das soll** one wonders what it's all about; **~ freuen/gedulden/wundern** to be pleased/patient/surprised; **~ schämen** to be ashamed of oneself ❷ *dat* one's; **~ etw einbilden** to imagine sth; **~ etw kaufen** to buy sth for oneself; **die Katze leckte ~ die Pfote** the cat licked its paw ❸ *pl* (*einander*) each other, one another; **~ lieben** to love each other ❹ *unpersönlich* **hier arbeitet es ~ gut** it's good to work here; **das Auto fährt ~ prima** the car drives really well ❺ + *prep* **wieder zu ~ kommen** to regain consciousness; **etw von ~ aus tun** to do sth of one's own accord; **er denkt immer nur an ~** he only ever thinks of himself

Sichel <-, -n> ['zɪ·çl̩] *f* ❶ (*Werkzeug*) sickle ❷ (*Gebilde, von Mond*) crescent

sicher ['zɪ·çɐ] **I.** *adj* ❶ (*gewiss*) certain, sure; *Zusage* definite; **sind Sie ~?** are you sure?; **es ist nicht ~, dass er kommt** it is not certain that he will come; ■ **sich** *dat* **einer S.** *gen* **~ sein** to be sure of sth; **so viel ist ~** that much is certain ❷ (*ungefährdet*) safe (**vor** + *dat* from); *Anlage, Arbeitsplatz* secure; **~ ist ~** you can't be too careful ❸ (*zuverlässig*) reliable; *Methode* foolproof ❹ (*geübt*) competent ❺ (*selbstsicher*) self-assured **II.** *adv* ❶ (*gewiss*) surely; **du hast ~ Recht** you are certainly right; **es ist ~ nicht das letzte Mal** this is surely not the last time; **[aber] ~!** (*fam*) sure!; **ich weiß das ganz ~** I know that for sure ❷ (*ungefährdet*) **sich** *akk* **~ fühlen** to feel safe; **etw ~ aufbewahren** to keep sth in a safe place

sicher|gehen *vi irreg sein* to make sure

Sicherheit <-, -en> *f* ❶ *kein pl* (*gesicherter Zustand*) safety; **die öffentliche ~** public safety; **etw in ~ bringen** to get sth to a safe place; **in ~ sein** to be safe ❷ *kein pl* (*Gewissheit*) certainty; **mit ~** for certain ❸ *kein pl* (*Gewandtheit*) competence ❹ (*Kaution*) surety

Sicherheitsabstand *m* safe distance

Sicherheitsbeamte(r), -beamtin *m, f* security officer

Sicherheitsbindung *f* safety binding

Sicherheitsgurt *m* seat [*or* safety] belt

sicherheitshalber *adv* to be on the safe side

Sicherheitskopie *f* COMPUT backup

Sicherheitsnadel *f* safety pin

Sicherheitsrat *m kein pl* Security Council

sicherlich *adv* surely

sichern ['zɪ·çɐn] *vt* ❶ (*schützen*) to safeguard (**gegen** + *akk* against) ❷ *Schusswaffe* to put a safety on ❸ (*absichern*) to protect; *Bergsteiger, Tatort, Tür* to secure; ■ **gesichert sein** to be protected ❹ (*sicherstellen*) to secure ❺ COMPUT to save

sicher|stellen *vt* ❶ (*in Gewahrsam nehmen*) to confiscate ❷ (*garantieren*) to guarantee

Sicherung <-, -en> *f* ❶ (*das Sichern*) securing, safeguarding ❷ ELEK fuse ❸ (*Schutzvorrichtung*) safety [catch] ❹ COMPUT backup

Sicherungskasten *m* fuse box

Sicherungskopie *f* COMPUT backup copy

Sicht <-, *selten* -en> [zɪçt] *f* ❶ (*Aussicht*) view; **du nimmst mir die ~** you're blocking my view; **die ~ beträgt heute nur 20 Meter** visibility is down to about 20 meters today; **auf kurze/mittlere/lange ~** (*fig*) in the short/medium/long term; **in ~ sein** to be in sight; **Land in ~!** land ahoy!; **etw ist in ~** (*fig*) sth is on the horizon ❷ (*Meinung*) [point of] view; **aus jds ~** from sb's point of view

sichtbar *adj* (*wahrnehmbar*) visible; (*offensichtlich*) apparent

sichten ['zɪ·çtn̩] *vt* ❶ (*ausmachen*) to sight ❷ (*durchsehen*) **die Akten ~** to look through the files

sichtlich *adv* **~ beeindruckt sein** to be visibly impressed

Sichtverhältnisse *pl* visibility

Sichtweite *f* visibility; **außer/in ~ sein** to be out of/in sight

sickern ['zɪ·kɐn̩] *vi sein* to seep (**aus** + *dat* from, **durch** + *akk* through)

sie [ziː] *pron pers, 3. pers* ❶ <*gen* ihrer, *dat* ihr, *akk* sie> *sing* she; **~ ist es!** it's her!; (*weibliche Sache bezeichnend*) it; (*Tier bezeichnend*) it; (*bei weiblichen Haustieren*) she ❷ <*gen* ihrer, *dat* ihnen, *akk* sie> *pl* they

Sie[1] <*gen* Ihrer, *dat* Ihnen, *akk* Sie> [ziː] *pron pers, 2. pers sing o pl* (*förmliche Anrede*) you

Sie[2] <-s> [ziː] *nt kein pl* **jdn mit ~ anreden** to address sb using the "Sie" form

Sieb <-[e]s, -e> [ziːp, *pl* 'ziː·bə] *nt* (*Küchensieb*) sieve; (*größer*) colander; (*Kaffeesieb, Teesieb*) strainer

Siebdruck *m* ❶ *kein pl* (*Druckverfahren*) silk-screen printing ❷ (*Druckerzeugnis*) silk-screen print

sieben[1] ['ziː·bn̩] *adj* seven; *s. a.* **acht[1]**

sieben[2] ['ziː·bn̩] *vt* to sieve

siebenfach, 7fach ['ziː·bn̩·fax] **I.** *adj* sevenfold; **die ~e Menge** seven times the amount

II. *adv* sevenfold, seven times

siebenhundert ['ziː·bn̩·'hʊn·dɐt] *adj* seven hundred

siebenmal ['ziː·bn̩·maːl] *adv* seven times; *s. a.* **achtmal**

siebentägig, 7-tägig[RR] *adj* seven-day *attr*

siebentausend ['ziː·bn̩·'tau·zn̩t] *adj* seven thousand

siebte(r, s) ['ziːp·tə, 'ziːp·tɐ, 'ziːp·təs] *adj* ❶ (*an siebter Stelle*) seventh; *s. a.* **achte(r, s) 1** ❷ (*Datum*) seventh, 7th; *s. a.* **achte(r, s) 2**

Siebtel <-s, -> ['ziːp·tl̩] *nt* seventh

siebzehn ['ziːp·tseːn] *adj* seventeen; *s. a.* **acht**[1]

siebzehnte(r, s) *adj* ❶ (*an siebzehnter Stelle*) seventeenth; *s. a.* **achte(r, s) 1** ❷ (*Datum*) seventeenth, 17th; *s. a.* **achte(r, s) 2**

siebzig ['ziːp·tsɪç] *adj* seventy; *s. a.* **achtzig 1, 2**

Siebzigerjahre *pl* **in den ~n** in the seventies

siebzigste(r, s) *adj* seventieth; *s. a.* **achte(r, s) 1**

siedeln ['ziː·dl̩n] *vi* to settle

sieden <siedete, gesiedet> ['ziː·dn̩] *vi* to boil

Siedepunkt *m* boiling point

Siedler(in) <-s, -> ['ziːd·lɐ] *m(f)* settler

Siedlung <-, -en> ['ziːd·lʊŋ] *f* ❶ (*Wohnhausgruppe*) housing development ❷ (*Ansiedlung*) settlement

Sieg <-[e]s, -e> [ziːk, *pl* 'ziː·gə] *m* victory (**über** +*akk* over)

Siegel <-s, -> ['ziː·gl̩] *nt* seal; (*privates a.*) signet

siegen ['ziː·gn̩] *vi* to win [sth]; **haushoch ~** to win hands down

Sieger(in) <-s, -> *m(f)* ❶ MIL victor ❷ SPORT winner; **der zweite ~** the runner-up

Siegerehrung *f* SPORT victory ceremony

Siegerpodest *nt* victory podium

Siegerurkunde *f* SPORT winner's certificate

siegesbewusst[RR] *adj s.* **siegessicher**

siegessicher *adj* certain of victory *pred;* **ein ~es Lächeln** a confident smile

Siegeszug *m* MIL triumphal procession; (*fig: gewaltiger Erfolg*) triumph

siegreich I. *adj* ❶ MIL victorious ❷ SPORT winning *attr,* successful **II.** *adv* in triumph

sieh [ziː], **siehe** ['ziː·ə] (*geh*) *imp sing von* **sehen**

siezen ['ziː·tsn̩] *vt* ■**jdn/sich ~** to address sb/each other using the "Sie" form

Signal <-s, -e> [zɪ·'gnaːl] *nt* ❶ (*Zeichen*) signal ❷ BAHN signal; **ein ~ überfahren** to run a signal ❸ *pl* (*geh: Ansätze*) signs; **~e setzen** to blaze a trail

signalisieren* [zɪ·gna·li·'ziː·rən] *vt* ❶ (*durch Signale übermitteln*) to signal ❷ (*zu verstehen geben*) to indicate

Signatur <-, -en> [zɪ·gna·'tuːɐ̯] *f* signature

signieren* [zɪ·'gniː·rən] *vt* to sign; (*bei einer Autogrammstunde*) to autograph; ■**signiert** signed, autographed

Silbe <-, -n> ['zɪl·bə] *f* syllable

Silbenrätsel *nt a word game in which words are made up from a given list of syllables*

Silbentrennung *f* hyphenation

Silber <-s> ['zɪl·bɐ] *nt kein pl* silver

Silberhochzeit *f* silver wedding anniversary

Silbermedaille *f* silver medal; **die ~ holen** to win [a] silver [*or* a silver medal]

silbern ['zɪl·bɐn] *adj* ❶ (*aus Silber bestehend*) silver ❷ (*Farbe*) silver[y]

silbrig ['zɪl·brɪç] **I.** *adj* silver[y] **II.** *adv* **~ glänzen** to have a silvery luster

Silhouette <-, -n> [zi·'lu̯ɛtə] *f* silhouette

Silikon <-s, -e> [zi·li·'koːn] *nt* silicone

Silizium <-s> [zi·'liː·tsi̯·ʊm] *nt kein pl* silicon

Silvester <-s, -> [zɪl·'vɛs·tɐ] *m o nt* New Year's Eve

simpel ['zɪm·pl̩] **I.** *adj* simple **II.** *adv* simply

Sims <-es, -e> [zɪms] *m o nt* (*Fenstersims*) windowsill; (*Kaminsims*) mantelpiece

simsen ['zɪm·zən] *vt, vi* TELEK (*fam*) to text, to send a text message

Simulant(in) <-en, -en> [zi·mu·'lant] *m(f)* malingerer

Simulation <-, -en> [zi·mu·la·'tsi̯oːn] *f* simulation

Simulator <-s, -toren> [zi·mu·'laː·toɐ̯, *pl* -'toː·rən] *m* simulator

simulieren* [zi·mu·'liː·rən] **I.** *vi* to malinger **II.** *vt* ❶ (*vortäuschen*) **eine Krankheit ~** to pretend to be sick ❷ SCI to [computer-]simulate

simultan [zi·mʊl·'taːn] **I.** *adj* simultaneous **II.** *adv* simultaneously, at the same time; **~ dolmetschen** to simultaneously interpret

sind [zɪnt] *1. und 3. pers pl von* **sein**

Sinfonie <-,-n> [zɪn·fo·'niː, *pl* -fo·'niː·ən] *f* symphony

Sinfonieorchester *nt* symphony orchestra

singen <sang, gesungen> ['zɪŋ·ən] *vi, vt* to sing

Single[1] <-, -[s]> ['zɪŋl̩] *f* (*Schallplatte*) single

Single[2] <-s, -s> ['zɪŋl̩] *m* (*Ledige[r]*) single person

Singular <-s, -e> ['zɪŋ·gu·laːɐ̯] *m* LING singular

Singvogel *m* songbird

sinken <sank, gesunken> ['zɪŋ·kn̩] *vi sein* ❶ (*versinken*) to sink; *Schiff* to go down ❷ (*herabsinken*) to descend ❸ (*niedersinken*) to drop, to fall; **ins Bett ~** to fall into bed ❹ (*abnehmen*) to go down, to abate; *Fieber, Preis* to fall ❺ (*schwinden*) to diminish, to decline; *Hoffnung* to sink; **den Mut ~ lassen** to lose courage

Sinn <-[e]s, -e> [zɪn] *m* ❶ *meist pl* (*Organ der Wahrnehmung*) sense; **bist du noch bei ~en?** (*geh*) have you taken leave of your senses?; **von ~en sein** to be out of one's mind ❷ *kein pl* (*Bedeutung*) meaning; **im wahrsten ~e des Wortes** in the truest sense of the word; **im übertragenen ~e** in the figurative sense; **in diesem ~e** in that respect ❸ (*Zweck*) point; **der ~ des Lebens** the meaning of life; **einen bestimmten ~ haben**

to have a particular purpose; **es hat keinen ~[, etw zu tun]** there's no point [in doing sth] ❹ *kein pl* (*Verständnis*) **~ für etw** *akk* **haben** to appreciate sth ❺ (*Intention, Gedanke*) inclination; **in jds** *dat* **~ handeln** to act according to sb's wishes; **was hast du mit ihm im ~?** what do you have in mind with him?; **sich** *dat* **etw aus dem ~ schlagen** (*fam*) to put sth out of one's mind

Sịnnbild *nt* symbol

sịnnbildlich I. *adj* symbolic II. *adv* symbolically

sinnen <sạnn, gesọnnen> ['zɪnən] *vi* ■ **auf etw** *akk* **~** to think of sth; **auf Rache ~** to plot revenge

Sịnnesorgan *nt* sense organ

Sịnnestäuschung *f* (*Illusion*) illusion; (*Halluzination*) hallucination

sịnngemäß I. *adj* **eine ~e Wiedergabe einer Rede** a summary of a speech II. *adv* in the general sense; **etw ~ wiedergeben** to give the gist of sth

sịnnlich I. *adj* ❶ (*sexuell*) carnal *form* ❷ (*sexuell verlangend*) sensual; (*stärker*) voluptuous ❸ (*gern genießend*) sensuous, sensual ❹ (*die Sinne ansprechend*) sensory, sensorial II. *adv* (*mit den Sinnen*) sensuously

Sịnnlichkeit <-> *f kein pl* sensuality

sịnnlos *adj* ❶ (*unsinnig*) senseless; *Bemühungen* futile; *Geschwätz* meaningless; **das ist doch ~!** that's pointless! ❷ (*pej: maßlos*) frenzied; *Hass, Wut* blind

Sịnnlosigkeit <-, -en> *f* senselessness, meaninglessness, futility

sịnnvoll I. *adj* ❶ (*zweckmäßig*) practical, appropriate ❷ (*Erfüllung bietend*) meaningful ❸ (*eine Bedeutung habend*) meaningful, coherent II. *adv* sensibly

Sintflut ['zɪnt·flu:t] *f* ■ **die ~** the Flood ▶ WENDUNGEN: **nach mir die ~** (*fam*) I don't care what happens after I leave

Sippe <-, -n> ['zɪ·pə] *f* ❶ SOZIOL [extended] family ❷ (*hum fam: Verwandtschaft*) family, clan *fam*

Sịppschaft <-, -en> *f* (*pej fam*) clan, relatives *pl*

Sirene <-, -n> [zi·'re:·nə] *f* siren

Sirenengeheul *nt* wail of a siren

Sirup <-s, -e> ['zi:·rʊp] *m* syrup

Sitte <-, -n> ['zɪtə] *f* ❶ (*Gepflogenheit*) custom; **es ist bei uns ~, ...** it is our custom ...; **nach alter ~** traditionally ❷ *meist pl* (*Manieren*) manners *npl;* (*moralische Normen*) moral standards *pl* ▶ WENDUNGEN: **andere Länder, andere ~n** other countries, other customs

sịttenwidrig *adj* immoral

sịttlich *adj* moral

Sịttlichkeitsverbrechen *nt* sex crime

Situation <-, -en> [zi·tu̯a·'tsi̯o:n] *f* situation; (*persönlich a.*) position

Sitz <-es, -e> [zɪts] *m* ❶ (*Sitzgelegenheit*) seat ❷ (*Amtssitz*) seat; *von Verwaltung* headquarters *+ sing/pl vb; von Unternehmen* head office

Sịtzbank *f* bench

sitzen <sạß, gesẹssen> ['zɪtsn̩] *vi haben o* SÜDD, ÖSTERR, SCHWEIZ *sein* ❶ (*sich gesetzt haben*) to sit; **gut ~** to be comfortable; **im S~** while seated, sitting down; **bitte bleiben Sie ~!** please don't get up! ❷ (*beschäftigt sein*) **an einem Aufsatz ~** to be laboring over an essay; **er sitzt im Vorstand** he has a seat on the board of directors ❸ (*fam: inhaftiert sein*) to do time ❹ (*befestigt sein*) to be [installed]; **locker/schief ~** to be loose/lopsided ❺ (*Passform haben*) *Hosen, Rock* to fit ❻ (*treffen, wirken*) *Schlag* to hit home ❼ SCH **~ bleiben** (*fam*) to repeat a grade ❽ (*nicht absetzen können*) **auf etw** *dat* **~ bleiben** to be left with sth ▶ WENDUNGEN: **sie hat <u>einen</u> ~** (*fam*) she's had one too many; **jdn ~ <u>lassen</u>** (*fam: im Stich lassen*) to leave sb in the lurch [*or sl* hanging]; (*versetzen*) to stand sb up; (*nicht heiraten*) to jilt sb; **das lasse ich nicht <u>auf</u> mir ~!** I won't stand for this/that!

Sịtzgelegenheit *f* seats *pl,* seating [accommodation]

Sịtzordnung *f* seating plan

Sịtzplatz *m* seat

Sịtzreihe *f* row [of seats]; (*in Theater*) tier

Sịtzstreik *m* sit-in

Sịtzung <-, -en> *f* ❶ (*Konferenz*) meeting; (*im Parlament*) [parliamentary] session ❷ (*Behandlung*) visit

Sịtzungssaal *m* conference hall

Sịtzverteilung *f* POL distribution of seats

Sizilien <-s> [zi·'tsi:·li̯ən] *nt* Sicily; *s. a.* **Deutschland**

Skala <-, Skalen *o* -s> ['ska:·la, *pl* 'ska:·lən] *f* ❶ (*Maßeinteilung*) scale ❷ (*Palette*) range

Skalp <-s, -e> [skalp] *m* scalp

Skalpell <-s, -e> [skal·'pɛl] *nt* scalpel

skalpieren* [skal·'pi:·rən] *vt* to scalp

Skandal <-s, -e> [skan·'da:l] *m* scandal

skandalös [skan·da·'lø:s] I. *adj* scandalous, outrageous II. *adv* outrageously, shockingly

Skandinavien <-s> [skan·di·'na:·vi̯ən] *nt* Scandinavia

Skandinavier(in) <-s, -> [skan·di·'na:·vi̯ɐ] *m(f)* Scandinavian

skandinavisch [skan·di·'na:·vɪʃ] *adj* Scandinavian

Skateboard <-s, -s> ['ske:t·bo:ɐ̯t] *nt* skateboard; **~ fahren** to skateboard

skaten ['ske:·tn̩] *vi* (*fam*) to ice-skate, to Rollerblade, to roller-skate, to skateboard

Skelett <-[e]s, -e> [ske·'lɛt] *nt* skeleton

Skepsis <-> ['skɛp·sɪs] *f kein pl* skepticism; **etw** *dat* **mit ~ begegnen** to be very skeptical about sth

skeptisch ['skɛp·tɪʃ] I. *adj* skeptical II. *adv* skeptically

Sketch, Sketsch^RR <-[es], -e[s]> [skɛtʃ] *m* sketch

Ski <-s, - *o* -er> [ʃi:, 'ʃi:ɐ] *m* ski; **~ laufen** to ski

Ski̱anzug *m* ski suit

S

Skier ['ʃiːɐ] *pl von* **Ski**
Skifahrer(in) *m(f)* skier
Skiläufer(in) *m(f)* skier
Skilehrer(in) *m(f)* ski instructor
Skilift *m* ski lift
Skinhead <-s, -s> ['skɪn·hɛt] *m* skinhead
Skipiste *f* ski run
Skispringen *nt kein pl* ski jumping
Skispringer(in) *m(f)* ski jumper
Skizze <-, -n> ['skɪ·tsə] *f* sketch
skizzenhaft I. *adj Zeichnung, Beschreibung* rough II. *adv* **etw ~ zeichnen** to sketch sth roughly
skizzieren* [skɪ·'tsiː·rən] *vt* ❶ (*umreißen*) *Plan* to outline ❷ KUNST (*als Skizze darstellen*) to sketch
Sklave, Sklavin <-n, -n> ['sklaː·və, 'sklaː·vɪn] *m, f* slave
Sklavenhandel *m kein pl* slave trade
Sklaverei <-, -en> [sklaː·və·'rai] *f* slavery *no art*
Sklerose <-, -n> [skle·'roː·zə] *f* sclerosis; **multiple ~** multiple sclerosis
Skorpion <-s, -e> [skɔr·'pi̯oːn] *m* ❶ ZOOL scorpion ❷ ASTROL Scorpio
Skript <-[e]s, -en> [skrɪpt] *nt* ❶ SCH lecture notes *pl* ❷ (*schriftliche Vorlage*) transcript ❸ FILM [movie] script
Skrupel <-s, -> ['skruː·pl̩] *m meist pl* scruple, qualms *pl*
skrupellos (*pej*) I. *adj* unscrupulous II. *adv* without scruple
Skrupellosigkeit <-> *f kein pl* (*pej*) unscrupulousness
Skulptur <-, -en> [skʊlp·'tuːɐ̯] *f* sculpture
skurril [skʊ·'riːl] *adj* bizarre
Slalom <-s, -s> ['slaː·lɔm] *m* slalom
Slang <-s> [slɛŋ] *m kein pl* ❶ (*Umgangssprache*) slang *no art* ❷ (*Fachjargon*) jargon
Slawe, Slawin <-n, -n> ['slaː·və, 'slaː·vɪn] *m, f* Slav; *s. a.* **Deutsche(r)**
slawisch ['slaː·vɪʃ] *adj* Slav[on]ic; *s. a.* **deutsch**
Slip <-s, -s> [slɪp] *m* panties *pl*
Slipeinlage *f* panty liner
Slogan <-s, -s> ['sloː·gn̩] *m* slogan
Slowakei <-> [slo·va·'kai] *f* ■**die ~** Slovakia; *s. a.* **Deutschland**
Slowenien <-s> [slo·'veː·ni̯ən] *nt* Slovenia; *s. a.* **Deutschland**
Slum <-s, -s> [slam] *m* slum
Smaragd <-[e]s, -e> [sma·'rakt] *m* emerald
Smog <-[s], -s> [smɔk] *m* smog
Smogalarm *m* smog alert
Smoking <-s, -s> ['smoː·kɪŋ] *m* tuxedo, dinner jacket
SMS <-, -> [ɛs·ʔɛm·'ɛs] *f* MEDIA, TELEK *Abk von* **Short Message Service** text [message], IM; **jdm eine ~ schicken** to text sb
Snob <-s, -s> [snɔp] *m* snob
snobistisch [sno·'bɪs·tɪʃ] *adj* snobby, snobbish
Snowboard <-s, -s> ['snoː·boːɐ̯t] *nt* snowboard
so [zoː] I. *adv* ❶ + *adj und adv* (*derart*) so; **~ viel [wie]** as much [as]; **das ist ~ weit richtig, aber ...** generally speaking that is right, but ...; **~ weit sein** (*fam*) to be ready; **~ wenig wie möglich** as little as possible; **es ist ~, wie du sagst** it is [just] as you say ❷ + *vb* (*derart*) **sie hat sich ~ darauf gefreut** she was really looking forward to it; **ich habe mich ~ über ihn geärgert!** I was so angry with him ❸ (*auf diese Weise*) like this/that, this/that way, thus *form;* **~ musst du es machen** this is how you have to do it; **~ ist das nun mal** (*fam*) that's the way things are; **~ ist es** that's [just] the way it is; **~, als ob ...** as if ...; **~ oder ~** either way, in the end; **und ~ weiter [und ~ fort]** et cetera[, et cetera]; **~ genannt** so-called ❹ (*solch*) **~ ein Buch haben wir nicht** we don't have a book like that; **~ etwas** such a thing; **~ etwas sagt man nicht** you shouldn't say such things ❺ (*fam: etwa*) **wir treffen uns ~ gegen 7 Uhr** we'll meet at around 7 o'clock ❻ (*fam*) **und/oder ~** or so; **ich gehe um 5 oder ~** I'm going around 5 or so ❼ (*fam: umsonst*) for nothing; **das können Sie ~ haben** you can have it [for free] II. *konj* ❶ (*konsekutiv*) ■**~ dass** [*o* **sodass**] so that ❷ (*obwohl*) **~ leid es mir auch tut** as sorry as I am III. *interj* ❶ (*also*) so, right; **~, jetzt gehen wir einkaufen** so, now let's go shopping ❷ (*ätsch*) so there! ❸ (*ach*) **~, ~!** (*fam*) is that a fact! *iron*
s.o. *Abk von* **siehe oben** see above
sobald [zo·'balt] *konj* as soon as
Socke <-, -n> ['zɔ·kə] *f* sock ►WENDUNGEN: **sich auf die ~n machen** (*fam*) to get a move on
Sockel <-s, -> ['zɔ·kl̩] *m* ❶ *von Statue* plinth, pedestal ❷ (*von Gebäude*) plinth, base course
Soda <-s> ['zoː·da] *nt kein pl* ❶ CHEM soda ❷ (*Sodawasser*) carbonated water
Sodbrennen [zoːt-] *nt* heartburn
soeben [zo·'ʔeː·bn̩] *adv* (*geh*) **er hat ~ das Haus verlassen** he just left the building
Sofa <-s, -s> ['zoː·fa] *nt* sofa
sofern [zo·'fɛrn] *konj* if, provided that
soff [zɔf] *imp von* **saufen**
sofort [zo·'fɔrt] *adv* immediately; **sie kam ~** she came right away; **ich mache es ~** I'll do it right now [*or* this instant]
Sofortbildkamera *f* instant camera
sofortig [zo·'fɔr·tɪç] *adj* immediate; **mit ~er Wirkung** with immediate effect
Sofortmaßnahme *f* immediate measure; **~n ergreifen** to take immediate action
Softie <-s, -s> ['zɔf·ti] *m* (*fam*) softie
Softporno ['sɔft-] *m* soft[-core] porn [movie]
Software <-, -s> ['sɔft·vɛːɐ̯] *f* software
Softwarepaket *nt* software package
sog [zoːk] *imp von* **saugen**
sog. *adj Abk von* **so genannt** so-called
Sog <-[e]s, -e> [zoːk] *m* suction
sogar [zo·'gaːɐ̯] *adv* even
Sohle <-, -n> ['zoː·lə] *f* sole
Sohn <-[e]s, Söhne> [zoːn, *pl* 'zøː·nə] *m* son

S

Soja <-s, Sojen> ['zoː·ja, *pl* 'zoː·jən] *meist sing f* soy
Sojabohne *f* soybean
Sojasoße *f* soy sauce
solang [zo·'laŋ], **solange** [zo·'laŋə] *konj* as long as
Solarenergie *f* solar energy
Solarium <-s, -rien> [zo·'laː·ri̯·ʊm, *pl* -'la·ri̯·ən] *nt* solarium
Solarzelle *f* solar cell
solch [zɔlç] *adj* such; ~ **ein Mann** such a man
solche(r, s) *adj* ❶ *attr* such; ~ **Frauen** women like that; **ich machte mir ~ Sorgen** I was really worried; **~n Kuchen mag ich nicht** I don't like that kind of cake; **sie hatte ~ Angst ...** she was so afraid ... ❷ *substantivisch* (*solche Menschen*) people like that; (*ein solcher Mensch*) a person like this/that; **als ~(r, s)** as such, in itself; **der Mensch als ~r** man as such; **es gibt ~ und ~ Kunden** there are customers and then there are customers
Sold <-[e]s> [zɔlt] *m kein pl* MIL pay
Soldat(in) <-en, -en> [zɔl·'daːt] *m(f)* soldier
Söldner(in) <-s, -> ['zœld·nɐ] *m(f)* mercenary
Soli ['zoː·li] *pl von* **Solo**
solid [zo·'liːt] *adj, adv s.* **solide**
solidarisch [zo·li·'daː·rɪʃ] **I.** *adj* **sich** *akk* [**mit jdm/etw**] ~ **erklären** to declare one's solidarity [with sb/sth] **II.** *adv* in solidarity
solidarisieren* [zo·li·da·ri·'ziː·rən] *vr* ■**sich** *akk* ~ to show [one's] solidarity
Solidarität <-> [zo·li·da·ri·'tɛːt] *f kein pl* solidarity
Solidaritätszuschlag *m* POL solidarity tax (*a tax to help finance the cost of the German reunification*)
solide [zo·'liː·də] **I.** *adj* ❶ (*haltbar, fest*) solid; *Kleidung* durable ❷ (*fundiert*) *Kenntnisse* sound, thorough ❸ (*untadelig*) *Leben* respectable ❹ (*seriös*) *Unternehmen* well-established *attr*; sound **II.** *adv* (*haltbar, fest*) solidly
Solist(in) <-en, -en> [zo·'lɪst] *m(f)* MUS soloist
Soll <-[s], -[s]> [zɔl] *nt* ❶ (*Sollseite*) debit side; ~ **und Haben** debit and credit ❷ (*Produktionsnorm*) target; **sein ~ erfüllen** to reach one's target
sollen ['zɔ·lən] **I.** *aux vb* <sollte, sollen> ❶ (*etw zu tun haben*) **du sollst herkommen, habe ich gesagt!** I said [you should] come here!; **man hat mir gesagt, ich soll Sie fragen** I was told to ask you; **was ~ wir machen?** what should we do? ❷ (*falls*) **sollte das passieren, ...** should that happen ... ❸ (*eigentlich müssen*) **du sollst dich schämen!** you should be ashamed [of yourself]; **das solltest du unbedingt sehen** you have to see this; **so soll es sein** that's how it ought to be ❹ (*angeblich sein, tun*) to be supposed to; **sie soll mitgemacht haben** she supposedly took part in it; **sie soll sehr reich sein** she is said to be very rich; **was soll das heißen?** what's that supposed to mean? ❺ (*dürfen*) **du hättest das nicht tun ~** you should not have done that ❻ *in der Vergangenheit* **es sollte ganz anders kommen** things were supposed to turn out quite differently **II.** *vi* <sollte, gesollt> ❶ (*eine Anweisung befolgen*) **soll er reinkommen? – ja, er soll** should he come in? — yes, he should ❷ (*müssen*) **du sollst sofort nach Hause** you should go home right away ❸ (*bedeuten*) **was soll der Blödsinn?** (*fam*) what's all this nonsense about?; **was soll das?** (*fam*) what's that supposed to mean?; **was soll's?** (*fam*) who cares?
Solo <-s, Soli> ['zoː·lo, *pl* 'zoː·li] *nt* MUS solo
somit [zo·'mɪt] *adv* therefore, hence *form*
Sommer <-s, -> ['zɔ·mɐ] *m* summer
Sommerferien *pl* summer vacation
sommerlich **I.** *adj* summer *attr*; **~es Wetter** summer weather **II.** *adv* like in summer; **sich ~ kleiden** to wear summer clothing
Sommersemester *nt* summer semester
Sommersprosse *f meist pl* freckle
Sommerurlaub <-(e)s, -e> *m* summer vacation
Sommerzeit *f* ❶ (*Jahreszeit*) summertime ❷ (*Uhrzeit*) summer time
Sonate <-, -n> [zo·'naː·tə] *f* sonata
Sonde <-, -n> ['zɔn·də] *f* ❶ MED (*Schlauchsonde*) tube; (*Operationssonde*) probe ❷ (*Raumsonde*) probe
Sonderangebot *nt* special offer; **etw im ~ haben** to have sth on sale
Sonderausgabe *f* ❶ MEDIA special edition ❷ *kein pl* ÖKON contingent expenses *pl*
sonderbar ['zɔn·dɐ·baːɐ̯] **I.** *adj* peculiar, strange, odd **II.** *adv* strangely
Sonderfall *m* special case
Sondergenehmigung *f* special authorization *no art*
sonderlich ['zɔn·dɐ·lɪç] **I.** *adj* ❶ *attr* (*besonders*) particular; **ohne ~es Interesse** without any particular interest ❷ (*seltsam*) peculiar, strange **II.** *adv* particularly; **nicht ~ begeistert** not particularly enthusiastic
Sonderling <-s, -e> ['zɔn·dɐ·lɪŋ] *m* oddball
Sondermarke *f* commemorative [stamp]
Sondermüll *m* hazardous waste
sondern ['zɔn·dɐn] *konj* but; **nicht sie war es, ~ er** it wasn't her, it was him
Sonderpreis *m* special [reduced] [*or* sale] price
Sonderregelung *f* special provision
Sonderschule *f* school for special education
Sonderstellung *f* special position
Sonderzug *m* special [*or* chartered] train
Sonett <-[e]s, -e> [zo·'nɛt] *nt* sonnet
Song <-s, -s> [zɔŋ] *m* song
Sonnabend ['zɔn·ʔaːbn̩t] *m* DIAL (*Samstag*) Saturday
sonnabends *adv* DIAL (*samstags*) [on] Saturdays
Sonne <-, -n> ['zɔnə] *f kein pl* sun; **die ~ geht auf/unter** the sun rises/sets
sonnen ['zɔ·nən] *vr* ❶ (*sonnenbaden*) ■**sich** *akk* ~ to sunbathe ❷ (*genießen*) ■**sich** *akk* **in etw** *dat* ~ to bask in sth

Sọnnenaufgang *m* sunrise, sunup
Sọnnenbad *nt* sunbathing; **ein ~ nehmen** to sunbathe
Sọnnenblume *f* sunflower
Sọnnenbrand *m* sunburn *no art*
Sọnnenbrille *f* sunglasses *npl,* shades *npl sl*
Sọnnencreme *f* suntan lotion
Sọnnenenergie *f* solar energy
Sọnnenfinsternis *f* solar eclipse
sonnenklar ['zɔ·nən·'klaːɐ̯] *adj* (*fam*) crystal-clear, clear as daylight *pred*
Sọnnenkollektor *m* solar panel
Sọnnenlicht *nt kein pl* sunlight
Sọnnenmilch *f* suntan lotion
Sọnnenöl *nt* suntan oil
Sọnnenschein *m* sunshine; **bei strahlendem ~** in the bright sunshine
Sọnnenschirm *m* sunshade; (*tragbar*) parasol
Sọnnenstich *m* sunstroke *no art*
Sọnnenstrahl *m* sunbeam
Sọnnensystem *nt* solar system
Sọnnenuhr *f* sundial
Sọnnenuntergang *m* sunset, sundown
sonnig ['zɔ·nɪç] *adj* sunny
Sonntag ['zɔn·taːk] *m* Sunday; *s. a.* **Dienstag**
sọnntäglich *adj* [regular] Sunday *attr*
Sọnntagnachmittag[RR] *m* Sunday afternoon; *s. a.* **Dienstag**
sọnntags *adv* [on] Sundays
sonst [zɔnst] *adv* ① (*andernfalls*) or [else], otherwise ② (*gewöhnlich*) usually; **du hast doch ~ keine Bedenken** you don't usually have any doubts; **kälter als ~** colder than usual ③ (*außerdem*) **~ noch Fragen?** any more questions?; **gibt es ~ noch etwas?** is there anything else?; ■ **~ keine(r,s)** nothing/nobody else; **~ nichts** nothing else; **~ was** whatever
sonstig ['zɔns·tɪç] *adj attr* (*weitere[s]*) other; **„Sonstiges"** "miscellaneous"; **und wie sind ihre ~en Leistungen?** and how is her performance otherwise?
sooft [zo·'ʔɔft] *konj* whenever
Sopran <-s, -e> [zo·'praːn] *m kein pl* soprano
Sorbet <-s, -s> ['zɔr·bɛt, zɔr·'beː] *m o nt* sherbe[r]t
Sorge <-, -n> ['zɔr·gə] *f* worry; **~n haben** to have problems; **es macht mir ~n, dass ...** it worries me that ...; **wir haben uns solche ~n gemacht!** we were so worried; **machen Sie sich deswegen keine ~n!** don't worry about that; **lassen Sie das meine ~ sein!** let me worry about that; **keine ~!** (*fam*) don't [you] worry
sorgen ['zɔr·gn̩] **I.** *vi* ① (*sich kümmern*) ■ **für jdn ~** to provide for [*or* look after] sb ② (*besorgen*) **für etw** *akk* **~** to get sth; **für die Musik ~** to take care of the music; **ich sorge dafür, dass ...** I'll see to it that ...; **dafür ist gesorgt** that's taken care of ③ (*bewirken*) **für Aufsehen ~** to cause a sensation **II.** *vr* ■ **sich** *akk* **um jdn/etw ~** to be worried about sb/sth
sọrgenfrei **I.** *adj* carefree, free of care *pred* **II.** *adv* free of care
Sọrgenkind *nt* problem child
sọrgenvoll **I.** *adj* (*besorgt*) worried **II.** *adv* worriedly, anxiously
Sọrgerecht *nt kein pl* custody
Sorgfalt <-> ['zɔrk·falt] *f kein pl* care
sọrgfältig **I.** *adj* careful **II.** *adv* carefully, with care
sorglos ['zɔrk·loːs] **I.** *adj* ① (*achtlos*) careless ② *s.* **sorgenfrei** **II.** *adv* ① (*achtlos*) carelessly ② (*sorgenfrei*) free of care
Sorte <-, -n> ['zɔr·tə] *f* ① (*Art*) kind, variety ② (*Marke*) brand
sortieren* [zɔr·'tiː·rən] *vt* to sort; **etw nach Farbe ~** to sort sth by color; **gestern habe ich meine Unterlagen sortiert** yesterday I sorted out my documents
Sortiment <-[e]s, -e> [zɔr·ti·'mɛnt] *nt* range [of products]
SOS <-, -> [ɛs·ʔoː·'ʔɛs] *nt* SOS; **~ funken** to put out an SOS
sosehr [zo·'zeːɐ̯] *konj* ■ **~ [... auch]** however much ..., no matter how much ...
Soße <-, -n> ['zoː·sə] *f* sauce; (*Bratensoße*) gravy
Soufflé, **Soufflee**[RR] <-s, -s> [zu·'fleː] *nt* KOCHK soufflé
soufflieren* [zu·'fliː·rən] *vi* THEAT to prompt
Sound <-s, -s> [saʊnd] *m* MUS sound
Soundkarte ['zaunt-] *f* COMPUT sound card
soundso ['zoː·ʔʊnt·zoː] **I.** *adv* (*fam*) such and such; **~ breit/groß** this wide/big; **~ viele** this many **II.** *adj* such and such; **auf Seite ~** on page such and such
Souterrain <-s, -s> [su·tɛ·'rɛ̃ː, 'zuː·tɛ·rɛ̃] *nt* basement
Souvenir <-s, -s> [zu·və·'niːɐ̯] *nt* souvenir
souverän [zu·və·'rɛːn] **I.** *adj* ① (*unabhängig*) sovereign *attr* ② (*überlegen*) superior **II.** *adv* with superior ease; **etw ~ machen** to do sth confidently
Souveränität <-> [zu·və·rɛ·ni·'tɛːt] *f kein pl* sovereignty; (*Überlegenheit*) supremacy
soviel [zo·'fiːl] *konj* as far as; **~ ich weiß ...** as far as I know ...; **~ ich auch trinke ...** no matter how much I drink ...
soweit [zo·'vait] *konj* as far as
sowie [zo·'viː] *konj* ① (*sobald*) as soon as, the moment [that] ② (*und auch*) as well as
sowieso [zo·vi·'zoː] *adv* anyway, anyhow
sowohl [zo·'voːl] *konj* ■ **~ ... als auch ...** both ... and ..., ... as well as ...
sozial [zo·'tsi̯aːl] **I.** *adj* ① (*gesellschaftlich*) social ② (*für Hilfsbedürftige gedacht*) welfare *attr* ③ (*gesellschaftlich verantwortlich*) public-spirited **II.** *adv* **~ schwache Familien** low-income families; **~ denken** to be socially minded
Sozialabbau *m kein pl* cuts in social services
Sozialabgaben *pl* social security contributions
Sozialamt *nt* Department of Social Services
Sozialarbeiter(in) *m(f)* social worker
Sozialdemokrat(in) *m(f)* social democrat
Sozialdemokratie *f kein pl* social democracy

S

sozialdemokratisch *adj* social democratic

Sozialfall *m* welfare case

Sozialhilfe *f kein pl* welfare

Sozialismus <-> [zo·tsi̯a·ˈlɪs·mʊs] *m kein pl* socialism

Sozialist(in) <-en, -en> [zo·tsi̯a·ˈlɪst] *m(f)* socialist

sozialistisch [zo·tsi̯a·ˈlɪstɪʃ] *adj* ❶ (*Sozialismus betreffend*) socialist ❷ ÖSTERR (*sozialdemokratisch*) social democratic

Sozialleistungen *pl* social security benefits

Sozialstaat *m* welfare state

Sozialwohnung *f* [housing] project

Soziologe, Soziologin <-n, -n> [zo·tsi̯o·ˈloː·gə, -ˈloː·gɪn] *m, f* sociologist

Soziologie <-> [zo·tsi̯o·lo·ˈgiː] *f kein pl* sociology

sozusagen [zoː·tsu·ˈzaː·gn̩] *adv* as it were, so to speak

Spachtel <-s, -> [ˈʃpa·xtl̩] *m* putty knife

Spagat <-[e]s, -e> [ʃpa·ˈgaːt] *m o nt* split, the splits *npl*

Spagetti[RR], **Spaghetti** [ʃpa·ˈgɛ·ti] *pl* spaghetti + *sing vb*

spähen [ˈʃpɛː·ən] *vi* ❶ (*suchend blicken*) **aus dem Fenster ~** to peer out [of] the window; ■ **durch etw** *akk* **~** to peek through sth ❷ (*Ausschau halten*) to look out (**nach** +*dat* for)

Spalt <-[e]s, -e> [ʃpalt] *m* gap; (*Riss*) crack; (*Felsspalt*) crevice; **die Tür einen ~ öffnen/offen lassen** to open the door slightly/leave the door ajar

Spalte <-, -n> [ˈʃpal·tə] *f* ❶ (*Öffnung*) fissure; (*Felsspalte a.*) crevice ❷ TYPO, MEDIA column

spalten [ˈʃpal·tn̩] **I.** *vt* <*pp* gespalten *o* gespaltet> ❶ (*zerteilen*) to split; *Holz a.* to chop ❷ (*trennen*) to divide **II.** *vr* <*pp* gespalten> ■ **sich** *akk* **~** ❶ (*der Länge nach reißen*) to split ❷ (*sich teilen*) to divide

Spaltung <-, -en> *f* ❶ (*Kernphysik*) splitting, fission ❷ (*Aufspaltung in Fraktionen*) division; (*von Partei a.*) split

Spamfilter [ˈspɛm-] *m* INET spam filter

Span <-[e]s, Späne> [ʃpaːn, *pl* ˈʃpɛː·nə] *m* (*Holzspan*) [wood] chip; (*Bohrspan*) swarf, turnings *pl*

Spanferkel [ˈʃpaːn·fɛr·kl̩] *nt* suckling pig

Spange <-, -n> [ˈʃpaŋə] *f* ❶ (*Haarspange*) barrette ❷ (*Zahnspange*) braces *pl,* retainer

Spanien <-s> [ˈʃpaː·ni̯ən] *nt* Spain; *s. a.* **Deutschland**

Spanier(in) <-s, -> [ˈʃpaː·ni̯ɐ] *m(f)* Spaniard; ■ **die ~** the Spanish; *s. a.* **Deutsche(r)**

spanisch [ˈʃpaː·nɪʃ] *adj* Spanish; *s. a.* **deutsch**

Spanisch [ˈʃpaː·nɪʃ] *nt dekl wie adj* Spanish; **auf S~** in Spanish; *s. a.* **Deutsch**

spann [ʃpan] *imp von* **spinnen**

Spannbetttuch[RR] *nt* fitted sheet

Spanne <-, -n> [ˈʃpanə] *f* ❶ (*Gewinnspanne*) [profit] margin ❷ (*Zeitspanne*) span

spannen [ˈʃpa·nən] **I.** *vt* ❶ (*straffen*) to tighten ❷ (*aufspannen*) to put up *sep;* **ein Seil zwischen etw** *akk* **~** to stretch a rope between sth ❸ (*anspannen*) ■ **ein Tier vor etw** *akk* **~** to harness an animal to sth **II.** *vr* ■ **sich** *akk* **~** *Seil* to become taut **III.** *vi* (*zu eng sitzen*) *Hose* to be [too] tight

spannend *adj* exciting; (*stärker*) thrilling

Spanner(in) <-s, -> *m(f)* (*sl: Voyeur*) peeping Tom

Spannung <-, -en> *f* ❶ *kein pl* (*gespannte Erwartung*) suspense; **etw mit ~ erwarten** to anxiously await sth ❷ *meist pl* (*Anspannung*) tension ❸ *kein pl* (*straffe Beschaffenheit*) tension, tautness ❹ ELEK voltage; **unter ~ stehen** to be live

Sparbuch *nt* bankbook

Sparbüchse *f* piggy bank

sparen [ˈʃpaː·rən] **I.** *vt* ❶ (*einsparen*) to save ❷ (*ersparen*) ■ **jdm/sich etw ~** to spare sb/oneself sth; **den Weg hätten wir uns ~ können** we could have saved ourselves that trip; **deine Ratschläge kannst du dir ~** [you can] keep your advice to yourself **II.** *vi* ❶ FIN (*Geld zurücklegen*) to save; ■ **für etw** *akk* **~** to save [up] for sth ❷ (*sparsam sein*) to economize (**an** +*dat* on)

Sparer(in) <-s, -> *m(f)* saver

Spargel <-s, -> [ˈʃpar·gl̩] *m* asparagus

Sparkasse *f* bank (*supported publicly by a commune or district*)

Sparkonto *nt* savings account

spärlich [ˈʃpɛːɐ̯·lɪç] **I.** *adj Haarwuchs, Vegetation* sparse; *Ausbeute, Reste* meager **II.** *adv* sparsely; **~ bekleidet** scantily dressed; **~ besucht** poorly attended

Sparmaßnahme *f* cost-cutting measure

Sparpackung *f* economy pack

Sparpreis *m* budget [*or* economy] price

sparsam [ˈʃpaːɐ̯·zaːm] **I.** *adj* ❶ (*wenig verbrauchend*) thrifty ❷ (*ökonomisch*) economical **II.** *adv* ❶ (*wenig verbrauchend*) thriftily, sparingly ❷ (*ökonomisch*) sparingly

Sparsamkeit <-> *f kein pl* thriftiness

Sparschwein *nt* piggy bank

Spartarif *m* TELEK, INET, TRANSP budget [*or* economy] rate

Sparte <-, -n> [ˈʃpar·tə] *f* ❶ (*Branche*) line of business ❷ (*Spezialbereich*) area, branch ❸ (*Rubrik*) section, column

Sparvertrag *m* savings agreement

Spaß <-es, Späße> [ʃpaːs, *pl* ˈʃpɛː·sə] *m* ❶ *kein pl* (*Vergnügen*) fun; **es macht mir ~, das zu tun** I enjoy doing that; **jdm den ~ verderben** to spoil sb's fun; **viel ~!** have fun! ❷ (*Scherz*) joke; **da hört der ~ auf** that's going a bit too far; **~ muss sein** (*fam*) there's no harm in a joke; **keinen ~ verstehen** to not have a sense of humor; **~ beiseite** joking apart; **[nur] ~ machen** to be [just] kidding ▸ WENDUNGEN: **ein teurer ~ sein** to be an expensive business

spaßen [ˈʃpaː·sn̩] *vi* to joke; **mit etw** *dat* **ist nicht zu ~** sth is no joking matter

spaßig [ˈʃpaː·sɪç] *adj* funny

Spaßverderber(in) <-s, -> *m(f)* spoilsport
Spaßvogel *m* joker
spät [ʃpɛːt] **I.** *adj* late; **am ~en Abend** late in the evening **II.** *adv* late; **du kommst zu ~** you're too late; **~ dran sein** to be [running] late ▶WENDUNGEN: **wie ~ ist es?** what time is it?; **wie ~ kommst du heute nach Hause?** what time are you coming home today?
Spaten <-s, -> [ˈʃpaː·tn̩] *m* spade
später [ˈʃpɛː·tɐ] **I.** *adj* later **II.** *adv* ❶ (*zeitlich danach*) later [on]; **bis ~!** see you later!; **nicht ~ als** not later than ❷ (*die Zukunft*) the future; **jeder sollte für ~ vorsorgen** everybody should make provisions for the future; **~ [ein]mal** at a later date, some other time
spätestens [ˈʃpɛː·təs·tn̩s] *adv* at the [very] latest
Spätfolge <-, -n> *f meist pl* long-term consequence
Spätschicht *f* late shift
Spätsommer *m* late summer
Spätvorstellung *f* late show[ing]
Spatz <-en *o* -es, -en> [ʃpats] *m* ORN sparrow
spazieren* [ʃpa·ˈtsiː·rən] *vi sein* to stroll, to walk; **den Hund ~ führen** to take the dog for a walk; **~ fahren** to go for a drive; **~ gehen** to go for a walk
Spazierfahrt *f* drive; **eine ~ machen** to go for a drive
Spaziergang <-gänge> *m* walk, stroll; **einen ~ machen** to go for a walk
Spaziergänger(in) <-s, -> *m(f)* stroller
Specht <-[e]s, -e> [ʃpɛçt] *m* woodpecker
Speck <-[e]s, -e> [ʃpɛk] *m* bacon
Spediteur(in) <-s, -e> [ʃpe·di·ˈtøːɐ̯] *m(f)* freight forwarder, shipper
Spedition <-, -en> [ʃpe·di·ˈtsi̯oːn] *f* (*Transportunternehmen*) trucking company; (*Umzugsunternehmen*) moving company
Speed <-s, -s> [spiːt] *nt* speed
Speer <-[e]s, -e> [ʃpeːɐ̯] *m* ❶ SPORT javelin ❷ (*Waffe*) spear
Speerwerfen *nt kein pl* SPORT the javelin
Speiche <-, -n> [ˈʃpai·çə] *f* spoke
Speichel <-s> [ˈʃpai·çl̩] *m kein pl* saliva
Speicher <-s, -> [ˈʃpai·çɐ] *m* ❶ (*Dachboden*) attic, loft; **auf dem ~** in the attic ❷ (*Lagerhaus*) storehouse ❸ COMPUT memory
Speicherfunktion *f* COMPUT memory function
Speicherkapazität *f* COMPUT memory capacity
Speicherkarte *f* COMPUT memory [*or* flash] card
speichern [ˈʃpai·çɐn] *vt, vi* ❶ COMPUT to save; **etw ~ unter ...** to save sth as ...; *Nummern in Handy* to store ❷ (*aufbewahren*) to store
Speicherplatz *m* COMPUT memory space; (*auf Festplatte*) disk space
Speicherung <-, -en> *f* COMPUT storage
Speise <-, -n> [ˈʃpai·zə] *f meist pl* meal
Speisekammer *f* pantry
Speisekarte *f* menu
speisen [ˈʃpai·zn̩] *vi* to dine, to eat
Speiseöl *nt* cooking oil
Speiseröhre *f* esophagus, gullet
Speisesaal *m* dining hall [*or* room]
Speisewagen *m* dining car
Spektakel[1] <-s, -> [ʃpɛk·ˈtaː·kl̩] *m* (*fam*) ❶ (*Lärm*) racket ❷ (*Ärger*) scene
Spektakel[2] <-s, -> [ʃpɛk·ˈtaː·kl̩] *nt* spectacle
spektakulär [ʃpɛk·ta·ku·ˈlɛːɐ̯] *adj* spectacular
Spekulant(in) <-en, -en> [ʃpe·ku·ˈlant] *m(f)* speculator
Spekulation <-, -en> [ʃpe·ku·la·ˈtsi̯oːn] *f* speculation; **[über etw** *akk*] **~en anstellen** to speculate [about sth]
spekulieren* [ʃpe·ku·ˈliː·rən] *vi* to speculate (**mit** +*dat* in, **auf** +*akk* on)
spendabel [ʃpɛn·ˈdaː·bl̩] *adj* generous
Spende <-, -n> [ˈʃpɛn·də] *f* donation
spenden [ˈʃpɛn·dn̩] *vt, vi* to donate; *Blut* to give
Spender <-s, -> [ˈʃpɛn·dɐ] *m* (*Dosierer*) dispenser
Spender(in) <-s, -> [ˈʃpɛn·dɐ] *m(f)* ❶ (*jd, der spendet*) don[at]or ❷ MED donor
Spenderausweis *m* donor card
spendieren* [ʃpɛn·ˈdiː·rən] *vt* (*fam*) ■ **[jdm] etw ~** to buy [sb] sth; **das Essen spendiere ich** [the] dinner's on me
Sperling <-s, -e> [ˈʃpɛr·lɪŋ] *m* sparrow
Sperma <-s, Spermen *o* -ta> [ˈʃpɛr·ma, ˈspɛr·ma, *pl* -ma·ta] *nt* sperm
Sperre <-, -n> [ˈʃpɛ·rə] *f* ❶ (*Sperrvorrichtung*) barrier ❷ (*Spielverbot*) ban
sperren [ˈʃpɛ·rən] **I.** *vt* ❶ SÜDD, ÖSTERR (*schließen*) to close off (**für** +*akk* to) ❷ (*blockieren*) to block; *Konto* to freeze; *Scheck* to stop payment on ❸ (*einschließen*) to lock [up] ❹ (*ein Spielverbot verhängen*) to ban **II.** *vr* ■ **sich** *akk* **~** to back away (**gegen** +*akk* from)
Sperrgebiet *nt* restricted area
Sperrholz *nt* plywood
Sperrmüll *m* bulky trash
Sperrstunde *f* closing time
Sperrung <-, -en> *f* ❶ (*Schließung*) closing off ❷ (*Blockierung*) blocking
Spesen [ˈʃpeː·zn̩] *pl* expenses *npl*
Spezialeffekt *m* special effect
Spezialgebiet *nt* special field
spezialisieren* [ʃpe·tsi̯a·li·ˈziː·rən] *vr* ■ **sich** *akk* **~** to specialize (**auf** +*akk* in)
Spezialisierung <-, -en> *f* specialization
Spezialist(in) <-en, -en> [ʃpe·tsi̯a·ˈlɪst] *m(f)* specialist
Spezialität <-, -en> [ʃpe·tsi̯a·li·ˈtɛːt] *f* specialty
speziell [ʃpe·ˈtsi̯ɛl] **I.** *adj* special **II.** *adv* [e]specially
Spezies <-, -> [ˈʃpeː·tsi̯ɛs, ˈsp-] *f* species +*sing vb*
spezifisch [ʃpe·ˈtsiː·fɪʃ] **I.** *adj* specific **II.** *adv* typically
Sphäre <-, -n> [ˈsfɛː·rə] *f* sphere
sphärisch [ˈsfɛː·rɪʃ] *adj* spherical
spicken [ˈʃpɪ·kn̩] *vt* ❶ KOCHK (*durchsetzen*) to lard ❷ (*fam: abschreiben*) to copy
Spickzettel *m* cheat sheet

Spiegel <-s, -> [ˈʃpiː·gl̩] *m* mirror
Spiegelbild *nt* mirror image
Spiegelei *nt* egg sunny side up
spiegeln [ˈʃpiː·gl̩n] **I.** *vi* to reflect **II.** *vr* ■ **sich** *akk* **in etw** *dat* ~ to be reflected in sth
Spiegelreflexkamera *f* reflex camera
Spiegelung <-, -en> [ˈʃpiː·gə·lʊŋ] *f* ❶ MED endoscopy ❷ (*Abbild*) reflection
Spiel <-[e]s, -e> [ʃpiːl] *nt* ❶ (*Gesellschafts-, Kinder-, Glücksspiel*) game ❷ (*im Baseball, Basketball, Fußball, Hockey*) game; (*im Tennis, Volleyball*) match; **die Olympischen ~e** the Olympic Games ▶ WENDUNGEN: **ein abgekartetes ~** (*fam*) a fix; **leichtes ~ haben** to have an easy job of it; **etw [mit] ins ~ bringen** to bring up *sep* sth; **[bei etw] im ~ sein** to be involved [in sth]; **jdn/etw aus dem ~ lassen** to keep sb/sth out of it; **etw aufs ~ setzen** to put sth on the line; **auf dem ~ stehen** to be at stake; **jdm das ~ verderben** (*fam*) to ruin sb's plans
Spielautomat *m* gambling machine
Spielbank *f* casino
spielen [ˈʃpiː·lən] **I.** *vt* to play ▶ WENDUNGEN: **was wird hier gespielt?** what's going on here? **II.** *vi* ❶ (*ein Spiel machen*) to play ❷ (*auftreten*) **in einem Stück ~** to star in a play; **gut/schlecht ~** to play well/poorly ❸ (*als Szenario haben*) **in Italien/im Mittelalter ~** to be set in Italy/in the Middle Ages ❹ SPORT to play ❺ (*Glücksspiel betreiben*) to gamble
spielend *adv* easily
Spieler(in) <-s, -> [ˈʃpiː·lɐ] *m(f)* ❶ (*Mitspieler*) player ❷ (*Glücksspieler*) gambler
spielerisch I. *adj* playful **II.** *adv* playfully
Spielfeld [ˈʃpiːl·fɛlt] *nt* [playing] field
Spielfilm *m* feature film
Spielhalle *f* arcade
Spielkamerad(in) *m(f)* playmate
Spielkarte *f* playing card
Spielkasino *nt* casino
Spielplan *m* schedule; THEAT program
Spielplatz *m* playground
Spielraum *m* leeway
Spielregel *f meist pl* rules *pl*
Spielsachen *pl* toys *pl*
Spielsucht *f* compulsive gambling
Spieluhr *f* music box
Spielverderber(in) <-s, -> *m(f)* spoilsport
Spielzeit *f* ❶ THEAT season ❷ SPORT playing time
Spielzeug *nt* toy
Spieß <-es, -e> [ʃpiːs] *m* ❶ (*Bratspieß*) spit; (*kleiner*) skewer ❷ MIL (*sl*) sarge ❸ (*Stoßwaffe*) spike ▶ WENDUNGEN: **wie am ~ brüllen** to scream at the top of one's lungs; **den ~ umdrehen** to turn the tables
Spießbürger(in) *m(f) s.* **Spießer**
spießbürgerlich *adj s.* **spießig**
spießen [ˈʃpiː·sn̩] *vt* ■ **etw auf etw** *akk* ~ to skewer sth on sth
Spießer(in) <-s, -> [ˈʃpiː·sɐ] *m(f)* (*fam*) narrow-minded person
spießig [ˈʃpiː·sɪç] *adj* (*fam*) narrow-minded
Spießigkeit <-> *f kein pl* (*pej fam*) narrow-mindedness
Spikes [ʃpaiks, sp-] *pl* (*an Schuhen*) spikes *pl;* (*an Reifen*) studs *pl*
Spinat <-[e]s> [ʃpiˈnaːt] *m kein pl* spinach
Spind <-[e]s, -e> [ʃpɪnt, *pl* ˈʃpɪn·də] *m* locker
Spindel <-, -n> [ˈʃpɪn·dl̩] *f* spindle
Spinne <-, -n> [ˈʃpɪ·nə] *f* spider
spinnen <spann, gesponnen> [ˈʃpɪ·nən] **I.** *vt* ❶ *Wolle* to spin ❷ *Geschichte* to invent **II.** *vi* (*fam: nicht bei Trost sein*) to be crazy [*or sl* nuts]; **sag mal, spinnt der?** is he out of his mind?
Spinnennetz *nt* spiderweb
Spinner(in) <-s, -> [ˈʃpɪ·nɐ] *m(f)* (*fam*) nutcase
Spinnerei <-, -en> [ʃpɪ·nə·ˈrai] *f* ❶ (*Betrieb*) spinning mill ❷ *kein pl* (*fam: Blödsinn*) nonsense
Spinnwebe <-, -n> *f* cobweb
Spion(in) <-s, -e> [ʃpi̯·oːn] *m(f)* spy
Spionage <-> [ʃpi̯o·ˈnaː·ʒə] *f kein pl* espionage
Spionageabwehr *f* counterespionage, counterintelligence
spionieren* [ʃpi̯o·ˈniː·rən] *vi* to spy
Spirale <-, -n> [ʃpi·ˈraː·lə] *f* ❶ (*gewundene Linie*) spiral ❷ MED IUD
spirituell [ʃpi·ri·ˈtu̯·ɛl, sp-] *adj* spiritual
Spirituosen [ʃpi·ri·ˈtu̯oː·zn̩, sp-] *pl* spirits *pl*
Spital <-s, Spitäler> [ʃpi·ˈtaːl, *pl* -ˈtɛː·lɐ] *nt* ÖSTERR, SCHWEIZ hospital
spitz [ʃpɪts] **I.** *adj* ❶ (*mit einer Spitze*) pointed; *Bleistift, Messer* sharp ❷ (*spitz zulaufend*) tapered; *Nase, Kinn* pointy ❸ *Bemerkung* sharp **II.** *adv* ❶ (*V-förmig*) tapered ❷ (*spitzzüngig*) sharply
Spitze <-, -n> [ˈʃpɪtsə] *f* ❶ (*spitzes Ende*) point ❷ (*vorderster Teil*) front ❸ (*erster Platz, höchste Stelle eines Turms, Berges*) top ❹ (*Höchstwert*) peak ❺ *pl* (*führende Leute*) *der Gesellschaft* the top; *eines Unternehmen* the heads ❻ MODE lace ▶ WENDUNGEN: **~ sein** (*fam*) to be great; **etw auf die ~ treiben** to take sth to extremes
Spitzel <-s, -> [ˈʃpɪtsl̩] *m* informer
spitzen [ˈʃpɪtsn̩] *vt* to sharpen
Spitzengeschwindigkeit *f* top speed
Spitzenklasse *f* elite, top of the line
Spitzenleistung *f* outstanding [*or* first-rate] performance
spitzenmäßig I. *adj* (*sl*) brilliant **II.** *adv* (*sl*) brilliantly
Spitzensportler(in) *m(f)* top athlete
spitzfindig *adj* hairsplitting
spitz|kriegen *vt* (*fam*) to catch on to
Spitzname *m* nickname
spitzwinkelig, spitzwinklig *adj Dreieck* acute
Spleen <-s, -s> [ʃpliːn, sp-] *m* (*fam*) eccentricity
Splitter <-s, -> [ˈʃplɪ·tɐ] *m* splinter
splittern *vi sein o haben* to splinter

S

splitternackt ['ʃplɪ·tɐ·'nakt] *adj* stark naked
sponsern ['ʃpɔn·zɐn, 'sp-] *vt* to sponsor

The **Sponsion** is an academic ceremony in Austria at which Master's degrees are awarded.

Sponsor, **Sponsorin** <-s, -soren> ['ʃpɔn·zɐ, 'sp-, ʃpɔn·'zoːr·ɪn, *pl* -'zoː·rən] *m, f* sponsor
Sponsoring <-s> ['ʃpɔn·zor·ɪŋ, 'sp-] *nt kein pl* sponsoring
spontan [ʃpɔn·'taːn, sp-] *adj* spontaneous
Spontaneität <-> [ʃpɔn·ta·nei·'tɛːt, sp-] *f kein pl* spontaneity
sporadisch [ʃpo·'raː·dɪʃ, sp-] *adj* sporadic
Sport <-[e]s, *selten* -e> [ʃpɔrt] *m* ❶ SPORT sport[s *pl*]; **~ treiben** to play sports ❷ SCH PE, gym ❸ MEDIA sports [news]; **~ sehen** to watch sports
Sportart *f* discipline, kind of sport
Sportbericht *m* sports report
Sportlehrer(in) *m(f)* PE [*or* gym] teacher
Sportler(in) <-s, -> ['ʃpɔrt·lɐ] *m(f)* athlete
sportlich ['ʃpɔrt·lɪç] **I.** *adj* ❶ (*den Sport betreffend*) sporting ❷ (*trainiert*) *Figur* athletic; *Mensch* sporty ❸ MODE casual **II.** *adv* ❶ SPORT (*in einer Sportart*) in sports ❷ (*flott*) casually
Sportplatz *m* [playing [*or* sports]] field
Sportveranstaltung *f* sports event
Sportverein *m* sports club
Sportwagen *m* AUTO sports car
Spot <-s, -s> [spɔt, ʃp-] *m* ❶ MEDIA commercial, ad *fam* ❷ ELEK spot
Spott <-[e]s> [ʃpɔt] *m kein pl* mockery
spottbillig ['ʃpɔt·'bɪ·lɪç] *adj* dirt cheap
spotten ['ʃpɔ·tn̩] *vi* to mock; ■**[über jdn/etw] ~** to make fun [of sb/sth]
Spötter(in) <-s, -> ['ʃpœ·tɐ] *m(f)* mocker
spöttisch ['ʃpœ·tɪʃ] *adj* mocking
sprach [ʃpraːx] *imp von* **sprechen**
sprachbegabt *adj* linguistically talented; ■**~ sein** to be good at languages
Sprachcomputer *m* computer with a voice synthesizer
Sprache <-, -n> ['ʃpraː·xə] *f* ❶ (*Kommunikationssystem*) language ❷ *kein pl* (*Sprechweise*) way of speaking ❸ *kein pl* (*das Sprechen*) speech; **etw zur ~ bringen** to bring up *sep* sth; **zur ~ kommen** to come up ▸ WENDUNGEN: **mit der ~ herausrücken** (*fam*) to come out with it; **jdm die ~ verschlagen** to leave sb speechless; **heraus mit der ~!** (*fam*) out with it!
Spracherkennung *f* COMPUT voice recognition
Sprachfehler *m* speech impediment
Sprachführer *m* phrase book
Sprachgefühl *nt kein pl* feel for language
Sprachkenntnisse *pl* language skills *pl*
Sprachkurs *m* language class [*or* course]
sprachlich **I.** *adj* linguistic **II.** *adv* ❶ LING grammatically ❷ (*stilistisch*) stylistically
sprachlos *adj* speechless
Sprachschule *f* language school
Sprachstörung *f* speech disorder
Sprachwissenschaft *f* linguistics + *sing vb*
sprang [ʃpraŋ] *imp von* **springen**
Spray <-s, -s> [ʃpreː, spreː] *m o nt* spray
Spraydose ['ʃpreː-, 'spreː-] *f* aerosol [*or* spray] can
Sprechanlage *f* intercom
sprechen <spricht, sprach, gesprochen> ['ʃprɛ·çn̩] **I.** *vi* ❶ (*reden*) to speak, to talk; **sprich nicht so laut** don't talk so loud; **sprich nicht in diesem Ton mit mir!** don't speak to me like that!; **wovon ~ Sie eigentlich?** what are you talking about?; **sein Benehmen spricht für sich [selbst]** his behavior speaks for itself; **mit sich selbst ~** to talk to oneself; **„hallo, wer spricht denn da?"** "hello, who's speaking?" ❷ (*empfehlen*) ■**für jdn/etw ~** to speak well for sb/sth; ■**gegen jdn/etw ~** to not be in sb's/sth's favor **II.** *vt* ❶ (*können*) to speak; **~ Sie Chinesisch?** can you speak Chinese? ❷ (*sich unterreden*) ■**jdn ~** to speak to sb ▸ WENDUNGEN: **nicht gut auf jdn zu ~ sein** to be on bad terms with sb; **für jdn/niemanden zu ~ sein** to be available for sb/to not be available for anyone; **wir ~ uns noch!** you haven't heard the last of this!
Sprecher(in) <-s, -> *m(f)* ❶ (*Wortführer*) spokesperson ❷ (*Beauftragter*) speaker ❸ RADIO, TV announcer; (*Nachrichtensprecher*) newscaster, anchorperson
Sprechstunde *f* office hours *pl*
Sprechstundenhilfe *f* receptionist
Sprechzimmer *nt* consultation room
spreizen ['ʃprai·tsn̩] *vt* to spread
sprengen[1] ['ʃprɛŋən] **I.** *vt* ❶ (*zur Explosion bringen*) to blow up *sep* ❷ (*bersten lassen*) to burst ❸ (*gewaltsam auflösen*) to break up *sep* **II.** *vi* to blast
sprengen[2] ['ʃprɛŋən] *vt Rasen* to water
Sprengkopf *m* warhead
Sprengkörper *m* explosive device
Sprengkraft *f kein pl* explosive force
Sprengsatz *m* explosive device
Sprengstoff *m* explosive
Sprengstoffanschlag *m* bomb attack
Sprengung <-, -en> *f* blasting
Spreu <-> [ʃprɔy] *f kein pl* AGR chaff
Sprichwort <-wörter> ['ʃprɪç·vɔrt, *pl* -vœrtɐ] *nt* proverb
sprichwörtlich *adj* proverbial
sprießen <spross *o* sprießte, gesprossen> ['ʃpriː·sn̩] *vi sein* BOT to sprout; *Haare* to grow
Springbrunnen *m* fountain
springen[1] <sprang, gesprungen> ['ʃprɪŋən] *vi sein* to shatter; (*einen Sprung bekommen*) to crack
springen[2] <sprang, gesprungen> ['ʃprɪŋən] *vi sein* to jump; (*in Sprüngen*) to leap; **er sprang hin und her** he jumped around ▸ WENDUNGEN: **etw ~ lassen** (*fam*) to fork out sth
Springflut *f* spring tide
Springreiten *nt* show jumping

Sprit <-[e]s> [ʃprɪt] *m kein pl* ❶ (*Benzin*) gas[oline] ❷ (*Schnaps*) booze

Spritze <-, -n> [ˈʃprɪ·tsə] *f* ❶ (*Injektionsspritze*) syringe, needle ❷ (*Injektion*) injection, shot

spritzen [ˈʃprɪ·tsn̩] **I.** *vi* ❶ *haben* (*in Tropfen*) to spray; *Fett* to spit; *Farbe* to splash ❷ *sein* (*im Strahl*) to spurt **II.** *vt haben* ❶ (*im Strahl verteilen*) to squirt ❷ (*bewässern*) to sprinkle ❸ (*injizieren*) to inject ❹ (*mit Bekämpfungsmittel besprühen*) to spray (**gegen** +*akk* against)

Spritzer <-s, -> *m* splash

spritzig [ˈʃprɪ·tsɪç] *adj* ❶ (*prickelnd*) tangy ❷ (*flott*) sparkling

Spritztour *f* spin

spröde [ˈʃprøː·də] *adj* ❶ (*unelastisch*) brittle ❷ (*rau*) rough; *Haar* brittle; *Lippen* chapped ❸ (*abweisend*) aloof

spross[RR], **sproß**[ALT] [ʃprɔs] *imp von* **sprießen**

Spross[RR] <-es, -e>, **Sproß**[ALT] <-sses, -sse> [ʃprɔs] *m* ❶ (*Schössling*) shoot ❷ (*Nachkomme*) offspring

Sprosse <-, -n> [ˈʃprɔ·sə] *f* rung, step

Spruch <-[e]s, Sprüche> [ʃprʊx, *pl* ˈʃprʏ·çə] *m* ❶ (*Ausspruch*) saying; (*Parole*) slogan ❷ (*Richterspruch*) verdict ▸ WENDUNGEN: **Sprüche klopfen** (*fam*) to talk big

Spruchband <-bänder> *nt* banner

Sprudel <-s, -> [ˈʃpruː·dl̩] *m* ❶ (*Mineralwasser*) sparkling mineral water ❷ ÖSTERR (*Erfrischungsgetränk*) soft drink

sprudeln [ˈʃpruː·dl̩n] *vi* ❶ *haben* (*aufschäumen*) to bubble, to foam ❷ *sein* (*heraussprudeln*) to bubble out

Sprühdose *f* aerosol [*or* spray] can

sprühen [ˈʃpryː·ən] **I.** *vt* to spray **II.** *vi* ❶ (*spritzen*) to spray ❷ (*lebhaft sein*) to sparkle; **vor Begeisterung ~** to bubble with excitement

Sprung <-[e]s, Sprünge> [ʃprʊŋ, *pl* ˈʃprʏŋə] *m* ❶ (*Riss*) crack ❷ (*Satz*) leap, jump; **einen ~ machen** to leap, to jump ▸ WENDUNGEN: [**mit etw** *dat*] **keine großen Sprünge machen können** (*fam*) to not be able to live it up [with sth]; **jdm auf die Sprünge helfen** to give sb a helping hand; **auf dem ~ sein** to be in a hurry; **auf einen ~** [**bei jdm**] **vorbeikommen** (*fam*) to pop in [to see sb]

Sprungbrett *nt* ❶ (*ins Wasser*) diving board ❷ (*Turngerät*) springboard

sprunghaft **I.** *adj* ❶ (*in Schüben erfolgend*) rapid; (*abrupt*) sudden ❷ (*unstet*) volatile, fickle **II.** *adv* in leaps and bounds; **~ ansteigen** to rise sharply

Sprungschanze *f* ski jump

Spucke <-> [ˈʃpʊ·kə] *f kein pl* (*fam*) spit ▸ WENDUNGEN: **jdm bleibt die ~ weg** sb is flabbergasted

spucken [ˈʃpʊ·kn̩] **I.** *vi* to spit **II.** *vt* to spit out *sep*

Spuk <-[e]s, -e> [ʃpuːk] *m* spook

spuken [ˈʃpuː·kn̩] *vi impers* to haunt; **hier spukt es** this place is haunted

Spülbecken *nt* sink

Spule <-, -n> [ˈʃpuː·lə] *f* (*Garnrolle*) bobbin; FILM spool; ELEK coil

Spüle <-, -n> [ˈʃpyː·lə] *f* [kitchen] sink

spulen [ˈʃpuː·lən] *vt, vi* to wind [on[to]]

spülen [ˈʃpyː·lən] **I.** *vi* ❶ *Geschirr* to do the dishes ❷ *Toilette* to flush **II.** *vt* ❶ (*abspülen*) to do [the dishes] ❷ (*schwemmen*) to rinse

Spülmaschine *f* dishwasher

Spülmittel *nt* dish soap

Spülstein *m* sink

Spülung <-, -en> *f* ❶ (*Wasserspülung*) flush ❷ (*Haarspülung*) conditioner

Spur <-, -en> [ʃpuːɐ̯] *f* ❶ (*Anzeichen*) trace; **~en der Verwüstung** signs of devastation; **~en hinterlassen** to leave traces; *Schicksal a.* to leave its mark; *Verbrecher a.* to leave clues; **jdm auf der ~ sein** to be on sb's trail; **auf der falschen/richtigen ~ sein** to be on the wrong/right track; **eine heiße ~** a firm lead; **jdm auf die ~ kommen** to be onto sb ❷ (*Fußspuren*) track[s *pl*], trail ❸ (*kleine Menge*) trace; *Knoblauch, etc.* touch; **eine ~ von Mitleid** a hint of pity ❹ (*Fahrstreifen*) lane; **aus der ~ geraten** to swerve out of one's/a lane

spürbar *adj* perceptible, noticeable

spüren [ˈʃpyː·rən] **I.** *vt* ❶ (*körperlich wahrnehmen*) to feel ❷ (*merken*) to sense; **jdn seine Verärgerung ~ lassen** to let sb know that one is annoyed; **etw zu ~ bekommen** to feel the brunt of sth **II.** *vi* ■ **~, dass ...** to sense that ...; ■ **jdn ~ lassen, dass ...** to leave sb with no doubt that ...

Spürhund *m* tracker dog

spurlos **I.** *adj* without a trace *pred* **II.** *adv* without [leaving] a trace; **die Scheidung ging nicht ~ an ihm vorüber** the divorce left its mark on him

Spurt <-s, -s *o* -e> [ʃpʊrt] *m* spurt

spurten [ˈʃpʊr·tn̩] *vi sein* to spurt

Spurweite <-, -n> *f* AUTO track; BAHN gauge

Squash <-> [skvɔʃ] *nt* squash

St. ❶ *Abk von* **Stück** pc[.], pcs[.] *pl* ❷ *Abk von* **Sankt** St., SS *pl*

Staat <-[e]s, -en> [ʃtaːt] *m* ❶ (*Land*) country ❷ (*staatliche Institutionen*) state ❸ *pl* (*USA*) ■ **die ~en** the States

Staatenbund <-bünde> *m* confederation [of states]

staatenlos *adj* stateless

Staatenlose(r) *f(m) dekl wie adj* stateless person

staatlich **I.** *adj* ❶ (*staatseigen*) state-owned; (*staatlich geführt*) state-run; **~e Einrichtungen** government facilities ❷ (*den Staat betreffend*) state *attr,* national ❸ (*aus dem Staatshaushalt stammend*) government *attr,* state *attr* **II.** *adv* **~ anerkannt** state-approved; SCH, UNIV state-accredited; **~ gefördert** government-sponsored; **~ geprüft** [state-]certified

Staatsakt *m* state ceremony

Staatsangehörige(r) *f(m) dekl wie adj* citizen

Staatsangehörigkeit *f* nationality

S

Staatsanwalt, -anwältin *m, f* district attorney
Staatsanwaltschaft <-, -en> *f* office of the district attorney, DA's office
Staatsbeamte(r), -beamtin *m, f* civil servant
Staatsbesuch *m* state visit
Staatsbürger(in) *m(f)* citizen
Staatsbürgerschaft *f* nationality, citizenship; **doppelte ~** dual citizenship
Staatschef(in) [-ʃɛf] *m(f)* head of state
Staatsdienst *m* civil service
Staatseigentum *nt* state [*or* government] property
Staatsexamen *nt* state exam[ination]; (*zur Übernahme in den Staatsdienst*) civil service exam[ination]

In Germany, some university courses of study, such as medicine, education, and law, end with one or two sets of **Staatsexamen** (state examinations), which are administered by university professors and government-approved examiners. The **Staatsexamen** is equivalent to the *Diplom* and the *Magister*.

Staatsfeind(in) *m(f)* enemy of the state
Staatsform *f* form of government
Staatsgebiet *nt* national territory
Staatsgeheimnis *nt* state secret
Staatsgewalt *f kein pl* state [*or* government[al]] authority
Staatshaushalt *m* national budget
Staatskosten *pl* public expenses *pl*
Staatsmann *m* statesman
Staatsminister(in) <-s, -> *m(f)* secretary of state
Staatsoberhaupt *nt* head of state
Staatspräsident(in) *m(f)* president [of a republic]
Staatsstreich *m* coup [d'état]
Staatstheater *nt* national theater
Staatsverschuldung *f* national debt
Stab <-[e]s, Stäbe> [ʃtaːp, *pl* 'ʃtɛː·bə] *m* ❶ (*runde Holzlatte*) rod; (*Gitterstab*) bar ❷ (*Stabhochsprungstab*) pole; (*Staffelstab*) baton ❸ (*beigeordnete Gruppe*) staff; *von Experten* panel
Stäbchen <-s, -> ['ʃtɛːp·çən] *nt* (*Essstäbchen*) chopstick
Stabhochsprung *m* pole vault
stabil [ʃta·'biːl, st-] *adj* ❶ (*strapazierfähig*) sturdy ❷ (*beständig*) *Preise, Zustand, Währung* stable ❸ (*nicht labil*) steady; *Gesundheit* sound
stabilisieren [ʃta·bi·li·'ziː·rən] *vt* to stabilize
Stabilisierung <-, -en> *f* stabilization
Stabilität <-> [ʃta·bi·li·'tɛːt, st-] *f kein pl* stability, solidity
Stabmixer *m* handheld blender
stach [ʃtaːx] *imp von* **stechen**
Stachel <-s, -n> ['ʃta·xl̩] *m* ❶ (*von Rose*) thorn; (*von Kakteen*) spine ❷ (*Giftstachel*) sting
Stachelbeere *f* gooseberry
Stacheldraht *m* barbed wire
stachelig ['ʃta·xə·lɪç] *adj* prickly; *Rosen* thorny; *Kakteen* spiny
Stachelschwein *nt* porcupine
stachlig ['ʃtax·lɪç] *adj s.* **stachelig**
Stadion <-s, Stadien> ['ʃtaː·di̯·ɔn, *pl* 'ʃtaː·di̯·ən] *nt* stadium, bowl
Stadium <-s, Stadien> ['ʃtaː·di̯·ʊm, *pl* 'ʃtaː·di̯·ən] *nt* stage; **im letzten ~** MED at a terminal stage
Stadt <-, Städte> [ʃtat, *pl* 'ʃtɛː·tə] *f* ❶ (*Ort*) town; (*Großstadt*) city; **am Rande der ~** at the edge of town ❷ (*Stadtverwaltung*) city/town council
Stadtbezirk *m* city/town district
Stadtbibliothek *f* city/town library
Städtchen <-s, -> ['ʃtɛːt·çən] *nt dim von* **Stadt** small town
Städtepartnerschaft *f* sister city arrangement
Städter(in) <-s, -> ['ʃtɛː·tɐ] *m(f)* city/town dweller
Stadtgebiet *nt* municipal area
Stadthalle *f* city/town hall
städtisch ['ʃtɛː·tɪʃ] *adj* ❶ (*kommunal*) municipal, city/town *attr* ❷ (*urban*) urban
Stadtkern *m* city/town center
Stadtmauer *f* city/town wall
Stadtmitte *f* downtown
Stadtplan *m* [street] map [of a city/town]
Stadtrand *m* edge of town, outskirts *npl* of the city
Stadtrat *m* city/town council
Stadtrundfahrt *f* sightseeing tour of a city/town
Stadtstaat *m* city-state
Stadtteil *m* district, part of town
Stadtverwaltung *f* city/town council
Stadtviertel *nt* district, part of town
Stadtwerke *pl* public utilities *pl*
Stadtzentrum *nt* city/town center
Staffel <-, -n> ['ʃta·fl̩] *f* ❶ (*Luftwaffeneinheit*) squadron; (*Formation*) echelon ❷ SPORT relay team ❸ TV season
Staffelei <-, -en> [ʃta·fə·'lai] *f* easel
Staffellauf *m* relay [race]
staffeln ['ʃta·fl̩n] *vt* ❶ (*einteilen*) to grade, to graduate ❷ (*formieren*) to stack [up *sep*]
Staffelung, Stafflung <-, -en> *f* ❶ (*Einteilung*) graduation ❷ SPORT *von Startzeiten* staggering
Stagnation <-, -en> [ʃta·gna·'tsi̯oːn, st-] *f* stagnation, stagnancy
stagnieren* [ʃta·'gniː·rən, st-] *vi* to stagnate
stahl [ʃtaːl] *imp von* **stehlen**
Stahl <-[e]s, -e *o* Stähle> [ʃtaːl, *pl* 'ʃtɛː·lə] *m* steel
Stahlbeton *m* reinforced concrete
Stahlhelm *m* steel helmet
Stahlindustrie *f kein pl* steel industry
Stahlwerk *nt* steel mill
stak [ʃtaːk] *imp von* **stecken**

Stall <-[e]s, Ställe> [ʃtal, *pl* ˈʃtɛ·lə] *m* (*Hühnerstall*) coop; (*Kaninchenstall*) hutch; (*Kuhstall*) cowshed, [cow] barn; (*Pferdestall*) stable; (*Schweinestall*) [pig]sty, [pig]pen

Stamm <-[e]s, Stämme> [ʃtam, *pl* ˈʃtɛ·mə] *m* ① (*Baumstamm*) [tree] trunk ② LING stem ③ (*Volksstamm*) tribe

Stammbaum *m* family tree

stammeln [ˈʃta·mln̩] *vi, vt* to stammer

stammen [ˈʃta·mən] *vi* ① (*gebürtig sein*) **aus Berlin ~** to come from Berlin; **woher ~ Sie?** where are you from [originally]? ② (*herrühren*) **aus dem 16. Jahrhundert ~** to date from the 16th century; **diese Unterschrift stammt nicht von mir** this isn't my signature

Stammgast *m* regular [guest]

Stammkneipe *f* usual [*or* favorite] bar

Stammkunde, -kundin *m, f* regular [customer]

Stammlokal *nt* usual [*or* favorite] café/restaurant/bar

Stammplatz *m* usual [*or* favorite] seat

Stammtisch *m* ① (*Tisch für Stammgäste*) table reserved for the regulars ② (*regelmäßiges Zusammentreffen*) [group of] regulars

> Most restaurants and bars have a **Stammtisch** (table reserved for regular customers).

stampfen [ˈʃtamp·fn̩] **I.** *vi* ① *haben* (*aufstampfen*) to stomp [one's foot] ② *sein* ■ **irgendwohin ~** to stomp off somewhere **II.** *vt haben* ① (*feststampfen*) to tamp [*or* pack] [down *sep*] ② (*zerstampfen*) to mash

stand [ʃtant] *imp von* **stehen**

Stand <-[e]s, Stände> [ʃtant, *pl* ˈʃtɛn·də] *m* ① (*das Stehen*) **aus dem ~** from a standing position ② (*Verkaufsstand*) stand ③ (*Anzeige*) reading; **laut ~ des Barometers** according to the barometer [reading] ④ *kein pl* (*Zustand*) state; **der ~ der Forschung** the [current] status of the research; **auf dem neuesten ~ der Technik** state of the art; **der ~ der Dinge** the [present] state of affairs; **sich auf dem neuesten ~ befinden** to be up-to-date ⑤ (*Spielstand*) score ⑥ SCHWEIZ (*Kanton*) canton

Standard <-s, -s> [ˈʃtan·dart, ˈst-] *m* standard

standardisieren* [ʃtan·dar·di·ˈziː·rən, st-] *vt* to standardize

Standbild *nt* statue

Stand-by-Betrieb [stɛndˈbɛɪ-] *m*, **Stand-by-Modus** *m* TECH standby; **im ~** on standby

Ständer <-s, -> [ˈʃtɛn·dɐ] *m* ① (*Gestell*) stand ② (*sl: erigierter Penis*) hard-on

Ständerat *m* SCHWEIZ upper house [*or* chamber] (*of the Swiss parliament*)

Standesamt *nt* justice of the peace['s office]

standesamtlich *adv* **sich ~ trauen lassen** to be married by the Justice of the Peace

Standesbeamte(r), -beamtin *m, f* Justice of the Peace

standesgemäß I. *adj* befitting one's social status *pred* **II.** *adv* **~ heiraten** to marry within one's social class

standhaft I. *adj* steadfast **II.** *adv* steadfastly

stand|halten [ˈʃtant·hal·tn̩] *vi irreg* ■ **[einer S.** *dat*] **~** to hold out against sth

ständig [ˈʃtɛn·dɪç] **I.** *adj* constant, permanent **II.** *adv* constantly, all the time

Standlicht *nt kein pl* parking lights *pl*

Standort <-[e]s, -e> *m* ① (*Unternehmenssitz*) location ② (*Standpunkt*) position

Standpauke *f* (*fam*) **jdm eine ~ halten** to lecture sb

Standpunkt *m* ① (*Meinung*) [point of] view, standpoint; **den ~ vertreten, dass ...** to take the view that ... ② (*Beobachtungsplatz*) vantage point, viewpoint

Standspur *f* (*Teil einer Fahrbahn*) shoulder

Standuhr *f* grandfather clock

Stange <-, -n> [ˈʃtaŋə] *f* ① (*Stab*) pole; (*kürzer*) rod ② (*Metallstange*) bar ③ *Zigaretten* carton ▶ WENDUNGEN: **bei der ~ bleiben** (*fam*) to keep at it; **eine [schöne] ~ Geld kosten** (*fam*) to cost a pretty penny; **von der ~** (*fam*) off the rack

StängelRR <-s, -> [ˈʃtɛŋl̩] *m* stalk, stem

stank [ʃtaŋk] *imp von* **stinken**

stänkern [ˈʃtɛŋ·kɐn] *vi* to stir things up

stanzen [ˈʃtan·tsn̩] *vt* ① (*ausstanzen*) to press ② (*einstanzen*) **Löcher in etw** *akk* **~** to punch holes in sth

Stapel <-s, -> [ˈʃtaː·pl̩] *m* ① (*geschichteter Haufen*) stack; (*unordentlicher Haufen*) pile ② NAUT **vom ~ laufen** to be launched

Stapellauf *m* NAUT launch[ing]

stapeln [ˈʃtaː·pl̩n] **I.** *vt* to stack [up *sep*] **II.** *vr* ■ **sich** *akk* **~** to pile up

stapfen [ˈʃtap·fn̩] *vi sein* ■ **durch etw** *akk* **~** to tramp through sth

Star[1] <-[e]s, -e> [ʃtaːɐ̯] *m* ① (*Vogel*) starling ② MED **[grauer] ~** cataract; **grüner ~** glaucoma

Star[2] <-s, -s> [ʃtaːɐ̯, st-] *m* (*berühmte Person*) star

starb [ʃtarp] *imp von* **sterben**

stark <stärker, stärkste> [ʃtark] **I.** *adj* ① (*kräftig*) strong ② (*mächtig*) powerful, strong ③ (*dick*) thick ④ *Hitze, Kälte* severe; *Regen* heavy; *Strömung* strong; *Sturm* violent ⑤ *Erkältung* bad; *Fieber* high ⑥ *Schlag* hard; *Druck* high ⑦ *Gefühle, Schmerzen* intense; *Bedenken* considerable; *Liebe* deep ⑧ (*leistungsfähig*) powerful ⑨ *Medikamente, Schnaps* strong **II.** *adv* ① (*heftig*) a lot; **~ regnen** to rain heavily ② (*erheblich*) **~ beschädigt** badly damaged; **~ bluten** to bleed profusely; **~ erkältet sein** to have a bad cold; **~ gewürzt** very spicy ③ (*in höherem Maße*) greatly, a lot; **~ vertreten** strongly represented

Stärke <-, -n> [ˈʃtɛr·kə] *f* ① (*Kraft*) strength ② (*Macht, von Motor*) power ③ (*Dicke*) thickness ④ (*zahlenmäßiges Ausmaß*) size; *Armee* strength ⑤ (*Fähigkeit*) **jds ~ sein** to be sb's strong point ⑥ CHEM starch

stärken ['ʃtɛr·kn̩] **I.** *vt* to strengthen **II.** *vi* ■ **~d** fortifying **III.** *vr* ■ **sich** *akk* ~ to fortify oneself
stark|machen[RR] *vr* (*fam*) ■ **sich** *akk* **für jdn/etw** ~ to stand up for sb/sth
Starkstrom *m* high voltage
Stärkung <-, -en> *f kein pl* strengthening
starr [ʃtar] **I.** *adj* ① (*steif*) rigid ② (*erstarrt*) stiff; ~ **vor Angst** paralyzed with fear; ~ **vor Kälte** numb with cold; **~er Blick** [fixed] stare ③ (*rigide*) inflexible; *Haltung* unbending **II.** *adv* ~ **an etw** *dat* **festhalten** to adhere to sth
starren ['ʃta·rən] *vi* ① (*starr blicken*) to stare ② (*bedeckt sein*) **vor Dreck** ~ to be covered with dirt
Starrsinn *m* stubbornness
starrsinnig *adj* stubborn
Start <-s, -s> [ʃtart, start] *m* ① LUFT takeoff; RAUM liftoff, launch ② SPORT start; **am ~ sein** (*von Läufern*) to be on the starting line; (*von Rennwagen*) to be on the starting grid ③ (*Beginn*) start; *Projekt* launch[ing]
Startbahn *f* LUFT runway
startbereit *adj* ① LUFT ready for takeoff *pred* ② SPORT ready to go *pred*
starten ['ʃtar·tn̩, 'st-] **I.** *vi sein* ① LUFT to take off; RAUM to lift off ② SPORT to start; ■ **für etw ~** to compete for [*or* represent] sth ③ (*beginnen*) to start; *Projekt* to be launched **II.** *vt haben* ① *Auto* to start; *Computer* to initialize, to boot [up *sep*]; COMPUT *Programm* to run ② (*beginnen lassen*) to launch, to start
Starterlaubnis *f* takeoff clearance
Starthilfe *f* ① (*Zuschuss*) initial aid ② AUTO **jdm ~ geben** to give sb a jump-start
Startkapital *nt* seed money
startklar *adj s.* **startbereit**
Startlinie *f* starting line
Startschuss[RR] *m* starting signal
Stasi <-> ['ʃtaː·zi] *f kein pl kurz für* **Staatssicherheit(sdienst)** *secret police of the former GDR*
Statik <-> ['ʃtaː·tɪk, 'st-] *f* ① *kein pl* (*Stabilität*) stability ② *kein pl* PHYS statics + *sing vb*
Station <-, -en> [ʃta·'tsi̯oːn] *f* ① (*Haltestelle*) stop ② (*Aufenthalt*) stopover; ~ **machen** to make a stop ③ (*Klinikabteilung*) ward ④ METEO, SCI, RADIO station
stationär [ʃta·tsi̯o·'nɛːɐ̯] **I.** *adj* MED inpatient *attr;* **ein ~er Aufenthalt** a stay in a hospital **II.** *adv* MED in the hospital
stationieren* [ʃta·tsi̯o·'niː·rən] *vt* ① (*installieren*) to station ② (*aufstellen*) to deploy
Stationierung <-, -en> *f* ① (*das Installieren*) stationing, posting ② (*Aufstellung*) deployment
Stationsarzt, -ärztin *m, f* departmental physician
Stationsschwester *f* senior nurse
statisch ['ʃtaː·tɪʃ, 'st-] *adj* ① BAU, ELEK static ② (*keine Entwicklung aufweisend*) in abeyance *pred*
Statist(in) <-en, -en> [ʃta·'tɪst] *m(f)* extra
Statistik <-, -en> [ʃta·'tɪs·tɪk] *f* statistics + *sing vb*
statistisch [ʃta·'tɪs·tɪʃ] **I.** *adj* statistical; **~e Zahlen** statistics **II.** *adv* statistically
Stativ <-s, -e> [ʃta·'tiːf, *pl* ʃta·'tiː·və] *nt* tripod
statt [ʃtat] **I.** *präp +gen* instead of **II.** *konj* (*anstatt*) instead of
stattdessen[RR] *adv* instead
Stätte <-, -n> ['ʃtɛ·tə] *f* place
statt|finden ['ʃtat·fɪn·dn̩] *vi irreg* to take place; *Veranstaltung a.* to be held
stattlich ['ʃtat·lɪç] *adj* ① (*imposant*) imposing ② (*beträchtlich*) considerable
Statue <-, -n> ['ʃtaː·tu̯ə, 'st-] *f* statue
Status <-, -> ['ʃtaː·tʊs, 'st-] *m* status, position
Statussymbol *nt* status symbol
Stau <-[e]s, -e *o* -s> [ʃtau] *m* ① (*Verkehrsstau*) traffic jam ② (*von Wasser etc.*) build-up
Staub <-[e]s, -e *o* Stäube> [ʃtaup, *pl* 'ʃtɔy·bə] *m kein pl* dust; ~ **saugen** to vacuum; ~ **wischen** to dust ▶ WENDUNGEN: **sich aus dem ~[e] machen** (*fam*) to bolt
stauben ['ʃtau·bn̩] *vi impers* **bei etw** *dat* **staubt es sehr** sth makes a lot of dust
staubig ['ʃtau·bɪç] *adj* dusty
staubsaugen <*pp* staubgesaugt>, **Staub saugen** <*pp* Staub gesaugt> *vi, vt* to vacuum
Staubsauger *m* vacuum [cleaner]
Staubtuch *nt* dust cloth
Staudamm *m* dam
Staude <-, -n> ['ʃtau·də] *f* HORT perennial [plant]
Staudensellerie *m kein pl* celery
stauen ['ʃtau·ən] **I.** *vt* to dam [up *sep*] **II.** *vr* ■ **sich** *akk* ~ ① (*sich anstauen*) to collect; (*von Wasser a.*) to rise ② (*Schlange bilden*) *Autos* to pile up
Staumeldung *f* traffic report
staunen ['ʃtau·nən] *vi* to be astonished (**über** +*akk* at); **da staunst du, was?** you weren't expecting that, were you?
Stausee *m* reservoir
Steak <-s, -s> [steːk, ʃteːk] *nt* steak
stechen <sticht, stach, gestochen> ['ʃtɛ·çn̩] **I.** *vi* ① (*pieksen*) to prick ② (*von Insekten*) to sting; *Mücken* to bite ③ (*mit spitzem Gegenstand eindringen*) to stab ④ KARTEN to take the trick **II.** *vt* to stab; (*Insekt*) to sting; *Mücken* to bite **III.** *vr* ■ **sich** *akk* ~ to prick oneself
stechend *adj* ① (*scharf*) sharp ② (*durchdringend*) *Schmerzen* stabbing ③ (*beißend*) *Geruch* acrid
Stechmücke *f* mosquito
Stechuhr *f* time clock
Steckbrief *m* "wanted" poster
Steckdose *f* [wall] socket, electrical outlet
stecken ['ʃtɛ·kn̩] **I.** *vi* <steckte *o geh* stak, gesteckt> ① (*festsitzen*) ■ **in etw** *dat* ~ to be stuck in sth; ~ **bleiben** to get stuck ② (*eingesteckt sein*) ■ **hinter/in/zwischen etw** *dat* ~ to be behind/in/among sth; **den Schlüssel ~ lassen** to leave the key in the

lock ③ (*verborgen sein*) **wo hast du denn gesteckt?** (*fam*) where have you been [hiding]?; **wo steckt er denn bloß wieder?** (*fam*) where did he disappear to again? ④ (*verwickelt sein*) [**tief**] **in der Arbeit ~** to be bogged down in [one's] work; **in einer Krise ~** to be in the middle of a crisis; **in Schwierigkeiten ~** to be in trouble ⑤ (*stocken*) **~ bleiben** *in einer Rede* to falter; *im Verkehr* to get stuck **II.** *vt* <steckte, gesteckt> ① (*schieben*) ■**etw hinter/in/unter etw** *akk* **~** to put sth behind/in[to]/under sth ② (*fam: befördern*) **jdn ins Bett ~** to put sb to bed; **jdn ins Gefängnis ~** to stick sb in prison ③ (*fam: investieren*) **Geld in eine Firma ~** to put money into a company; **viel Zeit in etw** *akk* **~** to devote a lot of time to sth

Stecker <-s, -> *m* plug

Stecknadel *f* pin

Steckrübe *f* rutabaga

Steg <-[e]s, -e> [ʃteːk] *m* ① (*schmale Holzbrücke*) footbridge ② (*Bootssteg*) dock, pier

Stegreif [ˈʃteːk·raif] *m* ■**etw aus dem ~ tun** to do sth off the cuff

Stehcafé *nt* stand-up cafe

stehen <stand, gestanden> [ˈʃteː·ən] **I.** *vi haben o* SÜDD, ÖSTERR, SCHWEIZ *sein* ① (*in aufrechter Stellung sein*) to stand ② (*hingestellt sein*) to be; **~ bleiben** to be left [behind]; **~ lassen** to leave; (*nicht anfassen*) to leave sth where it is; (*vergessen*) to leave sth behind; **alles ~ und liegen lassen** to drop everything ③ (*gedruckt sein*) **in einem Buch ~** to be in a book; **das steht auf Seite sechs** that's on page six; **wo steht das?** where does it say that?; **was steht in seinem Brief?** what does his letter say? ④ (*nicht mehr in Betrieb sein*) to have stopped; (*von Maschine a.*) to be at a standstill; **zum S~ kommen** to come to a stop ⑤ (*anhalten*) **~ bleiben** to stop; **wo steht das Auto?** where did you park the car? ⑥ (*nicht verzehren*) **das Essen ~ lassen** to leave the food untouched ⑦ (*von etw betroffen sein*) **unter Drogen ~** to be under the influence of drugs; **unter Schock ~** to be in a state of shock ⑧ (*passen zu*) **jdm** [**gut**] **~** to suit sb [well]; **das steht dir nicht** it doesn't suit you ⑨ (*einen bestimmten Spielstand haben*) **wie steht das Spiel?** what's the score? ⑩ (*allein lassen*) **jdn einfach ~ lassen** to walk out on sb ⑪ (*fam: fest sein*) *Termin, Abmachung* to be finally settled; (*fertig sein*) to be ready ⑫ (*unterstützen*) ■**zu jdm/etw ~** to stand by sb/sth ⑬ (*eingestellt sein*) **wie ~ Sie dazu?** what is your opinion on this? ⑭ (*unterstützen*) ■**hinter jdm/etw ~** to support sb/sth ⑮ (*anzeigen*) ■**auf etw** *dat* **~** to indicate sth; **die Ampel steht auf Rot** the traffic light is red ⑯ (*sl: gut finden*) ■**auf jdn ~** to be crazy about sb; **stehst du auf Techno?** are you into techno? ▶WENDUNGEN: **jdm steht etw bis hier** (*fam*) sb is sick and tired of sth **II.** *vi impers* ① (*sich darstellen*) **es steht gut/schlecht mit jdm/etw** it's looking good/bad for sb/sth ② (*gesundheitlich*) **es steht gut/schlecht um jdn** sb is in good/bad shape

Stehlampe *f* floor lamp

stehlen <stahl, gestohlen> [ˈʃteː·lən] **I.** *vt, vi* to steal; ■**das S~** stealing ▶WENDUNGEN: **jdm die Zeit ~** to take up sb's time; **das kann mir gestohlen bleiben!** (*fam*) to hell with it! **II.** *vr* to sneak; ■**sich** *akk* **von etw** *dat* **~** to sneak away from sth

Steiermark <-> [ˈʃtaie·mark] *f* ■**die ~** Styria

steif [ʃtaif] *adj* ① (*starr*) stiff; *Begrüßung* formal ② (*erigiert*) erect ▶WENDUNGEN: **etw ~ und fest behaupten** to stubbornly maintain sth

steif|halten *vt irreg* **die Ohren ~** to keep one's chin up

Steigbügel [ˈʃtaik-] *m* stirrup

steigen <stieg, gestiegen> [ˈʃtai·gn̩] **I.** *vi sein* ① (*klettern*) to climb; **durchs Fenster ~** to climb through the window; ■**auf etw** *akk* **~** to climb [up] sth ② (*besteigen*) ■**auf etw** *akk* **~** to get on[to] sth ③ (*einsteigen*) ■**in etw** *akk* **~** to get in[to] sth; **in einen Zug ~** to get on a train ④ (*aussteigen*) ■**aus etw** *dat* **~** to get out of sth; **aus einem Bus ~** to get off a bus ⑤ (*absteigen*) ■**von etw** *dat* **~** to get off [of] sth ⑥ (*sich aufwärts bewegen*) to rise [up]; **das Blut stieg ihm ins Gesicht** the blood rushed to his face; **der Sekt ist mir zu Kopf gestiegen** the sparkling wine has gone to my head ⑦ *Achtung* to rise; *Flut* to swell; *Preis, Wert* to increase; *Temperatur* to climb ⑧ (*sich intensivieren*) to increase; (*von Spannung, Ungeduld, a.*) to mount **II.** *vt sein* ■**Treppen ~** to climb [up] stairs

steigend *adj* ① (*sich erhöhend*) *Preise, Löhne* rising ② (*sich intensivierend*) *Spannung, Ungeduld* mounting

steigern [ˈʃtai·gen] **I.** *vt* ① (*erhöhen*) to increase (**auf** +*akk* to, **um** +*akk* by) ② (*verbessern*) to improve **II.** *vr* ① (*sich intensivieren*) ■**sich** *akk* **~** to increase; *Spannung a.* to mount ② (*seine Leistung verbessern*) ■**sich** *akk* **~** to improve

Steigerung <-, -en> *f* ① (*Erhöhung*) increase (+*gen* in), rise (+*gen* in) ② (*Verbesserung*) improvement (+*gen* to)

Steigung <-, -en> *f* ① (*ansteigende Strecke*) ascent ② (*Anstieg*) slope; **eine ~ von 10 %** a 10% gradient

steil [ʃtail] **I.** *adj* ① (*stark abfallend/ansteigend*) steep ② (*sehr rasch*) rapid **II.** *adv* steeply

Steilhang *m* steep slope

Steilküste *f* bluff

Stein <-[e]s, -e> [ʃtain] *m* ① (*Gesteinsstück*) stone, rock ② (*Obstkern*) stone ▶WENDUNGEN: **bei jdm einen ~ im Brett haben** (*fam*) to be in good with sb; **mir fällt ein ~ vom Herzen!** that's [taken] a load off [of] my mind!; **den ~ ins Rollen bringen** (*fam*) to start the ball rolling; **jdm ~e in den Weg legen** to put obstacles in sb's way

Steinbock *m* ❶ ZOOL ibex ❷ ASTROL Capricorn
Steinbruch *m* quarry
steinhart ['ʃtain·'hart] *adj* rock-hard, [as] hard as [a] rock *pred*
steinig ['ʃtai·nɪç] *adj* stony
steinigen ['ʃtai·nɪ·gn̩] *vt* to stone
Steinmetz(in) <-en, -en> ['ʃtain·mɛts] *m(f)* stonemason
Steinobst *nt* stone fruit[s *pl*]
Steinpilz *m* porcino
steinreich ['ʃtain·'raiç] *adj* filthy rich
Steinschlag *m* falling rocks *pl*
Steinzeit *f kein pl* ■ **die ~** the Stone Age
Steißbein *nt* ANAT coccyx
Stelle <-, -n> ['ʃtɛ·lə] *f* ❶ (*Platz*) place; (*genauer*) spot; **an dieser ~** in this place, here; (*fig*) at this point; **auf der ~ laufen** to run in place; **sich nicht von der ~ rühren** to not move [an inch]; **an anderer ~** elsewhere; **an erster/zweiter ~** in the first/second place ❷ (*umrissener Bereich*) spot; **fettige/rostige ~** grease/rust spot ❸ (*Abschnitt im Buch*) passage ❹ MATH digit; **eine Zahl mit sieben ~n** a seven-digit number ❺ (*Posten*) place; **an jds ~ treten** to take sb's place; **an ~ von etw** *dat* instead of sth; **an deiner ~ würde ich ...** if I were you, I would ... ❻ (*Arbeitsplatz*) job; **eine freie ~** a vacancy ▶ WENDUNGEN: **zur ~ sein** to be on hand; **auf der ~ treten** to not make any progress; **auf der ~** at once; **er war auf der ~ tot** he died instantly
stellen ['ʃtɛ·lən] **I.** *vt* ❶ (*hin-, abstellen*) to put; **das Auto in die Garage ~** to put the car in the garage; **den Wein kalt ~** to chill the wine ❷ (*aufrecht hinstellen*) to stand [up *sep*] ❸ (*einstellen*) **die Heizung höher/kleiner ~** to turn up/down *sep* the heat; **den Fernseher lauter/leiser ~** to turn the television up/down; **den Wecker auf 7 Uhr ~** to set the alarm for 7 o'clock ❹ (*zur Aufgabe zwingen*) ■ **jdn ~** to hunt down *sep* sb ❺ (*vorgeben*) *Aufgabe* to set; *Bedingungen* to stipulate; **[jdm] eine Frage ~** to ask [sb] a question ❻ (*richten*) **einen Antrag ~** to put forward a motion; **Forderungen ~** to make demands ❼ (*konfrontieren*) ■ **jdn vor etw** *akk* **~** to confront sb with sth ❽ (*zur Verfügung stellen*) ■ **[jdm] etw ~** to provide [sb with] sth ▶ WENDUNGEN: **auf sich** *akk* **selbst gestellt sein** to have to fend for oneself **II.** *vr* ❶ (*sich hinstellen*) ■ **sich** *akk* **~** to take up position ❷ (*entgegentreten*) ■ **sich** *akk* **jdm/einer S. ~** to face sb/sth ❸ (*sich melden*) **sich** *akk* **der Polizei ~** to turn oneself in to the police ❹ (*etw vorgeben*) **sich** *akk* **dumm/ahnungslos ~** to play dumb/innocent; **sich** *akk* **tot ~** to pretend to be dead
Stellenangebot *nt* job offer; **„~e"** "job market", "help wanted"
Stellenanzeige *f* job advertisement [*or fam* ad]
Stellenbeschreibung *f* job description
Stellengesuch *nt* "employment wanted" advertisement
Stellenvermittlung *f* ❶ (*das Vermitteln*) job placement ❷ (*Einrichtung*) employment agency
stellenweise *adv* in [some] places
Stellplatz *m* parking space
Stellung <-, -en> *f* ❶ (*Arbeitsplatz*) job ❷ (*Rang, Körperhaltung, Position*) position; **in ~ gehen** to take up position; **die ~ halten** to hold the fort ❸ (*Standpunkt*) **~ zu etw** *dat* **beziehen** to take a stand on sth; **~ zu etw** *dat* **nehmen** to express an opinion about/on sth
Stellungnahme <-, -n> *f* statement; **eine ~ [zu etw** *dat*] **abgeben** to make a statement [about sth]
stellvertretend I. *adj attr* (*vorübergehend*) acting *attr;* (*an zweiter Stelle stehen*) deputy *attr* **II.** *adv* ■ **~ für jdn** on sb's behalf
Stellvertreter(in) *m(f)* deputy, substitute
Stellvertretung *f* (*Stellvertreter*) deputy, substitute; **die ~ von jdm übernehmen** to stand in for sb
Stemmeisen *nt* chisel
stemmen ['ʃtɛ·mən] **I.** *vt* ❶ (*hochdrücken*) to lift ❷ (*stützen*) **die Arme in die Seiten ~** to put one's hands on one's hips **II.** *vr* ■ **sich** *akk* **gegen etw** *akk* **~** to brace oneself against sth
Stempel <-s, -> ['ʃtɛm·pl̩] *m* ❶ (*Gummistempel*) [rubber] stamp ❷ (*Stempelabdruck*) stamp ❸ (*Punzierung*) hallmark
stempeln ['ʃtɛm·pl̩n] *vt, vi* to stamp
Stengel[ALT] <-s, -> ['ʃtɛŋl̩] *m s.* **Stängel**
Steno <-> ['ʃteː·no] *f kein pl* (*fam*) *Abk von* **Stenografie**
Stenografie <-, -n> [ʃte·no·gra·'fiː] *f* shorthand, stenography
Stenogramm <-gramme> [ʃte·no·'gram] *nt* text written in shorthand
Stenographie <-, -n> [ʃte·no·gra·'fiː] *f s.* **Stenografie**
Stenotypist(in) <-en, -en> [ʃte·no·ty·'pɪst] *m(f)* stenographer
Steppdecke *f* comforter
Steppe <-, -n> ['ʃtɛ·pə] *f* steppe
Stepptanz[RR], **Steptanz**[ALT] ['ʃt-, 'st-] *m* tap dance
Sterbebett *nt* deathbed
Sterbehilfe *f kein pl* euthanasia
sterben <starb, gestorben> ['ʃtɛr·bn̩] *vi sein* to die (**an** +*dat* of); **daran wirst du [schon] nicht ~!** (*hum fam*) it won't kill you!; **ich sterbe vor Durst** (*fig*) I'm dying of thirst ▶ WENDUNGEN: **für jdn ist jd/etw gestorben** sb is finished with sb/sth; **er ist für mich gestorben** I'm finished with him
Sterberate *f* death rate
Sterbeurkunde *f* death certificate
sterblich ['ʃtɛrp·lɪç] *adj* (*geh*) mortal
Sterblichkeit <-> *f kein pl* mortality
Sterblichkeitsrate *f* mortality rate
Stereo <-> ['ʃteː·reo, 'st-] *nt kein pl* stereo
Stereoanlage *f* stereo [system]
stereotyp [ʃte·reo·'tyːp, st-] **I.** *adj* stereotype *attr,* stereotypical **II.** *adv* stereotypically

S

Stereotyp <-s, -e> [ʃte·reo·ˈtyːp, st-] *nt* stereotype

steril [ʃte·ˈriːl, st-] *adj* ❶ (*keimfrei*) sterile ❷ (*unfruchtbar*) infertile

Sterilisation <-, -en> [ʃte·ri·li·za·ˈtsi̯oːn, st-] *f* sterilization

sterilisieren* [ʃte·ri·li·ˈziː·rən] *vt* to sterilize; ■ **sich** *akk*~ **lassen** to get sterilized

Sterilität <-> [ʃte·ri·li·ˈtɛːt, st-] *f kein pl* ❶ (*Keimfreiheit*) sterility ❷ (*Unfruchtbarkeit*) infertility

Stern <-[e]s, -e> [ʃtɛrn] *m* star ▶ WENDUNGEN: **in den ~en stehen** to be written in the stars

Sternbild *nt* constellation

Sternenhimmel *m* starry sky

sternklar [ˈʃtɛrn·klaːɐ̯] *adj* starlit, starry

Sternschnuppe <-, -n> *f* shooting star

Sternwarte *f* observatory

Sternzeichen *nt* [star] sign

Stethoskop <-s, -e> [ʃte·to·ˈskoːp] *nt* stethoscope

stetig [ˈʃteː·tɪç] *adj* steady

stets [ʃteːts] *adv* at all times

Steuer¹ <-s, -> [ˈʃtɔy·ɐ] *nt* ❶ AUTO [steering] wheel; **hinterm ~ sitzen** (*fam*) to be behind the wheel ❷ NAUT helm; **am ~ stehen** to be at the helm

Steuer² <-, -n> [ˈʃtɔy·ɐ] *f* ÖKON tax; **etw von der ~ absetzen** to deduct sth from one's taxes

steuerbegünstigt *adj* tax-deductible

Steuerbelastung *meist sing f* tax burden

Steuerberater(in) *m(f)* tax consultant

Steuerbescheid *m* tax assessment

Steuerbetrug *m kein pl* tax evasion

Steuerbord [ˈʃtɔy·ɐ·bɔrt] *nt kein pl* starboard

Steuererhöhung *f* tax increase

Steuererklärung *f* tax return

Steuerermäßigung *f* FIN tax reduction

steuerfrei **I.** *adj* tax-exempt *attr,* exempt from tax *pred* **II.** *adv* without paying tax

Steuergelder *pl* taxes *pl,* tax revenue[s *pl*]

Steuerhinterziehung *f* tax evasion

Steuerklasse *f* tax category

steuerlich **I.** *adj* tax *attr* **II.** *adv* **~ absetzbar** tax-deductible; **etw ~ berücksichtigen** to deduct sth from one's taxes; **~ vorteilhaft sein** to carry tax benefits

Steuermann <-männer *o* -leute> [ˈʃtɔy·ɐ·man, *pl* -mɛ·nɐ, -lɔy·tə] *m* NAUT helmsman

steuern [ˈʃtɔy·ɐn] **I.** *vt* ❶ (*lenken*) to steer ❷ LUFT to fly ❸ (*regulieren*) to control **II.** *vi* AUTO to drive

steuerpflichtig *adj* ❶ (*zu versteuern*) taxable ❷ (*zur Steuerzahlung verpflichtet*) obligated to pay tax *pred*

Steuerprüfung *f* tax audit

Steuerrad *nt* wheel, helm

Steuerreform *f* tax reform

Steuerruder *nt* rudder

Steuersatz *m* tax rate

Steuersenkung *f* tax cut

Steuerung <-> *f kein pl* (*Regulierung*) control; (*das Lenken*) steering *no art*

Steuervergünstigung *f* tax concession

Steuerzahler(in) *m(f)* taxpayer

Steward <-s, -s> [ˈstjuː·ɐt, ˈʃt(j)uː·ɐt] *m* steward

Stewardess^RR <-, -en>, **Stewardeß**^ALT <-, -ssen> [ˈstjuː·ɐ·dɛs, stjuː·ɐ·ˈdɛs] *f* stewardess

Stich <-[e]s, -e> [ʃtɪç] *m* ❶ (*Messerstich*) stab; (*Stichwunde*) stab wound ❷ (*Insektenstich*) sting; (*Mückenstich*) bite ❸ (*stechender Schmerz*) stabbing pain ❹ (*Nadelstich*) stitch ❺ KUNST engraving ❻ (*Farbschattierung*) **ein ~ ins Rote** a tinge of red ▶ WENDUNGEN: **einen ~ haben** (*fam: verdorben sein*) to be spoiled; (*übergeschnappt sein*) to be nuts; **jdn im ~ lassen** to leave sb in the lurch [*or sl* hanging]

Stichelei <-, -en> [ʃtɪ·çə·ˈlai] *f* ❶ (*das Sticheln*) needling ❷ (*Bemerkung*) gibe, dig

sticheln [ˈʃtɪ·çl̩n] *vi* to make nasty remarks

stichhaltig *adj,* **stichhältig** *adj* ÖSTERR *Alibi* solid; *Argumentation* sound; *Beweis* conclusive; ■ **[nicht] ~ sein** to [not] hold water

Stichprobe *f* spot check; **~n machen** to carry out a spot check

Stichtag *m* deadline

Stichwahl *f* runoff [election]

Stichwort [ˈʃtɪç·vɔrt] *nt* ❶ (*Haupteintrag*) headword ❷ *meist pl* (*Wort als Gedächtnisstütze*) cue; (*Schlüsselwort*) keyword; **jdm das ~ geben** to give sb the cue; THEAT to cue in *sep* sb

stichwortartig *adv* briefly

Stichwunde *f* knife wound

sticken [ˈʃtɪ·kn̩] *vt, vi* to embroider

Stickerei <-, -en> [ʃtɪ·kə·ˈrai] *f* embroidery

stickig [ˈʃtɪ·kɪç] *adj* stuffy; *Luft* stale

Stickstoff [ˈʃtɪk·ʃtɔf] *m kein pl* nitrogen

Stiefbruder [ˈʃtiːf-] *m* stepbrother

Stiefel <-s, -> [ˈʃtiː·fl̩] *m* boot

Stiefelette <-, -n> [ʃtiː·fə·ˈlɛ·tə] *f* ankle boot

Stiefeltern *pl* stepparents *pl*

Stiefkind *nt* stepchild

Stiefmutter *f* stepmother

Stiefmütterchen *nt* BOT pansy

stiefmütterlich *adv* **jdn/etw ~ behandeln** to pay little attention to sb/sth

Stiefschwester *f* stepsister

Stiefsohn *m* stepson

Stieftochter *f* stepdaughter

Stiefvater *m* stepfather

stieg [ʃtiːk] *imp von* **steigen**

Stiel <-[e]s, -e> [ʃtiːl] *m* ❶ (*Handgriff*) handle; (*Besenstiel*) broomstick ❷ (*Blumenstiel*) stem, stalk

Stier <-[e]s, -e> [ʃtiːɐ̯] *m* ❶ (*Bulle*) bull ❷ ASTROL Taurus

stieren [ˈʃtiː·rən] *vi* to stare

Stierkampf *m* bullfight

stieß [ʃtiːs] *imp von* **stoßen**

Stift <-[e]s, -e> [ʃtɪft] *m* ❶ (*Stahlstift*) [steel] pin [*or* tack] ❷ (*zum Schreiben*) pen, pencil

stiften [ˈʃtɪf·tn̩] *vt* ❶ (*spenden*) to donate ❷ (*verursachen*) to cause; **Unruhe ~** to create

S

unrest

Stifter(in) <-s, -> ['ʃtɪf·tɐ] *m(f)* ❶ (*Spender*) don[at]or ❷ (*Gründer*) founder

Stịftung <-, -en> *f* ❶ (*Organisation*) foundation ❷ (*Schenkung*) donation

Stigmatisierung [ʃtɪg·ma·ti·'zi:·rʊŋ] *f* SOZIOL (*geh*) stigmatization

Sti̱l <-[e]s, -e> [ʃti:l, st-] *m* (*Ausdrucksform*) style; **das ist nicht unser ~** that's not the way we do things [around here] ▶ WENDUNGEN: **im <u>großen</u> ~** on a grand scale

Sti̱lbruch *m* inconsistency in style; KUNST, LING stylistic incongruity

sti̱lecht **I.** *adj* period *usu attr* **II.** *adv* in period style

stilisieren* [ʃti·li·'zi:·rən, st-] *vt* to stylize

stilịstisch **I.** *adj* stylistic **II.** *adv* stylistically

still [ʃtɪl] *adj* ❶ (*ruhig*) quiet, peaceful; **sei ~!** be quiet!; **in einer ~en Stunde** in a quiet moment ❷ (*geräuschlos*) silent; **es wurde ~ im Raum** the room went still ❸ (*verschwiegen*) *Vorwurf* silent ❹ (*unbewegt*) still; **etw ~ halten** to keep sth still ❺ (*heimlich*) **im S~en** in secret; **im S~en hoffen** to secretly hope ▶ WENDUNGEN: **<u>es</u> ist um ihn ~ geworden** you don't hear much about him anymore

Stille <-> ['ʃtɪ·lə] *f kein pl* ❶ (*Ruhe*) quiet; (*ohne Geräusch*) silence; **in aller ~** quietly ❷ (*Abgeschiedenheit*) peace

Stịlleben^ALT *nt s.* **Stillleben**

stịllegen^ALT <stịllgelegt> *vt s.* **stilllegen**

Stịllegung^ALT <-, -en> *f s.* **Stilllegung**

stillen ['ʃtɪ·lən] *vt* ❶ (*säugen*) to breastfeed ❷ (*befriedigen*) to satisfy; **den Durst ~** to quench sb's thirst ❸ (*aufhören lassen*) to stop; *Blutverlust* to stanch

stịll|halten *vi irreg* to keep still, to not move

Stillleben^RR ['ʃtɪl·le:bn̩] *nt* still life

stịll|legen^RR <stịllgelegt> *vt* to close [down *sep*]; ■**stillgelegt** closed [down]

Stịlllegung^RR <-, -en> *f* closure

sti̱llos *adj* lacking any definite style *pred*

Stịllschweigen *nt* silence; **über etw** *akk* **~ bewahren** to keep quiet about sth

stillschweigend ['ʃtɪl·ʃvai·gn̩t] **I.** *adj* tacit **II.** *adv* tacitly; **etw ~ billigen** to give sth one's tacit approval

stịll|sitzen *vi irreg sein o haben* to sit still

Stịllstand *m kein pl* standstill; **zum ~ kommen** (*zum Erliegen*) to come to a standstill; (*aufhören*) to stop

stịll|stehen *vi irreg sein o haben* ❶ (*außer Betrieb sein*) to stand idle; *Verkehr, Verhandlungen* to be at a standstill ❷ (*a. fig: sich nicht bewegen*) to stand still

Sti̱lmöbel *nt meist pl* period furniture

sti̱lvoll *adj* stylish

Stịmmband *nt meist pl* vocal cord

stịmmberechtigt *adj* entitled to vote *pred*

Stịmmbruch *m* **er war mit 12 im ~** his voice broke when he was 12

Stimme <-, -n> ['ʃtɪ·mə] *f* ❶ (*Art des Sprechens*) voice ❷ POL vote; **sich** *akk* **der ~ enthalten** to abstain ❸ (*Meinungsäußerung*) voice

stimmen¹ ['ʃtɪ·mən] *vi* ❶ (*zutreffen*) to be right; ■**es stimmt, dass ...** it is true that ...; **stimmt!** right! ❷ (*korrekt sein*) to be correct; **diese Rechnung stimmt nicht** there's something wrong with this bill; **da stimmt was nicht** there's something wrong here; **stimmt so** keep the change

stimmen² ['ʃtɪ·mən] *vt* MUS to tune

Stịmmengleichheit *f* tie

Stịmmenmehrheit *f* majority of votes; **jdn durch ~ besiegen** to outvote sb

Stịmmenthaltung *f* abstention

Stịmmgabel *f* tuning fork

stịmmhaft *adj* LING voiced

stịmmlos *adj* LING voiceless

Stịmmrecht *nt* right to vote

Stimmung <-, -en> *f* ❶ (*Gemütslage*) mood; ■**in der ~ sein** to be in the mood (**zu** +*dat* for); **in ~ kommen** to get in the [right] mood ❷ (*Atmosphäre*) atmosphere ❸ (*öffentliche Einstellung*) public opinion; **~ für/gegen etw** *akk* **machen** to stir up [public] opinion for/against sth

Stịmmzettel *m* ballot

stimulieren* [ʃti·mu·'li:·rən] *vt* to stimulate

stinken <stạnk, gestụnken> ['ʃtɪŋ·kn̩] *vi* ❶ (*unangenehm riechen*) to stink (**nach** +*dat* of) ❷ (*verdächtig sein*) **die Sache stinkt** the whole business stinks ❸ (*sl: zuwider sein*) ■**jdm stinkt etw** sb is sick and tired of sth

stinkfaul ['ʃtɪŋk·'faul] *adj* lazy as hell *pred fam*

stịnklangweilig *adj* boring as hell *pred fam*

stinksauer ['ʃtɪŋk·'zau·ɐ] *adj* **~ auf jdn sein** to be pissed off at/with sb

Stịnktier *nt* skunk

Stinkwut ['ʃtɪŋk·'vu:t] *f* rage; ■**eine ~ haben** to seethe with rage; ■**eine ~ auf jdn haben** to be furious with sb

Stipendiat(in) <-en, -en> [ʃti·pɛn·'di̯a:t] *m(f)* scholarship recipient

Stipendium <-s, -dien> [ʃti·'pɛn·di̯·ʊm, *pl* -di̯·ən] *nt* scholarship

Stippvisite ['ʃtɪp·vi·'zi:·tə] *f* (*fam*) quick visit; **bei jdm eine ~ machen** to pop by

Stirn <-, -en> [ʃtɪrn] *f* forehead; **die ~ runzeln** to frown ▶ WENDUNGEN: **jdm die ~ <u>bieten</u>** to stand up to sb

Stịrnband <-bänder> *nt* headband

Stịrnhöhle *f* sinus

Stịrnhöhlenentzündung *f* sinus infection

stö̱bern ['ʃtø:·bɐn] *vi* ■**in etw** *dat* **~** to rummage in sth

Stock¹ <-[e]s, Stöcke> [ʃtɔk, *pl* 'ʃtœ·kə] *m* ❶ (*Holzstange*) stick ❷ (*Topfpflanze*) plant

Stock² <-[e]s, -> [ʃtɔk] *m* floor, story; **der 1. ~** the second floor

stockbesoffen ['ʃtɔk·bə·'zɔ·fn̩] *adj* (*fam*) plastered *fam*

stockdunkel ['ʃtɔk·'dʊŋ·kl̩] *adj* pitch-dark

Stọ̈ckelschuh *m* high-heeled shoe

stocken ['ʃtɔ·kn̩] *vi* ❶ (*innehalten*) to falter

② (*zeitweilig stillstehen*) to come to a halt
stockend *adj* ① *Unterhaltung* flagging ② *Verkehr* stop-and-go
stocksauer [ˈʃtɔk·ˈzau·ɐ] *adj* (*fam*) ■ **~ sein** to be pissed off
Stockwerk *nt s.* **Stock²**
Stoff <-[e]s, -e> [ʃtɔf] *m* ① (*Textil*) material, fabric ② (*Material*) material ③ CHEM substance ④ (*thematisches Material*) material ⑤ (*Lehrstoff*) subject material ⑥ *kein pl* (*sl: Rauschgift*) dope
Stofftier *nt* stuffed animal
Stoffwechsel [-vɛksl] *m* metabolism
stöhnen [ˈʃtøː·nən] *vi* to moan; (*vor Schmerz*) to groan
Stollen <-s, -> [ˈʃtɔ·lən] *m* ① BERGB tunnel ② KOCHK stollen (*a sweet Christmas bread-like cake made with dried fruit, often filled with marzipan*)
stolpern [ˈʃtɔl·pɐn] *vi sein* to trip, to stumble
stolz [ʃtɔlts] *adj* proud
Stolz <-es> [ʃtɔlts] *m kein pl* pride; **jds ganzer ~ sein** to be sb's pride and joy
Stop^ALT <-s, -s> [ʃtɔp] *m s.* **Stopp**
stopfen [ˈʃtɔp·fn̩] **I.** *vt* ① (*hineinzwängen*) to stuff; *Loch* to fill ② (*mit Nadel und Faden*) to darn **II.** *vi* (*die Verdauung hemmen*) to cause constipation
Stopp^RR <-s, -s> [ʃtɔp] *m* stop; **ohne ~** without stopping
Stoppel <-, -n> [ˈʃtɔ·pl̩] *f meist pl* stubble
Stoppelbart *m* stubbly beard
stoppen [ˈʃtɔ·pn̩] *vt, vi* ① (*anhalten*) to stop ② (*Zeit nehmen*) to time
Stoppschild <-schilder> *nt* stop sign
Stoppuhr *f* stopwatch
Stöpsel <-s, -> [ˈʃtœp·sl̩] *m* stopper; (*für Badewanne*) plug
Storch <-[e]s, Störche> [ʃtɔrç, *pl* ˈʃtœr·çə] *m* stork
stören [ˈʃtøː·rən] **I.** *vt* ① (*unterbrechen*) to disturb; **jdn bei der Arbeit ~** to disturb sb while he/she is working; **entschuldigen Sie, wenn ich Sie störe** I'm sorry to bother you ② (*beeinträchtigen*) **jds Pläne ~** to interfere with sb's plans ③ (*unangenehm berühren*) **stört es Sie, wenn ich ...?** do you mind if I ...?; **das stört mich nicht** that doesn't bother me; **das stört mich!** that's getting on my nerves [*or* annoying [me]]! **II.** *vi* ① (*bei etw unterbrechen*) to disturb; **ich will nicht ~, aber ...** I'm sorry to bother you, but ... ② (*lästig sein*) to be irritating **III.** *vr* **er stört sich aber auch an allem** he lets absolutely everything bother him
stornieren* [ʃtɔr·ˈniː·rən] *vt* to cancel
Stornierung <-, -en> *f* ① HANDEL *eines Auftrags* cancellation ② FIN *einer Buchung* reversal, cancellation of an entry
störrisch [ˈʃtœ·rɪʃ] **I.** *adj* obstinate, stubborn **II.** *adv* obstinately, stubbornly
Störung <-, -en> *f* ① (*Unterbrechung*) interruption, disruption, disturbance ② (*Störsignale*) interference ③ (*technischer Defekt*) fault; (*Fehlfunktion*) malfunction
Störungsstelle *f* TELEK customer hotline
Story <-, -s> [ˈstoː·ri, ˈstɔ·ri] *f* story
Stoß <-es, Stöße> [ʃtoːs, *pl* ˈʃtøː·sə] *m* ① (*Schubs*) push; (*mit dem Ellbogen*) dig; (*mit der Faust*) punch; (*mit dem Fuß*) kick; **jdm einen ~ versetzen** to give sb a push etc. ② *einer Waffe* thrust ③ (*Erschütterung*) bump ④ (*Stapel*) pile, stack ► WENDUNGEN: **sich** *dat* **einen ~ geben** to pull oneself together
Stoßdämpfer *m* shock absorber
stoßen <stößt, stieß, gestoßen> [ˈʃtoː·sn̩] **I.** *vt* (*schubsen*) to push, to shove (**aus** +*dat* out of, **von** +*dat* off) **II.** *vr* ■ **sich** *akk* [**an etw** *dat*] **~** to hurt oneself [on sth]; [**sich** *dat*] **den Kopf ~** to bang one's head **III.** *vi* ① *sein* (*aufschlagen*) ■ **an/gegen etw** *akk* **~** to bump against/into sth; **mit dem Kopf an etw** *akk* **~** to bang one's head on sth ② *sein* (*grenzen*) ■ **an etw** *akk* **~** to border on sth ③ *sein* (*treffen*) ■ **zu jdm ~** to join sb ④ *sein* (*finden*) ■ **auf etw** *akk* **~** to find sth; **auf Erdöl ~** to strike oil; **ich stieß auf ein interessantes Gebäude** I came across an interesting building ⑤ *sein* (*konfrontiert werden*) **auf Ablehnung/Zustimmung ~** to meet with disapproval/approval ⑥ SCHWEIZ (*schieben*) to push, to shove
Stoßstange *f* bumper
stoßweise *adv* ① (*ruckartig*) in fits and starts ② (*in Stapeln*) in piles
Stoßzahn *m* tusk
Stoßzeit *f* ① (*Hauptverkehrszeit*) rush hour ② (*Hauptgeschäftszeit*) peak business hour[s *pl*], busy time of day
stottern [ˈʃtɔ·tɐn] *vi* ① (*stockend sprechen*) to stutter ② *Motor* to splutter
Stövchen <-s, -> [ˈʃtøːf·çən] *nt* [teapot/coffee pot] warmer
Str. *Abk von* **Straße** St.
Strafanstalt *f* penal institution
Strafanzeige *f* [criminal] charge
Strafarbeit *f* extra work (*assigned as punishment*)
Strafbank *f* SPORT penalty box
strafbar *adj* punishable [by law]; **sich** *akk* **~ machen** to make oneself liable to prosecution
Strafbefehl *m* penalty order (*requested by the office of the district attorney*)
Strafe <-, -n> [ˈʃtraː·fə] *f* ① (*Bestrafung*) punishment; JUR penalty; **zur ~** as a punishment ② (*Geldstrafe*) fine; (*Haftstrafe*) sentence; **seine ~ absitzen** to serve [out] one's sentence
strafen [ˈʃtraː·fn̩] *vt* ① (*bestrafen*) to punish; **mit dieser Arbeit/Frau bin ich wirklich gestraft** this work/woman is a real pain [in the neck] ② (*behandeln*) **jdn mit Verachtung ~** to treat sb with contempt
Straferlass^RR *m* remission of a sentence
straff [ʃtraf] **I.** *adj* ① (*fest gespannt*) taut, tight ② (*nicht schlaff*) firm **II.** *adv* tightly
straffällig *adj* JUR punishable, criminal *attr;* **ein**

~ er Jugendlicher a young offender; ■ **~ werden** to become a criminal
straffen [ˈʃtra·fn̩] *vt* ❶ (*straff anziehen*) to tighten ❷ (*kürzen*) *Artikel, Text* to shorten; (*präziser machen*) to tighten up *sep*
straffrei *adj* unpunished; **~ bleiben** to go unpunished
Straffreiheit *f kein pl* immunity from criminal prosecution
Strafgefangene(r) *f(m) dekl wie adj* prisoner
Strafgesetzbuch *nt* penal code
sträflich [ˈʃtrɛːf·lɪç] *adj* criminal *attr*
Sträfling <-s, -e> [ˈʃtrɛːf·lɪŋ] *m* prisoner
straflos *adj* unpunished
Strafmaß *nt* sentence
strafmildernd *adj* mitigating
strafmündig *adj* of the age of criminal responsibility
Strafporto *nt* postage due
Strafprozess[RR] *m* trial
Strafpunkt *m* SPORT penalty point
Strafraum *m* FBALL penalty area [*or* box]
Strafrecht *nt* criminal law
Strafstoß *m* SPORT penalty [kick]
Straftat *f* [criminal] offense
Straftäter(in) *m(f)* criminal, offender
Strafverfahren *nt* criminal proceedings *pl*
Strafversetzung *f* transfer for disciplinary reasons
Strafverteidiger(in) *m(f)* defense attorney
Strafvollzug *m* penal system
Strafvollzugsanstalt *f* penal institution
Strafzettel *m* ticket
Strahl <-[e]s, -en> [ʃtraːl] *m* ❶ (*Lichtstrahl*) ray [of light]; (*Sonnenstrahl*) sunbeam; (*konzentriertes Licht*) beam ❷ (*Wasserstrahl*) jet
strahlen [ˈʃtraː·lən] *vi* ❶ (*leuchten*) to shine ❷ (*Radioaktivität abgeben*) to be radioactive ❸ (*ein freudiges Gesicht machen*) to beam (**vor** +*dat* with) ❹ (*glänzen*) to shine
Strahlenbelastung *f* radiation, radioactive contamination
Strahlentherapie *f* radiotherapy
strahlenverseucht *adj* contaminated with radioactivity *pred*
Strahler <-s, -> *m* (*Leuchte*) spotlight, spot *fam*
Strahlung <-, -en> *f* PHYS radiation; **radioaktive ~** radioactivity
Strähnchen <-s, -> *nt meist pl* streaks *pl*; **~ machen lassen** to have highlights put in
Strähne <-, -n> [ˈʃtrɛː·nə] *f* strand; **eine weiße ~** a white streak
strähnig [ˈʃtrɛː·nɪç] *adj* straggly
stramm [ʃtram] **I.** *adj* ❶ (*straff*) tight; **etw ~ ziehen** to tighten sth ❷ (*kräftig*) strong, brawny, strapping *hum fam* ❸ (*drall*) taut; *Beine* sturdy ❹ *Marsch* brisk **II.** *adv* ❶ (*eng anliegend*) tightly ❷ (*fam: intensiv*) intensively; **~ marschieren** to march briskly
stramm|stehen *vi irreg* to stand at attention
strampeln [ˈʃtram·pl̩n] *vi* ❶ *haben* (*heftig treten*) to kick around ❷ *haben* (*fam: sich abmühen*) to struggle
Strand <-[e]s, Strände> [ʃtrant, *pl* ˈʃtrɛn·də] *m* beach
stranden [ˈʃtran·dn̩] *vi sein* (*auf Grund laufen*) to run aground ▶ WENDUNGEN: **irgendwo gestrandet sein** to be stranded somewhere
Strandgut *nt kein pl* flotsam and jetsam + *sing vb*
Strandkorb *m* beach chair

> **Strandkörbe** are a common sight on the beaches along the North Sea and Baltic Sea coasts. They are large, sturdy, two-seater chairs made of wickerwork and are designed with a hood and sides to protect the occupants from the harsh sunshine as well as the cold wind and rain, which are fairly common.

Strang <-[e]s, Stränge> [ʃtraŋ, *pl* ˈʃtrɛŋə] *m* ❶ (*dicker Strick*) rope ❷ (*Bündel von Fäden*) skein ▶ WENDUNGEN: **am gleichen ~ ziehen** to [all] pull together; **über die Stränge schlagen** (*fam*) to be out of control
strangulieren* [ʃtraŋ·gu·ˈliː·rən] *vt* to strangle
Strapaze <-, -n> [ʃtra·ˈpaː·tsə] *f* stress, strain
strapazieren* [ʃtra·pa·ˈtsiː·rən] **I.** *vt* ❶ (*stark beanspruchen*) to wear; (*abnutzen*) to wear out *sep* ❷ (*überbeanspruchen*) **jds Geduld ~** to tax sb's patience; **jds Nerven ~** to get on sb's nerves **II.** *vr* ■ **sich** *akk* [**bei etw** *dat*] **~** to overdo it [when doing sth], to wear oneself out
strapazierfähig *adj* durable
strapaziös [ʃtra·pa·ˈtsi̯øːs] *adj* strenuous
Straps <-es, -e> [ʃtraps] *m meist pl* garter
Straßburg <-s> [ˈʃtraːs·bʊrk] *nt* Strasbourg
Straße <-, -n> [ˈʃtraː·sə] *f* (*Verkehrsweg*) road; (*bewohnte Straße*) street; (*enge Straße auf dem Land*) lane ▶ WENDUNGEN: **auf die ~ gehen** to demonstrate; **auf der ~ sitzen** (*fam*) to be [out] on the streets; **auf offener ~** in broad daylight; **jdn auf die ~ setzen** (*fam*) to throw sb out
Straßenbahn *f* streetcar
Straßenbahnhaltestelle *f* streetcar stop
Straßenbahnlinie *f* streetcar line
Straßenbau *m kein pl* road construction *no art*
Straßenbelag *m* road surface
Straßenfest *nt* street party
Straßengraben *m* [roadside] ditch
Straßenkarte *f* road map
Straßenkehrer(in) <-s, -> *m(f)* street sweeper
Straßenkind *nt* street child [*or* urchin]
Straßenlaterne *f* street lamp [*or* light]
Straßenrand *m* roadside
Straßenschild *nt* street sign
Straßenseite *f* (*einer Straße*) roadside; (*eines Gebäudes*) side next to the road/street
Straßensperre *f* roadblock
Straßenstrich *m* (*fam*) red-light district
Straßenverhältnisse *pl* road conditions *pl*
Straßenverkehr *m* [road] traffic

Stratege, **Strategin** <-n, -n> [ʃtra·ˈteː·gə, st-, ˈʃtra·ˈteː·gɪn] *m, f* strategist

Strategie <-, -en> [ʃtra·te·ˈgiː, st-, *pl* -ˈgiː·ən] *f* strategy

strategisch [ʃtra·ˈteː·gɪʃ, st-] *adj* strategic

Stratosphäre [ʃtra·to·ˈsfɛː·rə, st-] *f kein pl* stratosphere

sträuben [ˈʃtrɔy·bn̩] *vr* ① (*sich widersetzen*) ■**sich** *akk* [**gegen etw** *akk*] ~ to resist [sth] ② (*sich aufrichten*) *Fell, Haar* to stand on end

Strauch <-[e]s, Sträucher> [ʃtraux, *pl* ˈʃtrɔy·çɐ] *m* shrub, bush

straucheln [ˈʃtrau·xl̩n] *vi sein* (*geh*) ① (*stolpern*) to stumble ② (*straffällig werden*) to go astray

Strauß¹ <-es, Sträuße> [ʃtraus, *pl* ˈʃtrɔy·sə] *m* bunch [of flowers], bouquet

Strauß² <-es, -e> [ʃtraus] *m* ostrich

streben [ˈʃtreː·bn̩] *vi* ① *haben* (*sich bemühen*) to strive (**nach** +*dat* for) ② *sein* (*geh: sich hinbewegen*) **zum Ausgang** ~ to make for the exit

Streber(**in**) <-s, -> [ˈʃtreː·bɐ] *m(f)* (*pej fam*) dweeb *sl*

strebsam [ˈʃtreːp·zaːm] *adj* industrious

Strecke <-, -n> [ˈʃtrɛ·kə] *f* ① (*Wegstrecke*) distance; **ich habe auf der ganzen ~ geschlafen** I slept the whole way; **auf halber ~** halfway; **über weite ~n** for long stretches ② BAHN stretch; **auf freier ~** between stations ▶ WENDUNGEN: **auf der ~ bleiben** *dat* (*fam*) to fall by the wayside; **jdn zur ~ bringen** to hunt sb down

strecken [ˈʃtrɛ·kn̩] **I.** *vt* ① (*recken*) to stretch; **den Finger** ~ to raise one's finger ② (*ergiebiger machen*) to stretch; *Drogen etc.* to dilute **II.** *vr* ■**sich** *akk* ~ to stretch

Streckenabschnitt *m* BAHN [rail] line

Streckennetz *nt* BAHN rail network

streckenweise *adv* in parts

Streich <-[e]s, -e> [ʃtraiç] *m* ① (*Schabernack*) prank; **ein böser** ~ a dirty trick; **jdm einen ~ spielen** to play a trick on sb ② (*geh: Schlag*) blow

streicheln [ˈʃtrai·çl̩n] *vt* to caress; *Katze, Hund* to pet

streichen <strich, gestrichen> [ˈʃtrai·çn̩] **I.** *vt haben* ① (*anmalen*) to paint ② (*schmieren*) to spread ③ (*ausstreichen*) to delete ④ (*zurückziehen*) *Auftrag, Projekt* to cancel; *Zuschüsse* to withdraw **II.** *vi* ① *haben* (*darüberfahren*) ■**über etw** *akk* ~ to stroke sth ② *sein* (*streifen*) to prowl

Streichholz *nt* match

Streichinstrument *nt* string[ed] instrument

Streichorchester *nt* string orchestra

Streichung <-, -en> *f* ① (*das Streichen*) deletion ② (*das Zurückziehen*) *von Auftrag, Projekt* cancellation; *von Zuschüssen* withdrawal

Streichwurst *f* spreadable sausage

Streife <-, -n> [ˈʃtrai·fə] *f* patrol; **auf ~ sein** to be on patrol

streifen [ˈʃtrai·fn̩] **I.** *vt haben* ① (*flüchtig berühren*) to touch; **der Schuss streifte ihn nur** the shot just grazed him ② (*flüchtig erwähnen*) **ein Thema nur** ~ to just touch on a subject ③ (*überziehen*) ■**etw auf/über etw** *akk* ~ to slip sth on/over sth ④ (*abstreifen*) ■**etw von etw** *dat* ~ to slip sth off [of] sth **II.** *vi sein* (*geh*) to roam

Streifen <-s, -> [ˈʃtrai·fn̩] *m* ① (*schmaler Abschnitt*) stripe ② (*schmales Stück*) strip

Streifenpolizist(**in**) *m(f)* police officer on patrol

Streifenwagen *m* patrol car

Streik <-[e]s, -s> [ʃtraik] *m* strike; **in den ~ treten** to go on strike

Streikbrecher(**in**) *m(f)* strikebreaker, scab *pej fam*

streiken [ˈʃtrai·kn̩] *vi* ① (*nicht arbeiten*) to be on strike, to strike ② (*hum fam: nicht funktionieren*) to call it quits ③ (*fam: sich weigern*) to go on strike

Streikende(**r**) *f(m) dekl wie adj* striker

Streikposten *m* picket; **~ aufstellen** to set up a picket line

Streikrecht *nt kein pl* right to strike

Streit <-[e]s, -e> [ʃtrait] *m* argument, dispute, fight; [**mit jdm**] ~ [**wegen etw** *dat*] **bekommen** to get into an argument [with sb] [about sth]; **~ haben/suchen** to have/be looking for an argument; **im** ~ during an argument

streiten <stritt, gestritten> [ˈʃtrai·tn̩] *vi, vr* to argue, to fight (**über** +*akk* about); ■**sich** *akk* **um etw** *akk* ~ to argue [*or* fight] over sth

Streiterei <-, -en> [ʃtrai·tə·ˈrai] *f* (*fam*) arguing

Streitfall *m* dispute, conflict; **im** ~ in case of dispute

Streitgespräch *nt* debate

streitig [ˈʃtrai·tɪç] *adj* disputed; JUR contentious; **jdm eine Stellung ~ machen** to challenge sb's position

Streitigkeit *f meist pl* dispute

Streitkräfte *pl* [armed] forces *pl*

streitlustig *adj* argumentative

Streitpunkt *m* POL contentious issue

streitsüchtig *adj* quarrelsome, contentious

streng [ʃtrɛŋ] **I.** *adj* ① (*auf Disziplin achtend*) strict ② (*unnachsichtig*) severe; *Kontrolle* strict ③ *Geruch* pungent ④ *Winter* severe ⑤ (*konsequent*) strict; **ich bin ~er Vegetarier/Moslem** I am a strict vegetarian/Muslim ⑥ SCHWEIZ (*anstrengend*) strenuous **II.** *adv* ① (*unnachsichtig*) strictly; **~ durchgreifen** to crack down ② (*durchdringend*) pungently; **was riecht hier so ~?** what's that strong smell?

Strenge <-> [ˈʃtrɛŋə] *f kein pl* ① (*Unnachsichtigkeit*) strictness ② (*Härte*) severity ③ *von Geschmack* sharpness; *von Geruch* pungency

strenggläubig *adj* strict; ■**~ sein** to be strictly religious

StressRR <-es, -e>, **Streß**ALT <-sses, -sse> [ʃtrɛs, st-] *m* stress; **~ haben** to experience stress; **im ~ sein/unter ~ stehen** to be under

S

stress; **ich bin voll im ~** I am completely stressed out

stressen ['ʃtrɛ·sn̩] *vt* to put under stress

stressig ['ʃtrɛ·sɪç] *adj* stressful

Streu <-> [ʃtrɔy] *f kein pl* litter

streuen ['ʃtrɔy·ən] **I.** *vt* ❶ (*hinstreuen*) to scatter, to spread ❷ (*verbreiten*) to spread **II.** *vi* (*Streumittel anwenden*) to put down sand; *Salz* to salt [the roads]

streunen *vi* ❶ *sein o haben* (*umherstreifen*) to roam around; **~de Hunde/Katzen** stray dogs/cats ❷ *sein* (*ziellos umherziehen*) to wander around; **durch die Straßen ~** to roam the streets

Streusel <-s, -> ['ʃtrɔy·zl̩] *nt* streusel

Streuselkuchen *m* streusel [cake]

strich [ʃtrɪç] *imp von* **streichen**

Strich <-[e]s, -e> [ʃtrɪç] *m* ❶ (*gezogene Linie*) line; **einen ~ [unter etw** *akk*] **ziehen** to draw a line [under sth] ❷ (*fam: Prostitution*) **auf den ~ gehen** to become a streetwalker ▶ WENDUNGEN: **nach ~ und Faden** (*fam*) good and proper; **jd/etw macht jdm einen ~ durch die Rechnung** sb/sth messes up sb's plans; **jdm gegen den ~ gehen** (*fam*) to go against the grain; **einen ~ unter etw** *akk* **ziehen** to put an end to sth; **unterm ~** (*fam*) at the end of the day

Strichcode [-ko:t] *m* bar code

stricheln ['ʃtrɪ·çl̩n] *vt* to sketch in *sep;* ■ **gestrichelte Linie** dotted line; *auf Straße* broken line

Stricher <-s, -> *m* (*sl*) young male prostitute

Strichkode [-ko:t] *f s.* **Strichcode**

Strichpunkt *m* semicolon

strichweise *adv* METEO here and there, in places

Strick <-[e]s, -e> [ʃtrɪk] *m* rope ▶ WENDUNGEN: **wenn alle ~e reißen** (*fam*) if all else fails

stricken ['ʃtrɪ·kn̩] *vi, vt* to knit

Strickgarn *nt* knitting yarn

Strickjacke *f* cardigan

Strickwaren *pl* knitwear

Strickzeug *nt* knitting

striegeln ['ʃtri:·gl̩n] *vt* to groom

Striemen <-s, -> ['ʃtri:·mən] *m* weal

strikt [ʃtrɪkt, st-] **I.** *adj* strict; *Weigerung* point-blank **II.** *adv* strictly; **~ gegen etw** *akk* **sein** to be totally against sth

Strip <-s, -s> [ʃtrɪp, st-] *m* (*sl*) strip[tease]

Striplokal ['strɪp·lo·ka:l] *nt* (*fam*) strip joint

Strippe <-, -n> ['ʃtrɪ·pə] *f* (*fam: Telefonleitung*) line

strippen ['ʃtrɪ·pn̩, 'st-] *vi* to strip

Striptease <-> ['ʃtrɪp·ti:s, 'st-] *m o nt kein pl* striptease

stritt [ʃtrɪt] *imp von* **streiten**

strittig ['ʃtrɪ·tɪç] *adj* contentious; *Fall* controversial; *Grenze* disputed; **der ~e Punkt** the point at issue; ■ **~ sein** to be in dispute

Stroh <-[e]s> [ʃtro:] *nt kein pl* straw

strohblond *adj Mensch* with sandy blonde hair; *Haare* sandy [blonde]

strohdumm *adj* (*fam*) brainless

Strohhalm *m* straw

Strohhut *m* straw hat

Strohmann *m* front man

Strom <-[e]s, Ströme> [ʃtro:m, *pl* 'ʃtrø:·mə] *m* ❶ ELEK electricity; **elektrischer ~** electric current; **grüner ~** green power ❷ (*großer Fluss*) [large] river ❸ (*Schwarm*) stream; **Ströme von Besuchern** streams of visitors ▶ WENDUNGEN: **in Strömen gießen** to pour [down] [rain]; **mit dem/gegen den ~ schwimmen** to swim with/against the current; **unter ~ stehen** (*elektrisch geladen sein*) to be live; (*überaus aktiv sein*) to be a live wire *fig*

stromabwärts [ʃtro:m·'ʔap·vɛrts] *adv* downstream

stromaufwärts [ʃtro:m·'ʔauf·vɛrts] *adv* upstream

Stromausfall *m* power outage

strömen ['ʃtrø:·mən] *vi sein* ❶ (*in Mengen fließen*) to pour (**aus** *+dat* out of) ❷ (*in Scharen eilen*) to stream (**aus** *+dat* out of); **die Touristen strömten zum Palast** the tourists flocked to the palace

Stromerzeugung *f* electricity generation

Stromkabel *nt* power line

Stromkreis *m* [electric[al]] circuit

Stromleitung *f* power supply line

stromlinienförmig [-li:·ni·ən-] *adj* streamlined

Strommast *m* high-voltage tower

Stromnetz *nt* power grid

Stromschnelle *f meist pl* rapids *npl*

Stromstärke *f* current [strength]

Stromstoß *m* electric shock

Stromtankstelle *f* electric vehicle [*or* EV] charging station

Strömung <-, -en> *f* ❶ (*fließendes Wasser*) current ❷ (*Tendenz*) trend

Stromverbrauch *m* power consumption

Stromversorgung *f* power supply

Stromzähler *m* electric meter

Strophe <-, -n> ['ʃtro:·fə] *f* verse

strubbelig ['ʃtrʊ·bə·lɪç], **strubblig** ['ʃtrʊb·lɪç] *adj* (*fam*) tousled; *Fell* tangled

Strudel <-s, -> ['ʃtru:·dl̩] *m* ❶ (*Wasserwirbel*) whirlpool; (*kleiner*) eddy ❷ (*Gebäck*) strudel

Struktur [ʃtrʊk·'tu:ɐ̯, strʊ-] *f* ❶ (*Aufbau*) structure ❷ (*von Stoff etc.*) texture

strukturell [ʃtrʊk·tu·'rɛl] *adj* structural

strukturieren* [ʃtrʊk·tu·'ri:·rən, st-] *vt* to structure

Strukturierung <-, -en> *f* ❶ *kein pl* (*das Strukturieren*) structuring ❷ (*Struktur*) structure; (*von Stoff etc.*) texture

strukturschwach *adj* economically underdeveloped

Strukturwandel *m* structural change

Strumpf <-[e]s, Strümpfe> [ʃtrʊmpf, *pl* 'ʃtrʏm·pfə] *m* ❶ (*Kniestrumpf*) knee-high; (*Socke*) sock ❷ (*Damenstrumpf*) stocking

Strumpfhalter <-s, -> *m* garter

S

Strụmpfhose *f* pantyhose, stockings; (*fester*) tights *npl*
struppig [ˈʃtrʊ·pɪç] *adj Haare* tousled; *Fell* shaggy
Stube <-, -n> [ˈʃtuː·bə] *f* DIAL (*Wohnzimmer*) living room; **die gute ~** the front room
Stubenarrest *m* **~ haben** (*fam*) to be confined to one's room
stubenrein *adj* housebroken
Stuck <-[e]s> [ʃtʊk] *m kein pl* stucco, cornices *pl*
Stück <-[e]s, -e *o nach Zahlenangaben* -> [ʃtʏk] *nt* ❶ (*einzelnes Teil*) piece; **ein ~ Kuchen** a piece of cake; **etw in ~e reißen** to tear sth to pieces; **~ für ~** bit by bit; **am ~** in one piece; **geschnitten oder am ~?** sliced or unsliced?; **5 Euro das** [*o* **pro**] **~** 5 euros each ❷ (*besonderer Gegenstand*) piece, item ❸ (*Abschnitt*) part; **ich begleite dich noch ein ~** I'll go part of the way with you; **ein ~ Acker/Land** part of a field/a plot of land ❹ THEAT play ❺ MUS piece ❻ **ein ziemliches ~ Arbeit** quite a job; **jds bestes ~** (*hum fam*) sb's pride and joy; **aus freien ~en** of one's own free will; **große ~e auf jdn halten** (*fam*) to think highly of sb
Stückpreis *m* unit price
stụ̈ckweise *adv* individually, separately
Student(in) <-en, -en> [ʃtu·ˈdɛnt] *m(f)* student
Studẹntenausweis *m* [college] student ID [card]
Studẹntenwerk *nt* student union
Studẹntenwohnheim *nt* residence hall
Studie <-, -n> [ˈʃtuː·di̯ə] *f* study
Studien [ˈʃtuː·di̯·ən] *pl von* **Studium**
Studienabbrecher(in) <-s, -> *m(f)* dropout *fam*
Studienabschluss^RR *m* degree
Studienfach *nt* subject
Studiengang *m* program
Studiengebühren *pl* tuition
Studienplatz *m a spot for a student at a university/college*
Studienrat, -rätin *m, f* ≈ school board member
Studienreise *f* study trip
studieren* [ʃtu·ˈdiː·rən] *vi, vt* to study; **sie studiert noch** she is still a student; **ich will ~** I want to go to college
Studio <-s, -s> [ˈʃtuː·di̯o] *nt* studio
Studium <-, Studien> [ˈʃtuː·di̯·ʊm, *pl* ˈʃtuː·di̯·ən] *nt* ❶ *an Universität* studies *pl;* **ein ~ aufnehmen** to begin one's studies ❷ (*eingehende Beschäftigung*) study ❸ *kein pl* (*genaues Durchlesen*) study; **das ~ der Akten ist noch nicht abgeschlossen** the files are still being scrutinized
Stufe <-, -n> [ˈʃtuː·fə] *f* ❶ (*Treppenabschnitt*) step; **~ um ~** step by step ❷ (*geh: Niveau*) level ❸ (*Abschnitt*) stage, phase
stufenförmig *adj* terraced
stufenlos I. *adj* continuously variable II. *adv* smoothly
Stufenschnitt *m* (*Frisur*) layered cut
stufenweise I. *adj* phased II. *adv* step by step
stufig [ˈʃtuː·fɪç] I. *adj Haarschnitt* layered II. *adv* in layers; **~ schneiden** to layer
Stuhl <-[e]s, Stühle> [ʃtuːl, *pl* ˈʃtyː·lə] *m* chair ▶ WENDUNGEN: **jdn vom ~ hauen** (*sl*) to bowl sb over; **sich zwischen zwei Stühle setzen** to fall between the cracks
Stuhlbein *nt* chair leg
Stuhlgang *m kein pl* MED (*geh*) bowel movement[s]
Stuhllehne *f* chair back
stumm [ʃtʊm] I. *adj* ❶ (*nicht sprechen könnend*) dumb ❷ (*schweigend*) silent; ■ **~ werden** to go silent ❸ LING silent II. *adv* silently
Stummel <-s, -> [ˈʃtʊ·ml̩] *m Glied* stump; *Bleistift, Kerze* stub
Stụmmfilm *m* silent movie
Stümper(in) <-s, -> [ˈʃtʏm·pɐ] *m(f)* (*pej*) incompetent
stumpf [ʃtʊmpf] *adj* ❶ (*nicht scharf*) blunt ❷ (*glanzlos*) dull ❸ (*abgestumpft*) apathetic
Stụmpfsinn *m kein pl* ❶ (*geistige Trägheit*) apathy ❷ (*Stupidität*) mindlessness, tedium
stụmpfsinnig *adj* ❶ (*geistig träge*) apathetic ❷ (*stupide*) mindless, tedious
Stunde <-, -n> [ˈʃtʊn·də] *f* ❶ (*60 Minuten*) hour; **nur noch eine knappe ~** just under an hour to go; **zu später ~** at a late hour; **in einer stillen ~** in a quiet moment; **eine Viertel~** a quarter of an hour, fifteen minutes; **eine halbe ~** half an hour; **eine Dreiviertel~** three-quarters of an hour, forty-five minutes; **anderthalb ~n** an hour and a half; **volle ~** on the hour; **der Zug fährt jede volle ~** the train departs every hour on the hour; **alle** [**halbe**] **~** every [half [an]] hour ❷ *kein pl* (*festgesetzter Zeitpunkt*) time, hour *form;* **bis zur ~** up to the present moment, as yet; **zur gewohnten ~** at the usual time ❸ (*Unterrichtsstunde*) lesson, period ❹ *meist pl* (*Zeitraum von kurzer Dauer*) times *pl;* **sich nur an die angenehmen ~n erinnern** to only remember the good times ❺ **die ~ der Wahrheit** the moment of truth; **jds große ~** sb's big moment; **jds letzte ~ hat geschlagen** sb's hour has come; **die ~ null** zero hour, the new beginning
stunden [ˈʃtʊn·dn̩] *vt* ■ **jdm etw ~** to give sb time to pay [for] sth
Stụndengeschwindigkeit *f* speed per hour; **bei einer ~ von 80 km** at a speed of 80 kmph
Stụndenkilometer *pl* kilometers *pl* per hour
stụndenlang I. *adj* lasting several hours *pred;* **nach ~em Warten** after hours of waiting II. *adv* for hours
Stụndenlohn *m* hourly wage
Stụndenplan *m* timetable, schedule
Stụndentakt *m* ■ **im ~** at hourly intervals
stụndenweise I. *adv* for an hour or two [at a time] II. *adj* for a few hours *pred*
stündlich [ˈʃtʏnt·lɪç] I. *adj* hourly II. *adv* hourly, every hour
Stupsnase *f* snub nose

S

stur [ʃtuːɐ̯] I. *adj* stubborn, obstinate II. *adv* ❶ (*ohne abzuweichen*) doggedly; **~ nach Vorschrift arbeiten** to work strictly according to regulations ❷ (*uneinsichtig*) obstinately; **sich** *akk* **~ stellen** (*fam*) to dig one's heels in

Sturheit <-> *f kein pl* stubbornness, obstinacy

Sturm <-[e]s, Stürme> [ʃtʊrm, *pl* ˈʃtʏr·mə] *m* ❶ (*starker Wind*) storm ❷ FBALL forward line; **im ~ spielen** to play forward ❸ (*heftiger Andrang*) rush (**auf** +*akk* for) ► WENDUNGEN: **gegen etw** *akk* **~ laufen** to be up in arms against sth; **~ läuten** to keep ringing the doorbell

stürmen [ˈʃtʏr·mən] I. *vi impers haben* ■ **es stürmt** it's really windy out II. *vi* ❶ *haben* SPORT to attack ❷ *sein* (*rennen*) to storm; **aus dem Haus ~** to storm out of the house III. *vt haben* ❶ (*erobern*) to storm ❷ (*fam: auf, in etw eindringen*) to storm; **die Bühne ~** to storm the stage

Stürmer(in) <-s, -> [ˈʃtʏr·mɐ] *m(f)* forward; FBALL striker

Sturmflut *f* storm tide

stürmisch [ˈʃtʏr·mɪʃ] I. *adj* ❶ METEO blustery; (*mit Regen*) stormy; **~e See** rough sea ❷ (*vehement*) tumultuous; *Mensch* impetuous; *Beziehung* passionate; **nicht so ~!** take it easy! II. *adv* tumultuously

Sturmwarnung *f* storm warning

Sturz <-es, Stürze> [ʃtʊrts, *pl* ˈʃtʏr·tsə] *m* ❶ (*Fall*) fall; **ein ~ der Temperatur** a drop in temperature ❷ **einer Regierung, eines Diktators** downfall

stürzen [ˈʃtʏr·tsn̩] I. *vi sein* ❶ (*fallen*) to fall; **vom Dach/Fahrrad ~** to fall off a roof/bicycle ❷ (*rennen*) to rush; **ins Zimmer ~** to burst into the room II. *vt haben* ❶ (*werfen*) **jdn/sich aus dem Fenster ~** to throw sb/oneself out the window ❷ POL (*absetzen*) ■ **jdn/etw ~** to bring sb/sth down; *Minister* to force to resign; *Diktator* to overthrow; *Regierung* to topple ❸ KOCHK (*aus der Form kippen*) to turn upside down III. *vr* ❶ (*sich werfen*) ■ **sich** *akk* **auf jdn ~** to pounce on sb; **die Gäste stürzten sich aufs kalte Büfett** the guests stormed the cold buffet ❷ (*sich mit etw belasten*) ■ **sich** *akk* **in etw** *akk* **~** to plunge into sth; **sich in große Unkosten ~** to go to great expense

Sturzflug *m* LUFT nosedive; ORN steep dive

Sturzhelm *m* crash helmet

Stute <-, -n> [ˈʃtuː·tə] *f* mare

Stütze <-, -n> [ˈʃtʏ·tsə] *f* ❶ (*Stützpfeiler*) support [pillar] ❷ (*Halt*) support, prop ❸ (*Unterstützung*) support ❹ (*sl: finanzielle Hilfe vom Staat*) welfare

stutzen¹ [ˈʃtʊ·tsn̩] *vi* to hesitate, to stop short

stutzen² [ˈʃtʊ·tsn̩] *vt* ❶ HORT to prune ❷ ZOOL to clip; **gestutzte Flügel** clipped wings ❸ (*kürzen*) to trim

stützen [ˈʃtʏ·tsn̩] I. *vt* ❶ (*Halt geben*) to support ❷ (*aufstützen*) ■ **etw auf etw** *akk* **~** to rest sth on sth ❸ (*gründen*) ■ **etw auf etw** *akk* **~** to base sth on sth ❹ (*untermauern*) to back up *sep; Theorie* to support II. *vr* ❶ (*sich aufstützen*) ■ **sich** *akk* **auf jdn/etw ~** to lean on sb/sth ❷ (*basieren*) ■ **sich** *akk* **auf etw** *akk* **~** to be based on sth

stutzig [ˈʃtʊ·tsɪç] *adj* **jdn ~ machen** to make sb suspicious; **~ werden** to begin to wonder

Stützpunkt *m* MIL base

stylen [ˈstai·lən] *vt* to design; *Haar* to style

Styropor® <-s> [ʃty·ro·ˈpoːɐ̯] *nt kein pl* Styrofoam®

s.u. *Abk von* **siehe unten** see below

Subjekt <-[e]s, -e> [zʊp·ˈjɛkt] *nt* subject

subjektiv [zʊp·jɛk·ˈtiːf, ˈzʊp-] *adj* subjective

Subjektivität <-> [zʊp·jɛk·ti·vi·ˈtɛːt] *f kein pl* subjectivity

Substantiv <-s, -e> [ˈzʊp·stan·tiːf] *nt* noun

Substanz <-, -en> [zʊp·ˈstants] *f* ❶ (*Material*) substance ❷ *kein pl* (*geh: Essenz*) essence

subtil [zʊp·ˈtiːl] *adj* subtle

subtrahieren* [zʊp·tra·ˈhiː·rən] *vt, vi* to subtract (**von** +*dat* from)

Subtraktion <-, -en> [zʊp·trak·ˈtsi̯oːn] *f* subtraction

Subunternehmer(in) <-s, -> [ˈzʊp·ʔʊn·tɐ·neː·mɐ] *m(f)* subcontractor

Subvention <-, -en> [zʊp·vɛn·ˈtsi̯oːn] *f* subsidy

subventionieren* [zʊp·vɛn·tsi̯o·ˈniː·rən] *vt* to subsidize

subversiv [zʊp·vɛr·ˈziːf] I. *adj* subversive II. *adv* subversively

Suchaktion *f* organized search

Suchbegriff *m* target word; COMPUT search key

Suchdienst *m* missing persons tracking service

Suche <-, -n> [ˈzuː·xə] *f* search (**nach** +*dat* for); **sich** *akk* **auf die ~ [nach jdm/etw] machen** to go in search [of sb/sth]; **auf der ~ [nach jdm/etw] sein** to be looking [for sb/sth]

suchen [ˈzuː·xn̩] I. *vt* ❶ (*zu finden versuchen*) ■ **etw ~** to look for sth; (*intensiver*) to search for sth; **du hast hier nichts zu ~!** you've got no business being here! ❷ (*nach etw trachten*) to seek; **den Nervenkitzel ~** to be looking for thrills II. *vi* to search, to look (**nach** +*dat* for)

Sucher <-s, -> *m* viewfinder

Suchfunktion *f* COMPUT search function

Suchlauf *m* search process

Suchmannschaft *f* search party

Suchmaschine *f* search engine

Sucht <-, Süchte> [zʊxt, *pl* ˈzʏç·tə] *f* ❶ (*Abhängigkeit*) addiction; **~ erzeugend** addictive ❷ (*Verlangen*) obsession; ■ **jds ~ nach etw** *dat* sb's craving for sth

Suchtgefahr *f* danger of addiction

süchtig [ˈzʏç·tɪç] *adj* ❶ (*abhängig*) addicted *pred;* **~ machen** to be addictive ❷ (*begierig*) ■ **~ sein** to be hooked (**nach** +*dat* on)

Süchtige(r) *f(m) dekl wie adj* addict

Suchtkranke(r) <-n, -n> *f(m) dekl wie adj* addict

Süd <-[e]s, -e> [zyːt] *m kein pl, kein art* south;

aus ~ from the South
Südafrika ['zy:t·'ʔa:f·ri·ka] *nt* South Africa; *s. a.* **Deutschland**
südafrikanisch ['zy:t·ʔafri·'ka:·nɪʃ] *adj* South African; *s. a.* **deutsch**
Südamerika ['zy:t·ʔa'me:·ri·ka] *nt* South America; *s. a.* **Deutschland**
südamerikanisch *adj* South American; *s. a.* **deutsch**
süddeutsch ['zy:t·dɔytʃ] *adj* Southern German; *s. a.* **deutsch**
Süddeutschland ['zy:t·dɔytʃ·lant] *nt* Southern Germany; *s. a.* **Deutschland**
Süden <-s> ['zy:·dn̩] *m kein pl, kein indef art* ❶ (*Himmelsrichtung*) south; *s. a.* **Norden 1** ❷ (*südliche Gegend*) south; **gen ~ ziehen** to fly south; *s. a.* **Norden 2**
Südeuropa <-s> ['zy:t·ʔɔy·'ro:·pa] *nt* Southern Europe
Südfrankreich *nt* South[ern] France, the south of France
Südfrucht *f* tropical fruit
Südhalbkugel *f* Southern Hemisphere
Südkorea ['zy:t·ko·'re:a], *nt* (*fam*) South Korea; *s. a.* **Deutschland**
Südküste *f* south[ern] coast
Südländer(in) <-s, -> ['zy:t·lɛn·dɐ] *m(f)* Southern European
südländisch *adj* Southern European
südlich ['zy:t·lɪç] **I.** *adj* ❶ (*Himmelsrichtung*) southern; *s. a.* **nördlich I 1** ❷ (*im Süden liegend*) southern; *s. a.* **nördlich I 2** ❸ (*von/nach Süden*) southward, southerly; *s. a.* **nördlich I 3 II.** *adv* ■ **~ von ...** south of ... **III.** *präp +gen* **~ der Stadt** [to the] south of the city/town
Südostasien [zy:t·ʔɔst·'ʔa:zi̯·ən] *nt* Southeast Asia
Südosten [zy:t·'ʔɔs·tn̩] *m kein pl, kein indef art* southeast
südöstlich [zy:t·'ʔœst·lɪç] **I.** *adj* ❶ (*im Südosten gelegen*) southeastern ❷ (*von/nach Südosten*) southeastward, southeasterly **II.** *adv* southeast **III.** *präp +gen* [to the] southeast of sth
Südpol ['zy:t·po:l] *m* ■ **der ~** the South Pole
Südsee ['zy:t·ze:] *f kein pl* ■ **die ~** the South Seas *pl,* the South Pacific
Südspanien <-s, -> *nt* South[ern] Spain
Südstaaten ['zy:t·ʃta:·tn̩] *pl* (*in den USA*) ■ **die ~** the South
Südwesten [zy:t·'vɛs·tn̩] *m kein pl, kein indef art* southwest
südwestlich [zy:t·'vɛst·lɪç] **I.** *adj* ❶ (*im Südwesten liegend*) southwestern ❷ (*von/nach Südwesten*) southwestward **II.** *adv* [to the] southwest **III.** *präp +gen* [to the] southwest of sth
Suff <-[e]s> [zʊf] *m kein pl* (*fam*) boozing; **im ~** while under the influence
suggerieren* [zʊ·ge·'ri:·rən] *vt* to suggest
suggestiv [zʊ·gɛs·'ti:f] *adj* suggestive
Sühne <-, -n> ['zy:·nə] *f* atonement
sühnen ['zy:·nən] *vt* ■ **etw ~** to atone for sth
Suite <-, -n> ['svi:·tə, zu·'i:tə] *f* suite
Sujet <-s, -s> [zy·'ʒe:] *nt* subject
sukzessiv [zʊk·tsɛ·'si:f] *adj* (*geh*) gradual
Sultan, Sultanin <-s, -e> ['zʊl·ta:n, 'zʊl·ta·nɪn, zʊl·'ta:·nɪn] *m, f* sultan *masc,* sultana *fem*
Summe <-, -n> ['zʊ·mə] *f* ❶ (*Additionsergebnis*) sum, total ❷ (*Betrag*) sum, amount
summen ['zʊ·mən] *vi, vt* to hum; *Biene* to buzz
summieren* [zʊ·'mi:·rən] **I.** *vt* to add up *sep* **II.** *vr* ■ **sich** *akk* **auf etw** *akk* **~** to amount [*or* add up] to sth
Sumpf <-[e]s, Sümpfe> [zʊmpf, *pl* 'zʏm·pfə] *m* marsh, swamp; (*Moor*) bog
Sumpffieber *nt* malaria
Sumpfgebiet *nt* marsh[land], swamp[land]
sumpfig ['zʊm·pfɪç] *adj* marshy, swampy
Sünde <-, -n> ['zʏn·də] *f* sin
Sündenbock *m* scapegoat
Sündenfall *m kein pl* ■ **der ~** the Fall [of Man]
Sünder(in) <-s, -> *m(f)* sinner
sündhaft ['zʏnt·haft] *adj* ❶ (*exorbitant hoch*) outrageous ❷ (*unmoralisch*) sinful
sündig ['zʏn·dɪç] *adj* ❶ REL sinful ❷ (*lasterhaft*) dissolute
sündigen ['zʏn·dɪ·gn̩] *vi* to sin
super ['zu:·pɐ] **I.** *adj* super **II.** *adv* great; **sie kann ~ singen** she's a great singer
Super <-s> ['zu:·pɐ] *nt kein pl* AUTO super, premium
Superlativ <-[e]s, -e> ['zu:·pɐ·la·ti:f] *m* superlative
Supermacht *f* superpower
Supermarkt ['zu:·pɐ·markt] *m* supermarket
superreich ['zu:·pɐ-] *adj* (*pej*) superrich
Superstar *m* superstar
Suppe <-, -n> ['zʊ·pə] *f* soup; **klare ~** consommé, broth ▶ WENDUNGEN: **die ~ auslöffeln müssen** (*fam*) to have to face the music
Suppenhuhn *nt* boiling chicken
Suppenlöffel *m* soup spoon
Suppenschüssel *f* soup tureen
Suppenteller *m* soup plate [*or* bowl]
Suppenwürfel *m* bouillon cube
Surfbrett ['zœɐ̯f-] *nt* ❶ (*zum Windsurfen*) windsurfer ❷ (*zum Wellensurfen*) surfboard
Surfen <-s> ['zø:ɐ̯·fn̩] *nt kein pl* surfing
surfen ['zœr·fn̩, 'zø:ɐ̯·fn̩] *vi* to surf; **im Internet ~** to surf the Internet
Surfer(in) <-s, -> *m(f)* surfer
Surrealismus <-> [zʊ·rea·'lɪs·mʊs, zʏr-] *m kein pl* surrealism
surrealistisch [zʊ·rea·'lɪs·tɪʃ, zʏr-] *adj Autor, Maler* surrealist; *Film, Buch* surrealistic
surren ['zʊ·rən] *vi Insekt* to buzz; *Motor* to hum
suspekt *adj* (*geh*) suspicious; ■ **jdm ~ sein** to look suspicious to sb
suspendieren* [zʊs·pɛn·'di:·rən] *vt* to suspend (**von** *+dat* from)
süß [zy:s] **I.** *adj* sweet **II.** *adv* ❶ (*mit Zucker*

zubereitet) with sugar; **ich trinke meinen Kaffee nie ~** I never take sugar with my coffee ❷ (*lieblich*) sweetly

süßen ['zy:·sn̩] *vt* to sweeten

Süßigkeit <-, -en> ['zy:·sɪç·kait] *f meist pl* sweets *pl,* candy

süßlich *adj* sickly sweet

süßsauer ['zy:s·'zau·ɐ] *adj* sweet-and-sour

Süßspeise *f* dessert

Süßstoff *m* sweetener

Süßwaren *pl* sweets *pl*

Süßwarengeschäft *nt* candy store

Süßwasser *nt* fresh water

Swimmingpool <-s, -s> ['svɪ·mɪŋ·pu:l] *m* swimming pool

Symbol <-s, -e> [zym·'bo:l] *nt* symbol

Symbolfigur *f* symbol[ic figure]

symbolisch [zym·'bo:·lɪʃ] *adj* symbolic

symbolisieren* [zym·bo·li·'zi:·rən] *vt* to symbolize

Symbolleiste *f* COMPUT toolbar

Symmetrie <-, -n> [zy·me·'tri:, *pl* -'tri:·ən] *f* symmetry

symmetrisch [zy·'me:·trɪʃ] *adj* symmetrical

Sympathie <-, -en> [zym·pa·'ti:, *pl* -'ti:·ən] *f* sympathy

Sympathisant(in) <-en, -en> [zym·pati·'zant] *m(f)* sympathizer

sympathisch [zym·'pa:·tɪʃ] *adj* nice, likeable; **sie war mir gleich ~** I liked her right away

sympathisieren* [zym·pa·ti·'zi:·rən] *vi* to sympathize

Symphonie <-, -en> [zym·fo·'ni:, *pl* -'ni:·ən] *f* symphony

Symposium <-s, -ien> [zym·'po:·zi̯·ʊm, *pl* -i̯·ən] *nt* symposium

Symptom <-s, -e> [zymp·'to:m] *nt* symptom (**für** +*akk* of)

Synagoge <-, -n> [zy·na·'go:·gə] *f* synagogue

synchron [zyn·'kro:n] **I.** *adj* synchronous **II.** *adv* synchronously

Synchronisation <-, -en> [zyn·kro·ni·za·'tsi̯o:n] *f* ❶ FILM, TV dubbing ❷ (*Abstimmung*) synchronization

synchronisieren* [zyn·kro·ni·'zi:·rən] *vt* ❶ FILM, TV to dub ❷ (*zeitlich abstimmen*) to synchronize

Syndrom <-s, -e> [zyn·'dro:m] *nt* syndrome

synonym [zy·no·'ny:m] *adj* synonym

Synonym <-s, -e> [zy·no·'ny:m] *nt* synonym

Syntax <-, -en> ['zyn·taks] *f* syntax

Synthese <-, -n> [zyn·'te:·zə] *f* synthesis

Synthesizer <-s, -> ['zyn·tə·sai·zɐ] *m* synthesizer

Synthetik <-> [zyn·'te:·tɪk] *nt kein pl* synthetic fiber; **das Hemd ist aus ~** the shirt is made of artificial fibers

synthetisch [zyn·'te:·tɪʃ] *adj* synthetic; **eine ~e Faser** a man-made fiber

Syphilis <-> ['zy:·fi·lɪs] *f kein pl* syphilis

System <-s, -e> [zys·'te:m] *nt* system; **~ in etw** *akk* **bringen** to bring some order to sth; **mit ~** systematically

Systematik <-, -en> [zys·te·'ma:·tɪk] *f* system

systematisch [zys·te·'ma:·tɪʃ] *adj* systematic

Systemfehler *m* system error

Szenarium <-s, -ien> [stse·'na:·ri̯·ʊm, *pl* -i̯·ən] *nt* (*a. fig*) scenario

Szene <-, -n> ['stse:·nə] *f* ❶ THEAT, FILM scene; **etw in ~ setzen** (*a. fig*) to stage sth; **sich** *akk* **in ~ setzen** (*fig*) to play to the gallery ❷ (*Krach*) scene; **eine ~ machen** to make a scene ❸ *kein pl* (*Milieu*) scene

Szeneladen *m* (*fam: Kneipe*) trendy bar; (*Disco oder Club*) trendy club

Szenenwechsel *m* change of scene

Szenerie <-, -n> [stse·nə·'ri:, *pl* -'ri:·ən] *f* ❶ (*Umgebung*) scenery ❷ FILM, LIT setting

Tt

T, t <-, - *o fam* -s, -s> [teː] *nt* T, t; **~ wie Theodor** T as in Tango

t *Abk von* **Tonne**

Tabak <-s, -e> [ˈtaː·bak, ˈta·bak] *m* tobacco

Tabakladen *m* tobacco store

Tabaksteuer *f* tobacco tax

Tabakwaren *pl* tobacco products *pl*

tabellarisch [ta·bɛ·ˈlaː·rɪʃ] **I.** *adj* tabular **II.** *adv* in tabular form

Tabelle <-, -n> [ta·ˈbɛ·lə] *f* table; SPORTS [league] standings

Tabellenführer(in) *m(f)* SPORTS league leader

Tabellenkalkulation *f* spreadsheet

Tablett <-[e]s, -s *o* -e> [ta·ˈblɛt] *nt* tray

Tablette <-, -n> [ta·ˈblɛ·tə] *f* pill

tabu [ta·ˈbuː] *adj inv* taboo

tabuisieren* [ta·bui·ˈziː·rən] *vt* ■**etw ~** to make sth [a] taboo [subject]

Tabula rasa [ˈtaː·bu·la ˈraː·za] *f kein pl* ▶ WENDUNGEN: **~ ~ machen** (*fam*) to make a clean sweep of sth

Tach(e)les [ˈta·x(ə·)ləs] ▶ WENDUNGEN: **[mit jdm] ~ reden** (*fam*) to talk turkey [with sb] *fam*

Tacho <-s, -s> [ˈta·xo] *m* (*fam*) *kurz für* **Tachometer** speedometer

Tachometer *m o nt* speedometer

Tadel <-s, -> [ˈtaː·dl̩] *m* ❶ (*Verweis*) reprimand, reproach ❷ (*Makel*) **ohne ~** faultless

tadellos **I.** *adj* (*einwandfrei*) perfect **II.** *adv* perfectly

tadeln *vt* ❶ (*zurechtweisen*) to reprimand, to reproach ❷ (*missbilligen*) ■**etw ~** to express one's disapproval of sth

Tadschikistan <-s> [ta·ˈdʒiː·kis·taːn] *nt* Tajikistan; *s. a.* **Deutschland**

Tafel <-, -n> [ˈtaː·fl̩] *f* ❶ (*Platte*) board; **eine ~ Schokolade** a bar of chocolate; (*Anzeigetafel*) SPORTS scoreboard; AVIAT, RAIL departure and arrivals [information] board; (*Gedenktafel*) plaque; SCH [black]board ❷ (*Bildtafel*) plate ❸ (*geh: festlicher Esstisch*) table

täfeln [tɛː·fl̩n] *vt* to panel

Täfelung <-, -en> *f* paneling

Tafelwasser *nt* table water

Tafelwein *m* table wine

Tag <-[e]s, -e> [ˈtaːk, *pl* ˈtaː·gə] *m* ❶ (*Abschnitt von 24 Stunden*) day; **ein freier ~** a day off; **den ganzen ~ [lang]** all day; **guten ~!** hello!, good afternoon/morning!; **~ für ~** every day, day after day; **von einem ~ auf den anderen** overnight; **eines [schönen] ~es** one [fine] day; **der Brief muss jeden ~ kommen** the letter should arrive any day now ❷ (*Datum*) day; **~ der offenen Tür** open house; **der ~ X** D-Day *fig;* **bis zum heutigen ~** up to the present day ❸ (*Tageslicht*) light; **es ist noch nicht ~** it's not light out yet; **am ~** during the day ❹ *pl* (*fam: Menstruation*) period ▶ WENDUNGEN: **es ist noch nicht aller ~e Abend** it's not over yet; **man soll den ~ nicht vor dem Abend loben** (*prov*) don't count your chickens before they're hatched; **etw kommt an den ~** sth comes to light; **in den ~ hinein leben** to live from day to day; **über/unter ~e** above/below ground

tagaus [taːk·ˈʔaus] *adv* **~, tagein** day in, day out

Tagebau *m kein pl* strip mining

Tagebuch *nt* ❶ (*tägliche Aufzeichnungen*) diary ❷ (*Terminkalender*) appointment book

Tagedieb(in) *m(f)* (*pej veraltet*) idler

Tagegeld *nt* ❶ (*tägliches Krankengeld*) daily disability pay ❷ (*tägliche Spesenpauschale*) per diem

tagein [taːk·ˈʔain] *adv s.* **tagaus**

tagelang **I.** *adj* lasting for days; **nach ~em Warten** after days of waiting **II.** *adv* for days

Tagelöhner(in) <-s, -> [ˈtaː·gə·løː·nɐ] *m(f)* (*veraltend*) day laborer

tagen¹ [ˈtaː·gn̩] *vi impers* (*geh*) **es tagt!** day is breaking!

tagen² *vi* to meet; **der Kongress tagt** Congress is in session

Tagesablauf *m* daily routine

Tagesanbruch *m* daybreak (**bei, nach, vor** at, after, before)

Tageseinnahmen *pl* day's receipts *npl*

Tagesfahrt *f* day trip

Tagesgericht *nt* special of the day

Tagesgeschäft *nt* BÖRSE day order

Tagesgespräch *nt* topic of the day

Tageskarte *f* ❶ (*Speisekarte*) menu of the day ❷ (*einen Tag gültige Eintrittskarte*) [one-]day pass

Tageslicht *nt kein pl* daylight (**bei** by/in); (*vor Einbruch der Dunkelheit*) before dark ▶ WENDUNGEN: **etw ans ~ bringen** to bring sth to light

Tagesmutter *f* nanny

Tagesordnung *f* agenda; **etw auf die ~ setzen** to put sth on the agenda; **auf der ~ stehen** to be on the agenda ▶ WENDUNGEN: **[wieder] zur ~ übergehen** to carry on [with business] as usual

Tagesumsatz *m* day's sales *pl*

Tageszeit *f* time [of day]

Tageszeitung *f* daily [[news]paper]

tageweise *adv* on a daily basis

täglich [ˈtɛːk·lɪç] **I.** *adj attr* daily **II.** *adv* daily

Tagschicht *f* day shift

tagsüber [ˈtaːks·ʔyːbɐ] *adv* during the day

Tagung <-, -en> *f* ❶ (*Fachtagung*) conference ❷ (*Sitzung*) meeting

Taifun <-s, -e> [tai·ˈfuːn] *m* typhoon

Taille <-, -n> [ˈtal·jə] *f* waist

tailliert [ta(l)·ˈjiːɐt] *adj* fitted at the waist

Taiwan <-s> [tai·ˈvaːn] *nt* Taiwan

Taiwaner(in) <-s, -> [tai·ˈvaː·nɐ] *m(f)* Taiwanese

taiwanisch [tai·ˈvaː·nɪʃ] *adj* Taiwanese; *s. a.* **deutsch**

Takt <-[e]s, -e> [ˈtakt] *m* ❶ MUS bar ❷ *kein pl* (*Rhythmus*) rhythm; **den ~ angeben** to beat time; **im ~** in time to sth ❸ *kein pl* (*Taktgefühl*) tact

Taktgefühl *nt* ❶ (*Feingefühl*) sense of tact ❷ MUS sense of rhythm

taktieren* [tak·ˈtiː·rən] *vi* to use tactics

Taktik <-, -en> [ˈtak·tɪk] *f* tactics *pl*

Taktiker(in) <-s, -> [ˈtak·ti·kɐ] *m(f)* tactician

taktisch [ˈtak·tɪʃ] **I.** *adj* tactic[al] **II.** *adv* tactically

taktlos *adj* tactless

Taktlosigkeit <-, -en> *f* ❶ *kein pl* (*taktlose Art*) tactlessness ❷ (*taktlose Aktion*) tactless act

Taktstock *m* baton

taktvoll *adj* tactful

Tal <-[e]s, Täler> [taːl, *pl* tɛː·lɐ] *nt* valley

Talar <-s, -e> [ta·ˈlaːɐ̯] *m* JUR robe; REL cassock; SCH gown

Talent <-[e]s, -e> [taː·ˈlɛnt] *nt* talent

talentiert [tal·ɛn·ˈtiːɐ̯t] **I.** *adj* talented **II.** *adv* in a talented way

Taler <-s, -> [ˈtaː·lɐ] *m* taler, thaler

Talisman <-s, -e> [ˈtaː·lɪs·man] *m* lucky charm

Talkshow[RR] <-, -s> [ˈtɔː·kʃoː] *f* talk show

Tamburin <-s, -e> [tam·bu·ˈriːn, ˈtam·bu·riːn] *nt* tambourine

Tampon <-s, -s> [ˈtam·pɔn, tam·ˈpoːn, tãˈpõː] *m* tampon

Tandem <-s, -s> [ˈtan·dɛm] *nt* tandem

Tang <-[e]s, -e> [ˈtaŋ] *m* seaweed

Tanga <-s, -s> [ˈtaŋ·ga] *m* thong

Tangente <-, -n> [taŋ·ˈgɛn·tə] *f* MATH tangent

tangieren* [taŋ·ˈgiː·rən] *vt* ❶ (*geh: streifen*) to touch upon ❷ (*geh: betreffen*) to affect; **jdn nicht ~** (*fam*) to not bother sb ❸ MATH ■ **etw ~** to be tangent to

Tango <-s, -s> [ˈtaŋ·go] *m* tango

Tank <-s, -s> [taŋk] *m* tank

tanken [ˈtaŋ·kn̩] **I.** *vi* (*Auto*) to get gas; (*Flugzeug*) to refuel **II.** *vt* ❶ (*als Tankfüllung*) ■ **etw ~** to fill up sth *sep* [with sth] ❷ (*fam: in sich aufnehmen*) **frische Luft/Sonne ~** to get some fresh air/sun ▶WENDUNGEN: **[ganz schön] getankt haben** (*fam*) to have drunk a fair share

Tanker <-s, -> [ˈtaŋ·kɐ] *m* tanker

Tankfüllung *f* tankful

Tanklastzug *m* tanker

Tanksäule *f* gas pump

Tankstelle *f* gas station

Tankwart(in) *m(f)* gas station attendant

Tanne <-, -n> [ˈta·nə] *f* fir

Tannenbaum *m* ❶ (*Weihnachtsbaum*) Christmas tree ❷ (*fam: Tanne*) fir [tree]

Tannennadel *f* pine needle

Tannenzapfen *m* pinecone

Tante <-, -n> [ˈtan·tə] *f* aunt

Tante-Emma-Laden [-ˈɛma-] *m* (*fam*) corner store

Tantieme <-, -n> [tãˈti̯eː·mə] *f* ❶ (*Absatzhonorar*) royalty ❷ *meist pl* (*Gewinnbeteiligung*) percentage of the profits

Tanz <-es, Tänze> [ˈtants, *pl* ˈtɛn·tsə] *m* dance

tänzeln [ˈtɛn·tsl̩n] *vi* ❶ *haben* (*auf und ab federn*) *Boxer* to dance; *Pferd* to prance ❷ *sein* (*sich leichtfüßig fortbewegen*) to skip

tanzen [ˈtan·tsn̩] **I.** *vi* ❶ *haben* (*einen Tanz ausführen*) to dance ❷ *sein* (*sich tanzend fortbewegen*) to dance ❸ *haben* (*hüpfen*) *Gläser, Würfel* to jump in the air; **das kleine Boot tanzte auf den Wellen** the little boat bobbed up and down on the waves; **ihm tanzte alles vor den Augen** the room was spinning before his eyes **II.** *vt haben* to dance

Tänzer(in) <-s, -> [ˈtɛn·tsɐ] *m(f)* dancer

Tanzfläche *f* dance floor

Tanzmusik *f* dance music

Tanzpartner(in) *m(f)* dance [*or* dancing] partner

Tanzschule *f* dance school

Tanzstunde *f* ❶ *kein pl* (*Kurs*) dance class ❷ (*Unterrichtsstunde*) dance [*or* dancing] lesson

Tapete <-, -n> [ta·ˈpeː·tə] *f* wallpaper

tapezieren* [ta·pe·ˈtsiː·rən] *vt* to wallpaper

tapfer [ˈtap·fɐ] *adj* brave

Tapferkeit <-> *f kein pl* courage

tappen [ˈta·pn̩] *vi* ❶ *sein* (*schwerfällig gehen*) **schlaftrunken tappte er zum Telefon** he shuffled drowsily to the phone ❷ *haben* (*tasten*) ■ **[nach etw** *dat*] **~** to feel [for sth]

tapsen [ˈtap·sn̩] *vi sein* (*fam*) *Kleinkind* to toddle; *Bär* to lumber

Tarantel <-, -n> [ta·ˈran·tl̩] *f* tarantula

Tarif <-[e]s, -e> [ta·ˈriːf] *m* ❶ (*gewerkschaftliche Gehaltsvereinbarung*) pay scale (**nach, über, unter** *+dat* according to, above, below) ❷ (*festgesetzter Einheitspreis*) charge

Tarifabschluss[RR] *m* wage agreement

Tarifgruppe *f* wage group

tariflich **I.** *adj* negotiated **II.** *adv* by negotiation

Tariflohn *m* standard wage

Tarifrunde *f* round of collective bargaining

Tarifverhandlung *f meist pl* collective bargaining negotiations *pl*

Tarifvertrag *m* collective bargaining agreement

tarnen [ˈtar·nən] *vt* ❶ MIL to camouflage (**gegen** *+akk* against) ❷ (*Identität wechseln*) ■ **etw [durch etw** *akk*] **~** to disguise sth [by doing sth]; ■ **sich** *akk* **[als jd] ~** to disguise oneself [as sb]

Tarnfarbe *f* camouflage paint

Tarnname *m* cover name

Tarnung <-, -en> *f* ❶ *kein pl* (*das Tarnen*) *a.* MIL camouflage ❷ (*tarnende Identität*) cover

Tasche <-, -n> [ˈta·ʃə] *f* ❶ (*Handtasche*) [hand]bag; (*Einkaufstasche*) [shopping] bag; (*Aktentasche*) briefcase ❷ (*in Kleidungsstü-*

cken) pocket ▸ WENDUNGEN: **jdm auf der ~ liegen** (*fam*) to live off [of] sb['s money]; **jdn in die ~ stecken** (*fam*) to be head and shoulders above sb; **in die eigene ~ wirtschaften** (*fam*) to line one's own pocket[s]
Taschenbuch *nt* paperback
Taschenbuchausgabe *f* paperback edition
Taschencomputer *m* hand-held computer
Taschendieb(in) *m(f)* pickpocket
Taschengeld *nt* allowance, spending money
Taschenlampe *f* [pocket] flashlight
Taschenmesser *nt* pocketknife
Taschenrechner *m* pocket calculator
Taschentuch *nt* handkerchief
Taschenuhr *f* pocket watch
Taskleiste ['task-] *f* COMPUT task bar
Tasse <-, -n> ['ta·sə] *f* cup; **eine ~ Tee** a cup of tea ▸ WENDUNGEN: **nicht alle ~n im Schrank haben** (*fam*) to have a screw loose
Tastatur <-, -en> [tas·ta·'tu:ɐ̯] *f* keyboard
Taste <-, -n> ['tas·tə] *f* (*Schreibmaschine*) key; (*Telefon*) button
tasten ['tas·tn̩] **I.** *vi* (*fühlend suchen*) to feel (**nach** +*dat* for) **II.** *vr* (*sich vortasten*) ■ **sich** *akk* **irgendwohin ~** to feel one's way somewhere **III.** *vt* ① (*fühlend wahrnehmen*) to feel ② (*per Tastendruck eingeben*) to enter; **taste eine 9** press [the] 9
Tasteninstrument *nt* keyboard instrument
Tastsinn *m kein pl* sense of touch
tat ['ta:t] *imp von* **tun**
Tat <-, -en> ['ta:t] *f* ① (*Handlung*) act; **eine gute ~** a good deed; **etw in die ~ umsetzen** to put sth into effect ② (*Straftat*) crime; **jdn auf frischer ~ ertappen** to catch sb redhanded *fig* ▸ WENDUNGEN: **in der ~** indeed
Tatbestand *m* ① (*Sachlage*) facts [of the matter] ② JUR elements of an offense
tatenlos *adj inv* idle; **~ zusehen** to stand back and do nothing
Täter(in) <-s, -> ['tɛ:·tɐ] *m(f)* perpetrator
tätig ['tɛ:·tɪç] *adj* ① (*beschäftigt*) employed; ■ **[irgendwo] ~ sein** to work [somewhere] ② *attr* (*tatkräftig*) active ③ (*aktiv*) active; ■ **[in etw** *dat*] **~ werden** (*geh*) to act [on sth]
Tätigkeit <-, -en> *f* ① (*Beschäftigung*) occupation ② *kein pl* (*Aktivität*) activity; **in ~ sein** to be operating
Tätigkeitsbereich *m* field of activity
Tatkraft *f kein pl* drive
tatkräftig *adj* active
tätlich ['tɛ:t·lɪç] *adj* violent (**gegen** +*akk* toward)
Tatmotiv *nt* motive
Tatort *m* scene of the crime
tätowieren* [tɛ·to·'vi:·rən] *vt* to tattoo
Tätowierung <-, -en> *f* ① (*eingeritztes Motiv*) tattoo ② *kein pl* (*das Tätowieren*) tattooing
Tatsache ['ta:t·za·xə] *f* fact; **~ ist [aber], dass ...** the fact of the matter is [however] that ... ▸ WENDUNGEN: **den ~n ins Auge sehen** to face the facts
tatsächlich ['ta:t·zɛç·lɪç, ta:t·'zɛç·lɪç] **I.** *adj inv, attr* (*wirklich*) actual *attr,* real **II.** *adv* ① (*in Wirklichkeit*) actually ② (*in der Tat*) really
tätscheln ['tɛ:t·ʃl̩n] *vt* to pat
Tatverdacht *m* suspicion
tatverdächtig *adj* under suspicion
Tatverdächtige(r) *f(m)* suspect
Tatwaffe *f* murder weapon
Tatze <-, -n> ['ta·tsə] *f* (*a. pej fam*) paw
Tatzeuge, -zeugin *m, f* JUR incident witness
Tau¹ <-[e]s> ['tau] *m kein pl* (*Tautropfen*) dew
Tau² <-[e]s, -e> ['tau] *nt* rope
taub ['taup] *adj* ① (*gehörlos*) deaf; **sich** *akk* **~ stellen** to turn a deaf ear ② (*gefühllos*) numb ③ *Nuss* empty; *Boden* barren; *Metall* dull
Taube <-, -n> ['tau·bə] *f* pigeon
Taubheit <-> *f kein pl* ① (*Gehörlosigkeit*) deafness ② (*Gefühllosigkeit*) numbness
taubstumm *adj* deaf and dumb
Taubstumme(r) *f(m)* deaf-mute
Taubstummensprache *f* sign language
tauchen [tau·xn̩] **I.** *vi* ① *haben o sein* (*untertauchen*) to dive (**nach** +*dat* for) ② *sein* (*auftauchen*) ■ **[aus etw** *dat*] **~** to emerge **II.** *vt haben* ① (*eintauchen*) to dip; **in [gleißendes] Licht getaucht** bathed in [glistening] light ② (*untertauchen*) to duck
Tauchen <-s> ['tau·xn̩] *nt kein pl* diving
Taucher(in) <-s, -> ['tau·xɐ] *m(f) a.* ORN diver
Taucheranzug *m* diving suit
Taucherbrille *f* diving goggles *npl*
Tauchsieder <-s, -> *m* immersion heater
tauen ['tau·ən] **I.** *vi* ① *haben* (*Tauwetter setzt ein*) ■ **es taut** it's thawing [*or* starting to thaw] ② *sein* ([*ab*]*schmelzen*) to melt **II.** *vt* to melt
Taufbecken *nt* baptismal font
Taufe <-, -n> ['tau·fə] *f* (*christliches Aufnahmeritual*) baptism ▸ WENDUNGEN: **etw aus der ~ heben** (*hum fam*) to launch sth
taufen ['tau·fn̩] *vt* ① (*die Taufe vollziehen*) to baptize ② (*in der Taufe benennen*) to christen ③ (*fam: benennen*) to christen
Täufling <-s, -e> *m* person to be baptized
Taufname *m* Christian name
Taufpate, -patin *m, f* godfather *masc,* godmother *fem*
taugen ['taugn̩] *vi* ① (*wert sein*) ■ **etw/viel/nichts ~** to be useful/very useful/useless ② (*geeignet sein*) to be suitable (**als/zu/für** for)
Taugenichts <-[es], -e> ['tau·gə·nɪçts] *m* (*veraltend*) good-for-nothing
tauglich ['tauk·lɪç] *adj* ① (*geeignet*) suitable ② MIL fit [for military service]
Tauglichkeit <-> *f kein pl* ① (*Eignung für einen Zweck*) suitability ② MIL fitness [for military service]
Taumel <-s> ['tau·ml̩] *m kein pl* (*geh*) ① (*Schwindelgefühl*) dizziness ② (*geh: Überschwang*) frenzy
taumeln ['tau·ml̩n] *vi sein* to stagger
Tausch <-[e]s, *selten* -e> [tauʃ] *m* swap, trade; **im ~ gegen [etw** *akk*] in exchange for

[sth]

tauschen ['tau·ʃn̩] **I.** *vt* ❶ (*gegeneinander einwechseln*) to swap [*or* trade] (**mit** +*dat* with, **gegen** +*akk* for) ❷ (*geh: austauschen*) to exchange **II.** *vi* to swap [*or* trade] ▶WENDUNGEN: **mit niemandem ~ wollen** to not wish to trade places with anyone

täuschen ['tɔy·ʃn̩] **I.** *vt* (*irreführen*) to deceive; ■**sich** *akk* **[von jdm/etw] nicht ~ lassen** to not be fooled [by sb/sth]; **wenn mich nicht alles täuscht ....** if I'm not completely mistaken ... **II.** *vr* (*sich irren*) ■**sich** *akk* ~ to be mistaken [*or* wrong] (**in** +*dat* about) **III.** *vi* (*irreführen*) to be deceptive

täuschend **I.** *adj inv* (*trügerisch*) deceptive; *Ähnlichkeit* striking **II.** *adv* (*trügerisch*) deceptively; **sie sieht ihrer Mutter ~ ähnlich** she bears a striking resemblance to her mother

Tauschgeschäft *nt* exchange

Täuschung <-, -en> ['tɔy·ʃʊŋ] *f* ❶ (*Betrug*) deception ❷ (*Irrtum*) error; **optische ~** optical illusion

Täuschungsmanöver *nt* ploy

tausend ['tauz·n̩t] *adj* ❶ (*Zahl*) a [*or* one] thousand ❷ (*fam: sehr viele*) thousands of ...

Tausend[1] <-s, -e o -> ['tauz·n̩t, *pl* -n̩·də] *nt* ❶ (*Einheit von 1000 Dingen*) a [*or* one] thousand ❷ *pl, auch kleingeschrieben* (*viele tausend*) thousands *pl* (**von** +*dat* of); **einige ~e ...** several thousand ...; **einer von ~** one in a thousand; **zu ~en** by the thousands

Tausend[2] <-, -en> ['tauzn̩t, *pl* -n̩·dn̩] *f* thousand

Tausender <-s, -> ['tau·zn̩·dɐ] *m* (*1000 als Bestandteil einer Zahl*) thousands

tausendfach, 1000fach ['tau·zn̩t·fax] **I.** *adj* thousandfold **II.** *adv* thousandfold, a thousand times over

Tausendfüßler <-s, -> ['tau·zn̩t·fy:s·lɐ] *m* centipede

tausendjährig, 1000-jährig[RR] ['tau·zn̩t·jɛ:·rɪç] *adj* ❶ (*Alter*) thousand-year-old *attr,* one thousand years old *pred; s. a.* **achtjährig 1** ❷ (*Zeitspanne*) thousand-year *attr; s. a.* **achtjährig 2**

tausendmal, 1000-mal[RR] ['tau·zn̩t·ma:l] *adv* ❶ a thousand times; *s. a.* **achtmal** ❷ (*fam: sehr viel, sehr oft*) a thousand times; **bitte ~ um Entschuldigung!** (*fam*) a thousand apologies!

Tausendstel ['tau·zn̩t·stl̩] *nt o* SCHWEIZ *m* thousandth

Tautropfen *m* dewdrop

Tauwasser *nt* melt water

Tauwetter *nt* thaw

Tauziehen *nt kein pl* (*a. fig*) tug of war

Taxameter <-s, -> [tak·sa·'me:·tɐ] *m* taximeter, clock *fam*

Taxe <-, -n> ['tak·sə] *f* ❶ (*Kurtaxe*) charge ❷ (*Schätzwert*) estimate ❸ DIAL (*Taxi*) taxi

Taxi <-s, -s> ['tak·si] *nt* taxi, cab

Taxifahrer(in) *m(f)* taxi [*or* cab] driver

Taxistand *m* taxi [*or* cab] stand

Tb <-, -s> [te:·'be:] *f,* **Tbc** <-, -s> [te:·be:·'tse:] *f Abk von* **Tuberkulose** TB

Team <-s, -s> [ti:m] *nt* team

Teamarbeit ['ti:m-] *f* teamwork

teamfähig ['ti:m-] *adj* able to work in a team

Technik <-, -en> ['teç·nɪk] *f* ❶ *kein pl* (*Technologie*) technology ❷ *kein pl* (*technische Ausstattung*) technical equipment ❸ *kein pl* (*technische Konstruktion*) technology ❹ (*besondere Methode*) technique ❺ ÖSTERR (*technische Hochschule*) college of technology

Techniker(in) <-s, -> ['teç·nɪ·kɐ] *m(f)* (*Fachmann der Technik*) engineer; *in der Kunst* technician

technisch ['teç·nɪʃ] **I.** *adj* ❶ *attr* (*technologisch*) technical ❷ (*technisches Wissen vermittelnd*) technical ❸ *Können, Probleme* technical **II.** *adv* technically

Technische Hochschule <-n -, -n -n> *f vocational college providing degree courses in technical and scientific subjects*

Technologie <-, -n> [tɛç·no·lo·'gi:] *f* technology

technologisch [tɛç·no·'lo:·gɪʃ] *adj* technological

Teddybär ['tɛ·di-] *m* teddy [bear]

Tee <-s, -s> [te:] *m* (*Getränk*) tea; (*aus Heilkräutern*) herbal tea; **eine Tasse ~** a cup of tea; **grüner/schwarzer ~** green/black tea ▶WENDUNGEN: **abwarten und ~ trinken** (*fam*) to wait and see

Teebeutel *m* tea bag

Teefilter *m* tea strainer

Teekanne *f* teapot

Teelicht *nt* tea candle

Teelöffel *m* ❶ (*Löffel*) teaspoon ❷ (*Menge*) teaspoon[ful]

Teen <-s, -s> [ti:n] *m,* **Teenager** <-s, -> ['ti:n·e:dʒɐ] *m* teenager

Teer <-[e]s, -e> [te:ɐ̯] *m* tar

teeren ['te:·rən] *vt* to tar

Teeservice *nt* tea set

Teflon® <-s> ['tɛf·lo:n] *nt kein pl* Teflon®

Teich <-[e]s, -e> [taiç] *m* pond

Teig <-[e]s, -e> [taik] *m* (*Hefe-, Rühr-, Nudelteig*) dough; (*Mürbe-, Blätterteig*) pastry; (*flüssig*) batter

Teigwaren *pl* (*geh*) pasta + *sing vb*

Teil[1] <-[e]s, -e> [tail] *m* ❶ (*Bruchteil*) part; **in zwei ~e zerbrechen** to break in two; **zum größten ~** for the most part; **zum ~** partly; (*gelegentlich*) on occasion ❷ (*Anteil*) share; **zu gleichen ~en** equally ❸ (*Bereich*) *einer Stadt* district; (*einer Strecke*) stretch; (*eines Gebäudes, einer Zeitung, eines Buches*) section ▶WENDUNGEN: **sich** *dat* **seinen ~ denken** (*fam*) to draw one's own conclusions

Teil[2] <-[e]s, -e> [tail] *nt* ❶ (*Einzelteil*) component ❷ (*sl: Ding*) thing

Teilansicht *f* partial view

teilbar *adj* ❶ (*aufzuteilen*) ■**[in etw** *akk***] ~ sein** to be able to be divided [into sth] ❷ MATH (*dividierbar*) ■**[durch etw** *akk***] ~ sein** to be

divisible [by sth]
Teilbereich *m* section
Teilbetrag *m* installment
Teilchen <-s, -> *nt dim von* **Teil**[1] **1** ① (*Partikel*) particle ② (*Kernphysik*) nuclear particle ③ KOCHK DIAL pastries *pl*
teilen ['tai·lən] **I.** *vt* ① (*aufteilen*) to share ② MATH (*dividieren*) to divide (**durch** +*akk* by) ③ (*trennen*) to separate **II.** *vr* ① (*sich aufteilen*) ■**sich** [**in etw** *akk*] ~ to split up [into sth] ② (*sich gabeln*) ■**sich** [**in etw** *akk*] ~ to fork [into sth] ③ (*unter sich aufteilen*) ■**sich** *dat* **etw** [**mit jdm**] ~ to share sth [with sb] ④ (*gemeinsam benutzen*) ■**sich** *dat* **etw** ~ to share sth **III.** *vi* (*abgeben*) to share
Teilhaber(in) <-s, -> *m(f)* partner
Teilnahme <-, -en> ['tail·naː·mə] *f* ① (*Beteiligung*) participation (**an** +*dat* in) ② (*geh: Mitgefühl*) sympathy ③ (*geh: Interesse*) interest
teilnahmslos *adj* apathetic
Teilnahmslosigkeit <-> *f kein pl* apathy
teil|nehmen *vi irreg* ① (*anwesend sein*) ■[**an etw** *dat*] ~ to attend [sth] ② (*sich beteiligen*) to participate (**an** +*dat* in); *Wettbewerb* to take part; *Kurs* to attend
Teilnehmer(in) <-s, -> *m(f)* ① (*Anwesender*) person present ② (*Beteiligter*) participant (**an** +*dat* in) ③ (*Telefoninhaber*) subscriber
teils ['tails] *adv* partly; **~, ~** (*fam*) yes and no
Teilstück *nt* part
Teilung <-, -en> *f* division
teilweise ['tail·vai·zə] **I.** *adv* partly **II.** *adj attr* partial
Teilzeitarbeit *f* part-time work
Teint <-s, -s> ['tɛ̃ː] *m* complexion
Telearbeit ['teːlə-] *f kein pl* telework
Telebanking ['teː·lə·bɛŋ·kɪŋ] *nt* home banking
Telefax ['teː·lə·faks] *nt* fax
Telefon <-s, -e> [te·le·'foːn, a. 'teː·le·foːn] *nt* telephone, phone *fam*
Telefonanschluss[RR] *m* [tele]phone connection
Telefonat <-[e]s, -e> [te·le·fo·'naːt] *nt* (*geh*) [tele]phone call
Telefonauskunft *f* directory assistance
Telefonbuch *nt* [tele]phone book
Telefongesellschaft *f* [tele]phone company
Telefongespräch *nt* [tele]phone call
Telefonhörer *m* [[tele]phone] receiver
telefonieren* [te·le·fo·'niː·rən] *vi* to be on the phone; ■**mit jdm** ~ to talk on the phone with sb
telefonisch **I.** *adj* [tele]phone **II.** *adv* by [tele]phone
Telefonkarte *f* calling card
Telefonleitung *f* [tele]phone line
Telefonnummer *f* [tele]phone number
Telefonrechnung *f* [tele]phone bill
Telefonzelle *f* phone booth
Telefonzentrale *f* switchboard
Telegraf <-en, -en> [te·le·'graːf] *m* telegraph
telegrafieren* [te·le·graː·'fiː·rən] *vi, vt* to telegraph
Telegramm <-s, -e> [te·le·'gram] *nt* telegram
Telegrammstil *m kein pl* telegraphese
Telegraph <-s, -en> *m s.* **Telegraf**
telegraphieren *vi, vt s.* **telegrafieren**
Telekom <-> ['teː·lə·kɔm] *f kein pl kurz für* **Deutsche Telekom AG**: ■**die** ~ *German Telecommunications Company*
Telekommunikation *f* telecommunication
Teleobjektiv *nt* telephoto lens
Telepathie <-> [te·le·pa·'tiː] *f kein pl* telepathy
Teleskop <-s, -e> [te·le·'skoːp] *nt* telescope
Teller <-s, -> ['tɛ·lɐ] *m* ① (*Geschirrteil*) plate; **flacher/tiefer** ~ dinner/soup plate ② (*Menge*) plate[ful]
Tellergericht *nt* KOCHK one-course meal
Tellerrand *m* ▶ WENDUNGEN: **über den ~ hinausschauen** (*fam*) to think outside the box; **über den ~ nicht hinausschauen** (*fam*) to not see farther than [the end of] one's nose
Tellerwäscher(in) *m(f)* dishwasher
Tempel <-s, -> ['tɛm·pl̩] *m* temple
Temperament <-[e]s, -e> [tɛm·pə·ra·'mɛnt] *nt* ① (*Wesensart*) temperament ② *kein pl* (*Lebhaftigkeit*) vivacity; ~ **haben** to be very lively
temperamentvoll **I.** *adj* lively, vivacious **II.** *adv* vivaciously
Temperatur <-, -en> [tɛm·pə·ra·'tuːɐ̯] *f* temperature; [**seine/die**] ~ **messen** to take one's temperature; [**erhöhte**] ~ **haben** to have a temperature
Temperaturanstieg *m* rise in temperature
Temperaturrückgang *m* drop in temperature
Temperaturschwankung *f* fluctuation in temperature
Tempo[1] <-s, -s> ['tɛm·po] *nt* ① (*Geschwindigkeit*) speed; **mit hohem ~** at high speed ② (*musikalisches Zeitmaß*) tempo
Tempo®[2] <-s, -s> *nt* (*fam: Papiertaschentuch*) tissue, Kleenex®
Tempolimit *nt* speed limit
Tendenz <-, -en> [tɛn·'dɛnts] *f* ① (*Trend*) trend ② (*Neigung*) tendency (**zu** +*dat* to)
tendenziell [tɛn·dɛn·'tsi̯ɛl] *adj inv* **es zeichnet sich eine ~e Entwicklung zum Besseren ab** trends indicate a change for the better
tendieren* [tɛn·'diː·rən] *vi* ① (*hinneigen*) to tend (**zu** +*dat* toward); ■**dazu ~, etw zu tun** to tend to do sth ② (*sich entwickeln*) ■[**irgendwohin**] ~ to have a tendency [to move in a certain direction]
Teneriffa [te·ne·'rɪ·fa] *nt* Tenerife
Tennis <-> ['tɛ·nɪs] *nt kein pl* tennis
Tennisball *m* tennis ball
Tennisplatz *m* ① (*Spielfeld*) tennis court ② (*Anlage*) outdoor tennis complex
Tennisschläger *m* tennis racket
Tennisspiel *nt* ① (*Sportart*) tennis ② (*Einzelspiel*) game of tennis
Tennisspieler(in) *m(f)* tennis player
Tenor <-s, Tenöre> [te·'noːɐ̯, *pl* te·'nøː·rə] *m*

T

MUS tenor

Teppich <-s, -e> ['tɛ·pɪç] *m* (*Fußbodenbedeckung*) carpet; (*klein*) rug; (*Wandteppich*) tapestry

Tẹppichboden *m* wall-to-wall carpeting

Termin <-s, -e> [tɛr·'mi:n] *m* ❶ (*verabredeter Zeitpunkt*) appointment; **sich** *dat* **einen ~ [für etw** *akk*] **geben lassen** to make an appointment [for sth]; **einen ~ vereinbaren/verpassen** to set up/miss an appointment ❷ (*festgelegter Zeitpunkt*) deadline

Terminal[1] <-s-, -s> ['tø:ɐ̯·min|] *nt* COMPUT terminal

Terminal[2] <-s, -s> ['tø:ɐ̯·mi·n|] *m o nt* LUFT, TRANSP terminal

Termindruck *m kein pl* time pressure, pressure to meet a deadline

termingerecht I. *adj* according to schedule II. *adv* on time

Terminkalender *m* [appointment] calendar, schedule

Terminologie <-, -n> [tɛr·mi·no·lo·'gi:, *pl* -'gi:·ən] *f* terminology

Terminplaner <-s, -> *m* ❶ (*Kalender*) [appointment] calendar, schedule ❷ TECH, COMPUT electronic organizer

Termite <-, -n> [tɛr·'mi:·tə] *f* termite

Terpentin <-s, -e> [tɛr·pɛn·'ti:n] *nt o* ÖSTERR *m* turpentine; (*Terpentinöl a.*) oil of turpentine

Terrain <-s, -s> [tɛ·'rɛ̃:] *nt* ❶ (*Gelände*) terrain ❷ (*a. fig:* [*Bau*]*grundstück*) site

Terrarium <-s, -rien> [tɛ·'ra:·ri̯·ʊm, *pl* -ri̯·ən] *nt* terrarium

Terrasse <-, -n> [tɛ·'ra·sə] *f* ❶ (*Freisitz*) terrace; (*Balkon*) [large] balcony ❷ (*Geländestufe*) terrace

Territorium <-s, -rien> [tɛ·ri·'to:·ri̯·ʊm, *pl* -ri̯·ən] *nt* territory

Terror <-s> ['tɛ·ro:ɐ̯] *m kein pl* ❶ (*terroristische Aktivitäten*) terrorism ❷ (*Furcht und Schrecken*) terror ❸ (*fam: Stunk*) huge fuss

Tẹrrorakt *m* act of terrorism

Tẹrroranschlag *m* terror[ist] attack

terrorisieren* [tɛ·ro·ri·'zi:·rən] *vt* ❶ (*fam: schikanieren*) to intimidate ❷ (*in Angst und Schrecken versetzen*) to terrorize

Terrorismus <-> [tɛ·ro·'rɪs·mʊs] *m kein pl* terrorism

Terrorist(in) <-en, -en> [tɛ·ro·'rɪst] *m(f)* terrorist

terroristisch *adj* terrorist *attr*

Terz <-, -en> ['tɛrts] *f* MUS third

Terzett <-[e]s, -e> [tɛr·'tsɛt] *nt* MUS trio

Tesafilm® ['te:·za·fɪlm] *m* Scotch tape®

Test <-[e]s, -s *o* -e> [tɛst] *m* test

Testament <-[e]s, -e> [tɛs·ta·'mɛnt] *nt* ❶ JUR will ❷ REL **Altes/Neues ~** Old/New Testament

testamentarisch [tɛs·ta·mɛn·'ta:·rɪʃ] I. *adj* testamentary II. *adv* in the will

Testamentseröffnung *f* reading of the will

Tẹstbild *nt* TV test pattern

testen ['tɛs·tn̩] *vt* to test (**auf** + *akk* for)

teuer ['tɔy·ɐ] I. *adj* ❶ (*viel kostend*) expensive ❷ (*geh: geschätzt*) dear II. *adv* (*zu einem hohen Preis*) expensively; **das hast du aber zu ~ eingekauft** you paid too much for that; **sich** *dat* **etw** *akk* **~ bezahlen lassen** to demand a high price for sth ▶ WENDUNGEN: **etw** *akk* **~ bezahlen müssen** to pay a high price for sth; **jdn ~ zu stehen kommen** to cost sb dearly

Teuerungsrate *f* rate of price increase

Teufel <-s, -> [tɔyf|] *m* ❶ *kein pl* (*Satan*) ■ **der ~** the Devil ❷ (*teuflischer Mensch*) devil ▶ WENDUNGEN: **in ~s Küche kommen** (*fam*) to get into a hell of a mess; **den ~ an die Wand malen** to imagine the worst; **geh zum ~!** (*fam*) go to hell!; **soll jdn [doch] der ~ holen** (*fam*) to hell with sb; **irgendwo ist der ~ los** (*fam*) all hell is breaking loose somewhere; **weiß der ~** (*fam*) who the hell knows

Teufelskreis *m* vicious circle

teuflisch ['tɔyf·lɪʃ] I. *adj* diabolical II. *adv* ❶ (*diabolisch*) diabolically ❷ (*fam: höllisch*) like hell

Text <-[e]s, -e> [tɛkst] *m* ❶ (*schriftliche Darstellung*) text ❷ (*Lied*) lyrics ❸ (*Wortlaut*) text; *einer Rede* script ▶ WENDUNGEN: **jdn aus dem ~ bringen** (*fam*) to confuse sb

texten ['tɛks·tn̩] I. *vt* to write II. *vi* to write songs; (*in der Werbung*) to write copy

Tẹxter(in) <-s, -> *m(f)* songwriter; (*in der Werbung*) copywriter

Textilfabrik *f* textile factory

Textilien [tɛks·'ti:·li̯·ən] *pl* textiles *pl*

Textilindustrie *f* textile industry

Tẹxtstelle *f* passage

Tẹxtverarbeitungsprogramm *nt* word processing program

TH <-, -s> [te'ha] *f Abk von* **Technische Hochschule**

Thai ['tai] *nt* Thai; *s. a.* **Deutsch**

Thailand ['tai·lant] *nt* Thailand

Thailänder(in) <-s, -> ['tai·lɛn·dɐ] *m(f)* Thai

thailändisch ['tai·lɛn·dɪʃ] *adj* Thai; *s. a.* **deutsch**

Theater <-s, -> [te·'a:·tɐ] *nt* ❶ (*Gebäude*) theater ❷ *kein pl* (*Schauspielkunst*) theater; **~ spielen** to act; **nur ~ sein** (*fam*) to be only an act ❸ *kein pl* (*fam: Umstände*) fuss; **[ein] ~ machen** to make a fuss

Theateraufführung *f* theater performance

Theaterbesucher(in) *m(f)* theatergoer

Theaterkarte *f* theater ticket

Theaterstück *nt* play

Theke <-, -n> ['te:·kə] *f* counter; (*in einem Lokal*) bar

Thema <-s, Themen *o* -ta> ['te:·ma, *pl* -mən, -ta] *nt* ❶ (*Gesprächsthema*) topic; **jdn vom ~ abbringen** to get [*or* throw] sb off the subject; **beim ~ bleiben** to stick to the subject; **ein ~ ist [für jdn] erledigt** (*fam*) a matter is closed [as far as sb is concerned] ❷ (*schriftliches Thema*) subject ❸ (*Bereich*) subject area ❹ MUS theme ▶ WENDUNGEN: **ein/kein ~ sein**

to be/not be an issue
Thematik <-> [te·ˈmaː·tɪk] *f kein pl* topic
Themen [ˈteː·mən] *pl von* **Thema**
Theologe, Theologin <-n, -n> [teo·ˈloː·gə] *m, f* theologian
Theologie <-, -n> [teo·lo·ˈgiː, *pl* -ˈgiː·ən] *f* theology
theologisch [teo·ˈloː·gɪʃ] **I.** *adj* theological **II.** *adv* ❶ (*in der Theologie*) in theological matters ❷ (*für die Theologie*) theologically
Theoretiker(in) <-s, -> [teo·ˈreː·ti·kɐ] *m(f)* theorist
theoretisch [teo·ˈreː·tɪʃ] **I.** *adj* theoretical **II.** *adv* theoretically
Theorie <-, -n> [teo·ˈriː, *pl* -ˈriː·ən] *f* theory
Therapeut(in) <-en, -en> [te·ra·ˈpɔyt] *m(f)* therapist
therapeutisch [te·ra·ˈpɔy·tɪʃ] **I.** *adj* therapeutic **II.** *adv* as therapy
Therapie <-, -n> [te·ra·ˈpiː, *pl* -ˈpiː·ən] *f* therapy
therapieren [te·ra·ˈpiː·rən] *vt* to treat
Thermalquelle [tɛr·ˈmaːl-] *f* thermal spring
Thermometer <-s, -> [tɛr·mo·ˈmeː·tɐ] *nt* thermometer
Thermometerstand *m* temperature
Thermoskanne [ˈtɛr·mɔs-] *f* thermos flask
Thermostat <-[e]s *o* -en, -e[n]> [tɛr·mo·ˈstaːt] *m* thermostat
These <-, -n> [ˈteː·zə] *f* (*geh*) thesis
Thriller <-s, -> [θrɪ·lɐ] *m* thriller
Thrombose <-, -n> [trɔm·ˈboː·sə] *f* thrombosis
Thron <-[e]s, -e> [ˈtroːn] *m* throne
Thronfolge *f* line of succession
Thronfolger(in) <-s, -> *m(f)* heir to the throne
Thunfisch [ˈtuːn·fɪʃ] *m* tuna [fish]
Thüringen <-s> [ˈtyː·rɪŋən] *nt* Thuringia
Thüringer(in) <-s, -> [ˈtyː·rɪŋɐ] *m(f)* Thuringian
thüringisch [ˈtyː·rɪŋɪʃ] *adj* Thuringian
Thymian <-s, -e> [ˈtyː·mi̯·aːn] *m* thyme
Tibet <-s> [ˈtiː·bɛt, ti·ˈbeːt] *nt* Tibet; *s. a.* **Deutschland**
ticken [ˈtɪkn̩] *vi* (*ein klickendes Geräusch machen*) to tick ▸ WENDUNGEN: **nicht richtig ~** (*sl*) to be off one's rocker *sl*
tief [ˈtiːf] **I.** *adj* ❶ (*eine große Tiefe/Dicke aufweisend*) deep; **ein Meter ~** a meter deep ❷ (*niedrig*) low ❸ MUS (*tief klingend*) low; *Stimme* deep ❹ (*intensiv empfunden*) intense ❺ (*tiefgründig*) profound ❻ (*mitten in etw liegend*) deep; **im ~sten Winter** in the middle of winter ❼ (*weit hineinreichend*) deep; *Ausschnitt* low **II.** *adv* ❶ (*weit eindringend*) deep; **~ greifend** far-reaching ❷ (*vertikal weit hinunter*) deep; **er stürzte 300 Meter ~** he fell 300 meters [down] ❸ (*dumpf tönend*) low; **zu ~ singen** to sing flat; **~ sprechen** to talk in a deep voice ❹ (*zutiefst*) deeply; **etw ~ bedauern** to deeply regret sth; **jdn ~ erschrecken** to frighten sb terribly ❺ (*intensiv*) deeply; **~ schlafen** to sleep soundly ❻ (*niedrig*) low; **~ liegend** low-lying; **~ stehend** (*fig*) low-level
Tief <-[e]s, -s> [ˈtiːf] *nt* ❶ METEO low ❷ (*depressive Phase*) low [point]
Tiefdruck *m kein pl* METEO low pressure
Tiefe <-, -n> [ˈtiː·fə] *f* ❶ (*Wassertiefe*) depth ❷ (*vertikal hinabreichende Ausdehnung*) depth; **der Schacht führt hinab bis in 1200 Meter ~** the shaft goes down to a depth of nearly 1200 meters ❸ (*horizontal hineinreichende Ausdehnung*) depth ❹ *kein pl* (*Intensität*) intensity; *einer Farbe* depth ❺ (*Tiefgründigkeit*) depth ❻ (*dunkler Klang*) deepness
Tiefebene *f* lowland plain
Tiefenschärfe *f kein pl* depth of field
Tiefenwirkung *f eines Kosmetikums* deep action; ■ **mit ~** deep-acting
Tiefgang *m* NAUT draft ▸ WENDUNGEN: **~ haben** to be profound
Tiefgarage *f* underground parking lot
tiefgefroren, tiefgekühlt *adj* frozen
tiefgreifend *adj s.* **tief II, 1**
Tiefkühlkost *f* frozen food
Tiefkühlschrank *m* freezer
Tiefkühltruhe *f* freezer chest
Tiefland [ˈtiːf·lant] *nt* lowlands *pl*
Tiefpunkt *m* low point
Tiefschlaf *m kein pl* deep sleep
Tiefschlag *m* ❶ (*schwerer Schicksalsschlag*) cruel stroke of fate ❷ SPORT blow below the belt
tiefsinnig *adj* profound
Tier <-[e]s, -e> [ˈtiːɐ̯] *nt* animal
Tierart *f* animal species + *sing vb*
Tierarzt, -ärztin *m, f* veterinarian, vet *fam*
Tiergarten *m* zoo
Tierhandlung *f* pet store
tierisch [ˈtiː·rɪʃ] **I.** *adj* ❶ (*bei Tieren anzutreffend*) animal *attr* ❷ (*sl: gewaltig*) **einen ~en Durst/Hunger haben** to be dying of thirst/hunger *fig* **II.** *adv* (*sl*) **~ schuften/schwitzen** to work/sweat like hell; **~ wehtun** to hurt like crazy, to kill *sl or fig*
Tierkreiszeichen *nt* zodiac sign
tierlieb *adj* animal-loving *attr;* ■ **~ sein** to be an animal lover
Tierpfleger(in) *m(f)* zookeeper
Tierquäler(in) <-s, -> *m(f)* person who is cruel to animals
Tierquälerei [tiːɐ̯·kvɛː·lə·ˈrai] *f* cruelty to animals
Tierschutz *m* protection of animals
Tierschützer(in) *m(f)* animal welfare activist
Tierversuch *m* animal testing [*or* experimentation]
Tiger <-s, -> [tiː·gɐ] *m* tiger
tilgen [ˈtɪlgn̩] *vt* (*geh*) ❶ FIN (*abtragen*) to pay off ❷ (*beseitigen*) to wipe out *sep;* ■ **etw** *akk* **von etw** *dat* **~** to erase sth from sth
Tilgung <-, -en> *f* (*geh*) ❶ FIN (*das Tilgen*) repayment ❷ (*Beseitigung*) deletion
Tinte <-, -n> [ˈtɪn·tə] *f* ink ▸ WENDUNGEN: **in der ~ sitzen** (*fam*) to be in a scrape
Tintenfisch *m* squid

T

Tintenstrahldrucker *m* ink-jet printer
TippRR, **Tip**ALT <-s, -s> ['tɪp] *m a.* SPORT tip; **guter/schlechter/sicherer Tipp** good/bad/safe bet
tippen[1] [tɪpn̩] **I.** *vi* ❶ (*Wettscheine ausfüllen*) to fill out betting slips; **im Lotto ~** to play the lottery ❷ (*fam: etw vorhersagen*) to guess; ■**auf jdn/etw ~** to put one's money on sb/sth; ■**darauf ~, dass ...** to bet that ... **II.** *vt* **eine Zahl ~** to play a number
tippen[2] [tɪ·pn̩] **I.** *vi* ❶ (*fam: Schreibmaschine schreiben*) to type ❷ (*kurz anstoßen*) to tap (**an/auf, gegen** +*akk* on, against) **II.** *vt* (*fam*) to type
Tippfehler *m* typo
Tippschein *m* lottery ticket
Tirol <-s> [ti·'ro:l] *nt* Tyrol
Tiroler(in) <-s, -> [ti·'ro:·lɐ] *m(f)* Tyrolean
Tisch <-[e]s, -e> [tɪʃ] *m* table ▶WENDUNGEN: **reinen ~ machen** to sort things out; **unter den ~ fallen** (*fam*) to fall by the wayside; **vom ~ sein** to be [all] cleared up; **sich** *akk* [**mit jdm**] **an einen ~ setzen** to come to the table [with sb]; **jdn über den ~ ziehen** (*fam*) to put one over [*or* pull a fast one] on sb
Tischbein ['tɪʃ·bain] *nt* table leg
Tischdecke *f* tablecloth
Tischgespräch *nt* table talk
Tischkante *f* table edge, edge of a table
Tischler(in) <-s -> ['tɪʃ·lɐ] *m(f)* carpenter
Tischlerei <-, -en> [tɪʃ·lə·'rai] *f* carpenter's workshop
Tischmanieren ['tɪʃ·ma·ni:·rən] *pl* table manners *pl*
Tischtennis *nt* table tennis, ping-pong
Tischtennisplatte *f* table-tennis [*or* ping-pong] table
Tischtennisschläger *m* table-tennis [*or* ping-pong] paddle
Titel <-s, -> ['ti:·tl̩] *m* ❶ (*Überschrift*) heading ❷ (*Namenszusatz*) [academic] title ❸ (*Adelstitel*) title ❹ MEDIA, SPORT title
Titelanwärter(in) *m(f)* title contender
Titelbild *nt* cover [picture]
Titelblatt *nt* ❶ (*Buchseite mit dem Titel*) title page ❷ *einer Zeitung* front page; *einer Zeitschrift* cover
Titelrolle *f* title role
Titelverteidiger(in) *m(f)* title holder
tja [tja] *interj* well
Toast[1] <-[e]s, -e *o* -s> ['to:st] *m* ❶ *kein pl* (*Toastbrot*) toast ❷ (*Scheibe Toastbrot*) ■**ein ~** a slice of toast
Toast[2] <-[e]s, -e *o* -s> ['to:st] *m* toast; **einen ~ auf jdn/etw ausbringen** to propose a toast to sb/sth
Toastbrot ['to:st-] *nt* white bread
toasten [to:s·tn̩] *vt* ■**etw ~** to toast sth
Toaster <-s, -> ['to:s·tɐ] *m* toaster
toben ['to:·bn̩] *vi* ❶ *haben* (*wüten*) ■[**vor etw** *dat*] **~** to be raging [with sth] ❷ *haben* (*ausgelassen spielen*) to romp [around] ❸ *sein* (*fam: sich ausgelassen fortbewegen*) ■**irgendwohin ~** to romp somewhere
tobsüchtig *adj* stark raving mad
Tobsuchtsanfall *m* (*fam*) fit of rage
Tochter <-, Töchter> ['tɔx·tɐ, *pl* 'tœçtɐ] *f* ❶ (*weibliches Kind*) daughter ❷ (*Tochterfirma*) subsidiary
Tochtergesellschaft *f* subsidiary [company]
Tod <-[e]s, -e> ['to:t] *m* death; **~ durch Ertrinken** death by drowning; **etw mit dem ~e bezahlen** *akk* (*geh*) to pay for sth with one's life ▶WENDUNGEN: **jdn/etw auf den ~ nicht ausstehen können** (*fam*) to be unable to stand sb/sth; **sich** *dat* **den ~ holen** (*fam*) to catch one's death [of cold]; **sich** *akk* **zu ~e langweilen** (*fam*) to be bored to death; **sich** *akk* **zu ~e schämen** (*fam*) to be utterly ashamed
todernst ['to:t·'ʔɛrnst] **I.** *adj* deadly serious **II.** *adv* in a deadly serious manner
Todesangst *f* ❶ (*fam: entsetzliche Angst*) mortal fear; **Todesängste ausstehen** (*fam*) to be scared to death ❷ (*Angst vor dem Sterben*) fear of death
Todesanzeige *f* obituary
Todesfall *m* death
Todesfolge *f kein pl* JUR **Körperverletzung mit ~** physical injury resulting in death
Todesgefahr *f* mortal danger
todesmutig **I.** *adj* [absolutely] fearless **II.** *adv* fearlessly
Todesopfer *nt* casualty
Todesstrafe *f* death penalty; **auf etw** *akk* **steht die ~** sth is punishable by death
Todestag *m* anniversary of sb's death
Todesursache *f* cause of death
Todesurteil *nt* death sentence
Todfeind(in) ['to:t·faint] *m(f)* mortal enemy
todkrank ['to:t·'kraŋk] *adj* terminally ill
todlangweilig ['to:t·'laŋ·vai·lɪç] *adj inv* so boring
tödlich ['tø:t·lɪç] **I.** *adj* ❶ (*den Tod verursachend*) deadly ❷ (*fam: absolut*) deadly; **das ist mein ~er Ernst** I'm dead serious **II.** *adv* ❶ (*mit dem Tod als Folge*) **~ verunglücken** to be killed in an accident ❷ (*fam: entsetzlich*) **sich** *akk* **~ langweilen** to be bored to death; **jdm ist ~ übel** sb feels really sick [to one's stomach]
todmüde ['to:t·'my:·də] *adj* (*fam*) dead tired
todsicher ['to:t·'zɪ·çɐ] **I.** *adj* (*fam*) dead certain; *Methode* sure-fire *fam* **II.** *adv* (*fam*) for sure
Todsünde *f* deadly sin
Toilette <-, -n> [to̯a·'lɛ·tə] *f* restroom, bathroom *fam;* **ich muss mal auf die ~** I need to go to the restroom; **öffentliche ~** public restroom
Toilettenartikel *pl* toiletries *pl*
Toilettenfrau *f* [female] bathroom attendant
Toilettenpapier *nt* toilet paper
tolerant [to·le·'rant] *adj* tolerant (**gegen, gegenüber** +*dat* of, toward)
Toleranz <-, en> [to·le·'rants] *f kein pl* (*geh*)

T

tolerance (**gegen, gegenüber** *+dat* of, toward)

Toleranzbereich *m* range of tolerance

tolerieren* [to·le·'riː·rən] *vt* (*geh*) to tolerate

toll ['tɔl] **I.** *adj* (*fam*) great **II.** *adv* ❶ (*wild*) wild; **ihr treibt es manchmal wirklich zu ~!** you [guys] really [do] go too far sometimes! ❷ (*fam: sehr gut*) very well

Tollpatsch[RR] <-es, -e> ['tɔl·patʃ] *m* (*fam*) clumsy fool

tollpatschig[RR] ['tɔl·pat·ʃɪç] **I.** *adj* clumsy **II.** *adv* **sich** *akk* **~ anstellen** to act clumsily

Tollwut *f* rabies

tollwütig *adj* ■**~ sein** ❶ ZOOL to have rabies ❷ (*rasend*) to be stark raving mad

Tolpatsch[ALT] <-es, -e> *m s.* **Tollpatsch**

tolpatschig[ALT] *adj, adv s.* **tollpatschig**

Tölpel <-s, -> ['tœl·pl̩] *m* (*fam*) fool

Tomate <-, -n> [to·'maː·tə] *f* (*Frucht o Strauch*) tomato ▶WENDUNGEN: **~n auf den Augen haben** (*fam*) to be blind; **du treulose ~!** (*fam*) you're a fine friend! *iron*

Tomatenketschup[RR], **Tomatenketchup** *nt* [tomato] ketchup [*or* catsup]

Tomatenmark *nt* tomato paste

Tomatensauce *f* tomato sauce

Tombola <-, -s *o* Tombolen> ['tɔm·bo·la, *pl* 'tɔm·bo·lən] *f* raffle

Tomographie, **Tomografie**[RR] <-, -n> [to·mo·gra·'fiː] *f* tomography

Ton[1] <-[e]s, -e> ['toːn] *m* clay

Ton[2] <-[e]s, Töne> ['toːn, *pl* 'tøː·nə] *m* ❶ (*hörbare Schwingung*) sound; **halber/ganzer ~** half/whole step ❷ FILM, RADIO, TV sound ❸ (*fam: Wort*) sound; **ich will keinen ~ mehr hören!** I don't want to hear another sound out of you!; **große Töne spucken** (*sl*) to brag about sth *fam;* **keinen ~ herausbringen** to not be able to utter a word ❹ (*Tonfall*) tone; **einen anderen ~ anschlagen** to change one's tune; **ich verbitte mir diesen ~!** I will not be spoken to like that! ❺ (*Farbton*) tone ▶WENDUNGEN: **der ~ macht die Musik** (*prov*) it's not what you say, but the way you say it; **den ~ angeben** to set the tone; **hast du Töne!** (*fam*) you can't be serious!

Tonart *f* ❶ MUS key ❷ (*Typ von Ton*[1]) type of clay

Tonaufnahme *f* sound recording

Tonband *nt* tape; **etw** *akk* **auf ~ aufnehmen** to tape sth

Tonbandgerät *nt* tape recorder

tönen ['tøː·nən] *vt* to tint; *Haare* to color

Tonfall *m* tone of voice

Tonfilm *m* sound film

Tongefäß *nt* earthenware vessel

Tonhöhe *f* pitch

Toningenieur, -ingenieurin [-ɪn·ʒe·ni̯øːɐ̯] *m, f* sound engineer

Tonlage *f* pitch

Tonleiter *f* scale

tonlos *adj* flat

Tonne <-, -n> ['tɔ·nə] *f* ❶ (*zylindrischer Behälter*) barrel ❷ (*Mülltonne*) garbage can; **grüne ~** recycling container for paper ❸ (*Gewichtseinheit*) ton ❹ (*fam: fetter Mensch*) fatso *sl*

tonnenweise *adv* by the ton

Tonstörung *f* sound interference

Techniker(in) *m(f)* sound technician

Tonträger *m* sound carrier

Tönung <-, -en> *f* ❶ (*das Tönen*) tinting ❷ (*Produkt für Haare*) hair color ❸ (*Farbton*) shade

Topf <-[e]s, Töpfe> ['tɔpf, *pl* 'tœp·fə] *m* ❶ (*Kochtopf*) pot, sauce pan ❷ (*Nachttopf*) bedpan ❸ (*Topf für Kleinkinder*) potty *fam* ▶WENDUNGEN: **alles in einen ~ werfen** to lump everything together

Töpfer(in) <-s, -> ['tœp·fɐ] *m(f)* potter

Töpferei <-, -en> [tœp·fə·'rai] *f* pottery

töpfern ['tœp·fɐn] **I.** *vi* to do pottery **II.** *vt* ■**etw ~** to make sth from clay

Töpferscheibe *f* potter's wheel

Töpferwaren *pl* pottery

Topflappen *m* pot holder

Topfpflanze *f* potted plant

Topmodel ['tɔp·mɔ·dl̩] *nt* supermodel

Tor <-[e]s, -e> ['toːɐ̯] *nt* ❶ (*breite Tür*) gate; *Garage* door ❷ (*Torbau*) gateway ❸ SPORT goal; **ein ~ schießen** to score a goal; **im ~ stehen** to be the goalkeeper [*or* goalie]

Torbogen *m* archway

Torf <-[e]s, -e> ['tɔrf] *m* peat

töricht ['tœ·rɪçt] **I.** *adj* (*geh*) foolish **II.** *adv* (*geh*) foolishly

torkeln ['tɔr·kl̩n] *vi sein* ❶ (*taumeln*) to reel ❷ (*irgendwohin taumeln*) to stagger

Torlinie *f* goal line

Tornado <-s, -s> [tɔr·'naː·do] *m* tornado, twister

Torpedo <-s, -s> [tɔr·'peː·do] *m* torpedo

Torschlusspanik[RR] *f* (*fam*) **~ haben** to be afraid of missing the boat

Torschütze, -schützin *m, f* scorer

Torte <-, -n> ['tɔr·tə] *f* torte, cake; (*Obstkuchen*) tart

Tortenboden *m* tart shell [*or* base]

Tortenheber <-s, -> *m* cake server

Torwart(in) *m(f)* goalkeeper, goalie

Toskana <-> [tɔs·'kaː·na] *f* Tuscany

tot ['toːt] *adj* ❶ (*gestorben*) dead; **sich** *akk* **~ stellen** to play dead; **~ umfallen** to drop dead ❷ (*abgestorben*) dead ❸ (*nicht mehr genutzt*) no longer in use

total [to·'taːl] *adj* total

Totalausverkauf *m* clearance sale

totalitär [to·ta·li·'tɛːɐ̯] **I.** *adj* totalitarian **II.** *adv* in a totalitarian manner

Totalschaden *m* write-off

Tote(r) ['toː·tə] *f(m)* (*toter Mensch*) dead person; (*Todesopfer*) fatality

töten ['tøː·tn̩] *vt* to kill

Totenkopf *m* ❶ ANAT skull ❷ (*Zeichen*) skull and crossbones

T

Totenschädel *m s.* **Totenkopf 1**
Totenschein *m* death certificate
totenstill ['toː·tn̩·'ʃtɪl] *adj* ■**es/alles ist** ~ it/everything is deadly silent
Totenwache *f* **die** ~ **halten** to hold the wake
tot|fahren *irreg vt* (*fam*) ■**jdn/etw** ~ to run over [and kill] sb/sth
Totgeburt *f* stillbirth
tot|lachen *vr* (*fam*) ■**sich** *akk* [**über etw/jdn**] ~ to die laughing [about sth/sb]
tot|schießen *vt irreg* (*fam*) ■**jdn/etw** ~ to shoot sb/sth dead
Totschlag *m kein pl* manslaughter
Totschlagargument *nt* (*pej fam*) dead-end argument
tot|schlagen *vt irreg* (*fam*) ■**jdn/etw** ~ to beat sb/sth to death
tot|schweigen *vt irreg* ❶ (*über etw nicht sprechen*) to hush up ❷ (*über jdn nicht sprechen*) ■**jdn** ~ to keep quiet about sb
Tötung <-, *selten* -en> *f* killing; **fahrlässige** ~ [involuntary] manslaughter
Tötungsversuch *m* JUR attempted murder
Toupet <-s, -s> [tu·'peː] *nt* toupee
toupieren* [tu·'piː·rən] *vt* ■**jdm/sich die Haare** ~ to tease sb's/one's hair
Tour <-, -en> [tuːɐ̯] *f* ❶ (*Geschäftsfahrt*) trip ❷ (*Ausflugsfahrt*) tour; **eine** ~ **machen** to go on a tour ❸ (*fam: Vorhaben*) wheeling and dealing *fam;* **jdm auf die dumme** ~ **kommen** to try to cheat sb ▶ WENDUNGEN: **auf** ~**en kommen** (*fam*) to get into high gear; **in einer** ~ (*fam*) nonstop
Tourismus <-> [tu·'rɪs·mʊs] *m kein pl* tourism
Tourist(in) <-en, -en> [tu·'rɪst] *m(f)* tourist
Touristik <-> [tu·'rɪs·tɪk] *f kein pl* tourism
touristisch *adj inv* touristic *attr*
Tournee <-, -n *o* -s> [tʊr·'neː, *pl* -'neːən] *f* tour; **auf** ~ **gehen/sein** to go/be on tour
toxisch ['tɔk·sɪʃ] *adj* toxic
Trab <-[e]s> [traːp] *m kein pl* trot ▶ WENDUNGEN: **jdn auf** ~ **bringen** (*fam*) to make sb get a move on
traben ['traː·bn̩] *vi* ❶ *haben o sein* (*im Trab laufen o reiten*) to trot ❷ *sein* (*sich im Trab irgendwohin bewegen*) to trot
Tracht <-, -en> [traxt] *f* ❶ (*Volkstracht*) traditional attire ❷ (*Berufskleidung*) uniform ▶ WENDUNGEN: **eine** ~ **Prügel** (*fam*) a walloping
trächtig ['trɛç·tiç] *adj Tier* pregnant
Tradition <-, -en> [tra·di·'tsi̯oːn] *f* tradition; **aus** ~ traditionally
traditionell [tra·di·tsi̯o·n'ɛl] *adj meist attr* traditional
traf [traːf] *imp von* **treffen**
Trafo <-[s], -s> ['traː·fo] *m* (*fam*) *kurz für* **Transformator** transformer
tragbar *adj* ❶ (*portabel konstruiert*) portable ❷ (*akzeptabel*) acceptable
träge ['trɛː·gə] **I.** *adj* ❶ (*schwerfällig*) lethargic ❷ PHYS, CHEM inert **II.** *adv* lethargically
tragen <trägt, trug, getragen> ['traː·gn̩] **I.** *vt* ❶ (*schleppen*) to carry ❷ (*mit sich führen*) ■**etw bei sich** *dat* ~: **tragen Sie Waffen bei sich?** do you have any weapons on you? ❸ (*anhaben*) to wear ❹ (*in bestimmter Weise frisiert sein*) **einen Bart** ~ to have a beard; **das Haar kurz/lang** ~ to have short/long hair ❺ (*stützen*) to support ❻ AGR, HORT to produce ❼ (*ertragen*) to bear ❽ (*für etw aufkommen*) to bear **II.** *vi* ❶ AGR, HORT to produce ❷ (*trächtig sein*) to be pregnant ❸ (*das Begehen aushalten*) to withstand weight ❹ MODE to wear; **sie trägt lieber kurz** she prefers to wear short clothing ▶ WENDUNGEN: **an etw** *dat* **schwer zu** ~ **haben** to have a heavy cross to bear with sth; **zum T~ kommen** to come into effect **III.** *vr* ❶ (*sich schleppen lassen*) **sich leicht/schwer** ~ to be easy/hard to carry ❷ MODE **die Hose trägt sich bequem** the pants are comfortable ❸ (*geh: in Erwägung ziehen*) ■**sich** *akk* **mit etw** *dat* ~ to contemplate sth ❹ FIN ■**sich** ~ to pay for itself
Träger <-s, -> *m* ❶ *meist pl* MODE strap; *Hose* suspenders *npl* ❷ BAU girder
Tragetasche *f* [tote] bag
Tragfläche *f* wing
Trägheit <-, *selten* -en> *f* ❶ *kein pl* (*Schwerfälligkeit*) sluggishness; (*Faulheit*) laziness ❷ PHYS inertia
Tragik <-> ['traː·gɪk] *f kein pl* tragedy
tragisch ['traː·gɪʃ] **I.** *adj* tragic; **es ist nicht** [**so**] ~ (*fam*) it's not the end of the world **II.** *adv* tragically; **nimm's nicht so** ~**!** (*fam*) don't take it to heart!
Tragödie <-, -n> [tra·'gøː·di̯ə] *f a.* LIT, THEAT tragedy
Tragweite *f* scale; (*einer Entscheidung, Handlung*) consequence
Trainer <-s, -> ['trɛː·nɐ] *m* SCHWEIZ tracksuit
Trainer(in) <-s, -> ['trɛː·nɐ] *m(f)* coach
trainieren* [trɛ·'niː·rən] **I.** *vt* ❶ (*durch Training üben*) to practice ❷ (*auf Wettkämpfe vorbereiten*) ■**jdn** ~ to coach sb **II.** *vi* ❶ (*üben*) to practice ❷ (*sich auf Wettkämpfe vorbereiten*) to train
Training <-s, -s> ['trɛː·nɪŋ] *nt* practice
Trainingsanzug ['trɛː·nɪŋs-] *m* tracksuit
Trakt <-[e]s, -e> ['trakt] *m* ARCHIT wing
Traktor <-s, -toren> ['trak·toːɐ̯, *pl* -'toː·rən] *m* tractor
Tram <-, -s o -s, -s> ['tram] *f o nt* SCHWEIZ streetcar
Trambahn *f* SÜDD streetcar
Trampel <-s, -> ['tram·pl̩] *m o nt* (*fam*) klutz
trampeln ['tram·pl̩n] *vi* ❶ *haben* (*stampfen*) **mit den Füßen** ~ to stamp one's feet ❷ *sein* (*sich trampelnd bewegen*) to stomp along; **sie trampelten die Treppe hinunter** they stomped down the stairs
Trampelpfad *m* trail
trampen [trɛmpn̩] *vi sein* to hitchhike
Tramper(in) <-s, -> ['trɛm·pɐ] *m(f)* hitchhiker
Trampolin <-s, -e> ['tram·po·liːn] *nt* trampoline

Tramway <-, -s> ['tram·vai] *f* ÖSTERR (*Straßenbahn*) streetcar
Trance <-, -n> ['trã:s(ə)] *f* trance
Träne <-, -n> ['trɛ:·nə] *f* tear; **in ~n aufgelöst** in tears; **den ~n nahe sein** to be close to tears; **jdm kommen die ~n** sb is starting to cry; **~n lachen** to laugh until one cries
tränen ['trɛ:·nən] *vi* to water
trank [traŋk] *imp von* **trinken**
tränken ['trɛŋ·kn̩] *vt* ❶ (*durchnässen*) to soak ❷ *Tier* to water
Transfer <-s, -s> [trans·'fe:ɐ̯] *m* transfer
Transformator <-s, -en> [trans·fɔr·'ma:·to:ɐ̯, *pl* -ma·'to:·rən] *m* transformer
Transistor <-s, -en> [tran·'zɪs·to:ɐ̯, *pl* -'to:·rən] *m* transistor
transitiv ['tran·zi·ti:f] *adj* LING transitive
Transitverkehr [tran·'zɪt-] *m* transit traffic
Transkription <-, -en> [trans·krɪp·'ts̯i̯o:n] *f* LING, MUS transcription
transparent [trans·pa·'rɛnt] *adj* transparent
Transparent <-[e]s, -e> [trans·pa·'rɛnt] *nt* banner
Transparenz <-> [trans·pa·'rɛnts] *f kein pl* (*geh*) transparency
Transplantation <-, -en> [trans·plan·ta·'tsi̯o:n] *f* transplant; (*Haut*) graft
transplantieren* [trans·plan·'ti:·rən] *vt* to transplant
Transport <-[e]s, -e> [trans·'pɔrt] *m* transport
Transporter <-s, -> [trans·'pɔr·tɐ] *m* ❶ (*Lieferwagen*) van ❷ LUFT cargo plane
transportfähig *adj* transportable
transportieren* [trans·pɔr·'ti:·rən] *vt* ❶ (*befördern*) to transport; (*Person*) to move ❷ FOTO to wind
Transportmittel *nt* means of transportation
Transportunternehmen *nt* trucking company
transsexuell [trans·zɛ·'ksu̯·ɛl] *adj* transsexual
Transvestit <-en, -en> [trans·vɛs·'ti:t] *m* transvestite
Trapez <-es, -e> [tra·'pe:ts] *nt* ❶ MATH trapezoid ❷ (*Artistenschaukel*) trapeze
trat [tra:t] *imp von* **treten**
Tratsch <-[e]s> [tra:tʃ] *m kein pl* (*fam*) gossip
tratschen ['tra:·tʃn̩] *vi* (*fam*) to gossip (**über** +*akk* about)
Traualtar *m* altar; [**mit jdm**] **vor den ~ treten** (*geh*) to walk down the aisle [with sb]
Traube <-, -n> ['trau·bə] *f* ❶ *meist pl* (*Weintraube*) grape *usu pl* ❷ (*Ansammlung*) cluster
Traubensaft *m* grape juice
Traubenzucker *m* glucose
trauen[1] ['trau·ən] *vt* ■**jdn ~** to join sb in marriage; ■**sich** *akk* **~ lassen** to marry
trauen[2] ['trau·ən] **I.** *vi* (*vertrauen*) to trust **II.** *vr* ■**sich** *akk* **~, etw** *akk* **zu tun** to dare to do sth
Trauer <-> ['trau·ɐ] *f kein pl* grief
Trauerfall *m* bereavement
Trauergottesdienst *m* funeral service
Trauerkleidung *f* mourning attire [*or* dress]
trauern ['trau·ɐn] *vi* to mourn (**um** +*akk* for)
Traum <-[e]s, Träume> ['traum, *pl* 'trɔy·mə] *m* dream; **es war immer mein ~, mal so eine Luxuslimousine zu fahren** I've always dreamed of driving a luxury car like this ▶ WENDUNGEN: **etw fällt jdm im ~ nicht ein** sb wouldn't dream of it; **aus der ~!** so much for that!
Trauma <-s, Traumen *o* -ta> ['trau·ma, *pl* 'trau·mən, -ta] *nt* trauma
traumatisch [trau·'ma:·tɪʃ] *adj* traumatic
Traumen *pl von* **Trauma**
träumen ['trɔy·mən] **I.** *vi* ❶ (*Träume haben*) to dream; **schlecht ~** to have bad dreams ❷ (*Wünsche*) ■**von jdm/etw ~** to dream about sb/sth; **jd hätte sich** *dat* **etw** *akk* **nie ~ lassen** sb never would have dreamed of [doing] sth; **jd hätte sich** *dat* **nie ~ lassen, dass ...** sb never would have thought it possible that ... ❸ (*abwesend sein*) to daydream **II.** *vt* to dream
Träumer(in) <-s, -> ['trɔy·mɐ] *m(f)* [day]dreamer
Träumerei <-, -en> [trɔy·mə·'rai] *f meist pl* dream *usu pl*
traumhaft *adj* (*fam*) dreamlike
Traumpaar *nt* perfect couple
traurig ['trau·rɪç] **I.** *adj* ❶ (*betrübt*) sad ❷ (*betrüblich*) sorry; **die ~e Tatsache ist, dass ...** the sad fact of the matter is that ... ❸ (*sehr bedauerlich*) ■[**es ist**] **~, dass ...** it's unfortunate that ..., unfortunately ... **II.** *adv* (*betrübt*) sadly ▶ WENDUNGEN: **mit etw** *dat* **sieht es ~ aus** sth doesn't look too good
Traurigkeit <-> *f kein pl* sadness
Trauring *m* wedding ring [*or* band]
Trauschein *m* marriage certificate
Trauung <-, -en> ['trau·ʊŋ] *f* marriage [*or* wedding] ceremony
Trauzeuge, -zeugin *m, f* best man, witness to a marriage
Treff <-s, -s> [trɛf] *m* (*fam*) ❶ (*Treffen*) get-together ❷ (*Treffpunkt*) meeting point
treffen <trifft, traf, getroffen> [trɛ·fn̩] **I.** *vt haben* ❶ (*mit jdm zusammenkommen*) to meet ❷ (*antreffen*) to find; **ich habe ihn zufällig in der Stadt getroffen** I bumped into him in town ❸ (*mit einem Wurf, Schlag etc. erreichen*) to hit ❹ (*innerlich bewegen*) ■**jdn mit etw** *dat* **~** to hit a sore spot with sb; ■**jdn ~** to affect sb; **sich** *akk* **durch etw** *akk* **getroffen fühlen** to take sth personally ❺ *Maßnahmen, Vorkehrungen* to take ❻ *Entscheidung* to make; **eine Abmachung ~** to have an agreement ❼ (*wählen*) **den richtigen Ton ~** to strike the right chord; **auf dem Foto bis du wirklich gut getroffen** that's a really good picture of you; **du hättest es auch schlechter ~ können** it could have been worse **II.** *vi* ❶ *sein* (*antreffen*) ■**auf jdn ~** to meet sb ❷ *haben* (*sein Ziel erreichen*) to meet, to hit ❸ *haben* (*verletzen*) to hurt **III.** *vr haben* ■**sich** *akk* [**mit jdm**] **~** to meet [sb]; **das trifft sich** [**gut**] that works out [great]
Treffen <-s, -> [trɛ·fn̩] *nt* meeting

T

treffend *adj* appropriate
Treffer <-s, -> *m* ❶ (*ins Ziel gegangener Schuss*) hit, bull's-eye ❷ (*Tor*) goal ❸ (*Gewinnlos*) winner
Trefferquote *f* hit ratio
Treffpunkt *m* meeting point
treiben <trieb, getrieben> ['trai·bn̩] **I.** *vt haben* ❶ (*durch Antreiben drängen*) to drive ❷ (*fortbewegen*) ■**jdn/etw [irgendwohin] ~** (*durch Wasser*) to wash sb/sth [somewhere]; (*durch Wind*) to blow sb/sth [somewhere] ❸ (*bringen*) ■**jdn zu etw** *dat* ~ to drive sb to sth; **jdn in den Wahnsinn ~** to drive sb mad; **jdn zur Eile ~** to rush sb ❹ *Nagel* to drive (**in** +*akk* into) ❺ TECH to propel ❻ (*fam: anstellen*) ■**etw ~** to be up to sth; **dass ihr mir bloß keinen Blödsinn treibt!** don't you [guys] try to pull any nonsense now! ❼ *Tiere* to drive ❽ BOT to sprout ❾ (*betreiben*) *Gewerbe* to carry out; *Handel* to trade ❿ (*fam*) **es zu bunt/wild ~** to go too far ⓫ (*sl: Sex haben*) **es [mit jdm] ~** to do it [with sb] **II.** *vi* ❶ *sein* (*sich fortbewegen*) to drift; ■**sich** *akk* **[von etw** *dat*] **~ lassen** to let oneself be carried along [by sth] ❷ *haben* BOT to sprout ❸ *haben* KOCHK to rise ❹ *haben* (*diuretisch wirken*) to have a diuretic effect ► WENDUNGEN: **sich** *akk* **~ lassen** to drift
Treiben <-s> ['trai·bn̩] *nt kein pl* ❶ (*pej: üble Aktivität*) dirty tricks ❷ (*geschäftige Aktivität*) hustle and bustle
Treibgas *nt* propellant
Treibhaus *nt* greenhouse
Treibhauseffekt *m kein pl* ■**der ~** the greenhouse effect
Treibholz *nt kein pl* driftwood
Treibstoff *m* fuel
Trend <-s, -s> ['trɛnt] *m* trend; **voll im ~ liegen** to be very popular at the moment
Trendsetter(in) <-s, -> *m(f)* trendsetter
Trendwende *f* change [of direction]
trennen ['trɛ·nən] **I.** *vt* ❶ (*abtrennen*) ■**etw von etw** *dat* ~ to cut sth off [of/from] sth; (*bei einem Unfall*) to sever sth from sth ❷ (*ablösen*) **die Knöpfe von etw** *dat* **~** to remove the buttons from sth ❸ (*auseinanderbringen*) to separate (**von** +*dat* from) ❹ (*teilen*) to separate (**von** +*dat* from) ❺ LING to divide **II.** *vr* ❶ (*getrennt weitergehen*) ■**sich** *akk* ~ to part company ❷ (*die Beziehung lösen*) ■**sich** *akk* **von jdm ~** to split up with sb ❸ (*von etw lassen*) ■**sich** *akk* **von etw** *dat* ~ to part with sth **III.** *vi* ■**[zwischen ihnen] ~** to differentiate [between them]
Trennung <-, -en> *f* ❶ (*Scheidung*) separation; **in ~ leben** to be separated ❷ (*Unterscheidung*) distinction ❸ LING division
Trennungsstrich *m* hyphen
Trennwand *f* partition [wall]
treppab [trɛp·'ʔap] *adv inv* downstairs; **trepp-auf, ~** up and down the stairs
treppauf [trɛp·'ʔauf] *adv inv* upstairs
Treppe <-, -n> ['trɛ·pə] *f* stairs *pl*
Treppenabsatz *m* landing
Treppengeländer *nt* handrail
Treppenhaus *nt* stairwell
Treppenstufe *f* step
Tresen <-s, -> ['tre:·zn̩] *m* ❶ (*Theke*) bar ❷ (*Ladentisch*) counter
Tresor <-s, -e> [tre·'zo:ɐ̯] *m* ❶ (*Safe*) safe ❷ (*Tresorraum*) strongroom
treten <tritt, trat, getreten> ['tre:·tn̩] **I.** *vt haben* ❶ (*mit dem Fuß stoßen*) to kick ❷ (*mit dem Fuß betätigen*) to step on; **die Bremse ~** to brake **II.** *vi* ❶ *haben* (*mit dem Fuß stoßen*) to kick; ■**nach jdm ~** to kick out at sb; **sie trat ihm in den Bauch** she kicked him in the stomach ❷ *sein* (*einen Schritt machen*) to step; **~ Sie bitte zur Seite** please step aside; **pass auf, wohin du trittst** watch where you step [*or* your step] ❸ *sein o haben* (*den Fuß setzen*) to tread (**auf** +*akk* on) ❹ *sein o haben* (*betätigen*) to step (**auf** +*akk* on); **auf die Bremse ~** to put on the brakes ❺ *sein* (*hervorkommen*) ■**aus etw** *dat* ~ to come out of sth; **der Fluss trat über seine Ufer** the river overflowed its banks; **Schweiß trat ihm auf die Stirn** sweat appeared on his forehead **III.** *vr* **sie trat sich einen Nagel in den Fuß** she stepped on a nail
Tretmine *f* antipersonnel mine
treu ['trɔy] **I.** *adj* ❶ (*loyal*) loyal; **sich** *dat* **selbst ~ bleiben** to remain true to oneself ❷ (*verlässlich*) loyal ❸ (*keinen Seitensprung machend*) faithful ❹ (*fig*) **der Erfolg blieb ihm ~** he had continued success **II.** *adv* ❶ (*loyal*) loyally ❷ (*treuherzig*) trustingly
Treue <-> ['trɔyə] *f kein pl* ❶ (*Loyalität, Verlässlichkeit*) loyalty ❷ (*monogames Verhalten*) fidelity; **jdm die ~ halten** to be faithful to sb
Treueschwur *m* ❶ (*Schwur, jdm treu zu sein*) vow to be faithful ❷ HIST (*Eid*) oath of allegiance
Treuhandgesellschaft *f* trust company
treulos **I.** *adj* ❶ *Ehemann* unfaithful ❷ (*ungetreu*) disloyal **II.** *adv* disloyally
Treulosigkeit <-> *f kein pl* disloyalty, unfaithfulness
Triangel <-s, -> ['tri:·aŋl̩] *m o* ÖSTERR *nt* triangle
Tribunal <-s, -e> [tri·bu·'na:l] *nt* (*geh*) tribunal
Tribüne <-, -n> [tri·'by:·nə] *f* stand
Tribut <-[e]s, -e> [tri·'bu:t] *m* HIST tribute
Trichter <-s, -> ['trɪç·tɐ] *m* ❶ (*Einfülltrichter*) funnel ❷ (*Explosionskrater*) crater
Trick <-s, -s> ['trɪk] *m* ❶ (*Täuschungsmanöver*) trick; **keine faulen ~s!** (*fam*) no funny business! ❷ (*Kunstgriff*) trick; **den ~ raushaben[, wie etw gemacht wird]** (*fam*) to get the hang of sth
Trickaufnahme *f* FILM special effect
Trickbetrüger(in) *m(f)* con artist [*or* man]
Trickfilm *m* cartoon [*or* animated] movie
trieb ['tri:p] *imp von* **treiben**
Trieb[1] <-[e]s, -e> ['tri:p, *pl* 'tri:·bə] *m* BOT shoot

Trieb² <-[e]s, -e> ['tri:p, *pl* 'tri:·bə] *m* ❶ (*innerer Antrieb*) drive ❷ (*Sexualtrieb*) sex[ual] drive

Triebkraft *f* ❶ (*fig*) driving force ❷ BOT germinating power

Triebtäter(in) *m(f)* sex offender

Triebverbrechen *nt* sex crime

Triebwerk *nt* engine

triefen <triefte *o geh* troff, getrieft> ['tri:·fn̩] *vi* ❶ (*rinnen*) to run; (*Auge*) to water; ■**aus etw** *dat* ~ to pour from [*or* out of] sth ❷ **vor Nässe** ~ to be dripping wet ❸ (*geh: strotzen*) ■**vor etw** *dat* ~ to be dripping with sth *fig*

trifft ['trɪft] *3. pers sing pres von* **treffen**

triftig ['trɪf·tɪç] **I.** *adj* good; *Argument, Grund* convincing **II.** *adv* convincingly; [**jdm etw** *akk*] ~ **begründen** to make a valid argument [to sb for [*or* about] sth]

Trikot¹ <-s> [tri·'ko:, 'trɪ·ko] *m o nt kein pl* (*dehnbares Gewebe*) tricot

Trikot² <-s, -s> [tri·'ko:, 'trɪ·ko] *nt* MODE, SPORT jersey

Trillerpfeife ['trɪ·lɐ-] *f* whistle

Trilogie <-, -n> [tri·lo·'gi:, *pl* -'gi:·ən] *f* trilogy

Trimm-dich-Pfad *m* fitness course

trimmen ['trɪ·mən] **I.** *vt* ❶ (*trainieren*) to train (**auf** +*akk* for) ❷ (*scheren*) to trim **II.** *vr* ■**sich** *akk* [**durch etw** *akk*] ~ to stay fit [by doing sth]

trinkbar *adj* drinkable

trinken <trank, getrunken> ['trɪŋ·kn̩] **I.** *vt* ❶ (*Flüssigkeit schlucken*) to drink; **möchten Sie lieber Kaffee oder Tee ~?** would you prefer coffee or tea [to drink]?; ■**etw zu ~** sth to drink; [**mit jdm**] **einen ~ gehen** (*fam*) to go for a drink [with sb] ❷ (*anstoßen*) ■**auf jdn/etw ~** to drink to sb/sth **II.** *vi* to drink

Trinker(in) <-s, -> *m(f)* drunk[ard]; (*Alkoholiker*) alcoholic

trinkfest *adj* ■**~ sein** to be able to hold one's alcohol

Trinkgeld *nt* tip; **~ geben** to give a tip

> Tipping is voluntary but usually expected, as the wages in the service industry are very low. If a customer is happy with the service, a **Trinkgeld** (tip) of 5–10% (around 15% in Austria) is standard in cafés and restaurants.

Trinkspruch *m* toast

Trinkwasser *nt* drinking water

Trinkwasseraufbereitung *f* drinking water purification

Trio <-s, -s> ['tri:o] *nt* trio

Trip <-s, -s> [trɪp] *m* ❶ (*fam: Ausflug*) trip ❷ (*sl: Drogenrausch*) trip *fam*; **auf einem ~ sein** to be tripping *fam*

tritt [trɪt] *3. pers sing pres von* **treten**

Tritt <-[e]s, -e> [trɪt] *m* ❶ (*Fußtritt*) kick; **jdm/etw einen ~ geben** to kick sb/sth ❷ *kein pl* (*Gang*) step ❸ (*Stufe*) step

Trittbrettfahrer(in) *m(f)* (*fam*) fare evader, freeloader; (*fig: Nachahmer*) copycat

Triumph <-[e]s, -e> [tri·'ʊmf] *m* triumph

Triumphbogen *m* triumphal arch

triumphieren* [tri·ʊm·'fi:·rən] *vi* (*geh*) ❶ (*frohlocken*) to rejoice; **höhnisch ~** to gloat ❷ (*erfolgreich sein*) to triumph (**über** +*akk* over)

triumphierend **I.** *adj* triumphant **II.** *adv* triumphantly

Triumphzug *m* triumphal procession

trocken ['trɔ·kn̩] **I.** *adj* ❶ (*ausgetrocknet*) dry ❷ (*nicht mehr nass*) dry; **im T~en** out of the rain ❸ *a.* METEO *Gebiet* dry ❹ *Wein* dry ❺ *Buch* dull; *Zahlen* dry ▶ WENDUNGEN: **auf dem T~en sitzen** (*fam*) to be broke **II.** *adv* **~ aufbewahren** to keep in a dry place; **sich** *akk* **~ rasieren** to use an electric razor, to dry shave

Trockenhaube *f* [salon] hair dryer

Trockenheit <-, *selten* -en> *f* ❶ (*Dürreperiode*) drought ❷ (*trockene Beschaffenheit*) *a. eines Gebietes* dryness

trocken|legen *vt* ❶ (*windeln*) **ein Baby ~** to change a baby['s diaper] ❷ (*entwässern*) to drain

Trockenobst *nt kein pl* dried fruit

trocken|reiben *vt irreg* ■**jdn/etw ~** to rub sb/sth dry

Trockenzeit *f* dry season

trocknen ['trɔk·nən] **I.** *vi sein* to dry **II.** *vt haben* ❶ (*trocken machen*) *a.* KOCHK to dry ❷ (*abtupfen*) **sie trocknete ihm den Schweiß von der Stirn** she wiped the sweat from his forehead; **komm, ich trockne dir die Tränen** come here and let me dry your tears

Trockner <-s, -> *m* drier

Trödel <-s> ['trø:·dl̩] *m kein pl* (*fam*) junk

Trödelei <-, -en> [trø:·də·'lai] *f* (*fam*) dilly-dallying

Trödelmarkt *m s.* **Flohmarkt**

trödeln ['trø:·dl̩n] *vi* ❶ *haben* (*langsam sein*) to dilly-dally ❷ *sein* (*langsam schlendern*) to [take a] stroll

Trödler(in) <-s, -> ['trø:d·lɐ] *m(f)* ❶ (*Altwarenhändler*) second-hand dealer ❷ (*fam: trödelnder Mensch*) dilly-dallier

troff ['trɔf] *imp von* **triefen**

trog ['tro:k] *imp von* **trügen**

Trog <-[e]s, Tröge> ['tro:k, *pl* 'trø:·gə] *m* trough

Troll <-s, -e> ['trɔl] *m* troll

Trolleybus ['trɔ·li·bʊs] *m bes* SCHWEIZ trolley bus

Trommel <-, -n> ['trɔ·ml̩] *f* MUS, TECH, COMPUT drum

Trommelfell *nt* eardrum

trommeln ['trɔ·ml̩n] **I.** *vi* to drum **II.** *vt* MUS **einen Rhythmus ~** to beat out a *sep* rhythm

Trommler(in) <-s, -> *m(f)* drummer

Trompete <-, -n> [trɔm·'pe:·tə] *f* trumpet

Trompeter(in) <-s, -> *m(f)* trumpeter

Tropen ['tro:pn̩] *pl* ■**die ~** the tropics *pl*

Tropenkrankheit *f* tropical disease

Tropenwald *m* tropical rain forest

Tropf <-[e]s, -e> ['trɔpf] *m* MED drip

tröpfeln ['trœp·fl̩n] **I.** *vi* ❶ *haben* (*ständig tropfen*) to drip ❷ *sein* (*rinnen*) to drip (**aus** +*dat* from) **II.** *vi impers* to drizzle **III.** *vt* ■ **etw auf/in etw** *akk* ~ to put sth onto/into sth

tropfen ['trɔp·fn̩] *vi* ❶ *haben* (*Tropfen fallen lassen*) to drip; (*Nase*) to run ❷ *sein* (*tropfenweise gelangen*) ■ **aus etw** *dat* [**irgendwohin**] ~ to drip from sth [somewhere]

Tropfen <-s, -> ['trɔp·fn̩] *m* ❶ (*kleine Menge Flüssigkeit*) drop; **bis auf den letzten ~** [down] to the last drop ❷ *pl* PHARM, MED drops *pl* ▶ WENDUNGEN: **ein ~ auf den heißen Stein** (*fam*) just a drop in the ocean

Tropfstein *m* ❶ (*Stalaktit*) stalactite ❷ (*Stalagmit*) stalagmite

Tropfsteinhöhle *f* cave with stalactites and stalagmites

Trophäe <-, -n> [tro·'fɛːə] *f* trophy

tropisch ['troː·pɪʃ] *adj* tropical

Trost <-[e]s> ['troːst] *m kein pl* ❶ (*Linderung*) consolation; **ein schwacher ~ sein** to be of little consolation; **das ist ein schöner ~** (*iron*) some comfort that is ❷ (*Zuspruch*) words of comfort; **jdm ~ spenden** to comfort sb ▶ WENDUNGEN: **nicht** [**ganz**] **bei ~ sein** (*fam*) to have taken leave of one's senses

trösten ['trøːs·tn̩] **I.** *vt* (*jds Kummer lindern*) to comfort; **sie war von nichts und niemandem zu ~** she was utterly inconsolable; ■ **etw tröstet jdn** sth is of consolation to sb **II.** *vr* ■ **sich** *akk* [**mit jdm**] ~ to find consolation [with sb]; ■ **sich** *akk* [**mit etw** *dat*] ~ to console oneself [with sth]

tröstlich *adj* comforting

trostlos *adj* ❶ (*deprimierend*) miserable ❷ (*öde und hässlich*) desolate; *Landschaft* bleak

Trostlosigkeit <-> *f kein pl* ❶ (*deprimierende Art*) miserableness ❷ (*triste Beschaffenheit*) desolateness

Trostpreis *m* consolation prize

Trott <-s> ['trɔt] *m kein pl* routine

Trottel <-s, -> ['trɔ·tl̩] *m* (*fam*) bonehead *sl*

trotten ['trɔ·tn̩] *vi sein* to trudge [along]

trotz ['trɔts] *präp* +*gen* despite

Trotz <-es> ['trɔts] *m kein pl* defiance; **aus ~** [**gegen jdn/etw**] out of spite [for sb/sth]; **jdm/einer S. zum ~** in defiance of sb/sth

Trotzalter *nt* difficult age, the terrible twos

trotzdem ['trɔts·deːm] *adv* nevertheless; (*aber*) still

trotzen ['trɔ·tsn̩] *vi* ■ **jdm/einer S. ~** (*die Stirn bieten*) to resist sb/brave sth; (*sich widersetzen*) to defy sb/sth; **einer Herausforderung ~** to meet a challenge

trotzig ['trɔ·tsɪç] *adj* defiant

Trotzkopf *m* (*fam: trotziges Kind*) [little] brat

trübe ['tryː·bə] *adj* ❶ (*unklar*) murky; *Saft, Urin* cloudy; *Glas, Spiegel* dull ❷ (*matt*) dim ❸ *Himmel* dull ❹ (*deprimierend*) bleak; *Stimmung* gloomy ▶ WENDUNGEN: **mit etw** *dat* **sieht es ~ aus** the prospects [for sth] are [looking] bleak

Trubel <-s> ['truː·bl̩] *m kein pl* hustle and bustle

trüben ['tryː·bn̩] **I.** *vt* ■ **etw ~** ❶ (*unklar machen*) to make sth murky [*or* cloudy] ❷ (*beeinträchtigen*) to cast a cloud over sth; *Beziehungen, ein Verhältnis* to strain **II.** *vr* ❶ (*unklar werden*) ■ **sich** *akk* ~ to become murky ❷ (*geh*) **sein Gedächtnis trübte sich im Alter** his memory is becoming cloudy in his old age

Trübsal ['tryːp·zaːl] *f kein pl* (*geh*) ❶ (*Betrübtheit*) grief ❷ (*Leid*) suffering ▶ WENDUNGEN: **~ blasen** (*fam*) to mope

trübselig *adj* ❶ (*betrübt*) miserable; *Miene* gloomy ❷ (*trostlos*) bleak

Trübsinn *m kein pl* gloom[iness]

Trübung <-, -en> *f* ❶ (*Veränderung zum Unklaren*) clouding ❷ (*Beeinträchtigung*) straining

Trüffel[1] <-, -n> ['tryfl̩] *f* (*Pilz*) truffle

Trüffel[2] <-, -n> ['try·fl̩] *f* (*gefüllte Praline*) truffle

trug ['ːk] *imp von* **tragen**

Trug <-[e]s> ['ːk] *m kein pl* (*Betrug*) delusion; **Lug und ~** lies and deception

Trugbild *nt* (*veraltend geh*) illusion

trügen <trog, getrogen> ['tryːgn̩] **I.** *vt* **wenn mich nicht alles trügt** unless I'm very much mistaken **II.** *vi* to be deceptive

trügerisch ['tryː·gə·rɪʃ] *adj* deceptive

Trugschluss[RR] *m* fallacy

Truhe <-, -n> ['truːə] *f* chest

Trümmer ['trʏ·mɐ] *pl* rubble; *eines Flugzeugs* wreckage; **in ~n liegen** to lie in ruins *pl*

Trümmerhaufen *m* pile of rubble

Trumpf <-[e]s, Trümpfe> ['trʊmpf, *pl* 'trʏm·pfə] *m* ❶ KARTEN trump [card]; **~ sein** to be trumps ❷ (*fig: entscheidender Vorteil*) trump card; **noch einen ~ in der Hand haben** to have another ace up one's sleeve

Trunk <-[e]s, Trünke> ['trʊŋk, *pl* 'trʏŋ·kə] *m* (*geh*) beverage

trunken ['trʊŋ·kn̩] *adj* (*geh*) ■ **~ vor etw** *dat* **sein** to be intoxicated with sth

Trunkenheit <-> *f kein pl* drunkenness; **~ am Steuer** drunk driving

Truppe <-, -n> ['trʊ·pə] *f* ❶ *kein pl* (*Soldaten an der Front*) combat unit ❷ (*Soldatenverband mit bestimmter Aufgabe*) squad ❸ (*gemeinsam auftretende Gruppe*) company

Truthahn ['truːt·haːn] *m* turkey

Tschad <-s> ['tʃat] *nt* Chad; *s. a.* **Deutschland**

Tscheche, Tschechin <-n, -n> ['tʃɛ·çə] *m, f* Czech; *s. a.* **Deutsche(r)**

Tschechien <-s> ['tʃɛ·çi̯ən] *nt* Czech Republic; *s. a.* **Deutschland**

tschechisch ['tʃɛ·çɪʃ] *adj* ❶ GEOG Czech; *s. a.* **deutsch 1** ❷ LING Czech; *s. a.* **deutsch 2**

Tschechische Republik *f* Czech Republic; *s. a.* **Deutschland**

tschüs, tschüss ['tʃʏs] *interj* (*fam*) bye

T-Shirt <-s, -s> ['tiː·ʃøːɐ̯t] *nt* T-shirt

TU <-, -s> [teː·'ʔuː] *f Abk von* **technische Universität** technical university

Tuba <-, Tuben> ['tuː·ba, *pl* 'tuː·bn̩] *f* tuba

Tube <-, -n> ['tuː·bə] *f* tube ▶ WENDUNGEN: **auf die ~ drücken** (*fam*) to step on it

Tuberkulose <-, -n> [tu·bɛr·ku·'loː·zə] *f* tuberculosis

Tuch[1] <-[e]s, Tücher> ['tuːx, *pl* 'tyː·çɐ] *nt* ❶ (*Kopftuch*) [head]scarf; (*Halstuch*) scarf ❷ (*dünne Decke*) cloth

Tuch[2] <-[e]s, -e> ['tuːx] *nt* (*textiles Gewebe*) cloth

tüchtig ['tʏç·tɪç] **I.** *adj* ❶ (*fähig*) capable; (*fleißig*) hard-working ❷ (*fam: groß*) big **II.** *adv* (*fam*) ❶ (*viel*) **~ anpacken** to [eagerly] help out; **~ essen** to eat heartily ❷ (*stark*) **~ regnen/schneien** to rain/snow hard

Tücke <-, -n> ['tʏkə] *f* ❶ *kein pl* (*Heimtücke*) malice; (*einer Tat*) maliciousness ❷ *kein pl* (*Gefährlichkeit*) dangerousness; (*von Krankheiten*) deadly ❸ (*Unwägbarkeiten*) ■**~n** *pl* vagaries *pl;* **seine ~n haben** to be temperamental ▶ WENDUNGEN: **das ist die ~ des Objekts** these things have a will of their own!

tückisch ['tʏ·kɪʃ] *adj* ❶ (*hinterhältig*) malicious ❷ (*heimtückisch*) pernicious ❸ (*gefährlich*) treacherous

tüfteln ['tʏf·tl̩n] *vi* (*fam*) to fiddle around (**an** +*dat* with)

Tugend <-, -en> ['tuː·gn̩t, *pl* -n̩·dən] *f* virtue

Tulpe <-, -n> ['tʊl·pə] *f* tulip

tummeln ['tʊ·ml̩n] *vr* ■**sich** *akk* **~** ❶ (*froh umherbewegen*) to romp [around] ❷ (*sich beeilen*) to hurry [up]

Tumor <-s, -en> ['tuː·moːɐ̯, tu·'moːɐ̯, *pl* tu·'moː·rən] *m* tumor

Tumult <-[e]s, -e> [tu·'mʊlt] *m* ❶ *kein pl* (*lärmendes Durcheinander*) commotion ❷ *meist pl* (*Aufruhr*) disturbance

tun <tat, getan> ['tuːn] **I.** *vt* ❶ + *unbestimmtem Objekt* (*machen*) to do; **was sollen wir bloß ~?** what the heck should we do?; **was tut er nur den ganzen Tag?** what does he do all day?; **noch viel ~ müssen** to still have a lot to do; **etw aus Liebe ~** to do sth out of love; **er tut nichts, als sich zu beklagen** he does nothing but complain; **~ und lassen können, was man will** to do as one pleases; **~, was man nicht lassen kann** (*fam*) to do sth if one has to; **so etwas tut man nicht!** you just don't do [things like] that! ❷ (*unternehmen*) ■**etw/nichts/einiges für jdn ~** to do something/nothing/a lot for sb; **was tut man nicht alles für seine Nichten und Neffen!** the things we do for our nephews and nieces!; **etw gegen etw** *akk* **~** *Beschwerden, Pickel, Belästigungen, Unrecht* to do sth about sth; **ich will versuchen, was sich da ~ lässt** I'll see what I can do [about it] [*or* do what I can] ❸ (*fam: legen o stecken*) ■**etw irgendwohin ~** to put sth somewhere ❹ (*fam*) **tut es dein altes Tonbandgerät eigentlich noch?** [by the way,] is your old tape recorder still working? ❺ (*fam: ausmachen*) **das tut nichts** it doesn't matter, no problem ❻ (*fam*) **für heute tut's das** that'll do for today ▶ WENDUNGEN: **was kann ich für Sie ~?** ÖKON can [*or* may] I help you?; **es** [**mit jdm**] **~** (*sl*) to do it [with sb] **II.** *vr impers* ■**etw/nichts/einiges tut sich** something/nothing/a lot is happening **III.** *vi* ❶ (*sich benehmen*) to act; **albern/dumm ~** to play dumb; **so ~, als ob** to pretend that; **er ist doch gar nicht wütend, er tut nur so** he's not angry at all; he's just pretending [to be] ❷ (*Dinge erledigen*) ■**zu ~ haben** to be busy ▶ WENDUNGEN: **es mit jdm zu ~ bekommen** (*fam*) to get into trouble with sb; **es mit jdm zu ~ haben** to be dealing with sb; **etw/nichts mit jdm/etw zu ~ haben** to have something/nothing to do with sb/sth **IV.** *aux vb modal* ❶ + *vorgestelltem Infinitiv* **singen tut sie ja gut** she sure is a good singer [*or* can sing] ❷ + *nachgestelltem Infinitiv* DIAL **ich tu nur schnell den Braten anbraten** I'll just quickly sear the roast; **tust du die Kinder ins Bett bringen?** will you [please] put the children to bed?; **er tut sich schrecklich ärgern** he's really getting worked up ❸ *konjunktivisch,* + *vorgestelltem Infinitiv* DIAL **deine Gründe täten mich schon interessieren** I would be interested to hear your reasons; **er täte zu gerne wissen, warum ...** he would love to know why ...

Tun <-s> ['tuːn] *nt kein pl* action; **ihr ganzes ~ und Trachten** everything she does

Tunesien <-s> [tu·'neː·ziən] *nt* Tunisia; *s. a.* **Deutschland**

Tunesier(in) <-s, -> [tu·'neː·ziɐ] *m(f)* Tunisian; *s. a.* **Deutsche(r)**

tunesisch [tu·'neː·zɪʃ] *adj* ❶ (*Tunesien betreffend*) Tunisian; *s. a.* **deutsch 1** ❷ LING Tunisian; *s. a.* **deutsch 2**

Tunfisch[RR] *m s.* **Thunfisch**

Tunnel <-s, - *o* -s> ['tʊnl̩] *m* tunnel; (*für Fußgänger*) pedestrian underpass

Tüpfelchen <-s, -> *nt* dot ▶ WENDUNGEN: **das ~ auf dem i** the final touch

tupfen ['tʊp·fn̩] *vt* ■**etw von etw** *dat* **~** to dab sth from sth; ■**sich** *dat* **etw ~** to dab one's sth

Tür <-, -en> ['tyːɐ̯] *f* door; **an die ~ gehen** to get the door ▶ WENDUNGEN: **zwischen ~ und Angel** (*fam*) in passing; **mit der ~ ins Haus fallen** (*fam*) to blurt it [right] out; [**bei jdm**] [**mit etw** *dat*] **offene ~en einrennen** to be preaching to the choir [with sth]; **jdm** [**fast**] **die ~ einrennen** (*fam*) to pester sb constantly; **vor der ~ sein** to be just around the corner; **jdn vor die ~ setzen** (*fam*) to kick sb out

Turban <-s, -e> ['tʊr·baːn] *m* turban

Turbine <-, -n> [tʊr·biː·nə] *f* turbine

Turbo <-s, -s> ['tʊrbo] *m* AUTO ❶ (*Turbolader*) turbocharger ❷ (*Auto mit Turbomotor*) turbo

turbulent [tʊr·bu·'lɛnt] **I.** *adj* turbulent; *Wochenende* tumultuous; **die Wochen vor**

T

Weihnachten waren reichlich ~ the weeks leading up to Christmas were really chaotic **II.** *adv* turbulently; **~ verlaufen** to be turbulent

Turbulenz <-, -en> [tʊr·bu·'lɛnts] *f a.* METEO turbulence

Türgriff *m* door handle, doorknob

Türke(in) <-n, -n> ['tʏr·kə] *m(f)* Turk; *s. a.* **Deutsche(r)**

Türkei <-> [tʏr·'kai] *f* ■**die ~** Turkey; *s. a.* **Deutschland**

türkis [tʏr·'kiːs] *adj* turquoise

türkisch ['tʏr·kɪʃ] *adj* ❶ (*die Türkei betreffend*) Turkish; *s. a.* **deutsch 1** ❷ LING Turkish; *s. a.* **deutsch 2**

Turm <-[e]s, Türme> ['tʊrm, *pl* 'tʏr·mə] *m* ❶ ARCHIT tower; (*spitzer Kirchturm*) spire, steeple ❷ SPORT (*Sprungturm*) diving platform ❸ (*Schachfigur*) castle

türmen[1] ['tʏr·mən] **I.** *vt haben* ■**etw [auf etw** *akk*] **~** to pile up sth *sep* [on sth] **II.** *vr* ■**sich** *akk* **[auf etw** *dat*] **~** to pile up [on sth]

türmen[2] ['tʏr·mən] *vi sein* (*fam*) ■**[aus etw** *dat*/**irgendwohin] ~** to storm [out of sth/toward sb/sth]; **aus dem Knast ~** to break out of jail

Turmspringen *nt kein pl* high diving

Turmuhr *f* [tower] clock

turnen ['tʊr·nən] **I.** *vi haben* ❶ SPORT to do gymnastics ❷ *sein* (*fam: sich flink bewegen*) to dash **II.** *vt haben* SPORT ■**etw ~** to do sth; **für diese fehlerfrei geturnte Übung erhielt er 9,9 Punkte** he received a score of 9.9 for this flawless routine

Turnen <-s> ['tʊr·nən] *nt kein pl* ❶ SPORT gymnastics + *sing vb* ❷ SCH physical education, PE

Turner(in) <-s, -> ['tʊr·nɐ] *m(f)* gymnast

Turngerät *nt* gymnastics equipment

Turnhalle *f* gymnasium, gym *fam*

Turnier <-s, -e> [tʊr·'niːɐ̯] *nt* ❶ SPORT (*längerer Wettbewerb*) tournament; *der Springreiter* show jumping competition ❷ HIST tournament

Turnschuh *m* tennis shoe

Turnübung *f* gymnastics exercise

Turnus <-, -se> ['tʊr·nʊs, *pl* -ʊ·sə] *m* ❶ (*regelmäßige Abfolge*) regular cycle; **für die Kontrollgänge gibt es einen festgesetzten ~** there is a set rotation for making the rounds; **im [regelmäßigen] ~ [von etw** *dat*] at regular intervals [of sth] ❷ ÖSTERR MED residency

Türöffner *m* automatic door opener

Türpfosten *m* doorjamb

Türschild *nt* nameplate

Türschloss[RR] *nt* door lock

Türschwelle *f* threshold

Türsteher *m* doorman

Tusche <-, -n> ['tʊ·ʃə] *f* Indian ink

tuscheln ['tʊ·ʃl̩n] *vi* (*heimlich reden*) ■**[über jdn/etw] ~** to gossip secretly [about sb/sth]

Tüte <-, -n> ['tyː·tə] *f* bag; **Suppe aus der ~** instant soup; **eine ~ Popcorn** a bag of popcorn ▶ WENDUNGEN: **[das] kommt nicht in die ~!** (*fam*) no way!

Tutor, Tutorin <-s, Tutoren> ['tuː·toːɐ̯, *pl* tu·'toː·rən] *m, f* (*Mentor*) tutor

TÜV <-s, -s> ['tʏf] *m Akr von* **Technischer Überwachungsverein** Technical Inspection Association (*performs vehicle inspections*); **jds/der ~ läuft ab** sb's/the annual car inspection needs to be renewed; **durch den ~ kommen** to get [a vehicle] through its inspection

> Every vehicle licensed for the public roadways must regularly undergo a **TÜV** inspection. When a vehicle passes the inspection, a *TÜV-Plakette* (sticker) valid for two years is attached to the vehicle's rear license plate.

TV <-[s], -s> [teː·'fau, a. tiː·'viː] *nt Abk von* **Television** TV

twittern ['tvɪ·tɐn] *vt, vi* INET to tweet, to post on Twitter

Typ <-s, -en> ['tyːp] *m* ❶ (*Ausführung*) model ❷ (*Art Mensch*) type [of person] *fam;* **was ist er für ein ~, dein neuer Chef?** what type of person is your new boss?; ■**der ~ ... sein, der ...** to be the type of ... who ...; **dein ~ ist nicht gefragt** (*fam*) we don't want your type [around] here ❸ (*sl: Kerl, Freund*) guy ❹ (*fam: merkwürdiger Mensch*) character; **was ist denn das für ein ~?** what a weirdo!

Type <-, -n> ['tyː·pə] *f* TYPO type

Typen ['tyː·pn̩] *pl von* **Typus**

typisch ['tyː·pɪʃ] **I.** *adj* typical; ■**~ für jdn sein** to be typical of sb; **[das ist] ~!** (*fam*) [that's] [just] typical! **II.** *adv* ■**~ jd** [that's] typical of sb; **~ Frau/Mann!** typical woman/man!; **~ amerikanisch/deutsch** typically American/German; **sein unterkühlter Humor ist ~ hamburgisch** his dry humor is typical of a person from Hamburg

Typus <-, Typen> ['tyː·pʊs, *pl* 'tyː·pn̩] *m* ❶ (*Menschenschlag*) race [*or* breed] [of people] ❷ (*geh: Typ*) type

Tyrann(in) <-en, -en> [ty·'ran] *m(f)* tyrant

tyrannisch [ty·'ra·nɪʃ] **I.** *adj* tyrannical **II.** *adv* tyrannically

tyrannisieren* [ty·ra·ni·'ziː·rən] *vt* ■**jdn ~** to tyrannize sb; ■**sich** *akk* **[von jdm/etw] ~ lassen** to [allow oneself to] be tyrannized [by sb/sth]

Uu

U, u <-, - *o fam* -s, -s> [uː] *nt* U, u; **~ wie Ulrich** U as in Uniform

u. *konj Abk von* **und**

u.a. ❶ *Abk von* **und andere(s)** and other things ❷ *Abk von* **unter anderem** among other things

U-Bahn [uː-] *f* ❶ (*Untergrundbahn*) subway ❷ (*U-Bahn-Zug*) [subway] train

U-Bahn-Station *f* subway station

übel ['yːbl̩] **I.** *adj* ❶ (*schlimm*) bad, nasty; *Affäre* ugly ❷ (*unangenehm*) nasty ❸ (*ungut*) bad ❹ (*verkommen*) rotten; *Stadtviertel* bad ❺ (*schlecht*) ■ **jdm ist/wird ~** sb feels nauseous **II.** *adv* ❶ (*unangenehm*) **was riecht hier so ~?** what's that awful smell [[in] here]?; **nicht ~** not that bad [at all] ❷ (*schlecht*) badly; **sich** *akk* **~ fühlen** to feel awful; **jdn ~ behandeln** to treat sb badly ❸ (*nachteilig*) **jdm etw ~ auslegen** to hold sth against sb

Übel <-s, -> ['yːbl̩] *nt* evil ▶ WENDUNGEN: **das kleinere ~** the lesser evil; **ein notwendiges ~** a necessary evil

Übelkeit <-, -en> *f* nausea

Übeltäter(in) *m(f)* wrongdoer

üben ['yːbn̩] **I.** *vt, vi a.* SPORT, MUS to practice **II.** *vr* ■ **sich** *akk* **in etw** *dat* **~** to practice sth

über ['yːbɐ] **I.** *präp* ❶ +*dat* (*oberhalb von*) above ❷ +*akk* (*quer hinüber*) over ❸ +*akk* (*höher als*) above, over ❹ +*akk* (*etw erfassend*) over; **ein Überblick ~ etw** an overview of sth ❺ +*akk* (*quer darüber*) over; **er strich ihr ~ das Haar/die Wange** he stroked her hair/cheek ❻ +*akk* (*jdn/etw betreffend*) about ❼ +*dat* (*zahlenmäßig größer als*) above ❽ (*durch jdn/etw*) through ❾ (*via*) via ❿ (*während*) over; **habt ihr ~ die Feiertage/das Wochenende schon was vor?** do you have anything planned for the holiday/weekend? ▶ WENDUNGEN: **~ alles** more than anything **II.** *adv* ❶ (*älter als*) over ❷ (*mehr als*) more than ▶ WENDUNGEN: **~ und ~** completely **III.** *adj* (*fam*) ❶ (*übrig*) ■ **~ sein** to be left; *Essen* to be left [over] ❷ (*überlegen*) **jdm auf einem bestimmten Gebiet ~ sein** to be better than sb in a certain field

überall [yːbɐ·ˈʔal] *adv* ❶ (*an allen Orten*) everywhere; (*an jeder Stelle*) all over [the place]; **~ wo** wherever ❷ (*wer weiß wo*) anywhere ❸ (*in allen Dingen*) everything; **er kennt sich** *akk* **~ aus** he knows something about everything ❹ (*bei jedermann*) everyone; **er ist ~ beliebt** everyone likes him

überallher [yːbɐ·ʔal·ˈheːɐ̯] *adv* ■ **von ~** from all over

überallhin [yːbɐ·ʔal·ˈhɪn] *adv* all over; **sie kann ~ verschwunden sein** she could have disappeared anywhere

Überangebot *nt* surplus (**an** +*dat* of)

überanstrengen* [yːbɐ·ˈʔan·ʃtrɛŋ·ən] **I.** *vt* ■ **etw ~** to put too great a strain on sth **II.** *vr* ■ **sich** *akk* **~** to overexert oneself

Überanstrengung *f* ❶ *kein pl* (*das Überbeanspruchen*) overstraining ❷ (*zu große Beanspruchung*) overexertion

überarbeiten* [yːbɐ·ˈʔar·bai·tn̩] **I.** *vt* to revise **II.** *vr* ■ **sich** *akk* **~** to overwork oneself

überaus [ˈyːbɐ·ʔaus] *adv* extremely

überbacken* [yːbɐ·ˈba·kn̩] *vt irreg* **etw mit Käse ~** to top sth with cheese and bake it

überbelasten* *vt* to overload

überbelichten* *vt* to overexpose

Überbevölkerung *f kein pl* overpopulation

überbewerten* *vt* ❶ (*zu gut bewerten*) to overvalue ❷ (*überbetonen*) to overestimate; **du überbewertest diese Äußerung** you're placing too much importance on this comment

überbieten* [yːbɐ·ˈbiː·tn̩] *irreg vt* ❶ SPORT to better (**um** +*akk* by); *Rekord* to break ❷ (*durch höheres Gebot übertreffen*) to outbid (**um** +*akk* by)

Überbleibsel <-s, -> [ˈyːbɐ·blaip·sl̩] *nt* (*fam*) ❶ (*Relikt*) relic ❷ (*Rest*) remnant

Überblick [ˈyːbɐ·blɪk] *m* view (**über** +*akk* of) ▶ WENDUNGEN: **einen ~ [über etw** *akk***] haben** to have an overview [of sth]; **den ~ [über etw** *akk***] verlieren** to lose track [of sth]

überblicken* [yːbɐ·ˈblɪ·kn̩] *vt* ❶ (*überschauen*) to look out over ❷ (*in der Gesamtheit einschätzen*) to have an overview of

überboten [yːbɐ·ˈboː·tn̩] *pp von* **überbieten**

überbracht [yːbɐ·ˈbraxt] *pp von* **überbringen**

überbringen* [yːbɐ·ˈbrɪ·ŋən] *vt irreg* to deliver

überbrücken* [yːbɐ·ˈbrʏ·kn̩] *vt* ❶ (*notdürftig bewältigen*) to get through; *Krise* to ride out ❷ (*ausgleichen*) to reconcile

überdachen* [yːbɐ·ˈdaxn̩] *vt* to roof over *sep*; ■ **überdacht** covered

überdacht [yːbɐ·ˈdaxt] *pp von* **überdachen**

überdauern* *vt* to survive

überdenken* [yːbɐ·ˈdɛŋ·kn̩] *vt irreg* to think over *sep*

Überdosis *f* overdose (**an** +*dat* of)

Überdruck *m* excess pressure

Überdruss[RR] <-es>, **Überdruß**[ALT] <-sses> [ˈyːbɐ·drʊs] *m kein pl* aversion; **aus ~ [an etw** *dat***]** out of an aversion [to sth]; **ich habe das nun schon bis zum ~ gehört** [by now] I've heard that ad nauseam

überdrüssig [ˈyːbɐ·drʏ·sɪç] *adj* ■ **jds/einer S.** *gen* **~ sein/werden** to be/grow tired of sb/sth

überdurchschnittlich **I.** *adj* above-average *attr,* above average *pred* **II.** *adv* above average

übereinander [yːbɐ·ʔai·ˈnan·dɐ] *adv* ❶ (*eins über dem anderen/das andere*) on top of each other ❷ (*über sich*) about each other

übereinander|schlagen *vt irreg* **die Beine ~**

U

to cross one's legs
überein|kommen [y:bɐ·ˈʔain·kɔ·mən] *vi irreg sein* to agree
Übereinkommen [y:bɐ·ˈʔain·kɔ·mən] *nt* agreement; **ein ~ erzielen** to reach an agreement (**in** +*dat* on)
überein|stimmen [y:bɐ·ˈʔain·ʃtɪ·mən] *vi* ❶ (*der gleichen Meinung sein*) to agree (**in** +*dat* on) ❷ (*sich gleichen*) ■[**mit etw** *dat*] ~ to match [sth]
übereinstimmend I. *adj* ❶ (*einhellig*) unanimous ❷ (*sich gleichend*) corresponding II. *adv* ❶ (*einhellig*) unanimously ❷ (*in gleicher Weise*) concurrently
Übereinstimmung *f* agreement (**in** +*dat* on)
überempfindlich I. *adj* oversensitive; MED hypersensitive (**gegen** +*akk* to) II. *adv* oversensitively; MED hypersensitively
überfahren* [y:bɐ·ˈfa:·rən] *vt irreg* ❶ (*niederfahren*) to run over *sep* ❷ (*nicht beachten*) **eine rote Ampel ~** to run a red light ❸ (*fam: übertölpeln*) ■**jdn ~** to railroad sb
Überfall *m* attack; (*Raubüberfall*) robbery
überfallen* [y:bɐ·ˈfal·ən] *vt irreg* ❶ (*angreifen*) to mug; *Bank* to rob; *Land* to attack; MIL to raid ❷ (*überkommen*) **Heimweh überfiel sie** she was overcome by homesickness ❸ (*überraschend besuchen*) to descend (+*akk* [up]on) ❹ (*bestürmen*) to bombard (**mit** +*dat* with)
überfällig *adj* ❶ TRANSP delayed; **der Zug ist seit 20 Minuten ~** the train is 20 minutes late ❷ (*längst zu tätigen*) overdue
überfliegen* [y:bɐ·ˈfli:·gn̩] *vt irreg* ❶ LUFT to fly over ❷ (*flüchtig ansehen*) to take a quick look at; *Text a.* to skim through
überflogen [y:bɐ·ˈflo:·gn̩] *pp von* **überfliegen**
ÜberflussRR *m kein pl* abundance; **im ~ vorhanden sein** to be in plentiful supply; **etw im ~ haben** to have plenty of sth ► WENDUNGEN: **zu allem ~** to top it all off
überflüssig *adj* superfluous; *Anschaffungen, Bemerkung* unnecessary
überfluten* [y:bɐ·ˈflu:·tn̩] *vt* (*a. fig*) to flood
Überflutung <-, -en> [y:bɐ·ˈflu:·tʊŋ] *f* flooding
überfordern* [y:bɐ·ˈfɔr·dɐn] *vt* to overtax, to be too much for; ■**überfordert sein** to be out of one's league
überfragt [y:bɐ·ˈfra:kt] *vt* **da bin ich ~** I don't know [the answer to that]
überführen*1 [y:bɐ·ˈfy:·rən] *vt* (*woandershin transportieren*) to transfer; *Leiche* to transport
überführen*2 [y:bɐ·ˈfy:·rən] *vt* JUR to convict; **jdn des Mordes ~** to convict sb of murder
überfüllt *adj* overcrowded
Überfunktion *f* MED hyperactivity
Übergabe *f* ❶ (*das Übergeben*) handing over ❷ MIL surrender
Übergang *m* ❶ (*an der Grenze*) border crossing [point] ❷ (*Wechsel*) transition ❸ *kein pl* (*Übergangszeit*) interim ❹ *kein pl* (*Zwischenlösung*) interim solution
Übergangsfrist *f* transition period
übergangslos *adv* seamless
Übergangslösung *f* temporary solution
Übergangsphase <-, -n> *f* transitional phase
Übergangszeit *f* ❶ (*Zeit zwischen zwei Phasen*) transition ❷ (*Zeit zwischen Jahreszeiten*) off-season
übergeben* [y:bɐ·ˈge:·bn̩] *irreg* I. *vt* ❶ (*überreichen*) ■[**jdm**] **etw ~** to hand over *sep* sth [to sb] ❷ (*ausliefern*) ■**jdn jdm ~** to hand over *sep* sb to sb ❸ MIL (*überlassen*) to surrender II. *vr* ■**sich** *akk* ~ to vomit
über|gehen1 [ˈy:bɐ·ge:·ən] *vi irreg sein* ❶ (*überwechseln*) to move on (**zu** +*dat* to); ■**dazu ~, etw zu tun** to move on to sth ❷ (*übertragen werden*) **in anderen Besitz ~** to become sb else's property ❸ (*einen anderen Zustand erreichen*) **in Fäulnis/Gärung/Verwesung ~** to begin to rot/ferment/decay ❹ (*verschwimmen*) ■**ineinander ~** to merge into one another
übergehen*2 [y:bɐ·ˈge:·ən] *vt irreg* ❶ (*nicht berücksichtigen*) to pass over *sep* ❷ (*nicht beachten*) to ignore ❸ (*auslassen*) to skip [over *sep*]
übergeordnet *adj* ❶ (*vorrangig*) superior ❷ (*vorgesetzt*) higher
übergeschnappt *adj* (*fam*) crazy
Übergewicht *nt kein pl* ❶ (*zu hohes Körpergewicht*) excess weight; **~ haben** to be overweight ❷ (*vorrangige Bedeutung*) predominance
übergewichtig *adj* overweight
überglücklich I. *adj* extremely happy, overjoyed *pred* II. *adv* **~ lächeln** to smile blissfully
über|greifen *vi irreg* to spread (**auf** +*akk* to)
Übergröße *f* extra large size
überhand|nehmen [y:bɐ·ˈhant-] *vi irreg* to get out of hand
über|hängen1 [ˈy:bɐ·hɛ·ŋən] *vt* ■**jdm/sich** *dat* **etw ~** to put sth around sb's/one's shoulders; **sich eine Tasche ~** to hang a bag over one's shoulder
über|hängen2 [ˈy:bɐ·hɛ·ŋən] *vi irreg* ❶ (*hinausragen*) to hang over ❷ (*vorragen*) to project
überhäufen* [y:bɐ·ˈhɔy·fn̩] *vt* ■**jdn mit etw** *dat* ~ (*a. fig*) to heap sth [up]on sb; **jdn mit Beschwerden ~** to inundate sb with complaints
überhaupt [y:bɐ·ˈhaupt] I. *adv* ❶ (*zudem*) **das ist ~ die Höhe!** this is insufferable! ❷ (*in Verneinungen*) ■**~ kein(e, r)** nobody/nothing/none at all; **~ kein Geld haben** to have no money at all; ■**~ nicht/nichts** not/nothing at all; ■**~ [noch] nie** never [at all]; ■**und ~, ...?** and anyway, ...?; **Sie bekommen nicht mehr als 4.200 Euro, wenn ~** you'll get no more than 4,200 euros, if that II. *part* (*eigentlich*) **was soll das ~?** what's that supposed to mean?; **wissen Sie ~, wer ich bin?** don't you even know who I am?
überheblich [y:bɐ·ˈhe:p·lɪç] I. *adj* arrogant II. *adv* arrogantly

U

Überheblichkeit <-> *f kein pl* arrogance

überhöht *adj* excessive; **mit ~er Geschwindigkeit fahren** to speed

überholen* [y:bɐ·ˈho:·lṇ] *vt* ❶ (*schneller vorbeifahren*) to pass ❷ (*übertreffen*) to surpass ❸ *Motor, Gerät* to overhaul

Überholspur *f* fast lane

überholt *adj* outdated

Überholverbot *nt* restriction on passing; (*Strecke*) no passing zone

überhören* [y:bɐ·ˈhø:·rən] *vt* ❶ (*nicht hören*) to not hear ❷ (*nicht hören wollen*) to ignore

überinterpretieren* *vt* to overinterpret

überirdisch [ˈy:bɐ·ʔɪr·dɪʃ] *adj* celestial *poet; Schönheit* divine

über|kochen [ˈy:bɐ·kɔ·xṇ] *vi sein* to boil over

überkommen* [y:bɐ·ˈkɔ·mən] *irreg vt* **es überkam mich plötzlich** it suddenly overcame me

überkreuzen* [y:bɐ·ˈkrɔy·tsṇ] **I.** *vt* (*verschränken*) **die Arme ~** to fold one's arms **II.** *vr* **sich ~de Linien** intersecting lines

überladen*¹ [y:bɐ·ˈla:·dṇ] *vt irreg* to overload

überladen² [y:bɐ·ˈla:·dṇ] *adj* ❶ (*zu stark beladen*) overloaded ❷ (*geh: überreich ausgestattet*) overornate; *Stil* florid

überlappen* [y:bɐ·ˈla·pṇ] **I.** *vi* to overlap **II.** *vr* ■ **sich ~** to overlap

überlassen* [y:bɐ·ˈla·sṇ] *vt irreg* ❶ (*zur Verfügung stellen, verkaufen*) ■ **jdm etw ~** to let sb have sth ❷ (*lassen*) ■ **jdm etw ~** to leave sth to sb; **ich überlasse dir die Wahl** it's your choice; **jdm ~ sein** to be up to sb ❸ (*preisgeben*) ■ **jdn jdm/etw ~** to leave sb to sb/sth; **sich** *dat* **selbst ~ sein** to be left to one's own devices

überlasten* [y:bɐ·ˈlas·tṇ] *vt* ❶ (*zu stark in Anspruch nehmen*) ■ **jdn ~** to overburden sb; ■ **etw ~** to overstrain sth ❷ (*zu stark belasten*) ■ **etw ~** to overload sth

Überlastung <-, -en> *f* ❶ (*zu starke Inanspruchnahme*) excess strain ❷ (*zu starke Belastung*) overloading

überlaufen*¹ [y:bɐ·ˈlau·fṇ] *vt irreg* ■ **etw überläuft jdn** sb is seized with sth; **es überlief mich kalt** a cold shiver ran down my spine

über|laufen² [ˈy:bɐ·lau·fṇ] *vi irreg sein* ❶ (*über den Rand fließen*) to overflow; *Tasse a.* to run over *a. poet* ❷ (*überkochen*) to boil over ❸ MIL to desert

überlaufen³ [y:bɐ·ˈlau·fṇ] *adj* overrun

Überläufer(in) *m(f)* MIL deserter

überleben* [y:bɐ·ˈle:·bṇ] **I.** *vt* ❶ (*lebend überstehen*) to survive ❷ (*lebend überdauern*) ■ **etw ~** to live through sth ❸ (*über jds Tod hinaus leben*) ■ **jdn ~** to outlive sb **II.** *vi* to survive

Überlebende(r) *f(m) dekl wie adj* survivor

Überlebenschance *f* chance of survival

überlegen*¹ [y:bɐ·ˈle:·gṇ] **I.** *vi, vt* to think [about it]; **nach kurzem/langem Ü~** after short/long deliberation; **ohne zu ~** without thinking; **das wäre zu ~** it is worth considering; **überleg [doch] mal!** just [stop and] think about it! **II.** *vr* ■ **sich** *dat* **etw ~** to consider sth; **sich etw reiflich ~** to give serious thought to sth; **ich will es mir noch einmal ~** I'll think it over again; **es sich [anders] ~** to change one's mind; **wenn man es sich recht überlegt** on second thought

über|legen² [ˈy:bɐ·le:·gṇ] *vt* ■ **jdm etw ~** to put sth over sb; **sich** *dat* **etw ~** to put on *sep* sth

überlegen³ [y:bɐ·ˈle:·gṇ] **I.** *adj* ❶ (*jdn weit übertreffend*) superior; *Sieg* convincing; ■ **jdm ~ sein** to be superior to sb (**auf/in** +*dat* in) ❷ (*herablassend*) superior **II.** *adv* ❶ (*mit großem Vorsprung*) convincingly ❷ (*herablassend*) superciliously *pej*

Überlegenheit <-> *f kein pl* superiority

überlegt [y:bɐ·ˈle:kt] **I.** *adj* [well-]considered **II.** *adv* with consideration, in a [carefully] thought-out manner

Überlegung <-, -en> *f* ❶ *kein pl* (*das Überlegen*) consideration, thought; **nach eingehender ~** after close reflection ❷ *pl* (*Erwägungen*) considerations *pl;* (*Bemerkungen*) observations *pl*

über|leiten *vi* to lead (**zu** +*dat* to)

Überleitung *f* transition

überliefern* [y:bɐ·ˈli:·fɐn] *vt* to hand down *sep*

Überlieferung *f* tradition; **mündliche ~** oral tradition

überlisten* [y:bɐ·ˈlɪs·tṇ] *vt* to outwit

überm [ˈy:bɐm] (*fam*) = **über dem** *s.* **über**

Übermacht *f kein pl* superiority; **in der ~ sein** to have the greater strength

übermächtig *adj* ❶ (*die Übermacht besitzend*) superior ❷ (*geh: alles beherrschend*) overpowering; *Verlangen* overwhelming

Übermaß *nt kein pl* ■ **das ~ einer S.** *gen* the excess[ive amount] of sth; ■ **ein ~ an/von etw** *dat* an excess[ive amount] of sth

übermäßig **I.** *adj* excessive; *Freude, Trauer* intense; *Schmerz* violent **II.** *adv* ❶ (*in zu hohem Maße*) excessively; **sich** *akk* **~ anstrengen** to try too hard ❷ (*unmäßig*) too much

übermenschlich *adj* superhuman

übermitteln* [y:bɐ·ˈmɪ·tḷn] *vt* ❶ (*überbringen*) ■ **jdm etw ~** to bring sth to sb ❷ (*zukommen lassen*) ■ **[jdm] etw ~** to convey sth [to sb] *form*

übermorgen [ˈy:bɐ·mɔr·gṇ] *adv* the day after tomorrow, in two days

übermüdet [y:bɐ·ˈmy:·dət] *adj* overtired; (*erschöpft a.*) overfatigued *form*

Übermüdung <-> *f kein pl* overtiredness; (*Erschöpfung a.*) overfatigue *form*

Übermut *m* high spirits *npl;* **aus ~** just for the hell of it *fam*

übermütig [ˈy:bɐ·my:·tɪç] **I.** *adj* high-spirited; (*zu dreist*) cocky *fam* **II.** *adv* boisterously

übern [ˈy:bɐn] (*fam*) = **über den** *s.* **über**

übernächste(r, s) [ˈy:bɐ·nɛ:çs·tə, -tɐ, -təs] *adj*

U

attr ~**s Jahr**/~ **Woche** the year/week after next, in two years/weeks; **die ~ Tür** two doors down

übernachten* [y:bɐ·ˈnax·tn̩] *vi* ■[**bei jdm**] ~ to spend the night [at sb's place]

übernächtigt [y:bɐ·ˈnɛç·tɪçt] *adj*, **übernächtig** [y:bɐ·ˈnɛç·tɪç] *adj* ÖSTERR worn out [from lack of sleep] *pred;* (*a. mit trüben Augen*) bleary-eyed

Übernachtung <-, -en> *f* ❶ *kein pl* (*das Übernachten*) spending the night [*or* a]; (*bei Kindern*) sleepover ❷ (*verbrachte Nacht*) overnight stay; **mit zwei ~en in Bangkok** with two nights in Bangkok; **~ mit Frühstück** bed and breakfast

Übernahme <-, -n> [ˈy:bɐ·na:·mə] *f* ❶ (*Inbesitznahme*) taking possession ❷ (*das Übernehmen*) assumption; *von Verantwortung a.* acceptance ❸ ÖKON takeover

übernatürlich *adj* supernatural

übernehmen* [y:bɐ·ˈne:·mən] *irreg* **I.** *vt* ❶ (*in Besitz nehmen*) to take; (*kaufen*) to buy; *Geschäft* to take over *sep* ❷ (*auf sich nehmen, annehmen*) to accept; *Auftrag, Verantwortung a.* to take on *sep; Kosten* to pay; *Verpflichtungen* to assume ❸ (*fortführen*) to take over *sep* ❹ (*verwenden*) to take ❺ (*weiterbeschäftigen*) to take over *sep;* **jdn ins Angestelltenverhältnis ~** to employ sb on a permanent basis **II.** *vr* ■**sich** *akk* ~ to take on too much

über|ordnen *vt* ■**jdn jdm ~** to place sb over sb; ■**etw einer S.** *dat* ~ to give sth precedence over sth

überprüfen* [y:bɐ·ˈpry:·fn̩] *vt* ❶ (*durchchecken*) to vet; *Papiere, Rechnung* to check (**auf** +*akk* for) ❷ (*die Funktion von etw nachprüfen*) to examine ❸ (*erneut bedenken*) to examine

Überprüfung *f* ❶ *kein pl* (*das Durchchecken*) vetting; (*das Kontrollieren*) check ❷ (*Funktionsprüfung*) check ❸ (*erneutes Bedenken*) review

überqueren* [y:bɐ·ˈkve:·rən] *vt* ❶ (*sich über etw hinweg bewegen*) to cross [over] ❷ (*über etw hinwegführen*) to lead over

überragen*[1] [y:bɐ·ˈra:·gn̩] *vt* ❶ (*größer sein*) to tower above (**um** +*akk* by); (*um ein kleineres Maß*) to be taller than ❷ (*übertreffen*) to outclass

über|ragen[2] [ˈy:bɐ·ra:·gn̩] *vi* (*überstehen*) to project

überraschen* [y:bɐ·ˈra·ʃn̩] *vt* ❶ (*unerwartet erscheinen*) to surprise (**mit** +*dat* with) ❷ (*ertappen*) ■**jdn bei etw** *dat* ~ to surprise sb doing sth; ■**jdn dabei ~, wie er etw tut** to catch sb doing sth ❸ (*überraschend erfreuen*) to surprise (**mit** +*dat* with); **lassen wir uns ~!** (*fam*) let's wait and see [what happens] ❹ (*erstaunen*) to surprise; (*stärker*) to astound (**mit** +*dat* with) ❺ (*unerwartet überfallen*) ■**jdn ~** to take sb by surprise; **vom Regen überrascht werden** to get caught in the rain

überraschend I. *adj* unexpected **II.** *adv* unexpectedly

überraschenderweise *adv* surprisingly

Überraschung <-, -en> *f* ❶ *kein pl* (*Erstaunen*) surprise; (*stärker*) astonishment ❷ (*etwas Unerwartetes*) surprise

Überraschungseffekt *m* surprise effect; *von Plan* element of surprise

Überreaktion *f* overreaction

überreden* [y:bɐ·ˈre:·dn̩] *vt* to persuade; ■**jdn zu etw** *dat* ~ to talk sb into [doing] sth

überreichen* [y:bɐ·ˈrai·çn̩] *vt* ■**jdm etw** ~ to hand over *sep* sth to sb; (*feierlich*) to present sth to sb

Überrest *m meist pl* remains *npl;* **jds sterbliche ~e** sb's [mortal] remains

überrunden* [y:bɐ·ˈrʊn·dn̩] *vt* ❶ SPORT to lap ❷ (*leistungsmäßig übertreffen*) to outstrip; *Schüler* to outperform

übers [ˈy:bɐs] (*fam*) = **über das** *s.* **über**

übersät [y:bɐ·ˈzɛ:t] *adj* covered

überschatten* [y:bɐ·ˈʃa·tn̩] *vt* to cast a shadow over

überschätzen* [y:bɐ·ˈʃɛ·tsn̩] **I.** *vt* to overestimate **II.** *vr* ■**sich** *akk* ~ to think too highly of oneself

überschaubar *adj* ❶ (*abschätzbar*) *Größe* manageable; *Kosten, Preis* clear; *Risiko* contained ❷ (*einen begrenzten Rahmen habend*) tightly structured

über|schäumen [ˈy:bɐ·ʃɔy·mən] *vi sein* ❶ (*mit Schaum überlaufen*) to foam over ❷ (*fig: ganz ausgelassen sein*) ■**vor etw** *dat* ~ to brim [over] with sth

überschlagen*[1] [y:bɐ·ˈʃla:·gn̩] *irreg* **I.** *vt* ❶ (*beim Lesen auslassen*) to skip [over] ❷ (*überschläglich berechnen*) to [roughly] estimate **II.** *vr* ❶ (*eine vertikale Drehung ausführen*) ■**sich** *akk* ~ *Mensch* to fall head over heels; *Fahrzeug* to overturn ❷ (*rasend schnell aufeinander folgen*) ■**sich** ~ to follow in quick succession ❸ (*besonders beflissen sein*) **sich** *akk* [**vor Freundlichkeit/Hilfsbereitschaft**] ~ to bend over backwards [to be friendly/helpful] ❹ (*schrill werden*) ■**sich** ~ to crack

über|schlagen[2] [ˈy:bɐ·ʃla:·gn̩] *irreg* **I.** *vt haben* **die Beine** ~ to cross one's legs; **mit übergeschlagenen Beinen sitzen** to sit cross-legged **II.** *vi sein* ❶ (*fig*) ■**in etw** *akk* ~ to turn into sth ❷ (*brechen*) to overturn; **die Wellen schlugen über** the waves broke ❸ (*übergreifen*) to spread (**auf** +*akk* to)

über|schnappen *vi sein* (*fam*) to crack up, to lose one's mind

überschneiden* [y:bɐ·ˈʃnai·dn̩] *vr irreg* ■**sich** ~ ❶ (*sich zeitlich überlappen*) to overlap (**um** +*akk* by) ❷ (*sich mehrfach kreuzen*) to intersect

überschreiben* [y:bɐ·ˈʃrai·bn̩] *vt irreg* ❶ (*betiteln*) to head ❷ (*darüberschreiben*) to write over; COMPUT to overwrite ❸ (*übertragen*) ■**jdm etw** ~ to sign over sth to sb

überschreiten* [y:bɐ·ˈʃrai·tn̩] *vt irreg* ❶ (*geh:

zu Fuß überqueren) to cross [over] ❷ (*über etw hinausgehen*) to exceed (**um** +*akk* by) ❸ (*sich nicht im Rahmen von etw halten*) to overstep

Überschrift *f* title; *Zeitung* headline

Überschuss[RR] *m* ❶ (*Reingewinn*) profit ❷ (*überschüssige Menge*) surplus (**an** +*dat* of)

überschüssig ['y:bɐ·ʃʏ·sɪç] *adj* surplus *attr*

überschütten* [y:bɐ·'ʃʏ·tn̩] *vt* ❶ (*übergießen*) ■ **etw mit etw** *dat* ~ to pour sth over sth ❷ (*bedecken*) to cover ❸ (*überhäufen*) to inundate; **jdn mit Geschenken/Komplimenten** ~ to shower sb with presents/compliments

überschwänglich[RR] **I.** *adj* effusive **II.** *adv* effusively

überschwemmen* [y:bɐ·'ʃvɛ·mən] *vt* ❶ (*überfluten*) to flood ❷ (*in Mengen hineinströmen*) to pour into ❸ (*mit großen Mengen eindecken*) to flood

Überschwẹmmung <-, -en> *f* flood[ing]

überschwenglich[ALT] ['y:bɐ·ʃvɛŋ·lɪç] *adj, adv s.* **überschwänglich**

Übersee ['y:bɐ·ze:] *kein art* ■ **aus** ~ from overseas; ■ **in/nach** ~ overseas

übersehbar [y:bɐ·'ze:·ba:ɐ̯] *adj* ❶ (*abschätzbar*) *Auswirkungen* containable; *Dauer, Kosten, Schäden* assessable; *Konsequenzen* clear; ■ **etw ist/ist noch nicht** ~ sth is in sight/sth is still not known ❷ (*mit Blicken zu erfassen*) visible

übersehen* [y:bɐ·'ze:·ən] *vt irreg* ❶ (*versehentlich nicht erkennen*) to overlook ❷ (*abschätzen*) to assess ❸ (*mit Blicken erfassen*) to have a view of

übersetzen*[1] [y:bɐ·'zɛ·tsn̩] *vt, vi* to translate; [**etw**] **aus dem Deutschen ins Englische** ~ to translate [sth] from German into English

über|setzen[2] ['y:bɐ·zɛ·tsn̩] **I.** *vt haben* ■ **jdn** ~ to ferry across *sep* sb **II.** *vi sein* to cross [over]

Übersẹtzer(in) <-s, -> *m(f)* translator

Übersẹtzung <-, -en> *f* ❶ (*übersetzter Text*) translation ❷ *pl selten* (*das Übersetzen*) translation ❸ TECH transmission ratio

Übersicht <-, -en> *f* ❶ *kein pl* (*Überblick*) overall view ❷ (*knappe Darstellung*) outline

übersichtlich I. *adj* ❶ (*rasch erfassbar*) clear ❷ (*gut zu überschauen*) open *attr;* ■ [**nicht**] ~ **sein** to [not] be clearly visible [from all sides]; (*wenig Deckung bietend*) to be exposed **II.** *adv* ❶ (*rasch erfassbar*) clearly ❷ (*gut überschaubar*) **etw** ~ **anlegen** to give sth an open layout

Übersichtlichkeit <-> *f kein pl* ❶ (*rasche Erfassbarkeit*) clarity ❷ (*übersichtliche Anlage*) openness

über|siedeln ['y:bɐ·zi:·dl̩n] *vi sein* to move (**in** +*akk* to, **nach** +*dat* to)

Übersiedler(in) *m(f)* migrant; (*Einwanderer*) immigrant; (*Auswanderer*) emigrant

übersinnlich *adj* paranormal

überspielen* [y:bɐ·'ʃpi:·lən] *vt* ❶ (*audiovisuell übertragen*) to record (**auf** +*akk* on[to]); **etw auf Kassette** ~ to tape sth ❷ (*verdecken*) to cover up *sep* (**durch** +*akk* with)

überspịtzt I. *adj* exaggerated **II.** *adv* in an exaggerated fashion

überspringen*[1] [y:bɐ·'ʃprɪ·ŋən] *vt irreg* ❶ (*über etw hinwegspringen*) to jump; *Mauer* to vault ❷ (*auslassen*) to skip [over] ❸ SCH *Klasse* to skip

über|springen[2] ['y:bɐ·ʃprɪ·ŋən] *vi irreg sein* ❶ (*sich übertragen*) *a.* MED to spread (**auf** +*akk* to) ❷ (*plötzlich übergreifen*) to spread quickly

überstehen*[1] [y:bɐ·'ʃte:·ən] *vt irreg* (*durchstehen*) to get through; *Krankheit, Operation* to get over; **die Belastung** ~ to hold out under the stress; **die nächsten Tage** ~ to make it through the next few days

über|stehen[2] ['y:bɐ·ʃte:·ən] *vi irreg sein o haben* (*herausragen*) to jut out, to project

übersteigen* [y:bɐ·'ʃtai·gn̩] *vt irreg* ❶ (*über etw klettern*) to climb over; *Mauer* to scale ❷ (*über etw hinausgehen*) to exceed

überstimmen* [y:bɐ·'ʃtɪ·mən] *vt* ❶ (*mit Stimmenmehrheit besiegen*) to outvote ❷ (*mit Stimmenmehrheit ablehnen*) to defeat

überstrapazieren* *vt* ❶ (*zu sehr ausnutzen*) to abuse ❷ (*zu oft verwenden*) to wear out *sep*

Überstunde *f* hour of overtime; ■ **~n** overtime

überstürzen* [y:bɐ·'ʃtʏr·tsn̩] **I.** *vt* ■ **etw** ~ to rush into sth **II.** *vr* ■ **sich** ~ to follow in quick succession

übertönen* *vt* to drown out *sep*

Übertopf *m* planter

übertragbar [y:bɐ·'tra:k·ba:ɐ̯] *adj* ❶ (*durch Infektion weiterzugeben*) communicable *form* (**auf** +*akk* to); (*durch Berührung*) contagious ❷ (*anderweitig anwendbar*) to be applicable (**auf** +*akk* to) ❸ (*von anderen zu benutzen*) ■ ~ **sein** to be transferable

übertragen*[1] [y:bɐ·'tra:·gn̩] *irreg* **I.** *vt* ❶ (*senden*) to broadcast ❷ (*geh: übersetzen*) to translate ❸ (*infizieren*) to communicate (**auf** +*akk* to) ❹ (*woanders eintragen*) to transfer (**auf** +*akk* to, **in** +*akk* into) ❺ (*übergeben*) *Besitz* to transfer (**auf** +*akk* to); ■ **jdm die Verantwortung** ~ to entrust sb with the responsibility ❻ (*überspielen*) to record (**auf** +*akk* on[to]) ❼ (*anwenden*) to apply (**auf** +*akk* to) ❽ TECH to transmit (**auf** +*akk* to) **II.** *vr* ❶ MED ■ **sich** [**auf jdn**] ~ to be communicated [to sb] ❷ (*ebenfalls beeinflussen*) ■ **sich auf jdn** ~ to spread to sb

übertragen[2] [y:bɐ·'tra:·gn̩] **I.** *adj* figurative **II.** *adv* figuratively

Übertragung <-, -en> *f* ❶ (*das Senden*) transmission; (*übertragene Sendung*) broadcast ❷ (*geh: das Übersetzen*) translation ❸ (*das Infizieren*) transmission ❹ (*das Eintragen an anderer Stelle*) carryover ❺ *von Verantwortung* entrusting ❻ JUR transfer; *von Rechten a.* assignment ❼ (*das Anwenden*) application (**auf** +*akk* to) ❽ *kein pl* TECH transmission (**auf** +*akk* to)

übertreffen* [y:bɐ·'trɛ·fn̩] *vt irreg* ❶ (*besser/größer sein*) to surpass (**an/in** +*dat* in)

U

❷ (*über etw hinausgehen*) to exceed (**um** +*akk* by)

übertreiben* [yːbɐˈtrai·bn̩] *irreg* **I.** *vi* to exaggerate **II.** *vt* to overdo; ■ **ohne zu ~** I'm not joking

Übertreibung <-, -en> *f* exaggeration

über|treten¹ [ˈyːbɐ·treː·tn̩] *vi irreg sein* ❶ (*konvertieren*) to convert (**zu** +*dat* to) ❷ SPORT to overstep

übertreten*² [yːbɐˈtreː·tn̩] *vt irreg Gesetz, Vorschrift* to break

Übertretung <-, -en> [yːbɐˈtreː·tʊŋ] *f* violation

übertrieben **I.** *adj* exaggerated; (*zu stark*) excessive **II.** *adv* excessively

überwachen* [yːbɐˈvaː·xn̩] *vt* ❶ (*heimlich kontrollieren*) to keep under surveillance; *Telefon* to bug ❷ (*durch Kontrollen sicherstellen*) to supervise; (*durch eine Kamera*) to monitor

Überwachung <-, -en> *f* ❶ (*das heimliche Kontrollieren*) surveillance; *eines Telefons* bugging ❷ (*das Überwachen*) supervision; (*durch eine Kamera*) monitoring

Überwachungskamera *f* security camera

Überwachungsstaat *m* police state

Überwachungssystem *nt* surveillance system

überwältigen* [yːbɐˈvɛl·tɪ·gn̩] *vt* ❶ (*bezwingen*) to overpower ❷ (*geh: übermannen*) ■ **etw überwältigt jdn** sth overwhelms sb

überwältigend *adj* overwhelming; *Schönheit* stunning; *Sieg* crushing

über|wechseln [ˈyːbɐ·vɛk·sl̩n] *vi sein* ❶ (*sich jd anderem anschließen*) to go over (**zu** +*dat* to); ■ **zu jdm ~** to go over to sb's side ❷ (*ausscheren*) ■ **auf etw** *akk* **~** to move [in]to sth ❸ (*umsatteln*) ■ **von etw** *dat* **zu etw** *dat* **~** to change from sth to sth

überweisen* [yːbɐˈvai·sn̩] *vt irreg* ❶ *Geld* to transfer ❷ *Patienten* to refer (**an** +*akk* to)

Überweisung <-, -en> *f* ❶ *von Geld* transfer ❷ *eines Patienten* referral (**an** +*akk* to); (*Überweisungsformular*) referral form

überwiegen* [yːbɐˈviː·gn̩] *irreg* **I.** *vi* to be predominant **II.** *vt* to outweigh

überwiegend [ˈyːbɐ·viː·gn̩t] **I.** *adj* predominant; *Mehrheit* vast **II.** *adv* mainly

überwinden* [yːbɐˈvɪn·dn̩] *irreg* **I.** *vt* ❶ (*nicht länger an etw festhalten*) to overcome ❷ (*im Kampf besiegen*) to defeat ❸ (*ersteigen*) to surmount **II.** *vr* ■ **sich** *akk* **~** to overcome one's feelings/inclinations etc.; ■ **sich** *akk* **zu etw** *dat* **~** to force oneself to do sth

Überwindung <-> *f kein pl* ❶ (*das Überwinden*) overcoming; *Minenfeld* negotiation ❷ (*Selbstüberwindung*) conscious effort; **jdn ~ kosten[, etw zu tun]** to take sb a lot of will power [to do sth]

überwintern* [yːbɐˈvɪn·tɐn] *vi* to [spend the] winter; *Pflanzen* to overwinter

überzählig *adj* (*überschüssig*) surplus *attr;* (*übrig*) spare

überzeugen* [yːbɐˈtsɔy·gn̩] **I.** *vt* to convince (**von** +*dat* of); (*umstimmen a.*) to persuade **II.** *vi* ❶ (*überzeugend sein*) to be convincing ❷ (*eine überzeugende Leistung zeigen*) ■ **bei etw** *dat* **~** to prove oneself in sth **III.** *vr* ■ **sich** *akk* **[selbst] ~** to convince oneself; **~ Sie sich selbst!** [go and] see for yourself!

überzeugend **I.** *adj* convincing; (*umstimmend a.*) persuasive **II.** *adv* convincingly

überzeugt *adj* convinced (**von** +*dat* of); **[sehr] von sich** *dat* **~ sein** to be [very] sure of oneself

Überzeugung <-, -en> [yːbɐˈtsɔy·gʊŋ] *f* convictions *npl;* **zu der ~ gelangen, dass ...** to become convinced that ...

überziehen*¹ [yːbɐˈtsiː·ən] *irreg vt* ❶ (*bedecken*) to cover; *Belag* to coat ❷ *Konto* to overdraw (**um** +*akk* by) ❸ (*überbeanspruchen*) to overrun (**um** +*akk* by) ❹ (*zu weit treiben*) ■ **etw ~** to carry sth too far; ■ **überzogen** exaggerated

über|ziehen² [ˈyːbɐ·tsiː·ən] *vt irreg* ❶ (*anlegen*) ■ **[sich** *dat*] **etw ~** to put on *sep* sth ❷ (*fam: schlagen*) **jdm eins [mit etw** *dat*] **~** to whack sb [with sth]

Überzug *m* ❶ (*überziehende Schicht*) coat[ing]; (*dünner*) film; (*Zuckerguss*) frosting ❷ (*Hülle*) cover

üblich [ˈyːp·lɪç] *adj* usual; **es ist bei uns hier [so] ~** that's the custom around here

U-Boot [ˈuːboːt] *nt* submarine

übrig [ˈyː·brɪç] *adj* remaining, rest of *attr;* (*andere a.*) other *attr;* ■ **die Ü~en** the remaining ones; ■ **das Ü~e** the rest; **es wird ihm nichts anderes ~ bleiben** he won't have any [other] choice; **[jdm] etw ~ lassen** to leave sth [for sb]; ■ **~ sein** to be left [over]

übrigens [ˈyː·brɪ·gn̩s] *adv* by the way

übrig|haben^RR *vt irreg* ■ **für jdn/etw nichts/viel ~** to be not at all/very interested in sb/sth

Übung <-, -en> [ˈyːbʊŋ] *f* ❶ *kein pl* (*das Üben*) practice; **das ist alles nur ~** it [all] comes with practice; **zur ~** for practice ❷ (*Übungsstück*) exercise ❸ SPORT exercise ❹ (*Probe für den Ernstfall*) drill ❺ (*Lehrveranstaltung*) lab (**zu** +*dat* on) ▶ WENDUNGEN: **~ macht den Meister** (*prov*) practice makes perfect

Ufer <-s, -> [ˈuːfɐ] *nt* (*Flussufer*) bank; (*Seeufer*) shore; **ans ~ schwimmen** to swim ashore

Ufo, UFO <-[s], -s> [ˈuːfo] *nt Abk von* **Unbekanntes Flugobjekt** UFO

Uganda <-> [uˈgan·da] *nt* Uganda; *s. a.* **Deutschland**

Ugander(in) <-s, -> [uˈgan·dɐ] *m(f)* Ugandan; *s. a.* **Deutsche(r)**

ugandisch [uˈgan·dɪʃ] *adj* Ugandan; *s. a.* **deutsch**

U-Haft [ˈuː-] *f* (*fam*) *s.* **Untersuchungshaft**

Uhr <-, -en> [uːɐ̯] *f* ❶ (*Instrument zur Zeitanzeige*) clock; (*Armbanduhr*) watch; **die ~ [auf Sommer-/Winterzeit] umstellen** to set the clock/one's watch [an hour forward/backward at daylight saving time]; **diese ~ geht nach/vor** this watch is slow/fast; ■ **rund um die ~** round-the-clock, 24 hours a day ❷ (*Zeitangabe*) o'clock; **15 ~** 3 o'clock [in the afternoon], 3 p.m.; **7 ~ 30** half past 7, seven thirty; **8 ~ 23** 23 minutes after 8, eight twenty-three; **10 ~ früh/abends/nachts** ten [o'clock] in the morning/in the evening/at night; **wie viel ~ ist es?** what time is it?; **um wie viel ~?** [at] what time?; **um 10 ~** at ten [o'clock]

Uhrmacher(in) <-s, -> *m(f)* watchmaker/clockmaker

Uhrwerk *nt* clockwork

Uhrzeigersinn *m* ■ **im ~** clockwise; ■ **gegen den ~** counterclockwise

Uhrzeit *f* time [of day]

Uhu <-s, -s> ['uːhu] *m* eagle owl

Ukraine <-> [ukra·'iːnə] *f* ■ **die ~** [the] Ukraine; *s. a.* **Deutschland**

Ukrainer(in) <-s, -> [ukra·'iːnɐ] *m(f)* Ukrainian; *s. a.* **Deutsche(r)**

ukrainisch [ukra·'iːnɪʃ] *adj* Ukrainian; *s. a.* **deutsch**

UKW <-> [uː·kaː·'veː] *f kein pl, ohne art Abk von* **Ultrakurzwelle** ≈ VHF

ulkig ['ʊl·kɪç] *adj* ❶ (*lustig*) funny ❷ (*seltsam*) odd

Ultimaten *pl von* **Ultimatum**

ultimativ [ʊl·ti·ma·'tiːf] **I.** *adj* ■ **eine ~e Forderung** an ultimatum **II.** *adv* in the form of an ultimatum; **jdn ~ auffordern, etw zu tun** to give sb an ultimatum to do sth

Ultimatum <-s, -s *o* Ultimaten> [ʊl·ti·'maː·tʊm, *pl* ʊl·ti·'maː·tən] *nt* ultimatum; **jdm ein ~ stellen** to give sb an ultimatum

Ultraschall ['ʊl·tra·ʃal] *m* ultrasound

Ultraschallgerät *nt* [ultrasound] scanner

Ultraschalluntersuchung *f* ultrasound

ultraviolett [ʊl·tra·vi̯o·'lɛt] *adj* ultraviolet

um [ʊm] **I.** *präp* +*akk* ❶ (*etw umgebend*) ■ **~ etw [herum]** around sth; **ganz um etw [herum]** all around sth ❷ (*gegen*) **~ Ostern/den 15./die Mitte des Monats [herum]** around Easter/the 15th/the middle of the month ❸ (*über*) **~ etw streiten** to argue about sth ❹ *Unterschiede im Vergleich ausdrückend* **~ einiges besser** quite a bit better; **~ einen Kopf größer/kleiner** taller/shorter by a head; **~ 10 cm länger/kürzer** 4 inches longer/shorter ❺ (*wegen*) ■ **~ jdn/etw** for sb/sth; ■ **~ jds/einer S.** *gen* **willen** for sb's sake/for the sake of sth; **~ meinetwillen** for my sake ❻ (*für*) **Minute ~ Minute** minute by minute ❼ (*nach allen Richtungen*) **~ sich** *akk* **schlagen/treten** to hit/kick out in all directions ❽ (*vorüber*) ■ **~ sein** to be over; *Zeit* to be up; *Frist* to expire **II.** *konj* ■ **~ etw zu tun** [in order] to do sth **III.** *adv* **~ die 80 Meter** about 250 feet

um|ändern *vt* to alter

umarmen* [ʊm·'ʔar·mən] *vt* to embrace; (*fester*) to hug

Umarmung <-, -en> *f* embrace, hug

Umbau *m kein pl* rebuilding, renovation; (*zu etw anderem a.*) conversion

um|bauen ['ʊm·bau·ən] **I.** *vt* to convert **II.** *vi* to renovate

um|benennen* *vt irreg* to rename

Umbenennung *f* renaming

um|besetzen* *vt* ❶ FILM, THEAT to recast ❷ POL to reassign

um|bestellen* *vt, vi* to change the order

um|biegen *irreg* **I.** *vt haben* ❶ (*durch Biegen krümmen*) to bend ❷ (*auf den Rücken biegen*) **jdm den Arm ~** to twist sb's arm [behind sb's back] **II.** *vi sein* ❶ (*kehrtmachen*) to turn back ❷ (*abbiegen*) **nach links/rechts ~** to take a left/right; *Pfad, Straße* to curve to the left/right

um|bilden *vt* to reshuffle, to reorganize

Umbildung *f* reshuffle, reorganization

um|binden ['ʊm·bɪn·dn̩] *vt irreg* ■ **jdm ein Tuch ~** to put a scarf around sb's neck; (*mit Knoten a.*) to tie a scarf around sb's neck; ■ **sich** *dat* **etw ~** to put [*or* tie] on *sep* sth

um|blättern *vi* to turn over

um|blicken *vr* ❶ (*nach hinten blicken*) ■ **sich** *akk* **~** to look back; ■ **sich** *akk* **nach jdm/etw ~** to turn around to look at sb/sth ❷ (*zur Seite blicken*) **sich** *akk* **nach links/rechts/allen Seiten ~** to look to the left/right/in all directions; (*vor Straßenüberquerung a.*) to look left/right/both ways

um|bringen *irreg* **I.** *vt* to kill; (*vorsätzlich a.*) to murder (**durch** +*akk* with); **jdn mit einem Messer ~** to stab sb to death **II.** *vr* ❶ ■ **sich** *akk* **~** to kill oneself ❷ **sich** *akk* **vor Freundlichkeit/Höflichkeit [fast] ~** to go out of one's way to be friendly/polite

Umbruch ['ʊm·brʊx] *m* radical change

um|buchen *vt* ❶ *Reise* to change one's booking/reservation (+*akk* for, **auf** +*akk* to); **den Flug auf einen anderen Tag ~** to change one's flight reservation to another day ❷ *Geld* to transfer (**auf** +*akk* to)

um|definieren* *vt* to redefine

um|denken *vi irreg* ■ **[in etw** *dat*] **~** to change one's ideas/views [of sth]

um|disponieren* *vi* to change one's plans

um|drehen **I.** *vt haben* ❶ (*auf die andere Seite drehen*) to turn over *sep* ❷ (*herumdrehen*) to turn **II.** *vr haben* ■ **sich** *akk* **~** to turn around **III.** *vi sein o haben* to turn around; *Mensch a.* to turn back

Umdrehung [ʊm·'dreː·ʊŋ] *f* AUTO revolutions *pl* [per minute/second]

Umdrehungszahl *f* number of revolutions [per minute/second]

umeinander [ʊm·ʔai·'nan·dɐ] *adv* about each other; **wir haben uns nie groß ~ gekümmert** we never really had much to do with each other

um|erziehen* ['ʊm·ɛɐ̯·tsiː·ən] *vt irreg* to reeducate

um|fahren[1] ['ʊm·faː·rən] *irreg vt* (*fam*)

❶ (*überfahren*) to run over *sep* ❷ *Baum etc.* to hit

umfahren*² [ʊm·ˈfaː·rən] *vt irreg* (*vor etw ausweichen*) to circumvent *form; Auto a.* to drive around

Umfahrung <-, -en> [ʊm·ˈfaː·rʊŋ] *f* ÖSTERR, SCHWEIZ bypass

ụm|fallen *vi irreg sein* ❶ (*umkippen*) to topple over; *Baum a.* to fall [down] ❷ (*zu Boden fallen*) to fall over; (*schwerfällig*) to slump to the floor/ground; **tot ~** to drop dead ❸ (*fam: die Aussage widerrufen*) to retract one's statement

Ụmfang <-[e]s, Ụmfänge> *m* ❶ (*Perimeter*) circumference; *eines Baums a.* girth ❷ (*Ausdehnung*) area ❸ (*Ausmaß*) **in großem ~** on a large scale; **in vollem ~** completely

ụmfangreich *adj* extensive; *Buch* thick

umfassen* [ʊm·ˈfa·sn̩] *vt* ❶ (*umschließen*) to clasp; (*umarmen*) to embrace ❷ (*aus etw bestehen*) to comprise

umfassend [ʊm·ˈfa·sn̩t] **I.** *adj* ❶ (*weitgehend*) extensive ❷ (*alles enthaltend*) full **II.** *adv* **~ über etw berichten** to report all the details of sth; **jdn ~ informieren** to keep sb informed about everything

Ụmfeld *nt* sphere

ụm|formen *vt* to transform

Ụmfrage *f* survey; POL [opinion] poll; **eine ~ machen** to conduct a survey (**zu** +*dat* on/about, **über** +*akk* on/about)

Ụmgang *m* ❶ (*gesellschaftlicher Verkehr*) dealings *pl;* **kein ~ für jdn sein** to not be fit company for sb ❷ (*Beschäftigung*) ■**jds ~ mit etw** *dat* sb's dealing[s] with sth

umgänglich [ˈʊm·gɛŋ·lɪç] *adj* friendly; (*entgegenkommend*) obliging

Ụmgangsformen *pl* [social] manners *pl*

Ụmgangssprache *f* ❶ LING colloquial speech; **die griechische ~** colloquial Greek ❷ (*übliche Sprache*) **in dieser Schule ist Französisch die ~** French is spoken at this school

ụmgangssprachlich *adj* colloquial

Ụmgangston *m* way of speaking

umgeben* [ʊm·ˈgeː·bn̩] *irreg* **I.** *vt* ❶ (*einfassen*) to surround ❷ (*sich rings erstrecken*) **etw von drei Seiten ~** to surround sth on three sides **II.** *vr* ■**sich** *akk* **mit jdm/etw ~** to surround oneself with sb/sth

Umgebung <-, -en> [ʊm·ˈgeː·bʊŋ] *f* ❶ (*umgebende Landschaft*) environment, surroundings *pl; einer Stadt a.* environs *npl;* (*Nachbarschaft*) vicinity ❷ (*jdn umgebender Kreis*) people around one

um|gehen¹ [ˈʊm·geː·ən] *vi irreg sein* ❶ (*behandeln*) to treat; **mit jdm nicht ~ können** to not know how to deal with sb; **mit etw** *dat* **gleichgültig/vorsichtig ~** to handle sth indifferently/carefully ❷ *Gerücht* to circulate

umgehen*² [ʊm·ˈgeː·ən] *vt irreg* (*vermeiden*) to avoid

umgehend [ˈʊm·geː·ənt] **I.** *adj* immediate **II.** *adv* immediately

Umgehung <-, -en> [ʊm·ˈgeː·ʊŋ] *f,* **Umgehungsstraße** *f* bypass

ụmgekehrt I. *adj* reverse *attr; Richtung* opposite; **in ~er Reihenfolge** in reverse order; (*rückwärts*) backward; [**es ist**] **gerade ~!** [it's] just the opposite! **II.** *adv* the other way around

Ụmgestaltung <-, -en> *f* reorganization; *von Gesetzeswerk, Verfassung* reformation; *eines Parks, Schaufensters* redesign

ụm|gewöhnen* *vr* ■**sich** *akk* **~** to readapt, to readjust

ụm|graben *vt irreg* to dig over *sep*

Ụmhang *m* cape

um|hängen [ˈʊm·hɛ·ŋən] *vt* ❶ (*umlegen*) ■**sich** *dat* **etw ~** to put on *sep* sth; ■**jdm etw ~** to wrap sth around sb ❷ (*woanders hinhängen*) ■**etw ~** to rehang sth, to hang sth somewhere else

Ụmhängetasche *f* shoulder bag

um|hauen [ˈʊm·hau·ən] *vt irreg* (*fam*) ❶ (*fällen*) to chop down *sep; Bäume* to fell ❷ (*völlig verblüffen*) to stagger ❸ (*lähmen*) to knock out *sep*

umher [ʊm·ˈheːɐ̯] *adv* around; **überall ~** everywhere; **weit ~** all around

umher|blicken [ʊm·ˈheːɐ̯·blɪ·kn̩] *vi* to glance around

umher|gehen *vi irreg sein* ■**in etw** *dat* **~** to walk around sth

umher|irren *vi sein* to wander around

umher|laufen *vi irreg sein* ■[**in etw** *dat*] **~** to walk around [sth]; (*rennen*) to run around [sth]

umhin|können [ʊm·ˈhɪn·kœ·nən] *vi irreg* **jd kann nicht umhin, etw zu tun** sb cannot avoid doing sth

ụm|hören *vr* ■**sich** *akk* **~** to ask around

umkämpft [ʊm·ˈkɛmpft] *adj* disputed

ụm|kehren I. *vi sein* to turn back **II.** *vt haben* to reverse

ụm|kippen I. *vi sein* ❶ (*seitlich umfallen*) to tip over; *Stuhl, Fahrrad* to fall over ❷ (*fam: bewusstlos zu Boden fallen*) to pass out ❸ (*sl: die Meinung ändern*) to come around ❹ ÖKOL to become polluted ❺ (*ins Gegenteil umschlagen*) *Laune* to change; ■**in etw** *akk* **~** to turn into sth **II.** *vt haben* to tip over *sep*

umklammern* [ʊm·ˈkla·mɐn] *vt* ■**jdn ~** to cling [on] to sb; ■**etw ~** to hold sth tight

ụm|klappen *vt* to fold down *sep*

Ụmkleidekabine *f* changing room

Ụmkleideraum *m* changing room

ụm|knicken I. *vi sein* ❶ (*brechen*) *Stab, Zweig* to snap ❷ (*zur Seite knicken*) [**mit dem Fuß**] **~** to twist one's ankle **II.** *vt haben* to snap; *Papier, Pappe* to fold over; *Pflanze, Trinkhalm* to bend [over]

ụm|kommen *vi irreg sein* ❶ (*sterben*) to be killed (**bei/in** +*dat* in) ❷ (*fam: verderben*) to go bad ❸ (*fam: es nicht mehr aushalten*) **vor Hunger/Durst ~** to be dying of hunger/thirst; **vor Langeweile ~** to be bored to death

Ụmkreis *m* vicinity; **im ~ von 100 Metern** within a radius of 100 Meters

umkreisen* [ʊm·ˈkrai·zn̩] *vt* ASTRON, RAUM to

U

orbit

ụm|krempeln *vt* ❶ (*aufkrempeln*) ■**sich** *dat* **etw** *akk* ~ to roll up *sep* sth; *Hosenbein* to turn up *sep* sth ❷ (*gründlich durchsuchen*) ■**etw** ~ to turn sth upside down ❸ (*grundlegend umgestalten*) ■**etw/jdn** ~ to shake up *sep* sth/sb

umlagern* [ʊm·ˈlaː·gen] *vt* to surround

Ụmland *nt kein pl* surrounding area

Umlauf [ˈʊm·lauf, *pl* ˈʊm·lɔy·fə] *m* ❶ ASTRON rotation ❷ (*internes Rundschreiben*) circular ❸ (*Weitergabe von Person zu Person*) **etw in ~ bringen** to circulate sth; *Gerücht, Lüge* to spread sth; (*etw kursieren lassen*) *Geld* to put into circulation

Ụmlaufbahn *f* orbit

Ụmlaut *m* umlaut

um|legen [ˈʊm·leː·gn̩] *vt* ❶ *Schalter* to turn ❷ (*um Körperteil legen*) ■**jdm/sich** *dat* **etw** ~ to put sth around sb/oneself ❸ (*flachdrücken*) to flatten ❹ (*fällen*) to bring down *sep* ❺ (*sl: umbringen*) ■**jdn** ~ to bump off *sep* sb ❻ ([*auf einen anderen Zeitpunkt*] *verlegen*) to reschedule (**auf** +*akk* for)

ụm|leiten *vt* to divert

Ụmleitung *f* detour

umliegend [ˈʊm·liː·gn̩t] *adj* surrounding

ụm|melden *vt, vr* **jdn/sich** *akk* ~ to notify the authorities of sb's/one's change of address

ụm|münzen *vt* (*pej fam*) to convert (**zu** +*dat* into)

ụm|organisieren* *vt* to reorganize

um|pflügen [ˈʊm·pflyː·gn̩] *vt* to plow up *sep*

ụm|programmieren* *vt* COMPUT to reprogram

umrahmen* [ʊm·ˈraː·mən] *vt* ❶ (*einrahmen*) to frame ❷ HORT to border

ụm|räumen I. *vi* to rearrange **II.** *vt Möbel, Zimmer* to rearrange; ■**etw** [**irgendwohin**] ~ to move sth [somewhere]

ụm|rechnen *vt* to convert (**in** +*akk* into)

Ụmrechnung *f* conversion

Ụmrechnungskurs *m* exchange rate

umreißen* [ʊm·ˈrai·sn̩] *vt irreg Situation, Lage* to outline; *Ausmaß, Kosten* to estimate

ụm|rennen *vt irreg* to [run into and] knock over

ỤmrissRR *m meist pl* contour, outline; **in ~en** in outline

umrịssen *adj* well-defined; **fest ~e Vorstellungen** clear-cut impressions

ụm|rühren *vi, vt* to stir

ums [ʊms] (*fam*) = **um das** *s.* **um**

ụm|satteln *vi* (*fam*) [**auf einen anderen Beruf**] ~ to change jobs

Ụmsatz *m* turnover

Ụmsatzsteuer *f* sales tax

ụm|schalten I. *vi* ❶ RADIO, TV to switch over; **auf einen anderen Kanal/Sender ~** to change the channel/station ❷ *Ampel* to change; **auf Rot/Gelb/Grün ~** to turn red/yellow/green ❸ (*fam: sich einstellen*) to shift gears *fig* (**auf** +*akk* to) **II.** *vt* RADIO, TV to switch (**auf** +*akk* to); **das Fernsehgerät/Radio ~** to change the TV channel/radio station

ụm|schauen *vr s.* **umsehen**

Ụmschlag *m* ❶ (*Briefumschlag*) envelope ❷ (*Schutzumschlag*) jacket ❸ MED compress ❹ *kein pl* ÖKON transfer

um|schlagen [ˈʊm·ʃlaː·gn̩] *irreg* **I.** *vt haben* ❶ *Kragen* to turn down *sep; Ärmel* to turn up *sep* ❷ (*umladen*) to transfer **II.** *vi sein* METEO to change

umschließen* [ʊm·ˈʃliː·sn̩] *vt irreg* ❶ (*umgeben, umzingeln*) to enclose ❷ (*umarmen*) **jdn/etw mit den Armen ~** to take sb/sth into one's arms ❸ (*eng anliegen*) ■**jdn/etw** ~ to fit sb/sth closely ❹ (*einschließen*) to include

umschlingen* [ʊm·ˈʃlɪŋ·ən] *vt irreg* ❶ (*eng umfassen*) to embrace; **jdn mit den Armen ~** to wrap one's arms around sb ❷ BOT to climb

umschlụngen *adj* **jdn** [**fest**] **~ halten** to hold sb [tightly] in one's arms

ụm|schnallen *vt* to buckle on *sep*

um|schreiben¹ [ˈʊm·ʃrai·bn̩] *vt irreg* ❶ (*grundlegend umarbeiten*) to rewrite ❷ (*im Grundbuch übertragen*) to transfer (**auf** +*akk* to)

umschreiben*² [ʊm·ˈʃrai·bn̩] *vt irreg* ❶ (*indirekt ausdrücken*) to talk around ❷ (*beschreiben*) to outline; (*in andere Worten fassen*) to paraphrase

ụm|schulen *vt* ❶ (*für andere Tätigkeit ausbilden*) to retrain (**zu** +*dat* as) ❷ (*auf andere Schule schicken*) to transfer to another school

Ụmschulung *f* ❶ (*Ausbildung für andere Tätigkeit*) retraining ❷ SCH transfer

Umschweife [ˈʊm·ʃvai·fə] *pl* **ohne ~** without mincing one's words; **keine ~!** stop beating about the bush!

Ụmschwung *m* ❶ (*plötzliche Veränderung*) drastic change ❷ SCHWEIZ (*umgebendes Gelände*) surrounding property

ụm|sehen *vr irreg* ❶ (*in Augenschein nehmen*) ■**sich** *akk* **irgendwo/bei jdm ~** to have a look around somewhere/in sb's home ❷ (*nach hinten blicken*) ■**sich** *akk* ~ to look back ❸ (*suchen*) ■**sich** *akk* **nach jdm/etw ~** to look around for sb/sth

um|setzen [ˈʊm·ze·tsn̩] *vt* ❶ (*an anderen Platz setzen*) to move ❷ (*umwandeln*) to convert (**in** +*akk* to); **etw in die Praxis ~** to put sth [in]to practice ❸ (*verkaufen*) to turn over

umsonst [ʊm·ˈzɔnst] *adv* ❶ (*gratis*) for free, free of charge ❷ (*vergebens*) in vain; ■**~ sein** to be pointless; **nicht ~** not without reason

umsorgen* [ʊm·ˈzɔr·gn̩] *vt* to look after

um|springen [ˈʊm·ʃprɪŋ·ən] *vi irreg sein* ❶ (*grob behandeln*) ■**mit jdm grob ~** to treat sb roughly ❷ METEO to veer around ❸ *Ampel* to change (**auf** +*akk* to)

Ụmstand *m* ❶ (*wichtige Tatsache*) fact; **mildernde Umstände** JUR mitigating circumstances; **den Umständen entsprechend** [**gut**] [as good] as can be expected under the circumstances; **unter diesen Umständen** under these circumstances; **unter Umständen** pos-

U

sibly ❷ *pl* (*Schwierigkeiten*) trouble; **bitte keine Umstände!** please don't go to any trouble! ▶ WENDUNGEN: **in anderen Umständen sein** to be expecting

umständlich ['ʊm·ʃtɛnt·lɪç] **I.** *adj* ❶ (*mit großem Aufwand verbunden*) laborious; *Anweisung, Beschreibung* elaborate; *Aufgabe, Reise* complicated; *Erklärung, Anleitung* long-winded; ■**~ sein** to be inconvenient ❷ (*unpraktisch veranlagt*) ■**~ sein** to be awkward **II.** *adv* ❶ (*weitschweifig*) long-windedly ❷ (*mühselig und aufwändig*) laboriously

Ụmstandskleid *nt* maternity dress

ụm|steigen *vi irreg sein* ❶ TRANSP to change ❷ (*überwechseln*) to switch [over] (**auf** +*akk* to)

um|stellen[1] ['ʊm·ʃtɛ·lən] **I.** *vt* ❶ (*anders hinstellen*) to move ❷ (*anders anordnen*) to reorder ❸ (*anders einstellen*) to switch over *sep* (**auf** +*akk* to); **die Uhr ~** to turn the clock back/forward ❹ (*zu etw anderem übergehen*) to convert (**auf** +*akk* to); **die Ernährung ~** to change one's diet **II.** *vi* (*zu etw anderem übergehen*) ■**auf etw** *akk* **~** to change over to sth **III.** *vr* (*sich anpassen*) ■**sich** *akk* **~** to adapt (**auf** +*akk* to)

umstellen*[2] [ʊm·'ʃtɛ·lən] *vt* (*umringen*) ■**jdn/etw ~** to surround sb/sth

Ụmstellung *f* ❶ (*Übergang*) change (**auf** +*akk* to); *Beheizung, Ernährung* conversion ❷ (*Anpassung*) adjustment

ụm|stimmen *vt* ■**jdn ~** to change sb's mind; ■**sich** *akk* **[von jdm] ~ lassen** to let oneself be persuaded [by sb]

umstritten [ʊm·'ʃtrɪ·tn̩] *adj* ❶ (*noch nicht entschieden*) disputed ❷ (*in Frage gestellt*) controversial

Ụmsturz *m* coup [d'état]

ụm|stürzen **I.** *vi sein* to fall **II.** *vt haben* to knock over *sep; politisches Regime etc.* to overthrow

Ụmtausch *m a.* FIN exchange

ụm|tauschen *vt* to exchange (**in/gegen** +*akk* for); *Währung* to change (**in** +*akk* into)

ụm|topfen *vt* to repot

um|wandeln ['ʊm·van·dl̩n] *vt* to convert (**in** +*akk* into); **wie umgewandelt sein** to be a changed person

Ụmwandlung *f* conversion

Ụmweg *m* detour

Umwelt ['ʊm·vɛlt] *f kein pl* environment

ụmweltbelastend *adj* damaging to the environment *pred*, environmentally harmful

Ụmweltbelastung *f* environmental damage

ụmweltbewusst[RR] *adj* environmentally aware

Ụmweltbewusstsein[RR] *nt kein pl* environmental consciousness

Ụmwelteinfluss[RR] *m* environmental impact

ụmweltfeindlich *adj* harmful to the environment

ụmweltfreundlich *adj* environmentally friendly

Ụmweltgefahr *f* environmental hazards *pl*

Ụmweltgefährdung *f* environmental threat

Ụmweltpolitik *f* environmental policy

Ụmweltschäden *pl* environmental damage

Ụmweltschutz *m* environmental protection

Ụmweltschützer(in) *m(f)* environmentalist

Umweltschụtzpapier *nt* recycled paper

Ụmweltverschmutzer(in) <-s, -> *m(f)* ❶ (*die Umwelt verschmutzender Mensch*) **ein ~ sein** to be environmentally irresponsible ❷ (*Quelle der Umweltverschmutzung*) pollutant

Ụmweltverschmutzung *f* pollution

ụmweltverträglich *adj* environmentally friendly

Ụmweltvorschrift *f* environmental regulation *usu pl*

Ụmweltzerstörung *f* destruction of the environment

umwerben* [ʊm·'vɛr·bn̩] *vt irreg* to woo

ụm|werfen *vt irreg* ❶ (*zum Umfallen bringen*) to knock over *sep* ❷ (*fam: fassungslos machen*) to bowl over *sep* ❸ (*zunichtemachen*) *Ordnung, Plan* to upset ❹ (*rasch umlegen*) ■**jdm etw ~** to throw sth on sb

um|ziehen ['ʊm·tsiː·ən] *irreg* **I.** *vi sein* to move [house] **II.** *vr* ■**sich** *akk* **~** to get changed

umzingeln* [ʊm·'tsɪŋ·l̩n] *vt* to surround; (*durch die Polizei*) to cordon off *sep*

Ụmzug *m* ❶ (*Wohnungswechsel*) move ❷ (*Parade*) parade

UN <-> [uː'ʔɛn] *pl Abk von* **Vereinte Nationen** UN

unabhängig ['ʊn·ʔap·hɛ·ŋɪç] *adj* ❶ (*von niemandem abhängig*) independent (**von** +*dat* of/from) ❷ (*ungeachtet*) ■**~ von etw** *dat* regardless of sth; **~ davon, ob/wann ...** regardless of whether/when ...; **~ voneinander** separately

Ụnabhängigkeit *f kein pl a.* POL independence (**von** +*dat* of/from)

unabsichtlich ['ʊn·ʔap·zɪçt·lɪç] **I.** *adj* unintentional; *Beschädigung* accidental **II.** *adv* accidentally

Ụnachtsamkeit *f* carelessness

unangebracht ['ʊn·ʔan·gə·braxt] *adj* ❶ (*nicht angebracht*) misplaced ❷ (*unpassend*) inappropriate

unangemessen ['ʊn·ʔan·gə·mɛ·sn̩] **I.** *adj* ❶ (*überhöht*) unreasonable ❷ (*nicht angemessen*) inappropriate **II.** *adv* unreasonably

unangenehm ['ʊn·ʔan·gə·neːm] **I.** *adj* ❶ (*nicht angenehm*) unpleasant ❷ (*peinlich*) ■**jdm ist etw ~** sb feels bad about sth ❸ (*unsympathisch*) unpleasant; **sie kann ganz schön ~ werden** she can get quite nasty **II.** *adv* unpleasantly

Unannehmlichkeit ['ʊn·ʔan·neːm·lɪç·kait] *f meist pl* trouble

unanständig ['ʊn·ʔan·ʃtɛn·dɪç] **I.** *adj* ❶ (*obszön*) dirty ❷ (*rüpelhaft*) rude **II.** *adv* rudely

unantastbar [ʊn·ʔan·'tast·baːɐ̯] *adj* sacrosanct

unappetitlich ['ʊn·ʔape·tiːt·lɪç] *adj* ❶ (*nicht

U

appetitlich) unappetizing ❷ (*ekelhaft*) disgusting

unartig ['ʊn·ʔaːɐ̯·tɪç] *adj* naughty

unaufdringlich ['ʊn·ʔauf·drɪŋ·lɪç] *adj* ❶ (*dezent*) unobtrusive ❷ (*nicht aufdringlich*) discrete

unauffällig ['ʊn·ʔauf·fɛ·lɪç] **I.** *adj* discrete **II.** *adv* discretely

unaufgefordert ['ʊn·ʔauf·gə·fɔr·dɐt] **I.** *adj* unsolicited; *Kommentar, Bemerkung* uninvited **II.** *adv* without having been asked; **~ eingesandte Manuskripte** unsolicited manuscripts

unaufhaltsam [ʊn·ʔauf·'halt·zaːm] **I.** *adj* unstoppable **II.** *adv* relentlessly

unaufhörlich [ʊn·ʔauf·'høːɐ̯·lɪç] **I.** *adj* constant **II.** *adv* ❶ (*fortwährend*) constantly ❷ (*ununterbrochen*) incessantly

unaufmerksam ['ʊn·ʔauf·mɛrk·zaːm] *adj* ❶ (*nicht aufmerksam*) inattentive ❷ (*nicht zuvorkommend*) thoughtless

Ụnaufmerksamkeit *f kein pl* ❶ (*unaufmerksames Verhalten*) inattentiveness ❷ (*unzuvorkommende Art*) thoughtlessness

unausgeglichen ['ʊn·ʔaus·gə·glɪ·çn̩] *adj* unbalanced; *Mensch* moody; *Wesensart* uneven

Ụnausgeglichenheit *f* moodiness

ụnausgewogen *adj* unbalanced

unausstehlich [ʊn·ʔaus·'ʃteː·lɪç] *adj* intolerable; *Mensch, Art a.* insufferable

unausweichlich [ʊn·ʔaus·'vaiç·lɪç] **I.** *adj* inevitable **II.** *adv* inevitably

unbarmherzig ['ʊn·barm·hɛr·tsɪç] **I.** *adj* merciless **II.** *adv* mercilessly

Ụnbarmherzigkeit *f* mercilessness

ụnbeabsichtigt **I.** *adj* (*versehentlich*) accidental; (*nicht beabsichtigt*) unintentional **II.** *adv* accidentally

unbeachtet ['ʊn·bə·ʔax·tət] **I.** *adj* overlooked *pred,* unnoticed **II.** *adv* without any notice

ụnbeaufsichtigt *adj* unattended

unbedenklich ['ʊn·bə·dɛŋk·lɪç] **I.** *adj* harmless; *Situation, Vorhaben* acceptable **II.** *adv* quite safely

unbedeutend ['ʊn·bə·dɔy·tn̩t] **I.** *adj* ❶ (*nicht bedeutend*) insignificant ❷ (*geringfügig*) minimal; *Änderung, Modifikation* minor **II.** *adv* insignificantly

unbedingt ['ʊn·bə·dɪŋt] **I.** *adj attr* absolute **II.** *adv* (*auf jeden Fall*) really; **erinnere mich ~ daran, sie anzurufen** [whatever you do,] don't forget to remind me to call her; **nicht ~** not necessarily; **~!** absolutely!

unbefangen ['ʊn·bə·faŋ·ən] **I.** *adj* ❶ (*unvoreingenommen*) objective; *Ansicht* unbiased ❷ (*nicht gehemmt*) uninhibited **II.** *adv* ❶ (*unvoreingenommen*) objectively ❷ (*nicht gehemmt*) uninhibitedly

Ụnbefangenheit *f kein pl* ❶ (*Unvoreingenommenheit*) objectiveness ❷ (*ungehemmte Art*) uninhibitedness

unbefriedigend ['ʊn·bə·friː·dɪ·gn̩t] **I.** *adj* unsatisfactory **II.** *adv* in an unsatisfactory way

unbefriedigt ['ʊn·bə·friː·dɪçt] *adj* unsatisfied; *Gefühl, Mensch* dissatisfied

unbefristet ['ʊn·bə·frɪs·tət] **I.** *adj* lasting for an indefinite period; *Aufenthaltserlaubnis, Visum* permanent; ■**~ sein** to be [valid] for an indefinite period **II.** *adv* indefinitely

unbefugt ['ʊn·bə·fuːkt] **I.** *adj* unauthorized **II.** *adv* without authorization

Ụnbefugte(r) *f(m) dekl wie adj* unauthorized person

unbegrenzt ['ʊn·bə·grɛntst] **I.** *adj* unlimited; *Vertrauen* boundless **II.** *adv* indefinitely

unbegründet ['ʊn·bə·grʏn·dət] *adj* ❶ (*grundlos*) unfounded; *Kritik, Maßnahme* unwarranted ❷ JUR unfounded

unbehaglich ['ʊn·bə·haːk·lɪç] **I.** *adj* uneasy **II.** *adv* uneasily

unbeherrscht ['ʊn·bə·hɛrʃt] **I.** *adj* uncontrolled; ■**~ sein** to lack self-control **II.** *adv* ❶ (*ohne Selbstbeherrschung*) without self-control ❷ (*gierig*) greedily

unbeholfen ['ʊn·bə·hɔl·fn̩] **I.** *adj* (*schwerfällig*) clumsy; (*wenig gewandt*) awkward **II.** *adv* clumsily

unbeirrbar [ʊn·bə·'ʔɪr·baːɐ̯] **I.** *adj* unwavering **II.** *adv* perseveringly

unbekannt ['ʊn·bə·kant] *adj* unknown; ■**jdm ~ sein** to be unknown to sb; *Gesicht, Name, Wort* to be unfamiliar to sb; **„~ verzogen"** "moved — address unknown"

Ụnbekannte(r) *f(m)* stranger

unbekümmert ['ʊn·bə·kʏ·mɐt] **I.** *adj* carefree **II.** *adv* in a carefree manner

unbelastet ['ʊn·bəlas·tət] **I.** *adj* ❶ (*frei*) ■**von etw** *dat* **~** [**sein**] [to be] free of sth ❷ FIN unencumbered **II.** *adv* freely

unbelehrbar ['ʊn·bə·leːɐ̯·baːɐ̯] *adj* obstinate

unbeliebt ['ʊn·bəliːpt] *adj* unpopular

unbenutzt ['ʊn·bə·nʊtst] *adj* unused; *Bett* not slept in; *Kleidung* unworn

unbeobachtet ['ʊn·bə·ʔoːbax·tət] *adj* unnoticed; *Gebäude, Platz* unwatched

unbequem ['ʊn·bə·kveːm] **I.** *adj* ❶ *Stuhl, Sofa* uncomfortable ❷ *Frage* awkward **II.** *adv* ❶ (*nicht bequem*) uncomfortably ❷ (*lästig*) awkwardly

unberechenbar [ʊn·bə·'rɛ·çn̩·baːɐ̯] *adj* ❶ (*nicht einschätzbar*) *Gegner, Mensch* unpredictable ❷ (*nicht vorhersehbar*) unforeseeable

unberechtigt ['ʊn·bə·rɛç·tɪçt] *adj* unfounded; *Vorwurf* unwarranted

unberücksichtigt ['ʊn·bə·rʏk·zɪç·tɪçt] *adj* unconsidered

unberührt ['ʊn·bə·ryːɐ̯t] *adj* ❶ (*im Naturzustand erhalten*) unspoiled ❷ (*nicht benutzt*) untouched

ụnbeschädigt *adj, adv* undamaged

unbeschränkt ['ʊn·bə·ʃrɛŋkt] *adj* unrestricted; *Macht* limitless; *Möglichkeiten* unlimited

unbeschreiblich ['ʊn·bɛ·ʃraip·lɪç] **I.** *adj* ❶ (*maßlos*) tremendous ❷ (*nicht zu beschreiben*) indescribable **II.** *adv* **sich** *akk* **~ freuen/ärgern** to be enormously happy/terribly angry

U

unbeschwert ['ʊn·bə·ʃveːɐ̯t] *adj* carefree
unbesiegbar [ʊn·bə·'ziːk·baːɐ̯] *adj* ❶ MIL (*a. fig*) invincible ❷ SPORT unbeatable
unbesonnen ['ʊn·bə·zɔ·nən] *adj Entschluss* rash; *Wesensart* impulsive
unbesorgt ['ʊn·bə·zɔrkt] **I.** *adj* unconcerned **II.** *adv* without worrying
unbeständig ['ʊn·bə·ʃtɛn·dɪç] *adj* ❶ METEO unsettled ❷ (*wankelmütig*) fickle
unbestechlich ['ʊn·bɛ·ʃtɛç·lɪç] *adj* ❶ (*nicht bestechlich*) incorruptible ❷ (*nicht zu täuschen*) unerring
unbestimmt ['ʊn·bə·ʃtɪmt] *adj* ❶ (*unklar*) vague ❷ (*nicht festlegbar*) indefinite; *Alter* uncertain; *Anzahl, Menge* indeterminate; *Grund, Zeitspanne* unspecified
unbestreitbar ['ʊn·bə·ʃtrait·baːɐ̯] **I.** *adj* unquestionable **II.** *adv* unquestionably
unbestritten ['ʊn·bɛ·ʃtrɪ·tn̩] **I.** *adj* ❶ (*nicht bestritten*) undisputed; *Argument* irrefutable ❷ JUR uncontested **II.** *adv* ❶ (*wie nicht bestritten wird*) unquestionably ❷ (*unstreitig*) unarguably
unbeteiligt ['ʊn·bə·tai·lɪçt] *adj* ❶ (*an etw nicht beteiligt*) uninvolved ❷ (*desinteressiert*) indifferent; (*in einem Gespräch*) uninterested
unbeweglich ['ʊn·bɛ·veːk·lɪç] *adj* ❶ (*starr*) fixed; *Konstruktion, Teil* immovable ❷ (*unveränderlich*) inflexible; *Gesichtsausdruck* rigid; (*fig*) unmoved
unbewohnbar [ʊn·bə·'voːn·baːɐ̯] *adj* uninhabitable
ụnbewohnt *adj* ❶ (*nicht besiedelt*) uninhabited ❷ (*nicht bewohnt*) unoccupied
unbewusst[RR] ['ʊn·bə·vʊst] **I.** *adj a.* PSYCH unconscious **II.** *adv* unconsciously
unbezahlbar [ʊn·bə·'tsaːl·baːɐ̯] *adj* ❶ (*nicht aufzubringen*) unaffordable ❷ (*äußerst nützlich*) invaluable ❸ (*immens wertvoll*) priceless
unblutig ['ʊn·bluː·tɪç] **I.** *adj* bloodless **II.** *adv* without bloodshed
unbrauchbar ['ʊn·braux·baːɐ̯] *adj* useless
und [ʊnt] *konj* and; ~ **dann?** then what?; (*nun*) well?; **na ~?** so what?
undankbar ['ʊn·daŋk·baːɐ̯] *adj* ❶ (*nicht dankbar*) ungrateful ❷ (*nicht lohnend*) thankless
undenkbar [ʊn·'dɛŋk·baːɐ̯] *adj* unthinkable
undeutlich ['ʊn·dɔyt·lɪç] **I.** *adj* ❶ (*nicht deutlich vernehmbar*) unclear ❷ (*nicht klar sichtbar*) blurred; *Schrift* illegible ❸ (*vage*) vague **II.** *adv* ❶ (*nicht deutlich vernehmbar*) unclearly; ~ **sprechen** to mumble ❷ (*nicht klar*) unclearly ❸ (*vage*) vaguely
undicht ['ʊn·dɪçt] *adj* (*luftdurchlässig*) not airtight; (*wasserdurchlässig*) not watertight
Unding ['ʊn·dɪŋ] *nt kein pl* **ein ~ sein**[, **etw zu tun**] to be absurd [to do sth]
undurchdringlich ['ʊn·dʊrç·drɪŋ·lɪç] *adj* ❶ (*kein Durchdringen ermöglichend*) impenetrable ❷ (*verschlossen*) inscrutable
undurchschaubar [ʊn·dʊrç·'ʃau·baːɐ̯] *adj* unfathomable; *Verbrechen* baffling; *Wesensart, Miene* enigmatic
undurchsichtig ['ʊn·dʊrç·zɪç·tɪç] *adj* ❶ (*nicht transparent*) nontransparent; *Glas* opaque ❷ (*fig*) *Geschäfte* shadowy ❸ (*fig: zweifelhaft*) obscure
uneben ['ʊn·ʔeːbn̩] *adj* uneven; *Straße* bumpy
Ụnebenheit <-, -en> *f* ❶ *kein pl* (*unebene Beschaffenheit*) unevenness ❷ (*unebene Stelle*) bump
unecht ['ʊn·ʔɛçt] *adj* ❶ (*imitiert*) fake *usu pej; Haar* artificial; *Zähne* false ❷ (*unaufrichtig*) false
unehelich ['ʊn·ʔeːə·lɪç] *adj Kind* illegitimate
uneigennützig ['ʊn·ʔai·gn̩·nʏ·tsɪç] *adj* selfless
uneingeschränkt ['ʊn·ʔain·gə·ʃrɛŋkt] **I.** *adj* absolute; *Handel* free; *Lob* unreserved **II.** *adv* absolutely, unreservedly
unempfindlich ['ʊn·ʔɛmp·fɪnt·lɪç] *adj* insensitive (**gegen** +*akk* to); (*durch Erfahrung*) hardened, seasoned; *Pflanze* hardy; *Material* practical
unendlich [ʊn·'ʔɛnt·lɪç] *adj* ❶ (*nicht überschaubar*) infinite ❷ (*unbegrenzt*) endless
Unẹndlichkeit <-> *f kein pl* infinity
unentbehrlich ['ʊn·ʔɛnt·beːɐ̯·lɪç] *adj* ❶ (*unbedingt erforderlich*) essential ❷ (*unverzichtbar*) indispensable
unentgeltlich ['ʊn·ʔɛnt·gɛlt·lɪç] **I.** *adj* free of charge; **die ~e Benutzung von etw** *dat* the free use of sth **II.** *adv* for free
unentschieden ['ʊn·ʔɛnt·ʃiː·dn̩] **I.** *adj* ❶ SPORT tied ❷ (*noch nicht entschieden*) undecided **II.** *adv* SPORT ~ **ausgehen** to end in a tie; ~ **spielen** to tie
Unentschieden <-s, -> ['ʊn·ʔɛnt·ʃiː·dn̩] *nt* SPORT tie
unentschlossen ['ʊn·ʔɛnt·ʃlɔ·sn̩] **I.** *adj* indecisive **II.** *adv* indecisively
Ụnentschlossenheit *f* indecision
unentschuldigt ['ʊn·ʔɛnt·ʃʊl·dɪçt] **I.** *adj* unexcused **II.** *adv* unexcused; ~ **fehlen** to cut class
unerbittlich [ʊn·ʔɛɐ̯·'bɪt·lɪç] *adj* ❶ (*nicht umzustimmen*) unrelenting ❷ (*gnadenlos*) merciless
unerfahren ['ʊn·ʔɛɐ̯·faː·rən] *adj* inexperienced
Ụnerfahrenheit *f* lack of experience
unerfreulich ['ʊn·ʔɛɐ̯·frɔy·lɪç] **I.** *adj* unpleasant; *Neuigkeiten, Nachrichten* bad; *Zwischenfall* unfortunate **II.** *adv* unpleasantly
unergründbar [ʊn·ʔɛɐ̯·'grʏnt·baːɐ̯], **unergründlich** [ʊn·ʔɛɐ̯·'grʏnt·lɪç] *adj* puzzling; *Blick, Lächeln* enigmatic
unerheblich ['ʊn·ʔɛɐ̯·heːp·lɪç] **I.** *adj* insignificant; ■ ~ **sein, ob ...** to be irrelevant whether ... **II.** *adv* insignificantly
unerhört ['ʊn·ɛɐ̯·'høːɐ̯t] *adj attr* ❶ (*pej: skandalös*) outrageous ❷ (*außerordentlich*) incredible
unerkannt ['ʊn·ʔɛɐ̯·kant] *adv* unrecognized
unerklärbar [ʊn·ʔɛɐ̯·'klɛːɐ̯·baːɐ̯], **unerklärlich** [ʊn·ʔɛɐ̯·'klɛːɐ̯·lɪç] *adj* inexplicable; ■ **jdm ist ~, warum/wie ...** sb cannot understand

why/how ...

unerlässlichRR, **unerläßlich**ALT [ʊn·ʔɛɐ̯·ˈlɛs·lɪç] *adj* essential

unerlaubt [ˈʊn·ʔɛɐ̯·laupt] **I.** *adj* unauthorized; JUR illegal **II.** *adv* without permission

unerledigt [ˈʊn·ʔɛɐ̯·leː·dɪçt] **I.** *adj* unfinished; *Antrag* incomplete; *Post* unanswered **II.** *adv* unfinished

unermüdlich [ʊn·ʔɛɐ̯·ˈmyːt·lɪç] **I.** *adj* tireless **II.** *adv* tirelessly

unerreichbar [ʊn·ʔɛɐ̯·ˈraiç·baːɐ̯] *adj* unattainable; (*telefonisch*) unavailable

unersättlich [ʊn·ʔɛɐ̯·ˈzɛt·lɪç] *adj* insatiable; *Wissensdurst* unquenchable

unerschrocken [ˈʊn·ʔɛɐ̯·ʃrɔ·kn̩] **I.** *adj* fearless **II.** *adv* fearlessly

unerschütterlich [ʊn·ʔɛɐ̯·ˈʃʏ·te·lɪç] **I.** *adj* unshakable **II.** *adv* unshakably

unerschwinglich [ʊn·ʔɛɐ̯·ˈʃvɪŋ·lɪç] *adj* exorbitant; ■ **für jdn ~ sein** to be beyond sb's means

unersetzlich [ʊn·ʔɛɐ̯·ˈzɛts·lɪç] *adj* indispensable; *Wertgegenstand* irreplaceable; *Schaden* irreparable

unerträglich [ʊn·ʔɛɐ̯·ˈtrɛːk·lɪç] **I.** *adj* ① (*nicht auszuhalten*) unbearable ② (*pej: unmöglich*) impossible **II.** *adv* ① (*nicht auszuhalten*) unbearably ② (*pej: unmöglich*) impossibly

unerwartet [ˈʊn·ʔɛɐ̯·var·tət] **I.** *adj* unexpected **II.** *adv* unexpectedly

unerwünscht [ˈʊn·ʔɛɐ̯·vʏnʃt] *adj* ① (*nicht willkommen*) unwelcome ② (*lästig*) undesirable

UNESCO <-> [uˈnɛs·ko] *f Akr von* **United Nations Educational, Scientific, and Cultural Organization** UNESCO

unfähig [ˈʊn·fɛː·ɪç] *adj* ① (*inkompetent*) incompetent ② (*nicht imstande*) incapable (**zu** +*dat* of)

Unfähigkeit *f kein pl* incompetence, inability

unfair [ˈʊn·fɛːɐ̯] **I.** *adj* unfair (**gegenüber** +*dat* to[ward]) **II.** *adv* unfairly

Unfall [ˈʊn·fal] *m* accident

Unfallchirurgie *f* emergency surgery

Unfallflucht *f* leaving the scene of an accident, hit-and-run

Unfallort *m* scene of an accident

Unfallstation *f* emergency room

Unfallstelle *f* scene of an accident

Unfallursache *f* cause of an accident

Unfallversicherung *f* accident insurance

unfassbarRR, **unfaßbar**ALT [ʊn·ˈfas·baːɐ̯], **unfasslich**RR, **unfaßlich**ALT [ʊn·ˈfas·lɪç] *adj* ① (*unbegreiflich*) incomprehensible; *Phänomen* incredible ② (*unerhört*) outrageous

unfehlbar [ʊn·ˈfeːl·baːɐ̯] **I.** *adj* infallible; *Geschmack* impeccable; *Gespür, Instinkt* unerring **II.** *adv* without fail

Unfehlbarkeit <-> *f kein pl* infallibility

unförmig [ˈʊn·fœr·mɪç] **I.** *adj* shapeless; (*groß*) cumbersome; *Gesicht* misshapen; *Bein* unshapely **II.** *adv* shapelessly

unfreiwillig [ˈʊn·frai·vɪ·lɪç] **I.** *adj* ① (*gezwungen*) compulsory ② (*unbeabsichtigt*) unintentional **II.** *adv* ■ **etw ~ tun** to be forced to do sth

unfreundlich [ˈʊn·frɔynt·lɪç] **I.** *adj* ① (*nicht liebenswürdig*) unfriendly ② (*unangenehm*) unpleasant; *Klima* inhospitable; *Jahreszeit, Tag* dreary; *Raum* cheerless **II.** *adv* **jdn ~ behandeln** to be unfriendly to sb

unfruchtbar [ˈʊn·frʊxt·baːɐ̯] *adj* MED infertile; AGR *a.* barren

Unfruchtbarkeit *f kein pl* ① MED infertility ② AGR barrenness

Unfug <-s> [ˈʊn·fuːk] *m kein pl* nonsense; **~ machen** to be up to no good

Ungar(in) <-n, -n> [ˈʊŋ·gar] *m(f)* Hungarian; *s. a.* **Deutsche(r)**

ungarisch [ˈʊŋ·ga·rɪʃ] *adj* Hungarian; *s. a.* **deutsch**

Ungarn <-s> [ˈʊŋ·garn] *nt* Hungary; *s. a.* **Deutschland**

ungebeten [ˈʊn·gə·beː·tn̩] **I.** *adj* unwelcome **II.** *adv* ① (*ohne eingeladen zu sein*) without being invited ② (*ohne aufgefordert zu sein*) without an invitation

ungebildet [ˈʊn·gə·bɪl·dət] *adj* uneducated

ungeboren [ˈʊn·gəboː·rən] *adj* unborn

ungebräuchlich [ˈʊn·gə·brɔyç·lɪç] *adj* uncommon, not in use *pred*

ungebunden [ˈʊn·gə·bʊn·dn̩] *adj* unattached

Ungeduld [ˈʊn·gə·dʊlt] *f* impatience

ungeduldig [ˈʊn·gə·dʊl·dɪç] **I.** *adj* impatient **II.** *adv* impatiently

ungeeignet [ˈʊn·gə·ʔaig·nət] *adj* unsuitable; ■ **~ sein** to be unsuited (**für** +*akk* for/to)

ungefähr [ˈʊn·gə·fɛːɐ̯] **I.** *adv* ① (*zirka*) approximately, about *fam;* **um ~ ...** *Zeit* at around ... ② (*etwa*) **~ da/hier** around there/here; **~ so** something like this/that ③ (*in etwa*) more or less **II.** *adj attr* approximate

ungefährlich [ˈʊn·gəfɛːɐ̯·lɪç] *adj* harmless; ■ **~ sein, etw zu tun** to be safe to do sth

ungeheuer [ˈʊn·gə·hɔy·ɐ] **I.** *adj* ① (*ein gewaltiges Ausmaß besitzend*) enormous ② (*größte Intensität o. Bedeutung besitzend*) tremendous **II.** *adv* ① (*äußerst*) terribly ② (*ganz besonders*) enormously

Ungeheuer <-s, -> [ˈʊn·gə·hɔy·ɐ] *nt* monster

ungehindert [ˈʊn·gə·hɪn·dɐt] **I.** *adj* unhindered **II.** *adv* without hindrance

ungehorsam [ˈʊn·gə·hoːɐ̯·zaːm] *adj* disobedient (**gegenüber** +*dat* toward)

Ungehorsam [ˈʊn·gə·hoːɐ̯·zaːm] *m* disobedience

ungeklärt [ˈʊn·gəklɛːɐ̯t] *adj, adv* ① (*nicht aufgeklärt*) unsolved ② *Abwässer* untreated

ungekürzt [ˈʊn·gə·kʏrtst] **I.** *adj* MEDIA unabridged; FILM uncut **II.** *adv* in its unabridged version; FILM in its uncut version

ungelegen [ˈʊn·gə·leː·gn̩] *adj* inconvenient; [**jdm**] **~ kommen** to be inconvenient [for sb]; (*zeitlich*) to be an inconvenient time [for sb]

ungelenkig [ˈʊn·gə·lɛŋ·kɪç] *adj* inflexible

ungelernt [ˈʊn·gə·lɛrnt] *adj attr* unskilled

ungelöst [ˈʊn·gə·løːst] *adj* unsolved; *Frage* unresolved

ungemein [ˈʊn·gə·main] I. *adj* immense II. *adv* immensely

ungemütlich [ˈʊn·gə·myːt·lɪç] *adj* ① (*nicht gemütlich*) uninviting ② (*unerfreulich*) uncomfortable ▶ WENDUNGEN: **~ werden** (*fam*) to become nasty

ungenau [ˈʊn·gə·nau] I. *adj* ① (*nicht exakt*) vague ② (*nicht korrekt*) inaccurate II. *adv* ① (*nicht exakt*) vaguely ② (*nicht korrekt*) incorrectly

Ụngenauigkeit <-, -en> *f* ① *kein pl* (*nicht exakte Beschaffenheit*) vagueness ② (*mangelnde Korrektheit*) inaccuracy

ungenießbar [ˈʊn·gə·niːs·baːɐ] *adj* ① (*nicht zum Genuss geeignet*) inedible; *Getränke* undrinkable ② (*schlecht schmeckend*) unpalatable ③ (*fam: unausstehlich*) unbearable

ungenügend [ˈʊn·gə·nyː·gn̩t] I. *adj* ① (*nicht ausreichend*) insufficient; *Information* inadequate ② SCH unsatisfactory, ≈ F II. *adv* insufficiently, inadequately

ungenutzt [ˈʊn·gə·nʊtst] *adj* unused; *materielle/personelle Ressourcen* unexploited; *Gelegenheit* missed

ungepflegt [ˈʊn·gə·pfleːkt] *adj Haus, Garten* neglected; *Person* unkempt

ungerade [ˈʊn·gə·raː·də] *adj* odd

ungerecht [ˈʊn·gə·rɛçt] I. *adj* unjust; ■ **~ sein** to be unfair (**gegen** +*akk* to); **ein ~er Richter** a partial judge II. *adv* unjustly, unfairly

ungerechtfertigt [ˈʊn·gə·rɛçt·fɛr·tɪçt] *adj* unjustified

Ụngerechtigkeit <-, -en> *f* injustice

ungern [ˈʊn·gɛrn] *adv* reluctantly

ungerührt [ˈʊn·gə·ryːɐ̯t] *adj, adv* unmoved

ungeschehen [ˈʊn·gə·ʃeː·ən] *adj* undone; **etw ~ machen** to undo sth

ungeschickt [ˈʊn·gə·ʃɪkt] *adj* ① (*unbeholfen*) clumsy; (*unbedacht*) careless ② DIAL, SÜDD (*unhandlich*) unwieldy; (*ungelegen*) awkward

ungeschoren [ˈʊn·gə·ʃoː·rən] I. *adj* unshorn II. *adv* unscathed; **~ davonkommen** to get away with it

ungesehen [ˈʊn·gə·zeː·ən] *adv* unseen, without being seen

ungesetzlich [ˈʊn·gə·zɛts·lɪç] *adj* unlawful

ungestört [ˈʊn·gə·ʃtøːɐ̯t] I. *adj* undisturbed; **~ sein wollen** to want to be left alone II. *adv* without being disturbed

ungestraft [ˈʊn·gə·ʃtraːft] *adv* with impunity; **~ davonkommen** to get away scot-free

ungestüm [ˈʊn·gə·ʃtyːm] I. *adj Art, Temperament* impetuous; *Wind* gusty; *Begrüßung* enthusiastic II. *adv* enthusiastically

ungesund [ˈʊn·gə·zʊnt] I. *adj* unhealthy II. *adv* unhealthily

ungeteilt [ˈʊn·gə·tailt] *adj* ① (*vollständig*) complete ② (*ganz*) **mit ~er Freude** with total pleasure

ungetrübt [ˈʊn·gə·tryːpt] *adj Freude, Glück* unclouded; *Tage, Zeit* perfect

Ungetüm <-[e]s, -e> [ˈʊn·gə·tyːm] *nt* monster

ungeübt [ˈʊn·gə·ʔyːpt] *adj* unpracticed; *Lehrlinge* inexperienced; ■ **in etw** *dat* **~ sein** to lack experience in sth

ungewiss[RR] [ˈʊn·gə·vɪs] *adj* uncertain

Ụngewissheit[RR] <-, -en> *f* uncertainty

ungewöhnlich [ˈʊn·gə·vøːn·lɪç] I. *adj* ① (*vom Üblichen abweichend*) unusual ② (*außergewöhnlich*) remarkable II. *adv* ① (*äußerst*) exceptionally ② (*in nicht üblicher Weise*) unusually

ungewohnt [ˈʊn·gə·voːnt] *adj* unusual

ungewollt [ˈʊn·gə·vɔlt] I. *adj* unintentional; *Schwangerschaft* unwanted II. *adv* unintentionally; **ich musste ~ grinsen** I couldn't help grinning

Ungeziefer <-s> [ˈʊn·gə·tsiː·fɐ] *nt kein pl* pests *pl*

ungezogen [ˈʊn·gə·tsoː·gn̩] I. *adj Kind* naughty; *Bemerkung* impertinent; ■ **~ sein** to be ill-mannered II. *adv* impertinently; **sich** *akk* **~ benehmen** to behave badly

ungezwungen [ˈʊn·gə·tsvʊ·ŋən] *adj* informal

Unglaube [ˈʊn·glau·bə] *m* ① (*Zweifel*) disbelief ② (*Gottlosigkeit*) unbelief

unglaubhaft [ˈʊn·glaup·haft] I. *adj* unbelievable II. *adv* unbelievably

ungläubig [ˈʊn·glɔy·bɪç] *adj* ① (*etw nicht glauben wollend*) disbelieving; **ein ~es Kopfschütteln** an incredulous shake of the head ② (*gottlos*) unbelieving

unglaublich [ˈʊn·glaup·lɪç] I. *adj* ① (*nicht glaubhaft*) unbelievable ② (*unerhört*) outrageous II. *adv* (*fam: überaus*) incredibly

unglaubwürdig [ˈʊn·glaup·vʏr·dɪç] I. *adj* implausible; *Zeuge* unreliable II. *adv* implausibly

ungleich [ˈʊn·glaiç] I. *adj* ① (*unterschiedlich*) *Bezahlung* unequal; *Belastung* uneven; *Paar* odd; *Gegenstände* dissimilar ② (*unterschiedliche Voraussetzungen*) unequal II. *adv* ① (*unterschiedlich*) unequally ② *vor komp* (*weitaus*) far III. *präp* +*dat* (*geh*) unlike

Ụngleichgewicht *nt* imbalance

ụngleichmäßig I. *adj* ① (*unregelmäßig*) irregular ② (*nicht zu gleichen Teilen*) uneven II. *adv* ① (*unregelmäßig*) irregularly ② (*ungleich*) unevenly

Unglück <-glücke> [ˈʊn·glʏk] *nt* ① *kein pl* (*Pech*) bad luck; **zu allem ~** to make matters worse ② (*katastrophales Ereignis*) disaster ③ *kein pl* (*Elend*) unhappiness ▶ WENDUNGEN: **ein ~ kommt selten allein** (*prov*) when it rains it pours

unglücklich [ˈʊn·glʏk·lɪç] I. *adj* ① (*betrübt*) unhappy ② (*ungünstig, ungeschickt*) unfortunate II. *adv* unfortunately; **~ verliebt sein** to be lovelorn

ụnglücklicherweise *adv* unfortunately

Ụnglücksfall *m* ① (*Unfall*) accident ② (*unglückliche Begebenheit*) mishap

Ungnade [ˈʊn·gnaː·də] *f* disgrace

ungnädig [ˈʊn·gnɛː·dɪç] I. *adj* ① (*gereizt, unfreundlich*) ungracious ② (*geh: verhängnisvoll*) fated; *Schicksal* cruel II. *adv* ungraciously

ungültig ['ʊn·gʏl·tɪç] *adj* ❶ (*nicht mehr gültig*) invalid; *Tor, Treffer* disallowed ❷ (*nichtig*) [null and] void
Ụngültigkeit *f* invalidity
ungünstig ['ʊn·gʏns·tɪç] *adj Zeit[punkt]* inconvenient; *Wetter* inclement
ungut ['ʊn·guːt] *adj* bad; *Verhältnis* strained ▶ WENDUNGEN: **nichts für ~!** no offense!
unhaltbar ['ʊn·halt·baːɐ̯] *adj* ❶ (*haltlos*) untenable ❷ (*unerträglich*) intolerable ❸ SPORT unstoppable
unhandlich ['ʊn·hant·lɪç] *adj* unwieldy
Unheil ['ʊn·hail] *nt* disaster; **großes/viel ~ anrichten** to wreak havoc
unheilbar ['ʊn·hail·baːɐ̯] I. *adj* incurable II. *adv* incurably
unheilvoll ['ʊn·hail·fɔl] *adj* fateful; *Blick* ominous
unheimlich ['ʊn·haim·lɪç] I. *adj* ❶ (*Grauen erregend*) eerie ❷ (*fam: unglaublich, sehr*) incredible ❸ (*fam: sehr groß, sehr viel*) terrific *fig* II. *adv* (*fam*) incredibly
unhöflich ['ʊn·høːf·lɪç] I. *adj* impolite II. *adv* impolitely
unhygienisch ['ʊn·hy·gi̯eː·nɪʃ] *adj* unhygienic
Uni <-, -s> ['ʊni] *f* (*fam*) *kurz für* **Universität** university
UNICEF <-> ['uːni·tsɛf] *f Akr von* **United Nations International Children's Emergency Fund** UNICEF
Uniform <-, -en> [uni·'fɔrm, 'ʊni·fɔrm] *f* uniform
Unikat <-[e]s, -e> [uni·'kaːt] *nt* ❶ (*einzigartiges Exemplar*) unique specimen ❷ (*einzigartiges Schriftstück*) unicum *spec*, unique copy [of a text]
Union <-, -en> [u'ni̯·oːn] *f* union
universal [uni·vɛr·'zaːl], **universell** [uni·vɛr·'zɛl] I. *adj* universal II. *adv* universally
Univẹrsen *pl von* **Universum**
Universität <-, -en> [uni·vɛr·zi·'tɛːt] *f* university
Universitätsbibliothek *f* university library
Universitätsstadt *f* university town
Universum <-s, Universen> [uni·'vɛr·zʊm] *nt* universe
unkenntlich ['ʊn·kɛnt·lɪç] *adj* unrecognizable; *Eintragung* indecipherable
Unkenntnis ['ʊn·kɛnt·nɪs] *f kein pl* ignorance
unklar ['ʊn·klaːɐ̯] I. *adj* ❶ (*unverständlich*) unclear ❷ (*ungeklärt*) unclear; [**sich** *dat*] **im U~en sein** to be uncertain (**über** +*akk* about); **jdn im U~en lassen** to leave sb in the dark (**über** +*akk* about) ❸ (*verschwommen*) indistinct; *Wetter* hazy; *Umrisse* blurred; *Erinnerungen* vague II. *adv* (*unverständlich*) unclearly
Ụnklarheit <-, -en> *f* ❶ *kein pl* (*Ungewissheit*) uncertainty ❷ (*Undeutlichkeit*) lack of clarity
unklug ['ʊn·kluːk] *adj* unwise
unkompliziert ['ʊn·kɔmp·li·tsiːɐ̯t] *adj* straightforward; *Fall* simple; *Mensch* uncomplicated
unkonzentriert ['ʊn·kɔn·tsɛn·triːɐ̯t] *adj* distracted
Unkosten ['ʊn·kɔs·tn̩] *pl* costs *npl*
Unkraut ['ʊn·kraut] *nt* weed
Ụnkrautbekämpfungsmittel *nt*, **Ụnkrautvernichter** <-s, -> *m* herbicide
unkritisch ['ʊn·kriː·tɪʃ] I. *adj Denken, Meinung* uncritical II. *adv* uncritically
unkündbar ['ʊn·kʏnt·baːɐ̯] *adj Stellung* tenured; *Vertrag* not subject to termination
unleserlich ['ʊn·leː·zɐ·lɪç] I. *adj Schrift* illegible II. *adv* illegibly
ụnlogisch I. *adj* illogical II. *adv* illogically
unlösbar [ʊn·'løːs·baːɐ̯], **unlöslich** [ʊn·'løːs·lɪç] *adj* ❶ (*nicht zu lösen*) *Problem* unsolvable; *Widerspruch* irreconcilable ❷ CHEM insoluble
Unlust ['ʊn·lʊst] *f kein pl* reluctance
unmäßig ['ʊn·mɛː·sɪç] I. *adj* excessive II. *adv* excessively
Unmenge ['ʊn·mɛ·ŋə] *f* enormous amount (**an** +*dat* of)
unmenschlich ['ʊn·mɛnʃ·lɪç] I. *adj* ❶ *Bedingungen, Verhältnisse* appalling, inhuman[e]; *Diktator, Grausamkeit* brutal ❷ *Hitze, Leid* tremendous II. *adv* ❶ (*grausam*) in an inhuman[e] manner ❷ (*entsetzlich*) appallingly
Ụnmenschlichkeit <-, -en> *f* ❶ *kein pl* (*Art*) inhumanity ❷ (*Tat*) inhuman act
unmerklich ['ʊn·mɛrk·lɪç] I. *adj* imperceptible II. *adv* imperceptibly
unmissverständlich[RR] ['ʊn·mɪs·fɛɐ̯·ʃtɛnt·lɪç] I. *adj* unequivocal; *Antwort* blunt II. *adv* unequivocally
unmittelbar ['ʊn·mɪ·tl̩·baːɐ̯] I. *adj* ❶ (*direkt*) direct ❷ (*räumlich/zeitlich nicht getrennt*) immediate; **ein ~er Nachbar** a next-door neighbor II. *adv* ❶ (*sofort*) immediately ❷ (*ohne Umweg*) directly ❸ (*direkt*) imminently; **etw ~ erleben** to experience sth first hand
unmodern ['ʊn·mo·dɛrn] I. *adj* old-fashioned II. *adv* in an old-fashioned way
unmöglich ['ʊn·møːk·lɪç] I. *adj* ❶ (*nicht machbar*) impossible; *Vorhaben* infeasible ❷ (*pej fam: nicht tragbar, lächerlich*) impossible II. *adv* (*fam*) not possibly
Ụnmöglichkeit *f kein pl* impossibility
unmoralisch ['ʊn·mo·raː·lɪʃ] *adj* immoral
unmotiviert ['ʊn·mo·ti·viːɐ̯t] I. *adj Person, Wutausbruch, Angriff* unmotivated, unprovoked II. *adv* without motivation; **~ loslachen** to start laughing for no reason
unmündig ['ʊn·mʏn·dɪç] *adj* ❶ (*noch nicht volljährig*) underage ❷ (*geistig unselbstständig*) dependent
unmusikalisch ['ʊn·mu·zi·kaː·lɪʃ] *adj* unmusical
unnachahmlich ['ʊn·naːx·ʔaːm·lɪç] *adj* inimitable
unnachgiebig ['ʊn·naːx·giː·bɪç] I. *adj* adamant II. *adv* adamantly
unnahbar [ʊn·'naː·baːɐ̯] *adj* unapproachable

unnatürlich [ˈʊn·na·tyːɐ̯·lɪç] *adj* ① (*nicht natürlich*) unnatural; (*abnorm*) abnormal ② (*gekünstelt*) artificial

unnormal [ˈʊn·nɔr·maːl] *adj* abnormal

unnötig [ˈʊn·nøː·tɪç] *adj* unnecessary

unnötigerweise *adv* unnecessarily

unnütz [ˈʊn·nʏts] **I.** *adj* useless **II.** *adv* needlessly

UNO <-> [ˈuː·no] *f Akr von* **United Nations Organization** UN

UNO-Friedenstruppen *pl* UN peacekeeping forces *npl*

unordentlich [ˈʊn·ʔɔr·dn̩t·lɪç] **I.** *adj* messy; *Schrift* sloppy **II.** *adv* messily; *schreiben* sloppily; ~ **arbeiten** to work carelessly

Unordnung [ˈʊn·ʔɔrd·nʊŋ] *f kein pl* mess

unparteiisch [ˈʊn·par·tai·ɪʃ] **I.** *adj* impartial **II.** *adv* impartially

unpassend [ˈʊn·pa·sn̩t] *adj* ① (*unangebracht*) inappropriate ② (*ungelegen*) inconvenient; *Augenblick* inopportune

unpersönlich [ˈʊn·pɛr·zøːn·lɪç] *adj* ① (*distanziert*) *Mensch* distant; *Gespräch, Art* impersonal ② LING impersonal

unpraktisch [ˈʊn·prak·tɪʃ] *adj* ① (*nicht handwerklich veranlagt*) unpractical ② (*nicht praxisgerecht*) impractical

unproblematisch [ˈʊn·pro·ble·maː·tɪʃ] **I.** *adj* unproblematic **II.** *adv* without problem

unpünktlich [ˈʊn·pʏŋkt·lɪç] **I.** *adj* ① (*generell nicht pünktlich*) unpunctual ② (*verspätet*) late **II.** *adv* late

Unpünktlichkeit *f* ① (*unpünktliche Art*) unpunctuality ② (*verspätetes Eintreffen*) late arrival

unrealistisch [ˈʊn·rea·lɪs·tɪʃ] **I.** *adj* unrealistic **II.** *adv* unrealistically

Unrecht [ˈʊn·rɛçt] *nt kein pl* ① (*unrechte Handlung*) wrong; **jdm ein ~ antun** to do sb an injustice ② (*dem Recht entgegengesetztes Prinzip*) **im ~ sein** to be [in the] wrong; **zu ~** wrongly

unrechtmäßig [ˈʊn·rɛçt·mɛː·sɪç] **I.** *adj* illegal **II.** *adv* illegally

unregelmäßig [ˈʊn·reː·gl̩·mɛː·sɪç] **I.** *adj* irregular **II.** *adv* irregularly

Unregelmäßigkeit <-, -en> *f* irregularity

unreif [ˈʊn·raif] *adj* ① AGR, HORT unripe, green ② *Person* immature

unrein [ˈʊn·rain] *adj* impure; *Haut* bad; *Teint* poor

Unruhe [ˈʊn·ruːə] *f* ① (*Ruhelosigkeit*) restlessness ② (*ständige Bewegung*) agitation ③ (*erregte Stimmung*) agitation; **~ stiften** to cause trouble ④ (*Aufstand*) ■ **~n** *pl* riots *pl*

Unruhestifter(in) <-s, -> *m(f)* troublemaker

unruhig [ˈʊn·ruː·ɪç] **I.** *adj* ① (*ständig gestört*) restless; *Zeit* troubled; (*ungleichmäßig*) uneven; *Herzschlag* irregular ② (*laut*) noisy ③ (*ruhelos*) agitated; *Leben* eventful; *Geist* restless; *Schlaf* fitful **II.** *adv* ① (*ruhelos*) anxiously ② (*unter ständigen Störungen*) restlessly

uns [ʊns] **I.** *pron pers* ① *dat von* **wir** [to/for] us; ■ **bei ~** at our house ② *akk von* **wir** us **II.** *pron refl* ① *akk o dat von* **wir** ourselves ② (*einander*) each other

unsachgemäß [ˈʊn·zax·gə·mɛːs] **I.** *adj* improper **II.** *adv* improperly

unsachlich [ˈʊn·zax·lɪç] *adj* unobjective

unsanft [ˈʊn·zanft] **I.** *adj* rough; *Erwachen* rude **II.** *adv* roughly

unsauber [ˈʊn·zau·bɐ] **I.** *adj* ① (*schmutzig*) dirty ② (*unordentlich, nachlässig*) careless; (*unpräzise*) unclear **II.** *adv* carelessly

unschädlich [ˈʊn·ʃɛːt·lɪç] *adj* harmless

unscharf [ˈʊn·ʃarf] **I.** *adj* ① (*ohne klare Konturen*) blurred ② (*nicht scharf*) out of focus ③ (*nicht präzise*) imprecise **II.** *adv* ① (*nicht präzise*) out of focus ② (*nicht exakt*) imprecisely

unschätzbar [ʊn·ˈʃɛts·baːɐ̯] *adj* inestimable; **etw ist von ~em Wert** sth is priceless

unscheinbar [ˈʊn·ʃain·baːɐ̯] *adj* inconspicuous

unschlagbar [ʊn·ˈʃlaːk·baːɐ̯] *adj* unbeatable (**in** +*dat* at)

unschlüssig [ˈʊn·ʃlʏ·sɪç] *adj* ① (*unentschlossen*) indecisive ② (*selten: nicht schlüssig*) undecided

Unschuld [ˈʊn·ʃʊlt] *f* ① (*Schuldlosigkeit*) innocence ② (*Reinheit*) purity; (*Naivität*) innocence ③ (*veraltend: Jungfräulichkeit*) virginity

unschuldig [ˈʊn·ʃʊl·dɪç] **I.** *adj* innocent **II.** *adv* ① JUR despite sb's/one's innocence ② (*arglos*) innocently

unselbständig [ˈʊn·zɛlp·ʃtɛn·dɪç], **unselbstständig**[RR] [ˈʊn·zɛlp·stʃtɛn·dɪç] *adj* dependent [on others]

unser [ˈʊn·zɐ] **I.** *pron poss, adjektivisch* our **II.** *pron pers gen von* **wir** (*geh*) of us

unsere(r, s) [ˈʊn·zə·rə, -zərɐ, -zə·rəs] *pron poss, substantivisch* (*geh*) ours

unsererseits [ˈʊn·zə·rɐ·ˈzaits] *adv* (*von uns aus*) on our part

unseresgleichen [ˈʊn·zɐs·ˈglai·çn̩] *pron inv* people *npl* like us

unseriös [ˈʊn·ze·ri̯·øːs] *adj Firma, Geschäftsmann* untrustworthy; *Angebot* dubious

unsicher [ˈʊn·zɪ·çɐ] **I.** *adj* ① (*gefährlich*) unsafe; *Gegend* dangerous ② (*gefährdet*) insecure, at risk *pred* ③ (*nicht selbstsicher*) unsure; *Blick* uncertain ④ (*unerfahren, ungeübt*) **sich** *akk* **~ fühlen** to feel unsure of oneself ⑤ (*schwankend*) unsteady; *Hand* shaky ⑥ (*ungewiss*) uncertain ⑦ (*nicht verlässlich*) unreliable *fam* **II.** *adv* ① (*schwankend*) unsteadily ② (*nicht selbstsicher*) **~ fahren** to drive with little confidence

Unsicherheit *f* ① *kein pl* (*mangelnde Selbstsicherheit*) insecurity ② *kein pl* (*mangelnde Verlässlichkeit*) unreliability ③ *kein pl* (*Ungewissheit*) uncertainty ④ (*Gefährlichkeit*) dangers *pl* ⑤ *meist pl* (*Unwägbarkeit*) uncertainty

unsichtbar [ˈʊn·zɪçt·baːɐ̯] *adj* invisible

Unsinn [ˈʊn·zɪn] *m kein pl* nonsense;

~ **machen** to mess around
unsinnig ['ʊn·zɪ·nɪç] **I.** *adj* ridiculous **II.** *adv* (*fam: unerhört*) terribly
Unsitte ['ʊn·zɪ·tə] *f* bad habit
unsittlich ['ʊn·zɪt·lɪç] **I.** *adj* indecent **II.** *adv* indecently
unsolide ['ʊn·zo·liː·də] *adj* dissolute; *Arbeit* shoddy; *Bildung* superficial; *Möbel* flimsy
unsozial ['ʊn·zo·tsi̯aːl] **I.** *adj* antisocial **II.** *adv* antisocially
unsportlich ['ʊn·ʃpɔrt·lɪç] **I.** *adj* ❶ *Person* unathletic ❷ (*nicht fair*) unsportsmanlike **II.** *adv* (*nicht fair*) **sich ~ verhalten** to behave in an unsportsmanlike way
unsterblich ['ʊn·ʃtɛrp·lɪç] **I.** *adj* ❶ (*ewig lebend*) immortal ❷ (*unvergänglich*) *Liebe* undying **II.** *adv* (*fam: über alle Maßen*) incredibly
Unstẹrblichkeit <-> *f kein pl* immortality
Unstimmigkeit <-, -en> ['ʊn·ʃtɪ·mɪç·kait] *f* ❶ *meist pl* (*Differenz*) differences *pl* ❷ (*Ungenauigkeit*) discrepancy
unsymmetrisch ['ʊn·zʏ·meː·trɪʃ] *adj* asymmetric
unsympathisch ['ʊn·zʏm·paː·tɪʃ] *adj* unpleasant
untätig ['ʊn·tɛː·tɪç] **I.** *adj* idle **II.** *adv* idly
untauglich ['ʊn·tauk·lɪç] *adj* unsuitable; MIL unfit
unteilbar [ʊn·'tail·baːɐ̯] *adj* indivisible
unten ['ʊn·tn̩] *adv* ❶ (*an einer tieferen Stelle*) down; **dort ~** down there; **weiter ~** farther down; **ich habe die Bücher ~ ins Regal gelegt** I put the books down below on the shelf; **~ links/rechts** on the bottom left/right ❷ (*Unterseite*) bottom ❸ (*in einem tieferen Stockwerk*) downstairs; **der Aufzug fährt nach ~** the elevator is going down ❹ (*in sozial niedriger Position*) bottom ❺ (*hinten im Text*) **siehe ~** see below ❻ (*am hinteren Ende*) at the bottom
unter ['ʊn·tɐ] **I.** *präp* ❶ +*dat* (*unterhalb von etw*) under, underneath; **~ freiem Himmel** outdoors ❷ +*akk* (*unterhalb von etw*) under; ■**sich** *akk* **~ einen Baum stellen** to stand under a tree ❸ +*dat* (*weniger, niedriger*) less; **~ dem Durchschnitt liegen** to be below average ❹ +*dat* (*zwischen*) among[st]; (*von*) among; **~ uns gesagt** between you and me; **~ anderem** among other things ❺ +*dat* (*begleitet von, hervorgerufen durch*) under; **~ Zwang** under duress; **~ Lebensgefahr** at risk to one's life; **~ der Bedingung, dass ...** on the condition that ...; **~ Umständen** possibly ❻ +*dat* (*in einem Zustand*) under; **~ Druck stehen** to be under pressure; **~ einer Krankheit leiden** to suffer from an illness ❼ +*dat* SÜDD (*während*) during; **~ der Woche** during the week **II.** *adv* ❶ (*jünger als*) under ❷ (*weniger als*) less than
Unterarm ['ʊn·tɐ·ʔarm] *m* forearm
ụnterbelichten* *vt* to underexpose
ụnterbewerten* *vt* to undervalue
ụnterbewusst^RR *adj* subconscious
Unterbewusstsein^RR ['ʊn·tɐ·bə·vʊst·zain] *nt* ■**das/jds ~** the/sb's subconscious; **im ~** subconsciously
ụnterbezahlt *adj* underpaid
unterbieten* [ʊn·tɐ·'biː·tn̩] *vt irreg* ❶ (*billiger sein*) to undercut (**um** +*akk* by) ❷ SPORT **einen Rekord ~** to break a record
unterbrechen* [ʊn·tɐ·'brɛ·çn̩] *vt irreg* ❶ (*vorübergehend beenden*) to interrupt ❷ (*räumlich auflockern*) to break up *sep*
Unterbrẹchung <-, -en> *f* interruption; **mit ~en** with breaks
unterbreiten* [ʊn·tɐ·'brai·tn̩] *vt* (*geh*) ❶ (*vorlegen*) ■**jdm etw ~** to present sth to sb ❷ (*informieren*) ■**jdm ~, dass ...** to advise sb that ...
ụnter|bringen *vt irreg* ❶ (*Unterkunft verschaffen*) ■**jdn ~** to put sb up; **die Kinder sind gut untergebracht** (*fig*) the children are being well looked after ❷ (*abstellen*) ■**etw ~** to put sth somewhere ❸ (*fam: eine Anstellung verschaffen*) ■**jdn ~** to get sb a job
Ụnterbringung <-, -en> *f* ❶ (*das Unterbringen*) accommodation ❷ (*Unterkunft*) accommodations *pl, no indef art*
Ụnterdruck <-drücke> *m* ❶ PHYS vacuum ❷ *kein pl* (*niedriger Blutdruck*) low blood pressure
unterdrücken* [ʊn·tɐ·'drʏ·kn̩] *vt* ❶ (*niederhalten*) ■**jdn ~** to oppress sb; ■**etw ~** to suppress sth ❷ (*zurückhalten*) to suppress
Unterdrụckung <-, -en> *f* ❶ *kein pl* (*das Unterdrücken*) *Bürger, Einwohner, Volk* oppression; *Aufstand, Unruhen* suppression ❷ (*das Unterdrücktsein*) oppression
untere(r, s) ['ʊn·tə·rə, -tə·rɐ, -tə·rəs] *adj attr* lower
untereinander [ʊn·tɐ·ʔai·'nan·dɐ] *adv* ❶ (*miteinander*) among yourselves/themselves etc.; **sich ~ helfen** to help each other ❷ (*eines unterhalb des anderen*) one below the other
ụnterentwickelt *adj* underdeveloped
ụnterernährt *adj* undernourished
Ụnterernährung *f* malnutrition
Unterführung [ʊn·tɐ·'fyː·rʊŋ] *f* underpass
Ụntergang *m* ❶ *Schiff* sinking ❷ *Sonne* setting ❸ (*Zerstörung*) destruction; **der ~ einer Zivilisation** the decline of a civilization
Untergebene(r) *f(m) dekl wie adj* subordinate
ụnter|gehen *vi irreg sein* ❶ (*versinken*) to sink; **im Lärm ~** (*fig*) to drown in noise ❷ *Sonne* to set ❸ (*zugrunde gehen*) to be destroyed
ụntergeordnet *adj* ❶ (*zweitrangig*) secondary ❷ (*subaltern*) subordinate
Ụntergeschoss^RR *nt* basement
Ụntergewicht *nt kein pl* insufficient weight; **~ haben** to be underweight
ụntergewichtig *adj* underweight
untergliedern* *vt* to subdivide (**in** +*akk* into)
Untergrund ['ʊn·tɐ·grʊnt] *m* ❶ GEOL subsoil ❷ *kein pl* (*politische Illegalität*) underground;

U

im ~ underground ❸ KUNST (*unterste Farbschicht*) undercoat

unterhalb ['ʊn·tɐ·halp] **I.** *präp +gen* (*darunter befindlich*) below **II.** *adv* (*tiefer gelegen*) below; *Fluss* downstream; ■ **~ von etw** *dat* below sth

Unterhalt <-[e]s> ['ʊn·tɐ·halt] *m kein pl* ❶ (*Lebensunterhalt*) keep; (*Unterhaltsgeld*) alimony ❷ (*Instandhaltung*) upkeep

unterhalten* [ʊn·tɐ·'hal·tn̩] *irreg* **I.** *vt* ❶ (*für jds Lebensunterhalt sorgen*) to support ❷ (*instand halten, pflegen*) to maintain ❸ (*betreiben*) to run ❹ (*die Zeit vertreiben*) to entertain **II.** *vr* ❶ (*sich vergnügen*) ■ **sich** *akk* **~** to keep oneself amused ❷ (*sprechen*) ■ **sich** *akk* **[mit jdm] ~** to talk [to sb] (**über** +*akk* about); **wir müssen uns mal ~** we need to have a talk

unterhaltend [ʊn·tɐ·'hal·tənt], **unterhaltsam** [ʊn·tɐ·'halt·za:m] *adj* entertaining

Ụnterhaltsanspruch *m* entitlement to [child/spousal] support

ụnterhaltsberechtigt *adj* entitled to [child/spousal] support

Ụnterhaltsberechtigte(r) *f(m) dekl wie adj* person entitled to [child/spousal] support

Ụnterhaltskosten *pl* ❶ JUR [child/spousal] support ❷ (*Instandhaltungskosten*) maintenance costs *npl* ❸ (*Betriebskosten*) operating costs *pl*

Ụnterhaltspflicht *f kein pl* obligation to pay maintenance

Ụnterhaltszahlung *f* alimony

Unterhaltung <-, -en> *f* ❶ *kein pl* (*Instandhaltung*) maintenance ❷ *kein pl* (*Betrieb*) running ❸ (*Gespräch*) conversation ❹ *kein pl* (*Zeitvertreib*) entertainment; **gute ~!** enjoy [yourselves]!

Unterhaus ['ʊn·tɐ·haus] *nt* lower house, ≈ House of Representatives

Unterhemd ['ʊn·tɐ·hɛmt] *nt* undershirt

Unterhose ['ʊn·tɐ·ho:·zə] *f* underwear

unterirdisch ['ʊn·tɐ·ʔɪr·dɪʃ] **I.** *adj* underground; *Fluss* subterranean **II.** *adv* underground

ụnter|kommen *vi irreg sein* ❶ (*eine Unterkunft finden*) ■ **bei jdm/irgendwo ~** to find accommodation at sb's house/somewhere ❷ (*fam: eine Anstellung bekommen*) ■ **[als etw] ~** to find a job [as sth]

Ụnterkörper *m* lower [part of the] body

unterkühlt *adj* ❶ (*mit niedriger Körpertemperatur*) suffering from hypothermia ❷ (*betont kühl, distanziert*) cool

Unterkunft <-, Unterkünfte> ['ʊn·tɐ·kʊnft, *pl* 'ʊn·tɐ·kʏnf·tə] *f* accommodation; **~ mit Frühstück** bed and breakfast; **~ und Verpflegung** room and board

Unterlage ['ʊn·tɐ·la:·gə] *f* ❶ (*etw zum Unterlegen*) mat ❷ *meist pl* (*Dokument*) document *usu pl*

Unterlass^RR, **Unterlaß**^ALT ['ʊn·tɐ·las] *m* **ohne ~** (*geh*) incessantly

unterlassen* [ʊn·tɐ·'la·sn̩] *vt irreg* ❶ (*nicht ausführen*) ■ **etw ~** to fail to do sth ❷ (*mit etw aufhören*) ■ **etw ~** to refrain from doing sth

unterlaufen* [ʊn·tɐ·'lau·fn̩] *irreg* **I.** *vt haben* (*umgehen*) to evade **II.** *vi sein* ❶ (*versehentlich vorkommen*) ■ **jdm unterläuft etw** sth happens to sb; **da muss mir ein Fehler ~ sein** I must have made a mistake ❷ (*fam: passieren*) ■ **jdm ~** to happen to sb

unter|legen[1] ['ʊn·tɐ·le:·gn̩] *vt* (*darunter platzieren*) to put under[neath]

unterlegen*[2] [ʊn·tɐ·'le:·gn̩] *vt* ❶ (*mit einer Unterlage versehen*) to underlay ❷ **einen Film mit Musik ~** to put music to a film

unterlegen[3] [ʊn·tɐ·'le:·gn̩] *adj* ❶ (*schwächer als andere*) inferior; **zahlenmäßig ~ sein** to be outnumbered ❷ SPORT ■ **jdm ~ sein** to be defeated by sb

Unterlegenheit <-, -en> *f pl selten* inferiority

Ụnterleib *m* [lower] abdomen

unterliegen* ['ʊn·tɐ·li:·gn̩] *vi irreg* ❶ *sein* (*besiegt werden*) ■ **[jdm] ~** to lose [to sb] ❷ *haben* (*unterworfen sein*) **einer Täuschung ~** to be the victim of deception; **der Schweigepflicht ~** to be bound to maintain confidentiality

Ụnterlippe *f* lower lip

unterm ['ʊn·tɐm] (*fam*) = **unter dem** *s.* **unter**

untermauern* [ʊn·tɐ·'mau·ɐn] *vt* ❶ *These, Behauptung* to support ❷ BAU to underpin

Untermiete ['ʊn·tɐ·mi:·tə] *f* ❶ (*Mieten eines Zimmers, einer Wohnung*) subtenancy; **zur ~ wohnen** to sublet [a room/apartment] ❷ (*das Untervermieten*) sublease; **jdn in ~ nehmen** to sublet a room/apartment to sb

Ụntermieter(in) *m(f)* subtenant

untern ['ʊn·tɐn] (*fam*) = **unter den** *s.* **unter**

unternehmen* [ʊn·tɐ·'ne:·mən] *vt irreg* ❶ (*in die Wege leiten*) ■ **etw/nichts ~** to take action/no action (**gegen** +*akk* against) ❷ (*Vergnügliches durchführen*) **wollen wir nicht etwas zusammen ~?** why don't we do something together? ❸ (*geh: machen*) **einen Ausflug ~** to take a trip; **einen Versuch ~** to make an attempt

Unternehmen <-s, -> [ʊn·tɐ·'ne:·mən] *nt* ❶ ÖKON company ❷ (*Vorhaben*) venture

Unternehmensberater(in) *m(f)* management consultant

Unternehmer(in) <-s, -> [ʊn·tɐ·'ne:·mɐ] *m(f)* entrepreneur

Unternehmungsgeist *m kein pl* entrepreneurial spirit

unternehmungslustig *adj* enterprising

Unteroffizier ['ʊn·tɐ·ʔɔfi·tsi:ɐ̯] *m* noncommissioned officer

ụnter|ordnen **I.** *vt* ❶ (*hintanstellen*) ■ **etw einer S.** *dat* **~** to put sth before sth ❷ (*jdm/einer Institution unterstellen*) ■ **jdm/einer S.** *dat* **untergeordnet sein** to be subordinate to sb/sth **II.** *vr* ■ **sich** *akk* **[jdm] ~** to take on a subordinate role [to sb]

Unterredung <-, -en> *f* discussion

Unterricht <-[e]s, -e> ['ʊn·tɐ·rɪçt] *m pl selten* lesson, class; **theoretischer/praktischer ~** theoretical/practical classes; **der ~ beginnt um zehn vor acht** classes begin at ten to eight; **im ~ sein** to be in class; **heute fällt der ~ in Mathe aus** there's no math class today

unterrichten* [ʊn·tɐ·'rɪç·tn̩] **I.** *vt* ❶ (*lehren*) to teach ❷ (*informieren*) to inform (**über** +*akk* about) **II.** *vi* (*als Lehrer tätig sein*) **in einem Fach ~** to teach a subject; **an welcher Schule ~ Sie?** which school do you teach at?

Ụnterrichtsfach *nt* subject

Ụnterrichtsstunde *f* lesson, class

Unterrock ['ʊn·tɐ·rɔk] *m* petticoat

unters ['ʊn·tɐs] (*fam*) = **unter das** *s.* **unter**

untersagen* [ʊn·tɐ·'zaː·gn̩] *vt* ■**jdm etw ~** to forbid sb to do sth; **das Rauchen ist in diesen Räumen untersagt** smoking is prohibited in these rooms

Untersatz ['ʊn·tɐ·zats] *m* mat

unterschätzen* [ʊn·tɐ·'ʃɛ·tsn̩] *vt* to underestimate

unterscheiden* [ʊn·tɐ·'ʃai·dn̩] *irreg* **I.** *vt* ❶ (*differenzieren*) to distinguish (**zwischen** +*dat* between); ■**etw von etw** *dat* **~** to tell sth from sth ❷ (*auseinanderhalten*) to tell the difference between; **ich kann die beiden nie ~** I can never tell the difference between the two; **Ulmen und Linden kann man leicht ~** you can easily tell elm trees from lime trees **II.** *vi* [**zwischen Dingen**] **~** to differentiate [between things] **III.** *vr* ■**sich** *akk* **von jdm/etw ~** to differ from sb/sth

Unterscheidung *f* distinction

Ụnterschenkel *m* lower leg; *Hähnchen* drumstick

Ụnterschicht *f* lower class

Unterschied <-[e]s, -e> ['ʊn·tɐ·ʃiːt] *m* difference; **einen/keinen ~** [**zwischen Dingen**] **machen** to draw a/no distinction [between things]; **im ~ zu dir bin ich vorsichtiger** unlike you, I'm more careful; **ohne ~** indiscriminately

unterschiedlich ['ʊn·tɐ·ʃiːt·lɪç] **I.** *adj* different; **~er Auffassung sein** to have different views **II.** *adv* differently

unterschlagen* [ʊn·tɐ·'ʃlaː·gn̩] *vt irreg* ❶ (*unrechtmäßig für sich behalten*) to misappropriate; *Geld* to embezzle; *Brief, Beweise* to withhold ❷ (*vorenthalten*) ■**jdm etw ~** to withhold sth from sb

Unterschlupf <-[e]s, -e> ['ʊn·tɐ·ʃlʊpf] *m* hideout; **bei jdm ~ suchen/finden** to look for/find shelter with sb

unterschreiben* [ʊn·tɐ·'ʃrai·bn̩] *irreg vt, vi* to sign

Unterschrift ['ʊn·tɐ·ʃrɪft] *f* ❶ (*eigene Signatur*) signature ❷ (*Bildunterschrift*) caption

Ụnterschriftenliste *f* petition

Unterseeboot ['ʊn·tɐ·zeː·boːt] *nt* submarine

Ụnterseite *f* underside

Untersetzer <-s, -> ['ʊn·tɐ·zɛ·tsɐ] *m* (*für Gläser*) coaster; (*für heisse Töpfe*) trivet

untersetzt [ʊn·tɐ·'zɛtst] *adj* stocky

unterste(r, s) ['ʊn·tɐs·tə, -tɐs·tɐ, -tɐs·təs] *adj superl von* **untere(r, s)** ▶WENDUNGEN: **das U~ zuoberst kehren** (*fam*) to turn everything upside down

unterstehen*[1] [ʊn·tɐ·'ʃteː·ən] *irreg* **I.** *vi* ■**jdm/einer S.** *dat* **~** to be subordinate to sb/sth; **der Abteilungsleiterin ~ 17 Mitarbeiter** seventeen employees report to the departmental head; **jds Befehl ~** to be under sb's command **II.** *vr* ■**sich** *akk* **~ etw zu tun** to have the audacity to do sth; **untersteh dich!** don't you dare!

unter|stehen[2] ['ʊn·tɐ·ʃteː·ən] *vi irreg haben* SÜDD, ÖSTERR, SCHWEIZ (*Schutz suchen*) to take shelter

unterstellen*[1] [ʊn·tɐ·'ʃtɛ·lən] *vt* ❶ (*unterordnen*) ■**jdm jdn/etw ~** to put sb in charge of sb/sth; **Sie sind ab sofort der Redaktion III unterstellt** from now on, you report to Editorial Department III ❷ (*unterschieben*) ■**jdm etw ~** to imply that sb has said/done sth ❸ (*annehmen*) to suppose

unter|stellen[2] ['ʊn·tɐ·ʃtɛ·lən] **I.** *vt* ❶ (*abstellen*) ■**etw irgendwo/bei jdm ~** to store sth somewhere/at sb's house; **ein Auto bei jdm ~** to leave one's car at sb's house ❷ (*darunterstellen*) **einen Eimer ~** to put a bucket underneath **II.** *vr* ■**sich** *akk* **~** to take shelter

Unterstẹllung *f* ❶ (*falsche Behauptung*) insinuation ❷ *kein pl* (*Unterordnung*) subordination

unterstreichen* [ʊn·tɐ·'ʃtrai·çn̩] *vt irreg* ❶ (*markieren*) to underline ❷ (*betonen*) to emphasize

unterstützen* [ʊn·tɐ·'ʃtʏ·tsn̩] *vt* ❶ (*helfen*) to support (**bei/in** +*dat* in) ❷ (*sich dafür einsetzen*) to back

Unterstụ̈tzung *f* ❶ *kein pl* (*Hilfe*) support ❷ (*finanzielle Hilfe*) financial aid; (*Arbeitslosenunterstützung*) unemployment benefit

untersuchen* [ʊn·tɐ·'zuː·xn̩] *vt* ❶ (*den Gesundheitszustand überprüfen*) to examine (**auf** +*akk* for) ❷ (*überprüfen*) to investigate; *Fahrzeug* to check ❸ (*genau betrachten*) to scrutinize ❹ (*durchsuchen*) to search (**auf** +*akk* for) ❺ (*aufzuklären suchen*) to investigate

Untersuchung <-, -en> *f* ❶ (*Überprüfung des Gesundheitszustandes*) [medical] examination ❷ (*Durchsuchung*) search ❸ (*Überprüfung*) investigation ❹ (*analysierende Arbeit*) investigation

Untersuchungsausschuss[RR] *m* investigating committee

Untersuchungsergebnis *nt* ❶ JUR findings *pl* ❷ MED results *pl*

Untersuchungshaft *f* custody; **in ~ sein** to be in detention pending trial

Untersuchungsrichter(in) *m(f)* magistrate judge

Untertan(in) <-en, -en> ['ʊn·tɐ·taːn] *m(f)* subject

Untertasse *f* saucer
unter|tauchen ['ʊn·tɐ·tau·xn̩] **I.** *vt haben* ■ **jdn ~** to dunk sb's head under the water **II.** *vi sein* ❶ (*tauchen*) to dive [under]; *U-Boot* to submerge ❷ (*sich verstecken*) to go underground; ■ **bei jdm ~** to hide out at sb's place; **im Ausland ~** to go underground abroad ❸ (*verschwinden*) ■ **irgendwo ~** to disappear somewhere
Unterteil ['ʊn·tɐ·tail] *nt o m* bottom part
unterteilen* [ʊn·tɐ·'tai·lən] *vt* ❶ (*einteilen*) to subdivide (**in** +*akk* into) ❷ (*aufteilen*) to partition (**in** +*akk* into)
Unterteilung <-, -en> *f* subdivision
Unterteller *m* SCHWEIZ, SÜDD saucer
Untertitel ['ʊn·tɐ·ti:·tl̩] *m* subtitle
untertreiben* [ʊn·tɐ·'trai·bn̩] *irreg* **I.** *vt* to understate **II.** *vi* to play sth down
untervermieten* *vt, vi* to sublet
unterversorgt *adj* undersupplied
Unterversorgung *f kein pl* shortage
Unterwäsche <-> ['ʊn·tɐ·vɛ·ʃə] *f kein pl* underwear
unterwegs [ʊn·tɐ·'ve:ks] *adv* on the way; **für ~** for the trip; **Herr Müller ist gerade nach München ~** Mr. Müller is on his way to Munich at the moment; **er hat mich von ~ angerufen** he called me while he was on the road
Unterwelt ['ʊn·tɐ·vɛlt] *f kein pl* underworld
unterwerfen* [ʊn·tɐ·'vɛr·fn̩] *irreg* **I.** *vt* ❶ (*unterjochen*) to subjugate ❷ (*unterziehen*) ■ **jdn einer S.** *dat* **~** to subject sb to sth **II.** *vr* ❶ (*sich fügen*) *einem Herrscher* to obey; **sich** *akk* **jds Willkür ~** to bow to sb's will ❷ (*sich unterziehen*) ■ **sich** *akk* **einer S.** *dat* **~** to submit to sth
Unterwerfung <-, -en> *f* subjugation
unterworfen *adj* ■ **jdm/einer S.** *dat* **~ sein** to be subject to sb/sth
unterzeichnen* [ʊn·tɐ·'tsaiç·nən] *vt* to sign
unterziehen*[1] [ʊn·tɐ·'tsi:·ən] *irreg* **I.** *vt* ■ **jdn/etw einer S.** *dat* **~** to subject sb/sth to sth **II.** *vr* ■ **sich** *akk* **einer S.** *dat* **~** to undergo sth
unter|ziehen[2] ['ʊn·tɐ·tsi:·ən] *vt irreg* to put on *sep* underneath; **Sie sollten sich** *dat* **einen Pullover ~** you should put a sweater on underneath
Untiefe ['ʊn·ti:·fə] *f* ❶ (*seichte Stelle*) shallow *usu pl* ❷ (*geh: große Tiefe*) depth *usu pl*
untragbar [ʊn·'tra:k·ba:ɐ̯] *adj* ❶ (*unerträglich*) unbearable ❷ (*nicht tolerabel*) intolerable
untrennbar [ʊn·'trɛn·ba:ɐ̯] *adj* inseparable
untreu ['ʊn·trɔy] *adj* unfaithful; ■ **jdm ~ sein** to be unfaithful to sb; **sich** *dat* **~ werden** (*geh*) to be untrue to oneself; **einer S.** *dat* **~ werden** to be disloyal to sth
Untreue *f* ❶ (*untreues Verhalten*) unfaithfulness ❷ JUR embezzlement
untröstlich [ʊn·'trø:st·lɪç] *adj* inconsolable
Untugend ['ʊn·tu:·gn̩t] *f* bad habit
untypisch *adj* untypical

U

unüberlegt ['ʊn·ʔy:bɐ·le:kt] **I.** *adj* rash **II.** *adv* rashly
unübersehbar [ʊn·ʔy:bɐ·'ze:·ba:ɐ̯] *adj* ❶ (*nicht zu übersehen*) obvious ❷ (*nicht abschätzbar*) incalculable; *Konsequenzen* unforeseeable
unübersichtlich ['ʊn·ʔy:bɐ·zɪçt·lɪç] *adj* ❶ (*nicht übersichtlich*) confusing ❷ (*schwer zu überblicken*) unclear
unübertroffen [ʊn·ʔy:bɐ·'trɔ·fn̩] *adj* unsurpassed; *Rekord* unbroken
unüberwindlich [ʊn·ʔy:bɐ·'vɪnt·lɪç] *adj* ❶ (*nicht abzulegen*) deep[-rooted] ❷ (*nicht zu meistern*) insurmountable ❸ (*unbesiegbar*) invincible
unüblich ['ʊn·ʔy:p·lɪç] **I.** *adj* uncustomary **II.** *adv* unusually
unumstößlich [ʊn·ʔʊm·'ʃtø:s·lɪç] **I.** *adj* irrefutable; *Entschluss* irrevocable **II.** *adv* irrefutably
unumstritten [ʊn·ʔʊm·'ʃtrɪ·tn̩] **I.** *adj* undisputed **II.** *adv* undisputedly
ununterbrochen ['ʊn·ʔʊn·tɐ·brɔ·xn̩] **I.** *adj* ❶ (*unaufhörlich andauernd*) incessant ❷ (*nicht unterbrochen*) uninterrupted **II.** *adv* incessantly
unveränderlich [ʊn·fɛɐ̯·'ʔɛn·dɐ·lɪç] *adj* unchanging
unverändert ['ʊn·fɛɐ̯·ʔɛn·dɐt] **I.** *adj* ❶ (*keine Änderungen aufweisend*) unrevised ❷ (*gleich bleibend*) unchanged; *Einsatz, Fleiß* unchanging **II.** *adv* **auch morgen ist es wieder ~ kalt** it will remain [just as] cold tomorrow
unverantwortlich [ʊn·fɛɐ̯·'ʔant·vɔrt·lɪç] **I.** *adj* irresponsible **II.** *adv* irresponsibly
unverbesserlich [ʊn·fɛɐ̯·'bɛ·sɐ·lɪç] *adj* incorrigible; *Optimist* incurable
unverbindlich ['ʊn·fɛɐ̯·bɪnt·lɪç] **I.** *adj* ❶ (*nicht verpflichtend*) not binding *pred* ❷ (*distanziert*) detached **II.** *adv* without obligation
unvereinbar [ʊn·fɛɐ̯·'ʔain·ba:ɐ̯] *adj* incompatible; *Gegensätze* irreconcilable
unverfälscht ['ʊn·fɛɐ̯·fɛlʃt] *adj* unadulterated
unverfroren ['ʊn·fɛɐ̯·fro:·rən] *adj* insolent
unvergänglich ['ʊn·fɛɐ̯·gɛŋ·lɪç] *adj* ❶ (*bleibend*) abiding; *Eindruck* lasting ❷ (*nicht vergänglich*) immortal
unvergesslich[RR] [ʊn·fɛɐ̯·'gɛs·lɪç] *adj* unforgettable
unvergleichlich [ʊn·fɛɐ̯·'glaiç·lɪç] **I.** *adj* incomparable **II.** *adv* incomparably
unverhältnismäßig ['ʊn·fɛɐ̯·hɛlt·nɪs·mɛ:·sɪç] *adv* excessively
unverhofft ['ʊn·fɛɐ̯·hɔft] **I.** *adj* unexpected **II.** *adv* unexpectedly; **sie besuchten uns ~** they paid us an unexpected visit
unverhüllt ['ʊn·fɛ·ɐ̯hʏlt] *adj* undisguised
unverkäuflich ['ʊn·fɛɐ̯·kɔyf·lɪç] *adj* not for sale *pred*
unverkennbar [ʊn·fɛɐ̯·'kɛn·ba:ɐ̯] *adj* unmistakable; ■ **~ sein/werden, dass ...** to be/become clear that ...
unverletzt ['ʊn·fɛɐ̯·lɛtst] *adj* unhurt

unvermeidbar [ʊn·fɛɐ̯·ˈmait·baːɐ̯] *adj* unavoidable
unvermeidlich [ʊn·fɛɐ̯·ˈmait·lɪç] *adj* unavoidable
unvermindert [ˈʊn·fɛɐ̯·mɪn·dɐt] **I.** *adj* undiminished **II.** *adv* unabated
unvermittelt [ˈʊn·fɛɐ̯·mɪ·tl̩t] **I.** *adj* sudden **II.** *adv* suddenly
Unvermögen [ˈʊn·fɛɐ̯·møː·gn̩] *nt kein pl* powerlessness; ■ **jds ~, etw zu tun** sb's inability to do sth
unvermutet [ˈʊn·fɛɐ̯·muː·tət] **I.** *adj* unexpected **II.** *adv* unexpectedly
Unvernunft [ˈʊn·fɛɐ̯·nʊnft] *f* stupidity
unvernünftig [ˈʊn·fɛɐ̯·nʏnf·tɪç] *adj* unreasonable
unveröffentlicht [ˈʊn·fɛɐ̯·ʔœfn̩t·lɪçt] *adj* unpublished
unverrichtet [ˈʊn·fɛɐ̯·rɪç·tət] *adj* **~er Dinge** without having achieved anything
unverschämt [ˈʊn·fɛɐ̯·ʃɛːmt] **I.** *adj* ❶ (*dreist*) impudent ❷ (*fam: unerhört*) outrageous **II.** *adv* ❶ (*dreist*) insolently; **~ lügen** to tell barefaced lies ❷ (*fam: unerhört*) outrageously
Ụnverschämtheit <-, -en> *f* ❶ *kein pl* (*Dreistigkeit*) insolence ❷ (*Bemerkung*) impertinent remark; [**das ist eine**] **~!** that's outrageous! ❸ (*Handlung*) impertinence
unverschuldet [ˈʊn·fɛɐ̯·ʃʊl·dət] *adj, adv* through no fault of one's own
unversehens [ˈʊn·fɛɐ̯·zeː·əns] *adv* unexpectedly
unversehrt [ˈʊn·fɛɐ̯·zeːɐ̯t] *adj* undamaged; *Mensch* unscathed
unversöhnlich [ˈʊn·fɛɐ̯·zøːn·lɪç] *adj* irreconcilable
unverständlich [ˈʊn·fɛɐ̯·ʃtɛnt·lɪç] *adj* ❶ (*akustisch nicht zu verstehen*) unintelligible ❷ (*unbegreifbar*) incomprehensible
Ụnverständnis *nt kein pl* lack of understanding
unversucht [ˈʊn·fɛɐ̯·zuːxt] *adj* **nichts ~ lassen** to leave no stone unturned
unverträglich [ˈʊn·fɛɐ̯·trɛːk·lɪç] *adj* indigestible
Ụnverträglichkeit *f* <-> *kein pl* ❶ MED intolerance ❷ (*Unvereinbarkeit*) incompatibility
unverwechselbar [ʊn·fɛɐ̯·ˈvɛk·sl̩·baːɐ̯] *adj* unmistakable
unverwundbar [ʊn·fɛɐ̯·ˈvʊnt·baːɐ̯] *adj* invulnerable
unverwüstlich [ʊn·fɛɐ̯·ˈvyːst·lɪç] *adj* tough; *Gesundheit* robust
unverzeihlich [ʊn·fɛɐ̯·ˈtsai·lɪç] *adj* inexcusable
unverzollt [ˈʊn·fɛɐ̯·tsɔlt] *adj* duty-free
unverzüglich [ʊn·fɛɐ̯·ˈtsyːk·lɪç] **I.** *adj* immediate **II.** *adv* immediately; **~ gegen jdn vorgehen** to take immediate action against sb
unvollendet [ˈʊn·fɔl·ʔɛn·dət] *adj* unfinished
unvollkommen [ˈʊn·fɔl·kɔ·mən] *adj* incomplete
Ụnvollkommenheit *f* imperfection
unvollständig [ˈʊn·fɔl·ʃtɛn·dɪç] **I.** *adj* incomplete **II.** *adv* incompletely
Ụnvollständigkeit *f* incompleteness
unvorbereitet [ˈʊn·foːɐ̯·bə·rai·tət] **I.** *adj* unprepared **II.** *adv* ❶ (*ohne sich vorbereitet zu haben*) without [any] preparation ❷ (*unerwartet*) unexpectedly
unvoreingenommen [ˈʊn·foːɐ̯·ʔain·gə·nɔ·mən] **I.** *adj* unbiased **II.** *adv* impartially
Ụnvoreingenommenheit *f* impartiality
unvorhergesehen [ˈʊn·foːɐ̯·heːɐ̯·gə·zeː·ən] **I.** *adj* unforeseen; *Besuch* unexpected **II.** *adv* unexpectedly
unvorsichtig [ˈʊn·foːɐ̯·zɪç·tɪç] **I.** *adj* ❶ (*unbedacht*) rash ❷ (*nicht vorsichtig*) careless **II.** *adv* ❶ (*unbedacht*) rashly ❷ (*nicht vorsichtig*) carelessly
ụnvorsichtigerweise *adv* carelessly
Ụnvorsichtigkeit <-, -en> *f* ❶ *kein pl* (*unbedachte Art*) rashness ❷ (*Bemerkung*) rash comment ❸ (*Handlung*) rash act
unvorstellbar [ʊn·foːɐ̯·ˈʃtɛl·baːɐ̯] **I.** *adj* inconceivable **II.** *adv* inconceivably
unvorteilhaft [ˈʊn·fɔr·tail·haft] **I.** *adj* ❶ (*nicht vorteilhaft aussehend*) unflattering ❷ (*nachteilig*) disadvantageous **II.** *adv* unflatteringly; **sich** *akk* **~ kleiden** to not dress well
Unwägbarkeit <-, -en> *f* unpredictability
unwahr [ˈʊn·vaːɐ̯] *adj* untrue, false
unwahrscheinlich [ˈʊn·vaːɐ̯·ʃain·lɪç] **I.** *adj* ❶ (*kaum denkbar*) unlikely; *Zufall* remarkable ❷ (*fam: unerhört*) incredible; *Mistkerl* absolute **II.** *adv* (*fam*) incredibly; **letzten Winter haben wir ~ gefroren** we froze our butts off last winter; **du hast ja ~ abgenommen!** you've lost a hell of a lot of weight!
Ụnwahrscheinlichkeit <-, -en> *f* improbability
unweigerlich [ˈʊn·vai·gɐ·lɪç] **I.** *adj attr* inevitable **II.** *adv* inevitably
unweit [ˈʊn·vait] *adv* ■ **~ von etw** *dat* not far from sth
Unwesen [ˈʊn·veː·zn̩] *nt kein pl* deplorable state of affairs; **sein ~ treiben** to up to no good
unwesentlich [ˈʊn·veː·zn̩t·lɪç] **I.** *adj* insignificant **II.** *adv* slightly
Unwetter <-s, -> [ˈʊn·vɛ·tɐ] *nt* thunderstorm
unwichtig [ˈʊn·vɪç·tɪç] *adj* unimportant
unwiderruflich [ʊn·viː·dɐ·ˈruːf·lɪç] **I.** *adj* irrevocable **II.** *adv* irrevocably
unwiderstehlich [ʊn·viː·dɐ·ˈʃteː·lɪç] *adj* irresistible
Unwille [ˈʊn·vɪ·lə] *m* displeasure
unwillig [ˈʊn·vɪ·lɪç] **I.** *adj* ❶ (*verärgert*) angry ❷ (*widerwillig*) reluctant **II.** *adv* reluctantly
unwillkürlich [ˈʊn·vɪl·kyːɐ̯·lɪç] **I.** *adj* involuntary **II.** *adv* involuntarily
unwirklich [ˈʊn·vɪrk·lɪç] *adj* unreal
unwirksam [ˈʊn·vɪrk·zaːm] *adj* ineffective
unwirsch [ˈʊn·vɪrʃ] *adj* curt
unwissend [ˈʊn·vɪ·sn̩t] *adj* (*über kein Wissen verfügend*) ignorant; (*ahnungslos*) unsuspecting

U

Unwissenheit <-> ['ʊn·vɪ·sn̩·hait] *f kein pl* ignorance
unwohl ['ʊn·vo:l] *adj* ■ **jdm ist ~** ① (*gesundheitlich nicht gut*) sb feels sick ② (*unbehaglich*) sb feels uneasy
Unwohlsein <-s> ['ʊn·vo:l·zain] *nt kein pl* [slight] nausea
unwürdig ['ʊn·vʏr·dɪç] *adj* ① (*nicht würdig*) unworthy ② (*schändlich*) disgraceful
unzählig [ʊn·'tsɛ:·lɪç] *adj* countless
unzeitgemäß ['ʊn·tsait·gə·mɛ:s] *adj* old-fashioned
unzerbrechlich ['ʊn·tsɛɐ̯·brɛç·lɪç] *adj* unbreakable
unzufrieden ['ʊn·tsu·fri:·dn̩] *adj* dissatisfied
Unzufriedenheit *f* dissatisfaction
unzugänglich ['ʊn·tsu:·gɛŋ·lɪç] *adj* ① (*schwer erreichbar*) inaccessible ② (*nicht aufgeschlossen*) unapproachable
unzulänglich ['ʊn·tsu:·lɛŋ·lɪç] **I.** *adj* inadequate; *Erfahrungen, Kenntnisse* insufficient **II.** *adv* inadequately
unzulässig ['ʊn·tsu:·lɛ·sɪç] *adj* inadmissible
unzumutbar ['ʊn·tsu:·mu:t·ba:ɐ̯] *adj* unreasonable
unzurechnungsfähig ['ʊn·tsu:·rɛç·nʊŋs·fɛ:·ɪç] *adj* of unsound mind *pred;* **jdn für ~ erklären** to certify [*or* declare] sb mentally incompetent
unzusammenhängend ['ʊn·tsu·za·mən·hɛŋ·ənt] *adj* incoherent
unzustellbar ['ʊn·tsu:·ʃtɛl·ba:ɐ̯] *adj* undeliverable
unzutreffend ['ʊn·tsu:·trɛ·fn̩t] *adj* inapplicable; (*falsch*) incorrect
unzuverlässig ['ʊn·tsu:·fɛɐ̯·lɛ·sɪç] *adj* unreliable
üppig ['ʏpɪç] *adj* ① (*schwellend*) voluptuous ② (*reichhaltig*) sumptuous ③ (*geh: in großer Fülle vorhanden*) luxuriant
Urahn(e) <-en, -en> ['u:ɐ̯·ʔa:n] *m(f)* ancestor
uralt ['u:ɐ̯·ʔalt] *adj* ① (*sehr alt*) very old ② (*schon lange existent*) ancient ③ (*fam: schon lange bekannt*) ancient; *Problem* old, perennial
Uran <-s> [u'ra:n] *nt kein pl* uranium
uraufführen ['u:ɐ̯·ʔauf·fy:·rən] *vt nur Infinitiv und pp* to première
Uraufführung *f* THEAT debut; *Film* première
Ureinwohner(in) *m(f)* indigenous person
Urenkel(in) ['u:ɐ̯·ʔɛŋ·kl̩] *m(f)* great-grandchild, great-grandson *masc,* great-granddaughter *fem*
Urgeschichte ['u:ɐ̯·gə·ʃɪç·tə] *f kein pl* prehistory
Urgroßeltern ['u:ɐ̯·gro:s·ʔɛl·tɐn] *pl* great-grandparents *pl*
Urgroßmutter ['u:ɐ̯·gro:s·mʊ·tɐ] *f* great-grandmother
Urgroßvater *m* great-grandfather
Urheber(in) <-s, -> ['u:ɐ̯·he:·bɐ] *m(f)* ① (*Autor*) author ② (*Initiator*) originator
Urheberrecht *nt* ① (*Recht des Autors*) copyright (**an** +*dat* on) ② (*urheberrechtliche Bestimmungen*) copyright law
urheberrechtlich **I.** *adj* copyright *attr* **II.** *adv* **~ geschützt** copyright[ed]
urig ['u:rɪç] *adj* (*fam*) ① (*originell*) eccentric ② (*Lokalkolorit besitzend*) with a local flavor *pred;* **dieses Lokal ist besonders ~** this bar has a real local flavor
Urin <-s, -e> [u'ri:n] *m* urine
urinieren* [ur·i'ni:·rən] *vi* (*geh*) to urinate
Urinprobe *f* urine sample
Urknall *m* big bang
urkomisch ['u:ɐ̯·'ko:·mɪʃ] *adj* hilarious
Urkunde <-, -n> ['u:ɐ̯·kʊn·də] *f* (*Auszeichnung*) certificate; (*rechtskräftig*) document
Urkundenfälschung *f* document forgery
Urlaub <-[e]s, -e> ['u:ɐ̯·laup] *m* vacation; **~ machen** to go on vacation; **in ~ sein** to be on vacation
Urlauber(in) <-s, -> *m(f)* vacationer
Urlaubsgeld *nt* vacation pay
urlaubsreif *adj* ■ **~ sein** to be ready for a vacation
Urlaubsreise *f* vacation trip
Urne <-, -n> ['ʊr·nə] *f* ① (*Graburne*) urn ② (*Wahlurne*) ballot box; **zu den ~n gehen** to go to the polls
Urnengang *m* election
Urologie <-> [uro·lo·'gi:] *f kein pl* urology
urplötzlich **I.** *adj attr* very sudden **II.** *adv* very suddenly
Ursache *f* reason; **die ~ für etwas sein** to be the cause of sth ▶ WENDUNGEN: **keine ~!** you're welcome
Ursprung ['u:ɐ̯·ʃprʊŋ] *m* origin
ursprünglich ['u:ɐ̯·ʃprʏŋ·lɪç] **I.** *adj* ① *attr* (*anfänglich*) original ② (*im Urzustand befindlich*) unspoiled ③ (*urtümlich*) ancient **II.** *adv* originally
Urteil <-s, -e> ['ʊr·tail] *nt* ① JUR judgment, verdict ② (*Meinung*) opinion (**über** +*akk* on)
urteilen ['ʊr·tai·lən] *vi* to pass judgment (**über** +*akk* on)
Urteilsbegründung *f* basis for a judgment
Urteilsspruch *m* verdict
Uruguay <-s> ['u:ru·gu̯ai] *nt* Uruguay; *s. a.* **Deutschland**
Uruguayer(in) <-s, -> ['u:ru·gu̯ai·ɐ] *m(f)* Uruguayan; *s. a.* **Deutsche(r)**
uruguayisch ['u:ru·gu̯ai·ɪʃ] *adj* Uruguayan; *s. a.* **deutsch**
Urwald ['u:ɐ̯·valt] *m* primeval [*or* virgin] forest
urwüchsig *adj* ① (*im Urzustand erhalten*) unspoiled ② (*unverbildet*) earthy ③ (*ursprünglich*) original
Urzeit *f* ■ **die ~** primeval times *pl* ▶ WENDUNGEN: **seit ~en** for eons; **vor ~en** eons ago
urzeitlich *adj* primeval
Urzustand *m kein pl* original state
USA [u:·ʔɛs·'ʔa:] *pl Abk von* **United States of America:** ■ **die ~** the US[A] + *sing vb*
US-amerikanisch [u:·'ʔɛs·ʔame·ri·ka:·nɪʃ] *adj* American, US
USB-Stick <-s, -s> [u·ʔɛs·'be·stɪk, ju·ʔɛs·

'bi-] *m* COMPUT flash drive
usw. *Abk von* **und so weiter** etc.
Utensil <-s, Utensilien> [utɛn·'ziːl, *pl* utɛn·'ziː·li̯·ən] *nt meist pl* utensil
Utopie <-, -n> [uto·'piː, *pl* -'piː·ən] *f* Utopia
utopisch [u'toː·pɪʃ] *adj* utopian
u. U. *Abk von* **unter Umständen** possibly
UV-Strahlen *pl* UV rays *pl*

Vv

V, v <-, - *o fam* -s, -s> [fau] *nt* V, v; **~ wie Viktor** V as in Victor
V *Abk von* **Volt** V
Vagabund(in) <-en, -en> [va·ga·'bʊnt] *m(f)* vagabond
vage ['vaː·gə] **I.** *adj* vague **II.** *adv* vaguely
Vagina <-, Vaginen> [va·'giː·na, 'vaː·gi·na] *f* vagina
Vakuum <-s, Vakuen *o* Vakua> ['vaː·ku·ʊm, *pl* 'vaː·ku·ən, 'vaː·kua] *nt* vacuum
vakuumverpackt *adj* vacuum-packed
Vamp <-s, -s> [vɛmp] *m* vamp
Vampir <-s, -e> [vam·'piːɐ̯] *m* vampire
Vandale, Vandalin <-n, -n> [van·'daː·lə, van·'daː·lɪn] *m, f* vandal
Vandalismus <-> [van·da·'lɪs·mʊs] *m kein pl* vandalism
Vanille <-, -en> [va·'nɪlə] *f* vanilla
variabel [va·'ri̯aː·bl̩] *adj* variable
Variable <-n, -n> [va·'ri̯aː·blə] *dekl wie adj f* variable
Variante <-, -n> [va·'ri̯an·tə] *f* ❶ (*Abwandlung*) variation ❷ (*veränderte Ausführung*) variant
Variation <-, -en> [va·ria·'tsi̯oːn] *f* variation
variieren* [va·ri·'iː·rən] *vi* to vary
Vase <-, -n> ['vaː·zə] *f* vase
Vater <-s, Väter> ['faː·tɐ, *pl* 'fɛ·tɐ] *m* father
Vaterland *nt* fatherland
väterlich ['fɛ·tɐ·lɪç] **I.** *adj* ❶ (*dem Vater gehörend*) **das ~e Geschäft** his/her father's business ❷ (*zum Vater gehörend*) paternal ❸ (*fürsorglich*) fatherly **II.** *adv* like a father
väterlicherseits *adv* on sb's father's side
Vaterschaft <-, -en> *f* paternity
Vaterschaftsklage *f* paternity suit
Vatertag *m* Father's Day
Vaterunser <-s, -> [faː·tɐ·'ʔʊn·zɐ] *nt* REL ■**das ~** the Lord's Prayer
Vati <-s, -s> ['faː·ti] *m* (*fam*) daddy
Vatikan <-s> [va·ti·'kaːn] *m* Vatican
V-Ausschnitt ['fau-] *m* V-neck; **ein Pullover mit ~** a V-neck sweater
v.Chr. *Abk von* **vor Christus** BC
Vegetarier(in) <-s, -> [ve·ge·'taː·ri̯·ɐ] *m(f)* vegetarian
vegetarisch [ve·ge·'ta·rɪʃ] **I.** *adj* vegetarian **II.** *adv* **sich** *akk* **~ ernähren** to be a vegetarian
Vegetation <-, -en> [ve·ge·ta·'tsi̯oːn] *f* vegetation
vegetieren* [ve·ge·'tiː·rən] *vi* to vegetate
Vehikel <-s, -> [ve·'hiː·kl̩] *nt* (*fam*) vehicle
Veilchen <-s, -> ['fail·çən] *nt* violet
Velo <-s, -s> ['veː·lo] *nt* SCHWEIZ (*Fahrrad*) bicycle, bike *fam*
Velours <-, -> [və·'luːɐ̯] *nt*, **Veloursleder** *nt* suede
Vene <-, -n> ['veː·nə] *f* vein
Venedig <-s> [ve·'neː·dɪç] *nt kein pl* Venice; *s. a.* **Deutschland**
Ventil <-s, -e> [vɛn·'tiːl] *nt* valve
Ventilator <-s, -toren> [vɛn·ti·'laː·toːɐ̯, *pl* -'toː·rən] *m* fan
Venus <-s> ['veː·nʊs] *f kein pl* Venus
verabreden* **I.** *vr* ■**sich** *akk* **[mit jdm] ~** to set up a date [*or* make plans] [with sb]; ■**[mit jdm] verabredet sein** to have plans [*or* a date] [with sb] **II.** *vt* ■**etw [mit jdm] ~** to arrange [*or* set up] sth [with sb]; ■**verabredet** agreed
Verabredung <-, -en> *f* ❶ (*Treffen*) meeting; (*Rendezvous*) date ❷ (*Vereinbarung*) arrangement
verabscheuen* *vt* to detest, to loathe
verabschieden* **I.** *vr* ■**sich** *akk* **~** to say goodbye (**von** + *dat* to) **II.** *vt Gesetz* to pass
verachten* *vt* ❶ (*verächtlich finden*) to despise ❷ (*nicht achten*) to scorn; **nicht zu ~ sein** [sth is] not to be sneezed at *fam*
verächtlich [fɛɐ̯·'ʔɛçt·lɪç] **I.** *adj* ❶ (*Verachtung zeigend*) contemptuous, scornful ❷ (*verabscheuungswürdig*) despicable **II.** *adv* contemptuously, scornfully
Verachtung *f* contempt, scorn
verallgemeinern* **I.** *vt* ■**etw ~** to generalize about sth **II.** *vi* to generalize
Verallgemeinerung <-, -en> *f* generalization
veralten* [fɛɐ̯·'ʔal·tn̩] *vi sein* to become obsolete; *Ansichten, Methoden* to become outdated; ■**veraltet** obsolete; *Reiseführer, Stadtplan* old
Veranda <-, Veranden> [ve·'ran·da, *pl* ve·'ran·dən] *f* veranda
veränderlich *adj a.* METEO variable
verändern* *vt, vr* to change
Veränderung *f* change; (*leicht*) alteration, modification
verängstigen* *vt* to frighten; ■**verängstigt** frightened, scared
veranlagt [fɛɐ̯·'ʔan·laːkt] *adj* **ein künstlerisch ~er Mensch** a person with an artistic disposition; **er ist praktisch ~** he is practically minded
Veranlagung <-, -en> *f* disposition; **eine ~ zu etw** *dat* **haben** to have a tendency toward sth

V

veranlassen* I. *vt* ① (*in die Wege leiten*) to arrange ② (*dazu bringen*) ■ **jdn zu etw** *dat* ~ to cause sb to do sth II. *vi* ■ **~, dass etw geschieht** to see to it that sth happens
Veranlassung <-, -en> *f* ① (*Einleitung*) **auf jds ~** at sb's instigation ② (*Anlass*) cause, reason
veranschaulichen* [fɛɐ̯·ˈʔan·ʃau·lɪ·çn̩] *vt* to illustrate
veranschlagen* *vt* to estimate (**mit** +*dat* at)
veranstalten* [fɛɐ̯·ˈʔan·ʃtal·tn̩] *vt* to organize
Veranstalter(in) <-s, -> *m(f)* organizer
Veranstaltung <-, -en> *f* ① *kein pl* (*das Durchführen*) organizing ② (*Ereignis*) event
Veranstaltungsort *m* venue
verantworten* I. *vt* ■ **etw ~** to take responsibility for sth II. *vr* ■ **sich** *akk* [**vor jdm**] ~ to answer [to sb] (**für** +*akk* for)
verantwortlich *adj* responsible
Verantwortliche(r) *f(m) dekl wie adj* person responsible, responsible party
Verantwortung <-, -en> *f* responsibility; **die ~ [für etw] tragen/übernehmen** to be responsible/take responsibility [for sth]; **auf eigene ~** on one's own responsibility, at one's own risk
verantwortungsbewusst[RR] I. *adj* responsible II. *adv* responsibly
verantwortungslos I. *adj* irresponsible II. *adv* irresponsibly
verantwortungsvoll *adj* responsible
verarbeiten* *vt* ① (*verwenden*) to use; *Lebensmittel, Rohstoffe* to process; ■ **etw zu etw** *dat* ~ to make sth into sth ② PSYCH to assimilate, to come to terms with
Verarbeitung <-, -en> *f* ① (*das Verarbeiten*) processing ② (*Fertigungsqualität*) workmanship
verärgern* *vt* to annoy
Verärgerung <-, -en> *f* annoyance
verarmen* [fɛɐ̯·ˈʔar·mən] *vi sein* to become poor; ■ **verarmt** impoverished
Verarmung <-, -en> *f* impoverishment
verarschen* [fɛɐ̯·ˈʔar·ʃn̩] *vt* (*derb*) ■ **jdn ~** to mess around with sb
verarzten* [fɛɐ̯·ˈʔaːɐ̯ts·tn̩] *vt* (*fam*) to treat
verausgaben* [fɛɐ̯·ˈʔaus·gaː·bn̩] *vr* ■ **sich** *akk* ~ (*körperlich*) to overexert; (*finanziell*) to overspend
Verb <-s, -en> [vɛrp] *nt* verb
verbal [vɛr·ˈbaːl] I. *adj* verbal II. *adv* verbally
Verband <-[e]s, Verbände> [fɛɐ̯·ˈbant, *pl* fɛɐ̯·ˈbɛn·də] *m* ① (*Bund*) association ② MED bandage, dressing
Verband(s)kasten *m* first-aid kit
verbannen* *vt* ① (*ins Exil schicken*) to banish ② (*ausmerzen*) to ban (**aus** +*dat* from)
Verbannung <-, -en> *f* exile, banishment
verbarrikadieren* I. *vt* to barricade II. *vr* ■ **sich** *akk* ~ to barricade oneself
verbauen* *vt* ① (*verderben*) to spoil, to ruin *a. fig* ② (*versperren*) *Aussicht* to block
verbergen* *vt irreg* to hide, to conceal (**vor** +*dat* from)

verbessern* I. *vt* ① (*besser machen*) to improve ② (*korrigieren*) to correct II. *vr* ■ **sich** *akk* ~ to improve
Verbesserung <-, -en> *f* ① (*qualitative Anhebung*) improvement ② (*Korrektur*) correction
verbeugen* *vr* ■ **sich** *akk* ~ to bow
Verbeugung *f* bow
verbiegen* *irreg vt, vr* to bend; ■ **verbogen** bent
verbieten <verbot, verboten> *vt* to forbid, to ban; (*offiziell*) to outlaw; ■ **jdm ~, etw zu tun** to forbid sb to do sth; **ich habe es dir doch verboten** I told you you weren't allowed to do that
verbilligen* *vt* to reduce [in price] (**um** +*akk* by)
verbinden*[1] *vt irreg* (*einen Verband anlegen*) ■ **jdn ~** to dress sb's wound[s]; ■ **etw ~** to dress sth
verbinden*[2] *irreg vt* ① (*zusammenfügen*) to join (**mit** +*dat* to) ② TELEK ■ **jdn [mit jdm] ~** to connect sb [to sb]; **falsch verbunden!** wrong number! ③ TRANSP to connect, to link ④ (*verknüpfen*) to combine; **das Nützliche mit dem Angenehmen ~** to combine business with pleasure ⑤ (*assoziieren*) ■ **etw [mit etw** *dat*] ~ to associate sth [with sth]
verbindlich [fɛɐ̯·ˈbɪnt·lɪç] I. *adj* ① (*bindend*) binding ② (*entgegenkommend*) friendly II. *adv* ① (*bindend*) **~ zusagen** to make a binding commitment ② (*entgegenkommend*) in a friendly manner
Verbindung *f* ① (*direkte Beziehung*) contact; **in ~ bleiben** to keep in touch; **~en zu jdm/etw haben** to have connections *pl* with sb/sth; **sich** *akk* **mit jdm in ~ setzen** to contact sb ② TELEK connection ③ TRANSP connection (**nach** +*dat* to) ④ (*Verknüpfung*) combination; **in ~ mit etw** *dat* in conjunction with sth ⑤ (*Zusammenhang*) **jdn mit etw** *dat* **in ~ bringen** to connect sb with sth; **in ~ mit** in connection with ⑥ CHEM compound ⑦ (*für Männer*) fraternity; (*für Frauen*) sorority
verbissen I. *adj* ① (*hartnäckig*) dogged ② (*verkrampft*) grim II. *adv* doggedly
verbitten* *vr irreg* ■ **sich** *dat* **etw ~** to not tolerate sth
verbittert I. *adj* embittered, bitter II. *adv* bitterly
Verbitterung <-, *selten* -en> *f* bitterness
verblassen* *vi sein* ① (*blasser werden*) to pale ② (*schwächer werden*) to fade
Verbleib <-[e]s> [fɛɐ̯·ˈblaip] *m kein pl* (*geh*) whereabouts *npl*
verbleiben* *vi irreg sein* ① (*eine Vereinbarung treffen*) **~ wir so, dass ...?** is it agreed that ...? ② (*geh: bleiben*) to remain
verbleichen *vi irreg sein* to fade
verbleit *adj* leaded
verblöden* [fɛɐ̯·ˈbløː·dn̩] *vi sein* (*fam*) to turn into a zombie
verblüffen* [fɛɐ̯·ˈblʏ·fn̩] *vt* to astonish
verblühen* *vi sein* to wilt

V

verbluten* *vi sein* to bleed to death
verbohrt *adj* obstinate
verborgen *adj* hidden
Verbot <-[e]s, -e> [fɛɐ̯·'bo:t] *nt* ban
verboten [fɛɐ̯·'bo:·tn̩] *adj* prohibited, forbidden; **hier ist das Parken ~!** you're not allowed to park here!
Verbotsschild *nt* sign prohibiting sth
Verbrauch *m kein pl* consumption (**an** +*dat* of)
verbrauchen* *vt Vorräte* to use up *sep,* to consume *form*
Verbraucher(in) <-s, -> *m(f)* consumer
verbraucherfreundlich *adj* consumer-friendly
Verbraucherschutz *m* consumer protection
verbraucht *adj* (*aufgebraucht*) exhausted; (*Mensch a.*) burned-out *fam*
verbrechen <verbrach, verbrochen> *vt* (*fam*) to be up to
Verbrechen <-s, -> *nt* crime
Verbrecher(in) <-s, -> *m(f)* criminal
verbrecherisch *adj* criminal
verbreiten* *vt, vr* to spread
verbreitern* [fɛɐ̯·'brai·tɐn] *vt* to widen
verbreitet *adj* popular; ■**[weit] ~ sein** to be [very] widespread
Verbreitung <-, -en> *f* ① *kein pl* (*das Verbreiten*) dissemination ② MEDIA distribution ③ MED spread
verbrennen* *irreg* **I.** *vt haben* ① (*in Flammen aufgehen lassen*) to burn ② (*versengen*) to scorch **II.** *vr haben* **sich** *dat* **die Zunge ~** to burn one's tongue; **sich** *dat* **die Finger [an etw** *dat*] **~** to burn one's fingers [on sth] **III.** *vi sein* to burn; ■**verbrannt** burned
Verbrennung <-, -en> *f* ① *kein pl* (*das Verbrennen*) burning ② MED burn
verbringen* *vt irreg* to spend
verbrochen *pp von* **verbrechen**
Verbrüderung <-, -en> *f* fraternization
verbrühen* *vt* to scald
verbuchen* *vt* to mark up *sep* (**als** +*akk* as)
verbummeln* *vt* (*fam*) ① (*vertrödeln*) to waste ② (*verlieren*) to misplace
verbünden* [fɛɐ̯·'bʏn·dn̩] *vr* ■**sich** *akk* **~** to form an alliance
Verbundenheit <-> *f kein pl* closeness
Verbündete(r) *f(m) dekl wie adj* ally
verbürgen* **I.** *vr* ■**sich** *akk* **für jdn/etw ~** to vouch for sb/sth **II.** *vt* to guarantee
verbüßen* *vt* JUR to serve
verchromt *adj* chrome-plated
Verdacht <-[e]s> [fɛɐ̯·'daxt] *m kein pl* suspicion; **~ erregen** to arouse suspicion; **jdn im ~ haben** to suspect sb
verdächtig [fɛɐ̯·'dɛç·tɪç] **I.** *adj* suspicious; **jdm ~ vorkommen** to seem suspicious to sb; **sich** *akk* **~ machen** to arouse suspicion **II.** *adv* suspiciously
Verdächtige(r) *f(m) dekl wie adj* suspect
verdächtigen* [fɛɐ̯·'dɛç·tɪ·gn̩] *vt* to suspect
verdammen* [fɛɐ̯·'da·mən] *vt* to condemn
verdammt *adj* ① (*sl: Ärger ausdrückend*) damned; **~!** damn! ② (*sehr groß*) **wir hatten ~es Glück!** we were damn lucky!
verdampfen* *vi sein* to evaporate
verdanken* *vt* ① (*durch etw erhalten*) **diesen Erfolg verdanke ich dir** thanks to you, this has been a success; **es ist ihnen zu ~, wenn ...** we should thank them if ... ② SCHWEIZ (*Dank aussprechen*) ■**[jdm] etw ~** to express one's thanks [to sb]
verdarb [fɛɐ̯·'darp] *imp von* **verderben**
verdauen* [fɛɐ̯·'dau·ən] *vt* ① *Nahrung* to digest ② *Niederlage etc.* to get over
verdaulich *adj* digestible; **gut/schwer ~** easy/hard to digest
Verdauung <-> *f kein pl* digestion
Verdauungsapparat *m* digestive system
Verdauungsstörung *f meist pl* indigestion
Verdeck <-[e]s, -e> *nt* convertible top
verdecken* *vt* ① (*die Sicht nehmen*) to cover [up *sep*] ② (*maskieren*) to conceal
verdeckt *adj* ① (*geheim*) undercover ② (*verborgen*) hidden
verderben <verdarb, verdorben> [fɛɐ̯·'dɛr·bn̩] **I.** *vt haben* ① (*moralisch korrumpieren*) to corrupt ② (*ruinieren*) to ruin ③ (*zunichtemachen*) *Spaß* to spoil ④ (*verscherzen*) **sie will es mit niemandem ~** she's always trying to please everyone **II.** *vi sein* to spoil; *Lebensmittel* to go bad
Verderben <-s> [fɛɐ̯·'dɛr·bn̩] *nt kein pl* doom
verderblich [fɛɐ̯·'dɛrp·lɪç] *adj* ① (*nicht lange haltbar*) perishable ② (*unheilvoll*) corrupting
verdeutlichen* [fɛɐ̯·'dɔyt·lɪ·çn̩] *vt* to explain
verdichten* **I.** *vt* PHYS to compress **II.** *vr* ■**sich** *akk* **~** *Eindruck, Gefühl* to intensify; *Verdacht* to grow
verdienen* **I.** *vt* ① (*als Verdienst bekommen*) to earn ② (*Gewinn machen*) to make (**an** +*dat* off of) ③ (*zustehen*) to deserve **II.** *vi* ① (*einen Verdienst bekommen*) to earn [money] ② (*Gewinn machen*) to make a profit (**an** +*dat* off of)
Verdienst¹ <-[e]s, -e> [fɛɐ̯·'di:nst] *m* FIN income, earnings *npl*
Verdienst² <-[e]s, -e> [fɛɐ̯·'di:nst] *nt* merit; **es ist sein ~, dass ...** it's thanks to him [*or* to his credit] that ...
Verdienstausfall *m* loss of earnings *pl*
verdient [fɛɐ̯·'di:nt] **I.** *adj* ① (*zustehend*) well-deserved; *Strafe* rightful ② (*Verdienste aufweisend*) of outstanding merit **II.** *adv* (*leistungsgemäß*) deservedly
verdirbt [fɛɐ̯·'dɪrpt] *3. pers sing pres von* **verderben**
verdonnern* *vt* (*fam*) ■**jdn [zu etw** *dat*] **~** ① (*verurteilen*) to sentence sb [to sth] ② (*anweisen*) to order sb [to do sth]
verdoppeln* **I.** *vt* ① (*erhöhen*) to double ② (*verstärken*) to redouble **II.** *vr* ■**sich** *akk* **~** to double
Verdoppelung, Verdopplung <-, -en> *f* doubling
verdorben [fɛɐ̯·'dɔr·bn̩] **I.** *pp von* **verderben** **II.** *adj* ① (*ungenießbar*) bad ② (*moralisch korrumpiert*) corrupt ③ MED **einen ~en Magen**

haben to have an upset stomach
verdorren* [fɛɐ̯·ˈdɔ·rən] *vi sein* to wither
verdrạngen* *vt* ① (*vertreiben*) to drive out ② (*unterdrücken*) *Erinnerung, Gefühl* to suppress
Verdrạngung <-, -en> *f* ① (*Vertreibung*) driving out ② (*Unterdrückung*) suppression
verdrẹckt *adj* filthy
verdrehen* *vt* ① (*wenden*) to twist; *Augen* to roll ② *Tatsachen* to distort ▶ WENDUNGEN: **jdm den Kopf** ~ to turn sb's head
verdreifachen* [fɛɐ̯·ˈdrai·fa·xn̩] I. *vt* to triple II. *vr* ■ **sich** *akk* ~ to triple
verdrẹschen* *vt irreg* (*fam*) to beat up *sep*
verdrießlich [fɛɐ̯·ˈdriːs·lɪç] *adj* (*geh*) ① *Gesicht* sullen; *Stimmung* morose ② (*misslich*) tiresome
verdrossen [fɛɐ̯·ˈdrɔ·sn̩] *adj* sullen, morose
verdrụcken* I. *vt* (*fam: verzehren*) to polish off *sep* II. *vr* (*fam: verschwinden*) ■ **sich** *akk* ~ to slip away
Verdruss[RR] <-es, -e>, **Verdruß**[ALT] <-sses, -sse> [fɛɐ̯·ˈdrʊs] *m meist sing* annoyance; **jdm ~ bereiten** to annoy sb
verdụften* *vi sein* (*fam*) to beat it
Verdụmmung <-> *f kein pl* dumbing down
verdụnkeln* I. *vt* ① (*abdunkeln*) to black out ② (*verdüstern*) to darken II. *vr* (*dunkler werden*) ■ **sich** *akk* ~ to darken
verdünnen* [fɛɐ̯·ˈdʏ·nən] *vt* to dilute
verdụnsten* *vi sein* to evaporate
Verdụnstung <-> *f kein pl* evaporation
verdụrsten* *vi sein* to die of thirst
verdutzt [fɛɐ̯·ˈdʊtst] I. *adj* (*fam*) ① (*verwirrt*) baffled, confused ② (*überrascht*) taken aback *pred* II. *adv* in a baffled manner
verehren* *vt* ① (*bewundernd*) to admire ② REL to worship
Verehrer(in) <-s, -> *m(f)* admirer
Verehrung *f kein pl* ① (*Bewunderung*) admiration ② REL worship
vereidigen* [fɛɐ̯·ˈʔai·dɪ·gn̩] *vt* to swear in *sep*
vereidigt [fɛɐ̯·ˈʔai·dɪçt] *adj* sworn; **gerichtlich** ~ certified before the court
Vereidigung <-, -en> *f* swearing in
Verein <-[e]s, -e> [fɛɐ̯·ˈʔain] *m* club, association; **eingetragener** ~ registered association; **gemeinnütziger** ~ charitable organization
vereinbar *adj* compatible (**mit** + *dat* with)
vereinbaren* [fɛɐ̯·ˈʔain·baː·rən] *vt* ① (*absprechen*) ■ **etw** [**mit jdm**] ~ to agree to [*or* arrange] sth [with sb] ② (*in Einklang bringen*) to reconcile; ■ **sich** *akk* ~ **lassen** to be compatible
Vereinbarung <-, -en> *f* ① *kein pl* (*das Vereinbaren*) arranging ② (*Abmachung*) agreement; **laut** ~ as agreed; **nach** ~ by arrangement
vereinen* *vt* to unite
vereinfachen* [fɛɐ̯·ˈʔain·fa·xn̩] *vt* to simplify
Vereinfachung <-, -en> *f* simplification
vereinheitlichen* [fɛɐ̯·ˈʔain·hait·lɪ·çn̩] *vt* to standardize
vereinigen* I. *vt* to unite; *Firmen, Organisationen* to merge II. *vr* ■ **sich** *akk* ~ to merge
vereinigt *adj* united
Vereinigung <-, -en> *f* ① (*Organisation*) organization ② *kein pl* (*Zusammenschluss*) amalgamation
vereinsamen* [fɛɐ̯·ˈʔain·zaː·mən] *vi sein* to become lonely
vereinsamt *adj* ① (*einsam*) lonely ② (*abgeschieden*) isolated
Vereinsamung <-> *f kein pl* loneliness
vereinzelt [fɛɐ̯·ˈʔain·ts̩lt] *adj* occasional
vereisen* I. *vi sein* to ice up; **eine vereiste Fahrbahn** an icy road II. *vt haben* (*lokal anästhesieren*) to freeze
vereiteln* [fɛɐ̯·ˈʔait̩ln] *vt* to thwart
vereitern* *vi sein* to go septic
verẹnden* *vi sein* to perish
verengen* [fɛɐ̯·ˈʔɛŋ·ən] *vr* ■ **sich** *akk* ~ *Pupillen* to contract; *Gefäße* to become constricted
verẹrben* I. *vt* ■ [**jdm**] **etw** ~ ① (*hinterlassen*) to leave [sb] sth ② (*durch Vererbung weitergeben*) to pass on *sep* sth [to sb]; (*schenken*) to hand down *sep* sth [to sb] II. *vr* ■ **sich** *akk* ~ to be hereditary
verẹrblich *adj* hereditary
verewigen* [fɛɐ̯·ˈʔeːvɪ·gn̩] I. *vr* ■ **sich** *akk* ~ to leave one's mark [for posterity] II. *vt* (*unsterblich machen*) to immortalize
verfahren*[1] [fɛɐ̯·ˈʔfaː·rən] *vi irreg sein* ① (*vorgehen*) to proceed ② (*umgehen*) ■ **mit jdm** ~ to deal with sb
verfahren*[2] [fɛɐ̯·ˈʔfaː·rən] *irreg* I. *vt Benzin* to use up *sep* II. *vr* ■ **sich** *akk* ~ to get lost [while driving]
verfahren[3] [fɛɐ̯·ˈʔfaː·rən] *adj* muddled; **völlig ~ sein** to be a total mess
Verfahren <-s, -> [fɛɐ̯·ˈʔfaː·rən] *nt* ① (*Methode*) process ② (*Gerichtsverfahren*) [legal [*or* criminal]] proceedings *npl*
Verfall [fɛɐ̯·ˈfal] *m kein pl* ① (*das Verfallen*) dilapidation ② (*das Ungültigwerden*) expiration ③ (*geh: Niedergang*) decline
Verfạlldatum *nt s.* **Verfallsdatum**
verfạllen*[1] *vi irreg sein* ① (*zerfallen*) to decay ② (*immer schwächer werden*) to deteriorate ③ (*ungültig werden*) *Ticket, Gutschein* to expire; *Anspruch* to lapse ④ (*erliegen*) ■ **jdm** ~ to be captivated by sb; ■ **einer S.** *dat* ~ to become addicted to sth
verfạllen[2] *adj* ① (*völlig baufällig*) dilapidated ② (*abgelaufen*) expired
Verfạllsdatum *nt* ÖKON ① (*der Haltbarkeit*) use-by date ② (*der Gültigkeit*) expiration date
verfälschen* *vt* ① (*falsch darstellen*) to distort ② (*in der Qualität mindern*) to adulterate (**durch** + *akk* with)
Verfälschung *f* ① (*das Verfälschen*) distortion ② (*Qualitätsminderung*) adulteration
verfänglich [fɛɐ̯·ˈfɛŋ·lɪç] *adj* embarrassing
verfärben* I. *vr* ■ **sich** *akk* ~ to change color; *Wäsche* to discolor II. *vt* to discolor
verfạssen* *vt* to write; *Gesetz, Urkunde* to draw up

V

Verfasser(in) <-s, -> [fɛɐ̯·ˈfa·sɐ] *m(f)* author

Verfassung *f* ① *kein pl* (*Zustand*) condition; (*körperlich*) state [of health]; (*seelisch*) state [of mind] ② POL constitution

Verfassungsgericht *nt* constitutional court

Verfassungsschutz *m* domestic intelligence agency

verfassungswidrig *adj* unconstitutional

verfaulen* *vi sein* to rot

Verfechter(in) *m(f)* advocate, champion

verfehlen* *vt* ① (*nicht treffen, verpassen*) to miss; ■**nicht zu ~ sein** to be impossible to miss ② (*nicht erreichen*) to not achieve; **das Thema ~** to be off the subject; **seinen Beruf ~** to miss one's calling

verfehlt *adj* ① (*misslungen*) unsuccessful ② (*unangebracht*) inappropriate

verfeinden* [fɛɐ̯·ˈfain·dn̩] *vr* ■**sich** *akk* ~ to fall out; ■**verfeindet sein** to be enemies; **verfeindete Staaten** enemy states

verfeinern* [fɛɐ̯·ˈfai·nɐn] *vt* ① KOCHK to improve ② (*raffinierter gestalten*) to refine

verfilmen* *vt* to film

Verfilmung <-, -en> *f* ① *kein pl* (*das Verfilmen*) filming ② (*Film*) film

verfinstern* [fɛɐ̯·ˈfɪns·tɐn] *vr* ■**sich** *akk* ~ to darken

Verflechtung <-, -en> *f* interconnection

verfliegen* *irreg* **I.** *vi sein* ① *Zorn* to pass; *Kummer* to vanish ② *Geruch* to evaporate **II.** *vr haben* ■**sich** *akk* ~ *Pilot* to lose one's bearings *pl; Flugzeug* to stray off course

verflixt [fɛɐ̯·ˈflɪkst] **I.** *adj* (*fam*) ① (*verdammt*) damn[ed] ② (*ärgerlich*) unpleasant **II.** *adv* (*fam: ziemlich*) damn[ed]

verfluchen* *vt* to curse

verflucht I. *adj* (*fam*) damn[ed] **II.** *adv* (*fam*) damn[ed]

verflüchtigen* [fɛɐ̯·ˈflʏç·tɪ·gn̩] *vr* ■**sich** *akk* ~ to evaporate

verflüssigen* [fɛɐ̯·ˈflʏ·sɪ·gn̩] *vt, vr* to liquefy

verfolgen* *vt* ① (*nachgehen*) to follow ② (*aus politischen etc. Gründen*) to persecute ③ (*zu erreichen suchen*) to pursue; **eine Absicht ~** to have sth in mind ④ (*belasten*) **vom Pech verfolgt sein** to be dogged by bad luck

Verfolger(in) <-s, -> *m(f)* pursuer

Verfolgte(r) [fɛɐ̯·ˈfɔlk·tə, -tɐ] *f(m) dekl wie adj* victim of persecution

Verfolgung <-, -en> *f* ① (*das Verfolgen*) pursuit ② (*aus politischen Gründen*) persecution ③ JUR prosecution

Verfolgungsjagd *f* pursuit, chase

Verfolgungswahn *m* persecution complex

verformen* **I.** *vt* to distort **II.** *vr* ■**sich** *akk* ~ to become distorted [*or* misshapen]

verfremden *vt* to alienate

Verfremdung <-, -en> *f* alienation

verfressen* *adj* (*pej sl*) [overly] greedy

verfrüht *adj* premature

verfügbar *adj* available

verfügen* **I.** *vi* ■**über etw** *akk* ~ to have sth at one's disposal **II.** *vt* (*anordnen*) to order

Verfügung <-, -en> *f* ① (*Anordnung*) order; **einstweilige ~** JUR temporary injunction ② (*Disposition*) ■**etw zur ~ haben** to have sth at one's disposal; ■**jdm zur ~ stehen** to be available to sb; ■**[jdm] etw zur ~ stellen** to make sth available [to sb]

verführen* *vt* ① (*verleiten*) to entice; (*sexuell*) to seduce ② (*hum: verlocken*) to tempt

Verführer(in) *m(f)* seducer *masc,* seductress *fem*

verführerisch [fɛɐ̯·ˈfyː·rə·rɪʃ] *adj* ① (*verlockend*) tempting ② (*aufreizend*) seductive

Verführung *f* ① (*Verleitung*) seduction; **~ Minderjähriger** JUR seduction of minors ② (*Verlockung*) temptation

Vergabe [fɛɐ̯·ˈgaː·bə] *f von Arbeit, Studienplätzen* allocation; *eines Auftrags, Preises* award

vergammeln* *vi sein Essen* to go bad

vergammelt <-er, -este> *adj* (*fam*) scruffy

vergangen *adj* past, former

Vergangenheit <-, *selten* -en> [fɛɐ̯·ˈgaŋən·hait] *f* ① *kein pl* (*Vergangenes*) past ② LING past [tense]

vergänglich [fɛɐ̯·ˈgɛŋ·lɪç] *adj* transient

Vergänglichkeit <-> *f kein pl* transience

vergasen* *vt* to gas

Vergaser <-s, -> *m* AUTO carburetor

vergaß [fɛɐ̯·ˈgaːs] *imp von* **vergessen**

vergeben* *irreg* **I.** *vi* to forgive **II.** *vt* ① (*verzeihen*) to forgive ② (*zuteilen*) to allocate sth (**an** +*akk* to); *Preis, Auftrag* to award

vergebens [fɛɐ̯·ˈgeː·bn̩s] **I.** *adj pred* in vain *pred* **II.** *adv s.* **vergeblich**

vergeblich [fɛɐ̯·ˈgeːp·lɪç] **I.** *adj* (*erfolglos bleibend*) futile **II.** *adv* (*umsonst*) in vain

Vergebung <-, -en> *f* forgiveness

vergehen* [fɛɐ̯·ˈgeː·ən] *irreg* **I.** *vi sein* ① (*verstreichen*) to go by, to pass ② (*schwinden*) to wear off; **igitt! da vergeht einem ja der Appetit** yuck! it's enough to make you lose your appetite ③ (*sich zermürben*) to die (**vor** +*dat* of); **vor Sehnsucht ~** to pine away **II.** *vr haben* ■**sich** *akk* **an jdm ~** to sexually assault sb

Vergehen <-s, -> [fɛɐ̯·ˈgeː·ən] *nt* offense

vergelten *vt irreg* ■**[jdm] etw ~** to repay sb for sth

Vergeltung <-, -en> *f* revenge

Vergeltungsmaßnahme *f* reprisal

Vergeltungsschlag *m* retaliatory strike

vergessen <vergisst, vergaß, vergessen> [fɛɐ̯·ˈgɛ·sn̩] **I.** *vt* ① (*nicht mehr daran denken*) to forget; **nicht zu ~ ...** keep [*or* bear] in mind that ... ② (*liegen lassen*) to leave behind **II.** *vr* (*die Beherrschung verlieren*) ■**sich** *akk* ~ to lose oneself

Vergessenheit <-> *f kein pl* oblivion

vergesslichRR, **vergeßlich**ALT [fɛɐ̯·ˈgɛs·lɪç] *adj* forgetful

VergesslichkeitRR <-> *f kein pl* forgetfulness

vergeuden* [fɛɐ̯·ˈgɔy·dn̩] *vt* to waste

vergewaltigen* [fɛɐ̯·gə·ˈval·tɪ·gn̩] *vt* to rape

Vergewaltigung <-, -en> *f* rape

vergewissern* [fɛɐ̯·gə·ˈvɪ·sn̩] *vr* ■ **sich** *akk* **~, dass ...** to make sure that ...
vergießen* *vt irreg* ① (*danebengießen*) to spill ② *Tränen, Blut* to shed
vergiften* *vt* to poison
Vergiftung <-, -en> *f kein pl* poisoning
vergilbt *adj* yellowed
Vergissmeinnicht[RR], **Vergißmeinnicht**[ALT] <-[e]s, -[e]> [fɛɐ̯·ˈgɪs·main·nɪçt] *nt* forget-me-not
vergisst[RR], **vergißt**[ALT] [fɛɐ̯·ˈgɪst] *3. pers sing pres von* **vergessen**
Vergleich <-[e]s, -e> [fɛɐ̯·ˈglaiç] *m* comparison; **im ~ [zu jdm/etw]** in comparison [with sb/sth], compared to [sb/sth] ▶WENDUNGEN: **der ~ hinkt** that's a poor comparison
vergleichbar *adj* comparable (**mit** +*dat* to/with)
vergleichen* *irreg vt* to compare (**mit** +*dat* to/with)
vergleichsweise *adv* comparatively; **das ist ~ wenig/viel** that is a little/a lot in comparison
vergnügen* [fɛɐ̯·ˈgny:·gn̩] *vr* ■ **sich** *akk* **~** to amuse [*or* enjoy] oneself
Vergnügen <-s, -> [fɛɐ̯·ˈgny:·gn̩] *nt* (*Freude*) enjoyment; (*Genuss*) pleasure ▶WENDUNGEN: **viel ~!** have a good time!
vergnügt [fɛɐ̯·ˈgny:kt] **I.** *adj* happy, cheerful **II.** *adv* happily, cheerfully
Vergnügungspark *m* amusement park
vergolden* [fɛɐ̯·ˈgɔl·dn̩] *vt* to gold-plate
vergöttern* [fɛɐ̯·ˈgœ·tɐn] *vt* to idolize
vergraben* *irreg* **I.** *vt* to bury **II.** *vr* ■ **sich** *akk* **in Arbeit ~** to bury oneself in work
vergrämt *adj* troubled
vergraulen* *vt* (*fam*) to scare away
vergreifen* *vr irreg* ① (*stehlen*) ■ **sich** *akk* **an etw** *dat* **~** to steal sth ② (*Gewalt antun*) ■ **sich** *akk* **an jdm ~** to assault sb ③ (*sich unpassend ausdrücken*) ■ **sich** *akk* **im Ton ~** to adopt the wrong tone
vergreisen [fɛɐ̯·ˈgrai·zn̩] *vi sein* ① (*senil werden*) to become senile ② *Bevölkerung* to age
vergriffen *adj Buch* out of print *pred; Ware* unavailable
vergrößern [fɛɐ̯·ˈgrø:·sɐn] **I.** *vt* ① *Fläche, Umfang* to extend, to enlarge (**um** +*akk* by, **auf** +*akk* to) ② *Distanz* to increase ③ *Firma* to expand ④ (*größer erscheinen lassen*) to magnify ⑤ FOTO to enlarge, to blow up *sep* **II.** *vr* ■ **sich** *akk* **~** (*anschwellen*) to become enlarged
Vergrößerung <-, -en> *f* ① (*das Vergrößern*) enlargement, increase; *einer Firma* expansion; (*technisch*) magnification ② (*vergrößertes Foto*) enlargement, blowup ③ (*Anschwellung*) enlargement
Vergrößerungsglas *m* magnifying glass
vergünstigt [fɛɐ̯·ˈgʏns·tɪçt] *adj* cheaper
Vergünstigung <-, -en> *f* ① (*finanzieller Vorteil*) perk ② (*Ermäßigung*) reduction, concession
vergüten* [fɛɐ̯·ˈgy:·tn̩] *vt* ■ **[jdm] etw ~** ① (*ersetzen*) to reimburse sb for sth ② (*bezahlen*) to pay sb for sth
Vergütung <-, -en> *f* ① (*das Ersetzen*) refund, reimbursement ② (*Geldsumme*) payment, remuneration; (*Honorar*) fee
verhaften* *vt* to arrest; **Sie sind verhaftet!** you're under arrest!
Verhaftete(r) *f(m) dekl wie adj* person under arrest
Verhaftung <-, -en> *f* arrest
verhallen* *vi sein* to fade away
verhalten*[1] [fɛɐ̯·ˈhal·tn̩] *vr irreg* ■ **sich** *akk* **~** ① (*sich benehmen*) to behave ② (*beschaffen sein*) to be; **die Sache verhält sich anders, als du denkst** it's not what you think
verhalten[2] [fɛɐ̯·ˈhal·tn̩] **I.** *adj* ① (*zurückhaltend*) restrained ② (*unterdrückt*) suppressed **II.** *adv* in a restrained manner
Verhalten <-s> [fɛɐ̯·ˈhal·tn̩] *nt kein pl* behavior
Verhaltensforschung *f kein pl* behavioral research
verhaltensgestört *adj* disturbed
Verhaltensstörung *f meist pl* behavioral problem
Verhaltensweise *f* behavior
Verhältnis <-ses, -se> [fɛɐ̯·ˈhɛlt·nɪs] *nt* ① (*Relation*) ratio; **in keinem ~ zu etw** *dat* **stehen** to bear no relation to sth; **im ~** in a ratio (**von** +*dat* of, **zu** +*dat* to); **im ~ [zu jdm]** compared to [sb] ② (*persönliche Beziehung*) relationship (**zu** +*dat* with); (*Affäre*) affair ③ *pl* (*Bedingungen*) conditions *pl* ④ *pl* (*Lebensumstände*) circumstances *pl;* **über seine ~se** *pl* **leben** to live beyond one's means *pl;* **klare ~se schaffen** to get things straightened out
verhältnismäßig *adv* relatively
Verhältniswort *nt* LING preposition
verhandeln* **I.** *vi* to negotiate **II.** *vt* ① (*aushandeln*) to negotiate ② JUR to hear
Verhandlung *f* ① *meist pl* (*das Verhandeln*) negotiations *npl* ② JUR trial, hearing
verhängen* *vt* ① (*zuhängen*) to cover (**mit** +*dat* with) ② SPORT (*aussprechen*) to award ③ (*verfügen*) to impose; *Ausnahmezustand* to declare
Verhängnis <-, -se> [fɛɐ̯·ˈhɛŋ·nɪs] *nt* disaster; **jdm zum ~ werden** to be sb's undoing
verhängnisvoll *adj* disastrous, fatal
verharmlosen* [fɛɐ̯·ˈharm·lo:·zn̩] *vt* to play down *sep*
Verharmlosung <-, -en> *f* playing down
verharren* *vi sein o haben* (*geh*) to pause
verhärten* **I.** *vt* to harden **II.** *vr* ■ **sich** *akk* **~** to become hardened
verhaspeln* *vr* ■ **sich** *akk* **~** to get [all] mixed up
verhasst[RR], **verhaßt**[ALT] [fɛɐ̯·ˈhast] *adj* hated
verhätscheln *vt* to spoil, to pamper
verhauen* <verhaute, verhauen> **I.** *vt* (*fam*) ① (*verprügeln*) to beat up *sep* ② SCH **ich habe den Aufsatz [gründlich] ~!** I've made a [complete] mess of the essay! **II.** *vr* (*fam: sich verkal-*

kulieren) ■**sich** *akk* ~ to slip up

verheddern* [fɛɐ̯ˈhɛ·dɐn] *vr* ■**sich** *akk* ~ ① (*sich verfangen*) to get tangled up ② (*sich versprechen*) to get [all] mixed up

verheerend I. *adj* devastating **II.** *adv* devastatingly; **sich** *akk* ~ **auswirken** to have a devastating effect

verheilen* *vi sein* to heal [up]

verheimlichen* [fɛɐ̯ˈhaim·lɪ·çn̩] *vt* ■[**jdm**] **etw** ~ to conceal sth [*or* keep sth secret] [from sb]; **ich habe nichts zu** ~ I have nothing to hide

verheiratet *adj* married; ■[**mit jdm**] ~ **sein** to be married [to sb]

verheißen* *vt irreg* to promise

verheißungsvoll I. *adj* promising; **wenig** ~ not very promising **II.** *adv* full of promise

verhelfen* *vi irreg* ■**jdm zu etw** *dat* ~ to help sb [to] achieve sth

verherrlichen* [fɛɐ̯ˈhɛr·lɪ·çn̩] *vt* to glorify

Verherrlichung <-, -en> *f* glorification

verheult *adj Augen* swollen from crying

verhexen* *vt* to bewitch

verhindern* *vt* to prevent

verhindert *adj* ■~ **sein** to be unable to come

verhöhnen* *vt* to mock

verhökern* *vt* (*fam*) to get rid of

Verhör <-[e]s, -e> [fɛɐ̯ˈhøːɐ̯] *nt* questioning, interrogation

verhören* **I.** *vt* (*offiziell befragen*) to question, to interrogate **II.** *vr* (*falsch hören*) ■**sich** *akk* ~ to mishear, to not hear correctly

verhüllen* *vt* to cover

verhungern* *vi sein* to starve [to death]

verhüten* *vt* to prevent; *Schwangerschaft* to use contraception

Verhütung <-, -en> *f* ① (*das Verhindern*) prevention ② (*Empfängnisverhütung*) contraception

Verhütungsmittel *nt* contraceptive

verifizieren* [ve·ri·fi·ˈtsiː·rən] *vt* to verify

verirren* *vr* ■**sich** *akk* ~ to get lost

verjagen* *vt* to chase away *sep*

verjähren* *vi sein* to pass the statute of limitations; ■**verjährt** barred by the statute of limitations

Verjährungsfrist *f* statute of limitations

verjubeln* *vt* to blow

verjüngen* [fɛɐ̯ˈjʏŋən] **I.** *vi* (*vitalisieren*) to make one feel younger **II.** *vt Haut* to rejuvenate **III.** *vr* ■**sich** *akk* ~ (*schmaler werden*) to narrow

Verjüngung <-, -en> *f* rejuvenation

verkabeln* *vt* to connect to the cable network

Verkabelung <-, -en> *f* connecting to the cable network

verkalken* *vi sein* ① (*Kalk einlagern*) to clog up; ■**verkalkt** clogged up ② *Arterien* to harden

verkalkulieren* *vr* ■**sich** *akk* ~ ① (*sich verrechnen*) to miscalculate ② (*sich irren*) to be mistaken

Verkalkung <-, -en> *f* ① (*das Verkalken*) clogging ② *von Arterien* hardening

verkannt *adj* unrecognized

verkappt *adj attr* disguised; **ein ~er Kommunist** a communist in disguise

verkatert [fɛɐ̯ˈkaː·tɐt] *adj* (*fam*) hung-over *pred*

Verkauf <-s, Verkäufe> [fɛɐ̯ˈkauf, *pl* fɛɐ̯ˈkɔy·fə] *m* ① (*das Verkaufen*) sale, selling; **zum ~ stehen** to be [up] for sale ② *kein pl* (*Verkaufsabteilung*) sales *no art, + sing/pl vb*

verkaufen* **I.** *vt* to sell (**an** +*akk* to); **zu ~ sein** to be for sale **II.** *vr* ■**sich** *akk* ~ to sell; **das Buch verkauft sich gut** the book is selling well

Verkäufer(in) [fɛɐ̯ˈkɔy·fɐ] *m(f)* ① (*in Geschäft*) sales assistant ② (*verkaufender Eigentümer*) seller; JUR vendor

verkäuflich *adj* for sale *pred*

Verkaufspreis *m* retail price

Verkaufszahlen *pl* sales figures *pl*

Verkehr <-[e]s> [fɛɐ̯ˈkeːɐ̯] *m kein pl* ① (*Straßenverkehr*) traffic ② (*Umgang*) contact, dealings *pl* ③ (*Handel*) **etw aus dem ~ ziehen** to withdraw sth from circulation ④ (*Geschlechtsverkehr*) intercourse

verkehren* **I.** *vi* ① *sein o haben* (*fahren*) to run; **der Zug verkehrt nur zweimal am Tag** the train only runs twice a day ② *haben* (*häufiger Gast sein*) to visit regularly ③ *haben* (*Umgang pflegen*) ■[**mit jdm**] ~ to associate [with sb] **II.** *vr haben* (*sich umkehren*) ■**sich** *akk* **in etw** *akk* ~ to turn into sth

Verkehrsampel *f* traffic lights *pl*

verkehrsberuhigt *adj* traffic-calmed

Verkehrschaos *nt* traffic mess

Verkehrsfunk *m* traffic report

verkehrsgünstig *adj* close to public transportation

Verkehrshinweis *m* traffic announcement

Verkehrskontrolle *f* police checkpoint

Verkehrslage *f* traffic [conditions *pl*]

Verkehrsmittel *nt* means + *sing/pl vb* of transportation; **öffentliches/privates** ~ public/private transportation

Verkehrsnetz *nt* transportation system

Verkehrspolizei *f* traffic police

Verkehrsregel *f* traffic regulation

Verkehrsschild *nt* traffic sign

verkehrssicher *adj Fahrzeug* safe; (*bes. Auto*) roadworthy

Verkehrssünder(in) *m(f)* (*fam*) traffic offender

Verkehrstote(r) *f(m) dekl wie adj* traffic fatality

Verkehrsverein *m* tourist [information] office

verkehrswidrig *adj* in violation of traffic regulations *pl*

Verkehrszeichen *nt s.* **Verkehrsschild**

verkehrt I. *adj* (*falsch*) wrong; **die ~e Richtung** the wrong direction; ■**der V~e** the wrong person **II.** *adv* wrong; ~ **herum** the wrong way around

verkennen* *vt irreg* (*falsch einschätzen*) to misjudge

V

verklagen* *vt* ■ **jdn** ~ to take sb to court; **jdn auf Schadenersatz** ~ to sue sb for damages

verkleiden* **I.** *vt* ① (*kostümieren*) to dress up *sep* ② (*überdecken*) to cover; (*innen*) to line **II.** *vr* ■ **sich** *akk* ~ to dress up

Verkleidung *f* ① (*zur Tarnung*) disguise; (*Kostüm*) costume ② (*Auskleidung*) lining

verkleinern* [fɛɐ̯ˈklai̯·nɐn] **I.** *vt* ① (*verringern*) to reduce ② FOTO to reduce; COMPUT to scale down **II.** *vr* ■ **sich** *akk* ~ ① (*sich verringern*) to be reduced in size ② (*schrumpfen*) to shrink

Verkleinerung <-, -en> *f* reduction

Verkleinerungsform *f* LING diminutive [form]

verklemmt *adj* uptight [about sex *pred*]

verklingen* *vi irreg sein* to fade away

verknacksen* *vt* **sich** *akk* **den Fuß** ~ to sprain one's ankle

verknallen* *vr* (*fam*) ■ **sich** *akk* ~ to fall head over heels in love (**in** +*akk* with)

Verknappung *f* shortage

verkneifen* *vr irreg* (*fam*) ■ **sich** *dat* **etw** ~ ① (*nicht offen zeigen*) to repress sth; **ich konnte mir ein Grinsen nicht** ~ I couldn't help grinning ② (*sich versagen*) to do without sth

verknittern* *vt* to crumple

verknoten* *vt* ■ **etw miteinander** ~ to knot together *sep* sth

verknüpfen* *vt* ① (*verknoten*) to tie [together *sep*] ② (*verbinden*) to combine ③ (*in Zusammenhang bringen*) to link (**mit** +*dat* to)

Verknüpfung <-, -en> *f* ① (*Verbindung*) combination ② (*Zusammenhang*) link, connection

verkochen* *vi sein* to get mushy *fam*

verkommen*[1] *vi irreg sein* ① (*verwahrlosen*) to decay; *Mensch* to go downhill ② (*herunterkommen*) to go to the dogs; ■ **zu etw** *dat* ~ to degenerate into sth

verkommen[2] *adj* ① (*verwahrlost*) degenerate ② (*im Verfall begriffen*) dilapidated

verkorksen* [fɛɐ̯ˈkɔrk·sn̩] *vt* (*fam*) ■ **etw/jdn** ~ to screw up *sep* sb/sth

verkorkst <-er, -este> *adj* screwed-up; *Magen* upset

verkörpern* [fɛɐ̯ˈkœr·pɐn] *vt* ① FILM, THEAT to play [the part of] ② (*personifizieren*) to personify

Verkörperung <-, -en> *f* ① *kein pl* FILM, THEAT portrayal ② (*Inbegriff*) personification ③ (*Abbild*) embodiment

verköstigen* [fɛɐ̯ˈkœs·tɪ·gn̩] *vt bes* ÖSTERR ■ **jdn** ~ to cater for sb

verkrachen* *vr* (*fam*) ■ **sich** *akk* ~ to fall out

verkracht *adj* (*fam*) failed

verkraften* [fɛɐ̯ˈkraf·tn̩] *vt* ■ **etw** ~ to cope with sth

verkrampfen* *vr* ■ **sich** *akk* ~ ① (*zusammenkrümmen*) to cramp [up] ② (*sich anspannen*) to tense [up]

verkrampft **I.** *adj* tense **II.** *adv* tensely

verkriechen* *vr irreg* ■ **sich** *akk* ~ to crawl away

V

verkrüppelt <-er, -este> *adj* ① *Pflanzen* stunted ② *Mensch, Körperteil* crippled

verkümmern* *vi sein* ① (*eingehen*) to [shrivel up and] die ② (*verloren gehen*) to wither away ③ (*die Lebenslust verlieren*) to waste away

verkünden* *vt* to announce; **ein Urteil** ~ to pronounce sentence; **Gutes/Unheil** ~ to bode/not bode well

verkündigen* *vt* to proclaim

Verkündigung *f* (*geh*) ① (*das Verkündigen*) announcement ② (*Proklamation*) proclamation

Verkündung <-, -en> *f* announcement; *von Urteil* pronouncement

verkuppeln* *vt* to pair off *sep*

verkürzen* **I.** *vt* ① (*kürzer machen*) to shorten (**auf** +*akk* to, **um** +*akk* by) ② (*zeitlich vermindern*) to reduce (**auf** +*akk* to, **um** +*akk* by); *Urlaub* to cut short *sep* **II.** *vr* ■ **sich** *akk* ~ to become shorter

Verkürzung *f* ① (*das Verkürzen*) shortening, cutting short ② (*zeitliche Verminderung*) reduction

verladen* *vt irreg* to load

Verladung *f* loading

Verlag <-[e]s, -e> [fɛɐ̯ˈlaːk, *pl* -ˈlaː·gə] *m* publisher, publishing house

verlagern* *vt* to move; **den Schwerpunkt** ~ to shift the emphasis

verlangen* **I.** *vt* ① (*fordern*) to demand (**von** +*dat* of); *Preis* to ask ② (*erfordern*) to require ③ (*erwarten*) to expect; **das ist nicht zu viel verlangt** that is not too much to expect **II.** *vi* ■ **nach etw** *dat* ~ ① (*fordern*) to demand sth ② (*um etw bitten*) to ask for sth

Verlangen <-s, -> *nt* ① (*dringender Wunsch*) desire (**nach** +*dat* for) ② (*Forderung*) demand; **auf** ~ [up]on demand; **auf ihr** ~ **[hin]** at her request

verlängern* [fɛɐ̯ˈlɛŋɐn] **I.** *vt* ① (*länger machen*) to lengthen, to extend (**um** +*akk* by) ② (*länger dauern lassen*) to extend; *Leben* to prolong; *Vertrag* to renew **II.** *vr* ■ **sich** *akk* ~ to increase (**um** +*akk* by), to become longer (**um** +*akk* by); *Leben, Leid* to be prolonged

Verlängerung <-, -en> *f* ① *kein pl* (*räumlich*) lengthening; (*durch ein Zusatzteil*) extension ② *kein pl* (*zeitliche*) extension ③ SPORT overtime

Verlängerungskabel *nt,* **Verlängerungsschnur** *f* extension cord

verlangsamen* [fɛɐ̯ˈlaŋ·zaː·mən] **I.** *vt* to slow down *sep* **II.** *vr* ■ **sich** *akk* ~ to slow [down]

Verlass[RR] <-es>, **Verlaß**[ALT] <-sses> [fɛɐ̯ˈlas] *m kein pl* ■ **auf jdn ist/ist kein** ~ you can/cannot rely on sb

verlassen*[1] *irreg* **I.** *vt* ① (*im Stich lassen*) to abandon ② (*hinausgehen, fortgehen*) to leave ③ (*verloren gehen*) ■ **jdn** ~ to desert sb; **der Mut verließ ihn** he lost [his] courage **II.** *vr* ■ **sich** *akk* **auf jdn/etw** ~ to rely on sb/sth; **worauf du dich** ~ **kannst!** you bet!, I guaran-

tee it!
verlassen[2] *adj* deserted; (*verwahrlost*) desolate
verlässlich[RR], **verläßlich**[ALT] [fɛɐ̯ˈlɛs·lɪç] *adj* reliable
Verlauf [fɛɐ̯ˈlauf] *m* course; **einen guten ~ nehmen** to go well; **im ~ der nächsten Monate** over the course of the next few months
verlaufen* *irreg* **I.** *vi sein* ❶ (*ablaufen*) **das Gespräch verlief nicht wie erhofft** the discussion didn't go as hoped ❷ (*sich erstrecken*) to run **II.** *vr* ■ **sich** *akk* ~ ❶ (*sich verirren*) to get lost ❷ (*auseinandergehen*) to disperse; (*panisch*) to scatter
Verlaufsform *f* LING continuous form
verleben* *vt* to spend
verlebt *adj* ruined, haggard
verlegen*[1] [fɛɐ̯ˈleː·gn̩] *vt* ❶ *Schlüssel etc.* to misplace ❷ *Termin* to postpone (**auf** +*akk* until) ❸ *Gleise, Teppich, Kabel* to lay ❹ *Buch* to publish ❺ *Patient, Abteilung* to transfer
verlegen[2] [fɛɐ̯ˈleː·gn̩] **I.** *adj* embarrassed; **er ist nie um eine Entschuldigung ~** he's never lost for an excuse **II.** *adv* in embarrassment
Verlegenheit <-, -en> *f kein pl* embarrassment
Verleger(in) <-s, -> *m(f)* publisher
Verlegung <-, -en> *f* ❶ (*Verschiebung*) rescheduling; (*auf einen späteren Zeitpunkt*) postponement ❷ TECH installation, laying ❸ (*Ortswechsel*) transfer
Verleih <-[e]s, -e> [fɛɐ̯ˈlai] *m* ❶ (*Unternehmen*) rental company ❷ *kein pl* (*das Verleihen*) renting out
verleihen* *vt irreg* ❶ (*verborgen*) to lend (**an** +*akk* to); (*gegen Geld*) to rent out *sep* ❷ (*jdn mit etw auszeichnen*) **jdm einen Preis ~** to award sb a prize ❸ (*geben*) to give; **die Wut verlieh ihm neue Kräfte** anger gave him new strength
Verleihung <-, -en> *f* ❶ (*das Verleihen*) lending; (*für Geld*) renting out ❷ (*Zuerkennung*) award
verleiten* *vt* ■ **jdn [zu etw** *dat*] ~ ❶ (*dazu bringen*) to persuade sb [to do sth] ❷ (*verführen*) to entice sb [to do sth]
verlernen* *vt* to forget; **das Tanzen ~** to forget how to dance
verlesen*[1] *irreg* **I.** *vt* (*vorlesen*) to read [aloud *sep*] **II.** *vr* ■ **sich** *akk* ~ to read sth wrong
verlesen*[2] *vt irreg* (*aussortieren*) to sort
verletzbar *adj s.* **verletzlich**
verletzen* [fɛɐ̯ˈlɛtsn̩] *vt* ❶ (*verwunden*) ■ **[sich/etw** *akk*] ~ to injure [*or* hurt] [oneself/sth] ❷ (*kränken*) to offend; *Gefühle* to hurt ❸ (*übertreten*) to violate
verletzend *adj* hurtful
verletzlich *adj* vulnerable
Verletzte(r) *f(m) dekl wie adj* injured person; (*Opfer*) casualty; ■ **die ~n** the injured + *pl vb*
Verletzung <-, -en> *f* ❶ MED injury ❷ *kein pl* (*Übertretung*) violation
verleugnen* *vt* to deny
verleumden* [fɛɐ̯ˈlɔym·dn̩] *vt* to slander; (*schriftlich*) to libel
Verleumdung <-, -en> *f* slander, libel
Verleumdungskampagne *f* smear campaign
verlieben* *vr* ■ **sich** *akk* ~ to fall in love (**in** +*akk* with); (*für jdn schwärmen*) to have a crush on sb
verliebt *adj* infatuated; ■ **~ sein** to be in love (**in** +*akk* with)
verlieren <verlor, verloren> [fɛɐ̯ˈliː·rən] **I.** *vt* to lose ▸ WENDUNGEN: **du hast hier nichts verloren** (*fam*) you have no business being here **II.** *vr* ■ **sich** *akk* ~ to disappear
Verlierer(in) <-s, -> *m(f)* loser
Verlies <-es, -e> [fɛɐ̯ˈliːs, *pl* ˈliː·zə] *nt* dungeon
verlinken* [fɛɐ̯ˈlɪŋ·kən] *vt* ■ **etw mit etw** *dat* ~ INET to link sth to sth
verloben* *vr* ■ **sich** *akk* ~ to get engaged (**mit** +*dat* to)
Verlobte(r) *f(m) dekl wie adj* fiancé *masc*, fiancée *fem*
Verlobung <-, -en> *f* engagement
verlocken* *vi* to tempt
verlockend *adj* tempting
Verlockung <-, -en> *f* temptation
verlogen [fɛɐ̯ˈloː·gn̩] *adj* ❶ (*lügnerisch*) lying *attr;* ~ **sein** *Behauptung* to be a lie; *Mensch* to be a liar ❷ (*heuchlerisch*) insincere, phony
verlor [fɛɐ̯ˈloːɐ̯] *imp von* **verlieren**
verloren [fɛɐ̯ˈloː·rən] **I.** *pp von* **verlieren** **II.** *adj* ■ **~ sein** to be finished; **sich ~ fühlen** to feel lost; ~ **gehen** to get lost
verlosen* *vt* to raffle
Verlosung *f* raffle, drawing
Verlust <-[e]s, -e> [fɛɐ̯ˈlʊst] *m* loss; **~e machen** to be losing money
vermachen* *vt* to bequeath
Vermächtnis <-ses, -se> [fɛɐ̯ˈmɛçt·nɪs] *nt* legacy
vermählen* [fɛɐ̯ˈmɛː·lən] *vr* ■ **sich** *akk* [**mit jdm**] ~ to marry [sb] *attr*
Vermählung <-, -en> *f* (*geh*) marriage, wedding
vermarkten* *vt* to market
Vermarktung <-, -en> *f* marketing
vermasseln* [fɛɐ̯ˈma·sl̩n] *vt* to mess up *sep*
vermehren* *vr* ■ **sich** *akk* ~ ❶ (*sich fortpflanzen*) to reproduce; (*stärker*) to multiply ❷ (*zunehmen*) to increase (**um** +*akk* by)
Vermehrung <-, -en> *f* ❶ (*Fortpflanzung*) reproduction; (*stärker*) multiplying ❷ (*das Anwachsen*) increase
vermeidbar *adj* avoidable
vermeiden* *vt irreg* to avoid; **sich nicht ~ lassen** to be inevitable
vermeintlich [fɛɐ̯ˈmaint·lɪç] **I.** *adj attr* supposed *attr* **II.** *adv* supposedly
Vermerk <-[e]s, -e> [fɛɐ̯ˈmɛrk] *m* note
vermerken* *vt* to make note of
vermessen*[1] [fɛɐ̯ˈmɛ·sn̩] *irreg* **I.** *vt* to measure; *Grundstück, Gebäude* to survey **II.** *vr* ■ **sich** *akk* ~ to measure [sth] wrong

V

vermessen[2] [fɛɐ̯·ˈmɛ·sn̩] *adj* presumptuous
Vermessenheit <-, -en> *f* presumption
vermiesen* [fɛɐ̯·ˈmiː·zn̩] *vt* (*fam*) ■[jdm] etw ~ to spoil sth [for sb]
vermieten* *vt* to rent out *sep* (**an** +*akk* to); **„zu ~“** “for rent”
Vermieter(in) *m(f)* landlord *masc,* landlady *fem*
vermindern* I. *vt* to reduce II. *vr* ■**sich** *akk* ~ to decrease, to diminish
Verminderung *f* reduction, decrease
vermischen* I. *vt* to mix; (*um eine bestimmte Qualität zu erreichen*) to blend II. *vr* ■**sich** *akk* [**miteinander**] ~ to mix
vermissen* *vt* ❶ (*das Fehlen bemerken*) ■**etw** ~ to have lost sth ❷ (*jds Abwesenheit bedauern*) ■**jdn** ~ to miss sb ❸ (*jds Abwesenheit feststellen*) **wir ~ unsere Tochter** our daughter is missing
Vermisstenanzeige[RR] *f* **eine ~ aufgeben** to report sb [as] missing
Vermisste(r)[RR], **Vermißte(r)**[ALT] *f(m) dekl wie adj* missing person
vermittelbar *adj* employable; **ältere Arbeitnehmer sind kaum mehr ~** it is almost impossible to find jobs for older people
vermitteln* I. *vt* ❶ (*beschaffen*) **jdm eine Stellung ~** to find sb a job; **jdn an eine Firma ~** to place sb with a company ❷ (*weitergeben*) to pass on *sep;* **jdm ein schönes Gefühl ~** to give sb a good feeling ❸ (*arrangieren*) to arrange II. *vi* to mediate
Vermittler(in) <-s, -> *m(f)* ❶ (*Schlichter*) mediator ❷ (*Unterhändler*) negotiator ❸ (*Makler*) agent
Vermittlung <-, -en> *f* ❶ (*Vermitteln*) *einer Stelle, Wohnung* finding ❷ (*Schlichtung*) mediation ❸ (*Telefonzentrale*) operator ❹ (*das Weitergeben*) imparting
Vermittlungsgebühr *f* commission
vermodern* *vi sein* to rot, to decay
Vermögen <-s, -> [fɛɐ̯·ˈmøː·gn̩] *nt* ❶ FIN assets *pl;* (*Geld*) capital; (*Eigentum*) property; (*Reichtum*) fortune, wealth ❷ *kein pl* (*geh: Fähigkeit*) ability
vermögend [fɛɐ̯·ˈmøː·gn̩t] *adj* wealthy
Vermögenssteuer *f* property tax
vermummt *adj* masked
vermuten* *vt* to suspect; **er wird in Paris vermutet** he is thought to be in Paris
vermutlich I. *adj attr* probable, likely II. *adv* probably
Vermutung <-, -en> *f* assumption
vernachlässigen* [fɛɐ̯·ˈnaːx·lɛ·sɪ·gn̩] *vt* ❶ (*sich nicht genügend kümmern*) to neglect ❷ (*unberücksichtigt lassen*) to ignore
Vernachlässigung <-, -en> *f* ❶ *kein pl* (*das Vernachlässigen*) neglect ❷ (*die Nichtberücksichtigung*) disregard
vernarben* *vi sein* to form a scar; ■**vernarbt** scarred
vernarren* *vr* (*fam*) ■**in jdn/etw vernarrt sein** to be crazy about sb/sth

V

vernehmen* *vt irreg* ❶ JUR to question ❷ (*geh: hören*) to hear
Vernehmen *nt* **dem ~ nach** from what one hears
Vernehmung <-, -en> *f* questioning
verneigen* *vr* ■**sich** *akk* ~ to bow
verneinen* [fɛɐ̯·ˈnai·nən] *vt* ❶ (*negieren*) to say no; **eine Frage ~** to answer a question in the negative ❷ (*leugnen*) to deny
Verneinung <-, -en> *f* LING negative
vernetzen *vt* ❶ COMPUT to network, to link up *sep* ❷ (*fig: verknüpfen*) ■[**mit etw** *dat*] **vernetzt sein** to be linked [up] [to sth]
vernetzt *adj* networked
Vernetzung <-, -en> *f* ❶ COMPUT networking ❷ (*Verflechtung*) network
vernichten* [fɛɐ̯·ˈnɪç·tn̩] *vt* ❶ (*zerstören*) to destroy ❷ (*ausrotten*) to exterminate
vernichtend I. *adj* devastating; *Niederlage* crushing II. *adv* **jdn ~ schlagen** to inflict a crushing defeat on sb
Vernichtung <-, -en> *f* ❶ (*Zerstörung*) destruction ❷ (*Ausrottung*) extermination
Vernichtungslager *nt* extermination camp
verniedlichen* [fɛɐ̯·ˈniːt·lɪ·çn̩] *vt* to play down *sep*
Vernissage <-, -n> [vɛr·nɪ·ˈsaːʒə] *f* private viewing
Vernunft <-> [fɛɐ̯·ˈnʊnft] *f kein pl* reason, common sense; **jdn zur ~ bringen** to bring sb to his/her senses
vernünftig [fɛɐ̯·ˈnʏnf·tɪç] I. *adj* ❶ (*klug*) reasonable, sensible ❷ (*fam: ordentlich*) proper; (*anständig, gut*) decent; **~e Preise** decent prices II. *adv* (*fam*) properly, decently
veröffentlichen* [fɛɐ̯·ˈʔœfn̩t·lɪ·çn̩] *vt* to publish
Veröffentlichung <-, -en> *f* publication
verordnen* *vt* ❶ (*verschreiben*) to prescribe ❷ (*geh: anordnen*) to decree
Verordnung <-, -en> *f* ❶ (*Verschreibung*) prescribing ❷ (*geh: Anordnung*) order, enforcement
verpachten* *vt* to lease (**an** +*akk* to)
Verpachtung <-, -en> *f* leasing
verpacken* *vt* to pack [up *sep*]; (*als Geschenk*) to wrap [up *sep*]
Verpackung <-, -en> *f* ❶ *kein pl* (*das Verpacken*) packing ❷ (*Hülle*) packaging
verpassen* *vt* ❶ (*versäumen*) to miss ❷ (*fam: aufzwingen*) ■**jdm etw ~** to give sb sth; **jdm einen Denkzettel ~** to give sb a warning
verpatzen* *vt* ■**etw ~** to make a mess of sth
verpennen* (*fam*) I. *vt* to miss II. *vi* to oversleep
verpesten* [fɛɐ̯·ˈpɛs·tn̩] *vt* to pollute
verpetzen* *vt* (*fam*) ■**jdn ~** to tell on sb
verpfänden* *vt* to pawn; *Grundstück, Haus* to mortgage
verpfeifen* *vt irreg* ■**jdn ~** to inform on sb
verpflanzen* *vt* ❶ (*umpflanzen*) to replant ❷ MED ■**jdm ein Organ ~** to give sb an organ transplant

verpflegen* *vt* ■**jdn ~** to look after sb
Verpflegung <-, *selten* -en> *f* ❶ *kein pl* (*das Verpflegen*) catering; **mit voller ~** with full board ❷ (*Nahrung*) food
verpflichten* [fɛɐ̯·ˈpflɪç·tn̩] **I.** *vt* ❶ (*eine Pflicht auferlegen*) ■**jdn** [**zu etw** *dat*] **~** to oblige sb to do sth ❷ (*einstellen*) ■**jdn** [**für etw** *akk*] ~ to hire sb [to do sth] **II.** *vr* ■**sich** *akk* **zu etw** *dat* ~ to commit oneself to doing sth
Verpflichtung <-, -en> *f* ❶ *meist pl* (*Pflichten*) duty; **seinen ~en nachkommen** to fulfill one's obligations; **finanzielle ~en** financial commitments ❷ *kein pl* (*das Engagieren*) engagement
verpfuschen* *vt* ■**etw ~** to make a mess of sth
verpissen *vr* (*vulg*) **verpiss dich!** get lost!, fuck off! *vulg*
verpixeln *vt* (*fam*) COMPUT ■**to be ~t** to be pixelated [*or* pixellated]
verplanen* *vt* ❶ (*falsch planen*) to plan poorly ❷ (*fam*) ■**verplant sein** to be booked [up]
verplappern* *vr* ■**sich** *akk* ~ to blab
verplempern* *vt* (*fam*) to waste
verpönt [fɛɐ̯·ˈpøːnt] *adj* deprecated
verprassen* *vt* to squander
verprügeln* *vt* to beat up *sep;* (*als Strafe*) to give sb a beating
verpuffen* *vi sein* ❶ (*plötzlich abbrennen*) to blow out ❷ (*ohne Wirkung bleiben*) to fizzle out
Verputz *m* plaster
verputzen* *vt* ❶ (*mit Putz versehen*) to plaster ❷ (*fam: aufessen*) to polish off *sep*
verqualmt <-er, -este> *adj* smoke-filled *attr,* full of smoke *pred*
verquollen *adj* swollen
verramschen* *vt* to sell dirt cheap
Verrat <-[e]s> [fɛɐ̯·ˈraːt] *m* ❶ *kein pl* betrayal (**an** +*dat* of) ❷ JUR treason
verraten <verriet, verraten> **I.** *vt* ❶ (*ausplaudern*) to give away *sep* ❷ (*Verrat üben, preisgeben*) to betray ❸ (*erkennen lassen*) to show **II.** *vr* ■**sich** *akk* ~ to give oneself away
Verräter(in) <-s, -> [fɛɐ̯·ˈrɛː·tɐ] *m(f)* traitor
verräterisch **I.** *adj* ❶ (*auf Verrat zielend*) treacherous ❷ (*etw andeutend*) meaningful, telltale *attr* **II.** *adv* meaningfully
verrechnen* **I.** *vr* ■**sich** *akk* ~ to miscalculate **II.** *vt* ■**etw mit etw** *dat* ~ to set off *sep* sth against sth
Verrechnungsscheck *m* a check [endorsed] for deposit only
verrecken* *vi sein* (*sl*) to die a miserable death ▶ WENDUNGEN: **nicht ums V~!** (*sl*) not on your life!
verregnet <-er, -este> *adj* spoiled by rain; *Tag* rainy
verreiben* *vt irreg* to rub in *sep*
verreisen* *vi sein* to go away; **geschäftlich verreist sein** to be away on business
verreißen* *vt irreg* to tear apart
verrenken* *vt* to twist; **sich** *dat* **ein Gelenk ~** to dislocate a joint
Verrenkung <-, -en> *f* distortion; *Gelenk* dislocation
verrichten* *vt* to perform
verriegeln* *vt* to bolt
verringern* [fɛɐ̯·ˈrɪŋɐn] **I.** *vt* to reduce (**um** +*akk* by) **II.** *vr* ■**sich** *akk* ~ to decrease
Verringerung <-> *f kein pl* reduction
verrosten* *vi sein* to rust
verrotten* [fɛɐ̯·ˈrɔ·tn̩] *vi sein* ❶ (*faulen*) to rot ❷ (*verwahrlosen*) to decay
verrücken* *vt* to move
verrückt [fɛɐ̯·ˈrʏkt] *adj* ❶ (*wahnsinnig*) nuts, crazy; **bist du ~?** are you out of your mind?; **jdn ~ machen** to drive sb crazy ❷ (*in starkem Maße*) **wie ~** like crazy ❸ (*ausgefallen*) crazy, wild ❹ (*versessen*) ■**~ nach etw/jdm sein** to be crazy about sth/sb
Verrückte(r) *f(m) dekl wie adj* lunatic
Verruf *m kein pl* **in ~ kommen** to fall into disrepute
verrufen *adj* disreputable
verrühren* *vt* to stir
verrutschen* *vi sein* to slip
Vers <-es, -e> [fɛrs, *pl* ˈfɛr·zə] *m* verse, lines *pl*
versagen* **I.** *vi* to fail, to choke *sl* **II.** *vt* ■**jdm etw ~** to refuse sb sth
Versagen <-s> *nt kein pl* failure; **menschliches ~** human error
Versager(in) <-s, -> *m(f)* failure
versalzen* *vt irreg* to put too much salt in/on
versammeln* **I.** *vr* ■**sich** *akk* ~ to gather, to assemble **II.** *vt* (*zusammenkommen lassen*) to call together; *Truppen* to rally
Versammlung *f* ❶ (*Zusammenkunft*) meeting ❷ (*versammelte Menschen*) assembly
Versand <-[e]s> [fɛɐ̯·ˈzant] *m kein pl* ❶ (*das Versenden*) dispatch ❷ (*Versandabteilung*) dispatch, distribution
Versandhandel *m* mail order *no art*
Versandhaus *nt* mail-order company
versauen* *vt* (*sl*) ❶ (*verdrecken*) to make filthy ❷ (*verderben*) to ruin
versäumen* *vt* to miss
verschaffen* *vt* ❶ (*beschaffen*) ■**jdm/sich etw ~** to get [a hold of] sth for sb/oneself ❷ (*vermitteln*) to earn; **jdm Respekt ~** to earn sb respect; **jdm eine Stellung ~** to get sb a job; **sich** *dat* **Gewissheit ~** to make certain
verschämt [fɛɐ̯·ˈʃɛːmt] *adj* shy, bashful
verschandeln* [fɛɐ̯·ˈʃan·dl̩n] *vt* to ruin
verschanzen* **I.** *vt* MIL to fortify **II.** *vr* ■**sich** *akk* ~ ❶ MIL to take up a fortified position ❷ (*verstecken*) to take refuge
verschärfen* **I.** *vr* ■**sich** *akk* ~ to get worse; *Krise* to intensify **II.** *vt* ❶ (*rigoroser machen*) to make more rigorous; *Strafe* to make more severe ❷ (*zuspitzen*) *Situation* to aggravate
Verschärfung <-, -en> *f* ❶ (*Zuspitzung*) intensification, worsening ❷ (*das Verschärfen*) tightening up
verschätzen* *vr* ■**sich** *akk* ~ to misjudge

V

verschenken* *vt* ① (*schenken*) to give away *sep* (**an** +*akk* to) ② (*ungenutzt lassen*) to waste

verscherbeln* *vt* to sell [off *sep*]

verscherzen* *vr* ■ **sich** *dat* **etw** ~ to lose sth; ■ **es sich** *dat* **mit jdm** ~ to have a falling out with sb

verscheuchen* *vt* to chase away *sep*

verschicken* *vt* to send

verschieben* *irreg* **I.** *vt* ① *Gegenstand* to move (**um** +*akk* by) ② *Termin* to postpone (**auf** +*akk* until, **um** +*akk* by) **II.** *vr* ■ **sich** *akk* ~ ① (*später stattfinden*) to be postponed ② (*verrutschen*) to slip

Verschiebung *f* postponement

verschieden [fɛɐ̯·ˈʃiː·dn̩] **I.** *adj* ① (*unterschiedlich*) different; (*mehrere*) various ② *attr* (*einige*) several *attr,* a few *attr;* ■ **V~es** various things *pl* **II.** *adv* differently

verschiedenartig *adj* different kinds of *attr,* diverse

Verschiedenheit <-, -en> *f* (*Unterschiedlichkeit*) difference; (*Unähnlichkeit*) dissimilarity

verschiedentlich [fɛɐ̯·ˈʃiː·dn̩t·lɪç] *adv* ① (*mehrmals*) several times, on several occasions ② (*vereinzelt*) occasionally

verschimmeln* *vi sein* to get moldy

verschissen *adj* (*sl*) **du hast bei mir ~!** I'm finished with you!

verschlafen*[1] *irreg* **I.** *vi* to oversleep **II.** *vt* ① (*fam*) to miss ② (*schlafend verbringen*) to sleep through

verschlafen[2] *adj* sleepy

Verschlag <-[e]s, -schläge> *m* shed

verschlagen*[1] *vt irreg* ① (*nehmen*) **jdm die Sprache ~** to leave sb speechless ② (*geraten*) **es hatte mich nach Argentinien ~** I ended up in Argentina

verschlagen[2] **I.** *adj* devious, sly *pej;* **ein ~er Blick** a furtive glance **II.** *adv* slyly; (*verdächtig*) shiftily

verschlampen* *vt* ■ **etw** ~ to manage to lose sth

verschlechtern* [fɛɐ̯·ˈʃlɛç·tɐn] **I.** *vt* to make worse **II.** *vr* ■ **sich** *akk* ~ to get worse, to worsen

Verschlechterung <-, -en> *f* worsening (+*gen* of)

verschleiern* [fɛɐ̯·ˈʃlai·ɐn] *vt* ① (*mit einem Schleier bedecken*) to cover with a veil ② (*verdecken*) to cover up *sep*

verschleiert *adj Gesicht* veiled

Verschleiß <-es, -e> [fɛɐ̯·ˈʃlais] *m* wear [and tear]

verschleißen <verschliss, verschlissen> *vi, vt sein* to wear out

verschleppen* *vt* ① (*deportieren*) to take away *sep* ② (*hinauszögern*) to prolong ③ MED to delay treatment

Verschleppung <-, -en> *f* ① (*Deportation*) taking away *sep* ② (*Hinauszögerung*) prolonging

verschleudern* *vt* to sell off *sep* cheaply

verschließen* *irreg* **I.** *vt* ① (*zumachen*) to close ② (*zuschließen*) to lock ③ (*wegschließen*) to lock away *sep* ④ (*versagt bleiben*) ■ **jdm verschlossen bleiben** to be closed off to sb **II.** *vr* ■ **sich** *akk* **einer S.** *dat* ~ to ignore sth

verschlimmern* **I.** *vt* to make worse **II.** *vr* ■ **sich** *akk* ~ to get worse; *Zustand, Lage a.* to deteriorate

Verschlimmerung <-, -en> *f* deterioration (+*gen* in)

verschlingen* *vt irreg Essen, Buch* to devour

verschliss[RR], **verschliß**[ALT] *imp von* **verschleißen**

verschlissen **I.** *pp von* **verschleißen** **II.** *adj* worn-out

verschlossen [fɛɐ̯·ˈʃlɔ·sn̩] *adj* ① (*zugemacht*) closed ② (*abgeschlossen*) locked ③ (*zurückhaltend*) reserved; (*schweigsam*) taciturn

verschlucken* **I.** *vt* ① (*hinunterschlucken*) to swallow ② (*undeutlich aussprechen*) to slur; (*nicht aussprechen*) to bite back **II.** *vr* ■ **sich** *akk* ~ to choke (**an** +*dat* on)

verschlungen **I.** *pp von* **verschlingen** **II.** *adj* entwined

Verschluss[RR], **Verschluß**[ALT] *m* ① *von Tasche, Brosche* clasp; **etw unter ~ halten** to keep sth under lock and key ② (*Deckel*) lid; *Flasche* top

verschlüsseln* [fɛɐ̯·ˈʃlʏ·sl̩n] *vt* to [en]code

verschmähen* *vt* to reject; (*stärker*) to scorn

verschmelzen* *irreg* **I.** *vi sein* to melt together **II.** *vt* (*löten*) to solder; (*verschweißen*) to weld

Verschmelzung <-, -en> *f* ① (*das Verschmelzen*) fusing ② ÖKON merger

verschmerzen* *vt* to get over

verschmieren* **I.** *vt* ① (*verstreichen*) to apply; *Creme etc.* to spread ② (*verwischen*) to smear ③ (*beschmieren*) to make dirty **II.** *vi* to smear, to get smeared

verschmutzen* **I.** *vt* to make dirty; ÖKOL to pollute **II.** *vi sein* to get dirty; ÖKOL to get polluted

Verschmutzung <-, -en> *f* ① *kein pl* dirt ② ÖKOL pollution

verschnaufen* *vi, vr* to take a breather

Verschnaufpause *f* breather; **eine ~ einlegen** to take a breather

verschneit *adj* snow-covered *attr;* ■ **~ sein** to be covered in snow

verschnörkelt *adj* adorned with flourishes

verschnupft [fɛɐ̯·ˈʃnʊpft] *adj* (*fam*) ■ **~ sein** ① (*erkältet*) to have a cold ② (*indigniert*) to be in a huff

verschnüren* *vt* to tie up *sep* [with a string]

verschollen [fɛɐ̯·ˈʃɔ·lən] *adj* missing; ■ **~ sein** to have disappeared

verschonen* *vt* to spare; **verschone mich mit den Einzelheiten!** spare me the details!; **von etw** *dat* **verschont bleiben** to escape sth

verschönern* [fɛɐ̯·ˈʃøː·nɐn] *vt* to brighten up *sep*

verschränken* *vt* **die Arme/Beine ~** to fold

one's arms/cross one's legs

verschreiben* *irreg* **I.** *vt* ■ **jdm etw ~** to prescribe sb sth (**gegen** +*akk* for) **II.** *vr* ❶ (*falsch schreiben*) ■ **sich** *akk* **~** to make a slip of the pen ❷ (*sich widmen*) ■ **sich** *akk* **einer S.** *dat* **~** to devote oneself to sth

verschreibungspflichtig *adj* available by prescription only *pred*

verschrieen [fɛɐ̯·ˈʃri·əːn], **verschrien** [fɛɐ̯·ˈʃriːn] *adj* notorious

verschrotten* *vt* to scrap

Verschrottung <-, -en> *f* scrapping

verschüchtert *adj* intimidated

verschulden* **I.** *vt* ■ **etw ~** to be to blame for sth **II.** *vi sein* ■ **verschuldet sein** to be in debt **III.** *vr* ■ **sich** *akk* **~** to get into debt

Verschulden <-s> *nt kein pl* fault

Verschuldung <-, -en> *f* (*Schulden*) debts *pl*

verschütten* [fɛɐ̯·ˈʃʏ·tən] *vt* ❶ (*danebenschütten*) to spill ❷ (*unter etw begraben*) to bury

verschwägert [fɛɐ̯·ˈʃvɛː·gɐt] *adj* related by marriage *pred*

verschweigen* *vt irreg* to keep secret (**vor** +*dat* from); *Informationen* to withhold; ■ **jdm ~, dass ...** to keep from sb the fact that ...

verschwenden* *vt* to waste

Verschwender(in) <-s, -> *m(f)* wasteful person; *Geld a.* spendthrift

verschwenderisch **I.** *adj* ❶ (*sinnlos ausgebend*) wasteful ❷ (*sehr üppig*) extravagant, sumptuous **II.** *adv* wastefully

Verschwendung <-, -en> *f* waste

verschwiegen [fɛɐ̯·ˈʃviː·gn̩] *adj* discreet

verschwimmen* *vi irreg sein* to become blurred

verschwinden* *vi irreg sein* ❶ (*nicht mehr da sein*) to disappear; ■ **verschwunden** [**sein**] [to be] missing; **etw in etw** *dat* **~ lassen** to slip sth into sth ❷ (*sich auflösen*) to vanish ❸ (*fam: sich davonmachen*) to disappear; **verschwinde!** beat it!, scram!

Verschwinden <-s> *nt kein pl* disappearance (↑ *gon* of)

verschwitzt <-er, -este> *adj* ❶ (*mit Schweiß durchsetzt*) sweaty ❷ (*fam: vergessen*) forgotten

verschwommen *adj* ❶ (*undeutlich*) blurred ❷ (*unklar*) hazy, vague

verschwören* *vr irreg* ■ **sich** *akk* **~** to conspire [*or* plot] (**gegen** +*akk* against)

Verschwörer(in) <-s, -> *m(f)* conspirator

Verschwörung <-, -en> *f* conspiracy, plot

versehen* [fɛɐ̯·ˈzeː·ən] *irreg vt* to provide; **etw mit einem Vermerk ~** to add a note to sth ▶ WENDUNGEN: **ehe man sich's versieht** before you know it

Versehen <-s, -> [fɛɐ̯·ˈzeː·ən] *nt* (*Irrtum*) mistake; (*Unachtsamkeit*) oversight; **aus ~** inadvertently; (*aufgrund einer Verwechslung a.*) by mistake

versehentlich [fɛɐ̯·ˈzeː·ənt·lɪç] *adv* inadvertently; (*aufgrund einer Verwechslung a.*) by mistake

versenden* *vt irreg o reg* to send

versengen* *vt* to singe

versenken* *vt* ❶ (*sinken lassen*) to sink ❷ (*einklappen, hinunterlassen*) to lower

Versenkung *f* (*das Versenken*) sinking, lowering ▶ WENDUNGEN: **aus der ~ auftauchen** (*fam*) to reemerge on the scene; **in der ~ verschwinden** to vanish from the scene

versessen [fɛɐ̯·ˈzɛ·sn̩] *adj* ■ **auf etw** *akk* **~ sein** to be crazy about sth; *Geld* to be obsessed with sth

versetzen* **I.** *vt* ❶ (*an eine andere Stelle*) to move; (*aus Berufsgründen*) to transfer ❷ SCH **einen Schüler ~** to move up *sep* [*or* promote] a student ❸ (*bringen*) **jdn in Begeisterung ~** to fill sb with enthusiasm; **jdn in Panik/Wut ~** to send sb into a panic/a rage ❹ (*verpfänden*) to pawn ❺ (*warten lassen*) ■ **jdn ~** to stand sb up ❻ (*mischen*) ■ **etw mit etw** *dat* **~** to mix sth with sth **II.** *vr* (*sich hineindenken*) ■ **sich** *akk* **in jdn ~** to put oneself in sb's place

Versetzung <-, -en> *f* ❶ (*beruflich*) transfer ❷ SCH moving up, promotion

verseuchen* [fɛɐ̯·ˈzɔy·çn̩] *vt* to contaminate; *Umwelt* to pollute

Verseuchung <-, -en> *f* contamination, pollution

versichern*[1] *vt* to insure

versichern*[2] *vt* ■ **jdm ~,** [**dass**] ... to assure sb [that] ...

Versicherte(r) *f(m) dekl wie adj* insured

Versichertenkarte *f* insurance card

Versicherung[1] *f* ❶ (*Vertrag*) insurance policy ❷ (*Gesellschaft*) insurance company

Versicherung[2] *f* (*Beteuerung*) assurance

Versicherungsanspruch *m* insurance claim

Versicherungsbetrug *m* insurance fraud

Versicherungsschutz *m kein pl* insurance coverage

Versicherungsvertreter(in) *m(f)* insurance agent

versickern* *vi sein* to seep away

versiegeln* *vt* to seal [up *sep*]

versiegen* *vi sein* to dry up

versilbern* [fɛɐ̯·ˈzɪl·bɐn] *vt* to silver-plate

versinken *vi irreg sein* to sink

Version <-, -en> [vɛr·ˈzi̯oːn] *f* version

Versklavung <-, -en> *f* enslavement

versöhnen* [fɛɐ̯·ˈzøː·nən] **I.** *vr* ■ **sich** *akk* **mit jdm ~** to make up with sb **II.** *vt* ❶ (*aussöhnen*) to reconcile ❷ (*besänftigen*) to mollify

Versöhnung <-, -en> *f* reconciliation

versorgen* *vt* ❶ (*betreuen*) ■ **jdn ~** to take care of [*or* look after] sb ❷ (*versehen*) to supply; ■ **sich** *akk* **mit etw** *dat* **~** to provide oneself with sth; **sich** *akk* **selbst ~** to look after oneself

Versorgung <-> *f kein pl* ❶ (*das Versorgen*) care ❷ (*das Ausstatten*) supply

verspäten* [fɛɐ̯·ˈʃpɛː·tn̩] *vr* ■ **sich** *akk* **~** to be [running] late

verspätet **I.** *adj* ① (*zu spät eintreffend*) delayed ② (*zu spät erfolgend*) late **II.** *adv* late; (*nachträglich*) belatedly

Verspätung <-, -en> *f* delay; ~ **haben** to be late; **mit einer Stunde ~ ankommen** to arrive an hour late

versperren* *vt* to block

verspielen* **I.** *vt* ① (*beim Glücksspiel verlieren*) to gamble away *sep* ② (*sich um etw bringen*) to squander **II.** *vr* ■ **sich** *akk* ~ to miss a note

verspielt *adj* playful

verspotten* *vt* to mock

versprechen* *irreg* **I.** *vt* to promise; **das Wetter verspricht schön zu werden** the weather looks promising **II.** *vr* ① (*sich erhoffen*) ■ **sich** *dat* **etw von jdm/etw** ~ to hope for sth from sb/sth; **ich versprach mir nicht viel davon** I didn't expect much ② (*falsch sprechen*) ■ **sich** *akk* ~ to misspeak

Versprechen <-s, -> *nt* promise

Versprecher <-s, -> *m* slip of the tongue

Versprechung <-, -en> *f meist pl* promise

verspritzen* *vt* to spray

versprühen* *vt* to spray; *Optimismus* to spread

verspüren* *vt* to feel

verstaatlichen* [fɛɐ̯·ˈʃtaːt·lɪ·çn̩] *vt* to nationalize

Verstaatlichung <-, -en> *f* nationalization

verstand [fɛɐ̯·ˈʃtant] *imp von* **verstehen**

Verstand <-[e]s> [fɛɐ̯·ˈʃtant] *m kein pl* reason; **bei klarem ~ sein** to be lucid; **jdn um den ~ bringen** to drive sb out of his/her mind; **du bist wohl nicht bei ~!** you're out of your mind!

verstanden *pp von* **verstehen**

verständig [fɛɐ̯·ˈʃtɛn·dɪç] *adj* (*vernünftig*) sensible; (*einsichtig*) cooperative; **sich ~ zeigen** to show a willingness to cooperate

verständigen* [fɛɐ̯·ˈʃtɛn·dɪ·gn̩] **I.** *vt* to notify (**von** +*dat* of) **II.** *vr* ■ **sich** *akk* ~ ① (*sich verständlich machen*) to communicate ② (*sich einigen*) to reach an agreement

Verständigung <-, *selten* -en> *f* ① (*Benachrichtigung*) notification ② (*Kommunikation*) communication ③ (*Einigung*) agreement, understanding

verständlich [fɛɐ̯·ˈʃtɛnt·lɪç] **I.** *adj* ① (*begreiflich*) understandable; **sich ~ machen** to make oneself understood ② (*gut zu hören*) clear, intelligible ③ (*leicht zu verstehen*) clear, comprehensible **II.** *adv* ① (*vernehmbar*) clearly ② (*verstehbar*) comprehensibly

verständlicherweise *adv* understandably

Verständnis <-ses, *selten* -se> [fɛɐ̯·ˈʃtɛnt·nɪs] *nt* ① (*Einfühlungsvermögen*) understanding; **für etw** *akk* **~ haben** to have sympathy for sth ② (*das Verstehen*) comprehension, understanding

verständnislos **I.** *adj* uncomprehending; **ein ~er Blick** a blank look **II.** *adv* uncomprehendingly, blankly

verständnisvoll *adj* understanding, sympathetic

verstärken* *vt* ① (*stärker machen*) to strengthen; (*durch stärkeres Material a.*) to reinforce ② (*intensivieren*) *Gefühle* to intensify ③ (*erhöhen*) to increase

Verstärker <-s, -> *m* TECH amplifier, amp *fam*

Verstärkung *f* ① (*das Verstärken*) strengthening ② (*Vergrößerung*) reinforcement ③ (*Erhöhung*) increase

verstauben* *vi sein* (*staubig werden*) to get dusty; (*unberührt liegen*) to gather dust

verstauchen* *vt* ■ **sich** *dat* **das Handgelenk** ~ to sprain one's wrist

verstauen* *vt* to pack [away *sep*]

Versteck <-[e]s, -e> [fɛɐ̯·ˈʃtɛk] *nt* hiding place

verstecken* *vt* to hide (**vor** +*dat* from)

Versteckspiel *nt* [game of] hide-and-seek

versteckt *adj* ① (*verborgen*) hidden; (*vorsätzlich a.*) concealed ② (*abgelegen*) secluded ③ (*unausgesprochen*) veiled

verstehen <verstand verstanden> **I.** *vt* ① (*hören*) to hear; **~ Sie mich gut?** can you hear me okay? ② (*begreifen*) to understand ③ (*können*) to understand; **sie ~ es zu kochen** they [certainly] know how to cook; **er versteht nichts von Musik** he doesn't know a thing about music ④ (*auslegen*) **was verstehst du unter teuer?** what's "expensive" to you?; **wie darf ich das ~?** how am I supposed to interpret that?; **dieser Brief ist als Drohung zu ~** this letter has to be taken as a threat **II.** *vr* ① (*auskommen*) ■ **sich** *akk* **mit jdm** ~ to get along with sb ② (*beherrschen*) ■ **sich** *akk* **auf etw** *akk* ~ to know all about sth ③ (*zu verstehen sein*) **etw versteht sich von selbst** sth goes without saying **III.** *vi* **verstehst du?** [do you] understand?, you know?

versteifen* *vr* ■ **sich** *akk* ~ ① (*auf etw beharren*) to insist (**auf** +*akk* on) ② MED to stiffen [up]

versteigern* *vt* to auction [off]

Versteigerung *f* auction

Versteinerung <-, -en> *f* fossil

verstellbar *adj* adjustable

verstellen* **I.** *vt* ① (*anders einstellen*) to adjust ② (*woandershin stellen*) to move ③ (*unzugänglich machen*) to block ④ (*verändern*) to disguise **II.** *vr* ■ **sich** *akk* ~ to put on an act

Verstellung *f* ① (*das Verstellen*) adjustment ② *kein pl* (*Heuchelei*) pretence

versteuern* *vt* ■ **etw** ~ to pay tax on sth

verstimmt *adj* ① MUS out of tune ② (*verärgert*) ■ **~ sein** to be disgruntled ③ *Magen* upset

verstockt *adj* obstinate

verstohlen [fɛɐ̯·ˈʃtoː·lən] **I.** *adj* furtive **II.** *adv* furtively

verstopfen* **I.** *vt* to block up *sep* **II.** *vi sein* to get blocked [up]

verstopft *adj* blocked, congested

Verstopfung <-, -en> *f* MED constipation; **~ haben** to be constipated

verstorben [fɛɐ̯·ˈʃtɔr·bn̩] *adj* deceased, late *attr*

Verstorbene(r) *f(m) dekl wie adj* deceased
verstört [fɛɐ̯·ˈʃtøːɐ̯t] **I.** *adj* distraught **II.** *adv* in distress
Verstoß [fɛɐ̯·ˈʃtoːs] *m* violation (**gegen** +*akk* of); JUR offense
verstoßen* *irreg* **I.** *vi* ■**gegen etw** *akk* ~ to violate sth **II.** *vt* ■**jdn** ~ to expel sb
verstrahlen *vt* to contaminate with radiation
verstreichen* *irreg* **I.** *vt Farbe* to apply; *Butter* to spread **II.** *vi sein Zeit* to pass [by]; *Zeitspanne a.* to elapse
verstreut *adj* (*einzeln liegend*) isolated; (*verteilt*) scattered
verstricken* **I.** *vt* ■**jdn in etw** *akk* ~ to involve sb in sth **II.** *vr* ■**sich** *akk* **in etw** *akk* ~ to get caught up in sth
verstümmeln* [fɛɐ̯·ˈʃtʏ·ml̩n] *vt* to mutilate; (*verkrüppeln*) to maim
Verstümmelung <-, -en> *f* mutilation
verstummen* [fɛɐ̯·ˈʃtʊ·mən] *vi sein* to fall silent
Versuch <-[e]s, -e> [fɛɐ̯·ˈzuːx] *m* ❶ (*Bemühen*) attempt, try ❷ (*Experiment*) experiment
versuchen* **I.** *vt* ❶ (*probieren*) to try; ■**es mit jdm/etw** ~ to give sb/sth a try ❷ (*neugierig*) ■**versucht sein, etw zu tun** to be tempted to do sth **II.** *vi* ■~**, etw zu tun** to try doing/to do sth **III.** *vr* ■**sich** *akk* **an/in etw** *dat* ~ to try one's hand at sth
Versuchskaninchen *nt* guinea pig
Versuchsperson *f* test subject
Versuchstier *nt* laboratory animal
versuchsweise *adv* on a trial basis
Versuchung <-, -en> *f* temptation; **jdn in ~ führen** to tempt sb; **in ~ geraten** to be tempted
versunken [fɛɐ̯·ˈzʊŋ·kn̩] *adj* ❶ (*untergegangen*) sunken *attr; Kultur* submerged ❷ (*vertieft*) ■**in etw** *akk* ~ **sein** to be absorbed in sth; **in Gedanken ~ sein** to be lost in thought
versüßen* *vt* to sweeten
vertagen* *vt* to adjourn (**auf** +*akk* until); *Entscheidung* to postpone
Vertagung *f* adjournment
vertauschen* *vt* to switch; (*unabsichtlich*) to mix up *sep*
verteidigen* [fɛɐ̯·ˈtai·dɪ·gn̩] *vt, vi* to defend
Verteidiger(in) <-s, -> *m(f)* ❶ JUR defense counsel ❷ SPORT defender
Verteidigung <-, -en> *f* defense
Verteidigungsministerium *nt* Defense Department
verteilen* **I.** *vt* ❶ (*austeilen*) to distribute (**an** +*akk* to) ❷ (*platzieren*) to place ❸ (*ausstreuen, verstreichen*) to spread (**auf** +*dat* on) **II.** *vr* (*sich verbreiten*) ■**sich** *akk* ~ to spread out
Verteilung *f* distribution
verteuern* [fɛɐ̯·ˈtɔy·ɐn] **I.** *vt* to increase the price (**um** +*akk* by) **II.** *vr* ■**sich** *akk* ~ to become more expensive
Verteuerung *f* price increase
verteufeln* [fɛɐ̯·ˈtɔy·fl̩n] *vt* to demonize, to condemn
vertiefen* [fɛɐ̯·ˈtiː·fn̩] **I.** *vt* to deepen **II.** *vr* ■**sich** *akk* **in etw** *akk* ~ to become absorbed in sth; **in Gedanken vertieft sein** to be deep in thought
Vertiefung <-, -en> *f* ❶ (*vertiefte Stelle*) depression; (*Boden a.*) hollow ❷ *kein pl* (*das Vertiefen*) deepening ❸ (*Festigung*) consolidation
vertikal [vɛr·ti·ˈkaːl] **I.** *adj* vertical **II.** *adv* vertically
vertippen* *vr* (*fam*) ■**sich** *akk* ~ to make a typo *fam*
vertonen* *vt* to set to music
vertrackt [fɛɐ̯·ˈtrakt] *adj* tricky
Vertrag <-[e]s, Verträge> [fɛɐ̯·ˈtraːk, *pl* -ˈtrɛː·gə] *m* contract; (*international*) treaty; **jdn unter ~ nehmen** to contract sb
vertragen* *irreg* **I.** *vt* ❶ (*aushalten*) to bear, to stand ❷ (*wegstecken können*) to tolerate ❸ (*fam: zu sich nehmen können*) **ich vertrage keinen Alkohol** alcohol doesn't agree with me ❹ (*fam: benötigen*) **das Haus könnte einen neuen Anstrich ~** the house could use a new coat of paint ❺ SCHWEIZ (*austragen*) to deliver **II.** *vr* ❶ (*auskommen*) ■**sich** *akk* **mit jdm** ~ to get along with sb ❷ (*zusammenpassen*) ■**sich** *akk* **mit etw** *dat* ~ to go with sth
vertraglich [fɛɐ̯·ˈtraːk·lɪç] **I.** *adj* contractual **II.** *adv* contractually, by contract; ~ **festgelegt werden** to be laid down in a contract
verträglich [fɛɐ̯·ˈtrɛːk·lɪç] *adj* ❶ (*umgänglich*) good-natured ❷ (*bekömmlich*) **gut/schwer** ~ easily digestible/hard to digest; *Medikament* well[-]/not well[-]tolerated
Verträglichkeit <-> *f kein pl* digestibility
VertragsabschlussRR *m* acceptance of the terms and conditions of a contract
Vertragsbruch *m* breach of contract
vertrauen* *vi* ■**jdm** ~ to trust sb; ■**auf jdn** ~ to trust in sb; **auf Gott** ~ to put one's trust in God; ■**darauf ~, dass ...** to be confident that ...
Vertrauen <-s> *nt kein pl* trust, confidence (**zu** +*dat* in); ~ **erweckend sein** to inspire confidence; **im ~ [gesagt]** [told] in [strict] confidence
Vertrauensbruch *m* breach of confidence
Vertrauensfrage *f* **es ist eine ~, ob ...** it is a question of trust whether ...; **die ~ stellen** POL to ask for a vote of confidence
Vertrauenssache *f* ❶ (*vertrauliche Angelegenheit*) confidential matter ❷ *s.* **Vertrauensfrage**
vertrauensvoll **I.** *adj* trusting, based on trust *pred* **II.** *adv* trustingly
Vertrauensvotum *nt* POL vote of confidence
vertrauenswürdig *adj* trustworthy
vertraulich **I.** *adj* ❶ (*geheim*) [**streng**] ~ [strictly] confidential ❷ (*freundschaftlich*) familiar, chummy *fam* **II.** *adv* confidentially
Vertraulichkeit <-, -en> *f* ❶ *kein pl* (*das Vertraulichsein*) confidentiality ❷ *pl* (*Zudringlich-*

keit) familiarity

verträumt *adj* ① (*idyllisch*) sleepy ② (*realitätsfern*) dreamy

vertraut *adj* ① (*wohlbekannt*) familiar; **sich** *akk* **mit etw** *dat* **~ machen** to familiarize oneself with sth; **sich mit dem Gedanken ~ machen, dass ...** to get used to the idea that ... ② (*eng verbunden*) close, intimate

Vertraute(r) *f(m) dekl wie adj* confidant *masc,* confidante *fem*

Vertrautheit <-, -en> *f* ① *kein pl* (*gute Kenntnis*) familiarity ② (*Verbundenheit*) closeness, intimacy

vertreiben*¹ *vt irreg* (*verjagen*) to drive away [*or* out] *sep*

vertreiben*² *vt irreg* (*verkaufen*) to sell

Vertreibung <-, -en> *f* expulsion

vertretbar *adj* ① (*zu vertreten*) tenable ② (*akzeptabel*) justifiable

vertreten*¹ *vt irreg* ① (*jdn vorübergehend ersetzen*) ■**jdn ~** to cover for sb; **durch jdn ~ werden** to be replaced by sb ② (*repräsentieren*) to represent ③ (*verfechten*) to support; *Ansicht* to take; *Meinung* to hold

vertreten*² *vr irreg* (*verstauchen*) **sich** *dat* **den Fuß ~** to twist one's ankle ▶ WENDUNGEN: **sich** *dat* **die Beine ~** to stretch one's legs

Vertreter(in) <-s, -> *m(f)* ① (*Stellvertreter*) deputy, stand-in ② (*Handelsvertreter*) sales representative ③ (*Repräsentant*) representative

Vertretung <-, -en> *f* ① (*das Vertreten*) deputizing; **die ~ von jdm übernehmen** to stand in for sb ② (*Stellvertreter*) deputy, stand-in; **eine diplomatische ~** a diplomatic mission ③ (*Handelsvertretung*) agency, branch

Vertrieb <-[e]s, -e> *m* ① *kein pl* (*das Vertreiben*) sale[s *pl*] ② (*Vertriebsabteilung*) sales department

Vertriebene(r) *f(m) dekl wie adj* deportee, displaced person

vertrocknen* *vi sein Vegetation* to dry out

vertrödeln* *vt* to idle away *sep*

vertrösten* *vt* to put off *sep* (**auf** +*akk* until)

vertun* *irreg vr* ■**sich** *akk* **~** to make a mistake

vertuschen* *vt* to hush up *sep*

verübeln* [fɛɐ̯·ˈʔyːbl̩n] *vt* ■**jdm etw ~** to hold sth against sb

verüben* *vt* to commit; **einen Anschlag auf jdn ~** to make an attempt on sb's life; **ein Attentat auf jdn ~** to assassinate sb

verunglimpfen* [fɛɐ̯·ˈʔʊn·glɪm·pfn̩] *vt* to denigrate

verunglücken* [fɛɐ̯·ˈʔʊn·glʏ·kn̩] *vi sein* to have an accident; **tödlich ~** to be killed in an accident

verunreinigen* *vt* (*mit schädlichen Stoffen*) to contaminate; *Umwelt* to pollute

verunsichern* [fɛɐ̯·ˈʔʊn·zɪ·çɐn] *vt* to unsettle

verunsichert <-er, -este> *adj* insecure

Verunsicherung <-, -en> *f* ① (*das Verunsichern*) unsettling ② (*verunsicherte Stimmung*) [feeling of] uncertainty

verunstalten* [fɛɐ̯·ˈʔʊn·ʃtal·tn̩] *vt* to disfigure

veruntreuen* [fɛɐ̯·ˈʔʊn·trɔy·ən] *vt* to embezzle

Veruntreuung <-, -en> *f* embezzlement

verursachen* [fɛɐ̯·ˈʔuːɐ̯·za·xn̩] *vt* to cause; [**jdm**] **Schwierigkeiten ~** to create difficulties [for sb]

Verursacher(in) <-s, -> *m(f)* cause; (*Person*) person responsible

verurteilen* *vt* ① (*für schuldig befinden*) to convict; ■**jdn zu etw** *dat* **~** to sentence sb to sth ② (*verdammen*) to condemn ③ (*bestimmt sein*) ■**zu etw** *dat* **verurteilt sein** to be condemned to sth; **zum Scheitern verurteilt sein** to be bound to fail

Verurteilte(r) *f(m) dekl wie adj* convicted man *masc* [*or fem* woman]

Verurteilung <-, -en> *f* conviction, sentencing

vervielfachen* [fɛɐ̯·ˈfiːl·fa·xn̩] **I.** *vt* to increase greatly **II.** *vr* ■**sich** *akk* **~** to multiply

vervielfältigen* [fɛɐ̯·ˈfiːl·fɛl·tɪ·gn̩] *vt* to duplicate; (*fotokopieren*) to photocopy

vervierfachen* [fɛɐ̯·ˈfiːɐ̯·fa·xn̩] *vt, vr* to quadruple

vervollkommnen* [fɛɐ̯·ˈfɔl·kɔm·nən] *vt* to perfect

vervollständigen* [fɛɐ̯·ˈfɔl·ʃtɛn·dɪ·gn̩] *vt* to complete

verwählen* *vr* TELEK ■**sich** *akk* **~** to dial the wrong number

verwahren* [fɛɐ̯·ˈvaː·rən] **I.** *vt* to keep safe **II.** *vr* ■**sich** *akk* **gegen etw** *akk* **~** to protest against sth

verwahrlosen* [fɛɐ̯·ˈvaːɐ̯·loː·zn̩] *vi sein* to fall into disrepair, to go to seed

verwahrlost <-er, -este> *adj* neglected

verwaist *adj inv* orphaned; (*fig: verlassen*) deserted, abandoned

verwalten* *vt* ① FIN, ADMIN to administer; *Besitz* to manage ② COMPUT to manage

Verwalter(in) <-s, -> *m(f)* administrator; *Gut* manager; *Nachlass* trustee

Verwaltung <-, -en> *f* ① *kein pl* (*das Verwalten*) administration, management ② (*Verwaltungsabteilung*) administration, admin *fam;* **städtische ~** municipal authority

Verwaltungsbezirk *m* administrative district

Verwaltungsgericht *nt* administrative court

verwandeln* **I.** *vt* ① (*umwandeln*) ■**jdn in etw** *akk* **~** to turn sb into sth; **er ist wie verwandelt** he is a changed person ② TECH to convert ③ (*anders erscheinen lassen*) to transform **II.** *vr* ■**sich** *akk* **in etw** *akk* **~** to turn into sth

Verwandlung *f* ① (*Umformung*) transformation ② TECH conversion

verwandt¹ [fɛɐ̯·ˈvant] *adj* related (**mit** +*dat* to); *Methoden* similar

verwandt² [fɛɐ̯·ˈvant] *pp von* **verwenden**

verwandte *imp von* **verwenden**

Verwandte(r) *f(m) dekl wie adj* relative, relation

Verwandtschaft <-, -en> *f* ① (*die Verwand-*

ten) relatives *pl* ❷ (*gemeinsamer Ursprung*) affinity

verwarnen* *vt* to warn

Verwarnung *f* warning, caution

verwaschen *adj* faded

verwechseln* [-'vɛk·sl̩n] *vt* ■ **etw ~** to get sth mixed up; ■ **jdn mit jdm ~** to confuse sb with sb

Verwechslung <-, -en> [-'vɛks·lʊŋ] *f* mix-up, confusion

verwegen [fɛɐ̯·'veː·gn̩] *adj* daring, bold

verwehren* *vt* ■ **jdm etw ~** to refuse sb sth

Verweigerer, Verweigerin <-s, -> *m, f* objector; (*Kriegsdienstverweigerer*) conscientious objector

verweigern* *vt, vi* to refuse; **jede Auskunft ~** to refuse to give any information; **einen Befehl ~** to refuse to obey an order

Verweigerung *f* refusal

verweilen* *vi* (*geh*) to stay; **vor einem Gemälde ~** to linger in front of a painting; **bei einem Gedanken ~** to dwell on a thought

verweint *adj Augen* red from crying; *Gesicht* tear-stained

Verweis <-es, -e> [fɛɐ̯·'vais] *m* ❶ (*Tadel*) reprimand; **jdm einen ~ erteilen** to reprimand sb ❷ (*Hinweis*) reference (**auf** +*akk* to); (*Querverweis*) cross-reference

verweisen* *irreg vt, vi* to refer (**an/auf** +*akk* to)

verwelken* *vi sein* to wilt

verwendbar *adj* usable

verwenden <verwendete *o* verwandte, verwendet *o* verwandt> *vt* to use (**für** +*akk* for)

Verwendung <-, -en> *f* use

Verwendungszweck *m* purpose

verwerfen* *irreg vt Plan, Vorschlag* to reject; *Gedanken* to dismiss

verwertbar *adj* usable

verwerten* *vt* ❶ (*ausnutzen, heranziehen*) to use ❷ (*nutzbringend anwenden*) to exploit

Verwertung <-, -en> *f* use

verwesen* [fɛɐ̯·'veː·zn̩] *vi sein* to rot, to decompose

Verwesung <-> *f kein pl* decomposition

verwetten* *vt* to gamble away *sep*

verwickeln* **I.** *vt* ■ **jdn in etw** *akk* **~** to involve sb in sth; **jdn in ein Gespräch ~** to engage sb in conversation **II.** *vr* ■ **sich** *akk* **~** to get tangled up

verwickelt *adj* complicated, intricate

Verwickelung <-, -en>, **Verwicklung** <-, -en> *f* ❶ (*Verstrickung*) entanglement ❷ *pl* (*Komplikationen*) complications *pl*

verwildern* *vi sein* ❶ *Garten* to become overgrown ❷ *Tier* to go wild

verwildert *adj* ❶ *Garten* overgrown ❷ *Tier* feral

verwirklichen* [fɛɐ̯·'vɪrk·lɪ·çn̩] **I.** *vt* to realize; *Idee, Plan* to put into practice; *Projekt* to carry out *sep* **II.** *vr* ■ **sich** *akk* **~** to fulfill oneself

Verwirklichung <-, -en> *f* realization

verwirren* *vt* to confuse

verwirrend <-er, -este> *adj* confusing

verwirrt <-er, -este> *adj* confused

Verwirrung <-, -en> *f* ❶ (*Verstörtheit*) confusion ❷ (*Chaos*) chaos

verwischen* **I.** *vt* ❶ (*verschmieren*) to smudge; *Farbe* to smear ❷ (*unkenntlich machen*) to cover [up *sep*] **II.** *vr* ■ **sich** *akk* **~** to become blurred; (*Erinnerung*) to fade

verwittern* *vi sein* to weather

verwittert **I.** *pp von* **verwittern** **II.** *adj* weathered

verwitwet [fɛɐ̯·'vɪt·vət] *adj* widowed

verwöhnen* [fɛɐ̯·'vøː·nən] *vt* to spoil

verwöhnt *adj* (*anspruchsvoll*) discriminating

verworren [fɛɐ̯·'vɔ·rən] *adj* confused

verwundbar *adj* vulnerable

verwunden* [fɛɐ̯·'vʊn·dn̩] *vt* to wound

verwunderlich *adj* odd, strange; **das ist nicht ~** that's not surprising

verwundert **I.** *adj* astonished, surprised (**über** +*akk* at) **II.** *adv* in amazement

Verwunderung <-> *f kein pl* amazement

verwundet *adj* (*fig a.*) wounded, hurt

Verwundete(r) *f(m) dekl wie adj* casualty, wounded person

Verwundung <-, -en> *f* wound

verwünschen* *vt* ❶ (*verfluchen*) to curse ❷ (*verzaubern*) to cast a spell on

verwurzelt *adj* rooted

verwüsten* *vt* to devastate; *Wohnung* to wreck; *Land* to ravage

Verwüstung <-, -en> *f meist pl* devastation

verzählen* *vr* ■ **sich** *akk* **~** to miscount

verzaubern* *vt* ❶ (*verhexen*) ■ **jdn ~** to cast a spell on sb; **jdn in einen Vogel ~** to turn sb into a bird ❷ (*betören*) to enchant

Verzauberung <-, -en> *f* enchantment

verzehnfachen* [fɛɐ̯·'tseːn·fa·xn̩] *vt, vr* to increase tenfold

Verzehr <-[e]s> [fɛɐ̯·'tseːɐ̯] *m kein pl* consumption

verzehren* **I.** *vt* ❶ (*essen*) to consume ❷ (*verbrauchen*) to use up **II.** *vr* ■ **sich** *akk* **nach jdm ~** to pine for sb

verzeichnen* *vt* to list; **einen Erfolg ~** to score a success

Verzeichnis <-ses, -se> *nt* list; (*Tabelle*) table; (*Computer*) directory

verzeihen <verzieh, verziehen> **I.** *vt* to forgive **II.** *vi* to excuse; *Unrecht, Sünde* to forgive; **~ Sie!** excuse me!, I beg your pardon!

Verzeihung <-> *f kein pl* forgiveness; [**jdn**] **um ~ bitten** to apologize [to sb]; **~!** sorry!

verzerren* **I.** *vt* ❶ (*verziehen, entstellen*) to distort ❷ *Muskel* to pull; *Sehne* to strain **II.** *vr* (*sich verziehen*) ■ **sich** *akk* **~** to become contorted

Verzerrung *f* distortion

verzetteln* *vr* ■ **sich** *akk* **~** to take on too much at once

Verzicht <-[e]s, -e> [fɛɐ̯·'tsɪ·çt] *m* **~ auf etw** *akk* **ueben** to forgo [*or* do without] sth

verzichten* [fɛɐ̯·'tsɪç·tn̩] *vi* to go without, to

V

forgo; ■ **auf etw** *akk* ~ to do without sth; *auf ein Amt, auf Eigentum* to relinquish sth; **auf sein Recht** ~ to waive one's right

verzieh *imp von* **verzeihen**

verziehen*¹ *irreg* **I.** *vi sein* (*umziehen*) to move **II.** *vr haben* (*verschwinden*) ■ **sich** *akk* ~ to disappear; *Gewitter* to pass; **verzieh dich!** beat it!, scram!

verziehen*² *irreg* **I.** *vt* to twist; **das Gesicht** [**vor Schmerz**] ~ to grimace [with pain] **II.** *vr* ■ **sich** *akk* ~ ① (*verzerren*) to contort, to twist ② (*verformen*) to become misshapen

verziehen³ *pp von* **verzeihen**

verzieren* *vt* to decorate

Verzierung <-, -en> *f* decoration; (*an Gebäuden*) ornamentation

verzinsen* *vt* **etw** [**mit 3 Prozent**] ~ to pay [3 Percent] interest on sth

verzocken *vt* to gamble away *sep*

verzogen [fɛɐ̯·'tsoː·gn̩] *adj* badly brought up; *Kinder* spoiled

verzögern* **I.** *vt* ① (*später erfolgen lassen*) to delay (**um** +*akk* by/for) ② (*verlangsamen*) to slow down **II.** *vr* (*später erfolgen*) ■ **sich** *akk* ~ to be delayed (**um** +*akk* by/for)

Verzögerung <-, -en> *f* delay, holdup *fam;* (*Verlangsamung*) slowing down

Verzögerungstaktik *f* stall tactics *pl*

verzollen* *vt* ■ **etw** ~ to pay customs on sth; **haben Sie etwas zu ~?** do you have anything to declare?

Verzug <-[e]s> *m kein pl* delay; [**mit etw** *dat*] **in ~ geraten** to fall behind [with sth]

verzweifeln* *vi sein* to despair (**an** +*dat* of)

verzweifelt **I.** *adj* ① (*völlig verzagt*) despairing; **ein ~es Gesicht machen** to look desperate; **ich bin völlig ~** I'm at my wits' end ② (*hoffnungslos*) desperate **II.** *adv* (*völlig verzagt*) despairingly, desperately

Verzweiflung <-> *f kein pl* (*Gemütszustand*) despair; (*Ratlosigkeit*) desperation; **jdn zur ~ bringen** to drive sb to despair

verzweigen* [fɛɐ̯·'tsvai·gn̩] *vr* ■ **sich** *akk* ~ to branch out; *Straße* to branch off

verzwickt [fɛɐ̯·'tsvɪkt] *adj* tricky

Vesper <-s, -> ['fɛs·pɐ] *f o nt* DIAL snack

Veteran <-en, -en> [ve·te·'raːn] *m* veteran

Veto <-s, -s> ['veː·to] *nt* veto

Vetorecht *nt* right of veto

Vetter <-s, -n> ['fɛ·tɐ] *m* cousin

Vetternwirtschaft *f kein pl* nepotism

vgl. *interj Abk von* **vergleiche** cf.

Viadukt <-[e]s, -e> [via·'dʊkt] *m o nt* viaduct

Vibration <-, -en> [vi·bra·'tsi̯oːn] *f* vibration

Vibrator <-s, -toren> [vi·'braː·toːɐ̯, *pl* -'toː·rən] *m* vibrator

vibrieren* [vi·'briː·rən] *vi* to vibrate

Video <-s, -s> ['viː·deo] *nt* video

Videoaufzeichnung *f* video recording

Videokamera *f* video camera

Videorecorder, **Videorekorder** <-s, -> *m* VCR, video recorder

Videotext *m kein pl* videotex[t]

Videoüberwachung *f* [monitoring by] closed-circuit television

Vieh <-[e]s> [fiː] *nt kein pl* ① AGR livestock; (*Rinder*) cattle ② (*fam: Tier*) animal, beast

Viehbestand *m* livestock

Viehhaltung <-> *f kein pl* animal husbandry

Viehzucht *f* cattle [*or* livestock] breeding

Viehzüchter(in) *m(f)* cattle [*or* livestock] breeder

viel [fiːl] **I.** *adj* <mehr, meiste> ① *sing, adjektivisch* a lot of; **er braucht ~ Geld** he needs lots of money; **~ Erfolg!** good luck!; **~ Spaß!** have a good time! ② *sing, + art, poss* **das ~e Essen ist mir nicht bekommen** all that food hasn't done me any good; **sein ~es Geld nützt ihm wenig** all his money is no good to him ③ *substantivisch* a lot, much; **ich habe zu ~ zu tun** I have too much to do; **obwohl er ~ weiß, ...** although he knows a lot, ... ④ *pl, adjektivisch* ■ **~e** a lot of, many; **und ~e andere** and many others; **~e deiner Bücher kenne ich schon** I know a lot of your books already ⑤ + *pl, substantivisch* (*eine große Anzahl*) ■ **~e** a lot; (*von Menschen a.*) many; **diese Ansicht wird von ~en vertreten** many people hold this view **II.** *adv* <mehr, am meisten> ① (*häufig*) a lot; **sie hat ihre Mutter immer ~ besucht** she used to visit her mother a lot; **~ diskutiert** much-discussed; **eine ~ befahrene Straße** a [very] busy street ② (*wesentlich*) a lot; **die Mütze ist ~ zu groß** the hat is way [*or* much] too big

vieldeutig *adj* ambiguous

vielfach ['fiːl·fax] **I.** *adj* ① (*mehrere Male so groß*) many times ② (*mehrfach*) multiple **II.** *adv* (*häufig*) frequently, in many cases; (*mehrfach*) many times

Vielfache(s) *nt dekl wie adj* multiple; **um ein ~s** many times over

Vielfalt <-> ['fiːl·falt] *f* diversity, [great] variety (**an** +*dat* of)

vielfältig ['fiːl·fɛl·tɪç] *adj* diverse, varied

Vielfraß <-es, -e> ['fiːl·fraːs] *m* glutton

vielleicht [fi·'laiçt] **I.** *adv* ① (*eventuell*) perhaps, maybe ② (*ungefähr*) about; **er ist ~ 30 Jahre alt** he is about 30 years old **II.** *part* ① (*bitte* [*mahnend*]) please; **würdest du mich ~ einmal ausreden lassen?** would you please let me finish what I'm saying for once? ② (*etwa*) by any chance; **erwarten Sie ~, dass ich Ihnen das Geld gebe?** I don't suppose you expect me to give you the money, do you? ③ (*wirklich*) really; **du erzählst ~ einen Quatsch** what are you talking about?

vielmals ['fiːl·maːls] *adv* **danke ~!** thank you very much!

vielmehr ['fiːl·meːɐ̯] *adv* rather; **ich bin ~ der Meinung, dass ...** I prefer to think that ...

vielseitig ['fiːl·zai·tɪç] **I.** *adj Mensch, Maschine* versatile; *Angebot, Arbeit* varied **II.** *adv* ① (*in vieler Hinsicht*) widely ② (*in verschiedener Weise*) **etw ist ~ anwendbar** sth can be used in a variety of ways

Vielzahl *f kein pl* ■ **eine ~ von etw** *dat* a large number of sth
vier [fiːɐ̯] *adj* four; *s. a.* **acht**[1] ▶ WENDUNGEN: **ein Gespräch unter ~ Augen führen** to have a private conversation
Vier <-, -en> [fiːɐ̯] *f* ❶ (*Zahl*) four ❷ (*Zeugnisnote*) **er hat in Deutsch eine ~** ≈ he got a D in German ▶ WENDUNGEN: **auf allen ~en** on all fours
Vierbeiner <-s, -> *m* four-legged friend *hum*
Viereck ['fiːɐ̯·ʔɛk] *nt* square; MATH quadrilateral
viereckig ['fiːɐ̯·ʔɛkɪç] *adj* rectangular
vierfach, 4fach **I.** *adj* fourfold; **die ~e Menge** four times the amount **II.** *adv* fourfold, four times over
vierhundert ['fiːɐ̯·'hʊn·dɐt] *adj* four hundred
Vierling <-s, -e> ['fiːɐ̯·lɪŋ] *m* quadruplet
viermal, 4-mal[RR] ['fiːɐ̯·maːl] *adv* four times; *s. a.* **achtmal**
Vierradantrieb *m* four-wheel drive
vierspurig *adj* four-lane *attr*
vierstellig *adj* **eine ~e Zahl** a four-digit number
viert ['fiːɐ̯t] *adv* **zu ~ sein** to be a party of four; **wir waren zu ~** there were four of us
viertausend ['fiːɐ̯·tau·zn̩t] *adj* four thousand
vierte(r, s) ['fiːɐ̯·tə -tɐ -təs] *adj* ❶ (*an vierter Stelle*) fourth; *s. a.* **achte(r, s) 1** ❷ (*Datum*) fourth, 4th; *s. a.* **achte(r, s) 2**
viertel ['fɪr·tl̩] *adj* quarter, fourth; **drei ~** three-quarters, three-fourths
Viertel[1] <-s, -> ['fɪr·tl̩] *nt* district, quarter
Viertel[2] <-s, -> ['fɪr·tl̩] *nt o* SCHWEIZ *m* ❶ (*der vierte Teil*) quarter ❷ (*15 Minuten*) **~ vor/nach drei** [a] quarter to [*or* of]/after three
Viertelfinale *nt* quarterfinal
Vierteljahr [fɪr·tl̩·'jaːɐ̯] *nt* three months, quarter *spec*
vierteljährlich ['fɪr·tl̩·jɛːɐ̯·lɪç] *adj, adv* quarterly
vierteln ['fɪr·tl̩n] *vt* to divide into quarters
Viertelstunde [fɪr·tl̩·'ʃtʊn·də] *f* quarter of an hour, fifteen minutes
viertens ['fiːɐ̯·tn̩s] *adv* fourth[ly], in the fourth place
vierzehn ['fɪr·tseːn] *adj* fourteen; **~ Tage** two weeks; *s. a.* **acht**[1]
vierzehntägig ['fɪr·tseːn-] *adj* two-week *attr*
vierzehntäglich *adj, adv* every two weeks
vierzehnte(r, s) *adj* ❶ (*an vierzehnter Stelle*) fourteenth; *s. a.* **achte(r, s) 1** ❷ (*Datum*) fourteenth, 14th; *s. a.* **achte(r, s) 2**
vierzig ['fɪr·tsɪç] *adj* forty; *s. a.* **achtzig 1, 2**
vierziger, 40er ['fɪr·tsɪ·gɐ] *adj attr* the forties, the 40s
vierzigste(r, s) *adj* fortieth; *s. a.* **achte(r, s) 1**
Vierzigstundenwoche *f* 40-hour week
Vietnam <-s> [vi̯ɛt·'nam] *nt* Vietnam; *s. a.* **Deutschland**
Vikar(in) <-s, -e> [vi·'kaːɐ̯] *m(f)* vicar
Villa <-, Villen> ['vɪla, *pl* 'vɪ·lən] *f* villa
violett [vi̯o·'lɛt] *adj* violet, purple
Violine <-, -n> [vi̯o·'liː·nə] *f* violin
Violinist(in) <-en, -en> [vi̯o·li·'nɪst] *m(f)* violinist
VIP <-, -s> [vɪp] *m Abk von* **very important person** VIP
Viren ['viː·rən] *pl von* **Virus**
Virensuchprogramm *nt* COMPUT antivirus software
virtuell [vɪr·'tu·ɛl] *adj* virtual
virtuos [vɪr·'tu̯·oːs] **I.** *adj* virtuoso **II.** *adv* in a virtuoso manner
Virus <-, Viren> ['viː·rʊs, *pl* 'viː·rən] *nt o m* virus
Virusinfektion *f* viral infection
Visa ['viː·za], **Visen** ['viː·zen] *pl von* **Visum**
Visier <-s, -e> [vi·'ziːɐ̯] *nt* ❶ (*Zielvorrichtung*) sight ❷ (*Klappe am Helm*) visor ▶ WENDUNGEN: **jdn/etw im ~ haben** to have one's sights on sb/sth
Vision <-, -en> [vi·'zi̯oːn] *f* vision; **~en haben** to be seeing things
Visite <-, -n> [vi·'ziː·tə] *f* (*Arztbesuch*) round
Visitenkarte [vi·'ziː·tən-] *f* business card
Viskose <-> [vɪs·'koː·zə] *f kein pl* viscose
visuell [vi·'zu̯·ɛl] *adj* visual
Visum <-s, Visa *o* Visen> ['viː·zʊm, *pl* 'viː·za, 'viː·zən] *nt* visa
vital [vi·'taːl] *adj* (*geh*) ❶ (*Lebenskraft besitzend*) lively, vigorous ❷ (*lebenswichtig*) vital
Vitalität <-> [vi·ta·li·'tɛt] *f kein pl* vitality, vigor
Vitamin <-s, -e> [vi·ta·'miːn] *nt* vitamin
Vitaminmangel *m* vitamin deficiency
Vitaminpräparat *nt* vitamin supplement
Vitrine <-, -n> [vi·'triː·nə] *f* (*Schaukasten*) display case; (*Glasvitrine*) glass cabinet
Vizekanzler(in) *m(f)* vice chancellor
Vizepräsident(in) *m(f)* vice president
Vogel <-s, Vögel> ['foː·gl̩, *pl* 'føː·gl̩] *m* ❶ (*Tier*) bird ❷ (*fam: auffallender Mensch*) **ein lustiger ~** a real joker; **ein seltsamer ~** a strange bird ▶ WENDUNGEN: **einen ~ haben** to have a screw loose
Vogelfutter *nt* bird food
vögeln ['føː·gl̩n] *vi* (*derb*) to screw
Vogelperspektive *f* bird's-eye view
Vogelscheuche <-, -n> *f* scarecrow
Vogelschutzgebiet *nt* bird refuge
Vokabel <-, -n> [vo·'kaː·bl̩] *f* word; **~n** *pl* **lernen** to memorize vocabulary words
Vokabular <-s, -e> [vo·ka·bu·'laːɐ̯] *nt* vocabulary
Vokal <-s, -e> [vo·'kaːl] *m* vowel
Volk <-[e]s, Völker> [fɔlk, *pl* 'fœl·kɐ] *nt* ❶ (*Nation*) nation, people ❷ *kein pl* (*fam: Menschenmenge*) masses *pl;* **das ~ aufwiegeln** to incite the masses; **sich unters ~ mischen** to mingle with the people ❸ *kein pl* (*untere Bevölkerungsschicht*) people *npl;* **ein Mann aus dem ~** a man of the people
Völkergemeinschaft *f* international community
Völkerkunde <-> *f kein pl* ethnology
Völkermord *m* genocide
Völkerrecht *nt kein pl* international law

V

Vọlkerwanderung *f* ① HIST migration of peoples ② (*fam*) mass exodus
Vọlksabstimmung *f* referendum
Vọlksfest *nt* folk festival

> A **Volksfest** is a traditional festival lasting several days with such attractions as a Ferris wheel, roller coasters, and beer tents. Possibly the most famous **Volksfest** is the *Oktoberfest* in Munich.

Vọlksheld(in) *m(f)* national hero
Vọlkshochschule *f* adult education center

> **Volkshochschulen** are autonomous, public education institutions. They offer a variety of courses on such subjects as computer science, foreign languages, philosophy, and dance. Classes are intended for people from all walks of life and nearly every age group. **Volkshochschulen** are becoming increasingly recognized as valid providers of additional vocational training.

Vọlkslied *nt* folk song
Vọlksmärchen *nt* folk tale
Vọlksmund *m kein pl* vernacular
Vọlksmusik *f* folk music
Vọlksschule *f* ÖSTERR (*Grundschule*) ≈ elementary school, *for children aged 6–10*
Vọlkssport *m* national sport
Vọlksstamm *m* tribe
Vọlkstanz *m* folk dance
volkstümlich ['fɔlks·tyːm·lɪç] *adj* traditional
Vọlkswirtschaft *f* national economy
vọlkswirtschaftlich I. *adj* economic II. *adv* economically
Vọlkswirtschaftslehre *f* economics *nsing*
Vọlkszählung *f* [national] census
voll [fɔl] I. *adj* ① (*gefüllt*) full; **das Glas ist ~ Wasser** the glass is full of water; **eine Hand ~ Reis** a handful of rice; **~ sein** (*fam: satt*) to be full ② (*vollständig*) full, whole; **etw in ~en Zügen genießen** to enjoy sth to the fullest; **ein ~er Erfolg** a total success; **jede ~e Stunde** every hour on the hour; **in ~er Größe** full-size; **bei ~em Bewusstsein** fully conscious ③ (*kräftig*) *Stimme* rich; *Haar* thick ④ (*sl: betrunken*) ■**~ sein** to be hammered ▶ WENDUNGEN: **sie nimmt ihn nicht für ~** she doesn't take him seriously; **aus dem V~en schöpfen** to draw on plentiful resources II. *adv* ① (*vollkommen*) completely ② (*uneingeschränkt*) fully; **~ und ganz** totally; **etw ~ ausnutzen** to take full advantage of sth; **er war nicht ~ da** he was not quite with it ③ (*mit aller Wucht*) right, smack; **der Wagen war ~ gegen den Pfeiler geprallt** the car ran smack into the pillar
vollauf ['fɔl·ʔauf] *adv* fully, completely
vọllautomatisch I. *adj* fully automatic II. *adv* fully automatically
Vọllbart *m* full beard
Vọllbeschäftigung *f kein pl* full-time employment
Vọllblut *nt* thoroughbred
vollbrịngen* *vt irreg* to accomplish; *Wunder* to perform
vọllbusig *adj* buxom, busty
vollenden* [fɔl·'ʔɛn·dn̩] *vt* to complete
vollẹndet *adj Redner* accomplished; *Schönheit* perfect
vollends ['fɔl·ɛnts] *adv* (*völlig*) completely, totally
Vollendung <-, -en> [fɔl·'ʔɛn·dʊŋ] *f* ① (*das Vollenden*) completion; **mit ~ des 50. Lebensjahres** on his/her fiftieth birthday ② *kein pl* (*Perfektion*) perfection
vọller *adj* ① (*voll bedeckt*) **ein Hemd ~ Flecken** a shirt covered with stains ② (*erfüllt*) full of; **ein Leben ~ Schmerzen** a life full of pain
Volleyball ['vɔli-] *m* volleyball
vollführen* [fɔl·'fyː·rən] *vt* to perform
Vọllgas *nt kein pl* full speed; **~ geben** to put one's foot down
vọllgestopft *adj Koffer* jam-packed
Vọllidiot(in) *m(f)* complete idiot
völlig ['fœ·lɪç] I. *adj* complete II. *adv* completely; **Sie haben ~ recht** you're absolutely right
volljährig ['fɔl·jɛː·rɪç] *adj* of age; ■**~ werden** to come of age
Vọlljährigkeit <-> *f kein pl* majority
Vọllkaskoversicherung *f* comprehensive car insurance [coverage]
vọllklimatisiert *adj* fully air-conditioned
vollkommen [fɔl·'kɔ·mən] I. *adj* ① (*perfekt*) perfect ② (*völlig*) complete II. *adv* completely
Vọllkornbrot *nt* whole-grain bread
Vollmacht <-, -en> ['fɔl·maxt] *f* ① (*Ermächtigung*) authorization; **jdm [die] ~ für etw** *akk* **geben** to authorize sb to do sth ② (*Schriftstück*) power of attorney; **eine ~ haben** to have power of attorney
Vọllmilch *f* whole milk
Vọllmilchschokolade *f* milk chocolate
Vọllmond *m kein pl* full moon; **bei ~** when there's a full moon
Vọllnarkose *f* general anesthetic
Vọllpension *f kein pl* [**mit**] **~** full board
Vọllrausch *m* drunken stupor
vọllschlank *adj* plump
vollständig ['fɔl·ʃtɛn·dɪç] I. *adj* complete, entire; **nicht ~** incomplete II. *adv* completely
Vọllständigkeit <-> *f kein pl* completeness; **der ~ halber** for the sake of completeness
vollstrecken* [fɔl·'ʃtrɛ·kn̩] *vt* to carry out; *Testament* to execute
Vollstrẹckung <-, -en> *f* execution
vọll|tanken *vt* to fill up
Vọlltreffer *m* ① (*direkter Treffer*) direct hit, bull's eye *fig fam*; **einen ~ landen** to land a good punch ② (*fam: voller Erfolg*) complete success
Vọllversammlung *f* general meeting

V

vollwertig *adj* ❶ **~e Kost** whole foods ❷ *Ersatz* fully adequate

Vollwertkost *f kein pl* whole foods *pl*

vollzählig ['fɔl·tsɛ:·lɪç] **I.** *adj* (*komplett*) complete, whole; ■ **~ sein** to be all present **II.** *adv* at full strength

vollziehen* [fɔl·'tsi:·ən] *irreg* **I.** *vt* to carry out *sep; Urteil* to execute; *Ehe* consummate **II.** *vr* ■ **sich** *akk* **~** to take place

Vollzug [fɔl·'tsu:k] *m kein pl* ❶ (*das Vollziehen*) execution ❷ (*Strafvollzug*) imprisonment

Vollzugsanstalt *f* penal institution

Vollzugsbeamte(r) *f(m) dekl wie adj* [prison] warden

Volontär(in) <-s, -e> [vo·lɔn·'tɛ:ɐ̯] *m(f)* intern, trainee

Volontariat <-[e]s, -e> [vo·lɔn·ta·'ri̯·a:t] *nt* ❶ (*Ausbildungszeit*) internship, period of training ❷ (*Stelle*) internship, trainee position

Volt <-[e]s, -> [vɔlt] *nt* volt

Volumen <-s, - *o* Volumina> [vo·'lu:·mən, *pl* vo·'lu:·mi·na] *nt* volume

vom [fɔm] = **von dem** from

von [fɔn] *präp +dat* ❶ *räumlich* (*ab, herkommend*) from; **~ woher...?** where ... from?, from where...?; **~ rechts** from the right; **~ diesem Fenster kann man alles sehen** you can see everything from this window; **~ unserem eigenen Garten** from our own garden; (*aus ... herab/heraus*) off; **er fiel ~ der Leiter** he fell off [*or* from] the ladder ❷ *räumlich* (*etw entfernend*) from, off; **die Wäsche ~ der Leine nehmen** to take the laundry off the line; **Schweiß ~ der Stirn wischen** to wipe sweat from one's brow ❸ *zeitlich* (*stammend*) from; **die Zeitung ~ gestern** yesterday's [news]paper; **ich kenne sie ~ früher** I know her from a long time ago; **~ jetzt an** from now on ❹ (*Urheber, Ursache*) **~ jdm gelobt werden** to be praised by sb; **~ wem ist dieses Geschenk?** who is this present from?; **~ wem weißt du das?** who told you that?; **~ wem ist dieser Roman?** who wrote this novel?; **das war nicht nett ~ dir!** that wasn't nice of you! ❺ *statt gen* (*Zugehörigkeit*) of; **die Musik ~ Beethoven** Beethoven's music ❻ (*Gruppenangabe*) of; **einer ~ vielen** one of many; **keiner ~ uns** none of us; **ein Student ~ mir** a student of mine, one of my students ❼ (*bei Maßangaben*) of; **eine Pause ~ zehn Minuten** a ten-minute break; **ein Abstand ~ zwei Metern** a distance of six feet ▶ WENDUNGEN: **~ wegen!** no way!

voneinander [fɔn·ʔai·'nan·dɐ] *adv* from each other; **die beiden Städte sind 25 Kilometer ~ entfernt** the two cities are 25 kilometers apart

vor [foːɐ̯] **I.** *präp* ❶ (*davor befindlich*) in front of; **sie ließ ihn ~ sich her gehen** she let him go in front of her; **~ sich hin summen** (*fam*) to hum to oneself; **8 km ~ der Stadt** 8 km outside of town; **~ etw** *dat* **davonlaufen** (*fig*) to run away from sth; **etw ~ sich** *dat* **haben** to have sth ahead of you ❷ (*in Bezug auf*) regarding, with regard to; **jdn ~ jdm warnen** to warn sb about sb ❸ (*eher*) before; **vor kurzem/hundert Jahren** a short time/a hundred years ago; **es ist zehn ~ zwölf** it is ten to twelve; **ich war ~ dir dran** I was before you ❹ (*bedingt durch*) with; **starr ~ Schreck** scared stiff; **~ Kälte zittern** to shiver [with cold] **II.** *adv* forward; **~ und zurück** forwards and backwards; **Freiwillige ~!** volunteers, take one step forward!

Vorabend <-s,-e> ['fo:ɐ̯·ʔa:bn̩t] *m* **am ~ [einer S.** *gen*] on the evening before [sth], on the eve [of sth]

Vorahnung *f* premonition

voran [fo·'ran] *adv* first; **der Lehrer geht ~** the teacher goes first

voran|bringen [fo·'ran·brɪŋ·ən] *vt irreg* to advance

voran|gehen *vi irreg sein* ❶ (*an der Spitze gehen*) ■ **jdm ~** to go ahead of sb ❷ *a. impers* (*Fortschritte machen*) to make progress; **die Arbeiten gehen zügig voran** the work is progressing rapidly ❸ (*einer Sache vorausgehen*) to precede

voran|kommen *vi irreg sein* ❶ (*vorwärtskommen*) to make headway ❷ (*Fortschritte machen*) to make progress; **wie kommt ihr voran mit der Arbeit?** how's your work coming along[, guys]?

Voranmeldung ['fo:ɐ̯·ʔan·mɛl·dʊŋ] *f* appointment, booking

voran|treiben *vt irreg* to push ahead

Vorarbeiter(in) *m(f)* foreman *masc,* forewoman *fem*

voraus [fo·'raus] *adv* in front, ahead; **jdm ~ sein** to be ahead of sb; **im V~** in advance

voraus|fahren *vi irreg sein* to go [*or* drive] on ahead

voraus|gehen [fo·'raus·ge:·ən] *vi irreg sein* to go on ahead; **einem Unwetter geht meistens ein Sturm voraus** bad weather is usually preceded by a storm

vorausgesetzt *adj* ■ **~, [dass] ...** provided [that] ...

Voraussage <-, -en> *f* prediction

voraus|sagen *vt* to predict

voraus|schicken *vt* ❶ (*vor jdm losschicken*) to send on ahead ❷ (*vorher sagen*) to say in advance

voraus|sehen *vt irreg* to foresee; **das war vorauszusehen!** that was to be expected!

voraus|setzen *vt* ❶ (*als selbstverständlich erachten*) to assume ❷ (*erfordern*) to require

Voraussetzung <-, -en> *f* ❶ (*Vorbedingung*) condition; ■ **~en** (*für eine Arbeit*) qualifications *npl;* **unter der ~, dass ...** on the condition that ...; **unter bestimmten ~en** under certain conditions ❷ (*Annahme*) assumption, premise

Voraussicht *f kein pl* foresight; **aller ~ nach** in all probability

voraussichtlich [fo·'raus·zɪçt·lɪç] **I.** *adj*

V

(*erwartet*) expected **II.** *adv* (*wahrscheinlich*) probably

voraus|zahlen *vt* to pay in advance

Vorauszahlung *f* advance payment

Vorbehalt <-[e]s, -e> ['foɐ̯·bə·halt] *m* reservation (**gegen** +*akk* about); **ohne ~** without reservation; **unter ~** with reservations *pl*

vor|behalten* *vt irreg* ■**sich** *dat* [**etw**] ~ to reserve [sth] for oneself; **Änderungen ~** subject to changes; **alle Rechte ~** all rights reserved

vorbehaltlos I. *adj* unreserved **II.** *adv* unreservedly, without reservation

vorbei [foːɐ̯·'bai] *adv* ❶ (*vorüber*) ■**an etw** *dat* ~ past sth; **wir sind schon an München ~** we already passed Munich; **schon wieder ~, ich treffe nie** missed again — I never hit the target ❷ (*vergangen*) ■**~ sein** to be over; **es ist drei Uhr ~** it's [already] past three o'clock; **aus und ~** over and done

vorbei|bringen *vt irreg* to drop off

vorbei|fahren *irreg vi sein* ❶ (*vorüberfahren*) to drive past; **im V~** while driving past ❷ (*kurz aufsuchen*) ■**bei etw** *dat* ~ *Supermarkt, Apotheke* to stop off at sth

vorbei|führen *vi* ■**an etw** *dat* ~ to lead past sth

vorbei|gehen [foːɐ̯·'bai·geː·ən] *vi irreg sein* ❶ (*vorübergehen*) to go past; (*überholen*) to pass; (*danebengehen*) *Schuss* to miss; **sie ging dicht an uns vorbei** she walked right past us ❷ (*aufsuchen*) to go to; **gehe doch bitte bei der Apotheke vorbei** please stop off at the drugstore ❸ (*vergehen*) **die Ferien gingen schnell ~** vacation went by fast

vorbei|kommen *vi irreg sein* ❶ (*passieren*) to pass ❷ (*besuchen*) to drop in (**bei** +*dat* at) ❸ (*vorbeigehen können*) to get past

vorbei|lassen *vt irreg* to let past; **lassen Sie uns bitte vorbei!** please let us through!

vorbei|reden *vi* **am Thema ~** to miss the point; **aneinander ~** to be talking at cross-purposes *pl*

vorbelastet *adj* at a disadvantage; **erblich ~ sein** to have a genetic predisposition

vor|bereiten* **I.** *vt* to prepare **II.** *vr* ■**sich** *akk* ~ to prepare oneself

Vorbereitung <-, -en> *f* preparation

Vorbesitzer(in) <-s, -> *m(f)* previous owner

vor|bestellen* *vt* to order in advance; **ich möchte zwei Karten ~** I'd like to reserve two tickets

V

Vorbestellung *f* advance booking

vorbestraft *adj* previously convicted (**wegen** +*dat* for/of); **nicht ~ sein** to not have a criminal record

Vorbestrafte(r) *f(m) dekl wie adj* person with a previous conviction

vor|beugen I. *vt* (*nach vorne beugen*) to bend forward **II.** *vi* (*Prophylaxe betreiben*) **einer Krankheit/Gefahr ~** to prevent an illness/danger **III.** *vr* ■**sich** *akk* ~ to lean forward

Vorbeugung <-, -en> *f* prevention; **zur ~ [gegen etw** *akk*] as a preventive measure [against sth]

Vorbild <-[e]s, -er> ['foːɐ̯·bɪlt] *nt* example; [**jdm**] **als ~ dienen** to serve as an example [for sb]

vorbildlich I. *adj* exemplary **II.** *adv* in an exemplary manner

Vorbote *m* harbinger, herald

vor|bringen *vt irreg Argument* to put forward; *Bedenken* to express; *Einwand* to raise

vorchristlich *adj attr* **in ~er Zeit** in pre-Christian times

Vordach *nt* canopy

vor|datieren* [foːɐ̯·da·tiː·rən] *vt* to post-date

Vọrderachse *f* front axle

Vọrderasien <-s> *nt* Near East

vordere(r, s) ['fɔr·də·rə, -rɐ, -rəs] *adj* front

Vọrdergrund *m a.* KUNST, FOTO foreground; **etw in den ~ stellen** to give priority to sth; **im ~ stehen** to be the center of attention; **in den ~ treten** to come to the fore

vọrdergründig I. *adj* superficial **II.** *adv* at first glance

Vọrdermann *m* ■**mein ~** the person in front of me

Vọrderrad *nt* front wheel

Vọrderradantrieb *m* front-wheel drive

Vọrderseite *f* front [side]

vorderste(r, s) ['fɔr·dɐ·stə, -stɐ, -stəs] *adj superl von* **vordere(r, s)** foremost; **die ~n Plätze** the seats at the very front

vor|drängeln, vor|drängen *vr* ■**sich** *akk* ~ to push one's way to the front

vor|dringen *vi irreg sein* to reach, to get as far as

vorehelich *adj attr* premarital

voreilig ['foːɐ̯·ʔai·lɪç] **I.** *adj* rash, over-hasty **II.** *adv* rashly, hastily

voreinander [foːɐ̯·ʔai'nan·dɐ] *adv* in front of each other; **Angst ~ haben** to be afraid of each other; **Geheimnisse ~ haben** to keep secrets from each other

voreingenommen ['foːɐ̯·ʔain·gə·nɔ·mən] *adj* prejudiced (**gegenüber** +*dat* against)

vor|enthalten* ['foːɐ̯·ʔɛnt·hal·tn̩] *vt irreg* ■[**jdm**] **etw ~** to withhold sth [from sb]

Vorentscheidung *f* preliminary decision

vorerst ['foːɐ̯·ʔeːɐ̯st] *adv* for the time being

Vorfahr(in) <-en, -en> ['foːɐ̯·faːɐ̯] *m(f)* ancestor

vor|fahren *irreg* **I.** *vi sein* ❶ (*vor ein Gebäude fahren*) to drive up ❷ (*ein Stück weiterfahren*) to move up ❸ (*früher fahren*) to drive on ahead **II.** *vt haben* (*vor ein Gebäude fahren*) *Wagen* to bring around

Vorfahrt ['foːɐ̯·faːɐ̯t] *f kein pl* right of way; **jdm die ~ nehmen** to not yield to sb

Vorfahrtsschild *nt* yield sign

Vorfahrtsstraße *f* main road

Vorfall *m* incident, occurrence

vor|fallen *vi irreg sein* to happen, to occur

Vorfeld *nt* ► WENDUNGEN: **im ~ von etw** *dat* in the run-up to sth

vor|finden *vt irreg* to find

Vorfreude *f* [excited] anticipation (**auf** +*akk* of)
vor|führen *vt* ① (*präsentieren*) *Gerät* to demonstrate; MODE to model ② (*darbieten*) to perform ③ JUR **jdn dem Richter ~** to bring sb before the judge
Vorführung *f* ① demonstration ② FILM screening
Vorgabe *f* ① *meist pl* (*Richtwert*) guideline ② SPORT head start
Vorgang <-gänge> *m* ① (*Geschehnis*) event ② (*Prozess*) process
Vorgänger(in) <-s, -> *m(f)* predecessor
Vorgarten *m* front yard
vor|geben *irreg* **I.** *vt* ① (*vorschützen*) to use as an excuse ② (*nach vorn geben*) to pass forward ③ (*festlegen*) to set in advance **II.** *vi* ■ ~ [, **dass ...**] to pretend [that ...]
Vorgebirge *nt* foothills *pl*
vorgefasst[RR], **vorgefaßt**[ALT] *adj* preconceived
vorgefertigt *adj* prefabricated
vor|gehen *vi irreg sein* ① (*vorausgehen*) to go on ahead ② (*zu schnell gehen*) to be fast; **meine Uhr geht fünf Minuten vor** my watch is five minutes fast ③ (*Priorität haben*) to have priority, to come first ④ (*Schritte ergreifen*) to take action ⑤ (*sich abspielen*) to be going on; **was ging in ihr vor?** what was going on inside her? ⑥ (*verfahren*) to proceed (**bei** +*dat* in/with)
Vorgehensweise *f* procedure
vorgelagert *adj* GEOG offshore
Vorgeschmack *m kein pl* foretaste
Vorgesetzte(r) *f(m) dekl wie adj* superior
vorgestern ['foːɐ̯·gɛs·tɐn] *adv* the day before yesterday; ~ **Morgen/Nacht** the morning/night before last
vor|haben ['foːɐ̯·haː·bn̩] *vt irreg* to have planned; **wir haben große Dinge mit Ihnen vor** we've got great plans for you; **hast du etwa vor, noch weiterzuarbeiten?** do you intend to keep on working?
Vorhaben <-s, -> ['foːɐ̯·haː·bn̩] *nt* plan, project
vor|halten *irreg* **I.** *vt* ■ **jdm etw ~** ① (*vorwerfen*) to reproach sb for sth ② (*davorhalten*) *Spiegel* to hold sth in front of sb **II.** *vi* to last
Vorhaltung *f meist pl* reproach; **jdm ~en machen** to reproach sb (**wegen** +*dat* for)
vorhanden ['foːɐ̯·'handn̩] *adj* ① (*verfügbar*) available; ■ ~ **sein** to be left ② (*existierend*) existing; ■ ~ **sein** to exist
Vorhang <-s, Vorhänge> ['foːɐ̯·haŋ, *pl* 'foːɐ̯·hɛŋə] *m* curtain
Vorhängeschloss[RR] *nt* padlock
Vorhaut *f* ANAT foreskin
vorher [foːɐ̯·'heːɐ̯] *adv* beforehand; **kurz ~** just before; **ich muss ~ noch essen** I have to eat first
vorher|bestimmen* *vt* to predetermine; ■ **vorherbestimmt sein** to be predestined
vorhergehend *adj* previous *attr;* preceding
vorherig [foːɐ̯·'heː·rɪç] *adj attr* prior; *Abmachung, Vereinbarung* previous
Vorherrschaft *f* POL hegemony, [pre]dominance
vor|herrschen *vi* to predominate
Vorhersage [foːɐ̯·'heːɐ̯·zaː·gə] *f* ① METEO forecast ② (*Voraussage*) prediction
vorher|sagen *vt* to predict
vorhersehbar *adj* foreseeable
vorher|sehen *vt irreg* to foresee
vorhin [foːɐ̯·'hɪn] *adv* a moment ago, just [now]
Vorhut <-, -en> *f* MIL vanguard
vorig ['foː·rɪç] *adj attr* last, previous
Vorjahr *nt* last year
vor|jammern *vt* ■ **jdm etw ~** to moan to sb
Vorkämpfer(in) *m(f)* pioneer
Vorkaufsrecht *nt* right of first refusal
Vorkehrung <-, -en> *f* precaution; **~en treffen** to take precautions
Vorkenntnis *f meist pl* previous experience
vor|knöpfen *vt* ■ **sich** *dat* **jdn ~** to give sb a good talking-to
vor|kochen *vt* KOCHK to precook
vor|kommen *vi irreg sein* ① (*passieren*) to happen; ■ **es kommt vor, dass ...** it can happen that ...; **das kann [schon mal] ~** these things [can] happen ② (*vorhanden sein*) to be found, to occur ③ (*erscheinen*) to seem; **jdm bekannt ~** to sound familiar to sb; **du kommst dir wohl sehr schlau vor?** you think you're real clever, don't you? ④ (*nach vorn kommen*) to come [up] to the front ⑤ (*zum Vorschein kommen*) [**hinter etw** *dat*] ~ to come out [from behind sth]
Vorkommen <-s, -> *nt* ① *kein pl* (*Auftreten*) incidence ② *meist pl* GEOL deposit
Vorkommnis <-ses, -se> ['foːɐ̯·kɔm·nɪs] *nt* incident, occurrence; **keine besonderen ~se** nothing out of the ordinary
Vorkriegszeit *f* prewar period
vor|laden *vt irreg* JUR to summon
Vorladung *f* JUR ① (*das Vorladen*) summoning ② (*Schreiben*) summons
Vorlage *f* ① *kein pl* (*das Vorlegen*) presentation ② (*Muster*) pattern ③ SCHWEIZ (*Vorleger*) mat
vor|lassen *vt irreg* ① (*den Vortritt lassen*) to let go first ② (*nach vorn durchlassen*) to let past
Vorläufer(in) *m(f)* precursor
vorläufig ['foːɐ̯·lɔy·fɪç] **I.** *adj* temporary; *Ergebnis* provisional; *Regelung* interim **II.** *adv* for the time being
vorlaut ['foːɐ̯·laut] *adj* cheeky, impertinent
vor|legen *vt* (*einreichen*) ■ [**jdm**] **etw ~** to present sth [to sb]; [**jdm**] **Beweise ~** to provide [sb with] evidence
vor|lesen *irreg* **I.** *vt* to read aloud *sep;* **soll ich dir den Artikel ~?** should I read you the article? **II.** *vi* to read aloud (**aus** +*dat* from)
Vorlesung *f* lecture (**über** +*akk* on)
Vorlesungsverzeichnis *nt* ≈ schedule of classes
vorletzte(r, s) ['foːɐ̯·lɛts·tə, -s·tɐ, -s·təs] *adj* ① (*vor dem Letzten liegend*) before last *pred;* **das ~ Treffen** the meeting before last ② (*in einer Aufstellung*) penultimate, next to last

Vorliebe [foːɐ̯·ˈliː·bə] *f* preference; **eine ~ für jdn/etw haben** to be particularly fond of sb/sth
vorlieb|nehmen [foːɐ̯·ˈliːp-] *vi irreg* ■**[mit jdm/etw]** ~ to make do [with sb/sth]
vor|liegen *vi irreg* ❶ (*eingereicht sein*) ■**jdm** ~ to have been received by sb; **uns liegen keine Beweise vor** we have no proof ❷ (*bestehen*) to be
vor|lügen *vt irreg* ■**jdm etw** ~ to lie to sb
vor|machen *vt* ❶ (*täuschen*) ■**jdm/sich etw** ~ to fool sb/oneself; **machen wir uns doch nichts vor** let's not kid ourselves ❷ (*demonstrieren*) ■**jdm etw** ~ to show sb [how to do] sth
Vormachtstellung *f kein pl* POL hegemony, supremacy
vormalig [ˈfoːɐ̯·maːl·ɪç] *adj attr* former
Vormarsch *m a.* MIL advance; **auf dem ~ sein** to be advancing; (*fig*) to be gaining ground
vor|merken *vt* **lassen Sie bitte zwei Zimmer** ~ please book two rooms for me; **ich habe mir den Termin vorgemerkt** I've made a note of the appointment
Vormittag [ˈfoɐ̯·mɪ·taːk] *m* morning; **am [frühen/späten]** ~ [early/late] in the morning
vormittags [ˈfoɐ̯·mɪ·taːks] *adv* in the morning
Vormund <-[e]s, -e *o* Vormünder> [ˈfoɐ̯·mʊnt, *pl* ˈfoɐ̯·myn·dɐ] *m* guardian
Vormundschaft <-, -en> [ˈfoɐ̯·mʊnt·ʃaft] *f* guardianship
vorn [fɔrn] *adv* at the front; ~ **im Bus** at the front of the bus; **nach** ~ to the front; **von** ~ (*von der Vorderseite her*) from the front; (*von Anfang an*) from the beginning; **von ~ bis hinten** (*fam*) from beginning to end; **jetzt kann ich wieder von ~ anfangen** now I have to start from scratch all over again
Vorname *m* first name
vorne *adv s.* **vorn**
vornehm [ˈfoːɐ̯·neːm] *adj* ❶ (*elegant*) elegant; *Mensch, Benehmen* distinguished ❷ (*luxuriös*) *Gegend, Restaurant* exclusive ▶ WENDUNGEN: ~ **tun** (*pej*) to put on airs
vor|nehmen *vt irreg* ❶ (*einplanen*) ■**sich** *dat* **etw** ~ to plan sth ❷ (*sich eingehend beschäftigen*) ■**sich** *dat* **etw** ~ to get to work on sth ❸ (*fam: sich vorknöpfen*) ■**sich** *dat* **jdn** ~ to give sb a good talking-to ❹ (*ausführen*) to carry out *sep;* **Änderungen** ~ to make changes
vornherein [ˈfɔrn·hɛ·rain] *adv* ■**von** ~ from the start
Vorort [ˈfoːɐ̯·ʔɔrt] *m* suburb
Vorplatz *m* forecourt
vorprogrammiert *adj* pre-programmed; (*vorbestimmt*) predetermined
Vorrang *m kein pl* ❶ (*Priorität*) priority (**vor** +*dat* over); **mit** ~ as a matter of priority ❷ ÖSTERR (*Vorfahrt*) right of way
vorrangig I. *adj* priority *attr,* of prime importance *pred;* ■~ **sein** to have priority **II.** *adv* as a matter of priority
Vorrat <-[e]s, Vorräte> [ˈfoːɐ̯·raːt, *pl* ˈfoːɐ̯·rɛ·tə] *m* stock, supply (**an** +*dat* of); **etw auf ~ kaufen** to stock up on sth; **Vorräte anlegen** to stock up on sth; **so lange der ~ reicht** while supplies last
vorrätig [ˈfoːɐ̯·rɛ·tɪç] *adj* in stock *pred;* **etw ~ haben** to have sth in stock
Vorratskammer *f* pantry
Vorrecht *nt* privilege
Vorreiter(in) *m(f)* pioneer
Vorrichtung <-, -en> *f* device, gadget
vor|rücken I. *vi sein* ❶ MIL to advance (**gegen** +*akk* on) ❷ (*nach vorn rücken*) to move forward **II.** *vt haben* to move forward
Vorruhestand *m* early retirement
Vorrunde *f* SPORT preliminary round
Vorsaison *f* low season
Vorsatz <-[e]s, Vorsätze> [ˈfoːɐ̯·zats, *pl* foːɐ̯·zɛ·tsə] *m* resolution; **den ~ fassen, etw zu tun** to resolve to do sth
vorsätzlich [ˈfoːɐ̯·zɛts·lɪç] **I.** *adj* deliberate, intentional **II.** *adv* deliberately, intentionally
Vorschau <-, -en> *f* FILM, TV trailer (**auf** +*akk* for), preview (**auf** +*akk* of)
Vorschein *m* **etw zum ~ bringen** (*finden*) to find sth; (*zeigen*) to produce sth; **zum ~ kommen** (*sich bei Suche zeigen*) to turn up; (*offenbar werden*) to come to light
vor|schieben *vt irreg* ❶ (*vorschützen*) to use as an excuse ❷ (*für sich agieren lassen*) ■**jdn** ~ to use sb as a front man/woman ❸ (*nach vorn schieben*) to push forward ❹ (*vor etw schieben*) *Riegel* to push across
vor|schießen *vt irreg Geld* to advance
Vorschlag *m* suggestion; **[jdm] einen ~ machen** to make a suggestion [to sb]; **auf jds ~ [hin]** on sb's recommendation
vor|schlagen *vt irreg* ❶ (*als Vorschlag unterbreiten*) to suggest ❷ (*empfehlen*) to recommend
Vorschlaghammer *m* sledgehammer
vor|schreiben *vt irreg* ■**jdm etw** ~ to stipulate sth to sb; **schreib mir nicht vor, was ich machen soll!** don't tell me what to do!
Vorschrift *f* ADMIN regulation, rule; (*Anweisung*) instructions *pl;* (*polizeilich*) orders *pl;* ~ **sein** to be the rule[s]; **jdm ~en machen** to tell sb what to do
vorschriftsmäßig *adj, adv* according to [the] regulations
Vorschub *m* **einer S.** *dat* ~ **leisten** to encourage sth
Vorschulalter *nt kein pl* preschool age; **im ~ sein** to be of preschool age
Vorschule *f* preschool

> In Switzerland, every child has the right to attend a **Vorschule** for at least one or two years. The **Vorschule** is voluntary and free. In most cantons, children attend such schools for 4–5 hours a day and are prepared for elementary school.

Vorschuss[RR] <-es, Vorschüsse>, **Vorschuß**[ALT] <-sses, Vorschüsse> ['foːɐ̯·ʃʊs] *m* advance

vor|schweben *vi* to have in mind

vor|sehen *irreg* **I.** *vr* ■ **sich** *akk* ~ to watch out (**vor** +*dat* for); **sieh dich vor!** watch it! **II.** *vt* ❶ (*eingeplant haben*) **das Geld war für den Urlaub vorgesehen** the money was intended for the vacation; ■ **jdn** ~ to designate sb; **Sie hatte ich für eine andere Aufgabe** ~ I had you in mind for a different job ❷ (*bestimmen*) to call for; (*in Gesetz, Vertrag*) to provide for **III.** *vi* (*bestimmen*) **es ist vorgesehen, [dass ...]** it is planned [that ...]

Vorsehung <-> ['foːɐ̯·zeːʊŋ] *f kein pl* providence

Vorsicht <-> ['foːɐ̯·zɪçt] *f kein pl* care; **etw ist mit ~ zu genießen** (*fam*) sth should be taken with a grain of salt; **mit** ~ carefully; **zur** ~ as a precaution; **~!** watch out!

vorsichtig **I.** *adj* ❶ (*umsichtig*) careful ❷ (*zurückhaltend*) cautious **II.** *adv* ❶ (*umsichtig*) carefully ❷ (*zurückhaltend*) cautiously

vorsichtshalber *adv* as a precaution, just to be on the safe side

Vorsichtsmaßnahme *f* precaution; **~n treffen** to take precautions

Vorsilbe *f* prefix

vor|singen *irreg vt* to sing first

vorsintflutlich ['foːɐ̯·zɪnt·fluːt·lɪç] *adj* (*fam*) ancient

Vorsitz ['foːɐ̯·zɪts] *m* chairmanship; **den ~ haben** to be chairman/-woman/-person; **den ~ bei etw** *dat* **haben** to chair sth

Vorsitzende(r) *f(m) dekl wie adj* chairman/-woman/-person

Vorsorge *f* provisions *pl;* **~ für etw** *akk* **treffen** to make provisions for sth

vor|sorgen *vi* to provide

Vorsorgeuntersuchung *f* medical checkup

vorsorglich **I.** *adj* precautionary **II.** *adv* as a precaution

Vorspann <-[e]s, -e> ['foːɐ̯·ʃpan] *m* FILM, TV opening credits *npl*

Vorspeise *f* starter, appetizer

Vorspiel *nt* ❶ MUS prelude; (*zur Probe*) audition ❷ (*vor dem Liebesakt*) foreplay

vor|spielen **I.** *vt* ❶ MUS to play ❷ (*vorheucheln*) to put on **II.** *vi* MUS to play

vor|sprechen *irreg* **I.** *vt* ■ **jdm etw** ~ to say sth for sb first **II.** *vi* (*offiziell aufsuchen*) ■ **bei jdm/etw** ~ to pay sb/sth a [formal] visit

Vorsprung *m* lead

Vorstadium *nt* early stage

Vorstadt *f* suburb

Vorstand *m* ❶ (*Geschäftsführung*) [management] board; (*einer Partei, eines Vereins*) [executive] committee ❷ (*Vorstandsmitglied*) director, board member; (*einer Partei*) executive; (*eines Vereins*) [member of the] executive [committee]

vor|stehen *vi irreg sein o haben* ❶ (*hervorragen*) to be prominent, to protrude ❷ (*Vorsteher sein*) ■ **einer S.** *dat* ~ to be the head of sth

Vorsteher(in) <-s, -> ['foːɐ̯·ʃteːɐ] *m(f)* head

vorstellbar *adj* conceivable, imaginable; **kaum** ~ almost inconceivable

vor|stellen **I.** *vt* ❶ (*gedanklich sehen*) ■ **sich** *dat* **etw** ~ to imagine sth; **das muss man sich mal ~!** just imagine [it]!; **unter dem Namen Schlüter kann ich mir nichts** ~ the name Schlüter doesn't mean a thing to me ❷ (*als angemessen betrachten*) ■ **sich** *dat* **etw** ~ to have sth in mind ❸ (*bekannt machen*) ■ **jdm jdn** ~ to introduce sb to sb ❹ (*präsentieren*) ■ **jdm etw** ~ to present sth to sb ❺ (*vorrücken*) *Uhr* to set forward **II.** *vr* ■ **sich** *akk* ~ ❶ (*bekannt machen*) to introduce oneself ❷ *bei Arbeitgeber* to have an interview

Vorstellung *f* ❶ (*gedankliches Bild*) idea; **in jds** ~ in sb's mind; **das Gehalt entspricht nicht ganz meinen ~en** the salary doesn't quite meet my expectations; **bestimmte ~en haben** to have certain ideas; **falsche ~en haben** to have false hopes ❷ THEAT performance; FILM screening ❸ (*Präsentation*) presentation

Vorstellungsgespräch *nt* interview

Vorstellungskraft *f kein pl,* **Vorstellungsvermögen** *nt kein pl* [powers *npl* of] imagination

vor|stoßen *irreg vi sein* to venture; *Truppen* to advance

Vorstrafe *f* previous conviction

vor|strecken *vt* ❶ (*leihen*) **jdm einen Geldbetrag** ~ to advance sb a sum of money ❷ (*nach vorn strecken*) to stretch forward; **den Arm/die Hand** ~ to stretch out one's arm/hand

Vorstufe *f* preliminary stage

Vortag *m* **am** ~ the day before; **vom** ~ from yesterday

vor|täuschen *vt Unfall* to fake; *Interesse* to feign

Vorteil <-s, -e> ['foːɐ̯·tail] *m* advantage; **er ist nur auf seinen ~ bedacht** he only ever thinks of his own interests; **im ~ sein** to have an advantage (**gegenüber** +*dat* over); **von ~ sein** to be advantageous (**für** +*akk* for/to)

vorteilhaft *adj* favorable (**für** +*akk* for); *Geschäft* lucrative, profitable

Vortrag <-[e]s, Vorträge> ['foːɐ̯·traːk, *pl* 'foːɐ̯·trɛːgə] *m* lecture; **einen ~ halten** to give a lecture (**über** +*akk* about/on)

vor|tragen *vt irreg* ❶ (*berichten*) to present; *Wunsch* to express ❷ (*rezitieren*) to recite; *Lied* to sing

vortrefflich [foːɐ̯·trɛf·lɪç] **I.** *adj* excellent; (*Gedanke, Idee a.*) splendid **II.** *adv* excellently

vor|treten *vi irreg sein* ❶ (*nach vorn treten*) to step forward ❷ (*vorstehen*) to jut out

Vortritt[1] *m* precedence, priority; ■ **jdm den ~ lassen** to let sb go first

Vortritt[2] *m kein pl* SCHWEIZ (*Vorfahrt*) right of way

vorüber [fo·'ryːbɐ] *adv* ■ ~ **sein** ❶ *räumlich* to have gone past ❷ *zeitlich* to be over;

Schmerz to be gone
vorüber|gehen [fo·ˈryː·bɐ·geː·ən] *vi irreg sein* to pass; *Schmerz* to go
vorübergehend I. *adj* temporary **II.** *adv* for a short time; ~ **geschlossen** temporarily closed
Vorurteil [ˈfoːɐ̯·ʔʊr·tail] *nt* prejudice; ~**e haben** to be prejudiced (**gegenüber** +*dat* against)
vorurteilslos I. *adj* unprejudiced **II.** *adv* without prejudice
Vorverkauf *m* advance sale
Vorverkaufsstelle *f* advance ticket office
vor|verlegen* *vt* to move up (**auf** +*akk* to)
Vorwahl *f* ❶ (*vorherige Auswahl*) pre-selection [process] ❷ POL primary [election] ❸ TELEK area code
vor|wählen *vt* TELEK to dial first
Vorwand <-[e]s, Vorwände> [ˈfoːɐ̯·vant, *pl* ˈfoːɐ̯·vɛn·də] *m* pretext, excuse; **unter einem** ~ on a pretext
vor|warnen *vt* to warn [in advance]
Vorwarnung *f* [advance] warning
vorwärts [ˈfoːɐ̯·vɛrts] *adv* forward; ~! onward!, move it!
vorwärts|bringen *vt irreg* ■**jdn** ~ to help sb make progress
Vorwärtsgang <-gänge> *m* forward gear
vorwärts|kommen *vi irreg sein* to make progress
Vorwäsche <-, -n> *f* prewash [cycle]
vor|waschen *vt irreg* to prewash
vorweg [foːɐ̯·ˈvɛk] *adv* ❶ (*zuvor*) beforehand ❷ (*an der Spitze*) in front
vorweg|nehmen [foːɐ̯·ˈvɛk·neː·mən] *vt irreg* to anticipate
vorweihnachtlich *adj* pre-Christmas
vor|weisen *vt irreg* ❶ (*nachweisen*) **Erfahrung ~ können** to have experience ❷ (*vorzeigen*) to show
vor|werfen *vt irreg* ❶ (*als Vorwurf vorhalten*) ■**jdm etw** ~ to reproach sb for [doing] sth; **sich** *dat* **nichts vorzuwerfen haben** to have a clear conscience ❷ (*als Futter hinwerfen*) ■**einem Tier etw** ~ to throw sth to an animal
vorwiegend *adv* predominantly, mainly
vorwitzig *adj* cocky
Vorwort <-worte> *nt* foreword, preface
Vorwurf <-[e]s, Vorwürfe> *m* reproach; ■**jdm Vorwürfe machen** to reproach sb (**wegen** +*dat* for)
vorwurfsvoll I. *adj* reproachful **II.** *adv* reproachfully
Vorzeichen *nt* ❶ (*Omen*) omen ❷ (*Anzeichen*) sign
vor|zeigen *vt* to show
Vorzeit [ˈfoːɐ̯·tsait] *f* prehistoric times
vorzeitig [ˈfoːɐ̯·tsai·tɪç] *adj* early; *Tod* untimely
vorzeitlich [ˈfoːɐ̯·tsait·lɪç] *adj* prehistoric
vor|ziehen *vt irreg* ❶ (*bevorzugen*) to prefer ❷ (*zuerst erfolgen lassen*) *Termin* to move up ❸ (*nach vorn ziehen*) to pull forward
Vorzimmer *nt* ❶ (*Sekretariat*) secretary's office ❷ ÖSTERR (*Diele*) hall
Vorzug <-[e]s, Vorzüge> [ˈfoːɐ̯·tsuːk, *pl* ˈfoːɐ̯·tsyː·gə] *m* ❶ (*gute Eigenschaft*) asset, merit ❷ (*Vorteil*) advantage ❸ (*Bevorzugung*) **einer S. den ~ geben** to prefer sth
vorzüglich [foːɐ̯·ˈtsyːg·lɪç] **I.** *adj* excellent, first-rate **II.** *adv* excellently; ~ **speisen** to have a sumptuous meal
Vorzugspreis *m* discount fare
vorzugsweise *adv* primarily
Votum <-s, Voten *o* Vota> [ˈvoː·tʊm, *pl* ˈvoː·tən, ˈvoː·ta] *nt* ❶ (*Entscheidung*) decision ❷ POL vote
Voyeur <-s, -e> [vo̯a·ˈjøːɐ̯] *m* voyeur
Voyeurismus <-> [vo̯a·ˈjøː·ɐ̯ɪs·mʊs] *m kein pl* voyeurism
voyeuristisch *adj* voyeuristic
vulgär [vʊl·ˈgɛːɐ̯] **I.** *adj* vulgar **II.** *adv* **sich ~ ausdrücken** to use vulgar language
Vulkan <-[e]s, -e> [vʊl·ˈkaːn] *m* volcano
Vulkanausbruch [vʊ-] *m* volcanic eruption
vulkanisch [vʊl·ˈkaː·nɪʃ] *adj* volcanic

Ww

W, w <-, - *o fam* -s, -s> [veː] *nt* W, w; **~ wie Wilhelm** W as in Whiskey
Waadt <-> [vaːt] *f* Vaud
Waage <-, -n> ['vaː·gə] *f* ① TECH scale ② *kein pl* ASTROL Libra
waagerecht ['vaː·gə·rɛçt] **I.** *adj* horizontal **II.** *adv* horizontally
Waagerechte <-n, -n> *f* horizontal [line]; **in der ~n** level
wabbelig ['va·bə·lɪç], **wabblig** ['vab·lɪç] *adj* wobbly
wach [vax] *adj* awake; ■ **~ werden** to wake up
Wache <-, -n> ['va·xə] *f* ① *kein pl* (*Wachdienst*) guard duty; **~ stehen** to be on guard duty ② (*Wachposten*) guard ③ (*Polizeiwache*) police station
wachen ['va·xn̩] *vi* ① (*Wache halten*) to keep watch ② ■ **über etw** *akk* **~** to ensure that sth is done
Wạchhund *m* watchdog
Wạchmann <-leute *o* -männer> *m* ① (*Wächter*) [night] watchman ② ÖSTERR (*Polizist*) policeman
wạch|rufen *vt irreg Erinnerungen* to evoke
Wachs <-es, -e> [vaks] *nt* wax
wachsam ['vax·zaːm] **I.** *adj* vigilant, watchful **II.** *adv* vigilantly, watchfully
Wạchsamkeit <-> *f kein pl* vigilance
wachsen[1] <wạchst, wụchs, gewạchsen> ['vak·sn̩] *vi sein* to grow (**um** *+akk* by); **in die Breite/Höhe ~** to grow broader/taller
wachsen[2] ['vak·sn̩] *vt* (*mit Wachs einreiben*) to wax
wạchst *3. pers sing pres von* **wachsen**[1]
Wachstum <-[e]s> ['vaks·tuːm] *nt kein pl* growth
Wachtel <-, -n> ['vax·tl̩] *f* quail
Wächter(in) <-s, -> ['vɛç·tɐ] *m(f)* ① (*einer Anstalt*) guard; (*Wachmann*) [night] watchman ② ([*moralischer*] *Hüter*) guardian
Wạch(t)turm *m* watchtower
wackelig ['va·kə·lɪç] *adj Konstruktion* rickety; *Stuhl* unsteady
Wạckelkontakt *m* loose connection
wackeln ['va·kl̩n] *vi* ① (*wackelig sein*) to wobble; *Konstruktion* to shake ② (*hin und her bewegen*) **mit dem Stuhl ~** to rock [in] one's chair; **mit dem Kopf ~** to shake one's head; **mit den Ohren ~** to wiggle one's ears
Wạckelpudding *m* (*fam*) jello
wacklig ['vak·lɪç] *adj s.* **wackelig**
Wade <-, -n> ['vaː·də] *f* calf
Waffe <-, -n> ['va·fə] *f* weapon; **zu den ~n greifen** to take up arms ▶ WENDUNGEN: **jdn mit seinen eigenen ~n schlagen** to beat sb at his own game
Waffel <-, -n> ['va·fl̩] *f* waffle
Wạffeleisen *nt* waffle iron
Wạffenbesitz *m* possession of firearms
Wạffenhandel *m* arms trade
Wạffenhändler *m* arms dealer
Wạffenruhe *f* ceasefire
Wạffenschein *m* gun license
Wạffenstillstand *m* armistice
wagemutig *adj* daring
wagen ['vaː·gn̩] **I.** *vt* ① (*riskieren*) to risk ② (*sich trauen*) ■ **es ~, etw zu tun** to dare [to] do sth ▶ WENDUNGEN: **wer nicht wagt, der nicht gewinnt** (*prov*) nothing ventured, nothing gained **II.** *vr* ■ **sich** *akk* **irgendwohin ~** to venture out to somewhere
Wagen <-, - *o* SÜDD, ÖSTERR Wägen> ['vaː·gn̩] *m* (*Auto, Zug*) car
Wagenheber <-s, -> *m* jack
Waggon <-s, -s> [va·'gõ, va·'gɔŋ] *m* RAIL car
waghalsig ['vaːk·hal·zɪç] *adj* daring
Wagnis <-ses, -se> ['vaːk·nɪs] *nt* ① (*riskantes Vorhaben*) risky venture ② (*Risiko*) risk
Wagon <-s, -s> [va·'gõ, va·'gɔŋ] *m s.* **Waggon**
Wahl <-, -en> [vaːl] *f* ① POL election; **zur ~ gehen** to [go to] vote ② (*Auswahl*) choice; **eine ~ treffen** to make a choice; **jdm die ~ lassen** to let sb choose; **jdm keine ~ lassen** to leave sb no choice
wahlberechtigt *adj* entitled to vote *pred*
Wahlbeteiligung *f* [voter] turnout
wählen ['vɛː·lən] *vi, vt* ① (*auswählen*) to choose ② POL to vote; ■ **jdn ~** to vote for sb; ■ **jdn zu etw** *dat* **~** to elect sb [as] sth ③ TELEK to dial
Wähler(in) <-s, -> *m(f)* voter
Wahlergebnis *nt* election result
wählerisch ['vɛː·lə·rɪʃ] *adj* particular, choos[e]y *fam;* (*Kunde*) discerning
Wahlgang *m* ballot
Wahlkampf *m* election campaign
wahllos ['vaːl·loːs] **I.** *adj* indiscriminate **II.** *adv* indiscriminately
Wahlniederlage *f* electoral defeat
Wahlplakat *nt* election poster
Wahlrecht *nt kein pl* [right to] vote; **das allgemeine ~** universal suffrage
Wahlsieg *m* election victory
Wahlspruch *m* motto, slogan
wahlweise *adv* as desired
Wahlwiederholung *f* TELEK automatic redial
Wahn <-[e]s> [vaːn] *m kein pl* ① (*irrige Vorstellung*) delusion ② (*Manie*) mania
Wahnsinn *m kein pl* ① (*Geisteskrankheit*) insanity ② (*fam: Unsinn*) madness; **~!** amazing!
wahnsinnig **I.** *adj* ① (*geisteskrank*) insane; **jdn ~ machen** (*fam*) to drive sb crazy ② (*fam: unsinnig*) crazy ③ *attr* (*fam: gewaltig*) terrible, dreadful **II.** *adv* (*fam: sehr*) terribly, dreadfully; **~ viel** a whole lot
Wahnsinnige(r) *f(m) dekl wie adj* lunatic
Wahnvorstellung *f* delusion

W

wahr [vaːɐ̯] *adj* ❶ (*zutreffend*) true ❷ *attr* (*wirklich*) real; ~ **werden** to become a reality; **etw** ~ **machen** to carry out sth ► WENDUNGEN: **das darf doch nicht** ~ **sein!** (*verärgert*) I don't believe this [is happening]!; (*entsetzt*) this can't be true!; **da ist etwas W~es dran** there is some truth in it; (*als Antwort*) you're right about that; **etw ist** [**auch**] **nicht das W~e** sth is not the real McCoy *fam*
wahren ['vaː·rən] *vt* ❶ (*erhalten*) to maintain; **die Form** ~ (*geh*) to maintain etiquette [*or* social graces] ❷ (*schützen*) to protect; **jds Interessen** ~ to look after sb's interests
während ['vɛː·rənt] **I.** *präp* +*gen* during **II.** *konj* ❶ (*zur selben Zeit*) while ❷ (*wohingegen*) whereas
währenddessen ['vɛː·rənt·'dɛ·sn̩] *adv* meanwhile, in the meantime
wahrhaben *vt* ■ **etw nicht** ~ **wollen** to not want to admit sth
wahrhaftig [vaːɐ̯·'haf·tɪç] *adv* really
Wahrheit <-, -en> ['vaːɐ̯·hait] *f* truth; **es mit der** ~ **nicht so genau nehmen** to stretch the truth
wahrlich ['vaːɐ̯·lɪç] *adv* really
wahrnehmbar *adj* perceptible; *Geräusch* audible
wahr|nehmen ['vaːɐ̯·neː·mən] *vt irreg* ❶ (*merken*) to perceive; *Geräusch, Geschmack* to detect ❷ (*nutzen*) *Gelegenheit* to take advantage of; *Interessen* to look after; *Termin* to keep
Wahrnehmung <-, -en> *f Geräusch* detection; *Geruch* perception
wahr|sagen ['vaːɐ̯·zaː·gn̩] *vi* to tell fortunes
Wahrsager(in) <-s, -> ['vaːɐ̯·zaː·gɐ] *m(f)* fortune teller
wahrscheinlich [vaːɐ̯·'ʃain·lɪç] **I.** *adj* probable, likely **II.** *adv* probably
Wahrscheinlichkeit <-, -en> *f* probability; **aller** ~ **nach** in all probability
Währung <-, -en> ['vɛː·rʊŋ] *f* currency
Währungspolitik *f* monetary policy
Währungsreform *f* currency reform
Währungsunion *f* monetary union; ■ **die Europäische** ~ the European Monetary Union
Wahrzeichen ['vaːɐ̯·tsai·çn̩] *nt* landmark
Waise <-, -n> ['vai·zə] *f* orphan
Waisenhaus *nt* orphanage
Waisenkind *nt* orphan
Waisenrente *f a living subsidy for a juvenile orphan*
Wal <-[e]s, -e> [vaːl] *m* whale
Wald <-[e]s, Wälder> [valt, *pl* 'vɛl·dɐ] *m* forest, woods *pl*
Wạldbrand *m* forest fire
Wạldlauf *m* cross-country run
Wạldschaden *m* damage to forests
Wạldsterben *nt* [forest] dieback
Wạldweg *m* forest path
Wales <-> [weɪlz] *nt* Wales; *s. a.* **Deutschland**
Walfang ['vaːl·faŋ] *m kein pl* whaling
Waliser(in) <-s, -> [va·'liː·zɐ] *m(f)* Welshman *masc*, Welshwoman *fem*; *s. a.* **Deutsche(r)**
walisisch [va·'liː·zɪʃ] *adj* Welsh; *s. a.* **deutsch**
Walisische <-n> [va·'liː·zɪ·ʃə] *nt* ■ **das** ~ Welsh, the Welsh language; *s. a.* **Deutsche**
Wall <-[e]s, Wälle> [val, *pl* 'vɛ·lə] *m* embankment; *Burg* rampart
Wạllfahrer(in) *m(f)* pilgrim
Wallfahrt ['val·faːɐ̯t] *f* pilgrimage
Wạllfahrtsort *m* place of pilgrimage
Wallis <-> ['va·lɪs] *nt* Valais (*Swiss Canton*)
Walliser(in) <-s, -> ['va·li·zɐ] *m(f)* inhabitant of Valais (*in Switzerland*)
Wạllung <-, -en> *f* (*Hitzewallung*) [hot] flash *usu pl* ► WENDUNGEN: **jdn in** ~ **bringen** to make sb's blood surge
Walnuss[RR] ['val·nʊs] *f* walnut
Wạlnussbaum[RR] *m* walnut [tree]

> The **Walpurgisnacht** is the eve of May 1st and, according to ancient German folklore, is the night of the Witches' Sabbat on the Blocksberg (that used to be called the Brocken), the highest peak in the Harz mountains of central Germany.

Walross[RR] <-es, -e>, **Walroß**[ALT] <-rosses, -rosse> ['val·rɔs] *nt* walrus
walten ['val·tn̩] *vi* (*geh*) ❶ (*herrschen*) to reign ❷ (*üben*) **Nachsicht** ~ **lassen** to show leniency
Walze <-, -n> ['val·tsə] *f* roller
wälzen ['vɛl·tsn̩] **I.** *vt* ❶ (*rollen*) to roll ❷ *Probleme* to turn over in one's mind ❸ *Bücher* to pore over **II.** *vr* ■ **sich** ~ to roll (**in** +*dat* in); **sie wälzte sich im Bett hin und her** she tossed and turned in bed
Walzer <-s, -> ['val·tsɐ] *m* waltz
Wampe <-, -n> ['vam·pə] *f* (*fam*) [beer] belly
wạnd *imp von* **winden**[1]
Wand <-, Wände> [vant, *pl* 'vɛn·də] *f* wall; **da könnte ich die Wände hochgehen!** (*fig fam*) that drives me up the wall!
Wandalismus <-> [van·da·'lɪs·mʊs] *m kein pl s.* **Vandalismus**
Wandel <-s> ['van·dl̩] *m kein pl* change
wandeln ['van·dl̩n] *vt, vr* ■ [**sich**] ~ to change
Wạnderausstellung *f* traveling exhibit
Wanderer, Wanderin <-s, -> ['van·də·rɐ] *m, f* hiker
Wạnderkarte *f* trail map
wandern ['van·dɐn] *vi sein* ❶ (*eine Wanderung machen*) to hike ❷ ZOOL to migrate ❸ (*fam*) **in den Müll** ~ to be thrown in the garbage
Wanderung <-, -en> ['van·də·rʊŋ] *f* hike
Wạndervogel *m* ❶ (*Zugvogel*) migratory bird ❷ (*hum*) avid hiker
Wạnderweg *m* [hiking] trail
Wạnderzirkus *m* traveling circus
Wandlung <-, -en> ['vand·lʊŋ] *f* change
Wạndschrank *m* built-in wall closet

wandte ['van·tə] *imp von* **wenden**

Wange <-, -n> ['va·ŋə] *f* cheek

wankelmütig ['vaŋ·kl̩·myː·tɪç] *adj* inconsistent

wanken ['vaŋ·kn̩] *vi* ❶ *haben* (*schwanken*) to sway ❷ *sein* (*wankend gehen*) to stagger

wann [van] *adv* when; **seit ~** since when; **~ [auch] immer** whenever

Wanne <-, -n> ['va·nə] *f* tub

Wanst <-[e]s, Wänste> [vanst, *pl* 'vɛns·tə] *m* belly

Wanze <-, -n> ['van·tsə] *f* bug

wappnen ['vap·nən] *vr* ■**sich** *akk* **[gegen etw] ~** to prepare oneself [for sth]

war [vaːɐ̯] *imp von* **sein**[1]

warb [varp] *imp von* **werben**

Ware <-, -n> ['vaː·rə] *f* article, product

Wa̲renangebot *nt* range of products

Wa̲renbestand *m* stock

Wa̲renhaus *nt* department store

Wa̲renlager *nt* warehouse

warf [varf] *imp von* **werfen**

warm <wạ̈rmer, wạ̈rmste> [varm] *adj* warm; **etw ~ halten** to keep sth warm; **etw ~ machen** to heat sth up; **den Motor ~ laufen lassen** to let the engine warm up; **mir ist zu ~** I'm hot ▶ WENDUNGEN: **etw wärmstens empfehlen** to highly recommend sth; **mit jdm ~ werden** to warm to sb

Wärme <-> ['vɛr·mə] *f kein pl* warmth

Wạ̈rmekraftwerk *nt* thermal power plant

wärmen ['vɛr·mən] **I.** *vt* to warm up; ■**sich [gegenseitig] ~** to keep each other warm **II.** *vi* to be warm

wạ̈rmer *adj komp von* **warm**

Wạ̈rmeregler *m* thermostat

Wạ̈rmflasche *f* hot-water bottle

Wạrmhaltekanne *f* thermos

wạrm|halten *vr irreg* ■**sich** *dat* **jdn ~** to maintain a good relationship with sb

Wạrmhalteplatte *f* hot plate

wạrmherzig *adj* warm-hearted

Wạrmmiete *f* rent including heat

Wạrmstart *m* COMPUT soft reset

wạ̈rmste(r, s) *adj superl von* **warm**

Warmwạsserversorgung *f* hot water supply

Wạrnblinkanlage *f* AUTO hazard lights *pl,* hazards *pl fam*

Wạrndreieck *nt* hazard warning triangle

warnen ['var·nən] *vt* to warn (**vor** +*dat* about)

Wạrnlicht *nt* AUTO hazard lights *pl,* harzards *pl fam*

Wạrnschild *nt* warning sign

Wạrnschuss[RR] *m* warning shot

Wạrnsignal *nt* warning signal

Wạrnstreik *m* warning strike

Wạrnung <-, -en> *f* warning (**vor** +*dat* about)

Warschau <-s> ['var·ʃau] *nt* Warsaw

Wạrtehalle *f* waiting room

Wạrteliste *f* waiting list

warten ['var·tn̩] **I.** *vi* to wait (**auf** +*akk* for); **auf sich ~ lassen** to be a long time [in] coming; **warte mal!** hold on!; **na warte!** just you wait! **II.** *vt Gerät* to service

Wärter(in) <-s, -> ['vɛr·tɐ] *m(f)* ❶ (*Gefängniswärter*) prison guard ❷ (*Tierpfleger*) keeper

Wạrteraum *m* waiting room

Wạrteschlange *f* line

Wạrtezeit *f* wait

Wạrtezimmer *nt* waiting room

Wạrtung <-, -en> *f* service, maintenance

warum [va·'rʊm] *adv* why

Warze <-, -n> ['var·tsə] *f* wart

was [vas] **I.** *pron interrog* what; **~ bedeutet das?** what does that mean?; **~ kostet das?** how much does that cost?; **~ ist?** what's up?; **~ für ein ...** what kind of ...; **~ für ein Glück!** what luck! **II.** *pron rel* what; **alles, ~ du willst** everything you want; **alles, ~ ich weiß** all [that] I know **III.** *pron indef* (*fam: etwas*) something; (*in Fragesätzen*) anything; **ist ~?** is anything wrong?; **gibt es ~ Neues?** have you heard anything [new]?; **kann ich ~ helfen?** is there anything I can do to help?

Wạschanlage *f* car wash

Wạschanleitung *f* washing instructions *pl*

wạschbar *adj* washable

Wạschbär *m* raccoon

Wạschbecken *nt* sink

Wạ̈sche <-> *f kein pl* ❶ (*das Waschen, Schmutzwäsche*) laundry, wash ❷ (*Unterwäsche*) underwear ❸ (*Haushaltswäsche*) linens *pl*

wạschecht *adj* ❶ (*typisch*) genuine, real ❷ (*nicht verbleichend*) colorfast

Wạ̈scheklammer *f* clothespin

Wạ̈schekorb *m* laundry basket

Wạ̈scheleine *f* [clothes]line

waschen <wạ̈scht, wu̲sch, gewạschen> ['va·ʃn̩] *vt* to wash

Wäscherei <-, -en> [vɛ·ʃə·'rai] *f* laundry

Wạ̈scheschrank *m* linen cupboard

Wạ̈scheständer *m* clotheshorse, drying rack

Wạ̈schetrockner <-s, -> *m* drier

Wạschküche *f* laundry room

Wạschlappen *m* ❶ (*Lappen*) washcloth ❷ (*fam: Feigling*) wimp

Wạschmaschine *f* washing machine

Wạschmittel *nt* detergent

Wạschpulver *nt* laundry powder

Wạschraum *m* laundry room

Wạschsalon *m* laundromat

Wạschstraße *f* car wash

wạ̈scht *3. pers sing pres von* **waschen**

Wasser <-s, - *o* Wässer> ['va·sɐ, *pl* 'vɛ·sɐ] *nt* water; **~ abweisend** water-repellent; **etw unter ~ setzen** to flood sth; **unter ~ stehen** to be flooded ▶ WENDUNGEN: **ins ~ fallen** to fall through; **das ~ bis zum Hals stehen haben** to be up to one's ears in debt; **sich über ~ halten** to keep oneself above water; **jdm läuft das ~ im Mund zusammen** (*fam*) sb's mouth is watering

Wạsseranschluss[RR] *m* water main connection

Wasserau̲fbereitungsanlage *f* water treat-

W

ment plant
Wasserball *m* ❶ *kein pl* (*Sport*) water polo ❷ (*Ball*) beach ball
Wasserbett *nt* waterbed
Wasserdampf *m* steam
wasserdicht *adj* watertight, waterproof
Wasserfall *m* waterfall
wasserfest *adj* waterproof, water-resistant
Wasserflugzeug *nt* seaplane
Wasserglas *nt* glass, tumbler
Wassergraben *m* ditch
Wasserhahn *m* [water] faucet
Wasserhärte *f* hardness of the water
wässerig ['vɛ·sə·rɪç] *adj s.* **wäss(e)rig**
Wasserkessel *m* KOCHK [tea]kettle; TECH boiler
Wasserkraft *f kein pl* water power
Wasserkraftwerk *nt* hydroelectric power station
Wasserleitung *f* water pipe
wasserlöslich *adj* water-soluble
Wassermann ['va·se·man] *m* ASTROL Aquarius
Wassermelone *f* watermelon
Wassermühle *f* water mill
wässern ['vɛ·sen] *vt* to water
Wasserpistole *f* water pistol
Wasserrohr *nt* water pipe
Wasserschaden *m* water damage
wasserscheu *adj* scared of water
Wasserschutzgebiet *nt* water protection area
Wasserschutzpolizei *f* river police
Wasserski *m* ❶ *kein pl* (*Sportart*) waterskiing ❷ (*Sportgerät*) waterski
Wasserspiegel *m* water level
Wassersport *m* water sports *pl*
Wassersportler(in) *m(f)* water sports enthusiast
Wasserspülung *f* flush
Wasserstand *m* water level
Wasserstrahl *m* jet of water
Wasserverbrauch *m* water consumption
Wasserverschmutzung *f* water pollution
Wasserversorgung *f* water supply
Wasserwaage *f* level
Wasserwerfer *m* water cannon
Wasserwerk *nt* waterworks + *sing/pl vb*
Wasserzähler *m* water meter
wäss(e)rigRR, **wäß(e)rig**ALT ['vɛs(ə)·rɪç] *adj Suppe* watery
waten ['va:·tn̩] *vi sein* to wade
Watsche <-, -n> ['va:·tʃə] *f*, **Watschen** <-, -> ['va:·tʃn̩] *f* ÖSTERR, SÜDD (*fam*) slap in the face
watscheln ['va:·tʃl̩n] *vi sein* to waddle
Watt[1] <-s, -> [vat] *nt* PHYS watt
Watt[2] <-[e]s, -en> [vat] *nt* mudflats *pl*

The **Watt** is a large area of tidal mudflats (similar to tideland in the USA) on the North Sea coast. At low tide, one can walk on the sandy seabed. At high tide, the **Watt** lies several feet underwater and flat-bottomed coastal ships sail over it.

Watte <-, -n> ['va·tə] *f* cotton wool
Wattenmeer *nt kein pl* mudflats *pl*
Wattestäbchen *nt* cotton swab, Q-tip®
wattieren* [va·'ti:·rən] *vt* to pad
WC <-s, -s> [ve·'tse] *nt Abk von* **watercloset** bathroom; (*public*) restroom
weben <webte *o geh* wob, gewebt *o geh* gewoben> ['ve:·bn̩] *vt, vi* to weave
Webseite *f* INET Web page
Webserver *m* INET Web server
Website <-, -s> ['wɛb·saɪt] *f* INET Web site
Wechsel <-s, -> ['vɛk·sl̩] *m* ❶ (*Änderung*) change; **in stündlichem ~** on an hourly rotation ❷ SPORT (*Spielerwechsel*) substitution, change
Wechselbeziehung *f* correlation, interrelation
Wechselgeld *nt kein pl* change
wechselhaft ['vɛk·sl̩-] *adj* changeable
Wechseljahre *pl* menopause; **in die ~ kommen** to reach menopause
Wechselkurs *m* exchange rate
wechseln ['vɛk·sl̩n] *vt, vi* to change
wechselnd *adj* changing; **mit ~em Erfolg** with varying [degrees of] success
wechselseitig *adj* mutual
Wechselstrom *m* alternating current
Wechselstube *f* exchange booth
wechselweise *adv* alternately
Wechselwirkung *f* interaction
wecken ['vɛ·kn̩] *vt* ❶ (*aufwecken*) to wake [up] ❷ (*hervorrufen*) to bring back *sep; Assoziationen* to create; *Interesse, Verdacht* to arouse
Wecken <-s, -> ['vɛ·kn̩] *m* ÖSTERR, SÜDD (*Brötchen*) loaf of bread
Wecker <-s, -> ['vɛ·kɐ] *m* alarm clock
wedeln ['ve:·dl̩n] *vi* ■ **mit etw** *dat* ~ to wave sth; *Schwanz* to wag
weder ['ve:·dɐ] *konj* ~ **... noch ...** neither ... nor ...; ~ **du noch er** neither you nor him; ~ **noch** neither
weg [vɛk] *adv* ❶ (*fort*) ■ ~ **sein** to have left, to be gone; ~ **mit dir!** go away!; **nichts wie ~ hier!** let's get out of here!; ~ **da!** [get] out of the way! ❷ (*fam: hinweggekommen*) ■ **über etw** *akk* ~ **sein** to have gotten over sth
Weg <-[e]s, -e> [ve:k, *pl* 've:·gə] *m* ❶ (*Pfad*) path ❷ (*unbefestigte Straße*) track ❸ (*Strecke*) way; **auf dem ~ sein** to be on one's way; **auf jds ~ liegen** to be on sb's way; **sich** *akk* **auf den ~ machen** to take off ❹ (*Methode*) way; **auf friedlichem ~e** by peaceful means ► WENDUNGEN: **auf dem ~e der Besserung sein** to be on the road to recovery; **jdm auf halbem ~e entgegenkommen** to meet sb halfway; **jdm/etw aus dem ~ gehen** to avoid sb/sth; **jdm über den ~ laufen** to run into sb; **etw in die ~e leiten** to arrange sth; **etw aus dem ~ räumen** to remove sth; **sich** *akk* **jdm in den ~ stellen** to block sb's path; **jdm nicht über den ~ trauen** to not trust sb for a second
weg|bekommen* *vt irreg* (*fam*) ❶ (*entfernen können*) to remove ❷ (*fortbewegen können*) to move away

W

Wegbereiter(in) <-s, -> *m(f)* forerunner, precursor
weg|bleiben *vi irreg sein* to stay away; **bleib nicht so lange weg!** don't stay out too long
weg|bringen *vt irreg* to take away
weg|denken *vt irreg* ■**sich** *dat* **etw ~** to imagine sth without sth
weg|drehen *vt* to turn away *sep*
weg|dürfen *vi irreg (fam)* to be allowed to go out
wegen ['ve:·gn̩] *präp +gen* ① *(aufgrund von)* because of, due to; ■**~ ihm** *(fam)* because of him ② *(bezüglich)* regarding
weg|fahren *irreg* **I.** *vi sein* ① *(abfahren)* to drive off, to leave ② *(verreisen)* to leave on a trip **II.** *vt haben (wegbringen)* to drive [*or* take] away
weg|fallen *vi irreg sein* to cease to apply
weg|fliegen *vi irreg sein* ① *Vogel* to fly away ② *Hut, Blätter* to be blown away, to fly off
weg|führen *vt, vi* to lead away
weg|geben *vt irreg* to give away *sep*
weg|gehen *vi irreg sein* ① *(fortgehen)* to walk away; *(fam: ausgehen)* to go out ② *(fam: sich entfernen lassen)* to go away; **der Fleck geht nicht weg** the stain won't come out
weggetreten *adj* **~ sein** to be miles away
weg|gießen *vt irreg* to pour away *sep*
weg|gucken *vi (fam) s.* **wegsehen**
weg|hören *vi* to stop listening
weg|jagen *vt* to drive away *sep*
weg|kommen *vi irreg sein (fam)* ① *(weggehen können)* to get away ② **mach, dass du wegkommst!** get out of here! ③ *(abhandenkommen)* to disappear ④ *(fam: abschneiden)* [**bei etw** *dat*] **gut/schlecht ~** to do/not do well [on sth]
Wegkreuzung *f* crossroads
weg|kriegen *vt (fam) s.* **wegbekommen**
weg|lassen *vt irreg* ① *(auslassen)* to leave out *sep* ② *(weggehen lassen)* to let go
weg|laufen *vi irreg sein* to run away (**vor** *+dat* from)
weg|legen *vt* ① *(beiseitelegen)* to put down *sep* ② *(aufbewahren)* to put aside *sep*
weg|machen *vt* to get rid of
weg|müssen *vi irreg* to have to go
weg|nehmen *vt irreg* ■**jdm etw ~** to take away sth *sep* from sb; ■**etw** [**von etw** *dat*] **~** to take sth *sep* [off sth]
Wegrand *m* side of the road
weg|rationalisieren* *vt* ■**jdn/etw ~** to downsize sb/sth
weg|räumen *vt* to clear away *sep*
weg|rennen *vi irreg sein (fam) s.* **weglaufen**
weg|rutschen *vi sein* to slip away
weg|schaffen *vt* to remove
weg|schauen *vi s.* **wegsehen**
weg|schicken *vt* ① *Person* to send away ② *Brief* to send off *sep*
weg|schieben *vt irreg* to push away *sep*
weg|schleppen *vt* to drag away *sep*
weg|schließen *vt irreg* to lock away *sep* (**vor** *+dat* from)
weg|schmeißen *vt irreg (fam) s.* **wegwerfen**
weg|schütten *vt s.* **weggießen**
weg|sehen *vi irreg* to look away
weg|setzen *vr* ■**sich ~** to move away
weg|stecken *vt* ① *(einstecken)* to put away *sep* ② *(verkraften)* to get over
weg|stellen *vt* to move out of the way
weg|stoßen *vt irreg* to push away *sep*; *(mit dem Fuß)* to kick away *sep*
weg|tragen *vt irreg* to carry away *sep*
weg|tun *vt irreg* ① *(wegwerfen)* to throw away *sep* ② *(weglegen)* to put down *sep*
wegweisend *adj Taten* pioneering; *Erfindung* revolutionary
Wegweiser <-s, -> *m* signpost
weg|werfen *vt irreg* to throw away *sep*
Wegwerfgesellschaft *f* throwaway society
Wegwerfpackung *f* disposable packaging
weg|wischen *vt* to wipe away *sep*
weg|ziehen *irreg* **I.** *vi sein* to move away; **aus Köln ~** to move from Cologne **II.** *vt haben* **die Hand ~** to pull away one's hand
Wehe[1] <-, -n> ['ve:·ə] *f (Schnee-, Sandwehe)* drift
Wehe[2] <-, -n> ['ve:·ə] *f meist pl (Geburtswehe)* contraction; **in den ~n liegen** to be in labor
wehen ['ve:·ən] *vi* ① *Wind* to blow ② *Haare* to blow around; *Fahne* to flutter
wehleidig *adj* oversensitive
wehmütig ['ve:·my:·tɪç] *adj (geh)* melancholy; *Erinnerung* nostalgic
Wehr [ve:ɐ̯] *f* **sich zur ~ setzen** to defend oneself
Wehrdienst *m kein pl* military service
wehrdiensttauglich *adj* fit for military service
Wehrdienstverweigerer *m* conscientious objector
wehren ['ve:·rən] *vr* ① *(sich widersetzen)* ■**sich** *akk* **gegen etw ~** to fight against sth ② *(sich sträuben)* ■**sich** *akk* **dagegen ~, etw zu tun** to resist doing sth
Wehrersatzdienst *m* alternative to military service
wehrlos I. *adj* defenseless (**gegen** *+akk* against) **II.** *adv* in a defenseless state; **etw** *dat* **~ gegenüberstehen** to be defenseless against sth
Wehrpflicht *f kein pl* mandatory military service
wehrpflichtig *adj* obliged to enlist for military service
wehrtauglich *adj* fit for military service
weh|tun *vt* to hurt
Weib <-[e]s, -er> [vaip, *pl* 'vai·bɐ] *nt* woman
Weibchen <-s, -> ['vaip·çən] *nt* female
Weiberheld *m (pej)* ladykiller *sl*
weiblich ['vaip·lɪç] *adj* ① *(fraulich)* feminine ② ANAT female ③ LING feminine
Weiblichkeit <-> *f kein pl* femininity
weich [vaiç] **I.** *adj* soft ► WENDUNGEN: **~ werden** to weaken **II.** *adv* softly

weichen <wịch, gewịchen> ['vai·çn̩] *vi sein* (*weggehen*) to go; **jdm nicht von der Seite ~** to not leave sb's side; **er wich nicht von der Stelle** he didn't budge from the spot
weichherzig *adj* soft-hearted
Weichkäse *m* soft cheese
weichlich *adj* weak
Weichling <-s, -e> ['vaiç·lɪŋ] *m* (*pej*) weakling
Weichteile *pl* ① (*knochenlose Körperteile*) soft parts [of one's body] *pl* ② (*fam: männliche Geschlechtsteile*) private parts *pl*
Weide <-, -n> ['vai·də] *f* ① BOT willow ② AGR meadow
Weideland *nt* pastureland
weiden ['vai·dn̩] **I.** *vi* (*grasen*) to graze **II.** *vr* ■ **sich an etw** *dat* **~** to feast one's eyes on sth; (*schadenfroh*) to revel in sth
weigern ['vai·gɐn] *vr* ■ **sich ~** to refuse
Weigerung <-, -en> *f* refusal
Weihnachten <-, -> ['vai·nax·tn̩] *nt* Christmas, Xmas *fam;* **fröhliche ~!** Merry Christmas!
weihnachtlich **I.** *adj* Christmassy, festive **II.** *adv* festively
Weihnachtsabend *m* Christmas Eve
Weihnachtsbaum *m* Christmas tree
Weihnachtsfeier *f* Christmas party
Weihnachtsfest *nt* Christmas
Weihnachtsgeld *nt* Christmas bonus
Weihnachtsgeschenk *nt* Christmas present
Weihnachtslied *nt* [Christmas] carol
Weihnachtsmann *m* Santa Claus, Father Christmas
Weihnachtsmarkt *m* Christmas market

> The **Weihnachtsmarkt** (Christmas market) is a staple of most cities at Christmastime where people can enjoy all sorts of special food, drink *Glühwein* (mulled wine), and purchase Christmas decorations, presents, and handicrafts. The most famous **Weihnachtsmarkt** in Germany takes place in Nürnberg (Nuremberg).

weil [vail] *konj* because, since
Weilchen <-s> *nt kein pl* ■ **ein ~** a little while
Weile <-> ['vai·lə] *f kein pl* while; **eine ganze ~** quite a while
Wein <-[e]s, -e> [vain] *m* ① (*Getränk*) wine ② *kein pl* (*Weinrebe*) [grape]vines *pl* ► WENDUNGEN: **jdm reinen ~ einschenken** to tell sb the truth
Weinbau *m kein pl* wine growing
Weinbaugebiet *nt* wine-growing area
Weinbeere *f* ① (*Traube*) grape ② SÜDD, ÖSTERR, SCHWEIZ (*Rosine*) raisin
Weinberg *m* vineyard
Weinbrand *m* brandy
weinen ['vai·nən] *vi* to cry (**um** +*akk* for)
weinerlich **I.** *adj* tearful **II.** *adv* tearfully
Weinflasche *f* wine bottle
Weinglas *nt* wine glass
Weingut *nt* winery
Weinkeller *m* wine cellar
Weinlese *f* grape harvest
Weinprobe *f* wine tasting
Weinrebe *f* grape[vine]
weinrot *adj* burgundy[-colored]
Weinstube *f* wine bar
Weintraube *f* grape
weise ['vai·zə] **I.** *adj* wise **II.** *adv* wisely
Weise <-, -n> ['vai·zə] *f* way; **auf diese/bestimmte ~** in this/a certain way; **in gewisser ~** in certain respects
weisen <wies, gewiesen> ['vai·zn̩] **I.** *vt* ① **jdm den Weg ~** to show sb the way ② **jdn aus dem Zimmer ~** to send sb out of the room ③ **etw von sich** *dat* **~** to reject sth **II.** *vi* ■ **irgendwohin ~** to point somewhere
Weisheit <-, -en> ['vais·hait] *f* ① *kein pl* (*Klugheit*) wisdom ② *meist pl* (*weiser Rat*) word *usu pl* of wisdom; **eine alte ~ sein** to be a wise old saying ► WENDUNGEN: **mit seiner ~ am Ende sein** to be at one's wits' end
Weisheitszahn *m* wisdom tooth
weis|machen *vt* ■ **jdm etw ~** to lead sb to believe sth
weiß[1] [vais] *adj* white
weiß[2] [vais] *3. pers sing pres von* **wissen**
weissagen **I.** *vi* ■ **jdm ~** to tell sb's fortune **II.** *vt* ■ **[jdm] etw ~** to prophesy sth [to sb]
Weissagung <-, -en> *f* prophecy
Weißbier *nt* Weissbier (*light, top-fermented beer*)
Weißbrot *nt* white bread
Weiße(r) *f(m) dekl wie adj* white, white man/woman; ■ **die ~n** white people
Weißglut *f* ► WENDUNGEN: **jdn zur ~ bringen** to make sb livid with rage
weißhaarig *adj* white-haired
Weißkohl *m,* **Weißkraut** *nt* SÜDD, ÖSTERR white cabbage
Weißrussland[RR] *nt* White Russia; *s. a.* **Deutschland**
Weißwein *m* white wine
Weißwurst *f* Bavarian veal sausage (*simmered and served midmorning with sweet mustard*)
weit [vait] **I.** *adj* ① (*räumlich/zeitlich ausgedehnt*) long; **bis dahin ist es noch ~** we still have a way to go before we get there ② (*breit*) wide, vast; (*Meer, Wüste*) open; (*Kleidung*) baggy; **~er werden** to widen **II.** *adv* ① (*eine große Strecke*) far, a long way; **8 km ~er** 8 km ahead; **am ~esten** farthest; **es noch ~ haben** to have a long way to go; **~ weg** far away; **von ~ her** from far away ② **etw ~ öffnen** to open sth wide ③ (*erheblich*) far; **~ besser** far better; **~ schöner** far more beautiful ④ **~ reichend** extensive; **~ verbreitet** widespread ⑤ (*zeitlich lang*) **~ nach etw** *dat* well after sth; **~ zurückliegen** to be a long time ago ► WENDUNGEN: **bei/von ~em** by/from far; **bei ~em nicht** not nearly; **~ und breit** for miles around; **jdn so ~ bringen, dass er etw tut** to

bring sb to the point of doing sth; ~ **hergeholt** far-fetched; **mit etw** *dat* **ist es nicht ~ her** sth is nothing much to write home about

weitab ['vait·'ʔap] *adv* far away; ■ **~ von etw** *dat* far from sth

weitaus ['vait·ʔaus] *adv* ❶ *vor komp* (*erheblich*) far, much; **~ schlechter sein** to be far [*or* much] worse ❷ *vor superl* (*bei weitem*) [by] far

Weitblick *m kein pl* (*Voraussicht*) farsightedness, vision

Weite[1] <-, -n> ['vai·tə] *f* ❶ (*weite Ausdehnung*) expanse, vastness ❷ (*Breite*) width

Weite[2] ['vai·tə] *nt* ▶ WENDUNGEN: **das ~ suchen** to take to one's heels

weiten ['vai·tn̩] **I.** *vt* MODE to widen **II.** *vr* ■ **sich** *akk* ~ to widen; (*Pupille*) to dilate

weiter ['vai·tɐ] *adv* ❶ (*sonst*) **wenn es ~ nichts ist, ...** well, if that's all ... ❷ (*weiterhin*) **~ bestehen** to continue to exist

weiter|arbeiten ['vai·tɐ·ʔar·bai·tn̩] *vi* to keep working (**an** +*dat* on)

weiter|bilden *vr* ■ **sich** *akk* **in etw** *dat* ~ to [further] develop one's knowledge of sth

Weiterbildung *f kein pl* continuing education

weiter|bringen *vt irreg* to help along

weitere(r, s) *adj* (*zusätzlich*) further, additional; **alles W~** everything else ▶ WENDUNGEN: **bis auf ~s** until further notice, for the time being; **ohne ~s** easily, just like that

weiter|empfehlen* *vt irreg* to recommend

weiter|entwickeln* *vt, vr* ■ [**sich** *akk*] ~ to develop further

Weiterentwicklung *f* further development

weiter|erzählen* *vt* to pass on *sep*

weiter|fahren *irreg vi sein* to continue driving; **nach München ~** to drive on to Munich

weiter|führen *vt* (*fortsetzen*) to continue

weiter|geben *vt irreg* to pass on *sep* (**an** +*akk* to)

weiter|gehen *vi irreg sein* ❶ (*seinen Weg fortsetzen*) to keep going ❷ (*seinen Fortgang nehmen*) to go on; **so kann es nicht ~** things can't go on like this

weiter|helfen *vi irreg* to keep helping; (*auf die Sprünge helfen*) to help along

weiterhin ['vai·tɐ·'hɪn] *adv* ❶ (*immer noch*) still ❷ (*außerdem*) furthermore, in addition

weiter|kommen *vi irreg sein* to get farther along

weiter|leben *vi* to live on

weiter|leiten *vt* to pass on *sep* (**an** +*akk* to)

weiter|machen *vi* to continue

weiter|sagen *vt* to pass on *sep*; **nicht ~!** don't tell anyone!

weiter|verarbeiten* *vt* to process (**zu** +*dat* into)

weitestgehend I. *adj* most extensive **II.** *adv* to the greatest possible extent

weitgehend I. *adj* (*umfassend*) extensive **II.** *adv* extensively, to a large extent

weitläufig ['vait·lɔy·fɪç] **I.** *adj* ❶ (*ausgedehnt*) extensive ❷ (*entfernt*) distant **II.** *adv* extensively, distantly

weiträumig I. *adj* spacious **II.** *adv* spaciously; **den Verkehr ~ umleiten** to divert [the] traffic around a wide area

weitreichend *adj* extensive

weitschweifig ['vait·ʃvai·fɪç] **I.** *adj* long-winded **II.** *adv* long-windedly, at great length

Weitsicht ['vait·zɪçt] *f* farsightedness, vision

weitsichtig ['vait·zɪç·tɪç] *adj* ❶ MED farsighted ❷ (*weitblickend*) ■ **~ sein** to be farsighted

Weitsichtigkeit <-> *f kein pl* MED farsightedness

Weitspringer(in) *m(f)* long jumper

Weizen <-s, -> ['vai·tsn̩] *m* wheat

Weizenbier *nt* Weissbier (*light, top-fermented beer*)

welche(r, s) I. *pron interrog* which **II.** *pron rel* (*der, die, das: Mensch*) who; (*Sache*) which **III.** *pron indef* ❶ (*etwas*) some; **wenn du Geld brauchst, kann ich dir ~s leihen** if you need money, I can lend you some ❷ *pl* (*einige*) some; ■ **~, die ...** some [people], who

welk [vɛlk] *adj* ❶ (*verwelkt*) wilted ❷ (*schlaff*) worn-out

welken ['vɛl·kn̩] *vi sein* to wilt

Wellblech *nt* corrugated iron

Welle <-, -n> ['vɛ·lə] *f* wave

wellen ['vɛ·lən] *vr* ■ **sich ~** to be/become wavy; (*Papier*) to crinkle

Wellenbad *nt* wave pool

Wellenbrecher <-s, -> *m* breakwater

Wellengang <-[e]s> *m kein pl* waves *pl*; **starker ~** heavy seas *pl*

Wellenlänge *f* PHYS wavelength

Wellenreiten *nt* surfing

Wellensittich *m* parakeet

wellig ['vɛ·lɪç] *adj* ❶ (*gewellt*) wavy ❷ (*wellenförmig*) uneven

Wellness[RR] <-> ['vɛl·nɛs] *f kein pl* ❶ (*Wohlbefinden*) well-being ❷ (*wohltuende Behandlung*) spa treatment

Wellnesshotel[RR] *nt* spa, health resort

Welpe <-n, -n> ['vɛl·pə] *m* puppy, whelp

Welt <-, -en> [vɛlt] *f* world; **auf der ~** in the world; **die ~ des Films** the world of film ▶ WENDUNGEN: **alle ~** (*fam*) the whole world; **in aller ~** all over the world; **die Dritte ~** the Third World; **auf die ~ kommen** to be born; **in einer anderen ~ leben** to live on another planet; **um nichts in der ~** not for the world

Weltall *nt* universe

Weltanschauung *f* worldview, philosophy of life

Weltausstellung *f* world's fair

weltberühmt *adj* world-famous

Weltbevölkerung *f kein pl* world population

weltbewegend *adj* earthshaking

Weltbürger(in) *m(f)* citizen of the world

Weltcup <-s, -s> [-kap] *m* World Cup

Weltenbummler(in) <-s, -> *m(f)* globetrotter

Welterfolg *m* worldwide success

weltfremd *adj* unworldly

Welthandel *m* global trade

Weltkarte *f* world map

Weltkrieg *m* world war; **der Erste/Zweite ~** World War I/II
Weltkugel *f* globe
weltlich ['vɛlt·lɪç] *adj* ❶ (*irdisch*) worldly ❷ (*profan*) mundane
Weltmacht *f* world power
Weltmeer *nt* ocean
Weltmeister(in) *m(f)* world champion (**in** +*dat* in)
Weltmeisterschaft *f* world championship
weltoffen *adj* cosmopolitan
Weltraum *m kein pl* [outer] space
Weltraumbehörde *f* space agency
Weltraumfähre *f* space shuttle
Weltraumstation *f* space station
Weltraumtourismus *m* ■ **der ~** space tourism
Weltreich *nt* empire
Weltreise *f* **eine ~ machen** to go on a trip around the world
Weltrekord *m* world record
Weltruhm *m* world[wide] fame
Weltschmerz *m kein pl* world-weariness
Weltsicherheitsrat *m* [United Nations] Security Council
Weltstadt *f* international city
Weltstar *m* international star
Weltuntergang *m* end of the world
Weltuntergangsstimmung *f* apocalyptic mood
Weltverbesserer, -verbesserin *m, f* (*pej*) do-gooder
weltweit I. *adj* global, worldwide **II.** *adv* globally
Weltwirtschaft *f* world economy
Weltwirtschaftsgipfel *m* world economic summit
Weltwirtschaftskrise *f* world economic crisis
Weltwunder *nt* **die sieben ~** the Seven Wonders of the World
wem [ve:m] **I.** *pron indef dat von* **wer** (*fam*) to/for somebody **II.** *pron interrog* who ... to, to whom *form;* **~ gehört dieser Schlüssel?** who does this key belong to?; **mit/von ~** with/from whom **III.** *pron rel* ■ **~ ..., [der]** ... the person to whom ..., the person who ... to
wen [ve:n] **I.** *pron indef akk von* **wer** (*fam*) somebody **II.** *pron interrog* who, whom; **an/für ~** to/for whom *form,* who ... to/for **III.** *pron rel* ■ **~ ..., [der]** ... the person who[m] ...; **an/für ~** to/for whom *form,* who ... to/for
Wende <-, -n> ['vɛn·də] *f* change, turn
Wendekreis *m* AUTO turning circle
Wendeltreppe *f* spiral staircase
wenden ['vɛn·dn̩] **I.** *vr* <wendete *o geh* wandte, gewendet *o geh* gewandt> ❶ (*sich drehen*) **sich nach links/rechts ~** to turn left/right ❷ (*kontaktieren*) ■ **sich [in etw *dat*] an jdn ~** to turn to sb [regarding sth] ❸ (*zielen*) ■ **sich an jdn ~** to be directed at sb ❹ (*entgegentreten*) ■ **sich gegen jdn ~** to turn against sb; ■ **sich gegen etw ~** to oppose sth ❺ (*sich verkehren*) **sich zum Besseren/Schlechteren ~** to take a turn for the better/worse **II.** *vt* <wendete, gewendet> (*umdrehen*) to turn over *sep* **III.** *vi* <wendete, gewendet> AUTO to turn
Wendeplatz *m* turnaround
Wendepunkt *m* turning point
wendig ['vɛn·dɪç] *adj* maneuverable
Wendung <-, -en> *f* ❶ (*Veränderung*) turn ❷ (*Redewendung*) expression
wenig ['ve:·nɪç] **I.** *pron indef* ❶ *sing* (*nicht viel*) little; **~ Zeit/Geld haben** to have little time/money; **zu ~ Freizeit** not enough free time; ■ **~ sein** to be not [very] much ❷ *pl* (*nicht viele*) ■ **~e** a few; **~e Stunden später** a few hours later; **das wissen nur ~e** only a few [people] know about it **II.** *adv* little; **~ interessant** of little interest; **zu ~ schlafen** to not get enough sleep
weniger ['ve:·nɪ·gɐ] **I.** *adj komp von* **wenig:** ■ **~ als ...** less ... than **II.** *pron indef* ❶ (*unzählbar*) *Zeit, Geld* less ❷ (*zählbar*) *Menschen, Bücher* fewer **III.** *adv* less; **~ bekannt sein** to be less known; **das ist ~ angenehm** that is not very pleasant
wenigste(r, s) I. *pron* ■ **die ~n** very few; ■ **das ~, was ...** the least that ... **II.** *adv* least; *pl* fewest; **am ~n** least of all
wenigstens ['ve:·nɪçs·tn̩s] *adv* at least
wenn [vɛn] *konj* ❶ (*falls*) if; **~ das so ist** if that's true [*or* the way it is] ❷ (*sobald*) as soon as
wenngleich [vɛn·'glaiç] *konj* although
wer <*gen* wessen, *dat* wem, *akk* wen> [ve:ɐ̯] **I.** *pron interrog* who; **~ von beiden?** which of the two? **II.** *pron rel* **~ das sagt, [der] lügt** whoever says that is lying **III.** *pron indef* (*fam*) somebody; (*in Fragesätzen*) someone, somebody; *fragend, verneinend* anyone, anybody; **da ist ~ für dich an der Tür** there's somebody at the door for you; **ist da ~?** is anyone there? ▶ WENDUNGEN: **~ <u>sein</u>** to be somebody *fam*
Werbeagentur *f* advertising agency
Werbeanzeige *f* advertisement
Werbebroschüre *f* promotional brochure
Werbefernsehen *nt* commercials *pl*
Werbefilm *m* promotional film
Werbegeschenk *nt* promotional gift
Werbekampagne *f* advertising campaign
werben <wirbt, warb, geworben> ['vɛr·bn̩] **I.** *vt* ■ **jdn [für etw] ~** to recruit sb [for sth] **II.** *vi* ❶ (*Reklame machen*) ■ **für etw ~** to advertise [*or* promote] sth ❷ (*zu erhalten suchen*) **um eine Frau ~** to woo a woman; **um neue Wähler ~** to try to attract new voters
Werbeslogan *m* advertising slogan
Werbespot *m* commercial
Werbetrommel *f* ▶ WENDUNGEN: **die ~ für jdn/etw <u>rühren</u>** to beat the drum for sb/sth
Werbeunterbrechung *f* TV commercial break
Werbung <-> *f kein pl* ❶ (*Reklame*) advertisement; **~ für etw machen** to advertise sth ❷ (*Werbespot*) commercial; (*Werbeprospekt*)

W

promotional brochure ③ (*Branche*) advertising

Werdegang *m* career

werden ['veːɐ̯·dn̩] **I.** *vi* <wird, wurde, geworden> *sein* ① (*seinen Zustand ändern*) to become, to get; **alt/älter ~** to get old/older; **kalt ~** to get cold; **es wird dunkel** it is getting dark; **es wird besser ~** it is going to get better; **es wird Sommer** summer is coming [*or* almost here]; **jdm wird heiß/übel** sb feels hot/sick; **sie ist gerade 98 geworden** she [has] just turned 98 ② (*eine Ausbildung machen*) ■**etw ~** to become sth; **sie will Ärztin werden** she wants to become a doctor; **was möchtest du einmal ~?** what do you want to be [when you grow up]? ③ (*sich entwickeln*) **Wirklichkeit/Mode ~** to become reality/fashionable; ■**zu etw** *dat* **~** to turn into sth; **es wird schon [wieder] ~** it'll turn out okay in the end **II.** *aux vb* ① *zur Bildung des Futurs* ■**etw tun ~** to be going to do sth; ■**es wird etw geschehen** sth is going to happen; ■**jd wird etw getan haben** sb will have done sth ② *zur Bildung des Konjunktivs* ■**jd würde etw tun** sb would do sth ③ *mutmaßend* **es wird gegen 20 Uhr sein** it's probably [*or* I'm guessing it's] about 8 o'clock **III.** *aux vb* <wird, wurde, worden> *sein zur Bildung des Passivs* **du wirst gerufen** you are being called; **gebissen ~** to be bitten; **sie wurde entlassen** she was laid off [*or* fired]; **das wird bei uns häufig gemacht** we do that a lot here

werfen <wirft, warf, geworfen> ['vɛr·fn̩] *vt, vi* ① (*schleudern*) to throw (**nach** *+dat* at) ② (*Junge gebären*) to throw *spec*, to give birth

Werft <-, -en> [vɛrft] *f* shipyard

Werk <-[e]s, -e> [vɛrk] *nt* ① (*Buch, Kunstwerk*) work ② (*Gesamtwerk*) works *pl* ③ **ans ~ gehen** to go to work; **am ~ sein** to be at work ④ (*Fabrik*) factory ▶ WENDUNGEN: **ein gutes ~ tun** to do a good deed

Werk(s)angehörige(r) *f(m) dekl wie adj* factory employee

Werksgelände *nt* factory premises *npl*

Werkstatt *f* ① (*Arbeitsraum*) workshop ② AUTO garage

Werktag *m* workday

werktags *adv* on workdays

werktätig ['vɛrk·tɛː·tɪç] *adj* **die ~e Bevölkerung** the working population

Werktätige(r) *f(m) dekl wie adj* working person

Werkzeug <-[e]s, -e> *nt* tool *usu pl*

Werkzeugkasten *m* toolbox

Wermutstropfen *m* (*geh*) a bitter pill

wert [veːɐ̯t] *adj* ① (*einen Wert besitzen*) ■**[jdm] etw ~ sein** to be worth sth [to sb] ② (*verdienen*) ■**einer S.** *gen* **~ sein** to be worthy of sth

Wert <-[e]s, -e> [veːɐ̯t] *m* ① (*Preis*) value; **im ~ steigen** to increase in value; **an ~ verlieren** to decrease in value; **im ~e von etw** worth sth ② *pl* (*Daten*) results *pl* ③ (*Wichtigkeit*) **~ auf etw** *akk* **legen** to think sth is important; **~ darauf legen, etw zu tun** to find it important to do sth ④ (*Wertvorstellung*) value ▶ WENDUNGEN: **das hat keinen ~** (*fam*) it's useless

Wertegemeinschaft *f* POL community of [shared] values

werten *vt* to rate

Wertewandel *m* change in values

wertfrei *adj* impartial

Wertgegenstand *m* valuable object; ■**Wertgegenstände** valuables

wertlos *adj* worthless

Wertmaßstab *m* standard

Wertsache *f meist pl* valuable object; ■**~n** valuables

Wertschätzung *f* esteem

Wertstoff *m* recyclable material

wertvoll *adj* valuable

Wertvorstellung *f meist pl* moral concept *usu pl*

Wesen <-s, -> ['veː·zn̩] *nt* ① (*Geschöpf*) being; (*tierisch*) creature ② *kein pl* (*Grundzüge*) nature

Wesensart *f* nature

Wesenszug *m* characteristic

wesentlich ['veː·zn̩t·lɪç] **I.** *adj* ① (*erheblich*) considerable ② (*wichtig*) essential; ■**das W~e** the essential part; **im W~en** essentially **II.** *adv* considerably

weshalb [vɛs·'halp] *adv* why

Wespe <-, -n> ['vɛs·pə] *f* yellow jacket

Wespenstich *m* yellow jacket sting

wessen ['vɛ·sn̩] *pron interrog gen von* **wer** whose

Wessi <-, -s> ['vɛ·si] *m o f* (*fam*) West German

> The expression **Wessi** emerged after reunification as a counterpart to the term *Ossi*. The citizens of the former East Germany use **Wessi** to describe — often pejoratively — their fellow citizens in the former West Germany.

West <-[e]s, -e> [vɛst] *m kein pl, kein art* west; **aus ~** from the west

westdeutsch ['vɛst·dɔytʃ] *adj* West German, in West Germany

Westdeutschland ['vɛst·dɔytʃ·lant] *nt* West Germany

Weste <-, -n> ['vɛs·tə] *f* vest

Westen <-s> ['vɛs·tn̩] *m kein indef art, kein pl* ① (*Himmelsrichtung*) west; *s. a.* **Norden**[1] ② (*westliche Gegend*) West; **der Wilde ~** the Wild West; *s. a.* **Norden**[2]

Westentasche *f* vest pocket

Western <-[s], -> ['vɛs·tɐn] *m* western

Westeuropa ['vɛst·ʔɔy·'roː·pa] *nt* Western Europe

westeuropäisch ['vɛst·ʔɔy·ro·'pɛː·ɪʃ] *adj* West European

Westfale, **Westfälin** <-n, -n> [vɛst·'faː·lə, vɛst·'fɛː·lɪn] *m, f* Westphalian

Westfalen <-s> [vɛst·'faː·lən] *nt* Westphalia

westfälisch [vɛst·ˈfɛː·lɪʃ] *adj* Westphalian
Wẹstküste *f* West Coast
westlich [ˈvɛst·lɪç] **I.** *adj* ❶ (*Himmelsrichtung*) western; *s. a.* **nördlich I 1** ❷ (*im Westen liegend*) western; *s. a.* **nördlich I 2** ❸ (*von/nach Westen*) westward, westerly; *s. a.* **nördlich I 3 II.** *adv* ■ ~ **von** to the west of **III.** *präp* +*gen* [to the] west of
Wẹstwind *m* west wind
weswegen [vɛs·ˈveː·gn̩] *adv* why
Wettbewerb <-[e]s, -e> [ˈvɛt·bə·vɛrp] *m* competition
Wẹttbewerber(in) *m(f)* competitor
wẹttbewerbsfähig *adj* competitive
Wette <-, -n> [ˈvɛ·tə] *f* bet; ■ **jede ~ eingehen, dass** to bet anything that; **die ~ gilt!** you're on!; **um die ~ essen/singen** to have an eating/singing contest; **um die ~ laufen** to race [each other]
Wetteifer <-s> [ˈvɛt·ʔai·fɐ] *m kein pl* competitiveness
wẹtteifern *vi* ■ **miteinander ~** to contend with each other
wetten [ˈvɛ·tn̩] *vi, vt* to bet (**auf** +*akk* on); ■ **[mit jdm] um etw ~** to bet [sb] sth; **[wollen wir] ~?** [do you] want to bet?
Wetter <-s> [ˈvɛ·tɐ] *nt kein pl* weather; **bei jedem ~** rain or shine
Wẹtterbericht *m* weather report
Wẹtterdienst *m* weather service
wẹtterfest *adj* weatherproof
wẹtterfühlig *adj* sensitive to weather changes *pred*
Wẹtterhahn *m* rooster weathervane
Wẹtterkarte *f* weather map
Wẹtterlage *f* weather situation
wettern [ˈvɛ·tɐn] *vi* ■ **[gegen jdn/etw] ~** to curse [sb/sth]
Wẹtterprognose *f* weather forecast
Wẹtterumschwung *m* sudden change in the weather
Wẹttervorhersage *f* weather forecast
Wẹttkampf *m* competition
Wẹttkämpfer(in) *m(f)* competitor, contestant
Wẹttlauf *m* race
wett|machen [ˈvɛt·ma·xn̩] *vt* ❶ (*aufholen*) to make up ❷ (*gutmachen*) to make up for
Wẹttrennen *nt* race
Wẹttrüsten <-s> *nt kein pl* arms race; **das atomare ~** the nuclear arms race
Wettstreit [ˈvɛt·ʃtrait] *m* competition
wetzen [ˈvɛ·tsn̩] **I.** *vt haben* ❶ (*schleifen*) to whet ❷ (*reiben*) to rub (**an** +*dat* on) **II.** *vi sein* (*fam: rennen*) to scoot [off]
WG <-, -s> [veː·ˈgeː] *f Abk von* **Wohngemeinschaft**
wich [vɪç] *imp von* **weichen**
wichsen [ˈvik·sn̩] **I.** *vi* (*vulg*) to jack [*or* jerk] off *vulg sl* **II.** *vt Schuhe* to polish
Wịchser <-s, -> *m* (*vulg*) jerk-off
wichtig [ˈvɪç·tɪç] *adj* important; **sich** *dat* **~ vorkommen** to be full of oneself
Wịchtigkeit <-> *f kein pl* importance, significance
wịchtig|machenRR *vr* ■ **sich** *akk* ~ to try to act important
Wịchtigmacher(in) <-s, -> *m(f)* ÖSTERR, **Wịchtigtuer(in)** <-s, -> [-tuːɐ] *m(f)* stuffed shirt
wịchtig|tunRR *vi, vr irreg* ■ **[sich]** ~ to act important
Wickel <-s, -> [ˈvɪ·kl̩] *m* (*Umschlag*) compress ▶ WENDUNGEN: **jdn beim ~ packen** (*fam*) to grab sb by the scruff of the neck
wickeln [ˈvɪ·kl̩n] *vt* ❶ (*binden*) to wrap (**um** +*akk* around, **in** +*akk* in); ■ **etw von etw** *dat* ~ to unwrap sth from sth ❷ *Baby* to change
Widder <-s, -> [ˈvɪ·dɐ] *m* ❶ ZOOL ram ❷ *kein pl* ASTROL Aries
widerborstig [ˈviː·dɐ·bɔrs·tɪç] *adj Mensch* contrary, unruly; *Haare* unmanageable
widerfahren* [viː·dɐ·ˈfaː·rən] *vi irreg sein* to happen, to befall
Widerhall <-s, -e> [ˈviː·dɐ·hal] *m* echo
widerlegen* [viː·dɐ·ˈleː·gn̩] *vt* to refute
widerlich [ˈviː·dɐ·lɪç] **I.** *adj* ❶ (*ekelhaft*) disgusting ❷ (*unsympathisch*) repulsive **II.** *adv* (*überaus*) *süß, kalt* awfully
widernatürlich [ˈviː·dɐ·na·tyːɐ̯·lɪç] *adj* perverted, unnatural
wi̲derrechtlich **I.** *adj* unlawful **II.** *adv* unlawfully
Widerrede [ˈviː·dɐ·reː·də] *f* **ohne ~** without protest; **keine ~!** don't argue [with me]!
widerrufen* [viː·dɐ·ˈruː·fn̩] *irreg vt* ❶ (*für ungültig erklären*) to revoke ❷ (*zurücknehmen*) to retract
Widersacher(in) <-s, -> [ˈviː·dɐ·za·xɐ] *m(f)* antagonist
widersetzen* [viː·dɐ·ˈzɛ·tsn̩] *vr* ■ **sich** *akk* **jdm ~** to resist sb; ■ **sich** *akk* **etw** *dat* ~ to refuse to comply with sth
widerspenstig [ˈviː·dɐ·ʃpɛns·tɪç] *adj* unruly; *Mensch, Pferd* stubborn; *Haar* unmanageable
wider|spiegeln [ˈviː·dɐ·ʃpiː·gl̩n] **I.** *vt* to mirror, to reflect **II.** *vr* **sich ~** to be reflected
widersprechen* [viː·dɐ·ˈʃprɛ·çn̩] *irreg* **I.** *vi* to contradict **II.** *vr* ■ **sich** *dat* ~ *Aussage, Angaben* to be contradictory
Widerspruch [ˈviː·dɐ·ʃprʊx] *m* ❶ *kein pl* (*das Widersprechen*) contradiction; **auf ~ stoßen** to meet with opposition ❷ (*Unvereinbarkeit*) inconsistency; **in ~ zu etw** *dat* **stehen** to conflict with sth
widersprüchlich [ˈviː·dɐ·ʃprʏç·lɪç] *adj* inconsistent; ■ **~ sein** to be contradictory
wi̲derspruchslos *adv* without protest
Widerstand <-[e]s, -stände> [ˈviː·dɐ·ʃtant, *pl* -ʃtɛn·də] *m* ❶ *kein pl* (*Gegenwehr*) opposition, resistance ❷ ELEK (*Schaltelement*) resistor
Wi̲derstandsbewegung *f* resistance movement; (*bewaffnet*) partisan movement
wi̲derstandsfähig *adj* resistant (**gegen** +*akk* to)
Wi̲derstandsfähigkeit *f kein pl* robustness; ■ **jds ~ gegen etw** sb's resistance to sth
Wi̲derstandskämpfer(in) *m(f)* resistance

W

fighter
Widerstandskraft *f s.* **Widerstandsfähigkeit**
widerstandslos *adv* without resistance
widerstehen* [viː·dɐ·ˈʃteː·ən] *vi irreg* ①(*standhalten*) to withstand ②(*nicht nachgeben*) *Person, Versuchung* to resist
widerstreben* [viː·dɐ·ˈʃtreː·bn̩] *vi* ■**jdm widerstrebt es, etw zu tun** sb is reluctant to do sth
Widerstreben <-s> [viː·dɐ·ˈʃtreː·bn̩] *nt kein pl* reluctance
widerwärtig [ˈviː·dɐ·vɛr·tɪç] **I.** *adj* disgusting; (*Kerl*) nasty **II.** *adv* disgustingly
Widerwille [ˈviː·dɐ·vɪlə] *m* distaste (**gegen** +*akk* for)
widerwillig **I.** *adj* reluctant **II.** *adv* reluctantly
widmen [ˈvɪt·mən] **I.** *vt* to dedicate to **II.** *vr* ①(*sich kümmern*) ■**sich** *akk* **jdm ~** to attend to sb ②(*sich beschäftigen*) ■**sich** *akk* **etw** *dat* ~ to devote oneself to sth
Widmung <-, -en> [ˈvɪt·mʊŋ] *f* dedication
widrig [ˈviː·drɪç] *adj* adverse; *Umstände, Verhältnisse* unfavorable
wie [viː] **I.** *adv* how; **~ geht es dir?** how are you?; **~ heißt er?** what's his name?; **~ war das Wetter?** what was the weather like?; **~ viel/viele** how much/many; **~ sehr** how much; **~ wär's mit ...?** how about ...? **II.** *konj* ①(*vergleichend*) **so alt/groß ~ ...** as big/old as ...; **er ist genau ~ du** he's just like you ②(*beispielsweise*) like
wieder [ˈviː·dɐ] *adv* again, once more; **~ mal** again; **Verhandlungen ~ aufnehmen** to resume negotiations; **Kontakt ~ aufnehmen** to reestablish contact; **etw ~ einführen** to reintroduce sth
Wiederaufbau [viː·dɐ·ˈʔauf·bau] *m kein pl* reconstruction
Wiederaufbereitung <-, -en> *f* recycling; (*von Atommüll*) reprocessing
Wiederaufnahme [viː·dɐ·ˈʔauf·naː·mə] *f von Verhandlungen* resumption; *von Kontakten* reestablishment
wieder|bekommen* *vt irreg* to get back
wieder|beleben* *vt* to revive
wiederbeschreibbar *adj CD* rewritable
wieder|bringen [ˈviː·dɐ·brɪ·ŋən] *vt irreg* to bring back *sep*
wieder|entdecken* *vt* to rediscover
wieder|erkennen* *vt irreg* to recognize; **nicht wiederzuerkennen sein** to be unrecognizable
Wiedereröffnung *f* reopening
wieder|erstatten* [ˈviː·dɐ·ʔɛɐ̯·ʃta·tn̩] *vt* to refund; ■**jdm etw ~** to reimburse sb for sth
wieder|finden *irreg* **I.** *vt* ①(*auffinden*) to find again ②*Fassung* to regain **II.** *vr* ■**sich ~** to turn up again; **der Schlüssel findet sich bestimmt wieder** the key is sure to turn up again
Wiedergabe <-, -n> [ˈviː·dɐ·gaː·bə] *f* ①(*Schilderung*) account, report ②PHOTO, TYPO reproduction
wieder|geben [ˈviː·dɐ·geː·bn̩] *vt irreg* ①(*zurückgeben*) to give back ②(*zitieren*) to quote
wieder|gewinnen* [ˈviː·dɐ·gə·vɪ·nən] *vt irreg* ①(*zurückgewinnen*) to reclaim ②(*wiedererlangen*) to regain
wieder|gut|machen *vt* **wie kann ich das nur je ~?** how can I ever repay you?
Wiedergutmachung <-, -en> *f* compensation
wieder|her|stellen [viː·dɐ·ˈheːɐ̯·ʃtɛ·lən] *vt* ①(*restaurieren*) to restore ②*Ordnung, Kontakt, Gesundheit* to reestablish
wiederholen*[1] [viː·dɐ·ˈhoː·lən] **I.** *vt* ①(*erneut sagen/machen*) to repeat ②*Lernstoff* to revise **II.** *vr* ■**sich ~** *Ereignis* to happen again; *Person* to repeat oneself
wieder|holen[2] [ˈviː·dɐ·hoː·lən] *vt* ■**jdn ~** to get sb back; ■[**jdm**] **etw ~** to bring sth back [for sb]
wiederholt **I.** *adj* repeated **II.** *adv* repeatedly
Wiederholung <-, -en> [viː·dɐ·ˈhoː·lʊŋ] *f* ①(*erneutes Tun*) repetition ②(*im Radio/TV*) repeat ③*von Lernstoff* review
Wiederholungstäter(in) *m(f)* repeat offender
wieder|kehren [ˈviː·dɐ·keː·rən] *vi sein* ①*Mensch* to return ②*Problem* to reoccur
wieder|kommen [ˈviː·dɐ·kɔ·mən] *vi irreg sein* ①(*zurückkommen*) to come back ②(*erneut kommen*) to come again; *Gelegenheit* to reoccur
wieder|sehen [ˈviː·dɐ·zeː·ən] *vt irreg* ①■**jdn ~** to see sb again ②■**sich** *akk* ~ to meet again
Wiedersehen <-s, -> [ˈviː·dɐ·zeː·ən] *nt* [another] meeting; (*nach längerer Zeit*) reunion; [**auf**] **~ sagen** to say goodbye
wiederum [ˈviː·dər·ʊm] *adv* ①(*abermals*) again ②(*andererseits*) on the other hand, though ③(*für jds Teil*) in turn
wieder|vereinigen* *vt* POL to reunify
Wiedervereinigung [ˈviː·dɐ·fɛɐ̯·ʔai·nɪ·gʊŋ] *f* POL reunification
wiederverwendbar *adj* reusable
Wiederverwendung *f* reuse
wieder|verwerten* *vt* to recycle
Wiederverwertung *f* recycling
Wiederwahl [ˈviː·dɐ·vaːl] *f* POL reelection
Wiege <-, -n> [ˈviː·gə] *f* cradle
wiegen[1] <wog, gewogen> [ˈviː·gn̩] *vt, vi* to weigh
wiegen[2] [ˈviː·gn̩] *vt* (*hin und her bewegen*) to rock; *Hüften* to sway
Wiegenlied *nt* lullaby
wiehern [ˈviː·ɐn] *vi* to neigh
Wien <-s> [viːn] *nt* Vienna
Wiener [ˈviː·nɐ] *adj attr* Viennese
wienern [ˈviː·nɐn] *vt* to polish
wies [viːs] *imp von* **weisen**
Wiese <-, -n> [viː·zə] *f* meadow
Wiesel <-s, -> [ˈviː·zl̩] *nt* weasel
wieso [vi·ˈzoː] *adv* why
wievielmal [vi·fiːl·ˈmaːl] *adv* how many times
wievielte(r, s) [ˈviː·fiːl·tə, -tɐ, -təs] *adj* ■**der/die/das ~ ...?** how many ...?, which...?; **den**

W

W~n haben wir heute? what's today's date?

wild [vɪlt] **I.** *adj* ① BOT, ZOOL wild ② *Kampf* frenzied ③ (*illegal*) illegal ④ (*sehr gereizt*) furious; **~ werden** to go wild ▶ WENDUNGEN: **halb so ~ sein** (*fam*) to not be important; **~ auf jdn/etw sein** (*fam*) to be crazy about sb/sth; **wie ~** (*fam*) wildly **II.** *adv* ① (*ungeordnet*) strewn around ② (*hemmungslos*) wildly, furiously ③ (*in freier Natur*) wild *pred*

Wild <-[e]s> [vɪlt] *nt kein pl* ① KOCHK game ② ZOOL wild animals

Wilderer, **Wilderin** <-s, -> ['vɪl·də·rɐ] *m, f* poacher

wildern ['vɪl·dɐn] *vi* to poach

wildfremd ['vɪlt·'frɛmt] *adj* completely strange

Wịldhüter(in) <-s, -> *m(f)* gamekeeper

Wịldkatze *f* wildcat

Wildnis <-, -se> ['vɪlt·nɪs] *f* wilderness

Wịldpark *m* wildlife park

Wịldschwein *nt* wild boar

Wildwestfilm [vɪlt·'vɛst-] *m* western

wịll *3. pers sing pres von* **wollen**²

Wille <-ns> ['vɪ·lə] *m kein pl* will; **seinen eigenen ~n haben** to have a mind of one's own; **guter/schlechter ~** good/ill will; **seinen ~n durchsetzen** to get one's way ▶ WENDUNGEN: **sein/ihr letzter ~** his/her last will and testament

willen ['vɪ·lən] *präp +gen* **um jds/einer S. ~** for the sake of sb/sth

wịllenlos *adj* spineless

Wịllenskraft *f kein pl* willpower

wịllensstark *adj* strong-willed

willig ['vɪ·lɪç] *adj* willing

willkommen [vɪl·'kɔ·mən] *adj* welcome; ■ **[jdm] ~ sein** to be welcomed [by sb]; **jdn ~ heißen** to welcome sb

Willkommen <-s, -> [vɪl·'kɔ·mən] *nt* welcome; **ein herzliches ~** a warm welcome

Willkür <-> ['vɪl·kyːɐ̯] *f kein pl* arbitrariness

willkürlich ['vɪl·kyːɐ̯·lɪç] **I.** *adj* arbitrary **II.** *adv* arbitrarily

wimmeln ['vɪ·ml̩n] *vi impers* ■ **es wimmelt von etw** *dat* it is teeming with sth; *Menschen* it is swarming with

wimmern ['vɪ·mɐn] *vi* to whimper

Wimper <-, -n> ['vɪm·pɐ] *f* [eye]lash ▶ WENDUNGEN: **ohne mit der ~ zu zucken** without batting an eyelid

Wịmperntusche *f* mascara

Wind <-[e]s, -e> [vɪnt, *pl* 'vɪn·də] *m* wind ▶ WENDUNGEN: **viel ~ um etw machen** to make a fuss about sth; **bei ~ und Wetter** rain or shine

Wịndböe *f* gust of wind

Winde <-, -n> ['vɪn·də] *f* TECH winch

Windel <-, -n> ['vɪn·dl̩] *f* diaper

wịndelweich *adv* **jdn ~ schlagen** to beat sb black and blue

winden¹ <wạnd, gewụnden> ['vɪn·dn̩] **I.** *vr* ■ **sich** *akk* **~** ① (*nach Ausflüchten suchen*) to attempt to wriggle out ② (*sich krümmen*) to writhe (**vor** *+dat* in); **sich vor Schmerzen ~** to writhe in pain ③ *Weg* to wind its way; *Bach* to meander ④ BOT to wind [itself] (**um** *+akk* around) **II.** *vt* ■ **etw um etw ~** to wind sth around sth

winden² ['vɪn·dn̩] *vi impers* ■ **es windet** it's windy

Wịndenergie *f* wind energy

wịndgeschützt **I.** *adj* sheltered [from the wind] **II.** *adv* in a sheltered place

Wịndgeschwindigkeit *f* wind speed

windig ['vɪn·dɪç] *adj* windy

Wịndjacke *f* windbreaker

Wịndkraftanlage *f*, **Wịndkraftwerk** *nt* wind [-driven] power plant

Wịndmühle *f* windmill

Wịndpark *m* wind farm

Wịndpocken *pl* chickenpox *sing*

Wịndrad *nt* wind turbine

wịndschief *adj* crooked

Wịndschutzscheibe *f* windshield

Wịndseite *f* windward side

Wịndstärke *f* wind force

wịndstill *adj* windless; ■ **~ sein** to be calm

Wịndstille *f* calm

Wịndstoß *m* gust of wind

windsurfen ['vɪnt·zøːɐ̯·fn̩] *vi* to windsurf

Wịndsurfer(in) *m(f)* windsurfer

Windsurfing ['vɪnt·zøːɐ̯·fɪŋ] *nt* windsurfing

Wink <-[e]s, -e> [vɪŋk] *m* ① (*Hinweis*) hint; **einen ~ bekommen** to receive a tip ② (*Handbewegung*) signal ▶ WENDUNGEN: **ein ~ mit dem Zaunpfahl** a broad hint

Winkel <-s, -> ['vɪŋ·kl̩] *m* ① MATH angle; **rechter ~** right angle ② (*Ecke*) corner ③ (*Bereich*) place, spot ▶ WENDUNGEN: **toter ~** blind spot

winkelig ['vɪŋ·kə·lɪç] *adj s.* **winklig**

winken <gewịnkt *o* DIAL gewụnken> ['vɪŋ·kn̩] **I.** *vi* to wave; ■ **mit etw** *dat* **~** to wave sth; **einem Taxi ~** to hail a taxi **II.** *vt* ■ **jdn zu sich** *dat* **~** to beckon sb over [to one's side]

winklig ['vɪŋk·lɪç] *adj* full of nooks and crannies; *Gasse* windy

winseln ['vɪn·zl̩n] *vi* to whimper; ■ **um etw ~** to plead for sth

Winter <-s, -> ['vɪn·tɐ] *m* winter

Wịntereinbruch *m* onset of winter

Wịnterfell *nt* winter coat

Wịnterferien *pl* winter vacation

wịnterfest *adj* suitable for winter; **ein Auto ~ machen** to get a car ready for winter

Wịntergarten *m* winter garden

Wịnterkleidung *f* winter clothes *pl*

winterlich ['vɪn·tɐ·lɪç] **I.** *adj* wintry; **~e Temperaturen** winter temperatures **II.** *adv* **~ gekleidet** dressed for winter

Wịntermantel *m* winter coat

Wịnterreifen *m* winter tire

Wịnterschlaf *m* hibernation; **~ halten** to hibernate

Wịnterschlussverkauf^RR *m* end-of-winter sale

Wịnterspeck *m kein pl* (*hum*) [layer of] winter fat, holiday pounds *pl fam*

Wịntersport *m* winter sport
Wịnterurlaub *m* winter vacation
Winzer(in) <-s, -> ['vɪn·tsɐ] *m(f)* wine grower
winzig ['vɪn·tsɪç] *adj* tiny; **~ klein** minute
Winzling <-s, -e> ['vɪnts·lɪŋ] *m* tiny thing
Wipfel <-s, -> ['vɪp·fl̩] *m* treetop
Wippe <-, -n> ['vɪ·pə] *f* seesaw
wippen ['vɪ·pn̩] *vi* to bob up and down (**auf** *+dat* on); (*auf einer Wippe*) to seesaw
wir <*gen* ụnser, *dat* ụns, *akk* ụns> [viːɐ̯] *pron pers* we; **~ nicht** not us
Wirbel <-s, -> ['vɪr·bl̩] *m* ① (*Rückenwirbel*) vertebra ② (*Haarwirbel*) cowlick ③ (*fam: Trubel*) turmoil
Wịrbelsäule *f* spinal column
Wịrbelsturm *m* whirlwind
wịrbt *3. pers sing pres von* **werben**
wịrd *3. pers sing pres von* **werden**
wịrft *3. pers sing pres von* **werfen**
wirken ['vɪr·kn̩] *vi* ① (*Wirkung haben*) to have an effect; (*beabsichtigten Effekt haben*) to work; **dieses Medikament wirkt sofort** this medicine takes effect immediately; **etw auf sich** *akk* **~ lassen** to take sth in ② (*erscheinen*) to seem, to appear
wirklich ['vɪrk·lɪç] **I.** *adj* real **II.** *adv* really
Wịrklichkeit <-, -en> *f* reality; **~ werden** to come true
wirksam ['vɪrk·zaːm] **I.** *adj* effective **II.** *adv* effectively
Wịrksamkeit <-> *f kein pl* effectiveness
Wịrkstoff *m* active ingredient
Wirkung <-, -en> ['vɪr·kʊŋ] *f* effect
wịrkungslos *adj* ineffective
wịrkungsvoll *adj* effective
wirr [vɪr] *adj* ① (*unordentlich*) tangled ② (*verworren*) weird ③ (*durcheinander*) confused
Wirren ['vɪ·rən] *pl* confusion *sing*
Wirrwarr <-s> ['vɪr·var] *m kein pl* ① (*Durcheinander*) confusion ② (*Unordnung*) tangle
Wirsing <-s> ['vɪr·zɪŋ] *m kein pl*, **Wịrsingkohl** *m* savoy cabbage
Wirt(in) <-[e]s, -e> [vɪrt] *m(f)* innkeeper, ≈ restaurant/tavern manager/owner
Wirtschaft <-, -en> ['vɪrt·ʃaft] *f* ① ÖKON economy ② (*Gastwirtschaft*) tavern, pub
wirtschaftlich ['vɪrt·ʃaft·lɪç] **I.** *adj* ① ÖKON economic ② (*sparsam*) economical **II.** *adv* economically
Wịrtschaftlichkeit <-> *f kein pl* economy
Wịrtschaftsabkommen *nt* economic agreement [*or* treaty]
Wịrtschaftsflüchtling *m* economic refugee
Wịrtschaftshilfe *f* economic aid
Wịrtschaftskriminalität *f* white-collar crime
Wịrtschaftslage *f* economic situation
Wịrtschaftsminister(in) *m(f)* Secretary of Commerce, Commerce Secretary
Wịrtschaftsministerium *nt* Department of Commerce, Commerce Department
Wịrtschaftspolitik *f* economic policy
Wịrtschaftssanktionen *pl* economic sanctions *pl*
Wịrtschaftswachstum *nt* economic growth
Wịrtschaftswissenschaft *f meist pl* economics *sing*
Wịrtschaftswissenschaftler(in) *m(f)* economist
Wịrtschaftswunder *nt* economic miracle

> Triggered by the currency reform of 1948, the **Wirtschaftswunder** was a period of dramatic recovery of the German economy during the post-war years. The **Wirtschaftswunder** led to renewed stability and prosperity in West Germany.

Wịrtschaftszweig *m* branch of industry
Wịrtshaus *nt* tavern, restaurant, inn
Wịrtsleute *pl the people, often husband and wife, who own and/or operate a restaurant/tavern*
Wisch <-[e]s, -e> [vɪʃ] *m* (*pej fam*) worthless official document [*or* form]
wischen ['vɪ·ʃn̩] *vt* ① (*abwischen*) to wipe ② SCHWEIZ (*fegen*) to sweep ▶ WENDUNGEN: [**von jdm**] **eine gewischt <u>bekommen</u>** (*fam*) to get whacked [by sb]
Wischiwaschi <-s> [vɪ·ʃi·'va·ʃi] *nt kein pl* (*fam*) wish-wash, drivel
Wịschlappen *m* cloth
wispern ['vɪs·pɐn] *vt, vi* to whisper
Wissbegier(de)[RR], **Wịßbegier(de)**[ALT] <-> ['vɪs·bə·giːɐ̯(·də)] *f kein pl* thirst for knowledge
wịssbegierig[RR], **wịßbegierig**[ALT] *adj* eager to learn
wissen <w<u>ei</u>ß, wụsste, gewụsst> ['vɪ·sn̩] *vt, vi* ① (*Kenntnis haben*) to know; **man kạnn nie ~!** you never know!; **jdn etw ~ lassen** to let sb know sth; **woher soll ich das ~?** how should I know that?; **wenn ich nur wüsste, ...** if only I knew ...; **soviel** [*o* **soweit**] **ich weiß** as far as I know ② (*sich erinnern*) **weißt du noch?** do you remember? ③ (*können*) **etw zu schätzen ~** to appreciate sth; **sich** *dat* **zu helfen ~** to be resourceful ▶ WENDUNGEN: **von jdm/etw nichts** [**mehr**] **~ <u>wollen</u>** (*fam*) to not want to have anything [more] to do with sb/sth
Wissen <-s> ['vɪ·sn̩] *nt kein pl* knowledge
Wissenschaft <-, -en> ['vɪ·sn̩·ʃaft] *f* science
Wịssenschaftler(in) <-s, -> *m(f)* scientist
wissenschaftlich ['vɪ·sn̩·ʃaft·lɪç] **I.** *adj* scientific; (*akademisch*) academic **II.** *adv* scientifically; (*akademisch*) academically
Wịssensdrang *m*, **Wịssensdurst** *m* thirst for knowledge
Wịssensgebiet *nt* field of knowledge
Wịssenslücke *f* gap in sb's knowledge
wịssenswert *adj* worth knowing
wissentlich ['vɪ·sn̩t·lɪç] **I.** *adj* deliberate **II.** *adv* deliberately, knowingly
wittern ['vɪ·tɐn] *vt* (*ahnen*) to suspect
Wịtterung <-, -en> *f* METEO weather

W

Witterungsverhältnisse *pl* weather conditions *pl*
Witwe <-, -n> ['vɪt·və] *f fem form von* **Witwer** widow *fem;* ~ **werden** to be widowed
Witwer <-s, -> ['vɪt·vɐ] *m* widower *masc;* ~ **werden** to be widowed
Witz <-es, -e> [vɪts] *m* ❶ (*Scherz*) joke; **einen ~ machen** to tell [*or fam* crack] a joke ❷ *kein pl* (*Esprit*) wit
Witzbold <-[e]s, -e> *m* joker
witzeln ['vɪ·ts̩ln] *vi* to joke (**über** +*akk* about)
Witzfigur *f* laughingstock
witzig ['vɪ·tsɪç] *adj* funny
witzlos *adj* pointless
WM <-, -s> *f Abk von* **Weltmeisterschaft** world championship; (*im Fußball*) World Cup
wo [vo:] **I.** *adv* ❶ (*räumlich*) where; **pass auf, ~ du hintrittst!** watch your step! [*or* where you're going!] ❷ (*zeitlich*) when; **zu dem Zeitpunkt, ~ ...** when ... **II.** *konj* (*zumal*) when, as; ~ **er doch wusste, dass ich keine Zeit hatte** when he knew that I had no time
woanders [vo·'ʔan·dɐs] *adv* somewhere else, elsewhere
woandershin [vo·'ʔan·dɐs·'hɪn] *adv* somewhere else
wob *imp von* **weben**
wobei [vo·'bai] *adv* ❶ *interrog* how; ~ **ist das passiert?** how did that happen? ❷ *rel* in which; ~ **mir gerade einfällt ...** which reminds me ...
Woche <-, -n> ['vɔ·xə] *f* week
Wochenblatt *nt* weekly
Wochenende ['vɔ·xn̩·ʔɛn·də] *nt* weekend; **schönes ~!** have a nice weekend!; **am ~** on the weekend
Wochenendhaus ['vɔ·xn̩·ʔɛnt·haus] *nt* weekend home
Wochenendticket [-tɪ·kət] *nt* TRANSP *discount train ticket for weekend travel*
Wochenkarte *f* TRANSP weekly pass
wochenlang ['vɔ·xn̩·laŋ] *adj, adv* for weeks
Wochenmarkt *m* weekly market
Wochentag *m* weekday; **was ist heute für ein ~?** what day of the week is it today?
wochentags ['vɔ·xn̩·ta:ks] *adv* on weekdays
wöchentlich ['vœ·çn̩t·lɪç] *adj, adv* weekly
Wochenzeitung *f* weekly [newspaper]
Wodka <-s, -s> ['vɔt·ka] *m* vodka
wodurch [vo·'dʊrç] *adv* ❶ *interrog* how ❷ *rel* which
wofür [vo·'fy:ɐ̯] *adv* ❶ *interrog* for what, what ... for; ~ **hast du denn so viel Geld bezahlt?** what did you pay so much money for? ❷ *rel* for which
wog [vo:k] *imp von* **wiegen**[1]
Woge <-, -n> ['vo:·gə] *f* wave ▶ WENDUNGEN: **wenn sich die ~n geglättet haben** when things have calmed down
wogegen [vo·'ge:·gn̩] *adv* ❶ *interrog* against what; ~ **hilft dieses Mittel?** what is this medicine for? ❷ *rel* against what/which
woher [vo·'he:ɐ̯] *adv* ❶ *interrog* where ... from; ~ **hast du dieses Buch?** where did you get this book [from]? ❷ *rel* from which, where ... [from]
wohin [vo·'hɪn] *adv* ❶ *interrog* where [to]; ~ **damit?** where should I put it? ❷ *rel* where
wohingegen [vo·hɪn·'ge:·gn̩] *konj* while, whereas
wohl [vo:l] *adv* ❶ (*gut, gesund*) well; **sich** *akk* **~ fühlen** to feel well; **sich** *akk* **irgendwo ~ fühlen** to feel at home somewhere ❷ (*gut*) **jdm ~ bekannt sein** to be well-known to sb; ~ **geformt** well-formed; *Körperteil* shapely; ~ **überlegt** well thought out ❸ (*wahrscheinlich*) probably; ~ **kaum** hardly ❹ ■**jdm ist ~ bei etw** *dat* sb is comfortable with sth; ■**jdm ist nicht ~ bei etw** *dat* sb is uneasy about sth ❺ (*zirka*) about ▶ WENDUNGEN: ~ **oder übel** whether you like it or not
Wohl <-[e]s> [vo:l] *nt kein pl* welfare, well-being; **auf jds ~ trinken** to drink to sb's health; **zum ~!** cheers!
wohlauf [vo:l·'ʔauf] *adj pred* ■~ **sein** to be well
Wohlbefinden <-s> *nt kein pl* well-being
Wohlbehagen <-s> *nt kein pl* feeling of well-being
wohlbehalten *adv* safe and sound
Wohlfahrtsstaat *m* welfare state
Wohlgefallen ['vo:l·gə·fa·lən] *nt* ▶ WENDUNGEN: **sich in ~ auflösen** (*fam*) to vanish into thin air
wohlgesinnt <wohlgesinnter, wohlgesinnteste> *adj* ■**jdm ~ sein** to be well-disposed toward sb
wohlhabend <wohlhabender, wohlhabendste> *adj* well-to-do
wohlig ['vo:·lɪç] **I.** *adj* (*behaglich*) pleasant **II.** *adv* (*genießerisch*) luxuriously
wohlklingend <wohlklingender, wohlklingendste> *adj* melodious
wohlmeinend <wohlmeinender, wohlmeinendste> *adj* well-meaning
wohlriechend <wohlriechender, wohlriechendste> *adj* fragrant
wohlschmeckend <wohlschmeckender, wohlschmeckendste> *adj* palatable
Wohlstand *m kein pl* affluence, prosperity
Wohlstandsgesellschaft *f* affluent society
Wohlstandsmüll *m* trash of the affluent [society]
Wohltat *f* ❶ *kein pl* (*Erleichterung*) relief ❷ (*Unterstützung*) good deed
Wohltäter(in) *m(f)* benefactor *masc,* benefactress *fem*
wohltätig *adj* charitable
Wohltätigkeit *f kein pl* charity
Wohltätigkeitsveranstaltung *f* charity event
Wohltätigkeitsverein *m* charity
wohltuend <wohltuender, wohltuendste> *adj* agreeable
wohlverdient *adj* well-earned; **seine ~e Strafe erhalten** to get one's just deserts
wohlweislich ['vo:l·vais·lɪç] *adv* very wisely

Wohlwollen <-s> ['vo:l·vɔ·lən] *nt kein pl* goodwill

wohlwollend <wohlwollender, wohlwollendste> **I.** *adj* benevolent **II.** *adv* benevolently

Wohnanlage *f* housing development

Wohnbezirk *m* residential district

Wohnblock *m* apartment building

Wohncontainer *m* temporary housing unit

wohnen ['vo:·nən] *vi* to live; (*im Hotel*) to stay

Wohnfläche *f* living space

Wohngebiet *nt* residential area

Wohngegend *f* residential area; **eine gute ~ sein** to be a nice area to live in

Wohngeld *nt* housing subsidy

Wohngemeinschaft *f* communal residence, shared house [*or* apartment]; **in einer ~ leben** to share a house/apartment with sb

Wohnhaus *nt* residential building

Wohnheim *nt* (*Studentenwohnheim*) residence hall, dormitory; (*Arbeiterwohnheim*) rooming house [for workers]

Wohnküche *f* eat-in kitchen

wohnlich ['vo:n·lɪç] *adj* cozy

Wohnmobil <-s, -e> *nt* camper

Wohnort *m* place of residence

Wohnraum *m kein pl* living space

Wohnsitz *m* ADMIN domicile; **erster ~** permanent residence; **ohne festen ~** without a fixed residence

Wohnung <-, -en> *f* apartment

Wohnungsbesetzer(in) <-s, -> *m(f)* squatter

Wohnungseigentümer(in) *m(f)* property owner

Wohnungseinrichtung *f* furnishings *pl*

Wohnungsmarkt *m* housing market

Wohnungsnot *f kein pl* serious housing shortage

Wohnungssuche *f* apartment hunting; **auf ~ sein** to be apartment hunting

Wohnungstür *f* front door

Wohnviertel *nt* residential area

Wohnwagen *m* (*zum Campen*) RV

Wohnzimmer *nt* living room

wölben ['vœl·bn̩] *vr* ■ **sich ~** ① (*sich biegen*) to bend ② ■ **sich über etw** *akk* **~** to arch over sth

Wölbung <-, -en> *f* (*Rundung*) bulge

Wolf <-[e]s, Wölfe> [vɔlf, *pl* 'vœl·fə] *m* wolf

Wolke <-, -n> ['vɔl·kə] *f* cloud ▶ WENDUNGEN: **aus allen ~n fallen** (*fam*) to be flabbergasted

Wolkenbruch *m* cloudburst

Wolkendecke *f* cloud cover

Wolkenkratzer *m* skyscraper

wolkenlos *adj* cloudless

wolkig ['vɔl·kɪç] *adj* cloudy

Wolldecke *f* [wool] blanket

Wolle <-, -n> ['vɔ·lə] *f* wool

wollen¹ ['vɔ·lən] *adj attr* (*aus Wolle*) wool

wollen² ['vɔ·lən] **I.** *aux vb* <will, wollte, wollen> *modal* ① (*zu tun beabsichtigen*) ■ **etw tun ~** to want to do sth; ■ **etw gerade tun ~** to be [just] about to do sth; ■ **etw haben ~** to want [to have] sth; **~ wir uns nicht setzen?** why don't we sit down? ② (*behaupten*) ■ **etw getan haben ~** to claim to have done sth; **und so jemand will Arzt sein!** and he calls himself a doctor! ③ *passivisch* **diese Aktion will gut vorbereitet sein** this operation has to be carefully planned **II.** *vi* <will, wollte, gewollt> ① (*den Willen haben*) to want; **ob du willst oder nicht** whether you like it or not; **wenn du willst** if you['d] like; **[ganz] wie du willst** whatever is good for you, as you wish ② (*gehen wollen*) ■ **irgendwohin ~** to want to go somewhere; **zu wem ~ Sie?** who[m] do you wish to see? **III.** *vt* <will, wollte, gewollt> ① (*haben wollen*) ■ **etw [von jdm] ~** to want sth [from sb]; **willst du lieber Tee oder Kaffee?** would you prefer tea or coffee?; **ich will, dass du jetzt sofort gehst!** I want you to go right now [*or* leave immediately] ② (*bezwecken*) ■ **etw mit etw** *dat* **~** to want sth with [*or* for] sth; **ohne es zu ~** without wanting to

Wolljacke *f* wool cardigan

Wollust <-, Wollüste> ['vɔ·lʊst, *pl* 'vɔ·lʏs·tə] *f* lust

wollüstig ['vɔ·lʏs·tɪç] *adj* lascivious

womit [vo·'mɪt] *adv* ① *interrog* with what, what ... with; **~ reinigt man Seidenhemden?** what do you use to clean silk shirts [with]?; **~ habe ich das verdient?** what did I do to deserve this? ② *rel* with which

womöglich [vo·'mø:k·lɪç] *adv* possibly

wonach [vo·'na:x] *adv* ① *interrog* what ... for, what ... of; **~ suchst du?** what are you looking for?; **~ riecht das hier?** what's that smell [in here]? ② *rel* which [*or* what] ... for, of which

Wonne <-, -n> ['vɔ·nə] *f* joy, delight

woran [vo·'ran] *adv* ① *interrog* (*an welchem/welchen Gegenstand*) what ... on, on what; **~ soll ich das befestigen?** what should I fasten this to? ② *interrog* (*an welchem/welchen Umstand*) what ... of, of what; **~ haben Sie ihn erkannt?** how did you recognize him?; **~ denkst du?** what are you thinking of?; **~ ist sie gestorben?** what did she die of? ③ *rel* (*an welchem/welchen Gegenstand*) on which; **das Seil, ~ der Kübel befestigt war, riss** the rope [that] the pail was fastened to broke ④ *rel* (*an welchem/welchen Umstand*) by which; **das ist das einzige, ~ ich mich noch erinnere** that's the only thing I can remember

worauf [vo·'rauf] *adv* ① *interrog* on what ..., what ... on; **~ wartest du noch?** what are you waiting for?; **~ stützen sich deine Behauptungen?** what do you base your claims on? ② *rel* on which; **das Bett, ~ wir liegen ...** the bed [that] we're lying on ...

woraufhin *adv* ① *interrog* for what reason ② *rel* whereupon, after which

woraus [vo·'raus] *adv* ① *interrog* what ... out of, out of what; **und ~ schließen Sie das?** and what do you base your conclusion[s] on? ② *rel* from which, what ... out of, out of which; **das Material, ~ die Socken beste-**

W

hen, kratzt the material [that] the socks are made of is itchy

worden *pp von* **werden**

worin [vo·ˈrɪn] *adv* ① *interrog* in what, what ... in; **~ besteht der Unterschied?** where is the difference? ② *rel* in which; **es gibt etwas, ~ sich Original und Fälschung unterscheiden** there is something that the original and the forgery do not have in common

Workaholic <-s, -s> [vøːɐ̯k·əˈhɔ·lɪk] *m* workaholic

Workshop <-s, -s> [ˈvøːɐ̯k·ʃɔp] *m* workshop

Wort <-[e]s, Wörter *o* -e> [vɔrt] *nt* ① LING word; **im wahrsten Sinne des ~es** in the true sense of the word ② *meist pl* (*Äußerung*) word *usu pl;* **mit anderen ~en** in other words; **etw in ~e fassen** to put sth into words; **jdm fehlen die ~e** sb is speechless; **kein ~ herausbringen** to not get a word out; **ein ernstes ~ mit jdm reden** to have a serious talk with sb; **kein ~ verstehen** to not understand a word; (*hören*) to be unable to hear a word ③ *kein pl* (*Ehrenwort*) **jdm sein ~ geben** to give sb one's word; **sein ~ brechen/halten** to break/keep one's word; **jdn beim ~ nehmen** to take sb's word for it; **das glaube ich dir aufs ~** I can believe it, trust me, I believe you ④ *kein pl* (*Rede[erlaubnis]*) **jdm das ~ abschneiden** to cut sb short; **jdm ins ~ fallen** to interrupt sb; **zu ~ kommen** to get a chance to speak; **das ~ an jdn richten** to address sb ▶ WENDUNGEN: **das <u>ist</u> ein ~!** [it's [*or* that's] a] deal!; **jdm das ~ im <u>Munde</u> herumdrehen** to twist sb's words

wortbrüchig *adj* treacherous

Wörtchen [ˈvœrt·çən] *nt* ▶ WENDUNGEN: **ein ~ <u>mitzureden</u> haben** (*fam*) to have a say in sth; **mit jdm noch ein ~ zu <u>reden</u> haben** (*fam*) to have a bone to pick with sb

Wörterbuch *nt* dictionary

Wortfetzen *pl* scraps of conversation *pl*

Wortführer(in) *m(f)* spokesperson, spokesman *masc,* spokeswoman *fem*

Wortgefecht *nt* battle of words

wortgewandt *adj* eloquent

wortkarg *adj* taciturn

Wortklauberei <-, -en> [vɔrt·klau·bə·ˈrai] *f* (*pej*) hairsplitting

wörtlich [ˈvœrt·lɪç] **I.** *adj* ① *Wiedergabe* word-for-word, verbatim ② *Übersetzung* literal **II.** *adv* ① *wiedergeben* word for word ② *übersetzen* literally

wortlos I. *adj* silent **II.** *adv* silently, without saying a word

Wortschatz *m* vocabulary

Wortspiel *nt* play on words

Wortstellung *f* word order

Wortwechsel *m* verbal exchange

wortwörtlich [ˈvɔrt·ˈvœrt·lɪç] **I.** *adj* word-for-word **II.** *adv* word for word

worüber [vo·ˈryː·bɐ] *adv* what ... about, about what; **~ habt ihr euch unterhalten?** what was it you talked about? [*or fam* did you guys talk about?]

worum [vo·ˈrʊm] *adv* what ... about; **~ handelt es sich?** what is it about?

worunter [vo·ˈrʊn·tɐ] *adv* what ... from; **~ leidet Ihre Frau?** what is your wife suffering from?

wovon [vo·ˈfɔn] *adv* what ... about; **~ bist du denn so müde?** what has made you so tired?; **~ soll ich leben?** what am I supposed to live on?

wovor [vo·ˈfoːɐ̯] *adv* what ... of; **~ fürchtest du dich denn?** what are you afraid of?

wozu [vo·ˈtsuː] *adv* why, how come, what ... for; **~ soll das gut sein?** what's the purpose of that?; **~ hast du das gemacht?** what did you do that for?

Wrack <-[e]s, -s> [vrak] *nt* ① (*Schiffswrack*) wreck; (*Flugzeug-, Autowrack*) wreckage ② (*pej: Mensch*) wreck

Wucher <-s> [ˈvuː·xɐ] *m kein pl* extortion; (*Zinsen*) usury; **das ist ~!** that's highway robbery!

Wucherer, Wucherin <-s, -> [ˈvuː·xə·rɐ] *m, f* (*pej*) profiteer, usurer

wuchern [ˈvuː·xɐn] *vi sein o haben* ① *Pflanze* to grow rampant ② *Geschwür* to proliferate

Wucherpreis *m* (*pej*) extortionate price

wuchs [vuːks] *imp von* **wachsen**[1]

Wucht <-> [vʊxt] *f kein pl* force; *eines Schlags* brunt; **mit voller ~** with full force ▶ WENDUNGEN: **eine ~ <u>sein</u>** (*fam*) to be smashing

wuchtig [ˈvʊx·tɪç] *adj* ① (*mit großer Wucht*) forceful; *Schlag* powerful ② (*massig*) massive

wühlen [ˈvyː·lən] **I.** *vi* ■ **in etw** *dat* **[nach etw** *dat*] **~** ① (*kramen*) to rummage through sth [for sth] ② (*graben, aufwühlen*) to root through sth [[looking] for sth]; **in jds Haaren ~** to tousle sb's hair **II.** *vr* ■ **sich** *akk* **durch etw ~** ① (*sich vorwärtsarbeiten*) to burrow one's way through sth ② (*fam: sich durcharbeiten*) to slog through sth

Wühltisch *m* discount table

Wulst [vʊlst, *pl* ˈvʏl·stə] *m* <-[e]s, Wülste>, *f* <-, Wülste> bulge

wulstig [ˈvʊls·tɪç] *adj* bulging; (*Lippen*) thick

wummern [ˈvʊ·mɐn] *vi* to boom

wund [vʊnt] **I.** *adj* sore **II.** *adv* **sich** *akk* **~ liegen** to get bedsores; **sich** *dat* **die Füße ~ laufen** to walk until one's feet are sore

Wunde <-, -n> [ˈvʊn·də] *f* wound

Wunder <-s, -> [ˈvʊn·dɐ] *nt* miracle; **wie durch ein ~** miraculously; **die ~ der Natur** the wonders of nature ▶ WENDUNGEN: **sein <u>blaues</u> ~ erleben** (*fam*) to be in for a nasty surprise; **es <u>ist</u> kein ~, dass ...** (*fam*) it is no wonder that ...; **~ <u>wirken</u>** (*fam*) to work wonders

wunderbar [ˈvʊn·dɐ·baːɐ̯] **I.** *adj* ① (*herrlich*) wonderful, marvelous ② (*wie ein Wunder*) miraculous **II.** *adv* (*fam*) wonderfully

Wunderheiler(in) <-s, -> *m(f)* miracle healer

Wunderkerze *f* sparkler

Wunderkind *nt* child prodigy

wunderlich ['vʊn·dɐ·lɪç] *adj* odd, strange
Wụndermittel *nt* miracle cure; (*Zaubertrank*) magic potion
wundern ['vʊn·dɐn] **I.** *vt* ■**jdn ~** to surprise sb; **das wundert mich** [**nicht**] I'm [not] surprised at that **II.** *vr* ■**sich** *akk* ~ to be surprised (**über** +*akk* at/about); **du wirst dich ~!** you'll be surprised!
wunderschön ['vʊn·dɐ·'ʃøːn] *adj* wonderful
wụndervoll *adj, adv s.* **wunderbar**
Wụndsalbe *f* ointment
Wụndstarrkrampf *m kein pl* tetanus
Wunsch <-[e]s, Wünsche> [vʊnʃ, *pl* 'vʏn·ʃə] *m* ① (*Verlangen*) wish; (*stärker*) desire; (*Bitte*) request; **jdm jeden ~ erfüllen** to grant sb's every wish; **auf jds ~** [**hin**] at/on sb's request ② *meist pl* (*Glückwunsch*) wish; **mit besten Wünschen** best wishes
Wụnschbild *nt* ideal
Wụnschdenken <-s> *nt kein pl* wishful thinking
wünschen ['vʏn·ʃn̩] *vt* ① (*als Geschenk erbitten*) ■**sich** *dat* **etw** [**von jdm**] ~ to ask for sth [from sb]; **was wünschst du dir?** what would you like? [*or* can I get [for] you?]; **nun darfst du dir etwas ~** now you can say what you'd like for a present ② (*erhoffen*) to wish; **ich wünschte, der Regen würde aufhören** I wish the rain would stop; ■**jdm etw ~** to wish sb sth; **jdm zum Geburtstag alles Gute ~** to wish sb a happy birthday; **ich will dir ja nichts Böses ~** I don't mean to wish you any harm; ■**~, dass** to hope that ③ (*haben wollen*) ■**sich** *dat* **etw ~** to want sth; **man hätte sich kein besseres Wetter ~ können** one couldn't have wished for better weather ▶ WENDUNGEN: **nichts/viel zu ~ übrig lassen** to leave nothing/much to be desired
wụ̈nschenswert *adj* desirable
Wụnschkind *nt* planned child
wụnschlos *adj* **~ glücklich sein** to be perfectly happy
Wụnschtraum *m* dream
Wụnschzettel *m* wish list
wurde ['vʊr·də] *imp von* **werden**
Würde <-> ['vʏr·də] *f kein pl* dignity
wụ̈rdevoll *adj* dignified
würdig ['vʏr·dɪç] **I.** *adj* ① (*ehrbar*) dignified ② (*wert, angemessen*) worthy; **einer S.** *gen* [**nicht**] **~ sein** to [not] be worthy of sth **II.** *adv* (*mit Würde*) with dignity; (*gebührend*) worthy
würdigen ['vʏr·dɪ·gn̩] *vt* ① (*anerkennend erwähnen*) to acknowledge ② (*schätzen*) **etw zu ~ wissen** to appreciate sth
Wụ̈rdigung <-, -en> *f* appreciation, acknowledgement
Wurf <-[e]s, Würfe> [vʊrf, *pl* 'vʏr·fə] *m* ① (*das Werfen*) throw; (*gezielter Wurf*) shot; (*vom Pitcher*) pitch; (*Kegeln*) bowl; (*Würfel*) throw; **zum ~ ausholen** to get ready to throw ② (*Tierjunge*) litter
Würfel <-s, -> ['vʏr·fl̩] *m* ① (*Spielwürfel*) dice *pl*, die ② (*Kubus*) cube; **etw in ~ schneiden** to dice sth ▶ WENDUNGEN: **die ~ sind gefallen** the die is cast
Wụ̈rfelbecher *m* shaker
würfeln ['vʏr·fl̩n] **I.** *vi* to throw the dice; ■**um etw** *akk* ~ to throw dice for sth **II.** *vt* ① (*Würfel werfen*) **eine Sechs ~** to throw a six ② (*in Würfel schneiden*) to dice
Wụ̈rfelspiel *nt* dice game
Wụ̈rfelzucker *m kein pl* sugar cube[s]
würgen ['vʏr·gn̩] **I.** *vt* ■**jdn ~** to strangle sb **II.** *vi* ■**an etw** *dat* ~ to choke on sth
Wurm <-[e]s, Würmer> [vʊrm, *pl* 'vʏr·mɐ] *m* worm ▶ WENDUNGEN: **da ist der ~ drin** (*fam*) there's something fishy about it
wurmen ['vʊr·mən] *vt* (*fam*) to bug; **das wurmt mich sehr** that really bugs me
wurmstichig ['vʊrm·ʃtɪ·çɪç] *adj Apfel* maggoty; *Holz* full of woodworms
wụrscht, wụrst *adj* ■**jdm ~ sein** (*fam*) to be all the same to sb
Wurst <-, Würste> [vʊrst, *pl* 'vʏr·stə] *f* sausage; (*Brotauflage*) cold cuts *pl* ▶ WENDUNGEN: **jetzt geht es um die ~** (*fam*) the moment of truth has come
Wụrstbrot *nt open sandwich with cold cuts*
Würstchen <-s, -> ['vʏrst·çən] *nt dim von* **Wurst** little sausage; **Frankfurter/Wiener ~** hot dog, frankfurter
Wụ̈rstchenbude *f*, **Wụ̈rstchenstand** *m* hot dog stand
Wụrstsalat *m* sausage salad
Wurzel <-, -n> ['vʊr·tsl̩] *f* (*a. fig*) root; **~n schlagen** (*a. fig*) to put down roots
wurzeln ['vʊr·tsl̩n] *vi* ■**in etw** *dat* ~ to be rooted in sth
würzen ['vʏr·tsn̩] *vt* to season
würzig ['vʏr·tsɪç] **I.** *adj* tasty **II.** *adv* tastily
Wụ̈rzstoff *m* flavoring
wusch [vuːʃ] *imp von* **waschen**
wuschelig ['vʊ·ʃə·lɪç] *adj* (*fam*) woolly, fuzzy *fam; Tier* shaggy
Wụschelkopf *m* (*fam*) moptop *sl*
wuschlig ['vʊʃ·lɪç] *adj s.* **wuschelig**
wuseln ['vuː·zl̩n] *vi* to bustle around
wụsste[RR], **wụßte**[ALT] *imp von* **wissen**
Wust <-[e]s> [vʊst] *m kein pl* (*fam*) pile; **ein ~ von Problemen** a load of problems
wüst [vyːst] **I.** *adj* ① (*öde*) waste, desolate ② (*fig: wild, derb*) vile, rude ③ (*unordentlich*) hopeless, terrible **II.** *adv* vilely, terribly; **jdn ~ beschimpfen** to curse at sb
Wüste <-, -n> ['vyːs·tə] *f* desert, wasteland *fig;* **die ~ Gobi** the Gobi Desert
Wüstenklima *nt kein pl* desert climate
Wüstling <-s, -e> ['vyːst·lɪŋ] *m* (*pej*) lecher
Wut <-> [vuːt] *f kein pl* fury, rage; **seine ~ an jdm/etw auslassen** to take one's anger out on sb/sth; **eine ~** [**auf jdn**] **haben** to be furious [with sb]; **vor ~ kochen** to seethe with rage
Wutanfall *m* fit of rage; (*Kind*) tantrum; **einen ~ bekommen** to lose one's temper
Wutausbruch *m* tantrum

wüten ['vyː·tn̩] *vi* to rage; *Sturm* to cause havoc
wütend **I.** *adj* furious, enraged; **auf jdn ~ sein** to be furious with sb **II.** *adv* furiously, in a rage
wutentbrannt *adv* in a fury
WWW <-[s]> [veː·veː·'veː] *nt* INET *Abk von* **World Wide Web** WWW

Xx

X, x <-, -> [ɪks] *nt* ❶ *(Buchstabe)* X, x; **~ wie Xanthippe** X as in X-ray ❷ *(eine unbestimmte Zahl)* x amount of; **~ Bücher** x number of books
x-Achse *f* x-axis
X-Beine ['ɪks·bai·nə] *pl* knock-knees *pl;* **~ haben** to be knock-kneed
x-beliebig [ɪks·bə·'liː·bɪç] **I.** *adj (fam)* any old; **jeder ~e Ort** any old place **II.** *adv (fam)* as often as one likes
x-fach ['ɪks·fax] **I.** *adj (fam)* umpteen; **die ~e Menge** n times the amount **II.** *adv (fam)* umpteen times
x-förmig[RR] *adj* X-shaped *pred*
x-mal ['ɪks·maːl] *adv (fam)* umpteen times
x-te(r, s) ['ɪks·tə, 'ɪks·tɐ, 'ɪks·təs] *adj (fam)* ■ **der/die/das ~** the umpteenth; **beim/zum ~n Mal** after/for the umpteenth time
Xylofon[RR], **Xylophon** <-s, -e> [ksy·lo·'foːn] *nt* xylophone

Yy

Y, y <-, - *o fam* -s, -s> ['ʏpsi·lɔn] *nt* Y, y; **~ wie Ypsilon** Y as in Yankee
y-Achse ['ʏpsi·lɔn·ʔaksə] *f* y-axis
Yacht <-, -en> [jaxt] *f* yacht
Yankee <-s, -s> ['jɛŋ·ki] *m (pej)* Yankee
Yoga <-[s]> ['joː·ga] *m o nt* yoga
Yoghurt <-s, -s> ['joː·gʊrt] *m o nt s.* **Joghurt**
Ypsilon <-[s], -s> ['ʏpsi·lɔn] *nt s.* **Y**
Yuppie <-s, -s> ['jʊ·pi] *m* yuppie

Zz

Z, z <-, -> [tsɛt] *nt* Z, z; **~ wie Zacharias** Z as in Zulu
zack [tsak] *interj* (*fam*) zap; **~, ~!** chop-chop!
Zacke <-, -n> ['tsa·kə] *f* point; *eines Kamms* tooth; *eines Berges* peak; *einer Gabel* prong
Zacken <-s, -> ['tsa·kn̩] *m* DIAL *s.* **Zacke**
zackig ['tsa·kɪç] *adj* ① (*gezackt*) jagged; *Stern* pointed ② (*schnell*) *Bewegungen* brisk; *Musik* upbeat
zaghaft ['tsa:k·haft] *adj* timid
Zaghaftigkeit *f* timidity
zäh [tsɛ:] **I.** *adj* ① (*eine feste Konsistenz aufweisend*) tough ② (*zähflüssig*) glutinous ③ (*hartnäckig*) tenacious; *Gespräch* long-drawn-out; *Verhandlungen* tough **II.** *adv* tenaciously
zähflüssig *adj* thick; (*fig*) *Verkehr* slow-moving
Zahl <-, -en> [tsa:l] *f* ① MATH number, figure; **eine ganze/gerade/ungerade/vierstellige ~** whole/even/odd/four-digit number ② *pl* (*Zahlenangaben*) numbers; (*Verkaufszahlen*) figures; **arabische/römische ~en** Arabic/Roman numerals ③ *kein pl* (*Anzahl*) number
zählbar *adj* countable
zahlen ['tsa:·lən] *vt, vi* to pay; **~ bitte!** the check please!
zählen ['tsɛ:·lən] **I.** *vt* ① (*addieren*) to count ② (*geh: dazurechnen*) ■**jdn/sich zu etw** *dat* **~** to regard sb/oneself as belonging to sth **II.** *vi* ① (*Zahlen aufsagen*) **bis zehn ~** to count to ten ② (*addieren*) to count; **falsch ~** to miscount ③ (*gehören*) to belong (**zu** +*dat* to) ④ (*sich verlassen*) to count (**auf** +*akk* on) ⑤ (*gültig sein*) to count
zahlenmäßig **I.** *adj* numerical **II.** *adv* (*an Anzahl*) in number
Zahlenschloss^RR^ *nt* combination lock
Zähler <-s, -> *m* ① TECH meter ② MATH numerator
zahllos *adj* countless
zahlreich **I.** *adj* ① (*sehr viele*) numerous ② (*eine große Anzahl*) large **II.** *adv* (*in großer Anzahl*) **~ erscheinen** to appear in large numbers
Zahlung <-, -en> *f* payment
Zählung <-, -en> *f* count
zahlungsfähig *adj* solvent
zahlungskräftig *adj* wealthy
Zahlungsmittel *nt* means of payment + *sing vb*
zahlungsunfähig *adj* insolvent
Zahlungsverkehr *m* payment transactions *pl*
Zahlwort <-wörter> *nt* numeral
zahm [tsa:m] *adj* tame
zähmen ['tsɛ:·mən] *vt* to tame
Zähmung <-, -en> *f* taming
Zahn <-[e]s, Zähne> [tsa:n, *pl* tsɛ:·nə] *m* ① (*Teil des Gebisses*) tooth; **Zähne bekommen** to be teething; **sich** *dat* **die Zähne putzen** to brush one's teeth; **sich** *dat* **einen ~ ziehen lassen** to have a tooth pulled ② (*fam: Tempo*) **einen ~ draufhaben** to drive at breakneck speed; **einen ~ zulegen** to step on it ►WENDUNGEN: **sich** *dat* **an jdm/etw die Zähne ausbeißen** (*fam*) to have a tough time with sb/sth; **jdm auf den ~ fühlen** (*fam*) to grill sb
Zahnarzt, -ärztin *m, f* dentist
zahnärztlich **I.** *adj* dental *attr* **II.** *adv* **~ behandelt werden** to have dental treatment
Zahnbehandlung *f* dental treatment
Zahnbelag *m kein pl* plaque
Zahnbürste *f* toothbrush
Zahncreme *f* toothpaste
zähneknirschend *adv* grinding one's teeth
zahnen ['tsa:·nən] *vi Baby* to teethe
Zahnfäule *f kein pl* tooth decay
Zahnfleisch *nt* gum[s *pl*]
Zahnfüllung *f* filling
Zahnlücke *f* gap between the teeth
Zahnpasta *f* toothpaste
Zahnpflege *f kein pl* dental hygiene
Zahnprothese *f* dentures *pl*
Zahnrad *nt* AUTO gearwheel; TECH cogwheel
Zahnradbahn *f* cog railway [*or* railroad]
Zahnschmelz *m* [tooth] enamel
Zahnschmerzen *pl* toothache
Zahnseide *f* dental floss
Zahnspange *f* braces *pl*
Zahnstein *m kein pl* tartar
Zahnstocher <-s, -> *m* toothpick
Zahnweh *nt kein pl* (*fam*) toothache
Zander <-s, -> ['tsan·dɐ] *m* pikeperch
Zange <-, -n> ['tsaŋə] *f* pliers *npl*, a pair of pliers; *Hummer, Krebs* pincers *npl;* MED forceps *npl;* (*für Zucker*) tongs *npl* ►WENDUNGEN: **jdn in die ~ nehmen** (*fam*) to give sb the third degree
Zank <-[e]s> [tsaŋk] *m kein pl* fight
zanken ['tsaŋ·kn̩] **I.** *vi* to fight **II.** *vr* ■**sich ~** to have a fight (**um** +*akk* over)
zänkisch ['tsɛŋ·kɪʃ] *adj* quarrelsome
Zäpfchen <-s, -> ['tsɛpf·çən] *nt* MED suppository
zapfen ['tsap·fn̩] *vt Bier* to draw
Zapfen <-s, -> ['tsap·fn̩] *m* ① BOT, ANAT cone ② (*Eiszapfen*) icicle
Zapfenstreich *m* (*Signal*) taps
Zapfhahn *m* tap
Zapfsäule *f* gas pump
zappelig ['tsa·pə·lɪç] *adj* ① (*sich unruhig bewegend*) fidgety ② (*voller Unruhe*) restless
zappeln ['tsa·pl̩n] *vi* to fidget ►WENDUNGEN: **jdn ~ lassen** (*fam*) to keep sb in suspense
zappen ['tsa·pn̩] *vi* TV (*sl*) to channel-surf
zapplig ['tsap·lɪç] *adj s.* **zappelig**
Zar(in) <-en, -en> [tsa:ɐ̯] *m(f)* czar *masc*, cza-

rina *fem*

zart [tsaːɐ̯t] *adj* ① (*mürbe*) tender; *Gebäck* delicate ② (*weich*) delicate; *Haut* soft ③ (*leicht*) mild; *Berührung, Andeutung* gentle; *Farbe, Duft* delicate

zartbitter *adj Schokolade* dark

zartgliederig [ˈtsaːɐt·gliː·də·rɪç], **zartgliedrig** [ˈtsaːɐt·gliːd·rɪç] *adj* (*fein*) dainty; (*zerbrechlich*) delicate

zärtlich [ˈtsɛːɐ̯t·lɪç] **I.** *adj* tender, affectionate **II.** *adv* tenderly, affectionately

Zärtlichkeit <-, -en> *f* ① *kein pl* (*zärtliches Wesen*) tenderness ② *pl* (*Liebkosung*) caresses *pl*; (*zärtliche Worte*) tender words *pl*

Zäsur <-, -en> [tsɛˈzuːɐ̯] *f* (*geh: Einschnitt*) break [with tradition]

Zauber <-s, -> [ˈtsau·bɐ] *m* ① (*magische Handlung*) magic; (*magische Wirkung*) spell; **einen ~ anwenden/aufheben** to cast/break a spell ② *kein pl* (*Faszination, Reiz*) charm

Zauberei <-, -en> [tsau·bə·ˈrai] *f kein pl* magic

Zauberer, Zauberin <-s, -> [ˈtsau·bə·rɐ, ˈtsau·bə·rɪn] *m, f* ① (*Magier*) sorcerer *masc*, sorceress *fem*, wizard ② (*Zauberkünstler*) magician

Zauberformel *f* magic words *npl*

zauberhaft *adj* enchanting; *Kleid* gorgeous; *Abend, Urlaub* splendid

Zauberkünstler(in) *m(f)* magician

Zauberkunststück *nt* magic trick

zaubern [ˈtsau·bɐn] **I.** *vt* ① (*erscheinen lassen*) to conjure (**aus** + *dat* from); **einen Hasen aus einem Hut ~** to pull a rabbit out of a hat ② (*a. fam: schaffen*) ■ **etw ~** to conjure up sth **II.** *vi* (*Magie anwenden*) to do magic; (*Zauberkunststücke vorführen*) to do magic tricks

Zauberspruch *m* magic spell

Zauberstab *m* magic wand

Zaum <-[e]s, Zäume> [tsaum, *pl* ˈtsɔy·mə] *m* bridle; **etw/jdn/sich in ~ halten** (*fig*) to keep sth/sb/oneself in check

zäumen [ˈtsɔy·mən] *vt* ■ **ein Tier ~** to bridle an animal

Zaun <-[e]s, Zäune> [tsaun, *pl* ˈtsɔy·nə] *m* fence

Zaungast <-gäste> *m* onlooker

Zaunkönig *m* wren

zausen [ˈtsau·zn̩] *vt Haar* to tousle

z. B. *Abk von* **zum Beispiel** e.g.

Zebra <-s, -s> [ˈtseː·bra] *nt* zebra

Zebrastreifen *m* pedestrian crossing, crosswalk

Zeche[1] <-, -n> [ˈtsɛ·çə] *f* BERGB coal mine

Zeche[2] <-, -n> [ˈtsɛ·çə] *f* (*Rechnung für Verzehr*) bill

Zechpreller(in) <-s, -> *m(f)* walkout

Zechtour *f* bar hop

Zecke <-, -n> [ˈtsɛ·kə] *f*, **Zeck** <-[e]s, -en> [tsɛk] *m* ÖSTERR (*fam*) tick

Zeckenbiss[RR] *m* tick bite

Zeh <-s, -en> [tseː] *m*, **Zehe** <-, -n> [ˈtseː·ə] *f* ① ANAT toe ② (*Knoblauchzehe*) clove

Zehennagel *m* toenail

Zehenspitze *f* tip of the toe; ■ **auf den ~n** on one's tiptoes

zehn [tseːn] *adj* ten; *s. a.* **acht**[1]

Zehn <-, -en> [tseːn] *f* ① (*Zahl*) ten ② KARTEN ten; *s. a.* **Acht**[1] ③ (*Verkehrslinie*) ■ **die ~** the [number] ten

Zehnerkarte *f* TRANSP ten-trip ticket; TOURIST ticket good for ten admissions

zehnfach, 10fach [ˈtseːn·fax] **I.** *adj* tenfold; **die ~e Menge** ten times the amount **II.** *adv* tenfold, ten times over

Zehnkampf [ˈtseːn·kampf] *m* decathlon

Zehnkämpfer(in) *m(f)* decathlete

zehnmal, 10-mal[RR] [ˈtseːn·maːl] *adv* ten times; *s. a.* **achtmal**

zehntausend [ˈtseːn·ˈtau·zn̩t] *adj* ① (*Zahl*) ten thousand ② (*sehr viele*) ■ **Z~e von ...** tens of thousands of ...

zehnte(r, s) [ˈtseːn·tə, ˈtseːn·tɐ, ˈtseːn·təs] *adj* ① (*nach dem neunten kommend*) tenth; *s. a.* **achte(r, s) 1** ② (*Datum*) tenth, 10th; *s. a.* **achte(r, s) 2**

zehntel [ˈtseːn·tl̩] *adj* tenth

Zehntel <-s, -> [ˈtseːn·tl̩] *nt* ■ **ein ~** a tenth

zehren [ˈtseː·rən] *vi* ① (*erschöpfen, schwächen*) ■ **an jdm/etw ~** to wear sb/sth out; **an jds Gesundheit ~** to ruin sb's health ② (*sich ernähren*) ■ **von etw** *dat* **~** to live on sth

Zeichen <-s, -> [ˈtsai·çn̩] *nt* ① (*Symbol*) symbol; (*Schriftzeichen*) character; (*Satzzeichen*) punctuation mark ② (*Markierung*) sign; **ein ~ auf etw** *akk* **machen** to mark sth [on sth] ③ (*Hinweis*) sign; (*Symptom*) symptom ④ (*Signal*) signal; **das ~ zu etw** *dat* **geben** to give the signal to do sth; **ein ~ setzen** to set an example; **zum ~, dass ...** to show that ... ⑤ ASTROL sign; **im ~ einer S.** *gen* **geboren sein** to be born under the sign of sth

Zeichenblock <-blöcke *o* -blocks> *m* sketch pad

Zeichenbrett *nt* drawing board

Zeichenerklärung *f* key; (*Landkarte*) legend

Zeichensetzung <-> *f kein pl* punctuation

Zeichensprache *f* sign language

Zeichentrickfilm *m* cartoon

zeichnen [ˈtsaiç·nən] **I.** *vt* ① KUNST, ARCHIT to draw ② (*schriftlich anerkennen*) **einen Scheck ~** to sign a check ③ (*mit Zeichen versehen*) to mark **II.** *vi* ① KUNST ■ **an etw** *dat* **~** to draw sth ② (*geh: verantwortlich sein*) **für etw** *akk* **[verantwortlich] ~** to be responsible for sth

Zeichner(in) <-s, -> *m(f)* ① KUNST draftsman *masc*, draftswoman *fem* ② FIN subscriber

zeichnerisch **I.** *adj* graphic; **~e Begabung** talent for drawing **II.** *adv* graphically

Zeichnung <-, -en> *f* ① KUNST drawing ② BOT, ZOOL markings *pl* ③ FIN subscription

Zeigefinger *m* index finger

zeigen [ˈtsai·gn̩] **I.** *vt* ① (*deutlich machen*) to show ② (*vorführen*) to show; **zeig mal, was du kannst!** (*fam*) let's see what you can do!; **es jdm ~** (*fam*) to show sb **II.** *vi* ① (*deuten*) to point (**auf** +*akk* at); **nach rechts/hinten ~** to point to the right/back ❷ (*erkennen lassen*) ■ **~, dass ...** to show that ... **III.** *vr* ❶ (*sich sehen lassen*) ■ **sich** [**jdm**] **~** to show oneself [to sb]; **komm, zeig dich mal!** come on, let me see what you look like; **sich von seiner besten Seite ~** to show oneself at one's best ❷ (*erkennbar werden*) ■ **sich ~** to appear

Zeiger <-s, -> ['tsai·gɐ] *m* (*Uhrzeiger*) hand

Zeigestock *m* pointer

Zeile <-, -n> ['tsai·lə] *f* ❶ (*geschriebene Reihe*) line; **jdm ein paar ~n schrieben** (*fam*) to drop sb a line; **zwischen den ~n lesen** to read between the lines ❷ (*Reihe*) row

zeit [tsait] *präp +gen* **~ meines Lebens** all my life

Zeit <-, -en> [tsait] *f* ❶ *kein pl* (*verstrichener zeitlicher Ablauf*) time; **mit der ~** in time; **~ raubend** time-consuming; **~ sparend** time-saving ❷ (*Zeitraum*) time; ■ **eine ~ lang** for a while; **die ganze ~** [**über**] the whole time; **in letzter ~** lately; **in nächster ~** in the near future; **auf unbestimmte ~** for an indefinite period; **~ gewinnen** to gain time; **zwei Tage ~ haben**[**, etw zu tun**] to have two days [to do sth]; **haben Sie einen Augenblick ~?** do you have a moment to spare?; **das hat noch ~** that can wait; **sich** [**mit etw** *dat*] **~ lassen** to take one's time [with sth]; **jdm die ~ stehlen** to waste sb's time; **jdn auf ~ beschäftigen** to employ sb on a temporary basis ❸ (*Zeitpunkt*) time; **es ist höchste Zeit, dass wir die Tickets kaufen** it's about time we bought the tickets; **seit dieser ~** since then; **von ~ zu ~** from time to time; **zur ~** at the moment; **zu jeder ~** [at] any time ❹ (*Epoche, Lebensabschnitt*) time, age; **die ~ der Aufklärung** the age of enlightenment; **für alle ~en** forever; **zu jener ~** at that time ❺ LING tense ❻ SPORT time; **eine gute ~ laufen** to run a good time

Zeitabschnitt *m* period [of time]

Zeitalter *nt* age; **in unserem ~** nowadays

Zeitansage *f* announcement of the time; TELEK telephone time service; RADIO time check

Zeitarbeit *f kein pl* temporary work

Zeitarbeitsfirma *f* temp agency

Zeitaufwand *m* expenditure of time; **mit großem ~ verbunden sein** to be extremely time-consuming

zeitaufwändig[RR] *adj* time-consuming

Zeitbombe *f* time bomb

Zeitdruck *m kein pl* time pressure

Zeiteinteilung *f* time management

Zeitgefühl *nt kein pl* sense of time

zeitgemäß *adj, adv* up-to-date, modern

Zeitgenosse, -genossin ['tsait·gə·nɔ·sə, -gənɔ·sɪn] *m, f* contemporary

zeitgenössisch ['tsait·gə·nœ·sɪʃ] *adj* contemporary

Zeitgeschichte *f kein pl* contemporary history

Zeitgewinn *m* timesaving

zeitgleich I. *adj* contemporaneous **II.** *adv* at the same time

zeitig ['tsai·tɪç] *adj, adv* early

Zeitkarte *f* TRANSP monthly/weekly/weekend pass

Zeitlang *f s.* **Zeit 2**

zeitlebens [tsait·'le:·bn̩s] *adv* all one's life

zeitlich I. *adj* chronological **II.** *adv* ❶ (*terminlich*) timewise *fam;* **~ zusammenfallen** to coincide; **etw ~ abstimmen** to synchronize sth ❷ (*vom Zeitraum her*) **~ begrenzt** for a limited time

zeitlos *adj* timeless; *Kleidung* classic; **~er Stil** style that doesn't go out of fashion

Zeitlupe *f kein pl* slow motion *no art*

Zeitlupentempo *nt* **im ~** in slow motion

Zeitnot *f kein pl* shortage of time; **in ~ sein** to be short of time

Zeitplan *m* schedule

Zeitpunkt *m* time; **zum jetzigen ~** at this moment in time

Zeitraffer <-s> *m kein pl* time-lapse photography

Zeitraum *m* period of time

Zeitrechnung *f* calendar; **vor unserer ~** before Christ, BC; **unserer ~** Anno Domini, AD

Zeitschrift ['tsait·ʃrɪft] *f* magazine; (*wissenschaftlich*) journal

Zeitspanne *f* period of time

Zeitumstellung *f* changing of the clocks

Zeitung <-, -en> ['tsai·tʊŋ] *f* newspaper

Zeitungsannonce *f* newspaper advertisement; (*Geburt, Tod, Ehe*) announcement

Zeitungsanzeige *f* newspaper advertisement

Zeitungsartikel *m* newspaper article

Zeitungsbericht *m* newspaper article

Zeitungsmeldung *f* newspaper report

Zeitungspapier *nt* newspaper

Zeitungsverkäufer(in) *m(f)* newspaper salesman

Zeitverschiebung *f* time difference

Zeitverschwendung *f kein pl* waste of time

Zeitvertrag *m* temporary contract

Zeitvertreib <-[e]s, -e> *m* pastime; **zum ~** to pass the time

zeitweise *adv* ❶ (*gelegentlich*) occasionally ❷ (*vorübergehend*) temporarily

zelebrieren* [tse·le·'bri:·rən] *vt* to celebrate

Zelle <-, -n> ['tsɛ·lə] *f* cell

Zellgewebe *nt* cell tissue

Zellkern *m* nucleus [of a cell]

Zellkultur *f* cell culture

Zellophan <-s> [tsɛ·lo·'fa:n] *nt kein pl s.* **Cellophan**

Zellstoff ['tsɛl·ʃtɔf] *m s.* **Zellulose**

Zellteilung *f* cell division

Zellulitis <-, Zellulitiden> [tsɛ·lu·'li:·tɪs, *pl* -'ti:·dn̩] *f meist sing* MED cellulitis

Zelluloid <-[e]s> [tsɛ·lu·'lɔyt] *nt kein pl* celluloid

Zellulose <-, -n> [tsɛ·lu·'lo:·zə] *f* cellulose

Zelt <-[e]s, -e> [tsɛlt] *nt* tent; (*Festzelt*) exhibit tent; (*Zirkuszelt*) big top; **ein ~ aufschlagen** to pitch a tent

zelten ['tsɛl·tn̩] *vi* to camp

Zeltlager *nt* camp
Zeltplane *f* tarpaulin, tarp *fam*
Zeltplatz *m* campsite
Zement <-[e]s, -e> [tse·'mɛnt] *m* cement
zementieren* [tse·mɛn·'tiː·rən] *vt* (*a. fig*) to cement
Zenit <-[e]s> [tse·'niːt] *m kein pl* zenith
zensieren* [tsɛn·'ziː·rən] *vt* ❶ SCH to grade ❷ (*der Zensur unterwerfen*) to censor
Zensor, Zensorin <-s, Zensoren> ['tsɛn·zoːɐ̯, tsɛn·'zoː·rɪn, *pl* tsɛn·'zoː·rən] *m, f* censor
Zensur <-, -en> [tsɛn·'zuːɐ̯] *f* ❶ SCH grade ❷ *kein pl* (*prüfende Kontrolle*) censorship
zensurieren* [tsɛn·zu·'riː·rən] *vt* ÖSTERR, SCHWEIZ *s.* **zensieren**
Zentimeter [tsɛn·ti·'meː·tɐ] *m o nt* centimeter
Zentner <-s, -> ['tsɛnt·nɐ] *m* 50 kg (*110 lbs*); ÖSTERR, SCHWEIZ 100 kg (*220 lbs*)
zentral [tsɛn·'traːl] **I.** *adj* central **II.** *adv* centrally
Zentralafrika *nt* Central Africa
Zentralamerika <-s> *nt* Central America
Zentralbank *f* FIN central bank; ■ **die Europäische ~** the European Central Bank
Zentrale <-, -n> [tsɛn·'traː·lə] *f* ❶ (*Hauptgeschäftsstelle: Bank, Firma*) head office; (*Militär, Polizei, Taxiunternehmen*) headquarters + *sing/pl vb;* (*Busse*) depot ❷ TELEK operator; *Firma* switchboard
Zentralheizung *f* central heating
zentralisieren* [tsɛn·tra·li·'ziː·rən] *vt* to centralize
Zentralnervensystem *nt* central nervous system
Zentralrat *m* central committee
Zentralverriegelung <-, -en> *f* power locks *npl*
Zentren *pl von* **Zentrum**
Zentrifugalkraft *f* centrifugal force
Zentrifuge <-, -n> [tsɛn·tri·'fuː·gə] *f* centrifuge
Zentripetalkraft *f kein pl* centripetal force
Zentrum <-s, Zentren> ['tsɛn·trʊm, *pl* 'tsɛn·trən] *nt* center
Zeppelin <-s, -e> ['tsɛ·pə·liːn] *m* blimp, zeppelin
Zepter <-s, -> ['tsɛp·tɐ] *nt* scepter
zerbeißen* [tsɛɐ̯·'bai·sn̩] *vt irreg* ❶ (*kaputtbeißen*) to chew; *Bonbon* to crunch ❷ (*überall stechen*) to bite
zerbomben* *vt* ■ **etw ~** to bomb sth to smithereens
zerbrechen* *irreg* **I.** *vt haben* (*in Stücke zerbrechen*) ■ **etw ~** to break sth [in]to pieces; *Glas, Teller* to smash; *Kette* to break **II.** *vi sein* ❶ (*entzweibrechen*) to break [in]to pieces ❷ (*in die Brüche gehen*) to be destroyed; *Partnerschaft* to break up ❸ (*seelisch zugrunde gehen*) ■ **an etw** *dat* **~** to be destroyed by sth
zerbrechlich *adj* ❶ (*leicht zerbrechend*) fragile ❷ (*geh: zart*) frail
zerbröckeln* **I.** *vt haben* to crumble **II.** *vi sein* to crumble
zerdrücken* *vt* ❶ (*zu einer Masse pressen*) to crush; *Kartoffeln* to mash ❷ *Zigarette* to put out *sep* ❸ *Stoff* to crease
Zeremonie <-, -n> [tse·re·mo·'niː, *pl* -'niː·ən] *f* ceremony
zeremoniell [tse·re·mo·'ni̯ɛl] **I.** *adj* (*geh*) ceremonial **II.** *adv* (*geh*) ceremonially
Zeremoniell <-s, -e> [tse·re·mo·'ni̯ɛl] *nt* (*geh*) ceremonial
Zerfall *m* ❶ *kein pl* (*das Auflösen*) disintegration; *Fassade, Gebäude* decay; *Leiche, Holz* decomposition ❷ *Land, Kultur* decline
zerfallen* *vi irreg sein* ❶ (*sich zersetzen*) *Fassade, Gebäude* to disintegrate; *Körper, Materie* to decompose; *Gesundheit* to decline ❷ (*auseinanderbrechen*) *Reich, Sitte* to decline ❸ (*sich gliedern*) ■ **in etw** *akk* **~** to fall into sth
zerfetzen* *vt* ❶ (*klein reißen*) ■ **etw ~** to tear sth to shreds ❷ (*zerreißen*) ■ **jdn/etw ~** to tear sb/sth to pieces
zerfleddern*, zerfledern* [tsɛɐ̯·'fleː·dɐn] *vt* (*fam*) ■ **etw ~** to cause sth to become ragged and worn
zerfließen* *vi irreg sein* ❶ (*sich verflüssigen*) *Butter, Make-up, Salbe* to run; *Eis* to melt ❷ (*fig*) **vor Mitleid ~** to be overcome with compassion
zerfranst *adj* frayed
zerfressen* *vt irreg* ❶ (*korrodieren*) to corrode ❷ (*durch Fraß/Wuchern zerstören*) to eat
zergehen* *vi irreg sein* to melt (**auf** + *dat* on)
zerkauen* *vt* ❶ (*zerkleinern*) to chew ❷ (*beschädigen*) to chew up *sep*
zerkleinern* [tsɛɐ̯·'klai·nɐn] *vt* to cut up *sep; Holz* to chop; *Pfefferkörner* to crush
zerknirscht [tsɛɐ̯·'knɪrʃt] *adj* remorseful
zerknittern* *vt* to crease
zerknüllen* *vt* to crumple up *sep*
zerkochen* *vi sein* to overcook
zerkratzen* *vt* to scratch
zerkrümeln* *vt* to crumble; *Erde* to loosen
zerlassen* *vt irreg Butter* to melt
zerlegen* *vt* ❶ KOCHK to cut [up *sep*]; *Braten* to carve ❷ (*auseinandernehmen*) to take apart *sep; Maschine* to dismantle; *Getriebe, Motor* to strip down *sep*
zerlumpt *adj* ragged; **~ sein** to be in tatters
zermalmen* *vt* to crush
zermürben* [tsɛɐ̯·'myr·bn̩] *vt* to wear down *sep*
zerquetschen* *vt* ❶ (*zermalmen*) to squash ❷ *Kartoffeln* to mash
Zerrbild *nt* distorted picture
zerreiben* *vt irreg* to crush
zerreißen* *irreg* **I.** *vt haben* ❶ (*in Stücke reißen*) ■ **etw ~** to tear sth to pieces ❷ (*durchreißen*) to tear; *Brief, Scheck* to tear up *sep* ❸ (*durchreißen*) to tear apart *sep* **II.** *vi sein* to tear; *Seil, Faden* to break
Zerreißprobe *f* real test
zerren ['tsɛ·rən] **I.** *vt* to drag **II.** *vi* to tug (**an** + *dat* at/on); **an den Nerven ~** to be

nerve-racking **III.** *vr* MED ■ **sich** *dat* **einen Muskel** ~ to pull a muscle

zerrinnen* *vi irreg sein* to melt away

Zerrung <-, -en> *f* MED (*Muskelzerrung*) pulled muscle; (*Sehnenzerrung*) pulled tendon

zerrütten* [tsɛɐ̯ˈrʏ·tn̩] *vt* to destroy; *Ehe* to ruin

zersägen* *vt* to saw up *sep*

zerschellen* *vi sein* to be smashed to pieces

zerschlagen*[1] *irreg* **I.** *vt* ❶ ■ **etw** ~ *Glas, Teller etc.* to smash sth to pieces ❷ (*zerstören*) to break up *sep; Angriff* to crush; *Plan* to shatter **II.** *vr* ■ **sich** ~ *Plan* to fall through

zerschlagen[2] *adj pred* shattered

zerschmettern* *vt* to shatter

zerschneiden* *vt irreg* ❶ (*in Stücke schneiden*) to cut up *sep* ❷ (*durchschneiden*) ■ **etw** ~ to cut sth in two

zersetzen* **I.** *vt Metall* to corrode **II.** *vr* (*sich auflösen*) ■ **sich** ~ to decompose

zerspalten* *vt* to split

zersplittern* **I.** *vt haben* to shatter; *Gruppe, Partei* to fragment **II.** *vi sein* to shatter; *Holz, Knochen* to splinter

zerspringen* *vi irreg sein* ❶ (*zerbrechen*) to shatter ❷ (*einen Sprung bekommen*) to crack

zerstampfen* *vt* ❶ (*zerkleinern*) to crush; *Kartoffeln* to mash ❷ (*zertreten*) to stamp on *sep*

zerstäuben* *vt* to spray

Zerstäuber <-s, -> *m* atomizer

zerstechen* *vt irreg* ❶ (*beschädigen*) ■ **etw** ~ to lay into sth with a knife ❷ *Mücken, Moskitos* ■ **jdn/etw** ~ to bite sb/sth [all over]; *Bienen* to sting sb/sth [all over]

zerstören* *vt* ❶ (*kaputtmachen*) to destroy ❷ (*zugrunde richten*) *Plan, Gesundheit* to ruin

zerstörerisch I. *adj* destructive **II.** *adv* destructively

Zerstörung <-, -en> *f* ❶ *kein pl* destruction ❷ (*Verwüstung*) devastation

zerstreuen* **I.** *vt* ❶ (*auseinandertreiben*) to disperse ❷ (*unterhalten*) ■ **jdn** ~ to take sb's mind off sth ❸ *Ängste, Sorgen* to dispel **II.** *vr* ■ **sich** ~ ❶ *Menge* to disperse ❷ (*sich auflösen*) to be dispelled

zerstreut *adj* ❶ (*gedankenlos*) absent-minded ❷ (*weit verteilt*) scattered

Zerstreutheit <-> *f kein pl* absent-mindedness

Zerstreuung <-, -en> *f* (*Unterhaltung*) diversion

zerstückeln* *vt* to cut up *sep; Leiche* to dismember; *Land* to carve up *sep*

zerteilen* *vt* to cut up *sep* (**in** +*akk* into)

Zertifikat <-[e]s, -e> [tsɛr·ti·fi·ˈka:t] *nt* certificate

zertreten* *vt irreg* to crush

zertrümmern* [tsɛɐ̯·ˈtrʏ·mɐn] *vt* to smash

zerwühlen* *vt Haare* to tousle; *Bett* to rumple

zerzausen* *vt Haare* to ruffle

zetern [ˈtse:·tɐn] *vi* (*pej*) to nag

Zettel <-s, -> [ˈtsɛ·tl̩] *m* piece of paper

Zeug <-[e]s> [tsɔyk] *nt kein pl* (*fam*) ❶ (*Sachen*) stuff; **altes** ~ junk ❷ (*Quatsch*) crap *fam* ▶ WENDUNGEN: **was das** ~ **hält** (*fam*) for all one is worth; **sich ins** ~ **legen** (*fam*) to put one's shoulder to the wheel

Zeuge, Zeugin <-n, -n> [ˈtsɔy·gə, ˈtsɔy·gɪn] *m, f* witness

zeugen[1] [ˈtsɔy·gn̩] *vt* ■ **jdn** ~ to father sb

zeugen[2] [ˈtsɔy·gn̩] *vi* ❶ (*auf etw schließen lassen*) ■ **von etw** *dat* ~ to show sth ❷ JUR to testify

Zeugenaussage *f* testimony

Zeugenstand *m* witness stand

Zeugnis <-ses, -se> [ˈtsɔyk·nɪs] *nt* ❶ SCH report card ❷ (*Empfehlung*) certificate of recommendation; (*Arbeitszeugnis*) reference

Zeugung <-, -en> *f* fathering

zeugungsfähig *adj* fertile

zeugungsunfähig *adj* sterile

z.H(d). *Abk von* **zu Händen** attn.

Zicke <-, -n> [ˈtsɪ·kə] *f* ❶ (*weibliche Ziege*) nanny goat ❷ (*pej fam: launische Frau*) bitch

zicken [ˈtsɪ·kən] *vi* (*sl*) to kick up a fuss

zickig [ˈtsɪ·kɪç] *adj* uptight, snotty

Zickzack [ˈtsɪk·tsak] *m* zigzag

Ziege <-, -n> [ˈtsi:·gə] *f* goat

Ziegel <-s, -> [ˈtsi:·gl̩] *m* ❶ (*Ziegelstein*) brick ❷ (*Dachziegel*) tile

Ziegeldach *nt* tiled roof

Ziegelstein *m* brick

Ziegenbart *m* goat's beard; (*hum fam: Spitzbart*) goatee

Ziegenbock *m* billy goat

Ziegenkäse *m* goat cheese

Ziegenpeter <-s, -> [ˈtsi:·gn̩·pe:·tɐ] *m* (*fam: Mumps*) mumps + *sing/pl vb*

ziehen <zog, gezogen> [ˈtsi:·ən] **I.** *vt haben* ❶ (*hinter sich her schleppen, zerren*) to pull; (*fester*) to drag; (*am Ärmel*) to tug ❷ (*bewegen*) *Choke, Starter* to pull out *sep; Handbremse* to put on *sep; Vorhänge* to draw; *Rollläden* to raise; **die Knie in die Höhe** ~ to raise one's knees; **die Stirn in Falten** ~ to knit one's brow ❸ (*herausziehen*) *Fäden, Zahn* to take out *sep; Revolver, Spielkarte* to draw ❹ (*züchten*) *Pflanzen* to grow; *Tiere* to breed ❺ *Kreis, Linie* to draw ❻ (*anziehen*) ■ **etw auf sich** *akk* ~ to attract sth; **jdn ins Gespräch** ~ to draw sb into the conversation ❼ (*zur Folge haben*) ■ **etw nach sich** *dat* ~ to have consequences **II.** *vi* ❶ *haben* (*zerren*) to pull (**an** +*dat* on) ❷ *sein* (*umziehen*) to move; ■ **zu jdm** ~ to move in with sb; **nach München** ~ to move to Munich ❸ *sein* (*einen bestimmten Weg einschlagen*) *Menschenmenge* to march; *Wanderer* to wander; *Rauch, Wolke* to drift; *Gewitter* to move; **durch die Stadt** ~ to wander through [the] town/the city; **in den Krieg** ~ to go to war ❹ *haben* (*saugen*) **an einer Zigarette** ~ to drag on a cigarette ❺ *haben Tee* to brew **III.** *vi impers haben* **es zieht** there is a draft **IV.** *vt impers haben* **es zog ihn in die weite Welt** he felt a strong urge to see the world; **was zieht dich hierhin?** what brings you here? **V.** *vr haben* ■ **sich** ~ *Gespräch, Verhandlungen* to drag on

Ziehen <-s> ['tsiː·ən] *nt kein pl* ache
Ziehharmonika *f* concertina
Ziehung <-, -en> *f* drawing
Ziel <-[e]s, -e> [tsiːl] *nt* ❶ (*angestrebtes Ergebnis*) goal, aim; **am ~ sein** to be at one's destination; **sich** *dat* **ein ~ setzen** to set a goal for oneself ❷ SPORT, MIL target; **ins ~ treffen** to hit the target ❸ (*Rennen*) finish; **durchs ~ gehen** to cross the finish line ❹ (*Reiseziel*) destination ▶ WENDUNGEN: **über das ~ hinausschießen** (*fam*) to overshoot the mark
zielbewusstRR, **zielbewußt**ALT **I.** *adj* purposeful **II.** *adv* purposefully
zielen ['tsiː·lən] *vi* ❶ (*anvisieren*) to aim (**auf** +*akk* at/for) ❷ (*gerichtet sein*) ■**auf jdn/etw ~** to be aimed at sb/sth
Zielfernrohr *nt* scope
Zielgerade *f* home stretch
Zielgruppe *f* target group
ziellos I. *adj* aimless **II.** *adv* aimlessly
Zielort *m* destination
Zielscheibe *f* target
Zielsetzung <-, -en> *f* aim
zielsicher *adj* unerring
zielstrebig ['tsiːl·ʃtreː·bɪç] **I.** *adj* single-minded **II.** *adv* single-mindedly
Zielstrebigkeit <-> *f kein pl* single-mindedness
ziemlich ['tsiːm·lɪç] **I.** *adj attr* (*beträchtlich*) considerable **II.** *adv* ❶ (*weitgehend*) quite ❷ (*beinahe*) almost; **so ~** more or less; **so ~ alles** just about everything; **so ~ dasselbe** pretty much the same
Zierde <-, -n> ['tsiːɐ̯·də] *f* decoration
zieren ['tsiː·rən] **I.** *vr* ■**sich ~** to make a fuss; *Mädchen* to act coyly; **ohne sich zu ~** without having to be pressed **II.** *vt* to adorn
zierlich ['tsiːɐ̯·lɪç] *adj* dainty
Zierpflanze *f* ornamental plant
Ziffer <-, -n> ['tsɪ·fɐ] *f* (*Zahlzeichen*) digit; (*Zahl*) figure; **römische/arabische ~n** Roman/Arabic numerals
Zifferblatt *nt* face
zig [tsɪç] *adj* (*fam*) umpteen; **~mal** umpteen times
Zigarette <-, -n> [tsi·ga·'rɛ·tə] *f* cigarette
Zigarettenpackung *f* cigarette pack
Zigarettenpause *f* cigarette break
Zigarettenstummel *m* cigarette butt
Zigarillo <-s, -s> [tsi·ga·'rɪ·lo] *m o nt* cigarillo
Zigarre <-, -n> [tsi·'ga·rə] *f* cigar
Zigeuner(in) <-s, -> [tsi·'gɔy·nɐ] *m(f)* Gypsy
zigmal ['tsɪç··maːl] *adv* (*fam*) umpteen times
Zikade <-, -n> [tsi·'kaː·də] *f* cicada
Zimmer <-s, -> ['tsɪ·mɐ] *nt* room; **~ frei haben** to have vacancies
Zimmerantenne *f* indoor antenna
Zimmerdecke *f* ceiling
Zimmermädchen *nt* [chamber]maid
Zimmermann <-leute> *m* carpenter
zimmern ['tsɪ·mɐn] *vt* ■**etw ~** to make sth from wood
Zimmerpflanze *f* house plant
Zimmerservice *m* room service
Zimmervermittlung *f* accommodations service
zimperlich ['tsɪm·pɐ·lɪç] *adj* prim, squeamish; (*empfindlich*) [hyper]sensitive
Zimt <-[e]s, -e> [tsɪmt] *m* cinnamon
Zink <-[e]s> [tsɪŋk] *nt kein pl* zinc
Zinke <-, -n> ['tsɪŋ·kə] *f eines Kamms, Rechens* tooth; *einer Gabel* prong
Zinn <-[e]s> [tsɪn] *nt kein pl* tin
zinnoberrot *adj* vermilion
Zins1 <-es, -en> [tsɪns] *m* FIN interest; **~en bringen** to earn interest; **zu hohen/niedrigen ~en** at a high/low rate of interest
Zins2 <-es, -e> [tsɪns] *m* SÜDD, ÖSTERR, SCHWEIZ (*Miete*) rent
Zinsertrag *m* interest yield
Zinseszins *m* compound interest
zinslos *adj* interest-free
Zipfel <-s, -> ['tsɪp·fl̩] *m* corner; *Hemd, Jacke* tail
Zipfelmütze *f* pointed cap
zirka ['tsɪr·ka] *adv* about
Zirkel <-s, -> ['tsɪr·kl̩] *m* ❶ (*Gerät*) compass ❷ (*Gruppe*) group
Zirkulation <-, -en> [tsɪr·ku·la·'tsi̯oːn] *f* circulation
zirkulieren* [tsɪr·ku·'liː·rən] *vi* to circulate
Zirkus <-, -se> ['tsɪr·kʊs] *m* circus; **mach nicht so einen ~!** (*fig fam*) don't make such a fuss!
Zirkuszelt *nt* big top
zirpen ['tsɪr·pn̩] *vi* ZOOL to chirp
zisch [tsɪʃ] *interj* hiss
zischen ['tsɪ·ʃn̩] *vi haben* to hiss; *Fett* to sizzle
Zischen <-s> ['tsɪ·ʃn̩] *nt kein pl* hiss
Zitadelle <-, -n> [tsi·ta·'dɛ·lə] *f* citadel
Zitat <-[e]s, -e> [tsi·'taːt] *nt* quotation
zitieren* [tsi·'tiː·rən] *vt* to quote
Zitrone <-, -n> [tsi·'troː·nə] *f* lemon
zitronengelb *adj* lemon-yellow
Zitronensaft *m* lemon juice
Zitronensäure *f kein pl* citric acid
Zitronenschale *f* lemon peel
Zitrusfrucht ['tsiː·trʊs-] *f* citrus fruit
zitterig ['tsɪ·tə·rɪç], **zittrig** ['tsɪt·rɪç] *adj* shaky
zittern ['tsɪ·tɐn] *vi* ❶ (*hin und her bewegen*) to shake (**vor** +*dat* with/in); **vor Angst ~** to tremble with fear; *Blätter, Gräser, Lippen* to tremble ❷ (*fig*) ■[**vor jdm/etw**] **~** to be terrified [of sb/sth]
zittrig ['tsɪt·rɪç] *adj s.* **zitterig**
Zivi <-s, -s> ['tsiː·vi] *m* (*fam*) *kurz für* **Zivildienstleistender**
zivil [tsi·'viːl] *adj* civilian
Zivil <-s> [tsi·'viːl] *nt kein pl* civilian clothes *npl*
Zivilbevölkerung *f* civilian population
Zivildienst *m kein pl community service as an alternative to military service*

Conscientious objectors in Germany are required to complete nine months of Zivil-

dienst (community service) — the time required for military service. In Germany, most *Zivildienstleistende*, or *Zivis*, care for the elderly, serve as drivers for the handicapped, or work as assistants in youth hostels. In Austria, **Zivildienst** lasts for 12 months. Since October 1996, community service has also been a valid option in Switzerland, with most conscientious objectors there working in the health-care field. In Switzerland, the length of service is 390 days.

Zivildienstleistender *m young man doing community service instead of military service*
Zivilgericht *nt* civil court
Zivilgesetzbuch *nt* SCHWEIZ (*Bürgerliches Gesetzbuch*) code of civil law
Zivilisation <-, -en> [tsi·vi·li·za·'tsi̯o:n] *f* civilization
zivilisieren* [tsi·vi·li·'zi:·rən] *vt* to civilize
zivilisiert I. *adj* civilized **II.** *adv* civilly
Zivilist(in) <-en, -en> [tsi·vi·'lɪst] *m(f)* civilian
Zivilprozess[RR] *m* civil action
Zivilrecht *nt* civil law
Zobel <-s, -> ['tso:·bl̩] *m* sable
zocken ['tsɔ·kn̩] *vi* (*sl*) to gamble
Zoff <-s> [tsɔf] *m kein pl* (*sl*) trouble
zog [tso:k] *imp von* **ziehen**
zögerlich ['tsø:·ɡɐ·lɪç] **I.** *adj* hesitant **II.** *adv* hesitantly
zögern ['tsø:·ɡɐn] *vi* to hesitate; **ohne zu ~** without hesitation
Zölibat <-[e]s, -e> [tsø·li·'ba:t] *nt o m* celibacy
Zoll[1] <-[e]s, -> [tsɔl] *m* (*Maß*) inch
Zoll[2] <-[e]s, Zölle> [tsɔl, *pl* 'tsœ·lə] *m* ❶ ÖKON customs *npl*, duty; ■ **für etw** *akk* **~ bezahlen** to pay customs on sth ❷ *kein pl* (*Zollverwaltung*) customs *npl*
Zollamt *nt* customs office
Zollbeamte(r), -beamtin *m, f* customs officer
zollen ['tsɔ·lən] *vt* (*geh*) to give; **jdm Anerkennung ~** to show one's appreciation for sb
Zollfahnder(in) <-s, -> *m(f)* customs investigator
Zollfahndung *f* customs investigation department
zollfrei *adj, adv* duty-free
Zollgebühren *pl* customs *npl*, duty
Zöllner <-s, -> ['tsœl·nɐ] *m* customs officer
zollpflichtig *adj* dutiable
Zollstock *m* ruler
Zone <-, -n> ['tso:·nə] *f* zone
Zoo <-s, -s> [tso:] *m* zoo
Zoologie <-> [tsoo·lo·'gi:] *f kein pl* zoology
zoologisch [tsoo·'lo:·gɪʃ] **I.** *adj* zoological **II.** *adv* zoologically
Zoom <-s, -s> [zu:m, tso:m] *nt* zoom lens
zoomen ['zu:·mən, 'tso:·mən] *vt* ■ **jdn/etw ~** to zoom in on sb/sth
Zopf <-[e]s, Zöpfe> [tsɔpf, *pl* tsœp·fə] *m* braid
Zorn <-[e]s> [tsɔrn] *m kein pl* anger
zornig ['tsɔr·nɪç] *adj* angry (**auf** +*akk* with/at)
Zote <-, -n> ['tso:·tə] *f* dirty joke
zottelig ['tsɔ·tə·lɪç] *adj* (*fam*) shaggy
z.T. *Abk von* **zum Teil** partly
zu [tsu:] **I.** *präp* +*dat* ❶ (*wohin*) to; **ich muss ~m Arzt** I have to go see a doctor; **~ Fuß/Pferd** on foot/horseback ❷ (*örtlich: Richtung*) **~m Meer/~r Stadtmitte hin** toward the sea/downtown; **das Zimmer liegt ~r Straße hin** the room faces the street ❸ (*neben*) ■ **~ jdm/etw** next to sb/sth; **setz dich ~ uns** [come and] sit with us ❹ *zeitlich* at; **~ Ostern/Weihnachten** at Easter/Christmas; **~m Wochenende fahren wir weg** we're going away on the weekend ❺ (*anlässlich*) **etw ~m Geburtstag bekommen** to get sth for one's birthday; **jdn ~m Essen einladen** to invite sb for a meal; **~ dieser Frage möchte ich Folgendes sagen** I would like to say the following regarding this question ❻ (*für etw bestimmt*) **das Zeichen ~m Aufbruch** the signal to leave; **mögen Sie Zucker ~m Kaffee?** do you take sugar with your coffee?; **~m Frühstück trinkt sie immer Tee** she always has tea with breakfast ❼ (*um etw herbeizuführen*) **~r Entschuldigung** in apology; **~ was soll das gut sein?** what is that [supposed to be good] for? ❽ + *substantiviertem Infinitiv* **nichts ~m Essen** nothing to eat; **etwas ~m Spielen** something to play with; **das ist ja ~m Lachen** that's ridiculous ❾ (*Veränderung*) **~ etw werden** to turn into sth; **~m Vorsitzenden gewählt werden** to be elected [to the post of] chairman ❿ (*Beziehung*) **Liebe ~ jdm** love for sb; **aus Freundschaft ~ jdm** because of one's friendship with sb; **meine Beziehung ~ ihr** my relationship with her ⓫ (*Verhältnis*) **im Verhältnis 1 ~ 4** in a 1:4 [*or* 1 to 4] ratio; **unsere Chancen stehen 50 ~ 50** we have a fifty-fifty chance; SPORT **sie gewannen mit 5 ~ 1** they won 5-1, 5 to 1 ⓬ (*Zugehörigkeit*) **wo ist der Korken ~ der Flasche?** where is the cork for this bottle?; **der Schlüssel ~ dieser Tür** the key to this door ⓭ *bei Mengenangaben* **~ drei Prozent** at three percent; **sechs [Stück] ~ fünfzig Cent** six for fifty cents; **~m halben Preis** at [*or* for] half price; **~m ersten Mal** for the first time ⓮ (*örtlich: Lage*) in; **~ Hause** at home; **~ seiner Rechten/Linken** on his right/left[-hand side] ⓯ (*in Wendungen*) **~m Beispiel** for example; **~r Belohnung/Strafe** as a reward/punishment; **~m Glück** luckily; **jdm ~ Hilfe kommen** to come to sb's aid; **~ Hilfe!** help!; **~r Probe** on a trial basis; SCHWEIZ **~r Hauptsache** mainly **II.** *adv* ❶ (*allzu*) too; **~ sehr** too much; **ich wäre ~ gern mitgefahren** I would have loved to have gone along ❷ (*geschlossen*) shut, closed; **Tür ~!** shut the door!; **mach die Augen ~** close your eyes ❸ (*fam: betrunken sein*) ■ **~ sein** to be drunk ❹ (*in Wendungen*) **nur ~!** go [right] ahead; **mach ~** hurry up **III.** *konj* ❶ + *Infinitiv* to;

■**etw ~ essen** sth to eat; **sie hat ~ gehorchen** she has to obey; **ohne es ~ wissen** without knowing it ❷ + *Partizip* ~ **bezahlende Rechnungen** outstanding bills; **nicht ~ unterschätzende Probleme** problems [that are] not to be underestimated
zuallererst [tsu·ˈʔalɐ·ʔeːɐ̯st] *adv* first of all
zuallerletzt [tsu·ˈʔalɐ·lɛtst] *adv* last of all
Zubehör <-[e]s, *selten* -e> [ˈtsuː·bə·høːɐ̯] *nt o m* equipment; (*Accessoires*) accessories *pl*
zu|beißen *vi irreg* to bite
zu|bereiten* *vt* ■**etw ~** to prepare sth
Zubereitung <-, -en> *f* preparation
zu|billigen *vt* ■**jdm etw ~** to grant sb sth
zu|binden *vt irreg Schuhe* to tie
zu|blinzeln *vi* ■**jdm ~** to wink at sb
zu|bringen *vt irreg Zeit* to spend
Zubringer <-s, -> *m* TRANSP (*Bus, Zug*) shuttle
Zucchini <-, -> [tsʊ·ˈkiː·ni] *f meist pl* zucchini
Zucht <-, -en> [tsʊxt] *f kein pl* (*Pflanzenzucht*) cultivation; (*Tierzucht*) breeding
züchten [ˈtsʏç·tn̩] *vt Pflanzen* to grow; *Tiere* to breed
Züchter(in) <-s, -> *m(f) Tierzüchter* breeder; *Pflanzenzüchter* grower
Zuchthaus *nt* HIST prison
Zuchthengst *m* stud horse
züchtigen [ˈtsʏç·tɪ·gn̩] *vt* (*geh*) to beat
Zuchtperle *f* cultured pearl
Zuchttier *nt* breeding animal
Züchtung <-, -en> *f kein pl* (*Pflanzenzüchtung*) cultivation; (*Tierzüchtung*) breeding
zucken [ˈtsʊ·kn̩] *vi* ❶ *haben* (*ruckartig bewegen*) *Augenlid* to flutter; *Mundwinkel* to twitch; **mit den Achseln ~** to shrug one's shoulders ❷ *haben Blitz* to flash
zücken [ˈtsʏ·kn̩] *vt Messer* to draw
Zucker[1] <-s, -> [ˈtsʊ·kɐ] *m* sugar
Zucker[2] <-s> [ˈtsʊ·kɐ] *m kein pl* MED diabetes
Zuckerbrot *nt* ▶ WENDUNGEN: **mit ~ und Peitsche** (*prov*) with the carrot and the stick
Zuckerguss[RR] *m* icing
Zuckerhut [ˈtsʊ·kɐ·huːt] *m* GEOL sugar loaf
zuckerkrank *adj* diabetic
Zuckerkranke(r) *f(m)* diabetic
Zuckerkrankheit *f* diabetes
zuckern [ˈtsʊ·kɐn] *vt* to sugar
Zuckerrohr *nt* sugar cane
Zuckerrübe *f* sugar beet
zuckersüß [ˈtsʊ·kɐ·ˈzyːs] *adj* as sweet as sugar *pred*
Zuckerwatte *f* cotton candy
Zuckung <-, -en> *f meist pl* twitch
zu|decken *vt* to cover [up *sep*]
zu|drehen *vt* ❶ (*verschließen*) to screw on *sep* ❷ (*abstellen*) to turn off *sep* ❸ (*festdrehen*) to tighten ❹ (*zuwenden*) **jdm den Rücken ~** to turn one's back on sb
zudringlich [ˈtsuː·drɪŋ·lɪç] *adj* pushy
Zudringlichkeit <-, -en> *f* ❶ *kein pl* (*zudringliche Art*) pushiness *pej* ❷ *meist pl* (*zudringliche Handlung*) advances *pl*
zu|dröhnen *vr* (*sl*) ■**sich ~** to be/become intoxicated; **sich mit Rauschgift ~** to get high [on drugs]
zu|drücken *vt* to press shut *sep*
zueinander [tsu·ʔai·ˈnan·dɐ] *adv* to each other; **~ passen** *Menschen* to suit each other; *Farben, Kleider* to go well together
zuerst [tsu·ˈʔeːɐ̯st] *adv* ❶ (*als Erster*) the first; (*als Erstes*) first ❷ (*anfangs*) at first ❸ (*zum ersten Mal*) for the first time
Zufahrt [ˈtsuː·faːɐ̯t] *f* entrance
Zufahrtsstraße *f* access road; (*zur Autobahn*) approach road
Zufall *m* coincidence; (*Schicksal*) chance; **etw dem ~ überlassen** to leave sth to chance
zu|fallen *vi irreg sein* ❶ *Tür* to close ❷ (*zuteilwerden*) ■**jdm ~** to go to sb
zufällig **I.** *adj* chance *attr* **II.** *adv* by chance; **rein ~** by pure chance; **jdn ~ treffen** to happen to meet sb; **wissen Sie ~, ob ...?** do you happen to know whether ...?
zufälligerweise *adv s.* **zufällig II**
Zufallstreffer *m* fluke *fam*
Zuflucht <-, -en> [ˈtsuː·flʊxt] *f* refuge ▶ WENDUNGEN: **jds letzte ~ sein** to be sb's last resort
Zufluchtsort *m* place of refuge
Zufluss[RR], **Zufluß**[ALT] *m* ❶ *kein pl* (*das Zufließen*) inflow ❷ (*Nebenfluss*) tributary
zu|flüstern *vt* ■**jdm etw ~** to whisper sth to sb
zufolge [tsu·ˈfɔl·gə] *präp* +*dat* (*geh*) according to
zufrieden [tsu·ˈfriː·dn̩] **I.** *adj* (*befriedigt*) satisfied (**mit** +*dat* with); (*glücklich*) contented (**mit** +*dat* with) **II.** *adv* with satisfaction; (*glücklich*) contentedly; **~ stellend** satisfactory
zufrieden|geben *vr irreg* ■**sich** [**mit etw** *dat*] **~** to be satisfied [with sth]
Zufriedenheit <-> *f kein pl* satisfaction; (*Glücklichsein*) contentedness
zufrieden|lassen *vt irreg* ■**jdn ~** to leave sb alone
zu|frieren *vi irreg sein* to freeze [over]
zu|fügen *vt* to cause; **jdm Schaden ~** to harm sb; **jdm Unrecht ~** to do sb an injustice
Zufuhr <-, -en> [ˈtsuː·fuːɐ̯] *f* supply
Zug[1] <-[e]s, Züge> [tsuːk, *pl* ˈtsyː·gə] *m* train ▶ WENDUNGEN: **der ~ ist abgefahren** (*fam*) you missed the boat
Zug[2] <-[e]s, Züge> [tsuːk, *pl* ˈtsyː·gə] *m* ❶ (*inhalierte Menge*) puff (**an** +*dat* on/at), drag *fam* (**an** +*dat* of/on); **einen ~ machen** to take a drag *fam* ❷ (*Schluck*) gulp ❸ *kein pl* (*Luftzug*) draft ❹ (*Spielzug*) move; **am ~ sein** to be sb's move ❺ (*Kolonne*) procession ❻ (*Gesichtszug*) feature ❼ (*Charakterzug*) characteristic ❽ (*Schritt*) ■**~ um ~** step by step; ■**in einem ~** in one stroke ❾ (*Umriss*) **in groben Zügen** in broad terms
Zugabe [ˈtsuː·gaː·bə] *f* MUS encore
Zugabteil *nt* train compartment
Zugang <-[e]s, Zugänge> [ˈtsuː·gaŋ, *pl* ˈtsuː·gɛŋə] *m* ❶ (*Eingang*) entrance ❷ *kein pl* (*Zutritt, Zugriff*) access (**zu** +*dat* to)

zugänglich ['tsuː·gɛŋ·lɪç] *adj* ❶ (*erreichbar*) accessible ❷ *Mensch* approachable; ■ **für etw** *akk* ~ **sein** to be receptive to sth

Zugbegleiter(in) *m(f)* BAHN conductor

Zugbrücke *f* drawbridge

zu|geben *vt irreg* to admit

zugegen [tsu·'geː·gn̩] *adj* (*geh*) ■ **bei etw** *dat* ~ **sein** to be present at sth

zu|gehen *irreg* **I.** *vi sein* ❶ *Tür* to shut ❷ (*zubewegen*) ■ **auf jdn/etw** ~ to approach sb/sth ❸ (*sich versöhnen*) ■ **aufeinander** ~ to become reconciled **II.** *vi impers sein* **auf ihren Partys geht es immer sehr lustig zu** her parties are always great fun

zu|gehören* *vi* (*geh*) ■ **jdm/etw** ~ to belong to sb/sth

zugehörig ['tsuː·gə·høː·rɪç] *adj attr* accompanying *attr*

Zugehörigkeit <-> *f kein pl* (*Verbundenheit*) affiliation (**zu** +*dat* to); **ein Gefühl der** ~ a sense of belonging

zugekifft ['tsuː·gəkɪft] *adj* (*sl*) stoned

zugeknöpft *adj* ❶ *Hemd* buttoned-up ❷ *Mensch* reserved

Zügel <-s, -> ['tsyː·gl̩] *m* reins *npl*

zügellos *adj* unrestrained

zügeln ['tsyː·gl̩n] **I.** *vt* ❶ (*im Zaum halten*) to rein in *sep* ❷ (*beherrschen*) to curb ❸ (*zurückhalten*) ■ **jdn/sich** ~ to restrain sb/oneself **II.** *vi sein* SCHWEIZ (*umziehen*) ■ [**irgendwohin**] ~ to move [somewhere]

Zugeständnis ['tsuː·gə·ʃtɛnt·nɪs] *nt* concession

zu|gestehen* *vt irreg* to concede

zugetan ['tsuː·gə·taːn] *adj* (*geh*) ■ **jdm/etw** ~ **sein** to be taken with sb/sth

Zugführer(in) *m(f)* BAHN conductor

zugig ['tsuː·gɪç] *adj* drafty

zügig ['tsyː·gɪç] **I.** *adj* ❶ (*rasch erfolgend*) speedy ❷ SCHWEIZ (*eingängig*) catchy **II.** *adv* rapidly

Zugkraft *f* ❶ PHYS tensile force *spec* ❷ *kein pl* (*Anziehungskraft*) appeal

zugkräftig *adj* appealing

zugleich [tsu·'glaiç] *adv* ❶ (*ebenso*) both ❷ (*gleichzeitig*) at the same time

Zugluft *f kein pl* draft

Zugmaschine *f* AUTO tractor

Zugpferd *nt* ❶ (*Tier*) draft horse ❷ (*besondere Attraktion*) crowd pleaser

zu|greifen *vi irreg* ❶ (*sich bedienen*) to help oneself ❷ COMPUT ■ **auf etw** *akk* ~ to access sth

Zugrestaurant *nt* dining car

Zugriff *m* COMPUT access (**auf** +*akk* to)

Zugriffsberechtigung *f* COMPUT access authorization

Zugriffsrecht *nt* COMPUT access rights *pl*

zugrunde, zu Grunde[RR] [tsu·'grʊn·də] *adv* [**an etw** *dat*] ~ **gehen** to be destroyed [by sth]; **einer S.** *dat* ~ **liegen** to form the basis of sth

Zugschaffner(in) *m(f)* train conductor

zu|gucken *vi* (*fam*) *s.* **zusehen**

zugunsten, zu Gunsten[RR] [tsu·'gʊns·tn̩] *präp* +*gen* in favor of

zugute|halten[RR] [tsu·'guː·tə-] *vt irreg* ■ **jdm etw** ~ to make allowances for sb's sth

zugute|kommen[RR] *vi irreg sein* ■ **jdm/etw** ~ to be for the benefit of sb/sth

Zugverbindung *f* train connection

Zugverkehr *m* train service

Zugvogel *m* migratory bird

Zugzwang *m* pressure to act

zu|haben *irreg vi* (*fam*) to be closed

zu|halten *irreg vt* ■ **etw** ~ to hold sth closed; ■ **jdm/sich den Mund** ~ to hold one's hand over sb's/one's mouth; **sich** *dat* **die Nase** ~ to hold one's nose

Zuhälter(in) <-s, -> ['tsuː·hɛl·tɐ] *m(f)* pimp

Zuhause <-s> [tsu·'hau·zə] *nt kein pl* home

zu|hören *vi* to listen (+*dat* to)

Zuhörer(in) *m(f)* listener; ■ **die** ~ (*Publikum*) the audience + *sing/pl vb;* (*Radiozuhörer a.*) the listeners

Zuhörerschaft *f kein pl* audience

zu|jubeln *vi* to cheer

zu|kehren *vt* **jdm den Rücken** ~ to turn one's back on sb

zu|klappen *vt, vi* to snap shut

zu|kleben *vt* to glue down *sep*

zu|knallen *vt, vi* (*fam*) to slam shut

zu|kneifen *vt irreg* ■ **etw** ~ to shut sth tight[ly]

zu|knöpfen *vt* ■ **etw** ~ to button up *sep* sth

zu|kommen *vi irreg sein* ❶ (*sich nähern*) ■ **auf jdn/etw** ~ to come toward sb/sth ❷ (*bevorstehen*) ■ **auf jdn** ~ to be in store for sb; **alles auf sich** ~ **lassen** to take things as they come ❸ (*geben*) **jdm etw** ~ **lassen** (*geh*) to send sb sth

Zukunft <-> ['tsuː·kʊnft] *f kein pl* ❶ (*das Bevorstehende*) future; **in ferner/naher** ~ in the distant/near future ❷ LING future [tense]

zukünftig ['tsuː·kʏnf·tɪç] **I.** *adj* future *attr* **II.** *adv* in future

Zukunftsaussichten *pl* future prospects *pl*

Zukunftsfähigkeit *f* forward compatibility

Zukunftsmusik *f* ▶ WENDUNGEN: ~ **sein** (*fam*) to be a long way off

Zukunftspläne *pl* plans *pl* for the future

Zukunftstechnologie *f* technology of the future

zukunft(s)weisend *adj* forward-looking

zu|lächeln *vi* ■ **jdm** ~ to smile at sb

Zulage <-, -n> ['tsuː·laː·gə] *f* bonus

zu|langen *vi* (*fam*) ❶ (*zugreifen*) to help oneself ❷ *Händler* to ask a fortune

zu|lassen *vt irreg* ❶ (*dulden*) to allow ❷ (*fam*) *Tür* to keep shut *sep* ❸ (*die Genehmigung erteilen*) ■ **jdn** ~ to admit sb (**zu** +*dat* to) ❹ (*anmelden*) to register

zulässig ['tsuː·lɛ·sɪç] *adj* permissible

Zulassung <-, -en> *f* ❶ *kein pl* (*Genehmigung*) authorization; (*Lizenz*) license; **die** ~ **entziehen** to revoke sb's license ❷ (*Anmeldung*) registration ❸ (*Fahrzeugschein*) [motor vehicle] registration

Zulassungsbeschränkung *f* admission restriction

Zulassungspapier *nt meist pl* registration papers *npl;* AUTO [motor vehicle] registration

zulassungspflichtig *adj* (*geh*) requiring licensing

Zulassungsprüfung *f* ADMIN, SCH entrance exam

Zulauf ['tsuː·lauf] *m* inlet

zu|laufen *vi irreg sein* ① (*zubewegen*) ■ **auf jdn/etw ~** to run toward sb/sth; (*direkt*) to run up to sb/sth ② *Haustier* **ein zugelaufener Hund/eine zugelaufene Katze** a stray [dog/cat]

zu|legen I. *vt* (*fam: zunehmen*) to put on *sep* ▶ WENDUNGEN: **einen Zahn ~** (*fam*) to step on it **II.** *vi* ① (*fam: zunehmen*) to put on weight ② (*fam: das Tempo steigern*) to get a move on; *Läufer* to increase the pace **III.** *vr* (*fam*) ■ **sich** *dat* **jdn/etw ~** to get oneself sb/sth

zuleide, zu Leide[RR] [tsu·'lai·də] *adv* **jdm etw/nichts ~ tun** (*veraltend*) to harm/not harm sb

zuletzt [tsu·'lɛtst] *adv* ① (*als Letzte[r]*) **~ eingetroffen** to be the last to arrive; **~ durchs Ziel gehen** to finish last ② (*zum Schluss*) **bis ~** until the end; **ganz ~** right at the end ③ (*letztmalig*) last; **nicht ~** not least [of all]

zuliebe [tsu·'liː·bə] *adv* ■ **jdm/etw ~** for sb['s sake]

Zulieferbetrieb *m,* **Zulieferer** <-s, -> *m* supplier

zu|liefern *vi* to supply

zum [tsʊm] = **zu dem** *s.* **zu**

zu|machen *vt, vi* ① (*verschließen*) to close; **eine Flasche/ein Glas ~** to put the top on a bottle/lid on a jar ② (*zukleben*) *Brief* to seal ③ (*zuknöpfen*) ■ **etw ~** to button [up *sep*] sth ④ (*den Betrieb einstellen*) to close [down *sep*]

zumal [tsu·'maːl] **I.** *konj* particularly as **II.** *adv* particularly

zu|mauern *vt* to wall up *sep*

zumindest [tsu·'mɪn·dəst] *adv* at least

zumutbar *adj* reasonable

zumute, zu Mute[RR] [tsu·'muː·tə] *adv* **mir ist so merkwürdig ~** I feel so strange; **mir ist nicht zum Scherzen ~** I'm not in a joking mood

zu|muten ['tsuː·muː·tn̩] *vt* ■ **jdm etw ~** to expect sth of sb; **jdm zu viel ~** to expect too much of sb; ■ **sich** *dat* **etw ~** to undertake sth; **sich zu viel ~** to overtax oneself

Zumutung *f* unreasonable demand; **das ist eine ~!** it's just too much!

zunächst [tsu·'nɛçst] *adv* ① (*anfangs*) initially ② (*vorerst*) for the moment

zu|nageln *vt* to nail up *sep*

zu|nähen *vt* to sew up *sep; Wunde* to stitch up

Zunahme <-, -n> ['tsuː·naː·mə] *f* increase

Zuname ['tsuː·naː·mə] *m* (*geh*) surname

zünden ['tsʏndn̩] *vi, vt* ① TECH to fire *spec* ② (*zu brennen anfangen*) to catch fire; *Streichholz* to light

zündend *adj Rede* stirring; *Idee* great

Zünder <-s, -> ['tsʏn·dɐ] *m* detonator

Zündholz <-es, -hölzer> *nt bes* SÜDD, ÖSTERR match

Zündholzschachtel *f* matchbox

Zündkabel *nt* ignition cable

Zündkerze *f* spark plug

Zündschlüssel *m* ignition key

Zündschnur *f* fuse

Zündung <-, -en> *f* ① AUTO ignition ② TECH firing

zu|nehmen *irreg vi* ① *Gewicht* to gain weight ② (*sich verstärken*) to increase

zunehmend I. *adj* increasing *attr; Verbesserung* growing *attr* **II.** *adv* increasingly

zu|neigen I. *vi* ■ **einer S.** *dat* **~** to be inclined toward sth **II.** *vr* **sich dem Ende ~** to draw to a close

Zuneigung *f* affection

Zunft <-, Zünfte> [tsʊnft, *pl* 'tsʏnf·tə] *f* HIST guild

zünftig ['tsʏnf·tɪç] *adj* (*veraltend fam*) proper

Zunge <-, -n> ['tsʊŋə] *f* tongue; **auf der ~ zergehen** to melt in one's mouth ▶ WENDUNGEN: **etw liegt jdm auf der ~** sth is on the tip of sb's tongue

züngeln ['tsʏŋl̩n] *vi* ① *Schlange* to dart its tongue in and out ② (*hin und her bewegen*) to dart

Zungenbrecher <-s, -> *m* (*fam*) tongue twister

Zungenkuss[RR] *m* French kiss

Zungenspitze *f* tip of the tongue

zunichte|machen[RR] [tsu·'nɪç·tə-] *vt* (*geh*) ■ **etw ~** to wreck sth; *Hoffnungen* to ruin sth

zu|nicken *vi* ■ **jdm ~** to nod to sb

zunutze, zu Nutze[RR] [tsu·'nʊ·tsə] *adv* **sich** *dat* **etw ~ machen** to make use of sth

zu|ordnen ['tsuː·ʔɔrd·nən] *vt* ■ **etw einer S.** *dat* **~** to assign sth to sth

Zuordnung *f* assignment

zu|packen *vi* ① (*zufassen*) to grip; (*schneller*) to make a grab ② (*mithelfen*) ■ **[mit] ~** to lend a [helping] hand

zupfen ['tsʊp·fn̩] *vt* ① (*ziehen*) ■ **jdn an etw** *dat* **~** to pluck at sb's sth; (*stärker*) to tug at sb's sth ② (*herausziehen*) ■ **etw aus/von etw** *dat* **~** to pull sth out of/off [of] sth; **sich die Augenbrauen ~** to pluck one's eyebrows

Zupfinstrument *nt* plucked instrument

zur [tsuːɐ̯, tsʊr] = **zu der** *s.* **zu**

Zürcher ['tsʏr·çɐ] *adj* Zurich *attr*

zurechnungsfähig *adj* JUR responsible for one's [own] actions *pred*

zurecht|biegen *vt irreg* ① (*in Form biegen*) to bend into shape ② (*fam*) ■ **jdn ~** to whip sb into shape; **etw wieder ~** to get sth straightened out again

zurecht|finden [tsu·'rɛçt·fɪn·dn̩] *vr irreg* ■ **sich irgendwo ~** to get used to a place; **sich in einer Großstadt ~** to find one's way around a city

zurecht|kommen *vi irreg sein* ① (*auskommen*) to get along (**mit** + *dat* with) ② (*klarkom-*

men) to cope (**mit** +*dat* with)

zurẹcht|legen *vr* ■ **sich** *dat* **etw** ~ (*sich etw griffbereit hinlegen*) to get sth ready; (*sich im Voraus überlegen*) to work out *sep* sth

zurẹcht|machen *vt* (*fam*) ① (*vorbereiten*) ■ **etw** ~ to get sth ready ② (*zubereiten*) ■ **etw** ~ to prepare sth ③ (*schminken*) ■ **sich** ~ to put on *sep* one's makeup ④ (*schick machen*) ■ **sich/jdn** ~ to get [oneself]/sb ready

zurẹcht|weisen *vt irreg* to reprimand (**wegen** +*gen* for)

zu|reden [ˈtsuːˑreːˑdn̩] *vi* ■ **jdm [gut]** ~ to encourage sb

Zürich <-s> [ˈtsyːˑrɪç] *nt* Zurich

zu|richten [ˈtsuːˑrɪçˑtn̩] *vt* **jdn übel** ~ to beat up *sep* sb badly; **etw übel** ~ to make a mess of sth

Zurschaustellung *f* (*meist pej*) flaunting

zurück [tsuˑˈrʏk] *adv* ① (*wieder da*) back; ■ ~ **sein** to be back (**von** +*dat* from) ② (*Rückfahrt, -flug*) return; **hin und ~ oder einfach?** round-trip or one-way? ▶ WENDUNGEN: **~!** back up!

zurụ̈ck|bekommen* *vt irreg* to get back *sep*

zurụ̈ck|beugen I. *vt* to lean back *sep* II. *vr* ■ **sich** ~ to lean back

zurụ̈ck|bezahlen* *vt* to repay, to pay back *sep*

zurụ̈ck|bilden *vr* ■ **sich** ~ to recede

zurụ̈ck|bleiben *vi irreg sein* ① (*nicht mitkommen*) to stay behind ② (*zurückgelassen werden*) to be left [behind] ③ (*nicht mithalten können*) to fall behind

zurück|blicken [tsuˑˈrʏkˑblɪˑkn̩] *vi* to look back (**auf** +*akk* on, at)

zurụ̈ck|bringen *vt irreg* to bring back *sep*

zurụ̈ck|denken *vi irreg* to think back (**an** +*akk* to)

zurụ̈ck|drängen *vt* to force back *sep*

zurụ̈ck|erobern* *vt* ① MIL to recapture ② POL (*erneut gewinnen*) to win back *sep*

zurụ̈ck|erstatten* *vt* ■ **[jdm] etw** ~ to refund [sb's] sth

zurụ̈ck|fahren *irreg* I. *vi sein* (*zum Ausgangspunkt fahren*) to drive back II. *vt* ① (*rückwärtsfahren*) to reverse ② (*mit dem Auto*) to drive back *sep* ③ (*reduzieren*) to cut back *sep*

zurụ̈ck|fallen *vi irreg sein* ① SPORT to fall behind ② (*zurückkehren*) ■ **in etw** *akk* ~ to lapse back into sth ③ (*darunterbleiben*) ■ **hinter etw** *akk* ~ to fall short of sth ④ (*angelastet werden*) ■ **auf jdn** ~ to reflect on sb

zurụ̈ck|finden *vi irreg* to find one's way back

zurụ̈ck|fordern *vt* ■ **etw** ~ to demand sth back (**von** +*dat* from)

zurụ̈ck|führen *vt* ① (*Ursache bestimmen*) ■ **etw auf etw** *akk* ~ to attribute sth to sth ② (*zum Ausgangsort zurückbringen*) ■ **jdn irgendwohin** ~ to take sb back somewhere

zurụ̈ck|geben *vt irreg* to return; **ein Kompliment** ~ to return a compliment

zurụ̈ckgeblieben *adj* slow

zurụ̈ck|gehen *vi irreg sein* ① (*zurückkehren*) to return, to go back ② (*abnehmen*) to go down ③ MED (*sich zurückbilden*) to go down; *Geschwulst* to be in recession

zurụ̈ck|gewinnen* *vt irreg* to win back

zurụ̈ckgezogen *adj, adv* secluded

zurụ̈ck|greifen *vi irreg* ■ **auf etw** *akk* ~ to fall back [up]on sth

zurụ̈ck|halten *irreg* I. *vr* ■ **sich** ~ ① (*sich beherrschen*) to restrain oneself ② (*reserviert sein*) to be reserved II. *vt* ① (*aufhalten*) to hold up *sep* ② (*abhalten*) ■ **jdn [von etw** *dat*] ~ to keep sb from doing sth

zurụ̈ckhaltend I. *adj* ① (*reserviert*) reserved ② (*vorsichtig*) cautious II. *adv* cautiously

Zurụ̈ckhaltung *f kein pl* reserve

zurụ̈ck|holen *vt* (*zurückbringen*) to bring back *sep*; (*in seinen Besitz*) to get back *sep*

zurụ̈ck|kehren *vi sein* to return (**zu** +*dat* to); **nach Hause** ~ to return home

zurụ̈ck|kommen *vi irreg sein* ① (*erneut zum Ausgangsort kommen*) to return; **nach Hause/aus dem Ausland** ~ to return home/from abroad ② (*erneut aufgreifen*) ■ **auf etw** *akk* ~ to come back to sth; ■ **auf jdn** ~ to get back to sb

zurụ̈ck|kriegen *vt* (*fam*) *s.* **zurückbekommen**

zurụ̈ck|lassen *vt irreg* to leave behind *sep*

zurụ̈ck|legen *vt* ① (*wieder hinlegen*) to put back *sep* ② (*reservieren*) ■ **jdm etw** ~ to set sth aside for sb ③ (*hinter sich bringen*) **5 km** ~ to go 5 km; (*zu Fuss a.*) to walk 5 km; (*mit dem Auto a.*) to drive 5 km ④ (*sparen*) to put away *sep*

zurụ̈ck|lehnen *vr* ■ **sich** ~ to lean back

zurụ̈ck|liegen *vi irreg* **etw liegt vier Jahre zurück** it's been four years since sth

zurụ̈ck|melden *vr* ■ **sich** ~ to be back

zurụ̈ck|nehmen *vt irreg* ① (*als Retour annehmen*) to take back *sep* ② (*widerrufen*) to take back *sep* ③ (*rückgängig machen*) to withdraw; **ich nehme alles zurück** I take it all back

zurụ̈ck|prallen *vi sein* ■ **von etw** *dat* ~ to bounce off [of] sth

zurụ̈ck|reichen *vi* ■ **irgendwohin** ~ to go back to sth; **ins 16. Jahrhundert** ~ to go back to the 16th century

zurụ̈ck|reisen *vi sein* to travel back

zurụ̈ck|rufen *irreg* I. *vt* ① (*zurück telefonieren*) to call back *sep* ② (*zurückbeordern*) to recall II. *vi* to call back

zurụ̈ck|schalten *vi* AUTO to downshift (**in** +*akk* into)

zurụ̈ck|schauen *vi* to look back (**auf** +*akk* on, at)

zurụ̈ck|schicken *vt* to send back *sep*

zurụ̈ck|schlagen *irreg* I. *vt* ① SPORT to hit back ② (*umschlagen*) to turn back *sep* II. *vi* ■ **auf jdn/etw** ~ to have an effect on sb/sth

zurụ̈ck|schrauben *vt* (*fam*) *Ansprüche* to lower (**auf** +*akk* to)

zurụ̈ck|schrecken *vi irreg sein* ① (*Bedenken*

Z

vor etw haben) to shrink (**vor** +*dat* from); **vor nichts** ~ (*völlig skrupellos sein*) to stop at nothing; (*keine Angst haben*) to not flinch at anything ② (*erschrecken*) to start back

zurück|schreiben *vt* to write back

zurück|sehnen *vr* **sich nach Hause** ~ to long to return home

zurück|setzen **I.** *vt* ① (*zurückstellen*) to put back *sep* ② (*zurückfahren*) to reverse ③ (*benachteiligen*) to neglect **II.** *vr* ■ **sich** ~ ① (*sich zurücklehnen*) to sit back ② (*den Platz wechseln*) **setzen wir uns einige Reihen zurück** let's sit a few rows back **III.** *vi* (*zurückfahren*) ■ [**mit etw** *dat*] ~ to reverse [sth]

zurück|spulen *vt* to rewind

zurück|stecken **I.** *vt* to put back *sep* **II.** *vi* to back down

zurück|stehen *vi irreg* ① (*weiter entfernt stehen*) to stand back ② (*hintangesetzt werden*) ■ [**hinter jdm**] ~ to be behind [sb]

zurück|stellen *vt* ① (*wieder hinstellen*) to put back *sep* ② (*nach hinten stellen*) to move back *sep* ③ *Heizung* to turn down *sep* ④ (*aufschieben*) to put back *sep;* (*verschieben*) to postpone; **die Uhr** ~ to turn back *sep* the clock ⑤ *Wünsche* to put aside ⑥ ÖSTERR (*zurückgeben*) to return

zurück|stoßen *vt irreg* to push away *sep*

zurück|stufen *vt* to downgrade

zurück|treten *vi irreg sein* ① (*nach hinten treten*) to step back (**von** +*dat* from) ② (*von einem Amt*) to resign

zurück|verfolgen* *vt* to trace back *sep*

zurück|versetzen* **I.** *vt* ■ **jdn** ~ to transfer sb back **II.** *vr* ■ **sich** ~ to be transported back

zurück|weichen *vi irreg sein* to draw back (**vor** +*dat* from)

zurück|weisen *vt irreg* ■ **jdn** ~ to turn away *sep* sb; ■ **etw** ~ to reject sth

Zurückweisung *f* rejection

zurück|werfen *vt irreg* ① (*jdm etw wieder zuwerfen*) ■ **etw** ~ to throw back *sep* sth ② (*Position verschlechtern*) **das wirft uns um Jahre zurück** that will set us back years

zurück|wollen **I.** *vi* (*fam*) to want to return **II.** *vi* ■ **etw** ~ to want sth back

zurück|zahlen *vt* ■ [**jdm**] **etw** ~ to repay [sb] sth

zurück|ziehen *irreg* **I.** *vt* ① (*nach hinten ziehen*) to pull back *sep; Vorhang* to draw back *sep* ② (*widerrufen*) to withdraw **II.** *vr* ■ **sich** ~ to withdraw (**aus** +*dat* from) **III.** *vi sein* **nach Hamburg** ~ to move back to Hamburg

Zuruf ['tsuː·ruːf] *m* call; (*nach Hilfe*) cry

zu|rufen *vt irreg* ■ **jdm etw** ~ to shout sth to sb

zurzeit [tsʊr·'tsait] *adv* at present

Zusage ['tsuː·zaː·gə] *f* acceptance

zu|sagen **I.** *vt* ■ [**jdm**] ~ to promise **II.** *vi* ■ [**jdm**] ~ ① (*die Teilnahme versichern*) to accept sb ② (*gefallen*) to appeal to sb

zusammen [tsu·'za·mən] *adv* ① (*gemeinsam*) together (**mit** +*dat* with); ■ **mit jdm ~ sein** to be with sb ② (*ein Paar sein*) ■ **~ sein** to be going out ③ (*insgesamt*) altogether

Zusammenarbeit *f kein pl* cooperation

zusammen|arbeiten *vi* ■ **mit jdm** ~ to cooperate [*or* work [together]] with sb

zusammen|bauen *vt* to assemble

zusammen|beißen *vt* **die Zähne** ~ to clench one's teeth

zusammen|binden *vt irreg* to tie together *sep*

zusammen|bleiben *vi irreg sein* to stay together; ■ **mit jdm** ~ to stay with sb

zusammen|brechen *vi irreg sein* to collapse

zusammen|bringen *vt irreg* ① (*in Kontakt bringen*) ■ **jdn** [**mit jdm**] ~ to introduce sb [to sb] ② (*anhäufen*) to amass

Zusammenbruch *m* collapse

zusammen|drängen **I.** *vr* ■ **sich** ~ to crowd [together] **II.** *vt* to concentrate

zusammen|drücken *vt* ① (*zerdrücken*) to crush ② (*aneinanderdrücken*) to press together

zusammen|fahren *vi irreg sein* to start; (*vor Schmerzen*) to flinch

zusammen|fallen *vi irreg sein* ① (*einstürzen*) ■ [**in sich**] ~ to collapse; *Gebäude a.* to cave in ② *Ereignisse* to coincide

zusammen|falten *vt* to fold [up *sep*]

zusammen|fassen **I.** *vt* ① (*resümieren*) to summarize ② (*vereinigen*) **die Bewerber in Gruppen** ~ to divide the applicants into groups; ■ **jdn/etw in etw** *dat* ~ to unite sb/sth into sth; ■ **etw unter etw** *dat* ~ to classify sth under sth **II.** *vi* to summarize; **..., wenn ich kurz ~ darf** to sum up, ...

Zusammenfassung *f* summary

zusammen|fließen *vi irreg sein* to flow together

zusammen|fügen **I.** *vt* to assemble; **die Teile eines Puzzles** ~ to piece together a jigsaw puzzle **II.** *vr* **die Teile fügen sich nahtlos zusammen** the parts fit together seamlessly

zusammen|führen *vt* to bring together *sep; eine Familie* to reunite

zusammen|gehören* *vi* ① (*zueinander gehören*) to belong together ② (*ein Ganzes bilden*) to go together; *Socken* to form a pair

zusammengehörig *adj pred* ① (*eng verbunden*) close ② (*zusammengehörend*) matching

Zusammengehörigkeit <-> *f kein pl* unity

Zusammengehörigkeitsgefühl *nt kein pl* sense of togetherness

zusammengesetzt *adj* compound *attr*

zusammengestöpselt [tsu·'za·mən·gə·ʃtœp·sl̩t] *adj* (*pej fam*) [hastily] thrown together

zusammengewürfelt *adj* mismatched

Zusammenhalt *m kein pl* solidarity

zusammen|halten *irreg* **I.** *vi* to stick together **II.** *vt* ① (*beisammenhalten*) **seine Gedanken** ~ to keep one's thoughts together; **sein Geld ~ müssen** to have to be careful with one's money ② (*verbinden*) to hold together

Zusammenhang <-[e]s, -hänge> *m* connection; (*Verbindung*) link (**zwischen** +*dat* between); **jdn/etw mit etw** *dat* **in ~ bringen**

to connect sb/sth with [*or* to] sth; **etw aus dem ~ reißen** to take sth out of context; **im ~ mit etw** *dat* in connection with [*or* to] sth; **im ~ mit etw** *dat* **stehen** to be connected with [*or* to] sth

zusạmmen|hängen *vi irreg* ❶ (*in Zusammenhang stehen*) ■ **mit etw** *dat* **~** to be connected with [*or* to] sth ❷ (*verbunden sein*) to be joined [together]

zusạmmenhängend I. *adj* ❶ (*kohärent*) coherent ❷ (*betreffend*) ■ **mit etw** *dat* **~** connected with [*or* to] sth II. *adv* coherently

zusạmmenhang(s)los I. *adj* incoherent II. *adv* incoherently

zusạmmen|heften *vt* to clip together *sep;* (*mit einem Hefter*) to staple together *sep*

zusạmmen|klappen I. *vt haben* to fold up *sep* II. *vi sein* (*a. fig fam*) to collapse

zusạmmen|knoten *vt* to tie together *sep*

zusạmmen|kommen *vi irreg sein* ❶ (*sich treffen*) to come together; ■ **mit jdm ~** to meet sb; **zu einer Besprechung ~** to get together for a discussion ❷ (*sich akkumulieren*) to combine; **heute kommt wieder alles zusammen!** it's another of those days! ❸ *Schulden* to mount [up]; *Spenden* to be collected

zusạmmen|krachen *vi sein* (*fam*) ❶ (*einstürzen*) *Brücke* to crash down; *Bett, Stuhl* to collapse with a crash; *Börse, Wirtschaft* to crash ❷ (*zusammenstoßen*) to smash together; *Auto a.* to crash [into each other]

zusạmmen|kratzen *vt* (*fam*) to scrape together *sep*

Zusammenkunft <-, -künfte> [tsu·ˈza·mən·kʊnft, *pl* -kʏnf·tə] *f* meeting

zusạmmen|läppern *vr* (*fam*) ■ **sich ~** to add up

zusạmmen|laufen *vi irreg sein* to meet (**in** +*dat* at), to converge (**in** +*dat* at); *Flüsse* to flow together; *Menschen* to gather

zusạmmen|leben *vi* to live together

Zusạmmenleben *nt kein pl* living together *no art*

zusạmmen|legen I. *vt* ❶ (*zusammenfalten*) to fold [up *sep*] ❷ (*vereinigen*) to combine (**mit** +*dat* into), to join II. *vi* (*Geld sammeln*) to pitch in

zusạmmen|nehmen *irreg* I. *vt* to summon [up *sep*]; **den Verstand ~** to get one's thoughts together; ■ **alles zusammengenommen** all in all II. *vr* ■ **sich ~** to control oneself

zusạmmen|passen *vi Menschen* to suit each other; **gut/schlecht ~** to be well-matched/a poor match; *Farben* to go together; *Kleidungsstücke* to match

zusạmmen|pferchen *vt* to herd together *sep*

Zusạmmenprall *m* collision

zusạmmen|prallen *vi sein* to collide

zusạmmen|pressen *vt* to press together *sep;* **die Faust ~** to clench one's fist; **zusammengepresste Lippen** pinched lips

zusạmmen|raufen *vr* (*fam*) ■ **sich ~** to get it together

zusạmmen|rechnen *vt* to add up *sep;* **alles zusammengerechnet** all in all

zusạmmen|reimen *vr* ■ **sich** *dat* **etw ~** to put two and two together from [doing] sth; **ich kann es mir einfach nicht ~** I just don't get it

zusạmmen|reißen *irreg vr* (*fam*) ■ **sich ~** to pull oneself together, to get a grip *fam*

zusạmmen|rücken I. *vi sein* (*enger aneinanderrücken*) to move up closer; (*enger zusammenhalten*) to join in a common cause II. *vt haben* ■ **etw ~** to move sth closer together

zusạmmen|rufen *vt irreg* to call together *sep;* **die Mitglieder ~** to convene [a meeting of] the members *form*

zusạmmen|sacken *vi sein* to collapse

zusạmmen|scheißen *vt irreg* (*derb*) ■ **jdn ~** to read sb the riot act *fig*

zusạmmen|schlagen *irreg vt irreg haben* ❶ (*verprügeln*) to beat up *sep* ❷ (*zertrümmern*) to smash [up *sep*]

zusạmmen|schließen *irreg* I. *vt* to lock together *sep* II. *vr* ■ **sich ~** ❶ (*sich vereinigen*) to join together ❷ (*sich verbinden*) to join forces

Zusạmmenschluss[RR], **Zusạmmenschluß**[ALT] *m* union; *Firmen* merger

zusạmmen|schrauben *vt* to screw together

zusạmmen|schreiben *vt irreg* ■ **etw ~** to write sth as one word

zusạmmen|schustern *vt* (*pej fam*) to throw together *sep*

Zusạmmensein <-s> *nt kein pl* meeting; (*zwanglos*) get-together

zusạmmen|setzen I. *vt* ❶ (*aus Teilen herstellen*) to assemble ❷ (*nebeneinandersetzen*) **Schüler/Tischgäste ~** to seat students/guests beside each other II. *vr* ❶ (*sich zueinandersetzen*) ■ **sich ~** to sit together; (*um etw zu besprechen*) to get together ❷ (*bestehen*) ■ **sich aus etw** *dat* **~** to be composed of sth

Zusạmmensetzung <-, -en> *f* ❶ (*Struktur*) composition; *Mannschaft* lineup ❷ (*Kombination der Bestandteile*) ingredients *pl; Rezeptur, Präparat* composition; *Teile* assembly

Zusạmmenspiel *nt kein pl* ❶ SPORT teamwork ❷ MUS ensemble playing ❸ (*fig*) interplay

zusạmmen|stauchen *vt* (*fam*) ❶ (*maßregeln*) ■ **jdn ~** to reprimand sb ❷ (*zusammendrücken*) ■ **etw ist zusammengestaucht** sth is crushed

zusạmmen|stecken I. *vt* to pin together *sep* II. *vi* (*fam*) **die beiden stecken aber auch immer zusammen!** the two of them are inseparable!

zusạmmen|stellen *vt* ❶ (*auf einen Fleck stellen*) to place side by side ❷ (*aufstellen*) to compile; *Delegation* to assemble

Zusạmmenstellung *f* compilation; (*Liste*) list

Zusạmmenstoß *m* ❶ (*Zusammenprall*) collision ❷ (*Auseinandersetzung*) clash

zusạmmen|stoßen *vi irreg sein* ❶ (*kollidieren*) to collide; ■ **mit jdm ~** to bump into sb ❷ (*aneinandergrenzen*) to adjoin

Z

zusammen|strömen *vi sein* to flock together
zusammen|stürzen *vi sein* to collapse
zusammen|tragen *vt irreg* to collect
zusammen|treffen *vi irreg sein* ❶ (*sich treffen*) to meet; ■ **mit jdm ~** to meet sb; (*unverhofft*) to encounter sb ❷ *Umstände* to coincide
Zusammentreffen *nt* ❶ (*Treffen*) meeting ❷ *von Umständen* coincidence
zusammen|treiben *vt* **Menschen/Tiere ~** to drive people/animals together
zusammen|trommeln *vt* (*fam*) **Anhänger/Mitglieder ~** to rally supporters/members
zusammen|tun *irreg* **I.** *vt* (*fam*) to put together **II.** *vr* (*fam*) ■ **sich ~** to get together
zusammen|wirken *vi* (*geh*) ❶ (*gemeinsam tätig sein*) to work together ❷ (*vereint wirken*) to combine
Zusammenwirken *nt kein pl* interaction
zusammen|zählen *vt* to add up *sep;* **alles zusammengezählt** all in all
zusammen|ziehen *irreg* **I.** *vi sein* to move in together **II.** *vr* ■ **sich ~** ❶ (*sich verengen*) to contract; *Schlinge* to tighten ❷ *Sturm, Unheil* to be brewing; *Wolken* to gather **III.** *vt* **die Augenbrauen ~** to frown
zusammen|zucken *vi sein* to start; (*vor Schmerz*) to flinch
Zusatz ['tsu:·zats] *m* ❶ (*zugefügter Teil*) appendix ❷ (*Nahrungszusatz*) additive; **ohne ~ von Farbstoffen** no artificial colors added
Zusatzgerät *nt* attachment; COMPUT peripheral [device]
zusätzlich ['tsu:·zɛts·lɪç] **I.** *adj* further *attr; Kosten* additional **II.** *adv* in addition; **jdn ~ belasten** to put extra pressure on sb
Zusatzstoff *m* additive
zu|schauen *vi s.* **zusehen**
Zuschauer(in) <-s, -> *m(f)* ❶ SPORT spectator; TV viewer ❷ FILM, THEAT ■ **die ~** the audience
Zuschauerraum *m* auditorium
Zuschauertribüne *f* stands *pl*
zu|schicken *vt* to send; ■ **sich** *dat* **etw ~ lassen** to send for sth
Zuschlag <-[e]s, Zuschläge> *m* ❶ (*Preisaufschlag*) surcharge ❷ (*zusätzliches Entgelt*) bonus
zu|schlagen *irreg* **I.** *vt haben* ❶ (*schließen*) to slam [shut] *sep; Buch* to close ❷ (*zuspielen*) **jdm den Ball ~** to kick [*or* hit] the ball to sb **II.** *vi* ❶ *haben* (*einen Hieb versetzen*) to strike ❷ *sein Tür* to slam shut
zu|schließen *irreg vt* to lock
zu|schnappen *vi* ❶ *haben* to snap ❷ *sein* to snap shut
zu|schneiden *vt irreg* ❶ MODE ■ **etw ~** to cut sth to size; *Stoff* to cut out *sep* ❷ (*fig*) ■ **auf jdn [genau] zugeschnitten sein** to be cut out for sb
zu|schnüren *vt* ❶ (*durch Schnüren verschließen*) to tie ❷ (*fig*) **die Angst schnürte ihr die Kehle zu** she was choked with fear
zu|schrauben *vt* to screw on *sep*
zu|schreiben *vt irreg* ❶ (*beimessen*) ■ **jdm etw ~** to attribute sth to sb ❷ (*zur Last legen*) **jdm/etw die Schuld an etw** *dat* **~** to blame sb/sth for sth
Zuschrift *f* (*geh*) reply
zuschulden, zu SchuldenRR [tsu·'ʃʊl·dn̩] *adv* **sich** *dat* **etwas/nichts ~ kommen lassen** to do something/nothing wrong
ZuschussRR <-es, Zuschüsse>, **Zuschuß**ALT <-sses, Zuschüsse> ['tsu:·ʃʊs, *pl* 'tsu:·ʃʏ·sə] *m* subsidy
zu|schütten **I.** *vt* to fill in *sep* **II.** *vr* (*fam*) ■ **sich ~** to get drunk
zu|sehen *vi irreg* ❶ (*mit Blicken verfolgen*) to watch ❷ (*etw geschehen lassen*) ■ **einer S.** *dat* **~** to sit back and watch sth; **tatenlos musste er ~, wie ...** he could only stand and watch while ... ❸ (*dafür sorgen*) ■ **~, dass ...** to see [to it] that ...
zusehends ['tsu:·ze:·ənts] *adv* noticeably
zu|senden *vt irreg s.* **zuschicken**
zu|setzen **I.** *vt* ■ **[einer S.** *dat*] **etw ~** to add sth [to sth] **II.** *vi* (*bedrängen*) ■ **jdm ~** to badger sb
zu|sichern *vt* ■ **jdm etw ~** to assure sb of sth; **jdm seine Hilfe ~** to promise to help sb
zu|sperren *vt* to lock
zu|spielen *vt* ❶ SPORT ■ **jdm den Ball ~** to pass the ball to sb ❷ (*zukommen lassen*) **etw der Presse ~** to leak sth [to the press]
zu|spitzen **I.** *vr* ■ **sich ~** to come to a head **II.** *vt* to sharpen
zu|sprechen *irreg* **I.** *vt* ❶ (*offiziell zugestehen*) ■ **jdm etw ~** to award sth to sb ❷ (*geh*) **jdm Mut/Trost ~** to encourage/comfort sb ❸ (*zuerkennen*) ■ **jdm/einer S. etw ~** to attribute sth to sb/sth **II.** *vi* (*geh*) **jdm ermutigend ~** to encourage sb
Zuspruch *m kein pl* (*geh*) ❶ (*Popularität, Anklang*) **sich großen ~s erfreuen** to be very popular ❷ (*Worte*) **ermutigender ~** words of encouragement
Zustand <-[e]s, Zustände> ['tsu:·ʃtant, *pl* 'tsu:·ʃtɛn·də] *m* ❶ (*Verfassung*) state, condition; **im wachen ~** while awake ❷ *pl* (*Verhältnisse*) conditions; **das ist doch kein ~!** what a disgrace!
zustande, zu StandeRR [tsu·'ʃtan·də] *adv* **etw ~ bringen** to manage [to do] sth; **die Arbeit ~ bringen** to get the work done; **eine Einigung ~ bringen** to reach an agreement; **~ kommen** to materialize; (*stattfinden*) to take place
zuständig ['tsu:·ʃtɛn·dɪç] *adj* responsible; **der ~e Beamte** the official in charge; **dafür ist er ~** that's his responsibility
Zuständigkeit <-, -en> *f* competence
zu|stecken *vt* ■ **jdm etw ~** to slip sb sth
zu|stehen *vi irreg* ❶ (*gehören*) ■ **etw steht jdm zu** sb is entitled to sth ❷ (*zukommen*) **es steht dir nicht zu, so über ihn zu reden** it's not for you to speak of him like that
zu|steigen *vi irreg sein* to get on; **noch jemand zugestiegen?** (*im Bus, Zug*) tickets

please!

zu|stellen *vt* ❶ (*form: überbringen*) ■ [**jdm**] **etw** ~ to deliver sth [to sb] ❷ (*fam: blockieren*) to block

Zustellung <-, -en> *f* delivery

zu|stimmen *vi* ■ [**jdm/einer S.** *dat*] ~ to agree [with sb/to sth]

zustimmend **I.** *adj* affirmative; **ein** ~**es Nicken** a nod of agreement **II.** *adv* in agreement

Zustimmung *f* agreement; (*Einwilligung*) consent

zu|stoßen *irreg* **I.** *vi sein* ■ **jdm** ~ to happen to sb **II.** *vt* **die Tür mit dem Fuß** ~ to kick the door shut

Zustrom *m kein pl* ❶ METEO inflow ❷ *von Menschen* influx, stream

zutage, zu Tage[RR] [tsu·ˈtaː·gə] *adj* **etw** ~ **bringen** to bring sth to light; ~ **treten** to come to light

Zutat <-, -en> [ˈtsuː·taːt] *f meist pl* ❶ (*Bestandteil*) ingredient ❷ (*benötigte Dinge*) necessaries *pl*

zu|teilen *vt* to allocate; **jdm eine Aufgabe/Rolle** ~ to assign a task/role to sb

Zuteilung *f* allocation; *von Mitarbeitern* assignment

zuteil|werden[RR] [tsu·ˈtail-] *vi* (*geh*) ■ **jdm wird etw zuteil** sb is given sth; ■ **jdm etw** ~ **lassen** to grant sb sth

zutiefst [tsu·ˈtiː·fst] *adv* deeply

zu|trauen *vt* **jdm viel Mut** ~ to believe sb has great courage; **sich** *dat* **nichts** ~ to have no self-confidence; **sich** *dat* **zu viel** ~ to take on too much; **das hätte ich dir nie zugetraut!** I never would have expected that from you!

Zutrauen <-s> *nt kein pl* confidence (**zu** +*dat* in)

zutraulich [ˈtsuː·trau·lɪç] *adj* trusting; *Hund* friendly

zu|treffen *vi irreg* ❶ (*richtig sein*) to be correct; (*wahr sein*) to be true ❷ (*anwendbar sein*) ■ **auf jdn** [**nicht**] ~ to [not] apply to sb; **genau auf jdn** ~ *Beschreibung* to fit sb['s description] perfectly

zutreffend **I.** *adj* ❶ (*richtig*) correct; **Z**~**es bitte ankreuzen** [please] check where applicable ❷ (*anwendbar*) **eine auf jdn** ~**e Beschreibung** a fitting description sb **II.** *adv* correctly

Zutritt *m kein pl* admission (**zu** +*dat* to); (*Zugang*) access; [**keinen**] ~ **zu etw** *dat* **haben** to [not] be admitted to sth; ~ **verboten!** [*o* **kein** ~**!**] no admittance

Zutun *nt* **ohne jds** ~ (*ohne jds Hilfe*) without sb's help; (*ohne jds Schuld*) through no fault of sb's own

zuverlässig [ˈtsuː·fɛɐ̯·lɛ·sɪç] *adj* reliable

Zuverlässigkeit <-> *f kein pl* reliability

Zuversicht <-> [ˈtsuː·fɛɐ̯·zɪçt] *f kein pl* confidence

zuversichtlich *adj* confident

zuvor [tsu·ˈfoːɐ̯] *adv* before; (*zunächst*) beforehand; **im Jahr** ~ the year before; **noch nie** ~ never before

zuvor|kommen *vi irreg sein* ❶ (*schneller handeln*) ■ **jdm** ~ to beat sb to it ❷ (*verhindern*) ■ **einer S.** *dat* ~ to forestall

zuvorkommend **I.** *adj* (*gefällig*) accommodating; (*höflich*) courteous **II.** *adv* (*gefällig*) obligingly; (*höflich*) courteously

Zuvorkommenheit <-> *f kein pl* courtesy

Zuwachs <-es, Zuwächse> [ˈtsuː·vaks, *pl* ˈtsuː·vɛk·sə] *m* increase

zu|wachsen *vi irreg sein* ❶ (*überwuchert werden*) to become overgrown ❷ *Wunde* to heal [over [*or* up]]

Zuwachsrate *f* growth rate

Zuwanderer, Zuwanderin *m, f* immigrant

zu|wandern *vi sein* to immigrate

Zuwanderung *f* immigration

zuwege, zu Wege[RR] [tsu·ˈveː·gə] *adv* **gut** ~ **sein** to be in good health; **etw** ~ **bringen** to achieve sth

zu|weisen *vt irreg* ■ **jdm etw** ~ *Aufgabe* to assign sth to sb

zu|wenden *irreg* **I.** *vt* **jdm das Gesicht/den Rücken** ~ to turn one's face toward/back on sb; **einer S.** *dat* **seine Aufmerksamkeit** ~ to turn one's attention to sth **II.** *vr* ■ **sich jdm/einer S.** ~ to devote oneself to sb/sth; **wollen wir uns dem nächsten Thema** ~**?** shall we go on to the next topic?

Zuwendung *f* ❶ *kein pl* (*intensive Hinwendung*) love and care ❷ (*Geld*) [financial] contribution

zuwider[1] [tsu·ˈviː·dɐ] *adv* ■ **jdm ist jd/etw** ~ sb finds sb/sth unpleasant; (*stärker*) sb loathes sb/sth

zuwider[2] [tsu·ˈviː·dɐ] *präp* ■ **einer S.** *dat* ~ contrary to sth; **allen Verboten** ~ in defiance of all bans

zu|winken *vi* ■ **jdm** ~ to wave to sb

zu|ziehen *irreg* **I.** *vt haben* ❶ *Schnur* to tighten ❷ *Gardinen* to draw; *Tür* to pull ❸ *Experten, Gutachter* to consult **II.** *vr haben* ❶ (*erleiden*) **sich** *dat* **eine Krankheit** ~ to catch a disease; **sich** *dat* **eine Verletzung** ~ to sustain an injury *form* ❷ (*einhandeln*) **sich** *dat* **jds Zorn** ~ to incur sb's wrath *form* ❸ (*sich eng zusammenziehen*) ■ **sich** ~ to tighten **III.** *vi sein* to move into the area

zuzüglich [ˈtsuː·tsyːg·lɪç] *präp* ■ ~ **einer S.** *gen* plus sth

zu|zwinkern *vi* ■ **jdm** ~ to wink at sb

zwang [tsvaŋ] *imp von* **zwingen**

Zwang <-[e]s, Zwänge> [tsvaŋ, *pl* ˈtsvɛ·ŋə] *m* ❶ (*Gewalt*) force; (*Druck*) pressure; **gesellschaftliche Zwänge** social constraints ❷ (*Notwendigkeit*) compulsion; **aus** ~ out of necessity

zwängen [ˈtsvɛŋ·ən] *vt* **Sachen in einen Koffer** ~ to cram things into a suitcase; **sich durch die Menge** ~ to force one's way through the crowd

zwanglos **I.** *adj* (*ungezwungen*) casual; (*ohne

Z

Förmlichkeit) informal **II.** *adv* (*ungezwungen*) casually; (*ohne Förmlichkeit*) informally
Zwangsarbeit *f kein pl* hard labor
Zwangseinweisung *f* compulsory hospitalization
Zwangsernährung *f* force-feeding *no indef art*
Zwangshandlung *f* compulsive act
Zwangsjacke *f* straitjacket
Zwangslage *f* predicament
zwangsläufig I. *adj* inevitable **II.** *adv* inevitably; **dazu musste es ja ~ kommen** it had to happen
Zwangsräumung *f* eviction
Zwangsversteigerung *f* foreclosure sale
Zwangsvorstellung *f* obsession
zwangsweise I. *adj* compulsory **II.** *adv* compulsorily
zwanzig ['tsvan·tsɪç] *adj* twenty; *s. a.* **achtzig 1, 2**
Zwanziger[1] <-s, -> ['tsvan·tsɪ·gɐ] *m* ❶ (*fam*) twenty-euro bill ❷ SCHWEIZ twenty-rappen coin
Zwanziger[2] ['tsvan·tsɪ·gɐ] *pl* ■ **die ~** the twenties; (*geschrieben a.*) the 20[']s; **in den ~n sein** to be in one's twenties
zwanzigjährig, 20-jährig[RR] ['tsvan·tsɪç·jɛː·rɪç] *adj* twenty-year-old *attr,* twenty years old *pred*
zwanzigste(r, s) ['tsvan·tsɪç·stə, -stɐ, -stəs] *adj* ❶ (*an zwanzigster Stelle*) twentieth; *s. a.* **achte(r, s) 1** ❷ (*Datum*) twentieth, 20th; *s. a.* **achte(r, s) 2**
zwar [tsvaːɐ̯] *adv* (*einschränkend*) **sie ist ~ 47, sieht aber wie 30 aus** she may be 47, but she looks like 30; **das mag ~ stimmen, aber ...** that may be true, but ...; ■ **und ~** namely
Zweck <-[e]s, -e> [tsvɛk] *m* ❶ (*Verwendungszweck*) purpose; **ein guter ~** a good cause ❷ (*Absicht*) aim; **seinen ~ verfehlen** to fail to achieve its/one's object; **zu welchem ~?** for what purpose? ❸ (*Sinn*) point; **das hat doch alles keinen ~!** there's no point in any of that ► WENDUNGEN: **der ~ heiligt die Mittel** (*prov*) the end justifies the means
Zwecke <-, -n> ['tsvɛ·kə] *f* DIAL (*Nagel*) nail; (*Reißzwecke*) thumbtack
zweckentfremden* *vt* to use for an unintended purpose
Zweckgemeinschaft *f* partnership of convenience
zwecklos *adj* futile
Zwecklosigkeit <-> *f kein pl* futility
zweckmäßig *adj* ❶ (*geeignet*) suitable ❷ (*sinnvoll*) appropriate
Zweckmäßigkeit <-, -en> *f* usefulness
zwecks [tsvɛks] *präp* (*geh*) ■ **~ einer S.** *gen* for the purpose of sth
zwei [tsvai] *adj* two; *s. a.* **acht**[1]
zweibändig *adj* two-volume *attr,* in two volumes *pred*
Zweibettzimmer *nt* double room
zweideutig ['tsvai·dɔy·tɪç] **I.** *adj* ambiguous; (*anrüchig*) suggestive **II.** *adv* ambiguously; (*anrüchig*) suggestively
Zweideutigkeit <-, -en> *f* ambiguity
zweidimensional I. *adj* two-dimensional **II.** *adv* in two dimensions
Zweidrittelmehrheit *f* two-thirds majority
zweieinhalb ['tsvai·ʔain·'halp] *adj* two-and-a-half
Zweierbeziehung *f* relationship
Zweieurostück *nt* two-euro coin
zweifach, 2fach ['tsvai·fax] **I.** *adj* **die ~e Menge** twice as much; **in ~er Ausfertigung** in duplicate **II.** *adv* **etw ~ ausfertigen** to issue sth in duplicate
Zweifamilienhaus [tsvai·fa·'miː·li̯ən·haus] *nt* two-family house
Zweifel <-s, -> ['tsvai·fl̩] *m* doubt; **da habe ich meine ~!** I'm not sure about that!; **jdm kommen ~** sb begins to doubt; **es steht außer ~, dass ...** it is beyond [all] doubt that ...
zweifelhaft *adj* ❶ (*anzuzweifeln*) doubtful ❷ (*pej*) dubious
zweifellos ['tsvai·fl̩·loːs] *adv* undoubtedly
zweifeln ['tsvai·fl̩n] *vi* ■ **an jdm/etw ~** to doubt sb/sth; ■ **[daran] ~, ob ...** to doubt whether ...
Zweifelsfall *m* ■ **im ~** if [*or* when] in doubt
Zweig <-[e]s, -e> [tsvaik] *m* ❶ (*Ast*) branch; (*kleiner*) twig ❷ (*Sparte*) branch ► WENDUNGEN: **auf keinen grünen ~ kommen** (*fam*) to get nowhere
zweigleisig ['tsvai·glai·zɪç] **I.** *adj* two-track *attr* **II.** *adv* ❶ on two tracks ❷ (*fig*) **~ fahren** to pursue a dual-track policy
Zweigniederlassung *f* subsidiary
Zweigstelle *f* branch office
zweihändig ['tsvai·hɛn·dɪç] *adj* two-handed
zweihundert ['tsvai·'hʊn·dɐt] *adj* two hundred
zweijährig, 2-jährig[RR] *adj* ❶ (*Alter*) two-year-old *attr,* two years old *pred; s. a.* **achtjährig 1** ❷ (*Zeitspanne*) two-year *attr,* two years *pred; s. a.* **achtjährig 2**
Zweikampf *m* duel
Zweiklassengesellschaft *f* SOZIOL, POL divided society
zweimal, 2-mal[RR] ['tsvai·maːl] *adv* twice, two times; **sich** *dat* **etw ~ überlegen** to think over *sep* sth carefully; *s. a.* **achtmal**
Zweirad *nt* (*Fahrrad*) bicycle; (*Motorrad*) motorcycle
zweireihig ['tsvai·rai·ɪç] *adj Anzug* double-breasted
zweischneidig ['tsvai·ʃnai·dɪç] *adj* two-edged ► WENDUNGEN: **ein ~es Schwert** a double-edged sword
zweiseitig *adj* two-page *attr;* **~ sein** to be two pages
zweisprachig ['tsvai·ʃpraː·xɪç] **I.** *adj* bilingual **II.** *adv* **~ erzogen sein** to be brought up speaking two languages
Zweisprachigkeit <-> *f kein pl* bilingualism form

Z

zweispurig *adj* two-lane *attr;* ■ **~ sein** to have two lanes
zweistellig *adj* two-digit *attr,* with two digits *pred*
zweistündig, **2-stündig**RR ['tsvai·ʃtʏn·dɪç] *adj* two-hour *attr,* lasting two hours *pred*
zweit [tsvait] *adv* **wir sind zu ~** there are two of us
zweitägig, **2-tägig**RR *adj* two-day *attr*
Zweitaktmotor *m* two-stroke engine
zweitausend ['tsvai·'tau·zn̩t] *adj* two thousand
zweitbeste(r, s) ['tsvait·'bɛs·tə, -'bɛs·tɐ, -'bɛs·təs] *adj* second best; ■ **Z~[r] werden** to finish second
zweite(r, s) ['tsvɛɪ·tə, 'tsvɛɪ·tɐ, 'tsvɛɪ·təs] *adj* ① *(hinsichtlich der Reihenfolge)* second, 2nd; **in der ~n Klasse sein** to be in second grade ② *(bei der Datumsangabe)* 2nd; **am ~n Mai** on May 2nd ③ *(hinsichtlich des Preises, des Prestiges)* second; **ein Fahrschein ~r Klasse** a second-class ticket; *s. a.* **achte(r, s) 2**
zweitens ['tsvai·tn̩s] *adv* secondly; *(bei Aufzählung a.)* second
zweitklassig *adj (pej)* second-rate
zweitrangig *adj s.* **zweitklassig**
Zweitschlüssel *m* duplicate key
Zweitstimme *f* second vote
Zweitürer *m* two-door [car]
Zweitwohnung *f* second home
Zwerchfell ['tsvɛr·çfɛl] *nt* diaphragm
Zwerg(in) <-[e]s, -e> [tsvɛrk, *pl* 'tsvɛr·gə] *m(f)* dwarf
Zwergwuchs *m* dwarfism
Zwetschge <-, -n> ['tsvɛtʃ·gə] *f* damson plum
Zwetschgenmus *nt* plum jam
Zwetschgenwasser *nt* plum brandy
Zwickel <-s, -> ['tsvɪ·kl̩] *m* MODE gusset
zwicken ['tsvɪ·kn̩] *vi, vt* to pinch
Zwickmühle *f* ▶ WENDUNGEN: **in der ~ sein** *(fam)* to be in a dilemma
Zwieback <-[e]s, -e *o* -bäcke> ['tsviː·bak, *pl* -bɛ·kə] *m* zwieback
Zwiebel <-, -n> ['tsviː·bl̩] *f* ① *(Gemüse)* onion ② *(Blumenzwiebel)* bulb
Zwiebelturm *m* cupola
Zwiegespräch *nt (geh)* tête-à-tête
Zwielicht ['tsviː·lɪçt] *nt kein pl* twilight
zwielichtig *adj (pej)* dubious
Zwiespalt ['tsviː·ʃpalt] *m kein pl (geh)* conflict
zwiespältig ['tsviː·ʃpɛl·tɪç] *adj* conflicting; *Charakter* ambivalent; *Gefühle* mixed
Zwietracht <-> ['tsviː·traxt] *f kein pl (geh)* discord
Zwilling <-s, -e> ['tsvɪ·lɪŋ] *m* ① *meist pl* twin ② *pl* ASTROL Gemini
Zwillingsbruder *m* twin brother
Zwillingspaar *nt* twins *pl*
Zwillingsschwester *f* twin sister
Zwinge <-, -n> ['tsvɪ·ŋə] *f* TECH [screw] clamp
zwingen <zwang, gezwungen> ['tsvɪ·ŋən] **I.** *vt* to force; ■ **gezwungen sein, etw zu tun** to be forced into doing [*or* to do] sth **II.** *vr* ■ **sich zu etw** *dat* **~** to force oneself to do sth
zwingend **I.** *adj* urgent; *Gründe* compelling **II.** *adv* **sich ~ ergeben** to follow conclusively
Zwinger <-s, -> ['tsvɪ·ŋɐ] *m* cage
zwinkern ['tsvɪŋ·kɐn] *vi* to blink; *mit einem Auge* to wink
Zwirn <-s, -e> [tsvɪrn] *m* thread
zwischen ['tsvɪ·ʃn̩] *präp* ① +*dat (räumlich: zwischen 2 Personen, Dingen)* between; *(zwischen mehreren: unter)* among[st] ② +*dat (zeitlich)* between ③ +*dat (Beziehung)* **~ dir und mir** between you and me
Zwischenaufenthalt *m* stopover
Zwischenbemerkung *f* interruption
Zwischenbericht *m* interim report
Zwischenbilanz *f* FIN interim balance
zwischendurch [tsvɪ·ʃn̩·'dʊrç] *adv* ① *zeitlich* in between times ② *örtlich* in between [them]
Zwischenfall *m* ① *(unerwartetes Ereignis)* incident ② *pl (Ausschreitungen)* serious incidents
Zwischenfrage *f* question [thrown in]
Zwischengröße *f* in-between size
Zwischenhändler(in) *m(f)* middleman
Zwischenlager *nt* temporary storage [facility]
zwischen|lagern *vt* to store [temporarily]
zwischenlanden *vi sein* to stop over
Zwischenlandung *f* stopover
zwischenmenschlich *adj* interpersonal
Zwischenprüfung *f* ≈ qualifying exams *npl*
Zwischenraum *m* ① *(Lücke)* gap ② *(zeitlicher Intervall)* interval
Zwischenruf *m* interruption; ■ **~e** heckling
Zwischenrunde *f* SPORT intermediate round
zwischenspeichern *vt* COMPUT to buffer
Zwischenstation *f* stop; **in einer Stadt ~ machen** to stop [off] in a town
Zwischenstück *nt* connecting [*or* middle] piece
Zwischenzeit *f* ■ **in der ~** [in the] meantime
zwischenzeitlich *adv* meanwhile
Zwischenzeugnis *nt (vorläufiges Schulzeugnis)* midterm report card
Zwist <-es, -e> [tsvɪst] *m (geh)* discord
zwitschern ['tsvɪt·ʃɐn] *vi, vt* to twitter, to chirp
Zwitter <-s, -> ['tsvɪ·tɐ] *m* hermaphrodite
zwo [tsvoː] *adj (fam)* two
zwölf [tsvœlf] *adj* twelve; *s. a.* **acht**[1]
Zwölffingerdarm [tsvœlf·'fɪŋɐ·darm] *m* duodenum
zwölfte(r, s) ['tsvœlf·tə, 'tsvœlf·tɐ, 'tsvœlf·təs] *adj attr* ① *(an zwölfter Stelle)* twelfth; *s. a.* **achte(r, s) 1** ② *(Datum)* twelfth, 12th; *s. a.* **achte(r, s) 2**
Zyankali <-s> [tsy̌·aːn·'kaː·li] *nt kein pl* potassium cyanide
zyklisch ['tsyː·klɪʃ] *adj* cyclical
Zyklon <-s, -e> [tsy·'kloːn] *m* cyclone
Zyklop <-en, -en> [tsy·'kloːp] *m* Cyclops
Zyklus <-, Zyklen> ['tsyː·klʊs, *pl* 'tsyː·klən] *m* cycle; *von Vorträgen* series
Zylinder <-s, -> [tsi·'lɪn·dɐ] *m* ① MATH, TECH cylinder ② *(Hut)* top hat

zylịnderförmig *adj s.* **zylindrisch**
Zylịnderkopf *m* cylinder head
zylindrisch [tsi·'lɪn·drɪʃ] *adj* cylindrical
Zyniker(in) <-s, -> ['tsyː·ni·kɐ] *m(f)* cynic
zynisch ['tsyː·nɪʃ] **I.** *adj* cynical **II.** *adv* cynically
Zypern ['tsyː·pɐn] *nt* Cyprus; *s. a.* **Deutschland**
Zypresse <-, -n> [tsy·'prɛ·sə] *f* cypress
Zyste <-, -n> ['tsʏs·tə] *f* cyst
z. Z(t). *Abk von* **zur Zeit** in sb's times

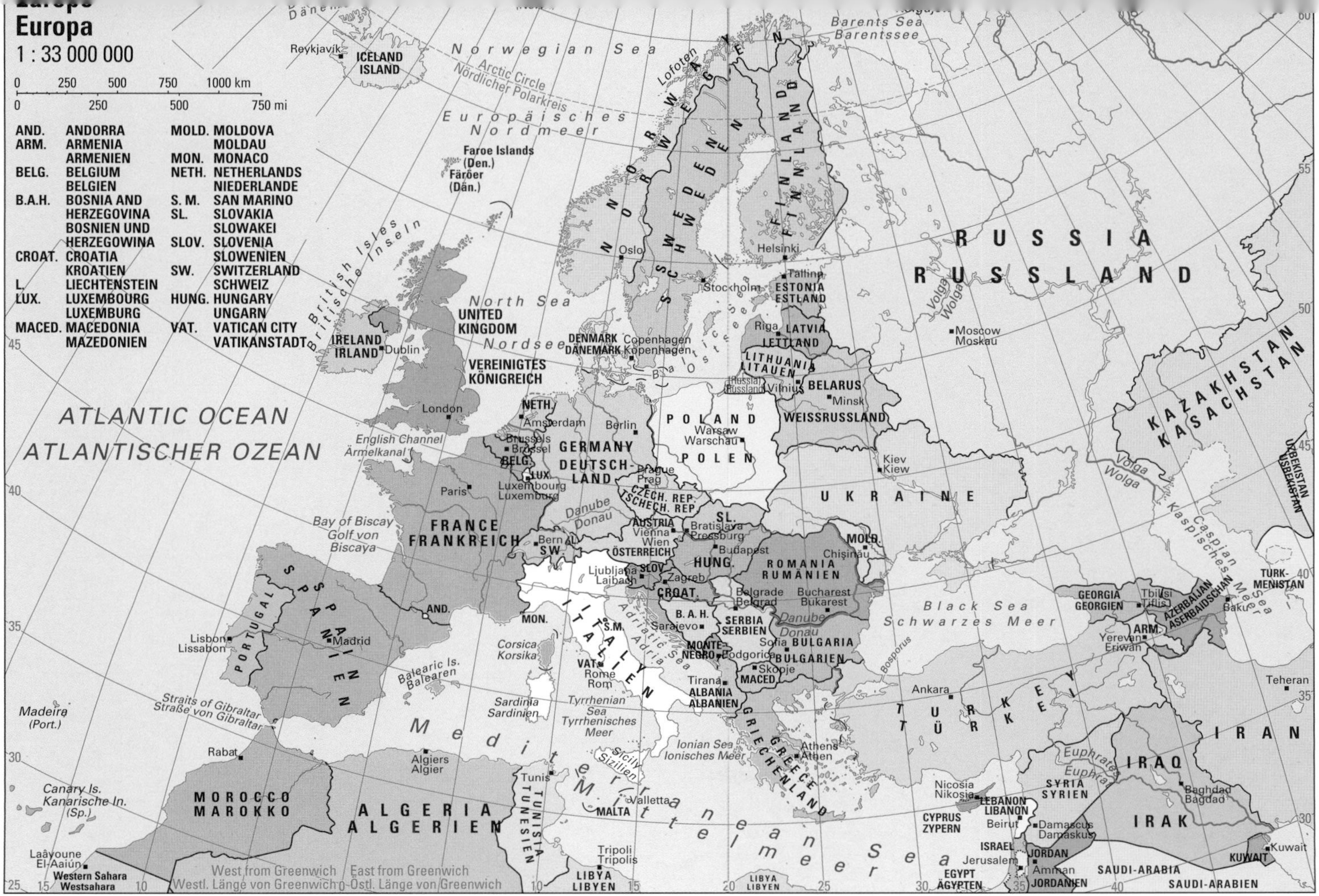

Europa
1 : 33 000 000
0 250 500 750 1000 km
0 250 500 750 mi
AND. ANDORRA
ARM. ARMENIA ARMENIEN
BELG. BELGIUM BELGIEN
B.A.H. BOSNIA AND HERZEGOVINA BOSNIEN UND HERZEGOWINA
CROAT. CROATIA KROATIEN
L. LIECHTENSTEIN
LUX. LUXEMBOURG LUXEMBURG
MACED. MACEDONIA MAZEDONIEN
MOLD. MOLDOVA MOLDAU
MON. MONACO
NETH. NETHERLANDS NIEDERLANDE
S. M. SAN MARINO
SL. SLOVAKIA SLOWAKEI
SLOV. SLOVENIA SLOWENIEN
SW. SWITZERLAND SCHWEIZ
HUNG. HUNGARY UNGARN
VAT. VATICAN CITY VATIKANSTADT
Norwegian Sea
Europäisches Nordmeer
Arctic Circle
Nördlicher Polarkreis
Barents Sea
Barentssee
Reykjavik
ICELAND
ISLAND
Faroe Islands (Den.)
Färöer (Dän.)
British Isles
Britische Inseln
North Sea
Nordsee
UNITED KINGDOM
VEREINIGTES KÖNIGREICH
IRELAND
IRLAND
Dublin
London
ATLANTIC OCEAN
ATLANTISCHER OZEAN
English Channel
Ärmelkanal
Bay of Biscay
Golf von Biscaya
Lofoten
NORWAY
NORWEGEN
SWEDEN
SCHWEDEN
FINLAND
FINNLAND
Oslo
Stockholm
Helsinki
Tallinn
ESTONIA
ESTLAND
Riga
LATVIA
LETTLAND
LITHUANIA
LITAUEN
Vilnius
Russia
Russland
BELARUS
WEISSRUSSLAND
Minsk
Baltic Sea
Ostsee
DENMARK
DÄNEMARK
Copenhagen
Kopenhagen
RUSSIA
RUSSLAND
Moscow
Moskau
Volga
Wolga
KAZAKHSTAN
KASACHSTAN
UZBEKISTAN
USBEKISTAN
NETH.
Amsterdam
Brussels
Brüssel
BELG.
LUX.
Luxembourg
Luxemburg
Berlin
GERMANY
DEUTSCHLAND
POLAND
POLEN
Warsaw
Warschau
Prague
Prag
CZECH. REP.
TSCHECH. REP.
Kiev
Kiew
UKRAINE
Paris
FRANCE
FRANKREICH
Danube
Donau
AUSTRIA
ÖSTERREICH
Vienna
Wien
Bratislava
Pressburg
SL.
Bern
SW.
Budapest
HUNG.
MOLD.
Chişinău
ROMANIA
RUMÄNIEN
Bucharest
Bukarest
Ljubljana
Laibach
SLOV.
Zagreb
CROAT.
Belgrade
Belgrad
B.A.H.
Sarajevo
SERBIA
SERBIEN
MONTE-NEGRO
Podgorica
Sofia
BULGARIA
BULGARIEN
Skopje
MACED.
Tirana
ALBANIA
ALBANIEN
ITALY
ITALIEN
S.M.
VAT.
Rome
Rom
MON.
AND.
Adriatic Sea
Adria
Corsica
Korsika
Sardinia
Sardinien
Tyrrhenian Sea
Tyrrhenisches Meer
Sicily
Sizilien
Valletta
MALTA
Ionian Sea
Ionisches Meer
GREECE
GRIECHENLAND
Athens
Athen
PORTUGAL
Lisbon
Lissabon
SPAIN
SPANIEN
Madrid
Balearic Is.
Balearen
Straits of Gibraltar
Straße von Gibraltar
Madeira (Port.)
Canary Is.
Kanarische In. (Sp.)
Rabat
MOROCCO
MAROKKO
Laâyoune
El-Aaiún
Western Sahara
Westsahara
Algiers
Algier
ALGERIA
ALGERIEN
Tunis
TUNISIA
TUNESIEN
Tripoli
Tripolis
LIBYA
LIBYEN
Mediterranean Sea
Mittelmeer
Black Sea
Schwarzes Meer
Bosporus
Ankara
TURKEY
TÜRKEI
GEORGIA
GEORGIEN
Tbilisi
Tiflis
AZERBAIJAN
ASERBAIDSCHAN
Baku
ARM.
Yerevan
Eriwan
Caspian Sea
Kaspisches Meer
TURKMENISTAN
Teheran
IRAN
IRAQ
IRAK
Baghdad
Bagdad
Euphrates
Euphrat
SYRIA
SYRIEN
Damascus
Damaskus
Nicosia
Nikosia
CYPRUS
ZYPERN
LEBANON
LIBANON
Beirut
ISRAEL
Jerusalem
JORDAN
JORDANIEN
Amman
EGYPT
ÄGYPTEN
SAUDI-ARABIA
SAUDI-ARABIEN
KUWAIT
Kuwait
West from Greenwich
Westl. Länge von Greenwich
East from Greenwich
Östl. Länge von Greenwich

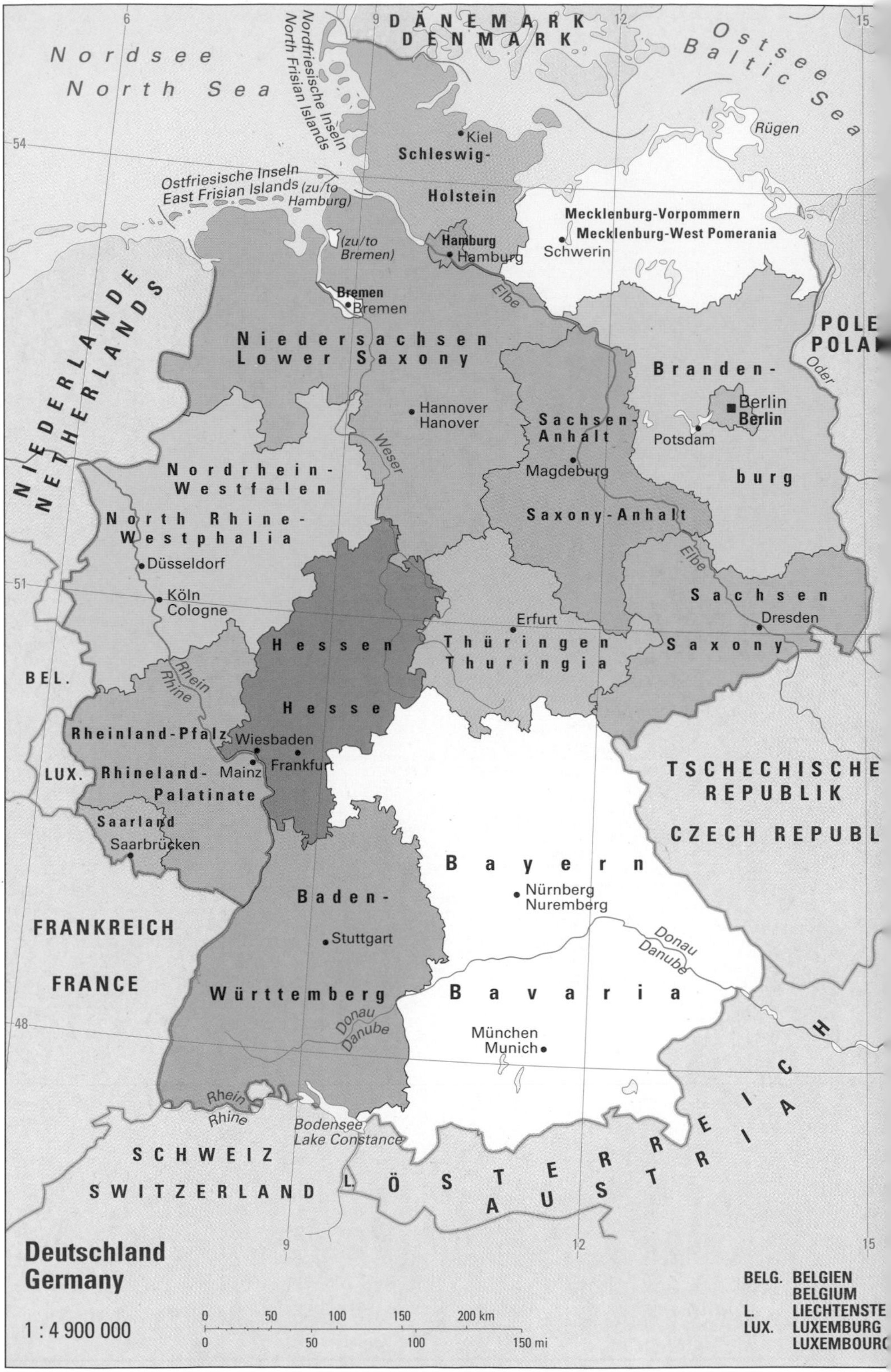
Nordsee
North Sea
DÄNEMARK
DENMARK
Ostsee
Baltic Sea
Nordfriesische Inseln
North Frisian Islands
Ostfriesische Inseln
East Frisian Islands (zu/to Hamburg)
Rügen
Kiel
Schleswig-Holstein
Hamburg
Hamburg
Mecklenburg-Vorpommern
Mecklenburg-West Pomerania
Schwerin
(zu/to Bremen)
Bremen
Bremen
Elbe
NIEDERLANDE
NETHERLANDS
Niedersachsen
Lower Saxony
POLE
POLA
Oder
Branden-burg
Berlin
Berlin
Potsdam
Hannover
Hanover
Sachsen-Anhalt
Saxony-Anhalt
Magdeburg
Weser
Nordrhein-Westfalen
North Rhine-Westphalia
Düsseldorf
Köln
Cologne
Sachsen
Saxony
Dresden
Erfurt
Hessen
Hesse
Thüringen
Thuringia
BEL.
Rhein
Rhine
Rheinland-Pfalz
Rhineland-Palatinate
Wiesbaden
Mainz
Frankfurt
LUX.
Saarland
Saarbrücken
TSCHECHISCHE REPUBLIK
CZECH REPUBL
Bayern
Bavaria
Nürnberg
Nuremberg
Baden-Württemberg
Stuttgart
FRANKREICH
FRANCE
Donau
Danube
München
Munich
Bodensee
Lake Constance
SCHWEIZ
SWITZERLAND
L.
ÖSTERREICH
AUSTRIA
Deutschland
Germany
1 : 4 900 000
0 50 100 150 200 km
0 50 100 150 mi
BELG. BELGIEN
BELGIUM
L. LIECHTENSTE
LUX. LUXEMBURG
LUXEMBOUR

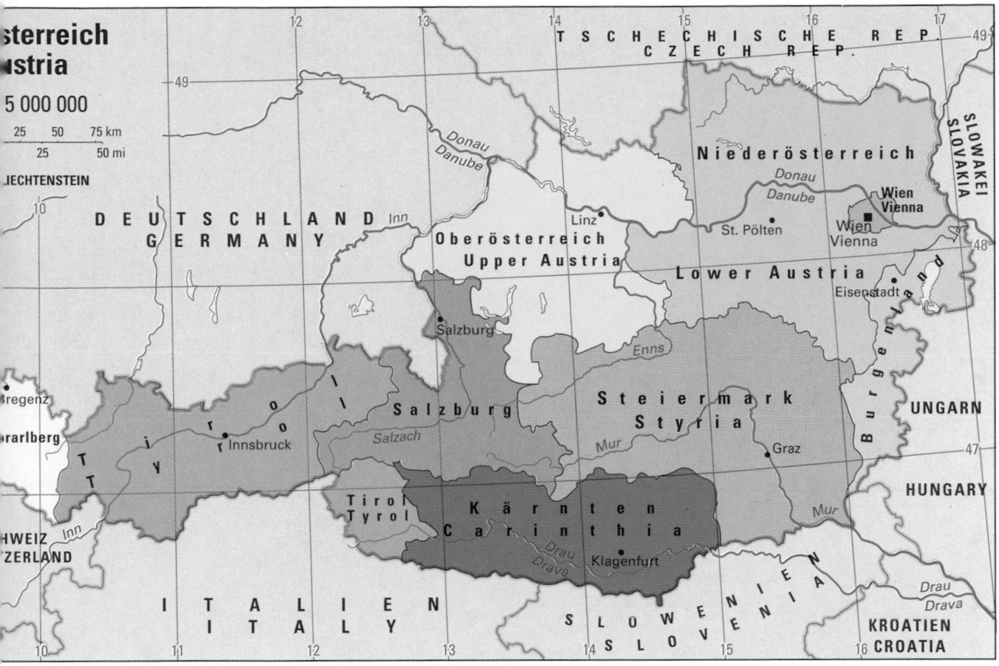
sterreich
ustria
5 000 000
25 50 75 km
25 50 mi
LIECHTENSTEIN
TSCHECHISCHE REP.
CZECH REP.
SLOWAKEI
SLOVAKIA
DEUTSCHLAND
GERMANY
Donau
Danube
Inn
Linz
Oberösterreich
Upper Austria
Niederösterreich
Lower Austria
St. Pölten
Wien
Vienna
Eisenstadt
Burgenland
Salzburg
Enns
Steiermark
Styria
UNGARN
HUNGARY
Bregenz
rarlberg
Tyrol
Tirol
Innsbruck
Salzach
Mur
Graz
Kärnten
Carinthia
Drau
Drava
Klagenfurt
HWEIZ
ZERLAND
ITALIEN
ITALY
SLOWENIEN
SLOVENIA
KROATIEN
CROATIA

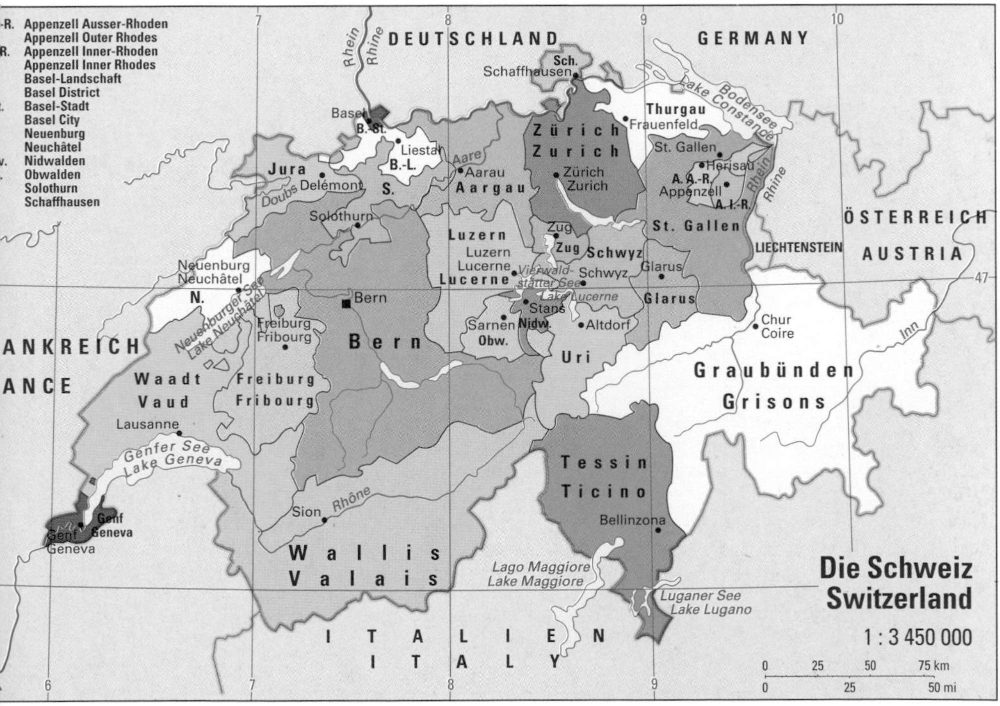
-R. Appenzell Ausser-Rhoden
Appenzell Outer Rhodes
R. Appenzell Inner-Rhoden
Appenzell Inner Rhodes
Basel-Landschaft
Basel District
Basel-Stadt
Basel City
Neuenburg
Neuchâtel
Nidwalden
Obwalden
Solothurn
Schaffhausen
Rhein
Rhine
DEUTSCHLAND
GERMANY
Sch.
Schaffhausen
Bodensee
Lake Constance
Basel
B.-St.
Liestal
B.-L.
Jura
Delémont
Doubs
S.
Aare
Aarau
Aargau
Zürich
Zurich
Thurgau
Frauenfeld
St. Gallen
Herisau
A.A.-R.
Appenzell
A.I.-R.
Solothurn
Luzern
Lucerne
Zug
Schwyz
Vierwaldstätter See
Lake Lucerne
Glarus
LIECHTENSTEIN
ÖSTERREICH
AUSTRIA
Neuenburg
Neuchâtel
N.
Neuenburger See
Lake Neuchâtel
Bern
Stans
Nidw.
Sarnen
Obw.
Altdorf
Uri
Chur
Coire
Inn
ANKREICH
ANCE
Freiburg
Fribourg
Waadt
Vaud
Graubünden
Grisons
Lausanne
Genfer See
Lake Geneva
Tessin
Ticino
Genf
Geneva
Sion
Rhône
Bellinzona
Wallis
Valais
Lago Maggiore
Lake Maggiore
Luganer See
Lake Lugano
ITALIEN
ITALY
Die Schweiz
Switzerland
1 : 3 450 000
0 25 50 75 km
0 25 50 mi

The English-Speaking World
Die englischsprachige Welt

1 : 94 500 000

0 1000 2000 3000 km

0 1000 2000 mi

Countries where English is the official language
Staaten, in denen Englisch die offizielle Landessprache ist

Countries where English is one of the official languages
Staaten, in denen Englisch eine der offiziellen Landesprachen ist

TSWANA
TSUANA
ish Virgin Islands
ische Jungferninseln (U. K.)
MEROON
MERUN
E GAMBIA
MBIA
raltar (U. K.)
m (USA)
thern Mariana Is.
rdliche Marianen (USA)

P. PAPUA NEW GUINEA
PAPUA NEUGUINEA
P. R. Puerto Rico (USA)
S. SINGAPORE
SINGAPUR
S. A. SOUTH AFRICA
SÜDAFRIKA
S. I. SOLOMON ISLANDS
SALOMONEN
S. L. SIERRA LEONE
ST K. ST KITTS AND NEVIS
ST. KITTS UND NEVIS

ST V. ST VINCENT AND THE GRENADINES
ST. VINCENT UND DIE GRENADINEN
U. UGANDA
U. A. E. UNITED ARAB EMIRATES
VEREINIGTE ARABISCHE EMIRATE
Z. ZAMBIA
SAMBIA
ZI. ZIMBABWE
SIMBABWE

Countries in the Pacific Ocean:
Staaten im Pazifischen Ozean:

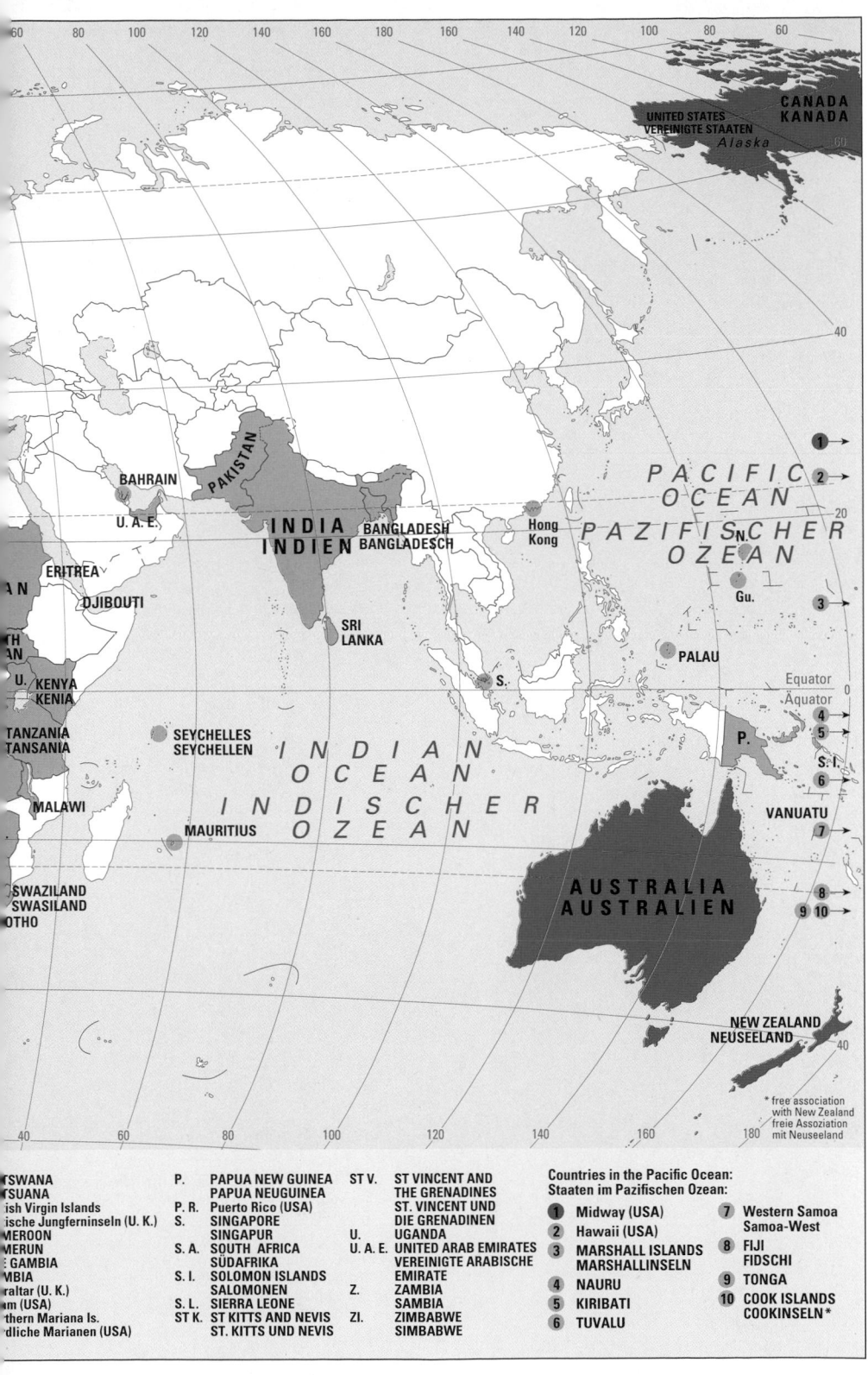

1. Midway (USA)
2. Hawaii (USA)
3. MARSHALL ISLANDS
MARSHALLINSELN
4. NAURU
5. KIRIBATI
6. TUVALU
7. Western Samoa
Samoa-West
8. FIJI
FIDSCHI
9. TONGA
10. COOK ISLANDS
COOKINSELN*

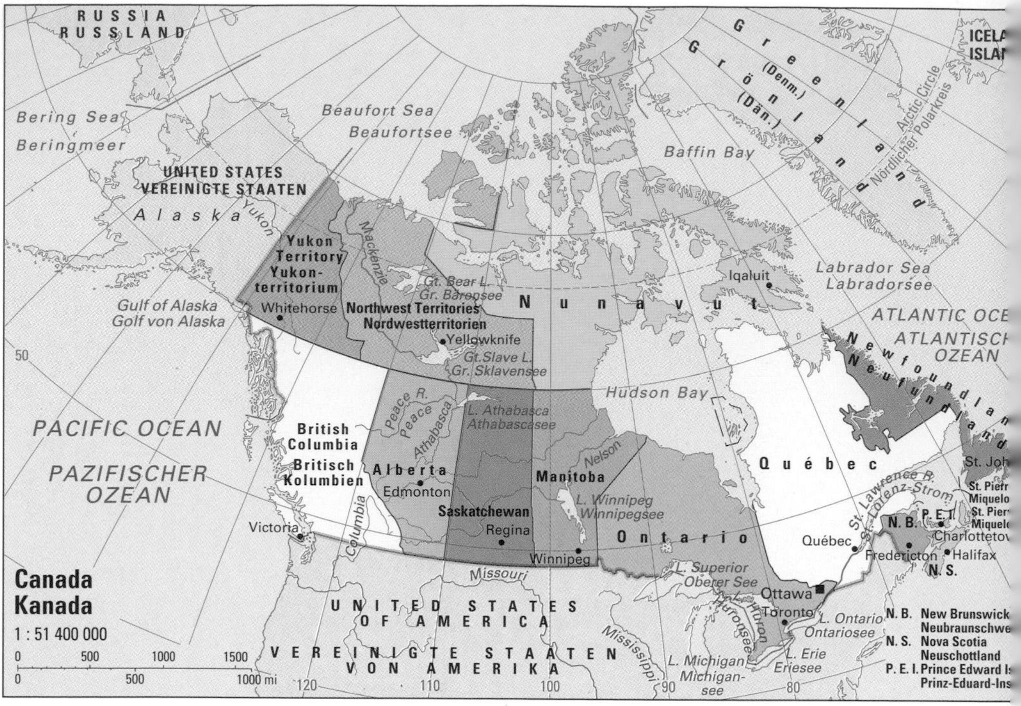
RUSSIA
RUSSLAND
Bering Sea
Beringmeer
UNITED STATES
VEREINIGTE STAATEN
Alaska
Yukon
Beaufort Sea
Beaufortsee
Greenland
Grönland
(Denm.)
(Dän.)
Baffin Bay
Arctic Circle
Nördlicher Polarkreis
ICELA
ISLA
Yukon Territory
Yukon-territorium
Mackenzie
Gt. Bear L.
Gr. Bärensee
Nunavut
Iqaluit
Labrador Sea
Labradorsee
Gulf of Alaska
Golf von Alaska
Whitehorse
Northwest Territories
Nordwestterritorien
Yellowknife
Gt. Slave L.
Gr. Sklavensee
ATLANTIC OCE
ATLANTISCH
OZEAN
Newfoundland
Neufundland
50
Hudson Bay
Peace R.
Peace
Athabasca
L. Athabasca
Athabascasee
PACIFIC OCEAN
British Columbia
Britisch Kolumbien
Alberta
Edmonton
Nelson
Manitoba
Québec
St. John
PAZIFISCHER OZEAN
L. Winnipeg
Winnipegsee
St. Lawrence R.
St.-Lorenz-Strom
St. Pierr
Miquelo
Saskatchewan
Victoria
Columbia
Regina
Ontario
N.B.
P.E.I.
Charlottetov
Québec
Fredericton
Halifax
N.S.
Winnipeg
L. Superior
Oberer See
Missouri
Canada
Kanada
1 : 51 400 000
0 500 1000 1500
0 500 1000 mi
UNITED STATES OF AMERICA
VEREINIGTE STAATEN VON AMERIKA
Ottawa
Toronto
Huronsee
L. Ontario
Ontariosee
L. Erie
Eriesee
L. Michigan
Michigansee
Mississippi
120 110 100 90 80
N.B. New Brunswick
Neubraunschwe
N.S. Nova Scotia
Neuschottland
P.E.I. Prince Edward Is
Prinz-Eduard-Ins

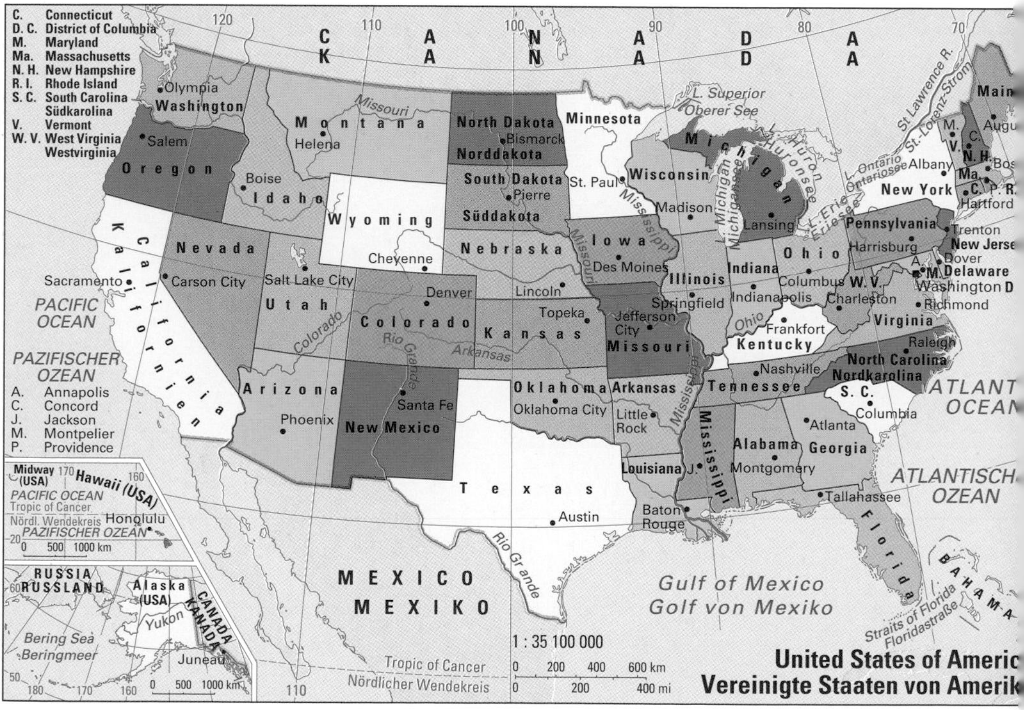
C. Connecticut
D.C. District of Columbia
M. Maryland
Ma. Massachusetts
N.H. New Hampshire
R.I. Rhode Island
S.C. South Carolina
Südkarolina
V. Vermont
W.V. West Virginia
Westvirginia
CANADA
KANADA
120 110 100 90 80 70
Olympia
Washington
Missouri
Montana
Helena
North Dakota
Bismarck
Norddakota
Minnesota
L. Superior
Oberer See
Michigan
L. Huron
Huronsee
St. Lawrence R.
St.-Lorenz-Strom
Maine
Augusta
Salem
Oregon
Boise
Idaho
South Dakota
Pierre
Süddakota
St. Paul
Wisconsin
Madison
Lansing
L. Michigan
Michigansee
L. Ontario
Ontariosee
Albany
New York
Boston
Hartford
P.
Wyoming
L. Erie
Eriesee
Pennsylvania
Harrisburg
Trenton
New Jersey
Dover
Delaware
Washington D.C.
California
Kalifornien
Nevada
Cheyenne
Nebraska
Iowa
Des Moines
Illinois
Indiana
Ohio
Columbus
W.V.
Charleston
Richmond
Virginia
Sacramento
Carson City
Salt Lake City
Utah
Denver
Colorado
Lincoln
Topeka
Kansas
Springfield
Jefferson City
Missouri
Indianapolis
Frankfort
Kentucky
Raleigh
North Carolina
Nordkarolina
PACIFIC OCEAN
PAZIFISCHER OZEAN
Colorado
Rio Grande
Arkansas
Arizona
Phoenix
Santa Fe
New Mexico
Oklahoma
Oklahoma City
Arkansas
Little Rock
Tennessee
Nashville
S.C.
Columbia
Mississippi
ATLANTIC OCEAN
Atlanta
Alabama
Georgia
Montgomery
A. Annapolis
C. Concord
J. Jackson
M. Montpelier
P. Providence
Texas
Louisiana
J.
Austin
Baton Rouge
Tallahassee
ATLANTISCHER OZEAN
Florida
Midway (USA)
Hawaii (USA)
PACIFIC OCEAN
Tropic of Cancer
Nördl. Wendekreis
Honolulu
PAZIFISCHER OZEAN
0 500 1000 km
MEXICO
MEXIKO
Rio Grande
Gulf of Mexico
Golf von Mexiko
BAHAMA
Straits of Florida
Floridastraße
RUSSIA
RUSSLAND
Alaska (USA)
CANADA
KANADA
Yukon
Bering Sea
Beringmeer
Juneau
0 500 1000 km
1 : 35 100 000
0 200 400 600 km
0 200 400 mi
Tropic of Cancer
Nördlicher Wendekreis
United States of America
Vereinigte Staaten von Amerika

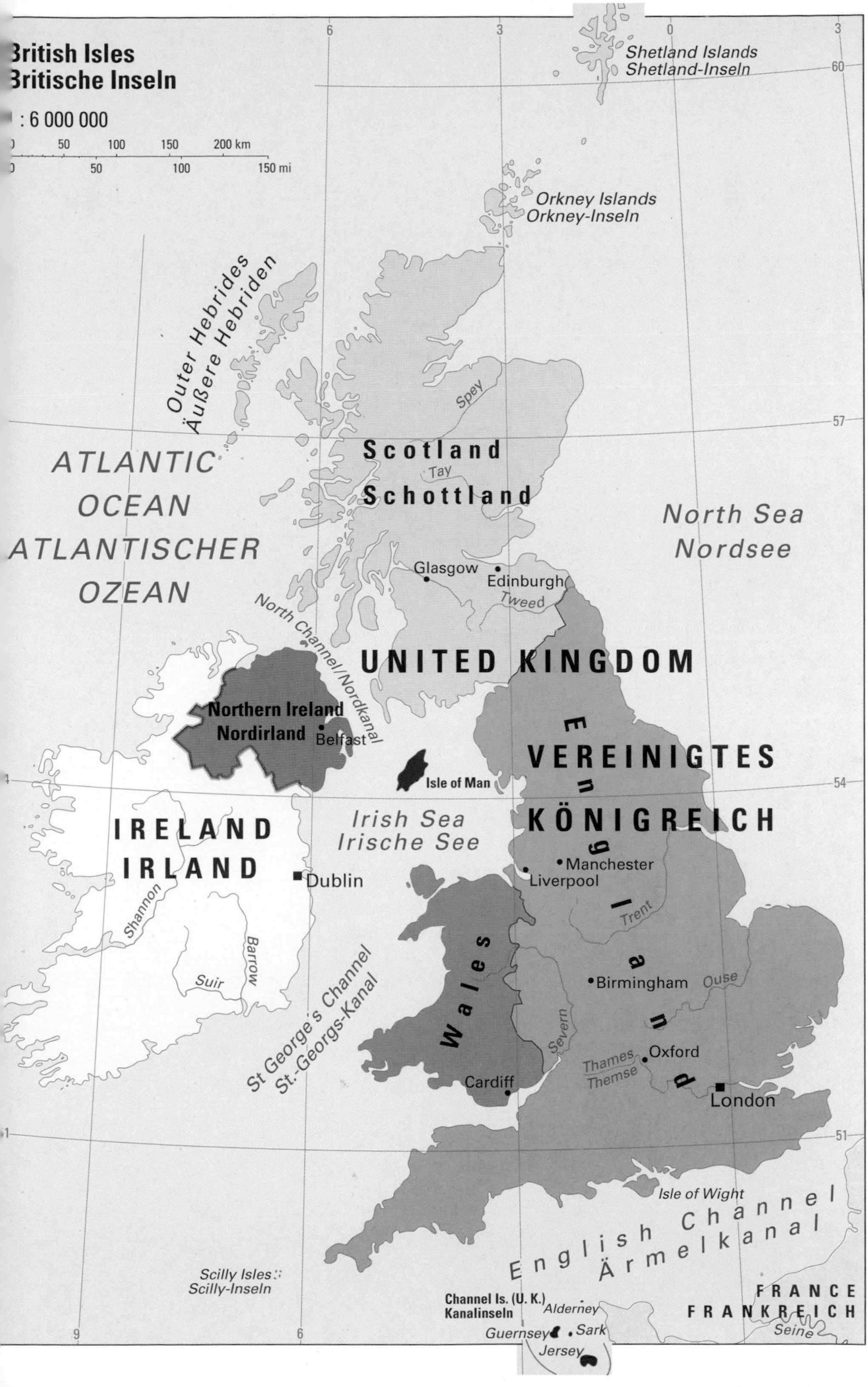

British Isles
Britische Inseln
1 : 6 000 000
0 50 100 150 200 km
0 50 100 150 mi
Shetland Islands
Shetland-Inseln
Orkney Islands
Orkney-Inseln
Outer Hebrides
Äußere Hebriden
Spey
ATLANTIC OCEAN
ATLANTISCHER OZEAN
Scotland
Schottland
Tay
North Sea
Nordsee
Glasgow
Edinburgh
Tweed
North Channel/Nordkanal
UNITED KINGDOM
Northern Ireland
Nordirland
Belfast
England
VEREINIGTES KÖNIGREICH
Isle of Man
IRELAND
IRLAND
Irish Sea
Irische See
Dublin
Manchester
Liverpool
Trent
Shannon
Barrow
Suir
Wales
Birmingham
Ouse
St George's Channel
St.-Georgs-Kanal
Severn
Oxford
Thames
Themse
Cardiff
London
Isle of Wight
English Channel
Ärmelkanal
Scilly Isles
Scilly-Inseln
Channel Is. (U. K.)
Kanalinseln
Alderney
Guernsey
Sark
Jersey
FRANCE
FRANKREICH
Seine

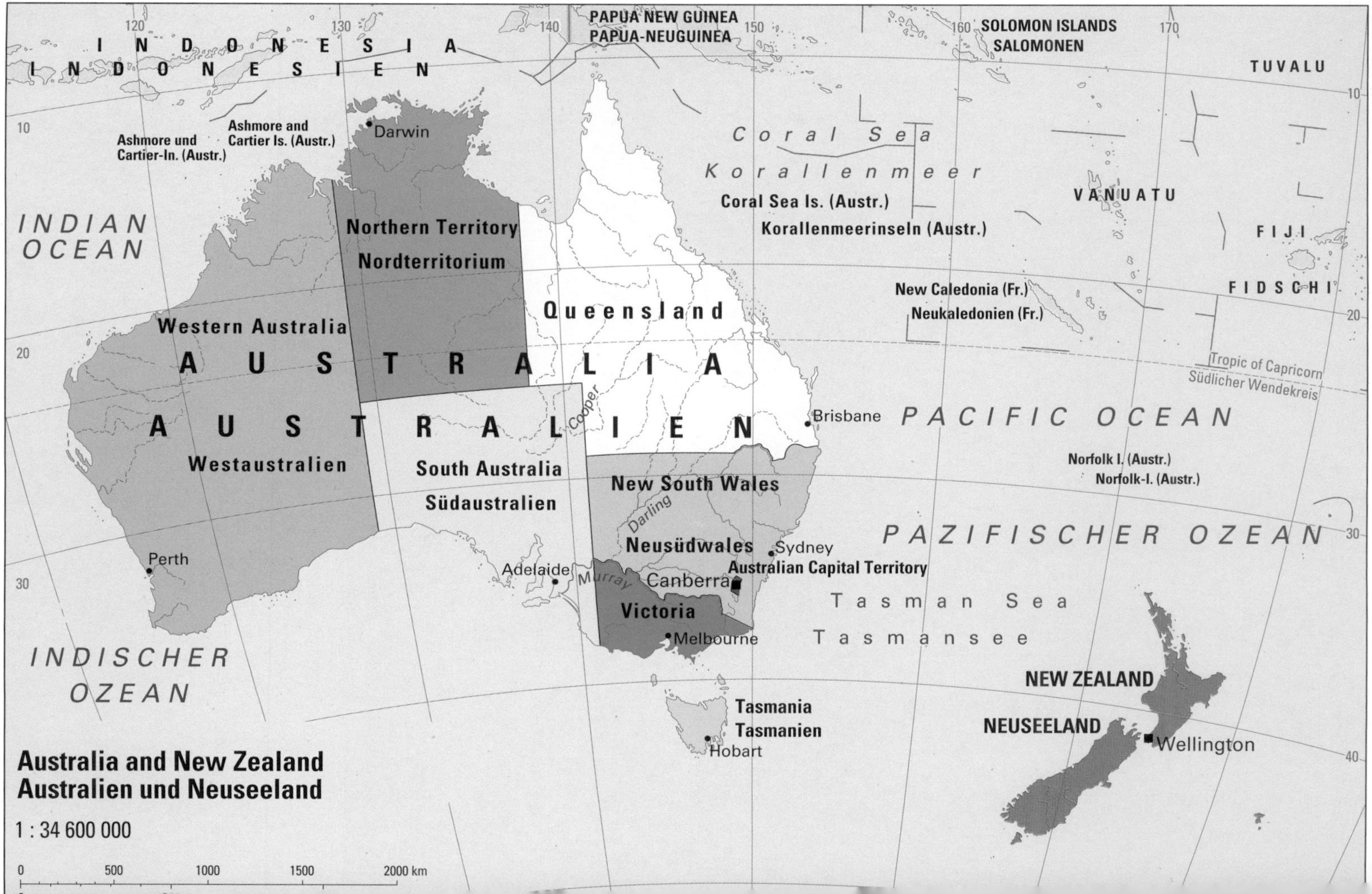
INDONESIA
INDONESIEN
PAPUA NEW GUINEA
PAPUA-NEUGUINEA
SOLOMON ISLANDS
SALOMONEN
TUVALU
Ashmore and Cartier Is. (Austr.)
Ashmore und Cartier-In. (Austr.)
Darwin
INDIAN OCEAN
Coral Sea
Korallenmeer
Coral Sea Is. (Austr.)
Korallenmeerinseln (Austr.)
VANUATU
FIJI
FIDSCHI
New Caledonia (Fr.)
Neukaledonien (Fr.)
Northern Territory
Nordterritorium
Queensland
Western Australia
AUSTRALIA
AUSTRALIEN
Westaustralien
South Australia
Südaustralien
Tropic of Capricorn
Südlicher Wendekreis
Cooper
Brisbane
PACIFIC OCEAN
Norfolk I. (Austr.)
Norfolk-I. (Austr.)
New South Wales
Darling
Neusüdwales
Sydney
Australian Capital Territory
Canberra
PAZIFISCHER OZEAN
Perth
Adelaide
Murray
Victoria
Melbourne
Tasman Sea
Tasmansee
INDISCHER OZEAN
NEW ZEALAND
NEUSEELAND
Wellington
Tasmania
Tasmanien
Hobart
0
500
1000
1500
2000 km

Australia and New Zealand
Australien und Neuseeland

1 : 34 600 000

Aa

A <*pl* -'s *or* -s>, **a** <*pl* -'s> [eɪ] *n* ❶ (*letter*) A *nt*, a *nt;* **~ as in Alpha** A wie Anton ❷ MUS A *nt*, a *nt;* **~ major** A-Dur *nt;* **~ minor** a-Moll *nt* ❸ (*school grade*) ≈ Eins *f;* **to get an ~** eine Eins schreiben

a [eɪ, ə], *before vowel* **an** [æn, ən] *art indef* ❶ (*undefined*) ein(e) ❷ *after neg* ■ **not ~** kein(e); **there was not ~ person to be seen** es war niemand zu sehen ❸ (*one*) ein(e); **can I have ~ knife and fork, please?** kann ich bitte Messer und Gabel haben?; **for half ~ mile** eine halbe Meile; **to count to ~ thousand** bis tausend zählen; **one and ~ half** eineinhalb ❹ *before profession, nationality* **she's ~ teacher** sie ist Lehrerin ❺ (*per*) **three times ~ day** dreimal täglich

aback [ə·'bæk] *adv* **to be taken ~** erstaunt sein; (*sad*) betroffen sein

abacus <*pl* -es> ['æb·ə·kəs] *n* MATH Abakus *m*

abandon [ə·'bæn·dən] **I.** *vt* ❶ (*leave*) verlassen; *baby* aussetzen; **to ~ sb to his/her fate** jdn seinem Schicksal überlassen ❷ (*leave behind*) zurücklassen; *car* stehen lassen ❸ (*give up*) aufgeben; *attempt* abbrechen; *plan* fallen lassen; *search* einstellen **II.** *n* **with ~** mit Leib und Seele

abandoned [ə·'bæn·dənd] *adj* ❶ (*discarded*) verlassen; *baby* ausgesetzt ❷ (*empty*) *building* leer stehend; *property* herrenlos

abashed [ə·'bæʃt] *adj* verlegen

abate [ə·'beɪt] *vi* (*form*) *rain* nachlassen; *storm, anger* abflauen; *pain, fever* abklingen

abattoir ['æb·ə·twar] *n* Schlachthof *m*

abbey ['æb·i] *n* Abtei[kirche] *f*

abbot ['æb·ət] *n* Abt *m*

abbreviate [ə·'bri·vi·eɪt] *vt* abkürzen; **Susan is often ~d to Sue** Susan wird oft mit Sue abgekürzt

abbreviation [ə·ˌbri·vɪ·'eɪ·ʃən] *n* Abkürzung *f*

ABC [ˌeɪ·bi·'si] *n* (*alphabet*) ABC *nt;* **as easy as ~** kinderleicht ▶ PHRASES: **the ~s of sth** das Einmaleins einer S. *gen*

abdicate ['æb·dɪ·keɪt] **I.** *vi monarch* abdanken **II.** *vt* **to ~ the throne** auf den Thron verzichten

abdication [ˌæb·dɪ·'keɪ·ʃən] *n* Abdankung *f*

abdomen ['æb·də·mən] *n* ❶ MED Unterleib *m* ❷ ZOOL Hinterleib *m*

abdominal [æb·'dam·ə·nəl] *adj* Unterleibs-; **~ wall** Bauchdecke *f*

abduction [æb·'dʌk·ʃən] *n* Entführung *f*

aberration [ˌæb·ə·'reɪ·ʃən] *n* (*deviation*) Abweichung *f*

abet <-tt-> [ə·'bet] *vt* unterstützen, Beihilfe leisten

abeyance [ə·'beɪ·əns] *n* **in ~** [vorübergehend] außer Kraft [gesetzt]

abhorrent [æb·'hɔr·ənt] *adj* abscheulich; **I find his cynicism ~** sein Zynismus ist mir zuwider

abide [ə·'baɪd] **I.** *vt* <abode *or* abided, abode *or* abided> *usu neg* (*not like*) ausstehen **II.** *vi* (*continue*) fortbestehen

◆ **abide by** *vt rules* befolgen; **to ~ by the law** sich an das Gesetz halten

abiding [ə·'baɪ·dɪŋ] *adj* beständig; *love* immer während; *values* bleibend

ability [ə·'bɪl·ɪ·t̬i] *n* ❶ (*capability*) Fähigkeit *f;* **to the best of my ~** so gut ich kann ❷ (*talent*) Talent *nt*

abject ['æb·dʒekt] *adj* ❶ (*extreme*) äußerste(r, s); *failure* komplett; *poverty* bitter ❷ (*humble*) unterwürfig; *apology a.* demütig; *failure* kläglich

ablaze [ə·'bleɪz] *adj* ❶ (*burning*) ■ **to be ~** in Flammen stehen ❷ (*bright*) **to be ~ with lights** hell erleuchtet sein ❸ (*fig: impassioned*) **to be ~ with anger** vor Zorn glühen

able ['eɪ·bəl] *adj* ❶ <more *or* better ~, most *or* best ~> (*can do*) ■ **to** [**not**] **be ~ to do sth** etw [nicht] tun können ❷ <abler *or* more ~, ablest *or* most ~> (*bright*) talentiert; *mind* fähig

able-bodied [ˌeɪ·bəl·'bad·ɪd] *adj* gesund; MIL [wehr]tauglich

ABM [eɪ·bi·'em] *n abbrev of* **antiballistic missile** Antiraketenrakete *f*

abnormal [æb·'nɔr·məl] *adj* anormal; *weather a.* ungewöhnlich

abnormality [ˌæb·nɔr·'mæl·ɪ·t̬i] *n* ❶ MED Anomalie *f* ❷ (*unusualness*) Abnormität *f; of a situation* Außergewöhnlichkeit *f*

aboard [ə·'bɔrd] *adv, prep* (*on plane, ship*) an Bord; (*on train*) im Zug; **all ~!** (*on train, bus*) alles einsteigen!; (*on plane, ship*) alle Mann an Bord!

abode [ə·'boʊd] *n* ❶ (*hum: home*) Wohnung *f* ❷ (*residence*) Wohnsitz *m;* **of no fixed ~** ohne festen Wohnsitz

abolish [ə·'bal·ɪʃ] *vt* abschaffen; *law* aufheben

abolition [æb·ə·'lɪʃ·ən] *n* Abschaffung *f; of a law* Aufhebung *f*

abominable [ə·'bam·ə·nə·bəl] *adj* furchtbar

abomination [ə·ˌbam·ə·'neɪ·ʃən] *n* ❶ (*loathing*) Abscheu *m* (**of** vor +*dat*) ❷ (*detestable thing*) Abscheulichkeit *f*

Aboriginal [ˌæb·ə·'rɪdʒ·ə·nəl] *adj* der Aborigines *nach n*

Aborigine [ˌæb·ə·'rɪdʒ·ə·ni] *n* Aborigine *m, f*

abort [ə·'bɔrt] *vt* ❶ (*prevent birth*) *baby, fetus* abtreiben; *pregnancy* abbrechen ❷ (*stop*) abbrechen

abortion [ə·'bɔr·ʃən] *n* Schwangerschaftsabbruch *m*, Abtreibung *f*

abortive [ə·'bɔr·t̬ɪv] *adj attempt* gescheitert; *plan* misslungen

abound [ə·'baʊnd] *vi* [sehr] zahlreich sein; **rumors ~ that ...** zahlreiche Gerüchte kursie-

A

ren, dass ...; ■ **to ~ in** reich sein an *+dat*

about [ə·ˈbaʊt] **I.** *prep* ❶ (*on the subject of*) über *+akk;* **anxiety ~ the future** Angst *f* vor der Zukunft; **what's that book ~?** worum geht es in dem Buch?; **to ask sb ~ sth/sb** jdn nach etw/jdm fragen ❷ (*affecting*) gegen *+akk;* **to do something ~ sth** etw gegen etw machen ❸ (*surrounding*) um *+akk* ❹ *after vb* (*expressing movement*) **to wander ~ the house** im Haus herumlaufen ▶ PHRASES: **how ~ sb/sth?** wie wäre es mit jdm/etw?; **what ~ it?** was ist damit? **II.** *adv* ❶ (*approximately*) ungefähr; **~ eight [o'clock]** [so] gegen acht [Uhr]; **~ two days ago** vor etwa zwei Tagen ❷ (*almost*) fast ❸ (*barely*) **we just ~ made it** wir haben es gerade noch [so] geschafft ❹ (*intending*) **we're just ~ to have supper** wir wollen gerade zu Abend essen ▶ PHRASES: **that's ~ all** [*or* **it**] das wär's

about-ˈface *n* ❶ *esp* MIL Kehrtwendung *f* ❷ (*fig*) **they've done a complete ~** sie haben ihre Meinung um 180° geändert

above [ə·ˈbʌv] **I.** *prep* ❶ (*over*) über *+dat;* **~ the spectators** über den Zuschauern ❷ (*greater than*) über *+akk;* **to be barely ~ freezing** kaum über dem Gefrierpunkt sein; **to be ~ and beyond all expectation[s]** weit über allen Erwartungen *dat* liegen ❸ (*more importantly than*) **they value freedom ~ all else** für sie ist die Freiheit wichtiger als alles andere; **~ all** vor allem ▶ PHRASES: **that's ~ me** das ist mir zu hoch **II.** *adv* ❶ (*on higher level*) oberhalb, darüber; **they live in the apartment ~** sie wohnen in der Wohnung darüber; (*above oneself*) sie wohnen in der Wohnung über mir/uns ❷ (*overhead*) **from ~** von oben ❸ (*in the sky*) am Himmel; **he looked up to the stars ~** er blickte hinauf zu den Sternen ❹ (*earlier in text*) oben; **the address given ~** die oben genannte Adresse **III.** *adj* obige(r, s); **the ~ address** die oben genannte Adresse **IV.** *n* ■ **the ~** (*thing*) das Obengenannte; (*person*) der/die Obengenannte

aboveˈboard *adj* (*fam*) einwandfrei

aboveˈmentioned *adj* oben genannte(r, s)

abracadabra [ˌæb·rə·kə·ˈdæb·rə] *interj* (*fam*) Simsalabim!

abrasion [ə·ˈbreɪ·ʒən] *n* (*injury*) Abschürfung *f*

abrasive [ə·ˈbreɪ·sɪv] **I.** *adj* ❶ (*rubbing*) abreibend; **~ cleaner** Scheuermittel *nt* ❷ (*unpleasant*) aggressiv **II.** *n* MECH Schleifmittel *nt*

abreast [ə·ˈbrest] *adv* ❶ (*side by side*) nebeneinander ❷ (*up to date*) **to keep ~ of sth** sich über etw *akk* auf dem Laufenden halten; **to keep sb ~ of sth** jdn über etw *akk* auf dem Laufenden halten

abridge [ə·ˈbrɪdʒ] *vt* kürzen

abroad [ə·ˈbrɔd] *adv* (*in foreign country*) im Ausland; **to go ~** ins Ausland fahren; **from ~** aus dem Ausland

abrupt [ə·ˈbrʌpt] *adj* ❶ (*sudden*) abrupt; *departure* plötzlich; **to come to an ~ end** ein jähes Ende finden ❷ (*brusque*) schroff

ABS [ˌeɪ·bi·ˈes] *n abbrev of* **antilock braking system** ABS *nt*

abs [æbs] *n* ANAT (*fam*) *pl short for* **abductors** Abduktionsmuskeln *pl*

abscess <*pl* -es> [ˈæb·ses] *n* Abszess *m*

abscond [əb·ˈskand] *vi* (*form: run away*) sich davonmachen; ■ **to ~ with sb** mit jdm durchbrennen *fam*

absence [ˈæb·səns] *n* ❶ (*nonappearance*) Abwesenheit *f;* (*from school, work*) Fehlen *nt* ❷ (*lack*) Fehlen *nt;* ■ **in the ~ of sth** in Ermangelung einer S. *gen* ▶ PHRASES: **~ makes the heart grow fonder** (*prov*) die Liebe wächst mit der Entfernung

absent **I.** *adj* [ˈæb·sənt] ❶ (*not there*) abwesend; **to be ~ from work/school** auf der Arbeit/in der Schule fehlen ❷ (*lacking*) ■ **to be ~** fehlen **II.** *vt* [əb·ˈsent] ■ **to ~ oneself** sich zurückziehen

absentee [ˌæb·sən·ˈti] *n* Abwesende(r) *f(m),* Fehlende(r) *f(m)*

absenteeism [ˌæb·sən·ˈti·ɪz·əm] *n* häufiges Fernbleiben

absent-ˈminded *adj* (*momentarily*) geistesabwesend; (*habitually*) zerstreut

absent-mindedness *n* (*momentary*) Geistesabwesenheit *f;* (*habitual*) Zerstreutheit *f*

absolute [ˈæb·sə·lut] *adj* ❶ absolut ❷ *angel* wahr; *disaster, mess* einzig; *idiot* ausgemacht; *nonsense* komplett; *ruler* unumschränkt; **in ~ terms** absolut gesehen

absolutely [ˌæb·sə·ˈlut·li] *adv* absolut; **you're ~ right** Sie haben vollkommen Recht; **~ not!** nein, überhaupt nicht!; **~ delicious** einfach köstlich; **~ nothing** überhaupt nichts; **to trust sb ~** jdm bedingungslos vertrauen

absolve [əb·ˈzalv] *vt from blame* freisprechen; *from sins* lossprechen

absorb [əb·ˈsɔrb] *vt* ❶ (*soak up*) aufnehmen; *attention* in Anspruch nehmen ❷ (*reduce*) *blow* abfangen; *light* absorbieren; *noise* dämpfen ❸ ■ **to be ~ed in sth** in etw *akk* vertieft sein

absorbent [əb·ˈsɔr·bənt] *adj* absorptionsfähig; *cotton, paper* saugfähig

absorbing [əb·ˈsɔr·bɪŋ] *adj* fesselnd; *problem* kniffelig

absorption [əb·ˈsɔrp·ʃən] *n* ❶ (*absorbing*) Aufnahme *f* ❷ (*engrossment*) Vertieftsein *nt*

abstain [əb·ˈsteɪn] *vi* ❶ (*eschew*) ■ **to ~ [from sth]** sich [einer S. *gen*] enthalten ❷ (*not vote*) sich der Stimme enthalten

abstention [əb·ˈsten·ʃən] *n* POL [Stimm]enthaltung *f*

abstinence [ˈæb·stə·nəns] *n* Abstinenz *f*

abstract **I.** *adj* [ˈæb·strækt] abstrakt; **~ noun** Abstraktum *nt* **II.** *n* ❶ (*summary*) Zusammenfassung *f* ❷ (*generalized form*) ■ **the ~** das Abstrakte; **in the ~** abstrakt **III.** *vt* [æb·ˈstrækt] (*summarize*) zusammenfassen

abstraction [əb·ˈstræk·ʃən] *n* ❶ (*generalization*) Abstraktion *f* ❷ (*distraction*) [Geistes|abwesenheit *f*

absurd [əb·ˈsɜrd] *adj* absurd; **don't be ~!** sei nicht albern!; **to look ~** lächerlich aussehen

absurdity [əb·ˈsɜr·dɪ·t̬i] *n* Absurdität *f*

abundance [ə·ˈbʌn·dəns] *n* Fülle *f;* **to have an ~ of sth** reich an etw *dat* sein; **in ~** in Hülle und Fülle

abundant [ə·ˈbʌn·dənt] *adj* reichlich; *harvest* reich; *vegetation* üppig

abuse I. *n* [ə·ˈbjus] ① (*affront*) [**verbal**] ~ Beschimpfung[en] *f*[*pl*]; **a term of ~** ein Schimpfwort *nt* ② (*mistreatment*) Missbrauch *m;* **child ~** Kindesmissbrauch *m* ③ (*misuse*) Missbrauch *m;* **drug ~** Drogenmissbrauch *m* **II.** *vt* [ə·ˈbjuz] ① (*verbally*) beschimpfen ② (*maltreat*) missbrauchen, misshandeln ③ (*exploit*) *authority, trust* missbrauchen; *kindness* ausnützen

abusive [ə·ˈbju·sɪv] *adj* ① (*insulting*) beleidigend; **~ language** Beleidigungen *pl* ② (*mistreating*) misshandelnd

abysmal [ə·ˈbɪz·məl] *adj* entsetzlich

abyss [ə·ˈbɪs] *n* (*a. fig*) Abgrund *m*

AC [ˌeɪ·ˈsi] *n* ① *abbrev of* **air conditioning** ② *abbrev of* **alternating current** WS

academic [ˌæk·ə·ˈdem·ɪk] **I.** *adj* akademisch; **~ year** Studienjahr *nt* **II.** *n* Lehrkraft *f* an der Universität

academy [ə·ˈkæd·ə·mi] *n* ① Akademie *f* ② (*school*) [höhere] Schule

accede [æk·ˈsid] *vi* ① (*agree*) ■ **to ~ to sth** etw *dat* zustimmen; *demands* nachgeben ② (*assume*) übernehmen; **to ~ to the throne** den Thron besteigen

accelerate [ək·ˈsel·ə·reɪt] **I.** *vi* ① (*go faster*) beschleunigen; *driver* Gas geben *fam* ② (*increase*) zunehmen **II.** *vt* beschleunigen

acceleration [ək·ˌsel·ə·ˈreɪ·ʃən] *n* Beschleunigung *f*

accelerator [ək·ˈsel·ə·reɪ·t̬ər] *n* (*in car*) Gas[pedal] *nt*

accent [ˈæk·sent] *n* ① LING Akzent *m* ② (*stress*) Betonung *f;* **to put the ~ on sth** etw in den Mittelpunkt stellen

accentuate [ək·ˈsen·tʃʊ·eɪt] *vt* ① betonen ② MUS, LING akzentuieren

accept [ək·ˈsept] *vt* ① (*take*) annehmen; *award* entgegennehmen; *bribe* sich bestechen lassen; **do you ~ credit cards?** kann man bei Ihnen mit Kreditkarte zahlen? ② (*believe*) glauben ③ (*acknowledge*) anerkennen; *blame* auf sich *akk* nehmen; *decision* akzeptieren; *fate* sich abfinden mit +*dat; responsibility* übernehmen; ■ **to ~** [**that**] ... akzeptieren, dass ...

acceptable [ək·ˈsep·tə·bəl] *adj* ① (*satisfactory*) akzeptabel (**to** für +*akk*) ② (*welcome*) willkommen

acceptance [ək·ˈsep·təns] *n* ① (*accepting*) Annahme *f; of idea* Zustimmung *f* ② (*positive answer*) Zusage *f;* **letter of ~** schriftliche Zusage ③ (*recognition*) Anerkennung *f*

accepted [ək·ˈsep·tɪd] *adj* anerkannt

access [ˈæk·ses] **I.** *n* Zugang *m;* (*to room, building*) Zutritt *m;* **the only ~ to the village is by boat** das Dorf ist nur mit dem Boot zu erreichen; **~ to information** Zugriff *m* auf Informationen **II.** *vt* COMPUT *data* zugreifen auf +*akk; file* öffnen

accessibility [æk·ˌses·ə·ˈbɪl·ɪ·t̬i] *n* Zugänglichkeit *f*

accessible [ək·ˈses·ə·bəl] *adj* ① (*approachable*) [leicht] erreichbar ② ■ **to be ~ to sb** jdm zugänglich sein

accession [æk·ˈseʃ·ən] *n* Antritt *m;* **~ to the throne** Thronbesteigung *f*

accessory [ək·ˈses·ə·ri] *n* ① FASHION Accessoire *nt* ② (*equipment*) Zubehör *nt* ③ (*criminal*) Helfershelfer(in) *m(f);* **he became an ~ to the crime** er machte sich am Verbrechen mitschuldig

accident [ˈæk·sɪ·dənt] *n* ① (*with injury*) Unfall *m;* **car ~** Verkehrsunfall *m* ② (*chance*) Zufall *m;* **by ~** zufällig ③ (*mishap*) Missgeschick *nt;* **by ~** aus Versehen ▶ PHRASES: **~s will happen** so was kommt vor

accidental [ˌæk·sɪ·ˈden·təl] *adj* ① (*unintentional*) unbeabsichtigt; **it was ~** es war ein Versehen ② (*chance*) zufällig

acclaim [ə·ˈkleɪm] **I.** *vt* ■ **to be ~ed** gefeiert werden **II.** *n* Anerkennung *f*

acclimate [ˈə·klaɪ·mɪt] *vt, vi* sich akklimatisieren (**to** an +*akk*); *to new conditions* sich gewöhnen

acclimation [ˌæk·lə·ˈmeɪ·ʃən], **acclimatization** [ə·ˌklaɪ·mə·t̬ɪ·ˈzeɪ·ʃən] *n* Akklimatisation *f;* **~ to a new environment** Eingewöhnung *f* in eine neue Umgebung

acclimatize [ə·ˈklaɪ·mə·taɪz] *vi, vt see* **acclimate**

accommodate [ə·ˈkam·ə·deɪt] *vt* (*have room for*) unterbringen; **the cabin ~s up to 6 people** die Hütte bietet Platz für bis zu 6 Personen

accommodating [ə·ˈkam·ə·deɪ·t̬ɪŋ] *adj* entgegenkommend

accommodation [ə·ˌkam·ə·ˈdeɪ·ʃən] *n* ① (*lodging*) ■ **~s** *pl* Unterkunft *f* ② (*compromise*) Einigung *f*

accompaniment [ə·ˈkʌm·pə·nɪ·mənt] *n* Begleitung *f;* **to be the perfect ~ to ...** ideal passen zu ...; **to the ~ of** begleitet von +*dat*

accompanist [ə·ˈkʌm·pə·nɪst] *n* MUS Begleiter(in) *m(f)*

accompany <-ie-> [ə·ˈkʌm·pə·ni] *vt* ① begleiten ② (*occur together*) ■ **to be accompanied by sth** mit etw *dat* einhergehen

accomplice [ə·ˈkam·plɪs] *n* Komplize *m,* Komplizin *f*

accomplish [ə·ˈkam·plɪʃ] *vt* schaffen; *goal* erreichen; *task* erledigen

accomplished [ə·ˈkam·plɪʃt] *adj* fähig; *actor* versiert; *performance* gelungen

accomplishment [ə·ˈkam·plɪʃ·mənt] *n* ① (*completion*) Vollendung *f; of a goal* Erreichen *nt; of a task* [erfolgreiche] Beendigung ② *usu pl* (*skill*) Fähigkeit *f* ③ (*achievement*)

Leistung *f*

accord [ə·ˈkɔrd] **I.** *n* ① (*treaty*) Vereinbarung *f* ② (*agreement*) Übereinstimmung *f* ▶ PHRASES: **of one's/its own ~** (*voluntarily*) von sich *dat* aus; (*without external cause*) von alleine **II.** *vt* gewähren

accordance [ə·ˈkɔr·dəns] *prep* **in ~ with** gemäß +*dat*

accordingly [ə·ˈkɔr·dɪŋ·li] *adv* ① (*appropriately*) [dem]entsprechend ② (*thus*) folglich

according to [ə·ˈkɔr·dɪŋ·tə] *prep* nach +*dat;* **~ the weather report** dem Wetterbericht zufolge

accordion [ə·ˈkɔr·di·ən] *n* Akkordeon *nt*

accost [ə·ˈkɔst] *vt* ansprechen; (*more aggressively*) anpöbeln

account [ə·ˈkaʊnt] *n* ① (*description*) Bericht *m;* **by** [*or* **from**] **all ~s** nach allem, was man so hört; **by his own ~** eigenen Aussagen zufolge ② (*bank service*) Konto *nt* (**with** bei +*dat*) ③ (*bill*) Rechnung *f* ④ (*records*) ■ **~s** *pl* [Geschäfts]bücher *pl;* **to keep the ~s** die Buchhaltung machen ⑤ (*consideration*) **to take into ~** berücksichtigen ⑥ (*reason*) ■ **on ~ of** aufgrund +*gen;* **on my ~** meinetwegen; **on no ~** auf keinen Fall ⑦ (*importance*) **to be of no ~** keinerlei Bedeutung haben ▶ PHRASES: **to be brought to ~** zur Rechenschaft gezogen werden; **to settle ~s with sb** mit jdm abrechnen

◆**account for** *vt* ① (*explain*) erklären; **there's no ~ing for taste**[**s**] über Geschmack lässt sich streiten ② (*represent*) ausmachen

accountability [ə·ˌkaʊn·tə·ˈbɪl·ɪ·t̬i] *n* Verantwortlichkeit *f* (**to** gegenüber +*dat,* **for** für +*akk*)

accountable [ə·ˈkaʊn·tə·bəl] *adj* verantwortlich

accountant [ə·ˈkaʊn·tənt] *n* [Bilanz]buchhalter(in) *m(f)*

accounting [ə·ˈkaʊn·t̬ɪŋ] *n* Buchhaltung *f*

accredit [ə·ˈkred·ɪt] *vt* ① (*approve*) ■ **to have been ~ed** *degree, school* anerkannt worden sein ② (*authorize*) ■ **to be ~ed to sb/sth** *ambassador* bei jdm/etw akkreditiert sein

acct. *n abbrev of* **account** Kto.

accumulate [ə·ˈkjum·jə·leɪt] *vt, vi* [sich] ansammeln

accumulation [ə·ˌkjum·jə·ˈleɪ·ʃən] *n* (*quantity*) Ansammlung *f; of sand* Anhäufung *f*

accuracy [ˈæk·jər·ə·si] *n* Genauigkeit *f*

accurate [ˈæk·jər·ɪt] *adj* ① (*precise*) genau ② (*correct*) richtig; *report* getreu

accusation [ˌæk·ju·ˈzeɪ·ʃən] *n* ① (*charge*) Anschuldigung *f;* LAW Anklage *f* (**of** wegen +*gen*); **to make** [*or* **level**] **an ~ against sb** jdn beschuldigen ② (*accusing*) Vorwurf *m*

accusative [ə·ˈkju·zə·t̬ɪv] *n* **~** [**case**] Akkusativ *m*

accusatory [ə·ˈkju·zə·tɔr·i] *adj look* anklagend; *tone* vorwurfsvoll

accuse [ə·ˈkjuz] *vt* ① (*charge*) ■ **to ~ sb** [**of sth**] jdn [wegen einer S. *gen*] anklagen ② (*claim*) ■ **to ~ sb of sth** jdn einer S. *gen* beschuldigen; **I'm often ~d of ...** mir wird oft vorgeworfen, dass ...

accused <*pl* -> [ə·ˈkjuzd] *n* ■ **the ~** die/der Angeklagte

accustomed [ə·ˈkʌs·təmd] *adj* ■ **to be ~ to sth** etw gewohnt sein; **to become** [*or* **get**] **~ to sth** sich an etw *akk* gewöhnen

AC/DC [ˌeɪ·si·ˈdi·si] **I.** *n abbrev of* **alternating current/direct current** WS/GS **II.** *adj* (*sl: bisexual*) bi *fam*

ace [eɪs] **I.** *n* (*all meanings*) Ass *nt;* **~ of spades** Pikass *nt* **II.** *adj* (*fam*) klasse **III.** *vt* (*fam*) **to ~ a test** einen Test mit Leichtigkeit bestehen

acetate [ˈæs·ɪ·teɪt] *n* CHEM Acetat *nt*

acetic ˈacid *n* Essigsäure *f*

ache [eɪk] **I.** *n* (*pain*) Schmerz[en] *m*[*pl*]; **~s and pains** Wehwehchen *pl* **II.** *vi* (*feel pain*) schmerzen; **I'm aching all over** mir tut alles weh

achieve [ə·ˈtʃiv] *vt* erreichen; *fame* erlangen; *success* erzielen; *victory* erringen

achievement [ə·ˈtʃiv·mənt] *n* ① (*feat*) Leistung *f* ② (*achieving*) Erreichen *nt*

acid [ˈæs·ɪd] **I.** *n* ① CHEM Säure *f* ② (*sl: LSD*) Acid *nt sl* **II.** *adj* ① CHEM sauer; **~ solution** saure Lösung ② (*sour*) sauer

acidic [ə·ˈsɪd·ɪk] *adj* ① CHEM säurehaltig ② (*sour*) sauer

acidity [ə·ˈsɪd·ɪ·t̬i] *n* ① CHEM Säuregehalt *m* ② (*sourness*) Säure *f*

acid ˈrain *n* saurer Regen

ˈacid test *n* ① CHEM Säureprobe *f* ② (*fig*) Feuerprobe *f*

acknowledge [ək·ˈnal·ɪdʒ] *vt* ① (*admit*) zugeben ② (*respect*) anerkennen; **he was generally ~d to be an expert** er galt allgemein als Experte ③ (*reply to*) *greeting* erwidern; *receipt* bestätigen

acknowledg(e)ment [ək·ˈnal·ɪdʒ·mənt] *n* ① (*admission*) Bekenntnis (**of** zu +*dat*); **~ of guilt** Schuldeingeständnis *nt* ② (*respect*) Anerkennung *f* ③ (*reply*) Erwiderung *f*

acne [ˈæk·ni] *n* Akne *f*

acorn [ˈeɪ·kɔrn] *n* Eichel *f*

acoustic [ə·ˈku·stɪk] *adj* akustisch

acoustic guiˈtar *n* Akustikgitarre *f*

acoustics [ə·ˈku·stɪks] *n* ① + *pl vb* (*of hall*) Akustik *f* ② + *sing vb* PHYS Akustik *f*

acquaint [ə·ˈkweɪnt] *vt* vertraut machen

acquaintance [ə·ˈkweɪn·təns] *n* ① (*friend*) Bekannte(r) *f(m)* ② (*relationship*) Bekanntschaft *f*

acquiesce [ˌæk·wɪ·ˈes] *vi* ■ **to ~** [**to sth**] [in etw *akk*] einwilligen

acquiescence [ˌæk·wɪ·ˈes·əns] *n* Einwilligung *f* (**to** in +*akk*)

acquire [ə·ˈkwaɪr] *vt* erwerben; *knowledge* sich *dat* aneignen; *reputation* bekommen; **to be an ~d taste** gewöhnungsbedürftig sein

acquisition [ˌæk·wɪ·ˈzɪʃ·ən] *n* ① (*purchase*) Anschaffung *f* ② (*acquiring*) Erwerb *m; of* *company* Übernahme *f; of knowledge* Aneignung *f*

acquit <-tt-> [ə·ˈkwɪt] *vt* ❶ (*free*) freisprechen ❷ (*perform*) **to ~ oneself well** seine Sache gut machen

acquittal [ə·ˈkwɪṭ·əl] *n* Freispruch *m* (**on** von +*dat*)

acre [ˈeɪ·kər] *n* (*unit*) ≈ Morgen *m*

acrid [ˈæk·rɪd] *adj smell* stechend; *smoke* beißend; *taste* bitter

acrimonious [ˌæk·rɪ·ˈmoʊ·ni·əs] *adj* erbittert

acrimony [ˈæk·rɪ·moʊ·ni] *n* Verbitterung *f; of argument* Schärfe *f*

acrobat [ˈæk·rə·bæt] *n* Akrobat(in) *m(f)*

acrobatic [ˌæk·rə·ˈbæṭ·ɪk] *adj* akrobatisch

acronym [ˈæk·rə·nɪm] *n* Akronym *nt*

across [ə·ˈkrɔs] **I.** *prep* ❶ (*on other side of*) über +*dat;* **~ town** am anderen Ende der Stadt ❷ (*from one side to other*) über +*akk;* **~ country** über Land ▸ PHRASES: **~ the** **board** allgemein **II.** *adv* ❶ (*to other side*) hinüber; (*from other side*) herüber ❷ (*on other side*) drüben; **~ from sb/sth** jdm/etw gegenüber ❸ (*wide*) breit; *of circle* im Durchmesser ▸ PHRASES: **to get one's point ~** sich verständlich machen

act [ækt] **I.** *n* ❶ (*deed*) Tat *f;* **~ of kindness** Akt *m* der Güte; **an ~ of God** höhere Gewalt; **to catch sb in the ~** jdn auf frischer Tat ertappen ❷ (*of a play*) Akt *m;* **one-~ play** Einakter *m* ❸ (*pretence*) Schau *f;* **to put on an ~** Theater spielen ▸ PHRASES: **to get in on the ~** mitmischen; **to get one's ~ together** sich am Riemen reißen **II.** *vi* ❶ (*take action*) handeln; (*proceed*) vorgehen; **to ~ [up]on sb's advice** jds Rat befolgen ❷ (*represent*) ■**to ~ for** [*or* **on behalf of**] **sb** jdn vertreten ❸ (*behave*) sich benehmen; ■**to ~ as if ...** so tun, als ob ... ❹ (*play*) spielen; (*be an actor*) Schauspieler(in) sein ❺ (*take effect*) ■**to ~ [on sth]** [auf etw *akk*] wirken **III.** *vt* ❶ THEAT spielen ❷ (*behave appropriate to*) **~ your age!** benimm dich gefälligst deinem Alter entsprechend! ▸ PHRASES: **to ~ a part** (*pej*) schauspielern; **to ~ the part** überzeugend sein

◆**act out** *vt* ❶ (*realize*) ausleben ❷ (*perform*) nachspielen

◆**act up** *vi* (*fam*) ❶ *person* Theater machen ❷ *thing* Ärger machen

acting [ˈæk·tɪŋ] **I.** *adj* stellvertretend **II.** *n* Schauspielerei *f*

action [ˈæk·ʃən] *n* ❶ (*activeness*) Handeln *nt;* (*proceeding*) Vorgehen *nt;* (*measures*) Maßnahmen *pl;* **decisive ~** ein entschlossenes Vorgehen; **course of ~** Vorgehensweise *f;* **to spring into ~** in Aktion treten; **to put into ~** in die Tat umsetzen; **to take ~** etwas unternehmen ❷ (*act*) Handlung *f,* Tat *f* ❸ FILM Action *f* ❹ (*combat*) Einsatz *m;* **to go into ~** ins Gefecht ziehen; **to be killed in ~** fallen; **to see ~** im Einsatz sein ❺ LAW Klage *f* ▸ PHRASES: **~s speak louder than words** (*prov*) Taten sagen mehr als Worte; **to want a piece of the ~** eine Scheibe vom Kuchen abhaben wollen

ˈaction-packed *adj* spannungsgeladen

activate [ˈæk·tə·veɪt] *vt* aktivieren; *alarm* auslösen

active [ˈæk·tɪv] *adj* aktiv; *children* lebhaft

actively [ˈæk·tɪv·li] *adv* aktiv

activist [ˈæk·tə·vɪst] *n* Aktivist(in) *m(f)*

activity [æk·ˈtɪv·ɪ·ṭi] *n* ❶ (*activeness*) Aktivität *f* ❷ *usu pl* (*pastime*) Aktivität *f;* **classroom activities** schulische Tätigkeiten

actor [ˈæk·tər] *n* Schauspieler *m*

actress <*pl* -es> [ˈæk·trɪs] *n* Schauspielerin *f*

actual [ˈæk·tʃʊ·əl] *adj* (*real*) eigentlich; *facts* konkret; **in ~ fact** tatsächlich

actually [ˈæk·tʃʊ·ə·li] *adv* ❶ (*in fact*) eigentlich ❷ (*really*) wirklich; **did you ~ say that?** hast du das tatsächlich gesagt?

actuate [ˈæk·tʃʊ·eɪt] *vt* in Gang setzen

acumen [ə·ˈkju·mən] *n* Scharfsinn *m;* **business ~** Geschäftssinn *m*

acupuncture [ˈæk·jʊ·pʌŋk·tʃər] *n* Akupunktur *f*

acute [ə·ˈkjut] *adj* ❶ (*serious*) akut; *anxiety* ernsthaft; *pain* heftig ❷ *hearing* fein; *sense of smell* ausgeprägt ❸ MATH *angle* spitz

acutely [ə·ˈkjut·li] *adv* ❶ (*extremely*) äußerst; **to be ~ aware of sth** sich *dat* einer S. *gen* sehr bewusst sein ❷ (*shrewdly*) scharfsinnig

ad [æd] *n* (*fam*) *short for* **advertisement** Anzeige *f*

AD [ˌeɪ·ˈdi] *adj abbrev of* **Anno Domini** n. Chr.

adamant [ˈæd·ə·mənt] *adj* unnachgiebig; ■**to be ~ about sth** auf etw *dat* beharren

Adam's ˈapple *n* Adamsapfel *m*

adapt [ə·ˈdæpt] **I.** *vt* ❶ (*modify*) anpassen (**to** an +*akk*); *machine* umstellen ❷ (*rewrite*) bearbeiten **II.** *vi* ■**to ~ [to sth]** sich [einer S. *dat*] anpassen

adaptable [ə·ˈdæp·tə·bəl] *adj* anpassungsfähig; *machine* vielseitig

adaptation [ˌæd·æp·ˈteɪ·ʃən] *n* ❶ (*adapting*) Anpassung *f* (**to** an +*akk*) ❷ (*modification*) Umbau *m* (**to** +*gen*); *of machine* Umstellung *f* (**to** auf +*akk*) ❸ (*composition*) Bearbeitung *f*

adapter, adaptor [ə·ˈdæp·tər] *n* ELEC Adapter *m*

add [æd] **I.** *vt* ❶ hinzufügen ❷ MATH ■**to ~ [together]** addieren; ■**to ~ sth to sth** etw zu etw *dat* [dazu]zählen **II.** *vi* addieren

◆**add up I.** *vi* ❶ (*fam: make sense*) **it doesn't ~ up** es macht keinen Sinn ❷ (*total*) ■**to ~ up to sth** *bill* sich auf etw *akk* belaufen ❸ (*accumulate*) *debt* sich anhäufen **II.** *vt* addieren

addendum <*pl* -da> [ə·ˈden·dəm] *n* ❶ (*addition*) Nachtrag *m* ❷ (*in book*) ■**addenda** *pl* Addenda *pl*

adder [ˈæd·ər] *n* Otter *f*

addict [ˈæd·ɪkt] *n* Süchtige(r) *f(m);* **drug ~** Drogenabhängige(r) *f(m)*

addicted [ə·ˈdɪk·tɪd] *adj* süchtig (**to** nach +*dat*)

addiction [ə·ˈdɪk·ʃən] *n* Sucht *f* (**to** nach +*dat*)

addictive [ə·ˈdɪk·tɪv] *adj* süchtig; ~ **substance** Suchtmittel *nt*

addition [ə·ˈdɪʃ·ən] *n* ❶ MATH Addition *f* ❷ (*attaching*) Hinzufügen *nt* (**to** an +*akk*) ❸ (*extra*) Ergänzung *f* ❹ ■ **in** ~ außerdem; ■ **in** ~ **to** zusätzlich zu +*dat*

additional [ə·ˈdɪʃ·ən·əl] *adj* zusätzlich; ~ **charge** Aufpreis *m*, Zuschlag *m*

additionally [ə·ˈdɪʃ·ən·əl·i] *adv* außerdem

additive [ˈæd·ɪ·t̬ɪv] *n* Zusatz *m*

address [ˈæd·res] **I.** *n* <*pl* -es> ❶ *a.* COMPUT Adresse *f* ❷ (*speech*) Rede *f* (**to** an +*akk*) **II.** *vt* ❶ (*write address*) adressieren (**to** an +*akk*) ❷ (*direct*) *remark* richten (**to** an +*akk*) ❸ (*speak to*) anreden

addressee [ˌæd·re·ˈsi] *n* Empfänger(in) *m(f)*; ~ **unknown** Empfänger unbekannt

adept [ə·ˈdept] *adj* geschickt (**at** in +*dat*)

adequacy [ˈæd·ɪ·kwə·si] *n* ❶ (*sufficiency*) Angemessenheit *f* ❷ (*suitability*) Tauglichkeit *f*

adequate [ˈæd·ɪ·kwət] *adj* ❶ (*sufficient*) ausreichend ❷ (*barely sufficient*) zulänglich

adhere [æd·ˈhɪr] *vi* ❶ (*stick*) kleben (**to** an +*akk*) ❷ (*follow*) *rules* sich halten (**to** an +*akk*)

adherence [æd·ˈhɪr·əns] *n* Festhalten *nt* (**to** an +*dat*); *of rule* Befolgung *f* (**to** +*gen*)

adherent [æd·ˈhɪr·ənt] *n* Anhänger(in) *m(f)*

adhesive [æd·ˈhi·sɪv] **I.** *adj* haftend **II.** *n* Klebstoff *m*

ad hoc [æd·ˈhak] *adv* ad hoc

adjacent [ə·ˈdʒeɪ·sənt] *adj* angrenzend; **her room was ~ to mine** ihr Zimmer lag neben meinem

adjectival [ˌædʒ·ɪk·ˈtaɪ·vəl] *adj* adjektivisch; ~ **ending** Adjektivendung *f*

adjective [ˈædʒ·ɪk·tɪv] *n* Adjektiv *nt*, Eigenschaftswort *nt*

adjoining [ə·ˈdʒɔɪ·nɪŋ] *adj* angrenzend

adjourn [ə·ˈdʒɜrn] **I.** *vt* (*interrupt*) unterbrechen; (*suspend*) verschieben; LAW vertagen **II.** *vi* (*stop temporarily*) eine Pause einlegen

adjudicate [ə·ˈdʒu·dɪ·keɪt] *vi, vt* ■ **to** ~ [**on**] **sth** über etw *akk* entscheiden; LAW über etw *akk* ein Urteil fällen

adjust [ə·ˈdʒʌst] **I.** *vt* ❶ (*set*) [richtig] einstellen; *lever* verstellen ❷ *clothing* in Ordnung bringen **II.** *vi* (*adapt*) ■ **to** ~ **to sth** sich an etw *akk* anpassen; (*feel comfortable with*) sich an etw *akk* gewöhnen

adjustable [ə·ˈdʒʌst·ə·bəl] *adj* verstellbar

adjustment [ə·ˈdʒʌst·mənt] *n* ❶ (*mental*) Anpassung *f*; **to make an ~ to sth** sich auf etw *akk* umstellen ❷ (*mechanical*) Einstellung *f*

ad-lib <-bb-> [ˌæd·ˈlɪb] *vi, vt* improvisieren

admin [ˈæd·mɪn] *n* (*fam*) ❶ *short for* **administration** ❷ COMPUT *short for* **administrator** Administrator(in) *m(f)*

administer [æd·ˈmɪn·ɪ·stər] *vt* ❶ (*manage*) verwalten ❷ (*dispense*) geben; (*issue*) ausgeben; **to ~ first aid** [**to sb**] [bei jdm] erste Hilfe leisten

administration [æd·ˌmɪn·ɪ·ˈstreɪ·ʃən] *n* ❶ Verwaltung *f* ❷ (*term in office*) Amtszeit *f* ❸ (*government*) Regierung *f*

administrative [æd·ˈmɪn·ɪ·streɪ·tɪv] *adj* administrativ, Verwaltungs-

administrator [æd·ˈmɪn·ɪ·streɪ·t̬ər] *n* ❶ (*person in charge*) Leiter(in) *m(f)* ❷ (*clerk*) Verwaltungsbeamte(r) *m*/-beamtin *f*

admirable [ˈæd·mər·ə·bəl] *adj* bewundernswert; *job* hervorragend

admiral [ˈæd·mər·əl] *n* Admiral(in) *m(f)*

admiration [ˌæd·mə·ˈreɪ·ʃən] *n* ❶ (*respect*) Hochachtung *f* (**for** vor +*dat*) ❷ (*wonderment*) Bewunderung *f*

admire [əd·ˈmaɪr] *vt* bewundern

admirer [əd·ˈmaɪr·ər] *n* ❶ (*with romantic interest*) Verehrer(in) *m(f)* ❷ (*supporter*) Anhänger(in) *m(f)*

admissible [æd·ˈmɪs·ə·bəl] *adj* zulässig

admission [æd·ˈmɪʃ·ən] *n* ❶ (*entering*) Eintritt *m*; (*acceptance*) Zutritt *m*; (*into university*) Zulassung *f*; (*into a hospital*) Einlieferung *f* ❷ (*entrance fee*) Eintritt[spreis] *m* ❸ (*acknowledgment*) Eingeständnis *nt*

admit <-tt-> [æd·ˈmɪt] **I.** *vt* ❶ (*acknowledge*) zugeben; *defeat* eingestehen ❷ (*allow entrance*) hereinlassen/hineinlassen; ■ **to ~ sb to the hospital** jdn ins Krankenhaus einliefern **II.** *vi* ■ **to ~ to sth** etw zugeben

admittance [æd·ˈmɪt·əns] *n* (*entrance*) Zutritt *m*; *to club* Aufnahme *f*; **"no ~"** „Betreten verboten"

admittedly [æd·ˈmɪt̬·ɪd·li] *adv* zugegebenermaßen

ado [ə·ˈdu] *n* großer Aufwand; **without further ~** ohne weitere Umstände

adolescence [ˌæd·əl·ˈes·əns] *n* Jugend[zeit] *f*

adolescent [ˌæd·əl·ˈes·ənt] **I.** *adj* ❶ (*of teenagers*) heranwachsend, jugendlich ❷ (*pej: immature*) pubertär **II.** *n* Jugendliche(r) *f(m)*

adopt [ə·ˈdapt] *vt* ❶ (*raise*) adoptieren ❷ (*sponsor*) die Patenschaft übernehmen ❸ (*put into practice*) annehmen; *pose* einnehmen; *strategy* verfolgen

adoption [ə·ˈdap·ʃən] *n* ❶ Adoption *f*; **to give up one's child to ~** sein Kind zur Adoption freigeben ❷ (*taking on*) Annahme *f*; *of a technology* Übernahme *f*; *of a method* Aneignung *f*

adorable [ə·ˈdɔr·ə·bəl] *adj* entzückend

adoration [ˌæd·ə·ˈreɪ·ʃən] *n* Verehrung *f*

adore [ə·ˈdɔr] *vt* ❶ (*love*) über alles lieben; (*admire*) aufrichtig bewundern ❷ (*like very much*) ■ **to ~ sb** für jdn schwärmen; **to ~ sth** etw wunderbar finden

adoring [ə·ˈdɔr·ɪŋ] *adj* (*loving*) liebend; (*devoted*) hingebungsvoll

adorn [ə·ˈdɔrn] *vt* schmücken

adornment [ə·ˈdɔrn·mənt] *n* ❶ (*ornament*) Schmuck *m* ❷ (*act*) Verschönerung *f*

adrenalin(e) [ə·ˈdren·ə·lɪn] *n* Adrenalin *nt*

adrift [ə·ˈdrɪft] **I.** *adv* **to cut ~** losmachen **II.** *adj* **to be ~** treiben

adroit [ə·ˈdrɔɪt] *adj* geschickt

adulation [ˌædʒ·ə·ˈleɪ·ʃən] *n* (*admiration*) Vergötterung *f;* (*flattery*) Schmeichelei *f*

adult [ə·ˈdʌlt] **I.** *n* ① (*grownup*) Erwachsene(r) *f(m);* ■**to be an ~** erwachsen sein ② (*animal*) ausgewachsenes Tier **II.** *adj* ① (*grown-up*) erwachsen; *animal* ausgewachsen; *behavior* reif ② (*sexually explicit*) [nur] für Erwachsene

adult eduˈcation *n* Erwachsenenbildung *f*

adulterate [ə·ˈdʌl·tə·reɪt] *vt* verfälschen; *wine* panschen

adultery [ə·ˈdʌl·tə·ri] *n* Ehebruch *m*

adulthood [ə·ˈdʌlt·hʊd] *n* (*state*) Erwachsensein *nt;* (*period*) Erwachsenenalter *nt*

advance [əd·ˈvæns] **I.** *vi* ① (*make progress*) Fortschritte machen ② (*move forward*) sich vorwärtsbewegen; MIL vorrücken **II.** *vt* ① (*develop*) voranbringen; *career* vorantreiben ② (*make earlier*) vorverlegen; *money* vorschießen **III.** *n* ① (*forward movement*) Vorrücken *nt* ② (*progress*) Fortschritt *m* ③ (*ahead of time*) **in ~** im Voraus; **thank you in ~** vielen Dank im Voraus ④ (*payment*) Vorschuss *m* (**on** auf +*akk*) **IV.** *adj* vorherig

advanced [əd·ˈvænst] *adj* ① (*in skills*) fortgeschritten; **~ mathematics** höhere Mathematik ② (*in development*) fortschrittlich ③ (*in time*) fortgeschritten; *age* vorgerückt

advancement [əd·ˈvæns·mənt] *n* ① (*improvement*) Verbesserung *f;* (*furtherance*) Förderung *f* ② (*in career*) Aufstieg *m*

advance ˈnotice *n* Vorankündigung *f*

advantage [əd·ˈvæn·tɪdʒ] *n* Vorteil *m;* **to take ~ of sb** (*pej*) jdn ausnutzen; **to take ~ of sth** (*approv*) etw nutzen

advantageous [ˌæd·væn·ˈteɪ·dʒəs] *adj* günstig

advent [ˈæd·vənt] *n* REL ■**A~** Advent *m*

adventure [æd·ˈven·tʃər] *n* Abenteuer *nt;* **to have an ~** ein Abenteuer erleben

adventurer [əd·ˈven·tʃər·ər] *n* Abenteurer(in) *m(f)*

adventurous [əd·ˈven·tʃər·əs] *adj* ① (*filled with adventures*) abenteuerlich ② (*daring*) abenteuerlustig

adverb [ˈæd·vɜrb] *n* Adverb *nt*

adverbial [æd·ˈvɜr·bi·əl] *adj* adverbial

adversary [ˈæd·vər·ser·i] *n* Gegner(in) *m(f)*

adverse [æd·ˈvɜrs] *adj* ungünstig; *criticism, effect* negativ; *conditions* widrig

adversity [æd·ˈvɜr·sɪ·t̬i] *n* Not *f*

advertise [ˈæd·vər·taɪz] **I.** *vt* ① Werbung machen für +*akk;* (*in a newspaper*) inserieren; (*on a bulletin board*) in einem Aushang anbieten ② (*announce*) ankündigen **II.** *vi* ① (*publicize*) werben ② (*in a newspaper*) inserieren; (*on a bulletin board*) einen Aushang machen; ■**to ~ for sb/sth** jdn/etw per Inserat suchen

advertisement [ˌæd·vər·ˈtaɪz·mənt] *n* Werbung *f;* (*in a newspaper*) Anzeige *f;* (*on a bulletin board*) Aushang *m;* **TV ~** Werbespot *m;* (*fig*) Reklame *f*

advertiser [ˈæd·vər·taɪ·zər] *n* Werbungtreibende(r) *f(m);* (*in a newspaper*) Inserent(in) *m(f)*

advertising [ˈæd·vər·ˌtaɪ·zɪŋ] *n* Werbung *f*

ˈadvertising agency *n* Werbeagentur *f*

ˈadvertising campaign *n* Werbekampagne *f*

advice [æd·ˈvaɪs] *n* (*recommendation*) Rat *m;* **some ~** ein Rat[schlag] *m;* **to seek legal ~** sich juristisch beraten lassen; **to take sb's ~** jds Rat[schlag] *m* befolgen

advisable [æd·ˈvaɪ·zə·bəl] *adj* ratsam

advise [æd·ˈvaɪz] **I.** *vt* beraten; ■**to ~ sb against sth** jdm von etw *dat* abraten; ■**to ~ sb to do sth** jdm [dazu] raten, etw zu tun **II.** *vi* raten; ■**to ~ against sth** von etw *dat* abraten; ■**to ~ on sth** bei etw *dat* beraten

adviser, advisor [əd·ˈvaɪ·zər] *n* Berater(in) *m(f)*

advisory [æd·ˈvaɪ·zə·ri] *adj* beratend; **~ committee** Beratungsausschuss *m*

advocate **I.** *vt* [ˈæd·və·keɪt] befürworten **II.** *n* [ˈæd·və·kət] ① Befürworter(in) *m(f)* ② LAW [Rechts]anwalt *m,* [Rechts]anwältin *f*

aerate [ˈer·eɪt] *vt* durchlüften; *soil* auflockern; *liquid* mit Kohlensäure versetzen

aerial [ˈer·i·əl] **I.** *adj* Luft- **II.** *n* Antenne *f*

aerobatics [ˌer·ə·ˈbæt̬·ɪks] *npl* ① (*maneuvers*) Flugkunststücke *pl* ② + *sing vb* (*stunt flying*) Kunstflug *m*

aerobics [ə·ˈroʊ·bɪks] *n* (*exercise*) Aerobic *nt*

aerodynamic [ˌer·oʊ·daɪ·ˈnæm·ɪk] *adj* aerodynamisch

aerodynamics [ˌer·oʊ·daɪ·ˈnæm·ɪks] *n* Aerodynamik *f*

aeronautic [ˈer·ə·nɔ·t̬ik] *adj* aeronautisch

aeronautics [ˌer·ə·ˈnɔ·t̬ɪks] *n* + *sing vb* Luftfahrt[technik] *f*

aerosol [ˈer·ə·sɔl] *n* ① (*mixture*) Aerosol *nt* ② (*spray container*) Spraydose *f*

aesthetic [es·ˈθet̬·ɪk] *adj* ästhetisch

aesthetics [es·ˈθet̬·ɪks] *n* Ästhetik *f*

afar [ə·ˈfar] *adv* **from ~** aus der Ferne

affable [ˈæf·ə·bəl] *adj* freundlich

affair [ə·ˈfer] *n* ① (*matter, event*) Angelegenheit *f;* **the state of ~s** der Stand der Dinge; **to handle sb's ~s** jds Geschäfte *pl* besorgen ② (*controversial situation, relationship*) Affäre *f*

affect [ə·ˈfekt] *vt* ① (*have effect on*) ■**to ~ sb/sth** sich auf jdn/etw auswirken; (*negatively*) **to ~ one's health** seiner Gesundheit schaden; (*concern*) jdn/etw betreffen ② (*move*) ■**to be ~ed by sth** von etw *dat* bewegt sein

affectation [ˌæf·ek·ˈteɪ·ʃən] *n* Affektiertheit *f*

affected [ə·ˈfek·tɪd] *adj* ① (*insincere*) affektiert ② (*influenced*) betroffen

affection [ə·ˈfek·ʃən] *n* Zuneigung *f* (**for** zu +*dat*)

affectionate [ə·ˈfek·ʃə·nɪt] *adj* liebevoll

affiliate [ə·ˈfɪl·i·eɪt] **I.** *vt* ■**to be ~d with sth** mit etw *dat* assoziiert sein; (*in subordinate position*) etw *dat* angeschlossen sein **II.** *n* Konzernunternehmen *nt*

affiliation [ə·ˌfɪl·i·ˈer·ʃən] *n* Angliederung *f;* **political ~s** politische Zugehörigkeit

affinity [ə·ˈfɪn·ɪ·t̬i] *n* ① (*solidarity*) Verbundenheit *f;* **to feel an ~ for sb** sich jdm verbunden fühlen ❷ (*similarity*) Gemeinsamkeit *f*

affirm [ə·ˈfɜrm] *vt* beteuern

affirmation [ˌæf·ər·ˈmeɪ·ʃən] *n* ❶ (*positive assertion*) Bekräftigung *f* ❷ (*declaration*) Beteuerung *f*

affirmative [ə·ˈfɜr·mə·t̬ɪv] **I.** *adj* zustimmend; *answer* positiv **II.** *n* Bejahung *f;* **to answer in the ~** mit Ja antworten **III.** *interj* **~!** jawohl!

affix [ə·ˈfɪks] *vt* (*attach*) befestigen (**to** an +*dat*); (*stick on*) ankleben (**to** an +*akk*); (*clip on*) anheften (**to** an +*akk*)

afflict [ə·ˈflɪkt] *vt* plagen; **he is ~ed with severe rheumatism** er leidet an schwerem Rheumatismus

affliction [ə·ˈflɪk·ʃən] *n* ❶ (*illness*) Leiden *nt* ❷ (*distress*) Kummer *m*

affluence [ˈæf·lʊ·əns] *n* Wohlstand *m*

affluent [ˈæf·lʊ·ənt] *adj* reich; **~ society** Wohlstandsgesellschaft *f*

afford [ə·ˈfɔrd] *vt* (*have money, time for*) sich *dat* leisten; **you can't ~ to miss this opportunity** diese Gelegenheit darfst du dir nicht entgehen lassen

affordable [ə·ˈfɔr·də·bəl] *adj* erschwinglich

affront [ə·ˈfrʌnt] **I.** *n* Beleidigung *f* **II.** *vt* beleidigen

Afghan [ˈæf·gæn] **I.** *n* ❶ (*person*) Afghane *m,* Afghanin *f* ❷ (*dog*) Afghane *m* **II.** *adj* afghanisch

Afghanistan [æf·ˈgæn·ɪ·stæn] *n* Afghanistan *nt*

afield [ə·ˈfild] *adv* entfernt

afloat [ə·ˈfloʊt] *adj* (*a. fig*) über Wasser; ■ **to be ~** schwimmen

afoot [ə·ˈfʊt] **I.** *adj* im Gange **II.** *adv* zu Fuß

aforementioned [ə·ˌfɔr·ˈmen·ʃənd], **aforesaid** [ə·ˈfɔr·sed] *adj* (*form*) oben erwähnt

afraid [ə·ˈfreɪd] *adj* ❶ (*frightened*) verängstigt; **to [not] be ~ [of sb/sth]** [keine] Angst haben [vor jdm/etw]; **to be ~ that ...** befürchten, dass ... ❷ (*expressing regret*) **I'm ~ not/so** leider nicht/ja

afresh [ə·ˈfreʃ] *adv* [noch einmal] von vorn

Africa [ˈæf·rɪ·kə] *n* Afrika *nt*

African [ˈæf·rɪ·kən] **I.** *n* Afrikaner(in) *m(f)* **II.** *adj* afrikanisch

African American [ˌæf·rɪ·kən·ə·ˈmer·ɪ·kən] *n* Afroamerikaner(in) *m(f)*

Afrikaans [ˌæf·rɪ·ˈkans] *n* Afrikaans *nt*

Afro-American [ˌæf·roʊ·ə·ˈmer·ɪ·kən] **I.** *n* Afroamerikaner(in) *m(f)* **II.** *adj* afroamerikanisch

after [ˈæf·tər] **I.** *prep* ❶ (*later time*) nach +*dat;* **~ lunch** nach dem Mittagessen; **[a] quarter ~ six** [um] Viertel nach Sechs ❷ (*in pursuit of*) ■ **to be ~ sb/sth** hinter jdm/etw her sein ❸ (*following*) nach +*dat* ❹ (*behind*) **he shut the door ~ them** er machte die Tür hinter ihnen zu ❺ **~ all** schließlich; (*in spite of*) trotz +*gen;* **he couldn't come ~ all** er konnte doch nicht kommen; **she promised it, ~ all** sie hat es immerhin versprochen **II.** *adv* danach; **shortly ~** kurz darauf

ˈaftereffect *n* Nachwirkung *f*

ˈafterlife *n* Leben *nt* nach dem Tod

ˈaftermath [-mæθ] *n* Folgen *pl;* ■ **in the ~ of** infolge +*gen*

afternoon [ˌæf·tər·ˈnun] *n* Nachmittag *m;* **good ~!** guten Tag!; **early/late ~** am frühen/späten Nachmittag; **this ~** heute Nachmittag; **in the ~** am Nachmittag, nachmittags; **on the ~ of May 23rd** am Nachmittag des 23. Mai; **on Wednesday ~** [am] Mittwochnachmittag

ˈaftershave *n* Aftershave *nt*

ˈaftershock *n usu pl* GEOL Nachbeben *nt*

ˈaftertaste *n* Nachgeschmack *m*

ˈafterthought *n* **as an ~** im Nachhinein; **sth was added as an ~** etw kam erst später hinzu

afterward, afterwards [ˈæf·tər·wərdz] *adv* (*later*) später; (*after something*) danach; **shortly ~** kurz danach

again [ə·ˈgen] *adv* ❶ (*as a repetition*) wieder; (*one more time*) noch einmal; **~ and ~** immer wieder; **what's her name ~?** wie ist noch mal ihr Name? ❷ (*anew*) noch einmal

against [ə·ˈgenst] **I.** *prep* gegen +*akk;* **~ one's better judgment** wider besseres Wissen; **the dollar rose ~ the euro** der Dollar stieg gegenüber dem Euro **II.** *adv* gegen; **only 14 voted ~** es gab nur 14 Gegenstimmen

age [eɪdʒ] **I.** *n* ❶ (*length of existence*) Alter *nt;* **he's about your ~** er ist ungefähr so alt wie du; **to be 45 years of ~** 45 [Jahre alt] sein; **sb looks their ~** man sieht jdm sein Alter an; **at the ~ of 80** mit achtzig [Jahren]; **at your ~** in deinem Alter; **to come of ~** volljährig werden ❷ (*era*) Zeitalter *nt;* **in this day and ~** heutzutage ❸ (*long time*) ■ **an ~** eine Ewigkeit, Ewigkeiten; **the meeting took ~s** die Besprechung dauerte ewig [lang] **II.** *vi* ❶ altern ❷ FOOD reifen **III.** *vt* ❶ FOOD reifen lassen; *wine* ablagern lassen ❷ (*make look older*) älter machen; *strain, suffering* altern lassen

ˈage bracket *n* Altersgruppe *f*

aged[1] [eɪdʒd] *adj* **children ~ 8 to 12** Kinder [im Alter] von 8 bis 12 Jahren

aged[2] [ˈeɪ·dʒɪd] **I.** *adj* (*old*) alt **II.** *n* ■ **the ~** *pl* die alten Menschen *pl*

age group *n* Altersgruppe *f*

ageless [ˈeɪdʒ·lɪs] *adj* zeitlos

ˈage limit *n* Altersgrenze *f*

agency [ˈeɪ·dʒən·si] *n* ❶ (*private business*) Agentur *f* ❷ (*of government*) Behörde *f*

agenda [ə·ˈdʒen·də] *n* ❶ (*for a meeting*) Tagesordnung *f* ❷ (*for action*) Programm *nt;* **to have a hidden ~** geheime Pläne haben

agent [ˈeɪ·dʒənt] *n* ❶ (*representative*) [Stell]vertreter(in) *m(f);* (*for artists, athletes*) Agent(in) *m(f)* ❷ (*of a secret service*) Agent(in) *m(f)*

aggravate [ˈæg·rə·veɪt] *vt* ❶ (*worsen*) verschlechtern ❷ (*fam: annoy*) auf die Nerven gehen

aggravating [ˈæg·rə·veɪ·t̬ɪŋ] *adj* (*fam: annoying*) ärgerlich

aggravation [ˌæg·rə·ˈveɪ·ʃən] *n* ① (*worsening*) Verschlimmerung *f* ② (*fam: annoyance*) Ärger *m*

aggregate [ˈæg·rɪ·gɪt] **I.** *n* Gesamtmenge *f* **II.** *adj* Gesamt-

aggression [ə·ˈgreʃ·ən] *n* Aggression *f;* **act of ~** Angriffshandlung *f*

aggressive [ə·ˈgres·ɪv] *adj* aggressiv; *salesman* aufdringlich

aggressor [ə·ˈgres·ər] *n* Angreifer(in) *m(f)*

aggrieved [ə·ˈgrivd] *adj* gekränkt (**at** wegen +*akk*)

aghast [ə·ˈgæst] *adj* entsetzt (**at** über +*akk*)

agile [ˈædʒ·əl] *adj* geschickt; *fingers* flink; *mind* rege

agility [ə·ˈdʒɪl·ɪ·t̬i] *n* Flinkheit *f*

aging [ˈeɪ·dʒɪŋ] *adj person* alternd; *machinery* veraltend

agitate [ˈædʒ·ɪ·teɪt] *vt* ① (*make nervous*) aufregen; ■ **to get ~d** sich aufregen ② (*shake*) schütteln; (*stir*) [um]rühren

agitation [ˌædʒ·ɪ·ˈteɪ·ʃən] *n* ① (*nervousness*) Aufregung *f* ② (*of a liquid*) [Auf]rühren *nt*

agitator [ˈædʒ·ɪ·teɪ·t̬ər] *n* (*person*) Agitator(in) *m(f)*

agnostic [æg·ˈnas·tɪk] **I.** *n* Agnostiker(in) *m(f)* **II.** *adj* agnostisch

ago [ə·ˈgoʊ] *adv* **a year ~** vor einem Jahr; **[not] long ~** vor [nicht] langer Zeit; **how long ~ was that?** wie lange ist das her?

agonize [ˈæg·ə·naɪz] *vi* ■ **to ~ about** [*or* **over**] **sth** sich über etw *akk* den Kopf zermartern

agonizing [ˈæg·ə·naɪ·zɪŋ] *adj* qualvoll; *pain* unerträglich

agony [ˈæg·ə·ni] *n* Todesqualen *pl;* ■ **to be in ~** große Schmerzen leiden

agree [ə·ˈgri] **I.** *vi* ① (*have same opinion*) zustimmen; **to ~ to sth** mit etw *dat* einverstanden sein; **to be unable to ~** sich nicht einigen können; ■ **to ~ with sb** mit jdm einer Meinung sein; ■ **to ~ on sth** über etw *akk* einer Meinung sein; *date* vereinbaren ② (*consent to*) zustimmen; **~d!** einverstanden!; **let's ~ to disagree** [*or* **differ**] ich fürchte, wir können uns nicht einigen ③ ■ **to ~ with sb** *food* jdm [gut] bekommen **II.** *vt* ■ **to ~ that ...** sich darauf einigen, dass ...

agreeable [ə·ˈgri·ə·bəl] *adj* ① (*pleasant*) angenehm; *weather* freundlich ② (*acceptable*) ■ **to be ~ to sb** für jdn akzeptabel sein

agreement [ə·ˈgri·mənt] *n* ① (*same opinion*) Übereinstimmung *f;* **to reach an ~** zu einer Einigung kommen; ■ **to be in ~ with sb** mit jdm übereinstimmen ② (*approval*) Zustimmung *f* ③ (*contract*) Vertrag *m*

agricultural [ˌæg·rɪ·ˈkʌl·tʃər·əl] *adj* landwirtschaftlich; **~ land** Agrarland *nt*

agriculture [ˈæg·rɪ·kʌl·tʃər] *n* Landwirtschaft *f*

aground [ə·ˈgraʊnd] **I.** *adv* **to run ~** auf Grund laufen **II.** *adj after n* auf Grund gelaufen

ah [a] *interj* (*in realization*) ach so; (*in happiness*) ah; (*in sympathy*) oh; (*in pain*) au[tsch]

aha [a·ˈha] *interj* (*in understanding*) aha; (*in glee*) haha

ahead [ə·ˈhed] *adv* ① (*in front*) vorn; **the road ~** die Straße vor uns; **full speed ~** volle Kraft voraus; **to go ~** *project* vorangehen ② (*more advanced*) **to be way ~ of sb** jdm um einiges voraus sein ③ (*in the future*) **he has a lonely year ~** es liegt ein einsames Jahr vor ihm; **to look ~** nach vorne sehen

AI [ˌeɪ·ˈaɪ] *n* ① COMPUT *abbrev of* **artificial intelligence** künstliche Intelligenz ② SCI *abbrev of* **artificial insemination** künstliche Befruchtung

aid [eɪd] **I.** *n* ① (*assistance*) Hilfe *f;* **to come to sb's ~** jdm zu Hilfe kommen ② (*helpful tool*) [Hilfs]mittel *nt;* **hearing ~** Hörgerät *nt* **II.** *vt* helfen +*dat* ► PHRASES: **to ~ and abet** LAW begünstigen

aide [eɪd] *n* ① (*advisor*) Berater(in) *m(f)* ② (*assistant*) Hilfskraft *f* (*im Unterricht*)

AIDS [eɪdz] *n abbrev of* **acquired immune deficiency syndrome** Aids *nt*

ailment [ˈeɪl·mənt] *n* Leiden *nt*

aim [eɪm] **I.** *vi* ① (*point*) zielen (**at** auf +*akk*) ② (*try to achieve*) ■ **to ~ at** [*or* **for**] **sth** etw zum Ziel haben; **to ~ for next week** nächste Woche anpeilen; **to ~ to please** gefallen wollen ► PHRASES: **to ~ high** hoch hinaus wollen **II.** *vt* ① (*point*) ■ **to ~ sth at sb/sth** mit etw *dat* auf jdn/etw zielen; **to ~ a camera at sb/sth** eine Kamera auf jdn/etw richten; **to ~ a punch at sb** nach jdm schlagen ② (*direct at*) *remark* richten (**at** an +*akk*) **III.** *n* ① (*skill*) Zielen *nt;* **to take ~** [**at sb/sth**] [auf jdn/etw] zielen ② (*goal*) Ziel *nt;* ■ **with the ~ of doing sth** in der Absicht, etw zu tun

aimless [ˈeɪm·lɪs] *adj* ziellos

ain't [eɪnt] (*sl*) ① = **am not, is not, are not** *see* **be** ② = **has not, have not** *see* **have**

air [er] **I.** *n* ① Luft *f;* **by ~** mit dem Flugzeug; **to be [up] in the ~** (*fig*) in der Schwebe sein ② TV, RADIO Äther *m;* **on/off the ~** auf Sendung/nicht mehr auf Sendung sein ③ (*facial expression*) Miene *f;* (*manner*) Auftreten *nt;* **she has an ~ of confidence [about her]** sie strahlt eine gewisse Selbstsicherheit aus **II.** *vt* ① (*ventilate*) lüften; *clothes* auslüften [lassen] ② (*express*) *feelings, thoughts* äußern ③ (*broadcast*) senden **III.** *vi* ① TV, RADIO gesendet werden ② (*ventilate*) auslüften

ˈair bag *n* Airbag *m*

ˈairbase *n* Luftwaffenstützpunkt *m*

ˈairborne *adj* ① (*transported by air*) in der Luft befindlich; *disease* durch die Luft übertragen; **~ troops** Luftlandetruppen *pl* ② (*flying*) ■ **to be ~** in der Luft sein

ˈair brake *n* AUTO Druckluftbremse *f;* AVIAT Luftbremse *f*

ˈair bubble *n* Luftblase *f*

ˈair-conditioned *adj* klimatisiert

ˈair conditioner *n* Klimaanlage *f*

ˈair conditioning *n* ① (*process*) Klimatisierung *f* ② (*device*) Klimaanlage *f*

ˈair-cooled *adj* luftgekühlt

A

'aircraft <*pl* -> *n* Luftfahrzeug *nt;* **commercial** ~ Verkehrsflugzeug *nt*
'aircraft carrier *n* Flugzeugträger *m*
'aircraft industry *n* Flugzeugindustrie *f*
'aircrew *n* Crew *f,* Flugpersonal *nt*
'air cushion *n* Luftkissen *nt*
'airfield *n* Flugplatz *m*
'air filter *n* Luftfilter *m*
'air force *n* Luftwaffe *f*
'air freight *n* Luftfracht *f*
'air hole *n* Luftloch *nt*
airless ['er·lɪs] *adj* stickig
'airlift I. *n* Luftbrücke *f* **II.** *vt sth in* über eine Luftbrücke befördern; *sb out* per Flugzeug evakuieren
airline *n* **budget** [*or* **no-frills**] ~ Billigfluglinie *f,* Billigflieger *m fam*
'airliner *n* Verkehrsflugzeug *nt*
'airmail I. *n* Luftpost *f* **II.** *vt* per Luftpost schicken
'airman *n* MIL Flieger *m*
airplane ['er·pleɪn] *n* Flugzeug *nt*
'airport *n* Flughafen *m;* ~ **tax** Flughafengebühr *f*
'air raid *n* Luftangriff *m*
'airsick *adj* luftkrank
'airspace *n* Luftraum *m*
'airstrip *n* Start- und Landebahn *f*
'airtight *adj* luftdicht; (*fig*) hieb- und stichfest
'air traffic *n* Flugverkehr *m;* **high volume of** ~ hohes Flugaufkommen
air traffic con'trol *n* ❶ (*job*) Flugsicherung *f* ❷ (*facility*) Flugleitung *f*
air traffic con'troller *n* Fluglotse *m,* Fluglotsin *f*
'airway *n* ❶ ANAT Luftröhre *f* ❷ *see* **airline**
airy ['er·i] *adj* ❶ ARCHIT luftig ❷ (*lacking substance*) leichtfertig
aisle [aɪl] *n* Gang *m; of church* Seitenschiff *nt* ▶ PHRASES: **to have sb rolling in the ~s** jdn dazu bringen, sich vor Lachen zu kugeln
ajar [ə·'dʒar] *adj* einen Spalt offen
AK *abbrev of* **Alaska**
aka [ˌeɪ·keɪ·'eɪ] *abbrev of* **also known as** alias
akin [ə·'kɪn] *adj* ■ ~ **to sth** etw *dat* ähnlich sein
AL, Ala. *abbrev of* **Alabama**
Alabama [ˌæl·ə·'bæm·ə] *n* Alabama *nt*
alarm [ə·'larm] **I.** *n* ❶ (*worry*) Angst *f;* **to give sb cause for** ~ jdm einen Grund zur Sorge geben ❷ (*signal*) Alarm *m* ❸ (*device*) Alarmanlage *f* **II.** *vt* ❶ (*worry*) beunruhigen; (*frighten*) erschrecken ❷ (*warn of danger*) alarmieren
'alarm clock *n* Wecker *m*
alarming [ə·'lar·mɪŋ] *adj* (*worrying*) beunruhigend; (*frightening*) erschreckend
alarmist [ə·'lar·mɪst] (*pej*) **I.** *adj* schwarzseherisch **II.** *n* Schwarzseher(in) *m(f)*
Alas. *abbrev of* **Alaska**
Alaska [ə·'læs·kə] *n* Alaska *nt*
Albania [æl·'beɪ·ni·ə] *n* Albanien *nt*
Albanian [æl·'beɪ·ni·ən] **I.** *n* ❶ (*person*) Albaner(in) *m(f)* ❷ (*language*) Albanisch *nt* **II.** *adj* albanisch
albatross <*pl* -es> ['æl·bə·trɔs] *n* Albatros *m*
albeit [ɔl·'bi·ɪt] *conj* wenn auch
albino [æl·'baɪ·noʊ] **I.** *adj* Albino- **II.** *n* Albino *m*
album ['æl·bəm] *n* Album *nt*
alcohol ['æl·kə·hɔl] *n* Alkohol *m*
alcohol-free [ˌæl·kə·hɔl·'fri] *adj* alkoholfrei
alcoholic [ˌæl·kə·'hɔ·lɪk] **I.** *n* Alkoholiker(in) *m(f)* **II.** *adj person* alkoholsüchtig; *drink* alkoholisch
alcoholism ['æl·kə·hɔ·lɪz·əm] *n* Alkoholismus *m*
alcove ['æl·koʊv] *n* (*niche*) Nische *f;* (*for sleeping*) Alkoven *m*
ale [eɪl] *n* Ale *nt*
alert [ə·'lɜrt] **I.** *adj* ❶ (*mentally*) aufgeweckt ❷ (*watchful*) wachsam; (*attentive*) aufmerksam; (*conscious*) bewusst **II.** *n* ❶ (*alarm*) Alarmsignal *nt* ❷ (*period of watchfulness*) Alarmbereitschaft *f;* **on full** ~ *army* in Gefechtsbereitschaft; ■ **to be on the** ~ [**for sth**] [vor etw] auf der Hut sein **III.** *vt* ■ **to** ~ **sb to** [*or* **of**] **sth** ❶ (*notify*) jdn auf etw *akk* aufmerksam machen ❷ (*warn*) jdn vor etw *dat* warnen
algae <*pl* -e> ['æl·gə] *n usu pl* Alge *f*
algebra ['æl·dʒə·brə] *n* Algebra *f*
Algeria [æl·'dʒɪr·i·ə] *n* Algerien *nt*
Algerian [æl·'dʒɪr·i·ən] **I.** *n* Algerier(in) *m(f)* **II.** *adj* algerisch
alias ['eɪ·li·əs] **I.** *n* Deckname *m* **II.** *adv* alias
alibi ['æl·ə·baɪ] *n* Alibi *nt*
alien ['eɪ·li·ən] **I.** *adj* ❶ (*foreign*) ausländisch ❷ (*strange*) fremd **II.** *n* ❶ (*foreigner*) Ausländer(in) *m(f)* ❷ (*from space*) Außerirdische(r) *f(m)*
alienate ['eɪ·li·ə·neɪt] *vt* befremden
alienation [ˌeɪ·li·ə·'neɪ·ʃən] *n* Entfremdung *f*
alight[1] [ə·'laɪt] *vi* ❶ (*from train, bus*) aussteigen (**from** aus +*dat*) ❷ *bird, butterfly* landen (**on** auf +*dat*); (*fig*) *eyes, glance* fallen (**on** auf +*akk*)
alight[2] [ə·'laɪt] *adj* (*on fire*) **to be** ~ brennen; **to set** ~ in Brand stecken
align [ə·'laɪn] *vt* ❶ (*move into line*) ■ **to** ~ **sth** [**with sth**] etw [auf etw *akk*] ausrichten ❷ (*move into position*) *wheels* die Spur einstellen ❸ (*fig: support*) ■ **to** ~ **oneself with sb/sth** sich hinter jdn/etw stellen
alignment [ə·'laɪn·mənt] *n* Ausrichten *nt;* **the wheels are in/out of** ~ die Spur ist richtig/falsch eingestellt
alike [ə·'laɪk] **I.** *adj* ❶ (*identical*) gleich ❷ (*similar*) ähnlich **II.** *adv* ❶ (*similarly*) gleich; **to look** ~ sich *dat* ähnlich sehen; **to think** ~ gleicher Ansicht sein ❷ (*both*) gleichermaßen
alimony ['æl·ɪ·moʊ·ni] *n* Unterhalt *m*
alive [ə·'laɪv] *adj* ❶ (*not dead*) lebendig, lebend; ■ **to be** ~ leben, am Leben sein; **to keep sb** ~ jdn am Leben erhalten; **to make sth come** ~ *story* etw lebendig werden lassen ❷ (*swarming*) **to be** ~ **with sth** von etw *dat* wimmeln

alkali <*pl* -s *or* -es> ['æl·kə·laɪ] *n* Alkali *nt*
alkaline ['æl·kə·laɪn] *adj* alkalisch
Allah ['æl·ə] *n* Allah
all-'around *adj* Allround-; ~ **athlete** Allroundsportler(in) *m(f)*
allay ['ə·leɪ] *vt* beschwichtigen; *suspicions* zerstreuen
all 'clear *n* Entwarnung *f;* **to give the** ~ Entwarnung geben
allegation [ˌæl·ɪ·'geɪ·ʃən] *n* Behauptung *f;* **to make an** ~ **against sb** jdn beschuldigen
allege [ə·'ledʒ] *vt* behaupten
alleged [ə·'ledʒd] *adj* angeblich
allegedly [ə·'ledʒ·ɪd·li] *adv* angeblich
allegiance [ə·'li·dʒəns] *n* Loyalität *f;* **to pledge** ~ **to sb** jdm Treue schwören
allegorical [ˌæl·ɪ·'gɔr·ɪk·əl] *adj* allegorisch
allegory ['æl·ɪ·gɔr·i] *n* Allegorie *f*
allergen ['æl·ər·dʒən] *n* Allergen *nt*
allergenic [æl·ər·'dʒen·ɪk] *adj* allergen
allergic [ə·'lɜr·dʒɪk] *adj* allergisch (**to** gegen +*akk*)
allergy ['æl·ər·dʒi] *n* Allergie *f* (**to** gegen +*akk*)
alleviate [ə·'li·vi·eɪt] *vt fears* abbauen; *pain* lindern; *stress* verringern
alley ['æl·i] *n* (*between buildings*) Gasse *f*
alliance [ə·'laɪ·əns] *n* Allianz *f;* **to form an** ~ ein Bündnis schließen
allied ['æl·aɪd] *adj* ❶ (*united*) verbündet; MIL alliiert ❷ (*related*) verwandt
alligator ['æl·ɪ·geɪ·t̬ər] *n* Alligator *m*
allocate ['æl·ə·keɪt] *vt* zuteilen; *funds* bereitstellen
allocation [ˌæl·ə·'keɪ·ʃən] *n usu sing* (*assignment*) Zuteilung *f;* (*distribution*) Verteilung *f; of funds* Bereitstellung *f*
allot <-tt-> [ə·'lat] *vt* zuteilen; *time* vorsehen
all-'out *adj* umfassend; ~ **attack** Großangriff *m*
allow [ə·'laʊ] *vt* ❶ (*permit*) erlauben; *access* gewähren; *goal* anerkennen; ~ **me** erlauben Sie; ■ **to** ~ **oneself sth** sich *dat* etw gönnen ❷ (*allocate*) einplanen
◆ **allow for** *vt* berücksichtigen; *error, delay* einkalkulieren
allowable [ə·'laʊ·ə·bəl] *adj* zulässig
allowance [ə·'laʊ·əns] *n* ❶ (*permitted amount*) Zuteilung *f* ❷ (*pocket money*) Taschengeld *nt* ❸ **to make** ~**s for sth** etw berücksichtigen; **to make** ~**s for sb** mit jdm nachsichtig sein ❹ (*additional pay*) Zulage *f;* **cost of living** ~ Teuerungszulage *f*
alloy ['æl·ɔɪ] *n* Legierung *f;* ~ **wheels** Alu-Felgen *pl*
all-'purpose *adj* Allzweck-
all 'right **I.** *adj* ❶ (*OK*) in Ordnung; **that's** ~ (*apologetically*) das macht nichts; (*you're welcome*) keine Ursache; **it was** ~**, nothing special** na ja, es war nichts Besonderes; **it'll be** ~ **to leave your car here** du kannst deinen Wagen ruhig hierlassen; ■ **to be** ~ **with sb** jdm recht sein ❷ (*healthy*) gesund; (*safe*) gut **II.** *interj* ❶ (*in agreement*) o.k., in Ordnung ❷ (*approv fam*) bravo **III.** *adv* ❶ (*doubtless*) auf jeden Fall ❷ (*quite well*) ganz gut
all-'round *adj see* **all-around**
All 'Saints' Day *n* Allerheiligen *nt*
alluring [ə·'lʊr·ɪŋ] *adj* (*attractive*) anziehend; (*enticing*) verführerisch
allusion [ə·'lu·ʒən] *n* Anspielung *f* (**to** auf +*akk*)
'all-weather *adj* Allwetter-
ally **I.** *n* ['æl·aɪ] Verbündete(r) *f(m);* HIST Alliierte(r) *m* **II.** *vt* <-ie-> [ə·'laɪ] ■ **to** ~ **oneself with** sich verbünden mit +*dat*
almanac ['ɔl·mə·næk] *n* Almanach *m*
almighty [ɔl·'maɪ·t̬i] *adj* ❶ REL allmächtig ❷ (*fam: huge*) Riesen-
almond ['a·mənd] *n* (*nut*) Mandel *f;* (*tree*) Mandelbaum *m*
almost ['ɔl·moʊst] *adv* fast, beinahe; **we're** ~ **there** wir sind gleich da
alms [amz] *npl* Almosen *pl*
aloe vera [ˌal·oʊ·'ver·ə] *n* Aloe vera *f*
alone [ə·'loʊn] *adj, adv* allein; **am I** ~ **in thinking that ...** bin ich als Einzige der Meinung, dass ...; **to leave sb** ~ jdn in Ruhe lassen ►PHRASES: **to go it** ~ sich selbständig machen; (*act independently*) etw im Alleingang machen
along [ə·'laŋ] **I.** *prep* entlang; *before n* +*dat;* **the trees** ~ **the river** die Bäume entlang dem Fluss; *after n* + *akk;* ~ **the way** unterwegs, auf dem Weg **II.** *adv* **you go ahead — I'll be** ~ **in a minute** geh du vor – ich komme gleich nach; ■ ~ **with** [zusammen] mit +*dat;* **to bring** ~ mitbringen
alongside [ə·'laŋ·saɪd] **I.** *prep* neben +*dat;* NAUT längsseits +*gen* **II.** *adv* daneben; **the truck pulled up** ~ der Laster fuhr heran
aloof [ə·'luf] **I.** *adj* zurückhaltend **II.** *adv* **to remain** ~ **[from sth]** sich [von etw *dat*] fernhalten
aloud [ə·'laʊd] *adv* laut
alphabet ['æl·fə·bet] *n* Alphabet *nt*
alphabetical [ˌæl·fə·'bet̬·ɪ·kəl] *adj* alphabetisch
alphabetize ['æl·fə·bɪ·taɪz] *vt* ■ **to** ~ **sth** etw *akk* alphabetisch ordnen
alphanumeric [ˌæl·fə·nu·'mer·ɪk] *adj* alphanumerisch
alpine ['æl·paɪn] **I.** *adj* alpin **II.** *n* BOT [Hoch]gebirgspflanze *f*
Alps [ælps] *npl* ■ **the** ~ die Alpen
already [ɔl·'red·i] *adv* ❶ schon ❷ (*fam: indicating impatience*) endlich
alright [ɔl·'raɪt] *adj, adv, interj see* **all right**
Alsace ['æl·sæs] *n* Elsass *nt*
Alsatian [æl·'seɪ·ʃən] *adj* elsässisch
also ['ɔl·soʊ] *adv* ❶ (*too*) auch ❷ (*furthermore*) außerdem
altar ['ɔl·tər] *n* Altar *m*
'altar boy *n* Ministrant *m*
alter ['ɔl·tər] **I.** *vt* ändern; **that doesn't** ~ **the fact that ...** das ändert nichts an der Tatsache, dass ... **II.** *vi* sich ändern

alteration [ˌɔl·tər·ˈeɪ·ʃən] *n* Änderung *f*

alternate I. *vi* [ˈɔl·tər·neɪt] abwechseln II. *vt* **he ~d working in the office with working at home** abwechselnd arbeitete er mal im Büro und mal zu Hause III. *adj* [ˈɔl·tɜr·nət] *attr, inv* ❶ (*by turns*) abwechselnd; **on ~ days** jeden zweiten Tag ❷ (*alternative*) alternativ

alternating [ˈɔl·tər·neɪ·t̬ɪŋ] *adj* alternierend

alternative [ɔl·ˈtɜr·nə·t̬ɪv] I. *n* Alternative *f* (**to** zu +*dat*) II. *adj* alternativ; **~ date** Ausweichtermin *m*

alternatively [ɔl·ˈtɜr·nə·t̬ɪv·li] *adv* stattdessen

alternator [ˈɔl·tər·neɪ·t̬ər] *n* [Drehstrom]generator *m*

although [ɔl·ˈðoʊ] *conj* obwohl

altimeter [æl·ˈtɪm·ɪ·t̬ər] *n* Höhenmesser *m*

altitude [ˈæl·tə·tud] *n* Höhe *f*; **at high ~** in großer Höhe

alto [ˈæl·toʊ] I. *n* ❶ (*singer*) Altist(in) *m(f)* ❷ (*vocal range*) Altstimme *f*; **to sing ~** Alt singen II. *adj* Alt-

altogether [ˌɔl·tə·ˈgeð·ər] *also adv* ❶ (*completely*) völlig, ganz ❷ (*in total*) insgesamt

altruistic [ˌæl·tru·ˈɪs·tɪk] *adj* altruistisch

aluminum [ə·ˈlu·mə·nəm] *n* Aluminium *nt*

aluminum ˈfoil *n* Alufolie *f*

alumna <*pl* -nae> [ə·ˈlʌm·nə] *n* Absolventin *f*

alumnus <*pl* -ni> [ə·ˈlʌm·nəs] *n* Absolvent *m*

always [ˈɔl·weɪz] *adv* ❶ (*at all times*) immer ❷ (*as last resort*) immer noch

am [əm, *stressed:* æm] *vi first pers. sing of* **be**

a.m. [ˌeɪ·ˈem] *abbrev of* **ante meridiem**: **at 6 ~** um sechs Uhr morgens

amalgam [ə·ˈmæl·gəm] *n* Mischung *f* (**of** aus +*dat*)

amalgamate [ə·ˈmæl·gə·meɪt] I. *vt companies* fusionieren; *departments* zusammenlegen II. *vi* sich zusammenschließen

amalgamation [ə·ˌmæl·gə·ˈmeɪ·ʃən] *n* Vereinigung *f*

amass [ə·ˈmæs] *vt* anhäufen

amateur [ˈæm·ə·tʃər] I. *n* Amateur(in) *m(f)*; (*pej*) Dilettant(in) *m(f)* II. *adj* Hobby-; SPORTS Amateur-; **~ theater** Laienspiel *nt*

amateurish [ˌæm·ə·ˈtʃɜr·ɪʃ] *adj* (*pej*) dilettantisch

amaze [ə·ˈmeɪz] *vt* erstaunen

amazement [ə·ˈmeɪz·mənt] *n* Verwunderung *f*

amazing [ə·ˈmeɪ·zɪŋ] *adj* ❶ (*very surprising*) erstaunlich ❷ (*fam: excellent*) toll

Amazon [ˈæm·ə·zan] *n* ■**the ~** [**River**] der Amazonas

ambassador [æm·ˈbæs·ə·dər] *n* (*of a country*) Botschafter(in) *m(f)* (**to** in +*dat*)

amber [ˈæm·bər] *n* ❶ (*fossil*) Bernstein *m* ❷ (*color*) Bernsteingelb *nt*

ambidextrous [ˌæm·bɪ·ˈdek·strəs] *adj* beidhändig

ambiguity [ˌæm·bɪ·ˈgju·ɪ·t̬i] *n* Zweideutigkeit *f*

ambiguous [æm·ˈbɪg·jʊ·əs] *adj* zweideutig, mehrdeutig; *feelings* gemischt

ambition [æm·ˈbɪʃ·ən] *n* ❶ (*wish to succeed*) Ehrgeiz *m* ❷ (*aim*) Ambition[en] *f[pl]*

ambitious [æm·ˈbɪʃ·əs] *adj* ehrgeizig; *target* hochgesteckt

ambivalent [æm·ˈbɪv·ə·lənt] *adj* zwiespältig; *attitude* ambivalent (**toward**[**s**] gegenüber +*dat*)

amble [ˈæm·bəl] *vi* schlendern

ambulance [ˈæm·bjʊ·ləns] *n* Krankenwagen *m*; **~ service** Rettungsdienst *m*

ambush [ˈæm·bʊʃ] I. *vt* ■**to be ~ed** aus dem Hinterhalt überfallen werden II. *n* Überfall *m* aus dem Hinterhalt; **to lie in ~ for sb** jdm auflauern

ameba <*pl* -s *or* -bae> [ə·ˈmi·bə] *n see* **amoeba**

amebic [ə·ˈmi·bɪk] *adj* Amöben-

ameliorate [ə·ˈmil·jə·reɪt] *vt* verbessern; *symptoms* lindern

amen [eɪ·ˈmen] *interj* Amen; **~ to that!** Gott sei's gedankt!

amenable [ə·ˈmi·nə·bəl] *adj* aufgeschlossen (**to** gegenüber +*dat*)

amend [ə·ˈmend] *vt* [ab]ändern

amendment [ə·ˈmend·mənt] *n* Änderung *f*; **the Fifth A~** der Fünfte Zusatzartikel [zur Verfassung]

amenities [ə·ˈmen·ə·t̬iz] *n* Freizeiteinrichtungen *pl*; **public ~** öffentliche Einrichtungen

America [ə·ˈmer·ɪ·kə] *n* Amerika *nt*; ■**the ~s** Nord-, Süd- und Mittelamerika *nt*

American [ə·ˈmer·ɪ·kən] I. *adj* amerikanisch II. *n* Amerikaner(in) *m(f)*

> Mit dem ersten Schuss, der in der Schlacht von Lexington und Concord 1775 fiel, *The shot heard 'round the world*, begann der amerikanische Unabhängigkeitskrieg, der **American Revolutionary War**, der 1781 mit dem Rückzug der englischen Armee bei der Schlacht von Yorktown endete.
> Die Amerikaner – unter der Führung von General George Washington – bekamen schließlich Unterstützung von Frankreich, Spanien und den Niederlanden im Krieg gegen die englischen Soldaten, die *redcoats* genannt wurden, und gegen die von letzteren angeheuerten deutschen Söldner. Diese Revolte gegen das wirtschaftliche System und die Einschränkung der individuellen Freiheiten in den amerikanischen Kolonien war mit der Anerkennung der Unabhängigkeit der Vereinigten Staaten von Amerika, die im Frieden von Paris 1783 protokolliert wurde, zu Ende.

American ˈIndian *n* Indianer(in) *m(f)*

Americanize [ə·ˈmer·ɪ·kə·naɪz] *vt* amerikanisieren

amethyst [ˈæm·ɪ·θɪst] I. *n* Amethyst *m* II. *adj* amethystfarben

amiable [ˈeɪ·mi·ə·bəl] *adj* freundlich

A

amicable [ˈæm·ɪ·kə·bəl] *adj* freundlich; *divorce* einvernehmlich; *settlement* gütlich

amid [ə·ˈmɪd], **amidst** [ə·ˈmɪdst] *prep* inmitten +*gen*

amino acid [ə·ˈmi·noʊ·ˈæs·ɪd] *n* Aminosäure *f*

amiss [ə·ˈmɪs] *adj* **there's something ~** etwas stimmt nicht

ammonia [ə·ˈmoʊn·jə] *n* ① (*gas*) Ammoniak *nt* ② (*liquid*) Salmiakgeist *m*

ammunition [ˌæm·jə·ˈnɪʃ·ən] *n* Munition *f*

amnesia [æm·ˈni·ʒə] *n* Amnesie *f*

amnesty [ˈæm·nɪ·sti] *n* Amnestie *f*

amoeba <*pl* -s *or* -bae> [ə·ˈmi·bə] *n* Amöbe *f*

amoebic [ə·ˈmi·bɪk] *adj* Amöben-

amok [ə·ˈmʌk] *adv see* **amuck**

among [ə·ˈmʌŋ], **amongst** [ə·ˈmʌŋst] *prep* ① (*between*) unter +*dat;* [**just**] **one ~ many** [nur] eine(r, s) von vielen; **~ other things** unter anderem ② (*in midst of*) inmitten +*gen*

amoral [ˌeɪ·ˈmɔr·əl] *adj* amoralisch

amorous [ˈæm·ər·əs] *adj* amourös; *look* verliebt

amortization [æm·ˌər·t̬ɪ·ˈzeɪ·ʃən] *n* Amortisation *f*

amortize [ə·ˈmɔr·taɪz] *vt* amortisieren

amount [ə·ˈmaʊnt] **I.** *n* (*quantity*) Menge *f; of land* Fläche *f; of money* Betrag *m* **II.** *vi* (*add up to*) ■**to ~ to sth** sich auf etw *akk* belaufen; (*fig*) etw *dat* gleichkommen

amp [æmp] ① *short for* **ampere** Ampere *nt* ② *short for* **amplifier** Verstärker *m*

ampere [ˈæm·pɪr] *n* Ampere *nt*

amphetamine [æm·ˈfet·ə·min] *n* Amphetamin *nt*

amphibian [æm·ˈfɪb·i·ən] *n* (*animal*) Amphibie *f*

amphibious [æm·ˈfɪb·i·əs] *adj* amphibisch; **~ vehicle** Amphibienfahrzeug *nt*

amphitheater [ˈæm·fəˌθi·ə·t̬ər] *n* Amphitheater *nt*

ample <-r, -st> [ˈæm·pəl] *adj* ① (*plentiful*) reichlich; (*enough*) genügend ② (*large*) groß

amplification [ˌæm·plə·fɪ·ˈkeɪ·ʃən] *n* (*making loud*) Verstärkung *f*

amplifier [ˈæm·plə·faɪ·ər] *n* Verstärker *m*

amplify <-ie-> [ˈæm·plə·faɪ] *vt* ① (*make louder*) verstärken ② (*enlarge upon*) weiter ausführen

amputate [ˈæm·pjʊ·teɪt] *vt, vi* amputieren

amputation [ˌæm·pjʊ·ˈteɪ·ʃən] *n* Amputation *f*

amputee [ˌæm·pjʊ·ˈti] *n* Amputierte(r) *f(m)*

amuck [ə·ˈmʌk] *adv* **to run ~** Amok laufen

amuse [ə·ˈmjuz] *vt* ① (*make laugh*) amüsieren; ■**to be ~d by sth** sich über etw *akk* amüsieren ② (*entertain*) unterhalten

amusement [ə·ˈmjuz·mənt] *n* Belustigung *f;* [**much**] **to her ~** [sehr] zu ihrem Vergnügen

aˈmusement park *n* Freizeitpark *m*

amusing [ə·ˈmju·zɪŋ] *adj* amüsant; **that's** [**not**] **very ~** das ist [nicht] sehr witzig

an [ən, *stressed:* æn] *art indef* ein(e) (*unbestimmter Artikel vor Vokalen oder stimmlosem h*); *see also* **a**

anabolic steroid [æn·ə·ˈbɔl·ɪk·ˈster·ɔɪd] *n* anaboles Steroid

anachronism [ə·ˈnæk·rə·nɪz·əm] *n* Anachronismus *m*

anachronistic [əˌnæk·rə·ˈnɪs·tɪk] *adj* anachronistisch

anagram [ˈæn·ə·græm] *n* Anagramm *nt*

anal [ˈeɪ·nəl] *adj* ① ANAT anal ② (*fam*) hyperordentlich

analgesic [ˌæn·əl·ˈdʒi·zɪk] **I.** *adj* schmerzlindernd **II.** *n* Analgetikum *nt*

analog [ˈæn·ə·lag] **I.** *n* Entsprechung *f* **II.** *adj* analog

analogous [ə·ˈnæl·ə·gəs] *adj* analog; ■**to be ~ to sth** etw *dat* entsprechen

analogy [ə·ˈnæl·ə·dʒi] *n* (*similarity*) Analogie *f;* **by ~** [**with**] in Analogie [zu +*dat*]

analysis <*pl* -ses> [ə·ˈnæl·ə·sɪs] *n* ① Analyse *f* ② PSYCH [Psycho]analyse *f*

analyst [ˈæn·ə·lɪst] *n* Analytiker(in) *m(f);* FIN Analyst(in) *m(f);* (*psychoanalyst*) Psychoanalytiker(in) *m(f)*

analytical [ˌæn·ə·ˈlɪt·ɪ·kəl] *adj* analytisch

analyze [ˈæn·ə·laɪz] *vt* analysieren

anarchic(**al**) [æn·ˈar·kɪk(əl)] *adj* anarchisch

anarchism [ˈæn·ər·kɪ·zəm] *n* Anarchismus *m*

anarchist [ˈæn·ər·kɪst] **I.** *n* Anarchist(in) *m(f)* **II.** *adj* anarchistisch

anarchy [ˈæn·ər·ki] *n* Anarchie *f*

anatomical [ˌæn·ə·ˈtam·ɪ·kəl] *adj* anatomisch

anatomy [ə·ˈnæt̬·ə·mi] *n* Anatomie *f*

ancestor [ˈæn·ses·tər] *n* Vorfahr[e] *m,* Vorfahrin *f*

ancestral [æn·ˈses·trəl] *adj* Ahnen-; *rights* angestammt

ancestry [ˈæn·ses·tri] *n* Abstammung *f*

anchor [ˈæŋ·kər] **I.** *n* ① Anker *m* ② TV Moderator(in) *m(f)* **II.** *vt* ① verankern ② *radio/TV program* moderieren **III.** *vi* vor Anker gehen

anchorage [ˈæŋ·kər·ɪdʒ] *n* Ankerplatz *m*

ˈanchorman *n* TV Moderator *m*

ˈanchorwoman *n* TV Moderatorin *f*

anchovy [ˈæn·tʃoʊ·vi] *n* An[s]chovis *f,* Sardelle *f*

ancient [ˈeɪn·ʃənt] *adj* alt; (*fam: very old*) uralt; **~ Rome** das antike Rom ▶ PHRASES: **to be ~ history** ein alter Hut sein

and [ænd, ənd] *conj* und; **nice ~ hot** schön heiß; **more ~ more** immer mehr; **~ so on** und so weiter; **let's wait ~ see** warten wir mal ab

Andes [ˈæn·diz] *npl* ■**the ~** die Anden *pl*

android [ˈæn·drɔɪd] *n* Androide *m*

anecdotal [ˌæn·ɪk·ˈdoʊt̬·əl] *adj* anekdotisch

anecdote [ˈæn·ɪk·doʊt] *n* Anekdote *f*

anemia [ə·ˈni·mi·ə] *n* Anämie *f*

anemic [ə·ˈni·mɪk] *adj* anämisch; (*fig*) saft- und kraftlos

anemone [ə·ˈnem·ə·ni] *n* Anemone *f*

anesthesia [ˌæn·ɪs·ˈθi·ʒə] *n* Anästhesie *f*

anesthesiologist [ˌæn·ɪs·ˌθi·zi·ˈɔl·ə·dʒɪst] *n* Anästhesist(in) *m(f) fachspr,* Narkosearzt, -ärztin *m, f*

anesthetic [ˌæn·ɪs·ˈθet̬·ɪk] **I.** *n* Betäubungsmittel *nt;* **under** ~ in Narkose **II.** *adj* betäubend

anesthetize [ə·ˈnes·θɪ·taɪz] *vt* betäuben

anew [ə·ˈnu] *adv* aufs Neue

angel [ˈeɪn·dʒl] *n* Engel *m*

angelic [æn·ˈdʒel·ɪk] *adj* engelhaft

anger [ˈæŋ·gər] **I.** *n* Ärger *m* (**at** über +*akk*); (*fury*) Wut *f* (**at** auf +*akk*); (*wrath*) Zorn *m* **II.** *vt* ärgern; (*more violently*) wütend machen

angina [æn·ˈdʒaɪ·nə], **angina pectoris** [æn·ˈdʒaɪ·nə·ˈpek·tər·ɪs] *n* MED Angina pectoris *f*

angle [ˈæŋ·gəl] *n* ❶ Winkel *m;* **at an ~ of 20°** in einem Winkel von 20° ❷ (*perspective*) Blickwinkel *m;* **from all ~s** von allen Seiten

angler [ˈæŋ·glər] *n* Angler(in) *m(f)*

anglicize [ˈæŋ·glɪ·saɪz] *vt* anglisieren

angling [ˈæŋ·glɪŋ] *n* Angeln *nt*

Anglophile [ˈæŋ·glə·faɪl] **I.** *n* Englandliebhaber(in) *m(f)* **II.** *adj* anglophil

Anglo-ˈSaxon I. *n* ❶ (*person*) Angelsachse *m,* Angelsächsin *f* ❷ (*language*) Angelsächsisch *nt* **II.** *adj* angelsächsisch

angora [æŋ·ˈgɔ·rə] *n* Angorawolle *f*

angry [ˈæŋ·gri] *adj* ❶ (*annoyed*) verärgert; (*stronger*) zornig; (*enraged*) wütend; **to make sb ~** jdn verärgern; (*stronger*) jdn wütend machen ❷ (*fig*) *sky* bedrohlich; *wound* böse

angst [æŋkst] *n* [neurotische] Angst

anguish [ˈæŋ·gwɪʃ] *n* Qual *f*

angular [ˈæŋ·gjʊ·lər] *adj* kantig; (*bony*) knochig

animal [ˈæn·ɪ·məl] *n* Tier *nt;* **~ fat** tierisches Fett

animal ˈkingdom *n* Tierreich *nt*

animal ˈrights *npl das Recht der Tiere auf Leben und artgerechte Haltung*

animate I. *adj* [ˈæn·ɪ·mət] belebt **II.** *vt* [ˈæn·ɪ·meɪt] beleben

animated [ˈæn·ɪ·meɪ·t̬ɪd] *adj* ❶ *discussion* lebhaft ❷ **~ cartoon** [Zeichen]trickfilm *m*

animation [ˌæn·ɪ·ˈmeɪ·ʃən] *n* ❶ (*energy*) Lebhaftigkeit *f* ❷ FILM Animation *f*

animator [ˈæn·ɪ·meɪ·t̬ər] *n* Trickfilmzeichner(in) *m(f)*

animosity [ˌæn·ɪ·ˈmas·ɪ·t̬i] *n* Feindseligkeit *f* (**toward**[**s**] gegenüber +*dat*)

anise [ˈæn·ɪs] *n* Anis *m*

aniseed [ˈæn·ɪ·sid] *n* Anis[samen] *m*

ankle [ˈæŋ·kəl] *n* [Fuß]knöchel *m*

ˈankle bone *n* Sprungbein *nt*

ˈankle-deep *adj* knöcheltief

ˈankle sock *n* Söckchen *nt*

annex I. *vt* [ə·ˈneks] annektieren **II.** *n* <*pl* -es> [ˈæn·eks] ❶ (*building*) Anbau *m* ❷ (*appendix*) *to a letter* Anlage *f; to an e-mail* Anhang *m*

annexation [ˌæn·ɪk·ˈseɪ·ʃən] *n* Annektierung *f*

annihilate [ə·ˈnaɪ·ə·leɪt] *vt* vernichten

annihilation [ə·ˌnaɪ·ə·ˈleɪ·ʃən] *n* Vernichtung *f*

anniversary [ˌæn·ə·ˈvɜr·sə·ri] *n* Jahrestag *m*

annotate [ˈæn·ə·teɪt] *vt* kommentieren

annotation [ˌæn·ə·ˈteɪ·ʃən] *n* ❶ (*act*) Kommentierung *f* ❷ (*note*) Kommentar *m*

announce [ə·ˈnaʊns] *vt* bekannt geben; *result* verkünden

announcement [ə·ˈnaʊns·mənt] *n* Bekanntmachung *f;* (*on train, at airport*) Durchsage *f;* (*on radio*) Ansage *f;* (*in newspaper*) Anzeige *f*

announcer [ə·ˈnaʊn·sər] *n* [Radio-/Fernseh]sprecher(in) *m(f)*

annoy [ə·ˈnɔɪ] *vt* ärgern

annoyance [ə·ˈnɔɪ·əns] *n* ❶ (*anger*) Ärger *m;* (*weaker*) Verärgerung *f* ❷ (*pest*) Ärgernis *nt*

annoying [ə·ˈnɔɪ·ɪŋ] *adj* ärgerlich; *habit* lästig

annual [ˈæn·jʊ·əl] **I.** *adj* jährlich; *event* alljährlich; **~ income** Jahreseinkommen *nt* **II.** *n* ❶ (*publication*) Jahrbuch *nt* ❷ (*plant*) einjährige Pflanze

annually [ˈæn·jʊ·ə·li] *adv* [all]jährlich

annuity [ə·ˈnu·ə·t̬i] *n* Jahresrente *f*

annul <-ll-> [ə·ˈnʌl] *vt* annullieren; *contract* auflösen

annulment [ə·ˈnʌl·mənt] *n* Annullierung *f; of a contract* Auflösung *f*

anode [ˈæn·oʊd] *n* Anode *f*

anodyne [ˈæn·ə·daɪn] *adj* (*pej*) einlullend; *music* unauffällig; *approach* neutral

anoint [ə·ˈnɔɪnt] *vt* (*with oil*) einölen

anomalous [ə·ˈnam·ə·ləs] *adj* anomal

anomaly [ə·ˈnam·ə·li] *n* ❶ (*irregularity*) Anomalie *f* ❷ (*state*) Absonderlichkeit *f*

anonymity [ˌæn·ə·ˈnɪm·ɪ·t̬i] *n* Anonymität *f*

anonymous [ə·ˈnan·ə·məs] *adj* anonym

anorak [ˈæn·ə·ræk] *n* (*jacket*) Anorak *m*

anorexia [ˌæn·ə·ˈrek·si·ə], **anorexia nervosa** [ˌæn·ə·ˈrek·si·ə nɜr·ˈvoʊ·sə] *n* Magersucht *f*

anorexic [ˌæn·ə·ˈrek·sɪk] **I.** *adj* magersüchtig **II.** *n* Magersüchtige(r) *f(m)*

another [ə·ˈnʌð·ər] **I.** *adj* ❶ (*one more*) noch eine(r, s); **~ piece of cake** noch ein Stück Kuchen ❷ (*similar to*) ein zweiter/zweites/eine zweite; **the Gulf War could have been ~ Vietnam** der Golfkrieg hätte ein zweites Vietnam sein können ❸ (*not the same*) ein anderer/anderes/eine andere; **that's ~ story** das ist eine andere Geschichte **II.** *pron* ❶ (*different one*) ein anderer/eine andere/ein anderes; **one way or ~** irgendwie ❷ (*additional one*) noch eine(r, s); **yet ~** noch eine(r, s) ❸ (*each other*) **one ~** einander

answer [ˈæn·sər] **I.** *n* ❶ (*reply*) Antwort *f* (**to** auf +*akk*); (*reaction a.*) Reaktion *f* ❷ MATH Ergebnis *nt;* **~ to a problem** Lösung *f* eines Problems **II.** *vt* ❶ (*reply*) beantworten, antworten auf +*akk; door* öffnen; **to ~ the telephone** ans Telefon gehen; ■**to ~ sb** jdm antworten ❷ MATH *problem* lösen **III.** *vi* antworten; **nobody ~ed** (*telephone*) es ist keiner rangegangen; (*doorbell*) es hat keiner aufgemacht

◆**answer for** *vt* Verantwortung tragen für +*akk*

◆**answer to** *vt* ❶ (*take orders*) ■**to ~ to sb** jdm Rede und Antwort stehen ❷ *description* entsprechen +*dat* ❸ **to ~ to the name of ...** auf den Namen ... hören

answerable [ˈæn·sər·ə·bəl] *adj* ❶ (*respon-*

sible) verantwortlich ❷ (*accountable*) **to be ~ to sb** jdm gegenüber haftbar sein

'answering machine *n* Anrufbeantworter *m*

ant [ænt] *n* Ameise *f*

antagonism [æn·'tæg·ə·nɪz·əm] *n* Feindseligkeit *f* (**toward**[**s**] gegenüber +*dat*)

antagonistic [æn·ˌtæg·ə·'nɪs·tɪk] *adj* ■ **to be ~ toward**[**s**] **sb** jdm gegenüber feindselig eingestellt sein

antagonize [æn·'tæg·ə·naɪz] *vt* sich *dat* zum Feind machen

Antarctic [ænt·'ark·tɪk] **I.** *n* ■ **the ~** die Antarktis **II.** *adj* antarktisch; *expedition, explorer* Antarktis-; **~ Circle** südlicher Polarkreis

Antarctica [ænt·'ark·tɪ·kə] *n* die Antarktis

anteater ['ænt·ˌi·t̬ər] *n* Ameisenbär *m*

antecedent [ˌæn·tɪ·'si·dənt] *n* (*forerunner*) Vorläufer(in) *m(f)*

antelope <*pl* -s *or* -> ['æn·t̬ɪ·loʊp] *n* Antilope *f*

antenna [æn·'ten·ə] *n* ❶ <*pl* -nae> *of an insect* Fühler *m* ❷ <*pl* -s> (*aerial*) Antenne *f*

anterior [æn·'tɪr·i·ər] *adj* vordere(r, s)

anteroom ['æn·tɪ·rum] *n* Vorzimmer *nt*

anthem ['æn·θəm] *n* Hymne *f*

anthill ['ænt·hɪl] *n* Ameisenhaufen *m*

anthology [æn·'θal·ə·dʒi] *n* Anthologie *f*

anthracite ['æn·θrə·saɪt] *n* Anthrazit *m*

anthropological [ˌæn·θrə·pə·'ladʒ·ɪ·kəl] *adj* anthropologisch

anthropologist [ˌæn·θrə·'pal·ə·dʒɪst] *n* Anthropologe *m,* Anthropologin *f*

anthropology [ˌæn·θrə·'pal·ə·dʒi] *n* Anthropologie *f*

anti ['æn·ti] **I.** *n* Gegner(in) *m(f)* **II.** *adj* ■ **to be ~** dagegen sein **III.** *prep* gegen +*akk*

anti'aircraft *adj* Flugabwehr- *f*

antibiotic [ˌæn·tɪ·baɪ·'at̬·ɪk] **I.** *n* Antibiotikum *nt* **II.** *adj* antibiotisch

'antibody *n* Antikörper *m*

anticipate [æn·'tɪs·ə·peɪt] *vt* ❶ (*expect*) erwarten; (*foresee*) vorhersehen ❷ (*act in advance*) vorgreifen

anticipation [æn·ˌtɪs·ə·'peɪ·ʃən] *n* (*expecting*) Erwartung *f;* (*pleasure in advance*) Vorfreude *f*

anti'climax *n* Enttäuschung *f;* LIT Antiklimax *m*

anticor'rosive *adj* Korrosionsschutz-

antics ['æn·tɪks] *npl* Kapriolen *pl*

anti'cyclone *n* Hochdruckgebiet *nt*

antide'pressant *n* Antidepressivum *nt*

antidote ['æn·tɪ·doʊt] *n* Gegenmittel *nt*

'antifreeze *n* Frostschutzmittel *nt*

antigen ['æn·tɪ·dʒən] *n* Antigen *nt*

'antihero *n* Antiheld *m*

anti'histamine *n* Antihistamin *nt*

antilock 'braking system *n* Antiblockiersystem *nt*

anti'oxidant *n* Antioxidationsmittel *nt*

antipathy [æn·'tɪp·ə·θi] *n* Antipathie *f*

antiperspirant [ˌæn·tɪ·'pɜr·spər·ənt] *n* Antitranspirant *nt*

Antipodes [æn·'tɪp·ə·diz] *npl* (*fam*) ■ **the ~** Australien *nt* und Neuseeland *nt*

antiquarian [ˌæn·tɪ·'kwer·i·ən] **I.** *n* Antiquitätensammler(in) *m(f)* **II.** *adj* antiquarisch

antiquated ['æn·tɪ·kweɪ·t̬ɪd] *adj* antiquiert

antique [æn·'tik] **I.** *n* (*iron a.*) Antiquität *f;* **~ dealer** Antiquitätenhändler(in) *m(f)* **II.** *adj* antik

antiquity [æn·'tɪk·wə·t̬i] *n* ❶ (*ancient times*) Altertum *nt* ❷ (*relics*) ■ **antiquities** *pl* Altertümer

anti'rust *adj* Rostschutz-

anti-'Semite *n* Antisemit(in) *m(f)*

anti-'Semitic *adj* antisemitisch

anti-'Semitism *n* Antisemitismus *m*

anti'septic **I.** *n* Antiseptikum *nt* **II.** *adj* antiseptisch; (*fig*) steril

anti'social *adj* ❶ (*harmful*) unsozial; (*alienated*) asozial ❷ (*not sociable*) ungesellig

anti'static *adj* antistatisch

anti'tank *adj* Panzerabwehr-

antithesis <*pl* -ses> [æn·'tɪθ·ə·sɪs] *n* Gegenteil *nt*

anti'toxin *n* Gegengift *nt*

antler ['ænt·lər] *n* Geweihstange *f;* **pair of ~s** Geweih *nt*

antonym ['æn·tə·nɪm] *n* Antonym *nt*

antsy ['ænt·si] *adj* (*fam*) *child* zappelig *fam*

anus ['eɪ·nəs] *n* Anus *m*

anvil ['æn·vɪl] *n* Amboss *m*

anxiety [æŋ·'zaɪ·ɪ·t̬i] *n* ❶ (*feeling of concern*) Sorge *f* ❷ (*concern*) Angst *f* ❸ (*desire*) Verlangen *nt*

anxious ['æŋk·ʃəs] *adj* ❶ (*concerned*) besorgt ❷ (*eager*) bestrebt; ■ **to be ~ for sth** ungeduldig auf etw *akk* warten

any ['en·i] **I.** *adj* ❶ (*in questions, conditional*) [irgend]ein(e); (*with uncountables*) etwas; **do you have ~ brothers or sisters?** haben Sie Geschwister?; **if I had ~ money ...** wenn ich [etwas] Geld hätte, ... ❷ (*with negative*) **I don't have ~ money** ich habe kein Geld ❸ (*every*) jede(r, s); **~ time** jederzeit; **in ~ case** (*whatever happens*) auf jeden Fall; (*anyway*) außerdem ❹ (*whichever you like*) jede(r, s) [beliebige]; (*with uncountables, pl n*) alle; (*not important which*) irgendein(e); (*with pl n*) irgendwelche; **~ number** beliebig viele **II.** *pron* ❶ (*some of many*) welche; (*one of many*) eine(r, s); **do you have ~ [at all]?** haben Sie [überhaupt] welche?; **did ~ of you hear anything?** hat jemand von euch etwas gehört? ❷ (*some of a quantity*) welche(r, s); **~ at all** überhaupt welche(r, s); **hardly ~** kaum etwas ❸ (*with negative*) **don't you have ~ at all?** haben Sie denn überhaupt keine? ❹ (*not important which*) irgendeine(r, s); (*replacing pl n*) irgendwelche; **~ will do** egal welche **III.** *adv* ❶ (*emphasizing*) noch; (*a little*) etwas; (*at all*) überhaupt; **if I have to stay here ~ longer, ...** wenn ich noch länger hierbleiben muss, ...; **are you feeling ~ better?** fühlst du dich [denn] etwas besser?; **~ more** noch mehr ❷ (*expressing termination*) **not ~ longer/more** nicht mehr

A

anybody ['en·ɪ·bad·i] *pron* ❶ (*each person*) jede(r, s) ❷ (*someone*) jemand; **does ~ else want coffee?** möchte noch jemand Kaffee?

anyhow ['en·ɪ·haʊ] *adv* ❶ (*in any case*) sowieso ❷ (*in a disorderly way*) irgendwie

anyone ['en·ɪ·wʌn] *pron see* **anybody**

anyplace ['en·ɪ·pleɪs] *adv* (*fam*) irgendwo

anything ['en·ɪ·θɪŋ] *pron* ❶ (*each thing*) alles ❷ (*something*) **is there ~ I can do to help?** kann ich irgendwie helfen?; **hardly ~** kaum etwas ❸ (*nothing*) **not ~** nichts; **not ~ like ...** nicht annähernd ...; **you don't have to sing or ~** du musst weder singen noch sonst was ▶ PHRASES: **[as]** ... **as** ~ ausgesprochen ...; **not for ~ [in the world]** um nichts in der Welt

anytime ['en·i·taɪm] *adv* jederzeit

anyway ['en·ɪ·weɪ] *adv,* **anyways** ['en·ɪ·weɪz] *adv* (*fam*) ❶ (*in any case*) sowieso; **what's he doing there ~?** was macht er dort überhaupt? ❷ (*well*) jedenfalls; **~!** na ja!

anywhere ['en·ɪ·wer] *adv* ❶ (*in any place*) überall; **~ else** irgendwo anders ❷ (*some place*) irgendwo; **I'm not getting ~** ich komme einfach nicht weiter; **to go ~** irgendwohin gehen; **miles from ~** am Ende der Welt

aorta [eɪ·'ɔr·t̬ə] *n* Aorta *f*

apart [ə·'part] *adv* ❶ (*not together*) auseinander; **to live ~** getrennt leben ❷ ■ **~ from** abgesehen von +*dat*

apartheid [ə·'part·heɪt] *n* Apartheid *f*

apartment [ə·'part·mənt] *n* Wohnung *f;* (*smaller*) Ap[p]art[e]ment *nt*

a'partment building, a'partment house *n* Wohnhaus *nt;* (*with smaller apartments*) Ap[p]art[e]menthaus *nt*

apathetic [ˌæp·ə·'θet̬·ɪk] *adj* apathisch

apathy ['æp·ə·θi] *n* Apathie *f*

ape [eɪp] **I.** *n* [Menschen]affe *m* **II.** *vt* nachahmen

aperitif [ə·ˌper·ə·'tif] *n* Aperitif *m*

aperture ['æp·ər·tʃʊr] *n* [kleine] Öffnung; PHOT Blende *f*

apex <*pl* -es *or* apices> ['eɪ·peks] *n* Spitze *f*

aphid ['eɪ·fɪd] *n* Blattlaus *f*

aphrodisiac [ˌæf·rə·'dɪ·zi·æk] *n* Aphrodisiakum *nt*

apiary ['eɪ·pɪ·er·i] *n* Bienenhaus *nt*

apiece [ə·'pis] *adv* das Stück; (*per person*) jeder

aplomb [ə·'plam] *n* Aplomb *m*

apocalypse [ə·'pak·ə·lɪps] *n* Apokalypse *f*

apocalyptic [ə·ˌpak·ə·'lɪp·tɪk] *adj* apokalyptisch

apologetic [ə·ˌpal·ə·'dʒet̬·ɪk] *adj* ❶ (*showing regret*) entschuldigend; ■ **to be ~ about** sich entschuldigen für +*akk* ❷ (*diffident*) bescheiden

apologetically [ə·ˌpal·ə·'dʒet̬·ɪk·li] *adv* entschuldigend; **to smile ~** zaghaft lächeln

apologize [ə·'pal·ə·dʒaɪz] *vi* sich entschuldigen (**to** bei +*dat*)

apology [ə·'pal·ə·dʒi] *n* Entschuldigung *f;* **to make an ~** um Entschuldigung bitten

apostle [ə·'pas·əl] *n* Apostel *m*

apostrophe [ə·'pas·trə·fi] *n* Apostroph *m*

> Die **Appalachian Mountains** (die Appalachen) erstrecken sich über ca. 2.000 Meilen (3.200 km) im östlichen Teil Nordamerikas von Neufundland/Kanada bis nach Alabama/USA. Da sie älter und somit zerklüfteter als die *Rocky Mountains* im Westen Nordamerikas sind, ist dieses Gebirge fabelhaft bewaldet und von Straßen und Wegen wie dem *Blue Ridge Parkway* und dem *Skyline Drive* durchzogen, die eine prächtige Landschaft zu bieten haben, oder dem *Appalachian Trail*, einem 2.175 Meilen (3.500 km) langen Wanderweg, der von Maine bis nach Georgia führt.

appall [ə·'pɔl] *vt* entsetzen; ■ **to be ~led at** [*or* **by**] **sth** über etw *akk* entsetzt sein

appalling [ə·'pɔ·lɪŋ] *adj* entsetzlich

apparatus [ˌæp·ə·'ræt̬·əs] *n* ❶ (*equipment*) [**piece of**] **~** Gerät *nt* ❷ (*system*) Apparat *m*

apparent [ə·'pær·ənt] *adj* ❶ (*obvious*) offensichtlich; **for no ~ reason** aus keinem ersichtlichen Grund ❷ (*seeming*) scheinbar

apparently [ə·'pær·ənt·li] *adv* ❶ (*obviously*) offensichtlich ❷ (*seemingly*) anscheinend

apparition [ˌæp·ə·'rɪʃ·ən] *n* (*ghost*) Erscheinung *f*

appeal [ə·'pil] **I.** *vi* ❶ (*attract*) ■ **to ~ to sb/sth** jdn/etw reizen; (*aim to please*) jdn/etw ansprechen ❷ (*protest formally*) Einspruch einlegen (**against** gegen +*akk*) ❸ (*plead*) bitten; **to ~ to sb's conscience** an jds Gewissen *nt* appellieren **II.** *n* ❶ (*attraction*) Reiz *m* ❷ (*formal protest*) Einspruch *m* (**against** gegen +*akk*); **Court of A~** Berufungsgericht *nt* ❸ (*request*) Appell *m;* **to make an ~** appellieren (**to** an +*akk*)

appealing [ə·'pi·lɪŋ] *adj* ❶ (*attractive*) attraktiv; *idea* verlockend; ■ **to be ~ [to sb]** [für jdn] verlockend sein ❷ (*beseeching*) flehend

appealingly [ə·'pi·lɪŋ·li] *adv* ❶ (*attractively*) reizvoll ❷ (*beseechingly*) flehend

appear [ə·'pɪr] *vi* ❶ (*become visible*) erscheinen; (*be seen a.*) sich *dat* zeigen; (*arrive a.*) auftauchen; (*come out a.*) herauskommen ❷ (*come out*) *film* anlaufen; *newspaper* erscheinen; (*perform*) auftreten ❸ (*seem*) scheinen; **to ~ [to be] calm** ruhig erscheinen

appearance [ə·'pɪr·əns] *n* ❶ (*instance of appearing*) Erscheinen *nt;* (*on TV, theater*) Auftritt *m;* **to make an ~** auftreten ❷ (*looks*) Aussehen *nt;* **neat ~** gepflegtes Äußeres ▶ PHRASES: **to all ~s** allem Anschein nach; **to keep up ~s** den Schein wahren

appease [ə·'piz] *vt* besänftigen

appeasement [ə·'piz·mənt] *n* Besänftigung *f*

A

append [ə·ˈpend] *vt* hinzufügen

appendicitis [ə·ˌpen·dɪ·ˈsaɪ·tɪs] *n* Blinddarmentzündung *f*

appendix [ə·ˈpen·dɪks] *n* ❶ <*pl* -es> (*body part*) Blinddarm *m* ❷ <*pl* -dices *or* -es> (*in book*) Anhang *m*

appetite [ˈæp·ə·taɪt] *n* Appetit *m;* **to give sb an ~** jdn hungrig machen

appetizer [ˈæp·ə·taɪ·zər] *n* (*before meal*) Vorspeise *f,* Appetithappen *m*

appetizing [ˈæp·ə·taɪ·zɪŋ] *adj* (*enticing*) appetitlich; (*fig: attractive*) reizvoll

applaud [ə·ˈplɔd] **I.** *vi* applaudieren, Beifall klatschen **II.** *vt* ❶ (*clap*) ■**to ~ sb** jdm applaudieren ❷ (*praise*) loben; *decision* begrüßen

applause [ə·ˈplɔz] *n* [**a round of**] ~ Applaus *m*

apple [ˈæp·əl] *n* Apfel *m*

ˈapple juice *n* Apfelsaft *m*

apple ˈpie *n* FOOD gedeckter Apfelkuchen

ˈapplesauce *n* Apfelmus *nt*

ˈapple tree *n* Apfelbaum *m*

appliance [ə·ˈplaɪ·əns] *n* Gerät *nt*

applicable [ə·ˈplɪ·kə·bəl] *adj* anwendbar (**to** auf +*akk*); (*on application form*) **not ~** nicht zutreffend

applicant [ˈæp·lɪ·kənt] *n* Bewerber(in) *m(f)* (**for** für +*akk*)

application [ˌæp·lɪ·ˈkeɪ·ʃən] *n* ❶ *for a job* Bewerbung *f* (**for** um +*akk*); *for a permit* Antrag *m* (**for** auf +*akk*) ❷ (*implementation*) Anwendung *f* ❸ (*coating*) Anstrich *m; of ointment* Auftragen *nt* ❹ COMPUT Anwendung *f*

appliˈcation form *n* (*for job*) Bewerbungsformular *nt;* (*for permit*) Antragsformular *nt*

applied [ə·ˈplaɪd] *adj* angewandt

apply <-ie-> [ə·ˈplaɪ] **I.** *vi* ❶ (*formally request*) ■**to ~** [**to sb**] [**for sth**] (*for a job*) sich [bei jdm] [um etw *akk*] bewerben; (*for permission, passport*) etw [bei jdm] beantragen ❷ (*pertain*) gelten; ■**to ~ to** betreffen **II.** *vt* ❶ (*put on*) anwenden (**to** auf +*akk*); *cream, makeup* auftragen ❷ (*use*) gebrauchen; *force* anwenden; *sanctions* verhängen; **to ~ the brakes** bremsen; **to ~ pressure to sth** auf etw *akk* drücken

appoint [ə·ˈpɔɪnt] *vt* ■**to ~ sb** [**to do sth**] jdn [dazu] berufen[, etw zu tun]; ■**to ~ sb** [**as**] **sth** jdn zu etw *dat* ernennen

appointed [ə·ˈpɔɪn·t̬ɪd] *adj* ❶ (*selected*) ernannt ❷ (*designated*) vereinbart

appointee [ə·pɔɪn·ˈti] *n* Ernannte(r) *f(m)*

appointment [ə·ˈpɔɪnt·mənt] *n* ❶ (*being selected*) Ernennung *f* (**as** zu +*dat*) ❷ (*selection*) Einstellung *f* ❸ (*official meeting*) Verabredung *f;* **dentist ~** Zahnarzttermin *m;* **by ~ only** nur nach Absprache

apportion [ə·ˈpɔr·ʃən] *vt* aufteilen; *blame* zuweisen

appraisal [ə·ˈpreɪ·zəl] *n* ❶ (*evaluation*) Bewertung *f,* Beurteilung *f* ❷ (*estimation*) [Ab]schätzung *f*

appraise [ə·ˈpreɪz] *vt* ❶ (*evaluate*) bewerten; *situation* einschätzen ❷ (*estimate*) schätzen

appreciable [ə·ˈpri·ʃə·bəl] *adj* beträchtlich; *difference* nennenswert

appreciate [ə·ˈpri·ʃi·eɪt] **I.** *vt* ❶ (*value*) schätzen; (*be grateful for*) zu schätzen wissen ❷ (*understand*) Verständnis haben für +*akk;* ■**to ~ that ...** verstehen, dass ... **II.** *vi* **to ~ in value** im Wert steigen

appreciation [ə·ˌpri·ʃi·ˈeɪ·ʃən] *n* ❶ (*gratitude*) Anerkennung *f* ❷ (*understanding*) Verständnis *nt* (**of** für +*akk*) ❸ (*increase in value*) [Wert]steigerung *f*

appreciative [ə·ˈpri·ʃə·t̬ɪv] *adj* ❶ (*grateful*) dankbar (**of** für +*akk*) ❷ (*showing appreciation*) anerkennend; *audience* dankbar

apprehend [ˌæp·rɪ·ˈhend] *vt* festnehmen

apprehension [ˌæp·rɪ·ˈhen·ʃən] *n* ❶ (*arrest*) Festnahme *f* ❷ (*anxiety*) Besorgnis *f*

apprehensive [ˌæp·rɪ·ˈhen·sɪv] *adj* besorgt; (*scared*) ängstlich; ■**to be ~ about sth** vor etw *dat* Angst haben

apprentice [ə·ˈpren·tɪs] *n* Auszubildende(r) *f(m)*

apprenticeship [ə·ˈpren·tɪs·ʃɪp] *n* ❶ (*training*) Ausbildung *f* ❷ (*period of training*) Lehrzeit *f*

approach [ə·ˈproʊtʃ] **I.** *vt* ❶ (*come closer*) ■**to ~ sb/sth** sich jdm/etw nähern; (*come toward*[*s*]) auf jdn/etw zukommen; **it's ~ing lunchtime** es geht auf Mittag zu ❷ (*ask*) ■**to ~ sb** jdn ansprechen (**about** wegen +*gen*); ■**to ~ sb for sth** jdn um etw *akk* bitten ❸ (*handle*) *problem, issue* angehen **II.** *vi* sich nähern **III.** *n* ❶ (*coming*) Nähern *nt;* **at the ~ of winter ...** wenn der Winter naht, ... ❷ (*preparation to land*) [Lande]anflug *m* ❸ (*method*) Ansatz *m* ❹ (*proposal*) Vorstoß *m;* **to make an ~ to sb** sich an jdn wenden

approachable [ə·ˈproʊ·tʃə·bəl] *adj person* umgänglich; *place* zugänglich

appropriate **I.** *adj* [ə·ˈproʊ·pri·ət] ❶ (*suitable*) angemessen, angebracht; *words* richtig ❷ (*relevant*) entsprechend **II.** *vt* [ə·ˈproʊ·pri·eɪt] sich *dat* aneignen

appropriation [ə·ˌproʊ·pri·ˈeɪ·ʃən] *n* Aneignung *f*

approval [ə·ˈpru·vəl] *n* ❶ (*consent*) Zustimmung *f* ❷ (*praise*) Anerkennung *f* ►PHRASES: **on ~** ECON zur Ansicht; (*to try*) zur Probe

approve [ə·ˈpruv] **I.** *vi* ❶ (*agree with*) ■**to ~ of sth** etw *dat* zustimmen ❷ (*like*) ■**to ~/not ~ of sb** etwas/nichts von jdm halten; ■**to ~ of sth** etw gutheißen **II.** *vt* (*permit*) genehmigen; (*consent to*) billigen; *minutes* annehmen

approved [ə·ˈpruvd] *adj* ❶ (*agreed*) bewährt ❷ (*sanctioned*) [offiziell] anerkannt

approving [ə·ˈpru·vɪŋ] *adj* zustimmend

approvingly [ə·ˈpru·vɪŋ·li] *adv* anerkennend, zustimmend

approx. *adv abbrev of* **approximately** ca.

approximate **I.** *adj* [ə·ˈprak·sɪ·mət] ungefähr; **~ number** [An]näherungswert *m* **II.** *vt* [ə·ˈprak·sɪ·meɪt] sich nähern **III.** *vi* [ə·ˈprak·sɪ·meɪt] ■**to ~ to sth** etw *dat* annähernd gleich-

A

kommen

approximately [ə·ˈprak·sɪ·mət·li] *adv* ungefähr

approximation [ə·ˌprak·sɪ·ˈmeɪ·ʃən] *n* Annäherung *f;* **that's only an ~** das ist nur eine grobe Schätzung

APR [ˌeɪ·pi·ˈar] *n* FIN *abbrev of* **annual percentage rate** Jahreszinssatz *m*

Apr. *n abbrev of* **April** Apr.

apricot [ˈeɪ·prɪ·kat] **I.** *n (fruit)* Aprikose *f,* Marille *f* ÖSTERR **II.** *adj* aprikosenfarben, apricot

April [ˈei·prəl] *n* April *m; see also* **February**

April 'Fools' Day *n* der erste April

apron [ˈeɪ·prən] *n* Schürze *f*

apropos [ˌæp·rə·ˈpoʊ] *adv, prep* apropos

apt [æpt] *adj* ① *(appropriate)* passend; *description, remark* treffend; *moment* geeignet ② *(likely)* ■**to be ~ to do sth** dazu neigen, etw zu tun

aptitude [ˈæp·tɪ·tud] *n* Begabung *f*

'aptitude test *n* Eignungstest *m*

aquarium <*pl* -s *or* -ria> [ə·ˈkwer·i·əm] *n* Aquarium *nt*

Aquarius [ə·ˈkwer·i·əs] *n* ASTROL Wassermann *m*

aquatic [ə·ˈkwæt̬·ɪk] *adj* Wasser-

AR *abbrev of* **Arkansas**

Arab [ˈær·əb] **I.** *n* Araber(in) *m(f)* **II.** *adj* arabisch

Arabian [ə·ˈrei·bi·ən] *adj* arabisch

Arabic [ˈær·ə·bɪk] **I.** *n* Arabisch *nt* **II.** *adj* arabisch

arable [ˈær·ə·bəl] *adj* **~ land** Ackerland *nt*

arbitrary [ˈar·bɪ·trer·i] *adj* willkürlich

arbitrate [ˈar·bɪ·treɪt] **I.** *vt* schlichten **II.** *vi* vermitteln

arbitration [ˌar·bɪ·ˈtreɪ·ʃən] *n* Schlichtung *f;* **to go to ~** einen Schlichter anrufen

arbitrator [ˈar·bɪ·treɪ·t̬ər] *n* Schlichter(in) *m(f)*

arbor [ˈar·bər] *n* Laube *f*

arc [ark] **I.** *n* Bogen *m* **II.** *vi* einen Bogen beschreiben

arcade [ær·ˈkeɪd] *n* ① *(for playing games)* Spielhalle *f* ② ARCHIT Arkade *f*

arch [artʃ] **I.** *n* Bogen *m;* **~ of the foot** Fußgewölbe *nt* **II.** *vi* sich wölben **III.** *vt back* krümmen; *eyebrows* heben

archaic [ar·ˈkeɪ·ɪk] *adj* veraltet

archangel [ˈark·eɪn·dʒl] *n* Erzengel *m*

arch'bishop *n* Erzbischof *m*

arch'diocese *n* Erzdiözese *f*

arch'enemy *n* Erzfeind(in) *m(f)*

archeological [ˌar·ki·ə·ˈladʒ·ɪ·kəl] *adj* archäologisch; **~ dig** [Aus]grabungsort *m*

archeologist [ˌar·ki·ˈal·ə·dʒɪst] *n* Archäologe *m,* Archäologin *f*

archeology [ˌar·ki·ˈal·ə·dʒi] *n* Archäologie *f*

archer [ˈar·tʃər] *n* Bogenschütze *m,* Bogenschützin *f*

archery [ˈar·tʃə·ri] *n* Bogenschießen *nt*

archipelago <*pl* -s *or* -es> [ˌar·kə·ˈpel·ə·goʊ] *n* Archipel *m*

architect [ˈar·kɪ·tekt] *n* Architekt(in) *m(f)*

architecture [ˈar·kɪ·tek·tʃər] *n* Architektur *f*

archive [ˈar·kaɪv] *n* Archiv *nt*

archivist [ˈar·kə·vɪst] *n* Archivar(in) *m(f)*

'archway *n* Torbogen *m*

'arc lamp, 'arc light *n* Bogenlampe *f*

Arctic [ˈark·tɪk] **I.** *n* ■**the ~** die Arktis **II.** *adj* arktisch; *expedition, explorer* Arktis-; **~ Circle** nördlicher Polarkreis; **~ Ocean** nördliches Eismeer

ardent [ˈar·dənt] *adj* leidenschaftlich; **~ admirer** glühender Verehrer/glühende Verehrerin

ardor [ˈar·dər] *n* Leidenschaft *f*

arduous [ˈar·dʒu·əs] *adj* anstrengend

are [ər, *stressed:* ar] *vi, vt see* **be**

area [ˈer·i·ə] *n* ① Gebiet *nt;* **~ of the brain** Hirnregion *f* ② *(surface measure)* Fläche *f* ③ *(approximately)* ■**in the ~ of ...** ungefähr ...

'area code *n* Vorwahl *f*

arena [ə·ˈri·nə] *n* Arena *f*

Argentina [ˌar·dʒən·ˈti·nə] *n* Argentinien *nt*

Argentine [ˈar·dʒən·tin], **Argentinean** [ˌar·dʒən·ˈtɪn·i·ən] **I.** *adj* argentinisch **II.** *n* Argentinier(in) *m(f)*

arguable [ˈar·gju·ə·bəl] *adj* fragwürdig

arguably [ˈar·gju·ə·bli] *adv* wohl

argue [ˈar·gju] **I.** *vi* ① *(disagree)* [sich] streiten; **don't ~ [with me]!** keine Widerrede! ② *(reason)* argumentieren; ■**to ~ for sth** sich für etw *akk* aussprechen **II.** *vt* erörtern; ■**to ~ that ...** dafür sprechen, dass ...

argument [ˈar·gjə·mənt] *n* ① *(heated discussion)* Auseinandersetzung *f* ② *(case)* Argument *nt*

argumentative [ˌar·gjə·ˈmen·t̬ə·t̬ɪv] *adj* streitsüchtig

aria [ˈa·ri·ə] *n* Arie *f*

arid [ˈær·ɪd] *adj* dürr

Aries [ˈer·iz] *n* ASTROL Widder *m*

arise <arose, arisen> [ə·ˈraɪz] *vi (come about)* sich ergeben; **should the need ~, ...** sollte es notwendig werden, ...

arisen [ə·ˈrɪz·ən] *pp of* **arise**

aristocracy [ˌær·ɪ·ˈstak·rə·si] *n* + *pl/sing vb* Aristokratie *f*

aristocrat [ə·ˈrɪs·tə·kræt] *n* Aristokrat(in) *m(f)*

aristocratic [e·ˌrɪs·tə·ˈkræt̬·ɪk] *adj* aristokratisch

arithmetic **I.** *n* [ə·ˈrɪθ·mɪ·tɪk] Arithmetik *f* **II.** *adj* [ˌer·ɪθ·ˈmet̬·ɪk] arithmetisch

Ariz. *abbrev of* **Arizona**

Arizona [ˌær·ɪ·ˈzoʊ·nə] *n* Arizona *nt*

ark [ark] *n* Arche *f*

Ark. *abbrev of* **Arkansas**

Arkansas [ˈar·kən·sɔ] *n* Arkansas *nt*

Der **Arlington National Cemetery** (Nationalfriedhof Arlington) befindet sich am Potomac River, südöstlich von Washington, D.C. Er hat eine Fläche von 1 Quadratmeile (2,6 km^2) und beherbergt die Gräber von mehr als 60.000 amerikanischen Soldaten sowie die bekannter amerikanischer Persönlichkeiten wie Präsident William Howard Taft, Präsident John F. Kennedy, General John J. Pershing, Admiral Robert E. Peary und schließlich das des „Unbekannten Soldaten", der das ganze Jahr rund um die Uhr bewacht wird.

arm¹ [arm] *n* ❶ ANAT, GEOG Arm *m;* **on one's ~** am Arm ❷ (*armrest*) Armlehne *f* ❸ (*division*) Abteilung *f* ▶ PHRASES: **to cost an ~ and a leg** Unsummen kosten; **to keep sb at ~'s length** jdn auf Distanz halten

arm² [arm] **I.** *vt* ❶ (*supply with weapons*) bewaffnen; ■**to ~ oneself** (*fig*) sich wappnen ❷ (*prime*) *bomb* scharf machen **II.** *n* ■**~s** *pl* ❶ (*weapons*) Waffen *pl;* **under ~s** kampfbereit ❷ (*heraldic insignia*) Wappen *nt*

'armband *n* Armbinde *f*

'armchair *n* Sessel *m;* **~ politician** Stammtischpolitiker(in) *m(f)*

armed [armd] *adj* bewaffnet

armed 'forces *npl* Streitkräfte *pl*

Armenia [ar·'mi·ni·ə] *n* Armenien *nt*

Armenian [ar·'mi·ni·ən] **I.** *adj* armenisch **II.** *n* ❶ (*person*) Armenier(in) *m(f)* ❷ (*language*) Armenisch *nt*

armful ['arm·fʊl] *n* Armvoll *m*

armhole ['arm·hoʊl] *n* Armloch *nt*

armistice ['ar·mə·stɪs] *n* Waffenstillstand *m*

armor ['ar·mər] *n* HIST Rüstung *f;* **suit of ~** Panzerkleid *nt;* **~ plate** Panzerplatte *f*

armored ['ar·mərd] *adj* gepanzert; **~ car** Panzer[späh]wagen *m*

armor-'plated *adj* gepanzert

'armpit *n* Achselhöhle *f*

'armrest *n* Armlehne *f*

'arms control *n* Abrüstung *f*

'arms race *n* Wettrüsten *nt*

army ['ar·mi] *n* ❶ Armee *f;* ■**the ~** das Heer; **to join the ~** zum Militär gehen ❷ (*fig*) Heer *nt*

aroma [ə·'roʊ·mə] *n* Duft *m*

aroma'therapy *n* Aromatherapie *f*

aromatic [ˌær·ə·'mæt̬·ɪk] *adj* aromatisch

arose [ə·'roʊz] *pt of* **arise**

around [ə·'raʊnd] **I.** *adv* ❶ (*on all sides*) rundum; **from miles ~** von weither; **he's the biggest crook ~** er ist der größte Gauner, den es gibt ❷ (*with circular motion*) umher; **to wave one's arms ~** mit den Armen [herum]fuchteln ❸ (*here and there*) herum; **to show sb ~** jdn herumführen; **to get ~** herumkommen ▶ PHRASES: **see you ~** bis demnächst mal **II.** *prep* ❶ um +*akk;* **~ the table** um den Tisch herum; **from all ~ the world** aus aller Welt ❷ ungefähr; **~ 12:15** um ungefähr 12.15 Uhr ❸ (*expressing location*) **she must be ~ here somewhere** sie muss hier irgendwo sein

arouse [ə·'raʊz] *vt* ❶ (*stir*) erwecken; *suspicion* erregen ❷ (*sexually excite*) erregen

arraign [ə·'reɪn] *vt* ■**to ~ sb** jdn vor Gericht stellen

arrange [ə·'reɪndʒ] **I.** *vt* ❶ (*organize*) arrangieren; *date* vereinbaren; *matters* regeln ❷ (*put in order*) ordnen; *flowers* arrangieren ❸ MUS arrangieren **II.** *vi* festlegen; ■**to ~ to do sth** etw vereinbaren; ■**to ~ for sb to do sth** etw für jdn organisieren

arrangement [ə·'reɪndʒ·mənt] *n* ❶ ■**~s** *pl* (*preparations*) Vorbereitungen *pl* ❷ (*agreement*) Abmachung *f;* **by [prior] ~** nach [vorheriger] Absprache ❸ (*ordering, a. music*) Arrangement *nt;* **an ~ of dried flowers** ein Gesteck *nt* von Trockenblumen

array [ə·'reɪ] **I.** *n* stattliche Reihe **II.** *vt* (*display*) aufreihen

arrears [ə·'rɪrz] *npl* Rückstände *pl;* **in ~** in Verzug

arrest [ə·'rest] **I.** *vt* (*apprehend*) verhaften **II.** *n* Verhaftung *f;* **to place under ~** in Haft nehmen

arresting [ə·'res·tɪŋ] *adj* (*striking*) faszinierend; *account* fesselnd; *performance* eindrucksvoll

arrival [ə·'raɪ·vəl] *n* ❶ (*at a destination*) Ankunft *f; of a baby* Geburt *f* ❷ (*person*) Ankommende(r) *f(m);* **new ~** Baby *nt*

arrive [ə·'raɪv] *vi* ❶ *bus* ankommen; *baby, mail, season* kommen; **to ~ at a conclusion** zu einem Schluss gelangen ❷ (*establish one's reputation*) es schaffen

arrogance ['ær·ə·gəns] *n* Arroganz *f*

arrogant ['ær·ə·gənt] *adj* arrogant

arrow ['ær·oʊ] *n* Pfeil *m*

'arrowhead *n* Pfeilspitze *f*

arsenic ['ar·sə·nɪk] *n* Arsen *nt*

arson ['ar·sən] *n* Brandstiftung *f*

art [art] *n* Kunst *f;* ■**the ~s** *pl* die Kunst

artefact ['ar·t̬ə·fækt] *n see* **artefact**

arteriosclerosis [ar·ˌtɪr·i·oʊ·sklə·'roʊ·səs] *n* Arterienverkalkung *f*

artery ['ar·t̬ə·ri] *n* ❶ ANAT Arterie *f* ❷ TRANSP Hauptverkehrsader *f*

arthritic [ar·'θrɪt̬·ɪk] *adj* arthritisch

arthritis [ar·'θraɪ·t̬ɪs] *n* Gelenkentzündung *f*

artichoke ['ar·t̬ɪ·tʃoʊk] *n* Artischocke *f*

article ['ar·t̬ɪ·kəl] *n* ❶ Artikel *m;* **~ of clothing** Kleidungsstück *nt* ❷ LAW Paragraph *m*

articulate I. *adj* [ar·'tɪk·jə·lət] ❶ *person* redegewandt ❷ *speech* verständlich **II.** *vt* [ar·'tɪk·jʊ·leɪt] ❶ (*express*) aussprechen; *idea* äußern ❷ (*pronounce*) artikulieren; *sound* bilden

artifact ['ar·tə·fækt] *n* Artefakt *nt*

artificial [ˌar·tə·'fɪʃ·əl] *adj* ❶ (*not natural*) künstlich; **~ color[ing]** Farbstoff *m;* **~ leg** Beinprothese *f;* **~ sweetener** Süßstoff *m* ❷ (*pej: not genuine*) aufgesetzt; *smile* unecht

artillery [ar·'tɪl·ə·ri] *n* Artillerie *f*

artisan ['ar·t̬ɪ·zən] *n* Handwerker(in) *m(f)*

artist ['ar·t̬ɪst] *n* Künstler(in) *m(f)*

artiste [ar·'tist] *n* THEAT, TV Artist(in) *m(f)*

artistic [ar·'tɪs·tɪk] *adj* künstlerisch; *arrange-*

A

ment kunstvoll

artistry ['ar·t̬ɪ·stri] *n* Kunstfertigkeit *f*

'artwork *n* ① (*work of art*) Kunstwerk *nt* ② (*illustrations*) Illustrationen *pl*

arty ['ar·t̬i], **artsy** ['art·si] *adj* gewollt bohemienhaft

Aryan ['er·i·ən] **I.** *n* Arier(in) *m(f)* **II.** *adj* arisch

as [æz, əz] **I.** *conj* ① (*while*) während ② (*in the way that, like*) wie; **do ~ I say!** mach, was ich sage!; **~ it were** sozusagen; **~ if** [*or* **though**] als ob; **~ if!** wohl kaum! ③ (*because*) weil ▶ PHRASES: **~ <u>for</u> ...** was ... betrifft; **~ <u>of</u>** ab; **~ <u>to</u> ...** was ... angeht **II.** *prep* als; **~ a child** als Kind; **dressed ~ a banana** als Banane verkleidet; **the news came ~ no surprise** die Nachricht war keine Überraschung; **such big names ~ ...** so große Namen wie ...; **~ a matter of principle** aus Prinzip **III.** *adv* ① (*in comparisons*) wie; ■ **[just] ~ ... ~ ...** [genau]so ... wie ...; **if you play ~ well ~ that, ...** wenn du so gut spielst, ... ② (*indicating an extreme*) **~ tall ~ 8 ft.** bis zu 8 Fuß hoch; **~ little ~** nur

asbestos [æs·'bes·təs] *n* Asbest *m*

ascend [ə·'send] **I.** *vt* hinaufsteigen; (*fig*) *throne* besteigen **II.** *vi* ① (*move upwards*) aufsteigen; *elevator* hinauffahren; **in ~ing order of importance** nach zunehmender Wichtigkeit ② (*lead up*) *path* hinaufführen

ascendancy, **ascendency** [ə·'sen·dən·si] *n* Vormachtstellung *f*

ascendant, ascendent [ə·'sen·dənt] *n* **to be in the ~** (*be gaining influence*) im Kommen sein; (*have supremacy*) beherrschenden Einfluss haben

ascent [ə·'sent] *n* ① (*upward movement*) Aufstieg *m; of a mountain* Besteigung *f* ② (*slope*) Anstieg *m*

ascertain [ˌæs·ər·'teɪn] *vt* feststellen

ascetic [ə·'set̬·ɪk] **I.** *n* Asket(in) *m(f)* **II.** *adj* asketisch

asexual [ˌeɪ·'sek·ʃu·əl] *adj* asexuell; *reproduction* ungeschlechtlich

ash[1] [æʃ] *n* (*from burning*) Asche *f;* ■ **~es** *pl* Asche *f kein pl;* **to reduce to ~es** völlig niederbrennen

ash[2] [æʃ] *n* (*tree*) Esche *f;* (*wood*) Eschenholz *nt*

ashamed [ə·'ʃeɪmd] *adj* ■ **to be ~ [of sb/sth]** sich [für jdn/etw] schämen; **that's nothing to be ~ of!** deswegen brauchst du dich [doch] nicht zu schämen!

ashore [ə·'ʃɔr] *adv* an Land; **to swim ~** ans Ufer schwimmen

'ashtray *n* Aschenbecher *m*

Ash 'Wednesday *n* Aschermittwoch *m*

Asia ['eɪ·ʒə] *n* Asien *nt*

Asia 'Minor *n* Kleinasien *nt*

Asian ['eɪ·ʒən] **I.** *n* Asiat *m,* Asiatin *f* **II.** *adj* asiatisch

Asiatic [ˌeɪ·ʒi·'æt̬·ɪk] (*esp pej*) **I.** *n* Asiat *m,* Asiatin *f* **II.** *adj* asiatisch

aside [ə·'saɪd] **I.** *adv* zur Seite; **to take sb ~** jdn beiseitenehmen; **to leave sth ~** etw [weg]lassen **II.** *n* Nebenbemerkung *f*

aside from *prep* abgesehen von +*dat*

ask [æsk] **I.** *vt* ① (*request information*) fragen; **to ~ a question [about sth]** [zu etw *dat*] eine Frage stellen; **may I ~ you a question?** darf ich Sie etwas fragen? ② (*request*) *favor* bitten [um +*dat*]; **she ~ed me for help** sie bat mich, ihr zu helfen ③ (*invite*) einladen **II.** *vi* ① (*request information*) fragen; **you may well ~** gute Frage; ■ **to ~ about sb/sth** nach jdm/etw fragen; **I was only ~ing!** war ja nur 'ne Frage! ② (*request*) bitten ③ (*fig: take a risk*) ■ **to be ~ing for sth** etw geradezu herausfordern; **you're ~ing for trouble** du willst wohl Ärger haben!

askew [ə·'skju] *adj, adv* schief

asking ['æs·kɪŋ] *n* **it's yours for the ~** du kannst es gerne haben

asleep [ə·'slip] *adj* ① (*sleeping*) ■ **to be ~** schlafen; **to fall ~** einschlafen ② (*numb*) eingeschlafen

asparagus [ə·'spær·ə·gəs] *n* Spargel *m*

aspect ['æs·pekt] *n* ① Aspekt *m* ② (*outlook*) Lage *f*

aspen ['æs·pən] *n* Espe *f*

aspersion [ə·'spɜr·ʒən] *n* **to cast ~s on sb** jdn verleumden

asphalt ['æs·fɔlt] **I.** *n* Asphalt *m* **II.** *vt* asphaltieren

asphyxia [æs·'fɪk·si·ə] *n* Asphyxie *f*

asphyxiate [əs·'fɪk·si·eɪt] *vi, vt* ersticken

asphyxiation [əs·ˌfɪk·sɪ·'eɪ·ʃən] *n* Erstickung *f*

aspiration [ˌæs·pə·'reɪ·ʃən] *n* Ambition *f*

aspire [ə·'spaɪr] *vi* anstreben; **to ~ to be president** danach trachten, Präsident zu werden

aspirin ['æs·pə·rɪn] *n* Aspirin *nt*

aspiring [ə·'spaɪr·ɪŋ] *adj* aufstrebend

ass[1] <*pl* -es> [æs] *n* Esel *m;* **to make an ~ of oneself** sich lächerlich machen

ass[2] <*pl* -es> [æs] *n* (*vulg: rear end*) Arsch *m* ▶ PHRASES: **<u>my</u> ~!** (*fam: emphatically not*) wahrlich nicht; **beautiful? beautiful my ~!** schön? wahrlich nicht!

assail [ə·'seɪl] *vt* ① (*attack*) angreifen ② **to be ~ed by doubts** von Zweifeln geplagt werden

assailant [ə·'seɪ·lənt] *n* Angreifer(in) *m(f)*

assassin [ə·'sæs·ɪn] *n* Mörder(in) *m(f);* (*esp political*) Attentäter(in) *m(f)*

assassinate [ə·'sæs·ə·neɪt] *vt* ■ **to ~ sb** ein Attentat auf jdn verüben

assassination [ə·ˌsæs·ə·'neɪ·ʃən] *n* Attentat *nt* (**of** auf +*akk*)

assault [ə·'sɔlt] **I.** *n* Angriff *m* (**on** auf +*akk*) **II.** *vt* angreifen

assemble [ə·'sem·bəl] **I.** *vi* sich versammeln **II.** *vt* zusammenbauen

assembly [ə·'sem·bli] *n* ① (*gathering*) Versammlung *f;* ■ **the A~** das Unterhaus ② TECH Montage *f;* **~ line** Fließband *nt*

assert [ə·'sɜrt] *vt* ① (*state firmly*) beteuern ② *independence* behaupten ③ (*act confidently*) ■ **to ~ oneself** sich durchsetzen

assertion [ə·ˈsɜr·ʃən] *n* ❶ (*claim*) Behauptung *f; of innocence* Beteuerung *f* ❷ *of authority* Geltendmachung *f*

assertive [ə·ˈsɜr·t̬ɪv] *adj* ■**to be ~** Durchsetzungsvermögen zeigen

assertiveness [ə·ˈsɜr·tɪv·nɪs] *n* Durchsetzungsvermögen *nt*

assess [ə·ˈses] *vt* ❶ (*evaluate*) einschätzen; *cost* veranschlagen; *damage* schätzen (**at** auf +*akk*) ❷ FIN ■**to be ~ed** *person, property* steuerlich geschätzt werden

assessment [ə·ˈses·mənt] *n* ❶ *of damage* Schätzung *f* ❷ *of tax* Veranlagung *f* ❸ (*evaluation*) Beurteilung *f*

assessor [ə·ˈses·ər] *n* Taxator(in) *m(f)*, Schätzer(in) *m(f)*

asset [ˈæs·et] *n* ❶ (*good quality*) Pluspunkt *m* ❷ (*valuable person*) Bereicherung *f;* (*useful thing*) Vorteil *m* ❸ FIN ■**~s** *pl* Vermögenswerte *pl*

assign [ə·ˈsaɪn] *vt* zuweisen; *task* zuteilen; ■**to ~ sb to do sth** jdn damit betrauen, etw zu tun

assignment [ə·ˈsaɪn·mənt] *n* (*task*) Aufgabe *f;* (*job*) Auftrag *m*

assimilate [ə·ˈsɪm·ə·leɪt] **I.** *vt* integrieren; *information* aufnehmen **II.** *vi* sich eingliedern

assimilation [ə·ˌsɪm·ə·ˈleɪ·ʃən] *n* (*integration*) Eingliederung *f*

assist [ə·ˈsɪst] *vt, vi* helfen (**with** bei +*dat*)

assistance [ə·ˈsɪs·təns] *n* Hilfe *f;* **can I be of any ~?** kann ich Ihnen irgendwie behilflich sein?

assistant [ə·ˈsɪs·tənt] **I.** *n* Assistent(in) *m(f);* (*in store*) Verkäufer(in) *m(f)* **II.** *adj* stellvertretend

associate I. *n* [ə·ˈsoʊ·ʃi·ət] (*friend*) Gefährte *m,* Gefährtin *f;* (*colleague*) Kollege *m,* Kollegin *f;* (*of criminals*) Komplize *m,* Komplizin *f;* **business ~** Geschäftspartner(in) *m(f)* **II.** *vt* [ə·ˈsoʊ·ʃi·eɪt] in Verbindung bringen; ■**to be ~d with sth** in Zusammenhang mit etw *dat* stehen **III.** *vi* verkehren

association [ə·ˌsoʊ·si·ˈeɪ·ʃən] *n* ❶ (*organization*) Vereinigung *f;* (*corporation*) Verband *m* ❷ (*involvement*) Verbundenheit *f;* **in ~ with** in Verbindung mit +*dat* ❸ (*mental connection*) Assoziation *f*

assorted [ə·ˈsɔr·t̬ɪd] *adj* gemischt; *colors* verschieden

assortment [ə·ˈsɔrt·mənt] *n* Sortiment *nt*

assume [ə·ˈsum] *vt* ❶ (*regard as true*) annehmen ❷ (*adopt*) annehmen; *role* übernehmen ❸ (*take on*) **to ~ office** sein Amt antreten; *power* ergreifen; *responsibility* übernehmen

assumed [ə·ˈsumd] *adj* **under an ~ name** unter einem Decknamen

assumption [ə·ˈsʌmp·ʃən] *n* (*supposition*) Annahme *f;* (*presupposition*) Voraussetzung *f;* **on the ~ that ...** wenn man davon ausgeht, dass ...

assurance [ə·ˈʃʊr·əns] *n* ❶ (*promise*) Zusicherung *f* ❷ (*self-confidence*) Selbstsicherheit *f*

assure [ə·ˈʃʊr] *vt* ❶ (*confirm certainty*) zusichern; ■**to ~ oneself of sth** sich *dat* etw sichern ❷ (*promise*) ■**to ~ sb of sth** jdm etw zusichern

assured [ə·ˈʃʊrd] *adj* ❶ (*confident*) selbstsicher ❷ (*certain*) sicher

assuredly [ə·ˈʃʊr·ɪd·li] *adv* ❶ (*confidently*) selbstsicher ❷ (*certainly*) sicher[lich]

asterisk [ˈæs·tə·rɪsk] **I.** *n* Sternchen *nt* **II.** *vt* mit einem Sternchen versehen

asteroid [ˈæs·tə·rɔɪd] *n* Asteroid *m*

asthma [ˈæz·mə] *n* Asthma *nt*

asthmatic [æz·ˈmæt̬·ɪk] **I.** *n* Asthmatiker(in) *m(f)* **II.** *adj* asthmatisch

astonish [ə·ˈstɑn·ɪʃ] *vt* erstaunen

astonished [ə·ˈstɑn·ɪʃt] *adj* erstaunt

astonishing [ə·ˈstɑn·ɪʃ·ɪŋ] *adj* erstaunlich

astonishment [ə·ˈstɑn·ɪʃ·mənt] *n* Erstaunen *nt;* **to stare in ~** verblüfft starren

astound [ə·ˈstaʊnd] *vt* verblüffen

astounding [ə·ˈstaʊn·dɪŋ] *adj* erstaunlich; *fact* verblüffend

astray [ə·ˈstreɪ] *adv* verloren; **to lead sb ~** (*fig*) jdn auf Abwege bringen

astride [ə·ˈstraɪd] *prep* rittlings auf +*dat*

astrologer [ə·ˈstrɑl·ə·dʒər] *n* Astrologe *m,* Astrologin *f*

astrological [ˌæs·trə·ˈlɑdʒ·ɪ·kəl] *adj* astrologisch

astrology [ə·ˈstrɑl·ə·dʒi] *n* Astrologie *f*

astronaut [ˈæs·trə·nɔt] *n* Astronaut(in) *m(f)*

astronomer [ə·ˈstrɑn·ə·mər] *n* Astronom(in) *m(f)*

astronomical [ˌæs·trə·ˈnɑm·ɪ·kəl] *adj* (*a. fig*) astronomisch

astronomy [ə·ˈstrɑn·ə·mi] *n* Astronomie *f*

astute [ə·ˈstut] *adj* scharfsinnig

asylum [ə·ˈsaɪ·ləm] *n* (*protection*) Asyl *nt;* **~ seeker** Asylbewerber(in) *m(f)*

asymmetric(al) [ˌeɪ·sɪ·ˈmet·rɪk(əl)] *adj* asymmetrisch

at [ət, æt] *prep* ❶ (*in location of*) an +*dat;* **~ the bakery** beim Bäcker; **~ home** zu Hause; **~ the party** auf der Party; **~ school** in der Schule; **~ work** bei der Arbeit ❷ (*during time of*) **~ night** in der Nacht, nachts; **~ 10:00 [a.m.]** um 10:00 Uhr; **~ the moment** im Moment; **~ this stage** bei diesem Stand; **several things ~ a time** mehrere Sachen auf einmal; **~ the time** zu diesem Zeitpunkt; **~ the same time** (*simultaneously*) zur gleichen Zeit; (*on the other hand*) auf der anderen Seite ❸ (*to amount of*) **~ a distance of 165 feet** auf eine Entfernung von 50 Metern; **~ 80 miles per hour** mit 80 Meilen pro Stunde; **~ a gallop** im Galopp; **~ regular intervals** in regelmäßigen Abständen ❹ (*in state of*) **~ war** im Krieg; **~ a disadvantage** im Nachteil; **~ fault** im Unrecht ❺ (*in ability to*) bei +*dat;* **good ~ math** gut in Mathematik ▶PHRASES: **~ all** überhaupt; **did she suffer ~ all?** hat sie denn gelitten?; **not ~ all** (*definitely not*) keineswegs

ate [eɪt] *pt of* **eat**

atheism ['eɪ·θi·ɪz·əm] *n* Atheismus *m*

atheist ['eɪ·θi·ɪst] **I.** *n* Atheist(in) *m(f)* **II.** *adj* atheistisch

Athens ['æθ·ənz] *n* Athen *nt*

athlete ['æθ·lit] *n* Athlet(in) *m(f)*

athletic [æθ·'leṭ·ɪk] *adj* athletisch, sportlich

athletics [æθ·'leṭ·ɪks] *n* SCH, UNIV [Schul]sport *m kein pl*

Atlantic [ət·'læn·tɪk] *n* ■**the ~ [Ocean]** der Atlantik

atlas <*pl* -es> ['æt·ləs] *n* Atlas *m*

ATM [ˌeɪ·ti·'em] *n abbrev of* **automated teller machine** Geldautomat *m*

atmosphere ['æt·mə·sfɪr] *n* Atmosphäre *f a. fig*

atmospheric [ˌæt·mə·'sfer·ɪk] *adj* ❶ atmosphärisch ❷ (*fig*) stimmungsvoll

atoll ['æt·ɔl] *n* Atoll *nt*

atom ['æṭ·əm] *n* PHYS Atom *nt;* (*fig*) Bisschen *nt*

'atom bomb *n* Atombombe *f*

atomic [ə·'tam·ɪk] *adj* Atom-, atomar

atomize ['æṭ·ə·maɪz] *vt* zerstäuben

atone [ə·'toʊn] **I.** *vi* ■**to ~ for sth** etw wiedergutmachen **II.** *vt* **to ~ one's sins** für seine Sünden büßen

atrocious [ə·'troʊ·ʃəs] *adj* grässlich; *weather, food* scheußlich; *conditions* grauenhaft

atrocity [ə·'tras·ɪ·ṭi] *n* Gräueltat *f*

attach [ə·'tætʃ] *vt* ❶ (*fix*) befestigen (**to** an +*dat*) ❷ (*connect*) verbinden (**to** mit +*dat*) ❸ (*send as enclosure*) ■**to ~ sth [to sth]** etw [etw *dat*] beilegen ❹ (*join*) ■**to ~ oneself to sb** sich jdm anschließen ❺ (*assign*) ■**to be ~ed to sth** etw *dat* zugeteilt sein

attaché [ˌæṭ·ə·'ʃeɪ] *n* Attaché *m*

atta'ché case *n* Aktenkoffer *m*

attachment [ə·'tætʃ·mənt] *n* ❶ (*fondness*) Sympathie *f;* **to form an ~ to sb** sich mit jdm anfreunden ❷ (*support*) Unterstützung *f* ❸ (*for appliances*) Zusatzgerät *nt* ❹ COMPUT Anhang *m*

attack [ə·'tæk] **I.** *n* ❶ (*assault*) Angriff *m* (**on** auf +*akk*) ❷ (*bout*) Anfall *m* **II.** *vt* ❶ angreifen; *by criminal* überfallen ❷ (*fig*) anpacken **III.** *vi* angreifen

attacker [ə·'tæ·kər] *n* Angreifer(in) *m(f)*

attain [ə·'teɪn] *vt* erreichen; *independence* erlangen

attainable [ə·'teɪn·ə·bəl] *adj* erreichbar

attainment [ə·'teɪn·mənt] *n* ❶ Leistung *f* ❷ ■**~s** *pl* (*accomplishments*) Fertigkeiten *pl*

attempt [ə·'tempt] **I.** *n* Versuch *m;* **make an ~ on sb's life** einen Mordanschlag auf jdn verüben **II.** *vt* versuchen

attend [ə·'tend] **I.** *vt* ❶ (*be present at*) besuchen; **to ~ a wedding** zu einer Hochzeit gehen ❷ (*care for*) [ärztlich] behandeln **II.** *vi* (*be present*) teilnehmen

attendance [ə·'ten·dəns] *n* ❶ (*being present*) Anwesenheit *f;* **in ~** anwesend ❷ (*number of people present*) Besucherzahl *f*

attendant [ə·'ten·dənt] *n* Aufseher(in) *m(f);* **flight ~** Flugbegleiter(in) *m(f)*

attention [ə·'ten·ʃən] *n* ❶ (*notice*) Aufmerksamkeit *m;* **~!** Achtung!; **to pay ~ to sb** jdm Aufmerksamkeit schenken; **to pay ~ to sth** auf etw *akk* achten ❷ (*care*) Pflege *f;* MED Behandlung *f* ❸ (*in letters*) **to sb's ~** zu Händen von ❹ MIL **to stand at ~** stillstehen

at'tention span *n* Konzentrationsvermögen *f*

attentive [ə·'ten·tɪv] *adj* ❶ (*caring*) fürsorglich ❷ (*paying attention*) aufmerksam

attic ['æṭ·ɪk] *n* Dachboden *m;* **in the ~** auf dem Dachboden

attitude ['æṭ·ɪ·tud] *n* (*way of thinking*) Haltung *f,* Einstellung *f*

attorney [ə·'tɜr·ni] *n* Anwalt *m,* Anwältin *f*

attorney 'general <*pl* attornies general> *n* Justizminister [und Generalstaatsanwalt], Justizministerin [und Generalstaatsanwältin] *m, f*

attract [ə·'trækt] *vt* anziehen; *attention* erregen; *criticism* stoßen auf

attraction [ə·'træk·ʃən] *n* ❶ PHYS Anziehungskraft *f* ❷ (*between people*) Anziehung *f;* **she felt an ~ to him** sie fühlte sich zu ihm hingezogen ❸ (*appeal*) Reiz *m*

attractive [ə·'træk·tɪv] *adj* attraktiv

attribute [ə·'trɪb·jut] **I.** *vt* [ə·'trɪb·jut] ❶ (*ascribe*) zurückführen (**to** auf +*dat*) ❷ (*give credit for*) zuschreiben (**to** +*dat*) **II.** *n* ['æt·rɪ·bjut] Eigenschaft *f*

attrition [ə·'trɪʃ·ən] *n* ❶ Zermürbung *f* ❷ *Personalabbau durch Einstellungsstopp*

auburn ['ɔ·bərn] *adj* rotbraun

auction ['ɔk·ʃən] **I.** *n* Auktion *f,* Versteigerung *f* **II.** *vt* ■**to ~ [off]** versteigern

auctioneer [ˌɔk·ʃə·'nɪr] *n* Auktionator(in) *m(f)*

audacious [ɔ·'deɪ·ʃəs] *adj* ❶ (*bold*) kühn ❷ (*impudent*) dreist

audaciousness [ɔ·'deɪ·ʃəs·nɪs], **audacity** [ɔ·'dæs·ɪ·ṭi] *n* ❶ (*boldness*) Kühnheit *f* ❷ (*impudence*) Dreistigkeit *f*

audible ['ɔ·də·bəl] *adj* hörbar

audience ['ɔ·di·əns] *n* ❶ (*at performance*) Publikum *nt; a.* THEAT Besucher *pl;* TV Zuschauer *pl;* RADIO [Zu]hörer *pl* ❷ (*formal interview*) Audienz *f* (**with** bei +*dat*)

audio ['ɔ·dɪ·oʊ] *adj* Audio-; **~ book** Hörbuch *nt*

audit ['ɔ·dɪt] **I.** *n* Rechnungsprüfung *f* **II.** *vt* ❶ [amtlich] prüfen ❷ UNIV *class* [nur] als Gasthörer besuchen

audition [ɔ·'dɪʃ·ən] **I.** *n* (*for actor*) Vorsprechen *nt;* (*for singer*) Vorsingen *nt;* (*for dancer*) Vortanzen *nt;* (*for instrumentalist*) Vorspielen *nt* **II.** *vi* vorsprechen, vorsingen, vortanzen **III.** *vt* vorsprechen/vorsingen/vortanzen lassen

auditor ['ɔ·də·ṭər] *n* Rechnungsprüfer(in) *m(f)*

auditorium <*pl* -s *or* -ria> [ˌɔ·də·'tɔr·i·əm] *n* THEAT Zuschauerraum *m;* (*hall*) Zuhörersaal *m;* (*for concerts*) Konzerthalle *f*

Aug. *n abbrev of* **August** Aug.

augment [ɔg·'ment] *vt* vergrößern; *income*

A

verbessern

August ['ɔ·gəst] *n* August *m; see also* **February**

aunt [ænt] *n* Tante *f*

au pair [oʊ·'per] *n* au pair *nt*

aura ['ɔr·ə] *n* Aura *f*

aural ['ɔr·əl] *adj* akustisch; MED aural

auspices ['ɔ·spɪ·sɪz] *npl* Schirmherrschaft *f*

auspicious [ɔ·'spɪʃ·əs] *adj* viel versprechend

austere [ɔ·'stɪr] *adj* ❶ (*without comfort*) karg; (*severely plain*) nüchtern; *room* schmucklos; (*ascetic*) asketisch ❷ (*joyless and strict*) streng

austerity [ɔ·'ster·ɪ·t̬i] *n* ❶ (*absence of comfort*) Rauheit *f* ❷ (*sparseness*) Kargheit *f;* (*asceticism*) Askese *f* ❸ (*strictness*) Strenge *f*

Australia [ɔ·'streɪl·jə] *n* Australien *nt*

Australian [ɔ·'streɪl·jən] **I.** *n* (*person*) Australier(in) *m(f)* **II.** *adj* australisch

Austria ['ɔ·stri·ə] *n* Österreich *nt*

Austrian ['ɔ·stri·ən] **I.** *n* (*person*) Österreicher(in) *m(f)* **II.** *adj* österreichisch

authentic [ɔ·'θen·tɪk] *adj* authentisch

authenticate [ɔ·'θen·tɪ·keɪt] *vt* [die Echtheit] bestätigen; LAW beglaubigen

authentication [ɔ·ˌθen·tɪ·'keɪ·ʃən] *n* Bestätigung *f* [der Echtheit]; LAW Beglaubigung *f*

authenticity [ˌɔ·θən·'tɪs·ɪ·t̬i] *n* Echtheit *f*

author ['ɔ·θər] *n* (*profession*) Schriftsteller(in) *m(f); of particular book* Autor(in) *m(f)*

authoritarian [ə·ˌθɔr·ə·'ter·i·ən] *adj* autoritär

authoritative [ə·'θɔr·ə·teɪ·t̬ɪv] *adj* ❶ (*definitive*) maßgebend ❷ (*commanding*) Respekt einflößend

authority [ə·'θɔr·ɪ·t̬i] *n* ❶ (*right of control*) Autorität *f;* **in ~** verantwortlich ❷ (*permission*) Befugnis *f;* (*to act on sb's behalf*) Vollmacht *f;* **to have the ~ to do sth** befugt/bevollmächtigt sein, etw zu tun; **on whose ~?** wer hat das genehmigt? ❸ (*expert*) **an ~ on microbiology** eine Autorität auf dem Gebiet der Mikrobiologie ❹ (*organization*) Behörde *f*

authorization [ˌɔ·θər·ɪ·'zeɪ·ʃən] *n* (*approval*) Genehmigung *f;* (*delegation of power*) Bevollmächtigung *f*

authorize ['ɔ·θə·raɪz] *vt* genehmigen; ■**to ~ sb** jdn bevollmächtigen

authorship ['ɔ·θər·ʃɪp] *n* Autorschaft *f*

autistic [ɔ·'tɪs·tɪk] *adj* autistisch

auto ['ɔ·t̬oʊ] **I.** *n* Auto *nt* **II.** *adj* ❶ (*concerning cars*) Auto- ❷ (*automatic*) automatisch; **~ restart** COMPUT Selbstanlauf *m*

autobiographical [ˌɔ·t̬ə·baɪ·ə·'græf·ɪ·kəl] *adj* autobiografisch

autobiography [ˌɔ·t̬ə·baɪ·'ag·rə·fi] *n* Autobiografie *f*

autocratic [ˌɔ·t̬ə·'kræt̬·ɪk] *adj* autokratisch

autograph ['ɔ·t̬ə·græf] **I.** *n* Autogramm *nt* **II.** *vt* signieren

automate ['ɔ·t̬ə·meɪt] *vt* automatisieren

automated 'teller machine *n* Geldautomat *m*

automatic [ˌɔ·t̬ə·'mæt̬·ɪk] **I.** *adj* automatisch; **~ washing machine** Waschautomat *m* **II.** *n* ❶ (*nonmanual machine*) Automat *m* ❷ (*rifle*) Selbstladegewehr *nt*

automatic 'pilot *n* Autopilot *m*

automatic 'teller machine *n see* **automated teller machine**

automation [ˌɔ·t̬ə·'meɪ·ʃən] *n* Automatisierung *f*

automobile ['ɔ·t̬ə·moʊ·bil] *n* Auto *nt*

automotive [ˌɔ·t̬ə·'moʊ·t̬ɪv] *adj attr, inv industry, trade, manufacturing* Auto-

autonomy [ɔ·'tan·ə·mi] *n* Autonomie *f*

autopsy ['ɔ·tap·si] *n* Autopsie *f*

autumn ['ɔ·t̬əm] *n* Herbst *m;* **in the ~** im Herbst

autumnal [ɔ·'tʌm·nəl] *adj* (*liter*) herbstlich

auxiliary [ɔg·'zɪl·jə·ri] **I.** *n* ❶ Hilfskraft *f;* (*soldier*) Soldat(in) *m(f)* der Hilfstruppen ❷ LING Hilfsverb *nt* **II.** *adj* Hilfs-; (*additional*) Zusatz-

avail [ə·'veɪl] *n* Nutzen *m;* **to no ~** vergeblich

available [ə·'veɪ·lə·bəl] *adj* ❶ (*free for use*) verfügbar; **in the time ~** in der vorhandenen Zeit; **to make ~** zur Verfügung stellen ❷ (*not busy*) abkömmlich ❸ ECON erhältlich; (*in stock*) lieferbar; *size* vorrätig

avalanche ['æv·ə·læntʃ] *n* Lawine *f*

avant-garde [ˌa·vant·'gard] **I.** *n* Avantgarde *f* **II.** *adj* avantgardistisch

avarice ['æv·ə·rɪs] *n* (*form*) Habgier *f*

Ave. *n abbrev of* **avenue**

avenge [ə·'vendʒ] *vt* rächen; ■**to ~ oneself on sb** sich an jdm rächen

avenue ['æv·ə·nu] *n* ❶ (*broad street*) Avenue *f* ❷ (*fig: possibility*) Weg *m*

average ['æv·ər·ɪdʒ] **I.** *n* Durchschnitt *m;* **on ~** im Durchschnitt; [**to be**] [**way**] **below ~** [weit] unter dem Durchschnitt [liegen]; **law of ~s** Gesetz *nt* der Serie **II.** *adj* durchschnittlich; **~ income** Durchschnittseinkommen *nt* **III.** *vt* im Durchschnitt betragen; **to ~ 40 hours a week** durchschnittlich 40 Stunden pro Woche arbeiten

averse [ə·'vɜrs] *adj* ■**to be ~ to sth** etw *dat* abgeneigt sein

aversion [ə·'vɜr·ʒən] *n* ❶ (*intense dislike*) Abneigung *f* (**to** gegen *+akk*) ❷ (*hated thing*) Gräuel *m*

avert [ə·'vɜrt] *vt* ❶ (*turn away*) abwenden ❷ (*prevent*) verhindern

avg. *n, adj abbrev of* **average**

aviation [ˌeɪ·vi·'eɪ·ʃən] *n* Luftfahrt *f;* **~ industry** Flugzeugindustrie *f*

avid ['æv·ɪd] *adj* eifrig, begeistert

avocado <*pl* -s *or* -es> [ˌæv·ə·'ka·doʊ] *n* Avocado *f*

avoid [ə·'vɔɪd] *vt* ❶ (*stay away from*) meiden ❷ (*prevent sth from happening*) vermeiden; **to narrowly ~ sth** etw *dat* knapp entgehen ❸ (*not hit*) ausweichen *+dat*

avoidable [ə·'vɔɪd·ə·bəl] *adj* vermeidbar

avoidance [ə·'vɔɪd·əns] *n* Vermeidung *f; of taxes* Umgehung *f*

await [ə·'weɪt] *vt* erwarten; **long ~ed** lang ersehnt

awake [ə·ˈweɪk] **I.** *adj* (*not asleep*) wach **II.** *vi* <awoke *or* awaked, awoken *or* awaked> (*stop sleeping*) erwachen **III.** *vt* <awoke *or* awaked, awoken *or* awaked> (*from sleep*) [auf]wecken

awakening [ə·ˈweɪ·kə·nɪŋ] *n* **rude ~** böses Erwachen

award [ə·ˈwɔrd] **I.** *vt* ■**to ~ sb sth** *damages* jdm etw zusprechen; *grant* jdm etw gewähren; *prize* jdm etw verleihen **II.** *n* ❶ (*prize*) Auszeichnung *f* ❷ (*compensation*) Entschädigung *f*

aware [ə·ˈwer] *adj* ❶ (*knowing*) ■**to be ~ of sth** sich *dat* einer S. *gen* bewusst sein; **as far as I'm ~** soviel ich weiß ❷ (*physically sensing*) ■**to be ~ of sb/sth** jdn/etw [be]merken ❸ (*well informed*) informiert; **environmentally ~** umweltbewusst

awareness [ə·ˈwer·nɪs] *n* Bewusstsein *nt*

awash [ə·ˈwaʃ] *adj* ❶ ■**to be ~** unter Wasser stehen ❷ (*fig*) ■**to be ~ with sth** voll von etw *dat* sein

away [ə·ˈweɪ] **I.** *adv* ❶ (*distant*) weg; **to be ~ on business** geschäftlich unterwegs sein; **~ from each other** voneinander entfernt; **two days ~** in zwei Tagen ❷ (*continuously*) dahin-; **you're dreaming your life ~** du verträumst noch dein ganzes Leben; **to be working ~** ständig am Arbeiten sein ❸ SPORTS auswärts **II.** *adj* SPORTS auswärts; **~ game** Auswärtsspiel *nt*

awe [ɔ] **I.** *n* Ehrfurcht *f*; **to hold sb in ~** großen Respekt vor jdm haben **II.** *vt* <awing> einschüchtern

ˈawe-inspiring *adj* Ehrfurcht gebietend

awesome [ˈɔ·səm] *adj* ❶ (*impressive*) beeindruckend ❷ (*intimidating*) beängstigend ❸ (*sl: very good*) spitze

awestruck [ˈɔ·ˌstrʌk], **awestricken** [ˈɔ·ˌstrɪk·ən] *adj* [von Ehrfurcht] ergriffen; *expression* ehrfurchtsvoll

awful [ˈɔ·fəl] *adj* ❶ (*extremely bad*) furchtbar; **what an ~ thing to say!** das war aber gemein von dir!; **to look ~** schrecklich aussehen ❷ (*great*) außerordentlich; **an ~ lot** eine riesige Menge

awfully [ˈɔ·fə·li] *adv* furchtbar; **~ good** besonders gut; **an ~ long way** ein schrecklich weiter Weg

awhile [ə·ˈhwaɪl] *adv* eine Weile

awkward [ˈɔk·wərd] *adj* ❶ (*difficult*) schwierig ❷ (*embarrassing*) peinlich; **to feel ~** sich unbehaglich fühlen ❸ (*inconvenient*) ungünstig ❹ (*clumsy*) unbeholfen

awning [ˈɔ·nɪŋ] *n* (*on building*) Markise *f*; (*on camper*) Vorzelt *nt*

awoke [ə·ˈwoʊk] *pt of* **awake**

awoken [ə·ˈwoʊ·kən] *pp of* **awake**

ax, axe [æks] **I.** *n* Axt *f* ▶ PHRASES: **to get the ~** *workers* entlassen werden; *projects* gestrichen werden **II.** *vt* *things* streichen; *people* entlassen

axis <*pl* axes> [ˈæk·sɪs] *n* Achse *f*

axle [ˈæk·səl] *n* Achse *f*

aye [aɪ] **I.** *interj* NAUT **~, ~, sir!** zu Befehl, Herr Kapitän! **II.** *n* POL Jastimme *f*

AZ *abbrev of* **Arizona**

azalea [ə·ˈzeɪl·jə] *n* Azalee *f*

Aztec [ˈæz·tek] **I.** *n* Azteke *m*, Aztekin *f* **II.** *adj* aztekisch; **~ language** Aztekisch *nt*

azure [ˈæʒ·ər] **I.** *n* Azur[blau] *nt* **II.** *adj* azur[blau]

Bb

B <*pl* -'s *or* -s>, **b** <*pl* -'s> [bi] *n* ① (*letter*) B *nt*, b *nt*; **~ as in Bravo** B wie Berta ② MUS H *nt*, h *nt* ③ (*school mark*) ≈ Zwei *f*; **to get a ~** eine Zwei schreiben

BA [ˌbi·ˈeɪ] *n abbrev of* **Bachelor of Arts** B.A.

babble [ˈbæb·əl] **I.** *n* ① (*confused speech*) Geplapper *nt* ② *of water* Plätschern *nt* **II.** *vi* ① (*talk incoherently*) plappern; *baby* babbeln ② *water* plätschern **III.** *vt* stammeln

babe [beɪb] *n* (*fam*) ① (*address*) Schatz *m* ② (*person*) Süße(r) *f(m)*

baboon [bæ·ˈbun] *n* Pavian *m*

baby [ˈbeɪ·bi] **I.** *n* ① (*child*) Baby *nt*; **to have a ~** ein Baby bekommen ② (*youngest person*) Jüngste(r) *f(m)* ③ (*fam: address*) Baby *nt* ▶ PHRASES: **to throw the ~ out with the bathwater** das Kind mit dem Bade ausschütten **II.** *adj* klein; **~ carrots** Babymöhren *pl* **III.** *vt* <-ie-> ■**to ~ sb** jdn wie ein kleines Kind behandeln

ˈbaby boom *n* Babyboom *m fam*

ˈbaby boomer *n* (*generation*) Nachkriegsgeneration *f kein pl*

ˈbaby carriage *n* Kinderwagen *m*

ˈbaby food *n* Babynahrung *f*

babyish [ˈbeɪ·bi·ɪʃ] *adj* kindisch

ˈbaby-sit I. *vi* babysitten *fam*; ■**to ~ for sb** bei jdm babysitten *fam* **II.** *vt* ■**to ~ sb** auf jdn aufpassen

ˈbabysitter *n* Babysitter(in) *m(f)*

ˈbaby tooth *n* Milchzahn *m*

bachelor [ˈbætʃ·ə·lər] *n* ① (*unmarried man*) Junggeselle *m* ② UNIV **B~ of Arts/Science** Bakkalaureus *m* der philosophischen/naturwissenschaftlichen Fakultät (*unterster akademischer Grad in englischsprachigen Ländern*)

bachelorette [ˌbætʃ·ə·lə·ˈret] *n* (*unmarried woman*) Junggesellin *f*

> Ein **Bachelor's degree** ist ein Universitätsabschluss, den Studenten in der Regel nach vier Jahren Studium an einem College oder einer Universität erhalten. Die wichtigsten Abschlüsse sind *B.A.* (*Bachelor of Arts*) für geisteswissenschaftliche Fächer und *B.S.* (*Bachelor of Science*) für naturwissenschaftliche Fächer. Die Studenten wählen ein oder zwei *majors* (Hauptfächer). In den ersten ein bis zwei Jahren werden allgemeinbildende Fächer absolviert und in den letzten beiden Jahren wird der Schwerpunkt auf die Hauptfächer gelegt.

bacillus <*pl* bacilli> [bə·ˈsɪl·əs] *n* Bazillus *m*

back [bæk] **I.** *n* ① (*of body*) Rücken *m*; **~ to ~** Rücken an Rücken ② *of building, page* Rückseite *f*; *of car* Heck *nt*; *of chair* Lehne *f*; (*in car*) Rücksitz[e] *m*[*pl*]; **at** [*or* **in**] **the ~ of the theater** hinten im Theater; **~ of the hand/head/leg** Handrücken *m*/Hinterkopf *m*/Wade *f* ▶ PHRASES: **to know sth like the ~ of one's hand** etw in- und auswendig kennen; **in the ~ of one's mind** im Hinterkopf **II.** *adj* ① (*rear*) Hinter-; **~ pocket** Gesäßtasche *f* ② (*of body*) Rücken- **III.** *adv* ① (*to previous place*) [wieder] zurück; **there and ~** hin und zurück; **~ and forth** hin und her ② (*to past*) **that was ~ in 1950** das war [schon] 1950; **two months ~** vor zwei Monaten **IV.** *vt* ① (*support*) unterstützen ② (*drive*) **she ~ed the car into the garage** sie fuhr rückwärts in die Garage **V.** *vi car* zurücksetzen

◆**back away** *vi* zurückweichen (**from** vor +*dat*)

◆**back down** *vi* nachgeben

◆**back off** *vi* sich zurückziehen; **~ off!** lass mich in Ruhe!

◆**back out I.** *vi* ① *of a commitment* einen Rückzieher machen ② AUTO rückwärts herausfahren **II.** *vt car* rückwärts herausfahren

◆**back up I.** *vi traffic* sich stauen **II.** *vt* ① (*support*) unterstützen; (*confirm*) bestätigen ② COMPUT sichern ③ (*reverse*) zurücksetzen

ˈbackbone *n* Rückgrat *nt a. fig*

back ˈdoor *n* Hintertür *f*

backer [ˈbæk·ər] *n* Förderer, Förderin *m, f*

ˈbackfire *vi* ① AUTO frühzünden ② (*go wrong*) fehlschlagen

background [ˈbæk·graʊnd] *n* ① Hintergrund *m*; **~ noise** Geräuschkulisse ② **with a ~ in ...** mit Erfahrung in ...

ˈbackhand *n* Rückhand *f*

backing [ˈbæk·ɪŋ] *n* ① (*support*) Unterstützung *f* ② (*stiffener*) Verstärkung *f*

back ˈissue *n* alte Ausgabe

ˈbacklash *n* Gegenreaktion *f*

ˈbacklog *n usu sing* Rückstand *m*

ˈbackpack I. *n* Rucksack *m* **II.** *vi* mit dem Rucksack reisen

ˈbackpacker *n* Rucksackreisende(r) *f(m)*

ˈback pay *n* (*of wages*) Lohnnachzahlung *f*; (*of salaries*) Gehaltsnachzahlung *f*

ˈback seat *n* ① Rücksitz *m* ② (*fig*) **to take a ~** in den Hintergrund treten

ˈbackside *n* (*fam*) Hintern *m*

ˈbackslash *n* Backslash *m*

ˈbackspace, ˈbackspace key *n* Backspace-Taste *f*

ˈbackstage I. *n* Garderobe *f* **II.** *adj, adv* hinter der Bühne

ˈbackstroke *n* Rückenschwimmen *nt*

ˈback talk *n* (*fam*) Widerrede *f*

ˈbacktrack *vi* ① (*go back*) [wieder] zurückgehen ② (*change opinion*) einlenken

ˈbackup [ˈbæk·ʌp] *n* ① (*support*) Unterstützung *f;* ~ **generator** Notstromaggregat *nt* ❷ COMPUT Sicherung *f,* Backup *nt*

backward ['bæk·wərd] *adj* ❶ (*facing rear*) rückwärtsgewandt; (*reversed*) Rück[wärts]-; **a ~ step** ein Schritt *m* nach hinten ❷ (*slow in learning*) zurückgeblieben ❸ (*underdeveloped*) rückständig

backward(s) ['bæk·wərd(z)] *adv* ❶ (*toward the back*) nach hinten ❷ (*in reverse*) rückwärts ❸ (*into past*) zurück

'backwater *n* ❶ (*of river*) stehendes Gewässer ❷ (*isolated place*) toter Fleck

back'yard *n* Hinterhof *m* ▶ PHRASES: **in one's <u>own</u> ~** vor der eigenen Haustür

bacon ['beɪ·kən] *n* [Schinken]speck *m*

bacteria [bæk·'tɪr·i·ə] *n pl of* **bacterium** Bakterien *pl*

bacterium <*pl* -ria> [bæk·'tɪr·i·əm] *n* Bakterie *f*

bad <worse, worst> [bæd] **I.** *adj* schlecht; *dream* böse; *smell* übel; *cold* schlimm; *storm* heftig; **~ at math** schlecht in Mathe; **~ blood** böses Blut; **~ language** Kraftausdrücke *pl;* **~ luck** Pech *nt;* **too ~** zu schade **II.** *adv* ❶ (*fam*) sehr ❷ (*in bad condition*) schlecht; **to go ~** sich verschlechtern; *food* schlecht werden **III.** *n* **to take the ~ with the good** auch das Schlechte in Kauf nehmen

badge [bædʒ] *n* Abzeichen *nt*

badger ['bædʒ·ər] **I.** *n* Dachs *m* **II.** *vt* bedrängen

badly <worse, worst> ['bæd·li] *adv* schlecht; **to be ~ in need of sth** etw dringend benötigen; **~ hurt** schwer verletzt

badminton ['bæd·mɪn·tən] *n* Federball *m*

baffle ['bæf·əl] *vt* verwirren

baffling ['bæf·əl·ɪŋ] *adj* (*confusing*) verwirrend; (*mysterious*) rätselhaft

bag [bæg] **I.** *n* ❶ (*container*) Tasche *f;* (*drawstring*) Beutel *m;* (*sack*) Sack *m;* **paper/plastic ~** Papier-/Plastiktüte *f* ❷ (*handbag*) Handtasche *f;* (*traveling*) Reisetasche *f;* **to pack one's ~s** die Koffer packen ❸ **to have ~s under one's eyes** Ringe unter den Augen haben **II.** *vt* <-gg-> eintüten

bagel ['beɪ·gəl] *n* Bagel *m*

baggage ['bæg·ɪdʒ] *n* Gepäck *nt*

'baggage allowance *n* Freigepäck *nt*

'baggage car *n* Gepäckwagen *m*

'baggage check *n* Gepäckkontrolle *f*

'baggage claim *n* Gepäckausgabe *f*

baggy ['bæg·i] *adj* [weit] geschnitten

'bag lady *n* Obdachlose *f*

'bagpipes *npl* Dudelsack *m*

Bahamas [bə·'ha·məz] *npl* ■ **the ~** die Bahamas

Bahamian [bə·'hæ·mi·ən] **I.** *n* Bahamaer(in) *m(f)* **II.** *adj* bahamaisch

bail [beɪl] **I.** *n* Kaution *f* **II.** *vt* (*release*) ■ **to ~ sb** jdn gegen Kaution freilassen

◆ **bail out I.** *vt* ❶ (*pay*) ■ **to ~ out ⇔ sb** für jdn [die] Kaution stellen ❷ (*help*) ■ **to ~ sb out** jdm aus der Klemme helfen **II.** *vi* ❶ (*jump*) [mit dem Fallschirm] abspringen ❷ (*fig*) aussteigen

bailiff ['beɪ·lɪf] *n* Justizwachtmeister(in) *m(f)*

bait [beɪt] **I.** *n* Köder *m a. fig;* **to take the ~** anbeißen **II.** *vt* ❶ (*put bait on*) mit einem Köder versehen ❷ (*harass*) *person* schikanieren

bake [beɪk] **I.** *vi* ❶ (*cook*) backen ❷ (*fam*) **it's baking outside** draußen ist es wie im Backofen **II.** *vt* ❶ (*cook*) [im Ofen] backen ❷ *pottery* brennen

baker ['beɪ·kər] *n* Bäcker(in) *m(f)*

bakery ['beɪ·kə·ri] *n* Bäckerei *f*

'baking powder *n* Backpulver *nt*

'baking soda *n* Natron *nt*

balance ['bæl·ənts] **I.** *n* ❶ Gleichgewicht *nt a. fig;* **to hang** [*or* **be**] **in the ~** (*fig*) in der Schwebe sein; **to strike a ~** den goldenen Mittelweg finden ❷ FIN Kontostand *m;* **~ of payments** Zahlungsbilanz *f* ❸ (*scale*) Waage *f* ❹ (*harmony*) Ausgewogenheit *f* **II.** *vt* ❶ (*compare*) abwägen ❷ (*keep steady*) balancieren ❸ (*achieve equilibrium*) ein Gleichgewicht herstellen ❹ FIN *account* ausgleichen **III.** *vi* ❶ (*a. fig: keep steady*) das Gleichgewicht halten ❷ FIN ausgeglichen sein

balanced ['bæl·ənst] *adj* ausgewogen; *personality* ausgeglichen

'balance sheet *n* Bilanz *f*

balcony ['bæl·kə·ni] *n* Balkon *m*

bald [bɔld] *adj* ❶ (*hairless*) glatzköpfig; **to go ~** eine Glatze bekommen ❷ *tire* abgefahren

baldly ['bɔld·li] *adv* unumwunden

baldness ['bɔld·nɪs] *n* Kahlheit *f*

bale [beɪl] **I.** *n* Ballen *m* **II.** *vt* bündeln

baleful ['beɪl·fʊl] *adj* böse

balk [bɔk] *vi* ❶ (*stop*) *horse* scheuen ❷ (*be unwilling*) zurückschrecken (**at** vor +*dat*)

Balkan States [ˌbɔl·kən·'steɪts] *npl* ■ **the ~** die Balkanstaaten

ball [bɔl] *n* ❶ Ball *m* ❷ (*ball-shaped*) *of yarn* Knäuel *m o nt; of dough* Kugel *f* ❸ **~ of the foot** Fußballen *m* ❹ (*dance*) Ball *m* ▶ PHRASES: **to be <u>on</u> the ~** auf Zack sein; **to <u>have</u> a ~** Spaß haben; **to <u>play</u> ~** (*cooperate*) mitmachen

ballad ['bæl·əd] *n* Ballade *f*

ballast ['bæl·əst] *n* ❶ Ballast *m* ❷ RAIL Schotter *m*

ball 'bearing *n* Kugellager *nt*

ballerina [ˌbæl·ə·'ri·nə] *n* Ballerina *f*

ballet [bæ·'leɪ] *n* Ballett *nt*

bal'let dancer *n* Balletttänzer(in) *m(f)*

'ball game *n* Baseballspiel *nt* ▶ PHRASES: **that's a whole <u>new</u> ~** das ist eine ganz andere Sache

ballistic [bə·'lɪs·tɪk] *adj* ballistisch ▶ PHRASES: **to <u>go</u> ~** (*fam*) ausflippen *fam*

balloon [bə·'lun] *n* Ballon *m*

ballot ['bæl·ət] **I.** *n* ❶ (*paper*) Stimmzettel *m* ❷ **secret ~** (*vote*) geheime Abstimmung; (*election*) Geheimwahl *f* **II.** *vi* abstimmen

'ballot box *n* Wahlurne *f*

'ballpark *n* Baseballstadion *nt* ▶ PHRASES: **<u>in</u> the ~ [of sth]** in der Größenordnung [von etw]

'ballplayer *n* Baseballspieler(in) *m(f)*

'ballpoint, ballpoint 'pen *n* Kugelschreiber *m*
'ballroom *n* Ballsaal *m*
ballroom 'dancing *n* Gesellschaftstanz *m*
balls ['bɔlz] *n pl* (*vulg, sl*) ❶ (*testicles*) Eier *pl derb* ❷ (*guts*) **to have the ~ to do sth** den Mumm haben, etw zu tun
balm [bam] *n* Balsam *m*
balmy ['ba·mi] *adj* mild
baloney [bə·'lɔʊ·ni] *n* ❶ (*bologna*) ≈ Fleischwurst *f* ❷ (*fam: nonsense*) Quatsch *m fam*
Baltic ['bɔl·tɪk] **I.** *adj* baltisch **II.** *n* ■**the ~** die Ostsee
bamboo [bæm·'bu] *n* Bambus *m*
bamboozle [bæm·'bu·zəl] *vt* (*fam*) ❶ (*confuse*) verwirren ❷ (*trick*) übers Ohr hauen
ban [bæn] **I.** *n* Verbot *nt;* **~ on smoking** Rauchverbot *nt* **II.** *vt* <-nn-> ■**to ~ sth** etw verbieten; ■**to ~ sb** jdn ausschließen
banal [bə·'nal] *adj* banal
banality [bə·'næl·ɪ·t̬i] *n* Banalität *f*
banana [bə·'næn·ə] *n* Banane *f*
banana re'public *n* (*pej*) Bananenrepublik *f usu pej*
band[1] [bænd] **I.** *n* ❶ *of metal, cloth* Band *nt* ❷ *of color* Streifen *m;* (*section a.*) Abschnitt *m* ❸ (*range*) Bereich *m* **II.** *vt* zusammenbinden
◆**band together** *vi* sich vereinigen
band[2] [bænd] *n* ❶ MUS (*modern*) Band *f;* (*traditional*) Kapelle *f* ❷ (*group*) *of criminals* Bande
bandage ['bæn·dɪdʒ] **I.** *n* Verband *m;* (*of cloth*) Binde *f;* (*for support*) Bandage *f* **II.** *vt limb* bandagieren; *wound* verbinden
'Band-Aid® *n* Hansaplast® *nt,* Pflaster *nt*
B & B [ˌbi·ən(d)·'bi] *n abbrev of* **bed and breakfast**
bandit ['bæn·dɪt] *n* Bandit(in) *m(f)*
'band member *n* Mitglied *nt* einer Kapelle/Band
'bandstand *n* Musikpavillon *m*
'bandwagon *n* ▶ PHRASES: **to jump on the ~** auf den fahrenden Zug aufspringen
'bandwidth *n* Bandbreite *f*
bandy ['bæn·di] *vt* ■**to be bandied about** verbreitet werden
bang [bæŋ] **I.** *n* ❶ (*loud sound*) Knall *m* ❷ (*blow*) Schlag *m* ❸ ■**~s** *pl* (*fringe*) [kurzer] Pony ▶ PHRASES: **to go over with a ~** ein echter Knaller sein **II.** *adv* **to go ~** [mit einem lauten Knall] explodieren **III.** *interj* ■**~!** peng! **IV.** *vi* Krach machen; *door* knallen **V.** *vt* (*hit*) *door* zuschlagen
◆**bang away** *vi* herumhämmern
Bangladeshi [bæŋ·glə·'deʃi] **I.** *n* Bangale, -in *m, f* **II.** *adj* bangalisch
bangle ['bæŋ·gəl] *n* Armreif[en] *m*
banish ['bæn·ɪʃ] *vt* verbannen (**from** aus +*dat*); *from country* ausweisen
banister ['bæn·ə·stər] *n usu pl* [Treppen]geländer *nt*
banjo <*pl* -s *or* -es> ['bæn·ʒoʊ] *n* Banjo *nt*
bank[1] [bæŋk] **I.** *n of river* Ufer *nt;* (*elevated area*) Abhang *m* **II.** *vi* AVIAT in die Querlage gehen **III.** *vt* AVIAT in die Querlage bringen
bank[2] [bæŋk] **I.** *n* ❶ (*financial institution*) Bank *f;* **in[to] the ~** auf die Bank ❷ (*storage place*) Bank *f* **II.** *vi* ■**to ~ with sb** bei jdm ein Konto haben **III.** *vt* [auf der Bank] einzahlen
◆**bank on** *vt* (*rely on*) zählen (auf +*dat*); (*expect*) rechnen (mit +*dat*)
'bank account *n* Bankkonto *nt*
'bank balance *n* Kontostand *m*
'bank book *n* Sparbuch *nt*
'bank charges *npl* Bankgebühren
banker ['bæŋ·kər] *n* ❶ (*in bank*) Banker(in) *m(f)* ❷ (*in games*) Bankhalter(in) *m(f)*
banking ['bæŋ·kɪŋ] *n* Bankwesen *nt;* **to be in ~** bei einer Bank arbeiten
bank 'manager *n* Filialleiter(in) *m(f)* einer Bank
'banknote *n* Banknote *f*
'bank robber *n* Bankräuber(in) *m(f)*
bankrupt ['bæŋk·rʌpt] **I.** *adj* bankrott; **to go ~** in Konkurs gehen **II.** *vt* [finanziell] ruinieren **III.** *n* Konkursschuldner(in) *m(f)*
bankruptcy ['bæŋk·rəp·si] *n* ❶ (*insolvency*) Konkurs *m* ❷ (*individual case*) Konkursfall *m*
'bank statement *n* Kontoauszug *m*
'bank transfer *n* Überweisung *f*
banner ['bæn·ər] *n* ❶ (*sign*) Transparent *nt* ❷ (*flag*) Banner *nt*
banquet ['bæŋ·kwət] **I.** *n* Bankett *nt* **II.** *vi* festlich speisen
bantam ['bæn·təm] *n* Bantamhuhn *nt*
banter ['bæn·tər] **I.** *n* scherzhaftes Gerede **II.** *vi* herumscherzen
baptism ['bæp·tɪz·əm] *n* Taufe *f*
baptismal [bæp·'tɪz·məl] *adj* Tauf-
Baptist ['bæp·tɪst] *n* Baptist(in) *m(f)*
baptize ['bæp·taɪz] *vt* taufen
bar [bar] **I.** *n* ❶ (*rod*) Stange *f; of cage* Gitterstab *m;* **to be behind ~s** hinter Schloss und Riegel sein; **to put sb behind ~s** jdn einlochen, jdn hinter Gitter bringen ❷ *of chocolate* Riegel *m; of soap* Stück *nt;* **~ of gold** Goldbarren *m* ❸ (*for drinking*) Lokal *nt,* Bar *f;* (*counter*) Bar *f,* Theke *f* ❹ LAW **to be admitted to the ~** als Anwalt/Anwältin [vor Gericht] zugelassen werden **II.** *vt* <-rr-> ❶ (*fasten*) verriegeln ❷ (*obstruct*) blockieren ❸ (*prohibit*) *something* verbieten; *somebody* ausschließen **III.** *prep* außer; **~ none** [alle] ohne Ausnahme
barb [barb] *n* ❶ *of hook, arrow* Widerhaken *m* ❷ (*insult*) Gehässigkeit *f*
barbarian [bar·'ber·i·ən] *n* Barbar(in) *m(f)*
barbaric [bar·'ber·ɪk] *adj* barbarisch
barbarity [bar·'ber·ɪ·t̬i] *n* Barbarei *f*
barbarous ['barbər·əs] *adj* grausam
barbecue ['bar·bɪ·kju] **I.** *n* (*utensil*) Grill *m;* (*event*) Grillparty *f* **II.** *vt* grillen

> Der Name, der einem Fest gegeben wird, bezieht sich häufig auf das, was dabei gegessen wird.

B

Ein **Barbecue**, auch *cookout* genannt, ist eine Art Grillparty.
Ein **clambake** wird im Normalfall am Strand ausgerichtet und besteht darin, dass Steine erhitzt und mit Seetang bedeckt werden. Anschließend kocht man darauf Venusmuscheln, Maiskolben, Kartoffeln, Hähnchen, Meeresfrüchte etc.
Bei einem **corn roast** röstet man Maiskolben über einem Holzfeuer. Man isst sie heiß, mit Butter und Salz.
Bei einem **pancake breakfast** werden amerikanische Pfannkuchen mit Butter oder Ahornsirup serviert.

barbed [barbd] *adj* ❶ *hook, arrow* mit Widerhaken *nach n* ❷ (*fig: hurtful*) bissig
barbed 'wire *n* Stacheldraht *m*
barber ['bar·bər] *n* [Herren]friseur *m*
'barbershop *n* Friseurgeschäft *nt*
barbiturate [bar·'bɪtʃ·ər·ɪt] *n* Barbiturat *nt*
'bar chart *n see* **bar graph**
'bar code *n* Strichcode *m*
bare [ber] **I.** *adj* ❶ (*unclothed*) nackt; **with one's ~ hands** (*fig*) mit seinen bloßen Händen ❷ (*uncovered*) *branch* kahl; *landscape* karg ❸ (*unadorned*) nackt; *room* karg ❹ (*basic*) **the ~ minimum** das absolute Minimum; **the ~ essentials** das Allernotwendigste **II.** *vt* entblößen; **to ~ one's heart/soul to sb** jdm sein Herz ausschütten
'bareback I. *adj rider* auf ungesatteltem Pferd *nach n* **II.** *adv* ohne Sattel
'barefaced *adj* unverschämt
'barefoot, bare'footed I. *adj* barfüßig **II.** *adv* barfuß
barely ['ber·li] *adv* ❶ (*hardly*) kaum ❷ (*scantily*) karg
barf [barf] (*fam*) **I.** *vi* kotzen *derb* **II.** *n* Kotze *f derb*
bargain ['bar·gɪn] **I.** *n* ❶ (*agreement*) Handel *m;* **to drive a hard ~** hart verhandeln ❷ (*good buy*) guter Kauf; **a real ~** ein echtes Schnäppchen **II.** *vi* (*negotiate*) [ver]handeln; (*haggle*) feilschen (**for** um +*akk*)
◆**bargain for** *vt* rechnen mit; **to get more than one ~ed for** eine unangenehme Überraschung erleben
bargain 'basement *n* Untergeschoss *nt* mit Sonderangeboten
barge [bardʒ] **I.** *n* (*for cargo*) Lastkahn *m* **II.** *vi* ■ **to ~ into sb** jdn anrempeln **III.** *vt* **to ~ one's way to the front** sich nach vorne drängeln
◆**barge in** *vi, vt* (*enter*) hinein-/hereinplatzen
◆**barge in on** *vt* (*interrupt*) ins Wort fallen
'bar graph, 'bar chart *n* Histogramm *nt*
baritone ['ber·ə·toʊn] *n* Bariton *m*
bark¹ [bark] *n* (*rind*) [Baum]rinde *f*
bark² [bark] **I.** *n* Bellen *nt;* (*fig*) Anblaffen *nt* **II.** *vi* bellen
◆**bark out** *vt* [barsch] bellen
barley ['bar·li] *n* Gerste *f*
'barmaid *n* Bardame *f*
'barman *n* Barmann *m*
barn [barn] *n* Scheune *f*
barnacle ['bar·nə·kəl] *n* Rankenfußkrebs *m*
'barnyard ['barn·jard] *n* [Bauern]hof *m*
barometer [bə·'ram·ə·t̬ər] *n* Barometer *nt*
baron ['bær·ən] *n* Baron *m,* Freiherr *m;* **press ~** Pressezar *m*
baroness ['bær·ə·nɪs] *n* Baronin *f*
baroque [bə·'roʊk] **I.** *adj* barock **II.** *n* ■ **the ~** der [*o* das] Barock
barracks ['bær·əks] *npl + sing/pl vb* Kaserne *f*
barrage [bə·'raʒ] *n* ❶ MIL Sperrfeuer *nt* ❷ (*fig*) **~ of questions** Schwall *m* von Fragen ❸ (*river barrier*) Wehr *nt*
barrel ['bær·əl] *n* ❶ (*container*) Fass *nt* ❷ (*measure*) Barrel *nt* ❸ *of gun* Lauf *m; of cannon* Rohr *nt*
barren ['bær·ən] *adj* ❶ unfruchtbar; *landscape* karg ❷ (*fig*) unproduktiv; *years* mager
barrette [bə·'ret] *n* Haarspange *f*
barricade ['bær·ə·keɪd] **I.** *n* Barrikade *f* **II.** *vt* verbarrikadieren
barrier ['bær·i·ər] *n* Barriere *f;* (*man-made*) Absperrung *f;* (*at railroad crossing*) Schranke *f*
barring ['bar·ɪŋ] *prep* ausgenommen; **~ any delays** wenn es keine Verspätungen gibt
barrio [ba·rioʊ] *n* Barrio *m* (*vorwiegend spanischsprachiges Viertel in amerikanischen Städten*)
barrow ['bær·oʊ] *n* (*wheelbarrow*) Schubkarren *m*
bartender ['bar·ten·dər] *n* Barkeeper *m*
barter ['bar·t̬ər] **I.** *n* Tausch[handel] *m* **II.** *vi* Tauschhandel [be]treiben; **to ~ for sth** um etw *akk* handeln **III.** *vt* ■ **to ~ sth for** etw tauschen gegen +*akk*
base¹ [beɪs] **I.** *n* ❶ (*bottom*) Fuß *m; of spine* Basis *f* ❷ (*HQ*) Hauptsitz *m;* MIL Basis *f* ❸ (*ingredient*) Hauptbestandteil *m* ❹ (*substrate*) Grundlage *f;* (*for painting*) Grundierung *f* ❺ SPORTS Base *f* ▶ PHRASES: **to touch ~** sich kurz mit jdm in Verbindung setzen **II.** *vt* ❶ ■ **to be ~d** *company* seinen Sitz haben; *soldier* stationiert sein ❷ (*taken from*) ■ **to be ~d on sth** auf etw *dat* basieren
base² [beɪs] *adj* ❶ (*immoral*) niederträchtig ❷ (*inferior*) *metal* unedel
'baseball *n* Baseball *m o nt*

Baseball ist eine traditionsreiche Ball- und Mannschaftssportart US-amerikanischer Herkunft. Zusammen mit American Football und Basketball zählt sie dort zu den beliebtesten Sportarten.
Zwei Mannschaften zu je neun Spielern haben abwechselnd das Schlagrecht (*offense*) und können *runs* (Punkte) erzielen, während die andere (*defense*) das Feld verteidigen und den Ball unter Kontrolle halten muss. Die Spieler der *offense* sind *at*

bat und versuchen *runs* zu machen, indem die Spieler vier *bases* (Bases) nacheinander berühren, die in einem *diamond* (Innenfeld) angeordnet sind. Der *pitcher* (Werfer) wirft den Ball und der *batter* (Schlagmann) der Gegenmannschaft versucht, den Ball mit seinem Schläger zu treffen. Trifft er den Ball und schlägt ihn zurück ins Feld, wird er zum *runner* (Läufer) und muss gegen den Uhrzeigersinn zur ersten Base rennen. Die Gegenseite, in diesem Fall die *defense*, kann das verhindern, wenn die Spieler den Ball schnell unter Kontrolle bekommen. Die Spieler der *defense* können ein *out* (Aus) des *batters* erzielen, indem sie den Ball direkt aus der Luft fangen oder ihn vom Boden aufnehmen und dem ersten Basemann zuwerfen, wenn dieser die erste Base berührt, bevor der *batter* dort ankommt. Gelingt es dem *pitcher* den Ball drei Mal so durch die *Strike Zone* (Fenster, durch das der *pitcher* den Ball werfen muss) zu werfen, dass der *batter* ihn nur schwach oder gar nicht schlagen kann, ist der Schlagmann ebenfalls *out*. Jeder *runner*, der nicht gerade eine Base berührt, ist auch *out*, wenn er von einem Feldspieler mit dem Ball selbst oder dem Handschuh berührt wird, in dem sich der Ball befindet (*tag out*). Wenn drei Schlagmänner oder Läufer *out* sind, wechseln die Teams die Seiten.
Ein Spielabschnitt heißt *inning* und ein Spiel besteht in der Regel aus neun solcher *innings*.

'base camp *n* Basislager *nt*
baseless ['beɪs·lɪs] *adj* unbegründet
'base rate *n* FIN Leitzins *m*
bash [bæʃ] (*fam*) **I.** *n* <*pl* -es> ❶ (*blow*) [heftiger] Schlag ❷ (*party*) **birthday ~** Geburtstagsparty **II.** *vi* ■ **to ~ into** zusammenstoßen mit +*dat* **III.** *vt* ■ **to ~ sb** jdn verhauen
bashful ['bæʃ·fəl] *adj* schüchtern
basic ['beɪ·sɪk] *adj* ❶ (*fundamental*) grundlegend; **~ requirements** Grundvoraussetzungen *pl;* ■ **the ~s** *pl* die Grundlagen; **to go back to** [**the**] **~s** zum Wesentlichen zurückkehren ❷ (*very simple*) [sehr] einfach
basically ['beɪ·sɪ·kə·li] *adv* im Grunde
basic 'salary *n* Grundgehalt *nt*
basil ['beɪ·zəl] *n* Basilikum *nt*
basilica [bə·'sɪl·ɪ·kə] *n* ARCHIT Basilika *f*
basin ['beɪ·sɪn] *n* ❶ (*in kitchen*) Schüssel *f;* (*washbasin*) Waschbecken *nt* ❷ GEOG Becken *nt*
basis <*pl* bases> ['beɪ·sɪs] *n* Basis *f;* ■ **to be the ~ for sth** als Grundlage für etw *akk* dienen; **on a regular ~** regelmäßig
bask [bæsk] *vi* ❶ **to ~ in the sun** sich in der Sonne aalen ❷ (*fig*) ■ **to ~ in sth** *success* sich in etw *dat* sonnen
basket ['bæs·kɪt] *n* Korb *m*
'basketball *n* Basketball *m*
'basket case *n* (*fam*) hoffnungsloser Fall
Basque [bæsk] **I.** *n* ❶ (*person*) Baske, -in *m, f* ❷ (*language*) Baskisch *nt* **II.** *adj* baskisch
bass¹ [beɪs] *n* MUS Bass *m*
bass² [bæs] *n* (*fish*) Barsch *m*
bassoon [bə·'sun] *n* Fagott *nt*
bastard ['bæs·tərd] *n* ❶ (*fam*) Dreckskerl *m;* **lucky ~** (*fam*) Glückspilz *m* ❷ (*pej old: illegitimate*) uneheliches Kind
baste¹ [beɪst] *vt* FOOD mit [Braten]saft beträufeln
baste² [beɪst] *vt* (*tack*) [an]heften
bastion ['bæs·tʃən] *n* Bollwerk *nt a. fig*
bat¹ [bæt] *n* ❶ (*animal*) Fledermaus *f* ❷ (*fam*) **old ~** alte Schrulle ▶ PHRASES: [**as**] **blind as a ~** blind wie ein Maulwurf
bat² [bæt] *vt* **to not ~ an eyelash** (*fig*) nicht mal mit der Wimper zucken
bat³ [bæt] **I.** *n* SPORTS Schläger *m* ▶ PHRASES: [**right**] **off the ~** prompt **II.** *vi, vt* <-tt-> SPORTS schlagen
batch <*pl* -es> [bætʃ] *n* Stapel *m; of bread* Schub *m*
bated ['beɪ·t̬ɪd] *adj* **with ~ breath** mit angehaltenem Atem
bath [bæθ] *n* ❶ (*washing*) Bad *nt;* **to take** [*or* **have**] **a ~** ein Bad nehmen, baden ❷ (*water*) Bad[ewasser] *nt;* **to run** [**sb**] **a ~** [jdm] ein Bad einlassen ❸ (*tub*) [Bade]wanne *f*
bathe [beɪð] **I.** *vi* ❶ (*take bath*) ein Bad nehmen ❷ (*swim*) schwimmen **II.** *vt* ❶ (*bath*) [sich] baden ❷ MED baden; **to ~ one's eyes** ein Augenbad machen ❸ (*fig: cover*) tauchen; **to be ~d in sweat** schweißgebadet sein
bather ['beɪ·ðər] *n* Badende(r) *f(m)*
bathing ['beɪ·ðɪŋ] *n* Baden *nt*
'bathing cap *n* Bademütze *f*
'bathing suit *n* (*top and bottom*) Badeanzug *m;* (*trunks*) Badehose *f*
'bathrobe *n* Bademantel *m*
'bathroom *n* Bad[ezimmer] *nt;* **to go to the ~** auf die Toilette gehen
'bath towel *n* Bade[hand]tuch *nt*
'bathtub *n* Badewanne *f*
baton [bə·'tan] *n* ❶ (*in conducting*) Taktstock *m* ❷ (*in relay races*) Staffelholz *nt*
battalion [bə·'tæl·jən] *n* Bataillon *nt*
batten ['bæt·ən] *n* Latte *f*
◆**batten down** *vt* mit Latten befestigen; **to ~ down the hatches** (*fig*) sich auf etwas gefasst machen
batter¹ ['bæt̬·ər] FOOD **I.** *n* [Back]teig *m* **II.** *vt* panieren
batter² ['bæt̬·ər] *n* SPORTS Schlagmann *m*
batter³ ['bæt̬·ər] **I.** *vt* ■ **to ~ sb** jdn verprügeln; ■ **to ~ sth** auf etw *akk* einschlagen **II.** *vi* schlagen; (*with fists*) hämmern
battered ['bæt̬·ərd] *adj* ❶ (*beaten*) misshandelt ❷ (*damaged*) böse zugerichtet; *car* verbeult; *equipment* schadhaft; *furniture, image*

ramponiert ③ (*covered in batter*) paniert

battering ['bæt̬·ər·ɪŋ] *n* ① (*attack*) Prügel *pl* ② (*fam: defeat*) Niederlage *f*

'battering ram *n* Rammbock *m*

battery ['bæt̬·ə·ri] *n* ① (*power*) Batterie *f*; **~-operated** [*or* **-powered**] batteriebetrieben ② MIL Batterie *f* ③ (*assault*) tätlicher Angriff

'battery charger *n* [Batterie]ladegerät *nt*

battle ['bæt̬·əl] **I.** *n* Kampf *m*; **~ of wills** Machtkampf *m* ► PHRASES: **to fight a losing ~** auf verlorenem Posten kämpfen **II.** *vi* kämpfen *a. fig* **III.** *vt* ■**to ~ sth** gegen etw *akk* [an]kämpfen

'battle-ax, **'battle-axe** *n* ① (*hist*) Streitaxt *f* ② (*fam: woman*) Schreckschraube *f*

'battle cry *n* Schlachtruf *m*

'battle dress *n* Kampfanzug *m*

'battlefield, **'battleground** *n* ① Schlachtfeld *nt* ② (*fig*) Reizthema *nt*

'battleship *n* Schlachtschiff *nt*

bauxite ['bɔk·saɪt] *n* Bauxit *m*

bawdy ['bɔ·di] *adj* schlüpfrig, zweideutig

bawl [bɔl] **I.** *vi* ① (*weep*) heulen, plärren ② (*bellow*) brüllen **II.** *vt* schreien

bay¹ [beɪ] *n* GEOG Bucht *f*; **the San Francisco B~** der Golf von San Francisco

bay² [beɪ] *n* (*for loading*) Ladeplatz *m*

bay³ [beɪ] **I.** *n* ► PHRASES: **at ~** in die Enge getrieben; **to keep sb at ~** sich *dat* jdn vom Leib halten **II.** *vi* bellen; HUNT melden

'bay leaf *n* FOOD Lorbeerblatt *nt*

bayonet [ˌbeɪ·ə·'net] **I.** *n* Bajonett *nt* **II.** *vt* mit dem Bajonett aufspießen

bay 'window *n* Erkerfenster *nt*

bazaar [bə·'zar] *n* Basar *m*

BBC [ˌbi·bi·'si] *n abbrev of* **British Broadcasting Corporation**: ■**the ~** die BBC

BC [ˌbi·'si] *adv abbrev of* **before Christ** v. Chr.

be <was, been> [bi] *vi + n/adj* ① (*describes*) sein; **what is that?** was ist das?; **she's a doctor** sie ist Ärztin; **what do you want to ~ when you grow up?** was willst du einmal werden, wenn du erwachsen bist?; **to ~ [all] for sth** [ganz] für etw *akk* sein ② (*location*) sein; *town, country* liegen; **the keys are in that box** die Schlüssel befinden sich in der Schachtel; **to ~ in a fix** in der Klemme stecken ③ (*do*) **to ~ on welfare** Sozialhilfe bekommen; **to ~ on a diet** auf Diät sein; **to ~ on the pill** die Pille nehmen; ■**to ~ up to sth** etw im Schild[e] führen ④ (*exist*) **to ~ or not to ~, that is the question** Sein oder Nichtsein, das ist die Frage; **there is/are ...** es gibt ... ⑤ (*expressing future*) **we are going to visit Europe in the spring** im Frühling reisen wir nach Europa; (*expressing future in past*) **she was never to see her brother again** sie sollte ihren Bruder nie mehr wiedersehen; **what are we to do?** was sollen wir tun?; (*in conditionals*) **if I were you, I'd ...** an deiner Stelle würde ich ... ⑥ (*impersonal use*) **what's it gonna ~?** (*what are you drinking*) was möchten Sie trinken?; (*please decide now*) was soll es denn [nun] sein?; **is it true that ...?** stimmt es, dass ...?; **as it were** sozusagen ⑦ (*expressing imperatives*) **~ quiet or I'll ...!** sei still oder ich ...!; **please ~ seated!** setzen Sie sich bitte! ⑧ (*expressing continuation*) **while I'm eating** während ich beim Essen bin; **it's raining** es regnet; **you're always complaining** du beklagst dich dauernd ⑨ (*expressing passive*) **to ~ asked** gefragt werden; **to ~ left speechless** sprachlos sein; **what is to ~ done?** was kann getan werden? ► PHRASES: **~ that as it may** wie dem auch sei; **so ~ it** so sei es; **to ~ off** (*go away*) weggehen

beach [bitʃ] **I.** *n* <*pl* -es> Strand *m* **II.** *vt* auf [den] Strand setzen

'beach ball *n* Wasserball *m*

'beachfront I. *n* Strandpromenade *f* **II.** *adj attr location, house, property* am Strand

'beachwear *n* Strandkleidung *f*

beacon ['bi·kən] *n* ① (*signal*) Leuchtfeuer *nt* ② (*fig: inspiration*) Leitstern *m*

bead [bid] *n* ① Perle *f* ② (*fig*) **~s of perspiration** Schweißtropfen *pl* ③ REL ■**~s** *pl* Rosenkranz *m*

beading ['bi·dɪŋ] *n* Perlstab *m*

beady ['bi·di] *adj* **~ eyes** [glänzende] Knopfaugen

beak [bik] *n* Schnabel *m*

beaker ['bi·kər] *n* SCI Becherglas *nt*

beam [bim] **I.** *n* ① (*light*) [Licht]strahl *m* ② (*rafter*) Balken *m* ③ SPORTS Schwebebalken *m* **II.** *vt* ausstrahlen **III.** *vi* strahlen

beaming ['bi·mɪŋ] *adj* strahlend

bean [bin] *n* (*seed*) Bohne *f*; (*pod*) [Bohnen]hülse *f*; **baked ~s** Baked Beans *pl*

'bean sprouts *npl* Sojabohnensprossen *pl*

bear¹ [ber] *n* (*animal*) Bär(in) *m(f)*

bear² <bore, born(e)> [ber] **I.** *vt* ① (*carry*) tragen; *gifts* mitbringen; (*liter*) *tidings* überbringen; **to ~ the blame** die Schuld auf sich *akk* nehmen ② (*endure*) ertragen; *suspense* aushalten; *criticism* vertragen ③ (*harbor*) **to ~ sb a grudge** einen Groll gegen jdn hegen ④ (*keep*) **I'll ~ that in mind** ich werde das berücksichtigen ⑤ (*give birth to*) gebären; **his wife bore him a son** seine Frau schenkte ihm einen Sohn ⑥ BOT **to ~ fruit** Früchte tragen *a. fig* **II.** *vi* ① (*tend*) **to ~ right** sich rechts halten ② (*be patient*) ■**to ~ with sb** mit jdm Geduld haben ③ (*approach*) ■**to ~ down on** zusteuern auf *+akk* ④ ■**to ~ on** (*be relevant*) betreffen; (*have effect on*) beeinflussen

◆**bear down** *vi* überwältigen

bearable ['ber·ə·bəl] *adj* erträglich

beard [bɪrd] *n* Bart *m*; **to have a ~** einen Bart tragen [*o* haben]

bearded ['bɪr·dɪd] *adj* bärtig

bearer ['ber·ər] *n* Überbringer(in) *m(f)*

bearing ['ber·ɪŋ] *n* ① NAUT Peilung *f*; ■**~s** *pl* (*position*) Lage *f*; (*direction*) Kurs *m*; **to lose one's ~s** die Orientierung verlieren ② (*deportment*) Benehmen *nt*; (*posture*) Haltung *f* ③ TECH Lager *nt*

'bearskin *n* (*fur*) Bärenfell *nt*

beast [bist] *n* ① (*animal*) Tier *nt;* **~ of burden** Lasttier *nt* ② (*person*) Biest *nt;* (*cruel*) Bestie *f*

beastly ['bist·li] *adj* (*nasty*) scheußlich, ekelhaft

beat [bit] **I.** *n* ① (*throb*) Schlag *m* ② (*act*) Schlagen *nt; of heart* Klopfen *nt* ③ MUS Takt *m* ④ *usu sing* (*patrol*) Runde *f* **II.** *adj* (*fam*) fix und fertig; **dead ~** total geschafft **III.** *vt* <beat, beaten *or* beat> ① (*hit*) schlagen; ■**to ~ sth** gegen/auf etw *akk* schlagen; *carpet* [aus]klopfen; **to ~ sb to death** jdn totschlagen; **to ~ a drum** trommeln ② FOOD schlagen ③ (*defeat*) schlagen, besiegen; (*outscore*) übertreffen; ■**to ~ sb to sth** jdm bei etw *dat* zuvorkommen; **you just can't ~ their prices** (*fam*) ihre Preise sind schlichtweg nicht zu unterbieten; **it ~s me how/why ...** (*fam*) es ist mir ein Rätsel, wie/warum ... ▶ PHRASES: **~ it!** (*fam*) hau ab! **IV.** *vi* <beat, beaten *or* beat> ① (*throb*) schlagen; *heart a.* klopfen, pochen; *drum* dröhnen ② (*strike*) ■**to ~ against/on sth** gegen etw *akk* schlagen ③ *rain* prasseln; *sun* [nieder]brennen; *waves* schlagen ▶ PHRASES: **to ~ around the bush** um den heißen Brei herumreden

◆**beat down I.** *vi rain* [her]niederprasseln; *sun* [her]niederbrennen **II.** *vt* herunterhandeln (**to** auf +*akk*)

◆**beat off I.** *vt* abwehren; MIL zurückschlagen **II.** *vi* (*vulg, sl*) sich *dat* einen runterholen *vulg*

◆**beat out** *vt* ① (*extinguish*) ausschlagen ② (*drum*) schlagen ▶ PHRASES: **to ~ sb's brains out** (*fam*) jdm den Schädel einschlagen

◆**beat up I.** *vt* verprügeln, zusammenschlagen **II.** *vi* ■**to ~ up on** verprügeln

beaten ['bit·ən] *adj* geschlagen; *metal* gehämmert ▶ PHRASES: **off the ~ track** abgelegen

beater ['bi·t̬ər] *n* (*for cooking*) Rührbesen *m*

beatify [bɪ·'æt̬·ə·faɪ] *vt* seligsprechen

beating ['bi·t̬ɪŋ] *n* ① (*smacking*) Prügel *pl* ② (*defeat*) Niederlage *f*

beatnik ['bit·nɪk] *n* Beatnik *m*

'beat poetry *n* Beatlyrik *f*

beautician [bju·'tɪʃ·ən] *n* Kosmetiker(in) *m(f)*

beautiful ['bju·t̬ə·fəl] *adj* ① (*attractive*) schön; **extremely ~** wunderschön ② (*uplifting*) herrlich, großartig

beautify ['bju·t̬ə·faɪ] *vt* verschönern; (*hum*) **to ~ oneself** sich schön machen

beauty ['bju·t̬i] *n* ① (*attractiveness*) Schönheit *f* ② (*woman*) Schönheit *f* ③ (*attraction*) **the ~ of our plan ...** das Schöne an unserem Plan ...

'beauty contest, 'beauty pageant *n* Schönheitswettbewerb *m*

'beauty parlor *n* Schönheitssalon *m,* Kosmetiksalon *m*

'beauty spot *n* (*on face*) Schönheitsfleck *m*

beaver ['bi·vər] **I.** *n* ① Biber *m* ② (*fig*) **eager ~** Arbeitstier *nt* **II.** *vi* (*fam*) **to ~ away** schuften

became [bɪ·'keɪm] *pt of* **become**

because [bɪ·'kɔz] **I.** *conj* weil; (*since*) da; (*for*) denn ▶ PHRASES: **just ~!** [einfach] nur so! **II.** *prep* ■**~ of** wegen +*gen*

beckon ['bek·ən] **I.** *vt* ■**to ~ sb over** jdn herüberwinken **II.** *vi* winken *a. fig*

become <became, become> [bɪ·'kʌm] **I.** *vi* werden; **to ~ extinct** aussterben; **what became of ...?** was ist aus ... geworden?; **to ~ interested in sb/sth** anfangen, sich für jdn/etw zu interessieren **II.** *vt* ① werden; **she wants to ~ an actress** sie will Schauspielerin werden ② (*look good*) ■**sth ~s sb** etw steht jdm

becoming [bɪ·'kʌm·ɪŋ] *adj dress, hat* vorteilhaft

bed [bed] *n* ① (*furniture*) Bett *nt;* **to go to ~** zu [*o* ins] Bett gehen ② (*flower patch*) Beet *nt* ③ (*base*) **sea~** Meeresgrund *m;* **served on a ~ of rice** auf Reis serviert ▶ PHRASES: **as you make your ~ so you must lie on it** (*prov*) wie man sich bettet, so liegt man

bed and 'breakfast *n* Übernachtung *f* mit Frühstück

'bedbug *n* [Bett]wanze *f*

'bedclothes *npl* Bettzeug *nt kein pl*

bedding ['bed·ɪŋ] *n* ① Bettzeug *nt* ② AGR [Ein]streu *f;* **~ plant** Freilandpflanze *f*

'bedfellow *n* Verbündete(r) *f(m);* **the priest and the politician made strange ~s** der Pfarrer und der Politiker gaben ein merkwürdiges Gespann ab

bedlam ['bed·ləm] *n* Chaos *nt*

'bed linen *n* Bettwäsche *f*

bedraggled [bɪ·'dræg·əld] *adj* durchnässt [und verdreckt]

'bedridden *adj* bettlägerig

'bedrock *n* Grundgestein *nt;* (*fig*) Fundament *nt*

'bedroom *n* Schlafzimmer *nt*

'bedside *n* Seite *f* des Bett[e]s; **to be at sb's ~** an jds Bett sitzen

bedside 'table *n* Nachttisch *m*

'bedsore *n* wund gelegene Stelle

'bedspread *n* Tagesdecke *f*

'bedstead *n* Bettgestell *nt*

'bedtime *n* Schlafenszeit *f;* **it's ~** Zeit fürs Bett!; **at ~** vor dem Schlafengehen

'bed-wetting *n* Bettnässen *nt*

bee [bi] *n* ① (*insect*) Biene *f* ② (*meet*) Treffen *nt;* **spelling ~** Buchstabierwettbewerb; **quilting ~** Patchworkkränzchen *nt* ▶ PHRASES: **to have a ~ in one's bonnet** einen Tick haben; **to be a busy ~** fleißig wie eine Biene sein

beech [bitʃ] *n* Buche *f*

'beechnut *n* Buchecker *f*

beef [bif] **I.** *n* ① (*meat*) Rindfleisch *nt;* **ground ~** Rinderhack[fleisch] *nt* ② (*fam: complaint*) Beschwerde *f* **II.** *vi* (*fam*) sich beschweren (**about** über +*akk*)

'beefcake *n* (*fam*) Muskelpakete *pl*

'beefsteak *n* Beefsteak *nt*

beefy ['bi·fi] *adj* ① (*fam: muscular*) muskulös ② (*like beef*) Rindfleisch-

'beehive *n* ① (*of bees*) Bienenstock *m;*

B

B

(*rounded*) Bienenkorb *m* ❷ (*hairstyle*) toupierte Hochfrisur

'**beekeeper** [-ˌki·pər] *n* Imker(in) *m(f)*

'**beeline** *n* **to make a ~ for sb/sth** schnurstracks auf jdn/etw zugehen

been [bɪn] *pp of* **be**

beep [bip] **I.** *vt* ❶ (*make brief noise*) **to ~ one's horn** hupen ❷ (*on pager*) ■ **to ~ sb** jdn anpiepen **II.** *vi* piepen; (*in car*) hupen **III.** *n* Piep[s]ton *m; of car* Hupen *nt*

beeper ['bi·pər] *n* Piepser *m*

beer [bɪr] *n* Bier *nt*

'**beer garden** *n* Biergarten *m*

'**beeswax** *n* Bienenwachs *nt*

beet [bit] *n* ❶ (*plant*) [Runkel]rübe *f* ❷ (*edible root*) Rote Bete

beetle ['biṭ·əl] *n* Käfer *m*

befit <-tt-> [bɪ·'fɪt] *vt* **as ~s a princess** wie es einer Prinzessin geziemt

before [bɪ·'fɔr] **I.** *prep* ❶ (*earlier*) vor +*dat;* **~ everything else** zuallererst; **~ long** in Kürze; **the day ~ yesterday** vorgestern ❷ (*in front of*) vor +*dat; with verbs of motion* vor +*akk;* **the letter K comes ~ L** der Buchstabe K kommt vor dem L; **the task ~ us** die Aufgabe, vor der wir stehen **II.** *conj* ❶ (*at previous time*) bevor; **just ~ ...** kurz bevor ...; **but ~ I knew it, she was gone** doch ehe ich mich versah, war sie schon verschwunden ❷ (*rather than*) bevor, ehe ❸ (*until*) bis; ■ **not ~** erst wenn ❹ (*so that ... do not*) damit; **stop that ~ you make a mess!** hör auf damit, bevor du eine Schweinerei veranstaltest! **III.** *adv* zuvor, vorher; **I have never seen that ~** das habe ich noch nie gesehen; **she has seen it all ~** sie kennt das alles schon; **~ and after** davor und danach **IV.** *adj after n* zuvor; **it had rained the day ~** tags zuvor hatte es geregnet

beforehand [bɪ·'fɔr·hænd] *adv* vorher

befriend [bɪ·'frend] *vt* ❶ (*become friends with*) sich anfreunden mit ❷ (*look after*) sich annehmen

beg <-gg-> [beg] **I.** *vt* (*request*) bitten; **to ~ sb's forgiveness** jdn um Verzeihung bitten; **I ~ your pardon** entschuldigen Sie bitte **II.** *vi* ❶ (*seek charity*) betteln (**for** um +*akk*) ❷ (*request*) ■ **to ~ of sb** jdn anflehen; **to ~ for mercy** um Gnade flehen ❸ *dog* Männchen machen

began [bɪ·'gæn] *pt of* **begin**

beggar ['beg·ər] **I.** *n* Bettler(in) *m(f)* **II.** *vt* ▶ PHRASES: **to ~ belief** [einfach] unglaublich sein

begin <-nn-, began, begun> [bɪ·'gɪn] *vt, vi* anfangen, beginnen; **I began this book two months ago** ich habe mit diesem Buch vor zwei Monaten angefangen; **to ~ work** mit der Arbeit beginnen; **I began to think he'd never come** ich dachte schon, er würde nie kommen; **she was ~ning to get angry** sie wurde allmählich wütend; **to ~ to roll/stutter** ins Rollen/Stottern kommen; **I don't know where to ~** ich weiß nicht, wo ich anfangen soll; **before school ~s** vor Schulanfang; **to ~ again** neu anfangen; **to ~ with, I want to ...** zunächst einmal möchte ich ...; **there were six of us to ~ with** anfangs waren wir noch zu sechst; **he began by saying ...** zunächst einmal sagte er ...

beginner [bɪ·'gɪn·ər] *n* Anfänger(in) *m(f)*

beginning [bɪ·'gɪn·ɪŋ] *n* ❶ (*starting point*) Anfang *m;* (*in time*) Beginn *m;* **at** [*or* **in**] **the ~** am Anfang, zu Beginn; **from ~ to end** (*place*) von vorn bis hinten; (*temporal*) von Anfang bis Ende ❷ ■ **~s** *pl* (*origin*) Anfänge *pl;* (*start*) erste Anzeichen ▶ PHRASES: **the ~ of the end** der Anfang vom Ende

begrudge [bɪ·'grʌdʒ] *vt* ■ **to ~ sb sth** jdm etw missgönnen; **I don't ~ him his freedom** ich gönne ihm seine Freiheit

begun [bɪ·'gʌn] *pp of* **begin**

behalf [bɪ·'hæf] *n* **on ~ of sb** [*or* **on sb's ~**] (*speaking for*) im Namen einer Person; (*as authorized by*) im Auftrag von jdm

behave [bɪ·'heɪv] **I.** *vi* ❶ *people* sich verhalten; **to ~ badly** sich schlecht benehmen; **~!** benimm dich! ❷ *object, substance* sich verhalten **II.** *vt* ■ **to ~ oneself** sich [anständig] benehmen

behavior [bɪ·'heɪv·jər] *n* ❶ *of person* Benehmen *nt,* Verhalten *nt;* **to be on one's best ~** sich von seiner besten Seite zeigen; **~ pattern** Verhaltensmuster *nt* ❷ *of car* [Fahr]verhalten *nt*

behavioral [bɪ·'heɪv·jər·əl] *adj* Verhaltens-

behead [bɪ·'hed] *vt* köpfen

behind [bɪ·'haɪnd] **I.** *prep* ❶ hinter +*dat; with verbs of motion* hinter +*akk;* **~ the wheel** hinterm Lenkrad; **to fall ~ sb** hinter jdn zurückfallen; **~ schedule** in Verzug ❷ (*fig*) **I'm ~ you all the way** ich stehe voll hinter dir; **who's ~ [all] this?** wer steckt dahinter? ▶ PHRASES: **~ the times** hinter der Zeit zurück[geblieben] **II.** *adv* hinten **III.** *adj* ❶ (*in arrears*) im Rückstand ❷ (*slow*) **to be [way] ~** [weit] zurück sein **IV.** *n* (*fam*) Hintern *m*

behold <beheld, beheld> [bɪ·'hoʊld] *vt* (*liter or old*) erblicken

beige [beɪʒ] *adj* beige[farben]

being ['bi·ɪŋ] **I.** *n* ❶ (*creature*) Wesen *nt* ❷ (*existence*) Dasein *nt;* **to come into ~** entstehen **II.** *adj* **for the time ~** vorerst **III.** *see* **be**

belated [bɪ·'leɪ·ṭɪd] *adj* verspätet; **~ birthday greetings** nachträgliche Geburtstagsgrüße

belch [beltʃ] **I.** *n* <*pl* -es> Rülpser *m* **II.** *vi* rülpsen **III.** *vt* ausstoßen; *volcano* ausspeien

belfry ['bel·fri] *n* Glockenturm *m* ▶ PHRASES: **to have bats in the ~** einen Vogel haben

Belgian ['bel·dʒən] **I.** *n* Belgier(in) *m(f)* **II.** *adj* belgisch

Belgium ['bel·dʒəm] *n* Belgien *nt*

belief [bɪ·'lif] *n* ❶ (*faith*) Glaube *m kein pl* (**in** an +*akk*); **to be beyond ~** [einfach] unglaublich sein ❷ (*view*) Überzeugung *f;* **it is my firm ~ that ...** ich bin der festen Überzeugung, dass ...; **to the best of my ~** nach bestem Wissen und Gewissen

believable [bɪ·ˈli·və·bəl] *adj* glaubwürdig

believe [bɪ·ˈliv] **I.** *vt* ① (*presume true*) glauben; **would you ~ it?** kannst du dir das vorstellen?; **I couldn't ~ my luck** ich konnte mein Glück [gar] nicht fassen; **I can't ~ how ...** ich kann gar nicht verstehen, wie ...; ■**to ~ sb to be sth** jdn für etw *akk* halten ② (*pretend*) **to make ~ [that]** ... so tun, als ob ... ▶ PHRASES: **seeing is believing** was ich sehe, glaube ich **II.** *vi* ① (*be certain of*) glauben (**in** an *+akk*) ② (*have confidence*) ■**to ~ in sb/sth** auf jdn/etw vertrauen ③ (*support sincerely*) ■**to ~ in sth** viel von etw *dat* halten ④ (*think*) glauben; **we have [every] reason to ~ that ...** wir haben [allen] Grund zu der Annahme, dass ...; **I ~ so** ich glaube schon

believer [bɪ·ˈli·vər] *n* ① REL Gläubige(r) *f(m)* ② (*enthusiast*) [überzeugter] Anhänger/[überzeugte] Anhängerin; **to be a [great] ~ in sth** [sehr] viel von etw *dat* halten

belittle [bɪ·ˈlɪt̬·əl] *vt* herabsetzen; *successes* schmälern

bell [bel] *n* ① (*for ringing*) Glocke *f;* (*small one*) Glöckchen *nt;* **door ~** [Tür]klingel *f* ② (*signal*) Läuten *nt kein pl,* Klingeln *nt kein pl;* **there's the ~ for lunch** es läutet zur Mittagspause ▶ PHRASES: **sth rings a ~ [with sb]** etw kommt jdm bekannt vor

ˈbellboy *n* [Hotel]page *m*

belligerent [bɪ·ˈlɪdʒ·ər·ənt] *adj* kampflustig

ˈbell jar *n* Glasglocke *f*

bellow [ˈbel·oʊ] **I.** *vt, vi* brüllen **II.** *n* Gebrüll *nt*

bellows [ˈbel·oʊz] *npl* Blasebalg *m*

belly [ˈbel·i] *n* Bauch *m*

ˈbellyache (*fam*) **I.** *n* Bauchschmerzen *pl,* Bauchweh *nt kein pl* **II.** *vi* jammern

ˈbelly button *n* (*fam*) [Bauch]nabel *m*

ˈbelly dancer *n* Bauchtänzerin *f*

ˈbellyflop *n* Bauchklatscher *m*

belong [bɪ·ˈlaŋ] *vi* ① (*be owned*) gehören (**to** *+dat*); (*be in right place*) hingehören; **where do these spoons ~?** wohin gehören diese Löffel? ② (*be welcome*) **you don't ~ here** Sie haben hier nichts zu suchen ③ (*fit in*) [dazu]gehören; **she doesn't really ~ here** sie passt eigentlich nicht hierher

belongings [bɪˈlaŋ·ɪŋz] *npl* Hab und Gut *nt kein pl;* **personal ~** persönliche Sachen

beloved [bɪ·ˈlʌv·ɪd] **I.** *n* Geliebte(r) *f(m)* **II.** *adj* geliebt

below [bɪ·ˈloʊ] **I.** *adv* ① (*lower*) unten, darunter; **down ~** NAUT unter Deck ② (*on page*) unten; **see ~** siehe unten **II.** *prep* ① unter *+dat; with verbs of motion* unter *+akk;* **~ average** unter dem Durchschnitt; **~ zero** *temperature* unter null ② (*south of*) unterhalb *+gen*

belt [belt] **I.** *n* ① (*for waist*) Gürtel *m;* **below the ~** unter der Gürtellinie ② (*conveyor*) Band *nt* ③ (*area*) Gebiet *nt;* **commuter ~** Einzugsbereich *m* [einer Großstadt]; **green ~** Grüngürtel *m* ▶ PHRASES: **to tighten one's ~** den Gürtel enger schnallen **II.** *vt* (*fam*) hauen; *ball* knallen

◆**belt out** *vt song* schmettern

bemoan [bɪ·ˈmoʊn] *vt* beklagen

bemused [bɪ·ˈmjuzd] *adj* verwirrt

bench <*pl* -es> [bentʃ] *n* ① Bank *f* ② LAW ■**the ~** die [Richter]bank

ˈbenchmark *n* ① (*standard*) Maßstab *m* ② (*in surveying*) Höhenmarke *f*

ˈbenchwarmer *n* SPORT (*substitute*) Ersatzspieler(in) *m(f)* (*der/die kaum eingesetzt wird*)

bend [bend] **I.** *n* ① (*in road*) Kurve *f;* (*in pipe*) Krümmung *f;* (*in river*) Biegung *f* ② ■**the ~s** *pl* MED die Caissonkrankheit *kein pl* ▶ PHRASES: **to go around the ~** (*fam*) durchdrehen **II.** *vi* <bent, bent> ① (*turn*) *road* biegen; **to ~ forward** sich vorbeugen; **to be bent double** sich krümmen ② (*be flexible*) sich biegen; *tree* sich neigen **III.** *vt* biegen; (*deform*) verbiegen; **to ~ the rules** (*fig*) sich nicht ganz an die Regeln halten

◆**bend back** **I.** *vt* zurückbiegen; **to ~ sth back into shape** etw wieder in [die ursprüngliche] Form bringen **II.** *vi* sich nach hinten beugen

◆**bend down** *vi* sich niederbeugen

◆**bend over** *vi* sich vorbeugen ▶ PHRASES: **to ~ over backwards** sich *dat* die allergrößte Mühe geben

beneath [bɪ·ˈniθ] **I.** *prep* unter *+dat; with verbs of motion* unter *+akk;* **to be ~ sb** (*lower rank than*) unter jdm stehen; (*lower standard than*) unter jds Würde sein **II.** *adv* unten, darunter

benediction [ˌben·ɪ·ˈdɪk·ʃən] *n* Segnung *f*

benefactor [ˈben·ə·fæk·tər] *n* Wohltäter(in) *m(f)*

beneficiary [ˌben·ə·ˈfɪʃ·i·ər·i] *n* Nutznießer(in) *m(f)*

benefit [ˈben·ə·fɪt] **I.** *n* ① (*advantage*) Vorteil *m;* (*profit*) Nutzen *m;* **to derive** [*or* **get**] **[much] ~ from sth** einen [großen] Nutzen aus etw *dat* ziehen; **to give sb the ~ of the doubt** im Zweifelsfall zu jds Gunsten entscheiden ② (*welfare*) Beihilfe *f;* **unemployment ~** Arbeitslosengeld *nt* **II.** *vi* <-t- *or* -tt-> ■**to ~ from sth** von etw *dat* profitieren, aus etw *dat* Nutzen ziehen **III.** *vt* <-t- *or* -tt-> ■**to ~ sb/sth** jdm/etw nützen

bent [bent] **I.** *pt, pp of* **bend** **II.** *n* Neigung *f;* ■**a [natural] ~ for sth** ein [natürlicher] Hang zu etw *dat* **III.** *adj* umgebogen; *wire* verbogen; *person* gekrümmt

benzene [ˈben·zin] *n* Benzol *nt*

bequeath [bɪ·ˈkwið] *vt* hinterlassen

bequest [bɪ·ˈkwest] *n* Vermächtnis *nt*

bereaved [bɪ·ˈrivd] **I.** *adj* trauernd **II.** *n* ■**the ~** *pl* die Hinterbliebenen

bereavement [bɪ·ˈriv·mənt] *n* (*death*) Trauerfall *m;* (*loss*) schmerzlicher Verlust

beret [bə·ˈreɪ] *n* Baskenmütze *f;* MIL Barett *nt*

Bermuda shorts [bər·ˌmju·də·ˈʃɔrts] *npl* Bermudas *pl*

B

berry [ˈber·i] *n* Beere *f*

berserk [bərˈsɜrk] *adj* außer sich *dat;* **to go ~** [fuchsteufels]wild werden

berth [bɜrθ] **I.** *n* ❶ (*for ship*) Liegeplatz *m* ❷ NAUT (*bed*) [Schlaf]koje *f;* RAIL Schlafwagenbett *nt* **II.** *vt, vi* festmachen

beset <-tt-, beset, beset> [bɪˈset] *vt usu passive* ■**to be ~ by sth** von etw *dat* bedrängt werden; *by worries* von etw *dat* geplagt werden

beside [bɪˈsaɪd] *prep* ❶ (*next to*) neben +*dat; with verbs of motion* neben +*akk* ❷ (*irrelevant to*) **~ the point** nebensächlich

besides [bɪˈsaɪdz] **I.** *adv* außerdem; **many more ~** noch viele mehr **II.** *prep* ❶ (*in addition to*) außer +*dat* ❷ (*except for*) abgesehen von +*dat*

besiege [bɪˈsidʒ] *vt* ❶ MIL (*surround*) belagern ❷ (*overwhelm*) überschütten

besotted [bɪˈsa·t̬ɪd] *adj* ■**~ with sb** in jdn völlig vernarrt

best [best] **I.** *adj superl of* **good** ❶ (*finest*) ■**the ~ ...** der/die/das beste ...; **the ~ days of my life** die schönste Zeit meines Lebens; **~ regards** [*or* **wishes**] viele [*o* herzliche] Grüße; **give my ~ wishes to your wife** richten Sie Ihrer Frau herzliche Grüße von mir aus ❷ (*most favorable*) **he is acting in her ~ interest**[s] er handelt nur zu ihrem Besten; **what's the ~ way to the train station?** wie komme ich am besten zum Bahnhof?; ■**to be ~** am besten sein ▶ PHRASES: **sb's ~ bet** (*fam*) **your ~ bet would be to take a taxi** am besten nehmen Sie ein Taxi **II.** *adv superl of* **well** am besten; **to do as one thinks ~** tun, was man für richtig hält; **~ of all** am allerbesten **III.** *n* ❶ (*finest person, thing*) ■**the ~** der/die/das Beste; **at its ~** vom Feinsten; **the ~ of friends** die besten Freunde; **in the ~ of health** bei bester Gesundheit; **to the ~ of my knowledge** meines Wissens; **at one's ~** (*performance*) in Höchstform; (*condition*) in bester Verfassung ❷ (*most favorable*) **all the ~!** (*fam*) alles Gute!; **at ~** bestenfalls ▶ PHRASES: **to make the ~ of things** [*or* **it**] das Beste daraus machen; **the ~ of both worlds** das Beste von beidem

bestiality [ˌbes·tʃiˈæl·ɪ·t̬i] *n* Bestialität *f*

best ˈman *n* Trauzeuge *m* (*des Bräutigams*)

bestˈseller *n* Bestseller *m*

bet [bet] **I.** *n* ❶ (*gamble*) Wette *f;* **to place** [*or* **make**] **a ~ on sth** auf etw *akk* wetten; **to make a ~ with sb** mit jdm wetten ❷ (*fig: guess*) Tipp *m;* **all ~s are off** alles ist möglich **II.** *vt, vi* <-tt-, bet *or* -ted, bet *or* -ted> wetten; **I ~ you 25 dollars that ...** ich wette mit dir um 25 Dollar, dass ... ▶ PHRASES: **you ~!** (*fam*) das kannst du mir aber glauben!

beta [ˈbeɪ·t̬ə] *n* Beta *nt*

ˈbeta-blocker *n* Betablocker *m*

betray [bɪˈtreɪ] *vt* ❶ (*be disloyal*) verraten; *trust* missbrauchen; ■**to ~ sb** (*be unfaithful*) jdm untreu sein; (*deceive*) jdn betrügen ❷ (*reveal*) *feelings* zeigen; *ignorance* verraten

betrayal [bɪˈtreɪ·əl] *n* Verrat *m; of trust* Enttäuschung *f*

better[1] [ˈbet̬·ər] **I.** *adj comp of* **good** ❶ (*superior*) besser; **~ luck next time** vielleicht klappt's ja beim nächsten Mal; **she is much ~ at tennis than I am** sie spielt viel besser Tennis als ich ❷ (*healthier*) besser; **to get ~** sich erholen ❸ (*most*) **the ~ part** der größte Teil; **the ~ part of sth** der Großteil einer S. *gen;* **the ~ part of an hour** fast eine Stunde [lang] **II.** *adv comp of* **well** ❶ (*in superior manner*) besser; **or ~ yet ...** oder noch besser ... ❷ (*to a greater degree*) mehr; *like* lieber; **she is much ~-looking** sie sieht viel besser aus; **to think ~ of sth** sich *dat* etw anders überlegen **III.** *n* ❶ (*improvement*) **to change for the ~** sich zum Guten wenden; **all** [*or* **so much**] **the ~** umso besser ❷ ■**one's ~s** *pl* (*hum dated*) *Leute, die über einem stehen* ▶ PHRASES: **to get the ~ of sb** über jdn die Oberhand gewinnen **IV.** *vt* verbessern; **to ~ oneself** (*improve social position*) sich verbessern; (*further one's knowledge*) sich weiterbilden

better[2] [ˈbet̬·ər] *n see* **bettor**

betting [ˈbet̬·ɪŋ] *n* Wetten *nt*

bettor [ˈbet̬·ər] *n jd, der eine Wette abschließt*

between [bɪˈtwin] **I.** *prep* zwischen +*dat; with verbs of motion* zwischen +*akk;* **halfway ~ Miami and Tampa** auf halbem Weg zwischen Miami und Tampa; **~ you and me** unter uns gesagt **II.** *adv* ■[**in**] **~** dazwischen

beverage [ˈbev·ər·ɪdʒ] *n* Getränk *nt*

bevy [ˈbev·i] *n* Schar *f*

beware [bɪˈwer] *vi, vt* sich in Acht nehmen (**of** vor +*dat*); **~!** Vorsicht!; **"~ of the dog"** „[Vorsicht,] bissiger Hund!"; ■**to ~ of doing sth** sich davor hüten, etw zu tun

bewilder [bɪˈwɪl·dər] *vt* verwirren

bewilderment [bɪˈwɪl·dər·mənt] *n* Verwirrung *f*

bewitch [bɪˈwɪtʃ] *vt* ❶ (*put under spell*) verzaubern ❷ (*enchant*) bezaubern

bewitching [bɪˈwɪtʃ·ɪŋ] *adj* bezaubernd

beyond [bɪˈjand] **I.** *prep* ❶ (*on the other side of*) über +*akk,* jenseits +*gen* ❷ (*after*) nach +*dat* ❸ (*further than*) über +*akk;* **to be ~ the reach of sb** außerhalb jds Reichweite sein; **to see ~ sth** über etw *akk* hinaus sehen ❹ (*surpassing*) **damaged ~ repair** irreparabel beschädigt; **~ help** nicht mehr zu helfen **II.** *adv* (*in space*) jenseits; (*in time*) darüber hinaus; **with the mountains ~** mit den Bergen dahinter; **to go ~** hinausgehen über +*akk*

biannual [ˌbaɪˈæn·jʊ·əl] *adj* halbjährlich; **~ report** Halbjahresbericht *m*

bias [ˈbaɪ·əs] **I.** *n usu sing* ❶ (*prejudice*) Vorurteil *nt* ❷ (*one-sidedness*) Befangenheit *f* (**against** gegenüber +*dat*) ❸ (*predisposition*) Neigung *f* (**in favor of, toward**[**s**] für +*akk*) **II.** *vt* <-ss- *or* -s-> ■**to ~ sth** etw einseitig darstellen; ■**to ~ sb against sth** jdn gegen etw *akk* einnehmen

biased ['baɪ·əst] *adj* voreingenommen
bib [bɪb] *n* Lätzchen *nt*
Bible ['baɪ·bəl] *n* Bibel *f*
biblical ['bɪb·lɪ·kəl] *adj* biblisch
bibliographer [ˌbɪb·lɪ·'ag·rə·fər] *n* Bibliograf(in) *m(f)*
bibliographic [ˌbɪb·lɪ·ə·'græf·ɪk], **bibliographical** [ˌbɪb·lɪ·ə·'græf·ɪ·kəl] *adj* bibliografisch
bibliography [ˌbɪb·li·'ag·rə·fi] *n* Bibliografie *f*
bicarbonate [ˌbaɪ·'kar·bə·nɪt], **bicarbonate of 'soda** *n* Natriumbikarbonat *nt;* (*in cooking*) Natron *nt*
bicentennial [baɪ·sen·'ten·ɪ·əl], **bicentenary** [baɪ·'sen·ten·ə·ri] *n* zweihundertjähriges Jubiläum
biceps <*pl* -> ['baɪ·seps] *n* Bizeps *m*
bicker ['bɪk·ər] *vi* sich zanken
bickering ['bɪk·ər·ɪŋ] *n* Gezänk *nt*
bicycle ['baɪ·sɪk·əl] *n* Fahrrad *nt;* **by ~** mit dem Fahrrad
bid¹ <-dd-, bid *or* bade, bid *or* bidden> [bɪd] *vt* **to ~ sb farewell** jdm Lebewohl sagen
bid² [bɪd] **I.** *n* ❶ (*offer*) Angebot *nt;* (*at auction*) Gebot *nt* ❷ (*attempt*) Versuch *m;* **to make a ~ for power** nach der Macht greifen **II.** *vi* <-dd-, bid, bid> ❶ (*offer money*) bieten ❷ (*tender*) ein Angebot unterbreiten; **to ~ on a contract** sich um einen Auftrag bewerben **III.** *vt* <-dd-, bid, bid> bieten
bidder ['bɪd·ər] *n* Bieter(in) *m(f);* **highest ~** Meistbietende(r) *f(m)*
bidding ['bɪd·ɪŋ] *n* Bieten *nt;* (*at auction*) Steigern *nt*
bide [baɪd] *vt* **to ~ one's time** den rechten Augenblick abwarten
bidet [bɪ·'deɪ] *n* Bidet *nt*
biennial [baɪ·'en·i·əl] **I.** *adj* zweijährlich **II.** *n* zweijährige Pflanze
big <-gg-> [bɪg] *adj* ❶ (*of size, amount*) groß; *meal* üppig; *tip* großzügig; **the ~ger the better** je größer, desto besser ❷ (*significant*) bedeutend; *decision* schwerwiegend ▶ PHRASES: **a ~ fish in a small pond** der Hecht im Karpfenteich
◆ **big up** *vt* (*sl*) ■ **to ~ up ⊂ sb/sth** jdn/etw groß herausbringen
bigamist ['bɪg·ə·mɪst] *n* Bigamist(in) *m(f)*
bigamy ['bɪg·ə·mi] *n* Bigamie *f*
Big 'Apple *n* (*fam*) ■ **the ~** New York *nt*
big 'business *n* ■ **to be ~** ein lukratives Geschäft sein
big 'cheese *n* (*fam*) hohes Tier *fam*
Big 'Easy *n* ■ **the ~** New Orleans *nt*
big 'game *n* Großwild *nt*
big 'government *n* (*pej*) übermächtige Regierung
bigot ['bɪg·ət] *n* Eiferer, Eiferin *m, f*
bigoted ['bɪg·ə·t̬ɪd] *adj* fanatisch
bigotry ['bɪg·ə·tri] *n* Fanatismus *m*
'big shot *n* (*fam*) hohes Tier
'big time *n* (*fam*) ■ **the ~** eine große Nummer *fam;* **to hit** [*or* **make**] **the ~** den großen Durchbruch schaffen
'big-time (*fam*) **I.** *adj attr criminal* berühmt-berüchtigt **II.** *adv* (*in a big way*) großartig
'big top *n* großes Zirkuszelt
'bigwig *n* (*fam*) hohes Tier
bike [baɪk] (*fam*) **I.** *n* ❶ (*bicycle*) [Fahr]rad *nt;* **by ~** mit dem [Fahr]rad ❷ (*motorcycle*) Motorrad *nt* **II.** *vi* mit dem Fahrrad fahren
biker ['baɪ·kər] *n* (*fam: bicycle rider*) Fahrradfahrer; (*motorcycle rider*) Motorradfahrer(in) *m(f);* (*in gang*) Rocker(in) *m(f)*
bikini [bɪ·'ki·ni] *n* Bikini *m*
bilateral [ˌbaɪ·'læt̬·ər·əl] *adj* bilateral
bile [baɪl] *n* ❶ Galle *f;* **~ duct** Gallengang *m meist pl* ❷ (*fig*) Bitterkeit *f*
bilingual [baɪ·'lɪŋ·gwəl] *adj* zweisprachig
bilious ['bɪl·jəs] *adj* ❶ MED **~ attack** Gallenkolik *f* ❷ (*fig: bad-tempered*) übellaunig
bill¹ [bɪl] **I.** *n* ❶ (*invoice*) Rechnung *f;* **could we have the ~, please?** zahlen bitte! ❷ (*money*) Geldschein *m;* [**one-**]**dollar ~** Dollarschein *m* ❸ (*placard*) Plakat *nt* ▶ PHRASES: **to fit the ~** der/die/das Richtige sein **II.** *vt* ■ **to ~ sb** jdm eine Rechnung ausstellen; ■ **to ~ sb for sth** jdm etw in Rechnung stellen
bill² [bɪl] *n of bird* Schnabel *m*
'billboard *n* Reklamefläche *f,* Plakatwand *f*
billet ['bɪl·ət] MIL **I.** *n* Quartier *nt* **II.** *vt usu passive* ■ **to be ~ed** einquartiert werden
'billfold *n* Brieftasche *f*
billiards ['bɪl·jərdz] *n + sing vb* Billard *nt*
billing ['bɪl·ɪŋ] *n* Programm *nt*
billion ['bɪl·jən] *n* Milliarde *f*
billow ['bɪl·oʊ] *vi cloth* sich blähen; *smoke* in Schwaden aufsteigen; *skirt* sich bauschen
'billy goat *n* Ziegenbock *m*
bimbo <*pl* -es *or* -s> ['bɪm·boʊ] *n* (*pej fam*) Puppe *f*
bin [bɪn] **I.** *n* ❶ **garbage ~** Mülleimer *m,* Mülltonne *f* ❷ (*for storage*) Behälter *m* **II.** *vt* einlagern
binary ['baɪ·nə·ri] *adj* binär
bind [baɪnd] **I.** *n* (*fam*) ❶ **to be a ~** lästig sein ❷ **to be in a ~** in der Klemme stecken **II.** *vi* <bound, bound> binden **III.** *vt* <bound, bound> (*fasten*) ■ **to ~ sb** jdn fesseln (**to** an +*akk*); ■ **to ~ sth** etw festbinden (**to** an +*akk*); *feet* einbinden
binder ['baɪn·dər] *n* Einband *m*
binding ['baɪn·dɪŋ] **I.** *n* ❶ (*covering*) Einband *m* ❷ (*act*) Binden *nt* ❸ (*on ski*) Bindung *f* **II.** *adj* verbindlich
binge [bɪndʒ] (*fam*) **I.** *n* Gelage *nt;* **shopping ~** Kaufrausch *m* **II.** *vi* ■ **to ~ on sth** sich mit etw *dat* vollstopfen
bingo ['bɪŋ·goʊ] **I.** *n* Bingo *nt* **II.** *interj* ■ **~!** bingo!
binoculars [bɪ·'nak·jə·lərz] *npl* [**pair of**] **~** Fernglas *nt*
bio'chemical *adj* biochemisch
bio'chemist *n* Biochemiker(in) *m(f)*
bio'chemistry *n* Biochemie *f*
biode'gradable *adj* biologisch abbaubar

biode'grade *vi* sich zersetzen
biodi'versity *n* Artenvielfalt *f*
bioengi'neering *n* Biotechnik *f*
'biofuel *n* Biotreibstoff *m*
'biogas *n* Biogas *nt*
biographer [baɪ·'ag·rə·fər] *n* Biograf(in) *m(f)*
biographical [ˌbaɪ·oʊ·'græf·ɪ·kəl] *adj* biografisch
biography [baɪ·'ag·rə·fi] *n* Biografie *f*
biological [ˌbaɪ·ə·'ladʒ·ɪ·kəl] *adj* biologisch
biologist [baɪ·'al·ə·dʒɪst] *n* Biologe, -in *m, f*
biology [baɪ·'al·ə·dʒi] *n* Biologie *f*
biomass ['baɪ·oʊ·ˌmæs] *n* Biomasse *f*
biopsy ['baɪ·ap·si] *n* Biopsie *f*
'biorhythm *n* Biorhythmus *m*
'biosphere *n* Biosphäre *f*
biotech'nology *n* Biotechnologie *f*
biotope ['baɪ·ə·toʊp] *n* Biotop *m o nt*
bipartisan [ˌbaɪ·'par·t̬ə·zən] *adj* von zwei Parteien getragen
biped ['baɪ·ped] *n* Zweifüß[l]er(in) *m(f)*
biplane ['baɪ·pleɪn] *n* Doppeldecker *m*
bipolar [ˌbaɪ·'poʊ·lər] *adj* bipolar
birch <*pl* -es> [bɜrtʃ] *n* Birke *f*
bird [bɜrd] *n* Vogel *m* ▶PHRASES: **a ~ in the hand is worth two in the bush** (*prov*) besser ein Spatz in der Hand als eine Taube auf dem Dach; **the early ~ gets** [*or* **catches**] **the worm** (*prov*) Morgenstunde hat Gold im Munde; [**strictly**] **for the ~s** (*fam*) für die Katz
'birdbath *n* Vogelbad *nt*
'birdcage *n* Vogelkäfig *m*
birdie ['bɜr·di] *n* ① (*esp childspeak*) Piepmatz *m* ② SPORT Federball *m*
bird of 'paradise <*pl* birds of paradise> *n* Paradiesvogel *m*
'birdseed *n* Vogelfutter *nt*
bird's-eye 'view *n* Vogelperspektive *f*
'birdwatching *n* das Beobachten von Vögeln
birth [bɜrθ] **I.** *n* ① (*event of being born*) Geburt *f*; **date of ~** Geburtsdatum *nt;* **to give ~ to a child** ein Kind zur Welt bringen ② (*family*) Abstammung *f*; **American by ~** gebürtiger Amerikaner/gebürtige Amerikanerin **II.** *vt* ① (*give birth to*) *baby* zur Welt bringen ② (*create*) *idea, project* hervorbringen
'birth certificate *n* Geburtsurkunde *f*
'birth control *n* Geburtenkontrolle *f*; **~ pill** Antibabypille *f*
birthday ['bɜrθ·deɪ] *n* Geburtstag *m;* **happy ~ [to you]!** alles Gute zum Geburtstag!
'birthday cake *n* Geburtstagstorte *f*
'birthday card *n* Geburtstagskarte *f*
'birthday party *n* Geburtstagsparty *f*
'birthday present *n* Geburtstagsgeschenk *nt*
'birthday suit *n* ▶PHRASES: **in one's ~** (*hum*) im Adamskostüm
'birthmark *n* Muttermal *nt*
'birthplace *n* Geburtsort *m*
'birth rate *n* Geburtenrate *f*
biscuit ['bɪs·kɪt] *n* ① (*bread type*) Brötchen *nt* ② **dog ~** Hundekuchen *m*

> **Biscuits and gravy**, eine Mahlzeit, die aus den Südstaaten stammt, werden in den USA oft zum Frühstück gegessen. Die *biscuits* sind eine Art flache Brötchen, die man mit *gravy* (Bratensoße) serviert.

bisect ['baɪ·sekt] *vt* zweiteilen
bisexual [ˌbaɪ·'sek·ʃʊ·əl] **I.** *n* Bisexuelle(r) *f(m)* **II.** *adj* bisexuell
bishop ['bɪʃ·əp] *n* ① REL Bischof *m* ② CHESS Läufer *m*
bison <*pl* -s *or* -> ['baɪ·sən] *n* ① (*American*) amerikanischer Bison ② (*European*) europäischer Bison, Wisent *m*
bit[1] [bɪt] *n* ① (*piece*) Stück *nt;* (*fig: some*) **~ of advice** Rat *m;* **~s of glass** Glasscherben *pl;* **~s of paper** Papierfetzen *pl;* **to smash sth to ~s** etw zerschmettern ② (*part*) Teil *m; of a story, film* Stelle *f;* **~ by ~** Stück für Stück ③ (*a little*) ■**a ~** ein bisschen; **just a ~** ein klein bisschen ④ (*quite*) ■**a ~** ziemlich; [**quite**] **a ~ of money** ziemlich viel Geld ⑤ (*short time*) **I'm just going out for a ~** ich gehe mal kurz raus ⑥ (*in negations*) ■**not a ~** kein bisschen
bit[2] [bɪt] *vt, vi pt of* **bite**
bit[3] [bɪt] *n* COMPUT Bit *nt*
bit[4] [bɪt] *n* (*for horse*) Gebiss *nt*
bitch [bɪtʃ] **I.** *n* <*pl* -es> ① (*pej fam: woman*) Miststück *nt* ② (*dog*) Hündin *f* **II.** *vi* (*fam*) ■**to ~ about sb/sth** über jdn/etw lästern
bitchy ['bɪtʃ·i] *adj* (*fam*) gehässig
bite [baɪt] **I.** *n* ① (*using teeth*) Biss *m; of insect* Stich *m;* **~ mark** Bisswunde *f;* **to have a ~ to eat** (*fam*) eine Kleinigkeit essen ② (*fig: sharpness*) Biss *m* ③ (*pungency*) Schärfe *f* **II.** *vt* <bit, bitten> beißen; *insect* stechen; **to ~ one's nails** an seinen Nägeln kauen; **to ~ one's tongue** sich *dat* auf die Zunge beißen *a. fig* **III.** *vi* <bit, bitten> *dog, snake* beißen; *insect* stechen
biting ['baɪ·t̬ɪŋ] *adj* beißend *a. fig*
bitten ['bɪt·ən] *vt, vi pp of* **bite**
bitter ['bɪt̬·ər] *adj* <-er, -est> ① (*sour*) *taste* bitter ② (*fig: painful*) bitter ③ (*resentful*) verbittert
bitterly ['bɪt̬·ər·li] *adv* bitter; **~ cold** bitterkalt; **~ disappointed** schwer enttäuscht
bitterness ['bɪt̬·ər·nɪs] *n* ① (*rancor*) Verbitterung *f* (**toward** gegenüber +*dat*) ② FOOD Bitterkeit *f*
bizarre [bɪ·'zar] *adj* bizarr; *behavior* seltsam
blab <-bb-> [blæb] (*fam*) **I.** *vt* ausplaudern **II.** *vi* plaudern; ■**to ~ to sb** jdm gegenüber nicht dichthalten
black [blæk] **I.** *adj* schwarz *a. fig;* **~ and blue** grün und blau **II.** *n* ① (*person*) Schwarze(r) *f(m)* ② (*color*) Schwarz *nt* ③ (*not in debt*) **in the ~** in den schwarzen Zahlen
◆**black out I.** *vi* [kurz] das Bewusstsein verlieren **II.** *vt* verdunkeln
'blackball *vt* ■**to ~ sb** (*vote against*) gegen jdn

stimmen; (*reject*) jdn ausschließen

blackberry ['blæk·ˌber·i] *n* Brombeere *f*

'blackbird *n* Amsel *f*

'blackboard *n* Tafel *f*

black 'box *n* AEROSP Flugschreiber *m*

blacken ['blæk·ən] **I.** *vt* ① (*make black*) schwärzen ② (*malign*) anschwärzen; **to ~ sb's name** dem Ruf einer Person schaden **II.** *vi* schwarz werden

black 'eye *n* blaues Auge

'blackhead *n* Mitesser *m*

black 'hole *n* schwarzes Loch *a. fig*

black 'ice *n* Glatteis *nt*

blackjack ['blæk·dʒæk] *n* CARDS Siebzehnundvier *nt*

'blacklist I. *vt* auf die schwarze Liste setzen **II.** *n* schwarze Liste

'blackmail I. *n* Erpressung *f;* **open to ~** erpressbar **II.** *vt* erpressen

'blackmailer *n* Erpresser(in) *m(f)*

black 'market *n* Schwarzmarkt *m*

black marke'teer *n* Schwarzhändler(in) *m(f)*

blackness ['blæk·nɪs] *n* Schwärze *f*

blackout ['blæk·aʊt] *n* ① (*unconsciousness*) Ohnmachtsanfall *m* ② ELEC [Strom]ausfall *m* ③ (*censor*) Sperre *f;* **news ~** Nachrichtensperre *f*

Black 'Sea *n* ■ **the ~** das Schwarze Meer

black 'sheep *n* (*fig*) schwarzes Schaf

'blacksmith *n* [Huf]schmied(in) *m(f)*

bladder ['blæd·ər] *n* [Harn]blase *f*

blade [bleɪd] *n* Klinge *f;* **~ of grass** Grashalm *m;* **~ of an oar** Ruderblatt *nt*

blame [bleɪm] **I.** *vt* ■ **to ~ sb/sth for sth** [*or* **sth on sb/sth**] jdm/etw die Schuld an etw *dat* geben; ■ **to ~ sb for doing sth** jdn beschuldigen, etw getan zu haben **II.** *n* ① (*guilt*) Schuld *f;* **to take the ~** die Schuld auf sich nehmen ② (*censure*) Tadel *m*

blameless ['bleɪm·lɪs] *adj* schuldlos; *life* untadelig

blanch [blæntʃ] **I.** *vi* erblassen **II.** *vt* ① (*cause to whiten*) bleichen ② (*parboil*) blanchieren

bland [blænd] *adj* fade; (*fig*) vage

blank [blæŋk] **I.** *adj* ① (*empty*) leer; **~ tape** Leerband *nt;* **my mind went ~** ich hatte ein Brett vor dem Kopf ② (*without emotion*) ausdruckslos; (*without comprehension*) verständnislos **II.** *n* ① (*empty space*) Leerstelle *f,* Lücke *f* ② (*mental void*) Gedächtnislücke *f* ▶ PHRASES: **to draw a ~** kein Glück haben **III.** *vt* ■ **to ~ out** ausstreichen

blanket ['blæŋ·kɪt] **I.** *n* [Bett]decke *f;* (*fig*) Decke *f* **II.** *vt* bedecken **III.** *adj* umfassend; *coverage* ausführlich

blankly ['blæŋk·li] *adv* (*without expression*) ausdruckslos; (*without comprehension*) verständnislos

blare [bler] **I.** *n* Geplärr[e] *nt* **II.** *vi radio* plärren; *music* dröhnen; *trumpets* schmettern

blaspheme ['blæs·fim] *vi* [Gott] lästern

blasphemy ['blæs·fə·mi] *n* Blasphemie *f*

blast [blæst] **I.** *n* ① (*explosion*) Explosion *f* ② (*air*) **~ of air** Luftstoß *m* ③ (*noise*) **~ of music** Schwall *m* Musik; **a ~ from the past** (*fam*) eine Begegnung mit der Vergangenheit; **at full ~** *radio* in voller Lautstärke ④ (*fam: fun*) tolle Zeit **II.** *vt* ① (*explode*) sprengen ② (*fig*) heftig angreifen

blasted ['blæs·tɪd] *adj attr* (*fam*) verdammt

'blast furnace *n* Hochofen *m*

blastoff ['blæst·af] *n* [Raketen]start *m*

blatant ['bleɪ·tənt] *adj* offensichtlich; *lie* unverfroren

blaze [bleɪz] **I.** *n* ① (*fire*) Brand *m* ② (*light*) Glanz *m;* (*fig*) **~ of color** Farbenpracht *f* **II.** *vi* glühen; *eyes* glänzen; *fire* [hell] lodern; *sun* brennen

◆**blaze away** *vi* ① (*shine*) [nicht aufhören zu] strahlen ② (*shoot*) drauflosfeuern

◆**blaze up** *vi* aufflammen

blazer ['bleɪ·zər] *n* Blazer *m*

blazing ['bleɪ·zɪŋ] *adj fire* lodernd; *argument* heftig; *sun* grell

bleach [blitʃ] **I.** *vt* bleichen **II.** *n* <*pl* -es> (*chemical*) Bleichmittel *nt;* (*for hair*) Blondierungsmittel *nt*

bleachers ['bli·tʃərz] *npl* unüberdachte [Zuschauer]tribüne

bleak [blik] *adj* kahl, öde; (*fig*) trostlos

bleary ['blɪr·i] *adj* (*sleepy*) verschlafen; **~ eyes** müde Augen

bleary-'eyed *adj* mit müden Augen *nach n;* **to look ~** verschlafen aussehen

bleat [blit] **I.** *vi sheep* blöken; *goat* meckern; *person* jammern **II.** *n of sheep* Blöken *nt; of goat* Meckern *nt*

bled [bled] *pt, pp of* **bleed**

bleed [blid] **I.** *vi* <bled, bled> bluten **II.** *vt* <bled, bled> ① (*hist: take blood*) ■ **to ~ sb** jdn zur Ader lassen ② *brakes, radiator* entlüften

bleeder ['bli·dər] *n* (*fam: hemophiliac*) Bluter(in) *m(f)*

bleep [blip] **I.** *n* TECH Piepton *m* **II.** *vi* piepsen **III.** *vt* **to ~ sb** jdn über einen Piepser rufen

blemish <*pl* -es> ['blem·ɪʃ] *n* Makel *m*

blend [blend] **I.** *n* Mischung *f; of wine* Verschnitt *m* **II.** *vt* [miteinander] vermischen **III.** *vi* ① (*match*) ■ **to ~ with sb/sth** zu jdm/etw passen; MUS mit jdm/etw harmonisieren ② (*not be noticeable*) ■ **to ~ into sth** mit etw *dat* verschmelzen

blender ['blen·dər] *n* Mixer *m*

bless <-ed *or* blest, -ed *or* blest> [bles] *vt* segnen ▶ PHRASES: **~ [him/her]!** der/die Gute!; **~ you!** (*after a sneeze*) Gesundheit!; (*as thanks*) das ist lieb von dir!

blessed ['bles·ɪd] *adj* gesegnet

blessing ['bles·ɪŋ] *n* Segen *m* ▶ PHRASES: **to count one's ~s** für das dankbar sein, was man hat

blew [blu] *pt of* **blow**

blight [blaɪt] **I.** *vt* vernichten; (*fig*) zunichtemachen **II.** *n* Pflanzenkrankheit *f;* (*fig*) Plage *f*

blind [blaɪnd] **I.** *n* ① (*for window*) Jalousie *f;*

B

B

roller ~ Rollo *nt* ❷ (*people*) ■ **the** ~ *pl* die Blinden ❸ (*shelter for concealing*) Tarnung *f* **II.** *vt* ❶ (*permanently*) blind machen; (*temporarily*) blenden; ~**ed by tears** blind vor Tränen ❷ (*fig: impress*) **to** ~ **sb with science** jdn mit seinem Wissen beeindrucken **III.** *adj* ❶ (*sightless*) blind; **to go** ~ blind werden ❷ (*fig: unable to perceive*) blind; ■ **to be** ~ **to sth** etw nicht bemerken ❸ (*fig: unprepared*) unvorbereitet ❹ (*fig: lacking judgment*) blind; *acceptance* bedingungslos ❺ (*concealed*) *curve* schwer einsehbar ▸ PHRASES: **to turn a** ~ **eye to sth** vor etw *dat* die Augen verschließen

blind 'alley *n* Sackgasse *f a. fig*

blinders ['blaɪn·dərz] *n pl* Scheuklappen *pl a. fig*

blindfold ['blaɪnd·foʊld] **I.** *n* Augenbinde *f* **II.** *vt* ■ **to** ~ **sb** jdm die Augen verbinden

blindfolded ['blaɪnd·foʊld·ɪd] *adj* mit verbundenen Augen; **to be able to do sth** ~ etw im Schlaf tun können

blinding ['blaɪnd·ɪŋ] *adj flash* blendend; *light a.* grell; *headache* rasend

blindman's 'bluff, blindman's 'buff *n* Blindekuh

blindness ['blaɪnd·nɪs] *n* Blindheit *f*

'blind spot *n* ❶ ANAT blinder Fleck ❷ TRANSP toter Winkel ❸ (*weakness*) Schwachpunkt *m*

blink [blɪŋk] **I.** *vt* **to** ~ **one's eyes** mit den Augen zwinkern; **to** ~ **back tears** die Tränen zurückhalten **II.** *vi* ❶ (*as protective reflex*) blinzeln; (*intentionally*) zwinkern ❷ *of light* blinken **III.** *n* Blinzeln *nt;* (*intentionally*) Zwinkern *nt* ▸ PHRASES: **to be on the** ~ (*fam*) kaputt sein

blinker ['blɪŋ·kər] *n* AUTO Blinker *m*

bliss [blɪs] *n* [Glück]seligkeit *f;* **what** ~**!** herrlich!

blissful ['blɪs·fəl] *adj* glückselig; *couple* glücklich; *smile* selig

blister ['blɪs·tər] **I.** *n* Blase *f* **II.** *vt* Blasen hervorrufen auf +*dat* **III.** *vi paint* Blasen werfen; *skin* Blasen bekommen

blistering ['blɪs·tər·ɪŋ] *adj* Wahnsinns-; *attack* massiv; *heat* brütend; *pace* mörderisch

blitz [blɪts] **I.** *n* ❶ (*air attack*) [plötzlicher] Luftangriff *m* ❷ (*fig*) **to have** [*or* **make**] **a** ~ **on sth** etw in Angriff nehmen **II.** *vt* ❶ **to** ~ **a city** Luftangriffe auf eine Stadt fliegen ❷ (*fig*) in Angriff nehmen

blitzed [blɪtst] *adj* (*sl: on alcohol*) voll; (*on drugs*) total zu

blizzard ['blɪz·ərd] *n* Schneesturm *m*

bloated ['bloʊ·t̬ɪd] *adj* ❶ (*swollen*) aufgedunsen ❷ (*overindulged*) vollgestopft

blob [blab] *n* ❶ (*spot*) Klecks *m* ❷ (*mass*) Klümpchen *nt*

bloc [blak] *n* POL Block *m*

block [blak] **I.** *n* ❶ (*lump*) Block *m;* ~ **of wood** Holzklotz *m* ❷ (*toy*) **building** ~ Bauklötzchen *nt* ❸ (*neighborhood*) [Häuser]block *m* ❹ SPORTS **starting** ~ Startblock *m* **II.** *vt* blockieren; *artery, pipeline* verstopfen; *exit, passage* versperren; *progress* aufhalten; *account* sperren; *ball* abblocken

◆**block off** *vt* [ver]sperren

◆**block up** *vt* (*obstruct*) blockieren; (*clog*) verstopfen

blockade [bla·'keɪd] **I.** *n* Blockade *f* **II.** *vt* abriegeln

blockage ['blak·ɪdʒ] *n* Verstopfung *f*

block 'capitals, block 'letters *npl* Blockbuchstaben; **in** ~ in Blockschrift

'blockhead *n* (*pej fam*) Strohkopf *m pej fam,* Trottel *m pej fam*

blond(e) [bland] **I.** *adj* blond **II.** *n* (*person*) Blonde(r) *f(m);* (*woman a.*) Blondine *f*

blood [blʌd] *n* Blut *nt* ▸ PHRASES: ~ **is thicker than water** (*prov*) Blut ist dicker als Wasser; **in cold** ~ kaltblütig; **to be after sb's** ~ es jdm heimzahlen wollen

'blood bank *n* Blutbank *f*

'bloodbath *n* Blutbad *nt*

'blood clot *n* Blutgerinnsel *nt*

'bloodcurdling *adj* markerschütternd

'blood donor *n* Blutspender(in) *m(f)*

'blood group *n* Blutgruppe *f*

'bloodhound *n* Bluthund *m*

bloodless ['blʌd·lɪs] *adj* ❶ (*without violence*) unblutig ❷ (*pale*) blutleer

'blood poisoning *n* Blutvergiftung *f*

'blood pressure *n* Blutdruck *m*

blood 'relative *n* Blutsverwandte(r) *f(m)*

'bloodshed *n* Blutvergießen *nt*

'bloodshot *adj* blutunterlaufen

'bloodstained *adj* blutbefleckt

'bloodstream *n* Blutkreislauf *m*

'bloodsucker *n* Blutsauger *m a. fig*

'blood sugar *n* Blutzucker *m*

'blood test *n* Bluttest *m*

'bloodthirsty *adj* blutrünstig

'blood transfusion *n* [Blut]transfusion *f*

'blood type *n* Blutgruppe *f*

'blood vessel *n* Blutgefäß *nt;* **to burst a** ~ (*fig*) ausflippen *fam*

bloody ['blʌd·i] *adj* blutig; **to give sb a** ~ **nose** jdm die Nase blutig schlagen

bloom [blum] **I.** *n* Blüte *f;* **to come into** ~ aufblühen **II.** *vi* ❶ (*produce flowers*) blühen ❷ (*fig: flourish*) seinen Höhepunkt erreichen

bloomer ['blu·mər] *n* ❶ (*plant*) Blüher ❷ (*person*) **early/late** ~ Früh-/ Spätzünder

blossom ['blas·əm] **I.** *n* [Baum]blüte *f* **II.** *vi* blühen *a. fig*

blot [blat] *n* ❶ (*mark*) Klecks *m* ❷ (*ugly feature*) ~ **on the landscape** Schandfleck *m* in der Landschaft

blotch <*pl* -es> [blatʃ] *n* Fleck *m*

blotchy ['blatʃ·i] *adj* fleckig

blotter ['blat̬·ər] *n* [Tinten]löscher *m*

'blotting paper *n* Löschpapier *nt*

blouse [blaʊs] *n* Bluse *f*

blow[1] [bloʊ] **I.** *vi* <blew, blown> ❶ *wind* wehen; **the window blew open** das Fenster wurde aufgeweht ❷ (*exhale*) blasen, pusten ❸ *whale* spritzen; **there she** ~**s!** Wal in Sicht!

④ (*break*) *fuse* durchbrennen; *gasket* undicht werden; *tire* platzen **II.** *vt* <blew, blown> ① (*propel*) blasen; *wind* wehen ② (*send*) **to ~ sb a kiss** jdm ein Küsschen zuwerfen ③ (*play*) blasen; **to ~ the whistle** (*start a game*) [das Spiel] anpfeifen; (*stop, end a game*) [das Spiel] abpfeifen ④ (*clear*) **to ~ one's nose** sich *dat* die Nase putzen ⑤ (*create*) **to ~ bubbles** [Seifen]blasen machen ⑥ (*destroy*) **we blew a tire** uns ist ein Reifen geplatzt; **to ~ a safe [open]** einen Safe [auf]sprengen ⑦ (*fam: squander*) *lead* verpulvern ⑧ (*fam: botch*) vermasseln **III.** *n* ① **to give your nose a [good] ~** sich *dat* [gründlich] die Nase putzen ② (*sl: cocaine*) Koks *m,* Schnee

◆**blow around** *vi* herumgewirbelt werden

◆**blow away I.** *vt* ① *wind* wegwehen ② (*fam: kill*) wegpusten ③ (*fig fam: impress*) ■**to ~ away** ⊂⊃ **sb** jdn [fast] umhauen *fig fam* ④ (*fam: defeat*) erledigen *fam* **II.** *vi* wegfliegen, verwehen

◆**blow back** *vi, vt* zurückwehen

◆**blow down I.** *vi* umgeweht werden **II.** *vt* umwehen

◆**blow in I.** *vi* ① *window* eingedrückt werden ② *sand* hineinwehen **II.** *vt* ① *window* eindrücken ② *sand* hineinwehen

◆**blow off I.** *vt* ① (*release*) *steam* ablassen ② (*fam*) ■**to ~ off** ⊂⊃ **sth** (*ignore*) etw nicht ernst nehmen; (*neglect*) etw sausen lassen *fam* ③ (*remove*) wegblasen; *wind* wegwehen ④ (*rip off*) wegreißen **II.** *vi* (*blow away*) weggeweht werden

◆**blow out I.** *vt* ① (*extinguish*) ausblasen ② **to ~ out** ⊂⊃ **one's brains** sich *dat* eine Kugel durch den Kopf jagen ③ (*fill*) *cheeks* aufblasen **II.** *vi* ① *candle* verlöschen ② *tire* platzen

◆**blow over I.** *vi* ① (*fall*) umstürzen ② (*die down*) *storm* sich legen **II.** *vt* umwerfen

◆**blow up I.** *vi* ① (*explode*) explodieren; (*fig: get angry*) an die Decke gehen ② (*come up*) *storm* [her]aufziehen **II.** *vt* ① (*inflate*) aufblasen ② (*fig: exaggerate*) hochspielen ③ (*enlarge*) vergrößern ④ (*destroy*) [in die Luft] sprengen

blow² [bloʊ] *n* ① (*hit*) Schlag *m;* **to come to ~s over sth** sich wegen einer S. *gen* prügeln ② (*setback*) [Schicksals]schlag *m;* **to take a ~** (*fam*) einen Tiefschlag erleiden; (*in confidence*) einen Knacks bekommen; **to come as a ~ [to** [*or* **for**] **sb]** ein schwerer Schlag [für jdn] sein ③ (*helping action*) **to strike a ~ for** [*or* **against**] **sth** eine Lanze für etw brechen

blow-by-'blow *adj, adv account, description* haarklein

'blow-dry I. *vt* <-ie-> fönen **II.** *n* Fönen *nt*

'blow dryer *n* Fön *m*

'blowhole *n* Atemloch *nt*

blown [bloʊn] *vt, vi pp of* **blow**

blowout ['bloʊ·aʊt] *n* ① (*of tire*) Platzen *nt* [eines Reifens] ② (*fam: meal*) Schlemmerei *f* ③ (*party*) Fete *f*

'blowpipe *n* Blasrohr *nt*

'blowtorch *n* Lötlampe *f*

'blowup I. *n* ① PHOT Vergrößerung *f* ② (*fam: argument*) Krach *m* **II.** *adj* aufblasbar

blubber ['blʌb·ər] *n* Speck *m a. fig*

bludgeon ['blʌdʒ·ən] **I.** *n* Schlagstock *m* **II.** *vt* verprügeln

blue [blu] **I.** *adj* <-r, -st> ① (*color*) blau ② (*depressed*) traurig ③ (*fam*) **~ movie** Pornofilm *m* ► PHRASES: **once in a ~ <u>moon</u>** alle Jubeljahre einmal **II.** *n* Blau *nt* ► PHRASES: **<u>out</u> of the ~** aus heiterem Himmel

'bluebell *n* [blaue Wiesen]glockenblume

'blueberry *n* Heidelbeere *f*

'blue chip *n* FIN Blue Chip *m*

blue-'collar *adj* **~ worker** Arbeiter(in) *m(f)*

'blueprint *n* Blaupause *f;* (*fig*) Plan *m*

blues [bluz] *npl* ① (*fam*) **to have the ~** melancholisch gestimmt sein ② (*music*) Blues *m*

bluff¹ [blʌf] **I.** *vi* bluffen **II.** *vt* täuschen; **to ~ one's way into sth** sich in etw *akk* hineinmogeln **III.** *n* Bluff *m;* **to call sb's ~** jdn bloßstellen

bluff² [blʌf] **I.** *n* (*bank*) Steilhang *m;* (*shore*) Steilküste *f* **II.** *adj manner* direkt

bluffer ['blʌf·ər] *n* Bluffer(in) *m(f)*

bluish ['blu·ɪʃ] *adj* bläulich

blunder ['blʌn·dər] **I.** *n* schwer[wiegend]er Fehler **II.** *vi* ① (*make a bad mistake*) einen groben Fehler machen ② ■**to ~ into sth** in etw *akk* hineinplatzen

blunt [blʌnt] **I.** *adj* ① (*not sharp*) stumpf ② (*outspoken*) direkt **II.** *vt* ① stumpf machen ② (*fig*) *enthusiasm* dämpfen

bluntly ['blʌnt·li] *adv* direkt

bluntness ['blʌnt·nɪs] *n* Direktheit *f*

blur [blɜr] **I.** *vi* <-rr-> verschwimmen **II.** *vt* <-rr-> verschwimmen lassen **III.** *n* undeutliches Bild; ■**to be a ~** verschwimmen; (*fig*) **it's all just a ~ to me now** ich erinnere mich nur noch vage daran

blurb [blɜrb] *n* Klappentext *m*

blurred [blɜrd], **blurry** ['blɜri] *adj* ① (*vague*) verschwommen; *picture* unscharf ② (*not clearly separated*) nicht klar voneinander getrennt

blush [blʌʃ] **I.** *vi* erröten **II.** *n* ① (*reddening of face*) (Scham-)röte ② (*makeup*) Rouge *nt*

blusher ['blʌʃ·ər] *n* Rouge *nt*

blushing ['blʌʃ·ɪŋ] *adj* errötend

bluster ['blʌs·tər] **I.** *vi* ① (*speak angrily*) poltern ② *wind* toben **II.** *n* Theater *nt*

BO [ˌbi·'oʊ] *n abbrev of* **body odor** Körpergeruch *m*

boa ['boʊ·ə] *n* Boa *f*

boar [bɔr] *n* Eber *m,* Keiler *m;* **wild ~** Wildschwein *nt*

board [bɔrd] **I.** *n* ① Brett *nt;* (*blackboard*) Tafel *f;* (*bulletin board*) Schwarzes Brett; (*sign*) [Aushänge]schild *nt;* (*floorboard*) Diele *f* ② ADMIN Behörde *f;* **~ of directors** Vorstand *m;* **B~ of Trade** Handelskammer *f;* **the school ~** der Schulbeirat ③ (*meals*) **room and ~** Kost und

B

Logis, Unterkunft und Verpflegung ❹ TRANSP **on ~** an Bord *a. fig* ▶ PHRASES: **across the ~** rundum; **to win across the ~** alles gewinnen **II.** *vt* ❶ ■**to ~ up** mit Brettern vernageln ❷ *plane, ship* besteigen; *bus, train* einsteigen **III.** *vi* ❶ SCH im Internat wohnen ❷ AVIAT **United flight 345 is now ~ing at Gate C22** die Passagiere für Flug 345 können jetzt über Gate C22 zusteigen

boarder ['bɔr·dər] *n* ❶ SCH Internatsschüler(in) *m(f)* ❷ (*lodger*) Pensionsgast *m*

'board game *n* Brettspiel *nt*

'boarding card *n* Bordkarte *f*

'boarding house *n* Pension *f*

'boarding pass *n* Bordkarte *f*

'boarding school *n* Internat *nt*

'board meeting *n of executives* Vorstandssitzung *f; of owners' representatives* Aufsichtsratssitzung *f*

'boardroom *n* Sitzungssaal *m*

'boardwalk *n* Uferpromenade *f* (*aus Holz*)

boast [boʊst] **I.** *vi* prahlen; ■**to ~ about** [*or* **of**] **sth** mit etw *dat* angeben **II.** *n* großspurige Behauptung

boastful ['boʊst·fəl] *adj* großspurig; ■**to be ~** prahlen

boat [boʊt] *n* Boot *nt;* (*bigger*) Schiff *nt;* **to travel by ~** mit dem Schiff fahren ▶ PHRASES: **to be in the same ~** im selben Boot sitzen; **to miss the ~** den Anschluss verpassen

'boathouse *n* Bootshaus *nt*

boating ['boʊ·t̬ɪŋ] *n* Bootfahren *nt*

'boatman *n* Bootsführer *m*

'boat race *n* Bootsrennen *nt*

'boat trip *n* Bootsfahrt *f*

bob[1] [bab] *n* Bubikopf *m*

bob[2] [bab] *n abbrev of* **bobsleigh** Bob *m*

bob[3] <-bb-> [bab] **I.** *vi* ❶ (*move*) ■**to ~** [**up and down**] sich auf und ab bewegen; ■**to ~** [**up**] [plötzlich] auftauchen *a. fig* ❷ (*curtsy*) knicksen **II.** *n* [angedeuteter] Knicks

bobbin ['bab·ɪn] *n* Spule *f*

'bobsled *n* Bob[sleigh] *m*

bode [boʊd] *vi, vt* **to ~ well** etwas Gutes bedeuten

bodice ['bad·ɪs] *n* Oberteil *nt*

bodily ['bad·əl·i] **I.** *adj* körperlich; [**great**] **~ harm** [schwere] Körperverletzung **II.** *adv* gewaltsam

body ['bad·i] *n* ❶ (*physical structure*) Körper *m;* **~ and soul** mit Leib und Seele ❷ (*organized group*) Gruppe *f;* **advisory ~** beratendes Gremium; **governing ~** Leitung *f* ❸ (*central part*) Hauptteil *m; of church* Hauptschiff *nt; of plane, ship* Rumpf *m* ❹ AUTO Karosserie *f* ❺ (*corpse*) Leiche *f;* (*of animal*) Kadaver *m;* SCI Körper *m;* **foreign ~** Fremdkörper *m* ❻ (*substance*) *of hair* Fülle *f* ▶ PHRASES: **over my dead ~** nur über meine Leiche

'body bag *n* Leichensack *m*

'bodybuilder *n* Bodybuilder(in) *m(f)*

'bodybuilding *n* Bodybuilding *nt*

'bodyguard *n* ❶ (*person*) Bodyguard *m* ❷ (*group*) Leibwache *f*

'body language *n* Körpersprache *f*

'body lotion *n* Körperlotion *f*

'body search *n* Leibesvisitation *f*

'body shop *n* AUTO Karosseriewerkstatt *f*

'bodysuit *n* Body[suit] *m*

'bodywork *n* AUTO Karosserie *f*

bog [bag] *n* Sumpf *m*

◆**bog down** *vt* ■**to be ~ged down** stecken bleiben; **to get ~ged down** sich verheddern *a. fig*

bogey ['boʊ·gi] *n* (*golf score*) Bogey *nt*

'bogeyman *n* Schreckgespenst *nt*

boggle ['bag·əl] **I.** *vi* sprachlos sein; **the mind ~s** man fasst sich an den Kopf **II.** *vt* **to ~ the mind** unglaublich sein

boggy ['bag·i] *adj* morastig

bogie *n see* **bogey**

bogus ['boʊ·gəs] *adj* unecht; *documents, name* falsch; **~ company** Scheinfirma *f*

bogy *n see* **bogey**

bohemian [boʊ·'hi·mi·ən] **I.** *n.* Bohemien *m* **II.** *adj* **~ life** Künstlerleben *nt*

boil [bɔɪl] **I.** *n* ❶ **to let sth come to a ~** etw aufkochen lassen ❷ MED Furunkel *m o nt* **II.** *vi* ❶ kochen; **to ~ dry** verkochen ❷ CHEM den Siedepunkt erreichen ❸ (*fig: be angry*) **to ~ with rage** vor Wut kochen; (*be hot*) **I'm ~ing** ich schwitze mich zu Tode **III.** *vt* ❶ (*heat*) kochen ❷ (*bring to boil*) zum Kochen bringen

◆**boil away** *vi, vt* verkochen

◆**boil down I.** *vi* (*reduce*) *sauce* einkochen ▶ PHRASES: **it all ~s down to ...** es läuft auf ... hinaus **II.** *vt* ❶ (*reduce*) einkochen ❷ (*fig: condense*) zusammenfassen

◆**boil over** *vi* ❶ überkochen ❷ (*fig*) *situation* außer Kontrolle geraten; *person* ausrasten

boiler ['bɔɪ·lər] *n* Boiler *m*

'boiler room *n* Kesselraum *m*

boiling ['bɔɪ·lɪŋ] *adj* ❶ *water* kochend ❷ *weather* sehr heiß; **I'm ~** ich komme um vor Hitze; **~** [**hot**] **weather** unerträgliche Hitze

'boiling point *n* Siedepunkt *m a. fig*

boisterous ['bɔɪ·stər·əs] *adj* ❶ (*rough*) wild; (*noisy*) laut ❷ (*exuberant*) übermütig

bold [boʊld] *adj* ❶ (*brave*) mutig; **to take a ~ step** ein Wagnis eingehen ❷ *colors* kräftig; *pattern* auffällig; *handwriting* schwungvoll; **~ type** Fettdruck *m*

boldness ['boʊld·nɪs] *n* Mut *m*

bolero [bə·'ler·oʊ] *n* Bolero *m*

bologna [bə·'loʊ·ni] *n* ≈ Fleischwurst *f*

bolster ['boʊl·stər] **I.** *n* Nackenrolle *f* **II.** *vt* ❶ (*prop up*) stützen ❷ (*increase*) erhöhen

bolt [boʊlt] **I.** *vi* ❶ (*move quickly*) rasen ❷ (*run away*) ausreißen; *horse* durchgehen **II.** *vt* ❶ (*gulp down*) ■**to ~** [**down** ◌] **sth** etw hinunterschlingen ❷ (*lock*) verriegeln ❸ (*fix*) ■**to ~ sth on**[**to**] **sth** etw mit etw *dat* verbolzen **III.** *n* ❶ **~ of lightning** Blitz[schlag] *m* ❷ (*lock*) Riegel *m* ❸ (*screw*) Schraubenbolzen *m* ❹ (*cloth*) [Stoff]ballen *m* ▶ PHRASES: **to**

be a ~ **from the** <u>**blue**</u> aus heiterem Himmel kommen

bomb [bam] I. *n* ❶ (*explosive*) Bombe *f* ❷ (*fam*) Flop ❸ (*sl: sb/sth great*) ■**the ~** das Coolste *sl*, das Fetteste *sl* II. *vt* bombardieren III. *vi* (*fam*) [völlig] danebengehen

bombard [bam·ˈbard] *vt* bombardieren *a. fig*

bombardment [bam·ˈbard·mənt] *n* Bombardierung *f*

bombastic [bam·ˈbæs·tɪk] *adj* bombastisch

bombed [bamd] *adj* (*sl: on drugs*) total zu; (*on alcohol*) voll

bomber [ˈbam·ər] *n* ❶ (*plane*) Bombenflugzeug *nt* ❷ (*person*) Bombenleger(in) *m(f)*

bombing [ˈbam·ɪŋ] *n* MIL Bombardierung *f*; (*terrorist attack*) Bombenanschlag *m*

ˈ**bombproof** *adj* bombensicher

ˈ**bombshell** *n* Bombe *f a. fig*; **to drop a ~** (*fig*) die Bombe platzen lassen

ˈ**bomb squad** *n* Bombenräumkommando *nt*

bona fide [ˌboʊ·nə·ˈfaɪd] *adj* echt; *offer* seriös

bonanza [bə·ˈnæn·zə] *n* Goldgrube *f*

bond [band] I. *n* ❶ (*emotional connection*) Bindung *f* ❷ FIN Schuldschein *m*; **government ~** Staatsanleihe *f* ❸ LAW schriftliche Verpflichtung ❹ CHEM Bindung *f* II. *vt* ❶ (*unite emotionally*) verbinden ❷ (*stick together*) ■**to ~ together** zusammenfügen III. *vi* haften

bondage [ˈban·dɪdʒ] *n* ❶ (*slavery*) Sklaverei *f* ❷ (*sexual act*) Fesseln *nt*

bone [boʊn] I. *n* ❶ Knochen *m*; *of fish* Gräte *f* ❷ (*material*) Bein *nt* ► PHRASES: **to work one's** <u>**fingers**</u> **to the ~** sich abrackern; **to be** <u>**close**</u> **to the ~** unter die Haut gehen; **to** <u>**feel**</u> **sth in one's ~s** etw instinktiv fühlen; **to** <u>**make**</u> **no ~s about sth** kein Geheimnis aus etw *dat* machen II. *vt fish* entgräten; *meat* ausbeinen

ˈ**bonehead** *n* (*fam*) Holzkopf *m*

ˈ**bone marrow** *n* Knochenmark *nt*

bonfire [ˈban·faɪr] *n* Freudenfeuer *nt*

bonkers [ˈbaŋ·kərz] *adj pred* (*fam*) verrückt

bonnet [ˈban·ɪt] *n* Mütze *f*; (*dated*) Haube *f*

bonus [ˈboʊ·nəs] *n* ❶ FIN Prämie *f*; **Christmas ~** Weihnachtsgratifikation *f*; **productivity ~** Ertragszulage *f*; **~ share** Gratisaktie *f* ❷ (*fig: sth extra*) Bonus *m*

bony [ˈboʊ·ni] *adj* ❶ (*with prominent bones*) knochig ❷ (*full of bones*) *fish* voller Gräten; *meat* knochig

boo [bu] I. *interj* ❶ (*to surprise*) huh ❷ (*to show disapproval*) buh II. *vi* buhen III. *vt* ausbuhen; **to ~ sb off the stage** jdn von der Bühne wegbuhen IV. *n* Buhruf *m*

boob [bub] *n usu pl* (*vulg, sl: breast*) **big ~s** große Titten *derb*

ˈ**booby prize** *n* Trostpreis *m*

ˈ**booby trap** *n* getarnte Bombe

book [bʊk] I. *n* ❶ Buch *nt*; **to be in the ~** im Telefonbuch stehen; **~ of stamps** Briefmarkenheftchen *nt* ❷ *pl* FIN ■**the ~s** die [Geschäfts]bücher *pl* ► PHRASES: **to do sth** <u>**by**</u> **the ~** etw nach Vorschrift machen; **to** <u>**throw**</u> **the ~ at sb** jdm gehörig den Kopf waschen II. *vt* ❶ (*reserve*) buchen; ■**to ~ sth for sb** etw für jdn reservieren; **to be fully ~ed** *hotel* ausgebucht sein ❷ LAW (*charge*) **to ~ sb** jdn verwarnen III. *vi* buchen, reservieren

◆**book up** *vi* buchen; ■**to be ~ed up** ausgebucht sein

bookable [ˈbʊk·ə·bəl] *adj* im Vorverkauf erhältlich

ˈ**bookbinding** *n* Buchbinderhandwerk *nt*

ˈ**bookcase** *n* Bücherschrank *m*

ˈ**book club** *n* Buchklub *m*

ˈ**bookend** *n* Buchstütze *f*

bookie [ˈbʊk·i] *n* (*fam*) Buchmacher(in) *m(f)*

booking [ˈbʊk·ɪŋ] *n* Reservierung *f*; **to make a ~** etw buchen

bookish [ˈbʊk·ɪʃ] *adj* ❶ (*studious*) streberhaft ❷ (*unworldly*) weltfremd

ˈ**bookkeeper** *n* Buchhalter(in) *m(f)*

ˈ**bookkeeping** *n* Buchhaltung *f*

booklet [ˈbʊk·lɪt] *n* Broschüre *f*

ˈ**bookmark** I. *n* (*in book, Internet*) Lesezeichen *nt* II. *vt* **to ~ a website** bei einer Webseite ein Lesezeichen setzen

ˈ**book review** *n* Buchbesprechung *f*

ˈ**bookseller** *n* Buchhändler(in) *m(f)*

ˈ**bookshelf** *n* Bücherregal *nt*

ˈ**bookshop** *n* Buchgeschäft *nt*

ˈ**bookstore** *n* Buchgeschäft *nt*

ˈ**bookworm** *n* Bücherwurm *m*

boom¹ [bum] ECON I. *vi* florieren II. *n* Boom *m*, Aufschwung *m* III. *adj* florierend; *town* aufstrebend

boom² [bum] I. *n* Dröhnen *nt kein pl* II. *vi* ■**to ~ [out]** dröhnen III. *vt* ■**to ~ [out ↻] sth** etw mit dröhnender Stimme befehlen

boom³ [bum] *n* ❶ (*barrier*) Baum *m* ❷ FILM, TV Galgen *m*

boomerang [ˈbu·mə·ræŋ] I. *n* Bumerang *m* II. *vi* (*fig*) ■**to ~ on sb** *plan* sich für jdn als Bumerang erweisen

boor [bʊr] *n* Rüpel *m*

boorish [ˈbʊr·ɪʃ] *adj* rüpelhaft

boost [bust] I. *n* Auftrieb *m* II. *vt* ansteigen lassen; *morale* heben; ELEC verstärken

booster [ˈbu·stər] *n* ❶ (*improvement*) Verbesserung *f*; **to be a confidence ~** das Selbstvertrauen heben ❷ MED **~ vaccination** [*or fam* **shot**] Auffrischungsimpfung *f*

ˈ**booster rocket** *n* Trägerrakete *f*

ˈ**booster seat** *n* AUTO Kindersitz *m*

boot [but] I. *n* ❶ (*shoe*) Stiefel *m* ❷ (*fam: kick*) Stoß *m*; **to get the ~** (*fig fam*) hinausfliegen; **to give sb the ~** (*fig fam*) jdn hinauswerfen ❸ AUTO **Denver ~** Wegfahrsperre *f* ► PHRASES: **to be too** <u>**big**</u> **for one's ~s** (*fam*) hochnäsig sein II. *vt* ■**to ~ sth** etw *dat* einen Tritt versetzen

◆**boot out** *vt* (*fam*) rausschmeißen

bootee [ˈbu·t̬i] *n* gestrickter Babyschuh

booth [buθ] *n* ❶ (*cubicle*) Kabine *f*; (*in restaurant*) Sitzecke *f* ❷ (*at fair*) Stand *m*

ˈ**bootleg** *adj* ❶ (*sold illegally*) geschmuggelt ❷ (*illegally made*) illegal hergestellt; **~ alco-**

B

hol schwarzgebrannter Alkohol; ~ **tapes** Raubkopien
'**bootmaker** *n* Schuhmacher(in) *m(f)*
booty[1] ['bu·ţi] *n* (*loot*) Beutegut *nt*
booty[2] ['bu·ţi] *n* (*fam*) Hintern *m*
booze [buz] (*fam*) **I.** *n* Alk *m;* **to be off the ~** nicht mehr trinken **II.** *vi* saufen
boozer ['bu·zər] *n* (*fam*) Säufer(in) *m(f)*
boozy ['bu·zi] *adj* (*fam*) versoffen
border ['bɔr·dər] **I.** *n* ❶ (*boundary*) Grenze *f;* ~ **dispute** Grenzstreit *m* ❷ (*edge*) Begrenzung *f; of picture* Umrahmung *f;* FASHION Borte *f* ❸ (*in garden*) Rabatte *f* **II.** *vt* ❶ (*be or act as frontier*) grenzen an +*akk* ❷ (*bound*) begrenzen
◆**border on** *vi* grenzen an *akk*
bordering ['bɔr·dər·ɪŋ] *adj* angrenzend
borderland ['bɔr·dər·lænd] *n* ❶ GEOG Grenzgebiet *nt* ❷ (*fig*) Grenzbereich *m*
borderline ['bɔr·dər·laɪn] **I.** *n* Grenze *f* **II.** *adj* Grenz-
bore[1] [bɔr] **I.** *n* ❶ (*thing*) langweilige Sache; **what a ~** wie langweilig ❷ (*person*) Langweiler(in) *m(f)* **II.** *vt* langweilen
bore[2] [bɔr] *pt of* **bear**
bore[3] [bɔr] **I.** *n* ❶ *of pipe* Innendurchmesser *m* ❷ *of gun* Kaliber *nt* **II.** *vt* bohren **III.** *vi* ■**to ~ through/into sth** etw durchbohren
bored [bɔrd] *adj* gelangweilt
boredom ['bɔr·dəm] *n* Langeweile *f*
boring ['bɔr·ɪŋ] *adj* langweilig
born [bɔrn] *adj* geboren; (*fig*) *idea* entstanden; **American-~** in Amerika geboren
'**born-again** *adj* überzeugt
borne [bɔrn] *vi pt of* **bear**
borough ['bɜr·oʊ] *n* Verwaltungsbezirk *m*
borrow ['bar·oʊ] **I.** *vt* ❶ (*take temporarily*) leihen; (*from library*) ausleihen ❷ LING entlehnen ❸ MATH borgen **II.** *vi* Geld leihen
borrower ['bar·oʊ·ər] *n* ❶ (*from bank*) Kreditnehmer(in) *m(f)* ❷ (*from library*) Entleiher(in) *m(f)*
borrowing ['bar·oʊ·ɪŋ] *n* ❶ (*taking temporarily*) Ausleihen *nt* ❷ LING Entlehnen *nt* ❸ FIN **public ~** Staatsverschuldung *f*
Bosnia ['baz·ni·ə] *n* Bosnien *nt*
Bosnian ['baz·ni·ən] **I.** *adj* bosnisch **II.** *n* Bosnier(in) *m(f)*
bosom ['bʊz·əm] *n usu sing* ❶ (*breasts*) Busen *m* ❷ (*fig*) **in the ~ of one's family** im Schoß der Familie
bosom 'buddy *n* Busenfreund(in) *m(f)*
boss [bas] **I.** *n* Chef(in) *m(f);* **to be one's own ~** sein eigener Herr sein **II.** *vt* ■**to ~ [around ◌] sb** jdn herumkommandieren
bossy ['ba·si] *adj* (*fam*) herrschsüchtig

Die **Boston Tea Party** 1773 war ein Akt des Misstrauens der Kolonien in Amerika gegenüber der britischen Kontrolle. Als Indianer verkleidete Kolonialisten, unter anderem auch Samuel Adams und Paul Revere, stiegen auf britische Boote und warfen hunderte von Teekisten über Bord, um dagegen zu protestieren, dass die Kolonien besteuert wurden, obwohl ihnen keine Sitze im britischen Parlament zustanden. Es handelt sich dabei um eines der Schlüsselereignisse, die zum Unabhängigkeitskrieg der USA gegen England führten.

botanical [bə·'tæn·ɪ·kəl] *adj* botanisch
botanist ['bat·ən·ɪst] *n* Botaniker(in) *m(f)*
botany ['bat·ən·i] *n* Botanik *f*
botch [batʃ] *vt* (*fam*) ■**to ~ [up ◌] sth** etw verpfuschen
both [boʊθ] **I.** *adj, pron* beide; ~ **sexes** Männer und Frauen; **a picture of ~ of us** ein Bild von uns beiden **II.** *adv* **to be competitive in terms of ~ quality and price** sowohl bei der Qualität als auch beim Preis wettbewerbsfähig sein; ~ **men and women** sowohl Männer als auch Frauen
bother ['bað·ər] **I.** *n* ❶ (*effort*) Mühe *f;* (*work*) Aufwand *m;* **to be not worth the ~** kaum der Mühe wert sein ❷ (*nuisance*) **to be a ~** lästig sein **II.** *vi* **shall I wait? — no, don't ~** soll ich warten? – nein, nicht nötig; **he hasn't even ~ed to write** er hat sich nicht mal die Mühe gemacht, zu schreiben **III.** *vt* ❶ (*worry*) beunruhigen; **what's ~ing you?** was hast du?; **you shouldn't let that ~ you** du solltest dir darüber keine Gedanken machen ❷ (*concern*) **it doesn't ~ me** das macht mir nichts aus ❸ (*disturb*) stören; **don't ~ me [with that]!** verschone mich [damit]!; **I'm sorry to ~ you, but ...** entschuldigen Sie bitte [die Störung], aber ... ❹ (*annoy*) belästigen; **my tooth is ~ing me** mein Zahn macht mir zu schaffen
bothersome ['bað·ər·səm] *adj* lästig
bottle ['baţ·əl] **I.** *n* Flasche *f;* **baby's ~** Fläschchen *nt* **II.** *vt* abfüllen
bottled ['baţ·əld] *adj* in Flaschen abgefüllt; ~ **beer** Flaschenbier *nt*
'**bottle-fed** *adj* mit der Flasche gefüttert
'**bottle-feed** *vt* mit der Flasche füttern
'**bottleneck** *n* Engpass *m a. fig*
'**bottle opener** *n* Flaschenöffner *m*
bottom ['baţ·əm] **I.** *n* ❶ (*lowest part*) Boden *m; on chair* Sitz *m; in valley* Talsohle *f;* **pajama ~s** Pyjamahose *f;* **rock ~** (*fig*) Tiefststand *m;* **from top to ~** von oben bis unten; **to sink to the ~** auf den Grund sinken ❷ (*end*) **at the ~ of the street** am Ende der Straße ❸ ANAT Hinterteil *nt* ▸ PHRASES: **to get to the ~ of sth** einer Sache *dat* auf den Grund gehen **II.** *adj* untere(r, s); **the ~ shelf** das unterste Regal **III.** *vi* ECON ■**to ~ out** seinen Tiefstand erreichen
bottomless ['baţ·əm·lɪs] *adj* ❶ (*without limit*) unerschöpflich ❷ (*fig: very deep*) unendlich; ~ **pit** Fass *nt* ohne Boden
bottom 'line *n usu sing* ❶ FIN Bilanz *f* ❷ (*fig:*

main point) Wahrheit *f*
botulism ['batʃ·ə·lɪz·əm] *n* MED Nahrungsmittelvergiftung *f*
bought [bɔt] *vt pt of* **buy**
boulder ['boʊl·dər] *n* Felsbrocken *m*
boulevard ['bʊl·ə·vard] *n* Boulevard *m*
bounce [baʊns] **I.** *n* ① *of ball* Aufprall ② (*spring*) Sprungkraft *f; hair* Elastizität ③ (*fig: vitality*) Schwung *m* **II.** *vi* ① *ball* aufspringen ② (*bob*) hüpfen ③ FIN (*fam*) *check* platzen **III.** *vt* ① aufspringen lassen; *baby* schaukeln ② FIN (*fam*) *check* platzen
◆**bounce back** *vi* ① (*rebound*) zurückspringen ② (*fig: recover*) wieder auf die Beine kommen
bouncer ['baʊn·sər] *n* Rausschmeißer(in) *m(f)*
bouncing ['baʊn·sɪŋ] *adj* lebhaft; **~ baby boy** strammer Junge
bouncy ['baʊn·si] *adj* ① *mattress* federnd ② (*lively*) frisch und munter
bound[1] [baʊnd] **I.** *vi* springen; *kangaroo* hüpfen **II.** *n* Sprung *m*
bound[2] [baʊnd] *vt usu passive* (*border*) ■**to be ~ed by sth** von etw *dat* begrenzt werden
bound[3] [baʊnd] *adj* ■**to be ~ for X** unterwegs nach X sein
bound[4] [baʊnd] **I.** *pt, pp of* **bind II.** *adj* **to be ~ to happen** zwangsläufig geschehen; **it was ~ to happen** das musste so kommen
boundary ['baʊn·də·ri] *n* Grenze *f*
boundless ['baʊnd·lɪs] *adj* grenzenlos
bounds [baʊndz] *npl* Grenzen *pl;* **to be out of ~s** *ball* im Aus sein; *area* Sperrgebiet sein
bounty ['baʊn·ti] *n* ① Kopfgeld *nt* ② (*liter: generosity*) Freigebigkeit *f*
bouquet [boʊ·'keɪ] *n* Bukett *nt*
bourbon ['bɜr·bən] *n* Bourbon *m*
bourgeois [bʊr·'ʒwa] *adj* bürgerlich, spießbürgerlich
bout [baʊt] *n* ① (*short attack*) Anfall *m;* **drinking ~** Trinkgelage *nt* ② (*in boxing*) Boxkampf *m;* (*in wrestling*) Ringkampf *m*
boutique [bu·'tik] *n* Boutique *f*
bovine ['boʊ·vaɪn] *adj* Rinder-
bow[1] [boʊ] *n* ① (*weapon*) Bogen *m* ② (*for instrument*) Bogen *m* ③ (*knot*) Schleife *f*
bow[2] [baʊ] **I.** *vi* sich verbeugen (**to** vor +*dat*) **II.** *vt* **to ~ one's head** den Kopf senken **III.** *n* ① (*bending over*) Verbeugung *f;* **to take a ~** sich [unter Applaus] verbeugen ② NAUT Bug *m*
◆**bow out** *vi* sich verabschieden
bowel ['baʊ·əl] *n usu pl* MED ■**~s** Darm *m*
'**bowel movement** *n* Stuhl[gang] *m*
bowl[1] [boʊl] *n* (*dish*) Schüssel *f;* (*shallower*) Schale *f;* **~ of soup** Tasse *f* Suppe; (*for doing dishes*) Spülschüssel *f*
bowl[2] [boʊl] SPORTS **I.** *vi* (*in alley*) bowlen, Bowling spielen; (*lawn bowling*) Bowls spielen **II.** *vt* SPORTS (*bowling*) werfen; (*lawn bowling*) rollen **III.** *n* Kugel *f*
◆**bowl over** *vt* umwerfen *a. fig*
bow-legged ['boʊ·ˌleg·ɪd] *adj* O-beinig
bowler ['boʊ·lər] *n* ① (*bowling*) Bowlingspieler(in) *m(f);* (*lawn bowling*) Bowlsspieler(in) *m(f)* ② (*hat*) Bowler *m,* Melone *f*
bowling ['boʊ·lɪŋ] *n* Bowling *nt*
'**bowling alley** *n* Bowlingbahn *f*
'**bowling green** *n* Rasenfläche *f* für Bowls
bowman ['boʊ·mən] *n* Bogenschütze *m*
'**bowstring** *n* Bogensehne *f*
bow 'tie *n* Fliege *f*
box[1] [baks] **I.** *vi* boxen **II.** *vt* ① ■**to ~ sb** gegen jdn boxen ② (*slap*) **to ~ sb's ears** jdn ohrfeigen
box[2] [baks] **I.** *n* ① (*container*) Kiste *f; carton* Karton *m; of candy, cigars, matches* Schachtel *f* ② (*space*) Kästchen *nt;* ■**the penalty ~** (*in soccer*) der Strafraum; (*in hockey*) Strafbank **II.** *vt* ■**to ~ [up** ◌**] sth** etw [in einen Karton/eine Schachtel] verpacken
◆**box in** *vt car* einparken; **to feel ~ed in** (*fig*) sich eingeengt fühlen
◆**box up** *vt* [in Kartons] einpacken
boxer ['bak·sər] *n* ① (*dog*) Boxer *m* ② (*person*) Boxer(in) *m(f)*
boxers ['bak·sərz], '**boxer shorts** *npl* Boxershorts *pl*
boxing ['bak·sɪŋ] *n* Boxen *nt*
'**boxing gloves** *npl* Boxhandschuhe *pl*
'**boxing match** *n* Boxkampf *m*
'**boxing ring** *n* Boxring *m*
'**box number** *n* Chiffre[nummer] *f*
'**box office** *n* Kasse *f* (*im Theater oder Kino*)
box 'spring *n* Sprungfederrahmen *m*
boy [bɔɪ] **I.** *n* ① Junge *m* ② (*fam: friends*) ■**the ~s** *pl* die Kumpels *pl* ▶ PHRASES: **the big ~s** die Großen; **~s will be ~s** Jungs sind nun mal so **II.** *interj* [**oh**] **~!** Junge, Junge!
boycott ['bɔɪ·kat] **I.** *vt* boykottieren **II.** *n* Boykott *m*
'**boyfriend** *n* Freund *m*
boyhood ['bɔɪ·hʊd] *n* Kindheit *f*
boyish ['bɔɪ·ɪʃ] *adj* jungenhaft
'**Boy Scout** *n* Pfadfinder *m*
bra [bra] *n* BH *m*
brace [breɪs] **I.** *n* (*for back*) Stützapparat *m;* (*for knee*) Kniestütze *f;* (*for teeth*) ■**~s** *pl* Zahnspange *f* **II.** *vt* ① (*prepare for*) ■**to ~ oneself for sth** sich auf etw *akk* vorbereiten ② (*support*) [ab]stützen; (*horizontally*) verstreben
bracelet ['breɪs·lɪt] *n* Armband *nt*
bracken ['bræk·ən] *n* Adlerfarn *m*
bracket ['bræk·ɪt] **I.** *n* ① *usu pl* (*in writing*) **in [round/square/angle] ~s** in [runden/eckigen/spitzen] Klammern ② (*class*) **age ~** Altersgruppe *f;* **income ~** Einkommensstufe *f;* **tax ~** Steuerklasse *f* ③ (*support*) [Winkel]stütze *f* **II.** *vt* in Klammern setzen
brackish ['bræk·ɪʃ] *adj* brackig
brag <-gg-> [bræg] *vi, vt* ■**to ~ [about sth]** [mit etw] prahlen
braid [breɪd] **I.** *n* ① (*on cloth*) Borte *f;* (*on uniform*) Litze *f;* (*with metal threads*) Tresse[n] *f[pl]* ② (*in hair*) Zopf *m* **II.** *vt, vi* flechten
Braille [breɪl] *n* Blindenschrift *f*

brain [breɪn] **I.** *n* ① *(organ)* Gehirn *nt;* ■ **~s** *pl* [Ge]hirn *nt* ② *(intelligence)* Verstand *m;* ■ **~s** *pl* Intelligenz *f kein pl; (fam)* Grips *m* ③ *(fam: intelligent person)* heller Kopf; **the best ~s** die fähigsten Köpfe ► PHRASES: **to have sth on the ~** *(fam)* immer nur an etw *akk* denken **II.** *vt (fam)* ■ **to ~ sb** jdm den Schädel einschlagen
'brainchild *n* genialer Einfall
'brain damage *n* [Ge]hirnschaden *m*
'brain dead *adj* [ge]hirntot
'brain death *n* [Ge]hirntod *m*
'brain drain *n* Braindrain *m*
brainless ['breɪn·lɪs] *adj* hirnlos
'brain scan *n* Computertomographie *f* des Schädels
'brainstorm I. *vi* ein Brainstorming machen **II.** *n (fam: idea)* Geistesblitz *m*
'brainstorming *n* Brainstorming *nt*
'brain tumor *n* [Ge]hirntumor *m*
'brainwash *vt* ■ **to ~ sb** jdn einer Gehirnwäsche unterziehen
'brainwashing *n* Gehirnwäsche *f*
'brainwave *n* Geistesblitz *m*
'brainwork *n* Kopfarbeit *f*
brainy ['breɪ·ni] *adj (fam)* gescheit
braise [breɪz] *vt* FOOD schmoren
brake [breɪk] **I.** *n* Bremse *f* **II.** *vi* bremsen
'brake fluid *n* Bremsflüssigkeit *f*
'brake shoe *n* Bremsklotz *f*
braking ['breɪ·kɪŋ] *n* Bremsen *nt*
'braking distance *n* Bremsweg *m*
bran [bræn] *n* Kleie *f*
branch [bræntʃ] **I.** *n* ① *of bough* Zweig *m; of trunk* Ast *m* ② **~ of a river** Flussarm *m* ③ *(office)* Zweigstelle *f,* Filiale *f* **II.** *vi* ① *(form branches)* Zweige treiben ② *(fig: fork)* sich gabeln
◆ **branch off I.** *vi* sich verzweigen **II.** *vt* **to ~ off a subject** vom Thema abkommen
◆ **branch out** *vi* seine Aktivitäten ausdehnen; *socially* gesellschaftlich mehr unternehmen; **to ~ out on one's own** sich selbstständig machen
'branch office *n* Filiale *f*
brand [brænd] **I.** *n* ① *(product)* Marke *f;* **store ~** Hausmarke *f* ② *(fig: type)* Art *f* ③ *(mark)* Brandzeichen *nt* **II.** *vt* ① *(label)* ■ **to be ~ed [as] sth** als etw gebrandmarkt sein ② *animal* mit einem Brandzeichen versehen
brandish ['bræn·dɪʃ] *vt* [drohend] schwingen
'brand name *n* Markenname *m*
brand 'new *adj* [funkel]nagelneu
brandy ['bræn·di] *n* Weinbrand *m*
brash [bræʃ] *adj* ① *(cocky)* dreist ② *(gaudy)* grell
brass [bræs] *n* ① *(metal)* Messing *nt* ② *+ sing/pl vb* MUS ■ **the ~** die Blechinstrumente *pl*
brass 'band *n* Blaskapelle *f*
brassy ['bræs·i] *adj* ① *(like brass)* messingartig ② *sound* blechern
brat [bræt] *n (hum o pej)* Balg *m o nt*
bravado [brə·'vɑ·doʊ] *n* Draufgängertum *nt*
brave [breɪv] **I.** *adj* ① *(fearless)* mutig ② *(stoical)* tapfer ► PHRASES: **to put on a ~ face** sich *dat* nichts anmerken lassen **II.** *vt* trotzen *+dat*
bravery ['breɪ·və·ri] *n* Tapferkeit *f,* Mut *m*
brawl [brɔl] **I.** *n* [lautstarke] Schlägerei **II.** *vi* sich [lautstark] schlagen
brawn [brɔn] *n* Muskelkraft *f*
brawny ['brɔ·ni] *adj (fam)* muskulös
bray [breɪ] **I.** *vi donkey* schreien; *person* kreischen **II.** *n* [Esels]schrei *m*
brazen ['breɪ·zən] *adj* unverschämt
brazier ['breɪ·zər] *n* ① *(pan)* [große, flache] Kohlenpfanne ② *(barbecue)* [Grill]rost *m*
Brazil [brə·'zɪl] *n* Brasilien *nt*
Brazilian [brə·'zɪl·jən] **I.** *n* Brasilianer(in) *m(f)* **II.** *adj* brasilianisch
Bra'zil nut *n* Paranuss *f*
breach [britʃ] **I.** *n* ① *(infringement)* Verletzung *f;* **~ of trust** Vertrauensbruch *m;* **~ of contract** Vertragsbruch *m;* **security ~** Verstoß *m* gegen die Sicherheitsbestimmungen ② *(estrangement)* Bruch *m* **II.** *vt* ① *(break)* verletzen; *contract* brechen ② *defense* durchbrechen
bread [bred] *n* Brot *nt* ► PHRASES: **to know which side one's ~ is buttered on** seinen Vorteil kennen
bread and 'butter *n* ① Butterbrot *nt* ② *(fig: income)* Lebensunterhalt *m; (job)* Broterwerb *m*
'breadbasket *n* ① *(container)* Brotkorb *m* ② *(region)* Kornkammer *f*
'breadbox *n* Brotkasten *m*
'breadcrumb *n* Brotkrume *f;* ■ **~s** *pl (for coating food)* Paniermehl *nt kein pl;* **to coat with ~s** panieren
breadth [bredθ] *n* ① Breite *f* ② *(fig)* Ausdehnung *f*
'breadwinner *n* Ernährer(in) *m(f)*
break [breɪk] **I.** *n* ① *(fracture)* Bruch *m* ② *(gap)* Lücke *f* ③ *(interruption)* Unterbrechung *f; (shorter)* Pause *f;* **coffee ~** Kaffeepause *f* ④ *(end of relationship)* **to make a clean ~** einen sauberen Schlussstrich ziehen ⑤ *(opportunity)* Chance *f* **II.** *vt* <broke, broken> ① *(shatter)* zerbrechen; *(into two pieces)* entzweibrechen; *(damage)* kaputtmachen; *window* einschlagen; *(fracture)* brechen; **to ~ one's arm** sich *dat* den Arm brechen ② *(momentarily interrupt)* unterbrechen; *fall* abfangen ③ *(put an end to)* brechen; *habit* aufgeben; **to ~ a deadlock** einen toten Punkt überwinden ④ *(violate) agreement* verletzen; *law* übertreten; *promise* brechen; *treaty* verstoßen (gegen *+akk*) ⑤ *code* entschlüsseln ⑥ *bad news* ■ **to ~ sth to sb** jdm etw mitteilen **III.** *vi* <broke, broken> ① *(stop working)* kaputtgehen; *(collapse)* zusammenbrechen; *(fall apart)* auseinanderbrechen; *(shatter)* zerbrechen ② *voice* **the boy's voice is ~ing** der Junge ist [gerade] im Stimmbruch ③ METEO *dawn, day* anbrechen; *storm* losbre-

chen ④ *news* bekannt werden ⑤ (*billiards*) anstoßen; (*boxing*) sich trennen ▶ PHRASES: **to ~ <u>even</u>** kostendeckend arbeiten; **to ~ <u>free</u>** ausbrechen

◆**break away** *vi* ① (*move away forcibly*) sich losreißen ② (*split off*) sich absetzen

◆**break down** **I.** *vi* ① (*stop working*) stehen bleiben; *engine* versagen ② (*dissolve*) sich auflösen; *marriage* scheitern ③ (*emotionally*) zusammenbrechen **II.** *vt* ① (*force open*) aufbrechen; (*with foot*) eintreten ② (*separate into parts*) aufgliedern; CHEM aufspalten; *figures* aufschlüsseln

◆**break in** **I.** *vi* ① (*enter by force*) einbrechen ② (*interrupt*) unterbrechen **II.** *vt* ① (*condition*) *shoes* einlaufen ② (*tame*) zähmen; (*train*) abrichten; *horse* zureiten

◆**break into** *vt* ① (*forcefully enter*) einbrechen in +*akk;* *car* aufbrechen ② (*start doing sth*) **to ~ into a run** [plötzlich] zu laufen anfangen

◆**break off** **I.** *vt* ① (*separate forcefully*) abbrechen ② (*terminate*) beenden; *engagement* lösen; *talks* abbrechen **II.** *vi* abbrechen

◆**break out** *vi* ① (*escape*) ausbrechen ② (*begin*) ausbrechen; *storm* losbrechen ③ **to ~ out in a rash** einen Ausschlag bekommen; **to ~ out in a sweat** ins Schwitzen kommen

◆**break through** *vi* ① (*make one's way*) sich durchdrängen ② (*be successful*) einschlagen

◆**break up** **I.** *vt* ① (*end*) beenden; *marriage* zerstören; (*dissolve*) auflösen ② (*split up*) aufspalten; *gang, monopoly* zerschlagen; *coalition* auflösen; *collection, family* auseinanderreißen; **~ it up, you two!** auseinander, ihr beiden! **II.** *vi* ① (*end relationship*) sich trennen ② (*come to an end*) enden; *meeting* sich auflösen; *marriage* scheitern ③ (*fall apart*) auseinandergehen; *coalition* auseinanderbrechen; *aircraft, ship* zerschellen; (*in air*) zerbersten

breakable ['breɪ·kə·bəl] *adj* zerbrechlich

breakage ['breɪ·kɪdʒ] *n* Bruch *m;* **~ must be paid for** zerbrochene Ware muss bezahlt werden

'**breakaway** **I.** *n* Lossagung *f;* (*splitting off*) Absplitterung *f* **II.** *adj* Splitter-

'**breakdown** *n* ① (*collapse*) Zusammenbruch *m;* (*failure*) Scheitern *nt;* (*decomposition*) Zersetzung *f* ② AUTO Panne *f* ③ (*list*) Aufgliederung *f,* Aufschlüsselung *f* ④ PSYCH [Nerven]zusammenbruch *m*

breaker ['breɪ·kər] *n* (*wave*) Brecher *m*

breakfast ['brek·fəst] *n* Frühstück *nt;* **to have** [*or* **eat**] **~** frühstücken

> In den USA ist das **breakfast** (Frühstück) eine wichtige Mahlzeit. Zum traditionellen Frühstück werden häufig Rühreier, gebratene oder hartgekochte Eier, Speck, *French toast*, *pancakes* (eine Art dicker Pfannkuchen), *waffles* (Waffeln), gebratene Würstchen, Bagels, Toast und *hash browns* (Bratkartoffeln aus geriebenen Kartoffeln) serviert. Für die Zubereitung von *French toast* werden Brotscheiben ohne Rinde oder Toastbrot in einer Masse aus Eiern, Milch und Zucker getränkt und anschließend in Butterschmalz goldbraun gebraten. Sie werden unter anderem mit Ahornsirup, Honig oder Marmelade gegessen.

'**break-in** *n* Einbruch *m*

'**breaking point** *n* Belastungsgrenze *f*

'**breakneck** *adj* **at ~ speed** mit halsbrecherischer Geschwindigkeit

'**breakout** *n* Ausbruch *m*

'**breakthrough** *n* Durchbruch *m* (**in** bei +*dat*)

'**breakup** *n* Auseinanderbrechen *nt;* *of marriage* Scheitern *nt;* *of group* Auflösung *f*

'**breakwater** *n* Wellenbrecher *m*

breast [brest] *n* ① (*mammary gland*) Brust *f;* (*bust*) Busen *m* ② (*of bird*) Brust *f* ▶ PHRASES: **to make a <u>clean</u> ~ of sth** etw gestehen

'**breastbone** *n* Brustbein *nt*

'**breast cancer** *n* Brustkrebs *m*

'**breastfeed** <-fed, -fed> *vi, vt* stillen

'**breast-feeding** *n* Stillen *nt*

breast '**pocket** *n* Brusttasche *f*

'**breaststroke** *n* Brustschwimmen *nt*

breath [breθ] *n* ① (*air*) Atem *m;* (*inhalation*) Atemzug *m;* **bad ~** Mundgeruch *m;* **out of ~** außer Atem; **to catch one's ~** [*or* **get one's ~ back**] verschnaufen; **to take a deep ~** tief Luft holen; **to take sb's ~ away** jdm den Atem rauben ② (*wind*) **~ of air** Hauch *m;* **to go out for a ~ of fresh air** frische Luft schnappen gehen

breathalyze ['breθ·ə·laɪz] *vt* blasen lassen

Breathalyzer® ['breθ·ə·laɪ·zər] *n* Alcotest® *m,* Alkoholtestgerät *nt*

breathe [brið] **I.** *vi* atmen; **to ~ again/more easily** (*fig*) [erleichtert] aufatmen ▶ PHRASES: **to ~ down sb's <u>neck</u>** jdm im Nacken sitzen **II.** *vt* ① (*exhale*) [aus]atmen; **to ~ a sigh of relief** erleichtert aufatmen ② (*whisper*) flüstern ▶ PHRASES: **to not ~ a <u>word</u>** kein Sterbenswörtchen sagen

breather ['bri·ðər] *n* [Verschnauf]pause *f*

breathing ['bri·ðɪŋ] *n* Atmung *f*

'**breathing apparatus** *n* Sauerstoffgerät *nt*

'**breathing room,** '**breathing space** *n* (*fig*) Bewegungsfreiheit *f*

breathless ['breθ·lɪs] *adj* atemlos

'**breathtaking** *adj* atemberaubend

'**breath test** *n* Alkoholtest *m*

bred [bred] *pt, pp of* **breed**

breeches ['brɪtʃ·ɪz] *npl* Kniehose *f;* **riding ~** Reithose *f*

breed [brid] **I.** *vt* <bred, bred> züchten; (*fig*) *crime* hervorbringen; *resentment* hervorrufen **II.** *vi* <bred, bred> sich fortpflanzen; *birds* brüten; *rabbits* sich vermehren **III.** *n* (*of animal*) Rasse *f;* (*of plant*) Sorte *f*

breeder ['bri·dər] *n* Züchter(in) *m(f)*

B

breeding ['bri·dɪŋ] *n* ① (*of animals*) Zucht *f* ② (*of people*) Erziehung *f*

'breeding ground *n* Brutstätte *f a. fig*

breeze [briz] **I.** *n* ① (*light wind*) Brise *f* ② (*fam: sth very easy*) Kinderspiel *nt* **II.** *vi* (*fam*) ■**to ~ through sth** etw spielend schaffen

breezy ['bri·zi] *adj* ① (*windy*) windig ② (*jovial*) unbeschwert

brevity ['brev·ɪ·t̬i] *n* Kürze *f*

brew [bru] **I.** *n* Gebräu *nt;* (*fig*) Mischung *f* **II.** *vi* (*fig*) *trouble* sich zusammenbrauen **III.** *vt* brauen

brewer ['bru·ər] *n* [Bier]brauer(in) *m(f)*

brewery ['bru·ə·ri] *n* Brauerei *f*

briar ['braɪ·ər] *n* Dornbusch *m*

bribe [braɪb] **I.** *vt* bestechen **II.** *n* Bestechung *f,* Schmiergeld *nt;* **to take a ~** sich bestechen lassen

bribery ['braɪ·bə·ri] *n* Bestechung *f*

bric-a-brac ['brɪk·ə·bræk] *n* Nippes *pl*

brick [brɪk] *n* Ziegel[stein] *m,* Backstein *m*

◆**brick up** *vt* zumauern

bricklayer *n* Maurer(in) *m(f)*

brick 'wall *n* [Ziegelstein]mauer *f,* [Backstein]mauer *f* ▶ PHRASES: **to be talking to a ~** gegen eine Wand reden

'brickwork *n* Mauerwerk *nt*

bridal ['braɪd·əl] *adj* (*of wedding*) Hochzeits-; (*of bride*) Braut-

bride [braɪd] *n* Braut *f*

bridegroom ['braɪd·ˌgrum] *n* Bräutigam *m*

'bridesmaid *n* Brautjungfer *f*

bridge [brɪdʒ] **I.** *n* ① Brücke *f* ② (*for teeth*) [Zahn]brücke *f* ③ *of nose* Nasenrücken *m* ④ *of glasses* Brillensteg *m;* (*of instrument*) Steg *m* ⑤ (*on ship*) Kommandobrücke *f* ⑥ (*card game*) Bridge *nt* **II.** *vt valley* eine Brücke schlagen (über +*akk*); (*fig*) *gap* überwinden

bridle ['braɪd·əl] **I.** *n* Zaumzeug *nt* **II.** *vt* aufzäumen **III.** *vi* ■**to ~ at sth** sich über etw *akk* entrüsten

'bridle path *n* Reitweg *m*

brief [brif] **I.** *adj* kurz; ■**to be ~** sich kurzfassen; **in ~** kurz gesagt **II.** *n* ① LAW Unterlagen *pl* zu einer Rechtssache ② ■**~s** *pl* (*for men*) Herrenunterhose *f;* (*for women*) Slip *m,* [Damen]schlüpfer *m* **III.** *vt* informieren

briefcase ['brif·keɪs] *n* Aktentasche *f*

briefing ['bri·fɪŋ] *n* ① (*meeting*) [Einsatz]besprechung *f* ② (*information*) Anweisung[en] *f[pl]*

briefly ['brif·li] *adv* kurz

briefness ['brif·nɪs] *n* Kürze *f*

brigade [brɪ·'geɪd] *n* Brigade *f*

bright [braɪt] **I.** *adj* ① (*shining*) *light* hell; (*blinding*) grell; *star* leuchtend; *sunshine* strahlend ② (*vivid*) **~ blue** strahlend blau; **~ red** leuchtend rot ③ (*intelligent*) intelligent; *child* aufgeweckt; *idea* glänzend *a. iron* ④ (*promising*) viel versprechend ▶ PHRASES: **to look on the ~ side [of sth]** etw positiv sehen **II.** *n* AUTO ■**~s** *pl* Fernlicht *nt*

brighten ['braɪt·ən] **I.** *vt* ① (*make brighter*) heller machen ② (*make more cheerful*) auflockern **II.** *vi* ■**to ~ [up]** ① (*become cheerful*) fröhlicher werden; *eyes* aufleuchten ② METEO sich aufklären

brightness ['braɪt·nɪs] *n of light* Helligkeit *f; of sun* Strahlen *nt; of eyes* Leuchten *nt*

brilliance ['brɪl·jəns] ① (*ability*) Brillanz *f;* (*intelligence*) Scharfsinn *m; of idea* Genialität *f* ② (*brightness*) *of sun* Strahlen *nt; of stars, eyes* Funkeln *nt; of snow* Glitzern *nt*

brilliant ['brɪl·jənt] *adj* ① (*shining*) *color, eyes* leuchtend; *smile, sun* strahlend ② (*intelligent*) *person* hoch begabt; *plan* brillant; *idea* glänzend

brim [brɪm] **I.** *n* ① *of hat* Krempe *f* ② (*top*) Rand *m;* **filled [*or* full] to the ~** randvoll **II.** *vi* <-mm-> **her eyes ~med with tears** ihr standen die Tränen in den Augen; **to be ~ming with confidence** vor Selbstbewusstsein nur so strotzen

brimful [ˌbrɪm·'fʊl] *adj* **~ of ideas** voller Ideen

brine [braɪn] *n* [Salz]lake *f*

bring <brought, brought> [brɪŋ] *vt* ① (*convey*) mitbringen; **I didn't ~ my keys with me** ich habe meine Schlüssel nicht mitgenommen; **to ~ sth to sb's attention** jdn auf etw *akk* aufmerksam machen; **to ~ news** Nachrichten überbringen ② (*cause to come, happen*) bringen; **to ~ sb luck** jdm Glück bringen; **so what ~s you here to Chicago?** was hat dich hier nach Chicago verschlagen?; (*fig*) **this ~s me to the second part of my talk** damit komme ich zum zweiten Teil meiner Rede ③ LAW **to ~ charges against sb** Anklage gegen jdn erheben

◆**bring about** *vt* verursachen

◆**bring along** *vt* mitbringen

◆**bring around** *vt* ① (*persuade*) überreden ② (*bring back to consciousness*) wieder zu Bewusstsein bringen ③ (*bring along*) mitbringen

◆**bring back** *vt* ① (*return*) zurückbringen ② (*reintroduce*) wieder einführen ③ (*call to mind*) *memories* wecken

◆**bring down** *vt* ① (*get down*) herunterbringen ② (*trip*) zu Fall bringen ③ (*shoot down*) abschießen ④ (*depose*) stürzen ⑤ (*reduce*) senken ▶ PHRASES: **to ~ the house ⌒ down** einen Beifallssturm auslösen

◆**bring forth** *vt* (*form, liter*) hervorbringen

◆**bring forward** *vt* vorverlegen

◆**bring in** *vt* ① (*fetch in*) hereinbringen; *harvest* einbringen ② (*introduce*) einführen ③ (*earn*) [ein]bringen

◆**bring off** *vt* zustande bringen

◆**bring on** *vt* herbeiführen; MED verursachen; **she brought disgrace on the whole family** sie brachte Schande über die ganze Familie

◆**bring out** *vt* ① (*get out*) herausbringen ② (*encourage*) ■**to ~ sb out of his/her shell** jdm die Hemmungen nehmen ③ COMM (*launch*) herausbringen

◆**bring over** *vt* ① (*take over*) herbeibringen

② *(persuade)* **to ~ sb over to one's side** jdn auf seine Seite bringen
◆**bring up** *vt* ① *(carry up)* heraufbringen ② *(rear)* großziehen ③ *(mention)* zur Sprache bringen; **to ~ up ⊂ sth for discussion** etw zur Diskussion stellen ④ COMPUT aufrufen ▶ PHRASES: **to ~ up the rear** das Schlusslicht bilden

brink [brɪŋk] *n* Rand *m a. fig*

briny ['braɪ·ni] *adj* salzig

briquet(te) [brɪ·'ket] *n* Brikett *nt*

brisk [brɪsk] *adj* ① *(quick)* zügig; *walk* stramm ② *(busy)* lebhaft ③ *wind* frisch

briskness ['brɪsk·nɪs] *n of pace* Zügigkeit *f; of trade* Lebhaftigkeit *f*

bristle ['brɪs·əl] **I.** *n* Borste *f;* *(on face)* [Bart]stoppel *f meist pl* **II.** *vi* ① *fur* sich sträuben ② *(fig)* ■**to ~ [at sth]** sich [über etw *akk*] empören

bristly ['brɪs·li] *adj* borstig; *chin* stoppelig

Brit [brɪt] *n (fam)* Brite, -in *m, f*

Britain ['brɪt·ən] *n* Großbritannien *nt*

British ['brɪṭ·ɪʃ] **I.** *adj* britisch **II.** *npl* ■**the ~** die Briten *pl*

British 'Isles *npl* **the ~** die Britischen Inseln

Briton ['brɪt·ən] *n* Brite, -in *m, f*

brittle ['brɪṭ·əl] *adj* ① *(fragile)* zerbrechlich; *bones* brüchig ② *(fig) laugh* schrill

broach [broʊtʃ] **I.** *vt subject* anschneiden **II.** *n* <*pl* -es> *see* **brooch**

broad [brɔd] *adj* ① *(wide)* breit; *expanse* weit ② *(general)* allgemein; *generalization* grob ③ *(wide-ranging)* weitreichend; *interests* vielseitig ▶ PHRASES: **in ~ daylight** am helllichten Tag[e]

'broadband *n* INET Breitband *nt*

broadcast ['brɔd·kæst] **I.** *n* Übertragung *f;* *(program)* Sendung *f* **II.** *vi, vt* <broadcast *or* broadcasted, broadcast *or* broadcasted> senden; *game* übertragen; *rumor* [überall] verbreiten

broadcaster ['brɔd·kæst·ər] *n* *(announcer)* Sprecher(in) *m(f);* *(host)* Moderator(in) *m(f)*

broadcasting ['brɔd·kæst·ɪŋ] *n* *(radio)* Rundfunk *m;* *(TV)* Fernsehen *nt*

broaden ['brɔd·ən] **I.** *vi* breiter werden **II.** *vt* ① *(make wider)* verbreitern ② *(fig)* vergrößern; *discussion* ausweiten; **to ~ one's mind** seinen Horizont erweitern

broadly ['brɔd·li] *adv* ① *(widely)* breit ② *(generally) agree* weitgehend; **~ speaking, ...** ganz allgemein gesehen, ...

broad-'minded *adj* tolerant

'broadsheet *n* großformatige [seriöse] Zeitung

'broadside *n* Breitseite *f a. fig*

> Der **Broadway** ist eine große Straße in New York, die sich durch den gesamten Stadtteil Manhattan zieht. In dieser Straße befindet sich in der Nähe des Times Square das berühmte Theaterviertel mit gleichem Namen. **Broadway** ist gleichbedeutend mit großer amerikanischer Schauspielkunst und es wurden dort so gut wie alle Theaterstücke aufgeführt, die auf irgendeine Weise wichtig sind. Stücke, die dort nicht gespielt werden, sind oft Experimentalstücke oder Niedrigbudget-Stücke, die *off-Broadway plays* genannt werden.

brocade [broʊ·'keɪd] *n* Brokat *m*

broccoli ['brak·ə·li] *n* Brokkoli *m*

brochure [broʊ·'ʃʊr] *n* Broschüre *f*

brogue[1] [broʊg] *n* LING *irischer oder schottischer Akzent*

brogue[2] [broʊg] *n* *(shoe)* Brogue *m*

broil [brɔɪl] *vt* grillen

broiler ['brɔɪ·lər] *n* *(stove part)* Bratrost *nt*

broke [broʊk] **I.** *pt of* **break** **II.** *adj pred* *(fam)* pleite

broken ['broʊ·kən] **I.** *pp of* **break** **II.** *adj* ① *arm* gebrochen; *bottle* zerbrochen; *watch* kaputt; **~ glass** Glasscherben *pl* ② **in ~ Spanish** in gebrochenem Spanisch

'broken-down *adj* ① *(not working)* kaputt ② *(dilapidated)* verfallen

broken'hearted *adj* untröstlich

broker ['broʊ·kər] **I.** *n* ① ECON [Börsen]makler(in) *m(f)* ② *(negotiator)* Vermittler(in) *m(f)* **II.** *vt* aushandeln

brokerage ['broʊ·kər·ɪdʒ] *n* ECON ① *(activity)* Maklergeschäft *nt* ② *(fee)* Maklergebühr *f*

bromide ['broʊ·maɪd] *n* CHEM Bromid *nt*

bromine ['broʊ·min] *n* CHEM Brom *nt*

bronchial ['braŋ·ki·əl] *adj* Bronchial-

bronchitis [braŋ·'kaɪ·ṭɪs] *n* Bronchitis *f*

bronco ['braŋ·koʊ] *n wildes Pferd im Westen der USA*

bronze [branz] **I.** *n* Bronze *f* **II.** *adj* **the B~ Age** die Bronzezeit; **~ medal** Bronzemedaille *f*

brooch <*pl* -es> [broʊtʃ] *n* Brosche *f*

brood [brud] **I.** *n* Brut *f a. fig* **II.** *vi* ■**to ~ on** [*or* **over**] **sth** über etw *dat* brüten

brooding ['bru·dɪŋ] *adj* ① *(thinking)* nachdenklich ② *(threatening) atmosphere* drückend; *sky* dunkel

brook [brʊk] *n* Bach *m*

broom [brum] *n* ① *(brush)* Besen *m* ② BOT Ginster *m*

'broom handle, broomstick ['brum·stɪk] *n* Besenstiel *m*

broth [brɔθ] *n* Brühe *f*

brothel ['braθ·əl] *n* Bordell *nt*

brother ['brʌð·ər] **I.** *n* ① Bruder *m;* **~s and sisters** Geschwister *pl* ② *(fam)* Kumpel *m* **II.** *interj* **oh, ~!** Mann!

brotherhood ['brʌð·ər·hʊd] *n* ① *(group)* Bruderschaft *f* ② *(feeling)* Brüderlichkeit *f*

'brother-in-law <*pl* brothers-in-law> *n* Schwager *m*

brotherly ['brʌð·ər·li] *adj* brüderlich

brought [brɔt] *pp, pt of* **bring**

brow [braʊ] *n* Stirn *f; of hill* Bergkuppe *f*

browbeat <-beat, -beaten> ['braʊ·bit] *vt* einschüchtern; ■**to ~ sb into doing sth** jdn so unter Druck setzen, dass er etw tut

brown [braʊn] **I.** *n* Braun *nt* **II.** *adj* braun **III.** *vt onion* [an]bräunen; *meat* anbraten

brown 'bread *n locker gebackenes Brot aus dunklerem Mehl, etwa wie Mischbrot*

brownie ['braʊ·ni] *n* FOOD *kleiner Schokoladenkuchen mit Nüssen*

Brownie ['braʊ·ni] *n* (*Girl Scout*) junge Pfadfinderin

'brownie point *n* (*hum fam*) Pluspunkt *m;* **to get ~s** Pluspunkte machen

brownish ['braʊ·nɪʃ] *adj* bräunlich

brown 'rice *n* ungeschälter Reis

'brownstone *n* ① (*stone*) rötlich brauner Sandstein ② (*house*) [rotbraunes] Sandsteinhaus

browse [braʊz] **I.** *vi* ① **to ~ through a magazine** eine Zeitschrift durchblättern ② **to ~ [around a store]** sich [in einem Geschäft] umsehen ③ (*graze*) grasen **II.** *vt* COMPUT etw durchsehen; **to ~ the Internet** im Internet surfen

browser ['braʊ·zər] *n* COMPUT Browser *m*

bruise [bruz] **I.** *n* blauer Fleck, Prellung *f;* (*on fruit*) Druckstelle *f* **II.** *vt* **to ~ one's arm** sich am Arm stoßen **III.** *vi* einen blauen Fleck bekommen; *fruit* Druckstellen bekommen

bruiser ['bru·zər] *n* (*pej fam*) Schläger[typ] *m*

brunch <*pl* -es> [brʌntʃ] *n* Brunch *m*

brunette [bru·'net] **I.** *n* Brünette *f* **II.** *adj* brünett

brunt [brʌnt] *n* **to bear the ~ of sth** etw am stärksten zu spüren bekommen

brush [brʌʃ] **I.** *n* <*pl* -es> ① (*for hair, cleaning*) Bürste *f;* (*broom*) Besen *m;* (*for painting*) Pinsel *m* ② (*act*) Bürsten *nt* ③ (*encounter*) Zusammenstoß *m;* **to have a ~ with the law** mit dem Gesetz in Konflikt geraten ④ (*brushwood*) Unterholz *nt* **II.** *vt* ① (*clean*) abbürsten; **to ~ one's hair** sich *dat* die Haare bürsten ② (*touch lightly*) leicht berühren ③ (*apply a substance*) bestreichen **III.** *vi* ■**to ~ against sb/sth** jdn/etw streifen; ■**to ~ by sb/sth** an jdm/etw vorbeieilen

◆**brush aside** *vt* ① (*move aside*) wegschieben ② (*dismiss*) *thing* abtun; *person* ignorieren

◆**brush away** *vt* wegwischen; *fly* verscheuchen; *tears* sich *dat* abwischen

◆**brush off** *vt* ① (*remove with brush*) abbürsten ② (*ignore*) *person* abblitzen lassen; *thing* zurückweisen

◆**brush up I.** *vi* ■**to ~ up on sth** etw auffrischen **II.** *vt* auffrischen

'brush-off *n* **to get the ~ from sb** von jdm einen Korb bekommen

'brushwood *n* Reisig *nt*

brusque [brʌsk] *adj* schroff

brusqueness ['brʌsk·nɪs] *n* Schroffheit *f*

Brussels ['brʌs·əlz] *n* Brüssel *nt*

Brussel(s) 'sprout *n* ■**~s** *pl* Rosenkohl *m kein pl*

brutal ['bruṭ·əl] *adj* brutal *a. fig; honesty* schonungslos; *truth* ungeschminkt

brutality [bru·'tæl·ɪ·ṭi] *n* Brutalität *f*

brutalize ['bruṭ·əl·aɪz] *vt* ① (*treat cruelly*) brutal behandeln ② (*make brutal*) brutalisieren

brute [brut] **I.** *n* ① (*savage*) Bestie *f* ② (*person*) brutaler Kerl **II.** *adj* **~ force** rohe Gewalt

brutish ['bru·ṭɪʃ] *adj* brutal

BS [ˌbi·es] *n* ① *abbrev of* **Bachelor of Science** Bakkalaureus *m* der Naturwissenschaften ② (*vulg*) *abbrev of* **bullshit**

BSE [ˌbi·es·'i] *n abbrev of* **bovine spongiform encephalopathy** BSE *f*

bubble ['bʌb·əl] **I.** *n* Blase *f* **II.** *vi* kochen *a. fig; coffee, stew* brodeln; *water, fountain* sprudeln; *champagne* perlen; (*make bubbling sound*) blubbern

◆**bubble over** *vi* ■**to ~ over with sth** vor etw *dat* [über]sprudeln

'bubble bath *n* Schaumbad *nt*

'bubblegum *n* Bubblegum *m o nt*

'bubble pack, 'bubble wrap *n* Luftpolsterfolie *f*

bubbly ['bʌb·li] **I.** *n* (*fam*) Schampus *m* **II.** *adj* ① *drink* sprudelnd ② *person* temperamentvoll

bubonic plague [bu·ˌban·ɪk·'pleɪg] *n* Beulenpest *f*

buccaneer [ˌbʌk·ə·'nɪr] *n* Seeräuber(in) *m(f)*

buck¹ [bʌk] *n* (*fam*) Dollar *m;* **to make a fast** [*or* **an easy**] **~** eine schnelle Mark machen

buck² [bʌk] **I.** *n* <*pl* - *or* -s> (*deer*) Bock *m;* (*rabbit*) Rammler *m* **II.** *vi* bocken

buck³ [bʌk] *n* (*fam*) **to pass the ~** [**to sb**] die Verantwortung [auf jdn] abwälzen

◆**buck up I.** *vi* [wieder] Mut fassen; **~ up!** Kopf hoch! **II.** *vt* aufmuntern

bucket ['bʌk·ɪt] *n* ① (*pail*) Eimer *m;* **champagne ~** Sektkübel *m* ② (*fam: large amounts*) ■**~s** *pl* Unmengen *pl* ► PHRASES: **to kick the ~** (*fam*) ins Gras beißen

'bucketful <*pl* -s *or* **bucketsful**> *n* Eimer *m*

buckle ['bʌk·əl] **I.** *n* Schnalle *f* **II.** *vt* ① *belt* [zu]schnallen ② (*bend*) verbiegen **III.** *vi* sich verbiegen; **my knees began to ~** ich bekam weiche Knie

◆**buckle up** *vi* (*fam*) AUTO sich anschnallen

buckshot *n* grobkörniger Schrot

buckskin ['bʌk·skɪn] *n* Wildleder *nt*

'buckwheat *n* Buchweizen *m*

bud [bʌd] **I.** *n* Knospe *f* **II.** *vi* <-dd-> knospen

Buddhism ['bu·dɪz·əm] *n* Buddhismus *m*

Buddhist ['bu·dɪst] **I.** *n* Buddhist(in) *m(f)* **II.** *adj* buddhistisch

budding ['bʌd·ɪŋ] *adj* (*fig*) angehend

buddy ['bʌd·i] *n* (*fam*) Kumpel *m*

budge [bʌdʒ] **I.** *vi* ① (*move*) sich [vom Fleck] rühren ② (*change mind*) nachgeben **II.** *vt* ① (*move*) [von der Stelle] bewegen ② (*cause to change mind*) umstimmen

budget ['bʌdʒ·ɪt] **I.** *n* Budget *nt;* ■**the B~** der öffentliche Haushalt[splan] **II.** *vi* ■**to ~ for sth** etw [im Budget] vorsehen **III.** *adj* preiswert; **~ travel** Billigreisen *pl*

B

buff[1] [bʌf] I. *n* ► PHRASES: **in the** ~ (*fam*) nackt II. *adj* ① (*color*) gelbbraun ② (*sl: fit*) muskulös III. *vt* ■**to** ~ **[up] sth** etw polieren
buff[2] [bʌf] *n* (*fam*) Fan *m*
buffalo <*pl* - *or* -oes> [ˈbʌf·ə·loʊ] *n* Büffel *m*
buffer [ˈbʌf·ər] *n* ① (*shock absorber*) Puffer *m* ② COMPUT Puffer *m*, Zwischenspeicher *m* ③ (*polisher*) Poliermaschine *f*
ˈbuffer zone *n* Pufferzone *f*
buffet[1] [bə·ˈfeɪ] *n* (*food*) Büfett *nt*
buffet[2] [ˈbʌf·ɪt] *vt* [heftig] hin und her bewegen
buffoon [bə·ˈfun] *n* Clown *m*
bug [bʌg] I. *n* ① (*insect*) ■~**s** *pl* Ungeziefer *nt kein pl*; **bed** ~ Bettwanze *f* ② (*fam*) MED Bazillus *m* ③ COMPUT (*fault*) Bug *m* ④ (*listening device*) Wanze *f* II. *vt* <-gg-> ① (*fam: annoy*) ■**to** ~ **sb** [**about sth**] jdm [mit etw *dat*] auf die Nerven gehen; **stop** ~**ging me!** hör auf zu nerven! ② (*install bugs*) verwanzen ③ (*eavesdrop on*) abhören
ˈbugbear *n* Ärgernis *nt*
buggy [ˈbʌg·i] *n* ① (*horse-drawn*) Pferdewagen *m*, leichter Einspänner *m* ② (*baby carriage*) Kinderwagen *m*, Buggy *m* ③ (*off-road vehicle*) Buggy *m*
bugle [ˈbju·gəl] *n* Horn *nt*
bugler [ˈbju·glər] *n* Hornist(in) *m(f)*
build [bɪld] I. *n* Körperbau *m* II. *vt* <built, built> ① (*construct*) bauen; *building a.* errichten; *fire* machen; *wall* ziehen ② (*fig*) aufbauen III. *vi* <built, built> ① (*construct*) bauen ② (*increase*) zunehmen; *tension* steigen
◆**build in** *vt* einbauen
◆**build on** *vt* ① (*develop*) bauen auf +*akk* ② (*add extension*) anbauen
◆**build up** I. *vt* aufbauen; *lead* ausbauen; *speed* erhöhen II. *vi* (*increase*) zunehmen; *traffic* sich verdichten; *backlog* größer werden; *pressure* sich erhöhen
builder [ˈbɪl·dər] *n* (*worker*) Bauarbeiter(in) *m(f)*; (*contractor*) Bauherr(in) *m(f)*
building [ˈbɪl·dɪŋ] *n* Gebäude *nt*
ˈbuilding contractor *n* Bauunternehmer(in) *m(f)*
ˈbuilding site *n* Baustelle *f*
ˈbuildup *n* ① (*increase*) Zunahme *f*; ~ **of traffic** Verkehrsverdichtung *f* ② (*accumulation*) Ansammlung *f* ③ (*hype*) Werbung *f* ④ (*preparations*) Vorbereitung *f*
built [bɪlt] *pp, pt of* **build**
built-in [ˈbɪlt·ɪn] *adj* eingebaut; ~ **cupboard** Einbauschrank *m*
built-up [ˈbɪlt·ʌp] *adj* ① *area* verbaut ② *heels* erhöht
bulb [bʌlb] *n* ① BOT Zwiebel *f* ② ELEC [Glüh]birne *f*
bulbous [ˈbʌl·bəs] *adj* knollig
Bulgaria [bʌl·ˈger·i·ə] *n* Bulgarien *nt*
Bulgarian [bʌl·ˈger·i·ən] I. *adj* bulgarisch II. *n* ① (*person*) Bulgare, -in *m, f* ② (*language*) Bulgarisch *nt*
bulge [bʌldʒ] I. *n* (*protrusion*) Wölbung *f*; (*in tire*) Wulst *m* II. *vi* sich runden; *eyes* hervortreten
bulging [ˈbʌldʒ·ɪŋ] *adj* ① (*full*) *container* zum Bersten voll; *stomach, wallet* prall gefüllt ② (*protruding*) *eyes* hervorquellend
bulimia [bu·ˈli·mi·ə] *n* Bulimie *f*
bulk [bʌlk] *n* ① (*mass*) Masse *f* ② (*size*) Ausmaß *nt* ③ (*quantity*) **in** ~ in großen Mengen ④ (*largest part*) Großteil *m*; **the** ~ **of the work** die meiste Arbeit
bulk ˈbuying *n* Großeinkauf *m*
bulky [ˈbʌl·ki] *adj* ① *luggage* sperrig ② *person* massig
bull [bʊl] *n* ① (*steer*) Stier *m*; **elephant, walrus also** Bulle *m* ② (*fig*) Bulle *m* ③ STOCKEX Haussier *m* ► PHRASES: **like a** ~ **in a china shop** wie ein Elefant im Porzellanladen; **to be** [**like**] **a red flag to a** ~ [wie] ein rotes Tuch sein
ˈbulldog *n* Bulldogge *f*
bulldoze [ˈbʊl·doʊz] *vt* ① (*level off*) einebnen; (*clear*) räumen; (*tear down*) abreißen ② (*fig*) **to** ~ **through** ⊂ **sth** etw durchboxen
bulldozer [ˈbʊl·doʊ·zər] *n* Bulldozer *m*
bullet [ˈbʊl·ɪt] *n* ① Kugel *f*; ~ **wound** Schusswunde *f* ② TYPO großer Punkt ► PHRASES: **to bite the** ~ in den sauren Apfel beißen
bulletin [ˈbʊl·ə·tɪn] *n* Bulletin *nt*; (*update*) [kurzer] Lagebericht; [**news**] ~ [Kurz]nachrichten *pl*
ˈbulletin board *n* schwarzes Brett, Pinnwand *f*
ˈbullet point *n* Stichpunkt *m*
ˈbulletproof *adj* kugelsicher
ˈbullfight *n* Stierkampf *m*
ˈbullfighter *n* Stierkämpfer(in) *m(f)*
ˈbullfrog *n* Ochsenfrosch *m*
bullion [ˈbʊl·jən] *n* **gold** ~ Goldbarren *pl*
bullock [ˈbʊl·ək] *n* Ochse *m*
ˈbullring *n* Stierkampfarena *f*
ˈbull's eye *n* Zentrum *nt* der Zielscheibe; **to hit the** ~ einen Volltreffer landen *a. fig*
ˈbullshit (*vulg, sl*) I. *n* Schwachsinn *m*; **don't give me that** ~ komm mir nicht mit so 'nem Scheiß *pej derb* II. *vt* <-tt-> verscheißern III. *vi* <-tt-> Scheiß erzählen *pej derb*
bully [ˈbʊl·i] I. *n* Rabauke *m* II. *vt* <-ie-> tyrannisieren; ■**to** ~ **sb into doing sth** jdn so weit einschüchtern, dass er etw tut
bulrush <*pl* -es> [ˈbʊl·rʌʃ] *n* [große] Binse
bulwark [ˈbʊl·wərk] *n* Bollwerk *nt*
bum [bʌm] (*fam*) I. *n* (*good-for-nothing*) Penner(in) *m(f)* II. *adj attr* mies; ~ **steer** Verschaukelung *f* III. *vt* <-mm-> ■**to** ~ **sth off sb** etw von jdm schnorren
◆**bum around** *vi* (*fam*) ① (*hang out*) herumgammeln *fam* ② (*travel*) herumziehen
◆**bum out** *vt* (*fam: disappoint*) ■**to** ~ **sb out** jdm die Stimmung vermiesen *fam*
bumblebee [ˈbʌm·bəl·bi] *n* Hummel *f*
bumbling [ˈbʌm·blɪŋ] *adj* tollpatschig; ~ **idiot** ausgemachter Volltrottel
bummer [ˈbʌm·ər] *n* (*sl*) ■**to be a** ~ saublöd sein *sl*
bump [bʌmp] I. *n* ① (*on head*) Beule *f*; (*in*

road) Unebenheit *f* ❷ (*light blow*) leichter Stoß ❸ (*thud*) Bums *m;* **to go ~** rumsen **II.** *vt* ❶ AUTO zusammenstoßen mit *+dat* ❷ ■ **to ~ oneself** sich [an]stoßen ❸ *usu passive* **to get ~ed from a flight** von der Passagierliste gestrichen werden **III.** *vi* ■ **to ~ along** entlangrumpeln

◆ **bump into** *vi* ■ **to ~ into sb** ❶ (*knock*) mit jdm zusammenstoßen; ■ **to ~ into sth** gegen etw *akk* stoßen ❷ (*fig: meet*) jdm [zufällig] in die Arme laufen

◆ **bump off** *vt* (*fam*) umlegen

bumper ['bʌm·pər] *n* Stoßstange *f;* RAIL Prellbock *m*

'**bumper car** *n* [Auto]skooter *m*

'**bumper sticker** *n* Autoaufkleber *m*

bumpkin ['bʌmp·kɪn] *n* **country ~** Bauerntölpel *m*

bumptious ['bʌmp·ʃəs] *adj* überheblich

bumpy ['bʌm·pi] *adj* holp[e]rig; *flight, ride* unruhig

bun [bʌn] *n* ❶ (*for burger*) Brötchen *nt* (*für Hamburger verwendetes weiches Brötchen*) ❷ (*hair style*) [Haar]knoten *m* ❸ (*fam: buttock*) ■ **~s** Po *m kein pl fam,* Hintern *m kein pl fam*

bunch <*pl* -es> [bʌntʃ] **I.** *n* ❶ (*group*) *of bananas* Büschel *m; of carrots, parsley, keys* Bund *m; of files* Bündel *nt; of flowers* Strauß *m; of people* Haufen *m;* **~ of grapes** Weintraube *f;* **a whole ~ of problems** jede Menge Probleme ❷ (*wad*) **in a ~** aufgebauscht ▶ PHRASES: **to be the best of the ~** der/die/das Beste von allen sein **II.** *vt* bündeln **III.** *vi* sich bauschen

bundle ['bʌn·dəl] **I.** *n* Bündel *nt* **II.** *vt* **to ~ sb into a car** jdn in ein Auto verfrachten

◆ **bundle up** **I.** *vt* bündeln **II.** *vi* sich warm einpacken

bung [bʌŋ] *n* Pfropfen *m*

bungalow ['bʌŋ·gə·loʊ] *n* Bungalow *m*

'**bungee jumping** ['bʌn·ˌdʒi-] *n* Bungeespringen *nt*

bungle ['bʌŋ·gəl] **I.** *vt* verpfuschen **II.** *vi* Mist bauen

bungler ['bʌŋ·gəl·ər] *n* (*pej*) Pfuscher(in) *m(f)*

bungling ['bʌŋ·gəl·ɪŋ] **I.** *n* Stümperei *f* **II.** *adj attr* ungeschickt; **~ idiot** ausgemachter Trottel

bunk [bʌŋk] **I.** *n* ❶ (*in boat*) Koje *f* ❷ (*part of bed*) **bottom/top ~** unteres/oberes Bett (*eines Etagenbetts*) **II.** *vi* (*fam*) ■ **to ~ [down]** sich aufs Ohr legen

'**bunk bed** *n* Etagenbett *nt*

bunker ['bʌŋ·kər] *n* Bunker *m*

bunny ['bʌn·i] *n* Häschen *nt*

'**bunny slope** *n* Anfängerhügel *m*

bunting ['bʌn·tɪŋ] *n* Schmücken *nt* mit Fähnchen

buoy [bɔɪ] **I.** *n* Boje *f* **II.** *vt* ■ **to ~ up ⊂ sb/sth** jdm/etw Auftrieb geben

buoyancy ['bɔɪ·jən·si] *n* Schwimmfähigkeit *f*

buoyant ['bɔɪ·jənt] *adj* ❶ (*able to float*) schwimmfähig ❷ (*cheerful*) **to be in a ~ mood** in bester Stimmung sein ❸ ECON lebhaft

burble ['bɜr·bəl] **I.** *vi water* plätschern **II.** *vt* brabbeln

burden ['bɜr·dən] **I.** *n* ❶ Last *f* ❷ (*fig*) Belastung *f* (**to** für *+akk*) **II.** *vt* ❶ (*load*) beladen ❷ (*bother*) belasten

burdensome ['bɜr·dən·səm] *adj* belastend

bureau <*pl* -x *or* -s> ['bjʊr·oʊ] *n* ❶ (*government department*) Amt *nt,* Behörde *f* ❷ (*office*) [Informations]büro *nt* ❸ (*chest of drawers*) Kommode *f*

bureaucracy [bjʊ·'rak·rə·si] *n* Bürokratie *f*

bureaucrat ['bjʊr·ə·kræt] *n* Bürokrat(in) *m(f)*

bureaucratic [ˌbjʊr·ə·'kræṭ·ɪk] *adj* bürokratisch

burger ['bɜr·gər] *n short for* **hamburger** [Ham]burger *m*

burglar ['bɜr·glər] *n* Einbrecher(in) *m(f)*

'**burglar alarm** *n* Alarmanlage *f*

burglarize ['bɜr·glə·raɪz] *vt* einbrechen in *+akk*

burglary ['bɜr·glə·ri] *n* Einbruch[diebstahl] *m*

burgundy ['bɜr·gən·di] **I.** *n* ❶ (*red wine*) Burgunder *m* ❷ (*red color*) Burgunderrot *nt* **II.** *adj* (*dark red*) burgunderrot

burial ['ber·i·əl] *n* Beerdigung *f;* **~ at sea** Seebestattung *f*

'**burial ground** *n* Friedhof *m*

burlap ['bɜr·læp] *n* Sackleinen *nt*

burlesque [bɜr·'lesk] *n* ❶ (*written*) Parodie *f* ❷ (*genre*) Burleske *f*

burly ['bɜr·li] *adj* kräftig [gebaut]

burn [bɜrn] **I.** *n* ❶ (*injury*) Verbrennung *f,* Brandwunde *f;* (*sunburn*) Sonnenbrand *m* ❷ (*damage*) Brandfleck *m* **II.** *vi* <burned *or* burnt, burned *or* burnt> ❶ (*be in flames*) brennen; *house* in Flammen stehen; **to ~ to death** verbrennen ❷ FOOD anbrennen ❸ (*sunburn*) einen Sonnenbrand bekommen **III.** *vt* <burned *or* burnt, burned *or* burnt> ❶ (*damage with heat*) verbrennen; *village* niederbrennen; **I ~t my tongue** ich habe mir die Zunge verbrannt; **to ~ one's fingers** (*a. fig*) sich *dat* die Finger verbrennen ❷ FOOD anbrennen lassen ❸ (*use up*) *calories* verbrennen; *oil* verbrauchen ❹ COMPUT brennen

◆ **burn away** **I.** *vi* herunterbrennen; (*continuously*) vor sich hinbrennen **II.** *vt* abbrennen

◆ **burn down** **I.** *vt* abbrennen **II.** *vi building* niederbrennen; *forest* abbrennen; *candle, fire* herunterbrennen

◆ **burn out** **I.** *vi* ❶ *fire, candle* herunterbrennen ❷ *rocket* ausbrennen ❸ *bulb* durchbrennen; (*slowly*) durchschmoren **II.** *vt* ❶ (*stop burning*) **the candle ~ed itself out** die Kerze brannte herunter ❷ (*person*) ■ **to ~ [oneself] out** sich völlig verausgaben

◆ **burn up** **I.** *vi* ❶ verbrennen ❷ (*fig: be feverish*) glühen ❸ *rocket* verglühen **II.** *vt* verbrauchen; *calories* verbrennen

burner ['bɜr·nər] *n* Brenner *m;* (*on stove*) Kochplatte *f*

burning ['bɜr·nɪŋ] **I.** *adj* ❶ (*on fire, stinging*)

brennend; *face* glühend ❷ (*fig: intense*) brennend ❸ (*controversial*) *issue* heiß diskutiert; *question* brennend **II.** *n* **there's a smell of ~** es riecht verbrannt
'burnout *n* ausgebrannter Mensch
burnt [bɜrnt] **I.** *vt, vi pt, pp of* **burn II.** *adj* (*completely*) verbrannt; (*partly*) *food* angebrannt; (*from sun*) verbrannt
burp [bɜrp] **I.** *n* Rülpser *m; of baby* Bäuerchen *nt* **II.** *vi* aufstoßen, rülpsen *fam; baby* ein Bäuerchen machen **III.** *vt baby* aufstoßen lassen
burr [bɜr] *n* BOT Klette *f*
burrow ['bɜr·oʊ] **I.** *n* Bau *m* **II.** *vt* graben **III.** *vi* einen Bau graben
bursar ['bɜr·sər] *n* Finanzverwalter(in) *m(f)*
burst [bɜrst] **I.** *n* **~ of speed** Spurt *m;* **~ of activity** plötzliche Geschäftigkeit **II.** *vi* <burst, burst> ❶ (*explode*) platzen *a. fig; bubble* zerplatzen; *dam* bersten ❷ (*fig*) ■ **to be ~ing to do sth** darauf brennen, etw zu tun ❸ (*be full*) *suitcase* zum Bersten voll sein; **to be ~ing with pride** vor Stolz platzen; **to be ~ing with energy** vor Kraft [nur so] strotzen **III.** *vt* <burst, burst> zum Platzen bringen; *balloon* platzen lassen; **the river ~ its banks** der Fluss trat über die Ufer
◆**burst in** *vi* herein-/hineinstürzen; **to ~ in on a meeting** in eine Versammlung hineinplatzen
◆**burst out** *vi* ❶ (*hurry out*) herausstürzen ❷ **to ~ out crying/laughing** in Tränen/Gelächter ausbrechen ❸ (*speak*) ■ **to ~ out with sth** mit etw losplatzen
◆**burst through** *vi* durchbrechen
bury <-ie-> ['ber·i] *vt person* begraben; *thing* vergraben *a. fig*
bus [bʌs] **I.** *n* <*pl* -es *or* -ses> [Omni]bus *m;* **to go by ~** mit dem Bus fahren **II.** *vt* <-ss- *or* -s-> mit dem Bus befördern
'busboy *n* Abräumer *m,* Hilfskellner *m*
'bus driver *n* Busfahrer(in) *m(f)*
bush <*pl* -es> [bʊʃ] *n* ❶ Busch *m;* **in the ~es** im Gebüsch *nt* ❷ (*in Africa, Australia*) Busch *m* ► PHRASES: **to beat about the ~** um den heißen Brei herumreden
bushel ['bʊʃ·əl] *n* ► PHRASES: **to hide one's light under a ~** sein Licht unter den Scheffel stellen
'Bushman *n see* **San**
bushy ['bʊʃ·i] *adj* buschig
busily ['bɪz·ɪ·li] *adv* eifrig; **~ working on sth** intensiv mit etw *dat* beschäftigt
business <*pl* -es> ['bɪz·nɪs] *n* ❶ (*commerce*) Handel *m;* **to do ~ with sb** mit jdm Geschäfte machen; **to go out of ~** das Geschäft aufgeben; **on ~** beruflich, dienstlich, geschäftlich ❷ (*profession*) Branche *f* ❸ (*company*) Unternehmen *nt* ❹ (*matter*) Angelegenheit *f;* **that's none of your ~** das geht dich nichts an; **to have no ~ doing sth** nicht das Recht haben, etw zu tun ► PHRASES: **~ before pleasure** (*prov*) erst die Arbeit, dann das Vergnügen; **to get down to ~** zur Sache kommen
'business address *n* Geschäftsadresse *f*
'business card *n* Visitenkarte *f*
'business class *n* Businessclass *f*
'business hours *npl* Geschäftszeiten *pl*
'business letter *n* Geschäftsbrief *m*
'businesslike *adj* geschäftsmäßig
'businessman *n* Geschäftsmann *m*
'business park *n* Industriepark *m*
'business trip *n* Dienstreise *f,* Geschäftsreise *f*
'businesswoman *n* Geschäftsfrau *f*
'busload *n* Busladung *f*
'bus station *n* Busbahnhof *m*
'bus stop *n* Bushaltestelle *f*
bust[1] [bʌst] *n* ❶ (*statue*) Büste *f* ❷ (*breasts*) Büste *f;* (*measurement*) Oberweite *f*
bust[2] [bʌst] (*fam*) **I.** *n* ❶ (*recession*) [wirtschaftlicher] Niedergang ❷ (*raid*) Razzia *f* **II.** *adj* ❶ (*broken*) kaputt ❷ (*bankrupt*) **to go ~** Pleite machen **III.** *vt* <bust *or* busted, bust *or* busted> ❶ (*break*) kaputtmachen ❷ (*arrest*) festnehmen
bustle ['bʌs·əl] **I.** *n* Getriebe *nt* **II.** *vi* **the street ~d with activity** auf der Straße herrschte reger Betrieb; ■ **to ~ about** herumwuseln
bustling ['bʌs·əl·ɪŋ] *adj place* belebt
busy ['bɪz·i] **I.** *adj* ❶ (*occupied*) beschäftigt; **I'm very ~ this week** ich habe diese Woche viel zu tun; **to keep oneself ~** sich beschäftigen ❷ (*active*) *day* arbeitsreich; *life* bewegt; *street* verkehrsreich; **the busiest time of year** die Jahreszeit, in der am meisten los ist ❸ TELEC besetzt **II.** *vt* <-ie-> ■ **to ~ oneself with sth** sich mit etw *dat* beschäftigen
'busybody *n* Wichtigtuer(in) *m(f)*
'busy signal *n* TELEC Besetztzeichen *nt*
but [bʌt] **I.** *conj* ❶ (*although, however*) aber; **~ [then,] I'm no expert** ich bin allerdings keine Expertin ❷ (*except*) als ❸ (*rather*) sondern; **not only ... ~ also ...** nicht nur[,] ... sondern auch ... **II.** *prep* außer; **nothing ~ trouble** nichts als Ärger **III.** *n* **no [ifs, ands, or] ~s about it** da gibt es kein Wenn und Aber ► PHRASES: **~ for** bis auf; **~ for the storm, ...** wäre der Sturm nicht gewesen, ...
butane ['bju·teɪn] *n* Butan[gas] *nt*
butch [bʊtʃ] *adj* maskulin
butcher ['bʊtʃ·ər] **I.** *n* Metzger(in) *m(f)* **II.** *vt* ❶ (*slaughter*) schlachten ❷ (*murder*) niedermetzeln ❸ (*screw up*) *one's lines* verpfuschen, verhauen
butchery ['bʊtʃ·ə·ri] *n* Abschlachten *nt*
butler ['bʌt·lər] *n* Butler *m*
butt [bʌt] **I.** *n* ❶ *of rifle* Kolben *m; of cigarette* Stummel *m* ❷ (*fam*) Hintern *m;* **to get off one's ~** seinen Hintern in Bewegung setzen ❸ (*hit with head*) Stoß *m* [mit dem Kopf] **II.** *vt* ■ **to ~ sb/sth** jdm/etw einen Stoß mit dem Kopf versetzen **III.** *vi person* mit dem Kopf stoßen; *goat* mit den Hörnern stoßen
butter ['bʌt̬·ər] **I.** *n* Butter *f* **II.** *vt* mit Butter bestreichen
◆**butter up** *vt* ■ **to ~ up** ↻ **sb** jdm Honig um

B

den Bart schmieren

'buttercup *n* Butterblume *f*

'butter dish *n* Butterdose *f*

'butterfingers <*pl* -> *n* (*fam*) Tollpatsch *m*

butterfly ['bʌt̬·ər·flaɪ] *n* ❶ Schmetterling *m* ❷ (*in swimming*) Butterfly *m* ► PHRASES: **to <u>have</u> butterflies** [**in one's stomach**] ein flaues Gefühl [im Magen] haben

'buttermilk *n* Buttermilch *f*

buttery ['bʌt̬·ə·ri] *adj* butt[e]rig

buttock ['bʌt̬·ək] *n* [Hinter]backe *f;* ■ **~s** *pl* Gesäß *nt*

button ['bʌt·ən] **I.** *n* ❶ Knopf *m* ❷ (*badge*) Button *m* ► PHRASES: **at the <u>push</u> of a ~** auf Knopfdruck; **to be <u>right</u> on the ~** den Nagel auf den Kopf treffen **II.** *vt garment* zuknöpfen **III.** *vi* **to ~ down the front/the back** sich vorn/hinten knöpfen lassen

◆**button up** *vt garment* zuknöpfen

'buttonhole I. *n* Knopfloch *nt* **II.** *vt* (*fam*) zu fassen kriegen

buttress <*pl* -es> ['bʌt·rɪs] **I.** *n* ARCHIT Strebepfeiler *m* **II.** *vt argument* untermauern

buxom ['bʌk·səm] *adj* vollbusig

buy [baɪ] **I.** *n* Kauf *m* **II.** *vt* <bought, bought> ❶ ■ **to ~ sb sth** [*or* **sth for sb**] jdm etw kaufen; ■ **to ~ sth from** [*or fam,* **off**] **sb** jdm etw abkaufen; *silence* erkaufen; *time* gewinnen ❷ (*fam: believe*) abkaufen

◆**buy off** *vt* kaufen, bestechen

◆**buy out** *vt company* aufkaufen; *person* auszahlen

◆**buy up** *vt* aufkaufen

buyer ['baɪ·ər] *n* Käufer(in) *m(f);* (*as job*) Einkäufer(in) *m(f)*

'buyout *n* Übernahme *f*

buzz [bʌz] **I.** *vi bee, buzzer* summen; *fly* brummen; *ears* dröhnen; **the room was ~ing with conversation** das Zimmer war von Stimmengewirr erfüllt **II.** *vt* (*fam: telephone*) anrufen **III.** *n* <*pl* -es> ❶ *of bee, buzzer* Summen *nt; of fly* Brummen *nt;* **~ of conversation** Stimmengewirr *nt* ❷ (*fam: call*) **to give sb a ~** jdn anrufen ❸ (*fam: high feeling*) Kick *m;* (*from alcohol*) Rausch *m*

◆**buzz off** *vi* (*fam*) abzischen

buzzard ['bʌz·ərd] *n* (*vulture*) Truthahngeier *m*

buzzer ['bʌz·ər] *n* Summer *m*

'buzzword *n* Schlagwort *nt*

by [baɪ] **I.** *prep* ❶ (*beside*) neben +*akk/dat;* **come and sit ~ me** komm und setz dich zu mir ❷ (*not later than*) bis +*akk;* **~ February 14**[**th**] [spätestens] bis zum 14.02.; **~ now** [*or* **this time**] inzwischen ❸ (*during*) bei +*dat;* **~ day/night** tagsüber/nachts ❹ (*happening progressively*) **little ~ little** nach und nach; **day ~ day** Tag für Tag ❺ (*agent*) von +*dat;* **a painting ~ Picasso** ein Gemälde von Picasso ❻ (*by means of*) durch +*akk,* mit +*dat;* **you turn it on ~ pressing this button** man schaltet es ein, indem man auf diesen Knopf drückt; **~ hand** mit der Hand; **~ boat/bus** mit dem Schiff/Bus; **~ chance** durch Zufall; **~ check** mit einem Scheck; **~ contrast** im Gegensatz; **to travel ~ sea** auf dem Seeweg reisen ❼ (*quantity*) **~ the hour** stundenweise; **~ the foot** fußweise; **~ the thousand** zu Tausenden ❽ (*margin*) um +*akk;* **to go up ~ 20%** um 20 % steigen **II.** *adv* ❶ (*past*) vorbei; **excuse me, I can't get ~** Entschuldigung, ich komme nicht vorbei ❷ **close ~** ganz in der Nähe ► PHRASES: **~ and <u>large</u>** im Großen und Ganzen; **~ <u>oneself</u>** (*alone*) allein; (*unaided*) selbst

bye [baɪ] *interj* (*fam*) tschüs

bye-bye [ˌbaɪ·'baɪ] *interj* (*fam*) tschüs

'bygone I. *adj attr* vergangen **II.** *n* ► PHRASES: **to <u>let</u> ~s be ~s** die Vergangenheit ruhen lassen

'bylaw *n* Gemeindeverordnung *f*

'bypass I. *n* ❶ TRANSP Umgehungsstraße *f* ❷ MED Bypass *m* **II.** *vt* ❶ (*detour*) umfahren ❷ (*not consult*) übergehen

'byproduct *n* Nebenprodukt *nt;* (*fig*) Begleiterscheinung *f*

'bystander *n* Zuschauer(in) *m(f)*

byte [baɪt] *n* COMPUT Byte *nt*

'byway *n* Nebenstraße *f,* Seitenweg *m*

'byword *n* Musterbeispiel *nt*

C c

C <*pl* -'s *or* -s>, **c** <*pl* -'s> [siː] *n* ① (*letter*) C *nt*, c *nt*; **~ as in Charlie** C wie Cäsar ② MUS C *nt*, c *nt*; **~ flat** ces *nt*, Ces *nt*; **~ sharp** Cis *nt*, cis *nt* ③ (*school grade*) ≈ Drei *f*; **to get a ~** eine Drei schreiben

C *after n abbrev of* **Celsius** C

CA *abbrev of* **California**

ca. *abbrev of* **circa** ca.

cab [kæb] *n* ① (*taxi*) Taxi *nt* ② (*of a truck*) Führerhaus *nt*

cabaret [ˌkæb·ə·'reɪ] *n* (*performance*) Varietee *nt*

cabbage ['kæb·ɪdʒ] *n* Kohl *m kein pl*, Kraut *nt kein pl bes* SÜDD

cabbie, cabby ['kæb·i], **'cabdriver** *n* Taxifahrer(in) *m(f)*

cabin ['kæb·ɪn] *n* ① (*wooden house*) [Block]hütte *f*; (*for vacation*) Ferienhütte *f* ② (*on ship*) Kabine *f*

cabinet ['kæb·ɪ·nɪt] *n* ① (*storage place*) Schrank *m* ② POL Kabinett *nt*

cable ['keɪ·bəl] *n* ① ELEC [Leitungs]kabel *nt*, Leitung *f* ② NAUT Tau *nt* ③ TV Kabelfernsehen *nt* ④ TELEC Telegramm *nt*

'cable car *n* Drahtseilbahn *f*; (*on street*) Kabelbahn *f*

'cable network *n* TV Kabelnetz *nt*

cable 'television, cable T'V *n* Kabelfernsehen *nt*

cache [kæʃ] *n* ① (*hiding place*) Versteck *nt*; **~ of weapons** geheimes Waffenlager ② COMPUT Cache *m*

cachet [kæ·'ʃeɪ] *n* Ansehen *nt*

cackle ['kæk·əl] **I.** *vi* gackern **II.** *n* ① (*chicken noise*) Gackern *nt kein pl* ② (*laughter*) Gegacker *nt*

cacophony [kə·'kaf·ə·ni] *n* (*form*) Missklang *m*

cactus <*pl* -es *or* cacti> ['kæk·təs] *n* Kaktus *m*

CAD [kæd] *n abbrev of* **computer-aided design** CAD *nt*

cadaver [kə·'dæv·ər] *n* (*form*) *of humans* Leiche *f*

caddie, caddy ['kæd·i] **I.** *n* Caddie *m* **II.** *vi* ■**to ~ for sb** jds Caddie sein

cadence ['keɪd·əns] *n* Tonfall *m*; (*rhythm*) Rhythmus *m*

cadet [kə·'det] *n* MIL Kadett *m*

Caesarean [sɪ·'ze·ri·ən] MED **I.** *adj* **~ section** Kaiserschnitt *m* **II.** *n* Kaiserschnitt *m*

café, cafe [kæ·'feɪ] *n* Café *nt*

cafeteria [ˌkæf·ɪ·'tɪr·i·ə] *n* Cafeteria *f*; UNIV Mensa *f*

caffeine [kæf·'in] *n* Koffein *nt*

cage [keɪdʒ] *n* Käfig *m*

cagey ['keɪ·dʒi] *adj* (*fam: secretive*) verschlossen

cajole [kə·'dʒoʊl] *vt* beschwatzen

cake [keɪk] **I.** *n* ① (*in baking*) Kuchen *m*; (*layered*) Torte *f* ② (*patty*) Küchlein *nt*; **fish ~** Fischfrikadelle *f* ▶ PHRASES: **a piece of ~** (*fam*) ein Klacks **II.** *vt* **~d with mud** dreckverkrustet

cal. *n abbrev of* **calorie** cal

calamity [kə·'læm·ə·ti] *n* Katastrophe *f*

calcium ['kæl·si·əm] *n* Kalzium *nt*

calculate ['kæl·kjə·leɪt] **I.** *vt* berechnen; (*estimate*) veranschlagen **II.** *vi* ■**to ~ [on sth]** [mit etw *dat*] rechnen

calculated ['kæl·kjə·leɪ·t̬ɪd] *adj* beabsichtigt; *risk* kalkuliert

calculating ['kæl·kjə·leɪ·t̬ɪŋ] *adj* berechnend

calculation [ˌkæl·kjə·'leɪ·ʃən] *n* ① MATH Berechnung *f*; **to do ~s** rechnen; (*estimate*) Schätzung *f* ② (*process*) Rechnen *nt* ③ (*pej: selfish planning*) Berechnung *f*

calculator ['kæl·kjə·leɪ·t̬ər] *n* Rechner *m*

calendar ['kæl·ən·dər] *n* Kalender *m*

calf <*pl* calves> [kæf] *n* ① (*animal*) Kalb *nt* ② ANAT Wade *f*

caliber ['kæl·ə·bər] *n* ① (*diameter*) Kaliber *nt* ② (*quality*) Niveau *nt*

Calif. *abbrev of* **California**

California [ˌkæl·ə·'fɔr·njə] *n* Kalifornien *nt*

call [kɔl] **I.** *n* ① (*on the telephone*) [Telefon]anruf *m*, [Telefon]gespräch *nt*; **to make a ~** telefonieren ② (*visit*) Besuch *m*; *of a doctor, nurse*; **house ~** Hausbesuch *m* ③ (*request to come*) **to be on ~** Bereitschaftsdienst haben ④ (*shout*) Ruf *m*; **a ~ for help** ein Hilferuf *m* ⑤ (*summoning*) Aufruf *m* (**for** zu +*dat*) **II.** *vt* ① (*on the telephone*) anrufen; ■**to ~ sb back** jdn zurückrufen ② (*name*) nennen; **what's that animal ~ed again?** wie heißt dieses Tier nochmal?; **to ~ sb names** jdn beschimpfen ③ (*summon*) [auf]rufen; **to ~ a doctor** einen Arzt kommen lassen; **to ~ sb into a room** jdn in ein Zimmer bitten ④ (*bring*) **to ~ attention to oneself** auf sich aufmerksam machen; **to ~ into question** in Frage stellen ⑤ LAW *witness* aufrufen; **to ~ sb as a witness** jdn als Zeugen benennen **III.** *vi* ① (*shout*) rufen; *animal* schreien; ■**to ~ to sb** jdm zurufen; **to ~ for sb** jdn rufen ② (*telephone*) anrufen; **who's ~ing, please?** wer ist am Apparat? ③ (*drop by*) vorbeischauen; (*return*) wiederkommen

◆**call away** *vt* wegrufen

◆**call back I.** *vt* zurückrufen **II.** *vi* zurückrufen

◆**call for** *vi* ① (*order*) *taxi, food* kommen lassen, bestellen ② (*shout*) **to ~ for help** um Hilfe rufen ③ (*demand*) **this ~s for a celebration** das muss gefeiert werden

◆**call in I.** *vt* ① (*consult*) *specialist, expert* hinzuziehen; (*ask to come*) kommen lassen ② (*report*) *results, score* ■**to ~ in** ↔ **sth** etw *akk* telefonisch durchgeben **II.** *vi* sich telefonisch melden; **to ~ in sick** sich telefonisch krankmelden

C

◆**call off** *vt* ❶ (*cancel*) *engagement* absagen; (*stop*) abbrechen ❷ (*order back*) *dog* zurückrufen
◆**call on** *vt* ■**to ~ on sb to do sth** jdn dazu auffordern, etw zu tun
◆**call out** *vt* ❶ (*shout*) rufen; **to ~ out ↻ sth to sb** jdm etw zurufen; ■**to ~ out ↻ sb's name** jdn [*o* jds Namen] aufrufen ❷ (*summon*) *fire department* alarmieren ❸ **to ~ sb out on strike** jdn zum Streik aufrufen
◆**call over** *vt* ■**to ~ sb over** jdn zu sich herüber-/hinüberrufen
◆**call up** *vt* ❶ (*telephone*) anrufen ❷ COMPUT aufrufen ❸ MIL einberufen
◆**call upon** *vi* ❶ (*appeal to*) ■**to ~ upon sb to do sth** jdn dazu auffordern, etw zu tun ❷ (*use*) in Anspruch nehmen; *courage* zusammennehmen
caller ['kɔ·lər] *n* ❶ (*on telephone*) Anrufer(in) *m(f)* ❷ (*visitor*) Besucher(in) *m(f)*
calligraphy [kə·'lɪg·rə·fi] *n* Kalligraphie *f*
'**call-in** *adj* **~ show** *Sendung, bei der sich das Publikum telefonisch beteiligen kann*
calling ['kɔ·lɪŋ] *n* ❶ (*profession*) Beruf *m* ❷ (*inner impulse*) Berufung *f*
'**calling card** *n* ❶ (*personal*) Visitenkarte *f*, Visitkarte *f* ÖSTERR ❷ TELEC *see* **phone card**
callous ['kæl·əs] *adj* hartherzig
calm [kam] **I.** *adj* ruhig **II.** *n* ❶ (*calmness*) Ruhe *f* ❷ METEO Windstille *f* ▶ PHRASES: **the ~ before the storm** die Ruhe vor dem Sturm **III.** *vt* beruhigen
◆**calm down** *vi, vt* beruhigen
calmness ['kalm·nɪs] *n* Ruhe *f*
calorie ['kæl·ə·ri] *n* Kalorie *f*; **low in ~s** kalorienarm
Cambodia [kæm·'boʊ·di·ə] *n* Kambodscha *nt*
camcorder ['kæm·kɔr·dər] *n* Camcorder *m*
came [keɪm] *vi pt of* **come**
camel ['kæm·əl] *n* Kamel *nt*
cameo <*pl* -os> ['kæm·i·oʊ] *n* ❶ (*stone*) Kamee *f* ❷ FILM Miniaturrolle *f*
camera ['kæm·ər·ə] *n* Kamera *f*
'**cameraman** *n* Kameramann *m*
'**camera-shy** *adj* kamerascheu
'**camerawoman** *n* Kamerafrau *f*
camomile ['kæm·ə·mil] *n* Kamille *f*
camouflage ['kæm·ə·ˌflaʒ] **I.** *n* (*a. fig*) Tarnung *f* **II.** *vt* (*a. fig*) tarnen
camp¹ [kæmp] **I.** *n* MIL [Feld]lager *nt*; **prison ~** Gefangenenlager *nt* **II.** *vi* ■**to ~ [out]** zelten; **to go ~ing** campen gehen
camp² [kæmp] *adj* ❶ (*pej: theatrical*) manieriert ❷ (*effeminate*) tuntenhaft
campaign [kæm·'peɪn] **I.** *n* ❶ Kampagne *f* ❷ (*for election*) [**election**] **~** Wahlkampf *m*; **~ pledge** Wahlversprechen *nt* ❸ MIL Feldzug *m* **II.** *vi* kämpfen, sich engagieren
campaigner [kæm·'peɪ·nər] *n* ❶ (*in election*) Wahlwerber(in) *m(f)* ❷ (*advocate*) Kämpfer(in) *m(f)*; **environmental ~** Umweltschützer(in) *m(f)*
camper ['kæm·pər] *n* ❶ (*person*) Camper(in) *m(f)* ❷ (*vehicle*) Wohnmobil *nt*
'**campfire** *n* Lagerfeuer *nt*
'**campground** *n* Campingplatz *m*
camping ['kæm·pɪŋ] *n* Camping *nt*; **to go ~** zelten gehen
'**campsite** *n* Campingplatz *m*
campus ['kæm·pəs] *n* Campus *m*; **on ~** auf dem Campus
can¹ <could, could> [kæn] *aux vb* (*be able to*) können; (*be allowed to*) dürfen; (*less formal*) können; **~ you hear me?** kannst du mich hören?, hörst du mich?; **you ~'t park here** hier dürfen [*o* können] Sie nicht parken; **you could [always] try** du könntest es ja mal versuchen; **you ~'t [*or* cannot] be serious!** das ist nicht dein Ernst!; **who ~ blame her?** wer will es ihr verdenken?; **no ~ do** tut mir leid
can² [kən] **I.** *n* ❶ (*container*) Dose *f*, Büchse *f*; **gasoline ~** Benzinkanister *m*; *of paint* Farbtopf *m* ❷ (*sl: bathroom*) Klo *nt* ▶ PHRASES: **in the ~** FILM im Kasten; **a ~ of worms** eine verzwickte Angelegenheit **II.** *vt* <-nn-> eindosen, in Dosen konservieren; *fruit* einmachen
Canada ['kæn·ə·də] *n* Kanada *nt*
Canadian [kə·'neɪ·di·ən] **I.** *n* Kanadier(in) *m(f)* **II.** *adj* kanadisch
canal [kə·'næl] *n* Kanal *m*
canary [kə·'ner·i] *n* Kanarienvogel *m*
Ca'nary Islands *npl* Kanarische Inseln
cancel <-l- *or* -ll-> ['kæn·səl] **I.** *vt* ❶ (*call off*) absagen; (*while in progress*) *game* abbrechen ❷ (*remove from schedule*) streichen ❸ (*annul*) annullieren; *check, reservation* stornieren; (*revoke*) *privileges* widerrufen ❹ (*discontinue*) beenden; *subscription* kündigen; COMPUT abbrechen **II.** *vi* absagen
cancellation [ˌkæn·sə·'leɪ·ʃən] *n* ❶ (*calling off*) Absage *f* ❷ (*from schedule*) Streichung *f* ❸ (*annulling*) Annullierung *f*; (*revocation*) Widerruf *m* ❹ (*discontinuation*) Kündigung *f*; *of a subscription* Abbestellung *f* ❺ FIN Stornierung *f*
cancer ['kæn·sər] *n* ❶ (*a. fig: disease*) Krebs *m*; **stomach ~** Magenkrebs *m*; **~ research** Krebsforschung *f* ❷ (*growth*) Krebsgeschwulst *f*
Cancer ['kæn·sər] *n* Krebs *m*
cancerous ['kæn·sər·əs] *adj* krebsartig
candelabra <*pl* - *or* -s> [ˌkæn·dəl·'a·brə] *n* Leuchter *m*
candid ['kæn·dɪd] *adj* offen
candidate ['kæn·dɪ·dət] *n* ❶ POL, SCH Kandidat(in) *m(f)* ❷ (*possible choice*) [möglicher] Kandidat
candied ['kæn·dɪd] *adj* kandiert
candle ['kæn·dəl] *n* Kerze *f* ▶ PHRASES: **to burn the ~ at both ends** Raubbau mit seiner Gesundheit treiben
'**candlelight** *n* Kerzenlicht *nt*
'**candlestick** *n* Kerzenständer *m*
candor ['kæn·dər] *n* Offenheit *f*
candy ['kæn·di] *n* Süßigkeiten *pl*; (*piece*) Bonbon *m o nt*

'candy bar *n* Schokoriegel *m*
'candy store *n* Süßwarenladen *m*
cane [keɪn] **I.** *n* ❶ (*of plant*) Rohr *nt;* ~ **sugar** Rohrzucker *m* ❷ (*stick*) [Rohr]stock *m* **II.** *vt* [mit einem Stock] züchtigen
canine ['keɪ·naɪn] *adj* (*of dogs*) Hunde-
canister ['kæn·ɪ·stər] *n* Behälter *m;* (*for oil, gasoline*) Kanister *m*
cannabis ['kæn·ə·bɪs] *n* Cannabis *m*
canned [kænd] *adj* FOOD Dosen-, konserviert; ~ **milk** Dosenmilch *f*
cannibal ['kæn·ɪ·bəl] *n* Kannibale *m,* Kannibalin *f*
cannibalism ['kæn·ɪ·bəl·ɪz·əm] *n* Kannibalismus *m*
canning ['kæn·ɪŋ] *n* Konservierung *f;* ~ **factory** Konservenfabrik *f*
cannon ['kæn·ən] *n* MIL Kanone *f*
'cannonball *n* Kanonenkugel *f*
'cannon fodder *n* Kanonenfutter *nt*
cannot ['kæn·at] *aux vb* = **can not** *see* **can**
canoe [kə·'nu] *n* Kanu *nt*
canoeing [kə·'nu·ɪŋ] *n* Paddeln *nt;* SPORTS Kanufahren *nt*
canoeist [kə·'nu·ɪst] *n* Kanufahrer(in) *m(f)*
canon¹ ['kæn·ən] *n* Grundregel *f*
canon² ['kæn·ən] *n* (*priest*) Kanoniker *m*
canonize ['kæn·ə·naɪz] *vt* heiligsprechen
'can opener *n* Dosenöffner *m*
canopy ['kæn·ə·pi] *n* ❶ (*awning*) Überdachung *f;* (*over throne, bed*) Baldachin *m* ❷ (*sunshade*) Sonnendach *nt*
can't [kænt] (*fam*) = **cannot** *see* **can**
cantaloupe ['kæn·t̬ə·loʊp] *n* Honigmelone *f*
cantankerous [kæn·'tæŋ·kər·əs] *adj* streitsüchtig
canteen [kæn·'tin] *n* (*flask*) Feldflasche
canter ['kæn·t̬ər] **I.** *n* (*gait*) Handgalopp *m* **II.** *vi* leicht galoppieren
cantilever ['kæn·t̬əl·i·vər] *n* ~ **bridge** Auslegerbrücke *f*
canvas <*pl* -es> ['kæn·vəs] *n* ❶ (*cloth*) Segeltuch *nt;* (*for painting*) Leinwand *f* ❷ (*painting*) [Öl]gemälde *nt*
canvass ['kæn·vəs] **I.** *vt* ❶ (*poll*) befragen ❷ POL werben **II.** *vi* POL ~ **for votes** um Stimmen werben
canvassing ['kæn·və·sɪŋ] *n* POL Wahlwerbung *f*
canyon ['kæn·jən] *n* Schlucht *f*
cap [kæp] **I.** *n* ❶ (*hat*) Mütze *f,* Kappe *f* ❷ (*top*) Verschlusskappe *f;* (*on tooth*) Schutzkappe *f;* **lens** ~ PHOT Objektivdeckel *m* ❸ (*limit*) Obergrenze *f* **II.** *vt* <-pp-> ❶ (*limit*) begrenzen ❷ (*cover*) bedecken; *teeth* überkronen
capability [ˌkeɪ·pə·'bɪl·ɪ·ti] *n* Fähigkeit *f*
capable ['keɪ·pə·bəl] *adj* ❶ (*competent*) fähig; *worker* tüchtig ❷ (*able*) fähig; ■ **to be ~ of doing sth** in der Lage sein, etw zu tun
capacity [kə·'pæs·ɪ·ti] *n* ❶ (*available space*) Fassungsvermögen *nt* ❷ (*maximum*) Kapazität *f;* **at full** ~ voll ausgelastet; **a ~ crowd** ein volles Haus ❸ (*position*) Funktion *f;* (*role*) Eigenschaft *f*
cape¹ [keɪp] *n* Umhang *m,* Cape *nt*
cape² [keɪp] *n* Kap *nt;* **C~ Horn** Kap Hoorn
caper¹ ['keɪ·pər] *n* (*sl: dubious activity*) krumme Sache, Ding
caper² ['keɪ·pər] *n usu pl* FOOD Kaper *f*
capillary ['kæp·ə·ler·i] *n* Kapillare *f*
capital ['kæp·ɪ·təl] *n* ❶ (*city*) Hauptstadt *f* ❷ (*letter*) Großbuchstabe *m* ❸ FIN Kapital *nt*
capital 'assets *npl* FIN Kapitalvermögen *nt kein pl*
capital 'city *n* Hauptstadt *f*
capital 'crime *n* Kapitalverbrechen *nt*
capital 'gains tax *n* Kapitalgewinnsteuer *f*
capital in'vestment *n* FIN Kapitalanlage *f*
capitalism ['kæp·ɪ·təl·ɪz·əm] *n* Kapitalismus *m*
capitalist ['kæp·ɪ·təl·ɪst] **I.** *n* Kapitalist(in) *m(f)* **II.** *adj* kapitalistisch
capitalization [ˌkæp·ɪ·təl·ɪ·'zeɪ·ʃən] *n* ❶ LING Großschreibung *f* ❷ FIN Kapitalisierung *f*
capitalize ['kæp·ɪ·tə·laɪz] *vt* ❶ LING großschreiben ❷ FIN kapitalisieren
capital 'letter *n* Großbuchstabe *m*
capital 'punishment *n* Todesstrafe *f*
Capitol ['kæ·pə·t̬əl] *n* ■ **the** ~ das Kapitol
Capitol 'Hill *n* Capitol Hill; **on** ~ im amerikanischen Kongress
capitulate [kə·'pɪtʃ·ə·leɪt] *vi* kapitulieren (**to** vor +*dat*)
capitulation [kə·ˌpɪtʃ·ə·'leɪ·ʃən] *n* Kapitulation *f* (**to** vor +*dat*)
cappuccino <*pl* -s> [ˌkæp·ə·'tʃi·noʊ] *n* Cappuccino *m*
capricious [kə·'prɪʃ·əs] *adj* (*liter*) *person* launisch
Capricorn ['kæp·rɪ·kɔrn] *n* Steinbock *m*
capsize ['kæp·saɪz] NAUT **I.** *vi* kentern **II.** *vt* zum Kentern bringen
capsule ['kæp·səl] *n* Kapsel *f*
captain ['kæp·tɪn] **I.** *n* Kapitän(in) *m(f);* (*in army*) Hauptmann *m* **II.** *vt* anführen; MIL befehligen
caption ['kæp·ʃən] *n* ❶ (*under illustration*) Bildunterschrift *f* ❷ TV, FILM (*for the hearing-impaired*) Untertitel *m* ❸ (*heading*) Überschrift *f*
captivate ['kæp·tə·veɪt] *vt* faszinieren
captive ['kæp·tɪv] **I.** *n* Gefangene(r) *f(m)* **II.** *adj* gefangen; **be taken** ~ gefangen genommen werden
captivity [kæp·'tɪv·ɪ·ti] *n* Gefangenschaft *f*
capture ['kæp·tʃər] **I.** *vt* ❶ (*take prisoner*) gefangen nehmen; *person* festnehmen; *city* einnehmen ❷ COMPUT erfassen **II.** *n of a person* Gefangennahme *f;* (*by police*) Festnahme *f; of a city* Einnahme *f*
car [kar] *n* ❶ (*vehicle*) Auto *nt,* Wagen *m;* **by** ~ mit dem Auto ❷ TRAIN Waggon *m,* Wagen *m;* **passenger** ~ Personenwagen *m*
carafe [kə·'ræf] *n* Karaffe *f*
caramel ['kar·məl] *n* ❶ (*toffee*) Karamellbonbon *nt* ❷ (*burnt sugar*) Karamell *m*
carat <*pl* -s *or* -> ['ker·ət] *n* Karat *nt*

C

caraway ['kær·ə·weɪ] *n* Kümmel *m*
carbohydrate [ˌkar·boʊ·'haɪ·dreɪt] *n* Kohle[n]hydrat *nt*
'car bomb *n* Autobombe *f*
carbon ['kar·bən] *n* CHEM Kohlenstoff *m*
carbonated ['kar·bə·neɪ·t̬ɪd] *adj* sprudelnd; ~ **beverage** Getränk *nt* mit Kohlensäure
'carbon copy *n* Durchschlag *m;* (*fig*) Ebenbild *nt*
carbon di'oxide *n* Kohlendioxid *nt*
carbon 'footprint *n* CO_2-Bilanz *f,* CO_2-Fußabdruck *m*
carbon mon'oxide *n* Kohlenmonoxid *nt*
'carbon paper *n* Kohlepapier *nt*
carbs *n pl* (*fam*) *see* **carbohydrates** Kohle[n]hydrat *nt*
carbuncle ['kar·bʌŋ·kəl] *n* MED Karbunkel *m*
carburetor ['kar·bə·reɪ·t̬ər] *n* AUTO Vergaser *m*
carcass <*pl* -es> ['kar·kəs] *n* ❶ (*of an animal*) Tierleiche *f;* (*of a meat animal*) Rumpf *m;* (*of poultry*) Gerippe *nt* ❷ (*of a vehicle*) [Auto]wrack *nt*
carcinogen [kar·'sɪn·ə·dʒen] *n* Krebserreger *m*
carcinogenic [ˌkar·sɪn·ə·'dʒen·ɪk] *adj* Krebs erregend
card [kard] *n* Karte *f;* (*postcard*) [Post]karte *f,* Ansichtskarte *f;* (*with a message*) [Glückwunsch]karte *f;* **anniversary** ~ Jubiläumskarte *f;* (*for games*) [Spiel]karte *f;* **[game of]** ~**s** *pl* Kartenspiel *nt;* **ID** ~ Ausweis *m* ► PHRASES: **to have a ~ up one's sleeve** noch etwas in petto haben; **to play one's ~s right** geschickt vorgehen; **in the ~s** zu erwarten
'cardboard *n* Pappe *f,* [Papp]karton *m*
cardiac ['kar·dɪ·æk] *adj* Herz-
cardigan ['kar·dɪ·gən] *n* Strickjacke *f*
cardinal ['kar·dɪn·əl] **I.** *n* ❶ REL Kardinal *m* ❷ ORN Rotkardinal *m* **II.** *adj* ~ **number** Kardinalzahl *f;* ~ **rule** Grundregel *f;* ~ **sin** Todsünde *f*
'card index *n* Kartei *f*
care [ker] **I.** *n* ❶ (*looking after*) Betreuung *f;* (*of children, the elderly*) Pflege *f;* (*in a hospital*) Versorgung *f;* **to take good ~ of sb/sth** jdn/etw schonen; **take ~ [of yourself]!** pass auf dich auf!; ■ **to take ~ of sth** für etw *akk* sorgen; **let me take ~ of it** lass mich das übernehmen; ~ **of ...** c/o ..., zu Händen von ... ❷ (*carefulness*) Sorgfalt *f;* **to do sth with ~** etw sorgfältig machen; **to handle sth with ~** mit etw *dat* vorsichtig umgehen; **"handle with ~"** „Vorsicht, zerbrechlich!" ❸ (*worry*) Sorge *f;* **to not have a ~ in the world** keinerlei Sorgen haben **II.** *vi* ❶ (*be concerned*) betroffen sein; **I think he really ~s a lot** ich glaube, es macht ihm eine ganze Menge aus; **for all I ~** meinetwegen; **who ~s?** (*it's not important*) wen interessiert das schon?; (*so what*) was soll's? ❷ (*want*) ■ **to ~ for sth** *drink, dessert* etw mögen ❸ (*look after*) ■ **to ~ for sb/sth** sich um jdn/etw kümmern **III.** *vt* ■ **sb does not ~ what/who/whether ...** jdm ist es egal, was/wer/ob ...
career [kə·'rɪr] **I.** *n* ❶ (*profession*) Beruf *m;* ~ **politician** Berufspolitiker(in) *m(f)* ❷ (*working life*) Karriere *f,* Laufbahn *f* **II.** *vi* rasen; **to ~ out of control** außer Kontrolle geraten
ca'reer woman *n* Karrierefrau *f*
'carefree *adj* sorgenfrei
careful ['ker·fəl] *adj* ❶ (*cautious*) vorsichtig; *driver* umsichtig; **to be ~ with sb/sth** mit jdm/etw *dat* vorsichtig umgehen; ■ **to be ~ [that [*or* to]] ...** darauf achten, dass ... ❷ (*meticulous*) sorgfältig; *analysis* umfassend; *consideration* reiflich; *examination* gründlich; *worker* gewissenhaft
carefulness ['ker·fəl·nɪs] *n* ❶ (*caution*) Vorsicht *f* ❷ (*meticulousness*) Sorgfalt *f*
careless ['ker·lɪs] *adj* ❶ (*lacking attention*) unvorsichtig; *driver* leichtsinnig ❷ (*unthinking*) *remark* unbedacht; *talk* gedankenlos ❸ (*not painstaking*) nachlässig
carelessness ['ker·lɪs·nɪs] *n* ❶ (*lack of care*) Nachlässigkeit *f* ❷ (*lack of carefulness*) Unvorsichtigkeit *f*
caress [kə·'res] **I.** *n* <*pl* -es> Streicheln *nt;* ■ ~**es** *pl* Zärtlichkeiten *pl* **II.** *vt* streicheln
'caretaker I. *n* Hausverwalter(in) *m(f)* **II.** *adj* ~ **government** Übergangsregierung *f*
cargo <*pl* -s *or* -es> ['kar·goʊ] *n* ❶ (*goods*) Fracht *f* ❷ (*load*) Ladung *f*
Caribbean [ˌker·ɪ·'bi·ən] **I.** *n* ■ **the** ~ die Karibik **II.** *adj* karibisch; **the ~ Islands** die Karibischen Inseln
caricature ['ker·ə·kə·tʃʊr] **I.** *n* Karikatur *f* **II.** *vt* (*draw*) karikieren; (*parody*) parodieren
caricaturist ['kær·ə·kə·tʃʊr·ɪst] *n* Karikaturist(in) *m(f)*
caring ['ker·ɪŋ] *adj* warmherzig; *person* fürsorglich; *society* sozial
'car insurance *n* Kfz-Versicherung *f*
'carjacking *n* Autoentführung *f*
carnage ['kar·nɪdʒ] *n* Gemetzel *nt*
carnal ['kar·nəl] *adj* sinnlich
carnation [kar·'neɪ·ʃən] *n* Nelke *f;* ~ **pink** zartrosa
carnival ['kar·nə·vəl] **I.** *n* ❶ (*festival*) Volksfest *nt* ❷ (*traveling amusement park*) Jahrmarkt *m* ❸ (*pre-Lent*) Karneval *m,* Fasching *m bes* SÜDD, ÖSTERR **II.** *adj* Fest-, Karnevals-; ~ **atmosphere** ausgelassene Stimmung
carnivore ['kar·nə·vɔr] *n* Fleischfresser *m*
carnivorous [kar·'nɪv·ər·əs] *adj* Fleisch fressend
carol ['ker·əl] *n* **[Christmas]** ~ Weihnachtslied *nt*
caroler ['ker·əl·ər] *n* Sternsinger(in) *m(f)*
carotene ['kær·ə·tin] *n* Karotin *nt*
carousel [ˌkær·ə·'sel] *n* ❶ (*merry-go-round*) Karussell *nt* ❷ AVIAT [Gepäck]ausgabeband *nt*
'car owner *n* Autobesitzer(in) *m(f)*
carp[1] [karp] *vi* meckern
carp[2] <*pl* - *or* -s> [karp] *n* Karpfen *m*
carpenter ['kar·pən·tər] *n* Zimmermann *m,* Schreiner(in) *m(f),* Tischler(in) *m(f)*

carpentry ['kar·pən·tri] *n* (*activity*) Zimmer-/Schreiner-/Tischlerhandwerk *nt*
carpet ['kar·pət] **I.** *n* Teppich *m a. fig;* (*fitted*) Teppichboden *m* **II.** *vt* [mit einem Teppich] auslegen
carpeting ['kar·pɪ·t̬ɪŋ] *n* Teppich[boden] *m*
'**carpet sweeper** *n* Teppichkehrer *m*
'**carpool** **I.** *n* Fahrgemeinschaft *f* **II.** *vi* eine Fahrgemeinschaft *akk* bilden, an einer Fahrgemeinschaft *dat* teilnehmen
'**car rental** *n* Autovermietung *f*
carriage ['ker·ɪdʒ] *n* Kutsche *f*
carrier ['kæ·ri·ər] *n* ❶ (*person*) Träger(in) *m(f)* ❷ MIL (*vehicle*) Transporter *m;* [**aircraft**] ~ Flugzeugträger *m* ❸ (*transportation company*) *for people* Personenbeförderungsunternehmen *nt;* *for freight* Transportunternehmen *nt,* Spedition *f;* (*by air*) Fluggesellschaft *f* ❹ (*entrepreneur, person*) Frachtunternehmer(in) *m(f),* Spediteur(in) *m(f)* ❺ MED [Über]träger(in) *m(f)* ❻ TELEC **wireless** ~ Mobilfunkanbieter *m*
carrion ['ker·i·ən] *n* Aas *nt*
carrot ['ker·ət] *n* ❶ (*vegetable*) Möhre *f,* Karotte *f,* Mohrrübe *f* NORDD, gelbe Rübe SÜDD, Rüebli *nt* SCHWEIZ ❷ (*fam: reward*) Belohnung *f;* **the ~ and [the] stick** Zuckerbrot und Peitsche
carry <-ie-> ['ker·i] **I.** *vt* ❶ (*bear*) tragen *a. fig;* ■**to ~ sth around** etw mit sich herumtragen; **to be carried downstream** flussabwärts treiben ❷ (*transport*) transportieren ❸ (*have, incur*) **to ~ a penalty** eine [Geld]strafe nach sich ziehen; **to ~ weight with sb** Einfluss auf jdn haben ❹ MED (*transmit*) übertragen; *electricity, oil* leiten ❺ *usu passive* (*approve*) *motion* annehmen ❻ MATH *numbers* übertragen; (*mentally*) behalten **II.** *vi* (*reach*) *sound* zu hören sein
◆**carry away** *vt* ❶ (*take away*) wegtragen; *current* wegtreiben; (*stronger*) [mit sich] fortreißen ❷ *usu passive* ■**to get carried away** (*be overcome by*) sich mitreißen lassen; (*be enchanted by*) hingerissen sein
◆**carry forward** *vt* FIN übertragen
◆**carry off** *vt* ❶ (*take away*) wegtragen; SPORTS vom Spielfeld tragen ❷ (*succeed*) hinbekommen
◆**carry on** **I.** *vt* ❶ (*continue*) fortführen; *discussion* fortsetzen; **to ~ on reading** weiterlesen ❷ (*conduct*) führen; **to ~ on one's work** arbeiten **II.** *vi* ❶ (*continue*) weitermachen (**with** mit +*dat*) ❷ (*fam: behave silly*) sich danebenbenehmen; (*make a fuss*) ein [furchtbares] Theater machen (**about** wegen +*gen*)
◆**carry out** *vt* ❶ hinaus-/heraustragen; *current* hinaustreiben ❷ (*perform*) durchführen; *order, plan* ausführen; *threat* wahr machen
◆**carry over** *vt* ❶ (*postpone*) verschieben (**until** auf +*akk*) ❷ FIN vortragen
◆**carry through** *vt* ❶ (*sustain*) durchbringen ❷ (*complete*) durchführen
'**carry-on** *adj attr* ~ **bag** Handgepäck *nt*

CARS [karz] *n no pl acr for* **Car Allowance Rebate System** Verschrottungsprämie *f,* Abwrackprämie *f*
cart [kart] **I.** *n* ❶ (*pulled vehicle*) Wagen *m,* Karren *m;* **luggage** ~ Gepäckwagen *m;* (*for serving*) Servierwagen *m* ❷ (*in supermarket*) Einkaufswagen *m* ▶ PHRASES: **to put the ~ before the horse** das Pferd beim Schwanz aufzäumen **II.** *vt* (*fam*) schleppen
carte blanche [ˌkart·'blanʃ] *n* **to give sb ~** jdm freie Hand geben
cartel [kar·'tel] *n* Kartell *nt*
cartilage ['kar·t̬əl·ɪdʒ] *n* MED Knorpel *m*
cartographer [kar·'tag·rə·fər] *n* Kartograph(in) *m(f)*
cartography [kar·'tag·rə·fi] *n* Kartographie *f*
carton ['kar·tən] *n* Karton *m;* (*small*) Schachtel *f;* **milk** ~ Milchtüte *f*
cartoon [kar·'tun] *n* ❶ (*drawing*) Cartoon *m o nt* ❷ FILM Zeichentrickfilm *m*
car'toonist *n* ❶ ART Karikaturist(in) *m(f)* ❷ FILM Trickzeichner(in) *m(f)*
cartridge ['kar·trɪdʒ] *n* ❶ (*for ink, ammunition*) Patrone *f* ❷ (*for film*) Kassette *f*
'**cartwheel** **I.** *n* SPORTS Rad *nt;* **to do** [*or* **turn**] **a ~** ein Rad schlagen **II.** *vi* Rad schlagen
carve [karv] **I.** *vt* ❶ (*cut a figure*) schnitzen; (*with a chisel*) meißeln; (*cut a pattern*) [ein]ritzen ❷ FOOD tranchieren **II.** *vi* tranchieren
carver ['kar·vər] *n* ❶ (*person*) Bildhauer(in) *m(f);* *wood* Holzschnitzer(in) *m(f)* ❷ (*carving knife*) Tranchiermesser *nt*
carving ['kar·vɪŋ] *n* ART *of wood* Schnitzerei *f;* *in/from stone* Skulptur *f*
'**carving knife** *n* Tranchiermesser *nt*
'**car wash** *n* Autowaschanlage *f*
cascade [kæs·'keɪd] **I.** *n* (*natural*) Wasserfall *m;* (*artificial*) Kaskade *f a. fig* **II.** *vi* sich ergießen
case[1] [keɪs] *n* ❶ (*situation, instance*) Fall *m;* **in ~ of [an] emergency** im Notfall; **in most ~s** meistens; **in ~ ...** falls ...; **in any ~** (*regardless*) jedenfalls ❷ LAW [Rechts]fall *m;* (*suit*) Verfahren *nt;* **there was no ~ against her** es lag nichts gegen sie vor ❸ MED Fall *m* ❹ LING Fall *m,* Kasus *m;* **to be in the accusative ~** im Akkusativ stehen
case[2] [keɪs] **I.** *n* ❶ (*small container*) Schatulle *f;* (*for hat*) Schachtel *f;* (*for eyeglasses*) Etui *nt;* (*for musical instrument*) Kasten *m;* (*for CD, umbrella*) Hülle *f* ❷ (*packaging plus contents*) *of beer* Kiste *f* ❸ (*suitcase*) Koffer *m* ❹ TYPO **written in lower/upper ~** klein-/großgeschrieben **II.** *vt* (*sl*) **to ~ the joint** sich *dat* den Laden mal ansehen
'**case study** *n* Fallstudie *f*
cash [kæʃ] **I.** *n* Bargeld *nt;* **to pay** [**by** [*or* **in**]] **~** bar bezahlen **II.** *vt* ■**to ~ [in] ↔ sth** etw einlösen; *chips* eintauschen
◆**cash in** *vi* ■**to ~ in on sth** von etw *dat* profitieren
'**cash crop** *n* *ausschließlich zum Verkauf bestimmte Agrarprodukte*

cashew ['kæʃ·u] *n* Cashewnuss *f*
'cash flow *n* Cashflow *m*
cashier [kæ·'ʃɪr] *n* Kassierer(in) *m(f)*
'cash machine *n* Geldautomat *m,* Bankomat *m* SCHWEIZ, ÖSTERR
cashmere ['kæʒ·mɪr] *n* FASHION Kaschmir *m*
'cash register *n* Registrierkasse *f*
casing ['keɪ·sɪŋ] *n* Hülle *f; of a machine* Verkleidung *f*
casino <*pl* -os> [kə·'si·noʊ] *n* [Spiel]kasino *nt*
cask [kæsk] *n* Fass *nt*
casket ['kæs·kɪt] *n* ① (*coffin*) Sarg *m* ② (*box*) Kästchen *nt*
casserole ['kæs·ə·roʊl] *n* ① (*baking dish*) Auflaufform *f,* Schmortopf *m* ② (*baked food*) **tuna/potato ~** Thunfisch-/Kartoffelauflauf
cassette [kə·'set] *n* Kassette *f*
cas'sette deck *n* Kassettendeck *nt*
cas'sette player, cas'sette recorder *n* Kassettenrecorder *m*
cast [kæst] **I.** *n* ① THEAT, FILM Besetzung *f* ② (*molded object*) [Ab]guss *m* ③ MED Gips[verband] *m* **II.** *vt* <cast, cast> ① (*throw*) werfen *a. fig; fishing line* auswerfen; **to ~ doubt on sth** etw zweifelhaft erscheinen lassen ② (*give*) *ballots, votes* abgeben ③ THEAT, FILM *part, role* besetzen; **to ~ a film** das Casting für einen Film machen; **to ~ sb in a role** jdm eine Rolle geben ④ (*make in a mold*) gießen
◆**cast away** *vt* (*discard*) wegwerfen
◆**cast off I.** *vt* losmachen **II.** *vi* ablegen
◆**cast out** *vt* vertreiben
castanet [ˌkæs·tə·'net] *n* Kastagnette *f*
castaway ['kæst·ə·weɪ] *n* Schiffbrüchige(r) *f(m)*
caste [kæst] *n* Kaste *f*
caster ['kæs·tər] *n* (*wheel*) Laufrolle *f*
casting ['kæs·tɪŋ] *n* ① (*mold*) Guss *m;* (*molding*) Gießen *nt* ② THEAT Casting *nt*
'casting vote *n* entscheidende Stimme
cast 'iron *n* Gusseisen *nt*
cast-'iron *adj* ① aus Gusseisen ② (*fig*) *alibi* wasserdicht; *guarantee* sicher
castle ['kæs·əl] *n* ① (*fortress*) Burg *f;* (*mansion*) Schloss *nt* ② (*fam*) CHESS Turm *m*
'castoff I. *n* ■ **~s** *pl* abgelegte Kleidung **II.** *adj* (*secondhand*) gebraucht; (*discarded*) abgelegt
castor ['kæs·tər] *n see* **caster**
castrate ['kæs·treɪt] *vt* kastrieren
casual ['kæʒ·u·əl] *adj* ① (*informal*) lässig, salopp; *clothing* leger; **~ shirt** Freizeithemd *nt* ② (*not planned*) zufällig; *acquaintance, glance* flüchtig ③ (*irregular*) gelegentlich; **~ sex** Gelegenheitssex *m*
casually ['kæʒ·u·əl·i] *adv* ① (*informally*) lässig, leger; **~ dressed** salopp gekleidet ② (*accidentally*) zufällig ③ (*without seriousness*) beiläufig
casualty ['kæʒ·u·əl·ti] *n* (*accident victim*) [Unfall]opfer *nt;* (*injured person*) Verletzte(r) *f(m);* (*dead person*) Todesfall *m*
cat [kæt] *n* Katze *f* ▶ PHRASES: **to be raining ~s and dogs** wie aus Eimern schütten
CAT [kæt] *n* MED *abbrev of* **computerized axial tomography** Computertomographie *f*
catalog ['kæt̬·əl·ag] **I.** *n* Katalog *m* **II.** *vt* katalogisieren
catalyst ['kæt̬·əl·ɪst] *n* ① AUTO, CHEM Katalysator *m* ② (*fig*) Auslöser *m*
catalytic [kæt·ə·'lɪt·ɪk] *adj* katalytisch
catamaran [ˌkæt̬·ə·mə·'ræn] *n* Katamaran *m*
catapult ['kæt̬·ə·pʌlt] **I.** *n* Katapult *nt* **II.** *vt* katapultieren
cataract ['kæt̬·ə·rækt] *n* ① MED grauer Star ② GEOG Katarakt *m*
catastrophe [kə·'tæs·trə·fi] *n* Katastrophe *f*
catastrophic [ˌkæt̬·ə·'straf·ɪk] *adj* katastrophal
'catcall I. *n* Hinterherpfeifen *nt* **II.** *vi* pfeifen
catch [kætʃ] **I.** *n* <*pl* -es> ① *of a ball* Fang *m;* **nice ~!** gut gefangen! ② (*fish*) Fang *m kein pl* ③ (*fastener*) Verschluss *m;* (*bolt*) Riegel *m;* (*hook*) Haken *m;* **window ~** Fensterverriegelung *f* ④ (*trick*) Haken *m* **II.** *vt* <caught, caught> ① (*intercept*) fangen; *light* einfangen; *person, liquid* auffangen ② (*capture*) *person* ergreifen; (*arrest*) festnehmen; *animal* fangen; *escaped animal* einfangen ③ (*surprise, get hold of*) erwischen; **to ~ sb in the act** jdn auf frischer Tat ertappen; **to be caught in a thunderstorm** von einem Gewitter überrascht werden; ■ **to ~ sb/oneself doing sth** jdn/sich bei etw *dat* ertappen ④ MED ■ **to ~ sth from sb** sich bei jdm mit etw *dat* anstecken; **to ~ [a] cold** sich erkälten ⑤ ■ **to ~ sth in sth** (*trap*) etw in etw *akk* einklemmen; (*entangle*) mit etw *dat* in etw *dat* hängen bleiben; ■ **to get caught [in sth]** sich [in etw *dat*] verfangen; (*fig: become involved*) in etw *akk* verwickelt werden; ■ **to get caught on sth** an etw *dat* hängen bleiben ⑥ (*take*) *bus/train* nehmen; (*arrive in time for*) kriegen ⑦ (*attract*) *attention* erregen; *imagination* anregen ⑧ (*notice*) bemerken; **to ~ sight** [*or* **a glimpse**] **of sb/sth** etw [kurz] sehen; (*by chance*) etw [zufällig] sehen; (*hear*) mitbekommen ▶ PHRASES: **to ~ <u>fire</u>** Feuer fangen; **to ~ sb off <u>guard</u>** jdn überrumpeln **III.** *vi* <caught, caught> ① (*entangle*) sich in etw *dat* verfangen; ■ **to ~ on sth** an etw *dat* hängen bleiben ② (*ignite*) **to get a fire to ~** ein Feuer zum Brennen bringen; *engine* zünden
◆**catch on** *vi* (*fam*) ① (*understand*) kapieren ② (*become popular*) sich durchsetzen
◆**catch up I.** *vi* ① (*reach*) ■ **to ~ up with** [*or* **to**] **sb** jdn einholen *a. fig;* **she's ~ing up!** sie holt auf! ② (*fig: complete*) ■ **to ~ up with** [*or* **on**] **sth** etw aufarbeiten; *sleep* nachholen **II.** *vt usu passive* **to get caught up [in sth]** sich [in etw *dat*] verfangen; (*fig*) in etw *akk* verwickelt werden
catcher ['kætʃ·ər] *n* Fänger(in) *m(f);* (*in baseball*) Catcher *m*
catching ['kætʃ·ɪŋ] *adj* ansteckend
'catch phrase *n* Slogan *m*
catchup ['kætʃ·əp] *n* FOOD *see* **ketchup**
catchy ['kætʃ·i] *adj* eingängig; **~ tune** Ohr-

wurm *m*
categorical [ˌkæt̬·ə·ˈɡɔr·ɪ·kəl] *adj* kategorisch
categorically [ˌkæt̬·ə·ˈɡɔr·ɪ·kli] *adv* **to ~ deny sth** etw kategorisch abstreiten
categorize [ˈkæt̬·ə·ɡə·raɪz] *vt* kategorisieren, einstufen
category [ˈkæt̬·ə·ɡɔr·i] *n* Kategorie *f*
cater [ˈkeɪ·t̬ər] *vi* ① (*provide food, drink*) für Speise und Getränke sorgen; *company* Speisen und Getränke liefern ② (*minister*) sich kümmern (**to** um *+akk*)
caterer [ˈkeɪ·t̬ər·ər] *n* (*company*) Cateringservice *m;* (*for parties*) Partyservice *m*
catering [ˈkeɪ·tər·ɪŋ] *n* ① (*trade*) Catering *nt* ② (*service*) Cateringservice *m;* (*for parties*) Partyservice *m*
caterpillar [ˈkæt̬·ər·pɪl·ər] *n* Raupe *f*
Caterpillar® *n* Raupenfahrzeug *nt*
ˈ**catfish** *n* <*pl* -> Seewolf *m*
ˈ**catgut** *n* MUS [Darm]saite *f*
cathedral [kə·ˈθi·drəl] *n* Kathedrale *f,* Dom *m,* Münster *nt*
cathode [ˈkæθ·oʊd] *n* Kat[h]ode *f*
Catholic [ˈkæθ·ə·lɪk] **I.** *n* Katholik(in) *m(f)* **II.** *adj* katholisch
Catholicism [kə·ˈθal·ə·sɪz·əm] *n* Katholizismus *m*
ˈ**cat litter** *n* Katzenstreu *f*
ˈ**catnap** (*fam*) **I.** *n* **to take a ~** ein Nickerchen machen **II.** *vi* <-pp-> kurz schlafen
catsup [ˈketʃ·əp] *n* FOOD *see* **ketchup**
cattle [ˈkæt̬·əl] *npl* Rinder *pl*
catty [ˈkæt̬·i] *adj* gehässig; *remark* bissig
ˈ**catwalk** *n* FASHION Laufsteg *m*
Caucasian [kɔ·ˈkeɪ·ʒən] **I.** *n* (*white person*) Weiße(r) *f(m)* **II.** *adj* ① (*white-skinned*) weiß ② (*of Caucasus*) kaukasisch
caught [kɔt] *pt, pp of* **catch**
cauldron [ˈkɔl·drən] *n* (*pot*) [großer] Kessel
cauliflower [ˈkɔ·lɪ·ˌflaʊ·ər] *n* Blumenkohl *m,* Karfiol *m* SÜDD, ÖSTERR
causal [ˈkɔ·zəl] *adj* (*form*) kausal
causality [kɔ·ˈzæl·ɪ·ti] *n* (*form*) Kausalität *f*
cause [kɔz] **I.** *n* ① (*of effect*) Ursache *f;* **~ of death** Todesursache *f* ② (*reason*) Grund *m;* **~ for concern** Anlass *m* zur Sorge; ■ **to be the ~ of sth** der Grund für etw *akk* sein ③ (*object of support*) Sache *f;* **a good ~** ein guter Zweck; **a lost ~** eine verlorene Sache **II.** *vt* verursachen; *trouble* stiften; ■ **to ~ sb to do sth** jdn veranlassen, etw zu tun; **the bright light ~d her to blink** das helle Licht ließ sie blinzeln
ˈ**cause** [kəz] *conj* (*fam*) *abbrev of* **because**
causeway [ˈkɔz·ˌweɪ] *n* Damm *m*
caustic [ˈkɔ·stɪk] *adj* ätzend *a. fig; humor* beißend
caution [ˈkɔ·ʃən] **I.** *n* ① (*carefulness*) Vorsicht *f;* **to treat sth with ~** etw mit Vorbehalt aufnehmen ② (*warning*) Vorwarnung *f* **II.** *vt* (*form*) ■ **to ~ sb [against sth]** jdn [vor etw] warnen
cautionary [ˈkɔ·ʃə·ner·i] *adj* warnend; **~ tale** Geschichte *f* mit einer Moral
cautious [ˈkɔ·ʃəs] *adj* (*careful*) vorsichtig; (*prudent*) umsichtig; *optimism* verhalten
cavalier [ˌkæv·ə·ˈlɪr] **I.** *n* Kavalier *m* **II.** *adj* unbekümmert
cavalry [ˈkæv·əl·ri] *n usu + pl vb* ■ **the ~** die Kavallerie
cave [keɪv] *n* Höhle *f*
◆**cave in** *vi* ① (*collapse*) einstürzen ② (*give in*) kapitulieren; ■ **to ~ in to sth** sich etw *dat* beugen
ˈ**caveman** *n* Höhlenmensch *m*
cavern [ˈkæv·ərn] *n* Höhle *f*
cavernous [ˈkæv·ər·nəs] *adj* ① (*cave-like*) höhlenartig ② (*fig*) *cheeks* hohl; *eyes* tiefliegend
caviar(e) [ˈkæv·i·ar] *n* Kaviar *m*
cavity [ˈkæv·ɪ·ti] *n* ① (*hole*) Loch *nt;* (*hollow space*) Hohlraum *m* ② MED (*in tooth*) Loch (im Zahn)
caw [kɔ] **I.** *n* Krächzen *nt* **II.** *vi* krächzen
cayenne [kaɪ·ˈen], **cayenne** ˈ**pepper** [kaɪ·ˈen-] *n* Cayennepfeffer *m*
CB [ˌsi·ˈbi] *n* RADIO *abbrev of* **citizens band** CB-Funk *m*
cc <*pl* - *or* -s> [ˌsi·ˈsi] *n abbrev of* **cubic centimeter** cm^3
CD [ˌsi·ˈdi] *n abbrev of* **compact disc** CD *f*
C'D player *n* CD-Spieler *m*
CD-ROM [ˌsi·di·ˈram] *n abbrev of* **compact disc read-only memory** CD-ROM *f*
CD-'ROM drive *n* CD-ROM-Laufwerk *nt*
cease [sis] (*form*) **I.** *vi* aufhören **II.** *vt* beenden; *fire* einstellen
ˈ**ceasefire** *n* Waffenruhe *f*
ceaseless [ˈsis·lɪs] *adj* endlos; *noise* ständig
cedar [ˈsi·dər] *n* Zeder *f*
ceiling [ˈsi·lɪŋ] *n* [Zimmer]decke *f;* (*fig*) Obergrenze *f*
celebrate [ˈsel·ɪ·breɪt] *vi, vt* feiern
celebrated [ˈsel·ɪ·breɪ·t̬ɪd] *adj* berühmt
celebration [ˌsel·ɪ·ˈbreɪ·ʃən] *n* Feier *f;* **cause for ~** Grund *m* zum Feiern
celebrity [sə·ˈleb·rɪ·t̬i] *n* ① (*person*) berühmte Persönlichkeit ② (*fame*) Ruhm *m*
celeriac [sə·ˈler·ɪ·æk] *n* [Knollen]sellerie *m o f*
celery [ˈsel·ə·ri] *n* [Stangen]sellerie *m o f*
celestial [sɪ·ˈles·tʃəl] *adj* ASTRON Himmels-
celibacy [ˈsel·ɪ·bə·si] *n* Zölibat *m o nt*
celibate [ˈsel·ɪ·bət] **I.** *n* Zölibatär *m* **II.** *adj* zölibatär
cell [sel] *n* ① BIOL Zelle *f* ② (*prison room*) Zelle *f* ③ (*fam*) *see* **cell phone**
cellar [ˈsel·ər] *n* Keller *m*
cellist [ˈtʃel·ɪst] *n* Cellist(in) *m(f)*
cello <*pl* -s> [ˈtʃel·oʊ] *n* Cello *nt*
cellophane [ˈsel·ə·feɪn] *n* Cellophan® *nt*
ˈ**cell phone** *n* Mobiltelefon *nt,* Handy *nt,* Natel *nt* SCHWEIZ
cellular [ˈsel·jʊ·lər] *adj* zellular
cellular ˈ**phone** *n* Mobiltelefon *nt,* Handy *nt*
cellulite [ˈsel·jə·laɪt] *n* Zellulitis *f*
celluloid [ˈsel·jʊ·lɔɪd] *n* Zelluloid *nt*

cellulose ['sel·jʊ·loʊs] *n* Zellulose *f*
Celsius ['sel·si·əs] *n* Celsius
Celtic ['kel·tik, 'sel·tɪk] *adj* keltisch
cement [sɪ·'ment] **I.** *n* Zement *m* **II.** *vt* ❶ (*with concrete*) betonieren; (*with cement*) zementieren ❷ (*a. fig: bind*) festigen
ce'ment mixer *n* Betonmischmaschine *f*
cemetery ['sem·ə·ter·i] *n* Friedhof *m*
censor ['sen·sər] **I.** *n* Zensor(in) *m(f)* **II.** *vt* zensieren
censorious [sen·'sɔr·i·əs] *adj* [übertrieben] kritisch
censorship ['sen·sər·ʃɪp] *n* Zensur *f*
censure ['sen·ʃər] **I.** *n* Tadel *m* **II.** *vt* tadeln
census ['sen·səs] *n* Zählung *f*
cent [sent] *n* Cent *m;* **to not be worth a** [**red**] ~ keinen Pfifferling wert sein
centenarian [ˌsen·tə·'ner·i·ən] *n* Hundertjährige(r) *f(m)*
centennial [sen·'teni·əl] *n* Hundertjahrfeier *f*
center ['sen·tər] **I.** *n* ❶ Zentrum *nt; of chocolates* Füllung *f;* POL Mitte *f* ❷ SPORTS (*in basketball, hockey*) Center *m;* (*in soccer*) Mittelfeldspieler(in) *m(f)* **II.** *vt* zentrieren **III.** *vi* ■ **to ~ upon sth** sich um etw *akk* drehen
'centerpiece *n* ❶ (*on table*) Tafelaufsatz *m;* (*in room*) Mittelstück *nt* ❷ (*central feature*) Kernstück *nt*
centigrade ['sen·tə·greɪd] *n* Celsius
centigram ['sen·tə·græm] *n* Zentigramm *nt*
centimeter ['sen·tə·ˌmi·t̬ər] *n* Zentimeter *m*
centipede ['sen·tə·pid] *n* Tausendfüßler *m*
central ['sen·trəl] *adj* ❶ (*in the middle*) zentral ❷ (*paramount*) wesentlich
centralization [ˌsen·trə·lɪ·'zeɪ·ʃən] *n* Zentralisierung *f*
centralize ['sen·trə·laɪz] *vt* zentralisieren
centrifugal [sen·'trɪf·jə·gəl] *adj* zentrifugal
century ['sen·tʃə·ri] *n* (*period*) Jahrhundert *nt;* **turn of the ~** Jahrhundertwende *f*
CEO [ˌsi·i·'oʊ] *n abbrev of* **chief executive officer** Generaldirektor(in) *m(f)*
ceramic [sə·'ræm·ɪk] *adj* keramisch
ceramics [sə·'ræm·ɪks] *n + sing vb* Keramik *f*
cereal ['sɪr·i·əl] *n* ❶ (*for breakfast*) Frühstückszerealien *pl* (*Cornflakes, Müsli ...*) ❷ Getreide *nt*
cerebral ['ser·ə·brəl] *adj* ❶ ANAT Gehirn- ❷ (*intellectual*) hochgeistig
ceremonial [ˌser·ə·'moʊ·ni·əl] **I.** *adj* zeremoniell **II.** *n* (*form*) Zeremoniell *nt*
ceremonious [ˌser·ə·'moʊ·ni·əs] *adj* förmlich
ceremony ['ser·ə·moʊ·ni] *n* Zeremonie *f,* Feier *f;* **to stand on ~** förmlich sein
certain ['sɜr·tən] **I.** *adj* ❶ (*sure*) sicher; (*unavoidable*) bestimmt; **to mean ~ death** den sicheren Tod bedeuten; **to make ~** [**that ...**] darauf achten[, dass ...]; **to make ~ of sth** sich einer S. *gen* vergewissern; ■ **for ~** ganz sicher ❷ (*particular*) **at a ~ age** in einem bestimmten Alter; **in ~ circumstances** unter gewissen Umständen **II.** *pron* (*form*) einige
certainly ['sɜr·tən·li] *adv* ❶ (*surely*) sicher[lich]; (*without a doubt*) bestimmt, gewiss ❷ (*gladly*) gern[e]; (*of course*) [aber] selbstverständlich; ~ **not** auf [gar] keinen Fall
certainty ['sɜr·tən·ti] *n* Gewissheit *f;* **with ~** mit Sicherheit
certifiable ['sɜr·t̬ə·'faɪ·ə·bəl] *adj* ❶ (*officially admissible*) nachweisbar ❷ (*psychologically ill*) unzurechnungsfähig
certificate [sər·'tɪf·ɪ·kət] *n* (*official document*) Urkunde *f;* (*attestation*) Bescheinigung *f;* **birth ~** Geburtsurkunde *f;* **death ~** Totenschein *m;* **marriage ~** Trauschein *m*
certification [ˌsɜr·t̬ə·fɪ·'keɪ·ʃən] *n* ❶ (*state*) Qualifikation *f;* (*process*) Qualifizierung *f* ❷ (*document*) Zertifikat *nt;* (*attestation*) Beglaubigung *f*
certified ['sɜr·t̬ə·faɪd] *adj* ❶ (*official*) *copy* beglaubigte Kopie ❷ (*trained*) ausgebildet, -meister, -in *m, f;* (*by the state*) staatlich anerkannt
certify <-ie-> ['sɜr·tə·faɪ] *vt* (*declare as true*) bescheinigen, bestätigen; LAW beglaubigen
cervical ['sɜr·vɪ·kəl] *adj* ANAT ❶ (*of neck*) zervikal ❷ (*of cervix*) Gebärmutterhals-
cervix <*pl* -es *or* -vices> ['sɜr·vɪks] *n* ANAT Gebärmutterhals *m*
cessation [se·'seɪ·ʃən] *n* (*form: end*) Ende *nt;* (*process*) Beendigung *f; of hostilities* Einstellung *f*
cesspit ['ses·pɪt], **cesspool** ['ses·pul] *n* Jauchegrube *f;* (*fig, pej*) Sumpf *m*
cf. ['si·ef] *vt* (*form*) *abbrev of* **compare** vgl.
CFC [ˌsi·ef·'si] *n abbrev of* **chlorofluorocarbon** FCKW *nt*
CFO [ˌsi·ef·'oʊ] *n abbrev of* **chief financial officer** Leiter(in) *m(f)* der Finanzabteilung
chafe [tʃeɪf] **I.** *vi* (*make sore*) sich [wund]scheuern; *hands* wund werden **II.** *vt* (*rub sore*) [wund]scheuern
chaff [tʃæf] *n* Spreu *f*
chain [tʃeɪn] **I.** *n* ❶ Kette *f; of prisoner;* ■ **~s** *pl* Fesseln *pl* ❷ (*fig: series*) Reihe *f; of mishaps* Verkettung *f; of shops* [Laden]kette *f;* **~ of command** Hierarchie *f* **II.** *vt* ■ **to ~** [**up**] [an]ketten (**to** an +*akk*)
'chain letter *n* Kettenbrief *m*
'chain mail *n* Kettenhemd *nt*
chain re'action *n* Kettenreaktion *f*
'chain saw *n* Kettensäge *f*
'chain smoker *n* Kettenraucher(in) *m(f)*
'chain store *n* Kettenladen *m*
chair [tʃer] **I.** *n* ❶ (*seat*) Stuhl *m;* **easy ~** Sessel *m;* ■ **the ~** (*sl*) der elektrische Stuhl ❷ UNIV (*professorship*) Lehrstuhl *m;* **to hold a ~** einen Lehrstuhl innehaben ❸ (*chairperson*) Vorsitzende(r) *f(m)* **II.** *vt* (*be leader*) ■ **to ~ sth** bei etw *dat* den Vorsitz führen
'chair lift *n* Sessellift *m*
'chairman *n* Vorsitzende(r) *m*
'chairmanship *n* Vorsitz *m*
'chairperson *n* Vorsitzende(r) *f(m)*
'chairwoman *n* Vorsitzende *f*
chalet [ʃæ·'leɪ] *n* Chalet *nt*

chalk [tʃɔk] **I.** *n* ① (*for writing*) Kreide *f* ② (*type of stone*) Kalkstein *m* **II.** *vt* mit Kreide schreiben/zeichnen
◆**chalk out** *vt design* entwerfen; *strategy* planen
◆**chalk up** *vt* ① (*achieve*) *victory* verbuchen können ② (*attribute*) ■**to ~ sth up to sth** etw einer S. zuschreiben
'**chalkboard** *n* Tafel *f*
chalky ['tʃɔk·i] *adj* ① (*of chalk*) kalk[halt]ig ② (*chalk-like*) kreideartig
challenge ['tʃæl·ɪndʒ] **I.** *n* Herausforderung *f;* **to find sth a ~** etw schwierig finden **II.** *vt* ① (*ask to compete*) herausfordern ② (*call into question*) *findings* in Frage stellen ③ (*stimulate*) *the imagination* anregen
challenger ['tʃæl·ɪn·dʒər] *n* Herausforderer *m,* Herausforderin *f;* **~ for a title** Titelanwärter(in) *m(f)*
challenging ['tʃæl·ɪn·dʒɪŋ] *adj* [heraus]fordernd
chamber ['tʃeɪm·bər] *n* ① (*old: room*) [Schlaf]gemach *nt geh* ② (*judge's offices*) ■**~s** Amtszimmer *nt* ③ (*cavity*) Kammer *f* ④ (*in a firearm*) Patronenlager
'**chambermaid** *n* Zimmermädchen *nt*
'**chamber music** *n* Kammermusik *f*
chameleon [kə·'mi·li·ən] *n* Chamäleon *nt a. fig*
chamois <*pl* -> ['ʃæm·i] *n* ① ZOOL Gämse *f* ② (*polishing cloth*) Fensterleder *nt*
champ [tʃæmp] *n short for* **champion** Champion *m*
champagne [ʃæm·'peɪn] *n* Champagner *m*
champion ['tʃæm·pi·ən] **I.** *n* ① SPORTS Champion *m;* **world ~** Weltmeister(in) *m(f);* **defending ~** Titelverteidiger(in) *m(f)* ② (*supporter*) Verfechter(in) *m(f)* (**of**) **II.** *vt* verfechten; *cause* eintreten (für +*akk*) **III.** *adj* **~ boxer** Boxchampion *m*
championship ['tʃæm·pi·ən·ʃɪp] *n* SPORTS Meisterschaft *f*
chance [tʃæns] **I.** *n* ① Zufall *m;* **by ~** zufällig ② (*prospect*) Chance *f;* **to have** [*or* **stand**] **a ~** eine Chance haben; **no ~!** (*fam*) niemals!; **the ~ of a lifetime** eine einmalige Chance ③ (*risk*) Risiko *nt;* **to take ~s** [*or* **a ~**] etwas riskieren **II.** *vt* (*fam*) riskieren; **to ~ it** sein Glück versuchen, es wagen
◆**chance on, chance upon** *vi person* zufällig treffen; *thing* zufällig stoßen (auf +*akk*)
chancellor ['tʃæn·sə·lər] *n* ① Kanzler(in) *m(f);* (*of federal state*) [Bundes]kanzler(in) *m(f)* ② UNIV (*president*) Rektor(in) *m(f)*
chancy ['tʃæn·si] *adj* riskant
chandelier [ˌʃæn·də·'lɪr] *n* Kronleuchter *m*
change ['tʃeɪndʒ] **I.** *n* ① (*alteration*) [Ver]änderung *f;* **~ of direction** Richtungsänderung *f a. fig;* **to be a ~ for the better/worse** eine Verbesserung/eine Verschlechterung darstellen ② (*substitution*) Wechsel *m;* **~ of scene** THEAT Szenenwechsel *m;* (*fig*) Tapetenwechsel *m* ③ (*variety*) Abwechslung *f;* **for a ~** zur Abwechslung ④ (*coins*) Kleingeld *nt;* (*money returned*) Wechselgeld *nt,* Retourgeld *nt* SCHWEIZ; **to have** [**the**] **right ~** es passend haben; **to give the wrong ~** falsch herausgeben **II.** *vi* ① (*alter*) sich [ver]ändern; *traffic light* umspringen; *weather* umschlagen; *wind* sich drehen; **nothing** [**ever**] **~s** alles bleibt beim Alten; **to ~ into sth** sich in etw *akk* verwandeln ② (*substitute, move*) ■**to ~** [**over**] **to sth** zu etw *dat* wechseln ③ TRANSP umsteigen ④ (*dress*) sich umziehen **III.** *vt* ① (*make different*) [ver]ändern; (*transform*) verwandeln; **to ~ one's mind** seine Meinung ändern ② (*exchange, move*) wechseln; **to ~ places with sb** mit jdm den Platz tauschen; (*fig*) mit jdm tauschen ③ (*make fresh*) *baby* [frisch] wickeln; *bed* neu beziehen; **to ~** [**one's**] **clothes** sich umziehen ④ (*money*) wechseln; **to ~ $100 into euros** $100 in Euros umtauschen ⑤ TRANSP *buses, trains* umsteigen
changeable ['tʃeɪn·dʒə·bəl] *adj* unbeständig; *moods* wechselnd
'**changeover** *n usu sing* Umstellung *f* (**to** auf +*akk*)
changing ['tʃeɪn·dʒɪŋ] *adj* wechselnd
channel ['tʃæn·əl] **I.** *n* ① RADIO, TV Programm *nt;* **cable ~** Kabelkanal *m;* **to change ~s** umschalten; **to turn** [**one's TV**] **to ~ four** ins vierte Programm umschalten ② (*waterway*) [Fluss]bett *nt;* (*artificial*) Kanal *m;* **the English C~** der Ärmelkanal ③ (*means*) Weg *m;* **to go through** [**the**] **official ~s** den Dienstweg gehen **II.** *vt* <-l- *or* -ll-> (*direct*) leiten; *one's energies, money* stecken
chant [tʃænt] **I.** *n* ① REL [Sprech]gesang *m* ② SPORTS Sprechchor *m* **II.** *vi* ① REL einen Sprechgesang anstimmen ② *crowd* im Sprechchor rufen **III.** *vt* ① REL (*sing*) singen ② SPORTS im Sprechchor rufen
chanterelle [ˌʃæn·t̬ə·'rel] *n* Pfifferling *m*
chaos ['keɪ·as] *n* Chaos *nt,* Durcheinander *nt*
chaotic [keɪ·'at̬·ɪk] *adj* chaotisch
chap <-pp-> [tʃæp] **I.** *vi skin* aufspringen **II.** *vt lips* aufspringen
chap. *n abbrev of* **chapter** Kap.
chapel ['tʃæp·əl] *n* Kapelle *f*
chaperon(**e**) ['ʃæp·ə·roʊn] **I.** *n* ① (*adult supervisor*) Aufsichtsperson *f* ② (*dated*) Anstandsdame *f* **II.** *vt* ① (*supervise*) beaufsichtigen ② (*dated: accompany*) begleiten
chaplain ['tʃæp·lɪn] *n* Kaplan *m*
Chap Stick® *n* ≈ Labello® *m*
chapter ['tʃæp·tər] *n* ① Kapitel *nt;* **to quote ~ and verse** den genauen Wortlaut [einer S. *gen*] wiedergeben ② (*of organization*) Zweig *m*
char <-rr-> [tʃar] *vi, vt* verkohlen
character ['ker·ək·t̬ər] *n* ① Charakter *m;* **out of ~** ungewöhnlich ② LIT [Roman]figur *f* ③ TYPO Zeichen *nt*
'**character actor** *n* Charakterdarsteller *m*
characteristic [ˌker·ək·tə·'rɪs·tɪk] **I.** *n* charakteristisches Merkmal **II.** *adj* charakteristisch;

■ **to be ~ of sth** typisch (**of** für +*akk*)
characteristically [ˌker·ək·tə·ˈrɪs·tɪk·li] *adv* typisch
characterization [ˌker·ək·tər·ɪ·ˈzeɪ·ʃən] *n* ❶ LIT [Personen]beschreibung *f;* FILM Darstellung *f* ❷ (*description*) Charakterisierung *f*
characterize [ˈker·ək·tə·raɪz] *vt* kennzeichnen (**as** als +*akk*)
charade [ʃə·ˈreɪd] *n* ❶ *usu pl* (*game*) Scharade *f* ❷ (*lie*) Farce *f*
charcoal [ˈtʃɑr·koʊl] *n* ❶ (*fuel*) Holzkohle *f* ❷ (*for drawing*) Kohle *f*
charge [tʃɑrdʒ] **I.** *n* ❶ (*cost*) Gebühr *f;* **free of ~** kostenlos ❷ LAW Anklage *f* (**of** wegen +*gen*); ■ **~s** *pl* Anklagepunkte *pl;* (*in civil cases*) Ansprüche *pl;* **to press ~s against sb** Anklage gegen jdn erheben ❸ (*responsibility*) Verantwortung *f;* **to be in ~** die Verantwortung tragen; **who's in ~ here?** wer ist hier zuständig?; **she's in ~ of the department** sie leitet die Abteilung; (*care*) Obhut *f;* **to be placed in sb's ~** in jds Obhut gegeben werden ❹ ELEC Ladung *f* ❺ (*attack*) Angriff *m* **II.** *vi* ❶ (*attack*) [vorwärts]stürmen; **~!** vorwärts! ❷ (*move quickly*) stürmen (**in, into** in +*akk*) **III.** *vt* ❶ (*demand payment*) berechnen; **how much do you ~ for that?** was [*o* wie viel] kostet das bei Ihnen?; ■ **to ~ sth to sb** jdm etw in Rechnung stellen ❷ LAW **to ~ sb with murder** jdn des Mordes anklagen ❸ ELEC *battery* aufladen
ˈ**charge account** *n* Kreditkonto *nt*
ˈ**charge card** *n* [Kunden]kreditkarte *f*
ˈ**charging station** *n* Ladestation *f;* (*for electric vehicles*) Stromtankstelle *f*
chariot [ˈtʃær·i·ət] *n* Streitwagen *m*
charisma [kə·ˈrɪz·mə] *n* Charisma *nt*
charitable [ˈtʃer·ɪ·tə·bəl] *adj* ❶ (*generous*) großzügig; (*uncritical*) gütig ❷ (*of charity*) karitativ; **~ organization** Wohltätigkeitsorganisation *f*
charity [ˈtʃer·ɪ·t̬i] *n* ❶ (*generosity*) Barmherzigkeit *f* ❷ (*assistance*) **the proceeds go to ~** die Erträge sind für wohltätige Zwecke bestimmt ❸ (*organization*) Wohltätigkeitsorganisation *f*
charm [tʃɑrm] **I.** *n* ❶ (*attractive quality*) Charme *m* ❷ (*jewelry*) Anhänger *m;* **lucky ~** Glücksbringer *m* ► PHRASES: **to <u>work</u> like a ~** (*fam*) gut funktionieren **II.** *vt* bezaubern
charmed [tʃɑrmd] *adj* ❶ (*delighted*) bezaubert ❷ (*fortunate*) vom Glück gesegnet; **to lead a ~ life** ein [richtiges] Glückskind sein
charmer [ˈtʃɑr·mər] *n* (*pej*) Schmeichler(in) *m(f)*
charming [ˈtʃɑr·mɪŋ] *adj* (*approv*) bezaubernd, reizend
charred [tʃɑrd] *adj* verkohlt
chart [tʃɑrt] **I.** *n* ❶ (*visual*) Diagramm *nt;* **medical ~** Krankenblatt *nt* ❷ MUS ■ **the ~s** *pl* die Charts **II.** *vt* (*plot*) aufzeichnen; (*record*) erfassen
charter [ˈtʃɑr·t̬ər] **I.** *n* ❶ (*constitution*) Charta *f;* (*of society*) Satzung *f* ❷ TRANSP Charter *m* **II.** *vt* chartern
ˈ**charter flight** *n* Charterflug *m*
chase [tʃeɪs] **I.** *n* ❶ (*pursuit*) Verfolgungsjagd *f;* **to give ~ [to sb/sth]** jdn/etw verfolgen ❷ HUNT Jagd *f* **II.** *vi* ■ **to ~ after sb** hinter jdm herlaufen **III.** *vt* ❶ (*pursue*) verfolgen ❷ (*scare away*) ■ **to ~ away** vertreiben, verjagen; ■ **to ~ off** verscheuchen
chasm [ˈkæz·əm] *n* Kluft *f a. fig*
chassis <*pl* -> [ˈʃæs·i] *n* Fahrgestell *nt*
chaste [tʃeɪst] *adj* (*form*) keusch
chastity [ˈtʃæs·tɪ·t̬i] *n* Keuschheit *f*
chat [tʃæt] **I.** *n* ❶ (*informal conversation*) Unterhaltung *f;* (*fam*) Schwatz *m;* **to have a ~ [with sb]** [mit jdm] quatschen ❷ COMPUT Chatten **II.** *vi* <-tt-> ❶ (*talk informally*) plaudern; (*fam*) quatschen ❷ COMPUT chatten
ˈ**chat room** *n* COMPUT Chatroom *m*
chatter [ˈtʃæt̬·ər] **I.** *n* Geschwätz *nt* **II.** *vi* ❶ (*converse*) plaudern ❷ (*make clacking noises*) *teeth* klappern; *machines* knattern
chatty [ˈtʃæt̬·i] *adj* (*fam: person*) gesprächig; *letter* unterhaltsam; (*pej*) geschwätzig
chauffeur [ˈʃoʊ·ˈfər] **I.** *n* Chauffeur(in) *m(f)* **II.** *vt* ■ **to ~ sb around** jdn herumfahren
chauvinism [ˈʃoʊ·vɪ·nɪz·əm] *n* Chauvinismus *m*
chauvinist [ˈʃoʊ·vɪ·nɪst] *n* Chauvinist(in) *m(f)*
chauvinistic [ˌʃoʊ·vɪ·ˈnɪs·tɪk] *adj* (*pej*) chauvinistisch
cheap [tʃip] *adj* billig *a. fig;* (*reduced*) ermäßigt ► PHRASES: **a ~ <u>shot</u>** ein Schuss *m* unter die Gürtellinie
cheapen [ˈtʃi·pən] *vt* schlechtmachen
cheaply [ˈtʃip·li] *adv* billig
cheapness [ˈtʃip·nɪs] *n* ❶ (*low price*) Billigkeit *f* ❷ (*fam: miserliness*) Geiz *m*
ˈ**cheapskate** *n* (*pej fam*) Geizkragen *m*
cheat [tʃit] **I.** *n* ❶ (*person*) Betrüger(in) *m(f);* (*in game*) Mogler(in) *m(f);* (*in school*) Schummler(in) *m(f)* ❷ (*fraud*) Täuschung *f* **II.** *vi* betrügen; ■ **to ~ on sb** jdn betrügen; (*on exam*) abschreiben, mogeln; (*in game*) mogeln (**at, in** bei +*dat*) **III.** *vt* (*treat dishonestly*) täuschen; (*financially*) betrügen (**out of** um +*akk*)
cheater [ˈtʃi·t̬ər] *n* (*in game*) Mogler(in) *m(f);* (*in school*) Schummler(in) *m(f)*
check [tʃek] **I.** *n* ❶ (*inspection*) Kontrolle *f* ❷ (*search for information*) Suchlauf *m* ❸ (*restraint*) Kontrolle *f;* **to keep sth in ~** etw unter Kontrolle halten ❹ (*mark*) Haken *m* ❺ CHESS Schach *nt;* **to be in ~** im Schach stehen ❻ FIN Scheck *m* (**for** über +*akk*); (*bill*) Rechnung *f* (**for** über +*akk*) ❼ (*pattern*) Karo[muster] *nt* **II.** *adj* Karo- **III.** *vt* ❶ (*inspect*) überprüfen ❷ (*prevent*) *attack* aufhalten ❸ CHESS Schach bieten ❹ (*mark off*) abhaken **IV.** *vi* ❶ (*examine*) nachsehen, nachschauen *bes* SÜDD, ÖSTERR, SCHWEIZ ❷ (*consult*) ■ **to ~ with sb** bei jdm nachfragen
◆**check in I.** *vi* (*at airport*) einchecken; (*at

hotel) sich [an der Rezeption] anmelden **II.** *vt* (*at airport*) *passengers* abfertigen; (*at hotel*) *guests* anmelden; *luggage* einchecken
◆**check off** *vt* abhaken
◆**check out I.** *vi* sich abmelden; **to ~ out of a room** ein [Hotel]zimmer räumen **II.** *vt* ❶ (*investigate*) untersuchen ❷ (*sl: observe*) **~ it out!** schau dir bloß mal das an!
◆**check up** *vi* ■**to ~ up on sb/sth** jdn/etw überprüfen [*o* kontrollieren]
'**checkbook** *n* Scheckheft *nt*
checked [tʃekt] *adj* kariert
'**checkerboard** *n* Damebrett *nt*
checkered ['tʃek·ərd] *adj* ❶ (*patterned*) kariert ❷ (*inconsistent*) *past, career* bewegt
'**check-in** ['tʃek·ɪn] *n* ❶ (*registration for flight*) Einchecken *nt,* Abfertigung *f* ❷ (*desk in airport*) Abfertigungsschalter *m;* (*in hotel*) Rezeption *f*
'**check-in counter**, '**check-in desk** *n* (*in airport*) Abfertigungsschalter *m;* (*in hotel*) Rezeption *f*
'**checking account** *n* Girokonto *nt*
'**checklist** *n* Checkliste *f*
'**checkmate I.** *n* ❶ CHESS Schachmatt *nt* ❷ (*fig*) das Aus **II.** *vt* CHESS schachmatt setzen
'**checkout** *n* Kasse *f*
'**checkpoint** *n* Kontrollpunkt *m*
'**check room** *n* (*for coats*) Garderobe *f;* (*for luggage*) Gepäckaufbewahrung *f*
'**checkup** *n* [Kontroll]untersuchung *f;* **to go [in] for a ~** einen Check-up machen lassen
cheddar ['tʃed·ər] *n* Cheddar[käse] *m*
cheek [tʃik] *n* ❶ (*of face*) Backe *f* ❷ (*impertinence*) Frechheit *f*
'**cheekbone** *n usu pl* Backenknochen *m*
cheeky ['tʃi·ki] *adj* frech
cheep [tʃip] **I.** *n* (*of bird*) Piepser *m;* (*act*) Piepen *nt* **II.** *vi* piep[s]en
cheer [tʃɪr] **I.** *n* ❶ (*shout*) Beifallsruf *m;* (*cheering*) Jubel *m;* **three ~s for the champion!** ein dreifaches Hoch auf den Sieger! ❷ (*source of joy*) Freude *f* **II.** *vi* ■**to ~ for sb** jdn anfeuern
◆**cheer on** *vt* anfeuern
◆**cheer up I.** *vi* **~ up!** Kopf hoch! **II.** *vt* aufmuntern
cheerful ['tʃɪr·fʊl] *adj* ❶ (*happy*) fröhlich, heiter ❷ (*bright*) heiter; *color, tune* fröhlich
cheerfully ['tʃɪr·fəl·i] *adv* vergnügt
cheerfulness ['tʃɪr·fəl·nɪs] *n* Fröhlichkeit *f*
cheering ['tʃɪr·ɪŋ] **I.** *n* Jubel *m* **II.** *adj* jubelnd
'**cheerleader** *n* Cheerleader *m*
cheers [tʃɪrz] *interj* (*fam*) prost
cheery ['tʃɪr·i] *adj* fröhlich
cheese [tʃiz] *n* Käse *m*
'**cheeseburger** *n* Cheeseburger *m*
'**cheesecake** *n* Käsekuchen *m*
'**cheesecloth** *n* indische Baumwolle
cheesy ['tʃi·zi] *adj* ❶ (*with cheese flavor*) käsig ❷ (*fam or pej: uncool*) abgedroschen *fam,* geschmacklos ❸ (*fam or pej: not genuine*) **~ grin** Zahnpastalächeln *nt*
cheetah ['tʃɪ·t̬ə] *n* Gepard *m*
chef [ʃef] *n* Koch *m,* Köchin *f*
chemical ['kem·ɪ·kəl] **I.** *n* (*substance*) Chemikalie *f;* (*additive*) chemischer Zusatz **II.** *adj* chemisch
chemist ['kem·ɪst] *n* Chemiker(in) *m(f)*
chemistry ['kem·ɪ·stri] *n* ❶ Chemie *f a. fig* ❷ (*composition*) chemische Zusammensetzung
chemotherapy [ˌki·moʊ·'θer·ə·pi] *n* Chemotherapie *f*
cherish ['tʃer·ɪʃ] *vt* hegen
cherry ['tʃer·i] *n* ❶ (*fruit*) Kirsche *f* ❷ (*tree*) Kirschbaum *m*
'**cherry blossom** *n* Kirschblüte *f*
cherry to'mato *n* Cocktailtomate *f*
cherub <*pl* -s *or* -im> ['tʃer·əb] *n* ART Putte *f,* Putto *m*
chervil ['tʃɜr·vɪl] *n* Kerbel *m*
chess [tʃes] *n* Schach[spiel] *nt*
'**chessboard** *n* Schachbrett *nt*
'**chessman**, '**chesspiece** *n* Schachfigur *f*
chest [tʃest] *n* ❶ (*torso*) Brust *f* ❷ (*trunk*) Truhe *f;* (*box*) Kiste *f* ▶ PHRASES: **to get sth off one's ~** sich *dat* etw von der Seele reden
chestnut ['tʃes·nʌt] **I.** *n* ❶ (*nut, tree*) Kastanie *f* ❷ **old ~** (*fam: joke*) Witz *m* mit Bart **II.** *adj* (*color*) kastanienbraun
chesty ['tʃes·ti] *adj* (*fam*) ❶ (*arrogant*) eingebildet ❷ *blonde* vollbusig
chew [tʃu] **I.** *n* ❶ (*act of chewing*) **to have a ~ on sth** auf etw *dat* herumkauen ❷ (*food*) Bissen *m* **II.** *vt, vi* kauen; **to ~ one's fingernails** an den Nägeln kauen ▶ PHRASES: **to bite off more than one can ~** sich zu viel zumuten
'**chewing gum** *n* Kaugummi *m o nt*
chewy ['tʃu·i] *adj meat* zäh; *toffee* weich
chic [ʃik] **I.** *n* Schick *m* **II.** *adj* schick
chick [tʃɪk] *n* ❶ (*baby chicken*) Küken *nt* ❷ (*sl: good-looking female*) Puppe *f*
chicken ['tʃɪk·ən] **I.** *n* ❶ (*farm bird*) Huhn *nt* ❷ (*meat*) Hähnchen *nt* ❸ (*pej sl: coward*) Angsthase *m;* **to play ~** eine Mutprobe machen ▶ PHRASES: **don't count your ~s before they're hatched** (*prov*) man soll den Tag nicht vor dem Abend loben **II.** *adj* (*pej sl*) feige
'**chicken broth** *n* Hühnerbrühe *f*
'**chickenfeed** *n* ❶ (*fodder*) Hühnerfutter *nt* ❷ (*sl: money*) nur ein paar Groschen
'**chickenpox** *n* Windpocken *pl*
'**chick flick** *n* (*sl*) Frauenfilm *f* (*Film mit besonders emotionaler Handlung*)
chickpea ['tʃɪk·pi] *n* Kichererbse *f*
chicory ['tʃɪk·ə·ri] *n* ❶ (*vegetable*) Chicorée *m o f* ❷ (*in drink*) Zichorie *f*
chief [tʃif] **I.** *n* ❶ (*head of organization*) Chef(in) *m(f)* ❷ (*leader of people*) Führer(in) *m(f);* (*head of clan*) Oberhaupt *nt;* (*head of tribe*) Häuptling *m* **II.** *adj* ❶ (*main*) Haupt- ❷ (*head*) **~ administrator** Verwaltungschef(in) *m(f)*
chief ex'ecutive *n* ❶ (*head of state*) Präsident(in) *m(f)* ❷ (*head of organization*)

~ [**officer**] Generaldirektor(in) *m(f)*

chief 'justice *n* Oberrichter(in) *m(f)*

chiefly ['tʃif·li] *adv* hauptsächlich

chieftain ['tʃif·tən] *n* (*head of a tribe*) Häuptling *m;* (*of a clan*) Oberhaupt *nt*

chiffon [ʃɪ·'fan] *n* Chiffon *m*

child <*pl* -dren> [tʃaɪld] *n* Kind *nt*

'child abuse *n* Kindesmisshandlung *f;* (*sexually*) Kindesmissbrauch *m*

'childbearing I. *n* [Kinder]gebären *nt* **II.** *adj* **of ~ age** im gebärfähigen Alter

'childbirth *n* Geburt *f*

'childcare *n* Kinderpflege *f;* (*social services department*) Kinderfürsorge *f;* (*for older children*) Jugendfürsorge *f*

childhood ['tʃaɪld·hʊd] *n* Kindheit *f*

childish ['tʃaɪl·dɪʃ] *adj* (*pej*) kindisch

childless ['tʃaɪld·lɪs] *adj* kinderlos

'childlike *adj* kindlich

child por'nography *n* Kinderpornographie *f*

'childproof *adj* kindersicher

children ['tʃɪl·drən] *n pl of* **child**

'child's play *n* **to be ~** ein Kinderspiel sein, kinderleicht sein

'child support *n* Unterhalt *m*

chili <*pl* -es> ['tʃɪl·i] *n* Chili *m*

chili con carne [ˌtʃɪ·li·kan·'kar·ni] *n* Chili con Carne *nt*

chill [tʃɪl] **I.** *n* (*coldness*) Kühle *f;* (*feeling of coldness*) Kältegefühl *nt* **II.** *vi* ❶ abkühlen ❷ (*fam: relax*) ~ [**out**] chillen *sl* **III.** *vt* [ab]kühlen [lassen]

chilling ['tʃɪl·ɪŋ] *adj* ❶ (*making cold*) eisig ❷ (*causing fear*) abschreckend

chill-out ['tʃɪl·aʊt] *adj attr room, area* Ruhe-

chilly ['tʃɪl·i] *adj* kühl, frisch *a. fig;* **to feel ~** frösteln

chime [tʃaɪm] **I.** *n* (*bell tones*) Geläute *nt;* (*single one*) Glockenschlag *m;* (*of doorbell*) Läuten *nt kein pl* **II.** *vi* klingen; *church bells* läuten

chimney ['tʃɪm·ni] *n* ❶ Schornstein *m;* (*of factory*) Schlot *m;* (*of stove*) Rauchfang *m* ❷ (*in rock*) Kamin *m*

'chimney sweep *n* Schornsteinfeger(in) *m(f)*

chimpanzee [tʃɪm·'pæn·zi] *n* Schimpanse *m*

chin [tʃɪn] *n* Kinn *nt* ▶ PHRASES: **to keep one's ~ up** sich nicht unterkriegen lassen

china ['tʃaɪ·nə] *n* ❶ (*porcelain*) Porzellan *nt* ❷ (*tableware*) Geschirr *nt*

China ['tʃaɪ·nə] *n* China *nt*

Chinese <*pl* -> [tʃaɪ·'niz] **I.** *n* ❶ (*person*) Chinese, -in *m, f;* ■ **the ~** *pl* die Chinesen ❷ (*language*) Chinesisch *nt* **II.** *adj* chinesisch

chink [tʃɪŋk] *n* Spalt *m;* **a ~ in sb's armor** (*fig*) jds Schwachstelle *f*

Chink [tʃiŋk] *n* (*pej sl*) Schlitzauge *nt*

chintzy ['tʃɪnt·si] *adj* (*sl or pej: of bad quality*) schäbig; (*cheap*) billig

'chin-up *n* (*exercise*) Klimmzug *m*

chip [tʃɪp] **I.** *n* ❶ (*broken-off piece*) Splitter *m;* (*of wood*) Span *m* ❷ (*crack*) ausgeschlagene Ecke; (*on blade*) Scharte *f;* **this cup has a ~ in it** diese Tasse ist angeschlagen ❸ *usu pl* FOOD **potato ~s** Chips *pl* ❹ COMPUT Chip *m* ▶ PHRASES: **to be a ~ off the old block** ganz der Vater/die Mutter sein; **when the ~s are down** wenn es drauf ankommt **II.** *vt* <-pp-> ❶ (*damage*) abschlagen; (*break off*) abbrechen ❷ SPORTS *ball, puck* chippen **III.** *vi* <-pp-> [leicht] abbrechen

◆**chip in I.** *vi* ❶ (*pay*) beisteuern ❷ (*help*) mithelfen **II.** *vt money* etw beisteuern

chipmunk ['tʃɪp·mʌŋk] *n* Backenhörnchen *nt*

chipped [tʃɪpt] *adj* abgeschlagen; (*of blade*) schartig; *plate* angeschlagen; *tooth* abgebrochen

chiropractor ['kaɪ·roʊ·ˌpræk·tər] *n* Chiropraktiker(in) *m(f)*

chirp [tʃɜrp] **I.** *n* Zwitschern *nt* **II.** *vi, vt* zwitschern

chisel ['tʃɪz·əl] **I.** *n* Meißel *m;* (*for wood*) Beitel *m* **II.** *vt* <-l- *or* -ll-> meißeln; *wood* hauen

chitchat ['tʃɪt·ˌtʃæt] *n* (*fam*) Geplauder *nt*

chivalrous ['ʃɪv·əl·rəs] *adj* ritterlich

chivalry ['ʃɪv·əl·ri] *n* Ritterlichkeit *f*

chive [tʃaɪv] *n* ■ **~s** *pl* Schnittlauch *m kein pl*

chloride ['klɔr·aɪd] *n* Chlorid *nt*

chlorinate ['klɔr·ɪ·neɪt] *vt* chloren

chlorine ['klɔr·in] *n* Chlor *nt*

chlorofluorocarbon [ˌklɔr·oʊ·ˌflʊr·oʊ·'kar·bən] *n* Fluorchlorkohlenwasserstoff *m*

chloroform ['klɔr·ə·fɔrm] *n* Chloroform *nt*

chlorophyll ['klɔr·ə·fɪl] *n* Chlorophyll *nt*

chock [tʃak] *n* Bremsklotz *m*

chock-'full *adj* (*fam: full*) proppenvoll, vollgestopft

chocolate ['tʃak·lət] *n* ❶ Schokolade *f;* **dark ~** Zartbitterschokolade *f* ❷ (*in fancy box*) Praline *f*

chocolate 'chip *n* Schokoladenstückchen *nt*

choice [tʃɔɪs] **I.** *n* ❶ (*selection*) Wahl *f;* **to make a ~** eine Wahl treffen ❷ (*variety*) **a wide ~ of sth** eine reiche Auswahl an etw *dat* **II.** *adj* ❶ (*top quality*) erstklassig ❷ (*iron: abusive*) *language* deftig; *words* beißend

choir ['kwaɪr] *n* Chor *m*

choke [tʃoʊk] **I.** *n* AUTO Choke *m* **II.** *vt* ❶ (*strangle*) erwürgen; (*suffocate*) ersticken ❷ (*block*) *pipe, gutter* verstopfen **III.** *vi* ❶ (*have problems breathing*) keine Luft bekommen; **to ~ to death** ersticken ❷ (*fail*) versagen

◆**choke back** *vt* unterdrücken

◆**choke off** *vt* drosseln

◆**choke up** *vt* überwältigen

choker ['tʃoʊ·kər] *n* (*necklace*) eng anliegende Halskette; (*ribbon*) Halsband *nt*

cholera ['kal·ər·ə] *n* Cholera *f*

cholesterol [kə·'les·tə·ral] *n* Cholesterin *nt*

chomp [tʃamp] **I.** *vt* kauen, mampfen **II.** *vi* ■ **to ~ on sth** auf etw draufbeißen ▶ PHRASES: **to ~ at the bit** vor Ungeduld fiebern

choose <chose, chosen> [tʃuz] **I.** *vt* [aus]wählen; **they chose her to lead the project** sie haben sie zur Projektleiterin gewählt **II.** *vi* (*select*) wählen; (*decide*) sich entscheiden; **you can ~ from these prizes** Sie können sich etwas unter diesen Preisen aussuchen ▶ PHRASES: **there is little to ~ between them** sie unterscheiden sich kaum

choosy ['tʃu·zi] *adj* (*fam*) wählerisch (**about** bei +*dat*)

chop [tʃap] **I.** *vt* <-pp-> ❶ (*cut*) ■ **to ~ sth** ⟲ [**up**] etw klein schneiden; *wood* hacken ❷ (*reduce*) kürzen **II.** *vi* <-pp-> hacken **III.** *n* ❶ (*cut of meat*) Kotelett *nt* ❷ (*blow*) Schlag *m*

◆ **chop down** *vt* fällen

◆ **chop off** *vt* abhacken

chopper ['tʃap·ər] *n* ❶ (*sl: helicopter*) Hubschrauber *m* ❷ (*sl: motorcycle*) Chopper *m* ❸ (*for meat*) Hackbeil *nt;* (*for wood*) Hackbeil *nt,* Häcksler *nt*

'chopping block *n* Hackklotz *m*

'chopping board *n* Hackbrett *nt*

choppy ['tʃap·i] *adj* NAUT bewegt

'chopstick *n usu pl* [Ess]stäbchen *nt*

choral ['kɔr·əl] *adj* Chor-

chord [kɔrd] *n* Akkord *m* ▶ PHRASES: **to strike a ~ with sb** jdn berühren

chore [tʃɔr] *n* Routinearbeit *f,* lästige Aufgabe

choreographer [ˌkɔr·ɪ·'ag·rə·fər] *n* Choreograf(in) *m(f)*

choreography [ˌkɔr·ɪ·'ag·rə·fi] *n* Choreografie *f*

chorus ['kɔr·əs] **I.** *n* <*pl* -es> ❶ (*refrain*) Refrain *m* ❷ (*group of singers*) Chor *m* **II.** *vi* im Chor sprechen

chose [tʃoʊz] *pt of* **choose**

chosen ['tʃoʊ·zən] *pp of* **choose**

chow [tʃaʊ] *n* (*sl: food*) Futter *nt*

chowder ['tʃaʊ·dər] *n sämige Suppe mit Fisch, Muscheln etc.*

Christ [kraɪst] **I.** *n* Christus *m* **II.** *interj* (*sl*) **~ almighty!** Herrgott noch mal!

christen ['krɪs·ən] *vt* ❶ (*give name to*) taufen; (*give nickname to*) einen Spitznamen geben ❷ (*use for first time*) einweihen

christening ['krɪs·ə·nɪŋ] *n* Taufe *f*

Christian ['krɪs·tʃən] **I.** *n* Christ(in) *m(f)* **II.** *adj* christlich *a. fig;* (*decent*) anständig

Christianity [ˌkrɪs·tʃi·'æn·ɪ·ţi] *n* Christentum *nt*

Christmas <*pl* -es *or* -ses> ['krɪs·məs] *n* Weihnachten *nt;* **Merry ~!** Frohe [*o* Fröhliche] Weihnachten!

'Christmas card *n* Weihnachtskarte *f*

'Christmas carol *n* Weihnachtslied *nt*

Christmas 'Day *n* erster Weihnachtsfeiertag

Christmas 'Eve *n* Heiligabend *m*

'Christmas tree *n* Weihnachtsbaum *m*

chrome [kroʊm], **chromium** ['kroʊ·mi·əm] *n* Chrom *nt;* **~-plated** verchromt

chromosome ['kroʊ·mə·soʊm] *n* Chromosom *nt*

chronic ['kran·ɪk] *adj* ❶ (*continual*) chronisch ❷ (*habitual*) *liar* notorisch

chronicle ['kran·ɪ·kəl] **I.** *vt* aufzeichnen **II.** *n* Chronik *f*

chronological [ˌkran·ə·'ladʒ·ɪ·kəl] *adj* chronologisch

chronology [krə·'nal·ə·dʒi] *n* Chronologie *f*

chrysalis <*pl* -es> ['krɪs·ə·lɪs] *n* BIOL Puppe *f*

chubby ['tʃʌb·i] *adj* pummelig; *face* pausbäckig

chuck [tʃʌk] *vt* (*fam*) ❶ (*throw*) schmeißen ❷ (*fam: discard*) *old clothes* wegschmeißen

◆ **chuck out** *vt* (*fam*) wegschmeißen

chuckle ['tʃʌk·əl] **I.** *n* Gekicher *nt kein pl* **II.** *vi* in sich hineinlachen

chug¹ [tʃʌg] **I.** *vi* <-gg-> tuckern **II.** *n* Tuckern *nt*

chug² [tʃʌg] (*sl*) **I.** *n* **to down sth in one ~** etw in einem Zug hinunterkippen **II.** *vt, vi* auf Ex trinken

chum [tʃʌm] *n* (*fam*) Freund(in) *m(f)*

chummy ['tʃʌm·i] *adj* (*fam*) freundlich

chump [tʃʌmp] *n* (*fam*) Trottel *m*

chump change *n* (*sl*) Kleingeld

chunk [tʃʌŋk] *n* ❶ (*thick lump*) Brocken *m;* **~ of bread** [großes] Stück Brot ❷ (*fig fam: large part of sth*) großer Batzen

chunky ['tʃʌŋ·ki] *adj person* stämmig; *peanut butter* mit ganzen Stücken; *garments* grob; *jewelry* klobig

church [tʃɜrtʃ] *n* <*pl* -es> Kirche *f;* **to go to** [*or* **attend**] **~** in die [*o* zur] Kirche gehen

'churchgoer *n* Kirchgänger(in) *m(f)*

churlish ['tʃɜr·lɪʃ] *adj* ungehobelt

churn [tʃɜrn] **I.** *n* Butterfass *nt;* **milk ~** Milchkanne *f* **II.** *vt milk* quirlen; *ground, sea* aufwühlen **III.** *vi* (*fig*) sich heftig drehen

chute¹ [ʃut] *n* Rutsche *f;* **garbage ~** Müllschlucker *m*

chute² [ʃut] *n short for* **parachute** Fallschirm *m*

CIA [ˌsi·aɪ·'eɪ] *n abbrev of* **Central Intelligence Agency** CIA *m o f*

> **The Central Intelligence Agency (CIA)** ist die Bezeichnung für den Geheimdienst der Vereinigten Staaten. Die CIA wurde am 18. September 1947 gegründet und hat ihren Hauptsitz in Langley, Virginia. Neben der **CIA** gibt es noch eine Vielzahl weiterer Geheimdienste.

cider ['saɪ·dər] *n* Apfelmost *m*

cigar [sɪ·'gar] *n* Zigarre *f*

ci'gar box *n* Zigarrenkiste *f*

cigarette [ˌsɪg·ə·'ret] *n* Zigarette *f;* (*fam*) Kippe *f,* Glimmstängel *m*

cigarette butt *n* Kippe *f*

ciga'rette case *n* Zigarettenetui *nt*

ciga'rette holder *n* Zigarettenspitze *f*

cinch <*pl* -es> [sɪntʃ] *n usu sing* ■ **a ~** ein Kinderspiel *nt*

cinder ['sɪn·dər] *n* Zinder *m;* ■ **~s** *pl* Asche *f kein pl;* **~ track** Aschenbahn *f*

'cinder block *n* Bimsstein *m*

C

Cinderella [ˌsɪn·də·ˈrel·ə] *n* Aschenputtel *nt*
cinema [ˈsɪn·ə·mə] *n* Kino *nt*
cinematic [ˌsɪn·ə·ˈmæt̬·ɪk] *adj* Film-
cinnamon [ˈsɪn·ə·mən] *n* Zimt *m*
cipher [ˈsaɪ·fər] *n* (*secret code*) [Geheim]code *m;* (*symbol*) Chiffre *f*
circa [ˈsɜr·kə] *prep* (*form*) circa
circle [ˈsɜr·kəl] **I.** *n* Kreis *m;* **to go around in ~s** sich im Kreis drehen *a. fig;* **vicious ~** Teufelskreis *m* **II.** *vt* ❶ (*draw*) umkringeln; **to [put a] ~ [around] sth** etw einkreisen ❷ (*walk around*) umkreisen **III.** *vi* kreisen
circuit [ˈsɜr·kɪt] *n* ❶ ELEC Schaltsystem *nt* ❷ (*circular route*) Rundgang *m* (**around/through** um/durch +*akk*); **the lecture ~** UNIV Vorlesung *f* ❸ SPORTS (*series of competitions*) (Turnier)runde *f*
ˈ**circuit board** *n* Schaltbrett *nt*
ˈ**circuit breaker** *n* Schutzschalter *m*
circuitous [sər·ˈkju·ə·t̬əs] *adj* umständlich; **~ route** Umweg *m*
circular [ˈsɜr·kjə·lər] **I.** *adj* [kreis]rund **II.** *n* Rundschreiben *nt;* (*advertisement*) Wurfsendung *f*
circular ˈsaw *n* Kreissäge *f*
circulate [ˈsɜr·kjə·leɪt] **I.** *vt news* in Umlauf bringen; *petition* herumgehen lassen **II.** *vi* zirkulieren; *rumors* kursieren
circulation [ˌsɜr·kjʊ·ˈleɪ·ʃən] *n* ❶ MED [Blut]kreislauf *m,* Durchblutung *f;* **poor ~** Durchblutungsstörungen *pl* ❷ (*copies sold*) Auflage *f* ► PHRASES: **to be back in ~** wieder mitmischen
circumcise [ˈsɜr·kəm·saɪz] *vt* beschneiden
circumcision [ˌsɜr·kəm·ˈsɪʒ·ən] *n* Beschneidung *f*
circumference [sər·ˈkʌm·fər·əns] *n* Umfang *m*
circumnavigate [ˌsɜr·kəm·ˈnæv·ɪ·geɪt] *vt* umfahren; (*by sailing boat*) umsegeln
circumspect [ˈsɜr·kəm·spekt] *adj* umsichtig
circumstance [ˈsɜr·kəm·stæns] *n* Umstände *pl;* **in [***or* **under] no/these ~s** unter keinen/diesen Umständen
circumstantial [ˌsɜr·kəm·ˈstæn·ʃəl] *adj* indirekt; **~ evidence** Indizienbeweis *m*
circumvent [ˌsɜr·kəm·ˈvent] *vt* umgehen
circus [ˈsɜr·kəs] *n* Zirkus *m a. fig*
cirrus <*pl* -ri> [ˈsɪr·əs] *n* METEO Zirrus *m*
cistern [ˈsɪs·tərn] *n* (*water container*) Wasserspeicher *m*
citadel [ˈsɪt̬·ə·dəl] *n* Zitadelle *f*
citation [saɪ·ˈteɪ·ʃən] *n* ❶ (*quotation*) Zitat *nt* ❷ (*commendation*) lobende Erwähnung ❸ LAW (*ticket*) **traffic ~** Strafzettel *m*
cite [saɪt] *vt* ❶ (*mention*) anführen ❷ (*quote*) zitieren ❸ LAW verwarnen; **to be ~ed for speeding** eine Verwarnung wegen erhöhter Geschwindigkeit bekommen
citizen [ˈsɪt̬·ɪ·zən] *n* [Staats]bürger(in) *m(f)*
citizens band ˈradio *n* CB-Funk *m*
citizenship [ˈsɪt̬·ɪ·zən·ʃɪp] *n* (*national status*) Staatsbürgerschaft *f*
citric [ˈsɪt·rɪk] *adj* Zitrus-; **~ acid** Zitronensäure *f*
citrus <*pl* - *or* -es> [ˈsɪt·rəs] *n* Zitrusgewächs *nt;* **~ fruit** Zitrusfrucht *f*
city [ˈsɪt̬·i] *n* [Groß]stadt *f*

> Viele amerikanische **cities** (Großstädte) haben Spitznamen. New York heißt *The Big Apple*. In Anspielung darauf nennen manche Los Angeles *The Big Orange*, andere bevorzugen den Namen *The City of Angels*. Chicago ist *The Windy City* und New Orleans heißt *The Big Easy*. *The City of Brotherly Love* bezieht sich auf Philadelphia. Denver wird wegen seiner Höhenlage *The Mile High City* genannt und Detroit wird als Sitz der Autoindustrie als *Motor City* bezeichnet. San Francisco hat den Spitznamen *The City by the Bay* und wird von den Einheimischen stolz „The City" genannt.

city ˈclerk *n* Magistratsbeamte(r), -beamtin *m, f*
city ˈcouncil *n* Stadtrat *m,* Stadtverwaltung *f*
city ˈhall *n* Rathaus *nt;* ■ **C~** Stadtverwaltung *f*
city ˈplanning *n* Stadtplanung *f*
cityscape [ˈsɪt̬·i·skeɪp] *n* Stadtbild *nt;* (*picture of town*) Stadtansicht *f*
ˈ**city slicker** *n* (*pej fam*) Großstädter(in) *m(f),* Großstadtsnob *m pej*
civic [ˈsɪv·ɪk] *adj* städtisch; (*of citizenship*) bürgerlich
civics [ˈsɪv·ɪks] *n + sing vb* SCH Gemeinschaftskunde *f*
civil [ˈsɪv·əl] *adj* ❶ (*nonmilitary*) zivil; (*of ordinary citizens*) bürgerlich ❷ (*courteous*) höflich
civil ˈcourt *n* Zivilgericht *nt*
civil deˈfense *n* Zivilschutz *m*
civil disoˈbedience *n* ziviler Ungehorsam
civil engiˈneer *n* Bauingenieur(in) *m(f)*
civilian [sɪ·ˈvɪl·jən] **I.** *n* Zivilist(in) *m(f)* **II.** *adj* Zivil-
civility [sɪ·ˈvɪl·ɪ·ti] *n* (*politeness*) Höflichkeit *f*
civilization [ˌsɪv·ə·lɪ·ˈzeɪ·ʃən] *n* Zivilisation *f*
civilize [ˈsɪv·ə·laɪz] *vt* zivilisieren
civil ˈlaw *n* Zivilrecht *nt*
civil ˈliberties *npl* [bürgerliche] Freiheitsrechte *pl*
civil ˈrights *npl* Bürgerrechte *pl*
civil ˈservant *n* [Staats]beamte(r) *m,* [Staats]beamte [*o* -in] *f*
civil ˈservice *n* öffentlicher Dienst
civil ˈunion *n* eingetragene Lebenspartnerschaft *f*
civil ˈwar *n* Bürgerkrieg *m*

> Im **Civil War** (1861–1865) (Sezessionskrieg) standen einander die 24 im Wesentlichen industriellen Nordstaaten, die gegen Sklaverei waren, und die 11 hauptsächlich land-

wirtschaftlichen Südstaaten, die die Sklavenhaltung beibehalten wollten, gegenüber. Die Südstaaten spalteten sich schließlich von den Nordstaaten ab und gründeten die *Confederate States of America* (die Konföderierten Staaten von Amerika). Der Krieg forderte mehr als 970.000 Opfer, darunter 620.000 Tote. Das ist der größte Verlust von Menschenleben in der amerikanischen Geschichte.

clack [klæk] *vi* klappern

claim [kleɪm] I. *n* ❶ (*assertion*) Behauptung *f* ❷ (*demand for money*) Forderung *f* ❸ (*right*) Anspruch *m* (**to** auf +*akk*) ❹ **insurance ~** Versicherungsanspruch *m* II. *vt* ❶ (*declare ownership*) auf etw *akk* Anspruch erheben, Besitzansprüche geltend machen; *luggage* abholen; *throne* beanspruchen ❷ (*demand in writing*) beantragen; *damages, a refund* fordern ❸ (*assert*) behaupten; *responsibility* übernehmen; *victory* für sich in Anspruch nehmen; *diplomatic immunity* sich berufen auf ❹ (*take violently*) *lives* fordern ❺ (*require*) *attention* in Anspruch nehmen

claimant ['kleɪ·mənt] *n* Anspruchsteller(in) *m(f)*; (*for benefits*) Antragsteller(in) *m(f)*

clairvoyant [ˌkler·'vɔɪ·ənt] I. *n* Hellseher(in) *m(f)* II. *adj* hellseherisch; ■**to be ~** hellsehen können

clam [klæm] I. *n* Venusmuschel *f* II. *vi* <-mm-> ■**to ~ up** keinen Piep[s] mehr sagen

clamber ['klæm·bər] *vi* klettern

clam 'chowder *n* [sämige] Muschelsuppe

clammy ['klæm·i] *adj* feuchtkalt

clamor ['klæm·ər] I. *vi* (*demand*) schreien (**for** nach +*dat*); (*protest*) protestieren II. *n* ❶ (*popular outcry*) Aufschrei *m*; (*demand*) lautstarke Forderung ❷ (*loud noise*) Lärm *m*

clamp [klæmp] I. *n* Klammer *f*; (*screwable*) Klemme *f* II. *vt* ❶ (*fasten together*) ■**to ~ sth to sth** [*or* **sth together**] etw zusammenklammern ❷ (*hold tightly*) fest halten; **he ~ed his hand over her mouth** er hielt ihr mit der Hand den Mund zu

◆**clamp down** *vi* scharf vorgehen (**on** gegen +*akk*)

clan [klæn] *n* ❶ (*group with common ancestors*) Clan *m* ❷ (*fam: group with shared aim*) Sippschaft *f pej*

clandestine [klæn·'des·tɪn] *adj* heimlich

clang [klæŋ] I. *vi* scheppern; *bell* [laut] läuten II. *vt* klappern mit, schlagen III. *n usu sing* Scheppern *nt*; *bell* [lautes] Läuten

clank [klæŋk] I. *vi* klirren; *chain* rasseln II. *vt* klirren mit III. *n usu sing* Klirren *nt*

clap [klæp] I. *n* ❶ (*act*) Klatschen *nt* ❷ (*noise*) Krachen *nt*; **~ of thunder** Donner[schlag] *m* II. *vt* <-pp-> ❶ **to ~ one's hands** [**together**] in die Hände klatschen ❷ (*place quickly*) **she ~ped her hand over her mouth** sie hielt sich schnell den Mund zu; **to ~ handcuffs on sb** jdm Handschellen anlegen III. *vi* <-pp-> [Beifall] klatschen

clapper ['klæp·ər] *n* Klöppel *m*

claptrap ['klæp·træp] *n* (*pej fam*) Unsinn *m*

claret ['kler·ət] *n* ❶ (*wine*) roter Bordeaux ❷ (*color*) Weinrot *nt*

clarification [ˌkler·ɪ·fɪ·'keɪ·ʃən] *n* Klarstellung *f*

clarify <-ie-> ['kler·ɪ·fai] *vt* klarstellen

clarinet [ˌkler·ə·'net] *n* Klarinette *f*

clarity ['kler·ɪ·ti] *n* Klarheit *f*

clash [klæʃ] I. *vi* ❶ (*come into conflict*) zusammenstoßen ❷ (*compete against*) aufeinandertreffen ❸ (*contradict*) im Widerspruch stehen ❹ (*be discordant*) nicht harmonieren; *colors* sich beißen II. *vt* *cymbals* gegeneinanderschlagen III. *n* <*pl* -es> ❶ (*hostile encounter*) Zusammenstoß *m* ❷ (*contest*) Aufeinandertreffen *nt* ❸ (*conflict*) Konflikt *m* ❹ (*incompatibility*) Unvereinbarkeit *f*

clasp [klæsp] I. *n* ❶ (*fastening device*) Verschluss *m* ❷ (*firm grip*) Griff *m* II. *vt* umklammern; **to ~ one's hands** die Hände ringen

'clasp knife *n* Klappmesser *nt*

class [klæs] I. *n* <*pl* -es> ❶ (*lesson*) [Unterrichts]stunde *f*; SPORTS Kurs[us] *m* ❷ (*pupils*) [Schul]klasse *f* ❸ (*stratum*) Klasse *f*, Schicht *f* ❹ (*category, quality*) Klasse *f* II. *vt* einstufen

class 'act *n* (*fam*) spitze

class-'conscious *adj* klassenbewusst

classic ['klæs·ɪk] I. *adj* klassisch II. *n* Klassiker *m*

classical ['klæs·ɪ·kəl] *adj* klassisch

classics ['klæs·ɪks] *n + sing vb* Altphilologie *f*

classification [ˌklæs·ə·fɪ·'keɪ·ʃən] *n* Klassifikation *f*

classified ['klæs·ɪ·faɪd] *adj* geheim; **~ advertisement** Kleinanzeige *f*

classify <-ie-> ['klæs·ɪ·faɪ] *vt* klassifizieren

classless ['klæs·lɪs] *adj* klassenlos

'classmate *n* Klassenkamerad(in) *m(f)*

'classroom *n* Klassenzimmer *nt*

classy ['klæs·i] *adj* erstklassig

clatter ['klæţ·ər] I. *vt* klappern mit II. *vi* ❶ (*rattle*) klappern ❷ *hooves* trappeln III. *n* Klappern *nt*; *hooves* Getrappel *nt*

clause [klɔz] *n* ❶ (*part of sentence*) Satzglied *nt* ❷ (*in a contract*) Klausel *f*

claustrophobia [ˌklɔ·strə·'foʊ·bi·ə] *n* Klaustrophobie *f*

claustrophobic [ˌklɔ·strə·'foʊ·bɪk] *adj person* klaustrophobisch

claw [klɔ] I. *n* Kralle *f*; *of birds of prey, big cats* Klaue[n] *f[pl]*; (*of sea creatures*) Schere[n] *f[pl]* II. *vt* [zer]kratzen

clay [kleɪ] *n* ❶ (*earth*) Lehm *m*; (*for pottery*) Ton *m* ❷ TENNIS Sand *m*

clean [klin] I. *adj* ❶ (*not dirty*) sauber; *sheets* frisch ❷ LAW **to have a ~ record** nicht vorbestraft sein ❸ *joke* anständig; *living* makellos ❹ MED *break* glatt *dat* II. *adv* ❶ (*so as to be unsoiled*) **to sweep sth ~** etw (gründlich) säubern ② (*without polluting*) **to burn ~** *fuel* sauber verbrennen ③ (*fam: completely*) total, glatt **III.** *vt* (*remove dirt*) sauber machen; *car* waschen; *floor* wischen; *furniture* reinigen; *shoes, teeth* putzen; *wound* reinigen **IV.** *vi* ① (*remove dirt*) reinigen ② (*become rid of dirt*) sich reinigen lassen **V.** *n* **to give sth a [good] ~** etw [gründlich] sauber machen; *shoes, teeth, room* [gründlich] putzen; *furniture, carpet* [gründlich] reinigen

◆**clean out** *vt* ① (*clean thoroughly*) [gründlich] sauber machen; (*with water*) auswaschen; (*throw away*) entrümpeln ② (*fam: take all resources*) *person* [wie eine Weihnachtsgans] ausnehmen; (*in games*) sprengen; **to be completely ~ed out** völlig blank sein

◆**clean up I.** *vt* ① (*make clean*) sauber machen; *building* reinigen; *room, mess* aufräumen ② (*fig*) säubern **II.** *vi* ① (*make clean*) aufräumen; (*freshen oneself*) sich frisch machen; ■ **to ~ up after sb** jdm hinterherräumen ② (*sl: make profit*) absahnen

'clean-cut *adj* anständig

cleaner ['kli·nər] *n* ① (*substance*) Reiniger *m* ② (*person*) Reinigungskraft *f*, Putzfrau *f*

cleaning ['kli·nɪŋ] *n* Reinigung *f*; **to do the ~** sauber machen

'cleaning lady, **'cleaning woman** *n* Putzfrau *f*

cleanliness ['klen·lɪ·nɪs] *n* Sauberkeit *f*

cleanly ['klen·li] *adv* sauber

cleanse [klenz] *vt* reinigen

cleanser ['klen·zər] *n* Reiniger *m*; (*for skin*) Reinigungscreme *f*

clean-'shaven *adj* glatt rasiert

'cleanup *n* Reinigung *f*

clear [klɪr] **I.** *adj* ① (*easily understandable*) *instructions* klar; (*definite*) eindeutig; *signs* deutlich; **to make oneself ~** sich deutlich ausdrücken ② (*unmistakable*) klar; **he's got a ~ lead** er führt eindeutig; ■ **to be ~ about sth** sich *dat* über etw *akk* im Klaren sein ③ (*transparent*) *glass* durchsichtig; *liquid* klar ④ (*unobstructed*) *path, view* frei ⑤ (*guilt-free*) *conscience* rein ⑥ (*distinct*) *picture* scharf; *sounds* klar; **to make oneself ~** sich verständlich machen ⑦ (*pure*) *complexion* rein ⑧ METEO klar **II.** *n* ■ **to be in the ~** außer Verdacht sein **III.** *adv* ① (*away from*) **to be thrown ~ of sth** aus etw *dat* herausgeschleudert werden ② (*distinctly*) **loud and ~** klar und deutlich **IV.** *vt* ① (*remove confusion*) **to ~ one's head** einen klaren Kopf bekommen ② (*remove obstruction*) [weg]räumen; **to ~ one's throat** sich räuspern ③ (*remove blemish*) reinigen ④ (*empty*) ausräumen; *building* räumen; *table, desks* abräumen ⑤ (*acquit*) freisprechen; *name* reinwaschen ⑥ (*give permission*) genehmigen; **to ~ a plane for takeoff** ein Flugzeug zum Start freigeben ⑦ (*earn after deductions*) Netto verdienen ⑧ FIN *debts* begleichen ⑨ COMPUT (*delete*) löschen ▶ PHRASES: **to ~ the <u>decks</u>** klar Schiff machen **V.** *vi* ① (*become transparent*) *water* sich klären ② (*weather*) sich [auf]klären; *fog* sich auflösen ③ FIN *check* freigeben

◆**clear away** *vt* wegräumen

◆**clear off** *vt* abräumen

◆**clear out I.** *vt* ausräumen; *attic* entrümpeln **II.** *vi* (*fam*) verschwinden

◆**clear up I.** *vt* ① (*explain*) klären; *mystery* aufklären ② (*fig: put in order*) *mess* aufräumen **II.** *vi* ① (*stop raining*) aufhören zu regnen; (*brighten up*) sich aufklären ② (*become cured*) verschwinden, sich legen

clearance ['klɪr·əns] *n* ① (*act of clearing*) Beseitigung *f*; *of slums* Sanierung *f* ② (*space*) Spielraum *m*; *of a door* lichte Höhe ③ (*official permission*) Genehmigung *f*; (*for takeoff*) Starterlaubnis *f*; (*for landing*) Landeerlaubnis *f*

'clearance sale *n* Räumungsverkauf *m*

'clear-cut *adj* ① (*sharply outlined*) scharf geschnitten; *features* markant ② (*not ambiguous*) klar; *case* eindeutig

clearing ['klɪr·ɪŋ] *n* Lichtung *f*

'clearinghouse *n* Abrechnungsstelle *f*

clearly ['klɪr·li] *adv* ① (*distinctly*) klar, deutlich ② (*obviously*) offensichtlich; (*unambiguously*) eindeutig; (*undoubtedly*) zweifellos

clearness ['klɪr·nɪs] *n* Klarheit *f*; (*unambiguousness*) Eindeutigkeit *f*

cleavage ['kli·vɪdʒ] *n* Dekolletee *nt*

cleaver ['kli·vər] *n* Hackbeil *nt*

clef [klef] *n* [Noten]schlüssel *m*

cleft [kleft] **I.** *adj* gespalten; **~ palate** Gaumenspalte *f* **II.** *n* Spalt *m*

clematis <*pl* -> ['klem·ə·ţəs] *n* Klematis *f*

clemency ['klem·ən·si] *n* Milde *f*

clench [klentʃ] *vt* [fest] umklammern; *fist* ballen; *teeth* fest zusammenbeißen; *between one's teeth* klemmen

clergy ['klɜr·dʒi] *n* + *sing/pl vb* ■ **the ~** die Geistlichkeit

'clergyman *n* Geistliche(r) *m*

'clergywoman *n* Geistliche *f*

cleric ['kler·ɪk] *n* Kleriker(in) *m(f)*

clerical ['kler·ɪ·kəl] *adj* ① (*of offices*) Büro-; **~ error** Versehen *nt* ② (*of the clergy*) geistlich

'clerical work *n* Büroarbeit *f*

clerk [klɜrk] *n* Büroangestellte(r) *f(m)*; **sales ~** Verkäufer(in) *m(f)*; (*hotel receptionist*) Empfangschef *m*/Empfangsdame *f*

clever ['klev·ər] *adj* ① (*intelligent*) klug; (*ingenious*) clever *a. pej*; *trick* raffiniert ② (*dexterous*) geschickt (**with** mit +*dat*) ③ *attr* (*quick-witted*) schlagfertig; *wit* scharf

cleverness ['klev·ər·nɪs] *n* ① (*intelligence*) Klugheit ② (*dexterity*) Geschicklichkeit *f* ③ (*quick-wittedness*) Schlauheit *f*

cliché [kli·'ʃeɪ] *n* Klischee *nt*

click [klɪk] **I.** *n* ① (*short, sharp sound*) Klicken *nt*; *of heels* Zusammenklappen *nt*; *of lock* Einschnappen *nt* ② COMPUT Klick *m* **II.** *vi* ① (*short, sharp sound*) klicken; *lock* einschnappen ② (*fam: become friendly*) sich auf Anhieb verstehen ③ (*fam: become under-*

standable) [plötzlich] klar werden ❹ COMPUT klicken; ■**to ~ on sth** etw anklicken **III.** *vt* ❶ (*make sound*) **to ~ one's fingers** [mit den Fingern] schnippen; *heels* zusammenklappen ❷ COMPUT anklicken

client ['klaɪ·ənt] *n* Kunde *m*, Kundin *f*; LAW Klient(in) *m(f)*

clientele [ˌklaɪ·ən·'tel] *n* Kundschaft *f*

cliff [klɪf] *n* Klippe *f*

'cliffhanger *n* Thriller *m*

climate ['klaɪ·mɪt] *n* Klima *nt a. fig*; **the ~ of opinion** die allgemeine Meinung

'climate change *n* Klimaveränderung *f*

climatic [klaɪ·'mæṯ·ɪk] *adj* klimatisch

climatology [ˌklaɪ·mə·'tal·ə·dʒi] *n* Klimatologie *f*

climax ['klaɪ·mæks] **I.** *n* ❶ (*culmination*) Höhepunkt *m* ❷ (*orgasm*) Orgasmus **II.** *vi* ❶ (*reach a high point*) einen Höhepunkt erreichen; ■**to ~ with sth** in etw *dat* gipfeln ❷ (*achieve orgasm*) einen Orgasmus haben

climb [klaɪm] **I.** *n* ❶ (*ascent*) Aufstieg *m a. fig* ❷ (*increase*) Anstieg *m* (**in** +*gen*) **II.** *vt* ❶ (*ascend*) **to ~ [up] a hill** auf einen Hügel [hinauf]steigen; **to ~ [up] a tree** auf einen Baum [hoch]klettern ❷ (*conquer*) ersteigen **III.** *vi* ❶ (*ascend*) [auf]steigen *a. fig*; ■**to ~ up** *path* sich hochschlängeln; *plant* hochklettern ❷ (*increase rapidly*) [an]steigen ❸ (*get out*) herausklettern (**out of** aus +*dat*)

◆**climb down** *vi* heruntersteigen; *from summit* absteigen; *from tree* herunterklettern (von +*dat*)

climber ['klaɪ·mər] *n* ❶ (*mountaineer*) Bergsteiger(in) *m(f)*; *of rock faces* Kletterer *m*, Kletterin *f* ❷ (*climbing plant*) Kletterpflanze *f*

climbing ['klaɪ·mɪŋ] **I.** *n mountains* Bergsteigen *nt*; *rock faces* Klettern *nt* **II.** *adj* Kletter-

clinch [klɪntʃ] **I.** *n* <*pl* -es> Umschlingung *f* **II.** *vt* entscheiden; *deal* perfekt machen

clincher ['klɪn·tʃər] *n* (*fam*) entscheidender Faktor

cling <clung, clung> [klɪŋ] *vi* ❶ (*hold tightly*) [sich] klammern (**to** an +*akk*) ❷ (*stick*) kleben; *smell* hängen bleiben

clinging ['klɪŋ·ɪŋ] *adj* ❶ (*close-fitting*) eng anliegend ❷ (*emotionally*) klammernd

clingy ['klɪŋ·i] *adj* ❶ (*pej: dependent*) klammernd ❷ FASHION *fabric* elastisch

clinic ['klɪn·ɪk] *n* MED Klinik *f*, Ärztepraxis *f*

clinical ['klɪn·ɪ·kəl] *adj* ❶ MED klinisch ❷ (*emotionless*) distanziert

clink[1] [klɪŋk] **I.** *vt, vi* klirren [mit]; *esp metal* klimpern [mit] **II.** *n* Klirren *nt*; *coins* Klimpern *nt*

clink[2] [klɪŋk] *n* (*sl: jail*) Kittchen *nt*

clip[1] [klɪp] **I.** *n* ❶ (*trim*) Haarschnitt *m* ❷ FILM Ausschnitt *m* ❸ (*fam: pace*) **at a fast ~** mit gewaltigem Tempo **II.** *vt* <-pp-> ❶ (*trim*) *dog* trimmen; *hedge* stutzen; *sheep* scheren; *nails* schneiden ❷ (*cut out*) *coupons* abtrennen, abschneiden ❸ (*fig: reduce*) verkürzen ► PHRASES: **to ~ sb's wings** (*fig*) jdm die Flügel stutzen

clip[2] [klɪp] **I.** *n* ❶ (*fastener*) Klipp *m*; (*for wires*) Klemme *f*; **hair ~** [Haar]spange *f*; **paper ~** Büroklammer *f* ❷ (*for gun*) Ladestreifen *m* **II.** *vt* <-pp-> (*attach*) *paper* anheften; *rope* klemmen (**to** an +*akk*); ■**to ~ together** zusammenklammern

'clipboard *n* Klemmbrett *nt*

clipped [klɪpt] *adj* (*trimmed*) *hedges* gestutzt

clipping ['klɪp·ɪŋ] *n* **nail ~s** abgeschnittene Nägel; **newspaper ~** Zeitungsausschnitt *m*

clique [klik] *n* (*pej*) Clique *f*

cliquish ['kli·kɪʃ], **cliquey** ['kli·ki] *adj* (*pej*) cliquenhaft

clitoris ['klɪṯ·ər·əs] *n* Klitoris *f*, Kitzler *m*

cloak [kloʊk] **I.** *n* ❶ (*garment*) Umhang *m* ❷ (*fig*) Deckmantel *m* **II.** *vt* verhüllen

'cloakroom *n* Garderobe *f*

clobber ['klab·ər] *vt* (*fam*) ❶ (*strike*) verprügeln; **to ~ sb [with sth]** jdm eins [mit etw *dat*] überziehen ❷ (*defeat*) vernichtend schlagen

clock [klak] **I.** *n* Uhr *f*; **to work against the ~** gegen die Zeit arbeiten; **around the ~** rund um die Uhr **II.** *vt* ❶ (*measure speed*) **the police ~ed him doing 90 miles per hour** die Polizei blitzte ihn mit 90 Meilen pro Stunde ❷ (*fam: strike*) ■**to ~ sb** jdm eine kleben

'clock face *n* Zifferblatt *nt*

◆**clock in, clock out** *vi* stechen

clock 'radio *n* Radiowecker *m*

'clock-watcher *n* (*pej*) *jd, der ständig auf die Uhr sieht*

clockwise ['klak·waɪz] *adj, adv* im Uhrzeigersinn

'clockwork *n* Uhrwerk *nt*; **everything is going like ~** alles läuft wie am Schnürchen; **as regular as ~** [so] pünktlich wie ein Uhrwerk

clod [klad] *n* Klumpen *m*

clog [klag] **I.** *n* Holzschuh *m*; (*modern*) Clog[s] *m[pl]* **II.** *vi, vt* <-gg-> ■**to ~ [up]** verstopfen

cloister ['klɔɪ·stər] *n usu pl* Kreuzgang *m*

clone [kloʊn] **I.** *n* Klon *m* **II.** *vt* klonen

cloning ['kloʊ·nɪŋ] *n* Klonen *nt*

close[1] [kloʊs] **I.** *adj* ❶ (*near*) nah[e]; **the ~st bar** die nächste Bar; ■**to be ~ to sth** in der Nähe einer S. *gen* liegen ❷ (*intimate*) eng; *relatives* nah; ■**to be ~ to sb** jdm [sehr] nahestehen ❸ (*almost equal*) knapp; **~ race** Kopf-an-Kopf-Rennen *nt* ❹ (*exact*) genau; **to pay ~ attention to sb** jdm gut zuhören; **to keep a ~ eye on sb/sth** jdn/etw gut im Auge behalten ❺ (*crowded*) *quarters* eng **II.** *adv* (*near*) nahe; **please come ~r** kommen Sie doch näher!; **she came ~ to getting the job** fast hätte sie die Stelle bekommen; **to hold sb ~** jdn fest an sich drücken; ■**~ together** dicht beieinander ► PHRASES: **cut it ~** knapp kalkulieren [*o* bemessen]

close[2] [kloʊz] **I.** *vt* ❶ (*shut*) schließen; *book, door, mouth* zumachen; *curtains* zuziehen; *road* sperren; *factory a.* stilllegen ❷ (*end*) abschließen; *bank account* auflösen; *meeting* beenden **II.** *vi* ❶ (*shut*) *wound* sich schließen;

door, lid zugehen; *shop* schließen; *eyes* zufallen ❷ (*shut down*) schließen; *shop* zumachen; *factory a.* stilllegen ❸ (*end*) zu Ende gehen; *meeting* schließen; **the Dow Jones ~d at 10,500** der Dow Jones schloss bei 10.500 [Punkten] **III.** *n* Ende *nt,* Schluss *m;* **to come to a ~** zu Ende gehen, enden

◆**close down I.** *vi business* schließen, zumachen; *factory* stillgelegt werden **II.** *vt* schließen; *factory* stilllegen

◆**close in** *vi* ■**to ~ in on sb/sth** sich jdm/etw nähern; (*surround*) jdn/etw umzingeln; *darkness* hereinbrechen

◆**close off** *vt* absperren

◆**close up I.** *vi* ❶ (*lock up*) abschließen ❷ (*shut*) *flower, oyster, wound* sich schließen ❸ (*get nearer*) *people* zusammenrücken; *troops* aufschließen **II.** *vt* [ab]schließen

closed [kloʊzd] *adj* geschlossen, zu; **behind ~ doors** (*fig*) hinter verschlossenen Türen

closed-'door *adj* geheim; **~ meeting** Besprechung *f* hinter verschlossenen Türen

'close-knit *adj family* eng verbunden

closely ['kloʊs·li] *adv* ❶ (*near*) dicht ❷ (*intimately*) eng ❸ (*exactly*) genau ❹ (*carefully*) sorgfältig

closeness ['kloʊs·nɪs] *n* ❶ (*nearness*) Nähe *f* ❷ (*intimacy*) Vertrautheit *f*

closet ['klaz·ɪt] *n* (*storage*) Abstellraum *m* ► PHRASES: **to come out of the ~** seine Homosexualität bekennen

'close-up *n* Nahaufnahme *f*

closing ['kloʊ·zɪŋ] **I.** *adj* abschließend; **~ argument** LAW Schlussplädoyer **II.** *n* ❶ (*bringing to an end*) Beenden *nt kein pl;* (*action of closing*) Schließung *f* ❷ (*end of business hours*) Geschäftsschluss *m*

'closing date *n* Schlusstermin *m;* (*for competition*) Einsendeschluss *m*

'closing time *n* (*for shop*) Ladenschluss *m;* (*for staff*) Feierabend *m;* (*for bars*) Sperrstunde *f*

closure ['kloʊ·ʒər] *n* ❶ *of institution* Schließung *f; of street* Sperrung *f; of mine* Stilllegung *f* ❷ **to have ~** (*conclusion*) etw verarbeiten

clot [klat] **I.** *n* MED [**blood**] ~ [Blut]gerinnsel *nt* **II.** *vi* <-tt-> gerinnen

cloth [klɔθ] *n* ❶ (*material*) Tuch *nt,* Stoff *m* ❷ (*for cleaning*) Lappen *m*

clothe [kloʊð] *vt* <clothed *or* clad, clothed *or* clad> [be]kleiden *a. fig*

clothes [kloʊz] *npl* Kleider *pl;* (*collectively*) Kleidung *f kein pl*

'clothes hanger *n* Kleiderbügel *m*

'clothesline *n* Wäscheleine *f*

'clothespin *n* Wäscheklammer *f*

clothing ['kloʊ·ðɪŋ] *n* Kleidung *f*

cloud [klaʊd] **I.** *n* Wolke *f; of insects* Schwarm *m;* **ash ~** Aschewolke *f* ► PHRASES: **every ~ has a silver lining** (*prov*) jedes Unglück hat auch sein Gutes; **to be under a ~** keinen guten Ruf haben **II.** *vt issue* verschleiern

◆**cloud over** *vi* ❶ *sky* sich bewölken ❷ (*fig*) *face* sich verfinstern

'cloudburst *n* Wolkenbruch *m*

clouded ['klaʊ·dɪd] *adj* ❶ (*cloudy*) bewölkt, bedeckt ❷ *liquid* trüb ❸ *mind* vernebelt, getrübt

cloudless ['klaʊd·lɪs] *adj* wolkenlos

cloudy ['klaʊ·di] *adj* ❶ (*overcast*) bewölkt, bedeckt ❷ *liquid* trüb

clout [klaʊt] *n* (*fam*) ❶ (*fam: influence*) Schlagkraft *f* ❷ (*hit*) Schlag *m*

clove [kloʊv] *n* ❶ Gewürznelke *f* ❷ **garlic ~** Knoblauchzehe *f*

clover ['kloʊ·vər] *n* Klee *m*

clown [klaʊn] **I.** *n* ❶ (*entertainer*) Clown *m* ❷ (*funny person*) Kasper *m;* (*pej*) Trottel *m* **II.** *vi* ■**to ~ around** herumalbern

club [klʌb] **I.** *n* ❶ (*group*) Klub *m,* Verein *m* ❷ (*nightclub*) Diskothek *f,* Klub *m* ❸ (*golf*) Schläger *m* ❹ (*weapon*) Knüppel *m* ❺ CARDS Kreuz *nt;* **queen of ~s** Kreuzdame *f* **II.** *vt* <-bb-> einknüppeln auf; **to ~ to death** erschlagen

clubbing ['klʌb·ɪŋ] *n* **to go ~** clubben gehen

club'foot *n* MED Klumpfuß *m*

'clubhouse *n* Klubhaus *nt*

club 'sandwich *n* Klubsandwich *nt*

club 'soda *n* Sodawasser *nt*

cluck [klʌk] *vi* gackern

clue [klu] *n* ❶ (*evidence*) Hinweis *m;* (*hint*) Tipp *m;* (*in criminal investigation*) Spur *f* ❷ (*idea*) Ahnung *f;* **I don't have a ~!** [ich hab'] keine Ahnung!

◆**clue in** *vt* ■**to ~ sb in [on sth]** jdn [über etw] informieren

clueless ['klu·lɪs] *adj* (*fam*) ahnungslos; ■**to be ~ about sth** von etw *dat* keine Ahnung haben

clump [klʌmp] **I.** *n* ❶ (*group*) Gruppe *f;* **~ of bushes** Gebüsch *nt* ❷ (*lump*) Klumpen *m* ❸ (*sound*) Sta[m]pfen *nt* **II.** *vi* ■**to ~ around** herumtrampeln

clumsiness ['klʌm·zɪ·nɪs] *n* Ungeschicktheit *f*

clumsy ['klʌm·zi] *adj* ❶ (*bungling*) ungeschickt, unbeholfen; *attempt* plump ❷ (*ungainly*) klobig

clung [klʌŋ] *pp, pt of* **cling**

clunk [klʌŋk] *n* dumpfes Geräusch

clunker ['klʌŋ·kər] *n* (*fam*) Klapperkiste *f*

cluster ['klʌs·tər] **I.** *n* Bündel *nt; of people* Traube *f; of eggs* Gelege *nt* **II.** *vi* ■**to ~ around sth** sich um etw *akk* scharen

clutch[1] [klʌtʃ] **I.** *vi* sich klammern (**at** an +*akk*) **II.** *vt* umklammern **III.** *n* ❶ *usu sing* AUTO Kupplung *f* ❷ (*control*) **to fall into the ~es of sb** jdm in die Klauen fallen

clutch[2] [klʌtʃ] *n* (*group*) **~ of eggs** Gelege *nt;* (*fig*) Schar *f*

'clutch bag *n* Unterarmtasche *f*

clutter ['klʌt̬·ər] **I.** *n* ❶ (*mess*) Durcheinander *nt* ❷ (*unorganized stuff*) Kram *m* **II.** *vt* durcheinanderbringen

◆**clutter up** *vt* ■**to be ~ed up** vollgestopft sein, übersät sein

cm <*pl* -> *n abbrev of* **centimeter** cm

c'mon [kə'man] (*fam*) *see* **come on**

CO [ˌsi·'oʊ] *n* ① GEOG *abbrev of* **Colorado** ② MIL *abbrev of* **Commanding Officer** Befehlshaber(in) *m(f)*

Co. [koʊ] *n abbrev of* **company**

c/o [ˌsi·'oʊ] *abbrev of* **care of** c/o, bei

coach [koʊtʃ] **I.** *n* ① SPORTS Trainer(in) *m(f)*; (*teacher*) Nachhilfelehrer(in) *m(f)* ② *horse-drawn* Kutsche *f*; RAIL [Eisenbahn]wagen *m* ③ (*private bus*) Reisebus *m* **II.** *vt* ① SPORTS trainieren ② (*help to learn*) Nachhilfe geben

coaching ['koʊtʃ·ɪŋ] *n* ① SPORTS Training *nt* ② (*teaching*) Nachhilfe *f*

coagulate [koʊ·'æg·jə·leɪt] **I.** *vi* gerinnen **II.** *vt* gerinnen lassen

coal [koʊl] *n* Kohle *f*

'**coal-black** *adj* kohlrabenschwarz

coalesce [koʊ·ə·'les] *vi* (*form*) sich verbinden

coalition [ˌkoʊ·ə·'lɪʃ·ən] *n* Koalition *f*

'**coal mine** *n* Kohlenbergwerk *nt*

'**coal miner** *n* Bergmann *m*

'**coal mining** *n* Kohle[n]bergbau *m*

coarse [kɔrs] *adj* ① (*rough*) grob ② (*vulgar*) derb

coarsely ['kɔrs·li] *adv* derb

coarsen ['kɔr·sən] **I.** *vt* rau machen **II.** *vi* rau werden

coarseness ['kɔrs·nɪs] *n* Grobheit *f*

coast [koʊst] **I.** *n* Küste *f*; **off the ~** vor der Küste ▶ PHRASES: **the ~ is clear** die Luft ist rein **II.** *vi* dahinrollen; **to ~ [along]** mühelos vorankommen

coastal ['koʊ·stəl] *adj* Küsten-

coaster ['koʊ·stər] *n* ① (*mat for glass*) Untersetzer *m* ② (*ship*) Küstenmotorschiff *nt* ③ (*roller coaster*) Achterbahn

'**coast guard,** '**Coast Guard** *n* Küstenwache *f*

'**coastline** *n* Küste[nlinie] *f*

coast-to-'coast *adj* von Küste zu Küste

coat [koʊt] **I.** *n* ① (*outer garment*) Mantel *m* ② (*animal's fur*) Fell *nt* ③ (*layer*) Schicht *f*; **~ of paint** Farbanstrich *m* **II.** *vt* überziehen; ■**to ~ sth with breadcrumbs** etw *akk* panieren

coated ['koʊ·t̬ɪd] *adj* überzogen; *tongue* belegt; *textiles* imprägniert; *glass* getönt

'**coat hanger** *n* Kleiderbügel *m*

coating ['koʊ·t̬ɪŋ] *n* Schicht *f*, Überzug *m*; *of paint* Anstrich *m*

co-author [koʊ·'ɔ·θər] **I.** *n* Mitautor(in) *m(f)* **II.** *vt* gemeinsam verfassen

coax [koʊks] *vt* ■**to ~ sb into doing sth** jdn dazu bringen, etw zu tun; **to ~ a smile out of sb** jdm ein Lächeln entlocken

coaxing ['koʊk·sɪŋ] **I.** *n* Zuspruch *m* **II.** *adj* schmeichelnd

cobble ['kab·əl] *n* Kopfstein *m*

◆**cobble together** *vt* zusammenschustern

cobbled ['kab·əld] *adj* **~ streets** Straßen *pl* mit Kopfsteinpflaster

cobbler[1] ['kab·lər] *n* (*sb who repairs shoes*) [Flick]schuster *m*

cobbler[2] ['kab·lər] *n* FOOD (*fruit pie*) **apple/peach ~** *Apfel-/Pfirsichauflauf mit Teigkruste*

'**cobblestone** *n* Kopfstein *m*

cobra ['koʊ·brə] *n* Kobra *f*

cobweb ['kab·web] *n* (*web*) Spinnennetz *nt*

cocaine [koʊ·'keɪn] *n* Kokain *nt*

cock [kak] **I.** *n* ① (*male chicken*) Hahn *m* ② (*gun part*) Gewehrhahn ③ (*vulg, sl: penis*) Schwanz *m* **II.** *vt* ① *head* auf die Seite legen; *ears* spitzen ② **to ~ a gun** den Hahn spannen

cock-a-doodle-doo [ˌkak·ə·ˌdu·dəl·'du] *n* Kikeriki *nt*

cockatoo <*pl* -s *or* -> ['kak·ə·'tu] *n* Kakadu *m*

cocked [kakt] *adj hat* aufgestülpt

cockeyed ['kak·aɪd] *adj* (*fam*) ① (*not straight*) schief ② (*ridiculous*) verrückt

'**cockfight** *n* Hahnenkampf *m*

cockiness ['kak·ɪ·nɪs] *n* Großspurigkeit *f*

cockle ['kak·əl] *n* Herzmuschel *f*

cockpit ['kak·pɪt] *n* Cockpit *nt*

cockroach ['kak·roʊtʃ] *n* Küchenschabe *f*

cocktail ['kak·teɪl] *n* Cocktail *m*

'**cocktail dress** *n* Cocktailkleid *nt*

'**cocktail lounge** *n* Cocktailbar *f*

'**cocktail stick** *n* Spießchen *nt*

cocky ['kak·i] *adj* (*fam*) großspurig

cocoa ['koʊ·koʊ] *n* Kakao *m*

coconut ['koʊ·kə·nʌt] *n* Kokosnuss *f*; **grated ~** Kokosraspel *pl*, Kokosette *nt* ÖSTERR

coconut 'milk *n* Kokosmilch *f*

coconut 'oil *n* Kokosöl *nt*

cocoon [kə·'kun] **I.** *n* Kokon *m* **II.** *vt* (*fig*) abschirmen

cod <*pl* - *or* -s> [kad] *n* Kabeljau *m*

coddle ['kad·əl] *vt* ① (*treat tenderly*) verhätscheln ② (*cook gently*) langsam köcheln lassen; *eggs* pochieren

code [koʊd] **I.** *n* ① (*ciphered language*) Kode *m*; **to write sth in ~** etw verschlüsseln ② LAW Kodex *m* **II.** *vt* chiffrieren

codeine ['koʊ·din] *n* Kodein *nt*

'**code name** *n* Deckname *m*

'**code number** *n* Kodenummer *f*; ADMIN Kennziffer *f*

code of 'conduct *n* Verhaltensregeln *pl*

'**code word** *n* Kennwort *nt*

codicil ['kad·ɪ·sɪl] *n* Kodizill *nt*

cod-liver 'oil *n* Lebertran *m*

co-ed [ˌkoʊ·'ed] *adj* SCH gemischt

coeducation [ˌkoʊ·edʒ·ʊ·'keɪ·ʃən] *n* Koedukation *f*

coefficient [ˌkoʊ·ɪ·'fɪʃ·ənt] *n* Koeffizient *m*

coerce [koʊ·'ɜrs] *vt* (*form*) ■**to ~ sb into doing sth** jdn dazu zwingen, etw zu tun

coercion [koʊ·'ɜr·ʒən] *n* (*form*) Zwang *m*

coexist [ˌkoʊ·ɪg·'zɪst] *vi* nebeneinander bestehen

coexistence [ˌkoʊ·ɪg·'zɪs·təns] *n* Koexistenz *f*

coffee ['kɔ·fi] *n* Kaffee *m*

'**coffee bean** *n* Kaffeebohne *f*

'**coffee break** *n* Kaffeepause *f*; **to take a ~** eine

C

Kaffeepause machen
'coffeecake *n* Kuchen *m*
'coffee cup *n* Kaffeetasse *f*
'coffee grinder *n* Kaffeemühle *f*
'coffee grounds *npl* Kaffeesatz *m kein pl*
'coffeehouse *n* Café *nt*
'coffeemaker *n* Kaffeemaschine *f*
'coffee mill *n* Kaffeemühle *f*
'coffeepot *n* Kaffeekanne *f*
'coffee shop *n* Café *nt*
'coffee table *n* Couchtisch *m*
coffer ['kɔ·fər] *n pl* (*money reserves*) Rücklagen *pl; of the state* Staatssäckel *nt*
coffin ['kɔ·fɪn] *n* Sarg *m*
cog [kag] *n* ❶ (*part of wheel*) Zahn *m* ❷ (*wheel*) Zahnrad *nt* ❸ (*fig*) Rädchen *nt*
cognac ['koʊn·jæk] *n* Cognac *m*
cognitive ['kag·nə·tɪv] *adj* (*form*) kognitiv; ~ **therapy** Kognitionstherapie *f*
cognoscenti [ˌkag·nə·'ʃen·ti] *npl* (*form*) Kenner(innen) *mpl(fpl)*
cohabit [koʊ·'hæb·ɪt] *vi* (*form*) zusammenleben; LAW in eheähnlicher Gemeinschaft leben
cohabitant [koʊ·'hæb·ɪ·tənt] *n* (*form*) Lebensgefährte, -gefährtin *m, f*
cohabitation [koʊ·ˌhæb·ɪ·'teɪ·ʃən] *n* Zusammenleben *nt;* LAW eheähnliche Gemeinschaft
cohere [koʊ·'hɪr] *vi* (*form*) zusammenhängen
coherence [koʊ·'hɪr·əns] *n* Zusammenhang *m*
coherent [koʊ·'hɪr·ənt] *adj* zusammenhängend
coherently [koʊ·'hɪr·ənt·li] *adv* zusammenhängend; *speak* verständlich
cohesion [koʊ·'hi·ʒən] *n* Zusammenhalt *m*
cohesive [koʊ·'hi·sɪv] *adj* geschlossen
cohesiveness [koʊ·'hi·sɪv·nɪs] *n* (*in physics*) Kohäsionskraft *f;* (*in group*) Zusammenhalt *m*
cohort ['koʊ·hɔrt] *n* ❶ (*subgroup*) [Personen]gruppe *f* ❷ (*pej: crony*) ■**~s** *pl* Konsorten *pl*
coil [kɔɪl] **I.** *n* ❶ (*wound spiral*) Rolle *f* ❷ ELEC Spule *f* **II.** *vi* sich winden **III.** *vt* aufwickeln; ■**to ~ oneself around sth** sich um etw *akk* winden
coiled [kɔɪld] *adj* gewunden; ~ **spring** Sprungfeder *f*
coin [kɔɪn] **I.** *n* Münze *f* **II.** *vt* ▶ PHRASES: **to ~ a phrase ...** ich will mal so sagen ...

> Die **coins** (Münzen) der USA haben spezielle Namen. Ein *dollar* besteht aus 100 *cents*. Eine Ein-Cent-Münze wird *penny* und eine Fünf-Cent-Münze *nickel* genannt. Eine Zehn-Cent-Münze wird als *dime* bezeichnet und eine 25-Cent-Münze als *quarter* (Vierteldollar).

coinage ['kɔɪ·nɪdʒ] *n* ❶ (*coins*) Münzen *pl* ❷ (*act*) Prägung *f* ❸ (*new word/phrase*) [Wort-]Prägung
coincide [ˌkoʊ·ɪn·'saɪd] *vi* ❶ (*happen at same time*) *events* zusammenfallen ❷ (*correspond*) *subjects* übereinstimmen ❸ (*concur*) übereinstimmen
coincidence [koʊ·'ɪn·sɪ·dəns] *n* ❶ (*chance happening*) Zufall *m* ❷ (*simultaneous occurrence*) *of events* Zusammenfallen *nt;* **bad ~** unglückliches Zusammentreffen ❸ (*concurrence*) *of opinion* Übereinstimmung *f*
coincidental [koʊ·ˌɪn·sɪ·'den·təl] *adj* zufällig
coincidentally [koʊ·ˌɪn·sɪ·'dən·təl·i] *adv* zufällig[erweise]
coke [koʊk] *n* (*sl*) Koks *m*
Coke® [koʊk] *n short for* **Coca Cola®** Cola *f*
col. [kal] *n abbrev of* **column** Sp.
Col. *n abbrev of* **colonel**
colander ['kʌl·ən·dər] *n* Sieb *nt*
cold [koʊld] **I.** *adj* kalt; **as ~ as ice** eiskalt; **to be** [*or* **feel**] **~** frieren; **I'm ~** mir ist kalt ▶ PHRASES: **to pour ~ water on sth** etw *dat* einen Dämpfer versetzen **II.** *n* ❶ (*low temperature*) Kälte *f;* **with ~** vor Kälte ❷ MED Erkältung *f,* Schnupfen *m;* **to have a ~** erkältet sein; **to catch a ~** sich erkälten
cold-blooded [ˌkoʊld·'blʌd·ɪd] *adj* kaltblütig
'cold call *n* unangemeldeter Vertreterbesuch
'cold cream *n* Cold Cream *f* (*halbfette Feuchtigkeitscreme*)
'cold cuts *npl* Aufschnitt *m kein pl*
'cold front *n* Kaltfront *f*
cold-'hearted *adj* kaltherzig
coldness ['koʊld·nɪs] *n* Kälte *f*
cold 'shoulder *n* (*fig*) **to give sb the ~** jdn schneiden
'cold snap *n* kurze Kälteperiode
'cold sore *n* Bläschenausschlag *m*
cold 'storage *n* **to put in ~** kühl lagern; (*fig*) auf Eis legen
cold 'sweat *n* kalter Schweiß
cold 'turkey *n* (*sl*) kalter Entzug
'cold war *n* kalter Krieg
coleslaw ['koʊl·slɔ] *n* Krautsalat *m*
colic ['kal·ɪk] *n* Kolik *f*
collaborate [kə·'læb·ə·reɪt] *vi* ❶ zusammenarbeiten (**on** an +*dat*) ❷ (*with enemy*) kollaborieren
collaboration [kə·ˌlæb·ə·'reɪ·ʃən] *n* ❶ Zusammenarbeit *f* ❷ (*with enemy*) Kollaboration *f*
collaborative [kə·'læb·ə·rə·tɪv] *adj effort* gemeinsam
collaborator [kə·'læb·ə·reɪ·t̬ər] *n* ❶ (*colleague*) Mitarbeiter(in) *m(f)* ❷ (*pej: traitor*) Kollaborateur(in) *m(f)*
collage [kə·'laʒ] *n* Collage *f*
collapse [kə·'læps] **I.** *vi* ❶ (*fall down*) *things, buildings* zusammenbrechen, einstürzen; *people* zusammenbrechen; **to ~ from exhaustion** zusammenklappen ❷ (*fail*) zusammenbrechen; *enterprise* zugrunde gehen; *hopes* sich zerschlagen; *prices* einbrechen; *society* zerfallen; *talks* scheitern **II.** *n* ❶ (*act of falling down*) Einsturz *m,* Zusammenbruch *m* ❷ (*failure*) Zusammenbruch *m* ❸ MED Kollaps *m*
collar ['kal·ər] **I.** *n* Kragen *m;* (*for animals*)

Halsband *nt* **II.** *vt* (*fam*) ■**to ~ sb** jdn schnappen

'collarbone *n* Schlüsselbein *nt*

collate [kə·'leɪt] *vt* ❶ (*analyze*) vergleichen ❷ (*arrange*) zusammenstellen

collateral [kə·'læṭ·ər·əl] *n* FIN [zusätzliche] Sicherheit

collateral 'damage *n* Kollateralschaden *m*

colleague ['kal·ig] *n* [Arbeits]kollege, -in *m, f*

collect [kə·'lekt] **I.** *adj* TELEC **~ call** R-Gespräch *nt* **II.** *adv* TELEC **to call [sb] ~** jdn per R-Gespräch anrufen **III.** *vi* (*gather*) sich versammeln; (*accumulate*) sich ansammeln **IV.** *vt* ❶ (*gather*) einsammeln; *money, stamps* sammeln ❷ (*pick up*) abholen

collectable [kə·'lek·tə·bəl] *adj, n see* **collectible**

col'lect call *n* R-Gespräch *nt*

collected [kə·'lek·tɪd] *adj* (*calm*) beherrscht

collectible [kə·'lek·tə·bəl] **I.** *adj* sammelbar **II.** *n* Sammlerstück *nt*

collection [kə·'lek·ʃən] *n* ❶ *of money, objects* Sammlung *f;* (*in church*) Kollekte *f;* **to start a ~ [for sb]** [für jdn] sammeln ❷ *of people* Ansammlung *f* ❸ FASHION Kollektion *f* ❹ (*act of collecting*) Abholung *f;* **garbage ~** Müllabfuhr *f;* (*from mailbox*) [Briefkasten]leerung *f*

collective [kə·'lek·tɪv] **I.** *adj* gemeinsam; *leadership* kollektiv; **~ interests** Gesamtinteressen *pl* **II.** *n* Gemeinschaft *f;* POL Kollektiv *nt;* ECON Genossenschaftsbetrieb *m*

collective 'bargaining *n* Tarifverhandlungen *pl*

collective 'noun *n* LING Sammelbegriff *m*

collector [kə·'lek·tər] *n* Sammler(in) *m(f);* **tax ~** Steuereintreiber(in) *m(f)*

col'lector's item *n* Sammlerstück *nt*

college ['kal·ɪdʒ] *n* ❶ (*institution of higher learning*) Universität *f,* College *nt,* Hochschule *f;* **art ~** Kunstakademie *f;* **to go to ~** auf die Universität gehen, studieren ❷ (*division of an institution*) Abteilung *f,* Fakultät *f*

> **College** entspricht in etwa dem Begriff Hochschule. Es bezeichnet häufig auch die Zeit an der *university* (Universität) bis zum Abschluss des *bachelor's degree*, normalerweise vier Jahre. **Colleges** können sowohl eigenständige Einrichtungen, die ausschließlich Undergraduate-Programme anbieten, als auch *schools* (Fakultäten) einer Universität sein. An diesen integrierten *colleges* werden ebenfalls *bachelor's degrees* vergeben, während die Universitäten *higher degrees* (höhere Abschlüsse) anbieten, wie *master's degrees* (entspricht etwa dem Magister) und *doctorates* oder *Ph. D.'s* (Promotionen). An *junior colleges* kann man die ersten zwei Collegejahre absolvieren oder einen technischen Beruf erlernen.

college 'graduate *n* Hochschulabsolvent(in) *m(f)*

college of education *n* Lehrerbildungsanstalt *f*

collide [kə·'laɪd] *vi* zusammenstoßen; ■**to ~ into sb/sth** mit jdm/etw zusammenprallen

collie ['kal·i] *n* Collie *m*

collision [kə·'lɪʒ·ən] *n* Zusammenstoß *m*

collocation [ˌkal·ə·'keɪ·ʃən] *n* LING Kollokation *f*

colloquial [kə·'loʊ·kwi·əl] *adj* umgangssprachlich; **~ language** Umgangssprache *f*

colloquialism [kə'loʊ·kwi·ə·lɪz·əm] *n* umgangssprachlicher Ausdruck

collude [kə·'lud] *vi* unter einer Decke stecken

collusion [kə·'lu·ʒən] *n* geheime Absprache; **to act in ~ with sb** mit jdm gemeinsame Sache machen

Colo. *abbrev of* **Colorado**

cologne [kə·'loʊn] *n* Eau *nt* de Cologne, Kölnischwasser *nt*

colon ['koʊ·lən] *n* ❶ ANAT Dickdarm *m* ❷ LING Doppelpunkt *m*

colonel ['kɜr·nəl] *n* Oberst *m*

colonial [kə·'loʊ·ni·əl] **I.** *adj* Kolonial- **II.** *n* Kolonist(in) *m(f)*

colonialism [kə·'loʊ·ni·ə·lɪz·əm] *n* Kolonialismus *m*

colonialist [kə·'loʊ·ni·ə·lɪst] **I.** *n* Kolonialist(in) *m(f)* **II.** *adj* kolonialistisch

colonist ['kal·ə·nɪst] *n* Kolonist(in) *m(f)*

colonization [ˌkal·ə·nɪ·'zeɪ·ʃən] *n* Kolonisation *f*

colonize ['kal·ə·naɪz] *vt* kolonisieren

colony ['kal·ə·ni] *n* Kolonie *f*

color ['kʌl·ər] **I.** *n* ❶ Farbe *f;* **~ photos** Farbfotos *pl* ❷ *of complexion* Gesichtsfarbe *f; of skin* Hautfarbe *f; of hair* Haarfarbe *f* ► PHRASES: **to pass with flying ~s** glänzend abschneiden; **to show one's true ~s** sein wahres Gesicht zeigen **II.** *vt* ❶ (*change color of*) färben ❷ (*distort*) beeinflussen **III.** *vi face* rot werden; *leaves* sich *akk* verfärben

Colorado [ˌkal·ərad·'oʊ] *n* Colorado *nt*

coloration [ˌkʌl·ə·'reɪ·ʃən] *n* Färbung *f*

'colorblind *adj* farbenblind

'colorblindness *n* Farbenblindheit *f*

colored ['kʌl·ərd] *adj* farbig; **~ pencil** [*or* **crayon**] Buntstift *m*

'colorfast *adj* farbecht

'color filter *n* Farbfilter *m o nt*

colorful ['kʌl·ər·fəl] *adj* ❶ (*full of color*) *paintings* farbenfroh; *clothing* bunt ❷ (*vivid*) lebendig; *description* anschaulich ❸ (*interesting*) [bunt] schillernd; *past* bewegt

coloring ['kʌl·ər·ɪŋ] *n* ❶ (*complexion*) Gesichtsfarbe *f* ❷ (*chemical*) Farbstoff *m*

colorless ['kʌl·ər·lɪs] *adj* farblos

color-safe ['kʌl·ər·seɪf] *adj detergent, bleach* mit Farbschutz *nach n;* **~ detergents** Colorwaschmittel *nt*

'color scheme *n* Farbzusammenstellung *f*

color 'television *n* Farbfernseher *m*

C

colossal [kə·ˈlas·əl] *adj* ungeheuer, riesig
colossus <*pl* -es *or* colossi> [kə·ˈlas·əs] *n* (*person*) Gigant(in) *m(f)*
colt [koʊlt] *n* [Hengst]fohlen *nt*

> **Columbus Day** ist der Jahrestag der Entdeckung der Neuen Welt durch den genuesischen Seefahrer Christoph Kolumbus am 12. Oktober 1492. In den USA wird seit 1971 der **Columbus Day** immer am zweiten Montag im Oktober gefeiert. In vielen amerikanischen Städten finden an diesem Tag *parades* (Umzüge) statt.

column [ˈkal·əm] *n* ① (*pillar*) Säule *f* ② JOURN (*article*) Kolumne *f*, Spalte *f* ③ (*vertical row*) Kolonne *f*, Reihe *f*
columnist [ˈkal·əm·nɪst] *n* Kolumnist(in) *m(f)*
coma [ˈkoʊ·mə] *n* MED Koma *nt*
comatose [ˈkoʊ·mə·toʊs] *adj* ① MED komatös ② (*fig*) apathisch
comb [koʊm] **I.** *n* Kamm *m* **II.** *vt* ① kämmen ② (*search thoroughly*) durchkämmen
combat [ˈkam·bæt] **I.** *n* Kampf *m* **II.** *vt* <-tt- *or* -t-> bekämpfen
combatant [kəm·ˈbæt·ənt] *n* Kämpfer(in) *m(f)*
combination [ˌkam·bə·ˈneɪ·ʃən] *n* Kombination *f* (**of** aus +*dat*)
combine¹ [kəm·ˈbaɪn] **I.** *vt* verbinden; **to ~ family life with a career** Familie und Karriere unter einen Hut bringen **II.** *vi* ① (*mix together*) sich verbinden ② (*work together*) sich verbünden
combine² [ˈkam·baɪn] *n* Mähdrescher *m*
combined [kəm·ˈbaɪnd] *adj* vereint; **~ total** Gesamtsumme *f*
combustible [kəm·ˈbʌs·tə·bəl] *adj* (*form*) ① brennbar ② (*fig*) reizbar
combustion [kəm·ˈbʌs·tʃən] *n* Verbrennung *f*
come [kʌm] *vi* <came, come> ① (*move towards*) kommen; **~ here for a second** kommst du mal einen Moment [her]?; **did you ~ straight from the airport?** kommen Sie direkt vom Flughafen?; ■**to ~ toward[s] sb** auf jdn zugehen ② (*arrive*) ankommen; **Christmas is coming** bald ist Weihnachten; **I think the time has ~ to ...** ich denke, es ist an der Zeit, ...; **in the year to ~** im kommenden Jahr; **I've ~ to read the gas meter** ich soll den Gaszähler ablesen; ■**to ~ for sb/sth** jdn/etw abholen ③ (*accompany someone*) mitkommen; **do you want to ~ to the bar with us?** kommst du mit einen trinken? ④ (*originate from*) stammen; **where is that awful smell coming from?** wo kommt dieser schreckliche Gestank her? ⑤ (*have priority*) **to ~ before sth** wichtiger als etw sein; **to ~ first** [bei jdm] an erster Stelle stehen ⑥ (*happen*) geschehen; **~ what may** komme, was wolle; **you could see it coming** das war ja zu erwarten; **how ~?** wieso? ⑦ (*be, become*) **to ~ under pressure** unter Druck geraten; **to ~ open** sich öffnen; *door* aufgehen; **all my dreams came true** all meine Träume haben sich erfüllt; **nothing came of it** daraus ist nichts geworden ▶ PHRASES: **~ again?** [wie] bitte?
◆**come about** *vi* (*happen*) passieren
◆**come across** *vi* ① (*by chance*) *person* [zufällig] begegnen +*dat; thing* [zufällig] stoßen (auf +*akk*) ② (*encounter*) **have you ever ~ across anything like this before?** ist dir so etwas schon einmal begegnet? ③ (*be evident*) *feelings* zum Ausdruck kommen ④ (*create an impression*) wirken
◆**come along** *vi* ① (*go too*) mitgehen, mitkommen; **I'll ~ along later** ich komme später nach ② (*progress*) Fortschritte machen; *person* sich gut machen; **how is the project coming along?** wie geht's mit dem Projekt voran? ③ (*improve*) vorankommen; **how's your English coming along?** wie geht's mit deinem Englisch voran?
◆**come apart** *vi* auseinanderfallen
◆**come around** *vi* ① (*regain consciousness*) [wieder] zu sich kommen ② (*change one's mind*) seine Meinung ändern; **to ~ around to sb's point of view** sich jds Standpunkt *m* anschließen
◆**come away** *vi* ① (*leave*) weggehen ② (*become detached*) sich lösen
◆**come back** *vi* ① (*return*) zurückkommen ② (*be remembered*) *name* wieder einfallen ③ SPORTS aufholen
◆**come by** *vi* ① (*visit*) vorbeikommen ② (*obtain*) kriegen; **how did you ~ by that black eye?** wie bist du denn zu dem blauen Auge gekommen?
◆**come down** *vi* ① (*fall*) fallen; *pants* rutschen ② (*collapse*) einstürzen; **the building will have to ~ down** das Gebäude muss abgerissen werden ③ (*move down*) herunterkommen ④ (*become less*) sinken ⑤ (*depend on*) ankommen (**to** auf +*akk*) ⑥ (*amount to*) hinauslaufen (**to** auf +*akk*) ⑦ (*be taken ill*) ■**to ~ down with sth** sich *dat* etw eingefangen haben; **to ~ down with the flu** die Grippe bekommen
◆**come forward** *vi* sich melden
◆**come in** *vi* ① (*enter*) hereinkommen; **~ in!** herein! ② (*arrive*) ankommen; *results* eintreffen; *ship* einlaufen; *train* einfahren; *plane* landen; *fruit, vegetables* geerntet werden; *tide* kommen; *money* reinkommen; *news* hereinkommen ③ (*become fashionable*) in Mode kommen ④ + *adj* (*be*) **to ~ in handy** gelegen kommen; **to ~ in useful** sich als nützlich erweisen ⑤ (*play a part*) **where do I ~ in?** welche Rolle spiele ich dabei?; **and that's where you ~ in** und hier kommst du dann ins Spiel ⑥ (*begin to participate*) sich *akk* einschalten; ■**to ~ in on sth** sich *akk* an etw *dat* beteiligen
◆**come into** *vi* (*inherit*) erben
◆**come off** *vi* ① (*become detached*) abgehen ② (*take place*) stattfinden ③ (*fam: succeed*)

klappen ④ (*end up*) abschneiden; **to always ~ off worse** immer den Kürzeren ziehen
◆**come on** *vi* ① (*hurry*) **~ on!** (*impatient*) komm jetzt [endlich]!, jetzt komm [endlich]!; (*encouraging*) komm schon!; (*expressing disbelief*) ach, komm!; (*annoyed*) jetzt hör aber auf! ② (*slowly advance*) *darkness, night* hereinbrechen, einsetzen ③ (*appear*) *actor* auftreten ④ (*begin*) *movie, show* anfangen; (*start to work*) *heat* angehen ⑤ (*sl: show sexual interest*) ■**to ~ on to sb** jdn anmachen, jdn angraben
◆**come out** *vi* ① (*go outside*) herauskommen; (*go out socially*) ausgehen ② (*be released*) *book, CD* herauskommen; (*onto the market*) auf den Markt kommen; *movie* anlaufen; **to ~ out of prison** aus dem Gefängnis kommen ③ (*become known*) bekannt werden ④ PHOT [gut] herauskommen ⑤ (*end up*) herauskommen, enden ⑥ (*tell*) ■**to ~ out with sth** *truth* mit etw *dat* herausrücken; **to ~ out with a remark** eine Bemerkung loslassen ⑦ (*appear*) *flowers, buds* herauskommen; *stars* zu sehen sein ⑧ (*reveal homosexuality*) sich outen ⑨ (*fade*) *stain* herausgehen ⑩ (*remove itself*) *tooth* herausfallen
◆**come over** *vi* ① (*to a place*) [her]überkommen; (*to sb's home*) vorbeischauen ② (*create impression*) wirken
◆**come through** *vi* ① (*become noticeable*) durchkommen ② (*survive*) überleben ③ (*help out*) **to ~ through [for sb]** für jdn da sein
◆**come to** *vi* ① (*regain consciousness*) [wieder] zu sich kommen ② (*amount to*) sich belaufen auf +*akk*; **your total ~s to 25 dollars** das macht 25 Dollar ③ (*reach*) **what is the world coming to?** wo soll das alles nur hinführen?; **he won't ~ to any harm** ihm wird nichts passieren; **to ~ to the conclusion ...** zu dem Schluss kommen, dass ...; **to ~ to nothing** zu nichts führen; **to ~ to the point** zum Punkt kommen ④ (*concern*) **when it ~s to traveling ...** wenn's ums Reisen geht, ...
◆**come under** *vi* ① (*be listed under*) stehen unter; **soups ~ under [the heading] "appetizers"** Suppen sind als Vorspeisen aufgeführt ② (*subject to*) **to ~ under fire** unter Beschuss geraten
◆**come up** *vi* ① (*to higher place*) hochkommen; *sun, moon* aufgehen; **do you ~ up to New England often?** kommen Sie oft nach New England? ② (*be mentioned*) aufkommen; *topic* angeschnitten werden; *name* erwähnt werden ③ (*happen unexpectedly*) [unerwartet] passieren ④ (*become vacant*) *job* frei werden ⑤ (*of plants*) herauskommen
◆**come upon** *vi thing* [zufällig] stoßen (auf +*akk*); *person* [zufällig] begegnen +*dat*
comeback ['kʌm·bæk] *n* ① (*return*) Comeback *nt* ② (*retort*) Reaktion *f*
comedian [kə·'mi·di·ən] *n* ① (*professional*) Komiker(in) *m(f)* ② (*amateur*) Clown *m*
comedienne [kə·ˌmi·di·'ən] *n* Komikerin *f*
comedown ['kʌm·daʊn] *n* (*fam*) Abstieg *m*
comedy ['kam·ə·di] *n* Komödie *f*
come-on ['kʌm·ɔn] *n* (*fam*) Anmache *f*
comet ['kam·ɪt] *n* Komet *m*
comeuppance [kʌm·'ʌp·əns] *n* **to get one's ~** die Quittung kriegen
comfort ['kʌm·fərt] **I.** *n* ① (*comfortable feeling*) Bequemlichkeit *f*; **the deadline is getting too close for ~** der Termin rückt bedrohlich näher ② (*consolation*) Trost *m* ③ (*pleasurable things in life*) ■**~s** *pl* Komfort *m kein pl* **II.** *vt* trösten
comfortable ['kʌm·fər·tə·bəl] *adj* ① (*offering comfort*) bequem; *house, room* komfortabel; *income* ausreichend; *temperature* angenehm ② (*at ease*) **to be** [*or* **feel**] **~** sich wohl fühlen; **are you ~?** sitzt du bequem?; **to make oneself ~** es sich *dat* bequem machen
comfortably ['kʌm·fər·tə·bli] *adv* ① (*in a comfortable manner*) bequem ② (*easily*) leicht ③ (*in financially stable manner*) **they are ~ off** es geht ihnen [finanziell] gut
comforter ['kʌm·fər·ṭər] *n* Oberbett *nt*, Federbett *nt*
comforting ['kʌm·fər·ṭɪŋ] *adj thoughts* beruhigend; *words* tröstend
comfy ['kʌm·fi] *adj* (*fam*) bequem
comic ['kam·ɪk] **I.** *n* ① (*strip*) ■**~s** *pl* Comicstrip *m* ② (*comedian*) *amateur* Clown *m*; *professional* Komiker(in) *m(f)* **II.** *adj* komisch
comical ['kam·ɪ·kəl] *adj* komisch
'comic book *n* Comicheft *nt*
'comic strip *n* Comic[strip] *m* (*in einer Zeitung*)
coming ['kʌm·ɪŋ] **I.** *adj* (*next*) kommend; (*approaching*) herannahend; *elections* anstehend; **this ~ Friday** nächsten Freitag **II.** *n* ① (*arrival*) Ankunft *f* ② **~s and goings** ein Kommen und Gehen *nt*
coming 'out <*pl* comings out> *n* Outing *nt*, Coming-out *nt*
comma ['kam·ə] *n* Komma *nt*
command [kə·'mænd] **I.** *vt* ① (*order*) ■**to ~ sb** jdm einen Befehl geben ② MIL ■**to ~ sth** den Oberbefehl über etw *akk* haben; *company* leiten; *ship* befehligen **II.** *vi* Befehle erteilen **III.** *n* ① (*order*) Befehl *m* ② (*authority*) Kommando *nt*; **to be in ~ of** befehligen; ■**to be at sb's ~** (*hum*) jdm zur Verfügung stehen ③ (*knowledge*) Beherrschung *f*
commandant ['kam·ən·dænt] *n* Kommandant(in) *m(f)*
commandeer [ˌkam·ən·'dɪr] *vt* beschlagnahmen
commander [kə·'mæn·dər] *n* ① MIL Kommandant(in) *m(f)* ② NAUT Fregattenkapitän(in) *m(f)*
commanding [kə·'mæn·dɪŋ] *adj* ① (*authoritative*) gebieterisch ② (*dominant*) *position, lead* beherrschend
com'mand key *n* COMPUT Befehlstaste *f*
commandment [kə·'mænd·mənt] *n* REL **the Ten C~s** die Zehn Gebote *pl*

com'mand module *n* Kommandokapsel *f*

commando <*pl* -s *or* -es> [kə·'mæn·doʊ] *n* MIL ❶ (*group*) Kommando *nt* ❷ (*member*) Angehörige(r) *f(m)* eines Kommandotrupps ▶ PHRASES: **to go** ~ (*fam or hum*) keine Unterwäsche tragen

commemorate [kə·'mem·ə·reɪt] *vt* gedenken +*gen*

commemoration [kə·ˌmem·ə·'reɪ·ʃən] *n* **in ~ of sb** zum Gedenken an jdn; **in ~ of sth** zur Erinnerung an etw *akk*

commemorative [kə·'mem·ər·ə·tɪv] *adj* **~ issue** Gedächtnisausgabe *f;* **~ plaque** Gedenktafel *f*

commence [kə·'mens] *vi* (*form*) beginnen, anfangen

commencement [kə·'mens·mənt] *n* (*form*) ❶ (*beginning*) Beginn *m,* Anfang *m* ❷ SCH, UNIV (*ceremony*) Abschlussfeier (*mit Verleihung der Diplome*)

commend [kə·'mend] *vt* ❶ (*praise*) loben ❷ (*recommend*) empfehlen

commendable [kə·'men·də·bəl] *adj* lobenswert

commendation [ˌkam·ən·'deɪ·ʃən] *n* ❶ (*praise*) Belobigung *f* ❷ (*honor*) Auszeichnung *f*

comment ['kam·ent] **I.** *n* Kommentar *m* **II.** *vi* einen Kommentar abgeben, bemerken; ■**to ~ on sth** sich zu etw *dat* äußern

commentary ['kam·ən·ter·i] *n* Kommentar *m* (**on** über +*akk*)

commentator ['kam·ən·teɪ·t̬ər] *n* Kommentator(in) *m(f),* Reporter(in) *m(f)*

commerce ['kam·ərs] *n* Handel *m*

commercial [kə·'mɜr·ʃəl] **I.** *adj* ❶ (*relating to commerce*) kaufmännisch, Handels-; (*engaged in commerce*) Güter- ❷ (*profit-orientated*) kommerziell **II.** *n* Werbespot *m*

commercialism [kə·'mɜr·ʃə·lɪz·əm], **commercialization** [kə·ˌmɜr·ʃə·lɪ·'zeɪ·ʃən] *n* Kommerzialisierung *f*

commercialize [kə·'mɜr·ʃə·laɪz] *vt* kommerzialisieren

commiserate [kə·'mɪz·ə·reɪt] *vi* mitfühlen

commiseration [kə·ˌmɪz·ə·'reɪ·ʃən] *n* ❶ (*sympathy*) Mitgefühl *nt* ❷ (*expression of sympathy*) ■**~s** *pl* Beileid *nt kein pl*

commission [kə·'mɪʃ·ən] **I.** *vt* (*order*) ■**to ~ sth** etw in Auftrag geben; ■**to ~ sb [to do sth]** jdn beauftragen[, etw zu tun] **II.** *n* ❶ (*order*) Auftrag *m* ❷ (*system of payment*) Provision *f* ❸ (*investigative body*) Kommission *f* ❹ **in/out of ~** *machine* in/außer Betrieb; *battleship* in/außer Dienst; (*fig*) außer Gefecht

commissioner [kə·'mɪʃ·ə·nər] *n* Beauftragte(r) *f(m);* **police ~** Polizeipräsident(in) *m(f)*

commit <-tt-> [kə·'mɪt] **I.** *vt* ❶ (*carry out*) begehen ❷ (*bind*) *money* bereitstellen; *soldiers* entsenden; ■**to ~ oneself to doing sth** sich verpflichten, etw zu tun **II.** *vi* (*bind oneself*) ■**to ~ to sth** sich auf etw *akk* festlegen

commitment [kə·'mɪt·mənt] *n* ❶ (*responsibility*) Verpflichtung *f* (**to** gegenüber +*dat*) ❷ (*dedication*) Engagement *nt* (**to** gegenüber +*dat*)

committed [kə·'mɪt̬·ɪd] *adj* ❶ (*obliged*) verpflichtet; ■**to be ~ to sth** auf etw *akk* festgelegt sein ❷ (*dedicated*) engagiert; *Christian* überzeugt; ■**to be ~ to sth** sich für etw *akk* engagieren

committee [kə·'mɪt̬·i] *n* + *sing/pl vb* Ausschuss *m,* Komitee *nt*

commode [kə·'moʊd] *n* ❶ (*euph: toilet*) Toilettenstuhl *m* ❷ (*chair with toilet*) Nachtstuhl *m* ❸ (*chest of drawers*) [dekorative] Kommode

commodity [kə·'mad·ɪ·ti] *n* (*product*) Ware *f;* (*raw material*) Rohstoff *m*

commodore ['kam·ə·dɔr] *n* (*in navy*) Kommodore *m*

common ['kam·ən] **I.** *adj* <-er, -est *or* more ~, most ~> ❶ (*often encountered*) üblich, gewöhnlich; *disease* weit verbreitet; *name* gängig ❷ (*normal*) normal; **it is ~ knowledge/practice ...** es ist allgemein bekannt/üblich ... ❸ (*shared*) gemeinsam; **by ~ consent** mit allgemeiner Einwilligung; **in ~** gemeinsam ❹ <-er, -est> (*pej: vulgar*) *behavior* vulgär **II.** *n* Gemeindeland *nt*

common de'nominator *n* gemeinsamer Nenner

commoner ['kam·ə·nər] *n* Bürgerliche(r) *f(m)*

commonly ['kam·ən·li] *adv* ❶ (*often*) häufig; (*usually*) gemeinhin; **a ~ held belief** eine weit verbreitete Annahme; **~ known as ...** oft auch ... genannt ❷ (*pej: vulgarly*) gewöhnlich

'commonplace **I.** *adj* ❶ (*normal*) alltäglich ❷ (*pej: trite*) banal **II.** *n* Gemeinplatz *m*

common 'sense *n* gesunder Menschenverstand

common 'stocks *npl* STOCKEX Stammaktien *pl*

commotion [kə·'moʊ·ʃən] *n* ❶ (*fuss*) Theater *nt* (**over** um +*akk*) ❷ (*noisy confusion*) Spektakel *m*

communal [kə·'mju·nəl] *adj* ❶ (*shared*) gemeinsam; **~ bathroom** Gemeinschaftsbad *nt* ❷ (*of religious communities*) Gemeinde-; **~ prayer** gemeinsames Gebet

commune ['kam·jun] *n* Kommune *f*

communicable [kə·'mju·nɪ·kə·bəl] *adj* vermittelbar; *disease* übertragbar

communicate [kə·'mju·nɪ·keɪt] **I.** *vt* ❶ (*pass on*) mitteilen; *knowledge* vermitteln ❷ *disease* übertragen auf +*akk* **II.** *vi* ❶ (*give information*) kommunizieren ❷ (*be in touch*) in Verbindung stehen; (*socially*) sich verstehen

communication [kə·ˌmju·nɪ·'keɪ·ʃən] *n* ❶ (*being in touch*) Kommunikation *f;* **~ gap** Informationslücke *f* ❷ (*passing on*) *of ideas* Vermittlung *f; of information* Übermittlung *f; of emotions* Ausdruck *m* ❸ (*form: thing communicated*) Mitteilung *f*

communicative [kə·'mju·nə·keɪ·tɪv] *adj* gesprächig; **~ skills** kommunikatives Talent

Communion [kəm·ˈjun·jən] *n* ■ **[Holy] ~** (*Protestant*) das [heilige] Abendmahl; (*Catholic*) die [heilige] Kommunion

communiqué [kə·ˌmju·nɪ·ˈkeɪ] *n* Kommuniqué *nt*

communism [ˈkam·jə·nɪz·əm] *n* Kommunismus *m*

communist [ˈkam·jə·nɪst] **I.** *n* Kommunist(in) *m(f)* **II.** *adj* kommunistisch

community [kə·ˈmju·nɪ·ti] *n* ① ADMIN Gemeinde *f* ② (*group*) **the business ~** die Geschäftswelt ③ (*public*) ■ **the ~** die Allgemeinheit

community ˈservice *n* gemeinnützige Arbeit

commute [kə·ˈmjut] **I.** *n* (*fam*) Pendelstrecke *f* **II.** *vi* pendeln

commuter [kə·ˈmju·t̬ər] *n* Pendler(in) *m(f)*

comˈmuter belt *n* städtischer Einzugsbereich

comˈmuter traffic *n* Pendelverkehr *m*

comˈmuter train *n* Pendlerzug *m*

compact [ˈkam·pækt] **I.** *adj* kompakt; *snow* fest; *style* knapp **II.** *vt* (*form: by a person*) festtreten; (*by a vehicle*) festfahren **III.** *n* ① (*cosmetics*) Puderdose *f* ② AUTO Kompaktwagen *m*

compact ˈdisc, compact ˈdisk *n* Compactdisc *f*

compactness [kəm·ˈpækt·nɪs] *n* Kompaktheit *f; of style* Knappheit *f*

companion [kəm·ˈpæn·jən] *n* (*person accompanying sb*) Begleiter(in) *m(f);* (*associate*) Gefährte, -in *m, f*

companionable [kəm·ˈpæn·jə·nə·bəl] *adj* angenehm

companionship [kəm·ˈpæn·jən·ʃɪp] *n* (*company*) Gesellschaft *f;* (*friendship*) Kameradschaft *f*

company [ˈkʌm·pə·ni] *n* ① COMM Firma *f,* Unternehmen *nt;* **shipping ~** Reederei *f;* **~ policy** Firmenpolitik *f* ② (*companionship*) Gesellschaft *f;* **to keep sb ~** jdm Gesellschaft leisten ③ (*visitors*) Besuch *m kein pl,* Gäste *pl* ④ THEAT (*group*) Schauspieltruppe *f;* MIL Kompanie *f*

comparable [ˈkam·pər·ə·bəl] *adj* vergleichbar (**to/with** mit +*dat*)

comparative [kəm·ˈper·ə·tɪv] **I.** *n* Komparativ *m* **II.** *adj* ① (*involving comparison*) vergleichend ② (*relative*) relativ

comparatively [kəm·ˈper·ə·tɪv·li] *adv* ① (*relatively*) verhältnismäßig ② (*by comparison*) im Vergleich

compare [kəm·ˈper] **I.** *vt* vergleichen (**to/with** mit); **to ~ notes on sth** (*fig*) Meinungen über etw *akk* austauschen **II.** *vi* vergleichbar sein; **to ~ favorably** vergleichsweise gut abschneiden

comparison [kəm·ˈper·ɪ·sən] *n* Vergleich *m;* **by ~ with** verglichen mit; **to draw** [*or* **make**] **a ~** einen Vergleich anstellen; **there's no ~ between them** man kann sie nicht vergleichen

compartment [kəm·ˈpart·mənt] *n* ① RAIL [Zug]abteil *nt,* Coupé *nt* ÖSTERR ② (*section*) Fach *nt*

compass <*pl* -es> [ˈkʌm·pəs] *n* ① (*for showing direction*) Kompass *m* ② (*for drawing circles*) Zirkel *m*

compassion [kəm·ˈpæʃ·ən] *n* **to feel ~ for** [*or* **toward**] **sb** Mitleid mit jdm haben; **to show ~ for** [*or* **toward**] **sb** Mitgefühl für jdn zeigen

compassionate [kəm·ˈpæʃ·ə·nɪt] *adj* mitfühlend

compatibility [kəm·ˌpæt̬·ə·ˈbɪl·ɪ·ti] *n* Vereinbarkeit *f;* COMPUT, MED Kompatibilität *f*

compatible [kəm·ˈpæt̬·ə·bəl] *adj* ① ■ **to be ~** zusammenpassen ② COMPUT, MED kompatibel ③ (*consistent*) vereinbar

compel <-ll-> [kəm·ˈpel] *vt* ■ **to ~ sb to do sth** jdn [dazu] zwingen, etw zu tun

compelling [kəm·ˈpel·ɪŋ] *adj reason* zwingend; *performance* fesselnd

compensate [ˈkam·pən·seɪt] **I.** *vt* [finanziell] entschädigen **II.** *vi* kompensieren; ■ **to ~ for sth** etw ausgleichen

compensation [ˌkam·pen·ˈseɪ·ʃən] *n* Entschädigung[sleistung] *f,* Schadenersatz *m*

compete [kəm·ˈpit] *vi* ■ **to ~** [**with sb**] [gegen jdn] kämpfen (**for** um +*akk*); **~ in a race** an einem Rennen teilnehmen

competence [ˈkam·pɪ·təns], **competency** [ˈkam·pɪ·tən·si] *n* ① (*ability*) Fähigkeiten *pl,* Kompetenz *f* ② LAW Zuständigkeit *f*

competent [ˈkam·pɪ·t̬ənt] *adj* ① (*capable*) fähig; (*qualified*) kompetent ② LAW zuständig

competition [ˌkam·pə·ˈtɪʃ·ən] *n* ① COMM (*state of competing*) Konkurrenz *f,* Wettbewerb *m;* ■ **to be in ~ with sb** mit jdm konkurrieren ② (*contest*) Wettbewerb *m* ③ (*competitor*) Konkurrent(in) *m(f)*

competitive [kəm·ˈpet̬·ɪ·t̬ɪv] *adj* ① (*characterized by competition*) konkurrierend; (*eager to compete*) kampfbereit; **~ sports** Leistungssport *m* ② COMM konkurrenzfähig, wettbewerbsfähig; **~ edge** Wettbewerbsvorteil *m*

competitiveness [kəm·ˈpet̬·ə·t̬ɪv·nɪs] *n* ① (*ambition*) Konkurrenzdenken *nt* ② COMM Wettbewerbsfähigkeit *f*

competitor [kəm·ˈpet̬·ɪ·t̬ər] *n* ① (*one who competes*) [Wettkampf]gegner(in) *m(f);* (*participant*) [Wettbewerbs]teilnehmer(in) *m(f)* ② COMM Konkurrent(in) *m(f)*

compilation [ˌkam·pə·ˈleɪ·ʃən] *n* ① (*act of compiling*) Zusammenstellung *f* ② (*collection*) Sammlung *f*

compile [kəm·ˈpaɪl] *vt* ① (*put together*) *list* erstellen ② (*gather*) *facts* zusammentragen ③ COMPUT kompilieren

compiler [ˌkəm·ˈpaɪ·lər] *n* ① Sammler(in) *m(f)* ② COMPUT Compiler *m*

complacence [kəm·ˈpleɪ·səns], **complacency** [kəm·ˈpleɪ·sən·si] *n* (*pej*) Selbstzufriedenheit *f*

complacent [kəm·ˈpleɪ·sənt] *adj* (*pej*) selbstzufrieden

complain [kəm·ˈpleɪn] *vi* klagen, sich beklagen (**about/of** über +*akk*)

complaint [kəm·ˈpleɪnt] *n* ① (*expression of displeasure*) Beschwerde *f,* Klage *f* ② LAW Klageschrift *f;* **to file** [*or* **make**] **a ~ against sb**

jdn verklagen, gegen jdn Anzeige erstatten ❸ COMM Mängelrüge *f*

complement ['kam·plɪ·mənt] **I.** *vt* ergänzen; **to ~ each other** sich [gegenseitig] ergänzen **II.** *n* ❶ Ergänzung *f* ❷ **a full ~ of staff** eine komplette Ersatzmannschaft

C

complementary [ˌkam·plə·'men·tə·ri] *adj* [einander] ergänzend

complete [kəm·'plit] **I.** *vt* ❶ (*add what is missing*) vervollständigen; *form* [vollständig] ausfüllen ❷ (*finish*) fertigstellen; *course* absolvieren; *studies* zu Ende bringen **II.** *adj* ❶ (*with nothing missing*) vollständig, komplett ❷ (*including*) **~ with** inklusive ❸ (*total*) absolut; *breakdown* total; *darkness, stranger, surprise* völlig; **a ~ fool** ein Vollidiot *m*

completely [kəm·'plit·li] *adv* völlig; **~ certain** absolut sicher; **to be ~ convinced** der vollen Überzeugung sein

completeness [kəm·'plit·nɪs] *n* Vollständigkeit *f*

completion [kəm·'pli·ʃən] *n* Fertigstellung *f*; **upon ~ of the project** nach Abschluss des Projekts

complex ['kam·pleks] **I.** *adj* komplex; (*complicated*) kompliziert; *issue, personality* vielschichtig; *plot* verwickelt **II.** *n* <*pl* -es> ❶ ARCHIT Komplex *m*; **sports and recreation ~** Sport- und Freizeitzentrum *nt* ❷ PSYCH Komplex *m* (**about** wegen +*dat*)

complexion [kəm·'plek·ʃən] *n* Teint *m*; **clear ~** reine Haut

complexity [kəm·'plek·sɪ·ti] *n* (*intricacy*) Komplexität *f*

compliance [kəm·'plaɪ·əns] *n* (*form: conformity*) Übereinstimmung *f*; **in ~ with the regulations** unter Einhaltung der Bestimmungen

compliant [kəm·'plaɪ·ənt] *adj* (*form*) gefügig

complicate ['kam·plɪ·keɪt] *vt* [noch] komplizierter machen

complicated ['kam·plɪ·keɪ·t̬ɪd] *adj* kompliziert

complication [ˌkam·plɪ·'keɪ·ʃən] *n* Komplikation *f*

compliment ['kam·plə·mənt] **I.** *n* Kompliment *nt*; **to pay sb a ~** jdm ein Kompliment machen ▶ PHRASES: **to be fishing for ~s** auf Komplimente aus sein **II.** *vt* ■ **to ~ sb** jdm ein Kompliment machen

complimentary [ˌkam·plə·'men·tə·ri] *adj* ❶ (*expressing a compliment*) schmeichelhaft ❷ (*free*) Frei-

comply [kəm·'plaɪ] *vi* sich fügen; **to ~ with the regulations** die Bestimmungen erfüllen

component [kəm·'poʊ·nənt] *n* [Bestand]teil *m*

compose [kəm·'poʊz] **I.** *vi* komponieren **II.** *vt* ❶ MUS komponieren ❷ LIT verfassen; *letter* aufsetzen ❸ (*comprise*) ■ **to be ~d of sth** aus etw *dat* bestehen

composed [kəm·'poʊzd] *adj* gefasst

composer [kəm·'poʊ·zər] *n* Komponist(in) *m(f)*

composite [kəm·'paz·ɪt] **I.** *n* Gemisch *nt* **II.** *adj* zusammengesetzt

composite sketch *n* Phantombild *nt*

composition [ˌkam·pə·'zɪʃ·ən] *n* ❶ (*in music*) Komponieren *nt*; (*in literature*) Verfassen *nt* ❷ (*piece*) Komposition *f* ❸ (*arrangement*) Gestaltung *f*; (*of painting*) Komposition *f* ❹ (*makeup*) Zusammenstellung *f*; CHEM Zusammensetzung *f*

compost ['kam·poʊst] **I.** *n* Kompost *m* **II.** *vt* kompostieren

composure [kəm·'poʊ·ʒər] *n* Fassung *f*

compound[1] **I.** *vt* [kam·'paʊnd, kəm-] verschlimmern **II.** *adj* ['kam·paʊnd] zusammengesetzt **III.** *n* ['kam·paʊnd] ❶ (*combination*) Mischung *f* ❷ CHEM Verbindung *f*

compound[2] ['kam·paʊnd] *n* MIL Truppenlager *nt*; **embassy ~** Botschaftsgelände *nt*

compound 'interest *n* FIN Zinseszins *m meist pl*

comprehend [ˌkam·prɪ·'hend] *vi, vt* begreifen, verstehen

comprehensible [ˌkam·prɪ·'hen·sə·bəl] *adj* verständlich (**to** für +*akk*)

comprehension [ˌkam·prɪ·'hen·ʃən] *n* Verständnis *nt*

comprehensive [ˌkam·prɪ·'hen·sɪv] *adj* umfassend; *answer* ausführlich; *list* vollständig

comprehensively [ˌkam·prɪ·'hen·sɪv·li] *adv* umfassend

compress[1] [kəm·'pres] *vt* ❶ (*squeeze together*) zusammendrücken ❷ (*condense*) zusammenfassen

compress[2] <*pl* -es> ['kam·pres] *n* MED Kompresse *f*

compressed [kəm·'prest] *adj* komprimiert

compression [kəm·'preʃ·ən] *n* Kompression *f*

compressor [kəm·'pres·ər] *n* Kompressor *m*, Verdichter *m*

comprise [kəm·'praɪz] *vt* (*form*) ■ **to ~ sth** aus etw *dat* bestehen

compromise ['kam·prə·maɪz] **I.** *n* Kompromiss *m*; **false ~** fauler Kompromiss **II.** *vi* Kompromisse eingehen **III.** *vt* etw *dat* schaden; ■ **to ~ oneself** sich kompromittieren

compromising ['kam·prə·maɪ·zɪŋ] *adj* kompromittierend

compulsion [kəm·'pʌl·ʃən] *n* Zwang *m*

compulsive [kəm·'pʌl·sɪv] *adj* ❶ (*obsessive*) zwanghaft; *liar* notorisch ❷ (*captivating*) fesselnd; **~ viewing** TV Pflichttermin *m*

compulsory [kəm·'pʌl·sə·ri] *adj* obligatorisch; **~ subject** Pflichtfach *nt*

compute [kəm·'pjut] *vt* berechnen ▶ PHRASES: **that doesn't ~** das ergibt keinen Sinn

computer [kəm·'pju·t̬ər] *n* Computer *m*

com'puter game *n* Computerspiel *nt*

computer 'graphics *n* + *sing/pl vb* Computergrafik *f*

computerization [kəm·ˌpju·t̬ər·ɪ·'zeɪ·ʃən] *n* ❶ (*equipping with computers*) Ausrüstung *f* mit Computern ❷ (*computer storage*) Computerisierung *f*

computerize [kəm·ˈpju·t̬ə·raɪz] **I.** *vt* ① (*store on computer*) [im Computer] speichern ② (*equip with computers*) computerisieren **II.** *vi* auf EDV umstellen

computer 'network *n* Rechnernetz *nt*

computer 'programmer *n* Programmierer(in) *m(f)*

computer 'science *n* Informatik *f*

computer 'scientist *n* Informatiker(in) *m(f)*

com'puter virus *n* Virus *m*

computing [kəm·ˈpju·t̬ɪŋ] *n* ① (*calculating*) Berechnen *nt* ② COMPUT EDV *f*

comrade [ˈkam·ræd] *n* ① POL Genosse, -in *m, f* ② (*friend*) Kamerad(in) *m(f)*

con¹ [kan] *n usu pl* (*fam*) **the pros and ~s** das Pro und Kontra

con² [kan] (*fam*) **I.** *vt* <-nn-> *person* reinlegen; **to ~ sb into believing** [*or* **thinking**] **that ...** jdm weismachen wollen, dass ... **II.** *n* (*trick*) Schwindel *m kein pl*

con³ [kan] *n* (*sl: convict*) Knacki *m sl*

'con artist *n* Schwindler(in) *m(f)*

concave [ˈkan·keɪv] *adj* konkav

conceal [kən·ˈsil] *vt* verbergen (**from** vor +*dat*)

concealment [kən·ˈsil·mənt] *n* Verheimlichung *f; of feelings* Verbergen *nt*

concede [kən·ˈsid] **I.** *vt* ① (*acknowledge*) zugeben; **to ~ defeat** sich geschlagen geben ② (*grant*) *privileges, rights* einräumen ③ SPORTS *point, match* abgeben **II.** *vi* sich geschlagen geben

conceit [kən·ˈsit] *n* Einbildung *f*

conceited [kən·ˈsi·t̬ɪd] *adj* eingebildet

conceivable [kən·ˈsiv·ə·bəl] *adj* vorstellbar

conceive [kən·ˈsiv] **I.** *vt* ① (*conceptualize*) kommen auf +*akk* ② (*imagine*) sich *dat* vorstellen ③ (*become pregnant with*) empfangen **II.** *vi* ① (*imagine*) ■**to ~ of sth** sich *dat* etw vorstellen ② (*become pregnant*) empfangen

concentrate [ˈkan·sən·treɪt] **I.** *vi* ① (*focus one's thoughts*) sich konzentrieren ② (*come together*) sich sammeln **II.** *vt* konzentrieren; **to ~ one's mind on sth** sich auf etw *akk* konzentrieren **III.** *n* Konzentrat *nt*

concentrated [ˈkan·sən·treɪ·t̬ɪd] *adj* konzentriert; *attack* geballt; *effort* gezielt

concentration [ˌkan·sən·ˈtreɪ·ʃən] *n* ① (*mental focus*) Konzentration *f* (**on** auf +*akk*) ② (*accumulation*) Konzentrierung *f; of troops* Zusammenziehung *f* ③ CHEM Konzentration *f*

concen'tration camp *n* Konzentrationslager *nt*

concept [ˈkan·sept] *n* ① (*abstract idea*) Vorstellung *f* ② (*plan*) Entwurf *m*, Konzept *nt* (**for** für +*akk*)

conception [kən·ˈsep·ʃən] *n* ① (*basic understanding*) Vorstellung *f* ② (*idea*) Idee *f*, Konzept *nt;* (*creation*) Konzeption *f* ③ BIOL Empfängnis *f*

conceptual [kən·ˈsep·tʃu·əl] *adj* begrifflich

concern [kən·ˈsɜrn] **I.** *n* ① (*interest*) Anliegen *nt*, Angelegenheit *f* ② (*worry*) Sorge *f*, Besorgnis *f* (**about** um +*akk*); **my ~ is that ...** ich mache mir Sorgen, dass ...; **there's no cause for ~** es besteht kein Grund zur Sorge ③ (*commercial enterprise*) Handelsunternehmen **II.** *vt* ① (*be about*) handeln von ② (*apply to, be sb's business*) angehen; (*affect*) betreffen; **as far as I'm ~ed** was mich betrifft ③ (*involve*) ■**to ~ oneself with sth** sich mit etw *dat* befassen ④ (*worry*) beunruhigen

concerning [kən·ˈsɜr·nɪŋ] *prep* bezüglich +*gen*

concert [ˈkan·sərt] *n* ① MUS Konzert *nt;* **in ~** live ② (*unity*) **to act in ~** an einem Strang ziehen

concerted [kən·ˈsɜr·tɪd] *adj* (*joint*) *effort* gemeinsam

concerto <*pl* -s *or* -ti> [kən·ˈtʃer·t̬oʊ] *n* Konzert *nt*

concession [kən·ˈseʃ·ən] *n* ① Zugeständnis *nt;* **as a ~** als Ausgleich; **to make no ~ to sb/sth** auf jdn/etw *akk* keine Rücksicht nehmen ② (*admission of defeat*) Eingeständnis *nt* [einer Niederlage] ③ ECON Konzession *f*

con'cession stand *n* Snacktheke *f*, Erfrischungstheke *f*

conciliation [kən·ˌsɪl·i·ˈeɪ·ʃən] *n* (*form*) ① (*reconciliation*) Besänftigung *f* ② (*mediation*) Schlichtung *f*

conciliatory [kən·ˈsɪl·i·ə·tɔr·i] *adj* versöhnlich; (*mediating*) beschwichtigend

concise [kən·ˈsaɪs] *adj* präzise; *answer* kurz und bündig; *style a.* knapp

conciseness [kən·ˈsaɪs·nɪs] *n*, **concision** [kən·ˈsɪʒ·ən] *n* Prägnanz *f*

conclude [kən·ˈklud] **I.** *vi* enden, schließen; **"that's all I have to say," he ~d** „mehr habe ich nicht zu sagen", meinte er abschließend **II.** *vt* ① (*finish*) [ab]schließen ② (*infer*) ■**to ~ [from sth] that ...** [aus etw] schließen, dass ...

concluding [kən·ˈklu·dɪŋ] *adj* abschließend; **~ remark** Schlussbemerkung *f*

conclusion [kən·ˈklu·ʒən] *n* ① (*end*) Abschluss *m; of a story* Schluss *m;* **in ~** zum Abschluss, abschließend ② (*decision*) **to come to a ~** einen Beschluss fassen ③ (*inference*) Schluss *m*, Schlussfolgerung *f;* **to draw** [*or* **reach**] **the ~ that ...** zu dem Schluss gelangen, dass ...

conclusive [kən·ˈklu·sɪv] *adj* ① (*convincing*) schlüssig ② (*decisive*) eindeutig; *evidence* stichhaltig

concoct [kən·ˈkakt] *vt dish* zusammenstellen; *drink* mixen; *excuse* sich *dat* zurechtbasteln; *story* sich *dat* ausdenken

concoction [kən·ˈkak·ʃən] *n* (*dish*) Kreation *f;* (*drink*) Gebräu *nt*

concourse [ˈkan·kɔrs] *n* Halle *f*

concrete [ˈkan·krit] **I.** *n* Beton *m* **II.** *adj* ① *surface* betoniert ② *proof* eindeutig ③ *suggestion* konkret **III.** *vt* betonieren

'concrete mixer *n* Betonmischmaschine *f*

concur <-rr-> [kən·ˈkɜr] *vi* übereinstimmen; **to ~ with sb's opinion** jds Meinung *f* zustimmen; ■**to ~ with sb** [**in** [*or* **on**] **sth**] jdm [in etw *dat*] beipflichten

concurrent [kən·ˈkʌr·ənt] *adj* gleichzeitig

concussion [kən·ˈkʌʃ·ən] *n* Gehirnerschütterung *f*

condemn [kən·ˈdem] *vt* ❶ verurteilen; (*fig*) verdammen ❷ (*declare unsafe*) für unbrauchbar erklären; *building* für unbewohnbar erklären

condemnation [ˌkan·dem·ˈneɪ·ʃən] *n* Verurteilung *f;* (*fig*) Verdammung *f*

condensation [ˌkan·den·ˈseɪ·ʃən] *n* ❶ (*process*) Kondensation *f* ❷ (*droplets*) Kondenswasser *nt*

condense [kən·ˈdens] **I.** *vt* ❶ (*concentrate*) *gas* komprimieren; *liquid* eindicken; **~d milk** Kondensmilch *f* ❷ (*form droplets from*) kondensieren ❸ (*shorten*) zusammenfassen **II.** *vi* kondensieren

condescending [ˌkan·dɪ·ˈsen·dɪŋ] *adj* herablassend

condiment [ˈkan·də·mənt] *n* Würzmittel *nt;* (*sauce*) Soße *f*

condition [kən·ˈdɪʃ·ən] **I.** *n* ❶ (*state*) Zustand *m; person* Verfassung *f;* **in good/bad ~** gut/schlecht in Schuss *fam* ❷ (*circumstances*) ■**~s** *pl* Bedingungen *pl* ❸ (*stipulation*) Bedingung *f;* ■**on the ~ that ...** unter der Bedingung, dass ... **II.** *vt* ❶ (*train*) konditionieren ❷ (*accustom*) gewöhnen; *hair* eine Pflegespülung machen

conditional [kən·ˈdɪʃ·ə·nəl] **I.** *adj* bedingt; ■**to be ~** [**up**]**on sth** von etw *dat* abhängen **II.** *n* LING ■**the ~** der Konditional

conditionally [kən·ˈdɪʃ·ə·nə·li] *adv* unter Vorbehalt

conditioner [kən·ˈdɪʃ·ə·nər] *n* (*for hair*) Pflegespülung *f*

condo [ˈkan·doʊ] *n* (*fam*) *short for* **condominium** Eigentumswohnung *f*

condolence [kən·ˈdoʊ·ləns] *n* ■**~s** Beileid *nt kein pl*

condom [ˈkan·dəm] *n* Kondom *nt,* Pariser *m sl*

condominium [ˌkan·də·ˈmɪn·i·əm] *n* (*owned apartment*) Eigentumswohnung *f*

condone [kən·ˈdoʊn] *vt* [stillschweigend] dulden

conducive [kən·ˈdu·sɪv] *adj* förderlich

conduct I. *vt* [ˌkən·ˈdʌkt] ❶ (*carry out*) durchführen; *negotiations* führen; *service* abhalten ❷ (*direct*) leiten; *orchestra* dirigieren; *traffic* [um]leiten ❸ ELEC leiten ❹ (*guide*) führen **II.** *vi* [ˌkən·ˈdʌkt] MUS dirigieren **III.** *n* [ˈkan·dʌkt] (*behavior*) Benehmen *nt,* Verhalten *nt*

conductive [kən·ˈdʌk·tɪv] *adj* ELEC leitfähig

conductor [kən·ˈdʌk·tər] *n* ❶ MUS Dirigent(in) *m(f)* ❷ PHYS Leiter *m* ❸ RAIL Schaffner(in) *m(f),* Zugführer(in) *m(f),* Zugbegleiter(in) *m(f)*

conduit [ˈkan·du·ɪt] *n* (*pipe*) [Rohr]leitung *f;* (*channel*) Kanal *m*

cone [koʊn] *n* ❶ MATH Kegel *m;* **traffic ~** Leitkegel *m;* **ice cream ~** Eistüte *f* ❷ BOT Zapfen *m*

confectioner [kən·ˈfek·ʃə·nər] *n* Süßwarenhändler(in) *m(f)*

confectioners' sugar *n* Puderzucker *m*

confectionery [kən·ˈfek·ʃə·ner·i] *n* (*candy*) Süßwaren *pl;* (*chocolate*) Konfekt *nt*

confederacy [kən·ˈfed·ər·ə·si] *n* Konföderation *f;* ■**the C~** HIST die Konföderierten Staaten *pl* von Amerika

confederate [kən·ˈfed·ər·ət] **I.** *n* Komplize, -in *m, f* **II.** *adj* HIST ■**C~** Südstaaten-

confederation [kən·ˌfed·ə·ˈreɪ·ʃən] *n* ❶ POL Bund *m* ❷ ECON Verband *m*

confer <-rr-> [kən·ˈfɜr] **I.** *vt* ■**to ~ sth** [**up**]**on sb** jdm etw verleihen; *rights* übertragen **II.** *vi* ■**to ~ with sb** sich mit jdm beraten

conference [ˈkan·fər·əns] *n* Konferenz *f,* Tagung *f* (**on** über +*akk*)

confess [kən·ˈfes] *vi, vt* ❶ (*admit*) zugeben; ■**to ~ to sth** etw gestehen ❷ REL beichten

confession [kən·ˈfeʃ·ən] *n* ❶ (*admission*) Geständnis *nt;* **to have a ~ to make** etw gestehen müssen ❷ REL Beichte *f*

confessional [kən·ˈfeʃ·ə·nəl] *n* Beichtstuhl *m*

confessor [kən·ˈfes·ər] *n* Beichtvater *m*

confetti [kən·ˈfeṭ·i] *n* Konfetti *nt*

confidant [ˈkan·fɪ·ˌdant] *n* Vertraute(r) *m*

confidante [ˈkan·fɪ·ˌdant] *n* Vertraute *f*

confide [kən·ˈfaɪd] **I.** *vt* gestehen; ■**to ~** [**to sb**] **that ...** jdm anvertrauen, dass ... **II.** *vi* ■**to ~ in sb** sich jdm anvertrauen

confidence [ˈkan·fɪ·dəns] *n* ❶ (*trust*) Vertrauen *nt;* **to have no ~ in sb** kein Vertrauen zu jdm haben; **in ~** im Vertrauen ❷ *kein pl* (*self-assurance*) Selbstvertrauen *nt* ❸ (*secrets*) ■**~s** *pl* Vertraulichkeiten *pl*

confident [ˈkan·fɪ·dənt] *adj* ❶ (*certain*) zuversichtlich; ■**to be ~ of sth** von etw *dat* überzeugt sein ❷ (*self-assured*) selbstbewusst

confidential [ˌkan·fɪ·ˈden·ʃəl] *adj* vertraulich

confidentially [ˌkan·fɪ·ˈden·ʃə·li] *adv* vertraulich

configuration [kən·ˌfɪg·jə·ˈreɪ·ʃən] *n* Konfiguration *f*

configure [kən·ˈfɪg·jər] *vt* konfigurieren

confine I. *vt* [kən·ˈfaɪn] ❶ (*restrict*) beschränken (**to** auf +*akk*) ❷ (*shut in*) einsperren **II.** *n* [ˈkan·faɪn] ■**the ~s** *pl* die Grenzen *pl*

confinement [kən·ˈfaɪn·mənt] *n* ❶ Einsperrung *f;* **solitary ~** Einzelhaft *f;* (*restriction*) Gebundenheit *f* ❷ MED Geburt *f*

confirm [kən·ˈfɜrm] **I.** *vt* ❶ (*verify*) bestätigen ❷ REL ■**to be ~ed** (*Catholic*) gefirmt werden; (*Protestant*) konfirmiert werden **II.** *vi* bestätigen

confirmation [ˌkan·fər·ˈmeɪ·ʃən] *n* ❶ (*verification*) Bestätigung *f* ❷ REL (*Catholic*) Firmung *f;* (*Protestant*) Konfirmation *f*

confirmed [kən·ˈfɜrmd] *adj* erklärt; *atheist* überzeugt; *bachelor* eingefleischt

confiscate [ˈkan·fɪ·skeɪt] *vt* beschlagnahmen

conflict I. *n* [ˈkan·flɪkt] ❶ (*clash*) Konflikt *m;* **to be in ~ with sb** mit jdm im Streit liegen ❷ (*battle*) Kampf *m* **II.** *vi* [kən·ˈflɪkt] ■**to ~**

with sth im Widerspruch zu etw *dat* stehen; *dates, events* sich überschneiden
conflicting [kən·'flɪk·tɪŋ] *adj* widersprüchlich; *claims* entgegengesetzt
conform [kən·'fɔrm] *vi* sich einfügen; (*agree*) übereinstimmen; ■ **to ~ to** [*or* **with**] **sth** etw *dat* entsprechen
conformist [kən·'fɔr·mɪst] **I.** *n* Konformist(in) *m(f)* **II.** *adj* konformistisch
conformity [kən·'fɔr·mɪ·t̬i] *n* (*uniformity*) Konformismus *m*
confound [kən·'faʊnd] *vt* ❶ (*astonish*) verblüffen ❷ (*confuse*) verwirren
confront [kən·'frʌnt] *vt* ❶ (*face*) ■ **to ~ sth** sich etw *dat* stellen; *danger* ins Auge sehen; *enemy* entgegentreten; ■ **to ~ sb** [**about sth**] jdn [wegen einer S. *gen*] zur Rede stellen ❷ (*compel to deal with*) konfrontieren
confrontation [ˌkan·frən·'teɪ·ʃən] *n* Konfrontation *f;* (*during inquiry*) Gegenüberstellung *f*
confrontational [ˌkan·frən·'teɪ·ʃə·nəl] *adj* herausfordernd
confuse [kən·'fjuz] *vt* ❶ (*perplex*) verwirren, durcheinanderbringen ❷ (*misidentify*) verwechseln
confused [kən·'fjuzd] *adj* ❶ *people* verwirrt, durcheinander ❷ *situation* verworren, konfus
confusing [kən·'fju·zɪŋ] *adj* verwirrend
confusion [kən·'fju·ʒən] *n* ❶ (*perplexity*) Verwirrung *f* ❷ (*mix-up*) Verwechslung *f* ❸ (*disorder*) Durcheinander *nt*
congeal [kən·'dʒil] *vi fat* fest werden
congenial [kən·'dʒin·jəl] *adj* angenehm; *people* sympathisch
congenital [kən·'dʒen·ɪ·t̬əl] *adj* angeboren; **~ defect** Geburtsfehler *m*
congested [kən·'dʒes·tɪd] *adj* ❶ (*overcrowded*) überfüllt; *road* verstopft ❷ MED verstopft
congestion [kən·'dʒes·tʃən] *n* ❶ (*overcrowding*) Überfüllung *f;* (*on roads*) Stau *m* ❷ MED **nasal ~** verstopfte Nase
conglomerate [kən·'glam·ə·reɪt] *n* Konglomerat *nt*
congratulate [kən·'grætʃ·ə·leɪt] *vt* ■ **to ~ sb** [**on sth**] (*wish well*) jdm [zu etw] gratulieren
congratulation [kən·ˌgrætʃ·ə·'leɪ·ʃən] *n* Gratulation *f,* Glückwunsch *m;* **~s!** herzlichen Glückwunsch!
congregate ['kaŋ·grɪ·geɪt] *vi* sich [ver]sammeln
congregation [ˌkaŋ·grɪ·'geɪ·ʃən] *n* REL [Kirchen]gemeinde *f*
congress ['kaŋ·gres] *n* Kongress *m;* **C~** POL der Kongress
congressional [kəŋ·'greʃ·ə·nəl] *adj* **~ elections** Wahlen *pl* zum US-Kongress
'congressman *n* [Kongress]abgeordneter *m*
'congresswoman *n* [Kongress]abgeordnete *f*
conical ['kan·ɪ·kəl] *adj* konisch, kegelförmig
conifer ['kan·ə·fər] *n* Nadelbaum *m*
coniferous [koʊ·'nɪf·ər·əs] *adj* Nadel-
conjecture [kən·'dʒek·tʃər] *n* Vermutung *f*
conjoined [kən·'dʒɔɪnd] *adj inv* (*form*) verbunden; **~** *twins* siamesische Zwillinge
conjugate ['kan·dʒə·geɪt] LING **I.** *vi* konjugiert werden **II.** *vt* konjugieren
conjugation [ˌkan·dʒə·'geɪ·ʃən] *n* LING Konjugation *f*
conjunction [kən·'dʒʌŋk·ʃən] *n* ❶ LING Bindewort *nt* ❷ (*combination*) ■ **in ~ with sth** in Verbindung mit etw *dat;* ■ **in ~ with sb** zusammen mit jdm
conjunctivitis [kən·ˌdʒʌŋk·tə·'vaɪ·t̬ɪs] *n* Bindehautentzündung *f*
conjure ['kan·dʒər] **I.** *vi* zaubern **II.** *vt* hervorzaubern
◆ **conjure up** *vt* ❶ (*produce*) *images, pictures* hervorzaubern; *meal* zaubern ❷ (*call upon*) beschwören
conjurer ['kan·dʒər·ər] *n* Zauberkünstler(in) *m(f)*
conjuring ['kan·dʒər·ɪŋ] *n* Zaubern *nt,* Zauberei *f*
conjuror *n see* **conjurer**
◆ **conk out** *vi* **to ~ out** (*fam*) kaputtgehen; (*completely*) den Geist aufgeben
'con man *n* Schwindler *m*
Conn. *abbrev of* **Connecticut**
connect [kə·'nekt] **I.** *vi* ❶ (*plug in*) ■ **to ~ to sth** an etw *akk* angeschlossen werden ❷ (*feel affinity*) ■ **to ~ with sb** sich auf Anhieb gut mit jdm verstehen ❸ (*become joined*) miteinander verbunden sein **II.** *vt* ❶ ELEC verbinden (**to/with** mit *+dat*); (*plug in*) anschließen (**to/with** an *+akk*) ❷ (*associate*) in Verbindung bringen; ■ **to be ~ed with sb/sth** mit jdm/etw *dat* zusammenhängen ❸ TELEC verbinden
Connecticut [kə·'net̬·ɪ·kəl] *n* Connecticut *nt*
connection [kə·'nek·ʃən] *n* ❶ (*joining, link*) Verbindung *f* (**to/with** mit *+dat*); ELEC Anschluss *m* (**to** an *+akk*); **to get a ~ through** [**to sb**] TELEC [zu jdm] durchkommen; **there was no ~ between the two phenomena** die beiden Phänomene hingen nicht zusammen ❷ TRANSP Verbindung *f;* (*connecting train, flight*) Anschluss *m* ❸ (*contacts*) ■ **~s** *pl* Beziehungen *pl* (**to/with** zu *+dat*) ❹ (*reference*) **in that/this ~** in diesem Zusammenhang *m*
connector [kə·'nek·tər] *n* ELEC Verbindungselement *nt*
conniving [kə·'naɪ·vɪŋ] *adj* hinterhältig
connoisseur [ˌkan·ə·'sɜr] *n* Kenner(in) *m(f)*
connotation [ˌkan·ə·'teɪ·ʃən] *n* Konnotation *f*
conquer ['kaŋ·kər] *vt person, disease* besiegen; *thing* erobern *a. fig; mountain* bezwingen ▶ PHRASES: **I came, I saw, I ~ed** (*saying*) ich kam, sah und siegte
conqueror ['kaŋ·kər·ər] *n* (*of sth*) Eroberer, Eroberin *m, f;* (*of sb*) Sieger(in) *m(f)* (**of** über *+akk*)
conquest ['kan·kwest] *n* ❶ *of a thing* Eroberung *f; of a person* Sieg *m* (**of** über *+akk*) ❷ (*climbing*) Bezwingung *f*

C

conscience ['kan·ʃəns] *n* Gewissen *nt;* **to do sth with a clear ~** ruhigen Gewissens etw tun
conscientious [ˌkan·ʃi·'en·ʃəs] *adj* ❶ (*thorough*) gewissenhaft; (*with sense of duty*) pflichtbewusst; *work* gründlich ❷ (*moral*) **on ~ grounds** aus Gewissensgründen
conscientiousness [ˌkan·ʃi·'en·ʃəs·nɪs] *n* (*thoroughness*) Gewissenhaftigkeit *f;* (*sense of duty*) Pflichtbewusstsein *nt*
conscientious ob'jector *n* Kriegsdienstverweigerer, -verweigerin *m, f*
conscious ['kan·ʃəs] *adj* ❶ MED ■ **to be** [**fully**] **~** bei [vollem] Bewusstsein sein ❷ (*deliberate*) *decision* bewusst ❸ (*aware*) bewusst; **fashion-~** modebewusst
consciousness ['kan·ʃəs·nɪs] *n* Bewusstsein *nt a. fig;* **to lose ~** das Bewusstsein verlieren
conscript I. *n* ['kan·skrɪpt] Wehrpflichtige(r) *m* II. *vt* [kən·'skrɪpt] *soldier* einziehen, einberufen
conscription [kən·'skrɪp·ʃən] *n* MIL Wehrpflicht *f;* (*act of conscripting*) Einberufung *f*
consecrate ['kan·sə·kreɪt] *vt* weihen
consecration [ˌkan·sə·'kreɪ·ʃən] *n* Weihe *f*
consecutive [kən·'sek·jə·t̬ɪv] *adj* (*following*) *days, months* aufeinanderfolgend; *numbers* fortlaufend
consecutively [kən·'sek·jə·t̬ɪv·li] *adv* hintereinander; **~ numbered** fortlaufend nummeriert
consensus [kən·'sen·səs] *n* Übereinstimmung *f;* **to reach a ~ on sth** sich in etw *dat* einigen
consent [kən·'sent] (*form*) I. *n* Zustimmung *f;* **by mutual ~** im gegenseitigen Einverständnis II. *vi* ■ **to ~ to sth** etw *dat* zustimmen; ■ **to ~ to do sth** einwilligen, etw zu tun
consequence ['kan·sɪ·kwəns] *n* ❶ (*result*) Folge *f,* Auswirkung *f;* **as a** [*or* **in**] **~** folglich; **as a ~ of sth** als Folge einer S. *gen* ❷ (*significance*) Bedeutung *f;* **of no ~** unwichtig
consequent ['kan·sɪ·kwənt], **consequential** [ˌkan·sɪ·'kwən·ʃəl] *adj* daraus folgend
consequently ['kan·sɪ·kwənt·li] *adv* folglich
conservation [ˌkan·sər·'veɪ·ʃən] *n* (*protection*) Schutz *m;* (*preservation*) Erhaltung *f*
conservationist [ˌkan·sər·'veɪ·ʃə·nɪst] *n* Naturschützer(in) *m(f);* **~ groups** Umweltschutzgruppen *pl*
conservative [kən·'sɜr·və·tɪv] I. *adj* ❶ (*in dress, opinion*) konservativ ❷ (*low*) *estimate* vorsichtig II. *n* POL Konservative(r) *f(m)*
conservatory [kən·'sɜr·və·tɔr·i] *n* ❶ (*for plants*) Wintergarten *m* ❷ MUS Konservatorium *nt*
conserve I. *vt* [kən·'sɜrv] (*save*) sparen; *strength* schonen II. *n* ['kan·sɜrv] Eingemachtes *nt kein pl*
consider [kən·'sɪd·ər] *vt* ❶ (*contemplate*) sich *dat* überlegen; ■ **to ~ doing sth** daran denken, etw zu tun ❷ (*look at*) betrachten; (*think of*) denken an +*akk;* (*take into account*) bedenken; **all things ~ed** alles in allem ❸ (*regard as*) ■ **to ~ sb/sth** [**as** [*or* **to be**]] **sth** jdn/etw für etw *akk* halten; ■ **to be ~ed** [**to be**] **sth** als etw gelten; **many ~ him the frontrunner for President** er gilt bei vielen als der nächste Präsident
considerable [kən·'sɪd·ər·ə·bəl] *adj* erheblich, beträchtlich
considerate [kən·'sɪd·ər·ɪt] *adj* rücksichtsvoll
consideration [kən·ˌsɪd·ə·'reɪ·ʃən] *n* ❶ (*thought*) Überlegung *f;* **to give sth one's ~** etw in Erwägung ziehen; ■ **to be under ~** geprüft werden ❷ (*account*) **to take into ~** berücksichtigen ❸ (*factor*) Gesichtspunkt *m* ❹ (*regard*) Rücksicht *f* (**for** auf +*akk*)
considered [kən·'sɪd·ərd] *adj opinion* wohl überlegt
considering [kən·'sɪd·ər·ɪŋ] I. *prep* ■ **~ how/what ...** wenn man bedenkt, wie/was ... II. *conj* ■ **~ that ...** dafür, dass ...
consignment [kən·'saɪn·mənt] *n* Warensendung *f;* **on ~** in Kommission
consist [kən·'sɪst] *vi* (*comprise*) ■ **to ~ of sth** aus etw *dat* bestehen
consistency [kən·'sɪs·tən·si] *n* ❶ (*firmness*) Konsistenz *f* ❷ (*constancy*) Beständigkeit *f*
consistent [kən·'sɪs·tənt] *adj* ❶ (*compatible*) vereinbar ❷ (*steady*) beständig; *way of doing sth* gleich bleibend; *improvement* ständig
consolation [ˌkan·sə·'leɪ·ʃən] *n* Trost *m*
conso'lation prize *n* Trostpreis *m*
console[1] [kən·'soʊl] *vt* trösten
console[2] ['kan·soʊl] *n* ❶ (*control desk*) Schaltpult *nt* ❷ COMPUT Konsole *f*
consolidate [kən·'sal·ə·deɪt] *vi, vt* ❶ (*unite*) [sich] vereinigen ❷ (*strengthen*) [sich] festigen
consolidated [kən·'sal·ə·deɪ·t̬ɪd] *adj* vereint
consolidation [kən·ˌsal·ə·'deɪ·ʃən] *n* ❶ (*merging*) Fusion *f* ❷ (*strengthening*) Festigung *f*
consonant ['kan·sə·nənt] *n* Konsonant *m*
consort I. *vi* [kən·'sɔrt] verkehren II. *n* ['kan·sɔrt] Gemahl(in) *m(f)*
consortium <*pl* -s *or* -tia> [kən·'sɔr·t̬i·əm] *n* Konsortium *nt*
conspicuous [kən·'spɪk·jʊ·əs] *adj* (*noticeable*) auffallend; (*clearly visible*) unübersehbar; *behavior, clothing* auffällig
conspiracy [kən·'spɪr·ə·si] *n* Verschwörung *f*
conspirator [kən·'spɪr·ə·t̬ər] *n* Verschwörer(in) *m(f)*
conspire [kən·'spaɪr] *vi* (*a. fig*) sich verschwören; ■ **to ~** [**together**] **to do sth** heimlich planen, etw zu tun
constant ['kan·stənt] I. *n* MATH Konstante *f* II. *adj* ❶ (*continuous*) ständig ❷ (*unchanging*) gleich bleibend; MATH konstant
constantly ['kan·stənt·li] *adv* ständig
constellation [ˌkan·stə·'leɪ·ʃən] *n* Sternbild *nt*
consternation [ˌkan·stər·'neɪ·ʃən] *n* Bestürzung *f;* **in ~** bestürzt
constipated ['kan·stə·peɪ·t̬ɪd] *adj* verstopft; **to be ~** [eine] Verstopfung haben
constipation ['kan·stə·'peɪ·ʃən] *n* Verstop-

fung *f*

constituency [kən·ˈstɪtʃ·u·ən·si] *n* POL Wahlkreis *m;* (*voters a.*) Wählerschaft *f* eines Wahlkreises

constituent [kən·ˈstɪtʃ·u·ənt] **I.** *n* ❶ (*voter*) Wähler(in) *m(f)* ❷ (*part*) Bestandteil *m* **II.** *adj* (*component*) einzeln; ~ **part** Bestandteil *m*

constitute [ˈkan·stɪ·tut] *vt* ❶ (*make up*) bilden ❷ (*form: be*) sein

constitution [ˌkan·stɪ·ˈtu·ʃən] *n* ❶ (*structure*) Zusammensetzung *f* ❷ POL Verfassung *f* ❸ (*health*) Konstitution *f*

> Die **Constitution** (Verfassung) der Vereinigten Staaten wurde 1787 geschrieben und trat 1789 in Kraft. Sie führte die Gewaltenteilung der amerikanischen Regierung in Legislative, Exekutive und Judikative ein. Die nach der Ratifizierung durch die ersten 13 amerikanischen Staaten seit 1789 rechtskräftige Verfassung ist die älteste schriftlich niedergelegte ihrer Art, die heute immer noch gültig ist. Der erste amerikanische Präsident, George Washington, wurde beim ersten Verfassungskongress am 6. April 1789 einstimmig gewählt.

constitutional [ˌkan·stɪ·ˈtu·ʃə·nəl] **I.** *adj* konstitutionell; ~ **right** Grundrecht *nt* **II.** *n* (*hum*) [regelmäßiger] Spaziergang *m*

constraint [kən·ˈstreɪnt] *n* ❶ (*compulsion*) Zwang *m* ❷ (*restriction*) Beschränkung *f*

constrict [kən·ˈstrɪkt] **I.** *vt* ❶ (*narrow*) verengen; (*squeeze*) einschnüren ❷ (*hinder*) behindern **II.** *vi* sich zusammenziehen

constriction [kən·ˈstrɪk·ʃən] *n* ❶ (*narrowing*) Verengung *f;* (*squeezing*) Einschnüren *nt* ❷ (*hindrance*) Behinderung *f*

construct [kən·ˈstrʌkt] *vt* ❶ (*build*) bauen; *dam* errichten ❷ (*develop*) *theory* entwickeln

construction [kən·ˈstrʌk·ʃən] *n* ❶ (*act of building*) Bau *m;* **the ~ industry** die Bauindustrie; ~ **site** Baustelle *f;* **under ~** im Bau ❷ (*how sth is built*) Bauweise *f* ❸ (*object*) Konstruktion *f;* (*architectural feature*) Bau *m,* Bauwerk *nt;* (*building*) Gebäude *nt*

constructive [kən·ˈstrʌk·tɪv] *adj* konstruktiv

constructor [kən·ˈstrʌk·tər] *n* (*tech*) Konstrukteur(in) *m(f);* ARCHIT Erbauer(in) *m(f)*

consul [ˈkan·səl] *n* Konsul(in) *m(f)*

consular [ˈkan·sə·lər] *adj* konsularisch; ~ **staff** Konsulatsbelegschaft *f*

consulate [ˈkan·sə·lət] *n* (*building*) Konsulat *nt*

consult [kən·ˈsʌlt] **I.** *vi* sich beraten **II.** *vt* ❶ (*ask*) ■**to ~ sb [about** [*or* **on**] **sth]** jdn [bezüglich einer S. *gen*] um Rat fragen; *doctor, lawyer, specialist* konsultieren, zu Rate ziehen ❷ (*look at*) *dictionary* nachschlagen in +*dat; oracle* befragen

consultancy [kən·ˈsʌl·tən·si] *n* (*company*) Beratungsdienst *m*

consultant [kən·ˈsʌl·tənt] *n* Berater(in) *m(f)*

consultation [ˌkan·sʌl·ˈteɪ·ʃən] *n* ❶ Beratung *f* (**on** über +*akk*); **in ~ with** in Absprache mit; *with lawyer, accountant* Rücksprache *f* ❷ MED Konsultation *f*

consulting [kən·ˈsʌl·tɪŋ] **I.** *n* Beratung *f* **II.** *adj* beratend

consume [kən·ˈsum] *vt* ❶ (*eat, drink*) konsumieren; *food a.* verzehren; (*fig*) **to be ~d by jealousy** vor Eifersucht [fast] vergehen ❷ *fire* zerstören ❸ (*use up*) verbrauchen

consumer [kən·ˈsu·mər] *n* Verbraucher(in) *m(f)*

consumerism [kən·ˈsu·mə·rɪz·əm] *n* Konsumdenken *nt*

consummate [ˈkan·sə·meɪt] *adj* (*form*) vollendet; ~ **athlete** Spitzensportler(in) *m(f); liar* ausgebufft

consumption [kən·ˈsʌm(p)·ʃᵊn] *n no pl* ❶ (*using up*) Verbrauch *m;* (*using*) Konsum *m;* **energy ~** Energieverbrauch ❷ (*eating, drinking*) Konsum *m; of food also* Verzehr *m;* **unfit for human ~** nicht für den menschlichen Verzehr geeignet ❸ (*fig: use*) **for internal ~** zur internen Nutzung ❹ *no pl* MED (*hist*) Schwindsucht *f*

contact [ˈkan·tækt] **I.** *n* ❶ (*communication*) Kontakt *m,* Verbindung *f;* **to be in ~ [with sb]** [mit jdm] in Verbindung stehen; **to make ~ with sb** sich mit jdm in Verbindung setzen ❷ (*person*) Kontaktperson *f;* **business ~s** Geschäftskontakte *pl* ❸ (*touch*) Kontakt *m;* **to come into ~ with sth** mit etw *dat* in Berührung kommen *a. fig* ❹ ELEC Kontakt *m* ❺ *see* **contact lens II.** *vt* ■**to ~ sb** sich mit jdm in Verbindung setzen; (*by phone*) jdn [telefonisch] erreichen

ˈcontact lens *n* Kontaktlinse *f*

contagious [kən·ˈteɪ·dʒəs] *adj* ansteckend *a. fig*

contain [kən·ˈteɪn] *vt* ❶ (*hold, include*) enthalten ❷ (*limit*) in Grenzen halten; (*hold back*) aufhalten; (*suppress*) zurückhalten; **she could barely ~ herself** sie konnte kaum an sich halten

container [kən·ˈteɪ·nər] *n* ❶ Behälter *m; of yogurt, cream* Becher *m* ❷ TRANSP Container *m*

containment [kən·ˈteɪn·mənt] *n* (*limitation*) Eindämmung *f*

contaminate [kən·ˈtæm·ə·neɪt] *vt* verunreinigen; (*with radioactivity, a. food*) verseuchen

contamination [kən·ˌtæm·ɪ·ˈneɪ·ʃən] *n* Verunreinigung *f;* (*by radioactivity, a. of food*) Verseuchung *f*

contemplate [ˈkan·tem·pleɪt] **I.** *vi* nachdenken **II.** *vt* ❶ (*consider*) in Erwägung ziehen; (*reflect upon*) über etw *akk* nachdenken; *suicide* denken an +*akk* ❷ (*gaze at*) betrachten

contemplation [ˌkan·tem·ˈpleɪ·ʃən] *n* ❶ (*thought*) Nachdenken *nt* (**of** über +*akk*) ❷ (*gazing*) Betrachtung *f*

C

C

contemplative [kən·ˈtem·plə·tɪv] *adj* ❶ (*reflective*) *mood* nachdenklich ❷ REL besinnlich; *life* beschaulich

contemporary [kən·ˈtem·pə·rer·i] **I.** *n* ❶ (*from same period*) Zeitgenosse, -in *m, f* ❷ (*of same age*) Altersgenosse, -in *m, f* **II.** *adj* zeitgenössisch

contempt [kən·ˈtempt] *n* ❶ (*scorn*) Verachtung *f;* (*disregard*) Geringschätzung *f* (**for** +*gen*); **to treat sb/sth with ~** jdn/etw mit Verachtung strafen ❷ LAW **~ [of court]** Missachtung *f* [des Gerichts]; **to hold sb in ~ of court** jdn wegen Missachtung des Gerichts festhalten

contemptuous [kən·ˈtemp·tʃu·əs] *adj* verächtlich; *look, remark a.* geringschätzig

contend [kən·ˈtend] **I.** *vi* ❶ (*compete*) kämpfen (**for** um +*akk*) ❷ (*cope*) ■**to ~ with sth** mit etw *dat* fertigwerden müssen **II.** *vt* ■**to ~ that ...** behaupten, dass ...

contender [kən·ˈten·dər] *n* Bewerber(in) *m(f)* (**for** für +*akk*), Anwärter(in) *m(f)* (**for** auf +*akk*)

content¹ [ˈkan·tent] *n* ❶ (*what is inside*) Inhalt *m* ❷ (*amount contained*) Gehalt (**of** an +*dat*); **to have a high/low fat ~** einen hohen/niedrigen Fettgehalt aufweisen

content² [kən·ˈtent] **I.** *adj* zufrieden **II.** *vt* **to be easily ~ed** leicht zufrieden zu stellen sein; ■**to ~ oneself with sth** sich mit etw *dat* zufriedengeben

contented [kən·ˈten·t̬ɪd] *adj* zufrieden

contention [kən·ˈten·ʃən] *n* ❶ (*dispute*) Streit *m* ❷ SPORTS **in/out of ~ for sth** [noch] im/aus dem Rennen um etw *akk*

contentious [kən·ˈten·ʃəs] *adj* umstritten

contentment [kən·ˈtent·mənt] *n* Zufriedenheit *f*

contents [ˈkan·tents] *npl* Inhalt *m;* **[table of] ~** Inhaltsverzeichnis *nt*

contest **I.** *n* [ˈkan·test] ❶ (*event*) Wettbewerb *m;* SPORTS Wettkampf *m;* **dance ~** Tanzturnier *nt* ❷ *a.* POL Wettstreit *m* (**for** um +*akk*) ▸ PHRASES: **no ~** ungleicher Kampf **II.** *vt* [kən·ˈtest] ❶ (*compete for*) kämpfen um ❷ (*dispute*) bestreiten; *decision* in Frage stellen

contestant [kən·ˈtes·tənt] *n* (*in a competition*) Wettbewerbsteilnehmer(in) *m(f);* SPORTS Wettkampfteilnehmer(in) *m(f);* (*on a game show*) Kandidat(in) *m(f)*

context [ˈkan·tekst] *n* Kontext *m;* **to take** [*or* **use**] **sth out of ~** etw aus dem Zusammenhang reißen

continent [ˈkan·tə·nənt] *n* GEOG Kontinent *m,* Erdteil *m*

continental [ˌkan·tə·ˈnən·təl] *adj* ❶ kontinental; **~ breakfast** kontinentales Frühstück ❷ (*of the colonies*) Kontinental-; **C~ Congress** Kontinentalkongress *m*

contingent [kən·ˈtɪn·dʒənt] **I.** *n* ❶ (*group*) Gruppe *f* ❷ MIL [Truppen]kontingent *nt* **II.** *adj* ■**to be ~ [up]on sth** von etw *dat* abhängig sein

continual [kən·ˈtɪn·ju·əl] *adj* ständig, andauernd

continually [kən·ˈtɪn·ju·əl·i] *adv* ständig, [an]dauernd

continuation [kən·ˌtɪn·ju·ˈeɪ·ʃən] *n* Fortsetzung *f*

continue [kən·ˈtɪn·ju] **I.** *vi* ❶ (*persist*) andauern; (*go on*) weitergehen; *rain* anhalten; (*in an activity*) weitermachen; ■**to ~ doing/to do sth** weiter[hin] etw tun; ■**to ~ with sth** mit etw *dat* weitermachen ❷ (*remain*) bleiben; **to ~ in power** an der Macht bleiben ❸ (*resume*) weitergehen; *speaking* fortfahren; ■**to ~ doing/to do sth** weiter[hin] etw tun; ■**to ~ with sth** mit etw *dat* weitermachen **II.** *vt* ❶ (*keep up, carry on*) fortführen; *an action* mit etw *dat* weitermachen; *career* weiterverfolgen; *education* fortsetzen ❷ (*resume*) fortsetzen; **~d on the following page** Fortsetzung *f* umseitig, auf der nächsten Seite weitergehen

continued [kən·ˈtɪn·jud] *adj* fortwährend; **~ existence** Weiterbestehen *nt*

continuity [ˌkan·tə·ˈnu·ɪ·t̬i] *n* ❶ (*consistency*) Kontinuität *f* ❷ FILM Drehbuch *nt*

continuous [kən·ˈtɪn·ju·əs] *adj* (*permanent*) ununterbrochen; (*steady*) stetig; (*unbroken*) durchgehend; *line a.* durchgezogen; *pain* anhaltend

contort [kən·ˈtɔrt] **I.** *vt* **to ~ one's body** sich verrenken **II.** *vi* (*in pain*) sich verzerren

contortion [kən·ˈtɔr·ʃən] *n* Verrenkung *f*

contortionist [kən·ˈtɔr·ʃə·nɪst] *n* Schlangenmensch *m*

contour [ˈkan·tʊr] *n* ❶ (*outline*) Kontur *f meist pl* ❷ GEOG **~ [line]** Höhenlinie *f*

contraband [ˈkan·trə·bænd] **I.** *n* Schmuggelware *f* **II.** *adj* geschmuggelt

contraception [ˌkan·trə·ˈsep·ʃən] *n* [Empfängnis]verhütung *f*

contraceptive [ˌkan·trə·ˈsep·tɪv] **I.** *n* Verhütungsmittel *nt* **II.** *adj* empfängnisverhütend

contract¹ **I.** *n* [ˈkan·trækt] Vertrag *m;* **to be under ~ [to** [*or* **with**] **sb]** [bei jdm] unter Vertrag stehen; **breach of ~** Vertragsbruch *m* **II.** *vt* (*formally agree to do*) vertraglich vereinbaren; ■**to ~ sb to do sth** jdn vertraglich dazu verpflichten, etw zu tun **III.** *vi* ■**to ~ to do sth** sich vertraglich verpflichten, etw zu tun

◆**contract out** *vt* vergeben (**to** an +*akk*)

contract² [kən·ˈtrækt] **I.** *vt* ❶ (*tense*) *muscles* zusammenziehen ❷ (*shrink*) *metal* zusammenschrumpfen ❸ MED bekommen; *pneumonia* sich *dat* zuziehen ❹ LING (*shorten*) *word, phrase* zusammenziehen, kontrahieren **II.** *vi* [kən·ˈtrækt] ❶ (*tense*) *muscles* sich zusammenziehen ❷ (*shrink*) sich *akk* zusammenziehen; *pupils* sich verengen

contraction [kən·ˈtræk·ʃən] *n* ❶ (*shrinkage*) Zusammenziehen *nt; of pupils* Verengung *f* ❷ *of a muscle* Kontraktion *f* ❸ LING Kontraktion *f*

contractor [ˈkan·træk·tər] *n* (*person*) Auftragnehmer(in) *m(f);* (*company*) beauftragte Fir-

ma; **building ~** Bauunternehmer *m*
contractual [kən·ˈtræk·tʃu·əl] *adj* vertraglich
contradict [ˌkan·trə·ˈdɪkt] *vt* ■**to ~ sb/sth** jdm/etw widersprechen; ■**to ~ oneself** sich *dat* [selbst] widersprechen
contradiction [ˌkan·trə·ˈdɪk·ʃən] *n* Widerspruch *m* (**of** gegen +*akk*)
contradictory [ˌkan·trə·ˈdɪk·tə·ri] *adj* widersprüchlich
contralto <*pl* -s *or* -ti> [kən·ˈtræl·toʊ] *n* ❶ (*singer*) Altist(in) *m(f)* ❷ (*voice*) Alt *m*
contraption [kən·ˈtræp·ʃən] *n* Apparat *m;* (*vehicle*) Vehikel *nt*
contrary [ˈkan·trer·i] **I.** *n* ■**the ~** das Gegenteil; **on the ~** ganz im Gegenteil **II.** *adj* ❶ (*conflicting*) *interests, opinions, views* entgegengesetzt; **~ to popular opinion** im Gegensatz zur allgemeinen Meinung ❷ (*opposite in direction*) *course, direction* entgegengesetzt ❸ (*argumentative*) widerspenstig
contrast I. *n* [ˈkan·træst] ❶ (*difference*) Gegensatz *m,* Kontrast *m* (**to/with** zu +*dat*); **to be in stark ~ to sth** in krassem Gegensatz zu etw *dat* stehen ❷ TV Kontrast *m* **II.** *vt* [kən·ˈtræst] ■**to ~ sth with sth** etw etw *dat* gegenüberstellen **III.** *vi* [kən·ˈtræst] kontrastieren
contrasting [kən·ˈtræs·tɪŋ] *adj* gegensätzlich; *colors/flavors* konträr; *techniques* unterschiedlich
contribute [kən·ˈtrɪb·jut] *vi, vt money, food, equipment* beisteuern; *ideas* beitragen; *article* schreiben (**to** für +*akk*); (*pay in*) *to retirement plan etc.* einen Beitrag leisten
contribution [ˌkan·trɪ·ˈbju·ʃən] *n* Beitrag *m* (**to/toward** zu +*dat*); (*to charity*) Spende *f* (**to/toward** für +*akk*)
contributor [kən·ˈtrɪb·jə·tər] *n* ❶ (*donor*) Spender(in) *m(f)* ❷ (*writer*) Mitarbeiter(in) *m(f)* (**to** bei +*dat*)
contributory [kən·ˈtrɪb·jə·tɔr·i] *adj* (*causing*) **to be a ~ factor to sth** ein Faktor sein, der zu etw *dat* beiträgt
contrive [kən·ˈtraɪv] **I.** *vt* ❶ (*devise*) sich *dat* ausdenken ❷ (*fabricate*) entwerfen, einfädeln **II.** *vi* ■**to ~ to do sth** es schaffen, etw zu tun
contrived [kən·ˈtraɪvd] *adj* (*pej: artificial*) gestellt, gekünstelt
control [kən·ˈtroʊl] **I.** *n* ❶ Kontrolle *f; of a country* Gewalt *f; of a company* Leitung *f;* **to be in ~ of sth** etw unter Kontrolle haben; *a territory* etw in seiner Gewalt haben; **out of ~** außer Kontrolle sein; **to get** [*or* **go**] **out of ~** außer Kontrolle geraten; **arms ~** Rüstungsbegrenzung *f;* **birth ~** Geburtenkontrolle *f* ❷ TECH Schalter *m,* Regler *m;* **~ panel** Schalttafel *f;* **volume ~** Lautstärkeregler *m* ❸ COMPUT Steuerung *f* **II.** *vt* <-ll-> ❶ (*direct*) kontrollieren; *car* steuern; *company* leiten ❷ TECH (*limit*) *valve, volume* regulieren; *inflation* eindämmen; *pain* in Schach halten ❸ *emotions* beherrschen; *temper* zügeln
controllable [kən·ˈtroʊl·əb·əl] *adj* kontrollierbar, steuerbar
controlled [kən·ˈtroʊld] *adj* ❶ kontrolliert; *voice* beherrscht ❷ MED verschreibungspflichtig
controller [kən·ˈtroʊ·lər] *n* ❶ (*director*) Leiter(in) *m(f);* (*of a radio station*) Intendant(in) *m(f);* (*supervisor*) Aufseher(in) *m(f)* ❷ AVIAT **air traffic** [*or* **flight**] **~** Fluglotse, Fluglotsin *m, f* ❸ FIN Controller(in) *m(f)*
controversial [ˌkan·trə·ˈvɜr·ʃəl] *adj* umstritten
controversy [ˈkan·trə·vɜr·si] *n* Kontroverse *f*
convalesce [ˌkan·və·ˈles] *vi* genesen
convalescence [ˌkan·və·ˈles·əns] *n* ❶ (*recovery*) Genesung *f* ❷ (*time*) Genesungszeit *f*
convalescent [ˌkan·və·ˈles·ənt] **I.** *n* Genesende(r) *f(m)* **II.** *adj* ❶ *person* genesend ❷ *for convalescents* Genesungs-
convection [kən·ˈvek·ʃən] *n* Konvektion *f*
con'vection oven *n* Heißluftherd *m*
convene [kən·ˈvin] (*form*) **I.** *vi* sich versammeln; *committee* zusammentreten **II.** *vt people* zusammenrufen; *committee, meeting* einberufen
convenience [kən·ˈvin·jəns] *n* ❶ (*comfort*) Annehmlichkeit *f;* **at your earliest ~** baldmöglichst ❷ (*device*) Annehmlichkeit *f;* **with all modern ~s** mit allem Komfort
con'venience store *n* Laden *m* an der Ecke
convenient [kən·ˈvin·jənt] *adj* ❶ (*useful*) zweckmäßig; (*comfortable*) bequem; *excuse* passend ❷ *date, time* passend, günstig ❸ (*accessible*) *location* günstig gelegen
convent [ˈkan·vənt] *n* [Nonnen]kloster *nt*
convention [kən·ˈven·ʃən] *n* ❶ (*custom*) Brauch *m;* (*social code*) Konvention *f;* **~ dictates that ...** es ist Brauch, dass ... ❷ (*agreement*) Abkommen *nt; on human rights* Konvention *f* ❸ (*assembly*) [Mitglieder]versammlung *f;* (*conference*) Konferenz *f;* **~ center** Tagungszentrum *nt*
conventional [kən·ˈven·ʃə·nəl] *adj* konventionell; **~ medicine** Schulmedizin *f*
converge [kən·ˈvɜrdʒ] *vi* ❶ *lines* zusammenlaufen ❷ *people* **to ~ on a city** scharenweise in eine Stadt kommen ❸ MATH konvergieren
convergence [kən·ˈvɜr·dʒəns] *n of lines* Zusammenlaufen *nt;* **point of ~** Schnittpunkt *m*
convergent [kən·ˈvɜr·dʒent] *adj* ❶ *lines* konvergent ❷ (*similar*) ähnlich; *opinions* konvergierend
conversation [ˌkan·vər·ˈseɪ·ʃən] *n* Gespräch *nt,* Unterhaltung *f;* **to be in** [*or* **have a**] **~** [**with sb**] sich [mit jdm] unterhalten; **to carry on** [*or* **hold**] **a ~** sich unterhalten, ein Gespräch führen; **to make ~** (*small talk*) Konversation machen
conversational [ˌkan·vər·ˈseɪ·ʃə·nəl] *adj* Gesprächs-, Unterhaltungs-; **~ tone** Plauderton *m*
conversationally [ˌkan·vər·ˈseɪ·ʃən·əl·i] *adv* im Plauderton
converse¹ [kən·ˈvɜrs] *vi* (*form*) sich *akk* unterhalten
converse² [ˈkan·vɜrs] (*form*) **I.** *n* ■**the ~** das

Gegenteil **II.** *adj* gegenteilig
conversely [kən·ˈvɜrs·li] *adv* umgekehrt
conversion [kən·ˈvɜr·ʒən] *n* ① (*change of form or function*) Umwandlung *f* (**into** in +*akk*); TECH Umrüstung *f* (**into** zu +*dat*) ② REL Konversion *f,* Übertritt *m,* Bekehrung *f* ③ MATH Umrechnung *f* ④ (*in football*) Conversion *f;* (*in hockey, soccer*) Verwandlung *f*
convert **I.** *n* [ˈkan·vɜrt] REL Bekehrte(r) *f(m),* Konvertit(in) *m(f);* **to become a ~ to Islam** zum Islam übertreten **II.** *vi* [kən·ˈvɜrt] ① REL übertreten; **he ~ed to his wife's religion** er nahm die Religion seiner Frau an ② (*change in function*) sich verwandeln lassen **III.** *vt* [kən·ˈvɜrt] ① REL (*a. fig*) bekehren ② (*change in form or function*) ■**to ~ sth [into]** etw umwandeln [in] +*akk;* ARCHIT etw umbauen [zu]; TECH etw umrüsten [zu] ③ (*calculate*) umrechnen; (*exchange*) umtauschen ④ (*in football*) *extra point* erfolgreich abschliessen; (*in hockey, soccer*) *penalty* verwandeln
converter [kən·ˈvɜr·t̬ər] *n* ① ELEC Umwandler *m* ② AUTO **catalytic ~** Katalysator *m*
convertible [kən·ˈvɜr·t̬ə·bəl] **I.** *n* Kabrio[lett] *nt,* Kabriole *nt* ÖSTERR **II.** *adj* ① (*changeable*) verwandelbar ② FIN konvertierbar
convex [ˈkan·veks] *adj* konvex
convey [kən·ˈveɪ] *vt* ① (*transport*) befördern ② (*transmit*) überbringen; (*impart*) vermitteln; (*make clear*) deutlich machen
conveyance [kən·ˈveɪ·əns] *n* (*form: vehicle*) Verkehrsmittel *nt*
conveyor [kən·ˈveɪ·ər] *n* ① **~ [belt]** Förderband *nt;* (*in factory*) Fließband *nt* ② (*bearer*) Überbringer(in) *m(f)*
convict **I.** *n* [ˈkan·vɪkt] Strafgefangene(r) *f(m)* **II.** *vi* [kən·ˈvɪkt] auf schuldig erkennen **III.** *vt* [kən·ˈvɪkt] verurteilen
conviction [kən·ˈvɪk·ʃən] *n* ① (*judgment*) Verurteilung *f* (**for** wegen +*dat*); **previous ~s** Vorstrafen *pl* ② (*belief*) Überzeugung *f;* **to have a deep ~ that ...** der festen Überzeugung sein, dass ...
convince [kən·ˈvɪns] *vt* überzeugen (**of** von +*dat*)
convincing [kən·ˈvɪn·sɪŋ] *adj* überzeugend
convoluted [ˌkan·və·ˈlut̬ɪd] *adj* (*form*) ① (*twisted*) verwickelt ② (*difficult*) *sentences* verschachtelt; *plot* verschlungen
convoy [ˈkan·vɔɪ] *n* Konvoi *m*
convulse [kən·ˈvʌls] **I.** *vi* **to ~ with laughter** sich vor Lachen biegen **II.** *vt* erschüttern; **to be ~d with laughter** sich vor Lachen biegen
convulsion [kən·ˈvʌl·ʃən] *n usu pl* Krampf *m;* **to go into ~s** Krämpfe bekommen
coo [ku] *vi* gurren
cook [kʊk] **I.** *n* Koch, Köchin *m, f* **II.** *vi* ① (*make meals*) kochen ② (*in water*) kochen; *fish, meat* garen; (*fry, roast*) braten ▶ PHRASES: **<u>what's</u> ~ing?** (*sl*) was ist los? **III.** *vt* ① (*make*) kochen; **how do you ~ this fish?** wie wird dieser Fisch zubereitet? ② (*heat*) kochen; *fish, meat* garen; (*fry, roast*) braten
ˈ**cookbook** *n* Kochbuch *nt*
cooker [ˈkʊ·kər] *n* BRIT ① (*stove*) Herd *m;* **induction ~** Induktionsherd *m* ② (*fam: cooking apple*) Kochapfel *m*
cookie [ˈkʊk·i] *n* ① (*crisp cake*) Keks *m,* Plätzchen *nt* ② (*sl: person*) **he's one tough ~** er ist eine harte Nuss ③ COMPUT Cookie *nt* ▶ PHRASES: **that's the way the ~ <u>crumbles</u>** (*saying*) so ist das nun mal im Leben
cooking [ˈkʊk·ɪŋ] *n* ① (*act*) Kochen *nt;* **to do the ~** kochen ② (*style*) **French ~** die französische Küche
cool [kul] **I.** *adj* ① (*pleasantly cold*) kühl; (*unpleasantly cold*) kalt; *clothing, material* luftig; *color* kühl ② (*calm*) ruhig, cool *sl;* (*levelheaded*) besonnen; **to keep a ~ head** einen kühlen Kopf bewahren ③ (*unfriendly, unfeeling*) *reception* kühl; (*not showing interest*) abweisend ④ (*fam: trendy, great*) cool *sl,* geil *sl* **II.** *interj* (*fam*) cool *sl,* geil *sl* **III.** *n* ① (*cold*) Kühle *f;* **in the ~ of the evening** in der Abendkühle ② (*calm*) Ruhe *f* **IV.** *vi* ① (*lose heat*) abkühlen (**to** auf +*akk*) ② (*die down*) *tempers* nachlassen **V.** *vt* ① (*make cold*) kühlen; (*cool down*) abkühlen ② (*sl: calm down*) **[just] ~ it!** reg dich ab!
cooler [ˈku·lər] *n* Kühlbox *f; for wine bottles* Kühler *m*
coolˈ**headed** *adj* besonnen
cooling [ˈku·lɪŋ] *adj* [ab]kühlend
coolly [ˈku·li] *adv* (*coldly*) kühl, distanziert; (*in a relaxed manner*) cool *sl,* gelassen
coolness [ˈkul·nɪs] *n* ① (*low temperature*) Kühle *f* ② (*unfriendliness*) Kühle *f,* Distanziertheit *f*
coop [kup] **I.** *n* Hühnerstall *m* **II.** *vt* ■**to ~ up** einsperren
co-op [ˈkoʊ·ap] *n abbrev of* **cooperative I**
cooperate [koʊ·ˈap·ə·reɪt] *vi* ① (*help*) kooperieren; (*comply a.*) mitmachen ② (*act jointly*) kooperieren, zusammenarbeiten (**in/with** bei +*dat*)
cooperation [koʊ·ˌap·ə·ˈreɪ·ʃən] *n* ① (*assistance*) Kooperation *f,* Mitarbeit *f* (**in/with** bei +*dat*) ② (*joint work*) Zusammenarbeit *f,* Kooperation *f* (**in/with** bei +*dat*)
cooperative [koʊ·ˈap·ər·ə·t̬ɪv] **I.** *n* Genossenschaft *f,* Kooperative *f* **II.** *adj* ① ECON genossenschaftlich, kooperativ; **~ farm** landwirtschaftliche Genossenschaft ② (*willing*) kooperativ
coordinate [ˌkoʊ·ˈɔr·dɪn·eɪt] **I.** *n usu pl* MATH Koordinate *f* **II.** *vi* [gut] zusammenarbeiten **III.** *vt* koordinieren
coordination [ˌkoʊ·ˌɔr·də·ˈneɪ·ʃən] *n* ① (*coordinating*) Koordination *f* ② (*cooperation*) Zusammenarbeit *f* ③ (*dexterity*) Sinn *m* für Koordination
coordinator [koʊ·ˈɔr·də·neɪ·t̬ər] *n* Koordinator(in) *m(f)*
cop [kap] **I.** *n* (*fam: police officer*) Bulle *m* **II.** *vt* <-pp-> **to ~ a plea** LAW *sich schuldig be-*

kennen und dafür eine mildere Strafe aushandeln

cope [koʊp] *vi* ❶ (*mentally*) zurechtkommen; **to ~ with a problem** ein Problem bewältigen ❷ (*physically*) gewachsen sein

Copenhagen ['koʊ·pən·ˌheɪ·gən, -'ha-] *n* Kopenhagen *nt*

copier ['kap·i·ər] *n* (*machine*) Kopiergerät *nt*

copilot ['koʊ·ˌpaɪ·lət] *n* Kopilot(in) *m(f)*

copious ['koʊ·pi·əs] *adj* zahlreich; **~ amounts of** Unmengen von

copper ['kap·ər] *n* (*metal*) Kupfer *nt*

copulate ['kap·jə·leɪt] *vi* kopulieren

copy ['kap·i] **I.** *n* ❶ (*duplicate*) Kopie *f;* (*of a document*) Abschrift *f;* (*of a photo*) Abzug *m* ❷ (*issue*) Exemplar *nt;* **hard ~** COMPUT [Computer]ausdruck *m* ❸ PUBL Manuskript *nt;* (*in advertising*) Werbetext *m* **II.** *vt* <-ie-> ❶ (*duplicate*) kopieren; (*write down*) **~ [down]** *from text* abschreiben; *from words* niederschreiben ❷ (*imitate*) *person* nachmachen; *style* nachahmen; *picture* abmalen ❸ (*plagiarize*) abschreiben *f* **III.** *vi* <-ie-> (*in school*) abschreiben

'copycat I. *n* (*pej fam*) Nachmacher(in) *m(f);* (*of written work*) Abschreiber(in) *m(f)* **II.** *adj* imitiert

'copyeditor *n* Manuskriptbearbeiter(in) *m(f);* (*for news media*) Redakteur(in) *m(f);* (*in a publishing house*) Lektor(in) *m(f)*

copy pro'tection *n* COMPUT Kopierschutz *m*

copyright ['kap·i·raɪt] **I.** *n* Copyright *nt,* Urheberrecht *nt;* **out of ~** nicht [mehr] urheberrechtlich geschützt **II.** *vt* urheberrechtlich schützen

'copywriter *n* [Werbe]texter(in) *m(f)*

coral ['kɔr·əl] *n* Koralle *f*

'coral reef *n* Korallenriff *nt*

cord [kɔrd] *n* ❶ (*for package*) Schnur *f;* **electrical ~** Kabel *nt* ❷ (*fam: pants*) ■ **~s** *pl* Cordhose *f*

cordial ['kɔr·dʒəl] **I.** *adj* ❶ (*friendly*) freundlich, herzlich; *relations* freundschaftlich ❷ (*form: fervent*) heftig; *dislike* tief **II.** *n* (*liqueur*) Likör *m*

cordless ['kɔrd·lɪs] *adj* schnurlos

cordon ['kɔr·dən] **I.** *n* Kordon *m* **II.** *vt* ■ **to ~ off** ◡ **sth** etw absperren

corduroy ['kɔr·də·rɔɪ] *n* ❶ (*material*) Cordsamt *m;* **~ jacket** Cordjacke *f* ❷ (*pants*) ■ **~s** *pl* Cordhose *f*

core [kɔr] **I.** *n* ❶ (*center*) *of apple* Kerngehäuse *nt; of rock* Innere[s] *nt; of planet* Mittelpunkt *m; of reactor* [Reaktor]kern *m* ❷ (*fig*) Kern *m;* **rotten to the ~** bis ins Mark verdorben ❸ ELEC Leiter *m* **II.** *adj* zentral **III.** *vt* entkernen

coriander ['kɔr·i·æn·dər] *n* Koriander *m*

cork [kɔrk] **I.** *n* ❶ (*material*) Kork *m* ❷ (*stopper*) Korken *m* **II.** *vt* zukorken

'corkscrew *n* Korkenzieher *m*

corn[1] [kɔrn] *n* FOOD Mais *m*

corn[2] [kɔrn] *n* MED Hühnerauge *nt*

> Der Mais, **corn**, kommt aus der „Neuen Welt". In den USA isst man gerne *corn on the cob* (Maiskolben) an Feiertagen oder bei einem Picknick. *Popcorn* wird eher bei einem Kinobesuch genossen. Aufgereiht auf einen Faden wird es auch gerne benutzt, um den Christbaum zu schmücken. Das *cornmeal* (Maismehl) wird dazu verwendet, *Indian pudding,* eine Süßspeise aus Maismehl und Melasse, oder *corn bread,* eine Art Maisbrot, zu machen.

'corncob *n* Maiskolben *m*

corner ['kɔr·nər] **I.** *n* ❶ Ecke *f;* **on the ~ [of the street]** an der Straßenecke; *of table* Kante *f;* **to fold the ~ of a page** ein Eselsohr machen; **the four ~s of the world** alle vier Himmelsrichtungen; **out of the ~ of one's eye** aus dem Augenwinkel ❷ (*in soccer*) Ecke *f,* Eckball *m* ▶ PHRASES: **to cut ~s** (*financially*) Kosten sparen; (*in procedure*) das Verfahren abkürzen; **to turn the ~** um die Ecke biegen **II.** *adj* Eck- **III.** *vt* ❶ (*trap*) in die Enge treiben ❷ COMM monopolisieren; *market* beherrschen **IV.** *vi vehicle* eine Kurve/Kurven nehmen; **to ~ well** gut in der Kurve liegen

'cornerstone *n* ARCHIT (*a. fig*) Eckstein *m*

cornet [kɔr·'net] *n* MUS Kornett *nt*

'corn flakes *npl* Cornflakes *pl*

'cornflower *n* Kornblume *f*

'cornstarch *n* Maisstärke *f*

corny ['kɔr·ni] *adj* (*fam: sentimental*) kitschig; (*dopey*) blöd

coronary ['kɔr·ə·ner·i] **I.** *n* Herzinfarkt *m* **II.** *adj* koronar, Herzkranz-

coronation [ˌkɔr·ə·'neɪ·ʃən] *n* Krönung[szeremonie] *f*

coroner ['kɔr·ə·nər] *n* Coroner *m* (*Beamter, der unter verdächtigen Umständen eingetretene Todesfälle untersucht*)

corp. [korp] *n* ❶ *short for* **corporation** ❷ *short for* **corporal**

corporal ['kɔr·pər·əl] *n* Unteroffizier *m*

corporate ['kɔr·pər·ət] *adj* (*of corporation*) körperschaftlich; **~ policy** Firmenpolitik *f*

corporate income tax *n* Körperschaftssteuer *f*

corporation [ˌkɔr·pə·'reɪ·ʃən] *n* COMM [Kapital]gesellschaft *f*

corps <*pl* -> [kɔr] *n* Korps *nt;* **medical ~** Sanitätstruppe *f*

corpse [kɔrps] *n* Leiche *f*

corpuscle ['kɔr·pʌs·əl] *n* Blutkörperchen *nt*

corral [kə·'ræl] **I.** *n* [Fang]gehege *nt* **II.** *vt* <-ll-> *animals* in den Korral treiben; ■ **to ~ sth off** etw absperren

correct [kə·'rekt] **I.** *vt* korrigieren; **I stand ~ed** ich nehme alles zurück **II.** *adj* (*accurate*) richtig; *proper a.* korrekt; **that is ~** das stimmt

correcting [kə·'rek·tiŋ] *n* SCH (*checking work*) Korrigieren *nt;* (*checking spelling*) Korrekturen *pl*

C

C

correction [kə·ˈrek·ʃən] *n* ❶ (*change*) Korrektur *f* ❷ (*improvement*) Verbesserung *f,* Berichtigung *f*
correctional [kə·ˈrek·ʃə·nəl] *adj* ~ **facility** *Strafanstalt für junge Straftäter*
corrective [kə·ˈrek·tɪv] **I.** *adj* ❶ (*counteractive*) korrigierend; ~ **surgery** Korrekturoperation *f* ❷ (*improving behavior*) Besserungs- **II.** *n* Korrektiv *nt*
correctly [kə·ˈrekt·li] *adv* korrekt, richtig
correctness [kə·ˈrekt·nɪs] *n* Korrektheit *f,* Richtigkeit *f*
correlate [ˈkɔr·ə·leɪt] *vi* sich *dat* entsprechen
correlation [ˌkɔr·ə·ˈleɪ·ʃən] *n* ❶ [Wechsel]beziehung *f,* Zusammenhang *m* ❷ (*in statistics*) Korrelation *f*
correspond [ˌkɔr·ə·ˈspand] *vi* ❶ (*be equivalent of*) entsprechen (**to** +*dat*); (*be same as*) übereinstimmen (**with** mit +*dat*) ❷ (*write*) korrespondieren
correspondence [ˌkɔr·ə·ˈspan·dəns] *n* (*letter writing*) Korrespondenz *f*
correspondent [ˌkɔr·ə·ˈspan·dənt] *n* ❶ (*of letters*) Briefeschreiber(in) *m(f)* ❷ (*journalist*) Berichterstatter(in) *m(f),* Korrespondent(in) *m(f)*
corresponding [ˌkɔr·ə·ˈspan·dɪŋ] *adj* ❶ (*same*) entsprechend ❷ (*accompanying*) dazugehörig
corridor [ˈkɔr·ɪ·dər] *n* ❶ (*inside*) Flur *m,* Gang *m,* Korridor *m* ❷ (*strip of land, air space*) Korridor *m*
corroborate [kə·ˈrab·ə·reɪt] *vt* bestätigen
corroboration [kə·ˌrab·ə·ˈreɪ·ʃən] *n* Bestätigung *f*
corrode [kə·ˈroʊd] **I.** *vi* korrodieren **II.** *vt metal* korrodieren; (*fig*) zerstören
corrosion [kə·ˈroʊ·ʒən] *n* ❶ Korrosion *f* ❷ (*fig*) Verfall *m*
corrosive [kə·ˈroʊ·sɪv] *adj* ❶ korrosiv; *acid* ätzend ❷ (*fig*) zerstörerisch
corrugated [ˈkɔr·ə·geɪ·t̬ɪd] *adj iron, cardboard* gewellt
corrupt [kə·ˈrʌpt] **I.** *adj* ❶ (*dishonest*) korrupt; (*bribable*) bestechlich ❷ (*ruined*) *text* entstellt; *file* unlesbar; *disk* kaputt **II.** *vt* ❶ (*debase ethically*) korrumpieren; (*morally*) [moralisch] verderben; (*influence by bribes*) bestechen ❷ (*change*) entstellen; *text* verfälschen ❸ COMPUT *data, file* ruinieren
corruption [kə·ˈrʌp·ʃən] *n* ❶ (*action*) *of moral standards* Korruption *f; of a text* Entstellung *f; of computer file* Zerstörung *f* ❷ (*dishonesty*) Unehrenhaftigkeit *f;* (*bribery*) Korruption *f* ❸ (*decay*) Zersetzung *f*
corset [ˈkɔr·sɪt] *n* (*undergarment*) Korsett *nt;* MED Stützkorsett *nt*
Corsica [ˈkɔr·sɪ·kə] *n* Korsika *nt*
Corsican [ˈkɔr·sɪ·kən] **I.** *adj* korsisch **II.** *n* ❶ (*person*) Korse, -in *m, f* ❷ (*language*) Korsisch *nt*
cosignatory [ˌkoʊ·ˈsɪg·nə·tɔr·i] *n* Mitunterzeichner(in) *m(f)*
cosmetic [kaz·ˈme·t̬ɪk] **I.** *n* Kosmetik *f;* **~s** *pl* Kosmetika *pl* **II.** *adj* kosmetisch *a. fig*
cosmic [ˈkaz·mɪk] *adj* kosmisch *a. fig*
cosmology [kaz·ˈmal·ə·dʒi] *n* Kosmologie *f*
cosmonaut [ˈkaz·mə·nɔt] *n* Kosmonaut(in) *m(f)*
cosmopolitan [ˌkaz·mə·ˈpal·ɪ·tən] *adj* kosmopolitisch
cosmos [ˈkaz·məs] *n* Kosmos *m*
cost [kɔst] **I.** *vt* ❶ <cost, cost> kosten ❷ <-ed, -ed> FIN ■ **to ~ [out]** *expenses* [durch]kalkulieren **II.** *n* ❶ (*price*) Preis *m,* Kosten *pl* (**of** für +*akk*); **at no extra ~** ohne Aufpreis; **to buy sth at ~** etw zum Selbstkostenpreis kaufen ❷ (*fig*) Aufwand *m kein pl;* **at no ~ to the environment** ohne Beeinträchtigung für die Umwelt; **at all ~[s]** [*or* **at any ~**] um jeden Preis ❸ ■ **~s** *pl* Kosten *pl* (**of** für +*akk*)
costar [ˌkoʊ·ˈstar] **I.** *n* einer der Hauptdarsteller; **to be sb's ~** neben jdm die Hauptrolle spielen **II.** *vt, vi* <-rr-> ■ **to ~ [with] sb** neben jdm die Hauptrolle spielen
cost-cutting *n* kostensenkend; **to be taking ~ measures** auf dem Spartrip sein
costly [ˈkɔst·li] *adj* kostspielig *a. fig*
costume [ˈkas·tum] *n* ❶ (*national dress*) Tracht *f;* **historical ~** historisches Kostüm ❷ (*decorative dress*) Kostüm *nt;* **to wear a witch['s] ~** Hexe verkleidet sein
cosy [ˈkoʊ·zi] *adj, vi see* **cozy**
cot [kat] *n* (*camping bed*) Feldbett *nt;* (*foldout bed*) Klappbett *nt*
cottage [ˈka·t̬ɪdʒ] *n* Cottage *nt*
cottage ˈcheese *n* Hüttenkäse *m*
cottage ˈindustry *n* Heimindustrie *f*
cotton [ˈkat·ən] **I.** *n* ❶ (*material, plant*) Baumwolle *f* ❷ (*thread*) Garn *nt* **II.** *adj* Baumwoll- **III.** *vi* (*fam: understand*) ■ **to ~ [on] to [sth]** [etw] kapieren
cotton ˈcandy *n* Zuckerwatte *f*
ˈcotton mill *n* Baumwollspinnerei *f*
ˈcottonseed *n* Baumwollsamen *m*
couch [kaʊtʃ] **I.** *n* <*pl* -es> Couch *f* **II.** *vt* formulieren
ˈcouch potato *n* (*fam*) Couchpotato *f,* Fernsehglotzer(in) *m(f)*
cougar [ˈku·gər] *n* ZOOL Puma *m*
cough [kɔf] **I.** *n* Husten *m* **II.** *vi* ❶ *person* husten; (*as warning*) hüsteln ❷ *motor* stottern **III.** *vt blood* husten
◆ **cough up I.** *vt* ❶ *blood* husten ❷ (*fam: pay*) herausrücken **II.** *vi* (*fam*) herausrücken
ˈcough drop *n* Hustenbonbon *nt*
ˈcough medicine *n* (*in liquid form*) Hustensaft *m*
cough syrup *n* Hustensaft *m*
could [kʊd] *pt, subjunctive of* **can**
council [ˈkaʊn·səl] *n* Rat *m;* **city ~** Stadtrat *m*
councilor, councillor [ˈkaʊn·sə·lər] *n* Ratsmitglied *nt;* **city ~** Stadtrat, -rätin *m, f*
counsel [ˈkaʊn·səl] **I.** *vt* <-l- *or* -ll-> empfehlen; ■ **to ~ sb about** [*or* **on**] **sth** jdn bei etw *dat* beraten; ■ **to ~ sb against sth** jdm von

etw *dat* abraten **II.** *n* (*lawyer*) Anwalt, Anwältin *m, f;* ~ **for the defense** Verteidiger(in) *m(f)*
counseling, counselling ['kaʊn·sə·lɪŋ] **I.** *n* psychologische Betreuung **II.** *adj* Beratungs-
counselor, counsellor ['kaʊn·sə·lər] *n* ① (*advisor*) Berater(in) *m(f)* ② (*lawyer*) Anwalt *m,* Anwältin *f*
count[2] [kaʊnt] **I.** *n* ① (*action of calculating*) Zählung *f;* POL Auszählung *f;* **to lose** ~ beim Zählen durcheinanderkommen; **on the** ~ **of three** bei drei ② (*total*) [An]zahl *f,* Ergebnis *nt* ③ LAW Anklagepunkt *m;* **on all** ~**s** in allen [Anklage]punkten ④ (*in boxing*) Auszählung ⑤ (*in baseball*) Count *m,* Zählung *f* ▸ PHRASES: **to be out for the** ~ k.o. sein **II.** *vt* ① (*number*) zählen; *change* nachzählen; ~ **[off]** abzählen ② (*consider*) **to** ~ **sb as a friend** jdn als Freund betrachten; **to** ~ **oneself lucky** sich glücklich schätzen ▸ PHRASES: **to** ~ **the cost [of sth]** [etw] bereuen **III.** *vi* zählen; ■**to** ~ **against sb** gegen jdn sprechen; ■**to be** ~**ed as sth** als etw gelten; **that's what** ~**s** darauf kommt es an
◆**count down** *vi* rückwärts bis null zählen; AEROSP den Countdown durchführen
◆**count on** *vi* zählen auf +*akk*
◆**count out** *vt* ① (*count one by one*) *money* abzählen ② (*fam: exclude*) ■**to** ~ **sb out** jdn nicht einplanen; **you can** ~ **me out** ich mache nicht mit ③ SPORTS *boxer* auszählen
count[2] [kaʊnt] *n* Graf *m*
countdown ['kaʊnt·daʊn] *n* Countdown *m* (**to** +*gen*)
countenance ['kaʊn·tə·nəns] **I.** *n* (*liter: face*) Antlitz *nt* **II.** *vt* (*form*) gutheißen; ■**to not** ~ **sth** etw nicht dulden
counter[1] ['kaʊn·tər] **I.** *vt* ausgleichen; *arguments* widersprechen; *orders* aufheben **II.** *vi* kontern **III.** *adv* entgegen; **to run** ~ **to sth** etw *dat* zuwiderlaufen
counter[2] ['kaʊn·tər] *n* ① (*service point*) Theke *f;* (*in bank, post office*) Schalter *m;* **[kitchen]** ~ [Küchen]arbeitsplatte *f;* **over the** ~ *medication* rezeptfrei; **under the** ~ (*fig*) unterm Ladentisch ② (*disc*) Spielmarke *f*
counter[3] ['kaʊn·tər] *n* (*person*) Zähler(in) *m(f);* (*machine*) Zählwerk *nt*
counter'act *vt* entgegenwirken +*dat; poison* neutralisieren
'counterattack I. *n* Gegenangriff *m* **II.** *vt* im Gegenzug angreifen **III.** *vi* zurückschlagen; SPORTS kontern
counterbalance I. *n* ['kaʊn·tər·ˌbæl·əns] Gegengewicht *nt* **II.** *vt* [ˌkaʊn·tər·'bæl·əns] ausgleichen; (*fig*) ein Gegengewicht zu etw *dat* darstellen
'countercharge *n* ① LAW Gegenklage *f* ② MIL Gegenattacke
counter'clockwise *adv* gegen den Uhrzeigersinn
counter'espionage *n* Spionageabwehr *f*
counterfeit ['kaʊn·tər·fɪt] **I.** *adj* gefälscht; ~ **money** Falschgeld *nt* **II.** *vt* fälschen **III.** *n* Fälschung *f*
counterin'telligence *n* Spionageabwehr *f*
'countermeasure *n* Gegenmaßnahme *f*
'counterpart *n* Gegenstück *nt,* Pendant *nt;* POL Amtskollege, -in *m, f*
counterpro'ductive *adj* kontraproduktiv
'countersign *vt* gegenzeichnen
counter'terrorism *n* Terrorismusbekämpfung *f*
countess <*pl* -es> ['kaʊn·tɪs] *n* Gräfin *f*
countless ['kaʊnt·lɪs] *adj* zahllos
country ['kʌn·tri] **I.** *n* ① (*nation*) Land *nt;* ~ **of origin** Herkunftsland *nt;* **native** ~ Heimat *f,* Heimatland *nt* ② (*rural areas*) **town and** ~ Stadt und Land; ■**in the** ~ auf dem Land ③ (*land*) Land *nt,* Gebiet *nt;* **open** ~ freies Land ④ (*music*) Countrymusic *f* **II.** *adj cottage, road* Land-; *customs* ländlich
country 'bumpkin *n* (*pej*) Bauerntölpel *m;* (*woman*) Bauerntrampel *m*
'country club *n* Country Club *m*
'countryman *n* **[fellow]** ~ Landsmann *m*
'country music *n* Countrymusic *f*
'countryside *n* Land *nt;* (*scenery*) Landschaft *f;* **through the** ~ (*not on roads*) querfeldein; (*avoiding towns*) über Land
'countrywide I. *adj* landesweit **II.** *adv* im ganzen Land
'countrywoman *n* **[fellow]** ~ Landsmännin *f*
county ['kaʊn·ti] *n* [Verwaltungs]bezirk *m*
county 'seat *n* Bezirkshauptstadt *f*
coup [ku] *n* ① (*unexpected achievement*) Coup *m* ② POL Staatsstreich *m*
coup de grâce <*pl* coups de grâce> [ˌku·də·'gras] *n* Gnadenstoß *m*
coup d'état <*pl* coups d'état> [ˌku·deɪ·'ta] *n* Staatsstreich *m*
coupé [ku:·'peɪ] *n* Coupé *nt*
couple ['kʌp·əl] **I.** *n* ① (*a few*) ■**a** ~ **of ...** einige ..., ein paar ...; **every** ~ **of days** alle paar Tage; **in a** ~ **more minutes** in wenigen Minuten; **the first** ~ **of weeks** die ersten Wochen ② (*two people*) Paar *nt* **II.** *vt* ① (*join*) koppeln (**to** mit +*dat*) ② *usu passive* (*put together*) ■**to be** ~**d with sth** mit etw *dat* verbunden sein
couplet ['kʌp·lɪt] *n* Verspaar *nt;* **rhyming** ~ Reimpaar *nt*
coupling ['kʌp·lɪŋ] *n* Kupplung *f*
coupon ['ku·pan] *n* Coupon *m,* Gutschein *m*
courage ['kʌr·ɪdʒ] *n* Mut *m;* **to have/lack the** ~ **to do sth** den Mut haben/nicht den Mut haben etw zu tun
courageous [kə·'reɪ·dʒəs] *adj* mutig
courier ['kʊr·i·ər] *n* Kurier(in) *m(f);* **motorcycle** ~ Motorradbote, -in *m, f*
course [kɔrs] **I.** *n* ① (*series*) *of classes* Kurs *m;* **to take a** ~ **[in sth]** einen Kurs [für etw] besuchen; **training** ~ Lehrgang *m;* MED ~ **[of treatment]** Behandlung *f* ② (*of aircraft, ship*) Kurs *m;* **to change** ~ den Kurs ändern; **off** ~ nicht auf Kurs; (*fig*) aus der Bahn geraten; **on** ~ auf Kurs; (*fig*) auf dem [richtigen] Weg

C

C

❸ (*of road*) Verlauf *m;* (*of river, history, justice*) Lauf *m;* **to change ~** einen anderen Verlauf nehmen ❹ (*way of acting*) ~ **[of action]** Vorgehen *nt;* **of the three ~s open to us ...** von den drei Wegen, die uns offenstehen, ... ❺ **in the ~ of sth** (*during*) im Verlauf einer S. *gen;* **in the normal ~ of events** normalerweise ❻ **[golf]** ~ Golfplatz *m* ❼ (*part of meal*) Gang *m* ▶ PHRASES: **in due ~** zu gegebener Zeit; **of ~** natürlich; **of ~ not** natürlich nicht; **to be par for the ~** normal sein; **to take its ~** seinen Weg gehen **II.** *vi* (*flow*) *tears* strömen

court [kɔrt] **I.** *n* ❶ (*judicial body*) Gericht *nt;* **to go to ~** vor Gericht gehen; **out of ~** außergerichtlich; **to take sb to ~** jdn vor Gericht bringen ❷ (*room*) Gerichtssaal *m* ❸ (*playing area*) [Spiel]platz *m;* **basketball ~** Basketballcourt *m;* **grass ~** Rasenplatz *m* ❹ (*of king, queen*) Hof *m* **II.** *vt* ❶ (*try to gain*) *fame, wealth* suchen ❷ (*ingratiate oneself*) hofieren ❸ (*dated: woo*) umwerben

courteous ['kɜr·t̬i·əs] *adj* höflich

courtesy ['kɜr·t̬ə·si] *n* ❶ (*politeness*) Höflichkeit *f* ❷ (*courteous gesture*) Höflichkeit *f* ▶ PHRASES: **~ of sb/sth** (*thanks to*) dank jdm/etw; (*with the permission of*) mit freundlicher Genehmigung von jdm/etw

'courthouse *n* Gerichtsgebäude *nt*

courtier ['kɔr·ti·ər] *n* Höfling *m*

court-'martial I. *n* <*pl* -s *or form* courts martial> Kriegsgericht *nt* **II.** *vt* <-l- *or* -ll-> vor ein Kriegsgericht stellen

'courtroom *n* Gerichtssaal *m*

courtship ['kɔrt·ʃɪp] *n* Werben *nt* (**of** um +*akk*)

'courtyard *n* Hof *m;* (*walled-in*) Innenhof *m;* ■ **in the ~** auf dem Hof

cousin ['kʌz·ɪn] *n* Vetter *m,* Cousin, Cousine *m, f*

cove [koʊv] *n* kleine Bucht

covenant ['kʌv·ə·nənt] **I.** *n* ❶ (*legal agreement*) vertragliches Abkommen; **restrictive ~** restriktive Vertragsklausel ❷ REL Bündnis *nt* **II.** *vt, vi* vertraglich vereinbaren

cover ['kʌv·ər] **I.** *n* ❶ (*covering*) Abdeckung *f;* (*sheath-like*) Hülle *f;* (*protective top*) Deckel *m;* (*for bed*) [Bett]decke *f;* (*for furniture*) [Schon]bezug *m;* (*tarp*) Plane *f;* ■ **the ~s** *pl* das Bettzeug ❷ (*of a book*) Einband *m;* *of a magazine* Titelseite *f,* Cover *nt* ❸ (*shelter*) Schutz *m;* **under ~ of darkness** im Schutze der Dunkelheit [*o* Nacht]; **to take ~** (*from rain*) sich unterstellen; (*from danger*) sich verstecken ❹ MIL Deckung *f* ▶ PHRASES: **never judge a book by its ~** man sollte niemals nur nach dem Äußeren urteilen **II.** *vt* ❶ (*put over*) bedecken; (*against dust a.*) überziehen; **to be ~ed [in** [*or* **with**] **sth]** [mit etw] bedeckt sein; **~ed in ink** voller Tinte ❷ (*to protect*) abdecken; **to ~ one's eyes with one's hands** die Augen mit den Händen bedecken ❸ (*to hide*) verdecken; (*fig*) *one's confusion* überspielen ❹ (*extend over*) sich erstrecken über +*akk;* (*fig*) zuständig sein ❺ (*travel*) fahren; **to ~ a lot of ground** eine große Strecke zurücklegen; (*make progress*) gut vorankommen *a. fig;* (*be wide-ranging*) sehr umfassend sein ❻ (*deal with*) sich befassen mit ❼ (*report on*) berichten über +*akk* ❽ (*insure*) versichern (**against/for** gegen +*akk*) ❾ MIL decken; **~ me!** gib mir Deckung! ❿ MUS *song* covern ▶ PHRASES: **to ~ one's tracks** seine Spuren verwischen **III.** *vi* ❶ (*substitute*) ■ **to ~ for sb** jdn vertreten ❷ **to ~ well** *paint* gut decken

◆ **cover up I.** *vt* ❶ (*protect*) ■ **to ~ [oneself] up** sich bedecken ❷ (*hide*) verdecken; *spot* abdecken ❸ (*keep secret*) vertuschen **II.** *vi* alles vertuschen; ■ **to ~ up for sb** jdn decken

coverage ['kʌv·ər·ɪdʒ] *n* ❶ (*reporting*) Berichterstattung *f* (**of** über +*akk*) ❷ (*dealing with*) Behandlung *f;* **to give comprehensive ~ of sth** etw ausführlich behandeln ❸ (*insurance*) Versicherungsschutz *m* ❹ (*staffing*) **to provide emergency ~** einen Notdienst aufrechterhalten

'coveralls *npl* Overall *m*

'cover charge *n* (*in a nightclub*) Eintritt *m;* (*in a restaurant*) Kosten *pl* für das Gedeck

covered ['kʌv·ərd] *adj* ❶ (*roofed over*) überdacht; **~ bridge** gedeckte [Holz]brücke; **~ wagon** Planwagen *m* ❷ (*insured*) versichert

'cover girl *n* Covergirl *nt*

covering ['kʌv·ər·ɪŋ] *n* Bedeckung *f;* **floor ~** Bodenbelag *m*

'cover letter *n* Begleitbrief *m,* Begleitschreiben *nt*

'cover story *n* Coverstory *f,* Titelgeschichte *f*

covert ['koʊ·vɜrt] *adj* verdeckt, geheim; *glance* verstohlen

'cover-up *n* Vertuschung *f*

cow [kaʊ] *n* Kuh *f a. pej* ▶ PHRASES: **until the ~s come home** bis in alle Ewigkeit

coward ['kaʊ·ərd] *n* Feigling *m*

cowardice ['kaʊ·ər·dɪs], **cowardliness** ['kaʊ·ərd·lɪ·nɪs] *n* Feigheit *f*

cowardly ['kaʊ·ərd·li] *adj* feige

'cowboy *n* Cowboy *m*

cower ['kaʊ·ər] *vi* kauern; **to ~ behind sb/sth** sich hinter jdn/etw ducken

'cowhide *n* Rindsleder *nt*

cowl [kaʊl] *n* (*hood*) Kapuze *f*

coworker ['koʊ·ˌwɜr·kər] *n* Mitarbeiter(in) *m(f)*

coxswain ['kak·sən] *n* Steuermann *m* (*beim Rudern*)

coy [kɔɪ] *adj* ❶ (*pretending to be shy*) geziert ❷ (*secretive*) geheimnistuerisch; ■ **to be ~ about sth** aus etw *dat* ein Geheimnis machen

coyote [kaɪ·'oʊ·t̬i] *n* (*animal*) Kojote *m*

coziness ['koʊ·zɪ·nɪs] *n* Gemütlichkeit *f*

cozy, cosy ['koʊ·zi] **I.** *adj* ❶ gemütlich, behaglich; (*nice and warm*) mollig warm; *atmosphere* heimelig; *relationship* traut ❷ (*pej*) bequem; **~ deal** Kuhhandel *m* **II.** *vi* <-ie-> ■ **to ~ up to sb/sth** ❶ (*snuggle up to*) sich an jdn/etw anschmiegen ❷ (*fam: ingratiate oneself*)

mit jdm/etw einen Kuhhandel machen
CPA [ˌsi·pi·ˈeɪ] *n* ECON, FIN *abbrev of* **certified public accountant** Wirtschaftsprüfer(in) *m(f)*
Cpl, **Cpl.**, **CPL.** *n short for* **corporal**
CPR [ˌsi·pi·ˈar] *n* MED *abbrev of* **cardiopulmonary resuscitation** CPR *f*
CPU [ˌsi·pi·ˈju] *n* COMPUT *abbrev of* **central processing unit** CPU *f*
crab[1] [kræb] *n* Krebs *m*
crab[2] [kræb] *vi* <-bb-> (*fam*) nörgeln
ˈ**crab apple** *n* Holzapfel[baum] *m*
crabby [ˈkræb·i] *adj* (*fam*) mürrisch
crack [kræk] **I.** *n* ❶ (*fissure*) Riss *m* ❷ (*narrow space*) Ritze *f;* **to open sth a ~** etw einen Spalt öffnen ❸ (*sharp noise*) *of a breaking branch* Knacken *nt; of breaking ice, thunder* Krachen *nt* ❹ (*sharp blow*) Schlag *m* ❺ (*illegal drug*) Crack *nt o m* ❻ (*attempt*) Versuch *m;* **to take a ~ at sth** etw. [mal] ausprobieren ▶ PHRASES: **at the ~ of dawn** im Morgengrauen **II.** *adj* erstklassig; **~ shot** Meisterschütze, -in *m, f;* **~ regiment** Eliteregiment *nt* **III.** *vt* ❶ (*break*) **to ~ sth** einen Sprung in eine S. *akk* machen ❷ (*open*) ■**to ~ sth** ⇔ **[open]** etw aufbrechen; *bottle* aufmachen; *egg* aufschlagen; *nuts, safe* knacken ❸ (*hit*) **to ~ one's head open** sich den Kopf aufschlagen ❹ (*make noise*) **to ~ one's knuckles** mit den Fingern knacken; **to ~ a whip** mit einer Peitsche knallen ▶ PHRASES: **to ~ a joke** einen Witz reißen **IV.** *vi* ❶ (*break*) [zer]brechen, zerspringen; *lips, paint* aufspringen, rissig werden ❷ (*break down*) zusammenbrechen; *voice* versagen ❸ (*make noise*) *ice, thunder* krachen; *shot, whip* knallen
◆**crack down** *vi* vorgehen (**on** gegen +*akk*)
◆**crack up I.** *vi* (*fam*) ❶ (*find sth hilarious*) lachen müssen ❷ (*have nervous breakdown*) zusammenbrechen; (*go crazy*) durchdrehen **II.** *vt* ❶ (*assert*) **it's not all it's ~ed up to be** es hält nicht alles, was es verspricht ❷ (*fam: amuse*) zum Lachen bringen; **it ~s me up** ich könnte mich kaputtlachen
ˈ**crackdown** *n* scharfes Vorgehen (**on** gegen +*akk*)
cracked [krækt] *adj* (*having cracks*) rissig; *cup, glass* gesprungen; *lips* aufgesprungen
cracker [ˈkræk·ər] *n* ❶ (*biscuit*) Kräcker *m* ❷ (*pej: poor white person*) *abwertende Bezeichnung für Weiße*
crackle [ˈkræk·əl] **I.** *vi* knistern *a. fig; telephone line* knacken **II.** *vt* ■**to ~ sth** mit etw *dat* knistern **III.** *n* (*on a telephone line, radio*) Knacken *nt; of paper* Knistern *nt; of fire a.* Prasseln *nt*
crackling [ˈkræk·lɪŋ] *n* ❶ *of paper* Knistern *nt;* (*of fire a.*) Prasseln *nt;* (*on the radio*) Knacken *nt* ❷ (*pork skin*) ■**~s** *pl* [Braten]kruste *f*
ˈ**crackpot I.** *n* (*fam*) Spinner(in) *m(f)* **II.** *adj* (*fam*) bescheuert
cradle [ˈkreɪ·dəl] **I.** *n* ❶ (*baby's bed*) Wiege *f a. fig* ❷ (*origin*) Ursprung *m* ❸ (*hanging platform*) Hängebühne *f* **II.** *vt* [sanft] halten; *sb's head* betten
craft [kræft] **I.** *n* ❶ <*pl* -> (*ship*) Schiff *nt;* (*boat*) Boot *nt;* (*plane*) Flugzeug *nt* ❷ (*trade*) Handwerk *nt kein pl;* (*handmade objects*) ■**~s** *pl* Kunsthandwerk *nt kein pl* ❸ (*skill*) Kunst *f* **II.** *vt* kunstvoll fertigen; **a cleverly ~ed poem** ein geschickt verfasstes Gedicht
craftiness [ˈkræf·tɪ·nɪs] *n* Gerissenheit *f*
ˈ**craftsman** *n* gelernter Handwerker; **master ~** Handwerksmeister *m*
crafty [ˈkræf·ti] *adj* schlau, gerissen
crag [kræg] *n* Felsmassiv *nt*
craggy [ˈkræg·i] *adj* zerklüftet; *features* markant
cram <-mm-> [kræm] **I.** *vt* stopfen; **six children were ~med into the back of the car** sechs Kinder saßen gedrängt auf dem Rücksitz des Autos **II.** *vi* büffeln, pauken
cramp [kræmp] **I.** *n* [Muskel]krampf *m;* **to get a ~** einen Krampf bekommen **II.** *vi* [sich] verkrampfen **III.** *vt* einengen ▶ PHRASES: **to ~ sb's style** (*hum*) jdn nicht zum Zug kommen lassen
cramped [kræmpt] *adj* beengt; **to be [pretty] ~ for space** [ziemlich] wenig Platz haben
cranberry [ˈkræn·ˌber·i] *n* Kranichbeere *f*
crane [kreɪn] **I.** *n* ❶ (*device*) Kran *m* ❷ (*bird*) Kranich *m* **II.** *vt* **to ~ one's neck** den Hals recken
crank [kræŋk] **I.** *n* ❶ MECH Kurbel *f* ❷ (*fam: eccentric*) Spinner(in) *m(f);* **~ call** Juxanruf *m* **II.** *vt* ❶ (*start*) *engine* ankurbeln ❷ (*make louder*) *music, volume* aufdrehen; **~ it!** Mach mal lauter!
◆**crank up** *vt* ❶ (*make louder*) *music, volume* aufdrehen ❷ (*start up*) *device, machine* ankurbeln
ˈ**crankshaft** *n* Kurbelwelle *f*
cranky [ˈkræŋ·ki] *adj* (*fam: grouchy*) mürrisch
cranny [ˈkræn·i] *n* Ritze *f*
crap [kræp] **I.** *vi* <-pp-> (*vulg*) kacken **II.** *n usu sing* (*vulg*) Scheiße *f a. fig;* **to take a ~** kacken **III.** *adj* (*fam*) mies
crappy [ˈkræp·i] *adj* (*vulg*) Scheiß-
crash [kræʃ] **I.** *n* <*pl* -es> ❶ (*accident*) Unfall *m; of plane* Absturz *m* ❷ (*noise*) Krach *m kein pl* ❸ COMM Zusammenbruch *m;* **stock market ~** Börsenkrach *m* ❹ COMPUT Absturz *m* **II.** *vi* ❶ (*have an accident*) *driver, car* verunglücken; *plane* abstürzen ❷ (*collide with*) ■**to ~ into sb/sth** mit etw/jdm zusammenstoßen ❸ (*make loud noise*) *cymbals, thunder* donnern; *door* knallen; (*move noisily*) poltern; **to come ~ing to the ground** auf den Boden knallen ❹ COMM *stock market* zusammenbrechen ❺ COMPUT abstürzen ❻ (*sl*) pennen **III.** *vt* ❶ (*damage in accident*) zu Bruch fahren; *plane* eine Bruchlandung machen; (*deliberately*) einen Unfall/Absturz absichtlich verursachen; **to ~ sth into sth** etw gegen eine S. *akk* fahren/in eine S. *akk* fliegen ❷ (*cause to make noise*) knallen ❸ (*fam: gatecrash*) **to ~ a party** uneingeladen zu einer Party kommen

C

'crash course *n* Intensivkurs *m,* Crashkurs *m*
crash 'diet *n* radikale Abmagerungskur, Crashdiät *f*
'crash helmet *n* Sturzhelm *m*
crash-'land *vi* bruchlanden
crash 'landing *n* Bruchlandung *f*
crass [kræs] *adj* krass, grob; *behavior* derb
crate [kreɪt] **I.** *n* (*open box*) Kiste *f;* (*for bottles*) [Getränke]kasten *m* **II.** *vt* ■**to ~ [up]** in eine Kiste einpacken
crater ['kreɪ·ṭər] *n* Krater *m; of bomb* Trichter *m*
crave [kreɪv] *vt* begehren; **to ~ attention** sich nach Aufmerksamkeit sehnen
craving ['kreɪ·vɪŋ] *n* heftiges Verlangen (**for** nach +*dat*)
crawfish ['krɔ·fɪʃ] *n* Languste *f*
crawl [krɔl] **I.** *vi* ① (*go on all fours*) krabbeln ② (*move slowly*) kriechen **II.** *n* ① (*slow pace*) **to move at a ~** im Schneckentempo fahren ② (*style of swimming*) Kraulen *nt*
crawler ['krɔ·lər] *n* ① (*tracked vehicle*) Raupe *f* ② COMPUT *Suchmaschine, die Internetseiten automatisch durchsucht* ③ ZOOL Kriechtier *nt*
crayfish ['kreɪ·fɪʃ] *n* Flusskrebs *m*
crayon ['kreɪ·an] **I.** *n* Buntstift *m* **II.** *vt* ■**to ~ [in]** ↻ **sth** etw [mit Buntstift] ausmalen
craze [kreɪz] *n* Mode[erscheinung] *f,* Fimmel *m pej;* ■**~ for sth** Begeisterung *f* für etw *akk*
crazed [kreɪzd] *adj* wahnsinnig
craziness ['kreɪ·zɪ·nɪs] *n* Verrücktheit *f*
crazy ['kreɪ·zi] **I.** *adj* verrückt (**about** nach +*dat*); **to drive sb ~** jdn zum Wahnsinn treiben **II.** *n* (*sl*) Verrückte(r) *f(m)*
creak [krik] **I.** *vi furniture* knarren; *door* quietschen; *bones* knirschen **II.** *n of furniture* Knarren *nt; of a door* Quietschen *nt; of bones* Knirschen *nt*
cream [krim] **I.** *n* ① FOOD Sahne *f,* Obers *nt* ÖSTERR; **~ of mushroom soup** Champignoncremesuppe *f* ② (*cosmetic*) Creme *f;* **to put ~ on [sb's] sth** [jdm] etw eincremen ③ (*color*) Creme *nt* ④ (*fig: the best*) Creme *f,* Elite *f;* **the ~ of the crop** das Beste vom Besten **II.** *adj* cremefarben **III.** *vt* (*beat*) cremig rühren; **~ed potatoes** Kartoffelpüree *nt*
cream 'cheese *n* [Doppelrahm]frischkäse *m*
'cream-colored *adj* cremefarben
creamy ['kri·mi] *adj* ① (*smooth*) cremig, sahnig ② (*off-white*) cremefarben
crease [kris] **I.** *n* (*fold*) [Bügel]falte *f* **II.** *vt* zerknittern **III.** *vi* knittern
create [kri·'eɪt] *vt* ① (*make*) erschaffen ② (*cause*) erzeugen; *confusion* stiften; *impression* erwecken; *sensation* erregen
creation [kri·'eɪ·ʃən] *n* ① (*making*) [Er]schaffung *f;* (*founding*) Gründung *f;* REL Schöpfung *f* ② (*product*) Produkt *nt,* Erzeugnis *nt;* FASHION Kreation *f;* (*of arts a.*) Werk *nt*
creative [kri·'eɪ·ṭɪv] *adj* kreativ, schöpferisch; **~ ability** [*or* **talent**] Kreativität *f*
creator [kri·'eɪ·ṭər] *n* Schöpfer(in) *m(f)*
creature ['kri·tʃər] *n* ① (*being*) Kreatur *f,* Wesen *nt;* **living ~s** Lebewesen *pl* ② (*person*) Kreatur *f,* Geschöpf *nt*
credence ['krid·əns] *n* (*form*) Glaube *m;* **to add** [*or* **lend**] **~ to sth** etw glaubwürdig machen
credentials [krɪ·'den·ʃəlz] *npl* ① (*documents*) Zeugnisse *pl* ② (*letter of recommendation*) Empfehlungsschreiben *nt*
credibility [ˌkred·ə·'bɪl·ɪ·ti] *n* Glaubwürdigkeit *f*
credible ['kred·ə·bəl] *adj* glaubwürdig
credit ['kred·ɪt] **I.** *n* ① (*recognition, praise*) Anerkennung *f;* (*respect*) Achtung *f;* (*honor*) Ehre *f;* (*standing*) Ansehen *nt;* **to do sb/sth ~** jdm/etw Ehre machen; **it is to sb's ~ that ...** es ist jds Verdienst, dass ... ② COMM Kredit *m;* **to buy sth on ~** etw auf Kredit kaufen ③ FIN Haben *nt* ④ (*contributors*) ■**~s** *pl* FILM, TV Abspann *m;* **opening/closing ~s** Vor-/Nachspann *m* ⑤ UNIV (*unit of study*) Credit [Point] *m,* Leistungspunkt *m* **II.** *vt* ① (*believe*) glauben ② (*attribute*) zuschreiben; **I ~ed her with far more determination than she showed** ich hatte ihr viel mehr Entschlossenheit zugetraut ③ FIN gutschreiben
creditable ['kred·ɪ·ṭə·bəl] *adj* ehrenwert; *result* verdient
'credit card *n* Kreditkarte *f*
'credit limit *n* Kredit[höchst]grenze *f*
creditor ['kred·ɪ·tər] *n* Gläubiger(in) *m(f)*
'credit rating *n* Kreditwürdigkeit *f kein pl*
'credit slip *n* Gutschrift *f*
credulous ['kredʒ·ə·ləs] *adj* (*form*) leichtgläubig
creed [krid] *n* Glaubensbekenntnis *nt*
creek [krik] *n* (*stream*) Bach *m;* (*tributary*) Nebenfluss *m* ▶ PHRASES: **to be up the ~ [without a paddle]** (*fam*) in der Patsche sitzen, in Teufels Küche kommen
creep [krip] **I.** *n* (*fam*) ① (*unpleasant person*) Mistkerl *m* ② (*unpleasant feeling*) ■**the ~s** *pl* das Gruseln *kein pl;* **that gives me the ~s** das ist mir nicht ganz geheuer **II.** *vi* <crept, crept> ① kriechen; *water* steigen ② (*fig*) **doubts began to ~ into people's minds** den Menschen kamen langsam Zweifel
◆**creep up** *vi* ① (*increase steadily*) [an]steigen ② (*sneak up on*) sich anschleichen *a. fig* (**behind/on** an +*akk*)
creeper ['kri·pər] *n* BOT (*along ground*) Kriechgewächs *nt;* (*up a wall*) Kletterpflanze *f*
creepy ['kri·pi] *adj* (*fam*) grus[e]lig, schaurig
creepy-'crawly [-'krɔ·li] *n* (*fam*) Krabbeltier *nt*
cremate ['kri·meɪt] *vt* verbrennen, einäschern
cremation [krɪ·'meɪ·ʃən] *n* Einäscherung *f*
crematorium <*pl* -s *or* -ria> [ˌkri·mə·'tɔr·i·əm], **crematory** ['kri·mə·tɔr·i] *n* Krematorium *nt*
crêpe [kreɪp] *n* ① FOOD Crêpe *f* ② (*fabric*) Krepp *m* ③ **~ rubber** Kreppgummi *m*
crept [krept] *pp, pt of* **creep**
crescendo [krɪ·'ʃen·doʊ] *n* ① MUS Crescendo *nt* ② (*fig*) Anstieg *m;* **to reach a ~** einen

Höhepunkt erreichen
crescent ['kres·ənt] *n* ❶ (*moon*) Mondsichel *f* ❷ *halbkreisförmige Straße*
crest [krest] I. *n* ❶ (*peak*) Kamm *m;* ~ **of a hill** Hügelkuppe *f;* ~ **of a wave** Wellenkamm *m* ❷ ZOOL *of a rooster* Kamm *m; of a bird* Schopf *m* ❸ (*insignia*) Emblem *nt;* **family** ~ Familienwappen *nt* II. *vt hill* erklimmen
'**crestfallen** *adj* niedergeschlagen
Crete [krit] *n* Kreta *nt*
cretin ['kri·tən] *n* (*pej fam*) Schwachkopf *m*
Creutzfeldt-Jakob disease [ˌkrɔɪts·felt·'jæ·kɔb-] *n* Creutzfeldt-Jakob-Syndrom *nt*
crevasse [krə·'væs] *n* Gletscherspalte *f*
crevice ['krev·ɪs] *n* Spalte *f*
crew [kru] I. *n* ❶ AVIAT, NAUT Crew *f,* Besatzung *f;* **ambulance/lifeboat** ~ Rettungsmannschaft *f;* **film** ~ Filmteam *nt;* **ground** ~ Bodenpersonal *nt* ❷ (*fam: gang*) Bande *f* II. *vt, vi* Mannschaftsmitglied sein; ■ **to** ~ **for sb** zu jds Mannschaft gehören
'**crew cut** *n* Bürstenschnitt *m*
'**crewman,** '**crewmember** *n* Besatzungsmitglied *nt*
crib [krɪb] *n* Kinderbett *nt,* Gitterbett *nt;* REL Krippe *f*
'**crib death** *n see* **sudden infant death syndrome**
crib sheet *n* (*fam*) SCH Spickzettel *m,* Schummler *m* ÖSTERR
cricket[1] ['krɪk·ɪt] *n* ZOOL Grille *f*
cricket[2] ['krɪk·ɪt] *n* SPORTS Kricket *nt*
crime [kraɪm] *n* ❶ (*illegal act*) Verbrechen *nt* ❷ (*criminality*) Kriminalität *f;* **to lead a life of** ~ das Leben eines/einer Kriminellen führen
'**crime prevention** *n* Verbrechensverhütung *f*
'**crime wave** *n* Welle *f* der Kriminalität
criminal ['krɪm·ə·nəl] I. *n* Verbrecher(in) *m(f)* II. *adj* ❶ (*illegal*) verbrecherisch; *behavior* kriminell; *offense* strafbar ❷ (*fig*) schändlich; **it's ~ to charge so much** es ist eine Schande, so viel Geld zu verlangen
criminality [ˌkrɪm·ə·'næl·ɪ·ti] *n* Kriminalität *f*
criminologist [ˌkrɪm·ə·'nal·ə·dʒɪst] *n* Kriminologe, -in *m, f*
criminology [ˌkrɪm·ə·'nal·ə·dʒi] *n* Kriminologie *f*
crimp [krɪmp] *vt* ❶ kräuseln ❷ **to ~ one's hair** sich *dat* das Haar wellen
crimson ['krɪm·zən] I. *n* Purpur[rot] *nt* II. *adj* purpurrot
cringe [krɪndʒ] *vi* ❶ (*cower*) sich ducken ❷ (*shiver*) schaudern; (*feel uncomfortable*) **we all ~d with embarrassment** das war uns allen furchtbar peinlich
crinkle ['krɪŋ·kəl] I. *vt* [zer]knittern II. *vi dress, paper* knittern; *face, skin* [Lach]fältchen bekommen III. *n* [Knitter]falte *f;* (*in hair*) Krause *f*
crinkly ['krɪŋ·kli] *adj* ❶ (*full of wrinkles*) *paper* zerknittert; *skin* knittrig ❷ (*wavy and curly*) gekräuselt
cripple ['krɪp·əl] I. *n* Krüppel *m* II. *vt person* zum Krüppel machen; *thing* gefechtsunfähig machen; (*fig*) lahmlegen
crippling ['krɪp·əl·ɪŋ] *adj debts* erdrückend; *pain* lähmend
crisis <*pl* -ses> ['kraɪ·sɪs] *n* Krise *f;* **to be in ~** in einer Krise stecken; ~ **of confidence** Vertrauenskrise *f*
crisis 'management *n* Krisenmanagement *nt*
crisp [krɪsp] I. *adj* ❶ (*hard and brittle*) knusprig; *snow* knirschend ❷ (*firm and fresh*) *apple, lettuce* knackig ❸ (*stiff and smooth*) *paper, tablecloth* steif; *banknote* druckfrisch ❹ (*quick and precise*) *manner, style* präzise; *answer, reply* knapp II. *n* ❶ (*easily crumbled state*) **burnt to a ~** verkohlt ❷ FOOD Obstdessert *nt* (*mit Streuseln überbacken*)
'**crispbread** *n* Knäckebrot *nt*
crispy ['krɪs·pi] *adj* (*approv*) knusprig
'**criss-cross** I. *vt* durchqueren II. *vi* sich kreuzen
criterion <*pl* -ria> [kraɪ·'tɪr·i·ən] *n* Kriterium *nt*
critic ['krɪt̬·ɪk] *n* Kritiker(in) *m(f)*
critical ['krɪt̬·ɪ·kəl] *adj* ❶ (*judgmental*) kritisch; ~ **success** Erfolg *m* bei der Kritik; ■ **to be ~ of sb** an jdm etwas auszusetzen haben ❷ (*crucial*) entscheidend ❸ MED kritisch
criticism ['krɪt̬·ɪ·sɪz·əm] *n* (*general*) Kritik *f;* (*specific*) Kritikpunkt *m*
criticize ['krɪt̬·ɪ·saɪz] I. *vt* kritisch beurteilen; ■ **to ~ sb/sth for sth** jdn/etw wegen einer S. *gen* kritisieren II. *vi* kritisieren
critter ['krɪt̬·ər] *n* (*fam*) ❶ (*creature*) Lebewesen *nt,* Kreatur *f* ❷ (*person*) Typ *m fam*
croak [kroʊk] I. *vi* ❶ *frog* quaken; *person* krächzen ❷ (*sl: die*) abkratzen II. *vt* krächzen III. *n of a crow, person* Krächzen *nt; of a frog* Quaken *nt*
Croatia [kroʊ·'eɪ·ʃə] *n* Kroatien *nt*
crochet [kroʊ·'ʃeɪ] *vi, vt* häkeln
crockery ['krak·ə·ri] *n* Geschirr *nt*
crocodile <*pl* - *or* -s> ['krak·ə·daɪl] *n* ZOOL Krokodil *nt;* ~ **skin** Krokodilleder *nt*
crocus ['kroʊ·kəs] *n* Krokus *m*
croissant [krwa·'saŋ] *n* Croissant *nt*
crony ['kroʊ·ni] *adj* (*pej fam*) Spießgeselle *m,* Haberer *m* ÖSTERR
crook [krʊk] I. *n* ❶ (*fam: rogue*) Gauner *m* ❷ (*of a shepherd*) Hirtenstab *m* II. *vt arm* beugen; *finger* krümmen
crooked ['krʊk·ɪd] *adj* ❶ (*fam: dishonest*) unehrlich; (*illegal*) krumm; *police officer, politician* korrupt; *salesman* betrügerisch ❷ (*not straight*) krumm; *grin, teeth* schief
crop [krap] I. *n* ❶ (*plant*) Feldfrucht *f;* (*harvest*) Ernte *f* ❷ (*short hair cut*) Kurzhaarschnitt *m* ❸ (*whip*) Reitgerte *f* II. *vt* <-pp-> ❶ (*cut short*) *hair* kurz schneiden ❷ PHOT zurechtschneiden
◆ **crop up** *vi* (*fam*) auftauchen; **something ~ped up** es ist etwas dazwischengekommen
'**crop rotation** *n* Fruchtfolge *f*
croquet [kroʊ·'keɪ] *n* Krocket[spiel] *nt*

C

cross [krɔs] **I.** *n* ① Kreuz *nt a. fig;* **to mark sth with a [red] ~** etw [rot] ankreuzen ② (*hybrid*) Kreuzung *f;* (*fig*) Mittelding *nt* (**between** zwischen +*dat*); (*person*) Mischung *f* (**between** aus +*dat*) ③ (*in soccer*) Flanke *f* **II.** *vt* ① (*cross over*) überqueren; (*a. on foot*) *bridge, road* gehen über; *border* passieren; *threshold* überschreiten; (*traverse*) durchqueren; **the bridge ~es the river** die Brücke führt über den Fluss ② (*in soccer*) flanken ③ (*place crosswise*) [über]kreuzen; *arms* verschränken; *legs* übereinanderschlagen ④ REL ■ **to ~ oneself** sich bekreuz[ig]en ⑤ (*breed*) kreuzen ▸ PHRASES: **to keep** [*or* **have**] **one's fingers ~ed** [**for sb**] [jdm] die Daumen drücken; **to ~ one's mind** jdm einfallen **III.** *vi* ① (*intersect*) sich kreuzen ② (*traverse a road*) die Straße überqueren; (*on foot*) über die Straße gehen; **to ~ into a country** die Grenze in ein Land passieren ③ (*meet*) **our paths have ~ed several times** wir sind uns schon mehrmals über den Weg gelaufen

◆ **cross off** *vt* streichen [von]

◆ **cross out** *vt* ausstreichen; ■ **to ~ out sth** etw [durch]streichen

◆ **cross over** *vi* hinübergehen, überqueren; (*on boat*) übersetzen

'crossbar *n* SPORT Querlatte *f; of bicycle* [Quer]stange *f*

'crossbow *n* Armbrust *f*

'crossbreed **I.** *n* ZOOL Kreuzung *f;* (*half-breed*) Mischling *m* **II.** *vt* kreuzen

'crosscheck *vt* nachprüfen

cross-'country **I.** *adj* Querfeldein-; **~ race** Geländerennen *nt;* **~ skiing** Langlauf *m* **II.** *adv* ① (*across a country*) quer durchs Land ② (*through countryside*) querfeldein

'crosscurrent *n* Gegenströmung *f*

cross-exami'nation *n* Kreuzverhör *nt;* **under ~** im Kreuzverhör

cross-ex'amine *vt* ■ **to ~ sb** jdn ins Kreuzverhör nehmen *a. fig*

'cross-eyed *adj* schielend; ■ **to be ~** schielen

'crossfire *n* Kreuzfeuer *nt;* **to be caught in the ~** ins Kreuzfeuer geraten *a. fig*

crossing ['krɔ·sɪŋ] *n* ① (*place to cross*) Übergang *m;* (*crossroads*) [Straßen]kreuzung *f* ② (*journey*) Überfahrt *f*

cross-'legged [ˌkrɔs·'leg·əd] **I.** *adj* **in a ~ position** mit gekreuzten Beinen **II.** *adv* **to sit ~** im Schneidersitz [da]sitzen

cross-'reference *n* Querverweis *m* (**to** auf +*akk*)

'crossroads <*pl* -> *n* Kreuzung *f;* (*fig*) Wendepunkt *m;* ■ **at a** [*or* **the**] **~** am Scheideweg

cross-'section *n* ① (*cut*) Querschnitt *m* (**of** durch +*akk*) ② (*sample*) repräsentative Auswahl

'crosswalk *n* Fußgängerübergang *m*

'crosswind *n* Seitenwind *m*

'crossword, 'crossword puzzle *n* Kreuzworträtsel *nt*

crotch [kratʃ] *n* Unterleib *m; of pants* Schritt *m*

crotchety ['kratʃ·ə·ti] *adj* (*fam*) quengelig

crouch [kraʊtʃ] **I.** *n usu sing* Hocke *f* **II.** *vi* sich kauern

crow[1] [kroʊ] *n* Krähe *f* ▸ PHRASES: **as the ~ flies** [in der] Luftlinie

crow[2] [kroʊ] *vi* <**crowed, crowed**> ① (*cry*) *rooster* krähen ② (*express happiness*) jauchzen; (*gloatingly*) triumphieren

'crowbar *n* Brecheisen *nt*

crowd [kraʊd] **I.** *n* ① (*throng*) [Menschen]menge *f;* SPORTS, MUS Zuschauermenge *f;* **to follow the ~** (*fig*) mit der Masse gehen ② (*fam: clique*) Clique *f;* **a bad ~** ein übler Haufen **II.** *vt* ① (*fill*) *stadium* füllen; *streets* bevölkern ② (*fam: pressure*) ■ **to ~ sb** jdn [be]drängen **III.** *vi* ■ **to ~ into sth** sich in etw *akk* hineindrängen

◆ **crowd out** *vt* herausdrängen

crowded ['kraʊ·dɪd] *adj* überfüllt; *schedule* übervoll

crown [kraʊn] **I.** *n* ① (*of a monarch, a. fin*) Krone *f* ② (*top of head*) Scheitel *m;* (*of hill*) Kuppe *f;* (*of tooth, tree, hat*) Krone *f* **II.** *vt* krönen; **to ~ sb world champion** jdn zum Weltmeister krönen; *teeth* überkronen

crown 'jewels *npl* Kronjuwelen *pl*

crown 'prince *n* Kronprinz *m*

'crow's feet *npl* (*wrinkles*) Krähenfüße *pl*

crucial ['kru·ʃəl] *adj* (*decisive*) entscheidend (**to** für +*akk*); (*critical*) kritisch; (*very important*) äußerst wichtig

crucible ['kru·sɪ·bəl] *n* TECH Schmelztiegel *m*

crucifix ['kru·sɪ·fɪks] *n* Kruzifix *nt*

crucifixion [ˌkru·sɪ·'fɪk·ʃən] *n* Kreuzigung *f*

crucify ['kru·sɪ·faɪ] *vt* kreuzigen; (*fig fam*) verreißen

crude [krud] **I.** *adj* ① (*rudimentary*) primitiv ② (*vulgar*) derb ③ (*unprocessed*) roh; **~ oil** Rohöl *nt* **II.** *n* Rohöl *nt*

cruel <-l- *or* -ll-> ['kru·əl] *adj* ① (*deliberately mean*) grausam; *remark* gemein ② (*harsh*) hart; *disappointment* schrecklich ▸ PHRASES: **to be ~ to be kind** (*saying*) jdm beinhart die Wahrheit sagen

cruelty ['kru·əl·ti] *n* Grausamkeit *f* (**to** gegen +*akk*); **~ to animals** Tierquälerei *f;* **~ to children** Kindesmisshandlung *f*

cruise [kruz] **I.** *n* Kreuzfahrt *f;* **to go on a ~** eine Kreuzfahrt machen **II.** *vi* ① (*take a cruise*) eine Kreuzfahrt machen; (*ship*) kreuzen ② (*travel at constant speed*) *airplane* [mit Reisegeschwindigkeit] fliegen; *car* [konstante Geschwindigkeit] fahren ③ (*fam: drive around aimlessly*) herumfahren **III.** *vt* (*sl*) **to ~ the bars** in den Bars aufreißen gehen

'cruise control *n* Temporegler *m*

cruiser ['kru·zər] *n* ① (*warship*) Kreuzer *m* ② (*pleasure boat*) Motoryacht *f* ③ *see* **squad car**

'cruise ship *n* Kreuzfahrtschiff *nt*

crumb [krʌm] *n* ① Krümel *m,* Brösel *m* ÖSTERR *a. nt; of bread a.* Krume *f* ② (*fig*) **a small ~ of comfort** ein kleiner Trost

crumble ['krʌm·bəl] **I.** *vt* zerkrümeln, zerbröckeln **II.** *vi* ① (*disintegrate*) zerbröckeln ② (*fig*) *empire* zerfallen; *opposition, relationship* [allmählich] zerbrechen; *resistance* schwinden; *support* abbröckeln

crummy ['krʌm·i] *adj* (*fam*) mies; *house* schäbig

crumple ['krʌm·pəl] **I.** *vt* zerknittern; *paper* zerknüllen, zusammenknüllen **II.** *vi* ① (*become wrinkled*) sich verziehen ② (*collapse*) zusammenbrechen

crunch [krʌntʃ] **I.** *n* ① *usu sing* (*noise*) Knirschen *nt kein pl* ② (*fam: difficult situation*) Krise *f* **II.** *vt* FOOD geräuschvoll verzehren **III.** *vi gravel, snow* knirschen

'crunch time *n* **it's ~** (*fam*) jetzt kommt es drauf an!

crunchy ['krʌn·tʃi] *adj apple* knackig; *cereal, toast* knusprig; *snow* verharscht

crusade [kru·'seɪd] **I.** *n* Kreuzzug *m;* ■ **the C~s** *pl* HIST die Kreuzzüge *pl* **II.** *vi* ■ **to ~ for/against sth** einen Kreuzzug für/gegen etw *akk* führen

crusader [kru·'seɪ·dər] *n* ① (*campaigner*) ■ **a ~ for/against sth** jd, der für/gegen etw *akk* zu Felde zieht ② HIST Kreuzritter *m*

crush [krʌʃ] **I.** *vt* ① (*compress*) zusammendrücken; (*causing serious damage*) zerquetschen; MED [sich] etw quetschen ② FOOD zerdrücken; *grapes* zerstampfen; *ice* zerstoßen ③ (*defeat*) vernichten; *hopes* zunichtemachen; *rebellion* niederschlagen; *resistance* zerschlagen **II.** *n* ① (*crowd*) Gedränge *nt* ② (*drink*) Fruchtsaft *m* mit zerstoßenem Eis ③ (*infatuation*) Schwarm *m;* **to have a ~ on sb** in jdn verknallt sein

crushing ['krʌʃ·ɪŋ] *adj* schrecklich; *blow* hart; *defeat* vernichtend

crust [krʌst] *n* Kruste *f;* (*pastry shell*) Boden *m*

crustacean [krʌ·'steɪ·ʃən] *n* Krustentier *nt*

crusty ['krʌs·ti] *adj bread* knusprig

crutch [krʌtʃ] *n* ① MED Krücke *f* ② (*fig*) Stütze *f*, Halt *m*

crux [krʌks] *n* Kernfrage *f*

cry <-ie-> [kraɪ] **I.** *n* ① (*act of shedding tears*) Weinen *nt* ② (*loud emotional utterance*) Schrei *m;* (*shout a.*) Ruf *m* (**for** nach +*dat*); **~ for help** Hilferuf *m;* **a ~ of pain** ein Schmerzensschrei *m* ③ ZOOL, ORN Schreien *nt kein pl,* Geschrei *nt kein pl* **II.** *vi* weinen (**for** nach +*dat*); *baby* schreien **III.** *vt* ① (*shed tears*) weinen ② (*exclaim*) rufen

◆**cry out I.** *vi* ① (*shout*) aufschreien ② (*fig: need*) schreien (**for** nach +*dat*) ▶ PHRASES: **for ~ing out loud** (*fam*) verdammt nochmal! **II.** *vt* rufen; (*scream*) schreien

crying ['kraɪ·ɪŋ] *n* Weinen *nt;* (*screaming*) Schreien *nt*

crypt [krɪpt] *n* Krypta *f*

cryptic ['krɪp·tɪk] *adj* rätselhaft; *message a.* geheimnisvoll; *look* unergründlich

crystal ['krɪs·təl] **I.** *n* ① CHEM Kristall *m* ② (*glass*) Kristallglas *nt* ③ (*on a watch, clock*) [Uhr]glas *nt* **II.** *adj* ① CHEM kristallin ② (*made of crystal*) Kristall-

crystal 'ball *n* Kristallkugel *f*

crystal 'clear *adj* ① (*transparent*) *water* kristallklar ② (*obvious*) glasklar; **she made it ~ that ...** sie stellte unmissverständlich klar, dass ...

crystalline ['krɪs·tə·laɪn] *adj* ① CHEM kristallin ② (*liter: crystal clear*) kristallklar

crystallize ['krɪs·tə·laɪz] **I.** *vi* CHEM kristallisieren; (*fig*) *feelings* fassbar werden **II.** *vt* (*fig*) herausbilden

CST [ˌsi·es·'ti] *n abbrev of* **Central Standard Time** Zentral Standardzeit *f*

CT *abbrev of* **Connecticut**

cub [kʌb] *n* ① ZOOL Junge[s] *nt* ② (*Cub Scout*) Wölfling *m*

Cuba ['kju·bə] *n* Kuba *nt*

cubbyhole ['kʌb·ɪ·hoʊl] *n* Kämmerchen *nt*

cube [kjub] **I.** *n* ① (*shape*) Würfel *m* ② MATH Kubikzahl *f* **II.** *vt* ① FOOD in Würfel schneiden ② MATH hoch drei nehmen; **2 ~d equals 8** 2 hoch 3 ist 8

cubic ['kju·bɪk] *adj* MATH Kubik-

cubicle ['kju·bɪ·kəl] *n* (*for working*) Arbeitsnische *f*

cuckoo ['ku·ku] **I.** *n* ORN Kuckuck *m* **II.** *adj* (*fam*) übergeschnappt

'cuckoo clock *n* Kuckucksuhr *f*

cucumber ['kju·kʌm·bər] *n* [Salat]gurke *f* ▶ PHRASES: **to be** [**as**] **cool as a ~** immer einen kühlen Kopf behalten

cuddle ['kʌd·əl] **I.** *n* [liebevolle] Umarmung **II.** *vt* liebkosen **III.** *vi* kuscheln

cuddly ['kʌd·əl·i] *adj* knudd[e]lig

cue[1] [kju] *n* (*billiards*) Queue *nt* ÖSTERR *a. m,* Billardstock *m*

cue[2] [kju] **I.** *n* THEAT Stichwort *nt;* (*fig a.*) Zeichen *nt;* **to take one's ~ from sb** jds Beispiel *nt* folgen ▶ PHRASES: [**right**] **on ~** wie gerufen **II.** *vt* ■ **to ~ in** ⟲ **sb** jdm das Stichwort geben

cuff[1] [kʌf] **I.** *n* ① (*of sleeve*) Manschette *f* ② (*of pants leg*) [Hosen]aufschlag *m* ③ (*fam*) LAW ■ **~s** *pl* Handschellen *pl* ▶ PHRASES: **off the ~** aus dem Stegreif **II.** *vt* ■ **to ~ sb** (*fam: handcuff*) jdm Handschellen anlegen

cuff[2] [kʌf] *vt* ■ **to ~ sb** (*strike*) jdm einen Klaps geben

'cuff link *n* Manschettenknopf *m*

cuisine [kwɪ·'zin] *n* Küche *f*

cul-de-sac <*pl* -s *or* culs-de-sac> ['kʌl·də·sæk] *n* Sackgasse *f a. fig*

culinary ['kʌl·ə·ner·i] *adj* kulinarisch; **~ skills** Kochkünste *pl*

cull [kʌl] **I.** *vt* ① (*select*) herausfiltern ② (*kill*) erlegen (*um den Bestand zu reduzieren*) **II.** *n* Abschlachten *nt kein pl;* (*fig*) Abschuss *m kein pl*

culminate ['kʌl·mɪ·neɪt] *vi* gipfeln (**in** in +*dat*)

culmination [ˌkʌl·mɪ·'neɪ·ʃən] *n* Höhepunkt *m*

culpable ['kʌl·pə·bəl] *adj* (*form*) schuldig; **to hold sb ~ for sth** jdm die Schuld an etw *dat* geben

culprit ['kʌl·prɪt] *n* Schuldige(r) *f(m)*; (*hum*) Missetäter(in) *m(f)*

cult [kʌlt] *n* Kult *m*

cultivate ['kʌl·tə·veɪt] *vt* ❶ *crops* anbauen; *land* bestellen ❷ (*fig form*) entwickeln; *accent, contacts* pflegen; *sb's talent* fördern

cultivated ['kʌl·tə·veɪ·t̬ɪd] *adj* ❶ *field* bestellt; *land, soil a.* bebaut ❷ (*fig*) kultiviert

cultivation [ˌkʌl·tə·'veɪ·ʃən] *n of crops, vegetables* Anbau *m; of land* Bebauung *m*, Bestellung *m*

cultivator ['kʌl·tə·veɪ·t̬ər] *n* Grubber *m*

cultural ['kʌl·tʃər·əl] *adj* kulturell

culture ['kʌl·tʃər] **I.** *n* Kultur *f* **II.** *vt* BIOL züchten

cultured ['kʌl·tʃərd] *adj* kultiviert

cumbersome ['kʌm·bər·səm] *adj luggage* unhandlich; *clothing* unbequem

cumin ['kju·mɪn] *n* Kreuzkümmel *m*

cumulative ['kju·mjə·lə·t̬ɪv] *adj* kumulativ; **~ total** Gesamtbetrag *m*

cunning ['kʌn·ɪŋ] **I.** *adj* (*ingenious*) *idea* clever, raffiniert; *person a.* schlau, gerissen **II.** *n* Cleverness *f*, Gerissenheit *f*

cup [kʌp] **I.** *n* ❶ (*container*) Tasse *f*; **a ~ of coffee/tea** eine Tasse Kaffee/Tee; (*of paper, plastic*) Becher *m* ❷ SPORTS Pokal *m*; **the World C~** die Weltmeisterschaft ❸ (*part of bra*) Körbchen *nt*; (*size*) Körbchengröße *f* ▶ PHRASES: **that's just** [*or* **not**] **my ~ of <u>tea</u>** das ist genau [*o* überhaupt nicht] mein Fall **II.** *vt* <-pp-> **to ~ one's hands** mit den Händen eine Schale bilden; **she ~ped her hands around her mug** sie legte die Hände um den Becher

cupboard ['kʌb·ərd] *n* Schrank *m*, Kasten *m* ÖSTERR

cupful <*pl* -s> ['kʌp·fʊl] *n* Tasse *f*

curator ['kjʊ·reɪ·t̬ər] *n* Konservator(in) *m(f)*

curb [kɜrb] **I.** *vt* zügeln; *expenditures* senken; *inflation* bremsen **II.** *n* ❶ (*concrete border*) Randstein *m* ❷ (*restraint*) Beschränkung *f*

curd [kɜrd] *n* Quark *m*

curdle ['kɜr·dəl] **I.** *vi* gerinnen ▶ PHRASES: **to make sb's <u>blood</u> ~** jdm das Blut in den Adern gerinnen lassen **II.** *vt* gerinnen lassen

cure [kjʊr] **I.** *vt* ❶ (*heal*) heilen *a. fig* (**of** von +*dat*); *cancer* besiegen ❷ FOOD haltbar machen; (*by smoking*) räuchern; (*by salting*) pökeln; (*by drying*) trocknen **II.** *n* ❶ (*remedy*) [Heil]mittel *nt* (**for** gegen +*akk*) ❷ (*recovery*) Heilung *f*; (*fig: solution*) Lösung *f*

'cure-all *n* Allheilmittel *nt* (**for** gegen +*akk*)

curfew ['kɜr·fju] *n* Ausgangssperre *f*

curiosity [ˌkjʊr·ɪ·'as·ɪ·ti] *n* ❶ (*desire to know*) Neugier[de] *f* ❷ (*object*) Kuriosität *f*

curious ['kjʊr·i·əs] *adj* ❶ (*inquisitive*) neugierig (**about** auf +*akk*); **to be ~ to see sb/sth** neugierig darauf sein, jdn/etw zu sehen ❷ (*peculiar*) seltsam, merkwürdig

curl [kɜrl] **I.** *n* ❶ (*loop of hair*) Locke *f* ❷ (*spiral*) Kringel *m* ❸ SPORTS Hantelübung *f* **II.** *vi* ❶ (*of hair*) sich locken ❷ (*of a road*) sich schlängeln **III.** *vt* ❶ **to ~ one's hair** sich *dat* Locken drehen ❷ *lips, leaves* kräuseln

curler ['kɜr·lər] *n* Lockenwickler *m*

curling ['kɜr·lɪŋ] *n* SPORTS Curling *nt*, Eisstockschießen *nt*

'curling iron *npl* Lockenstab *m*

curly ['kɜr·li] *adj leaves* gewellt, gekräuselt; *hair a.* lockig

currency ['kɜr·ən·si] *n* ❶ (*money*) Währung *f*; [**foreign**] **~** Devisen *pl* ❷ (*acceptance*) [weite] Verbreitung *f*; **to gain ~** sich verbreiten

current ['kɜr·ənt] **I.** *adj* gegenwärtig; *issue* aktuell; **in ~ use** gebräuchlich **II.** *n* ❶ (*of air, water*) Strömung *f*; **to swim against the ~** gegen dem Strom schwimmen *a. fig* ❷ ELEC Strom *m*

current af'fairs, current e'vents *npl* POL Zeitgeschehen *nt kein pl*

currently ['kɜr·ənt·li] *adv* zurzeit

curriculum vitae <*pl* -s *or* curricula vitae> [-'vi·taɪ] *n* Lebenslauf *m*

curry ['kɜr·i] *n* FOOD Curry *nt o m*

curse [kɜrs] **I.** *vi* fluchen **II.** *vt* ❶ (*swear at*) verfluchen ❷ (*put a magic spell on*) verwünschen; ■ **to be ~d with sth** mit etw *dat* geschlagen sein **III.** *n* Fluch *m*; **to put a ~ on sb** jdn verwünschen

cursed ['kɜr·sɪd] *adj* (*liter: under a curse*) verhext

cursive ['kɜr·sɪv] **I.** *adj* **~ writing** Schreibschrift *f* **II.** *n* Schreibschrift *f*; **to write sth in ~** etw in Schreibschrift schreiben

cursor ['kɜr·sər] *n* COMPUT Cursor *m*

cursory ['kɜr·sə·ri] *adj* (*form*) *glance* flüchtig; *examination* oberflächlich

curt [kɜrt] *adj* (*pej*) schroff, barsch

curtail [kər·'teɪl] *vt* ❶ (*reduce*) kürzen ❷ (*shorten*) verkürzen; *vacation* frühzeitig abbrechen

curtain ['kɜr·tən] *n* ❶ Vorhang *m*, Gardine *f* ❷ (*fig*) Schleier *m*, Vorhang *m*; **~ of smoke** Rauchwand *f*

'curtain call *n* THEAT Vorhang *m*; **to take a ~** einen Vorhang bekommen

curtsy, curtsey ['kɜrt·si] **I.** *vi* knicksen (**to** vor +*dat*) **II.** *n* [Hof]knicks *m*

curvature ['kɜr·və·tʃər] *n* Krümmung *f*; **~ of the spine** Rückgratverkrümmung *f*

curve [kɜrv] **I.** *n* ❶ (*bending line*) *of a figure, vase* Rundung *f*, Wölbung *f*; *of a road* Kurve *f*; *of a river* Bogen *m* ❷ MATH Kurve *f* **II.** *vi river, road* eine Kurve machen; *line* eine Kurve beschreiben **III.** *vt* biegen

cushion ['kʊʃ·ən] **I.** *n* ❶ (*pillow*) Kissen *nt*, Polster *m* ÖSTERR ❷ (*fig: buffer*) Polster *nt o* ÖSTERR *a. m*; **~ of air** Luftkissen *nt* **II.** *vt* dämpfen *a. fig*

cushy ['kʊʃ·i] *adj* (*pej fam*) bequem; *job* ruhig

custard ['kʌs·tərd] *n* (*dessert*) ≈ Vanillepudding *m*

custodial [kʌs·'toʊ·di·əl] *adj* ❶ (*janitorial*) pflegerisch ❷ LAW Wach-; **~ sentence** Freiheitsstrafe *f*

custodian [kʌs·ˈtoʊ·di·ən] *n* ① (*janitor*) Hausmeister(in) *m(f)* ② (*keeper*) Aufseher(in) *m(f)*; *of valuables* Hüter(in) *m(f)*

custody [ˈkʌs·tə·di] *n* ① (*guardianship*) Obhut *f*; LAW Sorgerecht *nt* (**of** für *+akk*) ② (*detention*) Haft *f*; **to keep sb in ~** jdn in Gewahrsam halten; **to take sb into ~** jdn verhaften

custom [ˈkʌs·təm] **I.** *n* ① (*tradition*) Brauch *m*, Sitte *f* ② (*usual behavior*) Gewohnheit *f* **II.** *adj attr* maßgeschneidert

customary [ˈkʌs·tə·mer·i] *adj* üblich

ˈcustom-built *adj* spezialangefertigt

customer [ˈkʌs·tə·mər] *n* ① (*buyer, patron*) Kunde, -in *m, f* ② (*fam: person*) Typ *m*

ˈcustomer number *n* Kundennummer *f*

customer ˈservice *n* Kundendienst *m*

customize [ˈkʌs·tə·maɪz] *vt* nach Kundenwünschen anfertigen

custom-ˈmade *adj* auf den Kunden zugeschnitten; *shirt* maßgeschneidert; *shoes* maßgefertigt

customs [ˈkʌs·təmz] *npl* Zoll *m*

ˈcustoms declaration *n* Zollerklärung *f*

ˈcustoms duties *npl* Zollabgaben *pl*

ˈcustoms officer, **ˈcustoms official** *n* Zollbeamte(r), -in *m, f*

ˈcustoms union *n* Zollunion *f*

cut [kʌt] **I.** *n* ① (*act*) Schnitt *m*; **my hair needs a ~** mein Haar muss geschnitten werden; **to make a ~ [in sth]** [in etw *akk*] einen Einschnitt machen ② (*piece of meat*) Stück *nt* ③ (*fit*) [Zu]schnitt *m*; *of shirt, pants* Schnitt *m* ④ (*wound*) Schnittwunde *f*; **to get a ~** sich schneiden ⑤ (*decrease*) Senkung *f*; **~ in production** Produktionseinschränkung *f*; **~ in staff** Personalabbau *m* ⑥ (*less spending*) ■ **~s** *pl* Kürzungen *pl* ⑦ *in film* Schnitt *m* ▶ PHRASES: **to be a ~ above sb/sth** jdm/etw um einiges überlegen sein **II.** *adj* ① (*sliced*) *bread* [auf]geschnitten; **~ flowers** Schnittblumen *pl* ② (*fitted*) *glass, gemstones* geschliffen **III.** *interj* FILM **~!** Schnitt! **IV.** *vt* <-tt-, cut, cut> ① (*slice*) schneiden; *bread* aufschneiden; *slice of bread* abschneiden; **to ~ sth in[to] several pieces** etw in mehrere Teile zerschneiden; **to ~ open** aufschneiden ② (*sever*) durchschneiden ③ (*trim*) [ab]schneiden; *hair, fingernails* schneiden; *grass* mähen; **to have [or get] one's hair ~** sich *dat* die Haare schneiden lassen ④ (*decrease*) *costs* senken; *prices* herabsetzen; *overtime* reduzieren; *wages* kürzen (**by** um *+akk*) ⑤ *film* kürzen; *scene* herausschneiden; **to ~ sb short** jdn unterbrechen ⑥ (*shape*) *diamond* schleifen ⑦ AUTO *corner* schneiden ⑧ *teeth* bekommen ⑨ CARDS abheben ⑩ COMPUT ausschneiden ▶ PHRASES: **to [not] ~ it** [k]ein hohes Niveau erreichen **V.** *vi* <-tt-, cut, cut> ① (*slice*) *knife* schneiden ② (*slice easily*) *material* sich schneiden lassen ③ (*take short cut*) eine Abkürzung nehmen ④ (*withdraw*) ■ **to ~ loose** sich trennen (**from** von *+dat*); (*fig*) alle Hemmungen verlieren ▶ PHRASES: **to ~ to the chase** (*fam*) auf den Punkt kommen; **to ~ and run** Reißaus nehmen

◆**cut across** *vi* ① (*to other side*) hinüberfahren ② (*take short cut*) durchqueren

◆**cut away** *vt* wegschneiden

◆**cut back I.** *vt* ① FIN kürzen; *production* zurückschrauben ② HORT zurückschneiden **II.** *vi* (*reduce*) ■ **to ~ back on sth** etw kürzen; **to ~ back on spending** die Ausgaben reduzieren

◆**cut down I.** *vt* ① (*fell*) *tree* umhauen ② (*reduce*) einschränken; *workforce* abbauen; *production* zurückfahren ③ (*abridge*) kürzen ▶ PHRASES: **to ~ sb down to size** jdn in seine Schranken verweisen **II.** *vi* ■ **to ~ down on sth** *smoking, spending* etw einschränken

◆**cut in I.** *vi* ① (*interrupt*) unterbrechen ② AUTO einscheren; ■ **to ~ in in front of sb** jdn schneiden ③ (*jump line*) sich vordränge[l]n; ■ **to ~ in on [or in front of] sb** sich vor jdn drängeln ④ (*activate*) sich einschalten **II.** *vt* ■ **to ~ sb in** (*share with*) jdn [am Gewinn] beteiligen

◆**cut into** *vi* ① (*slice*) anschneiden ② (*decrease*) *profits* verkürzen

◆**cut off** *vt* ① (*remove*) abschneiden; ■ **to ~ sth off [of] sth** etw von etw *dat* abschneiden ② (*silence*) unterbrechen; **to ~ sb off mid-sentence** jdm den Satz abschneiden ③ (*disconnect*) unterbinden; *electricity* abstellen; *gas supply* abdrehen; *phone conversation* unterbrechen ④ (*isolate*) abschneiden; ■ **to ~ oneself off** sich zurückziehen

◆**cut out I.** *vt* ① (*excise*) herausschneiden ② (*from paper*) ausschneiden ③ (*abridge*) streichen ④ (*fam: desist*) aufhören mit; **~ it [or that] out!** hör auf damit! ⑤ (*block*) *light* abschirmen ⑥ (*disinherit*) **to ~ sb out of one's will** jdn aus seinem Testament streichen ▶ PHRASES: **to have one's work ~ out for one** alle Hände voll zu tun haben; **to be ~ out for sth** für etw *akk* geeignet sein **II.** *vi* ① (*stop operating*) sich ausschalten; *plane's engine* aussetzen ② AUTO ausscheren; **to ~ out of traffic** plötzlich die Spur wechseln

◆**cut up** *vt* ① (*slice*) zerschneiden; *food for a child* klein schneiden ② (*injure*) ■ **to ~ up ⊂ sb** jdm Schnittwunden zufügen

cut-and-ˈdried *adj* ① (*fixed*) abgemacht; *decision* klar ② (*routine*) eindeutig; **~ solution** Patentlösung *f*

cutback [ˈkʌt·bæk] *n* Kürzung *f*

cute <-r, -st> [kjut] *adj* ① (*sweet*) süß, niedlich ② (*clever*) schlau

cuticle [ˈkju·t̬ə·kəl] *n* Nagelhaut *f*

cutlery [ˈkʌt·lə·ri] *n* Besteck *nt*

cutlet [ˈkʌt·lɪt] *n* ① (*meat*) Kotelett *nt* ② (*patty*) Frikadelle *f*

cutoff [ˈkʌt̬·ɔf] *n* ① (*limit*) Obergrenze *f* ② (*stop*) Beendigung *f*; **~ date** Endtermin *m*

ˈcutoffs *npl* abgeschnittene Jeans *f*

cutout [ˈkʌt̬·aʊt] **I.** *n* ① (*shape*) Ausschneidefigur *f* ② (*stereotype*) **cardboard ~** [Reklame]puppe *f* ③ (*switch*) Unterbrecher *m* **II.** *adj*

ausgeschnitten
'cut-price *adj goods* Billig-; *clothing* herabgesetzt
cutter ['kʌṭ·ər] *n* ❶ (*tool*) Schneider *m* ❷ (*person*) [Zu]schneider(in) *m(f);* FILM Cutter(in) *m(f)* ❸ NAUT Kutter *m*
'cutthroat *adj competition, pricing* gnadenlos
cutting ['kʌṭ·ɪŋ] **I.** *n* HORT Ableger *m* **II.** *adj* ❶ (*capable of severing*) *tool* schneidend ❷ (*abrasive*) *comment* scharf; *remark* bissig
cutting 'edge I. *n* ❶ (*blade*) Schneide *f* ❷ (*latest stage*) ■ **to be at the ~** an vorderster Front stehen **II.** *adj attr* supermodern, Hightech-
cyanide ['saɪ·ə·naɪd] *n* Zyanid *nt*
cybernetics [ˌsaɪ·bər·'neṭ·ɪks] *n + sing vb* Kybernetik *f*
cyberspace ['saɪ·bər·speɪs] *n* Cyberspace *m*
cycle¹ ['saɪ·kəl] *short for* **bicycle I.** *n* [Fahr]rad *nt* **II.** *vi* Rad fahren
cycle² ['saɪ·kəl] *n* Zyklus *m; of washing machine* Arbeitsgang *m;* **~ of life** Lebenskreislauf *m*
cyclical ['saɪ·klɪ·kəl, 'sɪk-] *adj* zyklisch
cyclist ['saɪ·klɪst] *n* Radfahrer(in) *m(f)*
cyclone ['saɪ·kloʊn] *n* METEO Zyklon *m*
cygnet ['sɪg·nɪt] *n* junger Schwan
cylinder ['sɪl·ɪn·dər] *n* ❶ AUTO, MATH Zylinder *m* ❷ TECH Walze *f* ❸ (*vessel*) Flasche *f*
cylindrical [sɪ·'lɪn·drɪ·kəl] *adj* zylindrisch
cymbal ['sɪm·bəl] *n usu pl* Beckenteller *m;* ■ **~s** Becken *nt*
cynic ['sɪn·ɪk] *n* Zyniker(in) *m(f)*
cynical ['sɪn·ɪ·kəl] *adj* zynisch
cynicism ['sɪn·ɪ·sɪz·əm] *n* Zynismus *m*
cypher *n see* **cipher**
cypress ['saɪ·prəs] *n* Zypresse *f*
Cyprus ['saɪ·prəs] *n* Zypern *nt*
cyst [sɪst] *n* MED Zyste *f*
cystitis [sɪ·'staɪ·ṭɪs] *n* Blasenentzündung *f*
czar [zar] *n* Zar *m;* **drug ~** Drogenzar *m*
czarina [za·'ri·nə] *n* Zarin *f*
Czech [tʃek] **I.** *n* ❶ (*person*) Tscheche, -in *m, f* ❷ (*language*) Tschechisch *nt* **II.** *adj* tschechisch
Czech Re'public *n* ■ **the ~** die Tschechische Republik

Dd

D <*pl* -'s *or* -s>, **d** <*pl* -'s> [di] *n* ❶ (*letter*) D *nt,* d *nt;* **~ as in Delta** D wie Dora ❷ MUS D *nt,* d *nt* ❸ (*school grade*) ≈ Vier *f;* **to get a ~** eine Vier schreiben
DA [ˌdi·'eɪ] *n* LAW *abbrev of* **district attorney**
dab [dæb] **I.** *vt* <-bb-> betupfen; **to ~ one's eyes** sich *dat* die Augen [trocken] tupfen **II.** *vi* <-bb-> ■ **to ~ at sth** etw betupfen
dabble ['dæb·əl] **I.** *vi* dilettieren; ■ **to ~ in** [*or* **with**] **sth** sich nebenbei mit etw *dat* beschäftigen **II.** *vt* **to ~ one's feet in the water** mit den Füßen im Wasser planschen
dad [dæd] *n* (*fam*) Papa *m*
daddy ['dæd·i] *n* (*fam*) Vati *m,* Papi *m*
daddy 'longlegs <*pl* -> *n* (*fam*) Weberknecht *m*
daffodil ['dæf·ə·dɪl] *n* Osterglocke *f*
daffy ['dæf·i] *adj* (*fam*) doof *pej sl,* blöd *fam,* bescheuert *sl*
dagger ['dæg·ər] *n* Dolch *m*
daily ['deɪ·li] **I.** *adj, adv* täglich; **~ routine** Alltagsroutine *f* **II.** *n* Tageszeitung *f*
dainty ['deɪn·ti] *adj* fein
dairy ['der·i] *n* ❶ (*company*) Molkerei *f;* **~ products** Molkereiprodukte *pl* ❷ (*farm*) Milchbetrieb *m;* **~ farmer** Milchbauer, Milchbäuerin *m, f*
daisy ['deɪ·zi] *n* Gänseblümchen *nt* ▶ PHRASES: **as fresh as a ~** putzmunter
dam [dæm] **I.** *n* [Stau]damm *m* **II.** *vt* <-mm-> stauen
damage ['dæm·ɪdʒ] **I.** *vt* ■ **to ~ sth** ❶ (*wreck*) *vehicle* etw [be]schädigen ❷ (*blemish*) *reputation* etw *dat* schaden **II.** *n* Schaden *m* (**to** an +*dat*); **brain ~** Gehirnschaden *m* ▶ PHRASES: **what's the ~?** (*fam*) was kostet der Spaß?
'damage limitation *n* ❶ POL Schadensbegrenzung *f* ❷ MIL Vermeidung *f* von Verlusten
damn [dæm] (*inf*) **I.** *interj* (*in anger*) ■ **~** [**it**]! verdammt [noch mal]!; [**oh**] **~!** [so ein] Mist!; (*in surprise*) Wahnsinn! **II.** *adj* ❶ (*cursed*) Scheiß- ❷ (*emph: extreme*) verdammt; **to be a ~ sight better** entschieden besser sein ❸ **not a ~ thing** überhaupt nichts **III.** *vt* ❶ (*curse*) verfluchen; **~ you!** hol dich der Teufel! ❷ (*condemn*) verurteilen ▶ PHRASES: **I'll be ~ed if I'm going to invite her** es fällt mir nicht im Traum ein, sie einzuladen **IV.** *adv* (*vulg*) verdammt **V.** *n* **to not give a ~ about sb/sth** sich nicht den Teufel um jdn/etw scheren *fam*
damnation [dæm·'neɪ·ʃən] **I.** *n* Verdammnis *f* **II.** *interj* verdammt!
damned [dæmd] **I.** *adj* (*vulg*) ❶ (*cursed*) Scheiß- ❷ (*emph: extreme*) verdammt **II.** *adv* (*vulg*) verdammt
damning ['dæm·ɪŋ] *adj comment* vernichtend; *evidence* erdrückend; *report* belastend
damp [dæmp] **I.** *adj* feucht **II.** *n* Feuchtigkeit *f*
dampen ['dæm·pən] *vt* ❶ (*wet*) befeuchten, anfeuchten ❷ (*suppress*) dämpfen
dampness ['dæmp·nɪs] *n* Feuchtigkeit *f*
dance [dæns] **I.** *vi, vt* tanzen *a. fig* **II.** *n* Tanz *m*
'dance music *n* Tanzmusik *f*

dancer ['dæn·sər] *n* Tänzer(in) *m(f)*
dancing ['dæn·sɪŋ] *n* Tanzen *nt*
dandelion ['dæn·də·laɪ·ən] *n* Löwenzahn *m*
dandruff ['dæn·drəf] *n* [Kopf]schuppen *pl*
Dane [deɪn] *n* Däne, -in *m, f*
danger ['deɪn·dʒər] *n* Gefahr *f;* **~! keep out!** Zutritt verboten! Lebensgefahr!; **to be in ~ of extinction** vom Aussterben bedroht sein; ■**to be in ~ of doing sth** Gefahr laufen, etw zu tun
dangerous ['deɪn·dʒər·əs] *adj* gefährlich
'**danger zone** *n* Gefahrenzone *f*
dangle ['dæŋ·gəl] **I.** *vi* herabhängen; *earrings* baumeln (**from** an *+dat*) **II.** *vt* ❶ (*swing*) **to ~ one's feet** mit den Füßen baumeln ❷ (*tempt with*) ■**to ~ sth before** [*or* **in front of**] **sb** jdm etw [verlockend] in Aussicht stellen
Danish ['deɪ·nɪʃ] **I.** *n* <*pl* -es> ❶ (*language*) Dänisch *nt* ❷ (*people*) ■**the ~** *pl* die Dänen ❸ (*cake*) *see* **Danish pastry II.** *adj* dänisch
Danish 'pastry *n* Blätterteiggebäck *nt*
dank [dæŋk] *adj* nasskalt
Danube ['dæn·jub] *n* ■**the ~** die Donau
dappled ['dæp·əld] *adj horse* scheckig; *light* gesprenkelt
dare [der] **I.** *vt* herausfordern; **I ~ you!** trau dich! **II.** *vi* sich trauen; ■**to ~** [**to**] **do sth** es wagen, etw zu tun ▶PHRASES: **don't you ~!** untersteh dich!; **I ~ say** (*supposing*) ich nehme an; (*confirming*) das glaube ich gern **III.** *n* Mutprobe *f;* ■**to do sth on a ~** etw als Mutprobe tun
'**daredevil** (*fam*) **I.** *n* Draufgänger(in) *m(f)* **II.** *adj* tollkühn; *stunt, tactics* halsbrecherisch
daring ['der·ɪŋ] **I.** *adj person* kühn, wagemutig; *action* waghalsig **II.** *n* Kühnheit *f*
dark [dark] **I.** *adj* ❶ (*unlit*) dunkel, finster; (*gloomy*) düster ❷ (*in color*) dunkel ❸ (*fig*) *chapter* dunkel; *look* finster **II.** *n* ■**the ~** die Dunkelheit; **to see in the ~** im Dunkeln sehen; **after ~** nach Einbruch der Dunkelheit ▶PHRASES: **to keep sb in the ~** jdn im Dunkeln lassen
'**Dark Ages** *npl* HIST ■**the ~** das frühe Mittelalter
darken ['dar·kən] **I.** *vi* ❶ *sky* dunkel werden ❷ *face, mood* sich verdüstern **II.** *vt* verdunkeln; *room* abdunkeln
dark 'horse *n* ❶ (*talent*) unbekannte Größe ❷ (*victor*) erfolgreicher Außenseiter
darkly ['dark·li] *adv* ❶ (*dimly*) dunkel, finster ❷ (*ominously*) böse
darkness ['dark·nɪs] *n* ❶ (*no light*) Dunkelheit *f* ❷ (*night*) Finsternis *f*
'**darkroom** *n* Dunkelkammer *f*
'**dark-skinned** <darker-, darkest-> *adj* dunkelhäutig
darling ['dar·lɪŋ] **I.** *n* Liebling *m,* Schatz *m,* Schätzchen *nt;* ■**to be sb's ~** jds Liebling *nt* sein **II.** *adj* entzückend
darn¹ [darn] **I.** *vt* stopfen **II.** *n* gestopfte Stelle
darn² [darn] *interj* (*euph*) *see* **damn**
dart [dart] **I.** *n* ❶ (*weapon*) Pfeil *m* ❷ SPORT Wurfpfeil *m;* **~s** *+ sing vb* (*game*) Darts *nt* **II.** *vi* flitzen
'**dartboard** *n* Dartscheibe *f*
dash [dæʃ] **I.** *n* <*pl* -es> ❶ (*rush*) Hetze *f;* **to make a ~ for the door** zur Tür stürzen ❷ SPORTS Kurzstreckenlauf *m* ❸ (*little bit*) ■**a ~** [**of**] ein kleiner Zusatz; *of spice* eine Messerspitze; *of salt* eine Prise; *of originality* ein Hauch von ❹ (*punctuation*) Gedankenstrich *m* **II.** *vi* (*hurry*) sausen; **I've got to ~** ich muss fort; **to ~ out of the room** aus dem Zimmer stürmen; ■**to ~ around** herumrennen; ■**to ~ off** davonjagen **III.** *vt* ❶ (*strike forcefully*) schleudern; **to ~ to pieces** zerschmettern ❷ (*destroy*) *hopes* zunichtemachen
'**dashboard** *n* Armaturenbrett *nt*
dashing ['dæʃ·ɪŋ] *adj* schneidig
data ['deɪ·t̬ə] *npl + sing/pl vb* Daten *pl*
'**database** *n* Datenbank *f*
data 'processing *n* Datenverarbeitung *f*
date¹ [deɪt] **I.** *n* ❶ (*calendar day*) Datum *nt;* **out of ~** überholt; **up to ~** *technology* auf dem neuesten Stand; *style* zeitgemäß ❷ (*on coins*) Jahreszahl *f* ❸ (*engagement*) *business* Termin *m; social* Verabredung *f; romantic* Date *nt;* **to make a ~** sich verabreden; **to go out on a ~** ausgehen ❹ (*person*) Date *nt* **II.** *vt* ❶ (*have relationship*) ■**to ~ sb** mit jdm gehen ❷ (*establish the age of*) datieren; **that sure ~s you!** daran merkt man, wie alt du bist!; **a letter ~d November 2nd** ein Brief vom 2. November **III.** *vi* ❶ (*have a relationship*) miteinander gehen ❷ (*go back to*) ■**to ~ from** [*or* **back to**] **sth** auf etw *akk* zurückgehen; *tradition* aus etw *dat* stammen
date² [deɪt] *n* FOOD Dattel *f*

> Beim **dating** (sich Verabreden) gibt es in den Vereinigten Staaten mehrere Ausdrücke, die die Beziehung zwischen einem Mädchen und einem Jungen beschreiben. *Seeing each other* heißt, dass sich zwei Menschen häufig treffen, sich dabei aber die Möglichkeit offen halten, auch mit anderen Partnern auszugehen. *Going out* weist darauf hin, dass sie einander regelmäßig sehen und dass ihre Beziehung ernst ist.

dated ['deɪ·t̬ɪd] *adj* überholt
'**dateline** *n* JOURN Datumszeile *f*
'**date rape** *n* Vergewaltigung *f* durch eine dem Opfer bekannte Person
'**date stamp** *n* Datumsstempel *m*
dative ['deɪ·t̬ɪv] **I.** *n* LING Dativ *m;* **to be in the ~** im Dativ stehen **II.** *adj* **the ~ case** der Dativ
daub [dɔb] **I.** *vt* beschmieren **II.** *n* Spritzer *m;* **~ of paint** Farbklecks *m*
daughter ['dɔ·t̬ər] *n* Tochter *f a. fig*
'**daughter-in-law** <*pl* daughters-> *n* Schwiegertochter *f*

D

daunt [dɔnt] *vt usu passive* entmutigen
daunting ['dɔn·tɪŋ] *adj* entmutigend
dawdle ['dɔd·əl] *vi* trödeln
dawdler ['dɔd·lər] *n* Trödler(in) *m(f)*
dawn [dɔn] **I.** *n* ❶ (*daybreak*) [Morgen]dämmerung *f;* **at [the break of] ~** bei Tagesanbruch, im Morgengrauen ❷ (*fig*) Anfang *m* **II.** *vi* ❶ (*start*) anbrechen *a. fig* ❷ (*become apparent*) bewusst werden, dämmern; **it suddenly ~ed on me that ...** auf einmal fiel mir siedend heiß ein, dass ...
day [deɪ] *n* Tag *m;* **ten ~s from now** heute in zehn Tagen; **any ~ [now]** jeden Tag; **from one ~ to the next** von heute auf morgen; **one ~** eines Tages; **the other ~** neulich; **some ~** irgendwann [einmal]; **from that ~ on[ward]** von dem Tag an; **the ~ after tomorrow** übermorgen; **the ~ before yesterday** vorgestern; **from ~ to ~** von Tag zu Tag; **to the ~** auf den Tag genau; **to this ~** bis heute; **these ~s** (*recently*) in letzter Zeit; (*nowadays*) heutzutage; (*at the moment*) zurzeit; **one of these ~s** eines Tages; (*soon*) demnächst [einmal]; **those were the ~s** das waren noch Zeiten; **in the good old** [*or* **ol'**] **~s** in der guten alten Zeit; **in those ~s** damals; **in this ~ and age** heutzutage ▶ PHRASES: **to call it a ~** Schluss machen [für heute]; **at the end of the ~** (*in the final analysis*) letzten Endes; (*eventually*) schließlich; **to make sb's ~** jds Tag retten; **to pass the time of ~** plaudern; **that will be the ~!** das möchte ich zu gern[e] einmal erleben!
'daybreak *n* **at ~** bei Tagesanbruch
'daycare *n of preschoolers* Vorschulkinderbetreuung *f; of the elderly* Altenbetreuung *f;* **~ center** (*for preschoolers*) Kindertagesstätte *f,* Kinderkrippe *f;* (*for the elderly*) Altentagesstätte *f*
'daydream I. *vi* vor sich *akk* hinträumen **II.** *n* Tagtraum *m*
'daylight *n* Tageslicht *nt;* **in broad ~** am hellichten Tag[e] ▶ PHRASES: **to scare the living ~s out of sb** jdn zu Tode erschrecken
daylight-'saving time *n* Sommerzeit *f*
'day shift *n* Tagschicht *f*
'daytime I. *n* Tag *m;* **in** [*or* **during**] **the ~** tagsüber **II.** *adj* Tages-
day-to-'day *adj* (*daily*) [tag]täglich; (*normal*) alltäglich; **on a ~ basis** tageweise
'day trip *n* Tagesausflug *m*
daze [deɪz] **I.** *n* Betäubung *f;* **in a ~** ganz benommen **II.** *vt* ■**to be ~d** wie betäubt sein
dazzle ['dæz·əl] **I.** *vt* ❶ (*blind*) blenden ❷ (*amaze*) verwundern **II.** *n* ❶ blendendes Licht ❷ (*fig*) Glanz *m*
'dazzled *adj* geblendet *a.fig,* überwältigt *fig*
DC [ˌdi·'si] *n* ❶ ELEC *abbrev of* **direct current** Gleichstrom *m* ❷ *abbrev of* **District of Columbia** D.C.
'D-Day *n no art* ❶ HIST *6. Juni 1944, Tag der Landung der Alliierten in der Normandie* ❷ (*fig*) der Tag X
DE *abbrev of* **Delaware**
dead [ded] **I.** *adj* ❶ (*not alive*) tot; **~ body** Leiche *f;* **to drop ~** tot umfallen ❷ *custom* ausgestorben; *feelings* erloschen; *fire, match, volcano* erloschen; *language* tot ❸ (*numb*) *limbs* taub ❹ (*deserted*) *city* [wie] ausgestorben; *party* öde ❺ (*fig fam: exhausted*) tot *fam,* kaputt *fam* ❻ (*not functioning*) *phone* tot ❼ (*fig: used up*) verbraucht; *batteries* leer ▶ PHRASES: **I wouldn't be caught ~ in that dress** so ein Kleid würde ich nie im Leben anziehen **II.** *adv* ❶ (*fam: totally*) absolut; **~ certain** todsicher *fam;* **~ drunk** stockbetrunken; **to be ~ set against sth** absolut gegen etw *akk* sein; **to be ~ set on sth** etw felsenfest vorhaben; **~ silent** totenstill; **~ tired** todmüde ❷ (*exactly*) genau; **~ on time** auf die Minute genau ▶ PHRASES: **to stop sth ~ in its tracks** etw völlig zum Stillstand bringen **III.** *n* ❶ (*people*) ■**the ~** *pl* die Toten ❷ (*in the middle*) **in the ~ of night** mitten in der Nacht; **in the ~ of winter** im tiefsten Winter
'deadbeat (*sl*) **I.** *n* ❶ (*chronic debtor*) Schnorrer(in) *m(f)* ❷ (*lazy person*) Faulpelz *m;* (*feckless person*) Gammler(in) *m(f)* **II.** *adj* säumig
'deadbolt *n* Schließriegel *m*
deaden ['ded·ən] *vt* ❶ (*numb*) *pain* abtöten *a. fig* ❷ (*diminish*) *sound* dämpfen
dead 'end *n* Sackgasse *f a. fig*
dead-'end *adj* **~ street** Sackgasse *f;* (*fig*) aussichtslos
dead 'heat *n* totes Rennen
'deadline *n* letzter Termin, Deadline *f*
deadlock ['ded·lak] *n* toter Punkt; **to end in a ~** an einem toten Punkt enden
deadly ['ded·li] **I.** *adj* ❶ (*capable of killing*) *weapons* tödlich ❷ (*implacable*) **~ enemies** Todfeinde *pl* ❸ (*pej fam: very boring*) todlangweilig ▶ PHRASES: **the seven ~ sins** die sieben Todsünden *pl* **II.** *adv* **~ serious** todernst
'deadpan *adj* ausdruckslos; *humor* trocken
Dead 'Sea *n* ■**the ~** das Tote Meer
'deadwood *n* ❶ BOT totes Holz ❷ (*fig*) Ballast *m*
deaf [def] **I.** *adj* (*unable to hear*) taub; (*hard of hearing*) schwerhörig; **to go ~** taub werden; ■**to be ~ to sth** (*fig*) taube Ohren für etw *akk* haben **II.** *n* ■**the ~** *pl* die Tauben
deafen ['def·ən] *vt* taub machen; (*fig*) betäuben
deafening ['def·ə·nɪŋ] *adj* ohrenbetäubend
deaf-'mute *n* Taubstumme(r) *f(m)*
deafness ['def·nɪs] *n* (*complete*) Taubheit *f;* (*partial*) Schwerhörigkeit *f*
deal [dil] **I.** *n* ❶ Menge *f;* **a great** [*or* **good**] **~** eine Menge ❷ (*in business*) Geschäft *nt,* Deal *m sl;* **we got a good ~ on that computer** mit dem Rechner haben wir ein gutes Geschäft gemacht; **to make a ~ with sb** mit jdm ein Geschäft abschließen ❸ (*general agreement*) Abmachung *f;* **it's a ~** abgemacht; **to make a ~ [with sb]** eine Vereinbarung [mit jdm] treffen ❹ (*treatment*) **a raw** [*or* **rough**] **~** eine ungerechte Behandlung ❺ CARDS Geben

nt ▶ PHRASES: **big ~!** (*fam*) was soll's?; **what's the big ~?** (*fam*) na und? **II.** *vi* <-t, -t> ❶ CARDS geben ❷ (*sl: sell drugs*) dealen **III.** *vt* <-t, -t> ❶ (*give*) ■ **to ~** [**out**] verteilen; **to ~ sb a blow** jdm einen Schlag versetzen *a. fig* ❷ (*sell*) ■ **to ~ sth** *drugs* mit etw *dat* dealen
◆**deal with** *vi* ❶ (*handle*) sich befassen mit, sich kümmern um; ■ **to ~ with sth** mit etw *dat* zurande kommen *fam*; ■ **to ~ with sb/sth** mit jdm/etw *dat* zurechtkommen ❷ (*treat*) handeln von ❸ (*do business*) Geschäfte machen mit

dealer ['di·lər] *n* ❶ COMM Händler(in) *m(f)*; *of drugs* Dealer(in) *m(f)* ❷ CARDS [Karten]geber(in) *m(f)*

dealership ['di·lər·ʃɪp] *n* Verkaufsstelle *f*

dealing ['di·lɪŋ] *n* ❶ ■ **~s** *pl* (*transactions*) Geschäfte *pl*; (*contact*) Umgang *m kein pl* ❷ (*way of behaving*) Verhalten *nt*; (*in business*) Geschäftsgebaren *nt*

dealt [delt] *pt, pp of* **deal**

dean [din] *n* Dekan(in) *m(f)*

dear [dɪr] **I.** *adj* ❶ (*much loved*) lieb; (*lovely*) *baby, kitten* süß; *thing a.* entzückend ❷ (*in letters*) **D~ Mr. Jones** Sehr geehrter Herr Jones; **D~ Jane** Liebe Jane ❸ (*costly*) teuer **II.** *interj* **~ me!** du liebe Zeit!; **oh ~!** du meine Güte! **III.** *n* ❶ (*nice person*) Schatz *m* ❷ (*term of endearment*) **my ~**[**est**] [mein] Liebling *m*

dearly ['dɪr·li] *adv* von ganzem Herzen; **to pay ~** (*fig*) teuer bezahlen

dearth [dɜrθ] *n* (*form*) Mangel *m* (**of** an +*dat*)

death [deθ] *n* Tod *m*; **to be bored to ~** sich zu Tode langweilen; **to be put to ~** getötet werden; **accidental ~** Tod durch Unfall ▶ PHRASES: **to be at ~'s door** an der Schwelle des Todes stehen; **to be the ~ of sb** jdn das Leben kosten; **to look like ~ warmed over** wie eine Leiche auf Urlaub aussehen

'**deathbed** *n* Sterbebett *nt*

'**deathblow** *n* Todesstoß *m*

'**death certificate** *n* Sterbeurkunde *f*

deathly ['deθ·li] *adj, adv* tödlich; **~ silence** Totenstille *f*

'**death penalty** *n* Todesstrafe *f*; **to receive the ~** zum Tode verurteilt werden

'**death rate** *n* Sterblichkeitsziffer *f*

death 'row *n* Todestrakt *m*

'**death sentence** *n* Todesurteil *nt*

'**death tax** *n see* **inheritance tax**

'**death trap** *n* Todesfalle *f*

debacle [dɪ·'ba·kəl] *n* Debakel *nt*

debar <-rr-> [dɪ·'bar] *vt* ausschließen

debase [dɪ·'beɪs] *vt* ❶ *thing* herabsetzen; *currency* schmälern ❷ *person* entwürdigen

debatable [dɪ·'beɪ·t̬ə·bəl] *adj* umstritten; ■ **it's ~ whether ...** es ist fraglich, ob ...

debate [dɪ·'beɪt] **I.** *n* Debatte *f* **II.** *vt, vi* debattieren

debauch [dɪ·'bɔtʃ] *vt* [sittlich] verderben

debauchery [dɪ·'bɔ·tʃə·ri] *n* Ausschweifungen *pl*

debilitate [dɪ·'bɪl·ɪ·teɪt] *vt* schwächen

debilitating [dɪ·'bɪl·ɪ·teɪ·t̬ɪŋ] *adj* schwächend

debility [dɪ·'bɪl·ɪ·t̬i] *n* Schwäche *f*

debit ['deb·ɪt] **I.** *n* Debet *nt*, Soll *nt*; **to be in ~** im Minus sein **II.** *vt* abbuchen

'**debit card** *n* Debitkarte *f*, Geldautomatenkarte *f*

debris [də·'bri] *n* Trümmer *pl*

debt [det] *n* Schuld *f*; **to be** [**heavily**] **in ~** [**to sb**] [große] Schulden [bei jdm] haben

'**debt collector** *n* Schuldeneintreiber(in) *m(f)*

debtor ['det̬·ər] *n* Schuldner(in) *m(f)*

'**debtor country**, '**debtor nation** *n* Schuldnerstaat *m*

debug <-gg-> [ˌdi·'bʌg] *vt* ■ **to ~ sth** ❶ COMPUT bei etw *dat* die Fehler beseitigen; **to ~ a program** ein Programm auf Viren hin absuchen ❷ (*remove hidden microphones*) etw entwanzen

debut [deɪ·'bju] **I.** *n of a performer* Debüt *nt* **II.** *vi* debütieren

debutante ['deb·ju·tant] *n* Debütantin *f a. fig*

Dec. *n abbrev of* **December** Dez.

decade ['dek·eɪd] *n* Jahrzehnt *nt*

decadence ['dek·ə·dəns] *n* Dekadenz *f*

decadent ['dek·ə·dənt] *adj* dekadent; (*hum*) üppig

decaf ['di·kæf] (*fam*) **I.** *adj abbrev of* **decaffeinated** entkoffeiniert, koffeinfrei **II.** *n abbrev of* **decaffeinated coffee** entkoffeinierter Kaffee

decaffeinated [ˌdi·'kæf·ɪ·neɪ·t̬ɪd] *adj* entkoffeiniert, koffeinfrei

decant [dɪ·'kænt] *vt* umfüllen

decanter [dɪ·'kæn·tər] *n* Karaffe *f*

decapitate [dɪ·'kæp·ɪ·teɪt] *vt* köpfen

decapitation [dɪ·ˌkæp·ɪ·'teɪ·ʃən] *n* Enthauptung *f*

decathlete [dɪ·'kæθ·lit] *n* Zehnkämpfer(in) *m(f)*

decathlon [dɪ·'kæθ·lan] *n* Zehnkampf *m*

decay [dɪ·'keɪ] **I.** *n* ❶ (*deterioration*) Verfall *m*; **to fall into ~** verfallen ❷ BIOL Verwesung *f*; BOT Fäulnis *f*; PHYS Zerfall *m*; **tooth ~** Zahnfäule *f* **II.** *vi* ❶ (*deteriorate*) verfallen ❷ BIOL verwesen, [ver]faulen; BOT verblühen; PHYS zerfallen

deceased [dɪ·'sist] (*form*) **I.** *n* <*pl* -> ■ **the ~** der/die Verstorbene, die Verstorbenen *pl* **II.** *adj* verstorben

deceit [dɪ·'sit] *n* Betrug *m*

deceitful [dɪ·'sit·fəl] *adj* [be]trügerisch

deceive [dɪ·'siv] *vt* betrügen; ■ **to ~ sb** jdn hintergehen; ■ **to ~ oneself** sich [selbst] täuschen; ■ **to be ~d by sth** von etw *dat* getäuscht werden

deceiver [dɪ·'si·vər] *n* Betrüger(in) *m(f)*

decelerate [di·'sel·ə·reɪt] *vi* sich verlangsamen; *vehicle, driver* langsamer fahren

December [dɪ·'sem·bər] *n* Dezember *m*; *see also* **February**

decency ['di·sən·si] *n* ❶ (*respectability*) Anstand *m*; (*goodness*) Anständigkeit *f* ❷ (*approved behavior*) ■ **decencies** *pl* Anstandsformen *pl*

decent ['di·sənt] *adj* ❶ (*socially acceptable*)

anständig ❷ (*good*) *person* nett ❸ (*appropriate*) angemessen; **to do the ~ thing** das [einzig] Richtige tun ❹ (*good-sized*) anständig; *helping* ordentlich ❺ (*acceptable*) *job, proposal* annehmbar ❻ (*fam: dressed*) angezogen
decentralization [di·ˌsen·trə·lɪ·ˈzeɪ·ʃən] *n* Dezentralisierung *f*
decentralize [di·ˈsen·trə·laɪz] *vt* dezentralisieren
deception [dɪ·ˈsep·ʃən] *n* Täuschung *f*
deceptive [dɪ·ˈsep·tɪv] *adj* täuschend
decibel [ˈdes·ə·bəl] *n* Dezibel *nt*
decide [dɪ·ˈsaɪd] **I.** *vi* sich entscheiden (**on** für +*akk*); ■**to ~ to do sth** beschließen [*o* sich entschließen], etw zu tun **II.** *vt* entscheiden; *sb's fate* entscheiden über +*akk*
decided [dɪ·ˈsaɪ·dɪd] *adj* (*definite*) entschieden; *dislike* ausgesprochen
deciduous [dɪ·ˈsɪdʒ·u·əs] *adj* **~ tree** Laubbaum *m*
decimal [ˈdes·ə·məl] *n* Dezimalzahl *f*, Dezimale *f*; **~ place** Dezimalstelle *f*; **~ point** Komma *nt*
decipher [dɪ·ˈsaɪ·fər] *vt* entziffern; *code* entschlüsseln
decision [dɪ·ˈsɪʒ·ən] *n* Entscheidung *f* (**about/on** über +*akk*), Entschluss *m*; **to come to** [*or* **reach**] **a ~** zu einer Entscheidung gelangen; **to make a ~** eine Entscheidung treffen
de'cision-making *n* Entscheidungsfindung *f*
decisive [dɪ·ˈsaɪ·sɪv] *adj* ❶ (*determining*) bestimmend; *battle* entscheidend; *part* maßgeblich ❷ (*firm*) *measure* entschlossen
deck [dek] **I.** *n* ❶ (*on a ship, bus*) Deck *nt*; **on ~** an Deck ❷ (*raised porch*) Veranda *f* ❸ CARDS **~ of cards** Spiel *nt* Karten ❹ MUS **tape ~** Tapedeck *nt* ▶ PHRASES: **to clear the ~s** klar Schiff machen; **to have all hands on ~** jede erdenkliche Unterstützung haben **II.** *vt* ❶ (*adorn*) ■**to ~ sth** [**out**] etw [aus]schmücken ❷ (*sl: knock down*) ■**to ~ sb** jdm eine verpassen
'deck chair *n* Liegestuhl *m*; (*on ship*) Deckchair *m*
declaration [ˌde·klə·ˈreɪ·ʃən] *n* Erklärung *f*; **to make a ~** eine Erklärung abgeben

> In der **Declaration of Independence**, der Unabhängigkeitserklärung, erklärten sich die 13 Kolonien Nordamerikas als unabhängig von Großbritannien, gaben sich selbst den Namen der 13 Vereinigten Staaten von Amerika und verteidigten die Gründe, die sie dazu gebracht hatten, so zu handeln. Die Erklärung wurde am 4. Juli 1776 durch den *Continental Congress* (Kontinentalkongress) ratifiziert und dieser Tag wird heute in den Vereinigten Staaten jedes Jahr als *Independence Day* (Unabhängigkeitstag) gefeiert.

declare [dɪ·ˈkler] **I.** *vt* ❶ (*make known*) verkünden; *intention* kundtun; *support* zusagen; **to ~ one's love for sb** jdm eine Liebeserklärung machen ❷ (*state*) erklären; **to ~ war on sb** jdm den Krieg erklären ❸ (*for customs, tax*) deklarieren; **do you have anything to ~?** haben Sie etwas zu verzollen? **II.** *vi* sich aussprechen
decline [dɪ·ˈklaɪn] **I.** *n* ❶ (*decrease*) Rückgang *m* ❷ (*deterioration*) Verschlechterung *f*; **industrial ~** Niedergang *m* der Industrie **II.** *vi* ❶ (*refuse*) ablehnen ❷ (*diminish*) *interest, popularity* sinken, nachlassen; *health* sich verschlechtern; *strength* abnehmen ❸ (*sink in position*) abfallen **III.** *vt* ❶ (*refuse*) ablehnen ❷ LING deklinieren, beugen
decode [ˌdi·ˈkoʊd] *vt* entschlüsseln
decoder [dɪ·ˈkoʊ·dər] *n* Decoder *m*
decompose [ˌdi·kəm·ˈpoʊz] *vi* sich zersetzen
decomposition [ˌdi·kam·pə·ˈzɪʃ·ən] *n* Zersetzung *f*
decompress [ˌdi·kəm·ˈpres] *vt, vi* dekomprimieren
decompression [ˌdi·kəm·ˈpreʃ·ən] *n* Dekompression *f*; COMPUT Entpacken *nt*
decongestant [ˌdi·kən·ˈdʒes·tənt] *n* abschwellendes Mittel, Mittel, das die Atemwege frei macht
decontaminate [ˌdi·kən·ˈtæm·ɪ·neɪt] *vt* entseuchen
decontamination [ˌdi·kən·ˌtæm·ɪ·ˈneɪ·ʃən] *n* Entseuchung *f*
decor [ˈdeɪ·kɔr] *n* Ausstattung *f*; THEAT Dekor *m o nt*
decorate [ˈdek·ə·reɪt] *vt* ❶ (*adorn*) schmücken; *cake, store window* dekorieren ❷ *usu passive* (*honor*) ■**to be ~** [**for sth**] [für etw *akk*] ausgezeichnet werden
decoration [ˌdek·ə·ˈreɪ·ʃən] *n* ❶ (*for party*) Dekoration *f*; (*for Christmas tree*) Schmuck *m kein pl* ❷ (*medal*) Auszeichnung *f*
decorative [ˈdek·ər·ə·t̬ɪv] *adj* dekorativ
decorum [dɪ·ˈkɔr·əm] *n* (*form*) Schicklichkeit *f*
decoy [ˈdi·kɔɪ] *n* Lockvogel *m*
decrease I. *vi* [dɪ·ˈkris] abnehmen, zurückgehen **II.** *vt* [dɪ·ˈkris] reduzieren; *production* drosseln **III.** *n* [ˈdi·kris] Abnahme *f*; *numbers* Rückgang *m*
decree [dɪ·ˈkri] **I.** *n* (*form*) Erlass *m* **II.** *vt* verfügen
decrepit [dɪ·ˈkrep·ɪt] *adj* klapprig
decriminalize [ˌdi·ˈkrɪm·ə·nə·laɪz] *vt* legalisieren
dedicate [ˈded·ɪ·keɪt] *vt* ■**to ~ sth to sb** jdm etw *akk* widmen; ■**to ~ oneself to sth** sich etw *dat* widmen
dedicated [ˈded·ɪ·keɪ·t̬ɪd] *adj* engagiert
dedication [ˌded·ɪ·ˈkeɪ·ʃən] *n* ❶ (*hard work*) Engagement *nt* (**to** für +*akk*) ❷ (*in book*) Widmung *f*
deduce [dɪ·ˈdus] *vt* folgern; ■**to ~ whether ...** feststellen, ob ...
deduct [dɪ·ˈdʌkt] *vt* abziehen; FIN ausgleichen;

to ~ sth from your taxes etw von der Steuer absetzen
deductible [dɪ·ˈdʌk·tə·bəl] *adj* absetzbar
deduction [dɪ·ˈdʌk·ʃən] *n* ❶ (*inference*) Schlussfolgerung *f* ❷ (*subtraction*) Abzug *m*
deed [did] *n* ❶ (*action*) Tat *f;* **dirty ~s** Drecksarbeit *f;* **to do a good ~** eine gute Tat vollbringen ❷ LAW Eigentumsurkunde *f*
deep [dip] **I.** *adj, adv* tief; *disappointment* schwer; *regret* groß; **the snow was 3 feet ~** der Schnee lag 3 Fuß hoch; **to take a ~ breath** tief Luft holen; **to be ~ in conversation** in ein Gespräch vertieft sein; **~ in debt** hoch verschuldet; **to be in ~ trouble** in großen Schwierigkeiten stecken; **~ blue** tiefblau; **~ space** äußerer Weltraum **II.** *n* (*liter*) ■ **the ~** die Tiefe
deepen [ˈdi·pən] **I.** *vt* ❶ (*make deeper*) tiefer machen ❷ (*intensify*) vertiefen **II.** *vi* ❶ *voice, water* tiefer werden ❷ (*intensify*) sich vertiefen; *crisis* sich verschärfen
ˈdeep freeze *n* Tiefkühlschrank *m;* (*chest*) Tiefkühltruhe *f*
deep-ˈfry *vt* frittieren
ˈdeep fryer *n* Fritteuse *f*
deeply [ˈdip·li] *adv* tief, äußerst; **to ~ regret sth** etw sehr bereuen
deep-ˈseated *adj* tief sitzend
deer <*pl* -> [dɪr] *n* Hirsch *m;* (*roe deer*) Reh *nt*
deface [dɪ·ˈfeɪs] *vt* verunstalten; *building* verschandeln
defamation [ˌdef·ə·ˈmeɪ·ʃən] *n* (*form*) Diffamierung *f*
defamatory [dɪ·ˈfæm·ə·tɔr·i] *adj* (*form*) diffamierend
defame [dɪ·ˈfeɪm] *vt* (*form*) diffamieren
default [dɪ·ˈfɔlt] **I.** *vi* ❶ (*fail to pay*) in Verzug geraten (**on** mit +*dat*) ❷ COMPUT ■ **to ~ to sth** standardmäßig eingestellt sein **II.** *n* ❶ *of contract* Nichterfüllung *f;* (*failure to pay debt*) Versäumnis *nt;* **in ~ of payment ...** bei Zahlungsverzug ... ❷ ■ **by ~** automatisch ❸ COMPUT Voreinstellung *f* **III.** *adj* Standard-; **~ program** Standardprogramm *nt*
defeat [dɪ·ˈfit] **I.** *vt* besiegen; (*at games, sports*) schlagen; *hopes* zerschlagen; *proposal, government bill* ablehnen **II.** *n* Niederlage *f*
defeatism [dɪ·ˈfi·t̬ɪ·zəm] *n* (*pej*) Defätismus *m,* Defaitismus *m* SCHWEIZ
defeatist [dɪ·ˈfi·t̬ɪst] **I.** *adj* defätistisch, defaitistisch SCHWEIZ **II.** *n* Defätist(in) *m(f),* Defaitist(in) *m(f)* SCHWEIZ
defecate [ˈdef·ə·keɪt] *vi* (*form*) den Darm entleeren
defecation [ˌdef·ə·ˈkeɪ·ʃən] *n* (*form*) Stuhlentleerung *f*
defect[1] [ˈdi·fekt] *n* Fehler *m;* TECH Defekt *m* (**in** an +*dat*)
defect[2] [dɪ·ˈfekt] *vi* POL überlaufen (**to** in +*akk*)
defection [dɪ·ˈfek·ʃən] *n* Flucht *f;* POL Überlaufen *nt*
defective [dɪ·ˈfek·tɪv] *adj* fehlerhaft; TECH defekt
defend [dɪ·ˈfend] *vt, vi* verteidigen; ■ **to ~ oneself** (*fight off*) sich wehren
defendant [dɪ·ˈfen·dənt] *n* LAW Angeklagte(r) *f(m)*
defense[1] [dɪ·ˈfens] *n* ❶ Verteidigung *f a. fig;* **~ witness** Zeuge, -in *m, f* der Verteidigung ❷ MED ■ **~s** *pl* Abwehrkräfte *pl*
defense[2] [ˈdɪ·fens] *n esp* SPORTS Abwehr *f;* **to play [on] ~** Abwehrspieler/Abwehrspielerin sein; CHESS Verteidigungsstellung *f*
defenseless [dɪ·ˈfens·lɪs] *adj* wehrlos
Deˈfense Secretary *n* Verteidigungsminister(in) *m(f)*
defensible [dɪ·ˈfen·sə·bəl] *adj* vertretbar
defensive [dɪ·ˈfen·sɪv] **I.** *adj* defensiv **II.** *n* Defensive *f;* **to be on the ~** in der Defensive sein
defer <-rr-> [dɪ·ˈfɜr] **I.** *vi* (*form*) ■ **to ~ to sb/sth** sich jdm/etw beugen; *to sb's judgment* sich fügen **II.** *vt* verschieben; FIN, LAW aufschieben; *decision* vertagen
deference [ˈdef·ər·əns] *n* (*form*) Respekt *m;* **in ~ to** aus Respekt vor
deferential [ˌdef·ə·ˈren·tʃəl] *adj* respektvoll
defiance [dɪ·ˈfaɪ·əns] *n* Aufsässigkeit *f;* ■ **in ~ of sb/sth** jdm/etw zum Trotz
defiant [dɪ·ˈfaɪ·ənt] *adj* aufsässig
deficiency [dɪ·ˈfɪʃ·ən·si] *n* Mangel *m* (**in** an +*dat*)
deficient [dɪ·ˈfɪʃ·ənt] *adj* unzureichend; ■ **to be ~ in sth** an etw *dat* mangeln
deficit [ˈdef·ɪ·sɪt] *n* Defizit *nt* (**in** in +*dat*)
defile [dɪ·ˈfaɪl] *vt* (*form*) beschmutzen; *tomb* schänden
define [dɪ·ˈfaɪn] *vt* ❶ (*give definition*) definieren (**by** über +*akk*) ❷ (*specify*) festlegen
definite [ˈdef·ə·nɪt] *adj* sicher; *answer* klar; *decision* definitiv; *improvement, increase* eindeutig; *place, time limit* bestimmt; **there's nothing ~ yet** es steht noch nichts fest; ■ **to be ~ about sth** sich *dat* einer S. *gen* sicher sein
definite ˈarticle *n* LING bestimmter Artikel
definitely [ˈdef·ɪ·nət·li] *adv* eindeutig; **to decide sth ~** etw endgültig beschließen
definition [ˌdef·ɪ·ˈnɪʃ·ən] *n* ❶ (*meaning*) Definition *f* ❷ (*distinctness*) Schärfe *f;* **to lack ~** unscharf sein
definitive [dɪ·ˈfɪn·ɪ·t̬ɪv] *adj* ❶ (*conclusive*) endgültig; *proof* eindeutig ❷ (*most authoritative*) ultimativ
deflate [dɪ·ˈfleɪt] **I.** *vt* ❶ Luft ablassen aus; *tire* die Luft aus einem Reifen lassen ❷ (*fig*) *hopes* zunichtemachen ❸ ECON *currency* deflationieren **II.** *vi* Luft verlieren
deflation [dɪ·ˈfleɪ·ʃən] *n* ECON Deflation *f*
deflationary [dɪ·ˈfleɪ·ʃən·er·i] *adj tactics* deflationär
deflect [dɪ·ˈflekt] **I.** *vt* ablenken; ■ **to ~ sth** etw ablenken; *ball* abfälschen; *blow* abwehren; PHYS *light* beugen; ■ **to ~ sb from doing sth** jdn davon abbringen, etw zu tun **II.** *vi* ■ **to ~ off sb/sth** *ball* von jdm/etw *dat* abprallen
deflection [dɪ·ˈflek·ʃən] *n* Ablenkung *f;* SPORTS

D

Abpraller *m*
defogger [ˌdi·ˈfɔ·gər] *n* AUTO Gebläse *nt*
deforest [ˌdi·ˈfɔr·ɪst] *vt* abholzen
deforestation [di·ˌfɔr·ɪ·ˈsteɪ·ʃən] *n* Abholzung *f*, Entwaldung *f*
deform [dɪ·ˈfɔrm] **I.** *vt* deformieren **II.** *vi* sich verformen
deformation [ˌdi·fɔr·ˈmeɪ·ʃən] *n* Deformation *f*, Verformung *f*
deformed [dɪ·ˈfɔrmd] *adj* verformt; *face* entstellt
deformity [dɪ·ˈfɔr·mɪ·t̬i] *n* Missbildung *f*
defraud [dɪ·ˈfrɔd] *vt* betrügen (**of** um +*akk*)
defray [dɪ·ˈfreɪ] *vt* (*form*) *costs* tragen
defrost [ˌdi·ˈfrɔst] *vt, vi* auftauen; *refrigerator* abtauen; *window, windshield* enteisen
deft [deft] *adj* geschickt
defunct [dɪ·ˈfʌŋkt] *adj* (*form*) gestorben; (*hum*) hinüber *fam; institution* ausgedient; *process* überholt
defy <-ie-> [dɪ·ˈfaɪ] *vt* ❶ (*disobey*) ■**to ~ sb/sth** sich jdm/etw widersetzen; (*fig: resist, withstand*) sich etw *dat* entziehen; **to ~ description** jeder Beschreibung spotten ❷ (*challenge*) *one's accusers* auffordern
deg. *n abbrev of* **degree**
degenerate I. *vi* [dɪ·ˈdʒen·ə·reɪt] degenerieren; ■**to ~ into sth** zu etw *dat* entarten **II.** *adj* [dɪ·ˈdʒen·ə·rət] degeneriert **III.** *n* [dɪ·ˈdʒen·ə·rət] *jd, der keine moralischen Werte mehr hat*
degeneration [dɪ·ˌdʒen·ə·ˈreɪ·ʃən] *n* Degeneration *f*
degrade [dɪ·ˈgreɪd] **I.** *vt* ❶ *person* erniedrigen ❷ CHEM abbauen **II.** *vi* CHEM ■**to ~ into sth** zu etw *dat* abgebaut werden
degree [dɪ·ˈgri] *n* ❶ (*amount*) Maß *nt;* (*extent*) Grad *m;* **a high ~ of skill** ein hohes Maß an Können; **by ~s** nach und nach; **to some ~** bis zu einem gewissen Grad ❷ MATH, METEO Grad *m* ❸ UNIV Abschluss *m;* (*document*) Abschlusszeugnis *nt*
dehumanize [ˌdi·ˈhju·mə·naɪz] *vt* entmenschlichen
dehydrate [ˌdi·haɪ·ˈdreɪt] **I.** *vt* ■**to ~ sb/sth** jdm/etw *dat* das Wasser entziehen; **to become ~d** austrocknen **II.** *vi* MED dehydrieren
dehydrated [ˌdi·haɪ·ˈdreɪ·t̬ɪd] *adj food* getrocknet; *skin* ausgetrocknet
dehydration [ˌdi·haɪ·ˈdreɪ·ʃən] *n* MED Dehydration *f*
deice [ˌdi·ˈaɪs] *vt* enteisen
deity [ˈdi·ə·t̬i] *n* Gottheit *f*
dejected [dɪ·ˈdʒek·tɪd] *adj* niedergeschlagen
dejection [dɪ·ˈdʒek·ʃən] *n* Niedergeschlagenheit *f*
Del. *abbrev of* **Delaware**
Delaware [ˈdel·ə·wer] *n* Delaware *nt*
delay [dɪ·ˈleɪ] **I.** *vt* ❶ (*postpone*) verschieben ❷ (*hold up*) **to be ~ed** [**by 10 minutes**] [zehn Minuten] Verspätung haben; **I was ~ed** ich wurde aufgehalten **II.** *vi* verschieben **III.** *n* Verzögerung *f;* TRANSP Verspätung *f*
delaying [dɪ·ˈleɪ·ɪŋ] *adj* verzögernd; **~ tactics** Verzögerungstaktiken *pl*
delectable [dɪ·ˈlek·tə·bəl] *adj food, drink* köstlich; (*esp hum*) *person* bezaubernd
delectation [ˌdi·lek·ˈteɪ·ʃən] *n* (*form or hum*) Vergnügen *nt*
delegate I. *n* [ˈdel·ɪ·gət] Delegierte(r) *f(m)* **II.** *vt* [ˈdel·ɪ·geɪt] ❶ (*appoint*) als Vertreter(in) [aus]wählen; ■**to ~ sb to do sth** jdn dazu bestimmen, etw zu tun ❷ (*assign*) ■**to ~ sth to sb** etw auf jdn übertragen; ■**to ~ sb to do sth** jdn zu etw *dat* ermächtigen **III.** *vi* [ˈdel·ɪ·geɪt] delegieren
delegation [ˌdel·ɪ·ˈgeɪ·ʃən] *n* Delegation *f*
delete [dɪ·ˈlit] **I.** *vt* ❶ (*in writing*) streichen (**from** aus +*dat*) ❷ COMPUT löschen **II.** *vi* löschen
deletion [dɪ·ˈli·ʃən] *n* Streichung *f*, Löschung *f; of a file* Löschen *nt*
deli [ˈdel·i] *n* (*fam*) *short for* **delicatessen** Feinkostgeschäft *nt;* (*in a supermarket*) *Frischtheke, an der Wurst- und Käseaufschnitt, frische Salate etc. verkauft werden*
deliberate I. *adj* [dɪ·ˈlɪb·ər·ət] ❶ (*intentional*) absichtlich; *decision, lie* bewusst ❷ (*careful*) *pace* vorsichtig **II.** *vi* [dɪ·ˈlɪb·ə·reɪt] (*form*) [gründlich] nachdenken (**on** über +*akk*) **III.** *vt* [dɪ·ˈlɪb·ə·reɪt] (*form: consider*) ■**to ~ whether ...** überlegen, ob ...
deliberately [dɪ·ˈlɪb·ər·ət·li] *adv* absichtlich
deliberation [dɪ·ˌlɪb·ə·ˈreɪ·ʃən] *n* ❶ (*carefulness*) Bedächtigkeit *f* ❷ (*form: consideration*) Überlegung *f*
delicacy [ˈdel·ɪ·kə·si] *n* ❶ FOOD Delikatesse *f* ❷ (*discretion*) Feingefühl *nt* ❸ (*fineness*) Feinheit *f; of features* Zartheit *f*
delicate [ˈdel·ɪ·kət] *adj* ❶ (*sensitive*) empfindlich; *china* zerbrechlich ❷ (*tricky*) heikel ❸ (*fine*) fein; *aroma, color* zart; **~ cycle** Feinwaschgang *m*
delicatessen [ˌdel·ɪ·kə·ˈtes·ən] *n* Feinkostgeschäft *nt*
delicious [dɪ·ˈlɪʃ·əs] *adj* köstlich, lecker
delight [dɪ·ˈlaɪt] **I.** *n* Freude *f;* **in ~** vor Freude **II.** *vt* erfreuen **III.** *vi* ■**to ~ in sth** Vergnügen bei etw *dat* empfinden
delighted [dɪ·ˈlaɪ·t̬ɪd] *adj* hocherfreut; *smile* vergnügt; ■**to be ~ to do sth** etw mit [großem] Vergnügen tun
delightful [dɪ·ˈlaɪt·fəl] *adj* wunderbar; *evening, village* reizend; *smile, person* charmant
delinquency [dɪ·ˈlɪŋ·kwən·si] *n* Straffälligkeit *f*
delinquent [dɪ·ˈlɪŋ·kwənt] **I.** *n* Delinquent(in) *m(f)* **II.** *adj* straffällig
delirious [dɪ·ˈlɪr·i·əs] *adj* ❶ im Delirium ❷ (*extremely happy*) *crowd* taumelnd
deliver [dɪ·ˈlɪv·ər] **I.** *vt* ❶ (*bring*) liefern; (*by mail*) zustellen; *newspapers* austragen; (*by car*) ausfahren; **to ~ a message to sb** jdm eine Nachricht überbringen ❷ (*recite*) *speech* halten; *verdict* verkünden ❸ (*direct*) *blow* geben; *rebuke* halten ❹ SPORTS *ball* werfen;

punch landen ❺ (*give birth*) zur Welt bringen; (*aid in giving birth*) entbinden **II.** *vi* ❶ (*supply*) liefern ❷ (*fulfill*) ■ **to ~ on sth** *promise* etw einhalten

deliverance [dɪ·ˈlɪv·ər·əns] *n* (*form*) Erlösung *f*

delivery [dɪ·ˈlɪv·ə·ri] *n* ❶ (*of goods*) Lieferung *f;* (*of mail*) Zustellung *f* ❷ (*manner of speaking*) Vortragsweise *f* ❸ (*birth*) Entbindung *f*

deˈlivery room *n* Kreißsaal *m*

deˈlivery van *n* Lieferwagen *m*

delta [ˈdel·tə] *n* Delta *nt*

delude [dɪ·ˈlud] *vt* täuschen; ■ **to ~ oneself** sich *dat* etwas vormachen

deluge [ˈdel·judʒ] **I.** *n* ❶ (*downpour*) Regenguss *m;* (*flood*) Flut *f* ❷ (*fig*) Flut *f* **II.** *vt* ■ **to be ~d** überflutet werden; (*fig*) überschüttet werden

delusion [dɪ·ˈlu·ʒən] *n* Täuschung *f;* **to suffer from** [*or* **be under**] **the ~ that ...** sich *dat* einbilden, dass ...

deluxe [dɪ·ˈlʌks] *adj* Luxus-

delve [delv] *vi* suchen (**for** nach +*dat*); **to ~ into sb's past** in jds Vergangenheit nachforschen

demagogue, **demagog** [ˈdem·ə·gɔg] *n* (*pej*) Demagoge, -in *m, f*

demand [dɪ·ˈmænd] **I.** *vt* ❶ (*insist upon*) verlangen ❷ (*need*) *skill, patience* erfordern **II.** *n* ❶ (*insistent request*) Forderung *f* (**for** nach +*dat*) ❷ (*requirement*) Bedarf *m;* COMM Nachfrage *f;* **in ~** gefragt ❸ (*expectations*) **to make ~s on sb/sth** Anforderungen *pl* an jdn/etw stellen; **she has a lot of ~s on her time** sie ist zeitlich sehr beansprucht

demanding [dɪ·ˈmæn·dɪŋ] *adj child, work* anstrengend; *job, person, test* anspruchsvoll

demarcation [ˌdi·mar·ˈkeɪ·ʃən] *n* Abgrenzung *f*

demean [dɪ·ˈmin] *vt* erniedrigen

demeaning [dɪ·ˈmi·nɪŋ] *adj* erniedrigend

demeanor [dɪ·ˈmi·nər] *n* (*form: behavior*) Verhalten *nt;* (*bearing*) Erscheinungsbild *nt*

demented [dɪ·ˈmen·tɪd] *adj* verrückt

demerit [dɪ·ˈmer·ɪt] *n* ❶ (*fault*) Schwäche *f* ❷ (*black mark*) Minuspunkt *m*

demilitarize [ˌdi·ˈmɪl·ɪ·tə·raɪz] *vt* entmilitarisieren

demise [dɪ·ˈmaɪz] *n* (*form*) Ableben *nt;* (*fig*) Niedergang *m*

demobilize [ˌdi·ˈmoʊ·bə·laɪz] **I.** *vt people* aus dem Kriegsdienst entlassen; *things* demobilisieren **II.** *vi* demobilisieren

democracy [dɪ·ˈmak·rə·si] *n* Demokratie *f*

democrat [ˈdem·ə·kræt] *n* Demokrat(in) *m(f)*

democratic [ˌdem·ə·ˈkræṭ·ɪk] *adj* demokratisch

democratization [dɪˌmak·rə·ṭɪ·ˈzeɪ·ʃən] *n* Demokratisierung *f*

democratize [dɪ·ˈmak·rə·taɪz] *vt* demokratisieren

demolish [dɪ·ˈmal·ɪʃ] *vt* ❶ *building* abreißen; *wall* einreißen ❷ (*refute, defeat*) zunichtemachen; *argument* widerlegen

demolition [ˌdem·ə·ˈlɪʃ·ən] *n* Abriss *m;* (*fig*) Widerlegung *f*

demon [ˈdi·mən] *n* (*evil spirit*) Dämon *m;* (*fig: wicked person*) Fiesling *m*

demonic [dɪ·ˈmɔn·ɪk] *adj* ❶ (*devilish*) dämonisch ❷ (*evil*) bösartig

demonstrable [dɪ·ˈman·strə·bəl] *adj* nachweislich

demonstrate [ˈdem·ən·streɪt] **I.** *vt* ❶ (*show*) zeigen; *operation* vorführen; *authority, knowledge* demonstrieren; *loyalty* beweisen ❷ (*prove*) nachweisen **II.** *vi* demonstrieren

demonstration [ˌdem·ən·ˈstreɪ·ʃən] *n* ❶ (*act of showing*) Demonstration *f,* Vorführung *f* ❷ (*proof*) Beweis *m* ❸ (*open expression*) *of one's feelings* Ausdruck *m* ❹ (*protest march*) Demonstration *f*

demonstrative [dɪ·ˈman·strə·ṭɪv] *adj* ❶ (*form: illustrative*) schlüssig ❷ (*expressing feelings*) offen ❸ LING ~ *pronoun* Demonstrativpronomen *nt*

demonstrator [ˈdem·ən·streɪ·ṭər] *n* ❶ (*of a product*) Vorführer(in) *m(f)* ❷ (*protester*) Demonstrant(in) *m(f)*

demoralize [dɪ·ˈmɔr·ə·laɪz] *vt* demoralisieren

demote [dɪ·ˈmoʊt] *vt* zurückstufen; MIL degradieren

demotion [dɪ·ˈmoʊ·ʃən] *n* MIL Degradierung *f*

demure [dɪ·ˈmjʊr] *adj* ❶ (*shy*) [sehr] schüchtern ❷ (*composed and reserved*) gesetzt

den [den] *n* ❶ (*lair*) Bau *m* ❷ (*study*) Arbeitszimmer *nt;* (*private room*) Bude *f,* Hobbyraum *m* ❸ (*children's playhouse*) Verschlag *m*

denial [dɪ·ˈnaɪ·əl] *n* ❶ (*statement*) Dementi *nt;* (*action*) Leugnen *nt kein pl* ❷ (*refusal*) Ablehnung *f* ❸ PSYCH **to be in ~** sich der Realität verschließen

denigrate [ˈden·ɪ·greɪt] *vt* verunglimpfen

denim [ˈden·ɪm] **I.** *n* ❶ (*material*) Denim® *m* ❷ (*fam*) ■ **~s** *pl* Jeans *f*[*pl*] **II.** *adj* Jeans-

Denmark [ˈden·mark] *n* Dänemark *nt*

denomination [dɪˌnam·ə·ˈneɪ·ʃən] *n* ❶ (*religious group*) Konfessionsgemeinschaft *f* ❷ (*unit of value*) Währungseinheit *f*

denominational [dɪˌnam·ə·ˈneɪ·ʃə·nəl] *adj* Konfessions-

denominator [dɪ·ˈnam·ə·neɪ·ṭər] *n* MATH Nenner *m*

denote [dɪ·ˈnoʊt] *vt* bedeuten

denouement [deɪ·ˈnu·maŋ] *n* (*form*) Ende *nt; film* Ausgang *m*

denounce [dɪ·ˈnaʊns] *vt* ❶ (*criticize*) anprangern ❷ (*accuse*) entlarven; ■ **to ~ sb to sb** jdn bei jdm denunzieren

dense <-r, -st> [dens] *adj* ❶ (*thick*) dicht ❷ (*fam: stupid*) dumm

densely [ˈdens·li] *adv* dicht

density [ˈden·sə·ṭi] *n* Dichte *f*

dent [dent] **I.** *n* ❶ (*hollow*) Beule *f,* Delle *f* ❷ (*fig*) Loch *nt* **II.** *vt* einbeulen

dental [ˈden·təl] *adj* Zahn-

D

dentist ['den·tɪst] *n* Zahnarzt, Zahnärztin *m, f*
dentistry ['den·tɪ·stri] *n* Zahnmedizin *f*
dentures ['den·tʃərz] *npl* [Zahn]prothese *f*
denunciation [dɪ·ˌnʌn·si·'eɪ·ʃən] *n* ① (*condemnation*) Anprangerung *f* ② LAW (*denouncing*) Denunziation *f*
Denver boot *n* Parkkralle *f*
deny <-ie-> [dɪ·'naɪ] *vt* ① (*declare untrue*) abstreiten; *accusation* zurückweisen ② (*refuse to grant*) ■**to ~ sth to sb** [*or* **sb sth**] jdm etw verweigern; *request* ablehnen
deodorant [di·'oʊ·dər·ənt] *n* Deo[dorant] *nt*
dep. [dep] *n* ① TRANSP *short for* **departure** Abf. *f*; *aircraft* Abfl. *m* ② *short for* **department** Abt.
depart [dɪ·'part] *vi* ① (*leave*) fortgehen; *plane* abfliegen, starten; *train* abfahren; *ship a.* ablegen ② (*differ*) abweichen (**from** von +*dat*)
department [dɪ·'part·mənt] *n* ① UNIV Institut *nt*; **the Philosophy D~** die philosophische Fakultät ② COMM Abteilung *f* ③ POL Ministerium *nt*; **State D~** Außenministerium *nt* ④ ADMIN Amt *nt*
departmental [ˌdi·part·'men·təl] *adj* ① UNIV Instituts- ② COMM Abteilungs- ③ POL Ministerial- ④ ADMIN Amts-
Department of De'fense *n* Verteidigungsministerium *nt*
Department of Motor 'Vehicles *n* Kfz-Zulassungsstelle *f*
de'partment store *n* Kaufhaus *nt*
departure [dɪ·'par·tʃər] *n* ① (*on a trip*) Abreise *f*, Abfahrt *f*; *plane* Abflug *m*; *ship* Ablegen *nt*, Abfahrt *f* ② (*deviation*) Abweichung *f*; *from policy* Abkehr *f*
de'parture lounge *n* Abfahrthalle *f*; AVIAT Abflughalle *f*
de'parture time *n* Abfahrtzeit *f*; AVIAT Abflugzeit *f*
depend [dɪ·'pend] *vi* ① (*rely on circumstance*) ■**to ~ [up]on sth** von etw *dat* abhängen; **that ~s** kommt darauf an ② (*get help from*) ■**to ~ [up]on sb/sth** von jdm/etw abhängig sein; *financially* finanziell auf jdn/etw angewiesen sein ③ (*rely on*) ■**to ~ [up]on sb/sth** sich auf jdn/etw verlassen
dependability [dɪ·ˌpen·də·'bɪl·ɪ·t̬i] *n* Zuverlässigkeit *f*, Verlässlichkeit *f*
dependable [dɪ·'pen·də·bəl] *adj* zuverlässig, verlässlich
dependence [dɪ·'pen·dəns] *n* Abhängigkeit *f*
dependency [dɪ·'pen·dən·si] *n* ① Abhängigkeit *f* ② (*dependent state*) Territorium *nt*
dependent [dɪ·'pen·dənt] **I.** *adj* ① (*conditional*) ■**to be ~ [up]on sth** von etw *dat* abhängen ② (*relying on*) ■**to be ~ [up]on sth** von etw *dat* abhängig sein; *help, goodwill* auf etw *akk* angewiesen sein **II.** *n* [finanziell] abhängige(r) Angehörige(r) *f(m)*
depict [dɪ·'pɪkt] *vt* (*form*) darstellen
depiction [dɪ·'pɪk·ʃən] *n* Darstellung *f*
deplete [dɪ·'plit] *vt* vermindern
depleted [dɪ·'pli·t̬ɪd] *adj* verbraucht
depletion [dɪ·'pli·ʃən] *n* Abbau *m*; *of resources, capital* Erschöpfung *f*
deplorable [dɪ·'plɔr·ə·bəl] *adj* beklagenswert; *conditions* erbärmlich
deplore [dɪ·'plɔr] *vt* ① (*disapprove*) verurteilen ② (*regret*) beklagen
deploy [dɪ·'plɔɪ] *vt* einsetzen
deployment [dɪ·'plɔɪ·mənt] *n* Einsatz *m*
depopulate [ˌdi·'pap·jə·leɪt] *vt* entvölkern
deport [dɪ·'pɔrt] *vt* ausweisen; *prisoner* deportieren
deportation [ˌdi·pɔr·'teɪ·ʃən] *n* Ausweisung *f*, Abschiebung *f*; *of prisoner* Deportation *f*
deportee [ˌdi·pɔr·'ti] *n* (*waiting to be deported*) Abzuschiebende(r) *f(m)*; (*already deported*) Abgeschobene(r) *f(m)*
deportment [dɪ·'pɔrt·mənt] *n* (*form*) Benehmen *nt*
depose [dɪ·'poʊz] *vt* absetzen; *monarch* entthronen
deposit [dɪ·'paz·ɪt] **I.** *vt* ① (*leave*) *person* absetzen; *thing* ablegen, abstellen; *luggage* deponieren ② (*in bank*) einzahlen; (*pay as first installment*) anzahlen **II.** *n* ① (*sediment*) Bodensatz *m*; (*layer*) Ablagerung *f*; (*underground layer*) Vorkommen *nt* ② (*in bank*) Einzahlung *f*; (*first installment*) Anzahlung *f*; (*security*) Kaution *f*; (*on a bottle*) Pfand *nt*
deposition [ˌdep·ə·'zɪʃ·ən] *n* ① (*form: removal from power*) Absetzung *f*; *of dictator* Sturz *m* ② LAW (*written statement*) Aussage *f*
depositor [dɪ·'paz·ə·t̬ər] *n* Anleger(in) *m(f)*
depot ['di·poʊ] *n* Depot *nt*
depraved [dɪ·'preɪvd] *adj* verdorben
depravity [dɪ·'præv·ɪ·t̬i] *n* Verdorbenheit *f*
deprecate ['dep·rɪ·keɪt] *vt* (*form*) ① (*show disapproval of*) missbilligen ② (*disparage*) schlechtmachen
deprecating ['dep·rə·keɪ·t̬ɪŋ] *adj* (*form*) ① (*strongly disapproving*) missbilligend; *stare* strafend ② (*disparaging*) herablassend; (*apologetic*) entschuldigend
depreciate [dɪ·'pri·ʃi·eɪt] **I.** *vi* an Wert verlieren **II.** *vt* entwerten
depreciation [dɪ·ˌpri·ʃi·'eɪ·ʃən] *n* Wertminderung *f*; *of currencies* Entwertung *f*
depress [dɪ·'pres] *vt* ① (*deject*) deprimieren ② (*reduce*) *prices* drücken ③ (*push*) *button, lever* niederdrücken; **to ~ a pedal** auf ein Pedal treten
depressant [dɪ·'pres·ənt] **I.** *n* Beruhigungsmittel *nt* **II.** *adj* beruhigend
depressed [dɪ·'prest] *adj* ① (*dejected*) deprimiert (**about, at, by, over** wegen +*gen*); **to feel ~** sich niedergeschlagen fühlen ② (*reduced*) *levels* reduziert, verringert ③ ECON *region, sector* heruntergekommen *fam*
depressing [dɪ·'pres·ɪŋ] *adj* deprimierend
depression [dɪ·'preʃ·ən] *n* ① (*sadness*) Depression *f*; **to suffer from ~** unter Depressionen leiden ② ECON Wirtschaftskrise *f* ③ METEO Tiefdruckgebiet *nt*
depressive [dɪ·'pres·ɪv] **I.** *n* Depressive(r) *f(m)*

II. *adj* depressiv
deprivation [ˌdep·rɪ·ˈveɪ·ʃən] *n* Entbehrung *f*
deprive [dɪ·ˈpraɪv] *vt* ■**to ~ sb [of] sth** jdm etw entziehen [*o* vorenthalten]
deprived [dɪ·ˈpraɪvd] *adj* sozial benachteiligt
dept. *n abbrev of* **department** Abt.
depth [depθ] *n* Tiefe *f a. fig;* **in the ~s of the forest** mitten im Wald; **in the ~s of despair** zutiefst verzweifelt; **in ~** gründlich ▶PHRASES: **to be** __**out**__ **of one's ~** für jdn zu hoch sein
ˈdepth charge *n* Wasserbombe *f*
deputation [ˌdep·jə·ˈteɪ·ʃən] *n* Abordnung *f*
deputize [ˈdep·jə·taɪz] *vi* ■**to ~ for sb** für jdn einspringen, jdn vertreten
deputy [ˈdep·jə·t̬i] **I.** *n* Stellvertreter(in) *m(f)* **II.** *adj* stellvertretend
derail [dɪ·ˈreɪl] *vt* ❶ *train* entgleisen lassen; ■**to be ~ed** entgleisen ❷ *plan, process* zum Scheitern bringen
derailment [dɪ·ˈreɪl·mənt] *n* Entgleisung *f*
deranged [dɪ·ˈreɪndʒd] *adj* geistesgestört
derby [ˈdɜr·bi] *n* ❶ SPORTS Derby *nt* ❷ (*hat*) Melone *f*
deregulate [di·ˈreg·jə·leɪt] *vt* ■**to ~ sth** etw deregulieren
deregulation [ˌdɪ·reg·jə·ˈleɪ·ʃən] *n* Deregulierung *f*
derelict [ˈder·ə·lɪkt] **I.** *adj* verlassen; **to lie ~** brachliegen **II.** *n* Obdachlose(r) *f(m)*
dereliction [ˌder·ə·ˈlɪk·ʃən] *n* ❶ (*negligence*) **~ of duty** Pflichtvernachlässigung *f* ❷ (*dilapidation*) Verwahrlosung *f*
deride [dɪ·ˈraɪd] *vt* (*form*) verspotten
derision [dɪ·ˈrɪʒ·ən] *n* Spott *m*
derisive [dɪ·ˈraɪ·sɪv] *adj* spöttisch
derisory [dɪ·ˈraɪ·sə·ri] *adj* ❶ (*derisive*) spöttisch ❷ (*ridiculously small*) lächerlich
derivation [ˌder·ɪ·ˈveɪ·ʃən] *n* ❶ (*origin*) Ursprung *m* ❷ (*process of evolving*) Ableitung *f*
derivative [dɪ·ˈrɪv·ə·t̬ɪv] **I.** *adj* (*pej*) nachgemacht **II.** *n* Ableitung *f,* Derivat *nt*
derive [dɪ·ˈraɪv] **I.** *vt* gewinnen; **sb ~s pleasure from doing sth** etw bereitet jdm Vergnügen **II.** *vi* ■**to ~ from sth** sich von etw *dat* ableiten [lassen]
dermatitis [ˌdɜr·mə·ˈtaɪ·t̬əs] *n* Hautreizung *f,* Dermatitis *f*
dermatologist [ˌdɜr·mə·ˈtal·ə·dʒɪst] *n* Dermatologe, -in *m, f,* Hautarzt, Hautärztin *m, f*
dermatology [ˌdɜr·mə·ˈtal·ə·dʒi] *n* Dermatologie *f*
derogatory [dɪ·ˈrag·ə·tɔr·i] *adj* abfällig
derrick [ˈder·ɪk] *n* ❶ (*crane*) Lastkran *m* ❷ (*over oil well*) Bohrturm *m*
desalinate [ˌdi·ˈsæl·ɪ·neɪt] *vt* entsalzen
desalination [di·ˌsæl·ɪ·ˈneɪ·ʃən] *n* Entsalzung *f*
descend [dɪ·ˈsend] **I.** *vi* ❶ (*go down*) *path* herunterführen; *person* heruntergehen ❷ (*be related*) ■**to be ~ed from sb/sth** von jdm/etw abstammen ❸ (*fall*) herabsinken ❹ (*fig: deteriorate*) ■**to ~ into sth** in etw *akk* umschlagen **II.** *vt* hinuntersteigen
descendant [dɪ·ˈsen·dənt] *n* Nachkomme *m*
descent [dɪ·ˈsent] *n* ❶ (*landing approach*) [Lande]anflug *m* ❷ (*way down*) Abstieg *m kein pl* ❸ (*fig: ancestry*) Abstammung *f*
describe [dɪ·ˈskraɪb] *vt* beschreiben; *experience* schildern
description [dɪ·ˈskrɪp·ʃən] *n* Beschreibung *f;* **of every ~** jeglicher Art
descriptive [dɪ·ˈskrɪp·tɪv] *adj* beschreibend
desecrate [ˈdes·ɪ·kreɪt] *vt* schänden
desecration [ˌdes·ɪ·ˈkreɪ·ʃən] *n* Schändung *f*
desegregate [ˌdi·ˈseg·rɪ·geɪt] *vt* **to ~ armed forces/schools/universities** die Rassentrennung in der Armee/in der Schule/an der Universität aufheben
desegregation [di·ˌseg·rɪ·ˈgeɪ·ʃən] *n* Aufhebung *f* der Rassentrennung
desensitize [ˌdi·ˈsen·sɪ·taɪz] *vt* ❶ (*make less sensitive to*) abstumpfen ❷ MED desensibilisieren
desert[1] [ˈdez·ərt] *n* Wüste *f a. fig;* **~ island** verlassene Insel
desert[2] [dɪ·ˈzɜrt] **I.** *vi* MIL desertieren **II.** *vt* verlassen
deserted [dɪ·ˈzɜr·t̬ɪd] *adj* verlassen; *of town* ausgestorben
deserter [dɪ·ˈzɜr·t̬ər] *n* Deserteur(in) *m(f)*
desertion [dɪ·ˈzɜr·ʃən] *n* Verlassen *nt;* MIL Desertion *f*
deserts [dɪ·ˈzɜrts] *npl* ■**to get one's [just] ~** seine Quittung bekommen
deserve [dɪ·ˈzɜrv] *vt* (*merit*) verdienen
deservedly [dɪ·ˈzɜr·vɪd·li] *adv* verdientermaßen
deserving [dɪ·ˈzɜr·vɪŋ] *adj* verdienstvoll; **a ~ cause** eine gute Sache
design [dɪ·ˈzaɪn] **I.** *vt* ❶ (*plan*) entwerfen; *books* gestalten; *cars* konstruieren ❷ (*intend*) ■**to be ~ed for sb** für jdn konzipiert sein; **these measures are ~ed to reduce pollution** diese Maßnahmen sollen die Luftverschmutzung verringern **II.** *n* ❶ (*plan or drawing*) Entwurf *m* ❷ (*art*) Design *nt; of building* Bauart *f; of machine* Konstruktion *f;* (*pattern*) Muster *nt* **III.** *adj* Konstruktions-
designate [ˈdez·ɪg·neɪt] **I.** *vt* ■**to ~ sb** jdn ernennen (**as** zu +*dat*); ■**to ~ sb to do sth** jdn mit etw *dat* beauftragen **II.** *adj after n* designiert
designated ˈdriver *n Person, die sich bereit erklärt, nüchtern zu bleiben und die Freunde sicher nach Hause zu fahren*
designation [ˌdez·ɪg·ˈneɪ·ʃən] *n* ❶ (*title*) Bezeichnung *f* ❷ (*act of designating*) Festlegung *f*
designer [dɪ·ˈzaɪ·nər] *n* Designer(in) *m(f)*
desirable [dɪ·ˈzaɪr·ə·bəl] *adj* ❶ (*worth having*) erstrebenswert; (*popular*) begehrt; *advantageous* erwünscht ❷ (*sexually attractive*) begehrenswert
desire [dɪ·ˈzaɪr] **I.** *vt* ❶ (*want*) wünschen ❷ (*be sexually attracted to*) begehren **II.** *n* ❶ (*strong wish*) Verlangen *nt;* (*stronger*) Sehnsucht *f;* (*request*) Wunsch *m* ❷ (*sexual*

D

need) Begierde *f*

desist [dɪ·ˈsɪst] *vi* (*form*) einhalten; **to ~ from doing sth** davon absehen, etw zu tun

desk [desk] *n* ❶ (*table for writing*) Schreibtisch *m* ❷ (*service counter*) Schalter *m*

ˈ**desk lamp** *n* Schreibtischlampe *f*

ˈ**desktop** *n* ❶ COMPUT Desktop *m* ❷ (*desk surface*) Tischoberfläche *f*

desolate [ˈdes·ə·lət] *adj* ❶ (*barren*) trostlos ❷ (*unhappy*) niedergeschlagen

desolation [ˌdes·ə·ˈleɪ·ʃən] *n* ❶ (*barrenness*) Trostlosigkeit *f* ❷ (*sadness*) Verzweiflung *f*

despair [dɪ·ˈsper] **I.** *n* (*feeling of hopelessness*) Verzweiflung *f*; **in ~** verzweifelt **II.** *vi* verzweifeln (**at, of** an +*dat*); **to ~ of doing sth** die Hoffnung aufgeben, etw zu tun

despairing [dɪ·ˈsper·ɪŋ] *adj* verzweifelt

despatch [dɪ·ˈspætʃ] *n, vt see* **dispatch**

desperate [ˈdes·pər·ɪt] *adj attempt* verzweifelt; (*great*) dringend; ■ **to be ~ for sth** etw dringendst brauchen

desperation [ˌdes·pə·ˈreɪ·ʃən] *n* Verzweiflung *f*; **in** [*or* **out of**] **~** aus Verzweiflung

despicable [dɪ·ˈspɪk·ə·bəl] *adj* abscheulich

despise [dɪ·ˈspaɪz] *vt* verachten

despite [dɪ·ˈspaɪt] *prep* trotz +*gen*

despondent [dɪ·ˈspan·dənt] *adj* niedergeschlagen

dessert [dɪ·ˈzɜrt] *n* Nachtisch *m*, Dessert *nt*

destabilization [ˌdi·ˈsteɪ·bə·lɪ·ˈzeɪ·ʃən] *n* Destabilisierung *f*

destabilize [ˌdi·ˈsteɪ·bə·laɪz] *vt* destabilisieren

destination [ˌdes·tə·ˈneɪ·ʃən] *n* Ziel *nt*; *of trip* Reiseziel *nt*; *of letter* Bestimmungsort *m*

destiny [ˈdes·tə·ni] *n* Schicksal *nt*

destitute [ˈdes·tɪ·tut] **I.** *adj* mittellos **II.** *n* ■ **the ~** *pl* die Bedürftigen

destitution [ˌdes·tɪ·ˈtu·ʃən] *n* Armut *f*

destroy [dɪ·ˈstrɔɪ] *vt* ❶ (*demolish*) *structure* zerstören ❷ (*do away with*) *possibility* vernichten ❸ (*kill*) auslöschen; *herd* abschlachten; *pet* einschläfern ❹ (*ruin*) zunichtemachen; *reputation* ruinieren

destroyer [dɪ·ˈstrɔɪ·ər] *n* MIL Zerstörer *m*

destructible [dɪ·ˈstrʌk·tə·bəl] *adj* zerstörbar

destruction [dɪ·ˈstrʌk·ʃən] *n* Zerstörung *f*; **mass ~** Massenvernichtung *f*

destructive [dɪ·ˈstrʌk·tɪv] *adj* zerstörerisch; *influence, person* destruktiv

destructiveness [dɪ·ˈstrʌk·tɪv·nɪs] *n of person* Zerstörungswut *f*; *of explosive* Sprengkraft *f*

desultory [ˈdes·əl·tɔr·i] *adj* (*form*) halbherzig

detach [dɪ·ˈtætʃ] *vt* abnehmen; (*without reattaching*) abtrennen

detachable [dɪ·ˈtætʃ·ə·bəl] *adj* abnehmbar

detached [dɪ·ˈtætʃt] *adj* ❶ (*separated*) abgelöst ❷ (*aloof*) distanziert

detachment [dɪ·ˈtætʃ·mənt] *n* ❶ (*aloofness*) Distanziertheit *f* ❷ (*of soldiers*) Einsatztruppe *f*

detail [dɪ·ˈteɪl] **I.** *n* ❶ (*item of information*) Detail *nt*, Einzelheit *f*; **further ~s** nähere Informationen; **to go into ~** ins Detail gehen, auf die Einzelheiten eingehen; **in ~** im Detail ❷ (*unimportant item*) Kleinigkeit *f* ❸ ■ **~s** *pl* (*vital statistics*) Personalien *pl* **II.** *vt* ❶ (*explain*) ausführlich erläutern ❷ (*specify*) einzeln aufführen

detailed [dɪ·ˈteɪld] *adj* detailliert; *description, report* ausführlich; *study* eingehend

detain [dɪ·ˈteɪn] *vt* ❶ LAW in Haft nehmen, inhaftieren ❷ (*form: delay*) aufhalten

detainee [ˌdi·teɪ·ˈni] *n* Häftling *m*

detect [dɪ·ˈtekt] *vt* ❶ (*discover presence of*) entdecken; *disease* feststellen; *mine* aufspüren; *smell* bemerken; *sound* wahrnehmen ❷ (*catch in act*) ertappen

detectable [dɪ·ˈtek·tə·bəl] *adj* feststellbar; *change* wahrnehmbar

detection [dɪ·ˈtek·ʃən] *n* ❶ Entdeckung *f*; *of cancer* Feststellung *f* ❷ (*by detective*) Ermittlungsarbeit *f*

detective [dɪ·ˈtek·tɪv] *n* ❶ (*police officer*) Kriminalbeamte(r) *m*, Kriminalbeamte [*o* -in] *f* ❷ (*private*) [Privat]detektiv(in) *m(f)*

detector [dɪ·ˈtek·tər] *n* Detektor *m*; **smoke ~** Rauchmelder *m*

detention [dɪ·ˈten·ʃən] *n* ❶ (*state*) Haft *f*; **to be kept in ~** in Haft gehalten werden; **to be kept in pretrial ~** in Untersuchungshaft sitzen *fam* ❷ (*act*) Festnahme *f* ❸ SCH Nachsitzen *nt kein pl*; **to get** [*or* **have**] **~** nachsitzen müssen

deˈtention center *n* Untersuchungsgefängnis *nt*

deter <-rr-> [dɪ·ˈtɜr] *vt* verhindern; (*put off*) *person* abschrecken, abhalten (**from** von +*dat*)

detergent [dɪ·ˈtɜr·dʒənt] *n* Reinigungsmittel *nt*; **laundry ~** Waschmittel *nt*

deteriorate [dɪ·ˈtɪr·i·ə·reɪt] *vi* ❶ (*become worse*) sich verschlechtern; *sales* zurückgehen ❷ (*disintegrate*) verfallen; *leather, wood* sich zersetzen; *rubber, leather* brüchig werden

deterioration [dɪ·ˌtɪr·i·ə·ˈreɪ·ʃən] *n* ❶ (*worsening*) Verschlechterung *f* ❷ ECON, TECH Qualitätsverlust *m* ❸ (*disintegration*) Verfall *m*; *of metal, wood* Zersetzung *f*

determination [dɪ·ˌtɜr·mɪ·ˈneɪ·ʃən] *n* ❶ (*resolve*) Entschlossenheit *f* ❷ (*determining*) Bestimmung *f*

determine [dɪ·ˈtɜr·mɪn] *vt* ❶ (*decide*) entscheiden; ■ **to ~ that ...** beschließen, dass ... ❷ (*find out*) ermitteln, feststellen, herausfinden ❸ (*influence*) bestimmen; **genetically ~d** genetisch festgelegt

determined [dɪ·ˈtɜr·mɪnd] *adj* entschlossen

deterrent [dɪ·ˈtɜr·ənt] **I.** *n* Abschreckung *f*, Abschreckungsmittel *nt* **II.** *adj* abschreckend

detest [dɪ·ˈtest] *vt* verabscheuen

dethrone [dɪ·ˈθroʊn] *vt* entthronen

detonate [ˈdet·ə·neɪt] *vi, vt* detonieren

detonation [ˌdet·ə·ˈneɪ·ʃən] *n* Detonation *f*

detonator [ˈdet·ə·neɪ·t̬ər] *n* [Spreng]zünder *m*

detour [ˈdi·tʊr] *n* ❶ TRANSP Umleitung *f*

❷ (*deviation*) Umweg *m*
detox ['di·taks] *n see* **detoxification** Entzug *m;* ■ **to be in ~** auf Entzug sein
detract [dɪ·'trækt] *vi* ■ **to ~ from sth** etw beeinträchtigen
detractor [dɪ·'træk·tər] *n* Kritiker(in) *m(f)*
detriment ['det·rə·mənt] *n* Nachteil *m*
detrimental [ˌdet·rɪ·'men·təl] *adj* schädlich
deuce [dus] *n* ❶ (*cards, dice*) Zwei *f* ❷ TENNIS Einstand *m*
devaluation [ˌdi·væl·ju·'eɪ·ʃən] *n* Abwertung *f*
devalue [ˌdi·'væl·ju] *vt* abwerten
devastate ['dev·ə·steɪt] *vt* vernichten; *region* verwüsten; (*fam*) umhauen
devastated ['dev·ə·steɪ·ṭɪd] *adj* völlig fertig *fam,* total down *sl*
devastating ['dev·ə·steɪ·ṭɪŋ] *adj* ❶ (*destructive*) verheerend, vernichtend *a. fig* ❷ (*fig fam: positively overwhelming*) umwerfend; *smile* unwiderstehlich; (*negatively*) niederschmetternd
devastation [ˌdev·ə·'steɪ·ʃən] *n* ❶ (*destruction*) Verwüstung *f* ❷ (*of person*) Verzweiflung *f*
develop [dɪ·'vel·əp] **I.** *vi* sich entwickeln (**into** zu +*dat*); *abilities* sich entfalten **II.** *vt* ❶ entwickeln; *habit* annehmen; *plan* ausarbeiten; *skills* weiterentwickeln ❷ ARCHIT erschließen [und bebauen] ❸ PHOT entwickeln
developed [dɪ·'vel·əpt] *adj* ❶ entwickelt ❷ ARCHIT erschlossen
developer [dɪ·'vel·ə·pər] *n* ❶ **late ~** Spätentwickler(in) *m(f)* ❷ (*person*) Bauunternehmer(in) *m(f);* (*company*) Baufirma *f,* Bauunternehmen *nt* ❸ PHOT Entwickler *m*
developing [dɪ·'vel·ə·pɪŋ] *adj* sich entwickelnd
development [dɪ·'vel·əp·mənt] *n* ❶ (*act, event, process*) Entwicklung *f* ❷ ARCHIT Bau *m;* (*area*) Baugebiet *nt;* (*buildings*) **housing ~** Siedlung *f;* **industrial ~** Industriegebiet *nt*
deviant ['di·vi·ənt] SOCIOL **I.** *n* **to be a** [**sexual**] **~** [im sexuellen Verhalten] von der Norm abweichen **II.** *adj behavior* abweichend
deviate ['di·vi·eɪt] *vi from norm* abweichen; *from route* sich entfernen
deviation [ˌdi·vi·'eɪ·ʃən] *n* Abweichung *f*
device [dɪ·'vaɪs] *n* ❶ (*machine*) Gerät *nt,* Vorrichtung *f* ❷ (*method*) Verfahren *nt;* **stylistic ~** Stilmittel *nt* ❸ (*bomb*) **incendiary ~** Brandsatz *m*
devil ['dev·əl] *n* ❶ Teufel *m;* ■ **the D~** der Teufel ❷ (*fig*) Teufel(in) *m(f)* ❸ (*fam: sly person*) alter Fuchs; (*daring person*) Teufelskerl *m* ❹ (*fam: affectionately*) **little ~** kleiner Schlingel *fam;* **lucky ~** Glückspilz *m* ► PHRASES: **to be between the ~ and the deep blue sea** sich in einer Zwickmühle befinden; **like the ~** wie besessen
devilish ['dev·ə·lɪʃ] *adj* teuflisch; *situation* verteufelt
devious ['di·vi·əs] *adj* ❶ (*dishonest*) *person* verschlagen; *plan* krumm ❷ (*roundabout*) gewunden; **to take a ~ route** einen Umweg fahren
devise [dɪ·'vaɪz] *vt* erdenken; *plan* aushecken
devoid [dɪ·'vɔɪd] *adj* ■ **to be ~ of sth** ohne etw sein
devolve [dɪ·'valv] (*form*) **I.** *vi* ❶ (*transfer*) übergehen ([**up**]**on** auf +*akk*) ❷ (*deteriorate*) entarten (**into** zu +*dat*) **II.** *vt* übertragen ([**up**]**on** auf +*akk*)
devote [dɪ·'voʊt] *vt* widmen; *one's time* opfern
devoted [dɪ·'voʊ·ṭɪd] *adj admirer* begeistert; *dog* anhänglich; *follower, friend* treu; *husband, mother* hingebungsvoll
devotee [ˌdev·ə·'ti] *n of an artist* Verehrer(in) *m(f); of a leader* Anhänger(in) *m(f); of a cause* Verfechter(in) *m(f); of music* Liebhaber(in) *m(f)*
devotion [dɪ·'voʊ·ʃən] *n* ❶ (*loyalty*) Ergebenheit *f* ❷ (*dedication*) Hingabe *f* (**to** an +*akk*) ❸ (*affection*) *of husband, wife* Liebe *f; of children* Anhänglichkeit *f; of an admirer* Verehrung *f*
devour [dɪ·'vaʊ·ər] *vt* verschlingen *a. fig*
devouring [dɪ·'vaʊ·ər·ɪŋ] *adj* verzehrend
devout [dɪ·'vaʊt] *adj* REL fromm; (*fig*) [sehr] engagiert; *hope, wish* sehnlich
dew [du] *n* Tau *m*
'dewdrop *n* Tautropfen *m*
dexterity [ˌdek·'ster·ɪ·ṭi] *n* ❶ (*of hands*) Geschicklichkeit *f* ❷ (*cleverness*) Gewandtheit *f;* (*of speech*) Redegewandtheit *f*
dexterous ['dek·stər·əs] *adj* gewandt; *fingers* geschickt
dextrose ['dek·stroʊs] *n* Traubenzucker *m*
dextrous ['dek·strəs] *adj see* **dexterous**
diabetes [ˌdaɪ·ə·'bi·ṭɪz] *n* Zuckerkrankheit *f*
diabetic [ˌdaɪ·ə·'beṭ·ɪk] **I.** *n* Diabetiker(in) *m(f)* **II.** *adj* ❶ (*having diabetes*) zuckerkrank ❷ (*for diabetics*) Diabetiker-
diabolical [ˌdaɪ·ə·'bal·ɪ·kəl] *adj* ❶ (*of Devil*) Teufels- ❷ (*evil*) teuflisch
diagnose [ˌdaɪ·əg·'noʊs] *vt* ❶ MED diagnostizieren ❷ (*discover*) erkennen; *fault, problem* feststellen
diagnosis <*pl* -ses> [ˌdaɪ·əg·'noʊ·sɪs] *n* ❶ *of a disease* Diagnose *f* ❷ *of a problem* Beurteilung *f*
diagnostic [ˌdaɪ·əg·'nas·tɪk] *adj.* diagnostisch
diagonal [daɪ·'æg·ə·nəl] **I.** *adj line* diagonal, schräg **II.** *n* Diagonale *f*
diagram ['daɪ·ə·græm] *n* schematische Darstellung; MATH Diagramm *nt*
dial ['daɪ·əl] **I.** *n of clock* Zifferblatt; *of instrument, radio* Skala *f; of telephone* Wählscheibe *f* **II.** *vi, vt* <-l- *or* -ll-> wählen; **to ~ the wrong number** sich verwählen
dialect ['daɪ·ə·lekt] *n* Dialekt *m*
dialing ['daɪ·əl·ɪŋ] *n* Wählen *nt*
dialogue, dialog ['daɪ·ə·lag] *n* Dialog *m*
'dial tone *n* Wählton *m*
dialysis [daɪ·'æl·ə·sɪs] *n* Dialyse *f*
diameter [daɪ·'æm·ə·ṭər] *n* Durchmesser *m*

diametrically [ˌdaɪ·ə·ˈmet·rɪ·kə·li] *adv* ~ **opposed** völlig entgegengesetzt
diamond [ˈdaɪ·ə·mənd] *n* ① (*stone*) Diamant *m* ② MATH Raute *f*, Rhombus *m* ③ CARDS Karo *nt*; **ace/king of ~s** Karoass *nt*/-könig *m* ④ (*fig: person*) **he's a ~ in the rough** er ist rau, aber herzlich
diamond anniˈversary *n* diamantene Hochzeit
diaper [ˈdaɪ·pər] *n* Windel *f*; **disposable ~** Wegwerfwindel *f*
diaphanous [daɪ·ˈæf·ə·nəs] *adj* (*liter*) durchscheinend
diaphragm [ˈdaɪ·ə·fræm] *n* Diaphragma *nt*, Pessar *nt*
diarrhea [ˌdaɪ·ə·ˈri·ə] *n* Durchfall *m*
diary [ˈdaɪ·ə·ri] *n* ① (*book*) Tagebuch *nt* ② (*schedule*) [Termin]kalender *m*
diatribe [ˈdaɪ·ə·traɪb] *n* (*form: verbal*) Schmährede *f*; (*written*) Schmähschrift *f*
dice [daɪs] **I.** *n* ① *pl of* **die** Würfel *m* ② (*game*) Würfelspiel *nt* ▶ PHRASES: **no** ~ (*sl*) kommt [überhaupt] nicht in Frage *fam*; (*of no use*) vergiss es *fam* **II.** *vt* FOOD würfeln
dicey [ˈdaɪ·si] *adj* (*fam*) riskant
dick [dɪk] *n* ① (*vulg: penis*) Schwanz *m* ② (*offensive: jerk*) Idiot *m pej*
Dictaphone® [ˈdɪk·tə·foʊn] *n* Diktaphon® *nt*
dictate [ˈdɪk·teɪt] **I.** *vt* ① (*command*) befehlen ② *a letter, memo* diktieren **II.** *vi* ① (*issue commands*) ■**to ~ to sb** jdm Vorschriften machen ② (*read aloud*) diktieren
dictation [dɪk·ˈteɪ·ʃən] *n* Diktat *nt*
dictator [ˈdɪk·teɪ·t̬ər] *n* ① POL (*a. fig*) Diktator *m* ② (*of text*) Diktierende(r) *f(m)*
dictatorial [ˌdɪk·tə·ˈtɔr·i·əl] *adj* diktatorisch
dictatorship [dɪk·ˈteɪ·t̬ər·ʃɪp] *n* Diktatur *f*
diction [ˈdɪk·ʃən] *n* Ausdrucksweise *f*
dictionary [ˈdɪk·ʃə·ner·i] *n* Wörterbuch *nt*
did [dɪd] *pt of* **do**
didactic [daɪ·ˈdæk·tɪk] *adj* didaktisch
diddle [ˈdɪd·əl] *vi* (*fam: tinker*) ■**to ~ [around] with sth** an etw *dat* [he]rummachen
didn't [ˈdɪd·ənt] = **did not** *see* **do**
die¹ <-y-> [daɪ] **I.** *vi* ① (*cease to live*) sterben, umkommen (**of** vor +*dat*); **to ~ of** [*or* **from**] **cancer** an Krebs sterben; **to ~ laughing** sich totlachen, sich kaputtlachen; **to ~ of hunger** verhungern; **to ~ of thirst** verdursten ② (*fig: end*) vergehen; *love* sterben ③ (*fam: stop functioning*) kaputtgehen; *engine* stehen bleiben; *battery* leer werden; *flame, light* [v]erlöschen ▶ PHRASES: **to be dying to do sth** darauf brennen, etw zu tun; **I'm dying to hear the news** ich bin wahnsinnig gespannt, die Neuigkeiten zu erfahren; **to be dying for sth** großes Verlangen nach etw *dat* haben **II.** *vt* sterben; **he ~d a lonely death** einsam sterben
◆**die away** *vi* schwinden; *anger, enthusiasm, wind* sich allmählich legen; *sound* verhallen
◆**die back** *vi* absterben
◆**die down** *vi noise* leiser werden; *rain, wind* schwächer werden; *storm* sich legen; *excitement* abklingen
◆**die off** *vi* aussterben; BOT absterben
◆**die out** *vi* aussterben
die² [daɪ] *n* <*pl* dice> (*for games*) Würfel *m* ▶ PHRASES: **the ~ is cast** die Würfel sind gefallen
ˈdiehard I. *n* (*pej*) Dickschädel *m* **II.** *adj* unermüdlich; *liberal* Erz-
diesel [ˈdi·zəl] *n* ① (*fuel*) Diesel[kraftstoff] *m*; **to run on ~** mit Diesel fahren ② (*vehicle*) Dieselfahrzeug *nt*, Diesel *m*
ˈdiesel engine *n* Dieselmotor *m*
ˈdiesel oil *n* Dieselöl *nt*
diet [ˈdaɪ·ət] **I.** *n* ① (*food and drink*) Nahrung *f*; **balanced ~** ausgewogene Kost ② MED Diät *f*, Schonkost *f*; **on a ~** auf Diät ③ (*plan for losing weight*) Diät *f*, Schlankheitskur *f*; **to go on a ~** eine Diät machen **II.** *vi* Diät halten **III.** *adj* Diät-
dietary [ˈdaɪ·ɪ·ter·i] *adj* ① (*of usual food*) Ernährungs-, Ess- ② (*of medical diet*) Diät-
dietary ˈfiber *n* Ballaststoffe *pl*
dieter [ˌdaɪ·ə·tər] *n Person, die eine Diät macht*
dietician, dietitian [ˌdaɪ·ə·ˈtɪʃ·ən] *n* Diätassistent(in) *m(f)*
ˈdiet pill *n* Schlankheitspille *f*
differ [ˈdɪf·ər] *vi* ① (*be unlike*) sich unterscheiden ② (*not agree*) verschiedener Meinung sein
difference [ˈdɪf·ər·əns] *n* ① Unterschied *m*; **to make all the ~** die Sache völlig ändern ② FIN Differenz *f*; MATH (*after subtraction*) Rest *m* ③ (*disagreement*) ~ [**of opinion**] Meinungsverschiedenheit *f*
different [ˈdɪf·ər·ənt] *adj* ① anders *präd*, andere(r, s) *attr*; ■**to be ~ from** [*or* **than**] **sb/sth** sich von jdm/etw unterscheiden ② (*unusual*) ungewöhnlich; **to do something ~** etwas Außergewöhnliches tun
differential [ˌdɪf·ə·ˈren·tʃəl] **I.** *n* ① MATH Differenzial *nt* ② MECH Differenzial[getriebe] *nt* ③ (*difference*) Unterschied *m*; ECON Gefälle *nt* **II.** *adj* ① (*different*) unterschiedlich; **~ treatment** Ungleichbehandlung *f* ② MATH, MECH Differenzial-
differentiate [ˌdɪf·ə·ˈren·tʃi·eɪt] *vi, vt* unterscheiden
differentiation [ˌdɪf·ə·ren·tʃi·ˈeɪ·ʃən] *n* Differenzierung *f*
difficult [ˈdɪf·ɪ·kəlt] *adj* schwierig, schwer; **to find it ~ to do sth** es schwer finden, etw zu tun; *job, trip* beschwerlich
difficulty [ˈdɪf·ɪ·kəl·ti] *n* ① (*effort*) **with ~** mit Mühe ② (*problematic nature*) *of a task* Schwierigkeit *f* ③ (*trouble*) Problem *nt*, Schwierigkeit *f*; **to have ~ doing sth** Schwierigkeiten dabei haben, etw zu tun
diffident [ˈdɪf·ɪ·dənt] *adj* (*form*) ① (*shy*) zaghaft ② (*reserved*) zurückhaltend
diffusion [dɪ·ˈfju·ʒən] *n* Verbreitung *f*; SOCIOL Ausbreitung *f*; CHEM, PHYS Diffusion *f*
dig [dɪg] **I.** *n* ① ARCHEOL Ausgrabung *f*

❷ (*thrust*) Stoß *m* ❸ (*fig: cutting remark*) Seitenhieb *m* (**at** auf +*akk*) **II.** *vi* <-gg-, dug, dug> graben (**for** nach +*dat*); **her nails dug into his palm** ihre Nägel gruben sich in seine Hand; **to ~ in one's pocket** in der Tasche graben **III.** *vt* <-gg-, dug, dug> ❶ (*with a shovel*) graben; *ditch* ausheben ❷ ARCHEOL ausgraben ❸ **to ~ sb in the ribs** jdn [mit dem Ellenbogen] anstoßen ❹ (*sl: enjoy*) ■ **to ~ sth** auf etw *akk* stehen *sl*

◆**dig in I.** *vi* ❶ MIL sich eingraben ❷ (*fam: start eating*) reinhauen *fam* **II.** *vt fertilizer* untergraben ▶ PHRASES: **to ~ in one's heels** auf stur schalten

◆**dig out** *vt* ausgraben *a. fig*

◆**dig up** *vt* ❶ (*turn over*) umgraben ❷ (*remove*) ausgraben; ARCHEOL freilegen ❸ (*fig: find out*) herausfinden

digest I. *vt* [daɪˈdʒest] ❶ verdauen *a. fig* ❷ CHEM auflösen **II.** *n* [ˈdaɪ·dʒest] Auswahl *f* (**of** aus +*dat*)

digestible [daɪˈdʒes·tə·bəl] *adj* verdaulich

digestion [daɪˈdʒes·tʃən] *n* Verdauung *f*

digger [ˈdɪg·ər] *n* (*sb who digs*) Gräber(in) *m(f);* ARCHEOL Ausgräber(in) *m(f)*

digit [ˈdɪdʒ·ɪt] *n* ❶ MATH Ziffer *f*; **three-~ number** dreistellige Zahl ❷ (*finger*) Finger *m;* (*toe*) Zehe *f*

digital [ˈdɪdʒ·ɪ·t̬əl] *adj* digital, Digital-

digital ˈradio *n* Digitalradio *nt*

digital ˈtelevision *n* Digitalfernsehen *nt*

digitize [ˈdɪdʒ·ɪ·taɪz] *vt* COMPUT digitalisieren

dignified [ˈdɪg·nɪ·faɪd] *adj* würdig, würdevoll; *silence* ehrfürchtig

dignify <-ie-> [ˈdɪg·nɪ·faɪ] *vt* Würde verleihen

dignitary [ˈdɪg·nə·ter·i] *n* Würdenträger(in) *m(f)*

dignity [ˈdɪg·nɪ·t̬i] *n* Würde *f*

digress [daɪˈgres] *vi* abschweifen

dike[1] [daɪk] *n* ❶ (*wall*) Deich *m* ❷ (*drainage channel*) [Abfluss]graben *m*

dike[2] *n* (*pej sl*) *see* **dyke**[2]

dilapidated [dɪˈlæp·ɪ·deɪ·t̬ɪd] *adj house* verfallen; *estate* heruntergekommen; *car* klapprig

dilate [ˈdaɪ·leɪt] **I.** *vi* sich weiten **II.** *vt* erweitern

dilation [daɪˈleɪ·ʃən] *n* Erweiterung *f*

dilemma [dɪˈlem·ə] *n* Dilemma *nt*

dilettante [ˌdɪl·ə·ˈtant] *n* <*pl* -s *or* -ti> Dilettant(in) *m(f)*

diligence [ˈdɪl·ɪ·dʒəns] *n* ❶ (*industriousness*) Fleiß *m;* (*enthusiasm*) Eifer *m* ❷ LAW (*carefulness*) Sorgfalt *f*

diligent [ˈdɪl·ɪ·dʒənt] *adj* ❶ (*hard-working*) fleißig; (*enthusiastic*) eifrig ❷ (*painstaking*) sorgfältig

dill [dɪl] *n* Dill *m*

dilly-dally <-ie-> [ˈdɪl·ɪ·dæl·i] *vi* (*pej fam*) schwanken

dilute [daɪˈlut] **I.** *vt* ❶ (*mix*) verdünnen ❷ (*fig*) abschwächen **II.** *adj* verdünnt

dilution [daɪˈlu·ʃən] *n* ❶ (*act*) Verdünnen *nt* ❷ (*liquid*) Verdünnung *f*

dim <-mm-> [dɪm] **I.** *adj* ❶ (*not bright*) schwach, trüb; (*poorly lit*) schumm[e]rig ❷ (*indistinct*) undeutlich; *recollection, shape* verschwommen ❸ (*fam: slow to understand*) schwer von Begriff **II.** *vt* abdunkeln; *headlights* abblenden; **to ~ the lights** das Licht dämpfen **III.** *vi lights* dunkler werden; *hopes* schwächer werden

dime [daɪm] *n* Dime *m,* Zehncentstück *nt* ▶ PHRASES: **a ~ a dozen** spottbillig

dimension [dɪˈmen·ʃən] *n* Dimension *f*

-dimensional [dɪˈmen·ʃə·nəl] *in compounds* (*1-, 2-, 3-*) -dimensional

diminish [dɪˈmɪn·ɪʃ] **I.** *vt* vermindern **II.** *vi* sich vermindern; *pain* nachlassen; *influence, value* abnehmen

diminutive [dɪˈmɪn·jə·t̬ɪv] **I.** *adj* ❶ (*tiny*) winzig ❷ LING diminutiv **II.** *n* LING Verkleinerungsform *f*

dimmer [ˈdɪm·ər], **dimmer switch** [ˈdɪm·ər-] *n* Dimmer *m,* Helligkeitsregler *m;* AUTO Abblendschalter *m*

dimness [ˈdɪm·nɪs] *n* ❶ (*lack of light*) Trübheit *f; of a lamp* Mattheit *f; of a memory* Undeutlichkeit *f; of an outline* Unschärfe *f; of a room* Düsterkeit *f* ❷ (*lack of intelligence*) Beschränktheit *f*

dimple [ˈdɪm·pəl] *n* (*in cheeks, chin*) Grübchen *nt*

dimpled [ˈdɪm·pəld] *adj* mit Grübchen; ■ **to be ~** Grübchen haben

din [dɪn] *n* (*liter*) Lärm *m;* **to make a ~** Krach machen

dine [daɪn] *vi* (*form*) speisen

diner [ˈdaɪ·nər] *n* ❶ (*person*) Speisende(r) *f(m);* (*in restaurant*) Gast *m* ❷ *Restaurant am Straßenrand mit Theke und Tischen* ❸ RAIL *see* **dining car**

In den USA ist ein **diner** eine Art Restaurant, das aus einer Theke und aus in Abteilen angeordneten Tischen besteht. Ursprünglich hatten die **diners** der 50er Hamburger, Pommes frites und weitere schnelle Gerichte im Sortiment. Heute sind sie für ihre Karten bekannt, die so lange wie ein Roman sind. Man kann dort ebenso Sandwiches, Steaks, Hähnchen und Eiergerichte bekommen. Viele **diners** werden von griechischen Immigranten geführt und bieten somit auch griechische Spezialitäten an.

dinghy [ˈdɪŋ·i] *n* Ding[h]i *nt*

dingy [ˈdɪn·dʒi] *adj* düster, schmuddelig; *color* trüb

dining car [ˈdaɪ·nɪŋˌ-] *n* RAIL Speisewagen *m*

ˈdining room *n* (*in house*) Esszimmer *nt;* (*in public building*) Speisesaal *m*

dinky [ˈdɪŋ·ki] *adj* (*fam or pej*) klein

dinner [ˈdɪn·ər] *n* ❶ (*evening meal*) Abendessen *nt;* DIAL (*warm lunch*) Mittagessen *nt;* **to**

go out for ~ essen gehen; **to make** ~ das Essen zubereiten; **for** ~ zum Essen ② (*formal meal*) Diner *nt*, Festessen *nt*

'dinner party *n* Abendgesellschaft *f* [mit Essen]

'dinner table *n* (*in house*) Esstisch *m;* (*at formal event*) Tafel *f*

'dinnertime *n* Essenszeit *f*

dinosaur ['daɪ·nə·sɔr] *n* Dinosaurier *m a. fig*

diocese ['daɪ·ə·sɪs] *n* Diözese *f*

dioxide [daɪ·'ak·saɪd] *n* Dioxyd *nt*

dioxin [daɪ·'ak·sɪn] *n* Dioxin *nt*

dip [dɪp] **I.** *n* ① (*dipping*) [kurzes] Eintauchen *kein pl* ② FOOD Dip *m* ③ (*brief swim*) kurzes Bad; **to go for a** ~ kurz reinspringen ④ *in the road* Vertiefung *f*, Senke *f* ⑤ (*sl: stupid person*) Idiot *m pej* **II.** *vi* <-pp-> ① (*go down*) [ver]sinken; (*lower*) sich senken ② (*decline*) fallen; *profits* zurückgehen ③ (*go under water*) eintauchen **III.** *vt* <-pp-> ① (*immerse*) [ein]tauchen; FOOD [ein]tunken ② (*put into*) [hinein]stecken; **to** ~ **[one's hand] into sth** [mit der Hand] in etw *akk* hineingreifen ③ (*lower*) senken; *flag* dippen

◆**dip into** *vi* ① (*study casually*) ■**to** ~ **into sth** *book* einen kurzen Blick auf etw *akk* werfen ② *savings* angreifen

diphtheria [dɪf·'θɪr·i·ə] *n* MED Diphtherie *f*

diphthong ['dɪf·θaŋ] *n* LING Doppellaut *m*

diploma [dɪ·'ploʊ·mə] *n* ① SCH, UNIV Diplom *nt* ② (*honorary document*) [Ehren]urkunde *f*

diplomacy [dɪ·'ploʊ·mə·si] *n* Diplomatie *f a. fig*

diplomat ['dɪp·lə·mæt] *n* Diplomat(in) *m(f) a. fig*

diplomatic [ˌdɪp·lə·'mæt̬·ɪk] *adj* diplomatisch *a. fig*

'dipstick *n* ① AUTO [Öl]messstab *m* ② (*sl: idiot*) Idiot(in) *m(f) pej*, Dummkopf *m pej*

dire ['daɪr] *adj* ① (*dreadful*) entsetzlich, furchtbar; *situation* aussichtslos; **in** ~ **straits** in einer ernsten Notlage ② (*ominous*) *warning, forecast* unheilvoll

direct [dɪ·'rekt] **I.** *adj* direkt; ~ **route** kürzester Weg; **the** ~ **opposite** das genaue Gegenteil **II.** *adv* direkt **III.** *vt* ① (*control*) leiten, führen; *traffic* regeln ② (*aim*) richten (**at, to** an +*akk*); *attention* lenken (**at, to** auf +*akk*); **to** ~ **a blow at sb** nach jdm schlagen ③ (*give directions*) ■**to** ~ **sb to sth** jdm den Weg zu etw *dat* zeigen ④ THEAT, FILM Regie führen bei; MUS dirigieren **IV.** *vi* THEAT, FILM Regie führen; MUS dirigieren

direct 'current *n* ELEC Gleichstrom *m*

direct 'hit *n* Volltreffer *m*

direction [dɪ·'rek·ʃən] *n* ① (*course taken*) Richtung *f;* **in the** ~ **of the bedroom** in Richtung Schlafzimmer; **sense of** ~ Orientierungssinn *m;* **to lack** ~ orientierungslos sein; **in opposite** ~**s** in entgegengesetzter Richtung; **to give sb** ~**s** jdm den Weg beschreiben ② (*supervision*) Leitung *f*, Führung *f* ③ (*instructions*) ■~**s** *pl* Anweisungen *pl*

directional [dɪ·'rek·ʃə·nəl] *adj* RADIO Richt-

directive [dɪ·'rek·tɪv] *n* [An]weisung *f*

directly [dɪ·'rekt·li] *adv* direkt; ~ **after/before ...** unmittelbar danach/davor ...

direct 'object *n* direktes Objekt

director [dɪ·'rek·tər] *n* ① ADMIN *of company* Direktor(in) *m(f); of information center* Leiter(in) *m(f);* **board of** ~**s** COMM Vorstand *m* ② (*member of board*) Mitglied *nt* des Board of Directors ③ FILM, THEAT Regisseur(in) *m(f); of orchestra* Dirigent(in) *m(f); of choir* Chorleiter(in) *m(f)*

directorate [dɪ·'rek·tər·ət] *n* ① ADMIN Direktorat *nt* ② (*board*) Direktorium *nt*

directorship [dɪ·'rek·tər·ʃɪp] *n* Direktorenstelle *f*

directory [dɪ·'rek·tə·ri] *n* **telephone** ~ Telefonbuch *nt;* (*list*) Verzeichnis *nt*

directory as'sistance *n* [Telefon]auskunft *f kein pl*

dirt [dɜrt] *n* ① (*filth*) Schmutz *m*, Dreck *m* ② (*soil*) Erde *f* ③ (*scandal*) **to dig for** ~ nach Skandalen suchen ▶ PHRASES: **to treat sb like** ~ jdn wie [den letzten] Dreck behandeln

dirt 'cheap I. *adj* (*fam*) spottbillig **II.** *adv* **to sell sth** ~ etw verschleudern

dirt 'road *n* Schotterstraße *f*

dirty ['dɜr·t̬i] **I.** *adj* ① (*unclean*) dreckig, schmutzig; *needle* benutzt ② (*fam: nasty*) gemein; *liar* dreckig; *rascal* gerissen ③ (*fam: lewd*) schmutzig; *language* vulgär ④ (*unfriendly*) **to give sb a** ~ **look** jdm einen bösen Blick zuwerfen **II.** *adv* ① (*dishonestly*) **to play** ~ unfair spielen ② (*obscenely*) **to talk** ~ sich vulgär ausdrücken **III.** *vt* beschmutzen

disability [ˌdɪs·ə·'bɪl·ɪ·t̬i] *n* Behinderung *f;* ~ **benefit** Erwerbsunfähigkeitsrente *f*

disable [dɪs·'eɪ·bəl] *vt person* arbeitsunfähig machen; *thing* funktionsunfähig machen

disabled [dɪs·'eɪ·bəld] **I.** *adj* ① (*handicapped*) behindert ② (*for the handicapped*) Behinderten- **II.** *n* ■**the** ~ *pl* die Behinderten

disadvantage [ˌdɪs·əd·'væn·tɪdʒ] **I.** *n* Nachteil *m;* (*state*) Benachteiligung *f;* **to put sb at a** ~ jdn benachteiligen **II.** *vt* benachteiligen

disadvantageous [ˌdɪs·ˌæd·væn·'teɪ·dʒəs] *adj* nachteilig

disaffected [ˌdɪs·ə·'fek·tɪd] *adj* (*form: dissatisfied*) unzufrieden; (*estranged*) entfremdet

disaffection [ˌdɪs·ə·'fek·ʃən] *n* (*form: dissatisfaction*) Unzufriedenheit *f;* (*estrangement*) Entfremdung *f*

disagree [ˌdɪs·ə·'gri] *vi* ① (*dissent*) nicht übereinstimmen; (*with plan, decision*) nicht einverstanden sein; (*with sb else*) anderer Meinung sein ② (*argue*) eine Auseinandersetzung haben ③ FOOD **I must have eaten something that** ~**d with me** ich muss etwas gegessen haben, das mir nicht bekommt

disagreeable [ˌdɪs·ə·'gri·ə·bəl] *adj* ① (*unpleasant*) unangenehm ② (*unfriendly*) unsympathisch

disagreement [ˌdɪs·ə·'gri·mənt] *n* ① (*lack of agreement*) Uneinigkeit *f* ② (*argument*) Mei-

nungsverschiedenheit *f* (**over/about** um/über +*akk*)
disallow [ˌdɪs·ə·ˈlaʊ] *vt* ❶ (*rule out*) nicht erlauben; SPORTS nicht anerkennen; *goal* annullieren ❷ LAW abweisen
disappear [ˌdɪs·ə·ˈpɪr] *vi* ❶ (*vanish*) verschwinden ❷ (*become extinct*) aussterben
disappearance [ˌdɪs·ə·ˈpɪr·əns] *n* ❶ (*vanishing*) Verschwinden *nt* ❷ (*becoming extinct*) Aussterben *nt*
disappoint [ˌdɪs·ə·ˈpɔɪnt] *vt* enttäuschen
disappointed [ˌdɪs·ə·ˈpɔɪn·t̬ɪd] *adj* enttäuscht (**at/about** über +*akk*, **in/with** mit +*dat*)
disappointing [ˌdɪs·ə·ˈpɔɪn·t̬ɪŋ] *adj* enttäuschend
disappointment [ˌdɪs·ə·ˈpɔɪnt·mənt] *n* Enttäuschung *f* (**at/about** über +*akk*, **in/with** mit +*dat*)
disapproval [ˌdɪs·ə·ˈpru·vəl] *n* Missbilligung *f*
disapprove [ˌdɪs·ə·ˈpruv] *vi* dagegen sein; ■ **to ~ of sth** etw missbilligen; ■ **to ~ of sb** jdn ablehnen
disarm [dɪs·ˈarm] **I.** *vt person* entwaffnen *a. fig; bomb* entschärfen **II.** *vi* abrüsten
disarmament [dɪs·ˈar·mə·mənt] *n* Abrüstung *f*
disarming [dɪs·ˈar·mɪŋ] *adj* entwaffnend
disarray [ˌdɪs·ə·ˈreɪ] *n* ❶ (*disorder*) Unordnung *f* ❷ (*confusion*) Verwirrung *f*
disaster [dɪ·ˈzæs·tər] *n* Katastrophe *f a. fig*
disastrous [dɪ·ˈzæs·trəs] *adj* katastrophal; *decision, impact* verhängnisvoll
disband [dɪs·ˈbænd] **I.** *vi* sich auflösen **II.** *vt meeting, club* auflösen
disbelief [ˌdɪs·bɪ·ˈlif] *n* Unglaube *m;* **she shook her head in ~** sie schüttelte ungläubig den Kopf
disbelieve [ˌdɪs·bɪ·ˈliv] *vt* (*form*) ■ **to ~ sb** jdm nicht glauben; ■ **to ~ sth** etw bezweifeln
disc [dɪsk] *n see* **disk**
discard [ˈdɪs·kard] *vt* ❶ (*throw away*) wegwerfen; (*fig*) *idea* fallen lassen ❷ CARDS abwerfen
ˈ**disc brake** *n* Scheibenbremse *f*
discern [dɪ·ˈsɜrn] *vt* (*form*) wahrnehmen
discernible [dɪ·ˈsɜr·nə·bəl] *adj* wahrnehmbar, erkennbar
discerning [dɪ·ˈsɜr·nɪŋ] *adj* urteilsfähig; *palate* fein; *reader* kritisch
discernment [dɪ·ˈsɜrn·mənt] *n* (*good judgment*) Urteilskraft *f*
discharge I. *vt* [dɪs·ˈtʃardʒ] ❶ (*release*) entlassen (**from** aus +*dat*); *soldier* verabschieden ❷ (*emit*) absondern; *sewage* ablassen ❸ (*shoot*) *weapon* abfeuern ❹ (*pay off*) *debt* begleichen ❺ PHYS entladen **II.** *vi* [dɪs·ˈtʃardʒ] ❶ (*pour out*) sich ergießen; *wound* eitern ❷ (*go off*) *bomb* hochgehen **III.** *n* [ˈdɪs·tʃardʒ] ❶ *of person* Entlassung *f* ❷ (*discharging of liquid*) Ausströmen *nt kein pl* ❸ (*liquid emitted*) Ausfluss *m kein pl; from wound* Absonderung *f* ❹ *of weapon* Abfeuern *nt kein pl* ❺ PHYS Entladung *f*
disciple [dɪ·ˈsaɪ·pəl] *n* Anhänger(in) *m(f);* (*of Jesus*) Jünger *m*
disciplinary [ˈdɪs·ə·plə·ner·i] *adj* Disziplinar-
discipline [ˈdɪs·ə·plɪn] **I.** *n* Disziplin *f* **II.** *vt* ❶ (*have self-control*) ■ **to ~ oneself** sich disziplinieren ❷ (*punish*) bestrafen
ˈ**disc jockey** *n* Diskjockey *m*
disclaim [dɪs·ˈkleɪm] *vt* abstreiten; *responsibility* ablehnen
disclaimer [dɪs·ˈkleɪ·mər] *n* Verzichtserklärung *f;* INET Disclaimer *n*
disclose [dɪs·ˈkloʊz] *vt* ❶ (*reveal*) bekannt geben ❷ (*uncover*) enthüllen
disclosure [dɪs·ˈkloʊ·ʒər] *n* (*form*) *of information, news* Bekanntgabe *f; of secret* Enthüllung *f*
disco [ˈdɪs·koʊ] *n short for* **discotheque** Disco *f,* Disko *f*
discolor [dɪs·ˈkʌl·ər] **I.** *vi* sich verfärben **II.** *vt* verfärben
discomfort [dɪs·ˈkʌm·fərt] *n* ❶ (*slight pain*) Beschwerden *pl* (**in** mit +*dat*) ❷ (*inconvenience*) Unannehmlichkeit *f*
disconcert [ˌdɪs·kən·ˈsɜrt] *vt* beunruhigen
disconnect [ˌdɪs·kə·ˈnekt] *vt* trennen; *electricity, gas, phone* abstellen
disconnected [ˌdɪs·kə·ˈnek·tɪd] *adj* ❶ (*turned off*) [ab]getrennt; (*left without supply*) abgestellt ❷ (*incoherent*) *speech* zusammenhang[s]los
disconsolate [dɪs·ˈkan·sə·lət] *adj* (*dejected*) niedergeschlagen; (*inconsolable*) untröstlich
discontent [ˌdɪs·kən·ˈtent] *n* Unzufriedenheit *f*
discontented [dɪs·kən·ˈten·t̬ɪd] *adj* unzufrieden (**with, about** mit +*dat*)
discontentment [dɪs·kən·ˈtent·mənt] *n see* **discontent**
discontinue [ˌdɪs·kən·ˈtɪn·ju] *vt* abbrechen; *product* auslaufen lassen; *service* einstellen; *subscription* kündigen; *visits* aufgeben
discord [ˈdɪs·kɔrd] *n* (*form*) Uneinigkeit *f,* Zwietracht *f*
discordant [dɪ·ˈskɔr·dənt] *adj* ❶ (*disagreeing*) entgegengesetzt; *views* gegensätzlich ❷ MUS disharmonisch
discotheque [ˈdɪs·kə·tek] *n* Diskothek *f*
discount I. *n* [ˈdɪs·kaʊnt] Rabatt *m;* **~ for cash** Skonto *nt o m* **II.** *vt* [dɪs·ˈkaʊnt] ❶ (*disregard*) unberücksichtigt lassen; *possibility* nicht berücksichtigen; *testimony* nicht einbeziehen ❷ (*reduce*) *article* herabsetzen; *price* reduzieren
ˈ**discount store** *n* Discountladen *m*
discourage [dɪ·ˈskɜr·ɪdʒ] *vt* ❶ (*dishearten*) entmutigen ❷ (*dissuade*) ■ **to ~ sth** von etw *dat* abraten; ■ **to ~ sb from doing sth** jdm davon abraten, etw zu tun ❸ (*stop*) abhalten; ■ **to ~ sb from doing sth** jdn davon abhalten, etw zu tun
discouragement [dɪ·ˈskɜr·ɪdʒ·mənt] *n* ❶ (*action*) Entmutigung *f;* (*feeling*) Mutlosigkeit *f* ❷ (*deterrence*) Abschreckung *f;* (*dissuasion*) Abraten *nt*

D

discouraging [dɪ·ˈskɜr·ɪdʒ·ɪŋ] *adj* entmutigend
discourteous [dɪs·ˈkɜr·t̬i·əs] *adj* (*form*) unhöflich
discover [dɪ·ˈskʌv·ər] *vt* ❶ (*find out*) herausfinden ❷ (*find first*) entdecken *a. fig* ❸ (*find*) finden
discoverer [dɪ·ˈskʌv·ə·rər] *n* Entdecker(in) *m(f)*

D

discovery [dɪ·ˈskʌv·ə·ri] *n* Entdeckung *f a. fig*
discredit [dɪs·ˈkred·ɪt] **I.** *vt* ❶ (*disgrace*) in Verruf bringen, diskreditieren ❷ (*cause to appear false*) unglaubwürdig machen **II.** *n* Misskredit *m*
discreet [dɪ·ˈskrit] *adj* ❶ (*unobtrusive*) diskret; *color, pattern* dezent ❷ (*tactful*) taktvoll
discrepancy [dɪ·ˈskrep·ən·si] *n* (*form*) Diskrepanz *f*
discrete [dɪ·ˈskrit] *adj* eigenständig
discretion [dɪ·ˈskreʃ·ən] *n* ❶ (*behavior*) Diskretion *f* ❷ (*good judgment*) **to use one's ~** nach eigenem Ermessen handeln
discriminate [dɪ·ˈskrɪm·ə·neɪt] *vi* ❶ (*differentiate*) unterscheiden ❷ (*be prejudiced*) diskriminieren; **to ~ in favor of sb** jdn bevorzugen; ■**to ~ against sb** jdn diskriminieren
discriminating [dɪ·ˈskrɪm·ə·neɪ·t̬ɪŋ] *adj* (*approv*) kritisch; *palate* fein
discrimination [dɪ·ˌskrɪm·ɪ·ˈneɪ·ʃən] *n* ❶ (*prejudice*) Diskriminierung *f* ❷ (*taste*) [kritisches] Urteilsvermögen ❸ (*ability to differentiate*) Unterscheidung *f*
discriminatory [dɪ·ˈskrɪm·ɪ·nə·tɔr·i] *adj* diskriminierend
discus <*pl* -es> [ˈdɪs·kəs] *n* SPORTS Diskus *m*; (*event*) Diskuswerfen *nt*
discuss [dɪ·ˈskʌs] *vt* ❶ (*talk about*) besprechen ❷ (*debate*) erörtern, diskutieren
discussion [dɪ·ˈskʌʃ·ən] *n* Diskussion *f*; **to be open to/under ~** zur Diskussion stehen
disˈcussion board *n* COMPUT, INET Diskussionsforum *nt*
disdain [dɪs·ˈdeɪn] **I.** *n* Verachtung *f* **II.** *vt* (*despise*) verachten; (*reject*) verschmähen
disdainful [dɪs·ˈdeɪn·fəl] *adj* (*form*) verächtlich
disease [dɪ·ˈziz] *n* Krankheit *f a. fig*
diseased [dɪ·ˈzizd] *adj* krank; *plant* befallen
disembark [ˌdɪs·ɪm·ˈbark] *vi* von Bord gehen
disembodied [ˌdɪs·ɪm·ˈbad·id] *adj* körperlos; *voice* geisterhaft
disenchant [ˌdɪs·ɪn·ˈtʃænt] *vt* ernüchtern
disengage [ˌdɪs·ɪn·ˈgeɪdʒ] **I.** *vt* ❶ ■**to ~ oneself** sich lösen ❷ MECH entkuppeln; **to ~ the clutch** auskuppeln ❸ MIL *troops* abziehen **II.** *vi* ❶ sich lösen ❷ MIL sich zurückziehen
disengagement [ˌdɪs·ɪn·ˈgeɪdʒ·mənt] *n* ❶ MECH Lösung *f*; *of a clutch* Auskuppeln *nt* ❷ MIL Absetzen *nt*
disentangle [ˌdɪs·ɪn·ˈtæŋ·gəl] *vt* ❶ (*untangle*) entwirren; (*fig*) herauslösen (**from** aus +*dat*) ❷ ■**to ~ oneself** sich befreien
disfavor [ˌdɪs·ˈfeɪ·vər] *n* Missfallen *nt*; **to fall into ~** in Ungnade fallen
disfigure [dɪs·ˈfɪg·jər] *vt* entstellen
disfigurement [dɪs·ˈfɪg·jər·mənt] *n* Entstellung *f*
disgorge [dɪs·ˈgɔrdʒ] *vt* ausspucken *a. fig*
disgrace [dɪs·ˈgreɪs] **I.** *n* Schande *f* **II.** *vt* Schande bringen (über +*akk*)
disgraced [dɪs·ˈgreɪst] *adj* beschämt
disgraceful [dɪs·ˈgreɪs·fəl] *adj* schändlich; *behavior* skandalös
disgruntled [dɪs·ˈgrʌn·təld] *adj* verstimmt (**with** über +*akk*)
disguise [dɪs·ˈgaɪz] **I.** *vt* ■**to ~ oneself** sich verkleiden; ■**to ~ sth** etw verbergen; *voice* verstellen **II.** *n* (*for body*) Verkleidung *f*; (*for face*) Maske *f*; **in ~** verkleidet
disgust [dɪs·ˈgʌst] **I.** *n* ❶ (*revulsion*) Ekel *m*; **sth fills sb with ~** etw ekelt jdn an ❷ (*indignation*) Empörung *f* (**at** über +*akk*); **in ~** entrüstet, empört **II.** *vt* ❶ (*sicken*) anwidern, anekeln ❷ (*appall*) entrüsten, empören
disgusted [dɪs·ˈgʌs·tɪd] *adj* ❶ (*sickened*) angeekelt, angewidert (**at, by** von +*dat*) ❷ (*indignant*) empört, entrüstet (**at, with** über +*akk*)
disgusting [dɪs·ˈgʌs·tɪŋ] *adj* ❶ (*repulsive*) widerlich ❷ (*unacceptable*) empörend
dish <*pl* -es> [dɪʃ] *n* ❶ (*for serving*) Schale *f*; (*plate*) Teller *m* ❷ (*containers and utensils*) ■**the ~es** *pl* das Geschirr *kein pl*; **to do** [*or* **wash**] **the ~es** [ab]spülen ❸ (*meal*) Gericht *nt*; **side ~** Beilage *f* ❹ TELEC Schüssel *f*
◆**dish out** *vt* ❶ (*give freely*) großzügig verteilen (**to** an +*akk*); **to ~ out punishment** [be]strafen ❷ (*serve*) *food* servieren
◆**dish up** *vt* (*fam*) auftischen
ˈ**dishcloth** *n* Geschirrtuch *nt*
dishearten [dɪs·ˈhar·tən] *vt* entmutigen
disheveled [dɪ·ˈʃev·əld] *adj* unordentlich; *hair* zerzaust
dishonest [dɪs·ˈan·ɪst] *adj* unehrlich
dishonesty [dɪs·ˈan·əs·ti] *n* Unehrlichkeit *f*
dishonor [dɪs·ˈan·ər] (*form*) **I.** *n* Schande *f* (**to** für *akk*) **II.** *vt* ❶ (*disgrace*) ■**to ~ sb/sth** dem Ansehen einer Person/Sache schaden ❷ (*not respect*) *agreement* verletzen; *promise* nicht einlösen
dishonorable [dɪs·ˈan·ər·ə·bəl] *adj* unehrenhaft
ˈ**dishtowel** *n* Geschirrtuch *nt*
ˈ**dishwasher** *n* ❶ (*machine*) Geschirrspülmaschine *f* ❷ (*person*) Tellerwäscher(in) *m(f)*
ˈ**dishwater** *n* Spülwasser *nt a. fig*
disillusion [ˌdɪs·ɪ·ˈlu·ʒən] **I.** *vt* desillusionieren **II.** *n* Ernüchterung *f*
disillusioned [dɪs·ɪ·ˈlu·ʒənd] *adj* desillusioniert
disillusionment [dɪs·ɪ·ˈlu·ʒən·mənt] *n* Ernüchterung *f* (**with** über +*akk*)
disinclination [ˌdɪs·ɪn·klɪ·ˈneɪ·ʃən] *n* Abneigung *f*
disinclined [ˌdɪs·ɪn·ˈklaɪnd] *adj* abgeneigt
disinfect [ˌdɪs·ɪn·ˈfekt] *vt* desinfizieren

disinfectant [ˌdɪs·ɪn·ˈfek·tənt] *n* Desinfektionsmittel *nt*
disingenuous [ˌdɪs·ɪn·ˈdʒen·ju·əs] *adj* (*form*) unaufrichtig
disinherit [ˌdɪs·ɪn·ˈher·ɪt] *vt* enterben
disintegrate [dɪs·ˈɪn·tə·greɪt] *vi* zerfallen; (*fig*) *marriage* zerbrechen
disintegration [dɪs·ˌɪn·tə·ˈgreɪ·ʃən] *n* Zerfall *m*
disinterested [dɪs·ˈɪn·trɪ·stɪd] *adj* (*impartial*) unparteiisch; ~ **party** Unbeteiligte(r) *f(m)*
disjointed [dɪs·ˈdʒɔɪn·tɪd] *adj* zusammenhanglos
disk, disc [dɪsk] *n* ① (*shape, object*) Scheibe *f;* MED Bandscheibe *f* ② MUS (*CD*) CD *f;* (*record*) [Schall]platte *f* ③ COMPUT Diskette *f;* ~ **drive** Laufwerk *nt*
ˈ**disk brake** *n see* **disc brake**
diskette [dɪs·ˈket] *n* Diskette *f*
ˈ**disk jockey** *n see* **disc jockey**
dislike [dɪs·ˈlaɪk] **I.** *vt* nicht mögen; *doing sth* nicht gern tun **II.** *n* Abneigung *f* (**of, for** gegen +*akk*)
dislocate [dɪs·ˈloʊ·keɪt] *vt* ■**to ~ sth** sich *dat* etw ausrenken
dislocation [ˌdɪs·loʊ·ˈkeɪ·ʃən] *n* Verrenkung *f; of shoulder* Auskugeln *nt kein pl*
dislodge [dɪs·ˈladʒ] *vt thing* lösen; *person* verdrängen
disloyal [dɪs·ˈlɔɪ·əl] *adj* illoyal (**to** gegenüber +*dat*)
dismal [ˈdɪz·məl] *adj* ① (*dreary*) düster, trostlos; *outlook, weather* trüb ② (*inadequate*) *performance* kläglich
dismantle [dɪs·ˈmæn·təl] *vt* zerlegen; (*fig*) demontieren
dismay [dɪs·ˈmeɪ] **I.** *n* Bestürzung *f* (**at/with** über +*akk*) **II.** *vt* schockieren
dismayed [dɪs·ˈmeɪd] *adj* bestürzt; *expression* betroffen (**at/with** über +*akk*)
dismember [dɪs·ˈmem·bər] *vt* zerstückeln
dismiss [dɪs·ˈmɪs] *vt* ① (*ignore*) abtun; *idea* aufgeben; **to ~ a thought [from one's mind]** sich *dat* einen Gedanken aus dem Kopf schlagen ② (*send away*) wegschicken; *class* gehen lassen ③ (*fire*) entlassen
dismissal [dɪs·ˈmɪs·əl] *n* ① (*disregard*) Abtun *nt* ② (*firing*) Entlassung *f* (**from** aus +*dat*) ③ *of an assembly* Auflösung *f*
dismissive [dɪs·ˈmɪs·ɪv] *adj* geringschätzig
dismount [dɪs·ˈmaʊnt] *vi* absteigen
disobedience [ˌdɪs·ə·ˈbi·di·əns] *n* Ungehorsam *m* (**to** gegenüber +*dat*)
disobedient [ˌdɪs·ə·ˈbi·di·ənt] *adj* ungehorsam
disobey [ˌdɪs·ə·ˈbeɪ] **I.** *vt person* nicht gehorchen; *orders* nicht befolgen; *rules* sich nicht halten an +*akk* **II.** *vi* ungehorsam sein
disorder [dɪs·ˈɔr·dər] *n* ① (*disarray*) Unordnung *f* ② MED [Funktions]störung *f;* **kidney ~** Nierenleiden *nt;* **skin ~** Hautirritation *f* ③ (*riot*) Aufruhr *m;* **civil ~** Bürgerunruhen *pl*
disorderly [dɪs·ˈɔr·dər·li] *adj* ① (*untidy*) unordentlich ② (*unruly*) aufrührerisch
disorganized [dɪs·ˈɔr·gə·naɪzd] *adj* schlecht organisiert
disorient [dɪs·ˈɔr·i·ent] *vt usu passive* ① (*lose bearings*) **to be/get** [*or* **become**] [**totally**] **~ed** [völlig] die Orientierung verloren haben/verlieren ② (*be confused*) ■**to be ~ed** orientierungslos sein
disown [dɪs·ˈoʊn] *vt* verleugnen; (*hum a.*) nicht mehr kennen
disparage [dɪ·ˈsper·ɪdʒ] *vt* diskreditieren
disparaging [dɪ·ˈsper·ɪdʒ·ɪŋ] *adj* geringschätzig
disparity [dɪ·ˈsper·ɪ·t̬i] *n* Ungleichheit *f*
dispassionate [dɪs·ˈpæʃ·ə·nɪt] *adj* objektiv
dispatch[1] [dɪ·ˈspætʃ] *n* <*pl* -es> ① (*something sent*) Sendung *f* ② (*sending*) Verschicken *nt; of a person* Entsendung *f* ③ (*press report*) [Auslands]bericht *m;* MIL [Kriegs]bericht
dispatch[2] [dɪ·ˈspætʃ] *vt* ① (*send*) *thing* senden; *person* entsenden ② (*kill*) töten
dispel <-ll-> [dɪ·ˈspel] *vt rumors* zerstreuen
dispensable [dɪ·ˈspen·sə·bəl] *adj* entbehrlich
dispensary [dɪ·ˈspen·sə·ri] *n* [Krankenhaus]apotheke *f*
dispensation [ˌdɪs·pen·ˈseɪ·ʃən] *n* (*form*) Befreiung *f;* REL Dispens *f*
dispense [dɪ·ˈspens] **I.** *vt* austeilen (**to** an +*akk*); *advice* erteilen; *medicine* ausgeben **II.** *vi* ■**to ~ with sth** auf etw *akk* verzichten
dispenser [dɪ·ˈspen·sər] *n* Automat *m*
dispersal [dɪ·ˈspɜr·səl] *n* ① (*scattering*) Zerstreuung *f; of a crowd* Auflösung *f;* (*migration*) Verbreitung *f* ② (*distribution*) Verstreutheit *f*
disperse [dɪ·ˈspɜrs] **I.** *vt* ① (*dispel*) auflösen; *crowd* zerstreuen ② (*distribute*) verteilen **II.** *vi crowd* auseinandergehen; *mist* sich auflösen
dispersion [dɪ·ˈspɜr·ʒən] *n* (*spread*) Verbreitung *f*
dispirited [dɪ·ˈspɪr·ɪ·t̬ɪd] *adj* entmutigt
displace [dɪs·ˈpleɪs] *vt* ① (*force out*) vertreiben ② (*replace*) ersetzen
displaced ˈperson *n* Heimatlose(r) *f(m)*
displacement [dɪs·ˈpleɪs·mənt] *n* ① (*expulsion*) Vertreibung *f* ② (*relocation*) Umsiedlung *f* ③ (*replacement*) Ablösung *f*
display [dɪ·ˈspleɪ] **I.** *vt* ① (*on a bulletin board*) aushängen; (*in a store window*) auslegen ② (*demonstrate*) *strength* zeigen **II.** *n* ① (*in a museum, store*) Auslage *f;* **to be on ~** ausgestellt sein ② (*demonstration*) Demonstration *f;* **~ of anger** Wutausbruch *m* ③ COMPUT Display *nt*
disˈplay case, disˈplay cabinet *n* Vitrine *f*
displease [dɪs·ˈpliz] *vt* ■**to ~ sb** jdm missfallen
displeasure [dɪs·ˈpleʒ·ər] *n* Missfallen *nt* (**at/with** über +*akk*)
disposable [dɪ·ˈspoʊ·zə·bəl] **I.** *adj* ① *articles* Wegwerf-; **~ razor** Einwegrasierer *m* ② FIN *income* verfügbar **II.** *n* ■**~s** *pl* Wegwerfartikel *pl*
disposal [dɪ·ˈspoʊ·zəl] *n* ① Beseitigung *f; of waste* Entsorgung *f* ② **garbage ~** Müllschlu-

cker *m* ❸ (*control*) Verfügung *f;* ■**to be at sb's ~** zu jds Verfügung stehen

dispose [dɪ·ˈspoʊz] *vt* (*form*) ■**to ~ sb to** [*or* **toward**] **sth** jdn zu etw *dat* bewegen
◆**dispose of** *vt* (*get rid of*) beseitigen; (*sell*) veräußern

disposed [dɪ·ˈspoʊzd] *adj* **to be** [*or* **feel**] **well ~ toward sb/sth** jdm/etw wohlgesinnt sein

disposition [ˌdɪs·pə·ˈzɪʃ·ən] *n* ❶ (*nature*) Art *f* ❷ (*tendency*) Veranlagung *f*

dispossess [ˌdɪs·pə·ˈzes] *vt* enteignen

disproportionate [ˌdɪs·prə·ˈpɔr·ʃə·nɪt] *adj* unangemessen

disprove [dɪs·ˈpruv] *vt* widerlegen

disputable [dɪ·ˈspju·t̬ə·bəl] *adj* strittig

dispute [dɪ·ˈspjut] **I.** *vt* ❶ (*argue*) sich streiten über +*akk* ❷ (*oppose*) bestreiten **II.** *vi* streiten **III.** *n* (*argument*) Streit *m* (**over** über +*akk*); **that is open to ~** darüber lässt sich streiten; **to be beyond ~** außer Frage stehen

disqualification [dɪs·ˌkwal·ə·fɪ·ˈkeɪ·ʃən] *n* Ausschluss *m;* SPORTS Disqualifikation *f*

disqualify <-ie-> [dɪs·ˈkwal·ə·faɪ] *vt* ausschließen; SPORTS disqualifizieren

disquiet [dɪs·ˈkwaɪ·ət] (*form*) **I.** *n* Besorgnis *f* (**about** um +*akk,* **over** über +*akk*) **II.** *vt* beunruhigen

disquieting [dɪ·ˈskwaɪ·ə·t̬ɪŋ] *adj* (*form*) beunruhigend

disregard [ˌdɪs·rɪ·ˈgard] **I.** *vt* ignorieren; ■**to ~ sb/sth** sich über jdn/etw hinwegsetzen **II.** *n* Gleichgültigkeit *f* (**for** gegenüber +*dat*); (*for a rule, the law*) Missachtung *f* (**for, of** +*gen*)

disrepair [ˌdɪs·rɪ·ˈper] *n* Baufälligkeit *f;* **to fall into ~** verfallen

disreputable [dɪs·ˈrep·jə·t̬ə·bəl] *adj* verrufen

disrepute [ˌdɪs·rɪ·ˈpjut] *n* Verruf *m kein pl*

disrespect [ˌdɪs·rɪ·ˈspekt] **I.** *n* Respektlosigkeit *f* (**for** gegenüber +*dat*); **to intend no ~** nicht respektlos sein wollen **II.** *vt* (*fam*) beleidigen

disrespectful [ˌdɪs·rɪ·ˈspekt·fəl] *adj* respektlos

disrupt [dɪs·ˈrʌpt] *vt* (*disturb*) stören

disruption [dɪs·ˈrʌp·ʃən] *n* ❶ (*interruption*) Unterbrechung *f* ❷ (*disrupting*) Störung *f*

disruptive [dɪs·ˈrʌp·tɪv] *adj* störend; **~ influence** Störelement *nt;* (*person*) Unruhestifter *m*

dissatisfaction [dɪs·ˌsæt̬·ɪs·ˈfæk·ʃən] *n* Unzufriedenheit *f*

dissatisfied [dɪs·ˈsæt̬·ɪs·faɪd] *adj* unzufrieden

dissect [dɪ·ˈsekt] *vt* ❶ (*cut open*) sezieren ❷ (*fig*) analysieren

dissection [dɪ·ˈsek·ʃən] *n* ❶ (*dissecting*) Sezieren *nt* ❷ (*instance*) Sektion *f* ❸ (*fig*) Analyse *f*

dissemble [dɪ·ˈsem·bəl] *vi* (*form*) sich verstellen

disseminate [dɪ·ˈsem·ɪ·neɪt] *vt* (*form*) verbreiten

dissemination [dɪ·ˌsem·ɪ·ˈneɪ·ʃən] *n* (*form*) Verbreitung *f*

dissension [dɪ·ˈsen·ʃən] *n* (*form*) Meinungsverschiedenheit[en] *m*[*pl*]

dissent [dɪ·ˈsent] **I.** *n* ❶ (*disagreement*) Meinungsverschiedenheit *f* ❷ (*protest*) Widerspruch *m* **II.** *vi* dagegen stimmen; (*disagree*) anderer Meinung sein

dissenter [dɪ·ˈsen·t̬ər] *n* Andersdenkende(r) *f(m);* POL Dissident(in) *m(f)*

dissertation [ˌdɪs·ər·ˈteɪ·ʃən] *n* Dissertation *f* (**on** über +*akk*)

disservice [ˌdɪs·ˈsɜr·vɪs] *n* **to do sb a ~** jdm einen schlechten Dienst erweisen

dissident [ˈdɪs·ɪ·dənt] **I.** *n* Dissident(in) *m(f)* **II.** *adj* regimekritisch

dissimilar [ˌdɪ·ˈsɪm·ɪ·lər] *adj* unterschiedlich

dissimilarity [ˌdɪ·ˌsɪm·ɪ·ˈler·ɪ·t̬i] *n* Unterschied *m*

dissipate [ˈdɪs·ɪ·peɪt] **I.** *vi* allmählich verschwinden; *crowd, mist* sich auflösen **II.** *vt* ❶ (*disperse*) auflösen ❷ (*squander*) verschwenden

dissipated [ˈdɪs·ɪ·peɪ·t̬ɪd] *adj* (*liter*) ausschweifend

dissipation [ˌdɪs·ɪ·ˈpeɪ·ʃən] *n* (*form*) ❶ (*squandering*) Verschwendung *f* ❷ (*indulgence*) Übermäßigkeit *f*

dissociate [dɪ·ˈsoʊ·ʃi·eɪt] *vt* getrennt betrachten; ■**to ~ oneself from sb/sth** sich von jdm/etw distanzieren

dissolute [ˈdɪs·ə·lut] *adj* (*liter*) *life* ausschweifend; *person* zügellos

dissolution [ˌdɪs·ə·ˈlu·ʃən] *n* ❶ (*annulment*) Auflösung *f* ❷ (*liter: debauchery*) Ausschweifung *f*

dissolve [dɪ·ˈzalv] **I.** *vi* ❶ (*be absorbed*) sich auflösen ❷ (*subside*) **to ~ in**[**to**] **tears** in Tränen ausbrechen ❸ (*dissipate*) verschwinden; *tension* sich lösen **II.** *vt* ❶ (*liquefy*) [auf]lösen ❷ (*annul*) auflösen; *marriage* scheiden

dissuade [dɪ·ˈsweɪd] *vt* abbringen

distance [ˈdɪs·təns] **I.** *n* ❶ (*route*) Strecke *f* ❷ (*linear measure*) Entfernung *f;* **within shouting ~** in Rufweite ❸ (*remoteness*) Ferne *f;* **from** [*or* **at**] **a distance** von weitem **II.** *vt* ■**to ~ oneself** sich distanzieren

ˈdistance learning *n* Fernunterricht *m*

distant [ˈdɪs·tənt] *adj* ❶ (*far away*) fern; **from the ~ past** aus der fernen Vergangenheit; (*fig*) *look* abwesend; *relative* entfernt ❷ (*aloof*) unnahbar

distantly [ˈdɪs·tənt·li] *adv* ❶ (*far away*) in der Ferne ❷ (*absently*) abwesend ❸ **~ related** entfernt verwandt (**to** mit +*dat*)

distaste [dɪs·ˈteɪst] *n* Widerwille *m* (**for** gegen +*akk*)

distasteful [dɪs·ˈteɪst·fəl] *adj* abscheulich

distend [dɪ·ˈstend] MED **I.** *vt* ■**to be ~ed** aufgebläht sein **II.** *vi* sich [auf]blähen

distill [dɪ·ˈstɪl] *vt* ❶ CHEM destillieren; *brandy* brennen ❷ (*fig*) zusammenfassen

distillation [ˌdɪs·tə·ˈleɪ·ʃən] *n* ❶ CHEM Destillation *f* ❷ (*fig*) Quintessenz *f*

distiller [dɪ·ˈstɪl·ər] *n* ❶ (*company*) Destillerie *f* ❷ (*person*) Destillateur *m*

distillery [dɪ·ˈstɪl·ə·ri] *n* Brennerei *f*
distinct [dɪ·ˈstɪŋkt] *adj* ① (*different*) verschieden; **as ~ from sth** im Unterschied zu etw *dat* ② (*clear*) deutlich
distinction [dɪ·ˈstɪŋk·ʃən] *n* ① (*difference*) Unterschied *m* ② (*eminence*) **of** [**great**] **~** von hohem Rang ③ (*award*) Auszeichnung *f*; ■ **with ~** ausgezeichnet
distinctive [dɪ·ˈstɪŋk·tɪv] *adj* charakteristisch
distinguish [dɪ·ˈstɪŋ·gwɪʃ] **I.** *vi* unterscheiden **II.** *vt* ① (*tell apart*) unterscheiden; (*positively*) abheben ② (*discern*) ausmachen [können] ③ (*excel*) ■ **to ~ oneself in sth** sich in etw *dat* auszeichnen
distinguishable [dɪ·ˈstɪŋ·gwɪʃ·ə·bəl] *adj* unterscheidbar
distinguished [dɪ·ˈstɪŋ·gwɪʃt] *adj* ① (*eminent*) *career* hervorragend; *person* von hohem Rang ② (*stylish*) distinguiert
distort [dɪ·ˈstɔrt] *vt* ① (*out of shape*) verzerren; *face* entstellen ② (*fig*) verdrehen; *history, the truth* verfälschen
distortion [dɪ·ˈstɔr·ʃən] *n* ① (*twisting*) Verzerrung *f*; *of a face* Entstellung *f* ② (*fig*) Verdrehung *f*
distract [dɪ·ˈstrækt] *vt* ablenken (**from** von +*dat*); **you're really ~ing me** du bringst mich völlig raus *fam*
distracted [dɪ·ˈstræk·tɪd] *adj* verwirrt; (*worried*) besorgt
distraction [dɪ·ˈstræk·ʃən] *n* ① (*disturbance*) Störung *f*; **sb finds sth a ~** etw stört jdn ② (*diversion*) Ablenkung *f* ③ (*confusion*) Aufregung *f*
distraught [dɪ·ˈstrɔt] *adj* verzweifelt, außer sich *dat*
distress [dɪ·ˈstres] **I.** *n* ① (*pain*) Leid *nt*; (*anguish*) Kummer *m*, Sorge *f* (**at** über +*akk*) ② (*despair*) Verzweiflung *f* ③ (*emergency*) Not *f* **II.** *vt* quälen
distressed [dɪ·ˈstrest] *adj* ① (*unhappy*) bekümmert ② (*shocked*) erschüttert (**at** über +*dat*) ③ (*old-looking*) *fabric* verwaschen; *jeans, furniture* Used-Look-
distressing [dɪ·ˈstres·ɪŋ], **distressful** [dɪ·ˈstres·fəl] *adj* ① (*worrying*) erschreckend ② (*painful*) schmerzlich
distribute [dɪ·ˈstrɪb·jut] *vt* verteilen; **widely ~d** weit verbreitet; *goods* vertreiben
distribution [ˌdɪs·trɪ·ˈbju·ʃən] *n* ① (*sharing*) Verteilung *f* ② (*scattering*) Verbreitung *f* ③ ECON Vertrieb *m*
distributor [dɪ·ˈstrɪb·jə·t̬ər] *n* ① COMM Vertriebsgesellschaft *f* ② AUTO Verteiler *m*
district [ˈdɪs·trɪkt] *n* (*area*) Gebiet *nt*; (*within a town/country*) Bezirk *m*
district atˈtorney *n* Staatsanwalt, Staatsanwältin *m, f*
district ˈcourt *n* [Bundes]bezirksgericht *nt*

> Der **District of Columbia** (oder **D. C.**) ist der amerikanische Regierungsbezirk. Washington D. C. ist Hauptstadt und Regierungssitz der Vereinigten Staaten. Der Bezirk wurde 1791 von dem ersten amerikanischen Präsidenten, George Washington, geschaffen, der die amerikanische Hauptstadt auf neutralem Gelände gründen wollte, das keinem Staat gehören sollte. Die ursprünglichen Pläne wurden von dem franko-amerikanischen Architekten und Ingenieur Pierre Charles L'Enfant umgesetzt. Das Weiße Haus, der Supreme Court und das Kapitol, der Sitz des Kongresses, befinden sich in Washington D. C.

distrust [dɪs·ˈtrʌst] **I.** *vt* misstrauen +*dat* **II.** *n* Misstrauen *nt* (**of** gegen +*akk*)
distrustful [dɪs·ˈtrʌst·fəl] *adj* misstrauisch (**of** gegen +*akk*)
disturb [dɪ·ˈstɜrb] **I.** *vt* ① (*interrupt*) stören ② (*worry*) beunruhigen **II.** *vi* stören; **"do not ~"** „bitte nicht stören"
disturbance [dɪ·ˈstɜr·bəns] *n* ① (*annoyance*) Belästigung *f* ② (*riot*) **to cause a ~** Unruhe stiften
disturbed [dɪ·ˈstɜrbd] *adj* ① (*worried*) beunruhigt ② PSYCH [geistig] verwirrt; **mentally ~** psychisch gestört
disturbing [dɪ·ˈstɜr·bɪŋ] *adj* beunruhigend
disuse [dɪs·ˈjus] *n* Nichtgebrauch *m*; **to fall into ~** nicht mehr benutzt werden
ditch [dɪtʃ] **I.** *n* <*pl* -es> Graben *m* **II.** *vt* (*fam*) ① (*discard*) wegwerfen; *getaway car* stehen lassen; *proposal, job* aufgeben ② (*get away from*) ■ **to ~ sb** jdn versetzen ③ *plane* im Bach landen **III.** *vi* AVIAT auf dem Wasser landen
dither [ˈdɪð·ər] **I.** *n* **in a ~** ganz aufgeregt **II.** *vi* schwanken
ditto [ˈdɪt̬·oʊ] *adv* (*likewise*) dito; (*me too*) ich auch
ditty [ˈdɪt̬·i] *n* [banales] Liedchen
divan [dɪ·ˈvan] *n* Diwan *m*
dive [daɪv] **I.** *n* ① (*into water*) [Kopf]sprung *m* ② *of a plane* Sturzflug *m* ③ (*sudden movement*) **to make a ~ at sb** auf jdn zuspringen ④ (*drop in price*) [Preis]sturz *m* ⑤ (*fam: dingy place*) Spelunke *f* **II.** *vi* <dived *or* dove, dived *or* dove> ① (*into water*) einen Kopfsprung ins Wasser machen; (*underwater*) tauchen ② *plane, bird* einen Sturzflug machen ③ (*move quickly*) ■ **to ~ for sth** nach etw *dat* hechten; **to ~ for cover** schnell in Deckung gehen
diver [ˈdaɪ·vər] *n* ① (*in ocean, lake*) Taucher(in) *m(f)*; SPORTS Turmspringer(in) *m(f)* ② (*bird*) Taucher *m*
diverge [dɪ·ˈvɜrdʒ] *vi* auseinandergehen
divergence [dɪ·ˈvɜr·dʒəns] *n* ① (*difference*) Divergenz *f* ② (*deviation*) Abweichung *f*
divergent [dɪ·ˈvɜr·dʒənt] *adj* ① (*differing*) abweichend; *opinions* auseinandergehend ② MATH divergent

diverse [dɪ·ˈvɜrs] *adj* ① (*varied*) vielfältig ② (*not alike*) unterschiedlich

diversification [dɪ·ˌvɜr·sɪ·fɪ·ˈkeɪ·ʃən] *n* Diversifikation *f*

diversify <-ie-> [dɪ·ˈvɜr·sɪ·faɪ] **I.** *vi* vielfältiger werden **II.** *vt* umfangreicher machen

diversion [dɪ·ˈvɜr·ʃən] *n* ① (*rerouting*) Verlegung *f;* **traffic ~** Umleitung *f* ② (*distraction*) Ablenkung *f*

diversity [dɪ·ˈvɜr·sɪ·t̬i] *n* Vielfalt *f*

divert [dɪ·ˈvɜrt] *vt* ① (*reroute*) verlegen; *traffic* umleiten ② (*reallocate*) *funds* anders einsetzen ③ (*distract*) ablenken

diverting [dɪ·ˈvɜr·t̬ɪŋ] *adj* unterhaltsam

divest [dɪ·ˈvest] *vt* ① (*deprive*) berauben ② (*sell*) verkaufen

divide [dɪ·ˈvaɪd] **I.** *n* ① (*gulf*) Kluft *f* ② (*boundary*) Grenze *f* ③ GEOG (*watershed*) Wasserscheide *f* **II.** *vt* ① (*split*) teilen ② (*share*) *profits* aufteilen ③ MATH teilen (**by** durch *+akk*) ④ (*separate*) trennen **III.** *vi* ① (*split*) sich teilen; **to ~ equally** [*or* **evenly**] in gleiche Teile zerfallen ② (*separate*) sich trennen ③ MATH dividieren

◆**divide off** *vt* [ab]teilen

◆**divide up I.** *vt* aufteilen **II.** *vi* sich teilen

divided [dɪ·ˈvaɪ·dɪd] *adj* uneinig

divided ˈhighway *n* Schnellstraße *f*

dividend [ˈdɪv·ɪ·dend] *n* FIN Dividende *f;* (*fig*) **to pay ~s** sich bezahlt machen

dividers [dɪ·ˈvaɪ·dərz] *npl* [**a pair of**] **~** [ein] Zirkel *m*

diˈviding line *n* Trennlinie *f*

divine [dɪ·ˈvaɪn] **I.** *adj* ① (*of God*) göttlich; **~ intervention** Gottes Hilfe; **~ right** heiliges Recht ② (*splendid*) himmlisch **II.** *vt* erraten; *future* vorhersehen

diving [ˈdaɪ·vɪŋ] *n* ① (*into water*) Tauchen *nt;* SPORTS Turmspringen *nt* ② (*underwater*) Tauchen *nt;* **to go ~** tauchen gehen

ˈdiving bell *n* Taucherglocke *f*

ˈdiving board *n* Sprungbrett *nt*

ˈdiving suit *n* Taucheranzug *m*

diˈvining rod *n* Wünschelrute *f*

divinity [dɪ·ˈvɪn·ɪ·t̬i] *n* ① (*godliness*) Göttlichkeit *f* ② (*god*) Gottheit *f*

divisible [dɪ·ˈvɪz·ə·bəl] *adj* teilbar (**by** durch *+akk*)

division [dɪ·ˈvɪʒ·ən] *n* ① (*sharing*) Verteilung *f* ② (*breakup*) Teilung *f* ③ MATH Division *f* ④ (*section*) Teil *m* ⑤ (*department*) Abteilung *f* ⑥ (*league*) Liga *f* ⑦ (*disagreement*) Meinungsverschiedenheit *f*

divisive [dɪ·ˈvaɪ·sɪv] *adj* entzweiend; **~ issue** Streitfrage *f*

divorce [dɪ·ˈvɔrs] **I.** *n* ① LAW Scheidung *f* ② (*fig*) Trennung *f* **II.** *vt* ① (*dissolve marriage*) ■**to ~ sb** [*or* **get ~d from sb**] sich von jdm scheiden lassen ② (*distance*) ■**to ~ oneself from sth** sich selbst von etw *dat* trennen **III.** *vi* sich scheiden lassen

divorcé [dɪ·ˈvɔr·seɪ] *n* Geschiedener *m*

divorced [dɪ·ˈvɔrst] *adj* ① (*no longer married*) geschieden ② (*out of touch*) ■**to be ~ from sth** keinen Bezug zu etw *dat* haben

divorcée [dɪ·ˌvɔr·ˈseɪ] *n* Geschiedene *f*

divulge [dɪ·ˈvʌldʒ] *vt* enthüllen; *information* weitergeben

dizziness [ˈdɪz·ɪ·nɪs] *n* Schwindel *m*

dizzy [ˈdɪz·i] *adj* ① (*unsteady*) schwindlig; **~ spells** Schwindelanfälle *pl* ② (*rapid*) atemberaubend ③ (*fam: scatterbrained*) dumm, einfältig

DJ [ˈdi·dʒeɪ] *n abbrev of* **disc jockey** DJ *m*

DMV [ˌdi·em·ˈvi] *n abbrev of* **Department of Motor Vehicles** Kfz-Zulassungsstelle *f*

DNA [ˌdi·en·ˈeɪ] *n abbrev of* **deoxyribonucleic acid** DNS *f*

do [du] **I.** *aux vb* <does, did, done> ① (*negating verb*) **Fred ~esn't like olives** Fred mag keine Oliven; **I ~n't want to go yet!** ich will noch nicht gehen!; **I ~n't smoke** ich rauche nicht ② (*forming question*) **~ you like children?** magst du Kinder?; **what did you say?** was hast du gesagt?; **~ I like cheese? — I love cheese!** ob ich Käse mag? – ich liebe Käse! ③ (*for emphasis*) **can I come? — please ~!** kann ich mitkommen? – aber bitte!; **you ~ look tired** du siehst wirklich müde aus; **~ tell me!** sag's mir doch! ④ (*replacing verb*) **she runs much faster than he ~es** sie läuft viel schneller als er; **who ate the cake? — I did!/didn't!** wer hat den Kuchen gegessen? – ich!/ich nicht!; **... so ~ I ...** ich auch; **so you ~n't like her — I ~!** du magst sie also nicht – doch! **II.** *vt* <does, did, done> ① tun, machen; **just ~ it!** mach's einfach!; **that was a stupid thing to ~** das war dumm!; **what did you ~ with my coat?** wo hast du meinen Mantel hingetan?; **what am I going to ~ with myself?** was soll ich nur die ganze Zeit machen?; **what are you going to ~ with that hammer?** was hast du mit dem Hammer vor?; **what ~es your father ~?** was macht dein Vater beruflich?; **today we're going to ~ Chapter 4** heute beschäftigen wir uns mit Kapitel 4; **to ~ the shopping** einkaufen; **to ~ the dishes** das Geschirr abspülen; **where ~ you get your hair done?** zu welchem Friseur gehst du?; **let me ~ the talking** überlass mir das Reden ② (*fam: finish*) **are you done?** bist du jetzt fertig? ③ (*travel*) fahren ④ (*suffice*) ■**to ~ sb** jdm genügen; **that'll ~ me nicely, thank you** das reicht mir dicke, danke! ⑤ (*put on*) *play* aufführen ⑥ (*impersonate*) nachmachen; (*fig*) **I hope she won't ~ a Helen and ...** ich hoffe, sie macht es nicht wie Helen und ... ⑦ (*fam: impress*) **that movie really did something to me** dieser Film hat mich wirklich beeindruckt ⑧ (*fam: serve*) *time in jail* sitzen ⑨ (*fam: cheat*) ■**to ~ sb out of sth** jdn übers Ohr hauen ⑩ (*vulg, sl: have sex with*) **to ~ it with sb** mit jdm schlafen *euph* ▶PHRASES: **that ~es it!** so, das war's jetzt! **III.** *vi* <does, did, done> ① (*behave*) tun; **to ~ well to do sth** gut daran tun, etw zu tun;

~ **as you're told** tu, was man dir sagt ❷ (*fare*) **sb is ~ing fine** jdm geht es gut; **mother and baby are ~ing well** Mutter und Kind sind wohlauf; **our daughter is ~ing well in school** unsere Tochter ist gut in der Schule ❸ (*fam: finish*) **I'm not done with you [just] yet** ich bin noch nicht fertig mit dir ❹ (*be acceptable, suffice*) **that'll ~** das ist o.k. so; **this will ~ just fine as a table** das wird einen guten Tisch abgeben; **will this room ~?** ist dieses Zimmer o.k. für Sie? ▶ PHRASES: **that will ~** jetzt reicht's aber!; **how ~ you ~?** (*form: as introduction*) angenehm **IV.** *n* ❶ (*allowed, not allowed*) **the ~s and ~n'ts** was man tun und was man nicht tun sollte ❷ (*fam: party*) Fete *f*

◆**do away with** *vi* ❶ (*discard*) abschaffen ❷ (*fam: kill*) um die Ecke bringen

◆**do over** *vt* noch einmal machen

◆**do up** *vt* ❶ (*dress*) ■**to ~ oneself up** sich zurechtmachen ❷ (*adorn*) herrichten; *house* renovieren ❸ (*close*) zumachen

◆**do with** *vi* ❶ (*fam: need*) brauchen; **I could ~ with some sleep** ich könnte jetzt etwas Schlaf gebrauchen ❷ (*be related to*) um etw *akk* gehen; **to have nothing to ~ with sth** mit etw *dat* nichts zu tun haben ❸ (*concern*) **sth has nothing to ~ with sb** etw geht jdn nichts an

◆**do without** *vi* ❶ (*not have*) auskommen ohne ❷ (*prefer not to have*) verzichten auf +*akk*

docile ['das·əl] *adj* sanftmütig

dock[1] [dak] **I.** *n* ❶ (*wharf*) Dock *nt;* ■**the ~s** *pl* die Hafenanlagen *pl;* **dry ~** Trockendock *nt* ❷ (*pier*) Kai *m* **II.** *vi* ❶ NAUT anlegen ❷ AEROSP andocken (**with** an +*akk*) **III.** *vt* ■**to ~ sth** etw eindocken; AEROSP etw aneinanderkoppeln

dock[2] [dak] *n* LAW Anklagebank *f*

dock[3] [dak] *vt* ❶ (*reduce*) kürzen (**by** um +*akk*); (*deduct*) abziehen ❷ (*cut off*) [den Schwanz] kupieren

docker ['dak·ər] *n* Hafenarbeiter(in) *m(f)*

docket ['dak·ɪt] *n* LAW Terminplan *m*

'dockyard *n* Werft *f*

doctor ['dak·tər] **I.** *n* ❶ (*medic*) Arzt, Ärztin *m, f;* **good morning, D~ Smith** guten Morgen, Herr/Frau Doktor Smith ❷ (*academic*) Doktor *m* ▶ PHRASES: **to be just what the ~ ordered** genau das Richtige sein **II.** *vt* ❶ (*falsify*) fälschen, frisieren ❷ (*poison*) vergiften

doctorate ['dak·tər·ət] *n* Doktor[titel] *m*

> Ein **doctorate** (Doktorwürde) oder ein **doctor's degree** (Doktortitel) in einem Fach ist der höchste akademische Grad, den man in der Regel für eine wissenschaftliche Arbeit von einer Universität verliehen bekommt. Der am häufigsten verliehene **doctorate** ist ein *Ph. D.* für eine Doktorarbeit in geisteswissenschaftlichen Fächern oder Musikwissenschaften. Weitere Doktorgrade sind: *J. D.* (*juris doctor, Doctor of Law*) (Doktor der Rechtswissenschaften), *M. D.* (*Doctor of Medicine*) (Doktor der Medizin) und *Th. D.* (*Doctor of Theology*) (Doktor der Theologie). Ein *honorary doctorate* oder *honorary Ph. D.* (Ehrendoktor) kann eine Universität einer Persönlichkeit von hohem Rang aufgrund wichtiger Veröffentlichungen oder sonstiger Arbeiten verleihen.

D

doctrine ['dak·trɪn] *n* ❶ (*set of beliefs*) Doktrin *f* ❷ (*belief*) Grundsatz *m*

document ['dak·jə·mənt] **I.** *n* Dokument *nt;* **travel ~s** Reisepapiere *pl* **II.** *vt* dokumentieren

documentary [ˌdak·jə·'men·tə·ri] **I.** *n* Dokumentation *f,* Dokumentarfilm *m* (**on/about** über +*akk*) **II.** *adj* ❶ (*factual*) dokumentarisch, Dokumentar- ❷ (*official*) urkundlich, Urkunden-

documentation [ˌdak·jə·men·'teɪ·ʃən] *n* ❶ (*proof*) [dokumentarischer] Nachweis ❷ COMPUT (*manual*) Informationsmaterial *nt*

doddering ['dad·ər·ɪŋ] *adj* (*fam*) tattrig

dodge [dadʒ] **I.** *vt* ❶ (*avoid*) *blow* ausweichen +*dat* ❷ (*evade*) sich entziehen; *military service* sich drücken vor; *question* ausweichend beantworten **II.** *vi* ausweichen **III.** *n* (*fam*) Trick *m*

dodger ['dadʒ·ər] *n* (*pej*) Drückeberger(in) *m(f)*

doe [doʊ] *n* ❶ (*deer*) Hirschkuh *f,* [Reh]geiß *f* ❷ (*hare or rabbit*) Häsin *f*

doer ['du·ər] *n* (*approv*) Macher *m*

does [dʌz] *vt, vi, aux vb 3rd pers. sing of* **do**

doesn't ['dʌz·ənt] = **does not** *see* **do I., II.**

dog [dɔg] **I.** *n* ❶ (*canine*) Hund *m* ❷ (*pej: nasty man*) **the [dirty] ~!** der [gemeine] Hund!; (*pej sl: ugly woman*) Bratze *f* ▶ PHRASES: **every ~ has its day** (*prov*) auch ein blindes Huhn findet mal ein Korn; **~ eat ~** jeder gegen jeden; **to go to the ~s** vor die Hunde gehen; **to work like a ~** arbeiten wie ein Pferd *fam* **II.** *vt* <-gg-> ❶ (*follow*) ständig verfolgen ❷ (*beset*) begleiten

'dog biscuit *n* Hundekuchen *m*

'dog collar *n* ❶ (*of a dog*) Hundehalsband *nt* ❷ (*fam: of a minister*) Halskragen *m* [eines Geistlichen]

'dog-eared *adj* mit Eselsohren

dogged ['dɔ·gɪd] *adj* verbissen, zäh

doggerel ['dɔ·gər·əl] *n* Knittelvers *m*

'doghouse *n* Hundehütte *f* ▶ PHRASES: **to be in the ~** in Ungnade gefallen sein

dogma ['dɔg·mə] *n* Dogma *nt*

dogmatic [dɔg·'mæt̬·ɪk] *adj* dogmatisch (**about** in +*dat*)

'dog race *n* Hunderennen *nt*

dog-'tired *adj* (*fam*) hundemüde

doing ['du·ɪŋ] *n* ❶ (*sb's work*) **to be sb's ~** jds Werk sein; **to take some [*or* a lot of] ~** ganz schön anstrengend sein ❷ *pl* (*activities*) ■ **~s** Tätigkeiten *pl*

do-it-yourself [ˌdu·ɪt·jər·ˈself] *n* Heimwerken *nt*

doldrums [ˈdoʊl·drəmz] *npl* (*fig*) **to be in the ~** (*be in low spirits*) deprimiert sein; (*be in stagnant state*) in einer Flaute stecken

dole [doʊl] *vt* ■ **to ~ out** sparsam austeilen (**to** an +*akk*)

doleful [ˈdoʊl·fəl] *adj* traurig

doll [dal] **I.** *n* ❶ (*toy*) Puppe *f* ❷ (*fam: attractive woman*) Puppe *f* **II.** *vt* ■ **to ~ oneself up** sich herausputzen

dollar [ˈdal·ər] *n* Dollar *m*

dollop [ˈdal·əp] *n* Klacks *m kein pl*

dolly [ˈdal·i] *n* ❶ TRANSP [Transport]wagen *m* ❷ (*esp childspeak: doll*) Püppchen *nt*

dolphin [ˈdal·fɪn] *n* Delphin *m*

dolt [doʊlt] *n* (*pej*) Tollpatsch *m*

domain [doʊ·ˈmeɪn] *n* ❶ Reich *nt*, Gebiet *nt* ❷ COMPUT Domäne *f*; TELEC Domain *f*

dome [doʊm] *n* Kuppel *f*

domed [doʊmd] *adj* gewölbt; **~ ceiling** Kuppeldach *nt*

domestic [də·ˈmes·tɪk] *adj* ❶ (*household*) häuslich; **~ appliance** [elektrisches] Haushaltsgerät ❷ ECON, POL inländisch, Inland[s]-; **~ policy** Innenpolitik *f*; **~ correspondent** Korrespondent(in) *m(f)* für Innenpolitik; **~ airline** Inlandsfluggesellschaft *f*; **~ market** Binnenmarkt *m*; **~ transportation** Binnentransport *m*; **gross ~ product** Bruttoinlandsprodukt *nt*

domesticate [də·ˈmes·tɪ·keɪt] *vt* ❶ (*tame*) zähmen ❷ (*accustom to home life*) häuslich machen

domesticity [ˌdoʊ·me·ˈstɪs·ɪ·t̬i] *n* Häuslichkeit *f*, häusliches Leben

domestic ˈviolence *n* Gewalt *f* in der Familie, häusliche Gewalt

domicile [ˈdam·ə·saɪl] (*form*) **I.** *n* Wohnsitz *m* **II.** *vi* **to be ~d in ...** in ... ansässig sein

dominance [ˈdam·ə·nəns] *n* ❶ (*superior position*) Vormacht[stellung] *f* ❷ (*being dominant*) Dominanz *f*, Vorherrschaft *f* (**over** über +*akk*)

dominant [ˈdam·ə·nənt] *adj* ❶ (*controlling*) *color, culture* vorherrschend; *issue, position* beherrschend; *personality* dominierend ❷ BIOL, MUS dominant

dominate [ˈdam·ə·neɪt] **I.** *vt* ❶ beherrschen ❷ PSYCH dominieren **II.** *vi* dominieren

domination [ˌdam·ə·ˈneɪ·ʃən] *n* ❶ (*state of dominating*) [Vor]herrschaft *f*; **world ~** Weltherrschaft *f* ❷ (*controlling position*) Vormachtstellung *f*

domineering [ˌdam·ə·ˈnɪr·ɪŋ] *adj* herrschsüchtig, herrisch

Dominican [də·ˈmɪn·ɪ·kən] **I.** *adj* ❶ REL Dominikaner- ❷ (*relating to Dominican Republic*) dominikanisch **II.** *n* Dominikaner(in) *m(f)*

dominion [də·ˈmɪn·jən] *n* ❶ (*form: sovereignty*) Herrschaft *f* (**over** über +*akk*) ❷ (*realm*) Herrschaftsgebiet *nt*

domino <*pl* -es> [ˈdam·ə·noʊ] *n* ❶ (*piece*) Dominostein *m* ❷ (*game*) ■ **~es** + *sing vb, no art* Domino[spiel] *nt*

don [dan] *n* (*sl*) Mafiaboss *m*

donate [ˈdoʊ·neɪt] *vt, vi* spenden (**to** für +*akk*)

donation [doʊ·ˈneɪ·ʃən] *n* ❶ (*contribution*) [Geld]spende *f*; (*endowment*) Stiftung *f*; LAW Schenkung *f*; **charitable ~s** Spenden *pl* für wohltätige Zwecke ❷ (*act of donating*) Spenden *nt*

done [dʌn] *pp of* **do**

donkey [ˈdaŋ·ki] *n* Esel *m a. fig*

donor [ˈdoʊ·nər] *n* Spender(in) *m(f)*; (*for large sums*) Stifter(in) *m(f)*; LAW Schenker(in) *m(f)*

don't [doʊnt] *see* **do not** *see* **do I., II.**

donut [ˈdoʊ·nʌt] *n see* **doughnut**

doodle [ˈdu·d̬l] **I.** *vi* vor sich *akk* hinkritzeln **II.** *n* Gekritzel *nt kein pl*

doom [dum] **I.** *n* ❶ (*grim destiny*) Verhängnis *nt kein pl*, [schlimmes] Schicksal ❷ (*disaster*) Unheil *nt* **II.** *vt* verdammen

doomed [dumd] *adj* ❶ (*destined to end badly*) verdammt ❷ (*condemned*) verurteilt

doomsday [ˈdumz·deɪ] *n* der Jüngste Tag

door [dɔr] *n* ❶ (*entrance*) Tür *f*; **out of ~s** im Freien, draußen ❷ (*house*) **two ~s away** zwei Häuser weiter; **next ~** nebenan; **~ to ~** von Tür zu Tür ❸ (*fig*) **to close the ~ on sth** etw ausschließen; **to open the ~ to sth** etw ermöglichen

ˈdoorbell *n* Türklingel *f*

ˈdoorframe *n* Türrahmen *m*

ˈdoorkeeper *n* Portier, Portiersfrau *m, f*

ˈdoorknob *n* Türknauf *m*

ˈdoorman *n* Portier *m*

ˈdoormat *n* ❶ (*thing*) Fußmatte *f*, Fußabstreifer *m bes* SÜDD ❷ (*fig, pej: person*) Waschlappen *m*

ˈdoornail *n* **as dead as a ~** mausetot

ˈdoorstep *n* (*step outside a house door*) Türstufe *f*; **right on one's ~** (*fig*) direkt vor der Haustür

door-to-ˈdoor *adj* von Haus zu Haus

ˈdoorway *n* [Tür]eingang *m*

doozy [ˈdu·zi] *n* (*sl: difficult job*) **to be a [real] ~** eine Heidenarbeit sein

dope [doʊp] **I.** *n* ❶ (*fam: illegal drug*) Rauschgift *nt*, Stoff *m sl* ❷ (*sl: stupid person*) Trottel *m* **II.** *vt* dopen

dopey [ˈdoʊ·pi] *adj* ❶ (*drowsy*) benebelt ❷ (*pej: stupid*) blöd

dorm [dɔrm] *n* Studentenwohnheim *nt*

dormant [ˈdɔr·mənt] *adj* ❶ (*inactive*) *volcano* untätig; *talents* brachliegend ❷ BOT, BIOL ■ **to be ~** ruhen; **to lie ~** schlafen; *seeds* ruhen

dormer [dɔr·mər], **dormer window** [dɔr·mər'-] *n* Mansardenfenster *nt*

dormitory [ˈdɔr·mɪ·tɔr·i] *n* ❶ (*student housing*) Studentenwohnheim *nt* ❷ (*sleeping quarters*) Schlafsaal *m*

dormouse [ˈdɔr·maʊs] *n* Haselmaus *f*

dorsal [ˈdɔr·səl] *adj* Rücken-

DOS [das] *n acr for* **disk operating system**

DOS *nt*
dosage ['doʊ·sɪdʒ] *n* (*size of dose*) Dosis *f*
dose [doʊs] **I.** *n* (*dosage*) Dosis *f a. fig* **II.** *vt* [medizinisch] behandeln
dossier ['dɑs·i·eɪ] *n* Dossier *nt*
DOT [ˌdi·oʊ·'ti] *n* (*fam*) *abbrev of* **Department of Transportation** Verkehrsministerium *nt*
dot [dɑt] **I.** *n* Punkt *m;* (*on material*) Tupfen *m* **II.** *vt* <-tt-> ❶ (*make a dot*) mit einem Punkt versehen ❷ *usu passive* (*scatter*) ■ **to be ~ted with sth** mit etw *dat* übersät sein
doting ['doʊ·t̬ɪŋ] *adj* vernarrt
dot-'matrix printer *n* Matrixdrucker *m*
double ['dʌb·əl] **I.** *adj* ❶ (*twice, two*) doppelt; **~ the price** doppelt so teuer; **my telephone number is: six, eight, two, five ~ oh three** meine Telefonnummer ist die sechs, acht, zwei, fünf, zweimal die Null, drei ❷ (*of two equal parts, layers*) Doppel-; **~ door**[**s**] (*with two parts*) Flügeltür *f;* (*twofold*) Doppeltür *f; pneumonia* doppelseitig; **~ life** Doppelleben *nt* **II.** *adv* ❶ (*twice as much*) doppelt so viel; **to charge sb ~** jdm das Doppelte berechnen ❷ (*two times*) **to see ~** doppelt sehen ❸ (*in the middle*) **to be bent ~** sich niederbeugen; (*with laughter, pain*) sich krümmen **III.** *n* ❶ (*double quantity*) ■ **the ~** das Doppelte [*o* Zweifache] ❷ (*whiskey, gin*) Doppelte(r) *m* ❸ (*duplicate person*) Doppelgänger(in) *m(f);* FILM Double *nt* ❹ SPORTS ■ **~s** *pl* Doppel *nt;* **mixed ~s** gemischtes Doppel ❺ (*in baseball*) Double *m* ▶ PHRASES: **on the ~** im Eiltempo **IV.** *vt* ❶ verdoppeln ❷ (*fold in two*) doppelt nehmen **V.** *vi* ❶ (*increase twofold*) sich verdoppeln ❷ (*serve a second purpose*) eine Doppelfunktion haben; FILM, THEAT (*play*) eine Doppelrolle spielen; **the kitchen table ~s as my desk** der Küchentisch dient auch als mein Schreibtisch ❸ (*in baseball*) einen Double schlagen
◆**double back** *vi* kehrtmachen
◆**double over** *vi* sich krümmen (**in, with** vor +*dat*)
◆**double up** *vi* ❶ (*bend over*) sich krümmen (**in, with** vor +*dat*) ❷ (*share a room*) sich *dat* ein Zimmer teilen
double-'barreled *adj* ❶ (*having two barrels*) doppelläufig ❷ (*having two purposes*) zweideutig
double 'bass *n* Kontrabass *m*
double 'bed *n* Doppelbett *nt*
double-'breasted *adj* zweireihig; **~ suit** Zweireiher *m*
double-'check *vt* noch einmal überprüfen
double 'chin *n* Doppelkinn *nt*
double-'click COMPUT **I.** *vt* doppelt anklicken **II.** *vi* doppelklicken
double-'cross[1] *vt* ■ **to ~ sb** mit jdm ein falsches Spiel treiben
double-'cross[2], **double 'cross** *n* <*pl* -es> Doppelspiel *nt*
double-'dealing (*pej*) **I.** *n* Betrügerei *f* **II.** *adj* betrügerisch
double-'decker *n* Doppeldecker *m*
double-'edged *adj* zweischneidig *a. fig*
double 'feature *n* FILM Doppelprogramm *nt*
double-'jointed *adj* äußerst gelenkig
double-'park *vt, vi* in der zweiten Reihe parken
double 'standard *n* Doppelmoral *f kein pl;* **to apply ~s** mit zweierlei Maß messen
double 'take *n* verzögerte Reaktion; ■ **to do a ~** zweimal hinschauen
double 'time *n* ❶ (*double pay*) doppelter Stundenlohn ❷ MIL Laufschritt *m*
doubly ['dʌb·li] *adv* doppelt
doubt [daʊt] **I.** *n* ❶ (*lack of certainty*) Zweifel *m* (**about** an +*dat*); ■ **to be in ~ about sth** über etw *akk* im Zweifel sein; **no ~** zweifellos; **open to ~** fraglich, unsicher; **to cast ~ on sth** etw in Zweifel ziehen ❷ (*feeling of uncertainty*) Ungewissheit *f,* Bedenken *pl* **II.** *vt* ❶ (*be unwilling to believe*) ■ **to ~ sb** jdm misstrauen; ■ **to ~ sth** Zweifel an etw *dat* haben ❷ (*call in question*) ■ **to ~ sb** jdm nicht glauben; **to ~ sb's abilities** an jds Fähigkeiten zweifeln ❸ (*feel uncertain*) ■ **to ~ that ...** bezweifeln, dass ...
doubtful ['daʊt·fəl] *adj* ❶ (*expressing doubt*) zweifelnd; **the expression on her face was ~** sie blickte skeptisch ❷ (*uncertain, undecided*) unsicher, unschlüssig; ■ **to be ~ about sth** über etw *akk* im Zweifel sein ❸ (*questionable*) fragwürdig, zweifelhaft
doubtless ['daʊt·lɪs] *adv* sicherlich
dough [doʊ] *n* ❶ (*for baking*) Teig *m* ❷ (*sl: money*) Knete *f,* Kohle *f*
doughnut ['doʊ·nʌt] *n* Donut *m*
doughy ['doʊ·i] *adj* teigig *a. fig*
dour [dʊr] *adj person* mürrisch; *face* düster; *expression* finster; *struggle* hart[näckig]
douse [daʊs] *vt* ❶ (*drench*) übergießen ❷ (*extinguish*) ausmachen; *fire* löschen
dove[1] [dʌv] *n* Taube *f a. fig*
dove[2] [doʊv] *vi pt of* **dive**
'dovetail I. *vi* übereinstimmen **II.** *vt* TECH *in wood* verschwalben; *in metal* verzinken **III.** *n* (*wood*) Schwalbenschwanz *m;* (*metal*) Zinken *m*
dowager ['daʊ·ə·dʒər] *n* [adlige] Witwe
dowdy ['daʊ·di] *adj* (*pej*) ohne jeden Schick
down[1] [daʊn] **I.** *adv* ❶ (*movement to a lower position*) hinunter; (*toward the speaker*) herunter; **"~!"** (*to a dog*) „Platz!" ❷ (*downwards*) nach unten; [**with one's**] **head ~** mit dem Kopf nach unten ❸ (*in a lower position*) unten; **~ there** dort unten ❹ (*in the south*) im Süden, unten *fam;* (*toward the south*) in den Süden, runter *fam* ❺ (*ill*) **to be ~ with sth** an etw *dat* erkrankt sein ❻ SPORTS im Rückstand ❼ (*including*) **from the mayor ~** angefangen beim Bürgermeister ❽ (*on paper*) **to have sth ~ in writing** [*or* **on paper**] etw schriftlich haben ❾ (*as initial payment*) als Anzahlung; **to pay** [*or* **put**] **100 dollars ~** 100 Dollar anzahlen ❿ (*in crossword puzzles*) senkrecht **II.** *prep* ❶ (*in a downward/downhill direc-*

D

tion) hinunter; (*toward the speaker*) herunter; **up and ~ the stairs** die Treppe rauf und runter; **she poured the milk ~ the sink** sie schüttete die Milch in den Abfluss ❷ **to come/go ~ the mountain** den Berg herunter-/hinuntersteigen ❸ (*along*) entlang; **go ~ the street** gehen Sie die Straße entlang; **~ the river** flussabwärts ❹ (*through time*) **~ the centuries** die Jahrhunderte hindurch **III.** *adj* ❶ (*moving downward*) abwärtsführend; **the ~ escalator** die Rolltreppe nach unten ❷ (*fam: unhappy*) niedergeschlagen, down *fam* ❸ (*not functioning*) außer Betrieb; *telephone lines* tot **IV.** *vt* ❶ (*knock down*) *person* zu Fall bringen ❷ (*shoot down*) *plane* abschießen **V.** *n* ❶ (*bad fortune*) **we've had our ups and ~s** wir haben schon Höhen und Tiefen durchgemacht ❷ (*in football*) Versuch *m* **VI.** *interj* **~ with the dictator!** nieder mit dem Diktator!

down² [daʊn] *n* (*soft feathers*) Daunen *pl*

down-and-'out I. *adj* heruntergekommen **II.** *n* (*pej*) Penner(in) *m(f)*

'downbeat *adj* (*sad*) pessimistisch, düster

'downcast *adj* ❶ (*sad*) niedergeschlagen ❷ (*looking down*) gesenkt

'downfall *n* ❶ (*ruin*) Untergang *m,* Fall *m fig; of government* Sturz *m* ❷ (*cause of ruin*) Ruin *m*

'downgrade I. *vt person* degradieren; *thing* herunterstufen **II.** *n* Gefälle *nt*

down'hearted *adj* niedergeschlagen

'downhill I. *adv* (*downwards*) bergab, abwärts; **to go ~** *person* heruntergehen; *vehicle* herunterfahren; *road, path* bergab führen; (*fig*) *person* bergab gehen; *situation* sich verschlechtern **II.** *adj* **it's all ~ from here** von hier geht es nur noch bergab; **to be ~ [all the way]** leichter werden

'download *vt* COMPUT herunterladen (**to** auf *+akk*)

down'market I. *adj* weniger anspruchsvoll, für den Massenmarkt **II.** *adv* auf den Massenmarkt ausgerichtet

down 'payment *n* Anzahlung *f*

down'play *vt* herunterspielen

'downpour *n* Regenguss *m,* Platzregen *m*

'downright I. *adj* völlig; *lie* glatt; *nonsense* komplett **II.** *adv* (*completely*) ausgesprochen; **~ dangerous** schlichtweg gefährlich

'downside *n* Kehrseite *f;* **the ~ of sth** die Kehrseite einer S. *gen*

'downsize *vi* ECON Personal abbauen

downsizing *n* ECON Entlassung *f* (*aus Arbeitsmangel oder Rationalisierungsgründen*)

'downstairs I. *adv* treppab, die Treppe hinunter, nach unten; **there's a man ~** unten steht ein Mann **II.** *adj* ❶ (*one floor down*) im unteren Stockwerk ❷ (*on the ground floor*) im Erdgeschoss **III.** *n* Erdgeschoss *nt*

'downstream I. *adv* stromabwärts **II.** *adj* stromabwärts gelegen

'downtime *n* MECH Ausfallzeit *f*

down-to-'earth *adj* nüchtern

'downtown I. *n* Innenstadt *f,* Zentrum *nt* **II.** *adj, adv* in der Innenstadt, im Zentrum; *go* in die Innenstadt, ins Zentrum

'downtrodden *adj* unterdrückt

'downturn *n* ECON Rückgang *m*

down 'under *adv* (*Australia*) in [*o* nach] Australien; (*New Zealand*) in [*o* nach] Neuseeland

downward ['daʊn·wərd] **I.** *adj* nach unten [gerichtet]; **on a ~ trend** im Abwärtstrend **II.** *adv* ❶ (*in/toward a lower position*) abwärts, nach unten, hinunter ❷ (*to a lower amount*) nach unten

downwards ['daʊn·wərdz] *adv see* **downward**

dowry ['daʊ·ri] *n* Mitgift *f*

dowse [daʊz] *vt see* **douse**

dowsing ['daʊ·zɪŋ] *n* Wünschelrutengehen *nt;* **~ rod** Wünschelrute *f*

doze [doʊz] **I.** *n* Nickerchen *nt* **II.** *vi* ■ **to ~ [off]** dösen

dozen ['dʌz·ən] *n* Dutzend *nt;* **half a ~** ein halbes Dutzend

Dr. *n abbrev of* **doctor** Dr.

drab <-bb-> [dræb] *adj* trist; *colors* trüb; *person* farblos; *surroundings* trostlos

draconian [drə·'koʊ·ni·ən] *adj* drakonisch

draft [dræft] **I.** *n* ❶ (*air current*) [Luft]zug *m kein pl;* **to sit in a ~** im Zug sitzen ❷ **on ~** vom Fass ❸ MIL Einberufung *f;* **~ card** (*hist*) Einberufungsbescheid *m* ❹ (*preliminary version*) **[first/rough] ~** [erster/roher] Entwurf *m* **II.** *adj* ❶ **~ animal** Zugtier *nt* ❷ **~ beer** Fassbier *nt* ❸ (*relating to military conscription*) Einberufungs-; **~ board** Wehrersatzbehörde *f* ❹ (*preliminary*) Entwurfs-; **~ contract** Vertragsentwurf *m* **III.** *vt* ❶ (*prepare*) entwerfen; *bill* verfassen; *contract* aufsetzen; *proposal* ausarbeiten ❷ MIL **to ~ sb into the army** jdn zum Wehrdienst einberufen

'draft dodger *n* (*shirker*) Drückeberger(in) *m(f);* (*conscientious objector*) Wehrdienstverweigerer, -in *m, f*

draftee [dræf·'ti] *n* Wehrpflichtige(r) *f(m)*

'draftsman *n* [technischer] Zeichner

drafty ['dræf·ti] *adj* zugig

drag [dræg] **I.** *n* ❶ PHYS Widerstand *m;* AVIAT Luftwiderstand *m;* NAUT Wasserwiderstand *m* ❷ (*fig: impediment*) Hemmschuh *m* ❸ (*fam: bore*) langweilige Sache; **what a ~!** so'n Mist! *sl* ❹ (*fam: puff*) Zug *m* ❺ (*fam: road*) **the main ~** die Hauptstraße ❻ (*fam: clothing of opposite sex*) Fummel *m;* **~ queen** *Künstler, der in Frauenkleidern auftritt* **II.** *vt* <-gg-> ❶ (*pull along the ground*) ziehen; **to ~ one's heels** [*or* **feet**] schlurfen; (*fig*) sich *dat* Zeit lassen; **to ~ sth behind oneself** etw hinter sich *dat* herziehen ❷ (*take despite resistance*) schleifen; **I don't want to ~ you away** ich will dich hier nicht wegreißen ❸ (*force*) ■ **to ~ sth out of sb** etw aus jdm herausbringen; **to ~ the truth out of sb** jdm die Wahrheit entlocken **III.** *vi* <-gg-> ❶ (*trail along*) schleifen ❷ (*pej: proceed tediously*) sich [da]hinziehen;

to ~ to a close schleppend zu Ende gehen
◆**drag along** *vi thing* wegschleppen; *person* mitschleppen; **to ~ oneself along** sich dahinschleppen
◆**drag down** *vt* ① (*force to lower level*) ■**to ~ sb/sth down** jdn/etw herunterziehen ② (*make depressed*) ■**to ~ sb down** jdn zermürben
◆**drag in** *vt person* hineinziehen; *thing* aufs Tapet bringen
◆**drag on** *vi* (*pej*) sich [da]hinziehen
◆**drag out** *vt* in die Länge ziehen
dragon ['dræg·ən] *n* ① (*mythical creature*) Drache *m* ② (*woman*) Drachen *m*
'dragonfly *n* Libelle *f*
drain [dreɪn] **I.** *n* ① (*pipe*) Rohr *nt;* (*under sink*) Abflussrohr *nt;* (*in road*) Gully *m;* **to go down the ~** (*fig*) vor die Hunde gehen, den Bach runtergehen *fam* ② (*constant outflow*) Belastung *f;* ■**to be a ~ on sth** *resources* eine Belastung für etw *akk* darstellen **II.** *vt* ① (*remove liquid*) entwässern; *liquid* ablaufen lassen; *vegetables* abgießen; *noodles/rice* abtropfen lassen; *abscess* drainieren ② (*form: empty*) austrinken ③ (*exhaust*) [völlig] auslaugen **III.** *vi* ① (*flow away*) ablaufen ② (*empty*) leeren ③ (*run out*) *enthusiasm* dahinschwinden
◆**drain away** *vi liquid* ablaufen; (*fig*) [dahin]schwinden
◆**drain off** *vt water* abgießen
drainage ['dreɪ·nɪdʒ] **I.** *n* ① (*water removal*) Entwässerung *f* ② (*system*) *for land* Entwässerungssystem *nt; for houses* Kanalisation *f* **II.** *adj* Entwässerungs-
'drain board *n* Abtropfbrett *nt*
'drainpipe *n* (*for rainwater*) Regenrohr *nt;* (*for sewage*) Abflussrohr *nt*
drake [dreɪk] *n* Enterich *m,* Erpel *m*
drama ['dra·mə] **I.** *n* ① (*theater art*) Schauspielkunst *f* ② (*play, dramatic event*) Drama *nt a. fig;* **television ~** Fernsehspiel *nt* ③ (*dramatic quality*) Dramatik *f* **II.** *adj* **~ critic** Theaterkritiker(in) *m(f)*
dramatic [drə·'mæt̬·ɪk] *adj* ① dramatisch ② (*pej: theatrical*) theatralisch ③ (*in theater*) **~ irony** tragische Ironie; **~ work** [Theater]stück *nt*
dramatics [drə·'mæt̬·ɪks] *npl* ① + *sing vb* (*art of acting*) Dramaturgie *f* ② (*usu pej: behavior*) theatralisches Getue
dramatist ['dræm·ə·t̬ɪst] *n* Dramatiker(in) *m(f)*
dramatization [ˌdræm·ə·t̬ɪ·'zeɪ·ʃən] *n* ① (*dramatizing of a work*) Dramatisierung *f;* THEAT Bühnenbearbeitung *f;* FILM Kinobearbeitung *f;* TV Fernsehbearbeitung *f* ② (*usu pej: exaggeration*) Dramatisieren *nt*
dramatize ['dræm·ə·taɪz] *vt* ① (*adapt*) bearbeiten ② (*usu pej: exaggerate*) dramatisieren
drank [dræŋk] *pt of* **drink**
drape [dreɪp] **I.** *vt* ① (*cover loosely*) bedecken (**in, with** mit + *dat*) ② (*place on*) drapieren, legen **II.** *n* ■**~s** *pl* Vorhänge *pl*
drastic ['dræs·tɪk] *adj* drastisch; *change, measures* radikal
draw [drɔ] **I.** *n* ① (*celebrity*) Publikumsmagnet *m;* (*popular film, play, etc.*) Kassenschlager *m* ② (*in chess, soccer*) Unentschieden *nt;* **to end in a ~** unentschieden ausgehen ③ (*drawing lots*) Verlosung *f* ④ (*inhalation*) Zug *m* **II.** *vt* <drew, -n> ① (*make a picture*) zeichnen; *line* ziehen ② (*depict*) darstellen ③ (*pull*) ziehen; (*close*) *curtains* zuziehen; (*open*) aufziehen ④ (*attract*) anlocken; **to ~ [sb's] attention [to sb/sth]** [jds] Aufmerksamkeit *f* [auf jdn/etw] lenken; **to ~ attention to oneself** sich in Szene setzen; ■**to feel ~n to** [*or* **toward**] **sb** sich zu jdm hingezogen fühlen ⑤ (*involve in*) ■**to ~ sb into sth** jdn in etw *akk* hineinziehen ⑥ (*elicit*) hervorrufen; *confession* entlocken ⑦ (*formulate*) *comparison* anstellen; *conclusion, parallel* ziehen ⑧ (*pull out*) *weapon* ziehen ⑨ (*earn, get from source*) beziehen, erhalten ⑩ (*select by chance*) ziehen, auslosen; **to ~ lots for sth** um etw *akk* losen ⑪ FIN *money* abheben; *check* ausstellen ⑫ (*inhale*) **to ~ a [deep] breath** [tief] Luft holen **III.** *vi* <drew, -n> ① (*make pictures*) zeichnen ② (*proceed*) sich bewegen; *vehicle, ship* fahren; **to ~ alongside** [*or* **even with**] **sb/sth** mit etw/jdm gleichziehen; **to ~ away** wegfahren ③ (*make use of*) ■**to ~ on sth** auf etw *akk* zurückgreifen; **she ~s on personal experience in her work** sie schöpft bei ihrer Arbeit aus persönlichen Erfahrungen ④ (*in chess, soccer*) unentschieden spielen
◆**draw in** *vt* ① (*involve*) hineinziehen ② (*inhale*) **to ~ in a [deep] breath** [tief] Luft holen
◆**draw on** *vi* ① (*pass slowly*) *evening, summer* vergehen; **as time drew on, ...** mit der Zeit ... ② (*form: approach* [*in time*]) **winter ~s on** der Winter naht ③ *cigarette* ziehen
◆**draw out** *vt* in die Länge ziehen; *vowels* dehnen
◆**draw together** **I.** *vt people* zusammenbringen; *things* zusammenziehen **II.** *vi* zusammenrücken
◆**draw up** *vt* aufsetzen; *agenda, list* aufstellen; *guidelines* festlegen; *plan* entwerfen; *proposal, questionnaire* ausarbeiten; *report* erstellen; *will* errichten
'drawback *n* Nachteil *m*
'drawbridge *n* Zugbrücke *f*
drawer [drɔr] *n* ① (*storage*) Schublade *f;* **chest of ~s** Kommode *f* ② (*hum*) ■**~s** *pl* (*underwear*) Unterwäsche *f*
drawing ['drɔ·ɪŋ] *n* ① (*art*) Zeichnen *nt* ② (*picture*) Zeichnung *f*
'drawing board *n* Zeichenbrett *nt;* **to go back to the ~** (*fig*) noch einmal von vorn anfangen
'drawing paper *n* Zeichenpapier *nt*
'drawing room *n* (*form*) Wohnzimmer *nt*
drawl [drɔl] **I.** *n* schleppende Sprache; **Texas ~** breites Texanisch **II.** *vi* schleppend sprechen
drawn [drɔn] *pp of* **draw** abgespannt

dread [dred] **I.** *vt* ■**to ~ sth** sich vor etw *dat* [sehr] fürchten; ■**to ~ doing sth** [große] Angst haben, etw zu tun **II.** *n* Furcht *f*

dreadful ['dred·fəl] *adj* ❶ (*awful*) schrecklich, furchtbar ❷ (*of very bad quality*) miserabel, erbärmlich

dreadfully ['dred·fə·li] *adv* ❶ (*in a terrible manner*) schrecklich, entsetzlich ❷ (*extremely*) schrecklich, furchtbar

dream [drim] **I.** *n* Traum *m a. fig;* **in your ~s!** du träumst wohl! **II.** *adj* Traum- **III.** *vi, vt* <dreamed *or* dreamt, dreamed *or* dreamt> träumen *a. fig;* ■**to not ~ of sth** nicht [einmal] im Traum an etw *akk* denken; **I wouldn't ~ of asking him for money!** es würde mir nicht im Traum einfallen, ihn um Geld zu bitten

◆**dream up** *vt* sich *dat* ausdenken

dreamer ['dri·mər] *n* Träumer(in) *m(f) a. fig*

dreamless ['drim·lɪs] *adj* traumlos

'**dreamlike** *adj* traumhaft

dreamt [dremt] *pt, pp of* **dream**

dreamy ['dri·mi] *adj* ❶ (*lost in thought*) verträumt ❷ (*fam: gorgeous*) zum Träumen

dreary ['drɪr·i] *adj* ❶ (*depressing*) trostlos; *day* trüb ❷ (*monotonous*) eintönig

dredge [dredʒ] **I.** *n* [Schwimm]bagger *m* **II.** *vt river* ausbaggern

dredger[1] ['dredʒ·ər] *n* (*digger*) [Schwimm]bagger *m*

dredger[2] ['dredʒ·ər] *n* FOOD Streuer

dregs [dregz] *npl* ❶ (*drink sediment*) [Boden]satz *m kein pl* ❷ (*fig*) Abschaum *m kein pl*

drench [drentʃ] *vt* durchnässen; **~ed in sweat** schweißgebadet

dress [dres] **I.** *n* <*pl* -es> ❶ (*woman's garment*) Kleid *nt* ❷ (*clothing*) Kleidung *f* **II.** *vi* ❶ (*put on clothing*) ■**to ~** [*or* **get ~ed**] sich anziehen ❷ (*wear clothing*) sich kleiden; **to ~ casually** sich leger anziehen **III.** *vt* ❶ (*put on clothing*) ■**to ~ sb/oneself** jdn/sich anziehen ❷ FOOD *salad* anmachen ❸ (*treat*) *wound* verbinden

◆**dress down I.** *vi* sich leger anziehen **II.** *vt* zurechtweisen

◆**dress up I.** *vi* ❶ (*wear nice clothes*) sich fein anziehen ❷ (*disguise oneself*) sich verkleiden **II.** *vt* ❶ (*in a costume*) verkleiden ❷ (*improve*) verschönern

dresser[1] ['dres·ər] *n* ❶ (*person*) **to be a stylish ~** jd sein, der sich modisch kleidet ❷ THEAT Garderobier(e) *m(f)*

dresser[2] ['dres·ər] *n* Kommode *f*

dressing ['dres·ɪŋ] *n* ❶ (*for salad*) Dressing *nt* ❷ (*for injury*) Verband *m* ❸ (*of clothes*) Anziehen *nt*

dressing-'down *n* (*fam*) Standpauke *f*

'**dressing room** *n* (*in theater*) [Künstler]garderobe *f;* SPORTS Umkleidekabine *f*

'**dressing table** *n* Schminktisch *m,* Frisierkommode *f*

'**dressmaker** *n* [Damen]schneider(in) *m(f)*

'**dressmaking** *n* Schneidern *nt*

dress re'hearsal *n* THEAT Generalprobe *f*

dress 'uniform *n* Galauniform *f*

dressy ['dres·i] *adj* (*fam*) ❶ (*stylish*) elegant ❷ (*requiring formal clothes*) vornehm

drew [dru] *pt of* **draw**

dribble ['drɪb·əl] **I.** *vi* ❶ (*trickle*) tropfen ❷ *baby* sabbern ❸ SPORTS dribbeln **II.** *vt* SPORTS dribbeln mit **III.** *n* ❶ (*saliva*) Sabber *m* ❷ SPORTS Dribbling *nt kein pl*

dried [draɪd] **I.** *pt, pp of* **dry II.** *adj* getrocknet; **~ fruit** Dörrobst *nt*

dried up *adj pred,* **dried-up** *adj attr* ausgetrocknet

drift [drɪft] **I.** *vi* treiben; *balloon* schweben; *mist, fog, clouds* ziehen; *snow* angeweht werden; **to ~ along** (*fig*) sich treiben lassen; **to ~ away** *people* davonschlendern; *fog* verwehen; **to ~ with the tide** mit dem Strom schwimmen **II.** *n* ❶ (*slow movement*) Strömen *nt* ❷ *of snow* Verwehung *f* ❸ (*slow trend*) Trend *m* ❹ (*general idea*) Kernaussage *f;* **to get** [*or* **catch**] **sb's ~** verstehen, was jd sagen will

◆**drift apart** *vi* einander fremd werden

◆**drift off** *vi* einschlummern

drifter ['drɪf·tər] *n* Gammler(in) *m(f)*

'**drift ice** *n* Treibeis *nt*

'**driftwood** *n* Treibholz *nt*

drill [drɪl] **I.** *n* ❶ (*tool*) Bohrer *m* ❷ (*exercise*) Übung *f;* MIL Drill *m* ❸ (*fam: routine procedure*) **to know the ~** wissen, wie es geht **II.** *vt* ❶ *holes* bohren; ■**to ~ through sth** etw durchbohren ❷ MIL, SCH drillen **III.** *vi* ❶ (*make holes*) bohren ❷ MIL exerzieren **IV.** *adj* Bohr-

'**drilling platform** *n* Bohrinsel *f*

drink [drɪŋk] **I.** *n* ❶ Getränk *nt;* **can I get you a ~?** kann ich Ihnen etwas zu trinken bringen?; **to have a ~** etw trinken ❷ (*alcoholic drink*) Drink *m,* Gläschen *nt* ❸ (*alcohol*) Alkohol *m;* **smelling of ~** mit einer [Alkohol]fahne; **to drive sb to ~** jdn zum Trinker/zur Trinkerin machen **II.** *vi, vt* <drank, drunk> trinken; **to not ~ and drive** nicht unter Alkoholeinfluss fahren; **I'll ~ to that** darauf trinke ich; (*fig*) dem kann ich nur zustimmen

◆**drink in** *vt* [begierig] in sich *akk* aufnehmen

drinkable ['drɪŋ·kə·bəl] *adj* trinkbar

drinker ['drɪŋ·kər] *n* Trinker(in) *m(f)*

drinking ['drɪŋ·kɪŋ] **I.** *n* Trinken *nt;* **this water is not for ~** das ist kein Trinkwasser **II.** *adj* Trink-; **~ bout** Sauftour *f*

'**drinking fountain** *n* Trinkwasserbrunnen *m*

'**drinking straw** *n* Trinkhalm *m*

'**drinking water** *n* Trinkwasser *nt*

drip [drɪp] **I.** *vi* <-pp-> (*continually*) tropfen; (*in individual drops*) tröpfeln **II.** *vt* <-pp-> [herunter]tropfen lassen; **to ~ blood** Blut verlieren **III.** *n* ❶ (*act of dripping*) Tropfen *nt; of rain* Tröpfeln *nt* ❷ (*drop*) Tropfen *m* ❸ MED Tropf *m* ❹ (*fam: fool*) Flasche *f pej fam,* Null *f pej fam*

drip-dry I. *vt* <-ie-> tropfnass aufhängen **II.** *vi clothes, dishes* abtropfen **III.** *adj* bügelfrei

dripping ['drɪp·ɪŋ] **I.** *adj* ❶ (*dropping drips*)

tropfend; ■**to be ~** tropfen ② (*extremely wet*) klatschnass ③ (*hum, iron: be covered with sth*) ■**to be ~ with sth** über und über mit etw *dat* behängt sein **II.** *adv* **~ wet** klatschnass **III.** *n* FOOD ■**~s** *pl* Schmalz *nt*

drive [draɪv] **I.** *n* ① (*trip*) Fahrt *f;* **to go for a ~** eine Spazierfahrt machen; **it is a 20-minute ~ to the airport** zum Flughafen sind es [mit dem Auto] 20 Minuten ② (*driveway*) Einfahrt *f;* (*to larger building*) Auffahrt *f;* (*approaching road*) Zufahrt[sstraße] *f* ③ TECH Antrieb *m* ④ (*energy*) Tatkraft *f;* (*élan, vigor*) Schwung *m,* Elan *m,* Drive *m;* (*motivation*) Tatendrang *m;* PSYCH Trieb *m* ⑤ (*campaign*) Aktion *f* ⑥ COMPUT Laufwerk *nt* **II.** *vt* <drove, -n> ① fahren; **to ~ a bus** einen Bus lenken; (*as a job*) Busfahrer(in) *m(f)* sein ② (*force onwards*) antreiben; **to ~ oneself too hard** (*fig*) sich *dat* zu viel zumuten; **he was ~n by greed** Gier bestimmte sein Handeln; **to ~ sb to suicide** jdn in den Selbstmord treiben; **to ~ sb mad/crazy** jdn wahnsinnig/verrückt machen ③ (*power*) *engine* antreiben; COMPUT treiben **III.** *vi* <drove, -n> ① fahren; **to learn to ~** den Führerschein machen ② *rain, snow* peitschen; *clouds* jagen

◆**drive along** *vt* entlangfahren

◆**drive around** *vi* herumfahren

◆**drive at** *vi* **what are you driving at?** worauf wollen Sie [eigentlich] hinaus?

◆**drive away** **I.** *vt* ① (*transport*) wegfahren ② (*expel*) vertreiben ③ (*fig: dispel*) zerstreuen **II.** *vi* wegfahren

◆**drive back** **I.** *vt* ① (*in a vehicle*) zurückfahren ② (*force back*) zurückdrängen; *animals* zurücktreiben; *enemy* zurückschlagen **II.** *vi* zurückfahren

◆**drive off** **I.** *vt* ① (*expel*) vertreiben ② (*repel*) zurückschlagen **II.** *vi* wegfahren

◆**drive out** **I.** *vt* hinausjagen; (*fig*) austreiben **II.** *vi* hinausfahren; (*come out*) herausfahren

◆**drive up** **I.** *vt prices* hochtreiben **II.** *vi* vorfahren

'**drive-in** **I.** *adj* Drive-in- **II.** *n* ① (*restaurant*) Drive-in *nt* ② (*movie theater*) Autokino *nt*

drivel ['drɪv·əl] *n* (*pej*) Gefasel *nt*

driven ['drɪv·ən] **I.** *pp of* **drive** **II.** *adj* ① (*very ambitious*) ehrgeizig ② (*powered*) angetrieben

driver ['draɪ·vər] *n* ① Fahrer(in) *m(f); of locomotive* Führer(in) *m(f);* **student ~** Fahrschüler(in) *m(f)* ② (*golf club*) Driver *m*

'**driver's license** *n* Führerschein *m*

driver's-side *adj attr* AUTO auf der Fahrerseite *nach n*

'**drive-through** **I.** *adj attr, inv* Drive-through- **II.** *n* Durchfahrt *f*

'**driveway** *n* (*to small building*) Einfahrt *f;* (*to larger building*) Auffahrt *f;* (*longer*) Zufahrt[sstraße] *f*

driving ['draɪ·vɪŋ] **I.** *n* (*of vehicle*) Fahren *nt* **II.** *adj* ① (*on road*) Fahr-; **~ conditions** Straßenverhältnisse *pl* ② (*lashing*) *rain* peitschend ③ (*powerfully motivating*) treibend; *ambition* stark

'**driving force** *n* treibende Kraft

'**driving instructor** *n* Fahrlehrer(in) *m(f)*

'**driving lesson** *n* Fahrstunde *f;* ■**~s** *pl* Fahrunterricht *m kein pl*

'**driving license** *n see* **driver's license**

'**driving school** *n* Fahrschule *f*

'**driving test** *n* Fahrprüfung *f*

drizzle ['drɪz·əl] **I.** *n* ① (*light rain*) Nieselregen *m* ② (*small amount of liquid*) ein paar Spritzer **II.** *vi impers* nieseln; **it's drizzling** es nieselt **III.** *vt* FOOD träufeln

drizzly ['drɪz·li] *adj* Niesel-; **it was a ~ afternoon** es hat den ganzen Nachmittag genieselt

droll [droʊl] *adj* drollig

drone[1] [droʊn] *n* ① (*male bee*) Drohne *f* ② AVIAT (*aircraft*) ferngesteuertes Flugzeug; (*missile*) ferngesteuerte Rakete

drone[2] [droʊn] **I.** *n* (*sound*) *of a machine* Brummen *nt; of insects* Summen *nt;* (*pej*) *of a person* Geleier *nt* **II.** *vi* ① (*make sound*) summen; *engine* brummen ② (*speak monotonously*) leiern

drool [drul] **I.** *vi* ① (*dribble*) sabbern ② (*fig*) ■**to ~ over sb/sth** von jdm/etw hingerissen sein **II.** *n* Sabber *m*

droop [drup] **I.** *vi* ① (*hang down*) schlaff herunterhängen; *flowers* die Köpfe hängen lassen; *eyelids* zufallen ② (*lack energy*) schlapp sein **II.** *n* Herunterhängen *nt; of body* Gebeugtsein *nt; of eyelids* Schwere *f*

droopy ['drup·i] *adj* [schlaff] herabhängend *attr*

drop [drap] **I.** *n* ① (*vertical distance*) Gefälle *nt;* (*difference in level*) Höhenunterschied *m* ② (*decrease*) Rückgang *m;* **~ in temperature** Temperaturrückgang *m* ③ *of liquid* Tropfen *m;* **~s of paint** Farbspritzer *pl;* ■**~s** *pl* MED Tropfen *pl* ④ (*collection point*) [Geheim]versteck *nt* **II.** *vt* <-pp-> ① (*cause to fall*) fallen lassen; *anchor* [aus]werfen; *bomb, leaflets* abwerfen; **to ~ a bombshell** (*fig*) eine Bombe platzen lassen ② (*lower*) senken ③ (*dismiss*) entlassen ④ (*give up*) aufgeben; *charges* fallen lassen; *demands* abgehen von; **to ~ everything** alles stehen und liegen lassen ⑤ (*abandon*) ■**to ~ sb** (*fig*) jdn fallen lassen; (*end a relationship*) mit jdm Schluss machen ⑥ (*fam: tell indirectly*) **to ~ [sb] a hint** [jdm gegenüber] eine Anspielung machen **III.** *vi* <-pp-> ① (*descend*) [herunter]fallen; *jaw* herunterklappen ② (*become lower*) *land* sinken; *prices, temperatures, water level* fallen ③ (*fam: become exhausted*) umfallen; **~ dead!** (*fam*) scher dich zum Teufel!

◆**drop behind** *vi* zurückfallen

◆**drop in** *vi* (*fam*) vorbeischauen (**on** bei +*dat*)

◆**drop off** **I.** *vt* (*fam*) *person* abliefern; *thing* absetzen **II.** *vi* ① (*fall off*) abfallen ② (*decrease*) zurückgehen; *support, interest* nachlassen ③ (*fam: fall asleep*) einschlafen

◆**drop out** *vi* ① (*give up membership*) ausscheiden; **to ~ out of college** das Studium abbrechen ② *of society* aussteigen

drop-down 'menu *n* COMPUT Pull-down-Menü *nt*

droplet ['drap·lət] *n* Tröpfchen *nt*

'dropout *n* ① (*from university*) [Studien]abbrecher(in) *m(f)*; (*from school*) Schulabgänger(in) *m(f)* ② (*from conventional lifestyle*) Aussteiger(in) *m(f)*

dropper ['drap·ər] *n* Tropfer *m*

droppings ['drap·ɪŋz] *npl of bird* Vogeldreck *m*; (*of horse*) Pferdeäpfel *pl*; *of rodents, sheep* Köttel *pl*

'drop shot *n* TENNIS Stopp[ball] *m*

dross [dras] *n* Schrott *m a. fig*

drought [draʊt] *n* Dürre[periode] *f*

drove [droʊv] *pt of* **drive**

drown [draʊn] **I.** *vt* ① (*kill*) ertränken; ■**to be ~ed** ertrinken ② (*make inaudible*) übertönen **II.** *vi* ertrinken *a. fig*

◆**drown out** *vt* niederschreien

drowse [draʊz] *vi* dösen

drowsy ['draʊ·zi] *adj* schläfrig; (*after waking up*) verschlafen

drudge [drʌdʒ] *n* (*person*) Kuli *m*

drudgery ['drʌdʒ·ə·ri] *n* Schufterei *f*

drug [drʌg] **I.** *n* ① (*medicine*) Medikament *nt* ② (*narcotic*) Droge *f*, Rauschgift *nt*; **to take** [*or* **do**] **~s** Drogen nehmen **II.** *vt* <-gg-> ① MED ■**to ~ sb** jdm Beruhigungsmittel verabreichen; ■**to ~ an animal** *ein Tier durch Verabreichung von Drogen langsam machen* ② (*secretly*) ■**to ~ sb** jdn unter Drogen setzen

'drug abuse *n* Drogenmissbrauch *m*

'drug addict *n* Drogensüchtige(r) *f(m)*

'drug addiction *n* Drogenabhängigkeit *f*

'drug czar *n* Drogenbeauftragte(r) der Regierung *f(m)*

'drug dealer *n* Drogenhändler(in) *m(f)*, Dealer(in) *m(f)*

drug-sniffing 'dog *n* Drogenspürhund *m*

'drug squad *n* Drogenfahndung *f*

'drugstore *n* Drogerie *f* [in der man auch Medikamente erhält]

'drug trafficker *n* Drogenhändler(in) *m(f)*

'drug trafficking *n* Drogenhandel *m*

druid ['dru·ɪd] *n* Druide *m*

drum [drʌm] **I.** *n* ① MUS Trommel *f*; ■**~s** *pl* (*drum kit*) Schlagzeug *nt* ② (*for storage, machine part*) Trommel *f*; **oil ~** Ölfass *nt* **II.** *vi* <-mm-> ① MUS trommeln; (*on a drum kit*) Schlagzeug spielen ② (*strike repeatedly*) trommeln (**on** auf +*akk*) **III.** *vt* <-mm-> (*fam*) ① (*make noise*) **to ~ one's fingers** [**on the table**] [mit den Fingern] auf den Tisch trommeln ② (*repeat*) ■**to ~ sth into sb** jdm etw einhämmern

'drumbeat *n* Trommelschlag *m*

drummer ['drʌm·ər] *n* MUS Trommler(in) *m(f)*; (*playing a drum kit*) Schlagzeuger(in) *m(f)*

'drumstick *n* ① MUS Trommelstock *m* ② FOOD Keule *f*, Schlegel *m* SÜDD, ÖSTERR

drunk [drʌŋk] **I.** *adj* ① (*inebriated*) betrunken; **blind** [*or* **dead**] **~** stockbetrunken; **to get ~** sich betrinken; **~ driving** Trunkenheit *f* am Steuer ② (*fig: overcome*) trunken **II.** *n* (*pej*) Betrunkene(r) *f(m)* **III.** *vt, vi pp of* **drink**

drunkard ['drʌŋ·kərd] *n* (*pej*) Trinker(in) *m(f)*

drunken ['drʌŋ·kən] *adj* (*pej*) ① *person* betrunken ② (*involving alcohol*) **~ brawl** Streit *m* zwischen Betrunkenen; **~ driving** Trunkenheit *f* am Steuer

drunkenness ['drʌŋ·kən·nɪs] *n* Betrunkenheit *f*

dry [draɪ] **I.** *adj* <-ier, -iest *or* -er, -est> ① trocken; **as ~ as a bone** knochentrocken ② (*without alcohol*) alkoholfrei **II.** *vt* <-ie-> trocknen; *fruit, meat* dörren; (*dry out*) austrocknen; (*dry up*) abtrocknen; **~ your eyes!** wisch dir die Tränen ab!; **to ~ one's hands** sich *dat* die Hände abtrocknen **III.** *vi* <-ie-> ① (*lose moisture*) trocknen ② (*dry up*) abtrocknen

◆**dry up I.** *vi* ① (*become dry*) austrocknen; *spring, well* versiegen ② (*dry the dishes*) abtrocknen ③ (*evaporate*) *liquid* trocknen ④ (*fig: run out*) *funds* schrumpfen; *source* versiegen; *supply* ausbleiben; *conversation* versiegen **II.** *vt* ① *dishes* abtrocknen ② (*dry out*) austrocknen

'dry-clean *vt* chemisch reinigen

'dry cleaner *n* Reinigung *f*

'dry cleaning *n* [chemische] Reinigung *f*

dryer ['draɪ·ər] *n* ① (*for laundry*) [Wäsche]trockner *m* ② (*for hair*) Fön *m*; (*overhead*) Trockenhaube *f*

dry 'ice *n* Trockeneis *nt*

dry 'land *n* Festland *nt*

dryness ['draɪ·nɪs] *n* ① Trockenheit *f* ② (*drought*) Dürre *f*

'dry rot *n* ① (*in wood*) Hausschwamm *m* ② (*in plants*) Trockenfäule *f*

DSL [ˌdi·es·'el] *n* INET, COMPUT, TELEC *acr for* **digital subscriber line** DSL *kein art*

DTP [ˌdi·ti·'pi] *n abbrev of* **desktop publishing** DTP *nt*

dual ['du·əl] *adj* (*double*) doppelt; (*two different*) zweierlei; **~ ownership** Miteigentümerschaft *f*; **~ role** Doppelrolle *f*

dub <-bb-> [dʌb] *vt* ① FILM synchronisieren; **to ~ into English** ins Englische übersetzen ② (*call*) ■**to ~ sb sth** jdn etw nennen

dubbing ['dʌb·ɪŋ] *n* FILM Synchronisation *f*

dubious ['du·bi·əs] *adj* ① (*questionable*) zweifelhaft, fragwürdig ② (*unsure*) unsicher; **to be ~ about** [*or* **as to**] **whether ...** bezweifeln, ob ...; **to feel ~ about sth** an etw *dat* zweifeln

duchess <*pl* -es> ['dʌtʃ·ɪs] *n* Herzogin *f*

duchy ['dʌtʃ·i] *n* Herzogtum *nt*

duck[1] [dʌk] *n* Ente *f* ▶ PHRASES: **to take to sth like a ~ to water** bei etw *dat* gleich in seinem Element sein

duck[2] [dʌk] **I.** *vi* ① **to ~** [**down**] sich ducken ② **to ~ under water** [unter]tauchen ③ **to ~ out of sight** sich verstecken **II.** *vt* ① **to ~ one's head** den Kopf einziehen; **to ~ one's**

head under water den Kopf unter Wasser tauchen ❷ (*avoid*) ■ **to ~ sth** etw *dat* ausweichen *a. fig*
duckling ['dʌk·lɪŋ] *n* ❶ (*animal*) Entenküken *nt*, Entchen *nt* ❷ (*meat*) junge Ente
duct [dʌkt] *n* ❶ (*pipe*) [Rohr]leitung *f*; **air ~** Luftkanal *m* ❷ ANAT **tear ~** Tränenkanal *m*
'**duct tape** *n* Panzerband *nt*
dud [dʌd] (*fam*) **I.** *n* ❶ (*bomb*) Blindgänger *m* ❷ (*useless thing*) **this pen is a ~** dieser Füller taugt nichts; (*failure*) Reinfall *m* ❸ (*fam: clothing*) ■ **~s** *pl* Klamotten *pl* **II.** *adj* (*worthless*) mies; *checks* gefälscht
dude [dud] *n* (*fam*) ❶ (*smartly dressed urbanite*) feiner Pinkel ❷ (*fellow*) Typ *m*, Kerl *m*; **what's up, ~?** wie geht's, Alter? *sl*
due [du] **I.** *adj* ❶ (*payable*) fällig; **~ date** Fälligkeitstermin *m* ❷ (*appropriate*) gebührend; **with ~ care** mit der nötigen Sorgfalt; **with** [**all**] **~ respect** bei allem [gebotenen] Respekt ❸ (*expected*) **in ~ course** zu gegebener Zeit; **~ date** (*for work due*) Abgabetermin *m*; (*for entries*) Einsendeschluss *m*; **their baby is ~ in January** sie erwarten ihr Baby im Januar ❹ (*because of*) ■ **~ to sth** wegen [*o* auf Grund] einer S. *gen*; ■ **to be ~ to sb/sth** jdm/etw zuzuschreiben sein **II.** *n* ❶ (*fair treatment*) **to give sb his/her ~** jdm Gerechtigkeit widerfahren lassen ❷ (*fees*) ■ **~s** *pl* Gebühren *pl* **III.** *adv* **~ north** genau nach Norden
duel ['du·əl] **I.** *n* Duell *nt* **II.** *vi* <-l- *or* -ll-> sich duellieren
duet [du·'et] *n* (*for instruments*) Duo *nt*; (*for voices*) Duett *nt*
duffel bag *n see* **duffle bag**
duffle bag ['dʌf·əl·ˌbæg] *n* Matchbeutel *m*; NAUT Seesack *m*
dug [dʌg] *pt, pp of* **dig**
'**dugout** *n* ❶ MIL Schützengraben *m* ❷ (*in baseball, soccer*) [überdachte] Spielerbank ❸ (*canoe*) Einbaum *m*
duke [duk] *n* Herzog *m*
dull [dʌl] **I.** *adj* ❶ (*pej: boring*) langweilig, eintönig; **as ~ as dishwater** stinklangweilig ❷ (*not bright*) *animal's coat* glanzlos; *weather* trüb; *color* matt; *light* schwach, trübe ❸ (*not sharp*) stumpf **II.** *vt* (*lessen*) schwächen; *pain* betäuben
dullness ['dʌl·nɪs] *n* Langweiligkeit *f*, Eintönigkeit *f*
duly ['du·li] *adv* ❶ (*appropriately*) gebührend ❷ (*at the expected time*) wie erwartet
dumb [dʌm] *adj* ❶ (*pej fam: stupid*) dumm ❷ (*mute*) stumm ▶ PHRASES: **to be** [**as**] **~ as a rock** (*pej*) dumm wie Bohnenstroh sein
'**dumbbell** *n* SPORTS Hantel *f*
'**dumbfound** *vt* verblüffen
'**dumbfounded** *adj* sprachlos
'**dumbstruck** *adj* sprachlos
'**dumbwaiter** *n* Speiseaufzug *m*, stummer Diener
dummy ['dʌm·i] **I.** *n* ❶ (*mannequin*) Schaufensterpuppe *f*; (*for crash tests*) Dummy *m*; (*for ventriloquist*) [Bauchredner]puppe *f* ❷ (*pej: fool*) Dummkopf *m* **II.** *adj* (*duplicate*) nachgemacht; (*false*) falsch **III.** *vi* (*fam*) ■ **to ~ up** dichthalten
dump [dʌmp] **I.** *n* ❶ (*for garbage*) Müll[abladeplatz *m*; (*fig, pej: messy place*) Dreckloch *nt*; (*badly run place*) Sauladen *m* ❷ (*storage place*) Lager *nt* ❸ COMPUT Speicherabzug *m* ▶ PHRASES: **down in the ~s** heruntergekommen **II.** *vt* ❶ (*offload*) abladen ❷ (*put down carelessly*) hinknallen ❸ (*fam: abandon*) *plan* fallen lassen; *sth unwanted* loswerden ❹ (*fam: end a relationship*) ■ **to ~ sb** jdm den Laufpass geben, mit jdm Schluss machen ❺ COMPUT ausgeben **III.** *vi* ❶ (*throw out garbage*) **"No ~ing"** „Müll abladen verboten“ ❷ (*fam: treat unfairly*) ■ **to ~ on sb** jdn fertigmachen
'**dumping ground** *n* Müll[ablade]platz *m*
dumpling ['dʌmp·lɪŋ] *n* Knödel *m*, Kloß *m*
'**dump truck** *n* Kipper *m*
dumpy ['dʌm·pi] *adj* pummelig
dunce [dʌns] *n* (*pej: poor pupil*) schlechter Schüler, schlechte Schülerin; (*stupid person*) Dummkopf *m*
dune [dun] *n* Düne *f*
dung [dʌŋ] *n* Dung *m*
dungarees [ˌdʌŋ·gə·'riz] *npl* Jeans[hose] *f*
dungeon ['dʌn·dʒən] *n* Verlies *nt*, Kerker *m*
dunk [dʌŋk] **I.** *vt* ❶ (*immerse*) [ein]tunken ❷ SPORTS *basketball* dunken **II.** *vi* SPORTS dunken **III.** *n* SPORTS Dunking *m*
duo ['du·oʊ] *n* Duo *nt*
duodenum <*pl* -na *or* -s> [ˌdu·ə·'di·nəm] *n* Zwölffingerdarm *m*
dupe [dup] **I.** *n* Betrogene(r) *f(m)* **II.** *vt* betrügen
duplex ['du·pleks] **I.** *n* <*pl* -es> ❶ (*two-family dwelling*) Doppelhaus *nt* ❷ (*apartment having two floors*) Maisonette[wohnung] *f* **II.** *adj* Doppel-
duplicate I. *vt* ['du·plɪ·keɪt] ■ **to ~ sth** eine zweite Anfertigung von etw *dat* machen; (*repeat an activity*) etw noch einmal machen **II.** *adj* ['du·plɪ·kət] Zweit-; **~ key** Nachschlüssel *m* **III.** *n* ['du·plɪ·kət] Duplikat *nt*; *of a document* Zweitschrift *f*; **in ~** in zweifacher Ausfertigung
duplicity [du·'plɪs·ɪ·t̬i] *n* (*pej: in speech*) Doppelzüngigkeit *f*; (*in behavior*) Doppelspiel *nt*
durability [ˌdʊr·ə·'bɪl·ɪ·t̬i] *n* ❶ (*endurance*) Dauerhaftigkeit *f* ❷ *of a product* Haltbarkeit *f*; *of a machine* Lebensdauer *f*
durable ['dʊr·ə·bəl] *adj* ❶ (*long-lasting*) strapazierfähig, dauerhaft ❷ ECON *goods* langlebig
duration [dʊ·'reɪ·ʃən] *n* Dauer *f*; *of a film* Länge *f*
duress [dʊ·'res] *n* (*form*) Zwang *m*, Nötigung *f*; **under ~** unter Zwang
during ['dʊr·ɪŋ] *prep* während +*gen*
dusk [dʌsk] *n* [Abend]dämmerung *f*
dusky ['dʌs·ki] *adj* dunkel
dust [dʌst] **I.** *n* Staub *m*; **covered in ~** (*out-*

D

D

side) staubbedeckt; (*inside*) völlig verstaubt ▸ PHRASES: **to let the ~ settle, to wait until the ~ has settled** [ab]warten, bis sich die Wogen wieder geglättet haben; **to bite the ~** ins Gras beißen **II.** *vt* ① (*clean*) *objects* abstauben; *rooms* Staub wischen in ② (*spread over finely*) bestäuben; (*using grated material*) bestreuen **III.** *vi* Staub wischen

'dust cover *n* (*for furniture*) Schonbezug *m;* (*for devices*) Abdeckhaube *f;* (*on a book*) Schutzumschlag *m;* (*for clothes*) Staubschutz *m kein pl*

duster ['dʌs·tər] *n* **feather ~** Staubwedel *m*

'dust jacket *n* Schutzumschlag *m*

'dust mite *n* Hausmilbe *f*

'dustpan *n* Schaufel *f*

'dust storm *n* Staubsturm *m*

'dustup *n* (*fam*) ① (*fight*) Schlägerei *f* ② (*dispute*) Krach *m*

dusty ['dʌs·ti] *adj* staubig; *objects* verstaubt

Dutch [dʌtʃ] **I.** *adj* holländisch, niederländisch **II.** *n* ① (*language*) Holländisch *nt,* Niederländisch *nt* ② (*people*) ■ **the ~** *pl* die Holländer **III.** *adv* **to go ~** getrennte Kasse machen

'Dutchman *n* Holländer *m*

'Dutchwoman *n* Holländerin *f*

dutiful ['du·t̬ɪ·fəl] *adj* ① *person* pflichtbewusst; (*obedient*) gehorsam ② *act* pflichtschuldig

duty ['du·t̬i] **I.** *n* ① (*obligation*) Pflicht *f;* **to do sth out of ~** etw aus Pflichtbewusstsein tun ② (*work*) Dienst *m;* **to be off ~** [dienst]frei haben; **to be on ~** Dienst haben; **to come/go on ~** seinen Dienst antreten ③ (*revenue*) Zoll *m* (**on** auf +*akk*); **customs duties** Zollabgaben *pl;* **to pay ~ on sth** etw verzollen **II.** *adj* (*nurse, officer*) diensthabend

duty-'free *adj* zollfrei

'duty roster *n* Dienstplan *m*

duvet [du·'veɪ] *n* Steppdecke *f,* Daunendecke *f*

DVD [ˌdi·vi·'di] *n abbrev of* **digital video disk** DVD *f*

DVR [ˌdi·vi·'·ar] *n abbrev of* **digital video recorder** digitaler Videorecorder

dwarf [dwɔrf] **I.** *n* <*pl* -s *or* dwarves> Zwerg(in) *m(f)* **II.** *adj* Zwerg- **III.** *vt* überragen; (*fig*) in den Schatten stellen

dwell <dwelt *or* dwelled, dwelt *or* dwelled> [dwel] *vi* ① (*reside*) wohnen ② (*think about*) nachdenken (**on** über +*akk*)

dweller ['dwel·ər] *n* (*form*) Bewohner(in) *m(f)*

dwelling ['dwel·ɪŋ] *n* (*form*) Wohnung *f*

dwelt [dwelt] *pp, pt of* **dwell**

dwindle ['dwɪn·dəl] *vi* abnehmen; *numbers* zurückgehen; *money, supplies* schrumpfen

dye [daɪ] **I.** *vt* färben **II.** *n* Färbemittel *nt*

dyed-in-the-'wool *adj* Erz-

dying ['daɪ·ɪŋ] *adj* sterbend; (*fig*) aussterbend

dyke¹ [daɪk] *n see* **dike¹**

dyke² [daɪk] *n* (*offensive sl: lesbian*) Lesbe *f*

dynamic [daɪ·'næm·ɪk] *adj* dynamisch

dynamics [daɪ·'næm·ɪks] *n* Dynamik *f*

dynamite ['daɪ·nə·maɪt] **I.** *n* Dynamit *nt a. fig* **II.** *vt* mit Dynamit sprengen

dynamo ['daɪ·nə·moʊ] *n* (*fig*) Energiebündel *nt*

dynasty ['daɪ·nə·sti] *n* Dynastie *f*

dysentery ['dɪs·ən·ter·i] *n* Ruhr *f*

dysfunctional [dɪs·'fʌŋk·ʃə·nəl] *adj* SOCIOL gestört

dyslexia [dɪ·'sleksiə] *n* Legasthenie *f*

dyslexic [dɪs·'lek·sɪk] *adj* legasthenisch

Ee

E <*pl* -'s *or* -s> [iː], **e** <*pl* -'s> [iː] *n* E *nt*, e *nt*; **~ as in Echo** E wie Emil

E *n* ① *abbrev of* **east** O ② (*in baseball*) *abbrev of* **error** Fehlpass *m*

each [itʃ] *adj, adv, pron* jede(r, s); **500 miles ~ way** 500 Meilen in eine Richtung; **~ [one] of the books** jedes einzelne Buch; **there are five leaflets — please take one of ~** hier sind fünf Broschüren – nehmen Sie bitte von jeder eine

each 'other *pron after vb* einander; **to be made for ~** füreinander bestimmt sein

eager <-er, -est *or* more ~, most ~> ['iː·gər] *adj* ① (*hungry*) begierig (**for** auf +*akk*) ② (*zealous*) eifrig; **~ to learn** lernbegierig ③ (*expectant*) *face* erwartungsvoll; *anticipation* gespannt

eagerness ['iː·gər·nəs] *n* Eifer *m*

eagle ['iː·gəl] *n* Adler *m*

'eagle-eyed *adj* scharfsichtig

ear^{1} [ɪr] *n* ANAT Ohr *nt*; **~, nose, and throat specialist** Hals-Nasen-Ohren-Arzt, -Ärztin *m, f*; **from ~ to ~** von einem Ohr zum anderen ▶ PHRASES: **to be up to one's ~s in work** bis über die Ohren in Arbeit stecken; **to keep one's ~ to the ground** auf dem Laufenden bleiben [*o* sein]; **to be all ~s** ganz Ohr sein; **sb's ~s are burning** jdm klingen die Ohren; **to have the ~ of sb** jds Vertrauen *nt* haben

ear^{2} [ɪr] *n* AGR Ähre *f*

'earache *n* Ohrenschmerzen *pl*

'eardrum *n* Trommelfell *nt*

'ear infection *n* Ohrenentzündung *f*

earl [ɜrl] *n* Graf *m*

'earlobe *n* Ohrläppchen *nt*

early <-ier, -iest *or* more ~, most ~> ['ɜr·li] **I.** *adj* ① (*in the day*) früh; **she usually has an ~ breakfast** sie frühstückt meistens zeitig; **the ~ hours** die frühen Morgenstunden; **~ morning call** Weckruf *m* ② (*of a period*) früh, Früh-; **she is in her ~ thirties** sie ist Anfang dreißig; **from an ~ age** von klein auf; **in the ~ 15th century** Anfang des 15. Jahrhunderts ③ (*ahead of time*) vorzeitig; (*comparatively early*) [früh]zeitig; **I took an earlier train** ich habe einen früheren Zug genommen; **to take ~ retirement** vorzeitig in den Ruhestand gehen **II.** *adv* ① (*in the day, of a period*) früh; **~ next week** Anfang nächster Woche ② (*ahead of time*) vorzeitig; (*prematurely*) zu früh; (*comparatively early*) [früh]zeitig

'earmark *vt* ① (*mark*) kennzeichnen ② (*allocate*) vorsehen; *money* bereitstellen

'earmuffs *npl* Ohrenschützer *pl*

earn [ɜrn] *vt* ① verdienen; *respect* gewinnen ② FIN (*yield*) einbringen

earned income ['ɜrnd·'ɪn·kʌm] *n* FIN Arbeitseinkommen *nt*

earner ['ɜr·nər] *n* ① (*person*) Verdiener(in) *m(f)* ② (*fam: income source*) Einnahmequelle *f*

earnest ['ɜr·nɪst] **I.** *adj* ernst[haft] **II.** *n* Ernst *m*; **in ~** ernst

earnestly ['ɜr·nɪst·li] *adv* ernsthaft

earnings ['ɜr·nɪŋz] *npl* Einkommen *nt*; *of business* Ertrag *m*

'earphone *n* Kopfhörer *m*

'earpiece *n* Hörer *m*

'earplug *n usu pl* Ohrenstöpsel *nt*

'earring *n* Ohrring *m*

'earshot *n* **[with]in/out of ~** in/außer Hörweite

earth [ɜrθ] *n* ① (*planet*) Erde *f*; **on ~** in der Welt; **how/what/who on earth ...** wie/was/wer um alles in der Welt ... ② (*soil*) Erde *f*, Boden *m* ▶ PHRASES: **to be down to ~** ein natürlicher und umgänglicher Mensch sein

> Der **Earth Day** (Tag der Erde), der in den USA zum ersten Mal 1970 stattfand, wird seit 1990 alljährlich am 22. April in über 150 Ländern begangen. Ziel der Kampagne ist es, insbesondere bei den jungen Menschen das Umweltbewusstsein zu verschärfen und auf die globale Gefährdung unserer Umwelt aufmerksam zu machen.
> Anlässlich des ersten Tages der Erde im Jahr 1970 kamen mehr als 20 Millionen Amerikaner aus dem ganzen Land in Colleges zusammen, um an umweltpolitischen „Teach-ins“ teilzunehmen. Initiiert wurden die Feierlichkeiten anlässlich des Tages der Erde von Senator Gaylord Nelson, einem Umweltaktivisten, um Unterstützung für die Umweltbewegung zu demonstrieren. Er ernannte Denis Hayes, einen Stanford Absolventen, zum Organisator der Festivitäten.
> In den USA finden am **Earth Day** zahlreiche öffentliche Veranstaltungen statt. Zu den beliebtesten gehören die Volksfeste, die typischerweise im Freien stattfinden.
> In der Woche oder dem Monat vor oder nach dem **Earth Day** werden so genannte „clean-ups“ organisiert, in denen z. B. lokale Müllsammelaktionen durchgeführt werden.

earthly ['ɜrθ·li] *adj* ① (*on Earth*) irdisch ② (*fam: possible*) möglich; **to be of no ~ use to sb** jdm nicht im Geringsten nützen

'earthquake *n* Erdbeben *nt*

'earthshaking, 'earthshattering *adj* welterschütternd

'earthworm *n* Regenwurm *m*

earthy <-ier, -iest *or* more ~, most ~> ['ɜr·θi] *adj* ❶ erdig ❷ (*coarse*) derb
'**earwax** *n* Ohrenschmalz *m*
'**earwig** *n* Ohrwurm *m*
ease [iz] **I.** *n* ❶ (*effortlessness*) Leichtigkeit *f* ❷ (*comfort*) **to be** [*or* **feel**] **at ~** sich wohl fühlen **II.** *vt* ❶ (*relieve*) *pain* lindern; *strain* mindern; **to ~ the tension** die Anspannung lösen; (*fig*) die Lage entspannen ❷ (*move*) **she ~d the lid off** sie löste den Deckel behutsam ab **III.** *vi* nachlassen; *tension* sich beruhigen
◆**ease off** *vi* ❶ (*decrease*) nachlassen ❷ (*leave alone*) ■**to ~ off on sb** jdn in Ruhe lassen
◆**ease up** *vi* ❶ (*abate*) nachlassen ❷ (*relax*) sich entspannen ❸ (*be less severe*) ■**to ~ up on sb** zu jdm weniger streng sein
easel ['i·zəl] *n* Staffelei *f*
easily ['i·zə·li] *adv* ❶ (*without difficulty*) leicht; (*effortlessly*) mühelos; **to win ~** spielend gewinnen ❷ (*by far*) ■**to be ~ the ...** + *superl* bei weitem der/die/das ... sein ❸ (*probably*) [sehr] leicht
easiness ['i·zɪ·nɪs] *n* Leichtigkeit *f;* (*effortlessness a.*) Mühelosigkeit *f; of question* Einfachheit *f*
east [ist] **I.** *n* ❶ (*direction*) Osten *m;* **to the ~** nach Osten ❷ (*part of region*) ■**the E~** der Osten **II.** *adj* östlich, Ost-; **~ wind** Ostwind *m* **III.** *adv* ostwärts, nach Osten; **~ of Hollywood** östlich von Hollywood
'**eastbound** *adj* nach Osten; **~ train** Zug *m* in Richtung Osten
Easter ['i·stər] *n* Ostern *nt*
'**Easter egg** *n* Osterei *nt*
easterly ['i·stər·li] **I.** *adj* östlich, Ost- **II.** *n* Ostwind *m*
eastern ['i·stərn] *adj* ❶ *location* östlich, Ost-; **the ~ seaboard** die Ostküste ❷ ■**E~** (*Asian*) orientalisch
easterner ['i·stər·nər] *n* Oststaatler(in) *m(f)*
easternmost ['i·stərn·moʊst] *adj* ■**the ~ ...** der/die/das östlichste ...
Easter 'Sunday *n* Ostersonntag *m*
Easter va'cation *npl* Osterferien *pl*
East 'Germany *n* HIST Ostdeutschland *nt*
eastward ['ist·wərd] **I.** *adj* östlich, nach Osten **II.** *adv* ostwärts, nach Osten
eastwards ['ist·wərdz] *adv see* **eastward II.**
easy <-ier, -iest *or* more ~, most ~> ['i·zi] **I.** *adj* ❶ (*simple*) leicht, einfach; **he is ~ to get along with** mit ihm kann man gut auskommen; **~ money** leicht verdientes Geld; **within ~ reach** leicht erreichbar ❷ (*effortless*) leicht, mühelos; *walk* bequem ❸ (*trouble-free*) angenehm; (*comfortable*) bequem; *life* sorglos ❹ (*sl: promiscuous*) promisk; **lady of ~ virtue** leichtes Mädchen **II.** *adv* ❶ (*cautiously*) vorsichtig; **to go ~ on sb** nicht zu hart mit jdm umgehen ❷ (*in a relaxed manner*) [**take it**] **~** [**now**]! immer mit der Ruhe!; **to take things** [*or* **it**] **~** (*fam: for one's health*) sich schonen; (*rest*) sich *dat* keinen Stress machen **III.** *interj* (*fam*) locker
'**easy-care** *adj* pflegeleicht
'**easy chair** *n* Sessel *m*
easy'going *adj* (*straightforward*) unkompliziert; (*relaxed*) gelassen
eat <ate, eaten> [it] **I.** *vt* essen; *animal* fressen; **to ~ breakfast** frühstücken ▶ PHRASES: **to ~ one's heart out** sich [vor Kummer] verzehren; **what's ~ing you?** was bedrückt dich? **II.** *vi* essen; *animal* fressen
◆**eat away** (**at**) *vt, vi* zerfressen; *river, sea* auswaschen
◆**eat into** *vi* ■**to ~ into sth** ❶ (*use up*) *savings, profit* etw angreifen ❷ (*corrode*) etw angreifen ❸ (*dig into*) sich in etw *akk* hineinfressen
◆**eat out** *vi* auswärts essen, essen gehen
◆**eat up I.** *vt* ❶ (*finish*) aufessen; *animal* auffressen ❷ (*consume*) *money, resources* verschlingen **II.** *vi* aufessen; *animals* auffressen
eaten ['i·t̬ən] *pp of* **eat**
eater ['i·t̬ər] *n* Esser(in) *m(f);* (*animal*) Fresser
eatery ['i·t̬ə·ri] *n* (*fam*) Esslokal *nt*
eating ['i·t̬ɪŋ] **I.** *n* das Essen **II.** *adj* Ess-
'**eating disorder** *n* Essstörung *f*
eau de cologne [ˌoʊ·də·kə·'loʊn] *n* Kölnischwasser *nt*
eaves [ivz] *npl* Dachvorsprung *m*
eavesdrop <-pp-> ['ivz·drap] *vi* [heimlich] lauschen; ■**to ~ on sb/sth** jdn/etw belauschen
eavesdropper ['ivz·drap·ər] *n* Lauscher(in) *m(f)*
ebb [eb] **I.** *n* ❶ Ebbe *f* ❷ (*fig*) **to be at a low ~** auf einem Tiefstand sein; *funds* knapp bei Kasse sein **II.** *vi* ❶ *tide* zurückgehen ❷ (*fig: lessen*) schwinden
ebony ['eb·ə·ni] *n* Ebenholz *nt*
EC [ˌi·'si] *n* HIST *abbrev of* **European Community**: ■**the ~** die EG
eccentric [ɪk·'sen·trɪk] **I.** *n* Exzentriker(in) *m(f)* **II.** *adj* exzentrisch; *clothes* ausgefallen
eccentricity [ˌek·sen·'trɪs·ə·ti] *n* Exzentrizität *f*
ecclesiastic [ɪ·ˌkli·zi·'æs·tɪk] (*form*) **I.** *n* Geistliche(r) *m* **II.** *adj inv* kirchlich, geistlich
ECG [ˌi·si·'dʒi] *n abbrev of* **electrocardiogram** EKG *nt*
echelon ['eʃ·ə·lan] *n* Rang *m*
echo ['ek·oʊ] **I.** *n* <*pl* -es> ❶ Echo *nt* ❷ (*fig*) Anklang *m* (**of** an +*akk*) **II.** *vi* ❶ [wider]hallen ❷ (*fig: repeat*) wiederholen **III.** *vt* ❶ (*copy*) wiedergeben; (*reflect*) widerspiegeln ❷ (*resemble*) ähneln ❸ (*parrot*) wiederholen
'**echo chamber** *n* Hallraum *m*
eclectic [ek·'lek·tɪk] *adj* eklektisch
eclipse [ɪ·'klɪps] **I.** *n* ❶ Finsternis *f* ❷ (*fig: decline*) Niedergang *m* **II.** *vt* ❶ verfinstern ❷ (*fig: overshadow*) in den Schatten stellen
ecological [ˌi·kə·'ladʒ·ɪ·kəl] *adj* ökologisch; **~ catastrophe** [*or* **disaster**] Umweltkatastrophe *f*
ecologically [ˌi·kə·'ladʒ·ɪk·li] *adv* ökologisch;

~ **friendly** umweltfreundlich

ecologist [i·ˈkal·ə·dʒɪst] *n* ① (*expert*) Ökologe, -in *m, f* ② POL Umweltbeauftragte(r) *f(m)*

ecology [i·ˈkal·ə·dʒi] *n* Ökologie *f*

e-commerce [ˈi·kam·ɜrs] *n short for* **electronic commerce** E-Commerce *m*

economic [ˌi·kə·ˈnam·ɪk] *adj* ① ökonomisch, wirtschaftlich; ~ **downturn/upturn** Konjunkturabschwächung *f*/-aufschwung *m* ② (*profitable*) rentabel

economical [ˌi·kə·ˈnam·ɪ·kəl] *adj* ① (*cost-effective*) wirtschaftlich, ökonomisch; *car* sparsam ② (*thrifty*) sparsam

economics [ˌi·kə·ˈnam·ɪks] *npl* ① + *sing vb* (*science*) Wirtschaftswissenschaft[en] *f*[*pl*]; (*management studies*) Betriebswirtschaft *f* ② (*economic aspects*) wirtschaftlicher Aspekt

economist [ɪ·ˈkan·ə·mɪst] *n* Wirtschaftswissenschaftler(in) *m(f)*; (*in industrial management*) Betriebswirtschaftler(in) *m(f)*

economize [ɪ·ˈkan·ə·maɪz] *vi* sparen (**on** an +*dat*)

economy [ɪ·ˈkan·ə·mi] *n* ① (*system*) Wirtschaft *f* ② (*thriftiness*) Sparsamkeit *f kein pl;* **to make economies** Einsparungen machen ③ (*sparing use*) Ökonomie *f*

eˈconomy class *n* Touristenklasse *f*

eˈconomy pack, eˈconomy size *n* Sparpackung *f*

ecosystem [ˈe·koʊ,-] *n* Ökosystem *nt*

ˈecotourism *n* Ökotourismus *m*

ˈecotourist *n* Ökotourist(in) *m(f)*

ˈeco-warrior *n* militanter Umweltschützer/militante Umweltschützerin

ecstasy [ˈek·stə·si] *n* ① (*bliss*) Ekstase *f* ② (*drug*) ■ **E~** Ecstasy *f*

ecstatic [ek·ˈstæt̬·ɪk] *adj* ekstatisch

ecumenical [ˌek·jʊ·ˈmen·ɪ·kəl] *adj* ökumenisch

eczema [ˈek·sə·mə] *n* Ekzem *nt*

eddy [ˈed·i] **I.** *vi* <-ie-> wirbeln; *water* strudeln **II.** *n* Wirbel *m; of water* Strudel *m*

edge [edʒ] **I.** *n* ① (*boundary*) Rand *m a. fig; of lake* Ufer *nt;* **the ~ of the table** die Tischkante ② (*sharp side*) Kante *f;* (*blade*) Schneide *f* ③ (*sharpness*) Schärfe *f;* **to take the ~ off sb's appetite** jdm den Appetit nehmen ④ (*superiority*) ■ **the ~** Überlegenheit *f;* **to have the ~ over sb** jdm überlegen sein ▶ PHRASES: **to live on the ~** ein extremes Leben führen **II.** *vt* **to ~ one's way forward** sich langsam vorwärtsbewegen **III.** *vi* **to ~ forward** langsam voranrücken

edgewise [ˈedʒ·waɪz] *adv* **to [not] get a word in edgewise** [nicht] zu Wort kommen

edgy [ˈedʒ·i] *adj* (*fam*) ① (*fam*) nervös ② *playing, piece of music* supermodern

edible [ˈed·ɪ·bəl] *adj* essbar, genießbar

edifice [ˈed·ɪ·fɪs] *n* Gebäude *nt*

edifying [ˈedɪ·faɪ·ɪŋ] *adj* erbaulich

edit [ˈed·ɪt] *vt* redigieren; COMPUT editieren; FILM, TV, RADIO cutten

◆ **edit out** *vt* [heraus]streichen; FILM, TV, RADIO herausschneiden

edition [ɪ·ˈdɪ·ʃən] *n* ① (*issue*) Ausgabe *f* ② (*broadcast*) Folge *f* ③ (*print run*) Auflage *f*

editor [ˈed·ɪ·tər] *n* ① (*of publication*) Herausgeber(in) *m(f)* ② (*of press department*) Redakteur(in) *m(f)* ③ FILM Cutter(in) *m(f)*

editorial [ˌed·ə·ˈtɔr·i·əl] **I.** *n* Leitartikel *m* **II.** *adj* Redaktions-, redaktionell; ~ **staff** Redaktion *f*

editor in chief [ˌed·ɪ·tər·ɪn·ˈtʃiːf] *n* (*of newspaper*) Chefredakteur(in) *m(f)*; (*at publishing house*) Herausgeber(in) *m(f)*

educate [ˈedʒ·ə·keɪt] *vt* ① (*teach*) unterrichten; (*train*) ausbilden ② (*enlighten*) aufklären

educated [ˈedʒ·ə·keɪ·t̬ɪd] *adj* gebildet; **to be Harvard-~** in Harvard studiert haben

education [ˌedʒ·ʊ·ˈkeɪ·ʃən] *n* ① (*teaching*) Bildung *f;* (*training*) Ausbildung *f* ② (*system*) Erziehungswesen *nt*

educational [ˌedʒ·ʊ·ˈkeɪ·ʃə·nəl] *adj* ① Bildungs-, pädagogisch; ~ **qualifications** schulische Qualifikationen ② (*enlightening*) lehrreich

education(al) ˈtheorist *n* Erziehungswissenschaftler(in) *m(f)*

educator [ˈedʒ·ə·keɪ·t̬ər] *n* Erzieher(in) *m(f)*

eel [il] *n* Aal *m*

eerie <-r, -st> [ˈɪr·i] *adj* unheimlich

effect [ɪ·ˈfekt] **I.** *n* ① (*consequence*) Auswirkung *f* ([**up**]**on** auf +*akk*), Folge *f* ([**up**]**on** für +*akk*) ② (*influence*) Einfluss *m* (**on** auf +*akk*) ③ (*force*) **to come into** [*or* **take**] **~** in Kraft treten ④ (*result*) Wirkung *f;* (*success*) Erfolg *m;* **in ~** eigentlich ⑤ (*summarizing*) **to say something to the ~ that ...** sinngemäß sagen, dass ... ⑥ FILM, THEAT, TV ■ **~s** *pl* Effekte *pl* **II.** *vt* bewirken

effective [ɪ·ˈfek·tɪv] *adj* ① (*competent*) fähig ② (*efficacious*) wirksam, effektiv; (*successful*) erfolgreich ③ (*in effect*) **~ January 1** mit Wirkung vom 1. Januar ④ (*real*) tatsächlich, wirklich

effectively [ɪ·ˈfek·tɪv·li] *adv* ① (*efficaciously*) wirksam, effektiv; (*successfully*) erfolgreich ② (*basically*) eigentlich

effectiveness [ɪ·ˈfek·tɪv·nəs] *n* Wirksamkeit *f,* Effektivität *f*

effeminate [ɪ·ˈfem·ə·nɪt] *adj* unmännlich

effervescence [ˌef·ər·ˈves·əns] *n* Sprudeln *nt*

effervescent [ˌef·ər·ˈves·ənt] *adj* sprudelnd *a. fig*

efficiency [ɪ·ˈfɪʃ·ən·si] *n* Leistungsfähigkeit *f; of person* Tüchtigkeit *f;* (*of machine*) Wirkungsgrad *m*

efficient [ɪ·ˈfɪʃ·ənt] *adj* ① (*productive*) leistungsfähig; *person* fähig, tüchtig ② (*economical*) wirtschaftlich

effigy [ˈef·ɪ·dʒi] *n* Bild[nis] *nt*

effluent [ˈef·lu·ənt] *n* Abwasser *nt*

effort [ˈef·ərt] *n* Mühe *f,* Anstrengung *f;* **to make an ~** (*physically*) sich anstrengen; (*mentally*) sich bemühen; **a poor ~** eine schwache Leistung

effortless ['ef·ərt·lɪs] *adj* mühelos; *grace* natürlich

effusive [ɪ·'fju·sɪv] *adj* überschwänglich

EFL [ˌi·ef·'el] *n abbrev of* **English as a Foreign Language** Englisch *nt* als Fremdsprache

e.g. [ˌi·'dʒi] *abbrev of* **exempli gratia** (**Latin: for the sake of example**) z. B.

egalitarian [ɪ·ˌgæl·ɪ·'ter·i·ən] **I.** *n* Verfechter(in) *m(f)* des Egalitarismus **II.** *adj* egalitär

e-generation [i·ˌdʒen·ə·'reɪ·ʃən] *n* Internetgeneration *f*

egg [eg] **I.** *n* ① Ei *nt* ② (*cell*) Eizelle *f* ▶ PHRASES: **to put all one's ~s in one basket** alles auf eine Karte setzen **II.** *vt* ■**to ~ on** ↻ **sb** jdn anstacheln

'egg cell *n* Eizelle *f*

'egghead *n* (*fam*) Eierkopf *m*

'eggplant *n* Aubergine *f*

'eggshell *n* Eierschale *f*

'egg timer *n* Eieruhr *f*

'egg white *n* Eiweiß *nt*

'egg yolk *n* Eigelb *nt*

ego ['i·goʊ] *n* Ego *nt*

egocentric [ˌi·goʊ·'sen·trɪk] *adj* egozentrisch

egoism ['i·goʊ·ɪz·əm] *n* Egoismus *m*

egoist ['i·goʊ·ɪst] *n* Egoist(in) *m(f)*

egoistic [ˌi·goʊ·'ɪs·tɪk] *adj* egoistisch

egotism ['i·goʊ·tɪz·əm] *n* Egotismus *m*

egotist ['i·goʊ·tɪst] *n* Egotist(in) *m(f)*

egotistic [ˌi·goʊ·'tɪs·tɪk] *adj* egoistisch

'ego trip *n* Egotrip *m*

Egypt ['i·dʒɪpt] *n* Ägypten *nt*

Egyptian [ɪ·'dʒɪp·ʃən] **I.** *n* Ägypter(in) *m(f)* **II.** *adj* ägyptisch

eh [eɪ] *interj* ■**~?** (*expressing confusion*) was?, hä?; (*inviting response to statement*) nicht [wahr]?

eiderdown ['aɪ·dər·daʊn] *n* [Eider]daunen *pl*

eight [eɪt] **I.** *adj* acht; **~ times three is 24** acht mal drei ist 24; **the score is ~ to three** es steht acht zu drei; **there are ~ of us** wir sind [zu] acht; **in packs of ~** in einer Achterpackung; **~ times** achtmal; **a family of ~** eine achtköpfige Familie; **~ and a quarter/half** achteinviertel/achteinhalb; **one in ~ [people]** jeder Achte; **at the age of ~** mit acht Jahren; **at ~ [o'clock]** um acht [Uhr]; **[at] about** [*or* **around**] **~ [o'clock]** gegen acht [Uhr]; **half past ~** halb neun; **at ~ thirty** um halb neun, um acht Uhr dreißig *gesprochen,* um 8.30 Uhr *geschrieben;* **at ~ twenty/forty-five** um zwanzig nach acht [*o* acht Uhr zwanzig]/Viertel vor neun [*o* drei viertel neun] **II.** *n* ① Acht *f;* **a figure ~** eine Acht ② CARDS Acht *f;* **~ of clubs** Kreuzacht *f*

eighteen [ˌeɪ·'tin] **I.** *adj* ① achtzehn; **there are ~ of us** wir sind achtzehn ② (*time*) **~ hundred hours** *spoken* achtzehn Uhr; **1800 hrs.** *written* 18:00 **II.** *n* Achtzehn *f; see also* **eight**

eighteenth [ˌeɪ·'tinθ] **I.** *adj* achtzehnte(r, s) **II.** *n* ■**the ~** der/die/das Achtzehnte

eighth [eɪtθ] **I.** *adj* achte(r, s); **the ~ person** der/die Achte; **every ~ person** jeder Achte; **in ~ place** an achter Stelle; **the ~ largest ...** der/die/das achtgrößte ... **II.** *n* ① (*order*) ■**the ~** der/die/das Achte; **~ [in line]** als Achter an der Reihe; **to be/finish ~ [in a race]** [bei einem Rennen] Achter sein/werden ② (*date*) ■**the ~ [of the month]** *spoken* der Achte [des Monats]; ■**the 8th [of the month]** *written* der 8. [des Monats]; **on February ~** [*or* **the ~ of February**] am achten Februar ③ (*in titles*) **Henry the E~** *spoken* Heinrich der Achte; **Henry VIII** *written* Heinrich VIII. ④ (*fraction*) Achtel *nt*

'eighth note *n* MUS Achtelnote *f*

'eight-hour *adj* achtstündig; **~ day** Achtstundentag *m*

eightieth ['eɪ·t̬ɪ·əθ] **I.** *adj* achtzigste(r, s) **II.** *n* ① (*order*) ■**the ~** der/die/das Achtzigste ② (*fraction*) achtzigstel *nt; see also* **eighth**

eighty ['eɪ·t̬i] **I.** *adj* achtzig; *see also* **eight II.** *n* ① Achtzig *f* ② (*age*) **in one's eighties** in den Achtzigern; **to be in one's early/mid-/late eighties** Anfang/Mitte/Ende achtzig sein ③ (*decade*) ■**the eighties** [*or written:* **80's**] *pl* die achtziger [*o* 80er] Jahre

Eire ['erə] *n* Eire *nt,* Irland *nt*

either ['i·ðər] **I.** *conj* **~ ... or ...** entweder ... oder ... **II.** *adv* ① + *neg* (*as well*) **she doesn't/hasn't ~** sie auch nicht ② + *neg* (*moreover*) **it's really good and not very expensive ~** es ist wirklich gut – und nicht einmal sehr teuer **III.** *adj* ① (*each of two*) **on ~ side** auf beiden Seiten ② (*one of two*) eine(r, s) [von beiden]; **~ way** so oder so **IV.** *pron* **~ of you** eine(r) von euch beiden

ejaculate [ɪ·'dʒæk·jʊ·leɪt] *vi, vt* ejakulieren

ejaculation [ɪ·ˌdʒæk·jʊ·'leɪ·ʃən] *n* Ejakulation *f*

eject [ɪ·'dʒekt] **I.** *vt person* hinauswerfen (**from, out of** aus +*dat*); *thing* auswerfen **II.** *vi* AVIAT den Schleudersitz betätigen

e'jector seat *n* Schleudersitz *m*

elaborate [ɪ·'læb·ər·ət] **I.** *adj design* kompliziert; *decorations* kunstvoll [gearbeitet]; *writing* ausgefeilt; *banquet* üppig; *plan* ausgeklügelt **II.** *vi* ins Detail gehen; ■**to ~ on sth** etw näher ausführen

elaboration [ɪ·ˌlæb·ə·'reɪ·ʃən] *n* ① *of style* Ausfeilung *f; of plan* Ausarbeitung *f* ② (*explanation*) [nähere] Ausführung

elapse [ɪ·'læps] *vi* vergehen

elastic [ɪ·'læs·tɪk] **I.** *adj* elastisch **II.** *n* elastisches Material, Gummi *m*

elastic 'band *n see* **rubber band**

elasticity [ˌe·læ·'stɪs·ə·ti] *n* Elastizität *f a. fig*

elated [ɪ·'leɪ·t̬ɪd] *adj* **to be ~ about** [*or* **at**] [*or* **by**] **sth** über etw *akk* hocherfreut sein

elation [ɪ·'leɪ·ʃən] *n* Hochstimmung *f*

elbow ['el·boʊ] **I.** *n* ① Ellbogen *m* ② (*fig: in pipe, river*) Knie *nt* **II.** *vt* **she ~ed him in the ribs** sie stieß ihm den Ellbogen in die Rippen; **to ~ sb out** jdn hinausdrängeln

'elbow grease *n* Muskelkraft *f*

'elbow room *n* ① Ellbogenfreiheit *f* ② (*fig*) Bewegungsfreiheit *f*

elder[1] ['el·dər] **I.** *n* Ältere(r) *f(m)*; **church/village** ~ Kirchen-/Dorfälteste(r) *f(m)* **II.** *adj* ältere(r, s); *statesman* erfahren

elder[2] ['el·dər] *n* BOT Holunder *m*

elderly ['el·dər·li] **I.** *adj* ältere(r, s), ältlich **II.** *n* ■**the** ~ *pl* ältere Menschen

eldest ['el·dɪst] **I.** *adj* älteste(r, s) **II.** *n* ■**the** ~ der/die Älteste

e-learning ['i·ˌlɜ·nɪŋ] *n no pl* E-Learning *nt*

elect [ɪ·'lekt] **I.** *vt* ❶ (*vote*) wählen (**to** in +*akk*); **to** ~ **sb as chairman** jdn zum Vorsitzenden wählen ❷ (*opt for*) ■**to** ~ **to do sth** sich [dafür] entscheiden, etw zu tun **II.** *adj* **the president-**~ der designierte Präsident

election [ɪ·'lek·ʃən] *n* Wahl *f*

e'lection booth *n* Wahlkabine *f*

e'lection campaign *n* Wahlkampf *m*

E'lection Day *n* Wahltag *m*

electioneering [ɪ·ˌlek·ʃə·'nɪr·ɪŋ] *n* Wahlpropaganda *f*

e'lection official *n* POL Wahlleiter(in) *m(f)*

e'lection platform *n* Wahlprogramm *nt*

e'lection returns *npl* Wahlergebnisse *pl*

e'lection speech *n* Wahlrede *f*

elective [ɪ·'lek·tɪv] **I.** *adj* Wahl- **II.** *n* SCH, UNIV Wahlfach *nt*

elector [ɪ·'lek·tər] *n* Wähler(in) *m(f)*

electoral [ɪ·'lek·tər·əl] *adj* Wahl-

electoral 'college *n* ❶ (*electors of a leader*) Wahlausschuss *m* ❷ (*of US president*) Wahlmännergremium *nt*

electorate [ɪ·'lek·tər·ət] *n* Wählerschaft *f*

electric [ɪ·'lek·trɪk] *adj* ❶ (*powered*) elektrisch; ~ **motor** Elektromotor *m* ❷ (*live*) Strom- ❸ (*fig: exciting*) elektrisierend; *atmosphere* spannungsgeladen; *performance* mitreißend

electrical [ɪ·'lek·trɪ·kəl] *adj* elektrisch

electrician [ɪ·ˌlek·'trɪʃ·ən] *n* Elektriker(in) *m(f)*

electricity [ɪ·ˌlek·'trɪs·ə·ti] *n* Elektrizität *f*, [elektrischer] Strom; **heated by** ~ elektrisch beheizt

electrify [ɪ·'lek·trɪ·faɪ] *vt* ❶ TECH elektrifizieren ❷ (*fig*) elektrisieren

electrocute [ɪ·'lek·trə·kjut] *vt* ❶ (*accidentally*) durch einen Stromschlag töten ❷ (*execute*) auf dem elektrischen Stuhl hinrichten

electrocution [ɪ·ˌlek·trə·'kju·ʃən] *n* ❶ (*accidentally*) Tötung *f* durch Stromschlag ❷ LAW Hinrichtung *f* durch den elektrischen Stuhl

electrode [ɪ·'lek·troʊd] *n* Elektrode *f*

electrolysis [ɪ·ˌlek·'tral·ə·sɪs] *n* Elektrolyse *f*

electro'magnet *n* Elektromagnet *m*

electromag'netic *adj* elektromagnetisch

electron [ɪ·'lek·tran] *n* Elektron *nt*

electronic [ɪ·ˌlek·'tran·ɪk] *adj* elektronisch

electronics [ɪ·ˌlek·'tran·ɪks] *n* ❶ + *sing vb* (*technology*) Elektronik *f kein pl* ❷ + *pl vb* (*parts*) Elektronik *f*

electroplate [ɪ·'lek·troʊ·pleɪt] *vt* galvanisieren; *cutlery* versilbern

elegance ['el·ɪ·gəns] *n* Eleganz *f*

elegant ['el·ɪ·gənt] *adj* elegant

elegy ['el·ə·dʒi] *n* Elegie *f*

element ['el·ə·mənt] *n* Element *nt*; **the criminal** ~ die Kriminellen *pl*

elemental [ˌel·ə·'men·təl] *adj* (*liter*) elementar

elementary [ˌel·ə·'men·tə·ri] *adj* elementar; *mistake* grob

ele'mentary school *n* Grundschule *f*

elephant ['el·ə·fənt] *n* Elefant *m*

elephantine [ˌel·ɪ·'fæn·taɪn] *adj* massig

elevate ['el·ə·veɪt] *vt* ❶ (*lift*) [empor]heben; (*raise*) erhöhen ❷ (*fig*) erheben

elevated ['el·ə·veɪ·t̬ɪd] *adj* ❶ (*raised*) erhöht, höher liegend ❷ (*important*) gehoben

elevation [ˌel·ɪ·'veɪ·ʃən] *n* ❶ (*raised area*) [Boden]erhebung *f* ❷ (*promotion*) Beförderung *f*

elevator ['el·ə·veɪ·t̬ər] *n* Aufzug *m*, Lift *m*

eleven [ɪ·'lev·ən] **I.** *adj* elf **II.** *n* Elf *f*; *see also* **eight**

eleventh [ɪ·'lev·ənθ] **I.** *adj* elfte(r, s) **II.** *n* ❶ **the** ~ der/die/das Elfte ❷ (*fraction*) Elftel *nt*; *see also* **eighth**

elf <*pl* elves> [elf] *n* Elf *m*, Elfe *f*

elicit [ɪ·'lɪs·ɪt] *vt* ❶ (*obtain*) ■**to** ~ **sth from sb** jdm etw entlocken ❷ (*provoke*) hervorrufen

eligibility [ˌel·ɪ·dʒə·'bɪl·ə·ti] *n* ❶ (*for job*) Eignung *f*; (*suitability*) Qualifikation *f* ❷ (*entitlement*) Berechtigung *f*

eligible ['el·ɪ·dʒə·bəl] *adj* ❶ (*qualified*) ■**to be** ~ in Frage kommen; ■**to be** ~ **for** [*or* **to**] **sth** für etw *akk* qualifiziert sein ❷ (*entitled*) ■**to be** ~ **for** [*or* **to**] **sth** zu etw *dat* berechtigt sein ❸ (*desirable*) begehrt

eliminate [ɪ·'lɪm·ɪ·neɪt] *vt* ❶ (*remove*) beseitigen; (*euph sl: murder*) eliminieren ❷ (*exclude*) ausschließen ❸ SPORTS ■**to be** ~**d** ausscheiden; ■**to be** ~**d by sb** gegen jdn ausscheiden

elimination [ɪ·ˌlɪm·ɪ·'neɪ·ʃən] *n* Beseitigung *f*; **process of** ~ Ausleseverfahren *nt*

elite [ɪ·'lit] **I.** *n* Elite *f* **II.** *adj* Elite-; ~ **university** Eliteuniversität *f*

elitism [ɪ·'li·tɪz·əm] *n* Elitedenken *nt*

elitist [ɪ·'li·tɪst] *adj* elitär

elk <*pl* - *or* -s> [elk] *n* Wapitihirsch *m*

ellipse [ɪ·'lɪps] *n* Ellipse *f*

elliptic(al) [ɪ·'lɪp·tɪ·k(əl)] *adj* elliptisch

elm [elm] *n* Ulme *f*

elocution [ˌel·ə·'kju·ʃən] *n* Sprechtechnik *f*

elongate [ɪ·'laŋ·geɪt] **I.** *vt* strecken **II.** *vi* länger werden

elope [ɪ·'loʊp] *vi* durchbrennen *fam*

elopement [ɪ·'loʊp·mənt] *n* Durchbrennen *nt fam*

eloquent ['el·ə·kwənt] *adj* sprachgewandt

else [els] *adv* ❶ (*other*) **I didn't tell anybody** ~ ich habe es niemand anders erzählt; **anyone** ~ **would have left** jeder andere wäre gegangen; **anywhere** ~ irgendwo anders; **she doesn't want to live anywhere** ~ sie will nirgendwo anders leben; **everybody** ~ alle anderen; **everything** ~ alles andere; **everywhere** ~ überall sonst; **nobody/nothing** ~

niemand/nichts anders; **someone ~** jemand anders; **something ~** etwas anderes; **somewhere ~** woanders; **how/what/where/who/why ~ ...?** wie/was/wo/wer/warum sonst ...? ❷ (*additional*) sonst noch; **I don't want anyone ~ to come but you** ich will, dass außer dir [sonst] keiner kommt; **there's nothing ~ for me to do here** es gibt hier nichts mehr für mich zu tun; **nobody/nothing ~** sonst niemand/nichts; **someone/something ~** sonst noch jemand/etwas; **somewhere ~** noch woanders ❸ (*otherwise*) sonst; **or ~!** (*fam*) sonst gibt's was!

elsewhere ['els·wer] *adv* woanders
elucidate [ɪ·'lus·ɪ·deɪt] **I.** *vt* erklären **II.** *vi* sich *akk* [auf]klären
elude [ɪ·'lud] *vt* ❶ ■ **to ~ sb** jdm entkommen ❷ (*fig*) ■ **to ~ sb/sth** sich jdm/etw entziehen
elusive [ɪ·'lu·sɪv] *adj* ❶ (*evasive*) ausweichend ❷ (*hard to find*) schwer zu fassen
elves [elvz] *n pl of* **elf**
emaciated [ɪ·'meɪ·ʃi·eɪ·t̬ɪd] *adj* [stark] abgemagert
e-mail ['i·meɪl] **I.** *n abbrev of* **electronic mail** E-Mail *f* **II.** *vt* [e-]mailen
emanate ['em·ə·neɪt] **I.** *vi heat, light* ausstrahlen; *odor* ausgehen; *documents* stammen **II.** *vt* ausstrahlen; *confidence* verströmen
emancipated [ɪ·'mæn·sə·peɪt̬·ɪd] *adj* ❶ SOCIOL emanzipiert ❷ POL frei[gelassen]
emancipation [ɪ·ˌmæn·sɪ·'peɪ·ʃən] *n* ❶ SOCIOL Emanzipation *f* ❷ POL Befreiung *f*
embalm [em·'bam] *vt* [ein]balsamieren
embankment [em·'bæŋk·mənt] *n* Damm *m; of road* [Straßen]damm *m,* Böschung *f; of river* Uferdamm *m*
embargo [em·'bar·goʊ] **I.** *n* <*pl* -es> Embargo *nt* **II.** *vt* ■ **to ~ sth** über etw *akk* ein Embargo verhängen
embark [em·'bark] *vi* ❶ (*board*) sich einschiffen ❷ (*begin*) ■ **to ~ [up]on sth** etw in Angriff nehmen
embarrass [em·'bær·əs] *vt* in Verlegenheit bringen
embarrassed [em·'bær·əst] *adj* verlegen; **to feel ~** verlegen sein
embarrassing [em·'bær·əsɪŋ] *adj* peinlich; *generosity* beschämend
embarrassment [em·'bær·əs·ment] *n* (*instance*) Peinlichkeit *f;* (*feeling*) Verlegenheit *f;* ■ **to be an ~ [to sb]** [jdm] peinlich sein; **to cause sb ~** jdn verlegen machen
embassy ['em·bə·si] *n* Botschaft *f*
embed <-dd-> [em·'bed] *vt* einlassen; (*fig*) verankern
embellish [em·'bel·ɪʃ] *vt* ❶ (*decorate*) schmücken ❷ (*fig*) *story* ausschmücken; *truth* beschönigen
embers ['em·bərz] *npl* Glut *f*
embezzle [ɪm·'bez·əl] *vt* unterschlagen
embezzlement [ɪm·'bez·əl·mənt] *n* Unterschlagung *f*
embezzler [em·'bez·lər] *n* Veruntreuer(in) *m(f)*
embitter [em·'bɪt̬·ər] *vt* verbittern
emblem ['em·bləm] *n* Emblem *nt*
embodiment [em·'bad·ɪ·mənt] *n* Verkörperung *f;* **the ~ of virtue** die Tugend selbst
embody [em·'bad·i] *vt* ❶ (*show*) zum Ausdruck bringen ❷ (*be incarnation of*) verkörpern
emboss [em·'bas] *vt* prägen
embrace [em·'breɪs] **I.** *vt* ❶ umarmen ❷ (*fig*) [bereitwillig] übernehmen; *idea* aufgreifen **II.** *n* Umarmung *f*
embroider [em·'brɔɪ·dər] *vt, vi* sticken; *cloth* besticken; (*fig*) *story* ausschmücken
embroidery [em·'brɔɪ·də·ri] *n* ❶ Stickerei *f* ❷ (*fig*) Ausschmückungen *pl*
embroil [ɪm·'brɔɪl] *vt* verwickeln
embryo ['em·bri·oʊ] *n* Embryo *m o* ÖSTERR *a. nt*
embryonic [ˌem·brɪ·'an·ɪk] *adj* embryonal; (*fig*) unentwickelt
emcee [em·'si] *n* (*fam*) Conférencier *m;* TV Showmaster *m*
emerald ['em·ər·əld] *n* Smaragd *m*
emerge [ɪ·'mɜrdʒ] *vi* ❶ (*come out*) herauskommen (**from** aus +*dat*); ■ **to ~ from behind sth** hinter etw *dat* hervorkommen ❷ (*surface*) auftauchen (**from** aus +*dat*) ❸ (*fig: become known*) sich herausstellen; *truth* an den Tag kommen
emergence [ɪ·'mɜr·dʒəns] *n* Auftauchen *nt* (**from** aus +*dat*); *of circumstances* Auftreten *nt; of country* Entstehung *f; of facts* Bekanntwerden *nt; of ideas, trends* Aufkommen *nt*
emergency [ɪ·'mɜr·dʒən·si] **I.** *n* ❶ Notfall *m* ❷ POL Notstand *m;* **state of ~** Ausnahmezustand *m* ❸ (*emergency room*) Notaufnahme *f* **II.** *adj* Not-; **~ measures** Krisenmaßnahmen
e'mergency brake *n* Notbremse *f*
e'mergency room, ER *n* Notaufnahme *f,* Unfallstation *f*
emergent [ɪ·'mɜr·dʒənt] *adj* aufstrebend
'emery board *n* Nagelfeile *f*
'emery paper *n* Schmirgelpapier *nt*
emetic [ɪ·'met̬·ɪk] *n* Brechmittel *nt*
emigrant ['em·ɪ·grənt] *n* Auswanderer, -in *m, f;* (*esp political*) Emigrant(in) *m(f)*
emigrate ['em·ɪ·greɪt] *vi* auswandern; (*esp political*) emigrieren
emigration [ˌem·ɪ·'greɪ·ʃən] *n* Auswanderung *f;* (*esp political*) Emigration *f*
eminence ['em·ɪ·nəns] *n* hohes Ansehen
eminent ['em·ɪ·nənt] *adj* [hoch] angesehen
eminently ['em·ɪ·nənt·li] *adv* überaus
emissary ['em·ɪ·ser·i] *n* Emissär(in) *m(f)*
emission [ɪ·'mɪʃ·ən] *n* Emission *f,* Abgabe *f; of gas, liquid, odor* Ausströmen *nt; of heat, light* Ausstrahlen *nt; of sparks* Versprühen *nt; of steam* Ablassen *nt*
emit <-tt-> [ɪ·'mɪt] *vt* abgeben; *fumes, smoke, cry* ausstoßen; *gas, odor* verströmen; *heat, radiation, sound* abgeben; *liquid* absondern;

rays aussenden; *sparks* [ver]sprühen; *steam* ablassen

emoticon [ɪ·ˈmoʊ·tɪ·kan] *n* INET Emoticon *nt*

emotion [ɪ·ˈmoʊ·ʃən] *n* Gefühl *nt*

emotional [ɪ·ˈmoʊ·ʃə·nəl] *adj* ❶ emotional; *decision* gefühlsmäßig; *experience* erregend; *reception* herzlich; *speech* gefühlsbetont; *voice* gefühlvoll ❷ PSYCH *development* seelisch; *blackmail* psychologisch; *person* leicht erregbar

emotionless [ɪ·ˈmoʊ·ʃən·lɪs] *adj* emotionslos; *face* ausdruckslos; *voice* gleichgültig

emotive [ɪ·ˈmoʊ·t̬ɪv] *adj* emotional; ~ **term** Reizwort *nt*

empathy [ˈem·pə·θi] *n* Empathie *f*

emperor [ˈem·pər·ər] *n* Kaiser *m*

emphasis <*pl* -ses> [ˈem·fə·sɪs] *n* Betonung *f*

emphasize [ˈem·fə·saɪz] *vt* betonen

emphatic [em·ˈfæt̬·ɪk] *adj* nachdrücklich; *denial* entschieden; *victory* deutlich

empire [ˈem·paɪr] *n* Imperium *nt a. fig*

empirical [em·ˈpɪr·ɪ·kəl] *adj* erfahrungsmäßig

employ [em·ˈplɔɪ] *vt* ❶ *worker* beschäftigen; (*staff*) einstellen ❷ (*fig: use*) anwenden; *means* einsetzen

employee [ˈem·plɔɪ·ˈi] *n* Angestellte(r) *f(m)*; (*vs employer*) Arbeitnehmer(in) *m(f)*; ■ **~s** *pl* (*in company*) Belegschaft *f*

employer [em·ˈplɔɪ·ər] *n* Arbeitgeber(in) *m(f)*

employment [em·ˈplɔɪ·mənt] *n* ❶ (*having work*) Beschäftigung *f;* (*taking on*) Anstellung *f;* **in ~** erwerbstätig ❷ (*profession*) Beruf *m* ❸ (*fig: use*) *of skill* Anwendung *f; of means* Einsatz *m; of concept* Verwendung *f*

emˈployment agency *n* Stellenvermittlung *f*

empower [em·ˈpaʊ·ər] *vt* ❶ (*strengthen*) [mental] stärken ❷ (*enable*) befähigen; (*authorize*) ermächtigen

empowerment [em·ˈpaʊ·ər·mənt] *n* Bevollmächtigung *f;* (*strengthening*) Stärkung *f*

empress <*pl* -es> [ˈem·prɪs] *n* Kaiserin *f*

emptiness [ˈemp·tɪ·nɪs] *n* Leere *f*

empty [ˈemp·ti] **I.** *adj* leer *a. fig; house* leer stehend; *seat* frei; *stomach* nüchtern **II.** *vt* <-ie-> [ent]leeren; (*pour*) schütten; *bottle* ausleeren **III.** *vi* <-ie-> sich leeren **IV.** *n* ■ **empties** *pl* Leergut *nt*

◆ **empty out I.** *vt* ausleeren, ausschütten (**into** in +*akk*) **II.** *vi* sich leeren

empty-ˈhanded *adj* mit leeren Händen *nach n*

empty-ˈheaded *adj* hohlköpfig

emu <*pl* - *or* -s> [ˈi·mju] *n* Emu *m*

emulate [ˈem·jʊ·leɪt] *vt* nacheifern +*dat*

emulation [ˌem·jʊ·ˈleɪ·ʃən] *n* Nacheifern *nt;* COMPUT Emulation *f*

emulsifier [ɪ·ˈmʌl·sɪ·faɪ·ər] *n* Emulgator *m*

emulsion [ɪ·ˈmʌl·ʃən] *n* ❶ (*mixture*) Emulsion *f* ❷ PHOT (*coating*) Fotoemulsion *f*

enable [ɪ·ˈneɪ·bəl] *vt* ❶ ■ **to ~ sb to do sth** jdm ermöglichen, etw zu tun ❷ COMPUT aktivieren

enact [ɪ·ˈnækt] *vt* ❶ LAW erlassen ❷ (*perform*) ausführen ❸ THEAT *part* spielen; *play* aufführen

enamel [ɪ·ˈnæm·əl] **I.** *n* ❶ (*substance*) Email *nt;* (*paint*) Emaillelack *m* ❷ (*dental*) Zahnschmelz *m* **II.** *vt* <-l- *or* -ll-> emaillieren

enamored [ɪ·ˈnæm·ərd] *adj* begeistert (**of, with** von +*dat*)

encampment [en·ˈkæmp·mənt] *n* Lager *nt*

encapsulate [ɪn·ˈkæp·sə·leɪt] *vt* ❶ ummanteln ❷ (*fig*) zusammenfassen

encase [en·ˈkeɪs] *vt* ■ **to be ~d** ummantelt sein; *waste* eingeschlossen sein

encephalitis [en·ˌsef·ə·ˈlaɪ·t̬ɪs] *n* Gehirnentzündung *f*

enchant [en·ˈtʃænt] *vt* (*delight*) entzücken; (*bewitch*) verzaubern

enchanting [en·ˈtʃæn·t̬ɪŋ] *adj* (*delightful*) bezaubernd; (*bewitching*) entzückend

encipher [en·ˈsaɪ·fər] *vt* chiffrieren

encircle [en·ˈsɜr·kəl] *vt* umgeben; MIL einkesseln, umzingeln

encl. *adj, n abbrev of* **enclosed, enclosure** Anl.

enclose [en·ˈkloʊz] *vt* ❶ (*surround*) umgeben; (*shut in*) einschließen ❷ *mail* beilegen

enclosure [en·ˈkloʊ·ʒər] *n* ❶ (*area*) eingezäuntes Grundstück; (*for animals*) Gehege *nt* ❷ (*item*) Anlage *f*

encode [en·ˈkoʊd] *vt* kodieren

encompass [en·ˈkʌm·pəs] *vt* umfassen

encore [ˈan·kɔr] *n* Zugabe *f*

encounter [en·ˈkaʊn·tər] **I.** *vt* ❶ (*experience*) stoßen (auf +*akk*) ❷ (*meet*) [unerwartet] treffen **II.** *n* Begegnung *f;* MIL Zusammenstoß *m*

encourage [en·ˈkɜr·ɪdʒ] *vt* ❶ (*give courage*) zusprechen +*dat;* (*give confidence*) ermutigen; (*give hope*) unterstützen ❷ (*urge*) ■ **to ~ sb to do sth** jdn [dazu] ermuntern, etw zu tun; (*advise*) jdm [dazu] raten, etw zu tun ❸ (*promote*) fördern

encouragement [en·ˈkɜr·ɪdʒ·mənt] *n* (*incitement*) Ermutigung *f;* (*urging*) Ermunterung *f;* SPORTS Anfeuerung *f;* (*support*) Unterstützung *f;* **to give sb ~** jdn ermutigen

encouraging [en·ˈkɜr·ɪdʒ·ɪŋ] *adj* ermutigend

encroach [en·ˈkroʊtʃ] *vi* ■ **to ~ [up]on sb** zu jdm vordringen; ■ **to ~ [up]on sth** in etw *akk* eindringen

encryption [ɪn·ˈkrɪp·ʃən] *n* Verschlüsselung *f*

encumber [en·ˈkʌm·bər] *vt* ■ **to be ~ed with sth** (*burdened*) mit etw *dat* belastet sein; (*impeded*) durch etw *akk* behindert sein

encyclopedia [en·ˌsaɪ·klə·ˈpi·di·ə] *n* Lexikon *nt*

encyclopedic [en·ˌsaɪ·klə·ˈpi·dɪk] *adj* universal

end [end] **I.** *n* ❶ Ende *nt;* (*completion*) Schluss *m;* **until the ~** bis zuletzt; **for hours on ~** stundenlang; **at the ~ of one's patience** mit seiner Geduld am Ende; **no ~ of trouble** reichlich Ärger; **~ to ~** der Länge nach; **on ~** hochkant ❷ *usu pl* (*aims*) Ziel *nt;* (*purpose*) Zweck *m* ❸ SPORTS [Spielfeld]hälfte *f* ► PHRASES: **to <u>become</u> an ~ in itself** [zum] Selbstzweck werden; **at the ~ of the <u>day</u>** [*or* **<u>in</u> the ~**] (*all*

E

considered) letzten Endes; (*finally*) schließlich; **to go off the deep ~** hochgehen; **to make ~s meet** mit seinem Geld zurechtkommen; **~ of story** [und] Schluss; **to throw sb in at the deep ~** jdn ins kalte Wasser werfen **II.** *vt* beenden **III.** *vi* enden; **to ~ in a tie** unentschieden ausgehen

◆**end up** *vi* ① (*in a place*) landen; **to ~ up in prison** [schließlich] im Gefängnis landen ② (*in a situation*) enden; ■**to ~ up doing sth** schließlich etw tun; **to ~ up teaching** schließlich Lehrer/Lehrerin werden

endanger [en·'deɪn·dʒər] *vt* gefährden; **an ~ed species** eine vom Aussterben bedrohte Art

endear [en·'dɪr] *vt* ■**to ~ oneself to sb** sich bei jdm beliebt machen

endearing [en·'dɪr·ɪŋ] *adj* lieb[enswert]; *smile* gewinnend

endeavor [en·'dev·ər] **I.** *vi* sich bemühen **II.** *n* Bemühung *f*

endemic [en·'dem·ɪk] *adj* endemisch

ending ['en·dɪŋ] *n* ① (*last part*) Ende *nt*, Schluss *m; of day* Abschluss *m; of story, book* Ausgang *m;* **happy ~** Happyend *nt* ② LING Endung *f*

endive ['en·daɪv] *n* ① Endivie *f* ② Chicorée *m*

endless ['end·lɪs] *adj* endlos; (*countless*) unzählig

endorse [en·'dɔrs] *vt* ① (*approve*) billigen; (*promote*) unterstützen ② (*sign*) **to ~ a check** einen Scheck auf der Rückseite unterschreiben

endorsement [en·'dɔrs·mənt] *n* ① (*support*) Billigung *f;* COMM Befürwortung *f* ② (*signature*) Giro *nt fachspr*

endow [en·'daʊ] *vt* ① (*give income to*) über eine Stiftung finanzieren; *prize* stiften ② (*give feature*) ■**to be ~ed with sth** mit etw *dat* ausgestattet sein

endowment [en·'daʊ·mənt] *n* FIN Stiftung *f*

end 'product *n* Endprodukt *nt;* (*fig*) Resultat *nt*

endurable [en·'dʊr·ə·bəl] *adj* erträglich

endurance [en·'dʊr·əns] *n* Ausdauer *f,* Durchhaltevermögen *nt*

endure [en·'dʊr] **I.** *vt* (*tolerate*) ertragen; (*suffer*) erleiden **II.** *vi* fortdauern

enduring [en·'dʊr·ɪŋ] *adj* dauerhaft

enema ['en·ə·mə] *n* MED Einlauf *m*

enemy ['en·ə·mi] **I.** *n* Feind(in) *m(f)* **II.** *adj* feindlich; **~ action** Feindeinwirkung *f*

energetic [ˌen·ər·'dʒeţ·ɪk] *adj* ① voller Energie *nach n,* energiegeladen, schwungvoll; (*resolute*) energisch ② (*overactive*) anstrengend

energize ['en·ər·dʒaɪz] *vt* ① ELEC unter Strom setzen ② (*fig*) neue Energie geben *+dat*

energy ['en·ər·dʒi] *n* ① (*vigor*) Energie *f,* Kraft *f* ② SCI Energie *f;* **~ crisis** Energiekrise *f;* **sources of ~** Energiequellen *pl*

enforce [en·'fɔrs] *vt* durchsetzen, erzwingen

enforcement [en·'fɔrs·mənt] *n* Erzwingung *f; of regulation* Durchsetzung *f; of law* Vollstreckung *f*

enfranchise [en·'fræn·tʃaɪz] *vt* ■**to ~ sb** jdm das Wahlrecht verleihen

engage [en·'geɪdʒ] **I.** *vt* ① (*employ*) anstellen ② (*involve*) **to ~ sb in a conversation** jdn in ein Gespräch verwickeln ③ (*mesh*) einschalten; TECH greifen ④ MIL angreifen **II.** *vi* ① ■**to ~ in sth** sich an etw *dat* beteiligen; **to ~ in conversation** sich unterhalten; **to ~ in espionage** Spionage betreiben ② TECH eingreifen

engaged [en·'geɪdʒd] *adj* ① (*fiancé*) verlobt; **to get ~** [**to sb**] sich [mit jdm] verloben ② TECH *gear* im Griff

engagement [en·'geɪdʒ·mənt] *n* ① (*to marry*) Verlobung *f* (**to** mit *+dat*) ② (*appointment*) Verabredung *f*

en'gagement ring *n* Verlobungsring *m*

engaging [en·'geɪ·dʒɪŋ] *adj* bezaubernd; *manner* einnehmend; *smile* gewinnend

engine ['en·dʒɪn] *n* Motor *m;* AVIAT Triebwerk *nt;* RAIL Lok[omotive] *f*

engineer [ˌen·dʒɪ·'nɪr] **I.** *n* ① Ingenieur(in) *m(f);* MIL Pionier *m;* **civil/electrical/mechanical ~** Bau-/Elektro-/Maschinenbauingenieur(in) *m(f)* ② (*train driver*) Lok[omotiv]führer(in) *m(f)* **II.** *vt* ① (*design*) konstruieren ② (*fig: contrive*) arrangieren

engineering [ˌen·dʒɪ·'nɪr·ɪŋ] *n* Technik *f,* Ingenieurwissenschaft *f;* (*mechanical engineering*) Maschinenbau *m*

England ['ɪŋ·glənd] *n* England *nt*

English ['ɪŋ·glɪʃ] **I.** *n* ① (*language*) Englisch *nt* ② (*people*) ■**the ~** *pl* die Engländer **II.** *adj* englisch; **~ department** UNIV Institut *nt* für Anglistik

'Englishman *n* Engländer *m*

English 'muffin *n flaches rundes Hefebrötchen, das halbiert getoastet und anschließend mit Butter* (*und ggf. Marmelade oder Erdnussbutter*) *gegessen wird*

'Englishwoman *n* Engländerin *f*

engrave [en·'greɪv] *vt* [ein]gravieren; (*on stone*) einmeißeln; (*on wood*) einschnitzen; (*fig*) sich *dat* einprägen

engraver [en·'greɪ·vər] *n* Graveur(in) *m(f);* (*of stone*) Steinhauer(in) *m(f);* (*of wood*) Holzschneider(in) *m(f)*

engraving [en·'greɪ·vɪŋ] *n* ① (*print*) Stich *m;* (*from wood*) Holzschnitt *m* ② (*design*) Gravierung *f,* Gravur *f* ③ (*art*) Gravierkunst *f*

engross [en·'groʊs] *vt* fesseln; **to be ~ed in sth** in etw *akk* vertieft sein

engulf [en·'gʌlf] *vt* verschlingen

enhance [ɪn·'hæns] *vt* (*improve*) verbessern; (*intensify*) hervorheben

enigma [ɪ·'nɪg·mə] *n* Rätsel *nt*

enjoy [en·'dʒɔɪ] *vt* genießen; **did you ~ the movie?** hat dir der Film gefallen?; ■**to ~ doing sth** etw gern[e] tun; ■**to ~ oneself** sich amüsieren; **~ yourself!** viel Spaß!

enjoyable [en·'dʒɔɪ·ə·bəl] *adj* angenehm, nett; (*entertaining*) unterhaltsam

enjoyment [en·'dʒɔɪ·mənt] *n* Vergnügen *nt,*

Spaß *m* (**of** an +*dat*)
enlarge [en·ˈlardʒ] **I.** *vt* vergrößern; (*expand*) erweitern **II.** *vi* ❶ (*grow*) sich vergrößern ❷ ■**to ~ [up]on sth** sich zu etw *dat* ausführlich äußern
enlargement [en·ˈlardʒ·mənt] *n* Vergrößerung *f;* (*expansion*) Erweiterung *f*
enlighten [en·ˈlaɪ·tən] *vt* aufklären
enlightened [en·ˈlaɪ·tənd] *adj* aufgeklärt
enlightenment [en·ˈlaɪ·tən·mənt] *n* ❶ PHILOS ■**the E~** die Aufklärung ❷ (*information*) aufklärende Information
enlist [en·ˈlɪst] **I.** *vi* MIL sich melden **II.** *vt person* anwerben; *support* gewinnen
enliven [en·ˈlaɪ·vən] *vt* beleben
en masse [an·ˈmæs] *adv* alle zusammen
enmesh [en·ˈmeʃ] *vt* ■**to become ~ed in sth** sich in etw *akk* verfangen *a. fig*
enmity [ˈen·mə·ti] *n* Feindschaft *f*
enormity [ɪ·ˈnɔr·mə·ti] *n* ungeheures Ausmaß; *of task* ungeheure Größe
enormous [ɪ·ˈnɔr·məs] *adj* enorm; *size* riesig; *mountain* gewaltig; *difficulties* ungeheuer
enough [ɪ·ˈnʌf] **I.** *adj* genug, genügend; **that should be ~** das dürfte reichen; **just ~ room** gerade Platz genug **II.** *adv* ❶ (*adequately*) genug; **are you warm ~?** ist es dir warm genug? ❷ (*quite*) **he seems nice ~** er scheint so weit recht nett zu sein; **strangely ~** seltsamerweise **III.** *pron* ❶ (*sufficient quantity*) genug; **there's ~ for everybody** es ist für alle genug da ❷ (*too much*) **that's ~!** jetzt reicht es!
enquire [en·ˈkwaɪr] *vi see* **inquire**
enquiry [en·ˈkwaɪr·i] *n see* **inquiry**
enrage [en·ˈreɪdʒ] *vt* wütend machen
enraged [en·ˈreɪdʒd] *adj* wütend
enrich [en·ˈrɪtʃ] *vt* ❶ (*improve*) bereichern ❷ (*make richer*) reich machen; ■**to ~ oneself** sich bereichern
enroll, enrol [en·ˈroʊl] **I.** *vi* sich einschreiben; *for course* sich anmelden **II.** *vt* aufnehmen
enrollment, enrolment [en·ˈroʊl·mənt] *n* ❶ (*act*) Einschreibung *f;* (*for course*) Anmeldung *f* ❷ (*students*) Studentenzahl *f*
en route [ˌan·ˈrut] *adv* unterwegs
ensemble [an·ˈsam·bəl] *n* Ensemble *nt*
ensign [ˈen·sən] *n* ❶ (*flag*) Schiffsflagge *f* ❷ MIL Fähnrich *m* zur See
enslave [en·ˈsleɪv] *vt* zum Sklaven machen
ensue [en·ˈsu] *vi* folgen
ensuing [en·ˈsu·ɪŋ] *adj* [darauf] folgend
ensure [en·ˈʃʊr] *vt* sicherstellen; (*guarantee*) garantieren
entail [en·ˈteɪl] *vt* mit sich bringen
entangle [en·ˈtæŋ·gəl] *vt* **to get** [*or* **become**] **~d in sth** sich in etw *dat* verfangen; (*fig*) sich in etw *akk* verwickeln
entanglement [en·ˈtæŋ·gəl·mənt] *n* Verfangen *nt;* (*fig*) Verwicklung *f*
enter [ˈen·tər] **I.** *vt* ❶ (*go into*) hineingehen in +*akk; building, room* betreten; *phase* eintreten in +*akk;* (*penetrate*) eindringen in +*akk* ❷ (*insert*) *data* eingeben; (*in register*) eintragen ❸ (*join*) beitreten +*dat;* ■**to ~ sb in sth** jdn für etw *akk* anmelden **II.** *vi* ❶ THEAT auftreten ❷ (*register*) ■**to ~ in sth** sich für etw *akk* [an]melden **III.** *n* COMPUT Eingabe *f*
◆**enter into** *vi* **to ~ into an alliance** ein Bündnis schließen; **to ~ into negotiations** in Verhandlungen eintreten
ˈ**enter key** *n* COMPUT Eingabetaste *f*
enterprise [ˈen·tər·praɪz] *n* ❶ Unternehmen *nt;* **private ~** Privatwirtschaft *f* ❷ (*initiative*) Unternehmungsgeist *m*
enterprising [ˈen·t̬ər·praɪ·zɪŋ] *adj* (*adventurous*) unternehmungslustig; (*ingenious*) einfallsreich; *idea* kühn
entertain [ˌen·tər·ˈteɪn] **I.** *vt* ❶ (*amuse*) unterhalten ❷ (*invite*) zu sich einladen; (*give meal*) bewirten **II.** *vi* Gäste haben
entertainer [ˌen·tər·ˈteɪ·nər] *n* Entertainer(in) *m(f)*
entertaining [ˌen·t̬ər·ˈteɪ·nɪŋ] **I.** *adj* unterhaltsam **II.** *n* **to do a lot of ~** häufig Leute bewirten
entertainment [ˌen·tər·ˈteɪn·mənt] *n* Unterhaltung *f*
enthrall [en·ˈθrɔl] *vt* packen
enthuse [en·ˈθuz] **I.** *vi* schwärmen (**about, over** von +*dat*) **II.** *vt* begeistern (**with** für +*akk*)
enthusiasm [en·ˈθu·zɪ·æz·əm] *n* Begeisterung *f*
enthusiast [ɪn·ˈθu·zɪ·æst] *n* Enthusiast(in) *m(f)*
enthusiastic [en·ˌθu·zɪ·ˈæs·tɪk] *adj* enthusiastisch, begeistert (**about** von +*dat*)
entice [en·ˈtaɪs] *vt* ■**to ~ sb [away from sth]** jdn [von etw *akk* weg]locken; ■**to ~ sb to do** [*or* **into doing**] **sth** jdn dazu verleiten, etw zu tun
entire [en·ˈtaɪr] *adj* (*whole*) ganz; (*complete*) vollständig
entirely [en·ˈtaɪr·li] *adv* ganz; *agree* völlig
entirety [en·ˈtaɪ·rə·t̬i] *n* Gesamtheit *f*
entitle [en·ˈtaɪ·t̬əl] *vt* ■**to be ~d to do sth** dazu berechtigt sein, etw zu tun
entitlement [en·ˈtaɪ·t̬əl·mənt] *n* (*right*) Berechtigung *f* (**to** zu +*dat*); (*claim*) Anspruch *m* (**to** auf +*akk*)
entity [ˈen·tə·ti] *n* Einheit *f*
entomology [ˌen·tə·ˈmal·ə·dʒi] *n* Insektenkunde *f*
entourage [ˌan·tʊ·ˈraʒ] *n* Gefolge *nt*
entrails [ˈen·treɪlz] *npl* Eingeweide *pl*
entrance[1] [ˈen·trəns] *n* ❶ (*door*) Eingang *m;* (*for vehicle*) Einfahrt *f* ❷ (*entering*) Eintritt *m* ❸ THEAT Auftritt *m;* **to make one's ~** auftreten *a. fig*
entrance[2] [en·ˈtræns] *vt* entzücken
ˈ**entrance exam(ination)** *n* SCH, UNIV Aufnahmeprüfung *f,* Zulassungstest *m*
ˈ**entrance fee** *n* Eintritt *m,* ÖSTERR *a.* Entree *nt;* (*for competition*) Teilnahmegebühr *f*
ˈ**entrance hall** *n* Eingangshalle *f*
ˈ**entrance requirement** *n* Aufnahmebedin-

gung *f*

entrant ['en·trənt] *n* Teilnehmer(in) *m(f)*

entreat [en·'trit] *vt* anflehen

entrepreneur [ˌan·trə·prə·'nɜr] *n* Unternehmer(in) *m(f)*

entrust [en·'trʌst] *vt* ■**to ~ sth to sb** [*or* **sb with sth**] jdm etw anvertrauen; **to ~ a task to sb** jdn mit einer Aufgabe betrauen

entry ['en·tri] *n* ❶ (*entering*) Eintritt *m;* (*by car*) Einfahrt *f;* (*into country*) Einreise *f;* (*into organization or activity*) Aufnahme *f;* **"no ~"** „Zutritt verboten" ❷ (*entrance*) Eingang *m;* (*by car*) Einfahrt *f* ❸ (*right of entry*) Zugang *m,* Zutritt *m* (**into** zu +*dat*) ❹ (*data*) Eintrag *m*

E

'entry fee *n* Eintritt *m,* ÖSTERR *a.* Entree *nt;* (*for competition*) Teilnahmegebühr *f;* (*for membership*) Aufnahmegebühr *f*

'entry form *n* Antragsformular *nt;* (*for competition*) Teilnahmeformular *nt*

'entry permit *n* Passierschein *m;* (*into country*) Einreiseerlaubnis *f,* Einreisegenehmigung *f*

entwine [en·'twaɪn] *vt* [miteinander] verflechten

enumerate [ɪ·'nu·mə·reɪt] *vt* aufzählen

enunciate [ɪ·'nʌn·si·eɪt] **I.** *vi* sich artikulieren; **to ~ clearly** deutlich sprechen **II.** *vt* aussprechen

envelop [en·'vel·əp] *vt* einhüllen

envelope ['en·və·loʊp] *n* Briefumschlag *m*

enviable ['en·vɪ·ə·bəl] *adj* beneidenswert

envious ['en·vi·əs] *adj* neidisch (**of** auf +*akk*)

environment [en·'vaɪ·ərn·mənt] *n* ❶ ECOL ■**the ~** die Umwelt ❷ (*surroundings*) Umgebung *f; social* Milieu *nt*

environmental [en·ˌvaɪ·ərn·'men·təl] *adj* Umwelt-

environmentalist [en·ˌvaɪ·ərn·'men·təl·ɪst] *n* Umweltschützer(in) *m(f)*

environmentally [en·ˌvaɪ·rən·'men·t̬əli] *adv* **~ damaging** umweltschädlich

environment-'friendly *adj* umweltfreundlich

envisage [en·'vɪz·ɪdʒ], **envision** [en·'vɪʒ·ən] *vt* sich *dat* vorstellen; ■**to ~ doing sth** vorhaben, etw zu tun

envoy ['an·vɔɪ] *n* Gesandte(r) *f(m);* **special ~** Sonderbeauftragte(r) *f(m)*

envy ['en·vi] **I.** *n* Neid *m* (**of** auf +*akk*); **to feel ~ toward sb** auf jdn neidisch sein; **he's the ~ of the school with his new car** die ganze Schule beneidet ihn um sein neues Auto **II.** *vt* <-ie-> ■**to ~ sb sth** [*or* **sb for sth**] jdn um etw *akk* beneiden

enzyme ['en·zaɪm] *n* Enzym *nt*

eon ['i·an] *n* Äon *m*

ephemeral [ɪ·'fem·ər·əl] *adj* kurzlebig

epic ['ep·ɪk] **I.** *n* Epos *nt* **II.** *adj* ❶ episch; *poem* erzählend; **~ poet** Epiker(in) *m(f)* ❷ (*fig*) schwierig und abenteuerlich; *struggle* heroisch; **~ proportions** unvorstellbare Ausmaße

epicenter ['ep·ɪ·sen·tər] *n* Epizentrum *nt*

epidemic [ˌep·ɪ·'dem·ɪk] **I.** *n* Epidemie *f* **II.** *adj* epidemisch *a. fig*

epilepsy ['ep·ɪ·lep·si] *n* Epilepsie *f*

epileptic [ˌep·ɪ·'lep·tɪk] **I.** *n* Epileptiker(in) *m(f)* **II.** *adj* epileptisch

epilogue, epilog ['ep·ɪ·lag] *n* Epilog *m*

Epiphany [ɪ·'pɪf·ə·ni] *n* Dreikönigsfest *nt*

episode ['ep·ɪ·soʊd] *n* ❶ (*event*) Episode *f* ❷ *of series* Folge *f*

episodic [ˌep·ɪ·'sad·ɪk] *adj* episodisch

epistle [ɪ·'pɪs·əl] *n* Epistel *f*

epitaph ['ep·ɪ·tæf] *n* Grabinschrift *f*

epitome [ɪ·'pɪt̬·ə·mi] *n* Inbegriff *m;* **the ~ of elegance** die Eleganz selbst

epitomize [ɪ·'pɪt̬·ə·maɪz] *vt* verkörpern

epoch ['ep·ək] *n* Epoche *f*

eponymous [ɪ·'pan·ə·məs] *adj* namensgebend

equable ['ek·wə·bəl] *adj* ausgeglichen

equal ['i·kwəl] **I.** *adj* ❶ (*same*) gleich; **of ~ size** gleich groß; **~ in volume** vom Umfang her gleich ❷ (*able*) **to be ~ to a task** einer Aufgabe gewachsen sein ▶ PHRASES: **all other things being ~** unter ansonsten gleichen Bedingungen **II.** *n* Gleichgestellte(r) *f(m);* **to have no ~** unübertroffen sein **III.** *vt* <-l- *or* -ll-> ❶ MATH ergeben ❷ (*match*) herankommen an +*akk; record* erreichen

equality [ɪ·'kwal·ə·t̬i] *n no pl* Gleichberechtigung *f;* **racial ~** Rassengleichheit *f;* ■**the E~ Act** EU das Allgemeine Gleichbehandlungsgesetz, das AGG

equalization [ˌi·kwə·lɪ·'zeɪ·ʃən] *n* Gleichmachung *f*

equalize ['i·kwə·laɪz] *vt* gleichmachen; *pressure* ausgleichen; *standards* einander angleichen

equally ['i·kwə·li] *adv* ebenso; **~ good** gleich gut; **to divide** [*or* **share**] **sth ~** etw gleichmäßig aufteilen

equal oppor'tunity *n* Chancengleichheit *f*

'equal sign *n* MATH Gleichheitszeichen *nt*

equanimity [ˌek·wə·'nɪm·ə·ti] *n* Gleichmut *m*

equate [ɪ·'kweɪt] **I.** *vt* gleichsetzen (**with** mit +*dat*) **II.** *vi* ■**to ~ to sth** etw *dat* entsprechen

equation [ɪ·'kweɪ·ʒən] *n* MATH Gleichung *f*

equator [ɪ·'kweɪ·t̬ər] *n* Äquator *m;* **on the ~** am Äquator

equatorial [ˌek·wə·'tɔr·i·əl] *adj* äquatorial

equestrian [ɪ·'kwes·tri·ən] **I.** *adj* Reit[er]- **II.** *n* Reiter(in) *m(f)*

equidistant [ˌi·kwɪ·'dɪs·tənt] *adj* gleich weit entfernt (**from** von +*dat*)

equilateral [ˌi·kwɪ·'læt̬·ər·əl] *adj* MATH gleichseitig

equilibrium [ˌi·kwɪ·'lɪb·ri·əm] *n* Gleichgewicht *nt*

equinox <*pl* -es> ['i·kwɪ·naks] *n* Tagundnachtgleiche *f*

equip <-pp-> [ɪ·'kwɪp] *vt* ❶ ausstatten; *with special equipment* ausrüsten ❷ (*fig*) rüsten

equipment [ɪ·'kwɪp·mənt] *n* Ausrüstung *f,* Ausstattung *f*

equitable ['ek·wɪ·tə·bəl] *adj* gerecht

equity ['ek·wə·ti] *n* ❶ (*fairness*) Gerechtigkeit *f* ❷ FIN Eigenkapital *nt;* ■**equities** *pl*

[Stamm]aktien *pl*

equivalence [ɪ·ˈkwɪv·ə·ləns] *n* Äquivalenz *f*

equivalent [ɪ·ˈkwɪv·ə·lənt] **I.** *adj* äquivalent, entsprechend; ■**to be ~ to sth** etw *dat* entsprechen **II.** *n* Äquivalent *nt* (**for, of** für +*akk*), Entsprechung *f*

equivocal [ɪ·ˈkwɪv·ə·kəl] *adj* ❶ (*ambiguous*) zweideutig ❷ (*dubious*) zweifelhaft

ER [ˌi·ˈar] *n abbrev of* **emergency room** Notaufnahme *f*

era [ˈɪr·ə] *n* Ära *f*

eradicate [ɪ·ˈræd·ɪ·keɪt] *vt* ausrotten

erase [ɪ·ˈreɪs] *vt* ❶ (*remove*) entfernen; *file* löschen; *memories* auslöschen ❷ (*rub out*) ausradieren

eraser [ɪ·ˈreɪ·sər] *n* Radiergummi *m*

erasure [ɪ·ˈreɪ·ʃər] *n* Löschung *f*

erect [ɪ·ˈrekt] **I.** *adj* aufrecht; *penis* erigiert **II.** *vt* ❶ (*build*) errichten ❷ (*upright*) aufstellen

erection [ɪ·ˈrek·ʃən] *n* ❶ (*building*) Errichtung *f* ❷ (*penis*) Erektion *f*

ergonomic [ˌɜr·gə·ˈnam·ɪk] *adj* ergonomisch

ermine [ˈɜr·mɪn] *n* Hermelin *nt*

erode [ɪ·ˈroʊd] **I.** *vt* ❶ GEOL erodieren; *water* auswaschen; *soil* abtragen ❷ CHEM zerfressen ❸ (*fig*) untergraben **II.** *vi* ❶ GEOL erodiert werden; *by water* ausgewaschen werden; *soil* abgetragen werden ❷ (*fig*) abnehmen

erogenous [ɪ·ˈradʒ·ə·nəs] *adj* erogen

erosion [ɪ·ˈroʊ·ʒən] *n* ❶ GEOL Erosion *f* ❷ (*fig*) [Dahin]schwinden *nt*

erotic [ɪ·ˈraṭ·ɪk] *adj* erotisch

eroticism [ɪ·ˈraṭ·ə·sɪz·əm] *n* Eroti[zi]smus *m*

err [ɜr] *vi* (*form*) sich irren; **to ~ on the side of caution** übervorsichtig sein

errand [ˈer·ənd] *n* Besorgung *f;* (*with message*) Botengang *m*

errant [ˈer·ənt] *adj* auf Abwegen *nach n*

erratic [ɪ·ˈræṭ·ɪk] *adj* ❶ (*inconsistent*) sprunghaft ❷ (*irregular*) unregelmäßig

erroneous [ɪ·ˈroʊ·ni·əs] *adj* falsch; *assumption* irrig

error [ˈer·ər] *n* Fehler *m,* Irrtum *m;* **in ~** aus Versehen; (*in baseball*) Fehlpass *m*

ˈerror message *n* COMPUT Fehlermeldung *f*

ˈerror-prone *adj* fehleranfällig

erudite [ˈer·jə·daɪt] *adj* gelehrt

erudition [ˌer·ju·ˈdɪʃ·ən] *n* Gelehrsamkeit *f*

erupt [ɪ·ˈrʌpt] *vi* ausbrechen; (*fig*) *person* explodieren

eruption [ɪ·ˈrʌp·ʃən] *n* Ausbruch *m a. fig*

escalate [ˈes·kə·leɪt] **I.** *vi* eskalieren, sich ausweiten; *incidents* stark zunehmen **II.** *vt* ausweiten

escalation [ˌes·kə·ˈleɪ·ʃən] *n* Eskalation *f,* Steigerung *f; of fighting* Ausweitung *f; of tension* Verschärfung *f*

escalator [ˈes·kə·leɪ·ṭər] *n* Rolltreppe *f*

escapade [ˌes·kə·ˈpeɪd] *n* Eskapade *f*

escape [ɪ·ˈskeɪp] **I.** *vi* ❶ (*flee*) fliehen; (*successfully*) entkommen; (*from cage, prison*) ausbrechen; *dog, cat* entlaufen; *bird* entfliegen; ■**to ~ from sb** vor jdm fliehen; (*successfully*) jdm entkommen; ■**to ~ from sth** aus etw *dat* fliehen; (*successfully*) aus etw *dat* entkommen ❷ (*avoid harm*) [mit dem Leben] davonkommen; **to ~ unhurt** unverletzt bleiben ❸ (*leak*) entweichen, austreten **II.** *vt* ❶ (*flee*) fliehen (aus +*dat*); (*successfully*) entkommen (aus +*dat*); (*fig*) **to ~ the fire** dem Feuer entkommen; ■**to ~ sb** vor jdm fliehen; (*successfully*) jdm entkommen ❷ (*avoid*) entgehen +*dat;* **she was lucky to ~ serious injury** sie hatte Glück, dass sie nicht ernsthaft verletzt wurde ❸ **to ~ sb's attention** [*or* **notice**] jds Aufmerksamkeit entgehen **III.** *n* ❶ (*act*) Flucht *f a. fig* (**from** aus +*dat*); *from prison* Ausbruch *m* ❷ (*avoidance*) Entkommen *nt;* **that was a lucky ~!** da haben wir wirklich noch einmal Glück gehabt!; **to have a narrow ~** gerade noch einmal davongekommen sein ❸ (*leak*) Austreten *nt kein pl,* Entweichen *nt kein pl*

eˈscape clause *n* Rücktrittsklausel *f*

escapee [ɪ·ˌskeɪ·ˈpi] *n* Entflohene(r) *f(m)*

eˈscape key *n* COMPUT Esc-Taste *f*

escapism [ɪ·ˈskeɪ·pɪz·əm] *n* Realitätsflucht *f*

escort **I.** *vt* [ɪs·ˈkɔrt, es·ˈkɔrt] eskortieren; MIL Geleitschutz geben +*dat;* **to ~ sb upstairs** jdn hinaufbringen **II.** *n* [ˈesk·ɔrt] ❶ (*companion*) Begleiter(in) *m(f),* Begleitung *f* ❷ (*guard*) Eskorte *f,* Begleitschutz *m*

esophagus <*pl* -agi *or* -es> [ɪ·ˈsaf·ə·gəs] *n* Speiseröhre *f*

esoteric [ˌes·ə·ˈter·ɪk] *adj* esoterisch

esp. *adv abbrev of* **especially** bes.

especially [ɪ·ˈspeʃ·ə·li] *adv* besonders

espionage [ˈes·pi·ə·naʒ] *n* Spionage *f*

espresso [ɪ·ˈspres·oʊ] *n* Espresso *m*

essay [ˈes·eɪ] *n* Essay *m o nt* (**on, about** über +*akk*)

essayist [ˈes·eɪ·ɪst] *n* Essayist(in) *m(f)*

essence [ˈes·əns] *n* ❶ PHILOS Wesen *nt* ❷ (*gist*) Wesentliche(s) *nt; of problem* Kern *m* ❸ FOOD Essenz *f,* Extrakt *m*

essential [ɪ·ˈsen·ʃəl] **I.** *adj* ❶ (*crucial*) unbedingt erforderlich; *vitamins* lebenswichtig ❷ (*basic*) essenziell; *element* wesentlich; *difference* grundlegend **II.** *n* ■**the ~s** *pl* das Wesentliche; **the bare ~s** das [Aller]nötigste

essentially [ɪ·ˈsen·ʃə·li] *adv* im Grunde [genommen]

EST [ˌi·es·ˈti] *n abbrev of* **Eastern Standard Time** Ostküsten Standardzeit *f*

est. *adj* ❶ *abbrev of* **estimated** ❷ *abbrev of* **established** gegr.

establish [ɪ·ˈstæb·lɪʃ] *vt* ❶ (*found*) gründen; *contact* aufnehmen; *dictatorship, monopoly* errichten; *precedent* schaffen; *priorities* setzen; *record* aufstellen; *relationship* aufbauen; *relations, rule of law* herstellen; *rule* aufstellen ❷ (*secure*) **to ~ one's authority over sb** sich *dat* Autorität gegenüber jdm verschaffen; **to ~ order** für Ordnung sorgen ❸ (*prove*) feststellen; *claim* nachweisen

established [ɪ·ˈstæb·lɪʃt] *adj* ❶ (*standard*)

E

fest; **it is ~ practice ...** es ist üblich, ... ❷ (*proven*) nachgewiesen; *fact* gesichert ❸ (*founded*) gegründet

establishment [ɪ·ˈstæb·lɪʃ·mənt] *n* ❶ (*institution*) Unternehmen *nt;* **educational ~** Bildungseinrichtung *f* ❷ (*ruling group*) ■**the ~** das Establishment ❸ (*founding*) Gründung *f*

estate [ɪ·ˈsteɪt] *n* ❶ (*landed property*) Gut *nt;* **country ~** Landgut *nt* ❷ LAW (*personal property*) [Privat]vermögen *nt*

esteem [ɪ·ˈstim] **I.** *n* Ansehen *nt;* **to hold sb in high ~** jdn hoch schätzen **II.** *vt* [hoch] schätzen

esthetic [es·ˈθeṭ·ɪk] *adj see* **aesthetic**

estimate **I.** *vt* [ˈes·tɪ·meɪt] [ein]schätzen **II.** *n* [ˈes·tɪ·mɪt] Schätzung *f;* ECON Kostenvoranschlag *m;* **conservative ~** vorsichtige Einschätzung

estimated [ˈes·tɪ·meɪ·ṭɪd] *adj* geschätzt; *arrival, departure* voraussichtlich

estimation [ˌes·tɪ·ˈmeɪ·ʃən] *n* ❶ (*opinion*) Einschätzung *f;* **in my ~** meiner Ansicht nach ❷ (*esteem*) Achtung *f*

estranged [ɪ·ˈstreɪndʒd] *adj* ❶ (*alienated*) entfremdet ❷ *couple* getrennt

estrogen [ˈes·trə·dʒən] *n* Östrogen *nt*

estuary [ˈes·tʃu·er·i] *n* Flussmündung *f*

ETA [ˌi·ti·ˈeɪ] *n abbrev of* **estimated time of arrival** voraussichtliche Ankunft

etc. *adv abbrev of* **et cetera** usw., etc.

etch [etʃ] *vt* ätzen; (*in metals*) radieren; (*in copper*) kupferstechen

eternal [ɪ·ˈtɜr·nəl] *adj* ewig *a. fig; complaints* endlos

eternally [ɪ·ˈtɜr·nə·li] *adv* ewig; (*fam*) unaufhörlich

eternity [ɪ·ˈtɜr·nə·ṭi] *n* Ewigkeit *f a. fig*

ethic [ˈeθ·ɪk] *n* Moral *f,* Ethos *nt*

ethical [ˈeθ·ɪkəl] *adj* ethisch

ethics [ˈeθ·ɪks] *n* Ethik *f*

ethnic [ˈeθ·nɪk] *adj* ❶ (*national*) ethnisch; **~ costumes** Landestrachten *pl* ❷ *food, restaurants* exotisch

etiquette [ˈeṭ·ɪ·kɪt] *n* Etikette *f*

etymology [ˌeṭ·ɪ·ˈmal·ə·dʒi] *n* Etymologie *f*

eulogy [ˈju·lə·dʒi] *n* ❶ (*at funeral*) Grabrede *f* ❷ (*praise*) Lobrede *f*

eunuch [ˈju·nək] *n* Eunuch *m*

euphemism [ˈju·fə·mɪz·əm] *n* Euphemismus *m*

euphemistic [ˌju·fə·ˈmɪs·tɪk] *adj* euphemistisch

euphoria [ju·ˈfɔr·i·ə] *n* Euphorie *f*

euphoric [ju·ˈfɔr·ɪk] *adj* euphorisch

euro [ˈjʊr·oʊ] *n* Euro *m*

euro ˈbailout fund, eurozone ˈbailout fund *n* FIN Euro-Rettungsschirm *m*

Eurocrat [ˈjʊr·ə·kræt] *n* Eurokrat(in) *m(f)*

Europe [ˈjʊr·əp] *n* Europa *nt*

European [ˌjʊr·ə·ˈpi·ən] **I.** *adj* europäisch **II.** *n* Europäer(in) *m(f)*

European ˈUnion *n* Europäische Union

euthanasia [ˌju·θə·ˈneɪ·ʒə] *n* Sterbehilfe *f*

evacuate [ɪ·ˈvæk·jʊ·eɪt] *vt* evakuieren; *area, building* räumen

evacuation [ɪ·ˌvæk·jʊ·ˈeɪ·ʃən] *n* Evakuierung *f;* (*of area, building*) Räumung *f*

evacuee [ɪ·ˌvæk·ju·ˈi] *n* Evakuierte(r) *f(m)*

evade [ɪ·ˈveɪd] *vt* ausweichen *+dat; the draft, responsibility* sich entziehen *+dat; police* entgehen *+dat; taxes* hinterziehen

evaluate [ɪ·ˈvæl·jʊ·eɪt] *vt* bewerten; *results* auswerten; *person* beurteilen

evaluation [ɪ·ˌvæl·jʊ·ˈeɪ·ʃən] *n* Schätzung *f; of experience* Einschätzung *f; of treatment* Beurteilung *f; of book* Bewertung *f*

evangelical [ˌi·væn·ˈdʒel·ɪ·kəl] *adj* evangelisch

evangelist [ɪ·ˈvæn·dʒə·lɪst] *n* Wanderprediger(in) *m(f)*

evaporate [ɪ·ˈvæp·ə·reɪt] **I.** *vt* verdampfen lassen **II.** *vi* verdunsten; (*fig*) sich in Luft auflösen

evaporation [ɪ·ˌvæp·ə·ˈreɪ·ʃən] *n* Verdunstung *f*

evasion [ɪ·ˈveɪ·ʒən] *n* ❶ (*excuse*) Ausweichen *nt* ❷ (*avoidance*) Umgehung *f;* **tax ~** Steuerhinterziehung *f*

evasive [ɪ·ˈveɪ·sɪv] *adj* ausweichend; **to take ~ action** ein Ausweichmanöver machen

eve [iv] *n* Vorabend *m*

Eve [iv] *n* Eva *f*

even [ˈi·vən] **I.** *adv* ❶ (*also*) selbst; **~ Chris was there** selbst Chris war da ❷ (*indeed*) sogar; **not ~** [noch] nicht einmal; **did he ~ read the letter?** hat er überhaupt den Brief gelesen? ❸ (*despite*) **~ if** [*or* **though**] **...** selbst wenn ...; **~ so** trotzdem; **~ then** trotzdem ❹ + *comp* **~ colder** noch kälter **II.** *adj* ❶ (*flat*) eben; *row* gerade; *two surfaces* auf gleicher Höhe; (*fig*) ausgeglichen ❷ (*equal*) gleich [groß]; *contest* ebenbürtig; *distribution* gleichmäßig; (*in race*) gleichauf; (*in points*) punktegleich; (*in standard*) gleich gut ❸ MATH gerade **III.** *vt* ebnen

◆**even out** **I.** *vt* ausgleichen **II.** *vi* sich ausgleichen; *prices* sich einpendeln

◆**even up** **I.** *vt* ausgleichen **II.** *vi* sich ausgleichen; *prices* sich einpendeln

evening [ˈiv·nɪŋ] **I.** *n* Abend *m;* **on Friday ~s** freitagabends **II.** *adj* Abend-

ˈevening dress *n* ❶ Abendkleid *nt* ❷ (*outfit*) Abendkleidung *f*

evenly [ˈi·vən·li] *adv* ❶ (*equally*) gleichmäßig ❷ (*calmly*) gelassen

evenness [ˈi·vən·nɪs] *n* Ebenheit *f*

event [ɪ·ˈvent] *n* ❶ (*occurrence*) Ereignis *nt;* **sporting ~** Sportveranstaltung *f* ❷ (*case*) Fall *m;* **in the ~ that ...** falls ...; **in any ~** auf jeden Fall ❸ SPORTS Wettkampf *m*

even-ˈtempered *adj* ausgeglichen

eventful [ɪ·ˈvent·fəl] *adj* ereignisreich

eventual [ɪ·ˈven·tʃʊ·əl] *adj* ❶ (*final*) schließlich; *cost* letztendlich ❷ (*possible*) etwaig

eventuality [ɪ·ˌven·tʃʊ·ˈæl·ə·ti] *n* Eventualität *f*

eventually [ɪ·ˈven·tʃʊ·ə·li] *adv* ❶ (*finally*) schließlich, endlich ❷ (*some day*) irgendwann

ever [ˈev·ər] *adv* ❶ (*at any time*) je[mals];

nothing ~ happens here hier ist nie was los; **have you ~ been to Los Angeles?** bist du schon einmal in Los Angeles gewesen?; **hardly ~** kaum; **worse than ~** schlimmer als je zuvor ❷ (*always*) **happily ~ after** glücklich bis ans Ende ihrer Tage; **~ since ...** seitdem ... ❸ (*of all time*) **the first performance ~** die allererste Darbietung ❹ (*as intensifier*) **how could anyone ~ ...?** wie kann jemand nur ...?; **when are we ~ going to get this finished?** wann haben wir das endlich fertig?

'everglade *n* Sumpfgebiet *nt;* ■ **the E~s** *pl* die Everglades *pl*

'evergreen I. *n* immergrüne Pflanze; (*tree*) immergrüner Baum II. *adj* immergrün; (*fig*) immer aktuell

everlasting [ˌev·ər·ˈlæs·tɪŋ] *adj* ❶ (*undying*) immerwährend; *gratitude* ewig; *happiness* dauerhaft ❷ (*unceasing*) endlos

every [ˈev·ri] *adj* ❶ (*each*) jede(r, s) ❷ (*as emphasis*) ganz und gar; **~ bit as ... as ...** genauso ... wie ...; **~ which way** (*fam*) in alle Richtungen

everybody [ˈev·ri·ˌbad·i], **everyone** [ˈev·rɪ·wʌn] *pron indef, + sing vb* jede(r); **~ but Jane** alle außer Jane; **~ else** alle anderen

'everyday *adj* alltäglich; **~ life** Alltagsleben *nt*

everyone [ˈev·rɪ·wʌn] *pron see* **everybody**

everything [ˈev·rɪ·θɪŋ] *pron indef* alles; **to blame ~ on sth/sb** [*or* **sth/sb for ~**] etw/jdm die ganze Schuld geben; **despite** [*or* **in spite of**] **~** trotz allem

everywhere [ˈev·rɪ·wer] *adv* überall; **~ else** überall sonst

evict [ɪ·ˈvɪkt] *vt* (*from home*) kündigen +*dat;* (*forcefully*) zur Räumung der Wohnung zwingen

eviction [ɪ·ˈvɪk·ʃən] *n* Zwangsräumung *f;* **~ order** Räumungsbefehl *m*

evidence [ˈev·ɪ·dəns] *n* ❶ (*proof*) Beweis[e] *m*[*pl*]; **to find no ~ of sth** keinen Anhaltspunkt für etw *akk* haben ❷ LAW Beweisstück *nt;* **to present ~** aussagen (**of** über +*akk,* **against** gegen +*akk*) ❸ (*be present*) ■ **to be** [**very much**] **in ~** [deutlich] sichtbar sein; **few police officers were in ~** nur ein geringes Polizeiaufgebot war zu erkennen

evident [ˈev·ɪ·dənt] *adj* offensichtlich, klar

evidently [ˈev·ɪ·dənt·li] *adv* offensichtlich

evil [ˈi·vəl] I. *adj* böse II. *n* Übel *nt;* **good and ~** das Gute und das Böse; **the lesser of two ~s** das kleinere von zwei Übeln

evocative [ɪ·ˈvak·ə·t̬ɪv] *adj* evokativ

evoke [ɪ·ˈvoʊk] *vt* hervorrufen; *suspicion* erregen; (*recall*) erinnern (an +*akk*); *memories* wachrufen

evolution [ˌev·ə·ˈlu·ʃən] *n* Evolution *f;* (*fig*) Entwicklung *f*

evolve [ɪ·ˈvalv] I. *vi* sich entwickeln II. *vt* entwickeln

ewe [ju] *n* Mutterschaf *nt*

ex <*pl* -es> [eks] *n* (*fam: spouse*) Ex-Mann, Ex-Frau *m, f;* (*lover*) Ex-Freund(in) *m(f)*

exacerbate [ɪg·ˈzæs·ər·beɪt] *vt* verschlimmern; *crisis* verschärfen

exact [ɪg·ˈzækt] I. *adj* genau; **the ~ opposite** ganz im Gegenteil II. *vt* fordern; *revenge* üben (**on** an +*dat*)

exactly [ɪg·ˈzækt·li] *adv* ❶ (*precisely*) genau; **~!** ganz genau! ❷ (*hardly*) ■ **not ~** eigentlich nicht, nicht gerade

exactness [ɪg·ˈzækt·nɪs] *n* Genauigkeit *f*

exaggerate [ɪg·ˈzædʒ·ə·reɪt] *vt, vi* übertreiben; *effect* verstärken

exaggerated [ɪg·ˈzædʒ·ə·reɪ·t̬ɪd] *adj* übertrieben

exaggeration [ɪg·ˌzædʒ·ə·ˈreɪ·ʃən] *n* Übertreibung *f;* **that's a bit of an ~** das ist ein bisschen übertrieben

exalt [ɪg·ˈzɔlt] *vt* ❶ (*praise*) preisen ❷ (*promote*) [in einen Stand] erheben

exaltation [ˌeg·zɔl·ˈteɪ·ʃən] *n* Begeisterung *f*

exalted [ɪg·ˈzɔl·tɪd] *adj* hoch

exam [ɪg·ˈzæm] *n* Prüfung *f,* Examen *nt*

examination [ɪg·ˌzæm·ɪ·ˈneɪ·ʃən] *n* ❶ (*test*) Prüfung *f;* UNIV Examen *nt* ❷ (*investigation*) Untersuchung *f; of evidence* Überprüfung *f;* **to be under ~** untersucht werden

examine [ɪg·ˈzæm·ɪn] *vt* ❶ (*test*) prüfen ❷ (*scrutinize*) untersuchen ❸ LAW verhören

examinee [ɪg·ˌzæm·ɪ·ˈni] *n* Examenskandidat(in) *m(f)*

examiner [ɪg·ˈzæm·ɪn·ər] *n* ❶ SCH, UNIV Prüfer(in) *m(f)* ❷ **medical ~** Gerichtsmediziner(in) *m(f)*

example [ɪg·ˈzæm·pəl] *n* Beispiel *nt;* **for ~** zum Beispiel; **to make an ~ of sb** an jdm ein Exempel statuieren, jdn exemplarisch bestrafen

exasperate [ɪg·ˈzæs·pə·reɪt] *vt* (*infuriate*) zur Verzweiflung bringen; (*irritate*) verärgern

exasperating [ɪg·ˈzæs·pə·reɪ·t̬ɪŋ] *adj* ärgerlich

exasperation [ɪg·ˌzæs·pə·ˈreɪ·ʃən] *n* Verzweiflung *f* (**at** über +*akk*)

excavate [ˈek·skə·veɪt] I. *vt* ❶ ARCHEOL ausgraben ❷ (*dig*) ausheben II. *vi* Ausgrabungen machen

excavation [ˌek·skə·ˈveɪ·ʃən] *n* ARCHEOL Ausgrabung *f;* (*digging*) Ausheben *nt*

excavator [ˈek·skə·veɪ·t̬ər] *n* Bagger *m*

exceed [ɪk·ˈsid] *vt* übersteigen; (*outdo*) übertreffen; *limit* überschreiten

exceedingly [ɪk·ˈsi·dɪŋ·li] *adv* äußerst

excel <-ll-> [ɪk·ˈsel] I. *vi* sich auszeichnen; ■ **to ~ at** [*or* **in**] **sth** sich bei etw *dat* hervortun II. *vt* ■ **to ~ oneself** sich *akk* selbst übertreffen

excellence [ˈek·sə·ləns] *n* Vorzüglichkeit *f; of performance* hervorragende Qualität

Excellency [ˈek·sə·lən·si] *n* (*form of address for certain high officials*) **His/Your ~** Seine/Eure Exzellenz

excellent [ˈek·sə·lənt] *adj* ausgezeichnet; *performance, quality* hervorragend

except [ɪk·ˈsept] I. *prep* ■ **~** [**for**] außer +*dat* II. *conj* ❶ (*only*) **I want to buy it, ~ I don't**

have any money (*fam*) ich will es kaufen, ich habe nur [*o* doch ich habe] kein Geld ② (*besides*) außer

excepting [ɪk·ˈsep·tɪŋ] *prep* außer +*dat*; **not ~** nicht ausgenommen

exception [ɪk·ˈsep·ʃən] *n* Ausnahme *f*; **without ~** ausnahmslos

exceptional [ɪk·ˈsep·ʃə·nəl] *adj* außergewöhnlich

exceptionally [ɪk·ˈsep·ʃə·nə·li] *adv* außergewöhnlich; **~ bright** ungewöhnlich intelligent

excerpt [ˈek·sɜrpt] *n* Auszug *m* (**from** aus +*dat*)

excess [ɪk·ˈses] **I.** *n* <*pl* -es> ① (*overindulgence*) Übermaß *nt* (**of** an +*dat*) ② (*surplus*) Überschuss *m* (**of** an +*dat*) **II.** *adj* Über-; **~ baggage** [*or* **luggage**] Übergepäck *nt*

excessive [ɪk·ˈses·ɪv] *adj* übermäßig; *claim* übertrieben

exchange [ɪks·ˈtʃeɪndʒ] **I.** *vt* austauschen; *in a store* umtauschen (**for** gegen +*akk*); *looks, words* wechseln **II.** *n* ① (*trade*) Tausch *m*; **in ~** dafür ② FIN Währung *f*; **foreign ~** Devisen *pl* ③ (*interchange*) Wortwechsel *m*; **~ of blows** Schlagabtausch *m*

exchangeable [ɪks·ˈtʃeɪndʒ·əbəl] *adj* austauschbar; *goods* umtauschbar; *token* einlösbar

exˈchange rate *n* Wechselkurs *m*

exˈchange student *n* SCH Austauschschüler(in) *m(f)*; UNIV Austauschstudent(in) *m(f)*

excise [ek·ˈsaɪz] *n* FIN **~ tax** Verbrauchssteuer *f* (**on** für +*akk*)

excitable [ɪk·ˈsaɪ·t̬ə·bəl] *adj* erregbar

excite [ɪk·ˈsaɪt] *vt* ① (*stimulate*) erregen; (*enthuse*) begeistern ② (*awaken*) hervorrufen; *curiosity* wecken; *imagination* anregen

excited [ɪk·ˈsaɪ·t̬ɪd] *adj* aufgeregt; (*thrilled*) begeistert; **to be ~ about sth** (*now*) von etw *dat* begeistert sein; (*in near future*) sich auf etw *akk* freuen

excitement [ɪk·ˈsaɪt·mənt] *n* Aufregung *f*

exciting [ɪk·ˈsaɪ·t̬ɪŋ] *adj* aufregend; *game, story* spannend; (*stimulating*) anregend

excl. *adj, prep abbrev of* **excluding, exclusive** exkl.

exclaim [ɪk·ˈskleɪm] **I.** *vi* **to ~ in delight** vor Freude aufschreien **II.** *vt* ausrufen

exclamation [ˌek·sklə·ˈmeɪ·ʃən] *n* Ausruf *m*

exclaˈmation point, exclaˈmation mark *n* Ausrufezeichen *nt*

exclude [ɪk·ˈsklud] *vt* ausschließen

excluding [ɪk·ˈsklu·dɪŋ] *prep* ausgenommen +*gen*

exclusion [ɪk·ˈsklu·ʒən] *n* Ausschluss *m* (**from** von +*dat*)

exclusive [ɪk·ˈsklu·sɪv] **I.** *adj* ① (*excluding*) ausschließlich ② (*select*) exklusiv; **for the ~ use of ...** nur für ... bestimmt **II.** *n* Exklusivbericht *m*

excommunicate [ˌeks·kə·ˈmju·nɪ·keɪt] *vt* exkommunizieren

excommunication [ˌeks·kə·ˌmju·nɪ·ˈkeɪ·ʃən] *n* Exkommunikation *f*

ex-con [eks·ˈka·n] *n* (*sl: ex-convict*) Knacki *m sl*

excrement [ˈek·skrə·mənt] *n* Kot *m*, Exkremente *pl*

excrete [ɪk·ˈskrit] **I.** *vt* ausscheiden **II.** *vi* Exkremente ausscheiden

excruciating [ɪk·ˈskru·ʃi·eɪ·t̬ɪŋ] *adj* ① (*painful*) schmerzhaft; *suffering* entsetzlich ② (*fig*) qualvoll

excursion [ɪk·ˈskɜr·ʒən] *n* Ausflug *m*

excusable [ɪk·ˈskju·zə·bəl] *adj* verzeihlich, entschuldbar

excuse **I.** *vt* [ɪk·ˈskjuz] ① (*forgive*) entschuldigen; (*make an exception*) hinwegsehen über +*akk*; ■**to ~ sb from sth** jdn von etw *dat* befreien ② (*attract attention*) **~ me!** entschuldigen Sie bitte!, Entschuldigung!; (*ask for repeat*) **~ me?** wie bitte? **II.** *n* [ɪk·ˈskjus] ① (*explanation*) Entschuldigung *f*; **doctor's ~** Krankmeldung *f* ② (*justification*) Ausrede *f*; (*cause, reason*) Anlass *m*

execute [ˈek·sɪ·kjut] *vt* ① (*perform*) durchführen; *maneuver, order, plan* ausführen ② (*kill*) hinrichten

execution [ˌek·sɪ·ˈkju·ʃən] *n* ① (*performing*) Durchführung *f* ② (*killing*) Hinrichtung *f*

executioner [ˌek·sɪ·ˈkju·ʃə·nər] *n* Scharfrichter *m*

executive [ɪg·ˈzek·jʊ·t̬ɪv] **I.** *n* (*manager*) leitender Angestellter/leitende Angestellte; **junior/senior ~** untere/höhere Führungskraft **II.** *adj* Exekutiv-; **~ editor** Chefredakteur(in) *m(f)*; **~ producer** leitender Produzent/leitende Produzentin

executive ˈbranch *n* POL Exekutivzweig *m*

executive comˈmittee *n* Vorstand *m*

executor [ɪg·ˈzek·jʊ·t̬ər] *n* LAW Testamentsvollstrecker(in) *m(f)*

exemplary [ɪg·ˈzem·plə·ri] *adj* vorbildlich; *punishment* exemplarisch

exemplify <-ie-> [ɪg·ˈzem·plɪ·faɪ] *vt person* erläutern; *thing* veranschaulichen

exempt [ɪg·ˈzempt] **I.** *vt* befreien; *from military service* freistellen **II.** *adj* befreit; **~ from duty** [*or* **tax**] gebührenfrei

exemption [ɪg·ˈzemp·ʃən] *n* Befreiung *f*; *from military service* Freistellung *f*

exercise [ˈek·sər·saɪz] **I.** *vt* ① (*physically*) trainieren; *dog* spazieren führen; *horse* bewegen ② (*use*) üben; *authority, control* ausüben; *caution* walten lassen; *right* geltend machen; *veto* einlegen; **to ~ tact** mit Takt vorgehen **II.** *vi* trainieren, sich bewegen **III.** *n* ① (*exertion*) Bewegung *f*; (*training*) Übung *f*; **to do ~s** Gymnastik machen ② MIL (*practice*) Übung *f*; SCH, UNIV Aufgabe *f* ③ ■**~s** *pl* Feierlichkeiten *pl* **IV.** *adj* Trainings-; **~ video** Übungsvideo *nt*

ˈexercise bike *n* Heimfahrrad *nt*

ˈexercise book *n* Heft *nt*

exerciser [ˈek·sər·saɪ·zər] *n* Trainingsgerät *nt*

exert [ɪg·ˈzɜrt] *vt* ① (*use*) *control* ausüben; *influence* geltend machen ② (*labor*) ■**to ~**

oneself sich anstrengen
exertion [ɪg·ˈzɜr·ʃən] *n* ❶ (*use*) Ausübung *f* ❷ (*strain*) Anstrengung *f*
exˈfoliating cream *n* Rubbelcreme *f*, Peeling *nt*
exhalation [ˌeks·hə·ˈleɪ·ʃən] *n* Ausatmen *nt*
exhale [eks·ˈheɪl] *vt, vi* ausatmen
exhaust [ɪg·ˈzɔst] **I.** *vt* ❶ (*tire*) ermüden; ■**to ~ oneself** sich strapazieren ❷ (*use up*) erschöpfen **II.** *n* ❶ ~ [**fumes**] Abgase *pl* ❷ (*tailpipe*) Auspuff *m*
exhausted [ɪg·ˈzɔs·tɪd] *adj* (*tired*) erschöpft; (*used up a.*) aufgebraucht
exhausting [ɪg·ˈzɔs·tɪŋ] *adj* anstrengend
exhaustion [ɪg·ˈzɔs·tʃən] *n* Erschöpfung *f*
exhaustive [ɪg·ˈzɔs·tɪv] *adj* erschöpfend; *inquiry* eingehend; *list* vollständig; *report* ausgiebig; *research* tief greifend
exˈhaust pipe *n* Auspuffrohr *nt*
exhibit [ɪg·ˈzɪb·ɪt] **I.** *n* ❶ (*display*) Ausstellungsstück *nt*, Ausstellung *f* ❷ LAW (*evidence*) Beweisstück *nt* **II.** *vt* ❶ (*display*) ausstellen ❷ (*manifest*) zeigen **III.** *vi* ausstellen
exhibition [ˌek·sɪ·ˈbɪʃ·ən] *n* (*display*) Ausstellung *f* (**about** über +*akk*); (*performance*) Vorführung *f*
exhibitionism [ˌek·sɪ·ˈbɪʃ·ə·nɪz·əm] *n* Exhibitionismus *m*
exhibitionist [ˌek·sɪ·ˈbɪʃ·ə·nɪst] *n* Exhibitionist(in) *m(f)*
exhibitor [ɪg·ˈzɪb·ɪ·tər] *n* Aussteller(in) *m(f)*
exhilarating [ɪg·ˈzɪl·ə·reɪ·t̬ɪŋ] *adj* ❶ (*thrilling*) berauschend; (*exciting*) aufregend ❷ (*energizing*) belebend
exhilaration [ɪg·ˈzɪl·ə·reɪ·ʃən] *n* Hochgefühl *nt*
exhumation [ˌeg·zju·ˈmeɪ·ʃən] *n* Exhumierung *f*
exhume [ɪg·ˈzum] *vt* exhumieren
exile [ˈek·saɪl] **I.** *n* ❶ (*banishment*) Exil *nt*, Verbannung *f* (**from** aus +*dat*); **to go into ~** ins Exil gehen ❷ (*person*) Verbannte(r) *f(m)*; **tax ~** Steuerflüchtling *m* **II.** *vt* verbannen
exist [ɪg·ˈzɪst] *vi* ❶ (*be*) existieren, bestehen ❷ (*live*) leben, existieren; (*survive*) überleben
existence [ɪg·ˈzɪs·təns] *n* ❶ (*state*) Existenz *f*, Bestehen *nt*; **to come into ~** entstehen ❷ (*life*) Leben *nt*, Existenz *f*; **means of ~** Lebensgrundlage *f*
existent [ɪg·ˈzɪs·tent] *adj* existent, vorhanden
existing [ɪg·ˈzɪs·tɪŋ] *adj* existierend, bestehend; *rules* gegenwärtig
exit [ˈeg·sɪt] **I.** *n* ❶ (*way out*) Ausgang *m* ❷ (*departure*) Weggehen *nt kein pl*, Abgang *m*; (*from room*) Hinausgehen *nt kein pl* ❸ (*road*) Ausfahrt *f*, Abfahrt *f* **II.** *vt* verlassen **III.** *vi* ❶ (*leave*) hinausgehen ❷ (*in car*) eine Ausfahrt nehmen
ˈexit visa *n* Ausreisevisum *nt*
exodus <*pl* -es> [ˈek·sə·dəs] *n* Auszug *m*; **general ~** allgemeiner Aufbruch
exonerate [ɪg·ˈzan·ə·reɪt] *vt* freisprechen; (*partially*) entlasten
exorbitant [ɪg·ˈzɔr·bə·tənt] *adj* überhöht
exorcism [ˈek·sɔr·sɪz·əm] *n* Exorzismus *m*
exorcist [ˈek·sɔr·sɪst] *n* Exorzist(in) *m(f)*
exorcize [ˈek·sɔr·saɪz] *vt* exorzieren
exotic [ɪg·ˈzat̬·ɪk] *adj* exotisch; (*fig*) fremdländisch
expand [ɪk·ˈspænd] **I.** *vi* ❶ (*increase*) zunehmen; *economy a.* expandieren; *population, trade* wachsen; *horizons, knowledge* sich erweitern ❷ PHYS sich ausdehnen **II.** *vt* ❶ (*enlarge*) erweitern ❷ PHYS ausdehnen ❸ (*elaborate*) weiter ausführen
expandable [ɪk·ˈspæn·də·bəl] *adj material* dehnbar; *business, project* entwicklungsfähig; *installation, system* ausbaufähig
expanse [ɪk·ˈspæns] *n* weite Fläche, Weite *f*; **~ of lawn** ausgedehnte Rasenfläche
expansion [ɪk·ˈspæn·ʃən] *n* ❶ (*increase*) *of knowledge* Erweiterung *f*; *of territory, economy* Expansion *f*; *of population, trade* Wachstum *nt*, Zunahme *f* ❷ PHYS Ausdehnung *f* ❸ (*elaboration*) Erweiterung *f*
expansionism [ɪk·ˈspæn·ʃə·nɪz·əm] *n* Expansionspolitik *f*
expansive [ɪk·ˈspæn·sɪv] *adj* ❶ (*sociable*) umgänglich; (*effusive*) überschwänglich; *personality* aufgeschlossen ❷ (*elaborated*) ausführlich
expatriate **I.** *n* [ek·ˈspeɪ·tri·ət] [ständig] im Ausland Lebende(r) *f(m)* **II.** *vt* [ek·ˈspeɪ·tri·eɪt] ausbürgern
expect [ɪk·ˈspekt] *vt* ❶ erwarten; **that was to be ~ed** das war zu erwarten; **to half ~ sth** fast mit etw *dat* rechnen; ■**to ~ to do sth** damit rechnen, etw zu tun ❷ (*fam: suppose*) glauben; **I ~ so** ich denke schon
expectancy [ɪk·ˈspek·tən·si] *n* Erwartung *f*; **air of ~** erwartungsvolle Atmosphäre; **with an air of ~** erwartungsvoll
expectant [ɪk·ˈspek·tənt] *adj* erwartungsvoll; *mother* werdend
expectation [ˌek·spek·ˈteɪ·ʃən] *n* Erwartung *f*
expedient [ɪk·ˈspi·di·ənt] *adj* ❶ (*useful*) zweckmäßig; (*advisable*) ratsam ❷ (*advantageous*) eigennützig
expedite [ˈek·spɪ·daɪt] *vt* ❶ (*hasten*) beschleunigen ❷ (*do*) schnell erledigen
expedition [ˌek·spɪ·ˈdɪʃ·ən] *n* Expedition *f*; MIL Feldzug *m*
expel <-ll-> [ɪk·ˈspel] *vt* ❶ (*evict*) ausschließen (**from** aus +*dat*); *from school, university* verweisen (**from** von +*dat*) ❷ (*force out*) vertreiben (**from** aus +*dat*) ❸ (*eject*) *breath* ausstoßen; *liquid* austreiben
expend [ɪk·ˈspend] *vt* ❶ (*spend*) *time, effort* aufwenden (**on** für +*akk*) ❷ (*use up*) aufbrauchen
expenditure [ɪk·ˈspen·dɪ·tʃər] *n* ❶ (*spending*) Ausgabe *f*; (*using*) *of energy, resources* Aufwand *m* (**of** an +*dat*) ❷ (*sum spent*) Ausgaben *pl*, Aufwendungen *pl* (**on** für +*akk*)
expense [ɪk·ˈspens] *n* ❶ [Un]kosten *pl*, Ausgaben *pl*; **at one's own ~** auf eigene Kosten

E

❷ ■ **~s** *pl* Spesen *pl* ❸ (*fig*) **at sb's ~** auf jds Kosten *pl;* **at the ~ of sth** auf Kosten einer S. *gen* ▶ PHRASES: **no ~s spared** [die] Kosten spielen keine Rolle

ex'pense account *n* Spesenrechnung *f*

expensive [ɪk·'spen·sɪv] *adj* teuer; *hobby* kostspielig

experience [ɪk·'spɪr·i·əns] **I.** *n* ❶ (*knowledge*) Erfahrung *f;* **to gain ~** Erfahrungen sammeln; **to learn by** [*or* **from**] **~** durch Erfahrung lernen ❷ (*event*) Erfahrung *f,* Erlebnis *nt;* **to have an ~** eine Erfahrung machen **II.** *vt* ❶ (*undergo*) erleben; (*endure*) kennen lernen, erfahren; *difficulties* stoßen auf +*akk* ❷ (*feel*) empfinden

experienced [ɪk·'spɪr·i·ənst] *adj* erfahren; *eye* geschult; ■ **to be ~ at** [*or* **in**] **sth** Erfahrung in etw *dat* haben

experiment **I.** *n* [ɪk·'sper·ɪ·mənt] Experiment *nt,* Versuch *m* (**on** an +*dat*/mit +*dat*); **by ~** durch Ausprobieren **II.** *vi* [ɪk·'sper·ɪ·ment] experimentieren, Versuche machen (**on** an +*dat*)

experimental [ɪk·ˌsper·ɪ·'men·təl] *adj* ❶ (*for experiment*) Versuchs- ❷ (*using experiments*) experimentell

experimentation [ɪk·ˌsper·ɪ·men·'teɪ·ʃən] *n* Experimentieren *nt*

expert ['ek·spɜrt] **I.** *n* Experte, -in *m, f,* Fachmann, Fachfrau *m, f;* LAW Sachverständige(r) *f(m);* **an ~ at doing sth** ein Experte *m*/ eine Expertin in etw *dat* **II.** *adj* ❶ (*specialized*) Fach-, fachmännisch; (*skilled*) erfahren; (*clever*) geschickt; *analysis* fachkundig ❷ (*excellent*) ausgezeichnet; *liar* perfekt

expertise [ˌek·spɜr·'tiz] *n* (*knowledge*) Fachkenntnis *f,* Sachverstand *m* (**in** in +*dat*); (*skill*) Können *nt*

expert 'knowledge *n* Fachkenntnis *f*

expert o'pinion *n* Expertenmeinung *f;* LAW Sachverständigengutachten *nt*

expert 'witness *n* LAW Sachverständige(r) *f(m)*

expiration [ˌek·spə·'reɪ·ʃən] *n* ❶ (*termination*) **~ date** *of drugs, food* Verfallsdatum *nt; of credit card, passport* Ablaufdatum *nt* ❷ (*exhalation*) Ausatmung *f*

expire [ɪk·'spaɪr] *vi* ❶ (*become invalid*) *passport* ablaufen; *contract, license* auslaufen; *coupon, ticket* verfallen, ablaufen ❷ (*die*) verscheiden

expiry [ɪk·'spaɪ·ri] *n* Ablauf *m*

explain [ɪk·'spleɪn] **I.** *vt* erklären; *reason, motive* erläutern; ■ **to ~ oneself** (*make clear*) sich [deutlich] ausdrücken; (*justify*) **you'd better ~ yourself** du solltest mir das erklären **II.** *vi* eine Erklärung geben

◆ **explain away** *vt* eine [einleuchtende] Erklärung für etw *akk* haben

explanation [ˌek·splə·'neɪ·ʃən] *n* Erklärung *f; of reason, motive* Erläuterung *f;* **in ~** [**of sth**] [*or* **by way of ~** [**for sth**]] als Erklärung [für etw *akk*]

explanatory [ɪk·'splæn·ə·tɔr·i] *adj* erklärend; *footnotes, statement, diagram* erläuternd

expletive ['ək·splɪ·t̬ɪv] *n* Kraftausdruck *m*

explicable [ek·'splɪk·ə·bəl] *adj* erklärbar

explicit [ɪk·'splɪs·ɪt] *adj* ❶ (*precise*) klar, deutlich; *agreement, order* ausdrücklich ❷ (*detailed*) eindeutig, unverhüllt

explode [ɪk·'sploʊd] **I.** *vi* explodieren *a. fig; tire* platzen; **to ~ in** [*or* **with**] **anger** vor Wut platzen **II.** *vt bomb* zünden; *container* sprengen; (*fig*) *argument* widerlegen

exploit **I.** *n* ['ek·splɔɪt] Heldentat *f* **II.** *vt* [ɪk·'splɔɪt] ❶ *worker* ausbeuten; *friend, thing* ausnutzen ❷ (*utilize*) nutzen

exploitation [ˌek·splɔɪ·'teɪ·ʃən] *n* ❶ *of workforce* Ausbeutung *f; of person, thing* Ausnutzung *f* ❷ (*use*) Nutzung *f*

exploration [ˌek·splɔ·'reɪ·ʃən] *n* ❶ (*journey*) Erforschung *f; of enclosed space* Erkundung *f* ❷ (*examination*) Untersuchung *f* (**of** von +*dat*)

exploratory [ɪk·'splɔr·ə·tɔr·i] *adj* Forschungs-; *drilling, well* Probe-; *operation* explorativ; **~ talks** Sondierungsgespräche *pl*

explore [ɪk·'splɔr] **I.** *vt* ❶ (*investigate*) erforschen, erkunden ❷ (*examine*) untersuchen **II.** *vi* sich umschauen

explorer [ɪk·'splɔr·ər] *n* Forscher(in) *m(f)*

explosion [ɪk·'sploʊ·ʒən] *n* Explosion *f a. fig*

explosive [ɪk·'sploʊ·sɪv] **I.** *adj* explosiv *a. fig; issue, situation* [hoch] brisant; **to have an ~ temper** zu Wutausbrüchen neigen **II.** *n* Sprengstoff *m kein pl*

exponent [ɪk·'spoʊ·nənt] *n* (*representative*) Vertreter(in) *m(f),* Exponent(in) *m(f);* (*advocate*) Verfechter(in) *m(f)*

export **I.** *vt, vi* [ɪk·'spɔrt] exportieren **II.** *n* ['ek·spɔrt] ❶ (*selling*) Export *m,* Ausfuhr *f* ❷ (*product*) Exportartikel *m*

exportable [ɪk·'spɔr·t̬ə·bəl] *adj* exportfähig

exportation [ˌek·spɔr·'teɪ·ʃən] *n* Export *m,* Ausfuhr *f*

'export business *n* Exportgeschäft *nt*

exporter [ɪk·'spɔr·t̬ər] *n* Exporteur *m;* (*person a.*) Exporthändler(in) *m(f);* (*company a.*) Exportfirma *f;* (*country*) Exportland *nt,* Ausfuhrland *nt*

'export goods *npl* Exportgüter *pl*

'export license *n* Ausfuhrgenehmigung *f,* Exportlizenz *f*

'export regulations *npl* Ausfuhrbestimmungen *pl*

'export trade *n* Exporthandel *m,* Außenhandel *m*

expose [ɪk·'spoʊz] *vt* ❶ (*bare*) freilegen; *nerves* bloßlegen ❷ (*subject*) *danger, ridicule* aussetzen (**to** +*dat*) ❸ (*reveal*) offenbaren; *scandal, plot* aufdecken; ■ **to ~ sb** jdn entlarven ❹ PHOT belichten

exposed [ɪk·'spoʊzd] *adj* ❶ (*unprotected*) ungeschützt; *position* exponiert ❷ (*bare*) freigelegt; *body part* unbedeckt ❸ PHOT belichtet

exposition [ˌek·spə·'zɪʃ·ən] *n* ❶ (*explanation*) Darlegung *f* ❷ (*show*) Ausstellung *f* ❸ LIT, MUS

Exposition *f*

exposure [ɪk·ˈspoʊ·ʒər] *n* ❶ (*being unprotected*) Aussetzung *f;* ~ **to radiation** Bestrahlung *f* ❷ (*contact*) Kontakt *m* (**to** mit +*dat*) ❸ (*contact with elements*) Ausgesetztsein *nt* ❹ (*revelation*) *of person* Entlarvung *f; of plot* Aufdeckung *f; of affair* Enthüllung *f* ❺ PHOT Belichtung[szeit] *f;* (*shot*) Aufnahme *f*

expound [ɪk·ˈspaʊnd] **I.** *vt* ❶ (*explain*) darlegen ❷ (*interpret*) erläutern **II.** *vi* ■**to ~ [up]on sth** etw darlegen

express [ɪk·ˈspres] **I.** *vt* ❶ (*communicate*) ausdrücken; (*say*) aussprechen; ■**to ~ oneself** sich ausdrücken ❷ MATH darstellen ❸ (*send*) per Express schicken **II.** *adj* ❶ (*rapid*) express; **by ~ delivery** per Eilzustellung, per Express ❷ (*precise*) bestimmt; (*explicit*) ausdrücklich; **for the ~ purpose** eigens zu dem Zweck **III.** *adv* per Express **IV.** *n* (*train*) Express[zug] *m,* Schnellzug *m,* ≈ ICE *m*

expression [ɪk·ˈspreʃ·ən] *n* Ausdruck *m,* Äußerung *f;* **to give ~ to sth** etw zum Ausdruck bringen; **freedom of ~** Freiheit *f* der Meinungsäußerung; (*on face*) [Gesichts]ausdruck *m*

expressionless [ɪk·ˈspreʃ·ən·lɪs] *adj* ausdruckslos

expressive [ɪk·ˈspres·ɪv] *adj* ausdrucksvoll; *voice* ausdrucksstark

expressly [ɪk·ˈspres·li] *adv* ❶ (*explicitly*) ausdrücklich ❷ (*particularly*) extra

ex'pressway *n* Schnellstraße *f*

expropriate [eks·ˈproʊ·pri·eɪt] *vt* ❶ (*dispossess*) enteignen ❷ (*appropriate*) sich *dat* [widerrechtlich] aneignen; *funds* veruntreuen

expropriation [eks·proʊ·pri·ˈeɪ·ʃən] *n* ❶ (*dispossessing*) Enteignung *f* ❷ (*appropriation*) [widerrechtliche] Aneignung; *of funds* Veruntreuung *f*

expulsion [ɪk·ˈspʌl·ʃən] *n from club* Ausschluss *m* (**from** aus +*dat*); *from country* Ausweisung *f* (**from** aus +*dat*); *from home* Vertreibung *f* (**from** aus +*dat*); *from school, university* Verweisung *f* (**from** von +*dat*)

exquisite [ˈek·skwɪ·zɪt] *adj* erlesen, exquisit

extemporaneous [ɪk·ˌstem·pə·ˈreɪ·ni·əs] *adj* improvisiert; *speech* aus dem Stegreif *nach n*

extemporize [ɪk·ˈstem·pə·raɪz] *vi* improvisieren

extend [ɪk·ˈstend] **I.** *vt* ❶ (*stretch*) ausstrecken; *rope* spannen ❷ (*prolong*) verlängern ❸ (*pull out*) verlängern; *ladder, table* ausziehen; *landing gear* ausfahren ❹ (*expand*) erweitern; *influence, business* ausdehnen ❺ (*build*) ausbauen **II.** *vi* sich erstrecken; *over time* sich hinziehen; **to ~ for miles** sich meilenweit hinziehen

extended [ɪk·ˈsten·dɪd] *adj* verlängert; *bulletin* umfassend

extension [ɪk·ˈsten·ʃən] **I.** *n* ❶ (*stretching*) *of extremities* Ausstrecken *nt; of muscles* Dehnung *f* ❷ (*lengthening*) Verlängerung *f;* **~ table** Ausziehtisch *m* ❸ (*expansion*) Erweiterung *f,* Vergrößerung *f; of influence, power* Ausdehnung *f;* **by ~** im weiteren Sinne ❹ (*prolongation*) Verlängerung *f* ❺ (*addition*) Anbau *m; to building* Erweiterungsbau *m* (**to** an +*dat*) ❻ (*phone line*) Nebenanschluss *m;* (*number*) [Haus]apparat *m* ❼ (*offering*) Bekundung *f* **II.** *adj* UNIV Fern-

ex'tension cord *n* Verlängerungskabel *nt*

ex'tension ladder *n* Ausziehleiter *f*

extensive [ɪk·ˈsten·sɪv] *adj* ❶ (*large*) ausgedehnt; *grounds* weitläufig ❷ (*far-reaching*) weitreichend ❸ (*large-scale*) *bombing* schwer; *damage* beträchtlich; *knowledge* breit; *repairs* umfangreich

extensively [ɪk·ˈsten·sɪv·li] *adv* ❶ (*for the most part*) weitgehend ❷ (*considerably*) beträchtlich; *damaged* erheblich ❸ (*thoroughly*) gründlich; (*in detail*) ausführlich; **to use sth ~** von etw *dat* ausgiebig Gebrauch machen

extent [ɪk·ˈstent] *n* ❶ (*size*) Größe *f,* Ausdehnung *f;* (*length*) Länge *f* ❷ (*range*) Umfang *m* ❸ (*degree*) Grad *m kein pl,* Maß *nt kein pl;* **to a certain ~** in gewissem Maße; **to a great** [*or* **large**] **~** in hohem Maße, weitgehend

exterior [ɪk·ˈstɪr·i·ər] **I.** *n* ❶ (*outside*) Außenseite *f; of building* Außenfront *f* ❷ (*appearance*) Äußere *nt* **II.** *adj* Außen-

exterminate [ɪk·ˈstɜr·mɪ·neɪt] *vt* ausrotten, vernichten; *vermin, weeds* vertilgen

extermination [ɪk·ˌstɜr·mɪ·ˈneɪ·ʃən] *n* Ausrottung *f,* Vernichtung *f; of vermin, weeds* Vertilgung *f*

external [ɪk·ˈstɜr·nəl] *adj* ❶ (*exterior*) äußerlich; *angle, pressure, world* Außen- ❷ (*from outside*) äußere(r, s) ❸ (*on surface*) äußerlich; **for ~ use only** nur zur äußerlichen Anwendung ❹ (*foreign*) auswärtig; **~ affairs** Außenpolitik *f*

externalize [ɪk·ˈstɜr·nə·laɪz] *vt* nach außen verlagern

extinct [ɪk·ˈstɪŋkt] *adj* ❶ (*died out*) ausgestorben; *custom, empire, people* untergegangen; *language* tot; **to become ~** aussterben ❷ (*inactive*) erloschen; **to become ~** *volcano* erlöschen

extinction [ɪk·ˈstɪŋk·ʃən] *n* ❶ (*dying out*) Aussterben *nt; of custom, empire, people* Untergang *m;* (*deliberate act*) Ausrottung *f* ❷ (*inactivity*) *volcano* Erlöschen *nt*

extinguish [ɪk·ˈstɪŋ·gwɪʃ] *vt* [aus]löschen; *candle* ausmachen

extinguisher [ɪk·ˈstɪŋ·gwɪʃ·ər] *n* Feuerlöscher *m*

extort [ɪk·ˈstɔrt] *vt* erzwingen; *money* erpressen

extortion [ɪk·ˈstɔr·ʃən] *n* Erzwingung *f; of money* Erpressung *f;* **that's sheer ~!** das ist ja Wucher!

extortionate [ɪk·ˈstɔr·ʃə·nɪt] *adj* ❶ (*exorbitant*) übermäßig; **~ prices** Wucherpreise *pl* ❷ (*using force*) erpresserisch

extra [ˈek·strə] **I.** *adj* zusätzlich; **some ~ money** etwas mehr Geld; **to take ~ care** besonders vorsichtig sein; ~ **charge** Aufschlag *m* **II.** *adv* ❶ (*more*) mehr; **to charge ~** einen Aufpreis verlangen; **postage and handling ~** zuzüglich Porto und Versand ❷ (*especially*) besonders; **I'll try ~ hard** ich werde mich ganz besonders anstrengen **III.** *n* ❶ ECON (*perk*) Zusatzleistung *f;* AUTO Extra *nt* ❷ (*charge*) Aufschlag *m* ❸ (*actor*) Statist(in) *m(f)* ❹ PUBL (*special edition*) Sonderausgabe *f*

extract **I.** *vt* [ɪk·ˈstrækt] ❶ (*remove*) [heraus]ziehen (**from** aus +*dat*); *bullet* entfernen; *tooth* ziehen ❷ (*obtain*) gewinnen (**from** aus +*dat*); *oil* fördern; *confession* abringen; *information* herausquetschen **II.** *n* [ˈek·strækt] ❶ (*excerpt*) Auszug *m* (**from** aus +*dat*) ❷ (*concentrate*) Extrakt *m*

extraction [ɪk·ˈstræk·ʃən] *n* ❶ (*removal*) Herausziehen *nt; of bullet* Entfernen *nt; of tooth* [Zahn]ziehen *nt* ❷ (*obtainment*) Gewinnung *f; of oil* Förderung *f; of confession* Abringen *nt*

extracurricular [ˌek·strə·kə·ˈrɪk·jə·lər] *adj* ❶ SCH, UNIV außerhalb des Stundenplans *nach n* ❷ (*fig*) außerplanmäßig

extradite [ˈek·strə·daɪt] *vt* ausliefern (**from** von +*dat,* **to** an +*akk*)

extradition [ˌek·strə·ˈdɪʃ·ən] *n* Auslieferung *f*

extramarital [ˌek·strə·ˈmer·ɪ·t̬əl] *adj* außerehelich

extraneous [ɪk·ˈstreɪ·ni·əs] *adj* ❶ (*external*) von außen *nach n;* ~ **substance** Fremdstoff *m* ❷ (*unrelated*) sachfremd

extraordinary [ɪk·ˈstrɔr·də·ner·i] *adj* außerordentlich, außergewöhnlich; *achievement* herausragend; *coincidence* merkwürdig; *success* erstaunlich

extrapolate [ek·ˈstræp·ə·leɪt] *vt* extrapolieren

extrasensory [ˌek·strə·ˈsen·sə·ri] *adj* übersinnlich

extraterrestrial [ˈek·strə·tə·ˈres·tri·əl] **I.** *adj* außerirdisch **II.** *n* außerirdisches [Lebe]wesen

extravagance [ɪk·ˈstræv·ə·gəns] *n* ❶ (*excess*) Verschwendungssucht *f;* (*expenditure*) Verschwendung *f* ❷ (*treat*) Luxus *m kein pl*

extravagant [ɪk·ˈstræv·ə·gənt] *adj* ❶ (*flamboyant*) extravagant ❷ (*luxurious*) üppig; *lifestyle* aufwendig; **to have ~ taste** einen teuren Geschmack haben ❸ (*wasteful*) verschwenderisch

extravaganza [ɪk·ˌstræv·ə·ˈgæn·zə] *n* opulente Veranstaltung

extreme [ɪk·ˈstrim] **I.** *adj* ❶ (*utmost*) äußerste(r, s); *difficulties, weather* extrem; *relief* außerordentlich ❷ (*radical*) radikal, extrem **II.** *n* Extrem *nt;* **to go from one ~ to the other** von einem Extrem ins andere fallen

In den USA werden die nicht-traditionellen Sportarten wie das Bungee-Jumping, das Paragliding oder das Freiklettern **extreme sports** oder **alternative sports** genannt. Andere Sportarten wie Heliskiing, Canyoning, Wakeboarding und Rennrodeln zählen ebenfalls zu den **extreme sports**. Es handelt sich um Sportarten von großer Schnelligkeit, die sehr modisch sind, weil sie für gefährlich und exzentrisch gehalten werden.

extremely [ɪk·ˈstrim·li] *adv* äußerst; **I'm ~ sorry** es tut mir außerordentlich leid

extremism [ɪk·ˈstri·mɪz·əm] *n* Extremismus *m*

extremist [ɪk·ˈstri·mɪst] **I.** *n* Extremist(in) *m(f)* **II.** *adj* radikal

extremity [ɪk·ˈstrem·ə·t̬i] *n* ❶ (*end*) äußerstes Ende ❷ (*fingers and toes*) ■ **extremities** *pl* Extremitäten *pl*

extricate [ˈek·strɪ·keɪt] *vt* befreien (**from** aus +*dat*)

extrovert [ˈek·strə·vɜrt] *n* extravertierter Mensch

extroverted [ˈek·strə·vɜr·tɪd] *adj* extravertiert

extrude [ek·ˈstrud] *vt* herauspressen

exuberance [ɪg·ˈzu·bər·əns] *n of person* Überschwänglichkeit *f; of feelings* Überschwang *m*

exuberant [ɪg·ˈzu·bər·ənt] *adj person* überschwänglich, ausgelassen; *mood* überschäumend

exude [ɪg·ˈzud] *vt* ausscheiden; *aroma* verströmen; *pus, resin* absondern; (*fig*) *confidence* ausstrahlen

exult [ɪg·ˈzʌlt] *vi* frohlocken (**at, in, over** über +*akk*)

exultant [ɪg·ˈzʌl·tənt] *adj* jubelnd; *laugh* triumphierend

exultation [ˌek·sʌl·ˈteɪ·ʃən] *n* Jubel *m* (**at** über +*akk*)

eye [aɪ] **I.** *n* ❶ Auge *nt;* **a black ~** ein blaues Auge; **as far as the ~ can see** so weit das Auge reicht ❷ (*in needle*) Öhr *nt;* **~ of a needle** Nadelöhr *nt* ❸ (*eyelet*) Öse *f* ▶ PHRASES: **to <u>cry</u> one's ~s out** sich *dat* die Augen ausheulen; **to <u>have</u> one's ~ on sb/sth** jdn/etw im Auge behalten, ein [wachsames] Auge auf jdn/etw haben; **to <u>have</u> a good ~ for sth** ein Auge für etw *akk* haben; **to <u>keep</u> an** [*or* **one's**] **~ on sb/sth** ein [wachsames] Auge auf jdn/etw haben; **to <u>keep</u> one's ~s open** [*or* **peeled**] die Augen offen halten; **to <u>open</u> sb's ~s** [**to sth**] jdm die Augen [für etw] öffnen; **with one's ~s <u>shut</u>** mit geschlossenen Augen; **to not <u>take</u> one's ~s off sb/sth** (*admire*) kein Auge von jdm/etw abwenden; (*guard*) jdn/etw keine Minute aus den Augen lassen; **to <u>turn</u> a blind ~** [**to sth**] [bei etw] beide Augen zudrücken **II.** *adj* Augen-; **~ specialist** Augenarzt, -ärztin *m, f* **III.** *vt* <-d, -d, -ing *or* eying> beäugen; ■ **to ~ sb up and down** (*carefully*) jdn von oben bis unten mustern; (*with desire*) mit begehrlichen Blicken betrachten

ˈ**eyeball** **I.** *n* Augapfel *m* **II.** *vt* (*fam*) ❶ (*watch*) mit einem durchdringenden Blick ansehen ❷ (*measure*) nach Augenmaß einschätzen

ˈ**eyebrow** *n* Augenbraue *f*

ˈ**eye-catching** *adj* auffallend

'eye contact *n* **to make ~ [with sb]** Blickkontakt [mit jdm] aufnehmen
'eyedrops *n pl* Augentropfen *pl*
'eyeful *n* **to get an ~ of dust** Staub ins Auge bekommen ▶PHRASES: **to get an ~ of sth** einen Blick auf etw *akk* werfen
'eyeglasses *npl* Brille *f*
'eyeglasses case *n* Brillenetui *nt*
'eyelash *n* Wimper *f*
eyelet ['aɪ·lɪt] *n* Öse *f*
'eyelid *n* Augenlid *nt*
'eyeliner *n* Eyeliner *m*
'eye opener *n* ■ **to be an ~ for sb** (*enlightening*) jdm die Augen öffnen; (*startling*) alarmierend für jdn sein
'eyepiece *n* Okular *nt*
'eye shadow *n* Lidschatten *m*
'eyesight *n* Sehvermögen *nt,* Sehkraft *f*
'eyesore *n* Schandfleck *m*
'eyestrain *n* Überanstrengung *f* der Augen
'eyetooth *n* Augenzahn *m;* (*fig*) **I'd give my eyeteeth for that** ich würde alles darum geben
'eyewash *n* ❶ Augenwasser *nt* ❷ (*fam: nonsense*) Blödsinn *m*
eye'witness *n* Augenzeuge, -in *m, f*
eyrie ['er·i, 'ɪr·i] *n* ORN *see* **aerie**

F

Ff

F <*pl* -'s *or* -s>, **f** <*pl* -'s> [ef] *n* ❶ (*letter*) F *nt,* f *nt;* **~ as in Foxtrot** F wie Friedrich ❷ MUS F *nt,* f *nt* ❸ SCH (*grade*) ≈ Sechs *f,* ≈ ungenügend
fable ['feɪ·bəl] *n* Fabel *f*
fabled ['feɪ·bld] *adj* legendär
fabric ['fæb·rɪk] *n* ❶ (*textile*) Stoff *m* ❷ *of building* Bausubstanz *f*
fabricate ['fæb·rɪ·keɪt] *vt* ❶ (*manufacture*) herstellen ❷ (*pej: make up*) erfinden
fabulous ['fæb·jə·ləs] *adj* (*terrific*) fabelhaft, sagenhaft, toll *fam; meal* hervorragend
façade [fə·'sad] *n* Fassade *f a. fig*
face [feɪs] **I.** *n* ❶ Gesicht *nt a. fig;* **with a smile on one's ~** mit einem Lächeln im Gesicht; **with a puzzled/worried look on one's ~** mit ratlosem/besorgtem Gesicht [*o* ratloser/besorgter Miene]; **~ down/up** mit dem Gesicht nach unten/oben; **to look sb in the ~** jdm in die Augen schauen; **to shut the door in sb's ~** jdm die Tür vor der Nase zuschlagen; **~ to ~** von Angesicht zu Angesicht; **to come ~ to ~ with sth** direkt mit etw *dat* konfrontiert werden; **to speak to sb ~ to ~** mit jdm persönlich sprechen; **I don't want to see your ~ in here again!** (*fam*) ich will dich hier nie wieder sehen! ❷ *of a building* Fassade *f; of a cliff, mountain* Wand *f; of a clock, watch* Zifferblatt *nt; of a playing card* Bildseite *f* ❸ (*reputation*) **to lose/save ~** das Gesicht verlieren/wahren ▶PHRASES: **to disappear [*or* be wiped] off the ~ of the earth** wie vom Erdboden verschluckt sein; **get out of my face!** (*fam*) lass mich in Ruhe!; **in the ~ of sth** (*despite*) trotz einer S. *gen;* **on the ~ of it** auf den ersten Blick; **to show one's ~** sich blicken lassen **II.** *vt* ❶ (*look toward*) *person* ■ **to ~ sb/sth** sich jdm/etw zuwenden; **to ~ the audience** sich dem Publikum zuwenden; ■ **to ~ [*or* sit facing] sb** jdm gegenübersitzen; ■ **to ~ [*or* sit facing] sth** mit dem Gesicht zu etw *dat* sitzen ❷ (*look toward*) *room, window* [hinaus]gehen (auf +*akk*); **my bedroom ~s the street** mein Schlafzimmer geht auf die Straße; (*be situated across from*) gegenüber liegen +*dat* ❸ (*be confronted*) ■ **to be ~ed with sth** sich einer S. +*dat* gegenübersehen; **the nation is facing a crisis** die Nation steht vor einer Krise ❹ (*confront*) ■ **to ~ sth/sb** etw/jdm ins Auge sehen; **it's time we ~d [the] facts** es wird Zeit, dass wir den Tatsachen ins Auge sehen ❺ (*bear*) ertragen; **he can't ~ work today** er ist heute nicht imstande zu arbeiten ▶PHRASES: **to ~ the music** für die Folgen geradestehen **III.** *vi* ❶ (*point*) **to ~ backward[s]/east** nach hinten/Osten zeigen; **a seat facing forward[s]** TRANSP ein Sitz in Fahrtrichtung ❷ (*look onto*) **to ~ south** *room, window* nach Süden [hinaus]gehen; *house, garden* nach Süden liegen ❸ (*look*) *person* blicken; **to sit facing away from sb/sth** mit dem Rücken zu jdm/etw sitzen; **facing forward[s]** mit dem Gesicht nach vorne
◆**face down I.** *vt* ■ **to ~ down** ↔ **sb/sth** jdm/etw [energisch] entgegentreten **II.** *vi* nach unten zeigen
◆**face out** *vi* nach außen zeigen
◆**face up I.** *vi* ■ **to ~ up to sth/sb** etw/jdm ins Auge sehen; **to ~ up to one's problems** sich seinen Problemen stellen **II.** *vi* nach oben zeigen
'face cream *n* Gesichtscreme *f*
'facelift *n* [Face]lifting *nt;* (*fig*) Renovierung *f;* **to have a ~** sich liften lassen
'face pack *n* Gesichtsmaske *f*
'face powder *n* Gesichtspuder *m*
facet ['fæs·ɪt] *n* Facette *f a. fig*
facetious [fə·'si·ʃəs] *adj* (*usu pej*) [gewollt] witzig
face-to-'face *adj* persönlich
face 'value *n* Nennwert *m;* **to take sth at ~** etw für bare Münze nehmen
facial ['feɪ·ʃəl] **I.** *adj* Gesichts- **II.** *n* [kosmetische] Gesichtsbehandlung

facile <-r, -st *or* more ~, most ~> ['fæs·ɪl] *adj* (*pej*) ① *person* oberflächlich ② (*superficially easy*) [allzu] einfach

facilitate [fə·'sɪl·ɪ·teɪt] *vt* erleichtern

facilitator [fə·'sɪl·ɪ·teɪ·t̬ər] *n* Vermittler(in) *m(f)*

facility [fə·'sɪl·ə·t̬i] *n* ① (*ease*) Leichtigkeit *f* ② (*natural ability*) Begabung *f* (**for** für +*akk*) ③ (*building and equipment*) Einrichtung *f,* Anlage *f;* **sports ~** Sportanlage *f;* **bathroom ~** Toilette *f*

facsimile [fæk·'sɪm·ə·li] *n* Faksimile *nt*

fact [fækt] *n* ① (*truth*) Wirklichkeit *f* ② (*single truth*) Tatsache *f;* **the ~ [of the matter] is that ...** Tatsache ist, dass ... ▶ PHRASES: **in** [*or* as **a matter of**] ~ genau genommen

'**fact-finding** *adj* Untersuchungs-; **~ mission** Erkundungsmission *f*

faction ['fæk·ʃən] *n* POL ① (*dissenting group*) [Splitter]gruppe *f* ② (*disagreement*) interne Unstimmigkeiten

factor ['fæk·t̬ər] *n* Faktor *m;* **to be a contributing ~ in sth** zu etw *dat* beitragen; **by a ~ of four** um das Vierfache

factory ['fæk·tə·ri] *n* Fabrik *f;* (*plant*) Werk *nt*

factory 'farm *n* [voll] automatisierter landwirtschaftlicher Betrieb

factory 'farming *n* [voll] automatisierte Viehhaltung

factual ['fæk·tʃu·əl] *adj* sachlich; **~ error** Sachfehler *m*

faculty ['fæk·əl·ti] *n* ① SCH, UNIV Lehrkörper *m* ② (*natural ability*) Fähigkeit *f;* **to have [all] one's faculties** im [Voll]besitz seiner [geistigen] Kräfte sein; (*skill*) Talent *nt*

fad [fæd] *n* Modeerscheinung *f;* **the latest ~** der letzte Schrei

fade [feɪd] **I.** *vi* ① (*lose color*) ausbleichen, verblassen ② (*lose intensity*) nachlassen; **the light is fading** (*at end of day*) es wird dunkel; *sound* verklingen; *smile* vergehen; *color* verbleichen ③ (*disappear*) verschwinden; FILM, TV ausgeblendet werden; **day slowly ~d into night** der Tag ging langsam in die Nacht über **II.** *vt* ausbleichen

◆**fade away** *vi* (*disappear gradually*) *courage, hope* schwinden; *memories* verblassen; *dreams, plans* zerrinnen; *beauty* verblühen

◆**fade in** FILM, TV **I.** *vi* eingeblendet werden **II.** *vt* einblenden

◆**fade out** **I.** *vi* ausgeblendet werden **II.** *vt* ausblenden

fag [fæg] *n* (*pej fam: homosexual*) Schwule(r) *m*

faggot ['fæg·ət] *n* (*pej fam*) Schwule(r) *m*

fail [feɪl] **I.** *vi* ① (*not succeed*) *person* versagen; *attempt, plan* scheitern, fehlschlagen; **if all else ~s** zur Not ② (*not do*) ■**to ~ to do sth** versäumen, etw zu tun; **to ~ in one's duty [to sb]** seiner Pflicht [jdm gegenüber] nicht nachkommen; **I ~ to see what ...** ich verstehe nicht, was ... ③ SCH, UNIV durchfallen ④ *brakes* versagen; *generator, harvest* ausfallen ⑤ (*become weaker*) nachlassen; *health* schwächer werden; *heart, voice* versagen ⑥ (*go bankrupt*) bankrottgehen **II.** *vt* ① (*not pass*) durchfallen; **she ~d her driving test** sie ist bei der Fahrprüfung durchgefallen; *course, subject* nicht bestehen; ■**to ~ sb** (*not grant a passing grade*) jdn durchfallen lassen ② (*let down*) im Stich lassen; **words ~ me** mir fehlen die Worte **III.** *n* negative Prüfungsarbeit; **is this one a pass or a ~?** hat dieser Kandidat bestanden oder ist er durchgefallen? ▶ PHRASES: **without** ~ auf jeden Fall

failing ['feɪ·lɪŋ] **I.** *adj* **~ eyesight** Sehschwäche *f;* **to be in ~ health** eine angeschlagene Gesundheit haben **II.** *n* Schwäche *f* **III.** *prep* mangels +*gen;* ■**~ that** ansonsten

'**fail-safe** *adj* abgesichert

failure ['feɪl·jər] *n* ① (*lack of success*) Scheitern *nt,* Versagen *nt; of bank/business* Bankrott *m; of crop* Missernte *f;* **~ rate** SCH, UNI Durchfallquote *f;* **to end in ~** scheitern ② (*unsuccessful thing*) Misserfolg *m; person* Versager(in) *m(f)* ③ (*omission*) Unterlassung *f* ④ MED, TECH Versagen *nt kein pl; of an engine* Ausfall *m*

faint [feɪnt] **I.** *adj* ① (*slight*) *light, color, smile, voice* matt; *sound, suspicion, hope* leise; *scent, pattern* zart; *smell, memory, taste* schwach; *chance* gering; **to not have the ~est idea** nicht die geringste Ahnung haben ② (*unclear*) *line* undeutlich ③ (*physically weak*) **to feel ~** sich schwach fühlen; **to be ~ with hunger/exhaustion** vor Hunger/Erschöpfung fast umfallen **II.** *vi* ohnmächtig werden **III.** *n* **in a [dead] ~** ohnmächtig

faint-'hearted *adj* zaghaft; **to be not for the ~** nichts für schwache Nerven sein

faintly ['feɪnt·li] *adv* ① (*weakly*) leicht, schwach ② (*not clearly*) schwach; **~ visible** schwach zu sehen ③ (*slightly*) leicht, etwas; **to ~ resemble sth** entfernt an etw *akk* erinnern

fair[1] [fer] **I.** *adj* ① (*reasonable*) fair; *salary* angemessen; (*legitimate*) berechtigt; **you're not being ~** das ist unfair; **[that's] ~ enough!** (*fam: agreed*) dagegen ist nichts einzuwenden!; **it's ~ to say that ...** man kann [wohl] sagen, dass ... ② (*just, impartial*) gerecht, fair; **to get one's ~ share** seinen Anteil bekommen; ■**to be ~ to/toward[s] sb** jdm gegenüber gerecht sein ③ (*large*) ziemlich; **there's still a ~ bit of work to do** es gibt noch einiges zu tun ④ (*good*) ziemlich gut; **she's got a ~ chance of winning** ihre Gewinnchancen stehen ziemlich gut ⑤ (*pale*) *skin* hell; *hair* blond ⑥ (*clear*) *weather, sky* heiter **II.** *adv* (*according to rules*) **to play ~** fair sein; SPORTS fair spielen ▶ PHRASES: **~ and square** klar und deutlich, ganz klar

fair[2] [fer] *n* ① (*carnival*) Jahrmarkt *m,* Rummel[platz] *m bes* NORDD, Kirmes *f* NORDD, MITTELD, Kir[ch]tag *m* ÖSTERR ② (*trade, industry*) Messe *f;* (*agriculture*) [Vieh]markt *m*

fair 'game *n* (*fig*) Freiwild *nt*

'fairground *n* Rummel[platz] *m bes* NORDD

fair-'haired <fairer-, fairest- *or* more ~, most ~> *adj* blond

fairly ['fer·li] *adv* ❶ (*quite*) ziemlich; ~ **recently** vor kurzem ❷ (*justly*) fair; *divide up* gerecht

fair-'minded <fairer-, fairest- *or* more ~, most ~> *adj* unvoreingenommen

fairness ['fer·nɪs] *n* ❶ (*justice*) Fairness *f*, Gerechtigkeit *f*; **in** [**all**] ~ fairerweise ❷ *of hair, skin* Helligkeit *f*

fair 'play *n* Fairplay *nt*

fairy ['fer·i] *n* ❶ Fee *f* ❷ (*offensive fam: homosexual*) Tunte *f meist pej fam*

'fairy tale *n* Märchen *nt a. fig*

'fairy-tale *adj* Märchen-

faith [feɪθ] *n* ❶ (*trust*) Vertrauen *nt* (**in** zu +*dat*); **to put one's ~ in sb/sth** auf jdn/etw vertrauen ❷ REL Glaube *m* (**in** an +*akk*) ❸ (*sincerity*) **to act in good ~** in gutem Glauben handeln

faithful ['feɪθ·fəl] **I.** *adj* ❶ (*loyal*) treu; ■ **to be ~ to sb/sth** jdm/etw treu sein ❷ REL gläubig ❸ (*accurate*) originalgetreu; *account* detailliert; ■ **to be ~ to sth** einer S. *dat* gerecht werden **II.** *n* ■ **the ~** *pl* die Gläubigen *pl*

faithfully ['feɪθ·fəl·i] *adv* ❶ (*loyally*) treu; **to serve sb ~** jdm treue Dienste leisten ❷ (*exactly*) genau; *reproduce* originalgetreu

'faith healer *n* Gesundbeter(in) *m(f)*

fake [feɪk] **I.** *n* ❶ (*counterfeit object*) Fälschung *f*; (*dummy*) Attrappe *f* ❷ (*impostor*) Hochstapler(in) *m(f)* **II.** *adj* Kunst-; *antique* falsch; *jewel* imitiert; *passport* gefälscht; ~ **tan** künstliche Bräune *f* (*mittels Selbstbräuner getönte Haut*) **III.** *vt* ❶ (*make a copy*) fälschen ❷ (*pretend*) vortäuschen; *illness* simulieren; **to ~ it** (*fam*) so tun als ob **IV.** *vi* (*pretend*) markieren, so tun als ob

falcon ['fæl·kən] *n* Falke *m*

fall [fɔl] **I.** *n* ❶ (*tumble, drop*) Fall *m*; (*harder*) Sturz *m*; **she broke her leg in the ~** sie brach sich bei dem Sturz das Bein; **the bushes broke his ~** die Büsche haben seinen Sturz abgefangen ❷ (*decrease*) Rückgang *m* (**in** +*gen*); *in support* Nachlassen *nt* (**in** +*gen*); *in a level a.* Sinken *nt* (**in** +*gen*); ~ **in pressure** Druckabfall *m*; ~ **in value** Wertverlust *m* ❸ (*downfall*) *of a city* Einnahme *f*; *of a dictator, regime* Sturz *m*; **the ~ of the Roman Empire** der Untergang des Römischen Reiches ❹ (*autumn*) Herbst *m* ► PHRASES: **to take a** [*or* **the**] **~ for sb/sth** für jdn/etw die Schuld auf sich *akk* nehmen **II.** *adj* Herbst- **III.** *vi* <fell, fallen> ❶ (*drop, tumble*) fallen; (*harder*) stürzen; *person* hinfallen; (*harder*) stürzen; *tree, post* umfallen; (*harder*) umstürzen; **to ~ to one's death** in den Tod stürzen; **to ~ flat on one's face** auf die Nase fallen; **to ~ to one's knees** auf die Knie fallen; **to ~ down dead** tot umfallen ❷ (*hang*) fallen; **her hair fell to her waist** ihr Haar reichte ihr bis zur Taille ❸ (*descend*) fallen; *darkness* hereinbrechen; *silence* eintreten ❹ (*decrease*) sinken, fallen; **church attendance has ~en dramatically** die Anzahl der Kirchenbesucher ist drastisch zurückgegangen ❺ (*be*) **the accent ~s on the second syllable** der Akzent liegt auf der zweiten Silbe ❻ (*become*) **to ~ asleep** einschlafen; **to ~ ill** krank werden ❼ (*enter a particular state*) **to ~ into debt** sich verschulden; **to ~ out of favor** [**with sb**] [bei jdm] nicht mehr gefragt sein; **to ~ in love** [**with sb/sth**] sich [in jdn/etw] verlieben

◆**fall apart** *vi* ❶ (*disintegrate*) auseinanderfallen; *clothing* sich auflösen ❷ (*fig: fail*) auseinanderfallen; *system* zusammenbrechen; *organization* sich auflösen; *marriage* auseinandergehen ❸ (*fig: not cope*) *person* zusammenbrechen

◆**fall away** *vi* ❶ (*detach itself*) abfallen ❷ (*slope*) abfallen ❸ (*decrease*) sinken, zurückgehen

◆**fall back** *vi* ❶ (*move back*) zurückweichen; MIL sich zurückziehen; SPORTS *in a race* zurückfallen ❷ (*resort to*) *thing* zurückgreifen ([**up**]**on** auf +*akk*); *person* zurückkommen ([**up**]**on** auf +*akk*)

◆**fall behind** *vi* ❶ (*slow*) zurückfallen ❷ (*achieve less*) zurückbleiben; (*at school*) hinterherhinken; ■ **to ~ behind with sth** mit etw *dat* in Verzug geraten ❸ SPORTS (*in a race*) zurückfallen

◆**fall down** *vi* ❶ (*drop, tumble*) hinunterfallen; (*topple*) *person* hinfallen; (*harder*) stürzen; *object* umfallen; (*harder*) umstürzen; ■ **to ~ down sth** etw hinunterfallen; *hole, well* hineinfallen in +*akk* ❷ (*collapse*) einstürzen; *tent* zusammenfallen; ■ **to be ~ing down** abbruchreif sein

◆**fall for** *vt* ❶ (*love*) *person* sich verlieben in +*akk* ❷ (*be deceived by*) *trick* hereinfallen auf +*akk*

◆**fall in** *vi* ❶ (*drop*) hineinfallen ❷ (*collapse*) einstürzen ❸ MIL (*take up a position*) [in Reih und Glied] antreten; ■ **to ~ in behind sb** hinter jdm herlaufen; ■ **to ~ in with sb** sich jdm anschließen

◆**fall off** *vi* ❶ ■ **to ~ off sth** von etw *dat* fallen ❷ (*decrease*) zurückgehen, sinken ❸ (*detach itself*) abfallen, herunterfallen; *wallpaper* sich lösen

◆**fall on** *vi* ❶ (*attack*) ■ **to ~ on sb** über jdn herfallen ❷ (*be assigned to*) ■ **to ~ on sb** jdm zufallen ❸ (*be directed at*) ■ **to ~ on sb** jdn treffen; *suspicion* auf jdn fallen

◆**fall out** *vi* ❶ (*drop*) herausfallen; *teeth, hair* ausfallen ❷ (*argue*) ■ **to ~ out** [**with sb**] sich [mit jdm] [zer]streiten

◆**fall over** *vi* ❶ (*topple*) *person* hinfallen; (*harder*) stürzen; *object* umfallen; (*harder*) umstürzen ❷ (*trip*) ■ **to ~ over sth** über etw *akk* fallen

◆**fall through** *vi* scheitern; *plan* ins Wasser fallen

◆**fall to** *vi* (*be assigned to*) ■ **to ~ to sb** jdm

zufallen
fallacious [fə·ˈleɪ·ʃəs] *adj* (*form*) abwegig
fallacy [ˈfæl·ə·si] *n* Irrtum *m*
fallen [ˈfɔ·lən] **I.** *adj* ❶ (*on the ground*) *apple* abgefallen; *leaf* heruntergefallen; *tree* umgestürzt ❷ (*overthrown*) *dictator* gestürzt; (*disgraced*) *idol* einstig; *angel* gefallen **II.** *n* (*liter*) **the ~** *pl* die Gefallenen *pl*
ˈfall guy *n* (*sl*) Prügelknabe *m*
fallible [ˈfæl·ə·bəl] *adj person* fehlbar; *thing* fehleranfällig
ˈfall-off *n* Rückgang *m* (**in** +*gen*)
fallopian tube [fə·ˈloʊ·pi·ən·ˈtub] *n* ANAT Eileiter *m*
ˈfallout *n* ❶ radioaktive Strahlung; **~ shelter** Atombunker *m* ❷ (*fig*) Konsequenzen *pl* (**from** +*gen*)
fallow [ˈfæl·oʊ] *adj* ❶ AGR (*not planted*) brachliegend ❷ (*unproductive*) ruhig
false [fɔls] *adj* falsch; *bottom* doppelt; *imprisonment* unrechtmäßig; *optimism* trügerisch; **~ start** Fehlstart *m a. fig*
falsehood [ˈfɔls·hʊd] *n* Unwahrheit *f*
falseness [ˈfɔls·nɪs] *n* ❶ (*inaccuracy*) Unkorrektheit *f* ❷ (*insincerity*) Falschheit *f*
false ˈteeth *n pl* Gebiss *nt*
falsetto [fɔl·ˈseṭ·oʊ] *n* Kopfstimme *f*
falsification [ˌfɔl·sɪ·fɪ·ˈkeɪ·ʃən] *n* Fälschung *f*
falsify <-ie-> [ˈfɔl·sɪ·faɪ] *vt* fälschen
falter [ˈfɔl·tər] *vi* ❶ stocken ❷ (*fig*) nachlassen; **without ~ing** ohne zu zögern
faltering [ˈfɔl·tər·ɪŋ] *adj* zögerlich; *economy* stagnierend; *step* stockend; **in a ~ voice** mit stockender Stimme
fame [feɪm] *n* Ruhm *m*
famed [feɪmd] *adj* berühmt
familiar [fə·ˈmɪl·jər] *adj* ❶ (*well-known*) vertraut; *faces* bekannt ❷ (*acquainted*) ■ **to be ~ with sth/sb** etw/jdn kennen ❸ (*informal*) vertraulich; **the ~ form [of the second person]** LING die Du-Form ❹ (*too friendly*) allzu vertraulich, plumpvertraulich
familiarity [fə·ˌmɪl·i·ˈer·ə·ṭi] *n* ❶ (*well-known quality*) Vertrautheit *f* ❷ (*knowledge*) Kenntnis *f* (**with** in +*dat*) ❸ (*overfriendliness*) Vertraulichkeit *f* ► PHRASES: **~ breeds contempt** (*prov*) allzu große Vertrautheit erzeugt Verachtung
familiarize [fə·ˈmɪl·jə·raɪz] *vt* ■ **to ~ oneself/sb with sth** sich/jdn mit etw *dat* vertraut machen; *with work* sich/jdn einarbeiten (**with** in +*akk*)
family [ˈfæm·ə·li] **I.** *n* Familie *f*; **we've got ~ coming to visit** wir bekommen Familienbesuch; **to keep sth in the ~** etw in Familienbesitz behalten; *keep sth secret* etw für sich behalten **II.** *adj* Familien-
family ˈdoctor *n* Hausarzt, Hausärztin *m, f*
famine [ˈfæm·ɪn] *n* Hungersnot *f*
famished [ˈfæm·ɪʃt] *adj* (*fam*) ausgehungert
famous [ˈfeɪ·məs] *adj* berühmt ► PHRASES: **~ last words** wer's glaubt, wird selig!
famously [ˈfeɪ·məs·li] *adv* (*as is well known*) bekanntermaßen
fan[1] [fæn] *n* (*enthusiast, admirer*) Bewunderer, Bewunderin *m, f*; **a football/baseball ~** ein Football-/Baseballfan; **I'm a big ~ of your work** ich schätze Ihre Arbeit sehr
fan[2] [fæn] **I.** *n* ❶ (*hand-held*) Fächer *m* ❷ (*electric*) Ventilator *m* **II.** *vt* <-nn-> ■ **to ~ sb/oneself** jdm/sich Luft zufächeln; *flames* anfachen; (*fig*) schüren
fanatic [fə·ˈnæṭ·ɪk] **I.** *n* ❶ (*pej: obsessed*) Fanatiker(in) *m(f)* ❷ (*enthusiast*) **fitness ~** ein Fitnessfan *m* **II.** *adj* fanatisch
fanatical [fə·ˈnæṭ·ɪ·kəl] *adj* ❶ (*obsessed*) besessen (**about** von +*dat*); *support* bedingungslos ❷ (*enthusiastic*) total begeistert (**about** von +*dat*)
fanaticism [fə·ˈnæṭ·ɪ·sɪz·əm] *n* (*pej*) Fanatismus *m*
ˈfan belt *n* AUTO Keilriemen *m*
fanciful [ˈfæn·sɪ·fəl] *adj* ❶ (*unrealistic*) unrealistisch ❷ *person* überspannt
ˈfan club *n* Fanclub *m*
fancy [ˈfæn·si] **I.** *adj* ❶ (*elaborate*) *decorations* aufwändig; *pattern* ausgefallen; *hairdo* kunstvoll; *car* schick; (*fig*) *talk* geschwollen; **nothing ~** nichts Ausgefallenes ❷ (*whimsical*) versponnen; **don't you go filling his head with ~ ideas** setz ihm keinen Floh ins Ohr **II.** *n* ❶ (*liking*) Vorliebe *f*; **to take a ~ to sth/sb** Gefallen an etw/jdm finden ❷ (*whim*) Laune *f*; **when the ~ takes him** wenn ihm gerade danach ist **III.** *vt* <-ie-> (*imagine, think*) **Dick fancies himself as a singer** Dick bildet sich ein, ein großer Sänger zu sein; **~ that!** stell dir das [mal] vor!
fancy-ˈfree *adj* sorglos
fanfare [ˈfæn·fer] *n* Fanfare *f*
fang [fæŋ] *n* Fang[zahn] *m*; *of a snake* Giftzahn *m*
ˈfan mail *n* Fanpost *f*
fanny [ˈfæn·i] *n* (*fam*) Hintern *m*
fantasize [ˈfæn·tə·saɪz] *vi* fantasieren
fantastic [fæn·ˈtæs·tɪk] *adj* ❶ (*fam: wonderful*) fantastisch, toll; **to look ~** *person* umwerfend aussehen ❷ (*fam: extremely large*) enorm, unwahrscheinlich viel ❸ (*unbelievable*) unwahrscheinlich
fantasy [ˈfæn·tə·si] *n* Fantasie *f*; ■ **to have fantasies about [doing] sth** von etw *dat* träumen; LIT Fantasy *f*
fanzine [ˈfæn·zin] *n* Fanmagazin *nt*
far <farther *or* further, farthest *or* furthest> [far] **I.** *adv* ❶ (*in space*) weit; **how much farther is it?** wie weit ist es denn noch?; **do you have ~ to travel to work?** haben Sie es weit zu Ihrer Arbeitsstelle?; **~ and wide** weit und breit ❷ (*in time*) weit; **some time ~ in the future** irgendwann in ferner Zukunft; **~ into the night** bis spät in die Nacht hinein; **to plan further ahead** weiter voraus planen; **as ~ back as I can remember ...** so weit ich zurückdenken kann ... ❸ (*in progress*) weit; **to not get very ~ with [doing] sth** mit etw

dat nicht besonders weit kommen ❹ (*much*) weit, viel; ~ **better** viel besser; **by** ~ bei weitem ▶ PHRASES: **as** ~ **as** (*in space*) bis; **as** ~ **as the eye can see** so weit das Auge reicht; (*in degree*) **as** ~ **as I know** soweit ich weiß; ~ **and away** mit Abstand; **I'd** ~ **rather ...** ich würde viel lieber ...; ~ **from it!** weit gefehlt; ~ **be it from me ...** es liegt mir fern ...; **sb will go** ~ jd wird es zu etwas bringen; **sth won't go very** ~ etw wird nicht lange vorhalten; **a hundred dollars won't go very** ~ mit hundert Dollar kommt man nicht weit; **so** ~, **so good** so weit, so gut; **so** ~ (*until now*) bisher; (*to a limited extent*) **only so** ~ nur bedingt **II.** *adj* ❶ (*further away*) **at the** ~ **end** am anderen Ende ❷ (*distant*) fern; **in the** ~ **distance** in weiter Ferne ▶ PHRASES: **to be a** ~ **cry from sth/sb** mit etw/jdm nicht zu vergleichen sein

faraway ['far·ə·weɪ] *adj* ❶ (*distant*) fern; *sound* weit entfernt ❷ (*dreamy*) *look* verträumt

farce [fars] *n* Farce *f*

farcical ['far·sɪ·kəl] *adj* absurd

fare [fer] *n* ❶ (*money*) Fahrpreis *m* ❷ (*traveler in a taxi*) Taxifahrgast *m*

Far 'East *n* ■ **the** ~ der Ferne Osten

farewell [ˌfer·'wel] **I.** *interj* (*form*) leb wohl; **to bid** [*or* **say**] ~ **to sb/sth** sich von jdm/etw verabschieden **II.** *n* Abschied *m* **III.** *adj* Abschied[s]-; **a** ~ **party** eine Abschiedsparty

far-'fetched *adj* weit hergeholt

far-'flung *adj* ❶ (*widespread*) weitläufig ❷ (*remote*) abgelegen

farm [farm] **I.** *n* Bauernhof *m;* **chicken** ~ Hühnerfarm *f* **II.** *vt* bebauen **III.** *vi* Land bebauen; **the family still** ~**s in California** die Familie hat immer noch Farmland in Kalifornien

◆ **farm out** *vt* *work* abgeben (**to** an +*akk*); *children* anvertrauen +*dat*

farmer ['far·mər] *n* Bauer, Bäuerin *m, f*

'farmhand *n* Landarbeiter(in) *m(f)*

'farmhouse *n* Bauernhaus *nt*

'farmland *n* Ackerland *nt*

'farmstead *n* Farm *f*

'farmyard *n* Hof *m*

'far-off *adj* ❶ (*distant*) fern; (*remote*) [weit] entfernt ❷ (*time*) fern

far-'reaching *adj* weit reichend

'farsighted *adj* ❶ (*hyperopic*) weitsichtig ❷ (*shrewd*) *decision* weitsichtig; *person* vorausschauend

fart [fart] **I.** *n* ❶ (*vulg*) Furz *m* ❷ (*pej: person*) Sack *m* **II.** *vi* (*vulg*) furzen

farther ['far·ðər] **I.** *adv comp of* **far** weiter; **how much** ~ **is it to the airport?** wie weit ist es noch zum Flughafen? **II.** *adj comp of* **far**: **at the** ~ **end** am anderen Ende; *see also* **further**

farthest ['far·ðɪst] **I.** *adv superl of* **far** am weitesten; **the** ~ **east** am weitesten östlich **II.** *adj superl of* **far** am weitesten; **the** ~ **place** der am weitesten entfernte Ort

fascinate ['fæs·ə·neɪt] *vt* faszinieren

fascinating ['fæs·ə·neɪ·t̬ɪŋ] *adj* faszinierend

fascination [ˌfæs·ə·'neɪ·ʃən] *n* Faszination *f;* **to watch in** ~ fasziniert zusehen

fascism ['fæʃ·ɪz·əm] *n* Faschismus *m*

fascist ['fæʃ·ɪst] **I.** *n* Faschist(in) *m(f)* **II.** *adj* faschistisch

fashion ['fæʃ·ən] **I.** *n* ❶ (*style*) Mode *f;* **to be in/come into** ~ in Mode sein/werden; **to be/go out of** ~ aus der Mode sein/kommen ❷ (*clothes*) ■ ~**s** *pl* Mode *f* ❸ ~ [*or* **the** ~ **industry**] die Modebranche **II.** *vt* ausarbeiten

fashionable ['fæʃ·ə·nə·bəl] *adj* modisch, schick; ■ **to be/become** ~ in Mode sein/werden

'fashion designer *n* Modedesigner(in) *m(f)*

'fashion show *n* Modenschau *f*

fast¹ [fæst] **I.** *adj* ❶ (*quick*) schnell; **to be a** ~ **runner** schnell laufen ❷ *clock, watch* ■ **to be** ~ vorgehen ❸ (*permanent*) *color* waschecht **II.** *adv* ❶ (*at speed*) schnell ❷ (*firmly*) fest; **to be** ~ **asleep** tief schlafen

fast² [fæst] **I.** *vi* fasten **II.** *n* Fastenzeit *f;* **to break one's** ~ das Fasten brechen

fasten ['fæs·ən] **I.** *vt* ❶ (*close*) schließen; *coat* zumachen; **to** ~ **one's seat belt** sich anschnallen ❷ (*secure*) befestigen (**on, to** an +*dat*); (*with glue*) festkleben; (*with rope*) festbinden **II.** *vi* (*close*) sich schließen lassen; **this dress** ~**s at the back** dieses Kleid wird hinten zugemacht

◆ **fasten down** *vt* befestigen

◆ **fasten up** **I.** *vt* zumachen; *buttons* zuknöpfen **II.** *vi* zugemacht werden

fastener ['fæs·ə·nər] *n* Verschluss *m*

fast 'food *n* Fast Food *nt*

fast-'forward *vt, vi* vorspulen

fastidious [fə·'stɪd·i·əs] *adj* ❶ wählerisch; *taste* anspruchsvoll; **to be very** ~ **about doing sth** sehr sorgsam darauf bedacht sein, etw zu tun ❷ (*pej*) pingelig

fat [fæt] **I.** *adj* <-tt-> ❶ (*fleshy*) dick, fett *pej;* *animal* fett ❷ (*thick*) dick ❸ (*substantial*) *profits* fett ❹ (*fam: little*) **do you think he'll win? —** ~ **chance!** glaubst du er wird gewinnen? – keine Chance! **II.** *n* Fett *nt;* **layer of** ~ Fettschicht *f*

fatal ['feɪt̬·əl] *adj* ❶ (*lethal*) tödlich ❷ (*disastrous*) fatal; ~ **blow** Todesstoß *m*

fatalism ['feɪt̬·əl·ɪz·əm] *n* Fatalismus *m*

fatalist ['feɪt̬·əl·ɪst] *n* Fatalist(in) *m(f)*

fatality [feɪ·'tæl·ə·t̬i] *n* Todesopfer *nt*

fatally ['feɪ·t̬əl·i] *adv* ❶ (*mortally*) tödlich; ~ **ill** sterbenskrank ❷ (*disastrously*) hoffnungslos; **his reputation was** ~ **damaged** sein Ansehen war für immer geschädigt

'fat cat *n* (*pej*) Bonze *m*

fate [feɪt] *n* Schicksal *nt;* **a twist of** ~ eine Fügung des Schicksals

fated ['feɪ·t̬ɪd] *adj* **to be** ~ **to fail** zum Scheitern verurteilt sein

fateful ['feɪt·fəl] *adj* schicksalhaft; *decision* verhängnisvoll

'fat-free *adj* fettfrei

F

'fathead *n* (*fam*) Schafskopf *m*

father ['fa·ðər] **I.** *n* Vater *m;* **on one's ~'s side** väterlicherseits **II.** *vt* **to ~ a child** ein Kind zeugen

fatherhood ['fa·ðər·hʊd] *n* Vaterschaft *f*

'father-in-law <*pl* fathers-> *n* Schwiegervater *m*

'fatherland *n* Vaterland *nt*

fatherless ['fa·ðər·lɪs] *adj* vaterlos

fatherly ['fa·ðər·li] *adj* väterlich

fathom ['fæð·əm] **I.** *n* Faden *m* (*= ca. 1,8 m*) **II.** *vt* begreifen

fathomless ['fæð·əm·lɪs] *adj* unergründlich

fatigue [fə·'tig] **I.** *n* ❶ Ermüdung *f;* **donor ~** Nachlassen *nt* der Spendenfreudigkeit ❷ MIL ■ **~s** *pl* (*uniform*) Arbeitskleidung *f kein pl* **II.** *vt, vi* ermüden

fatten ['fæt·ən] *vt animal* mästen; *person* aufpäppeln

fattening ['fæt·ən·ɪŋ] *adj* **to be ~** dick machen

fatty ['fæt̬·i] **I.** *adj* ❶ (*containing fat*) *food* fetthaltig, fett ❷ (*consisting of fat*) Fett-; **~ acid** Fettsäure *f;* **~ tissue** Fettgewebe *nt* **II.** *n* (*pej fam*) Dickerchen *nt*

fatuous ['fætʃ·u·əs] *adj* (*form*) albern

faucet ['fɔ·sɪt] *n* Wasserhahn *m*

fault [fɔlt] **I.** *n* ❶ (*responsibility*) Schuld *f;* **it's your own ~** du bist selbst schuld daran; **to find ~ with sb/sth** etw an jdm/etw auszusetzen haben; **through no ~ of his own** ohne sein eigenes Verschulden ❷ (*weakness*) Fehler *m;* **his main ~** seine größte Schwäche ❸ (*defect*) Fehler *m,* Defekt *m;* **a ~ on the line** eine Störung in der Leitung ❹ TENNIS Fehler *m* **II.** *vt* ■ **to ~ sb/sth** [einen] Fehler an jdm/etw finden

faultless ['fɔlt·lɪs] *adj* fehlerfrei; *performance a.* fehlerlos

faulty ['fɔl·ti] *adj* ❶ (*unsound*) fehlerhaft ❷ (*defective*) defekt

fauna ['fɔ·nə] *n + sing/pl vb* Fauna *f*

favor ['feɪ·vər] **I.** *n* ❶ (*approval*) **in ~ of** für; ■ **to be in ~** dafür sein; **all those in ~, ...** alle, die dafür sind, ...; **to fall out of ~** in Ungnade fallen ❷ (*advantage*) **in ~ of** für; **to reject sb/sth in ~ of sb/sth** jdm/etw gegenüber jdm/etw den Vorzug geben; **to rule in sb's ~** SPORTS für jdn entscheiden ❸ (*kind act*) Gefallen *m kein pl;* **do it as a ~ to me** tu es mir zuliebe; **to do sb a ~** [*or* **a ~ for sb**] jdm einen Gefallen tun **II.** *vt* ❶ (*prefer*) vorziehen ❷ (*approve*) gutheißen; ■ **to ~ doing sth** es gutheißen, etw zu tun ❸ (*be partial*) bevorzugen; SPORTS favorisieren

favorable ['feɪ·vər·ə·bəl] *adj* ❶ (*approving*) positiv, zustimmend; *impression* sympathisch; **in a ~ light** mit Wohlwollen ❷ (*advantageous*) günstig (**to** für *+akk*)

favored ['feɪ·vərd] *adj* ❶ (*preferred*) bevorzugt ❷ (*privileged*) begünstigt

favorite ['feɪ·vər·ɪt] **I.** *adj* Lieblings- **II.** *n* ❶ (*best-liked*) *person* Liebling *m; thing;* **which one's your ~?** welches magst du am liebsten?; ■ **to be a ~ with sb** bei jdm sehr beliebt sein ❷ (*contestant*) Favorit(in) *m(f)* ❸ (*privileged person*) Liebling *m*

favoritism ['feɪ·vər·ɪ·tɪz·əm] *n* (*pej*) Begünstigung *f*

fawn¹ [fɔn] *vi* (*pej*) ■ **to ~ over sb** vor jdm katzbuckeln

fawn² [fɔn] **I.** *n* ❶ (*deer*) Rehkitz *nt* ❷ (*brown*) Rehbraun *nt* **II.** *adj* rehbraun

fawning ['fɔ·nɪŋ] *adj* (*pej*) kriecherisch; *review* schmeichelhaft

fax [fæks] **I.** *n* Fax *nt;* **by ~** per Fax **II.** *vt* faxen

'fax machine *n* Fax[gerät] *nt*

FBI [ˌef·bi·'aɪ] *n abbrev of* **Federal Bureau of Investigation** FBI *nt*

> Das **FBI, the Federal Bureau of Investigation,** ist die Bundeskriminalpolizei. Die Amtsträger heißen *FBI agents* oder *federal agents*. Gegründet wurde die Behörde am 26. Juli 1908 und hat ihren Hauptsitz in Washington D. C. Sein Einsatzschwerpunkt dient der Aufrechterhaltung von Recht und Gesetz und dem Schutz vor terroristischen Aktivitäten.

fear [fɪr] **I.** *n* ❶ (*dread*) Angst *f,* Furcht *f;* **to have a ~ of sth** vor etw *dat* Angst haben; ■ **for ~ that ...** aus Angst, dass ...; **in ~ of one's life** in Todesangst ❷ (*worry*) **~s for sb's safety** Sorge *f* um jds Sicherheit; **sb's worst ~s** jds schlimmste Befürchtungen **II.** *vt* ❶ (*dread*) fürchten; **nothing to ~** nichts zu befürchten ❷ (*form: regret*) ■ **to ~** [**that**] ... befürchten, dass ... **III.** *vi* ■ **to ~ for sb/sth** sich *dat* um jdn/etw Sorgen machen; **to ~ for sb's life** um jds Leben fürchten

fearful ['fɪr·fəl] *adj* ❶ (*anxious*) ängstlich; **she was ~ of what he might say** sie hatte Angst davor, was er sagen würde; **~ of causing a scene, ...** aus Angst, eine Szene auszulösen, ... ❷ (*terrible*) schrecklich

fearless ['fɪr·lɪs] *adj* furchtlos

fearsome ['fɪr·səm] *adj* Furcht einflößend

feasibility [ˌfi·zə·'bɪl·ɪ·t̬i] *n* Machbarkeit *f; of plan* Durchführbarkeit *f;* **~ study** Machbarkeitsstudie *f*

feasible ['fi·zə·bəl] *adj* ❶ (*practicable*) durchführbar; **technically ~** technisch machbar ❷ (*possible*) möglich ❸ (*fam: plausible*) glaubhaft

feast [fist] **I.** *n* Festessen *nt;* **~ for the ears/eyes** Ohrenschmaus *m*/Augenweide *f* **II.** *vi* schlemmen; ■ **to ~ on sth** sich an etw *dat* gütlich tun

feat [fit] *n* ❶ (*brave deed*) Heldentat *f* ❷ (*skillful action*) [Meister]leistung *f;* **~ of engineering** technische Großtat; **no mean ~** keine schlechte Leistung

feather ['feð·ər] *n* Feder *f* ► PHRASES: **a ~ in sb's cap** etwas, worauf jd stolz sein kann; **to ~ one's** [**own**] **nest** seine Schäfchen ins Trockene bringen

'featherweight *n* Federgewicht *nt*

feathery ['feð·ə·ri] *adj* (*covered with feathers*) gefiedert; (*like a feather*) fed[e]rig

feature ['fi·tʃər] **I.** *n* ❶ (*aspect*) Merkmal *nt,* Kennzeichen *nt;* **special ~** Besonderheit *f* ❷ (*of face*) ■ **~s** *pl* Gesichtszüge *pl* ❸ FILM, TV (*report*) Sonderbeitrag *m* (**on** *+gen*); (*film*) Spielfilm *m* **II.** *vt* ❶ (*show*) aufweisen ❷ (*star*) **featuring sb** mit jdm in der Hauptrolle ❸ (*report*) ■ **to ~ sth** über etw *akk* groß berichten **III.** *vi* ❶ (*appear*) vorkommen; **to ~ high on the list** ganz oben auf der Liste stehen ❷ (*act*) *in a film* [mit]spielen

featureless ['fi·tʃər·lɪs] *adj* ohne Besonderheiten

Feb. *n abbrev of* **February** Febr.

February ['feb·ru·er·i] *n* Februar *m,* Feber *m* ÖSTERR; **at the beginning of** [*or* **in early**] **~** Anfang Februar; **at the end of** [*or* **in late**] **~** Ende Februar; **in the middle of ~** Mitte Februar; **in the first/second half of ~** in der ersten/zweiten Februarhälfte; **for the whole of ~** den ganzen Februar über; **last/next/this ~** vergangenen [*o* letzten]/kommenden [*o* nächsten]/diesen Februar; **to be in ~** in den Februar fallen; **in/during ~** im Februar; **on ~ 14**[**th**] am 14. Februar; **on Friday, ~ 14**[**th**] am Freitag, dem [*o* den] 14. Februar

feces ['fi·siz] *npl* (*form*) Fäkalien *pl*

Fed [fed] *n* (*fam*) ❶ (*bank*) Zentralbankrat *m* ❷ (*police*) FBI-Agent(in) *m(f)*

federal ['fed·ər·əl] *adj* föderativ; **~ republic** Bundesrepublik *f;* **~ law** Bundesgesetz *nt;* **~ income tax** nationale Einkommenssteuer

federalism ['fed·ər·ə·lɪz·əm] *n* Föderalismus *m*

federalist ['fed·ər·ə·lɪst] **I.** *n* Föderalist(in) *m(f)* **II.** *adj* föderalistisch

federation [ˌfed·ə·'reɪ·ʃən] *n* Föderation *f*

'fed up *adj* (*fam*) ■ **to be ~ up** [**with sb/sth**] die Nase voll haben [von jdm/etw]

fee [fi] *n* Gebühr *f;* **legal ~s** Rechtskosten *pl;* **membership ~**[**s**] Mitgliedsbeitrag *m*

feeble <-r, -st> ['fi·bəl] *adj* schwach; *attempt* müde; *joke, excuse* lahm

feeble-'minded *adj* schwachsinnig

feebleness ['fi·bəl·nɪs] *n* Schwäche *f*

feed [fid] **I.** *n* ❶ (*fodder*) Futter *nt* ❷ TECH (*supply*) Zufuhr *f* **II.** *vt* <fed, fed> ❶ (*give food to*) ■ **to ~ sb** jdm zu essen geben; *animal, invalid* füttern; *baby* füttern; (*with bottle*) die Flasche geben; *plant* düngen; ■ **to ~ sth to an animal** etw an ein Tier verfüttern; **the baby can ~ himself now** das Baby kann jetzt allein essen ❷ (*provide food for*) ernähren; **that's not going to ~ ten people** das reicht nicht für zehn Personen ❸ (*thread*) führen; *rope* fädeln; **to ~ paper into a printer** Papier nachfüllen in einen Drucker; (*to ~ a parking meter*) Münzen in eine Parkuhr einwerfen ❹ (*give*) versorgen; *information* geben **III.** *vi* <fed, fed> (*eat*) *animal* weiden; *baby* gefüttert werden

◆**feed off, feed on** *vi* ❶ (*eat*) sich ernähren von ❷ (*fig: gain strength from*) genährt werden von

'feedback *n* ❶ (*opinion*) Feedback *nt* ❷ ELEC Rückkopplung *f*

feeder ['fi·dər] *n* (*device*) Zuführapparat *m*

'feeding *n* (*meal*) *for baby* Mahlzeit *f; for animals* Fütterung *f*

feel [fil] **I.** *vt* <felt, felt> ❶ (*sense, touch*) fühlen; **to ~ one's age** sein Alter spüren; **to ~ nothing for sb** für jdn nichts empfinden; **I had to ~ my way along the wall** ich musste mich die Wand entlangtasten ❷ (*think*) halten; **what do you ~ about it?** was hältst du davon?; ■ **to ~ that ...** der Meinung sein, dass ... **II.** *vi* <felt, felt> ❶ + *adj* (*have a feeling*) sich fühlen; **my mouth ~s dry** mein Mund fühlt sich trocken an; **my eyes ~ sore** meine Augen brennen; **how do you ~ about it?** was sagst du dazu?; **how does it ~ to be world champion?** wie fühlt man sich als Weltmeister?; **to ~ angry** wütend sein; **to ~ better/sick** sich besser/krank fühlen; **to ~ foolish** sich *dat* dumm vorkommen; **to ~ free to do sth** etw ruhig tun; **~ free to visit any time you like** du kannst uns gern jederzeit besuchen; **sb ~s hot** jdm ist heiß; ■ **to ~ as if one were doing sth** das Gefühl haben, etw zu tun; ■ **to ~ like sth** sich *akk* wie etw fühlen; **to ~ like an idiot** sich *dat* wie ein Idiot vorkommen; **to ~ like one's old self** [**again**] [wieder] ganz der/die Alte sein; **what does it ~ like?** was für ein Gefühl ist das?; **to ~ for sb** mit jdm fühlen ❷ + *adj* (*seem*) scheinen ❸ (*search*) tasten (**for** nach *+dat*) ❹ (*want*) ■ **to ~ like sth** zu etw *dat* Lust haben; ■ **to ~ like doing sth** Lust haben auf *+akk* etw **III.** *n* ❶ (*texture*) **the ~ of wool** das Gefühl von Wolle; **to recognize sth by the ~ of it** etw beim Anfassen erkennen ❷ (*touch*) Berühren *nt;* (*by holding*) Anfassen *nt* ❸ (*talent*) Gespür *nt;* **to get the ~ for sth** ein Gespür für etw bekommen; **~ for language** Sprachgefühl *nt*

◆**feel up I.** *vt* (*fam*) begrapschen **II.** *vi* ■ **to ~ up to sth** sich etw *dat* gewachsen fühlen

feeler ['fi·lər] *n usu pl* Fühler *m*

'feel-good *adj* ein Wohlgefühl erzeugend

feeling ['fi·lɪŋ] *n* ❶ Gefühl *nt* (**of** *+gen*/von *+dat*); **to cause bad ~s** böses Blut verursachen; **~ of tension** angespannte Stimmung; **no hard ~s!** nichts für ungut!; **to have a ~ that ...** das Gefühl haben, dass ... ❷ (*opinion*) Ansicht *f* (**about/on** über *+akk*); **what are your ~s about ...?** wie denken Sie über ...?

feet [fit] *n pl of* **foot**

feign [feɪn] *vt* vortäuschen

feline ['fi·laɪn] *adj* (*of cats*) Katzen-; (*catlike*) katzenartig

fell[1] [fel] *pt of* **fall**

fell[2] [fel] *vt* ❶ (*cut down*) fällen ❷ (*knock down*) ■ **to ~ sb** jdn niederstrecken

fellow ['fel·oʊ] **I.** *n* ❶ (*fam: man*) Kerl *m*

② (*graduate student*) Fellow *m* **II.** *adj* ~ **citizen** Mitbürger(in) *m(f)*; ~ **countryman** Landsmann *m*, Landsmännin *f*; ~ **countrymen** *pl* Landsleute; ~ **sufferer** Leidensgenosse, -in *m, f*
fellowship ['fel·oʊ·ʃɪp] *n* ① (*group*) Gesellschaft *f* ② (*graduate position*) Fellowship *f* ③ (*award*) Stipendium *nt*
felon ['fel·ən] *n* LAW [Schwer]verbrecher(in) *m(f)*
felony ['fel·ə·ni] *n* [Schwer]verbrechen *nt*
felt¹ [felt] *pt, pp of* **feel**
felt² [felt] *n* Filz *m*
'felt tip, felt tip 'pen *n* Filzstift *m*
female ['fi·meɪl] **I.** *adj* weiblich **II.** *n* ① (*animal*) Weibchen *nt* ② (*woman*) Frau *f*
feminine ['fem·ə·nɪn] **I.** *adj* feminin, weiblich **II.** *n* Femininum *nt*
femininity [ˌfem·ə·'nɪn·ɪ·t̬i] *n* Weiblichkeit *f*
feminism ['fem·ə·nɪz·əm] *n* Feminismus *m*
feminist ['fem·ə·nɪst] **I.** *n* Feminist(in) *m(f)* **II.** *adj* feministisch
fence [fens] **I.** *n* ① (*barrier*) Zaun *m* ② (*in horse race*) Hindernis *nt* ③ (*sl: criminal*) Hehler(in) *m(f)* ▶ PHRASES: **to sit on the** ~ neutral bleiben **II.** *vi* fechten **III.** *vt* einzäunen
fencer ['fen·sər] *n* Fechter(in) *m(f)*
fencing ['fen·sɪŋ] *n* ① SPORTS Fechten *nt* ② (*barrier*) Einzäunung *f* ③ (*materials*) Einzäunungsmaterial *nt*
fend [fend] *vi* (*care*) ■ **to** ~ **for oneself** für sich selbst sorgen
◆ **fend off** *vt* ■ **to** ~ **off** ○ **sb/sth** jdn/etw abwehren; *criticism* zurückweisen
fender ['fen·dər] *n* AUTO Kotflügel *m*
fennel ['fen·əl] *n* Fenchel *m*
ferment I. *vt* [fər·'ment] ① CHEM fermentieren ② (*form: arouse*) schüren **II.** *vi* [fər·'ment] gären **III.** *n* ['fɜr·mənt] (*form*) Unruhe *f*
fermentation [ˌfɜr·mən·'teɪ·ʃən] *n* Gärung *f*
fern [fɜrn] *n* Farn *m*
ferocious [fə·'roʊ·ʃəs] *adj* wild; *fighting* heftig; *heat* brütend
ferociousness [fə'roʊ·ʃəs·nɪs], **ferocity** [fə·'ras·ə·t̬i] *n* Wildheit *f; of attack, storm* Heftigkeit *f*
ferret ['fer·ɪt] **I.** *n* Frettchen *nt* **II.** *vi* (*fam*) ■ **to** ~ [**around**] [**for sth**] [nach etw] wühlen
Ferris wheel ['fer·ɪs·ˌhwil] *n* Riesenrad *nt*
ferry ['fer·i] **I.** *n* Fähre *f* **II.** *vt* <-ie-> ① (*across water*) **to** ~ [**across** [*or* **over**]] übersetzen ② (*transport*) befördern; **to** ~ **sb around** jdn herumfahren
'ferryman *n* Fährmann *m*
fertile ['fɜr·t̬əl] *adj* fruchtbar; (*fig*) *imagination* lebhaft
fertility [fər·'tɪl·ɪ·t̬i] *n* Fruchtbarkeit *f*
fertilization [ˌfɜr·t̬əl·ɪ·'zeɪ·ʃən] *n* Befruchtung *f*
fertilize ['fɜr·t̬əl·aɪz] *vt* ① AGR düngen ② BIOL befruchten
fertilizer ['fɜr·t̬əl·aɪ·zər] *n* Dünger *m*
fervent ['fɜr·vənt] *adj* (*form*) ① *hope* inbrünstig ② *supporter* glühend
fervor ['fɜr·vər] *n* (*form*) Leidenschaft *f*
fester ['fes·tər] *vi* ① MED eitern ② (*fig*) gären
festival ['fes·tɪ·vəl] *n* ① (*event*) Festival *nt* ② (*holy day*) Fest *nt*
festive ['fes·tɪv] *adj* festlich
festivity [fes·'tɪv·ɪ·t̬i] *n* ① (*celebrations*) ■ **festivities** *pl* Feierlichkeiten *pl* ② (*festiveness*) Feststimmung *f*
festoon [fe·'stun] *vt* [mit Girlanden] schmücken
fetal ['fi·t̬l] *adj* fetal
fetch [fetʃ] **I.** *vt* ① (*get, collect*) abholen ② (*be sold for*) erzielen **II.** *vi* ~**!** bring [es] her!
fetching ['fetʃ·ɪŋ] *adj* schick
fetid ['fet̬·ɪd] *adj* übel riechend
fetish ['fet̬·ɪʃ] *n* Fetisch *m*
fetishist ['fet̬·ɪʃ·ɪst] *n* Fetischist(in) *m(f)*
fetter ['fet̬·ər] *vt* ① fesseln; *horse* anbinden ② (*fig: restrict*) einschränken
fetus ['fi·t̬əs] *n* Fetus *m*
feud [fjud] **I.** *n* Fehde *f* (**over** wegen +*akk*) **II.** *vi* in Fehde liegen
feudal ['fjud·əl] *adj* Feudal-
fever ['fi·vər] *n* ① (*temperature*) Fieber *nt kein pl* ② (*excitement*) Aufregung *f*; **baseball** ~ Baseballfieber *nt*; **at** ~ **pitch** fieberhaft
feverish ['fi·vər·ɪʃ] *adj* ① (*ill*) fiebrig ② (*frantic*) fieberhaft
few [fju] **I.** *adj* ① (*some*) **a** ~ ein paar, einige; **can I have a** ~ **words with you?** kann ich mal kurz mit dir sprechen?; **quite a** ~ ziemlich viele ② (*not many*) wenige; ~**er people** weniger Menschen; **he's a man of** ~ **words** er sagt nie viel; **as** ~ **as ...** nur ... ▶ PHRASES: ~ **and far between** dünn gesät **II.** *pron* ① (*some*) **a** ~ **of us** einige von uns; **quite a** ~ eine ganze Menge ② (*not many*) wenige; **the** ~ **who came ...** die paar, die kamen, ...; ~ **of the houses** nur wenige Häuser; **there were too** ~ **of us** wir waren nicht genug **III.** *n* (*minority*) ■ **the** ~ *pl* die Minderheit, die Wenigen; **I was one of the lucky** ~ **who ...** ich gehörte zu den wenigen Glücklichen, die ...
fiancé [ˌfi·an·'seɪ] *n* Verlobte(r) *m*
fiancée [ˌfi·an·'seɪ] *n* Verlobte *f*
fiasco <*pl* -es *or* -s> [fɪ·'æs·koʊ] *n* Fiasko *nt*
fib [fɪb] (*fam*) **I.** *vi* <-bb-> schwindeln; ■ **to** ~ **to sb** jdn anschwindeln **II.** *n* Schwindelei *f*
fibber ['fɪb·ər] *n* (*fam*) Schwindler(in) *m(f)*
fiber ['faɪ·bər] *n* ① (*thread*) Faden *m*; (*for cloth*) Faser *f* ② ANAT Faser *f* ③ FOOD Ballaststoffe *pl*
'fiberglass *n* ① (*plastic*) glasfaserverstärkter Kunststoff ② (*fabric*) Glasfaser *f*
fiber optic 'cable *n* Glasfaserkabel *nt*
fiber 'optics *n* + *sing vb* TELEC, COMPUT Glasfasertechnik *f*; MED, PHYS [Glas]faseroptik *f*
fibula <*pl* -s *or* -lae> ['fɪb·jə·lə, *pl* -li] *n* Wadenbein *nt*
fickle ['fɪk·l] *adj* (*pej*) ① (*vacillating*) wankelmütig ② (*not loyal*) untreu
fiction ['fɪk·ʃən] *n* ① LIT Erzählliteratur *f* ② (*fabrication*) Erfindung *f*

fictional ['fɪk·ʃə·nəl] *adj* erfunden; *character* fiktiv
fictitious [fɪk·'tɪʃ·əs] *adj* ① (*false*) falsch ② (*imaginary*) [frei] erfunden; *character* fiktiv
fiddle ['fɪd·l] **I.** *n* (*fam*) MUS Fidel *f* ▶ PHRASES: [as] fit as a ~ kerngesund **II.** *vi* ① MUS geigen ② (*finger*) herumspielen; ■ **to ~ with sth** an etw *dat* herumfummeln ③ (*tinker*) ■ **to ~ [around] with sth** an etw *dat* herumbasteln
fiddler ['fɪd·lər] *n* (*fam*) Geiger(in) *m(f)*
fiddling ['fɪd·lɪŋ] *adj* belanglos
fidelity [fɪ·'del·ɪ·t̬i] *n* Treue *f* (**to** gegenüber +*dat*)
fidget ['fɪdʒ·ɪt] *vi* zappeln
fidgety ['fɪdʒ·ɪ·t̬i] *adj* zapp[e]lig
field [fild] **I.** *n* ① (*meadow*) Wiese *f;* (*pasture*) Weide *f;* (*for crops*) Feld *nt,* Acker *m* ② SPORTS (*playing area*) [Spiel]feld *nt,* Platz *m;* (*contestants*) [Teilnehmer]feld *nt* ③ (*area of knowledge*) Gebiet *nt* ④ MATH, PHYS Feld *nt* **II.** *vi* SPORTS als Fänger *m* spielen, fielden **III.** *vt* ① (*stop*) *ball* fangen, fielden ② (*handle*) *questions* parieren; *phone calls* abweisen
'**field day** *n* ① [Schul]sportfest *nt* ② (*fig*) **to have a ~** seinen großen Tag haben
fielder ['fil·dər] *n* SPORTS Fielder(in) *m(f),* Fänger(in) *m(f)*
'**field events** *npl* SPORTS Sprung- und Wurfdisziplinen *pl*
'**field glasses** *npl* Feldstecher *m*
'**field mouse** *n* Feldmaus *f*
'**field trip** *n* Exkursion *f*
'**fieldwork** *n* Feldforschung *f*
fiend [find] *n* ① (*devil*) Teufel *m* ② (*fig fam: enthusiast*) Fanatiker, -in *m, f*
fiendish ['fin·dɪʃ] *adj* teuflisch
fierce [fɪrs] *adj* ① *animal* wild ② *attack, competition* scharf; *debate* hitzig; *fighting* erbittert; *opposition* entschlossen; *winds* tobend
fierceness ['fɪrs·nɪs] *n* ① (*hostility*) Wildheit *f* ② (*intensity*) Intensität *f* ③ (*destructiveness*) Heftigkeit *f*
fiery ['faɪr·i] *adj* ① (*burning*) glühend ② (*spicy*) feurig ③ (*passionate*) leidenschaftlich
fifteen [ˌfɪf·'tin] **I.** *adj* fünfzehn; **~ hundred hours** *spoken* fünfzehn Uhr; **1500 hours** *written* 15:00 **II.** *n* Fünfzehn *f; see also* **eight**
fifteenth [fɪf·'tinθ] **I.** *adj* fünfzehnte(r, s) **II.** *n* ① (*order*) ■ **the ~** der/die/das Fünfzehnte ② (*date*) ■ **the ~** der Fünfzehnte ③ (*fraction*) Fünfzehntel *nt*
fifth [fɪfθ] **I.** *adj* fünfte(r, s); **every ~ person** jeder Fünfte **II.** *n* ① (*order*) ■ **the ~** der/die/das Fünfte ② (*date*) **the ~** der Fünfte ③ (*fraction*) Fünftel *nt* ④ (*gear*) fünfter Gang **III.** *adv* fünftens; *see also* **eighth**
fiftieth ['fɪf·ti·əθ] **I.** *adj* fünfzigste(r, s) **II.** *n* ① (*order*) ■ **the ~** der/die/das Fünfzigste ② (*fraction*) Fünfzigstel *nt* **III.** *adv* fünfzigstens; *see also* **eighth**
fifty ['fɪf·ti] **I.** *adj* fünfzig **II.** *n* ① (*number*) Fünfzig *f* ② (*paper money*) Fünfziger *m; see also* **eight**

fig [fɪg] *n* FOOD Feige *f*
fig. [fɪg] **I.** *n abbrev of* **figure** Abb. *f* **II.** *adj abbrev of* **figurative** fig.
fight [faɪt] **I.** *n* ① Kampf *m* (**against/for** gegen/um +*akk*); (*brawl*) Rauferei *f;* (*involving fists*) Schlägerei *f;* **to give up without a ~** kampflos aufgeben; **to put up a ~** sich wehren ② MIL Gefecht *nt* **II.** *vi* <fought, fought> ① kämpfen; *children* sich raufen; ■ **to ~ with sb** (*against*) gegen jdn kämpfen; (*on same side*) an jds Seite *f* kämpfen; **to ~ for air/one's life** nach Luft ringen/um sein Leben kämpfen ② (*argue*) sich streiten (**about/over** um +*akk*) **III.** *vt* <fought, fought> ① kämpfen (**against** gegen +*akk*); *battle* schlagen; *crime, fire* bekämpfen; *disease* ankämpfen gegen; *duel* austragen; **to ~ one's way to the top** sich an die Spitze kämpfen ② (*in boxing*) boxen gegen +*akk*
◆**fight back** **I.** *vi* zurückschlagen; (*defend oneself*) sich zur Wehr setzen **II.** *vt tears* unterdrücken
◆**fight off** *vt* ■ **to ~ off ⊂ sb** jdn abwehren; *reporter* abwimmeln; ■ **to ~ off ⊂ sth** etw bekämpfen
fighter ['faɪ·t̬ər] *n* ① Kämpfer(in) *m(f)* ② (*boxer*) Boxer(in) *m(f)* ③ (*plane*) Kampfflugzeug *nt*
fighting ['faɪ·t̬ɪŋ] **I.** *n* ① (*hostilities*) Kämpfe *pl* ② (*fist fights*) Schlägereien *pl* **II.** *adj* kämpferisch
figment ['fɪg·mənt] *n* **a ~ of sb's imagination** reine Einbildung
figurative ['fɪg·jər·ə·t̬ɪv] *adj* (*metaphorical*) bildlich; LING figurativ; *sense* übertragen
figuratively ['fɪg·jər·ə·t̬ɪv·li] *adv* bildlich, figurativ
figure ['fɪg·jər] **I.** *n* ① (*shape*) Figur *f* ② (*person*) Gestalt *f;* (*personality*) Persönlichkeit *f* ③ MATH (*digit*) Ziffer *f;* (*numeral*) Zahl *f;* **he is good with ~s** er ist ein guter Rechner; **column of ~s** Zahlenreihe *f* ④ (*amount of money*) Betrag *m* **II.** *vt* ① (*envisage*) voraussehen; (*predict*) voraussagen; (*estimate*) schätzen ② (*consider*) verstehen **III.** *vi* ① (*feature*) eine Rolle spielen ② (*count on*) ■ **to ~ on sth** mit etw *dat* rechnen ③ (*make sense*) **that** [*or* **it**] **~s** das hätte ich mir denken können
◆**figure out** *vt* ① (*work out*) herausfinden; MATH ausrechnen ② (*understand*) begreifen; ■ **to ~ out ⊂ sth/sb** etw/jdn verstehen; **we're still trying to ~ out why/how ...** wir versuchen immer noch herauszukriegen, warum/wie ...
figure 'eight *n* SPORT Achter *m*
'**figurehead** *n* Galionsfigur *f a. fig*
'**figure skater** *n* Eiskunstläufer(in) *m(f)*
'**figure skating** *n* Eiskunstlauf *m*
filament ['fɪl·ə·mənt] *n* ① (*fiber*) Faden *m* ② ELEC Glühfaden *m* ③ BOT Filament *nt*
file[1] [faɪl] **I.** *n* ① (*folder*) [Akten]hefter *m;* (*loose-leaf*) [Akten]mappe *f* ② (*database*) Akte *f* (**on** über +*akk*); **to keep sth on ~** etw

aufbewahren ③ COMPUT Datei *f* **II.** *vt* ① (*put in folder*) ablegen, abheften; (*in order*) einordnen ② (*submit*) abgeben; JOURN einsenden; LAW einreichen **III.** *vi* LAW **to ~ for bankruptcy** einen Konkursantrag stellen; **to ~ for divorce** die Scheidung beantragen

◆**file away** *vt* ■**to ~ away ↻ sth** etw zu den Akten legen

file² [faɪl] **I.** *n* (*line*) Reihe *f;* **in single ~** im Gänsemarsch **II.** *vi* nacheinander gehen

file³ [faɪl] **I.** *n* (*tool*) Feile *f* **II.** *vt* (*smooth*) feilen; ■**to ~ down** abfeilen

filet [fɪ·ˈleɪ, ˈfɪ·leɪ] *n, vt see* **fillet**

filibuster [ˈfɪl·ɪ·bʌs·tər] **I.** *n* Obstruktion *f* **II.** *vi* Obstruktion betreiben *geh*

filing [ˈfaɪ·lɪŋ] *n* ① (*archiving*) Ablage *f* ② (*registration*) Einreichung *f* ③ COMPUT Archivierung *f*

ˈfiling cabinet *n* Aktenschrank *m*

fill [fɪl] **I.** *n* **to have one's ~ of sth** genug von etw *dat* haben **II.** *vt* ① (*make full*) füllen; *pipe* stopfen; *tooth* plombieren; *gap* schließen; *vacancy* besetzen ② (*pervade*) *building, room* erfüllen ③ (*cause to feel*) **to ~ sb with fear/joy** jdn mit Furcht/Freude erfüllen **III.** *vi* sich füllen; **their eyes ~ed with tears** sie hatten Tränen in den Augen, ihnen traten [die] Tränen in die Augen

◆**fill in I.** *vt* ① (*inform*) ■**to ~ in ↻ sb [on sth]** jdn [über etw *akk*] informieren ② (*seal*) [aus]füllen; *cracks* zuspachteln ③ (*complete*) *form* ausfüllen; *name and address* eintragen **II.** *vi* ■**to ~ in [for sb]** [für jdn] einspringen

◆**fill out I.** *vt* ausfüllen **II.** *vi* (*expand*) sich ausdehnen; (*gain weight*) fülliger werden

◆**fill up I.** *vt* ① (*make full*) *bucket* vollfüllen ② (*occupy entire space*) ausfüllen; **the painting ~s up the entire wall** das Bild füllt die gesamte Wand aus ③ AUTO volltanken **II.** *vi* ① (*become full*) sich füllen ② AUTO [voll]tanken

filler [ˈfɪl·ər] *n* ① (*for cracks*) Spachtelmasse *f;* **wood ~** Porenfüller *m* ② (*for adding bulk*) Füllmaterial *nt*

fillet [ˈfɪl·ɪt], **filet** [fɪ·ˈleɪ, ˈfɪ·leɪ] **I.** *n* FOOD Filet *nt* **II.** *vt* ① (*remove bones*) *fish* entgräten; *meat* entbeinen ② (*cut into pieces*) filetieren

filling [ˈfɪl·ɪŋ] **I.** *n* ① (*material*) Füllmasse *f* ② (*for teeth*) Füllung *f* ③ FOOD Füllung *f;* (*in a sandwich*) Belag *m* **II.** *adj* sättigend

ˈfilling station *n* Tankstelle *f*

fillip [ˈfɪl·ɪp] *n* ■**to give sb a ~** jdn anspornen

film [fɪlm] **I.** *n* ① FILM, PHOT Film *m* ② (*layer*) Schicht *f;* **~ of oil** Ölfilm *m* **II.** *adj* Film- **III.** *vt* filmen; *book* verfilmen; *scene* drehen **IV.** *vi* filmen, drehen

filter [ˈfɪl·tər] **I.** *n* Filter *m* **II.** *vt* ① (*process, purify*) filtern ② (*fig*) selektieren **III.** *vi light, sound* dringen (**into** in +*akk*)

◆**filter out I.** *vi* (*leak*) durchsickern **II.** *vt* herausfiltern (**from** aus +*dat*)

◆**filter through** *vi light* durchscheinen; *liquid* durchsickern; *sound* durchdringen; (*fig*) *reports* durchsickern

filth [fɪlθ] *n* ① (*dirt*) Dreck *m,* Schmutz *m* ② (*pej: obscenity*) Schmutz *m,* Obszönitäten *pl*

filthy [ˈfɪl·θi] *adj* ① (*dirty*) schmutzig, dreckig *fam,* verdreckt *pej fam* ② (*bad-tempered*) *look* vernichtend; *temper* aufbrausend ③ (*pej fam: obscene*) schmutzig; *language* obszön; *habit* widerlich

filtration [fɪl·ˈtreɪ·ʃən] *n* Filterung *f*

fin [fɪn] *n* Flosse *f*

final [ˈfaɪ·nəl] **I.** *adj* ① (*last*) letzte(r, s); **in the ~ analysis** letzten Endes; **~ chapter** Schlusskapitel *nt;* SPORTS End-; **~ score** Endstand *m;* **~ round** Endrunde *f* ② (*decisive*) endgültig; **to have the ~ say [on sth]** [bei etw] das letzte Wort haben; **that's ~!** und damit basta! **II.** *n* ① (*concluding match*) Endspiel *nt,* Finale *nt* ② (*test*) ■**~s** *pl* UNIV [Schluss]examen *nt;* SCH Abschlussprüfung *f*

finale [fɪ·ˈnæl·i] *n* Finale *nt;* (*fig*) [krönender] Abschluss

finalist [ˈfaɪ·nə·lɪst] *n* Finalist(in) *m(f)*

finality [faɪ·ˈnæl·ɪ·t̬i] *n* ① (*irreversibility*) Endgültigkeit *f* ② (*determination*) Entschiedenheit *f*

finalize [ˈfaɪ·nə·laɪz] *vt* ① (*complete*) zum Abschluss bringen ② (*agree on*) endgültig festlegen

finally [ˈfaɪ·nə·li] *adv* ① (*at long last*) schließlich; (*expressing relief*) endlich ② (*in conclusion*) abschließend, zum Schluss

finance [ˈfaɪ·næns] **I.** *n* ① (*money management*) Finanzwirtschaft *f* ② (*money*) ■**~s** *pl* Geldmittel *pl,* Finanzen *pl* **II.** *vt* finanzieren

ˈfinance company *n* Finanzierungsgesellschaft *f*

financial [faɪ·ˈnæn·ʃəl] *adj* finanziell, Finanz-; **~ resources** Geldmittel *pl*

financial ˈaid *n* Stipendium *nt*

finch <*pl* -es> [fɪntʃ] *n* Fink *m*

find [faɪnd] **I.** *n* (*thing*) Fund *m;* (*person*) Entdeckung *f* **II.** *vt* <found, found> finden; *money for sth* aufbringen; **she was found unconscious** sie wurde bewusstlos aufgefunden; ■**to ~ oneself** (*in a place*) sich befinden; (*discover one's true nature*) zu sich selbst finden; ■**to ~ sb/sth [to be sth]** jdn/etw [als etw] empfinden; **to ~ sb guilty** jdn für schuldig erklären; ■**to ~ that ...** feststellen, dass ...; (*come to realize*) sehen, dass ...; **I wish I could ~ more time for reading** ich wünschte, ich hätte mehr Zeit zum Lesen; **she found her boyfriend a job** sie besorgte ihrem Freund eine Stelle

◆**find out I.** *vt* ① (*detect*) erwischen ② (*discover*) herausfinden **II.** *vi* dahinterkommen; ■**to ~ out about sb/sth** (*get information*) sich über jdn/etw informieren; (*learn*) über jdn/etw etwas erfahren

finder [ˈfaɪn·dər] *n of sth lost* Finder(in) *m(f); of sth unknown* Entdecker(in) *m(f)*

finding [ˈfaɪn·dɪŋ] *n* ① (*discovery*) Entdeckung *f* ② (*result of inquiry*) [Urteils]spruch *m;*

usu pl (*result of investigation*) Ergebnis *nt*
fine[1] [faɪn] **I.** *adj* ❶ (*acceptable*) in Ordnung; **seven's ~ by me** sieben [Uhr] passt mir gut ❷ (*excellent*) glänzend; *food* ausgezeichnet; *wine* erlesen ❸ (*slender, cut small*) fein; *slice* dünn ❹ METEO schön ❺ (*subtle*) fein; **~r points** Feinheiten *pl;* **not to put too ~ a point on it ...** um ganz offen zu sein ... **II.** *adv* ❶ (*all right*) fein, [sehr] gut ❷ (*thinly*) fein
fine[2] [faɪn] **I.** *n* (*punishment*) Geldstrafe *f;* (*for minor offenses*) Bußgeld *nt* **II.** *vt person* zu einer Geldstrafe verurteilen; (*for minor offenses*) ein Bußgeld verhängen gegen *+akk*
fine 'art *n,* **fine 'arts** *npl* schöne Künste
fineness ['faɪn·nɪs] *n* Feinheit *f*
fine 'print *n* ■ **the ~** das Kleingedruckte
finery ['faɪ·nə·ri] *n* Staat *m*
finesse [fɪ·'nes] **I.** *n* ❶ (*delicacy*) Feinheit *f* ❷ (*skill*) Geschick *nt* **II.** *vt* deichseln
fine-tooth 'comb, fine-toothed 'comb *n* ▶ PHRASES: **to go through** [*or* **over**] **sth with a ~** etw sorgfältig unter die Lupe nehmen
fine-'tune *vt* ■ **to ~ sth** etw fein abstimmen
finger ['fɪŋ·gər] **I.** *n* Finger *m* ▶ PHRASES: **to keep one's ~s crossed** [**for sb**] [jdm] die Daumen drücken; **to not lift** [*or* **raise**] **a ~** keinen Finger rühren; **to put one's ~ on sth** etw genau ausmachen **II.** *vt* ❶ (*touch*) anfassen; (*play with*) befingern; **to ~ the strings** in die Saiten greifen ❷ (*fam: inform on*) verpfeifen (**to** bei *+dat*) ❸ (*choose*) aussuchen
fingering ['fɪŋ·gər·ɪŋ] *n* MUS ❶ (*technique*) Fingertechnik *f* ❷ (*marking*) Fingersatz *m*
'fingernail *n* Fingernagel *m*
'fingerprint I. *n* Fingerabdruck *m* **II.** *vt* ■ **to ~ sb** jdm die Fingerabdrücke abnehmen
'fingertip *n* Fingerspitze *f* ▶ PHRASES: **to have sth at one's ~s** etw perfekt beherrschen
finish ['fɪn·ɪʃ] **I.** *n* ❶ (*final stage*) Ende *nt; of race* Endspurt *m,* Finish *nt;* (*finishing line*) Ziel *nt* ❷ (*final treatment*) letzter Schliff; (*sealing, varnishing*) Finish *nt* ▶ PHRASES: **a fight to the ~** ein Kampf *m* bis zur Entscheidung **II.** *vi* enden, aufhören; (*conclude*) schließen; **are you ~ed yet?** (*iron*) bist du endlich fertig?; **to ~ second** als Zweiter fertig sein; SPORTS Zweiter werden; ■ **to ~ with sth** etw nicht mehr brauchen; ■ **to ~ with sb** Schluss machen mit jdm; **are you ~ed with the screwdriver?** brauchst du den Schraubenzieher noch? **III.** *vt* ❶ (*bring to end*) beenden; *book* zu Ende lesen; *sentence* zu Ende sprechen; ■ **to ~ doing sth** mit etw *dat* fertig sein ❷ SCH abschließen ❸ (*bring to completion*) **to ~ sth** etw fertigstellen; (*give final treatment*) etw *dat* den letzten Schliff geben ❹ *food* aufessen; *drink* austrinken
◆**finish off I.** *vt* ❶ (*get done*) fertigstellen ❷ (*make nice*) den letzten Schliff geben ❸ (*beat*) bezwingen; (*tire out*) schaffen; (*sl: murder*) erledigen **II.** *vi* ❶ (*end*) abschließen ❷ (*get work done*) fertig werden
◆**finish up I.** *vi* fertig werden **II.** *vt food* aufessen; *drink* austrinken
finished ['fɪn·ɪʃt] *adj* ❶ fertig; ■ **~ with sth** mit etw *dat* fertig; **the ~ product** das Endprodukt ❷ **beautifully ~** wunderbar bearbeitet ❸ (*ruined*) erledigt; *career* zu Ende
'finish line *n* SPORTS Ziellinie *f*
finite ['faɪ·naɪt] *adj* begrenzt; MATH endlich; LING *verb* finit
Finland ['fɪn·lənd] *n* Finnland *nt*
Finn [fɪn] *n* Finne, -in *m, f*
Finnish ['fɪn·ɪʃ] **I.** *n* Finnisch *nt* **II.** *adj* finnisch; **the ~ people** die Finnen
fiord [fjɔrd] *n* Fjord *m*
fir [fɜr] *n* Tanne *f*
fire ['faɪr] **I.** *n* ❶ Feuer *nt;* **to play with ~** mit dem Feuer spielen *a. fig* ❷ (*destructive burning*) Brand *m;* **~ prevention** Brandschutz *m;* **destroyed by ~** völlig abgebrannt; **to be on ~** brennen, in Flammen stehen; **to catch ~** Feuer fangen, in Brand geraten; **to set sth on ~** etw in Brand stecken ❸ MIL Feuer *nt,* Beschuss *m;* ■ **to be/come under ~** beschossen werden; (*fig*) unter Beschuss geraten; **to open ~** das Feuer eröffnen **II.** *vt* ❶ (*shoot*) abfeuern; *shot* abgeben; *gun* schießen; (*fig*) **to ~ questions at sb** jdn mit Fragen bombardieren ❷ (*dismiss*) feuern ❸ (*excite*) *person* begeistern, anregen; *imagination* beflügeln ❹ (*bake in kiln*) brennen **III.** *vi* ❶ (*shoot*) feuern, schießen (**at** auf *+akk*) ❷ (*start up*) zünden; (*be operating*) funktionieren
◆**fire away** *vi* losschießen *a. fig*
◆**fire off** *vt* abfeuern
◆**fire up** *vt person* begeistern (**about** für *+akk*); **engine** zünden
'fire alarm *n* ❶ (*instrument*) Feuermelder *m* ❷ (*sound*) Feueralarm *m*
'firearm *n* Schusswaffe *f*
'fireball *n* Feuerball *m;* ASTRON Feuerkugel *f*
'firebomb I. *n* Brandbombe *f* **II.** *vt* ■ **to ~ sth** eine Brandbombe auf etw *akk* werfen
'firebrand *n* Brandfackel *f;* (*fig*) Aufwiegler(in) *m(f)*
'firecracker *n* Kracher *m*
'fire department *n* Feuerwehr *f*
'fire drill *n* Feueralarmübung *f*
'fire-eater *n* Feuerschlucker(in) *m(f)*
'fire engine *n* Feuerwehrauto *nt,* [Feuer]löschfahrzeug *nt*
'fire escape *n* (*staircase*) Feuertreppe *f;* (*ladder*) Feuerleiter *f*
'fire exit *n* Notausgang *m*
'fire extinguisher *n* Feuerlöscher *m*
'firefighter *n* Feuerwehrmann, -frau *m, f*
'firefly *n* Leuchtkäfer *m*
'fire house *n see* **fire station**
'fire hydrant *n* Hydrant *m*
'fire insurance *n* Feuerversicherung *f*
'fireman *n* Feuerwehrmann *m*
'fireplace *n* Kamin *m*
'firepower *n* Feuerkraft *f*
'fireproof I. *adj* feuerfest **II.** *vt* feuerfest machen

F

'fireside *n* [offener] Kamin
'fire station *n* Feuerwache *f*
'firewall *n* ① ARCHIT Brandmauer *f* ② COMPUT Firewall *f*
'firewater *n* (*fam*) Feuerwasser *nt*
'firewoman *n* Feuerwehrfrau *f*
'firewood *n* Brennholz *nt*
'firework *n* ① Feuerwerkskörper *m* ② ■ **~s** *pl* (*display*) Feuerwerk *nt;* (*fig*) [Riesen]krach *m kein pl*
firing ['faɪr·ɪŋ] *n* ① (*shooting*) Abfeuern *nt; of a rocket* Abschießen *nt;* **~ practice** Schießübung *f* ② (*dismissal*) Rauswurf *m* ③ (*in a kiln*) Brennen *nt*
'firing line *n* (*fig*) Schusslinie *f*
'firing squad *n* Exekutionskommando *nt*
firm¹ [fɜrm] **I.** *adj* fest; COMM stabil; *basis* sicher; *offer* verbindlich; *undertaking* definitiv; ■ **to be ~ with sb** jdm gegenüber bestimmt auftreten **II.** *adv* fest; **to hold** [*or* **stand**] **~** standhaft bleiben **III.** *vi* sich stabilisieren
firm² [fɜrm] *n* Firma *f,* Unternehmen *nt*
firmness ['fɜrm·nɪs] *n* ① (*solidity*) Festigkeit *f* ② (*resoluteness*) Entschlossenheit *f*
first [fɜrst] **I.** *adj* erste(r, s); **~ thing tomorrow** morgen als Allererstes; [**right of**] **~ refusal** FIN Vorkaufsrecht *nt* ▶ PHRASES: **in the ~ place** (*at beginning*) zunächst [einmal]; (*from the beginning*) von vornherein; (*most importantly*) in erster Linie; **~ things ~** eins nach dem anderen **II.** *adv* ① (*before doing something else*) zuerst; ■ **~ of all** zu[aller]erst ② (*before other things, people*) als Erste(r, s); **head ~** mit dem Kopf voraus ▶ PHRASES: **~ and foremost** vor allem **III.** *n* ① ■ **the ~** der/die/das Erste; ■ **to be the ~ to do sth** etw als Erster/Erste tun ② (*start*) ■ **at ~** anfangs; **from the** [**very**] **~** von Anfang an ③ AUTO der erste Gang
first 'aid *n* erste Hilfe; **~ kit** Verbandskasten *m*
'firstborn I. *adj* erstgeboren **II.** *n* Erstgeborene(r) *f(m)*
'first-class *adj* ① (*best quality*) Erste[r]-Klasse- ② (*approv: wonderful*) erstklassig
first class *adv* erster Klasse
first 'cousin *n* Cousin(e) *m(f)* ersten Grades
first-degree 'burn *adj* Verbrennung *f* ersten Grades
first-degree 'murder *adj* schwerer Mord
first 'floor *n* Erdgeschoss *nt*
'firsthand¹ *adj attr* aus erster Hand; **to experience sth ~** etw am eigenen Leib erfahren
first'hand² *adv* aus erster Hand
first 'lady *n* ■ **the ~** die First Lady
firstly ['fɜrst·li] *adv* erstens
'first name *n* Vorname *m*
first 'person *n* LING **the ~** die erste Person
first-'rate *adj* erstklassig
first 'strike *n* MIL Erstschlag *m*
fiscal ['fɪs·kəl] *adj* fiskalisch
fiscal 'policy *n* Finanzpolitik *f*
fiscal 'year *n* Geschäftsjahr *nt*
fish [fɪʃ] **I.** *n* <*pl* -es *or* -> Fisch *m* ▶ PHRASES: **to have bigger ~ to fry** Wichtigeres zu tun haben; **to drink like a ~** wie ein Loch saufen **II.** *vi* ① (*catch fish*) fischen; (*with rod*) angeln (**for** auf +*akk*) ② (*look for*) herumsuchen; ■ **to ~ for sth** (*fig*) nach etw *dat* suchen; **to ~ for compliments** sich *dat* gerne Komplimente machen lassen; **to ~ for information** auf der Suche nach Informationen sein **III.** *vt* befischen
'fish bone *n* [Fisch]gräte *f*
'fishbowl *n* [Gold]fischglas *nt* ▶ PHRASES: **to be** [*or* **live**] **in a ~** auf dem Präsentierteller sitzen *fam o pej*
'fisherman *n* (*professional*) Fischer *m;* (*for hobby*) Angler *m*
fishery ['fɪʃ·ə·ri] *n* Fischfanggebiet *nt*
'fishhook *n* Angelhaken *m*
fishing ['fɪʃ·ɪŋ] *n* (*catching fish*) Fischen *nt;* (*with rod*) Angeln *nt*
'fishing line *n* Angelleine *f,* Angelschnur *f*
'fishing rod *n* Angel[rute] *f*
'fishing tackle *n* (*for industry*) Fischereigeräte *pl;* (*for sport*) Angelgeräte *pl*
'fish stick *n* Fischstäbchen *nt*
fishy ['fɪʃ·i] *adj* ① (*tasting of fish*) fischig; (*like fish*) fischartig ② (*pej fam: dubious*) verdächtig; **there is something ~ about that** daran ist irgendetwas faul
fission ['fɪʃ·ən] *n* PHYS [Kern]spaltung *f;* BIOL [Zell]teilung *f*
fissure ['fɪʃ·ər] *n* ① Spalte *f* ② (*fig*) Spaltung *f*
fist [fɪst] *n* Faust *f*
fit¹ [fɪt] **I.** *adj* <-tt-> ① (*suitable*) geeignet; **~ for human consumption** [*or* **to eat**] zum Verzehr geeignet; **that's all he's ~ for** das ist alles, wozu er taugt ② (*up to*) fähig; **~ to work** arbeitsfähig ③ (*appropriate*) angebracht; **do as you think ~** tun, was Sie für richtig halten ④ (*healthy*) fit **II.** *n* ① FASHION Sitz *m;* **these shoes are a good ~** diese Schuhe passen gut ② TECH Passung *f* **III.** *vt* <fitted *or* fit, fitted *or* fit> ① (*be the right size*) ■ **to ~ sb** jdm passen ② (*be appropriate*) ■ **to ~ sb/sth** sich für jdn/etw eignen ③ (*correspond with*) ■ **to ~ sth** etw *dat* entsprechen; **the punishment should always ~ the crime** die Strafe sollte immer dem Vergehen angemessen sein; **the key ~s the lock** der Schlüssel passt ins Schloss ④ (*make correspond*) ■ **to ~ sth to sth** etw einer S. *dat* anpassen ⑤ (*install*) montieren ⑥ (*position as required*) einpassen ⑦ (*supply*) ■ **to ~ sth with sth** etw mit etw *dat* versehen **IV.** *vi* <fitted *or* fit, fitted> ① (*be correct size*) passen, sitzen; **~ well** gut sitzen; ■ **to ~ into sth** in etw *akk* hineinpassen ② (*agree*) *facts* übereinstimmen
◆**fit in I.** *vi* ① (*get along well*) sich einfügen ② (*conform*) dazupassen; **this doesn't ~ in with my plans** das passt mir nicht in den Plan **II.** *vt* einschieben
fit² [fɪt] *n* Anfall *m;* **to be in ~s of laughter** sich kaputtlachen; **to have a ~** (*lose consciousness*) in Ohnmacht fallen; (*fig: lose temper*) einen Anfall bekommen

fitful [ˈfɪt·fəl] *adj* unbeständig; *sleep* unruhig

fitness [ˈfɪt·nɪs] *n* ① (*health*) Fitness *f* ② (*competence*) Eignung *f*

fitted [ˈfɪt̬·ɪd] *adj* (*tailor-made*) maßgeschneidert; (*close-fitting*) *jacket* tailliert

fitter [ˈfɪt̬·ər] *n* TECH [Maschinen]schlosser(in) *m(f)*

fitting [ˈfɪt̬·ɪŋ] **I.** *adj* passend; **it is ~ that ...** es schickt sich, dass ... **II.** *n* Anprobe *f*

five [faɪv] **I.** *adj* fünf **II.** *n* ① (*number, symbol*) Fünf *f;* **~ o'clock shadow** nachmittäglicher Stoppelbart ② (*five minutes*) **to take ~** (*fam*) sich *dat* eine kurze Pause genehmigen; *see also* **eight**

ˈfivefold *adj, adv* fünffach

fiver [ˈfaɪ·vər] *n* (*fam*) Fünfdollarschein *m*

fix [fɪks] **I.** *n* ① (*fam: dilemma*) Klemme *f* ② (*sl: drugs*) Schuss *m,* Fix *m* ③ NAUT, AVIAT (*position*) Position *f;* **to take a ~ on sth** etw orten **II.** *vt* ① (*repair*) reparieren, in Ordnung bringen ② (*fasten*) festmachen (**to** an +*akk*) ③ (*decide*) festlegen; *rent* festsetzen ④ (*arrange*) arrangieren ⑤ (*fam: prepare*) **to ~ one's hair** sich frisieren; **shall I ~ you something?** soll ich dir was zu essen machen? ⑥ (*sl: take revenge on*) ■**to ~ sb** es jdm heimzahlen ⑦ (*concentrate*) *eyes, thoughts* richten (**on** auf +*akk*); **he ~ed me with a disapproving stare** er durchbohrte mich mit missbilligenden Blicken **III.** *vi* (*sl*) *drugs* fixen

◆**fix on** *vt* ■**to ~ on** [*or* **upon**] **sth** sich auf etw *akk* festlegen

◆**fix up** *vt* ① (*supply*) ■**to ~ sb** ↻ **up** jdn versorgen; (*with a date*) jdm eine Verabredung arrangieren ② (*arrange*) arrangieren; *time to meet* vereinbaren ③ (*fam: repair*) in Ordnung bringen; *house* renovieren

fixation [fɪk·ˈseɪ·ʃən] *n* PSYCH Fixierung *f* (**with** auf +*akk*)

fixed [fɪkst] *adj* fest; *gaze* starr; *idea* fix; **how are you ~ for cash?** wie steht's bei dir mit Geld?

fixer [ˈfɪk·sər] *n* (*fam: person*) Schieber(in) *m(f)*

fixture [ˈfɪks·tʃər] *n* eingebautes Teil; ■**~s** *pl* Ausstattung *f,* Einrichtungsgegenstände *pl;* **to be a permanent ~** (*fig, hum*) zum [lebenden] Inventar gehören

fizz [fɪz] **I.** *vi* ① (*bubble*) sprudeln ② (*make sound*) zischen **II.** *n* Sprudeln *nt;* **the tonic water has lost its ~** in dem Tonic Water ist keine Kohlensäure mehr

◆**fizzle out** *vi* verpuffen

fjord [fjɔrd] *n* Fjord *m*

FL, Fla. *abbrev of* **Florida**

flabbergast [ˈflæb·ər·gæst] *vt* ■**to be ~ed** völlig platt sein

flabby [ˈflæb·i] *adj* schwabbelig; (*fig*) schlapp

flag [flæg] **I.** *n* ① (*pennant*) Fahne *f;* (*national*) Flagge *f* ② (*marker*) Markierung *f* **II.** *vt* <-gg-> ① (*mark*) markieren ② (*signal to*) **to ~** [**down**] anhalten **III.** *vi* <-gg-> *enthusiasm* abflauen; *interest* nachlassen; *person* ermüden; *strength* erlahmen

> Der **Flag Day** gedenkt des 14. Juni 1777, als der *Second Continental Congress* (zweiter Kontinentalkongress) die *Stars and Stripes* (Flagge der Vereinigten Staaten von Amerika) zur Nationalfahne ernannte. Allerdings ist der 14. Juni kein nationaler Feiertag, obwohl die Amerikaner diese Fahne als wichtigstes Symbol für ihr Land ansehen.

ˈflagpole, **ˈflagstaff** *n* Fahnenmast *m,* Flaggenmast *m*

flagrant [ˈfleɪ·grənt] *adj* offenkundig

ˈflagship *n* Flaggschiff *nt a. fig;* **~ store** Hauptgeschäft *nt*

ˈflagstaff *n see* **flagpole**

flail [fleɪl] **I.** *n* Dreschflegel *m* **II.** *vi* heftig um sich schlagen; ■**to ~ around** herumfuchteln **III.** *vt* **to ~ one's arms** wild mit den Armen fuchteln

flair [fler] *n* ① (*talent*) Talent *nt;* **to have a ~ for languages** sprachbegabt sein ② (*style*) Stil *m*

flak [flæk] *n* ① Flakfeuer *nt* ② (*fig*) scharfe Kritik

flake [fleɪk] **I.** *n* ① *of chocolate* Raspel *f; of metal* Span *m; of pastry* Krümel *m; of skin* [Haut]schuppe *f; of snow* Schneeflocke *f; of soap* Seifenflocke *f* ② (*sl: odd person*) Spinner(in) *m(f)* **II.** *vi skin* sich schuppen; *paint* abblättern; *plaster* abbröckeln

◆**flake out** *vi* (*fam*) nicht dran denken

flaky [ˈfleɪ·ki] *adj* ① (*with layers*) flockig; *pastry* blättrig; *paint* bröcklig; *skin* schuppig ② (*sl: unreliable*) schusselig, hirnlos *pej fam*

flamboyant [flæm·ˈbɔɪ·ənt] *adj* extravagant; *colors* prächtig

flame [fleɪm] **I.** *n* ① Flamme *f a. fig;* **to burst into ~s** in Brand geraten ② INET beleidigende E-Mail **II.** *vi* brennen; (*fig*) glühen **III.** *vt* (*sl*) COMPUT per E-Mail beleidigen

flaming [ˈfleɪ·mɪŋ] **I.** *adj color* flammend **II.** *n* INET *heftiges Beleidigen beim Chatten im Internet*

flamingo <*pl* -s *or* -es> [flə·ˈmɪŋ·goʊ] *n* Flamingo *m*

flammable [ˈflæm·ə·bəl] *adj* leicht entflammbar; **highly ~** feuergefährlich

flan [flæn] *n Kuchen mit einer Füllung aus Vanillepudding*

flange [flændʒ] *n* Flansch *m*

flank [flæŋk] **I.** *n* Flanke *f* **II.** *vt* flankieren

flannel [ˈflæn·l] *n* Flanell *m*

flap [flæp] **I.** *vt* <-pp-> **to ~ one's wings** mit den Flügeln schlagen; (*in short intervals*) flattern mit **II.** *vi* <-pp-> (*flutter*) flattern; *wings* schlagen **III.** *n* ① (*flutter*) Flattern *nt* ② *of cloth* Futter *nt;* **pocket ~** Taschenklappe *f* ③ (*fam: commotion*) helle Aufregung

flapjack [ˈflæp·dʒæk] *n* Pfannkuchen *m*

flare [fler] **I.** *n* ① (*signal*) Leuchtkugel *f* ② (*of pants*) Schlag *m* **II.** *vi* ① (*burn up*) aufflammen ② FASHION aufweiten ③ *nostrils* sich blähen
◆ **flare up** *vi* ① auflodern *a. fig; person* aufbrausen ② MED sich bemerkbar machen

'flare-up *n* ① Auflodern *nt a. fig* ② MED [erneuter] Ausbruch

flash [flæʃ] **I.** *n* <*pl* -es> ① (*light*) [Licht]blitz *m; of jewelry, metal* [Auf]blitzen *nt kein pl;* ~ **of lightning** Blitz *m* ② (*fig*) ~ **of inspiration** Geistesblitz *m* ③ PHOT Blitz *m;* **to use** [**a**] ~ mit Blitzlicht fotografieren ▶ PHRASES: **like a** ~ blitzartig; **in a** ~ im Nu **II.** *adj* ① (*sudden*) Blitz-; ~ **frost** Blitzeis *nt;* ~ **mob** TELEC, INET Flashmob *m* ② (*pej fam: showy*) protzig **III.** *vt* ① *light* aufleuchten lassen ② (*pej fam: flaunt*) ■**to** ~ **sth around** mit etw protzen **IV.** *vi* ① (*shine*) blitzen ② (*fig: appear*) kurz auftauchen ③ (*move*) ■**to** ~ **by** [*or* **past**] vorbeirasen

'flashback *n* ① FILM Rückblende *f* ② CHEM [Flammen]rückschlag *m*

'flashbulb *n* PHOT Blitz[licht]lampe *f*

'flash card *n* SCH Zeigekarte *f*

flasher ['flæʃ·ər] *n* ① AUTO ■~**s** *pl* (*hazard lights*) Lichthupe *f* ② (*exhibitionist*) Exhibitionist *m*

flash 'flood *n* flutartige Überschwemmung

'flashlight *n* ① Taschenlampe *f* ② PHOT Blitzlicht *nt*

'flashpoint *n* ① CHEM Flammpunkt *m* ② (*fig: trouble spot*) Unruheherd *m*

flashy ['flæʃ·i] *adj* protzig

flask [flæsk] *n* ① (*bottle*) [bauchige] Flasche; *for wine* Ballonflasche *f; for spirits* Flachmann *m* ② CHEM [Glas]kolben *m*

flat[1] [flæt] **I.** *adj* <-tt-> ① (*horizontal*) flach; *path, surface* eben; *face, nose* platt ② (*not carbonated*) *drinks* schal ③ (*deflated*) *tire* platt; *person* niedergeschlagen ④ COMM, ECON (*slack*) *market* flau; (*fixed*) *rate* Einheits-, Pauschal- ⑤ MUS *key* mit B-Vorzeichen *nach n; note* [um einen Halbton] erniedrigt; (*unintentionally*) zu tief [gestimmt] **II.** *adv* <-tt-> ① (*horizontally*) flach; **to fall** ~ **on one's face** der Länge nach hinfallen ② (*level*) platt; **to knock sth** ~ *wall, building* etw platt walzen ③ (*fam: absolutely*) rundheraus, glattweg ④ MUS zu tief ▶ PHRASES: **to fall** ~ (*fail*) *attempt* scheitern; *performance* durchfallen; *joke* nicht ankommen **III.** *n* ① (*level surface*) flache Seite; ~ **of the hand** Handfläche *f* ② (*level ground*) Ebene *f;* **salt** ~**s** *pl* Salzwüste *f* ③ (*tire*) Platte(r) *m*

flat[2] [flæt] *n* [Etagen]wohnung *f*

flat 'feet *npl* Plattfüße *pl*

flat-'footed *adj* plattfüßig; **to be** ~ Plattfüße haben

flatly ['flæt·li] *adv* ① (*dully*) ausdruckslos ② (*absolutely*) glatt[weg]

flatness ['flæt·nɪs] *n* Flachheit *f; of ground, track* Ebenheit *f*

'flat rate I. *n* Pauschaltarif *m,* Pauschale *f;* INET, TELEC Flatrate *f* **II.** *adj* Pauschal-; TELEC, INET Flatrate-

flatten ['flæt·n] *vt* ① (*level*) flach machen; *ground, path* eben machen; *dent* ausbeulen; ■**to** ~ **oneself against sth** sich platt gegen etw *akk* drücken ② (*knock down*) *thing* einebnen; *tree* umlegen; *person* niederstrecken

flatter[1] ['flæt̬·ər] *vt* ■**to** ~ **sb** jdm schmeicheln; **don't** ~ **yourself!** bilde dir ja nichts ein!

flatter[2] ['flæt̬·ər] *adj comp of* **flat**

flatterer ['flæt̬·ə·rər] *n* Schmeichler(in) *m(f)*

flattering ['flæt̬·ə·rɪŋ] *adj* (*approv*) schmeichelhaft; (*pej*) schmeichlerisch

flattery ['flæt̬·ə·ri] *n* Schmeicheleien *pl*

flatulence ['flætʃ·ə·ləns] *n* (*form*) Blähung[en] *f*[*pl*]

flaunt [flɔnt] *vt* (*esp pej*) zur Schau stellen

flautist ['flɔ·t̬ɪst] *n* Flötist(in) *m(f)*

flavor ['fleɪ·vər] **I.** *n* ① (*taste*) [Wohl]geschmack *m,* Aroma *nt;* (*particular taste*) Geschmacksrichtung *f,* Sorte *f* ② (*fig*) Anflug *m* **II.** *vt* würzen

flavoring ['fleɪ·vər·ɪŋ] *n* Aroma *nt,* Geschmacksstoff *m*

flaw [flɔ] **I.** *n* Fehler *m,* Mangel *m;* TECH Defekt *m* **II.** *vt usu passive* beeinträchtigen

flawed [flɔd] *adj* fehlerhaft; *diamond* unrein; **his argument is deeply** ~ seine Argumentation hat große Schwachstellen

flawless ['flɔ·lɪs] *adj* fehlerlos; *beauty* makellos; *behavior* einwandfrei; *diamond* lupenrein; *performance* vollendet

flax [flæks] *n* Flachs *m*

flay [fleɪ] *vt* ① *animal* [ab]häuten ② (*fig*) *person* auspeitschen

flea [fli] *n* Floh *m*

'flea market *n* Flohmarkt *m*

fleck [flek] **I.** *n* Fleck[en] *m* **II.** *vt* sprenkeln

fled [fled] *vi, vt pp, pt of* **flee**

fledged [fledʒd] *adj* **fully** ~ flügge *a. fig*

fledg(e)ling ['fledʒ·lɪŋ] **I.** *n* Jungvogel *m* **II.** *adj* neu, Jung-

flee <fled, fled> [fli] **I.** *vi* (*run away*) fliehen (**from** vor); (*seek safety*) flüchten **II.** *vt country* fliehen (aus +*dat*); *danger* fliehen [*o* flüchten] (vor +*dat*)

fleece [flis] **I.** *n* ① *of sheep* Schaffell *nt,* Vlies *nt* ② (*fabric*) Flausch *m,* weicher Wollstoff ③ (*clothing*) Vliesjacke *f* **II.** *vt* ① *sheep* scheren ② (*fig fam: cheat*) schröpfen, ausnehmen

fleet [flit] *n* ① NAUT Flotte *f* ② AVIAT Staffel *f* ③ (*group of vehicles*) Fuhrpark *m; of cars* Wagenpark *m*

fleeting ['fli·t̬ɪŋ] *adj* flüchtig; *beauty* vergänglich; *opportunity* kurzfristig

Flemish ['flem·ɪʃ] **I.** *adj* flämisch **II.** *n* Flämisch *nt*

flesh [fleʃ] *n* Fleisch *nt; of fruit* [Frucht]fleisch *nt* ▶ PHRASES: **to be** [**only**] ~ **and blood** auch [nur] ein Mensch sein; **to make one's** ~ **crawl** das Gruseln lernen; **in the** ~ in Person
◆ **flesh out** *vt* weiterentwickeln

'flesh-colored *adj* fleischfarben

'flesh wound *n* Fleischwunde *f*

flew [flu] *vi, vt pp, pt of* **fly**
flex [fleks] I. *vt* beugen; *muscles* [an]spannen; **to ~ one's muscles** (*fig*) seine Muskeln spielen lassen II. *vi* sich beugen; *muscles* sich [an]spannen III. *n* [Anschluss]kabel *nt*
flexibility [ˌflek·sə·ˈbɪl·ɪ·t̬i] *n* ❶ Biegsamkeit *f; of material* Elastizität *f* ❷ (*fig*) Flexibilität *f*
flexible [ˈflek·sə·bəl] *adj* ❶ biegsam ❷ (*fig*) flexibel; **~ working hours** gleitende Arbeitszeit
flextime [ˈfleks·taɪm] *n* Gleitzeit *f*
flick [flɪk] I. *n* ❶ (*movement*) kurze Bewegung; *of switch* Klicken *nt; of whip* Schnalzen *nt; of wrist* kurze Drehung ❷ (*fam: movie*) Film *m,* Streifen *m fam* II. *vt* ❶ (*move*) ■**to ~ sth** etw mit einer schnellen Bewegung ausführen; *whip* schnalzen mit; **to ~ the light switch off** das Licht ausknipsen ❷ (*remove*) wegwedeln; *with fingers* wegschnippen
flicker [ˈflɪk·ər] I. *vi* ❶ (*shine unsteadily*) flackern; *TV* flimmern; *eyelids* zucken; *tongue* züngeln ❷ (*fig*) aufkommen; *hope* aufflackern II. *n* ❶ Flackern *nt kein pl; of TV pictures* Flimmern *nt kein pl; of eyelids* Zucken *nt kein pl* ❷ (*fig*) Anflug *m;* **a ~ of hope** ein Hoffnungsschimmer *m*
flier [ˈflaɪ·ər] *n* ❶ Flieger(in) *m(f);* **frequent ~** Vielflieger(in) *m(f)* ❷ (*leaflet*) Flugblatt *nt*
flight¹ [flaɪt] *n* ❶ (*flying*) Flug *m;* **to take ~** auffliegen ❷ (*group*) *of birds, insects* Schwarm *m; of migrating birds* [Vogel]zug *m; of aircraft* [Flieger]staffel *f* ❸ (*series*) *of stairs* Treppe *f;* **we live three ~s up** wir wohnen drei Treppen hoch
flight² [flaɪt] *n* (*fleeing*) Flucht *f*
ˈ**flight attendant** *n* Flugbegleiter(in) *m(f)*
ˈ**flight deck** *n* ❶ (*on plane*) Cockpit *nt* ❷ (*on ship*) Flugdeck *nt*
flightless [ˈflaɪt·lɪs] *adj* flugunfähig
ˈ**flight number** *n* Flugnummer *f*
ˈ**flight path** *n of an aircraft* Flugweg *m; of an object* Flugbahn *f*
ˈ**flight recorder** *n* Flugschreiber *m*
flighty [ˈflaɪ·t̬i] *adj* (*usu pej*) flatterhaft
flimsiness [ˈflɪm·zɪ·nɪs] *n* ❶ *of material* mangelnde Festigkeit; *of a structure* mangelnde Stabilität ❷ *of a fabric, paper* Dünnheit *f* ❸ (*fig*) *of an excuse* Fadenscheinigkeit *f*
flimsy [ˈflɪm·zi] *adj* ❶ *construction* instabil, unsolide ❷ *clothing* dünn, leicht ❸ (*fig*) *excuse* schwach
flinch [flɪntʃ] *vi* (*wince*) [zusammen]zucken
fling [flɪŋ] I. *n* ❶ (*throw*) [mit Schwung ausgeführter] Wurf ❷ (*fig: good time*) ausgelassene Zeit; (*relationship*) **to have a ~ with sb** mit jdm etwas haben II. *vt* <flung, flung> werfen; **to ~ open** aufreißen; ■**to ~ oneself at sb/sth** sich auf jdn/etw stürzen; (*fig*) sich jdm an den Hals werfen; ■**to ~ oneself into sth** (*fig*) sich in etw *akk* stürzen
◆**fling off** *vt clothing* abwerfen *a. fig; blanket* wegstoßen
◆**fling on** *vt* (*fam*) sich *dat* überwerfen
flint [flɪnt] *n* Feuerstein *m*
flip [flɪp] I. *vt* <-pp-> ❶ (*turn on/off*) *switch* drücken ❷ (*turn over*) umdrehen; *coin* werfen; *pancake* wenden (*durch Hochwerfen*) II. *vi* <-pp-> ❶ ■**to ~ [over]** sich [schnell] [um]drehen; *vehicle* sich überschlagen ❷ (*fig sl*) ausflippen ❸ (*with coin*) eine Münze werfen (**for** um +*akk*) III. *n* ❶ (*throw*) Werfen *nt* ❷ (*movement*) Ruck *m;* **to have a [quick] ~ through sth** etw im Schnellverfahren tun
ˈ**flip chart** *n* Flipchart *m o nt*
ˈ**flip-flop** I. *n* ❶ (*shoe*) Badelatsche *f* ❷ (*fam: reversal of opinion*) plötzlicher Gesinnungswandel II. *vi* ständig seine Meinung ändern
flippancy [ˈflɪp·ən·si] *n* Leichtfertigkeit *f*
flippant [ˈflɪp·ənt] *adj* leichtfertig
flipper [ˈflɪp·ər] *n* [Schwimm]flosse *f*
ˈ**flip side** *n* ❶ B-Seite *f* ❷ (*fig*) Kehrseite *f*
flirt [flɜrt] I. *vi* ❶ flirten ❷ (*fig*) spielen II. *n* [gern] flirtende(r) Mann/Frau
flirtation [flɜr·ˈteɪ·ʃən] *n* Flirt *m*
flirtatious [flɜr·ˈteɪ·ʃəs] *adj* kokett
flit <-tt-> [flɪt] *vi* ❶ huschen *a. fig;* (*fly*) flattern ❷ (*fig*) sich stürzen; **to ~ through one's mind** einem durch den Kopf schießen
float [floʊt] I. *n* ❶ (*for fishing*) [Kork]schwimmer *m* ❷ (*for swimming*) Schwimmkork *m* ❸ TECH Schwimmer *m* ❹ (*drink*) **Coke ~** (*Coca-Cola mit Eiskugeln im hohen Glas serviert*) ❺ (*in parade*) Festzugswagen *m* II. *vi* ❶ (*be buoyant*) schwimmen, oben bleiben ❷ (*move in liquid or gas*) *objects* treiben; *people* sich treiben lassen ❸ (*move in air*) *clouds* ziehen; *leaves* segeln; *sound* dringen III. *vt* ❶ ECON *business* gründen; *currency* freigeben ❷ (*on water*) treiben lassen; *logs* flößen; *ship* zu Wasser lassen ❸ (*fig*) *idea* zur Diskussion stellen
◆**float around** *vi* (*fig*) *rumor* in Umlauf sein; *objects* [he]rum[f]liegen; *person* sich herumtreiben
floatation [floʊ·ˈteɪ·ʃən] *n see* **flotation**
floating [ˈfloʊ·t̬ɪŋ] *adj* ❶ (*in water*) schwimmend, treibend; *crane, dock* Schwimm- ❷ (*fluctuating*) *population* mobil; **~ voter** Wechselwähler, -in *m, f*
flock [flak] I. *n of animals* Herde *f; of people, birds* Schar *f,* Schwarm *m* II. *vi* sich scharen; ■**to ~ to sth** zu etw *dat* in Scharen kommen
floe [floʊ] *n* Eisscholle *f*
flog <-gg-> [flag] *vt* auspeitschen (**for** wegen +*akk*)
flogging [ˈflag·ɪŋ] *n* Auspeitschen *nt kein pl*
flood [flʌd] I. *n* ❶ (*excess water*) Überschwemmung *f,* Hochwasser *nt kein pl;* ■**the F~** REL die Sintflut ❷ (*tide*) **~ [tide]** Flut *f* II. *vt* ❶ (*overflow*) überschwemmen *a. fig; room* unter Wasser setzen ❷ AUTO *engine* absaufen lassen III. *vi* ❶ *place* überschwemmt werden, unter Wasser stehen; *river* über die Ufer treten ❷ (*fig*) strömen; **as soon as the gates were opened, the people ~ed in** sobald die Tore geöffnet wurden, strömten die Leute herein
ˈ**floodgate** *n* Schleusentor *nt;* **to open the ~s**

[**to sth**] (*fig*) [etw *dat*] Tür und Tor öffnen
'floodlight *n* Flutlicht *nt*
'floodlit *adj building* angestrahlt; *stadium* in Flutlicht getaucht
floor [flɔr] **I.** *n* ❶ (*surface*) [Fuß]boden *m;* GEOG Boden *m* ❷ (*story*) Stock *m,* Stockwerk *nt,* Etage *f;* **first ~** Erdgeschoss *nt* **II.** *vt* ❶ zu Boden schlagen ❷ (*fig*) umhauen
'floorboard *n* Diele *f*
flooring ['flɔr·ɪŋ] *n* Boden[belag] *m*
'floor lamp *n* Stehlampe *f*
'floor plan *n* Grundriss *m* (*eines Stockwerks*)
flop [flap] **I.** *vi* <-pp-> ❶ (*move*) sich fallen [*o* plumpsen] lassen ❷ (*fail*) ein Flop sein; *performance* durchfallen **II.** *n* ❶ (*movement*) Plumps *m* ❷ (*failure*) *thing* Flop *m; person* Niete *f*
'flophouse *n* (*cheap hotel*) Absteige *f*
floppy ['flap·i] **I.** *adj* schlaff; *hair* [immer wieder] herabfallend; **~ ears** Schlappohren *pl* **II.** *n* COMPUT (*fam*) Floppy [Disk] *f*
floppy 'disk *n* COMPUT Floppy Disk *f*
flora ['flɔr·ə] *n* Flora *f*
floral ['flɔr·əl] *adj* Blumen-
florid ['flɔr·ɪd] *adj* ❶ (*form: ruddy*) kräftig rot ❷ (*fig, usu pej: very ornate*) überladen; *style* blumig; *prose, rhetoric* schwülstig
Florida ['flɔr·ɪ·də] *n* Florida *nt*
florist ['flɔr·ɪst] *n* Florist(in) *m(f)*; ■ **~** [**shop**] Blumengeschäft *nt*
floss [flas] **I.** *n* Zahnseide *f* **II.** *vt* **to ~ one's teeth** seine Zähne mit Zahnseide reinigen
flotation [floʊ·'teɪ·ʃən] *n* ECON *of a business* Gründung *f;* **stock-market ~** Börsengang *m*
flotilla [floʊ·'tɪl·ə] *n* Flottille *f*
flotsam ['flat·səm], **flotsam and 'jetsam** *n* Treibgut *nt;* (*ashore*) Strandgut *nt*
flounce [flaʊnts] *vi* rauschen
flounder[1] <*pl* - *or* -s> ['flaʊn·dər] *n* (*flatfish*) Flunder *f*
flounder[2] ['flaʊn·dər] *vi* ❶ stolpern; *in mud, snow* waten; *in water* [herum]rudern ❷ (*fig: be in difficulty*) sich abmühen; (*be confused*) nicht weiterwissen
flour ['flaʊ·ər] *n* Mehl *nt*
flourish ['flɜr·ɪʃ] **I.** *vi* blühen; COMM blühen, florieren **II.** *vt* herumfuchteln mit *dat,* schwingen **III.** *n* (*movement*) schwungvolle Bewegung; (*gesture*) überschwängliche Geste; **the team produced a late ~** die Mannschaft brachte gegen Ende noch einmal Bewegung ins Spiel
flourishing ['flɜr·ɪʃ·ɪŋ] *adj* (*a. fig*) *plants* prächtig; *business, market* blühend, florierend
flout [flaʊt] *vt* [offen] missachten
flow [floʊ] **I.** *vi* fließen *a. fig; air, light, warmth* strömen; *conversation* in Gang kommen; **many rivers ~ into the North Sea** viele Flüsse münden in die Nordsee **II.** *n usu sing* Fluss *m a. fig;* (*volume*) Durchflussmenge *f;* **~ of goods** Güterverkehr *m;* **to stop the ~ of blood** das Blut stillen ▶ PHRASES: **to go <u>against</u>/<u>with</u> the ~** gegen den/mit dem Strom schwimmen
'flow chart, 'flow diagram *n* Flussdiagramm *nt*
flower ['flaʊ·ər] **I.** *n* ❶ BOT (*plant*) Blume *f;* (*blossom*) Blüte *f;* **to be in ~** blühen ❷ (*fig*) Blüte *f* **II.** *vi* blühen *a. fig*
'flower arrangement *n* Blumengesteck *nt*
'flower bed *n* Blumenbeet *nt*
'flowerpot *n* Blumentopf *m*
flowery ['flaʊ·ə·ri] *adj* ❶ *material* geblümt ❷ (*fig*) *language* blumig
flowing ['floʊ·ɪŋ] *adj* flüssig; *clothing, movement* fließend; *hair* wallend
flown [floʊn] *vi, vt pp of* **fly**
fl. oz. *n abbrev of* **fluid ounce** 29,57 cm^3
flu [flu] *n short for* **influenza** Grippe *f*
flub [flʌb] *vt* (*fam*) **to ~ sth** etw vermasseln [*o* ÖSTERR *a.* verhauen] *fam;* **to ~ one's lines** seinen Text verpatzen
fluctuate ['flʌk·tʃʊ·eɪt] *vi* schwanken; ECON fluktuieren
fluctuation [ˌflʌk·tʃʊ·'eɪ·ʃən] *n* Schwankung *f;* ECON Fluktuation *f*
flue [flu] *n* Abzugsrohr *nt;* (*in chimney*) Rauchabzug *m;* (*for furnace*) Flammrohr *nt*
fluency ['flu·ən·si] *n* Fluss *m; of style* Flüssigkeit *f; of foreign language* Beherrschung *f; of articulation* Gewandtheit *f*
fluent ['flu·ənt] *adj in a foreign language* fließend; *style, movements* flüssig; *rhetoric* gewandt; **to be ~ in a language** eine Sprache fließend beherrschen [*o* sprechen]
fluff [flʌf] **I.** *n* ❶ (*particle*) Fusseln *pl* ❷ ORN, ZOOL Flaum *m* **II.** *vt* vermasseln; **to ~ an exam/a test** ein Examen/eine Prüfung verhauen
fluffy ['flʌf·i] *adj* ❶ (*soft*) *feathers* flaumig; *pillows* flaumig weich; *towels* flauschig; *animal* kuschelig [weich] ❷ (*light*) *clouds* aufgelockert; *food, hair* locker; *egg whites* schaumig
fluid ['flu·ɪd] **I.** *n* Flüssigkeit *f;* **bodily ~s** Körpersäfte *pl* **II.** *adj* ❶ flüssig ❷ (*fig: changeable*) veränderlich
fluid 'ounce *n* 29,57 cm^3
flung [flʌŋ] *pp, pt of* **fling**
flunk [flʌŋk] *vt* (*fam*) durchfallen in +*dat*
fluorescence [flɔ·'res·əns] *n* Fluoreszenz *f*
fluorescent [flɔ·'res·ənt] *adj* fluoreszierend; **~ light** Neonlicht *nt*
fluoride ['flɔr·aɪd] *n* Fluorid *nt*
flurry ['flɜr·i] *n* ❶ METEO **snow ~** [Schnee]schauer *m* ❷ (*excitement*) Unruhe *f;* **~ of excitement** große Aufregung
flush[1] [flʌʃ] *adj* ❶ (*flat*) eben; **~ with sth** mit etw *dat* auf gleicher Ebene ❷ (*fam: rich*) reich
flush[2] [flʌʃ] **I.** *vi* ❶ (*blush*) erröten (**with** vor +*dat*) ❷ (*empty*) spülen; **the toilet won't ~** die Spülung geht nicht **II.** *vt* spülen; **to ~ [sth down] the toilet** [etw die Toilette hinunter]spülen **III.** *n* ❶ *usu sing* (*blush*) Röte *f kein pl* ❷ (*emptying*) Spülen *nt kein pl*
◆**flush out** *vt* ❶ (*cleanse*) ausspülen ❷ (*drive out*) hinaustreiben
flushed [flʌʃt] *adj* rot im Gesicht

fluster ['flʌs·tər] *vt* nervös machen

flute [flut] *n* Flöte *f*

flutist ['flu·t̬ɪst] *n* Flötist(in) *m(f)*

flutter ['flʌt̬·ər] **I.** *vi* flattern **II.** *vt* flattern lassen; *wings* schlagen mit; *eyelashes* klimpern mit **III.** *n* Flattern *nt kein pl*

flux [flʌks] *n* **in a state of ~** im Fluss

fly [flaɪ] **I.** *vi* <flew, flown> ① *(through the air)* fliegen; **he flew across the Atlantic** er überflog den Atlantik ② *(in the air) flag* wehen ③ *(speed)* sausen; **the door flew open** die Tür flog auf **II.** *vt* <flew, flown> ① *(pilot, transport)* fliegen ② *(raise) flag* wehen lassen; *kite* steigen lassen **III.** *n* ① *(insect)* Fliege *f* ② *(zipper)* Hosenschlitz *m* ▶ PHRASES: **the ~ in the ointment** das Haar in der Suppe; **to be a ~ on the wall** Mäuschen sein **IV.** *adj* <-er, -est> *(sl)* cool

◆**fly in** *vi, vt* einfliegen (**from** aus +*dat*)

'fly-by-night *adj (pej fam)* zweifelhaft

flyer ['flaɪ·ər] *n see* **flier**

flying ['flaɪ·ɪŋ] **I.** *n* Fliegen *nt* **II.** *adj* fliegend

'flyover *n* Luftparade *f*

'flypaper *n* Fliegenpapier *nt*

'flywheel *n* TECH Schwungrad *nt*

FM [ˌef·'em] *n abbrev of* **frequency modulation** FM

foal [foʊl] **I.** *n* Fohlen *nt* **II.** *vi* fohlen

foam [foʊm] **I.** *n* ① *(bubbles)* Schaum *m* ② *(plastic)* Schaumstoff *m* **II.** *vi* schäumen

foam 'rubber *n* Schaumgummi *m*

fob [fab] **I.** *n* ① *(for watch)* Uhrkette *f* ② *(for keys)* Schlüsselanhänger *m* **II.** *vt* <-bb-> ■**to ~ sb off with sth** jdn mit etw *dat* abspeisen; ■**to ~ sth off on sb** jdm etw andrehen

focal ['foʊ·kəl] *adj* im Brennpunkt stehend; **~ point** Brennpunkt *m*

focus <*pl* -es *or form* foci> ['foʊ·kəs, *pl* 'foʊ·saɪ] **I.** *n* ① *(center)* Mittelpunkt *m,* Brennpunkt *m;* **to be the ~ of attention** im Mittelpunkt stehen ② **in/out of ~** scharf/nicht scharf eingestellt **II.** *vi* <-s- *or* -ss-> ① *(concentrate)* sich konzentrieren (**[up]on** auf +*akk*) ② *(see)* klar sehen **III.** *vt* <-s- *or* -ss-> ① *(concentrate) attention, energy* konzentrieren (**on** auf +*akk*) ② *(direct) camera, telescope* scharf einstellen (**on** auf +*akk*); *eyes* richten (**on** auf +*akk*)

fodder ['fad·ər] *n* Futter *nt*

foe [foʊ] *n (liter)* Feind *m*

fog [fag] *n* Nebel *m*

'fogbound *adj airport* wegen Nebels geschlossen; *plane* durch Nebel festgehalten

fogey ['foʊ·gi] *n (fam) see* **fogy**

foggy ['fa·gi] *adj* neblig

'foghorn *n* Nebelhorn *nt*

'fog lamp, 'fog light *n* Nebelscheinwerfer *m*

fogy ['foʊ·gi] *n (fam)* Mensch *m* mit verstaubten Ansichten

foible ['fɔɪ·bəl] *n usu pl* Eigenart *f kein pl*

foil[1] [fɔɪl] *n* ① *(sheet)* Folie *f* ② *(sword)* Florett *nt*

foil[2] [fɔɪl] *vt thing* verhindern; *coup, person* vereiteln; *plan* durchkreuzen

foist [fɔɪst] *vt* ■**to ~ sth [up]on sb** jdm etw aufzwingen

fold [foʊld] **I.** *n (crease)* Falte *f* **II.** *vt* ① *(bend)* falten (**into** zu +*dat*); *letter* zusammenfalten; *umbrella* zusammenklappen; *arms, hands* verschränken ② *(enclose) letter* **to ~ sth into sth** etw in etw einwickeln ③ FOOD *(mix)* heben (**into** unter +*akk*) **III.** *vi* ① *(bend)* zusammenklappen ② *(fail)* eingehen ③ *(give up)* **to ~ under pressure** bei Druck nachgeben [*o* sich beugen]

◆**fold up** *vt, vi* zusammenfalten

folder ['foʊl·dər] *n* ① Mappe *f* ② COMPUT Ordner *m*

folding ['foʊl·dɪŋ] *adj* **~ bed** Klappbett *nt;* **~ door** Falttür *f;* **~ seat** Klappsitz *m;* **~ top** Verdeck *nt*

foliage ['foʊ·lɪ·ɪdʒ] *n* Laub *nt*

folk [foʊk] **I.** *n* ① *pl (fam: people)* Leute *pl* ② *pl (parents)* Eltern *pl* ③ *(music)* Folk *m* **II.** *adj* ① *(traditional)* Volks- ② *(connected with folk music)* Folk-

'folk dance *n* Volkstanz *m*

'folklore *n* Folklore *f*

'folk music *n* Folk *m*

'folk song *n* Volkslied *nt*

folksy ['foʊk·si] *adj (fam)* volkstümlich

'folk tale *n* Volkssage *f*

follow ['fal·oʊ] **I.** *vt* ① *(take same route as)* folgen +*dat* ② *(pursue)* verfolgen ③ *(happen next)* folgen auf +*akk* ④ *(succeed) person* nachfolgen +*dat* ⑤ *(obey)* befolgen; *(go along with)* folgen +*dat; guidelines* sich halten an +*akk; conscience* gehorchen +*dat* ⑥ *(understand)* folgen +*dat* **II.** *vi* ① *(take the same route, happen next)* folgen; **in the hours that ~ed ...** in den darauffolgenden Stunden ...; **he was being ~ed** er wurde verfolgt ② *(result)* sich ergeben (**from** aus +*dat*); *(be the consequence)* die Folge sein

◆**follow through I.** *vt* zu Ende verfolgen **II.** *vi* SPORTS durchschwingen

◆**follow up I.** *vt* ① *(investigate)* weiterverfolgen; *rumor* nachgehen +*dat;* MED nachuntersuchen ② *(do next)* ■**to ~ up** ↔ **sth with** [*or* **by doing**] **sth** etw *dat* etw folgen lassen **II.** *vi* ■**to ~ up with sth** etw folgen lassen

follower ['fal·oʊ·ər] *n* Anhänger(in) *m(f)*

following ['fal·oʊ·ɪŋ] **I.** *adj* folgende(r, s); **on the ~ day** am nächsten Tag **II.** *n* ① + *pl vb (listed)* ■**the ~** *persons* folgende Personen; *objects* Folgendes ② *usu sing (fans)* Anhänger *pl* **III.** *prep* nach +*dat*

'follow-up I. *n* Fortsetzung *f* (**to** von +*dat*) **II.** *adj visit, interviews* Folge-; **~ treatment** Nachbehandlung *f*

folly ['fal·i] *n (stupidity)* Dummheit *f*

fond [fand] *adj hope* kühn; *memories* teuer; *smile* liebevoll; ■**to be ~ of sb/sth** jdn/etw gerne mögen; ■**to be ~ of doing sth** etw gerne machen

fondle ['fan·dl] *vt* streicheln

fondness ['fand·nɪs] *n* Vorliebe *f*
font¹ [fant] *n* TYPO Schriftart *f*
font² [fant] *n* (*basin*) Taufbecken *nt*
food [fud] *n* ❶ (*eatables*) Essen *nt*, Nahrung *f*; **cat ~** Katzenfutter *nt* ❷ (*foodstuff*) Nahrungsmittel *pl*
'**food chain** *n* Nahrungskette *f*
'**food poisoning** *n* Lebensmittelvergiftung *f*
'**food processor** *n* Küchenmaschine *f*
'**foodstuff** *n* Nahrungsmittel *pl*
fool [ful] **I.** *n* (*idiot*) Dummkopf *m*, Trottel *m*; **to make a ~ of oneself** sich zum Narren machen; **he's no ~** er ist nicht blöd ▶ PHRASES: **a ~ and his money are soon parted** (*prov*) Dummheit und Geld lassen sich nicht vereinen **II.** *adj* (*fam*) blöd **III.** *vt* täuschen; ■**to ~ sb into doing sth** jdn [durch einen Trick] dazu bringen, etw zu tun **IV.** *vi* einen Scherz machen
◆**fool around** *vi* ❶ (*carelessly*) herumspielen ❷ (*amusingly*) herumblödeln ❸ (*fam: sexually*) ■**to ~ around with sb** es mit jdm treiben *sl*
foolhardy ['ful·har·di] *adj* (*pej*) verwegen; *attempt* tollkühn
foolish ['fu·lɪʃ] *adj* töricht; **to look ~** sich blamieren
'**foolproof** *adj* idiotensicher
foot [fʊt] **I.** *n* <*pl* feet> [*pl* fi:t] ❶ (*limb*) Fuß *m*; **what size are your feet?** welche Schuhgröße haben Sie?; **to be [back/quick] on one's feet** [wieder/schnell] auf den Beinen sein; **he can barely put one ~ in front of the other** er hat Schwierigkeiten beim Laufen; **to put one's feet up** die Füße hochlegen; **to set ~ in sth** einen Fuß in etw *akk* setzen; **at sb's feet** zu jds Füßen; **on ~** zu Fuß ❷ <*pl* foot *or* feet> (*length*) Fuß *m* (= *0,3048 Meter*) ❸ <*pl* feet> (*base*) Fuß *m*; *of page* Ende *nt*; **at the ~ of the bed** am Fußende des Betts ▶ PHRASES: **to get off on the right/wrong foot** einen guten/schlechten Start haben; **to land on one's feet** Glück haben; **to put one's ~ down** (*insist*) ein Machtwort sprechen; **to put one's ~ in one's mouth** ins Fettnäpfchen treten **II.** *vt* (*fam*) *bill* bezahlen
footage ['fʊt̬·ɪdʒ] *n* Filmmaterial *nt*
foot-and-'mouth disease *n* Maul- und Klauenseuche *f*
football ['fʊt·bɔl] *n* ❶ (*game*) [American] Football *m* ❷ (*ball*) Football *m*

Der amerikanische **football** ist anders als der europäische Fußball, der in den USA **soccer** genannt wird. Zwei Mannschaften mit je elf Spielern versuchen den eiförmigen Lederball über die gegnerische Grundlinie zu bringen. Die höchste Punktzahl kann durch einen *touchdown* erreicht werden. Dieser zählt sechs Punkte. Ein *touchdown* kann erzielt werden, indem der Ball über die Grundlinie des Gegners getragen wird oder in der *end zone* (Endzone) gefangen wird. Wird der Ball durch die gegnerischen Torstangen geschossen, spricht man von einem *field goal*. Jede der vier Spielzeiten à 15 Minuten fängt mit einem *kickoff* an, d. h. ein Spieler tritt den Ball und seine Gegenspieler versuchen diesen mit den Händen zu fangen, um damit hinter die Grundlinie zu gelangen. Die Gegenseite stoppt den Spieler mit dem Ball durch *tackling*, wobei man ihn mit den Armen festhält und zu Boden drückt. Wird der Spieler zu Boden gebracht oder verlässt er das Spielfeld (*player out of bounds*), ist der Spielzug beendet.

'**footbridge** *n* Fußgängerbrücke *f*
footer ['fʊt̬·ər] *n* TYPO Fußzeile *f*
'**foothills** *npl* Vorgebirge *nt sing*
'**foothold** *n* Halt *m* [für die Füße] ▶ PHRASES: **to gain a ~** Fuß fassen
footing ['fʊt̬·ɪŋ] *n* ❶ (*foothold*) Halt *m* ❷ (*basis*) **on [an] equal ~** auf gleicher Basis
'**footlights** *npl* Rampenlicht *nt kein pl*
'**footloose** *adj* ungebunden
'**footman** *n* Lakai *m*
'**footnote** *n* ❶ Fußnote *f* ❷ (*fig*) Anmerkung *f*
'**footpath** *n* Fußweg *m*
'**footprint** *n* Fußabdruck *m*
'**footrest** *n* Fußstütze *f*
'**footstep** *n* Schritt *m* ▶ PHRASES: **to follow in sb's ~** in jds Fußstapfen treten
'**footstool** *n* Fußbank *f*, Schemel *m* SÜDD, ÖSTERR
'**footwear** *n* Schuhe *pl*
'**footwork** *n* Beinarbeit *f*
for [fɔr] **I.** *conj* denn **II.** *prep* ❶ für; **to be all ~ sth** ganz für etw *akk* sein; **to make it easy ~ sb** es jdm einfach machen; **luckily ~ me** zu meinem Glück; **what did you do that ~?** wozu hast du das getan?; **what do you use these ~?** wozu brauchst du diese?; **that's not ~ eating** das ist nicht zum Essen; **to apply ~ a job** sich um eine Stelle bewerben; **I feel sorry ~ her** sie tut mir leid; **to head ~ home** sich auf den Heimweg machen, auf dem Heimweg sein; **to prepare ~ sth** sich auf etw *akk* vorbereiten; **to run ~ the bus** laufen, um den Bus zu kriegen; **say hi ~ me** grüß ihn/sie von mir; **to trade sth ~ sth** etw gegen etw *akk* [ein]tauschen; **to work ~ sb/sth** bei jdm/etw arbeiten; **~ my part** was mich betrifft; **a check ~ 100 dollars** eine Scheck über 100 Dollar; **if it hadn't been ~ him, ...** ohne ihn ...; **~ your information** zu Ihrer Information; **he's only in it ~ the money** er tut es nur wegen des Geldes; **to be arrested ~ murder** wegen Mordes verhaftet werden; **~ various reasons** aus verschiedenen Gründen; **~ rent/sale** zu vermieten/verkaufen; **what's the Spanish word ~ "vegetarian"?** was heißt „Vegetarier" auf Spanisch? ❷ (*with time, distance*) **to practice ~ half an hour** eine halbe Stunde

üben; ~ **the next two days** in den beiden nächsten Tagen; ~ **a while** eine Weile; **I'm just going out ~ a while** ich gehe mal kurz raus; ~ **a long time** seit langem; **I hadn't seen him ~ such a long time** ich hatte ihn schon so lange nicht mehr gesehen; ~ **some time** seit längerem; ~ **the time being** für den Augenblick; ~ **the first time** zum ersten Mal; ~ **a mile** eine Meile ③ (*despite*) trotz; ~ **all that** trotz alledem

forbade [fər·ˈbæd] *pt of* **forbid**

forbid <-dd-, forbad(e), forbidden> [fər·ˈbɪd] *vt* ■ **to ~ sb sth** jdm etw verbieten; ■ **to ~ sb from doing** [*or* **to do**] **sth** jdm verbieten, etw zu tun

forbidden [fər·ˈbɪd·ən] **I.** *adj* verboten **II.** *pp of* **forbid**

forbidding [fər·ˈbɪd·ɪŋ] *adj* abschreckend

force [fɔrs] **I.** *n* ① (*power*) Kraft *f;* (*intensity*) Stärke *f; of a blow* Wucht *f;* **to be come into** [*or* **take**] ~ in Kraft treten ② (*violence*) Gewalt *f;* **by** ~ mit Gewalt ③ (*group*) Truppe *f;* **police** ~ Polizei *f;* **armed ~s** Streitkräfte *pl* ▶ PHRASES: **to join ~s** zusammenhelfen **II.** *vt* (*compel*) zwingen; *confession* erzwingen; *door, lock* aufbrechen; **to ~ one's way** sich *dat* seinen Weg bahnen; ■ **to ~ sth on sb** jdm etw aufzwingen

◆**force back** *vt* ① (*repel*) zurückdrängen; (*fig*) *tears* unterdrücken ② (*push back*) zurückdrücken

◆**force down** *vt* ① *plane* zur Landung zwingen ② *food* hinunterwürgen

◆**force open** *vt* mit Gewalt öffnen; *door, window* aufbrechen

forced [fɔrst] *adj* ① (*imposed*) erzwungen; ~ **labor** Zwangsarbeit *f;* ~ **landing** Notlandung ② *smile* gezwungen

ˈ**force-feed** *vt* zwangsernähren

forceful [ˈfɔrs·fəl] *adj attack* kraftvoll; *personality* stark

forceps [ˈfɔr·seps] *npl* [**a pair of**] ~ [eine] Zange

forcible [ˈfɔr·sə·bəl] *adj* gewaltsam

forcibly [ˈfɔr·sə·bli] *adv* gewaltsam

ford [fɔrd] **I.** *n* Furt *f* **II.** *vt* durchqueren; (*on foot*) durchwaten

fore [fɔr] **I.** *adj* vordere(r, s) **II.** *n* Vordergrund *m;* ■ **to come to the ~** in den Vordergrund treten

forearm [ˈfɔr·arm] *n* Unterarm *m*

forebears [ˈfɔr·berz] *npl* (*form*) Vorfahren *pl*

foreboding [fɔr·ˈboʊ·dɪŋ] *n* (*liter*) [düstere] Vorahnung

forecast [ˈfɔr·kæst] **I.** *n* ① (*prediction*) Prognose *f* ② **weather ~** [Wetter]vorhersage *f* **II.** *vt* <-cast *or* -casted, -cast *or* -casted> METEO vorhersagen; ECON prognostizieren

forecaster [ˈfɔr·kæst·ər] *n* ECON Prognostiker(in) *m(f);* METEO Meteorologe *m/*Meteorologin *f*

ˈ**forefinger** *n see* **index finger**

ˈ**forefront** *n* **at the ~** an der Spitze

forego <-went, -gone> [fɔr·ˈgoʊ] *vt see* **forgo**

foregoing [ˈfɔr·goʊ·ɪŋ] *adj* (*form*) vorhergehend

foregone con'clusion *n* ausgemachte Sache

ˈ**foreground** *n* Vordergrund *m*

ˈ**forehand** *n* Vorhand *f*

forehead [ˈfɔr·hed] *n* Stirn *f*

foreign [ˈfɔr·ɪn] *adj* ① (*from another country*) ausländisch, fremd; ~ **countries** Ausland *nt kein pl* ② (*involving other countries*) ~ **policy** Außenpolitik *f* ③ (*not belonging*) fremd; ~ **body** Fremdkörper *m*

foreign af'fairs *npl* Außenpolitik *f kein pl*

foreign corre'spondent *n* Auslandskorrespondent(in) *m(f)*

foreigner [ˈfɔr·ɪ·nər] *n* Ausländer(in) *m(f)*

foreign ex'change *n* Devisen *pl*

ˈ**foreman** *n* ① (*workman*) Vorarbeiter *m;* (*fam or fig*) Boss *m* ② LAW Sprecher *m* (*der Geschworenen*)

foremost [ˈfɔr·moʊst] *adj* führend

forensic [fə·ˈren·sɪk] *adj* forensisch

ˈ**foreplay** *n* Vorspiel *nt*

ˈ**forerunner** *n* (*predecessor*) Vorläufer(in) *m(f)*

foresee <-saw, -seen> [fɔr·ˈsi] *vt* vorhersehen

foreseeable [fɔr·ˈsi·ə·bəl] *adj* absehbar; **in the ~ future** in absehbarer Zeit

fore'shadow *vt* ■ **to be ~ed** [**by sth**] [durch etw] angedeutet werden

ˈ**foresight** *n* Weitblick *m;* ■ **to have the ~ to do sth** so vorausschauend sein, etw zu tun

ˈ**foreskin** *n* Vorhaut *f*

forest [ˈfɔr·ɪst] *n* Wald *m a. fig;* **the Black F~** der Schwarzwald

forestall [fɔr·ˈstɔl] *vt* zuvorkommen *+dat*

forester [ˈfɔr·ɪ·stər] *n* Förster(in) *m(f)*

ˈ**forest fire** *n* Waldbrand *m*

ˈ**forest ranger** *n* Förster(in) *m(f)*

forestry [ˈfɔr·ɪ·stri] *n* Forstwirtschaft *f*

foretaste [ˈfɔr·teɪst] *n usu sing* Vorgeschmack *m*

foretell <-told, -told> [fɔr·ˈtel] *vt* vorhersagen

forever [fɔr·ˈev·ər] *adv* ① (*for all time*) ewig *a. fig* ② (*continually*) ständig; ■ **to be ~ doing sth** etw ständig machen

forewarn [fɔr·ˈwɔrn] *vt* vorwarnen ▶ PHRASES: **~ed is forearmed** (*prov*) bist du gewarnt, bist du gewappnet

ˈ**foreword** *n* Vorwort *nt*

forfeit [ˈfɔr·fɪt] **I.** *vt* (*surrender*) einbüßen; *right* verwirken **II.** *n* (*in a game*) Pfand *nt*

forgave [fər·ˈgeɪv] *n pt of* **forgive**

forge [fɔrdʒ] **I.** *n* ① (*furnace*) Glühofen *m* ② (*workshop*) Schmiede *f* **II.** *vt* ① (*heat and shape*) schmieden ② (*fig: develop*) etw mühsam schaffen ③ (*copy*) fälschen

◆**forge ahead** *vi* ① (*progress*) [rasch] Fortschritte machen ② (*take lead*) die Führung übernehmen

forger [ˈfɔr·dʒər] *n* Fälscher(in) *m(f)*

forgery [ˈfɔr·dʒə·ri] *n* ① (*copy*) Fälschung *f* ② (*crime*) Fälschen *nt*

forget <-got, -gotten *or* -got> [fər·ˈget] *vt, vi*

vergessen; **to ~ the past** die Vergangenheit ruhen lassen; ■**to ~ about sth/sb** jdn/etw vergessen

forgetful [fər·ˈget·fəl] *adj* vergesslich

forˈget-me-not *n* BOT Vergissmeinnicht *nt*

forgive <-gave, -given> [fər·ˈgɪv] *vt* ■**to ~ sb [for] sth** jdm etw verzeihen; *sin* vergeben; ■**to ~ sb for doing sth** jdm verzeihen, dass er/sie etw getan hat; **to ~ and forget** vergeben und vergessen

forgiven [fər·ˈgɪv·ən] *pp of* **forgive**

forgiveness [fər·ˈgɪv·nɪs] *n* ❶ (*pardon*) Vergebung *f* ❷ (*forgiving quality*) Versöhnlichkeit *f*

forgiving [fər·ˈgɪv·ɪŋ] *adj* versöhnlich

forgo <-went, -gone> [fɔr·ˈgoʊ] *vt* verzichten auf *akk*

forgot [fər·ˈgat] *pt of* **forget**

forgotten [fər·ˈgat·n] **I.** *pp of* **forget II.** *adj* vergessen

fork [fɔrk] **I.** *n* ❶ (*tool*) Gabel *f* ❷ (*division*) Gabelung *f; in road* Abzweigung *f; of tree* Astgabel *f* **II.** *vt* mit einer Gabel bearbeiten **III.** *vi* ❶ (*divide*) sich gabeln ❷ (*go*) **to ~ left/right** nach links/rechts abzweigen

◆**fork out** *vt* **to ~ out 40 dollars** 40 Dollar springen lassen *fam*

forked [fɔrkt] *adj* gegabelt; *tongue* gespalten; **~ lightning** Linienblitz *m* ▶ PHRASES: **to speak with ~ tongue** mit gespaltener Zuge reden

ˈforklift *n* Gabelstapler *m*

forlorn [fɔr·ˈlɔrn] *adj person* einsam; *place* verlassen; *hope* schwach

form [fɔrm] **I.** *n* ❶ (*type, variety*) Form *f*, Art *f; of a disease* Erscheinungsbild *nt; of energy* Typ *m;* **art ~** Kunstform *f;* **~ of exercise** Sportart *f;* **life ~** Lebensform *f* ❷ (*particular way*) Form *f*, Gestalt *f;* **the training program takes the ~ of a series of workshops** die Schulung wird in Form einer Serie von Workshops abgehalten; **in some ~ or other** auf die eine oder andere Art ❸ (*document*) Formular *nt;* **application ~** Bewerbungsbogen *m;* **printed ~** Vordruck *m* ❹ (*shape*) Form *f; of a person* Gestalt *f* ❺ (*physical/mental condition*) Form *f*, Kondition *f;* **to be in peak ~** in Höchstform sein ❻ (*past performance*) Form *f;* **true to ~** wie zu erwarten ❼ (*procedure*) Form *f;* **a matter of ~** eine Formsache **II.** *vt* ❶ (*shape*) formen *a. fig* (**into** zu +*dat*); GEOG **to be ~ed from** entstehen aus ❷ (*arrange, constitute*) bilden; **they ~ed themselves into three lines** sie stellten sich in drei Reihen auf ❸ (*set up*) gründen; *committee, government* bilden; *friendships* schließen; *relationship* eingehen; **to ~ an alliance with sb** sich mit jdm verbünden **III.** *vi* sich bilden; *idea* Gestalt annehmen; ■**to ~ into sth** sich zu etw *dat* formen

formal [ˈfɔr·məl] *adj* ❶ (*ceremonious*) formell; **~ wear** Gesellschaftskleidung *f* ❷ (*serious*) förmlich ❸ (*official*) offiziell; *education* ordentlich

formality [fɔr·ˈmæl·ɪ·t̬i] *n* ❶ (*ceremoniousness*) Förmlichkeit *f* ❷ (*matter of form*) Formalität *f*, Formsache *f*

formalize [ˈfɔr·mə·laɪz] *vt* ❶ (*make official*) *agreement* formell bekräftigen ❷ (*give shape to*) *thoughts* ordnen

formally [ˈfɔr·məl·i] *adv* ❶ (*ceremoniously*) formell ❷ (*officially*) offiziell

format [ˈfɔr·mæt] **I.** *n* Format *nt* **II.** *vt* <-tt-> formatieren

formation [fɔr·ˈmeɪ·ʃən] *n* ❶ Bildung *f* ❷ GEOL, MIL Formation *f*

formative [ˈfɔr·mə·t̬ɪv] *adj* prägend

former [ˈfɔr·mər] **I.** *adj* ❶ (*previous*) ehemalig, früher ❷ (*first of two*) erstere(r, s) **II.** *n* ■**the ~** der/die/das Erstere

formerly [ˈfɔr·mər·li] *adv* früher

formidable [ˈfɔr·mɪ·də·bəl] *adj* ❶ (*difficult*) schwierig; (*tremendous*) kolossal; *obstacle* ernstlich; *person, opponent* Furcht erregend ❷ (*powerful*) eindrucksvoll

ˈform letter *n* Briefvorlage *f*

formula <*pl* -s *or* -e> [ˈfɔr·mjʊ·lə, *pl* -li] *n* ❶ Formel *f* ❷ FOOD Babymilchpulver *nt*

formulate [ˈfɔr·mjʊ·leɪt] *vt* ❶ (*draw up*) ausarbeiten; *law* formulieren; *theory* entwickeln ❷ (*articulate*) formulieren

formulation [ˌfɔr·mjʊ·ˈleɪ·ʃən] *n* ❶ (*drawing up*) Entwicklung *f; of law* Fassung *f* ❷ (*articulation*) Formulierung *f*

fort [fɔrt] *n* Fort *nt* ▶ PHRASES: **to hold the ~** die Stellung halten

forte I. *n* [ˈfɔr·teɪ, fɔrt] *usu sing* Stärke *f* **II.** *adv* [ˈfɔr·teɪ] MUS forte

forth [fɔrθ] *adv* **back and ~** vor und zurück; **to set ~** ausziehen ▶ PHRASES: **[and so on] and so ~** und so weiter [und so fort]

forthcoming [ˌfɔrθ·ˈkʌm·ɪŋ] *adj* ❶ (*planned*) bevorstehend ❷ (*coming out soon*) in Kürze erscheinend; *film* in Kürze anlaufend ❸ (*informative*) mitteilsam

forthright [ˈfɔrθ·raɪt] *adj* direkt

fortieth [ˈfɔr·t̬i·əθ] **I.** *adj* vierzigste(r, s) **II.** *n* ❶ (*order*) ■**the ~** der/die/das Vierzigste ❷ (*fraction*) Vierzigstel *nt; see also* **eighth**

fortification [ˌfɔr·t̬ə·fɪ·ˈkeɪ·ʃən] *n* ❶ (*reinforcing*) Befestigung *f* ❷ (*structures*) ■**~s** *pl* Befestigungsanlagen *pl*

fortify <-ie-> [ˈfɔr·t̬ə·faɪ] *vt* ❶ MIL befestigen ❷ ■**to ~ oneself** sich stärken

fortnight [ˈfɔrt·naɪt] *n* (*liter*) zwei Wochen, vierzehn Tage

fortress <*pl* -es> [ˈfɔr·trɪs] *n* Festung *f*

fortuitous [fɔr·ˈtu·ɪ·t̬əs] *adj* (*form*) zufällig

fortunate [ˈfɔr·tʃə·nɪt] *adj* glücklich; ■**to be ~** Glück haben

fortunately [ˈfɔr·tʃə·nɪt·li] *adv* zum Glück; **~ for him** zu seinem Glück

fortune [ˈfɔr·tʃən] *n* ❶ (*money*) Vermögen *nt* ❷ (*form: luck*) Schicksal *nt;* **good/bad ~** Glück/Pech *nt;* **to tell sb's ~** jds Schicksal vorhersagen

ˈfortune teller *n* Wahrsager(in) *m(f)*

forty [ˈfɔr·t̬i] **I.** *adj* vierzig **II.** *n* Vierzig *f; see also* **eight**

forum ['fɔr·əm] *n* Forum *nt*
forward ['fɔr·wərd] **I.** *adv* (*toward front*) nach vorn[e]; (*onwards*) vorwärts; **to lean ~** sich vorlehnen; **from that day ~** von jenem Tag an **II.** *adj* ❶ (*toward front*) Vorwärts-; **~ pass** (*in football*) Vorwärtspass *m;* (*in rugby*) Vorpass *m* ❷ (*near front*) vordere(r, s) ❸ (*of future*) *planning* Voraus- *f;* **~ buying** Terminkauf *m* **III.** *n* SPORTS Stürmer(in) *m(f)* **IV.** *vt* weiterleiten (**to** an +*akk*)
forwarding ad'dress *n* Nachsendeadresse *f*
'forward-looking *adj* vorausschauend
forwards ['fɔr·wərdz] *adv see* **forward**
forwent [fɔr·'went] *pt of* **forgo**
fossil ['fas·əl] *n* Fossil *nt;* **~ fuel** fossiler Brennstoff
fossilized ['fas·ə·laɪzd] *adj* versteinert
foster ['fa·stər] **I.** *vt* ❶ *child* aufziehen, in Pflege nehmen ❷ (*encourage*) fördern **II.** *vi* ein Kind in Pflege nehmen **III.** *adj* Pflege-
'foster child *n* Pflegekind *nt*
'foster father *n* Pflegevater *nt*
'foster mother *n* Pflegemutter *nt*
fought [fɔt] *pt, pp of* **fight**
foul [faʊl] **I.** *adj* ❶ (*disgusting*) abscheulich; *smell* faul; *taste* schlecht ❷ (*polluted*) verpestet; *air* stinkend; *water* schmutzig ❸ (*unpleasant*) *mood* fürchterlich; *language* anstößig **II.** *n* SPORTS Foul *nt* (**on** an +*dat*) **III.** *vt* ❶ (*pollute*) verschmutzen ❷ SPORTS foulen
foul-'mouthed *adj* unflätig
foul 'play *n* ❶ (*criminal activity*) Verbrechen *nt* ❷ SPORTS Foulspiel *nt*
found[1] [faʊnd] *pt, pp of* **find**
found[2] [faʊnd] *vt* gründen
foundation [faʊn·'deɪ·ʃən] *n* ❶ (*basis*) Fundament *nt a. fig* (**of, for** zu +*dat*); **to be without ~** (*fig*) der Grundlage entbehren ❷ (*establishing*) Gründung *f* ❸ (*of makeup*) **~ [cream]** Grundierung *f*
foun'dation stone *n* Grundstein *m*
founder[1] ['faʊn·dər] *n* Gründer(in) *m(f)*
founder[2] ['faʊn·dər] *vi* ❶ (*sink*) sinken ❷ (*fig: fail*) scheitern
Founding 'Fathers *npl* Gründerväter *pl*
foundry ['faʊn·dri] *n* Gießerei *f*
fount [faʊnt] *n* Quelle *f*
fountain ['faʊn·tən] *n* ❶ Brunnen *m* ❷ (*fig: spray*) Schwall *m*
'fountain pen *n* Füllfederhalter *m,* Füllfeder *f bes* ÖSTERR, SÜDD, SCHWEIZ
four [fɔr] **I.** *adj* vier **II.** *n* ❶ (*number, symbol*) Vier *f* ❷ (*hands and knees*) **on all ~s** auf allen Vieren; *see also* **eight** ❸ SPORTS (*in rowing*) Vierer *m*
'four-by-four *n* AUTO allrad-/vierradangetriebenes Auto
'fourfold *adj, adv* vierfach; **to increase ~** um das Vierfache steigen
four-'footed *adj* vierfüßig
four'handed *adj inv* ❶ (*for four people*) für vier Personen ❷ (*for two pianists*) vierhändig
four-leaf 'clover *n* vierblättriges Kleeblatt
four-letter 'word *n* Schimpfwort *nt*
'foursome *n* Vierergruppe *f;* (*golf*) Vierer *m*
fourteen [ˌfɔr·'tin] **I.** *adj* vierzehn; **~ hundred hours** *spoken* vierzehn Uhr; **1400 hours** *written* 14:00 **II.** *n* Vierzehn *f; see also* **eight**
fourteenth [ˌfɔr·'tinθ] **I.** *adj* vierzehnte(r, s) **II.** *n* ❶ (*fraction*) Vierzehntel *nt* ❷ (*date*) ■ **the ~** der Vierzehnte ❸ (*order*) ■ **the ~** der/die/das Vierzehnte
fourth [fɔrθ] **I.** *adj* vierte(r, s) **II.** *n* ❶ (*order*) **the ~** der/die/das Vierte ❷ (*date*) **the ~** der Vierte ❸ (*fraction*) Viertel *nt* ❹ AUTO vierter Gang **III.** *adv* viertens; *see also* **eighth**

> Der **Fourth of July** oder **Independence Day** (der amerikanische Unabhängigkeitstag) ist der höchste amerikanische nichtkonfessionelle Feiertag zum Gedenken an die *Declaration of Independence* (Unabhängigkeitserklärung), in der die amerikanischen Kolonien am 4. Juli 1776 ihre Unabhängigkeit von Großbritannien erklärten. Man trifft sich zu Picknicks, Familienfeiern und professionellen Baseballspielen. Als Höhepunkt des Tages findet in vielen Städten ein großes Feuerwerk statt.

four-wheel 'drive **I.** *n* Allrad-/Vierradantrieb *m* **II.** *adj* mit Allrad-/Vierradantrieb
fowl <*pl* - *or* -s> [faʊl] *n* Geflügel *nt kein pl*
fox [faks] **I.** *n* ❶ (*animal*) Fuchs *m a. fig;* (*fur*) Fuchspelz *m* ❷ (*sl: attractive woman*) scharfe Braut *pej sl;* (*attractive man*) heißer Typ *pej sl* **II.** *vt* ❶ (*trick*) täuschen ❷ (*baffle*) verblüffen
'foxglove *n* BOT Fingerhut *m*
'foxhunt *n* Fuchsjagd *f*
'foxtrot **I.** *n* Foxtrott *m* **II.** *vi* <-tt-> Foxtrott tanzen
foxy ['fak·si] *adj* ❶ (*crafty*) gerissen ❷ (*fam: sexy*) sexy
foyer ['fɔɪ·ər] *n* ❶ (*of public building*) Foyer *nt* ❷ (*of house*) Diele *f*
fracas <*pl* **-es**> ['freɪ·kəs] *n* lautstarke Auseinandersetzung
fraction ['fræk·ʃən] *n* ❶ (*number*) Bruchzahl *f,* Bruch *m* ❷ (*proportion*) Bruchteil *m;* (*fig*) **by a ~** um Haaresbreite ❸ (*a little*) **a ~** ein bisschen
fractional ['fræk·ʃə·nəl] *adj* minimal
fractious ['fræk·ʃəs] *adj* reizbar, grantig SÜDD, ÖSTERR; *child* quengelig
fracture ['fræk·tʃər] **I.** *vt, vi* brechen **II.** *n* Bruch *m*
fragile ['frædʒ·əl] *adj* ❶ (*breakable*) zerbrechlich ❷ (*unstable*) brüchig; *agreement, peace* unsicher; *health* schwach
fragility [frə·'dʒɪl·ɪ·ţi] *n* ❶ (*delicacy*) Zerbrechlichkeit *f* ❷ (*weakness*) Brüchigkeit *f; of an agreement* Unsicherheit *f*
fragment ['fræg·ment] **I.** *n* ❶ (*broken piece*) Splitter *m* ❷ (*incomplete piece*) Brocken *m*

II. *vi* zerbrechen *a. fig;* (*burst*) zerbersten
fragmentary ['fræg·mən·ter·i] *adj* bruchstückhaft
fragrance ['freɪ·grəns] *n* Duft *m*
fragrant ['freɪ·grənt] *adj* duftend
frail [freɪl] *adj person* gebrechlich; *thing* schwach
frailty ['freɪl·ti] *n* ❶ (*of person*) Gebrechlichkeit *f; of thing* Zerbrechlichkeit *f* ❷ (*moral weakness*) Schwäche *f*
frame [freɪm] **I.** *n* ❶ (*of picture*) Bilderrahmen *m* ❷ (*of door, window*) Rahmen *m* ❸ (*of eyeglasses*) ■ **~s** *pl* Brillengestell *nt* ❹ (*support*) Rahmen *m a. fig* ❺ (*body*) Körper *m* ❻ (*of film*) Bild *nt* **II.** *vt* ❶ (*put in framework*) einrahmen ❷ (*form framework*) umrahmen ❸ (*fam: falsely incriminate*) verleumden, anschwärzen
'frame-up *n* (*fam*) abgekartetes Spiel
'framework *n* ❶ Gerüst *nt* ❷ (*fig*) Rahmen *m*
franc [fræŋk] *n* Franc *m;* [**Swiss**] ~ [Schweizer] Franken *m*
France [fræns] *n* Frankreich *nt*
franchise ['fræn·tʃaɪz] *n* Franchise *nt*
Franciscan [fræn·'sɪs·kən] *n* REL Franziskaner(in) *m(f)*
Franco- ['fræŋ·koʊ] *in compounds* französisch-; **~-German** deutsch-französisch
frank¹ [fræŋk] **I.** *adj* aufrichtig; ■ **to be ~** [**with sb**] [**about sth**] ehrlich [zu jdm] [über etw *akk*] sein **II.** *vt* ❶ (*put stamp on*) *envelope* frankieren ❷ (*cancel stamp*) freistempeln
frank² [fræŋk] *n* (*fam: frankfurter*) Frankfurter *f*
frankencorn ['fræŋ·kᵊn·kɔrn] *n no pl* (*pej fam*) Genmais *m,* Horrormais *m sl*
frankincense ['fræŋ·kɪn·sens] *n* Weihrauch *m*
frankly ['fræŋk·li] *adv* offen
frantic ['fræn·tɪk] *adj* ❶ (*distracted*) verrückt (**with** vor +*dat*) ❷ (*hurried*) hektisch
fraternal [frə·'tɜr·nəl] *adj* brüderlich
fraternity [frə·'tɜr·nɪ·ṭi] *n* ❶ (*feeling*) Brüderlichkeit *f* ❷ (*group*) Vereinigung *f* ❸ UNIV Burschenschaft *f*
fraternize ['fræt·ər·naɪz] *vi* sich verbrüdern
fratricide ['fræt·rə·saɪd] *n* Brudermord *m*
fraud [frɔd] *n* ❶ (*deceit*) Betrug *m* ❷ (*trick*) Schwindel *m* ❸ (*deceiver*) Betrüger(in) *m(f)*
fraudulent ['frɔ·dʒə·lənt] *adj* betrügerisch
fraught [frɔt] *adj* **to be ~ with difficulties** voller Schwierigkeiten stecken
fray [freɪ] *vi* ❶ (*come apart*) ausfransen ❷ (*become strained*) anspannen
freak [frik] **I.** *n* ❶ (*abnormal thing*) etwas Außergewöhnliches; **a ~ of nature** eine Laune der Natur ❷ (*abnormal person*) Missgeburt *f* ❸ (*fanatic*) Freak *m* **II.** *vi* (*fam*) ausflippen
◆ **freak out** (*fam*) **I.** *vi* ausflippen **II.** *vt* ausflippen lassen
freckle ['frek·əl] *n usu pl* Sommersprosse *f*
freckled ['frek·əld] *adj* sommersprossig
free [fri] **I.** *adj* ❶ frei; **~ of pain** schmerzfrei; **~ speech** Redefreiheit *f;* ■ **to be ~ of sb/sth** jdn/etw los sein; ■ **to be ~** [**to do sth**] Zeit haben[, etw zu tun]; **you are ~ to come and go as you please** Sie können kommen und gehen, wann Sie wollen; **to break ~** [**of** [*or* **from**] **sth**] sich [aus etw] befreien *a. fig;* **to break ~** [**of** [*or* **from**] **sb**] sich [von jdm] losreißen *a. fig;* **to set ~** freilassen *a. fig;* **to walk ~** straffrei ausgehen ❷ (*costing nothing*) frei; **~ copy** Freiexemplar *nt* ▶ PHRASES: **there's no such thing as a ~ lunch** nichts ist umsonst **II.** *adv* frei, gratis; **~ of charge** kostenlos **III.** *vt* freilassen; *hands* frei machen; *person, animal* befreien (**from** von +*dat*)
◆ **free up** *vt* freimachen
freebie ['fri·bi] *n* (*fam*) Werbegeschenk *nt*
freedom ['fri·dəm] *n* Freiheit *f;* **~ of information** freier Informationszugang; **~ of movement** Bewegungsfreiheit *f;* **~ of speech** Redefreiheit *f*
'free fall *n* freier Fall; **to go into** [**a**] **~** (*fig*) ins Bodenlose fallen
'free-for-all *n* allgemeines Gerangel
'freehand **I.** *adj* Freihand- **II.** *adv* freihändig
free 'kick *n* SPORTS Freistoß *m*
freelance ['fri·læns] **I.** *n* Freiberufler(in) *m(f)* **II.** *adj, adv* freiberuflich **III.** *vi* frei[beruflich] arbeiten
'freeload *vi* (*pej*) schnorren (**off** bei +*dat*)
'freeloader *vi* (*pej*) Schnorrer(in) *m(f)*
freely ['fri·li] *adv* ❶ (*unrestrictedly*) frei ❷ (*without obstruction*) ungehindert ❸ (*frankly*) offen ❹ (*generously*) großzügig
'freeman *n* ❶ (*hist: not slave*) freier Mann ❷ (*honorary citizen*) Ehrenbürger *m*
'Freemason *n* Freimaurer *m*
free 'port *n* Freihafen *m*
'free-range *adj* Freiland-; **~ eggs** Eier *pl* aus Freilandhaltung
free 'speech *n* Redefreiheit *f*
free'standing *adj* frei stehend
'freestyle *n* Freistil *m*
free 'trade *n* Freihandel *m*
'freeware *n* COMPUT Gratissoftware *f,* Freeware *f*
'freeway *n* Fern[verkehrs]straße *f*
'freewheel *vi* **to ~** [**downhill**] im Freilauf [den Hügel hinunter]fahren
free 'will *n* freier Wille; ■ **to do sth of one's own ~** etw aus freien Stücken tun
freeze [friz] **I.** *n* ❶ METEO Frost *m* ❷ ECON Einfrieren *nt* **II.** *vi* <froze, frozen> ❶ (*become solid*) *water* gefrieren; *pipes, food in freezer* einfrieren; *lake* zufrieren; **to ~ solid** festfrieren ❷ (*a. fig: get very cold*) [sehr] frieren; **to ~ to death** erfrieren ❸ (*be still*) erstarren **III.** *vt* <froze, frozen> ❶ (*turn to ice*) gefrieren lassen ❷ (*preserve*) einfrieren ❸ *image* festhalten; *film* anhalten ❹ ECON einfrieren
◆ **freeze up** *vi* einfrieren
freezer ['fri·zər] *n* (*upright*) Gefrierschrank *m;* (*chest*) Gefriertruhe *f,* Tiefkühltruhe *f*
freezer bag *n* Kühltasche *f*
freezing ['fri·zɪŋ] **I.** *adj* frostig; **it's ~** es ist eis-

kalt; **I'm** ~ mir ist eiskalt **II.** *n* ❶ (*32°F*) Gefrierpunkt *m* ❷ (*preserving*) Einfrieren *nt*

'freezing point *n* Gefrierpunkt *m*

freight [freɪt] **I.** *n* ❶ (*goods*) Frachtgut *nt* ❷ (*transportation*) Fracht *f;* **to send sth [by]** ~ etw als Fracht senden ❸ (*charge*) Frachtgebühr *f* **II.** *adv* als Fracht **III.** *vt* als Frachtgut befördern

'freight car *n* Güterwagen *m*

freighter ['freɪ·t̬ər] *n* ❶ (*ship*) Frachter *m* ❷ (*plane*) Frachtflugzeug *nt*

'freight train *n* Güterzug *m*

French [frentʃ] **I.** *adj* französisch **II.** *n* ❶ (*language*) Französisch *nt* ❷ (*people*) ■**the** ~ *pl* die Franzosen

French 'doors *npl* Verandatür *f*

'French fries *npl* Pommes frites *pl*

French 'horn *n* Waldhorn *nt*

'Frenchman *n* Franzose *m*

French 'toast *n* FOOD armer Ritter, Fotzelschnitte *f* SCHWEIZ

'Frenchwoman *n* Französin *f*

frenetic [frə·'net̬·ɪk] *adj* hektisch

frenzied ['fren·zɪd] *adj* fieberhaft; *attack, barking* wild; *crowd* aufgebracht

frenzy ['fren·zi] *n* Raserei *f;* **media** ~ Medienspektakel *nt*

frequency ['fri·kwən·si] *n* ❶ Häufigkeit *f;* **with increasing** ~ immer öfter ❷ RADIO Frequenz *f*

frequent ['fri·kwənt] **I.** *adj* ['frik·wənt] (*often*) häufig; (*regular*) regelmäßig **II.** *vt* [fri·'kwent] häufig besuchen

frequently ['fri·kwənt·li] *adv* häufig

fresco <*pl* -s *or* -es> ['fres·koʊ] *n* Fresko *nt*

fresh [freʃ] *adj* ❶ frisch *a. fig;* ~ **start** Neuanfang *m;* ~ **water** Süßwasser *nt;* **like a breath of** ~ **air** (*fig*) erfrischend [anders]; **to get a breath of** ~ **air** frische Luft schnappen ❷ (*fam: cheeky*) frech; (*forward*) zudringlich

freshen ['freʃ·ən] **I.** *vt drink* auffüllen; *makeup* auffrischen; *room* durchlüften **II.** *vi* frischer werden; *wind* auffrischen

freshman ['freʃ·mən] *n* ❶ (*college student*) Studienanfänger *m* ❷ (*ninth-grade high school student*) Gymnasiast *m* im ersten Jahr

> Ein **Freshman** ist in den USA ein Schüler der 9. Klasse, ein *Sophomore* ein Schüler der 10. Klasse, ein *Junior* ein Schüler der 11. Klasse und ein *Senior* ein Schüler der 12. Klasse. Das sind die üblichen Bezeichnungen der *High-School*-Jahre, auch wenn die *High School* in vielen Gegenden jetzt erst mit der 10. Klasse beginnt. Diese Begriffe werden außerdem auch für Studenten in den vier Collegejahren verwendet.

freshness ['freʃ·nɪs] *n* Frische *f*

'freshwater *adj* Süßwasser-

fret¹ [fret] *vi* <-tt-> sich *dat* Sorgen machen

fret² [fret] *n* MUS Bund *m*

friar ['fraɪ·ər] *n* Mönch *m*

friction ['frɪk·ʃən] *n* ❶ (*force*) Reibung *f* ❷ (*disagreement*) Reiberei[en] *f[pl]*

Friday ['fraɪ·di] *n* Freitag *m; see also* **Tuesday**

fridge [frɪdʒ] *n* (*fam*) Kühlschrank *m*

fried [fraɪd] *adj* (*of food*) gebraten; ~ **potatoes** Bratkartoffeln *pl*

fried 'egg *n* Spiegelei *nt*

friend [frend] *n* Freund(in) *m(f);* **to make** ~**s [with sb]** sich [mit jdm] anfreunden

friendless ['frend·lɪs] *adj* ohne Freund[e]

friendly ['frend·li] *adj* ❶ (*showing friendship*) freundlich; ■**to be** ~ **with sb** mit jdm befreundet sein ❷ (*of place, atmosphere*) angenehm ❸ (*allied*) freundlich gesinnt; *country* befreundet

friendship ['frend·ʃɪp] *n* Freundschaft *f*

fries [fraɪz] *npl* Pommes frites *pl*

frigate ['frɪg·ət] *n* Fregatte *f*

frigging ['frɪg·ɪŋ] *adj attr, inv* (*sl*) verdammte(r, s) *fam*

fright [fraɪt] *n* ❶ (*feeling*) Angst *f* ❷ *usu sing* (*experience*) Schrecken *m;* **to get a** ~ erschrecken

frighten ['fraɪt·ən] **I.** *vt* ■**to** ~ **sb** jdm Angst machen; **to** ~ **the [living] daylights out of sb** jdn furchtbar erschrecken **II.** *vi* erschrecken
◆**frighten away** *vt* abschrecken

frightened ['fraɪt·ənd] *adj* verängstigt; ■**to be** ~ **[that]** ... Angst haben, [dass] ...; ■**to be** ~ **of sth/sb** sich vor etw/jdm fürchten

frightening ['fraɪt·ən·ɪŋ] *adj* Furcht erregend

frightful ['fraɪt·fəl] *adj* (*liter*) ❶ (*bad*) entsetzlich ❷ (*extreme*) schrecklich, furchtbar

frigid ['frɪdʒ·ɪd] *adj* ❶ (*of manner*) frostig ❷ (*sexually*) frigid[e]

frigidity [frɪ·'dʒɪd·ɪ·t̬i] *n* ❶ (*of manner, temperature*) Kälte *f* ❷ (*of sexuality*) Frigidität *f*

frill [frɪl] *n* ❶ (*cloth*) Rüsche *f* ❷ (*fig fam: extras*) ■~**s** *pl* Schnickschnack *m*

frilly ['frɪl·i] *adj* mit Rüschen, Rüschen-

fringe [frɪndʒ] **I.** *n* ❶ (*edging*) Franse *f* ❷ (*of area*) Rand *m a. fig* **II.** *vt usu passive* umgeben; *cloth* umsäumen **III.** *adj* ~ **benefits** zusätzliche Leistungen *pl*

frisk [frɪsk] **I.** *vi* ■**to** ~ **[around]** herumtollen **II.** *vt* abtasten (**for** nach +*dat*)

frisky ['frɪs·ki] *adj* ausgelassen; *horse* lebhaft

fritter¹ ['frɪt̬·ər] *vt* ■**to** ~ **away** ↔ **sth** etw vergeuden; *money* verschleudern; *time* vertrödeln

fritter² ['frɪt̬·ər] *n* Fettgebackenes *nt* (*mit Obst-/Gemüsefüllung*)

frivolity [frɪ·'val·ɪ·t̬i] *n* (*lack of seriousness*) Frivolität *f*

frivolous ['frɪv·ə·ləs] *adj* ❶ (*pej*) *person* leichtfertig ❷ (*pej: unimportant*) belanglos

frizzy ['frɪz·i] *adj* gekräuselt

fro [froʊ] *adv* **to and** ~ hin und her

frock [frak] *n* (*liter*) Kleid *nt*

frog [frag] *n* Frosch *m*

frolic ['fral·ɪk] *vi* <-ck-> herumtollen

F

from [frʌm] *prep* ① (*off*) von; (*out of, made of, originating in*) aus ② (*as seen from*) ~ **here** von hier [aus]; ~ **my point of view** aus meiner Sicht ③ (*as starting location*) von; ~ **the north** von Norden; ~ **Washington to Florida** von Washington nach Florida ④ (*as starting time*) von, ab; ~ **tomorrow on[ward]** ab morgen; ~ **start to finish** vom Anfang bis zum Ende; ~ **time to time** ab und zu ⑤ (*as starting condition*) bei; ~ **25 to 200** von 25 auf 200; ~ **Latin** aus dem Lateinischen ⑥ (*considering*) aufgrund, wegen; ~ **the evidence** aufgrund des Beweismaterials ⑦ (*caused by*) an *+dat;* **he died ~ his injuries** er starb an seinen Verletzungen; **she suffers ~ arthritis** sie leidet unter Arthritis; **the risk ~ radiation [exposure]** das Risiko einer Verstrahlung ⑧ (*indicating protection*) vor; **to protect sb ~ sth** jdn vor etw *dat* schützen ⑨ (*indicating prevention*) vor; **the truth was kept ~ the public** die Wahrheit wurde vor der Öffentlichkeit geheim gehalten; **to prevent sb ~ doing sth** jdn davon abhalten, etw zu tun ⑩ (*indicating distinction*) von; **his opinion is different ~ mine** unsere Meinungen sind unterschiedlich

front [frʌnt] **I.** *n* ① *usu sing* (*forward-facing part*) Vorderseite *f; of building* Front *f; of sweater* Vorderteil *m;* **to lie on one's ~** auf dem Bauch liegen ② (*front area*) ■**the ~** der vordere Bereich; ■**at the ~** vorn[e] ③ (*ahead of*) ■**in ~** vorn[e]; ■**in ~ of sth/sb** vor etw/jdm; ■**to be in ~** SPORTS in Führung liegen ④ (*in advance*) ■**up ~** im Voraus ⑤ (*fig: deception*) Fassade *f oft pej;* **it's a ~ for the Mafia** das ist nur eine Deckadresse für die Mafia ⑥ MIL, METEO, POL Front *f* **II.** *adj* (*at the front*) vorder[st]e(r, s); ~ **wheel** Vorderrad *nt;* ~ **teeth** Schneidezähne *pl* **III.** *vt* ① (*be head of*) vorstehen *+dat* ② (*fam: advance*) *money* vorstrecken

frontage [ˈfrʌn·tɪdʒ] *n* [Vorder]front *f*

frontal [ˈfrʌn·təl] *adj* Frontal-; ~ **view** Vorderansicht *f*

front ˈdoor *n* Vordertür *f; of a house* Haustür *f*

frontier [frʌn·ˈtɪr] *n* (*outlying areas*) ■**the ~** *der ehemalige Wilde Westen der USA*

front ˈline *n* ① MIL Frontlinie *f* ② (*fig*) vorderste Front

front ˈpage *n* Titelseite *f*

ˈfront-page *adj* auf der Titelseite *nach n;* ~ **story** Titelgeschichte *f*

ˈfront-runner *n* Spitzenreiter(in) *m(f) a. fig*

front-wheel ˈdrive **I.** *n* Vorderradantrieb *m* **II.** *adj* mit Vorderradantrieb *nach n*

front ˈyard *n* Vorhof *m,* Vorgarten *m*

frost [frast] **I.** *n* Frost *m* **II.** *vt* FOOD glasieren

ˈfrostbite *n* Erfrierung *f*

ˈfrostbitten *adj* erfroren

frosted [ˈfra·stɪd] *adj* ① FOOD glasiert ② (*opaque*) ~ **glass** Milchglas *nt*

frosting [ˈfra·stɪŋ] *n* FOOD Glasur *f*

frosty [ˈfra·sti] *adj* ① (*very cold*) frostig; (*covered with frost*) vereist ② (*unfriendly*) frostig; *atmosphere* kühl

froth [fraθ] **I.** *n* Schaum *m* **II.** *vi* schäumen; **to ~ at the mouth** Schaum vor dem Mund haben; (*fig*) vor Wut schäumen **III.** *vt* ■**to ~ [up]** aufschäumen

frothy [ˈfra·θi] *adj* schaumig

frown [fraʊn] **I.** *vi* ① (*showing displeasure*) die Stirn runzeln; ■**to ~ on** [*or* **upon**] **sth** etw missbilligen ② (*in thought*) nachdenklich die Stirn runzeln **II.** *n* Stirnrunzeln *nt kein pl*

froze [froʊz] *pt of* **freeze**

frozen [ˈfroʊ·zn] **I.** *pp of* **freeze** **II.** *adj* ① (*of water*) gefroren ② FOOD [tief]gefroren; ~ **food** Tiefkühlkost *f* ③ (*fig: of person*) erfroren

frugal [ˈfru·gəl] *adj* ① (*economical*) sparsam; *lifestyle* genügsam ② *meal* karg, frugal

fruit [frut] **I.** *n* Frucht *f a. fig;* (*collectively*) Obst *nt* **II.** *vi* [Früchte] tragen

ˈfruitcake *n* ① Früchtebrot *nt* ② (*sl: eccentric*) Spinner(in) *m(f)*

fruitful [ˈfrut·fəl] *adj* fruchtbar *a. fig*

fruition [fru·ˈɪʃ·ən] *n* Verwirklichung *f;* **to come to** [*or* **reach**] **~** verwirklicht werden

fruitless [ˈfrut·lɪs] *adj* fruchtlos

fruit ˈsalad *n* Obstsalat *m*

fruity [ˈfru·t̬i] *adj* ① (*of taste*) fruchtig ② (*sl: crazy*) verrückt

frumpish [ˈfrʌm·pɪʃ], **frumpy** [ˈfrʌm·pi] *adj* altmodisch

frustrate [ˈfrʌs·treɪt] *vt* ① (*annoy*) frustrieren ② (*prevent*) hindern

frustrated [ˈfrʌs·treɪ·t̬ɪd] *adj* frustriert

frustrating [ˈfrʌs·treɪ·t̬ɪŋ] *adj* frustrierend

frustration [frʌ·ˈstreɪ·ʃən] *n* Frustration *f;* **to work off one's ~** seinen Frust abreagieren

fry[1] [fraɪ] **I.** *vt* <-ie-> braten **II.** *vi* <-ie-> braten

fry[2] [fraɪ] *npl* junger Fisch ▶ PHRASES: <u>**small**</u> ~ kleine Fische; (*person*) kleiner Fisch

frying pan [ˈfraɪ·ɪŋ-] *n* Bratpfanne *f*

ft. *n abbrev of* **feet, foot** ft

fuck [fʌk] (*vulg*) **I.** *n* ① (*act*) Fick *m* ② (*used as expletive*) **who gives a ~?** wen interessiert es schon? **II.** *interj* Scheiße! **III.** *vt* ① (*have sex with*) vögeln; **go ~ yourself!** verpiss dich!, schleich dich! *bes* SÜDD, ÖSTERR ② (*damn*) **[oh] ~ it!** verdammte Scheiße!; **~ you!** leck mich am Arsch! **IV.** *vi* ① (*have sex*) ficken ② (*play mind games*) ■**to ~ with sb** jdn verscheißern

◆**fuck off** *vi* (*vulg*) sich verpissen

fucker [ˈfʌk·ər] *n* (*vulg*) ① (*person*) Arsch *m* ② (*thing*) Scheiß *m*

fucking [ˈfʌk·ɪŋ] *adj, adv* (*vulg*) verdammt, Scheiß-; **to be ~ useless** zu gar nichts taugen; (*sl*) echt, verflixt; **you must be ~ crazy!** du musst verrückt sein, verdammt!

ˈfuckup *n* (*vulg, sl*) ① (*mess*) Scheiß *m pej derb;* (*confusion*) Durcheinander *nt* ② (*person*) Tollpatsch *m*

fudge [fʌdʒ] **I.** *n* ① (*candy*) Fondant *m o nt* ② (*nonsense*) Unsinn *m* **II.** *vt, vi figures* frisieren *fam*

fuel [ˈfju·əl] **I.** *n* Brennstoff *m;* (*for engines*) Kraftstoff *m,* Treibstoff *m* **II.** *vt* <-l- *or* -ll->

① ■ **to be ~ed [by sth]** [mit etw] betrieben werden ② (*fig*) nähren; *resentment* schüren; *speculation* anheizen

'fuel consumption *n* Brennstoffverbrauch *m;* TRANSP Treibstoffverbrauch *m*

'fuel gauge *n* Tankanzeige *f*

fuel-injection 'engine *n* Einspritzmotor *m*

'fuel pump *n* Kraftstoffpumpe *f*

'fuel rod *n* Brennstab *m*

fugitive ['fju·dʒɪ·t̬ɪv] **I.** *n* Flüchtige(r) *f(m)* **II.** *adj* flüchtig

fulfill [fʊl·'fɪl] *vt* ① (*satisfy*) erfüllen; *ambition* erreichen; *potential* ausschöpfen ② (*carry out*) nachkommen *+dat; contract, promise* erfüllen; *function* einnehmen

fulfillment [fʊl·'fɪl·mənt] *n* Erfüllung *f*

full [fʊl] **I.** *adj* voll; (*after eating*) satt; *explanation* vollständig; *life* ausgefüllt; *skirt* weit; *theater* ausverkauft; *wine* vollmundig; ■ **to be ~ of sth** (*enthusiastic*) von etw *dat* ganz begeistert sein; **to be ~ of oneself** eingebildet sein; **with one's mouth ~** mit vollem Mund; **[at] ~ speed** mit voller Geschwindigkeit; **in ~ swing** voll im Gang; **in ~ view of** direkt vor den Augen *+gen* **II.** *adv* ① (*completely*) voll ② (*very*) sehr; **to know ~ well [that ...]** sehr gut wissen, [dass ...] **III.** *n* **in ~** zur Gänze

'fullback *n* (*in football*) Fullback *m;* (*in soccer, rugby*) Außenverteidiger(in) *m(f)*

full-'blooded *adj* ① (*of descent*) reinrassig ② (*vigorous*) kraftvoll

full-'blown *adj disease* voll ausgebrochen; *scandal* ausgewachsen

full-'bodied *adj food* voll; *wine* vollmundig

full-'fledged *adj* ① *bird* flügge ② *person* ausgebildet

full-'frontal *adj* völlig nackt

full-'grown *adj* ausgewachsen

full-'length **I.** *adj film* abendfüllend; *gown, skirt* bodenlang; *mirror* groß **II.** *adv* **to lie ~ on the floor** sich der Länge nach auf den Boden legen [*o* der Länge nach auf dem Boden liegen]

full 'moon *n* Vollmond *m*

fullness ['fʊl·nɪs] *n* ① (*being full*) Völle *f* ② (*plumpness*) Fülle *f a. fig*

'full-page *adj* ganzseitig

'full-scale *adj* ① (*original size*) in Originalgröße *nach n* ② (*all-out*) umfassend; *war* ausgewachsen

full 'stop *n* **to come to a ~** zum Stillstand *m* kommen

full 'time *n* (*in soccer*) Spielende *nt*

'full-time **I.** *adj* Ganztags-; **~ job** Vollzeitbeschäftigung *f* **II.** *adv* ganztags

fully ['fʊl·i] *adv* ① (*completely*) völlig; **~ booked** ausgebucht ② (*in detail*) detailliert

fumble ['fʌm·bəl] **I.** *vi* ① ■ **to ~ [around** [*or* **about**]] **with sth** an etw *dat* [herum]fingern; ■ **to ~ [around** [*or* **about**]] **for sth** nach etw *dat* tasten ② SPORTS den Ball fallen lassen, fumblen **II.** *vt ball* fallen lassen, fumblen **III.** *n* SPORTS [Ballannahme]fehler *m,* Fumble *m*

fume [fjum] *vi* vor Wut schäumen

fumes [fjumz] *n pl* Dämpfe *pl; of car* Abgase *pl*

fumigate ['fju·mɪ·geɪt] *vt building, room* ausräuchern

fun [fʌn] **I.** *n* Spaß *m;* **it was lots of ~** es hat viel Spaß gemacht; **to be full of ~** immer unternehmungslustig sein; **for ~ [***or* **for the ~ of it]** nur [so] zum Spaß; **in ~** im Spaß; **have ~!** viel Spaß!; **to make ~ of sb** sich über jdn lustig machen; **to spoil sb's ~** jdm den Spaß verderben **II.** *adj* (*fam*) lustig

function ['fʌŋk·ʃən] **I.** *n* ① (*task*) *of a person* Aufgabe *f* ② MATH Funktion *f* ③ (*ceremony*) Feier *f;* (*social event*) Veranstaltung *f* **II.** *vi* funktionieren; ■ **to ~ as sth** *thing* als etw dienen; *person* als etw fungieren

functional ['fʌŋk·ʃə·nəl] *adj* ① (*with purpose*) funktional ② (*operational*) funktionstüchtig; ■ **to be ~** funktionieren

functionary ['fʌŋk·ʃə·ner·i] *n* Funktionär(in) *m(f)*

'function key *n* COMPUT Funktionstaste *f*

fund [fʌnd] **I.** *n* ① (*stock*) Fonds *m;* **disaster ~** Notfonds *m* ② (*money*) ■ **~s** *pl* [finanzielle] Mittel; **to allocate ~s** Gelder bewilligen ③ (*fig: supply*) Vorrat *m* (**of** an *+dat*) **II.** *vt* finanzieren

fundamental [ˌfʌn·də·'men·t̬əl] *adj* grundlegend (**to** für *+akk*); *difference* wesentlich; *question* entscheidend; **~ right** Grundrecht *nt*

fundamentalism [ˌfʌn·də·'men·t̬əl·ɪz·əm] *n* Fundamentalismus *m*

fundamentalist [ˌfʌn·də·'men·t̬əl·ɪst] **I.** *n* Fundamentalist(in) *m(f)* **II.** *adj* fundamentalistisch

fundamentally [ˌfʌn·də·'ment·əl·i] *adv* ① (*basically*) im Grunde ② (*in all important aspects*) grundsätzlich

funding ['fʌnd·ɪŋ] *n* Finanzierung *f*

'fundraiser *n* ① (*person*) Spendenbeschaffer(in) *m(f)* ② (*event*) Wohltätigkeitsveranstaltung *f*

'fundraising **I.** *adj* Wohltätigkeits-; **~ campaign** Spendenaktion *f* **II.** *n* Geldbeschaffung *f*

funeral ['fju·nər·əl] *n* Beerdigung *f*

'funeral director *n* Leichenbestatter(in) *m(f)*

'funeral home *n* Bestattungsinstitut *nt,* Bestattungsunternehmen *nt*

'funeral march *n* MUS Trauermarsch *m*

'funeral parlor *n see* **funeral home**

'funeral pyre *n* Scheiterhaufen *m*

funereal [fju·'nɪr·i·əl] *adj* gedrückt; *music* getragen

fungicide ['fʌn·dʒɪ·saɪd] *n* Fungizid *nt*

fungus <*pl* -es *or* -gi> ['fʌŋ·gəs, *pl* -gaɪ] *n* Pilz *m*

funicular [fju·'nɪk·ju·lər], **funicular 'railway** *n* Seilbahn *f*

funk [fʌŋk] *n* ① (*fam: depression*) **in a ~** deprimiert ② MUS Funk *m*

funky ['fʌŋ·ki] *adj* (*sl*) ① (*hip*) flippig ② MUS funkig

'fun-loving *adj* lebenslustig

funnel ['fʌn·əl] **I.** *n* ① (*tool*) Trichter *m* ② (*on* *ship*) Schornstein *m* **II.** *vt* <-l- *or* -ll-> ❶ (*pour*) [mit einem Trichter] einfüllen ❷ (*fig: direct*) zuleiten **III.** *vi people* drängen; *liquids* fließen; *gases* strömen

funnies [ˈfʌn·iz] *npl* ■ **the ~** der Witzteil (*einer Zeitung*)

funny [ˈfʌn·i] **I.** *adj* ❶ (*amusing*) lustig, witzig, komisch; **there's a ~ side to everything** alles hat auch seine komischen Seiten ❷ (*strange*) komisch, merkwürdig, seltsam; **to have a ~ feeling that ...** so eine Ahnung haben, dass ... ❸ (*dishonest*) verdächtig; **~ business** krumme Sachen ▶ PHRASES: **~ ha-ha or ~ peculiar** [*or* **weird**]**?** lustig oder merkwürdig? **II.** *adv* (*fam*) komisch, merkwürdig

F

ˈfunny bone *n* (*fam*) Musikantenknochen *m*

fur [fɜr] *n* ❶ (*on animal*) Fell *nt* ❷ FASHION Pelz *m*

fur ˈcoat *n* Pelzmantel *m*

furious [ˈfjʊr·i·əs] *adj* ❶ (*angry*) *person* [sehr] wütend; *argument* heftig; ■ **to be ~ with sb/about** [*or* **at**] **sth** wütend auf jdn/über etw *akk* sein ❷ (*intense*) *storm* heftig; **at a ~ pace** in rasender Geschwindigkeit; **fast and ~** rasant; **the questions came fast and ~** die Fragen kamen Schlag auf Schlag

furl [fɜrl] *vt* einrollen

furnace [ˈfɜr·nɪs] *n* ❶ (*industrial*) Hochofen *m*, Schmelzofen *m* ❷ (*domestic*) [Haupt]heizung *f*

furnish [ˈfɜr·nɪʃ] *vt* ❶ (*provide furniture*) einrichten ❷ (*supply*) liefern; ■ **to ~ sb with sth** jdn mit etw *dat* versorgen

furnished [ˈfɜr·nɪʃt] *adj house* eingerichtet; *apartment, room* möbliert

furnishings [ˈfɜr·nɪ·ʃɪŋz] *npl* Einrichtung *f*

furniture [ˈfɜr·nɪ·tʃər] *n* Möbel *pl;* **piece** [*or* **item**] **of ~** Möbelstück *nt*

furor [ˈfjʊr·ɔr] *n* ❶ (*uproar*) Aufruhr *m* ❷ (*excitement*) Wirbel *m* (**over** um +*akk*)

furrow [ˈfɜr·oʊ] *n* ❶ (*groove*) Furche *f* ❷ (*wrinkle*) Falte *f*

furry [ˈfɜr·i] *adj* (*short fur*) pelzig; (*long fur*) wollig; *tongue* belegt

further [ˈfɜr·ðər] **I.** *adj comp of* **far** ❶ (*additional*) weiter; **until ~ notice** bis auf weiteres ❷ (*more distant*) weiter [entfernt] **II.** *adv comp of* **far** ❶ (*to a greater degree*) weiter; **I wouldn't go any ~ than that** mehr möchte ich nicht sagen; **to take sth ~** mit etw *dat* weitermachen; (*pursue*) *matter* etw weiterverfolgen ❷ (*more*) [noch] weiter; **I have nothing ~ to say** ich habe nichts mehr zu sagen.; **to make sth go ~** *food* etw strecken ❸ (*more distant*) weiter; **nothing could be ~ from my mind** nichts liegt mir ferner; **~ back** (*in place*) weiter zurück; (*in time*) früher **III.** *vt* fördern

furthermore [ˈfɜr·ðər·mɔr] *adv* außerdem

furthest [ˈfɜr·ðɪst] **I.** *adj superl of* **far** ❶ (*fig*) extremste(r, s) ❷ am weitesten entfernte(r, s) **II.** *adv superl of* **far** am weitesten; **that's the ~ I can see** weiter [entfernt] erkenne ich nichts mehr

furtive [ˈfɜr·t̬ɪv] *adj glance* verstohlen; *action* heimlich; *manner* verschlagen

fury [ˈfjʊr·i] *n* ❶ (*rage*) Wut *f;* **in a ~** wütend ❷ (*intensity*) Ungestüm *nt; of a storm* Heftigkeit *f*

fuse[1] [fjuz] **I.** *n* (*device*) *of a bomb* Zündvorrichtung *f;* (*string*) Zündschnur *f* ▶ PHRASES: **sb has a short ~** jd wird schnell wütend **II.** *vt* **to ~ a bomb** eine Bombe mit einer Zündvorrichtung versehen

fuse[2] [fjuz] **I.** *n* Sicherung *f;* **to blow a ~** die Sicherung einer S. *gen* zum Durchbrennen bringen **II.** *vi* sich vereinigen **III.** *vt* verbinden; (*with heat*) verschmelzen

ˈfuse box *n* Sicherungskasten *m*

fuselage [ˈfju·sə·lɑʒ] *n* [Flugzeug]rumpf *m*

fusion [ˈfju·ʒən] *n* Verschmelzung *f kein pl a. fig;* **nuclear ~** Kernfusion *f*

fuss [fʌs] **I.** *n* ❶ (*excitement*) [übertriebene] Aufregung ❷ (*attention*) [übertriebener] Aufwand, Getue *nt pej;* **to make** [*or* **kick up**] **a ~** einen Aufstand machen **II.** *vi* (*be nervously active*) [sehr] aufgeregt sein; ■ **to ~ over sb/sth** (*treat with excessive attention*) für jdn/etw einen großen Aufwand betreiben; (*overly worry*) sich *dat* übertriebene Sorgen um jdn/etw machen

ˈfussbudget *n* (*fam*) **to be a ~** penibel sein

fussy [ˈfʌs·i] *adj* ❶ (*pej: about things*) pingelig; (*about food*) mäkelig; (*about people*) [zu] wählerisch ❷ (*pej: overly decorated*) [zu] verspielt, überladen

futile [ˈfju·t̬əl] *adj* sinnlos; (*pointless*) nutzlos; *attempt* vergeblich

futility [fju·ˈtɪl·ɪ·t̬i] *n* Sinnlosigkeit *f*

futon [ˈfu·tɑn] *n* Futon *nt*

future [ˈfju·tʃər] **I.** *n usu sing* ❶ (*in time*) Zukunft *f;* ■ **in the ~** in Zukunft; **to have no ~** keine Zukunft[saussichten] haben; **there's no ~ for me in this company** in dieser Firma habe ich keine Aussichten ❷ LING **~ tense** Futur *nt* **II.** *adj* zukünftig; *generations* kommend; *use* später

future ˈperfect *n* vollendetes Futur, Futur II

ˈfutures market *n* ECON Terminbörse *f*

futuristic [ˌfju·tʃə·ˈrɪs·tɪk] *adj* futuristisch

fuze [fjuz] *n, vt see* **fuse**[1]

fuzz[1] [fʌz] *n* ❶ (*fluff*) Fussel[n] *pl* ❷ (*fluffy hair*) Flaum *m*

fuzz[2] [fʌz] *n* (*sl: police*) ■ **the ~** die Bullen *pl*

fuzzy [ˈfʌz·i] *adj* ❶ (*fluffy*) flaumig ❷ (*frizzy*) wuschelig ❸ (*distorted*) verschwommen, unscharf

FYI *adv* (*fam*) *abbrev of* **for your information** z. K.

Gg

G <*pl* -'s *or* -s>, **g** <*pl* -'s> [dʒi] *n* ❶ (*letter*) G *nt,* g *nt;* ~ **as in Golf** G wie Gustav ❷ MUS G *nt,* g *nt;* ~ **flat** Ges *nt,* ges *nt;* ~ **sharp** Gis *nt,* gis *nt*

G *adj inv* FILM *abbrev of* **General Audiences: rated** ~ jugendfrei

GA, **Ga.** *abbrev of* **Georgia**

gab [gæb] **I.** *vi* <-bb-> (*pej fam*) quatschen **II.** *n* **to have the gift of** ~ überzeugend reden können

gabble ['gæb·əl] **I.** *vi* quasseln **II.** *vt* herunterrasseln

gable ['geɪ·bəl] *n* Giebel *m*

gadget ['gædʒ·ɪt] *n* [praktisches] Gerät

Gaelic ['geɪ·lɪk] **I.** *n* Gälisch *nt* **II.** *adj* gälisch

gaffe [gæf] *n* Fauxpas *m*

gaffer ['gæf·ər] *n* FILM, TV ≈ Filmtechniker *m*

gag [gæg] **I.** *n* ❶ (*for mouth*) Knebel *m* ❷ (*joke*) Gag *m* **II.** *vt* <-gg-> ■**to** ~ **sb** jdn knebeln; (*fig*) jdm einen Maulkorb verpassen **III.** *vi* ■**to** ~ **[on sth]** [an etw *dat* herum]würgen

gaga ['ga·ga] *adj* (*fam*) vertrottelt

gage [geɪdʒ] *n, vt see* **gauge**

gaggle ['gæg·əl] *n* ~ **of geese** Gänseherde *f*

'**gag order** *n* (*fam*) Nachrichtensperre *f*

gaiety ['geɪ·ə·t̬i] *n* Fröhlichkeit *f*

gaily ['geɪ·li] *adv* ❶ (*happily*) fröhlich ❷ (*brightly*) freundlich; ~ **colored** farbenfroh

gain [geɪn] **I.** *n* ❶ (*increase*) Zunahme *f kein pl; in speed* Erhöhung *f kein pl;* **weight** ~ Gewichtszunahme *f* ❷ (*advantage*) Vorteil *m* **II.** *vt* ❶ (*obtain*) gewinnen; *access, entry* sich *dat* verschaffen; *experience* sammeln; *independence* erlangen; *recognition* finden; *victory* erringen; **to** ~ **control of sth** etw unter [seine] Kontrolle bekommen ❷ (*increase*) ■**to** ~ **sth** an etw *dat* gewinnen; *self-confidence* entwickeln; **to** ~ **ground/popularity** an Boden/Beliebtheit gewinnen; **to** ~ **speed** schneller werden; **to** ~ **weight** zunehmen **III.** *vi* ❶ (*increase*) zunehmen; *prices, numbers* [an]steigen ❷ (*profit*) profitieren; **they would** ~ **by reducing their prices/improving their customer service** sie würden von einer Ermäßigung ihrer Preise/einer Verbesserung ihres Kundendienstes profitieren

gainful ['geɪn·fəl] *adj* ~ **employment** Erwerbstätigkeit *f*

gait [geɪt] *n* Gang *m kein pl; of a horse* Gangart *f*

gala ['geɪ·lə] *n* (*social event*) Gala *f*

galactic [gə·'læk·tɪk] *adj* galaktisch

galaxy ['gæl·ək·si] *n* (*star system*) Galaxie *f*

gale [geɪl] *n* Sturm *m*

gall [gɔl] *n* ANAT Galle *f;* ~ **bladder** Gallenblase *f* ▶ PHRASES: **to <u>have</u> the** ~ **to do sth** die Frechheit besitzen, etw zu tun

gallant ['gæl·ənt] *adj* ❶ (*chivalrous*) charmant ❷ (*brave*) tapfer

galleon ['gæl·i·ən] *n* Galeone *f*

gallery ['gæl·ə·ri] *n* Galerie *f*

galley ['gæl·i] *n* ❶ (*kitchen*) *of a ship* Kombüse *f; of an airplane* Bordküche *f* ❷ (*hist: ship*) Galeere *f*

gallivant [,gæl·ə·'vænt] *vi* (*fam*) ■**to** ~ **around** sich herumtreiben

gallon ['gæl·ən] *n* Gallone *f*

gallop ['gæl·əp] **I.** *vi* galoppieren **II.** *n usu sing* Galopp *m;* **to break into a** ~ in Galopp verfallen

gallows ['gæl·oʊz] *n* + *sing vb* Galgen *m;* **to send sb to the** ~ jdn an den Galgen bringen

'**gallstone** *n* Gallenstein *m*

galore [gə·'lɔr] *adj after n* im Überfluss

galvanize ['gæl·və·naɪz] *vt* ❶ TECH galvanisieren ❷ (*fig*) wachrütteln; **to** ~ **sb into action** jdn veranlassen aktiv zu werden

gambit ['gæm·bɪt] *n* ❶ (*in chess*) Gambit *nt* ❷ (*tactic, remark*) Schachzug *m;* **opening** ~ *Satz, mit dem man ein Gespräch anfängt*

gamble ['gæm·bəl] **I.** *n usu sing* Risiko *nt* **II.** *vi* ❶ (*bet*) [um Geld] spielen; **to** ~ **on horses** auf Pferde wetten; **to** ~ **on the stock market** an der Börse spekulieren ❷ (*take a risk*) ■**to** ~ **on/that ...** sich darauf verlassen, dass ...

gambler ['gæm·blər] *n* Spieler(in) *m(f)*

gambling ['gæm·bəlɪŋ] *n* Glücksspiel *nt*

game[1] [geɪm] **I.** *n* Spiel *nt;* **a** ~ **of chess/tennis** eine Partie Schach/Tennis; **what's your** ~**?** (*fig fam*) was soll das?; **to play** ~**s with sb** (*fig*) mit jdm spielen ▶ PHRASES: **to <u>beat</u> sb at their own** ~ jdn mit seinen eigenen Waffen schlagen; **to <u>give</u> the** ~ **<u>away</u>** alles verraten; **<u>two</u> can play at that** ~ was du kannst, kann ich schon lange; **the** ~**'s <u>up</u>** das Spiel ist aus **II.** *adj* bereit

game[2] [geɪm] *n* (*animal*) Wild *nt;* **big** ~ Großwild *nt*

'**gamekeeper** *n* Wildhüter(in) *m(f)*

'**game show** *n* Spielshow *f;* (*quiz show*) Quizsendung *f*

gaming ['geɪ·mɪŋ] *n* Spielen *nt*

gander ['gæn·dər] *n* (*goose*) Gänserich *m*

gang [gæŋ] **I.** *n of criminals* Bande *f; of youths* Gang *f; of friends* Clique *f; of workers, prisoners* Kolonne *f* **II.** *vi* ■**to** ~ **up** sich zusammentun; ■**to** ~ **up on sb** sich gegen jdn verbünden

gangling ['gæŋ·glɪŋ] *adj* schlaksig

'**gangplank** *n* Landungssteg *m,* Landungsbrücke *f*

gangrene ['gæŋ·grin] *n* MED Brand *m*

gangster ['gæŋ·stər] *n* Gangster(in) *m(f)*

gang '**warfare** *n* Bandenkrieg *m*

'**gangway** **I.** *n* ❶ NAUT, AERO Gangway *f* ❷ *see* **gangplank** **II.** *interj* (*fam*) ~**!** Platz da!

G

gantry [ˈgæn·tri] *n* Gerüst *nt;* (*for crane*) Portal *nt*

gap [gæp] *n* ① (*empty space*) Lücke *f a. fig* ② (*difference*) Unterschied *m;* **age ~** Altersunterschied *m*

gape [geɪp] *vi* glotzen; ■**to ~ at sb/sth** jdn/etw [mit offenem Mund] anstarren

gaping [ˈgeɪ·pɪŋ] *adj* weit geöffnet; *wound* klaffend; *hole* gähnend

garage [gə·ˈrɑʒ] *n* ① (*for cars*) Garage *f* ② (*repair shop*) [Kfz-]Werkstatt *f*

ga'rage sale *n privater Flohmarkt in der Garage*

garbage [ˈgɑr·bɪdʒ] *n* ① (*trash*) Müll *m a. fig* ② (*pej: nonsense*) Blödsinn *m*

'garbage can *n* Mülleimer *m*

'garbage man *n* Müllmann *m fam,* Kehrichtmann *m* SCHWEIZ

'garbage truck *n* Müllauto *m,* Kehrichtwagen *m* SCHWEIZ

garble [ˈgɑr·bəl] *vt* durcheinanderbringen; *message* verdrehen

garden [ˈgɑr·dən] *n* Garten *m;* ■**~s** *pl* Gartenanlage *f,* Gärten *pl*

gardener [ˈgɑrd·nər] *n* Gärtner(in) *m(f)*

gardening [ˈgɑrd·nɪŋ] *n* Gartenarbeit *f;* **~ tools** Gartengeräte *pl*

gargantuan [gɑr·ˈgæn·tʃu·ən] *adj* riesig

gargle [ˈgɑr·gəl] *vi* gurgeln

gargoyle [ˈgɑr·gɔɪl] *n* Wasserspeier *m*

garish [ˈger·ɪʃ] *adj* (*pej*) knallbunt

garland [ˈgɑr·lənd] **I.** *n* Kranz *m;* **~ of roses** Rosenkranz *m* **II.** *vt* bekränzen

garlic [ˈgɑr·lɪk] *n* Knoblauch *m;* **~ bread** Knoblauchbrot *nt*

garment [ˈgɑr·mənt] *n* Kleidungsstück *nt*

garnish [ˈgɑr·nɪʃ] **I.** *vt food* garnieren **II.** *n* <*pl* -es> Garnierung *f*

garrison [ˈger·ə·sən] *n* Garnison *f*

garrulous [ˈger·ə·ləs] *adj* schwatzhaft

garter [ˈgɑr·t̬ər] *n* Strumpfband *nt,* Strumpfhalter *m*

gas [gæs] **I.** *n* <*pl* -es *or* -sses> ① (*not solid or liquid*) Gas *nt;* **natural ~** Erdgas *nt* ② (*fam: gasoline*) Benzin *nt;* **to step on the ~** (*fig*) Gas geben ③ (*fam: flatulence*) Blähungen *pl* **II.** *vt* <-ss-> vergasen **III.** *vi* <-ss-> (*fam*) quatschen

'gasbag *n* (*pej sl*) Quasselstrippe *f*

'gas chamber *n* Gaskammer *f*

gaseous [ˈgæs·i·əs] *adj* gasförmig

'gas gauge *n* Benzinuhr *f*

'gas guzzler *n* (*fam*) Benzinfresser *m fam,* Benzinschlucker *m fam*

'gas-guzzling *adj* (*fam*) benzinfressend

gash [gæʃ] **I.** *n* <*pl* -es> *on the body* [tiefe] Schnittwunde; *in cloth* [tiefer] Schlitz **II.** *vt* aufschlitzen

'gas heating *n* [zentrale] Gasheizung

gasket [ˈgæs·kɪt] *n* Dichtung *f*

'gas lamp *n* Gaslampe *f*

'gas mask *n* Gasmaske *f*

'gas meter *n* Gaszähler *m*

gasoline [ˈgæs·ə·lin] *n* Benzin *nt*

'gas oven *n* Gasherd *m*

gasp [gæsp] **I.** *vi* (*pant*) keuchen; (*catch one's breath*) tief einatmen; ■**he ~ed in pain** ihm stockte der Atem vor Schmerz; **to ~ for air** nach Luft schnappen **II.** *vt* hervorstoßen; **"I thought you were dead," she ~ed** „ich dachte du wärst tot," stieß sie atemlos hervor **III.** *n* hörbares Lufteinziehen; **he gave a ~ of amazement** ihm blieb vor Überraschung die Luft weg ▶ PHRASES: **the last ~** der letzte Atemzug

'gas pedal *n* Gaspedal *nt*

'gas pipe *n* Gasleitung *f*

'gas pump *n* Zapfsäule *f*

'gas station *n* Tankstelle *f*

'gas stove *n* Gasherd *m;* (*small*) Gaskocher *m*

gassy [ˈgæs·i] *adj* (*fam*) *digestive system* gebläht

gastric [ˈgæs·trɪk] *adj* MED Magen-

gastronomic [ˌgæs·trə·ˈnɑm·ɪk] *adj* kulinarisch

gastronomy [gæ·ˈstrɑn·ə·mi] *n* Gastronomie *f*

gate [geɪt] *n* ① (*at an entrance*) Tor *nt;* (*at an airport*) Flugsteig *m,* Gate *nt;* (*to a yard, courtyard*) Pforte *f* ② SPORTS **starting ~** Startmaschine *f* ③ (*spectators*) Zuschauerzahl *f*

'gatecrash *vt* (*fam*) reinplatzen (**in** +*akk*)

'gatecrasher *n* (*fam*) un[ein]geladener Gast

'gatekeeper *n* Pförtner(in) *m(f)*

'gateway *n* ① Eingangstor *nt* ② (*fig*) Tor *nt*

'gateway drug *n* Einstiegsdroge *f*

gather [ˈgæð·ər] **I.** *vt* ① (*collect*) sammeln; **to ~ intelligence** sich *dat* [geheime] Informationen beschaffen ② FASHION kräuseln ③ (*increase*) **to ~ speed** schneller werden ④ (*understand*) verstehen; ■**to ~ from sth that ...** aus etw *dat* schließen, dass ...; ■**to ~ from sb that ...** von jdm erfahren haben, dass ... **II.** *vi* (*come together*) sich sammeln; *people* sich versammeln; (*accumulate*) sich ansammeln; *storm* heraufziehen

gathering [ˈgæð·ər·ɪŋ] **I.** *n* Versammlung *f;* **family ~** Familientreffen *nt* **II.** *adj clouds, storm* heraufziehend; *darkness, gloom* zunehmend

gauche [goʊʃ] *adj* unbeholfen

gaudy [ˈgɔ·di] *adj* knallig

gauge [geɪdʒ] **I.** *n* ① (*device*) Messgerät *nt;* (*for tools*) [Mess]lehre *f;* (*for water level*) Pegel *m* ② (*thickness*) *of metal, plastic* Stärke *f; of a wire, tube* Dicke *f;* (*diameter*) *of a gun, bullet* Durchmesser *m* ③ RAIL Spurweite *f* **II.** *vt* ① (*measure*) messen ② (*judge*) beurteilen; (*estimate*) [ab]schätzen

gaunt [gɔnt] *adj* hager; (*from illness*) ausgemergelt

gauntlet [ˈgɔnt·lɪt] *n* [Stulpen]handschuh *m* ▶ PHRASES: **to run the ~** Spießruten laufen; **to throw down the ~** den Fehdehandschuh hinwerfen *geh*

gauze [gɔz] *n* (*fabric*) Gaze *f*

gave [geɪv] *pt of* **give**

gavel ['gæv·əl] *n* Hammer *m*
gawk [gɔk] *vi* (*fam*) glotzen; ■**to ~ at sb/sth** jdn/etw anglotzen
gawky ['gɔ·ki] *adj* schlaksig, linkisch, unbeholfen
gay [geɪ] **I.** *adj* ① (*homosexual*) schwul, gay; **~ bar** Schwulenlokal *nt;* **~ community** Schwulengemeinschaft *f* ② (*liter: cheerful*) fröhlich, heiter **II.** *n* Schwule(r) *m,* Gay *m*
gaze [geɪz] **I.** *vi* starren; **to ~ into the distance/out of the window** ins Leere/aus dem Fenster starren; ■**to ~ at sb/sth** jdn/etw anstarren **II.** *n* Blick *m*
gazelle [gə·'zel] *n* Gazelle *f*
gazette [gə·'zet] *n* Blatt *nt,* Anzeiger *m*
GB [ˌdʒi·'bi] *n* <pl -> ① *abbrev of* **gigabyte** GByte *nt* ② *abbrev of* **Great Britain** GB
GDP [ˌdʒi·di·'pi] *n abbrev of* **gross domestic product** BIP *nt*
gear [gɪr] **I.** *n* ① TECH Gang *m;* **to shift ~s** schalten ② (*equipment*) Ausrüstung *f;* (*clothes*) Kleidung *f,* Sachen *pl fam* **II.** *vt* ausrichten (**to** auf +*akk*) **III.** *vi* ■**to ~ [oneself] up** sich einstellen (**for** auf +*akk*)
'gearbox *n* Getriebe *nt*
'gearshift *n* Schalthebel *m,* Schaltknüppel *m; on a bicycle* Gangschaltung *f*
GED [ˌdʒi·i·'di] *n abbrev of* **general equivalency diploma** ≈ SfE *f* (*Kurs zur Erlangung der US-Hochschulreife auf dem zweiten Bildungsweg*)
gee [dʒi] *interj* (*fam*) Mannomann
geezer ['gi·zər] *n* (*fam*) [**old**] ~ Alte(r) *m*
gel [dʒel] **I.** *n* Gel *nt* **II.** *vi* <-ll-> ① gelieren ② (*fig*) Form annehmen
gelatin, **gelatine** ['dʒel·ət·in] *n* ① (*colorless substance*) Gelatine *f* ② (*fruit-flavored dessert*) Wackelpudding *m*
gelding ['gel·dɪŋ] *n* (*castrated horse*) Wallach *m*
gem [dʒem] *n* ① (*jewel*) Edelstein *m* ② (*very good thing*) Juwel *nt;* **a ~ of a car/house** ein klasse Auto/prunkvolles Haus
Gemini ['dʒem·ɪ·naɪ] *n* ASTROL Zwillinge *pl;* **to be a ~** [ein] Zwilling sein
gen. [dʒen] *n* ① *short for* **general** allgem. ② *short for* **generation** Gen.
gender ['dʒen·dər] *n* Geschlecht *nt*
gene [dʒin] *n* Gen *nt*
genealogical [ˌdʒi·ni·ə·'ladʒ·ɪ·kəl] *adj* genealogisch; **~ tree** Stammbaum *m*
genealogist [ˌdʒi·nɪ·'æl·ə·dʒɪst] *n* Genealoge, -in *m, f*
genealogy [ˌdʒi·nɪ·'æl·ə·dʒi] *n* Genealogie *f*
'gene bank *n* Genbank *f*
general ['dʒen·ər·əl] **I.** *adj* allgemein; **~ idea** ungefähre Vorstellung; **~ impression** Gesamteindruck *m;* **~ meeting** Vollversammlung *f;* **it is ~ practice** es ist allgemein üblich; ■**the ~ view is that ...** die allgemein verbreitete Meinung ist, dass ...; **in ~** [*or* **as a ~ rule**] im Allgemeinen; **to be in ~ use** allgemein benutzt werden **II.** *n* MIL General(in) *m(f)*
General A'merican *n* die amerikanische Standardsprache
general anes'thetic *n* Vollnarkose *f*
General As'sembly *n* [UNO-]Vollversammlung *f*
general de'livery *n* postlagernd
general e'lection *n* Parlamentswahlen *pl*
generality [ˌdʒen·ə·'ræl·ə·ṭi] *n* (*general statement*) **to talk in generalities** (*generalize*) verallgemeinern; **to talk about/of generalities** sich über Allgemeines unterhalten
generalization [ˌdʒen·ər·ə·lɪ·'zeɪ·ʃən] *n* Verallgemeinerung *f*
generalize ['dʒen·ər·ə·laɪz] *vi, vt* ■**to ~ [about sth]** [etw] verallgemeinern
generally ['dʒen·ər·ə·li] *adv* ① (*usually*) normalerweise, im Allgemeinen ② (*mostly*) im Allgemeinen, im Großen und Ganzen ③ (*widely, not in detail*) allgemein; **~ speaking** im Allgemeinen
general prac'titioner *n* Arzt *m*/Ärztin *f* für Allgemeinmedizin, praktischer Arzt/praktische Ärztin
general 'public *n* **the ~** die Allgemeinheit, die Öffentlichkeit
general-'purpose *adj attr, inv* Allgemein-, Universal-
general 'staff *n* MIL Generalstab *m*
general 'store *n* Gemischtwarenladen *m*
general 'strike *n* Generalstreik *m*
generate ['dʒen·ə·reɪt] *vt controversy, enthusiasm* hervorrufen; *electricity* erzeugen; *income* erzielen; *jobs* schaffen
generation [ˌdʒen·ə·'reɪ·ʃən] *n* ① (*set*) Generation *f;* **the next/younger/older ~** die nächste/jüngere/ältere Generation; **the ~ gap** der Generationsunterschied ② (*production*) Erzeugung *f*
generator ['dʒen·ə·reɪ·ṭər] *n* ① (*dynamo*) Generator *m* ② (*producer*) **~ of new ideas** Ideenlieferant(in) *m(f)*
generic [dʒɪ·'ner·ɪk] *adj* ① (*general*) generisch; **~ term** Oberbegriff *m;* BIOL Gattungsbegriff *m* ② (*not name-brand*) *drug, food, product* markenlos
generosity [ˌdʒen·ə·'ras·ə·ṭi] *n* Großzügigkeit *f*
generous ['dʒen·ər·əs] *adj person* großzügig, freigebig; (*contribution, gesture, tip*) großzügig; *portion, helping* groß
genesis <pl -ses> ['dʒen·ə·sɪs, *pl* -siz] *n usu sing* ① (*form: origin*) Ursprung *m* ② REL **G~** das erste Buch Mose
gene 'therapy *n usu sing* Gentherapie *f*
genetic [dʒɪ·'neṭ·ɪk] *adj* genetisch; **~ disease** Erbkrankheit *f*
genetically 'modified *adj inv crop, food* genmanipuliert
geneticist [dʒɪ·'neṭ·ə·sɪst] *n* Genetiker(in) *m(f)*
genetics [dʒɪ·'neṭ·ɪks] *n* Genetik *f*
genial ['dʒi·ni·əl] *adj* freundlich
genie <*pl* -nii *or* -s> ['dʒi·ni, *pl* -niaɪ] *n*

G

Geist *m* (*aus einer Flasche oder Lampe*)

genitalia [dʒen·ɪ·ˈteɪ·li·ə] *npl* (*form*), **genitals** [ˈdʒen·ə·t̬əlz] *npl* Geschlechtsorgane *pl*

genitive [ˈdʒen·ɪ·t̬ɪv] *n* Genitiv *m;* **to be in the ~** im Genitiv stehen; **~ case** Genitiv *m*

genius <*pl* -es *or* -nii> [ˈdʒin·jəs, *pl* -niaɪ] *n* ① (*person*) Genie *nt;* **to be a ~ with numbers** genial rechnen können ② (*intelligence, talent*) Genialität *f*

genocide [ˈdʒen·ə·saɪd] *n* Völkermord *m*

genre [ˈʒɑːn·rə] *n* Genre *nt*

gent [dʒent] *n* (*hum fam*) *short for* **gentleman** Gentleman *m*

genteel [dʒen·ˈtil] *adj* vornehm

gentian [ˈdʒen·tiən] *n* Enzian *m*

gentile [ˈdʒen·taɪl] *n* Nichtjude *m,* Nichtjüdin *f*

gentle [ˈdʒen·təl] *adj* sanft; *hint* zart; *slope* leicht; **~ exercise** leichte sportliche Betätigung; ■ **to be ~ with sb** behutsam mit jdm umgehen

gentleman [ˈdʒen·təl·mən] *n* ① (*polite man*) Gentleman *m;* **a perfect ~** ein wahrer Gentleman ② (*man*) Herr *m*

gentlemanly [ˈdʒen·təl·mən·li] *adj* gentlemanlike

gentleness [ˈdʒen·təl·nɪs] *n* Sanftheit *f*

gentry [ˈdʒen·tri] *n* [**landed**] **~** niederer [Land]adel

genuine [ˈdʒen·ju·ɪn] *adj* ① (*not fake*) echt ② (*sincere*) ehrlich

genus <*pl* -nera> [ˈdʒi·nəs, *pl* -nə·rə] *n* BIOL Gattung *f*

geographer [dʒi·ˈag·rə·fər] *n* Geograph(in) *m(f)*

geographic(al) [ˌdʒi·ə·ˈgræf·ɪk(əl)] *adj* geographisch

geography [dʒi·ˈag·rə·fi] *n* ① (*study*) Erdkunde *f,* Geographie *f* ② (*layout*) Geographie *f*

geological [ˌdʒi·ə·ˈladʒ·ɪ·kəl] *adj* geologisch

geologist [dʒi·ˈal·ə·dʒɪst] *n* Geologe, -in *m, f*

geology [dʒi·ˈal·ə·dʒi] *n* Geologie *f*

geometric(al) [ˌdʒi·ə·ˈmet·rɪk(əl)] *adj* geometrisch

geometry [dʒi·ˈam·ə·tri] *n* Geometrie *f*

geophysical [ˌdʒi·oʊ·ˈfɪz·ɪ·kəl] *adj* geophysikalisch

geophysics [ˌdʒi·oʊ·ˈfɪz·ɪks] *n* Geophysik *f*

Georgia [ˈdʒɔr·dʒə] *n* Georgia *nt*

geothermal [ˌdʒi·oʊ·ˈθɜr·məl] *adj* geothermisch

geranium [dʒi·ˈreɪ·ni·əm] *n* Geranie *f*

geriatric [ˌdʒer·i·ˈæt·rɪk] **I.** *adj* geriatrisch; **~ nurse** Altenpfleger(in) *m(f)* **II.** *n* alter Mensch

geriatrics [ˌdʒer·i·ˈæt·rɪks] *n + sing vb* Altersheilkunde *f*

germ [dʒɜrm] *n* ① MED, BIOL Keim *m;* **to spread ~s** Keime verbreiten ② (*fig*) **the ~ of an idea** der Ansatz einer Idee

German [ˈdʒɜr·mən] **I.** *n* ① (*person*) Deutsche(r) *f(m)* ② (*language*) Deutsch *nt* **II.** *adj* deutsch

Germanic [dʒər·ˈmæn·ɪk] *adj* [indo]germanisch

German ˈmeasles *n + sing vb* Röteln *pl*

German ˈshepherd *n* (*dog*) Schäferhund *m*

Germany [ˈdʒɜr·mə·ni] *n* Deutschland

ˈgerm-free *adj* keimfrei

germicide [ˈdʒɜr·mə·saɪd] *n* keimtötendes Mittel

germinate [ˈdʒɜr·mə·neɪt] **I.** *vi* keimen **II.** *vt* zum Keimen bringen

germination [ˌdʒɜr·mə·ˈneɪ·ʃən] *n* Keimen *nt*

germ ˈwarfare *n* Bakterienkrieg *m*

gerrymander [ˈdʒer·ə·ˌmæn·dər] **I.** *vi* POL die Wahlbezirksgrenzen manipulieren **II.** *vt* POL **to ~ election/voting districts** Wahlkreisverschiebungen vornehmen

gerund [ˈdʒer·ənd] *n* LING Gerundium *nt*

gestation [dʒe·ˈsteɪ·ʃən] *n* ① *of humans* Schwangerschaft *f; of animals* Trächtigkeit *f* ② (*fig*) *of idea, project* Reifwerden *nt*

gesticulate [dʒe·ˈstɪk·jə·leɪt] *vi* (*form*) gestikulieren

gesticulation [dʒe·ˌstɪk·jə·ˈleɪ·ʃən] *n* (*form*) Gestik *f*

gesture [ˈdʒes·tʃər] **I.** *n* Geste *f;* **a ~ of defiance** eine trotzige Geste **II.** *vi, vt* deuten; **she ~d in the direction of the beach** sie deutete zum Strand hin

get <got, got *or* gotten> [get] **I.** *vt* ① (*obtain*) erhalten; **to ~ time off** frei bekommen; **where did you ~ your cell phone?** woher hast du dein Handy? ② (*receive*) bekommen ③ (*experience*) erleben; **to ~ a surprise** überrascht sein; **I got quite a shock** ich habe einen ganz schönen Schock bekommen; **she ~s a lot of pleasure out of** [*or* **from**] **it** es bereitet ihr viel Freude ④ (*deliver*) ■ **to ~ sth to sb** jdm etw bringen; ■ **to ~ sb/sth somewhere** jdn/etw irgendwohin bringen ⑤ MED (*fam: contract*) sich *dat* holen; **to ~ the flu** sich *dat* die Grippe einfangen; **to ~ food poisoning** sich *dat* eine Lebensmittelvergiftung zuziehen ⑥ (*go and obtain*) ■ **to ~** [**sb**] **sth** [*or* **sth for sb**] jdm etw besorgen; **can I ~ you a drink?** möchtest du was trinken? ⑦ TRANSP (*travel with*) *plane, taxi* nehmen; (*catch*) erwischen ⑧ (*fam: answer*) *door* aufmachen; **to ~ the telephone** ans Telefon gehen ⑨ (*fam: pay for*) bezahlen ⑩ + *pp* (*cause to be*) **to ~ sth confused** etw verwechseln; **to ~ sth finished** etw fertig machen ⑪ (*induce*) ■ **to ~ sb/sth to do sth** jdn/etw dazu bringen, etw zu tun ⑫ (*hear, understand*) verstehen; **to ~ the message** [*or* **picture**] [es] kapieren ⑬ (*prepare*) *meal* zubereiten **II.** *vi* ① (*become*) werden; **I got cold** mir wurde kalt; **~ well soon!** gute Besserung!; **to ~ used to sth** sich an etw *akk* gewöhnen; **to ~ to like sth** etw langsam mögen; **to ~ married** heiraten ② (*reach*) kommen; **to ~ home** nach Hause kommen ③ (*have opportunity*) ■ **to ~ to do sth** die Möglichkeit haben, etw zu tun ④ (*must*) ■ **to have got to do sth** etw machen müssen

◆ **get across** *vt* verständlich machen

◆**get along** *vi* ❶ (*be friends*) sich verstehen ❷ (*continue*) ■**to ~ along with sth** *job, project* weitermachen ❸ (*progress*) ■**to ~ along in sth** *a new environment, job, position* in etw Fortschritte machen [*o* vorankommen]

◆**get around** I. *vi* ❶ ■**to ~ around to [doing] sth** es schaffen, etw zu tun ❷ (*travel*) herumkommen ❸ *news* sich verbreiten II. *vt* ❶ (*evade*) *the law* umgehen ❷ (*deal with*) *a problem* angehen

◆**get at** *vi* ❶ (*reach*) rankommen (an +*akk*) ❷ (*fam: suggest*) ■**to ~ at sth** auf etw *akk* hinauswollen ❸ (*discover*) ■**to ~ at sth** etw aufdecken ❹ (*fam: bribe*) bestechen

◆**get away** *vi* ❶ (*leave*) fortkommen, wegkommen ❷ (*escape*) ■**to ~ away [from sb/sth]** jdm/etw entkommen ❸ (*avoid punishment*) ■**to ~ away with sth** mit etw *dat* ungestraft davonkommen; **you'll never ~ away with it!** das wird nicht gut gehen! ❹ (*succeed*) ■**to ~ away with sth** mit etw *dat* durchkommen; (*will I ~ away with wearing the same hat I wore to Peter's wedding?*) kann ich es mir erlauben, denselben Hut zu tragen, den ich an Peters Hochzeit anhatte? ▸ PHRASES: **to ~ away with <u>murder</u>** sich *dat* alles erlauben können

◆**get back** I. *vt* (*actively*) zurückholen; *strength* zurückgewinnen; (*passively*) zurückbekommen II. *vi* ❶ (*return*) zurückkommen ❷ ■**to ~ back to [doing] sth** zu etw *dat* wieder zurückgehen; **to ~ back to sleep** wieder einschlafen ❸ (*contact*) ■**to ~ back to sb** sich wieder bei jdm melden

◆**get behind** *vi* ❶ (*support*) unterstützen ❷ (*be slow*) in Rückstand geraten

◆**get by** *vi* ■**to ~ by [on/with sth]** mit etw *dat* auskommen

◆**get down** I. *vt* ❶ (*remove*) runternehmen (**from, off** von +*dat*) ❷ (*depress*) fertigmachen II. *vi* ❶ (*descend*) herunterkommen (**from, off** von +*dat*); *from the table* aufstehen ❷ (*bend down*) sich runterbeugen; (*kneel down*) niederknien ❸ (*start*) ■**to ~ down to [doing] sth** sich an etw *akk* machen

◆**get in** I. *vt* ❶ (*say*) *word* einwerfen ❷ (*fam: find time for*) reinschieben ❸ (*bring inside*) hereinholen II. *vi* ❶ (*arrive*) ankommen ❷ (*return*) zurückkehren; **to ~ in from work** von der Arbeit heimkommen ❸ (*become elected*) an die Macht kommen

◆**get into** I. *vi* ❶ (*enter*) [ein]steigen in +*akk* ❷ (*have interest for*) sich interessieren für II. *vt* (*become involved in*) *argument* verwickelt werden in +*akk*

◆**get off** I. *vi* ❶ (*exit*) *bus, train* aussteigen ❷ (*dismount*) absteigen ❸ (*evade punishment*) davonkommen ❹ (*go*) **to ~ off to bed** schlafen gehen; **to ~ off to school** zur Schule losgehen/-fahren ❺ (*sl: experience excitement*) **to ~ off on sth** bei etw *dat* ausflippen *fam* ❻ (*vulg: have orgasm*) den Höhepunkt erreichen II. *vt* ❶ (*remove*) nehmen von; **to ~ sb off sth** *bus, train, plane* herausbringen aus; *boat, roof* herunterholen von ❷ LAW freibekommen ❸ (*send to sleep*) [los]schicken; **to ~ sb off to sleep** jdn in den Schlaf wiegen

◆**get on** I. *vt* (*put on*) anziehen; *hat* aufsetzen; *lid* drauftun II. *vi* ❶ (*be friends*) sich verstehen ❷ (*continue*) weitermachen ❸ (*age*) alt werden; **to be ~ting on [in years]** an Jahren zunehmen ❹ (*criticize*) ■**to ~ on sb** auf jdm herumhacken ❺ (*nag*) **to ~ on sb to do sth** jdn dazu drängen, etw zu tun

◆**get out** I. *vi* ❶ (*become known*) *secret* herauskommen; *news* durchsickern ❷ (*socialize*) unter Leuten sein II. *vt* ❶ (*bring out*) rausbringen (**of** aus +*dat*) ❷ (*remove*) herausbekommen; *money* abheben

◆**get over** I. *vi* ❶ ■**to ~ over sb/sth** über jdn/etw hinwegkommen; *illness* sich erholen von; **I can't ~ over the way he behaved** ich komme nicht darüber hinweg, wie er sich verhalten hat ❷ ■**to ~ sth over [with]** etw hinter sich *akk* bringen II. *vt idea* rüberbringen

◆**get through** I. *vi* ❶ (*make oneself understood*) ■**to ~ through to sb that/how ...** jdm klarmachen, dass/wie ... ❷ (*contact*) ■**to ~ through to sb** *on the phone* zu jdm durchkommen II. *vt* ❶ (*use up*) aufbrauchen ❷ (*finish*) *work* erledigen ❸ (*survive*) *bad times* überstehen

◆**get together** *vi* sich treffen

◆**get up** I. *vt* ❶ (*climb*) hinaufsteigen ❷ (*gather*) *courage* aufbringen; *speed* sich beschleunigen ❸ (*fam: wake*) wecken II. *vi* ❶ (*get out of bed*) aufstehen ❷ (*stand up*) sich erheben

'**getaway** *n* (*fam*) ❶ (*escape*) Flucht *f*; **to make a ~** entwischen ❷ (*vacation*) Trip *m*

'**get-together** *n* (*fam*) Treffen *nt*

'**getup** *n* (*fam: outfit*) Kluft *f*

geyser ['gaɪ·zər] *n* Geysir *m*

ghastly ['gæst·li] *adj* ❶ (*fam: frightful*) *report* schrecklich ❷ **~ [white/pale]** totenbleich ❸ (*unwell*) grässlich, scheußlich

gherkin ['gɜr·kɪn] *n* Essiggurke *f*

ghetto <*pl* -s *or* -es> ['get̬·oʊ] *n* G[h]etto *nt*

ghost [goʊst] I. *n* Geist *m* ▸ PHRASES: **to <u>give</u> up the ~** den Geist aufgeben II. *vt* **his autobiography was ~ed** seine Autobiografie wurde von einem Ghostwriter geschrieben

ghostly ['goʊst·li] *adj* ❶ (*ghost-like*) geisterhaft ❷ (*eerie*) *voice* gespenstisch

'**ghost town** *n* Geisterstadt *f*

'**ghostwriter** *n* Ghostwriter *m*

ghoul [gul] *n* Ghul *m*

G'I *n* (*fam: soldier*) GI *m*

giant ['dʒaɪ·ənt] I. *n* Riese *m a. fig* II. *adj* riesig; **to make ~ strides** (*fig*) große Fortschritte machen

gibber ['dʒɪb·ər] *vi* stammeln

gibberish ['dʒɪb·ər·ɪʃ] *n* (*pej*) ❶ (*spoken*) Gestammel *nt* ❷ (*written*) Quatsch *m*

gibbon ['gɪb·ən] *n* ZOOL Gibbon *m*

gibe [dʒaɪb] I. *n* Stichelei *f*, verletzende Be-

G

merkung **II.** *vi* ■**to ~ at sb/sth** über jdn/etw spötteln **III.** *vt* sticheln

giblets ['dʒɪb·lɪts] *npl* Innereien *pl*

giddy ['gɪd·i] *adj* ❶ (*silly*) ausgelassen ❷ (*dizzy*) schwind(e)lig

gift [gɪft] *n* ❶ (*present*) Geschenk *nt a. fig* ❷ (*donation*) Spende *f* ❸ (*talent*) Talent *nt;* **to have a ~ for languages** sprachbegabt sein

'**gift certificate** *n* Geschenkgutschein *m*

gifted ['gɪft·ɪd] *adj* begabt; *musician* begnadet

'**gift horse** *n* ▶ PHRASES: **never look a ~ in the mouth** (*prov*) einem geschenkten Gaul guckt man nicht ins Maul

'**gift shop** *n* Geschenkartikelladen *m*

gig [gɪg] **I.** *n* Gig *m* **II.** *vi* <-gg-> auftreten

gigabyte ['gɪg·ə·baɪt] *n* COMPUT Gigabyte *nt*

gigantic [dʒaɪ·'gæn·tɪk] *adj* gigantisch; **~ bite** Riesenbissen *m*

giggle ['gɪg·əl] **I.** *vi* kichern (**at** über +*akk*) **II.** *n* Gekicher *nt kein pl*

gill [gɪl] *n usu pl* Kieme *f* ▶ PHRASES: **to look green around the ~s** grün im Gesicht sein

gilt [gɪlt] **I.** *adj* vergoldet **II.** *n* Vergoldung *f*

gimmick ['gɪm·ɪk] *n* (*esp pej*) ❶ (*trick*) Trick *m;* **advertising/sales ~** Werbetrick *m*/Verkaufstrick *m* ❷ (*attraction*) Attraktion *f*

gimmicky ['gɪm·ɪk·i] *adj* (*pej*) marktschreierisch

gin [dʒɪn] *n* (*drink*) Gin *m*

ginger ['dʒɪn·dʒər] **I.** *n* ❶ (*spice*) Ingwer *m* ❷ (*color*) gelbliches Braun **II.** *adj* gelblich braun

ginger 'ale *n* Gingerale *nt*

'**gingerbread** *n* Lebkuchen *m*

gingerly ['dʒɪn·dʒər·li] *adv* behutsam

Gipsy *n see* **Gypsy**

giraffe <*pl* -s *or* -> [dʒə·'ræf] *n* Giraffe *f*

girder ['gɜr·dər] *n* Träger *m*

girdle ['gɜr·dəl] *n* (*corset*) Korsett *nt*

girl [gɜrl] *n* Mädchen *nt;* (*girlfriend*) Freundin *f*

'**girlfriend** *n* Freundin *f*

girlie, girly ['gɜr·li] *adj* (*fam*) mädchenhaft; **~ magazines** Girlie-Zeitschriften

girlish ['gɜr·lɪʃ] *adj* mädchenhaft

'**Girl Scout** *n* Pfadfinderin *f*

girth [gɜrθ] *n* ❶ (*circumference*) Umfang *m;* **in ~** an Umfang ❷ (*saddle strap*) Sattelgurt *m*

gist [dʒɪst] *n* ■**the ~** das Wesentliche; **to get the ~ of sth** den Sinn von etw *dat* verstehen

give [gɪv] **I.** *vt* <gave, given> ❶ ■**to ~ sb sth** jdm etw geben; (*as present*) jdm etw schenken; (*donate*) jdm etw spenden; **to ~ sb a cold** jdn mit seiner Erkältung anstecken; **~n the choice** wenn ich die Wahl hätte; **to ~ sb his/her due** jdm Ehre erweisen; **to ~ sb encouragement** jdn ermutigen; **to ~ a speech** eine Rede halten; **to ~ sb/sth a bad name** jdn/etw in Verruf bringen; **to ~ sb the news of** [*or* **about**] **sth** jdm etw mitteilen; **to ~ sb permission** [**to do sth**] jdm die Erlaubnis erteilen[, etw zu tun]; **he couldn't ~ me a reason why ...** er konnte mir auch nicht sagen, warum ...; **don't ~ me that!** (*fig*) komm mir doch nicht damit!; **~ her my best wishes** grüß' sie schön von mir! ❷ (*emit*) **to ~ a cry/groan** aufschreien/aufstöhnen ❸ (*produce*) *result, number* ergeben; *warmth* spenden ❹ (*do*) **to ~ sb a** [**dirty**] **look** jdm einen vernichtenden Blick zuwerfen; **to ~ a shrug** mit den Schultern zucken **II.** *vi* <gave, given> ❶ (*donate*) spenden (**to** für +*akk*); **to ~ and take** [gegenseitige] Kompromisse machen ❷ (*bend, yield*) nachgeben; *knees* weich werden; *rope* reißen ▶ PHRASES: **it is better to ~ than to receive** (*prov*) Geben ist seliger denn Nehmen; **to ~ as good as one gets** Gleiches mit Gleichem vergelten **III.** *n* Nachgiebigkeit *f;* (*elasticity*) Elastizität *f;* **to not have any/much ~ in it** nicht [sehr] nachgeben; (*elasticity*) nicht [sehr] elastisch sein

◆**give away** *vt* ❶ (*offer for free*) verschenken ❷ *bride* zum Altar führen ❸ (*fig: lose*) *game* verschenken ❹ (*betray*) *secret, hiding place* verraten; ■**to ~ oneself away** sich verraten ▶ PHRASES: **to ~ the game away** alles verraten

◆**give back** *vt* zurückgeben (**to** +*dat*)

◆**give in I.** *vi* ❶ (*to pressure*) nachgeben (**to** +*dat*); **to ~ in to temptation** der Versuchung erliegen ❷ (*surrender*) aufgeben **II.** *vt* (*hand in*) abgeben; *document* einreichen

◆**give off** *vt* abgeben; *smell, smoke* ausströmen

◆**give out I.** *vi* ❶ (*run out*) ausgehen; *energy* zu Ende gehen; **then her patience gave out** dann war es mit ihrer Geduld vorbei ❷ (*stop working*) versagen **II.** *vt* ❶ (*distribute*) verteilen (**to** an +*akk*); *pencils, books* austeilen ❷ (*announce*) verkünden ❸ (*emit*) von sich *dat* geben

◆**give over** *vt* ❶ (*set aside*) ■**to be given over to sth** für etw *akk* beansprucht werden ❷ (*hand over*) übergeben

◆**give up I.** *vi* aufgeben **II.** *vt* ❶ (*quit*) aufgeben; *habit* ablegen; *relationship* fallen lassen; ■**to ~ up doing sth** mit etw *dat* aufhören ❷ (*surrender*) überlassen; *rights, territory* abtreten; **to ~ oneself up** [**to the police**] sich *akk* [der Polizei] stellen ❸ (*consider lost*) **to ~ sb up for dead** jdn für tot halten

give-and-'take *n* ❶ (*compromise*) Geben und Nehmen *nt* ❷ (*debate*) Meinungsaustausch *m*

'**giveaway I.** *n* ❶ (*fam: telltale sign*) **to be a dead ~** alles verraten ❷ (*freebie*) Werbegeschenk *nt* **II.** *adj* ❶ (*low*) **~ price** Schleuderpreis *m* ❷ (*free*) kostenlos; **~ newspaper** Gratiszeitung *f*

given ['gɪv·ən] **I.** *n* gegebene Tatsache; **to take sth as a ~** etw als gegeben annehmen **II.** *adj* ❶ (*certain*) gegeben ❷ (*specified*) festgelegt ❸ (*accustomed*) **to be ~ to doing sth** gewöhnt sein, etw zu tun **III.** *prep* **~ sth** angesichts einer S. *gen;* **~ the circumstances** unter diesen Umständen **IV.** *pp of* **give**

'**given name** *n* Vorname *m*

giver ['gɪv·ər] *n* Spender(in) *m(f)*

glacial ['gleɪ·ʃəl] *adj* ❶ (*left by glacier*) glazial

❷ (*a. fig: freezing*) eisig

glacier [ˈgleɪ·ʃər] *n* Gletscher *m*

glad <-dd-> [glæd] *adj* froh; **to be ~ about sth** sich über etw *akk* freuen; ■**to be ~ of sth** über etw *akk* froh sein; **I'd be ~ to help you** ich würde dir gerne helfen

gladden [ˈglæd·ən] *vt* (*form*) erfreuen

glade [gleɪd] *n* (*liter*) Lichtung *f*

gladiator [ˈglæd·i·eɪ·t̬ər] *n* Gladiator *m*

gladly [ˈglæd·li] *adv* gerne

gladness [ˈglæd·nɪs] *n* Freude *f*

ˈ**glad rags** *npl* (*hum*) Festkleidung *f*

glamor [ˈglæm·ər] *n see* **glamour**

glamorize [ˈglæm·ə·raɪz] *vt* verherrlichen

glamorous [ˈglæm·ə·rəs] *adj* glamourös

glamour [ˈglæm·ər] *n* Glanz *m*

glance [glæns] **I.** *n* Blick *m;* **at first ~** auf den ersten Blick; **to see at a ~** mit einem Blick erfassen **II.** *vi* ■**to ~ at sth** auf etw *akk* schauen; **to ~ through a letter** einen Brief überfliegen

◆**glance off** *vi* abprallen

gland [glænd] *n* Drüse *f*

glare [gler] **I.** *n* ❶ (*stare*) wütender Blick ❷ (*light*) grelles Licht **II.** *vi* (*stare*) ■**to ~ [at sb]** [jdn an]starren

glaring [ˈgler·ɪŋ] *adj* ❶ (*staring*) stechend ❷ (*blinding*) blendend; *light* grell ❸ (*obvious*) *mistake* eklatant; *weakness* krass; *injustice* himmelschreiend

glass [glæs] *n* ❶ Glas *nt;* **pane of ~** Glasscheibe *f;* **a ~ of water** ein Glas *nt* Wasser ❷ *pl* (*spectacles*) **[a pair of] ~es** [eine] Brille *f;* **to wear ~es** eine Brille tragen

ˈ**glass blower** *n* Glasbläser(in) *m(f)*

ˈ**glassful** *n* Glas *nt* voll

ˈ**glassware** *n* Glaswaren *pl*

ˈ**glassworks** *n + sing vb* Glasfabrik *f*

glassy [ˈglæs·i] *adj* ❶ *surface* spiegelglatt ❷ *eyes* glasig

Glaswegian [glæs·ˈwi·dʒən] **I.** *n* (*person*) Glasgower(in) *m(f)* **II.** *adj* aus Glasgow *nach n*

glaze [gleɪz] **I.** *n* (*on food, pottery*) Glasur *f* **II.** *vt* ❶ *food, pottery* glasieren ❷ (*fit with glass*) verglasen **III.** *vi* ■**to ~ [over]** *eyes* glasig werden

gleam [glim] **I.** *n* Schimmer *m* **II.** *vi* schimmern

gleaming [ˈglim·ɪŋ] *adj* glänzend

glean [glin] *vt* in Erfahrung bringen

glee [gli] *n* Entzücken *nt;* (*gloating joy*) Schadenfreude *f*

gleeful [ˈgli·fəl] *adj* ausgelassen; (*gloating*) schadenfroh

glen [glen] *n* Schlucht *f*

glib <-bb-> [glɪb] *adj person* zungenfertig; *answer, remark* unbedacht

glide [glaɪd] *vi* ❶ (*move smoothly*) hingleiten ❷ (*fly*) gleiten

glider [ˈglaɪ·dər] *n* (*plane*) Segelflugzeug *nt*

gliding [ˈglaɪ·dɪŋ] *n* Segelfliegen *nt*

glimmer [ˈglɪm·ər] **I.** *vi* schimmern **II.** *n* Schimmer *m kein pl;* **~ of hope/light** Hoffnungs-/Lichtschimmer *m*

glimpse [glɪmps] **I.** *vt* flüchtig sehen **II.** *n* [kurzer/flüchtiger] Blick

glint [glɪnt] **I.** *vi* glitzern **II.** *n* Glitzern *nt*

glisten [ˈglɪs·ən] *vi* glitzern, glänzen

glitch [glɪtʃ] *n* ❶ (*fam: fault*) Fehler *m;* **computer ~** Computerstörung *f* ❷ (*setback*) Verzögerung *f*

glitter [ˈglɪt̬·ər] **I.** *vi* glitzern; *eyes* funkeln ▶ PHRASES: **all that ~s is not <u>gold</u>** (*prov*) es ist nicht alles Gold, was glänzt **II.** *n* ❶ (*sparkling*) Glitzern *nt; of eyes* Funkeln *nt* ❷ (*decoration*) Glitter *m*

glittering [ˈglɪt̬·ər·ɪŋ] *adj* ❶ (*sparkling*) glitzernd ❷ (*impressive*) *career* glanzvoll

glitz [glɪts] *n* Glanz *m*

glitzy [ˈglɪt·si] *adj* glanzvoll

gloat [gloʊt] *vi* sich hämisch freuen; ■**to ~ over sth** sich an etw *dat* weiden

global [ˈgloʊ·bᵊl] *adj* ❶ (*worldwide*) global; **~ warming** globale Erwärmung ❷ (*complete*) umfassend ▶ PHRASES: **to <u>go</u> ~** (*fam*) auf den Weltmarkt vorstoßen

globalization [ˌgloʊ·bə·lɪ·ˈzeɪ·ʃən] *n* Globalisierung *f*

globalize [ˈgloʊ·bə·laɪz] *vt* globalisieren

global ˈwarming *n* Erwärmung *f* der Erdatmosphäre

globe [gloʊb] *n* ❶ (*Earth*) ■**the ~** die Erde; **to circle the ~** die Welt umreisen ❷ (*map*) Globus *m*

ˈ**globetrotter** *n* Globetrotter(in) *m(f),* Weltenbummler(in) *m(f)*

gloom [glum] *n* ❶ (*depression*) Hoffnungslosigkeit *f* ❷ (*darkness*) Düsterheit *f;* **to emerge from the ~** aus dem Dunkel auftauchen

gloominess [ˈglu·mi·nəs] *n* ❶ (*depression*) Hoffnungslosigkeit *f* ❷ (*darkness*) Düsterheit *f*

gloomy [ˈglu·mi] *adj* ❶ (*dismal*) trostlos; *thoughts* trübe ❷ (*dark*) düster

glorification [ˌglɔr·ə·fə·ˈkeɪ·ʃən] *n* Verherrlichung *f*

glorify <-ie-> [ˈglɔr·ə·faɪ] *vt* ❶ (*make seem better*) verherrlichen ❷ (*honor*) ehren; REL [lob]preisen

glorious [ˈglɔr·i·əs] *adj* ❶ (*illustrious*) *victory* glorreich ❷ (*splendid*) prachtvoll; *weather* herrlich

glory [ˈglɔr·i] **I.** *n* ❶ (*honor*) Ruhm *m* ❷ (*splendor*) Herrlichkeit *f,* Pracht *f* **II.** *vi* <-ie-> ■**to ~ in [doing] sth** etw genießen

gloss [glas] *n* ❶ (*shine*) Glanz *m;* **in ~ or matte** glänzend oder matt; **to put a ~ on sth** etw [besonders] hervorheben ❷ (*cosmetic*) **lip ~** Lipgloss *nt* ❸ *see* **gloss paint**

◆**gloss over** *vt* schönfärben

glossary [ˈglas·ə·ri] *n* Glossar *nt*

ˈ**gloss paint** *n* Glanzlack *m*

glossy [ˈglas·i] **I.** *adj* glänzend; **~ magazine** Hochglanzmagazin *nt* **II.** *n* (*photo*) [Hoch]glanzabzug *m*

glove [glʌv] *n usu pl* Handschuh *m;* **to fit like a ~** wie angegossen passen

ˈ**glove box,** ˈ**glove compartment** *n* AUTO

G

Handschuhfach *nt*

glow [gloʊ] **I.** *n* Leuchten *nt; of a lamp, the sun* Scheinen *nt; of a cigarette, the sunset* Glühen *nt; of fire* Schein *m;* **a healthy ~** eine gesunde Farbe **II.** *vi* ① (*shed light*) leuchten; *fire, light* scheinen ② (*be red and hot*) glühen; **the embers ~ed dimly in the fireplace** die Glut glimmte im Kamin ③ (*fig: look radiant*) strahlen; **to ~ with health** vor Gesundheit strotzen; **to ~ with pride** vor Stolz schwellen

glower ['glaʊ·ər] *vi* verärgert aussehen; ■**to ~ at sb** jdn zornig anstarren

glowing ['gloʊ·ɪŋ] *adj* ① (*radiating light*) *candle* leuchtend; *cigarette* glühend ② (*radiant*) leuchtend ③ (*very positive*) begeistert; *review* überschwänglich

'glowworm *n* Glühwürmchen *nt*

glucose ['glu·koʊs] *n* Traubenzucker *m*

glue [glu] **I.** *n* Klebstoff *m* **II.** *vt* ① kleben; ■**to ~ sth together** etw zusammenkleben ② (*fig*) ■**to be ~d to sth** an etw *dat* kleben; **we were ~d to the television** wir klebten am Fernsehen; **to be ~d to the spot** wie angewurzelt dastehen

'glue sniffing *n* Schnüffeln *nt*

'glue stick *n* Klebestift *m*

glum <-mm-> [glʌm] *adj* niedergeschlagen; *expression* mürrisch; *face* bedrückt

glut [glʌt] *n* Überangebot *nt;* **an oil ~** eine Ölschwemme

gluten ['glu·tən] *n* Gluten *nt*

glutinous ['glut·ən·əs] *adj* klebrig

glutton ['glʌt·ən] *n* ① (*pej: overeater*) Vielfraß *m* ② (*fig: enthusiast*) Unersättliche(r) *f(m);* **~ for punishment** Masochist(in) *m(f)*

gluttony ['glʌt·ən·i] *n* Gefräßigkeit *f*

gnarled [narld] *adj branch* knorrig; *finger* knotig

gnash [næʃ] *vt* **to ~ one's teeth** mit den Zähnen knirschen

gnat [næt] *n* [Stech]mücke *f*

gnaw [nɔ] **I.** *vi* nagen *a. fig* (**on, at, away at** an +*dat*) **II.** *vt* ① (*chew*) ■**to ~ sth** an etw *dat* kauen ② (*fig*) **to be ~ed by guilt** von Schuld geplagt sein

gnawing ['nɔ·ɪŋ] **I.** *adj* nagend **II.** *n* Nagen *nt*

gnome [noʊm] *n* Gnom *m;* [**garden**] **~** Gartenzwerg *m*

GNP [ˌdʒi·en·'pi] *n abbrev of* **Gross National Product** BSP *nt*

go [goʊ] **I.** *vi* <goes, went, gone> ① (*proceed*) gehen; *vehicle, train* fahren; *plane* fliegen; **we have a long way to ~** wir haben noch einen weiten Weg vor uns; ■**to ~ toward[s] sb/sth** auf jdn/etw zugehen; **to ~ home** nach Hause gehen; **to ~ to the hospital/a party/prison/the bathroom** ins Krankenhaus/auf eine Party/ins Gefängnis/auf die Toilette gehen ② (*travel*) reisen; **to ~ on vacation** in Urlaub gehen; **to ~ to Italy** nach Italien fahren; **to ~ on a trip** verreisen, eine Reise machen; **to ~ by plane** fliegen; **to ~ abroad** ins Ausland gehen ③ (*disappear*) verschwinden; **to ~ missing** verschwinden; **where did my keys go?** wo sind meine Schlüssel hin?; **my toothache's gone!** meine Zahnschmerzen sind weg!; **half of my salary ~es on rent** die Hälfte meines Gehaltes geht für die Miete drauf; **there ~es another one!** und wieder eine/einer weniger!; **the president will have to ~** der Präsident wird seinen Hut nehmen müssen ④ (*leave*) gehen; **let's ~!** los jetzt! ⑤ (*do*) **to ~ biking/shopping/swimming etc.** Rad fahren/einkaufen/schwimmen etc. gehen; **to ~ looking for sb/sth** jdn/etw suchen gehen ⑥ (*attend*) **to ~ to church** in die Kirche gehen; **to ~ to the doctor** zum Arzt gehen; **to ~ to school/college** in die Schule/auf die Universität gehen ⑦ + *adj* (*become*) werden; **to ~ bankrupt** bankrottgehen; **to ~ haywire** (*out of control*) außer Kontrolle geraten; (*malfunction*) verrücktspielen; **to ~ public** an die Öffentlichkeit treten; STOCKEX an die Börse gehen; **to ~ to sleep** einschlafen; **my mind went completely blank** ich hatte voll ein Brett vorm Kopf! ⑧ + *adj* (*be*) sein; **to ~ hungry** hungern; **to ~ thirsty** dursten; **to ~ unnoticed** unbemerkt bleiben ⑨ (*turn out*) gehen; **how did your party ~?** und, wie war deine Party?; **how are things ~ing?** und, wie läuft's?; **to ~ according to plan** nach Plan laufen; **to ~ from bad to worse** vom Regen in die Traufe kommen; **to ~ wrong** schieflaufen ⑩ (*pass*) vergehen; **only two days to ~ ...** nur noch zwei Tage ... ⑪ (*fail*) kaputtgehen; *hearing, memory* nachlassen; *rope* reißen ⑫ (*die*) sterben ⑬ (*belong*) hingehören; **the silverware ~es in this drawer** das Besteck gehört in diese Schublade ⑭ (*lead*) *path, road* führen ⑮ (*extend*) gehen; **the meadow ~es all the way down to the stream** die Weide erstreckt sich bis hinunter zum Bach ⑯ (*function*) *business* laufen; **to get/keep sth ~ing** etw in Gang bringen/halten; **come on! keep ~ing!** ja, weiter!; **to keep a conversation ~ing** eine Unterhaltung am Laufen halten; **to keep a fire ~ing** ein Feuer am Brennen halten ⑰ (*have recourse*) gehen; **to ~ to the police** zur Polizei gehen; **to ~ to war** in den Krieg ziehen ⑱ (*match, be compatible*) ■**to ~ together** [*or* **with sth**] zu etw passen; **these two colors don't ~ together** [**at all**] diese beiden Farben beißen sich ⑲ (*fit*) **will anything else ~ into the suitcase?** wird all das noch in den Koffer passen? ⑳ (*be accepted*) **anything ~es** alles ist erlaubt; **that ~es for all of you** das gilt für euch alle! ㉑ (*fam: use the bathroom*) **I really have to ~** ich muss ganz dringend mal! ▶ PHRASES: **there you ~** bitte schön!; **sb will ~ a long way** jd wird es weit bringen; **that ~es without saying** das versteht sich von selbst **II.** *aux vb future tense* ■**to be ~ing to do sth** etw tun werden; **we are ~ing to have a party tomorrow** wir geben morgen eine Party **III.** *vt* <goes, went, gone> ① (*travel*) *northern/southern route* nehmen ② (*fam: say*) **she ~es to me: I never want to see you again!** sie sagt zu mir: ich will dich nie wiedersehen! **IV.** *n* <*pl* -es> ① (*turn*) **you've had your ~ already!** du warst schon dran!; **can I have a ~?** darf ich mal? ② (*attempt*) Versuch *m;* **to give sth a ~** etw versuchen; **in one ~** auf einen Schlag ③ (*energy*) Antrieb *m;* **full of ~** voller Elan ▶ PHRASES: **from the word ~** von Anfang an; **to make a ~ of sth** mit etw *dat* Erfolg haben **V.** *adj* [start]klar; **all systems [are] ~** alles klar

◆**go about** *vt* ① (*be occupied with*) **to ~ about one's business** seinen Geschäften nachgehen ② (*deal with*) *problem* angehen

◆**go after** *vi* ① (*in succession*) ■**to ~ after sb/sth** nach jdm/etw gehen ② (*chase*) ■**to ~ after sb** jdn verfolgen

◆**go against** *vi* ① (*be negative for*) ■**to ~ against sb** zu jds Ungunsten *pl* ausgehen; **the jury's decision went against the defendant** die Entscheidung der Jury fiel gegen den Angeklagten aus ② (*contradict*) **that ~es against everything I believe in** das geht gegen all das, woran ich glaube ③ (*disobey*) ■**to ~ against sb** sich jdm widersetzen

◆**go ahead** *vi* ① (*go before*) vorgehen; (*in vehicle*) vorausfahren; (*in sports*) in Führung gehen ② (*proceed*) vorangehen; *event* stattfinden; **~ ahead, try it!** komm, versuch's doch einfach!; ■**to ~ ahead with sth** etw durchführen

◆**go along** *vi* ① (*on foot*) entlanggehen; (*in vehicle*) entlangfahren ② (*accompany*) mitgehen [*o* mitkommen] ③ (*agree*) ■**to ~ along with sth/sb** etw/jdm zustimmen; (*join in*) sich etw/jdm anschließen

◆**go around** *vi* ① (*travel around*) **they went around Europe for two months** sie reisten zwei Monate lang durch Europa ② (*visit*) **to ~ around and see sb** [*or* **to sb's house**] bei jdm vorbeischauen ③ (*be in circulation*) *rumor, illness* [he]rumgehen ④ (*do repeatedly*) ■**to ~ around doing sth** etw ständig tun ⑤ (*move in a curve*) herumgehen um +*akk; vehicle* herumfahren um +*akk;* (*circumnavigate*) umrunden; **to ~ around the block** um den Block laufen; **to ~ around the world** eine Weltreise machen ▶ PHRASES: **what ~es around, comes around** (*saying*) alles rächt sich früher oder später

◆**go at** *vi* ① (*attack*) ■**to ~ at sb [with sth]** auf jdn [mit etw *dat*] losgehen; (*fig: eat ravenously*) ■**to ~ at sth** über etw *akk* herfallen ② (*work hard*) ■**to ~ at sth** sich an etw *akk* machen; **to ~ at it** loslegen

◆**go away** *vi* ① (*travel*) weggehen; (*for vacation*) wegfahren ② (*leave*) [weg]gehen; **~ away!** geh' weg! ③ (*disappear*) verschwinden

◆**go back** *vi* ① (*return*) zurückgehen; *school* wieder anfangen; **there's no ~ing back now** jetzt gibt es kein Zurück mehr; ■**to ~ back to sb** zu jdm zurückkehren; **to ~ back to the beginning** noch mal von vorne anfangen; **to ~ back to normal** sich wieder normalisieren; ■**to ~ back to doing sth** wieder mit etw *dat* anfangen ② (*move backwards*) zurückgehen ③ (*not fulfill*) **to ~ back on one's promise** sein Versprechen nicht halten

◆**go beyond** *vi* ■**to ~ beyond sth** ① (*proceed past*) an etw *dat* vorübergehen ② (*exceed*) über etw *akk* hinausgehen

◆**go by** *vi* ① (*move past*) vorbeigehen; *vehicle* vorbeifahren ② (*of time*) vergehen; **in days gone by** (*form*) in früheren Tagen ③ (*be guided by*) ■**to ~ by sth** nach etw *dat* gehen; **to ~ by the book** sich an die Vorschriften halten; **~ing by what they said ...** nach dem, was sie gesagt haben ...; **if this is anything to ~ by ...** wenn man danach gehen kann ...

◆**go down** *vi* ① (*move downward*) hinuntergehen; *sun, moon* untergehen; *ship a.* sinken; *plane* abstürzen; *boxer* zu Boden gehen; *curtain* fallen; **to ~ down on all fours** sich auf alle viere begeben ② (*decrease*) *attendance, wind* nachlassen; *crime rate, fever, water level* zurückgehen; *prices, taxes, temperature* sinken; *currency* fallen; *tire* Luft verlieren ③ (*break down*) *computer* ausfallen ④ (*be defeated*) verlieren (**to** gegen +*akk*); *a.* SPORTS unterliegen; **to ~ down fighting** kämpfend untergehen ⑤ (*on foot*) entlanggehen; (*in vehicle*) entlangfahren; **she was ~ing down the road on her bike** sie fuhr auf ihrem Fahrrad die Straße entlang; **to ~ down a list** eine Liste [von oben nach unten] durchgehen ⑥ (*extend*) hinunterreichen; **the tree's roots ~ down six feet** die Wurzeln des Baumes reichen sechs Fuß in die Tiefe ⑦ (*be received*) **to [not] ~ down well [with sb]** [bei jdm] [nicht] gut ankommen ⑧ (*be recorded*) **to ~ down in history** in die Geschichte eingehen

◆**go for** *vi* ① (*fetch*) holen; *food etc.* besorgen; **to ~ for a newspaper** eine Zeitung holen gehen ② (*try to achieve*) **~ for it!** nichts wie ran!; **if I were you, I'd ~ for it** an deiner Stelle würde ich zugreifen ③ (*attack*) **to ~ for the jugular** (*fig*) an die Gurgel springen *fam* ④ (*be true for*) **that ~es for me too** das gilt auch für mich ⑤ (*fam: like*) ■**to ~ for sth/sb** auf etw/jdn stehen ⑥ (*do*) **to ~ for a drive** [ein bisschen] rausfahren

◆**go in** *vi* ① (*enter*) hineingehen ② (*fit*) hineinpassen ③ (*fam: be understood*) in den Kopf gehen

◆**go into** *vi* ① gehen in +*akk;* **to ~ into action** in Aktion treten; **to ~ into a coma** ins Koma fallen; **to ~ into effect** in Kraft treten; **to ~ into labor** [die] Wehen bekommen; **to ~ into reverse** in den Rückwärtsgang schalten ② (*examine*) ■**to ~ into sth** etw erörtern; **I don't want to ~ into that now** ich möchte jetzt nicht darauf eingehen; **to ~ into detail** ins Detail gehen ③ (*join*) **to ~ into the Army**

zur Armee gehen; **to ~ into the hospital** ins Krankenhaus gehen
◆**go off** *vi* ① (*stop working*) *lights* ausgehen; *electricity* ausfallen ② (*ring*) *alarm* losgehen; *alarm clock* klingeln ③ (*detonate*) *bomb* hochgehen; *gun* losgehen ④ (*leave*) weggehen ⑤ (*diverge*) abgehen; *road* abzweigen (**to** nach +*dat*); **to ~ off the subject** vom Thema abschweifen ⑥ (*criticize*) ■**to ~ off on sb** an jdm herumnörgeln
◆**go on** *vi* ① (*go further*) weitergehen; *vehicle* weiterfahren; **to ~ on ahead** vorausgehen; *vehicle* vorausfahren ② (*extend*) sich erstrecken; *time* voranschreiten; **it'll get warmer as the day ~es on** im Laufe des Tages wird es wärmer ③ (*continue*) weitermachen; *fighting* anhalten; *negotiations* andauern; ■**to ~ on with sth** etw fortsetzen, mit etw *dat* fortfahren; **I can't ~ on** ich kann nicht mehr; **to ~ on trying** es weiter versuchen; **to ~ on working** weiterarbeiten ④ (*continue speaking*) weiterreden; (*speak incessantly*) unaufhörlich reden; **sorry, please ~ on** Entschuldigung, bitte fahren Sie fort; **he went on to say that ...** dann sagte er, dass ...; **to be always ~ing on [about sth]** andauernd [über etw *akk*] reden ⑤ (*happen*) passieren; **what's ~ing on here?** was geht denn hier vor? ⑥ (*move on, proceed*) **he went on to become a teacher** später wurde er Lehrer ⑦ *lights* angehen ⑧ (*as encouragement*) **~ on, have another drink** na komm, trink noch einen; **~ on!** los, mach schon!; **~ on, tell me!** jetzt sag' schon! ⑨ (*start, embark on*) anfangen; **to ~ on a diet** auf Diät gehen; **to ~ on welfare** stempeln gehen; **to ~ on the pill** die Pille nehmen; **to ~ on strike** in [den] Streik treten ⑩ (*base conclusions on*) ■**to ~ on sth** sich auf etw *akk* stützen; **we don't have anything to ~ on** wir haben keine Anhaltspunkte ⑪ (*belong on*) gehören auf +*akk* ⑫ (*be nearly*) **be ~ing on nine o'clock/ninety** auf neun Uhr/die neunzig zugehen
◆**go out** *vi* ① (*leave home*) [hinaus]gehen; **to ~ out to work** arbeiten gehen; **to ~ out jogging** joggen gehen; **to ~ out horseback riding** ausreiten ② (*enjoy social life*) ausgehen; **to ~ out to eat** essen gehen ③ (*date*) ■**to ~ out with sb** mit jdm gehen ④ (*be extinguished*) *fire* ausgehen; *light a.* ausfallen ⑤ (*be sent out*) verschickt werden; MEDIA **to ~ out on the air** ausgestrahlt werden; (*be issued*) verteilt werden ⑥ (*recede*) *tide* zurückgehen; **when the tide ~es out ...** bei Ebbe ... ⑦ (*become unfashionable*) unmodern werden, aus der Mode kommen; *custom* aussterben
▶PHRASES: **to ~ all out** sich ins Zeug legen
◆**go over** *vi* ① (*cross*) hinübergehen; (*in vehicle*) hinüberfahren; *border, river, street* überqueren; *cliff* stürzen über +*akk* ② (*fig: change*) ■**to ~ over to sth** zu etw *dat* übergehen; POL zu etw *dat* überwechseln; REL zu etw *dat* übertreten; **to ~ over to the enemy** zum Feind überlaufen ③ (*examine*) durchgehen; *apartment, car* durchsuchen ④ (*exceed*) überschreiten; **to ~ over a time limit** überziehen ⑤ (*redraw*) nachzeichnen; *line* nachziehen ⑥ (*be received*) **to [not] ~ over well [with sb]** [nicht] gut ankommen [bei jdm]
◆**go through** *vi* ① (*pass in and out of*) durchgehen; *vehicle* durchfahren ② (*experience*) durchmachen ③ (*use up*) aufbrauchen; *money* ausgeben ④ (*look over*) durchsehen ⑤ (*be approved*) *plan* durchgehen; *bill, divorce* durchkommen; *business deal* [erfolgreich] abgeschlossen werden ⑥ (*carry out*) ■**to ~ through with sth** durchziehen; **he has to ~ through with it now** jetzt gibt es kein Zurück mehr für ihn
◆**go together** *vi* ① (*harmonize*) zusammenpassen ② (*date*) miteinander gehen
◆**go under** *vi* ① (*sink*) untergehen ② (*fail*) *person* scheitern; *business* eingehen ③ (*move below*) ■**to ~ under sth** unter etw *akk* druntergehen; **the road ~es under the railroad bridge** die Straße führt unter der Eisenbahnbrücke durch
◆**go up** *vi* ① (*move higher*) hinaufgehen; (*on a ladder*) hinaufsteigen; *curtain* hochgehen; *balloon* aufsteigen ② (*increase*) steigen; **everything is ~ing up!** alles wird teurer! ③ (*approach*) ■**to ~ up to sb/sth** auf jdn/etw zugehen ④ (*move as far as*) ■**to ~ up to sth** [bis] zu etw *dat* hingehen; (*in vehicle*) [bis] zu etw *dat* [hin]fahren ⑤ (*extend to*) **to ~ up to sth** bis zu etw hochreichen; (*of time*) bis zu einer bestimmten Zeit gehen ⑥ (*be built*) entstehen ⑦ (*ascend*) *mountain, street* ansteigen
▶PHRASES: **to ~ up against sb** sich jdm widersetzen; (*in a fight*) es mit jdm aufnehmen
◆**go with** *vt* ① (*accompany*) ■**to ~ with sb** mit jdm mitgehen ② (*date*) ■**to ~ with sb** mit jdm gehen ③ (*be associated with*) einhergehen mit ④ (*belong*) ■**to ~ with sth** zu etw *dat* gehören ⑤ (*harmonize*) passen zu
◆**go without** *vi* ■**to ~ without sth** ohne etw auskommen; **to ~ without breakfast/sleep** nicht frühstücken/schlafen

goad [goʊd] *vt* ① (*spur*) ■**to ~ sb [to sth]** jdn [zu etw] antreiben ② (*provoke*) ■**to ~ sb into [doing] sth** jdn dazu anstacheln, etw zu tun

go-ahead ['goʊ·ə·hed] *n* Erlaubnis *f* (**for** zu +*dat*); **to give/get the ~** grünes Licht geben/erhalten

goal [goʊl] *n* ① (*aim*) Ziel *nt* ② SPORTS Tor *nt;* **to play in ~** im Tor stehen

goalie ['goʊ·li] *n* (*fam*), '**goalkeeper** ['goʊl·ˌki·pər] *n* Tormann, -frau *m, f*

'**goal line** *n* Torlinie *f*

'**goalpost** *n* Torpfosten *m*

goat [goʊt] *n* Ziege *f;* **~'s milk** Ziegenmilch *f*
▶PHRASES: **to get sb's ~** jdn auf die Palme bringen

goatee [goʊ·'ti] *n* Spitzbart *m*

gobble ['gab·əl] **I.** *vi turkey* kollern **II.** *vt* (*fam*) [hinunter]schlingen

gobbledegook ['gab·əl·di·ˌguk], **gobbledygook** *n* (*pej fam*) Kauderwelsch *nt*
go-between ['goʊ·bə·ˌtwin] *n* Vermittler(in) *m(f)*; (*between lovers*) Liebesbote, -in *m, f*
goblet ['gab·lət] *n* Kelch *m*
goblin ['gab·lɪn] *n* Kobold *m*
'go-cart *n* Gokart *m*
god [gad] *n* Gott *m*
God [gad] *n* Gott *m;* **to believe in ~** an Gott glauben; **my ~!** mein Gott!; **~ forbid!** Gott bewahre!; **~ knows where Bob is!** weiß der Himmel, wo Bob steckt!; **thank ~!** Gott sei Dank!
god-'awful *adj* (*fam*) beschissen
'godchild *n* Patenkind *nt*
'goddamn (*vulg*) **I.** *adj* (*emphasizing annoyance*) gottverdammt **II.** *interj* verdammt
'goddaughter *n* Patentochter *f*
goddess <*pl* -es> ['gad·ɪs] *n* Göttin *f;* **screen ~** [Film]diva *f*
'godfather *n* (*male godparent*) Patenonkel *m; a. Mafia leader* Pate *m*
'god-fearing *adj* gottesfürchtig
'godforsaken *adj* (*pej*) gottverlassen
godless ['gad·lɪs] *adj* gottlos
godlike ['gad·laɪk] *adj* göttlich
'godmother *n* Patentante *f,* Patin *f;* **fairy ~** gute Fee
'godsend *n* (*fam*) Gottesgeschenk *nt*
'godson *n* Patensohn *m*
goer ['goʊ·ər] *n* (*fam: person or thing that goes*) Geher *m*
goes [goʊz] *3rd pers. sing of* **go**
go-getter [ˌgoʊ·'get̬·ər] *n* Tatmensch *m*
go-getting ['goʊ·ˌget̬·ɪŋ] *adj* tatkräftig
goggle ['gag·əl] **I.** *vi* (*fam*) glotzen; ■**to ~ at sb/sth** jdn/etw anglotzen **II.** *n* **[a pair of] ~s** [eine] [Schutz]brille; **ski ~s** Skibrille *f;* **swimming ~s** Schwimmbrille *f*
going ['goʊ·ɪŋ] **I.** *n* ❶ (*act of leaving*) Gehen *nt* ❷ (*departure*) Weggang *m* ❸ (*conditions*) **easy/rough ~** günstige/ungünstige Bedingungen; **while the ~ is good** solange es gut läuft ▶ PHRASES: **when the ~ gets tough, the tough get ~** was uns nicht umbringt, macht uns nur noch härter **II.** *adj* ❶ (*current*) aktuell; **what's the ~ rate for babysitters nowadays?** wie viel zahlt man heutzutage üblicherweise für einen Babysitter? ❷ (*in action*) am Laufen; **to keep sth ~** etw in Gang halten; **~ concern** gutgehendes Unternehmen ❸ (*available*) vorhanden; **it's the best thing ~** es ist das Beste, was es gibt
going-'over <*pl* goings-over> *n* **to give sth a [good] ~** (*search thoroughly*) etw gründlich durchsuchen; (*clean thoroughly*) etw gründlich reinigen
goings-'on *npl* Vorfälle *pl*
gold [goʊld] *n* Gold *nt* ▶ PHRASES: **[as] good as ~** mustergültig
'gold digger *n* Goldgräber *m;* **she's a ~** (*fig*) sie ist nur auf Geld aus
'gold dust *n* Goldstaub *m*
golden ['goʊl·dən] *adj* golden *a. fig;* **~ brown** goldbraun; **~ anniversary** goldene Hochzeit
'goldfish *n* Goldfisch *m*
gold 'leaf *n* Blattgold *nt*
gold 'medal *n* Goldmedaille *f*
'gold mine *n* Goldmine *f;* (*fig*) Goldgrube *f*
gold 'plating *n* Vergoldung *f*
'goldsmith *n* Goldschmied(in) *m(f)*
golf [galf] *n* Golf *nt;* **a round of ~** eine Runde Golf
'golf ball *n* Golfball *m*
'golf club *n* ❶ (*implement*) Golfschläger *m* ❷ (*association*) Golfclub *m*
'golf course *n* Golfplatz *m*
golfer ['gal·fər] *n* Golfer(in) *m(f)*
golly ['gal·i] *interj* (*fam*) Donnerwetter
gondola ['gan·də·lə] *n* Gondel *f*
gondolier [ˌgan·də·'lɪr] *n* Gondoliere *m*
gone [gɔn] **I.** *pp of* **go II.** *adj* ❶ (*no longer there*) weg; (*used up*) verbraucht ❷ (*dead*) tot; **to be too far ~** dem Tode zu nah sein
goner ['gɔ·nər] *n* (*fam*) **to be a ~** (*be bound to die*) es nicht mehr lange machen; (*be irreparable*) hoffnungslos kaputt sein
gong [gaŋ] *n* Gong *m*
gonna ['gan·ə] (*sl*) *see* **going to: what you ~ do about it?** was willst du dagegen machen?
gonorrhea [ˌgan·ə·'ri·ə] *n* Tripper *m*
goo [gu] *n* (*fam*) Schmiere *f*
good [gʊd] **I.** *adj* <better, best> ❶ gut; *weather* schön; (*healthy*) *appetite, leg* gesund; **~ morning** guten Morgen; **have a ~ day!** schönen Tag noch!; **to have a ~ time** [viel] Spaß haben; **it's ~ to see you again** schön, dich wiederzusehen; **~ dog!** braver Hund!; **to do a ~ job** gute Arbeit leisten; **it's a ~ thing ...** zum Glück ...; **~ luck!** viel Glück!; **~ sense** Geistesgegenwart *f;* **in ~ time** rechtzeitig; ■**to be ~ at sth** gut in etw *dat* sein; **he's a ~ runner** er ist ein guter Läufer; **she speaks ~ Spanish** sie spricht gut Spanisch; **he's not very ~ at math** er ist nicht besonders gut in Mathe; **to be ~ for nothing** zu nichts taugen; **sb looks ~ in sth** etw steht jdm; ■**to be ~ with children** mit Kindern gut umgehen können; **too ~ to be true** zu schön, um wahr zu sein ❷ (*kind, understanding*) **it was very ~ of you to help us** es war sehr lieb von dir, uns zu helfen ❸ (*thorough*) gut; **to have a ~ cry** sich richtig ausweinen; **to have a ~ laugh** ordentlich lachen; **to have a ~ look at sth** sich *dat* etw genau ansehen ❹ (*substantial*) beträchtlich; **to make ~ money** gutes Geld verdienen; **a ~ deal of ...** jede Menge ... ❺ (*able to provide*) **he is always ~ for a laugh** er ist immer gut für einen Witz ❻ ■**as ~ as ...** (*almost*) so gut wie ...; **they as ~ as called me a liar** sie nannten mich praktisch eine Lügnerin ▶ PHRASES: **it's as ~ as it gets** besser wird's nicht mehr; **to make ~** zu Geld kommen **II.** *n* ❶ (*moral force*) Gute *nt;* **~ and evil** Gut und Böse; **to be up to no ~** nichts Gutes im Schilde führen

❷ (*benefit*) Wohl *nt;* **this will do you a world of ~** das wird Ihnen unglaublich guttun; **to do more harm than ~** mehr schaden als nützen; **for the ~ of his health** seiner Gesundheit zuliebe; **for one's own ~** zu seinem eigenen Besten; **a lot of ~ that'll do [you]!** das wird [dir] ja viel nützen! ❸ (*ability*) ■ **to be no ~ at sth** etw nicht gut können

goodbye [gʊ(d)·'baɪ], **good-by** I. *interj* auf Wiedersehen; **to say ~ to sb/sth** sich von jdm/etw verabschieden; **to kiss sb ~** jdm einen Abschiedskuss geben; **to kiss sth ~** (*fig*) etw abschreiben II. *n* Abschied *m;* **to say one's ~s** sich verabschieden

'good-for-nothing I. *n* (*pej*) Taugenichts *m* II. *adj* (*pej*) nichtsnutzig

Good 'Friday *n no art* Karfreitag *m*

good-humored [ˌgʊd·'hju·mərd] *adj* fröhlich

good-'looking *adj* <more ~, most ~ *or* better-looking, best-looking> gut aussehend

good 'looks *npl* gutes Aussehen

good-'natured *adj* gutmütig

goodness ['gʊd·nɪs] *n* ❶ Güte *f* ❷ FOOD Wertvolle(s) *nt* ❸ (*for emphasis*) **for ~' sake** du liebe Güte; **thank ~** Gott sei Dank

goods [gʊdz] *npl* Waren *pl,* Güter *pl;* **sporting ~** Sportartikel *pl;* **manufactured ~** Fertigprodukte *pl* ▶ PHRASES: **sb/sth comes up with the ~** jd/etw hält, was er/es verspricht

'good-sized *adj* [recht] groß

'goodwill I. *n* ❶ guter Wille (**towards** gegenüber +*dat*); **feeling/gesture of ~** Atmosphäre *f*/Geste *f* des guten Willens ❷ ECON Goodwill *m* II. *adj* **a ~ gesture** eine Geste des guten Willens; **~ mission** Goodwillreise *f*

goody ['gʊd·i] I. *n* ❶ (*desirable object*) tolle Sache ❷ FOOD Leckerbissen *m* II. *interj* (*usu childspeak*) spitze

gooey ['gu·i] *adj* (*fam*) ❶ (*sticky*) klebrig ❷ (*fig, pej*) schmalzig

goof [guf] (*fam*) I. *n* ❶ (*silly person*) Idiot *m pej fam,* Trottel *m pej fam* ❷ (*mistake*) Patzer *m* II. *vi* ■ **to ~ [up]** Mist bauen

◆ **goof around** *vt* ❶ (*clown around*) herumblödeln *fam* ❷ (*do nothing productive*) herumhängen *sl*

◆ **goof up** (*fam*) I. *vt* vermasseln II. *vi* Mist bauen

goofy ['gu·fi] *adj* (*fam*) doof

goose [gus] *n* <*pl* geese> Gans *f* ▶ PHRASES: **to kill the ~ that lays the golden egg** den Ast absägen, auf dem man sitzt; **to cook sb's ~** jdm die Suppe versalzen

'goose bumps *npl,* **goose flesh** *n,* **'goose pimples** *npl* Gänsehaut *f kein pl*

'goose-step *vi* <-pp-> im Stechschritt marschieren

goose step *n* Stechschritt *m*

gopher ['goʊ·fər] *n* Ziesel *m*

gore¹ [gɔr] *vt* aufspießen

gore² [gɔr] *n* Blut *nt*

gorge¹ [gɔrdʒ] *n* Schlucht *f*

gorge² [gɔrdʒ] *vi* sich vollessen

gorgeous ['gɔr·dʒəs] *adj* ❶ (*very beautiful*) herrlich, großartig; **the bride looked ~** die Braut sah zauberhaft aus ❷ (*very pleasurable*) ausgezeichnet, fabelhaft

gorilla [gə·'rɪl·ə] *n* Gorilla *m a. fig*

gory ['gɔr·i] *adj* blutig; *film* blutrünstig

gosh [gaʃ] *interj* (*fam*) Mensch

gosling ['gaz·lɪŋ] *n* Gänseküken *nt*

gospel ['gas·pəl] *n* ❶ **the G~ according to Saint Mark** [*or* **St Mark's Gospel**] das Evangelium nach Markus ❷ (*music*) Gospel *nt*

gossamer ['gas·ə·mər] I. *n* Spinnfäden *pl* II. *adj* hauchdünn

gossip ['gas·əp] I. *n* (*usu pej*) ❶ (*rumors*) Klatsch *m;* **idle ~** leeres Geschwätz; **the latest ~** der neueste Tratsch ❷ (*pej: person*) Tratschbase *f* II. *vi* ❶ (*chatter*) schwatzen ❷ (*spread rumors*) tratschen

'gossip column *n* Klatschspalte *f*

gossipy ['gas·ə·pi] *adj* schwatzhaft; **~ person** Klatschmaul *nt*

got [gat] *pt, pp of* **get**

Gothic ['gaθ·ɪk] *adj* ❶ ARCHIT, TYPO gotisch ❷ LIT Schauer-

gotta ['gaṭ·ə] (*fam*) = [**have**] **got to** müssen; ■ **to ~ do sth** etw tun müssen; **I ~ go now** ich muss jetzt los *fam;* **he's ~ be kidding** das kann er nicht ernst meinen

gotten ['gat·ən] *pp of* **got**

gouge [gaʊdʒ] I. *n* (*indentation*) Rille *f* II. *vt* ❶ (*cut out*) ■ **to ~ out** aushöhlen; *eye* ausstechen ❷ (*fam: overcharge*) ■ **to ~ sb** jdn betrügen

goulash ['gu·laʃ] *n* Gulasch *nt*

gourd [gɔrd] *n* Kürbisflasche *f*

gourmand [gʊr·'mand] *n* Schlemmer(in) *m(f)*

gourmet [gʊr·'meɪ] *n* Feinschmecker(in) *m(f)*

gout [gaʊt] *n* Gicht *f*

Gov. *n* ❶ *abbrev of* **government** ❷ *abbrev of* **governor**

govern ['gʌv·ərn] I. *vt* ❶ POL, LING regieren ❷ (*regulate*) regeln; ■ **to be ~ed by sth** durch etw *akk* bestimmt werden II. *vi* regieren

governess <*pl* -es> ['gʌv·ər·nɪs] *n* (*hist*) Gouvernante *f*

governing ['gʌv·ərn·ɪŋ] *adj* regierend; **~ body** Vorstand *m*

government ['gʌv·ərn·mənt] *n* Regierung *f,* Staat *m;* **local ~** Kommunalverwaltung *f;* **~ agency** Behörde *f;* **~ department** Regierungsstelle *f;* **~ grant** staatlicher Zuschuss; **~ policy** Regierungspolitik *f;* **~ spending** Staatsausgaben *pl;* **~ securities** staatliche Wertpapiere *pl;* **~ subsidy** Subvention *f*

governmental [ˌgʌv·ərn·'men·təl] *adj* Regierungs-, staatlich

governor ['gʌv·ər·nər] *n* POL Gouverneur *m*

gown [gaʊn] *n* ❶ FASHION Kleid *nt* ❷ MED Kittel *m;* **surgical ~** Operationskittel *m*

GP [ˌdʒi·'pi] *n* MED *abbrev of* **general practitioner**

GPS ['dʒi·pi·es] *acr for* **global navigation system** (*fam*) Navi *nt fam,* Navigationsgerät *nt*

grab [græb] **I.** *n* (*snatch*) Griff *m* ▶ PHRASES: **to be** <u>**up**</u> **for ~s** zu haben sein **II.** *vt* <-bb-> ① [sich *dat*] schnappen; ■ **to ~ sb by the arm** jdn am Arm packen; ■ **to ~ hold of sb/sth** jdn/etw festhalten ② (*fig*) *attention* erregen; *opportunity* wahrnehmen; **to ~ a bite** [**to eat**] schnell einen Happen essen; **to ~ some sleep** [ein wenig] schlafen **III.** *vi* <-bb-> (*snatch*) grapschen; ■ **to ~ at sth** nach etw *dat* greifen

grace [greɪs] **I.** *n* ① (*of movement*) Grazie *f* ② (*of appearance*) Anmut *f* ③ (*of behavior*) Anstand *m kein pl;* **social ~s** gesellschaftliche Umgangsformen ④ *a.* REL (*favor*) Gnade *f;* **to fall from ~** in Ungnade fallen ⑤ (*prayer*) Tischgebet *nt;* **to say ~** ein Tischgebet sprechen **II.** *vt* (*form*) ① (*honor*) beehren ② (*adorn*) schmücken

graceful [ˈgreɪs·fəl] *adj* ① (*in movement*) graziös, anmutig ② (*in appearance*) elegant

graceless [ˈgreɪs·lɪs] *adj* taktlos

gracious [ˈgreɪ·ʃəs] **I.** *adj* ① (*kind*) liebenswürdig; (*merciful*) gnädig ② (*dignified*) würdevoll **II.** *interj* [**good** [*or* **goodness**]] **~** [**me**] [du] meine Güte

grade [greɪd] **I.** *n* ① (*rank*) Rang *m* ② (*of salary*) Gehaltsstufe *f* ③ SCH (*score*) Note *f;* (*class*) Klasse *m* ④ (*gradient*) Neigung *f;* [**gentle/steep**] **~** (*upwards*) [geringe/starke] Steigung; (*downwards*) [schwaches/starkes] Gefälle ▶ PHRASES: **to** <u>**make**</u> **the ~** den Anforderungen gerecht werden **II.** *vt* ① SCH, UNIV benoten ② (*categorize*) einteilen

> Das übliche Notensystem der USA, das **grading system**, verwendet die Buchstaben A, B, C, D, E und F, wobei das E nie benützt wird. A ist die beste Note, und F (*Fail*) bedeutet durchgefallen. Die Buchstaben können auch mit einem Plus oder Minus versehen werden. Wer zum Beispiel ein A+ erhält, hat eine außerordentlich gute Leistung erbracht.

grader [ˈgreɪ·dər] *n* SCH **the second ~s** die Schüler(innen) *mpl(fpl)* der zweiten Klasse

ˈ**grade school** *n* Grundschule *f*

gradient [ˈgreɪ·di·ənt] *n* Neigung *f;* [**gentle/steep**] **~** (*upwards*) [leichte/starke] Steigung; (*downwards*) [schwaches/starkes] Gefälle

gradual [ˈgrædʒ·u·əl] *adj* ① (*not sudden*) allmählich ② (*not steep*) sanft

gradually [ˈgrædʒ·u·ə·li] *adv* ① (*not suddenly*) allmählich ② (*not steeply*) sanft

graduate **I.** *n* [ˈgrædʒ·u·ət] ① UNIV Absolvent(in) *m(f);* **college ~** Hochschulabsolvent(in) *m(f);* **~ student** Student(in) *m(f)* mit Universitätsabschluss (*Studenten mit einem „Bachelor's Degree", die eine weitere Stufe zur Erlangung des „Master's Degrees" absolvieren*) ② SCH Schulabgänger(in) *m(f)* **II.** *vi* [ˈgrædʒ·u·eɪt] ① UNIV einen akademischen Grad erwerben; **to ~ with honors** seinen Abschluss mit Auszeichnung machen ② SCH die Abschlussprüfung bestehen; **to ~ from high school** das Abitur machen ③ (*complete training*) die Ausbildung abschließen; UNIV das Studium abschließen **III.** *vt* [ˈgrædʒ·u·eɪt] ① (*calibrate*) einteilen ② (*award degree*) ■ **to ~ sb** jdn graduieren

graduated [ˈgrædʒ·uəɪ·ṭɪd] *adj salaries, charges* gestaffelt

graduation [ˌgrædʒ·u·ˈeɪ·ʃən] *n* ① SCH, UNIV (*completion of studies*) [Studien]abschluss *m* ② (*ceremony*) Abschlussfeier *f*

graffiti [grə·ˈfi·ṭi] *n* Graffiti *nt*

graft [græft] **I.** *n* ① MED Transplantat *nt* ② HORT (*shoot*) Pfropfreis *m* ③ (*corruption*) Schiebung *f* **II.** *vt* ① MED übertragen (**on**[**to**] auf +*akk*) ② HORT aufpfropfen (**on**[**to**] auf +*akk*)

Grail [greɪl] *n* [**Holy**] **~** Heiliger Gral

grain [greɪn] *n* ① (*particle*) Korn *nt,* Körnchen *nt;* **~ of sand/wheat** Sand-/Weizenkorn *nt* ② (*crop*) Getreide *nt* ③ (*texture*) *of wood, marble* Maserung *f* ▶ PHRASES: **to** <u>**go**</u> **against the ~** jdm gegen den Strich gehen *fam*

gram [græm] *n* Gramm *nt*

grammar [ˈgræm·ər] *n* Grammatik *f;* **to be good/bad ~** grammatikalisch richtig/falsch sein

ˈ**grammar book** *n* Grammatik *f*

ˈ**grammar school** *n* Grundschule *f*

grammatical [grə·ˈmæṭ·ɪ·kəl] *adj* grammati[kali]sch

grand [grænd] **I.** *adj* ① (*splendid*) prächtig, großartig; **to make a ~ entrance** einen großen Auftritt haben ② (*excellent*) großartig ③ (*large, far-reaching*) **~ ambitions/ideas** große Pläne/Ideen; **on a ~ scale** in großem Rahmen **II.** *n* ① <*pl* -> (*fam: one thousand dollars*) Mille *f* ② <*pl* -s> (*grand piano*) Flügel *m;* **baby/concert ~** Stutz-/Konzertflügel *m*

grandad [ˈgræn·dæd] *n* (*fam*) *see* **granddad**

ˈ**grandchild** *n* Enkelkind *nt*

ˈ**granddad** *n* (*fam*) ① (*grandfather*) Opa *m,* Opi *m* ② (*pej: old man*) Opa *m,* Alter *m*

ˈ**granddaughter** *n* Enkeltochter *f*

grandeur [ˈgræn·dʒər] *n* Größe *f; of scenery, music* Erhabenheit *f;* **delusions of ~** Größenwahn *m*

ˈ**grandfather** *n* Großvater *m*

grandiose [ˈgræn·di·oʊs] *adj* grandios

grand ˈ**jury** *n* Anklagejury *f*

grandly [ˈgrænd·li] *adv* ① (*splendidly*) prachtvoll ② (*pej: over-importantly*) prahlerisch

ˈ**grandma** *n* (*fam*) Oma *f,* Omi *f*

ˈ**grandmother** *n* Großmutter *f*

ˈ**grandpa** *n* (*fam*) Opa *m,* Opi *f*

grand piˈ**ano** *n* [Konzert]flügel *m*

ˈ**grandson** *n* Enkel[sohn] *m*

ˈ**grandstand** **I.** *n* [Haupt]tribüne *f* **II.** *vi* Effekthascherei betreiben

grand ˈ**sum, grand** ˈ**total** *n* Gesamtsumme *f*

granite [ˈgræn·ɪt] *n* Granit *m*

grannie [ˈgræn·i], **granny** [ˈgræn·i] *n* (*fam*)

Oma *f*, Omi *f*

grant [grænt] **I.** *n* ❶ UNIV Stipendium *nt* ❷ (*from authority*) Zuschuss *m oft pl;* (*subsidy*) Subvention *f* **II.** *vt* ❶ (*allow*) ■ **to ~ sb sth** jdm etw gewähren; *favor* jdm etw erweisen; *money* jdm etw bewilligen; *permission, visa* jdm etw erteilen; **to ~ sb a request** jds Anliegen *nt* stattgeben ❷ (*admit*) zugeben; **~ed, ...** zugegeben, ... ▶ PHRASES: **to take sth for ~ed** etw für selbstverständlich halten; (*not appreciate*) etw als [allzu] selbstverständlich betrachten

granular ['græn·jə·lər] *adj* körnig

granulated ['græn·jə·leɪ·t̬ɪd] *adj* granuliert; **~ sugar** Kristallzucker *m*

granule ['græn·jul] *n* Körnchen *nt;* ■ **~s** *pl* Granulat *nt*

grape [greɪp] **I.** *n* [Wein]traube *f;* **a bunch of ~s** eine [ganze] Traube **II.** *adj* Trauben-

'grapefruit <*pl* - *or* -s> ['greɪp·frut] *n* Grapefruit *f*

'grapevine *n* Weinstock *m* ▶ PHRASES: **I heard [it] on the ~ that ...** es ist mir zu Ohren gekommen, dass ...

graph [græf] *n* Diagramm *nt,* Graph *m;* **temperature ~** Temperaturkurve *f;* **~ paper** Millimeterpapier *nt*

graphic ['græf·ɪk] *adj* ❶ (*diagrammatic*) grafisch ❷ (*vividly descriptive*) anschaulich; **in ~ detail** haarklein ❸ ART Grafik-; **~ design** Grafikdesign *nt*

graphics ['græf·ɪks] *npl* Grafik *f;* **~ card** Grafikkarte *f*

graphite ['græf·aɪt] *n* Graphit *m*

grapple ['græp·əl] *vi* ■ **to ~ with sb** mit jdm ringen; **to ~ with a problem** mit einem Problem zu kämpfen haben

grasp [græsp] **I.** *n* ❶ (*grip*) Griff *m* ❷ (*fig: attainability*) Reichweite *f;* **to be within sb's ~** zum Greifen nahe sein ❸ (*fig: understanding*) Verständnis *nt;* **to have a good ~ of a subject** ein Fach gut beherrschen **II.** *vt* ❶ (*take firm hold*) [fest] [er]greifen; **to ~ sb by the arm/hand** jdn am Arm/an der Hand fassen ❷ (*fig: understand*) begreifen **III.** *vi* ❶ ■ **to ~ at sth** nach etw *dat* greifen ❷ (*fig*) **to ~ at the opportunity** die Gelegenheit beim Schopfe packen

grasping ['græs·pɪŋ] *adj* (*fig, pej*) habgierig

grass <*pl* -es> [græs] **I.** *n* ❶ Gras *nt;* (*lawn*) Rasen *m;* **to put cattle out to ~** [das] Vieh auf die Weide treiben ❷ (*sl: marijuana*) Gras *nt sl* ▶ PHRASES: **the ~ is always greener on the other side of the fence** (*prov*) die Kirschen in Nachbars Garten schmecken immer süßer **II.** *vt* mit Gras bepflanzen

'grasshopper *n* Heuschrecke *f*

'grassland *n* Grasland *nt*

grass'roots *npl* (*ordinary people*) Volk *nt kein pl;* *of a party, organization* Basis *f kein pl;* **~ opinion** Volksmeinung *f*

'grass snake *n* Grasnatter *f*

grassy ['græs·i] *adj* grasbewachsen

grate [greɪt] **I.** *n* Kamin *m* **II.** *vi* ❶ (*annoy*) *noise* in den Ohren wehtun; **to ~ on sb['s nerves]** jdm auf die Nerven gehen ❷ (*rasp*) kratzen; ■ **to ~ against one another** gegeneinanderreiben **III.** *vt* FOOD reiben; *vegetables* raspeln

grateful ['greɪt·fəl] *adj* dankbar

grater ['greɪ·t̬ər] *n* Reibe *f*

gratification [ˌgræt̬·ə·fɪ·'keɪ·ʃən] *n* Genugtuung *f;* **sexual ~** sexuelle Befriedigung

gratify <-ie-> ['græt̬·ə·faɪ] *vt* ❶ *usu passive* (*please*) ■ **to be gratified at [*or* by] sth** über etw *akk* [hoch] erfreut sein ❷ (*satisfy*) befriedigen

gratifying ['græt̬·ə·faɪ·ɪŋ] *adj* erfreulich

grating ['greɪ·t̬ɪŋ] **I.** *n* Gitter *nt* **II.** *adj* ❶ (*grinding*) knirschend; (*rasping*) kratzend ❷ (*annoying*) nervtötend

gratitude ['græt̬·ə·tud] *n* Dankbarkeit *f*

gratuitous [grə·'tu·ɪ·t̬əs] *adj* ❶ (*free*) kostenlos ❷ (*pej: unnecessary*) überflüssig; **~ bad language** unnötige Kraftausdrücke; (*unjustifiable*) grundlos

gratuity [grə·'tu·ɪ·t̬i] *n* ❶ (*tip*) Trinkgeld *nt* ❷ (*bribe*) **illegal ~** Bestechungsgeld *nt*

grave [greɪv] **I.** *n* Grab *nt* ▶ PHRASES: **from beyond the ~** aus dem Jenseits **II.** *adj* ernst; *crisis* schwer; *mistake* gravierend; *news* schlimm; *reservations* schwerwiegend

'gravedigger *n* Totengräber(in) *m(f)*

gravel ['græv·əl] *n* Kies *m;* **~ road** Schotterstraße *f*

gravelly ['græv·ə·li] *adj* ❶ *soil* kieshaltig ❷ (*fig*) *voice* rau

'gravel pit *n* Kiesgrube *f*

gravely ['greɪv·li] *adv* ernst; **~ ill** schwer krank; **to be ~ mistaken** sich schwer irren

'grave robber *n* Grabräuber(in) *m(f)*

'gravestone *n* Grabstein *m*

'graveyard *n* Friedhof *m*

gravitate ['græv·ɪ·teɪt] *vi* ■ **to ~ to[ward] sth/sb** von etw/jdm angezogen werden

gravitation [ˌgræv·ɪ·'teɪ·ʃən] *n* ❶ (*movement*) ■ **~ to[ward] sth** Bewegung *f* zu etw *dat* hin ❷ (*attracting force*) Schwerkraft *f*

gravity ['græv·ɪ·t̬i] *n* ❶ PHYS Schwerkraft *f* ❷ (*seriousness*) Ernst *m;* *of speech* Ernsthaftigkeit *f*

gravy ['greɪ·vi] *n* ❶ [Braten]soße *f* ❷ (*fig sl: easy money*) leicht verdientes Geld

'gravy boat *n* Sauciere *f,* Soßenschüssel *f*

'gravy train *n* (*fig*) **to get on the ~** sich *dat* ein Stück vom Kuchen abschneiden

gray [greɪ] **I.** *n* (*color*) Grau *nt* **II.** *adj* grau *a. fig; face* [asch]grau; *horse* [weiß]grau

'gray matter *n* (*fam*) graue Zellen *pl*

graze¹ [greɪz] **I.** *vi* grasen, weiden **II.** *vt animals* weiden lassen; *meadow* abgrasen

graze² [greɪz] **I.** *n* Schürfwunde *f* **II.** *vt* streifen; **to ~ one's knee/elbow** sich *dat* das Knie/den Ellbogen aufschürfen

grease [gris] **I.** *n* ❶ (*fat*) Fett *nt;* **~ mark** Fettfleck *m* ❷ (*lubricating oil*) Schmierfett *nt* **II.** *vt*

[ein]fetten; MECH schmieren ▶ PHRASES: **like ~d lightning** wie ein geölter Blitz

'greasepaint *n* THEAT Fettschminke *f*

greasy ['gri·si] *adj hair, skin* fettig; *fingers, objects a.* schmierig; *food* fett; (*slippery*) glitschig

great [greɪt] **I.** *adj* ❶ (*very big*) groß; **a ~ deal of time** eine Menge Zeit; **to a ~ extent** im Großen und Ganzen ❷ (*famous*) groß; (*important*) bedeutend; (*outstanding*) überragend ❸ (*inf: wonderful*) großartig, hervorragend, toll; **to feel not all that ~** sich gar nicht gut fühlen; **we had a ~ time at the party** wir haben uns auf der Party großartig amüsiert; ■ **to be ~ at [doing] sth** etw sehr gut können **II.** *adv* (*extremely*) sehr; **~ big/long** riesengroß/-lang **III.** *n* (*person*) Größe *f;* (*in titles*) **Alexander/Catherine the G~** Alexander der Große/Katharina die Große

'great-aunt *n* Großtante *f*

Great 'Britain *n* Großbritannien *nt*

Greater ['greɪṱ·ər] (*in cities*) **~ Los Angeles** Großraum *m* Los Angeles

great-'grandchild *n* Urenkel(in) *m(f)*

Great 'Lakes *npl* GEOG ■ **the ~** die Großen Seen

Die **Great Lakes** (die Großen Seen), die entlang der Grenze zwischen den Vereinigten Staaten und Kanada liegen, stellen die größte Gruppe an Süßwasserseen auf der Erde und in Form des Sankt-Lorenz-Stroms das größte Süßwassersystem der Erde dar. Die dieses innere Meer bildenden Seen heißen – von Westen nach Osten: Oberer See, Michigansee, Huronsee, Eriesee und Ontariosee. Zwischen dem Eriesee und dem Ontariosee befinden sich die großartigen Niagarafälle, deren eine Seite auf US-Gebiet liegt, während die andere Hälfte zu Kanada gehört.

greatly ['greɪt·li] *adv* sehr; **~ impressed** tief beeindruckt; **to ~ regret** zutiefst bedauern

greatness ['greɪt·nɪs] *n* Bedeutsamkeit *f*

Die **Great Plains** (Große Ebenen) waren einst großflächige Steppen, die von Alberta und Saskatchewan im Westen Kanadas bis nach New Mexiko und Texas reichten. Die Bebauung dieser Steppen hat daraus eine der wichtigsten Getreideregionen der Welt gemacht.

great-'uncle *n* Großonkel *m*

Grecian ['gri·ʃən] *adj* griechisch

Greece [gris] *n* Griechenland *nt*

greed [grid], **greediness** ['gri·dɪ·nɪs] *n* Gier *f* (**for** nach *+dat*)

greedy ['gri·di] *adj* gierig; (*for money, things*) habgierig; ■ **to be ~ for sth** (*fig*) gierig nach etw *dat* sein; **~ pig** (*pej*) Vielfraß *m*

Greek [grik] **I.** *n* ❶ (*person*) Grieche, -in *m, f* ❷ (*language*) Griechisch *nt;* **ancient ~** Altgriechisch *nt;* **modern ~** Neugriechisch *nt* **II.** *adj* griechisch ▶ PHRASES: **it's all ~ to me** das sind alles böhmische Dörfer für mich

green [grin] **I.** *n* ❶ (*color*) Grün *nt* ❷ FOOD ■ **~s** *pl* Blattgemüse *nt kein pl* ❸ (*area of grass*) **bowling ~** *Rasenfläche zum Bowlen* **II.** *adj* ❶ grün; **~ with envy** grün vor Neid ❷ (*environmental*) grün, umweltfreundlich, ökologisch; **~ issues** *pl* Umweltschutzfragen

'greenback *n* (*fam*) Dollar[schein] *m,* Dollar[bank]note *f*

'green card *n* Aufenthaltserlaubnis *f* mit Arbeitsgenehmigung

greenery ['gri·nə·ri] *n* Grün *nt*

'greengrocer *n* Obst- und Gemüsehändler(in) *m(f)*

'greenhouse *n* Gewächshaus *nt;* **~ effect** Treibhauseffekt *m*

greenish ['gri·nɪʃ] *adj* grünlich

greenness ['grin·nɪs] *n* Grün[e] *nt*

'Green Party *n + sing vb* die Grünen *pl*

green 'pepper *n* grüne Paprikaschote

greet [grit] *vt* ❶ (*welcome*) [be]grüßen; (*receive*) empfangen; **to ~ each other [by shaking hands]** sich [mit Handschlag] begrüßen; **a scene of chaos ~ed us** ein chaotischer Anblick bot sich uns dar ❷ (*react*) ■ **to ~ sth with sth** auf etw *akk* mit etw *dat* reagieren

greeting ['gri·ṱɪŋ] *n* Begrüßung *f;* ■ **~s** *pl* Grüße *pl;* **birthday ~s** Geburtstagsglückwünsche *pl*

gregarious [grɪ·'ger·i·əs] *adj* gesellig

gremlin ['grem·lɪn] *n* Kobold *m*

grenade [grə·'neɪd] *n* Granate *f*

grew [gru] *pt of* **grow**

grey [greɪ] *adj see* **gray**

'greyhound *n* Windhund *m*

greying, graying ['greɪ·ɪŋ] *adj* ergrauend; **~ hair** leicht ergrautes Haar

greyish, grayish ['greɪ·ɪʃ] *adj* gräulich

grid [grɪd] *n* ❶ (*grating*) Gitter *nt* ❷ (*pattern*) Gitternetz *nt* ❸ ELEC Netz *nt*

griddle ['grɪd·əl] **I.** *n* Heizplatte *f* **II.** *vt* auf einer Heizplatte zubereiten

gridiron ['grɪd·aɪ·ərn] *n* ❶ (*metal grid*) [Grill]rost *m* ❷ SPORTS Footballfeld *nt*

gridlock ['grɪd·lak] *n* ❶ (*traffic jam*) Verkehrskollaps *m;* **to cause ~** den [gesamten] Verkehr lahmlegen ❷ (*impasse*) Arbeitshemmnis *f*

grief [grif] *n* ❶ (*sadness*) tiefe Trauer, Kummer *m* ❷ (*fam: trouble*) **to cause ~** für Ärger sorgen

grievance ['gri·vəns] *n* ❶ (*complaint*) Beschwerde *f* ❷ (*sense of injustice*) Groll *m kein pl*

grieve [griv] **I.** *vi* bekümmert sein; ■ **to ~ for sb** um jdn trauern; ■ **to ~ over sth** über etw *akk* betrübt sein **II.** *vt* ■ **to ~ sb** (*distress*) jdm Kummer bereiten; (*make sad*) jdn traurig ma-

G

chen

grievous ['gri·vəs] *adj* schwer; *danger* groß

grill [grɪl] **I.** *n* (*over charcoal*) [Grill]rost *m;* (*restaurant*) Grillrestaurant *nt* **II.** *vt* ① grillen ② (*fig fam: interrogate*) ausquetschen

grille [grɪl] *n* Gitter *nt*

grilling ['grɪl·ɪŋ] *n* (*fig fam*) strenges Verhör

grim [grɪm] *adj* ① (*forbidding*) grimmig, verbissen ② (*very unpleasant*) *apartment, picture* trostlos; *landscape* unwirtlich; *news* entsetzlich; *outlook* düster; *reminder* bitter; *situation* schlimm; **things were looking ~** die Lage sah langsam düster aus

grimace ['grɪm·əs] **I.** *n* Grimasse *f* **II.** *vi* **to ~ [with pain]** das Gesicht [vor Schmerz] verziehen

grime [graɪm] *n* Schmutz *m*

grimy ['graɪ·mi] *adj* schmutzig

grin [grɪn] **I.** *n* Grinsen *nt kein pl* **II.** *vi* grinsen ▶ PHRASES: **to ~ and <u>bear</u> it** gute Miene zum bösen Spiel machen

grind [graɪnd] **I.** *n* (*fam*) **the daily ~** der tägliche Trott; **to be a real ~** sehr mühsam sein **II.** *vt* <ground, ground> ① (*crush*) mahlen; *meat* fein hacken; **to ~ sth [in]to a powder** etw fein zermahlen; **to ~ one's teeth** mit den Zähnen knirschen ② (*sharpen*) schleifen **III.** *vi* <ground, ground> **to ~ to a halt** *machine* [quietschend] zum Stehen kommen; *production* stocken; *negotiations* sich festfahren

◆**grind down** *vt* ① (*file*) abschleifen; *mill* zerkleinern ② (*mentally wear out*) zermürben; (*oppress*) unterdrücken

◆**grind out** *vt* (*produce continuously*) ununterbrochen produzieren

grinder ['graɪn·dər] *n* ① (*mill*) Mühle *f* ② (*sharpener*) Schleifmaschine *f* ③ (*mincer*) Fleischwolf *m*

grindstone ['graɪnd·stoʊn] *n* Schleifstein *m* ▶ PHRASES: **to keep one's <u>nose</u> to the ~** sich [bei der Arbeit] ranhalten

gringo ['grɪŋ·goʊ] *n* (*pej*) Gringo *m pej*

grip [grɪp] **I.** *n* Griff *m kein pl a. fig;* **to be in the ~ of sth** von etw *dat* betroffen sein; **to get to ~s with sth** etw in den Griff bekommen; **to get/keep a ~ on oneself** sich zusammenreißen/sich im Griff haben; **to lose one's ~ on reality** den Bezug zur Realität verlieren **II.** *vt* <-pp-> ① packen ② (*fig*) packen; (*interest deeply*) fesseln **III.** *vi* <-pp-> greifen

gripe [graɪp] (*fam*) **I.** *n* Nörgelei *f* **II.** *vi* nörgeln

gripping ['grɪp·ɪŋ] *adj* packend, fesselnd

grisly ['grɪz·li] *adj* grausig

gristle ['grɪs·əl] *n* Knorpel *m*

grit [grɪt] **I.** *n* ① (*small stones*) Splitt *m;* (*for icy roads*) Streusand *m* ② (*fig: courage*) Schneid *m* **II.** *vt* <-tt-> ① *roads* streuen ② **to ~ one's teeth** die Zähne zusammenbeißen *a. fig*

gritty ['grɪt̬·i] *adj* ① (*like grit*) grob[körnig] ② (*full of grit*) sandig

grizzled ['grɪz·əld] *adj* ergraut

grizzly ['grɪz·li] **I.** *adj* gräulich **II.** *n* Grizzlybär *m*

groan [groʊn] **I.** *n* Stöhnen *nt kein pl* **II.** *vi* ① *person* [auf]stöhnen; ■**to ~ about sth** (*fig*) sich über etw *akk* beklagen ② *thing* ächzen

grocer ['groʊ·sər] *n* Lebensmittelhändler(in) *m(f)*

groceries ['groʊ·sə·riz] *npl* Lebensmittel *pl*

groggy ['grag·i] *adj* angeschlagen

groin [grɔɪn] *n* ANAT Leiste *f;* (*euph: genitals*) Weichteile *pl fam*

groom [grum] **I.** *n* ① (*bridegroom*) Bräutigam *m* ② (*for horses*) Pferdepfleger(in) *m(f)* **II.** *vt* (*clean fur*) das Fell pflegen; *horse* striegeln

groove [gruv] *n* Rille *f*

groovy ['gru·vi] *adj* (*sl*) klasse *fam,* cool *fam*

grope [groʊp] **I.** *n* (*fam*) Befummeln *nt kein pl* **II.** *vi* ■**to ~ for sth** nach etw *dat* tasten **III.** *vt* ① **to ~ one's way** sich *dat* tastend seinen Weg suchen ② (*fam*) ■**to ~ sb** jdn befummeln

gross [groʊs] **I.** *n* <*pl* - *or* -es> (*a group of 144*) Gros *nt;* **by the ~** en gros **II.** *adj* ① (*disgusting*) ekelhaft; (*very fat*) fett; (*big and ugly*) abstoßend ② FIN Brutto-; **~ national product** Bruttosozialprodukt *nt* ③ (*extreme*) **~ error** grober Fehler **III.** *vt* FIN brutto einnehmen

grossly ['groʊs·li] *adv* extrem

grotesque [groʊ·'tesk] *adj* grotesk

grotto <*pl* -es *or* -s> ['grat̬·oʊ] *n* Grotte *f*

grouch [graʊtʃ] **I.** *n* <*pl* -es> ① (*person*) Nörgler(in) *m(f)* ② (*complaint*) Beschwerde *f* **II.** *vi* [herum]nörgeln (**about** an +*dat*)

grouchy ['graʊ·tʃi] *adj* griesgrämig

ground[1] [graʊnd] **I.** *n* ① [Erd]boden *m,* Erde *f;* **above/below ~** über/unter der Erde; MIN über/unter Tage; **to get off the ~** *plane* abheben; (*fig fam*) *project* in Gang kommen; *plan* verwirklicht werden; **to get sth off the ~** (*fig fam*) etw realisieren ② (*area of land*) [ein Stück] Land *nt;* **waste ~** brachliegendes Land; **to gain/lose ~** MIL Boden gewinnen/verlieren; (*fig*) an Boden gewinnen/verlieren ③ ELEC (*earth*) Erdung *f* ④ (*fig: area of discussion*) **to find common ~** Gemeinsamkeiten entdecken; **to be on familiar/safe ~** sich auf vertrautem/sicherem Boden bewegen; **to go back over the same ~** sich *akk* wiederholen ⑤ *pl* ■**~s** (*area around large house*) Gelände *nt,* Anlage *f* ⑥ *pl* ■**~s** (*reasons*) Grund *m;* **~s for divorce** Scheidungsgrund *m* ▶ PHRASES: **to <u>break</u> new ~** Neuland betreten; **to <u>fall</u> on stony ~** auf taube Ohren stoßen; **to <u>shift</u> one's ~** seinen Standpunkt ändern; **to <u>work</u> oneself into the ~** sich kaputtmachen **II.** *vt* ① ■**to be ~ed** *pilot* Flugverbot haben; (*fig inf*) Hausarrest haben; NAUT auflaufen ② (*be based*) ■**to be ~ed upon sth** auf etw *dat* basieren; ■**to be ~ed in sth** (*have its origin*) von etw *dat* herrühren; **to be [well] ~ed** [wohl]begründet sein ③ ELEC erden

ground[2] [graʊnd] **I.** *vt pt of* **grind II.** *adj* gemahlen **III.** *n* ■**~s** *pl* [Boden]satz *m kein pl*

'groundbreaking *adj* bahnbrechend

'ground control *n* AVIAT Bodenkontrolle *f*
'ground crew *n* AVIAT Bodenpersonal *nt kein pl*
ground 'floor *n* Erdgeschoss *nt,* Parterre *nt* ► PHRASES: **to get in on the ~ [of sth]** von Anfang an [bei etw *dat*] dabei sein
'ground frost *n* Bodenfrost *m*
groundhog ['graʊnd·hag] *n* Waldmurmeltier *nt*
'Groundhog Day *n* Murmeltiertag *m*

> In den Vereinigten Staaten wird der 2. Februar **Groundhog Day** genannt. An diesem Tag kann man anhand des Verhaltens des aus seinem Bau kommenden *groundhog* (Murmeltier) vorhersagen, ob der Frühling verfrüht oder verspätet eintreffen wird. Sieht es seinen Schatten, erschrickt das Murmeltier und kehrt in den Bau zurück, was bedeutet, dass der Winter noch weitere sechs Wochen dauern wird. Ist der Himmel jedoch bedeckt, sodass es seinen Schatten nicht erkennen kann, bleibt es im Freien, weil der Frühling vor der Tür steht.

grounding ['graʊnd·ɪŋ] *n* Grundlagen *pl*
groundless ['graʊnd·lɪs] *adj* grundlos
'ground rules *npl* Grundregeln *pl*
'groundskeeper *n* Platzwart *m;* ■ **~s** *pl* Wartungspersonal *nt*
'ground staff *n* AVIAT Bodenpersonal *nt*
'groundswell *n* (*fig*) Anschwellen *nt*
'groundwater *n* Grundwasser *nt*
'groundwork *n* Vorarbeit *f*
group [grup] **I.** *n* ❶ Gruppe *f;* **~s of four or five** Vierer- oder Fünfergruppen *pl* ❷ ECON Konzern *m* **II.** *adj* Gruppen- **III.** *vt* gruppieren; (*classify*) ordnen; (*divide up*) einteilen **IV.** *vi* sich gruppieren; **to ~ together** sich zusammentun
groupie ['gru·pi] *n* (*fam*) Groupie *nt*
grouping ['gru·pɪŋ] *n* Gruppierung *f*
group 'practice *n* Gemeinschaftspraxis *f*
group 'therapy *n* Gruppentherapie *f*
grouse[1] <*pl* -> [graʊs] *n* Raufußhuhn *nt;* **black ~** Birkhuhn *nt*
grouse[2] [graʊs] (*fam*) **I.** *n* Meckerei *f* **II.** *vi* meckern
grove [groʊv] *n* Wäldchen *nt;* **olive ~** Olivenhain *m*
grovel <-l- *or* -ll-> ['grav·əl] *vi* ❶ (*behave obsequiously*) ■ **to ~ [before sb]** [vor jdm] zu Kreuze kriechen, katzbuckeln ❷ (*crawl*) kriechen
grow <grew, grown> [groʊ] **I.** *vi* wachsen; **to ~ taller/wiser** größer/weiser werden; *popularity, sales* zunehmen; **soccer's popularity continues to ~** Fußball wird immer populärer; **to ~ to like sth** langsam beginnen, etw zu mögen **II.** *vt* ❶ (*cultivate*) anbauen; *flowers* züchten; **to ~ sth from seed** etw aus Samen ziehen ❷ (*let grow*) *hair* wachsen lassen; **furry animals ~ a thicker coat in winter** Pelztiere bekommen im Winter ein dichteres Fell
◆ **grow apart** *vi* **to ~ apart from sb** sich jdm [allmählich] entfremden
◆ **grow into** *vi* hineinwachsen in +*akk*
◆ **grow out of** *vi* ■ **to ~ out of sth** aus etw *dat* herauswachsen; **to ~ out of a habit** eine Angewohnheit ablegen
◆ **grow up** *vi* (*become adult*) erwachsen werden; **when I ~ up I'm going to ...** wenn ich erwachsen bin, werde ich ...
grower ['groʊ·ər] *n* ❶ (*plant*) **a slow ~** eine langsam wachsende Pflanze ❷ AGR **coffee ~** Kaffeepflanzer(in) *m(f);* **fruit ~** Obstbauer, -bäuerin *m, f*
growing ['groʊ·ɪŋ] **I.** *n* Anbau *m* **II.** *adj* ❶ *boy, girl* im Wachstumsalter; **~ pains** Wachstumsschmerzen *pl;* (*fig*) Anfangsschwierigkeiten *pl* ❷ (*increasing*) zunehmend
growl [graʊl] **I.** *n of animal* Knurren *nt kein pl; of machine* Brummen *nt kein pl* **II.** *vi* knurren; ■ **to ~ at sb** jdn anknurren
grown [groʊn] **I.** *adj* erwachsen; **fully ~** ausgewachsen **II.** *pp of* **grow**
grownup ['groʊn·ʌp] *n* (*fam*) Erwachsene(r) *f(m)*
grown-up ['groʊn·ʌp] *adj* (*fam*) erwachsen
growth [groʊθ] *n* ❶ Wachstum *nt;* **~ industry** Wachstumsindustrie *f* ❷ MED Geschwulst *f*
grub [grʌb] **I.** *n* ❶ (*larva*) Larve *f* ❷ (*fam: food*) Fressalien *pl fam* **II.** *vi* <-bb-> **to ~ around [for sth]** [nach etw *dat*] wühlen
grubby ['grʌb·i] *adj* (*fam*) schmudd[e]lig; *hands* schmutzig; (*fig*) schäbig
grudge [grʌdʒ] **I.** *n* Groll *m kein pl;* **to have [*or* hold] a ~ against sb** einen Groll gegen jdn hegen **II.** *vt* ■ **to ~ sb sth** jdm etw missgönnen
grudging ['grʌdʒ·ɪŋ] *adj* widerwillig
grudgingly ['grʌdʒ·ɪŋ·li] *adv* widerwillig
gruel ['gru·əl] *n* Haferschleim *m*
grueling ['gru·lɪŋ] *adj time* aufreibend, zermürbend; *journey* strapaziös
gruesome ['gru·səm] *adj* grausig, schauerlich
gruff [grʌf] *adj* barsch
grumble ['grʌm·bəl] **I.** *n* Gemurre *nt kein pl* **II.** *vi* murren; ■ **to ~ about sth/sb** über etw/jdn schimpfen
grumpy ['grʌm·pi] *adj* (*fam*) mürrisch, brummig, grantig
grunt [grʌnt] **I.** *n* ❶ (*sound*) Grunzen *nt kein pl* ❷ MIL gemeiner Soldat/gemeine Soldatin **II.** *vi* grunzen
G-string ['dʒi·strɪŋ] *n* ❶ (*clothing*) String-Tanga *m* ❷ MUS G-Saite *f*
guarantee [ˌger·ən·'ti] **I.** *n* Garantie *f;* **to give sb one's ~** jdm etw garantieren; **money-back ~** Rückerstattungsgarantie *f;* **two-year ~** Garantie *f* auf 2 Jahre **II.** *vt* garantieren; ■ **to ~ sb sth** jdm etw zusichern; ■ **to ~ that ...** gewährleisten, dass ...
guarantor [ˌger·ən·'tɔr] *n* Garant(in) *m(f);* LAW Bürge, -in *m, f*

guard [gard] **I.** *n* ① (*person*) Wache *f;* (*sentry*) Wach[t]posten *m;* **prison** ~ Gefängniswärter(in) *m(f);* **security** ~ Sicherheitsbeamte(r) *f(m),* -beamtin *f;* **to be on** ~ Wache halten ② (*group of guards*) Garde *f;* ~ **of honor** Ehrengarde *f* ③ (*defensive stance*) Deckung *f;* **to be on one's** ~ **[against sth/sb]** (*fig*) [vor etw/jdm] auf der Hut sein; **to be caught off [one's]** ~ [von einem Schlag] unvorbereitet getroffen werden; (*fig*) auf etw *akk* nicht vorbereitet sein ④ (*protective device*) Schutz *m* **II.** *vt* (*keep watch*) bewachen; **heavily** ~**ed** scharf bewacht; (*protect*) [be]schützen (**against** vor +*dat*) **III.** *vi* ■**to** ~ **against sth** sich vor etw *dat* schützen

'guard dog *n* Wachhund *m*

'guard duty *n* Wachdienst *m;* **to be on** ~ **duty** Wachdienst haben

guarded ['gar·dɪd] *adj* (*reserved*) zurückhaltend; (*cautious*) vorsichtig

'guardhouse *n* Wache *f*

guardian ['gar·di·ən] *n* ① LAW Vormund *m* ② (*form: protector*) Hüter(in) *m(f)*

guardian 'angel *n* Schutzengel *m a. fig*

guardianship ['gar·di·ən·ʃɪp] *n* LAW Vormundschaft *f*

'guard rail *n* [Schutz]geländer *nt*

'guardroom *n* Wachstube *f*

'guardsman *n* (*member of National Guard*) Gardesoldat *m*

gubernatorial [ˌgu·bər·nə·'tɔr·i·əl] *adj inv* Gouverneurs-

gue(r)rilla [gə·'rɪl·ə] *n* Guerillakämpfer(in) *m(f);* ~ **warfare** Guerillakrieg *m*

guess [ges] **I.** *n* <*pl* -es> Vermutung *f;* (*estimate*) Schätzung *f;* **I'll give you three** ~**es** dreimal darfst du raten; **lucky** ~ Glückstreffer *m;* **to take a** ~ raten; **at a** ~ grob geschätzt; **my** ~ **is that ...** ich vermute, dass ... ▶ PHRASES: **it's anyone's** ~ weiß der Himmel **II.** *vi* ① (*conjecture*) [er]raten; **to keep sb** ~**ing** jdn auf die Folter spannen; ■**to** ~ **at sth** etw raten; (*estimate*) etw schätzen ② (*suppose*) denken; (*suspect*) annehmen; **I** ~ **you're right** du wirst wohl recht haben **III.** *vt* raten; ~ **where I'm calling from** rate mal, woher ich anrufe; ~ **what?** stell dir vor!; **to keep sb** ~**ing** jdn im Ungewissen lassen

guessing game ['ges·ɪŋ·ˌgeɪm] *n* Ratespiel *nt a. fig*

guesstimate ['ges·tɪ·mət] *n* (*fam*) grobe Schätzung

guesswork ['ges·wɜrk] *n* Spekulation *f oft pl*

guest [gest] **I.** *n* Gast *m* ▶ PHRASES: **be my** ~ nur zu! **II.** *vi* als Gaststar auftreten; **to** ~ **on an album** als Gaststar an einem Album mitwirken

'guesthouse *n* Gästehaus *nt,* Pension *f*

'guestroom *n* Gästezimmer *nt*

guidance ['gaɪ·dəns] *n* ① (*advice*) Beratung *f;* (*direction*) [An]leitung *f* ② (*steering system*) Steuerung *f;* ~ **system** (*of rocket*) Lenksystem *nt;* (*of missile*) Leitstrahlsystem *nt*

guide [gaɪd] **I.** *n* ① (*person*) Führer(in) *m(f); a.* TOURIST Fremdenführer(in) *m(f);* **tour** ~ Reiseführer(in) *m(f)* ② (*book*) Reiseführer *m* ③ (*indication*) Anhaltspunkt *m* **II.** *vt* ① (*show*) ■**to** ~ **sb** jdn führen *a. fig;* (*show the way*) jdm den Weg zeigen ② (*instruct*) anleiten ③ (*steer*) führen; **the plane was** ~**d in to land** das Flugzeug wurde zur Landung eingewiesen

'guidebook *n* Reiseführer *m*

guided ['gaɪ·dɪd] *adj* ① (*led by a guide*) geführt; ~ **tour** Führung *f* ② (*automatically steered*) [fern]gelenkt; ~ **missile** Lenkflugkörper *m*

'guide dog *n* Blindenhund *m*

'guideline *n usu pl* Richtlinie *f*

guiding hand ['gaɪ·dɪŋ·'hænd] *n* (*fig*) leitende Hand

guiding 'principle *n* Richtschnur *f*

guild [gɪld] *n of merchants* Gilde *f; of craftsmen* Innung *f,* Zunft *f*

guile [gaɪl] *n* Arglist *f*

guillotine ['gɪl·ə·tin] *n* HIST Guillotine *f,* Fallbeil *nt*

guilt [gɪlt] *n* Schuld *f;* **feelings of** ~ Schuldgefühle *pl*

guiltless ['gɪlt·lɪs] *adj* schuldlos

'guilt-ridden *adj* von Schuldgefühlen geplagt

guilty ['gɪl·ti] *adj* schuldig; ~ **conscience** schlechtes Gewissen; **to feel** ~ **about sth** ein schlechtes Gewissen wegen einer S. *gen* haben; **he is** ~ **of theft** er hat sich des Diebstahls schuldig gemacht; **to prove sb** ~ jds Schuld *f* beweisen

'guinea pig *n* Meerschweinchen *nt;* (*fig*) Versuchskaninchen *nt*

guise [gaɪz] *n* ① (*appearance*) Gestalt *f;* **in the** ~ **of a monk** als Mönch verkleidet ② (*pretense*) Vorwand *m;* **under the** ~ **of friendship** unter dem Deckmantel der Freundschaft

guitar [gɪ·'tar] *n* Gitarre *f*

guitarist [gɪ·'tar·ɪst] *n* Gitarrist(in) *m(f)*

gulch [gʌltʃ] *n* Schlucht *f*

gulf [gʌlf] *n* ① GEOG Golf *m;* **the G~ of Mexico** der Golf von Mexiko; **the G~ states** die Golfstaaten *pl;* ■**the Persian G~** der Persische Golf; **the G~ stream** der Golfstrom ② (*huge difference*) [tiefe] Kluft

gull [gʌl] *n* Möwe *f*

gullet ['gʌl·ɪt] *n* ANAT Speiseröhre *f*

gullible ['gʌl·ə·bəl] *adj* leichtgläubig

gully ['gʌl·i] *n* [enge] Schlucht *f;* (*channel*) Rinne *f*

gulp [gʌlp] **I.** *n* [großer] Schluck; **to get a** ~ **of air** Luft holen **II.** *vt* [hinunter]schlucken; *liquid* hinunterstürzen **III.** *vi* ① (*with emotion*) schlucken ② (*breathe*) **to** ~ **for air** nach Luft schnappen

gum¹ [gʌm] **I.** *n* ① (*sticky substance*) Gummi *nt;* (*on stamps etc.*) Gummierung *f;* (*glue*) Klebstoff *m* ② (*candy*) Kaugummi *m o nt* **II.** *vt* <-mm-> kleben; ■**to** ~ **down** zukleben

gum² [gʌm] *n* ANAT ■~**[s]** Zahnfleisch *nt kein pl*

gumbo ['gʌm·boʊ] *n* (*okra*) Okraschote *f*

gummy[1] ['gʌm·i] *adj* (*sticky*) klebrig

gummy[2] ['gʌm·i] *adj* (*without teeth*) zahnlos

gumption ['gʌmp·ʃən] *n* (*fam*) Grips *m*

gun [gʌn] **I.** *n* ① (*weapon*) [Schuss]waffe *f;* (*cannon*) Geschütz *nt;* (*pistol*) Pistole *f;* (*revolver*) Revolver *m;* (*rifle*) Gewehr *nt;* **big ~** Kanone *f;* (*fig*) hohes Tier ② SPORTS Startpistole *f;* **to jump the ~** einen Frühstart verursachen; (*fig*) voreilig handeln ③ MECH Pistole *f* ▶ PHRASES: **to <u>stick</u> to one's ~s** auf seinem Standpunkt beharren **II.** *vt* <-nn-> (*fam*) *engine* hochjagen

◆**gun down** *vt* niederschießen

'**gun barrel** *n of a rifle* Gewehrlauf *m; of a pistol* Pistolenlauf *m*

'**gunfight** *n* Schießerei *f*

'**gunfire** *n* Schießerei *f*

'**gun license** *n* Waffenschein *m*

'**gunman** *n* Bewaffnete(r) *m*

gunner ['gʌn·ər] *n* Artillerist *m*

'**gunpoint** *n* **at ~** mit vorgehaltener Waffe

'**gunpowder** *n* Schießpulver *nt*

'**gunrunner** *n* Waffenschmuggler(in) *m(f)*

'**gunrunning** *n* Waffenschmuggel *m*

'**gunshot** *n* (*shot*) Schuss *m;* **~ wound** Schusswunde *f*

gunslinger ['gʌn·ˌslɪŋ·ər] *n* (*hist*) Pistolenheld(in) *m(f)*

gurgle ['gɜr·gəl] **I.** *n* Glucksen *nt; of water* Gluckern *nt* **II.** *vi baby* glucksen; *water* gluckern

gush [gʌʃ] **I.** *n* Schwall *m;* (*fig*) Erguss *m* **II.** *vi* ① (*flow out*) [hervor]strömen; (*at high speed*) [hervor]schießen ② (*praise*) [übertrieben] schwärmen; ■**to ~ over sth** über etw *akk* ins Schwärmen geraten

gusher ['gʌʃ·ər] *n* [natürlich sprudelnde] Ölquelle

gushing ['gʌʃ·ɪŋ] *adj* schwärmerisch

gust [gʌst] **I.** *n* [Wind]stoß *m,* Bö[e] *f* **II.** *vi* böig wehen

gusto ['gʌs·toʊ] *n* ■**with ~** mit Begeisterung

gusty ['gʌs·ti] *adj* böig

gut [gʌt] **I.** *n* ① (*fam: abdomen*) Bauch *m;* **beer ~** Bierbauch *m* ② (*fam: courage*) ■**~s** *pl* Mumm *m kein pl* ③ (*intestine*) Darm[kanal] *m* ④ (*for instruments, rackets*) Darmsaite *f* ▶ PHRASES: **to <u>bust</u> a ~** sich abrackern **II.** *vt* <-tt-> ① *animal* ausnehmen ② (*destroy by fire*) ■**to be ~ed** [völlig] ausbrennen **III.** *adj* (*fam*) *feeling* instinktiv; *reaction* gefühlsmäßig, spontan

gutsy ['gʌt·si] *adj* mutig

gutter ['gʌt̬·ər] *n of road* Rinnstein *m;* (*of roof*) Dachrinne *f;* (*fig*) Gosse *f*

guttural ['gʌt̬·ər·əl] *adj* kehlig; LING guttural

guy [gaɪ] *n* ① (*fam: man*) Kerl *m,* Typ *m* ② *pl* (*fam: people*) **are you ~s coming to lunch?** kommt ihr [mit] zum Essen? ③ (*rope*) **~** [**rope**] Spannseil *nt;* (*for tent*) Zeltschnur *f*

guzzle ['gʌz·əl] *vt* (*fam: drink*) in sich *akk* hineinkippen

gym [dʒɪm] *n* ① *short for* **gymnasium** Turnhalle *f* ② *short for* **P.E.**

gymnasium <*pl* -s *or* -sia> [dʒɪm·'neɪ·zi·əm, *pl* -zi·ə] *n* Turnhalle *f*

gymnast ['dʒɪm·næst] *n* Turner(in) *m(f)*

gymnastic [dʒɪm·'næs·tɪk] *adj* turnerisch, Turn-

gymnastics [dʒɪm·'næs·tɪks] *npl* Turnen *nt kein pl;* **mental ~** (*fig*) Gehirnakrobatik *f*

'**gym shoes** *npl* Turnschuhe *pl*

gynecological [ˌgaɪ·nə·kə·'ladʒ·ɪ·kəl] *adj* gynäkologisch

gynecologist [ˌgaɪ·nə·'kal·ə·dʒɪst] *n* Gynäkologe, -in *m, f,* Frauenarzt, Frauenärztin *m, f*

gynecology [ˌgaɪ·nə·'kal·ə·dʒi] *n* Gynäkologie *f*

Gypsy ['dʒɪp·si] *n* Zigeuner(in) *m(f)*

gyrate ['dʒaɪ·reɪt] *vi* sich drehen; (*fig: dance*) [aufreizend] tanzen

gyration [ˌdʒaɪ·'reɪ·ʃən] *n* Drehung *f*

gyroscope ['dʒaɪ·rə·skoʊp] *n* NAUT, AVIAT Gyroskop *nt*

G

Hh

H <*pl* -'s *or* -s>, **h** <*pl* -'s> [eɪtʃ] *n* H *nt,* h *nt;* **~ as in Hotel** H wie Heinrich
habit ['hæb·ɪt] *n* ① (*repeated action*) Gewohnheit *f;* **a bad ~** eine schlechte [An]gewohnheit; **to get into/out of the ~ of [doing] sth** sich *dat* etw angewöhnen/abgewöhnen ② (*fam: drug addiction*) **to have a heroin ~** heroinsüchtig sein ③ (*nun's clothing*) Habit *m o nt*
habitable ['hæb·ɪ·t̬ə·bəl] *adj* bewohnbar
habitat ['hæb·ɪ·tæt] *n* Lebensraum *m*
habitation [ˌhæb·ɪ·'teɪ·ʃən] *n* [Be]wohnen *nt;* **unfit for human ~** menschenunwürdig
habitual [hə·'bɪtʃ·u·əl] *adj* ① (*constant*) ständig ② (*usual*) gewohnt

hack¹ [hæk] **I.** *vt* ① (*chop*) hacken; **to ~ sb/sth to pieces** jdn/etw zerstückeln ② COMPUT ■**to ~ sth** in etw *akk* eindringen ③ (*sl: cope with*) aushalten; **he can't ~ it** er bringt's einfach nicht **II.** *vi* ① (*chop*) ■**to ~ [away] at sth** auf etw *akk* einhacken ② COMPUT ■**to ~ into sth** in etw *akk* eindringen
hack² [hæk] *n* ① (*pej fam: writer*) Schreiberling *m* ② (*fam: taxi*) Taxi *nt;* (*taxi driver*) Taxifahrer(in) *m(f)*
hacker ['hæk·ər] *n* COMPUT Hacker(in) *m(f)*
hackles ['hæk·əlz] *npl* [aufstellbare] Nackenhaare ▶ PHRASES: **to raise sb's ~** jdn auf die Palme bringen *fam*
hackneyed ['hæk·nɪd] *adj* (*pej*) abgedroschen *fam*
'**hacksaw** *n* Bügelsäge *f*
had [hæd, *unstressed:* həd] **I.** *vt* ① *pt, pp of* **have** ② (*fam*) **to have ~ it** (*want to stop*) genug haben; (*to be broken*) kaputt sein **II.** *adj* (*fam*) ■**to be ~** [he]reingelegt werden
haddock <*pl* -> ['hæd·ək] *n* Schellfisch *m*
hadn't ['hæd·ənt] = **had not** *see* **have**
hag [hæg] *n* (*pej: witch*) Hexe *f;* (*old woman*) hässliches altes Weib
haggard ['hæg·ərd] *adj* ausgezehrt, verhärmt
haggle ['hæg·əl] *vi* ① (*bargain*) ■**to ~ [over sth]** [um etw *akk*] feilschen ② (*argue*) ■**to ~ over sth** [sich] über etw *akk* streiten
Hague [heɪg] *n* GEOG ■**The ~** Den Haag *kein art*
hail¹ [heɪl] **I.** *n* Hagel *m* **II.** *vi* hageln
hail² [heɪl] *vt* ① (*form: call*) zurufen; *taxi* rufen ② (*acclaim*) zujubeln; ■**to ~ sb/sth as sth** jdn/etw als etw bejubeln
'**hailstone** *n* Hagelkorn *nt*
hair [her] *n* ① (*single strand*) Haar *nt;* **to lose by a ~** (*fig*) ganz knapp verlieren ② (*on head*) Haar *nt,* Haare *pl;* (*on body*) Behaarung *f* ▶ PHRASES: **to <u>let</u> one's ~ down** sich gehen lassen
'**hairbrush** *n* Haarbürste *f*
'**hair care** *n* Haarpflege *f*
'**hair conditioner** *n* Pflegespülung *f*
'**haircut** *n* Haarschnitt *m,* Frisur *f;* **to get [*or* have] a ~** sich *dat* die Haare schneiden lassen
'**hairdo** *n* [kunstvolle] Frisur
'**hairdresser** *n* Friseur *m,* Friseuse *f*
'**hairdressing** *n* ① (*profession*) Friseurberuf *m* ② (*action*) Frisieren *nt*
'**hair drier,** '**hair dryer** *n* Föhn *m;* (*with hood*) Trockenhaube *f*
hairless ['her·lɪs] *adj* unbehaart; *person* glatzköpfig
'**hairline** *n* Haaransatz *m*
hairline '**crack** *n* Haarriss *m*
'**hairnet** *n* Haarnetz *nt*
'**hairpiece** *n* Haarteil *nt*
'**hairpin** *n* Haarnadel *f*
hairpin '**turn** *n* Haarnadelkurve *f*
'**hair-raising** *adj* (*fam*) haarsträubend
'**hair remover** *n* Enthaarungsmittel *nt*
'**hair restorer** *n* Haarwuchsmittel *nt*
'**hairsplitting** (*pej*) **I.** *n* Haarspalterei *f* **II.** *adj* haarspalterisch
'**hairspray** *n* Haarspray *nt*
'**hairstyle** *n* Frisur *f*
'**hairstylist** *n* Friseur *m,* Friseuse *f*
hairy ['her·i] *adj* ① (*having much hair*) haarig ② (*fig fam: dangerous*) haarig; *situation* brenzlig
hale [heɪl] *adj* **~ and hearty** gesund und munter
half [hæf] **I.** *n* <*pl* halves> ① (*fifty percent*) Hälfte *f;* **~ the amount** der halbe Betrag; **~ an apple** ein halber Apfel; **three and a ~ pounds** eineinhalb [*o* DIAL anderthalb] Kilo; **to cut sth in ~ [*or* into halves]** etw halbieren; **to fold in ~** zur Mitte falten ② SPORTS (*period*) Spielhälfte *f,* Halbzeit *f;* (*halfback*) Läufer(in) *m(f)* ▶ PHRASES: **given ~ a <u>chance</u>** wenn man die Möglichkeit hätte; **to <u>go</u> halves [on sth]** (*fam*) sich *dat* die Kosten [für etw *akk*] teilen **II.** *adj* halbe(r, s); **~ a percent** ein halbes Prozent **III.** *adv* ① (*almost*) fast ② (*partially*) halb; **it wasn't ~ as good** das war bei weitem nicht so gut; **~ asleep** halb wach ③ (*time*) **[at] ~ past nine** [um] halb zehn
'**halfback** *n* SPORTS Läufer(in) *m(f);* (*in rugby*) Halbspieler(in) *m(f)*
half-'**baked** *adj* (*fig fam*) unausgereift
'**half-breed** *n* (*offensive: person*) Mischling *m*
'**half brother** *n* Halbbruder *m*
'**half dozen, half a** '**dozen** *n* ein halbes Dutzend
half-'**empty** *adj* halb leer
half-'**full** *adj* halb voll
half-'**hearted** *adj* halbherzig
half-'**mast** *n* ■**at ~** auf halbmast
half '**moon** *n* Halbmond *m*
'**half note** *n* MUS halbe Note
half-'**price** *adj, adv* zum halben Preis
'**half rest** *n* MUS halbe Pause
'**half sister** *n* Halbschwester *f*

half-'timbered *adj* Fachwerk-
'halftime SPORTS **I.** *n* Halbzeit *f;* (*break*) Halbzeitpause *f* **II.** *adj* Halbzeit-
half'way I. *adj* halb; **at the ~ point of the race** nach der Hälfte des Rennens **II.** *adv* in der Mitte; **Philadelphia is ~ between Washington, D.C. and New York** Philadelphia liegt auf halber Strecke zwischen Washington, D.C. und New York; **~ through dinner** mitten beim Abendessen; **to meet sb ~** (*fig*) jdm [auf halbem Weg] entgegenkommen; **~ up** auf halber Höhe; **we went ~ up the mountain** wir bestiegen den Berg zur Hälfte
'half-wit *n* (*pej*) Dummkopf *m*
half-'yearly *adj, adv* halbjährlich
hall [hɔl] *n* ❶ (*room leading to other rooms*) Korridor *m,* Diele *f,* Flur *m* ❷ (*large building*) Halle *f;* (*public room*) Saal *m;* **assembly ~** Aula *f;* **city ~** Rathaus *nt* ❸ (*large country house*) Herrenhaus *nt*
hallmark ['hɔl·mark] *n* Kennzeichen *nt*
hallowed ['hæl·oʊd] *adj* [als heilig] verehrt; *ground* geweiht; *traditions* geheiligt
Halloween [ˌhæl·ə·'win] *n* Halloween *nt*

Halloween ist am 31. Oktober, dem Tag vor *All Saints' Day* oder *All Hallows* (Allerheiligen) und wird seit alters her mit Geistern und Hexen in Verbindung gebracht. In den USA verkleiden sich Kinder an diesem Abend und gehen mit einem Sack in der Hand von Tür zu Tür. Wenn die Bewohner ihre Haustür aufmachen, rufen sie *Trick or treat!*: Man soll ihnen einen *treat* (Süßigkeit) geben oder man bekommt einen *trick* (Streich) gespielt.

hallucinate [hə·'lu·sɪ·neɪt] *vi* halluzinieren
hallucination [hə·ˌlu·sɪ·'neɪ·ʃən] *n* Halluzination *f*
hallucinogenic [hə·ˌlu·sɪ·noʊ·'dʒen·ɪk] *adj* halluzinogen
'hallway *n* Korridor *m,* Diele *f,* Flur *m*
halo <*pl* -s *or* -es> ['heɪ·loʊ] *n* ❶ REL Heiligenschein *m* ❷ (*circle*) Ring *m;* **~ of light** Lichtkranz *m*
halogen 'bulb *n* Halogenglühbirne *f*
halt [hɔlt] **I.** *n* ❶ (*stoppage*) Stillstand *m;* **to grind to a ~** (*fig*) zum Erliegen kommen ❷ (*break*) Pause *f;* MIL Halt *m* **II.** *vt* zum Stillstand bringen; *fight* beenden **III.** *vi* ❶ (*stop*) zum Stillstand kommen ❷ (*break*) eine Pause machen; MIL Halt machen
halter ['hɔl·tər] *n* ❶ (*for animals*) Halfter *nt* ❷ FASHION *see* **halter-top**
'halter-top FASHION **I.** *n* rückenfreies Oberteil (*mit Nackenverschluss*) **II.** *adj* rückenfrei
halting ['hɔl·tɪŋ] *adj* zögernd; *speech* stockend
halve [hæv] **I.** *vt* ❶ (*cut in two*) halbieren ❷ (*lessen by 50 percent*) um die Hälfte reduzieren **II.** *vi* sich halbieren

ham [hæm] **I.** *n* ❶ FOOD Schinken *m* ❷ THEAT (*pej*) Schmierenkomödiant(in) *m(f)* ❸ (*fam*) **radio ~** Amateurfunker(in) *m(f)* **II.** *adj* ❶ (*made with ham*) Schinken- ❷ (*incompetently acting*) Schmieren-; **~ actor** Schmierenkomödiant(in) *m(f)* **III.** *vt* THEAT, FILM **to ~ it up** übertrieben agieren
hamburger ['hæm·bɜr·gər] *n* FOOD ❶ (*cooked*) Hamburger *m* ❷ (*raw*) Hackfleisch *nt*
ham-'fisted, ham-'handed *adj* (*pej*) ungeschickt
hamlet ['hæm·lət] *n* Weiler *m*
hammer ['hæm·ər] **I.** *n* ❶ (*tool*) Hammer *m* ❷ SPORTS [Wurf]hammer *m;* **[throwing] the ~** das Hammerwerfen **II.** *vt* ❶ (*hit*) *nail* einschlagen; *ball* [kräftig] schlagen; **to ~ sth into sb** (*fig*) jdm etw einhämmern ❷ (*fam: defeat*) **New England ~ed Pittsburgh 35-3** New England war Pittsburgh mit 35:3 haushoch überlegen ❸ (*criticize*) *film* niedermachen ▶ PHRASES: **to ~ sth <u>home</u>** etw *dat* Nachdruck verleihen **III.** *vi* hämmern *a. fig;* ■**to ~ at** [*or* **on**] **sth** gegen etw *akk* hämmern
◆**hammer in** *vt* ❶ (*hit*) *nail* einschlagen; (*fig*) *ball* hämmern ❷ (*fig*) ■**to ~ sth into sb** *fact* jdm etw einbläuen
◆**hammer out** *vt* ❶ *dent* ausbeulen ❷ *settlement* aushandeln; *difficulties* bereinigen; *plan, details* ausarbeiten
hammock ['hæm·ək] *n* Hängematte *f*
hamper[1] ['hæm·pər] *n* [Deckel]korb *m;* (*for food*) Präsentkorb *m;* (*for dirty laundry*) Wäschekorb *m*
hamper[2] ['hæm·pər] *vt* behindern
hamster ['hæm·stər] *n* Hamster *m*
hamstring ['hæm·strɪŋ] **I.** *n* ANAT Kniesehne *f* **II.** *vt* <-strung, -strung> *usu passive* (*fig*) **to be hamstrung** lahmgelegt sein
hand [hænd] **I.** *n* ❶ ANAT Hand *f;* **get your ~s off!** Hände weg!; **~s up!** Hände hoch!; **to be good with one's ~s** geschickte Hände haben; **to get one's ~s dirty** (*a. fig*) sich *dat* die Hände schmutzig machen; **by ~** (*manually*) von Hand; (*by messenger*) durch einen Boten; **on [one's] ~s and knees** auf allen vieren ❷ (*control*) **to be in good/safe ~s** in guten/sicheren Händen sein; **to fall into the wrong ~s** in die falschen Hände geraten; **to turn one's ~ to sth** sich an etw *akk* machen; ■**at ~** (*current, needing attention*) vorliegend; (*close*) in Reichweite; **to get out of ~** *situation* außer Kontrolle geraten; *children* nicht mehr zu bändigen sein ❸ (*assistance*) **to give** [*or* **lend**] **sb a ~** jdm helfen ❹ (*manual worker*) Arbeiter(in) *m(f);* (*sailor*) Matrose *m* ❺ (*on clock, watch*) Zeiger *m* ❻ (*applause*) **to give sb a big ~** jdm einen großen Applaus spenden ▶ PHRASES: **to live from ~ to <u>mouth</u>** von der Hand in den Mund leben; **to only have one <u>pair</u> of ~s** auch nur zwei Hände haben; **to keep a <u>firm</u> ~ on sth** etw fest im Griff behalten; **on the <u>one</u> ~ ... on the other [~] ...**

einerseits ... andererseits; **to get one's ~s on sb** jdn zu fassen kriegen; **to win ~s down** spielend gewinnen **II.** *vt* ■ **to ~ sb sth** jdm etw [über]geben ▶ PHRASES: **you've got to ~ it to sb** man muss es jdm lassen

◆**hand back** *vt* zurückgeben

◆**hand down** *vt* ① (*pass on*) weitergeben; *tradition* überliefern ② (*pronounce*) *decision, verdict* fällen

◆**hand in** *vt* einreichen; *homework* abgeben; *weapon* aushändigen

◆**hand on** *vt* ■ **to ~ sth** ↻ **on** [**to sb**] etw [an jdn] weitergeben; (*through family*) [jdm] etw vererben

◆**hand out** *vt* (*distribute*) *papers, test* austeilen (**to** an +*akk*); *homework, advice* geben (**to** +*dat*)

◆**hand over** *vt* ① (*pass*) herüberreichen; (*away from one*) hinüberreichen; (*present, transfer authority*) übergeben (**to** +*dat*); *check* überreichen ② TV, RADIO weitergeben (**to** an +*akk*)

'**handbag** *n* Handtasche *f*

'**handball** *n* ① (*team handball*) Handball *m* ② (*in soccer*) Handspiel *nt*

'**handbook** *n* Handbuch *nt*

'**hand brake** *n see* **emergency brake**

'**handcuff I.** *vt* ■ **to ~ sb** jdm Handschellen anlegen **II.** *n* ■ **~s** *pl* Handschellen *pl*

'**handful** *n* ① (*quantity*) Handvoll *f;* **a ~ of hair** ein Büschel *nt* Haare; (*small number*) **a ~ of people** wenige Leute ② (*person*) Nervensäge *f*

'**hand grenade** *n* Handgranate *f*

'**handgun** *n* Handfeuerwaffe *f*

hand-'held *adj attr* tragbar

handicap ['hæn·dɪ·kæp] **I.** *n* ① SPORTS Handicap *nt;* (*race*) Vorgaberennen *nt* ② (*disadvantage*) Handicap *nt* **II.** *vt* <-pp-> (*disadvantage*) benachteiligen

handicapped ['hæn·dɪ·kæpt] *adj* behindert

handicraft ['hæn·dɪ·kræft] **I.** *n* [Kunst]handwerk *nt kein pl* **II.** *adj* handwerklich

handiwork ['hæn·dɪ·wɜrk] *n* [Mach]werk *nt;* (*approv*) Meisterwerk *nt*

handkerchief ['hæŋ·kər·tʃɪf] *n* Taschentuch *nt*

handle ['hæn·dəl] **I.** *n* (*handgrip*) Griff *m; of a pot, basket* Henkel *m; of a door* Klinke *f; of a handbag* Bügel *m; of a broom, comb* Stiel *m; of a pump* Schwengel *m* ▶ PHRASES: **to fly off the ~** hochgehen **II.** *vt* ① (*grasp*) anfassen; **"~ with care"** „Vorsicht, zerbrechlich!" ② (*work on*) bearbeiten; *luggage* abfertigen; (*be in charge of*) zuständig sein für +*akk;* **to ~ sb's affairs** sich um jds Angelegenheiten kümmern ③ (*deal with*) umgehen mit +*dat,* behandeln **III.** *vi + adv* sich handhaben lassen; **this car ~s really well** dieser Wagen fährt sich wirklich gut

handlebar 'mustache *n* Schnauzbart *m*

'**handlebars** *npl* Lenkstange *f*

handler ['hænd·lər] *n* ① (*responsible person*) **baggage ~** Gepäckmann ② (*dog trainer*) Hundeführer(in) *m(f)*

handling ['hænd·lɪŋ] *n* ① (*act of touching*) Berühren *nt* ② (*treatment*) Handhabung *f* (**of** +*gen*); *of person* Behandlung *f* (**of** +*gen*), Umgang *m* (**of** mit +*dat*); *of a theme* [literarische] Abhandlung ③ (*processing of material*) Verarbeitung *f* (**of** +*gen*); (*treating of material*) Bearbeitung *f* (**of** mit +*dat*)

'**hand luggage** *n* Handgepäck *nt*

hand'made *adj* handgearbeitet; *paper* handgeschöpft

'**hand-me-down** *n* abgelegtes Kleidungsstück

'**handout** *n* ① (*money*) Almosen *nt* ② (*leaflet*) Flugblatt *nt; for students* Arbeitsblatt *nt*

'**handover** *n* Übergabe *f*

hand-'picked *adj* handverlesen *a. fig*

'**handrail** *n on stairs* Geländer *nt; on ship* Reling *f*

'**handsaw** *n* Handsäge *f*

'**handset** *n* TELEC Hörer *m*

'**handshake** *n* Händedruck *m*

handsome ['hæn·səm] *adj* ① (*attractive*) gut aussehend ② (*approv: larger than expected*) *number* beachtlich; **a ~ sum** eine stolze Summe

hands-'on *adj* ① (*non-delegating*) interventionistisch ② (*practical*) praktisch

'**handspring** *n* Handstandüberschlag *m*

'**handstand** *n* Handstand *m*

'**handwriting** *n* Handschrift *f*

'**handwritten** *adj* handgeschrieben

handy ['hæn·di] *adj* ① (*user-friendly*) praktisch, nützlich, geschickt SÜDD; (*easy to handle*) handlich ② (*convenient*) nützlich; *excuse* passend; **to come in ~** [**for sb/sth**] [jdm/etw] gelegen kommen ③ (*conveniently close*) *thing* griffbereit, greifbar; *spot* in der Nähe, leicht erreichbar; ■ **to be ~** *spot* günstig liegen ④ (*skillful*) geschickt; ■ **to be ~ with sth** mit etw *dat* gut umgehen können

'**handyman** *n* Heimwerker(in) *m(f)*

hang [hæŋ] **I.** *n* ① *of drapery* Fall *m; of clothes* Sitz *m* ② (*fig fam*) **to get the ~ of sth** bei etw *dat* den [richtigen] Dreh herausbekommen **II.** *vt* <hung, hung> ① (*mount*) aufhängen (**on** an +*dat*) ② (*decorate*) behängen ③ <-ed, -ed> (*execute*) [auf]hängen ④ (*let droop*) *head* hängen lassen; **to ~ one's head in shame** beschämt den Kopf senken **III.** *vi* ① <hung, hung> (*be suspended*) hängen (**from** an +*dat*); (*fall*) *clothes* fallen; ■ **to ~ down** herunterhängen ② <hanged, hanged> (*die by execution*) hängen ③ <hung, hung> (*remain in air*) *mist, smell* hängen ④ <hung, hung> (*listen carefully*) **to ~ on sb's** [**every**] **word** an jds Lippen hängen ⑤ <hung, hung> (*keep*) ■ **to ~ onto sth** etw behalten ▶ PHRASES: **to ~ in there** am Ball bleiben

◆**hang around** *vi* ① (*loiter*) herumlungern, rumhängen *fam* ② (*waste time*) herumtrödeln *fam*

◆**hang back** *vi* ① (*be slow*) sich zurückhalten; (*hesitate*) zögern ② (*stay behind*) zurück-

bleiben
◆**hang on** *vi* ① (*fam: persevere*) durchhalten ② (*grasp*) ■**to ~ on to sth** sich an etw *dat* festhalten; (*stronger*) sich an etw *akk* klammern ③ (*wait briefly*) warten; (*on the telephone*) dranbleiben; **~ on, ...** Moment mal, ...; **~ on!** (*annoyed*) Moment!
◆**hang out** I. *vt* heraushängen; *laundry* aufhängen II. *vi* ① (*project*) heraushängen ② (*sl: loiter*) [he]rumhängen; (*waste time*) herumtrödeln; (*live*) hausen; **where does he ~ out these days?** wo treibt er sich zurzeit herum? ▶ PHRASES: **to <u>let</u> it all ~ out** die Sau rauslassen *fam*
◆**hang together** *vi argument* schlüssig sein
◆**hang up** I. *vi* ① (*dangle*) hängen ② (*finish phone call*) auflegen II. *vt* ① (*suspend*) aufhängen ② *phone* auflegen

hangar ['hæŋ·ər] *n* AVIAT Hangar *m*

hangdog ['hæŋ·dɔg] *adj* **to have a ~ look on one's face** ein Gesicht wie vierzehn Tage Regenwetter machen

hanger ['hæŋ·ər] *n* [Kleider]bügel *m*

hanger-'on <*pl* **hangers-on**> *n* (*pej: follower*) Trabant(in) *m(f) pej*

'hang glider *n* (*person*) Drachenflieger(in) *m(f)*; (*device*) Drachen *m*

'hang-gliding *n* Drachenfliegen *nt*

hanging ['hæŋ·ɪŋ] I. *n* ① (*execution*) Hinrichtung *f* durch den Strang ② (*decorative fabric*) Behang *m*; (*curtain*) Vorhang *m* II. *adj* hängend

'hangman *n* ① (*executioner*) Henker *m* ② (*game*) Galgen *m*

'hangnail *n* ANAT Niednagel *m*

'hangout *n* (*fam*) Stammlokal *nt*, Treff *m*

'hangover *n* ① (*from drinking*) Kater *m* ② (*relic*) Überbleibsel *nt*

'hang-up *n* (*fam*) Komplex *m* (**about** wegen +*gen*)

hanker ['hæŋ·kər] *vi* sich sehnen (**after** nach +*dat*)

hankie, hanky ['hæŋ·ki] *n* (*fam*) *short for* **handkerchief** Taschentuch *nt*

hanky-panky [ˌhæŋ·ki·'pæŋ·ki] *n* (*fam*) ① (*groping*) Gefummel *nt kein pl* ② (*shifty business*) Mauschelei *f*

haphazard [hæp·'hæz·ərd] *adj* ① (*disorganized*) unüberlegt ② (*arbitrary*) willkürlich

happen ['hæp·ən] *vi* ① (*occur*) geschehen, passieren; *event* stattfinden; *process* vor sich gehen; **these things ~** das kann vorkommen; **it's all ~ing** (*fam*) es ist ganz schön was los ② (*by chance*) ■**to ~ to do sth** zufällig etw tun; **it just so ~s that ...** wie's der Zufall will, ...; **as it ~ed ...** wie es sich so traf, ...; **as it ~s** tatsächlich ③ (*indicating contradiction*) **I ~ to think he's right** ich glaube trotzdem, dass er Recht hat

happening ['hæp·ə·nɪŋ] *n usu pl* (*occurrence*) Ereignis *nt*; (*unplanned occurrence*) Vorfall *m*; (*process*) Vorgang *m*

happily ['hæp·ɪ·li] *adv* ① (*contentedly*) glücklich; (*cheerfully*) fröhlich; **and they all lived ~ ever after** und sie lebten glücklich und zufrieden bis an ihr Lebensende; (*fairytale ending*) und wenn sie nicht gestorben sind, dann leben sie noch heute ② (*willingly*) gern

happiness ['hæp·ɪ·nɪs] *n* Glück *nt*; (*contentment*) Zufriedenheit *f*; (*cheerfulness*) Fröhlichkeit *f*

happy ['hæp·i] *adj* ① (*pleased*) glücklich; (*contented*) zufrieden; (*cheerful*) fröhlich; ■**to be ~ about** [*or* **with**] **sb/sth** mit jdm/etw zufrieden sein; ■**to be ~ that ...** froh [darüber] sein, dass ... ② (*willing*) ■**to be ~ to do sth** etw gerne tun; **I'd be ~ to!** aber gern! ③ (*in greetings*) **~ birthday** alles Gute zum Geburtstag; **a ~ New Year** ein glückliches neues Jahr

happy-go-'lucky *adj* sorglos, unbekümmert

happy 'medium *n* goldene Mitte

harass [hə·'ræs] *vt* (*intimidate*) schikanieren; (*pester*) ständig belästigen

harassment [hə·'ræs·mənt] *n* (*intimidation*) Schikane *f*; (*pestering*) Belästigung *f*; **sexual ~** sexuelle Belästigung

harbor ['har·bər] I. *n* Hafen *m* II. *vt* ① (*keep in hiding*) ■**to ~ sb** jdm Unterschlupf gewähren ② *feelings, grudge* hegen

hard [hard] I. *adj* ① (*solid*) hart; [**as**] **~ as a rock** steinhart ② (*tough*) *person* zäh, hart ③ (*difficult*) schwierig; **she had a ~ time** [**of it**] es war eine schwere Zeit für sie; **to find sth ~ to believe** etw kaum glauben können ④ (*laborious*) anstrengend; **to be ~ work** harte Arbeit sein; *studies* anstrengend sein; *text* schwer zu lesen sein ⑤ (*harmful*) ■**to be ~ on sth** etw stark strapazieren; ■**to be ~ on sb** hart für jdn sein ⑥ *water, drug* hart; *frost, winter* streng; *voice* schroff ⑦ (*reliable*) sicher; **~ facts** (*verified*) gesicherte Fakten; (*blunt*) nackte Tatsachen ▶ PHRASES: **~ and <u>fast</u>** fest; *rule* verbindlich II. *adv* ① (*solid*) hart; **frozen ~** *soil* hart gefroren; **to set ~** *glue* hart werden; *concrete* fest werden ② (*vigorously*) fest[e], kräftig; *fight, work* hart; *rain* stark; **think ~!** denk mal genau nach!; **to try ~** sich sehr bemühen ③ (*severely*) schwer

'hardback *adj, n see* **hardcover**

'hardboard *n* Hartfaserplatte *f*

hard-'boiled *adj* ① *egg* hart gekocht ② (*fig*) hart gesotten

hard 'copy *n* COMPUT Ausdruck *m*

'hard-core, hardcore *adj* ① (*loyal*) *fan, supporter* eingefleischt ② (*explicit*) hart

'hardcover I. *adj* gebunden II. *n* gebundenes Buch

hard 'currency *n* harte Währung

'hard disk *n* COMPUT Festplatte *f*

'hard drive *n* COMPUT Festplatte *f*

hard-'earned *adj* ehrlich verdient; *pay* sauer verdient

harden ['har·dən] I. *vt* ① (*make harder*) härten; *arteries* verhärten ② (*make tougher*) *attitude* verhärten; ■**to ~ sb** [**to sth**] jdn [gegen etw *akk*] abhärten II. *vi* ① (*become hard*) sich

H

verfestigen, hart werden ❷ (*become tough*) sich verhärten; *face* sich versteinern

hard 'feelings *npl* **no ~?** alles klar?

hard-'fought *adj* ❶ *battle, match* hart ❷ *victory* hart erkämpft

'hard hat *n* ❶ (*helmet*) [Schutz]helm *m* ❷ (*fam: worker*) Bauarbeiter(in) *m(f)*

hard-'headed *adj* nüchtern

hard-'hearted *adj* hartherzig

hard-'hitting *adj* sehr kritisch

hard 'labor *n* Zwangsarbeit *f*

hard'liner *n* POL Hardliner *m*

hardly ['hard·li] *adv* ❶ (*scarcely*) kaum; **~ ever** so gut wie nie ❷ (*certainly not*) wohl kaum; (*as a reply*) bestimmt nicht

hardness ['hard·nɪs] *n* Härte *f*

hard-'nosed *adj* nüchtern; *person* abgebrüht

hard of'hearing *adj* schwerhörig

hard-'pressed *adj* bedrängt

hard 'sell *n* aggressive Verkaufsmethoden *pl*

hardship ['hard·ʃɪp] *n* Not *f*

'hardware *n* ❶ (*tools*) Eisenwaren *pl;* (*household items*) Haushaltswaren *pl* ❷ COMPUT Hardware *f*

'hardwood *n* Hartholz *nt*

hard-'working *adj* fleißig

hardy ['har·di] *adj* ❶ (*tough*) zäh; (*toughened*) abgehärtet ❷ BOT winterhart

hare <*pl* -s *or* -> [her] *n* [Feld]hase *m*

'harebrained *adj* verrückt

'harelip *n* MED Hasenscharte *f*

harem ['her·əm] *n* Harem *m*

harm [harm] **I.** *n* Schaden *m;* **there's no ~ in asking** Fragen kostet nichts; **to mean no ~** es nicht böse meinen; **to do more ~ than good** mehr schaden als nützen **II.** *vt* ■**to ~ sth** etw *dat* Schaden zufügen; ■**to ~ sb** jdm schaden; (*hurt*) jdn verletzen

harmful ['harm·fəl] *adj* schädlich; *words* verletzend

harmless ['harm·lɪs] *adj* harmlos

harmonic [har·'man·ɪk] *adj* harmonisch

harmonica [har·'man·ɪ·kə] *n* Mundharmonika *f*

harmonious [har·'moʊ·ni·əs] *adj* harmonisch *a. fig*

harmonization [ˌhar·mə·nɪ·'zeɪ·ʃən] *n* Harmonisierung *f a. fig*

harmonize ['har·mə·naɪz] **I.** *vt* ❶ MUS harmonisieren ❷ (*fig*) aufeinander abstimmen **II.** *vi* harmonieren *a. fig*

harmony ['har·mə·ni] *n* Harmonie *f a. fig;* **in ~** *live* in Eintracht [miteinander]; *sing* mehrstimmig; **in ~ with nature** im Einklang mit der Natur

harness ['har·nɪs] **I.** *n* <*pl* -es> (*for animal*) Geschirr *nt;* (*for person*) Gurtzeug *nt;* (*for baby*) Laufgeschirr *nt* **II.** *vt* ❶ *animal* anschirren; *person* anschnallen ❷ (*fig*) nutzen

harp [harp] *n* Harfe *f*

harpoon [har·'pun] **I.** *n* Harpune *f* **II.** *vt* harpunieren

harpsichord ['harp·sɪ·kɔrd] *n* Cembalo *nt*

harrowing ['her·oʊ·ɪŋ] *adj* grauenvoll

harsh [harʃ] *adj* ❶ rau; *winter* streng; *light* grell; *sound* schrill; *tone of voice* barsch ❷ (*severe*) hart; (*critical*) scharf; ■**to be ~ on sb** streng mit jdm sein

harvest ['har·vɪst] **I.** *n* Ernte *f; of grapes* Lese *f;* (*season*) Erntezeit *f* **II.** *vt* ernten; *shellfish* fangen

has [hæz, həz] *3rd pers sing of* **have**

has-been ['hæz·bɪn] *n* (*pej fam*) ehemalige Größe

hash¹ [hæʃ] *n* ❶ FOOD Haschee *nt* ❷ (*fam: shambles*) **to make a ~ of sth** etw vermasseln

hash² [hæʃ] *n* (*fam*) *see* **hashish**

hash 'browns *npl* Kartoffelpuffer *pl,* ≈ Rösti *pl* SÜDD, SCHWEIZ

hashish ['hæʃ·iʃ], **hasheesh** *n* Hasch *nt*

hasn't ['hæz·ənt] = **has not** *see* **have**

hassle ['hæs·əl] **I.** *n* (*fam*) Mühe *f kein pl;* **it's just too much [of a] ~** es ist einfach zu umständlich **II.** *vt* (*fam: pester*) schikanieren; (*harass*) bedrängen

haste [heɪst] *n* Eile *f;* (*rush*) Hast *f;* **to make ~** sich beeilen ▶PHRASES: **~ makes <u>waste</u>** (*prov*) eile mit Weile

hasten ['heɪ·sən] **I.** *vt person* drängen; *thing* beschleunigen **II.** *vi* sich beeilen

hasty ['heɪ·sti] *adj* ❶ (*hurried*) eilig, hastig *pej;* **to beat a ~ retreat** (*fam*) sich schnell aus dem Staub machen ❷ (*rash*) übereilt; (*badly thought out*) voreilig

hat [hæt] *n* Hut *m;* (*of fur, wool*) Mütze *f* ▶PHRASES: **to <u>pick</u> sb out of a ~** jdn zufällig auswählen

hatch¹ <*pl* -es> [hætʃ] *n* ❶ (*opening*) Durchreiche *f* ❷ NAUT Luke *f*

hatch² [hætʃ] **I.** *vi* schlüpfen **II.** *vt* ausbrüten *a. fig*

hatchback ['hætʃ·bæk] *n* ❶ (*door*) Heckklappe *f* ❷ (*vehicle*) Wagen *m* mit Heckklappe

hatchet ['hætʃ·ɪt] *n* Beil *nt* ▶PHRASES: **to <u>bury</u> the ~** das Kriegsbeil begraben

hate [heɪt] **I.** *n* Hass *m;* **to give sb a look of ~** jdn hasserfüllt ansehen **II.** *vt* hassen; **I ~ going to the dentist** ich hasse es, zum Zahnarzt zu gehen; **I ~ to say it, but ...** es fällt mir äußerst schwer, das sagen zu müssen, aber ...; **to ~ sb's guts** (*fig*) jdn wie die Pest hassen

'hate crime *n* LAW *Verbrechen, das aus [Rassen]hass oder Vorurteilen begangen wird*

hatred ['heɪ·trɪd] *n* Hass *m* (**of/for** auf +*akk*)

hatter ['hæt̬·ər] *n* ▶PHRASES: **to be as <u>mad</u> as a ~** total verrückt sein

'hat trick *n* Hattrick *m*

haughty ['hɔ·t̬i] *adj* (*pej*) überheblich

haul [hɔl] **I.** *n* ❶ (*quantity caught*) Ausbeute *f* (**of** von, an +*dat*); (*fig*) Beute *f* ❷ (*distance covered*) Strecke *f;* **over [*or* in] the long/short ~** lang-/kurzfristig **II.** *vt* ❶ (*pull*) ziehen; *sth heavy* schleppen ❷ (*transport*) befördern ◆**haul off** *vt* wegziehen; (*more brutally*) wegzerren; **to ~ sb off to jail** (*fig*) jdn ins Gefängnis werfen

hauler ['hɔ·lər] *n* **freight ~** Transportunternehmen *nt,* Spedition[sfirma] *f*

haunt [hɔnt] **I.** *vt* ① *ghost* spuken in *+dat* ② *memories* heimsuchen **II.** *n* (*place*) Treffpunkt *m;* (*bar*) Stammlokal *nt*

haunted ['hɔn·ṭɪd] *adj* ① (*with ghosts*) **~ house** Gespensterhaus *nt;* **this house is ~!** in diesem Haus spukt es! ② (*troubled*) *look* gehetzt

haunting ['hɔn·ṭɪŋ] *adj* ① (*disturbing*) quälend ② (*stirring*) sehnsuchtsvoll

have [hæv, həv] **I.** *aux vb* <has, had, had> ① (*forming past tenses*) **he has never been to San Francisco before** er war noch nie zuvor in San Francisco; **we had been swimming** wir waren schwimmen gewesen ② (*render*) ■**to ~ sth done** etw tun lassen; **to ~ one's hair cut** sich *dat* die Haare schneiden lassen ③ (*must*) ■**to ~ to do sth** etw tun müssen; **what time do we ~ to be there?** wann müssen wir dort sein? ④ (*form: if*) **had I/he etc. done sth, ...** hätte ich/er etc. etw getan, ..., wenn ich/er etc. etw getan hätte, ...; **if only I'd known this** wenn ich das nur gewusst hätte **II.** *vt* <has, had, had> ① (*possess*) ■**to ~ sth** etw haben; **he has green eyes** er hat grüne Augen; **I don't ~ a car** ich habe kein Auto; **~ a nice day!** viel Spaß!; (*to customers*) einen schönen Tag noch!; **to ~ the light/radio on** das Licht/Radio anhaben ② (*engage in*) *bath* nehmen; *nap, party, walk* machen; **to ~ a talk with sb** mit jdm sprechen ③ (*consume*) *food* essen; *cigarette* rauchen; **to ~ lunch** zu Mittag essen; **~ some more coffee** nimm doch noch etwas Kaffee ④ (*receive*) erhalten; **thanks for having us** danke für Ihre Gastfreundschaft; **to let sb ~ sth back** jdm etw zurückgeben ⑤ (*be obliged*) ■**to ~ sth to do** etw tun müssen ⑥ (*give birth to*) **to ~ a baby** ein Baby bekommen ⑦ (*induce*) ■**to ~ sb do sth** jdn [dazu] veranlassen, etw zu tun; ■**to ~ sb/sth doing sth** jdn/etw dazu bringen, etw zu tun; **he'll ~ it working in no time** er wird es im Handumdrehen zum Laufen bringen ►PHRASES: **to ~ had <u>it</u>** (*be broken*) hinüber sein; (*be exhausted*) fix und fertig sein; **to ~ had <u>it</u> with sb/sth** von jdm/etw die Nase voll haben; **and <u>what</u> ~ you** und wer weiß was noch; **to ~ something <u>against</u> sb/sth** etwas gegen jdn/etw [einzuwenden] haben **III.** *n* (*fam*) ■**the ~s** *pl* **the ~s and the ~-nots** die Besitzenden und die Besitzlosen

◆**have around** *vt* zur Hand haben

◆**have back** *vt* (*object*) zurückhaben; (*person*) wieder nehmen

◆**have in** *vt* (*call to do*) ■**to ~ sb in** [**to do sth**] jdn kommen lassen[, um etw zu tun] ►PHRASES: **to ~ it <u>in</u> for sb** jdn auf dem Kieker haben

◆**have on** *vt* ① (*wear*) *clothes* tragen ② (*carry*) ■**to ~ sth on one** etw bei sich *dat* haben, etw mit sich *dat* führen ③ (*know about*) ■**to ~ sth on sb/sth** *evidence, facts* etw über jdn/etw [in der Hand] haben

◆**have out** *vt* ① (*remove*) sich *dat* herausnehmen lassen; **he had his wisdom teeth out yesterday** ihm sind gestern die Weisheitszähne gezogen worden ② (*fam: argue*) ■**to ~ it out** [**with sb**] es [mit jdm] ausdiskutieren

◆**have over** *vt* ■**to ~ sb over** jdn zu sich *dat* einladen

haven ['heɪ·vən] *n* Zufluchtsort *m*

haven't ['hæv·ənt] = **have not** *see* **have**

havoc ['hæv·ək] *n* Verwüstungen *pl;* **to play ~ with sth** (*fig*) etw völlig durcheinanderbringen

Hawaii [hə·'waɪ·i] *n* Hawaii *nt*

hawk [hɔk] **I.** *n* ① (*bird*) Habicht *m;* (*fig*) **to watch sb like a ~** jdn nicht aus den Augen lassen ② POL Falke *m* **II.** *vt* ■**to ~ sth** etw auf der Straße verkaufen; (*door to door*) mit etw *dat* hausieren gehen

hawker ['hɔ·kər] *n* Hausierer(in) *m(f);* (*in the street*) fliegender Händler

'hawk-eyed *adj* ■**to be ~** Adleraugen haben

hawthorn ['hɔ·θɔrn] *n* Weißdorn *m*

hay [heɪ] *n* Heu *nt* ►PHRASES: **to make ~ while the <u>sun</u> shines** (*prov*) das Eisen schmieden, solange es heiß ist

'hay fever *n* Heuschnupfen *m*

'haystack *n* Heuhaufen *m*

'haywire *adj* (*fam*) **to go ~** verrücktspielen

hazard ['hæz·ərd] *n* Gefahr *f;* **fire ~** Brandrisiko *nt*

'hazard lights *npl* AUTO Warnblinkanlage *f*

hazardous ['hæz·ər·dəs] *adj* (*dangerous*) gefährlich; (*risky*) riskant

haze [heɪz] **I.** *n* ① (*mist*) Dunst[schleier] *m* ② (*fig*) Benommenheit *f* **II.** *vt* schikanieren

hazel ['heɪ·zəl] **I.** *adj* haselnussbraun **II.** *n* Hasel[nuss]strauch *m*

'hazelnut *n* Haselnuss *f*

hazy ['heɪ·zi] *adj* ① (*with haze*) dunstig, diesig ② (*confused, unclear*) unklar; (*indistinct*) verschwommen

he [hi] **I.** *pron pers* (*male person*) er; (*unspecified person*) er/sie/es **II.** *n* Er *m*

head [hed] **I.** *n* ① Kopf *m;* **she's got a good ~ for figures** sie kann gut mit Zahlen umgehen; **to use one's ~** seinen Verstand benutzen ② (*unit*) **a** [*or* **per**] **~** pro Kopf; **to win by a ~** mit einer Kopflänge Vorsprung gewinnen ③ (*top, front part*) *of bed, table* Kopfende *nt; of nail, coin, match* Kopf *m; of line* Anfang *m* ④ (*leader*) Chef(in) *m(f); of a project, department* Leiter(in) *m(f); of church, family, state* Oberhaupt *nt* ⑤ (*beer foam*) Blume *f* ⑥ (*accumulated amount*) **~ of steam** Dampfdruck *m* ►PHRASES: **to have one's ~ in the <u>clouds</u>** in höheren Regionen schweben; **to be ~ over <u>heels</u> in love** bis über beide Ohren verliebt sein; **to not be able to make ~s or <u>tails</u> of sth** aus etw *dat* nicht schlau werden; **to <u>bite</u> sb's ~ off** jdm den Kopf abreißen; **to <u>come</u> to a ~** sich zuspitzen; **to <u>go</u> to sb's ~**

jdm zu Kopf steigen; **to have one's ~ screwed on right** ein patenter Mensch sein **II.** *adj* leitend **III.** *vt* ❶ (*be at the front of*) anführen ❷ (*be in charge of*) *organization* leiten ❸ (*in soccer*) *ball* köpfen **IV.** *vi* **he ~ed straight for the fridge** er steuerte direkt auf den Kühlschrank zu; **to ~ [for] home** sich auf den Heimweg machen

◆**head back** *vi* zurückgehen; *with transport* zurückfahren

◆**head off I.** *vt* (*intercept*) abfangen **II.** *vi* ■ **to ~ off to[ward] sth** sich zu etw *dat* begeben

◆**head out** *vi* losziehen

◆**head up** *vt* leiten

'headache *n* Kopfschmerzen *pl;* (*fig*) Problem *nt*

'headband *n* Stirnband *nt*

head 'chef *n* Küchenchef(in) *m(f)*

'head cold *n* Kopfgrippe *f*

'headdress <*pl* -es> *n* Kopfschmuck *m*

header ['hed·ər] *n* ❶ (*at top of page*) Kopfzeile *f* ❷ (*in email*) Header *m* ❸ (*in soccer*) Kopfball *m*

head'first *adv* kopfüber; (*fig*) **to rush ~ into [doing] sth** sich Hals über Kopf in etw *akk* [hinein]stürzen

'headhunt *vt* (*fam*) abwerben

'headhunter *n* Headhunter(in) *m(f)*

heading ['hed·ɪŋ] *n* ❶ (*title*) Überschrift *f* ❷ (*division*) Kapitel *nt;* (*keyword*) Stichwort *nt*

'headlamp *n* Scheinwerfer *m*

headless ['hed·lɪs] *adj* kopflos ▶ PHRASES: **to run around like a ~ chicken** wie ein aufgeregtes Huhn hin und her laufen

'headlight *n* Scheinwerfer *m*

'headline I. *n* Schlagzeile *f* **II.** *vt* ❶ (*provide with headline*) mit einer Schlagzeile versehen ❷ (*star*) anführen

'headliner *n* Hauptattraktion *f;* **the ~ is ...** der Star des Abends ist ...

'headlong I. *adv* ❶ (*headfirst*) kopfüber ❷ (*recklessly*) überstürzt **II.** *adj* überstürzt

'headmaster *n* Schulleiter *m,* Rektor *m*

'headmistress *n* Schulleiterin *f,* Rektorin *f*

head 'office *n* Zentrale *f*

head-'on I. *adj* Frontal- **II.** *adv* frontal; (*fig*) direkt

'headphones *npl* Kopfhörer *m*

'headquarters *npl + sing/pl vb* MIL Hauptquartier *nt;* (*of company*) Hauptsitz *m;* (*of the police*) Polizeidirektion *f*

'headrest *n* Kopfstütze *f*

'headroom *n* lichte Höhe; *for ceiling* Kopfhöhe *f;* (*in cars*) Kopffreiheit *f*

'headscarf *n* Kopftuch *nt*

'headset *n* Kopfhörer *m*

head 'start *n* Vorsprung *m;* **to give sb a ~** jdm einen Vorsprung lassen

'headstone *n* Grabstein *m*

'headstrong *adj* eigensinnig

head-to-'head I. *adj contest* Kopf-an-Kopf- **II.** *adv* **to go ~** gegeneinander antreten

'headwaters *n pl* Quellgewässer *pl*

'headway *n* **to make ~** [gut] vorankommen (**in** bei *+dat,* **with** mit *+dat*)

'headwind *n* Gegenwind *m*

'headword *n* LING Stichwort *nt*

heady ['hed·i] *adj* berauschend

heal [hil] **I.** *vt* heilen; *differences* beilegen **II.** *vi* heilen *a. fig*

healing ['hi·lɪŋ] **I.** *adj attr experience, process* heilsam; **~ properties** Heilwirkung *f;* (*stronger*) Heilkräfte *pl* **II.** *n* Heilung *f;* (*of wounds*) Verheilen *nt*

health [helθ] *n* Gesundheit *f;* **to your ~!** Pros[i]t!

'health care *n* Gesundheitsfürsorge *f*

'health center *n* Ärztehaus *nt*

'health club *n* Fitnessclub *m*

'health farm *n* Gesundheitsfarm *f*

'health food *n* Reformkost *f*

'health food store *n* Naturkostladen *m,* Bioladen *m;* (*more formal*) Reformhaus *nt*

'health hazard *n* Gesundheitsrisiko *nt;* **smoking is a ~** Rauchen gefährdet die Gesundheit

'health insurance *n* Krankenversicherung *f;* **~ company** Krankenkasse *f*

'health service(s) *n* Gesundheitsdienst

healthy ['hel·θi] *adj* gesund *a. fig; profit* ordentlich; (*promoting good health*) gesundheitsfördernd

heap [hip] **I.** *n* ❶ (*pile*) Haufen *m a. fig;* **to collapse in a ~** zu Boden sacken ❷ (*fam: large amount*) ■ **~s** jede Menge (**of** *+gen*) **II.** *vt* aufhäufen; (*fig*) **to ~ criticism on sb** massive Kritik an jdm üben; **to ~ praise on sb** jdn überschwänglich loben

hear <heard, heard> [hɪr] **I.** *vt* ❶ (*perceive*) hören; **Jane ~d him go out** Jane hörte, wie er hinausging ❷ LAW *case* verhandeln ▶ PHRASES: **to be ~ing things** sich *dat* etwas einbilden; **I must be ~ing things!** ich hör' wohl nicht richtig! **II.** *vi* hören (**about/of** von *+dat*); **have you ~d about Jane getting married?** hast du schon gehört, dass Jane heiratet? ▶ PHRASES: **~ ~!** ja, genau!

heard [hɜrd] *pt, pp of* **hear**

hearing ['hɪr·ɪŋ] *n* ❶ (*ability to hear*) Gehör *nt;* **to be hard of ~** schwerhörig sein ❷ (*range of ability*) **within [sb's] ~** in [jds] Hörweite *f* ❸ (*official examination*) Anhörung *f*

'hearing aid *n* Hörgerät *nt*

'hearing-impaired *adj* schwerhörig

hearsay ['hɪr·seɪ] *n* Gerüchte *pl*

hearse [hɜrs] *n* Leichenwagen *m*

heart [hart] *n* ❶ ANAT Herz *nt* ❷ (*fig*) Herz *nt;* **my ~ goes out to her** ich fühle mit ihr; **from the bottom of one's ~** aus tiefstem Herzen; **to one's ~'s content** nach Herzenslust; **the ~ of the matter** der Kern der Sache; **to not have the ~ to do sth** es nicht übers Herz bringen, etw zu tun; **to put one's ~ in[to] sth** sich voll für etw *akk* einsetzen; **to have one's ~ set on sth** sein [ganzes] Herz an etw *akk* hängen ❸ (*courage*) Mut *m;* **to lose ~** den Mut

verlieren ④ CARDS ■ ~s *pl* Herz *nt kein pl;* **queen of ~s** Herzdame *f* ▶ PHRASES: **at** ~ im Grunde seines/ihres Herzens; **by** ~ auswendig; **to have a change of** ~ sich anders besinnen; **in my** ~ **of ~s** im Grunde meines Herzens
'heartache *n* Kummer *m*
'heart attack *n* Herzinfarkt *m;* (*not fatal*) Herzanfall *m;* (*fatal*) Herzschlag *m a. fig*
'heartbeat *n* Herzschlag *m*
'heartbreak *n* großer Kummer
'heartbreaking *adj* herzzerreißend
'heartbroken *adj* todunglücklich, untröstlich
'heartburn *n* Sodbrennen *nt*
'heart disease *n* Herzkrankheit *f*
heartening ['har·tə·nɪŋ] *adj* ermutigend
'heart failure *n* Herzversagen *nt*
'heartfelt *adj* (*strongly felt*) tief empfunden; (*sincere*) aufrichtig
hearth [harθ] *n* Kamin *m*
heartily ['har·ṱɪ·li] *adv* ① (*enthusiastically*) herzlich; *applaud* begeistert; *eat* herzhaft ② (*extremely*) von [ganzem] Herzen
'heartland *n of region* Kerngebiet *nt,* Herz *nt*
heartless ['hart·lɪs] *adj* herzlos
'heart murmur *n* Herzgeräusch[e] *nt*[*pl*]
'heart-rending *adj* herzzerreißend
'heartstrings *npl* **to tug at sb's** ~ jdm ans Herz gehen
'heartthrob *n* (*fam*) Schwarm *m*
heart-to-'heart I. *adj* [ganz] offen **II.** *n* **to have a** ~ sich aussprechen
'heart transplant *n* Herztransplantation *f*
'heartwarming *adj* herzerfreuend
hearty ['har·ṱi] *adj* ① (*warm*) herzlich ② (*large*) *breakfast* herzhaft, kräftig; *appetite* gesund ③ (*unreserved*) uneingeschränkt
heat [hit] **I.** *n* ① (*warmth*) Wärme *f;* (*high temperature*) Hitze *f;* **to cook sth on low** ~ etw bei schwacher Hitze kochen ② PHYS [Körper]wärme *f* ③ SPORTS Vorlauf *m* ④ ZOOL Brunst *f; of dogs, cats* Läufigkeit *f; of horses* Rossen *nt;* ■ **in** ~ brünstig; *deer* brunftig; *cat* rollig; *dog* läufig; *horse* rossig ▶ PHRASES: **if you can't stand the ~, get out of the kitchen** (*prov*) wenn es dir zu viel wird, dann lass es lieber sein **II.** *vt* erhitzen, heiß machen; *food* aufwärmen; *house, room* heizen; *pool* beheizen **III.** *vi* warm werden
◆ **heat up I.** *vt* heiß machen; *food* aufwärmen; *house, room* [auf]heizen **II.** *vi room* warm werden; *engine* warm laufen; (*fig*) *discussion* sich erhitzen; *pace* sich steigern; *situation* sich verschärfen
heated ['hi·ṱɪd] *adj* ① (*emotional*) hitzig; *discussion* heftig ② (*warm*) erhitzt; *room* geheizt; *pool, seats* beheizt
heatedly ['hi·ṱɪd·li] *adv* hitzig; *discuss* heftig
heater ['hi·ṱər] *n* [Heiz]ofen *m,* Heizgerät *nt;* (*in car*) Heizung *f;* **water** ~ Boiler *m*
heath [hiθ] *n* Heide *f*
heathen ['hi·ðən] **I.** *n* Heide *m,* Heidin *f* **II.** *adj* heidnisch
heather ['heð·ər] *n* Heidekraut *nt*
heating ['hi·ṱɪŋ] *n* ① (*action*) Heizen *nt; of room, house* [Be]heizen *nt; of substances* Erwärmen *nt;* PHYS Erwärmung *f* ② (*appliance*) Heizung *f;* ~ **engineer** Heizungsmonteur(in) *m(f)*
'heat pump *n* Wärmepumpe *f*
'heat rash *n* Hitzeausschlag *m*
'heat-resistant *adj* hitzebeständig; *ovenware* feuerfest
'heat-seeking *adj* MIL wärmesuchend
'heat shield *n* Hitzeschild *m*
'heat stroke *n* Hitzschlag *m*
'heat treatment *n* Wärmebehandlung *f*
'heatwave *n* Hitzewelle *f*
heave [hiv] **I.** *n* Ruck *m* **II.** *vt* ① (*move*) [hoch]hieven ② (*utter*) *sigh of relief* ausstoßen **III.** *vi* ① (*pull*) hieven ② (*move*) sich heben und senken; *chest, sea* wogen; *ship* schwanken
heaven ['hev·ən] *n* Himmel *m a. fig;* **it's ~!** (*fam*) es ist himmlisch!; **to go to** ~ in den Himmel kommen ▶ PHRASES: **what/why in ~'s name ...?** was/warum in Gottes Namen ...?; **for ~'s sake!** um Himmels willen!; **good ~s!** du lieber Himmel!; ~ **forbid!** Gott bewahre!
heavenly ['hev·ən·li] *adj* himmlisch
heavily ['hev·ɪ·li] *adv* ① (*to great degree*) stark; *gamble* leidenschaftlich; *invest* groß; *sleep* tief; ~ **armed** schwer bewaffnet ② (*with weight*) schwer; *move* schwerfällig; ~ **built** kräftig gebaut ③ (*severely*) schwer; **to snow** ~ stark schneien
heavy ['hev·i] **I.** *adj* ① (*weighty*) schwer *a. fig; fine* hoch ② (*excessive*) *frost, rain, drinker, smoker etc.* stark; **to be under ~ fire** MIL unter schwerem Beschuss stehen ③ (*fig: oppressive*) drückend; *weather* schwül ④ (*difficult*) schwierig; *breathing* schwer; ■ **to be ~ going** schwierig sein ⑤ (*dense*) *beard* dicht; *clouds* schwer; *coat* dick; *schedule* voll; *traffic* stark **II.** *n* ① (*sl: thug*) Schläger[typ] *m* ② THEAT Schurke *m,* Schurkin *f*
heavy-'duty *adj* ① robust; *clothes* strapazierfähig ② (*fam: intense*) intensiv, heftig
heavy-'handed *adj* ungeschickt
heavy-'hearted *adj* bedrückt
heavy 'industry *n* Schwerindustrie *f*
heavy 'metal *n* ① (*metal*) Schwermetall *nt* ② (*music*) Heavymetal *m*
'heavyweight I. *n* Schwergewicht *nt a. fig* **II.** *adj* ① SPORTS im Schwergewicht *nach n* ② (*weighty*) schwer ③ (*fig: important*) *person* prominent
Hebrew ['hi·bru] **I.** *n* ① (*person*) Hebräer(in) *m(f)* ② (*language*) Hebräisch *nt* **II.** *adj* hebräisch
heck [hek] *interj* (*euph sl*) **where the ~ have you been?** wo, zum Teufel, bist du gewesen?; **it's a ~ of a walk from here** es ist ein verdammt langer Weg von hier aus
heckle ['hek·əl] **I.** *vi* dazwischenrufen **II.** *vt speaker* durch Zwischenrufe stören

H

heckler ['hek·lər] *n* Zwischenrufer(in) *m(f)*
hectare ['hek·ter] *n* Hektar *m o nt*
hectic ['hek·tɪk] *adj* hektisch
he'd [hid] = **he had/he would** *see* **have I, II, would**
hedge [hedʒ] **I.** *n* ❶ BOT Hecke *f* ❷ (*fig*) Schutzwall *m;* FIN Absicherung *f* **II.** *vt* ▶ PHRASES: **to ~ one's bets** nicht alles auf eine Karte setzen **III.** *vi* ❶ (*avoid*) ausweichen ❷ FIN sich absichern
'hedgehog *n* Igel *m*
heebie-jeebies ['hi·bɪ·'dʒi·bɪz] *npl* (*sl*) **to get the ~** Zustände kriegen
heed [hid] (*form*) **I.** *vt* beachten **II.** *n* Beachtung *f;* **to pay ~ to** [*or* **take ~ of**] **sth** auf etw *akk* achten
heedless ['hid·lɪs] *adj* (*form*) achtlos; ■**to be ~ of sth** etw nicht beachten
heel [hil] **I.** *n* ❶ ANAT Ferse *f;* **~ of the hand** Handballen *m* ❷ *of shoe* Absatz *m; of sock* Ferse *f* ▶ PHRASES: **to dig one's ~s in** sich auf die Hinterbeine stellen **II.** *interj* ■**~!** bei Fuß! **III.** *vt a shoe* einen neuen Absatz machen ▶ PHRASES: **well ~ed** gut betucht
hefty ['hef·ti] *adj* ❶ (*strong*) kräftig; (*heavy*) schwer ❷ (*large*) mächtig; *workload* hoch ❸ (*considerable*) *price, fine* hoch, saftig *fam*
heifer ['hef·ər] *n* Färse *f*
height [haɪt] *n* ❶ (*top to bottom*) Höhe *f; of a person* [Körper]größe *f;* **to be 20 feet in ~** 20 Fuß hoch sein ❷ (*high places*) ■**~s** *pl* Höhen *pl;* **fear of ~s** Höhenangst *f* ❸ (*fig*) Höhepunkt *m;* **at the ~ of one's power** auf dem Gipfel seiner Macht
heighten ['haɪ·tən] *vt* verstärken; *awareness, tension* steigern
heir [er] *n* Erbe *m,* Erbin *f;* **~ to the throne** Thronfolger(in) *m(f)*
heiress <*pl* -es> ['er·ɪs] *n* Erbin *f*
heirloom ['er·lum] *n* Erbstück *nt*
heist [haɪst] *n* Raub[überfall] *m*
held [held] *vt, vi pt, pp of* **hold**
helicopter ['hel·ɪ·kap·tər] *n* Hubschrauber *m*
helipad ['hel·ɪ·pæd] *n* Hubschrauberlandeplatz *m*
'heliport *n* Heliport *m,* Hubschrauberlandeplatz *m*
helium ['hi·li·əm] *n* Helium *nt*
hell [hel] **I.** *n* ❶ (*not heaven*) Hölle *f;* **to go to ~** in die Hölle kommen ❷ (*fig fam*) **to ~ with it!** ich hab's satt!; **to not have a chance** [*or* **hope**] **in ~** nicht die leiseste Hoffnung haben; **to scare the ~ out of sb** jdn zu Tode erschrecken ❸ (*fam: for emphasis*) **he's one ~ of a guy!** er ist echt total in Ordnung!; **they had a ~ of a time** (*negative*) es war die Hölle für sie; (*positive*) sie hatten einen Heidenspaß; **a ~ of a lot** verdammt viel; [**as**] **cold as ~** saukalt ▶ PHRASES: **come ~ or high water** komme, was wolle; **to give sb ~** (*scold*) jdm die Hölle heißmachen; (*make life unbearable*) jdm das Leben zur Hölle machen; **go to ~!** scher dich zum Teufel! **II.** *interj* **what the ~ are you doing?** was zum Teufel machst du da?; **get the ~ out of here, will you?** mach, dass du rauskommst! ▶ PHRASES: **like ~!** nie im Leben!; **what the ~!?** was soll's!, was zum Teufel! *sl*
he'll [hil] = **he will/he shall** *see* **will, shall**
'hell-bent *adj* fest entschlossen
'hellfire *n* Höllenfeuer *nt*
hellish ['hel·ɪʃ] *adj* höllisch *a. fig; cold, heat* mörderisch; *day* grässlich; *experience* schrecklich
hellishly ['hel·ɪʃ·li] *adv* (*fam*) ❶ (*dreadfully*) höllisch ❷ (*extremely*) verdammt
hello [hə·'loʊ] **I.** *n* Hallo *nt;* **to say ~ to sb** jdn [be]grüßen **II.** *interj* hallo!
helm [helm] *n* Ruder *nt a. fig*
helmet ['hel·mɪt] *n* Helm *m*
helmsman ['helmz·mən] *n* Steuermann, -frau *m, f*
help [help] **I.** *n* Hilfe *f;* (*financial*) Unterstützung *f;* **a lot of ~ you are!** (*iron*) du bist mir eine schöne Hilfe!; **to cry for ~** nach Hilfe schreien **II.** *interj* ■**~!** Hilfe! **III.** *vi* helfen (**with** bei +*dat*); **is there any way that I can ~?** kann ich irgendwie behilflich sein? **IV.** *vt* ❶ (*assist*) ■**to ~ sb** jdm helfen (**with** bei +*dat*); **her local knowledge ~ed her** ihre Ortskenntnisse haben ihr genützt SÜDD [*o* NORDD genutzt]; **can I ~ you?** (*in shop*) kann ich Ihnen behilflich sein?; **to ~ sb through a difficult time** jdm eine schwierige Zeit hinweghelfen ❷ (*improve*) verbessern; (*alleviate*) lindern ❸ (*prevent*) **I can't ~ it!** ich kann nichts dagegen machen!; **I can't ~ thinking that ...** ich denke einfach, dass ...; **not if I can ~ it** nicht, wenn ich es irgendwie verhindern kann; ■**sth can't be ~ed** etw ist nicht zu ändern ❹ (*take*) ■**to ~ oneself** sich bedienen; ■**to ~ oneself to sth** sich *dat* etw nehmen; *thief* sich an etw *dat* bedienen **V.** *adj* Hilfe-
◆**help along** *vt* ■**to ~ sb along** jdm [auf die Sprünge] helfen; ■**to ~ sth along** etw vorantreiben
◆**help out I.** *vt* ■**to ~ out** ↔ **sb** jdm [aus]helfen **II.** *vi* aushelfen; ■**to ~ out with sth** bei etw *dat* helfen
◆**help up** *vt* ■**to ~ sb up** jdm aufhelfen
helper ['hel·pər] *n* Helfer(in) *m(f);* (*assistant*) Gehilfe *m,* Gehilfin *f*
helpful ['help·fəl] *adj person* hilfsbereit; *tool, suggestion* hilfreich; **to be ~** [**to sb**] [jdm] helfen
helping ['hel·pɪŋ] **I.** *n of food* Portion *f* **II.** *adj* hilfreich; **to give** [*or* **lend**] **sb a ~ hand** jdm helfen
'helping verb *n* LING *see* **auxiliary verb**
helpless ['help·lɪs] *adj* hilflos; (*powerless*) machtlos
'helpline *n* Notruf *m*
helter-skelter [ˌhel·tər·'skel·tər] **I.** *adj* hektisch **II.** *adv* Hals über Kopf
hem[1] [hem] **I.** *n* Saum *m* **II.** *vt* <-mm-> säumen
◆**hem in** *vt* ❶ (*surround*) umgeben ❷ (*fig*)

einengen; **to feel ~med in** sich eingeengt fühlen

hem² [hem] *vi* ▶ PHRASES: **to ~ and haw** herumdrucksen

'he-man *n* (*fam*) Heman *m*

hemisphere ['hem·ɪ·sfɪr] *n* GEOG, ASTRON [Erd]halbkugel *f*

hemline ['hem·laɪn] *n* [Kleider]saum *m;* **~s are up** die Röcke sind kurz

hemophiliac [ˌhi·moʊ·'fɪl·i·æk] *n* MED Bluter(in) *m(f)*

hemorrhage ['hem·ər·ɪdʒ] **I.** *n* MED [starke] Blutung **II.** *vi* MED [stark] bluten

hemorrhoids ['hem·ər·ɔɪdz] *npl* MED Hämorrhoiden *pl*

hemp [hemp] *n* Hanf *m*

hen [hen] *n* ZOOL Henne *f,* Huhn *nt*

hence [hens] *adv* ❶ *after n* (*from now*) von jetzt an; **four weeks ~** in vier Wochen ❷ (*therefore*) daher

henceforth [ˌhens·'fɔrθ], **henceforward** [ˌhens·'fɔr·wərd] *adv* (*form*) von nun an

henchman ['hentʃ·mən] *n* Handlanger *m*

henna ['hen·ə] *n* Henna *f o nt*

'henpecked *adj* **~ husband** Pantoffelheld *m;* ■ **to be ~** unter dem Pantoffel stehen

hepatitis [ˌhep·ə·'taɪ·t̬ɪs] *n* Leberentzündung *f*

heptathlon [hep·'tæθ·lan] *n* Siebenkampf *m*

her [hɜr] **I.** *pron pers* sie *in akk,* ihr *in dat;* **it was ~** sie war's **II.** *adj poss* ihr(e, n); (*ship, country, boat, car*) sein(e, n); **what's ~ name?** wie heißt sie?

herald ['her·əld] **I.** *n* (*messenger*) Bote *m,* Botin *f;* (*newspaper*) Bote *m* **II.** *vt* (*form*) ankündigen

heraldic [hə·'ræl·dɪk] *adj* Wappen-

heraldry ['her·əl·dri] *n* Wappenkunde *f*

herb [ɜrb] *n* [Gewürz]kraut *nt meist pl;* (*for medicine*) [Heil]kraut *nt meist pl*

herbal ['ɜr·bəl] *adj* Kräuter-

herbalist ['ɜr·bə·lɪst] *n* (*dealer*) Kräuterhändler(in) *m(f);* (*healer*) Kräuterheilkundige(r) *f(m)*

herbicide ['hɜr·bɪ·saɪd] *n* Unkrautvertilgungsmittel *nt*

herbivorous [hɜr·'bɪv·ər·əs] *adj* Pflanzen fressend

Herculean [ˌhɜr·kju·'li·ən] *adj* übermenschlich; **~ task** Herkulesarbeit *f*

Hercules ['hɜr·kjə·liz] *n* Herkules *m a. fig*

herd [hɜrd] **I.** *n* ❶ (*group of animals*) Herde *f; of wild animals* Rudel *nt* ❷ (*pej: group of people*) Herde *f,* Masse *f* **II.** *vt* treiben
◆**herd together** **I.** *vt animals* zusammentreiben; *people* zusammenpferchen **II.** *vi* sich zusammendrängen

'herd instinct *n* Herdentrieb *m*

'herdsman *n* Hirt[e] *m*

here [hɪr] **I.** *adv* hier; (*with movement*) hierher, hierhin; **come ~!** komm [hier]her!; **give it ~!** (*fam*) gib mal her!; **~ you are!** (*presenting*) bitte schön!; (*finding*) hier bist du!; **~ I am!** hier bin ich!; **~ comes the train** da kommt der Zug; **~ goes!** (*fam*) los geht's!; **~'s to you!** auf Ihr/dein Wohl!; **~ and now** [jetzt] sofort; **from ~ on in** [*or* **out**] von jetzt an **II.** *interj* **~!** (*to this place*) hier!; **~, don't cry/worry!** na komm, weine nicht/mach dir keine Sorgen!

hereabout [ˌhɪr·ə·'baʊt], **hereabouts** [ˌhɪr·ə·'baʊts] *adv* hier [in dieser Gegend]

hereditary [hə·'red·ɪ·ter·i] *adj* erblich; *disease* angeboren; *succession* gesetzlich

heredity [hə·'red·ɪ·t̬i] *n* (*transmission of characteristics*) Vererbung *f;* (*genetic makeup*) Erbgut *nt*

heresy ['her·ə·si] *n* Ketzerei *f*

heretic ['her·ə·tɪk] *n* Ketzer(in) *m(f)*

heretical [hə·'ret̬·ɪ·kəl] *adj* ketzerisch

here'with *adv* (*form*) anbei, hiermit; **enclosed ~** beiliegend

heritage ['her·ɪ·t̬ɪdʒ] *n* Erbe *nt*

hermaphrodite [hər·'mæf·roʊ·daɪt] *n* Zwitter *m*

hermetically [hər'met̬·ɪ·kə·li] *adv* hermetisch

hermit ['hɜr·mɪt] *n* Eremit(in) *m(f) a. fig,* Einsiedler(in) *m(f) a. fig*

hermitage ['hɜr·mɪ·t̬ɪdʒ] *n* Einsiedelei *f*

'hermit crab *n* Einsiedlerkrebs *m*

hernia <*pl* -s *or* -niae> ['hɜr·ni·ə] *n* MED Bruch *m*

hero <*pl* -es> ['hɪr·oʊ] *n* Held(in) *m(f)*

heroic [hɪ·'roʊ·ɪk] **I.** *adj* (*brave*) heldenhaft; *attempt* kühn; **~ deed** Heldentat *f* **II.** *n* ■ **~s** *pl* Heldentaten *pl*

heroin ['her·oʊ·ɪn] *n* Heroin *nt*

heroine ['her·oʊ·ɪn] *n* Heldin *f*

heroism ['her·oʊ·ɪz·əm] *n* Heldentum *nt;* **act of ~** heldenhafte Tat

heron <*pl* -s *or* -> ['her·ən] *n* Reiher *m*

herpes ['hɜr·piz] *n* MED Herpes *m*

herring <*pl* -s *or* -> ['her·ɪŋ] *n* Hering *m*

'herringbone *n* Fischgrätenmuster *nt*

hers [hɜrz] *pron pers* (*of person/animal*) ihre(r, s); **a good friend of ~** eine gute Freundin von ihr

herself [hɜr·'self] *pron reflexive* ❶ *after vb, prep* sich *in akk o dat* ❷ (*emph: personally*) selbst; **she talks to ~ when she works** sie spricht bei der Arbeit mit sich [selbst]; **she told me ~** sie hat es mir selbst erzählt ❸ (*alone*) **[all] by ~** ganz alleine

he's [hiz] = **he is/he has** *see* **be, have I, II**

hesitant ['hez·ɪ·tənt] *adj person* unschlüssig; *reaction, answer, smile* zögernd; *speech* stockend

hesitantly ['hez·ɪ·tənt·li] *adv act* unentschlossen; *smile* zögernd; *speak* stockend

hesitate ['hez·ɪ·teɪt] *vi* ❶ (*wait*) zögern; **don't ~ to call me** ruf mich einfach an ❷ (*falter*) stocken

hesitation [ˌhez·ɪ·'teɪ·ʃən] *n* (*indecision*) Zögern *nt,* Unentschlossenheit *f;* (*reluctance*) Bedenken *pl;* **without [the slightest] ~** (*indecision*) ohne [einen Augenblick] zu zögern; (*reluctance*) ohne [den geringsten] Zweifel

H

heterogeneous [ˌhet̬·ər·ə·ˈdʒi·ni·əs] *adj* uneinheitlich

heterosexual [ˌhet̬·ə·roʊ·ˈsek·ʃu·əl] **I.** *adj* heterosexuell **II.** *n* Heterosexuelle(r) *f(m)*

hexagon [ˈhek·sə·gan] *n* Sechseck *nt*

hexagonal [hek·ˈsæg·ə·nəl] *adv* sechseckig

hey [heɪ] *interj* (*fam*) he!

heyday [ˈheɪ·deɪ] *n usu sing* Glanzzeit *f*

HEV [ˌeɪtʃ·i·ˈvi] *n abbrev of* **hybrid electric vehicle** Hybridauto *nt,* Hybridfahrzeug *nt*

HI *abbrev of* **Hawaii**

hi [haɪ] *interj* hallo!

hibernate [ˈhaɪ·bər·neɪt] *vi* Winterschlaf halten

hibernation [ˌhaɪ·bər·ˈneɪ·ʃən] *n* Winterschlaf *m*

hiccup, hiccough [ˈhɪk·ʌp] **I.** *n* ① (*sound, attack*) Schluckauf *m;* **to have the ~s** einen Schluckauf haben ② (*fig: setback*) Schwierigkeit *f meist pl* **II.** *vi* schlucksen

hick [hɪk] *n* (*pej fam*) Provinzler(in) *m(f) pej fam*

hickory [ˈhɪk·ə·ri] *n* Hickory[baum] *m*

hid [hɪd] *vt pt of* **hide**

hidden [ˈhɪd·ən] **I.** *vt pp of* **hide II.** *adj* versteckt; *agenda* heimlich; *reserves* still; *talent* verborgen

hide[1] [haɪd] **I.** *vt* <hid, hidden> ① (*keep out of sight*) verstecken (**from** vor +*dat*); (*cover*) verhüllen ② (*keep secret*) *emotions* verbergen (**from** vor +*dat*); *facts* verheimlichen (**from** vor +*dat*) ③ (*block*) verdecken; **hidden from view** nicht zu sehen **II.** *vi* <hid, hidden> sich verstecken (**from** vor +*dat*)

◆**hide away I.** *vt* verstecken **II.** *vi* sich verstecken

◆**hide out, hide up** *vi* sich versteckt halten

hide[2] [haɪd] *n* (*skin*) Haut *f a. fig;* (*with fur*) Fell *nt;* (*leather*) Leder *nt*

ˈhide-and-go-seek, ˈhide-and-seek *n* Versteckspiel *nt;* **to play ~** Verstecken spielen

ˈhideaway *n* (*fam*) Versteck *nt a. fig*

hideous [ˈhɪd·i·əs] *adj* ① (*ugly*) grässlich, scheußlich ② (*terrible*) schrecklich, furchtbar

ˈhideout *n* Versteck *nt*

hiding [ˈhaɪ·dɪŋ] *n* (*concealment*) **to be in ~** sich versteckt halten; **to go into ~** untertauchen

hierarchy [ˈhaɪ·rar·ki] *n* Hierarchie *f*

hieroglyph [ˌhaɪ·roʊ·ˈglɪf] *n* Hieroglyphe *f*

hieroglyphic [ˌhaɪ·roʊ·ˈglɪf·ɪk] *n usu pl* ■ **~s** Hieroglyphen *pl*

hi-fi [ˈhaɪ·faɪ] **I.** *n short for* **high fidelity** Hi-Fi-Anlage *f* **II.** *adj short for* **high-fidelity** Hi-Fi-

high [haɪ] **I.** *adj* ① *building, speed, rank* hoch *präd,* hohe(r, s) *attr; winds* stark; *marks* gut; *hopes, altitude* groß; **~ in calories** kalorienreich; **to be ~ in calcium** viel Kalzium enthalten; **friends in ~ places** wichtige Freunde; **~ and mighty** (*pej*) herablassend ② (*on drugs*) high ▶ PHRASES: **~ time** höchste Zeit **II.** *adv* hoch; (*fig*) **emotions were running ~** die Gemüter erhitzten sich ▶ PHRASES: **~ and low** überall **III.** *n* ① (*high[est] point*) Höchststand *m* ② METEO Hoch *nt*

high ˈbeams *npl* AUTO Fernlicht *nt*

ˈhighbrow *adj* hochgeistig

ˈhighchair *n* Hochstuhl *m*

ˈhigh-class *adj* erstklassig; *product* hochwertig

ˈhigh court *n see* **Supreme Court**

high-ˈdensity *adj* ① COMPUT mit hoher Dichte ② (*closely packed*) kompakt; **~ housing** dicht bebautes Wohngebiet

higher eduˈcation *n* (*learning*) Hochschulbildung *f;* (*system*) Hochschulwesen *nt*

higher-ˈup *n* (*fam*) hohes Tier

highˈflier *n* (*fig*) Überflieger(in) *m(f)*

high-ˈflown *adj* hochtrabend

high ˈfrequency *n* Hochfrequenz *f*

highˈhanded *adj* selbstherrlich

highˈhandedness *n* Selbstherrlichkeit *f*

high ˈheels *npl* ① (*shoes*) hochhackige Schuhe ② (*parts of a shoe*) hohe Absätze

ˈhigh jinks, hijinks *npl* Ausgelassenheit *f kein pl*

ˈhigh jump *n* Hochsprung *m*

highlands [ˈhaɪ·ləndz] *npl* Hochland *nt kein pl*

ˈhigh-level *adj* auf höchster Ebene *nach n*

ˈhigh life *n* exklusives Leben; ■ **the ~** die Prasserei

ˈhighlight I. *n* ① (*best part*) Höhepunkt *m* ② (*in hair*) ■ **~s** *pl* Strähnchen *pl* **II.** *vt* ① (*draw attention to*) hervorheben, unterstreichen; *text* markieren ② (*dye*) **to have one's hair ~ed** sich *dat* Strähnchen machen lassen

ˈhighlighter *n* ① (*pen*) Textmarker *m* ② (*cosmetics*) Highlighter *m*

highly [ˈhaɪ·li] *adv* hoch-; **~ amusing** ausgesprochen amüsant; **~ contagious** hoch ansteckend; **~-strung** nervös; **to think ~ of someone** eine hohe Meinung von jdm haben

High ˈMass *n* Hochamt *nt*

Highness [ˈhaɪ·nɪs] *n* ■ **Her/His/Your ~** Ihre/Seine/Eure Hoheit

high-perˈformance *adj* Hochleistungs-

high-ˈpitched *adj* ① *voice* hoch ② *roof* steil

ˈhigh point *n* Höhepunkt *m*

high-ˈpowered *adj* ① *machine* Hochleistungs-; *car* stark; *computer* leistungsstark ② (*influential*) einflussreich; *delegation* hochrangig

high-ˈpressure I. *adj* ① METEO, TECH Hochdruck-; **~ area** Hochdruckgebiet *nt* ② ECON **~ sales techniques** aggressive Verkaufstechniken **II.** *vt* unter Druck setzen

high ˈpriest *n* REL Hohe(r) Priester *m;* (*fig*) Doyen *m*

high ˈprofile *n* **to have a ~** gerne im Rampenlicht stehen

high-ˈprofile *adj* **she's a ~ politician** sie ist eine Politikerin, die im Rampenlicht steht

high-ˈprotein *adj* eiweißreich

high-ˈranking *adj* hochrangig

high-resoˈlution *adj* mit hoher Auflösung

ˈhigh-rise, high-rise ˈbuilding *n* Hochhaus *nt*

high-'risk *adj* hochriskant; **to be in a ~ category** einer Risikokategorie angehören

'high school *n* Highschool *f*, ≈ Gymnasium *nt*

high 'seas *npl* hohe See; **on the ~** auf hoher See

high 'season *n* Hochsaison *f*

high-speed 'train *n* Hochgeschwindigkeitszug *m*

high-'spirited *adj* ausgelassen; *horse* temperamentvoll

high 'spirits *npl* Hochstimmung *f kein pl*

'high spot *n* Höhepunkt *m*

'hightail *vi, vt* (*fam*) **to ~ [it]** abhauen

high-'tech *adj* Hightech-

high tech'nology *n* Hightech *nt*, Hochtechnologie *f*

high 'tide *n* Flut *f*; **at ~** bei Flut

high 'treason *n* Hochverrat *m*

high-'water mark *n* Hochwassermarke *f*

'highway I. *n* Highway *m* **II.** *adj* Straßen-; **~ fatalities** Verkehrstote *pl*

'highwayman *n* (*hist*) Straßenräuber *m*

hijack ['haɪ·dʒæk] **I.** *vt* entführen; (*fig*) klauen *fam* **II.** *n* Entführung *f*

hijacker ['haɪ·dʒæk·ər] *n* Entführer(in) *m(f)*

hijacking ['haɪ·dʒæk·ɪŋ] *n* Entführung *f*

hijinks *n pl see* **high jinks**

hike [haɪk] **I.** *n* ❶ (*long walk*) Wanderung *f*; (*fam*) **that was quite a ~** das war ein ganz schöner Marsch [*o* ÖSTERR Hatscher] ❷ (*fam: increase*) Erhöhung *f* **II.** *vi* wandern **III.** *vt* (*fam*) erhöhen

hiker ['haɪ·kər] *n* Wanderer *m*, Wanderin *f*

hiking ['haɪ·kɪŋ] *n* Wandern *nt*; (*in hilly countryside*) Bergwandern *nt*

hilarious [hɪ·'ler·i·əs] *adj* urkomisch, zum Brüllen

hilarity [hɪ·'ler·ɪ·t̬i] *n* Ausgelassenheit *f*; **to cause ~** Heiterkeit erregen

hill [hɪl] *n* ❶ (*elevation*) Hügel *m*; (*higher*) Berg *m* ❷ (*slope*) Steigung *f* ►PHRASES: **to be over the ~** mit einem Fuß im Grab stehen

hillbilly ['hɪl·bɪl·i] *n* Hinterwäldler(in) *m(f)*, Hillbilly *m*

'hillside *n* Hang *m*

'hilltop I. *n* Hügelkuppe *f* **II.** *adj farm* auf einem Hügel gelegen

hilly ['hɪl·i] *adj* hügelig

hilt [hɪlt] *n* ❶ (*handle*) Griff *m*; *of a dagger, sword* Heft *nt* ❷ (*fig*) **[up] to the ~** hundertprozentig

him [hɪm] *pron object* ihn *in akk*, ihm *in dat*; **who? ~?** wer? der?; **you have more than ~** du hast mehr als er

Himalayas [ˌhɪm·ə·'leɪ·əz] *npl* GEOG Himalaja *m*

himself [hɪm·'self] *pron reflexive* ❶ *after vb, prep* sich *in akk o dat* ❷ (*emph: personally*) selbst; **he talks to ~ when he works** er spricht bei der Arbeit mit sich [selbst]; **he told me ~** er hat es mir selbst erzählt ❸ (*alone*) **[all] by ~** ganz alleine

hind [haɪnd] *adj* hintere(r, s); **~ leg** Hinterbein *nt*; *of game* Hinterlauf *m*

hinder ['hɪn·dər] *vt* behindern

Hindi ['hɪn·di] *n* Hindi *nt*

'hindquarters *npl* Hinterteil *nt*; *of a horse* Hinterhand *f*

hindrance ['hɪn·drəns] *n* Behinderung *f*; **sb is more of a ~ than a help** jd stört mehr, als dass er/sie hilft

'hindsight *n* **in** [*or* **with** [**the benefit of**]] **~** im Nachhinein

Hindu ['hɪn·du] **I.** *n* Hindu *m o f* **II.** *adj* hinduistisch, Hindu-

Hinduism ['hɪn·du·ɪz·əm] *n* Hinduismus *m*

hinge [hɪndʒ] **I.** *n* Angel *f*; *of a chest, gate* Scharnier *nt* **II.** *vi* ■**to ~ [up]on sb/sth** von jdm/etw abhängen

hint [hɪnt] **I.** *n* ❶ *usu sing* (*trace*) Spur *f*; **he gave me no ~ that ...** er gab mir nicht den leisesten Wink, ob ...; **at the slightest ~ of trouble** beim leisesten Anzeichen von Ärger ❷ (*allusion*) Andeutung *f*; **OK, I can take a ~** OK, ich verstehe schon; **to drop a ~** eine Andeutung machen ❸ (*advice*) Hinweis *m*, Tipp *m* **II.** *vt* ■**to ~ that ...** andeuten, dass ... **III.** *vi* andeuten; ■**to ~ at sth** auf etw *akk* anspielen

hip [hɪp] **I.** *n* ❶ ANAT Hüfte *f*; *of pants* Hüftweite *f*; **to dislocate a ~** sich *dat* die Hüfte ausrenken ❷ BOT **[rose] ~** Hagebutte *f* **II.** *adj* (*fam*) hip

'hipbone *n* ANAT Hüftknochen *m*

'hip flask *n* Flachmann *m*

hippie ['hɪp·i] *n* Hippie *m*

hippo ['hɪp·oʊ] *n* (*fam*) *short for* **hippopotamus**

hippopotamus <*pl* -es *or* -mi> [ˌhɪp·ə·'pat̬·ə·məs] *n* Nilpferd *nt*

hippy ['hɪp·i] *n see* **hippie**

hire [haɪr] **I.** *n* (*fam: employee*) Angestellte(r) *f(m)* **II.** *vt* (*act of employing*) einstellen; **to ~ a gunman** einen Killer anheuern
◆**hire out** *vt* **to ~ oneself ⊃ out** seine Dienste anbieten

his [hɪz] **I.** *pron pers* seine(r, s); **some friends of ~** einige seiner Freunde **II.** *adj poss* (*of person*) sein(e); **what's ~ name?** wie heißt er?

Hispanic [hɪs·'pæn·ɪk] **I.** *adj* hispanisch **II.** *n* Hispanoamerikaner(in) *m(f)*

hiss [hɪs] **I.** *vi* zischen; *cat, person* fauchen; ■**to ~ at sb** jdn anfauchen **II.** *vt* ❶ (*utter*) fauchen ❷ (*disapprove of*) ■**to ~ sb/sth** *singer, actor, speaker* jdn/etw auszischen **III.** *n* <*pl* -es> Zischen *nt kein pl*; *of cat* Fauchen *nt kein pl*; *of tape* Rauschen *nt kein pl*

historian [hɪ·'stɔr·i·ən] *n* Historiker(in) *m(f)*

historic [hɪ·'stɔr·ɪk] *adj* historisch

historical [hɪ·'stɔr·ɪ·kəl] *adj* geschichtlich, historisch; **~ accuracy** Geschichtstreue *f*

history ['hɪs·tə·ri] **I.** *n* ❶ (*past events*) Geschichte *f*; **to make ~** Geschichte schreiben ❷ (*fig*) **to be ~** *person* vergessen sein, passé sein *fam*; **ancient ~** kalter Kaffee *fam* ❸ *usu sing* (*background*) Vorgeschichte *f*; **her family**

H

has a ~ of heart problems Herzprobleme liegen bei ihr in der Familie **II.** *adj book, class* Geschichts-

histrionic [ˌhɪs·trɪ·ˈan·ɪk] *adj* theatralisch

hit [hɪt] **I.** *n* ① (*blow*) Schlag *m* ② (*shot*) Treffer *m;* **to suffer a direct ~** direkt getroffen werden ③ (*success, in baseball*) Hit *m;* **to be a** [**big**] **~ with sb** bei jdm gut ankommen ④ (*sl: of drug*) Schuss *m* ⑤ (*fam: murder*) Mord *m* ⑥ INET Besuch *m* einer Webseite, Hit *m* ⑦ COMPUT (*in database*) Treffer *m* **II.** *vt* <-tt-, hit, hit> ① (*strike*) schlagen; **to ~ sb below the belt** jdm einen Schlag unter die Gürtellinie versetzen *a. fig;* **to ~ sb where it hurts** (*a. fig*) jdn an einer empfindlichen Stelle treffen ② (*come in contact, strike note*) treffen *a. fig; by missile;* ■ **to be ~** getroffen werden; **the house was ~ by lightning** in das Haus schlug der Blitz ein ③ (*press*) *button* drücken; *key* drücken auf *+akk* ④ (*crash into*) stoßen (gegen *+akk*); **their car ~ a tree** ihr Auto krachte gegen einen Baum; **the glass ~ the floor** das Glas schlug auf den Boden [auf] ⑤ SPORTS treffen; (*score*) *basket* erzielen ⑥ (*fam: arrive at*) **my sister ~ 40 last week** meine Schwester wurde letzte Woche 40; **to ~ the headlines** in die Schlagzeilen kommen; **to ~ rock bottom** einen historischen Tiefstand erreichen ⑦ (*encounter*) stoßen auf *+akk;* **to ~ a traffic jam** in einen Stau geraten; **to ~ trouble** in Schwierigkeiten geraten **III.** *vi* ① (*strike*) ■ **to ~** [**at sb/sth**] [nach jdm/etw] schlagen; **to ~ hard** kräftig zuschlagen ② (*attack*) ■ **to ~ at sb** jdn attackieren *a. fig* ③ (*occur*) *storm* toben

◆**hit back** *vi* zurückschlagen; ■ **to ~ back at sb** jdm Kontra geben

◆**hit off** *vt* ■ **to ~ it off** [**with sb**] (*fam*) sich prächtig [mit jdm] verstehen

◆**hit on** *vt* ① (*think of*) kommen auf *+akk* ② (*sl: make sexual advances*) ■ **to ~ on sb** jdn anmachen

◆**hit up** *vt* (*fam*) **to ~ up** ○ **sb** [**for money**] jdn [um Geld] anhauen

◆**hit upon** *vt idea* kommen auf *+akk*

hit-and-ˈmiss *adj* zufällig; **a ~ affair** [reine] Glückssache

hit-and-ˈrun **I.** *n* AUTO Fahrerflucht *f* **II.** *adj driver* unfallflüchtig; **~ accident** Unfall *m* mit Fahrerflucht

hitch [hɪtʃ] **I.** *n* <*pl* -es> (*difficulty*) Haken *m;* **a technical ~** ein technisches Problem; **to go off without a ~** reibungslos ablaufen **II.** *vt* ① (*fasten*) festmachen (**to** an *+dat*); *trailer* anhängen (**to** an *+akk*); *animal* festbinden ② (*fam: hitchhike*) **to ~ a ride** [*or* **lift**] trampen, per Anhalter fahren ③ (*sl: marry*) **to get ~ed** heiraten **III.** *vi* (*fam*) trampen

◆**hitch up** *vt* ① (*fasten*) festmachen (**to** an *+dat*); *trailer* anhängen (**to** an *+akk*); **to ~ a horse up to a cart** ein Pferd vor einen Wagen spannen ② (*pull up*) *pants* hochziehen

hitcher [ˈhɪtʃ·ər] *n* Anhalter(in) *m(f),* Tramper(in) *m(f)*

ˈhitchhike *vi* per Anhalter fahren, trampen

ˈhitchhiker *n* Anhalter(in) *m(f),* Tramper(in) *m(f)*

ˈhitchhiking *n* Trampen *nt*

hi-ˈtech *adj see* **high-tech**

hither [ˈhɪð·ər] *adv* (*liter*) **~ and thither** hierhin und dorthin

hitherto [ˌhɪð·ər·ˈtu] *adv* (*form*) bisher

ˈhit man *n* Killer *m*

HIV [ˌeɪtʃ·aɪ·ˈvi] *n abbrev of* **human immunodeficiency virus** HIV *nt*

hive [haɪv] *n* ① (*beehive*) Bienenstock *m* ② (*busy place*) Ameisenhaufen *m fig*

HMO [ˌeɪtʃ·em·ˈoʊ] *n abbrev of* **health maintenance organization** *eine in der Regel vom Arbeitgeber getragene, preisgünstige Krankenversicherung mit begrenzter Ärzteauswahl*

hoagie [ˈhoʊ·gi] *n* Riesensandwich *nt*

hoard [hɔrd] **I.** *n* (*of money, food*) Vorrat *m* (**of** an *+dat*); (*treasure*) Schatz *m;* **~ of weapons** Waffenlager *nt* **II.** *vt* horten; *food a.* hamstern **III.** *vi* Vorräte anlegen

hoarse [hɔrs] *adj* heiser

hoarseness [ˈhɔrs·nɪs] *n* Heiserkeit *f*

hoary [ˈhɔr·i] *adj* (*fig liter*) uralt; **a ~ joke** ein alter Hut

hoax [hoʊks] **I.** *n* (*deception*) Täuschung *f;* (*joke*) Streich *m;* (*false alarm*) blinder Alarm **II.** *adj* vorgetäuscht **III.** *vt* [he]reinlegen; **to ~ sb into believing** [*or* **thinking**] **sth** jdm etw weismachen

hoaxer [ˈhoʊks·ər] *n jd, der falschen Alarm auslöst*

hobble [ˈhab·əl] **I.** *vi* hinken, humpeln; **to ~ around on crutches** mit Krücken herumlaufen **II.** *n* (*awkward walk*) Hinken *nt kein pl,* Humpeln *nt kein pl*

hobby [ˈhab·i] *n* Hobby *nt*

ˈhobbyhorse *n* Steckenpferd *nt*

hobnob <-bb-> [ˈhab·nab] *vi* (*fam*) verkehren

hobo <*pl* -s *or* -es> [ˈhoʊ·boʊ] *n* (*tramp*) Penner(in) *m(f),* Sandler(in) *m(f)* ÖSTERR

hock¹ [hak] *n* ZOOL Sprunggelenk *nt; of a horse* Fesselgelenk *nt;* (*meat*) Hachse *f,* Haxe *f* SÜDD, ÖSTERR

hock² [hak] **I.** *n* (*fam*) ① (*in debt*) **to be in ~** Schulden haben ② (*pawned*) **in ~** verpfändet **II.** *vt* verpfänden

hockey [ˈhak·i] *n* [Eis]hockey *nt;* **~ stick** Hockeyschläger *m*

hodgepodge [ˈhadʒ·padʒ] *n* Mischmasch *m* (**of** aus *+dat*)

hoe [hoʊ] **I.** *n* Hacke *f* **II.** *vt, vi* hacken

hog [hɔg] **I.** *n* Schwein *nt* ▶ PHRASES: **to go the whole ~** ganze Sache machen **II.** *vt* <-gg-> (*fam*) ■ **to ~ sb/sth** jdn/etw in Beschlag nehmen *akk;* **to ~ the road** die ganze Straße [für sich *akk*] beanspruchen

hoist [hɔɪst] **I.** *vt* hochheben; *flag, sail* hissen; **he ~ed her onto his shoulders** er hievte sie auf seine Schultern **II.** *n* Winde *f*

hold [hoʊld] **I.** *n* ① (*grasp*) Halt *m kein pl;* **to**

catch [*or* **get** [a]] **~ of sb/sth** jdn/etw ergreifen; **to keep ~ of sth** etw festhalten; **to take ~** (*fig*) *fire, epidemic* übergreifen ❷ SPORTS Griff *m* (**on** an *+akk*) ❸ (*delay*) **to be on ~** auf Eis liegen *fig;* TELEC in der Warteschleife sein; **to put on ~** *project, plans* auf Eis legen *fig;* TELEC *caller* in die Warteschleife schalten ❹ (*control*) **to have a** [**strong**] **~ on** [*or* **over**] **sb** [starken] Einfluss auf jdn haben ❺ NAUT, AVIAT Frachtraum *m* **II.** *vt* <held, held> ❶ (*grasp*) ■**to ~ sb/sth** [**tight** [*or* **tightly**]] jdn/etw [fest]halten; **to ~ the door open for sb** jdm die Tür aufhalten; **to ~ sth in place** etw halten ❷ (*keep*) halten; **to ~ sb's attention** [*or* **interest**] jdn fesseln; **to ~ sb hostage** jdn als Geisel halten; **to ~ its value** seinen Wert behalten; **to ~ sb to his/her word** jdn beim Wort nehmen ❸ (*delay, stop*) zurückhalten; PHOT **OK, ~ it!** gut, bleib so!; **to ~ one's breath** die Luft anhalten; TELEC **to ~ the line** am Apparat bleiben ❹ (*contain*) fassen; COMPUT speichern; **this room ~s 40 people** dieser Raum bietet 40 Personen Platz; **this hard disk ~s 13 gigabytes** diese Festplatte hat ein Speichervolumen von 13 Gigabyte

◆**hold against** *vt* ■**to ~ sth against sb** jdm etw vorwerfen

◆**hold back I.** *vt* (*stop*) aufhalten; (*impede development*) hindern; *information* geheim halten; *tears* zurückhalten **II.** *vi* (*refrain*) **to ~ back from doing sth** etw unterlassen

◆**hold down** *vt* (*keep near the ground*) niederhalten; (*keep low*) *levels, prices* niedrig halten

◆**hold forth** *vi* ■**to ~ forth** [**about sth**] sich [über etw *akk*] auslassen

◆**hold in** *vt emotions* zurückhalten; *fear* unterdrücken; *stomach* einziehen

◆**hold off I.** *vt* ❶ MIL *enemy* abwehren ❷ (*postpone*) verschieben **II.** *vi* warten; **the rain held off all day** es hat den ganzen Tag nicht geregnet

◆**hold on** *vi* ❶ (*affix, attach*) ■**to be held on by** [*or* **with**] **sth** mit etw *dat* befestigt sein ❷ (*manage to keep going*) durchhalten ❸ (*wait*) **~ on!** Moment bitte!

◆**hold onto** *vt* ❶ (*grasp*) festhalten ❷ (*keep*) behalten

◆**hold out I.** *vt* ausstrecken **II.** *vi* ❶ (*manage to resist*) durchhalten; **to ~ out for sth** auf etw *dat* bestehen ❷ (*refuse to give information*) **to ~ out on sb** jdm etw verheimlichen

◆**hold over** *vt* ❶ (*defer*) aufschieben ❷ (*extend*) verlängern

◆**hold to** *vt* **can I ~ you to that?** bleibst du bei deinem Wort?

◆**hold together** *vi, vt* zusammenhalten

◆**hold under** *vt* unterdrücken

◆**hold up I.** *vt* ❶ (*raise*) hochhalten; *hand* heben ❷ (*support*) stützen ❸ (*delay*) aufhalten; **the letter was held up in the mail** der Brief war bei der Post liegen geblieben **II.** *vi* ❶ (*endure*) durchhalten, aushalten ❷ (*remain convincing*) standhalten; *alibi* keine Widersprüche aufweisen; **to ~ up in court** vor Gericht standhalten

holder ['hoʊl·dər] *n* ❶ (*device*) Halter *m* ❷ (*person*) Besitzer(in) *m(f);* **account ~** Kontoinhaber(in) *m(f);* **record ~** Rekordhalter(in) *m(f)*

holding ['hoʊl·dɪŋ] *n* ❶ (*land*) Pachtbesitz *m* ❷ FIN Beteiligung *f;* ■**~s** *pl* Anteile *pl;* **~ company** Dachgesellschaft *f*

'holdup *n* ❶ (*crime*) Raubüberfall *m* ❷ (*delay*) Verzögerung *f;* **what's the ~?** was ist?

hole [hoʊl] **I.** *n* ❶ (*gap*) Loch *nt a. fig; of fox, rabbit* Bau *m* ❷ (*fig: fault*) **to pick ~s** [**in sth**] [etw] kritisieren ❸ (*fig fam: difficulty*) **to get sb out of a ~** jdm aus der Patsche helfen **II.** *vt* (*in golf*) einlochen

◆**hole up** *vi* (*fam*) sich verkriechen

holiday ['hal·ɪ·deɪ] *n* Feiertag *m;* ■**the ~s** *die Zeit zwischen Thanksgiving und Neujahr* ► PHRASES: **Happy ~s!** Frohe Weihnachten!

holiness ['hoʊ·lɪ·nɪs] *n* Heiligkeit *f*

Holland ['hal·ənd] *n* Holland *nt*

holler ['hal·ər] **I.** *vi, vt* (*fam*) brüllen **II.** *n* (*fam*) Schrei *m*

hollow ['hal·oʊ] **I.** *adj* ❶ (*empty, sunken*) hohl; *cheeks* eingefallen ❷ (*fig*) wertlos; *laughter* ungläubig; *victory* schal **II.** *n* ❶ (*hole*) Senke *f* ❷ (*valley*) Tal *nt* **III.** *vt* ■**to ~** [**out**] aushöhlen

holly ['hal·i] *n* Stechpalme *f*

holocaust ['hal·ə·kɔst] *n* ❶ (*destruction*) Inferno *nt* ❷ (*genocide*) Massenvernichtung *f;* ■**the H~** der Holocaust

hologram ['hal·ə·græm] *n* Hologramm *nt*

holster ['hoʊl·stər] *n* [Pistolen]halfter *nt o f*

holy ['hoʊ·li] *adj* heilig

Holy Com'munion *n* ❶ (*service*) heilige Kommunion ❷ (*bread and wine*) heiliges Abendmahl

Holy 'Father *n* ■**the ~** der Heilige Vater

Holy 'Scripture *n* ■**the ~** die Heilige Schrift

Holy 'Spirit *n* ■**the ~** der Heilige Geist

'holy water *n* Weihwasser *nt*

homage ['ham·ɪdʒ] *n* Huldigung *f* (**to** *+gen*); **to pay ~** [**to sb**] [jdm] huldigen

home [hoʊm] **I.** *n* ❶ (*abode*) Zuhause *nt;* **a ~ away from ~** ein zweites Zuhause; **to leave ~** [von zu Hause] ausziehen; **to make oneself at ~** es sich *dat* gemütlich machen; **at ~** zu Hause, zuhause ÖSTERR, SCHWEIZ ❷ (*house*) Haus *nt;* (*apartment*) Wohnung *f;* **starter ~** erstes eigenes Heim ❸ (*institution*) Heim *nt* ❹ (*place of origin*) Heimat *f; of people a.* Zuhause *nt kein pl* ❺ SPORTS **at ~** zu Hause ❻ COMPUT (*for the cursor*) Ausgangsstellung *f;* (*on the key*) **"~"** „Pos. 1" ► PHRASES: **to feel at ~ with sb** sich bei jdm wohl fühlen; **~ sweet ~** (*saying*) trautes Heim, Glück allein **II.** *adv* ❶ (*at one's abode*) zu Hause, zuhause ÖSTERR, SCHWEIZ, daheim *bes* SÜDD, ÖSTERR, SCHWEIZ; (*to one's abode*) nach Hause, nachhause ÖSTERR, SCHWEIZ; **hi! I'm ~!** hallo! ich bin

H

wieder da! ❷ (*to one's origin*) **to go/return ~** in seine Heimat zurückgehen/zurückkehren ❸ (*to sb's understanding*) **to bring sth ~ [to sb]** [jdm] etw klarmachen; **to drive it ~ that ...** unmissverständlich klarmachen, dass ... **III.** *vi* ■**to ~ in on sth** genau auf etw *akk* zusteuern; (*fig*) [sich *dat*] etw herausgreifen

'home address *n* Heimatadresse *f*, Privatanschrift *f*

'home advantage *n* Heimvorteil *m*

home-'baked *adj* selbst gebacken

home 'banking *n* Homebanking *nt*

home'brew *n* selbst gebrautes Bier

'homecoming *n* ❶ (*return*) Heimkehr *f kein pl* ❷ (*reunion*) Ehemaligentreffen *nt;* **~ queen** *Schönheitskönigin beim Ehemaligentreffen*

H

Homecoming ist in den USA ein wichtiges Fest an der High School und an der Universität. Das Fest findet gewöhnlich Ende September oder Anfang Oktober statt. An diesem Tag kommen die Absolventen und es wird eine große Party gefeiert. Üblicherweise kommt die Footballmannschaft zu einem Heimspiel „nach Hause" und eine beliebte Schülerin/Studentin und ein beliebter Schüler/Student werden zur *Homecoming Queen* bzw. zum *Homecoming King* gekürt.

home 'cooking *n* Hausmannskost *f*

home eco'nomics *n + sing vb* Hauswirtschaft[slehre] *f*

'home game *n* Heimspiel *nt*

home-'grown *adj* aus dem eigenen Garten, aus eigenem Anbau

home 'help *n* Haushaltshilfe *f*

'homeland *n* (*origin*) Heimat *f*, Heimatland *nt;* **~ security** innere Sicherheit, Heimatschutz *m*

homeless ['hoʊm·lɪs] **I.** *adj* heimatlos; ■**to be ~** obdachlos sein **II.** *n* **the ~** *pl* die Obdachlosen *pl*

'homeless shelter *n* Obdachlosenheim *nt*

'home loan *n* Hypothek *f*

homely ['hoʊm·li] *adj* ❶ (*pej: ugly*) unansehnlich ❷ (*plain*) schlicht aber gemütlich

home'made *adj* hausgemacht; *cake* selbst gebacken; *jam* selbst gemacht

'homemaker *n* Hausmann, -frau *m, f*

homeopath ['hoʊ·mi·oʊ·pæθ] *n* Homöopath(in) *m(f)*

homeopathic [ˌhoʊ·mi·oʊ·'pæθ·ɪk] *adj* homöopathisch

homeopathy [ˌhoʊ·mi·'ap·ə·θi] *n* Homöopathie *f*

'homeowner *n* Hausbesitzer(in) *m(f)*

'home page *n* COMPUT Homepage *f*

home 'plate *n* (*in baseball*) Homeplate *f*, Schlagmal *nt*

home 'rule *n* [politische] Selbstverwaltung

home 'run *n* (*in baseball*) *Punkt bringender Lauf um alle vier Male beim Baseball*

home'school *vt* jdm Hausunterricht erteilen

home'schooling *n* Unterricht *m* zu Hause

'homesick *adj* **to be** [*or* **feel**] **~ [for sth]** [nach etw *dat*] Heimweh haben

'homesickness *n* Heimweh *nt*

homestead ['hoʊm·sted] *n* Eigenheim *nt*

home'stretch *n* Zielgerade *f a. fig*

'home team *n* Heimmannschaft *f*

home'town *n* Heimatstadt *f*

home 'truth *n* bittere Wahrheit

homeward ['hoʊm·wərd] **I.** *adv* heimwärts, nach Hause **II.** *adj* heimwärts; **~ journey** Heimreise *f*

homewards ['hoʊm·wərdz] *adv* heimwärts

'homework *n* Hausaufgaben *pl a. fig*

'homeworker *n* Heimarbeiter(in) *m(f)*

homey ['hoʊ·mi] *adj* (*cozy*) heimelig

homicidal [ˌham·ɪ·'saɪ·dəl] *adj* gemeingefährlich

homicide ['ham·ɪ·saɪd] *n* LAW ❶ (*murdering*) Mord *m* ❷ (*death*) Mordfall *m;* **~ squad** Mordkommission *f*

homing ['hoʊ·mɪŋ] *adj* **~ instinct** Heimfindevermögen *nt;* **~ device** Peilsender *m*

homogenize [hə·'madʒ·ə·naɪz] *vt* homogenisieren

homophobia [ˌhoʊ·mə·'foʊ·bi·ə] *n* Homophobie *f*

homosexual [ˌhoʊ·mə·'sek·ʃu·əl] (*form*) **I.** *adj* homosexuell **II.** *n* Homosexuelle(r) *f(m)*

homosexuality [ˌhoʊ·mə·sek·ʃu·'æl·ə·t̬i] *n* Homosexualität *f*

Hon. *adj abbrev of* **Honorable** geehrt, ehrenhaft

Honduras [han·'dʊr·əs] *n* Honduras *nt*

honest ['an·ɪst] *adj* ❶ (*truthful*) ehrlich ❷ (*trusty*) redlich

honestly ['an·ɪst·li] **I.** *adv* ehrlich **II.** *interj* ❶ (*promising*) [ganz] ehrlich! ❷ (*disapproving*) also ehrlich!

honesty ['an·ɪ·sti] *n* Ehrlichkeit *f* ▶ PHRASES: **~ is the best policy** (*prov*) ehrlich währt am längsten

honey ['hʌn·i] *n* ❶ (*from bees*) Honig *m* ❷ (*fam: sweet person*) Schatz *m;* (*sl: attractive young woman*) Schnecke *f sl*, Schnitte *f sl*

'honeybee *n* [Honig]biene *f*

'honeycomb *n* (*wax*) Bienenwabe *f;* (*food*) Honigwabe *f;* **~ pattern** Wabenmuster *nt*

honeydew 'melon *n* Honigmelone *f*

'honeymoon I. *n* ❶ (*after marriage*) Flitterwochen *pl* ❷ *usu sing* (*fig*) Schonfrist *f* **II.** *vi* **they are ~ing in the Bahamas** sie verbringen ihre Flitterwochen auf den Bahamas

honk [haŋk] **I.** *n* ❶ *of goose* Schrei *m* ❷ *of horn* Hupen *nt* **II.** *vi* ❶ *goose* schreien ❷ *horn* hupen **III.** *vt* **to ~ one's horn** auf die Hupe drücken; **to ~ one's horn at sb** jdn anhupen

honor ['an·ər] **I.** *n* ❶ Ehre *f;* ■**in ~ of sb/sth** zu Ehren einer Person/einer S. *gen* ❷ (*award*) Auszeichnung *f* **II.** *vt* ❶ *person* ehren ❷ (*fulfill*) *obligation* erfüllen

honorable ['an·ər·əb·əl] *adj* (*worthy*) ehrenhaft; *agreement* ehrenvoll; *person* ehrenwert
honorary ['an·ə·rer·i] *adj* ehrenamtlich
'**honor roll** *n* SCH, UNIV Ehrenrolle *f*

Die Namen der Schüler und Studenten, die besonders gute Abschlussnoten erzielt haben, werden in den Schüler- bzw. Universitätszeitungen, manchmal sogar in der Tageszeitung, veröffentlicht. Diese Liste nennt sich **honor roll** oder, hauptsächlich in Universitäten *dean's list*. Die Schüler, deren Namen in dieser Liste auftauchen, werden oft bevorzugt, wenn sie sich um Zulassung bei einer Universität oder um einen Arbeitsplatz in einem Unternehmen bewerben.

'**honors degree** *n* UNIV *akademischer Grad mit Prüfung im Spezialfach*
hood¹ [hʊd] *n* ❶ (*head covering*) Kapuze *f* ❷ AUTO [Motor]haube *f* ❸ (*shield*) Haube *f*; **stove ~** Abzugshaube *f*
hood² [hʊd] *n* (*gangster*) Kriminelle(r) *f(m)*
hood³ [hʊd] *n* (*sl*) Nachbarschaft *f*
hoodlum ['hud·ləm] *n* ❶ (*gangster*) Kriminelle(r) *f(m)* ❷ (*thug*) Rowdy *m*
hoodwink ['hʊd·wɪŋk] *vt* hereinlegen
hoof [hʊf] **I.** *n* <*pl* hooves *or* -s> Huf *m* **II.** *vt* (*fam*) **to ~ it** laufen
hook [hʊk] **I.** *n* Haken *m*; **to leave the phone off the ~** den Telefonhörer nicht auflegen ▶ PHRASES: **by ~ or by crook** auf Biegen und Brechen; **to be off the ~** aus dem Schneider sein; **to let sb off the ~** jdn herauspauken **II.** *vt* ❶ (*fasten*) festhaken (**to** an +*dat*) ❷ (*grab with hook*) **she ~ed the shoe out of the water** sie angelte den Schuh aus dem Wasser ❸ *fish* an die Angel bekommen ❹ (*in baseball, golf*) *ball* einen Linksdrall verpassen
◆**hook up I.** *vt* ❶ (*connect*) anschließen (**to** an +*akk*) ❷ (*fasten*) zumachen ❸ (*hang*) aufhängen ❹ (*make meet*) ■**to ~ sb ↔ up [with sb]** jdn [mit jdm] verkuppeln **II.** *vi* ❶ (*connect*) ■**to ~ up [to sth]** sich [an etw *akk*] anschließen ❷ (*sl: get together*) **to ~ up [with sb]** sich [mit jdm] treffen ❸ (*sl: have sex*) **to ~ up [with sb]** [mit jdm] Sex haben
hooked [hʊkt] *adj* ❶ (*curved*) hakenförmig; **~ nose** Hakennase *f* ❷ (*addicted*) abhängig ❸ (*interested*) ■**to be ~** total begeistert sein; **to be ~ on sb** total verrückt nach jdm sein; **to be ~ on sth** von einer S. völlig besessen sein
hooker ['hʊk·ər] *n* (*fam*) Nutte *f sl*
hooky ['hʊk·i] *n* (*fam*) **to play ~** die Schule schwänzen
hooligan ['hu·lɪ·gən] *n* Hooligan *m*
hooliganism ['hu·lɪ·gən·ɪz·əm] *n* Rowdytum *nt*
hoop [hup] *n* ❶ (*ring*) Reifen *m* ❷ (*earring*) ringförmiger Ohrring
hooray [hə·'reɪ] *interj see* **hurray**
hoot [hut] **I.** *n* ❶ (*owl call*) Schrei *m* ❷ (*outburst*) **to give a ~ of laughter** losprusten ▶ PHRASES: **to be a [real] ~** zum Brüllen sein **II.** *vi* ❶ *owl* schreien ❷ (*utter*) **to ~ with laughter** in johlendes Gelächter ausbrechen
hooter ['hu·t̬ər] *n* (*vulg*) ■**~s** *pl* (*woman's breasts*) Hupen *pl*
hop¹ [hap] **I.** *vi* <-pp-> ❶ (*jump*) hüpfen; *bunny* hoppeln ❷ SPORTS springen **II.** *vt* <-pp-> ❶ (*jump*) springen über +*akk* ❷ (*fam: board*) steigen in +*akk* **III.** *n* ❶ (*jump*) Hüpfer *m* ❷ (*fam: trip*) **[short] ~** [Katzen]sprung *m* ❸ (*fam: flight stage*) Flugabschnitt *m*
◆**hop in/on** *vi, vt* (*fam*) einsteigen
◆**hop off/out** *vi, vt* (*fam*) aussteigen
hop² *n* [hap] BOT ❶ (*vine*) Hopfen *m* ❷ (*in brewing*) ■**~s** *pl* [Hopfen]dolden *pl*
hope [hoʊp] **I.** *n* Hoffnung *f*; **I don't hold out much ~ of ...** ich habe nicht sehr viel Hoffnung, dass ...; **to give up ~** die Hoffnung aufgeben; **to live in ~** hoffen; **in the ~ of doing sth** in der Hoffnung, etw zu tun **II.** *vi* hoffen (**for** auf +*akk*); **it's good news, I ~** hoffentlich gute Nachrichten; **to ~ for the best** das Beste hoffen
hopeful ['hoʊp·fəl] **I.** *adj* zuversichtlich; ■**to be ~ of sth** auf etw *akk* hoffen **II.** *n usu pl* viel versprechende Personen *pl*
hopefully ['hoʊp·fəl·i] *adv* ❶ (*in hope*) hoffnungsvoll ❷ (*it is hoped*) hoffentlich
hopeless ['hoʊp·lɪs] *adj* hoffnungslos; *situation* aussichtslos; ■**to be ~** (*fam: incompetent*) ein hoffnungsloser Fall sein; **I'm ~ at cooking** wenn es um's Kochen geht, bin ich eine absolute Null
hopelessly ['hoʊp·lɪs·li] *adv* hoffnungslos; **he's ~ in love with her** er hat sich bis über beide Ohren in sie verliebt
hopping ['hap·ɪŋ] *adj* (*fam*) auf hundertachtzig; **to be ~ mad at sb** stinksauer auf jdn sein
hopscotch ['hap·skatʃ] *n* Himmel und Hölle *nt*
horde [hɔrd] *n* Horde *f*; **~s of fans** eine riesige Fangemeinde
horizon [hə·'raɪ·zən] *n* Horizont *m*; **on the ~** am Horizont; (*fig*) in Sicht
horizontal [ˌhɔr·ɪ·'zan·təl] **I.** *adj* horizontal, waag[e]recht **II.** *n* ■**the ~** die Horizontale
hormone ['hɔr·moʊn] *n* Hormon *nt*
horn [hɔrn] **I.** *n* ❶ ZOOL Horn *nt* ❷ MUS Horn *nt* ❸ AUTO Hupe *f* **II.** *vi* ■**to ~ in on sth** bei etw *dat* mitmischen
hornet ['hɔr·nɪt] *n* Hornisse *f*
'**horn-rimmed** *adj* **~ glasses** Hornbrille *f*
horny ['hɔr·ni] *adj* ❶ (*hard*) hornartig; (*of horn*) aus Horn *nach n* ❷ (*fam: sexually excited*) geil; **to feel ~** spitz sein
horoscope ['hɔr·ə·skoʊp] *n* Horoskop *nt*
horrendous [hɔ·'ren·dəs] *adj* schrecklich; *conditions* entsetzlich; *losses, prices* horrend
horrible ['hɔr·ə·bəl] *adj* schrecklich, furchtbar; *weather* scheußlich; (*unkind*) gemein

horrid ['hɔr·ɪd] *adj* fürchterlich; (*unkind*) gemein
horrific [hɔ·'rɪf·ɪk] *adj* ❶ (*shocking*) entsetzlich, grausig ❷ (*extreme*) *losses, prices* horrend
horrify <-ie-> ['hɔr·ə·faɪ] *vt* entsetzen
horror ['hɔr·ər] *n* (*feeling*) Entsetzen *nt,* Grauen *nt* (**at** über +*akk*); **in ~** entsetzt
hors d'oeuvre <*pl* - *or* -s> [ˌɔr·'dɜrv] *n* ❶ (*appetizer*) Hors d'oeuvre *nt* ❷ (*canapés*) Appetithäppchen *nt*
horse [hɔrs] *n* Pferd *nt;* **~ and buggy** Pferdewagen *m;* **to eat like a ~** fressen wie ein Scheunendrescher ▶ PHRASES: **to hear sth** [**straight**] **from the ~'s mouth** etw aus erster Hand haben; **you can lead a ~ to water, but you can't make him** [*or* **it**] **drink** (*prov*) man kann jdn nicht zu seinem Glück zwingen; **to beat** [*or* **flog**] **a dead ~** sich *dat* die Mühe sparen können; **to hold one's ~s** die Luft anhalten; **hey! hold your ~s! not so fast!** he, nun mal langsam, nicht so schnell!

H

'horseback *n* **on ~** zu Pferd
'horse chestnut *n* Rosskastanie *f*
'horse-drawn *adj* von Pferden gezogen; **~ carriage** Pferdekutsche *f*
'horsefly *n* [Pferde]bremse *f*
'horsehair *n* Rosshaar *nt*
'horseman *n* Reiter *m*
'horsemanship *n* Reitkunst *f*
'horseplay *n* wilde Ausgelassenheit
'horsepower <*pl* -> *n* Pferdestärke *f;* **a 10-~ engine** ein Motor *m* mit 10 PS
'horse race *n* Pferderennen *nt*
'horse racing *n* Pferderennsport *m*
'horseradish *n* Meerrettich *m*
'horseshoe *n* Hufeisen *nt*
'horse trailer, 'horse van *n* Pferdetransporter *m*
'horsewoman *n* Reiterin *f*
hors(e)y ['hɔr·si] *adj* (*fam*) ❶ (*devoted to horses*) pferdenärrisch ❷ (*pej: ugly*) pferdeähnlich
horticultural [ˌhɔr·t̬ɪ·'kʌl·tʃər·əl] *adj* Gartenbau-
horticulture ['hɔr·t̬ɪ·ˌkʌl·tʃər] *n* Gartenbau *m*
hose [hoʊz] *n* Schlauch *m*
◆**hose down, hose off** *vt* ■**to ~ sth** ⊂ **down** [*or* **off**] etw [mit einem Schlauch] abspritzen
hosiery ['hoʊ·ʒə·ri] *n* Strumpfwaren *pl*
hospice ['has·pɪs] *n* Hospiz *nt*
hospitable ['has·pɪ·t̬ə·bəl] *adj* ❶ (*friendly*) gastfreundlich ❷ (*pleasant*) angenehm
hospital ['has·pɪ·t̬əl] *n* Krankenhaus *nt,* Spital *nt* SCHWEIZ; **to have to go to the ~** ins Krankenhaus müssen
hospitality [ˌhas·pɪ·'tæl·ɪ·t̬i] **I.** *n* ❶ (*welcome*) Gastfreundschaft *f* ❷ (*food*) Bewirtung *f* **II.** *adj* **~ suite** Loge *f,* Veranstaltungsraum *m,* Hospitality Suite *f*
hospitalization [ˌhas·pɪ·t̬ə·lɪ·'zeɪ·ʃən] *n* ❶ (*admittance*) Krankenhauseinweisung *f* ❷ (*treatment*) Krankenhausaufenthalt *m*
hospitalize ['has·pɪ·t̬ə·laɪz] *vt* ❶ (*admit*) ■**to be ~d** ins Krankenhaus eingewiesen werden ❷ (*beat up*) ■**to ~ sb** jdn krankenhausreif schlagen
host[1] [hoʊst] **I.** *n* ❶ (*party giver*) Gastgeber(in) *m(f)* ❷ TV Showmaster(in) *m(f)* ❸ BIOL Wirt *m* ❹ COMPUT Hauptrechner *m* **II.** *adj* **~ country** Gastland *nt;* **~ family** Gastfamilie *f* **III.** *vt* ❶ (*stage*) ausrichten ❷ TV präsentieren, moderieren
host[2] [hoʊst] *n usu sing* ■**a** [**whole**] **~ of ...** jede Menge ...
hostage ['has·tɪdʒ] *n* Geisel *f;* **to take sb ~** jdn als Geisel nehmen
hostel ['has·təl] *n* Wohnheim *nt;* [**youth**] **~** Jugendherberge *f*
hostess <*pl* -es> ['hoʊ·stɪs] *n* ❶ (*at home, on TV*) Gastgeberin *f* ❷ (*at restaurant*) Wirtin *f* ❸ (*in nightclub*) Animierdame *f* ❹ (*at exhibition*) Hostess *f*
hostile ['has·təl] *adj* ❶ (*unfriendly*) feindselig ❷ (*difficult*) hart, widrig; *climate, environment* rau ❸ ECON, MIL feindlich
hostility [ha·'stɪl·ɪ·t̬i] *n* ❶ Feindseligkeit *f;* **to show ~ to**[**ward**] **sb** sich jdm gegenüber feindselig verhalten; **~ to technology** Technikfeindlichkeit *f* ❷ MIL ■**hostilities** *pl* Feindseligkeiten *pl*
hot [hat] **I.** *adj* <-tt-> ❶ (*temperature*) heiß; **she was ~** ihr war heiß ❷ (*spicy*) *food* scharf ❸ (*fam: good*) **my Spanish is not all that ~** mein Spanisch ist nicht gerade umwerfend; **~ tip** heißer Tipp ❹ (*fam: dangerous*) *situation* brenzlig; *stolen items* heiß; **to be too ~ to handle** ein heißes Eisen sein ❺ (*new and exciting*) heiß; **~ gossip** das Allerneueste ❻ (*sl: sexy*) echt geil ▶ PHRASES: **to be all ~ and bothered** ganz aufgeregt sein **II.** *n* ▶ PHRASES: **to have the ~s for sb** scharf auf jdn sein
hot-'air balloon *n* Heißluftballon *m*
'hotbed *n* (*fig*) **a ~ of crime** eine Brutstätte für Kriminalität
hot-'blooded *adj* (*easy to anger*) hitzköpfig; (*passionate*) heißblütig
'hot dog *n* (*sausage*) Wiener Würstchen *nt;* (*in a bun*) Hotdog *m*
hotel [hoʊ·'tel] *n* Hotel *nt*
hotel 'industry *n* Hotelgewerbe *nt*
'hotfoot *vt* (*fam*) **to ~ it home** schnell nach Hause rennen
'hothead *n* Hitzkopf *m*
hot'headed *adj* hitzköpfig
hot'headedness *n* Hitzigkeit *f*
'hothouse *n* ❶ (*for plants*) Treibhaus *nt* ❷ (*fig: for development*) fruchtbarer Boden
'hotline *n* Hotline *f;* POL heißer Draht
hotly ['hat·li] *adv* heftig; **~ contested** heiß umkämpft
'hotplate *n* (*for cooking*) Kochplatte *f;* (*food warmer*) Warmhalteplatte *f*
hot po'tato *n* POL (*fig*) heißes Eisen
'hotrod *n* (*fam*) hochfrisiertes Auto

'hot seat *n* ❶ (*fig*) Schleudersitz *m;* **to be in the ~** (*in the spotlight*) im Rampenlicht stehen ❷ (*sl*) elektrischer Stuhl
'hotshot *n* (*fam*) Kanone *f*
'hot spot *n* ❶ (*popular place*) heißer Schuppen ❷ (*area of conflict*) Krisenherd *m* ❸ COMPUT drahtloser Internetzugangspunkt
hot 'stuff *n* ❶ (*fam: skillful*) ■ **to be ~** ein Ass sein ❷ (*sl: sexy woman*) heiße Braut, Schnecke *f sl;* (*sexy man*) heißer Typ, Schmacko *m sl*
hot-'tempered *adj* heißblütig
'hot tub *n* Jacuzzi® *m*
hot-'water bottle *n* Wärmflasche *f*
'hot-wire *vt* (*fam*) *car* kurzschließen
hound [haʊnd] **I.** *n* [Jagd]hund *m* **II.** *vt* jagen
hour [aʊr] *n* Stunde *f;* **it's about 3 ~s' walk from here** von hier sind es etwa 3 Stunden zu Fuß; **24 ~s a day** 24 Stunden am Tag; **50 miles an** [*or* **per**] **~** 50 Meilen pro Stunde; **~s of business** Öffnungszeiten *pl;* **to be paid by the ~** pro Stunde bezahlt werden; **to work long ~s** lange arbeiten; **at all ~s** zu jeder Tages- und Nachtzeit; **for ~s** stundenlang
'hour hand *n* Stundenzeiger *m*
hourly ['aʊr·li] *adj, adv* stündlich; **~ rate** Stundensatz *m*
house I. *n* [haʊs] Haus *nt;* **Sam's playing at Mary's ~** Sam spielt bei Mary; **the White H~** das Weiße Haus; **to play to a full ~** THEAT vor vollem Haus spielen; **in ~** im Hause; **on the ~** auf Kosten des Hauses ▶ PHRASES: **to get along like a ~ on fire** ausgezeichnet miteinander auskommen **II.** *adj* [haʊs] Haus-; **~ red/white** Rot-/Weißwein *m* der Hausmarke **III.** *vt* [haʊz] *person* unterbringen; *criminal* Unterschlupf gewähren +*dat; thing* beherbergen; (*encase*) verkleiden
'house arrest *n* Hausarrest *m*
'houseboat *n* Hausboot *nt*
'housebreak *vt* stubenrein machen
'housebreaker *n* Einbrecher(in) *m(f)*
'housebreaking *n* Einbruch *m*
'housebroken *adj* stubenrein
'house call *n* Hausbesuch *m*
'housecoat *n* Hausmantel *m*
'housefly *n* Stubenfliege *f*
'household I. *n* Haushalt *m* **II.** *adj appliance* Haushalts-; *expenses, task, waste* häuslich; **~ goods** Hausrat *m;* **~ budget** Haushaltsgeld *nt*
'householder *n* Hauseigentümer(in) *m(f)*
'house-hunt *vi* nach einem Haus suchen
'househusband *n* Hausmann *m*
'housekeeper *n* Haushälter(in) *m(f)*
'housekeeping *n* ❶ (*act*) Haushalten *nt* ❷ (*cleaning personnel*) Reinigungspersonal *nt*
House of Repre'sentatives *n* ■ **the ~** das Repräsentantenhaus
'houseplant *n* Zimmerpflanze *f*
house-to-'house *adj, adv* von Haus zu Haus; **a ~ search** eine Fahndung von Haus zu Haus
'housewarming, 'housewarming party *n* Einweihungsparty *f*
'housewife *n* Hausfrau *f*
'housework *n* Hausarbeit *f*
housing ['haʊ·zɪŋ] *n* ❶ (*living quarters*) Wohnungen *pl* ❷ (*casing*) Gehäuse *nt*
'housing conditions *npl* Wohnbedingungen *pl*
'housing development *n* Wohnsiedlung *f*
'housing market *n* Wohnungsmarkt *m*
'housing project *n* Sozialwohnungen *pl*
HOV [ˌeɪtʃ·oʊ·'vi] *n* AUTO *abbrev of* **high occupancy vehicle** Fahrzeug *nt* mit mindestens zwei Insassen; **~ lane** Fahrspur *f* für Fahrzeuge mit mindestens zwei Insassen
hovel ['hʌv·əl] *n* armselige Hütte; (*fig*) Bruchbude *f*
hover ['hʌv·ər] *vi* ❶ (*stay in air*) schweben; *hawk a.* stehen ❷ (*fig: be near*) **the waiter ~ed over our table** der Kellner hing ständig an unserem Tisch herum; **to ~ in the background** sich im Hintergrund herumdrücken; **to ~ on the brink of disaster** am Rande des Ruins stehen
'hovercraft <*pl* - *or* -s> *n* Luftkissenboot *nt*
how [haʊ] **I.** *adv* wie; **~ are you?** wie geht es Ihnen?; **~'s work?** was macht die Arbeit?; **~'s that?** (*comfortable?*) wie ist das?; (*do you agree?*) passt das?; **~ do you do?** (*meeting sb*) Guten Tag/Abend!; **~ come?** wie das?; **~ do you know that?** woher weißt du das?; **~ about a movie?** wie wäre es mit Kino?; **and ~!** und ob [*o* wie]!; **~'s that for an excuse!** ist das nicht eine klasse Ausrede!; **~ far/many** wie weit/viele; **~ much** wie viel; **~ much is it?** wie viel [*o* was] kostet es? **II.** *n* **the ~**[**s**] **and why**[**s**] das Wie und Warum
howdy ['haʊ·di] *interj* (*fam*) Tag *fam*
however [haʊ·'ev·ər] **I.** *adv* ❶ (*showing contradiction*) jedoch; **I love ice cream —~, I am trying to lose weight, so ...** ich liebe Eis – ich versuche jedoch gerade abzunehmen, daher ... ❷ + *adj* (*to whatever degree*) egal wie ❸ (*by what means*) wie um alles ...; **~ did you manage to get so dirty?** wie hast du es bloß geschafft, so schmutzig zu werden? **II.** *conj* ❶ (*in any way*) wie auch immer; **~ you do it, ...** wie auch immer du es machst, ... ❷ (*nevertheless*) jedoch; **there may, ~, be other reasons** es mag jedoch auch andere Gründe geben
howl [haʊl] **I.** *n of animal, wind* Heulen *nt kein pl; of person* Geschrei *nt kein pl;* **~ of pain** Schmerzensschrei *m* **II.** *vi* ❶ *animal, wind* heulen; *person* schreien ❷ (*fam: laugh*) brüllen
howler ['haʊ·lər] *n* (*mistake*) Schnitzer *m*
howling ['haʊ·lɪŋ] **I.** *adj* ❶ *animal, wind* heulend; *person* schreiend ❷ (*fam: great*) riesig; **~ success** Riesenerfolg *m* **II.** *n of animal, wind* Heulen *nt; of person* Geschrei *nt*
hp [ˌeɪtʃ·'pi] *n abbrev of* **horsepower** PS; **a 4 ~ engine** ein Motor *m* mit 4 PS
HQ [ˌeɪtʃ·'kju] *n abbrev of* **headquarters**
HR *n abbrev of* **human resources** Personalab-

H

teilung *f*

hr. *n abbrev of* **hour** Std.

ht. *n abbrev of* **height**

hub [hʌb] *n* ① TECH Nabe *f* ② (*of airline*) Basis *f* ③ (*fig: center*) Zentrum *nt*

hubbub ['hʌb·ʌb] *n* (*noise*) Lärm *m;* (*commotion*) Tumult *m*

hubby ['hʌb·i] *n* (*hum fam*) [Ehe]mann *m*

hubcap ['hʌb·kæp] *n* Radkappe *f*

huckleberry ['hʌk·əl·ber·i] *n* amerikanische Heidelbeere

huddle ['hʌd·əl] **I.** *n* ① (*close group*) [wirrer] Haufen; *of people* Gruppe *f* ② (*in football*) **to make** [*or* **form**] **a ~** die Köpfe zusammenstecken **II.** *vi* sich [zusammen]drängen

◆**huddle together** *vi* sich zusammenkauern; **to ~ together for warmth** sich wärmesuchend aneinanderschmiegen

◆**huddle up** *vi* sich zusammenkauern

hue [hju] *n* Farbe *f;* (*shade*) Schattierung *f;* (*complexion*) Gesichtsfarbe *f* ▶ PHRASES: **~ and cry** Gezeter *nt*

huff [hʌf] **I.** *vi* **to ~ and puff** schnaufen und keuchen **II.** *n* (*fam*) **to be in a ~** eingeschnappt sein; **to go off in a ~** beleidigt abziehen

huffy ['hʌf·i] *adj* ① (*easily offended*) empfindlich ② (*in a huff*) beleidigt

hug [hʌg] **I.** *vt* <-gg-> ① (*with arms*) umarmen ② (*fig*) **the dress ~ged her body** das Kleid lag eng an ihrem Körper an; **to ~ the shore** sich dicht an der Küste halten **II.** *vi* <-gg-> sich umarmen **III.** *n* Umarmung *f;* **to give sb a ~** jdn umarmen

huge [hjudʒ] *adj* ① (*big*) riesig; **~ success** Riesenerfolg *m* ② (*impressive*) gewaltig; *costs* immens

hugely ['hjudʒ·li] *adv* ungeheuer

hulk [hʌlk] *n* ① (*ship*) alter [Schiffs]rumpf; (*car*) Wrack *nt;* (*building*) Ruine *f* ② (*person*) Brocken *m*

hulking ['hʌl·kɪŋ] *adj* massig; (*clumsy*) ungeschlacht

hull [hʌl] *n* [Schiffs]rumpf *m*

hum [hʌm] **I.** *vi* <-mm-> ① (*make sound*) brausen; *engine* brummen; *small machine* surren; *bee* summen; *crowd* murmeln ② (*fig*) voller Leben sein ③ (*sing*) summen **II.** *vt* <-mm-> summen **III.** *n* Brausen *nt; of machinery* Brummen *nt; of insects* Summen *nt; of a conversation* Gemurmel *nt; of a small machine* Surren *nt*

human ['hju·mən] **I.** *n* Mensch *m* **II.** *adj* menschlich; **~ relationships** die Beziehungen *pl* des Menschen

humane [hju·'meɪn] *adj* human

humanitarian [hju·ˌmæn·ɪ·'ter·i·ən] **I.** *n* Menschenfreund(in) *m(f)* **II.** *adj* humanitär

humanities [hju·'mæn·ɪ·tiz] *npl* ■**the ~** die Geisteswissenschaften *pl*

humanity [hju·'mæn·ɪ·t̬i] *n* ① (*people*) die Menschheit; **crimes against ~** Verbrechen *pl* gegen die Menschheit ② (*quality*) Menschlichkeit *f;* **to treat sb with ~** jdn human behandeln

humanize ['hju·mə·naɪz] *vt* ① (*make acceptable*) humanisieren ② (*give human character*) vermenschlichen

humanly ['hju·mən·li] *adv* menschlich; **to do everything ~ possible** alles Menschenmögliche tun

human 'nature *n* die menschliche Natur

human 'race *n* ■**the ~** die menschliche Rasse

human 'resources *npl* ① + *sing vb* (*department*) Personalabteilung *f* ② (*staff*) Arbeitskräfte *pl*

human 'rights *npl* Menschenrechte *pl*

humble ['hʌm·bəl] **I.** *adj* <-r, -st> ① (*modest*) bescheiden; **of ~ birth** von niedriger Geburt ② (*respectful*) demütig **II.** *vt* ■**to be ~d by sth** durch etw *akk* gedemütigt werden

humbug ['hʌm·bʌg] *n* Humbug *m*

humdrum ['hʌm·drʌm] *adj* langweilig, fad[e]

humid ['hju·mɪd] *adj* feucht

humidifier [hju·'mɪd·ɪ·faɪ·ər] *n* Luftbefeuchter *m*

humidify <-ie-> [hju·'mɪd·ɪ·faɪ] *vt* befeuchten

humidity [hju·'mɪd·ɪ·t̬i] *n* [Luft]feuchtigkeit *f*

humiliate [hju·'mɪl·i·eɪt] *vt* ① (*humble*) demütigen ② (*embarrass*) blamieren

humiliating [hju·'mɪl·i·eɪ·t̬ɪŋ] *adj* erniedrigend; *defeat, experience* demütigend

humiliation [hju·ˌmɪl·i·'eɪ·ʃən] *n* Demütigung *f*

humility [hju·'mɪl·ɪ·t̬i] *n* Demut *f;* (*modesty*) Bescheidenheit *f*

humor ['hju·mər] **I.** *n* Humor *m;* **his speech was full of ~** seine Rede war voller Witz **II.** *vt* ■**to ~ sb** (*indulge*) jdm seinen Willen lassen; (*keep happy*) jdn bei Laune halten *fam*

humorist ['hju·mər·ɪst] *n* Humorist(in) *m(f)*

humorless ['hju·mər·lɪs] *adj* humorlos

humorous ['hju·mər·əs] *adj person* humorvoll; *book, program, situation* lustig; *idea, thought* witzig

hump [hʌmp] **I.** *n* ① (*hill*) kleiner Hügel; (*in street*) Buckel *m* ② (*on camel*) Höcker *m;* (*on a person*) Buckel *m* ▶ PHRASES: **to be over the ~** über den Berg sein **II.** *vt* (*vulg, sl: have sex with*) bumsen

'humpback *n* ① (*person*) Buck[e]lige(r) *f(m)* ② (*back*) Buckel *m* ③ (*whale*) Buckelwal *m*

'humpbacked *adj person* bucklig; *bridge* gewölbt

Hun [hʌn] *n* HIST Hunne *m,* Hunnin *f*

hunch [hʌntʃ] **I.** *n* <*pl* -es> ① (*feeling*) Gefühl *nt;* **to have a ~ that ...** das [leise] Gefühl haben, dass ... ② (*hump*) Buckel *m* **II.** *vi* sich krümmen **III.** *vt shoulders* hochziehen; **to ~ one's back** einen Buckel machen

'hunchback *n* ① (*person*) Bucklige(r) *f(m)* ② (*back*) Buckel *m*

hundred ['hʌn·drəd] **I.** *n* ① <*pl* -> (*number*) Hundert *f;* **~s of cars** Hunderte von Autos; **~s and ~s** Hunderte und aber Hunderte; **eight ~** achthundert ② <*pl* -> (*miles per hour*) **to**

drive a ~ hundert fahren ③ (*with centuries*) **the eighteen ~s** das neunzehnte Jahrhundert **II.** *adj* hundert; **a ~ miles** [ein]hundert Meilen; **a ~ percent** hundertprozentig; **a ~ and five** [ein]hundert[und]fünf

'hundredfold *adv* hundertfach; **sales have increased a ~** der Verkauf ist um das Hundertfache gestiegen

hundredth ['hʌn·drədθ] **I.** *n* ① (*in line*) Hundertste(r) *f(m)* ② (*fraction*) Hundertstel *nt* **II.** *adj* ① (*in series*) hundertste(r, s); **for the ~ time** zum hundertsten Mal ② (*in fraction*) hundertstel

hung [hʌŋ] **I.** *pt, pp of* **hang II.** *adj* **~ jury** *Jury, die zu keinem Mehrheitsurteil kommt*

Hungarian [hʌŋ·'ger·i·ən] **I.** *n* ① (*person*) Ungar(in) *m(f)* ② (*language*) Ungarisch *nt* **II.** *adj* ungarisch

Hungary ['hʌŋ·gə·ri] *n* Ungarn *nt*

hunger ['hʌŋ·gər] **I.** *n* Hunger *m a. fig;* **to die of ~** verhungern **II.** *vi* ■**to ~ after** [*or* **for**] **sth** nach etw *dat* hungern

hung 'over *adj* (*from drinking*) verkatert

hungry ['hʌŋ·gri] *adj* hungrig *a. fig;* **to go ~** hungern; ■**to be ~** Hunger haben; **~ for power** machthungrig; **~ for knowledge** wissensdurstig

hunk [hʌŋk] *n* ① (*piece*) Stück *nt* ② (*fam: man*) **a ~ of a man** ein Bild *nt* von einem Mann

hunky-dory [-'dɔ·ri] *adj* (*fam*) prima

hunt [hʌnt] **I.** *n* ① (*chase*) Jagd *f* ② (*search*) Suche *f;* **on the ~ for sb/sth** auf der Suche nach jdm/etw sein **II.** *vt* ① (*chase to kill*) jagen ② (*search for*) Jagd machen auf *+akk;* **the police are ~ing the terrorists** die Polizei fahndet nach den Terroristen **III.** *vi* ① (*chase to kill*) jagen ② (*search*) suchen; ■**to ~ through sth** etw durchsuchen

hunter ['hʌn·tər] *n* (*person*) Jäger(in) *m(f)*

hunting ['hʌn·tɪŋ] *n* ① HUNT Jagen *nt,* Jagd *f;* **to go ~** auf die Jagd gehen ② (*search*) Suche *f*

'hunting ground *n* Jagdrevier *nt*

'hunting license *n* Jagdschein *m*

'hunting season *n* Jagdzeit *f*

'huntsman *n* Jäger *m*

hurdle ['hɜr·dəl] **I.** *n* Hürde *f a. fig;* SPORTS ■**~s** *pl* (*for people*) Hürdenlauf *m;* **the American won the 400 meter ~s** der Amerikaner siegte über 400 Meter Hürden **II.** *vt* überspringen

hurdler ['hɜrd·lər] *n* Hürdenläufer(in) *m(f)*

hurl [hɜrl] **I.** *vt* schleudern; **to ~ abuse at sb** jdm Beschimpfungen an den Kopf werfen; **to ~ oneself into sth** sich in etw *+akk* stürzen **II.** *vi* (*sl*) kotzen

hurly-burly ['hɜr·li·bɜr·li] *n* Rummel *m*

hurrah [hə·'ra], **hurray** [hə·'reɪ] *interj* hurra

hurricane ['hɜr·ɪ·keɪn] *n* Orkan *m;* (*tropical*) Hurrikan *m;* **~-force wind** orkanartiger Wind

hurried ['hɜr·id] *adj* hastig; *departure* überstürzt

hurry ['hɜr·i] **I.** *n* Eile *f;* **what's [all] the ~?** wozu die Eile?; **there's no [big] ~** es hat keine Eile, es eilt nicht; **to leave in a ~** hastig aufbrechen; **to need sth in a ~** etw sofort brauchen **II.** *vi* <-ie-> sich beeilen; **there's no need to ~** lassen Sie sich ruhig Zeit **III.** *vt* <-ie-> ■**to ~ sb** jdn hetzen

◆**hurry along I.** *vi* sich beeilen **II.** *vt person* [zur Eile] antreiben; *process* beschleunigen

◆**hurry away, hurry off I.** *vi* schnell weggehen **II.** *vt* schnell wegbringen

◆**hurry out I.** *vi* hinauseilen **II.** *vt* schnell hinausbringen

◆**hurry up I.** *vi* sich beeilen; **~ up!** beeil dich! **II.** *vt person* zur Eile antreiben; *process* beschleunigen

hurt [hɜrt] **I.** *vi* <hurt, hurt> ① (*be painful*) wehtun ② (*do harm*) schaden *a. fig* **II.** *vt* <hurt, hurt> ① (*a. fig: cause pain*) ■**to ~ sb** jdm wehtun; (*injure*) jdn verletzen; **she was ~ by his refusal to apologize** dass er sich absolut nicht entschuldigen wollte, hat sie gekränkt; ■**to ~ oneself** sich verletzen; **to ~ one's leg** sich *dat* am Bein wehtun ② (*harm*) ■**to ~ sb/sth** jdm/etw schaden; **to ~ sb's pride** jds Stolz verletzen **III.** *adj* ① (*in pain*) verletzt ② (*fig*) *feelings* verletzt; *look, voice* gekränkt **IV.** *n* (*pain*) Schmerz *m;* (*injury*) Verletzung *f;* (*fig*) Kränkung *f*

hurtful ['hɜrt·fəl] *adj* verletzend

hurtle ['hɜr·təl] *vi* rasen

husband ['hʌz·bənd] *n* Ehemann *m;* **~ and wife** Mann und Frau

hush [hʌʃ] **I.** *n* Stille *f* **II.** *interj* ■**~!** pst! **III.** *vt* zum Schweigen bringen; (*soothe*) beruhigen

◆**hush up** *vt* vertuschen

hush-'hush *adj* (*fam*) [streng] geheim

'hush money *n* (*fam*) Schweigegeld *nt*

husk [hʌsk] **I.** *n* Schale *f; of corn* Hüllblatt *nt* **II.** *vt corn* schälen

husky¹ ['hʌs·ki] *adj* ① *voice* rau ② *person* kräftig [gebaut]

husky² ['hʌs·ki] *n* (*dog*) Husky *m,* Schlittenhund *m*

hussy ['hʌs·i] *n* (*pej, hum*) Flittchen *nt*

hustle ['hʌs·əl] **I.** *vt* ① (*hurry*) ■**to ~ sb somewhere** jdn irgendwohin treiben ② (*coerce*) ■**to ~ sb into doing sth** jdn [be]drängen, etw zu tun **II.** *vi* ① (*work quickly*) schnell erledigen; **to ~ for business** sich fürs Geschäft ins Zeug legen ② SPORTS (*play aggressively*) stoßen *fam* **III.** *n* Gedränge *nt;* **~ and bustle** geschäftiges Treiben

hustler ['hʌs·lər] *n* ① (*swindler*) Betrüger(in) *m(f)* ② (*prostitute*) Strichjunge *m,* Strichmädchen *nt*

'hustling *n* (*prostitution*) [Straßen]prostitution *f*

hut [hʌt] *n* Hütte *f*

hutch [hʌtʃ] *n* Käfig *m;* (*for rabbits*) Stall *m*

hybrid ['haɪ·brɪd] **I.** *n* ① BOT, ZOOL Kreuzung *f* ② AUTO Hybrid *m* **II.** *adj* ① BOT, ZOOL Misch-, hybrid ② AUTO hybrid, Hybrid-; **~ powertrain** Hybridantrieb *m;* **~ electric vehicle** Hybridauto *nt*

hydrant [ˈhaɪ·drənt] *n* Hydrant *m*

hydraulic [haɪ·ˈdra·lɪk] *adj inv* hydraulisch

hydraulics [haɪ·ˈdra·lɪks] *n + sing vb* Hydraulik *f*

hydrocarbon [ˌhaɪ·drə·ˈkar·bən] *n* Kohlenwasserstoff *m*

hydroelectric [ˌhaɪ·droʊ·ɪ·ˈlek·trɪk] *adj* hydroelektrisch; ~ **power plant** Wasserkraftwerk *nt*

hydrofoil [ˈhaɪ·drə·fɔɪl] *n* Tragflächenboot *nt*

hydrogen [ˈhaɪ·drə·dʒən] *n* Wasserstoff *m;* ~ **bomb** Wasserstoffbombe *f*

hydroponics [ˌhaɪ·drə·ˈpan·ɪks] *n + sing vb* BOT Hydrokultur *f*

hyena [haɪ·ˈi·nə] *n* Hyäne *f*

hygiene [ˈhaɪ·dʒin] *n* Hygiene *f;* **personal ~** Körperpflege *f*

hygienic [ˌhaɪ·dʒi·ˈen·ɪk] *adj* hygienisch

H

hymn [hɪm] *n* ❶ REL Kirchenlied *nt* ❷ (*praise*) Hymne *f*

hymnal [ˈhɪm·nəl], **hymnbook** [ˈhɪm·bʌk] *n* Gesangbuch *nt*

hype [haɪp] **I.** *n* Reklameaufwand *m;* (*deception*) Werbemasche *f;* **media ~** Medienrummel *m* **II.** *vt book, film* [in den Medien] hochjubeln

hyper [ˈhaɪ·pər] *adj* (*fam*) aufgedreht, hyper *sl*

hyperactive [ˌhaɪ·pər·ˈæk·tɪv] *adj* hyperaktiv

hyperbola [haɪ·ˈpɜr·bə·lə] *n* MATH Hyperbel *f*

hyperbole [haɪ·ˈpɜr·bə·li] *n* LIT Hyperbel *f*

hyperˈsensitive *adj* überempfindlich; ■ **to be ~ to sth** auf etw *akk* überempfindlich reagieren

hyphen [ˈhaɪ·fən] *n* (*between words*) Bindestrich *m;* (*at end of line*) Trennstrich *m*

hyphenate [ˈhaɪ·fə·neɪt] *vt* mit Bindestrich schreiben

hypnosis [hɪp·ˈnoʊ·sɪs] *n* Hypnose *f;* ■ **to be under ~** sich in Hypnose befinden

hypnotherapy [ˌhɪp·noʊ·ˈθer·ə·pi] *n* MED Hypnotherapie *f*

hypnotic [hɪp·ˈnaṭ·ɪk] *adj* (*causing hypnosis*) hypnotisierend; (*referring to hypnosis*) hypnotisch

hypnotist [ˈhɪp·nə·tɪst] *n* Hypnotiseur(in) *m(f)*

hypnotize [ˈhɪp·nə·taɪz] *vt* hypnotisieren *a. fig*

hypochondria [ˌhaɪ·pə·ˈkan·dri·ə] *n* Hypochondrie *f*

hypochondriac [ˌhaɪ·pə·ˈkan·drɪ·æk] *n* Hypochonder(in) *m(f)*

hypocrisy [hɪ·ˈpak·rə·si] *n* Heuchelei *f,* Scheinheiligkeit *f*

hypocrite [ˈhɪp·ə·krɪt] *n* Heuchler(in) *m(f),* Scheinheilige(r) *f(m)*

hypocritical [ˌhɪp·ə·ˈkrɪṭ·ɪ·kəl] *adj* heuchlerisch, scheinheilig

hypodermic [ˌhaɪ·pə·ˈdɜr·mɪk] *adj* subkutan; ~ **syringe** Injektionsspritze *f*

hypotenuse [ˌhaɪ·ˈpat·ə·nus] *n* MATH Hypotenuse *f*

hypothermia [ˌhaɪ·poʊ·ˈθɜr·mi·ə] *n* Unterkühlung *f*

hypothesis <*pl* -ses> [haɪ·ˈpaθ·ɪ·sɪs] *n* Hypothese *f*

hypothetical [ˌhaɪ·pə·ˈθeṭ·ɪ·kəl] *adj* hypothetisch

hysterectomy [ˌhɪs·tə·ˈrek·tə·mi] *n* MED Hysterektomie *f*

hysteria [hɪ·ˈster·i·ə] *n* Hysterie *f*

hysteric [hɪ·ˈster·ɪk] *adj* hysterisch

hysterical [hɪ·ˈster·ɪk·əl] *adj* ❶ (*emotional*) hysterisch ❷ (*fam: hilarious*) ausgelassen heiter

I

I[1] *<pl* -'s *or* -s>, **i** *<pl* -'s> [aɪ] *n* (*letter*) I *nt,* i *nt;* **~ as in India** I wie Ida
I[2] [aɪ] *pron personal* ich; **~ for one ...** ich meinerseits ...
IA, Ia. *abbrev of* **Iowa**
ibex *<pl* -es> ['aɪ·beks] *n* Steinbock *m*
ice [aɪs] **I.** *n* Eis *nt* ▸PHRASES: **to break the ~** das Eis zum Schmelzen bringen; **to put sth on ~** etw auf Eis legen **II.** *vt* glasieren ◆**ice over** *vi road* vereisen; *lake* zufrieren
'Ice Age *n* Eiszeit *f*
'iceberg *n* Eisberg *m*
'icebound *adj ship* eingefroren; *harbor* zugefroren
'icebox *n* Kühlschrank *m*
'icebreaker *n* ① (*ship*) Eisbrecher *m* ② (*entertainment*) *Spiel zur Auflockerung der Atmosphäre*
'ice cap *n* Eiskappe *f* (*an den Polen*)
ice-'cold *n* eiskalt
'ice cream *n* Eiscreme *f*
'ice-cream maker *n* Eismaschine *f*
'ice cube *n* Eiswürfel *m*
iced [aɪst] *adj inv* ① (*frozen*) eisgekühlt ② *cake* glasiert
'ice floe *n* Eisscholle *f*
'ice hockey *n* Eishockey *nt*
Iceland ['aɪs·lənd] *n* Island *nt*
Icelander ['aɪs·lən·dər] *n* Isländer(in) *m(f)*
Icelandic [aɪs·'læn·dɪk] **I.** *n* Isländisch *nt* **II.** *adj* isländisch
'ice pack *n* ① (*for swelling*) Eisbeutel *m* ② (*sea ice*) Packeis *nt*
'ice pick *n* Eispickel *m*
'ice rink *n* Schlittschuhbahn *f,* Eisbahn *f*
'ice skate *n* Schlittschuh *m*
'ice-skate *vi* Schlittschuh laufen, eislaufen
'ice skating *n* Schlittschuhlaufen *nt*
icicle ['aɪ·sɪ·kəl] *n* Eiszapfen *m*
icing ['aɪ·sɪŋ] *n* Zuckerguss *m* ▸PHRASES: **to be the ~ on the cake** (*pej: unnecessary*) [bloß] schmückendes Beiwerk sein; (*approv: unexpected extra*) das Sahnehäubchen sein *fam*
icon ['aɪ·kan] *n* ① (*painting*) Ikon *nt* ② COMPUT Symbol *nt,* Icon *nt*
icy ['aɪ·si] *adj* ① (*cold*) eisig [kalt]; *road* vereist ② (*hostile*) frostig
ID[1] [ˌaɪ·'di] *n abbrev of* **identification** Ausweis *m*
ID[2], **Id.** *n abbrev of* **Idaho**
I'd [aɪd] = **I would, I had** *see* **would, have I., II.**
Idaho ['aɪ·də·hoʊ] *n* Idaho *nt*
I'D card *n* [Personal]ausweis *m*
idea [aɪ·'di·ə] *n* ① (*notion*) Vorstellung *f;* **what gave you that ~?** wie kommst du denn [bloß] darauf? [*o* auf die Idee?]; **don't get any ~s** (*fam*) komm nicht auf dumme Gedanken!; **don't give him any ~s** (*fam*) bring ihn nicht auf dumme Gedanken! ② (*suggestion*) Idee *f;* **to toy with the ~ of doing sth** mit der Idee spielen, etw zu tun ③ (*knowledge*) Begriff *m;* **to have an ~ of sth** eine Vorstellung von etw *dat* haben; **to have no ~** keine Ahnung haben
ideal [aɪ·'di·əl] **I.** *adj inv* ideal **II.** *n* Ideal *nt*
idealism [aɪ·'di·ə·lɪz·əm] *n* Idealismus *m*
idealist [aɪ·'di·ə·lɪst] *n* Idealist(in) *m(f)*
idealistic [ˌaɪ·di·ə·'lɪs·tɪk] *adj* idealistisch
idealize [aɪ·'di·ə·laɪz] *vt* idealisieren
ideally [aɪ·'di·li] *adv inv* ① idealerweise ② (*perfectly*) genau richtig
identical [aɪ·'den·tɪ·kəl] *adj* identisch (**to** mit +*dat*)
identifiable [aɪ·ˌden·tə·'faɪ·ə·bəl] *adj* erkennbar; *substance* nachweisbar
identification [aɪ·ˌden·tə·fɪ·'keɪ·ʃən] *n* ① *of person, criminal* Identifizierung *f; of problem, goals* Identifikation *f;* (*of virus, plant*) Bestimmung *f* ② (*sympathy*) Identifikation *f* (**with** mit +*dat*)
identifi'cation papers *npl* Ausweispapiere *pl*
identify <-ie-> [aɪ·'den·tə·faɪ] **I.** *vt* ① (*recognize*) identifizieren ② (*name*) ▪**to ~ sb** jds Identität *f* feststellen **II.** *vi* ▪**to ~ with sb** sich mit jdm identifizieren; ▪**to be identified with sth** mit etw *dat* in Verbindung gebracht werden
identity [aɪ·'den·tə·t̬i] *n* Identität *f*
i'dentity card *n* [Personal]ausweis *m*
ideological [ˌaɪ·di·ə·'ladʒ·ɪ·kəl] *adj* ideologisch
ideology [ˌaɪ·di·'al·ə·dʒi] *n* Ideologie *f*
idiom ['ɪd·i·əm] *n* LING ① (*phrase*) [idiomatische] Redewendung ② (*language*) Idiom *nt;* (*dialect*) Dialekt *m*
idiomatic [ˌɪd·i·ə·'mæt̬·ɪk] *adj* idiomatisch
idiot ['ɪd·i·ət] *n* Idiot(in) *m(f)*
idiotic [ˌɪd·i·'at̬·ɪk] *adj* idiotisch; *idea* hirnverbrannt
idle ['aɪ·dəl] **I.** *adj* ① (*lazy*) faul ② (*inactive*) *people* untätig; *moment* müßig; *machine* außer Betrieb *präd* ③ (*unfounded*) *chatter* hohl; *fears* unbegründet; *rumors* rein; *threats* leer **II.** *vi engine* leerlaufen
idleness ['aɪ·dəl·nɪs] *n* Müßiggang *m;* (*inactivity*) Untätigkeit *f*
idol ['aɪ·dəl] *n* ① (*model*) Idol *nt* ② REL Götzenbild *nt*
idolatry [aɪ·'dal·ə·tri] *n* Götzenanbetung *f;* (*fig*) Vergötterung *f*
idolize ['aɪ·də·laɪz] *vt* vergöttern
idyllic [aɪ·'dɪl·ɪk] *adj* idyllisch
i.e. [ˌaɪ·'i] *n abbrev of* **id est** d.h.
if [ɪf] **I.** *conj* ① (*in case*) wenn, falls; **even ~ ...** selbst [dann,] wenn ...; ▪**~ ..., then ...** wenn ..., dann ... ② (*whether*) ob ③ (*although*) wenn auch ▸PHRASES: **barely/hardly/rarely ... ~ at all** kaum ..., wenn

überhaupt; ~ <u>**ever**</u> wenn [überhaupt] je[mals] **II.** *n* Wenn *nt;* **there's a big ~ hanging over the project** über diesem Projekt steht noch ein großes Fragezeichen ► PHRASES: **no ~s, ands, or <u>buts</u>** kein Wenn und Aber *fam*
iffy ['ɪf·i] *adj* (*fam*) ungewiss
igloo ['ɪg·lu] *n* Iglu *m o nt*
ignite [ɪg·'naɪt] **I.** *vi* Feuer fangen; ELEC zünden **II.** *vt* (*form*) anzünden; (*arouse*) entfachen
ignition [ɪg·'nɪʃ·ən] *n* Zündung *f*
ig'nition key *n* Zündschlüssel *m*
ig'nition switch <-es> *n* Zündschalter *m*
ignoble [ɪg·'noʊ·bəl] *adj* schändlich
ignominy ['ɪg·nə·mɪn·i] *n* Schande *f*
ignoramus [ˌɪg·nə·'reɪ·məs] *n* Ignorant(in) *m(f)*
ignorance ['ɪg·nər·əns] *n* Unwissenheit *f* (**about** über *+akk*)
ignorant ['ɪg·nər·ənt] *adj* unwissend; ■ **to be ~ about** [*or* **of**] **sth** von etw *dat* keine Ahnung haben *fam*
ignore [ɪg·'nɔr] *vt* ignorieren
iguana [ɪ·'gwa·nə] *n* Leguan *m*
IL *abbrev of* **Illinois**
ill [ɪl] **I.** *adj inv* ① (*sick*) krank; **to be critically ~** in Lebensgefahr schweben ② (*bad*) schlecht; (*harmful*) schädlich; (*unfavorable*) unerfreulich; *effects* negativ; **~ health** angegriffene Gesundheit **II.** *adv inv* (*badly*) schlecht; **to bode ~** nichts Gutes verheißen; **to speak ~ of sb** schlecht über jdn sprechen
Ill. *abbrev of* **Illinois**
I'll [aɪl] = **I will** *see* **will**
ill-ad'vised *adj* unklug
ill at 'ease *adj* unbehaglich
ill-con'ceived *adj* schlecht durchdacht
illegal [ɪ·'li·gəl] **I.** *adj* illegal **II.** *n* Illegale(r) *f(m)*
illegal 'immigrant *n* illegaler Einwanderer/illegale Einwanderin
illegality [ˌɪl·ɪ·'gæl·ə·t̬i] *n* Illegalität *f*
illegible [ɪ·'ledʒ·ə·bəl] *adj* unleserlich
illegitimate [ˌɪl·ɪ·'dʒɪt̬·ɪ·mət] *adj inv* ① *child* unehelich ② (*unauthorized*) unrechtmäßig
ill-e'quipped *adj* schlecht ausgestattet; ■ **to be ~ to do sth** für etw *akk* nicht die nötigen Mittel haben; (*unable*) nicht über die notwendigen Kenntnisse verfügen, um etw tun zu können
ill-'fitting *adj* schlecht sitzend *attr*
ill-'gotten *adj attr* unrechtmäßig erworben
illicit [ɪ·'lɪs·ɪt] *adj* [gesetzlich] verboten
ill-in'formed *adj* falsch informiert; (*ignorant*) schlecht informiert
Illinois [ˌɪl·ə·'nɔɪ] *n* Illinois *nt*
illiteracy [ɪ·'lɪt̬·ər·ə·si] *n* Analphabetismus *m*
illiterate [ɪ·'lɪt̬·ər·ɪt] **I.** *adj* des Lesens und Schreibens unkundig; ■ **to be ~** Analphabet/Analphabetin sein **II.** *n* Analphabet(in) *m(f)*
illness ['ɪl·nɪs] *n* Krankheit *f*
illogical [ɪ·'ladʒ·ɪ·kəl] *adj* unlogisch
illogicality [ɪ·ˌladʒ·ɪ·'kæl·ɪ·t̬i] *n* Mangel *m* an Logik
ill-'tempered *adj* (*at times*) schlecht gelaunt; (*by nature*) mürrisch
ill-'timed *adj* ungelegen
ill-'treat *vt* misshandeln
ill-'treatment *n* Misshandlung *f*
illuminate [ɪ·'lu·mə·neɪt] *vt* erhellen; (*spotlight*) beleuchten; (*fig*) erläutern
illuminating [ɪ·'lu·mə·neɪ·t̬ɪŋ] *adj* aufschlussreich
illumination [ɪ·ˌlu·mə·'neɪ·ʃən] *n* Beleuchtung *f*
illusion [ɪ·'lu·ʒən] *n* Illusion *f;* **to create the ~ of sth** die Illusion von etw *dat* hervorrufen
illusive [ɪ·'lu·sɪv], **illusory** [ɪ·'lu·sə·ri] *adj* ① (*deceptive*) illusorisch ② (*imaginary*) imaginär
illustrate ['ɪl·ə·streɪt] *vt* ① illustrieren ② (*fig: explain*) aufzeigen
illustration [ˌɪl·ə·'streɪ·ʃən] *n* ① Illustration *f* ② (*fig: example*) Beispiel *nt* ③ ART (*in books*) Buchmalerei *f*
illustrator ['ɪl·ə·streɪ·t̬ər] *n* Illustrator(in) *m(f)*
illustrious [ɪ·'lʌs·tri·əs] *adj person* berühmt; *deed* glanzvoll
ill 'will *n* Feindseligkeit *f;* **to bear sb ~** einen Groll auf jdn haben
I'm [aɪm] = **I am** *see* **be**
image ['ɪm·ɪdʒ] *n* ① (*likeness*) Ebenbild *nt* ② (*picture*) Bild *nt;* (*sculpture*) Skulptur *f* ③ (*mental picture*) Vorstellung *f* ④ (*reputation*) Image *nt*
imagery ['ɪm·ɪdʒ·ri] *n* LIT Bildersprache *f*
imaginable [ɪ·'mædʒ·ə·nə·bəl] *adj* erdenklich
imaginary [ɪ·'mædʒ·ə·ner·i] *adj* imaginär
imagination [ɪ·ˌmædʒ·ə·'neɪ·ʃən] *n* Fantasie *f;* **not by any stretch of the ~** beim besten Willen nicht
imaginative [ɪ·'mædʒ·ə·nə·t̬ɪv] *adj* fantasievoll
imagine [ɪ·'mædʒ·ɪn] *vt* ① ■ **to ~ sb/sth** sich *dat* jdn/etw vorstellen ② (*suppose*) sich *dat* denken; **I can't ~ what you mean** ich weiß wirklich nicht, was du meinst ③ (*suffer illusion*) glauben ► PHRASES: **~ <u>that!</u>** stell dir das mal vor!
imaging ['ɪm·ɪdʒ·ɪŋ] *n* COMPUT digitale Bildverarbeitung
imbalance [ˌɪm·'bæl·əns] *n* Ungleichgewicht *nt*
imbecile ['ɪm·bə·sɪl] *n* (*fam*) Idiot(in) *m(f) pej fam*
IMF [ˌaɪ·em·'ef] *n abbrev of* **International Monetary Fund:** ■ **the ~** der IWF
imitate ['ɪm·ɪ·teɪt] *vt* imitieren; *style* kopieren
imitation [ˌɪm·ɪ·'teɪ·ʃən] **I.** *n* ① (*mimicry*) Imitation *f* ② (*copy*) Kopie *f* **II.** *adj leather, silk* Kunst-; *pearl, gold, silver* unecht
imitative ['ɪm·ɪ·teɪ·t̬ɪv] *adj* ① (*copying*) imitierend ② (*onomatopoeic*) lautmalerisch
imitator ['ɪm·ɪ·teɪ·t̬ər] *n* Nachahmer(in) *m(f); of voices* Imitator(in) *m(f)*
immaculate [ɪ·'mæk·jʊ·lət] *adj* (*neat*) makellos; (*flawless*) perfekt; *lawn* säuberlich gepflegt
immaterial [ˌɪm·ə·'tɪr·i·əl] *adj inv* unwesent-

lich

immature [ˌɪm·ə·ˈtʃʊr] *adj* ❶ *person* unreif; (*childish*) kindisch *meist pej* ❷ (*undeveloped*) unreif; (*sexually*) nicht geschlechtsreif; *plan* unausgereift

immaturity [ˌɪm·ə·ˈtʃʊr·ə·t̬i] *n* Unreife *f*

immeasurable [ɪ·ˈmeʒ·ər·ə·bəl] *adj inv* (*limitless*) grenzenlos; (*great*) *influence* riesig; *effect* gewaltig

immediate [ɪ·ˈmi·di·ɪt] *adj* ❶ umgehend; *consequences* unmittelbar; **to take ~ effect** augenblicklich wirken ❷ *attr* (*close*) unmittelbar; **sb's ~ family** jds nächste Angehörige; **sb's ~ friends** jds engste Freunde ❸ (*current*) unmittelbar; *concerns, problems, needs* dringend

immediately [ɪ·ˈmi·di·ɪt·li] *adv* ❶ (*at once*) sofort, gleich ❷ (*closely*) direkt, unmittelbar

immemorial [ˌɪm·ə·ˈmɔr·i·əl] *adj inv* uralt; **from time ~** seit Urzeiten

immense [ɪ·ˈmens] *adj inv* riesig, enorm

immensely [ɪ·ˈmens·li] *adv inv* extrem, ungeheuer; *important* immens

immensity [ɪ·ˈmen·sə·t̬i] *n* ❶ Größe *f* ❷ *usu pl* (*boundlessness*) Endlosigkeit *f kein pl*

immerse [ɪ·ˈmɜrs] *vt* ❶ (*dip*) eintauchen ❷ ■ **to ~ oneself in sth** sich in etw *akk* vertiefen

immersion [ɪ·ˈmɜr·ʒən] *n* ❶ (*dipping*) Eintauchen *nt,* Untertauchen *nt;* (*baptizing*) Ganztaufe *f* ❷ (*total involvement*) Vertiefung *f fig*

immigrant [ˈɪm·ɪ·grənt] **I.** *n* Einwanderer *m*/Einwanderin *f,* Immigrant(in) *m(f)* **II.** *adj attr* Immigranten-, Einwanderer-

immigrate [ˈɪm·ɪ·greɪt] *vi* einwandern, immigrieren

immigration [ˌɪm·ɪ·ˈgreɪ·ʃən] *n* ❶ (*action*) Einwanderung *f,* Immigration *f* ❷ (*authority*) Grenzkontrolle *f,* ≈ Grenzschutz *m* (*an Flughäfen*)

imminent [ˈɪm·ɪ·nənt] *adj* bevorstehend *attr; danger* drohend

immobile [ɪ·ˈmoʊ·bəl] *adj* bewegungslos; (*sit*) regungslos; (*unable to move*) unbeweglich

immobility [ˌɪ·moʊ·ˈbɪl·ɪ·t̬i] *n* Bewegungslosigkeit *f,* Unbewegtheit *f;* (*due to damage*) Bewegungsunfähigkeit *f*

immobilize [ɪ·ˈmoʊ·bə·laɪz] *vt* ❶ lahmlegen; *machine* betriebsuntauglich machen; (*fig*) *fear* lähmen ❷ *patient, broken limb* ruhigstellen

immoderate [ɪ·ˈmad·ər·ɪt] *adj* (*form*) maßlos; *demands* übertrieben

immodest [ɪ·ˈmad·ɪst] *adj* ❶ (*conceited*) eingebildet ❷ (*indecent*) *clothing* unanständig

immoral [ɪ·ˈmɔr·əl] *adj* unmoralisch

immortal [ɪ·ˈmɔr·t̬əl] **I.** *adj inv* ❶ (*undying*) unsterblich ❷ (*unforgettable*) unvergesslich **II.** *n* Unsterbliche(r) *f(m)*

immortality [ˌɪ·mɔr·ˈtæl·ɪ·t̬i] *n* Unsterblichkeit *f*

immortalize [ɪ·ˈmɔr·t̬ə·laɪz] *vt* verewigen

immovable [ɪ·ˈmu·və·bəl] *adj inv* ❶ (*stationary*) unbeweglich ❷ (*unchanging*) unerschütterlich; *belief* fest; *opposition* starr

immune [ɪ·ˈmjun] *adj pred* ❶ immun *a. fig* (**to** gegen/für +*akk*) ❷ (*safe*) sicher (**from** vor +*dat*)

im'mune system *n* Immunsystem *nt*

immunity [ɪ·ˈmju·nɪ·t̬i] *n* ❶ Immunität *f* ❷ (*fig: invulnerability*) Unempfindlichkeit *f*

immunize [ˈɪm·jə·naɪz] *vt* immunisieren

immunodeficiency [ˌɪm·jə·noʊ·dɪ·ˈfɪʃ·ən·si] *n* MED Immunschwäche *f*

immunological [ˌɪm·jə·noʊ·ˈladʒ·ɪ·kəl] *adj* immunologisch *fachspr*

immunologist [ˌɪm·jʊ·ˈnal·ə·dʒɪst] *n* Immunologe, -in *m, f fachspr*

imp [ɪmp] *n* Kobold *m*

impact I. *n* [ˈɪm·pækt] ❶ (*contact*) Aufprall *m;* (*force*) Wucht *f;* (*of bullet/meteor*) Einschlag *m* ❷ (*fig: effect*) Auswirkung[en] *f[pl];* **to have an ~ on sb** Eindruck bei jdm machen **II.** *vt* [ɪm·ˈpækt] beeinflussen **III.** *vi* ❶ (*land*) aufschlagen ❷ (*affect*) ■ **to ~ on sb/sth** jdn/etw beeinflussen

impacted [ɪm·ˈpæk·tɪd] *adj* ❶ *inv tooth, bone* eingeklemmt ❷ (*affected*) betroffen

impair [ɪm·ˈper] *vt* (*disrupt*) behindern; *ability* beeinträchtigen; (*damage*) schaden +*dat,* schädigen

impaired [ɪm·ˈperd] *adj* geschädigt; **~ hearing/vision** Hör-/Sehbehinderung *f*

impale [ɪm·ˈpeɪl] *vt usu passive* aufspießen (**on** auf +*akk*)

impart [ɪm·ˈpart] *vt* ■ **to ~ sth** [**to sb/sth**] ❶ (*communicate*) [jdm/etw] etw vermitteln ❷ (*bestow*) [jdm/etw] etw verleihen

impartial [ɪm·ˈpar·ʃəl] *adj* unparteiisch

impartiality [ɪm·ˌpar·ʃɪ·ˈæl·ə·t̬i] *n* Unvoreingenommenheit *f*

impassable [ɪm·ˈpæs·ə·bəl] *adj inv road* unpassierbar; (*fig*) *problem* unüberwindlich

impasse [ˈɪm·pæs] *n* Sackgasse *f a. fig;* **to reach an ~** sich festfahren

impassioned [ɪm·ˈpæʃ·ənd] *adj* leidenschaftlich

impassive [ɪm·ˈpæs·ɪv] *adj* (*not showing emotion*) ausdruckslos; (*not sympathizing*) gleichgültig

impatience [ɪm·ˈpeɪ·ʃəns] *n* ❶ (*eagerness*) Ungeduld *f* ❷ (*intolerance*) Unduldsamkeit *f*

impatient [ɪm·ˈpeɪ·ʃənt] *adj* ungeduldig (**with** gegenüber +*dat*); (*intolerant*) intolerant (**of** gegenüber +*dat*)

impeach [ɪm·ˈpitʃ] *vt* anklagen (**for** wegen +*gen*); *president, official* wegen Amtsmissbrauchs anklagen

impeachment [ɪm·ˈpitʃ·mənt] *n* Amtsenthebungsverfahren *nt*

impeccable [ɪm·ˈpek·ə·bəl] *adj inv* makellos; *manners* tadellos; *performance* perfekt; *reputation* untadelig; *taste* ausgesucht

impede [ɪm·ˈpid] *vt* behindern

impediment [ɪm·ˈped·ɪ·mənt] *n* ❶ (*hindrance*) Hindernis *nt* (**to** für +*akk*) ❷ MED Behinderung *f;* **speech ~** Sprachfehler *m*

impel <-ll-> [ɪm·ˈpel] *vt* [an]treiben; (*force*) nötigen
impending [ɪm·ˈpend·ɪŋ] *adj attr, inv* bevorstehend; (*menacing*) drohend
impenetrable [ɪm·ˈpen·ɪ·trə·bəl] *adj* ❶ unüberwindlich; (*dense*) undurchdringlich; *fog* dicht ❷ (*fig: incomprehensible*) unverständlich
imperative [ɪm·ˈper·ə·t̬ɪv] **I.** *adj* unbedingt erforderlich **II.** *n* ❶ [Sach]zwang *m;* (*obligation*) Verpflichtung *f;* (*factor*) Erfordernis *f* ❷ LING ■**the ~** der Imperativ
imperceptible [ˌɪm·pər·ˈsep·tə·bəl] *adj* unmerklich
imperfect [ɪm·ˈpɜr·fɪkt] **I.** *adj* (*flawed*) fehlerhaft; (*incomplete*) unvollkommen; (*insufficient*) unzureichend **II.** *n* LING ■**the ~** der Imperfekt
imperfection [ˌɪm·pər·ˈfek·ʃən] *n* ❶ (*flaw*) Fehler *m,* Mangel *m* ❷ (*faultiness*) Unvollkommenheit *f,* Fehlerhaftigkeit *f*
imperial [ɪm·ˈpɪr·i·əl] *adj inv* ❶ (*of empire*) Reichs-; (*of emperor*) kaiserlich, Kaiser-; (*imperialistic*) imperialistisch ❷ (*grand*) prächtig ❸ *measures, weights* britisch
imperialism [ɪm·ˈpɪr·i·ə·lɪz·əm] *n* Imperialismus *m*
imperialist [ɪm·ˈpɪr·i·ə·lɪst] **I.** *n* Imperialist(in) *m(f)* **II.** *adj* imperialistisch
imperious [ɪm·ˈpɪr·i·əs] *adj* herrisch
impermanent [ɪm·ˈpɜr·mə·nənt] *adj* (*transitory*) unbeständig; (*temporary*) zeitlich begrenzt
impermeable [ɪm·ˈpɜr·mi·ə·bəl] *adj inv* undurchlässig
impersonal [ˌɪm·ˈpɜr·sə·nəl] *adj a.* LING unpersönlich; (*anonymous*) anonym
impersonate [ɪm·ˈpɜr·sə·neɪt] *vt* ■**to ~ sb** (*mimic*) jdn imitieren; (*pretend*) sich als jdn ausgeben
impersonator [ɪm·ˈpɜr·sə·neɪ·t̬ər] *n* Imitator(in) *m(f)*
impertinence [ɪm·ˈpɜr·t̬ə·nəns] *n* Unverschämtheit *f,* Frechheit *f*
impertinent [ɪm·ˈpɜr·t̬ə·nənt] *adj* unverschämt
impervious [ɪm·ˈpɜr·vi·əs] *adj* ❶ *inv* undurchlässig; **~ to fire/heat** feuer-/hitzebeständig; **~ to water** wasserdicht ❷ (*fig: unaffected*) immun (**to** gegenüber +*dat*)
impetuous [ɪm·ˈpetʃ·u·əs] *adj* impulsiv; *nature* hitzig; *decision, remark* unüberlegt
impetus [ˈɪm·pɪ·təs] *n* ❶ (*push*) Anstoß *m;* (*drive*) Antrieb *m* ❷ (*momentum*) Schwung *m*
impinge [ɪm·ˈpɪndʒ] *vi* (*affect*) ■**to ~ on sb/sth** sich *akk* [negativ] auf jdn/etw auswirken
impious [ˈɪm·pi·əs] *adj* pietätlos; (*blasphemous*) gotteslästerlich
impish [ˈɪm·pɪʃ] *adj child* lausbubenhaft; *look, grin* verschmitzt; *remark, trick* frech
implacable [ɪm·ˈplæk·ə·bəl] *adj* unversöhnlich; (*relentless*) unnachlässig; *enemy, opponent* unerbittlich
implacably [ɪm·ˈplæk·ə·bli] *adv* unnachgiebig; (*relentlessly*) unermüdlich
implant **I.** *n* [ˈɪm·plænt] Implantat *nt* **II.** *vt* [ɪm·ˈplænt] einpflanzen
implausible [ɪm·ˈplɔ·zə·bəl] *adj* unglaubwürdig
implement **I.** *n* [ˈɪm·plɪ·mənt] Gerät *nt;* (*tool*) Werkzeug *nt* **II.** *vt* [ˈɪm·plɪ·ment] einführen; *plan* in die Tat umsetzen
implementation [ˌɪm·plɪ·men·ˈteɪ·ʃən] *n* Einführung *f*
implicate [ˈɪm·plɪ·keɪt] *vt* ❶ (*involve*) ■**to ~ sb in sth** jdn mit etw *dat* in Verbindung bringen; **to be ~d in a crime** in ein Verbrechen verwickelt sein ❷ (*imply*) andeuten
implication [ˌɪm·plɪ·ˈkeɪ·ʃən] *n* ❶ (*involvement*) Verwicklung *f* ❷ (*intimation*) Implikation *f geh* ❸ *usu pl* (*effect*) Auswirkung[en] *f[pl]*
implicit [ɪm·ˈplɪs·ɪt] *adj* ❶ (*suggested*) indirekt ❷ *attr, inv* (*total*) bedingungslos; *confidence* unbedingt
implicitly [ɪm·ˈplɪs·ɪt·li] *adv* ❶ implizit ❷ (*fully*) völlig, bedingungslos
implied [ɪm·ˈplaɪd] *adj inv* indirekt
implode [ɪm·ˈploʊd] *vi* implodieren; (*fig*) zusammenbrechen
implore [ɪm·ˈplɔr] *vt* anflehen
imploring [ɪm·ˈplɔr·ɪŋ] *adj* flehend
implosion [ɪm·ˈploʊ·ʒən] *n* Implosion *f fachspr*
imply <-ie-> [ɪm·ˈplaɪ] *vt* andeuten
impolite [ˌɪm·pə·ˈlaɪt] *adj* unhöflich; (*stronger*) unverschämt
impoliteness [ˌɪm·pə·ˈlaɪt·nɪs] *n* Unhöflichkeit *f;* (*stronger*) Unverschämtheit *f*
impolitic [ɪm·ˈpal·ə·tɪk] *adj* (*form*) undiplomatisch
imponderable [ɪm·ˈpan·də·rə·bəl] **I.** *adj inv question, theory* unergründbar; *impact, effect* nicht einschätzbar **II.** *n usu pl* Unwägbarkeit[en] *f[pl]*
import **I.** *vt* [ɪm·ˈpɔrt] ❶ *goods* importieren (**from** aus +*dat*); *ideas, customs* übernehmen (**from** von +*dat*) ❷ COMPUT importieren **II.** *vi* [ɪm·ˈpɔrt] importieren (**from** aus +*dat*) **III.** *n* [ˈɪm·pɔrt] Import *m*
importance [ɪm·ˈpɔr·təns] *n* Bedeutung *f,* Wichtigkeit *f*
important [ɪm·ˈpɔr·tənt] *adj* ❶ wichtig ❷ (*influential*) bedeutend
importantly [ɪm·ˈpɔr·tənt·li] *adv* wichtig; (*self-importantly*) wichtigtuerisch
importation [ˌɪm·pɔr·ˈteɪ·ʃən] *n* Import *m*
ˈimport duty *n* [Import]zoll *m*
importune [ˌɪm·pɔr·ˈtun] *vt* ■**to ~ sb** (*harass*) jdn bedrängen
impose [ɪm·ˈpoʊz] **I.** *vt* (*implement*) durchsetzen; (*order*) verhängen; *law* verfügen; *taxes;* **on person** auferlegen (**on** auf +*dat*); (*on goods*) erheben (**on** auf +*akk*) **II.** *vi* ■**to ~ on sb** sich jdm aufdrängen
imposing [ɪm·ˈpoʊ·zɪŋ] *adj* beeindruckend;

person stattlich

imposition [ˌɪm·pə·ˈzɪʃ·ən] *n* ❶ (*implementation*) Einführung *f; of penalties, sanctions* Verhängen *nt* ❷ (*inconvenience*) Belastung *f;* (*annoyance*) Aufdringlichkeit *f*

impossibility [ɪm·ˌpas·ə·ˈbɪl·ə·ṭi] *n* ❶ (*thing*) Ding *nt* der Unmöglichkeit ❷ (*quality*) Unmöglichkeit *f*

impossible [ɪm·ˈpas·ə·bəl] **I.** *adj inv* ❶ unmöglich ❷ (*difficult*) *person* unerträglich **II.** *n* ■ **the ~** das Unmögliche; **to ask the ~** Unmögliches verlangen

impossibly [ɪm·ˈpas·ə·bli] *adv inv* unvorstellbar

impostor, imposter [ɪm·ˈpas·tər] *n* Hochstapler(in) *m(f)*

impotence [ˈɪm·pə·təns] *n* Machtlosigkeit *f;* (*sexual*) Impotenz *f*

impotent [ˈɪm·pə·tənt] *adj* ❶ machtlos ❷ *inv* (*sexually*) impotent

impound [ɪm·ˈpaʊnd] *vt* beschlagnahmen

impoverish [ɪm·ˈpav·ər·ɪʃ] *vt* ❶ arm machen ❷ (*fig*) *soil* auslaugen

impoverished [ɪm·ˈpav·ər·ɪʃt] *adj* arm; (*fig*) verarmt

impracticable [ɪm·ˈpræk·tɪ·kə·bəl] *adj* undurchführbar

impractical [ɪm·ˈpræk·tɪ·kəl] *adj* unpraktisch; (*unfit*) untauglich; (*unrealistic*) nicht anwendbar

imprecise [ˌɪm·prɪ·ˈsaɪs] *adj* ungenau

impregnable [ɪm·ˈpreg·nə·bəl] *adj* ❶ uneinnehmbar ❷ (*fig: unbeatable*) unschlagbar

impregnate [ɪm·ˈpreg·neɪt] *vt usu passive* ❶ *animal, egg* befruchten ❷ (*saturate*) imprägnieren

impresario [ˌɪm·prə·ˈsar·i·oʊ] *n* Impresario *m; for artists* Agent(in) *m(f)*

impress [ɪm·ˈpres] **I.** *vt* ❶ beeindrucken ❷ (*convince*) ■ **to ~ sth [up]on sb** jdn von etw *dat* überzeugen **II.** *vi* Eindruck machen, imponieren; **to fail to ~** keinen [guten] Eindruck machen

impression [ɪm·ˈpreʃ·ən] *n* ❶ (*opinion*) Eindruck *m;* **to be under the ~ that ...** den Eindruck haben, dass ... ❷ (*feeling*) Eindruck *m;* **to make a good ~ [on sb]** einen guten Eindruck [auf jdn] machen ❸ (*imitation*) Imitation *f;* **to do an ~ of sb/sth** jdn/etw imitieren

impressionable [ɪm·ˈpreʃ·ə·nə·bəl] *adj* [leicht] beeinflussbar

impressionism [ɪm·ˈpreʃ·ə·nɪz·əm] *n* Impressionismus *m*

impressionist [ɪm·ˈpreʃ·ə·nɪst] **I.** *n* ❶ Impressionist(in) *m(f)* ❷ (*imitator*) Imitator(in) *m(f)* **II.** *adj inv* impressionistisch

impressionistic [ɪm·ˌpreʃ·ə·ˈnɪs·tɪk] *adj* impressionistisch

impressive [ɪm·ˈpres·ɪv] *adj* beeindruckend

imprint **I.** *vt* [ɪm·ˈprɪnt] *usu passive* ❶ (*emboss*) prägen ❷ (*print*) drucken (**on** auf +*akk*); **to ~ sth on sb's mind** (*fig*) jdm etw einprägen **II.** *n* [ˈɪm·prɪnt] ❶ (*mark*) Abdruck *m; on coin, leather* Prägung *f; on paper, cloth* [Auf]druck *m;* (*fig*) Spuren *pl* ❷ (*in publishing*) Impressum *nt*

imprison [ɪm·ˈprɪz·ən] *vt usu passive* (*put in prison*) inhaftieren; (*sentence to prison*) zu einer Gefängnisstrafe verurteilen

imprisonment [ɪm·ˈprɪz·ən·mənt] *n* Haft *f;* (*esp in war*) Gefangenschaft *f*

improbability [ˌɪm·prab·ə·ˈbɪl·ɪ·ṭi] *n* Unwahrscheinlichkeit *f*

improbable [ɪm·ˈprab·ə·bəl] *adj* unwahrscheinlich; (*dubious*) unglaubhaft

impromptu [ɪm·ˈpramp·tu] *adj inv* spontan

improper [ɪm·ˈprap·ər] *adj* ❶ (*not correct*) falsch; (*showing bad judgment*) fälschlich ❷ (*inappropriate*) unpassend; (*indecent*) unanständig; *conduct* unschicklich

impropriety [ˌɪm·prə·ˈpraɪ·ə·ṭi] *n* Unanständigkeit *f*

improve [ɪm·ˈpruv] **I.** *vt* verbessern **II.** *vi* besser werden, sich verbessern; ■ **to ~ on sth** etw [noch] verbessern; **you can't ~ on that!** da ist keine Steigerung mehr möglich!

improvement [ɪm·ˈpruv·mənt] *n* ❶ (*instance*) Verbesserung *f* ❷ (*activity*) Verbesserung *f; of illness* Besserung *f;* **room for ~** Steigerungsmöglichkeiten *pl* ❸ **[home] ~[s]** Renovierungsarbeiten *pl* (*Ausbau- und Modernisierungsarbeiten am eigenen Heim*)

improvisation [ɪm·ˌprav·ɪ·ˈzeɪ·ʃən] *n* Improvisation *f*

improvise [ˈɪm·prə·vaɪz] *vt, vi* improvisieren

imprudent [ɪm·ˈpru·dənt] *adj* leichtsinnig

impudence [ˈɪm·pjʊ·dəns] *n* Unverschämtheit *f*

impudent [ˈɪm·pjʊ·dənt] *adj* unverschämt

impulse [ˈɪm·pʌls] *n* ❶ (*urge*) *a.* ELEC Impuls *m;* **to have an** [*or* **a sudden**] **~ to do sth** plötzlich den Drang verspüren, etw zu tun ❷ (*motive*) Antrieb *m*

impulsive [ɪm·ˈpʌl·sɪv] *adj* impulsiv; (*spontaneous*) spontan

impunity [ɪm·ˈpju·nɪ·ṭi] *n* Straflosigkeit *f;* LAW Straffreiheit *f;* **to do sth with ~** etw ungestraft tun

impure [ɪm·ˈpjʊr] *adj* (*unclean*) unrein, unsauber; (*contaminated*) *water* verunreinigt; *drugs* gestreckt; *medication* nicht rein

impurity [ɪm·ˈpjʊr·ɪ·ṭi] *n* ❶ (*quality*) Verunreinigung *f* ❷ (*element*) Verschmutzung *f*

impute [ɪm·ˈpjut] *vt* ■ **to ~ sth to sb** jdm etw unterstellen

in [ɪn] **I.** *prep* ❶ (*describing location*) in +*dat;* **he is deaf ~ his left ear** er hört auf dem linken Ohr nichts; **to ride ~ a car** [im] Auto fahren; **~ the hospital** im Krankenhaus; **~ the street** auf der Straße ❷ (*into*) in +*akk;* **to get ~ the car** ins Auto steigen ❸ (*describing state*) **he cried out ~ pain** er schrie vor Schmerzen; **~ anger** im Zorn; **difference ~ quality** Qualitätsunterschied *m;* **to [not] be ~ doubt** [nicht] zweifeln; **~ horror** voller Entsetzen; **to be ~ love [with sb]** [in jdn] verliebt sein; **to fall ~ love [with sb]** sich [in jdn] verlieben; **to be ~ a good mood** guter Laune sein; ~ **secret** heimlich ❹ ~ **French** auf Französisch ❺ (*during*) **she assisted the doctor ~ the operation** sie assistierte dem Arzt bei der Operation; ~ **the end** am Ende; ~ **March** im März; ~ **the morning** morgens ❻ (*describing job*) **she works ~ publishing** sie arbeitet bei einem Verlag ❼ (*wearing*) **the woman ~ the hat** die Frau mit dem Hut; ~ **disguise** verkleidet; ~ **the nude** nackt; **to be ~ uniform** Uniform tragen ❽ + *-ing* (*while*) ~ **attempting to save the child, he nearly lost his own life** bei dem Versuch, das Kind zu retten, kam er beinahe selbst um; ~ **doing so** dabei, damit ❾ (*state, condition*) **he's about six foot ~ height** er ist ca. sechs Fuß groß; **to be equal ~ weight** gleich viel wiegen; ~ **total** insgesamt ❿ (*of every*) pro; **one ~ ten people** jeder zehnte ⓫ *see a. n* **she had no say ~ the decision** sie hatte keinen Einfluss auf die Entscheidung; **to have confidence ~ sb** jdm vertrauen ▶ PHRASES: ~ **all** insgesamt; ~ **between** dazwischen **II.** *adv inv* ❶ (*to speaker*) herein; **come ~!** herein!; **to come ~** *tide* kommen; **to get ~** *train, bus* eintreffen ❷ (*submitted*) **to hand sth ~** etw abgeben ▶ PHRASES: **to let sb ~ on sth** jdn in etw *akk* einweihen **III.** *adj inv* ❶ *pred* (*there*) da; (*at home*) zu Hause; **to have a quiet evening ~** einen ruhigen Abend zu Hause verbringen ❷ (*in fashion*) in ❸ *pred* (*submitted*) **the application must be ~ by May 31** die Bewerbung muss bis zum 31. Mai eingegangen sein ▶ PHRASES: **to be ~ for sth** (*be in serious trouble*) dran sein; **to be ~ on sth** über etw *akk* Bescheid wissen **IV.** *n* (*connection*) Kontakt[e] *m*[*pl*] ▶ PHRASES: **to know the ~s and outs of sth** sich in einer S. *gen* genau auskennen

I

IN *abbrev of* **Indiana**

inability [ˌɪn·ə·ˈbɪl·ɪ·t̬i] *n* Unfähigkeit *f*

inaccessible [ˌɪn·æk·ˈses·ə·bəl] *adj* (*hard to enter*) unzugänglich; (*hard to understand*) unverständlich

inaccuracy [ɪn·ˈæk·jər·ə·si] *n* Ungenauigkeit *f*

inaccurate [ɪn·ˈæk·jər·ɪt] *adj* (*inexact*) ungenau; (*wrong*) falsch

inaction [ɪn·ˈæk·ʃən] *n* Untätigkeit *f*

inactive [ɪn·ˈæk·tɪv] *adj* untätig, inaktiv

inactivity [ˌɪn·æk·ˈtɪv·ɪ·t̬i] *n* Untätigkeit *f*

inadequacy [ɪn·ˈæd·ɪ·kwə·si] *n* ❶ (*trait*) Unzulänglichkeit[en] *f*[*pl*] ❷ (*quality*) Unzulänglichkeit *f*; **feelings of ~** Minderwertigkeitsgefühle *pl*

inadequate [ɪn·ˈæd·ɪ·kwɪt] *adj* unangemessen; **woefully ~** völlig unzulänglich

inadmissible [ˌɪn·əd·ˈmɪs·ə·bəl] *adj inv* unzulässig

inadvertent [ˌɪn·əd·ˈvɜr·tənt] *adj* (*careless*) unachtsam; (*erroneous*) versehentlich

inadvisable [ˌɪn·əd·ˈvaɪ·zə·bəl] *adj* nicht empfehlenswert

inane [ɪn·ˈeɪn] *adj* geistlos; (*silly*) dämlich

inanimate [ɪn·ˈæn·ɪ·mət] *adj inv* leblos; (*immobile*) bewegungslos

inapplicable [ɪn·ˈæp·lɪ·kə·bəl] *adj inv* unanwendbar; *answer, question* unzutreffend

inappropriate [ˌɪn·ə·ˈproʊ·pri·ɪt] *adj* ungeeignet; *time* unpassend; (*inconvenient*) ungelegen; (*out of place*) unangebracht

inarticulate [ˌɪn·ar·ˈtɪk·jʊ·lɪt] *adj* ❶ (*unable to express oneself*) **she was ~ with rage** die Wut verschlug ihr die Sprache ❷ (*unclear*) undeutlich; *speech* zusammenhangslos

inattention [ˌɪn·ə·ˈten·ʃən] *n* Unaufmerksamkeit *f*; (*negligence*) Achtlosigkeit *f*

inattentive [ˌɪn·ə·ˈten·tɪv] *adj* unaufmerksam; (*careless*) achtlos

inaudible [ɪn·ˈɔ·də·bəl] *adj* unhörbar

inaugural [ɪn·ˈɔ·gjʊ·rəl] *adj attr, inv* ❶ Einweihungs-; (*opening*) Eröffnungs- ❷ POL Antritts-

inaugurate [ɪn·ˈɔ·gjʊ·reɪt] *vt* ❶ (*induct into office*) **to ~ sb** jdn in sein Amt einführen ❷ (*start*) *new era* einläuten; *policy* [neu] einführen

inauguration [ɪn·ˌɔ·gjʊ·ˈreɪ·ʃən] *n* ❶ (*induction*) Amtseinführung *f* ❷ *of monument, stadium* Einweihung *f*; *of era, policy* Einführung *f*

inauspicious [ˌɪn·ɔ·ˈspɪʃ·əs] *adj* ungünstig

in-be'tween **I.** *adj attr, inv* Zwischen-, Übergangs- **II.** *n* Zwischending *nt*

inboard [ˈɪn·bɔrd] *adj attr* NAUT innenbords

inborn [ˈɪn·bɔrn] *adj inv personality trait* angeboren; *physical trait* vererbt

'in box *n* COMPUT Posteingangsordner *m*

inbred [ˈɪn·bred] *adj inv* ❶ durch Inzucht erzeugt ❷ (*inherent*) angeboren; *charm, talent* naturgegeben

inbreeding [ˈɪn·bri·dɪŋ] *n* Inzucht *f*

Inc. *adj after n, inv* ECON *abbrev of* **incorporated** [als Kapitalgesellschaft] eingetragen

incalculable [ɪn·ˈkæl·kjʊ·lə·bəl] *adj* ❶ *inv* (*high*) unabsehbar; *costs* unüberschaubar ❷ (*inestimable*) nicht zu ermessen *präd*, unvorstellbar; *value* unschätzbar

incandescent [ˌɪn·kən·ˈdes·ənt] *adj inv* (*lit*) [weiß]glühend *attr*, leuchtend hell

incantation [ˌɪn·kæn·ˈteɪ·ʃən] *n* ❶ (*activity*) Beschwörung *f* ❷ (*spell*) Zauberspruch *m*

incapability [ɪn·ˌkeɪ·pə·ˈbɪl·ɪ·t̬i] *n* Unfähigkeit *f*

incapable [ɪn·ˈkeɪ·pə·bəl] *adj* unfähig (**of** zu +*dat*)

incapacitate [ˌɪn·kə·ˈpæs·ɪ·teɪt] *vt* außer Gefecht setzen

incapacity [ˌɪn·kə·ˈpæs·ə·t̬i] *n* Unfähigkeit *f*

incarcerate [ɪn·ˈkar·sə·reɪt] *vt* einkerkern

incarnate [ɪn·ˈkar·nɪt] *adj after n, inv* **evil ~** das personifizierte Böse

incarnation [ˌɪn·kar·ˈneɪ·ʃən] *n* ❶ (*human form*) Verkörperung *f* ❷ (*lifetime*) Inkarnation *f*

incendiary [ɪn·ˈsen·di·er·i] **I.** *adj* ❶ *attr, inv* Brand- ❷ (*fig: inciting*) aufstachelnd *attr*, aufrührerisch **II.** *n* (*bomb*) Brandbombe *f*; (*device*) Brandmittel *nt*

incense[1] [ˈɪn·sens] *n* (*substance*) Räuchermittel *nt;* (*smoke*) wohlriechender Rauch; (*in church*) Weihrauch *m*

incense[2] [ɪn·ˈsens] *vt* empören

incensed [ɪn·ˈsenst] *adj* empört

incentive [ɪn·ˈsen·tɪv] **I.** *n* Anreiz *m* **II.** *adj attr, inv* Vorteile bringend

in'centive plan *n* Prämiensystem *nt*

inception [ɪn·ˈsep·ʃən] *n* Anfang *m;* (*of company*) Gründung *f*

incessant [ɪn·ˈses·ənt] *adj inv* ununterbrochen

incest [ˈɪn·sest] *n* Inzest *m*

incestuous [ɪn·ˈses·tʃu·əs] *adj* inzestuös

inch [ɪntʃ] **I.** *n* <*pl* -es> ❶ (*measurement*) Zoll *m* (*2,54 cm*) ❷ (*body size*) ■ **~es** *pl* Körpergröße *f* ❸ (*distance*) Zollbreit *m,* Zentimeter *m;* **to miss sb/sth by ~es** jdn/etw [nur] um Haaresbreite verfehlen **II.** *vi* sich [ganz] langsam bewegen **III.** *vt* [ganz] vorsichtig bewegen

incidence [ˈɪn·sɪ·dəns] *n* Auftreten *nt*

incident [ˈɪn·sɪ·dənt] *n* ❶ (*occurrence*) [Vor]fall *m* ❷ (*story*) Begebenheit *f*

incidental [ˌɪn·sɪ·ˈden·təl] *adj* ❶ (*related*) begleitend *attr,* verbunden; (*secondary*) nebensächlich ❷ (*by chance*) zufällig; (*in passing*) beiläufig

incidentally [ˌɪn·sɪ·ˈden·təl·i] *adv inv* ❶ (*by the way*) übrigens ❷ (*in passing*) nebenbei; (*accidentally*) zufällig

incinerate [ɪn·ˈsɪn·ə·reɪt] *vt* verbrennen

incinerator [ɪn·ˈsɪn·ə·reɪ·t̬ər] *n* Verbrennungsanlage *f;* (*for garbage*) Müllverbrennungsanlage *f;* (*for bodies*) [Verbrennungs]ofen *m*

incise [ɪn·ˈsaɪz] *vt* einritzen; (*in wood*) einschnitzen; (*in metal, stone*) eingravieren; *wound* aufschneiden

incision [ɪn·ˈsɪʒ·ən] *n* MED [Ein]schnitt *m*

incisive [ɪn·ˈsaɪ·sɪv] *adj* (*clear*) klar; *remark* schlüssig; (*clear-thinking*) scharfsinnig; *mind* [messer]scharf

incisor [ɪn·ˈsaɪ·zər] *n* Schneidezahn *m*

incite [ɪn·ˈsaɪt] *vt* aufstacheln; *revolt, riot* anzetteln

incitement [ɪn·ˈsaɪt·mənt] *n* Anstiftung *f*

inclination [ˌɪn·klɪ·ˈneɪ·ʃən] *n* ❶ (*tendency*) Neigung *f,* Hang *m kein pl* ❷ (*slope*) Neigung *f; of head* Neigen *nt*

incline I. *vi* [ɪn·ˈklaɪn] ❶ (*tend*) tendieren (**toward**[**s**] zu +*dat*) ❷ (*lean*) sich neigen **II.** *vt* [ɪn·ˈklaɪn] ❶ *usu passive* (*dispose*) ■ **to be ~d that way** dazu neigen; ■ **to be ~d to do sth** dazu neigen, etw zu tun ❷ *head* neigen **III.** *n* [ˈɪn·klaɪn] (*slope*) Neigung *f; of hill, mountain* [Ab]hang *m*

inclined [ɪn·ˈklaɪnd] *adj pred* bereit; **to be ~ to agree** eher zustimmen; **to be politically ~** eine Anlage für Politik haben

include [ɪn·ˈklud] *vt* (*contain*) beinhalten; (*add*) beifügen; ■ **to be ~d in sth** in etw *akk* eingeschlossen sein; **everything is ~d** alles ist inklusive; ■ **to ~ sb/sth in sth** jdn/etw in etw *akk* einbeziehen

including [ɪn·ˈklu·dɪŋ] *prep* einschließlich; **~ everything** alles inbegriffen

inclusion [ɪn·ˈklu·ʒən] *n* Einbeziehung *f*

inclusive [ɪn·ˈklu·sɪv] *adj* (*comprehensive*) [all]umfassend

incognito [ˌɪn·kag·ˈni·toʊ] *adv inv* inkognito

incoherent [ˌɪn·koʊ·ˈhɪr·ənt] *adj* zusammenhanglos

income [ˈɪn·kʌm] *n* Einkommen *nt; of company* Einnahmen *pl*

'income bracket *n* Einkommensstufe *f,* Lohnklasse *f* SCHWEIZ

'income tax *n* Einkommensteuer *f*

incoming [ˈɪn·ˌkʌm·ɪŋ] *adj attr, inv* ankommend; **~ call** [eingehender] Anruf; **~ freshman** *Studienanfänger an einer amerikanischen Hochschule oder Highschool;* (*immigrating*) zuwandernd; (*recently elected*) neu [gewählt]

incomings [ˈɪn·ˌkʌm·ɪŋz] *npl* Einkommen *nt; of company* Einnahmen *pl*

incommunicado [ˌɪn·kəˌmju·nɪ·ˈkad·oʊ] **I.** *adj pred, inv* nicht erreichbar **II.** *adv inv* isoliert

incomparable [ɪn·ˈkam·pər·ə·bəl] *adj inv* (*different*) unvergleichbar; (*superior*) unvergleichlich

incompatibility [ˌɪn·kəm·ˌpæt̬·ə·ˈbɪl·ɪ·t̬i] *n* Unvereinbarkeit *f;* COMPUT Inkompatibilität *f fachspr*

incompatible [ˌɪn·kəm·ˈpæt̬·ə·bəl] *adj* unvereinbar (**with** mit +*dat*); *machinery, computers* inkompatibel; *blood type* unverträglich; *colors* nicht kombinierbar; ■ **to be ~** *persons* nicht zusammenpassen

incompetence [ɪn·ˈkam·pə·təns], **incompetency** [ɪn·ˈkam·pə·tən·si] *n* Inkompetenz *f*

incompetent [ɪn·ˈkam·pə·tənt] *adj* ❶ (*incapable*) inkompetent, ungeeignet (**for** für +*akk*) ❷ LAW unzuständig

incomplete [ˌɪn·kəm·ˈplit] *adj inv* unvollständig; (*unfinished*) unfertig

incomprehensible [ˌɪn·kam·prɪ·ˈhen·sə·bəl] *adj* unverständlich; *act, event* unbegreiflich

inconceivable [ˌɪn·kən·ˈsi·və·bəl] *adj inv* undenkbar, unvorstellbar

inconclusive [ˌɪn·kən·ˈklu·sɪv] *adj argument* nicht überzeugend; *results, test* ergebnislos; *evidence* unzureichend

incongruous [ɪn·ˈkaŋ·grʊ·əs] *adj* (*inappropriate*) unpassend; (*inconsistent*) widersprüchlich

inconsequential [ɪn·ˈkan·sɪ·ˈkwen·ʃəl] *adj* (*illogical*) unlogisch; (*unimportant*) unbedeutend

inconsiderable [ˌɪn·kən·ˈsɪd·ər·ə·bəl] *adj* unbeträchtlich

inconsiderate [ˌɪn·kən·ˈsɪd·ər·ɪt] *adj* (*disregarding*) rücksichtslos (**toward**[**s**] gegenüber +*dat*); (*insensitive*) gedankenlos; *remark* taktlos

inconsistency [ˌɪn·kən·ˈsɪs·tən·si] *n* ❶ (*contradiction*) Unvereinbarkeit *f;* (*in text*) Unstimmigkeit *f* ❷ (*inconstancy*) Unbeständigkeit *f*

inconsistent [ˌɪn·kən·ˈsɪs·tənt] *adj* ❶ (*contradicting*) widersprüchlich ❷ (*erratic*) unbeständig

inconsolable [ˌɪn·kən·ˈsoʊ·lə·bəl] *adj inv* untröstlich

inconspicuous [ˌɪn·kən·ˈspɪk·jʊ·əs] *adj* unauffällig

incontestable [ˌɪn·kən·ˈtes·tə·bəl] *adj inv* unbestreitbar; *evidence* unwiderlegbar

incontinent [ɪn·ˈkan·tə·nənt] *adj* MED inkontinent

inconvenience [ˌɪn·kən·ˈvin·jəns] **I.** *n* ❶ (*trouble*) Unannehmlichkeit[en] *f*[*pl*] ❷ (*troublesome thing*) Unannehmlichkeit *f* **II.** *vt* ■ **to ~ sb** jdm Unannehmlichkeiten bereiten

inconvenient [ˌɪn·kən·ˈvin·jənt] *adj time* ungelegen; *place* ungünstig [gelegen]

incorporate [ɪn·ˈkɔr·pə·reɪt] *vt* ❶ (*integrate*) einfügen; *company, region* eingliedern; *food* [hin]zugeben ❷ (*contain*) enthalten

incorporation [ɪn·ˌkɔr·pə·ˈreɪ·ʃən] *n* Einfügung *f,* Eingliederung *f,* Einbeziehung *f; region* Eingemeindung *f; food* Zugabe *f*

incorrect [ˌɪn·kə·ˈrekt] *adj* ❶ (*untrue*) falsch; *calculation* fehlerhaft; *diagnosis* unkorrekt ❷ (*improper*) unkorrekt; *behavior* unangebracht

incorrigible [ɪn·ˈkɔr·ə·dʒə·bəl] *adj inv* unverbesserlich

incorruptible [ˌɪn·kə·ˈrʌp·tə·bəl] *adj inv* unbestechlich; (*virtuous*) integer

increase I. *vi* [ɪn·ˈkriːs] *prices, rates* [an]steigen; *pain, troubles* zunehmen; *population, wealth* anwachsen **II.** *vt* [ɪn·ˈkriːs] erhöhen; (*strengthen*) verstärken; (*enlarge*) vergrößern **III.** *n* [ˈɪn·kriːs] Anstieg *m,* Zunahme *f; in production* Steigerung *f;* **to be on the ~** ansteigen; (*multiply*) [mehr und] mehr werden; (*magnify*) [immer] größer werden

increasing [ɪn·ˈkris·ɪŋ] *adj inv* steigend, zunehmend

increasingly [ɪn·ˈkris·ɪŋ·li] *adv inv* zunehmend, immer

incredible [ɪn·ˈkred·ə·bəl] *adj* ❶ unglaublich ❷ (*fam: very good*) fantastisch

incredibly [ɪn·ˈkred·ɪbli] *adv* ❶ (*strangely*) erstaunlicherweise; (*surprisingly*) überraschenderweise ❷ + *adj* (*very*) unglaublich

incredulity [ˌɪn·krɪ·ˈdu·lɪ·t̬i] *n* (*disbelief*) [ungläubiges] Staunen; (*bewilderment*) Fassungslosigkeit *f*

incredulous [ɪn·ˈkredʒ·ə·ləs] *adj* (*disbelieving*) ungläubig; (*bewildered*) fassungslos

increment [ˈɪŋ·krə·mənt] *n* (*division*) Stufe *f; on scale* [Grad]einteilung *f;* **by ~s** stufenweise

incremental [ˌɪŋ·krə·ˈmən·təl] *adj inv* stufenweise

incriminate [ɪn·ˈkrɪm·ɪ·neɪt] *vt* beschuldigen

incriminating [ɪn·ˈkrɪm·ɪ·neɪt̬·ɪŋ] *adj* belastend

incubate [ˈɪn·kjʊ·beɪt] **I.** *vt* ❶ *egg* [be]brüten; (*hatch*) ausbrüten; *bacteria, cells* heranzüchten ❷ (*fig*) *idea, plan* ausbrüten **II.** *vi egg* bebrütet werden; *idea, plan* reifen

incubation [ˌɪn·kjʊ·ˈbeɪ·ʃən] *n* ❶ [Be]brüten *nt; for hatching* Ausbrüten *nt* ❷ (*time*) Brut[zeit] *f; for diseases* Inkubation[szeit] *f*

incubator [ˈɪn·kjʊ·beɪ·t̬ər] *n* (*for eggs*) Brutapparat *m;* (*for babies*) Brutkasten *m*

incumbent [ɪn·ˈkʌm·bənt] **I.** *adj attr, inv* amtierend **II.** *n* Amtsinhaber(in) *m(f)*

incur <-rr-> [ɪn·ˈkɜr] *vt* ❶ hinnehmen müssen; *debt* machen; *losses* erleiden; **to ~ costs** Kosten haben ❷ (*bring on*) hervorrufen; **to ~ the anger of sb** jdn verärgern

incurable [ɪn·ˈkjʊr·ə·bəl] *adj inv* unheilbar; *habit* nicht ablegbar

incursion [ɪn·ˈkɜr·ʃən] *n* [feindlicher] Einfall

Ind. *abbrev of* **Indiana**

indebted [ɪn·ˈdet̬·ɪd] *adj pred* ❶ (*obliged*) [zu Dank] verpflichtet; ■ **to be ~ to sb for sth** jdm für etw *akk* dankbar sein ❷ (*owing*) verschuldet

indebtedness [ɪn·ˈdet̬·ɪd·nɪs] *n* (*personal*) Verpflichtung *f;* (*financial*) Verschuldung *f*

indecency [ɪn·ˈdi·sən·si] *n* ❶ (*impropriety*) Ungehörigkeit *f* ❷ (*assault*) sexueller Übergriff (**against** auf +*akk*)

indecent [ɪn·ˈdi·sənt] *adj* ❶ (*improper*) ungehörig; (*unseemly*) unschicklich; (*inappropriate*) unangemessen ❷ (*lewd*) unanständig; *proposal* unsittlich

indecipherable [ˌɪn·dɪ·ˈsaɪ·fər·ə·bəl] *adj inv* (*illegible*) unlesbar; *handwriting* kaum zu entziffern; (*incomprehensible*) unverständlich

indecision [ˌɪn·dɪ·ˈsɪʒ·ən] *n* Unentschlossenheit *f*

indecisive [ˌɪn·dɪ·ˈsaɪ·sɪv] *adj* ❶ (*wishy-washy*) unentschlossen; *person* nicht entscheidungsfreudig ❷ (*inconclusive*) unschlüssig

indeed [ɪn·ˈdid] **I.** *adv inv* ❶ (*for emphasis*) wirklich; (*actually*) tatsächlich ❷ (*affirmation*) allerdings ❸ (*for strengthening*) ja **II.** *interj* [ja,] wirklich, ach, wirklich

indefatigable [ˌɪn·dɪ·ˈfæt̬·ɪ·gə·bəl] *adj inv* unermüdlich

indefensible [ˌɪn·dɪ·ˈfen·sə·bəl] *adj* ❶ (*unjustifiable*) unentschuldbar; (*unacceptable*) untragbar; *behavior* unmöglich ❷ MIL nicht zu halten *präd*

indefinable [ˌɪn·dɪ·ˈfaɪ·nə·bəl] *adj* undefinierbar

indefinite [ɪn·ˈdef·ə·nɪt] *adj* ❶ *inv* (*unknown*) unbestimmt ❷ (*vague*) unklar; *answer* nicht eindeutig; *date, time* offen; *plans, ideas* vage

indefinite ˈarticle *n* unbestimmter Artikel

indefinitely [ɪn·ˈdef·ən·ət·li] *adv* ❶ *inv* auf unbestimmte Zeit ❷ (*vaguely*) vage

indelible [ɪn·ˈdel·ə·bəl] *adj inv* ❶ *ink* unlöschbar; *colors, stains* unlöslich ❷ (*fig: permanent*) unauslöschlich

indemnify <-ie-> [ɪn·ˈdem·nɪ·faɪ] *vt* ❶ (*insure*) versichern ❷ (*compensate*) entschädigen

indemnity [ɪn·ˈdem·nɪ·t̬i] *n* ❶ (*insurance*) Versicherung *f* ❷ (*compensation with liability*) Schaden[s]ersatz *m;* (*without liability*) Entschädigung *f*
indent I. *vi* [ɪn·ˈdent] TYPO einrücken **II.** *vt* [ɪn·ˈdent] ❶ TYPO einrücken ❷ (*depress*) eindrücken; *metal* einbeulen **III.** *n* [ˈɪn·dent] TYPO Einzug *m*
indentation [ˌɪn·den·ˈteɪ·ʃən] *n* ❶ TYPO Einzug *m* ❷ (*depression*) Vertiefung *f; in cheek, head* Kerbe *f; in metal* Beule *f*
independence [ˌɪn·dɪ·ˈpen·dəns] *n* ❶ (*autonomy*) Unabhängigkeit *f* ❷ (*absence of influence*) Unabhängigkeit *f;* (*impartiality*) Unparteilichkeit *f* ❸ (*self-reliance*) Selbstständigkeit *f*
Indeˈpendence Day *n amerikanischer Unabhängigkeitstag*
independent [ˌɪn·dɪ·ˈpen·dənt] **I.** *adj* ❶ *inv* (*autonomous*) unabhängig (**from** von +*dat*) ❷ (*uninfluenced*) unabhängig (**of** von +*dat*); (*impartial*) unparteiisch ❸ (*unassisted*) selbstständig **II.** *n* POL Parteilose(r) *f(m)*
in-depth [ˈɪn·depθ] *adj attr* gründlich; *investigation* eingehend; *report* detailliert
indescribable [ˌɪn·dɪ·ˈskraɪ·bə·bəl] *adj* unbeschreiblich
indestructible [ˌɪn·dɪ·ˈstrʌk·tə·bəl] *adj* unzerstörbar; *toy* unverwüstlich
indeterminable [ˌɪn·dɪ·ˈtɜr·mɪn·ə·bəl] *adj* unbestimmbar, undefinierbar
indeterminate [ˌɪn·dɪ·ˈtɜr·mə·nɪt] *adj* ❶ (*immeasurable*) unbestimmt ❷ (*vague*) unklar; (*indistinct*) *color* unbestimmbar; *period* ungewiss
index <*pl* -es *or* indices> [ˈɪn·deks, *pl* ˈɪn·dɪ·siz] **I.** *n* ❶ <*pl* -es> (*in book*) Index *m;* (*of sources*) Quellenverzeichnis *nt;* (*in library*) Katalog *m;* **card ~** Kartei *f* ❷ <*pl* -dices *or* -es> ECON Index *m fachspr* ❸ <*pl* -dices *or* -es> (*indicator*) Anzeichen *nt* (**of** für +*akk*) **II.** *vt* ❶ (*create index*) ■ **to ~ sth** *in book* etw mit einem Verzeichnis versehen ❷ (*record in index*) ■ **to ~ sth** *in book* etw in ein Verzeichnis aufnehmen
indexation [ˌin·dek·ˈseɪ·ʃən] *n* ECON Indexierung *f fachspr*
ˈindex card *n* Karteikarte *f*
ˈindex finger *n* Zeigefinger *m*
India [ˈɪn·di·ə] *n* Indien *nt*
India ˈink *n* Tusche *f*
Indian [ˈɪn·di·ən] **I.** *adj* ❶ (*Asian*) indisch ❷ (*native American*) indianisch, Indianer- **II.** *n* ❶ (*Asian*) Inder(in) *m(f)* ❷ (*native American*) Indianer(in) *m(f)*
Indiana [ɪn·ˌdi·ˈæn·ə] *n* Indiana *nt*
Indian ˈcorn *n* FOOD Mais *m,* ÖSTERR *a.* Kukuruz *m*
Indian ˈfile *n see* **single file**
Indian ˈOcean *n* ■ **the ~** der Indische Ozean
Indian ˈsummer *n* Altweibersommer *m*
indicate [ˈɪn·dɪ·keɪt] *vt* ❶ (*show*) zeigen; (*register*) anzeigen ❷ (*imply*) auf etw *akk* hindeuten ❸ (*point to*) ■ **to ~ sb/sth** auf jdn/etw hindeuten
indication [ˌɪn·dɪ·ˈkeɪ·ʃən] *n* ❶ (*sign*) [An]zeichen *nt* (**of** für +*akk*), Hinweis *m* (**of** auf +*akk*); **he hasn't given any ~ of his plans** er hat nichts von seinen Plänen verlauten lassen ❷ (*reading*) *on gauge, meter* Anzeige *f*
indicative [ɪn·ˈdɪk·ə·tɪv] *adj* hinweisend *attr;* ■ **to be ~ of sth** etw erkennen lassen
indicator [ˈɪn·dɪ·keɪ·t̬ər] *n* ❶ (*evidence*) Indikator *m fachspr; of fact, trend* deutlicher Hinweis ❷ TECH (*gauge, meter*) Anzeiger *m;* (*needle*) Zeiger *m*
indices [ˈɪn·dɪ·siz] *n pl of* **index I. 2,3**
indict [ɪn·ˈdaɪt] *vt* anklagen
indictment [ɪn·ˈdaɪt·mənt] *n* ❶ LAW (*accusation*) Anklage[erhebung] *f;* (*bill*) Anklageschrift *f* ❷ (*fig: negative assessment*) Anzeichen *nt* (**of** für +*akk*)
indie [ˈɪn·di] *adj inv short for* **independent** *film, music* Indie-
indifference [ɪn·ˈdɪf·ər·əns] *n* Gleichgültigkeit *f* (**to[ward]** gegenüber +*dat*)
indifferent [ɪn·ˈdɪf·ər·ənt] *adj* ❶ (*uninterested*) gleichgültig (**to** gegenüber +*dat*); (*unmoved*) ungerührt (**to** von +*dat*) ❷ (*mediocre*) [mittel]mäßig
indigenous [ɪn·ˈdɪdʒ·ə·nəs] *adj inv* [ein]heimisch; **to be ~ to North America** in Nordamerika heimisch sein
indigestible [ˌɪn·dɪ·ˈdʒes·tə·bəl] *adj* (*a. fig*) schwer verdaulich; (*bad*) ungenießbar
indigestion [ˌɪn·dɪ·ˈdʒes·tʃən] *n* Magenverstimmung *f;* (*chronic*) Verdauungsstörung[en] *f[pl]*
indignant [ɪn·ˈdɪg·nənt] *adj* empört (**at/about** über +*akk*)
indignation [ˌɪn·dɪg·ˈneɪ·ʃən] *n* Empörung *f* (**at/about** über +*akk*)
indignity [ɪn·ˈdɪg·nɪ·t̬i] *n* Demütigung *f;* (*cause a.*) Erniedrigung *f*
indigo [ˈɪn·dɪ·goʊ] **I.** *n* (*blue dye*) Indigo *m o nt* **II.** *adj* (*dark blue*) indigoblau
indirect [ˌɪn·dɪ·ˈrekt] *adj* ❶ indirekt; **~ remark** Anspielung *f* ❷ *benefits, consequences* mittelbar
indirect ˈobject *n* LING indirektes Objekt, Dativobjekt *nt*
indirect ˈtax *n* FIN indirekte Steuer
indiscernible [ˌɪn·dɪ·ˈsɜr·nə·bəl] *adj* nicht wahrnehmbar; (*invisible*) nicht erkennbar
indiscreet [ˌɪn·dɪ·ˈskrit] *adj* indiskret; (*tactless*) taktlos
indiscretion [ˌɪn·dɪ·ˈskreʃ·ən] *n* ❶ Indiskretion *f;* (*tactlessness*) Taktlosigkeit *f* ❷ (*act*) Indiskretion *f;* (*thoughtless*) unüberlegte Handlung
indiscriminate [ˌɪn·dɪ·ˈskrɪm·ə·nɪt] *adj* ❶ (*unthinking*) unüberlegt; (*uncritical*) unkritisch ❷ (*random*) wahllos
indispensable [ˌɪn·dɪ·ˈspen·sə·bəl] *adj* unentbehrlich (**for/to** für +*akk*)
indisposed [ˌɪn·dɪ·ˈspoʊzd] *adj pred, inv*

❶ (*ill*) unpässlich; *artist, singer* indisponiert *geh* ❷ (*averse*) **to be ~ to do sth** nicht gewillt sein, etw zu tun
indisputable [ˌɪn·dɪ·ˈspju·t̬ə·bəl] *adj inv* unbestreitbar; *evidence* unanfechtbar; *skill, talent* unbestritten
indistinct [ˌɪn·dɪ·ˈstɪŋkt] *adj* ❶ (*mumbled*) undeutlich; (*blurred*) verschwommen ❷ (*unclear*) unklar; *memory* verschwommen
indistinguishable [ˌɪn·dɪ·ˈstɪŋ·gwɪ·ʃə·bəl] *adj inv* nicht unterscheidbar; (*imperceptible*) nicht wahrnehmbar
individual [ˌɪn·dɪ·ˈvɪdʒ·u·əl] **I.** *n* ❶ Einzelne(r) *f(m),* Individuum *nt geh* ❷ (*original person*) [selbstständige] Persönlichkeit **II.** *adj* ❶ *attr, inv* (*separate*) einzeln ❷ (*particular*) individuell
individualism [ˌɪn·dɪ·ˈvɪdʒ·u·ə·lɪz·əm] *n* Individualismus *m*
individualist [ˌɪn·dɪ·ˈvɪdʒ·u·ə·lɪst] *n* Individualist(in) *m(f)*
individualistic [ˌɪn·dɪ·ˌvɪdʒ·u·ə·ˈlɪs·tɪk] *adj* individualistisch *geh*
individuality [ˌɪn·dɪ·ˌvɪdʒ·u·ˈæl·ə·t̬i] *n* ❶ Individualität *f* ❷ ■ **individualities** *pl* (*characteristics*) Eigenarten *pl;* (*tastes*) Geschmäcker *pl*
individualize [ˌɪn·dɪ·ˈvɪdʒ·u·ə·laɪz] *vt* ❶ (*adapt*) nach individuellen Bedürfnissen ausrichten ❷ (*make distinctive*) individuell[er] gestalten
individually [ˌɪn·dɪ·ˈvɪdʒ·u·ə·li] *adv* ❶ *inv* einzeln ❷ (*distinctively*) individuell; (*distinctly*) eigen[tümlich]
indivisible [ˌɪn·dɪ·ˈvɪz·ə·bəl] *adj inv* unteilbar
indoctrinate [ɪn·ˈdak·trɪ·neɪt] *vt* indoktrinieren *geh o pej* (**in/with** mit +*dat*)
indoctrination [ɪn·ˌdak·trɪ·ˈneɪ·ʃən] *n* Indoktrination *f geh o pej;* (*process*) Indoktrinierung *f geh o pej*
indolence [ˈɪn·də·ləns] *n* Trägheit *f*
indolent [ˈɪn·də·lənt] *adj* träge
indomitable [ɪn·ˈdam·ə·tə·bəl] *adj* unbezähmbar; *courage* unerschütterlich; *spirit* unbeugsam; *will* unbändig
Indonesia [ˌɪn·də·ˈni·ʒə] *n* Indonesien *nt*
Indonesian [ˌɪn·də·ˈni·ʒən] **I.** *adj* indonesisch **II.** *n* ❶ Indonesier(in) *m(f)* ❷ (*language*) Indonesisch *nt*
indoor [ˌɪn·ˈdɔr] *adj attr, inv* ❶ (*inside*) Innen-; **~ plant** Zimmerpflanze *f;* SPORTS Hallen- ❷ (*for use inside*) Haus-, für zu Hause *nach n;* SPORTS Hallen-, für die Halle *nach n*
indoors [ˌɪn·ˈdɔrz] *adv inv* (*to inside*) herein/hinein, nach drinnen; (*in building*) drinnen; (*in house*) im Haus
indubitably [ɪn·ˈdu·bɪ·tə·bli] *adv inv* zweifellos
induce [ɪn·ˈdus] *vt* ❶ (*persuade*) ■ **to ~ sb to do sth** jdn dazu bringen, etw zu tun ❷ (*cause*) hervorrufen ❸ MED (*initiate*) *birth, labor* einleiten
inducement [ɪn·ˈdus·mənt] *n* Anreiz *m;* (*verbal*) Überredung *f*
induct [ɪn·ˈdʌkt] *vt usu passive* ❶ **to be ~ed into office** in ein Amt eingesetzt werden ❷ MIL **to be ~ed [into the Army]** eingezogen werden
induction [ɪn·ˈdʌk·ʃən] *n* ❶ (*into office*) [Amts]einführung *f;* (*into organization*) Aufnahme *f* (**into** in +*akk*); **~ into the military** Einberufung *f* [zum Wehrdienst] ❷ MED (*initiation*) Einführung *f* ❸ ELEC, PHYS, TECH Induktion *f fachspr; of engine* Ansaugung *f;* **~ range** [*or* **stove**] Induktionsherd *m*
in'duction coil *n* ELEC Induktionsspule *f fachspr*
indulge [ɪn·ˈdʌldʒ] **I.** *vt* ❶ (*allow*) nachgeben +*dat;* **to ~ sb's every wish** jdm jeden Wunsch erfüllen ❷ (*spoil*) verwöhnen **II.** *vi* ❶ (*enjoy*) sich *dat* einen genehmigen *fam o euph;* (*too much drink*) einen über den Durst trinken *fam o euph;* (*too much food*) sich den Magen/Bauch vollschlagen ❷ (*in activity*) ■ **to ~ in sth** in etw *dat* schwelgen
indulgence [ɪn·ˈdʌl·dʒəns] *n* ❶ (*treat, pleasure*) Luxus *m; food, drink, activity* Genuss *m* ❷ (*in food, drink, pleasure*) Frönen *nt;* (*in alcohol*) übermäßiger Alkoholgenuss *f;* **self-~** [ausschweifendes] Genießen
indulgent [ɪn·ˈdʌl·dʒənt] *adj* ❶ (*lenient*) nachgiebig (**toward[s]** gegenüber +*dat*) ❷ (*tolerant*) nachsichtig
industrial [ɪn·ˈdʌs·tri·əl] *adj* industriell; *product, city* Industrie-; *training, development* betrieblich; **~ area** Industriegebiet *nt;* **~ output** Industrieproduktion *f*
industrialism [ɪn·ˈdʌs·tri·ə·lɪz·əm] *n* Industrialismus *m*
industrialist [ɪn·ˈdʌs·tri·ə·lɪst] *n* Industrielle(r) *f(m)*
industrialization [ɪn·ˌdʌs·tri·ə·lɪ·ˈzeɪ·ʃən] *n* Industrialisierung *f*
industrialize [ɪn·ˈdʌs·tri·ə·laɪz] **I.** *vi country* zum Industriestaat werden; *area* Industrie ansiedeln **II.** *vt* industrialisieren; **to ~ an area** auf einem Gebiet eine Industrie ansiedeln
industrial 'park *n* Industriepark *m*
Industrial Revo'lution *n* HIST ■ **the ~** die Industrielle Revolution
industrious [ɪn·ˈdʌs·tri·əs] *adj* (*hard-working*) fleißig; (*busy*) eifrig
industry [ˈɪn·dəs·tri] *n* ❶ (*manufacturing*) Industrie *f* ❷ (*trade*) Branche *f*
inedible [ɪn·ˈed·ə·bəl] *adj* ❶ (*uneatable*) nicht essbar ❷ (*disgusting*) ungenießbar *pej*
ineducable [ɪn·ˈedʒ·ə·kə·bəl] *adj* schwer erziehbar; (*handicapped*) lernbehindert
ineffective [ˌɪn·ɪ·ˈfek·tɪv] *adj measure* unwirksam; *person* untauglich
ineffectual [ˌɪn·ɪ·ˈfek·tʃʊ·əl] *adj* ineffektiv *geh*
inefficiency [ˌɪn·ɪ·ˈfɪʃ·ən·si] *n* Ineffizienz *f geh; of person* Inkompetenz *f; of measure* Unwirksamkeit *f; of attempt* Erfolglosigkeit *f*
inefficient [ˌɪn·ɪ·ˈfɪʃ·ənt] *adj* ❶ *organization, person* unfähig; *system* ineffizient; (*unproductive*) unwirtschaftlich ❷ (*wasteful*) unrationell

inelegant [ˌɪn·ˈel·ɪ·gənt] *adj* ❶ unelegant; *setting, look* ohne [jeden] Schick *nach n; speech* holprig ❷ (*unrefined*) ungeschliffen; (*clumsy*) plump

ineligible [ɪn·ˈel·ɪdʒ·ə·bəl] *adj inv* (*for benefits*) nicht berechtigt (**for** zu +*dat*); (*for office*) nicht wählbar (**for** in +*dat*)

inept [ɪn·ˈept] *adj* unbeholfen (**at** in +*dat*); (*unskilled*) ungeschickt (**at** in +*dat*); *comment* unangebracht; *leadership* unfähig; *performance* stümperhaft; *remark* unpassend

inequality [ˌɪn·ɪ·ˈkwal·ɪ·t̬i] *n* Ungleichheit *f*

inequitable [ɪn·ˈek·wɪ·tə·bəl] *adj* (*form*) ungerecht

inequity [ɪn·ˈek·wɪ·t̬i] *n* (*form*) Ungerechtigkeit *f*

inert [ɪn·ˈɜrt] *adj* ❶ (*still*) unbeweglich ❷ (*slow*) träge; (*not vigorous*) kraftlos

inertia [ˌɪn·ˈɜr·ʃə] *n* ❶ (*stillness*) Unbeweglichkeit *f* ❷ (*idleness*) Trägheit *f*

inescapable [ˌɪn·ɪ·ˈskeɪ·pə·bəl] *adj inv* unvermeidlich; *fate* unentrinnbar; (*undeniable*) unleugbar; *truth* unbestreitbar

inessential [ˌɪn·ɪ·ˈsen·ʃəl] **I.** *adj inv* nebensächlich **II.** *n usu pl* Nebensächlichkeit *f*

inestimable [ɪn·ˈes·tɪ·mə·bəl] *adj* unschätzbar

inevitable [ɪn·ˈev·ɪ·tə·bəl] **I.** *adj inv* unvermeidlich; *result* zwangsläufig **II.** *n* ■ **the ~** das Unvermeidbare

inexact [ˌɪn·ɪg·ˈzækt] *adj* ungenau

inexcusable [ˌɪn·ɪk·ˈskju·zə·bəl] *adj* unverzeihlich

inexhaustible [ˌɪn·ɪg·ˈzɔs·tə·bəl] *adj* unerschöpflich

inexpensive [ˌɪn·ɪk·ˈspen·sɪv] *adj* preisgünstig; (*cheap*) billig

inexperience [ˌɪn·ɪk·ˈspɪr·i·əns] *n* Unerfahrenheit *f*

inexperienced [ˌɪn·ɪk·ˈspɪr·i·ənst] *adj* unerfahren; ■ **to be ~ in sth** mit etw *dat* nicht vertraut sein; *in skill* in etw *dat* nicht versiert sein; ■ **to be ~ with sth** sich mit etw *dat* nicht auskennen

inexpert [ɪn·ˈek·spɜrt] *adj* laienhaft; *attempt* stümperhaft; *handling* unsachgemäß

inexplicable [ˌɪn·ək·ˈsplɪk·ə·bəl] *adj inv* unerklärlich

inextricable [ˌɪn·ɪk·ˈstrɪk·ə·bəl] *adj* ❶ unentwirrbar; (*inseparable*) unlösbar ❷ (*inescapable*) unentrinnbar

inextricably [ˌɪn·ɪk·ˈstrɪk·ə·bli] *adv* untrennbar; **to be ~ linked with sb/sth** untrennbar mit jdm/etw verbunden sein

infallibility [ɪn·ˌfæl·ə·ˈbɪl·ɪ·t̬i] *n* Unfehlbarkeit *f*

infallible [ɪn·ˈfæl·ə·bəl] *adj inv* unfehlbar

infamous [ˈɪn·fə·məs] *adj* berüchtigt

infamy [ˈɪn·fə·mi] *n* Verrufenheit *f*

infancy [ˈɪn·fən·si] *n* früh[[e]st]e Kindheit; (*fig*) Anfangsphase *f*

infant [ˈɪn·fənt] **I.** *n* Säugling *m* **II.** *adj* **~ daughter** kleines Töchterchen

infanticide [ɪn·ˈfæn·tə·saɪd] *n* Kindestötung *f fachspr*

infantile [ˈɪn·fən·taɪl] *adj* (*pej*) kindisch *meist pej*

infant morˈtality *n* Säuglingssterblichkeit *f*

infantry [ˈɪn·fən·tri] **I.** *n* ■ **the ~** + *sing/pl vb* die Infanterie **II.** *adj* Infanterie-

ˈinfantryman *n* Infanterist *m*

infatuated [ɪn·ˈfætʃ·u·eɪ·t̬ɪd] *adj* vernarrt (**with** in +*akk*), verknallt *fam* (**with** in +*akk*)

infect [ɪn·ˈfekt] *vt* ❶ (*contaminate*) infizieren ❷ (*fig*) *with enthusiasm* anstecken

infection [ɪn·ˈfek·ʃən] *n* Infektion *f*; **throat ~** Halsentzündung *f*

infectious [ɪn·ˈfek·ʃəs] *adj* ansteckend *a. fig.*

infer <-rr-> [ɪn·ˈfɜr] *vt* schließen (**from** aus +*dat*); **from these facts we can ~ that ...** aus diesen Tatsachen können wir die Schlussfolgerung ziehen, dass ...

inference [ˈɪn·fər·əns] *n* ❶ (*conclusion*) Schluss *m* ❷ (*concluding*) [Schluss]folgern *nt*

inferior [ɪn·ˈfɪr·i·ər] **I.** *adj* ❶ minderwertig; *mind* unterlegen ❷ (*lower*) *in rank* [rang]niedriger; *in status* untergeordnet **II.** *n* ■ **~s** *pl* Untergebene *pl*

inferiority [ɪn·ˌfɪr·i·ˈɔr·ɪ·t̬i] *n* ❶ Minderwertigkeit *f*; *of work* schlechte Qualität ❷ *of rank* Unterlegenheit *f*

inferiˈority complex *n* Minderwertigkeitskomplex *m*

infernal [ɪn·ˈfɜr·nəl] *adj* ❶ *inv* höllisch, Höllen- ❷ *attr* (*fam: annoying*) grässlich

inferno [ɪn·ˈfɜr·noʊ] *n* flammendes Inferno

infertile [ɪn·ˈfɜr·t̬əl] *adj inv* unfruchtbar

infertility [ˌɪn·fər·ˈtɪl·ə·t̬i] *n* Unfruchtbarkeit *f*

infest [ɪn·ˈfest] *vt* befallen (**with** von +*dat*); (*haunt*) heimsuchen

infestation [ˌɪn·fes·ˈteɪ·ʃən] *n* ❶ (*state*) Verseuchung *f* ❷ (*instance*) Befall *m* (**of** durch +*akk*); **~ of rats** Rattenplage *f*

infidel [ˈɪn·fɪ·del] *n* Ungläubige(r) *f(m)*

infidelity [ˌɪn·fɪ·ˈdel·ɪ·t̬i] *n* ❶ (*disloyalty*) Verrat *m* (**to** gegenüber/an +*dat*); (*sexual*) Untreue *f* (**to** an +*dat*) ❷ (*sexual peccadillos*) ■ **infidelities** *pl* Seitensprünge *pl*

infighting [ˈɪn·faɪ·tɪŋ] *n* interne Machtkämpfe *pl*

infiltrate [ɪn·ˈfɪl·treɪt] *vt* ❶ unterwandern; *building, enemy lines* eindringen (in +*akk*); *agent, spy* einschleusen (**into** in +*akk*) ❷ *idea, theory* durchdringen

infiltration [ˌɪn·fɪl·ˈtreɪ·ʃən] *n* ❶ Unterwanderung *f*; MIL Infiltration *f fachspr* ❷ (*influence*) starke Einflussnahme

infiltrator [ˈɪn·fɪl·treɪ·t̬ər] *n* Eindringling *m*

infinite [ˈɪn·fə·nɪt] *adj inv* ❶ unendlich; *space* unbegrenzt ❷ (*great*) grenzenlos ❸ MATH unendlich

infinitely [ˈɪn·fən·ɪt·li] *adv inv* ❶ unendlich; **~ small** winzig klein ❷ (*much*) unendlich viel

infinitesimal [ˌɪn·fɪn·ɪ·ˈtes·ɪ·məl] *adj* winzig

infinitive [ɪn·ˈfɪn·ɪ·tɪv] **I.** *n* Infinitiv *m* **II.** *adj attr, inv* Infinitiv-; **~ form** Grundform *f*, Infinitiv *m*

infinity [ɪn·ˈfɪn·ɪ·t̬i] *n* ❶ das Unendliche;

■ **to ~** [bis] ins Unendliche ❷ Unendlichkeit *f;* **into ~** [bis] in die Unendlichkeit
infirm [ɪn·ˈfɜrm] **I.** *adj* ❶ *(ill)* gebrechlich ❷ *(old: weak)* schwach **II.** *n* ■ **the ~** *pl* die Kranken und Pflegebedürftigen
infirmary [ɪn·ˈfɜr·mə·ri] *n* ❶ Krankenhaus *nt* ❷ *(smaller)* Krankenzimmer *nt; (in prison)* Krankenstation *f*
infirmity [ɪn·ˈfɜr·mɪ·t̬i] *n* ❶ *(state)* Gebrechlichkeit *f* ❷ *(illness)* Gebrechen *nt geh*
inflame [ɪn·ˈfleɪm] *vt* ❶ *(arouse)* entfachen ❷ *(anger)* aufbringen; *(stronger)* erzürnen; *with anger* in Wut versetzen; *with desire* mit Verlangen erfüllen
inflammable [ɪn·ˈflæm·ə·bəl] *adj* ❶ [leicht] entzündbar ❷ *(fig) temperament* explosiv; **a highly ~ situation** eine höchst brisante Situation
inflammation [ˌɪn·flə·ˈmeɪ·ʃən] *n* Entzündung *f*
inflammatory [ɪn·ˈflæm·ə·tɔr·i] *adj* ❶ entzündlich, Entzündungs- ❷ *(provoking)* hetzerisch; POL aufrührerisch
inflatable [ɪn·ˈfleɪ·t̬ə·bəl] *adj inv* aufblasbar
inflate [ɪn·ˈfleɪt] **I.** *vt* ❶ aufblasen; *(with pump)* aufpumpen ❷ *(exaggerate)* aufblähen *pej* ❸ *(raise)* in die Höhe treiben **II.** *vi* sich mit Luft füllen
inflated [ɪn·ˈfleɪ·t̬ɪd] *adj inv* ❶ aufgeblasen ❷ *(exaggerated)* aufgebläht *pej;* **to have an ~ opinion of oneself** ein übersteigertes Selbstwertgefühl haben ❸ *(higher)* überhöht
inflation [ɪn·ˈfleɪ·ʃən] *n* ❶ ECON Inflation *f* ❷ Aufblasen *nt; (with pump)* Aufpumpen *nt*
inflationary [ɪn·ˈfleɪ·ʃə·ne·ri] *adj* FIN inflationär, Inflations-
inflect [ɪn·ˈflekt] *vt* ❶ LING beugen ❷ *(modulate)* modulieren
inflection [ɪn·ˈflek·ʃən] *n* ❶ LING Beugung *f* ❷ *(modulation)* Modulation *f fachspr*
inflexibility [ɪn·ˌflek·sə·ˈbɪ·lɪ·t̬i] *n* ❶ Inflexibilität *f geh; (stiffness)* Steifheit *f* ❷ *(stubbornness)* Sturheit *f*
inflexible [ɪn·ˈflek·sə·bəl] *adj* ❶ *(fixed)* starr; *ideas, person* unbeugsam, unflexibel ❷ *(stiff)* steif
inflict [ɪn·ˈflɪkt] *vt* ❶ *(impose)* zufügen *+dat; penalty* auferlegen *+dat;* **to ~ one's views on sb** jdm seine Ansichten aufzwingen ❷ *(usu hum)* **to ~ oneself on sb** sich jdm aufdrängen
influence [ˈɪn·flu·əns] **I.** *n* ❶ Einfluss *m;* **to be an ~ on sb/sth** [einen] Einfluss auf jdn/etw ausüben ❷ *(power)* Einfluss *m* (**on** auf *+akk*); **to be/fall under sb's ~** unter jds Einfluss stehen/geraten; **to exert one's ~** seinen [ganzen] Einfluss geltend machen **II.** *vt* beeinflussen; **easily ~d** beeinflussbar
influential [ˌɪn·flu·ˈen·ʃəl] *adj* einflussreich
influenza [ˌɪn·flʊ·ˈen·zə] **I.** *n* Grippe *f* **II.** *adj* Grippe-
influx [ˈɪn·flʌks] *n* Zustrom *m* (**of** an *+dat*); *of capital* Zufuhr *f* (**of** an *+dat*)
infomercial [ˌɪn·foʊ·ˈmɜr·ʃəl] *n* TV, MEDIA Infomercial *nt fachspr (als Informationssendung getarntes Werbevideo)*
inform [ɪn·ˈfɔrm] **I.** *vt* informieren; *police* benachrichtigen **II.** *vi* ■ **to ~ against/on sb** jdn verpfeifen, jdn anzeigen
informal [ɪn·ˈfɔr·məl] *adj* ❶ informell; *atmosphere, party* zwanglos; *(casual)* leger ❷ *(unofficial)* inoffiziell
informality [ˌɪn·fɔr·ˈmæl·ə·t̬i] *n* ❶ Zwanglosigkeit *f* ❷ *(unofficial nature)* inoffizieller Charakter
informant [ɪn·ˈfɔr·mənt] *n* Informant(in) *m(f)*
information [ˌɪn·fər·ˈmeɪ·ʃən] **I.** *n* ❶ Information *f;* **a piece of ~** eine Information; **a lot of ~** viele Informationen *pl* ❷ *(phone service)* Auskunft *f* **II.** *adj* Informations-; COMPUT Daten-
information reˈtrieval COMPUT **I.** *n* Wiederauffinden *nt* von Informationen, Informationsabruf *m* **II.** *adj* **~ system** Informationsaufrufsystem *nt*
inforˈmation science *n usu pl* Informatik *f kein pl*
information techˈnology *n* Informationstechnologie *f*
informative [ɪn·ˈfɔr·mə·t̬ɪv] *adj* informativ
informed [ɪn·ˈfɔrmd] *adj* [gut] informiert; *opinion* fundiert; **to keep sb ~** jdn auf dem Laufenden halten
informer [ɪn·ˈfɔr·mər] *n* Informant(in) *m(f),* Spitzel(in) *m(f)*
infotainment [ˈɪn·foʊ·teɪn·mənt] *n* Infotainment *nt*
infrared [ˈɪn·frə·ˈred] *adj inv* infrarot
infrastructure [ˈɪn·frə·ˌstrʌk·tʃər] *n* Infrastruktur *f*
infrequent [ɪn·ˈfri·kwənt] *adj* selten
infringe [ɪn·ˈfrɪndʒ] **I.** *vt* verletzen; *law* verstoßen (**against** gegen *+akk*) **II.** *vi* ■ **to ~ [up]on sth** etw verletzen; *area* in etw *akk* eindringen; *territory* auf etw *akk* übergreifen
infringement [ɪn·ˈfrɪndʒ·mənt] *n* ❶ *(action)* Verstoß *m; of law* Gesetzesverstoß *m; of rules* Regelverletzung *f; esp* SPORTS Regelverstoß *m* ❷ *(violation)* Übertretung *f*
infuriate [ɪn·ˈfjʊr·i·eɪt] *vt* wütend machen
infuse [ɪn·ˈfjuz] **I.** *vt* ❶ *(fill)* erfüllen ❷ *tea, herbs* aufgießen **II.** *vi* ziehen
infusion [ɪn·ˈfju·ʒən] *n* ❶ *(input)* Einbringen *nt;* ECON Infusion *f fachspr* ❷ *(brew)* Aufguss *m* ❸ *(brewing)* Aufgießen *nt*
ingenious [ɪn·ˈdʒin·jəs] *adj* ideenreich; *idea, method, plan* ausgeklügelt; *device* raffiniert
ingenuity [ˌɪn·dʒɪ·ˈnu·ə·t̬i] *n* Einfallsreichtum *m; of idea, plan, solution* Genialität *f; of device* Raffiniertheit *f*
ingenuous [ɪn·ˈdʒen·jʊ·əs] *adj* ❶ *(naive)* naiv ❷ *(honest)* offen
ingoing [ˈɪn·goʊ·ɪŋ] *adj attr, inv* eingehend
ingot [ˈɪŋ·gət] *n* Ingot *m fachspr; of gold, silver* Barren *m*
ingrained [ˌɪn·ˈgreɪnd] *adj* ❶ fest sitzend *attr;* **~ with dirt** stark verschmutzt ❷ *(fig: deep)* tief sitzend *attr,* fest verankert

ingratiate [ɪn·ˈɡreɪ·ʃi·eɪt] *vt no passive* ■**to ~ oneself** [**with sb**] sich [bei jdm] einschmeicheln

ingratitude [ɪn·ˈɡræt̬·ə·tud] *n* Undankbarkeit *f*

ingredient [ɪn·ˈɡri·di·ənt] *n* ① Zutat *f* ② (*component*) Bestandteil *m*

ˈin-group *n* angesagte Clique

ingrown [ˈɪn·ɡroʊn] *adj usu attr, inv* eingewachsen

inhabit [ɪn·ˈhæb·ɪt] *vt* bewohnen

inhabitable [ɪn·ˈhæb·ɪ·t̬ə·bəl] *adj* bewohnbar

inhabitant [ɪn·ˈhæb·ɪ·tənt] *n* Einwohner(in) *m(f)*

inhale [ɪn·ˈheɪl] *vt, vi* einatmen; *smoker* inhalieren

inhaler [ɪn·ˈheɪ·lər] *n* Inhalator *m*

inherent [ɪn·ˈhɪr·ənt] *adj* innewohnend *attr;* ■**to be ~ in sth** etw *dat* eigen sein

inherit [ɪn·ˈher·ɪt] **I.** *vt* erben (**from** von +*dat*); (*fig*) übernehmen (**from** von +*dat*) **II.** *vi* erben

inheritable [ɪn·ˈher·ɪ·t̬ə·bəl] *adj inv* vererbbar

inheritance [ɪn·ˈher·ɪ·təns] *n* ① Erbe *nt kein pl* (**from** von +*dat*) ② (*inheriting*) Erben *nt; of characteristics* Vererben *nt*

inhibit [ɪn·ˈhɪb·ɪt] *vt* ① (*restrict*) hindern ② (*deter*) hemmen

inhibition [ˌɪn·hə·ˈbɪʃ·ən] *n* ① *usu pl* Hemmung *f* ② (*inhibiting*) Einschränken *nt;* (*prevention*) Verhindern *nt*

inhospitable [ɪn·ˈhas·pɪ·t̬ə·bəl] *adj* ① (*unwelcoming*) ungastlich ② (*unpleasant*) unwirtlich

in-ˈhouse I. *adj attr, inv* hauseigen **II.** *adv inv* intern, im Hause

inhuman [ɪn·ˈhju·mən] *adj* ① (*cruel*) unmenschlich ② (*nonhuman*) unmenschlich; (*superhuman*) übermenschlich

inhumane [ˌɪn·hju·ˈmeɪn] *adj* inhuman; (*barbaric*) barbarisch

inhumanity [ˌɪn·hju·ˈmæn·ə·t̬i] *n* Grausamkeit *f;* (*barbarity*) Barbarei *f*

inimitable [ɪ·ˈnɪm·ɪ·t̬ə·bəl] *adj* unnachahmlich

iniquity [ɪ·ˈnɪk·wə·t̬i] *n* ① Bosheit *f;* (*unfairness*) Ungerechtigkeit *f;* (*sinfulness*) Verderbtheit *f veraltend geh* ② (*act*) Untat *f;* (*unfair*) Ungerechtigkeit *f;* (*sin*) Sünde *f*

initial [ɪ·ˈnɪʃ·əl] **I.** *adj attr, inv* anfänglich, erste(r, s) **II.** *n* Initiale *f* **III.** *vt* <-l- *or* -ll-> ■**to ~ sth** seine Initialen unter etw *akk* setzen

initialize [ɪ·ˈnɪʃ·ə·laɪz] *vt* COMPUT initialisieren

initially [ɪ·ˈnɪʃ·ə·li] *adv inv* anfangs, zunächst

initiate [ɪ·ˈnɪʃ·i·eɪt] *vt* ① (*start*) in die Wege leiten ② (*teach*) einweihen (**into** in +*akk*) ③ (*admit*) einführen (**into** in +*akk*); (*officially*) [feierlich] aufnehmen (**into** in +*akk*)

initiation [ɪ·ˌnɪʃ·ɪ·ˈeɪ·ʃən] *n* ① (*start*) Einleitung *f* ② (*introduction*) Einführung *f* (**into** in +*akk*); *of member* Aufnahme *f* (**into** in +*akk*); (*ritual*) Initiation *f* (**into** in +*akk*)

initiative [ɪ·ˈnɪʃ·ə·tɪv] *n* ① [Eigen]initiative *f;* **to use one's ~** eigenständig handeln ② (*action*) Initiative *f*

initiator [ɪ·ˈnɪʃ·i·əɪ·t̬ər] *n* Urheber(in) *m(f),* Initiator(in) *m(f)*

inject [ɪn·ˈdʒekt] *vt* ① spritzen (**into** in +*akk*) ② (*fig: introduce*) ■**to ~ sth into sth** etw in etw *akk* [hinein]bringen; **to ~ cash into sth** Geld zu etw *dat* zuschießen *fam* ③ TECH einspritzen

injection [ɪn·ˈdʒek·ʃən] *n* ① Spritze *f* ② (*extra*) **an ~ of cash** eine Geldspritze *fam;* **an ~ of optimism** ein Schuss *m* Optimismus ③ TECH Einspritzung *f*

inˈjection molding *n* Spritzguss *m*

ˈin-joke *n* Insiderwitz *m fam*

injunction [ɪn·ˈdʒʌŋk·ʃən] *n* ① LAW [gerichtliche] Verfügung ② (*instruction*) Ermahnung *f*

injure [ˈɪn·dʒər] *vt* ① (*wound*) verletzen; **to ~ one's back** sich *dat* den Rücken verletzen ② (*damage*) schaden +*dat*

injured [ˈɪn·dʒərd] **I.** *adj* ① (*wounded*) verletzt ② (*offended*) verletzt **II.** *n* ■**the ~** *pl* die Verletzten *pl*

injury [ˈɪn·dʒə·ri] *n* Verletzung *f*

injustice [ɪn·ˈdʒʌs·tɪs] *n* Ungerechtigkeit *f*

ink [ɪŋk] **I.** *n* Tinte *f;* ART Tusche *f;* (*for stamp*) Farbe *f;* TYPO Druckfarbe *f;* (*for newspapers*) Druckerschwärze *f* **II.** *vt* TYPO einfärben

ink-jet ˈprinter *n* Tintenstrahldrucker *m*

inkling [ˈɪŋk·lɪŋ] *n* ① (*suspicion*) Ahnung *f* ② (*hint*) Hinweis *m*

ˈink pad *n* Stempelkissen *nt*

ˈink stain *n* Tintenfleck *m;* (*on paper*) Tintenklecks *m*

inky [ˈɪŋ·ki] *adj* ① tintenbefleckt ② (*dark*) pechschwarz

inlaid [ˈɪn·leɪd] **I.** *adj inv* mit Intarsien *nach n* **II.** *vt pt, pp of* **inlay**

inland I. *adj* [ˈɪn·lənd] *usu attr, inv* Binnen- **II.** *adv* [ˈɪn·lænd] (*direction*) ins Landesinnere; (*place*) im Landesinneren

in-laws [ˈɪn·lɔz] *npl* Schwiegereltern *pl*

inlay I. *n* [ˈɪn·leɪ] ① Einlegearbeit[en] *f[pl]* ② (*for tooth*) Inlay *nt* **II.** *vt* <-laid, -laid> [ɪnˈ·leɪ] *usu passive* einlegen

inlet [ˈɪn·let] *n* ① GEOG [schmale] Bucht; (*of sea*) Meeresarm *m* ② TECH Einlass[kanal] *m;* (*pipe*) Zuleitung *f*

inmate [ˈɪn·meɪt] *n* Insasse, -in *m, f*

inn [ɪn] *n* Gasthaus *nt*

innards [ˈɪn·ərdz] *npl* (*fam*) Eingeweide *pl;* FOOD Innereien *pl*

innate [ɪ·ˈneɪt] *adj* natürlich, angeboren

inner [ˈɪn·ər] *adj inv, usu attr* ① (*inside*) Innen-, innere(r, s) *attr* ② (*emotional*) innere(r, s) *attr;* **~ life** Innenleben *nt*

inner ˈcity *n* Innenstadt *f,* [Stadt]zentrum *nt*

innermost [ˈɪn·ər·moʊst] *adj attr, inv* ① innerste(r, s) ② (*secret*) geheimste(r, s), intimste(r, s)

ˈinner tube *n* Schlauch *m*

inning [ˈɪn·ɪŋ] *n* SPORTS (*in baseball*) Inning *nt*

innocence [ˈɪn·ə·səns] *n* Unschuld *f*

innocent [ˈɪn·ə·sənt] **I.** *adj* ① unschuldig ② (*uninvolved*) unbeteiligt; **an ~ victim** ein unschuldiges Opfer ❸ (*harmless*) unschuldig; *mistake* unbeabsichtigt ❹ (*artless*) unschuldig **II.** *n* **to be an ~** naiv sein

innocuous [ɪ·'nak·jʊ·əs] *adj* harmlos

innovate ['ɪn·ə·veɪt] *vi* ❶ Neuerungen einführen; (*be creative*) kreativ sein ❷ (*change*) sich erneuern

innovation [ˌɪn·ə·'veɪ·ʃən] *n* ❶ Neuerung *f;* (*new product*) Innovation *f* ❷ (*creating*) [Ver]änderung *f*

innovative ['ɪn·ə·veɪ·t̬ɪv] *adj* ❶ innovativ ❷ (*creative*) kreativ

innovator ['ɪn·ə·veɪ·t̬ər] *n* Erneuerer, Erneuerin *m, f*

innuendo <*pl* -s *or* -es> [ˌɪn·ju·'en·doʊ] *n* ❶ (*insinuation*) Anspielung *f* (**about** auf *+akk*) ❷ (*remark*) Zweideutigkeit *f*

innumerable [ɪ·'nu·m͡ər·ə·bəl] *adj inv* unzählig

innumerate [ɪ·'nu·mər·ət] *adj* ■ **to be ~** nicht rechnen können

inoculate [ɪ·'nak·jə·leɪt] *vt* impfen (**against** gegen *+akk*)

inoculation [ɪ·ˌnak·jə·'leɪ·ʃən] *n* Impfung *f*

inoffensive [ˌɪn·ə·'fen·sɪv] *adj* unauffällig

inoperable [ˌɪn·'ap·ər·ə·bəl] *adj* ❶ *inv* MED inoperabel ❷ (*not working*) nicht funktionsfähig; (*impractical*) undurchführbar

inoperative [ˌɪn·'ap·ər·ə·t̬ɪv] *adj inv* ❶ (*invalid*) ungültig; **to be/become ~** außer Kraft sein/treten ❷ (*not working*) nicht funktionsfähig

inopportune [ˌɪn·ˌap·ər·'tun] *adj* ❶ (*inconvenient*) ungünstig ❷ (*unsuitable*) unpassend

inorganic [ˌɪn·ɔr·'gæn·ɪk] *adj inv* CHEM anorganisch

'inpatient *n* stationärer Patient/stationäre Patientin

input ['ɪn·pʊt] **I.** *n* ❶ Beitrag *m;* (*of work*) [Arbeits]aufwand *m* ❷ ELEC Anschluss *m* ❸ COMPUT (*data*) Input *m;* (*entering*) Eingabe *f* **II.** *adj* COMPUT Eingabe- **III.** *vt* <-tt-, ~, ~> COMPUT eingeben; (*with scanner*) einscannen

inquest ['ɪn·kwest] *n* gerichtliche Untersuchung [der Todesursache]; (*fig*) Untersuchung *f*

inquire [ɪn·'kwaɪr] *vt, vi* sich erkundigen (**about, as to** nach *+dat*); ■ **to ~ into sth** etw untersuchen

inquiry [ɪn·'kwaɪ·ri] *n* ❶ (*question*) Anfrage *f,* Erkundigung *f* ❷ (*investigation*) Untersuchung *f;* **to make inquiries** Nachforschungen anstellen

inquisition [ˌɪn·kwɪ·'zɪʃ·ən] *n* ❶ Verhör *nt* ❷ HIST ■ **the I~** die Inquisition

inquisitive [ɪn·'kwɪz·ɪ·t̬ɪv] *adj* ❶ wissbegierig; (*curious*) neugierig; *look, face* fragend *attr; child* fragelustig ❷ (*prying*) neugierig

inroad ['ɪn·roʊd] *n usu pl* ❶ (*progress*) **to make ~s [into sth]** [bei etw *dat*] weiterkommen ❷ (*raid*) **to make ~s on sth** in etw *akk* einfallen ❸ (*cut*) **to make ~s into sth** *money, savings* tiefe Löcher in etw *akk* reißen; *object, pile* sich an etw *dat* vergreifen *fam*

inrush ['ɪn·rʌʃ] *n usu sing of water* Einbruch *m; of people* Zustrom *m*

insane [ɪn·'seɪn] *adj* ❶ (*mentally ill*) geistesgestört ❷ (*fam: crazy*) verrückt

insanitary [ɪn·'sæn·ɪ·ter·i] *adj* unhygienisch

insanity [ɪn·'sæn·ɪ·t̬i] *n* Wahnsinn *a. fig*

insatiable [ɪn·'seɪ·ʃə·bəl] *adj* unstillbar; *person* unersättlich

inscribe [ɪn·'skraɪb] *vt* ❶ (*write*) schreiben (**in, on** in, auf *+akk*); (*engrave*) eingravieren (**in, on** in, auf *+akk*); (*chisel*) einmeißeln (**in, on** in, auf *+akk*) ❷ (*dedicate*) ■ **to ~ sth to sb** jdm etw widmen

inscription [ɪn·'skrɪp·ʃən] *n* Inschrift *f;* (*in book*) Widmung *f*

inscrutable [ɪn·'skru·t̬ə·bəl] *adj* undurchdringlich; *person* undurchschaubar

insect ['ɪn·sekt] *n* Insekt *nt*

insecticide [ɪn·'sek·tɪ·saɪd] *n* Insektenvernichtungsmittel *nt*

insecure [ˌɪn·sɪ·'kjʊr] *adj* ❶ unsicher ❷ (*loose*) nicht fest; (*unsafe*) unstabil

insecurity [ˌɪn·sɪ·'kjʊr·ə·t̬i] *n* Unsicherheit *f*

inseminate [ɪn·'sem·ɪ·neɪt] *vt* besamen; *woman* [künstlich] befruchten

insemination [ɪn·ˌsem·ɪ·'neɪ·ʃən] *n* Befruchtung *f; of animals* Besamung *f*

insensible [ɪn·'sen·sə·bəl] *adj* ❶ *inv* (*unconscious*) bewusstlos ❷ (*numb*) gefühllos; (*to pain*) [schmerz]unempfindlich

insensitive [ɪn·'sen·sɪ·t̬ɪv] *adj* ❶ (*uncaring*) gefühllos; *remark* taktlos ❷ *usu pred* (*numb*) unempfindlich (**to** gegenüber *+dat*)

inseparable [ɪn·'sep·rə·bəl] *adj* ❶ *friends* unzertrennlich ❷ (*connected*) untrennbar [miteinander verbunden]

insert I. *vt* [ɪn·'sɜrt] ■ **to ~ sth [into sth]** ❶ etw [in etw *akk*] [hinein]stecken; *coins* etw [in etw *akk*] einwerfen ❷ (*write*) etw [in etw *akk*] einfügen; (*on form*) etw [in etw *akk*] eintragen **II.** *n* ['ɪn·sɜrt] ❶ (*advertisement*) Werbebeilage[n] *f[pl]* ❷ (*in shoe*) Einlage *f;* (*in clothing*) Einsatz *m*

insertion [ɪn·'sɜr·ʃən] *n* ❶ Einlegen *nt,* Einsetzen *nt;* (*into slot*) Einführen *nt; of coins* Einwurf *m;* (*of words*) Ergänzung *f* ❷ (*thing*) Zusatz *m*

'in-service *adj attr* **~ training** [innerbetriebliche] Fortbildung

inside [ɪn·'saɪd] **I.** *n* ❶ Innere *nt;* **from the ~** von innen ❷ *of hand, door* Innenseite *f;* SPORTS Innenbahn *f* ❸ (*mind*) **who knows what she was feeling on the ~** wer weiß, wie es in ihr aussah **II.** *adv inv* ❶ innen ❷ (*indoors*) innen; (*direction*) hinein/herein; (*in house*) im Haus; (*into house*) ins Haus ❸ (*fam: jailed*) hinter Gittern *fam* **III.** *adj attr, inv* ❶ Innen-, innere(r, s) ❷ (*indoor*) Innen- **IV.** *prep* ■ **~ sth** (*direction*) in etw *akk* [hinein]; (*location*) in etw *dat;* (*within*) **he finished it ~ of two hours** er war in weniger als zwei Stunden damit fertig

insider ['ɪn·ˌsaɪ·dər] *n* Insider(in) *m(f)*

insidious [ɪn·ˈsɪd·i·əs] *adj* heimtückisch

insight [ˈɪn·saɪt] *n* ① (*perception*) Einsicht *f*, Einblick *m* (**into** in +*akk*); **to gain an ~ into sb/sth** jdn/etw verstehen lernen ② (*understanding*) Verständnis *nt*

insignia <*pl* - *or* -s> [ɪn·ˈsɪg·ni·ə] *n* Insignien *nt*

insignificance [ˌɪn·sɪg·ˈnɪf·ɪ·kəns] *n* Belanglosigkeit *f*

insignificant [ˌɪn·sɪg·ˈnɪf·ɪ·kənt] *adj* unbedeutend; *remark* belanglos; *sum, difference* geringfügig

insincere [ˌɪn·sɪn·ˈsɪr] *adj* unaufrichtig; *person* falsch; *smile, praise* unecht; *flattery* heuchlerisch

insinuate [ɪn·ˈsɪn·jʊ·eɪt] *vt* ① (*imply*) andeuten ② (*maneuver*) ■ **to ~ oneself into sth** sich in etw *akk* [ein]schleichen

insinuation [ɪn·ˌsɪn·jʊ·ˈeɪ·ʃən] *n* Unterstellung *f*

insipid [ɪn·ˈsɪp·ɪd] *adj* ① (*dull*) stumpfsinnig ② (*bland*) fade

insist [ɪn·ˈsɪst] **I.** *vi* ① (*demand*) bestehen ([**up**]**on** auf +*dat*) ② (*persist*) ■ **to ~ [up]on doing sth** sich nicht von etw *dat* abbringen lassen ③ (*maintain*) ■ **to ~ [up]on sth** auf etw *dat* beharren **II.** *vt* ■ **to ~ that ...** ① (*claim*) fest behaupten, dass ... ② (*demand*) darauf bestehen, dass ...

insistence [ɪn·ˈsɪs·təns] *n* Bestehen *nt* (**on** auf +*dat*)

insistent [ɪn·ˈsɪs·tənt] *adj* ① (*determined*) beharrlich ② (*forceful*) nachdrücklich

insofar as [ˌɪn·soʊ·ˈfar·əz] *adv inv* soweit

insole [ˈɪn·soʊl] *n* Einlegesohle *f*; (*part of shoe*) Innensohle *f*

insolence [ˈɪn·sə·ləns] *n* Unverschämtheit *f*

insolent [ˈɪn·sə·lənt] *adj* unverschämt

insoluble [ɪn·ˈsal·jə·bəl] *adj inv* ① unlösbar ② *minerals* nicht löslich

insolvency [ɪn·ˈsal·vən·si] *n* Zahlungsunfähigkeit *f*

insolvent [ɪn·ˈsal·vənt] *adj inv* zahlungsunfähig

insomnia [ɪn·ˈsam·ni·ə] *n* Schlaflosigkeit *f*

insomniac [ɪn·ˈsam·ni·æk] *n* **to be an ~** an Schlaflosigkeit leiden

inspect [ɪn·ˈspekt] *vt* untersuchen; (*officially*) kontrollieren

inspection [ɪn·ˈspek·ʃən] *n* [Über]prüfung *f*; (*official*) Kontrolle *f*

inspector [ɪn·ˈspek·tər] *n* ① Inspektor(in) *m(f)*; **tax ~** Steuerprüfer(in) *m(f)* ② (*police*) Inspektor(in) *m(f)*

inspiration [ˌɪn·spə·ˈreɪ·ʃən] *n* ① Inspiration *f*; **to lack ~** fantasielos sein ② (*inspirer*) Inspiration *f*

inspire [ɪn·ˈspaɪr] *vt* ① inspirieren ② (*arouse*) hervorrufen (**in** bei +*dat*); **they don't ~ me with confidence** sie wirken nicht Vertrauen erweckend auf mich

inspired [ɪn·ˈspaɪrd] *adj* ① *poet, athlete* inspiriert ② (*excellent*) großartig ③ (*motivated*) motiviert

instability [ˌɪn·stə·ˈbɪl·ə·t̬i] *n* ① Instabilität *f a. fig* ② PSYCH Labilität *f*

install [ɪn·ˈstɔl] *vt* ① *machinery* aufstellen; *computer, heating* installieren; *bathroom, kitchen* einbauen; *wiring, pipes* verlegen; *phone, washing machine* anschließen ② (*ceremonially*) einsetzen; **to ~ sb as mayor** jdn als Bürgermeister in sein Amt einführen ③ (*position*) **to ~ oneself at a desk** sich einen Schreibtisch aussuchen

installation [ˌɪn·stə·ˈleɪ·ʃən] *n* ① *of machinery* Aufstellen *nt*; *of appliance, heating* Installation *f*; *of kitchen, bathroom* Einbau *m*; *of wiring, pipes* Verlegung *f*; *of phone, washing machine* Anschluss *m* ② (*facility*) Anlage *f* ③ ART Installation *f*

installment [ɪn·ˈstɔl·mənt] *n* ① (*part*) Folge *f* ② (*payment*) Rate *f*

inˈstallment purchase *n* Ratenkauf *m*

instance [ˈɪn·stəns] *n* ① (*case*) Fall *m* ② **for ~** zum Beispiel

instant [ˈɪn·stənt] **I.** *n* ① Moment *m*, Augenblick *m*; **this ~** sofort ② (*as soon as*) ■ **the ~ ...** sobald ... **II.** *adj inv* ① sofortige(r, s) *attr*; **to take ~ effect** sofort wirken ② (*in bags*) Tüten-; (*in cans*) Dosen-; **~ coffee** Pulverkaffee *m*

instantaneous [ˌɪn·stən·ˈteɪ·ni·əs] *adj inv* unmittelbar

instantaneously [ˌɪn·stən·ˈteɪ·ni·əs·li] *adv inv* sofort, unmittelbar

instantly [ˈɪn·stənt·li] *adv inv* sofort

instant ˈreplay *n* TV Wiederholung *f*

instead [ɪn·ˈsted] **I.** *adv inv* stattdessen **II.** *prep* ■ **~ of sth/sb** [an]statt einer S./einer Person *gen*; ■ **~ of doing sth** [an]statt etw zu tun

instep [ˈɪn·step] *n* ① (*of foot*) Spann *m* ② (*of shoe*) Blatt *nt*

instigate [ˈɪn·stɪ·geɪt] *vt* ① (*start*) einleiten ② (*incite*) anzetteln

instigation [ˌɪn·stɪ·ˈgeɪ·ʃən] *n* Anregung *f* (**of** zu +*dat*); (*incitement*) Anstiftung *f* (**of** zu +*dat*)

instill [ɪn·ˈstɪl] *vt feeling* einflößen (**into** +*dat*); *knowledge* beibringen (**into** +*dat*)

instinct [ˈɪn·stɪŋkt] *n* ① (*natural response*) Instinkt *m*; **to have an ~ for sth** einen Riecher für etw *akk* haben *fam* ② (*innate behavior*) Instinkt *m*; **to do sth by/on ~** etw instinktiv tun

instinctive [ɪn·ˈstɪŋk·tɪv] *adj* instinktiv; (*innate*) natürlich, angeboren

institute [ˈɪn·stɪ·tut] **I.** *n* Institut *nt* **II.** *vt* ① (*establish*) einführen ② (*initiate*) einleiten; *legal action* anstrengen

institution [ˌɪn·stɪ·ˈtu·ʃən] *n* ① Einführung *f* ② (*building*) Heim *nt*, Anstalt *f* ③ (*organization*) Einrichtung *f*

institutional [ˌɪn·stɪ·ˈtu·ʃə·nəl] *adj* ① (*pej*) Anstalts-, Heim- ② (*organizational*) institutionell; (*established*) institutionalisiert, etabliert

institutionalize [ˌɪn·stɪ·ˈtu·ʃə·nə·laɪz] *vt* ① ■ **to ~ sb** jdn in ein Heim einweisen ② ■ **to**

~ **sth** etw institutionalisieren *geh*

instruct [ɪn·ˈstrʌkt] *vt* ❶ (*teach*) ■ **to ~ sb in sth** jdm etw beibringen ❷ (*order*) anweisen

instruction [ɪn·ˈstrʌk·ʃən] *n* ❶ *usu pl* (*order*) Anweisung *f* ❷ (*teaching*) Unterweisung *f;* **to give sb ~ in sth** jdm etw beibringen ❸ (*directions*) ■ **~s** *pl* Anweisung[en] *f;* **~s for use** Gebrauchsanweisung *f*

in'struction book, in'struction manual *n* Handbuch *nt; for device* Gebrauchsanweisung *f*

instructive [ɪn·ˈstrʌk·tɪv] *adj* lehrreich, aufschlussreich

instructor [ɪn·ˈstrʌk·tər] *n* ❶ (*teacher*) Lehrer(in) *m(f)* ❷ (*at university*) Dozent(in) *m(f)*

instrument [ˈɪn·strə·mənt] *n* ❶ Instrument *nt* ❷ (*means*) Mittel *nt*

instrumental [ˌɪn·strə·ˈmen·təl] *adj* ❶ *inv* MUS instrumental ❷ (*influential*) förderlich; **he was ~ in bringing about much-needed reforms** er war maßgeblich daran beteiligt, längst überfällige Reformen in Gang zu setzen

instrumentation [ˌɪn·strə·men·ˈteɪ·ʃən] *n* ❶ MUS Arrangement *nt* ❷ TECH Instrumente *pl*

'instrument panel *n* AUTO Armaturenbrett *nt;* AVIAT, NAUT Instrumententafel *f*

insubordinate [ˌɪn·sə·ˈbɔr·dən·ɪt] *adj* ungehorsam, aufsässig

insubstantial [ˌɪn·səb·ˈstæn·ʃəl] *adj* ❶ *argument, evidence* fadenscheinig; *plot, meal* dürftig ❷ (*small*) [sehr] klein

insufferable [ɪn·ˈsʌf·rə·bəl] *adj* unerträglich; *person* unausstehlich

insufficiency [ˌɪn·sə·ˈfɪʃ·ən·si] *n* Mangel *m* (**of** an +*dat*)

insufficient [ˌɪn·sə·ˈfɪʃ·ənt] *adj inv* zu wenig *präd,* unzureichend

insular [ˈɪn·sə·lər] *adj* (*parochial*) provinziell

insularity [ˌɪn·sə·ˈler·ə·t̬i] *n* Provinzialität *f*

insulate [ˈɪn·sə·leɪt] *vt* ❶ ELEC isolieren ❷ (*fig: shield*) [be]schützen (**from** vor +*dat*)

insulating [ˈɪn·sə·leɪ·t̬ɪŋ] *adj* Isolier-

'insulating tape *n* Isolierband *nt*

insulation [ˌɪn·sə·ˈleɪ·ʃən] *n* ❶ Isolierung *f* ❷ (*fig: protection*) Schutz *m*

insulin [ˈɪn·sə·lɪn] **I.** *n* Insulin *nt* **II.** *adj* Insulin-

insult I. *vt* [ɪn·ˈsʌlt] beleidigen **II.** *n* [ˈɪn·sʌlt] ❶ (*remark*) Beleidigung *f* ❷ (*affront*) **to be an ~ to sb's intelligence** jds Intelligenz beleidigen ▶ PHRASES: **to add ~ to <u>injury</u>** um dem Ganzen die Krone aufzusetzen

insuperable [ɪn·ˈsu·pər·ə·bəl] *adj* unüberwindlich

insupportable [ˌɪn·sə·ˈpɔr·t̬ə·bəl] *adj* unerträglich

insurance [ɪn·ˈʃʊr·əns] **I.** *n* ❶ Versicherung *f;* **to take out ~ [against sth]** sich [gegen etw *akk*] versichern ❷ (*payout*) Versicherungssumme *f* ❸ (*premium*) [Versicherungs]prämie *f* **II.** *adj* Versicherungs-

in'surance agent *n* Versicherungsmakler(in) *m(f)*

in'surance company *n* Versicherung[sgesellschaft] *f*

in'surance policy *n* ❶ Versicherungspolice *f* ❷ (*fig: alternative*) **as an ~** zur Sicherheit

in'surance premium *n* [Versicherungs]prämie *f*

insure [ɪn·ˈʃʊr] **I.** *vt* versichern (**against** gegen +*akk*) **II.** *vi* ❶ (*protect*) sich absichern (**against** gegen +*akk*) ❷ (*take insurance*) sich versichern (**with** bei +*dat*)

insured [ɪn·ˈʃʊrd] **I.** *adj* versichert **II.** *n* <*pl* -> ■ **the ~** der/die Versicherte

insurer [ɪn·ˈʃʊr·ər] *n* Versicherung[sgesellschaft] *f*

insurgency [ɪn·ˈsɜr·dʒən·si] *n* Unruhen *pl*

insurgent [ɪn·ˈsɜr·dʒənt] *n* POL *Parteimitglied, das sich der Parteidisziplin nicht beugt*

insurmountable [ˌɪn·sər·ˈmaʊn·tə·bəl] *adj inv* unüberwindlich

insurrection [ˌɪn·sə·ˈrek·ʃən] *n* Aufstand *m*

intact [ɪn·ˈtækt] *adj usu pred* ❶ (*whole*) intakt ❷ (*fig: morally*) unversehrt

intake [ˈɪn·teɪk] **I.** *n* ❶ (*act*) Aufnahme *f;* **~ of breath** Luftholen *nt* ❷ (*amount*) aufgenommene Menge; **~ of calories** Kalorienzufuhr *f* ❸ (*people*) Aufnahmequote *f* **II.** *adj inv* TECH Ansaug-, Saug-

intangible [ɪn·ˈtæn·dʒə·bəl] *adj* nicht greifbar; *emotion* unbestimmbar

integer [ˈɪn·tɪ·dʒər] *n* MATH ganze Zahl

integral [ˈɪn·tɪ·grəl] *adj* ❶ (*central*) wesentlich ❷ (*whole*) vollständig ❸ (*built-in*) eingebaut

integrate [ˈɪn·tɪ·greɪt] **I.** *vt* integrieren (**into** in +*akk*); ■ **to ~ sth [with sth]** etw [auf etw *akk*] abstimmen **II.** *vi* sich integrieren

integrated [ˈɪn·tɪ·greɪ·t̬ɪd] *adj* einheitlich; *person* integriert (**in** in +*akk*); **~ school** (*hist*) Schule *f* ohne Rassentrennung

integrated 'circuit, I 'C *n* ELEC integrierter Schaltkreis

integration [ˌɪn·tɪ·ˈgreɪ·ʃən] *n* ❶ (*assimilation*) Integration *f;* **~ of disabled people** Eingliederung *f* von Behinderten ❷ (*fusion*) Zusammenschluss *m;* (*combination*) Kombination *f*

integrity [ɪn·ˈteg·rə·t̬i] *n* ❶ (*uprightness*) Integrität *f* ❷ (*unity*) Einheit[lichkeit] *f*

intellect [ˈɪn·təl·ekt] *n* ❶ Verstand *m,* Intellekt *m* ❷ (*person*) großer Denker/große Denkerin

intellectual [ˌɪn·tə·ˈlek·tʃʊ·əl] **I.** *n* Intellektuelle(r) *f(m)* **II.** *adj* intellektuell, geistig

intelligence [ɪn·ˈtel·ə·dʒəns] **I.** *n* ❶ Intelligenz *f* ❷ (*department*) Geheimdienst *m* ❸ (*information*) [nachrichtendienstliche] Informationen; **according to our latest ~** unseren letzten Meldungen zufolge **II.** *adj* Nachrichten-; **~ report** Geheimdienstbericht *m*

in'telligence agency *n* Geheimdienst *m*

in'telligence test *n* Intelligenztest *m*

intelligent [ɪn·ˈtel·ə·dʒənt] *adj* klug, intelligent

intelligentsia [ɪn·ˌtel·ə·ˈdʒen·si·ə] *n* ■ **the ~**

die Intellektuellen *pl*

intelligible [ɪn·ˈtel·ɪ·dʒə·bəl] *adj* verständlich; *writing* leserlich

intend [ɪn·ˈtend] *vt* ① (*plan*) beabsichtigen; **I don't think she ~ed me to hear the remark** ich glaube nicht, dass ich die Bemerkung hören sollte ② (*intimate*) ■ **to be ~ed** beabsichtigt sein; **no disrespect ~ed** [das] war nicht böse gemeint ③ *usu passive* (*destine*) ■ **to be ~ed for sth** für etw *akk* gedacht sein

intended [ɪn·ˈten·dɪd] *adj* vorgesehen, beabsichtigt; LAW geplant

intense [ɪn·ˈtens] *adj* ① (*forceful*) intensiv; *odor* stechend; *cold* bitter; *desire, heat* glühend; *excitement* groß; *feeling, friendship* tief; *hatred* rasend; *love* leidenschaftlich; *pain* heftig ② (*serious*) ernst

intensify <-ie-> [ɪn·ˈten·sɪ·faɪ] **I.** *vt* intensivieren; *conflict* verschärfen; *fears* verstärken; *pressure* erhöhen **II.** *vi heat* stärker werden; *feeling, competition a.* zunehmen

intensity [ɪn·ˈten·sə·t̬i] *n* Stärke *f; of feelings* Intensität *f; of explosion, anger* Heftigkeit *f*

intensive [ɪn·ˈten·sɪv] *adj* intensiv; *analysis* gründlich; *bombardment* heftig

intensive ˈcare *n* Intensivpflege *f;* **to be in ~** auf der Intensivstation sein

intent [ɪn·ˈtent] **I.** *n* Absicht *f;* ■ **with ~ to do sth** mit dem Vorsatz, etw zu tun **II.** *adj* ① (*absorbed*) aufmerksam; ■ **to be ~ on sth** sich auf etw *akk* konzentrieren ② (*determined*) ■ **to be ~ on sth** auf etw *akk* versessen sein; ■ **to be ~ on doing sth** fest entschlossen sein, etw zu tun

intention [ɪn·ˈten·ʃən] *n* Absicht *f;* **it wasn't my ~ to exclude you** ich wollte Sie nicht ausschließen; **full of good ~s** voller guter Vorsätze

intentional [ɪn·ˈten·ʃə·nəl] *adj* absichtlich

interact [ɪn·tər·ˈækt] *vi* aufeinander einwirken

interaction [ˌɪn·tər·ˈæk·ʃən] *n* Wechselwirkung *f; of groups, people* Interaktion *f*

interactive [ˌɪn·tər·ˈæk·tɪv] *adj* interaktiv

interbreed <-bred, -bred> [ˌɪn·tər·ˈbrid] **I.** *vt* kreuzen **II.** *vi* sich kreuzen

intercede [ˌɪn·tər·ˈsid] *vi* ■ **to ~ [with sb on behalf of sb]** sich [bei jdm für jdn] einsetzen; **to ~ in an argument** in einem Streit vermitteln

intercept [ˌɪn·t̬ər·ˈsept] *vt* abfangen; **~ a call** eine Fangschaltung legen; **to ~ a pass** SPORTS einen Pass abfangen

interception [ˌɪn·tər·ˈsep·ʃən] *n* Abfangen *nt; of calls* Abhören *nt*

interceptor [ˌɪn·tər·ˈsep·tər] *n* MIL Abfangjäger *m*

intercession [ˌɪn·tər·ˈseʃ·ən] *n* Fürsprache *f,* Vermittlung *f*

interchange **I.** *n* [ˈɪn·tər·tʃeɪndʒ] ① Austausch *m* ② (*road*) [Autobahn]kreuz *nt* **II.** *vt* [ˌɪn·tər·ˈtʃeɪndʒ] austauschen **III.** *vi* [ˌɪn·tər·ˈtʃeɪndʒ] [aus]wechseln

interchangeable [ˌɪn·tər·ˈtʃeɪn·dʒə·bəl] *adj* austauschbar; *word* synonym

intercity [ˌɪn·tər·ˈsɪt·i] *adj attr, inv transportation* Intercity-

intercollegiate [ˌɪn·tər·kə·ˈli·dʒɪt] *adj inv* zwischen Colleges *nach n;* **~ championships** Meisterschaften *pl* der Colleges

intercom [ˈɪn·tər·kam] *n* [Gegen]sprechanlage *f;* (*for doors*) [Tür]sprechanlage *f*

intercontinental [ˌɪn·tər·ˌkan·tə·ˈnen·təl] *adj inv* interkontinental

intercourse [ˈɪn·tər·kɔrs] *n* ① (*sex*) [Geschlechts]verkehr *m* ② (*dealings*) Umgang *m;* **social ~** gesellschaftlicher Verkehr

interdenominational [ˌɪn·tər·dɪ·ˌnam·ə·ˈneɪ·ʃə·nəl] *adj* interkonfessionell

interdepartmental [ˌɪn·tər·ˌdi·part·ˈmen·təl] *adj* zwischen den Abteilungen *nach n*

interdependence [ˌɪn·tər·di·ˈpen·dəns] *n* gegenseitige Abhängigkeit, Interdependenz *f geh*

interdependent [ˌɪn·tər·di·ˈpen·dənt] *adj* voneinander abhängig, interdependent *geh*

interdict [ˌɪn·tər·ˈdɪkt] LAW **I.** *n* Verbot *nt* **II.** *vt* verbieten

interdisciplinary [ˌɪn·tər·ˈdɪs·ə·plɪ·ner·i] *adj inv* SCH fachübergreifend, interdisziplinär

interest [ˈɪn·trɪst] **I.** *n* ① Interesse *nt* (**in** an +*dat*); (*hobby*) Hobby *nt;* **to lose ~ in sb/sth** das Interesse an jdm/etw verlieren; **vested ~** eigennütziges Interesse; ■ **to be in sb's ~** in jds Interesse liegen ② (*advantage*) **in the ~ of safety** aus Sicherheitsgründen; **Jane is acting in the ~ of her daughter** Jane vertritt die Interessen ihrer Tochter ③ (*importance*) Interesse *nt;* **buildings of historical ~** historisch interessante Gebäude; **to be of ~ to sb** für jdn von Interesse sein ④ FIN Zinsen *pl;* **rate of ~** Zinssatz *m* **II.** *vt* interessieren (**in** für +*akk*)

interested [ˈɪn·trɪ·stɪd] *adj* ① (*concerned*) interessiert; **I'd be ~ to learn more about it** ich würde gerne mehr darüber erfahren; **to be ~ in sth/sb** sich für etw/jdn interessieren ② (*involved*) beteiligt; *witness* befangen

interest-ˈfree *adj* FIN zinslos; *credit* unverzinslich

interesting [ˈɪn·trɪ·stɪŋ] *adj* interessant

interface **I.** *n* [ˈɪn·tər·feɪs] Schnittstelle *f; a.* COMPUT, TECH Interface *nt* **II.** *vi* [ˌɪn·tər·ˈfeɪs] ■ **to ~ with sb** mit jdm in Verbindung treten **III.** *vt* [ˈɪn·tər·feɪs] COMPUT, TECH koppeln

interfere [ˌɪn·tər·ˈfɪr] *vi* ① (*meddle*) ■ **to ~ [in sth]** sich [in etw *akk*] einmischen ② (*hit*) ■ **to ~ with one another** aneinanderstoßen

interference [ˌɪn·tər·ˈfɪr·əns] *n* ① (*meddling*) Einmischung *f* ② RADIO, TECH Störung *f*

interim [ˈɪn·tər·ɪm] **I.** *n* Zwischenzeit *f;* **in the ~** in der Zwischenzeit **II.** *adj attr, inv* vorläufig; **~ government** Übergangsregierung *f*

interior [ɪn·ˈtɪr·i·ər] **I.** *adj attr, inv* ① (*inside*) Innen- ② (*country*) Inlands-, Binnen- **II.** *n* ① (*inside*) Innere *nt* ② POL ■ **the I~** das Innere; **the Department of the I~** das Innen-

ministerium; **Secretary of the I~** Innenminister(in) *m(f)*
interior de'signer *n* Innenarchitekt(in) *m(f)*
interject [ˌɪn·tər·'dʒekt] **I.** *vt* einwerfen **II.** *vi* dazwischenreden
interjection [ˌɪn·tər·'dʒek·ʃən] *n* ❶ (*interruption*) Zwischenbemerkung *f* ❷ LING Interjektion *f*
interlace [ˌɪn·tər·'leɪs] **I.** *vt* kombinieren **II.** *vi* sich ineinander verflechten
interloper ['ɪn·tər·loʊ·pər] *n* Eindringling *m*
interlude ['ɪn·tər·lud] *n* Abschnitt *m;* (*between acts*) Pause *f*
intermediary [ˌɪn·tər·'mi·di·er·i] **I.** *n* Vermittler(in) *m(f)* **II.** *adj inv* vermittelnd; **~ role** Vermittlerrolle *f;* **~ stage** Zwischenstadium *nt*
intermediate [ˌɪn·tər·'mi·di·ɪt] *adj inv* ❶ (*level*) mittel; (*between two things*) Zwischen- ❷ (*level of skill*) Mittel-; **~ course** Kurs *m* für fortgeschrittene Anfänger/Anfängerinnen
intermezzo <*pl* -s *or* -zi> [ˌɪn·tər·'met·soʊ, *pl* -t·si] *n* Intermezzo *nt*
interminable [ɪn·'tɜr·mɪ·nə·bəl] *adj* endlos
intermission [ˌɪn·tər·'mɪʃ·ən] *n* Pause *f*
intermittent [ˌɪn·tər·'mɪt·ənt] *adj* periodisch
intern I. *vt* [ɪn·'tɜrn] internieren **II.** *vi* [ɪn·'tɜrn] ein Praktikum absolvieren **III.** *n* ['ɪn·tɜrn] Praktikant(in) *m(f);* [**hospital**] ~ Assistenzarzt, Assistenzärztin *m, f*
internal [ɪn·'tɜr·nəl] *adj inv* innere(r, s); (*within company*) innerbetrieblich; (*within country*) Binnen-; *investigation, memo* intern; **~ affairs** innere Angelegenheiten *pl*
internalize [ɪn·'tɜːr·nə·laɪz] *vt* verinnerlichen
Internal 'Revenue Service *n* ■**the ~** ≈ das Finanzamt
international [ˌɪn·tər·'næʃ·ə·nəl] *adj* international; **~ flight** Auslandsflug *m;* **~ game** Länderspiel *nt*
International Court of 'Justice *n* Internationaler Gerichtshof
internationalize [ˌɪn·tər·'næʃ·ə·nə·laɪz] *vt* internationalisieren
International 'Monetary Fund *n* Internationaler Währungsfonds
International O'lympic Committee *n* Internationales Olympisches Komitee
internee [ˌɪn·tɜr·'ni] *n* Internierte(r) *f(m)*
Internet ['ɪn·tər·net] **I.** *n* Internet *nt;* **to surf** [*or* **browse**] **the ~** im Internet surfen; **on the ~** im Internet **II.** *adj* Internet-
Internet 'banking *n* Internetbanking *nt*
internist [ɪn·'tɜr·nɪst] *n* Internist(in) *m(f)*
internment [ɪn·'tɜrn·mənt] *n* Internierung *f*
in'ternment camp *n* Internierungslager *nt*
interpersonal [ˌɪn·tər·'pɜr·sə·nəl] *adj inv* zwischenmenschlich; **~ skills** soziale Kompetenz
interplanetary [ˌɪn·tər·'plæn·ə·ter·i] *adj inv* interplanetarisch
interplay ['ɪn·tər·pleɪ] *n* Zusammenspiel *nt* (**of** von +*dat*), Wechselwirkung *f* (**between** zwischen +*dat*)
Interpol ['ɪn·tər·pal] *n no art* Interpol *f*
interpolate [ɪn·'tɜr·pə·leɪt] *vt* einfügen; *opinion* einfließen lassen
interpret [ɪn·'tɜr·prɪt] **I.** *vt* ❶ (*explain*) interpretieren; (*understand*) auslegen ❷ (*perform*) wiedergeben; *role* auslegen **II.** *vi* dolmetschen
interpretation [ɪn·ˌtɜr·prɪ·'teɪ·ʃən] *n* Interpretation *f; of rules* Auslegung *f; of dream* Deutung *f*
interpreter [ɪn·'tɜr·prɪ·t̬ər] *n* Dolmetscher(in) *m(f)*
interpreting [ɪn·'tɜr·prɪ·tɪŋ] *n* Dolmetschen *nt*
interrelate [ˌɪn·tər·rɪ·'leɪt] **I.** *vi* zueinander in Beziehung stehen **II.** *vt* verbinden
interrogate [ɪn·'ter·ə·geɪt] *vt* (*question*) verhören
interrogation [ɪn·ˌter·ə·'geɪ·ʃən] *n* Verhör *nt*
interrogator [ɪn·'ter·ə·geɪ·t̬ər] *n* Vernehmungsbeamte(r) *m,* Vernehmungsbeamte [*o* -beamtin] *f*
interrogatory [ˌɪn·tə·'rag·ə·tɔr·i] *adj inv* fragend *attr*
interrupt [ˌɪn·tə·'rʌpt] **I.** *vt* unterbrechen; (*rudely*) ins Wort fallen **II.** *vi* unterbrechen
interruption [ˌɪn·tə·'rʌp·ʃən] *n* Unterbrechung *f*
intersect [ˌɪn·tər·'sekt] **I.** *vt* durchziehen; *line* schneiden; ■**to be ~ed by sth** *roads* etw kreuzen **II.** *vi* sich schneiden; *roads* sich kreuzen
intersection [ˌɪn·tər·'sek·ʃən] *n* ❶ Schnittpunkt *m* ❷ (*junction*) [Straßen]kreuzung *f*
intersperse [ˌɪn·tər·'spɜrs] *vt* ■**to ~ sth with sth** etw in etw *akk* einstreuen; **to be ~d throughout the text** über den ganzen Text verteilt sein
interstate ['ɪn·tər·'steɪt] **I.** *adj attr, inv* zwischenstaatlich **II.** *n* [Bundes]autobahn *f*
interstate 'highway *n* [Bundes]autobahn *f*
intertwine [ˌɪn·tər·'twaɪn] **I.** *vt usu passive* ■**to be ~d with sth** [miteinander] verflochten sein; *plots, destinies* miteinander verknüpft sein **II.** *vi* sich [ineinander] verschlingen
interval ['ɪn·tər·vəl] *n* ❶ (*gap*) Abstand *m* ❷ (*break*) Pause *f; a.* MUS Intervall *nt*
intervene [ˌɪn·tər·'vin] *vi* ❶ einschreiten; **to ~ on sb's behalf** sich für jdn einsetzen ❷ (*interrupt*) sich einmischen
intervening [ˌɪn·t̬ər·'vin·ɪŋ] *adj attr, inv* dazwischenliegend *attr;* **in the ~ period** in der Zwischenzeit
intervention [ˌɪn·tər·'ven·ʃən] *n* Eingreifen *nt*
interventionist [ˌɪn·tər·'ven·ʃə·nɪst] POL **I.** *adj inv* interventionistisch *fachspr* **II.** *n* Interventionist(in) *m(f) fachspr*
interview ['ɪn·tər·vju] **I.** *n* ❶ (*with media*) Interview *nt* (**with** mit +*dat*) ❷ (*for job*) Vorstellungsgespräch *nt* ❸ (*talk*) Unterredung *f;* (*with police*) Verhör *nt* **II.** *vt* (*by reporter*) interviewen; (*for job*) ein Vorstellungsgespräch führen (**with** mit +*dat*); (*by police*) befragen **III.** *vi* (*for job*) ein Vorstellungsgespräch führen
interviewee [ˌɪn·tər·vju·'i] *n* Interview-

te(r) *f(m)*; (*by police*) Befragte(r) *f(m)*; **job ~** Kandidat(in) *m(f)*

interviewer ['ɪn·tər·vju·ər] *n* (*reporter*) Interviewer(in) *m(f)*; (*in job interview*) Leiter(in) *m(f)* des Vorstellungsgesprächs

interweave <-wove, -woven> [ˌɪn·tər·'wiv] **I.** *vt* [miteinander] verweben; (*fig*) [miteinander] vermischen **II.** *vi* sich verschlingen

intestate [ɪn·'tes·teɪt] *adj usu pred, inv* LAW ■ **to be ~** kein Testament besitzen

intestine [ɪn·'tes·tɪn] *n usu pl* Darm *m*, Eingeweide *pl*

intimacy ['ɪn·tə·mə·si] *n* Intimität *f*; (*euph: sexual*) Intimitäten *pl*

intimate ['ɪn·tə·mɪt] *adj* ❶ (*close*) eng, vertraut; *atmosphere* gemütlich; *friend* eng; *relationship* intim ❷ (*detailed*) gründlich; *knowledge* umfassend ❸ (*private*) **~ details** intime Einzelheiten

intimation [ˌɪn·tə·'meɪ·ʃən] *n* Anzeichen *nt* (**of** für +*akk*)

intimidate [ɪn·'tɪm·ɪ·deɪt] *vt* einschüchtern

intimidating [ɪn·'tɪm·ɪ·deɪt̬·ɪŋ] *adj* beängstigend; *manner* einschüchternd

intimidation [ɪn·ˌtɪm·ɪ·'deɪ·ʃən] *n* Einschüchterung *f*

into ['ɪn·tə, -tu] *prep* ❶ (*to inside*) in +*akk*; **to go ~ town** in die Stadt gehen ❷ (*toward*) in +*akk*; **she looked ~ the mirror** sie sah in den Spiegel ❸ (*through time*) **sometimes we work late ~ the evening** manchmal arbeiten wir bis spät in den Abend ❹ (*fam: interested*) **to be ~ sth/sb** an etw/jdm interessiert sein; **what kind of music are you ~?** auf welche Art von Musik stehst du? ❺ *see a. vb* (*persuading*) **they tried to talk their father ~ buying them bikes** sie versuchten, ihren Vater dazu zu überreden, ihnen Fahrräder zu kaufen ❻ (*transition*) **her novels have been translated ~ nineteen languages** ihre Romane sind in neunzehn Sprachen übersetzt worden ❼ (*wear*) **I can't get ~ these pants anymore** ich komme nicht mehr in diese Hose rein

intolerable [ɪn·'tal·ər·ə·bəl] *adj* unerträglich

intolerance [ɪn·'tal·ər·əns] *n* ❶ (*impatience*) Intoleranz *f* (**of** gegenüber +*dat*) ❷ (*incompatibility*) Überempfindlichkeit *f*; MED Intoleranz *f* (**of** gegenüber +*dat*)

intolerant [ɪn·'tal·ər·ənt] *adj* ❶ (*impatient*) intolerant ❷ MED überempfindlich (**of** gegenüber +*dat*)

intonation [ˌɪn·tə·'neɪ·ʃən] *n usu sing* LING Intonation *f fachspr*

intoxicant [ɪn·'tak·sɪ·kənt] *n* Rauschmittel *nt*

intoxicate [ɪn·'tak·sɪ·keɪt] **I.** *vi* eine berauschende Wirkung haben **II.** *vt* berauschen *a. fig*, betrunken machen; (*fig*) *idea* begeistern

intoxicating [ɪn·'tak·sɪ·keɪ·t̬ɪŋ] *adj* berauschend *a. fig*

intoxication [ɪn·ˌtak·sɪ·'keɪ·ʃən] *n* ❶ (*from alcohol, drugs*) Rausch *m a. fig* ❷ MED Vergiftung *f*

intractable [ˌɪn·'træk·tə·bəl] *adj* unbeugsam; *problem, partygoer* hartnäckig; *pupil* widerspenstig; *situation* verfahren

intramural [ˌɪn·trə·'mjʊr·əl] *adj inv* innerhalb der Universität *nach n*, universitätsintern

Intranet [ˌɪn·trə·'net] *n* Intranet *nt*

intransigent [ɪn·'træn·sə·dʒənt] *adj attitude* unnachgiebig; *position* unversöhnlich

intransitive [ɪn·'træn·sɪ·t̬ɪv] *adj inv* intransitiv

intrauterine [ˌɪn·trə·'ju·t̬ər·ɪn] *adj inv* intrauterin

intravenous [ˌɪn·trə·'vi·nəs] *adj inv* intravenös

intrepid [ɪn·'trep·ɪd] *adj* unerschrocken

intricacy ['ɪn·trɪ·kə·si] *n* ❶ (*complexity*) Kompliziertheit *f* ❷ (*elaborateness*) ■ **intricacies** *pl* Feinheiten *pl*

intricate ['ɪn·trɪ·kɪt] *adj* kompliziert; *plot* verschlungen; *question* verzwickt

intrigue I. *vt* [ɪn·'trig] (*fascinate*) faszinieren; (*arouse curiosity*) neugierig machen; ■ **to be ~d by sth** von etw *dat* fasziniert sein **II.** *vi* [ɪn·'trig] intrigieren **III.** *n* ['ɪn·trig] Intrige *f* (**against** gegen +*akk*)

intriguing [ɪn·'tri·gɪŋ] *adj* faszinierend

intrinsic [ɪn·'trɪn·sɪk] *adj* innewohnend; *part* wesentlich

introduce [ˌɪn·trə·'dus] *vt* ❶ (*acquaint*) ■ **to ~ sb [to sb]** jdn [jdm] vorstellen ❷ (*launch*) einführen ❸ (*announce*) vorstellen; MUS einleiten; *program* ankündigen

introduction [ˌɪn·trə·'dʌk·ʃən] *n* ❶ (*announcement*) Vorstellung *f*, Bekanntmachen *nt* ❷ (*launch*) Einführung *f* ❸ (*preface*) Vorwort *nt*; MUS Einleitung *f*

introductory [ˌɪn·trə·'dʌk·tə·ri] *adj inv* ❶ (*preliminary*) einleitend ❷ (*inaugural*) einführend

intro'ductory course *n* Einführungskurs *m*

introspection [ˌɪn·trə·'spek·ʃən] *n* Selbstbeobachtung *f*

introspective [ˌɪn·trə·'spek·tɪv] *adj* verinnerlicht

introvert ['ɪn·trə·ˌvɜrt] *n* introvertierter Mensch

introverted ['ɪn·trə·ˌvɜr·t̬ɪd] *adj* introvertiert

intrude [ɪn·'trud] *vi* ❶ (*meddle*) stören, sich einmischen (**into** in +*akk*) ❷ (*encroach*) **am I intruding?** störe ich gerade?; ■ **to ~ on sb's privacy** in jds Privatsphäre eindringen

intruder [ɪn·'tru·dər] *n* Eindringling *m*; (*thief*) Einbrecher(in) *m(f)*

intrusion [ɪn·'tru·ʒən] *n* (*interruption*) Störung *f*; (*encroachment*) Verletzung *f*

intrusive [ɪn·'tru·sɪv] *adj* aufdringlich

intuition [ˌɪn·tu·'ɪʃ·ən] *n* Intuition *f*

intuitive [ɪn·'tu·ɪ·t̬ɪv] *adj* intuitiv

inundate ['ɪn·ən·deɪt] *vt* überschwemmen *a. fig*

invade [ɪn·'veɪd] **I.** *vt* ❶ **to ~ a country** in ein Land einmarschieren ❷ (*fig: breach*) **to ~ sb's privacy** jds Privatsphäre verletzen **II.** *vi* einfallen

invader [ɪn·'veɪ·dər] *n* Angreifer(in) *m(f)*; (*encroacher*) Eindringling *m*

invalid¹ ['ɪn·və·lɪd] **I.** *n* Invalide(r) *m(f)* **II.** *adj*

I

invalide, körperbehindert
invalid² [ɪn·ˈvæl·ɪd] *adj inv* (*void*) ungültig; (*unsound*) nicht stichhaltig; *theory* nicht begründet
invalidate [ɪn·ˈvæl·ɪ·deɪt] *vt* unwirksam machen; LAW für nichtig erklären; *argument* widerlegen; *judgment* aufheben; *results* annullieren; *theory* entkräftigen
invalidity [ˌɪn·və·ˈlɪd·ə·t̬i] *n* ❶ (*bedridden*) Invalidität *f* ❷ (*unsound*) [Rechts]ungültigkeit *f* ❸ (*void*) **~ of a contract** Nichtigkeit *f* eines Vertrags
invaluable [ɪn·ˈvæl·ju·ə·bəl] *adj inv* unbezahlbar; *source* unverzichtbar
invariable [ɪn·ˈver·i·ə·bəl] *adj inv* unveränderlich
invariably [ɪn·ˈver·i·ə·bli] *adv inv* ausnahmslos
invasion [ɪn·ˈveɪ·ʒən] *n* ❶ Invasion *f* ❷ (*interference*) Eindringen *nt kein pl*
invent [ɪn·ˈvent] *vt* ❶ (*create*) erfinden ❷ (*fabricate*) erdichten; *excuse* sich *dat* ausdenken
invention [ɪn·ˈven·ʃən] *n* ❶ (*creation*) Erfindung *f* ❷ (*creativity*) Einfallsreichtum *m* ❸ (*fabrication*) Erfindung *f*
inventive [ɪn·ˈven·tɪv] *adj* einfallsreich; *design* originell; *illustration* fantasievoll
inventiveness [ɪn·ˈven·tɪv·nɪs] *n* Einfallsreichtum *m*
inventor [ɪn·ˈven·tər] *n* Erfinder(in) *m(f)*
inventory [ˈɪn·vən·tɔr·i] **I.** *n* ❶ (*list*) Inventar *nt* ❷ (*stock*) [Lager]bestand *m;* **to take ~** Inventur machen **II.** *adj* Bestands-
inverse [ɪn·ˈvɜrs] **I.** *adj attr, inv* umgekehrt **II.** *n* Gegenteil *nt*
inversion [ɪn·ˈvɜr·ʒən] *n* Umkehrung *f*
invert [ɪn·ˈvɜrt] *vt* umkehren
invertebrate [ɪn·ˈvɜr·t̬ə·brɪt] **I.** *n* wirbelloses Tier **II.** *adj* wirbellos
invest [ɪn·ˈvest] **I.** *vt* investieren **II.** *vi* ■ **to ~ in sth** [sein Geld] in etw *akk* investieren; **to ~ in a new washing machine** sich *dat* eine neue Waschmaschine zulegen
investigate [ɪn·ˈves·tɪ·geɪt] *vt* untersuchen; *explore* erforschen
investigation [ɪn·ˌves·tɪ·ˈgeɪ·ʃən] *n* Untersuchung *f; of affair* [Über]prüfung *f;* (*by police*) Ermittlung *f;* (*inquiry*) Nachforschung *f*
investigative [ɪn·ˈves·tɪ·geɪ·t̬ɪv] *adj* Forschungs-, Untersuchungs-, Ermittlungs-
investigator [ɪn·ˈves·tɪ·geɪ·t̬ər] *n* (*form*) Ermittler(in) *m(f);* (*in pending proceedings*) Untersuchungsführer(in) *m(f)*
investment [ɪn·ˈvest·mənt] **I.** *n* ❶ (*act*) Investierung *f* ❷ (*instance*) Investition *f;* (*share*) Einlage *f* **II.** *adj* Anlage-, Investitions-, Investment-
in'vestment bank *n* FIN Investmentbank *f*
in'vestment fund *n* Investmentfonds *m*
investor [ɪn·ˈves·t̬ər] *n* [Kapital]anleger(in) *m(f)*, Investor(in) *m(f) fachspr*
inveterate [ɪn·ˈvet̬·ər·ɪt] *adj attr custom, prejudice* tief verankert; *optimist* unverbesserlich; *prejudice* hartnäckig
invidious [ɪn·ˈvɪd·i·əs] *adj* ❶ (*unpleasant*) unerfreulich ❷ (*unjust*) ungerecht
invigorate [ɪn·ˈvɪg·ə·reɪt] *vt* ❶ stärken ❷ (*fig: stimulate*) beleben
invigorating [ɪn·ˈvɪg·ə·reɪ·t̬ɪŋ] *adj* ❶ stärkend; *climate, food* kräftigend ❷ (*fig: stimulating*) belebend; *conversation* anregend; *walk* erfrischend
invincible [ɪn·ˈvɪn·sə·bəl] *adj* ❶ (*unbeatable*) unschlagbar ❷ (*insuperable*) unüberwindlich
invisible [ɪn·ˈvɪz·ə·bəl] *adj inv* ❶ unsichtbar ❷ (*hidden*) verborgen
invitation [ˌɪn·vɪ·ˈteɪ·ʃən] *n* ❶ (*request*) Einladung *f* (**to** zu +*dat*) ❷ (*incitement*) Aufforderung *f* (**to** zu +*dat*) ❸ (*chance*) Gelegenheit *f*
invite **I.** *n* [ˈɪn·vaɪt] (*fam*) Einladung *f* (**to** zu +*dat*) **II.** *vt* [ɪn·ˈvaɪt] ❶ (*to party*) einladen ❷ (*request*) ■ **to ~ sb to do sth** jdn auffordern, etw zu tun ❸ (*fig: cause*) herausfordern; **to ~ trouble** Unannehmlichkeiten hervorrufen
inviting [ɪn·ˈvaɪ·t̬ɪŋ] *adj* ❶ *sight, weather* einladend; *appearance, fashion* ansprechend ❷ (*tempting*) verlockend; *gesture, smile* einladend
in vitro [ɪn·ˈvi·troʊ] *inv* **I.** *adj* künstlich, In-vitro- **II.** *adv* künstlich, in vitro *fachspr*
in vitro fertili'zation *n* künstliche Befruchtung
invoice [ˈɪn·vɔɪs] **I.** *vt* ■ **to ~ sb** jdm eine Rechnung ausstellen **II.** *n* [Waren]rechnung *f* (**for** für +*akk*)
invoke [ɪn·ˈvoʊk] *vt* ❶ (*call on*) **to ~ God's name** Gottes Namen anrufen ❷ (*call forth*) [herauf]beschwören
involuntary [ɪn·ˈval·ən·ter·i] *adj inv* ❶ unfreiwillig; *kindness* gezwungen; *loyalty* erzwungen ❷ (*unintentional*) unbeabsichtigt
involve [ɪn·ˈvalv] *vt* ❶ (*include*) beinhalten; (*encompass*) umfassen; (*entail*) mit sich bringen; (*mean*) bedeuten ❷ (*affect*) betreffen; **that doesn't ~ her** sie hat damit nichts zu tun; **this incident ~s us all** dieser Zwischenfall geht uns alle an ❸ (*bring in*) ■ **to ~ sb in sth** jdn an etw *dat* beteiligen; (*unwillingly*) jdn in etw *akk* verwickeln; **I don't want to get ~d** ich will damit nichts zu tun haben ❹ *usu passive* ■ **to be ~d in sth** (*be busy*) mit etw *dat* zu tun haben; (*be engrossed*) von etw *dat* gefesselt sein; ■ **to be ~d with sb** (*have to do with*) mit jdm zu tun haben; (*relationship*) mit jdm eine Beziehung haben; (*affair*) mit jdm ein Verhältnis haben
involved [ɪn·ˈvalvd] *adj* kompliziert; *story* verworren; *style* komplex; *affair* verwickelt
involvement [ɪn·ˈvalv·mənt] *n* ❶ (*participation*) Beteiligung *f* (**in** an +*dat*), Verwicklung *f* (**in** in +*dat*) ❷ (*intricacy*) Verworrenheit *f*, Kompliziertheit *f;* (*complexity*) Komplexität *f* ❸ (*relationship*) Verhältnis *nt*
invulnerable [ɪn·ˈvʌl·nər·ə·bəl] *adj inv* ❶ (*immune*) unverwundbar, unverletzbar *fig* ❷ (*unassailable*) *position* unangreifbar; *right* unverletzlich; *argument* unwiderlegbar

inward [ˈɪn·wərd] **I.** *adj inv* ❶ (*ingoing*) nach innen gehend ❷ (*incoming*) Eingangs-, eingehend ❸ (*usu fig: internal*) innere(r, s), innerlich **II.** *adv* einwärts, nach innen
inwardly [ˈɪn·wərd·li] *adv* ❶ (*to inside*) nach innen ❷ (*internally*) innerlich, im Innern
inwards [ˈɪn·wərdz] *adv inv* ❶ (*to inside*) einwärts, nach innen ❷ (*spiritually*) im Innern
IOC [ˌaɪ·oʊˈsi] *n + sing/pl vb abbrev of* **International Olympic Committee:** ■**the ~** das IOC
iodine [ˈaɪ·ə·daɪn] *n* Jod *nt*
ion [ˈaɪ·ən] *n* Ion *nt*
iota [aɪˈoʊ·t̬ə] *n usu neg* Jota *nt;* **not an ~** kein bisschen
IOU [ˌaɪ·oʊˈju] *n* (*fam*) *abbrev of* **I owe you** Schuldschein *m*
Iowa [ˈaɪ·ə·wə] *n* Iowa *nt*
IPA [ˌaɪ·piˈeɪ] *n abbrev of* **International Phonetic Alphabet** internationales phonetisches Alphabet
IPO [ˌaɪ·piˈoʊ] *n* FIN *abbrev of* **initial public offering** Erstemission *f*
IQ [ˌaɪˈkju] *n abbrev of* **intelligence quotient** IQ *m*
IRA [ˌaɪ·arˈeɪ] *n* ❶ FIN *abbrev of* **Individual Retirement Account** [steuerbegünstigte] Altersvorsorge ❷ *abbrev of* **Irish Republican Army:** ■**the ~** die IRA
Iran [ɪˈræn] *n* [der] Iran
Iranian [ɪˈreɪ·ni·ən] **I.** *n* Iraner(in) *m(f)* **II.** *adj* iranisch
Iraq [ɪˈrak] *n* [der] Irak
Iraqi [ɪˈrak·i] **I.** *n* Iraker(in) *m(f)* **II.** *adj* irakisch
irascible [ɪˈræs·ə·bəl] *adj* aufbrausend
irate [aɪˈreɪt] *adj* wütend
Ireland [ˈaɪr·lənd] *n* Irland *nt*
iridescent [ˌɪr·ɪˈdes·ənt] *adj* irisierend
iris <*pl* -es> [ˈaɪ·rɪs] *n* ❶ BOT Schwertlilie *f,* Iris *f* ❷ ANAT Regenbogenhaut *f,* Iris *f*
Irish [ˈaɪ·rɪʃ] **I.** *adj* irisch **II.** *n pl* ■**the ~** die Iren *pl*
ˈIrishman *n* Ire *m*
ˈIrishwoman *n* Irin *f*
ˈiris recognition *n* Iriserkennung *f* (*zur Identifizierung einer Person*)
irk [ɜrk] *vt* ärgern
iron [ˈaɪ·ərn] **I.** *n* ❶ Eisen *nt* ❷ (*appliance*) [Bügel]eisen *nt* ❸ (*club*) Golfschläger *m* ▶ PHRASES: **to have many/other ~s in the fire** viele/andere Eisen im Feuer haben **II.** *adj* Eisen-; (*fig: strict*) eisern **III.** *vt, vi* bügeln
ˈIron Age I. *n* Eisenzeit *f* **II.** *adj* eisenzeitlich
iron ˈcurtain *n* ❶ (*hist*) ■**the I~ C~** der Eiserne Vorhang ❷ (*fig: barrier*) Abschottung *f*
ironic [aɪˈran·ɪk] *adj* ironisch
ironing [ˈaɪ·ər·nɪŋ] *n* ❶ (*pressing*) Bügeln *nt* ❷ (*laundry*) Bügelwäsche *f*
ˈironing board *n* Bügelbrett *nt*
iron ˈlung *n* eiserne Lunge
iron ˈore *n* Eisenerz *nt*
ˈironwork *n* ❶ (*decoration*) Eisenwerk *nt* ❷ (*part*) Eisenkonstruktion *f* ❸ (*goods*) Eisenzeug *nt*
ˈironworks *n + sing/pl vb* Eisenhütte *f*
irony [ˈaɪ·rə·ni] *n* Ironie *f*
irrational [ɪˈræʃ·ə·nəl] *adj* ❶ (*unreasonable*) irrational; (*not sensible*) unvernünftig; *suggestion* unsinnig ❷ (*illogical*) irrational
irreconcilable [ɪˌrek·ənˈsaɪ·lə·bəl] *adj inv* ❶ (*opposed*) *ideas, views* unvereinbar; **~ accounts/facts** sich völlig widersprechende Berichte/Tatsachen ❷ (*implacable*) unversöhnlich
irrecoverable [ˌɪr·ɪˈkʌv·ər·ə·bəl] *adj inv damages, losses* unersetzbar, nicht wiedergutzumachend; *treasure, paradise* unwiederbringlich [verloren]
irrefutable [ɪˈref·jə·t̬ə·bəl] *adj inv* ❶ *argument, evidence* unwiderlegbar ❷ (*incontestable*) unbestreitbar
irregular [ɪˈreg·jə·lər] *adj* ❶ (*asymmetrical*) unregelmäßig; *surface* uneben ❷ (*unorthodox*) *conduct* regelwidrig; *document* nicht ordnungsmäßig; *action* ungesetzlich; (*improper*) ungebührlich; *dealings* zwielichtig
irregularity [ɪˌreg·jəˈler·ɪ·t̬i] *n* ❶ (*asymmetry*) Unregelmäßigkeit *f; of surface* Unebenheit *f* ❷ *of conduct* Regelwidrigkeit *f; of action* Ungesetzlichkeit *f*
irrelevance [ɪˈrel·ə·vəns], **irrelevancy** [ɪˈrel·ə·vən·si] *n* Unerheblichkeit *f; of details* Bedeutungslosigkeit *f*
irrelevant [ɪˈrel·ə·vənt] *adj* belanglos, unerheblich
irreparable [ɪˈrep·ər·ə·bəl] *adj inv* irreparabel; *damage, loss* unersetzlich
irreplaceable [ˌɪr·ɪˈpleɪ·sə·bəl] *adj inv* unersetzlich; *resources* nicht erneuerbar
irrepressible [ˌɪr·ɪˈpres·ə·bəl] *adj* ❶ (*impossible to restrain*) *curiosity, desire* unbezähmbar; *anger, joy* unbändig ❷ (*incorrigible*) unverwüstlich, unerschütterlich
irreproachable [ˌɪr·ɪˈproʊ·tʃə·bəl] *adj inv* untadelig; *conduct, quality* einwandfrei
irresistible [ˌɪr·ɪˈzɪs·tə·bəl] *adj* ❶ (*powerful*) unwiderstehlich; *argument* schlagend ❷ (*lovable*) *appearance* äußerst anziehend; *personality* überaus einnehmend ❸ (*enticing*) äußerst verführerisch
irresolute [ɪˈrez·ə·lut] *adj* ❶ (*doubtful*) unentschlossen; *reply* unklar ❷ (*lethargic*) entschlusslos
irrespective [ˌɪr·ɪˈspek·tɪv] *adv inv* ■**~ of sth** ohne Rücksicht auf etw *akk,* ungeachtet einer S. *gen;* **~ of what ...** unabhängig davon, was ...
irresponsible [ˌɪr·ɪˈspan·sə·bəl] *adj* ❶ (*inconsiderate*) unverantwortlich; *person* verantwortungslos ❷ LAW (*inadequate*) unzurechnungsfähig
irretrievable [ˌɪr·ɪˈtri·və·bəl] *adj inv* (*impossible to recover*) *losses* unersetzlich; (*impossible to retrieve*) *treasure* unwiederbringlich
irreverent [ɪˈrev·ər·ənt] *adj* respektlos; (*religiously*) pietätlos *geh*

irreversible [ˌɪr·ɪ·ˈvɜr·sə·bəl] *adj inv* ❶ *development* nicht umkehrbar, irreversibel; *decision* unwiderruflich ❷ TECH *engine* in einer Richtung laufend
irrevocable [ɪ·ˈrev·ə·kə·bəl] *adj inv* unwiderruflich, endgültig, unumstößlich
irrigate [ˈɪr·ɪ·geɪt] *vt* bewässern
irrigation [ˌɪr·ɪ·ˈgeɪ·ʃən] **I.** *n* Bewässerung *f; of crops* Berieselung *f* **II.** *adj* Bewässerungs-
irritable [ˈɪr·ɪ·tə·bəl] *adj* reizbar, gereizt; *organ, tissue* [über]empfindlich
irritant [ˈɪr·ɪ·tənt] *n* ❶ (*substance*) Reizstoff *m* ❷ (*annoyance*) Ärgernis *nt*
irritate [ˈɪr·ɪ·teɪt] *vt* ❶ (*anger*) [ver]ärgern ❷ (*inflame*) **to ~ skin** Hautreizungen hervorrufen
irritating [ˈɪr·ɪ·teɪṭ·ɪŋ] *adj* ärgerlich, lästig; *conduct* irritierend
irritation [ˌɪr·ɪ·ˈteɪ·ʃən] *n* ❶ (*annoyance*) Ärger *m*, Verärgerung *f* ❷ (*nuisance*) Ärgernis *nt* ❸ (*inflammation*) Reizung *f;* **to cause ~** eine Reizung hervorrufen
IRS [ˌaɪ·ar·ˈes] *n* FIN *abbrev of* **Internal Revenue Service** Finanzamt *nt*
is [ɪz] *aux vb 3rd pers sing of* **be**
ISBN [ˌaɪ·es·bi·ˈen] *n abbrev of* **International Standard Book Number** ISBN-Nummer *f*
ISDN [ˌaɪ·es·di·ˈen] *n* TELEC *abbrev of* **integrated services digital network** ISDN
Islam [ɪz·ˈlam] *n* [der] Islam
Islamic [ɪz·ˈlam·ɪk] *adj inv* islamisch
island [ˈaɪ·lənd] *n* ❶ (*in sea*) Insel *f a. fig* ❷ (*on road*) Verkehrsinsel *f*
islander [ˈaɪ·lən·dər] *n* Insulaner(in) *m(f)*
isle [aɪl] *n* (*liter*) Eiland *nt*
isn't [ˈɪz·ənt] = **is not** *see* **be**
isobar [ˈaɪ·soʊ·bar] *n* Isobare *f*
isolate [ˈaɪ·sə·leɪt] *vt* ❶ (*set apart*) trennen (**from** von +*dat*); ■**to ~ oneself** sich absondern (**from** von +*dat*) ❷ CHEM, BIOL (*separate*) **to ~ a substance** eine Substanz isolieren ❸ (*identify*) **to ~ a problem** ein Problem gesondert betrachten
isolated [ˈaɪ·sə·leɪ·ṭɪd] *adj* ❶ (*outlying*) abgelegen; (*detached*) *building, house* frei stehend ❷ (*solitary*) einsam [gelegen]; *village* abgeschieden ❸ (*excluded*) *country* isoliert
isolation [ˌaɪ·sə·ˈleɪ·ʃən] **I.** *n* ❶ (*separation*) Isolation *f;* **~ from noise** Isolierung *f* gegen Schall ❷ (*remoteness*) *of building, house* Abgelegenheit *f* ❸ (*solitariness*) *of village* Einsamkeit *f* ❹ (*loneliness*) Isolation *f* **II.** *adj block, cell* Isolations-; *resistor, switch* Trenn-
isolationism [ˌaɪ·sə·ˈleɪ·ʃə·nɪz·əm] *n* Isolationismus *m*
iso'lation ward *n* Isolierstation *f*
isosceles triangle [aɪ·ˈsas·ə·liz·ˌtraɪ·æŋ·gəl] *n* gleichschenkliges Dreieck
isotope [ˈaɪ·sə·toʊp] *n* CHEM Isotop *nt*
ISP [ˌaɪ·es·ˈpi] *n* INET, TELEC *abbrev of* **Internet service provider** ISP *m*
Israel [ˈɪz·ri·əl] *n* Israel *nt*
Israeli [ɪz·ˈreɪ·li] **I.** *n* Israeli *m o f* **II.** *adj* israelisch
Israelite [ˈɪz·ri·ə·laɪt] *n* Israelit(in) *m(f)*
issue [ˈɪʃ·u] **I.** *n* ❶ (*topic*) Thema *nt;* (*question*) Frage *f;* (*dispute*) Streitfrage *f;* (*affair*) Angelegenheit *f;* (*problem*) Problem *nt;* **that's not the ~!** darum geht es doch gar nicht!; **the point at ~** der strittige Punkt; **side ~** Nebensache *f;* **to address an ~** ein Thema ansprechen; **to avoid the ~** [dem Thema] ausweichen; **to make an ~ of sth** etw aufbauschen; **to raise an ~** eine Frage aufwerfen ❷ (*edition*) Ausgabe *f;* **date of ~** Erscheinungsdatum *nt* ❸ (*circulation*) Auflage *f* ❹ (*provision*) Ausgabe *f; of shares* Emission *f; of fund, loan* Auflegung *f; of check, document* Ausstellung *f* **II.** *vt* ❶ (*produce*) ausstellen; *currency* in Umlauf bringen; *bonds* ausgeben; *newsletter* veröffentlichen; *command* erteilen; *ultimatum* stellen; *statement* abgeben; **to ~ an arrest warrant** einen Haftbefehl erlassen ❷ (*supply with*) ■**to ~ sb with sth** jdn mit etw *dat* ausstatten; (*distribute to*) etw an jdn austeilen
it [ɪt] *pron* ❶ (*unknown thing*) es; (*known thing*) er/es/sie; **a room with two beds in ~** ein Raum mit zwei Betten darin ❷ (*in time phrases*) **what time is ~?** wie spät ist es?; **what date/day is ~?** welchen Tag haben wir heute? ❸ (*distance*) es; **~'s a day's walk to get to town from the farm** die Stadt liegt einen Tagesmarsch von dem Bauernhaus entfernt ❹ *subject* (*referring to following*) **~'s common to have that problem** dieses Problem ist weit verbreitet; **~'s true I don't like Stephanie** es stimmt, ich mag Stephanie nicht; **~'s important that you see a doctor** du solltest unbedingt zu einem Arzt gehen; **~'s a shame I can't come** es ist schade, dass ich nicht kommen kann; **I like ~ in the fall when the weather is crisp and bright** ich mag den Herbst, wenn das Wetter frisch und klar ist ❺ (*in passive with verbs of opinion*) **~ is said that ...** es heißt, dass ... ❻ (*emph*) **~ was Paul who came here in September, not Bob** Paul kam im September, nicht Bob ❼ (*situation*) **~ appears that we have lost** mir scheint, wir haben verloren; **~ takes me an hour to get dressed in the morning** ich brauche morgens eine Stunde, um mich anzuziehen; **if ~'s convenient** wenn es Ihnen/dir passt ❽ (*right thing*) **that's exactly ~ — what a great find!** das ist genau das – ein toller Fund!; **that's ~!** das ist es! ❾ (*the end*) **that's ~** das war's ▶PHRASES: **go for ~!** hopp-auf!; **go for ~, girl!** (*encouragement*) du schaffst es, Mädchen!; **this is ~** jetzt geht's los; **that's ~** das ist der Punkt
IT [ˌaɪ·ˈti] *n* COMPUT *abbrev of* **information technology** IT *f*
Italian [ɪ·ˈtæl·jən] **I.** *n* ❶ (*person*) Italiener(in) *m(f)* ❷ (*language*) Italienisch *nt* **II.** *adj* italienisch
italic [ɪ·ˈtæl·ɪk] *adj* TYPO kursiv
italicize [ɪ·ˈtæl·ɪ·saɪz] *vt* TYPO kursiv drucken

italics [ɪ·ˈtæl·ɪks] *npl* TYPO Kursivschrift *f*

Italy [ˈɪt̬·ə·li] *n* Italien *nt*

itch [ɪtʃ] **I.** *n* <*pl* -es> Juckreiz *m;* MED Hautjucken *nt;* **I've got an ~ on my back** es juckt mich am Rücken **II.** *vi* ❶ (*prickle*) jucken ❷ (*fig fam: desire*) ■**to be ~ing to do sth** ganz wild darauf sein, etw zu tun; **to be ~ing for a fight** auf Streit aus sein

itchy [ˈɪtʃ·i] *adj* ❶ (*rough*) *clothes* kratzig; *wool* kratzend ❷ (*having itch*) juckend; **I've got an ~ scalp** meine Kopfhaut juckt

item [ˈaɪ·t̬əm] *n* ❶ (*article*) Punkt *m;* (*in catalog*) Artikel *m;* (*in ledger, on list*) Posten *m;* **~ of furniture** Möbelstück *nt;* **luxury ~** Luxusartikel *m;* **~ by ~** Punkt für Punkt ❷ (*topic*) Thema *m;* (*on agenda*) Punkt *m* ❸ (*fig fam: couple*) Beziehungskiste *f;* **are you two an ~ or just friends?** habt ihr beiden etwas miteinander, oder seid ihr nur Freunde?

itemize [ˈaɪ·tə·maɪz] *vt* näher angeben; *costs* aufgliedern; **I asked the telephone company to ~ my phone bill** ich bat die Telefongesellschaft, mir eine detaillierte Telefonrechnung auszustellen

itinerant [aɪ·ˈtɪn·ər·ənt] *adj* ❶ (*migrant*) Wander-, Saison- ❷ (*traveling*) reisend, Wander-, fahrend *hist*

itinerary [aɪ·ˈtɪn·ə·rer·i] *n* ❶ (*course*) Reiseroute *f* ❷ (*outline*) Reiseplan *m*

it'll [ˈɪt̬·əl] = **it will/it shall** *see* **will**[1], **shall**

its [ɪts] *pron poss* sein(e)/ihr(e)

it's [ɪts] = **it is/it has** *see* **be/have I., II.**

itself [ɪt·ˈself] *pron reflexive* ❶ *after vb, after prep* sich [selbst] ❷ (*specifically*) **the store ~ opened 15 years ago** das Geschäft selbst öffnete vor 15 Jahren ❸ (*alone*) **to keep sth to ~** etw geheim halten; [**all**] **by ~** [ganz] allein ▶ PHRASES: **in ~** selbst; **creativity in ~ is not enough to make a successful company** Kreativität allein genügt nicht, um eine erfolgreiche Firma aufzubauen

IUD [ˌaɪ·ju·ˈdi] *n abbrev of* **intrauterine device** Intrauterinpessar *nt*

IV [ˌaɪ·ˈvi] *adj abbrev of* **intravenous** intravenös; **~ injection** intravenöse Injektion

I've [aɪv] = **I have** *see* **have I., II.**

IVF [ˌaɪ·vi·ˈef] *n abbrev of* **in vitro fertilization** IVF *f*

ivory [ˈaɪ·və·ri] **I.** *n* Elfenbein *nt* **II.** *adj* elfenbeinern, Elfenbein-; **~-colored** elfenbeinfarben

ˈIvory Coast *n* ■**the ~** die Elfenbeinküste

ivory ˈtower *n* Weltabgeschiedenheit *f;* **to live in an ~** im Elfenbeinturm leben

ivy [ˈaɪ·vi] *n* Efeu *m*

Ivy ˈLeague I. *n* ■**the ~** *Eliteuniversitäten im Nordosten der USA* **II.** *n modifier* der Ivy League angehörende Eliteuniversitäten

J

Jj

J <*pl* -'s *or* -s>, **j** <*pl* -'s> [dʒeɪ] *n* J *nt,* j *nt;* **~ as in Juliet** J wie Julius

jab [dʒæb] **I.** *n* ❶ (*poke*) Stoß *m* ❷ (*boxing*) Gerade *f* **II.** *vt* <-bb-> (*poke or prick*) stechen; **he jabbed the needle into my arm** er stach mir mit der Nadel in den Arm **III.** *vi* <-bb-> ❶ (*poke*) schlagen; (*boxing*) eine [kurze] Gerade schlagen ❷ (*thrust at*) **she jabbed at me [with a stick]** sie stach [mit einem Stock] auf mich ein; **he jabbed at the words [with his pencil]** er tippte [mit seinem Stift] auf die Wörter

jabber [ˈdʒæb·ər] (*pej*) **I.** *n* Geplapper *nt fam* **II.** *vi* quasseln *fam* (**about** über +*akk*)

jabbering [ˈdʒæb·ər·ɪŋ] *n see* **jabber I**

jack [dʒæk] *n* ❶ (*tool*) Hebevorrichtung *f;* AUTO Wagenheber *m* ❷ CARDS Bube *m*

◆**jack off** *vi* (*vulg*) wichsen

◆**jack up I.** *vt* ❶ (*raise a heavy object*) hochheben; *car* aufbocken ❷ (*fig fam: raise*) erhöhen; *prices, rent* in die Höhe treiben **II.** *vi* (*sl*) fixen *fam*

jackal [ˈdʒæk·əl] *n* Schakal *m*

jackass [ˈdʒæk·æs] *n* ❶ (*donkey*) Esel *m* ❷ (*fam: idiot*) Esel *m pej,* Depp *m* SÜDD, ÖSTERR, SCHWEIZ *pej*

jackboot [ˈdʒæk·but] *n* Schaftstiefel *m*

jackdaw [ˈdʒæk·dɔ] *n* Dohle *f*

jacket [ˈdʒæk·ɪt] *n* ❶ FASHION Jacke *f* ❷ (*of a book*) Schutzumschlag *m*

jackhammer [ˈdʒæk·ˌhæm·ər] *n* Presslufthammer *m*

ˈjack-in-the-box *n* Schachtelmännchen *nt;* (*fig*) Hampelmann *m*

ˈjackknife I. *n* ❶ (*knife*) Klappmesser *nt* ❷ SPORTS Hechtsprung *m* **II.** *vi* **the truck ~d on the icy road** der Lastwagen stellte sich auf der vereisten Straße quer

jack-of-ˈall-trades *n* (*able to do many jobs*) Alleskönner(in) *m(f)*

ˈjack-o'-lantern *n* Kürbislaterne *f*

ˈjackpot *n* Hauptgewinn *m;* **to hit the ~** den Hauptgewinn ziehen; (*fig fam: have luck*) das große Los ziehen; (*have success*) einen Bombenerfolg haben

Jacuzzi® [dʒə·ˈku·zi] *n* Whirlpool *m*

jade [dʒeɪd] **I.** *n* ❶ (*precious green stone*) Jade *m o f;* **a ~ vase** eine Vase aus Jade ❷ (*color*) Jadegrün *nt* **II.** *adj* jadegrün

jaded [ˈdʒeɪ·dɪd] *adj* (*dulled*) übersättigt

jagged [ˈdʒæg·ɪd] *adj* gezackt; *coastline, rocks* zerklüftet; *cut, tear* ausgefranst; (*fig*) *nerves* angeschlagen

jaguar [ˈdʒæg·war] *n* Jaguar *m*

jail [dʒeɪl] **I.** *n* Gefängnis *nt;* **to go to ~** ins Gefängnis kommen **II.** *vt* einsperren
'jailbird *n* (*fam*) Knastbruder *m*
'jailbreak *n* Gefängnisausbruch *m*
jailer, jailor ['dʒeɪ·lər] *n* Gefängnisaufseher(in) *m(f)*
jalopy [dʒə·'lap·i] *n* (*hum fam*) [Klapper]kiste *f*
jam¹ [dʒæm] *n* Marmelade *f*
jam² [dʒæm] **I.** *n* ❶ (*fam: awkward situation*) Klemme *f;* **to be in a ~** in der Klemme sitzen ❷ (*obstruction*) *of people* Gedränge *nt; of traffic* Stau *m* **II.** *vt* <-mm-> ❶ (*block*) verklemmen; *switchboard* überlasten; **to ~ sth open** etw aufstemmen ❷ (*cram inside*) [hinein]zwängen (**into** in +*akk*); **he jammed the bags into the trunk of the car** er stopfte die Taschen in den Kofferraum **III.** *vi* <-mm-> (*become stuck*) sich verklemmen; *brakes* blockieren
◆**jam on** *vt* (*put on firmly*) ■**to ~ sth ↔ on** etw fest aufsetzen
◆**jam up** *vt* blockieren; *pipe* verstopfen
Jamaica [dʒə·'meɪ·kə] *n* Jamaika *nt*
Jamaican [dʒə·'meɪ·kən] **I.** *n* Jamaikaner(in) *m(f)* **II.** *adj* jamaikanisch
jamb [dʒæm] *n* ARCHIT [Tür]pfosten *m,* [Fenster]pfosten *m*
jamboree [ˌdʒæm·bə·'ri] *n* (*large social gathering*) großes Fest
'jam-packed *adj* (*fam*) *bus, store* gerammelt voll; *bag, box* randvoll; *suitcase* vollgestopft
'jam session *n* (*fam*) Jamsession *f*
Jan. *n abbrev of* **January** Jan.
jangle ['dʒæŋ·gəl] **I.** *vt* ❶ (*rattle*) ■**to ~ sth** [mit etw *dat*] klirren; *keys* rasseln ❷ (*fig: upset*) **to ~ sb's nerves** jdm auf die Nerven gehen **II.** *vi* klirren; *bells* bimmeln **III.** *n see* **jangling**
jangling ['dʒæŋ·gəl·ɪŋ] *n of bells* Bimmeln *nt; of keys* Klirren *nt*
janitor ['dʒæn·ɪ·t̬ər] *n* Hausmeister(in) *m(f)*
January ['dʒæn·ju·er·i] *n* Januar *m,* Jänner *m* ÖSTERR, SÜDD, SCHWEIZ; *see also* **February**
Japan [dʒə·'pæn] *n* Japan *nt*
Japanese [ˌdʒæp·ə·'niz] **I.** *n* <*pl* -> ❶ (*person*) Japaner(in) *m(f)* ❷ (*language*) Japanisch *nt* **II.** *adj* japanisch
jar¹ [dʒar] *n* (*of glass*) Glas[gefäß] *nt;* (*of metal, of clay without handle*) Topf *m*
jar² [dʒar] **I.** *vt* <-rr-> (*send a shock through*) erschüttern **II.** *vi* <-rr-> (*be incongruous*) nicht harmonieren; *colors* sich beißen; *opinions* sich widersprechen
jargon ['dʒar·gən] *n* [Fach]jargon *m*
jarring ['dʒar·ɪŋ] *adj colors* grell; *voice, laugh* schrill; (*inharmonious*) nicht miteinander im Einklang
jasmine ['dʒæs·mɪn] *n* Jasmin *m*
jaundice ['dʒɔn·dɪs] *n* Gelbsucht *f*
jaundiced ['dʒɔn·dɪst] *adj* ❶ (*affected with jaundice*) gelbsüchtig ❷ (*fig: bitter*) verbittert; *view* zynisch
jaunt [dʒɔnt] *n* Ausflug *m*
jaunty ['dʒɔn·ti] *adj* flott; *grin* fröhlich; *step* schwungvoll
javelin ['dʒæv·lɪn] *n* ❶ (*light spear*) Speer *m* ❷ (*athletic event*) Speerwerfen *nt*
jaw [dʒɔ] **I.** *n* ❶ (*body part*) Kiefer *m;* **lower/upper ~** Unter-/Oberkiefer *m;* **her ~ dropped** [**in amazement**] (*fig*) ihr fiel [vor Staunen] der Unterkiefer herunter *fam* ❷ (*large mouth and teeth*) ■**~s** *pl* Rachen *m a. fig* **II.** *vi* (*pej fam*) quasseln; ■**to ~ with sb** mit jdm quatschen
'jawbone *n* Kieferknochen *m*
'jawbreaker *n* ❶ FOOD großes, rundes, steinhartes Bonbon ❷ (*fam: tongue twister*) Zungenbrecher *m*
jay [dʒeɪ] *n* Eichelhäher *m*
'jaywalker *n* unachtsamer Fußgänger/unachtsame Fußgängerin
'jaywalking *n* unachtsames Überqueren einer Straße
jazz [dʒæz] *n* ❶ (*music*) Jazz *m* ❷ (*pej fam: nonsense*) Quatsch *m fam* ▶ PHRASES: **and all that ~** (*fam*) und all so was
◆**jazz up** *vt* (*fam*) ❶ MUS (*adapt for jazz*) verjazzen ❷ (*fig: brighten or enliven*) aufpeppen
jazzy ['dʒæz·i] *adj* ❶ (*of or like jazz*) Jazz-, jazzartig ❷ (*approv fam: bright and colorful*) *colors* knallig; *piece of clothing* poppig
jealous ['dʒel·əs] *adj* ❶ (*resentful*) eifersüchtig (**of** auf +*akk*) ❷ (*envious*) neidisch; ■**to be ~ of sb** auf jdn neidisch sein; **she was jealous of her brother's success** sie beneidete ihren Bruder um seinen Erfolg
jealousy ['dʒel·ə·si] *n* ❶ (*resentment*) Eifersucht *f* ❷ (*envy*) Neid *m*
jeans [dʒinz] *npl* Jeans[hose] *f;* **a pair of ~** eine Jeans[hose]
jeep [dʒip] *n* Jeep *m,* Geländewagen *m*
jeer [dʒɪr] **I.** *vt* ausbuhen *fam* **II.** *vi* (*make rude comments*) spotten (**at** über +*akk*); (*laugh*) höhnisch lachen; (*boo*) buhen **III.** *n* höhnische Bemerkung
Jehovah [dʒɪ·'hoʊ·və] *n* Jehova *m*
jell [dʒel] *vi see* **gel**
jellied ['dʒel·id] *adj inv* in Aspik eingelegt
Jell-O® ['dʒel·oʊ] *n* Wackelpudding *m fam*
jelly ['dʒel·i] *n* ❶ FOOD Gelee *m o nt* ❷ (*substance*) Gelee *nt*
'jellybean *n* [bohnenförmiges] Geleebonbon
'jellyfish *n* ❶ (*sea animal*) Qualle *f* ❷ (*pej fam: weak, cowardly person*) Waschlappen *m*
jeopardize ['dʒep·ər·daɪz] *vt* gefährden; *career, future* aufs Spiel setzen
jeopardy ['dʒep·ər·di] *n* Gefahr *f;* **in ~** in Gefahr
jerk [dʒɜrk] **I.** *n* ❶ (*sudden sharp movement*) Ruck *m;* (*pull*) Zug *m* ❷ (*pej sl: an annoying person*) Trottel *m fam,* Depp *m* SÜDD *fam* **II.** *vi* zucken; **to ~ upwards** hochschnellen; **to ~ to a halt** abrupt zum Stillstand kommen **III.** *vt* (*move sharply*) ■**to ~ sb/sth** jdn/etw mit einem Ruck ziehen; (*fig*) reißen (**out of** aus +*dat*)

◆**jerk off** *vi* (*vulg*) wichsen

jerkin ['dʒɜr·kɪn] *n* ärmellose Jacke

jerky ['dʒɜr·ki] **I.** *adj movement* ruckartig; *speech* abgehackt **II.** *n* luftgetrocknetes Fleisch

jerry-built ['dʒer·i·bɪlt] *adj attr* (*pej*) schlampig gebaut *fam*

jersey ['dʒɜr·zi] *n* ① (*garment*) Pullover *m* ② (*sports team shirt*) Trikot *nt* ③ (*cloth*) Jersey *m*

jest [dʒest] *n* (*form*) ① (*utterance*) Scherz *m* ② (*mood*) Spaß *m;* **to do/say sth in ~** etw im Spaß tun/sagen

jester ['dʒes·tər] *n* HIST **court ~** Hofnarr *m*

Jesuit ['dʒez·u·ɪt] **I.** *n* Jesuit *m* **II.** *adj* jesuitisch, Jesuiten-

Jesus ['dʒi·zəs], **Jesus Christ** [ˌdʒi·zəs 'kraɪst] **I.** *n* Jesus *m,* Jesus Christus *m* **II.** *interj* (*pej sl*) Mensch! *fam*

jet [dʒet] **I.** *n* ① AVIAT [Düsen]jet *m* ② (*thin stream*) Strahl *m* ③ (*nozzle*) Düse *f* **II.** *vi* <-tt-> mit einem Jet fliegen, jetten *fam;* **to ~ off to Europe** nach Europa jetten [*o* düsen] *fam*

'jet-black *adj inv* pechschwarz

jet 'engine *n* Düsentriebwerk *nt*

jet 'fighter *n* Düsenjäger *m*

'jetfoil *n* Tragflügelboot *nt*

'jet lag *n* Jetlag *m*

'jet plane *n* Düsenflugzeug *nt*

jet-pro'pelled *adj* mit Düsenantrieb *nach n*

jetsam ['dʒet·səm] *n see* **flotsam**

'jet set *n* (*fam*) Jetset *m*

jettison ['dʒeṭ·ɪ·sən] *vt* ① (*discard, abandon*) fallen lassen; *employee* entlassen ② (*drop*) *from a ship* über Bord werfen; *from a plane* abwerfen

jetty ['dʒeṭ·i] *n* (*pier*) Pier *m*

Jew [dʒu] *n* Jude, Jüdin *m, f*

jewel ['dʒu·əl] *n* ① (*precious stone*) Edelstein *m,* Juwel *m o nt* ② (*watch part*) Stein *m*

jeweler, jeweller ['dʒu·ə·lər] *n* Juwelier(in) *m(f)*

jewelry ['dʒu·əl·ri] *n* Schmuck *m*

Jewish ['dʒu·ɪʃ] *adj inv* jüdisch

jib [dʒɪb] *n* ① NAUT Klüver *m* ② TECH *of crane* Ausleger[arm] *m*

jibe [dʒaɪb] *n, vi see* **gibe**

jiffy ['dʒɪf·i] *n* (*fam*) Augenblick *m;* **in a ~** gleich

jig [dʒɪg] **I.** *vt* <-gg-> schütteln **II.** *vi* <-gg-> (*move around*) **to ~ about/up and down** herumhopsen/herumspringen **III.** *n* (*dance*) *a.* MUS Gigue *f*

jigger ['dʒɪg·ər] **I.** *n* (*container*) Messbecher *m* für Alkohol **II.** *vt* fälschen

jiggle ['dʒɪg·əl] **I.** *vt* ■**to ~ sth** mit etw *dat* wackeln; ■**to ~ sth around** etw schütteln **II.** *vi* wippen, hüpfen

'jigsaw *n* ① (*hand-operated*) Laubsäge *f;* (*electric*) Stichsäge *f* ② (*puzzle*) Puzzle[spiel] *nt*

jihad [dʒɪ·'had] *n* Dschihad *m*

jilt [dʒɪlt] *vt* ■**to ~ sb** jdn sitzen lassen; **he jilted her for her best friend** er hat sie wegen ihrer besten Freundin sitzen gelassen

jimmy ['dʒɪm·i] **I.** *n* Brecheisen *nt* **II.** *vt* <-ie-> ■**to ~ open** ⊂ **sth** etw aufbrechen

jingle ['dʒɪŋ·gəl] **I.** *vt bells* klingeln lassen; **to ~ coins** mit Münzen klimpern; **to ~ keys** mit Schlüsseln klirren **II.** *vi bells* bimmeln; *coins* klimpern; *keys* klirren **III.** *n* ① (*metallic ringing*) *of bells* Bimmeln *nt; of coins* Klimpern *nt; of keys* Klirren *nt* ② (*in advertisements*) Jingle *m*

jingoism ['dʒɪŋ·goʊ·ɪz·əm] *n* (*pej*) Chauvinismus *m*

jingoistic [ˌdʒɪŋ·goʊ·'ɪs·tɪk] *adj* (*pej*) chauvinistisch

jinx [dʒɪŋks] **I.** *n* Unglück *nt;* **to put a ~ on sb/sth** jdn/etw verhexen **II.** *vt* verhexen

jitters ['dʒɪṭ·ərz] *npl* (*fam*) Bammel *m kein pl; of an actor* Lampenfieber *nt;* **to get the ~** Muffensausen kriegen

jittery ['dʒɪṭ·ər·i] *adj* (*fam*) nervös

jive [dʒaɪv] **I.** *n* ① (*dance*) Jive *m;* (*music*) Swingmusik *f* ② (*sl: dishonest talk*) Gewäsch *nt fam* **II.** *vi* Jive tanzen; ■**to ~ to sth** auf etw *akk* Jive tanzen

job [dʒab] *n* ① (*employment*) Stelle *f;* **full-time ~** Vollzeitstelle *f;* **part-time ~** Teilzeitstelle *f;* **he has a part-time/full-time ~** er arbeitet halbtags/ganztägig; **to be out of a ~** arbeitslos sein; **to give up one's ~** kündigen; **to lose one's ~** seinen Arbeitsplatz verlieren; **she applied for a ~ at a travel agency** sie bewarb sich um eine Stelle bei einem Reisebüro ② (*piece of work*) Arbeit *f;* (*task*) Aufgabe *f;* **nose ~** (*fam*) Nasenkorrektur *f;* **to do a good ~ on sth** bei etw *dat* gute Arbeit leisten ③ (*fam: object*) Ding *nt* ④ (*sl: crime*) Ding *nt fam* ⑤ (*duty*) Aufgabe *f;* **she's only doing her ~** sie tut nur ihre Pflicht

'job application *n* Bewerbung *f*

jobber ['dʒab·ər] *n* Großhändler(in) *m(f)*

'job creation *n* Arbeitsbeschaffung *f*

'job cuts *npl* Stellenabbau *m kein pl,* Arbeitsplatzabbau *m kein pl*

'job description *n* Stellenbeschreibung *f*

'job hunt *n* (*fam*) Stellensuche *f*

'job interview *n* Bewerbungsgespräch *nt*

jobless ['dʒab·lɪs] **I.** *adj inv* arbeitslos **II.** *n* ■**the ~** *pl* die Arbeitslosen *pl*

'job market *n* Arbeitsmarkt *m*

'job-sharing *n* Arbeitsplatzteilung *f*

'job title *n* Berufsbezeichnung *f*

jockey ['dʒak·i] **I.** *n* Jockey *m* **II.** *vi* ■**to ~ for sth** um etw *akk* konkurrieren

jockstrap ['dʒak·stræp] *n* Suspensorium *nt*

jocular ['dʒak·jə·lər] *adj* (*form*) lustig; *comment* witzig; *person* heiter

jodhpurs ['dʒad·pərz] *npl* Reithose *f;* **a pair of ~** eine Reithose

jog [dʒag] **I.** *n* ① (*run*) Dauerlauf *m;* **to go for a ~** joggen gehen *fam* ② *usu sing* (*push, knock*) Stoß *m* **II.** *vi* <-gg-> joggen **III.** *vt* <-gg-> [an]stoßen ▶ PHRASES: **to ~ sb's memory** jds Gedächtnis *nt* nachhelfen

jogger ['dʒaɡ·ər] *n* Jogger(in) *m(f)*

jogging ['dʒaɡ·ɪŋ] *n* Joggen *nt*

john [dʒan] *n* ① (*fam: bathroom*) Klo *nt* ② (*sl: prostitute's client*) Freier *m fam*

join [dʒɔɪn] **I.** *vt* ① (*connect*) ■**to ~ sth** [**to sth**] etw [mit etw *dat*] verbinden; (*add*) etw [an etw *akk*] anfügen; **to ~ parts together** Teile zusammenfügen ② (*offer company*) ■**to ~ sb** sich zu jdm gesellen; **would you like to ~ us for dinner?** möchtest du mit uns zu Abend essen? ③ (*enroll*) beitreten; *club, party* Mitglied werden; **to ~ the army** Soldat werden ④ (*participate*) ■**to ~ sth** bei etw *dat* mitmachen; **let's ~ the dancing** lass uns mittanzen ⑤ (*support*) ■**to ~ sb in** [**doing**] **sth** jdm bei etw *dat* zur Seite stehen **II.** *vi* ① (*connect*) ■**to ~** [**with sth**] sich [mit etw *dat*] verbinden ② (*cooperate*) ■**to ~ with sb in doing sth** sich mit jdm *dat* zusammenschließen, um etw zu tun ③ (*enroll*) beitreten, Mitglied werden **III.** *n* (*seam*) Verbindung[sstelle] *f*

◆**join in I.** *vi* teilnehmen; (*in game*) mitspielen; (*in song*) mitsingen **II.** *vt* ■**to ~ in sth** bei etw *dat* mitmachen

◆**join up I.** *vi* ① MIL zum Militär gehen ② (*meet*) ■**to ~ up with sb** sich mit jdm zusammentun **II.** *vt* ■**to ~ up ↻ sth** etw [miteinander] verbinden; *parts* etw zusammenfügen

joiner ['dʒɔɪ·nər] *n* (*fam: outgoing person*) geselliger Typ

joint [dʒɔɪnt] **I.** *adj inv* gemeinsam; **~ undertaking** Gemeinschaftsunternehmen *nt;* **~ winners** zwei Sieger/Siegerinnen **II.** *n* ① (*connection*) Verbindungsstelle *f* ② ANAT Gelenk *nt;* **to put sth out of ~** etw ausrenken ③ (*fam: cheap bar, restaurant*) Laden *m* ④ (*cannabis cigarette*) Joint *m sl* ▸ PHRASES: **to be out of ~** aus den Fugen sein

joint ac'count *n* Gemeinschaftskonto *nt*

joint com'mittee *n* gemischter Ausschuss

jointed ['dʒɔɪn·tɪd] *adj inv* (*having joints*) gegliedert; **double-~** extrem gelenkig

jointly ['dʒɔɪnt·li] *adv inv* gemeinsam

joint 'owner *n* Miteigentümer(in) *m(f); of a company* Mitinhaber(in) *m(f)*

joint-stock 'company *n* Aktiengesellschaft *f*

joint 'venture *n* Joint Venture *nt*

joist [dʒɔɪst] *n* [Quer]balken *m*

joke [dʒoʊk] **I.** *n* ① (*action*) Spaß *m;* (*trick*) Streich *m;* (*amusing story*) Witz *m;* **dirty ~** Zote *f;* **to crack/tell ~s** Witze reißen *fam*/erzählen; **to make a ~ of sth** (*ridicule*) etw ins Lächerliche ziehen; **the ~ was on me** der Spaß ging auf meine Kosten ② (*fam: ridiculous thing or person*) Witz *m* **II.** *vi* scherzen; **you must be joking!** das meinst du doch nicht im Ernst!; ■**to ~ about sth** sich über etw *akk* lustig machen

joker ['dʒoʊ·kər] *n* ① (*person*) Spaßvogel *m* ② CARDS Joker *m*

joking ['dʒoʊk·ɪŋ] **I.** *adj* scherzhaft **II.** *n* Scherzen *nt;* **~ aside** Spaß beiseite

jokingly ['dʒoʊk·ɪŋ·li] *adv* im Scherz

jollity ['dʒal·ə·t̬i] *n* Fröhlichkeit *f*

jolly ['dʒal·i] **I.** *adj* ① (*happy*) lustig, vergnügt ② (*enjoyable or cheerful*) lustig **II.** *n* **to get one's jollies from** [*or* **out of**] **sth** (*fam or pej*) sich *dat* einen Spaß daraus machen, etw zu tun

Jolly 'Roger *n* Totenkopfflagge *f*

jolt [dʒoʊlt] **I.** *n* ① (*sudden jerk*) Stoß *m,* Ruck *m* ② (*shock*) Schlag *m;* **to wake up with a ~** aus dem Schlaf hochschrecken **II.** *vt* ① (*jerk*) durchrütteln; **the train stopped suddenly and we were ~ed forwards** der Zug hielt plötzlichen und wir wurden nach vorne geschleudert ② (*fig: shock*) **to ~ sb into action** jdn zum Handeln veranlassen **III.** *vi vehicle* rumpeln

josh [dʒaʃ] (*fam*) **I.** *vt* ■**to ~ sb** [**about sth**] jdn [wegen einer S. *gen*] aufziehen **II.** *vi* Spaß machen, scherzen

joss stick ['dʒas-] *n* Räucherstäbchen *nt*

jostle ['dʒas·əl] **I.** *vt* anrempeln; SPORTS rempeln **II.** *vi* ① (*push*) [sich *akk*] drängeln *fam* ② (*compete*) ■**to ~ for sth** *business, influence* um etw *akk* konkurrieren

jot [dʒat] **I.** *n* **not a ~ of truth** nicht ein Körnchen Wahrheit **II.** *vt* <-tt-> notieren

◆**jot down** *vt* ■**to ~ down ↻ sth** etw notieren

jottings ['dʒat̬·ɪŋz] *npl* Notizen *pl*

journal ['dʒɜr·nəl] *n* ① (*periodical*) Zeitschrift *f;* (*newspaper*) Zeitung *f* ② (*diary*) Tagebuch *nt*

journalism ['dʒɜr·nə·lɪz·əm] *n* Journalismus *m*

journalist ['dʒɜr·nə·lɪst] *n* Journalist(in) *m(f)*

journalistic [ˌdʒɜr·nə·'lɪs·tɪk] *adj* journalistisch

journey ['dʒɜr·ni] *n* Reise *f*

'journeyman *n* ① (*experienced workman*) Fachmann *m* ② (*qualified workman*) Geselle *m*

joust [dʒaʊst] **I.** *vi* einen Turnierzweikampf austragen **II.** *n* Turnierzweikampf *m*

jovial ['dʒoʊ·vi·əl] *adj* ① (*friendly*) *person* freundlich; *welcome* herzlich ② (*cheerful*) *mood* heiter; *chat, evening* nett

joviality [ˌdʒoʊ·vɪ·'æl·ə·t̬i] *n* ① (*friendliness*) Freundlichkeit *f* ② (*cheerfulness*) Fröhlichkeit *f*

jowl [dʒaʊl] *n usu pl* (*hanging flesh*) Kinnbacke *f*

joy [dʒɔɪ] *n* Freude *f,* Vergnügen *nt;* **one of the ~s of the job** einer der erfreulichen Aspekte dieses Berufs; **her singing is a ~ to listen to** ihrem Gesang zuzuhören ist ein Genuss; **to jump for ~** einen Freudensprung machen

joyful ['dʒɔɪ·fəl] *adj face, person* fröhlich; *event, news* freudig

joyless ['dʒɔɪ·lɪs] *adj childhood, time* freudlos; *expression, news* traurig; *marriage* unglücklich

joyous ['dʒɔɪ·əs] *adj* (*liter*) *event, news* freudig; *person, voice* fröhlich

'joy ride I. *n* [waghalsige] Spritztour (*in einem*

gestohlenen Auto) **II.** *vi* [waghalsige] Spritztour unternehmen (*in einem gestohlenen Auto*)

'joystick *n* AVIAT Steuerknüppel *m;* COMPUT Joystick *m*

JP *n abbrev of* **Justice of the Peace**

Jr. *adj after n, inv short for* **junior** jun.

jubilant ['dʒu·bɪ·lənt] *adj* glücklich; *crowd* jubelnd *attr; expression, voice* triumphierend *attr; face* freudestrahlend *attr*

jubilation [ˌdʒu·bɪ·'leɪ·ʃən] *n* Jubel *m*

jubilee ['dʒu·bə·li] *n* Jubiläum *nt*

Judaism ['dʒu·di·ɪz·əm] *n* Judaismus *m,* Judentum *nt*

judder ['dʒʌd·ər] **I.** *vi* ruckeln **II.** *n* Ruckeln *nt*

judge [dʒʌdʒ] **I.** *n* ❶ LAW Richter(in) *m(f)* ❷ (*at a competition*) Preisrichter(in) *m(f);* (*in boxing, gymnastics, wrestling*) Punktrichter(in) *m(f);* (*in track and field, swimming*) Kampfrichter(in) *m(f)* ❸ (*expert*) *of literature, wine* Kenner(in) *m(f);* **to be a good ~ of character** ein guter Menschenkenner sein **II.** *vi* ❶ (*decide*) urteilen; **~ing by his comments, he seems to have been misinformed** seinen Äußerungen nach zu urteilen, ist er falsch informiert worden ❷ (*estimate*) schätzen **III.** *vt* ❶ (*decide*) beurteilen ❷ (*estimate*) schätzen ❸ (*decide the winner*) ■**to ~ sth** bei etw *dat* Kampfrichter sein ▶ PHRASES: **you can't ~ a book by its cover** (*saying*) man kann eine Sache nicht nach dem äußeren Anschein beurteilen

judg(e)ment ['dʒʌdʒ·mənt] *n* ❶ LAW Urteil *nt;* **to pass ~ [on sb/sth]** (*a. fig*) ein Urteil [über jdn/etw] fällen ❷ (*opinion*) Urteil *nt;* **error of ~** Fehleinschätzung *f;* **against one's better ~** wider besseres Wissen

judgmental [dʒʌdʒ·'men·təl] *adj* (*pej*) [vorschnell] wertend *attr;* ■**to be ~ about sb** ein [vorschnelles] Urteil über jdn fällen

judicial [dʒu·'dɪʃ·əl] *adj inv* gerichtlich; **~ authorities** Justizbehörden *pl;* **~ review** gerichtliche Überprüfung (*der Vorinstanzentscheidung*), Normenkontrolle *f* (*Prüfung der Gesetze auf ihre Verfassungsmäßigkeit*)

judiciary [dʒu·'dɪʃ·i·er·i] *n* ■**the ~** (*people*) der Richterstand; (*system*) das Gerichtswesen

judicious [dʒu·'dɪʃ·əs] *adj choice, person* klug; *decision* wohl überlegt

judiciously [dʒu·'dɪʃ·əs·li] *adj* klug

judo ['dʒu·doʊ] *n* Judo *nt*

jug [dʒʌg] *n* Krug *m*

juggernaut ['dʒʌg·ər·nɔt] *n* (*pej: overwhelming force*) verheerende Gewalt

juggle ['dʒʌg·əl] **I.** *vt* ■**to ~ sth** ❶ (*toss and catch*) mit etw *dat* jonglieren; **it is quite hard to ~ children and a career** (*fig*) es ist ziemlich schwierig, Familie und Beruf unter einen Hut zu bringen ❷ (*fig, pej: manipulate*) etw manipulieren **II.** *vi* ❶ (*toss and catch*) jonglieren ❷ (*fig, pej: manipulate*) ■**to ~ with sth** *facts, information* etw manipulieren

juggler ['dʒʌg·lər] *n* Jongleur(in) *m(f)*

jugular ['dʒʌg·jə·lər], **jugular vein** [ˌdʒʌg·jə·lər'-] *n* Drosselvene *f fachspr* ▶ PHRASES: **to go for the ~** (*fig*) an die Gurgel springen *fam*

juice [dʒus] *n* ❶ (*of fruit, vegetables*) Saft *m;* **lemon ~** Zitronensaft *m* ❷ *pl* (*liquid in meat*) [Braten]saft *m kein pl* ❸ (*fam: electricity*) Saft *m sl*

juiced-'up *adj attr* aufgepeppt *fam*

juicy ['dʒu·si] *adj* ❶ (*succulent*) saftig ❷ (*fam: plentiful*) saftig; *profit* fett ❸ (*fam: suggestive*) *joke, story* schlüpfrig; *details, scandal* pikant

juju ['dʒu·dʒu] *n* Karma *nt*

jukebox ['dʒuk·baks] *n* Jukebox *f*

Jul. *n abbrev of* **July**

julep ['dʒu·ləp] *n* Julep *m o nt* (*alkoholisches Eisgetränk, oft mit Pfefferminze*)

July [dʒu·'laɪ] *n* Juli *m; see also* **February**

jumble ['dʒʌm·bəl] **I.** *n* (*a. fig: chaos*) Durcheinander *nt a. fig; of clothes, papers* Haufen *m* **II.** *vt* in Unordnung bringen

jumbo ['dʒʌm·boʊ] **I.** *adj attr* Riesen- **II.** *n* (*fam*) AVIAT Jumbo *m*

jumbo 'jet *n* Jumbojet *m*

jump [dʒʌmp] **I.** *n* ❶ (*leap*) Sprung *m,* Satz *m;* **high/long jump** SPORTS Hoch-/Weitsprung *m* ❷ (*fig: rise*) Sprung *m; in prices, temperatures* [sprunghafter] Anstieg; *in profits* [sprunghafte] Steigerung ❸ (*step*) Schritt *m* ❹ (*shock*) [nervöse] Zuckung; **to wake up with a ~** aus dem Schlaf hochfahren ❺ (*hurdle*) Hindernis *nt* **II.** *vi* ❶ (*leap*) springen; **to ~ to one's feet** aufspringen; **to ~ up and down** herumspringen *fam;* ■**to ~ in[to] sth** *car, water* in etw *akk* [hinein]springen ❷ (*rise*) sprunghaft ansteigen, in die Höhe schnellen ❸ (*be startled*) einen Satz machen; **to make sb ~** jdn erschrecken ▶ PHRASES: **to ~ to conclusions** voreilige Schlüsse ziehen **III.** *vt* ❶ (*leap over*) überspringen ❷ (*skip*) *line, page, stage* überspringen ❸ (*start too soon*) *a.* SPORTS **to ~ the gun** einen Fehlstart verursachen; AUTO **to ~ a (red) light** (*fam*) eine Ampel überfahren ▶ PHRASES: **to ~ the gun** (*fam*) überstürzt handeln

◆**jump at** *vi* (*accept*) ■**to ~ at sth** *idea, suggestion* sofort auf etw *akk* anspringen *fam; offer* sich auf etw *akk* stürzen

◆**jump in** *vi* ❶ (*leap in*) hineinspringen; (*into vehicle*) einsteigen ❷ (*interrupt*) dazwischenreden

◆**jump out** *vi* ❶ (*leave*) **to ~ out of bed** aus dem Bett springen ❷ (*fig: stand out*) ■**to ~ out at sb** jdm sofort auffallen

◆**jump up** *vi* aufspringen

jumper¹ ['dʒʌm·pər] *n* (*person*) Springer(in) *m(f);* (*horse*) Springpferd *nt*

jumper² ['dʒʌm·pər] *n* (*pinafore*) Trägerkleid *nt*

'jumper cables *npl* Starthilfekabel *nt*

jumping 'jack *n* (*exercise*) Hampelmann *m*

'jump jet *n* Senkrechtstarter *m*

'jump rope *n* Springseil *nt*

'jump-start *vt* **to ~ sb's car** jdm Starthilfe geben

'jump suit *n* Overall *m*
jumpy ['dʒʌm·pi] *adj* (*fam*) ❶ (*nervous*) nervös ❷ (*easily frightened*) schreckhaft ❸ (*unsteady*) *market* unsicher
Jun. *n abbrev of* **June**
junction ['dʒʌŋk·ʃən] *n* (*road*) Kreuzung *f;* (*freeway*) Autobahnkreuz *nt*
June [dʒun] *n* Juni *m; see also* **February**
jungle ['dʒʌŋ·gəl] *n* (*a. fig*) Dschungel *m*
junior ['dʒun·jər] **I.** *adj* ❶ *inv* (*younger*) junior *nach n* ❷ *attr, inv* SPORTS Junioren-, Jugend- ❸ *attr, inv* SCH ~ **college** Juniorencollege *nt* (*die beiden ersten Studienjahre umfassende Einrichtung*); ~ **high school** Aufbauschule *f* (*umfasst in der Regel die Klassenstufen 6–9*) ❹ (*low rank*) untergeordnet; ~ **officer** rangniedriger Offizier, rangniedrige Offizierin; ~ **partner** Juniorpartner(in) *m(f)* **II.** *n* ❶ (*son*) Sohn *m* ❷ (*younger*) Jüngere(r) *f(m);* **he's two years my** ~ er ist zwei Jahre jünger als ich ❸ SCH, UNIV (*third-year student*) Student (in) *m(f)* im vorletzten Studienjahr ❹ (*low-ranking person*) unterer Angestellter/untere Angestellte
juniper ['dʒu·nɪ·pər] *n* Wacholder *m*
junk[1] [dʒʌŋk] **I.** *n* ❶ (*worthless stuff*) Ramsch *m fam;* (*fig, pej*) Mist *m;* (*literature*) Schund *m* ❷ (*sl: heroin*) Stoff *m* **II.** *vt* (*fam*) wegschmeißen
junk[2] [dʒʌŋk] *n* NAUT Dschunke *f*
'junk food *n* Schnellgerichte *pl;* (*pej*) ungesundes Essen
junkie ['dʒʌŋ·ki] *n* (*sl*) Fixer(in) *m(f) fam;* **fitness** ~ (*hum*) Fitnessfreak *m*
'junk mail *n* Wurfsendungen *pl,* Reklame *f*
'junk shop *n* Trödelladen *m*
'junkyard *n* Schrottplatz *m*
junta ['hʊn·tə] *n* Junta *f*
Jupiter ['dʒu·pɪ·t̬ər] *n no art* Jupiter *m*
jurisdiction [ˌdʒʊr·ɪs·'dɪk·ʃən] *n* Gerichtsbarkeit *f*
jurisprudence [ˌdʒʊr·ɪs·'pru·dəns] *n* LAW Rechtswissenschaft *f*
juror ['dʒʊr·ər] *n* LAW Geschworene(r) *f(m)*
jury ['dʒʊr·i] *n* ❶ LAW ■ **the** ~ die Geschworenen *pl* ❷ (*competition*) Jury *f;* SPORTS Kampfgericht *nt* ▶ PHRASES: **the** ~ **is still out** das letzte Wort ist noch nicht gesprochen
just I. *adv* [dʒʌst] *inv* ❶ (*in a moment*) gleich; **we're** ~ **about to leave** wir wollen gleich los; **I was** ~ **going to call you** ich wollte dich eben anrufen ❷ (*directly*) direkt, gleich; ~ **after getting up** gleich nach dem Aufstehen ❸ (*recently*) gerade [eben], [so]eben ❹ (*now*) gerade; ■ **to be** ~ **doing sth** gerade dabei sein, etw zu tun ❺ (*exactly*) genau; **that's** ~ **what I was going to say** genau das wollte ich gerade sagen; **that's** ~ **it!** das ist es ja gerade!; ~ **now** gerade; ~ **then** gerade in diesem Augenblick; ~ **as well** ebenso gut; ~ **as/when ...** gerade in dem Augenblick, als ... ❻ (*only*) nur, bloß *fam;* (*simply*) einfach; **she's** ~ **a baby** sie ist noch ein Baby; ~ **for fun** nur [so] zum Spaß; **[not]** ~ **anybody** [nicht] einfach irgendjemand ❼ (*barely*) gerade noch/mal; ~ **in time** gerade noch rechtzeitig ❽ *with imperatives* ~ **imagine!** stell dir das mal vor!; ~ **look at this!** schau dir das mal an! ▶ PHRASES: ~ **a minute!** (*please wait*) einen Augenblick [bitte]!; (*as interruption*) Moment [mal]!; **it's** ~ **one of those things** (*saying*) so etwas passiert eben **II.** *adj* [dʒʌst] ❶ (*fair*) gerecht (**to** gegenüber +*dat*) ❷ (*justified*) *punishment* gerecht; **to have** ~ **cause to do sth** einen triftigen Grund haben, etw zu tun ▶ PHRASES: **to get one's** ~ **deserts** bekommen, was man verdient hat
justice ['dʒʌs·tɪs] *n* ❶ (*fairness*) Gerechtigkeit *f;* **to do sth** ~ etw *dat* gerecht werden ❷ (*administration of the law*) Justiz *f;* **a miscarriage of** ~ ein Justizirrtum *m* ❸ (*judge*) Richter(in) *m(f)*
Justice of the 'Peace *n* Friedensrichter(in) *m(f)*
justifiable [ˌdʒʌs·tə·'faɪ·ə·bəl] *adj* zu rechtfertigen *präd,* berechtigt
justification [ˌdʒʌs·tə·fɪ·'keɪ·ʃən] *n* Rechtfertigung *f*
justified ['dʒʌs·tə·faɪd] *adj* gerechtfertigt, berechtigt; **you were totally** ~ **in complaining** du hast dich völlig zu Recht beschwert
justify <-ie-> ['dʒʌs·tə·faɪ] *vt* rechtfertigen; **that does not** ~ **his being late** das entschuldigt nicht, dass er zu spät gekommen ist; ■ **to** ~ **oneself to sb** sich jdm gegenüber rechtfertigen
justly ['dʒʌst·li] *adv* zu Recht; **to act** ~ gerecht handeln
jut <-tt-> [dʒʌt] *vi* vorstehen
◆**jut out** *vi* herausragen, hervorstehen; *chin* vorspringen
jute [dʒut] *n* Jute *f*
juvenile ['dʒu·və·naɪl] **I.** *adj* ❶ (*youth*) Jugend-, jugendlich ❷ (*pej: childish*) kindisch **II.** *n* Jugendliche(r) *f(m)*
juvenile de'linquent *n* jugendlicher Straftäter/jugendliche Straftäterin
juxtapose ['dʒʌk·stə·poʊz] *vt* nebeneinanderstellen; *ideas* einander gegenüberstellen

Kk

K <*pl* -'s *or* -s>, **k** <*pl* -'s> [keɪ] *n* K *nt,* k *nt;* **~ as in Kilo** K wie Kaufmann
K¹ <*pl* -> *n* (*fam*) 1.000 Dollar
K² <*pl* -> *n abbrev of* **kilobyte** KB
K³ <*pl* -> *n abbrev of* **karat** kt.
kale [keɪl] *n* [Grün]kohl *m*
kaleidoscope [kə·ˈlaɪ·də·skoʊp] *n* (*a. fig*) Kaleidoskop *nt*
kamikaze [ˌkɑ·mɪ·ˈkɑ·zi] *adj attr* Kamikaze-
kangaroo <*pl* -s *or* -> [ˌkæŋ·gə·ˈru] *n* Känguru *nt*
Kans. *abbrev of* **Kansas**
Kansas [ˈkæn·zəs] *n* Kansas *nt*
kaolin, kaoline [ˈkeɪ·ə·lɪn] *n* Kaolin *m o nt*
karaoke [kær·i·ˈoʊ·ki] *n* Karaoke *nt*
karat [ˈker·ət] *n* Karat *nt*
karate [kə·ˈrɑ·t̬i] *n* Karate *nt*
karma [ˈkɑr·mə] *n* Karma *nt*
kayak [ˈkaɪ·æk] *n* Kajak *m o selten a. nt*
ˈkayaking *n* Kajakfahren *nt*
KB *n abbrev of* **kilobyte** KB
kebab [kə·ˈbɑb] *n* Kebab *m*
keel [kil] *n* NAUT Kiel *m*
◆**keel over** *vi* ❶ NAUT kentern ❷ (*fam: swoon*) umkippen
keen [kin] *adj* ❶ (*enthusiastic*) leidenschaftlich; ■**to not be ~ on [doing] sth** etw nicht [tun] wollen, etw nicht gerne tun ❷ (*perceptive*) *mind, eyesight* scharf ❸ (*extreme*) *competition* scharf; *desire* heftig; *interest* lebhaft ❹ (*piercing*) *wind* schneidend ❺ (*sharp*) *blade* scharf
keep [kip] **I.** *n* [Lebens]unterhalt *m;* **to earn one's ~** seinen Lebensunterhalt verdienen **II.** *vt* <kept, kept> ❶ (*hold onto*) behalten; *bills, receipts* aufheben ❷ (*store*) *medicine, money* aufbewahren; **where do you ~ your cups?** wo sind die Tassen? ❸ (*detain*) aufhalten; **to ~ sb waiting** jdn warten lassen ❹ (*prevent*) ■**to ~ sb from doing sth** jdn davon abhalten, etw zu tun ❺ (*maintain*) **to ~ one's balance** das Gleichgewicht halten; **to ~ sb/sth under control** jdn/etw unter Kontrolle halten; **to ~ count of sth** etw mitzählen; **to ~ sb/sth in mind** jdn/etw im Gedächtnis behalten; **to ~ one's mouth shut** den Mund halten; **to ~ time** *watch* richtig gehen; MUS Takt halten; **to ~ track of sb/sth** jdn/etw im Auge behalten; **to ~ sb awake** jdn wach halten; **to ~ sb/sth warm** jdn/etw warm halten ❻ (*guard*) bewachen; *watch* halten ❼ (*not reveal*) ■**to ~ sth from sb** jdm etw *akk* vorenthalten; *secret* hüten ❽ (*stick to*) *appointment, treaty* einhalten; *oath, promise* halten ❾ (*make records*) **to ~ a record of sth** über etw *akk* Buch führen; *diary* führen **III.** *vi* <kept, kept> ❶ (*stay fresh*) *food* sich halten ❷ (*wait*) Zeit haben; **your questions can ~ until later** deine Fragen können noch warten ❸ (*stay*) bleiben; **to ~ to the left/right** sich links/rechts halten; **to ~ quiet** still sein ❹ (*continue*) **don't ~ asking silly questions** stell nicht immer so dumme Fragen; ■**to ~ at sth** mit etw *dat* weitermachen ❺ (*stop oneself*) ■**to ~ from doing sth** etw unterlassen ❻ (*adhere to*) ■**to ~ to sth** an etw *dat* festhalten; (*not digress*) bei etw *dat* bleiben; **to ~ to an agreement** sich an eine Vereinbarung halten; **to ~ to a schedule** einen Zeitplan einhalten
◆**keep away I.** *vi* ■**to ~ away [from sb/sth]** sich [von jdm/etw] fernhalten **II.** *vt* ■**to ~ sb/sth away [from sb/sth]** jdn/etw [von jdm/etw] fernhalten
◆**keep back I.** *vi* zurückbleiben; (*stay at distance*) Abstand halten **II.** *vt* ❶ (*restrain*) zurückhalten ❷ (*prevent advance*) ■**to ~ back** ⊂ **sb** jdn aufhalten; ■**to ~ sb back from doing sth** jdn daran hindern, etw zu tun ❸ (*withhold*) *information* verschweigen; *payment* einbehalten
◆**keep down I.** *vi* unten bleiben, sich ducken **II.** *vt* ❶ (*suppress*) unterdrücken ❷ *food* bei sich *dat* behalten ▶ PHRASES: **~ it down!** sei still!
◆**keep in** *vt one's anger, feelings* zurückhalten
◆**keep off** *vt* ❶ (*not touch*) **to ~ one's hands off sb/sth** die Hände von jdm/etw lassen; **"Keep Off The Grass"** „Betreten des Rasens verboten" ❷ (*fam: not consume*) **to ~ off the booze** das Trinken lassen ❸ (*not talk about*) **to ~ off a subject** ein Thema vermeiden; **to ~ one's mind off sth** sich von etw *dat* ablenken
◆**keep on I.** *vi* (*continue*) ■**to ~ on doing sth** etw weiter[hin] tun **II.** *vt* **~ your jacket on — it's cold** behalte den Mantel an, es ist kalt
◆**keep out** *vi* draußen bleiben; **"Keep Out"** „Zutritt verboten"; ■**to ~ out of sth** etw nicht betreten; (*fig*) sich aus etw *dat* heraushalten
◆**keep together** *vt* zusammenhalten ▶ PHRASES: **~ it together!** bleib bei der Sache!
◆**keep up I.** *vt* ❶ (*maintain*) fortführen; *conversation* in Gang halten; **~ it up!** [nur] weiter so!; **to ~ one's spirits up** den Mut nicht sinken lassen; **to ~ one's strength up** sich bei Kräften halten ❷ (*hold up*) hoch halten; **these poles ~ the tent up** diese Stangen halten das Zelt aufrecht ❸ (*not let sleep*) wach halten **II.** *vi* ❶ (*not fall behind*) ■**to ~ up with sb/sth** mit jdm/etw mithalten ❷ (*continue*) *noise, rain* andauern, anhalten; *courage, strength* bestehen bleiben
keeper [ˈki·pər] *n in a zoo* Wärter(in) *m(f)*
keeping [ˈki·pɪŋ] *n* ❶ (*guarding*) Verwahrung *f;* (*care*) Obhut *f* ❷ (*obeying*) Einhalten *nt,* Befolgen *nt;* **in ~ with an agreement**

entsprechend einer Vereinbarung
keepsake ['kip·seɪk] *n* Andenken *nt*
keg [keg] *n* kleines Fass
kelp [kelp] *n* Seetang *m*
kennel ['ken·əl] *n* ❶ (*dog boarding*) Hundepension *f* ❷ (*doghouse*) Hundehütte *f*
Kentucky [kən·'tʌk·i] *n* Kentucky *nt*
Kenya ['ken·jə] *n* Kenia *nt*
Kenyan ['ken·jən] **I.** *n* Kenianer(in) *m(f)* **II.** *adj* kenianisch
kept [kept] *vt, vi pt, pp of* **keep**
kernel ['kɜr·nəl] *n* ❶ (*fruit center*) Kern *m;* (*grain center*) Getreidekorn *nt* ❷ (*fig*) **a ~ of truth** ein Körnchen *nt* Wahrheit
kerosene, kerosine ['ker·ə·sin] *n* Kerosin *nt*
kestrel ['kes·trəl] *n* Turmfalke *m*
ketchup ['ketʃ·əp] *n* Ketschup *m o nt*
kettle ['keṭ·əl] *n* [Wasser]kessel *m* ▶ PHRASES: **to be a [whole] different ~ of fish** etwas ganz anderes sein
'**kettledrum** *n* [Kessel]pauke *f*
key[1] [ki] **I.** *n* ❶ (*a. fig: for a lock*) Schlüssel *m* ❷ (*button*) *of a computer, piano* Taste *f* ❸ (*to symbols*) Zeichenerklärung *f* ❹ MUS Tonart *f* **II.** *adj factor, figure, role* Schlüssel-; **~ contribution** Hauptbeitrag *m*
key[2] [ki] *n* [Korallen]riff *nt;* **the Florida ~s** die Florida Keys
◆**key in** *vt* **to ~ in text** Text eingeben
◆**key up** *vt* **to be all ~ed up** völlig überdreht sein
'**keyboard I.** *n* ❶ (*of a computer*) Tastatur *f;* (*of a piano*) Klaviatur *f* ❷ (*musical instrument*) Keyboard *nt* **II.** *vt, vi* tippen
keyboard 'instrument *n* Tasteninstrument *nt*
'**keyhole** *n* Schlüsselloch *nt*
'**key money** *n* Kaution *f*
'**keynote** *n* Hauptthema *nt; of a speech* Grundgedanke *m,* Parteilinie *f*
'**keynote address,** '**keynote speech** *n* programmatische Rede
'**keypad** *n* Tastenfeld *nt*
'**key ring** *n* Schlüsselring *m*
'**keystone** *n* (*fig: crucial part*) Grundpfeiler *m*
'**keyword** *n* ❶ (*important word*) Schlüsselwort *nt* ❷ (*for identifying*) Kennwort *nt*
kg *n abbrev of* **kilogram** kg
khaki ['kæk·i] **I.** *n* (*cloth*) Khaki[stoff] *m* **II.** *adj* ❶ (*of khaki material*) Khaki- ❷ (*color*) khakifarben
kHz *n abbrev of* **kilohertz** kHz
KIA [ˌkeɪ·aɪ·'eɪ] *adj abbrev of* **killed in action** gef.
kibbutz [kɪ·'bʊts] *n* Kibbuz *m*
kick [kɪk] **I.** *n* ❶ (*with foot*) [Fuß]tritt *m,* Stoß *m;* (*in sports*) Schuss *m; of a horse* Tritt *m;* **a ~ in the teeth** (*fig*) ein Schlag *m* ins Gesicht ❷ (*fam: exciting feeling*) Nervenkitzel *m;* **to do sth for ~s** etw wegen des Nervenkitzels tun ❸ (*gun jerk*) Rückstoß *m* **II.** *vt* ❶ (*hit with foot*) [mit dem Fuß] treten; **to ~ a ball** einen Ball schießen ❷ (*get rid of*) *habit* aufgeben *fam* ▶ PHRASES: **to ~ the bucket** ins Gras beißen; **to ~ sb when he/she is down** jdm den Rest geben **III.** *vi* (*with foot*) treten (**at** nach +*dat*); *horse* ausschlagen ▶ PHRASES: **to be alive and ~ing** gesund und munter sein
◆**kick around I.** *vi* (*fam*) [he]rumliegen **II.** *vt* ❶ (*with foot*) ■**to ~ sth around** etw [in der Gegend] herumkicken *fam;* **to ~ a ball around** einen Ball hin- und herspielen ❷ (*consider*) **to ~ an idea around** (*fam*) eine Idee [ausführlich] bekakeln
◆**kick back I.** *vt* zurücktreten; *ball* zurückschießen; **to ~ money back to sb** (*fam*) sich mit Geld bei jdm *dat* revanchieren **II.** *vi* ❶ (*fam: relax*) [he]rumliegen ❷ (*recoil*) einen Rückstoß haben
◆**kick in I.** *vt* ❶ (*with foot*) *door, window* eintreten ❷ (*contribute*) dazugeben, beisteuern *fam* **II.** *vi* ❶ (*start*) *drug, measure* wirken; *device, system* anspringen ❷ (*to contribute*) ■**to ~ in for sth** einen Beitrag zu etw *dat* leisten
◆**kick off I.** *vi* beginnen, anfangen; (*in soccer, football*) anstoßen **II.** *vt* (*start, launch*) beginnen
◆**kick out** *vt* hinauswerfen
◆**kick over I.** *vi car* anfahren **II.** *vt* ■**to ~ over** ⊂ **sth** etw umrempeln *fam*
◆**kick up** *vi* **to ~ up dust** (*a. fig*) Staub aufwirbeln; **to ~ up a fuss** (*fig*) einen Wirbel machen *fam*
'**kickback** *n* (*bribe*) Schmiergeld *nt*
kicker ['kɪk·ər] *n* (*in football*) Fußballspieler(in) *m(f);* (*in soccer*) Freistoßnehmer(in) *m(f)*
'**kickoff** *n* (*in football, in soccer*) Anstoß *m*
kid [kɪd] **I.** *n* ❶ (*child*) Kind *nt;* (*young person*) Jugendliche(r) *f(m);* (*male*) Bursche *m;* (*female*) Mädchen *nt;* **~ brother/sister** kleiner Bruder/kleine Schwester ❷ (*young goat*) Zicklein *nt* **II.** *vi* <-dd-> (*fam*) Spaß machen; **just ~ding!** war nur Spaß!; **no ~ding?** ohne Scherz? **III.** *vt* (*fam*) ■**to ~ sb** jdn verulken
kiddie ['kɪd·i] **I.** *n* (*fam*) Kleine(r) *f(m)* **II.** *adj attr, inv bike, seat* Kinder-
kidnap ['kɪd·næp] **I.** *vt* <-pp-> entführen **II.** *n* Entführung *f*
kidnapper ['kɪd·næp·ər] *n* Entführer(in) *m(f)*
kidnapping ['kɪd·næp·ɪŋ] *n* Entführung *f*
kidney ['kɪd·ni] *n* ANAT, FOOD Niere *f*
'**kidney bean** *n* Kidneybohne *f*
'**kidney donor** *n* Nierenspender(in) *m(f)*
'**kidney failure** *n* Nierenversagen *nt*
kidney-'shaped *adj* nierenförmig
'**kidney stone** *n* Nierenstein *m*
kill [kɪl] **I.** *n* ❶ (*act*) *of animal* **to make a ~** eine Beute schlagen ❷ HUNT [Jagd]beute *f* **II.** *vi* (*end life*) *criminal* töten; *disease* tödlich sein **III.** *vt* ❶ (*end life*) umbringen *a. fig;* **to ~ sb by drowning/strangling** jdn ertränken/erwürgen; **to ~ sb with a gun/a knife** jdn erschießen/erstechen; **to be ~ed in an accident** bei einem Unfall ums Leben kommen ❷ (*destroy*)

K

zerstören; **to ~ the smell of sth** einer S. *dat* den Geruch [völlig] nehmen ③ (*spoil*) *fun, joke* [gründlich] verderben ④ (*stop*) *engine, lights* ausmachen; *pain* stillen; *plan, project* fallen lassen ⑤ (*fam: amuse*) **to ~ oneself with laughter** sich totlachen ⑥ (*fig fam: hurt*) ■ **to ~ sb** jdn umbringen; **my shoes are ~ing me!** meine Schuhe bringen mich noch mal um! ⑦ (*fig fam: overtax*) **to ~ oneself doing sth** sich mit etw *dat* umbringen; **I'm going to finish it if it ~s me!** ich werde es zu Ende bringen, und wenn ich draufgehe! ▶ PHRASES: **to ~ time** (*spend time*) sich *dat* die Zeit vertreiben; (*waste time*) die Zeit totschlagen; **to ~ two birds with one stone** (*prov*) zwei Fliegen mit einer Klappe schlagen

◆ **kill off** *vt* ① (*destroy*) *disease, species* ausrotten ② **to ~ off** ⊂ **a character** eine Romanfigur sterben lassen

killer ['kɪl·ər] **I.** *n* ① (*person*) Mörder(in) *m(f)*; (*thing*) Todesursache *f* ② (*agent*) Vertilgungsmittel *nt*; **weed ~** Unkrautvertilgungsmittel *nt* **II.** *adj attr, inv* (*deadly*) *flu, virus* tödlich; *hurricane, wave* mörderisch

'killer whale *n* Schwertwal *m*

killing ['kɪl·ɪŋ] **I.** *n* ① (*act*) Tötung *f*; (*case*) Mord[fall] *m* ② (*fig fam: lots of money*) **to make a ~** einen Mordsgewinn machen **II.** *adj attr, inv* ① (*causing death*) tödlich ② (*fig: difficult*) mörderisch *fam*

killjoy ['kɪl·dʒɔɪ] *n* Spielverderber(in) *m(f)*

kiln [kɪln] *n* [Brenn]ofen *m*

kilo ['ki·loʊ] *n* Kilo *nt*

kilobyte ['kɪl·ə·baɪt] *n* Kilobyte *nt*

kilogram ['kɪl·ə·græm] *n* Kilogramm *nt*

kilometer [kɪ·'lam·ɪ·t̬ər] *n* Kilometer *m*

kilowatt ['kɪl·ə·wat] *n* Kilowatt *nt*

kilt [kɪlt] *n* Kilt *m*

kilter ['kɪl·tər] *n* ■ **to be out of ~** aus dem Gleichgewicht sein

kimono [kə·'moʊ·nə] *n* Kimono *m*

kind[1] [kaɪnd] *adj* ① (*generous, helpful*) nett; **with ~ regards** (*in a letter*) mit freundlichen Grüßen ② (*gentle*) ■ **to be ~ to sb/sth** jdn/etw schonen; **this shampoo is ~ to your hair** dieses Shampoo pflegt dein Haar auf schonende Weise

kind[2] [kaɪnd] **I.** *n* ① (*group*) Art *f*; **he's not that ~ of person** so einer ist der nicht *fam*; **all ~s of animals** alle möglichen Tiere; **to be one of a ~** einzigartig sein; **his/her ~** (*pej*) so jemand [wie er/sie] ② (*limited*) **I guess you could call this success of a ~** man könnte das, glaube ich, als so etwas wie einen Erfolg bezeichnen ③ (*similar*) **nothing of the ~** nichts dergleichen **II.** *adv* ■ **~ of** irgendwie; **to be ~ of interesting** irgendwie interessant sein

kindergarten ['kɪn·dər·gar·dən] *n* SCH Vorschule *f*

kind-'hearted *adj* gütig

kindle ['kɪn·dəl] *vt fire* anzünden; (*fig*) *imagination* wecken

kindly ['kaɪnd·li] **I.** *adj person* freundlich; *smile, voice* sanft **II.** *adv* ① (*in a kind manner*) freundlich; **to not take ~ to sb/sth** sich nicht mit jdm/etw anfreunden können ② (*please*) freundlicherweise; **you are ~ requested to leave the building** Sie werden freundlich[st] gebeten, das Gebäude zu verlassen

kindness <*pl* -es> ['kaɪnd·nɪs] *n* ① (*attitude*) Freundlichkeit *f*; **to treat sb with ~** freundlich zu jdm sein ② (*act*) Gefälligkeit *f*

kinetic [kɪ·'net̬·ɪk] *adj inv* kinetisch

kinfolk ['kɪn·foʊk] *n + pl vb* Verwandtschaft *f*

king [kɪŋ] *n* (*male ruler, in cards, chess*) König *m*

kingdom ['kɪŋ·dəm] *n* ① (*country*) Königreich *nt* ② (*domain*) Reich *nt*; **animal ~** Tierreich *nt*

'kingfisher *n* Eisvogel *m*

kingly ['kɪŋ·li] *adj* majestätisch

'kingpin *n* (*fig: important person*) Hauptperson *f*

'king-size(d) *adj inv* extragroß

kink [kɪŋk] *n* ① (*twist*) *in hair* Welle *f*; *in a pipe* Knick *m*; *in a rope, hose* Knoten *m* ② (*problem*) Haken *m fam* ▶ PHRASES: **to iron out the ~s** die Mängel ausbügeln *fam*

kinky ['kɪŋ·ki] *adj* ① (*tightly curled*) *hair* kraus ② (*unusual*) spleenig; **~ sex** Sex *m* der anderen Art

kiosk ['ki·ask] *n* Kiosk *m*

kiss [kɪs] **I.** *n* <*pl* -es> Kuss *m*; **to blow sb a ~** jdm eine Kusshand zuwerfen **II.** *vi* [sich] küssen; **to ~ and tell** mit intimen Enthüllungen an die Öffentlichkeit gehen **III.** *vt* küssen; **to ~ sb goodbye** jdm einen Abschiedskuss geben ▶ PHRASES: **to ~ sb's ass** (*vulg*) jdm in den Arsch kriechen *derb*

kit [kɪt] *n* ① (*set*) Ausrüstung *f*; (*for a model*) Bausatz *m*; **first-aid ~** Verbandskasten *m* ② (*outfit*) Ausrüstung *f*

'kit bag *n* Kleidersack *m*

kitchen ['kɪtʃ·ɪn] *n* Küche *f*

kitchenette [ˌkɪtʃ·ɪ·'net] *n* Kochnische *f*

kitchen 'knife *n* Küchenmesser *nt*

kitchen 'sink *n* Spüle *f* ▶ PHRASES: **everything but the ~** aller nur mögliche Krempel *fam*

kitchen 'table *n* Küchentisch *m*

kite [kaɪt] *n* Drachen *m* ▶ PHRASES: **go fly a ~!** (*fam*) mach die Fliege! *sl*; **to be as high as a ~** (*drunk*) sternhagelvoll sein *fam*; (*high*) völlig zugedröhnt sein *sl*

kitsch [kɪtʃ] **I.** *n* (*pej*) Kitsch *m* **II.** *adj* kitschig

kitten ['kɪt·ən] *n* (*young cat*) Kätzchen *nt*

kitty ['kɪt̬·i] *n* ① (*childspeak: kitten*) Miezekatze *f*; **here, ~ ~!** komm, miez, miez! ② (*money*) gemeinsame Kasse; (*in games*) [Spiel]kasse *f*

'Kitty Litter® *n* Katzenstreu *f*

kiwi ['ki·wi] *n* (*bird, fruit*) Kiwi *m*

KKK [ˌkeɪ·keɪ·'keɪ] *n abbrev of* **Ku Klux Klan**

Kleenex® ['kli·neks] *n* Tempo[taschentuch]® *nt*

kleptomania [ˌklep·toʊ·'meɪ·ni·ə] *n* Kleptomanie *f*

kleptomaniac [ˌklep·toʊ·'meɪ·ni·æk] *n* Klep-

K

tomane *m,* Kleptomanin *f*

km *n abbrev of* **kilometer** km

knack [næk] *n* ❶ (*trick*) Kniff *m;* **to get the ~ of sth** herausfinden, wie etw geht *fam* ❷ (*talent*) Geschick *nt;* **to have a ~ for sth** (*a. iron*) ein Talent für etw *akk* haben

knapsack ['næp·sæk] *n* Rucksack *m*

knead [nid] *vt dough* kneten

knee [ni] **I.** *n* Knie *nt;* **to get down on one's ~s** niederknien; **to put sb across one's ~** jdn übers Knie legen *fam;* **to put sb on one's ~** jdn auf den Schoß nehmen ▶ PHRASES: **to <u>bring</u> sb to their ~s** jdn in die Knie zwingen *geh* **II.** *vt* ■ **to ~ sb** jdn mit dem Knie stoßen

'kneecap I. *n* Kniescheibe *f* **II.** *vt* <-pp-> ■ **to ~ sb** jdm die Kniescheibe zerschießen

knee-'deep *adj inv* knietief; ■ **to be ~ in sth** (*fig*) knietief in etw *dat* stecken

knee-'high¹ *adj inv* kniehoch; **~ grass** kniehohes Gras

'knee-high² *n* Kniestrumpf *m,* SCHWEIZ *a.* Kniesocke *f*

'knee-jerk I. *n* Knie[sehnen]reflex *m* **II.** *adj reaction* automatisch

K

kneel <knelt *or* kneeled, knelt *or* kneeled> [nil] *vi* knien; ■ **to ~ before sb** vor jdm niederknien

knelt [nelt] *pt of* **kneel**

knew [nu] *pt of* **know**

knickknack ['nɪk·næk] *n usu pl* (*fam*) Schnickschnack *m*

knife [naɪf] **I.** *n* <*pl* knives> Messer *nt* ▶ PHRASES: **to go <u>under</u> the ~** MED unters Messer kommen *fam* **II.** *vt* ■ **to ~ sb** auf jdn einstechen

'knife-edge *n* Messerschneide *f;* **to be on a ~** (*fig*) auf Messers Schneide stehen

'knifepoint *n* Messerspitze *f;* **at ~** mit vorgehaltenem Messer

knifing ['naɪ·fɪŋ] *n* Messerstecherei *f*

knight [naɪt] **I.** *n* ❶ (*hist: soldier*) Ritter *m* ❷ CHESS Springer *m* **II.** *vt* ■ **to ~ sb** jdn zum Ritter schlagen

knighthood ['naɪt·hʊd] *n* Ritterstand *m*

knit [nɪt] **I.** *n* (*stitch*) Strickart *f* **II.** *vi* <knitted *or* knit, knitted *or* knit> ❶ (*with yarn*) stricken; (*do basic stitch*) eine rechte Masche stricken ❷ (*heal*) *broken bone* zusammenwachsen **III.** *vt* <knitted *or* knit, knitted *or* knit> (*with yarn*) stricken ▶ PHRASES: **to ~ one's <u>brows</u>** die Augenbrauen zusammenziehen [*o* Stirn runzeln]

◆**knit together I.** *vi* ❶ (*combine*) sich zusammenfügen ❷ (*heal*) *broken bone* zusammenwachsen **II.** *vt* (*by knitting*) zusammenstricken

knitter ['nɪt̬·ər] *n* Stricker(in) *m(f)*

knitting ['nɪt̬·ɪŋ] *n* ❶ (*action*) Stricken *nt* ❷ (*product*) Gestrickte(s) *nt;* (*unfinished*) Strickzeug *nt*

'knitting needle *n* Stricknadel *f*

'knitwear *n* Stricksachen *pl*

knob [nab] *n of a door* Griff *m; of a radio* [Dreh]knopf *m*

knobby ['nab·i] *adj* knubbelig; *tree, wood* astreich

knock [nak] **I.** *n* ❶ (*sound*) Klopfen *nt;* **there was a ~ on the door** es hat [an der Tür] geklopft ❷ (*blow*) Schlag *m* ❸ (*fam: criticism*) **he's taken a few ~s** er musste sich einiges anhören **II.** *vi* ❶ (*strike noisily*) klopfen; **to ~ at the door** an die Tür klopfen ❷ (*collide with*) stoßen (**into/against** gegen +*akk*) ❸ TECH *engine, pipes* klopfen ▶ PHRASES: **to ~ on <u>wood</u>** dreimal auf Holz klopfen **III.** *vt* ❶ (*hit*) ■ **to ~ sth** gegen etw *akk* stoßen ❷ (*blow*) ■ **to ~ sb** jdm einen Schlag versetzen; (*less hard*) jdm einen Stoß versetzen; **to ~ sb unconscious** jdn bewusstlos schlagen ❸ (*drive*) ■ **to ~ sth out of sb** jdm etw austreiben; **to ~ some sense into sb** jdn zur Vernunft bringen ❹ (*fam: criticize*) ■ **to ~ sb/sth** jdn/etw schlechtmachen

◆**knock around I.** *vi* (*fam: travel aimlessly*) [he]rumziehen **II.** *vt* ❶ (*beat*) ■ **to ~ sb around** jdn verprügeln ❷ (*travel through*) **to ~ around Europe** in Europa herumreisen

◆**knock back** *vt* (*fam: drink quickly*) hinunterkippen

◆**knock down** *vt* ❶ (*cause to fall*) umstoßen; (*with a car, motorcycle*) umfahren ❷ (*demolish*) niederreißen ❸ (*reduce*) *price* herunterhandeln

◆**knock off I.** *vt* ❶ (*cause to fall off*) hinunterstoßen ❷ (*produce quickly*) schnell erledigen; (*easily*) etw mit links machen *fam* ❸ (*fam: stop*) **~ it off!** hör auf damit!; **to ~ off work early** früh Feierabend machen ❹ (*fam: rob*) **to ~ off a bank** eine Bank ausräumen ❺ (*sl: copy*) klauen *fam* **II.** *vi* (*fam*) Schluss machen

◆**knock out** *vt* ❶ (*render unconscious*) ■ **to ~ out ⊂ sb** jdn bewusstlos werden lassen; (*in a fight*) jdn k.o. schlagen ❷ (*forcibly remove*) **to ~ out two teeth** sich *dat* zwei Zähne ausschlagen ❸ (*eliminate*) ausschalten; **to be ~ed out of a competition** aus einem Wettkampf ausscheiden ❹ (*render useless*) außer Funktion setzen ❺ (*fam: produce quickly*) hastig entwerfen ❻ (*fam: astonish and impress*) umhauen

◆**knock over** *vt* (*cause to fall*) umstoßen; (*with a bike, car*) umfahren

◆**knock up** *vt* (*sl*) schwängern

'knockabout *adj attr, inv* THEAT, FILM Klamauk-; *comedy, humor* burlesk

'knockdown *adj attr, inv* ❶ (*very cheap*) supergünstig *sl;* **~ price** Schleuderpreis *m fam* ❷ (*physically violent*) **a ~ fight** eine handfeste Auseinandersetzung

knocker ['nak·ər] *n* ❶ (*on door*) Türklopfer *m* ❷ *pl* (*sl: breast*) ■ **big ~s** dicke Titten *derb*

knock-'kneed *adj* X-beinig; ■ **to be ~** X-Beine haben

'knockout I. *n* K.o. *m* **II.** *adj* **~ blow** K.-o.-Schlag *m*

knoll [noʊl] *n* Anhöhe *f*

knot [nat] **I.** *n* ❶ (*in rope, material*) Knoten *m*

❷ (*in hair*) [Haar]knoten *m* ❸ (*in wood*) Ast *m* ❹ (*of people*) Knäuel *m o nt* ▶ PHRASES: **to tie the ~** heiraten **II.** *vt* <-tt-> knoten; *a tie* binden **III.** *vi* <-tt-> *muscles* sich verspannen; *stomach* sich zusammenkrampfen

knotty ['naṭ·i] *adj* ❶ (*full of knots*) *wood* astreich; *branch, stick* knotig ❷ (*difficult*) *problem* kompliziert

know [noʊ] **I.** *vt* <knew, known> ❶ (*have information, knowledge*) wissen; *facts, results* kennen; **do you ~ where the post office is?** können Sie mir bitte sagen, wo die Post ist?; **I ~ what I am talking about** ich weiß, wovon ich rede; ■**to ~ how to do sth** wissen, wie man etw macht; **to ~ the alphabet** das Alphabet können; **to ~ sth by heart** etw auswendig können; **to let sb ~ sth** jdn etw wissen lassen ❷ (*be certain*) ■**to not ~ whether ...** sich *dat* nicht sicher sein, ob ...; **to ~ for a fact that ...** ganz sicher wissen, dass ... ❸ (*be acquainted with*) ■**to ~ sb** jdn kennen; **she ~s Philadelphia well** sie kennt sich in Philadelphia gut aus; **surely you ~ me better than that!** du solltest mich eigentlich besser kennen!; **to ~ sb by name** jdn dem Namen nach kennen; **to get to ~ sb/each other** jdn/sich kennen lernen ❹ (*have understanding*) verstehen; **do you ~ what I mean?** verstehst du, was ich meine? ❺ (*experience*) **I've never ~n anything like this** so etwas habe ich noch nie erlebt ❻ (*be able to differentiate*) **to ~ right from wrong** Gut und Böse unterscheiden können ▶ PHRASES: **to ~ no bounds** keine Grenzen kennen; **to ~ the score** wissen, was gespielt wird; **to ~ a thing or two about sth** sich mit etw *dat* auskennen **II.** *vi* <knew, known> ❶ (*have knowledge*) [Bescheid] wissen; **ask Kate — she's sure to ~** frag Kate, sie weiß es bestimmt; **as far as I ~** so viel ich weiß; **how should I ~?** wie soll ich das wissen? ❷ (*fam: understand*) begreifen; **I don't ~ why you can't ever be on time** ich begreife einfach nicht warum du nie pünktlich sein kannst ▶ PHRASES: **you ought to ~ better** du solltest es eigentlich besser wissen

'know-how *n* Know-how *nt*

knowing ['noʊ·ɪŋ] *adj* wissend *attr; look, smile* viel sagend

knowingly ['noʊ·ɪŋ·li] *adv* ❶ (*meaningfully*) viel sagend ❷ (*with full awareness*) bewusst

know-it-all ['noʊ·ɪṭ·ɔl] *n* (*pej fam*) Besserwisser(in) *m(f) pej*

knowledge ['nal·ɪdʒ] *n* ❶ (*body of learning*) Kenntnisse *pl* (**of** in +*dat*); **~ of French** Französischkenntnisse *pl;* **to have a thorough ~ of sth** ein fundiertes Wissen in etw *dat* besitzen ❷ (*acquired information, awareness*) Wissen *nt;* **to be common ~** allgemein bekannt sein

knowledg(e)able ['nal·ɪ·dʒə·bəl] *adj* (*well informed*) sachkundig; (*experienced*) bewandert

known [noʊn] **I.** *vt, vi pp of* **know II.** *adj* ❶ (*publicly recognized*) bekannt; **it is a little-/well-~ fact that ...** es ist nur wenigen/allgemein bekannt, dass ... ❷ (*understood*) bekannt; **no ~ reason** kein erkennbarer Grund ❸ (*tell publicly*) **to make sth ~** etw bekannt machen

knuckle ['nʌk·əl] *n* ❶ ANAT [Finger]knöchel *m* ❷ (*cut of meat*) Hachse *f,* Haxe *f* SÜDD; **~ of pork** Schweinshaxe *f* SÜDD

◆**knuckle down** *vi* (*start working hard*) sich dahinterklemmen

◆**knuckle under** *vi* (*submit*) sich fügen

KO [ˌkeɪ·'oʊ] **I.** *n abbrev of* **knockout** K.o. *m* **II.** *vt* <KO'd, KO'd> *abbrev of* **knock out:** ■**to ~ sb** jdn k.o. schlagen

koala *n,* **koala bear** [koʊ·'al·ə-] *n* Koala[bär] *m*

kooky ['ku·ki] *adj* (*sl*) ausgeflippt

Koran [kə·'ræn] *n* ■**the ~** der Koran

Korea [kə·'ri·ə] *n* Korea *nt;* **North/South ~** Nord-/Südkorea *nt*

Korean [kə·'ri·ən] **I.** *adj inv* koreanisch **II.** *n* ❶ (*inhabitant*) Koreaner(in) *m(f)* ❷ LING Koreanisch *nt*

kosher ['koʊ·ʃər] *adj* (*a. fig*) koscher; **to keep ~** [weiterhin] koscher leben

kowtow [ˌkaʊ·'taʊ] *vi* (*fam*) ■**to ~ to sb** vor jdm katzbuckeln

Kremlin ['krem·lɪn] *n* ■**the ~** der Kreml

KS *abbrev of* **Kansas**

kudos ['ku·doʊz] *npl* Ansehen *nt kein pl*

kudzu ['kud·zu] *n* Kopoubohne *f,* Kudzu *nt*

Ku Klux Klan ['ku·'klʌks·'klæn] *n + sing/pl vb* ■**the ~** der Ku-Klux-Klan

kung fu [ˌkʊŋ·'fu] *n* Kung-Fu *nt*

Kurd [kɜrd] *n* Kurde *m,* Kurdin *f*

Kurdish ['kɜr·dɪʃ] **I.** *adj inv* kurdisch **II.** *n* LING Kurdisch *nt*

Kurdistan [ˌkɜr·dɪ·'stæn] *n* Kurdistan *nt*

Kuwait [kʊ·'weɪt] *n* Kuwait *nt*

Kuwaiti [kʊ·'weɪ·ṭi] **I.** *adj inv* kuwaitisch **II.** *n* ❶ (*inhabitant*) Kuwaiter(in) *m(f)* ❷ LING Kuwaitisch *nt*

kW <*pl* -> *n abbrev of* **kilowatt** kW

Kwanzaa, Kwanza ['kwan·zə] *n von Amerikanern afrikanischer Herkunft vom 26. Dezember bis 1. Januar gefeiertes, nicht-religiöses Fest*

KY, Ky. *abbrev of* **Kentucky**

L l

L <*pl* -'s *or* -s>, **l** <*pl* -'s> [el] *n* L *nt*, l *nt*; **~ as in Lima** L wie Ludwig

l [el] **I.** *n* ❶ *abbrev of* **left** l. ❷ <*pl* -> *abbrev of* **liter** l ❸ <*pl* ll> TYPO *abbrev of* **line** Z. **II.** *adj inv abbrev of* **left** l., L **III.** *adv inv abbrev of* **left** l.

L. *n abbrev of* **lake**

LA, **La.** *abbrev of* **Louisiana**

lab [læb] *n short for* **laboratory** Labor *nt*

label ['leɪ·bəl] **I.** *n* ❶ (*on bottles*) Etikett *nt*; (*in clothes*) Schild[chen] *nt* ❷ (*brand name*) Marke *f*; **record ~** Schallplattenlabel *nt*; (*company*) Plattenfirma *f* ❸ (*set description*) Bezeichnung *f* **II.** *vt* <-l- *or* -ll-> ❶ (*affix labels*) etikettieren; (*mark*) kennzeichnen; (*write on*) beschriften ❷ (*categorize*) etikettieren; **to be ~ed as a criminal** als Krimineller/Kriminelle abgestempelt werden

labeling, **labelling** ['leɪ·bəl·ɪŋ] *n* Etikettierung *f*; (*marking*) Kennzeichnung *f*; (*with a price*) Auszeichnung *f*

labor ['leɪ·bər] **I.** *n* ❶ (*work*) Arbeit *f*; **division of ~** Arbeitsteilung *f*; **manual ~** körperliche Arbeit ❷ (*workers*) Arbeitskräfte *pl*; **skilled ~** ausgebildete Arbeitskräfte ❸ (*childbirth*) Wehen *pl*; **to go into ~** Wehen bekommen **II.** *adj* ECON Arbeits-; **~ legislation** arbeitsrechtliche Vorschriften **III.** *vi* ❶ (*toil*) hart arbeiten, sich abmühen, schuften ❷ (*struggle to do*) sich [ab]quälen, sich abplagen (**over** mit +*dat*)

laboratory ['læb·rə·ˌtɔr·i] *n* Labor[atorium] *nt*

'laboratory assistant *n* Laborant(in) *m(f)*

'labor camp *n* Arbeitslager *nt*

> **Labor Day**, der amerikanische Tag der Arbeit, wird nicht am 1. Mai, sondern am ersten Montag im September gefeiert und ist schon seit 1894 ein Nationalfeiertag.

'labor dispute *n* Arbeitskampf *m*

laborer ['leɪb·ər·ər] *n* Hilfsarbeiter(in) *m(f)*

'labor force *n* + *sing/pl vb* (*population*) Arbeiterschaft *f*; (*staff*) Belegschaft *f*

labor-in'tensive *adj* arbeitsintensiv

laborious [lə·'bɔr·i·əs] *adj* ❶ (*onerous*) mühsam ❷ (*industrious*) arbeitsam

'labor market *n* Arbeitsmarkt *m*

'labor pains *npl* MED Wehen *pl*

'labor-saving *adj* arbeitssparend

'labor shortage *n* Arbeitskräftemangel *m*

'labor ward *n* Kreißsaal *m*

Labrador ['læb·rə·dɔr], **Labrador re'triever** *n* Labrador[hund] *m*

labyrinth ['læb·ə·rɪnθ] *n* Labyrinth *nt*; (*fig liter*) Verwicklung *f*

lace [leɪs] **I.** *n* ❶ (*cloth*) Spitze *f*; (*edging*) Spitzenborte *f* ❷ (*cord*) Band *nt*; **shoe ~s** Schnürsenkel *pl bes* NORDD, MITTELD, Schuhbänder *pl* DIAL **II.** *vt* ❶ (*fasten*) *shoes* zubinden; *corset* zuschnüren ❷ (*add drug*) einen Schuss [Rauschmittel] dazugeben (in +*akk*)

◆ **lace up** *vt* zuschnüren

lacerate ['læs·ə·rəɪt] *vt* (*tear*) aufreißen

laceration [ˌlæs·ə·'reɪ·ʃən] *n* ❶ (*tearing*) Verletzung *f* ❷ (*injury*) Fleischwunde *f*; (*by tearing*) Risswunde *f*; (*by cutting*) Schnittwunde *f*; (*by biting*) Bisswunde *f*

'lace-ups *npl* Schnürschuhe *pl*

lack [læk] **I.** *n* Mangel *m* (**of** an +*dat*); **~ of judgment** mangelndes Urteilsvermögen; **~ of funds** fehlende Geldmittel; **~ of sleep** Schlafmangel *m* **II.** *vt* ■ **to ~ sth** etw nicht haben; **what we ~ in this house is ...** was uns in diesem Haus fehlt, ist ...

lackadaisical [ˌlæk·ə·'deɪ·zɪ·kəl] *adj* lustlos

lackey ['læk·i] *n* (*hist or a. pej*) Lakai *m*

lacking ['læk·ɪŋ] *adj pred* ■ **to be ~ in sth** an etw *dat* mangeln

lackluster ['læk·ˌlʌs·tər] *adj* ❶ (*lacking vitality*) langweilig ❷ (*dull*) trüb[e]

laconic [lə·'kan·ɪk] *adj* ❶ (*terse*) lakonisch ❷ (*taciturn*) wortkarg

lacquer ['læk·ər] **I.** *n* Lack *m* **II.** *vt* lackieren

lacrosse [lə·'kras] *n* SPORTS Lacrosse *nt*

ladder ['læd·ər] *n* ❶ (*device*) Leiter *f*; **to go up a ~** auf eine Leiter steigen ❷ (*hierarchy*) [Stufen]leiter *f*

laden ['leɪ·dən] *adj* beladen

'ladies' room *n* Damentoilette *f*

ladle ['leɪ·dəl] **I.** *n* [Schöpf]kelle *f* **II.** *vt* austeilen

lady ['leɪ·di] *n* ❶ (*woman*) Frau *f*; **cleaning ~** Putzfrau *f*; **old ~** alte Dame ❷ (*with social status*) Dame *f* ❸ (*form: polite address*) **ladies and gentlemen!** meine [sehr verehrten] Damen und Herren!

'ladybug *n* Marienkäfer *m*

'ladylike *adj* damenhaft

lag [læg] **I.** *n* (*lapse*) Rückstand *m*; (*falling behind*) Zurückbleiben *nt kein pl*; **time ~** Zeitabstand *m*; (*delay*) Verzögerung *f* **II.** *vi* <-gg-> zurückbleiben (**behind** hinter +*dat*); *sales* schleppend laufen

lagoon [lə·'gun] *n* Lagune *f*

laid [leɪd] *pt, pp of* **lay**

laid-'back *adj* (*fam: relaxed*) locker; (*calm*) gelassen

lain [leɪn] *pp of* **lie**

lair [ler] *n* ❶ HUNT Lager *nt fachspr; of fox* Bau *m; of small animals* Schlupfwinkel *m* ❷ (*hiding place*) Schlupfwinkel *m oft pej*

laissez-faire [ˌle·seɪ·'fer] *n* Laisser-faire *nt geh*

lake [leɪk] *n* See *m*

lam [læm] *n* (*fam*) **to be on the ~** auf der Flucht sein

lama ['la·mə] *n* REL Lama *m*

lamb [læm] **I.** *n* ❶ (*sheep*) Lamm *nt*; (*fig*)

Schatz *m fam* ② (*meat*) Lamm[fleisch] *nt* **II.** *vi* lammen

lambast(e) [læm·ˈbæst] *vt* heftig kritisieren

ˈlambskin *n* Lammfell *nt*

ˈlambswool **I.** *n* Lammwolle *f* **II.** *adj* Lambswool-

lame [leɪm] *adj* ① (*handicapped*) lahm ② (*weak*) lahm *pej fam; argument, excuse* schwach

lameness [ˈleɪm·nɪs] *n* Lähmung *f;* (*fig: weakness*) Lahmheit *f*

lament [lə·ˈment] **I.** *n* Klagelied *nt* (**for** über +*akk*) **II.** *vt* ■**to ~ sth** über etw *akk* klagen; ■**to ~ sb** um jdn trauern

lamentable [lə·ˈmən·tə·bəl] *adj* beklagenswert; *work* erbärmlich

laminate **I.** *n* [ˈlæm·ɪ·nɪt] Laminat *nt* **II.** *vt* [ˈlæm·ɪ·neɪt] beschichten **III.** *adj attr, inv* beschichtet

laminated [ˈlæm·ɪ·neɪ·t̬ɪd] *adj inv* geschichtet; (*with plastic*) beschichtet; **~ glass** Verbundglas *nt*

lamp [læmp] *n* Lampe *f;* **street ~** Straßenlaterne *f*

lampoon [læm·ˈpun] **I.** *n* Spottschrift *f* **II.** *vt* verspotten

ˈlamppost *n* Laternenpfahl *m*

lamprey [ˈlæm·pri] *n* ZOOL Neunauge *nt*

ˈlampshade *n* Lampenschirm *m*

LAN [læn] *n acr for* **local area network** LAN *nt;* **wireless ~** WLAN *nt;* **~ party** LAN-Party *f*

lance [læns] **I.** *n* Lanze *f* **II.** *vt* MED aufschneiden

land [lænd] **I.** *n* ① Land *nt;* **to travel by ~** auf dem Landweg reisen ② (*ground*) Land *nt;* (*soil*) Boden *m;* **agricultural ~** Ackerland *nt;* **piece** [*or* **plot**] **of ~** (*for building*) Grundstück *nt;* (*for development*) Bauland *nt;* (*for farming*) Stück *nt* Land ③ (*countryside*) ■**the ~** das Land ④ (*nation*) Land *nt;* (*fig: world*) Welt *f* **II.** *adj attr, inv* ① MIL, AGR Boden- ② (*real estate*) Grundstücks- ③ *crab, wind* Land- **III.** *vi* ① AVIAT, AEROSP landen (**on** auf +*dat*) ② NAUT *vessel* anlegen; *people* an Land gehen ③ (*come down*) landen (**in, on, outside** in, auf, außerhalb +*dat*); **to ~ on one's feet** auf den Füßen landen; (*fig*) [wieder] auf die Füße fallen ④ (*fam: end up*) landen; **to ~ in jail** im Gefängnis landen **IV.** *vt* ① *plane* landen; *boat, fish* an Land ziehen ② (*unload*) an Land bringen; *cargo* löschen; *passengers* von Bord [gehen] lassen; *troops* anlanden ③ (*fam: obtain*) *job* an Land ziehen *fig* ④ (*fam: cause to end up*) bringen; **to ~ sb in trouble** jdm Ärger einhandeln

landed [ˈlæn·dɪd] *adj attr, inv* **~ gentry** + *sing/pl vb* niederer Landadel

ˈlandfall *n* NAUT (*land reached*) Landungsort *m;* (*sighting*) Sichten *nt* von Land

ˈlandfill *n* ① (*waste disposal*) Geländeanfüllung *f* (*mit Müll*) ② (*site*) Deponiegelände *nt*

ˈland forces *npl* MIL Landstreitkräfte *pl*

landing [ˈlæn·dɪŋ] *n* ① *of stairs* Treppenabsatz *m* ② *of ship, plane* Landung *f;* **emergency ~** Notlandung *f* ③ SPORTS (*coming to rest*) Landung *f*

ˈlanding craft *n* MIL Landungsboot *nt*

ˈlanding gear *n* Fahrgestell *nt*

ˈlanding strip *n* Landebahn *f*

ˈlandlady *n* (*owner*) Hausbesitzerin *f;* (*leaser*) Vermieterin *f; of apartments a.* Hauswirtin *f*

landless [ˈlænd·lɪs] *adj inv* ohne Landbesitz *nach n,* landlos

ˈlandlocked *adj inv* von Land umgeben; **~ country** Binnenstaat *m*

ˈlandlord *n* (*owner*) Hausbesitzer *m;* (*leaser*) Vermieter *m; of apartments a.* Hauswirt *m*

ˈlandmark *n* ① (*point of recognition*) Erkennungszeichen *nt* ② (*event*) Meilenstein *m*

ˈlandmine *n* MIL Landmine *f*

ˈlandowner *n* Grundbesitzer(in) *m(f)*

ˈlandscape **I.** *n* Landschaft *f* **II.** *adj attr, inv* ① (*rural*) Landschafts- ② TYPO (*format*) **in ~ format** im Querformat **III.** *vt* [landschafts]gärtnerisch gestalten

ˈlandscape architect *n* Landschaftsarchitekt(in) *m(f)*

landscape ˈarchitecture *n* Landschaftsgärtnerei *f*

ˈlandslide **I.** *n* ① (*of earth, rock*) Erdrutsch *m* ② (*majority*) Erdrutsch[wahl]sieg *m;* **to win by a ~** mit einer überwältigenden Mehrheit siegen **II.** *adj attr, inv* **~ victory** Erdrutsch[wahl]sieg *m*

lane [leɪn] *n* ① (*road*) Gasse *f,* enge Straße ② *of freeway* [Fahr]spur *f;* SPORTS Bahn *f;* **bike ~** Fahrradweg *m*

language [ˈlæŋ·gwɪdʒ] *n* ① Sprache *f;* **native ~** Muttersprache *f;* **foreign ~** Fremdsprache *f* ② (*words*) Sprache *f;* (*style a.*) Ausdrucksweise *f;* **bad ~** Schimpfwörter *pl* ③ (*specialized*) Fachsprache *f;* (*expressions*) Fachausdrücke *pl*

ˈlanguage laboratory *n* Sprachlabor *nt*

ˈlanguage learning *n* Erlernen *nt* von Fremdsprachen

languid [ˈlæŋ·gwɪd] *adj* ① (*weak*) schwach, matt ② (*listless*) *mood* gelangweilt ③ (*sluggish*) träge

languish [ˈlæŋ·gwɪʃ] *vi* schmachten *geh;* **to ~ in jail** im Gefängnis schmoren *fam*

languor [ˈlæŋ·gər] *n* (*pleasant*) wohlige Müdigkeit; (*unpleasant*) Mattigkeit *f*

lank [læŋk] *adj* ① *hair* strähnig ② *person* hager

lanky [ˈlæŋ·ki] *adj* hoch aufgeschossen

lanolin(e) [ˈlæn·ə·lɪn] *n* Lanolin *nt*

lantern [ˈlæn·tərn] *n* Laterne *f*

lanyard [ˈlæn·jərd] *n* ① (*cord*) Kordel *f* ② NAUT Taljereep *nt*

Laos [laʊs] *n* Laos *nt*

lap¹ [læp] *n* Schoß *m* ▶ PHRASES: **to live in the ~ of luxury** ein Luxusleben führen, wie Gott in Frankreich leben

lap² [læp] **I.** *n* ① SPORTS Runde *f;* **~ of honor** Ehrenrunde *f* ② (*fig: stage*) Etappe *f* **II.** *vt*

<-pp-> (*overtake*) überrunden **III.** *vi* hängen (**over** über +*akk*)

lap³ [læp] **I.** *vt* ① (*drink*) lecken, schlecken SÜDD, ÖSTERR ② (*hit*) *waves* [sanft] gegen etw *akk* schlagen **II.** *vi waves* [sanft] schlagen (**against** gegen +*akk*)

◆**lap up** *vt* ① (*drink*) [auf]lecken, [auf]schlecken SÜDD, ÖSTERR ② (*fig: accept*) [gierig] aufsaugen *fig*

'lapdog *n* ① (*dog*) Schoßhündchen *nt* ② (*fig: person*) Spielball *m*

lapel [lə·'pel] *n* Revers *nt*

lapis lazuli [ˌlæp·ɪs·'læz·ə·li] *n* ① (*gem*) Lapislazuli *m* ② (*color*) Ultramarin *nt kein pl*

Lapland ['læp·lænd] *n* Lappland *nt*

Laplander ['læp·læn·dər] *n* Lappländer(in) *m(f)*

lapse [læps] **I.** *n* ① (*error*) Versehen *nt;* (*moral*) Fehltritt *m;* **~ of concentration** Konzentrationsmangel *m;* **~ of judgment** Fehleinschätzung *f;* **~ of memory** Gedächtnislücke *f* ② (*time*) Zeitspanne *f;* **after a ~ of a few days** nach Verstreichen einiger Tage **II.** *vi* ① (*fail*) *attention, concentration* abschweifen; *quality, standard* nachlassen ② (*end*) ablaufen; *contract a.* erlöschen; *subscription* auslaufen ③ (*pass into*) verfallen (**into** in +*akk*); (*revert to*) ■**to ~ [back] into sth** in etw *akk* zurückfallen; **to ~ into a coma** ins Koma fallen

lapsed [læpst] *adj attr, inv* ① (*former*) *Catholic* vom Glauben abgefallen; *member* ehemalig ② (*discontinued*) abgelaufen

'laptop, laptop com'puter *n* Laptop *m*

larceny ['lar·sə·ni] *n* JUR Diebstahl *m*

larch <*pl* -es> [lartʃ] *n* Lärche *f;* (*wood a.*) Lärchenholz *nt kein pl*

lard [lard] **I.** *n* Schweineschmalz *nt* **II.** *vt* (*a. fig*) spicken

large [lardʒ] **I.** *adj* ① *size* groß ② *quantity, extent* groß, beträchtlich; **a ~ amount of work** viel Arbeit; **the ~st ever** der/die/das bisher Größte ▶ PHRASES: **~r than <u>life</u>** überlebensgroß; (*fig*) *persons* aufgeschlossen; **<u>by</u> and ~** im Großen und Ganzen **II.** *n* ■**at ~** ① (*free*) auf freiem Fuß ② (*general*) im Allgemeinen

largely ['lardʒ·li] *adv* größtenteils

largeness ['lardʒ·nɪs] *n* (*size*) Größe *f;* (*extensiveness*) Umfang *m*

'large-scale *adj usu attr* ① (*extensive*) umfangreich; **~ manufacturer** Großerzeuger *m* ② (*made large*) in großem Maßstab *nach n;* **a ~ map** eine Karte mit großem Maßstab

largess(e) [lar·'dʒes] *n* Großzügigkeit *f*

lariat ['ler·i·ət] *n* Lasso *nt*

lark¹ [lark] *n* (*bird*) Lerche *f*

lark² [lark] *n* (*fam*) Spaß *m;* **for a ~** aus Jux *fam*

larkspur ['lark·spɜr] *n* Rittersporn *m*

larva <*pl* -vae> ['lar·və] *n* Larve *f*

laryngitis [ˌler·ɪn·'dʒaɪ·ṭɪs] *n* Kehlkopfentzündung *f*

larynx <*pl* -es *or* -ynges> ['ler·ɪŋks] *n* Kehlkopf *m*

lasagna, lasagne [lə·'zan·jə] *n* Lasagne *f;* (*pasta a.*) Lasagneblätter *pl*

lascivious [lə·'sɪv·i·əs] *adj* lüstern *geh*

laser ['leɪ·zər] *n* Laser *m*

'laser beam *n* Laserstrahl *m*

'laser printer *n* Laserdrucker *m*

lash¹ [læʃ] **I.** *n* <*pl* -es> ① (*whip*) Peitsche *f;* (*whip part*) Peitschenriemen *m* ② (*stroke*) Peitschenhieb *m* ③ (*eyelash*) [Augen]wimper *f* **II.** *vt* ① (*whip*) auspeitschen ② (*strike*) ■**to ~ sth** gegen etw *akk* schlagen; *rain* gegen etw prasseln ③ (*criticize*) ■**to ~ sb** heftige Kritik an jdm üben ④ (*wag*) **to ~ its tail** *animal* mit dem Schwanz schlagen **III.** *vi* ① (*strike*) schlagen (**at** gegen +*akk*); (*fig*) *rain, wave* peitschen (**at** gegen +*akk*) ② (*criticize*) ■**to ~ into sb** jdn anfahren [*o* anbrüllen]

◆**lash down I.** *vi rain* niederprasseln **II.** *vt* ■**to ~ down** ↔ **sth** etw festbinden

◆**lash out** *vi* ① (*attack physically*) ■**to ~ out at sb [with sth]** [mit etw *dat*] auf jdn einschlagen ② (*attack verbally, in writing*) ■**to ~ out at sb/sth** jdn/etw scharf kritisieren; (*criticize severely*) ■**to ~ out against sb/sth** jdn/etw heftig attackieren

lash² *vt* (*tie*) [fest]binden (**to** an +*dat*)

lashing ['læʃ·ɪŋ] *n* Peitschenhieb *m;* **to give sb a tongue ~** (*fig*) jdm ordentlich die Meinung sagen *fam*

lassitude ['læs·ɪ·tud] *n* Energielosigkeit *f*

lasso ['læs·oʊ] **I.** *n* <*pl* -s *or* -es> Lasso *nt* **II.** *vt* mit einem Lasso einfangen

last¹ [læst] **I.** *adj inv* ① *attr* (*after all the others*) ■**the ~ ...** der/die/das letzte ...; **to come ~** als Letzte(r) *f(m)* kommen; **next to ~** vorletzte(r, s); **the second/third to ~ door** die vor-/drittletzte Tür; **the ~ one** der/die/das Letzte; **she was the ~ one to arrive** sie kam als Letzte an ② (*lowest in order, rank*) letzte(r, s); ■**to be ~** Letzte(r) *f(m)* sein; **to come in ~** (*in a race, competition*) Letzte(r) *f(m)* werden ③ *attr* (*final, remaining*) letzte(r, s); **at the ~ moment** im letzten Moment; **at long ~** schließlich und endlich ④ *attr* (*most recent, previous*) letzte(r, s); **~ night** gestern Abend; **the week before ~** vorletzte Woche ▶ PHRASES: **to <u>have</u> the ~ laugh** zuletzt lachen *fig;* (*show everybody*) es allen zeigen; **sth is on its ~ <u>legs</u>** (*fam*) etw macht es nicht mehr lange; **to be the ~ <u>straw</u>** das Fass [endgültig] zum Überlaufen bringen *fig* **II.** *adv inv* ① (*after the others*) als Letzte(r, s) ② (*most recently*) *popular* das letzte Mal, zuletzt ③ (*lastly*) zuletzt, zum Schluss; **~ but not least** nicht zuletzt **III.** *n* <*pl* -> ① (*one after all the others*) ■**the ~** der/die/das Letzte; **she was the ~ to arrive** sie kam als Letzte ② (*only one left, final one*) **the ~** der/die/das Letzte ③ (*most recent, previous one*) ■**the ~** der/die/das Letzte; **the ~ we heard from her, ...** als wir das letzte Mal von ihr hörten, ... ④ *usu sing* SPORTS (*last position*) letzte Position ⑤ (*fam: end*) **you haven't heard the ~ of this!** das letzte Wort ist hier noch nicht gesprochen!; **to see the ~ of sth** (*fam*) etw nie wieder sehen müssen; **at ~** endlich

last[2] [læst] **I.** *vi* ❶ (*go on for*) *battle, game* [an]dauern ❷ (*endure*) *car, machine* halten; *enthusiasm, intentions* anhalten; *supplies etc.* ausreichen; **to make sth ~** etw sparsam verwenden; **he wouldn't ~ five minutes in the military!** er würde keine fünf Minuten beim Militär überstehen! **II.** *vt* (*serve*) *car, machine* halten; *supplies etc.* [aus]reichen; **to ~ [sb] a lifetime** ein Leben lang halten

last[3] [læst] *n* Leisten *m*

'last-ditch *adj attr* [aller]letzte(r, s)

lasting ['læs·tɪŋ] *adj* dauerhaft, andauernd; *impression* nachhaltig

lastly ['læst·li] *adv* schließlich

last-'minute *adj* in letzter Minute *nach n;* **~ booking** Last-Minute-Buchung *f*

'last name *n* Nachname *m,* Familienname *m*

latch [lætʃ] **I.** *n* Riegel *m* **II.** *vt* verriegeln
◆**latch on to, latch onto** *vi* ❶ (*become enthusiastic about*) ■**to ~ on to sth** *concept, idea* auf etw abfahren *fam* ❷ (*attach oneself to*) ■**to ~ on to sb/sth** sich an jdn/etw hängen

'latchkey child *n* Schlüsselkind *nt*

late [leɪt] **I.** *adj* <-r, -st> ❶ (*behind time*) verspätet *attr;* ■**to be ~** *bus, flight, train* Verspätung haben; *person* zu spät kommen, sich verspäten; ■**to be ~ for sth** zu spät zu etw *dat* kommen ❷ (*in the day*) spät; **let's go home - it's getting ~** lass uns nach Hause gehen, es ist schon spät ❸ *attr* (*towards the end*) spät; **in the ~ afternoon/evening** spät am Nachmittag/Abend; **~ October** Ende Oktober; **to be in one's ~ thirties** Ende dreißig sein ❹ *attr* (*dead*) verstorben ❺ *attr* (*former*) früher, ehemalig **II.** *adv* <-r, -s> ❶ (*after the expected time*) spät; **the train arrived ~** der Zug hatte Verspätung; **to stay up ~** bis spät aufbleiben; **to work ~** Überstunden machen; **the letter arrived two days ~** der Brief ist zwei Tage zu spät angekommen ❷ (*at an advanced time*) **we talked ~ into the night** wir haben bis spät in die Nacht geredet; **~ in the afternoon** am späten Nachmittag; **~ in the day** spät [am Tag]; (*fig: at the very last moment*) im [aller]letzten Augenblick; **it's rather ~ in the day to do sth** (*fig*) es ist schon beinahe zu spät, um etw zu tun; **too ~ in the day** (*a. fig*) zu spät

'latecomer *n* Nachzügler(in) *m(f)*

lately ['leɪt·li] *adv* kürzlich, in letzter Zeit, neuerdings

lateness ['leɪt·nɪs] *n* Verspätung *f*

'late-night *adj attr, inv* Spät-

latent ['leɪ·tənt] *adj inv* ❶ (*hidden*) verborgen ❷ SCI latent

later ['leɪ·t̬ər] **I.** *adj comp of* **late** ❶ *attr* (*at future time*) *date, time* später; **a ~ version of the text** eine neuere Version des Texts ❷ *pred* (*less punctual*) später **II.** *adv comp of* **late** ❶ (*at later time*) später, anschließend; **no ~ than nine o'clock** nicht nach neun Uhr; **see you** [*or fam* **ya**] **~!** bis später! ❷ (*afterwards*) später, danach

lateral ['læt̬·ər·əl] *adj esp attr* seitlich, Seiten-, Neben-; *thinking* unorthodox

latest ['leɪ·t̬ɪst] **I.** *adj superl of* **late**: ■**the ~ ...** der/die/das jüngste [*o* letzte] ...; **her ~ movie** ihr neuester Film **II.** *n* **have you heard the ~?** hast du schon das Neueste gehört?; (*most recent info*) **what's the ~ on that story?** wie lauten die neuesten Entwicklungen in dieser Geschichte? **III.** *adv* **at the** [**very**] **~** bis [aller]spätestens

latex ['leɪ·teks] *n* Latex *m*

latex 'paint *n* Dispersionsfarbe *f*

lathe [leɪð] *n* Drehbank *f*

lather ['læð·ər] **I.** *n* ❶ (*soap*) [Seifen]schaum *m* ❷ (*sweat*) Schweiß *m;* (*on horse*) Schaum *m* **II.** *vi* schäumen **III.** *vt* einseifen

Latin ['læt·ən] **I.** *n* Latein *nt* **II.** *adj* ❶ LING lateinisch ❷ (*of Latin origin*) Latein-

Latina [lə·'ti·nə] **I.** *n* Latina *f* **II.** *adj* lateinamerikanisch

Latino [lə·'ti·noʊ] **I.** *n* Latino *m* **II.** *adj* lateinamerikanisch

latitude ['læt̬·ɪ·tud] *n* Breite *f,* Breitengrad *m*

latrine [lə·'trin] *n* Latrine *f*

latter ['læt̬·ər] **I.** *adj attr* ❶ (*second*) zweite(r, s) ❷ (*near the end*) spätere(r, s); **in the ~ part of the year** in der zweiten Jahreshälfte **II.** *pron* ■**the ~** der/die/das Letztere

lattice ['læt̬·ɪs] *n* Gitter[werk] *nt*

Latvia ['læt·vi·ə] *n* Lettland *nt*

Latvian ['læt·vi·ən] **I.** *n* ❶ (*person*) Lette, -in *m, f* ❷ (*language*) Lettisch *nt kein pl* **II.** *adj* lettisch

laud [lɔd] *vt* (*form*) preisen *geh*

laudable ['lɔ·də·bəl] *adj* lobenswert

laugh [læf] **I.** *n* ❶ (*sound*) Lachen *nt kein pl* ❷ (*fam: activity*) **to have a good ~** sich köstlich amüsieren *m;* **to do sth for a ~** etw [nur] aus Spaß tun **II.** *vi* ❶ (*express amusement*) lachen (**at** über +*akk*); **to make sb ~** jdn zum Lachen bringen ❷ (*fig: scorn*) ■**to ~ at sb/sth** sich über jdn/etw lustig machen; ■**to ~ at sb** (*find funny*) über jdn lachen; (*find ridiculous*) jdn auslachen ▶PHRASES: **to ~ in sb's face** jdn auslachen; **no ~ing matter** nicht zum Lachen; **he who ~s last ~s best** (*prov*) wer zuletzt lacht, lacht am besten
◆**laugh off** *vt* mit einem Lachen abtun

laughable ['læf·ə·bəl] *adj* lächerlich *pej,* lachhaft *pej*

laughing gas ['læf·ɪŋ-] *n* Lachgas *nt*

'laughing stock *n* ■**to be a ~** die Zielscheibe des Spotts sein

laughter ['læf·tər] *n* Gelächter *nt,* Lachen *nt*

launch[1] [lɔntʃ] **I.** *n* ❶ (*of boat*) Stapellauf *m;* (*of rocket, spacecraft*) Start *m* ❷ (*presentation*) Präsentation *f* **II.** *vt* ❶ (*send out*) *boat* zu Wasser lassen; *ship* vom Stapel lassen; *balloon* steigen lassen; *missile, torpedo* abschießen;

rocket, spacecraft starten; *satellite* in den Weltraum schießen ❷ (*begin*) beginnen; *campaign, show* starten; *inquiry* anstellen; **to ~ an attack** zum Angriff übergehen; **to ~ an invasion** [in ein Land] einfallen ❸ (*hurl*) ■ **to ~ oneself at sb** sich auf jdn stürzen

◆ **launch into** *vi* ■ **to ~ into sth** sich [begeistert] in etw *akk* stürzen; **to ~ into a verbal attack** eine Schimpfkanonade loslassen

launch² [lɔnʃ] *n* (*boat*) Barkasse *f*

'**launching pad**, '**launch pad** *n* ❶ Abschussrampe *f* ❷ (*fig*) Anfang *m*

launder ['lɔn·dər] *vt* ❶ (*wash*) waschen [und bügeln] ❷ (*fig: disguise*) weißwaschen *fam; money* waschen *sl*

Laundromat® ['lɔn·drə·mæt] *n* Waschsalon *m*

laundry ['lɔn·dri] *n* ❶ (*dirty clothes*) Schmutzwäsche *f;* **to do the ~** Wäsche waschen ❷ (*washed clothes*) frische Wäsche ❸ (*place*) Wäscherei *f*

'**laundry basket** *n* Wäschekorb *m*

'**laundry hamper** *n see* **laundry basket**

'**laundry service** *n* ❶ (*facility*) Wäscheservice *m* ❷ (*business*) Wäscherei *f*

laureate ['lɔr·i·ɪt] *n* Preisträger(in) *m(f)*

laurel ['lɔr·əl] *n* ❶ (*tree*) Lorbeer[baum] *m* ❷ *pl* (*wreath*) ■ **~s** Lorbeeren *pl* ▶ PHRASES: **to rest on one's ~s** sich auf seinen Lorbeeren ausruhen

lava ['la·və] *n* Lava *f;* (*stone*) Lavagestein *nt*

lavatory ['læv·ə·tɔr·i] *n* Toilette *f*

lavender ['læv·ən·dər] **I.** *n* Lavendel *m* **II.** *adj* lavendelfarben

lavish ['læv·ɪʃ] **I.** *adj* ❶ *meal* üppig; *banquet, reception* aufwendig ❷ (*generous*) großzügig, verschwenderisch; *praise* überschwänglich; *promises* großartig **II.** *vt* ■ **to ~ sth on sb** jdn mit etw *dat* überhäufen; **to ~ great effort on sth** viel Mühe in etw *akk* stecken

law [lɔ] *n* ❶ (*rule*) Gesetz *nt* ❷ (*system*) ■ **the ~** das Gesetz; **against the ~** illegal; **to break the ~** das Gesetz brechen ❸ (*subject*) Jura *kein art* ▶ PHRASES: **the ~ of the jungle** das Gesetz des Stärkeren; **sb is a ~ unto himself/herself** jd lebt nach seinen eigenen Gesetzen

'**law-abiding** *adj citizen* gesetzestreu

'**lawbreaker** *n* Gesetzesbrecher(in) *m(f)*

'**law court** *n* Gericht *nt*

'**law enforcement** *n* Gesetzesvollzug *m;* **in most countries, ~ is in the hands of the police** in den meisten Ländern ist es Aufgabe der Polizei, für die Einhaltung der Gesetze zu sorgen

law firm, **law office** *n* Anwaltsbüro *nt,* Kanzlei *f*

lawful ['lɔ·fəl] *adj* gesetzlich; *heir, owner* gesetzmäßig

lawless ['lɔ·lɪs] *adj* ❶ (*without laws*) gesetzlos ❷ (*illegal*) gesetzwidrig

'**lawmaker** *n* Gesetzgeber(in) *m(f)*

lawn¹ [lɔn] *n* Rasen *m*

lawn² [lɔn] *n* (*cotton*) Batist *m;* (*linen*) Linon *m*

'**lawn bowling** *n* Bowls *pl*

'**lawnmower** *n* Rasenmäher *m*

'**law school** *n* juristische [*o* ÖSTERR juridische] Fakultät

'**law student** *n* Jurastudent(in) *m(f),* Jusstudent(in) *m(f)* ÖSTERR, SCHWEIZ

'**lawsuit** *n* Klage *f,* Prozess *m*

lawyer ['lɔ·jər] *n* Rechtsanwalt, -anwältin *m, f*

lax [læks] *adj* ❶ (*careless*) lax *oft pej; discipline, security* mangelnd ❷ (*lenient*) locker

laxative ['læk·sə·t̬ɪv] **I.** *n* Abführmittel *nt* **II.** *adj attr* abführend

laxity ['læk·sɪ·t̬i] *n* Laxheit *f*

lay¹ [leɪ] **I.** *vt* <laid, laid> ❶ (*spread*) legen (**on** auf +*akk*), breiten (**over** über +*akk*) ❷ (*produce*) **to ~ an egg** ein Ei legen ❸ (*put down*) verlegen; **to ~ the foundations of a building** das Fundament für ein Gebäude legen; **to ~ the foundations for sth** (*fig*) das Fundament zu etw *dat* legen; **to ~ the blame on sb** (*fig*) jdn für etw *akk* verantwortlich machen ❹ (*prepare*) *trap* [auf]stellen; *plans* schmieden; *bomb, fire* legen ❺ (*render*) **to ~ sth bare** etw offenlegen; **to ~ sb/sth open to criticism** jdn/etw der Kritik aussetzen ❻ (*present*) ■ **to ~ sth before sb** jdm etw vorlegen ❼ (*vulg, sl: have sex*) ■ **to ~ sb** jdn umlegen *vulg;* **to get laid** flachgelegt werden *sl* ▶ PHRASES: **to ~ hands on sb** Hand an jdn legen; **to ~ eyes on** [erstmals] zu sehen bekommen; **to ~ sth to rest** etw beschwichtigen **II.** *vi* <laid, laid> *hen* [Eier] legen **III.** *n* ❶ (*shape*) **the ~ of the land** (*fig*) die Lage; **to find out the ~ of the land** (*fig*) die Lage sondieren ❷ (*vulg, sl: sex partner*) **to be a good ~** gut im Bett sein *fam;* **to be an easy ~** leicht zu haben sein *fam*

◆ **lay aside** *vt* ❶ (*put away, save*) beiseitelegen ❷ (*fig: abandon*) auf Eis legen *fam* ❸ (*fig: forget*) *one's differences* beilegen ❹ (*reserve*) beiseitelegen

◆ **lay down** *vt* ❶ (*deposit*) hinlegen (**on** auf +*akk*) ❷ *weapons* niederlegen ❸ (*decide on*) *rules* festlegen; (*establish*) aufstellen ▶ PHRASES: **to ~ down the law** [**about sth**] [über etw *akk*] Vorschriften machen

◆ **lay into** *vi* (*fam*) ❶ ■ **to ~ into sb** (*physically*) jdn angreifen; (*verbally*) jdn zur Schnecke machen *fam* ❷ (*eat*) ■ **to ~ into sth** etw verschlingen

◆ **lay off I.** *vt* kündigen; ■ **to ~ off** ○ **sb** jdn entlassen **II.** *vi* aufhören; **to ~ off smoking** das Rauchen aufgeben

◆ **lay on** *vt* ❶ (*apply*) auftragen ❷ (*sl: berate*) **to ~ it on sb** jdn zur Schnecke machen *fam*

◆ **lay out** *vt* ❶ (*arrange*) planen; *schedule, phases* organisieren ❷ *map* ausbreiten (**on** auf +*dat*) ❸ *usu passive* (*design*) ■ **to be laid out** angeordnet sein; *garden* angelegt sein ❹ (*explain*) *rules* ■ **to ~ out** ○ **sth** [**for sb**] [jdm] etw erklären

◆ **lay up** *vt usu passive* **to be laid up** [**in bed**] **with the flu** mit einer Grippe im Bett liegen

lay² [leɪ] *adj attr, inv* ❶ (*amateur*) laienhaft

② *clergy* weltlich, Laien-
lay³ [leɪ] *pt of* **lie**
layer ['leɪ·ər] **I.** *n* ① Schicht *f;* ■ **~s** *pl* (*in hair*) Stufen *pl* ② (*fig: level*) Stufe *f; administrative* Ebene *f* **II.** *vt* ■ **to ~ sth [with sth]** etw [abwechselnd mit etw *dat*] in Schichten anordnen
layered ['leɪ·ərd] *adj inv* Stufen-, Schicht-
layette [leɪ·'et] *n* Babyausstattung *f*
'layman *n* Laie *m*
'layoff *n* (*from work*) *temporary* vorübergehende Entlassung; *permanent* Entlassung *f*
'layout *n* ① (*plan*) *of building* Raumaufteilung *f; of road, town* Plan *m* ② (*of text*) Layout *nt* ③ (*arrangement*) Anordnen *nt*
'layover *n* Aufenthalt *m;* (*of plane*) Zwischenlandung *f*
laze [leɪz] *vi* faulenzen
laziness ['leɪ·zɪ·nɪs] *n* Faulheit *f*
lazy ['leɪ·zi] *adj* ① (*unwilling*) faul; (*lacking pep*) träge; **~ as hell** stinkfaul ② (*relaxed*) müßig *geh;* **I had a wonderful, ~ weekend** ich hatte ein herrliches, erholsames Wochenende
'lazybones *n* + *sing vb* (*pej*) Faulenzer(in) *m(f)*
lb. <*pl* - *or* -s> *n abbrev of* **pound** Pfd.
LCD [ˌel·si·'di] *n abbrev of* **liquid crystal display** LCD *nt*
lead¹ [lid] **I.** *vt* <led, led> ① (*command*) führen; *delegation, discussion, inquiry* leiten ② (*guide*) führen (**into, over, through** in, über, durch +*akk,* **to** zu +*dat*); **to ~ sb astray** jdn auf Abwege führen ③ (*go in advance*) **to ~ the way** vorangehen; (*in car*) voranfahren; **to ~ the way in sth** (*fig*) bei etw *dat* an der Spitze stehen ④ ECON, SPORTS (*be ahead of*) anführen ▶ PHRASES: **to ~ sb down the garden path** (*fam*) jdn an der Nase herumführen **II.** *vi* <led, led> ① (*command*) die Leitung innehaben ② (*be guide*) vorangehen; **to ~ from the front** (*fig*) den Ton angeben ③ (*be directed toward*) ■ **to ~ somewhere/nowhere** irgendwohin/nirgendwohin führen ④ (*cause to happen*) ■ **to ~ to sth** zu etw *dat* führen ⑤ (*be in the lead*) führen; SPORTS in Führung liegen **III.** *adj* **~ singer** Leadsänger; **~ violinist** erster Geiger/erste Geigerin **IV.** *n* ① THEAT, FILM Hauptrolle *f* ② *usu sing* (*precedent, example*) Beispiel *nt* ③ (*front position*) Führung *f;* ■ **to be in the ~** führend sein; SPORTS in Führung liegen; **to take over the ~** sich an die Spitze setzen ④ (*advance position*) Vorsprung *m* ⑤ (*clue*) Hinweis *m* ⑥ (*leash*) Leine *f* ⑦ ELEC (*wire*) Kabel *nt*
◆**lead off I.** *vt* ① (*initiate*) ■ **to ~ off ⊂ sth [with sth]** etw [mit etw *dat*] eröffnen ② (*take away*) ■ **to ~ off ⊂ sb** jdn wegführen **II.** *vi* ① (*begin*) beginnen ② *road* wegführen; **to ~ off to the left/right** nach links/rechts abgehen
◆**lead on** *vt* (*pej*) ■ **to ~ on ⊂ sb** ① (*deceive*) jdm etw vormachen, jdn hinhalten ② (*entice*) jdn anstiften
◆**lead up to** *vi* ■ **to ~ up to sth** ① (*precede*) etw *dat* vorangehen ② (*approach*) *subject, topic* hinführen (zu +*dat*)
lead² [led] **I.** *n* ① (*metal*) Blei *nt* ② (*of pencil*) Mine *f* **II.** *adj* Blei-
leaded ['led·əd] **I.** *adj inv* ① AUTO *gasoline* verbleit ② ARCHIT *windows* bleiverglast **II.** *n* verbleites Benzin
leaden ['led·ən] *adj* ① (*of color*) bleiern ② (*heavy*) bleischwer; *facial expression* starr
leader ['li·dər] *n* ① (*head*) Leiter(in) *m(f),* Führer(in) *m(f)* ② (*competitor*) Erste(r) *f(m)* ③ (*most successful*) Führende(r) *f(m)* ④ MUS (*conductor*) Dirigent(in) *m(f)*
leadership ['li·dər·ʃɪp] **I.** *n* ① (*action*) Führung *f* ② (*position*) Leitung *f,* Führung *f,* Führerschaft *f* **II.** *adj* Führungs-
lead-free ['led·fri] *adj* bleifrei
leading ['li·dɪŋ] *adj attr* führend
leading 'edge I. *n* ① *of wing* Flügelvorderkante *f* ② *of development* ■ **to be at the ~ [of sth]** auf dem neuestem Stand [einer S. *gen*] sein **II.** *adj attr, inv* ■ **leading-edge** Spitzen-, Hightech-
leading 'lady *n* Hauptdarstellerin *f*
leading 'light *n* führende Persönlichkeit
leading 'man *n* Hauptdarsteller *m*
leading 'question *n* Suggestivfrage *f*
lead pencil [led'-] *n* Bleistift *m*
'lead poisoning *n* Bleivergiftung *f*
lead singer [lid'-] *n* Leadsänger(in) *m(f)*
lead 'story *n* Leitartikel *m*
'lead time *n* (*in production*) Vorlaufzeit *f;* (*for completion*) Realisierungszeit *f*
leaf [lif] **I.** *n* <*pl* leaves> ① *of plant* Blatt *nt* ② (*foliage*) Laub *nt* ▶ PHRASES: **to shake like a ~** wie Espenlaub zittern **II.** *vi* <-s, -ed> ■ **to ~ through sth** etw durchblättern
leaflet ['lif·lɪt] **I.** *n* (*for advertising*) Prospekt *m* ÖSTERR *a. nt;* (*for instructions*) Merkblatt *nt;* (*for political use*) Flugblatt *nt;* (*brochure*) Broschüre *f* **II.** *vi* <-t-> (*in street*) auf der Straße Prospekte/Flugblätter/Broschüren verteilen; (*by mail*) per Post Werbematerial/Broschüren verschicken
leafy ['li·fi] *adj* ① (*of place*) belaubt ② HORT Blatt-, blattartig
league [lig] **I.** *n* ① (*group*) Bund *m* ② SPORTS Liga *f* ③ (*fig: class*) Klasse *f;* ■ **to be out of sb's ~** eine Nummer zu groß für jdn sein **II.** *adj* SPORTS Liga-
leak [lik] **I.** *n* Leck *nt;* **gas ~** undichte Stelle in der Gasleitung **II.** *vi bucket, hose, container* undicht sein; *boat, ship* lecken; *faucet* tropfen; *tire* Luft verlieren; *pen* klecksen, patzen ÖSTERR **III.** *vt* ① *gas, liquid* austreten lassen ② (*fig: disclose*) *information* durchsickern lassen
leakage ['li·kɪdʒ] *n* ① *of gas* Ausströmen *nt; of liquid* Auslaufen *nt; of water* Versickern *nt* ② (*fig: disclosure*) Durchsickern *nt*
leaky ['li·ki] *adj* leck
lean¹ [lin] **I.** *vi* <leaned, leaned> ① (*incline*) sich beugen; (*prop*) sich lehnen; ■ **to ~ for-**

ward sich nach vorne lehnen; ■**to ~ on sb/sth** sich an jdn/etw [an]lehnen; **to ~ out of a window** sich aus einem Fenster [hinaus]lehnen ❷ (*fig: opinion*) neigen; **I ~ toward the view that ...** ich neige zur Ansicht, dass ... **II.** *vt* <leaned, leaned> lehnen (**against, on** an, auf +*akk*)

◆**lean on** *vi* ❶ (*rely on*) sich verlassen (auf +*akk*) ❷ (*fam: put under pressure*) unter Druck setzen

◆**lean over** *vi* sich beugen (über +*akk*)

lean² [lin] *adj* ❶ (*not fat*) mager; *person a.* schlank ❷ (*not excessive*) *budget* schmal *fig;* (*efficient*) effizient

leaning ['li·nɪŋ] *n esp pl* Neigung *f geh* (**for, toward** zu +*dat*)

'lean-to *n* ❶ (*annex*) Anbau *m* ❷ (*shelter*) Schuppen *m,* [*mit Pultdach*]

leap [lip] **I.** *n* ❶ (*jump*) Sprung *m;* (*longer*) Satz *m* ❷ (*fig: increase*) Sprung *m* (**in** bei +*dat*) **II.** *vi* <leaped *or* leapt, leaped *or* leapt> ❶ (*jump*) springen (**across, over** über +*akk,* **from** von +*dat*); ■**to ~ on sb/sth** sich auf jdn/etw stürzen ❷ (*rush*) **to ~ to sb's defense** (*fig*) zu jds Verteidigung eilen ❸ (*fig: be enthusiastic*) **to ~ at the chance to do sth** die Chance ergreifen, etw zu tun; **to ~ with joy** vor Freude einen Luftsprung machen ❹ (*fig: increase*) *prices, temperatures* in die Höhe schießen **III.** *vt* <leaped *or* leapt, leaped *or* leapt> springen (über +*akk*), überspringen

◆**leap out** *vi* ❶ (*jump out*) herausspringen (**of** aus +*dat*); (*from behind sth*) hervorspringen ❷ (*fig: grab attention*) ■**to ~ out at sb** jdm ins Auge springen

◆**leap up** *vi* aufspringen

'leapfrog I. *n* Bockspringen *nt* **II.** *vt* <-gg-> ❶ (*vault*) einen Bocksprung machen (über +*akk*) ❷ (*go around*) umgehen; (*fig: skip*) überspringen **III.** *vi* <-gg-> (*vault*) ■**to ~ over sb/sth** über jdn/etw einen Bocksprung machen

leapt [lept] *vt, vi pt, pp of* **leap**

'leap year *n* Schaltjahr *nt*

learn [lɜrn] **I.** *vt* <learned *or* learnt, learned *or* learnt> lernen; ■**to ~ how to do sth** lernen, wie man etw tut ▶PHRASES: **to ~ sth by heart** etw auswendig lernen **II.** *vi* <learned *or* learnt, learned *or* learnt> ❶ (*master*) lernen (**about** über +*akk*); **to ~ from one's mistakes** aus seinen Fehlern lernen ❷ (*become aware*) ■**to ~ about sth** von etw *dat* erfahren

learner ['lɜr·nər] *n* Lernende(r) *f(m);* **to be a quick ~** schnell lernen

learning ['lɜr·nɪŋ] *n* ❶ das Lernen ❷ (*education*) Bildung *f;* (*scholarliness*) Gelehrsamkeit *f*

'learning disability *n* Lernstörung *f;* (*more severe*) Lernbehinderung *f*

learnt [lɜrnt] *vt, vi pt, pp of* **learn**

lease [lis] **I.** *vt* ❶ (*grant use*) vermieten (**to** an +*akk*); *land, property* verpachten ❷ (*rent*) mieten; *land, property* pachten; *equipment* leasen **II.** *n of apartment, house* Mietvertrag *m; of land, property* Pachtvertrag *m; of equipment* Leasingvertrag *m*

'leasehold *n* (*renting of property*) Pachtbesitz *m*

leash [liʃ] **I.** *n* ❶ (*cord*) Leine *f;* (*for children*) Laufgurt *m;* **to be kept on a ~** an einer Leine geführt werden ❷ (*fig: restraint*) *on emotions, feelings* Zügel *m* **II.** *vt* ❶ *dog* anleinen ❷ (*fig: restrain*) *emotions, feelings* zügeln

leasing ['li·sɪŋ] *n* ❶ (*granting of use*) *of land* Verpachten *nt; of apartment, house* Vermieten *nt;* (*of equipment*) Leasing *nt* ❷ (*renting*) *of land* Pachten *nt; of apartment, house* Mieten *nt; of equipment* Leasen *nt*

least [list] **I.** *adv inv* am wenigsten; **the ~ little thing** die kleinste Kleinigkeit; **~ of all** am allerwenigsten; **no one believed her, ~ of all the police** niemand glaubte ihr, schon gar nicht die Polizei **II.** *adj det* (*tiniest amount*) geringste(r, s); ■**at ~** (*minimum*) mindestens, wenigstens; (*if nothing else*) wenigstens, zumindest

leather ['leð·ər] **I.** *n* Leder *nt* **II.** *adj inv* Leder-

leathery ['leð·ə·ri] *adj* ❶ (*tough*) led[e]rig; *hands, skin* ledern ❷ *meat* zäh

leave [liv] **I.** *n* ❶ (*farewell*) Abschied *m;* **to take one's ~** sich verabschieden ❷ (*permission*) Erlaubnis *f* ❸ (*off work*) Urlaub *m;* **maternity ~** Mutterschaftsurlaub *m;* **to go on ~** in Urlaub gehen **II.** *vt* <left, left> ❶ (*depart*) verlassen; (*train*) abfahren ❷ (*permanently*) *husband, wife* verlassen; *job* aufgeben; **to ~ home** von zu Hause weggehen; **to ~ school** die Schule beenden ❸ (*not take*) [zurück]lassen (**with** bei +*dat*); *message, note* hinterlassen ❹ (*forget*) vergessen ❺ *footprints, stains* hinterlassen ❻ (*cause to remain*) **to ~ sb better off** jdn in einer besseren Situation zurücklassen; **to ~ sth open** etw offen lassen ❼ (*not change*) lassen ❽ (*not eat*) übrig lassen ❾ (*bequeath*) *money, assets* hinterlassen ❿ (*not discuss*) *question, subject* lassen; **let's ~ it at that** lassen wir es dabei bewenden ⓫ (*assign*) ■**to ~ sth to sb** *decision* jdm etw überlassen ▶PHRASES: **to ~ nothing to chance** nichts dem Zufall überlassen; **to ~ sb to their own devices** jdn sich *dat* selbst überlassen; **to ~ a lot to be desired** viel zu wünschen übrig lassen; **to ~ sb alone** jdn in Ruhe lassen **III.** *vi* <left, left> [weg]gehen; *vehicle* abfahren; **the bus has [already] left** der Bus ist schon weg; *plane* abfliegen

◆**leave behind** *vt* ❶ (*not take*) zurücklassen ❷ *traces* hinterlassen ❸ (*fig: forget on purpose*) ■**to ~ behind** ↔ **sth** etw hinter sich *dat* lassen

◆**leave off** *vt* ❶ (*omit*) auslassen; **to ~ sb's name off a list** jds Namen nicht in eine Liste aufnehmen ❷ (*not put on*) **to ~ a lid off sth** keinen Deckel auf etw *akk* geben ❸ (*not wear*) **to ~ off** ↔ **one's coat** seinen Mantel nicht an-

ziehen
◆**leave out** *vt* ① (*omit*) auslassen; *facts, scenes* weglassen; (*accidentally*) vergessen, übersehen ② (*exclude*) ausschließen
◆**leave over** *vt usu passive* ■**to be left over [from sth]** [von etw *dat*] übrig geblieben sein
leaven [ˈlev·ən] *vt usu passive* ① *bread, dough* gehen lassen ② (*fig: lighten*) ■**to be ~ed by sth** mit etw *dat* aufgelockert werden
leavening [ˈlev·ən·ɪŋ] *n* ① (*rising agent*) Gärmittel *nt;* (*sourdough*) Sauerteig *m* ② (*liter: sth that enlightens*) Auflockerung *f*
leaves [livz] *n pl of* **leaf**
leaving [ˈli·vɪŋ] *n* Abreise *f*
lecher [ˈletʃ·ər] *n* Wüstling *m*
lecherous [ˈletʃ·ər·əs] *adj* geil *oft pej*
lechery [ˈletʃ·ə·ri] *n* Geilheit *f oft pej;* (*desire*) Lüsternheit *f*
lectern [ˈlek·tərn] *n* [Redner]pult *nt;* REL Lektionar *nt fachspr*
lecture [ˈlek·tʃər] **I.** *n* ① (*speech*) Vortrag *m* (**on, about** über +*akk*); UNIV Vorlesung *f* (**on** über +*akk*) ② (*criticism*) Standpauke *f fam* **II.** *vi* ① UNIV eine Vorlesung halten (**in, on** über +*akk*) ② (*criticize*) belehren (**about** über +*akk*) **III.** *vt* ■**to ~ sb on** [*or* **about**] **sth** ① (*give speech*) jdm über etw *akk* einen Vortrag halten; UNIV vor jdm über etw *akk* eine Vorlesung halten ② (*criticize*) jdm wegen einer S. eine Standpauke halten *fam;* (*advise*) jdm über etw *akk* einen Vortrag halten *fam*
ˈ**lecture hall** *n* Hörsaal *m*
lecturer [ˈlek·tʃər·ər] *n* ① (*speaker*) Redner(in) *m(f)* ② (*university*) Dozent(in) *m(f);* (*untenured*) Lehrbeauftragte(r) *f(m)*
ˈ**lecture tour** *n* Vortragsreise *f*
led [led] *pt, pp of* **lead**
ledge [ledʒ] *n* Sims *m o nt;* (*of rock*) Felsvorsprung *m*
ledger [ˈledʒ·ər] *n* FIN Hauptbuch *nt*
lee [li] *n* Windschatten *m;* GEOG, NAUT Lee *f o nt fachspr*
leech <*pl* -es> [litʃ] **I.** *n* ① (*worm*) Blutegel *m* ② (*person*) Blutsauger(in) *m(f)* **II.** *vi* ■**to ~ on sb/sth** (*rely on*) von jdm/etw abhängen; (*exploit*) bei jdm/etw schmarotzen *pej*
leek [lik] *n* Lauch *m*
leer [lɪr] **I.** *vi* ■**to ~ at sb** jdm anzügliche Blicke zuwerfen **II.** *n* anzügliches Grinsen
leeway [ˈli·weɪ] *n* Spielraum *m*
left[1] [left] **I.** *n* ① (*direction*) **from ~ to right** von links nach rechts ② (*turn*) **to make a ~** [nach] links abbiegen; (*street*) **the second ~** die zweite Straße links ③ (*side*) ■**the ~** die linke Seite; POL die Linke; **my sister is third from the ~** meine Schwester ist die Dritte von links; ■**on** [*or* **to**] **sb's ~** zu jds Linken, links von jdm **II.** *adj* ① *inv* linke(r, s) ② (*political*) linke(r, s), linksgerichtet **III.** *adv inv* (*direction*) nach links; (*side*) links; **to keep ~** sich links halten ▶ PHRASES: **~, right and <u>center</u>** überall
left[2] [left] *pt, pp of* **leave**
ˈ**left-hand** *adj attr* (*on left side*) linke(r, s)
left-ˈhanded I. *adj* ① *person* linkshändig; **she is ~** sie ist Linkshänderin ② *attr tool* Linkshänder- ③ *screw* linksdrehend; BIOL linksgedreht **II.** *adv* SPORTS **to bat/throw ~** mit links schlagen/werfen
left-ˈhander *n* (*person*) Linkshänder(in) *m(f)*
leftist [ˈlef·tɪst] **I.** *adj* linke(r, s), linksorientiert **II.** *n* Linke(r) *f(m)*
ˈ**leftovers** *npl* ① (*food*) Reste *pl* ② (*parts*) Überreste *pl*
left ˈwing *n* ■**the ~** ① POL die Linke ② MIL, SPORTS der linke Flügel
left-ˈwing *adj* linksgerichtet, links *präd*
left-ˈwinger *n* Linke(r) *f(m)*
leg [leg] *n* ① (*limb, support*) Bein *nt;* **table ~** Tischbein *nt* ② (*meat*) Keule *f,* Schlegel *m* SÜDD, ÖSTERR ③ *of clothes* [Hosen]bein *nt* ④ (*stage*) Etappe *f;* (*round*) Runde *f* ⑤ (*fam*) **to have ~s** (*remain popular*) langfristig halten; (*succeed*) klappen *fam* ▶ PHRASES: **to be on one's <u>last</u> ~s** auf dem letzten Loch pfeifen *sl;* **to <u>give</u> sb a ~ up** (*fam: help to climb*) jdm hinaufhelfen; (*fig: give advantage to*) jdm unter die Arme greifen; **to <u>pull</u> sb's ~** (*fam*) jdn auf den Arm nehmen
legacy [ˈleg·ə·si] *n* ① LAW Vermächtnis *nt,* Erbe *nt a. fig* ② (*sth from past*) Alt-
legal [ˈli·gəl] *adj* ① (*permitted by law*) legal ② (*statutory*) gesetzlich [vorgeschrieben] ③ (*under law*) rechtmäßig ④ (*of courts*) gerichtlich; (*of lawyers*) juristisch ⑤ (*of paper*) *nordamerikanische Standardgröße für Papierformat: 21,6 cm x 35,6 cm*
legal ˈaid *n* [unentgeltlicher] Rechtsbeistand
legalese [ˌli·gəl·ˈiz] *n* (*pej fam*) Juristenjargon *m oft pej*
legality [li·ˈgæl·ɪ·t̬i] *n* Legalität *f,* Gesetzmäßigkeit *f*
legalization [ˌli·gə·lɪ·ˈzeɪ·ʃən] *n* Legalisierung *f geh*
legalize [ˈli·gə·laɪz] *vt* legalisieren *geh*
legally [ˈli·gə·li] *adv* ① (*permissible*) legal ② (*required*) **~ obliged** gesetzlich verpflichtet ③ (*according to the law*) rechtmäßig
ˈ**legal pad** *n* Schreibblock *m*
legation [lɪ·ˈgeɪ·ʃən] *n* ① (*group*) Gesandtschaft *f* ② (*building*) Gesandtschaftsgebäude *nt*
legend [ˈledʒ·ənd] *n* ① (*saga*) Sage *f;* (*about saint*) Legende *f* ② (*person*) Legende *f,* legendäre Gestalt
legendary [ˈledʒ·ən·der·i] *adj* ① *inv* (*mythical*) sagenhaft; (*in legend*) legendär ② (*famous*) legendär; ■**to be ~ for sth** für etw *akk* berühmt sein
leggings [ˈleg·ɪŋz] *npl* ① (*tight-fitting*) Leggings *pl* ② (*protective*) Überhose *f*
leggy [ˈleg·i] *adj* (*of woman*) langbeinig, mit langen Beinen *nach n*
legible [ˈledʒ·ə·bəl] *adj* lesbar
legion [ˈli·dʒən] **I.** *n* HIST Legion *f;* (*soldiers*) Armee *f;* **the** [**Foreign**] **L~** die Fremdenlegion **II.** *adj pred, inv* unzählig

legionnaire [ˌli·dʒə·ˈner] *n* [Fremden]legionär *m*

Legion'naires' disease *n* die Legionärskrankheit

legislate [ˈledʒ·ɪ·sleɪt] **I.** *vi* ein Gesetz erlassen (**against** gegen +*akk*) **II.** *vt* gesetzlich regeln

legislation [ˌledʒ·ɪ·ˈsleɪ·ʃən] *n* ① (*laws*) Gesetze *pl;* **a piece of ~** ein Gesetz *nt;* (*proposed*) ein Gesetzentwurf *m* ② (*lawmaking*) Gesetzgebung *f*

legislative [ˈledʒ·ɪ·sleɪ·t̬ɪv] *adj esp attr* gesetzgebend; **~ period** Legislaturperiode *f*

legislator [ˈledʒ·ɪ·sleɪ·t̬ər] *n* Gesetzgeber(in) *m(f)*

legislature [ˈledʒ·ɪ·sleɪ·tʃər] *n* Legislative *f;* **member of the ~** Parlamentsmitglied *nt*

legitimacy [lə·ˈdʒɪt̬·ə·mə·si] *n* ① (*rightness*) Rechtmäßigkeit *f* ② (*of birth*) Ehelichkeit *f*

legitimate I. *adj* [lə·ˈdʒɪt̬·ə·mɪt] ① (*legal*) rechtmäßig ② (*reasonable*) gerechtfertigt; *complaint, grievance* begründet ③ *child* ehelich **II.** *vt* [lə·ˈdʒɪt̬·ə·meɪt] ① (*make legal*) für rechtsgültig erklären ② (*make acceptable*) anerkennen

legitim(at)ize [lə·ˈdʒɪt̬·ə·m(ə·t)aɪz] *vt* ① (*make legal*) für rechtsgültig erklären ② (*make acceptable*) legitimieren

'legroom *n* Beinfreiheit *f*

legume [lə·ˈgjum] *n* BOT Hülsenfrucht *f*

leisure [ˈli·ʒər] **I.** *n* Freizeit *f;* **to lead a life of ~** ein müßiges Leben führen ▶ PHRASES: **at [one's] ~** in aller Ruhe; **call me at your ~** rufen Sie mich an, wenn es Ihnen gelegen ist **II.** *adj* Freizeit-; **~ time** Freizeit *f*

leisurely [ˈli·ʒər·li] **I.** *adj* ruhig, geruhsam; **at a ~ pace** gemessenen Schrittes *geh; picnic, breakfast* gemütlich **II.** *adv* gemächlich

'leisurewear *n* Freizeit[be]kleidung *f*

lemming [ˈlem·ɪŋ] *n* Lemming *m*

lemon [ˈlem·ən] **I.** *n* ① (*fruit*) Zitrone *f* ② (*color*) Zitronengelb *nt* ③ AUTO (*fam: defective car*) Montagsauto *nt* **II.** *adj* **~ [yellow]** zitronengelb

lemonade [ˌlem·ə·ˈneɪd] *n* Zitronenlimonade *f*

'lemon peel, 'lemon rind *n* Zitronenschale *f*

lend <lent, lent> [lend] **I.** *vt* ① (*loan*) leihen ② (*be suitable*) ■**to ~ itself to sth** sich für etw *akk* eignen ▶ PHRASES: **to ~ an ear to sb/sth** jdm/etw zuhören; **to ~ a hand** helfen **II.** *vi* ■**to ~ to sb** jdm Geld leihen; *bank* jdm Kredit gewähren

lender [ˈlen·dər] *n* Verleiher(in) *m(f);* (*of money*) Kreditgeber(in) *m(f)*

lending [ˈlen·dɪŋ] *n* Leihen *nt*

'lending library *n* Leihbibliothek *f*

length [leŋkθ] *n* ① (*measurement*) Länge *f;* **6 feet in ~** 6 Fuß lang ② (*piece*) Stück *nt; of cloth, wallpaper* Bahn *f* ③ (*winning distance*) Länge *f* [Vorsprung] ④ (*duration*) Dauer *f;* **the ~ of a film** die Länge eines Films; **at ~** (*in detail*) ausführlich; **at great ~** in aller Ausführlichkeit; (*finally*) nach langer Zeit ▶ PHRASES: **to go to any ~s** vor nichts zurückschrecken; **to go to great ~s** sich *dat* alle Mühe geben

lengthen [ˈleŋk·θən] **I.** *vt* verlängern; *clothes* länger machen **II.** *vi* [immer] länger werden

lengthwise [ˈleŋkθ·waɪz], **lengthways** [ˈleŋkθ·weɪz] **I.** *adv inv* der Länge nach **II.** *adj inv* Längs-

lengthy [ˈleŋk·θi] *adj* ① (*long time*) [ziemlich] lange; *applause* anhaltend; *delay* beträchtlich ② (*tedious*) *treatment* langwierig; *explanation* umständlich

lenience [ˈli·ni·əns], **leniency** [ˈli·ni·ən·si] *n* Nachsicht *f,* Milde *f*

lenient [ˈli·ni·ənt] *adj* nachsichtig, milde

lens <*pl* -es> [lenz] *n* Linse *f; of camera, telescope a.* Objektiv *nt; of glasses* Glas *nt;* **[contact] ~** Kontaktlinse *f*

lent [lent] *vt, vi pt, pp of* **lend**

lentil [ˈlen·təl] *n* Linse *f*

Leo [ˈli·oʊ] *n* ASTRON, ASTROL ① *no art* der Löwe ② (*person*) Löwe *m;* **she is a ~** sie ist Löwe

leopard [ˈlep·ərd] *n* Leopard(in) *m(f)*

leotard [ˈli·ə·tard] *n* Trikot *nt;* (*for gymnastics a.*) Turnanzug *m*

leper [ˈlep·ər] *n* MED Leprakranke(r) *f(m),* Aussätzige(r) *f(m) a. fig*

leprosy [ˈlep·rə·si] *n* Lepra *f*

lesbian [ˈlez·bi·ən] **I.** *n* Lesbierin *f,* Lesbe *f* **II.** *adj inv* lesbisch

lesbianism [ˈlez·bi·ə·nɪz·əm] *n* lesbische Liebe

lesion [ˈli·ʒən] *n* Verletzung *f*

less [les] **I.** *adv comp of* **little** weniger; **the ~ ... the better** je weniger ..., umso besser; **much ~ complicated** viel einfacher; **~ and ~** immer weniger **II.** *adj* ① *comp of* **little** weniger ② *non-standard* (*fewer*) weniger **III.** *pron indef* ① weniger; **a lot ~** viel weniger; **I've been seeing ~ of her lately** ich sehe sie in letzter Zeit weniger; **~ of a problem** ein geringeres Problem ② *non-standard* (*fewer*) weniger ▶ PHRASES: **no ~ than ...** nicht weniger als ..., bestimmt ... **IV.** *prep* ■**~ sth** minus [*o* abzüglich] einer S. *gen*

lessen [ˈles·ən] **I.** *vi* schwächer werden; *fever* sinken; *pain* nachlassen **II.** *vt* verringern

lesser [ˈles·ər] *adj attr, inv* ① (*smaller*) geringer; **to a ~ degree** in geringerem Maße; **the ~ of two evils** das kleinere Übel ② (*minor*) unbedeutend

lesson [ˈles·ən] *n* ① (*at school*) Stunde *f;* ■**~s** *pl* Unterricht *m kein pl* (**in** in +*dat*); **guitar ~s** Gitarrenunterricht *m* ② (*experience*) Lehre *f,* Lektion *f;* **to teach sb a ~** jdm eine Lektion erteilen ③ (*exercise*) Lektion *f*

lest [lest] *conj* (*form*) ① (*for fear that*) damit ... nicht ... ② (*in case*) falls

let[1] [let] *vt* <-tt-, let, let> ① (*allow*) ■**to ~ sth/sb do sth** etw/jdn tun lassen; **to ~ one's hair grow** sich *dat* die Haare [lang] wachsen lassen; **to ~ sb go** (*allow to depart*) jdn gehen lassen; (*release from grip*) jdn loslassen; (*from captivity*) jdn freilassen; (*fire from job*) jdn entlassen; **I'll ~ you go** (*on the phone*) ich will Sie nicht länger aufhalten; **to ~ sth go** (*neglect*) etw vernachlässigen; (*let pass*) etw durchgehen lassen ② (*give permission*) ■**to ~ sb do sth** jdn etw tun lassen ③ (*make*) **to ~ sb know sth** jdn etw wissen lassen ④ (*in suggestions*) **~'s go out to dinner!** lass uns Essen gehen!; **~ us consider all the possibilities** wollen wir einmal alle Möglichkeiten ins Auge fassen ⑤ (*when thinking*) **~'s see, ...** also, ...; **~ me think [for a second]** Moment [mal], ... ► PHRASES: **~ alone ...** geschweige denn ...; **~ it rip** (*fam*) es [mal so richtig] krachen lassen *fam*

◆**let down** *vt* ① ■**to ~ down ⊂ sb** (*disappoint*) jdn enttäuschen; (*fail to support*) jdn im Stich lassen ② (*lower*) ■**to ~ down ⊂ sth** etw herunterlassen ► PHRASES: **to ~ one's hair down** sich gehen lassen

◆**let in** *vt* ① (*allow to enter*) hereinlassen; (*let through*) durchlassen; ■**to ~ oneself in** aufschließen ② (*allow to know*) ■**to ~ sb in on sth** *secret* jdn in etw *akk* einweihen

◆**let into** *vt* ■**to ~ sb/sth into sth** jdn/etw in etw *akk* lassen

◆**let off** *vt* ① (*not punish*) **to ~ sb off with a warning** jdn mit einer Verwarnung davonkommen lassen ② TRANSP (*allow to exit*) aussteigen lassen ③ (*emit*) ausstoßen; *bad smell* verbreiten; **to ~ off steam** (*a. fig*) Dampf ablassen ④ (*fire*) *shot, volley* abgeben

◆**let on** *vi* (*fam*) ■**to ~ on about sth [to sb]** [jdm] etwas von etw *dat* verraten

◆**let out** **I.** *vt* ① (*release*) herauslassen; **I'll ~ myself out** ich finde selbst hinaus ② (*emit*) ausstoßen; **to ~ out ⊂ a groan/shriek** [auf]stöhnen/aufschreien ③ (*widen*) *clothes* weiter machen; *seam* auslassen **II.** *vi* enden; **when does school ~ out for the summer?** wann beginnen die Sommerferien?

◆**let through** *vt* durchlassen

◆**let up** *vi* (*fam*) ① (*decrease*) aufhören; *rain a.* nachlassen; *fog, weather* aufklaren ② (*ease up*) nachlassen; (*give up*) lockerlassen *fam*

let² [let] *n* SPORTS Netzball *m*

lethal ['li·θəl] *adj* tödlich; **this knife looks pretty ~** dieses Messer sieht ziemlich gefährlich aus

lethargic [lɪ·'θar·dʒɪk] *adj* ① (*not energetic*) lethargisch ② (*apathetic*) lustlos

lethargy ['leθ·ər·dʒi] *n* ① (*no energy*) Lethargie *f* ② (*apathy*) Teilnahmslosigkeit *f*

letter ['leṭ·ər] **I.** *n* ① (*message*) Brief *m* (**from** von +*dat*, **to** an +*akk*); **love ~** Liebesbrief *m*; **to inform sb by ~** jdn schriftlich verständigen; **~ of recommendation** Empfehlungsschreiben *nt* ② (*of alphabet*) Buchstabe *m*; **in large [or capital] ~s** in Großbuchstaben **II.** *adj* (*of paper*) *nordamerikanische Standardgröße für Papierformat: 21,6 cm x 27,9 cm*

'letter bomb *n* Briefbombe *f*

'letterhead *n* ① (*header*) Briefkopf *m* ② (*paper*) Geschäfts-/Firmenbriefpapier *nt*

lettering ['leṭ·ər·ɪŋ] *n* Beschriftung *f*

lettuce ['leṭ·ɪs] **I.** *n* (*plant*) Blattsalat *m*; (*with firm head*) Kopfsalat *m* **II.** *adj attr, inv* Salat-

leukemia [lu·'ki·mi·ə] *n* Leukämie *f*

level ['lev·əl] **I.** *adj* ① (*plane*) horizontal, waag[e]recht ② (*flat*) eben ③ *pred* (*at equal height*) auf gleicher Höhe (**with** mit +*dat*) ④ (*calm*) *voice* ruhig; **in a ~ voice** mit ruhiger Stimme; *look* fest; **to keep a ~ head** einen kühlen Kopf bewahren **II.** *n* ① (*quantity, standard*) Niveau *nt*; (*height*) Höhe *f*; **above/below sea ~** über/unter dem Meeresspiegel ② (*extent*) Ausmaß *nt* ③ (*story*) Stockwerk *nt*; **on ~ four** im vierten Stock ④ (*rank*) Ebene *f* ⑤ (*social, intellectual, moral*) Niveau *nt* ⑥ (*liquid-filled tube*) Wasserwaage *f* **III.** *vt* <-l- *or* -ll-> ① (*flatten*) *ground* [ein]ebnen; *wood* [ab]schmirgeln; (*raze*) *building, town* dem Erdboden gleichmachen ② (*direct*) *pistol, rifle* richten (**at** auf +*akk*); (*fig*) **to ~ accusations against sb** Beschuldigungen gegen jdn erheben

◆**level off, level out** **I.** *vi* ① (*after dropping*) *plane* sich fangen; *pilot* das Flugzeug abfangen; (*after rising*) horizontal fliegen ② (*steady*) sich einpendeln; (*become equal*) sich angleichen ③ *path, road* flach werden **II.** *vt* [ein]ebnen; (*fig*) ausgleichen

◆**level with** *vi* (*fam*) ■**to ~ with sb** ehrlich zu jdm sein; ■**to ~ with sb about sth** jdm etw gestehen

level-'headed *adj* ① (*sensible*) vernünftig ② (*calm*) ruhig

lever ['lev·ər] **I.** *n* ① TECH Hebel *m*; (*for heavy objects*) Brechstange *f* ② (*fig: threat*) Druckmittel *nt* **II.** *vt* ■**to ~ sth up** etw aufstemmen

leverage ['lev·ər·ɪdʒ] *n* ① TECH Hebelkraft *f* ② (*fig: pressure*) Einfluss *m*; **to exert ~ on sb** Druck *m* auf jdn ausüben ③ FIN Hebelwirkung *f*

levitate ['lev·ɪ·teɪt] **I.** *vi* schweben **II.** *vt* schweben lassen

levity ['lev·ɪ·ṭi] *n* Ungezwungenheit *f*

levy ['lev·i] **I.** *n* Steuer *f*, Abgaben *pl*; **to impose a ~ on sth** eine Steuer auf etw *akk* erheben **II.** *vt* <-ie-> erheben; *fine, tax* auferlegen (**on** +*dat*)

lewd [lud] *adj* ① (*indecent*) unanständig; *ballad, comments* anzüglich; *behavior* anstößig; *gesture* obszön ② (*lecherous*) lüstern

lewdness ['lud·nɪs] *n* unzüchtiges Verhalten

lexical ['lek·sɪ·kəl] *adj inv* lexikalisch

lexicographer [,lek·sɪ·'kag·rə·fər] *n* Lexikograph(in) *m(f)*

lexicography [,lek·sɪ·'kag·rə·fi] *n* Lexikographie *f*

lexicology [,lek·sɪ·'kal·ə·dʒi] *n* Lexikologie *f*

lexicon ['lek·sɪ·kan] *n* Wörterbuch *nt*

liability [,laɪ·ə·'bɪl·ɪ·ṭi] *n* ① (*responsibility*) Haftung *f* ② FIN ■**liabilities** *pl* Verbindlichkeiten *pl* ③ (*handicap*) Belastung *f*

liable ['laɪ·ə·bəl] *adj* ① JUR haftbar ② (*likely*) ■**to be ~ to do sth** Gefahr laufen, etw zu tun ③ (*prone*) ■**to be ~ to sth** anfällig für etw *akk* sein

liaise [lɪ·ˈeɪz] *vi* ■**to ~ with sb/sth** ❶ (*establish contact*) eine Verbindung zu jdm/etw herstellen; (*be go-between*) als Verbindungsstelle zu jdm/etw fungieren ❷ (*cooperate*) mit jdm/etw zusammenarbeiten

liaison [ˈli·eɪ·zan] *n* ❶ (*contact*) Verbindung *f;* **to work in close ~ with sb** mit jdm eng zusammenarbeiten ❷ (*person*) Kontaktperson *f* ❸ (*affair*) Verhältnis *nt*

liar [ˈlaɪ·ər] *n* Lügner(in) *m(f)*

libel [ˈlaɪ·bəl] JUR **I.** *n* Verleumdung *f* **II.** *vt* <-l- *or* -ll-> verleumden

libelous, libellous [ˈlaɪ·bə·ləs] *adj* verleumderisch

liberal [ˈlɪb·ər·əl] **I.** *adj* ❶ (*tolerant*) liberal; *attitude, church, person a.* tolerant, aufgeschlossen ❷ (*progressive*) liberal, fortschrittlich ❸ (*generous*) großzügig; *portion* groß **II.** *n* Liberale(r) *f(m)*

liberal ˈarts I. *n pl* ■**the ~** die Geisteswissenschaften *pl* **II.** *adj* geisteswissenschaftlich; **~ degree** Abschluss *m* in Geisteswissenschaften

liberalism [ˈlɪb·ər·ə·lɪz·əm] *n* Liberalismus *m*

liberality [ˌlɪb·ə·ˈræl·ɪ·t̬i] *n* Großzügigkeit *f,* Freigebigkeit *f*

liberalization [ˌlɪb·ər·ə·lɪ·ˈzeɪ·ʃən] *n* Liberalisierung *f*

liberalize [ˈlɪb·ər·ə·laɪz] *vt* liberalisieren

liberate [ˈlɪb·ə·reɪt] *vt* ❶ (*free*) befreien (**from** von +*dat*) ❷ (*fam: steal*) ■**to ~ sth** etw mitgehen lassen

liberation [ˌlɪb·ə·ˈreɪ·ʃən] *n* Befreiung *f* (**from** von +*dat*)

liberator [ˈlɪb·ər·eɪ·t̬ər] *n* Befreier(in) *m(f)*

liberty [ˈlɪb·ər·t̬i] *n* ❶ (*freedom*) Freiheit *f;* **to be at ~** frei sein ❷ (*incorrect behavior*) **to take liberties with sb** sich *dat* bei jdm Freiheiten herausnehmen ❸ (*form: rights*) ■**liberties** *pl* Grundrechte *pl*

libido [lɪ·ˈbi·doʊ] *n* Libido *f*

Libra [ˈli·brə] *n* ASTRON, ASTROL ❶ die Waage ❷ (*person*) Waage *f;* **she is a ~** sie ist Waage

Libran [ˈli·brən] **I.** *n* **to be a ~** Waage sein **II.** *adj* Waage-

librarian [laɪ·ˈbrer·i·ən] *n* Bibliothekar(in) *m(f)*

library [ˈlaɪ·brer·i] **I.** *n* Bibliothek *f;* (*public a.*) Bücherei *f;* **public ~** Leihbücherei *f* **II.** *adj attr, inv* Bibliotheks-; (*from public library a.*) Bücherei-; **~ book** Leihbuch *nt;* **~ card** Leseausweis *m*

libretto [lɪ·ˈbret̬·oʊ] *n* Libretto *nt*

lice [laɪs] *n pl of* **louse**

license [ˈlaɪ·səns] **I.** *n* ❶ (*permit*) Genehmigung *f,* Erlaubnis *f;* (*formal*) Lizenz *f;* **driver's ~** Führerschein *m* ❷ Freiheit *f;* **to give sb/sth ~ to do sth** jdm/etw gestatten, etw zu tun **II.** *vt* ■**to ~ sb to do sth** jdm die Lizenz erteilen, etw zu tun; ■**to be ~d to do sth** berechtigt sein, etw zu tun

licensed [ˈlaɪ·sənst] *adj inv* zugelassen

licensee [ˌlaɪ·sən·ˈsi] *n* (*form*) Lizenznehmer(in) *m(f)*

ˈlicense plate *n* Nummernschild *nt*

ˈlicense plate number *n* Kfz-Kennzeichen *nt,* Kraftfahrzeugkennzeichen *nt*

licensing [ˈlaɪ·sən·sɪŋ] *n* Lizenzvergabe *f*

licentious [laɪ·ˈsen·ʃəs] *adj* [sexuell] ausschweifend

lichen [ˈlaɪ·kən] *n* Flechte *f*

lick [lɪk] **I.** *n* Lecken *nt kein pl,* Schlecken *nt kein pl* **II.** *vt* ❶ lecken; *lollipop* schlecken (an +*dat*); *plate* ablecken; *stamp* [mit der Zunge] befeuchten ❷ (*fam: beat*) ■**to ~ sb** jdn [doch glatt] in die Tasche stecken

licking [ˈlɪk·ɪŋ] *n* (*fam*) **to give sb a [good] ~** (*beating*) jdm eine Tracht Prügel verpassen *fam;* (*defeat*) jdn haushoch schlagen

licorice [ˈlɪk·ər·ɪʃ] *n* ❶ (*food*) Lakritze *f* ❷ (*plant*) Süßholz *nt*

lid [lɪd] *n* ❶ (*cover*) Deckel *m* ❷ (*eyelid*) Lid *nt*

lie[1] [laɪ] **I.** *n* Lage *f* **II.** *vi* <-y-, lay, lain> ❶ (*repose*) liegen; **to ~ on the ground** auf dem Boden liegen; **to ~ awake** wach [da]liegen ❷ (*become horizontal*) sich hinlegen ❸ (*be in particular state*) **to ~ in wait** auf der Lauer liegen; **to ~ dying** im Sterben liegen ❹ (*remain*) liegen bleiben ❺ (*be situated*) liegen; **to ~ to the east/north of sth** im Osten/Norden einer S. *gen* liegen ❻ (*weigh*) **to ~ heavily on sb's mind** jdn schwer bedrücken ►PHRASES: **to ~ low** (*escape search*) untergetaucht sein; (*avoid notice*) sich unauffällig verhalten

◆**lie around** *vi* ❶ (*be situated*) [he]rumliegen *fam* ❷ (*be lazy*) herumgammeln *fam*

◆**lie ahead** *vi* ❶ (*in space, position*) ■**to ~ ahead [of sb]** vor jdm liegen ❷ (*in time*) bevorstehen

◆**lie back** *vi* ❶ (*recline*) sich zurücklegen ❷ (*fig: relax*) sich entspannen

◆**lie behind** *vi* ❶ (*be cause of*) ■**to ~ behind sth** etw *dat* zugrunde liegen ❷ (*be past*) ■**to ~ behind sb** hinter jdm liegen

◆**lie down** *vi* sich hinlegen

lie[2] [laɪ] **I.** *vi* <-y-> lügen; ■**to ~ about sth** falsche Angaben über etw *akk* machen; ■**to ~ about sb** über jdn die Unwahrheit erzählen; ■**to ~ to sb** jdn belügen **II.** *n* Lüge *f;* **to be an outright ~** glatt gelogen sein *fam;* **to tell ~s** Lügen erzählen

ˈlie detector *n* Lügendetektor *m*

lieu [lu] *n* **in ~ of sth** an Stelle einer S. *gen*

Lieut. *n attr abbrev of* **Lieutenant** Lt.

lieutenant [lu·ˈten·ənt] *n* ❶ MIL Leutnant *m* ❷ LAW ≈ Polizeihauptwachtmeister(in) *m(f)*

lieutenant ˈgovernor *n* POL Vizegouverneur *m*

life <*pl* lives> [laɪf] **I.** *n* ❶ [das] Leben; **it's a matter of ~ and death!** es geht um Leben und Tod!; **to save sb's ~** jdm das Leben retten; **to take one's own ~** sich *dat* [selbst] das Leben nehmen ❷ (*quality, force*) Leben *nt;* **I love ~** ich liebe das Leben ❸ (*mode or aspect of existence, living things collectively*) das Leben; **family ~** das Familienleben; **plant ~** die Pflanzenwelt ❹ (*energy*) Lebendigkeit *f;* **to be full of ~** vor Leben [nur so] sprühen; **to bring sth to ~** etw lebendiger machen ⑤ (*biography*) Biografie *f* ⑥ (*time until death*) das/sein Leben; ■ **for ~** *friendship* lebenslang; **a job for ~** eine Stelle auf Lebenszeit; (*prison sentence*) **to be doing/get ~** lebenslänglich sitzen *fam*/bekommen ⑦ (*duration*) *of device, battery* Lebensdauer *f; of a contract* Laufzeit *f* ▶ PHRASES: **to frighten the ~ out of sb** jdn zu Tode erschrecken; **that's ~!** so ist das Leben [eben]! **II.** *adj* **~ drawing** Aktzeichnung *f*

'lifeboat *n* Rettungsboot *nt*

'life cycle *n* Lebenszyklus *m*

'life expectancy *n* Lebenserwartung *f*

'life form *n* Lebewesen *f*

'lifeguard *n* (*at swimming pool*) Bademeister(in) *m(f);* (*on beach*) Rettungsschwimmer(in) *m(f)*

life im'prisonment *n* lebenslängliche Freiheitsstrafe

'life insurance *n* Lebensversicherung *f*

'life jacket *n* Schwimmweste *f*

lifeless ['laɪf·lɪs] *adj* ① (*inanimate*) *body* leblos; *planet* unbelebt, ohne Leben *nach n* ② (*dull*) *game, story* langweilig; *person* teilnahmslos; *hair* stumpf; *performance* lahm *fam*

'lifelike *adj* lebensecht; *imitation a.* naturgetreu

'lifeline *n* ① (*rope*) Rettungsleine *f* ② (*fig: vital link*) [lebenswichtige] Verbindung ③ (*on palm*) Lebenslinie *f*

'lifelong *adj attr, inv* lebenslang

'life preserver *n* (*life jacket*) Schwimmweste *f;* (*life buoy*) Rettungsboje *m;* (*life belt*) Rettungsring *m*

lifer ['laɪ·fər] *n* ① (*fam: prisoner*) Lebenslängliche(r) *f(m) fam* ② (*soldier*) Berufssoldat(in) *m(f)*

'life raft *n* Rettungsfloß *nt;* (*dinghy*) Schlauchboot *nt*

'lifesaver *n* ① (*fam: thing*) die Rettung *fig;* (*person*) [Lebens]retter(in) *m(f) fig* ② (*life preserver*) Rettungsring *m*

life 'sentence *n* lebenslängliche Freiheitsstrafe

'life-size(d) *adj* in Lebensgröße *nach n,* lebensgroß

'lifespan *n* Lebenserwartung *f kein pl; of thing* Lebensdauer *f kein pl; of project* Laufzeit *f*

'lifestyle *n* Lebensstil *m*

'life support system *n* MED ① (*machine*) lebenserhaltender Apparat ② (*biological*) Lebenserhaltungssystem *nt*

'life-threatening *adj disease, illness* lebensbedrohend; *situation* lebensgefährlich

'lifetime I. *n usu sing* ① (*time one is alive*) Lebenszeit *f;* **once in a ~** einmal im Leben; **to last a ~** *objects, devices* ein Leben lang halten; *memories, good luck* das ganze Leben [lang] andauern ② (*time sth exists*) Lebensdauer *f kein pl* ▶ PHRASES: **the chance of a ~** eine einmalige Chance **II.** *adj* lebenslang, auf Lebenszeit *nach n;* **~ guarantee** Garantie *f* auf Lebenszeit

'life vest *n see* **life jacket**

lift [lɪft] **I.** *n* ① (*for skiers*) Skilift *m* ② (*act of lifting*) [Hoch]heben *nt kein pl* ③ MECH Hubkraft *f;* AVIAT Auftrieb *m* ④ (*ride*) Mitfahrgelegenheit *f;* **to give sb a ~** jdn [im Auto] mitnehmen ⑤ (*fig: positive feeling*) **to give sb a ~** jdn aufmuntern **II.** *vt* ① (*raise*) [hoch]heben; (*slightly*) anheben; ■ **to ~ sb/sth out of sth** jdn/etw aus etw *dat* [heraus]heben ② (*direct upward*) *eyes* aufschlagen; *head* heben; **to ~ one's eyes from sth** von etw *dat* aufsehen ③ (*airlift*) fliegen; *supplies, troops* auf dem Luftweg transportieren ④ *usu pass* (*in surgery*) *face, breasts* straffen lassen, liften ⑤ (*end*) *ban, restrictions* aufheben ⑥ (*fam: steal, plagiarize*) klauen **III.** *vi* ① (*be raised*) sich heben ② (*disperse*) *cloud, fog* sich auflösen

◆**lift off** *vi* ① (*leave earth*) abheben ② (*come off*) sich hochheben lassen

◆**lift up** *vt* hochheben; **to ~ up a lid** einen Deckel hochklappen

'liftoff *n* AEROSP Start *m*

ligament ['lɪg·ə·mənt] *n* ANAT Band *nt;* **to tear a ~** sich *dat* einen Bänderriss zuziehen

ligature ['lɪg·ə·tʃər] **I.** *n* ① (*bandage*) Binde *f;* MED Ligaturfaden *m fachspr* ② TYPO (*character*) Ligatur *f;* (*stroke*) [Feder-/Pinsel]strich *m* **II.** *vt* abbinden

light¹ [laɪt] **I.** *n* ① (*brightness*) Licht *nt;* (*daylight*) [Tages]licht *nt;* **is there enough ~?** ist es hell genug?; **by the ~ of the candle** im Schein der Kerze ② (*source of brightness*) Licht *nt;* (*lamp*) Lampe *f;* **to turn the ~ off** das Licht ausschalten ③ (*fire*) Feuer *nt;* (*flame*) [Kerzen]flamme *f;* **have you got a ~?** Entschuldigung, haben Sie [vielleicht] Feuer? ④ *usu pl* (*traffic light*) Ampel *f* ⑤ (*fig: perspective*) **try to look at it in a new ~** versuch es doch mal aus einer anderen Perspektive zu sehen; **to show sth in a good ~** etw in einem guten Licht erscheinen lassen ▶ PHRASES: **to come to ~** ans Licht kommen **II.** *adj* ① (*bright*) hell; **it's slowly getting ~** es wird allmählich hell ② (*pale*) hell; (*stronger*) blass- **III.** *vt* <lit *or* lighted, lit *or* lighted> ① (*illuminate*) erhellen; *stage, room* beleuchten ② (*ignite*) *candle, match, fire* anzünden **IV.** *vi* <lit *or* lighted, lit *or* lighted> ① (*burn*) brennen ② (*fig: become animated*) *eyes, etc.* aufleuchten

◆**light up I.** *vt* ① (*illuminate*) *hall, room* erhellen; *street* beleuchten ② *cigar, pipe* anzünden ③ (*make animated*) *eyes* aufleuchten lassen; *face* erhellen **II.** *vi* ① (*become illuminated*) aufleuchten ② (*smoke*) sich *dat* eine [Zigarette] anstecken *fam* ③ (*become animated*) *eyes* aufleuchten *fig*

light² [laɪt] **I.** *adj* ① (*not heavy, not sturdily built*) leicht ② (*for small loads*) Klein-; **~ airplane** Kleinflugzeug *nt* ③ (*of food and drink*) leicht; (*low-fat*) fettarm; *pastries* locker ④ (*porous*) *soil* locker ⑤ (*low in intensity*) *wind* leicht; ~ **rain** Nieselregen *m* ⑥ (*easily done*) *sentence* mild; *housework* leicht ⑦ (*gentle*) leicht; *kiss* zart; (*soft*) *touch* sanft ⑧ (*not serious*) leicht *attr;* ~ **reading** Unterhaltungslektüre *f* ▶ PHRASES: **to make ~ of sth** etw bagatellisieren **II.** *adv* **to travel** ~ mit leichtem Gepäck reisen

'light bulb *n* Glühbirne *f*

lighten¹ ['laɪ·tən] **I.** *vi* heller werden, sich aufhellen **II.** *vt* **to ~ one's hair** sich *dat* die Haare heller färben

lighten² ['laɪ·tən] **I.** *vt* ① (*make less heavy*) leichter machen ② (*fig: make easier*) erleichtern; **to ~ sb's burden** jdm etw abnehmen ③ (*fig: make less serious*) aufheitern; *situation* auflockern; *mood* heben **II.** *vi* leichter werden ◆**lighten up** *vi* ~ **up, would you?** mach bitte nicht so ein Gesicht

lighter ['laɪ·t̬ər] *n* Feuerzeug *nt*

light-'fingered *adj* ① (*thievish*) langfing[e]rig *oft hum* ② (*dexterous*) geschickt

light-'footed *adj* leichtfüßig

light'headed *adj* (*faint*) benommen; (*dizzy*) schwind[e]lig; (*ebullient*) aufgekratzt *fam*

light'hearted *adj* (*carefree*) unbeschwert; (*happy*) heiter

'lighthouse *n* Leuchtturm *m*

lighting ['laɪ·t̬ɪŋ] *n* Beleuchtung *f;* (*equipment*) Beleuchtungsanlage *f*

lightly ['laɪt·li] *adv* ① (*not seriously*) leichtfertig; **to not take sth** ~ etw nicht leichtnehmen ② (*gently*) leicht; (*not much*) wenig; **I tapped ~ on the door** ich klopfte leise an [die Tür] ③ (*slightly*) leicht; ~ **cooked vegetables** *Gemüse, das nur ganz kurz gegart wird* ④ LAW (*leniently*) mild; **to get off ~** glimpflich davonkommen

lightness¹ ['laɪt·nɪs] *n* (*brightness*) Helligkeit *f*

lightness² ['laɪt·nɪs] *n* ① (*not heaviness*) Leichtheit *f* ② (*gracefulness*) Leichtigkeit *f*, Behändigkeit *f* ③ (*no seriousness*) Leichtigkeit *f*

lightning ['laɪt·nɪŋ] **I.** *n* Blitz *m;* **thunder and ~** Blitz und Donner; **to be [as] quick as ~** blitzschnell sein *fam;* **to be struck by ~** vom Blitz getroffen werden **II.** *adj attr* **to do sth with ~ speed** etw in Windeseile machen

'lightning rod *n* Blitzableiter *m a. fig*

'light pen *n* COMPUT Lichtstift *m*

'lightweight **I.** *n* ① SPORTS Leichtgewicht *nt* ② (*boxer*) Leichtgewichtler(in) *m(f)* **II.** *adj* ① SPORTS Leichtgewichts-, im Leichtgewicht *nach n* ② (*weighing little*) leicht ③ (*trivial*) bedeutungslos, trivial

'light year *n* ① ASTRON Lichtjahr *nt* ② *usu pl* (*fam: long distance*) **to be ~s ahead** Lichtjahre voraus sein

lignite ['lɪg·naɪt] *n* Braunkohle *f*

likable ['laɪ·kə·bəl] *adj* liebenswert

like¹ [laɪk] **I.** *vt* ① (*enjoy*) mögen; **how do you ~ my new shoes?** wie gefallen dir meine neuen Schuhe?; ■**to ~ doing sth** etw gern[e *fam*] tun; ■**to ~ sb** (*find attractive*) jdn attraktiv finden; (*be sexually attracted by*) etw wollen von jdm ② (*want*) wollen; **whether you ~ it or not** ob es dir passt oder nicht; **would you ~ a drink?** möchten Sie etwas trinken?; **I'd ~ to go to Moscow for my vacation** ich würde gern[e *fam*] nach Moskau in Urlaub fahren ③ (*prefer*) **I ~ to get up early** ich stehe gern[e *fam*] früh auf **II.** *vi* **as you ~** wie Sie wollen; **we can leave now if you ~** wir können jetzt gehen, wenn du möchtest **III.** *n* ■ **~s** *pl* Neigungen *pl*

like² [laɪk] **I.** *prep* ① (*similar to*) wie; ~ **most people** wie die meisten Leute; ~ **father, ~ son** wie der Vater, so der Sohn; **what does it taste ~?** wie schmeckt es?; **it feels ~ ages since we last spoke** ich habe das Gefühl, wir haben schon ewig nicht mehr miteinander gesprochen; **he looks ~ his brother** er sieht seinem Bruder ähnlich; **there's nothing ~ a good cup of coffee** es geht doch nichts über eine gute Tasse Kaffee; **that's just ~ him!** das sieht ihm ähnlich! ② *after n* (*such as*) wie; **materials ~ cotton and wool** Naturmaterialien wie Baum- oder Schafwolle ▶ PHRASES: **it looks ~ rain** es sieht nach Regen aus **II.** *conj* (*fam*) ① (*the same as*) wie; **let's go swimming in the lake ~ we used to** lass uns im See schwimmen gehen wie früher ② (*as if*) als ob; **she acts ~ she's the boss** sie tut so, als sei sie die Chefin **III.** *n* **I have not seen his ~ for many years** [so] jemanden wie ihn habe ich schon seit vielen Jahren nicht mehr gesehen; **have you ever seen the ~?** hast du so was schon gesehen? **IV.** *adv inv* (*fam*) **I was ~, "what are you guys doing here?"** ich sagte nur, „was macht ihr hier eigentlich?"

likeable ['laɪ·kə·bəl] *adj see* **likable**

likelihood ['laɪk·li·hʊd] *n* Wahrscheinlichkeit *f;* **there is a great ~ that ...** es ist sehr wahrscheinlich, dass ...; **in all ~** aller Wahrscheinlichkeit nach

likely ['laɪk·li] **I.** *adj* <-ier, -iest *or* more ~, most ~> wahrscheinlich; **please remind me, because I'm ~ to forget** erinnere mich bitte unbedingt daran, sonst vergesse ich es wahrscheinlich **II.** *adv* <more ~, most ~> **very ~** sehr wahrscheinlich; **as ~ as not** höchstwahrscheinlich

like-'minded *adj* gleich gesinnt

liken ['laɪ·kən] *vt* vergleichen (**to** mit +*dat*)

likeness <*pl* -es> ['laɪk·nɪs] *n* ① (*resemblance*) Ähnlichkeit *f* (**to** mit +*dat*) ② (*semblance*) Gestalt *f*

likewise ['laɪk·waɪz] *adv inv* ebenfalls, gleichfalls; **to do ~** es genauso machen

liking ['laɪ·kɪŋ] *n* Vorliebe *f;* (*for person*) Zuneigung *f;* **to develop a ~ for sth** eine Vorliebe für etw *akk* entwickeln ▶ PHRASES: **for one's ~** für jds Geschmack

lilac ['laɪ·læk] **I.** *n* ① (*bush*) Flieder *m* ② (*color*) Lila *nt* **II.** *adj* lila

lilt [lɪlt] **I.** *n* ① *of voice* singender Tonfall ② (*song*) fröhliches Lied **II.** *vt, vi* trällern

lily ['lɪl·i] *n* Lilie *f*

'lily pad *n* Seerosenblatt *nt*
limb [lɪm] *n* ❶ ANAT Glied *nt;* ■ **~s** Gliedmaßen *pl* ❷ BOT Ast *m* ▶ PHRASES: **to risk life and ~** [**to do sth**] Kopf und Kragen riskieren[, um etw zu tun] *fam;* **to be out on a ~** [ganz] allein dastehen
limber ['lɪm·bər] **I.** *adj* <-er, -est *or* more ~, most ~> ❶ (*supple*) geschmeidig ❷ (*flexible*) gelenkig **II.** *vi* ■ **to ~ up** sich warm machen
limbo¹ ['lɪm·boʊ] *n* ❶ REL die Vorhölle ❷ (*waiting*) Schwebezustand *m;* **to be in ~** *plan, project* in der Schwebe sein; *person* in der Luft hängen *fam*
limbo² ['lɪm·boʊ] **I.** *n* (*dance*) Limbo **II.** *vi* (*dance*) Limbo tanzen
lime¹ [laɪm] *n* (*fruit*) Limette *f;* (*tree*) Limonenbaum *m*
lime² [laɪm] **I.** *n* Kalk *m* **II.** *vt* kalken
'limelight *n* Rampenlicht; **to be in the ~** im Rampenlicht stehen
limerick ['lɪm·ər·ɪk] *n* Limerick *m*
'limestone *n* Kalkstein *m*
limit ['lɪm·ɪt] **I.** *n* ❶ (*utmost*) [Höchst]grenze *f;* **boundary** Grenze *f;* **there's no ~ to her ambition** ihr Ehrgeiz kennt keine Grenzen; **to overstep the ~** zu weit gehen ❷ *of person* Grenze[n] *f*[*pl*]; **to know one's ~s** seine Grenzen kennen; **to reach one's ~** an seine Grenze[n] kommen ❸ (*restriction*) Beschränkung *f; of blood alcohol* Promillegrenze *f;* **age ~** Altersgrenze *f;* **speed ~** [zulässige] Höchstgeschwindigkeit ❹ MATH (*value*) Grenzwert *m* ▶ PHRASES: **to be off ~s** [**to sb**] [für jdn] gesperrt sein **II.** *vt* ❶ (*reduce*) einschränken ❷ (*restrict*) einschränken, begrenzen (**to** auf +*akk*); ■ **to ~ oneself to sth** sich auf etw *akk* beschränken
limitation [ˌlɪm·ɪ·'teɪ·ʃən] *n* ❶ Begrenzung *f,* Beschränkung *f* ❷ *usu pl* (*shortcomings*) ■ **~s** Grenzen *pl*
limited ['lɪm·ɪ·t̬ɪd] *adj* ❶ (*restricted*) begrenzt; **she's had very ~ movement in her legs since the accident** seit dem Unfall kann sie ihre Beine nur sehr eingeschränkt bewegen ❷ (*having limits*) begrenzt (**to** auf +*akk*)
limited lia'bility company *n* ≈ Gesellschaft *f* mit beschränkter Haftung
limitless ['lɪm·ɪt·lɪs] *adj inv* grenzenlos
limousine ['lɪm·ə·zin] *n* [Luxus]limousine *f*
limp [lɪmp] **I.** *vi* hinken; (*fig*) mit Müh und Not vorankommen **II.** *n* Hinken *nt;* **to walk with a ~** hinken **III.** *adj* ❶ (*not stiff*) schlaff; *cloth, material* weich; *leaves, flowers* welk ❷ (*weak*) schlapp; *efforts* halbherzig; *handshake* lasch; *response* schwach; *voice* matt
limpid ['lɪm·pɪd] *adj eyes, water* klar
linchpin ['lɪntʃ·pɪn] *n* ❶ (*pin*) Achsnagel *m* ❷ (*essential element*) Stütze *f,* das A und O *fam*
linden ['lɪn·dən] *n* Linde *f*
line¹ [laɪn] **I.** *n* ❶ (*mark, contour*) *a.* SPORTS Linie *f;* **dividing ~** Trennungslinie *f;* **straight ~** gerade Linie; MATH Gerade *f* ❷ (*wrinkle*) Falte *f* ❸ (*boundary*) Grenze *f;* **to cross the ~** die Grenze überschreiten *fig,* zu weit gehen ❹ (*cord*) Leine *f;* (*string*) Schnur *f* ❺ TELEC [Telefon]leitung *f;* (*connection*) Anschluss *m;* **please hold the ~!** bitte bleiben Sie am Apparat! ❻ (*of words, poem*) Zeile *f;* **to drop sb a ~** jdm ein paar Zeilen schreiben ❼ (*row*) Reihe *f* ❽ (*people waiting*) Schlange *f;* **to be first in ~** an erster Stelle stehen; (*fig*) ganz vorne dabei sein; **to get in ~** sich anstellen; **to stand** [*or* **wait**] **in ~** Schlange stehen ❾ (*range*) Sortiment *nt;* FASHION Kollektion *f* ▶ PHRASES: **right down the ~** voll und ganz; **to be out of ~** *behavior* aus dem Rahmen fallen; *person* sich danebenbenehmen; **to put sth on the ~** etw aufs Spiel setzen **II.** *vt* ❶ *usu passive* (*mark*) ■ **to be ~d** *paper* liniert sein ❷ (*make rows*) **to ~ the streets** die Straßen säumen *geh*
◆ **line up I.** *vt* ❶ (*put in row*) ■ **to ~ up** ↻ **sth** etw in einer Reihe aufstellen ❷ (*organize*) **do you have anyone ~d up to do the catering?** haben Sie jemanden für das Catering engagiert? **II.** *vi* ❶ (*stand in row*) sich [in einer Reihe] aufstellen; MIL, SPORTS antreten ❷ (*wait*) sich anstellen
line² [laɪn] *vt* ❶ (*cover*) *clothing* füttern; *drawers* von innen auslegen; *pipes* auskleiden ❷ (*fam: fill*) **to ~ one's pockets** [**with sth**] sich *dat* die Taschen [mit etw *dat*] füllen
lineage ['lɪn·i·ɪdʒ] *n* Abstammung *f*
linear ['lɪn·i·ər] *adj* ❶ (*of line*) Linien- ❷ (*of length*) Längen- ❸ (*sequential*) geradlinig
linear e'quation *n* MATH lineare Gleichung
linen ['lɪn·ɪn] *n* Leinen *nt;* **bed ~** Bettwäsche *f*
liner¹ ['laɪ·nər] *n* NAUT Liniendampfer *m;* **ocean ~** Ozeandampfer *m*
liner² ['laɪ·nər] *n* (*lining*) Einsatz *m*
'linesman *n* SPORTS Linienrichter *m*
'lineup *n* ❶ LAW Gegenüberstellung *f* ❷ SPORTS [Mannschafts]aufstellung *f;* (*in baseball*) Lineup *f fachspr* ❸ (*group*) *of performers* Besetzung *f; of endorsements* Gruppierung *f*
linger ['lɪŋ·gər] *vi* ❶ (*persist*) anhalten; **the smell ~ed in the kitchen for days** der Geruch hing tagelang in der Küche; **to ~ in the memory** im Gedächtnis bleiben ❷ (*tarry*) trödeln, verweilen
lingerie [ˌlan·ʒə·'reɪ] *n* [Damen]unterwäsche *f*
lingering ['lɪŋ·gər·ɪŋ] *adj attr* ❶ (*lasting*) verbleibend; *fears* [fort]bestehend; *regrets* nachhaltig; *suspicion* [zurück]bleibend; **I still have ~ doubts** ich habe noch immer so meine Zweifel ❷ (*long*) lang, ausgedehnt; *death* schleichend; *illness* langwierig; *kiss* innig
lingo <*pl* -s *or* -es> ['lɪŋ·goʊ] *n* (*esp hum fam*) ❶ (*language*) Sprache *f* ❷ (*jargon*) Jargon *m;* (*specialized*) Kauderwelsch *nt*
linguist ['lɪŋ·gwɪst] *n* ❶ (*specialist*) Linguist(in) *m(f)* ❷ (*fluent speaker*) Sprachkundige(r) *f(m)*
linguistic [lɪŋ·'gwɪs·tɪk] *adj inv* sprachlich; *science* linguistisch
linguistics [lɪŋ·'gwɪs·tɪks] *n* + *sing vb* die

Sprachwissenschaft
lining ['laɪ·nɪŋ] *n* ① (*fabric*) Futter *nt; of coat* Innenfutter *nt; of dress* Unterrock *m* ② *of stomach* Magenschleimhaut *f; of brake* Bremsbelag *m*
link [lɪŋk] **I.** *n* ① (*connection*) Verbindung *f* (**between** zwischen +*dat*); (*between people, nations*) Beziehung *f* (**between** zwischen +*dat*) ② INET, COMPUT Link *m fachspr* ③ *of chain* [Ketten]glied *nt;* **~ in a chain** [**of events**] (*fig*) Glied *nt* in der Kette [der Ereignisse] **II.** *vt* ① (*connect*) verbinden ② (*clasp*) **to ~ arms** sich unterhaken; **to ~ hands** sich an den Händen fassen **III.** *vi* sich zusammenfügen lassen
links [lɪŋks] *npl* (*golf course*) Golfplatz *m*
'linkup *n* Verbindung *f* (**between** zwischen +*dat*)
linoleum [lɪ·'noʊ·li·əm] *n* Linoleum *nt*
linseed ['lɪn·sid] *n* Leinsamen *m*
'linseed oil *n* Leinöl *nt*
lint [lɪnt] *n* ① (*fluff*) Fussel *f,* Fluse *f* NORDD ② MED Mull *m*
lion ['laɪ·ən] *n* ① Löwe *m* ② ASTROL Löwe *m* ▶ PHRASES: **the ~'s den** die Höhle des Löwen; **the ~'s share** der Löwenanteil
lioness <*pl* -es> ['laɪ·ə·nes] *n* Löwin *f*
lionize ['laɪ·ə·naɪz] *vt* ■**to ~ sb** jdn feiern
lip [lɪp] *n* ① Lippe *f* ② (*rim*) Rand *m; of pitcher* Schnabel *m* ③ (*fam: cheek*) Unverschämtheiten *pl*
'lip balm *n* ① (*cream*) Lippenpflege *f* ② (*stick*) Lippenpomade *f*
'lip gloss *n* Lipgloss *m*
liposuction ['lɪp·oʊ·ˌsʌk·ʃən] *n* Fettabsaugen *nt*
'lip-read <-read, -read> *vi* von den Lippen ablesen
'lip service *n* (*pej*) Lippenbekenntnis *nt;* **to pay ~ to sb/sth** ein Lippenbekenntnis zu etw/jdm ablegen
'lipstick *n* Lippenstift *m*
liquefy <-ie-> ['lɪk·wə·faɪ] **I.** *vt* ① CHEM verflüssigen ② FIN *assets* verfügbar machen **II.** *vi* CHEM sich verflüssigen
liqueur [lɪ·'kɜr] *n* Likör *m*
liquid ['lɪk·wɪd] **I.** *adj* ① (*watery*) flüssig, Flüssig-; **~ soap** Seifenlotion *f* ② (*clear*) *eyes* glänzend; *luster* schimmernd ③ *attr* CHEM *hydrogen, oxygen* verflüssigt ④ *inv* FIN [frei] verfügbar **II.** *n* Flüssigkeit *f*
liquidate ['lɪk·wɪ·deɪt] **I.** *vt* ① ECON, FIN *company, firm* auflösen; *assets* verfügbar machen; *debts* tilgen ② (*kill*) ■**to ~ sb** jdn liquidieren *geh* **II.** *vi* ECON liquidieren
liquidation [ˌlɪk·wɪ·'deɪ·ʃən] *n* ① FIN *of company, firm* Auflösung *f; of debts* Tilgung *f;* **to go into ~** in Liquidation gehen ② (*killing*) Liquidierung *f geh*
liquidity [lɪ·'kwɪd·ɪ·t̬i] *n* ① CHEM Flüssigkeit *f* ② FIN Liquidität *f fachspr*
liquidize ['lɪk·wɪ·daɪz] *vt food* pürieren
liquify ['lɪk·wə·faɪ] *vi, vt see* **liquefy**
liquor ['lɪk·ər] **I.** *n* Alkohol *m;* **he can't hold his ~** er verträgt keinen Alkohol; **hard ~** Schnaps *m* **II.** *vt* (*fam*) ■**to ~ sb up** jdn abfüllen
'liquor store *n* Wein- und Spirituosengeschäft *nt*
lisp [lɪsp] **I.** *n* Lispeln *nt kein pl* **II.** *vi, vt* lispeln
list[1] [lɪst] **I.** *n* Liste *f;* **~ of names** Namensliste *f;* (*in books*) Namensverzeichnis *nt;* **shopping ~** Einkaufszettel *m;* **to put sb/sth on a ~** jdn/etw auf eine Liste setzen **II.** *vt* auflisten; **to be ~ed in the phone book** im Telefonbuch stehen
list[2] [lɪst] NAUT **I.** *vi* Schlagseite haben **II.** *n* Schlagseite *f*
listen ['lɪs·ən] **I.** *vi* ① (*hear*) zuhören; ■**to ~ to sb/sth** jdm/etw zuhören; **~ to this!** hör dir das an! *fam;* **to ~ carefully** [ganz] genau zuhören; **to ~ to the radio** Radio hören ② (*heed*) zuhören; **don't ~ to them** hör nicht auf sie ③ (*attempt to hear*) **will you please ~ for the phone** [**to ring**]? könntest du bitte aufpassen, ob das Telefon klingelt? **II.** *n* **have a ~ to this!** hör dir das an!
◆**listen in** *vi* (*secretly*) mithören; (*without participating*) mitanhören
listener ['lɪs·nər] *n* ① (*in conversation*) Zuhörer(in) *m(f)* ② (*at lecture, concert*) Hörer(in) *m(f);* (*to radio*) [Radio]hörer(in) *m(f)*
listing ['lɪs·tɪŋ] *n* ① (*list*) Auflistung *f* ② (*entry in list*) Eintrag *m* ③ (*program*) ■**~s** *pl* Veranstaltungskalender *m;* **television ~s** Fernsehprogramm *nt*
listless ['lɪst·lɪs] *adj* ① (*unenergetic*) *person* teilnahmslos; (*fig*) *economy* stagnierend ② (*unenthusiastic*) lustlos; *performance* ohne Schwung *nach n,* schlaff
lit [lɪt] *vi, vt pt, pp of* **light**
litany ['lɪt·ə·ni] *n* REL Litanei *f a. fig*
liter ['li·t̬ər] *n* Liter *m o nt* (**per** pro +*akk*); **two ~s** [**of milk**] zwei Liter [Milch]
literacy ['lɪt̬·ər·ə·si] *n* Lese- und Schreibfähigkeit *f;* **computer ~** Computerkenntnisse *pl*
literal ['lɪt̬·ər·əl] *adj* ① (*word-for-word*) wörtlich; **~ meaning/sense** eigentliche Bedeutung ② (*unexaggerated*) buchstäblich, im wahrsten Sinne des Wortes *präd; truth* rein
literally ['lɪt̬·ər·ə·li] *adv* ① (*word-for-word*) [wort]wörtlich ② (*actually*) buchstäblich
literary ['lɪt̬·ə·rer·i] *adj attr criticism, prize* Literatur-; *language, style* literarisch; **~ career** Schriftstellerkarriere *f*
literary 'criticism *n* Literaturkritik *f*
literate ['lɪt̬·ər·ɪt] *adj* ① (*able to read and write*) ■**to be ~** lesen und schreiben können ② (*well-educated*) gebildet; **to be computer-~** sich mit Computern auskennen
literature ['lɪt̬·ər·ə·tʃər] *n* ① (*works*) Literatur *f;* **nineteenth-century ~** die Literatur des 19. Jahrhunderts ② (*specialized*) Fachliteratur *f* (**on/about** über +*akk*) ③ (*printed matter*) Informationsmaterial *nt*
lithe [laɪð] *adj* geschmeidig

lithium ['lɪθ·i·əm] *n* Lithium *nt*
lithograph ['lɪθ·ə·græf] *n* Lithographie *f*
lithography [lɪ·'θag·rə·fi] *n* Lithographie *f*
Lithuania [ˌlɪθ·ʊ·'eɪ·ni·ə] *n* Litauen *nt*
Lithuanian [ˌlɪθ·ʊ·'eɪ·ni·ən] **I.** *n* ❶ (*person*) Litauer(in) *m(f)* ❷ (*language*) Litauisch *nt* **II.** *adj inv* litauisch
litigant ['lɪt̬·ɪ·gənt] *n* LAW prozessführende Partei
litigate ['lɪt̬·ɪ·geɪt] LAW **I.** *vi* prozessieren **II.** *vt* ■**to ~ sth** um etw *akk* prozessieren
litigation [ˌlɪt̬·ɪ·'geɪ·ʃən] *n* LAW Prozess *m*
litigious [lɪ·'tɪdʒ·əs] *adj* LAW prozessfreudig *iron*
litmus ['lɪt·məs] *n* Lackmus *m o nt*
'litmus paper *n* Lackmuspapier *nt*
'litmus test *n* ❶ CHEM Lackmustest *m* ❷ (*fig: indication*) entscheidendes [An]zeichen (**of** für +*akk*)
litter ['lɪt̬·ər] **I.** *n* ❶ (*trash*) Müll *m,* Abfall *m* ❷ ZOOL Wurf *m;* **~ of kittens** Wurf *m* kleiner Kätzchen **II.** *vt* ❶ (*make untidy*) **dirty clothes ~ed the floor** dreckige Wäsche lag über den Boden verstreut ❷ *usu passive* (*fig: fill*) ■**to be ~ed with sth** mit etw *dat* übersät sein
'litter box *n* Katzenklo *nt*
'litterbug *n* (*fam*) Umweltverschmutzer(in) *m(f)*
little ['lɪt̬·əl] **I.** *adj* ❶ (*small*) klein; (*for emphasis*) richtige(r, s), kleine(r, s) ❷ (*young*) klein; **~ sister** kleine Schwester ❸ *attr, inv distance* kurz; *duration* wenig, bisschen **II.** *adv* ❶ (*somewhat*) ■**a ~** ein wenig ❷ (*hardly*) wenig; **~ did she know that ...** sie hatte ja keine Ahnung davon, dass ...; **[a] ~ more than an hour ago** vor kaum einer Stunde **III.** *pron sing* ❶ (*small quantity*) ■**a ~** ein wenig (**of** von +*dat*) ❷ (*not much*) wenig; **as ~ as possible** möglichst wenig; **the ~ ...** das wenige ... ❸ (*short time*) **it's a ~ after six** es ist kurz nach sechs ▶ PHRASES: **precious ~** herzlich wenig
liturgy ['lɪt̬·ər·dʒi] *n* Liturgie *f*
live¹ [lɪv] **I.** *vi* ❶ (*be alive*) leben; **will she ~?** wird sie überleben? ❷ (*spend life*) leben; **to ~ in fear/luxury** in Angst/Luxus leben ❸ (*subsist*) leben (**by** von +*dat*) ❹ (*reside*) wohnen; **where do you ~?** wo wohnst du?; **to ~ in the country** auf dem Land wohnen ▶ PHRASES: **you'll ~ to regret that!** das wirst du noch bereuen! **II.** *vt* **to ~ [one's] life to the fullest** das Leben in vollen Zügen genießen; **to ~ one's own life** sein eigenes Leben leben ▶ PHRASES: **to ~ a lie** mit einer Lebenslüge leben; **to ~ the life of Riley** (*fam*) wie Gott in Frankreich leben
◆**live down** *vt* ■**to ~ down** ↻ **sth** über etw *akk* hinwegkommen; *mistakes* über etw *akk* Gras wachsen lassen
◆**live for** *vi* ■**to ~ for sth** für etw *akk* leben ▶ PHRASES: **to ~ for the moment** ein sorgloses Leben führen
◆**live off, live off of** *vi* ❶ (*depend on*) ■**to ~ off sb** auf jds Kosten leben ❷ (*support oneself*) ■**to ~ off sth** *inheritance, pension* von etw *dat* leben
◆**live on** *vi* ❶ (*continue*) weiterleben; *tradition* fortbestehen; **to ~ on in memory** in Erinnerung bleiben ❷ (*support oneself*) ■**to ~ on sth** von etw *dat* leben
◆**live out** *vt* **to ~ out** ↻ **one's dreams** seine [Wunsch]träume verwirklichen; **to ~ out** ↻ **one's days** seine Tage verbringen
◆**live through** *vi* überstehen; **to ~ through an experience** eine Erfahrung durchmachen
◆**live together** *vi* zusammenleben; *residents* zusammenwohnen
◆**live up** *vt* **to ~ it up** (*fam*) die Puppen tanzen lassen *fam*
◆**live up to** *vi* **to ~ up to sb's expectations** jds Erwartungen gerecht werden; **to ~ up to one's reputation** seinem Ruf gerecht werden
◆**live with** *vi* ❶ (*cohabit*) zusammenleben ❷ (*tolerate*) sich abfinden (mit +*dat*)
live² [laɪv] **I.** *adj inv* ❶ *attr* (*living*) lebend; **~ animals** echte Tiere ❷ MUS, RADIO, TV live; **~ broadcast** Liveübertragung *f* ❸ ELEC geladen; **~ wire** Hochspannungskabel *nt* ❹ (*unexploded*) *ammunition* scharf **II.** *adv inv* MUS, RADIO, TV live
livelihood ['laɪv·li·hʊd] *n* Lebensunterhalt *m;* **to lose one's ~** seine Existenzgrundlage verlieren
liveliness ['laɪv·lɪ·nɪs] *n of story* Lebendigkeit *f; of person* Lebhaftigkeit *f*
lively ['laɪv·li] *adj* ❶ (*energetic*) lebhaft; *child, eyes, tune* munter; *nature* aufgeweckt; *imagination* rege(r, s); *mind* wach; **~ place** *ein Ort, an dem immer etwas los ist* ❷ (*bright*) *colors* hell; (*garish*) grell ❸ (*enduring*) *tradition* lebendig ❹ (*brisk*) rege; *pace* flott
liven ['laɪ·vən] **I.** *vt* ■**to ~ up** ↻ **sth** Leben in etw *akk* bringen; **to ~ up a room** ein Zimmer etwas aufpeppen *fam;* ■**to ~ up** ↻ **sb** jdn aufmuntern **II.** *vi* ■**to ~ up** *person* aufleben; *party, game* in Schwung kommen
liver ['lɪv·ər] *n* Leber *f*
'liver damage *n* Leberschaden *m*
'liverwurst *n* Leberwurst *f*
livery ['lɪv·ə·ri] *n* FASHION Livree *f*
'livestock *n* Vieh *nt,* Viehbestand *m*
live wire *n* ❶ ELEC unter Strom stehende Leitung ❷ (*fig fam*) Feger *m*
livid ['lɪv·ɪd] *adj* (*fam*) wütend
living ['lɪv·ɪŋ] **I.** *n* ❶ *usu sing* (*livelihood*) Lebensunterhalt *m;* **to do sth for a ~** mit etw *dat* seinen Lebensunterhalt verdienen ❷ (*lifestyle*) Lebensstil *m;* **standard of ~** Lebensstandard *m* ❸ *pl* ■**the ~** die Lebenden *pl* **II.** *adj inv* ❶ (*alive*) lebend *attr;* **we didn't see a ~ soul on the streets** wir sahen draußen auf der Straße keine Menschenseele; **~ creatures** Lebewesen *pl* ❷ (*in use*) lebendig; *language* lebend ▶ PHRASES: **to scare the ~ daylights out of sb** jdn zu Tode erschrecken; **to be in ~ memory** [noch] in [lebendiger] Erinnerung

L

sein

'**living conditions** *n* Lebensbedingungen *pl*

'**living quarters** *npl* Wohnbereich *m;* MIL Quartier *nt*

'**living room** *n* Wohnzimmer *nt*

'**living space** *n* (*for personal accommodation*) Wohnraum *m*

living 'will *n* LAW *Willenserklärung eines Patienten, die seine medizinische Behandlung festlegt*

lizard ['lɪz·ərd] **I.** *n* Eidechse *f* **II.** *adj attr, inv* aus Eidechsenleder *nach n*

llama ['la·mə] *n* Lama *nt*

load [loʊd] **I.** *n* ❶ (*amount carried*) Ladung *f;* **the maximum ~ for this elevator is 1000 pounds** der Aufzug hat eine Tragkraft von maximal 453 kg ❷ (*burden*) Last *f* ❸ (*fam: lots*) **a ~ of work** ein Riesenberg *m* an Arbeit; (*plenty*) ■ **~s** jede Menge; **what a ~ of garbage!** (*pej*) nichts als blanker Unsinn! *fam* ▶ PHRASES: **get a ~ of this!** (*fam*) hör dir das an! **II.** *adv* ■ **~s** *pl* (*fam*) tausendmal *fam* **III.** *vt* ❶ (*fill*) laden; *container* beladen; *dishwasher* einräumen; *washing machine* füllen ❷ (*fig: burden*) aufladen; **to ~ sb with responsibility** jdm sehr viel Verantwortung aufladen ❸ (*insert*) *CD, DVD, film* einlegen **IV.** *vi* [ver]laden

◆**load down** *vt thing* schwer beladen; *person* zu viel aufbürden +*dat*

◆**load up I.** *vt* aufladen; **let's ~ up the car and hit the road** lass uns die Sachen ins Auto laden und losfahren; **to ~ up ⊂ a container** einen Container beladen **II.** *vi* beladen

loaded ['loʊ·dɪd] *adj* ❶ (*carrying load*) beladen ❷ *gun* geladen ❸ (*excessive*) überladen (**with** mit +*dat*); **to be ~ with calories** eine Kalorienbombe sein ❹ *pred* (*fam: rich*) steinreich ❺ *pred* (*fam: drunk*) besoffen *fam* ❻ (*biased*) **~ question** Fangfrage *f*

'**loading dock** *n* Laderampe *f*

loaf[1] <*pl* loaves> [loʊf] *n* ❶ (*bread*) Brot *nt;* (*unsliced a.*) Brotlaib *m* ❷ (*bread-shaped object*) Kasten-

loaf[2] [loʊf] *vi* faulenzen; **to ~ around** herumgammeln *fam*

loafer ['loʊ·fər] *n* Faulenzer(in) *m(f) pej*

Loafer® ['loʊ·fər] *n* FASHION [leichter] Halbschuh

loam [loʊm] *n* ❶ (*soil*) Lehmerde *f* ❷ (*for bricks*) Lehm *m*

loan [loʊn] **I.** *n* ❶ (*money*) Kredit *m;* **to take out a ~** ein Darlehen aufnehmen ❷ (*act*) Ausleihe *f kein pl,* Verleihen *nt kein pl;* **to be on ~** verliehen sein **II.** *vt* leihen

'**loanword** *n* Lehnwort *nt*

loath [loʊθ] *adj pred* ■ **to be ~ to do sth** etw ungern tun

loathe [loʊð] *vt thing* nicht ausstehen können; *person* verabscheuen

loathing ['loʊ·ðɪŋ] *n* (*hate*) Abscheu *m;* (*hatred*) Hass *m;* **to fill sb with ~** jdn mit Ekel erfüllen; **to have a ~ for sb/sth** jdn/etw verabscheuen

loathsome ['loʊð·səm] *adj* abscheulich; *suggestion, action* abstoßend

loaves [loʊvz] *n pl of* **loaf**

lob [lab] **I.** *vt* <-bb-> lobben; **to ~ a ball** im Lob spielen **II.** *n* ❶ (*stroke*) Lobspiel *nt kein pl* ❷ (*ball*) Lob *m*

lobby ['lab·i] **I.** *n* ❶ ARCHIT Eingangshalle *f;* **hotel ~** Hotelfoyer *nt* ❷ POL Lobby *f* **II.** *vi* <-ie-> ■ **to ~ for/against sth** seinen Einfluss [mittels eines Interessensverbandes] für/gegen etw *akk* geltend machen **III.** *vt* <-ie-> ■ **to ~ sb/sth [to do sth]** jdn/etw beeinflussen[, etw zu tun]

lobbyist ['lab·i·ɪst] *n* Lobbyist(in) *m(f)*

lobe [loʊb] *n* Lappen *m; of ear* Ohrläppchen *nt; of brain* Gehirnlappen *m; of liver* Leberlappen *m*

lobster ['lab·stər] *n* Hummer *m*

local ['loʊ·kəl] **I.** *adj* ❶ (*neighborhood*) hiesig, örtlich; **~ politics** Kommunalpolitik *f;* **~ radio station** Lokalsender *m;* **~ branch** Filiale *f; of bank, shop* Zweigstelle *f;* **~ bar** Stammkneipe *f* ❷ MED lokal **II.** *n* ❶ *usu pl* (*inhabitant*) Ortsansässige(r) *f(m)* ❷ (*trade union*) örtliches Gewerkschaftsbüro

local anes'thetic *n* örtliche Betäubung

'**local call** *n* Ortsgespräch *nt*

locale [loʊ·'kæl] *n* Örtlichkeit *f*

local 'government *n of city* Stadtverwaltung *f; of community* Kommunalverwaltung *f*

locality [loʊ·'kæl·ɪ·t̬i] *n* Gegend *f*

localization [ˌloʊ·kə·lɪ·'zeɪ·ʃən] *n* Lokalisation *f*

localize ['loʊ·kə·laɪz] *vt* ❶ (*decentralize*) *government* dezentralisieren ❷ (*confine*) *bleeding* eingrenzen ❸ (*pinpoint*) lokalisieren *geh*

local 'newspaper *n* Lokalblatt *nt*

'**local time** *n* Ortszeit *f*

local 'train *n* Nahverkehrszug *m*

locate ['loʊ·keɪt] **I.** *vt* ❶ (*find*) ausfindig machen; *plane, sunken ship* orten ❷ (*situate*) bauen; **our office is ~d at the end of the road** unser Büro befindet sich am Ende der Straße; **to be centrally ~d** zentral liegen **II.** *vi* sich niederlassen

location [loʊ·'keɪ·ʃən] *n* ❶ (*place*) Lage *f; company* Standort *m* ❷ FILM Drehort *m* ❸ (*act*) Positionsbestimmung *f; of tumor* Lokalisierung *f*

lock[1] [lak] **I.** *n* ❶ (*fastener*) Schloss *nt;* **bicycle ~** Fahrradschloss *nt* ❷ NAUT Schleuse *f* ❸ (*wrestling*) Fesselgriff *m* ▶ PHRASES: **to be under ~ and key** hinter Schloss und Riegel sitzen *fam* **II.** *vt* ❶ (*fasten*) abschließen; *suitcase* verschließen ❷ *usu passive* (*entangle*) sich verhaken; **to be ~ed in an embrace** sich eng umschlungen halten **III.** *vi* ❶ (*become secured*) schließen ❷ (*become fixed*) binden

◆**lock away** *vt* ❶ (*secure*) wegschließen ❷ (*imprison*) einsperren *fam;* ■ **to ~ oneself away [in one's office]** sich [in seinem Büro] einschließen

◆**lock on** *vi* MIL **to ~ on to a target** ein genaues Ziel ausmachen
◆**lock out** *vt* aussperren
◆**lock up I.** *vt* ❶ (*shut, secure*) abschließen; *documents, money* wegschließen ❷ (*put in custody*) ■**to ~ up ↻ sb** LAW jdn einsperren *fam,* jdn einlochen *sl;* MED jdn in eine geschlossene Anstalt bringen **II.** *vi* abschließen, zuschließen

lock² [lak] *n* (*curl*) [Haar]locke *f*
locker ['lak·ər] *n* Schließfach *nt;* MIL, SCH, SPORTS Spind *m*
'**locker room** *n* Umkleideraum [mit Schließfächern] *m*
locket ['lak·ɪt] *n* Medaillon *nt*
'**lockjaw** *n* Wundstarrkrampf *m*
'**lockout** *n* Aussperrung *f*
'**locksmith** *n* Schlosser(in) *m(f)*
'**lockup** *n* Gefängnis *nt;* (*for drunks*) Ausnüchterungszelle *f*
locomotion [ˌloʊ·kə·'moʊ·ʃən] *n* Fortbewegung *f*
locomotive [ˌloʊ·kə·'moʊ·t̬ɪv] **I.** *n* Lokomotive *f* **II.** *adj attr, inv* Fortbewegungs-
locust ['loʊ·kəst] *n* Heuschrecke *f*
lode [loʊd] *n* MIN Ader *f a. fig*
lodge [ladʒ] **I.** *n* ❶ (*house*) Hütte *f* ❷ (*in resort*) Lodge *f* ❸ (*meeting hall*) Loge *f* **II.** *vt* ❶ (*submit*) *objection, complaint* einlegen; *protest* erheben ❷ (*fix*) hineinstoßen ❸ (*accommodate*) ■**to ~ sb** jdn [bei sich *dat*] unterbringen **III.** *vi* ❶ (*become fixed*) stecken bleiben ❷ (*live*) logieren, [zur Untermiete] wohnen (**with** bei +*dat*)
lodger ['ladʒ·ər] *n* Untermieter(in) *m(f)*
lodging ['ladʒ·ɪŋ] *n* Unterkunft *f*
loft [laft] *n* ❶ (*attic*) Speicher *m,* Estrich *m* SCHWEIZ; (*for living*) Dachwohnung *f,* Loft *m* ❷ (*in church*) **organ/choir ~** Empore *f* (*für die Orgel/den* [*Kirchen*] *chor*)
lofty ['laf·ti] *adj* ❶ (*high*) hoch [aufragend]; *heights* schwindelnd ❷ (*noble*) erhaben; *goals* hoch gesteckt; *ambitions* hochfliegend; *ideals* hohe(r, s)
log¹ [lɔg] **I.** *n* ❶ (*branch*) [gefällter] Baumstamm; (*trunk*) [Holz]block *m;* (*firewood*) [Holz]scheit *nt* ❷ (*record*) NAUT Logbuch *nt;* AVIAT Bordbuch *nt* ❸ (*systematic record*) Aufzeichnungen *pl;* **police ~** Polizeibericht *m* **II.** *vt* <-gg-> ❶ (*enter into record*) aufzeichnen; *phone calls* registrieren ❷ *forest* abholzen; *trees* fällen **III.** *vi* <-gg-> Bäume fällen
log² [lɔg] *n short for* **logarithm** Logarithmus *m*
◆**log in** *vi* sich einloggen
◆**log off** *vi* sich ausloggen
◆**log on** *vi* sich einloggen (**to** in +*akk*)
◆**log out** *vi* sich ausloggen (**of** aus +*dat*)
loganberry ['loʊ·gən·ber·i] *n* ❶ (*fruit*) Loganbeere *f* ❷ (*plant*) Loganbeerstrauch *m*
'**logbook** *n* NAUT Logbuch *nt;* AVIAT Bordbuch *nt*
log 'cabin *n* Blockhaus *nt*
logger ['lɔ·gər] *n* Holzfäller(in) *m(f)*
loggerheads ['lɔ·gər·hedz] *npl* ■**to be at ~** [**with sb**] [mit jdm] im Streit liegen
logic ['ladʒ·ɪk] *n* ❶ (*reasoning*) Logik *f;* **flawed ~** ein unlogischer Gedankengang; **to defy ~** gegen jede Logik verstoßen ❷ COMPUT, ELEC Logik *f*
logical ['ladʒ·ɪ·kəl] *adj* ❶ *inv* logisch ❷ (*sensible*) vernünftig ❸ (*clear thinking*) **I was incapable of ~ thought** ich konnte keinen klaren Gedanken fassen
logistics [loʊ·'dʒɪs·tɪks] *n + sing/pl vb* Logistik *f*
'**logjam** *n* ❶ (*logs*) Anstauung *f* von Floßholz ❷ (*deadlock*) toter Punkt; **to break a ~** wieder aus einer Sackgasse herauskommen
logo ['loʊ·goʊ] *n* Logo *m o nt*
'**logrolling** *n* (*fam*) POL Kuhhandel *m*
loin [lɔɪn] *n usu pl* Lende *f*
'**loincloth** *n* Lendenschurz *m*
loiter ['lɔɪ·t̬ər] *vi* ❶ (*idle*) **to ~** [**around**] herumhängen *fam,* herumlungern *fam* ❷ (*dawdle*) [herum]trödeln
loiterer ['lɔɪ·t̬ər·ər] *n* Herumtreiber(in) *m(f) pej fam*
loll [lal] *vi* (*idle*) lümmeln; (*sit*) faul dasitzen; (*lie*) faul daliegen; (*stand*) faul herumstehen
lollipop ['lal·i·pap] *n* Lutscher *m,* ÖSTERR *a.* Schlecker *m,* Schleckstängel *m* SCHWEIZ, Lolli *m fam*
lone [loʊn] *adj attr, inv* ❶ (*solitary*) einsam ❷ *father, parent* allein erziehend
loneliness ['loʊn·lɪ·nɪs] *n* Einsamkeit *f*
lonely <-ier, -iest *or* more ~, most ~> ['loʊn·li] *adj* ❶ (*alone*) einsam; **to feel ~** sich einsam fühlen ❷ (*unfrequented*) abgeschieden; *street* still
loner ['loʊ·nər] *n* Einzelgänger(in) *m(f)*
lonesome ['loʊn·səm] *adj* ❶ (*alone*) einsam; **to feel ~** sich einsam fühlen ❷ (*unfrequented*) abgelegen
long¹ [lɔŋ] **I.** *adj* ❶ (*in space*) lang; *distance, trip* weit; (*elongated*) lang, länglich; (*fam: tall*) groß, lang *fam;* (*fig*) **to have come a ~ way** von weit her gekommen sein ❷ (*in time*) lang; (*tedious*) lang[wierig]; **each session is an hour ~** jede Sitzung dauert eine Stunde; **a ~ day** ein langer [und anstrengender] Tag; *friendship* langjährig; *memory* gut; **it was a ~ time before I received a reply** es dauerte lange, bis ich [eine] Antwort bekam; **to work ~ hours** einen langen Arbeitstag haben ❸ (*in scope*) lang; *book* dick ▶ PHRASES: **in the ~ run** auf lange Sicht [gesehen] **II.** *adv* ❶ (*for a long time*) lang[e]; **have you been waiting ~?** wartest du schon lange?; **I won't be ~** (*before finishing*) ich bin gleich fertig; (*before appearing*) ich bin gleich da ❷ (*at a distant time*) lange; **~ ago** vor langer Zeit; **not ~ before that** kurz davor ❸ (*after implied time*) lange; **how much ~er will it take?** wie lange wird es noch dauern?; **he no ~er wanted to go there** er wollte nicht mehr dorthin ▶ PHRASES: **as ~ as ...** (*during*) solange ...; (*provided that*) vorausgesetzt, dass ... **III.** *n* (*long time*) eine

L

lange Zeit; **have you been waiting for ~?** wartest du schon lange? ▶PHRASES: **before [very] ~** schon [sehr] bald; **the ~ and the short of it** kurz gesagt

long[2] [lɔŋ] *vi* sich sehnen (**for** nach +*dat*); ■**to ~ to do sth** sich danach sehnen, etw zu tun

long[3] *n* GEOG *abbrev of* **longitude** Länge *f*

long-'distance I. *adj attr, inv* ① (*between places*) Fern-, Weit-; **~ flight** Langstreckenflug *m;* **~ relationship** *Beziehung zwischen zwei weit voneinander entfernt wohnenden Partnern* ② SPORTS *runner* Langstrecken- **II.** *adv inv* **to call ~** ein Ferngespräch führen; **to travel ~** eine Fernreise machen

longevity [lan·ˈdʒev·ɪ·t̬i] *n* Langlebigkeit *f*

'long-haired <longer-, longest-> *adj* langhaarig; *animals* Langhaar-

'longhand *n* Langschrift *f;* **to write sth in ~** etw mit der Hand schreiben

long 'haul *n* ① (*long distance*) Langstreckentransport *m* ② (*long time*) **to be in sth for the ~** sich langfristig für etw *akk* engagieren; **over the ~** auf lange Sicht

long-'haul *adj* **~ flight** Langstreckenflug *m*

'longhorn *n* (*breed of cattle*) Longhorn *nt*

longing [ˈlɔŋ·ɪŋ] **I.** *n* Sehnsucht *f,* Verlangen *nt* (**for** nach +*dat*) **II.** *adj attr* sehnsüchtig

longish [ˈlɔŋ·ɪʃ] *adj inv* (*fam*) ziemlich lang

longitude [ˈlan·dʒɪ·tud] *n* GEOG Länge *f*

longitudinal [ˌlan·dʒɪ·ˈtu·dən·əl] *adj inv* ① (*lengthwise*) Längs- ② GEOG Längen-, Longitudinal-

'long johns *npl* (*fam*) lange Unterhose

'long jump *n* SPORTS Weitsprung *m*

long-'lasting *adj* strapazierfähig

'long-life *adj inv batteries* langlebig, mit langer Lebensdauer *after n*

long-'lived <longer-, longest-> *adj* langlebig; *feud* seit langem bestehend

'long-lost *adj attr, inv* lang verloren geglaubt; *person* lang vermisst geglaubt

long-'range *adj* ① (*in distance*) Langstrecken- ② (*long-term*) langfristig

'long shot *n usu sing* ■**to be a ~** ziemlich aussichtslos sein; **[not] by a ~** (*fam*) bei weitem [nicht]

long-'standing *adj* seit langem bestehend; *argument* seit langem anhaltend; *friendship, relationship* langjährig

long-'suffering *adj* langmütig

'long-term *adj attr* langfristig; **~ memory** Langzeitgedächtnis *nt;* **~ strategy** Langzeitstrategie *f*

long-'winded *adj* langatmig

loofa, loofah [ˈlu·fə] *n* ① (*plant*) Luffa *f* ② (*sponge*) Luffaschwamm *m*

look [lʊk] **I.** *n* ① (*glance*) Blick *m;* **to get a good ~ at sb/sth** jdn/etw genau sehen können; **to give sb a ~** jdn ansehen; (*glimpse*) jdm einen Blick zuwerfen; **to have** [*or* **take**] **a ~ around [for sth]** sich [nach etw *dat*] umsehen ② (*on face*) [Gesichts]ausdruck *m,* Miene *f* ③ (*examination*) Betrachtung *f;* **to have** [*or* **take**] **a ~ at sth** sich *dat* etw ansehen; (*search*) **to have** [*or* **take**] **a ~ around for sb/sth** nach jdm/etw suchen ④ (*appearance*) Aussehen *nt;* **I don't like the ~[s] of it** das gefällt mir [gar] nicht; **good ~s** *of person* gutes Aussehen ⑤ FASHION Look *m* ▶PHRASES: **if ~s could kill** wenn Blicke töten könnten **II.** *interj* (*explanatory*) schau mal *fam,* pass mal auf *fam;* (*protesting*) hör mal *fam* **III.** *vi* ① (*glance*) schauen; **to ~ away/the other way** wegsehen ② (*search*) suchen; (*in an encyclopedia*) nachschlagen ③ (*appear*) **she doesn't ~ her age** man sieht ihr ihr Alter nicht an; **to ~ tired** müde aussehen; **it ~s very unlikely that ...** es scheint sehr unwahrscheinlich, dass ...; ■**to ~ like sb/sth** jdm/etw ähnlich sehen; **it ~s like rain** es sieht nach Regen aus ④ (*face*) blicken (**onto** auf +*akk*); *room, window* [hinaus]gehen (**onto** auf +*akk*)

◆**look after** *vi* (*care for*) ■**to ~ after sb/sth** sich um jdn/etw kümmern; **to ~ after one's own interests** seine eigenen Interessen verfolgen; (*keep eye on*) ■**to ~ after sb/sth** auf jdn/etw aufpassen

◆**look ahead** *vi* ① (*glance*) nach vorne sehen ② (*fig: plan*) vorausschauen

◆**look around** *vi* ① (*glance*) sich umsehen ② (*search*) ■**to ~ around for sb/sth** sich nach jdm/etw umsehen ③ (*examine*) sich *dat* ansehen; *house* besichtigen

◆**look at** *vi* ① (*glance*) ansehen ② (*examine*) ■**to ~ at sth/sb** sich *dat* etw/jdn ansehen ③ (*regard*) ■**to ~ at sth** etw betrachten; **he ~s at things differently than you do** er sieht die Dinge anders als du

◆**look back** *vi* ① (*glance*) zurückschauen ② (*remember*) zurückblicken (**on, over, at** auf +*akk*) ▶PHRASES: **sb never ~ed back** für jdn ging es bergauf

◆**look down** *vi* ① (*glance*) nach unten sehen; ■**to ~ down at/on sb/sth** zu jdm/etw hinuntersehen ② (*fig: despise*) ■**to ~ down [up]on sb/sth** auf jdn/etw herabsehen ③ (*examine*) **to ~ down a list** eine Liste von oben bis unten durchgehen

◆**look for** *vi* ① (*seek*) ■**to ~ for sb/sth** nach jdm/etw suchen; **to ~ for a job** Arbeit suchen ② (*anticipate*) jdn/etw erwarten

◆**look forward** *vi* ① (*glance*) nach vorne sehen ② (*anticipate*) sich freuen (**to** auf +*akk*)

◆**look in** *vi* ① (*glance*) hineinsehen ② (*visit*) ■**to ~ in [on sb]** [bei jdm] vorbeischauen *fam*

◆**look into** *vi* ■**to ~ into sth** ① (*glance*) in etw *akk* [hinein]sehen ② (*examine*) etw untersuchen; **to ~ into a complaint** eine Beschwerde prüfen

◆**look on** *vi* ① (*watch*) zusehen ② (*regard*) **to ~ on sth with disquiet** etw mit Unbehagen betrachten

◆**look out** *vi* ① (*take care*) aufpassen; ■**to ~ out for sb/sth** sich vor jdm/etw in Acht nehmen ② (*watch*) Ausschau halten (**for** nach +*dat*) ③ (*face*) blicken (**onto, over** auf +*akk*);

room, window hinausgehen (**onto, over** auf +*akk*)

◆**look over** **I.** *vi* ① (*glance*) blicken (über +*akk*); **to ~ over to sb/sth** zu jdm/etw hinübersehen ② (*offer view*) blicken (über +*akk*); *window, room* [hinaus]gehen (auf +*akk*) **II.** *vt* ① (*view*) besichtigen; (*inspect, survey*) inspizieren ② (*examine*) durchsehen; *letter* überfliegen; ■**to ~ over** ⊂ **sb** jdn mustern

◆**look through** *vi* ① (*glance*) ■**to ~ through sth** durch etw *akk* [hindurch]sehen ② (*peruse*) durchsehen; *article* [kurz] überfliegen; *magazine* durchblättern

◆**look to** *vi* ① (*rely on*) ■**to ~ to sb** sich auf jdn verlassen ② (*anticipate*) **to ~ to the future** in die Zukunft blicken

◆**look toward(s)** *vi* ① (*glance*) ■**to ~ toward sth/sb** zu etw/jdm sehen ② (*face*) ■**to ~ toward sth** auf etw *akk* blicken; *room, window* auf etw *akk* [hinaus]gehen

◆**look up** **I.** *vi* ① (*glance*) ■**to ~ up at sb/sth** zu jdm/etw hinaufsehen; ■**to ~ up [from sth]** [von etw *dat*] aufsehen ② (*improve*) besser werden **II.** *vt* ① (*fam: visit*) ■**to ~ up** ⊂ **sb** bei jdm vorbeischauen ② (*search for*) nachschlagen; *phone number* heraussuchen

◆**look upon** *vi see* **look on 1**

◆**look up to** *vi* ■**to ~ up to sb** aufsehen (zu +*dat*)

'**lookalike** *n* Doppelgänger(in) *m(f)*

looker ['lʊk·ər] *n* (*fam*) **to be a ~** gut aussehen

'**lookout** *n* ① (*post*) Beobachtungsposten *m* ② (*person*) Wache *f* ③ (*watch*) **to keep a ~ [for sb/sth]** [nach jdm/etw] Ausschau halten; (*search*) **to be on the ~ [for sb/sth]** auf der Suche [nach jdm/etw] sein

loom¹ [lum] *vi* ① (*come into view*) [drohend] auftauchen ② (*be ominously near*) sich drohend abzeichnen; *storm* sich zusammenbrauen *a. fig; difficulties* sich auftürmen; **to ~ large** eine große Rolle spielen

loom² [lum] *n* Webstuhl *m*

loony ['lu·ni] (*fam*) **I.** *n* Irre(r) *f(m)* **II.** *adj* verrückt

loop [lup] **I.** *n* ① (*shape*) Schleife *f; of string, wire* Schlinge *f; of river, tape, in skating* Schleife *f; of belt* Schlaufen *pl* ② COMPUT [Programm]schleife *f* ③ (*contraceptive*) Spirale *f* **II.** *vt* **~ the rope over the bar** schling das Seil um die Stange **III.** *vi* eine Schleife machen; *road, stream* sich schlängeln

'**loophole** *n* ① LAW Gesetzeslücke *f;* **to exploit a ~** eine Gesetzeslücke nutzen ② (*slit*) Schießscharte *f*

loose [lus] **I.** *adj* ① (*relaxed, not tight*) locker; *papers* los; *skin* schlaff; **~ cash/coins** Kleingeld *nt;* **to come ~** sich lösen; **to work itself ~** sich lockern ② *hair* offen ③ (*not confined*) frei; **to break ~** *person, dog* sich losreißen ④ (*not exact*) ungefähr *attr;* (*not strict*) lose; *adaptation, translation* frei; *discipline* mangelhaft ⑤ *clothing* weit, locker ⑥ (*indiscreet*) **~ tongue** loses Mundwerk *fam* ▸PHRASES: **to hang ~** (*fam*) cool bleiben **II.** *n* LAW **to be on the ~** frei herumlaufen **III.** *vt* ① (*set free*) freilassen ② (*untie*) lösen

'**loose-leaf** *adj attr, inv* Loseblatt-; **~ binder** Ringbuch *nt*

loosely ['lus·li] *adv* ① (*not tightly*) lose; **to hang ~** schlaff herunterhängen ② (*not exactly*) ungefähr; **~ speaking** grob gesagt; **~ translated** frei übersetzt

loosen ['lu·sən] **I.** *vt* ① *collar* aufmachen; *tie* lockern ② (*relax*) *grip, muscles* lockern ③ (*weaken*) *ties* lockern; *relationship* [langsam] lösen ▸PHRASES: **to ~ sb's tongue** jdm die Zunge lösen **II.** *vi* sich lockern

loot [lut] **I.** *n* ① MIL Kriegsbeute *f;* (*plunder*) [Diebes]beute *f* ② (*fam: money*) Zaster *m;* (*valued objects*) Geschenke *pl* **II.** *vt* ① (*plunder*) [aus]plündern ② (*steal*) stehlen **III.** *vi* plündern

looting ['lu·t̬ɪŋ] *n* Plünderei *f*

lop [lap] *vt* <-pp-> ① *tree* stutzen ② (*eliminate*) streichen; *budget* kürzen

◆**lop off** *vt* ① *branches* abhacken ② (*reduce*) *expenses* [ver]kürzen

lope [loʊp] *vi* in großen Sätzen springen; *hare* hoppeln

'**lopsided** *adj* schief; (*fig*) *victory* einseitig

loquacious [loʊ·'kweɪ·ʃəs] *adj* redselig

lord [lɔrd] *n* ① (*nobleman*) Lord *m* ② (*fam: powerful man*) Herr *m*

Lord [lɔrd] *n* REL ■**the ~** der Herr

lordship ['lɔrd·ʃɪp] *n* ① (*form of address*) **His/Your L~** Seine/Euer Lordschaft ② (*dominion*) Herrschaft *f*

lore [lɔr] *n* [überliefertes] Wissen

lose <lost, lost> [luz] **I.** *vt* ① (*forfeit*) verlieren; ■**to ~ sth to sb** etw an jdn verlieren; **to ~ one's breath** außer Atem kommen ② (*through death*) **she lost her son in the fire** ihr Sohn ist beim Brand umgekommen ③ *usu passive* ■**to be lost** *things* verschwunden sein; *victims* umgekommen sein; *plane, ship* verloren sein ④ (*waste*) *opportunity* versäumen; *time* verlieren; **to ~ no time in doing sth** etw sofort tun ⑤ *watch, clock* **to ~ time** nachgehen ⑥ (*not find*) *person, thing* verlieren; (*mislay*) verlegen; **to ~ one's way** sich verirren ⑦ (*not win*) verlieren ⑧ (*forget*) *language, skill* verlernen ▸PHRASES: **to ~ heart** den Mut verlieren; **to ~ it** (*fam*) durchdrehen; **to ~ sleep over sth** sich *dat* wegen einer S. *gen* Sorgen machen; **to ~ touch [with sb]** den Kontakt [zu jdm] verlieren; **to ~ track [of sth]** (*not follow*) [etw *dat*] [geistig] nicht folgen können; (*not remember*) **I've lost track of the number of times he's asked me for money** ich weiß schon gar nicht mehr, wie oft er mich um Geld gebeten hat **II.** *vi* ① (*be beaten*) verlieren (**to** gegen +*akk*) ② (*earn too little*) ein Verlustgeschäft sein ▸PHRASES: **you can't ~** du kannst nur gewinnen

◆**lose out** *vi* ① (*be deprived*) schlecht wegkommen *fam;* ■**to ~ out in sth** bei etw *dat* den Kürzeren ziehen *fam* ② (*be beaten*) ■ **to ~ out to sb/sth** jdm/etw unterliegen

loser [ˈlu·zər] *n* ① (*defeated person*) Verlierer(in) *m(f)* ② (*fam: habitually*) Verlierer[typ] *m*

losing [ˈlu·zɪŋ] *adj attr* Verlierer-

loss <*pl* -es> [lɔs] *n* Verlust *m* ▶ PHRASES: **to be at a ~** nicht mehr weiterwissen

lost [lɔst] **I.** *pt, pp of* **lose II.** *adj inv* ① (*unable to find way*) ■ **to be ~** sich verirrt haben; **to get ~** sich verirren; (*on foot*) sich verlaufen haben; (*using vehicle*) sich verfahren haben ② (*misplaced*) **to get ~ [in the mail/shuffle]** [in der Post/in dem Haufen] verschwinden ③ *pred* (*helpless*) **to feel ~** sich verloren fühlen; ■ **to be ~** (*not understand*) nichts verstehen; ■ **to be ~ without sb/sth** ohne jdn/etw verloren sein ④ (*perished, destroyed*) *soldiers* gefallen; *planes, ships, tanks* zerstört ⑤ (*not won*) *battle, contest* verloren ▶ PHRASES: **get ~!** (*fam*) hau ab!, zieh Leine! *sl;* **the joke's ~ on him** er versteht den Witz nicht

lost and 'found *n* Fundbüro *nt*

lot [lat] **I.** *pron* ① (*much, many*) ■ **a ~** viel/viele; **a ~ of people** viele [*o* eine Menge] Leute ② (*many things*) ■ **~s [of sth]** + *sing/pl vb* viel [*o fam* jede Menge] [etw]; **there's ~s to do here** es gibt hier jede Menge zu tun *fam;* **~s and ~s of people** wahnsinnig viele Leute *fam* ③ (*everything*) ■ **the [whole] ~** alles **II.** *adv* (*fam*) ■ **a ~** viel; **thanks a ~!** vielen Dank!; **we go on vacation a ~** wir machen oft Urlaub **III.** *n* ① (*land*) Stück *nt* Land; **parking ~** Parkplatz *m* ② (*object to determine sth*) **to draw ~s** Lose ziehen ③ (*movie studio*) Filmgelände ④ (*at auction*) **to bid on a ~** ein Gebot abgeben ⑤ (*fam: group*) Haufen *m*

loth [loʊθ] *adj see* **loath**

lotion [ˈloʊ·ʃən] *n* Lotion *f;* **suntan ~** Sonnenöl *nt*

lottery [ˈlaṭ·ə·ri] **I.** *n* Lotterie *f* **II.** *adj* **~ ticket** Lotterielos *nt*

lotus <*pl* -es> [ˈloʊ·ṭəs] *n* BOT Lotos *m*

'lotus position *n* Lotossitz *m*

loud [laʊd] **I.** *adj* ① (*audible*) laut ② (*garish*) auffällig; *colors* grell, schreiend **II.** *adv* laut; **~ and clear** laut und deutlich; **to laugh out ~** lauthals loslachen

'loudmouth *n* (*fam*) Großmaul *nt*

loudness [ˈlaʊd·nɪs] *n* Lautstärke *f*

'loudspeaker *n* Lautsprecher *m*

Louisiana [lu·ˌi·zi·ˈæn·ə] *n* Louisiana *nt*

lounge [laʊndʒ] **I.** *n* Lounge *f;* **departure ~** Abflughalle *f* **II.** *vi* (*lie*) [faul] herumliegen; (*sit*) [faul] herumsitzen; (*stand*) [faul] herumstehen

◆**lounge around** *vi* (*lie*) [faul] herumliegen; (*sit*) [faul] herumsitzen; (*stand*) [faul] herumstehen

'lounge chair *n* Klubsessel *m*

'lounge lizard *n* (*sl*) Salonlöwe, Salonlöwin *m, f*

louse I. *n* [laʊs] ① <*pl* lice> (*parasite*) Laus *f* ② <*pl* -s> (*fam: person*) miese Type *pej* **II.** *vt* [laʊz] (*fam*) ■ **to ~ up** ⊂ **sth** etw vermasseln

lousy [ˈlaʊ·zi] *adj* ① (*fam: bad*) lausig; **I'm ~ at math** in Mathe bin ich eine absolute Null ② *pred* (*fam: ill*) **to feel ~** sich hundeelend [*o* mies] fühlen ③ (*infested*) verlaust ④ (*inadequate*) armselig, dürftig; **a ~ 20 dollars** lumpige 20 Dollar

louver [ˈlu·vər] *n* Jalousie *f;* (*slat*) Lamelle *f* [einer Jalousie]

lovable [ˈlʌv·ə·bəl] *adj* liebenswert

love [lʌv] **I.** *n* ① (*affection*) Liebe *f;* **to show sb lots of ~** jdm viel Liebe geben; **to be head over heels in ~** bis über beide Ohren verliebt sein; **to be in ~** verliebt sein; **to fall in ~ with sb** sich in jdn verlieben ② (*interest*) Leidenschaft *f;* (*with activities*) Liebe *f;* **she has a great ~ of music** sie liebt die Musik sehr ③ TENNIS null **II.** *vt* (*be in love with*) lieben; (*greatly like*) sehr mögen; **I would ~ a cup of tea** ich würde [sehr] gerne eine Tasse Tee trinken **III.** *vi* lieben; (*like*) gern mögen; **I would ~ for you to come to dinner tonight** ich würde mich freuen, wenn du heute zum Abendessen kämst

'love affair *n* [Liebes]affäre *f*

'lovebird *n* ① ORN Unzertrennliche(r) *f(m)* ② (*fam*) ■ **~s** *pl* Turteltauben *pl*

love-'hate relationship *n* Hassliebe *f*

loveless [ˈlʌv·lɪs] *adj* (*unloved*) *childhood, marriage* ohne Liebe *nach n*

'love letter *n* Liebesbrief *m*

'love life *n* Liebesleben *nt kein pl*

loveliness [ˈlʌv·lɪ·nɪs] *n* Schönheit *f*

lovely [ˈlʌv·li] *adj* ① (*beautiful*) schön; *house* wunderschön; **to look ~** reizend aussehen ② (*fam: pleasant*) wunderbar, herrlich ③ (*charming*) nett, liebenswürdig

'lovemaking *n* [körperliche] Liebe

lover [ˈlʌv·ər] *n* ① (*partner*) Liebhaber(in) *m(f);* ■ **~s** *pl* Liebespaar *nt sing* ② (*fan*) Liebhaber(in) *m(f)* (**of** von +*dat*); **sports ~** Sportfan *m*

'lovesick *adj* **to be ~** Liebeskummer haben

'love song *n* Liebeslied *nt*

'love story *n* Liebesgeschichte *f*

loving [ˈlʌv·ɪŋ] *adj* (*feeling love*) liebend; (*showing love*) liebevoll

low[1] [loʊ] **I.** *adj* ① (*not high*) niedrig; *neckline, voice* tief; *slope* flach ② (*in number*) gering, wenig; *blood pressure* niedrig; **~ in calories** kalorienarm ③ (*depleted*) knapp; *stocks* gering; **to be ~** zur Neige gehen ④ (*not intense*) niedrig; *light* gedämpft ⑤ (*not good*) *morale* schlecht; *quality* minderwertig; *self-esteem* gering; **to have a ~ opinion of sb** von jdm nicht viel halten; **~ visibility** schlechte Sicht ⑥ (*not important*) niedrig, gering; **to be a ~ priority** nicht so wichtig sein **II.** *adv* ① (*in height*) niedrig; **to be cut ~** *dress, blouse* tief ausgeschnitten sein ② (*to low level, not high-pitched*) tief; **turn the oven on ~** stell den Ofen auf kleine Hitze **III.** *n* ① (*low level*) Tiefpunkt *m* ② METEO

Tief *nt*

low[2] [loʊ] **I.** *n* Muhen *nt* **II.** *vi* muhen

low-'alcohol *adj* alkoholarm

'lowbrow (*pej*) **I.** *adj book, film* geistig anspruchslos, seicht; *person* einfach, schlicht **II.** *n* Banause *m*

low-cal ['loʊ·kæl] *adj* (*fam*), **low-'calorie** *adj* kalorienarm

'low-cost *adj* billig

'low-cut *adj dress* tief ausgeschnitten, mit tiefem Ausschnitt *nach n*

'lowdown *n* (*fam*) ■**the** ~ ausführliche Informationen; **to get the ~ on sth** über etw *akk* aufgeklärt werden

lower[1] ['loʊ·ər] **I.** *adj inv* ① (*less high*) niedriger; (*below*) untere(r, s), Unter- ② (*less in hierarchy*) *status, rank, animal* niedere(r, s), untere(r, s) **II.** *vt* ① (*move down*) herunterlassen; *hem* herauslassen; *lifeboat* zu Wasser lassen; **she ~ed herself into a chair** sie ließ sich auf einem Stuhl nieder; **to ~ one's eyes** die Augen niederschlagen ② (*decrease*) verringern; *rates, voice* senken; *quality* mindern; **to ~ one's sights** seine Ansprüche zurückschrauben ③ (*demean*) ■**to ~ oneself to do sth** sich herablassen, etw zu tun **III.** *vi* sinken; *voice* leiser werden

lower[2] [laʊr] *vi person* ein finsteres Gesicht machen; *light* dunkler werden; *sky* sich verfinstern; ■**to ~ at sb** jdn finster ansehen

lower 'house *n* Unterhaus *nt*

low-'fat *adj* fettarm

low-'key *adj* unauffällig, zurückhaltend; *color* gedämpft; **to keep sth ~** vermeiden, dass etw Aufsehen erregt

lowland ['loʊ·lənd] *n* ① Flachland *nt* ② ■**the ~s** *pl* das Tiefland

'low-level *adj* ① (*not high*) tief ② (*of low status*) niedrig, auf unterer Ebene *nach n;* (*unimportant*) nebensächlich, unbedeutend; *job* niedrig; *official* klein *meist pej* ③ COMPUT niedere(r, s)

lowly ['loʊ·li] *adj* ① (*ordinary*) einfach; *status* niedrig ② (*modest*) bescheiden

lowness ['loʊ·nɪs] *n* ① (*in height*) Niedrigkeit *f; of neckline* Tiefe *f* ② (*low pitch*) *of note* Tiefe *f; of voice* Gedämpftheit *f* ③ (*shortage*) *of supplies* Knappheit *f*

low-'pitched *adj* tief

low 'pressure *n* PHYS Niederdruck *m;* METEO Tiefdruck *m*

low 'profile *n* Zurückhaltung *f;* **to keep a ~** sich zurückhalten; (*fig*) im Hintergrund bleiben

'low season *n* Nebensaison *f*

low-'spirited *adj* niedergeschlagen

low-'tech *adj* [technisch] einfach, Lowtech-

low 'tide *n* Niedrigwasser *nt; of sea* Ebbe *f*

loyal ['lɔɪ·əl] *adj* (*faithful*) treu (**to** +*dat*); (*showing loyalty*) loyal

loyalist ['lɔɪ·ə·lɪst] **I.** *n* Loyalist(in) *m(f)* **II.** *adj attr, inv* loyal[istisch], regierungstreu

loyalty ['lɔɪ·əl·ti] *n* ① (*faithfulness*) Treue *f* (**to** zu +*dat*); (*state of being loyal*) Loyalität *f* (**to** gegenüber +*dat*) ② (*feelings*) ■**loyalties** *pl* Loyalitätsgefühle *pl*

'loyalty card *n* Kundenkarte *f*

lozenge ['laz·əndʒ] *n* ① MED Pastille *f* ② MATH Raute *f*

LP [ˌel·'pi] *n abbrev of* **long-playing record** LP *f*

LSD [ˌel·es·'di] *n abbrev of* **lysergic acid diethylamide** LSD *nt*

lube [lub] (*fam*) **I.** *n see* **lubricant II.** *vt see* **lubricate**

lubricant ['lu·brɪ·kənt] *n* MED Gleitmittel *nt; a.* TECH Schmiermittel *nt*

lubricate ['lu·brɪ·keɪt] *vt* ① (*grease*) schmieren ② (*make slippery*) [ein]ölen

lubrication [ˌlu·brɪ·'keɪ·ʃən] *n* Schmieren *nt*

lubricator ['lu·brɪ·ˌkeɪ·t̬ər] *n* TECH ① (*substance*) Abschmierfett *nt* ② (*device*) Schmiergerät *nt*

lucid ['lu·sɪd] *adj* ① (*unambiguous*) klar; (*easy to understand*) einleuchtend, verständlich ② (*clear-thinking*) klar

luck [lʌk] **I.** *n* ① (*fortune*) Glück *nt;* **as ~ would have it** wie es der Zufall wollte; **just my ~!** Pech gehabt!; **to be out of ~** kein Glück haben; **to try one's ~** sein Glück versuchen ② (*success*) Erfolg *m;* **did you have any ~ finding the book?** ist es dir gelungen, das Buch zu finden? **II.** *vi* (*fam*) ■**to ~ into sth** etw durch Zufall ergattern

luckily ['lʌ·kɪ·li] *adv* glücklicherweise

luckless ['lʌk·lɪs] *adj* (*unfortunate*) glücklos; (*unsuccessful*) erfolglos

lucky ['lʌk·i] *adj* ① (*fortunate*) glücklich; **~ her!** die Glückliche!; **to count oneself ~** sich glücklich schätzen ② (*bringing fortune*) glückbringend, Glücks-

lucrative ['lu·krə·t̬ɪv] *adj* einträglich

ludicrous ['lu·dɪ·krəs] *adj* (*ridiculous*) lächerlich; (*absurd*) absurd

lug[1] [lʌg] *n* (*handle*) Halterung *f*

lug[2] [lʌg] *vt* <-gg-> (*carry*) schleppen; (*pull*) zerren; ■**to ~ sth along** etw herumschleppen

luggage ['lʌg·ɪdʒ] *n* [Reise]gepäck *nt;* **piece of ~** Gepäckstück *nt*

'luggage rack *n* Gepäckablage *f*

lugubrious [lə·'gu·bri·əs] *adj* (*liter*) schwermütig

lukewarm [ˌluk·'wɔrm] *adj inv* ① (*tepid*) lau[warm] ② (*fig: unenthusiastic*) *reception* mäßig

lull [lʌl] **I.** *vt* ① (*soothe*) *suspicions, fears* zerstreuen; **to ~ sb to sleep** jdn in den Schlaf lullen ② (*trick*) einlullen; **to ~ sb into a false sense of security** jdn in trügerischer Sicherheit wiegen **II.** *vi* sich legen; *storm* nachlassen; *sea* sich beruhigen **III.** *n* [Ruhe]pause *f;* ECON Flaute *f*

lullaby ['lʌl·ə·baɪ] *n* Schlaflied *nt*

lumber[1] ['lʌm·bər] *n* (*timber*) Bauholz *nt*

lumber[2] ['lʌm·bər] *vi person* schwerfällig gehen; *tank* rollen; *cart, wagon* [dahin]rumpeln;

animal trotten; *bear* [behäbig] tapsen
lumberjack ['lʌm·bər·dʒæk] *n* Holzfäller(in) *m(f)*
'**lumberyard** *n* Holzlager *nt*
luminary ['lu·mə·ner·i] *n* Leuchte *f fam,* Koryphäe *f geh;* (*in film, theater*) Berühmtheit *f*
luminosity [ˌlu·mə·'nas·ɪ·t̬i] *n* ❶ (*brightness*) Helligkeit *f; of lamp* Leuchtkraft *f;* PHYS Lichtstärke *f* ❷ (*fig*) *of artist* Brillanz *f*
luminous ['lu·mə·nəs] *adj* ❶ (*bright*) leuchtend *a. fig,* strahlend *a. fig* ❷ (*phosphorescent*) phosphoreszierend, Leucht-
lump [lʌmp] **I.** *n* ❶ (*chunk*) Klumpen *m* ❷ (*swelling*) Schwellung *f;* (*in breast*) Knoten *m;* (*in body*) Geschwulst *f* ► PHRASES: **to have a ~ in one's** <u>**throat**</u> einen Kloß im Hals haben **II.** *vt* ❶ (*combine*) ■**to ~ sth with sth** etw mit etw *dat* zusammentun *fam* ❷ (*fam: endure*) **you'll just have to like it or ~ it** damit musst du dich eben abfinden
lump 'sum *n* Einmalzahlung *f*
lumpy ['lʌm·pi] *adj liquid* klumpig; *figure* plump; *surface* uneben
lunacy ['lu·nə·si] *n* ❶ (*insanity*) [geistige] Unzurechnungsfähigkeit ❷ (*foolishness*) Wahnsinn *m fam*
lunar ['lu·nər] *adj attr, inv* Mond-, lunar *fachspr*
lunatic ['lu·nə·tɪk] **I.** *n* ❶ Geistesgestörte(r) *f(m);* LAW [geistig] Unzurechnungsfähige(r) *f(m)* ❷ (*fool*) Verrückte(r) *f(m) fam* **II.** *adj* verrückt *fam;* MED geistesgestört; LAW [geistig] unzurechnungsfähig
lunch [lʌntʃ] **I.** *n* <*pl* -es> ❶ (*noon meal*) Mittagessen *nt;* **to have ~** zu Mittag essen ❷ (*noon break*) Mittagspause *f;* **to be out to ~** in der Mittagspause sein ► PHRASES: **to be** <u>**out**</u> **to ~** (*fam or hum*) nicht ganz richtig im Kopf sein *fam* **II.** *vi* zu Mittag essen
'**lunch break** *n* Mittagspause *f*
luncheon ['lʌn·tʃən] *n* (*form*) Mittagessen *nt*
'**luncheon meat** *n* Frühstücksfleisch *nt*
'**lunch hour** *n* Mittagspause *f*
'**lunchtime I.** *n* (*noon*) Mittagszeit *f;* (*break*) Mittagspause *f;* **at ~** mittags **II.** *adj attr, inv* Mittags-
lung [lʌŋ] *n* Lungenflügel *m;* ■**the ~s** *pl* die Lunge[n *pl*]
'**lung cancer** *n* Lungenkrebs *m*
lunge [lʌndʒ] **I.** *n* Satz *m* nach vorn; (*in fencing*) Ausfall *m* **II.** *vi* ■**to ~ at sb** sich auf jdn stürzen; ■**to ~ forward** einen Satz nach vorne machen; (*in fencing*) einen Ausfall machen
lupin(e) ['lu·pɪn] *n* Lupine *f*
lurch¹ [lɜrtʃ] **I.** *n* <*pl* -es> Ruck *m a. fig* **II.** *vi crowd, person* torkeln; *car, ship* schlingern
lurch² [lɜrtʃ] *n* **to leave sb in the ~** jdn im Stich lassen
lure [lʊr] **I.** *vt* [an]locken; ■**to ~ sb away from sth** jdn von etw *dat* weglocken **II.** *n* ❶ (*attraction*) Reiz *m* ❷ (*decoy*) Köder *m a. fig;* HUNT Lockvogel *m a. fig*
lurid ['lʊr·ɪd] *adj* ❶ (*glaring*) grell [leuchtend]; *colors* schreiend ❷ (*sensational*) reißerisch *pej; cover, article* reißerisch aufgemacht *pej; details* schmutzig; **to describe sth in ~ detail** etw drastisch schildern
lurk [lɜrk] *vi* lauern *a. fig;* (*fig*) stecken (**behind** hinter +*dat*); **to ~ beneath the surface** (*fig*) unter der Oberfläche schlummern
luscious ['lʌʃ·əs] *adj* ❶ (*sweet*) *taste, smell* [herrlich] süß; *fruit* saftig [süß]; *cake, wine* köstlich; *color* satt ❷ (*voluptuous*) *curves* üppig; *lips* voll
lush¹ [lʌʃ] *adj* ❶ *grass* saftig [grün]; *growth, vegetation* üppig ❷ (*luxurious*) *car, décor* luxuriös; (*voluptuous*) *color* satt
lush² [lʌʃ] *n* <*pl* -es> (*fam*) Säufer(in) *m(f) pej sl*
lust [lʌst] **I.** *n* ❶ (*sexual drive*) Lust *f* (**for** nach +*dat*) ❷ (*desire*) Begierde *f* (**for** nach +*dat*); (*greed*) Gier *f* (**for** nach +*dat*) **II.** *vi* ■**to ~ after sb** jdn begehren *geh;* ■**to ~ after sth** gierig nach etw *dat* sein
luster ['lʌs·tər] *n* ❶ (*shine*) Glanz *m* ❷ (*fig: grandeur*) Glanz *m*
lustful ['lʌst·fəl] *adj* lüstern *geh*
lusty ['lʌs·ti] *adj* (*strong and healthy*) *person* gesund [und munter]; *cry* laut
lute [lut] *n* Laute *f*
Lutheran ['lu·θər·ən] REL **I.** *n* Lutheraner(in) *m(f)* **II.** *adj inv* lutherisch
Luxembourg ['lʌk·səm·bɜrg] *n* Luxemburg *nt*
Luxembourger ['lʌk·səm·bɜr·gər] *n* Luxemburger(in) *m(f)*
luxuriant [lʌg·'ʒʊr·i·ənt] *adj* (*abundant*) üppig; (*adorned*) prunkvoll; *hair* voll
luxuriate [lʌg·'ʒʊr·i·eɪt] *vi* sich aalen
luxurious [lʌg·'ʒʊr·i·əs] *adj* ❶ (*with luxuries*) luxuriös, Luxus- ❷ (*self-indulgent*) genüsslich; (*decadent*) genusssüchtig
luxury ['lʌk·ʃər·i] **I.** *n* ❶ (*self-indulgence*) Luxus *m* ❷ (*luxurious item*) Luxus[artikel] *m* **II.** *adj attr, inv* Luxus-
Lycra® ['laɪ·krə] **I.** *n* Lycra® *nt* **II.** *adj leggings, shirt* Lycra-, aus Lycra *nach n*
lye [laɪ] *n* Lauge *f*
lying¹ ['laɪ·ɪŋ] *vi present participle of* **lie**
lying² ['laɪ·ɪŋ] **I.** *adj attr, inv* verlogen, lügnerisch **II.** *n* Lügen *nt*
lymph [lɪmf] *n* Lymphe *f*
lymphatic [lɪm·'fæt̬·ɪk] **I.** *adj inv* lymphatisch *fachspr,* Lymph[o]- **II.** *n* Lymphgefäß *nt*
'**lymph gland**, '**lymph node** *n* Lymphknoten *m*
lynch [lɪntʃ] *vt* lynchen
lynchpin ['lɪntʃ·pɪn] *n see* **linchpin**
lynx <*pl* -es *or* -> [lɪŋks] *n* Luchs *m*
lyre [laɪr] *n* Leier *f*
lyric ['lɪr·ɪk] **I.** *adj inv* lyrisch **II.** *n* ■**~s** *pl* [Lied]text *m*
lyrical ['lɪr·ɪ·kəl] *adj* ❶ *poetry* lyrisch ❷ (*emotional*) gefühlvoll, schwärmerisch
lyricism ['lɪr·ɪ·ˌsɪz·əm] *n* ❶ LIT, MUS Lyrik *f;* (*passage*) Lyrismus *m fachspr* ❷ (*sentiment*) Gefühlsregung *f*
lyricist ['lɪr·ɪ·sɪst] *n* Texter(in) *m(f)*

L

Mm

M <*pl* -'s *or* -s>, **m** <*pl* -'s> [em] *n* (*letter*) M *nt,* m *nt;* ~ **as in Mike** M wie Martha

M [em] **I.** *n* <*pl* -> *abbrev of* **million** Mill., Mio. **II.** *adj* FASHION *abbrev of* **medium** M

m I. *n* <*pl* -> ❶ *abbrev of* **mile** ❷ *abbrev of* **meter** m ❸ *abbrev of* **minute** Min. **II.** *adj* ❶ *abbrev of* **male** männl. ❷ *abbrev of* **masculine** m ❸ *abbrev of* **married** verh.

MA [ˌem·'eɪ] *n* ❶ *abbrev of* **Master of Arts** ❷ *abbrev of* **Massachusetts**

ma [ma] *n* (*fam: mother*) Mama *f*

Mac [mæk] *n* COMPUT (*fam*) *short for* **Macintosh®** Mac *m*

macabre [mə·'kab·rə] *adj* makaber

macaroni [ˌmæk·ə·'roʊ·ni] *n* Makkaroni *pl*

macaroni and 'cheese *n* Käsemakkaroni *pl*

mace[1] [meɪs] *n* (*hist: weapon*) Keule *f;* (*with spikes*) Morgenstern *m*

mace[2] [meɪs] *n* BOT, FOOD Mazis *m*

Mace® [meɪs] **I.** *n* ≈ Tränengas *nt* **II.** *vt* mit Tränengas besprühen

Macedonia [ˌmæs·ə·'doʊ·ni·ə] *n* Makedonien *nt,* Mazedonien *nt*

Macedonian [ˌmæs·ə·'doʊ·ni·ən] **I.** *n* Makedonier(in) *m(f),* Mazedonier(in) *m(f)* **II.** *adj* makedonisch, mazedonisch

Mach [mak] *n* AEROSP, PHYS Mach *nt*

machete [mə·'ʃet̬·i] *n* Machete *f*

machine [mə·'ʃin] **I.** *n* ❶ (*mechanical device*) Maschine *f,* Apparat *m;* (*fig: person*) Maschine *f;* **by** ~ maschinell ❷ (*automobile, plane*) Maschine *f* **II.** *vt* (*produce*) maschinell herstellen

ma'chine gun *n* Maschinengewehr *nt*

machine-'readable *adj* COMPUT (*by device*) maschinenlesbar; (*by computer*) computerlesbar

machinery [mə·'ʃi·nə·ri] *n* ❶ (*machines*) Maschinen *pl* ❷ (*mechanism*) Mechanismus *m;* (*system*) Apparat *m*

ma'chine tool *n* Werkzeugmaschine *f*

machinist [mə·'ʃi·nɪst] *n* (*machine operator*) Maschinist(in) *m(f)*

macho ['matʃ·oʊ] *adj* (*pej fam*) machohaft, Macho-

mackerel <*pl* -s *or* -> ['mæk·rəl] *n* Makrele *f*

macro ['mæk·roʊ] *n* COMPUT Makro *nt*

macrobiotic [ˌmæk·roʊ·baɪ·'at̬·ɪk] *adj* makrobiotisch

macroeconomics [ˌmæk·roʊ·ˌek·ə·'nam·ɪks] *n* + *sing vb* Makroökonomie *f*

mad <-dd> [mæd] *adj* ❶ (*fam: angry*) sauer; **he's ~ as hell at you** er ist stinksauer auf dich; **to make sb ~** jdn rasend machen ❷ (*fam: insane*) wahnsinnig, verrückt; **to go ~** den Verstand verlieren; **to drive sb ~** jdn um den Verstand bringen, jdn verrückt machen ❸ (*frantic*) wahnsinnig *fam;* **like ~** wie verrückt ❹ (*fam: enthusiastic*) verrückt (**about** nach +*dat*)

Madagascar [ˌmæd·ə·'gæs·kər] *n* Madagaskar *nt*

madam ['mæd·əm] *n* ❶ (*form of address*) gnädige Frau; (*in titles*) **M~ President** Frau Präsidentin; **Dear M~, ...** (*in letter*) Sehr geehrte gnädige Frau, ... ❷ *of brothel* Bordellwirtin *f*

mad 'cow disease *n* Rinderwahnsinn *m*

madden ['mæd·n] *vt* (*drive crazy*) um den Verstand bringen; (*anger*) maßlos ärgern

maddening ['mæd·n·ɪŋ] *adj* äußerst ärgerlich; *habit* nervend

made [meɪd] **I.** *pp, pt of* **make II.** *adj* **to have [got] it ~** es geschafft haben *fam*

made-to-'measure *adj* maßgeschneidert

made-'up *adj* ❶ (*imaginary*) ausgedacht ❷ (*wearing makeup*) geschminkt

'madhouse *n* (*fig fam: chaotic place*) Irrenhaus *nt*

madly ['mæd·li] *adv* ❶ (*insanely*) wie verrückt ❷ (*fam: frantically*) wie ein Verrückter/eine Verrückte ❸ (*fam: very much*) wahnsinnig

'madman *n* (*fig fam*) Verrückter *m*

madness ['mæd·nɪs] *n* ❶ (*insanity*) Wahnsinn *m,* Geisteskrankheit *f geh* ❷ (*folly*) Wahnsinn *m fam,* Verrücktheit *f*

'madwoman *n* (*fig fam*) Verrückte *f fam*

mafia ['ma·fiə] *n* + *sing/pl vb* Mafia *f*

mag [mæg] *n* (*fam*) *short for* **magazine** Blatt *nt*

magazine ['mæg·ə·zin] *n* ❶ (*publication*) Zeitschrift *f* ❷ (*gun part*) Magazin *nt*

maggot ['mæg·ət] *n* Made *f*

Magi ['meɪ·dʒaɪ] *npl* ■ **the** ~ die Weisen aus dem Morgenland, die Heiligen Drei Könige

magic ['mædʒ·ɪk] **I.** *n* ❶ (*sorcery*) Magie *f,* Zauber *m* ❷ (*tricks*) Zaubertrick[s] *m[pl]*; **to do ~** zaubern ❸ (*extraordinariness*) Zauber *m* **II.** *adj* ❶ (*supernatural*) magisch, Zauber-; **they had no ~ solution** sie konnten keine Lösung aus dem Ärmel zaubern ❷ (*extraordinary*) *moment* zauberhaft, wundervoll; *powers* magisch

magical ['mædʒ·ɪk·əl] *adj* ❶ (*magic*) magisch, Zauber- ❷ (*extraordinary*) *moment* zauberhaft, wundervoll; *powers* magisch

magically ['mæ·dʒɪk·li] *adv* ❶ (*by magic*) wie von Zauberhand, wie durch ein Wunder ❷ (*extraordinarily*) wundervoll, zauberhaft

magic 'carpet *n* fliegender Teppich

magician [mə·'dʒɪʃ·ən] *n* Zauberer *m*/Zauberin *f,* Magier(in) *m(f) geh;* (*on stage*) Zauberkünstler(in) *m(f)*

magistrate ['mædʒ·ɪ·streɪt] *n* **to appear before a ~** vor einem Schiedsgericht erscheinen

magnanimous [mæg·'næn·ə·məs] *adj* großmütig *geh; generosity* überwältigend

magnate ['mæg·neɪt] *n* Magnat *m*

magnesium [mæg·ˈni·zi·əm] *n* Magnesium *nt*
magnet [ˈmæg·nɪt] *n* Magnet *m*
magnetic [mæg·ˈneṭ·ɪk] *adj* ❶ *iron, steel* magnetisch; ~ **strip** Magnetstreifen *m* ❷ (*fig*) *effect, attraction* unwiderstehlich; *smile, charm* anziehend
magˈnetic field *n* Magnetfeld *nt*
magnetic ˈpole *n* Magnetpol *m*
magnetism [ˈmæg·nə·tɪz·əm] *n* ❶ (*phenomenon*) Magnetismus *m;* (*charge*) magnetische Kräfte *pl* ❷ *of person* Ausstrahlung *f*
magnetize [ˈmæg·nə·taɪz] *vt* ❶ PHYS magnetisieren ❷ (*fig*) faszinieren
magnification [ˌmæg·nɪ·fɪ·ˈkeɪ·ʃən] *n* Vergrößerung *f*
magnificence [mæg·ˈnɪf·ɪ·səns] *n* Großartigkeit *f,* Größe *f*
magnificent [mæg·ˈnɪf·ɪ·sənt] *adj house, concert* wunderbar, großartig
magnify <-ie-> [ˈmæg·nɪ·faɪ] *vt* (*make bigger*) vergrößern; (*make worse*) *problem* verschlimmern
ˈmagnifying glass *n* Lupe *f*
magnitude [ˈmæg·nɪ·tud] *n* ❶ (*size*) Größe *f; of project, loss* Ausmaß *nt; of earthquake* Stärke *f; of problem* Tragweite *f* ❷ (*importance*) Bedeutung *f*
magnolia [mæg·ˈnoʊl·jə] *n* Magnolie *f*
magpie [ˈmæg·paɪ] *n* (*bird*) Elster *f*
mahogany [mə·ˈhag·ə·ni] *n* ❶ (*tree*) Mahagonibaum *m* ❷ (*wood*) Mahagoni[holz] *nt*
maid [meɪd] *n* (*servant*) Dienstmädchen *nt;* (*in hotel*) Zimmermädchen *nt*
maiden [ˈmeɪ·dən] **I.** *n* (*old*) Jungfer *f* **II.** *adj attr* ❶ (*unmarried*) unverheiratet ❷ (*first*) Jungfern-
ˈmaiden name *n* Mädchenname *m*
mail¹ [meɪl] **I.** *n* Post *f;* **today's/this morning's** ~ die Post von heute; **to send sth through** [*or* **in**] **the** ~ etw mit der Post [ver]schicken **II.** *vt* (*at post office*) *letter, package* aufgeben; (*in mailbox*) einwerfen; ■**to** ~ **sth to sb** jdm etw [mit der Post] schicken
mail² [meɪl] *n* (*armor*) Panzer *m;* **chain** ~ Kettenpanzer *m*
ˈmailbag *n* Postsack *m;* **since the controversial program aired, ABC's ~ has been bulging** seit der umstrittenen Sendung quillt der Briefkasten der ABC über
ˈmailbox *n* Briefkasten *m,* Postkasten *m bes* NORDD
ˈmailing list *n* Adressenliste *f,* Mailingliste *f*
ˈmailman *n* Briefträger *m,* Postbote *m*
ˈmail order *n* [Direkt]versand *m;* (*by catalog*) Katalogbestellung *f*
maim [meɪm] *vt* (*mutilate*) verstümmeln; (*cripple*) zum Krüppel machen
main [meɪn] **I.** *adj attr* Haupt-; ~ **concern** wichtigstes Anliegen **II.** *n* TECH **water/gas** ~ Wasser-/Gashauptleitung *f*
main ˈdrag *n* (*fam*) Haupt[einkaufs]straße *f*
Maine [meɪn] *n* Maine *nt*
ˈmainframe *n* Hauptrechner *m*
ˈmainland *n* ■**the** ~ das Festland
mainly [ˈmeɪn·li] *adv* hauptsächlich, in erster Linie
ˈmainspring *n* Triebfeder *f a. fig*
ˈmainstay *n of economy* Stütze *f; of boat* Hauptstag *m*
ˈmainstream **I.** *n* ■**the** ~ (*fig*) der Mainstream; **to enter the ~ of politics** am alltäglichen politischen Alltag[sgeschäft] teilnehmen **II.** *adj* Mainstream-; *book, film, music* kommerziell
ˈmain street *n* Haupt[einkaufs]straße *f*
maintain [meɪn·ˈteɪn] *vt* ❶ (*keep*) [bei]behalten; *law and order, status quo* aufrechterhalten; *dignity, sanity* bewahren; **to ~ the lead** in Führung bleiben; ■**to ~ a good relationship with sb** sich mit jdm gutstellen ❷ (*in good condition*) instand halten ❸ (*provide for*) *child, family* unterhalten ❹ (*claim*) behaupten; *innocence* beteuern
maintenance [ˈmeɪn·tə·nəns] **I.** *n* ❶ *of relations, peace* Beibehaltung *f,* Wahrung *f* ❷ *of car, lawn* Pflege *f; of building, monument* Instandhaltung *f; of machine* Wartung *f;* ~ **department** Wartungsabteilung *f* ❸ (*maintenance costs*) Unterhaltung *f* **II.** *adj attr* Wartungs-, Instandhaltungs-
majestic [mə·ˈdʒes·tɪk] *adj* majestätisch; *proportions* stattlich; *movements* gemessen; *music, march* getragen
majesty [ˈmædʒ·ɪ·sti] *n* ❶ (*royal title*) [**Her/His/Your**] **M~** [Ihre/Seine/Eure] Majestät ❷ (*beauty*) *of sunset* Herrlichkeit *f; of person* Würde *f; of music* Erhabenheit *f,* Anmut *f*
major [ˈmeɪ·dʒər] **I.** *adj* ❶ *attr* (*important*) bedeutend, wichtig; (*main*) Haupt-; (*large*) groß ❷ *attr* (*serious*) *crime* schwer; *illness* schwerwiegend; **to undergo ~ surgery** sich einer größeren Operation unterziehen **II.** *n* ❶ MIL (*officer rank*) Major(in) *m(f)* ❷ UNIV (*primary subject*) Hauptfach *nt;* (*person studying*) **she was a philosophy ~** sie hat Philosophie im Hauptfach studiert **III.** *vi* UNIV **to ~ in physics** Physik als Hauptfach studieren
major ˈgeneral *n* Generalmajor(in) *m(f)*
majority [mə·ˈdʒɔr·ɪ·ṭi] **I.** *n* ❶ + *sing/pl vb* (*greater part*) Mehrheit *f;* **in the ~ of cases** in der Mehrzahl der Fälle; **the ~ of** [**the**] **votes** die Stimmenmehrheit ❷ POL (*winning margin*) [Stimmen]mehrheit *f* **II.** *adj attr* POL Mehrheits-
make [meɪk] **I.** *n* ❶ ECON (*brand*) Marke *f* ❷ (*pej*) **to be on the ~** geldgierig sein **II.** *vt* <made, made> ❶ (*produce*) machen; (*manufacture*) herstellen; *movie* drehen; **this sweater is made of wool** dieser Pullover ist aus Wolle; ■**to be made for sb/sth** für etw/jdn [wie] geschaffen sein ❷ (*prepare*) *bed, dinner* machen; **to ~ coffee** Kaffee kochen ❸ (*become*) **I don't think he will ever ~ a good lawyer** ich glaube, aus ihm wird nie ein guter Rechtsanwalt [werden]; **to ~** [**for**] **fascinating reading** faszinierend zu lesen sein ❹ (*cause*) machen; **the wind is making my**

M

eyes water durch den Wind fangen meine Augen an zu tränen; **to ~ sb laugh** jdn zum Lachen bringen ⑤ (*force*) ■ **to ~ sb do sth** jdn zwingen, etw zu tun ⑥ + *adj* (*cause to be*) machen; **to ~ sth public** etw veröffentlichen; **to ~ oneself understood** sich verständlich machen ⑦ (*perform*) *mistake, progress, suggestion* machen; *appointment* vereinbaren; *deal* schließen; *decision* fällen; *speech, presentation* halten; **to ~ a call** anrufen; **to ~ an effort** sich anstrengen; **to ~ a move** (*in game*) einen Zug machen; (*with* [*a part of*] *one's body*) sich bewegen; **to ~ a promise** etw versprechen; **to ~ way** den Weg frei machen ⑧ (*amount to*) **five plus five ~s ten** fünf und fünf ist zehn ⑨ (*earn, get*) **he ~s 50,000 dollars a year** er verdient 50.000 Dollar im Jahr; **to ~ friends** Freundschaften schließen; **to ~ a killing** einen Riesengewinn machen; **to ~ a name for oneself** sich *dat* einen Namen machen ⑩ (*fam: reach*) **could you ~ a meeting at 8 a.m.?** schaffst du ein Treffen um 8 Uhr morgens?; **the fire made the front page** das Feuer kam auf die Titelseite; **to ~ the finals** sich für das Finale qualifizieren; **to ~ it** es schaffen ⑪ (*render perfect*) **this film has made his career** der Film machte ihn berühmt; **that ~s my day!** das freut mich unheimlich!; **you've got it made!** du hast ausgesorgt! **III.** *vi* <made, made> (*pretend*) **he made as if to leave the room** er machte Anstalten, das Zimmer zu verlassen; ■ **to ~ like ...** so tun, als ob ... ▶ PHRASES: **to ~ <u>do</u> without sth** ohne etw auskommen

◆**make for** *vi* ① (*head for*) zugehen (auf +*akk*); (*by car or bus*) zufahren (auf +*akk*); **the kids made for the woods to hide** die Kinder rannten auf den Wald zu, um sich zu verstecken ② (*promote*) **constant arguing doesn't ~ for a good relationship** ständiges Streiten ist einer guten Beziehung nicht gerade förderlich

◆**make of** *vt* ① (*understand*) **I don't know what to ~ of it** ich weiß nicht, wie ich das deuten soll; **I can't ~ anything of this book** ich verstehe dieses Buch nicht ② (*think*) **what do you ~ of his speech?** was hältst du von seiner Rede?; **I don't know what to ~ of her** ich weiß nicht, wie ich sie einschätzen soll

◆**make off** *vi* (*fam*) ① (*leave*) abhauen ② (*steal*) ■ **to ~ off with sth** etw mitgehen lassen *fam*

◆**make out I.** *vi* (*fam*) ① (*manage*) *person* zurechtkommen; *business* sich [positiv] entwickeln ② (*sl: kiss passionately*) [he]rummachen, [he]rumfummeln (**with** mit +*dat*) **II.** *vt* ① (*write out*) ausschreiben; *check* ausstellen; *will* verfassen ② (*see*) *writing, numbers* entziffern; *distant object* ausmachen; (*hear*) verstehen

◆**make over** *vt* (*change appearance*) *house* umändern; *person* verändern

◆**make up I.** *vt* ① (*invent*) ■ **to ~ up ⟲ sth: she made the whole thing up** sie hat das alles nur erfunden ② (*prepare*) fertig machen; *prescription* zusammenstellen ③ (*put on makeup*) ■ **to ~ oneself up** sich schminken ④ (*compensate*) *deficit* ausgleichen; **to ~ up time** Zeit wieder gutmachen; *train* Zeit wieder herausfahren; (*repay favor*) ■ **to ~ it up to sb** jdm gegenüber etw wiedergutmachen ⑤ *usu passive* (*comprise*) ■ **to ~ up ⟲ sth** etw ausmachen; **the book is made up of a number of different articles** das Buch besteht aus vielen verschiedenen Artikeln ⑥ (*decide*) **to ~ up one's mind** sich entscheiden **II.** *vi* sich versöhnen (**with** mit +*dat*); **kiss and ~ up** küsst euch und vertragt euch wieder

◆**make up for** *vt* entschädigen (für +*akk*); *mistake* etw wiedergutmachen; (*pay for*) etw wettmachen; **to ~ up for lost time** verlorene Zeit wieder aufholen

'make-believe I. *n* Fantasie *f*, Illusion *f* **II.** *adj* Fantasie- **III.** *vi* <made-, made-> ■ **to ~** [**that**] ... sich *dat* vorstellen, dass ...

maker ['meɪ·kər] *n* (*manufacturer*) ■ **the ~** Hersteller(in) *m(f)*, Produzent(in) *m(f)*

'makeshift I. *adj* Not-, behelfsmäßig **II.** *n* [Not]behelf *m*

'makeup *n* ① (*cosmetics*) Make-up *nt*; **to put on ~** sich schminken ② *of group, population* Zusammensetzung *f* ③ (*character*) Persönlichkeit *f*

'makeup artist *n* Visagist(in) *m(f)*

making ['meɪ·kɪŋ] *n* ① (*production*) Herstellung *f*; **her problems with that child are of her own ~** ihre Probleme mit diesem Kind hat sie selbst verschuldet ② (*qualities, ingredients*) ■ **~s** *pl* Anlagen *pl*; **she has the ~s of a great violinist** sie hat das Zeug zu einer großartigen Geigerin

maladjusted [ˌmæl·ə·'dʒʌs·tɪd] *adj* verhaltensgestört

Malagasy [ˌmæl·ə·'gæs·i] **I.** *adj* madagassisch **II.** *n* Madagasse *m*, Madagassin *f*

malaise [mæ·'leɪz] *n* Unbehagen *nt*

malaria [mə·'ler·i·ə] *n* Malaria *f*

Malawi [mə·'la·wi] *n* Malawi *nt*

Malawian [mə·'la·wi·ən] **I.** *n* Malawier(in) *m(f)* **II.** *adj* malawisch

Malaysia [mə·'leɪ·ʒə] *n* Malaysia *nt*

Malaysian [mə·'leɪ·ʒən] **I.** *n* Malaysier(in) *m(f)* **II.** *adj* malaysisch

Maldives ['mæl·daɪvz] *npl* ■ **the ~** die Malediven

male [meɪl] **I.** *adj* männlich; **~-dominated** von Männern dominiert **II.** *n* (*person*) Mann *m*; (*animal*) Männchen *nt*

malevolent [mə·'lev·ə·lənt] *adj* (*liter: evil*) bösartig; (*spiteful*) gehässig

malformation [ˌmæl·fɔr·'meɪ·ʃən] *n* Missbildung *f*

malfunction [ˌmæl·'fʌŋk·ʃən] **I.** *vi* (*not work properly*) nicht funktionieren; (*stop working*) ausfallen **II.** *n* Ausfall *m*; *of liver, kidney* Funktionsstörung *f*

Mali ['ma·li] *n* Mali *nt*
Malian ['ma·li·ən] **I.** *n* Malier(in) *m(f)* **II.** *adj* malisch
malice ['mæl·ɪs] *n* Boshaftigkeit *f*
malicious [mə·'lɪʃ·əs] *adj* boshaft, niederträchtig; *look* hasserfüllt
malignant [mə·'lɪg·nənt] *adj* MED bösartig
malinger [mə·'lɪŋ·gər] *vi* sich krank stellen
malingerer [mə·'lɪŋ·gər·ər] *n* Simulant(in) *m(f)*
mall [mɔl] *n* [überdachtes] Einkaufszentrum
mallard <*pl* -s *or* -> ['mæl·ərd] *n* Stockente *f*
malleable ['mæl·i·ə·bəl] *adj metal* formbar; *clay* geschmeidig; (*fig*) *person* gefügig
mallet ['mæl·ɪt] *n* (*hammer*) [Holz]hammer *m;* (*in croquet*) Krockethammer *m*
malnutrition [ˌmæl·nu·'trɪʃ·ən] *n* Unterernährung *f*
malpractice [ˌmæl·'præk·tɪs] *n* (*faulty work*) Berufsvergehen *nt;* (*criminal misconduct*) [berufliches] Vergehen; **medical ~** ärztlicher Kunstfehler
malt [mɔlt] **I.** *n* ① (*grain*) Malz *nt;* **~ whiskey** Malzwhisky *m* ② (*malted milk*) Malzmilch *f;* **chocolate ~** *Schokoladenshake mit Zusatz von Malzextrakt* **II.** *vt* **to ~ barley** Gerste mälzen
Malta ['mɔl·tə] *n* Malta *nt*
Maltese [ˌmɔl·'tiz] **I.** *adj* maltesisch **II.** *n* ① (*person*) Malteser(in) *m(f)* ② (*language*) Maltesisch *nt,* das Maltesische
mammal ['mæm·əl] *n* Säugetier *nt,* Säuger *m*
'mammary gland *n* Milchdrüse *f*
mammography [mə·'mag·rə·fi] *n* Mammographie *f*
mammoth ['mæm·əθ] **I.** *n* Mammut *nt* **II.** *adj* (*fig*) Mammut-, riesig
man [mæn] **I.** *n* <*pl* men> ① (*male adult*) Mann *m;* **men's clothing** Herrenkleidung *f;* **the men's [room]** die Herrentoilette ② (*person*) Mensch *m;* **to be sb's right-hand ~** jds rechte Hand sein ③ (*mankind*) der Mensch, die Menschheit; **this is one of the most dangerous substances known to ~** das ist eine der gefährlichsten Substanzen, die bisher bekannt sind ④ (*particular type*) **he's a ~ of his word** er ist jemand, der zu seinem Wort steht; **to be a family ~** ein Familienmensch *m* sein; **a ~ of letters** (*writer*) ein Schriftsteller *m;* (*scholar*) ein Gelehrter *m* ⑤ *pl* (*soldiers, workers*) Männer *pl,* Leute *pl* **II.** *interj* (*fam: to emphasize*) Mensch, Mann; (*in enthusiasm*) Mann, Manometer; (*in anger*) Mann **III.** *vt* <-nn-> *fortress, picket lines* besetzen; *phones, guns* bedienen; *ship* bemannen
manacle ['mæn·ə·kəl] **I.** *n* ■ **~s** *pl* Handschellen *pl,* Ketten *pl* **II.** *vt* in Ketten legen
manage ['mæn·ɪdʒ] **I.** *vt* ① (*run*) leiten ② (*control*) steuern; (*administer*) verwalten; (*organize*) organisieren; **to ~ one's time/resources** sich *dat* seine Zeit/Ressourcen richtig einteilen ③ (*accomplish*) schaffen; *distance, task* bewältigen; **you ~d it very well** das hast du sehr gut gemacht; **to ~ a smile** ein Lächeln zustande bringen ④ (*cope with*) ■ **to ~ sth** mit etw *dat* zurechtkommen **II.** *vi* ① (*succeed*) es schaffen; (*cope, survive*) zurechtkommen; **can you ~? — yes, I can ~** geht's? – danke, es geht schon; **we'll ~!** wir schaffen das schon! ② (*get by*) ■ **to ~ on/without sth** mit etw *dat*/ohne etw *akk* auskommen
manageable ['mæn·ɪ·dʒə·bəl] *adj* ① (*doable*) *job* leicht zu bewältigen; *task* überschaubar ② (*controllable*) kontrollierbar; **~ hair** leicht zu frisierendes Haar ③ (*feasible*) erreichbar; *deadline* realistisch; ■ **to be ~** machbar sein
management ['mæn̩·ɪdʒ·mənt] *n* ① *of business* Management *nt,* [Geschäfts]führung *f,* [Unternehmens]leitung *f* ② (*managers*) [Unternehmens]leitung *f,* Management *nt; of hospital, theater* Direktion *f;* **senior ~** oberste Führungsebene, Vorstand *m* ③ (*handling*) Umgang *m* (**of** mit +*dat*); *of finances* Verwalten *nt*
management 'buyout *n* Management-Buy-out *nt* (*Übernahme einer Firma durch die leitenden Direktoren*)
management con'sultant *n* Unternehmensberater(in) *m(f)*
management 'skills *npl* Führungsqualitäten *pl*
'management studies *n* + *sing/pl vb* Betriebswirtschaft[slehre] *f*
manager ['mæn·ɪ·dʒər] *n* ① (*business executive*) Geschäftsführer(in) *m(f);* (*in big business, of performer*) Manager(in) *m(f);* (*of department*) Abteilungsleiter(in) *m(f)* ② (*chief adviser*) **campaign ~** Wahlkampfleiter *m* ③ SPORTS (*coach*) [Chef]trainer(in) *m(f)*
managerial [ˌmæn·ə·'dʒɪr·i·əl] *adj* Manager-; **at ~ level** auf Führungsebene; **~ skills** Führungsqualitäten *pl*
managing di'rector *n* [Haupt]geschäftsführer(in) *m(f)*
mandarin ['mæn·də·rɪn] *n* ① (*fruit*) Mandarine *f* ② (*hist: Chinese official*) Mandarin *m*
Mandarin ['mæn·də·rɪn] *n* LING Mandarin *nt*
mandate ['mæn·deɪt] **I.** *n usu sing* (*authority*) Mandat *nt;* (*command*) Verfügung *f;* **electoral ~** Wählerauftrag *m* **II.** *vt* (*order*) anordnen; (*authorize*) ein Mandat erteilen (für +*akk*)
mandatory ['mæn·də·tɔr·i] *adj* ① (*required by law*) gesetzlich vorgeschrieben ② (*obligatory*) obligatorisch; **to be ~ for sb** jds Pflicht sein
mandolin ['mæn·də·lɪn] *n* MUS Mandoline *f*
mane [meɪn] *n* Mähne *f*
'man-eater *n* ① (*animal*) *Tier, das Menschen tötet* ② (*hum fam: woman*) männermordender Vamp
maneuver [mə·'nu·vər] **I.** *n* ① *usu pl* (*military exercise*) Manöver *nt* ② (*planned move*) Manöver *nt;* (*fig*) Schachzug *m* ③ **to have room for ~** Spielraum haben **II.** *vt* ① (*move*) manövrieren; *vehicle* lenken ② (*pressure sb*) ■ **to ~ sb into [doing] sth** jdn [durch geschickte Ma-

növer] dazu bringen, etw *akk* zu tun **III.** *vi* ❶ (*move*) manövrieren; **this car ~s well at high speed** dieses Auto lässt sich bei hoher Geschwindigkeit gut fahren ❷ (*plan*) taktieren

maneuverability [mə·ˌnu·vər·ə·ˈbɪl·ɪ·t̬i] *n* Beweglichkeit *f,* Manövrierfähigkeit *f*

maneuverable [mə·ˈnu·vər·ə·bəl] *adj* beweglich; *ship, vessel* manövrierfähig

manganese [ˈmæŋ·gə·niz] *n* Mangan *nt*

manger [ˈmeɪn·dʒər] *n* (*old*) Futtertrog *m;* (*in bible*) Krippe *f*

mangle [ˈmæŋ·gəl] *vt* ❶ *usu passive* (*crush*) zerstören; *limbs* verstümmeln; *car, metal* zerdrücken ❷ (*ruin*) entstellen

mango <*pl* -s *or* -es> [ˈmæŋ·goʊ] *n* Mango *f*

mangrove [ˈmæn·groʊv] *n* Mangrovenbaum *m*

mangy [ˈmeɪn·dʒi] *adj* ❶ (*suffering from mange*) räudig ❷ (*fam: shabby*) schäbig *pej*

manhandle [ˈmæn·hæn·dəl] *vt* (*handle roughly*) grob behandeln

ˈmanhole *n* Einstieg *m;* (*shaft*) Einstiegsschacht *m*

ˈmanhole cover *n* Einstiegsverschluss *m*

manhood [ˈmæn·hʊd] *n* ❶ (*adulthood*) Erwachsenenalter *nt* (*eines Mannes*); **to reach ~** ins Mannesalter kommen, zum Manne werden ❷ (*manliness*) Männlichkeit *f* ❸ (*hum: penis*) Männlichkeit *f euph*

ˈman-hour *n* Arbeitsstunde *f*

ˈmanhunt *n* [Ring]fahndung *f;* (*after criminal*) Verbrecherjagd *f*

mania [ˈmeɪ·ni·ə] *n* ❶ (*pej: obsessive enthusiasm*) Manie *f,* Besessenheit *f* ❷ MED (*obsessive state*) Wahn[sinn] *m;* (*state of excessive activity*) Manie *f*

maniac [ˈmeɪ·ni·æk] *n* (*fam: crazy person*) Verrückte(r) *f(m),* Irre(r) *f(m)*

maniacal [mə·ˈnaɪ·ə·kəl] *adj* (*crazy*) verrückt, irrsinnig

manic [ˈmæn·ɪk] *adj* erregt, manisch; (*highly energetic*) wild

manic deˈpression *n* manische Depression

manic deˈpressive **I.** *n* Manisch-Depressive(r) *f(m)* **II.** *adj* manisch-depressiv

manicure [ˈmæn·ɪ·kjʊr] **I.** *n* Maniküre *f* **II.** *vt* **to ~ one's nails** sich *dat* die Nägel maniküren

manicurist [ˈmæn·ɪ·kjʊr·ɪst] *n* Handpflegerin *f*

manifest [ˈmæn·ɪ·fest] **I.** *adj* offenkundig, deutlich erkennbar **II.** *vt* zeigen; **the illness ~ed itself as ...** die Krankheit äußerte sich durch ... **III.** *n* TRANSP (*list of passengers*) Passagierliste *f;* (*cargo list*) [Ladungs]manifest *nt*

manifestation [ˌmæn·ɪ·fe·ˈsteɪ·ʃən] *n* ❶ (*sign*) Zeichen *nt* (**of** für +*akk*) ❷ (*displaying*) Zeigen *nt geh;* MED Manifestation *f fachspr*

manifestly [ˈmæn·ɪ·fest·li] *adv* offenkundig, offensichtlich

manifesto <*pl* -s *or* -es> [ˌmæn·ɪ·ˈfes·toʊ] *n* Manifest *nt*

manifold [ˈmæn·ɪ·foʊld] **I.** *adj* (*liter*) vielfältig, vielseitig **II.** *n* TECH Verteilerrohr *nt*

Manil(l)a ˈenvelope [mə·ˈnɪl·ə-] *n* Briefumschlag *m* aus Manilapapier

manipulate [mə·ˈnɪp·jə·leɪt] *vt* ❶ (*esp pej: manage cleverly*) ■**to ~ sb/sth** geschickt mit jdm/etw umgehen; (*influence*) jdn/etw beeinflussen [*o* manipulieren] ❷ (*with hands*) handhaben; (*adjust*) einstellen; *machine* bedienen; COMPUT *text* bearbeiten

manipulation [mə·ˌnɪp·jə·ˈleɪ·ʃən] *n* ❶ (*esp pej: clever management*) Manipulation *f;* (*falsification*) Verfälschung *f* ❷ (*handling*) Handgriff *m;* (*adjustment*) Einstellung *f* (**of** an +*dat*)

manipulative [mə·ˌnɪp·jə·ˈlə·t̬ɪv] *adj* (*esp pej*) manipulativ

manipulator [mə·ˈnɪp·jə·leɪ·t̬ər] *n* (*esp pej*) Manipulant(in) *m(f)*

mankind [ˌmæn·ˈkaɪnd] *n* Menschheit *f*

manliness [ˈmæn·lɪ·nɪs] *n* Männlichkeit *f*

manly [ˈmæn·li] *adj* männlich

man-ˈmade *adj* künstlich

manna [ˈmæn·ə] *n* Manna *nt;* **~ from heaven** ein wahrer Segen

manned [mænd] *adj* AEROSP bemannt

mannequin [ˈmæn·ɪ·kɪn] *n* (*in store display*) Schaufensterpuppe *f*

manner [ˈmæn·ər] *n* ❶ (*way*) Weise *f,* Art *f;* **in a ~ of speaking** sozusagen ❷ (*behavior to others*) Betragen *nt,* Verhalten *nt* ❸ (*polite behavior*) ■**~s** *pl* Manieren *pl;* **it's bad ~s to ...** es gehört sich nicht, ...

mannered [ˈmæn·ərd] *adj* (*pej*) ❶ (*affected*) affektiert ❷ (*in behavior*) gekünstelt

mannerism [ˈmæn·ə·rɪz·əm] *n* Eigenart *f*

mannish [ˈmæn·ɪʃ] *adj* (*esp pej: of woman*) männlich

manor [ˈmæn·ər] *n* (*country house*) Landsitz *m,* Herrenhaus *nt*

ˈmanpower *n* Arbeitskräfte *pl*

mansion [ˈmæn·ʃən] *n* Villa *f;* (*manor house*) Herrenhaus *nt*

manslaughter [ˈmæn·slɔ·t̬ər] *n* Totschlag *m*

mantel [ˈmæn·təl] *n* Kaminsims *m o nt*

mantis [ˈmæn·tɪs] *n* Fangheuschrecke *f;* [**praying**] ~ Gottesanbeterin *f*

ˈman-to-man *adj* von Mann zu Mann

mantra [ˈmæn·trə] *n* ❶ (*for meditation*) Mantra *nt* ❷ (*catchphrase*) Slogan *m*

manual [ˈmæn·jʊ·əl] **I.** *adj* ❶ (*done with hands*) manuell, Hand-; ~ **labor** körperliche Arbeit ❷ (*hand-operated*) manuell, Hand-; ~ **transmission** AUTO Schaltgetriebe *nt* **II.** *n* (*book*) Handbuch *nt;* **training ~** Lehrbuch *nt*

manually [ˈmæn·jʊ·ə·li] *adv* manuell

manufacture [ˌmæn·jʊ·ˈfæk·tʃər] **I.** *vt* ❶ (*produce commercially*) herstellen ❷ (*fabricate*) erfinden **II.** *n* Herstellung *f*

manufacturer [ˌmæn·jʊ·ˈfæk·tʃər·ər] *n* Hersteller *m*

manufacturing [ˌmæn·jə·ˈfæk·tʃər·ɪŋ] **I.** *adj* Herstellungs-, Produktions-; ~ **industry** verarbeitende Industrie **II.** *n* Fertigung *f*

manure [mə·ˈnʊr] *n* Dung *m*

M

manuscript ['mæn·jʊ·skrɪpt] *n* ❶ (*author's script*) Manuskript *nt;* (*of famous person*) Autograph *nt fachspr* ❷ (*handwritten text*) Manuskript *nt,* Handschrift *f*

many ['men·i] *pron* (*a great number*) viele; **too ~** zu viele; **as ~ as ...** so viele wie ...; **as ~ as 6,000 people may have been infected with the disease** bereits 6.000 Menschen können mit der Krankheit infiziert sein; **~ a time** oft

many-'sided *adj* vielseitig; (*complex*) vielschichtig

Maori ['maʊ·ri] **I.** *n* Maori *m o f* **II.** *adj* Maori-, maorisch

map [mæp] **I.** *n* ❶ GEOG [Land]karte *f; of town, city* Stadtplan *m;* **road ~** Straßenkarte *f* ❷ (*simple diagram*) Plan *m,* Zeichnung *f* ▸ PHRASES: **to put sb/sth on the ~** jdn/etw bekannt machen **II.** *vt* <-pp-> kartographieren *fachspr*

◆ **map out** *vt* genau festlegen; *route* planen; **his future is all ~ped out for him** seine ganze Zukunft ist bereits fest vorgeplant

maple ['meɪ·pəl] *n* ❶ (*tree*) Ahorn *m* ❷ (*wood*) Ahorn *m,* Ahornholz *nt*

'maple leaf *n* Ahornblatt *nt*

maple 'sugar *n* Ahornzucker *m*

maple 'syrup *n* Ahornsirup *m*

mar <-rr-> [mar] *vt* stören; **to ~ the beauty of sth** etw verunstalten

Mar. *n abbrev of* **March**

marathon ['mær·ə·θan] *n* ❶ (*race*) Marathon[lauf] *m;* **~ runner** Marathonläufer(in) *m(f)* ❷ (*very long event*) Marathon *nt fam*

marauder [mə·'rɔ·dər] *n* (*raider*) Plünderer(in) *m(f)*

marauding [mə·'rɔ·dɪŋ] *adj attr* plündernd; *animal* auf Raubzug *nach n*

marble ['mar·bəl] *n* ❶ (*stone*) Marmor *m* ❷ (*for games*) Murmel *f* ▸ PHRASES: **to lose one's ~s** (*fam*) verrückt werden

'marble cake *n* Marmorkuchen *m*

marbled ['mar·bəld] *adj* marmoriert

march [martʃ] **I.** *n* <*pl* -es> ❶ MIL Marsch *m;* **a 10-mile ~** ein Marsch *m* über 16 Meilen; **to be on the ~** marschieren ❷ (*demonstration*) Demonstration *f;* **to go on a ~** demonstrieren gehen **II.** *vi* marschieren **III.** *vt* ❶ (*walk in step*) **to ~ 12 miles** 12 Meilen marschieren ❷ (*force to walk*) ■ **to ~ sb off** jdn wegführen; *police* jdn abführen

March <*pl* -es> [martʃ] *n* März *m; see also* **February**

Mardi Gras ['mar·di·ˌgra] *n* (*carnival on Shrove Tuesday*) ≈ Fastnachtsdienstag *m,* Karneval *m*

> **Mardi Gras** (Fetter Dienstag) ist das amerikanische Äquivalent zu Karneval oder Fasching. Dieses Fest geht zurück auf die französischen Kolonisten in New Orleans (im späteren Staat Louisiana). In Biloxi/Mississippi und Mobile/Alabama finden die beiden größten Feste statt. Das Fest in New Orleans ist jedoch das bekannteste. Dort feiern die *krewes* (Karnevalsvereine) während der Saison viele Partys und Bälle und veranstalten am Faschingsdienstag einen Umzug.

mare [mer] *n* Stute *f*

margarine ['mar·dʒər·ɪn] *n* Margarine *f*

margin ['mar·dʒɪn] *n* ❶ (*outer edge*) Rand *m;* TYPO [Seiten]rand *m* ❷ (*amount*) Differenz *f,* Abstand *m;* **to win by a wide ~** mit einem großen Vorsprung gewinnen ❸ (*provision*) Spielraum *m;* SCI Streubereich *m;* **a ~ of error** eine Fehlerspanne; **profit ~** Gewinnspanne *f*

marginal ['mar·dʒə·nəl] *adj* ❶ (*slight*) geringfügig; **to be of ~ importance** relativ unbedeutend sein ❷ (*insignificant*) nebensächlich

marginalize ['mar·dʒɪ·nə·laɪz] *vt* an den Rand drängen

marigold ['mær·ɪ·goʊld] *n* Studentenblume *f*

marijuana, marihuana [ˌmær·ɪ·'wa·nə] *n* Marihuana *nt*

marina [mə·'ri·nə] *n* Jachthafen *m*

marinade [ˌmær·ɪ·'neɪd] *n* Marinade *f*

marinate ['mær·ɪ·neɪt] *vt* marinieren

marine [mə·'rin] **I.** *adj attr* ❶ (*of sea*) Meeres-, See- ❷ (*of shipping*) Schiffs- ❸ (*naval*) Marine- **II.** *n* Marineinfanterist *m;* ■ **the ~s** die Marineinfanterie

marine bi'ologist *n* Meeresbiologe *m*/-biologin *f*

Ma'rine Corps *n* Marineinfanteriekorps *nt*

marionette [ˌmær·i·ə·'net] *n* Marionette *f*

marital ['mær·ɪ·t̬əl] *adj* ehelich, Ehe-; **~ status** Familienstand *m*

maritime ['mær·ɪ·taɪm] *adj* ❶ (*form: of sea*) Meer[es]-, See-; (*of ships*) Schifffahrts- ❷ (*near coast*) Küsten-

maritime 'law *n* Seerecht *nt*

marjoram ['mar·dʒər·əm] *n* Majoran *m*

mark [mark] **I.** *n* ❶ (*spot, stain*) Fleck *m;* (*on the skin*) Mal *nt;* (*scratch*) Kratzer *m;* (*trace*) Spur *f;* (*scar*) Narbe *f;* (*fingerprint, footprint*) Abdruck *m* ❷ (*identifying feature*) [Kenn]zeichen *nt,* Merkmal *nt* ❸ (*indication*) Zeichen *nt;* **a ~ of respect** ein Zeichen *nt* des Respekts ❹ (*sign to indicate position*) Markierung *f* ❺ (*a. fig: target*) Ziel *nt,* Zielscheibe *f;* **to be wide of the ~** das Ziel um Längen verfehlen ▸ PHRASES: **to leave its/one's ~ on sb/sth** seine Spuren bei jdm/etw hinterlassen **II.** *vt* ❶ (*stain*) schmutzig machen ❷ (*indicate*) markieren ❸ (*label*) beschriften; (*indicate the price of*) auszeichnen ❹ (*characterize*) kennzeichnen; (*mean*) bedeuten ❺ (*commemorate*) ■ **to ~ sth** an etw *akk* erinnern; **a concert to ~ the 10th anniversary** ein Konzert aus Anlass des zehnten Jahrestages ❻ SPORTS *opponent* decken **III.** *vi* (*get dirty*) schmutzig

werden; (*scratch*) Kratzer bekommen
◆**mark down** *vt* ❶ (*reduce the price of*) heruntersetzen ❷ (*give a lower grade*) ■**to ~ down** ○ **sb** jdm eine schlechtere Note geben ❸ (*jot down*) notieren
◆**mark off** *vt* (*separate off*) abgrenzen
◆**mark out** *vt* abstecken, markieren
◆**mark up** *vt* (*increase the price of*) heraufsetzen; *stocks* aufwerten
marked [markt] *adj* ❶ (*clear*) deutlich, ausgeprägt; (*striking*) auffallend, markant; *characteristic* herausstechend; **in ~ contrast to sth** im krassen Gegensatz zu etw *dat* ❷ (*with distinguishing marks*) markiert, gekennzeichnet
markedly ['mar·kəd·li] *adv* deutlich; **to be ~ different** sich deutlich unterscheiden
marker ['mar·kər] *n* ❶ (*sign or symbol*) [Kenn]zeichen *nt*, Marke *f* ❷ (*felt tip pen*) Filzstift *m*
market ['mar·kɪt] **I.** *n* Markt *m*; **housing ~** Wohnungsmarkt *m*; **stock ~** Börse *f*; **the open ~** der freie Markt; **to put sth on the ~** etw auf den Markt bringen **II.** *vt* (*sell*) vermarkten, verkaufen; (*put on market*) auf den Markt bringen
marketable ['mar·kɪ·t̬ə·bəl] *adj* marktfähig; *commodities* marktgängig
market 'forces *npl* Marktkräfte *pl*
marketing ['mar·kɪ·t̬ɪŋ] *n* Marketing *nt*, Vermarktung *f*
market 'leader *n* Marktführer *m*
'marketplace *n* ❶ (*place*) Marktplatz *m* ❷ (*commercial environment*) Markt *m*
market 'research *n* Marktforschung *f*
market 'researcher *n* Marktforscher(in) *m(f)*
marking ['mar·kɪŋ] *n* ■**~s** *pl* Markierungen *pl*, Kennzeichnungen *pl*; *on animals* Zeichnung *f kein pl*
marksman ['marks·mən] *n* Schütze *m*; **police ~** Scharfschütze *m*
marksmanship ['marks·mən·ʃɪp] *n* Treffsicherheit *f*
markswoman ['marks·wʊm·ən] *n* Schützin *f*; **police ~** Scharfschützin *f*
markup ['mark·ʌp] *n* [Kalkulations]aufschlag *m*
marmalade ['mar·mə·leɪd] *n* Orangenmarmelade *f*
maroon[1] [mə·'run] *vt* (*abandon*) aussetzen; **many people were ~ed in their cars by the blizzard** viele Menschen wurden von dem Schneesturm in ihren Autos eingeschlossen
maroon[2] [mə·'run] **I.** *n* (*color*) Kastanienbraun *nt*, Rötlichbraun *nt* **II.** *adj* kastanienbraun, rötlichbraun
marquee [mar·'ki] *n beleuchtete Werbetafel über Kino-/Theatereingängen*
marriage ['mær·ɪdʒ] *n* ❶ (*wedding*) Heirat *f*; (*at church*) Trauung *f* ❷ (*relationship*) Ehe *f* (**to** mit +*dat*); **she has two daughters by her first ~** sie hat zwei Töchter aus erster Ehe; **to have a happy ~** eine glückliche Ehe führen ❸ (*fusion*) Verbindung *f*; (*of companies*) Zusammenschluss *m*, Fusion *f*
marriageable ['mer·ɪdʒ·ə·bəl] *adj* heiratsfähig
'marriage certificate *n* Heiratsurkunde *f*
'marriage contract *n* Ehevertrag *m*
marriage counseling *n* Eheberatung *f*
marriage counselor *n* Eheberater(in) *m(f)*
'marriage license *n* Heiratserlaubnis *f*
marriage of con'venience *n* Vernunftehe *f*; (*not consummated*) Scheinehe *f*
'marriage vow *n usu pl* Ehegelübde *nt geh*
married ['mer·id] *adj* verheiratet; **~ couple** Ehepaar *nt*; **to get ~ [to sb]** [jdn] heiraten
marrow ['mær·oʊ] *n* (*of bone*) [Knochen]mark *nt*
marry ['mær·i] **I.** *vt* ❶ (*wed*) heiraten ❷ (*officiate at ceremony*) trauen, verheiraten ❸ (*combine*) verbinden (**to/with** mit +*dat*) **II.** *vi* heiraten; **to ~ into a wealthy family** in eine reiche Familie einheiraten
Mars [marz] *n* Mars *m*
marsh <*pl* -es> [marʃ] *n* Sumpf *m*, Sumpfland *nt*
marshal ['mar·ʃəl] **I.** *n* ❶ (*federal agent*) Gerichtsdiener(in) *m(f)*; **police ~** Polizeidirektor(in) *m(f)*; **fire ~** Branddirektor(in) *m(f)* ❷ MIL (*army officer*) Marschall *m* **II.** *vt* <-l- *or* -ll-> (*bring together*) *supporters* mobilisieren; **to ~ one's forces** MIL die Streitkräfte zusammenziehen; (*fig*) seine Kräfte mobilisieren
'marshland *n* Sumpfland *nt*
marshmallow ['marʃ·mel·oʊ] *n* ❶ (*food*) Marshmallow *nt* ❷ (*sl: weak person*) Weichei *nt sl o pej*
marshy ['mar·ʃi] *adj* sumpfig
marsupial [mar·'su·pi·əl] *n* Beuteltier *nt*
martial 'arts *npl* SPORTS Kampfsport *m kein pl*, Kampfsportarten *pl*
martial 'law *n* Kriegsrecht *nt*
Martian ['mar·ʃən] **I.** *adj* Mars- **II.** *n* Marsmensch *m*
Martinique [ˌmar·tən·'ik] *n* Martinique *nt*
martyr ['mar·t̬ər] **I.** *n* Märtyrer(in) *m(f)* **II.** *vt usu passive* ■**to be ~ed [for sth]** [für etw *akk*] [den Märtyrertod] sterben
martyrdom ['mar·t̬ər·dəm] *n* (*being a martyr*) Märtyrertum *nt*; (*suffering*) Martyrium *nt a. fig*; (*death*) Märtyrertod *m*
marvel ['mar·vəl] **I.** *n* (*wonderful thing*) Wunder *nt* **II.** *vi* <-l- *or* -ll-> (*wonder*) sich wundern (**at** über +*akk*); (*admire*) bewundern; ■**to ~ that ...** staunen, dass ...
marvelous ['mar·və·ləs] *adj* wunderbar, großartig
Marxism ['mark·sɪz·əm] *n* Marxismus *m*
Marxist ['mark·sɪst] **I.** *n* Marxist(in) *m(f)* **II.** *adj* marxistisch
Maryland ['mer·ə·lənd] *n* Maryland *nt*
marzipan ['mar·zɪ·pæn] *n* Marzipan *nt o m*
masc. *adj abbrev of* **masculine**
mascara [mæ·'skær·ə] *n* Wimperntusche *f*
mascot ['mæs·kat] *n* Maskottchen *nt*
masculine ['mæs·kjə·lɪn] *adj* männlich, maskulin

M

masculinity [ˌmæs·kjə·ˈlɪn·ɪ·t̬i] *n* Männlichkeit *f*
mash [mæʃ] **I.** *n* (*mixture*) Brei *m;* (*brewing*) Maische *f* **II.** *vt* zerdrücken, [zer]stampfen
◆ **mash up** *vt food* zerdrücken
mashed poˈtatoes *n pl* Kartoffelbrei *m,* [Kartoffel]püree *nt*
mask [mæsk] **I.** *n* ❶ (*for face*) Maske *f* ❷ (*pretense*) Maske *f,* Fassade *f* **II.** *vt* verbergen, verstecken
masked [mæskt] *adj* maskiert
masking tape [ˈmæs·kɪŋ-] *n* Tesakrepp® *nt*
masochism [ˈmæs·ə·kɪz·əm] *n* Masochismus *m*
masochist [ˈmæs·ə·kɪst] *n* Masochist(in) *m(f)*
masochistic [ˌmæs·ə·ˈkɪs·tɪk] *adj* masochistisch
mason [ˈmeɪ·sən] *n* ❶ (*stonemason*) Steinmetz(in) *m(f)* ❷ (*bricklayer*) Maurer(in) *m(f)*
Masonic [mə·ˈsan·ɪk] *adj* Freimaurer-, freimaurerisch
masonry [ˈmeɪ·sən·ri] *n* ❶ (*bricks*) Mauerwerk *nt* ❷ (*work*) Maurerhandwerk *nt*
masquerade [ˌmæs·kə·ˈreɪd] **I.** *n* Maskerade *f* **II.** *vi* ■ **to ~ as sb/sth** sich als jdn/etw ausgeben
mass [mæs] **I.** *n* ❶ *usu sing* (*formless quantity*) Masse *f;* **a ~ of dough** ein Teigklumpen *m* ❷ *usu sing* (*large quantity*) Menge *f;* **a ~ of contradictions** eine Reihe von Widersprüchen ❸ PHYS Masse *f* ❹ (*common people*) ■ **the ~es** *pl* **music for the ~** Musik für die breite Masse **II.** *vi crowd* sich ansammeln; *troops* aufmarschieren
Mass [mæs] *n* REL, MUS Messe *f*
Mass. *abbrev of* **Massachusetts**
Massachusetts [ˌmæs·ə·ˈtʃu·sɪts] *n* Massachusetts *nt*
massacre [ˈmæs·ə·kər] **I.** *n* ❶ (*killing*) Massaker *nt* ❷ (*defeat*) [verheerende] Niederlage, Desaster *nt* **II.** *vt* ❶ (*kill*) massakrieren ❷ (*defeat*) vernichtend schlagen; (*hum*) auseinandernehmen *sl*
massage [mə·ˈsadʒ] **I.** *n* Massage *f;* **to give sb a ~** jdn massieren **II.** *vt* ❶ (*rub*) massieren; **to ~ cream into the skin** Creme einmassieren; **to ~ sb's ego** (*fig*) jdm schmeicheln ❷ (*alter*) *figures, statistics* manipulieren
masˈsage parlor *n* (*for sex*) Massagesalon *m euph*
masseur [mæ·ˈsɜr] *n* Masseur *m*
masseuse [mæ·ˈsɜz] *n* Masseurin *f*
massive [ˈmæs·ɪv] *adj* riesig, enorm; *heart attack* schwer
mass ˈmarket *n* Massenmarkt *m*
mass-ˈmarket *adj attr* Massen-
mass ˈmedia *n + sing/pl vb* ■ **the ~** die Massenmedien *pl*
mass ˈmurder *n* Massenmord *m*
mass ˈmurderer *n* Massenmörder(in) *m(f)*
mass-proˈduce *vt* serienmäßig herstellen
mass proˈduction *n* Massenproduktion *f*
mass ˈtransit *n* öffentliche Verkehrsmittel

M

mast [mæst] *n* ❶ NAUT [Schiffs]mast *m* ❷ (*flag pole*) [Fahnen]mast *m* ❸ RADIO, TV Sendeturm *m*
mastectomy [ˌmæs·ˈtek·tə·mi] *n* Mastektomie *f*
master [ˈmæs·tər] **I.** *n* ❶ (*of slave, servant*) Herr *m;* (*of dog*) Herrchen *nt* ❷ (*expert*) Meister(in) *m(f);* **he was a ~ of disguise** er war ein Verwandlungskünstler ❸ (*original*) Original *nt* **II.** *vt* ❶ (*cope with*) meistern; **to ~ one's fear of flying** seine Flugangst überwinden ❷ (*become proficient*) beherrschen
master ˈbedroom *n* großes Schlafzimmer
ˈmaster class *n* Meisterklasse *f*
master ˈcraftsman *n* Handwerksmeister(in) *m(f)*
masterful [ˈmæs·tər·fəl] *adj* ❶ (*authoritative*) bestimmend, dominant ❷ (*skillful*) meisterhaft, meisterlich
ˈmaster key *n* Generalschlüssel *m*
masterly [ˈmæs·tər·li] *adj* meisterhaft, Meister-
ˈmastermind **I.** *n* führender Kopf **II.** *vt* federführend leiten; **she ~ed the takeover bid** das Übernahmeangebot war von ihr geplant worden
Master of ˈArts *n* ≈ Magister Artium *m*
Master of ˈCeremonies *n* ❶ (*at celebration*) Zeremonienmeister *m* ❷ TV Showmaster(in) *m(f)*
Master of ˈScience ■ **to have a ~** ≈ ein Diplom *nt* in einer Naturwissenschaft haben
ˈmasterpiece *n* Meisterwerk *nt,* Meisterstück *nt*
ˈmaster plan *n* Grundplan *m*
ˈmaster race *n* Herrenrasse *f*
Master's, Master's degree [ˈmæs·tərz-] *n* ≈ Magister *m;* **to study for one's ~** ≈ seinen Magister machen

Ein **Master's degree** ist ein wissenschaftliches Vertiefungsstudium, das nach dem *Bachelor's degree* in ein oder zwei Jahren an einer Universität absolviert werden kann. Der *M. A.* (*Master of Arts*) und der *M. S.* (*Master of Science*) sind die beiden häufigsten Abschlüsse.
Berufsbezogene Studienfächer wie z. B. Rechtswissenschaften und Medizin werden ebenfalls nur an den Universitäten angeboten. Diese Abschlüsse werden als „professional degrees" bezeichnet und die Studiendauer hierfür beträgt zwischen zwei und vier Jahren. Dazu zählt auch der bekannte *M. B. A.* (*Master of Business Administration*), für den man ein oder zwei Jahre studieren muss.

ˈmasterstroke *n* Glanzstück *nt*
ˈmaster switch *n* Hauptschalter *m*
ˈmasterwork *n see* **masterpiece**
mastery [ˈmæs·tə·ri] *n* ❶ (*domination*) Herr-

schaft *f* ❷ (*expertise*) Meisterschaft *f* (**of** in +*dat*)

mastiff ['mæs·tɪf] *n* englische Dogge

masturbate ['mæs·tər·beɪt] *vi* masturbieren

masturbation [ˌmæs·tər·'beɪ·ʃən] *n* Masturbation *f*

mat [mæt] **I.** *n* ❶ (*for floor*) Matte *f;* (*for furniture*) Untersetzer *m;* (*decorative mat*) Deckchen *nt* ❷ (*thick layer*) **a ~ of hair** dichtes Haar; (*on the head*) eine Mähne *fam* **II.** *vt* <-tt-> *usu passive* ■ **to be ~ted with sth** mit etw *dat* bedeckt sein

match¹ [mætʃ] **I.** *n* <*pl* -es> ❶ *usu sing* (*complement*) **to be a good ~** gut zusammenpassen ❷ (*one of pair*) Gegenstück *nt* ❸ *usu sing* (*equal*) ebenbürtiger Gegner/ebenbürtige Gegnerin (**for** für +*akk*); **to be no ~ for sb** sich mit jdm nicht messen können; **to have met one's ~** seine bessere Hälfte gefunden haben *fam o hum* ❹ SPORTS Spiel *nt;* **tennis ~** Tennisspiel; CHESS Partie *f;* **boxing ~** Boxkampf *m* ❺ COMPUT (*hit*) Treffer *m* **II.** *vi* (*harmonize*) zusammenpassen; (*make pair*) zusammengehören; **a dress with accessories to ~** ein Kleid mit dazu passenden Accessoires **III.** *vt* ❶ (*complement*) passen (zu +*dat*) ❷ (*find complement*) ■ **to ~ sth [with sth]** etw [auf etw *akk*] abstimmen; **I'm trying to ~ the names on the list with the faces on the photograph** ich versuche die Namen auf dieser Liste den Gesichtern auf dem Foto zuzuordnen ❸ (*correspond to*) ■ **to ~ sth** etw *dat* entsprechen, zu etw *dat* passen

◆ **match up I.** *vi* ❶ (*be aligned*) aufeinander abgestimmt sein ❷ (*meet standard*) ■ **to ~ up to sth** an etw *akk* heranreichen, etw *dat* entsprechen **II.** *vt* (*find complement*) **to ~ up** ↻ **socks** die zusammengehörigen Socken finden

match² <*pl* -es> [mætʃ] *n* (*for lighting*) Streichholz *nt*

'matchbox *n* Streichholzschachtel *f*

matching ['mætʃ·ɪŋ] *adj attr* [zusammen]passend

'matchmaker *n* (*marriage broker*) Heiratsvermittler(in) *m(f)*

match 'point *n* TENNIS Matchball *m*

'matchstick *n* Streichholz *nt*

mate¹ [meɪt] **I.** *n* ❶ (*sexual partner*) Partner(in) *m(f);* BIOL Sexualpartner(in) *m(f)* ❷ (*ship's officer*) Schiffsoffizier *m;* **second ~** Zweiter Offizier **II.** *vi* BIOL *animals* sich paaren (**with** mit +*dat*) **III.** *vt* **to ~ two animals** zwei Tiere miteinander paaren

mate² [meɪt] CHESS **I.** *n* [Schach]matt *nt* **II.** *vt* [schach]matt setzen

material [mə·'tɪr·i·əl] **I.** *n* ❶ (*substance*) Material *nt a. fig;* **raw ~** Rohmaterial *nt;* **to be college ~** (*hum*) das Zeug zum Studieren haben ❷ (*type of cloth*) Stoff *m,* Stoffart *f* ❸ (*information*) [Informations]material *nt,* Unterlagen *pl* ❹ (*equipment*) ■ **~s** *pl* Material *nt;* **writing ~s** Schreibzeug *nt* **II.** *adj* ❶ (*physical*) materiell; **~ damage** Sachschaden *m* ❷ (*important*) wesentlich, wichtig; ■ **to be ~ to sth** für etw *akk* relevant sein; **~ witness** Hauptzeuge *m,* Hauptzeugin *f*

materialism [mə·'tɪr·i·ə·lɪz·əm] *n* Materialismus *m*

materialist [mə·'tɪr·i·ə·lɪst] *n* Materialist(in) *m(f)*

materialistic [mə·ˌtɪr·i·ə·'lɪs·tɪk] *adj* materialistisch

materialize [mə·'tɪr·i·ə·laɪz] *vi* ❶ (*become fact*) *hope, dream* sich verwirklichen, in Erfüllung gehen; *plan, promise* in die Tat umgesetzt werden ❷ (*take physical form*) erscheinen

maternal [mə·'tɜr·nəl] *adj* ❶ (*motherly*) mütterlich, Mutter- ❷ (*of mother's family*) mütterlicherseits *nach n*

maternity [mə·'tɜr·nɪ·t̬i] *n* Mutterschaft *f*

ma'ternity clothes *npl* Umstandskleidung *f kein pl*

ma'ternity dress *n* Umstandskleid *nt*

ma'ternity leave *n* Mutterschaftsurlaub *m*

ma'ternity ward *n* Entbindungsstation *f*

math [mæθ] *n* (*fam*) *short for* **mathematics** Mathe *f*

mathematical [ˌmæθ·ə·'mæt̬·ɪ·kəl] *adj* mathematisch

mathematician [ˌmæθ·ə·mə·'tɪʃ·ən] *n* Mathematiker(in) *m(f)*

mathematics [ˌmæθ·ə·'mæt̬·ɪks] *n* + *sing vb* Mathematik *f*

matinee [mæt·ə·'neɪ] *n* Matinee *f;* (*afternoon performance*) Frühvorstellung *f*

mating ['meɪ·t̬ɪŋ] *n* Paarung *f*

matrices ['meɪ·trɪ·siz] *n pl of* **matrix**

matriculate [mə·'trɪk·jə·leɪt] *vi* UNIV sich immatrikulieren

matriculation [mə·ˌtrɪk·jə·'leɪ·ʃən] *n* UNIV Immatrikulation *f*

matrimonial [ˌmæt·rə·'moʊ·ni·əl] *adj* (*form*) Ehe-, ehelich

matrimony ['mæt·rə·moʊ·ni] *n* Ehe *f;* **to be joined in holy ~** in den heiligen Stand der Ehe treten

matrix <*pl* -es *or* -ices> ['meɪ·trɪks] *n* (*rectangular arrangement*) Matrix *f*

matron ['meɪ·trən] *n* ❶ (*middle-aged woman*) Matrone *f meist pej* ❷ **prison ~** Gefängnisaufseherin *f*

matronly ['meɪ·trən·li] *adj* (*esp hum*) matronenhaft *meist pej*

matte [mæt] *adj* matt

matted ['mæt̬·ɪd] *adj* verflochten; *hair* verfilzt

matter ['mæt̬·ər] **I.** *n* ❶ (*material*) Materie *f;* **printed ~** Gedrucktes *nt,* Drucksache[n] *f[pl];* **reading ~** Lesestoff *m* ❷ (*affair*) Angelegenheit *f,* Sache *f;* **this is a ~ for the police** das sollte man der Polizei übergeben; **to get to the heart of the ~** zum Kern der Sache vordringen; **a ~ of urgency** etwas Dringendes ❸ (*question*) Frage *f;* **as a ~ of fact** (*by the way*) übrigens; (*expressing agreement or disagreement*) in der Tat; **it's a ~ of life and death** es geht um Leben und Tod; **a ~ of taste**

M

eine Geschmacksfrage ④ (*topic*) Thema *nt;* **the subject ~ of the book** das Thema des Buches; **it's no laughing ~** das ist nicht zum Lachen ⑤ (*problem*) **is anything the ~?** stimmt etwas nicht?; **what's the ~ with you?** was ist los mit dir?; **no ~ what/when ...** egal, was/wann ... ⑥ (*state of affairs*) ■ **~s** *pl* die Situation [*o* Lage]; **to take ~s into one's own hands** die Dinge selbst in die Hand nehmen **II.** *vi* (*be of importance*) von Bedeutung sein; **that's the only thing that ~s** das ist das Einzige, was zählt; **it really ~s to me** das ist wirklich wichtig für mich; **it doesn't ~** das ist egal, das macht nichts

matter-of-'fact *adj* ① (*emotionless*) sachlich, nüchtern ② (*straightforward*) geradeheraus *präd,* direkt

matter-of-'factly *adv* ① (*without emotion*) sachlich, nüchtern ② (*straightforwardly*) direkt, geradeheraus

matting ['mæt̬·ɪŋ] *n* (*tangling*) Verflechten *nt;* (*of wool*) Verfilzen *nt*

mattress <*pl* -es> ['mæt·rɪs] *n* Matratze *f*

mature [mə·'tʃʊr] **I.** *adj* ① (*adult*) erwachsen; *animal* ausgewachsen; (*like an adult*) reif ② (*ripe*) reif; *wine* ausgereift **II.** *vi* ① (*physically*) erwachsen werden, heranreifen; (*mentally and emotionally*) reifer werden ② FIN (*become payable*) fällig werden ③ (*develop fully*) *idea, plan* ausreifen **III.** *vt* FOOD reifen lassen

maturity [mə·'tʃʊr·ɪ·t̬i] *n* ① (*adulthood*) Erwachsensein *nt;* (*wisdom*) Reife *f; of animals* Ausgewachsensein *nt;* **to reach ~** (*of person*) erwachsen werden; (*of animal*) ausgewachsen sein ② (*developed form*) Reife *f,* Vollendung *f* ③ FIN Fälligkeit *f*

maudlin ['mɔd·lɪn] *adj* [weinerlich] sentimental

maul [mɔl] *vt* ① (*wound*) verletzen; (*attack*) anfallen ② (*criticize*) heruntermachen, verreißen *fam*

Mauritania [ˌmɔr·ɪ·'teɪ·ni·ə] *n* Mauretanien *nt*

Mauritanian [ˌmɔr·ɪ·'teɪ·ni·ən] **I.** *n* Mauretanier(in) *m(f)* **II.** *adj* mauretanisch

Mauritian [mɔ·'rɪʃ·iən] **I.** *n* Mauritier(in) *m(f)* **II.** *adj* mauritisch

Mauritius [mɔ·'rɪʃ·i·əs] *n* Mauritius *nt*

mausoleum [ˌmɔ·sə·'li·əm] *n* Mausoleum *nt*

mauve [moʊv] *adj* mauve

maverick ['mæv·ər·ɪk] *n* (*unorthodox independent person*) Einzelgänger(in) *m(f),* Alleingänger(in) *m(f)*

mawkish ['mɔ·kɪʃ] *adj* (*pej*) rührselig, sentimental

max [mæks] (*fam*) **I.** *n short for* **maximum** max. **II.** *adv* **it'll cost you 40 dollars ~** das wird dich maximal 40 Dollar kosten

◆**max out** *vt* (*fam*) ■ **to ~ out** ⊂ **sth** *credit card* etw ausschöpfen

maxim ['mæk·sɪm] *n* Maxime *f*

maximal ['mæk·sɪ·məl] *adj* maximal

maximize ['mæk·sɪ·maɪz] *vt* maximieren

maximum ['mæk·sɪ·məm] **I.** *adj attr* maximal, Höchst- **II.** *n* <*pl* -ima *or* -s> Maximum *nt* **III.** *adv* maximal

maximum-security 'prison *n* Hochsicherheitsgefängnis *nt*

may <*3rd pers. sing* may, might, might> [meɪ] *aux vb* ① (*indicating possibility*) können; **there ~ be side effects from the drug** diese Arznei kann Nebenwirkungen haben; **I ~ be overreacting, but ...** mag sein, dass ich überreagiere, aber ... ② (*be allowed*) dürfen, können; **~ I ask you a question?** darf ich Ihnen [mal] eine Frage stellen? ③ (*expressing wish*) mögen; **~ she rest in peace** möge sie in Frieden ruhen *form*

May [meɪ] *n* Mai *m; see also* **February**

maybe ['meɪ·bi] *adv* ① (*perhaps*) vielleicht, möglicherweise; **~ we should start again** vielleicht sollten wir noch mal anfangen ② (*approximately*) circa, ungefähr

'mayday *n* Mayday *kein art* (*internationaler Notruf*)

'May Day *n* der Erste Mai, Maifeiertag *m*

'mayfly *n* Eintagsfliege *f*

mayhem ['meɪ·hem] *n* Chaos *nt*

mayo ['meɪ·oʊ] *n* (*fam*) *short for* **mayonnaise** Mayo *f*

mayonnaise [ˌmeɪ·ə·'neɪz] *n* Mayonnaise *f*

mayor ['meɪ·ər] *n* Bürgermeister(in) *m(f),* Oberbürgermeister(in) *m(f)*

maze [meɪz] *n* Labyrinth *nt*

MBA [ˌem·bi·'eɪ] *n abbrev of* **Master of Business Administration** MBA *m*

MC [ˌem·'si] *n abbrev of* **Master of Ceremonies**

MD [ˌem·'di] *n* ① *abbrev of* **Maryland** ② *abbrev of* **Doctor of Medicine** Dr. med.

me [mi] *pron object* (*1st person singular*) mir *in dat,* mich *in akk;* **why are you looking at ~?** warum siehst du mich an?; **it wasn't ~ who offered to go, it was him** ich wollte nicht gehen, er wollte; **hi, it's ~** hallo, ich bin's; **you have more than ~** du hast mehr als ich; **between you and ~** unter uns [gesagt] ► PHRASES: **dear ~!** du liebe Güte!; **silly ~!** bin ich dumm!

ME, Me. *abbrev of* **Maine**

meadow ['med·oʊ] *n* Wiese *f*

meager ['mi·gər] *adj* mager, dürftig

meal[1] [mil] *n* Mahlzeit *f,* Essen *nt;* **to go out for a ~** essen gehen

meal[2] [mil] *n* AGR [grobes] Mehl

'meal ticket *n* ① (*voucher*) Essensmarke *f* ② (*means of living*) Einnahmequelle *f*

'mealtime *n* Essenszeit *f*

mealy ['mi·li] *adj* mehlig

'mealy-mouthed *adj* (*pej*) ausweichend; *excuses* fadenscheinig; *expressions* schönfärberisch

mean[1] [min] *adj* ① (*unkind*) gemein, fies *fam* ② (*vicious*) aggressiv; (*dangerous*) gefährlich; *dog* bissig ③ (*bad*) schlecht; **no ~ feat** eine Meisterleistung

M

mean² <meant, meant> [min] *vt* ① (*signify*) *word, symbol* bedeuten; **no ~s no** nein heißt nein ② (*intend to convey*) *person* meinen; **what do you ~ by that?** was willst du damit sagen? ③ (*be sincere*) **I ~ what I say** ich meine es ernst, was ich sage ④ (*intend*) wollen; **he didn't ~ any harm** er wollte nichts Böses; **I've been ~ing to call you for weeks** ich will dich schon seit Wochen anrufen; **it was ~t to be a surprise** das sollte eine Überraschung sein; **to ~ business** es ernst meinen; **to ~ well** es gut meinen; **to be ~t for each other** füreinander bestimmt sein ⑤ (*result in*) bedeuten, heißen *fam*

mean³ [min] **I.** *n* (*average*) Mittel *nt;* (*average value*) Mittelwert *m;* (*fig*) Mittelweg *m* **II.** *adj* durchschnittlich

meander [mɪ·'æn·dər] **I.** *n* Windung *f,* Krümmung *f* **II.** *vi* ① (*flow in curves*) sich schlängeln [*o* winden] ② (*wander*) [umher]schlendern

meandering [mɪ·'æn·dər·ɪŋ] **I.** *adj* ① (*flowing in curves*) gewunden ② (*rambling*) abschweifend **II.** *n* ■ **~s** *pl* Gefasel *nt kein pl*

meanie ['mi·ni] *n* (*fam*) **to be a ~** gemein sein

meaning ['mi·nɪŋ] *n* ① (*sense*) Bedeutung *f;* **the ~ of life** der Sinn des Lebens; **what is the ~ of this?** was soll das heißen? ② (*importance*) Bedeutung *f,* Sinn *m;* **to have ~ for sb** jdm etwas bedeuten

meaningful ['mi·nɪŋ·fəl] *adj* ① (*important*) bedeutsam, wichtig; **she seems to find it difficult to form a ~ relationship** sie hat Schwierigkeiten, sich auf eine tiefer gehende Beziehung einzulassen ② (*implying something*) bedeutungsvoll, viel sagend

meaningless ['mi·nɪŋ·lɪs] *n* (*without importance*) bedeutungslos; (*nonsensical*) sinnlos; (*empty*) nichts sagend

meanness ['min·nɪs] *n* Gemeinheit *f,* Gehässigkeit *f*

means <*pl* -> [minz] *n* ① (*method*) Weg *m;* (*possibility*) Möglichkeit *f;* (*device*) Mittel *nt;* **~ of transport** Transportmittel *nt;* **~ of support** Einkommen *nt;* **to use all ~ at one's disposal** alle verfügbaren Mittel nutzen ② (*income*) ■ **~** *pl* Geldmittel *pl;* **to live beyond one's ~** über seine Verhältnisse leben ▶ PHRASES: **the end justifies the ~** (*prov*) der Zweck heiligt die Mittel; **by all ~** (*form*) unbedingt; (*of course*) selbstverständlich; **by no ~** keineswegs, auf keinen Fall

meant [ment] *pt, pp of* **mean**

'meantime *n* **in the ~** inzwischen, in der Zwischenzeit

meanwhile ['min·hwaɪl] *adv* inzwischen, unterdessen, mittlerweile

meany ['mi·ni] *n* (*fam*) *see* **meanie**

measles ['mi·zəlz] *n + sing vb* Masern *pl*

measly ['mi·zli] *adj* (*fam or pej*) mickrig, schäbig

measurable ['meʒ·ər·ə·bəl] *adj* messbar; *perceptible* nachweisbar, erkennbar, merklich

measure ['meʒ·ər] **I.** *n* ① (*unit*) Maß *nt,* Maßeinheit *f;* **a ~ of length** ein Längenmaß *nt* ② (*degree*) Maß *nt,* Grad *m;* **there was some ~ of truth in what he said** an dem, was er sagte, war etwas Wahres dran; **in large ~** in hohem Maß ③ (*measuring instrument*) Messgerät *nt;* (*ruler, indicator*) Messstab *m;* (*container*) Messbecher *m* ④ *usu pl* (*action*) Maßnahme *f* ▶ PHRASES: **for good ~** (*in addition*) zusätzlich, noch dazu; (*to ensure success*) sicherheitshalber **II.** *vt* [ab]messen **III.** *vi* messen

◆**measure out** *vt* ① (*take measured amount*) abmessen ② (*discover size*) ausmessen

◆**measure up I.** *vt* ■ **to ~ up ↻ sb** jdn einschätzen **II.** *vi* den Ansprüchen genügen; ■ **to ~ up to sth** an etw *akk* heranreichen, etw *dat* entsprechen

measured ['meʒ·ərd] *adj* gemäßigt; *voice, tone* bedächtig; *response* wohl überlegt; *pace* gemäßigt

measurement ['meʒ·ər·mənt] *n* ① (*size*) ■ **sb's ~s** *pl* jds Maße *pl,* jds Größe *f;* **chest ~** Brustumfang *m* ② (*measuring*) Messung *f,* Messen *nt*

measuring cup ['meʒ·ər·ɪŋ-] *n* Messbecher *m*

'measuring spoon *n* Messlöffel *m*

meat [mit] *n* Fleisch *nt;* (*fig: subject matter*) Substanz *f*

'meatball *n* Fleischklößchen *nt*

'meat cleaver *n* Fleischerbeil *nt*

'meat grinder *n* Fleischwolf *m*

'meat loaf *n* Hackbraten *m*

Mecca ['mek·ə] *n* Mekka *nt a. fig*

mechanic [mɪ·'kæn·ɪk] *n* Mechaniker(in) *m(f)*

mechanical [mɪ·'kæn·ɪk·əl] *adj* ① *machines* mechanisch, Maschinen-; (*technical*) technisch; (*by machine*) maschinell ② (*machine-like*) mechanisch, automatisch

mechanical engi'neer *n* Maschinenbauer(in) *m(f);* (*engineer*) Maschinenbauingenieur(in) *m(f)*

mechanical engi'neering *n* Maschinenbau *m*

mechanical 'pencil *n* Drehbleistift *m*

mechanics [mɪ·'kæn·ɪks] *n* ① *+ sing vb* AUTO, TECH Technik *f,* Mechanik *f* ② *+ pl vb* (*fam: practicalities*) Mechanismus *m*

mechanism ['mek·ə·nɪz·əm] *n* ① (*working parts*) Mechanismus *m* ② (*method*) Mechanismus *m,* Methode *f;* **defense ~** Abwehrmechanismus *m*

mechanize ['mek·ə·naɪz] *vt* mechanisieren

med I. *adj* (*fam*) *see* **medical II.** *n* (*fam*) ■ **~s** *pl* Medizin *f*

med. I. *n abbrev of* **medicine II.** *adj* ① *abbrev of* **medieval** ma. ② *abbrev of* **medium**

medal ['med·əl] *n* [Ehren]medaille *f,* Orden *m,* Auszeichnung *f;* SPORTS Medaille *f*

medalist ['med·əl·ɪst] *n* Medaillengewinner(in) *m(f)*

medallion [mə·'dæl·jən] *n* Medaillon *nt*

meddle ['med·əl] *vi* sich einmischen (**in** in *+akk*); ■ **to ~ with sth** sich mit etw *dat* abgeben

M

media [ˈmi·di·ə] *n* ① *pl of* **medium** ② + *sing/pl vb* (*the press*) ■**the ~** die Medien *pl;* **~ coverage** Berichterstattung *f;* **a ~ event** ein Medienereignis *nt*

mediaeval [ˌmi·di·ˈi·vəl] *adj see* **medieval**

ˈ**median** (**strip**) *n* Mittelstreifen *m*

ˈ**media studies** *npl* ≈ Kommunikationswissenschaft *f*

mediate [ˈmi·di·eɪt] **I.** *vi* vermitteln **II.** *vt* aushandeln

mediation [ˌmi·di·ˈeɪ·ʃən] *n* Vermittlung *f*

mediator [ˈmi·di·eɪ·t̬ər] *n* Vermittler(in) *m(f)*

medic [ˈmed·ɪk] *n* (*fam*) ① MIL, NAUT Sanitäter(in) *m(f)* ② (*doctor*) Doktor *m fam*

Medicaid [ˈmed·ɪ·keɪd] *n Gesundheitsfürsorgeprogramm in den USA für einkommensschwache Gruppen*

medical [ˈmed·ɪ·kəl] **I.** *adj facilities, research* medizinisch; *advice, care, treatment* ärztlich; **~ attention** ärztliche Behandlung **II.** *n* (*fam*) ärztliche Untersuchung; **to have a ~** sich ärztlich untersuchen lassen

ˈ**medical certificate** *n* ärztliches Attest

medical examiˈnation *n* ärztliche Untersuchung

ˈ**medical history** *n* Krankengeschichte *f*

Medicare [ˈmed·ɪ·ker] *n* staatliche Gesundheitsfürsorge [für Senioren]

medicate [ˈmed·ɪ·keɪt] *vt usu passive* (*treat with drug*) ■**to be ~d** medikamentös behandelt werden

M

medication [ˌmed·ɪ·ˈkeɪ·ʃən] *n* MED ① (*medicine*) Medikamente *pl;* **to be on ~ for sth** Medikamente gegen etw *akk* [ein]nehmen ② (*treatment*) medikamentöse Behandlung

medicinal [mə·ˈdɪs·ə·nəl] *adj* medizinisch; **~ herbs** Heilkräuter *pl*

medicine [ˈmed·ɪ·sɪn] *n* ① (*for illness*) Medizin *f,* Medikamente *pl;* **to take [one's] ~** [seine] Medizin einnehmen ② (*substance*) Medikament *nt;* **cough ~** Hustenmittel *nt* ③ (*medical science*) Medizin *f;* **herbal ~** Kräuterheilkunde *f;* **to practice ~** den Arztberuf ausüben

ˈ**medicine cabinet**, ˈ**medicine chest** *n* Hausapotheke *f*

ˈ**medicine man** *n* ① (*tribal healer*) Medizinmann *m* ② (*hum fam: doctor*) Medizinmann *m*

medieval [ˌmi·di·ˈi·vəl] *adj* mittelalterlich

mediocre [ˌmi·di·ˈoʊ·kər] *adj* mittelmäßig

mediocrity [ˌmi·di·ˈak·rɪ·t̬i] *n* ① (*state*) Mittelmäßigkeit *f* ② (*person*) Null *f pej*

meditate [ˈmed·ɪ·teɪt] **I.** *vi* ① (*think deeply*) nachdenken (**on/about** über +*akk*) ② (*as spiritual exercise*) meditieren **II.** *vt* (*form: plan*) planen; (*consider*) erwägen

meditation [ˌmed·ɪ·ˈteɪ·ʃən] *n* ① (*spiritual exercise*) Meditation *f* ② (*serious thought*) Nachdenken *nt,* Überlegen *nt* (**on/about** über +*akk*) ③ (*reflections*) ■**~s** *pl* Überlegungen *pl*

Mediterranean [ˌmed·ɪ·tə·ˈreɪ·ni·ən] **I.** *n* Mittelmeer *nt* **II.** *adj climate* mediterran; **~ cooking** Mittelmeerküche *f*

medium [ˈmi·di·əm] **I.** *adj* ① (*average*) durchschnittlich, mittel; **of ~ height** von mittlerer Größe ② FOOD *steak* halb durch **II.** *n* <*pl* -s *or* -dia> ① (*means*) Medium *nt,* Mittel *nt;* PUBL, TV Medium *nt;* **advertising ~** Werbeträger *m* ② (*art material*) Medium *nt* ③ <*pl* -s> (*spiritualist*) Medium *nt*

medium-ˈrare *adj* FOOD englisch

ˈ**medium-size**(**d**) *adj* mittelgroß

medley [ˈmed·li] *n* ① (*mixture*) Gemisch *nt* ② (*of tunes*) Medley *nt*

meek [mik] **I.** *adj* ① (*gentle*) sanftmütig ② (*pej: submissive*) unterwürfig **II.** *n* REL ■**the ~** die Sanftmütigen

meet [mit] **I.** *n* (*sporting event*) Sportveranstaltung *f,* [sportliche] Begegnung **II.** *vt* <met, met> ① (*by chance*) treffen; **I met her in the street** ich bin ihr auf der Straße begegnet ② (*by arrangement*) ■**to ~ sb** sich mit jdm treffen ③ (*collect*) abholen; **a bus ~s every train** zu jedem Zug gibt es einen Anschlussbus ④ (*make acquaintance of*) kennen lernen ⑤ (*fulfill*) erfüllen; *deadline* einhalten; *demands* befriedigen; *obligation* nachkommen ▶ PHRASES: **to ~ one's death** den Tod finden; **to make ends ~** über die Runden kommen; **to ~ sb halfway** jdm auf halbem Weg entgegenkommen **III.** *vi* <met, met> ① (*by chance*) sich begegnen ② (*by arrangement*) sich treffen; **to ~ for a drink** sich auf einen Drink treffen ③ (*get acquainted*) sich kennen lernen; **no, we haven't met** nein, wir kennen uns noch nicht ④ SPORTS aufeinandertreffen ⑤ (*join*) zusammentreffen; *roads, lines* zusammenlaufen; *counties, states* aneinandergrenzen

◆**meet with** *vi* ① (*have meeting*) treffen ② (*experience*) *problems* stoßen (auf +*akk*); **to ~ with approval** Beifall finden; **to ~ with success** Erfolg haben

meeting [ˈmi·t̬ɪŋ] *n* ① (*organized gathering*) Versammlung *f,* Sitzung *f,* Besprechung *f;* **to attend a ~** an einer Besprechung teilnehmen; **to hold a ~** eine Besprechung abhalten ② (*coming together of friends*) Treffen *nt*

ˈ**meeting point** *n* ① (*place to gather*) Treffpunkt *m* ② (*point of contact*) Schnittpunkt *m*

mega [ˈmegə] *adj* (*fam*) Riesen-, Mega-

mega- [ˈmegə] *in compounds* (*fam*) + *adj* mega- *fam;* **~-cool** megacool *sl,* geil *sl*

ˈ**megabucks** *npl* (*fam*) Schweinegeld *nt kein pl sl*

ˈ**megabyte** *n* Megabyte *nt*

ˈ**megahertz** *n* Megahertz *nt*

megalomania [ˌmeg·ə·loʊ·ˈmeɪ·ni·ə] *n* (*lust for power*) Größenwahn *m pej*

megalomaniac [ˌmeg·ə·loʊ·ˈmeɪ·ni·æk] *n* (*power-hungry person*) Größenwahnsinnige(r) *f(m) pej*

ˈ**megaphone** *n* Megaphon *nt*

ˈ**megawatt** *n* Megawatt *nt*

melancholy [ˈmel·ən·kal·i] **I.** *n* Melancholie *f,* Schwermut *f* **II.** *adj* melancholisch, schwermütig

melee ['meɪ·leɪ] *n usu sing* ❶ (*confused fight*) Handgemenge *nt* ❷ (*muddle*) Gedränge *nt*
mellow ['mel·oʊ] **I.** *adj* <-er, -est *or* more ~, most ~> ❶ (*relaxed*) *person* abgeklärt, locker *fam* ❷ (*not harsh*) sanft; *color* dezent; *light* gedämpft; *flavor* mild; *wine* lieblich **II.** *vi* ❶ (*become more easygoing*) umgänglicher werden ❷ (*become softer*) *colors* weicher werden; *flavor* milder werden **III.** *vt* ❶ (*make more easygoing*) *person* umgänglicher machen ❷ (*make softer*) abschwächen
melodic [mə·'lad·ɪk] *adj* melodisch
melodrama ['mel·oʊ·dra·mə] *n* THEAT (*a. fig*) Melodrama *nt*
melodramatic [ˌmel·oʊ·drə·'mæt̬·ɪk] *adj* melodramatisch
melody ['mel·ə·di] *n* Melodie *f*
melon ['mel·ən] *n* Melone *f*
melt [melt] **I.** *n* ❶ (*thaw*) Schneeschmelze *f* ❷ FOOD **patty ~** *Sandwich mit geschmolzenem Käse* **II.** *vi* ❶ (*turn into liquid*) schmelzen; **to ~ in the mouth** auf der Zunge zergehen ❷ (*change gradually*) ■**to ~ into sth** in etw *akk* übergehen; (*disappear*) sich in etw *dat* auflösen **III.** *vt* ❶ (*make liquid*) schmelzen ❷ (*fig: make tender*) *heart* erweichen
'**meltdown** *n* ❶ TECH [Ein]schmelzen *nt;* (*in nuclear power plant*) Durchbrennen *nt* ❷ (*fam: collapse*) Zusammenbruch *m*
'**melting point** *n* Schmelzpunkt *m*
'**melting pot** *n* (*fig*) Schmelztiegel *m*
member ['mem·bər] *n* (*of group*) Angehörige(r) *f(m); of club, party* Mitglied *nt;* **~ of staff** Mitarbeiter(in) *m(f)*
membership ['mem·bər·ʃɪp] *n* ❶ (*people*) ■**the ~** die Mitglieder *pl;* (*number of people*) Mitgliederzahl *f* ❷ (*being member*) Mitgliedschaft *f* ❸ (*fee*) Mitgliedsbeitrag *m*
'**membership card** *n* Mitgliedsausweis *m*
membrane ['mem·breɪn] *n* Membran *f,* Häutchen *nt; of cell* Zellmembran *f*
memento <*pl* -s *or* -es> [mə·'men·toʊ] *n* Andenken *nt* (**of** an +*akk*)
memo ['mem·oʊ] *n short for* **memorandum** Memo *nt*
memoir ['mem·war] *n* ❶ (*personal account*) Erinnerungen *pl* ❷ (*autobiography*) ■**~s** *pl* Memoiren *pl*
'**memo pad** *n* Notizblock *m*
memorabilia [ˌmem·ər·ə·'bɪl·i·ə] *npl* Souvenirs *pl*
memorable ['mem·ər·ə·bəl] *adj* unvergesslich; *achievement* beeindruckend
memorandum <*pl* -s *or* -da> [ˌmem·ə·'ræn·dəm] *n* ❶ (*form: message*) Mitteilung *f* ❷ (*document*) Memorandum *nt*
memorial [mə·'mɔr·i·əl] *n* Denkmal *nt;* MIL Ehrenmal *nt*
Me'morial Day *n* Volkstrauertag *m*

Der **Memorial Day** (Volkstrauertag) ist seit 1971 ein gesetzlicher Feiertag, an dem man der Gefallenen aller US-Kriege gedenkt. Dieser Tag wird am letzten Montag im Mai gefeiert. Man ehrt die gefallenen Soldaten mit Paraden, Gedenkgottesdiensten, sowie Gedenkfeiern in Kirchen, Schulen, an Kriegsdenkmälern und auf öffentlichen Plätzen.

memorize ['mem·ə·raɪz] *vt facts* sich *dat* einprägen; *poem, song* auswendig lernen
memory ['mem·ə·ri] *n* ❶ (*ability to remember*) Gedächtnis *nt* (**for** für +*akk*); **if my ~ serves me right** wenn mein Gedächtnis mich nicht täuscht; **within living/sb's ~** so weit man/jd zurückdenken kann ❷ (*remembered event*) Erinnerung *f* (**of** an +*akk*); **to bring back memories** Erinnerungen wachrufen; **in ~ of** zur Erinnerung an +*akk* ❸ COMPUT Speicher *m*
'**memory bank** *n* COMPUT Speicherbank *f*
men [men] *n pl of* **man**
menace ['men·əs] **I.** *n* ❶ (*threat*) Drohung *f* ❷ (*danger*) Bedrohung *f* ❸ (*annoying person*) Nervensäge *f fam* **II.** *vt* bedrohen
menacing ['men·ɪs·ɪŋ] *adj attr* drohend
menacingly ['men·ɪs·ɪŋ·li] *adv* drohend
mend [mend] **I.** *vt* (*repair*) reparieren; *socks* stopfen ▶ PHRASES: **to ~ one's ways** sich bessern **II.** *vi* gesund werden *a. fig; bone* heilen **III.** *n* ▶ PHRASES: **to be on the ~** auf dem Weg der Besserung sein
menial ['mi·ni·əl] *adj* niedrig; **~ labor** Hilfsarbeit *f*
meningitis [ˌmen·ɪn·'dʒaɪ·t̬ɪs] *n* Gehirnhautentzündung *f,* Meningitis *f fachspr*
menopause ['men·ə·pɔz] *n* Wechseljahre *pl,* Menopause *f fachspr*
'**men's room** *n* Herrentoilette *f*
menstruate ['men·stru·eɪt] *vi* menstruieren *geh*
menstruation [ˌmen·stru·'eɪ·ʃən] *n* Menstruation *f geh,* Periode *f*
mental ['men·təl] *adj* ❶ (*of the mind*) geistig, mental; **~ process** Denkprozess *m* ❷ (*psychological*) psychisch, seelisch; **~ illness** Geisteskrankheit *f;* **~ state** seelische Verfassung ❸ (*fam: crazy*) verrückt, übergeschnappt; ■**to be ~ about sb/sth** nach jdm/etw verrückt sein
'**mental hospital** *n* psychiatrische Klinik
mentality [men·'tæl·ɪ·t̬i] *n* Mentalität *f*
mentally ['men·təl·i] *adv* ❶ (*psychologically*) psychisch ❷ (*intellectually*) geistig; **~ disabled** geistig behindert
menthol ['men·θɔl] *n* Menthol *nt*
mention ['men·ʃən] **I.** *n* (*reference*) Erwähnung *f;* **to get a ~** erwähnt werden **II.** *vt* erwähnen; **don't ~ it!** gern geschehen!; **not to ~ ...** ganz zu schweigen von ...
menu ['men·ju] *n* ❶ (*in restaurant*) Speisekarte *f* ❷ COMPUT Menü *nt*
'**menu bar** *n* COMPUT Menüleiste *f*

meow [mi·'aʊ] **I.** *n* Miauen *nt* **II.** *vi* miauen
mercenary ['mɜr·sə·ner·i] **I.** *n* (*soldier*) Söldner *m* **II.** *adj* ① (*pej: motivated by gain*) gewinnsüchtig, geldgierig ② MIL Söldner-
merchandise ['mɜr·tʃən·daɪz] ECON **I.** *n* Handelsware *f* **II.** *vt* vermarkten
merchant ['mɜr·tʃənt] *n* Händler(in) *m(f),* Kaufmann *m,* Kauffrau *f*
merchant ma'rine *n* Handelsmarine *f*
'merchant ship *n* Handelsschiff *nt*
merciful ['mɜr·sɪ·fəl] *adj* ① (*forgiving*) gnädig ② (*fortunate*) **her death came as a ~ release** der Tod war für sie eine Erlösung
merciless ['mɜr·sɪ·lɪs] *adj* ① (*showing no mercy*) gnadenlos, mitleidlos ② (*relentless*) unnachgiebig
mercury ['mɜr·kjə·ri] *n* (*metal*) Quecksilber *nt*
Mercury ['mɜr·kjə·ri] *n* ASTRON Merkur *m*
mercy ['mɜr·si] *n* (*compassion*) Mitleid *nt,* Erbarmen *nt;* (*forgiveness*) Gnade *f;* **to beg for ~** um Gnade bitten; **to show [no] ~** [kein] Erbarmen haben ▶ PHRASES: **to be <u>at</u> the ~ of sb** jdm auf Gnade oder Ungnade ausgeliefert sein
mere [mɪr] *adj* nur, nichts als
merely ['mɪr·li] *adv* nur, bloß *fam*
merge [mɜrdʒ] **I.** *vi* ① (*join*) zusammenkommen; *roads* zusammenlaufen ② ECON *companies, organizations* fusionieren ③ (*fuse*) verschmelzen (**with/into** mit +*dat*); ■ **to ~ into each other** ineinander übergehen ④ AUTO **to ~ left/right** sich links/rechts einordnen **II.** *vt* zusammenlegen; *companies* zusammenschließen
merger ['mɜr·dʒər] *n* ECON Fusion *f*
meridian [mə·'rɪd·i·ən] *n* GEOG (*line of longitude*) Meridian *m,* Längenkreis *m*
meringue [mə·'ræŋ] *n* Baiser *nt,* Meringe *f,* Meringue *f* SCHWEIZ
merit ['mer·ɪt] **I.** *n* ① (*worthiness*) Verdienst *nt;* **she won her promotion on ~ alone** sie ist allein auf Grund ihrer Leistung befördert worden ② (*good quality*) gute Eigenschaft, Vorzug *m* ③ (*advantage*) Vorteil *m* **II.** *vt* verdienen
mermaid ['mɜr·meɪd] *n* Seejungfrau *f*
merriment ['mer·ɪ·mənt] *n* ① (*laughter and joy*) Fröhlichkeit *f* ② (*amusement*) Heiterkeit *f*
merry ['mer·i] *adj* fröhlich; **M~ Christmas** Frohe [*o* Fröhliche] Weihnachten
'merry-go-round *n* (*fairground ride*) Karussell *nt*
mesh [meʃ] **I.** *n* Geflecht *nt* **II.** *vi* ① (*join*) *gears* ineinandergreifen ② (*mix*) sich mischen
mesmerize ['mez·mə·raɪz] *vt* faszinieren
mess <*pl* -es> [mes] *n* ① *usu sing* (*messy state*) Unordnung *f,* Durcheinander *nt;* (*dirty state*) Schweinerei *f;* **you look like a complete ~!** du siehst ja schlimm aus! ② *usu sing* (*disorganized state*) Chaos *nt;* ■ **to be a ~** chaotisch sein; **to be in a ~** sich in einem schlimmen Zustand befinden; **he made a complete ~ of the invitations** (*fam*) he hat die Einladungen total vermasselt ▶ PHRASES: **a <u>fine</u> ~ you've gotten us into!** (*iron*) jetzt haben wir die Bescherung!
◆**mess around** *vi* ① (*behave foolishly*) herumblödeln *fam,* Unfug treiben ② (*waste time*) herumspielen ③ (*tinker*) herumspielen, herumfummeln (**with** an +*dat*) ④ ■ **to ~ around with sb** (*playfully*) jdn verarschen *derb;* (*unfairly*) mit jdm umspringen[, wie es einem gefällt]
◆**mess up** *vt* (*fam*) ① (*botch up*) verpfuschen, versauen; *plan* vermasseln ② (*make messy*) in Unordnung bringen
◆**mess with** *vi* ① (*get involved with*) ■ **to ~ with sb** sich mit jdm einlassen; (*cause trouble to*) jdn schlecht behandeln; **don't ~ with me!** verarsch mich bloß nicht! *derb* ② (*play with*) ■ **to ~ with sth** mit etw *dat* herumspielen; (*tamper*) an etw *dat* herumspielen
message ['mes·ɪdʒ] *n* (*communication*) Nachricht *f,* Botschaft *f;* **could you give him a ~ from me, please?** könntest du ihm bitte etwas [*o* eine Nachricht] von mir ausrichten?; **to get/leave a ~** eine Nachricht erhalten/hinterlassen ▶ PHRASES: **to <u>get</u> the ~** (*fam*) kapieren
messenger ['mes·ɪn·dʒər] *n* Bote *m,* Botin *f*
'mess hall *n* Kasino *nt*
messiah [mə·'saɪ·ə] *n usu sing* ① REL ■ **M~** Messias *m,* Erlöser *m* ② (*fig*) Messias *m*
messy ['mes·i] *adj* ① (*untidy*) unordentlich; *person* schlampig ② (*dirty*) schmutzig, dreckig ③ (*unpleasant*) unerfreulich
met [met] *vt, vi pt of* **meet**
metabolic [ˌmet̬·ə·'bal·ɪk] *adj* metabolisch *fachspr,* Stoffwechsel-
metabolism [mɪ·'tæb·ə·lɪz·əm] *n* Stoffwechsel *m,* Metabolismus *m fachspr*
metal ['met̬·əl] **I.** *n* Metall *nt;* **precious ~** Edelmetall *nt* **II.** *adj* aus Metall *nach n*
metallic [mə·'tæl·ɪk] *adj* ① (*like metal*) metallisch; **~ paint** Metalleffektlack *m* ② (*containing metal*) metallhaltig
metallurgy ['mət̬·əl·ɜr·dʒi] *n* Metallurgie *f*
'metalwork *n* ① (*craft*) Metallarbeit *f* ② (*objects*) Metallarbeiten *pl*
'metalworker *n* Metallarbeiter(in) *m(f)*
metamorphosis <*pl* -phoses> [ˌmet̬·ə·'mɔr·fə·sɪs] *n* Metamorphose *f geh,* Verwandlung *f*
metaphor ['met̬·ə·fɔr] *n* ① (*figure of speech*) Metapher *f* (**for** für +*akk*) ② (*figurative language*) bildhafte Sprache
metaphoric(al) [ˌmet̬·ə·'fɔr·ɪk(əl)] *adj* metaphorisch
mete [mit] *vt* ■ **to ~ out** ◯ **sth [to sb]** [jdm] etw auferlegen; **to ~ out punishment to sb** jdn bestrafen; (*physical*) jdn züchtigen
meteor ['mi·t̬i·ər] *n* Meteor *m*
meteoric [ˌmi·t̬i·'ɔr·ɪk] *adj* ① ASTRON Meteor-, meteorisch ② (*rapid*) kometenhaft
meteorite ['mi·t̬i·ə·raɪt] *n* Meteorit *m*
meteorological [ˌmi·t̬i·ər·ə·'ladʒ·ɪ·kəl] *adj* meteorologisch
meteorologist [ˌmi·t̬i·ə·'ral·ə·dʒɪst] *n* Meteo-

rologe *m,* Meteorologin *f*
meteorology [ˌmi·ti·ə·ˈral·ə·dʒi] *n* Meteorologie *f*
meter¹ [ˈmi·t̬ər] *n* Messuhr *f,* Zähler *m;* [**parking**] ~ Parkuhr *f;* **to read the ~** den Zähler ablesen
meter² [ˈmi·t̬ər] *n* (*unit of measurement*) Meter *m;* **the 1500 ~s** der 1500-Meter-Lauf
meter³ [ˈmi·t̬ər] *n* (*poetic rhythm*) Metrum *nt fachspr,* Versmaß *nt*
methane [ˈmeθ·eɪn] *n* Methan *nt*
methanol [ˈmeθ·ə·nɔl] *n* Methanol *nt*
method [ˈmeθ·əd] *n* ❶ (*way of doing sth*) Methode *f,* Art und Weise *f;* TECH Verfahren *nt* ❷ (*order*) System *nt*
methodical [mə·ˈθad·ɪ·kəl] *adj* ❶ (*ordered*) methodisch, systematisch ❷ (*careful*) sorgfältig
Methodist [ˈmeθ·ə·dɪst] **I.** *n* Methodist(in) *m(f)* **II.** *adj* methodistisch
methodology [ˌmeθ·ə·ˈdal·ə·dʒi] *n* ❶ (*theory of methods*) Methodologie *f geh* ❷ (*system*) Methodik *f*
methyl alcohol [ˌmeθ·əl·ˈæl·kə·hɔl] *n see* **methanol**
meticulous [mɪ·ˈtɪk·jʊ·ləs] *adj* peinlich genau, akribisch *geh;* ~ **detail** kleinstes Detail
metric [ˈmet·rɪk] *adj* metrisch
metro [ˈmet·roʊ] *adj attr short for* **metropolitan** Stadt-
metronome [ˈmet·rə·noʊm] *n* Metronom *nt geh*
metropolis [mə·ˈtrap·ə·lɪs] *n* (*form*) ❶ (*large city*) Metropole *f geh* ❷ (*chief city*) Hauptstadt *f*
metropolitan [ˌmet·rə·ˈpal·ə·tən] *adj* (*of large city*) weltstädtisch; ~ **area** Metropolregion *f*
mettle [ˈmet̬·əl] *n* (*form: inner strength*) Durchhaltevermögen *nt;* **to show one's ~** zeigen, was in einem steckt
mew [mju] **I.** *n* Miauen *nt* **II.** *vi* miauen
Mexican [ˈmek·sɪ·kən] **I.** *n* (*person*) Mexikaner(in) *m(f)* **II.** *adj* mexikanisch
Mexico [ˈmek·sɪ·koʊ] *n* Mexiko *nt*
Mexico ˈCity *n* Mexiko City *nt*
mg *n* <*pl* -> *abbrev of* **milligram** mg
MHz *n* <*pl* -> *abbrev of* **megahertz** MHz
MI *abbrev of* **Michigan**
mica [ˈmaɪ·kə] *n* Glimmererde *f*
mice [maɪs] *n pl of* **mouse**
Mich. *abbrev of* **Michigan**
Michigan [ˈmɪʃ·ɪ·gən] *n* Michigan *nt*
ˈMickey Mouse *adj attr* (*pej fam*) Scherz- *fam;* ~ **computer** Spielzeugcomputer *m;* **a ~ job** ein Witz *m* von einem Job
microbe [ˈmaɪ·kroʊb] *n* Mikrobe *f*
microbiˈology [ˌmaɪ·kroʊ-] *n* Mikrobiologie *f*
ˈmicrochip *n* Mikrochip *m*
ˈmicroclimate *n* Mikroklima *nt*
microcosm [ˈmaɪ·kroʊ·kaz·əm] *n* Mikrokosmos *m*
microelecˈtronics *n + sing vb* Mikroelektronik *f*
ˈmicrofiche *n* Mikrofiche *nt o m*
ˈmicrofilm *n* Mikrofilm *m*
micrometer [maɪˈkrɔ·mɪ·t̬ər] *n* (*measuring device*) Mikrometer *nt*
Micronesia [ˌmaɪ·kroʊ·ˈni·ʒə] *n* Mikronesien *nt*
microˈorganism *n* Mikroorganismus *m*
ˈmicrophone *n* Mikrofon *nt*
ˈmicroprocessor *n* Mikroprozessor *m*
microscope [ˈmaɪ·krə·skoʊp] *n* Mikroskop *nt;* **to put sth under the ~** (*fig*) etw unter die Lupe nehmen
microscopic [ˌmaɪ·krə·ˈskap·ɪk] *adj* ❶ (*fam: tiny*) winzig; **to look at sth in ~ detail** etw haargenau prüfen ❷ (*visible with microscope*) mikroskopisch klein ❸ (*using microscope*) *analysis, examination* mikroskopisch
ˈmicrowave I. *n* ❶ (*oven*) Mikrowellenherd *m,* Mikrowelle *f* ❷ (*wave*) Mikrowelle *f* **II.** *vt* in der Mikrowelle kochen/erwärmen
midˈday *n* Mittag *m;* **at ~** mittags, um die Mittagszeit
middle [ˈmɪd·əl] **I.** *n* ❶ (*center, division, between things*) Mitte *f; of fruit, nuts* Innere[s] *nt;* (*center part*) *of book, film, story* Mittelteil *m* ❷ (*in time, space*) mitten; **in the ~ of the road/room/table** mitten auf der Straße/im Zimmer/auf dem Tisch; **in the ~ of the night** mitten in der Nacht; **in the ~ of nowhere** (*fig*) am Ende der Welt; **in the ~ of 1985/the century** Mitte 1985/des Jahrhunderts; **to be in one's ~ forties** in den Mittvierzigern sein; **to be in the ~ of eating** (*busy with*) mitten dabei sein zu essen ❸ (*fam: waist*) Taille *f;* (*belly*) Bauch *m* **II.** *adj attr* mittlere(r, s)
middle ˈage *n* mittleres Alter
middle-ˈaged *adj* mittleren Alters *nach n*
Middle ˈAges *n* ■**the ~** *pl* das Mittelalter
ˈmiddlebrow (*pej*) **I.** *adj* für den [geistigen] Durchschnittsmenschen **II.** *n* [geistiger] Durchschnittsmensch
middle ˈclass *n* ■**the ~** der Mittelstand; **upper ~** gehobener Mittelstand
ˈmiddle-class *adj* Mittelstands-, mittelständisch
Middle ˈEast *n* ■**the ~** der Nahe Osten
ˈmiddleman *n* ❶ ECON (*person*) Zwischenhändler(in) *m(f);* (*wholesaler*) ■**the ~** der Zwischenhandel ❷ (*go-between*) Mittelsmann *m*
middle ˈname *n* zweiter Vorname
middle-of-the-ˈroad *adj* ❶ (*moderate*) *opinions, views* gemäßigt ❷ (*pej: boring*) *film, music* mittelmäßig
ˈmiddleweight *n* SPORTS ❶ (*division*) Mittelgewicht *nt* ❷ (*boxer*) Mittelgewichtler(in) *m(f)*
middling [ˈmɪd·lɪŋ] *adj* (*fam*) ❶ (*average*) mittlere(r, s) ❷ (*not very good*) mittelmäßig
Midˈeast *n* ■**the ~** der Nahe [*o* Mittlere] Osten
midge [mɪdʒ] *n* [kleine] Mücke
midget [ˈmɪdʒ·ɪt] **I.** *n* (*dwarf*) Liliputaner(in) *m(f);* (*child*) Knirps *m fam,* Zwerg *m*

hum **II.** *adj* (*small*) winzig, Mini-

midlife 'crisis *n* Midlife-Crisis *f*

'midnight *n* Mitternacht *f;* **at ~** um Mitternacht

'midpoint *n usu sing* Mittelpunkt *m;* MATH Mittelwert *m*

midriff ['mɪd·rɪf] *n,* **midsection** ['mɪd·sek·ʃən] *n* Taille *f*

midst [mɪdst] *n* (*presence*) **he was lost in their ~** er kam sich unter ihnen verloren vor; (*in middle of*) **in the ~ of chaos** mitten im Chaos

mid'summer *n* Hochsommer *m*

mid'term **I.** *n* ❶ (*midpoint*) *of political office* Halbzeit *f* der Amtsperiode; *of school year* Schulhalbjahr *nt; of pregnancy* Hälfte *f* der Schwangerschaftszeit; UNIV *of semester* Semesterhälfte *f; of trimester* Trimesterhälfte *f* ❷ (*midterm exams*) ■ **~s** *pl* Halbjahresprüfungen *pl* **II.** *adj* **~ elections** Zwischenwahlen *pl*

midway ['mɪd·ˌweɪ] **I.** *adv* auf halbem Weg; **the projector broke ~ through the film** mitten im Film ging der Projektor kaputt **II.** *adj attr* auf halbem Weg **III.** *n Mittelweg einer Ausstellung oder eines Jahrmarktes, an dem sich die Hauptattraktionen befinden*

mid'week *n* Wochenmitte *f*

midwife ['mɪd·waɪf] *n* Hebamme *f*

mid'winter *n* Mitte *f* des Winters; (*winter solstice*) Wintersonnenwende *f*

might¹ [maɪt] *n* ❶ (*authority*) Macht *f* ❷ (*strength*) Kraft *f;* MIL Stärke *f*

might² [maɪt] **I.** *pt of* **may** **II.** *aux vb* ❶ (*expressing possibility*) **I ~ go to the movies tonight** vielleicht gehe ich heute Abend ins Kino; (*could*) **someone called at six; it ~ have been him** um sechs rief jemand an, das könnte er gewesen sein; (*expressing probability*) **if he keeps studying so hard, he ~ even get an A on his final exam** wenn er weiterhin so eifrig lernt, könnte er sogar die Bestnote bei den Abschlussprüfungen bekommen ❷ (*form: polite form of may*) **~ I ...?** dürfte ich [vielleicht] ...?; **~ I make a suggestion?** dürfte ich vielleicht einen Vorschlag machen?; **I thought you ~ like to join me for dinner** ich dachte, du hättest vielleicht Lust, mit mir zu Abend zu essen

mightily ['maɪ·t̬ɪ·li] *adv* (*with effort*) mit aller Kraft [*o* Macht]; (*fig: majestically, imposingly*) gewaltig

mighty ['maɪ·t̬i] **I.** *adj* (*powerful, large*) *river, dinosaur, army* gewaltig; *king, country* mächtig; *warrior, giant* stark **II.** *adv* (*fam*) sehr; **that was ~ nice of you** das war wirklich nett von dir

migraine ['maɪ·greɪn] *n* Migräne *f*

migrant ['maɪ·grənt] **I.** *n* ❶ (*person*) Zuwanderer *m,* Zuwanderin *f* ❷ (*bird*) Zugvogel *m* **II.** *adj* **~ birds** Zugvögel *pl;* **~ worker** Wanderarbeiter(in) *m(f)*

migrate ['maɪ·greɪt] *vi* ❶ (*change habitat*) wandern, umherziehen; **to ~ south** *birds* nach Süden ziehen ❷ (*move*) *populations, customers* abwandern; *cells, chemicals* gelangen (**into** in +*akk*)

migration [maɪ·'greɪ·ʃən] *n* ❶ (*change of habitat*) Wanderung *f; of birds* Zug *m* ❷ (*for work*) *people* Abwanderung *f;* (*permanent*) Umzug *m*

migratory ['maɪ·grə·tɔr·i] *adj* ❶ *animals* Wander-; **~ bird** Zugvogel *m* ❷ (*of behavior*) Wander-; **~ patterns** Migrationsverhalten *nt*

mike [maɪk] *n* (*fam*) *short for* **microphone** Mikro *nt*

mild [maɪld] *adj* ❶ (*gentle*) *person, breeze* sanft; *soap, laundry detergent* schonend; (*not severe*) *shock, surprise* leicht; *criticism* schwach; *punishment, weather, climate* mild; *reproach* leise ❷ MED (*not strong*) leicht, schwach; (*not serious*) *fever, infection* leicht ❸ (*not strong in flavor*) *cheese, whiskey* mild; *cigarette* leicht

mildew ['mɪl·du] **I.** *n* Schimmel *m;* (*on plants*) Mehltau *m* **II.** *vi* schimmeln; (*plants*) von Mehltau befallen sein

mildly ['maɪld·li] *adv* ❶ (*gently*) leicht; *speak, smile* sanft; *clean* schonend; (*not severely*) milde ❷ (*slightly*) *surprised, worried, annoyed* leicht ❸ (*as an understatement*) **to put it ~** um es [mal] milde auszudrücken

mildness ['maɪld·nɪs] *n* ❶ *of person* Sanftmut *f* ❷ *of criticism, weather* Milde *f;* MED *of disease, symptoms* Leichtigkeit *f*

mile [maɪl] *n* ❶ (*distance*) Meile *f;* **we could see for ~s and ~s** wir konnten meilenweit sehen; **a nautical ~** eine Seemeile; **to miss sth by a ~** etw meilenweit verfehlen ❷ (*fam: far from*) **to be ~s from the truth** weit von der Wahrheit entfernt sein; **to be a ~ off** meilenweit danebenliegen

mileage, milage ['maɪ·lɪdʒ] *n* ❶ (*gasoline efficiency*) Kraftstoffverbrauch *m;* **his car gets good ~** sein Auto verbraucht wenig Kraftstoff ❷ (*distance traveled*) Meilenstand *m*

'milepost *n* Meilenpfosten *m;* (*fig*) Meilenstein *m*

'milestone *n* (*a. fig*) Meilenstein *m*

militant ['mɪl·ɪ·tənt] **I.** *adj* militant **II.** *n* Kämpfer(in) *m(f);* POL militantes Mitglied

militarism ['mɪl·ɪ·tə·rɪz·əm] *n* Militarismus *m;* (*when overly aggressive*) Kriegstreiberei *f*

militaristic [ˌmɪl·ɪ·tə·'rɪs·tɪk] *adj* militaristisch

militarize ['mɪl·ɪ·tə·raɪz] *vt* militarisieren

military ['mɪl·ɪ·ter·i] *n pl* ■ **the ~** das Militär

'military academy *n* ❶ (*for cadets*) Militärakademie *f* ❷ (*for pupils*) *sehr strenge Privatschule*

military po'lice *npl* ■ **the ~** die Militärpolizei

military 'service *n* Wehrdienst *m*

militia [mɪ·'lɪʃ·ə] *n* Miliz *f*

milk [mɪlk] **I.** *n* Milch *f;* (*breast milk*) Muttermilch *f;* (*in coconuts*) Kokosmilch *f;* **whole ~** Vollmilch *f;* **skim ~** entrahmte Milch **II.** *vt* ❶ (*get milk*) *cow, goat* melken ❷ (*exploit*) melken, schröpfen *fam;* **to ~ sb for all he/she** [*or* **sth for all it**] **is worth** jdn/etw nach Strich und Faden ausnehmen, jdm/etw den letzten Pfennig aus der Tasche ziehen

milk 'chocolate *n* Milchschokolade *f*

'milkman *n* Milchmann *m*

'milk shake *n* Milchshake *m*

milky ['mɪl·ki] *adj* ❶ (*with milk*) mit Milch *nach n* ❷ (*not clear*) *glass, water* milchig; *skin* sanft

Milky 'Way *n* ■ **the ~** die Milchstraße

mill [mɪl] **I.** *n* ❶ (*building*) Mühle *f* ❷ (*machine*) Mühle *f* ❸ (*factory*) Fabrik *f;* **cotton ~** Baumwollspinnerei *f;* **steel ~** Stahlwerk *nt* **II.** *vt grain* mahlen; *metal* walzen

millennium <*pl* -s *or* -nia> [mɪ·'len·i·əm] *n* ❶ (*1000 years*) Jahrtausend *nt,* Millennium *nt geh* ❷ (*anniversary*) Jahrtausendfeier *f*

miller ['mɪl·ər] *n* Müller(in) *m(f)*

millet ['mɪl·ət] *n* Hirse *f*

millibar ['mɪl·ɪ·bar] *n* Millibar *nt*

milligram ['mɪl·ɪ·græm] *n* Milligramm *nt*

milliliter ['mɪl·ɪ·ˌli·t̬ər] *n* Milliliter *m*

millimeter ['mɪl·ɪ·ˌmi·t̬ər] *n* Millimeter *m*

million ['mɪl·jən] *n* ❶ (*1,000,000*) Million *f;* **a ~ dollars** eine Million Dollar; **eight ~** [**people**] acht Millionen [Menschen] ❷ (*fam: countless number*) **I've already heard that story a ~ times** diese Geschichte habe ich schon tausendmal gehört; **~s of people** Unmengen von Menschen; **~s and ~s of years ago** vor Millionen und Abermillionen von Jahren

millionaire [ˌmɪl·jə·'ner] *n* Millionär *m*

millipede ['mɪl·ɪ·pid] *n* Tausendfüßler *m*

'millstone *n* Mühlstein *m*

mime [maɪm] **I.** *n* ❶ (*technique*) Pantomime *f* ❷ THEAT (*actor*) Pantomime *m,* Pantomimin *f;* (*performance*) Pantomime *f; by ordinary person* Nachahmung *f* **II.** *vt* THEAT pantomimisch darstellen; (*mimic*) mimen

mimic ['mɪm·ɪk] **I.** *vt* <-ck-> ❶ (*imitate*) nachahmen; (*when teasing*) nachäffen *pej* ❷ (*be similar*) *plant, animal* nachahmen; *drug, disease* ähneln, gleichen **II.** *n* Imitator(in) *m(f)*

mimicry ['mɪm·ɪk·ri] *n* Nachahmung *f;* (*by plant, animal*) Mimikry *f fachspr*

min. I. *n* ❶ *abbrev of* **minimum** Min. ❷ *abbrev of* **minute** Min. **II.** *adj abbrev of* **minimum** min.

minaret [ˌmɪn·ə·'ret] *n* Minarett *nt*

mince [mɪns] *vt* FOOD *meat* hacken; (*in grinder*) durch den Fleischwolf drehen; *garlic, onions* klein schneiden ▶ PHRASES: **to not ~** [**one's**] **words** kein Blatt vor den Mund nehmen

'mincemeat *n süße Gebäckfüllung aus Dörrobst und Gewürze*

mincer ['mɪn·sər] *n* Fleischwolf *m*

mind [maɪnd] **I.** *n* ❶ (*brain, intellect*) Geist *m;* (*sanity a.*) Verstand *m;* **she's one of the greatest ~s of today** sie ist einer der größten Köpfe unserer Zeit; **to have a logical ~** logisch denken können; **to use one's ~** seinen Verstand gebrauchen; **to be out of one's ~** den Verstand verloren haben ❷ (*thoughts*) Gedanken *pl;* **the idea never entered my ~** auf diesen Gedanken wäre ich gar nicht gekommen; **what's on your ~?** woran denkst du?; **to bear sth in ~** etw nicht vergessen; **to have sb/sth in ~** an jdn/etw denken; **to have a lot of things on one's ~** viele Sorgen haben; **to take sb's ~ off sth** jdn auf andere Gedanken bringen ❸ (*intention*) **to know one's** [**own**] **~** wissen, was man will; **to make up one's ~** sich entscheiden; **to set one's ~ to sth** sich *dat* etw in den Kopf setzen ❹ *usu sing* (*opinion*) Meinung *f,* Ansicht *f;* **to give sb a piece of one's ~** jdm seine Meinung sagen; **to change one's ~** es sich *dat* anders überlegen ▶ PHRASES: **to be <u>bored</u> out of one's ~** sich zu Tode langweilen; **to be <u>out</u> of one's ~** (*crazy*) übergeschnappt sein **II.** *vt* ❶ (*be careful of, look after*) aufpassen (auf +*akk*) ❷ (*care about*) **don't ~ me** kümmere dich nicht um mich; **~ your own business!** kümmer dich um deine eigenen Angelegenheiten!; **I don't ~ the heat** die Hitze macht mir nichts aus ❸ (*fam: object*) **would you ~ holding this for me?** würden Sie das [kurz] für mich halten?; **do you ~ if I smoke?** stört es Sie, wenn ich rauche?; **I wouldn't ~ a cup of coffee** gegen eine Tasse Kaffee hätte ich nichts einzuwenden ▶ PHRASES: **~ <u>you</u>** allerdings **III.** *vi* ❶ (*care*) sich *dat* etwas daraus machen; **I don't ~** das ist mir egal; **never ~!** [ist doch] egal!; **never ~ her — what about you?** jetzt vergiss sie doch mal – was ist mit dir? ❷ (*object*) etwas dagegen haben; **do you ~ if I ...?** stört es Sie, wenn ich ...?; **if you don't ~ ...** wenn du nichts dagegen hast, ... ▶ PHRASES: **<u>never</u> ~ ...** geschweige denn ...

'mind-bending *adj* (*fam*) *puzzle* knifflig

'mind-blowing *adj* (*sl*) irre *fam*

'mind-boggling *adj* (*fam*) irrsinnig *fam,* verrückt

minded ['maɪn·dɪd] *adj pred* ❶ (*inclined*) **to be mathematically ~** eine mathematische Neigung haben ❷ (*enthusiastic*) begeistert; **romantically ~** romantisch veranlagt

mindful ['maɪnd·fəl] *adj pred* ❶ (*be concerned about*) **to be ~ of sb's feelings** jds Gefühle berücksichtigen ❷ (*have understanding*) **to be ~ of the problems** sich *dat* der Probleme bewusst sein

mindless ['maɪnd·lɪs] *adj* ❶ (*pointless*) sinnlos; *violence, jealousy* blind ❷ (*not intellectual*) *job, talk, work* geistlos; *entertainment* anspruchslos

'mind reader *n* Gedankenleser(in) *m(f)*

'mindset *n* Denkart *f*

mine[1] [maɪn] **I.** *n* ❶ (*excavation*) Bergwerk *nt;* (*fig: valuable source*) Fundgrube *f* ❷ MIL (*explosive*) Mine *f* **II.** *vt* ❶ (*obtain resources*) *coal, iron, diamonds* abbauen, fördern; *gold* schürfen ❷ (*plant mines*) **to ~ an area** ein Ge-

M

biet verminen **III.** *vi* **to ~ for gold** nach Gold graben
mine² [maɪn] *pron poss* (*belonging to me*) meine(r, s); **she's an old friend of ~** sie ist eine alte Freundin von mir
'mine detector *n* Minensuchgerät *nt*
'minefield *n* Minenfeld *nt;* (*fig*) gefährliches Terrain
miner ['maɪ·nər] *n* Bergarbeiter(in) *m(f)*
mineral ['mɪn·ər·əl] *n* ❶ (*inorganic substance, in nutrition*) Mineral *nt* ❷ (*when obtained by mining*) [Gruben]erz *nt,* Mineral *nt*
'mineral deposits *npl* Erzlagerstätten *pl*
mineralogist [ˌmɪn·ə·'ral·ə·dʒɪst] *n* Mineraloge *m,* Mineralogin *f*
'mineral water *n* Mineralwasser *nt;* (*carbonated*) Sprudel *m*
'minesweeper *n* NAUT Minenräumer *m*
mingle ['mɪŋ·gəl] **I.** *vt usu passive* mischen; **the excitement of starting a new job is always ~ed with a certain amount of fear** Die Aufregung beim Beginn in einem neuen Job ist immer mit einer gewissen Portion Angst vermischt **II.** *vi* ❶ (*socialize*) sich untereinander vermischen; **to ~ with the guests** sich unter die Gäste mischen ❷ (*mix*) sich vermischen
mini- ['mɪni] *in compounds* Mini-
miniature ['mɪn·i·ə·tʃər] **I.** *adj attr* Miniatur- *f* **II.** *n* Miniatur *f*
'minibus *n* Kleinbus *m*
minimal ['mɪn·ɪ·məl] *adj* minimal, Mindest-; **with ~ effort** mit möglichst wenig Anstrengung
minimize ['mɪn·ɪ·maɪz] *vt* ❶ (*reduce*) auf ein Minimum beschränken, minimieren ❷ (*underestimate*) schlechtmachen; *feelings, concerns* herunterspielen
minimum ['mɪn·ɪ·məm] **I.** *n* <*pl* -s *or* -ima> Minimum *nt;* **to keep sth to a ~** etw so niedrig wie möglich halten **II.** *adj* ❶ (*lowest possible*) Mindest-; **~ requirements** Mindestanforderungen *pl* ❷ (*very low*) Minimal-, minimal
minimum-security 'prison *n* offenes Gefängnis
minimum 'wage *n* Mindestlohn *m*
mining ['maɪ·nɪŋ] **I.** *n* Bergbau *m* **II.** *adj attr* Bergbau-, Bergwerks-
'mining engineer *n* Bergbauingenieur(in) *m(f)*
minion ['mɪn·jən] *n* (*pej*) Speichellecker(in) *m(f)*
'miniskirt *n* Minirock *m*
minister ['mɪn·ɪ·stər] **I.** *n* ❶ (*protestant priest*) Pfarrer(in) *m(f)* ❷ (*in government*) Minister(in) *m(f)* **II.** *vi* (*be of service*) zu Diensten sein (**to** +*dat*)
ministerial [ˌmɪn·ɪ·'stɪr·i·əl] *adj* Minister-, ministeriell
ministry ['mɪn·ɪ·stri] *n* ❶ (*priesthood*) ■**the ~** der geistliche Stand ❷ (*in government*) Ministerium *nt*
'minivan *n* Minivan *m*
mink [mɪŋk] *n* <*pl* - *or* -s> ❶ (*animal*) Nerz *m* ❷ (*fur*) Nerz *m;* (*coat*) Nerz[mantel] *m*
Minn. *abbrev of* **Minnesota**
Minnesota [ˌmɪn·ɪ·'soʊ·t̬ə] *n* Minnesota *nt*
minor ['maɪ·nər] **I.** *adj* ❶ (*small, not serious*) *detail, criticism* nebensächlich; *character, plot* unbedeutend; *crime, violation* geringfügig; *improvement, repair* unwichtig; *accident, incident, illness* leicht; *interest, hobby, operation* klein ❷ (*low-ranking*) *official, politician* untergeordnet **II.** *n* ❶ (*underage person*) Minderjährige(r) *f(m)* ❷ MUS Moll *nt;* **D ~** d-Moll
minority [maɪ·'nɔr·ɪ·t̬i] *n* Minderheit *f;* **in a ~ of cases** in wenigen Fällen; **to be in the ~** in der Minderheit sein
minstrel ['mɪn·strəl] *n* (*hist: entertainer*) Spielmann *m;* (*singer*) Minnesänger *m*
mint¹ [mɪnt] **I.** *n* ❶ (*coin factory*) Münzanstalt *f,* Prägeanstalt *f* ❷ (*fam: lots of money*) **to make a ~** einen Haufen Geld machen *fam* **II.** *vt money* prägen; *gold, silver* münzen **III.** *adj attr coin* neu geprägt; (*fig*) nagelneu *fam;* **in ~ condition** in tadellosem Zustand
mint² [mɪnt] *n* ❶ (*herb*) Minze *f* ❷ (*candy*) Pfefferminz[bonbon] *nt*
minuet [ˌmɪn·ju·'et] *n* Menuett *nt*
minus ['maɪ·nəs] **I.** *prep* MATH minus; **what is 57 ~ 39?** was ist 57 minus 39? **II.** *n* <*pl* -es> ❶ (*minus sign*) Minus[zeichen] *nt* ❷ (*disadvantage*) Minus *nt* **III.** *adj attr* ❶ (*disadvantage*) **~ point** Minuspunkt *m* ❷ (*number*) minus; **~ ten [degrees] Fahrenheit** minus zehn Grad Fahrenheit
minuscule ['mɪn·ə·skjul] *adj* winzig
minute¹ ['mɪn·ɪt] **I.** *n* ❶ (*sixty seconds*) Minute *f* ❷ (*short time*) Moment *m,* Minute *f;* **[wait] just a ~!** (*for delay*) einen Moment noch!; (*in disbelief*) Moment mal! ❸ (*specific point in time*) Minute *f;* **to do sth at the last ~** etw in letzter Minute tun; **this ~** sofort **II.** *adj attr* **~ hand** Minutenzeiger *m;* **~ steak** Minutensteak *nt*
minute² [maɪ·'nut] *adj* ❶ (*small*) winzig; **in ~ detail** bis ins kleinste Detail ❷ (*meticulous*) minuziös
minutely [maɪ·'nut·li] *adv* minuziös, bis ins kleinste Detail
miracle ['mɪr·ə·kəl] *n* Wunder *nt a. fig;* **don't expect me to work ~s** erwarte keine Wunder von mir
miraculous [mɪ·'ræk·jə·ləs] *adj* wunderbar; **to make a ~ recovery** wie durch ein Wunder genesen
mirage [mə·'raʒ] *n* Fata Morgana *f;* (*fig*) Trugbild *nt,* Illusion *f*
mire [maɪr] *n* ❶ (*a. fig: swamp*) Sumpf *m* ❷ (*deep mud*) Morast *m,* Schlamm *m*
mirror ['mɪr·ər] **I.** *n* ❶ (*looking glass*) Spiegel *m* ❷ (*reflection*) Spiegelbild *nt* **II.** *vt* widerspiegeln
mirror 'image *n* Spiegelbild *nt*
mirth [mɜrθ] *n* (*merriment*) Fröhlichkeit *f;* (*laughter*) Heiterkeit *f*
misadventure [ˌmɪs·əd·'ven·tʃər] *n* (*form,*

M

liter: unlucky event) Missgeschick *nt*
misapprehension [ˌmɪs·æprɪ·ˈhen·ʃən] *n* Missverständnis *nt*
misappropriate [ˌmɪs·ə·ˈproʊ·pri·eɪt] *vt funds* veruntreuen
misappropriation [ˌmɪs·ə·ˌproʊ·prɪ·ˈeɪ·ʃən] *n of money* Unterschlagung *f*, Veruntreuung *f*
misbehave [ˌmɪs·bɪ·ˈheɪv] *vi* (*behave badly*) *adult* sich schlecht benehmen; *child* ungezogen sein; (*malfunction*) *machine* nicht richtig funktionieren
misbehavior [ˌmɪs·bɪ·ˈheɪv·jər] *n by adult* schlechtes Benehmen; *by child* Ungezogenheit *f*
misc. *adj short for* **miscellaneous** verschiedene(r, s)
miscalculate [ˌmɪs·ˈkæl·kjə·leɪt] *vt* ❶ MATH falsch berechnen ❷ (*misjudge*) falsch einschätzen
miscalculation [ˌmɪs·ˌkæl·kjə·ˈleɪ·ʃən] *n* ❶ MATH Fehlkalkulation *f* ❷ (*in planning*) Fehleinschätzung *m*
miscarriage [ˈmɪs·ˌkær·ɪdʒ] *n* ❶ MED Fehlgeburt *f* ❷ LAW ~ **of justice** Justizirrtum *m*
miscarry <-ie-> [ˈmɪs·ˌkær·i] *vi* (*in pregnancy*) eine Fehlgeburt haben
miscellaneous [ˌmɪs·ə·ˈleɪ·ni·əs] *adj* verschiedene(r, s), diverse(r, s); *collection, crowd* bunt; *short stories, poems* vermischt, verschiedenerlei
miscellany [ˈmɪs·ə·leɪ·ni] *n* (*mixture*) Auswahl *f*, [An]sammlung *f* (**of** von +*dat*)
mischief [ˈmɪs·tʃɪf] *n* Unfug *m*; **to be full of ~** nur Unfug im Kopf haben; **to keep sb out of ~** jdn davon abhalten, Dummheiten zu machen; **to mean ~** Unfrieden stiften wollen
mischievous [ˈmɪs·tʃə·vəs] *adj* ❶ (*naughty*) immer zu Streichen aufgelegt; **~ child** Schlingel *m* ❷ (*malicious*) boshaft; *rumors* bösartig
misconceived [ˌmɪs·kən·ˈsivd] *adj* ❶ (*misunderstood*) falsch verstanden ❷ (*ill-judged*) falsch eingeschätzt, missdeutet
misconception [ˌmɪs·kən·ˈsep·ʃən] *n* falsche Vorstellung (**about** von +*dat*), Irrglaube *m*
misconduct [ˌmɪs·ˈkan·dʌkt] *n* (*bad behavior*) schlechtes Benehmen; MIL schlechte Führung; **professional ~** standeswidriges Verhalten; **sexual ~** sexuelle Verfehlung
misconstrue [ˌmɪs·kən·ˈstru] *vt* missdeuten, missverstehen, falsch auslegen; **to ~ sth as sth** etw fälschlicherweise als etw auslegen
misdeed [ˌmɪs·ˈdid] *n* (*form*) Untat *f*
misdemeanor [ˌmɪs·dɪ·ˈmi·nər] *n* ❶ (*minor bad action*) [leichtes] Vergehen, [leichter] Verstoß, [geringfügige] Verfehlung ❷ LAW geringfügiges Vergehen, Bagatelldelikt *nt*
misdirect [ˌmɪs·dɪ·ˈrekt] *vt* ❶ (*send in wrong direction*) in die falsche Richtung schicken; *letter* falsch adressieren; *luggage, shipment* fehlleiten ❷ (*aim wrongly*) *hockey puck* in die falsche Richtung lenken
miser [ˈmaɪ·zər] *n* Geizhals *m*, Geizkragen *m*
miserable [ˈmɪz·rə·bəl] *adj* ❶ (*unhappy*) unglücklich, elend; **to make life ~** [**for sb**] [jdm] das Leben unerträglich machen ❷ *attr* (*bad-tempered*) griesgrämig; (*repulsive*) unausstehlich; (*fam: as insult*) mies, Mist- ❸ *attr* (*wretched*) erbärmlich, jämmerlich; **a ~ failure** ein kompletter Misserfolg
miserably [ˈmɪz·ər·ə·bli] *adv* ❶ (*unhappily*) traurig, niedergeschlagen ❷ (*extremely*) schrecklich, furchtbar ❸ (*utterly*) jämmerlich, kläglich
miserliness [ˈmaɪ·zər·li·nɪs] *n* Geiz *m*, Knaus[e]rigkeit *f pej fam*, Kleinlichkeit *f*
miserly [ˈmaɪ·zər·li] *adj* geizig, knaus[e]rig, kleinlich
misery [ˈmɪz·ə·ri] *n* ❶ (*suffering*) Elend *nt*, Not *f* ❷ (*unhappiness*) Jammer *m* ▶ PHRASES: **to make sb's life a ~** jdm das Leben zur Qual [*o* Hölle] machen
misfire I. *vi* [mɪs·ˈfaɪr] *engine* eine Fehlzündung haben; *gun* versagen **II.** *n* [ˈmɪs·faɪr] (*of engine*) Fehlzündung *f*, Aussetzer *m fam;* (*of gun*) Versager *m*
misfit [ˈmɪs·fɪt] *n* Außenseiter(in) *m(f)*, Eigenbrötler(in) *m(f)*
misfortune [ˌmɪs·ˈfɔr·tʃən] *n* ❶ (*bad luck*) Pech *nt*, Unglück *nt* ❷ (*mishap*) Missgeschick *nt kein pl*
misgiving [ˌmɪs·ˈgɪv·ɪŋ] *n* ❶ (*doubt*) Befürchtung *f*, Bedenken *nt meist pl* (**about** wegen +*gen*) ❷ ungutes Gefühl; **to be filled with ~** böse Ahnungen haben
misguided [mɪs·ˈgaɪ·dɪd] *adj attempt, measures* unsinnig; *effort, policy* verfehlt; *enthusiasm, idealism* falsch, unangebracht; *people* fehlgeleitet, irregeleitet; **to be ~ in sth** mit etw *dat* falschliegen
mishandle [ˌmɪs·ˈhæn·dəl] *vt* (*mismanage*) falsch behandeln; *business* schlecht führen; *investigation* [grobe] Fehler machen (bei +*dat*); *situation* falsch umgehen (mit +*dat*)
mishap [ˈmɪs·hæp] *n* Unfall *m*, Panne *f*
mishear [ˌmɪs·ˈhɪr] **I.** *vt* <-heard, -heard> falsch hören **II.** *vi* <-heard, -heard> sich verhören
mishmash [ˈmɪʃ·mæʃ] *n* Mischmasch *m fam*, Durcheinander *nt* (**of** von +*dat*)
misinform [ˌmɪs·ɪn·ˈfɔrm] *vt* falsch informieren
misinterpret [ˌmɪs·ɪn·ˈtɜr·prɪt] *vt* missverstehen; *evidence, statement, text* falsch interpretieren; *gesture, remark* falsch deuten
misinterpretation [ˌmɪs·ɪn·tɜr·prɪ·ˈteɪ·ʃən] *n* Missverständnis *nt*, Fehlinterpretation *f*
misjudge [ˌmɪs·ˈdʒʌdʒ] *vt prospects, situation* falsch einschätzen [*o* beurteilen]; *amount, distance* falsch schätzen
misjudgment [mɪs·ˈdʒʌdʒ·mənt] *n* ❶ (*wrong assessment*) falsche Einschätzung [*o* Beurteilung]; *of damage, size, sum* falsche Schätzung ❷ (*wrong decision*) Fehlentscheidung *f*, Fehlurteil *nt*
mislay <-laid, -laid> [ˌmɪs·ˈleɪ] *vt* verlegen
mislead <-led, -led> [ˌmɪs·ˈlid] *vt* ❶ (*deceive*)

M

täuschen, irreführen ❷ (*lead astray*) verführen, verleiten
misleading [mɪs·ˈli·dɪŋ] *adj* irreführend
mismanage [ˌmɪs·ˈmæn·ɪdʒ] *vt* falsch umgehen (mit +*dat*); *business* schlecht führen; *estate, finances* schlecht verwalten
mismanagement [ˌmɪs·ˈmæn·ɪdʒ·mənt] *n* schlechte Verwaltung [*o* Führung]; ~ **of the economy** schlechte Wirtschaftspolitik
misnomer [ˌmɪs·ˈnoʊ·mər] *n* ❶ (*wrong name*) falscher Name ❷ (*inappropriate name*) unzutreffender Name, unzutreffende Bezeichnung
misogynist [mɪ·ˈsadʒ·ə·nɪst] **I.** *n* Frauenfeind *m* **II.** *adj* frauenfeindlich
misogynistic [mɪ·ˌsadʒ·ə·ˈnɪstɪk] *adj* frauenfeindlich
misplace [ˌmɪs·ˈpleɪs] *vt* verlegen
misprint [ˈmɪs·ˌprɪnt] *n* Druckfehler *m*
mispronounce [ˌmɪs·prə·ˈnaʊns] *vt* falsch aussprechen
mispronunciation [ˌmɪs·prə·ˌnʌn·sɪ·ˈeɪ·ʃən] *n* ❶ (*incorrectness*) falsche Aussprache ❷ (*mistake*) Aussprachefehler *m*
misread <-read, -read> [ˌmɪs·ˈrid] *vt* ❶ (*read incorrectly*) *word, text* falsch lesen ❷ (*misinterpret*) *instructions, signal* falsch verstehen, missverstehen
misrepresent [ˌmɪs·ˌrep·rɪ·ˈzent] *vt* falsch darstellen; ■**to ~ sb as sb/sth** jdn fälschlicherweise als jd/etw hinstellen; **to ~ facts** Tatsachen entstellen; LAW falsche Tatsachen vorspiegeln
misrepresentation [ˌmɪs·ˌrep·rɪ·zen·ˈteɪ·ʃən] *n* ❶ (*false account*) falsche Darstellung; LAW falsche Angabe; **a ~ of facts** LAW eine Vorspiegelung falscher Tatsachen ❷ (*false representation*) falsche Wiedergabe
miss¹ [mɪs] **I.** *n* <*pl* -es> (*failure*) Fehlschlag *m*, Misserfolg *m*; SPORTS (*in basketball*) Fehlwurf *m*; (*in soccer, hockey*) Fehlschuss *m* **II.** *vi* nicht treffen; *projectile a.* danebengehen; *person, weapon a.* danebenschießen **III.** *vt* ❶ (*not hit*) verfehlen, nicht treffen ❷ (*not meet*) *bus, train* verpassen; *deadline* nicht [ein]halten ❸ (*be absent*) versäumen, verpassen; **to ~ school** in der Schule fehlen ❹ (*not use*) *opportunity* verpassen; **his new film is too good to ~** seinen neuen Film darf man sich einfach nicht entgehen lassen ❺ (*not see*) übersehen ❻ (*not hear*) nicht mitbekommen; (*deliberately*) überhören ❼ (*not notice*) nicht bemerken; (*deliberately*) übersehen; **Susan doesn't ~ much** Susan entgeht einfach nichts ❽ (*notice loss, long for*) vermissen
◆**miss out** *vi* zu kurz kommen; **you really ~ed out** da ist dir echt was entgangen *fam*; ■**to ~ out on sth** *chance, opportunity* sich *dat* etw entgehen lassen, etw *akk* verpassen
miss² [mɪs] *n* ■**M~** Fräulein *nt*; **M~ America** Miss Amerika
Miss. *abbrev of* **Mississippi**
misshapen [ˌmɪs·ˈʃeɪ·pən] *adj* (*out of shape*) unförmig
missile [ˈmɪs·əl] *n* MIL (*fired object*) [Raketen]geschoss *nt*, Projektil *nt*, Flugkörper *m*, Rakete *f*
ˈ**missile base** *n* Raketenstützpunkt *m*
ˈ**missile launcher** *n* [Raketen]abschussrampe *f*; (*vehicle*) Raketenwerfer *m*
missing [ˈmɪs·ɪŋ] *adj* ❶ (*disappeared*) *thing* verschwunden; *person* vermisst; (*not there*) fehlend; **when did you notice that the money was ~ from your account?** wann haben Sie bemerkt, dass das Geld nicht mehr auf Ihrem Konto war?; **to report sb/sth ~** jdn/etw als vermisst melden ❷ MIL (*absent*) verschollen; **~ in action** [nach Kampfeinsatz] vermisst
missing ˈ**link** *n* ❶ (*in evolution*) unbekannte Zwischenstufe; (*in investigation*) fehlendes Beweisstück ❷ (*connector*) Bindeglied *nt* (**between** zwischen +*dat*)
missing ˈ**person** *n* Vermisste(r) *f(m)*
mission [ˈmɪʃ·ən] *n* ❶ (*task*) Einsatz *m*, Mission *f* ❷ (*goal*) Ziel *nt* ❸ (*group sent*) Delegation *f*
missionary [ˈmɪʃ·ə·ner·i] *n* Missionar(in) *m(f)*
mission conˈ**trol** *n* Bodenkontrolle *f*
Mississippi [mɪs·ɪ·ˈsɪ·pi] *n* Mississippi *nt*

> Der **Mississippi River** (Mississippi) ist der drittlängste Wasserweg der Welt nach dem Amazonas und dem Nil. Von der Quelle im Itascasee/Minnesota bis zur Mündung in den Golf von Mexiko bei New Orleans/Louisiana, legt er 2.350 Meilen (3.781 km) zurück. Er fließt von Nord nach Süd über 1.245.000 Quadratmeilen (3.225.000 km²) Land und durchquert zehn Staaten bis er ins Mississippidelta mündet.

Missouri [mɪ·ˈzʊr·i] *n* Missouri *nt*
misspell <-spelled *or* -spelt, -spelled> [ˌmɪs·ˈspel] *vt* (*spell wrongly*) falsch buchstabieren
misspelling [mɪsˈspel·ɪŋ] *n* ❶ (*spelling mistake*) Rechtschreibfehler *m* ❷ (*wrong spelling*) falsches Buchstabieren
misspent [ˌmɪs·ˈspent] *adj* verschwendet, vergeudet
mist [mɪst] **I.** *n* ❶ (*light fog*) [leichter] Nebel, Dunst *m* ❷ (*condensation*) Beschlag *m*; (*vapor*) Hauch *m* ❸ (*blur*) Schleier *m* **II.** *vi* *eyes* feucht werden; *vision* sich trüben
mistake [mɪ·ˈsteɪk] **I.** *n* Fehler *m*, Irrtum *m*, Versehen *nt*; **there must be some ~** da kann etwas nicht stimmen; **spelling ~** Rechtschreibfehler *m*; **by ~** aus Versehen, versehentlich; **my ~** meine Schuld **II.** *vt* <-took, -taken> falsch verstehen; **there's no mistaking a painting by Picasso** ein Gemälde von Picasso ist unverwechselbar
mistaken [mɪ·ˈsteɪ·kən] **I.** *pp of* **mistake** **II.** *adj* *announcement* irrtümlich; *idea* falsch;

M

~ **identity** Personenverwechslung *f;* ■ **to be ~** sich irren (**about** in +*dat*); **to be very much ~** sich sehr täuschen; **unless I'm very much ~ ...** wenn mich nicht alles täuscht ...
Mister ['mɪs·tər] *n* ① (*Mr.*) Herr *m* ② (*a. iron fam: form of address*) Chef *m;* **hey, ~!** he, Sie da! *fam*
mistime [ˌmɪs·'taɪm] *vt* zeitlich falsch berechnen; SPORTS schlecht timen *fam*
mistletoe ['mɪs·əl·toʊ] *n* Mistel *f*
mistook [mɪ·'stʊk] *pt of* **mistake**
mistranslate [ˌmɪs·'træn·zleɪt] *vt* falsch übersetzen
mistreat [ˌmɪs·'trit] *vt* misshandeln
mistress <*pl* -es> ['mɪs·trɪs] *n* ① (*sexual partner*) Geliebte *f* ② (*animal owner*) Frauchen *nt*
mistrial ['mɪs·ˌtraɪ·əl] *n* ① (*misconducted trial*) fehlerhaftes Gerichtsverfahren ② (*inconclusive trial*) Gerichtsverfahren *nt* ohne Urteilsspruch
mistrust [ˌmɪs·'trʌst] **I.** *n* Misstrauen *nt* **II.** *vt* misstrauen
mistrustful [ˌmɪs·'trʌst·fəl] *adj* misstrauisch (**of** gegenüber +*dat*)
misty ['mɪs·ti] *adj* ① (*slightly foggy*) [leicht] neblig, dunstig ② (*blurred*) undeutlich, verschwommen; *eyes* verschleiert
misunderstand <-stood, -stood> [ˌmɪs·ˌʌn·dər·'stænd] **I.** *vt* missverstehen **II.** *vi* sich irren
misunderstanding [ˌmɪs·ʌn·dər·'stæn·dɪŋ] *n* ① (*misinterpretation*) Missverständnis *nt* ② (*quarrel*) Meinungsverschiedenheit *f*
misuse **I.** *n* [ˌmɪs·'jus] (*wrong use*) *of funds, position* Missbrauch *m,* falscher Gebrauch [*o* Umgang]; *of machinery* falsche Bedienung **II.** *vt* [ˌmɪs·'juz] ① (*use wrongly*) *funds, position* missbrauchen, falsch gebrauchen ② (*handle wrongly*) *machinery* falsch bedienen
mite [maɪt] *n* Milbe *f*
mitigate ['mɪt̬·ɪ·geɪt] *vt* (*form*) *misery, pain* lindern; *anger, sentence* mildern; ECON *loss* mindern
mitigation [ˌmɪt̬·ɪ·'geɪ·ʃən] *n* Linderung *f,* Milderung *f*
mitten ['mɪt·ən] *n* Fäustling *m*
mix [mɪks] **I.** *n* ① (*combination*) Mischung *f;* **a ~ of people** eine bunt gemischte Gruppe ② (*premixed ingredients*) Fertigmischung *f;* **sauce ~** Fertigsauce *f* **II.** *vi* ① (*combine*) sich mischen [lassen]; (*go together*) zusammenpassen ② (*make contact with people*) unter Leute gehen; *host* sich unter die Gäste mischen **III.** *vt* ① (*blend ingredients*) [miteinander] [ver]mischen; *dough* anrühren; *drinks* mixen; *ingredients* miteinander verrühren; *paint* mischen ② (*combine*) **to ~ love with toughness** Liebe und Strenge miteinander verbinden ③ *sound tracks* mischen
◆**mix in** **I.** *vi* sich einfügen **II.** *vt* untermischen
◆**mix up** *vt* ① (*mistake for another*) verwechseln ② (*bewilder, put in wrong order*) durcheinanderbringen ③ (*combine ingredients*) vermischen; *dough* anrühren ④ *usu passive* (*be involved with*) ■ **to be/get ~ed up in sth** in etw *akk* verwickelt sein/werden
mixed [mɪkst] *adj* (*positive and negative*) gemischt, unterschiedlich; **~ blessing** kein reiner Segen
mixed 'doubles *npl* SPORTS gemischtes Doppel
mixed e'conomy *n* gemischte Wirtschaftsform
mixer ['mɪk·sər] *n* ① (*machine*) Mixer *m,* Mixgerät *nt* ② (*drink*) ~ [**drink**] Mixgetränk *nt*
mixture ['mɪks·tʃər] *n* ① (*combination*) Mischung *f; of ingredients* Gemisch *nt* ② (*mixed fluid substance*) Mischung *f,* Mixtur *f;* AUTO Gemisch *nt* ③ (*act of mixing*) Mischen *nt,* Vermengen *nt;* (*state after mixing*) Gemisch *nt,* Gemenge *nt*
'mix-up *n* (*confused state*) Durcheinander *nt,* Verwirrung *f;* **there seems to have been a slight ~ with your reservation** mit Ihrer Reservierung muss einiges durcheinandergegangen sein
ml <*pl* - *or* mls> *n abbrev of* **milliliter** ml
MLB [ˌem·el·'bi] *n* SPORTS *abbrev of* **Major League Baseball** MLB *f*
mm *n abbrev of* **millimeter** mm
MN *abbrev of* **Minnesota**
mnemonic [nɪ·'man·ɪk] *n* Gädachtnisstütze *f,* Eselsbrücke *f fam*
MO [ˌem·'oʊ] *n* ① *abbrev of* **Missouri** ② *abbrev of* **modus operandi** ③ *abbrev of* **Medical Officer** Stabsarzt *m,* Stabsärztin *f* ④ *abbrev of* **money order**
mo. [moʊ] *n abbrev of* **month**
moan [moʊn] **I.** *n* (*groan*) Stöhnen *nt; of the wind* Heulen **II.** *vi* ① (*groan*) stöhnen; *wind* heulen ② (*complain*) klagen, sich beschweren (**at** bei +*dat*), jammern, quengeln (**about** über +*akk*)
moat [moʊt] *n* Burggraben *m*
mob [mab] **I.** *n* ① (*usu pej: crowd*) Mob *m;* **angry ~** aufgebrachte Menge; **a ~ of protesters** eine protestierende Menschenmenge ② POL (*pej: the common people*) ■ **the ~** die breite Masse; (*the lowest classes*) der Mob, der Pöbel ③ (*criminal gang*) Verbrecherbande *f,* Gang *f;* ■ **the M~** die Mafia **II.** *vt* <-bb-> ① (*surround*) umringen ② (*crowd around*) ■ **to ~ sth** *courtroom, entrance* etw umlagern; (*crowd into*) *fairground, park* in etw *akk* strömen
mobile ['moʊ·bəl] **I.** *adj* ① (*able to move*) beweglich ② (*flexible*) beweglich, wendig ③ (*changeable*) lebhaft, wechselhaft ④ (*in a vehicle*) mobil, fahrbar; ■ **to be ~** motorisiert sein **II.** *n* (*ceiling decoration*) Mobile *nt*
mobile 'home *n* [großer] Wohnwagen *m,* Trailer *m*
mobility [moʊ·'bɪl·ɪ·t̬i] *n* ① (*ability to move*) *of the body* Beweglichkeit *f,* Mobilität *f* ② (*social mobility*) Mobilität *f*
mobilization [ˌmoʊ·bə·lɪ·'zeɪ·ʃən] *n* ① (*for war*) Mobilmachung *f,* Mobilisierung *f* ② (*or-*

ganization) Mobilisierung *f*, Aktivierung *f*
mobilize ['moʊ·bə·laɪz] **I.** *vt* ❶ (*prepare for war*) *army* mobilisieren ❷ (*organize*) *supporters, support* aktivieren, mobilisieren ❸ (*put to use*) einsetzen; *helicopters, snowplows* zum Einsatz bringen **II.** *vi* MIL mobil machen
mob 'rule *n* Herrschaft *f* der Straße
mobster ['mab·stər] *n* (*fam*) Gangster *m*
moccasin ['mak·ə·sɪn] *n* Mokassin *m*
mocha ['moʊ·kə] *n* Mokka *m*
mock [mak] **I.** *adj* ❶ (*not real*) nachgemacht, Schein-; *fear, horror, sympathy* gespielt ❷ (*practice*) Probe-, simuliert **II.** *vi* spotten, höhnen **III.** *vt* (*ridicule*) lächerlich machen, verspotten
mockery ['mak·ə·ri] *n* ❶ (*ridicule*) Spott *m*, Hohn *m* ❷ (*travesty*) Farce *f* ▶ PHRASES: **to make a ~ of sb/sth** jdn/etw zum Gespött machen
mocking ['mak·ɪŋ] *adj laugh, laughter* spöttisch, höhnisch
'mockingbird *n* ORN Spottdrossel *f*
'mock-up *n* Attrappe *f*
mode [moʊd] *n* ❶ (*way*) Weise *f*, Methode *f*; **~ of operation** Betriebsart *f* ❷ MATH häufigster Wert ❸ COMPUT, TECH (*operation*) Betriebsart *f*, Modus *m*
model ['mad·əl] **I.** *n* ❶ (*representation*) Modell *nt*; COMPUT [schematische] Darstellung, Nachbildung *f*, Simulation *f* ❷ (*example*) Modell *nt*, Vorbild *nt* ❸ (*perfect example*) Muster *nt* ❹ *fashion* Model *nt* ❺ (*version, for painter*) Modell *nt* **II.** *vt* <-ll-> ❶ (*make figure*) modellieren ❷ (*on computer*) [schematisch] darstellen, nachbilden, simulieren ❸ (*show clothes*) vorführen
modem ['moʊ·dəm] *n* Modem *nt*
moderate I. *adj* ['mad·ər·ət] ❶ (*neither large nor small*) *amount, quantity, size* mittlere(r, s); *improvement, increase* leicht, nicht allzu groß; *prices, speed* angemessen, normal; *income* durchschnittlich ❷ (*not excessive*) mäßig, gemäßigt; *drinker, eater* mäßig, maßvoll; LAW *sentence* mild **II.** *n* ['mad·ər·ət] POL Gemäßigte(r) *f(m)* **III.** *vt* ['mad·ər·eɪt] ❶ (*make less extreme*) mäßigen; *voice* senken ❷ (*preside over*) den Vorsitz führen **IV.** *vi* ❶ (*abate*) lindern ❷ (*act as moderator*) moderieren
moderation [ˌmad·ə·'reɪ·ʃən] *n* ❶ (*restraint*) Mäßigung *f*; **in ~** in Maßen ❷ (*making moderate*) *demands* Abschwächung *f*; *sentence* Milderung *f*.
moderator ['mad·ə·reɪ·t̬ər] *n* ❶ (*mediator*) Vermittler(in) *m(f)* ❷ (*of discussion*) Moderator(in) *m(f)*
modern ['mad·ərn] *adj* ❶ (*contemporary*) modern ❷ (*not ancient or medieval*) modern, neuzeitlich; **~ Europe** Europa *nt* der Neuzeit; **the ~ world** die heutige Welt
modernize ['mad·ər·naɪz] **I.** *vt* modernisieren **II.** *vi* modern werden
modest ['mad·ɪst] *adj* ❶ (*not boastful*) bescheiden, zurückhaltend ❷ (*fairly small*) *income, increase* bescheiden, mäßig ❸ (*not elaborate*) *furniture, house* einfach
modesty ['mad·ɪ·sti] *n* ❶ (*without boastfulness*) Bescheidenheit *f*, Zurückhaltung *f* ❷ (*chasteness*) Anstand *m*, Sittsamkeit *f*
modicum ['mad·ɪ·kəm] *n* ■**a ~** ein bisschen [*o* wenig]
modification [ˌmad·ɪ·fɪ·'keɪ·ʃən] *n* ❶ (*change*) Modifikation *f*, [Ab]änderung *f* ❷ (*alteration*) *of engine* Modifikation *f*
modifier ['mad·ɪ·faɪ·ər] *n* LING näher bestimmendes Wort; (*as an adjective*) Beiwort *nt*; (*as an adverb*) Umstandswort *nt*
modify <-ie-> ['mad·ɪ·faɪ] *vt* ❶ (*change*) [ver]ändern ❷ (*alter*) *engine* modifizieren
modular ['madʒ·ə·lər] *adj* modular, Baukasten-
modulate ['madʒ·ə·leɪt] *vt* ❶ (*regulate*) anpassen, abstimmen ❷ (*adjust pitch*) *tone, voice* modulieren ❸ (*soften*) *noise, voice* dämpfen; *effect, impression* abschwächen
modulation [ˌmadʒ·ə·'leɪ·ʃən] *n* ❶ (*adaptation*) Anpassung *f*, Abstimmung *f* ❷ ELEC, RADIO Modulation *f*, Aussteuerung *f*
module ['madʒ·ul] *n* ❶ (*unit*) Modul *nt*, Baustein *m* ❷ AEROSP **space ~** Raumschiffmodul *nt*
mohair ['moʊ·her] *n* Mohair *m*
moist [mɔɪst] *adj* feucht; *cake* saftig
moisten ['mɔɪ·sən] *vt* anfeuchten
moisture ['mɔɪs·tʃər] *n* Feuchtigkeit *f*
moisturize ['mɔɪs·tʃə·raɪz] *vt* befeuchten; **to ~ one's skin** seine Haut mit Feuchtigkeitscreme einreiben
moisturizer ['mɔɪs·tʃə·raɪ·zər] *n* Feuchtigkeitscreme *f*
molar ['moʊ·lər] *n* ❶ ANAT Backenzahn *m* ❷ ZOOL Mahlzahn *m*
molasses [moʊ·'læs·ɪz] *n* Melasse *f*
mold¹ [moʊld] **I.** *n* ❶ (*shape*) Form *f* ❷ (*fig*) Typ *m*; **to be cast in the same ~** aus dem gleichen Holz geschnitzt sein; **to break the ~ [of sth]** neue Wege in etw *dat* gehen **II.** *vt* formen; ■**to ~ sb into sth** jdn zu etw *dat* machen
mold² [moʊld] *n* BOT Schimmel *m*
molding ['moʊl·dɪŋ] *n* ARCHIT Fries *m*; (*stucco*) Stuck *m kein pl*; ART [Zier]leiste *f*
moldy ['moʊl·di] *adj food* schimmelig, verschimmelt; ■**to get ~** [ver]schimmeln
mole¹ [moʊl] *n* ANAT [kleines] Muttermal
mole² [moʊl] *n* ZOOL Maulwurf *m*
molecular [mə·'lek·jə·lər] *adj* molekular, Molekular-
molecule ['mal·ɪ·kjul] *n* Molekül *nt*
molehill ['moʊl·hɪl] *n* Maulwurfshügel *m*
molest [mə·'lest] *vt* ❶ (*annoy*) belästigen ❷ (*attack sexually*) [sexuell] belästigen; ■**to ~ sb** jdn sexuell missbrauchen
mollify <-ie-> ['mal·ə·faɪ] *vt* ❶ (*pacify*) besänftigen, beschwichtigen ❷ (*reduce*) *demands* mäßigen; *anger* mildern
mollusk, mollusc ['mal·əsk] *n* Molluske *f*, Weichtier *nt*
Molotov cocktail [ˌmal·ə·tɔf·'kak·teɪl] *n* Molo-

M

towcocktail *m*

molt [moʊlt] *vi birds* [sich] mausern; *cats, dogs* haaren; *snakes, insects, crustaceans* sich häuten

molten ['moʊl·tən] *adj* geschmolzen; **~ bath** TECH Schmelzbad *nt*

mom [mam] *n* Mama *f,* Mutti *f bes* NORDD

mom-and-pop store *n* Tante-Emma-Laden *m fam*

moment ['moʊ·mənt] *n* ❶ (*very short time*) Moment *m,* Augenblick *m;* **just a ~, please** nur einen Augenblick, bitte; **not a ~ too soon** gerade noch rechtzeitig; **at any ~** jeden Augenblick; **in a ~** gleich, sofort ❷ (*specific time*) Zeitpunkt *m;* **a ~ in time** ein historischer Augenblick; ■**at the ~** im Augenblick, momentan ▶PHRASES: **to have one's ~s** [auch] seine guten Augenblicke haben

momentarily [ˌmoʊ·mən·'ter·ɪ·li] *adv* ❶ (*briefly*) kurz, momentan, eine Weile; **to pause ~** kurz innehalten ❷ (*very soon*) gleich, augenblicklich, in wenigen Augenblicken

momentary ['moʊ·mən·ter·i] *adj* ❶ (*brief*) kurz ❷ (*constant*) *fear* ständig

momentous [moʊ·'men·təs] *adj* bedeutsam, weitreichend, folgenschwer; *day* bedeutend

momentum [moʊ·'men·təm] *n* (*force*) Schwung *m,* Wucht *f;* **to gain ~** in Schwung kommen; **to give ~ to sth** etw in Schwung bringen

momma ['ma·mə] *n* (*childspeak*) Mama *f*

mommy ['mam·i] *n* (*childspeak*) Mama *f,* Mami *f,* Mutti *f bes* NORDD

Monaco ['man·ə·koʊ] *n* Monaco *nt*

monarch ['man·ərk] *n* Monarch(in) *m(f),* Herrscher(in) *m(f)*

monarchist ['man·ər·kɪst] *n* Monarchist(in) *m(f)*

monarchy ['man·ər·ki] *n* Monarchie *f*

monastery ['man·ə·ster·i] *n* [Mönchs]kloster *nt*

monastic [mə·'næs·tɪk] *adj* REL (*concerning monks*) mönchisch, Mönchs-; (*concerning monasteries*) klösterlich, Kloster-

Monday ['mʌn·di] *n* Montag *m; see also* **Tuesday**

monetary ['man·ə·ter·i] *adj* ECON Geld-, Währungs-

money ['mʌn·i] *n* ❶ (*cash*) Geld *nt;* **to be short on ~** knapp bei Kasse sein *fam;* **to put ~ into sth** Geld in etw *akk* stecken *fam;* **to spend ~** Geld ausgeben ❷ (*fam: pay*) Bezahlung *f,* Verdienst *m;* **they earn good ~ in that company** bei dieser Firma verdient man gutes Geld ▶PHRASES: **easy ~** leicht verdientes Geld; **~ doesn't grow on trees** (*prov*) Geld wächst nicht einfach nach

'moneybags <pl -> *n* (*hum, pej fam*) Geldsack *m*

moneyed ['mʌn·id] *adj* (*form*) vermögend, wohlhabend

'moneymaker *n* ❶ (*person*) erfolgreicher Geschäftsmann/erfolgreiche Geschäftsfrau ❷ (*profitable business*) gewinnbringendes Geschäft, Bombengeschäft *nt fam* ❸ (*profitable product*) Verkaufsschlager *m fam,* Renner *m fam*

'money market *n* Geldmarkt *m*

'money order *n* Postanweisung *f,* Zahlungsanweisung *f*

Mongol ['maŋ·gəl] **I.** *n* ❶ (*person*) Mongole *m,* Mongolin *f* ❷ (*language*) Mongolisch *nt,* das Mongolische **II.** *adj* mongolisch

Mongolia [maŋ·'goʊ·li·ə] *n* Mongolei *f*

Mongolian [maŋ·'goʊ·li·ən] **I.** *adj* mongolisch **II.** *n* ❶ (*person*) Mongole *m,* Mongolin *f* ❷ (*language*) Mongolisch *nt*

mongrel ['maŋ·grəl] **I.** *n* ❶ BOT, ZOOL (*result of crossing*) Kreuzung *f* ❷ (*esp pej: dog breed*) Promenadenmischung *f hum o pej,* Töle *f* NORDD **II.** *adj* Misch-; **~ species** Kreuzung *f*

monitor ['man·ɪ·t̬ər] **I.** *n* ❶ (*screen*) Bildschirm *m,* Monitor *m;* **color ~** Farbbildschirm *m,* Farbmonitor *m* ❷ POL (*observer*) Beobachter(in) *m(f)* ❸ (*device*) Anzeigegerät *nt,* Monitor *m* **II.** *vt* ❶ (*check*) beobachten, kontrollieren, überprüfen ❷ RADIO, TELEC, TV (*view, listen in on*) *device, person* abhören, mithören ❸ (*maintain quality, keep under surveillance*) *person, device* überwachen

monk [mʌŋk] *n* Mönch *m*

monkey ['mʌŋ·ki] *n* Affe *m*

◆**monkey around** *vi* (*fam*) ❶ (*waste time*) ■**to ~ around with sb** mit jdm seine Zeit verschwenden; (*waste sb's time*) jdm die Zeit stehlen ❷ (*pej: play*) ■**to ~ around with sth** mit etw *dat* herumspielen

'monkey business *n* ❶ (*silliness*) Blödsinn *m,* Unfug *m* ❷ (*trickery*) krumme Touren *pl,* faule Tricks *pl*

'monkey wrench *n* Universal[schrauben]schlüssel *m*

mono¹ ['man·oʊ] *n* (*fam*) *see* **infectious mononucleosis**

mono² ['man·oʊ] **I.** *n* MUS Mono *nt* **II.** *adj* Mono-

monochrome ['man·oʊ·kroʊm] *adj* ❶ PHOT (*black and white*) Schwarzweiß- ❷ (*using one color*) einfarbig, monochrom

monocle ['man·ə·kəl] *n* (*hist*) Monokel *nt*

monogamous [mə·'nag·ə·məs] *adj* monogam

monogamy [mə·'nag·ə·mi] *n* Monogamie *f*

monogram ['man·ə·græm] *n* Monogramm *nt*

monolingual [ˌman·oʊ·'lɪŋ·gwəl] *adj* einsprachig

monolith ['man·ə·lɪθ] *n* ❶ ARCHEOL (*single block*) Monolith *m* ❷ (*fig: sth huge*) Koloss *m; building* monumentales Gebäude; *organization* gigantische Organisation

monolithic [ˌman·ə·'lɪθ·ɪk] *adj* ❶ ARCHEOL monolithisch ❷ (*fig: huge*) *building, structure* monumental

monologue, monolog ['man·ə·lag] *n a.* THEAT Monolog *m*

monopolize [mə·'nap·ə·laɪz] *vt* ❶ ECON (*control*) monopolisieren, [allein] beherrschen

M

❷ (*keep for oneself*) ganz für sich *akk* beanspruchen, mit Beschlag belegen; *conversation* an sich *akk* reißen
monopoly [mə·ˈnap·ə·li] *n* Monopol *nt;* ■**to have a ~ on sth** ein Monopol auf etw *akk* haben
monorail [ˈman·oʊ·reɪl] *n* Einschienenbahn *f*
monosodium glutamate [ˌman·oʊ·soʊ·di·əm·ˈglu·t̬ə·meɪt] *n* CHEM [Mono]natriumglutamat *nt,* Glutamat *nt*
monosyllabic [ˌman·ə·sɪ·ˈlæb·ɪk] *adj* ❶ LING einsilbig ❷ (*pej: taciturn*) wortkarg, kurz angebunden
monotone [ˈman·ə·toʊn] *n* ❶ (*tone*) gleich bleibende Stimmlage, monotoner Klang ❷ (*single tone*) gleich bleibender Ton; **to speak in a ~** monoton sprechen
monotonous [mə·ˈnat·ən·əs] *adj* eintönig, monoton
monotony [mə·ˈnat·ən·i] *n* Monotonie *f,* Eintönigkeit *f*
monoxide [mə·ˈnak·saɪd] *n* Monoxid *nt*
monsoon [man·ˈsun] *n* ❶ (*wind*) Monsun *m* ❷ (*season of heavy rain*) ■**the ~[s]** der Monsun *kein pl*
monster [ˈman·stər] **I.** *n* ❶ (*imaginary creature*) Monster *nt,* Ungeheuer *nt* ❷ (*unpleasant person*) Scheusal *nt,* Ungeheuer *nt a. hum,* Monster *nt;* (*inhuman person*) Unmensch *m* ❸ (*fam: huge thing*) Ungetüm *nt,* Monstrum *nt* **II.** *adj attr* (*fam: huge*) ungeheuer, Mords- *fam*
monstrosity [man·ˈstras·ɪ·t̬i] *n* (*hugeness*) Riesengröße *f;* (*outrageousness*) Ungeheuerlichkeit *f;* (*awfulness*) Scheußlichkeit *f*
monstrous [ˈman·strəs] *adj* ❶ (*huge*) ungeheuer, monströs ❷ (*awful*) scheußlich; *cruelty* abscheulich
Mont. *abbrev of* **Montana**
montage [man·ˈtaʒ] *n* Montage *f*
Montana [man·ˈtæn·ə] *n* Montana *nt*
month [mʌnθ] *n* Monat *m;* **to take a two-~ vacation** zwei Monate Urlaub nehmen
monthly [ˈmʌnθ·li] **I.** *adj* monatlich, Monats- **II.** *adv* monatlich, einmal im Monat **III.** *n* Monatsschrift *f,* monatlich erscheinende Zeitschrift
monument [ˈman·jə·mənt] *n* ❶ (*fig: memorial*) Mahnmal *nt* ❷ (*historical structure*) Denkmal *nt,* Monument *nt;* **historic ~** Baudenkmal *nt*
monumental [ˌman·jə·ˈmen·təl] *adj* ❶ (*tremendous*) gewaltig, kolossal, eindrucksvoll ❷ ART (*large-scale*) monumental ❸ (*of monuments*) Gedenk-, Denkmal-
moo [mu] **I.** *n* Muhen *nt kein pl* **II.** *interj* muh **III.** *vi* muhen
mood [mud] *n* Laune *f,* Stimmung *f;* **in a good ~** gut gelaunt; **to be in a talkative ~** zum Erzählen aufgelegt sein; **to not be in the ~ to do sth** zu etw *dat* keine Lust haben
moodiness [ˈmu·dɪ·nɪs] *n* (*sullenness*) Missmut *m,* Verdrossenheit *f;* (*grumpiness*) Übellaunigkeit *f;* (*gloominess*) Trübsinnigkeit *f*
moody [ˈmu·di] *adj* ❶ (*temperamental*) launisch ❷ (*sullen*) missmutig, verdrossen; (*grumpy*) übel [*o* schlecht] gelaunt
moon [mun] **I.** *n* ASTRON Mond *m;* **full ~** Vollmond *m* ► PHRASES: **to be over the ~ about sth** über etw *akk* überglücklich sein **II.** *vt* (*sl*) ■**to ~ sb** [jdm] seinen nackten Hintern zeigen **III.** *vi* ■**to ~ over sb/sth** von jdm/etw träumen
ˈ**moonbeam** *n* Mondstrahl *m*
ˈ**moon boots** *npl* Moonboots *pl* (*dicke Synthetik-Winterstiefel*)
ˈ**moonlight** **I.** *n* (*moonshine*) Mondlicht *nt* **II.** *vi* <-lighted> (*fam: work at a second job*) schwarzarbeiten
ˈ**moonlit** *adj attr* (*lighted*) mondhell; **~ room** Zimmer *nt* im Mondlicht
ˈ**moonshine** *n* ❶ (*moonlight*) Mondschein *m* ❷ (*fam: liquor*) schwarzgebrannter Alkohol
ˈ**moonstone** *n* Mondstein *m*
moor¹ [mʊr] NAUT **I.** *vt* festmachen, vertäuen *fachspr* **II.** *vi* festmachen
moor² [mʊr] *n* Heideland *nt,* [Hoch]moor *nt*
mooring [ˈmʊr·ɪŋ] *n* NAUT (*berth*) Liegeplatz *m*
moose <*pl* -> [mus] *n* Elch *m*
moot [mut] *adj* (*open to debate*) strittig; **~ point** Streitfrage *f*
mop [map] **I.** *n* ❶ (*for cleaning*) Mopp *m* ❷ (*wiping*) **to give sth a ~** etw moppen ❸ (*mass of hair*) **she tied back her unruly ~ with a large ribbon** sie hielt ihr widerspenstiges Wuschelhaar hinten mit einem großen Band zusammen; (*sl: hairdo*) Frisur *f* **II.** *vt* <-pp-> ❶ (*clean with mop*) feucht wischen ❷ (*wipe*) **to ~ one's face** sich *dat* den Schweiß vom Gesicht wischen
mope [moʊp] *vi* Trübsal blasen, dumpf vor sich *akk* hinbrüten
◆**mope around** *vi* (*fam*) trübsinnig herumschleichen
moped [ˈmoʊ·ped] *n* Moped *nt*
moral [ˈmɔr·əl] **I.** *adj* ❶ (*ethical*) moralisch, ethisch ❷ (*virtuous*) *person* moralisch, anständig **II.** *n* ❶ (*of story*) Moral *f* ❷ (*standards of behavior*) ■**~s** *pl* Moralvorstellungen *pl,* moralische Grundsätze
morale [mə·ˈræl] *n* Moral *f,* Stimmung *f*
morality [mə·ˈræl·ɪ·t̬i] *n* ❶ (*moral principles*) moralische Grundsätze ❷ (*moral system*) Ethik *f*
moralize [ˈmɔr·ə·laɪz] *vi* moralisieren; ■**to ~ about sth** über etw *akk* Moral predigen
moratorium <*pl* -s *or* -ria> [ˌmɔr·ə·ˈtɔr·i·əm] *n* ❶ (*period of waiting*) Wartefrist *f* ❷ COMM Moratorium *nt*
morbid [ˈmɔr·bɪd] *adj* (*unhealthy*) morbid, krankhaft; (*gruesome*) makaber
more [mɔr] **I.** *adj comp of* **many, much** noch mehr; **two ~ days until Christmas** noch zwei Tage bis Weihnachten; **we can't take any ~ calls** wir können keine weiteren Anrufe entgegennehmen; **some ~ coffee?** noch et-

M

was Kaffee?; ~ **and** ~ **people are buying things on the Internet** immer mehr Leute kaufen Sachen im Internet **II.** *pron* ❶ (*greater amount*) mehr; **tell me** ~ erzähl' mir mehr; ~ **and** ~ **came** es kamen immer mehr; **she's** ~ **of a poet than a musician** sie ist eher Dichterin als Musikerin; **is there any** ~**?** ist noch etwas da?; **no** ~ nichts weiter; (*countable*) keine mehr ❷ **all the** ~ **...** umso mehr ...; **the** ~ **the better** je mehr, desto besser; **the** ~ **he drank, the** ~ **violent he became** je mehr er trank, desto gewalttätiger wurde er **III.** *adv* ❶ (*forming comparatives*) **let's find a** ~ **sensible way of doing it** wir sollten eine vernünftigere Lösung finden; **it's becoming** ~ **and** ~ **likely that she'll resign** es wird immer wahrscheinlicher, dass sie zurücktritt; ~ **importantly** wichtiger noch ❷ (*to a greater extent*) mehr; **you should listen** ~ **and talk less** du solltest besser zuhören und weniger reden; **we'll be** ~ **than happy to help** wir helfen sehr gerne; **to think** ~ **of sb** eine höhere Meinung von jdm haben ❸ (*longer*) **to be no** ~ *times* vorüber sein; *person* gestorben sein ▶ PHRASES: ~ **or less** (*all in all*) mehr oder weniger; (*approximately*) ungefähr; ~ **often than not** meistens

moreover [mɔr·'oʊ·vər] *adv* (*form*) zudem, ferner

morgue [mɔrg] *n* Leichen[schau]haus *nt*

Mormon ['mɔr·mən] **I.** *n* Mormone *m*, Mormonin *f* **II.** *adj* mormonisch, Mormonen-

morning ['mɔr·nɪŋ] **I.** *n* Morgen *m*, Vormittag *m*; **all** ~ den ganzen Vormittag; **tomorrow** ~ morgen Vormittag; **yesterday** ~ gestern Morgen **II.** *interj* (*fam*) Morgen!; **good** ~**!** guten Morgen!

'morning sickness *n* morgendliche Übelkeit

morning 'star *n* ASTRON (*planet*) Morgenstern *m*

Moroccan [mə·'rak·ən] **I.** *n* Marokkaner(in) *m(f)* **II.** *adj* marokkanisch

Morocco [mə·'rak·oʊ] *n* Marokko *nt*

moron ['mɔr·an] *n* (*pej fam*) Trottel *m*

moronic [mɔ·'ran·ɪk] *adj* (*pej fam*) blöde

morose [mə·'roʊs] *adj* mürrisch, griesgrämig

morphine ['mɔr·fin] *n* Morphium *nt*

Morse [mɔrs], **Morse 'code** *n* Morsezeichen *pl*, Morsealphabet *nt*

morsel ['mɔr·səl] *n* ❶ (*of food*) Bissen *m*, Happen *m*, Häppchen *pl* ❷ (*fig: small bit*) ■ **a** ~ ein bisschen

mortal ['mɔr·t̬əl] **I.** *adj* ❶ (*subject to death*) sterblich ❷ (*human*) menschlich ❸ (*fatal*) tödlich ❹ (*intense*) Todes-, höchste(r, s); **to be in** ~ **fear** sich zu Tode ängstigen **II.** *n* (*liter*) Sterbliche(r) *f(m)*; **ordinary** ~ (*hum*) Normalsterbliche(r) *f(m)*

mortality [mɔr·'tæl·ɪ·t̬i] *n* Sterblichkeit *f*

mortar ['mɔr·t̬ər] *n* ❶ ARCHIT, TECH (*mixture*) Mörtel *m* ❷ CHEM Mörser *m*; ~ **and pestle** Mörser *m* und Stößel *m*

'mortarboard *n* UNIV (*cap*) [quadratisches] Barett

'mortar shell *n* Mörsergranate *f*

mortgage ['mɔr·gɪdʒ] **I.** *n* (*amount*) Hypothek *f*; **to pay off a** ~ eine Hypothek tilgen **II.** *vt* hypothekarisch belasten

mortician [mɔr·'tɪʃ·ən] *n* Leichenbestatter(in) *m(f)*

mortification [ˌmɔr·t̬ə·fɪ·'keɪ·ʃən] *n* (*form*) ❶ (*humiliation*) Kränkung *f*, Demütigung *f* ❷ (*shame*) Beschämung *f*, Scham *f*

mortify <-ie-> ['mɔr·t̬ə·faɪ] *vt usu passive* ■ **to be mortified** (*be humiliated*) gedemütigt sein; (*be ashamed*) sich schämen; (*be embarrassed*) sich ärgern

mortuary ['mɔr·tʃu·er·i] *n* Leichen[schau]haus *nt*

mosaic [moʊ·'zeɪ·ɪk] *n* Mosaik *nt*

Moscow ['mas·kaʊ] *n* Moskau *nt*

Moslem ['maz·ləm] *adj, n see* **Muslim**

mosque [mask] *n* Moschee *f*

mosquito <*pl* -es *or* -s> [mə·'ski·t̬oʊ] *n* Moskito *m*; ~ **net** Moskitonetz *nt*

moss <*pl* -es> [mas] *n* (*plant*) Moos *nt*

mossy ['mas·i] *adj* ❶ (*overgrown with moss*) bemoost, moosbedeckt ❷ (*resembling moss*) moos-, moosartig

most [moʊst] **I.** *pron* ❶ (*largest quantity*) ■ **the** ~ am meisten; **what's the** ~ **you've ever won at cards?** was war das meiste, das du beim Kartenspielen gewonnen hast?; **at the** [**very**] ~ [aller]höchstens ❷ *pl* (*the majority*) die Mehrheit ❸ (*best*) ■ **the** ~ höchstens; **the** ~ **I can do is try** ich kann nicht mehr tun als es versuchen; **to make the** ~ **of sth** das Beste aus etw *dat* machen **II.** *adj* ❶ (*greatest in amount, degree*) am meisten ❷ (*majority of, nearly all*) die meisten ▶ PHRASES: **for the** ~ **part** im Allgemeinen **III.** *adv* ❶ (*forming superlative*) *im Deutschen durch Superlativ ausgedrückt;* **that's what I'm** ~ **afraid of** davor habe ich die meiste Angst; ~ **easily**/**rapidly** am leichtesten/schnellsten ❷ (*form: extremely*) höchst, äußerst, überaus *geh;* ~ **certainly** ganz bestimmt; ~ **likely** höchstwahrscheinlich ❸ (*to the greatest extent*) am meisten; **at** ~ höchstens; ~ **of all, I hope that ...** ganz besonders hoffe ich, dass ...

mostly ['moʊst·li] *adv* ❶ (*usually*) meistens ❷ (*mainly*) größtenteils, im Wesentlichen ❸ (*chiefly*) hauptsächlich, in der Hauptsache

motel [moʊ·'tel] *n* Motel *nt*

moth [mɔθ] *n* Motte *f*, Nachtfalter *m*

'mothball I. *n* Mottenkugel *f* **II.** *vt usu passive* ❶ (*put away for a while*) *battleship* einmotten ❷ (*postpone*) auf Eis legen

'moth-eaten *adj* ❶ (*eaten into*) mottenzerfressen ❷ (*outmoded*) *ideas, theories* verstaubt

mother ['mʌð·ər] **I.** *n* Mutter *f* ▶ PHRASES: **the** ~ **of all ...** der/die/das allergrößte ...; (*the most extreme: worst*) der/die/das Schlimmste aller *gen* ...; (*best*) herausragend; **the** ~ **of all battles** die Mutter aller Schlachten **II.** *vt* bemuttern

mother 'country *n* (*home country*) Vaterland *nt,* Heimatland *nt*

motherhood ['mʌð·ər·hʊd] *n* Mutterschaft *f*

'mother-in-law <*pl* mothers- *or* -s> *n* Schwiegermutter *f*

motherly ['mʌð·ər·li] *adj* mütterlich; ~ **love** Mutterliebe *f*

mother-of-'pearl *n* Perlmutt *nt*

'Mother's Day *n* Muttertag *m*

mother 'tongue *n* Muttersprache *f*

motif [moʊ·'tif] *n* ❶ LIT, MUS (*theme*) [Leit]motiv *nt,* Leitgedanke *m* ❷ (*design*) Motiv *nt*

motion ['moʊ·ʃən] **I.** *n* ❶ (*movement*) Bewegung *f,* Gang *m;* **in slow** ~ in Zeitlupe ❷ POL (*proposal*) Antrag *m;* **to defeat a** ~ einen Antrag ablehnen; **to pass a** ~ einen Antrag annehmen **II.** *vt* ■ **to** ~ **sb to do sth** jdn durch einen Wink auffordern, etw zu tun; **she** ~**ed us to sit down** sie bedeutete uns, Platz zu nehmen **III.** *vi* ■ **to** ~ **to sb to do sth** jdn durch einen Wink auffordern, etw zu tun

motionless ['moʊ·ʃən·lɪs] *adj* bewegungslos, reg[ungs]los

motion 'picture *n* [Spiel]film *m*

motivate ['moʊ·t̬ə·veɪt] *vt* ❶ (*provide with motive*) **they are** ~**d by a desire to help people** ihre Handlungsweise wird von dem Wunsch bestimmt, anderen zu helfen ❷ (*arouse interest*) motivieren, anregen; ■ **to** ~ **sb to do sth** jdn dazu bewegen [*o* veranlassen], etw zu tun

motivation [ˌmoʊ·t̬ə·'veɪ·ʃən] *n* ❶ (*reason*) Begründung *f,* Veranlassung *f* (**for** für +*akk*) ❷ (*drive*) Antrieb *m,* Motivation *f*

motive ['moʊ·t̬ɪv] **I.** *n* Motiv *nt,* Beweggrund *m* (**for** für +*akk*); **ulterior** ~ tieferer Beweggrund **II.** *adj attr* PHYS, TECH (*creating motion*) bewegend, Antriebs-

motley ['mat·li] *adj attr* (*a. pej: heterogeneous*) bunt [gemischt]

motor ['moʊ·t̬ər] **I.** *n* Antriebsmaschine *f,* [Verbrennungs]motor *m,* Triebwerk *nt* **II.** *adj attr* ❶ ANAT Bewegungs-, Muskel-, motorisch *fachspr* ❷ (*for motor vehicles*) Auto-

'motorbike *n* (*fam*) Motorrad *nt*

'motorboat *n* Motorboot *nt*

'motorcycle *n* Motorrad *nt*

'motorcycling *n* Motorradfahren *nt*

'motorcyclist *n* Motorradfahrer(in) *m(f)*

motoring ['moʊ·t̬ər·ɪŋ] *n* Fahren *nt*

motorist ['moʊ·t̬ər·ɪst] *n* Kraftfahrer(in) *m(f),* Automobilist(in) *m(f)* ÖSTERR, SCHWEIZ

motorized ['moʊ·t̬ə·raɪzd] *adj* motorisiert; ~ **wheelchair** elektrisch betriebener Rollstuhl

'motor racing *n* Autorennsport *m*

'motor scooter *n* Motorroller *m*

'motor vehicle *n* Kraftfahrzeug *nt*

mottled ['mat̬·əld] *adj* ❶ (*pej: blotchy*) *complexion, skin* fleckig ❷ (*diversified in shade*) *wood, marble* gemasert

motto <*pl* -s *or* -es> ['mat̬·oʊ] *n* Motto *nt*

mound [maʊnd] *n* ❶ (*pile*) Haufen *m;* (*small hill*) Hügel *m;* (*in baseball*) **pitcher's** ~ Mound *m* ❷ (*large quantity*) Masse *f,* Haufen *m fam*

mount [maʊnt] **I.** *n* ❶ (*horse*) Pferd *nt* ❷ (*backing, setting*) *of picture, photo* Halterung *f; of jewel* Fassung *f* ❸ (*mountain*) Berg *m;* **M~ Everest** Mount Everest *m;* **M~ Etna/Kilimanjaro/Vesuvius** der Ätna/Kilimandscharo/Vesuv; **M~ Fuji** Fudschisan *m* **II.** *vt* ❶ (*get on to ride*) [auf]steigen (auf +*akk*) ❷ (*fix securely*) aufhängen; **to** ~ **a camera on a tripod** eine Kamera auf ein Stativ montieren ❸ (*go up*) hochsteigen; *stairs* hochgehen ❹ (*organize*) organisieren; *attack, campaign* starten ❺ (*fasten for display*) befestigen; **to** ~ **sth in a frame** etw rahmen **III.** *vi* ❶ (*increase*) wachsen, [an]steigen, größer werden ❷ (*get on a horse*) aufsteigen

mountain ['maʊn·tən] *n* Berg *m; pl a.* Gebirge *nt*

mountaineer [ˌmaʊn·tə·'nɪr] *n* Bergsteiger(in) *m(f)*

mountaineering [ˌmaʊn·tə·'nɪr·ɪŋ] *n* Bergsteigen *nt*

mountainous ['maʊn·tə·nəs] *adj* gebirgig, bergig; (*fig*) riesig

'mountain range *n* Gebirgszug *m*

mounted ['maʊn·tɪd] *adj* beritten *geh*

mounting ['maʊn·t̬ɪŋ] **I.** *n* ❶ (*on a horse*) Besteigen *nt* ❷ (*display surface*) *of photograph, picture* Halterung *f; of machine* Sockel *m;* (*frame*) Rahmen *m* **II.** *adj attr* (*increasing*) wachsend, steigend

> Zwischen 1927 und 1941 wurden in die Granitfelsen des **Mount Rushmore** oder Mount Rushmore/Süddakota die 60 Fuß (18 m) hohen Büsten der Präsidenten George Washington, Thomas Jefferson, Theodore Roosevelt und Abraham Lincoln eingehauen. Sie stehen für die 150 Anfangsjahre der amerikanischen Geschichte und sind eine Hommage an die Geburt, die Entwicklung und den Erhalt der Vereinigten Staaten von Amerika.

mourn [mɔrn] *vi, vt* trauern (**for** um +*akk*)

mourner ['mɔr·nər] *n* Trauernde(r) *f(m);* (*nonrelative*) Trauergast *m*

mournful ['mɔrn·fəl] *adj* (*sad*) traurig, melancholisch; (*gloomy*) trübsinnig; *lamenting* klagend

mourning ['mɔr·nɪŋ] *n* (*grieving*) Trauer *f;* ■ **to be in** ~ [**for sb**] [um jdn] trauern; (*wear black clothes*) Trauer tragen

mouse <*pl* mice> [maʊs] *n* ZOOL, COMPUT Maus *f*

'mouse pad *n* COMPUT Mauspad *nt*

'mousetrap *n* Mausefalle *f*

mousse [mus] *n* ❶ FOOD Mousse *f* ❷ (*cosmetics*) Schaum *m;* **styling** ~ Schaumfestiger *m*

moustache ['mʌs·tæʃ] *n see* **mustache**

mousy ['maʊ·si] *adj* ❶ (*dull color*) farblos; *hair* mausgrau ❷ (*shy*) schüchtern; (*uncharismatic*) unscheinbar

mouth [maʊθ] *n* ❶ (*of human*) Mund *m; of animal* Maul *nt;* **to have a big ~** (*fig*) ein großes Mundwerk haben *fam* ❷ (*opening*) Öffnung *f; of cave* Eingang *m; of volcano* Krater *m; of river* Mündung *f*

mouthful ['maʊθ·fʊl] *n* ❶ *of food* Bissen *m; of drink* Schluck *m* ❷ (*hum fam: unpronounceable word*) Zungenbrecher *m*

'mouthpiece *n of musical instrument, snorkel* Mundstück *nt; of telephone* Sprechmuschel *f*

mouth-to-'mouth, mouth-to-mouth resusci'tation *n* Mund-zu-Mund-Beatmung *f*

'mouthwash *n* Mundwasser *nt*

'mouth-watering *adj* [sehr] appetitlich, köstlich

mouthy ['maʊ·θi] *adj* (*pej fam*) großmäulig *pej fam;* **she's ~** sie hat ein freches Mundwerk

movable ['mu·və·bəl] *adj* beweglich; *heavy objects* verschiebbar

move [muv] **I.** *n* ❶ (*movement*) Bewegung *f;* **to be on the ~** unterwegs sein; (*fig*) *country* sich im Umbruch befinden; **to make a ~** (*fam: leave*) sich auf den Weg machen; (*act*) etwas unternehmen; (*start*) loslegen *fam;* **to make no ~** sich nicht rühren ❷ (*step*) Schritt *m;* (*measure*) Maßnahme *f;* **to make the first ~** den ersten Schritt tun ❸ (*in games*) Zug *m;* CHESS [Schach]zug *m;* **it's your ~** du bist dran ❹ (*change of residence*) Umzug *m;* (*change of job*) Stellenwechsel *m;* (*transfer*) Versetzung *f* ▶ PHRASES: **to get a ~ on** (*fam*) sich beeilen; **to make a ~ on sb** (*fam*) jdn anmachen **II.** *vi* ❶ (*change position*) sich bewegen; (*go*) gehen; (*drive*) fahren; **no one ~d** keiner rührte sich; **to ~ [out of the way]** aus dem Weg gehen; **to begin to ~** sich in Bewegung setzen ❷ (*change*) **that's my final decision, and I am not going to ~ [on it]** das ist mein letztes Wort und dabei bleibt es; **to ~ off a subject** das Thema wechseln ❸ (*progress*) vorankommen; **to ~ forward** Fortschritte machen ❹ (*change address*) umziehen; (*change job*) [den Arbeitsplatz] wechseln ❺ (*fam: leave*) gehen, aufbrechen; **we have to get moving** wir müssen los **III.** *vt* ❶ (*change position of*) bewegen; (*place somewhere else*) woanders hinstellen; (*push somewhere else*) verrücken; (*clear*) wegräumen; (*rearrange*) *furniture* umstellen; (*transport*) befördern ❷ (*reschedule*) verlegen, verschieben ❸ (*transfer*) verlegen; (*to another job, class*) versetzen ❹ (*cause emotions*) bewegen; (*stronger*) ergreifen; **to ~ sb to tears** jdn zu Tränen rühren

move around I. *vi* ❶ (*go around*) herumgehen ❷ (*travel*) umherreisen ❸ (*change jobs*) oft wechseln; (*change house*) oft umziehen **II.** *vt* ❶ (*change position of*) [hin und her] bewegen; (*place somewhere else*) hin und her räumen; *furniture* umstellen ❷ (*fam: at work*) **to ~ sb ⊂ around** jdn oft versetzen

◆**move along I.** *vt* ■**to ~ sb ⊂ along** jdn zum Weitergehen bewegen **II.** *vi* ❶ (*walk farther on*) weitergehen; (*run farther on*) weiterlaufen; (*drive farther on*) weiterfahren ❷ (*make room*) aufrücken, Platz machen

◆**move away I.** *vi* ❶ (*leave*) weggehen; *vehicle* wegfahren ❷ (*move to new house*) wegziehen; (*leave home*) von zu Hause ausziehen **II.** *vt* wegräumen; (*push away*) wegrücken

◆**move down I.** *vi* ❶ (*change position*) sich nach unten bewegen; (*slip down*) runterrutschen *fam;* (*make room*) aufrücken; SPORTS *team* absteigen (**from** aus +*dat*) ❷ (*change value*) *shares, prices* fallen **II.** *vt* (*change position of*) nach unten bewegen; (*place lower down*) nach unten stellen; (*everything*) nach unten räumen

◆**move in I.** *vi* ❶ (*enter a new home*) einziehen; ■**to ~ in with sb** zu jdm ziehen ❷ (*take control*) **government officials have ~d in to settle the dispute** man hat Regierungsbeamte eingesetzt, um den Streit zu beenden ❸ (*advance to attack*) anrücken; **to ~ in on enemy territory** auf feindliches Gebiet vorrücken; **to ~ in for the kill** zum tödlichen Schlag ausholen **II.** *vt* ❶ (*change position of*) nach innen bewegen; (*push in*) nach innen rücken; (*take inside*) hineinbringen ❷ (*send*) einsetzen; *troops, police* einrücken lassen

◆**move off I.** *vi* sich in Bewegung setzen; (*walk*) losgehen; (*run*) loslaufen, losrennen **II.** *vt* wegräumen

◆**move on I.** *vi* ❶ (*continue a trip*) sich wieder auf den Weg machen; (*walk*) weitergehen; (*run*) weiterlaufen; (*drive*) weiterfahren ❷ (*advance*) sich weiterentwickeln; (*progress in career*) beruflich weiterkommen ❸ (*change subject*) ■**to ~ on to sth** zu etw *dat* übergehen; **can we move ~ to the next item?** können wir zum nächsten Punkt kommen? **II.** *vt* (*cause to leave*) zum Weitergehen auffordern; (*in a vehicle*) zum Weiterfahren auffordern; (*force to leave*) vertreiben

◆**move out I.** *vi* ❶ (*stop inhabiting*) ausziehen ❷ (*cease involvement*) ■**to ~ out [of sth]** sich [von etw *dat*] zurückziehen ❸ (*leave*) *troops* abziehen **II.** *vt* ❶ (*clear*) wegräumen; (*take outside*) hinausbringen ❷ (*make leave*) *tenant* kündigen; *troops* abziehen; **we were all ~d out of the danger zone** wir mussten alle das Gefahrengebiet räumen

◆**move over I.** *vi* ❶ (*make room*) Platz machen, aufrücken ❷ (*switch*) ■**to ~ over to sth** zu etw *dat* übergehen **II.** *vt* herüberschieben; (*put aside*) zur Seite räumen; (*push aside*) zur Seite rücken; (*turn*) umdrehen

◆**move toward** *vi* ■**to ~ toward sth** sich etw *dat* [an]nähern

◆**move up I.** *vi* ❶ (*advance*) aufrücken; (*to the next grade*) versetzt werden; (*professionally, socially*) aufsteigen; SPORTS *team* aufsteigen (**from** aus +*dat*) ❷ (*make room*) Platz ma-

M

chen, aufrücken ③ (*increase*) *prices* steigen **II.** *vt* (*change position of*) nach oben bewegen; (*place higher up*) nach oben stellen; (*everything*) nach oben räumen

movement ['muv·mənt] *n* ① (*change of position*) Bewegung *f;* **after the accident he had no ~ in his legs** nach seinem Unfall konnte er seine Beine nicht bewegen ② (*general activity*) Bewegung *f;* FIN, STOCKEX Schwankung[en] *f*[*pl*] ③ (*interest group*) Bewegung *f* ④ MUS (*part of symphony*) Satz *m* ⑤ (*tendency*) Tendenz *f,* Trend *m* (**toward**[**s**] [hin] zu +*dat*) ⑥ (*mechanism*) *of clock, watch* Uhrwerk *nt*

movie ['mu·vi] *n* [Kino]film *m;* ■**the ~s** *pl* das Kino; **to be in the ~s** (*fam*) im Filmgeschäft sein

'**movie camera** *n* Filmkamera *f*

'**moviegoer** *n* Kinogänger(in) *m(f)*

'**movie star** *n* Filmstar *m*

'**movie theater** *n* Kino *nt*

moving ['mu·vɪŋ] **I.** *n* Umziehen *nt* **II.** *adj* ① *attr* MECH beweglich ② (*causing emotion*) bewegend, ergreifend ③ (*related to a move*) *expenses, van* Umzugs-

mow <mowed, mowed *or* mown> [moʊ] **I.** *vi* (*cut grass, grain*) mähen **II.** *vt lawn* mähen; *field* abmähen

mower ['moʊ·ər] *n* Rasenmäher *m;* (*on a farm*) Mähmaschine *f*

mown [moʊn] **I.** *pp of* **mow II.** *adj* gemäht; *field* abgemäht

mpg [ˌem·pi·'dʒi] *abbrev of* **miles per gallon: to get 40 ~** 40 Meilen pro Gallone fahren

mph [ˌem·pi·'eɪtʃ] *abbrev of* **miles per hour: to do 50 ~** 50 Meilen pro Stunde fahren

Mr. ['mɪs·tər] *n* (*title for man*) Herr *m*

Mrs. ['mɪs·ɪz] *n* (*title for married woman*) Frau, Fr.

MS [ˌem·'es] *n* ① *abbrev of* **Master of Science** ② *abbrev of* **Mississippi** Mississippi *m* ③ *abbrev of* **multiple sclerosis** MS *f*

Ms. [mɪz] *n* (*title for woman, married or unmarried*) Fr., Frau (*Alternativbezeichnung zu Mrs und Miss, die sowohl für verheiratete wie unverheiratete Frauen zutrifft*)

ms [ˌem·'es] *n* ① *abbrev of* **manuscript** Mskr. ② *abbrev of* **millisecond** ms

MSG [ˌem·es·'dʒi] *n* CHEM *abbrev of* **monosodium glutamate**

MST [ˌem·es·'ti] *n abbrev of* **Mountain Standard Time** Mountain Standardzeit *f*

MT *abbrev of* **Montana**

Mt. *n abbrev of* **mount I. 3**

much [mʌtʃ] **I.** *adj* <more, most> + *sing* viel; **there wasn't ~ mail** es kam nicht viel Post; **how ~ ...?** wie viel ...?; **twice as ~** doppelt so viel **II.** *pron* ① (*relative amount*) viel; **however ~ you dislike her ...** wie unsympathisch sie dir auch sein mag, ...; **he left without so ~ as an apology** er ging ohne auch nur ein Wort der Entschuldigung ② (*great deal*) viel; **~ of what you say is right** vieles von dem, was Sie sagen, ist richtig ③ *with neg* (*pej: poor example*) **he's not ~ to look at** er sieht nicht gerade umwerfend aus ④ (*larger part*) **~ of the day** der Großteil des Tages **III.** *adv* <more, most> ① (*greatly*) sehr; **~ to our surprise** zu unserer großen Überraschung; **to not be ~ good at sth** in etw *dat* nicht sehr gut sein ② (*nearly*) fast; **~ the same** fast so ③ (*specifying degree*) **I like him as ~ as you do** ich mag ihn genauso sehr wie du; **I wanted to meet you so ~** ich wollte dich unbedingt treffen; **thank you very ~** herzlichen Dank ④ (*often*) häufig; **do you see ~ of her?** siehst du sie öfters? **IV.** *conj* (*although*) auch wenn, wenngleich *geh;* **~ as I like you, ...** so gern ich dich auch mag, ...

muck [mʌk] *n* ① (*dirt*) Dreck *m fam;* (*waste*) Müll *m* ② (*euph: excrement*) Haufen *m fam*

muckraker ['mʌk·reɪ·kər] *n* (*pej*) Skandalreporter(in) *m(f)*

mucus ['mju·kəs] *n* Schleim *m*

mud [mʌd] *n* Schlamm *m*

muddle ['mʌd·əl] **I.** *n* ① *usu sing* (*confused state*) Durcheinander *nt* ② (*mix-up*) Durcheinander *nt,* Kuddelmuddel *nt* **II.** *vi* ■**to ~ along** vor sich *akk* hin wursteln *fam*

muddy ['mʌd·i] **I.** *vt* ① (*make dirty*) verschmutzen, schmutzig machen ② (*fig: confuse*) undurchsichtig machen **II.** *adj* schlammig; (*dirty*) schmutzig; *ground, snow* matschig

'**mud flap** *n of car* Kotflügel *m; of bicycle* Schutzblech *nt*

'**mudpack** *n* Gesichtsmaske *f*

'**mudslide** *n* Schlammlawine *f*

mudslinging ['mʌd·slɪŋ·ɪŋ] *n* (*fig*) Schlammschlacht *f fam*

muff[1] [mʌf] *vt* (*fam*) vermasseln

muff[2] [mʌf] *n* FASHION Muff *m*

muffin ['mʌf·ɪn] *n* Muffin *nt* (*kleiner, hoher, runder, meist süßer Kuchen aus Rührteig*)

muffle ['mʌf·əl] *vt* dämpfen; (*fig*) [ab]schwächen

muffler ['mʌf·lər] *n* (*silencer*) *of car* Auspufftopf *m*

mug[1] [mʌg] *n* (*cup*) Becher *m* (*mit Henkel*)

mug[2] [mʌg] **I.** *n* (*pej: face*) Visage *f,* Fresse *f sl* **II.** *vt* <-gg-> (*rob*) überfallen und ausrauben **III.** *vi* (*pose*) **to ~ for the camera** ein Fotogesicht aufsetzen

mugger ['mʌg·ər] *n* [Straßen]räuber(in) *m(f)*

mugging ['mʌg·ɪŋ] *n* [Straßen]raub *m,* Überfall *m* (*auf offener Straße*)

muggy ['mʌg·i] *adv weather* schwül

mulberry ['mʌl·ber·i] *n* ① (*fruit*) Maulbeere *f* ② (*tree*) Maulbeerbaum *m*

mule[1] [mjul] *n* (*animal*) Maultier *nt*

mule[2] [mjul] *n* (*shoe*) halboffener Schuh; (*slipper*) Pantoffel *m*

mull [mʌl] *vt* ① (*spice*) **~ed wine** Glühwein *m* ② (*ponder*) ■**to ~ sth** [**over**] sich *dat* etw durch den Kopf gehen lassen

mullet ['mʌl·ɪt] *n* ① (*fish*) Meeräsche *f* ② (*fam: hairstyle*) Vokuhila *m sl*

mullion [ˈmʌl·jən] *n* ARCHIT Längspfosten *m;* ■ **~s** *pl* Stabwerk *nt*
multiˈcolored *adj* mehrfarbig
multiˈcultural *adj* multikulturell
multiˈlateral *adj* POL multilateral *geh*
multiˈlayered *adj* vielschichtig
multiˈlingual *adj* mehrsprachig
multiˈmedia I. *n* Multimedia *f* II. *adj* multimedial
multimillionˈaire *n* Multimillionär(in) *m(f)*
multiˈnational I. *n* multinationaler Konzern, Multi *m fam* II. *adj* multinational
multiplayer [ˈmʌl·ti·pleɪ·ər] *adj attr computer game* Multiplayer-, für mehrere Spieler *nach n*
multiple [ˈmʌl·ţə·pəl] I. *adj attr* vielfach, vielfältig II. *n* Vielfache[s]
multiplex [ˈmʌl·tə·pleks] *n* Multiplex-Kino *nt*
multiplication [ˌmʌl·tə·plɪ·ˈkeɪ·ʃən] *n* Multiplikation *f*
multiplier [ˈmʌl·tə·plaɪ·ər] *n* Multiplikator *m*
multiply <-ie-> [ˈmʌl·tə·plaɪ] I. *vt* multiplizieren (**by** mit *+dat*) II. *vi* sich vermehren; (*through reproduction a.*) sich fortpflanzen
multiˈpurpose *adj* multifunktional, Mehrzweck-
multiˈracial *adj* gemischtrassig; **~ society** *Gesellschaft, die aus den Angehörigen verschiedener Rassengruppen besteht*
multiˈtalented *adj* **~ individual** Multitalent *nt*
multiˈtasking I. *n* COMPUT Ausführen *nt* mehrerer Programme, Multitasking *nt* II. *adj attr* (*fig*) gleichzeitig mehreren Aufgaben nachkommend *attr*
multitude [ˈmʌl·tɪ·tud] *n* ❶ (*great number*) Vielzahl *f* ❷ (*crowd*) ■ **the ~s** *pl* die Allgemeinheit
mum [mʌm] *adj* (*fam: silent*) still; **... — ~'s the word** (*as a response*) ... – von mir erfährt keiner was; (*telling sb*) ... – und kein Wort darüber; **to keep ~** den Mund halten
mumble [ˈmʌm·bəl] *vi* (*speak unclearly*) nuscheln; (*speak quietly*) murmeln
mumbo jumbo [ˌmʌm·boʊ·ˈdʒʌm·boʊ] *n* (*fam*) Quatsch *m*
mummify <-ie-> [ˈmʌm·ə·faɪ] *vt* mumifizieren
mummy [ˈmʌm·i] *n* Mumie *f*
mumps [mʌmps] *n + sing vb* Mumps *m;* **to have the ~** Mumps haben
munch [mʌntʃ] *vi, vt* mampfen
mundane [mʌn·ˈdeɪn] *adj* profan *geh;* (*unexciting*) *problem, question* banal; (*routine*) *activity, task* alltäglich
municipal [mju·ˈnɪs·ə·pəl] *adj* städtisch, Stadt-, kommunal, Kommunal-; **~ elections** Kommunalwahlen *pl,* Gemeinderatswahlen *pl*
municipality [mju·ˌnɪs·ə·ˈpæl·ɪ·ţi] *n* (*political unit*) Gemeinde *f,* Kommune *f;* (*town-sized a.*) Stadt *f*
munitions [mju·ˈnɪʃ·ənz] *npl* (*weapons*) Waffen *pl;* (*weapons and ammunition*) Kriegsmaterial *nt kein pl;* (*ammunition*) Munition *f kein pl*
mural [ˈmjʊr·əl] I. *n* Wandgemälde *nt* II. *adj* Wand-
murder [ˈmɜr·dər] I. *n* ❶ (*crime*) Mord *m,* Ermordung *f* (**of** an *+dat*); **mass ~** Massenmord *m;* **to commit ~** einen Mord begehen ❷ (*fig: difficult thing*) **it's ~ trying to find a parking space around here** es ist wirklich schier unmöglich, hier in der Gegend einen Parkplatz zu finden II. *vt* ermorden, umbringen *a. fig*
murderer [ˈmɜr·dər·ər] *n* Mörder(in) *m(f)*
murderous [ˈmɜr·dər·əs] *adj* (*cruel*) mordlüstern, blutrünstig; (*evil*) *look, hatred* tödlich
murky [ˈmɜr·ki] *adj* düster; *night* finster; *water* trübe; (*fig*) *past* dunkel
murmur [ˈmɜr·mər] I. *vi, vt* murmeln II. *n* Gemurmel *nt kein pl,* Raunen *nt kein pl;* **a ~ of agreement** ein zustimmendes Raunen
muscle [ˈmʌs·əl] *n* ❶ (*contracting tissue*) Muskel *m* ❷ (*fig: influence*) Stärke *f*
◆ **muscle in** *vi* sich [rücksichtslos] einmischen; ■ **to ~ in on sth** sich irgendwo [mit aller Gewalt] hineindrängeln
ˈmuscle-bound *adj* (*pej*) [äußerst] muskulös
ˈmuscleman *n* Muskelprotz *m*
muscular [ˈmʌs·kjə·lər] *adj* ❶ (*relating to muscles*) muskulär, Muskel- ❷ (*with well-developed muscles*) muskulös
muse [mjuz] I. *vi* nachgrübeln, nachdenken (**about/on** über *+akk*) II. *n* (*female inspirer*) Muse *f;* (*artistic inspiration*) Inspiration *f*
museum [mju·ˈzi·əm] *n* Museum *nt*
mush [mʌʃ] *n* (*fam*) ❶ FOOD Brei *m,* Mus *nt;* **to turn to ~** zu Brei werden ❷ (*sentimentality*) **that film was just romantic ~** der Film war so eine richtige Schnulze
mushroom [ˈmʌʃ·rum] *n* Pilz *m*
mushy [ˈmʌʃ·i] *adj* ❶ (*pulpy*) breiig ❷ (*soppily romantic*) schnulzig
music [ˈmju·zɪk] *n* ❶ (*pattern of sounds*) Musik *f;* **to put on [some] ~** [etwas] Musik auflegen ❷ (*notes*) Noten *pl*
musical [ˈmju·zɪ·kəl] I. *adj* musikalisch, Musik- II. *n* Musical *nt*
ˈmusic box *n* Spieluhr *f*
musician [mju·ˈzɪʃ·ən] *n* Musiker(in) *m(f)*
ˈmusic stand *n* Notenständer *m*
musk [mʌsk] *n* Moschus *m*
musket [ˈmʌs·kɪt] *n* Muskete *f*
muskrat [ˈmʌs·kræt] *n* Moschusratte *f*
Muslim [ˈmʌz·ləm] I. *n* Moslem(in) *m(f),* Muslim(in) *m(f)* II. *adj* moslemisch, muslimisch
muslin [ˈmʌz·lɪn] *n* Musselin *m*
muss [mʌs] I. *n* Unordnung *f,* Durcheinander *nt* II. *vt* durcheinanderbringen; *wind* zerzausen
mussel [ˈmʌs·əl] *n* [Mies]muschel *f*
must [mʌst] I. *aux vb* ❶ (*be obliged, be required*) müssen; **for security reasons, all bags ~ be left at the cloakroom** lassen Sie bitte aus Sicherheitsgründen alle Handtaschen in der Garderobe; ■ **~ not** [*or* **~n't**] nicht dürfen; **you ~n't say anything to anyone about**

this matter darüber darfst du mit niemandem sprechen ② (*should*) **you really ~ read this book** dieses Buch sollten Sie wirklich einmal lesen ③ (*be certain to*) müssen; **she ~ be wondering where I am** sie wird sich bestimmt fragen, wo ich abgeblieben bin ④ (*be necessary*) müssen; **you ~n't worry too much about it** jetzt mach dir deswegen nicht so viele Sorgen **II.** *n* Muss *nt kein pl;* ■ **to be a ~** ein Muss *nt* sein; **this book is a ~!** dieses Buch muss man gelesen haben!

mustache ['mʌs·tæʃ] *n* Schnurrbart *m*

mustang ['mʌs·tæŋ] *n* Mustang *m*

mustard ['mʌs·tərd] *n* Senf *m*

muster ['mʌs·tər] **I.** *vt* ① (*bring together*) *soldiers* [zum Appell] antreten lassen ② (*gather*) *courage* aufbringen **II.** *vi* (*come together*) sich versammeln, antreten; *troop* [zum Appell] antreten

'must-have *adj attr* (*fam*) unentbehrlich; **be fashionable this fall with this pair of ~ boots** gehen Sie diesen Herbst mit der Mode - dazu gehören unbedingt diese Stiefel!

mustn't ['mʌs·ənt] *short for* **must not** *see* **must**

'must-see I. *n* **this film is a ~** diesen Film muss man gesehen haben **II.** *adj* sehenswert; **~ TV** *Fernsehsendung, die man unbedingt sehen muss*

musty ['mʌs·ti] *adj book* mod[e]rig; *room, smell* muffig

M

mutant ['mju·tənt] *n* Mutant(e) *m(f)*

mutation [mju·'teɪ·ʃən] *n* Veränderung *f,* Mutation *f fachspr*

mute [mjut] **I.** *n* ① (*person*) Stumme(r) *f(m)* ② MUS (*quieting device*) Dämpfer *m* **II.** *vt sound, noise* dämpfen **III.** *adj* stumm

muted ['mju·tɪd] *adj* (*not loud*) gedämpft; (*fig*) schweigend, stumm; *colors* gedeckt

mutilate ['mju·t̬ə·leɪt] *vt* verstümmeln; (*fig*) verschandeln

mutilation [ˌmju·t̬ə·'leɪ·ʃən] *n* Verstümmelung *f;* (*fig*) Verschandelung *f*

mutineer [ˌmju·tən·'ɪr] *n* Meuterer(in) *m(f)*

mutinous ['mju·tə·nəs] *adj* meuterisch; *shareholders* rebellisch

mutiny ['mju·tɪ·ni] **I.** *n* Meuterei *f* **II.** *vi* <-ie-> meutern

mutter ['mʌt̬·ər] **I.** *vi* ① (*mumble*) ■ **to ~ [to oneself]** irgendetwas [vor sich *akk* hin]murmeln ② (*grumble*) ■ **to ~ about sth** über etw *akk* murren **II.** *vt* (*complain softly*) brummen, murmeln; **to ~ sth to sb under one's breath** jdm etw zuraunen

mutton ['mʌt·ən] *n* Hammel *m,* Hammelfleisch *nt*

mutual ['mju·tʃu·əl] *adj* gegenseitig, beiderseitig; *friends, interests* gemeinsam; *agreement* wechselseitig; **the feeling is ~** das [Gefühl] beruht auf Gegenseitigkeit

'mutual fund *n* FIN offener Investmentfond

mutually ['mju·tʃu·ə·li] *adv* gegenseitig, für beide [Seiten]; **to be ~ exclusive** sich gegenseitig ausschließen

Muzak® ['mju·zæk] *n* Musikberieselung *f*

muzzle ['mʌz·əl] **I.** *n* ① (*animal mouth*) Schnauze *f,* Maul *nt* ② (*mouth covering*) Maulkorb *m* ③ (*gun end*) Mündung *f* **II.** *vt animal* einen Maulkorb anlegen; (*fig*) *person, press* mundtot machen

MW *n* PHYS *abbrev of* **megawatt** MW *nt*

my [maɪ] **I.** *adj poss* mein(e); **~ brother and sister** mein Bruder und meine Schwester; **I hurt ~ foot** ich habe mir den Fuß verletzt; **I need a car of ~ own** ich brauche ein eigenes Auto **II.** *interj* ach, oh; **~ ~** na, so was

myopic [maɪ·'ap·ɪk] *adj* (*form or fig*) kurzsichtig

myrrh [mɜr] *n* Myrrhe *f*

myrtle ['mɜr·t̬əl] *n* Myrte *f*

myself [maɪ·'self] *pron reflexive* ① (*direct object of verb*) mir *+dat,* mich *+akk;* **I caught sight of ~ in the mirror** ich sah mich im Spiegel; **yes, I thought to ~, it's time to take a vacation** ja, dachte ich mir, es ist Zeit für einen Urlaub ② (*emph form: I, me*) ich; **people like ~** Menschen wie ich ③ (*emph: me personally*) ich persönlich; **I wrote it ~** ich schrieb es selbst; ■ **to see [sth] for ~** [etw] selbst sehen ④ (*me alone*) **I never get an hour to ~** ich habe nie eine Stunde für mich; **I live by ~** ich lebe alleine; **[all] by ~** [ganz] alleine

mysterious [mɪ·'stɪr·i·əs] *adj* geheimnisvoll, mysteriös

mystery ['mɪs·tə·ri] *n* (*secret*) Geheimnis *nt;* (*puzzle*) Rätsel *nt;* **that's a ~ to me** das ist mir schleierhaft

mystic ['mɪs·tɪk] **I.** *n* Mystiker(in) *m(f)* **II.** *adj* ① (*inspiring sense of mystery*) geheimnisvoll, mysteriös ② (*relating to mysticism*) mystisch

mystical ['mɪs·tɪ·kəl] *adj* mystisch

mystification [ˌmɪs·tɪ·fɪ·'keɪ·ʃən] *n* ① (*puzzlement*) Verwunderung *f,* Verblüffung *f* ② (*intentional confusion*) Verwirrung *f,* Verwirrspiel *nt*

mystify <-ie-> ['mɪs·tə·faɪ] *vt* ■ **to ~ sb** jdn vor ein Rätsel stellen

myth [mɪθ] *n* ① (*ancient story*) Mythos *m* ② (*pej: false idea*) Ammenmärchen *nt*

mythical ['mɪθ·ɪ·kəl] *adj* ① (*fictional*) sagenhaft, legendär ② (*supposed*) gedacht, imaginär

mythological [ˌmɪθ·ə·'ladʒ·ɪ·kəl] *adj* mythologisch

mythology [mɪ·'θal·ə·dʒi] *n* Mythologie *f;* (*fig*) Ammenmärchen *nt*

Nn

N <*pl* -'s *or* -s>, **n** <*pl* -'s> [en] *n* N *nt,* n *nt;* **~ as in November** N wie Nordpol

N I. *n abbrev of* **North** N *m* **II.** *adj abbrev of* **North, Northern** nördl.

n *n* ① *abbrev of* **noun** Subst. ② *abbrev of* **neuter** nt

nab <-bb-> [næb] *vt* (*fam*) stibitzen

nag[1] [næg] **I.** *vi* <-gg-> [herum]nörgeln (**at** an +*dat*) **II.** *vt* <-gg-> ■**to ~ sb** (*urge*) jdm [ständig] zusetzen; (*annoy*) jdn nicht in Ruhe lassen **III.** *n* (*fam: person*) Nörgler(in) *m(f);* (*annoying*) Nervensäge *f*

nag[2] [næg] *n* (*horse*) [alte Schind]mähre

nagging ['næg·ɪŋ] **I.** *n* Nörgelei *f* **II.** *adj* ① (*criticizing*) nörgelnd ② (*persistent*) quälend

nail [neɪl] **I.** *n* ① (*small metal spike*) Nagel *m* ② (*body part*) [Finger-/Zeh]nagel *m;* **to bite one's ~s** an den Fingernägeln kauen; **to cut one's ~s** sich *dat* die Nägel schneiden **II.** *vt* ① (*fasten*) nageln (**to** an +*akk*) ② (*sl: catch*) *police* schnappen *fam; newspapers* drankriegen *fam*

'nail-biting I. *n* Nägelkauen *nt* **II.** *adj* nervenzerreißend; *film* spannend

'nail clippers *npl* Nagelknipser *m*

'nail file *n* Nagelfeile *f*

'nail polish *n* Nagellack *m*

'nail polish remover *n* Nagellackentferner *m*

'nail scissors *npl* Nagelschere *f*

naïve, naive [na·'iv] *adj* (*esp pej*) naiv *pej*

naked ['neɪ·kɪd] *adj* (*a. fig*) nackt; *aggression* unverhüllt; *ambition* blank; *flame* offen; **to the ~ eye** für das bloße Auge

nakedness ['neɪ·kɪd·nɪs] *n* Nacktheit *f*

namby-pamby [ˌnæm·bi·'pæm·bi] *adj attr* (*pej fam: weak*) *person* verweichlicht

name [neɪm] **I.** *n* ① (*title*) Name *m;* **my ~'s Peter** ich heiße Peter; **what's your ~?** wie heißen Sie?; **first/last ~** Vor-/Nachname *m;* **to call sb ~s** jdn beschimpfen; **in the ~ of ...** im Namen von ... ② (*reputation*) Name *m,* Ruf *m;* **to make a ~ for oneself** sich *dat* einen Namen machen **II.** *vt* ① (*call*) **they ~d their little boy Philip** sie nannten ihren kleinen Sohn Philip ② (*list*) nennen

'name-dropping *n* Namedropping *nt* (*das Angeben mit berühmten Persönlichkeiten, die man kennt*)

nameless ['neɪm·lɪs] *adj inv* namenlos

namely ['neɪm·li] *adv inv* nämlich

'nameplate *n of a person* Namensschild *nt;* (*on door*) Türschild *nt; of company* Firmenschild *nt*

'namesake *n* Namensvetter *m*

nana ['naen·ə] *n* (*fam*) Omi *f*

nanny ['næn·i] *n* Kindermädchen *nt*

'nanny goat *n* Geiß *f*

nanosecond ['nan·ə·ˌsek·ənd] *n* Nanosekunde *f*

nap [næp] **I.** *n* Nickerchen *nt;* **to take a ~** ein Nickerchen machen **II.** *vi* <-pp-> (*fam*) ein Nickerchen machen

napalm ['neɪ·pam] *n* Napalm *nt*

napkin ['næp·kɪn] *n* Serviette *f*

narc, nark [nark] *n* (*sl: narcotics agent*) Rauschgiftfahnder(in) *m(f)*

narcissus <*pl* -es *or* -issi *or* -> [nar·'sɪs·əs] *n* Narzisse *f*

narcosis [nar·'koʊ·sɪs] *n* Narkose *f*

narcotic [nar·'kaṭ·ɪk] **I.** *n* ① (*drug*) Rauschgift *nt* ② MED (*drug causing sleepiness*) Narkotikum *nt* **II.** *adj* ① (*affecting the mind*) berauschend ② MED narkotisch; (*sleep-inducing*) einschläfernd

narrate ['nær·eɪt] *vt* ① (*provide commentary*) erzählen ② (*give account of*) schildern

narration [næ·'reɪ·ʃən] *n* Schilderung *f; of a story, tale* Erzählung *f*

narrative ['nær·ə·ṭɪv] *n* (*form*) ① (*story*) Erzählung *f* ② (*description of events*) Schilderung *f*

narrator ['nær·eɪ·ṭər] *n* Erzähler(in) *m(f)*

narrow ['nær·oʊ] **I.** *adj* ① (*thin*) eng, schmal ② (*pej: limited*) **to have a ~ mind** engstirnig sein ③ (*small*) *margin, victory* knapp **II.** *vi* enger werden, sich verengen; (*fig*) *gap, difference* sich schließen **III.** *vt* verengen; (*fig*) beschränken; *eyes* zusammenkneifen

narrowly ['nær·oʊ·li] *adv* (*barely*) knapp

narrow-'minded *adj* engstirnig

NASA ['næs·ə] *n abbrev of* **National Aeronautics and Space Administration** NASA *f*

Die **National Aeronautics and Space Administration**, üblicherweise **NASA** genannt, ist eine Regierungsorganisation, die sich mit Forschungen zur Luft- und Raumfahrt befasst. Nach ihrer Gründung am 29. Juli 1958 war sie für die Organisation der berühmten *Apollo 11 Mission* verantwortlich, dank der Neil Armstrong am 20. Juli 1969 der erste Mann auf dem Mond war. Zu den neueren Missionen der NASA zählen die Mission *Mars Exploration Rovers*, die 2003 mit dem Ziel ins Leben gerufen wurde, die Marsoberfläche mit Hilfe zweier Roboter, Spirit und Opportunity, zu erkunden und die Mission *Deep Impact*, die am 12. Januar 2005 gestartet wurde, um den mittels eines „Impaktors" herbeigeführten Krater auf dem Kometen 9P/Tempel 1 und die beim Einschlag ausgestoßenen Substanzen von der Raumsonde aus erforschen zu können.

nasal ['neɪ·zəl] *adj* ❶ (*concerning nose*) Nasen- ❷ *voice* nasal
nastiness ['næs·tɪ·nɪs] *n* Gemeinheit *f*
nasturtium [nə·'stɜr·ʃəm] *n* [Kapuziner]kresse *f*
nasty ['næs·ti] *adj* ❶ (*mean*) *person* gemein; *trick, surprise* böse ❷ (*bad*) *smell* scheußlich, widerlich; *scare, shock* furchtbar ❸ (*dangerous*) *accident* gefährlich ❹ (*serious*) schlimm, böse; **to turn ~** *situation, person, animal* unangenehm werden
natal ['neɪ·t̬əl] *adj* Geburts-
nation ['neɪ·ʃən] *n* ❶ (*country, state*) Nation *f*, Land *nt;* **all across the ~** im ganzen Land ❷ (*people*) Volk *nt;* **the Apache N~** der Stamm der Apachen
national ['næʃ·ə·nəl] **I.** *adj inv* ❶ (*of a nation, nationwide*) *matter, organization* national; *flag, team* National-; **~ government** Landesregierung *f;* [**in the**] **~ interest** [im] Staatsinteresse *nt* ❷ (*particular to a nation*) Landes-, Volks- **II.** *n* Staatsangehörige(r) *f(m);* **foreign ~** Ausländer(in) *m(f)*
national 'anthem *n* Nationalhymne *f*
national 'debt *n* Staatsverschuldung *f*
National 'Guard *n* Nationalgarde *f*
national 'holiday *n* (*work-free*) gesetzlicher Feiertag; (*in celebration of a nation*) Nationalfeiertag *m*
nationalism ['næʃ·ə·nə·lɪz·əm] *n* (*usu pej*) Nationalismus *m*
nationalist ['næʃ·ə·nə·lɪst] **I.** *adj* nationalistisch **II.** *n* Nationalist(in) *m(f)*
nationalistic [ˌnæʃ·ə·nə·'lɪs·tɪk] *adj* (*usu pej*) nationalistisch
nationality [ˌnæʃ·ə·'næl·ə·t̬i] *n* ❶ (*esp cultural*) Nationalität *f* ❷ (*legal*) Staatsangehörigkeit *f*
nationalization [ˌnæʃ·ə·nə·lɪ·'zeɪ·ʃən] *n* Verstaatlichung *f*
nationalize ['næʃ·ə·nə·laɪz] *vt company, steel industry* verstaatlichen
national 'park, National 'Park *n* Nationalpark *m*
nation-'state *n* Nationalstaat *m*
'nationwide I. *adv* landesweit, im ganzen Land **II.** *adj inv coverage, strike, campaign* landesweit
native ['neɪ·t̬ɪv] **I.** *adj inv* ❶ (*of one's birth*) beheimatet; **~ country** Heimatland *nt;* **~ language** Muttersprache *f* ❷ (*indigenous*) *customs, traditions* einheimisch; *population* eingeboren ❸ BOT, ZOOL *animal, plant* beheimatet, einheimisch **II.** *n* (*local inhabitant*) Einheimische(r) *f(m);* **a ~ of Mexico** ein gebürtiger Mexikaner/eine gebürtige Mexikanerin; (*indigenous*) Eingeborene(r) *f(m)*
Native A'merican I. *n* amerikanischer Ureinwohner/amerikanische Ureinwohnerin **II.** *adj* **~ history** Geschichte der amerikanischen Ureinwohner

Die Mehrheit der Spezialisten sind sich darin einig, dass die **Native Americans**, die Indianer Nordamerikas, aus Asien auswanderten, die Bering-Meeresenge überquerten und sich in Südkanada und den USA verteilt hatten, lange vor der Entdeckung der Neuen Welt durch die europäischen Entdecker. Sie werden in sieben Kulturzonen gegliedert, von den Eskimos im hohen Norden bis zu den Seminolen der Everglades in Florida und ihr jeweiliger Lebensstil zeugt von ihrer sehr engen Verbindung mit ihrer Umwelt.

native-'born *adj* gebürtig
native 'speaker *n* Muttersprachler(in) *m(f)*
Nativity [nə·'tɪv·ə·t̬i] *n* ■ **the ~** die Geburt Christi
na'tivity play *n* Krippenspiel *nt*
NATO ['neɪ·t̬oʊ] *n acr for* **North Atlantic Treaty Organization** NATO *f*
natural ['nætʃ·ər·əl] **I.** *adj* ❶ (*not artificial*) *flavor, ingredients* natürlich; *color, curls, dye, fertilizer* Natur- ❷ (*as in nature*) *harbor, reservoir, camouflage* natürlich; *fabric, wood* naturbelassen; **~ state** Naturzustand *m* ❸ (*caused by nature*) natürlich; **to die of ~ causes** eines natürlichen Todes sterben; **~ disaster** Naturkatastrophe ❹ BIOL, SOCIOL *father, mother, parents* leiblich ❺ (*normal*) natürlich, normal **II.** *n* ❶ (*approv fam*) Naturtalent *nt* ❷ MUS Auflösungszeichen *nt*
natural 'gas *n* Erdgas *nt*
natural 'history *n* Naturgeschichte *f;* (*as topic of study*) Naturkunde *f*
naturalism ['nætʃ·ər·ə·lɪz·əm] *n* Naturalismus *m*
naturalist ['nætʃ·ər·ə·lɪst] *n* Naturforscher(in) *m(f)*
naturalistic [ˌnætʃ·ər·ə·'lɪs·tɪk] *adj* ART, LIT, PHILOS naturalistisch
naturalization [ˌnætʃ·ər·ə·lɪ·'zeɪ·ʃən] *n* Einbürgerung *f*
naturalize ['nætʃ·ər·ə·laɪz] **I.** *vt* einbürgern **II.** *vi* BOT, ZOOL ■ **to become ~d** heimisch werden
naturally ['nætʃ·ər·ə·li] *adv* ❶ (*of course*) natürlich; (*as expected*) verständlicherweise ❷ (*without aid*) natürlich ❸ (*without special training*) natürlich; **dancing comes ~ to him** Tanzen fällt ihm leicht; **driving doesn't come ~ to me** Autofahren liegt mir nicht
natural re'sources *npl* Bodenschätze *pl*
natural 'sciences *npl* Naturwissenschaft *f*
natural se'lection *n* natürliche Auslese
nature ['neɪ·tʃər] *n* ❶ *no art* (*natural environment*) Natur *f;* **to let ~ take its course** der Natur ihren Lauf lassen ❷ (*innate qualities*) Art *f;* **what is the ~ of your problem?** worum handelt es sich bei Ihrem Problem?; **by ~** von Natur aus ❸ (*character*) Naturell *nt*, Art *f*
nature conser'vation *n* Naturschutz *m*
'nature lover *n* Naturfreund(in) *m(f)*
'nature preserve *n* Naturschutzgebiet *nt*

N

'nature study *n* Naturkunde *f*
'nature trail *n* Naturlehrpfad *m*
naturism ['neɪ·tʃə·rɪz·əm] *n* Freikörperkultur *f*
naturist ['neɪ·tʃə·rɪst] *n* Anhänger(in) *m(f)* der Freikörperkultur
naught [nɔt] *pron* **to be [all] for ~** umsonst sein
naughty ['nɔ·t̬i] *adj* ❶ (*badly behaved*) *children* ungezogen; (*iron*) *adults* ungehörig ❷ (*hum fam: sinful*) unanständig
nausea ['nɔ·zi·ə] *n* Übelkeit *f;* (*fig*) Ekel *m*
nauseate ['nɔ·zi·eɪt] *vt usu passive* (*form*) ■ **to ~ sb** bei jdm Übelkeit verursachen; ■ **to be ~d by sth** (*fig, pej*) von etw *dat* angeekelt sein
nauseating ['nɔ·zi·eɪ·t̬ɪŋ] *adj* Übelkeit erregend *attr;* (*fig, pej*) Ekel erregend *attr*
nauseous ['nɔ·ʃəs] *adj* ❶ (*having nausea*) **she is ~** ihr ist übel ❷ (*fig: causing nausea*) widerlich
nautical ['nɔ·t̬ɪ·kəl] *adj inv* nautisch; **~ chart** Seekarte *f;* **~ mile** Seemeile *f*
naval ['neɪ·vəl] *adj inv* (*of a navy*) Marine-; (*of ships*) Schiffs-, See-; **~ base** Flottenstützpunkt *m;* **~ warfare** (*war*) Seekrieg *m;* (*warring*) Seekriegsführung *f*
nave [neɪv] *n* ARCHIT Hauptschiff *nt*
navel ['neɪ·vəl] *n* ANAT Nabel *m*
navigable ['næv·ɪ·gə·bəl] *adj* (*passable*) schiffbar
navigate ['næv·ɪ·geɪt] **I.** *vt* ❶ (*steer*) navigieren ❷ (*traverse*) befahren; (*pass through*) durchfahren ❸ (*pilot*) steuern; AUTO lenken **II.** *vi* NAUT, AVIAT navigieren; AUTO *driver* fahren; *passenger* lotsen
navigation [ˌnæ·vɪ·'geɪ·ʃən] *n no pl* ❶ (*navigating*) Navigation *f;* **~ system** Navigationssystem *nt*
navigational [ˌnæv·ɪ·'geɪ·ʃə·nəl] *adj inv* Navigations-
navigator ['næv·ɪ·geɪ·t̬ər] *n* Navigator(in) *m(f);* AUTO Beifahrer(in) *m(f)*
navy ['neɪ·vi] **I.** *n* ❶ (*armed forces*) ■ **the N~** die Marine ❷ (*color*) Marineblau *nt* **II.** *adj inv* marineblau
Nazi ['nat·si] *n* (*hist or pej*) Nazi *m*
Nazism ['nat·sɪz·əm], **Naziism** ['nat·si·ɪz·əm] *n* (*hist*) Nazismus *m*
NB [ˌen·'bi] *adv abbrev of* **nota bene** NB
NC, N.C. *abbrev of* **North Carolina**
NCO [ˌen·si·'oʊ] *n abbrev of* **noncommissioned officer** Uffz. *m*
ND, N.D. *abbrev of* **North Dakota**
NE *abbrev of* **Nebraska**
near [nɪr] **I.** *adj* ❶ (*close in space*) nahe, in der Nähe; **where's the ~est phone booth?** wo ist die nächste Telefonzelle? ❷ (*close in time*) nahe ❸ (*most similar*) **he rounded up the sum to the ~est dollar** er rundete die Summe auf den nächsten Dollar auf ❹ *attr* (*close to being*) **that's a ~ certainty/impossibility** das ist so gut wie sicher/unmöglich ▶ PHRASES: **to be a ~ miss** knapp danebengehen **II.** *adv* ❶ (*close in space*) nahe; **do you live somewhere ~?** wohnst du hier irgendwo in der Nähe? ❷ (*close in time*) nahe; **the time is drawing ~** die Zeit rückt näher ❸ (*almost*) beinahe, fast; **nowhere ~** bei weitem nicht **III.** *prep* ❶ (*in proximity to*) nahe [bei] +*dat;* **do you live ~ here?** wohnen Sie hier in der Nähe? ❷ (*almost time of*) **I'm nowhere ~ finishing the book** ich habe das Buch noch längst nicht ausgelesen ❸ (*close to a state*) **we came ~ to being killed** wir wären beinahe getötet worden ❹ (*similar in quantity or quality*) **this color is ~est [to] the original** diese Farbe kommt dem Original am nächsten **IV.** *vt* ■ **to ~ sth** sich etw *dat* nähern **V.** *vi* sich nähern, näher rücken
nearby [ˌnɪr·'baɪ] **I.** *adj* nahe gelegen **II.** *adv* in der Nähe
Near 'East *n* Naher Osten
nearly ['nɪr·li] *adv inv* fast, beinahe
near'sighted *adj* kurzsichtig
near'sightedness *n* Kurzsichtigkeit *f*
neat [nit] *adj* ❶ (*well-maintained*) ordentlich; *appearance, beard* gepflegt; **~ and tidy** sauber und ordentlich ❷ (*approv fam: very good*) toll ❸ *inv* (*undiluted*) pur
neaten ['ni·tən] *vt* in Ordnung bringen
neatly ['nit·li] *adv* ❶ (*tidily*) sauber, ordentlich ❷ (*skillfully*) geschickt
neatness ['nit·nɪs] *n* Ordentlichkeit *f,* Sauberkeit *f*
Nebr. *abbrev of* **Nebraska**
Nebraska [nə·'bræs·kə] *n* Nebraska *nt*
nebula <*pl* -lae *or* -s> ['neb·jə·lə, *pl* -li] *n* ASTRON Nebel *m*
nebulous ['neb·jə·ləs] *adj* nebelhaft; *fear, promise* vage
necessarily [ˌnes·ɪ·'ser·ə·li] *adv inv* (*consequently*) notwendigerweise; (*inevitably*) unbedingt; (*of necessity*) zwangsläufig; **not ~** nicht unbedingt
necessary ['nes·ɪ·ser·i] *adj* nötig, notwendig; **strictly ~** unbedingt nötig; **it's not ~ [for you] to shout** du brauchst nicht zu schreien
necessitate [nə·'ses·ɪ·teɪt] *vt* erfordern
necessity [nə·'ses·ə·t̬i] *n* ❶ (*being necessary*) Notwendigkeit *f* ❷ (*necessary thing*) **bare ~** Grundbedarf *m;* **the necessities of life** das Lebensnotwendige
neck [nek] *n* ❶ ANAT Hals; (*nape*) Nacken *m* ❷ FASHION Kragen *m;* (*neckline*) Ausschnitt *m* ❸ (*narrow part*) Hals *m* ▶ PHRASES: **to be breathing down sb's ~** jdm im Nacken sitzen; **~ and ~** Kopf an Kopf
'neckband *n* Halsbündchen *nt*
necklace ['nek·lɪs] *n* [Hals]kette *f*
'neckline *n* Ausschnitt *m*
'necktie *n* Krawatte *f*
nectar ['nek·tər] *n* Nektar *m*
nectarine [ˌnek·tə·'rin] *n* Nektarine *f*
née [neɪ] *adj pred, inv* geborene
need [nid] **I.** *n* ❶ (*requirement*) Bedarf *m* (**for** an +*dat*); **to be in ~ of sth** etw brauchen; **to have no ~ of sth** etw nicht brauchen

N

❷ (*necessity*) Notwendigkeit *f;* **if ~ be** falls nötig ❸ (*yearning*) Bedürfnis *nt;* **I'm in ~ of some fresh air** ich brauche etwas frische Luft ❹ (*poverty*) Not; **to be in ~** in Not sein **II.** *vt* ❶ (*require*) brauchen; **your pants ~ washing** deine Hose müsste mal gewaschen werden ❷ (*must*) ■**to ~ to do sth** etw tun müssen **III.** *aux vb* **~ I say more?** (*iron*) muss ich noch mehr sagen?; **you ~n't worry** du brauchst dir keine Gedanken zu machen

needed ['nid·ɪd] *adj inv* notwendig, nötig; **much-~** dringend nötig

needle ['ni·dəl] **I.** *n* ❶ (*for sewing*) Nadel *f;* **knitting ~** Stricknadel *f* ❷ MED, BOT Nadel *f* ❸ (*pointer*) Nadel *f* ▶ PHRASES: **it's like looking for a ~ in a haystack** das ist, als würde man eine Stecknadel im Heuhaufen suchen **II.** *vt* ärgern

needless ['nid·lɪs] *adj inv* unnötig; **~ to say ...** selbstverständlich ...

needn't ['ni·dənt] = **need not** *see* **need III.**

needy ['ni·di] **I.** *adj* (*poor*) bedürftig, Not leidend *attr* **II.** *n* ■**the ~** *pl* die Bedürftigen *pl*

negate [nɪ·'geɪt] *vt* (*nullify*) zunichtemachen; (*deny*) verneinen

negative ['neg·ə·t̬ɪv] **I.** *adj* (*all meanings*) negativ; **~ answer** ablehnende Antwort; **to be ~ about sth/sb** etw/jdm gegenüber negativ eingestellt sein **II.** *n* ❶ (*negation*) Verneinung *f;* **in the ~** abschlägig; LING in der Verneinungsform ❷ PHOT Negativ *nt* ❸ MATH **two ~s make a positive** zweimal minus macht plus

negatively ['neg·ə·t̬ɪv·li] *adv* negativ; (*saying no*) ablehnend

negativism ['neg·ə·t̬ɪ·vɪz·əm], **negativity** [ˌneg·ə·'tɪv·ə·t̬i] *n* Negativität *f*

neglect [nɪ·'glekt] **I.** *vt* vernachlässigen; ■**to ~ to do sth** [es] versäumen, etw zu tun **II.** *n* (*lack of care*) Vernachlässigung *f;* (*disrepair*) Verwahrlosung *f;* **to be in a state of ~** verwahrlost sein

neglected [nɪ·'glekt·ɪd] *adj* (*uncared for*) verwahrlost; (*overlooked*) vernachlässigt

neglectful [nɪ·'glekt·fəl] *adj* nachlässig (**of** gegenüber +*dat*); *parents* pflichtvergessen; **to be ~ of sth** etw vernachlässigen

negligee, negligée [ˌneg·lə·'ʒeɪ] *n* Negligee *nt*

negligence ['neg·lɪ·dʒəns] *n* (*lack of care*) Nachlässigkeit *f;* (*neglect*) Vernachlässigung *f;* LAW (*form*) Fahrlässigkeit *f*

negligible ['neg·lɪ·dʒə·bəl] *adj* unbedeutend; *amount* geringfügig

negotiable [nɪ·'goʊ·ʃi·ə·bəl] *adj* ❶ (*discussable*) verhandelbar ❷ (*traversable*) passierbar; *road* befahrbar ❸ FIN übertragbar

negotiate [nɪ·'goʊ·ʃi·eɪt] **I.** *vt* ❶ (*discuss*) aushandeln; *loan, treaty* abschließen ❷ (*traverse*) passieren; (*fig: surmount*) *problems* überwinden **II.** *vi* verhandeln (**for/on** über +*akk*)

negotiation [nɪ·ˌgoʊ·ʃi·'eɪ·ʃən] *n* Verhandlung *f*

negotiator [nɪ·'goʊ·ʃi·eɪ·t̬ər] *n* Unterhändler(in) *m(f)*

neigh [neɪ] **I.** *n* Wiehern *nt kein pl* **II.** *vi* wiehern

neighbor ['neɪ·bər] **I.** *n* (*person*) Nachbar(in) *m(f);* (*fig: country*) Nachbarland *nt;* (*fig: fellow citizen*) Nächste(r) *f(m)* **II.** *vi* [an]grenzen (**on** an +*akk*)

neighborhood ['neɪ·bər·hʊd] *n* ❶ (*district*) Viertel *nt;* (*people*) Nachbarschaft *f* ❷ (*vicinity*) Nähe *f kein pl* ❸ (*fig: approximately*) **in the ~ of a thousand dollars** um [die] tausend Dollar

neighborhood 'watch *n* Nachbarschaftswachdienst *m*

neighboring ['neɪ·bər·ɪŋ] *adj attr, inv* (*nearby*) benachbart, Nachbar-; (*bordering*) angrenzend

neighborliness ['neɪ·bər·lɪ·nɪs] *n* gutnachbarliche Art

neighborly ['neɪ·bər·li] *adj* (*community-friendly*) gutnachbarlich; (*kindly*) freundlich

neither ['ni·ðər] **I.** *adv inv* ❶ (*not either*) weder; **~ ... nor ...** [**nor ...**] weder ... noch ... [oder ...] ❷ (*a. not*) auch nicht ▶ PHRASES: **to be ~ here nor there** völlig nebensächlich sein **II.** *adj attr, inv* keine(r, s) von beiden **III.** *pron* (*not either of two*) keine(r, s) von beiden; **we've got two TVs, but ~ works right** wir haben zwei Fernseher, aber keiner funktioniert richtig **IV.** *conj* ❶ (*not either*) ■**~ ... nor ...** weder ... noch ❷ *after neg* (*also not*) weder; **I can't be at the meeting, and ~ can Andrew** ich kann nicht zum Treffen kommen und Andrew auch nicht

neoclassical [ˌni·oʊ·'klæs·ɪ·kəl] *adj* klassizistisch

neo-conservative [ˌni·oʊ·kən·'sɜr·və·t̬ɪv] *adj* neokonservativ (*mit Bezug auf die konservative Reagan-Ära*)

Neolithic [ˌni·oʊ·'lɪθ·ɪk] *adj inv* neolithisch; **~ Period** Neolithikum *nt*

neon ['ni·an] *n* Neon *nt;* **~ light** Neonlampe *f;* **~ sign** Leuchtreklame *f*

neo-Nazi [ˌni·oʊ·'nat·si] *n* Neonazi *m*

nephew ['nef·ju] *n* Neffe *m*

nepotism ['nep·ə·tɪz·əm] *n* (*pej*) Vetternwirtschaft *f*

nerd [nɜrd] *n* (*sl: geek*) Streber(in) *m(f) pej;* (*loser*) Depp *m bes* SÜDD, ÖSTERR, SCHWEIZ *pej;* **computer ~** Computerfreak *m sl*

nerdy ['nɜrd·i] *adj* (*fam*) doof

nerve [nɜrv] *n* ❶ ANAT Nerv *m* ❷ (*courage*) Mut *m;* **to lose one's ~** die Nerven verlieren ❸ (*nervousness*) ■**~s** *pl* Nervosität *f kein pl;* (*stress*) Nerven *pl* ❹ (*impudence*) Frechheit *f* ▶ PHRASES: **to get on sb's ~s** (*fam*) jdm auf die Nerven [*o* den Wecker] gehen

'nerve cell *n* Nervenzelle *f*

'nerve center *n* Nervenzentrum *nt a. fig*

'nerve gas *n* Nervengas *nt*

'nerve-racking, 'nerve-wracking *adj* nervenaufreibend

nervous ['nɜr·vəs] *adj* (*high-strung*) nervös; (*tense*) aufgeregt; (*fearful*) ängstlich; ■**to be ~**

N

about sth wegen etw *dat* nervös sein
nervous 'breakdown *n* Nervenzusammenbruch *m*
nervously ['nɜr·vəs·li] *adv* nervös; (*overexcitedly*) aufgeregt; (*timidly*) ängstlich
nervousness ['nɜr·vəs·nɪs] *n* (*nervous state*) Nervosität *f;* (*fear*) Angst *f* (**about** vor +*dat*)
'nervous system *n* Nervensystem *nt*
nervy ['nɜr·vi] *adj* (*pej*) unverschämt
nest [nest] **I.** *n* ❶ (*a. fig: of animals*) Nest *nt* ❷ (*pej: den*) Schlupfwinkel *m;* (*of criminals*) Brutstätte *f fig* **II.** *vi* ORN nisten
'nest egg *n* (*fig*) Notgroschen *m*
nesting ['nest·ɪŋ] *adj attr, inv* ❶ (*of sets*) ineinanderstapelbar ❷ (*of nests*) Nist-; ~ **box** Nistkasten *m*
nestle ['nes·əl] **I.** *vt* **she ~d the baby lovingly in her arms** sie hielt das Baby liebevoll in ihren Armen **II.** *vi* ❶ (*person*) ■**to ~ up to sb** sich an jdn anschmiegen ❷ (*object*) ■**to ~ in sth** in etw *akk* eingebettet sein
nestling ['nest·lɪŋ] *n* ORN Nestling *m*
Net [net] *n* INET, COMPUT ■**the ~** das Netz
net¹ [net] **I.** *n* Netz *nt a. fig;* **fishing ~** Fischernetz *nt* **II.** *vt* <-tt-> ❶ (*catch*) *fish* mit einem Netz fangen; (*fig*) *criminals* fangen ❷ TENNIS **to ~ a return** einen Return ins Netz schlagen
net² [net] **I.** *adj inv* ❶ *a.* FIN netto, rein, Netto-, Rein-; ~ **profit** Reingewinn *m;* ~ **salary** Nettolöhne *pl* ❷ *attr* (*fig: final*) End-; ~ **result** Endergebnis *nt* **II.** *vt* ❶ (*after tax*) netto verdienen ❷ (*realize*) netto einnehmen
Netherlands ['neð·ər·ləndz] *n* ■**the ~** die Niederlande *pl*
netiquette ['neṭ·ɪ·ˌket] *n* COMPUT Netiquette *f*
'Netspeak *adj* COMPUT Internet-Jargon *m*
netting ['neṭ·ɪŋ] *n* (*material*) Netzgewebe *nt;* (*structure*) Netzwerk *nt*
nettle ['neṭ·əl] *n* Nessel *f;* **stinging ~s** Brennnesseln *pl*
network ['net·ˌwɜk] **I.** *n* ❶ (*structure*) Netz[werk] *nt* ❷ (*fig: people*) Netz *nt* ❸ TELEC [Kommunikations]netzwerk *nt;* **cable ~** Kabelnetz *nt;* **telephone ~** Telefonnetz *nt;* **television** [*or* **TV**] **~** Sendernetz *nt* ❹ ECON Netz *nt* ❺ TRANSP **rail[road] ~** [Eisen]bahnnetz *nt* ❻ INET Netzwerk *nt;* **social ~** soziales Netzwerk, Social Network *nt* **II.** *vt* (*link*) *also* COMPUT vernetzen (**to** mit) **III.** *vi* Kontakte knüpfen und nutzen, netzwerken; ■**to ~ with sb** mit jdm Kontakt knüpfen
'networker *n* Networker(in) *m(f)*
networking ['net·ˌwɜrk·ɪŋ] *n* ❶ (*making contacts*) Kontaktknüpfen *nt* ❷ COMPUT Vernetzen *nt*
neural ['nʊr·əl] *adj attr, inv* ❶ ANAT Nerven-, neural *fachspr* ❷ COMPUT **~ network** Neuronennetz *nt*
neuralgia [nʊ·'ræl·dʒə] *n* Neuralgie *f*
neurological [ˌnʊr·ə·'ladʒ·ɪ·kəl] *adj inv* neurologisch
neurologist [nʊ·'ral·ə·dʒɪst] *n* Neurologe *m,* Neurologin *f*
neurology [nʊ·'ral·ə·dʒi] *n* Neurologie *f*
neuron ['nʊr·an] *n* Neuron *nt*
neuroscience [ˌnʊr·oʊ·'saɪ·əns] *n* Neurobiologie *f*
neurosis <*pl* -ses> [nʊ·'roʊ·sɪs, *pl* -siz] *n* Neurose *f*
neurosurgeon [ˌnʊr·oʊ·'sɜr·dʒən] *n* Neurochirurg(in) *m(f)*
neurosurgery [ˌnʊr·oʊ·'sɜr·dʒə·ri] *n* Neurochirurgie *f*
neurotic [nʊ·'raṭ·ɪk] **I.** *n* Neurotiker(in) *m(f)* **II.** *adj* neurotisch
neuter ['nu·ṭər] **I.** *adj* sächlich; ~ **noun** Neutrum *nt* **II.** *vt male animal* kastrieren
neutral ['nu·trəl] **I.** *adj* neutral **II.** *n* ❶ (*country*) neutrales Land; (*person*) Neutrale(r) *f(m)* ❷ AUTO Leerlauf *m;* **in ~** im Leerlauf
neutrality [nu·'træl·ə·ṭi] *n* Neutralität *f*
neutralization [ˌnu·trə·lɪ·'zeɪ·ʃən] *n* Neutralisierung *f*
neutralize ['nu·trə·laɪz] *vt* (*nullify*) neutralisieren; *bomb* entschärfen; (*weaken*) *smell* abschwächen; *strong taste* mildern
neutron ['nu·tran] *n* Neutron *nt;* **~ bomb** Neutronenbombe *f*
Nev. *abbrev of* **Nevada**
Nevada [nə·'vad·ə] *n* Nevada *nt*
never ['nev·ər] *adv inv* nie, niemals; **~ again!** nie wieder!; **~ before** noch nie [zuvor]; **~ ever** (*fam*) nie im Leben; **~ mind!** mach' dir nichts draus! *fam*
never-'ending *adj* endlos
never-'never land *n* (*fam*) Fantasiewelt *f*
nevertheless [ˌnev·ər·ðə·'les] *adv* dennoch, nichtsdestoweniger
new [nu] **I.** *adj* neu; **that's nothing ~!** das ist nichts Neues!; **~ boy/girl/kid** (*a. fig: in school*) Neue(r) *f(m);* **I'm ~ around here** ich bin neu hier **II.** *n* ■**the ~** das Neue
newbie ['nu·bi] *n* COMPUT Anfänger(in) *m(f)*
'newborn I. *adj attr, inv* neugeboren **II.** *n* ■**the ~** *pl* die Neugeborenen *pl*
'newcomer *n* (*new arrival*) Neuankömmling *m;* (*stranger*) Fremde(r) *f(m);* **I'm a ~ to Miami** ich bin neu in Miami
new'fangled *adj inv* (*fam*) neumodisch
'newfound *adj* neu[entdeckt]
New Hampshire [ˌnu·'hæmp·ʃər] *n* New Hampshire *nt*
newish ['nu·ɪʃ] *adj inv* (*fam*) relativ neu
New Jersey [ˌnu·'dʒɜr·zi] *n* New Jersey *nt*
newly ['nu·li] *adv inv* kürzlich, neulich; **~ married** jungverheiratet; **~ painted** frisch gestrichen
'newlywed I. *n* Jungverheiratete(r) *f(m)* **II.** *adj* jungverheiratet
New Mexico [ˌnu·'mek·sɪ·koʊ] *n* New Mexico *nt*
new 'moon *n* Neumond *m*
new po'tatoes *npl* neue Kartoffeln *pl*
news [nuz] *n* ❶ (*new information*) Neuigkeit *f;* **to be bad ~ [for sb/sth]** (*fig*) schlecht [für

N

jdn/etw] sein; **to break the ~ to sb** jdm die schlechte Nachricht überbringen ❷ (*media*) Nachrichten *pl;* **to be in the ~** in den Schlagzeilen sein; **on the ~** (*in TV, radio*) in den Nachrichten

ˈ**news agency** *n* Nachrichtenagentur *f*

ˈ**newscast** *n* Nachrichtensendung *f*

ˈ**newscaster** *n* Nachrichtensprecher(in) *m(f)*

ˈ**news conference** *n* Pressekonferenz *f*

ˈ**newsflash** *n* Kurzmeldung *f*

ˈ**newsgroup** *n* INET Newsgroup *f*

ˈ**news item** *n* Nachricht *f*

ˈ**newsletter** *n* Rundschreiben *nt*

ˈ**newspaper** *n* ❶ (*journal*) Zeitung *f;* **daily ~** Tageszeitung *f* ❷ (*material*) Zeitungspapier *nt*

ˈ**newsprint** *n* Zeitungspapier *nt*

ˈ**news release** *n* Presseerklärung *f*

ˈ**news report** *n* Meldung *f*

ˈ**newsroom** *n* Nachrichtenredaktion *f*

ˈ**newsstand** *n* Zeitungsstand *m*

ˈ**newsworthy** *adj* berichtenswert

newt [nut] *n* ZOOL Wassermolch *m*

New ˈTestament *n* **the ~** das Neue Testament

new ˈwave *n* ❶ FILM, TV, THEAT (*movement*) ≈ neue Welle ❷ (*fresh outbreak*) **a ~ of layoffs/violence** eine neue Entlassungswelle/Welle der Gewalt

New ˈYear *n* Neujahr *nt kein pl;* **Happy ~** gutes neues Jahr; ■**the ~** das neue Jahr; (*first weeks*) der Jahresbeginn

New ˈYear's *n* (*fam: January 1*) Neujahrstag *m;* (*December 31*) Silvester *nt*

New Year's ˈDay *n* Neujahr *nt,* Neujahrstag *m*

New Year's ˈEve *n* Silvester *nt*

New York [ˌnu·ˈjɔrk] *n* New York *nt*

New Zealand [ˌnu·ˈzi·lənd] *n* Neuseeland *nt*

New Zealander [ˌnu·ˈzi·lənd·ər] *n* Neuseeländer(in) *m(f)*

next [nekst] **I.** *adj inv* ❶ (*coming immediately after*) nächste(r, s); **~ month** nächsten Monat; **[the] ~ time** nächstes Mal ❷ (*next in order, space*) nächste(r, s), folgende(r, s); **in the ~ room** im Raum nebenan; **the week after ~** die übernächste Woche; **who's ~?** wer ist der/die Nächste? **II.** *adv inv* ❶ (*subsequently*) dann, gleich darauf; **so what happened ~?** was geschah als Nächstes? ❷ (*second*) zweit-; **the ~ best thing** die zweitbeste Sache ❸ (*to one side*) ■**~ to sth/sb** neben etw/jdm ❹ (*almost*) ■**~ to ...** beinahe ..., fast ...; **~ to impossible** beinahe unmöglich; **~ to nothing** fast gar nichts ❺ (*again*) das nächste Mal; **when I come ~** wenn ich das nächste Mal komme ▶ PHRASES: **what ~?** und was kommt dann? **III.** *n* (*following one*) der/die/das Nächste; **the week after ~** übernächste Woche

next ˈdoor I. *adv* nebenan **II.** *adj pred, inv buildings* nebenan *nach n; people* benachbart; *neighbor* direkt

next-ˈgen *adj* (*fam*) *short for* **next-generation** futuristisch

next of ˈkin *n + sing/pl vb* nächste(r) Angehörige(r)

NH, N.H. *abbrev of* **New Hampshire**

nib [nɪb] *n* [Schreib]feder *f*

nibble [ˈnɪb·əl] **I.** *n* Bissen *m* **II.** *vt* knabbern **III.** *vi* ❶ (*snack*) knabbern; ■**to ~ on sth** an etw *dat* herumknabbern ❷ (*eat into*) ■**to ~ away at sth** an etw *dat* nagen *fig*

Nicaragua [ˌnɪk·ə·ˈrag·wə] *n* Nicaragua *nt*

Nicaraguan [ˌnɪk·ə·ˈrag·wən] **I.** *n* Nicaraguaner(in) *m(f)* **II.** *adj* nicaraguanisch

nice [naɪs] *adj* (*approv*) ❶ nett; (*pleasant*) schön, angenehm; *neighborhood* freundlich; **~ to meet you!** es freut mich, Sie/dich kennen zu lernen!; **~ work!** (*fam*) gute Arbeit! ❷ (*amiable*) nett, freundlich ❸ (*intensifier*) schön; **~ and big** schön groß

nice-ˈlooking *adj* (*person*) gut aussehend, hübsch; (*thing*) hübsch

nicely [ˈnaɪs·li] *adv* ❶ (*pleasantly*) nett, hübsch ❷ (*well*) gut, nett; **that'll do ~** das reicht völlig

nicety [ˈnaɪ·sə·ṭi] *n* (*etiquette*) ■**niceties** *pl* Gepflogenheiten *pl*

niche [nɪtʃ] *n* Nische *f*

nick [nɪk] **I.** *n* (*chip*) Kerbe *f* ▶ PHRASES: **[just] in the ~ of time** gerade noch rechtzeitig **II.** *vt* (*chip*) einkerben; (*cut*) einschneiden

nickel [ˈnɪk·əl] *n* ❶ (*metal*) Nickel *nt* ❷ (*coin*) Fünfcentstück *nt*

nickel-ˈplated *adj* vernickelt

nickname [ˈnɪk·neɪm] **I.** *n* Spitzname *m;* (*affectionate*) Kosename *m* **II.** *vt* **the campsite has been ~d "Tent City" by visiting reporters** der Campingplatz wurde von besuchenden Reportern scherzhaft „Zeltstadt" genannt

nicotine [ˈnɪk·ə·ṭin] *n* Nikotin *nt;* **~ patch** Nikotinpflaster *nt*

niece [nis] *n* Nichte *f*

nifty [ˈnɪf·ti] *adj* (*approv fam: stylish*) elegant; (*skillful*) geschickt

niggardly [ˈnɪg·ərd·li] *adj* (*pej*) ❶ (*stingy*) geizig ❷ (*meager*) dürftig; *donation, supply* armselig

niggle [ˈnɪg·əl] **I.** *vi* ❶ (*criticize*) nörgeln ❷ (*worry*) beunruhigen, nagen *fig* (**at** an *+dat*) **II.** *vt* ■**to ~ sb** (*nag*) an jdm herumnörgeln; (*worry*) jdn beschäftigen

niggling [ˈnɪg·lɪŋ] *adj attr* (*troubling*) nagend *fig*

night [naɪt] *n* ❶ (*darkness*) Nacht *f;* **to spend the ~ with sb** (*as a friend, relation*) bei jdm übernachten; (*sexually*) die Nacht mit jdm verbringen; **at ~** nachts ❷ (*evening*) Abend *m;* **to have a ~ out** [abends] ausgehen; **by ~** abends ❸ THEAT, FILM **opening ~** Premiere *f*

ˈ**night blindness** *n* Nachtblindheit *f*

ˈ**nightcap** *n* (*drink*) Schlaftrunk *m*

ˈ**nightclothes** *npl* Nachtwäsche *f kein pl;* (*pajamas*) Schlafanzug *m*

ˈ**nightclub** *n* Nachtklub *m*

ˈ**night cream** *n* Nachtcreme *f*

ˈ**night depository** *n* Nachttresor *m*

'nightdress, **'nightgown**, *fam* **nightie** ['naɪ·t̬i] *n* Nachthemd *nt*

nightingale ['naɪ·t̬ɪŋ·geɪl] *n* Nachtigall *f*

'nightlife *n* Nachtleben *nt*

'nightlight *n* Nachtlicht *nt*

nightly ['naɪt·li] **I.** *adv inv* jede Nacht **II.** *adj inv* (*each night*) [all]abendlich; (*nocturnal*) nächtlich

nightmare ['naɪt·mer] *n* Alptraum *m*

nightmarish ['naɪt·mer·ɪʃ] *adj* (*horrific*) alptraumhaft; (*distressing*) grauenhaft

night-'night *interj* (*esp childspeak*) [gute] Nacht

'night nurse *n* Nachtschwester *f*

'night owl *n* (*fam*) Nachteule *f hum*

nights [naɪts] *adv inv* nachts; **to work ~** nachts arbeiten

'night school *n* Abendschule *f*

'night shift *n* Nachtschicht *f*

'nightshirt *n* [Herren]nachthemd *nt*

'nightspot *n* (*fam*) Nachtklub *m*

'nightstand *n* Nachttisch *m*

'nightstick *n* Schlagstock *m*

'night table *n* Nachttisch *m*

'nighttime *n* Nacht[zeit] *f*

'night watch *n* Nachtwache *f*

night 'watchman *n* Nachtwächter *m*

'nightwear *n* Nachtwäsche *f*

nihilism ['naɪ·ə·lɪz·əm] *n* Nihilismus *m*

nihilistic [ˌnaɪ·ə·'lɪs·tɪk] *adj* nihilistisch

Nikkei Index [nɪ·'keɪ-] *n, n* Nikkei Index *m*

nil [nɪl] *n* Nichts *nt*, Null *f*

nimble ['nɪm·bəl] *adj* (*usu approv: agile*) gelenkig, beweglich; (*quick*) flink; (*quick-witted*) [geistig] beweglich

NIMBY <*pl* -s> ['nɪm·bi] *n* (*pej*) *acr for* **not in my back yard** *Person, die sich gegen umstrittene Bauvorhaben in der eigenen Nachbarschaft stellt, aber nichts dagegen hat, wenn diese woanders realisiert werden*

nine [naɪn] **I.** *adj* neun; **~ times out of ten** in neun von zehn Fällen ▶ PHRASES: **the whole ~ yards** (*fam*) ganz und gar **II.** *n* Neun *f* ▶ PHRASES: **be dressed** [*fam* **up**] **to the ~s** in Schale [geworfen] sein

9-11, 9/11 [naɪn·ɪ·'lev·ən] *n* der 11. September (*Terrorangriffe am 11.9.2001 auf das World Trade Center in New York und das Pentagon in Washington*)

nineteen [ˌnaɪn·'tin] **I.** *n* Neunzehn *f* **II.** *adj* neunzehn

nineteenth [ˌnaɪn·'tinθ] **I.** *n* ❶ (*after 18th*) Neunzehnte(r,s) *f(m,nt)* ❷ (*fraction*) Neunzehntel *nt* **II.** *adj* neunzehnte(r,s) **III.** *adv* an neunzehnter Stelle

nineties ['naɪn·t̬iz] *npl* ❶ (*temperature*) **temperatures in the ~** Temperaturen um neunzig Grad Fahrenheit ❷ (*decade*) ■**the ~** die Neunziger *pl*

ninetieth ['naɪn·t̬i·əθ] **I.** *n* ❶ (*after 89th*) Neunzigste(r,s) *f(m,nt)* ❷ (*fraction*) Neunzigstel *nt* **II.** *adj* neunzigste(r,s) **III.** *adv* an neunzigster Stelle

'nine-to-five **I.** *adv* **to work ~** von neun bis fünf [Uhr] arbeiten **II.** *adj* **a ~ schedule** ein Achtstunden[arbeits]tag *m*

ninety ['naɪn·ti] **I.** *n* Neunzig *f* **II.** *adj* neunzig

ninja ['nɪn·dʒə] *n* ❶ HIST, MIL Ninja *m* ❷ SPORTS Ninjutsu-Schüler(in) *m(f)*

ninth [naɪnθ] **I.** *n* ❶ (*after 8th*) Neunte(r,s) *f(m,nt)* ❷ (*fraction*) Neuntel *nt* **II.** *adj* neunte(r,s) **III.** *adv* an neunter Stelle

nip¹ [nɪp] **I.** *vt* <-pp-> (*bite*) beißen; (*pinch*) zwicken ▶ PHRASES: **to ~ sth in the bud** etw im Keim ersticken **II.** *vi* <-pp-> beißen *dat* **III.** *n* ❶ (*pinch*) Kniff *m;* (*bite*) Biss *m* ❷ (*chill*) Kälte *f;* **there's a ~ in the air** es ist frisch

nip² [nɪp] *n* (*fam: sip*) Schluck *m*

nipple ['nɪp·əl] *n* ❶ ANAT Brustwarze *f* ❷ (*of baby bottle*) Sauger *m*

nippy ['nɪp·i] *adj* (*fam*) kühl

nirvana [nɪr·'va·nə] *n* Nirwana *nt;* (*fig*) Traumwelt *f*

nit [nɪt] *n* Nisse *f*

nitpick ['nɪt·pɪk] *vi* (*fam: find fault*) kleinlich sein

nitpicker ['nɪt·pɪk·ər] *n* (*pej: faultfinder*) Kleinigkeitskrämer(in) *m(f)*

nitpicking ['nɪt·pɪk·ɪŋ] **I.** *adj* (*pej fam*) pingelig **II.** *n* (*pej fam*) Krittelei *f*

nitrate ['naɪ·treɪt] *n* Nitrat *nt*

nitric ['naɪ·trɪk] *adj* Stickstoff-; **~ acid** Salpetersäure *f*

nitrite ['naɪ·traɪt] *n* Nitrit *nt*

nitrogen ['naɪ·trə·dʒən] *n* Stickstoff *m*

nitroglycerin(e) [ˌnaɪ·troʊ·'glɪs·ər·ɪn] *n* Nitroglyzerin *nt*

nitrous ['naɪ·trəs] *adj* Stickstoff-, stickstoffhaltig; **~ oxide** Lachgas *nt*

nitty-gritty [ˌnɪt̬·i·'grɪt̬·i] *n* (*fam*) **to get down to the ~** zur Sache kommen

nitwit ['nɪt·wɪt] *n* (*pej fam: stupid person*) Schwachkopf *m*

nix [nɪks] **I.** *vt* (*fam*) ablehnen **II.** *adv inv* (*fam*) nichts, nix *fam*

NJ, N.J. *abbrev of* **New Jersey**

NM, N.M. *abbrev of* **New Mexico**

no [noʊ] **I.** *adj* ❶ (*not any*) kein(e); **~ one** keiner; **to be of ~ interest** unwichtig sein ❷ (*on signs*) **"~ parking"** „Parken verboten" ❸ *with gerund* (*impossible*) **there's ~ denying** es lässt sich nicht leugnen **II.** *adv* ❶ *inv* (*not at all*) nicht; **~ less than sb/sth** nicht weniger als jd/etw ❷ (*negation*) nein ❸ (*doubt*) nein, wirklich nicht **III.** *n* <*pl* -es *or* -s> ❶ (*negation*) Nein *nt kein pl;* (*refusal*) Absage *f* ❷ (*negative vote*) Neinstimme *f* **IV.** *interj* ❶ (*refusal*) nein ❷ (*surprise*) **~! I don't believe it!** nein! das kann ich nicht glauben! *fam* ❸ (*distress*) **oh, ~!** oh nein!

Noah's ark [ˌnoʊ·əz·'ark] *n* die Arche Noah

Nobel Prize [ˌnoʊ·bel·'-] *n* Nobelpreis *m;* **~ winner** Nobelpreisträger(in) *m(f)*

nobility [noʊ·'bɪl·ə·t̬i] *n* ❶ (*aristocracy*) ■**the ~** der Adel ❷ (*approv: character*) hohe Gesinnung

N

noble ['noʊ·bəl] **I.** *adj* ❶ (*aristocratic*) ad[e]lig ❷ (*approv: estimable*) *ideals, motives, person* edel *geh,* nobel *geh* **II.** *n* Ad[e]lige(r) *f(m)*
'nobleman *n* Ad[e]liger *m,* Edelmann *m hist*
'noblewoman *n* Ad[e]lige *f,* Edelfrau *f hist*
nobly ['noʊ·bli] *adv* nobel *geh,* edel *geh*
nobody ['noʊ·bad·i] **I.** *pron indef pronoun, sing* (*no people*) niemand, keiner; ~ **else** niemand anders **II.** *n* <*pl* -dies> (*sb of no importance*) Niemand *m kein pl,* Nobody *m*
no-brainer ['noʊ·breɪ·nər] *n* (*fam*) ■ **to be a ~** ein Kinderspiel sein
nocturnal [nak·'tɜr·nəl] *adj inv* (*of the night*) nächtlich *attr,* Nacht-; ZOOL (*active at night*) nachtaktiv
nod [nad] **I.** *n usu sing* Nicken *nt kein pl;* **to get the ~** (*fig*) grünes Licht bekommen **II.** *vt* <-dd-> ❶ **to ~ one's head** mit dem Kopf nicken ❷ **to ~ a farewell to sb** jdm zum Abschied zunicken **III.** *vi* <-dd-> (*as signal*) nicken
◆**nod off** *vi* (*involuntarily*) einnicken; (*voluntarily*) ein Nickerchen machen
nodding ['nad·ɪŋ] *adj* ❶ (*head*) nickend ❷ (*fleeting*) *acquaintance* flüchtig
node [noʊd] *n* Knoten *m;* (*intersection*) Schnittpunkt *m;* COMPUT Schnittstelle *f*
nodule ['nadʒ·ul] *n* Knötchen *nt;* GEOL Klümpchen *nt*
no-'fault *adj attr, inv* Vollkasko-
no-'fly zone *n* Flugverbotszone *f*
no-'frills *adj attr, inv shop* [schlicht und] einfach; **~ service** Service *m* ohne Extras; **~ travel** Pauschalreise *f*
no-go 'area, no-go 'zone *n* ❶ (*prohibited*) verbotene Zone ❷ MIL Sperrgebiet *nt*
no-holds-barred [ˌnoʊ·ˌhoʊldz·'bard] *adj attr, inv* uneingeschränkt; *fight, report* schonungslos
nohow ['noʊ·haʊ] *adv inv* (*fam*) keinesfalls, auf gar keinen Fall
no-'iron *adj inv clothes* bügelfrei
noise [nɔɪz] *n* ❶ (*loudness*) Lärm *m,* Krach *m* ❷ (*sound*) Geräusch *nt* ▶ PHRASES: **to <u>make</u> ~** Aufsehen *nt* erregen
'noise barrier *n* Lärmschutzwand *f*
noiseless ['nɔɪz·lɪs] *adj inv breath, flight* geräuschlos, lautlos
'noise pollution *n* Lärmbelästigung *f*
noise prevention *n* Lärmvermeidung *f*
noisy ['nɔɪ·zi] *adj* ❶ (*making noise*) laut ❷ (*full of noise*) laut; **crowded and ~ bar** überfüllte und sehr laute Kneipe
nomad ['noʊ·mæd] *n* Nomade *m,* Nomadin *f;* (*fig*) Wandervogel *m hum*
nomadic [noʊ·'mæd·ɪk] *adj* nomadisch, Nomaden-
'no-man's-land *n* ❶ MIL Niemandsland *nt* ❷ (*limbo*) Schwebezustand *m*
nominal ['nam·ə·nəl] *adj* ❶ (*titular*) dem Namen nach *nach n,* nominell ❷ (*small*) *sum of money* gering
nominally ['nam·ə·nə·li] *adv* dem Namen nach, nominell
nominate ['nam·ə·neɪt] *vt* ❶ (*propose*) nominieren ❷ (*appoint*) ■ **to ~ sb [as] sth** jdn zu etw *dat* ernennen
nomination [ˌnam·ə·'neɪ·ʃən] *n* ❶ (*proposal*) Nominierung *f* (**for** für +*akk*) ❷ (*appointment*) Ernennung *f* (**to** zu +*dat*)
nominative ['nam·ə·nə·tɪv] **I.** *n* ■ **the ~** der Nominativ **II.** *adj inv* Nominativ-; **to be in the ~ case** im Nominativ stehen
nominee [ˌnam·ə·'ni] **I.** *n* Kandidat(in) *m(f);* **Oscar ~s** Oscar-Anwärter *pl* **II.** *adj attr, inv* nominiert
nonagenarian [ˌnan·ə·dʒə·'ner·i·ən] **I.** *n* ■ **to be a ~** in den Neunzigern sein **II.** *adj inv* in den Neunzigern *nach n*
nonag'gression *n* Gewaltverzicht *m;* **~ pact/treaty** Nichtangriffspakt *m*
nonalco'holic *adj inv drink, beer* alkoholfrei
nonat'tendance *n* (*at school, a hearing*) Abwesenheit *f*
nonchalant [ˌnan·ʃə·'lant] *adj* gleichgültig
noncom'batant *n* MIL Zivilist(in) *m(f)*
noncommissioned 'officer *n* MIL Unteroffizier(in) *m(f)*
noncommittal [ˌnan·kə·'mɪţ·əl] *adj letter, tone* unverbindlich
noncom'pliance *n with an order* Nichtbeachtung *f; with a wish* Nichterfüllung *f*
noncon'formist I. *adj* nonkonformistisch **II.** *n* Nonkonformist(in) *m(f)*
noncon'tributory *adj inv* beitragsfrei
noncoope'ration *n* Kooperationsverweigerung *f* (**with** in Bezug auf +*akk*)
nondeposit 'bottle *n* Einwegflasche *f*
nondescript [ˌnan·dɪ·'skrɪpt] *adj person, building* unscheinbar; *color, taste* undefinierbar
none [nʌn] **I.** *pron* ❶ (*not any*) keine(r, s); **~ of it matters anymore** das spielt jetzt keine Rolle mehr; **~ of the brothers** +*sing/pl vb* keiner der Brüder; **~ of us** +*sing/pl vb* niemand von uns; **~ at all** gar keine(r, s) ❷ (*no person, no one*) **~ other than ...** kein Geringer/keine Geringere als ... ▶ PHRASES: **to be ~ of sb's <u>business</u>** jdn nichts angehen; **to be <u>second</u> to ~** unvergleichlich sein **II.** *adv* kein bisschen; **~ too pleased** (*form*) nicht sonderlich erfreut
nonentity [nan·'en·tə·ţi] *n* (*pej: nobody*) ■ **a ~** ein Niemand *m*
nones'sential I. *adj inv* überflüssig, unnötig **II.** *n* unnötige Sache
none'vent *n* (*fam*) *in one's life* Enttäuschung *f; party* Reinfall *m*
nonex'istence *n* Nichtvorhandensein *nt*
nonex'istent *adj inv* nicht vorhanden
non'fat *adj food* fettfrei
non'fiction I. *n* Sachliteratur *f* **II.** *adj* Sachliteratur-; **~ author** Sachbuchautor(in) *m(f);* **~ books** Sachbücher *pl*
non'flammable *adj inv material* nicht entflammbar

nonne'gotiable *adj inv* ❶ LAW *terms, conditions* nicht verhandelbar ❷ FIN *document, bill of exchange* nicht übertragbar
'no-no <*pl* -es> *n* (*fam*) Unding *nt;* **that's a ~!** das macht man nicht!
nonplus <-ss-> [ˌnan·'plʌs] *vt* verblüffen
nonpol'luting *adj inv byproduct* ungiftig
nonpro'ductive *adj inv* unproduktiv; (*ineffective*) unwirksam; FIN *investment* nicht Gewinn bringend *attr*
non'profit I. *adj inv* nicht gewinnorientiert II. *n* gemeinnützige Organisation
nonprolife'ration POL I. *n* Nichtverbreitung *f* II. *adj attr* Nichtverbreitungs-
nonre'fundable *adj inv payment* nicht zurückzahlbar
nonrenewable 'resources *npl* nicht erneuerbare Energien *pl*
non'resident I. *adj inv* ❶ (*not local*) auswärtig ❷ COMPUT nicht resident II. *n* Nichtortsansässige(r) *f(m)*
nonre'turnable *adj inv* nicht zurücknehmbar
nonsense ['nan·sens] I. *n* ❶ (*absurdity*) Unsinn *m,* Quatsch *m* ❷ (*misbehavior*) Unfug *m* ❸ (*showing disapproval*) Blödsinn *m* II. *adj attr, inv* (*meaningless*) unsinnig, sinnlos III. *interj* ■ **~!** Quatsch!, Unsinn!
nonsensical [ˌnan·'sen·sɪ·kəl] *adj idea, plan* unsinnig
non'shrink *adj material, clothing* einlaufsicher
non'slip *adj inv surface* rutschfest
non'smoker *n* Nichtraucher(in) *m(f)*
non'smoking *adj inv section* Nichtraucher-
non'starter *n* (*idea*) Reinfall *m*
non'stick *adj inv* antihaftbeschichtet
non'stop I. *adj inv* Nonstop- II. *adv* nonstop; *talk, rain* ununterbrochen
non'taxable *adj inv income* steuerfrei
non'toxic *adj inv material, substance* ungiftig
non'verbal *adj inv communication* nonverbal
non'violent *adj inv protest* gewaltfrei
noob [nub] *n* COMPUT, INET Newbie *m fam*
noodle ['nu·dəl] *n* ❶ (*food*) Nudel *f;* ■ **~s** *pl* Pasta *f* ❷ (*fam: head*) **to use one's ~** seinen Verstand benutzen
noogie ['nu·gi] *n* (*sl*) ■ **to give sb a ~** jdm eine Kopfnuss geben
nook [nʊk] *n* Nische *f,* Ecke *f* ► PHRASES: **[in] every ~ and <u>cranny</u>** in allen Ecken und Winkeln
noon [nun] *n* Mittag *m;* ■ **about ~** um die Mittagszeit
no one ['noʊ·wʌn] *pron see* **nobody**
noose [nus] *n* Schlinge *f a. fig*
nope [noʊp] *adv inv* (*sl*) nö *fam*
nor [nɔr] *conj* noch; **neither ... ~ ...** weder ... noch ...
Nordic ['nɔr·dɪk] *adj inv country, person* nordisch
norm [nɔrm] *n* Norm *f*
normal ['nɔr·məl] I. *adj* ❶ (*ordinary*) *person, day* normal ❷ (*usual*) *behavior* normal (**for** für +*akk*); **as [is] ~** wie üblich ❸ (*fit*) gesund; **to be absolutely ~** völlig gesund sein II. *n* Normalzustand *m;* **the temperature was above ~** die Temperatur war höher als normal; **to return to ~** sich normalisieren
normalize ['nɔr·mə·laɪz] I. *vt* ❶ (*make normal*) *blood pressure* normalisieren ❷ *esp* COMPUT abgleichen II. *vi situation, relations* sich normalisieren
normally ['nɔr·mə·li] *adv* ❶ *inv* (*usually*) normalerweise ❷ (*in a normal way*) normal
north [nɔrθ] I. *n* ❶ (*direction*) Norden *m;* ■ **in the ~** im Norden; ■ **to the ~** nach Norden [hin] ❷ (*region*) ■ **the N~** der Norden II. *adj inv* nördlich, Nord-; **~ of Massachusetts** nördlich von Massachusetts III. *adv inv* nordwärts
North 'Africa *n* Nordafrika *nt*
North 'African I. *n* Nordafrikaner(in) *m(f)* II. *adj inv history, culture* nordafrikanisch
North A'merica *n* Nordamerika *nt*
North A'merican I. *n* Nordamerikaner(in) *m(f)* II. *adj inv* nordamerikanisch
North Carolina [ˌnɔrθ·ˌkær·ə·'laɪ·nə] *n* Nordkarolina *nt*
North Dakota [ˌnɔrθ·ˌdə·'koʊ·də] *n* Norddakota *nt*
north'east I. *n* ❶ (*direction*) Nordosten *m;* ■ **to the ~ [of ...]** nordöstlich [von ...] ❷ (*region*) ■ **the N~** der Nordosten II. *adj inv* nordöstlich, Nordost-; **~ wind** Wind *m* von Nordost III. *adv inv* nordostwärts (**of** von +*dat*)
north'eastern *adj attr, inv* nordöstlich, Nordost-
northerly ['nɔr·ðər·li] *adj* nördlich, Nord-
northern ['nɔr·ðərn] *adj attr, inv* nördlich
northerner ['nɔr·ðər·nər] *n* Nordstaatler(in) *m(f);* (*fig, hum*) Nordlicht *nt*
Northern 'Ireland *n* Nordirland *nt*
North 'Pole *n* ■ **the ~** der Nordpol
North 'Sea *n* ■ **the ~** die Nordsee
northward ['nɔrθ·wərd] *inv* I. *adj migration* nach Norden *nach n,* Nord-; **~ direction** nördliche Richtung II. *adv* nach Norden
north'west I. *n* Nordwesten *m;* ■ **to the ~ [of sth]** nordwestlich [von etw *dat*] II. *adj inv* nordwestlich, Nordwest-; **~ wind** Wind *m* von Nordwest III. *adv inv* nach Nordwesten
Norway ['nɔr·weɪ] *n* Norwegen *nt*
Norwegian [nɔr·'wi·dʒən] I. *n* ❶ (*person*) Norweger(in) *m(f)* ❷ (*language*) Norwegisch *nt* II. *adj inv* norwegisch, Norwegisch-
nose [noʊz] I. *n* ❶ (*organ*) Nase *f;* **to blow one's ~** sich *dat* die Nase putzen ❷ (*front*) Schnauze *f fam; of aircraft* Flugzeugnase *f* ► PHRASES: **to <u>stick</u> one's ~ into sth** (*fam*) seine Nase in etw *akk* hineinstecken II. *vi* **to ~ forward** sich vorsichtig vorwärtsbewegen III. *vt* **to ~ one's way 'forward/in/out/up** sich vorsichtig seinen Weg vorwärts-/hinein-/hinaus-/hinaufbahnen
◆ **nose around** I. *vi* (*fam*) herumstöbern *fam* II. *vt* ■ **to ~ around sth** in etw *dat* herumstöbern

◆**nose out** *vt* (*discover*) *secrets, details* herausfinden
'**nosebleed** *n* Nasenbluten *nt*
'**nosedive** **I.** *n* ❶ AVIAT Sturzflug *m* ❷ (*fig*) Einbruch *m* **II.** *vi* ❶ AVIAT im Sturzflug heruntergehen ❷ FIN *prices, economy* einbrechen
'**nose job** *n* MED (*fam*) Nasenkorrektur *f*
'**nose ring** *n* Nasenring *m*
nosey ['noʊ·zi] *adj* (*pej*) *see* **nosy**
nosh [naʃ] (*fam*) **I.** *n* (*snack*) **to have a ~** einen Happen zu sich *dat* nehmen **II.** *vi* ■**to ~ on sth** etw futtern
no-'smoking *adj area* Nichtraucher-
nostalgia [na·'stæl·dʒə] *n* Nostalgie *f*
nostalgic [na·'stæl·dʒɪk] *adj* nostalgisch
no-'strike agreement *n* Streikverbotsabkommen *nt*
nostril ['nas·trəl] *n of a person* Nasenloch *nt; of a horse* Nüster *f*
nosy ['noʊ·zi] *adj* (*pej*) neugierig
not [nat] *adv inv* ❶ *after aux vb* nicht; **it's ~ unusual** das ist nicht ungewöhnlich ❷ *in tag question* **it's cold, isn't it?** es ist kalt, nicht [wahr]? ❸ *before noun* kein, nicht; **it's a girl, ~ a boy** es ist ein Mädchen, kein Junge ❹ *before infin* nicht; **he asked me ~ to do it** er hat mich gebeten, es nicht zu tun ❺ *before predeterminer* nicht; **~ all children like swimming** nicht alle Kinder schwimmen gerne ❻ *before adj, adv* (*meaning opposite*) nicht; **~ much** nicht viel ▶ PHRASES: **~ at all!** (*polite answer*) überhaupt nicht!; (*denying vehemently*) überhaupt nicht!

N

notable ['noʊ·t̬ə·bəl] *adj* ❶ (*eminent*) *collection, philosopher* bedeutend ❷ (*remarkable*) *achievement, success* beachtlich, bemerkenswert
notably ['noʊ·t̬ə·bli] *adv* ❶ (*particularly*) insbesondere, vor allem ❷ (*perceptibly*) merklich, auffallend
notary 'public <*pl* -ies public> [ˌnoʊ·t̬ə·ri-] *n* Notar(in) *m(f)*
notation [noʊ·'teɪ·ʃən] *n* ❶ MATH, MUS Notation *f* ❷ (*note*) Notiz *f*
notch <*pl* -es> [natʃ] *n* ❶ (*indentation*) Einkerbung *f* ❷ (*in belt*) Loch *nt*
note [noʊt] **I.** *n* ❶ (*record*) Notiz *f;* **to leave a ~** eine Nachricht hinterlassen; **to make a ~ [of sth]** [sich *dat*] eine Notiz [von etw *dat*] machen ❷ (*attention*) **to take ~ of sth** von etw *dat* Notiz nehmen ❸ MUS Note *f* **II.** *vt* ❶ (*notice*) wahrnehmen; (*pay attention to*) beachten; ■**to ~ that ...** zur Kenntnis nehmen, dass ... ❷ (*remark*) anmerken; (*point out*) feststellen
'**notebook** *n* ❶ (*book*) Notizbuch *nt* ❷ COMPUT Notebook *nt*
noted ['noʊ·t̬ɪd] *adj attr* bekannt (**for** für +*akk*)
'**notepad** *n* ❶ (*pad*) Notizblock *m* ❷ COMPUT Notepad *nt*
'**notepaper** *n* Briefpapier *nt*
noteworthy ['noʊt·ˌwɜr·ði] *adj conclusions, results* beachtenswert; **nothing ~** nichts Besonderes
not-for-'profit *adj organization, company* nicht auf Gewinn ausgerichtet *attr*
nothing ['nʌθ·ɪŋ] **I.** *pron indef* ❶ (*not anything*) nichts, nix *fam;* **all or ~** alles oder nichts; **~ else** nichts weiter, sonst nichts ❷ (*of no importance*) nichts; **to mean ~ to sb** jdm nichts bedeuten; **it's ~** (*fam*) nicht der Rede wert ❸ (*zero*) Null *f* ❹ SPORTS (*no points*) null ▶ PHRASES: **[all] for ~** [vollkommen] umsonst; **to be ~ less/more than ...** nichts Geringeres/weiter sein, als ...; **there's ~ to it** (*easy*) dazu gehört nicht viel; (*not true*) da ist nichts dran *fam* **II.** *adj attr, inv* (*fam*) *activity* belanglos **III.** *n* (*fam*) ❶ (*person*) Niemand *m* ❷ (*thing*) Unwichtigkeit *f* **IV.** *adv inv* überhaupt nicht; **to look ~ like sb/sth** jdm/etw nicht ähnlich sehen
nothingness ['nʌθ·ɪŋ·nɪs] *n* (*emptiness*) Nichts *nt*
notice ['noʊ·t̬ɪs] **I.** *vt* ❶ (*see*) bemerken; (*catch*) mitbekommen; (*perceive*) wahrnehmen ❷ (*pay attention to*) beachten; (*take note of*) zur Kenntnis nehmen; ■**to ~ sb/sth** (*become aware of*) auf jdn/etw aufmerksam werden; (*realize*) jdn/etw [be]merken **II.** *n* ❶ (*attention*) Beachtung *f;* **to bring sth to sb's ~** jdn auf etw *akk* aufmerksam machen; **to take ~ of sb/sth** von jdm/etw Notiz nehmen; **to take no ~ of the fact that ...** die Tatsache ignorieren, dass ... ❷ (*poster*) Plakat *nt* ❸ (*information in advance*) **at a moment's ~** jederzeit; **until further ~** bis auf weiteres ❹ (*to end an arrangement*) **to give [one's] ~** kündigen
noticeable ['noʊ·t̬ɪs·ə·bəl] *adj improvement, increase* merklich
'**noticeboard** *n* Aushang *m,* schwarzes Brett
notification [ˌnoʊ·t̬ə·fɪ·'keɪ·ʃən] *n* Mitteilung *f*
notify <-ie-> ['noʊ·t̬ə·faɪ] *vt* ■**to ~ sb [of sth]** jdn [über etw *akk*] unterrichten; ■**to ~ sb that ...** jdn benachrichtigen, dass ...
notion ['noʊ·ʃən] *n* ❶ (*belief*) Vorstellung *f;* (*vague idea*) Ahnung *f* (**of** von +*dat*) ❷ (*whim*) Vorstellung *f*
notional ['noʊ·ʃə·nəl] *adj* (*form*) fiktiv; *payment* nominell
notoriety [ˌnoʊ·t̬ə·'raɪ·ə·t̬i] *n* [traurige] Berühmtheit (**for** wegen +*gen*)
notorious [noʊ·'tɔr·i·əs] *adj temper, thief* notorisch; *criminal* berüchtigt
nougat ['nu·gət] *n* Nougat *nt*
nought [nɔt] *pron see* **naught**
noun [naʊn] *n* Hauptwort *nt,* Substantiv *nt*
nourish ['nɜr·ɪʃ] *vt* ❶ (*feed*) ernähren ❷ (*enrich*) *skin* pflegen
nourishing ['nɜr·ɪʃ·ɪŋ] *adj* ❶ (*healthy*) *food, drink* nahrhaft ❷ (*rich*) *cream* reichhaltig
nourishment ['nɜr·ɪʃ·mənt] *n* ❶ (*food*) Nahrung *f* ❷ (*vital substances*) Nährstoffe *pl*
Nov. *n abbrev of* **November** Nov.
novel[1] ['nav·əl] *n* (*book*) Roman *m;* **detec-**

tive ~ Kriminalroman *m*

novel² ['nav·əl] *adj* (*new*) neuartig; *way, approach, idea* neu

novelist ['nav·ə·lɪst] *n* Romanautor(in) *m(f)*

novelty ['nav·əl·ti] *n* ❶ (*new thing*) Neuheit *f* ❷ (*newness*) Neuartigkeit *f* ❸ (*trinket*) Krimskrams *m;* (*funny*) Scherzartikel *m*

November [noʊ·'vem·bər] *n* November *m; see also* **February**

novice ['nav·ɪs] *n* ❶ (*learner*) Anfänger(in) *m(f)* ❷ REL Novize *m,* Novizin *f*

now [naʊ] **I.** *adv inv* ❶ (*at present*) jetzt; **until** ~ bis jetzt ❷ (*at once*) [**right**] ~ jetzt, sofort, gleich ❸ (*up to present*) jetzt, nun; **for two years** ~ seit zwei Jahren ❹ (*short time ago*) **just** ~ gerade eben ❺ (*occasionally*) [**every**] ~ **and then** ab und zu ❻ (*soothing*) ~, ~, **don't cry** aber, aber, nicht weinen ▶PHRASES: [**it's/it was**] ~ **or** <u>**never**</u> (*saying*) jetzt oder nie **II.** *n* Jetzt *nt;* **that's all for** ~ das ist für den Augenblick alles; **from ~ on** ab sofort **III.** *conj* ~ **that ...** jetzt, wo ...

nowadays ['naʊ·ə·deɪz] *adv inv* heutzutage

nowhere ['noʊ·hwer] **I.** *adv inv* nirgends, nirgendwo; ~ **to be seen** nirgends zu sehen; **from** [*or* **out of**] ~ aus dem Nichts *a. fig* **II.** *n* Nirgendwo *nt* **III.** *adj attr* (*fam*) ausweglos

noxious ['nak·ʃəs] *adj* (*form: toxic*) *chemicals, fumes* giftig

nozzle ['naz·əl] *n* Düse *f; of gasoline pump* [Zapf]hahn *m*

nuance ['nu·ans] *n* Nuance *f*

nub [nʌb] *n* (*crux*) Kernpunkt *m;* **the ~ of the matter** der springende Punkt

nuclear ['nu·kli·ər] *adj inv* ❶ (*of energy*) Kern-, Atom- ❷ MIL nuklear, atomar; ~**-free zone** atomwaffenfreie Zone

nuclear 'family *n* Kernfamilie *f*

nuclear 'medicine *n* Nuklearmedizin *f*

nuclear 'power plant *n* Kernkraftwerk *nt,* Atomkraftwerk *nt*

nuclear re'actor *n* Atomreaktor *m*

nucleus <*pl* -clei *or* -es> ['nu·kli·əs, *pl* -klaɪ] *n* Kern *m*

nude [nud] **I.** *adj inv* nackt; ~ **model** Aktmodel *nt* **II.** *n* ❶ ART Akt *m* ❷ (*nakedness*) **in the** ~ nackt

nudge [nʌdʒ] **I.** *vt* ❶ (*push*) stoßen ❷ (*fig: urge*) ■**to ~ sb into** [**doing**] **sth** jdn zu etw *dat* drängen **II.** *n* ❶ (*push*) Schubs *m* ❷ (*encouragement*) Anstoß *m*

nudism ['nu·dɪz·əm] *n* Freikörperkultur *f*

nudist ['nu·dɪst] *n* Nudist(in) *m(f)*

nudity ['nu·də·ṭi] *n* Nacktheit *f*

nugget ['nʌg·ɪt] *n* ❶ (*lump*) Klumpen *m;* **gold** ~ Goldnugget *nt* ❷ FOOD **chicken** ~ Hähnchennugget *nt*

nuisance ['nu·səns] *n* ❶ (*pesterer*) Belästigung *f,* Plage *f;* **to make a ~ of oneself** lästig werden ❷ (*annoyance*) Ärger *m;* **what a ~!** wie ärgerlich! ❸ LAW **public** ~ öffentliches Ärgernis

nuke [nuk, njuk] (*sl*) **I.** *vt* ❶ MIL atomar angreifen ❷ FOOD (*in microwave*) etw warm machen **II.** *n* (*bomb*) Atombombe *f*

null, null and 'void [nʌl-] *adj pred, inv* LAW null und nichtig

nullify <-ie-> ['nʌl·ɪ·faɪ] *vt* (*invalidate*) für ungültig erklären

numb [nʌm] **I.** *adj* ❶ *limbs* taub; ~ **with cold** taub vor Kälte; **to go** ~ *limbs* einschlafen ❷ (*torpid*) benommen ❸ (*shocked*) **to be ~ with grief** vor Schmerz wie betäubt sein **II.** *vt* ❶ (*deprive of feeling*) *limbs* taub machen ❷ (*lessen*) **to ~ the pain** den Schmerz betäuben

number¹ ['nʌm·bər] **I.** *n* ❶ MATH Zahl *f* ❷ (*symbol*) Zahl *f* ❸ (*identifying number*) Nummer *f* ❹ + *sing/pl vb* (*amount*) [An]zahl *f;* **in huge ~s** in riesigen Stückzahlen ❺ + *sing/pl vb* (*several*) **for a ~ of reasons** aus vielerlei Gründen ❻ (*issue*) Ausgabe *f* ❼ (*performance*) Auftritt *m;* (*music*) Stück *nt* **II.** *vt* ❶ (*mark in series*) nummerieren ❷ (*count*) abzählen

number² ['nʌm·ər] *adj comp of* **numb**

numbering ['nʌm·bər·ɪŋ] *n* Nummerierung *f*

numberless ['nʌm·bər·lɪs] *adj* (*esp liter*) zahllos, unzählig

numbness ['nʌm·nɪs] *n* ❶ *of limbs* Taubheit *f* ❷ (*torpor*) Benommenheit *f*

numbskull *n see* **numskull**

numeral ['nu·mər·əl] *n* Ziffer *f*

numerate ['nu·mər·ɪt] *adj* rechenfähig

numerical [nu·'mer·ɪ·kəl] *adj inv* numerisch; **in ~ order** in numerischer Reihenfolge

numeric 'keypad *n* COMPUT Ziffernblock *m*

numerous ['nu·mər·əs] *adj* zahlreich

numskull ['nʌm·skʌl] *n* Hohlkopf *m pej fam*

nun [nʌn] *n* Nonne *f*

nuptial ['nʌp·ʃəl] **I.** *adj* (*form, liter*) ehelich; ~ **vows** Ehegelöbnis *nt* **II.** *n pl* Hochzeit *f*

nurse [nɜrs] **I.** *n* ❶ (*in a hospital*) [Kranken]schwester *f;* (*male*) Krankenpfleger *m* ❷ (*nanny*) Kindermädchen *nt* **II.** *vt* ❶ (*care for*) pflegen; **to ~ sb back to health** jdn wieder gesund pflegen ❷ (*breastfeed*) stillen ❸ (*harbor*) *feeling, grudge* hegen (**for, against** für, gegen +*akk*) **III.** *vi* (*work as a nurse*) in der Krankenpflege arbeiten

nursery ['nɜr·sə·ri] *n* ❶ (*daycare*) Kindergarten *m;* (*preschool*) Vorschule *f* ❷ (*room*) Kinderzimmer *nt* ❸ HORT Gärtnerei *f;* (*for trees*) Baumschule *f*

'nursery rhyme *n* Kinderreim *m;* (*song*) Kinderlied *nt*

'nursery school *n* Vorschule *f*

nursing ['nɜr·sɪŋ] **I.** *n* ❶ (*taking care*) [Kranken]pflege *f;* **to go into** ~ Krankenpfleger(in) werden ❷ (*feeding*) Stillen *nt* **II.** *adj* ❶ (*caring*) Krankenpflege-; ~ **profession** Krankenpflegeberuf *m* ❷ (*feeding*) ~ **mothers** stillende Mütter

'nursing home *n* ❶ (*for old people*) Pflegeheim *nt* ❷ (*for convalescents*) Genesungsheim *nt*

N

nurture ['nɜr·tʃər] *vt* (*form*) ① (*raise*) aufziehen; *plant* hegen ② (*encourage*) fördern
nut [nʌt] *n* ① (*fruit*) Nuss *f* ② TECH Mutter *f* ③ (*fam: crazy person*) Bekloppte(r) *f(m) sl* ④ (*fam: fool*) Verrückte(r) *f(m)* ▶ PHRASES: **the ~s and bolts of sth** die fundamentalen Grundlagen einer S. *gen;* **to go ~s** durchdrehen
'nutcracker *n* Nussknacker *m*
'nut house *n* (*sl*) Klapsmühle *f fam*
nutmeg ['nʌt·meg] *n* ① (*fruit*) Muskatnuss *f* ② (*spice*) Muskat *m*
nutrient ['nu·tri·ənt] **I.** *n* Nährstoff *m* **II.** *adj* BIOL, FOOD Nährstoff-
nutrition [nu·'trɪʃ·ən] *n* ① (*eating*) Ernährung *f* ② (*science*) Ernährungswissenschaft *f*
nutritional [nu·'trɪʃ·ən·əl] *adj* Ernährungs-; **~ supplement** Nahrungsergänzung *f*
nutritionist [nu·'trɪʃ·ə·nɪst] *n* Ernährungswissenschaftler(in) *m(f)*
nutritious [nu·'trɪʃ·əs] *adj* nährstoffreich; (*nourishing*) nahrhaft
nuts [nʌts] *adj pred* ① (*crazy*) ■**to be ~** verrückt sein ② (*angry*) ■**to go ~** ausrasten ③ (*enthusiastic*) ■**to be ~ about sb/sth** verrückt nach jdm/etw sein
'nutshell *n* Nussschale *f* ▶ PHRASES: **in a ~** kurz gesagt
nutty ['nʌṭ·i] *adj* ① (*full of nuts*) mit vielen Nüssen *nach n* ② (*tasting like nuts*) *taste, aroma* nussig ③ (*fam: crazy*) *idea, person* verrückt
nuzzle ['nʌz·əl] **I.** *vt* [sanft] berühren **II.** *vi* ■**to ~ in[to] sth** *dogs, horses* die Schnauze in etw *akk* drücken
NV *abbrev of* **Nevada**
NY, N.Y. *abbrev of* **New York**
nylon ['naɪ·lan] *n* Nylon *nt*
nymph [nɪmf] *n* Nymphe *f*
nymphomaniac [ˌnɪm·fə·'meɪ·ni·æk] *n* (*pej*) Nymphomanin *f*
NZ *n abbrev of* **New Zealand**

Oo

O

O <*pl* -'s *or* -s>, **o** <*pl* -'s> [oʊ] *n* ① (*letter*) O *nt*, o *nt;* **~ as in Oscar** O wie Otto ② (*zero*) Null *f;* **my phone number is three, ~, five, one, one, two, eight** meine Telefonnummer ist drei, null, fünf, eins, eins, zwo, acht
O. *abbrev of* **Ohio**
oaf [oʊf] *n* (*pej fam*) ① (*clumsy person*) Tölpel *m fam* ② (*stupid person*) Dummkopf *m fam*
oafish ['oʊ·fɪʃ] *adj* (*pej fam*) ① (*rude*) *person, behavior* rüpelhaft ② (*clumsy*) *person* tölpelig *fam*
oak [oʊk] *n* ① (*tree*) Eiche *f* ② (*wood*) Eiche *f,* Eichenholz *nt*
oar [ɔr] *n* (*paddle*) Ruder *nt*
oasis <*pl* -ses> [oʊ·'eɪ·sɪs, *pl* -siz] *n* (*a. fig*) Oase *f*
oat [oʊt] *n* Hafer *m;* ■**~s** *pl* (*hulled grain*) Haferkörner *pl;* (*rolled*) Haferflocken *pl*
oath [oʊθ] *n* ① (*promise*) Eid *m;* **to be under ~** unter Eid stehen; **to declare under ~** unter Eid aussagen; **to take an ~ on sth** einen Eid auf etw *akk* schwören ② (*dated: curse*) Fluch *m*
'oatmeal I. *n* (*hot cereal*) Haferbrei *m* **II.** *adj* (*containing oatmeal*) Hafer-
obedience [oʊ·'bi·di·əns] *n* Gehorsam *m* (**to** gegenüber +*dat*)
obedient [oʊ·'bi·di·ənt] *adj* gehorsam; *child, dog a.* folgsam
obelisk ['ab·ə·lɪsk] *n* Obelisk *m*
obese [oʊ·'bis] *adj* fett *pej; esp* MED fettleibig
obesity [oʊ·'bi·sə·ṭi] *n* Fettheit *f pej; esp* MED Fettleibigkeit *f*
obey [oʊ·'beɪ] **I.** *vt* (*comply with*) gehorchen; **to ~ the law** sich an das Gesetz halten; *orders, rules* befolgen **II.** *vi* gehorchen
obituary [oʊ·'bɪtʃ·u·er·i] *n* Nachruf *m*
object¹ ['ab·dʒɪkt] *n* ① (*thing*) *a.* LING Objekt *nt* ② *usu sing* (*aim*) Zweck *m* ③ *usu sing* (*form: focus, subject*) Gegenstand *m* ▶ PHRASES: **money is no ~** Geld spielt keine Rolle
object² [əb·'dʒekt] *vi* ① (*oppose, disapprove*) dagegen sein; (*mind, dislike*) etwas dagegen haben; ■**to ~ to sth** (*oppose, disapprove*) gegen etw *akk* sein; (*dislike, mind*) etwas gegen etw *akk* haben ② (*protest*) protestieren
objection [əb·'dʒek·ʃən] *n* Einwand *m,* Widerspruch *m*
objectionable [əb·'dʒek·ʃə·nə·bəl] *adj* (*offensive*) anstößig; *smell, sight* übel
objective [əb·'dʒek·tɪv] **I.** *n* (*aim*) Ziel *nt* **II.** *adj* ① (*unbiased*) objektiv ② (*actual*) sachlich
objectively [əb·'dʒek·tɪv·li] *adv* (*without bias*) objektiv
objectivity [ˌab·dʒek·'tɪv·ə·ṭi] *n* ① (*impartiality*) Objektivität *f* ② (*actuality*) Sachlichkeit *f*
'object lesson *n* (*approv*) Paradebeispiel *nt* (**in** für +*akk*)
objector [əb·'dʒek·tər] *n* Gegner(in) *m(f)* (**to** +*gen*)
obligated ['ab·lɪ·geɪ·ṭɪd] *adj pred* (*form*) ■**to be ~ to do sth** dazu verpflichtet sein, etw zu tun
obligation [ˌab·lə·'geɪ·ʃən] *n* Verpflichtung *f* (**to** gegenüber +*dat*)
obligatory [ə·'blɪg·ə·tɔr·i] *adj inv* obligatorisch *a. hum*
oblige [ə·'blaɪdʒ] **I.** *vt* ① (*force*) ■**to ~ sb to**

do sth jdn zwingen, etw zu tun; ■**to be/feel ~d to do sth** verpflichtet sein/sich *akk* verpflichtet fühlen, etw zu tun ❷ (*please*) ■**to ~ sb [by doing sth]** jdm [durch etw *akk*] einen Gefallen erweisen; **I'd be much ~d if you/he ...** ich wäre Ihnen/ihm sehr dankbar, wenn Sie/er... **II.** *vi* helfen; **I'll be happy to ~** ich werde bereitwillig helfen

obliging [ə·ˈblaɪ·dʒɪŋ] *adj* (*approv*) *behavior* entgegenkommend; *character, person* zuvorkommend

oblique [oʊ·ˈblik] *adj* ❶ (*indirect*) indirekt ❷ (*slanting*) *line* schief ❸ ANAT *muscle* schräg

obliterate [ə·ˈblɪt̬·ə·reɪt] *vt* ❶ (*destroy*) vernichten ❷ (*efface*) verwischen; *view* verdecken

obliteration [ə·ˌblɪt̬·ə·ˈreɪ·ʃən] *n* ❶ (*destruction*) Auslöschung *f,* Vernichtung *f* ❷ (*effacing*) Verwischung *f*

oblivion [ə·ˈblɪv·i·ən] *n* ❶ (*obscurity*) Vergessenheit *f* ❷ (*unconsciousness*) Besinnungslosigkeit *f*

oblivious [ə·ˈblɪv·i·əs] *adj* ■**to be ~ of** [*or* **to**] **sth** sich *dat* einer S. *gen* nicht bewusst sein; (*not notice*) etw gar nicht bemerken

oblong [ˈab·laŋ] **I.** *n* Rechteck *nt* **II.** *adj inv* rechteckig

obnoxious [əb·ˈnak·ʃəs] *adj* (*pej*) widerlich; *person a.* unausstehlich

oboe [ˈoʊ·boʊ] *n* Oboe *f*

oboist [ˈoʊ·boʊ·ɪst] *n* Oboist(in) *m(f)*

obscene [əb·ˈsin] *adj* ❶ (*offensive*) obszön; *joke* zotig; *language* vulgär ❷ (*immoral*) schamlos

obscenity [əb·ˈsen·ə·t̬i] *n* ❶ *of behavior, language* Obszönität *f* ❷ (*obscene word*) Obszönität *f;* **to use an ~** einen ordinären Ausdruck benutzen

obscure [əb·ˈskjʊr] **I.** *adj* ❶ (*unknown*) *author, place, origins* unbekannt ❷ (*unclear*) unbestimmt; *reasons, comment, text* schwer verständlich; **for some ~ reason** aus irgendeinem unerfindlichen Grund **II.** *vt* ❶ (*block*) **heavy clouds were obscuring the sun** schwere Wolken verdunkelten die Sonne; *view* versperren ❷ (*make unclear*) ■**to ~ sth** etw unklar machen

obscurity [əb·ˈskjʊr·ə·t̬i] *n* ❶ (*anonymity*) Unbekanntheit *f;* (*of no importance*) Unbedeutendheit *f;* **to sink into ~** in Vergessenheit geraten ❷ (*lack of clarity*) Unverständlichkeit *f,* Unklarheit *f*

obsequious [əb·ˈsi·kwi·əs] *adj* (*pej form*) *person, manner* unterwürfig (**to** gegenüber +*dat*)

observable [əb·ˈzɜr·və·bəl] *adj inv* wahrnehmbar

observance [əb·ˈzɜr·vəns] *n* (*form*) ❶ REL (*practice*) Einhaltung *f* ❷ (*obedience*) Beachtung *f; law* Befolgung *f*

observant [əb·ˈzɜr·vənt] *adj* (*approv: sharp-eyed*) aufmerksam

observation [ˌab·zər·ˈveɪ·ʃən] *n* ❶ (*close watch*) Beobachtung *f;* LAW (*surveillance*) Überwachung *f* ❷ (*act of noticing*) Beobachtung *f;* **powers of ~** Beobachtungsgabe *f* ❸ (*remark*) Bemerkung *f* (**about** über +*akk*)

obserˈvation post *n* Beobachtungsposten *m*

obserˈvation tower *n* Aussichtsturm *m*

observatory [əb·ˈzɜr·və·tɔr·i] *n* Observatorium *nt*

observe [əb·ˈzɜrv] **I.** *vt* ❶ (*watch closely*) beobachten; *by police* überwachen ❷ (*study by watching*) *stars, animals* beobachten, observieren ❸ (*form: notice*) bemerken; **to ~ sb do[ing] sth** bemerken, wie jd etwas tut; ■**to ~ that ...** feststellen, dass ... ❹ (*form: remark*) bemerken ❺ (*form: obey*) *ceasefire, neutrality* einhalten; *law, order* befolgen; **to ~ the speed limit** sich an die Geschwindigkeitsbegrenzung halten **II.** *vi* zusehen; ■**to ~ how ...** beobachten, wie ...

observer [əb·ˈzɜr·vər] *n* (*watcher*) Beobachter(in) *m(f);* (*spectator*) Zuschauer(in) *m(f)*

obsess [əb·ˈses] **I.** *vt* verfolgen; **to be ~ed by sb/sth** von jdm/etw besessen sein **II.** *vi* ■**to ~ over** [*or* **about**] **sth** sich *akk* ständig mit etw befassen

obsession [əb·ˈseʃ·ən] *n* ❶ (*preoccupation*) Manie *f,* Besessenheit *f;* **to have an ~ with sth** von etw *dat* besessen sein ❷ PSYCH (*distressing idea*) Zwangsvorstellung *f*

obsessive [əb·ˈses·ɪv] **I.** *adj* zwanghaft; **~ behavior** Zwangsverhalten *nt* **II.** *n* Besessene(r) *f(m)*

obsolescence [ˌab·sə·ˈles·əns] *n* Veralten *nt; law* Überalterung *f*

obsolete [ˌab·sə·ˈlit] *adj inv* veraltet; *design* altmodisch; *law* nicht mehr gültig; *method* überholt

obstacle [ˈab·stə·kəl] *n* Hindernis *nt*

ˈobstacle course *n* Hindernisstrecke *f*

obstetrician [ˌab·stə·ˈtrɪʃ·ən] *n* Geburtshelfer(in) *m(f)*

obstetrics [əb·ˈstet·rɪks] *n* Obstetrik *f fachspr*

obstinacy [ˈab·stə·nə·si] *n* Hartnäckigkeit *f*

obstinate [ˈab·stə·nɪt] *adj* hartnäckig; *person* eigensinnig; *refusal* stur

obstreperous [əb·ˈstrep·ər·əs] *adj* (*form*) aufmüpfig

obstruct [əb·ˈstrʌkt] *vt* ❶ (*block*) blockieren; **to ~ sb's airway** jds Atemwege *pl* verstopfen; *path* versperren; *pipe* verstopfen; *progress* behindern ❷ SPORTS ■**to ~ sb** jdn sperren

obstruction [əb·ˈstrʌk·ʃən] *n* ❶ (*blockage*) Blockierung *f; of pipes* Verstopfung *f;* MED Verstopfung *f;* **to cause an ~** *for traffic* den Verkehr behindern ❷ (*interference*) LAW, A. BASEBALL Behinderung *f;* SPORTS Sperre *f;* **~ of justice** Behinderung *f* der Rechtspflege

obstructive [əb·ˈstrʌk·tɪv] *adj* (*pej*) hinderlich; ■**to be ~** *thing* hinderlich sein; *person* sich querstellen *fam*

obtain [əb·ˈteɪn] *vt* ■**to ~ sth [from sb]** (*to be given*) etw [von jdm] bekommen; (*to go and get*) sich *dat* etw [von jdm] verschaffen; **iron is ~ed from iron ore** Eisen wird aus Eisenerz gewonnen; **to ~ information** sich *dat* Informationen verschaffen; *permission* erhalten

obtainable [əb·ˈteɪ·nə·bəl] *adj inv* erhältlich

obtrusive [əb·ˈtru·sɪv] *adj* ❶ (*conspicuous*) zu auffällig ❷ *question* indiskret; *smell* penetrant

obtuse [ab·ˈtus] *adj* ❶ MATH (*angle*) stumpf ❷ (*form*) *person* begriffsstutzig

obvious [ˈab·vi·əs] **I.** *adj* offensichtlich; *comparison, objection, solution* naheliegend; *displeasure* deutlich; *distress* sichtlich; *hints* eindeutig; *lie* offenkundig; **to make sth ~** etw deutlich werden lassen; ■**to be ~ [that] ...** offenkundig sein, dass ... **II.** *n* **to state the ~** etw längst Bekanntes sagen

obviously [ˈab·viəs·li] *adv* offensichtlich; **he was ~ very upset** er war sichtlich sehr aufgebracht; **this camera is ~ defective** diese Kamera ist offenbar defekt

occasion [ə·ˈkeɪ·ʒən] **I.** *n* ❶ (*particular time*) Gelegenheit *f,* Anlass *m;* (*event*) Ereignis *nt;* **on this particular ~** dieses eine Mal; **on another ~** ein anderes Mal; **on several ~s** mehrmals; **on ~** gelegentlich; **on the ~ of sth** anlässlich einer S. ❷ (*opportunity*) Gelegenheit *f* **II.** *vt* hervorrufen, verursachen

occasional [ə·ˈkeɪ·ʒə·nəl] *adj inv* gelegentlich

occasionally [ə·ˈkeɪ·ʒə·nə·li] *adv inv* gelegentlich; **to see sb ~** jdn ab und zu treffen

occidental [ˌak·sə·ˈden·təl] *adj inv* (*form, poet*) abendländisch *liter*

occult [ə·ˈkʌlt] **I.** *n* ■**the ~** das Okkulte **II.** *adj* okkult; *powers* übersinnlich

occupancy [ˈak·jə·pən·si] *n* (*form*) Bewohnen *nt*

occupant [ˈak·jə·pənt] *n* (*form: tenant*) Bewohner(in) *m(f);* (*passenger*) Insasse, -in *m, f*

occupation [ˈak·jə·ˈpeɪ·ʃən] *n* ❶ (*form: profession*) Beruf *m* ❷ (*form: pastime*) Beschäftigung *f* ❸ MIL Besetzung *f*

occupational [ˌak·jə·ˈpeɪ·ʃə·nəl] *adj* Berufs-, beruflich

occupational ˈhazard *n* Berufsrisiko *nt*

occupational ˈtherapy *n* Beschäftigungstherapie *f*

occupier [ˈak·jə·paɪ·ər] *n* ❶ (*tenant*) Bewohner(in) *m(f)* ❷ (*conqueror*) Besatzer(in) *m(f)*

occupy <-ie-> [ˈak·ju·paɪ] *vt usu passive* ❶ (*fill*) ausfüllen; (*live in*) bewohnen; *room* belegen ❷ (*take control of*) besetzen; **~ing forces** Besatzungstruppen *pl*

occur <-rr-> [ə·ˈkɜr] *vi* ❶ (*take place*) geschehen; *accident* sich ereignen; *change* stattfinden; *symptom* auftreten; **that ~s very rarely** das kommt sehr selten vor ❷ (*come to mind*) ■**to ~ to sb** jdm einfallen; ■**to ~ to sb that ...** jdm in den Sinn kommen, dass ...; **it never ~red to his parents to ask** seine Eltern kamen nie auf den Gedanken, [danach] zu fragen

occurrence [ə·ˈkɜr·əns] *n* ❶ (*event*) Vorfall *m,* Vorkommnis *nt,* Ereignis *nt* ❷ (*incidence*) Vorkommen *nt; disease* Auftreten *nt*

ocean [ˈoʊ·ʃən] *n* Ozean *m,* Weltmeer *nt,* Meer *nt;* **Indian O~** Indischer Ozean

Oceania [ˌoʊ·ʃi·ˈeɪ·ni·ə] *n* Ozeanien *nt*

oceanography [ˌoʊ·ʃə·ˈnag·rə·fi] *n* Ozeanographie *f*

ocelot [ˈas·ə·lat] *n* Ozelot *m*

ocher, ochre [ˈoʊ·kər] *n* Ocker *m o nt*

o'clock [ə·ˈklak] *adv inv* **two ~** zwei Uhr

Oct. *n abbrev of* **October** Okt.

octagon [ˈak·tə·gan] *n* Achteck *nt*

octagonal [ak·ˈtæg·ə·nəl] *adj inv* achteckig

octane [ˈak·teɪn] *n* (*chemical*) Oktan *nt;* (*number*) Oktanzahl *f*

octave [ˈak·tɪv] *n* Oktave *f*

octet [ak·ˈtet] *n* MUS (*group of eight*) Oktett *nt*

October [ak·ˈtoʊ·bər] *n* Oktober *m; see also* **February**

octogenarian [ˌak·toʊ·dʒɪ·ˈner·i·ən] *n* Achtzigjährige(r) *f(m)*

octopus <*pl* -es *or* -pi> [ˈak·tə·pəs, *pl* -pə·sɪz, -paɪ] *n* Tintenfisch *m;* (*large*) Krake *f*

OD [ˌoʊ·ˈdi] (*sl*) *abbrev of* **overdose I.** *vi* ■**to ~ on sth** eine Überdosis einer S. *gen* nehmen *fig* **II.** *n* Überdosis *f*

odd [ad] **I.** *adj* ❶ (*strange*) merkwürdig, seltsam; *person, thing a.* eigenartig ❷ *inv* MATH ungerade ❸ (*occasional*) gelegentlich; *jobs* Gelegenheits- ❹ *attr; inv shoe, sock* einzeln **II.** *n* ■**~s** *pl* (*probability*) **the ~s are 3 to 1** die Chancen stehen 3 zu 1; ■**the ~s are ...** es ist sehr wahrscheinlich, dass ...; **the ~s on/against sb doing sth** die Chancen, dass jd etw tut/nicht tut; **what are the odds on him being late again?** wie stehen die Chancen, dass er wieder zu spät kommt? ▶ PHRASES: **against all the ~s** entgegen allen Erwartungen; **to be at ~s with sb** mit jdm uneins sein; **to be at ~s with sth** mit etw *dat* nicht übereinstimmen; **~s and ends** Krimskrams *m kein pl*

oddball [ˈad·bɔl] (*fam*) **I.** *n* Verrückte(r) *f(m)* **II.** *adj attr* verrückt

oddity [ˈad·ə·ṭi] *n* ❶ (*strange person*) komischer Kauz *fam* ❷ (*strange thing*) Kuriosität *f*

oddly [ˈad·li] *adv* seltsam; **~ enough** merkwürdigerweise

ode [oʊd] *n* Ode *f* (**to** an +*akk*)

odious [ˈoʊ·di·əs] *adj* (*form*) *crime* abscheulich; *person* abstoßend

odometer [oʊ·ˈdam·ə·tər] *n* Kilometerzähler *m*

odor [ˈoʊ·dər] *n* Geruch *m*

odorless [ˈoʊ·dər·ləs] *adj inv* (*form*) geruchlos

odyssey [ˈad·ɪ·si] *n usu sing* (*liter or a. fig*) Odyssee *f*

OECD [ˌoʊ·i·si·ˈdi] *n abbrev of* **Organization for Economic Cooperation and Development** OECD *f*

of [ʌv, əv] *prep* ❶ *after n* (*expressing relationship*) von; **the employees ~ the company** die Angestellten des Unternehmens; **the destruction ~ the rain forest** die Zerstörung des

Regenwalds; **the works ~ Shakespeare** die Werke Shakespeares; **an admirer ~ Picasso** ein Bewunderer Picassos; **a friend ~ mine** ein Freund von mir; **the cause ~ the disease** die Krankheitsursache; **the smell ~ roses** Rosenduft *m* ② *after n* (*relating a part to the whole*) von; **both ~ us** wir beide; **all ~ us** wir alle; **most ~ them** die meisten von ihnen; **a third ~ the people** ein Drittel der Leute; **there were ten ~ us on the trip** wir waren auf der Reise zu zehnt; **one ~ the smartest** eine(r) der Schlauesten; **I liked the green one best ~ all** am besten gefiel mir der grüne; **I hate this kind ~ party** ich hasse diese Art von Party ③ *after n* (*expressing quantities*) **a bunch ~ parsley** ein Bund Petersilie *nt;* **a cup ~ coffee** eine Tasse Kaffee; **two pounds ~ apples** ein Kilo Äpfel *nt;* **a lot ~ money** eine Menge Geld; **a piece ~ cake** ein Stück Kuchen ④ *after vb, n* (*consisting of*) aus; **a sweater made ~ the finest lambswool** ein Pullover aus feinster Schafswolle ⑤ (*expressing cause*) **to die ~ sth** an etw *dat* sterben ⑥ *after vb* (*concerning*) **he was accused ~ fraud** er wurde wegen Betrugs angeklagt; **speaking ~ sb/sth, ...** wo wir gerade von jdm/etw sprechen, ...; *after adj;* **to be unsure ~ oneself** sich seiner selbst nicht sicher sein; **to be afraid ~ sb/sth** vor jdm/etw Angst haben; **to be fond ~ swimming** gerne schwimmen; **to be sick ~ sth** etw satthaben; *after n;* **memories ~ sb/sth** Erinnerungen an jdn/etw; **to be in search ~ sb/sth** auf der Suche nach jdm/etw sein; **thoughts ~ revenge** Rachegedanken *pl* ⑦ *after n* (*expressing position*) von; **north/south ~** nördlich/südlich von; **in the back ~ the car** hinten im Auto; **on the corner ~ the street** an der Straßenecke ⑧ (*expressing age*) von; **at the age ~ six** im Alter von sechs Jahren; **he's a man ~ about 50** er ist um die 50 Jahre alt ⑨ *after n* (*in time phrases*) **the eleventh ~ March** der elfte März; (*to*) vor; **it's a quarter ~ five** es ist viertel vor fünf ⑩ *after vb* (*expressing removal*) **to get rid ~ sb** jdn loswerden; *after adj;* **free ~ charge** kostenlos

off [ɔf] **I.** *prep* ① (*indicating removal*) von; **I can't get this paint ~ my hands** ich bekomme diese Farbe nicht von meinen Händen ab; **he wiped the dust ~ the table** er wischte den Staub von dem Tisch; **he cut a piece ~ the cheese** er schnitt ein Stück Käse ab; **to be ~ the air** RADIO, TV nicht mehr senden; **~ the record** nicht für die Öffentlichkeit bestimmt; **~ the subject** nicht zum Thema gehörend ② *after vb* (*moving down*) hinunter [von]; (*towards sb*) herunter [von]; **they jumped ~ the cliff** sie sprangen von der Klippe; **the boy fell ~ his bike** der Junge fiel von seinem Fahrrad herunter ③ (*away from*) [weg] von; (*at sea*) vor +*dat;* **six miles ~ the coast of Florida** sechs Meilen vor der Küste Floridas; **to lead ~ sth** von etw *dat* wegführen; **we live just ~ the main street** wir wohnen gleich bei der Hauptstraße; **far/a long way ~ sth** weit entfernt von etw *dat;* **we're still a long way ~ finishing** wir sind noch weit vom Ende entfernt ④ (*absent from*) **to be ~ work** am Arbeitsplatz fehlen ⑤ (*fam: refraining from*) **to stay ~ alcohol/drugs** die Finger vom Alkohol/von Drogen lassen ⑥ (*from source*) **to get/buy sth ~ sb** (*fam*) etw von jdm bekommen/kaufen **II.** *adv inv* ① (*not on*) aus; **to switch/turn sth ~** etw ausschalten ② (*away*) weg-; **to go/drive ~** weggehen/-fahren; **I didn't get ~ to a very good start this morning** der Tag hat für mich nicht gut angefangen; **I'm ~ now — see you tomorrow** ich gehe jetzt – wir sehen uns morgen; **to see sb ~** jdn verabschieden ③ (*removed*) ab-; **I'll take my jacket ~** ich ziehe meine Jacke aus; **to come ~** *button* abgehen ④ (*distant in time*) entfernt; **to be/not be far ~** weit weg/nicht weit weg sein ⑤ (*discounted*) reduziert; **to get money ~** Rabatt bekommen; **there's 40% ~ this week on all winter coats** diese Woche gibt es ein Preisnachlass von 40 % auf alle Wintermäntel **III.** *adj inv* ① (*not working*) außer Betrieb; (*switched ~*) aus[geschaltet]; *faucet* zugedreht; *heating* abgestellt ② (*not at work*) ■**to be ~** freihaben; **to take some time ~** einige Zeit freinehmen ③ (*provided for*) **sb is well/not well ~** jdm geht es [finanziell] gut/schlecht

'offbeat *adj* unkonventionell; *music* synkopisch; *sense of humor* ausgefallen; *taste* extravagant

off-'center *adj* nicht in der Mitte *präd*

off-'color *adj* ① (*somewhat obscene*) schlüpfrig ② (*somewhat sick*) unpässlich

'off day *n* schlechter Tag

off-'duty *adj* ■**to be ~** dienstfrei haben; **an ~ police officer** ein Polizist *m* außer Dienst

offend [ə·'fend] **I.** *vi* (*commit a criminal act*) eine Straftat begehen **II.** *vt* (*insult*) beleidigen; (*hurt*) kränken; **to be easily ~ed** schnell beleidigt sein

offender [ə·'fen·dər] *n* [Straf]täter(in) *m(f)*

offense [ə·'fens] *n* ① LAW (*crime*) Straftat *f* ② (*upset feelings*) Beleidigung *f;* **to cause ~** Anstoß erregen; **to cause ~ to sb** (*hurt*) jdn kränken; (*insult*) jdn beleidigen; **to take ~ [at sth]** [wegen einer S. *gen*] gekränkt/beleidigt sein ③ SPORTS (*attack*) Angriff *m*

offensive [ə·'fen·sɪv] **I.** *adj* ① (*causing offense*) anstößig; *joke* anzüglich; *remark* unverschämt ② *smell* übel **II.** *n* MIL Angriff *m;* **to go on the ~** in die Offensive gehen

offer ['ɔ·fər] **I.** *n* ① (*proposal*) Angebot *nt* ② ECON Angebot *nt;* **to make an ~ for sth** ein Gebot für etw *akk* abgeben **II.** *vt* ① (*present for acceptance*) anbieten ② (*put forward*) vorbringen; *congratulations* aussprechen; *explanation* abgeben; *information* geben; *suggestion* unterbreiten ③ (*bid*) bieten **III.** *vi* sich

O

bereit erklären

offering ['ɔ·fər·ɪŋ] *n usu pl* Spende *f;* **sacrificial** ~ Opfergabe *f*

off'hand I. *adj* ① (*uninterested*) gleichgültig ② (*informal*) lässig; ~ **remark** nebenbei fallen gelassene Bemerkung II. *adv* ohne weiteres, aus dem Stand

office ['ɔ·fɪs] *n* ① (*room*) Büro *nt;* (*of company*) Geschäftsstelle *f; of lawyer* Kanzlei *f* ② POL (*authoritative position*) Amt *nt;* **to be in** ~ an der Macht sein; **to come into** ~ sein Amt antreten

'office building *n* Bürohaus *nt,* Bürogebäude *nt*

office e'quipment *n* Büroeinrichtung *f*

'office hours *npl* Geschäftszeit[en] *f[pl]*

officer ['ɔ·fɪ·sər] *n* ① MIL Offizier(in) *m(f)* ② (*office holder*) Beamte(r) *m,* Beamte [*o* -in] *f;* [**police**] ~ Polizeibeamte(r) *f(m),* Polizist(in) *m(f)*

'office supplies *npl* Bürobedarf *m kein pl*

'office worker *n* Büroangestellte(r) *f(m)*

official [ə·'fɪʃ·əl] I. *n* ① (*holding public office*) Amtsperson *f,* Beamte(r) *m,* Beamte [*o* -in] *f* ② (*responsible person*) Funktionsträger(in) *m(f)* ③ SPORTS Schiedsrichter, -in *m, f* II. *adj inv* ① (*relating to an office*) offiziell, amtlich; (*on business*) dienstlich; ~ **residence** Amtssitz *m* ② (*authorized*) offiziell; *inquiry, record* amtlich; *strike* regulär ③ (*officially announced*) amtlich bestätigt; ~ **statement** amtliche Erklärung

officialdom [ə·'fɪʃ·əl·dəm] *n* (*pej: bureaucracy*) Bürokratie *f*

officially [ə·'fɪʃ·ə·li] *adv inv* offiziell

officiate [ə·'fɪʃ·i·eɪt] *vi* (*form*) amtieren (**at** bei); **to** ~ **at a game** SPORTS ein Spiel pfeifen

officious [ə·'fɪʃ·əs] *adj* (*pej*) ① (*bossy*) schikanierend ② (*interfering*) aufdringlich

offing ['ɔ·fɪŋ] *n* ■ **to be in the** ~ bevorstehen

off-'key *adj* ① (*out of tune*) verstimmt ② (*fig: inopportune*) unangebracht

off'key *adv* falsch

off-'limits *adj inv, pred* ■ **to be** ~ **to sb** für jdn tabu sein

off'line *adj inv* offline

'offload *vt* ① (*unload*) ausladen ② (*get rid of*) loswerden *fam;* **to** ~ **the responsibility** [**onto sb**] die Verantwortung [auf jdn] abladen ③ COMPUT *data* umladen

off-'peak *adj inv* ① *telephone call* außerhalb der Hauptsprechzeiten *nach n* ② TOURIST ~ **travel** Reise *f* außerhalb der Hauptreisezeit

off-'piste I. *adv inv* abseits der Skipiste II. *adj inv* abseits der Skipiste *nach n*

'off-season *n* ■ **the** ~ die Nebensaison

offset ['ɔf·set] *vt* <-set, -set> *usu passive* (*compensate for*) ■ **to be** ~ **by** [**doing**] **sth** durch etw *akk* ausgeglichen werden

off'shore I. *adj inv* ① (*at sea*) küstennah ② *inv* FIN Auslands- II. *adv* (*of wind movement*) von der Küste her; **to fish** ~ vor der Küste fischen

off-'site *adj inv* Außen-

offspring <*pl* -> ['ɔf·sprɪŋ] *n* ① (*animal young*) Junge(s) *nt* ② (*a. hum: person's child*) Nachkomme *m;* (*children*) Nachkommen *pl*

off'stage I. *adj inv* (*behind the stage*) hinter der Bühne *nach n* II. *adv* ① (*away from the stage*) hinter der Bühne; **to walk** ~ von der Bühne abgehen ② (*privately*) privat

off-street 'parking *n Parken auf Parkplätzen außerhalb des Stadtzentrums*

off-the-'cuff I. *adj inv* spontan *f* II. *adv* aus dem Stegreif

off-the-'rack *adj inv* Konfektions-, von der Stange *nach n*

off-'white *n* gebrochenes Weiß

often ['ɔ·fən] *adv* oft; ■ **it's not** ~ **that ...** es kommt selten vor, dass ...; **every so** ~ gelegentlich

'oftentimes *adv* (*fam*) häufig, oft

ogle ['oʊ·gəl] I. *vi* gaffen *pej* II. *vt* angaffen *pej*

ogre ['oʊ·gər] *n* Menschenfresser *m;* (*fig fam*) Scheusal *nt pej*

OH *abbrev of* **Ohio**

oh[1] [oʊ] *interj* ① (*to show surprise, disappointment, pleasure*) oh; ~ **damn!** verdammt! *pej fam;* ~ **dear!** oje!; ~ **well** na ja ② (*by the way*) ach, übrigens

oh[2] [oʊ] *n* (*in phone numbers*) Null *f*

Ohio [oʊ·'haɪ·oʊ] *n* Ohio *nt*

oil [ɔɪl] I. *n* ① (*lubricant*) Öl *nt* ② (*petroleum*) [Erd]öl *nt* ③ FOOD [Speise]öl *nt* ④ ■ ~**s** *pl* (*oil-based paints*) Ölfarben *pl* II. *vt* (*lubricate*) ölen

'oilcan *n* Ölkännchen *nt*

'oil change *n* Ölwechsel *m*

'oilcloth *n* Wachstuch *nt*

'oil company *n* Ölfirma *f,* Erdölgesellschaft *f*

'oil crisis *n* Ölkrise *f*

'oil field *n* Ölfeld *nt*

oiliness ['ɔɪ·lɪ·nɪs] *n* ① Fettigkeit *f* ② (*fig: of behavior*) aalglatte Art *pej*

'oil lamp *n* Öllampe *f*

'oil painting *n* Ölbild *nt*

'oil pipeline *n* Ölpipeline *f*

'oil production *n* [Erd]ölförderung *f*

'oil rig *n* Bohrinsel *f*

'oilskin *n* ① (*waterproof cloth*) Öltuch *nt* ② (*waterproof clothing*) ■ ~**s** *pl* Ölzeug *nt kein pl*

'oil slick *n* Ölteppich *m*

'oil tanker *n* Öltanker *m*

'oil well *n* Ölquelle *f*

oily ['ɔɪ·li] *adj* ① *substance, food* ölig ② *hair, skin* fettig ③ (*fig: obsequious*) schmierig *pej fam*

oink [ɔɪŋk] I. *vi* grunzen II. *n* Grunzen *nt*

ointment ['ɔɪnt·mənt] *n* Salbe *f*

OK, okay [ˌoʊ·'keɪ] (*fam*) I. *adj* ① *pred, inv* (*acceptable*) okay; **if it's** ~ **with you, ...** wenn es dir recht ist, ... ② *pred, inv* (*healthy*) *person* in Ordnung; **are you** ~**? you look a bit pale** geht es dir gut? du siehst etwas blass aus ③ *pred, inv* (*not outstanding*) ganz gut, nicht schlecht ④ *pred, inv* (*have no problems*) **to be**

~ **for money/work** genug Geld/Arbeit haben ⑤ (*pleasant*) **to be an ~ guy** ein prima Kerl sein **II.** *interj* okay; **~ then** also gut **III.** *vt* ■**to ~ sth** zu etw *dat* sein Okay geben **IV.** *n* **to give** [**sth**] **the ~** das Okay [zu etw *dat*] geben **V.** *adv inv* gut; **did you get there ~?** bist du dort gut angekommen?

OK *abbrev of* **Oklahoma**

Okla. *abbrev of* **Oklahoma**

Oklahoma [ˌoʊ·klə·ˈhoʊ·mə] *n* Oklahoma *nt*

okra [ˈoʊk·rə] *n* Okra *f*

old [oʊld] **I.** *adj* ① *person, animal, object* alt; **to grow ~** alt werden ② *after n* (*denoting an age*) alt; **three years ~** drei Jahre alt ③ *attr, inv* (*former*) ehemalig; *job* alt ④ *attr, inv* (*fam*) **any ~ present/computer/thing** irgendein Geschenk/irgendeinen Computer/irgendwas ▶ PHRASES: **you can't teach an ~ dog new tricks** (*prov*) der Mensch ist ein Gewohnheitstier **II.** *n* ■**the ~** *pl* die Alten *pl;* **young and ~** Jung und Alt **III.** *in compounds* **a twenty-one-year-~** ein Einundzwanzigjähriger/eine Einundzwanzigjährige

old ˈage *n* Alter *nt*

old-ˈfashioned *adj* (*esp pej*) altmodisch

old ˈlady *n* ① (*elderly female*) alte Dame ② (*fam: one's wife, mother*) ■**the/sb's ~** die/jds Alte

old ˈman *n* ① (*elderly male*) alter Mann, Greis *m* ② (*fam: husband, father*) ■**the/sb's ~** der Alte/jds Alter *fam*

old ˈmaster *n* alter Meister

ˈold school I. *n* (*approv*) **he's from the ~** er ist [noch] einer der alten Schule **II.** *adj* der alten Schule *nach n*

Old ˈTestament *n* ■**the ~** das Alte Testament

old-ˈtimer *n* (*fam*) ① (*old man*) Oldie *m hum fam* ② (*long-time worker*) alter Hase *fam*

old ˈwives' tale *n* Ammenmärchen *nt*

oleander [ˌoʊ·li·ˈæn·dər] *n* Oleander *m*

olfactory [al·ˈfæk·tə·ri] *adj inv* Geruchs-, olfaktorisch *fachspr*

olive [ˈal·ɪv] *n* ① (*fruit*) Olive *f* ② (*tree*) Olivenbaum *m*

ˈolive branch *n* (*fig: symbol of peace*) Ölzweig *m*

ˈolive grove *n* Olivenhain *m*

ˈolive oil *n* Olivenöl *nt*

Olympiad [oʊ·ˈlɪm·pɪ·æd] *n* Olympiade *f*

Olympian [oʊ·ˈlɪm·pi·ən] **I.** *adj inv* olympisch **II.** *n* (*Olympic Games competitor*) Olympionike, -in *m, f*

Olympic [oʊ·ˈlɪm·pɪk] *adj attr, inv* olympisch; **~ stadium** Olympiastadion *nt*

Olympic ˈGames, Olympics [oʊ·ˈlɪm·pɪks] *n pl* ■**the ~** die Olympischen Spiele

ombudsman [ˈam·bədz·mən] *n* Ombudsmann *m*

omelet, omelette [ˈam·lət] *n* Omelett *nt*

omen [ˈoʊ·men] *n* Omen *nt*

ominous [ˈam·ə·nəs] *adj* unheilvoll

omission [oʊ·ˈmɪʃ·ən] *n* Auslassung *f*

omit <-tt-> [oʊ·ˈmɪt] **I.** *vt* auslassen; (*ignore*) übergehen **II.** *vi* ■**to ~ to do sth** es unterlassen, etw zu tun

omnipotent [am·ˈnɪp·ə·t̬ənt] *adj inv* allmächtig

omnipresent [ˌam·nɪ·ˈprez·ənt] *adj inv* (*widespread*) omnipräsent *geh;* (*everywhere*) überall

omnivorous [am·ˈnɪv·ər·əs] *adj inv* ① (*eating plants and meat*) alles fressend *attr* ② (*fig: voracious*) unstillbar

on [an] **I.** *prep* ① (*on top of*) auf +*dat;* **the book's ~ the desk/table** das Buch liegt auf dem Tisch/Stuhl ② *with verbs of motion* (*onto*) auf +*akk;* **to go out ~ the balcony** auf die Terrasse hinausgehen; **let's hang the picture ~ the wall** lass uns das Bild an die Wand hängen ③ (*indicating position*) an +*dat,* auf +*dat;* **to lie ~ the beach** am Strand liegen; **to lie ~ one's back** auf dem Rücken liegen; **he had a scratch ~ his arm** er hatte einen Kratzer am Arm; **~ the left/right** auf der linken/rechten Seite ④ (*indicating contact*) an +*dat;* **I hit my head ~ the shelf** ich stieß mir den Kopf am Regal an; **to stumble ~ sth** über etw *akk* stolpern ⑤ (*about*) über +*akk;* **a debate ~ the crisis** eine Debatte über die Krise; **he needs some advice ~ how to dress** er braucht ein paar Tipps, wie er sich anziehen soll; **essays ~ a wide range of issues** Aufsätze zu einer Vielzahl von Themen; **to congratulate sb ~ sth** jdn zu etw *dat* gratulieren ⑥ (*based on*) auf ... hin; **he was acting ~ a hunch** er handelte nach Gefühl; **~ account of** wegen; **to rely ~ sb/sth** sich auf jdn/etw verlassen ⑦ (*against*) auf +*akk;* **the attack ~ the village** der Angriff auf das Dorf; **to place restrictions ~ sb/sth** jdm/etw Beschränkungen auferlegen; **to place a limit ~ sth** etw begrenzen ⑧ (*indicating a medium*) auf +*dat;* **what's ~ TV tonight?** was kommt heute Abend im Fernsehen?; **to put sth down ~ paper** etw aufschreiben; **to come out ~ video** als Video herauskommen ⑨ (*in the course of*) auf +*dat;* **~ the way to town** auf dem Weg in die Stadt ⑩ (*travelling by*) in +*dat,* mit +*dat;* **~ foot/horseback** zu Fuß/auf dem Pferd ⑪ (*indicating date*) an +*dat;* **~ Friday** am Freitag; **~ Thursdays** donnerstags ⑫ (*engaged in*) bei; **~ business** geschäftlich; **to work ~ sth** an etw *dat* arbeiten ⑬ (*regularly taking*) **to be ~ medication** Medikamente einnehmen; **he survived ~ berries and roots** er überlebte von Beeren und Wurzeln ⑭ (*connected to*) an +*dat;* **to be ~ the phone** am Telefon sein **II.** *adv inv* ① (*in contact with*) auf; **to screw sth ~** etw anschrauben ② (*on body*) an; **to try sth ~** etw anprobieren; **with nothing ~** nackt ③ (*indicating continuance*) weiter; **if the line's busy, keep ~ trying!** wenn besetzt ist, probier es weiter!; **he talked ~ and ~** er redete pausenlos ④ (*in forward direction*) vorwärts; **from that day ~** von diesem Tag an; **to move ~** (*move forward*) weitergehen ⑤ (*scheduled*) geplant; **I have a lot going ~ this week** ich habe mir für diese Woche eine Menge vorgenommen ⑥ (*functioning*) an; **to leave the light ~** das Licht anlassen; **to switch/turn sth ~** etw einschalten ⑦ (*aboard*) **to get ~** *bus, train* einsteigen; *horse* aufsitzen ▶ PHRASES: **~ and off** ab und zu *fam;* **you're ~!** abgemacht! *fam*

once [wʌns] **I.** *adv inv* ① (*one time*) einmal; **~ a week** einmal pro Woche; **just this ~** nur dieses eine Mal ② (*in the past*) einst *geh,* früher; **~ upon a time ...** (*liter*) es war einmal ... ▶ PHRASES: **at ~** (*simultaneously*) auf einmal; (*immediately*) sofort; **for ~** ausnahmsweise; **~ more** (*one more time*) noch einmal; (*again, as before*) wieder; **~ or twice** ein paar Mal; **[every] ~ in a while** hin und wieder **II.** *conj* (*as soon as*) sobald

'once-over *n* (*fam*) ① (*cursory examination*) **to give sb/sth a/the ~** jdn/etw flüchtig ansehen ② (*cursory cleaning*) **to give sth a/the ~** etw rasch putzen

oncoming ['an·kʌm·ɪŋ] *adj attr, inv* (*approaching*) [heran]nahend; *vehicle* entgegenkommend; **~ traffic** Gegenverkehr *m*

one [wʌn] **I.** *n* ① (*unit*) eins; **a hundred and ~** einhundert[und]eins ② (*numeral*) Eins *f* **II.** *adj inv* ① *attr* (*not two*) ein(e); **~ hundred** einhundert; **~ million** eine Million; **~ third** ein Drittel *nt* ② *attr* (*one of a number*) ein(e); **he can't tell ~ wine from another** er schmeckt bei Weinen keinen Unterschied ③ *attr* (*single, only*) einzige(r, s); **we should paint the bedroom all ~ color** wir sollten das Schlafzimmer nur in einer Farbe streichen ④ *attr* (*some future*) irgendein(e); **~ day** irgendwann ⑤ *attr* (*some in the past*) ein(e); **~ day/evening/night** eines Tages/Abends/Nachts ⑥ *attr* (*emph fam: noteworthy*) **his mother is ~ generous woman** seine Mutter ist eine wirklich großzügige Frau ⑦ (*identical*) ein(e); **to be of ~ mind** einer Meinung sein; **~ and the same** ein und der-/die-/dasselbe ▶ PHRASES: **~ way or another** (*somehow*) irgendwie **III.** *pron* ① (*single item*) eine(r, s); **which cake would you like? — the ~ at the front** welchen Kuchen möchten Sie? – den vorderen; **not a single ~** kein Einziger/keine Einzige/kein Einziges; **~ at a time** immer nur eine(r, s); **~ after another** eine(r, s) nach dem/der anderen; **this/that ~** diese(r, s)/jene(r, s) ② (*single person*) eine(r); **she thought of her loved ~s** sie dachte an ihre Lieben; **~ after another** eine/einer nach der/dem anderen; **~ by ~** nacheinander; **she's ~ of my favorite writers** sie ist eine meiner Lieblingsautoren; **to be ~ of many/a few** eine(r) von vielen/wenigen sein ③ (*expressing alternatives, comparisons*) **~ or the other** der/die/das eine oder der/die/das andere ④ (*form: any person, most people*) man; (*I*) ich; **~ gets the impression that ...** man hat den Eindruck, dass ...; **it takes ~'s breath away** es raubt einem den Atem ▶ PHRASES: **to be ~ of the family** zur Familie gehören *fig;* **to be ~ up on sb** jdn übertrumpfen; **in ~s and twos** (*in small numbers*) immer nur ein paar; (*alone or in a pair*) allein oder paarweise

'one-armed *adj* einarmig; **~ bandit** (*fam*) einarmiger Bandit

'one-eyed *adj attr, inv* einäugig

one-'handed I. *adv* mit einer Hand **II.** *adj inv attr* einhändig

'one-horse town *n* (*inf*) Kaff *nt fam*

one-'legged *adj attr, inv* einbeinig

one-'liner *n* Einzeiler *m*

'one-man *adj attr, inv* ① (*consisting of one person*) Einmann-; **~ band** Einmannband *f fig,* Einmannbetrieb *m* ② (*designed for one person*) für eine Person *nach n*

one-night 'stand *n* ① (*sexual relationship*) Abenteuer *nt* für eine Nacht ② (*performance*) einmaliges Gastspiel

'one-piece, one-piece 'swimsuit *n* Einteiler *m*

onerous ['an·ər·əs] *adj* (*form*) ① (*very difficult*) *duty* schwer; *responsibility* schwerwiegend ② LAW [er]drückend

oneself [wʌn·'self] *pron reflexive* ① *after vb, after prep* (*direct object*) sich ② (*personally*) selbst; **to see/read sth for ~** etw selbst sehen/lesen ③ (*alone*) **to have sth to ~** etw für sich haben; **[all] by ~** [ganz] alleine

one-'sided *adj* einseitig

'one-time *adj attr, inv* ① (*former*) ehemalig ② (*happening only once*) einmalig

one-track 'mind *n* **to have a ~** immer nur eins im Kopf haben

one-'upmanship *n* (*fam*) *die Kunst, anderen immer um eine Nasenlänge voraus zu sein*

one-way 'street *n* Einbahnstraße *f*

one-way 'ticket *n* einfache Fahrkarte, Einzelfahrschein *m*

ongoing ['an·goʊ·ɪŋ] *adj inv* laufend *attr,* im Gang *präd*

onion ['ʌn·jən] *n* Zwiebel *f*

online [ˌan·'laɪn] COMPUT **I.** *adj inv* online, Online- **II.** *adv inv* online

onlooker ['an·lʊk·ər] *n* (*a. fig*) Zuschauer(in) *m(f)*

only ['oʊn·li] **I.** *adj attr, inv* einzige(r, s); **the ~ one** der/die/das Einzige; **the ~ way** die einzige Möglichkeit **II.** *adv inv* ① (*exclusively*) nur; **for members ~** nur für Mitglieder ② (*just*) erst ③ (*merely*) nur, bloß; **not ~ ..., but also ...** nicht nur ..., sondern auch ... ④ (*unavoidably*) nur, unweigerlich; **the situation can ~ get better/worse** die Situation kann sich nur verbessern/verschlechtern ⑤ (*to express wish*) **if ~ ...** wenn nur ... ▶ PHRASES: **you ~ live once** (*saying*) man lebt nur einmal **III.** *conj* ① (*however*) aber, jedoch; **he's a good athlete, ~ he smokes too much** er ist ein guter Sportler, bloß raucht er zu viel ② (*in addition*) **not ~ can she sing, she can dance and play the piano, too** sie kann nicht nur singen, sie kann auch tanzen und Klavier spielen

onrush <*pl* **-es**> ['an·rʌʃ] *n* ❶ (*of emotion*) Ansturm *m* ❷ (*of people*) Ansturm *m*

onset ['an·set] *n* Beginn *m* (**of** *+gen*); **~ of winter** Wintereinbruch *m*

onshore ['an·ʃɔr] *inv* **I.** *adj* Küsten-; **~ wind** auflandiger Wind *fachspr* **II.** *adv* an Land; (*blow*) landwärts

on-'site *inv* **I.** *adj* vor Ort *nach n,* Vor-Ort- **II.** *adv* vor Ort

onslaught ['an·slɔt] *n* (*a. fig: attack*) Ansturm *m* (**on** auf *+akk*)

onstage [ˌan·'steɪdʒ, ˌɔn-] **I.** *adj* auf der Bühne **II.** *adv* auf die Bühne

on-the-job 'training *n* Ausbildung *f* am Arbeitsplatz

onto, on to ['an·tu] *prep after vb* auf *+akk;* **to get ~ a horse/bike** auf ein Pferd/Fahrrad [auf]steigen; **to get ~ a bus/train** in einen Bus/einen Zug einsteigen; **to load sth ~ sth** etw auf etw *akk* laden ▶ PHRASES: **to be ~ sb/sth** jdm/etw auf der Spur sein; **to get ~ sb about sth** jdn wegen etw *dat* erinnern

onus ['oʊ·nəs] *n* (*form*) Verantwortung *f* (**of** für); **the ~ is on sb [to do sth]** es liegt an jdm [, etw zu tun]

onward ['an·wərd] *inv* **I.** *adj attr* (*of trip*) Weiter- **II.** *adv* ❶ (*into the future*) **from that day/time ~** von diesem Tag/dieser Zeit an ❷ (*of direction*) weiter

onyx ['an·ɪks] *n* Onyx *m*

oodles ['u·dəlz] *npl* (*fam*) Unmengen *pl* (**of** an/von *+dat*)

oomph [ʊmf] *n* (*fam*) ❶ (*power*) Kraft *f; of a car* Leistung *f* ❷ (*pizzazz*) Pep *m*

oops [ups] *interj* (*fam*) hoppla

ooze [uz] **I.** *n* Schlamm *m* **II.** *vi* (*seep out*) tropfen (**from** aus); *blood, water* sickern; *mud* quellen; **to ~ with blood/oil** vor Blut/Öl triefen **III.** *vt* ❶ (*seep out*) absondern ❷ (*fig: overflow with*) *charisma, charm* ausstrahlen; *sex appeal* versprühen

opacity [oʊ·'pæs·ə·t̬i] *n* (*nontransparency*) Lichtundurchlässigkeit *f*

opal ['oʊ·pəl] *n* Opal *m*

opalescent [ˌoʊ·pə·'les·ənt] *adj* schillernd; (*like an opal*) opalisierend

opaque [oʊ·'peɪk] *adj* (*not transparent*) undurchsichtig; *of wax* lichtundurchlässig; *of window, liquid* trüb

OPEC ['oʊ·pek] *n acr for* **Organization of Petroleum Exporting Countries** OPEC *f*

open ['oʊ·pən] **I.** *adj* ❶ *inv* (*not closed*) offen, geöffnet, auf *präd; book* aufgeschlagen; *flower* aufgeblüht; *map* auseinandergefaltet; **wide ~** [sperrangel]weit geöffnet; **to burst ~** *bag, case* aufgehen ❷ *inv, pred* (*for customers, visitors*) *shop, bar, museum* geöffnet, offen ❸ *inv* (*not yet decided*) *case, decision, question* offen; **to keep an ~ mind** unvoreingenommen bleiben; **to keep one's options ~** sich *dat* alle Möglichkeiten offenhalten ❹ *inv* (*not enclosed*) offen; **to be in the ~ air** an der frischen Luft sein; **on the ~ road** auf freier Strecke ❺ *inv a.* SPORTS (*accessible to all*) offen, öffentlich zugänglich; **the competition is ~ to anyone** an dem Wettbewerb kann jeder teilnehmen; **to have ~ access to sth** freien Zugang zu etw *dat* haben ❻ *inv, pred* (*frank*) *person* offen; ■**to be ~ with sb** offen zu jdm sein ❼ *inv, pred* (*exposed*) offen, ungeschützt; **to be ~ to attack** Angriffen ausgesetzt sein; **to be ~ to criticism** kritisierbar sein ▶ PHRASES: **to be an ~ book** *person* [wie] ein offenes Buch sein; *thing* ein Kinderspiel sein **II.** *vi* ❶ (*from closed*) sich öffnen, aufgehen; **the door ~s much more easily now** die Tür lässt sich jetzt viel leichter öffnen ❷ (*for business*) *cafe, shop, museum* öffnen; (*for the first time*) eröffnen ❸ (*start*) *piece of writing or music, story* beginnen, anfangen ❹ (*begin run*) *film* anlaufen; *play* Premiere haben **III.** *vt* ❶ (*change from closed*) *book, magazine, newspaper* aufschlagen; *box, window, bottle* aufmachen; *curtains* aufziehen; *eyes, letter* öffnen; *map* auffalten; (*a. fig*) *mouth* aufmachen ❷ (*set up*) *bank account, business* eröffnen ❸ (*declare ready for use*) *building* einweihen ▶ PHRASES: **to ~ sb's eyes to sb/sth** jdm die Augen über jdn/etw öffnen **IV.** *n* ❶ (*out of doors*) ■**[out] in the ~** draußen; (*in the open air*) im Freien ❷ (*not secret*) **to bring sth out into the ~** etw publik machen; **to come out into the ~** ans Licht kommen ❸ SPORTS (*competition*) ■**O~** [offene] Meisterschaft

◆**open out I.** *vi* ❶ (*move apart*) sich ausbreiten ❷ (*unfold*) *map* sich auffalten lassen; *flower* aufblühen, sich öffnen ❸ (*grow wider*) sich erweitern; *street, river* breiter werden; (*grow bigger*) sich vergrößern **II.** *vt* (*unfold*) **to ~ out ⊂ a map/newspaper** eine [Land]karte auseinanderfalten/eine Zeitung aufschlagen

◆**open up I.** *vi* ❶ (*start business*) *shop, store, etc.* eröffnen ❷ (*start shooting*) das Feuer eröffnen, losfeuern ❸ (*become more confiding*) *person* sich öffnen **II.** *vt* ❶ (*from closed*) *canal, pipe* passierbar machen; *car, house, store* aufschließen; *door, window* aufmachen ❷ (*make available*) ■**to ~ up ⊂ sth [to sb/sth]** [jdm/etw] etw zugänglich machen ❸ (*expand*) erweitern

'open-air *adj inv* im Freien *nach n;* **~ stage** Freilichtbühne *f*

open-'ended *adj inv* mit offenem Ausgang *nach n; question* ungeklärt

opener ['oʊ·pə·nər] *n* (*opening device*) Öffner *m*

open-'faced *adj inv sandwich* belegt

open-heart 'surgery *n* Operation *f* am offenen Herzen

opening ['oʊ·pə·nɪŋ] **I.** *n* ❶ (*action*) Öffnen *nt,* Aufmachen *nt* ❷ (*hole*) Öffnung *f;* (*in traffic*) Lücke *f;* (*in woods*) Lichtung *f* ❸ (*opportunity*) günstige Gelegenheit; (*job*) freie Stelle ❹ (*introduction*) *of a novel, film* An-

O

fang *m* ❺ (*inauguration*) Eröffnung *f* ❻ (*available appointment*) freier Termin **II.** *adj attr, inv* Anfangs-; *balance, bid, ceremony* Eröffnungs-; ~ **night** THEAT Premierenabend *m*
'opening hours *npl* Öffnungszeiten *pl*
'opening time *n* Öffnungszeit *f*
openly ['oʊ·pən·li] *adv* ❶ (*frankly*) offen ❷ *inv* (*publicly*) öffentlich
open 'market *n* offener Markt
open-'minded *adj* (*to new ideas*) aufgeschlossen; (*not prejudiced*) unvoreingenommen
open-'mouthed *adj inv* ❶ *pred* (*with open mouth*) mit offenem Mund ❷ *attr* (*shocked*) [sichtlich] betroffen
openness ['oʊ·pən·nəs] *n* ❶ (*frankness*) Offenheit *f* ❷ (*in character*) offenes Wesen ❸ (*lack of obstruction*) *of view, expanse* Weitläufigkeit *f*
opera ['ap·rə] *n* Oper *f*
operable ['ap·ər·ə·bəl] *adj* ❶ (*functioning*) funktionsfähig; AUTO fahrtüchtig ❷ MED *tumor, cancer* operabel
'opera glasses *npl* Opernglas *nt*
'opera house *n* Opernhaus *nt*
operate ['ap·ə·reɪt] **I.** *vi* ❶ (*work, run*) funktionieren ❷ (*perform surgery*) ■**to ~ on sb/sth** jdn/etw operieren ❸ (*do business*) operieren *geh* **II.** *vt* ❶ (*work*) bedienen ❷ (*manage*) betreiben
operating ['ap·ə·reɪ·t̬ɪŋ] **I.** *n* MED Operieren *nt* **II.** *adj attr, inv* ❶ (*in charge*) Dienst habend ❷ MED Operations-
'operating room *n* MED Operationssaal *m*
'operating system, OS [ˌoʊ·'es] *n* COMPUT Betriebssystem *nt*

O

operation [ˌap·ə·'reɪ·ʃən] *n* ❶ (*way of functioning*) Funktionsweise *f*; **day-to-day ~** gewöhnlicher Betriebsablauf ❷ (*functioning state*) Betrieb *m*; LAW Wirksamkeit *f*; **to come into ~** *machine* in Gang kommen; *plan, rule, law* in Kraft treten ❸ (*process*) Vorgang *m* ❹ (*activity*) Unternehmung *f*; MIL Operation *f*; **rescue ~** Rettungsaktion *f*; **undercover ~** MIL verdeckte Operation ❺ (*surgery*) Operation *f* ❻ MATH Operation *f*
operational [ˌap·ə·'reɪ·ʃə·nəl] *adj inv* ❶ (*in business*) betrieblich, Betriebs- *pl* ❷ (*functioning*) betriebsbereit
operative ['ap·ər·ə·t̬ɪv] **I.** *n* ❶ (*in a factory*) [Fach]arbeiter(in) *m(f)* ❷ (*secret agent*) Geheimagent(in) *m(f)* **II.** *adj inv* (*functioning*) in Betrieb *präd*; *regulations* gültig
operator ['ap·ə·reɪ·t̬ər] *n* ❶ (*worker*) Bediener(in) *m(f)*; **machine ~** Maschinist(in) *m(f)* ❷ (*switchboard worker*) Telefonist(in) *m(f)*; (*at telephone company*) ≈ Vermittlung *f* ❸ (*company*) Unternehmer(in) *m(f)*; **tour ~** Reiseveranstalter(in) *m(f)*
operetta [ˌap·ə·'ret̬·ə] *n* Operette *f*
ophthalmic [af·'θæl·mɪk] *adj attr, inv* Augen-, ophthalmisch *fachspr*
ophthalmologist [ˌaf·θəl·'mal·ə·dʒɪst] *n* Augenarzt, -ärztin *m, f*

opiate ['oʊ·pi·ɪt] *n* Opiat *nt*
opinion [ə·'pɪn·jən] *n* ❶ (*belief*) Meinung *f*, Ansicht *f*; **public ~** die öffentliche Meinung ❷ (*view on topic*) Einstellung *f*, Standpunkt *m* (**on** zu); **difference of ~** Meinungsverschiedenheit *f*; **just a matter of ~** reine Ansichtssache; **to have a high/low ~ of sb/sth** von jdm/etw eine hohe/keine gute Meinung haben; **to express an ~ on sth** seine Meinung zu etw *dat* äußern; **in my ~** meiner Meinung nach
opinionated [ə·'pɪn·jə·neɪ·t̬ɪd] *adj* (*pej*) rechthaberisch
o'pinion poll *n* Meinungsumfrage *f*
opium ['oʊ·pi·əm] *n* Opium *nt*; **~ den** Opiumhöhle *f*
opossum <*pl* -s *or* -> [ə·'pas·əm] *n* Opossum *nt*
opponent [ə·'poʊ·nənt] *n* POL Widersacher(in) *m(f)*; SPORTS Gegner(in) *m(f)*
opportune [ˌap·ər·'tun] *adj* angebracht; *chance* passend; *moment* geeignet
opportunism [ˌap·ər·'tu·nɪz·əm] *n* Opportunismus *m*
opportunist [ˌap·ər·'tu·nɪst] **I.** *n* Opportunist(in) *m(f)* **II.** *adj* (*pej*) opportunistisch
opportunity [ˌap·ər·'tu·nə·t̬i] *n* ❶ (*occasion*) Gelegenheit *f*; **a window of ~** eine Chance; **at every ~** bei jeder Gelegenheit; **to get the ~ to do** [*or* **of doing**] **sth** die Chance erhalten, etw zu tun ❷ (*for advancement*) Möglichkeit *f*
oppose [ə·'poʊz] *vt* ❶ (*disapprove*) ablehnen ❷ (*resist*) ■**to ~ sb/sth** sich jdm/etw widersetzen; (*actively*) gegen jdn/etw vorgehen ❸ SPORTS ■**to ~ sb** gegen jdn antreten
opposed [ə·'poʊzd] *adj pred* ❶ (*against*) ■**to be ~ to sth** gegen etw *akk* sein ❷ (*contrasted*) ■**as ~ to sth** im Gegensatz zu etw *dat*
opposing [ə·'poʊz·ɪŋ] *adj attr* entgegengesetzt; (*in conflict*) einander widersprechend; *opinion* gegensätzlich; *team* gegnerisch
opposite ['ap·ə·zɪt] **I.** *n* Gegenteil **II.** *adj inv* ❶ (*contrary*) *interests* gegensätzlich ❷ (*facing*) gegenüberliegend; *directions* entgegengesetzt; *after n*; **who owns that store ~?** wem gehört der Laden gegenüber? **III.** *adv inv* gegenüber; **she asked the man sitting ~ what time it was** sie fragte den ihr gegenübersitzenden Mann nach der Uhrzeit **IV.** *prep* (*across from*) gegenüber
opposition [ˌap·ə·'zɪʃ·ən] *n* ❶ (*resistance*) Widerstand *m* (**to** gegen) ❷ (*party not in power*) Opposition[spartei] *f*; (*opposing team*) gegnerische Mannschaft ❸ (*contrast*) Gegensatz *m*; ■**in ~ to sth** im Gegensatz zu etw *dat*
oppress [ə·'pres] *vt* (*subjugate*) unterdrücken
oppression [ə·'preʃ·ən] *n* (*subjugation*) Unterdrückung *f*
oppressive [ə·'pres·ɪv] *adj* ❶ (*harsh*) *regime* unterdrückerisch; *taxes* drückend ❷ (*stifling*) *heat, weather* drückend
oppressor [ə·'pres·ər] *n* Unterdrücker(in) *m(f)*

opt [apt] *vi* ■ **to ~ for sth** sich für etw *akk* entscheiden
◆**opt in** *vi* sich beteiligen
◆**opt out** *vi* nicht mitmachen; (*withdraw*) aussteigen *fam*
optic ['ap·tɪk] *adj attr, inv* Seh-
optical ['ap·tɪ·kəl] *adj inv* optisch
optician [ap·'tɪʃ·ən] *n* Optiker(in) *m(f)*
optics ['ap·tɪks] *npl + sing vb* Optik *f kein pl*
optimal ['ap·tɪ·məl] *adj inv* optimal
optimism ['ap·tə·mɪz·əm] *n* Optimismus *m*
optimist ['ap·tə·mɪst] *n* Optimist(in) *m(f)*
optimistic [ˌap·tə·'mɪs·tɪk] *adj* optimistisch
optimize ['ap·tə·maɪz] *vt* optimieren
optimum ['ap·tə·məm] **I.** *n* <*pl* -tima *or* -s> Optimum *nt* **II.** *adj inv* optimal
option ['ap·ʃən] *n* ① (*choice*) Wahl *f;* (*possibility*) Möglichkeit *f;* **to not be an ~** nicht in Frage kommen ② (*freedom to choose*) Wahlmöglichkeit *f*
optional ['ap·ʃə·nəl] *adj inv* wahlfrei
optometrist [ap·'tam·ɪ·trɪst] *n* Augenoptiker(in) *m(f)*
opulence ['ap·jə·ləns] *n* ① (*wealth*) Wohlstand *m* ② (*luxury*) Luxus
opulent ['ap·jə·lənt] *adj* ① (*affluent*) wohlhabend; *lifestyle* aufwendig ② (*luxurious*) luxuriös
OR *n abbrev of* **Oregon**
or [ɔr] *conj* ① (*as a choice*) oder ② (*otherwise*) sonst; **~ else** sonst; ■ **either ... ~ ...** entweder...[,] oder ③ (*and a. not*) ■ **not ... ~ ...** weder ... noch ... ④ (*a. called*) beziehungsweise
oracle ['ɔr·ə·kəl] *n* ① (*place*) Orakel *nt* ② (*person*) Seher(in) *m(f)* ③ (*fig: adviser*) Autorität *f*
oral ['ɔr·əl] **I.** *adj inv* ① (*spoken*) mündlich ② MED, PSYCH oral **II.** *n* ■ **~s** *pl* mündliches Examen
orange ['ɔr·ɪndʒ] **I.** *n* ① (*fruit*) Orange *f* ② (*color*) Orange *nt* **II.** *adj* orange[farben]
orangeade [ˌɔr·ɪndʒ·'eɪd] *n* Orangenlimonade *f*
'**orange juice** *n* Orangensaft *m*
'**orange peel** *n* Orangenschale *f*
orangutan [ɔ·'ræŋ·ə·tæn], **orangoutang** [ɔ·'ræŋ·ə·tæŋ] *n* Orang-Utan *m*
oration [ɔ·'reɪ·ʃən] *n* (*speech*) [feierliche] Rede
orator ['ɔr·ə·ṱər] *n* Redner(in) *m(f)*
oratorical [ˌɔr·ə·'tɔr·ɪ·kəl] *adj inv* rednerisch
oratorio [ˌɔr·ə·'tɔr·i·oʊ] *n* MUS Oratorium *nt*
orb [ɔrb] *n* ① (*spherical body*) kugelförmiger Körper ② (*hist: of a king*) Reichsapfel *m hist*
orbit ['ɔr·bɪt] **I.** *n* ① (*constant course*) Umlaufbahn *f;* **in ~ around the earth** in einer Erdumlaufbahn ② (*trip around*) Umkreisung *f* ③ (*fig: influence*) [Einfluss]bereich *m* **II.** *vi* kreisen **III.** *vt* (*circle around*) umkreisen
orbital ['ɔr·bɪ·ṱəl] *adj inv* orbital
orchard ['ɔr·tʃərd] *n* Obstgarten *m*
orchestra ['ɔr·kɪ·strə] *n* (*musicians*) Orchester *nt*
orchestral [ɔr·'kes·trəl] *adj inv* Orchester-, orchestral
'**orchestra pit** *n* Orchestergraben *m*
'**orchestra seats** *npl* Parkett *nt*
orchestrate ['ɔr·kɪ·streɪt] *vt* ① (*arrange for orchestra*) orchestrieren ② (*fig*) *event* organisieren
orchestration [ˌɔr·kɪ·'streɪ·ʃən] *n* ① (*of music*) Orchestration *f* ② (*of an event*) Organisation *f*
orchid ['ɔr·kɪd] *n* Orchidee *f*
ordain [ɔr·'deɪn] *vt* ① (*to the ministry*) ordinieren ② (*decree*) bestimmen
ordeal [ɔr·'dil] *n* ① (*fig: painful experience*) Zerreißprobe *f* ② (*torture*) Qual *f*
order ['ɔr·dər] **I.** *n* ① (*neatness*) Ordnung *f;* **to put sth in ~** etw ordnen ② (*sequence*) Reihenfolge *f;* **word ~** Wortstellung *f;* **in alphabetical/chronological ~** in alphabetischer/chronologischer Reihenfolge; **to be out of ~** durcheinandergeraten sein ③ (*command*) Befehl *m;* LAW Verfügung *f;* **doctor's ~s** ärztliche Anweisung ④ COMM (*request for product*) Bestellung *f;* (*request to make sth a.*) Auftrag *m;* (*in restaurant*) Bestellung *f* ⑤ (*correct behavior*) Ordnung *f;* (*discipline*) Disziplin *f;* **to be in ~** in Ordnung sein; **to restore ~** die Ordnung wiederherstellen ⑥ (*condition*) Zustand *f;* **to be in working ~** (*ready for use*) funktionsbereit sein; (*functioning*) funktionieren; **to be out of ~** (*not working*) nicht funktionieren; (*not ready for use*) nicht betriebsbereit sein; **"out of ~"** „außer Betrieb" ⑦ (*intention*) ■ **in ~ to do sth** um etw zu tun ⑧ REL (*society*) [geistlicher] Orden *m* ⑨ (*medal*) Orden *m* ▸ PHRASES: **to be the ~ of the day** an der Tagesordnung sein **II.** *vi* bestellen; **are you ready to ~?** möchten Sie schon bestellen? **III.** *vt* ① (*decide, decree*) anordnen ② (*command*) befehlen ③ COMM (*request from company or in restaurant*) bestellen
◆**order around** *vt* herumkommandieren *fam*
'**order form** *n* Bestellformular *nt*
orderly ['ɔr·dər·li] **I.** *n* ① (*hospital attendant*) ≈ [Kranken]pfleger(in) *m(f);* (*unskilled*) Hilfskraft *f* (*in Betreuungseinrichtungen*) ② MIL (*carrier of orders*) Ordonnanz *f geh* **II.** *adj* ① (*methodical*) geordnet; (*neat*) ordentlich; *room* aufgeräumt ② (*well-behaved*) gesittet; *demonstration* friedlich
ordinal, ordinal number ['ɔr·də·nəl-] *n* Ordinalzahl *f*
ordinary ['ɔr·də·ner·i] **I.** *adj* gewöhnlich, normal **II.** *n* (*normal state*) **out of the ~** außergewöhnlich; **nothing out of the ~** nichts Ungewöhnliches
ordnance ['ɔrd·nəns] *n* MIL Geschütze *pl*
ordure ['ɔr·dʒər] *n* Mist *m*
ore [ɔr] *n* Erz *nt*
Ore. *n abbrev of* **Oregon**
oregano [ə·'reg·ə·noʊ] *n* Oregano *nt*
Oregon ['ɔr·ɪ·gən] *n* Oregon *nt*
organ ['ɔr·gən] *n* ① MUS Orgel *f* ② ANAT Organ *nt*
'**organ donor** *n* Organspender(in) *m(f)*
'**organ grinder** *n* Drehorgelspieler(in) *m(f)*

O

organic [ɔr·'gæn·ɪk] *adj* ❶ (*of bodily organs*) organisch ❷ (*living*) organisch ❸ AGR, ECOL biologisch, Bio-; ~ **fruit** Obst *nt* aus biologischem Anbau; ~ **farming methods** biologische Anbaumethoden; ~ **label** Bio-Siegel *nt;* ~ **supermarket** Biosupermarkt *m*
organism ['ɔr·gə·nɪz·əm] *n* Organismus *m*
organist ['ɔr·gə·nɪst] *n* Organist(in) *m(f)*
organization [ˌɔr·gə·nɪ·'zeɪ·ʃən] *n* ❶ (*action*) Organisation *f* ❷ (*association, company*) Organisation *f*
organizational [ˌɔr·gə·nɪ·'zeɪ·ʃə·nəl] *adj inv* organisatorisch
organi'zation chart *n* ECON Organisationsplan *m*
Organization for Economic Cooperation and De'velopment *n* ■**the** ~ die Organisation für wirtschaftliche Zusammenarbeit und Entwicklung
Organization of Petroleum Exporting 'Countries *n* die Organisation Erdöl exportierender Länder
organize ['ɔr·gə·naɪz] *vt* ❶ (*into a system*) *activities* organisieren; *books, files* ordnen; *space* aufteilen ❷ (*prepare*) vorbereiten; *committee, search party, team* zusammenstellen
organized ['ɔr·gə·naɪzd] *adj* organisiert
organized 'crime *n* organisiertes Verbrechen
organizer ['ɔr·gə·naɪ·zər] *n* ❶ (*book*) Terminplaner *m* ❷ (*person*) Organisator(in) *m(f)*
orgasm ['ɔr·gæz·əm] **I.** *n* Orgasmus *m* **II.** *vi* einen Orgasmus haben
orgasmic [ɔr·'gæs·mɪk] *adj* orgastisch *geh;* (*fig fam*) aufregend
orgy ['ɔr·dʒi] *n* Orgie *f*
orient ['ɔr·i·ənt] **I.** *n* GEOG ■**the O~** der Orient **II.** *vt* ❶ (*position*) ■**to ~ sth** etw *dat* eine Richtung geben ❷ (*determine position*) ■**to ~ oneself** [**by sth**] sich [nach etw *dat*] orientieren ❸ (*familiarize*) ■**to ~ oneself** sich zurechtfinden
oriental [ˌɔr·i·'en·təl] **I.** *adj inv* orientalisch **II.** *n* (*a. pej*) ■**O~** Orientale, -in *m, f*
orientate ['ɔr·i·en·teɪt] **I.** *vt see* **orient II.** *vi* (*face or turn to east*) sich nach Osten drehen
orientation [ˌɔr·i·en·'teɪ·ʃən] *n* ❶ (*being oriented*) Orientierung; **to lose one's ~** die Orientierung verlieren *f* ❷ (*tendency*) Ausrichtung *f* ❸ (*attitude*) Orientierung *f;* **political ~** politische Gesinnung; **sexual ~** sexuelle Neigung ❹ (*introduction*) Einweisung *f,* Einführung *f*
orienteering [ˌɔr·i·en·'tɪr·ɪŋ] *n* Orientierungslauf *m*
orifice ['ɔr·ə·fɪs] *n* Öffnung *f*
origin ['ɔr·ə·dʒɪn] *n* ❶ (*beginning, source*) Ursprung *m; of a river* Quelle *f;* ■**in ~** ursprünglich ❷ (*place sth/sb comes from*) Herkunft *f kein pl;* (*ancestry a.*) Abstammung *f kein pl*
original [ə·'rɪdʒ·ɪ·nəl] **I.** *n* Original *nt* **II.** *adj inv* ❶ (*first*) ursprünglich; **the ~ version** die Originalversion; *of a book* die Originalausgabe ❷ (*unique*) originell; (*innovative*) bahnbrechend; (*creative*) kreativ ❸ (*from creator*) original; **an ~ Rembrandt** ein echter Rembrandt; ~ **painting** Original *nt*
originality [ə·ˌrɪdʒ·ɪ·'næl·ə·ţi] *n* Originalität *f*
originally [ə·'rɪdʒ·ɪ·nə·li] *adv inv* ❶ (*at first*) ursprünglich ❷ (*uniquely*) außergewöhnlich
originate [ə·'rɪdʒ·ɪ·neɪt] **I.** *vi* entstehen, seinen Anfang nehmen; ■**to ~ from sth** aus etw *dat* stammen **II.** *vt* hervorbringen; (*invent*) erfinden
originator [ə·'rɪdʒ·ɪ·neɪţər] *n* Urheber, -in *m, f;* (*founder*) Gründer, -in *m, f;* (*inventor*) Erfinder, -in *m, f*
ornament ['ɔr·nə·mənt] **I.** *n* ❶ (*pretty object*) Ziergegenstand *m;* (*figurine*) Figürchen *nt* ❷ (*adornment*) Schmuck *m;* (*decoration*) Dekoration *f* **II.** *vt* dekorieren
ornamental [ˌɔr·nə·'men·təl] *adj* Zier-, dekorativ
ornamentation [ˌɔr·nə·men·'teɪ·ʃən] *n* (*form*) ❶ (*thing*) Verzierung *f;* ART Ornament *nt* ❷ (*act*) Verzieren *nt;* (*of a room, text*) Ausschmückung *f*
ornate [ɔr·'neɪt] *adj object* prunkvoll; *music* ornamentreich; *language, style* kunstvoll; (*pej*) geschraubt
ornithologist [ˌɔr·nə·'θal·ə·dʒɪst] *n* Ornithologe, -in *m, f fachspr*
ornithology [ˌɔr·nə·'θal·ə·dʒi] *n* Ornithologie *f fachspr*
orphan ['ɔr·fən] **I.** *n* Waise *f* **II.** *vt* ■**to be ~ed** [zur] Waise werden
orphanage ['ɔr·fə·nɪdʒ] *n* Waisenhaus *nt*
orthodontist [ˌɔr·θə·'dan·tɪst] *n* Kieferorthopäde, -in *m, f*
orthodox ['ɔr·θə·daks] *adj* ❶ (*generally accepted*) herkömmlich; (*not innovative*) starr ❷ (*strictly religious*) strenggläubig ❸ REL **Greek/Russian ~** griechisch/russisch orthodox; **the O~ Church** die christlich orthodoxe Kirche
orthodoxy ['ɔr·θə·dak·si] *n* ❶ (*practice*) verbreitete Denkweise ❷ (*quality*) Rechtgläubigkeit *f*
orthographic [ˌɔr·θə·'græf·ɪk] *adj inv* orthographisch *geh,* Rechtschreib-
orthography [ɔr·'θag·rə·fi] *n* Orthographie *f geh*
orthopedic [ˌɔr·θə·'pi·dɪk] *adj* orthopädisch
orthopedics [ˌɔr·θə·'pi·dɪks] *n + sing vb* Orthopädie *f kein pl*
orthopedist [ˌɔr·θə·'pi·dɪst] *n* Orthopäde, -in *m, f*
OS [ˌoʊ·'es] *n* COMPUT *abbrev of* **operating system**
oscillate ['as·ə·leɪt] *vi* (*swing*) schwingen
oscillation [ˌas·ə·'leɪ·ʃən] *n* (*movement*) Schwingung *f*
oscilloscope [ə·'sɪl·ə·skoʊp] *n* Schwingungsmesser *m*
osmosis [az·'moʊ·sɪs] *n* BIOL, CHEM Osmose *f fachspr;* ■**by ~** durch Osmose
osprey ['as·pri] *n* Fischadler *m*

O

ossify <-ie-> ['as·ə·faɪ] *vi* (*a. fig: become bone*) verknöchern

ostensible [a·'sten·sə·bəl] *adj attr, inv* angeblich

ostensibly [a·'sten·səb·li] *adv inv* angeblich

ostentation [ˌas·tən·'teɪ·ʃən] *n* Großtuerei *f*

ostentatious [ˌas·tən·'teɪ·ʃəs] *adj* prahlerisch; *lifestyle* protzig; *gesture* demonstrativ

osteoarthritis [ˌas·ti·oʊ·ar·'θraɪ·t̬ɪs] *n* Arthrose *f*, Osteoarthritis *f fachspr*

osteoporosis [ˌas·ti·oʊ·pə·'roʊ·sɪs] *n* MED Osteoporose *f fachspr*

ostracism ['as·trə·sɪz·əm] *n* Ächtung *f*

ostracize ['as·trə·saɪz] *vt* (*exclude*) ächten

ostrich ['as·trɪtʃ] *n* ORN Strauß *m*

other ['ʌð·ər] **I.** *adj det* ① (*different*) andere(r, s); **some ~ time** ein anderes Mal; **in ~ words** mit anderen Worten; **~ people** andere [Leute] ② (*not long ago*) **the ~ day** neulich; **the ~ evening** neulich abends ③ (*additional*) andere(r, s), weitere(r, s) ④ (*alternative*) andere(r, s); **on the ~ hand** andererseits; **every ~** jede(r, s) zweite ⑤ (*not being exact*) **some time or ~** irgendwann [einmal]; **someone or ~** irgendwer **II.** *pron* (*the remaining one*) ■**the ~** der/die/das andere; **hold the racket in one hand and the ball in the ~** halte den Schläger in einer Hand und den Ball in der anderen; **one or the ~** eines davon; **one or [the] ~ of sth** eine(r, s) von etw *dat;* **the ~s** die anderen

otherwise ['ʌð·ər·waɪz] **I.** *adv inv* ① (*differently*) anders; **unless you let me know ~, ...** sofern ich nichts Gegenteiliges von dir höre, ... ② (*except for this*) sonst ③ (*alternatively*) **to be ~ engaged** anderweitig zu tun haben **II.** *conj* andernfalls

otter ['at̬·ər] *n* Otter *m*

ouch [aʊtʃ] *interj* aua, autsch

ought [ɔt] *aux vb* ① (*indicating duty*) ■**sb ~ to do sth** jd sollte etw tun; **we ~ not to have agreed** wir hätten nicht zustimmen sollen; **it ~ not to be allowed** das sollte nicht erlaubt sein ② (*indicating probability*) **we ~ to be home by 7 o'clock** um sieben müssten wir eigentlich zu Hause sein; **ten minutes ~ to be enough time** zehn Minuten müssten eigentlich genügen ③ (*indicating advice*) ■**sb ~ to do sth** jd sollte etw tun

ounce [aʊns] *n* Unze *f;* **if he's got an ~ of common sense, ...** wenn er auch nur einen Funken gesunden Menschenverstand hat, ...

our [aʊr] *adj poss* unser(e)

ours [aʊrz] *pron poss* (*belonging to us*) unsere(r, s); **he's a cousin of ~** er ist ein Cousin von uns

ourselves [aʊr·'selvz] *pron reflexive* ① *after vb, after prep* (*direct object*) uns; **we enjoyed ~ at the party very much** wir hatten großen Spaß bei der Party ② (*emph: personally*) wir persönlich; **we invented it ~** wir erfanden das selbst; **to see sth for ~** etw selbst sehen

oust [aʊst] *vt* (*expel*) vertreiben; (*by taking their position*) verdrängen

out [aʊt] **I.** *adj inv, pred* ① (*not at a place*) ■**to be ~** nicht da sein; (*more formally*) abwesend sein; (*not at home*) nicht zu Hause sein; **to be ~ and about** unterwegs sein; (*after an illness*) wieder auf den Beinen sein ② (*outside*) ■**to be ~** draußen sein; **they're ~ in the yard** sie sind draußen im Garten; *prisoner* [wieder] draußen sein *fam* ③ (*visible*) ■**to be ~** *sun, moon, stars* am Himmel stehen; (*in blossom*) blühen; *tree a.* in Blüte stehen; (*available*) erhältlich sein; (*on the market*) auf dem Markt sein ④ (*known*) ■**to be ~** heraus sein; *secret* gelüftet sein; *news* bekannt sein; *homosexual;* ■**to be ~** sich geoutet haben *fam* ⑤ (*finished*) aus; **school will be ~ in June** die Schule endet im Juni; **before the month/year is ~** vor Ende des Monats/Jahres ⑥ SPORTS ■**to be ~** (*not playing*) nicht [mehr] im Spiel sein; (*in cricket, baseball*) aus sein; (*outside a boundary*) *ball, player* im Aus sein ⑦ (*fam*) ■**to be ~** (*unacceptable, not possible*) unmöglich sein; (*unfashionable*) out sein ⑧ (*off*) *light, TV* aus; *fire a.* erloschen ⑨ (*asleep*) ■**to be ~** schlafen; (*unconscious*) bewusstlos sein ⑩ *tide* **the tide is ~** es ist Ebbe **II.** *adv inv* ① (*not in sth*) außen; (*not in a room, apartment*) draußen; (*outdoors*) draußen, im Freien; **to keep sb/sth ~** jdn/etw nicht hereinlassen ② (*outwards*) heraus; (*seen from inside*) hinaus; (*facing the outside*) nach außen; (*out of a room, building a.*) nach draußen; **get ~!** raus hier! *fam;* **to turn sth inside ~** etw umstülpen; *clothes* etw auf links drehen ③ (*away from home, for a social activity*) **to eat ~** im Restaurant essen; **to go ~** ausgehen ④ (*removed*) [he]raus; (*extinguished*) aus; **to put a fire ~** ein Feuer löschen; **to cross sth ~** etw ausstreichen ⑤ (*fully, absolutely*) **burned ~** (*a. fig*) ausgebrannt; *fuse* durchgebrannt; *candle* heruntergebrannt ⑥ (*aloud*) **to call ~ to sb** jdm zurufen; **to cry ~ in pain** vor Schmerzen aufschreien ⑦ (*to an end, finished*) **to die ~** aussterben; (*fig*) *applause* verebben ⑧ (*unconscious*) **to knock sb ~** jdn bewusstlos schlagen; **to pass ~** in Ohnmacht fallen ⑨ (*open*) **to open sth ~** (*unfold*) etw auseinanderfalten; (*spread out*) etw ausbreiten; (*extend*) *furniture* etw ausziehen ⑩ **the tide is going ~** die Ebbe setzt ein ⑪ (*at a distant place*) draußen; **~ at sea** auf See **III.** *vt* ■**to ~ sb** *homosexual* jdn outen *fam* **IV.** *prep* (*fam*) aus +*dat;* **to run ~ the door** zur Tür hinausrennen

'out-and-out *adj attr, inv* ausgemacht, durch und durch *nach n*

'outback *n* Hinterland *nt* [Australiens]; **to live in the ~** im [australischen] Busch leben

out'bid <-bid, -bid> *vt* überbieten

'outboard, outboard 'motor *n* Außenbordmotor *m*

'outbreak *n of a disease, hostilities, a war* Ausbruch *m*

'outburst *n* Ausbruch *m;* **an ~ of anger** ein

O

Wutanfall *m*

'outcast *n* Ausgestoßene(r) *f(m);* **social ~** gesellschaftlicher Außenseiter/gesellschaftliche Außenseiterin

out'class *vt* in den Schatten stellen

'outcome *n* Ergebnis *nt*

'outcrop *n* GEOL Felsnase *f*

'outcry *n* lautstarker Protest (**over** gegen); **to provoke a public ~** einen Sturm der Entrüstung in der Öffentlichkeit auslösen

out'dated *adj* veraltet; *ideas, views* überholt

out'distance *vt* ■ **to ~ sb** jdn hinter sich *dat* lassen

out'do <-did, -done> *vt* übertreffen

'outdoor *adj inv clothes* für draußen *nach n;* **~ swimming pool** Freibad *nt*

outdoors [ˌaʊt·'dɔrz] **I.** *n + sing vb* **in the great ~** in der freien Natur **II.** *adv* im Freien

outdoorsy [ˌaʊt·'dɔr·zi] *adj* (*fam*) ■ **to be ~** gern in der freien Natur [*o* an der frischen Luft] sein

outer ['aʊ·t̬ər] *adj inv* ① (*external*) äußerlich, Außen- ② (*far from center*) äußere(r, s), Außen-

outermost ['aʊ·t̬ər·moʊst] *n attr, inv* äußerste(r, s); *layer* oberst

'outfield *n* Outfield *nt*

'outfit I. *n* ① (*clothes*) Kleidung *f;* **cowboy ~** Cowboykostüm *nt;* **wedding ~** Hochzeitsgarderobe *f* ② (*fam: group*) Verein *m;* (*company*) Laden *m;* (*musicians, sports team*) Truppe *f* **II.** *vt* <-tt-> ■ **to ~ sb with sth** jdn mit etw *dat* ausrüsten

'outfitter *n* (*for outdoor pursuits*) **sports ~** Sportgeschäft *nt*

'outflow *n* Ausfluss *m*

out'going *adj* ① (*approv: extrovert*) kontaktfreudig ② *attr* (*retiring*) [aus]scheidend

out'grow <-grew, -grown> *vt* ① (*become too big for*) ■ **to ~ sth** aus etw *dat* herauswachsen ② (*leave behind*) ■ **to ~ sth** einer S. *gen* entwachsen

'outgrowth *n* Auswuchs *m a. fig;* (*development*) *of an idea, a theory* Weiterentwicklung *f*

'outhouse *n* (*bathroom*) Außentoilette *f*

outing ['aʊ·t̬ɪŋ] *n* ① (*trip*) Ausflug *m;* **to go on an ~** einen Ausflug machen ② (*revealing homosexuality*) Outing *nt*

outlandish [aʊt·'læn·dɪʃ] *adj* sonderbar; *behavior, ideas a.* bizarr; *clothing* skurril; *prices* horrend

out'last *vt* überdauern; ■ **to ~ sb** jdn überleben

outlaw ['aʊt·lɔ] **I.** *n* (*criminal*) Bandit(in) *m(f);* (*fugitive from law*) Geächtete(r) *f(m)* **II.** *vt* für ungesetzlich erklären

'outlay *n* Aufwendungen *pl*

'outlet *n* ① ELEC Steckdose *f* ② (*exit*) Ausgang *m; for water* Abfluss *m;* AUTO, TECH *exhaust* Abluftstutzen *m* ③ (*means of expression*) Ventil *nt fig,* Ausdrucksmöglichkeit *f* ④ (*store*) Verkaufsstelle *f;* **fast-food ~** Schnellrestaurant *nt;* **factory ~** Fabrikverkauf *m*

'outline I. *n* ① (*brief description*) Übersicht *f* (**of** über); *for a novel* Entwurf *m* ② (*contour*) Umriss *m* **II.** *vt* ■ **to ~ sth** ① (*draw*) die Umrisse von etw *dat* zeichnen ② (*summarize*) etw [kurz] umreißen

out'live *vt* (*live longer than*) ■ **to ~ sb** jdn überleben; ■ **to ~ sth** etw überdauern; **the system had ~d its usefulness** das System hatte ausgedient

'outlook *n* ① (*view*) Aussicht *f* ② (*future prospect*) Aussicht[en] *f[pl]* ③ (*attitude*) Einstellung *f*

'outlying *adj attr region, town* abgelegen

outma'neuver *vt* ausmanövrieren

outmoded [ˌaʊt·'moʊ·dɪd] *adj* (*pej*) altmodisch; *ideas* überholt

out'number *vt* zahlenmäßig überlegen sein; ■ **to be ~ed** in der Unterzahl sein; (*in vote*) überstimmt sein

'out of *prep* ① *after vb* (*towards outside*) aus ② *after vb* (*situated away from*) außerhalb; **she's ~ the office at the moment** sie ist zurzeit nicht an ihrem [Arbeits]platz; *after n* außerhalb; **five miles ~ San Francisco** fünf Meilen außerhalb von San Francisco ③ *after vb* (*from*) von; **he copied his essay straight ~ a textbook** er schrieb seinen Aufsatz wörtlich aus einem Lehrbuch ab; **she had to pay for it ~ her own pocket** sie musste es aus der eigenen Tasche bezahlen ④ (*excluded from*) aus; **I'm glad to be ~ it** ich bin froh, dass ich das hinter mir habe; **to be ~ the question** nicht in Frage kommen ⑤ *after n* (*ratio of*) von; **nine times ~ ten** neun von zehn Malen; **no one got 20 ~ 20 on the test** niemand bekam alle 20 möglichen Punkte für den Test ⑥ (*without*) **they were ~ luck** sie hatten kein Glück [mehr]; **to run ~ cash** kein Bargeld mehr haben; **to be ~ work** ohne Arbeit sein ⑦ (*beyond*) außer; **~ reach/sight/earshot** außer Reichweite/Sicht[weite]/ Hörweite; **~ focus** *photo* unscharf; *camera, microscope* unscharf eingestellt; **get ~ the way!** aus dem Weg! ▶ PHRASES: **to get ~ <u>hand</u>** außer Kontrolle geraten; **~ sight, ~ <u>mind</u>** aus den Augen, aus dem Sinn; **~ <u>place</u>** fehl am Platz

out-of-court 'settlement *n* LAW außergerichtliche Einigung

out of 'date *adj pred,* **'out-of-date** *adj attr* veraltet; *clothing* altmodisch; *furniture* antiquiert; *ideas* überholt

out of the 'way *adj pred,* **'out-of-the-way** *adj attr spot, place* abgelegen

'outpatient *n* ambulanter Patient/ambulante Patientin

out'play *vt* ■ **to ~ sb** besser spielen als jd

'outpost *n* ① MIL (*guards*) Außenposten *m;* (*base*) Stützpunkt *m* ② (*remote branch*) Außenposten *m; of a company* Außenstelle *f*

'outpouring *n* (*of emotion*) Ausbruch *m*

'output I. *n* ECON Ausstoß *m;* COMPUT Ausgabe *f;* ELEC Leistung *f* **II.** *vt image, data* ausgeben

'outrage I. *n* ❶ Empörung *f* (**at** über); **to express** ~ sich entsetzt zeigen ❷ (*deed*) Schandtat *f;* (*crime*) Verbrechen *nt;* (*disgrace*) Schande *f kein pl* **II.** *vt* (*arouse indignation*) ■ **to** ~ **sb** jdn erzürnen; ■ [**to be**] ~**d by sth** entrüstet über etw *akk* [sein]

outrageous [aʊt·'reɪ·dʒəs] *adj* ❶ (*terrible*) empörend; (*unacceptable*) unerhört; (*shocking*) schockierend ❷ (*unusual and shocking*) außergewöhnlich; *outfit a.* gewagt ❸ (*exaggerated*) ungeheuerlich; *story, statement a.* unwahrscheinlich; *lie* schamlos; *prices* horrend

'outreach I. *n* soziales Engagement **II.** *adj* ~ **work** soziales Engagement; ~ **program** Programm *nt* zur sozialen Unterstützung

'outrigger *n* NAUT Ausleger *m;* (*boat*) Auslegerboot *nt*

'outright I. *adj attr, inv* ❶ (*total*) total; *disaster* absolut; *nonsense* komplett ❷ (*undisputed*) offensichtlich; *winner, victory* eindeutig **II.** *adv inv* ❶ (*totally*) total ❷ (*clearly*) eindeutig ❸ (*directly*) offen ❹ (*immediately*) sofort; **to be killed** ~ auf der Stelle tot sein

out'run <-ran, -run, -nn-> *vt* ■ **to** ~ **sb** jdm davonlaufen; ■ **to** ~ **sth** über etw *akk* hinausgehen

'outset *n* Anfang *m;* ■ **from the** ~ von Anfang an

out'shine <-shone *or* -shined, -shone *or* -shined> *vt* (*be better than*) ■ **to** ~ **sb** jdn in den Schatten stellen

out'side I. *n* ❶ (*exterior*) Außenseite *f; of a fruit* Schale *f;* ■ **from the** ~ (*fig*) von außen ❷ (*external appearance*) ■ **on the** ~ äußerlich ❸ (*not within boundary*) ■ **on the** ~ draußen **II.** *adj attr, inv* ❶ (*outer*) *door, entrance* äußere(r, s); ~ **seat** Sitz *m* am Gang; ~ **wall** Außenmauer *f* ❷ (*external*) außenstehend; **the world** ~ die Welt draußen ❸ (*very slight*) *chance, possibility* minimal **III.** *adv* ❶ (*not in building*) außen ❷ (*in open air*) im Freien **IV.** *prep* ❶ (*beyond*) außerhalb (**of** von) ❷ (*apart from*) ausgenommen

outside 'line *n* Telefonleitung *f* für externe Gespräche

outsider [ˌaʊt·'saɪ·dər] *n* ❶ (*not a member*) Außenstehende(r) *f(m)* ❷ (*outcast, in sports*) Außenseiter(in) *m(f)*

'outsize *adj attr, inv* (*very large*) übergroß; ~ **clothes** Kleidung *f* in Übergrößen

outskirts ['aʊt·skɜrts] *npl* Stadtrand *m*

'outsource *vt work, production* auslagern, outsourcen *fachspr*

outsourcing ['aʊt·ˌsɔr·sɪŋ] *n* Outsourcing *nt fachspr; of staff* Beschäftigung *f* betriebsfremden Personals; *of production* Produktionsauslagerung *f*

outspoken [ˌaʊt·'spoʊ·kən] *adj* offen; *criticism* unverblümt; *opponent* entschieden

out'standing *adj* ❶ (*excellent*) außergewöhnlich; *effort, contribution* bemerkenswert; *actor, student, performance* brillant; *ability* außerordentlich; *achievement* überragend ❷ (*clearly noticeable*) auffallend ❸ (*not dealt with*) unerledigt; *problems* ungelöst

out'stay *vt stay too long* **to** ~ **one's welcome** länger bleiben, als man erwünscht ist

outstretched [ˌaʊt·'stretʃt] **I.** *adj pred, inv* ausgestreckt; *arms a.* ausgebreitet **II.** *adj attr, inv hands, legs* ausgestreckt

out'strip <-pp-> *vt* ❶ (*surpass*) übertreffen; (*go faster*) überholen ❷ (*be greater*) übersteigen

out'vote *vt* überstimmen

outward ['aʊt·wərd] **I.** *adj attr* ❶ (*exterior*) äußere(r, s), Außen-; (*superficial*) äußerlich; **an** ~ **show of confidence** ein demonstratives Zurschaustellen von Zuversicht ❷ (*going out*) ausgehend; ~ **flight** Hinflug *m* **II.** *adv* nach außen; **the door opens** ~ die Tür geht nach außen auf

outwardly ['aʊt·wərd·li] *adv inv* äußerlich, nach außen hin

outwards ['aʊt·wərdz] *adv inv* nach außen

out'weigh *vt* (*in importance*) ■ **to** ~ **sth** etw wettmachen; **the advantages** ~ **the disadvantages** die Vorteile überwiegen die Nachteile

out'wit <-tt-> *vt* austricksen

out'work *vt* (*work harder than*) schneller arbeiten

oval ['oʊ·vəl] **I.** *n* Oval *nt* **II.** *adj* oval

Oval 'Office *n* POL ■ **the** ~ das Oval Office (*Büro des US-Präsidenten*)

ovary ['oʊ·və·ri] *n* Eierstock *m,* Ovarium *nt fachspr*

ovation [oʊ·'veɪ·ʃən] *n* Applaus *m*

oven ['ʌv·ən] *n* [Back]ofen *m,* Backrohr *nt* ÖSTERR; **microwave** ~ Mikrowelle *f*

'oven mitt *n* Topfhandschuh *m*

'ovenproof *adj inv* hitzebeständig

'oven-ready *adj inv* bratfertig, backfertig

over ['oʊ·vər] **I.** *adv inv, pred* ❶ (*across*) hinüber; ~ **here** hier herüber; (*on the other side*) drüben; ~ **there** dort drüben; **to move** [**sth**] ~ [etw] [beiseite]rücken ❷ (*another way up*) **to turn** ~ umdrehen; **to turn a page** ~ [eine Seite] umblättern ❸ (*downwards*) **to fall** ~ hinfallen; **to knock sth** ~ etw umstoßen ❹ (*finished*) ■ **to be** ~ vorbei sein; **to get sth** ~ **and done with** etw hinter sich *akk* bringen ❺ (*remaining*) übrig; **left** ~ übrig gelassen ❻ (*again*) noch einmal; ~ **and** ~ immer wieder ❼ (*more*) mehr; **people aged 65 and** ~ Menschen, die 65 Jahre und älter sind **II.** *prep* ❶ (*across*) über ❷ (*on the other side of*) über ❸ (*above*) über; (*moving above*) über; **a flock of geese passed** ~ eine Schar von Gänsen flog über uns hinweg ❹ (*everywhere*) [überall] in; (*moving everywhere*) durch; **all** ~ **the world** in der ganzen Welt ❺ (*during*) in, während; ~ **the years, he became more and more depressed** mit den Jahren wurde er immer deprimierter; **she fell asleep** ~ **her homework** sie nickte bei ihren Hausaufgaben ein ❻ (*through*) **he told me** ~ **the phone** er sagte es mir am Telefon ⑦ (*more than*) über; **this shirt cost me ~ $50!** dieses Hemd hat mich über 50 Dollar gekostet! ⑧ *after vb* (*to check*) durch; **could you go ~ my essay again?** kannst du nochmal meinen Aufsatz durchschauen ⑨ (*past*) **to be/get ~ sb/sth** über jdn/etw hinweg sein/kommen

overa'bundant *adj inv* übermäßig

over'act *vi* THEAT übertreiben

overall I. *n* ['oʊ·vər·ɔl] ■ **~s** *pl* Latzhose *f* **II.** *adj* ['oʊ·vər·ɔl] *attr* ① (*general*) Gesamt-, allgemein ② (*over all others*) Gesamt-; **~ commander** Oberkommandierende(r) *f(m); majority* absolut **III.** *adv* [ˌoʊ·vər·'ɔl] *inv* insgesamt

over'arching *adj attr, inv* [mit]umfassend

over'bearing *adj* (*pej: arrogant*) anmaßend; (*authoritative*) herrisch

over'blown *adj* (*overdone*) geschraubt

'overboard *adv inv* NAUT über Bord ▶ PHRASES: **to go ~** zu weit gehen, es übertreiben

over'book I. *vt usu passive* ■ **to be ~ed** überbucht sein **II.** *vi* zu viele Buchungen vornehmen

over'burden *vt* überlasten

over'cast *adj sky* bedeckt; *weather* trüb

over'charge I. *vt* (*charge too much*) ■ **to ~ sb [for sth]** jdm [für etw *akk*] zu viel berechnen **II.** *vi* zu viel berechnen

'overcoat *n* Mantel *m*

over'come <-came, -come> **I.** *vt* ① *crisis, opposition, fear* überwinden; *temptation* widerstehen; *enemy forces* besiegen ② *usu passive* (*render powerless*) ■ **to be ~ by sth** *sleep, emotion, grief* von etw *dat* überwältigt werden; *fumes, exhausts* von etw *dat* ohnmächtig werden **II.** *vi* siegen

over'compensate *vi* ■ **to ~ for sth** etw *akk* überkompensieren

over'confident *adj* (*extremely self-assured*) übertrieben selbstbewusst; (*too optimistic*) übertrieben zuversichtlich

over'cook *vt* (*in water*) verkochen; (*in oven*) verbraten

over'crowded *adj* überfüllt; *profession* überlaufen; *town* übervölkert

overde'veloped *adj a.* PHOT überentwickelt

over'do <-did, -done> *vt* ① (*overexert oneself*) **to ~ it** sich überanstrengen; (*overindulge*) es übertreiben; (*go too far*) zu weit gehen ② (*use too much*) ■ **to ~ sth** von etw *dat* zu viel verwenden

over'done *adj* (*overcooked*) *in water* verkocht; *in oven* verbraten

overdose I. *n* ['oʊ·vər·doʊs] Überdosis *f*; **drug ~** Überdosis *f* Drogen **II.** *vi* [ˌoʊ·vər·'doʊs] eine Überdosis nehmen

'overdraft *n* Kontoüberziehung *f*

over'draw <-drew, -drawn> *vt* **to ~ one's account** sein Konto überziehen

over'dress *vi* sich zu fein anziehen

'overdrive *n* ① AUTO, TECH Schongang *m* ② (*fig: effort*) ■ **to be in ~** auf Hochtouren laufen

over'due *adj usu pred* überfällig

over 'easy *adj, adv usu pred* **~ egg** *auf beiden Seiten gebratenes Spiegelei*

over'eat <-ate, -eaten> *vi* zu viel essen

over'emphasize *vt* überbetonen

overestimate [ˌoʊ·vər·'es·tə·meɪt] *vt* (*estimate too much*) überschätzen

overex'cited *adj usu pred* ■ **to be/become ~** ganz aufgeregt sein/werden

overex'pose *vt* ■ **to be ~d** ① PHOT überbelichtet sein ② *usu passive* (*overpublicize*) *person* zu sehr im Rampenlicht der Öffentlichkeit stehen; **to be ~d to risks** zu starken Risiken ausgesetzt sein

overex'posure *n* ① PHOT Überbelichtung *f* ② (*in the media*) *of person* zu große Präsenz

overex'tend *vt* ■ **to ~ oneself [on sth]** sich [bei etw *dat*] [finanziell] übernehmen

overflow I. *n* ['oʊ·vər·floʊ] ① (*act of spilling*) Überlaufen *nt* ② (*overflowing liquid*) überlaufende Flüssigkeit ③ (*outlet*) Überlauf *m* ④ (*surplus*) Überschuss *m* (**of** an +*dat*) **II.** *vi* [ˌoʊ·vər·'floʊ] *river, tank* überlaufen; **to be ~ing with ideas** vor Ideen sprühen **III.** *vt* [ˌoʊ·vər·'floʊ] ■ **to ~ sth** *container, tank* etw zum Überlaufen bringen

over'grown *adj* ① (*with plants*) überwuchert ② (*usu pej: childish*) **he is just an ~ schoolboy** er ist wie ein großer Schuljunge

overhang [ˌoʊ·vər·'hæŋ] *vt* <-hung, -hung> (*project over*) ■ **to ~ sth** über etw *akk* hinausragen; ARCHIT über etw *akk* hervorstehen

overhaul I. *n* ['oʊ·vər·hɔl] [Generalüberholung *f*; (*revision*) Überarbeitung *f* **II.** *vt* [ˌoʊ·vər·'hɔl] ① (*repair*) überholen ② (*improve*) überprüfen; (*reform*) überarbeiten

overhead I. *n* ['oʊ·vər·hed] ① (*running costs of business*) laufende Geschäftskosten ② (*transparency*) Folie *f* **II.** *adj* ['oʊ·vər·hed] *attr, inv* ① (*above head level*) Hoch-; ELEC oberirdisch ② (*taken from above*) *photo* von oben nach *n* **III.** *adv* [ˌoʊ·vər·'hed] in der Luft; **a plane circled ~** ein Flugzeug kreiste über uns

over'hear <-heard, -heard> **I.** *vt* ■ **to ~ sth** etw zufällig mithören; ■ **to ~ sb** jdn unabsichtlich belauschen **II.** *vi* unabsichtlich mithören

over'heat I. *vt* überhitzen **II.** *vi* sich überhitzen *a. fig; motor a.* heiß laufen

overin'dulge I. *vt* ■ **to ~ oneself** sich zu sehr gehen lassen **II.** *vi* (*eat too much*) sich *dat* den Bauch vollschlagen *fam;* (*drink too much*) sich volllaufen lassen *fam*

overjoyed [ˌoʊ·vər·'dʒɔɪd] *adj pred* überglücklich (**at** über +*akk*)

'overkill *n* (*pej: excessiveness*) Übermaß *nt*

overland I. *adj* ['oʊ·vər·lænd] *attr* Überland-, Land-; **~ trip** Reise *f* auf dem Landweg **II.** *adv* [ˌoʊ·vər·'lænd] *inv* auf dem Landweg

overlap I. *n* ['oʊ·vər·læp] ① (*overlapping part*) Überlappung *f* ② (*similarity*) Überschneidung *f* **II.** *vi* <-pp-> [ˌoʊ·vər·'læp] ① (*lie edge over edge*) sich überlappen ② (*be partly similar*) sich überschneiden; ■ **to ~ with sth** sich teilweise mit etw *dat* decken **III.** *vt* <-pp-> [ˌoʊ·vər·ˈlæp] ■**to ~ sth** ①(*place edge over edge*) etw *akk* überlappen lassen ②(*partly duplicate*) etw ineinander übergehen lassen

overload I. *n* [ˈoʊ·vər·loʊd] ①ELEC Überlast[ung] *f;* TRANSP Übergewicht *nt* ②(*excess*) Überbelastung *f;* **information ~** Überangebot *nt* an Informationen **II.** *vt* [ˌoʊ·vər·ˈloʊd] (*overburden*) *vehicle* überladen; *road, system, person, equipment* überlasten

overlook I. *n* [ˈoʊ·vər·lʊk] Aussichtspunkt *m* **II.** *vt* [ˌoʊ·vər·ˈlʊk] ①(*look out onto*) überblicken ②(*not notice*) übersehen; (*ignore*) übergehen

overly [ˈoʊ·vər·li] *adv inv* allzu

over'night I. *adj* ①*attr, inv* (*for a night*) Nacht-, Übernachtungs-; **~ stay** Übernachtung *f* ②(*for next day*) *delivery, package* über Nacht ③(*sudden*) ganz plötzlich; **~ success** Blitzerfolg *m* **II.** *adv inv* ①(*until next day*) in der Nacht, über Nacht ②(*fig: suddenly*) in kurzer Zeit, über Nacht

'overpass *n* Überführung *f*

over'pay <-paid, -paid> *vt* ①(*overremunerate*) überbezahlen ②(*pay more than required*) für etw *akk* zu viel bezahlen

over'populated *adj* überbevölkert

overpopu'lation *n* Überbevölkerung *f*

over'power *vt* überwältigen

over'powering *adj* überwältigend; *smell* durchdringend

overpro'duce *vt* ■**to ~ sth** von etw *dat* zu viel produzieren

over'rated *adj* (*pej*) überbewertet

over'reach *vt* ■**to ~ oneself** sich übernehmen

overre'act *vi* überreagieren; ■**to ~ to sth** auf etw *akk* unangemessen reagieren

overre'action *n* Überreaktion *f* (**to** auf +*akk*)

over'ride I. *n* ①(*device*) Übersteuerung *f;* **manual ~** Automatikabschaltung *f* ②(*cancellation*) Außerkraftsetzen *nt* **II.** *vt* <-rid, -ridden> ①(*outweigh*) überwiegen ②(*cancel*) *veto* aufheben ③(*control*) abschalten

over'riding *adj attr, inv* vorrangig

over'rule *vt* überstimmen; *decision* aufheben; *objection* zurückweisen

over'run I. *vt* <-ran, -run> ①MIL (*occupy*) überrollen ②(*spread over*) sich in etw *dat* ausbreiten; ■**to be ~ with sth** von etw *dat* wimmeln; *market* von etw *dat* überschwemmt werden ③(*exceed*) *budget* überschreiten **II.** *vi* <-ran, -run> (*exceed time*) überziehen

overseas I. *adj* [ˈoʊ·vər·siz] *attr, inv* (*abroad*) Übersee-, in Übersee *nach n;* (*destined for abroad*) Übersee-, nach Übersee *nach n;* (*from abroad*) Übersee-, aus Übersee *nach n* **II.** *adv* [ˌoʊ·vər·ˈsiz] *inv* (*in foreign country*) im Ausland; (*to foreign country*) ins Ausland

over'see <-saw, -seen> *vt* beaufsichtigen; *project* leiten

overseer [ˈoʊ·vər·ˌsi·ər] *n* Aufseher, -in *m, f*

over'sell <-sold, -sold> *vt* ■**to ~ sth** (*overhype*) etw zu sehr anpreisen

over'shadow *vt* ①(*make insignificant*) in den Schatten stellen ②(*cast gloom over*) überschatten

'overshoe *n* Überschuh *m*

over'shoot <-shot, -shot> *vt* ■**to ~ sth** über etw *akk* hinausschießen; **the plane overshot the runway** das Flugzeug schoss über die Rennbahn hinaus ▶PHRASES: **to ~ the mark** über das Ziel hinausschießen

'oversight *n* (*mistake*) Versehen *nt;* ■**by an ~** aus Versehen

over'simplify <-ie-> *vt* grob vereinfachen

'oversize, 'oversized *adj* überdimensional

over'sleep <-slept, -slept> *vi* verschlafen

over'spend <-spent, -spent> **I.** *vi* zu viel [Geld] ausgeben **II.** *vt* überziehen; *budget, target* überschreiten

over'staffed *adj* überbesetzt

over'state *vt* übertreiben; **to ~ a case** einen Fall übertrieben darstellen

over'stay *vt* **to ~ a visa** ein Visum überschreiten; **to ~ one's welcome** jds Gastfreundschaft *f* überbeanspruchen

over'step <-pp-> *vt* überschreiten ▶PHRASES: **to ~ the mark** zu weit gehen

over'supply I. *n* (*supply*) Überangebot *nt* (**of** an); (*excess inventory*) Überbestand *m* (**of** an) **II.** *vt* <-ie-> *usu passive* ■**to be oversupplied with sth** einen zu großen Vorrat an etw *dat* haben

overt [ˈoʊ·vɜrt] *adj* offenkundig; *racism, sexism* unverhohlen

over'take <-took, -taken> *vt* ①(*pass from behind*) überholen; (*catch up*) einholen ②(*surpass*) überholen *fig*

over'tax *vt* ①FIN ■**to ~ sb** jdn überbesteuern ②(*exhaust*) überfordern

over-the-'counter *adj attr, inv* ①(*without prescription*) *drugs, medications, remedies* rezeptfrei ②FIN außerbörslich

over-the-'top *adj inv* (*fam*) übertrieben, exzessiv *geh*

overthrow I. *n* [ˈoʊ·vər·θroʊ] (*removal from power*) Sturz *m* **II.** *vt* <-threw, -thrown> [ˌoʊ·vər·ˈθroʊ] ①(*topple*) stürzen; **to ~ a regime** ein Regime zu Fall bringen ②SPORTS ■**to ~ sb** für jdn zu weit werfen

'overtime I. *n* ①(*extra work*) Überstunden *pl;* **to do ~** Überstunden machen ②SPORTS (*extra time*) Verlängerung *f* **II.** *adv* **to work ~** Überstunden machen

over'tired *adj inv* übermüdet

'overtone *n* ①(*implication*) Unterton *m* ②MUS Oberton *m*

overture [ˈoʊ·vər·tʃər] *n* (*introductory music*) Ouvertüre *f* (**to** zu) ▶PHRASES: **to make ~s to sb** jdm ein Angebot machen

over'turn I. *vi* umstürzen; *car* sich überschlagen; *boat* kentern **II.** *vt* ①(*turn upside down*) umstoßen; *boat* zum Kentern bringen ②(*reverse*) revidieren; *government* stürzen

over'value *vt* (*give excessively high value to*) überbewerten

'overview *n* Überblick *m* (**of** über +*akk*)
overweight [ˌoʊ·vər·ˈweɪt] *adj* zu schwer; *person a.* übergewichtig
overwhelm [ˌoʊ·vər·ˈwelm] *vt* ❶ (*affect powerfully*) überwältigen ❷ (*overpower*) überwältigen; *enemy* besiegen
overwhelming [ˌoʊ·vər·ˈwel·mɪŋ] *adj* (*very powerful*) überwältigend; *desire, need* unwiderstehlich; *grief* unermesslich; *joy* groß
overwork **I.** *n* [ˈoʊ·vər·wɜrk] Überarbeitung *f* **II.** *vi* [ˌoʊ·vər·ˈwɜrk] sich überarbeiten **III.** *vt* [ˌoʊ·vər·ˈwɜrk] ❶ (*give too much work*) ■**to ~ sb** jdn [mit Arbeit] überlasten ❷ (*overuse*) ■**to ~ sth** etw überstrapazieren
ovulate [ˈav·ju·leɪt] *vi* [einen] Eisprung haben
ovulation [ˌav·ju·ˈleɪ·ʃən] *n* Eisprung *m*
ovum <*pl* -va> [ˈoʊ·vəm, *pl* -və] *n* Eizelle *f*
ow [aʊ] *interj* au
owe [oʊ] *vt* ❶ (*be in debt*) schulden; **to ~ sb an explanation** jdm eine Erklärung schuldig sein; **to ~ sb thanks/gratitude** jdm zu Dank verpflichtet sein ❷ (*be indebted*) ■**to ~ sth to sb** jdm etw verdanken; **I ~ it all to my parents** ich habe alles meinen Eltern zu verdanken
owing [ˈoʊ·ɪŋ] *adj inv, pred* ausstehend
'owing to *prep* (*form*) ■**~ sth** wegen einer S. *gen*
owl [aʊl] *n* Eule *f;* **barn ~** Schleiereule *f*
own [oʊn] **I.** *pron* (*belonging, relating to*) **his time is his ~** er kann über seine Zeit frei verfügen; **to make sth [all] one's ~** sich *dat* etw [ganz] zu eigen machen; **to have ideas of one's ~** eigene Ideen haben ►PHRASES: **to <u>come</u> into one's ~** (*show qualities*) zeigen, was in einem steckt *fam;* (*get recognition*) die verdiente Anerkennung erhalten; **[all] <u>on</u> one's/its ~** [ganz] allein[e] **II.** *adj attr, inv* ❶ (*belonging to, individual*) eigene(r, s) ❷ (*for oneself*) **you'll have to get your ~ dinner** du musst dich selbst um das Abendessen kümmern; **to make up one's ~ mind** sich +*akk* entscheiden ►PHRASES: **to <u>do</u> one's ~ thing** (*fam*) tun, was man will; **in one's ~ <u>right</u>** (*not due to others*) aus eigenem Recht; (*through one's talents*) aufgrund der eigenen Begabung **III.** *vt* (*possess*) besitzen; ■**to be ~ed by sb** jdm gehören
◆**own up** *vi* es zugeben; ■**to ~ up to sth** etw zugeben
owner [ˈoʊ·nər] *n* Besitzer(in) *m(f)*
owner-'occupied *adj inv* vom Eigentümer/von der Eigentümerin selbst bewohnt
ownership [ˈoʊ·nər·ʃɪp] *n* (*have power over*) Besitz *m* (**of** +*gen*)
ox <*pl* -en> [aks] *n* Ochse *m;* **~ cart** Ochsenkarren *m*
oxidation [ˌak·sɪ·ˈdeɪ·ʃən] *n* Oxidation *f*
oxide [ˈak·saɪd] *n* Oxyd *nt*
oxidize [ˈak·sɪ·daɪz] *vi, vt* oxidieren
oxtail 'soup *n* Ochsenschwanzsuppe *f*
oxyacetylene [ˌak·si·ə·ˈset̬·ə·lin] *n* Azetylensauerstoff *m*
oxygen [ˈak·sɪ·dʒən] *n* Sauerstoff *m*
'oxygen mask *n* Sauerstoffmaske *f*
'oxygen tent *n* Sauerstoffzelt *nt*
oxymoron [ˌak·sɪ·ˈmɔr·an] *n* Oxymoron *nt*
oyster [ˈɔɪ·stər] *n* ❶ (*shellfish*) Auster[nmuschel] *f* ❷ FOOD Auster *f* ►PHRASES: **the <u>world</u> is sb's ~** jdm steht die Welt offen
oz, oz. <*pl* -> *n abbrev of* **ounce**
ozone [ˈoʊ·zoʊn] *n* ❶ (*chemical*) Ozon *nt* ❷ (*fam: clean air*) saubere [frische] Luft
'ozone layer *n* Ozonschicht *f*

Pp

P <*pl* -'s *or* -s>, **p** <*pl* -'s> [pi] *n* p *nt,* P *nt;* ~ **as in Papa** P wie Paula

p. [pi] *n* <*pl* pp> *abbrev of* **page** S.

p [pi] *adv* MUS *abbrev of* **piano** p

PA, Pa. *n abbrev of* **Pennsylvania**

pace [peɪs] **I.** *n* ① (*speed*) Tempo *nt;* **to set the** ~ das Tempo vorgeben ② (*step*) Schritt *m;* **to keep ~ with sb/sth** mit jdm/etw Schritt halten **II.** *vt* (*walk back and forth across*) **to ~ the room** das Zimmer auf und ab gehen **III.** *vi* gehen

'pacemaker *n* ① (*for heart*) [Herz]schrittmacher *m* ② SPORTS (*speed setter*) Schrittmacher(in) *m(f)*

Pacific [pə·'sɪf·ɪk] **I.** *n* ■ **the** ~ der Pazifik **II.** *adj inv* pazifisch, Pazifik-

pacification [ˌpæs·ə·fɪ·'keɪ·ʃən] *n* Befriedung *f*

pacifier ['pæs·ə·faɪ·ər] *n* (*for baby*) Schnuller *m*

pacifism ['pæs·ə·fɪz·əm] *n* Pazifismus *m*

pacifist ['pæs·ə·fɪst] **I.** *n* Pazifist(in) *m(f)* **II.** *adj* pazifistisch

pacify <-ie-> ['pæs·ə·faɪ] *vt* ① (*calm*) beruhigen ② (*establish peace*) befrieden

pack [pæk] **I.** *n* ① (*packet*) Packung *f;* (*box*) *of cigarettes etc.* Schachtel *f* ② (*backpack*) Rucksack *m;* (*bundle*) Bündel *nt;* (*bag*) Beutel *m* ③ *of cards* [Karten]spiel *nt* ④ (*group*) Gruppe *f; of wolves* Rudel *nt; of dogs* Meute *f a. fig, pej* **II.** *vi* ① (*for a trip*) packen ② (*be suitable for storage*) **to ~/not ~ well** gut/nicht gut hineinpassen ③ (*become compacted*) *snow* fest werden **III.** *vt* ① (*put into a container*) *articles, goods* [ein]packen; (*for transport*) verpacken; (*in units for sale*) abpacken ② (*fill*) packen ③ (*put in wrapping*) einpacken (**in** in +*akk*) ④ (*a. fig: cram*) vollpacken (**with** mit +*dat*); ■ **to be ~ed [with people]** gerammelt voll [mit Leuten] sein *fam* ⑤ (*compress*) zusammenpressen ⑥ (*fam*) *pistol* dabei haben, (bei sich) tragen

◆**pack away** *vt* wegpacken

◆**pack in** *vt* ① (*cram in*) hineinstopfen; *people, animals* hineinpferchen ② (*put in*) einpacken; (*for transport*) verpacken; (*in units for sale*) abpacken ► PHRASES: **to ~ it in** (*fam: stop working*) **let's ~ it in for the day** machen wir Feierabend für heute

◆**pack into** **I.** *vt* ① (*put*) [ein]packen; (*for transport*) verpacken; (*in units for sale*) abpacken ② (*cram*) [hinein]stopfen ③ (*fig: fit*) [hinein]packen **II.** *vi* (*throng*) hineindrängen *akk*

◆**pack off** *vt* (*fam*) wegschicken; **to ~ sb off to boarding school** jdn in ein Internat stecken

◆**pack up** **I.** *vt* zusammenpacken, einpacken **II.** *vi* (*fam*) **to ~ up and go home** Feierabend machen; **to ~ up and leave** seine Sachen packen und gehen

package ['pæk·ɪdʒ] **I.** *n* ① (*parcel, set*) Paket *nt* ② (*pack*) *of cookies etc.* Packung *f* **II.** *vt* ① (*pack*) verpacken, einpacken ② (*fig*) präsentieren

packaged [pæk·ɪdʒd] *adj food* verpackt

'package deal *n* Pauschalangebot *nt*

'package tour *n* Pauschalurlaub *m*

packaging ['pæk·ɪ·dʒɪŋ] *n* Verpackung *f*

packer ['pæk·ər] *n* [Ver]packer(in) *m(f)*

packet ['pæk·ɪt] *n* Packung *f,* Schachtel *f*

packing ['pæk·ɪŋ] *n* ① (*action*) Packen *nt* ② (*material*) Verpackung *f*

pact [pækt] *n* Pakt *m*

pad¹ [pæd] **I.** *n* ① (*wad*) Pad *m o nt* ② (*protector, for shaping*) Polster *nt;* SPORTS **knee** ~ Knieschoner *m* ③ (*of paper*) Block *m* ④ (*on animal's foot*) Ballen *m* ⑤ AEROSP, AVIAT **launch** ~ Abschussrampe *f* ⑥ (*sl: apartment*) Bude *f* **II.** *vt* <-dd-> [aus]polstern

pad² [pæd] *vi* trotten; (*walk softly*) tappen

padded ['pæd·ɪd] *adj inv* [aus]gepolstert; *bra* wattiert; *envelope* gefüttert

padding ['pæd·ɪŋ] *n* ① (*protective material*) Polsterung *f* ② (*superfluous material*) Füllwerk *nt*

paddle¹ ['pæd·əl] **I.** *n* (*with two blades*) Paddel *nt;* (*with one blade*) Stechpaddel *nt* **II.** *vt* (*row*) **to ~ a boat** ein Boot mit Paddeln vorwärtsbewegen **III.** *vi* ① (*row*) paddeln ② (*swim*) paddeln

paddle² ['pæd·əl] *vi* planschen

paddy ['pæd·i] *n* Reisfeld *nt*

padlock ['pæd·lak] **I.** *n* Vorhängeschloss *nt* **II.** *vt* [mit einem Vorhängeschloss] verschließen

pagan ['peɪ·gən] *n* ① (*polytheist*) Heide, -in *m, f* ② (*unbeliever*) Ungläubige(r) *f(m)*

page¹ [peɪdʒ] **I.** *n* ① (*single sheet*) Blatt *nt;* COMPUT (*single side*) Seite *f* ② (*fig: important event*) Kapitel *nt* **II.** *vi* COMPUT ■ **to ~ up/down** auf der Seite nach oben/unten gehen

page² [peɪdʒ] **I.** *n* ① (*hist: knight's attendant*) Knappe *m* ② (*Congressional intern*) Praktikant(in) *m(f), im amerikanischen Kongress* **II.** *vt* (*over loudspeaker*) ausrufen; (*by pager*) anpiepsen, über einen Piepser rufen

pageant ['pædʒ·ənt] *n* ① (*show*) **beauty** ~ Schönheitswettbewerb *m* ② (*play*) Historienspiel *nt*

pageantry ['pædʒ·ən·tri] *n* Pomp *m*

pageboy ['peɪdʒ·bɔɪ] *n* Pagenschnitt *m*

pager ['peɪ·dʒər] *n* Pager *m,* Piepser *m*

pagination [ˌpædʒ·ə·'neɪ·ʃən] *n* Seitennummerierung *f*

pagoda [pə·'goʊ·də] *n* Pagode *f*

paid [peɪd] **I.** *pt, pp of* **pay** **II.** *adj attr, inv* bezahlt

pail [peɪl] *n* Eimer *m*

pain [peɪn] **I.** *n* ① (*feeling*) Schmerz *m;* **a ~ in one's leg/side** Schmerzen *pl* im Bein/in der Seite ❷ (*physical suffering*) Schmerz[en] *m[pl]*; **to be in ~** Schmerzen haben; (*mental suffering*) Leid *nt* ❸ (*effort*) ■ **~s** *pl* Mühe *f;* **to go to great ~s to do sth** keine Mühe scheuen, etw zu tun ▶ PHRASES: **to be a ~ in the ass** (*fam*) eine Nervensäge sein; **no ~, no gain** ohne Fleiß kein Preis **II.** *vt* ■ **it ~s sb to do sth** es tut jdm leid, etw zu tun

pained [peɪnd] *adj expression, look* gequält

painful ['peɪn·fəl] *adj* ❶ (*causing physical pain*) schmerzhaft; *death* qualvoll ❷ (*upsetting*) schmerzlich

painfully ['peɪn·fəl·i] *adv* ❶ (*suffering pain*) unter Schmerzen ❷ (*unpleasantly*) schmerzlich ❸ (*with great effort*) quälend

'painkiller *n* Schmerzmittel *nt*

painless ['peɪn·lɪs] *adj* ❶ *inv* (*without pain*) schmerzlos ❷ (*fig: without trouble*) schmerzlos; *solution* einfach

painstaking ['peɪnz·ˌteɪ·kɪŋ] *adj* [sehr] sorgfältig; *care* äußerst

paint [peɪnt] **I.** *n* ❶ (*substance*) Farbe *f;* (*on car, furniture a.*) Lack *m* ❷ (*art color*) ■ **~s** *pl* Farben *pl;* **oil ~s** Ölfarben *pl* **II.** *vi* ❶ ART malen; **to ~ in oils** mit Ölfarben malen ❷ (*decorate rooms*) streichen **III.** *vt* ❶ (*make picture*) malen ❷ (*decorate*) *house* anstreichen; *room, wall* streichen ❸ (*fig: describe*) beschreiben; **to ~ a picture of sth** etw schildern

'paintbrush *n* [Farb]pinsel *m*

painter ['peɪn·tər] *n* ❶ (*artist*) [Kunst]maler(in) *m(f)* ❷ (*sb who paints buildings*) Maler(in) *m(f)*

painting ['peɪn·tɪŋ] *n* ❶ (*picture*) Bild *nt* ❷ (*art*) Malerei *f* ❸ (*house decorating*) Streichen *nt*

'paint thinner *n* Verdünner *m*

'paintwork *n of a house, room, wall* Anstrich *m*

pair [per] **I.** *n* ❶ (*two items*) Paar *nt;* **a ~ of gloves** ein Paar *nt* Handschuhe ❷ (*two-part item*) Paar *nt;* **a ~ of glasses** eine Brille; **a ~ of pants** eine Hose ❸ (*two people, a. couple*) Paar *nt;* **in ~s** paarweise **II.** *vt usu passive* ■ **to be ~ed with sb/sth** mit jdm/etw ein Paar bilden

◆**pair off I.** *vi* einen Partner/eine Partnerin finden **II.** *vt* ■ **to ~ sb off [with sb]** jdn [mit jdm] verkuppeln *fam*

pajamas [pə·'dʒa·məz] *npl* Pyjama *m;* **a pair of ~** ein Pyjama *m*

Pakistan ['pæk·ɪ·stæn] *n* Pakistan *nt*

Pakistani [ˌpæk·ɪ·'sta·ni] **I.** *n* Pakistani *m,* Pakistaner(in) *m(f)* **II.** *adj inv* pakistanisch

pal [pæl] *n* (*fam*) Kumpel *m;* ■ **to be ~s with sb** mit jdm [sehr] gut befreundet sein

palace ['pæl·əs] *n* Palast *m*

palatable ['pæl·ə·t̬ə·bəl] *adj* ❶ (*of food, drink*) schmackhaft ❷ (*fig: acceptable*) akzeptabel

palate ['pæl·ət] *n* Gaumen *m*

palatial [pə·'leɪ·ʃəl] *adj* prachtvoll

pale [peɪl] **I.** *adj* blass **II.** *vi* ❶ (*go white*) bleich werden ❷ (*seem unimportant*) **to ~ into** insignificance unwichtig erscheinen

paleness ['peɪl·nɪs] *n* Blässe *f*

Palestine ['pæl·ə·staɪn] *n* Palästina *nt*

Palestinian [ˌpæl·ə·'stɪn·i·ən] **I.** *n* Palästinenser(in) *m(f)* **II.** *adj inv* palästinensisch

palette ['pæl·ɪt] *n* ART ❶ (*for mixing paint*) Palette *f* ❷ (*range of colors*) [Farb]palette *f*

palisade [ˌpæl·ə·'seɪd] *n* ❶ (*fence*) Palisade *f* ❷ (*cliffs*) ■ **~s** *pl* Steilufer *nt*

pall¹ [pɔl] *n* ❶ (*for coffin*) Sargtuch *nt* ❷ (*cloud*) [Rauch]wolke *f*

pall² [pɔl] *vi* an Reiz verlieren

'pallbearer *n* Sargträger(in) *m(f)*

pallet ['pæl·ɪt] *n* Palette *f*

palliative ['pæl·i·ə·t̬ɪv] **I.** *n* (*drug*) Schmerzmittel *nt* **II.** *adj inv* (*pain-relieving*) schmerzstillend *attr,* palliativ *fachspr*

pallid ['pæl·ɪd] *adj* ❶ (*very pale*) fahl ❷ (*lacking verve*) fad[e]

pallor ['pæl·ər] *n* Blässe *f*

palm¹ [pam] *n* Handfläche *f;* **to read sb's ~** jdm aus der Hand lesen

palm² [pam] *n* (*tree*) Palme *f*

◆**palm off** *vt* ■ **to ~ off ⊂ sth on sb** jdm etw andrehen *fam*

Palm 'Sunday *n* Palmsonntag *m*

palpable ['pæl·pə·bəl] *adj* ❶ (*obvious*) offenkundig, deutlich ❷ (*tangible*) spürbar, greifbar

palpitations [ˌpæl·pə·'teɪ·ʃənz] *npl* Herzklopfen *nt kein pl;* **to have ~** (*fig*) einen [Herz]anfall bekommen

palsy ['pɔl·zi] *n* Lähmung *f;* **cerebral ~** Kinderlähmung *f*

paltry ['pɔl·tri] *adj* ❶ (*small*) armselig; *sum* lächerlich ❷ (*contemptible*) billig *pej*

Pampas ['pæm·pəz] *n + sing/pl vb* Pampa *f*

pamper ['pæm·pər] *vt* verwöhnen

pamphlet ['pæm·flɪt] *n* [kleine] Broschüre *f,* Faltblatt *nt;* POL Flugblatt *nt*

pan¹ [pæn] **I.** *n* Pfanne *f* **II.** *vt* <-nn-> (*fam: criticize*) verreißen **III.** *vi* <-nn-> **to ~ for gold** Gold *nt* waschen

pan² [pæn] **I.** *vi* **to ~ to the left/right** nach links/rechts schwenken **II.** *vt camera* abfahren

◆**pan out** *vi* ❶ (*develop*) sich entwickeln ❷ (*succeed*) klappen *fam*

panacea [ˌpæn·ə·'si·ə] *n* Allheilmittel *nt*

panache [pə·'næʃ] *n* Elan *m,* Schwung *m*

Panama ['pæn·ə·ma] *n* Panama *nt*

Panama Ca'nal *n* ■ **the ~** der Panamakanal

Panamanian [ˌpæn·ə·'meɪ·ni·ən] **I.** *n* Panamaer(in) *m(f)* **II.** *adj inv* panamaisch

'pancake *n* Pfannkuchen *m*

pancreas <*pl* -es> ['pæŋ·kri·əs] *n* Bauchspeicheldrüse *f*

panda ['pæn·də] *n* Panda *m*

pandemonium [ˌpæn·də·'moʊ·ni·əm] *n* ❶ (*noisy confusion*) Chaos *nt* ❷ (*fig: uproar*) Tumult *m*

pander ['pæn·dər] *vi* (*pej*) ■ **to ~ to sth** etw *dat* nachgeben

pane [peɪn] *n* [Fenster]scheibe *f*

panel ['pæn·əl] **I.** *n* ❶ (*wooden*) [Holz]pa-

P

neel *nt;* (*metal*) Blech *nt* ❷ FASHION (*part of garment*) [Stoff]streifen *m* ❸ **instrument** ~ AVIAT Instrumentenbrett *nt;* AUTO Armaturenbrett *nt* ❹ (*team*) Team *nt* **II.** *vt* <-l- *or* -ll-> täfeln (**with** mit +*dat*)

paneling ['pæn·ə·lɪŋ] *n* [Holz]täfelung *f*

panelist ['pæn·ə·lɪst] *n* (*on expert team*) Mitglied *nt* [einer Expertengruppe]

pang [pæŋ] *n* [plötzliches] Schmerzgefühl; **hunger ~s** nagender Hunger

'panhandle I. *n* ❶ (*on pan*) Pfannenstiel *m* ❷ GEOG Landzipfel *m* **II.** *vi* schnorren

'panhandler *n* (*fam*) Schnorrer(in) *m(f)*

panic ['pæn·ɪk] **I.** *n* ❶ (*overwhelming fear*) Panik *f* ❷ (*hysterical fear*) panische Angst **II.** *vi* <-ck-> in Panik geraten **III.** *vt* ■ **to ~ sb** unter jdm Panik auslösen

panicky ['pæn·ɪ·ki] *adj* panisch

'panic-stricken *adj* von Panik ergriffen

panorama [ˌpæn·ə·'ræm·ə] *n* Panorama *nt;* (*fig*) Überblick *m* (**of** über +*akk*)

panoramic [ˌpæn·ə·'ræm·ɪk] *adj* Panorama-

pansy ['pæn·zi] *n* ❶ (*flower*) Stiefmütterchen *nt* ❷ (*pej sl: effeminate male*) Weichei *nt;* (*male homosexual*) Homo *m*

pant¹ [pænt] **I.** *vi* (*breathe rapidly*) keuchen **II.** *n* (*breath*) Keuchen *nt kein pl*

pant² [pænt] *n* FASHION ■ **~s** *pl* **a pair of ~s** eine [lange] Hose ► PHRASES: **to scare the ~s off** [**of**] **sb** (*fam*) jdm einen Riesenschrecken einjagen; **to be caught with one's ~s down** (*fam*) auf frischer Tat ertappt werden

panther <*pl* - *or* -s> ['pæn·θər] *n* ❶ (*leopard*) Panther *m* ❷ *see* **mountain lion**

panties ['pæn·tiz] *npl* (*fam*) [Damen]slip *m,* [Damen]schlüpfer *m*

pantomime ['pæn·tə·maɪm] **I.** *n* Pantomime *f* **II.** *vt* pantomimisch darstellen

pantry ['pæn·tri] *n* Vorratskammer *f*

'pants leg *n* Hosenbein *nt*

'pantsuit, 'pants suit *n* Hosenanzug *m*

'pantyhose *npl* Strumpfhose *f*

'panty liner *n* Slipeinlage *f*

papa ['pa·pə] *n* (*childspeak fam*) Papa *m*

papacy ['peɪ·pə·si] *n* ❶ (*pope's jurisdiction*) ■ **the ~** das Pontifikat ❷ *usu sing* (*pope's tenure*) Pontifikat *nt*

papal ['peɪ·pəl] *adj inv* päpstlich, Papst-

paparazzi [ˌpa·pa·'ra·tsi] *npl* Paparazzi *pl*

papaya [pə·'paɪ·ə] *n* Papaya *f*

paper ['peɪ·pər] **I.** *n* ❶ (*for writing*) Papier *nt;* **a piece** [*or* **sheet**] **of ~** ein Blatt *nt* Papier; **recycled ~** Altpapier *nt* ❷ (*newspaper*) Zeitung *f* ❸ (*wallpaper*) Tapete *f* ❹ *usu pl* (*document*) Dokument *nt;* (*credentials*) [Ausweis]papiere *pl* **II.** *vt* tapezieren

'paperback *n* Taschenbuch *nt*

paper 'bag *n* Papiertüte *f*

'paperboy *n* Zeitungsjunge *m*

'paper chase *n* Schnitzeljagd *f*

'paper clip *n* Büroklammer *f*

paper 'cup *n* Pappbecher *m*

'papergirl *n* Zeitungsmädchen *nt*

'paper mill *n* Papierfabrik *f*

'paper money *n* Papiergeld *nt*

'paper route *n* Zeitungszustellung *f;* **to have a ~** Zeitungen austragen

paper-'thin *adj, adv inv* hauchdünn

paper 'towel *n* Papierhandtuch *nt,* Küchenrolle *f*

'paperweight *n* Briefbeschwerer *m*

'paperwork *n* Schreibarbeit *f;* **to do ~** [den] Papierkram machen *fam*

papery ['peɪ·pə·ri] *adj plaster* bröckelig; *skin* pergamenten

papier-mâché [ˌpeɪ·pər·mə·'ʃeɪ] *n* Pappmaschee *nt*

paprika [pæ·'pri·kə] *n* Paprika *m*

'Pap smear *n* MED Abstrich *m*

papyrus <*pl* -es *or* -ri> [pə·'paɪ·rəs] *n* ❶ Papyrusstaude *f* ❷ (*paper*) Papyrus *m*

par [par] *n* ❶ (*standard*) **above/below ~** über/unter dem Durchschnitt ❷ (*equality*) ■ **to be on** [**a**] **~ with sb/sth/each other** jdm/etw/einander ebenbürtig sein ❸ (*in golf*) Par *nt*

par. ['perə] *n short for* **paragraph** Absatz *m*

parable ['pær·ə·bəl] *n* Parabel *f*

parabola <*pl* -s *or* -lae> [pə·'ræb·ə·lə] *n* MATH Parabel *f*

parabolic [ˌpær·ə·'bal·ɪk] *adj inv* (*like a parabola*) parabolisch, Parabol-

parachute ['pær·ə·ʃut] **I.** *n* Fallschirm *m* **II.** *vi* mit dem Fallschirm abspringen

'parachute jump *n* Fallschirmabsprung *m*

parachutist ['pær·ə·ʃu·t̬ɪst] *n* Fallschirmspringer(in) *m(f)*

parade [pə·'reɪd] **I.** *n* ❶ (*procession*) Parade *f;* **victory ~** Siegeszug *m* ❷ MIL [Truppen]parade *f* **II.** *vi* ❶ (*walk in procession*) einen Umzug machen ❷ MIL marschieren ❸ (*show off*) ■ **to ~ around** auf und ab stolzieren **III.** *vt* ❶ MIL (*assemble*) *troops* aufmarschieren lassen ❷ (*march*) **to ~ the streets** durch die Straßen marschieren ❸ (*fig: show off*) stolz vorführen; (*fig*) *knowledge, wealth* zur Schau tragen

paradise ['pær·ə·daɪs] *n* Paradies *nt*

paradox <*pl* -es> ['pær·ə·daks] *n* Paradox[on] *nt geh*

paradoxical [ˌpær·ə·'dak·sɪ·kəl] *adj* paradox

paraffin ['pær·ə·fɪn] *n,* **paraffin wax** *n* Paraffin *nt*

paragon ['pær·ə·gan] *n* (*perfect example*) Muster[beispiel] *nt;* **a ~ of virtue** (*iron*) ein Ausbund *m* an Tugend

paragraph ['pær·ə·græf] *n* ❶ (*text*) Absatz *m* ❷ (*newspaper article*) [kurze] Zeitungsnotiz

parakeet ['pær·ə·kit] *n* Sittich *m*

paralegal [ˌpe·rə·'li·gəl] *n* juristische Hilfskraft, Anwaltsassistent(in) *m(f)*

parallel ['pær·ə·lel] **I.** *adj inv* ❶ *inv lines* parallel ❷ (*corresponding*) **~ example** Parallelbeispiel *nt* **II.** *n* ❶ (*similarity*) Parallele *f;* **to draw a ~** einen Vergleich ziehen ❷ MATH Parallele *f* ❸ GEOG **~** [**of latitude**] Brei-

P

tenkreis *m* **III.** *vt* (*correspond to*) entsprechen; (*be similar to*) ähneln **IV.** *adv inv* parallel; **to run ~ to sth** zu etw *dat* parallel verlaufen

parallel 'bars *npl* Barren *m*

parallel 'line *n* Parallele *f*

paralysis <*pl* -ses> [pə·ˈræl·ə·sɪs] *n* Lähmung *f a. fig*

paralyze [ˈpær·ə·laɪz] *vt* ① MED (*a. fig*) lähmen ② (*bring to halt*) lahmlegen

paralyzed [ˈper·ə·laɪzd] *adj* ① MED gelähmt ② (*brought to halt*) lahmgelegt; (*blocked*) blockiert

paramedic [ˌpær·ə·ˈmed·ɪk] *n* Sanitäter(in) *m(f)*

parameter [pə·ˈræm·ə·t̬ər] *n usu pl* ① SCI Bestimmungsfaktor *m* ② (*set of limits*) ■**~s** *pl* Leitlinien *pl*

paramount [ˈpær·ə·maʊnt] *adj inv* (*form: having priority*) vorrangig

paranoia [ˌpær·ə·ˈnɔɪ·ə] *n* PSYCH Paranoia *f geh*

paranoid [ˈpær·ə·nɔɪd] *adj* ① PSYCH paranoid ② (*mistrustful*) wahnhaft; ■**to be ~ about sth/sb** in ständiger Angst vor etw/jdm leben

paranormal [pær·ə·ˈnɔr·məl] **I.** *adj* übernatürlich; *powers* übersinnlich **II.** *n* ■**the ~** übernatürliche Erscheinungen

paraphernalia [ˌpær·ə·fər·ˈneɪl·jə] *n pl, + sing/pl vb* Zubehör *nt kein pl;* (*pej*) Brimborium *nt kein pl fam*

paraphrase [ˈpær·ə·freɪz] *vt text* umschreiben; *person* frei zitieren

paraplegic [ˌpær·ə·ˈpli·dʒɪk] **I.** *adj inv* doppelseitig gelähmt **II.** *n* doppelseitig Gelähmte(r) *f(m)*

parasite [ˈpær·ə·saɪt] *n* Parasit *m a. fig*

parasitic(al) [ˌper·ə·ˈsɪt̬·ɪk(əl)] *adj* ① BIOL parasitär ② (*fig, pej*) *person* schmarotzerhaft

parasol [ˈpær·ə·sɔl] *n* Sonnenschirm *m*

paratrooper [ˈpær·ə·ˌtru·pər] *n* Fallschirmjäger(in) *m(f)*

paratroops [ˈpær·ə·trups] *npl* Fallschirmtruppen *pl*

parboil [ˈpar·bɔɪl] *vt* **to ~ food** Lebensmittel kurz vorkochen (*um sie dann weiterzuverarbeiten*)

parcel [ˈpar·səl] **I.** *n* (*for mailing*) Paket *nt;* (*small parcel*) Päckchen *nt* **II.** *vt* <-l- *or* -ll-> einpacken

parcel 'post *n* Paketpost *f*

parch [partʃ] *vt, vi* austrocknen

parched [partʃt] *adj* ① (*dried out*) vertrocknet, verdorrt; *throat* ausgedörrt ② *attr* (*fig fam: very thirsty*) ■**to be ~ [with thirst]** am Verdursten sein

Parcheesi® [par·ˈtʃi·zi] *n* Mensch-ärgere-dich-nicht[-Spiel] *nt*

parchment [ˈpartʃ·mənt] *n* Pergament *nt*

pardon [ˈpar·dən] **I.** *n* LAW Begnadigung *f* **II.** *vt* ① (*forgive*) verzeihen, entschuldigen ② LAW begnadigen **III.** *interj* (*apology*) **I beg your ~!** [*or* **~ me!**] Entschuldigung!, tut mir Leid!; (*request for repetition*) wie bitte?; (*reply to offensiveness*) na, hören Sie mal!

pardonable [ˈpar·dən·ə·bəl] *adj* verzeihlich

pare [per] *vt* ① (*trim*) [ab]schneiden; *fruit* schälen ② (*reduce gradually*) reduzieren

◆**pare down** *vt* reduzieren

parent [ˈper·ənt] **I.** *n of a child* Elternteil *m;* ■**~s** Eltern *pl;* **single ~** Alleinerziehende(r) *f(m)* **II.** *adj* ① (*of parents*) *group* Eltern- ② (*of organizations*) *company* Mutter-

parentage [ˈper·ən·tɪdʒ] *n* ① (*descent*) Abstammung *f* ② (*fig*) Herkunft *f*

parental [pə·ˈren·təl] *adj inv* elterlich, Eltern-; **~ neglect** Vernachlässigung *f* durch die Eltern

parent 'company *n* Muttergesellschaft *f*

parenthesis <*pl* -ses> [pə·ˈren·θə·sɪs] *n* ① *usu pl* (*round brackets*) [runde] Klammern ② (*explanation*) eingeschobener Satz[teil]

parenthood [ˈper·ənt·hʊd] *n* Elternschaft *f*

parenting [ˈper·ən·tɪŋ] *n* Verhalten *nt* als Eltern, Kindererziehung *f*

parent 'teacher association *n* Eltern-Lehrer-Organisation *f*

pariah [pə·ˈraɪ·ə] *n* Paria *m*

'paring knife *n* Schälmesser *nt*

parish [ˈpær·ɪʃ] *n* ① REL [Pfarr]gemeinde *f* ② POL (*county*) Gemeinde *f*

parishioner [pə·ˈrɪʃ·ə·nər] *n* Gemeindemitglied *nt*

parity [ˈpær·ɪ·t̬i] *n* ① (*equality*) Gleichheit *f* ② FIN, MATH, PHYS Parität *f fachspr*

park [park] **I.** *n* Park *m;* **~ grounds** Parkanlagen *pl* **II.** *vt* ① AUTO [ein]parken ② (*fig fam: position*) abladen; **to ~ oneself** sich [irgendwo] hinpflanzen **III.** *vi* parken

parka [ˈpar·kə] *n* Parka *m*

parking [ˈpar·kɪŋ] *n* ① (*action*) Parken *nt* ② (*space*) Parkplatz *m*

'parking garage *n* Parkhaus *nt*

'parking lot *n* Parkplatz *m*

'parking meter *n* Parkuhr *f*

'parking permit *n* Parkerlaubnis *f*

'parking place, 'parking space *n* Parkplatz *m*

'parking ticket *n* Strafzettel *m* für unerlaubtes Parken

'parkland *n* Parklandschaft *f*

'park ranger *n* Parkaufseher(in) *m(f)*

'parkway *n* Schnellstraße *f*

parliament [ˈpar·lə·mənt] *n* ① (*institution*) ■**P~** Parlament *nt* ② (*period*) Legislaturperiode *f*

parliamentary [ˌpar·lə·ˈmen·tə·ri] *adj inv* parlamentarisch

parlor [ˈpar·lər] *n* Salon *m;* **funeral ~** Bestattungsinstitut *nt*

'parlor game *n* Gesellschaftsspiel *nt*

'parlormaid *n* (*hist*) Stubenmädchen *nt*

Parmesan, Parmesan cheese [ˈpar·mə·zan-] *n* Parmesan[käse] *m*

parochial [pə·ˈroʊ·ki·əl] *adj* ① *inv* REL Gemeinde-, Pfarr- ② (*pej: provincial*) provinziell; (*narrow-minded*) kleinkariert

parochial 'school *n* Konfessionsschule *f*

parody ['pær·ə·di] **I.** *n* (*a. pej: imitation*) Parodie *f* (**of** auf +*akk*) **II.** *vt* <-ie-> parodieren

parole [pə·'roʊl] **I.** *n* bedingte Haftentlassung **II.** *vt usu passive* Hafturlaub gewähren; ■**to be ~d** bedingt [aus der Haft] entlassen werden

parquet [par·'keɪ] *n* Parkett *nt*

parrot ['pær·ət] **I.** *n* (*bird*) Papagei *m* **II.** *vt* (*pej*) nachplappern, nachäffen

parry ['pær·i] **I.** *vt* <-ie-> ① (*deflect*) *blow, thrust* abwehren ② (*fig: evade*) *questions* [geschickt] ausweichen; *criticism* [schlagfertig] abwehren **II.** *vi* <-ie-> parieren

parse [pars] *vt* ① LING *sentence* grammatisch analysieren ② COMPUT **to ~ a text** einen Text parsen *fachspr*

parsimonious [ˌpar·sə·'moʊ·ni·əs] *adj* (*pej form*) knauserig

parsimoniousness [par·sə·'moʊ·ni·əs·nɪs], **parsimony** ['par·sə·moʊ·ni] *n* (*pej form*) Knauserigkeit *f*

parsley ['pars·li] *n* Petersilie *f*

parsnip ['pars·nɪp] *n* Pastinak *m*

parson ['par·sən] *n* Pastor(in) *m(f)*

part [part] **I.** *n* ① (*not the whole*) Teil *m;* **it's all ~ of growing up** das gehört [alles] zum Erwachsenwerden dazu; **to be an essential ~ of sth** ein wesentlicher Bestandteil einer S. *gen* sein; **for the most ~** zum größten Teil; **body ~** Körperteil *m* ② *a.* TECH (*component*) Teil *nt; of a machine* Bauteil *nt;* [**spare**] **~s** Ersatzteile *pl* ③ (*unit*) [An]teil *m* ④ FILM, TV Folge *f* ⑤ *usu pl* GEOG Gegend *f;* **around these ~s** (*inf*) in dieser Gegend; **in this ~ of the world** hierzulande ⑥ THEAT (*a. fig*) Rolle *f;* **leading/supporting ~** Haupt-/Nebenrolle *f* ⑦ MUS Part *m,* Stimme *f* ⑧ *of hair* Scheitel *m* **II.** *adj attr* Teil-, Mit- **III.** *adv inv* teils, teilweise **IV.** *vi* ① (*separate*) sich trennen ② (*become separated*) *curtains, seams* aufgehen; *lips* sich öffnen; *paths* sich trennen **V.** *vt* ① (*separate*) trennen ② (*keep separate*) trennen (**from** von +*dat*) ③ *hair* scheiteln ► PHRASES: **to ~ <u>company</u>** sich trennen

◆**part with** *vi* ■**to ~ with sth** sich von etw *dat* trennen

partake [par·'teɪk] *vi* <-took, -taken> (*form or hum*) **to ~ of drink/food** etw mittrinken/mitessen

parted ['par·t̬ɪd] *adj inv* ① (*opened*) **~ lips** leicht geöffnete Lippen ② (*separated*) getrennt (**from** von +*dat*) ③ *hair* **her hair is ~ on the side** sie trägt einen Seitenscheitel

partial ['par·ʃəl] *adj inv* ① (*incomplete*) Teil-; **their success was only ~** sie hatten nur teilweise Erfolg; *paralysis* partiell ② (*biased*) parteiisch ③ *pred* (*be fond of*) ■**to be ~ to sth** eine Vorliebe für etw *akk* haben

partiality [ˌpar·ʃi·'æl·ɪ·t̬i] *n* ① (*bias*) Parteilichkeit *f,* Voreingenommenheit *f* ② (*liking*) ■**to have a ~ for sth** eine Vorliebe für etw *akk* haben

partially ['par·ʃəl·i] *adv inv* teilweise

participant [par·'tɪs·ə·pənt] *n* Teilnehmer(in) *m(f)*

participate [par·'tɪs·ə·peɪt] *vi* teilnehmen (**in** an +*dat*)

participation [par·ˌtɪs·ə·'peɪ·ʃən] *n* Teilnahme *f* (**in** an +*dat*)

participle ['par·tɪ·sɪ·pəl] *n* Partizip *nt*

particle ['par·tɪ·kəl] *n* ① (*minute amount*) Teilchen *nt;* **dust ~** Staubkörnchen *nt* ② (*fig: smallest amount*) Spur *f*

particular [pər·'tɪk·jə·lər] **I.** *adj* ① *attr* (*individual*) bestimmt ② *attr* (*special*) besondere(r, s); **no ~ reason** kein bestimmter Grund ③ *pred* (*fussy*) eigen; (*demanding*) anspruchsvoll (**about** hinsichtlich +*gen*); **to be ~ about one's appearance** sehr auf sein Äußeres achten **II.** *n* (*information*) ■**~s** *pl* Einzelheiten *pl;* **to take down sb's ~** jds Personalien aufnehmen ► PHRASES: **<u>nothing</u> in ~** nichts Besonderes; **<u>in</u> ~** insbesondere

particularly [pər·'tɪk·jə·lər·li] *adv* besonders, vor allem

par'ticulate filter *n* Partikelfilter *m o nt;* **diesel ~** Rußpartikelfilter *m o nt*

parting ['par·t̬ɪŋ] **I.** *n* ① (*departure*) Abschied *m* ② (*separation*) Trennung *f* **II.** *adj attr, inv* Abschieds-

parting 'shot *n* letztes [sarkastisches] Wort

partisan ['par·t̬ɪ·zən] **I.** *n* ① (*supporter*) *of a party* Parteigänger(in) *m(f)* ② MIL Partisan(in) *m(f)* **II.** *adj* parteiisch, voreingenommen

partition [par·'tɪʃ·ən] **I.** *n* ① POL Teilung *f* ② (*structure*) Trennwand *f* **II.** *vt* ① POL [auf]teilen ② (*divide*) [unter]teilen

partly ['part·li] *adv inv* zum Teil, teils, teilweise

partner ['part·nᵊr] **I.** *n* ① (*owner*) Teilhaber(in) *m(f);* (*in a law firm*) Sozius *m* ② (*in dancing*) [Tanz]partner(in) *m(f);* (*in sports*) Partner(in) *m(f)* ③ (*spouse*) Ehepartner(in) *m(f);* (*unmarried*) [Lebens]partner(in) *m(f)* **II.** *vt usu passive* ■**to be ~ed with sb** jdn als Partner haben

partnership ['part·nᵊr·ʃɪp] *n* ① *no pl* (*condition*) Partnerschaft *f* ② (*company*) [offene] Handelsgesellschaft; *of lawyers* Sozietät *f* ③ (*relationship*) **domestic ~** Lebenspartnerschaft *f*

'partnership agreement *n* Gesellschaftsvertrag *m*

part of 'speech <*pl* parts-> *n* LING Wortart *f*

partridge <*pl* - *or* -s> ['par·trɪdʒ] *n* Rebhuhn *nt*

part-'time **I.** *adj* Teilzeit-, Halbtags- **II.** *adv* **to work ~** halbtags arbeiten

part-time 'job *n* Teilzeitarbeit *f*

part-'timer *n* Halbtagskraft *f*

party ['par·t̬i] **I.** *n* ① (*celebration*) Party *f* ② POL Partei *f* ③ (*group*) [Reise]gruppe *f;* **search ~** Suchtrupp *m* ④ (*fam: person*) Person *f* **II.** *adj* ① (*of a party*) Party- ② POL Partei- **III.** *vi* <-ie-> (*fam*) feiern

party 'line *n* ① POL Parteilinie *f* ② TELEC Gemeinschaftsanschluss *m*

P

party 'politics *n + sing/pl vb* Parteipolitik *f*

parvenu ['par·və·nu] *n* (*pej form*) Parvenü *m*

pass [pæs] **I.** *n* <*pl* -es> ① (*road*) Pass *m;* **mountain ~** [Gebirgs]pass *m* ② SPORTS (*of a ball*) Pass *m;* (*for a goal*) Vorlage *f* (*für ein Tor*) ③ (*fam: sexual advance*) **to make a ~ at sb** sich an jdn ranmachen ④ SCH, UNIV (*grade*) „Bestanden" ⑤ (*permit*) Passierschein *m;* (*for a festival*) Eintrittskarte *m;* (*for public transportation*) **weekly/monthly/annual ~** Wochen-/Monats-/Jahreskarte *f;* (*for train a.*) Netzkarte *f* **II.** *vt* ① (*go past*) ■**to ~ sb/sth** an jdm/etw vorbeigehen; (*in car*) an jdm/etw vorbeifahren ② (*overtake*) überholen ③ (*exceed*) *limit* überschreiten ④ (*hand to*) ■**to ~ sb sth** [*or* **to ~ sth to sb**] jdm etw geben; ■**to be ~ed to sb** auf jdn übergehen ⑤ SPORTS **to ~ the ball to sb** jdm den Ball zuspielen ⑥ (*succeed*) *exam, test* bestehen, ablegen ⑦ *usu passive esp* POL (*approve*) ■**to be ~ed** *law* verabschiedet werden ⑧ MED (*form: excrete*) **to ~ blood** absondern, ausscheiden ▸ PHRASES: **to ~ the buck to sb/sth** (*fam*) die Verantwortung auf jdn/etw abwälzen **III.** *vi* ① (*move by*) vorbeigehen, vorbeikommen; *road* vorbeiführen; *parade* vorbeiziehen; *car* vorbeifahren; **to ~ unnoticed** unbemerkt bleiben ② (*overtake*) überholen ③ (*go away*) vorübergehen, vorbeigehen ④ (*euph: die*) entschlafen *euph geh* ⑤ SPORTS (*of a ball*) zuspielen ⑥ SCH (*succeed*) bestehen ⑦ (*go by*) *time* vergehen ⑧ (*not answer*) passen [müssen] ⑨ (*forgo*) ■**to ~ on sth** auf etw *akk* verzichten ⑩ (*be accepted as*) **I don't think you'll ~ for 18** keiner wird dir abnehmen, dass du 18 bist

◆**pass along I.** *vt* ■**to ~ along ↻ sth** etw weitergeben **II.** *vi* vorbeigehen

◆**pass around** *vt* herumreichen

◆**pass away** *vi* ① (*euph: die*) entschlafen *geh* ② (*fade*) nachlassen; *anger* verrauchen

◆**pass by I.** *vi* ① *time* vergehen ② (*go past*) [an jdm/etw] vorbeigehen; (*in vehicle*) [an jdm/etw] vorbeifahren **II.** *vt* ① (*miss sb*) ■**sth ~es sb by** etw geht an jdm vorbei ② (*go past*) ■**to ~ by ↻ sb/sth** an jdm/etw vorübergehen

◆**pass down** *vt* ① *usu passive* (*bequeath*) ■**to be ~ed down** *tradition* weitergegeben werden; *songs, tales* überliefert werden ② (*hand down*) hinunterreichen

◆**pass off** *vt* ■**to ~ oneself off as sb** sich *akk* als jd ausgeben; ■**to ~ sth off as sth** etw *akk* als etw ausgeben

◆**pass on** *vt* ① *information, news* weitergeben ② *disease* übertragen ③ *usu passive* ■**to be ~ed on** *clothes, traditions* weitergegeben werden; *fortune* [weiter]vererbt werden; *stories* überliefert werden

◆**pass out I.** *vi* in Ohnmacht fallen, bewusstlos werden **II.** *vt* (*hand out*) verteilen

◆**pass over** *vt* ① *usu passive* (*not promote*) ■**to be ~ed over [for promotion]** [bei der Beförderung] übergangen werden ② (*disregard*) übergehen ③ *plane, birds* fliegen (über +*akk*)

◆**pass through** *vi* (*travel through*) durchreisen; (*on foot*) durchgehen; (*on bicycle*) durchfahren

◆**pass up** *vt* ■**to ~ up ↻ sth** sich *dat* etw entgehen lassen

passable ['pæs·ə·bəl] *adj* ① (*traversable*) passierbar, befahrbar ② (*satisfactory*) [ganz] passabel; **only ~** nur so leidlich

passage ['pæs·ɪdʒ] *n* ① (*narrow corridor*) Gang *m,* Flur *m;* **underground ~** Unterführung *f* ② (*long path*) Durchgang *m* ③ LIT (*excerpt*) [Text]passage *f;* MUS Stück *nt* ④ (*way of escape*) Durchlass *m* ⑤ (*progression*) *of time* Voranschreiten *nt; of troops* Durchzug *m; of a plane* Überfliegen *nt; of fire* ungehindertes Sichausbreiten ⑥ (*journey by sea*) Überfahrt, Schiffsreise

'passageway *n* Korridor *m,* [Durch]gang *m*

'passbook *n* Sparbuch *nt*

passenger ['pæs·ən·dʒər] **I.** *n* (*on a bus, subway*) Fahrgast *m;* (*on an airline*) Passagier(in) *m(f);* (*on a train*) Reisende(r) *f(m);* (*in a car*) Mitfahrer(in) *m(f),* Insasse, -in *m, f* **II.** *adj plane, ship, transportation* Passagier-; **~ elevator/traffic** Personenaufzug *m*/-verkehr *m; car, truck* Beifahrer-; **~ side** Beifahrerseite *f*

'passenger seat *n* (*in car, truck*) Beifahrersitz *m;* (*on motorcycle*) Soziussitz *m*

passer-by <*pl* passers-> [ˌpæs·ər·'baɪ] *n* Passant(in) *m(f)*

passing ['pæs·ɪŋ] **I.** *adj attr* ① *inv vehicle* vorbeifahrend; *pedestrian* vorbeigehend; **with each ~ day** mit jedem weiteren Tag[, der vergeht] ② *glance, thought* flüchtig; **a ~ fancy** nur so eine Laune ③ *remark* beiläufig ④ *inv resemblance* gering **II.** *n* ① (*euph: death*) Ableben *nt geh* ② (*end*) Niedergang *m;* **the ~ of an era** das Ende einer Ära ③ (*going by*) Vergehen *nt;* **with the ~ of the years** [*or* **time**] im Lauf der Jahre ④ SPORTS Passen *nt*

passion ['pæʃ·ən] *n* ① (*love, strong emotion*) [große] Leidenschaft; **crime of ~** Verbrechen *nt* aus Leidenschaft; **to hate sb/sth with a ~** jdn/etw aus tiefstem Herzen hassen ② (*fancy*) Vorliebe *f;* **to have a ~ for doing sth** etw leidenschaftlich gerne tun

passionate ['pæʃ·ə·nɪt] *adj* leidenschaftlich

'passion fruit *n* Passionsfrucht *f*

'passion play *n* Passionsspiel *nt*

passive ['pæs·ɪv] **I.** *n* LING Passiv *nt* **II.** *adj* ① *role* passiv; *victim* hilflos ② (*submissive*) unterwürfig; **to be too ~** sich *dat* zu viel gefallen lassen ③ *inv* LING passiv, passivisch

passiveness [pæ·'sɪv·nɪs] *n* (*inactivity*) Passivität *f;* (*apathy*) Teilnahmslosigkeit *f*

'passkey *n* ① *see* **master key** ② *see* **skeleton key**

Passover ['pæs·ˌoʊ·vər] *n* Passah[fest] *nt*

passport ['pæs·pɔrt] *n* [Reise]pass *m;* (*fig*) Schlüssel *m* (**to** zu +*dat*)

P

'passport control *n* Passkontrolle *f*
'passport holder *n* [Reise]passinhaber(in) *m(f)*
'password *n* Parole *f,* Losungswort *nt;* FIN Kennwort *nt;* COMPUT Passwort *nt*
past [pæst] **I.** *n* ❶ (*not present*) Vergangenheit *f;* (*past life*) Vorleben *nt* ❷ LING (*in grammar*) Vergangenheit[sform] *f* **II.** *adj inv* ❶ *attr* (*preceding*) vergangen; (*former*) frühere(r, s); **for the ~ five weeks** während der letzten fünf Wochen ❷ (*over*) vorüber, vorbei **III.** *adv inv* **to go ~ sb/sth** an jdm/etw vorbeigehen; *vehicle* an jdm/etw vorbeifahren **IV.** *prep* ❶ (*to other side*) an ... vorbei; **to drive ~** vorbeifahren; (*at other side*) hinter, nach; **just ~ the post office** gleich hinter der Post ❷ (*after the hour of*) nach; **it's a quarter ~ five** es ist Viertel nach Fünf ❸ (*beyond*) **the meat was ~ the expiration date** das Fleisch hatte das Verfallsdatum überschritten
pasta ['pas·tə] *n* Nudeln *pl*
paste [peɪst] **I.** *n* ❶ (*soft substance*) Paste *f* ❷ (*sticky substance*) Kleister *m* ❸ FOOD (*mixture*) Teig *m* **II.** *vt* ❶ (*affix*) kleben (**on[to]** auf +*akk*) ❷ COMPUT einfügen
pastel [pæ·'stel] **I.** *n* ❶ ART (*material*) Pastellkreide *f;* (*drawing*) Pastell *nt* ❷ (*color*) Pastellton *m* **II.** *adj inv* pastellfarben
pasteurizatlon [ˌpæs·tʃər·ɪ·'zeɪ·ʃən] *n* Pasteurisation *f*
pasteurize ['pæs·tʃə·raɪz] *vt usu passive* pasteurisieren
pastime ['pæs·taɪm] *n* Zeitvertreib *m*
pastor ['pæs·tər] *n* Pfarrer *m,* Pastor *m*
pastoral ['pæs·tər·əl] *adj inv* ❶ REL pastoral, seelsorgerisch ❷ LIT, ART idyllisch, Schäfer-; *scene* ländlich
past 'participle *n* Partizip Perfekt *nt*
past 'perfect, past 'perfect tense *n* Plusquamperfekt *nt*
pastry ['peɪ·stri] *n* ❶ (*dough*) [Kuchen]teig *m* ❷ (*cake*) Gebäckstück *nt*
'pastry chef, 'pastry cook *n* Konditor(in) *m(f)*
past 'tense *n* Vergangenheit *f*
pasture ['pæs·tʃər] *n* Weide *f;* **to put animals out to ~** Tiere auf die Weide treiben; **new ~s** (*fig*) neue Aufgaben, etwas Neues
pasty ['pæs·ti] *adj* (*pej*) *complexion* bleich, käsig *fam*
pat [pæt] **I.** *vt* <-tt-> tätscheln; **to ~ sb/oneself on the back** (*fig*) jdm/sich selbst auf die Schulter klopfen **II.** *n* ❶ (*tap*) [freundlicher] Klaps, Tätscheln *nt kein pl* ❷ (*small amount*) Klümpchen *nt;* **a ~ of butter** ein Stückchen *nt* Butter
patch [pætʃ] **I.** *n* <*pl* -es> ❶ (*piece of fabric*) Flicken *m;* (*for an eye*) Augenklappe *f;* (*bandage*) Pflaster *nt* ❷ (*spot*) Fleck[en] *m;* ■ **in ~es** stellenweise ❸ (*plot of land*) **vegetable ~** [kleines] Gemüsebeet **II.** *vt* (*cover*) flicken
◆**patch up** *vt* ❶ (*repair*) zusammenflicken *fam* ❷ (*fig: conciliate*) **to ~ up an argument** einen Streit beilegen

'patchwork I. *n* ❶ (*needlework*) Patchwork *nt* ❷ (*fig: mishmash*) Flickwerk *nt* **II.** *adj* Flicken-; **~ quilt** Patchworkdecke *f*
patchy ['pætʃ·i] *adj* ❶ METEO ungleichmäßig; **~ fog** stellenweise Nebel ❷ (*fig: inconsistent*) großen Qualitätsschwankungen unterworfen, von sehr unterschiedlicher Qualität *nach n, präd; knowledge* lückenhaft
pâté [pa·'teɪ] *n* Pastete *f*
patent ['pæt·ənt] **I.** *n* LAW Patent *nt* (**on** auf +*akk*); **to take out a ~ on sth** [sich *dat*] etw patentieren lassen **II.** *adj* ❶ *attr, inv* (*copyrighted*) Patent-, patentiert ❷ (*form: blatant*) offenkundig **III.** *vt* **to ~ an invention** eine Erfindung patentieren lassen
patented ['pæt·ən·tɪd] *adj inv* (*copyrighted*) patentiert
patent 'leather *n* Lackleder *nt*
'patent office *n* Patentamt *nt*
paternal [pə·'tɜr·nəl] *adj* ❶ *attr* (*on the father's side*) väterlich; **~ ancestors** Vorfahren *pl* väterlicherseits ❷ (*fatherly*) väterlich
paternalism [pə·'tɜr·nə·lɪz·əm] *n* Paternalismus *m*
paternalistic [pə·ˌtɜr·nəl·'ɪs·tɪk] *adj* paternalistisch
paternity [pə·'tɜr·nəɪ̯ti] *n* (*form: fatherhood*) Vaterschaft *f*
pa'ternity leave *n* Vaterschaftsurlaub *m*
pa'ternity suit *n* Vaterschaftsprozess *m*
path [pæθ] *n* ❶ (*way*) Weg *m,* Pfad *m;* **to clear a ~** einen Weg bahnen; *of a person* Lebensweg *m;* **to cross sb's ~** jdm über den Weg laufen ❷ (*direction*) Weg *m; of a bullet* Bahn *f;* **to block sb's ~** jdm den Weg verstellen
pathetic [pə·'θeṭ·ɪk] *adj* ❶ (*heart-rending*) Mitleid erregend ❷ (*pej: pitiful*) jämmerlich; *attempt* kläglich; *answer, reply* dürftig; *excuse* schwach
'pathfinder *n* (*person*) Wegbereiter(in) *m(f);* (*thing*) bahnbrechende Neuerung
pathological [ˌpæθ·ə·'ladʒ·ɪ·kəl] *adj* ❶ (*fam*) krankhaft; *liar* notorisch ❷ *inv* UNIV, MED Pathologie-; *analysis, examination* pathologisch
pathologist [pə·'θal·ə·dʒɪst] *n* Pathologe, -in *m, f*
pathology [pə·'θal·ə·dʒi] *n* ❶ (*study of illnesses*) Pathologie *f* ❷ (*disease characteristics*) Krankheitsbild *nt*
pathos ['peɪ·θas] *n* Pathos *nt geh*
'pathway *n* ❶ (*a. fig: route*) Weg *m a. fig* ❷ MED, BIOL Leitungsbahn *f*
patience ['peɪ·ʃəns] *n* Geduld *f*
patient ['peɪ·ʃənt] **I.** *adj* geduldig; ■ **to be ~ with sb** mit jdm Geduld haben **II.** *n* MED Patient(in) *m(f)*
patina ['pæt·ən·ə] *n* ❶ CHEM, SCI, TECH Film *m;* (*on copper, brass*) Patina *f;* (*verdigris*) Grünspan *m;* (*sheen*) Firnis *m* ❷ (*fig form: veneer*) Fassade *f*
patio ['pæṭ·i·oʊ] **I.** *n* (*veranda*) Terrasse *f,* Veranda *f* **II.** *adj* (*veranda*) Veranda-; (*courtyard*)

P

Innenhof-; ~ **furniture** Gartenmöbel *pl*

patriarch ['peɪ·tri·ark] *n* ① (*father figure*) Familienoberhaupt *nt* ② (*bishop*) Patriarch *m* ③ (*founder*) Vater *m*

patriarchal [ˌpeɪ·trɪ·'ar·kəl] *adj* patriarchalisch

patrician [pə·'trɪʃ·ən] *adj* ① (*aristocratic*) aristokratisch; (*pej*) vornehm *iron* ② *inv* (*hist: of Roman aristocracy*) patrizisch, Patrizier-

patricide ['pæt·rə·saɪd] *n* Vatermord *m*

patriot ['peɪ·tri·ət] *n* Patriot(in) *m(f)*

patriotic [ˌpeɪ·tri·'aṱ·ɪk] *adj* patriotisch

patriotism ['peɪ·tri·ə·tɪz·əm] *n* Patriotismus *m*

patrol [pə·'troʊl] **I.** *vi* <-ll-> patrouillieren **II.** *vt* <-ll-> abpatrouillieren **III.** *n* Patrouille *f;* **highway** ~ *Polizei, die die Highways überwacht*

pa'trol car *n* Streifenwagen *m*

pa'trol duty *n* Streifendienst *m*

pa'trolman *n* Streifenpolizist(in) *m(f),* Polizeiwachtmeister(in) *m(f)*

patron ['peɪ·trən] *n* ① (*form: customer*) [Stamm]kunde *m* ② (*benefactor*) Schirmherr *m;* ~ **of the arts** Mäzen(in) *m(f)* der [schönen] Künste

patronage ['peɪ·trə·nɪdʒ] *n* ① (*support*) Schirmherrschaft *f* ② (*trade*) Kundschaft *f*

patronize ['peɪ·trə·naɪz] *vt* ① (*form: frequent*) ■ **to ~ sth** [Stamm]kunde bei etw *dat* sein ② (*pej: treat condescendingly*) ■ **to ~ sb** jdn herablassend behandeln

patronizing ['peɪ·trə·naɪ·zɪŋ] *adj* (*pej*) *attitude* herablassend; *look, tone* gönnerhaft, von oben herab *präd*

patron 'saint *n* Schutzpatron(in) *m(f)*

patter ['pæṱ·ər] **I.** *n of rain* Prasseln *nt; of feet* Getrippel *nt* **II.** *vi feet* trippeln; *rain* prasseln

pattern ['pæṱ·ərn] **I.** *n* ① (*structure*) Muster *nt* ② FASHION (*for sewing*) Schnitt *m* **II.** *vt* ■ **to ~ sth on sth** etw nach dem Vorbild einer S. *gen* gestalten; ■ **to ~ oneself after sb** jdm nacheifern

patterned ['pæṱ·ərnd] *adj inv* gemustert

patty ['pæṱ·i] *n* Pastetchen *nt;* **burger** ~ Fleischbratling *m*

paunch <*pl* -es> [pɔntʃ] *n* Bauch *m,* Wanst *m fam*

paunchy ['pɔn·tʃi] *adj* dickbäuchig

pauper ['pɔ·pər] *n* Arme(r) *f(m)*

pause [pɔz] **I.** *n* Pause *f* **II.** *vi* eine [kurze] Pause machen; *speaker* innehalten **III.** *vt* anhalten

pave [peɪv] *vt usu passive* ① (*cover*) pflastern; **the streets are ~d with gold** (*fig*) das Geld liegt auf der Straße ② (*fig: ease*) **to ~ the way for sth** etw *dat* den Weg ebnen

pavement ['peɪv·mənt] *n* Asphalt *m*

pavilion [pə·'vɪl·jən] *n* ① (*ornamental building*) Pavillon *m* ② (*at an exhibition*) [Messe]pavillon *m*

paving ['peɪ·vɪŋ] *n* das Pflastern

'paving stone *n* Pflasterstein *m*

paw [pɔ] **I.** *n* Pfote *f; of a big cat, bear* Pranke *f;* (*hum fam*) Pfote *f sl* **II.** *vt* ① (*scrape*) **to ~ the ground** scharren ② (*fam: touch*) begrabschen **III.** *vi dog* scharren; *bull, horse* mit den Hufen scharren

pawn¹ [pɔn] *vt* verpfänden

pawn² [pɔn] *n* CHESS Bauer *m;* (*fig*) Marionette *f*

'pawnbroker *n* Pfandleiher(in) *m(f)*

'pawnbroking *n* Pfandleihe *f*

'pawnshop *n* Pfandleihe *f*

pay [peɪ] **I.** *n* (*wages*) Lohn *m;* (*salary*) Gehalt *nt; of a civil servant* Bezüge *pl; of a soldier* Sold *m* **II.** *vt* <paid, paid> ① (*give*) [be]zahlen; ■ **~ out** etw [aus]zahlen; **to ~ [in] cash/in dollars/money** [in] bar/in Dollar/Geld [be]zahlen; **to ~ dividends** *investment* Dividenden ausschütten; *company* Dividenden ausbezahlen; (*fig*) sich auszahlen ② (*give money for/to, settle*) bezahlen; **to ~ one's dues** (*debts*) seine Schulden bezahlen; *into an account* einzahlen (auf +*akk*); (*fig: obligations*) seine Schuldigkeit tun ③ (*fig: suffer the consequences*) **to ~ the price [for sth]** [für etw *akk*] bezahlen ④ (*bestow*) **to ~ attention** Acht geben *akk;* **to ~ [sb] a compliment** [jdm] ein Kompliment machen ▶ PHRASES: **to ~ one's way** finanziell unabhängig sein **III.** *vi* <paid, paid> ① (*give money*) [be]zahlen ② (*be worthwhile*) sich auszahlen; (*be profitable*) rentabel sein; ■ **it ~s to do sth** es lohnt sich, etw zu tun ③ (*fig: suffer*) ■ **to ~ [for sth]** [für etw *akk*] bezahlen; **to ~ with one's life** mit dem Leben bezahlen

◆**pay back** *vt* ① (*give back*) zurückzahlen; *debts* bezahlen; *money* zurückgeben ② (*fig: for revenge*) ■ **to ~ sb back for sth** jdm etw heimzahlen

◆**pay off I.** *vt* ① (*repay*) abbezahlen; (*settle*) *debt* [vollständig] begleichen; *mortgage* tilgen ② (*give money to*) aus[be]zahlen; (*fam: bribe*) ■ **to ~ off ⊂ sb** jdn kaufen **II.** *vi* (*fig fam*) sich auszahlen

◆**pay out I.** *vt* ① (*spend*) ausgeben ② (*give out*) aus[be]zahlen **II.** *vi* FIN **to ~ out [on a policy]** [be]zahlen

◆**pay up I.** *vi* [be]zahlen **II.** *vt* [vollständig] zurückzahlen; *debt* [vollständig] begleichen

payable ['peɪ·ə·bəl] *adj attr, inv* zahlbar; (*due*) fällig

'paycheck *n* Lohnscheck *m*

'payday *n* Zahltag *m*

payee [peɪ·'i] *n* Zahlungsempfänger(in) *m(f)*

payer ['peɪ·ər] *n* Zahler(in) *m(f);* **fee** ~ Gebührenzahler(in) *m(f)*

paying ['peɪ·ɪŋ] *adj attr, inv* zahlend

'payload *n* ① TRANSP, AEROSP Nutzlast *f* ② MIL Bombenlast *f*

'paymaster *n* Zahlmeister(in) *m(f)*

payment ['peɪ·mənt] *n* ① (*sum*) Zahlung *f;* (*fig*) Lohn *m* ② (*act of paying*) Bezahlung *f*

'payoff *n* ① (*fam: reward*) Lohn *m* ② (*fam: bribe*) Bestechung *f;* **to receive a ~ from sb** von jdm bestochen werden ③ FIN (*amount to pay off loan*) Abbezahlung *f*

'payout *n* FIN Ausschüttung *f*

pay-per-'view *n* Pay-per-View *nt* (*System, bei*

dem der Zuschauer nur für die Sendungen zahlt, die er auch tatsächlich gesehen hat)
'pay phone *n* Münzfernsprecher *m*
'pay raise *n* (*for white-collar worker*) Gehaltserhöhung *f;* (*for blue-collar worker*) Lohnerhöhung *f*
'payroll *n usu sing* (*for white-collar worker*) Gehaltsliste *f;* (*for blue-collar worker*) Lohnliste *f*
pay T'V *n* (*fam*) Pay-TV *nt*
PBS [ˌpi·bi·'es] *n abbrev of* **Public Broadcasting Service** *amerikanischer Fernsehsender*
PC [ˌpi·'si] **I.** *n* ① *abbrev of* **personal computer** PC *m* ② *abbrev of* **political correctness II.** *adj inv abbrev of* **politically correct** pc
p.c. [ˌpi·'si] *n abbrev of* **percent** p.c.
PDA [ˌpi·ˌdi·'eɪ] *n abbrev of* **personal digital assistant** PDA *m*
PE [ˌpi·'i] *n abbrev of* **physical education**
pea [pi] *n* Erbse *f*
peace [pis] *n* ① (*not war*) Frieden *m* ② (*social order*) Ruhe *f,* Frieden *m;* **to make one's ~ with sb** sich mit jdm versöhnen ③ (*tranquillity*) **~ of mind** Seelenfrieden *m;* **to leave sb in ~** jdn in Frieden lassen; **to be at ~ with the world** mit sich und der Welt im Einklang sein
peaceable ['pi·sə·bəl] *adj* friedlich; *person* friedliebend
'peace conference *n* Friedenskonferenz *f*
peaceful ['pis·fəl] *adj* friedlich; *nation a.* friedfertig; (*calm*) ruhig; *person* friedliebend
'peace'keeping I. *n* Friedenssicherung *f* **II.** *adj* Friedens-; **~ force** Friedenstruppe *f*
'peace-loving *adj* friedliebend
'peacemaker *n* Frieden[s]stifter(in) *m(f)*
'peacemaking *n* Befriedung *f geh*
'peace march *n* Friedensdemonstration *f*
'peace movement *n* Friedensbewegung *f*
'peace offering *n* Friedensangebot *nt*
'peace pipe *n* Friedenspfeife *f*
'peace settlement *n* Friedensabkommen *nt*
'peacetime *n* Friedenszeiten *pl*
'peace treaty *n* Friedensvertrag *m*
peach [pitʃ] **I.** *n* <*pl* -es> (*fruit*) Pfirsich *m;* (*tree*) Pfirsichbaum *m* **II.** *adj inv* (*peach-colored*) pfirsichfarben
peachy ['pitʃ·i] *adj* (*fam*) wunderbar, toll
peacock ['pi·kak] *n* Pfau *m*
pea-'green I. *n* Erbsengrün *nt* **II.** *adj inv* erbsengrün
peak [pik] **I.** *n* ① (*mountain top*) Gipfel *m* ② (*highest point*) Gipfel *m; of a curve, line* Scheitelpunkt *m;* **to reach a ~** den Höchststand erreichen **II.** *vi career* den Höhepunkt erreichen; *athletes* [seine] Höchstleistung erbringen; *skill* zur Perfektion gelangen; *figures, rates, production* den Höchststand erreichen **III.** *adj* ① (*busiest*) Haupt-; **~ viewing time** Hauptsendezeit *f* ② (*best, highest*) Spitzen-; **~ productivity** maximale Produktivität
peaked¹ [pikt] *adj inv* (*pointed*) spitz
peaked² [pikt] *adj* (*sickly*) kränklich, abgespannt
peal [pil] **I.** *n* (*sound*) Dröhnen *nt kein pl;* **~ of bells** Glockengeläut[e] *nt kein pl* **II.** *vi bells* läuten
peanut ['pi·nʌt] *n* ① (*nut*) Erdnuss *f* ② (*fam: very little*) ■ **~s** *pl* Klacks *m;* **to pay ~s** einen Hungerlohn zahlen
'peanut butter *n* Erdnussbutter *f*
pear [per] *n* (*fruit*) Birne *f;* (*tree*) Birnbaum *m*
pearl [pɜrl] *n* ① (*jewel*) Perle *f;* **string of ~s** Perlenkette *f* ② (*fig: a drop*) Tropfen *m,* Perle *f*
'pearl diver *n* Perlentaucher(in) *m(f)*
pearly ['pɜr·li] *adj* perlmuttartig; (*adorned with pearls*) mit Perlen besetzt; (*pearl-colored*) perlweiß
peasant ['pez·ənt] *n* ① (*small farmer*) [Klein]bauer, [Klein]bäuerin *m, f* ② (*offensive fam*) Bauer *m*
peasantry ['pez·ən·tri] *n* [Klein]bauernstand *m*
peat [pit] *n* Torf *m*
'peat bog *n* Torfmoor *nt*
pebble ['peb·əl] *n* Kieselstein *m*
pebbly ['peb·li] *adj* steinig
pecan [pɪ·'kan] *n* (*nut*) Pekannuss *f;* (*tree*) Hickory[baum] *m*
peck [pek] **I.** *n* ① (*bite*) Picken *nt kein pl* ② (*fam: quick kiss*) Küsschen *nt* **II.** *vt* ① (*bite*) hacken (nach +*dat*); **to ~ a hole** ein Loch picken ② (*fam: kiss quickly*) **to ~ sb on the cheek** jdn flüchtig auf die Wange küssen **III.** *vi* ① (*with the beak*) picken; ■ **to ~ at sth** etw aufpicken ② (*nibble*) **to ~ at one's food** in seinem Essen herumstochern
pecker ['pek·ər] *n* (*vulg: penis*) Schwanz *m*
'pecking order *n* Hackordnung *f*
pectin ['pek·tɪn] *n* Pektin *nt*
pectoral ['pek·tər·əl] *adj* Brust-, pektoral *fachspr*
peculiar [pɪ·'kjul·jər] *adj* ① (*strange*) seltsam, merkwürdig ② (*belonging to, special*) *to sb* typisch (für +*akk*); *to sth* eigen[tümlich] +*dat*
peculiarity [pɪ·ˌkju·li·'ær·ɪ·ţi] *n* ① (*strangeness*) Eigenartigkeit *f* ② (*strange habit*) Eigenheit *f* ③ (*idiosyncrasy*) Besonderheit *f,* Eigenart *f*
peculiarly [pɪ·'kjul·jər·li] *adv* ① (*strangely*) eigenartig, seltsam ② *inv* (*especially*) besonders
pedal ['ped·əl] **I.** *n* Pedal *nt* **II.** *vt* <-l- *or* -ll-> **to ~ a bicycle** Rad fahren **III.** *vi* <-l- *or* -ll-> Rad fahren; **she ~ed through the city** sie radelte durch die Stadt **IV.** *adj* Tret-
pedant ['ped·ənt] *n* Pedant(in) *m(f)*
pedantic [pə·'dæn·tɪk] *adj* pedantisch
pedantry ['ped·ən·tri] *n* Pedanterie *f a. pej*
peddle ['ped·əl] *vt* ■ **to ~ sth** ① (*esp pej: sell*) etw verscherbeln *pej;* **to ~ sth door to door** mit etw *dat* hausieren gehen ② (*pej: spread*) *lies* mit etw *dat* hausieren gehen
peddler ['ped·lər] *n* ① (*drug dealer*) Drogenhändler(in) *m(f)* ② (*dated: traveling salesman*) Hausierer(in) *m(f)* ③ (*pej*) **~ of gossip** Klatschmaul *nt;* **~ of lies** Lügenmaul *nt*
pedestal ['ped·ɪ·stəl] **I.** *n* Sockel *m* **II.** *adj* So-

ckel-, Stand-; ~ **desk** Stehpult *nt*

pedestrian [pə·'des·tri·ən] **I.** *n* Fußgänger(in) *m(f)* **II.** *adj inv* ❶ *bridge, tunnel, underpass* Fußgänger- ❷ *(form)* langweilig; *speech* trocken

pedestrian crossing *n* Zebrastreifen *m*

pedestrianize [pə·'des·tri·ə·naɪz] *vt* in eine Fußgängerzone umwandeln

pedestrianized [pɪ·'des·tri·ə·naɪzd] *adj inv* Fußgänger-; ~ **area** Fußgängerzone *f*

pedestrian 'mall *n* Fußgängerzone *f*

pediatric [ˌpi·di·'æt·rɪk] *adj inv* pädiatrisch; ~ **hospital** Kinderkrankenhaus *nt*

pediatrician [ˌpi·di·ə·'trɪʃ·ən] *n* Kinderarzt, -ärztin *m, f*

pediatrics [ˌpi·dɪ·'æt·rɪks] *npl + sing vb* Kinderheilkunde *f*

pedicure ['ped·ɪ·kjʊr] *n* Pediküre *f*

pedicurist ['ped·ɪ·kjʊr·ɪst] *n* Fußpfleger(in) *m(f)*

pedigree ['ped·ɪ·gri] *n* ❶ *(genealogy)* Stammbaum *m* ❷ *(background)* Laufbahn *f* ❸ *(history of idea)* Geschichte *f*

pedigreed ['ped·ɪ·grid] *adj dog, cattle, horse* reinrassig, mit Stammbaum *nach n*

pedometer [pɪ·'dam·ə·t̬ər] *n* Pedometer *nt*

pedophile ['ped·ə·faɪl] *n* Pädophile(r) *m*

pee [pi] *(fam)* **I.** *n* ❶ *(urine)* Pipi *nt Kindersprache* ❷ *(act)* Pinkeln *nt;* **to have to take a ~** pinkeln gehen müssen *sl;* **to go ~** *(esp childspeak)* Pipi machen **II.** *vi* pinkeln *fam;* **to ~ in one's pants** in die Hose[n] machen **III.** *vt* ■**to ~ one's pants** in die Hose[n] machen

peek [pik] **I.** *n* *(brief look)* flüchtiger Blick; *(furtive look)* heimlicher Blick **II.** *vi* blinzeln; ■**to ~ into sth** in etw *akk* hineinspähen; ■**to ~ over sth** über etw *akk* gucken

◆**peek out** *vi* hervorgucken; ■**to ~ out from behind sth** *person* hinter etw *dat* hervorgucken

peel [pil] **I.** *n* *(skin of fruit)* Schale *f* **II.** *vt fruit* schälen; **to ~ the paper off sth** etw auswickeln ►PHRASES: **to keep one's eyes ~ed for sth** *(fam)* nach etw *dat* die Augen offen halten **III.** *vi paint, rust, wallpaper* sich lösen; *skin* sich schälen

◆**peel off** **I.** *vt* schälen; *clothing* abstreifen; *adhesive strip* abziehen **II.** *vi* *(come off)* sich lösen

peeler ['pi·lər] *n* *(utensil)* Schäler *m*

peelings ['pi·lɪŋz] *npl* Schalen *pl*

peep[1] [pip] **I.** *n usu sing* ❶ *(bird sound)* Piep[ser] *m;* **to make a ~** piepsen ❷ *(answer, statement)* Laut *m;* **to not hear [so much as] a ~ out of [*or* from] sb** keinen Mucks von jdm hören **II.** *vi* piepsen

peep[2] [pip] **I.** *n* *(look)* [verstohlener] Blick; **to have a ~ at sth** auf etw *akk* einen kurzen Blick werfen **II.** *vi* ❶ *(look)* verstohlen blicken (**at** auf *+akk*), einen Blick werfen (**into** in *+akk*), spähen (**through** durch *+akk*) ❷ *(appear)* hervorkommen (**through** durch *+akk*)

◆**peep out** *vi toe, finger* herausgucken

P

'peephole *n* Guckloch *nt,* Spion *m*

peeping 'Tom *n* Voyeur *m,* Spanner *m fam*

peer[1] [pɪr] *vi* *(look closely)* spähen; **to ~ over one's glasses** über die Brille schauen; **to ~ over sb's shoulder** jdm über die Schulter gucken

peer[2] [pɪr] *n* *(equal)* Gegenstück *nt;* **to have no ~s** unvergleichlich sein; **to be liked by one's ~s** unter seinesgleichen beliebt sein

peerless ['pɪr·lɪs] *adj inv* *(form)* unvergleichlich

peeved [pivd] *adj* *(fam)* sauer; ■**to be ~ at sb for sth** wegen einer S. *gen* auf jdn sauer sein

peevish ['pi·vɪʃ] *adj* mürrisch

peg [peg] **I.** *n* *(hook)* Haken *m;* *(stake)* Pflock *m* **II.** *vt* <-gg-> ■**to ~ sth** ❶ *(bind down)* etw mit Haken sichern ❷ *(hold at certain level)* etw fixieren; **to ~ prices** Preise stützen ❸ *(classify)* ■**to ~ sb as sth** jdn als etw *akk* abstempeln

pejorative [pɪ·'dʒɔr·ə·t̬ɪv] *adj* *(form)* abwertend

Pekinese <*pl* - *or* -s> [ˌpi·kə·'niz] *n* *(dog)* Pekinese *m*

pelican ['pel·ɪ·kən] *n* Pelikan *m*

pellet ['pel·ɪt] *n* ❶ *(ball)* Kugel *f* ❷ *(gunshot)* Schrot *nt o m kein pl* ❸ *(rabbit/sheep excrement)* Kötel *m*

pelt[1] [pelt] *n* *(animal skin)* Fell *nt;* *(fur)* Pelz *m*

pelt[2] [pelt] *vt* ❶ *(bombard)* ■**to ~ sb with sth** jdn mit etw *dat* bewerfen ❷ *(hurl)* ■**to ~ sth at sb** etw nach jdm schleudern ❸ *(strike repeatedly)* niederprasseln

pelvic ['pel·vɪk] *adj attr, inv* Becken-

pelvis <*pl* -es> ['pel·vɪs] *n* Becken *nt*

pen[1] [pen] **I.** *n* *(writing utensil)* Feder *f;* **ballpoint ~** Kugelschreiber *m;* **fountain ~** Füller *m,* Füllfeder *f* ÖSTERR, SÜDD, SCHWEIZ **II.** *vt* <-nn-> schreiben

pen[2] [pen] **I.** *n* *(enclosed area)* Pferch *m* **II.** *vt* <-nn-> *usu passive* ■**to be ~ned** eingesperrt sein

◆**pen in** *vt* ❶ *animal* einsperren; ■**to be ~ned in** *people* eingeschlossen sein ❷ *usu passive* *(fig)* **to feel ~ned in by sth** sich von etw *dat* eingeengt fühlen

pen[3] [pen] *n* *(fam)* *short for* **penitentiary** Knast *m fam*

penal ['pi·nəl] *adj inv attr* *(of punishment)* Straf-; ~ **code** Strafgesetz *nt*

penalize ['pi·nə·laɪz] *vt* ❶ *(punish)* ■**to ~ sb [for sth]** jdn [für etw *akk*] bestrafen ❷ *(cause disadvantage)* benachteiligen

penalty ['pen·əl·ti] *n* ❶ LAW *(a. fig)* Strafe *f;* **minimum ~** Mindeststrafe *f* ❷ *(disadvantage)* Preis *m* ❸ *(fine)* [Extra]gebühr *f*

'penalty area *n* Strafraum *m*

'penalty box *n* ❶ *(in soccer)* Strafraum *m* ❷ *(in hockey)* Strafbank *f*

'penalty clause *n* [restriktive] Vertragsklausel

'penalty kick *n* **to award a ~** *(in soccer)* einen Elfmeter geben

'penalty shot *n* **to award a ~** *(in hockey)* einen Strafschuss verhängen; (*in soccer*) einen Elfmeter geben

penance ['pen·əns] *n* Buße *f*

penchant ['pen·tʃənt] *n usu sing* (*usu pej*) Neigung *f;* **to have a ~ for sth** einen Hang zu etw *dat* haben

pencil ['pen·səl] **I.** *n* (*writing utensil*) Bleistift *m;* FASHION **eyeliner ~** Eyelinerstift *m* **II.** *adj* ❶ **~-thin** *person* dünn wie ein Bleistift ❷ (*made by pencil*) **~ drawing** Bleistiftzeichnung *f* ❸ (*very narrow*) **~ moustache** dünner Oberlippenbart **III.** *vt* <-l- *or* -ll-> mit Bleistift schreiben

◆**pencil in** *vt* vormerken

'pencil case *n* Federmäppchen *nt,* Federpennal *nt* ÖSTERR

'pencil sharpener *n* [Bleistift]spitzer *m*

pendant ['pen·dənt] *n* Anhänger *m*

pending ['pen·dɪŋ] **I.** *adj inv* LAW anhängig; *deal* bevorstehend; *lawsuit* schwebend **II.** *prep* (*form*) **~ an investigation** bis zu einer Untersuchung

pendulum ['pen·dʒə·ləm] **I.** *n* Pendel *nt* **II.** *adj* Pendel-; (*swinging*) schwingend

penetrate ['pen·ɪ·treɪt] *vt* ■**to ~ sth** ❶ (*move into*) in etw *akk* eindringen ❷ (*spread through*) *smell* etw durchdringen ❸ MED *vein* etw durchstechen

penetrating ['pen·ɪ·treɪ·t̬ɪŋ] *adj* durchdringend *attr; analysis* eingehend; *observation* scharfsinnig; *scream* markerschütternd

penetration [ˌpen·ɪ·'treɪ·ʃən] *n* ❶ (*act*) Eindringen *nt kein pl* (**of** in +*akk*) ❷ (*sexual act*) Penetration *f*

penguin ['peŋ·gwɪn] *n* Pinguin *m*

penicillin [ˌpen·ɪ·'sɪl·ɪn] *n* Penicillin *nt*

peninsula [pə·'nɪn·sə·lə] *n* Halbinsel *f*

penis <*pl* -es *or* -nes> ['pi·nɪs] *n* Penis *m*

penitence ['pen·ɪ·təns] *n* (*repentance*) Reue *f*

penitent ['pen·ɪ·tənt] **I.** *n* REL reuiger Sünder/reuige Sünderin **II.** *adj* (*form*) reumütig

penitentiary [ˌpen·ɪ·'ten·tʃə·ri] *n* Gefängnis *nt*

'penknife *n* Taschenmesser *nt*

'pen name *n* Pseudonym *nt*

pennant ['pen·ənt] **I.** *n* (*flag*) Wimpel *m;* SPORTS Siegeswimpel *m* **II.** *adj* SPORTS **~ race** *Kampf um die Meisterschaft*

penniless ['pen·i·lɪs] *adj* mittellos

Pennsylvania [ˌpen·sɪl·'veɪ·ni·ə] *n* Pennsylvania *nt*

penny <*pl* -nies> ['pen·i] *n* Penny *m;* **to not cost a ~** nichts kosten ▶ PHRASES: **to be worth every ~** sein Geld wert sein

'penny-pinching I. *n* Pfennigfuchserei *f pej fam* **II.** *adj inv* geizig

'pen pal *n* Brieffreund(in) *m(f)*

pension ['pen·ʃən] *n* (*retirement money*) Rente *f;* (*for civil servants*) Pension *f;* **to draw a ~** Rente beziehen

'pension fund *n* Pensionskasse *f*

'pension plan *n* Altersversorgungsplan *m,* Altersversorgung *f*

pensive ['pen·sɪv] *adj* nachdenklich; *person* ernsthaft; *silence* gedankenverloren

pentagon ['pen·tə·gan] *n* Fünfeck *nt*

Pentagon ['pen·tə·gan] *n* ■**the ~** das Pentagon

> Das **Pentagon** befindet sich in Arlington in Virginia, in der Nähe von Washington D.C. Seinen Namen hat es aufgrund seiner fünfeckigen Form erhalten. Seit der Einweihung am 15. Januar 1943 ist dort das *United States Department of Defense* (das US-amerikanische Verteidigungsministerium) untergebracht. Es arbeiten mehr als 25.000 Menschen, Zivilisten und Militärs in diesem weitläufigen Gebäude, in dem mehr als 28 Kilometer an Korridoren vorhanden sind.

pentameter [pen·'tæm·ə·t̬ər] *n usu sing* LIT Pentameter *m fachspr*

pentathlete [pen·'tæθ·lit] *n* Fünfkämpfer(in) *m(f)*

pentathlon [pen·'tæθ·lan] *n* Fünfkampf *m*

Pentecost ['pen·t̬ɪ·kast] *n* REL ❶ (*Christian*) Pfingsten *nt* ❷ (*Jewish*) jüdisches Erntefest

penthouse ['pent·haʊs] *n* Penthaus *nt*

'pent-up *adj inv emotions* aufgestaut

penury ['pen·jʊ·ri] *n* (*form*) Armut *f*

peony ['pi·ə·ni] *n* Pfingstrose *f*

people ['pi·pəl] **I.** *n* ❶ *pl* (*persons*) Leute *pl,* Menschen *pl;* **rich ~** die Reichen *pl;* **the right ~** die richtigen Leute ❷ *pl* (*citizens, nation*) Volk *nt* ❸ (*comprising a race, tribe*) ■**~s** *pl* Völker *pl* **II.** *adj* **a ~ person** ein geselliger Mensch; **~ skills** Menschenkenntnis *f kein pl*

pep [pep] **I.** *n* (*fam*) Elan *m,* Schwung *m* **II.** *vt* <-pp-> ■**to ~ sb** ↻ **up** jdn in Schwung bringen; ■**to ~ sth** ↻ **up** aufpeppen (**with** mit +*dat*); **to ~ up business** das Geschäft ankurbeln

pepper ['pep·ər] **I.** *n* ❶ (*spice*) Pfeffer *m;* **black ~** schwarzer Pfeffer ❷ (*vegetable*) Paprika *f* **II.** *vt* ❶ (*add pepper*) pfeffern ❷ (*pelt*) **to ~ sb with bullets** jdn mit Kugeln durchsieben; **to be ~ed with mistakes** vor Fehlern strotzen

'peppercorn *n* Pfefferkorn *nt*

'pepper mill *n* Pfeffermühle *f*

'peppermint *n* ❶ (*plant*) Pfefferminze *f* ❷ (*candy*) Pfefferminz[bonbon] *nt*

pepperoni [pep·ə·'roʊ·ni] *n* Salami *f*

'pepper shaker *n* Pfefferstreuer *m*

peppery ['pep·ə·ri] *adj* (*with pepper flavor*) pfeffrig; (*full of pepper*) gepfeffert; *dish* scharf

'pep pill *n* Aufputschmittel *nt*

'pep talk *n* Motivationsgespräch *nt*

peptic ['pep·tɪk] *adj inv* ANAT Verdauungs-, peptisch *fachspr*

per [pɜr] *prep* ❶ (*for every*) pro ❷ (*in every*) pro ❸ (*according to*) **as ~ usual** wie gewöhnlich

P

per annum [pər·ˈæn·əm] *adv inv* (*form*) per annum

per capita [pər·ˈkæp·ɪ·t̬ə] *inv* (*form*) **I.** *adv* pro Person **II.** *adj attr* Pro-Kopf-

perceivable [pər·ˈsi·və·bəl] *adj* wahrnehmbar

perceive [pər·ˈsiv] *vt* ❶ (*see*) wahrnehmen; (*sense*) empfinden ❷ (*regard*) betrachten; **how do the French ~ the British?** wie sehen die Franzosen die Engländer?

percent [pər·ˈsent] **I.** *n* Prozent *nt;* **what ~ ...?** wie viel Prozent ...? **II.** *adv inv* -prozentig; **I'm 100 ~ sure that ...** ich bin mir hundertprozentig sicher, dass ... **III.** *adj attr, inv* **50 ~** 50-prozentig

percentage [pər·ˈsen·tɪdʒ] **I.** *n* ❶ (*rate*) Prozentsatz *m;* **what ~ ...?** wie viel Prozent ...? ❷ (*advantage*) Vorteil *m* **II.** *adj* Prozent-; **on a ~ basis** prozentual

perˈcentage point *n* Prozentpunkt *m*

perceptible [pər·ˈsep·tə·bəl] *adj* wahrnehmbar

perception [pər·ˈsep·ʃən] *n usu sing* Wahrnehmung *f kein pl; of a concept* Auffassung *f kein pl*

perceptive [pər·ˈsep·tɪv] *adj* einfühlsam; *observer* aufmerksam; *analysis, remark* scharfsinnig

perch¹ [pɜrtʃ] **I.** *n* <*pl* -es> ❶ (*for birds*) Sitzstange *f* ❷ (*high location*) Hochsitz *m* **II.** *vi bird* sitzen (**on** auf +*dat*); *person* thronen (**on** auf +*dat*) **III.** *vt* ■**to ~ sth somewhere** etw auf etw *akk* stecken; ■**to ~ oneself on sth** sich auf etw *dat* niederlassen

perch² <*pl* - *or* -es> [pɜrtʃ] *n* (*fish*) Flussbarsch *m*

percolate [ˈpɜr·kə·leɪt] **I.** *vt* filtrieren; **to ~ coffee** Filterkaffee zubereiten **II.** *vi* ❶ (*filter through*) *water* durchsickern; *sand* durchrieseln; *coffee* durchlaufen ❷ (*fig fam: spread*) durchsickern

percolator [ˈpɜr·kə·leɪ·t̬ər] *n* Kaffeemaschine *f*

percussion [pər·ˈkʌʃ·ən] **I.** *n* Percussion *f,* Schlagzeug *nt* **II.** *adj* MUS Schlag-

percussionist [pər·ˈkʌʃ·ə·nɪst] *n* Schlagzeuger(in) *m(f)*

peregrine ˈfalcon *n* Wanderfalke *m*

peremptory [pə·ˈremp·tə·ri] *adj inv* ❶ (*autocratic*) gebieterisch ❷ LAW End-; **~ challenge** *Ablehnung eines Geschworenen ohne Angabe der Gründe*

perennial [pə·ˈren·i·əl] **I.** *n* mehrjährige Pflanze **II.** *adj attr, inv* ❶ (*lasting through many years*) mehrjährig ❷ (*constant*) immer während; (*repeated*) immer wiederkehrend *attr; beauty, truth* unsterblich

perfect **I.** *adj* [ˈpɜr·fɪkt] *inv* vollkommen, perfekt; *calm* völlig **II.** *vt* [pər·ˈfekt] perfektionieren **III.** *n* [ˈpɜr·fɪkt] LING Perfekt *nt;* **future ~** vollendete Zukunft; **past ~** Plusquamperfekt *nt*

perfection [pər·ˈfek·ʃən] *n* Perfektion *f,* Vollkommenheit *f*

perfectionist [pər·ˈfek·ʃə·nɪst] *n* Perfektionist(in) *m(f)*

perfectly [ˈpɜr·fɪkt·li] *adv inv* vollkommen, perfekt; **you know ~ well what I'm talking about** du weißt ganz genau, wovon ich rede; **~ clear** absolut klar *fam;* **to be ~ honest ...** ehrlich gesagt, ...

perforate [ˈpɜr·fə·reɪt] *vt* perforieren; (*once*) durchstechen

perforated [ˈpɜr·fə·reɪ·t̬ɪd] *adj inv* perforiert; **~ eardrum** geplatztes Trommelfell

perforation [ˌpɜr·fə·ˈreɪ·ʃən] *n* ❶ (*hole in sth*) Loch *nt;* (*set of holes*) Perforation *f* ❷ (*act*) Perforieren *nt*

perform [pər·ˈfɔrm] **I.** *vt* ❶ (*entertain*) vorführen; *play, opera, ballet, symphony* aufführen; (*sing*) singen; (*on an instrument*) spielen ❷ *duty, function* erfüllen; *task* verrichten ❸ *surgical procedure* durchführen; *ceremony, ritual* vollziehen **II.** *vi* ❶ (*on stage*) auftreten; (*sing*) singen; (*play*) spielen ❷ (*function*) funktionieren; *car* laufen; (*respond*) sich fahren; **to ~ well** gut funktionieren ❸ (*do, act*) **how did she ~?** wie war sie?; **to ~ well** gut sein

performance [pər·ˈfɔr·məns] **I.** *n* ❶ (*entertaining, showing*) Vorführung *f; of a play, opera, ballet* Aufführung *f; of a part* Darstellung *f; of a song, musical piece* Darbietung *f;* (*show, event*) Vorstellung *f;* **to give a ~** eine Vorstellung geben ❷ (*capability, effectiveness, level of achievement*) Leistung *f;* **high ~** hohe Leistung ❸ (*execution*) ■**the ~ of sth** die Ausführung einer S. *gen;* **the ~ of a duty** die Erfüllung einer Pflicht ❹ (*fam: fuss*) Theater *nt kein pl fig, pej* **II.** *adj evaluation, problem, results* Leistungs-; **~ bonus** Leistungsprämie *f*

performer [pər·ˈfɔr·mər] *n* ❶ (*artist*) Künstler(in) *m(f);* (*actor*) Darsteller(in) *m(f)* ❷ (*achiever*) **to be a poor ~ [in school]** ein schlechter Schüler/eine schlechte Schülerin sein

perfume **I.** *n* [ˈpɜr·fjum] ❶ (*scented liquid*) Parfüm *nt* ❷ *of a flower* Duft *m* **II.** *vt* [pər·ˈfjum] parfümieren

perfunctory [pər·ˈfʌŋk·tə·ri] *adj* flüchtig; *examination* oberflächlich

perhaps [pər·ˈhæps] *adv inv* ❶ (*maybe*) vielleicht; **~ so** ja, vielleicht ❷ (*approximately*) etwa, ungefähr

peril [ˈper·əl] *n* (*form: danger*) Gefahr *f;* (*risk*) Risiko *nt;* **to be in ~** in Gefahr sein

perilous [ˈper·ə·ləs] *adj* (*form: dangerous*) gefährlich; (*risky*) riskant

perimeter [pə·ˈrɪm·ə·t̬ər] *n* ❶ (*border*) Grenze *f* ❷ MATH Umfang *m*

period [ˈpɪr·i·əd] **I.** *n* ❶ (*length of time*) Zeitspanne *f,* Periode *f;* **he was unemployed for a long ~ [of time]** er war lange [Zeit] arbeitslos; **for a ~ of three months** für die Dauer von drei Monaten ❷ SCH (*lesson*) Stunde *f* ❸ (*time in life, history, development*) Zeit *f;* (*distinct time*) Zeitabschnitt *m;* (*phase*) Phase *f;* **incubation ~** Inkubationszeit *f;* **~ of**

office Amtszeit *f* ❹ (*fam: menstruation*) Periode *f* ❺ LING (*a. fig*) Punkt *m* **II.** *adj furniture, clothing, novel* historisch

periodic [ˌpɪr·i·ˈad·ɪk] *adj attr, inv* periodisch *geh,* regelmäßig wiederkehrend

periodical [ˌpɪr·i·ˈad·ɪ·kəl] **I.** *n* Zeitschrift *f;* (*specialist journal a.*) Periodikum *nt fachspr* **II.** *adj attr, inv* periodisch *geh,* regelmäßig wiederkehrend

periodic ˈtable *n* CHEM Periodensystem *nt fachspr*

peripheral [pə·ˈrɪf·ər·əl] **I.** *adj inv* ❶ (*minor*) unbedeutend, unwesentlich ❷ (*at the edge*) Rand-, peripher *geh* **II.** *n* COMPUT Peripherie *f fachspr*

periscope [ˈper·ɪ·skoʊp] *n* Periskop *nt*

perish [ˈper·ɪʃ] *vi* (*form, liter: die*) sterben, umkommen; (*be destroyed*) untergehen *a. fig*

perishable [ˈper·ɪʃ·ə·bəl] *adj food* [leicht] verderblich

perjure [ˈpɜr·dʒər] *vt* ■**to ~ oneself** einen Meineid schwören

perjury [ˈpɜr·dʒə·ri] *n* Meineid *nt;* **to commit ~** einen Meineid schwören

perk [pɜrk] *n* ❶ (*additional benefit*) Vergünstigung *f* ❷ (*advantage*) Vorteil *m*

◆**perk up** **I.** *vi* ❶ (*cheer up*) aufleben; (*become more awake, livelier a.*) munter werden ❷ (*increase, recover*) steigen, sich erholen; *share prices* fester tendieren **II.** *vt* ❶ (*cheer up*) aufheitern ❷ (*energize*) aufmuntern

perky [ˈpɜr·ki] *adj* ❶ (*lively*) munter ❷ (*overly confident*) keck

perm[1] [pɜrm] *n short for* **permanent** Dauerwelle *f*

perm[2] [pɜrm] *vt* **to ~ hair** Dauerwellen machen; **~ed hair** Dauerwellen *pl*

permafrost [ˈpɜr·mə·frɔst] *n* Dauerfrost[boden] *m*

permanence [ˈpɜr·mə·nəns], **permanency** [ˈpɜr·mə·nən·si] *n* Beständigkeit *f*

permanent [ˈpɜr·mə·nənt] *adj inv* permanent, ständig; *agreement* unbefristet; *relationship* dauerhaft; *marker, ink* wasserfest; **~ address** fester Wohnsitz; **~ appointment** Ernennung *f* auf Lebenszeit; **~ damage** bleibender Schaden

permeable [ˈpɜr·mi·ə·bəl] *adj* (*a. fig form*) durchlässig *a. fig;* **~ to water** wasserdurchlässig

permeate [ˈpɜr·mi·eɪt] **I.** *vt* durchdringen **II.** *vi* (*form*) ■**to ~ into/through sth** etw durchdringen

permissible [pər·ˈmɪs·ə·bəl] *adj inv* gestattet, zulässig

permission [pər·ˈmɪʃ·ən] *n* Erlaubnis *f;* (*from an official body*) Genehmigung *f;* **with sb's written ~** mit jds schriftlichem Einverständnis

permissive [pər·ˈmɪs·ɪv] *adj* (*pej*) nachgiebig; (*sexually*) freizügig

permissiveness [pər·ˈmɪs·ɪv·nɪs] *n* Toleranz *f;* [**sexual**] **~** sexuelle Freizügigkeit

permit **I.** *n* [ˈpɜr·mɪt] Genehmigung *f;* **building ~** Baugenehmigung *f;* **export ~** Exporterlaubnis *f* **II.** *vt* <-tt-> [pər·ˈmɪt] ❶ (*allow, give permission*) gestatten, erlauben ❷ (*make possible*) ■**to ~ sb to do sth** jdm ermöglichen, etw zu tun **III.** *vi* [pər·ˈmɪt] (*allow*) erlauben, gestatten; **weather ~ting** vorausgesetzt, das Wetter spielt mit

permitted [pər·ˈmɪt̬·ɪd] *adj inv* zulässig

permutation [ˌpɜrm·ju·ˈteɪ·ʃən] *n a.* MATH (*rearrangement*) Umstellung *f*

pernicious [pər·ˈnɪʃ·əs] *adj* ❶ (*form*) schädlich ❷ MED bösartig, perniziös *fachspr*

peroxide [pə·ˈrak·saɪd] **I.** *n* Peroxyd *nt* **II.** *vt* mit Peroxyd behandeln; *hair* bleichen

perpendicular [ˌpɜr·pən·ˈdɪk·ju·lər] **I.** *adj inv* senkrecht (**to** zu +*dat*), perpendikular *fachspr* **II.** *n* Senkrechte *f;* MATH, ARCHIT ■**the ~** das Lot

perpetrate [ˈpɜr·pə·treɪt] *vt* (*form*) begehen

perpetration [ˌpɜr·pə·ˈtreɪ·ʃən] *n* LAW (*form*) Begehen *nt; of crime a.* Verübung *f*

perpetrator [ˈpɜr·pə·treɪ·t̬ər] *n* (*form*) Täter(in) *m(f);* **~ of fraud** Betrüger(in) *m(f)*

perpetual [pər·ˈpetʃ·u·əl] *adj attr, inv* ❶ (*everlasting*) immer während, ständig ❷ (*occurring repeatedly*) fortgesetzt, wiederholt

perpetuate [pər·ˈpetʃ·u·eɪt] *vt* aufrechterhalten

perpetuity [ˌpɜr·pə·ˈtu·ɪ·t̬i] *n* (*form*) Ewigkeit *f;* **in ~** auf ewig; LAW lebenslänglich

perplex [pər·ˈpleks] *vt* (*confuse*) verwirren; (*puzzle*) verblüffen

perplexed [pər·ˈplekst] *adj* perplex; (*confused a.*) verwirrt; (*puzzled a.*) verblüfft

perplexity [pər·ˈplek·sɪ·t̬i] *n* (*puzzlement*) Verblüffung *f;* (*confusion*) Verwirrung *f*

persecute [ˈpɜr·sɪ·kjut] *vt usu passive* verfolgen; ■**to be ~d for sth** wegen einer S. *gen* verfolgt werden

persecution [ˌpɜr·sɪ·ˈkju·ʃən] *n usu sing* Verfolgung *f*

persecutor [ˈpɜr·sɪ·kju·t̬ər] *n* Verfolger(in) *m(f)*

perseverance [ˌpɜr·sə·ˈvɪr·əns] *n* Beharrlichkeit *f,* Ausdauer *f*

persevere [ˌpɜr·sə·ˈvɪr] *vi* nicht aufgeben, beharrlich bleiben; ■**to ~ with sth** an etw *dat* festhalten; (*continue*) mit etw *dat* weitermachen; *project, crusade, program* etw [unbeirrt] fortsetzen

persevering [ˌpɜr·sə·ˈvɪr·ɪŋ] *adj* beharrlich, ausdauernd

Persia [ˈpɜr·ʒə] *n* (*hist*) Persien *nt*

Persian [ˈpɜr·ʒən] **I.** *adj inv* persisch **II.** *n* ❶ (*person*) Perser(in) *m(f)* ❷ (*language*) Persisch *nt* ❸ (*cat*) Perserkatze *f*

persist [pər·ˈsɪst] *vi* ❶ (*continue to exist*) andauern; *cold, heat, rain* anhalten; *habit, tradition* fortbestehen ❷ (*to not give up*) beharrlich bleiben ❸ (*continue*) ■**to ~ in doing sth** nicht aufhören, etw zu tun; ■**to ~ with sth** mit etw *dat* weitermachen; *project, crusade, program* etw unbeirrt fortsetzen

persistence [pər·ˈsɪs·təns] *n* ❶ (*continuation*)

P

Anhalten *nt* ❷ (*perseverance*) Hartnäckigkeit *f*

persistent [pər·'sɪs·tənt] *adj* ❶ *difficulties* anhaltend; *cough, rumor, request* hartnäckig ❷ (*constant*) unaufhörlich; *demand* ständig

persnickety [pər·'snɪk·ɪ·t̬i] *adj* (*pej: fussy*) pingelig *fam*, kleinlich

person <*pl* people *or form* -s> ['pɜr·sən] *n* (*human*) Person *f*, Mensch *m*; **not a single ~ came** kein Mensch kam; **cat ~** Katzenliebhaber(in) *m(f)*; **night ~** Nachtmensch *m*

persona <*pl* -nae *or* -s> [pər·'soʊ·nə] *n* Fassade *f meist pej*

personal ['pɜr·sə·nəl] *adj* ❶ (*of a particular person*) persönlich; *private a.* privat; **~ belongings** persönliches Eigentum; **~ data** Personalien *pl*; **~ quality** Charaktereigenschaft *f* ❷ (*direct, done in person*) persönlich; **to make a ~ appearance** persönlich erscheinen ❸ (*offensive*) persönlich; **nothing ~, but ...** es geht nicht gegen Sie persönlich, aber ...

'personal ad *n* Kontaktanzeige *f*

personal com'puter *n* Personal Computer *m*

personal digital as'sistant *n* PDA *m*, [handflächengroßer] Taschencomputer

personality [ˌpɜr·sə·'næl·ɪ·t̬i] **I.** *n* (*character, a celebrity*) Persönlichkeit *f*, Charakter *m* **II.** *adj problem, test, trait* Persönlichkeits-

personally ['pɜr·sə·nə·li] *adv* persönlich

personal 'pronoun *n* Personalpronomen *nt*

personify [pər·'san·ə·faɪ] *vt* personifizieren; (*be the personification of a.*) verkörpern

personnel [ˌpɜr·sə·'nel] *n* ❶ *pl* (*employees*) Personal *nt kein pl* ❷ (*human resources department*) Personalabteilung *f*

person'nel department *n* Personalabteilung *f*

person'nel director *n* Personalchef(in) *m(f)*

personnel 'manager *n* Personalchef(in) *m(f)*

perspective [pər·'spek·tɪv] *n* (*viewpoint*) Perspektive *f*; **from a historical ~** aus geschichtlicher Sicht; **in ~** perspektivisch; **to see sth in a new ~** etw aus einem neuen Blickwinkel sehen; **to get sth in ~** etw nüchtern betrachten

perspicacious [ˌpɜr·spɪ·'keɪ·ʃəs] *adj* (*form: astute*) scharfsinnig; (*far-sighted*) weitblickend

perspiration [ˌpɜr·spə·'reɪ·ʃən] *n* Schweiß *m*

perspire [pər·'spaɪr] *vi* schwitzen

persuade [pər·'sweɪd] *vt* (*talk sb into*) überreden (**to** zu +*dat*); (*convince*) überzeugen (von +*dat*)

persuasion [pər·'sweɪ·ʒən] *n usu sing* ❶ (*talking into*) Überredung *f*; (*convincing*) Überzeugung *f* ❷ (*conviction*) Überzeugung *f*; (*hum*) **to be of the Catholic/Protestant ~** katholischen/protestantischen Glaubens sein

persuasive [pər·'sweɪ·sɪv] *adj* überzeugend

pert [pɜrt] *adj* ❶ (*attractively small*) wohl geformt ❷ (*impudent*) frech ❸ (*neat and jaunty*) adrett

pertinent ['pɜr·tən·ənt] *adj* (*form*) relevant; *argument* stichhaltig; *question* sachdienlich; ■**to be ~ to sth** für etw *akk* relevant sein; *remark* treffend

perturb [pər·'tɜrb] *vt* (*form*) beunruhigen

Peru [pə·'ru] *n* Peru *nt*

perusal [pə·'ru·zəl] *n* (*form*) Durchlesen *nt*

peruse [pə·'ruz] *vt* (*form: read*) durchlesen; (*check*) durchsehen; (*study*) studieren

Peruvian [pə·'ru·vi·ən] **I.** *adj inv* peruanisch **II.** *n* Peruaner(in) *m(f)*

pervasive [pər·'veɪ·sɪv] *adj* (*form: penetrating*) durchdringend *attr*; (*widespread*) weit verbreitet

perverse [pər·'vɜrs] *adj* (*pej: deliberately unreasonable*) abwegig; *person* eigensinnig; *delight* diebisch

perversion [pər·'vɜr·ʒən] *n* (*pej*) ❶ (*unnatural behavior*) Perversion *f* ❷ (*corruption*) Pervertierung *f geh*; **~ of justice** Rechtsbeugung *f*

pervert **I.** *n* ['pɜr·vɜrt] (*pej: sexual deviant*) Perverse(r) *f(m)* **II.** *vt* [pər·'vɜrt] (*pej*) ❶ *person* verderben ❷ *truth* verdrehen

perverted [pər·'vɜr·t̬ɪd] *adj* ❶ (*sexually deviant*) pervers ❷ (*distorted*) verdreht

pesky ['pes·ki] *adj* (*fam*) verdammt *fam*; **~ fly** lästige Fliege; **~ kid** nerviges Kind

pessimism ['pes·ə·mɪz·əm] *n* Pessimismus *m* (**over, about** hinsichtlich +*gen*)

pessimist ['pes·ə·mɪst] *n* Pessimist(in) *m(f)*

pessimistic [ˌpes·ə·'mɪs·tɪk] *adj* pessimistisch

pest [pest] *n* ❶ (*destructive animal*) Schädling *m* ❷ (*fig fam: annoying person*) Nervensäge *f fam*; (*annoying thing*) Plage *f*

'pest control *n* ❶ (*removal*) Schädlingsbekämpfung *f* ❷ (*service*) Kammerjäger *m*

pester ['pes·tər] *vt* belästigen; ■**to ~ sb for sth** jdm mit etw *dat* keine Ruhe lassen; (*beg*) jdn um etw *akk* anbetteln; ■**to ~ sb to do sth** jdn drängen, etw zu tun

pesticide ['pes·tə·saɪd] *n* Schädlingsbekämpfungsmittel *nt*

pestilent ['pes·tə·lənt], **pestilential** [ˌpes·tə·'len·ʃəl] *adj inv* ❶ (*deadly*) tödlich ❷ (*fig: morally destructive*) verderblich

pestle ['pes·əl] *n* Stößel *m*

pet [pet] **I.** *n* ❶ (*animal*) Haustier *nt* ❷ (*pej: favorite*) Liebling *m* ❸ (*fam: nice person*) Schatz *m* **II.** *adj* ❶ (*concerning animals*) Tier-; **~ cat** Hauskatze *f* ❷ *project, theory, charity* Lieblings-; **to be one's ~ peeve** jdm ein Gräuel sein **III.** *vt* <-tt-> streicheln

petal ['pet̬·əl] *n* Blütenblatt *nt*

peter ['pi·t̬ər] *vi* ■**to ~ out** zu Ende gehen; *conversation, interest* sich totlaufen; *storm* abklingen; *trail, track, path* sich verlieren

petite [pə·'tit] *adj inv* (*approv*) *person* zierlich

petition [pə·'tɪʃ·ən] **I.** *n* ❶ (*signed document*) Petition *f* (**against, for** gegen, für +*akk*) ❷ LAW (*written request*) Gesuch *nt* **II.** *vi* LAW (*request formally*) einen Antrag stellen (**for** auf +*akk*) **III.** *vt* ■**to ~ sb for sth** jdn um etw *akk* ersuchen *form*; ■**to ~ sb to do sth** jdn ersuchen, etw *akk* zu tun

petitioner [pə·'tɪʃ·ən·ər] *n* ❶ (*collecting signatures*) Unterschriftensammler(in) *m(f)* ❷ LAW Kläger(in) *m(f)*

pet 'name *n* Kosename *m*

pet 'peeve *n* Ärgernis *nt*
petrified ['pet·rə·faɪd] *adj inv* ❶ (*fossilized*) versteinert ❷ (*terrified*) gelähmt *fig;* ▪ **to be ~ of sth** vor etw *dat* panische Angst haben; **to be ~ with fear** vor Angst wie gelähmt sein
petrify ['pet·rə·faɪ] **I.** *vi* versteinern **II.** *vt* (*terrify*) schreckliche Angst einjagen +*dat*
petrochemical [ˌpet·roʊ·'kem·ɪ·kəl] **I.** *n* petrochemisches Produkt **II.** *adj attr, inv* petrochemisch
petroleum [pə·'troʊ·li·əm] *n* Erdöl *nt*
pettiness ['peṭ·i·nɪs] *n* ❶ (*insignificance*) Belanglosigkeit *f;* (*triviality*) Trivialität *f* ❷ (*small-mindedness*) Kleinlichkeit *f pej*
petting ['peṭ·ɪŋ] *n* ❶ (*stroking*) Streicheln *nt* ❷ (*sexual fondling*) Petting *nt*
petty ['peṭ·i] *adj* (*pej*) ❶ (*insignificant*) unbedeutend; (*trivial*) trivial ❷ (*small-minded*) kleinkariert ❸ LAW (*on a small scale*) geringfügig
petty 'cash *n* Portokasse *f*
'petty officer *n* NAUT ≈ Marineunteroffizier *m*
petulant ['petʃ·ə·lənt] *adj* (*pej*) verdrießlich; *child* bockig; *look* verdrossen
petunia [pə·'tun·jə] *n* Petunie *f*
pew [pju] *n* Kirchenbank *f*
pewter ['pju·ṭər] *n* Zinn *nt*
PG [ˌpi·'dʒi] *adj inv abbrev of* **parental guidance: to be rated ~** bedingt jugendfrei sein; **~-13** frei ab 13
pH [ˌpi·'eɪtʃ] *n usu sing* pH-Wert *m*
phalanx <*pl* -es *or* phalanges> ['feɪ·læŋks] *n* (*form*) Phalanx *f*
phallic ['fæl·ɪk] *adj inv* phallisch
phallus <*pl* -es *or* -li> ['fæl·əs] *n* Phallus *m geh*
phantom ['fæn·təm] **I.** *n* Geist *m,* Gespenst *nt* **II.** *adj attr, inv* ❶ (*ghostly*) Geister- ❷ (*caused by mental illusion*) Phantom-
pharaoh ['fer·oʊ] *n* Pharao *m*
pharmaceutical [ˌfar·mə·'su·ṭɪ·kəl] *adj attr, inv* pharmazeutisch
pharma'ceutical industry *n* Pharmaindustrie *f*
pharmacist ['far·mə·sɪst] *n* Apotheker(in) *m(f),* Drogist(in) *m(f)*
pharmacology [ˌfar·mə·'kal·ə·dʒi] *n* Pharmakologie *f*
pharmacy ['far·mə·si] *n* ❶ (*drugstore*) Apotheke *f* ❷ (*profession*) Pharmazie *f*
phase [feɪz] **I.** *n* Phase *f;* **developmental ~** Entwicklungsphase *f;* **to go through a ~** eine Phase durchlaufen **II.** *vt usu passive* (*implement*) stufenweise durchführen; (*introduce*) stufenweise einführen; (*coordinate*) synchronisieren
◆ **phase in** *vt* stufenweise einführen
◆ **phase out** *vt* auslaufen lassen
phat [fæt] *adj* (*sl*) toll, krass *sl*
PhD [ˌpi·eɪtʃ·'di] *n abbrev of* **Doctor of Philosophy** Dr., Doktor *m;* **~ dissertation** Doktorarbeit *f*
pheasant <*pl* -s *or* -> ['fez·ənt] *n* Fasan *m*
phenomena [fə·'nam·ə·nə] *n pl of* **phenomenon**
phenomenal [fə·'nam·ə·nəl] *adj* (*great*) phänomenal
phenomenon <*pl* -mena *or* -s> [fə·'nam·ə·nan] *n* Phänomen *nt geh*
phew [fju] *interj* (*fam*) puh
philatelist [fɪ·'læṭ·ə·lɪst] *n* Philatelist(in) *m(f) geh*
philately [fɪ·'læṭ·ə·li] *n* Philatelie *f*
philharmonic [ˌfɪl·har·'man·ɪk] *adj attr, inv* philharmonisch; **the Vienna ~ Orchestra** die Wiener Philharmoniker *pl*
Philippines ['fɪl·ə·pinz] *npl* ▪ **the ~** die Philippinen *pl*
philistine ['fɪl·ɪ·stin] (*pej*) **I.** *n* Banause *m* **II.** *adj inv* banausisch
philology [fɪ·'lal·ə·dʒi] *n* Philologie *f*
philosopher [fɪ·'las·ə·fər] *n* Philosoph(in) *m(f)*
philosophic(al) [ˌfɪl·ə·'saf·ɪk(əl)] *adj* ❶ PHILOS philosophisch ❷ (*calm*) gelassen
philosophize [fɪ·'las·ə·faɪz] *vi* philosophieren
philosophy [fɪ·'las·ə·fi] *n* Philosophie *f*
phish [fɪʃ] *vi* INET phischen (*im Internet persönliche Daten und Passwörter auskundschaften, um die Betroffenen zu bestehlen*)
phlegm [flem] *n* Schleim *m*
phlegmatic [fleg·'mæṭ·ɪk] *adj* (*calm*) gleichmütig
phobia ['foʊ·bi·ə] *n* Phobie *f*
phoenix ['fi·nɪks] *n usu sing* Phönix *m*
phone [foʊn] **I.** *n* Telefon *nt;* **to answer the ~** ans Telefon gehen; **to pick up the ~** abheben; **to speak [to sb] on the ~** [mit jdm] telefonieren; **on the ~** am Telefon **II.** *vt* anrufen **III.** *vi* telefonieren
◆ **phone back I.** *vt* zurückrufen **II.** *vi* zurückrufen
◆ **phone in I.** *vi* anrufen, sich telefonisch melden; **to ~ in sick** sich telefonisch krankmelden **II.** *vt information* telefonisch durchgeben
◆ **phone up** *vt* anrufen
'phone book *n* Telefonbuch *nt*
'phone booth *n* Telefonzelle *f*
'phone card *n* Telefon[kredit]karte *f*
phonetic [fə·'neṭ·ɪk] *adj inv* LING phonetisch *fachspr*
phonetics [fə·'neṭ·ɪks] *n + sing vb* LING Phonetik *f kein pl fachspr*
phony, phoney ['foʊ·ni] (*pej*) **I.** *adj* (*fam*) *accent, smile* aufgesetzt, künstlich; *address* falsch; *documents* gefälscht **II.** *n* (*impostor*) Hochstapler(in) *m(f);* (*pretender*) Schwindler(in) *m(f);* (*fake*) Fälschung *f*
phooey ['fu·i] *interj* (*hum fam*) pfui
phosphate ['fas·feɪt] *n* Phosphat *nt*
phosphorescence [ˌfas·fə·'res·əns] *n* Phosphoreszenz *f*
phosphorescent [ˌfas·fə·'res·ənt] *adj* phosphoreszierend
phosphorus ['fas·fər·əs] *n* Phosphor *m*
photo ['foʊ·ṭoʊ] *n short for* **photograph** Foto *nt*

P

'photo album *n* Fotoalbum *nt*
'photocopier *n* [Foto]kopierer *m*
'photocopy I. *n* [Foto]kopie *f* II. *vt* [foto]kopieren
photo 'finish *n* SPORTS Fotofinish *nt fachspr*
photogenic [ˌfoʊ·ţoʊ·ˈdʒen·ɪk] *adj* fotogen
photograph [ˈfoʊ·ţə·græf] I. *n* Fotografie *f*, Foto *nt*; **aerial** ~ Luftaufnahme; **to take a** ~ [**of sb/sth**] [jdn/etw] fotografieren, ein Foto [von jdm/etw] machen *f* II. *vt* fotografieren III. *vi* **to** ~ **well** gut auf Fotos aussehen
photographer [fə·ˈtag·rə·fər] *n* Fotograf(in) *m(f)*
photographic [ˌfoʊ·ţə·ˈgræf·ɪk] *adj inv* fotografisch; ~ **equipment** Fotoausrüstung *f*
photography [fə·ˈtag·rə·fi] *n* Fotografie *f*
photo'journalism *n* Fotojournalismus *m*
photo oppor'tunity *n* Fototermin *m*
photo'sensitive *adj* lichtempfindlich
photo'synthesis *n* BIOL, CHEM Photosynthese *f*
phrasal 'verb *n* LING Phrasal Verb *nt* (*Grundverb mit präpositionaler oder adverbialer Ergänzung*)
phrase [freɪz] I. *n* ❶ (*words*) Satz *m*; (*idiomatic expression*) Ausdruck *m* ❷ MUS (*series of notes*) Phrase *f fachspr* II. *vt* formulieren
'phrase book *n* Sprachführer *m*
phraseology [ˌfreɪ·zi·ˈal·ə·dʒi] *n* Ausdrucksweise *f*
pH value [ˈpi·eɪtʃ·,-] *n* pH-Wert *m*
physical [ˈfɪz·ɪ·kəl] I. *adj* ❶ *condition, love* körperlich, physisch *geh*; **to have a** ~ **disability** körperbehindert sein; ~ **contact** Körperkontakt *m*; ~ **attraction** körperliche Anziehung ❷ *inv* (*material*) physisch; *object, world* stofflich II. *n* MED Untersuchung *f*
physical edu'cation *n* Sport[unterricht] *m*
physically [ˈfɪz·ɪ·kəl·i] *adv* ❶ (*concerning the body*) körperlich; **it's just not** ~ **possible** das ist schon rein physisch nicht möglich; ~ **disabled** körperbehindert ❷ (*not imagined*) wirklich
physical 'therapist *n* Physiotherapeut(in) *m(f) fachspr*, Krankengymnast(in) *m(f)*
physical 'therapy *n* Physiotherapie *f fachspr*
physician [fɪ·ˈzɪʃ·ən] *n* Arzt, Ärztin *m, f*
physicist [ˈfɪz·ɪ·sɪst] *n* Physiker(in) *m(f)*
physics [ˈfɪz·ɪks] *n + sing vb* Physik *f*
physiological [ˌfɪz·i·ə·ˈladʒ·ɪ·kəl] *adj inv* physiologisch
physiologist [ˌfɪz·i·ˈal·ə·dʒɪst] *n* Physiologe, -in *m, f*
physiology [ˌfɪz·i·ˈal·ə·dʒi] *n* Physiologie *f*
physique [fɪ·ˈzik] *n* Körperbau *m*; (*appearance*) Figur *f*
pianist [ˈpi·æn·ɪst] *n* Klavierspieler(in) *m(f)*; (*professional*) Pianist(in) *m(f)*
piano [pi·ˈæn·oʊ] *n* Klavier *nt*, Piano *nt*; **to play** [**the**] ~ Klavier spielen; ■**on the** ~ am Klavier
piazza [pɪ·ˈat·sə] *n* Marktplatz *m*
piccolo [ˈpɪk·ə·loʊ] *n* Pikkoloflöte *f*
pick[1] [pɪk] I. *n* ❶ (*choice*) Auswahl *f*; **to have** [**the**] **first** ~ die erste Wahl haben; **to take one's** ~ sich *dat* etw aussuchen ❷ + *sing/pl vb* (*best*) ■**the** ~ **of sth** *of things* das Beste; *of people* die Elite II. *vt* ❶ (*select*) aussuchen; ■**to** ~ **sb/sth** [**for sth**] jdn/etw [für etw *akk*] aussuchen; **to** ~ **sth/sb at random** jdn/etw [völlig] willkürlich aussuchen ❷ (*harvest*) pflücken; *mushrooms* sammeln ❸ (*scratch*) ■**to** ~ **sth** an etw *dat* kratzen; **to** ~ **one's nose** in der Nase bohren ❹ (*take*) ■**to** ~ **sth from/off** [**of**] **sth** etw aus/von etw *dat* nehmen ❺ (*open without key*) *lock* knacken ❻ MUS *guitar* zupfen III. *vi* ❶ (*be choosy*) aussuchen ❷ (*toy with*) ■**to** ~ **at one's food** in seinem Essen herumstochern ❸ (*scratch*) ■**to** ~ **at sth** an etw *dat* [herum]kratzen
◆**pick off** *vt* (*shoot*) ■**to** ~ **off** ↔ **sb/sth** jdn/etw einzeln abschießen
◆**pick on** *vi* (*bully*) herumhacken (auf +*dat*)
◆**pick out** *vt* ❶ (*select*) aussuchen; **to** ~ **out the best things for oneself** sich *dat* selbst das Beste herauspicken ❷ (*recognize*) erkennen
◆**pick over, pick through** *vt* ■**to** ~ **sth** ↔ **over** etw gut durchsehen
◆**pick up** I. *vt* ❶ (*lift*) aufheben; **to** ~ **up the phone** [den Hörer] abnehmen; (*make phone call*) anrufen ❷ (*acquire*) erwerben; **to** ~ **up a bargain** ein Schnäppchen machen; **to** ~ **up an illness** sich mit einer Krankheit anstecken ❸ (*collect*) abholen; *passengers* aufnehmen ❹ (*sl: for sexual purposes*) ■**to** ~ **up** ↔ **sb** jdn abschleppen ❺ (*detect*) *mistakes* wahrnehmen ❻ (*on radio*) *signal* empfangen ❼ (*increase*) **to** ~ **up speed** schneller werden; (*fig*) sich verstärken; *winds* sich auffrischen ❽ (*fam: earn*) *award, prize* verdienen ❾ (*fam: pay for*) **to** ~ **up the tab** die Rechnung bezahlen II. *vi* ❶ (*improve*) sich bessern, besser werden; *numbers* steigen ❷ (*resume*) **to** ~ **up where one left off** da weitermachen, wo man aufgehört hat ❸ (*increase*) *winds* sich auffrischen
pick[2] [pɪk] *n* (*pickax*) Spitzhacke *f*
'pickax, 'pickaxe *n* Spitzhacke *f*
picker [ˈpɪk·ər] *n* (*of crops*) Erntehelfer(in) *m(f)*; **cotton** ~ Baumwollpflücker(in) *m(f)*
picket [ˈpɪk·ɪt] I. *n* ❶ (*stake*) Palisade *f* ❷ (*striker*) Streikposten *m*; (*blockade*) Streikblockade *f* II. *vt* (*in a strike*) Streikposten aufstellen (vor +*dat*); (*demonstrate at*) demonstrieren (vor +*dat*); (*blockade*) blockieren III. *vi* demonstrieren
picket 'fence *n* Palisadenzaun *m*
'picket line *n* Streikpostenkette *f*
pickings [ˈpɪk·ɪŋz] *npl* **rich** ~ schnelles Geld; **slim** ~ magere Ausbeute
pickle [ˈpɪk·əl] I. *n* ❶ FOOD saure Gurke ❷ (*fam: predicament*) **to be caught in a** ~ in der Patsche sitzen II. *vt* FOOD einlegen
pickled [ˈpɪk·əld] *adj* ❶ *inv* (*preserved*) eingelegt ❷ (*fig fam: drunk*) besoffen
'pick-me-up *n* (*fam*) Muntermacher *m*

'pickpocket *n* Taschendieb(in) *m(f)*

'pickup *n* ❶ (*pickup truck*) (offener) Kleintransporter ❷ (*fam: acceleration power*) Beschleunigung *f* ❸ (*fam: improvement*) Verbesserung *f* ❹ (*fam: casual sexual acquaintance*) Eroberung *f hum*

'pickup truck *n* (offener) Kleintransporter

picky ['pɪk·i] *adj* (*pej fam*) pingelig; *eater* wählerisch

picnic ['pɪk·nɪk] **I.** *n* Picknick *nt;* **to go on a ~** ein Picknick machen **II.** *vi* <-ck-> picknicken

pictorial [pɪk·'tɔr·i·əl] *adj inv* (*done as picture*) Bild-; (*done like picture*) bildhaft; *book, brochure* illustriert

picture ['pɪk·tʃər] **I.** *n* ❶ (*painting, drawing*) Bild *nt; photograph a.* Foto *nt* ❷ (*on TV screen*) [Fernseh]bild *nt* ❸ FILM **motion ~** Film ❹ (*fig: impression*) Bild *nt;* **this is not an accurate ~** das ist eine Verdrehung der Tatsachen; **mental ~** Vorstellung *f* ❺ (*embodiment*) ■ **the [very] ~ of sth** der Inbegriff einer S. *gen* ▶ PHRASES: **to be in the ~** (*informed*) im Bilde sein; (*involved*) beteiligt sein; **to get the ~** etw verstehen **II.** *vt* (*imagine*) sich *dat* vorstellen; (*depict*) darstellen **III.** *vi* ■ **to ~ to oneself how ...** sich *dat* vorstellen, wie ...

'picture book *n* (*for children*) Bilderbuch *nt;* (*for adults*) Buch *nt* mit Illustrationen

'picture frame *n* Bilderrahmen *m*

'picture library *n* Bildarchiv *nt*

picturesque [ˌpɪk·tʃə·'resk] *adj scenery* malerisch, pittoresk *geh; language* bildhaft

'picture window *n* Panoramafenster *nt*

piddle ['pɪd·əl] *vi* (*vulg*) pinkeln

piddling ['pɪd·lɪŋ] *adj* (*pej vulg*) lächerlich

pidgin ['pɪdʒ·ɪn] **I.** *n* LING Pidgin *nt fachspr* **II.** *adj attr, inv* Pidgin-; **~ German** gebrochenes Deutsch

pie [paɪ] *n* [Obst]torte *f;* **spinach ~** Spinatpastete *f*

piece [pis] **I.** *n* ❶ (*bit*) Stück *nt;* (*part*) Teil *nt o m; of bread* Scheibe *f; of cake* Stück *nt; of glass;* **a ~ of broken glass** eine Glasscherbe; **[all] in one ~** heil; **to break sth in[to]** [*or* **to**] **~s** etw in Stücke brechen; **to fall** [*or* **go**] **to ~s** (*fig*) kaputtgehen; *person* zusammenbrechen; *marriage* zerbrechen; ■ **~ by ~** Stück für Stück ❷ (*item, coin*) Stück *nt;* **~ of baggage** Gepäckstück *nt;* **~ of paper** Blatt *nt* Papier; (*non-physical*) **a ~ of advice** ein Rat *m;* **a ~ of evidence** ein Beweis *m* ❸ (*in chess*) Figur *f;* (*in backgammon, checkers*) Stein *m* ❹ ART, LIT, MUS, THEAT Stück *nt,* Werk *nt;* JOURN Beitrag *m* ❺ (*sl: gun*) Knarre *f fam* ▶ PHRASES: **a ~ of the action** ein Stück *nt* des Kuchens; **to be a ~ of cake** (*fam*) kinderleicht sein; **to give sb a ~ of one's mind** (*fam*) jdm [mal gehörig] die Meinung sagen **II.** *vt* ■ **to ~ together** ⊂ **sth** etw zusammensetzen; (*reconstruct*) etw rekonstruieren

'piecemeal *inv* **I.** *adv* (*bit by bit*) Stück für Stück, stück[chen]weise; (*in fits and starts*) unsystematisch **II.** *adj* (*bit by bit*) stück[chen]weise; (*in fits and starts*) unsystematisch

'piece rate *n* Akkordlohn *m*

'piecework *n* Akkordarbeit *f*

pier [pɪr] *n* ❶ NAUT Pier *m o fachspr f,* Hafendamm *m;* (*dock*) Landungsbrücke *f,* Pier *m* ❷ ARCHIT (*wall support*) Trumeau *m;* (*pillar*) Pfeiler *m*

pierce [pɪrs] *vt* (*make hole in*) durchstechen; (*penetrate*) eindringen (in +*akk*); (*forcefully*) durchstoßen; (*break through*) durchbrechen; **to have ~d ears** Ohrlöcher haben

piercing ['pɪr·sɪŋ] **I.** *adj* ❶ (*loud*) durchdringend; (*pej*) *voice a.* schrill ❷ (*cold*) eisig ❸ (*penetrating*) *eyes, gaze, look* durchdringend, stechend; *question, reply, wit* scharf **II.** *n* (*hole in body*) Piercing *nt*

piety ['paɪ·ə·t̬i] *n* Frömmigkeit *f*

pig [pɪg] *n* ❶ (*animal*) Schwein *nt* ❷ (*fam: greedy person*) Vielfraß *m* ❸ (*pej fam: bad person*) Schwein *nt* ❹ FOOD **~ in a blanket** *in Teig gebackene Wurst*

◆ **pig out** *vi* (*fam*) ■ **to ~ out [on sth]** sich [mit etw *dat*] vollstopfen

pigeon ['pɪdʒ·ən] *n* Taube *f*

'pigeonhole I. *n* [Post]fach *nt,* Ablage *f;* **to put sb/sth in a ~** (*fig*) jdn/etw in eine Schublade stecken **II.** *vt* (*categorize*) in eine Schublade stecken

'pigeon-toed *adj inv* mit einwärtsgerichteten Füßen *nach n;* ■ **to be ~** über den großen Onkel gehen *veraltend fam*

piggish ['pɪg·ɪʃ] *adj* (*pej*) *behavior, manners* schweinisch; *appetite* verfressen

piggy ['pɪg·i] *n* (*fam or childspeak*) Schweinchen *nt*

'piggyback I. *n* **to give sb a ~ [ride]** jdn huckepack nehmen **II.** *vi* huckepack machen

'piggy bank *n* Sparschwein *nt,* Sparbüchse *f; for collection* Sammelbüchse *f*

pig'headed *adj* (*pej*) stur, starrköpfig

'pig iron *n* Roheisen *nt*

piglet ['pɪg·lɪt] *n* Ferkel *nt*

pigment ['pɪg·mənt] *n* Pigment *nt*

pigmentation [ˌpɪg·men·'teɪ·ʃən] *n* Pigmentation *f*

Pigmy ['pɪg·mi] *n, adj see* **Pygmy**

'pigskin I. *n* ❶ (*hide*) Schweinshaut *f* ❷ (*leather*) Schweinsleder *nt* ❸ SPORTS (*fam*) Leder *nt* (*Ball beim American Football*) **II.** *adj bag, belt etc.* Schweinsleder-, schweinsledern

'pigsty *n* (*pej, a. fig*) Schweinestall *m,* Saustall *m pej sl*

'pigtail *n* Zopf *m*

pike¹ [paɪk] *n* MIL, HIST (*weapon*) Spieß *m,* Pike *f*

pike² [paɪk] *n* ZOOL Hecht *m*

pike³ [paɪk] *n short for* **turnpike** Mautstraße *f* ▶ PHRASES: **sth comes down the ~** etw kommt auf uns zu; **it looks like there's a whole lot of trouble coming down the ~** es sieht so aus, als ob da gewaltig Ärger auf uns zukommt

pile¹ [paɪl] **I.** *n* ❶ (*stack*) Stapel *m;* (*fam: heap*)

P

Haufen *m* ❷ (*fam: accumulation*) *of trouble, work* Menge *f* ❸ (*sl: fortune*) Vermögen *nt* **II.** *vt* stapeln (**on[to]** auf +*dat*) **III.** *vi* (*fam*) **to ~ on to the bus** sich in den Bus reindrücken
◆**pile in** *vi* in etw *akk* [hinein]strömen; (*forcefully*) sich in etw *akk* [hinein]drängen
◆**pile on** *vt* anhäufen; **you're really piling on the compliments tonight** du bist ja heute Abend so großzügig mit Komplimenten *hum*
◆**pile up I.** *vi debts, problems* sich anhäufen; (*get more frequent*) sich häufen **II.** *vt* anhäufen
pile² [paɪl] *n* ARCHIT Pfahl *m*
pile³ [paɪl] *n* (*fabric surface*) Flor *m*
'pile driver *n* Ramme *f fachspr*
piles [paɪlz] *npl* (*fam*) *see* **hemorrhoids**
'pile-up *n* ❶ (*fam: crash*) Massenkarambolage *f* ❷ (*accumulation*) Anhäufung *f,* Berg *m fig*
pilfer ['pɪl·fər] *vt, vi* klauen
pilgrim ['pɪl·grɪm] *n* Pilger(in) *m(f)*
pilgrimage ['pɪl·grə·mɪdʒ] *n* REL Pilgerfahrt *f;* (*esp Christian*) Wallfahrt *f* (**to** nach +*dat*)
pill [pɪl] *n* ❶ (*tablet*) Tablette *f* ❷ (*contraceptive*) ■**the ~** die Pille; **to be on the ~** die Pille nehmen
pillage ['pɪl·ɪdʒ] **I.** *vt, vi* (*form*) plündern **II.** *n* (*form*) Plündern *nt*
pillar ['pɪl·ər] *n* ❶ (*column*) Pfeiler *m,* Säule *f* ❷ (*fig: mainstay*) Stütze *f*
'pillbox *n* ❶ (*for tablets*) Pillendose *f* ❷ (*hat*) Pillbox *f o m fachspr*
pillory ['pɪl·ə·ri] **I.** *vt* <-ie-> an den Pranger stellen *a. fig* **II.** *n* Pranger *m*
pillow ['pɪl·oʊ] **I.** *n* ❶ (*for bed*) [Kopf]kissen *nt* ❷ (*decorative cushion*) Kissen *nt* **II.** *vt* **to ~ one's head on sth** seinen Kopf auf etw *akk* legen
'pillowcase *n* [Kopf]kissenbezug *m*
pilot ['paɪ·lət] **I.** *n* ❶ AVIAT Pilot(in) *m(f);* NAUT Lotse, -in *m, f* ❷ TV Pilotfilm *f* ❸ TECH (*pilot light*) Zündflamme *f* **II.** *vt* ❶ AVIAT, NAUT *aircraft* fliegen; *ship* lotsen ❷ (*fig: guide*) durchbringen **III.** *adj usu attr, inv* Pilot-; **a ~ test** ein erster Test
pilot lamp *n* Kontrolllampe *f*
'pilot light *n* ❶ (*flame*) Zündflamme *f* ❷ *see* **pilot lamp**
'pilot program *n* Testreihe *f;* (*model project*) Pilotprojekt *nt*
'pilot's license *n* Pilotenschein *m*
pimento [pɪ·'men·toʊ], **pimiento** [pɪ·'mjen·toʊ] *n* ❶ (*sweet red pepper*) [rote] Paprika ❷ (*spice*) Piment *m o nt*
pimp [pɪmp] **I.** *n* Zuhälter *m* **II.** *vi* als Zuhälter arbeiten; ■**to ~ for sb** jds Zuhälter *m* sein
pimple ['pɪm·pəl] *n* Pickel *m;* (*pustule*) Pustel *f*
pimply ['pɪm·pli] *adj* pickelig
pin [pɪn] **I.** *n* ❶ (*sharp object*) Nadel *f* ❷ (*for clothing*) [Ansteck]nadel *f;* (*brooch*) Brosche *f* **II.** *vt* <-nn-> ❶ (*attach with pin*) befestigen (**[up]on/[on]to** an +*dat*) ❷ (*hold firmly*) **to ~ sb to the floor** jdn auf den Boden drücken; **to be ~ned behind the steering wheel** hinter dem Lenkrad eingeklemmt sein ❸ (*attach blame unfairly*) ■**to ~ sth on sb** etw auf jdn schieben
◆**pin down** *vt* ❶ (*define exactly*) genau definieren; (*locate precisely*) genau bestimmen ❷ (*make decide*) ■**to ~ down** ⊂ **sb [to sth]** jdn [auf etw *akk*] festnageln ❸ (*hold fast*) ■**to ~ down** ⊂ **sb** jdn fest halten
◆**pin up** *vt* anstecken; *hair* hochstecken; **to ~ up pictures** Bilder an die Wand hängen
PIN [pɪn] *n abbrev of* **personal identification number** PIN
pinafore ['pɪn·ə·fɔr] *n* [große] Schürze
'pinball *n* Flipper *m*
pincer ['pɪn·sər] *n* ❶ *usu pl* ZOOL Schere *f,* Zange *f* ❷ (*tool*) ■**~s** *pl* [Kneif]zange *f,* [Beiß]zange *f*
pinch [pɪntʃ] **I.** *vt* ❶ (*nip*) kneifen, zwicken BES. SÜDD, ÖSTERR; (*squeeze*) quetschen ❷ (*sl: steal*) klauen **II.** *vi* kneifen, zwicken; *boots, shoes, slippers* drücken **III.** *n* <*pl* -es> ❶ (*nip*) Kneifen *nt,* Zwicken *nt* ❷ (*small quantity*) Prise *f;* **a ~ of sugar** eine Prise Zucker ▶ PHRASES: **to take sth with a ~ of salt** etw mit Vorsicht genießen
pinched [pɪntʃt] *adj* verhärmt
pinch-'hit *vi* ❶ SPORT einspringen ❷ (*fig*) ■**to ~ for sb** für jdn einspringen
pinch 'hitter *n* ❶ SPORT Ersatzspieler(in) *m(f)* ❷ (*fig*) Ersatz *m,* Lückenbüßer(in) *m(f)*
'pincushion *n* Nadelkissen *nt*
pine¹ [paɪn] **I.** *n* ❶ (*tree*) Kiefer *f* ❷ (*wood*) Kiefer *f,* Kiefernholz *nt* **II.** *adj board, chair, table* aus Kiefer[nholz] *nach n*
pine² [paɪn] *vi* sich sehnen (**for** nach +*dat*)
pineapple ['paɪn·æp·əl] *n* Ananas *f*
'pinecone *n* Kiefernzapfen *m*
'pine needle *n* Kiefernnadel *f*
ping [pɪŋ] **I.** *n* ❶ (*sound*) [kurzes] Klingeln ❷ AUTO **engine ~** Motorklingeln *nt* **II.** *vi* ❶ (*make sound*) [kurz] klingeln; *glass* klirren; (*click*) klicken ❷ AUTO *engine* klingeln
Ping-Pong ['pɪŋ·,paŋ] *n* (*fam*) Tischtennis *nt,* Pingpong *nt*
'pinhead *n* ❶ (*of pin*) Stecknadelkopf *m* ❷ (*pej fam: simpleton*) Blödmann *m*
pinion ['pɪn·jən] *n* TECH Ritzel *nt*
pink [pɪŋk] **I.** *n* Rosa *nt,* Pink *nt* **II.** *adj* (*pale red*) rosa, pink; *cheeks* rosig
pinkie ['pɪŋ·ki] *n* (*fam*) kleiner Finger
pinking shears ['pɪŋ·kɪŋ-] *npl* Zickzackschere *f*
pink slip *n* (*fam*) ❶ (*notice*) Kündigung *f* ❷ AUTO (*ownership document*) Kraftfahrzeugbrief *m*
pinnacle ['pɪn·ə·kəl] *n* ❶ *usu pl of a mountain* Berggipfel *m* ❷ ARCHIT (*on a building*) Fiale *f fachspr* ❸ *usu sing* (*culmination*) *of a career* Höhepunkt *m*
'pinpoint I. *vt* [genau] feststellen **II.** *adj attr, inv* sehr genau, haargenau; **~ accuracy** hohe Genauigkeit; *of missile, shot* hohe Zielgenauigkeit **III.** *n* winziger Punkt

P

'pinprick *n* Nadelstich *m*
'pinstripe *n* (*pattern*) Nadelstreifen *m*
pint [paɪnt] *n* Pint *nt* (*0,473 l*)
'pintsize(d) *adj* (*fam*) winzig; (*fig*) unbedeutend
'pinup *n* ❶ (*picture*) [Star]poster *nt o m* ❷ (*fam: person*) **he's the latest teenage ~** er ist der neueste Teenagerschwarm
pioneer [ˌpaɪ·ə·'nɪr] **I.** *n* Pionier(in) *m(f)* **II.** *vt* den Weg bereiten (für *+akk*)
pioneering [ˌpaɪ·ə·'nɪr·ɪŋ] *adj* bahnbrechend; (*innovative*) innovativ
pious ['paɪ·əs] *adj* ❶ REL (*devout*) fromm ❷ (*commendable*) gut gemeint
pip [pɪp] *n* ❶ (*on playing card*) Farbe *f* ❷ HORT Kern *m*
pipe [paɪp] **I.** *n* ❶ TECH (*tube*) Rohr *nt;* (*small tube*) Röhre *f; for gas, water* Leitung *f* ❷ (*for smoking*) Pfeife *f* ❸ MUS (*instrument*) Flöte *f;* (*in organ*) [Orgel]pfeife *f* **II.** *vt* ❶ (*transport*) *gas, oil, water* leiten ❷ (*speak shrilly*) piepsen; (*loudly*) kreischen **III.** *vi* piepsen; *esp women* zwitschern *oft hum;* (*loudly*) kreischen
◆**pipe down** *vi* (*fam: be quiet*) den Mund halten; (*be quieter*) leiser sein
◆**pipe up** *vi* den Mund aufmachen
'pipe cleaner *n* Pfeifenreiniger *m*
'pipeline *n* Pipeline *f;* **in the ~** (*fig*) in Planung
piper ['paɪ·pər] *n* Dudelsackspieler(in) *m(f)*
piping ['paɪ·pɪŋ] **I.** *n* Paspel *f;* (*on furniture*) Kordel *f;* FOOD Spritzgussverzierung *f* **II.** *adv* **~ hot** kochend heiß
piquant ['pi·kənt] *adj* pikant; (*fig: stimulating*) interessant
pique [pik] **I.** *n* Ärger *m* **II.** *vt* verärgern; **to ~ sb's curiosity** jds Neugier *f* wecken
piracy ['paɪ·rə·si] *n* ❶ (*at sea*) Piraterie *f,* Seeräuberei *f,* Freibeuterei *f* ❷ (*of copyrights*) Raubkopieren *nt;* **video ~** Videopiraterie *f*
pirate ['paɪ·rət] **I.** *n* ❶ (*buccaneer*) Pirat(in) *m(f),* Seeräuber(in) *m(f)* ❷ (*plagiarizer*) Raubkopierer(in) *m(f)* **II.** *adj attr, inv video, CD* raubkopiert **III.** *vt* eine Raubkopie machen (von *+dat*)
pirouette [ˌpɪr·u·'et] **I.** *n* Pirouette *f* **II.** *vi* eine Pirouette drehen
Pisces <*pl* -> ['paɪ·siz] *n* ASTROL ❶ (*sign*) Fische *pl* ❷ (*person*) Fisch *m*
piss [pɪs] (*vulg*) **I.** *n* ❶ (*urine*) Pisse *f derb* ❷ *usu sing* (*action*) Pinkeln *nt fam;* **to take a ~** schiffen *derb* **II.** *vi* pinkeln *fam* **III.** *vt* ■ **to ~ oneself** in die Hose machen
pissed [pɪst] *adj* (*vulg*) [stink]sauer
pissed off [pɪst·ɔf] *adj* ■ **to be ~ at sb** auf jdn sauer sein
pistachio [pɪ·'stæʃ·i·oʊ] *n* Pistazie *f*
pistol ['pɪs·təl] *n* Pistole *f*
piston ['pɪs·tən] *n* Kolben *m*
pit¹ [pɪt] **I.** *n* ❶ (*hole in ground*) Grube *f* ❷ (*mine*) Bergwerk *nt* ❸ (*scar*) Narbe *f;* TECH (*hollow*) Loch *nt;* MED (*in body*) Grube *f,* Höhle *f* ❹ MUS (*orchestral area*) Orchestergraben *m* ❺ SPORTS ■ **the ~s** *pl* die Boxen *pl* ❻ (*sl: the worst*) ■ **the ~s** *pl* das Allerletzte **II.** *vt* <-tt-> ❶ *usu passive* (*marked*) ■ **sth is ~ted [with sth]** etw ist [von etw *dat*] zerfurcht ❷ (*place in competition*) ■ **to ~ sb/sth against sb/sth** *products* etw/jdn gegen etw/jdn ins Rennen schicken; ■ **to ~ oneself against sb/sth** sich mit jdm/etw messen
pit² [pɪt] FOOD **I.** *n* Kern *m* **II.** *vt* <-tt-> entkernen
pita, pita bread ['pi·t̬ə-] *n* Pitabrot *nt*
pitch¹ [pɪtʃ] **I.** *n* <*pl* -es> ❶ (*delivery from pitcher*) Pitch *m,* Wurf *m* ❷ (*tone*) Tonhöhe *f;* (*of a voice*) Stimmlage *f;* (*of an instrument*) Tonlage *f;* (*volume*) Lautstärke *f* ❸ (*persuasion*) [**sales**] **~** [Verkaufs]sprüche *pl a. pej fam* ❹ (*slope*) Schräge *f,* Neigung *f* **II.** *vt* ❶ (*throw*) pitchen, werfen ❷ (*set up*) aufstellen; *tent* aufschlagen ❸ MUS *instrument* stimmen; *song* anstimmen; *note* treffen ❹ (*target*) ■ **to ~ sth at sb** etw auf jdn ausrichten; ■ **to be ~ed at sb** *book, film* sich an jdn richten ❺ (*set*) **to ~ sth at a certain level** etw auf einem bestimmten Niveau ansiedeln ❻ *usu passive* (*slope*) **to be ~ed at 30°** eine Neigung von 30° haben **III.** *vi* ❶ SPORTS (*in baseball*) pitchen, werfen ❷ (*oscillate*) *ship* stampfen *fachspr;* AVIAT absacken
◆**pitch in** *vi* (*fam: contribute*) mit anpacken; (*financially*) zusammenlegen
pitch² [pɪtʃ] *n* (*sticky substance*) Pech *nt*
'pitch-black *adj inv* pechschwarz
pitcher¹ ['pɪtʃ·ər] *n* SPORTS (*in baseball*) Pitcher(in) *m(f) fachspr*
pitcher² ['pɪtʃ·ər] *n* (*jug*) [Henkel]krug *m*
'pitchfork *n* (*for hay*) Heugabel *f;* (*for manure*) Mistgabel *f*
'pitfall *n usu pl* Falle *f; of a subject* Hauptschwierigkeit *f*
pith [pɪθ] *n* ❶ (*of orange, grapefruit, etc.*) weiße Innenhaut ❷ (*in plants*) Mark *nt*
pithy ['pɪθ·i] *adj* ❶ (*succinct*) prägnant ❷ (*of citrus fruits*) dickschalig
pitiable ['pɪt̬·i·ə·bəl] *adj* ❶ (*arousing pity*) bemitleidenswert; (*terrible*) schrecklich ❷ (*pathetic*) lächerlich
pitiful ['pɪt̬·ɪ·fəl] *adj* ❶ (*arousing pity*) bemitleidenswert; *conditions etc.* schrecklich; *sight* traurig ❷ (*unsatisfactory*) jämmerlich
pitiless ['pɪt̬·ɪ·lɪs] *adj* erbarmungslos, unbarmherzig
'pit stop *n* ❶ AUTO Boxenstopp *m* ❷ *usu sing* (*hum: journey break*) Reiseunterbrechung *f*
pittance ['pɪt·əns] *n usu sing* (*pej*) Hungerslohn *m*
pituitary, **pituitary gland** [pɪ·'tu·ɪ·ter·i-] *n* ANAT Hirnanhangsdrüse *f*
pity ['pɪt̬·i] **I.** *n* ❶ (*compassion*) Mitleid *nt;* **to feel ~ for sb** mit jdm Mitleid haben ❷ (*shame*) **what a ~!** wie schade!; ■ **to be a ~** schade sein **II.** *vt* <-ie-> Mitleid haben (mit *+dat*)
pitying ['pɪt̬·i·ɪŋ] *adj* mitleidig; (*condescending*) herablassend
pivot ['pɪv·ət] **I.** *n* ❶ MECH, TECH (*shaft*)

[Dreh]zapfen *m* ❷ (*fig: focal point*) Dreh- und Angelpunkt *m* **II.** *vi* ■ **to ~ around sth** ❶ (*a. fig: revolve*) kreisen (um +*akk*) ❷ (*fig: depend on*) abhängen (von +*dat*)

pivotal [ˈpɪv·ə·t̬əl] *adj* Schlüssel-, Haupt-

pixel [ˈpɪk·səl] *n* Pixel *nt fachspr*

pixelate, pixellate [ˈpɪk·sə·leɪt] *vt* COMPUT verpixeln

pixie [ˈpɪk·si] *n* Kobold *m*

pizza [ˈpit·sə] *n* Pizza *nt*

placard [ˈplæk·ard] *n* Plakat *nt;* (*at demonstrations a.*) Transparent *nt*

placate [ˈpleɪ·keɪt] *vt* (*soothe*) beruhigen; (*appease*) beschwichtigen

place [pleɪs] **I.** *n* ❶ (*location*) Ort *m;* **this is the exact ~!** das ist genau die Stelle!; **this café is a nice ~** dieses Café ist echt nett *fam;* **~ of birth** Geburtsort *m;* **~ of work** Arbeitsplatz *m;* **in ~s** stellenweise ❷ (*home*) **I'm looking for a ~ to live** ich bin auf Wohnungssuche; **your ~ or mine?** zu dir oder zu mir? ❸ (*fig: position, rank*) Stellung *f;* **to put sb in his/her ~** jdm zeigen, wo es lang geht *fam;* **if I were in your ~ ...** ich an deiner Stelle ..., wenn ich du wäre ... ❹ (*proper position*) ■ **to be in ~** an seinem Platz sein; (*fig: completed*) fertig sein; *arrangements* abgeschlossen; **the chairs were all in ~** die Stühle waren alle dort, wo sie sein sollten; **suddenly it all fell into ~** (*fig*) plötzlich machte alles Sinn; **to be out of ~** nicht an der richtigen Stelle sein; *person* fehl am Platz[e] sein ❺ MATH (*in decimals*) Stelle *f* ❻ (*job, position*) Stelle *f;* (*seat, on team*) Platz *m;* **to take the ~ of sb** jds Platz *m* einnehmen; **to keep sb's ~** jdm den Platz freihalten ❼ (*ranking*) Platz *m,* Position *f;* **to take first ~** (*fig*) an erster Stelle kommen ▶ PHRASES: **in the <u>first</u> ~** (*at first*) zuerst; (*at all*) überhaupt; **in the <u>first</u>/<u>second</u> ~** (*firstly, secondly*) erstens/zweitens; **to <u>go</u> ~s** (*fam*) weit kommen, es zu etw *dat* bringen; **to <u>take</u> ~** stattfinden **II.** *vt* ❶ (*position*) ■ **to ~ sth somewhere** etw irgendwohin stellen; (*lay*) etw irgendwohin legen; **to ~ an ad in the paper** eine Anzeige in die Zeitung setzen; **to ~ a bet on sth** auf etw *akk* wetten ❷ (*impose*) *embargo* verhängen (**on** über +*akk*); **to ~ a limit on sth** etw begrenzen ❸ (*ascribe*) **to ~ the blame on sb** jdm die Schuld geben; **to ~ one's faith in sb/sth** sein Vertrauen in jdn/etw setzen; **to ~ importance on sth** auf etw *akk* Wert legen ❹ (*put in certain condition*) **to ~ sb under arrest** jdn festnehmen; **to ~ sb under surveillance** jdn unter Beobachtung stellen ❺ (*appoint to a position*) **to ~ sb in charge [of sth]** jdm die Leitung [von etw *dat*] übertragen ❻ (*accommodate*) ■ **to ~ sb/sth somewhere** jdn/etw irgendwo unterbringen [*o* SCHWEIZ platzieren] ❼ (*recognize*) *face, person, voice, accent* einordnen **III.** *vi* SPORTS sich platzieren; (*finish first or second*) **to bet [a horse] to ~** eine Platzwette abschließen

placebo [plə·ˈsi·boʊ] *n* MED Placebo *nt;* (*fig*) Ablenkungsmanöver *nt*

ˈplace kick *n* SPORTS Place-Kick *m,* Platzkick *m*

ˈplace mat *n* Set *nt o m,* Platzdeckchen *nt*

placement [ˈpleɪs·mənt] **I.** *n* ❶ (*being placed*) Platzierung *f;* *of building* Lage *f* ❷ (*by job service*) Vermittlung *f;* (*job itself*) Stelle *f* **II.** *adj attr, inv* Einstufungs-; **~ service** Stellenvermittlung *f*

ˈplace name *n* Ortsname *m*

placenta <*pl* -s *or* -tae> [plə·ˈsen·tə] *n* Plazenta *f*

placid [ˈplæs·ɪd] *adj* ruhig, friedlich; *person a.* gelassen

plagiarism [ˈpleɪ·dʒə·rɪz·əm] *n* geistiger Diebstahl

plagiarize [ˈpleɪ·dʒə·raɪz] **I.** *vt* ■ **to ~ sth** etw plagiieren *form* **II.** *vi* abschreiben (**from** aus +*dat*)

plague [pleɪg] **I.** *n* ❶ (*disease*) Seuche *f;* ■ **the ~** die Pest; **to avoid sb/sth like the ~** jdn/etw wie die Pest meiden ❷ *of insects* Plage *f* **II.** *vt* bedrängen; (*irritate*) ärgern; ■ **to be ~d with sth** von etw *dat* geplagt werden

plaice <*pl* -> [pleɪs] *n* Doggerscharbe *f*

plaid [plæd] **I.** *n* FASHION Schottenmuster *nt* **II.** *adj attr, inv* kariert

plain [pleɪn] **I.** *adj* ❶ (*simple, uncomplicated*) einfach; (*not flavored*) natur *nach n;* **~ and simple** ganz einfach ❷ (*clear*) klar, offensichtlich; **to make sth ~** etw klarstellen; **to make oneself plain** sich klar ausdrücken ❸ (*unattractive*) unscheinbar **II.** *adv* ❶ (*simply*) ohne großen Aufwand ❷ (*fam: downright*) einfach **III.** *n* GEOG Ebene *f*

ˈplainclothes *adj attr, inv* Zivil-, in Zivil

plainly [ˈpleɪn·li] *adv* ❶ (*simply*) einfach, schlicht ❷ (*clearly*) deutlich, klar; (*obviously*) offensichtlich

plainness [ˈpleɪn·nɪs] *n* ❶ (*simplicity*) Einfachheit *f,* Schlichtheit *f* ❷ (*obviousness*) Eindeutigkeit *f,* Klarheit *f* ❸ (*unattractiveness*) Unscheinbarkeit *f,* Unansehnlichkeit *f*

plain ˈsailing *n* (*fig*) ■ **to be ~** wie geschmiert laufen *fam*

plainˈspoken *adj* **he's very ~** er ist sehr direkt

plaintiff [ˈpleɪn·tɪf] *n* Kläger(in) *m(f)*

plaintive [ˈpleɪn·tɪv] *adj* klagend; (*wistful*) melancholisch; *voice* traurig

plan [plæn] **I.** *n* ❶ *a.* ECON (*detailed scheme*) Plan *m;* **to go according to ~** wie geplant verlaufen ❷ (*intention*) Plan *m,* Absicht *f;* **what are your ~s for this weekend?** was hast du dieses Wochenende vor? ❸ (*diagram*) Plan *m;* (*drawing*) ■ **~s** *pl* Pläne *pl* **II.** *vt* <-nn-> ❶ (*draft, envisage*) planen ❷ (*prepare*) vorbereiten ❸ (*intend*) vorhaben **III.** *vi* ❶ (*prepare*) planen; **to ~ for retirement** Vorkehrungen für das Rentenalter treffen ❷ ■ **to ~ on sth** (*expect*) mit etw *dat* rechnen; (*intend*) etw vorhaben

plane[1] [pleɪn] **I.** *n* ❶ (*aircraft*) Flugzeug *nt;* **by ~** mit dem Flugzeug ❷ MATH Ebene *f* ❸ (*surface*) Fläche *f* ❹ (*level*) Ebene *f,* Niveau *nt*

II. *adj attr, inv* flach, eben
plane² [pleɪn] **I.** *n* Hobel *m* **II.** *vt* hobeln; (*until smooth*) abhobeln
plane³ [pleɪn] *n* (*tree*) Platane *f*
'plane crash *n* Flugzeugunglück *nt*
planet ['plæn·ɪt] *n* Planet *m;* **to be from a different ~** (*fig*) aus einer anderen Welt sein
planetary ['plæn·ɪ·ter·i] *adj inv* planetarisch *geh*
plank [plæŋk] *n* ❶ (*timber*) Brett *nt,* Latte *f;* (*in house*) Diele *f;* NAUT Planke *f* ❷ (*fig: support element*) Pfeiler *m*
plankton ['plæŋk·tən] *n* Plankton *nt*
planner ['plæ·nər] *n* Planer(in) *m(f)*
planning ['plæ·nɪŋ] **I.** *n* Planung *f* **II.** *adj* Planungs-; **in the ~ stage[s]** in der Planung[sphase]
plant [plænt] **I.** *n* ❶ (*organism*) Pflanze *f;* **house ~** Zimmerpflanze *f* ❷ (*factory*) Werk *nt,* Betrieb *m* ❸ (*machinery*) Maschinen *pl* **II.** *vt* ❶ (*put in earth*) pflanzen ❷ (*lodge*) platzieren; **to ~ oneself on the sofa** (*fam*) sich aufs Sofa pflanzen ❸ (*fam: frame*) [heimlich] platzieren; ■**to ~ sth on sb** jdm etw unterschieben
plantain ['plæn·tɪn] *n* FOOD, BOT Kochbanane *f*
plantation [plæn·'teɪ·ʃən] *n* ❶ (*estate*) Plantage *f* ❷ (*plants*) Pflanzung *f;* (*trees*) Schonung *f*
planter ['plæn·tər] *n* ❶ (*plantation owner*) Pflanzer(in) *m(f)* ❷ (*container*) Blumentopf *m;* (*stand*) Blumenständer *m* ❸ (*machine*) Pflanzmaschine *f;* (*for sowing*) Sämaschine *f*
plaque [plæk] *n* ❶ (*plate*) Tafel *f;* **brass ~** Messingschild *nt;* **commemorative ~** Gedenktafel *f* ❷ MED [Zahn]belag *m*
plasma ['plæz·mə] **I.** *n no pl* MED, PHYS, ASTRON Plasma *nt* **II.** *adj cell, donation, donor* Plasma-; **~screen** Plasmabildschirm *m*
plaster ['plæs·tər] **I.** *n* ❶ ARCHIT [Ver]putz *m* ❷ *see* **plaster of Paris II.** *vt* ❶ (*mortar*) verputzen; **the rain had ~ed her hair to her head** (*fig*) durch den Regen klebte ihr das Haar am Kopf ❷ (*fam: put all over*) vollkleistern
'plaster cast *n* ❶ ART Gipsabguss *m* ❷ *see* **cast I. 3**
plastered ['plæs·tərd] *adj pred* (*fam*) stockbesoffen; **to get ~** sich zusaufen
plaster of 'Paris *n* Gips *m*
plastic ['plæs·tɪk] **I.** *n* ❶ (*material*) Plastik *nt kein pl* ❷ (*industry*) ■**~s** *pl* Kunststoffindustrie *f* ❸ (*fam: credit cards*) Plastikgeld *nt* **II.** *adj* ❶ *inv* (*of plastic*) Plastik- ❷ (*pej: artificial*) künstlich; (*false a.*) unecht; *smile* aufgesetzt ❸ (*malleable*) formbar
plastic 'bag *n* Plastiktüte *f*
plastic 'bullet *n* Gummigeschoss *nt*
plastic ex'plosive *n* Plastiksprengstoff *m*
plastic 'money *n* Plastikgeld *nt fam*
plastic 'surgery *n* Schönheitschirurgie *f*
'plastic wrap *n* Frischhaltefolie *f*
plate [pleɪt] **I.** *n* ❶ (*dish*) Teller *m* ❷ (*metal layer*) Überzug *m;* **chrome ~** Verchromung *f;* **gold ~** Vergoldung *f* ❸ AUTO **license ~** Nummernschild *nt* **II.** *vt* überziehen
plateau <*pl* -s *or* -x> [plæ·'toʊ] *n* ❶ GEOG (*upland*) [Hoch]plateau *nt* ❷ ECON (*flat period*) Stagnation *f;* (*stabilization*) Stabilisierung *f;* **to reach a ~** stagnieren
plated ['pleɪ·t̬ɪd] *adj inv* überzogen; **~ with chrome/gold/silver** verchromt/vergoldet/versilbert
plateful ['pleɪt·fʊl] *n* Teller *m;* **a ~ of lasagna** ein Teller *m* [voll] Lasagne
plate 'glass *n* Flachglas *nt fachspr*
platform ['plæt·fɔrm] *n* ❶ (*elevated area*) Plattform *f;* (*raised structure*) Turm *m* ❷ RAIL Bahnsteig *m* ❸ (*stage*) Podium *nt* ❹ (*opportunity to voice views*) Plattform *f*
platform 'shoes *npl* Plateauschuhe *pl*
plating ['pleɪ·t̬ɪŋ] *n* Überzug *m;* **chrome/gold/silver ~** Verchromung/Vergoldung/Versilberung *f*
platinum ['plæt·nəm] *n* Platin *nt*
platitude ['plæt̬·ɪ·tud] *n* (*pej*) Plattitüde *f geh*
platonic [plə·'tan·ɪk] *adj* platonisch
platoon [plə·'tun] *n* MIL Zug *m*
platter ['plæt̬·ər] *n* ❶ (*serving dish*) Platte *f* ❷ (*meal*) Platte *f;* (*main course*) Teller *m;* **seafood ~** Meeresfrüchteplatte
plausibility [ˌplɔ·zə·'bɪl·ɪ·t̬i] *n* Plausibilität *f; of an argument* Schlagkraft *f*
plausible ['plɔ·zə·bəl] *adj* plausibel; *person* glaubhaft
play [pleɪ] **I.** *n* ❶ (*recreation*) Spiel *nt;* **to be at ~** spielen ❷ SPORTS (*action during game*) Spiel *nt* ❸ SPORTS (*move*) Spielzug *m* ❹ THEAT [Theater]stück *nt;* **radio ~** Hörspiel *nt* ❺ (*space for movement*) Spielraum *m* **II.** *vi* ❶ MUS, SPORTS spielen; **to ~ for money** um Geld spielen ❷ THEAT *actor* spielen ❸ (*move*) **a smile ~ed across his lips** ein Lächeln spielte um seine Lippen ▶ PHRASES: **to ~ for time** versuchen, Zeit zu gewinnen **III.** *vt* ❶ (*take part in*) spielen; **to ~ cards** Karten spielen ❷ (*compete against*) ■**to ~ sb** gegen jdn spielen ❸ MUS spielen; **to ~ the violin** Geige spielen ❹ *CD, tape* [ab]spielen; **to ~ one's stereo** seine Anlage anhaben ❺ MUS, THEAT **to ~ a part** eine Rolle spielen; **to ~ the lead** die Hauptrolle spielen ❻ (*pretend to be*) **to ~ cowboys and indians** Cowboy und Indianer spielen ❼ (*gamble*) **to ~ the stock market** an der Börse spekulieren ❽ (*perpetrate*) **to ~ a trick on sb** jdn hochnehmen *fig fam;* (*practical joke*) [jdm] einen Streich spielen ❾ (*execute*) **to ~ a shot** schießen; (*in pool*) stoßen; ■**to ~ the ball** den Ball spielen ▶ PHRASES: **to ~ ball** (*sl*) mitspielen *fam;* **to ~ one's cards right** geschickt taktieren; **to ~ havoc with sth** etw durcheinanderbringen; **to ~ dumb** sich taub stellen; **to ~ it safe** auf Nummer sicher gehen
◆**play along** *vi* ■**to ~ along with sth** etw [zum Schein] mitmachen
◆**play around** *vi* ❶ (*mess around*) *children*

spielen; **stop ~ing around!** hör mir dem Blödsinn auf! *fam* ❷ (*pej fam: pretend to be attracted to*) ■**to ~ around with sb** mit jdm [herum]spielen ❸ (*experiment*) ■**to ~ around with sth** mit etw *dat* [herum]spielen; (*try out*) etw ausprobieren; **to ~ around with ideas** etw in Gedanken durchspielen

◆**play back** *vt* noch einmal abspielen

◆**play down** *vt* herunterspielen

◆**play off** *vt* ■**to ~ off** ↻ **sb against sb** jdn gegen jdn ausspielen

◆**play on** *vi* ❶ (*exploit*) ■**to ~ on sth** etw ausnutzen ❷ MUS, SPORTS (*keep playing*) weiterspielen

◆**play out** **I.** *vt* ❶ *usu passive* (*take place*) ■**to be ~ed out** *scene* sich abspielen ❷ (*act out*) umsetzen ❸ (*play to end*) *a play, scene* [zu Ende] spielen; **to ~ out the last few seconds** SPORTS die letzten Sekunden spielen **II.** *vi* zu Ende gehen

◆**play through** *vt* MUS [von Anfang bis Ende] [durch]spielen; **to ~ through a series of pieces** eine Reihe von Stücken spielen

◆**play up** **I.** *vt* hochspielen **II.** *vi* (*fam*) ■**to ~ up to sb** sich bei jdm einschmeicheln

◆**play upon** *vi* (*form*) *see* **play on**

◆**play with** **I.** *vi* ❶ (*entertain oneself with*) ■**to ~ with sth** mit etw *dat* spielen ❷ (*play together*) ■**to ~ with sb** mit jdm spielen ❸ (*manipulate nervously*) ■**to ~ with sth** mit etw *dat* herumspielen *fam* ❹ (*consider*) **to ~ with an idea** mit einem Gedanken spielen **II.** *vt* (*vulg, fam*) ■**to ~ with oneself** an sich *dat* herumspielen

'**playback** *n* ❶ (*pre-recorded version*) Playback *nt* ❷ (*replaying*) Wiederholung *f* einer Aufnahme

'**playbill** *n* ❶ (*poster*) Theaterplakat *nt* ❷ (*program*) Theaterprogramm *nt*

'**playboy** *n* (*usu pej*) Playboy *m*

player ['pleɪ·ər] *n* ❶ SPORTS Spieler(in) *m(f)*; **baseball ~** Baseballspieler(in) *m(f)* ❷ (*musical performer*) Spieler(in) *m(f)*; **cello ~** Cellist(in) *m(f)* ❸ (*playback machine*) **CD ~** CD-Player *m* ❹ POL (*participant*) ■**to be a ~** eine Rolle spielen; **a key ~** Schlüsselfigur *f* ❺ (*sl: cool person*) Hecht *m sl*

playful ['pleɪ·fəl] *adj* ❶ (*not serious*) spielerisch, scherzhaft ❷ (*frolicsome*) verspielt; **he was in a ~ mood** er war zum Spielen/Scherzen aufgelegt

'**playground** *n* Spielplatz *m*

'**playhouse** *n* ❶ (*theater*) Theater *nt* ❷ (*toy house*) Spielhaus *nt* (*für Kinder*)

playing card ['pleɪ·ɪŋ-] *n* Spielkarte *f*

playing field ['pleɪ·ɪŋ-] *n* Sportplatz *m*, [Spiel]feld *nt*

'**playmate** *n* (*for child*) Spielkamerad(in) *m(f)*

'**playoff** **I.** *n* Play-off *nt* **II.** *adj* **~ game** Playoff-Spiel *nt*, Entscheidungsspiel *nt*

'**playpen** *n* Laufstall *m*

'**playroom** *n* Spielzimmer *nt*

'**playsuit** *n* Spielanzug *m*

'**plaything** *n* ❶ (*toy*) Spielzeug *nt* ❷ (*pej*) *of force, power* Spielball *m fig*; **to treat sb as a ~** jdn wie eine Sache behandeln

'**playtime** *n* (*in school*) Pause *f*

'**playwright** *n* Dramatiker(in) *m(f)*

plaza ['pla·zə] *n* ❶ (*open square*) Marktplatz *m* ❷ (*for shopping*) [**shopping**] **~** Einkaufszentrum *nt*

plea [pli] *n* ❶ (*appeal*) Appell *m*; (*entreaty*) [flehentliche] Bitte; **to make a ~ for mercy** um Gnade bitten ❷ LAW [Sach]einwand *m*; **to enter a ~** eine Einrede erheben

'**plea bargaining** *n* LAW *Vereinbarung zwischen Staatsanwalt und Angeklagtem, der sich zu einem geringeren Straftatbestand bekennen soll*

plead <pleaded *or* pled, pleaded *or* pled> [plid] **I.** *vi* ❶ (*implore*) [flehentlich] bitten, flehen; **to ~ for forgiveness** um Verzeihung bitten; ■**to ~ with sb** [**to do sth**] jdn anflehen [, etw zu tun] ❷ LAW (*as advocate*) plädieren; (*speak for*) ■**to ~ for sb** jdn verteidigen ❸ + *adj* LAW (*answer charge*) **to ~ guilty** sich schuldig bekennen **II.** *vt* ❶ (*claim*) behaupten; **to ~ ignorance** sich auf Unkenntnis berufen; **to ~ insanity** LAW auf Unzurechnungsfähigkeit plädieren ❷ (*argue for*) **to ~ a case** LAW eine Sache vor Gericht vertreten

pleading ['pli·dɪŋ] *adj* flehend

pleasant ['plez·ənt] *adj* ❶ *day, experience* angenehm, schön; *chat, smile* nett ❷ (*friendly*) freundlich (**to** zu +*dat*), liebenswürdig

pleasantry ['plez·ən·tri] *n usu pl* Kompliment *nt*

please [pliz] **I.** *interj* ❶ (*in requests*) bitte ❷ (*when accepting sth*) ja, bitte; **more potatoes? — ~** noch Kartoffeln? – gern; **may I ...? — ~ do** darf ich ...? – selbstverständlich **II.** *vt* (*make happy*) ■**to ~ sb** jdm gefallen; **I'll do it to ~ you** ich mache es nur dir zuliebe; **to be hard to ~** schwer zufrieden zu stellen sein **III.** *vi* ❶ (*be agreeable*) **eager to ~** [unbedingt] gefallen wollen ❷ (*wish*) **to do as one ~s** machen, was man möchte

pleased [plizd] *adj* ❶ (*happy*) froh, erfreut; (*content*) zufrieden; ■**to be ~ about sth** sich über etw *akk* freuen; ■**to be ~ that ...** froh sein, dass ... ❷ (*willing*) **I'm ~ to help** ich helfe wirklich gerne

pleasing ['pli·zɪŋ] *adj* angenehm; **to be ~ to the ear** hübsch klingen

pleasurable ['pleʒ·ər·ə·bəl] *adj* angenehm

pleasure ['pleʒ·ər] *n* ❶ (*enjoyment*) Freude *f*, Vergnügen *nt*; **to give sb ~** jdm Freude bereiten; **to take ~ in doing sth** Vergnügen daran finden, etw *akk* zu tun ❷ (*source of enjoyment*) Freude *f*; **please don't mention it; it was a ~** nicht der Rede wert, das habe ich doch gern getan

pleat [plit] *n* Falte *f*

pled [pled] *vi, vt pt, pp of* **plead**

pledge [pledʒ] **I.** *n* ❶ (*promise*) Versprechen *nt*; **to make a ~ that ...** geloben, dass ...

❷ (*token*) **a ~ of loyalty** ein Unterpfand *nt* der Treue ❸ (*promise of donation*) Spendenzusage *f* ❹ LAW (*deposit*) Pfand *nt* **II.** *vt* versprechen; **to ~ allegiance to one's country** den Treueid auf sein Land leisten

plentiful ['plen·tɪ·fəl] *adj* reichlich *präd;* **~ supply** großes Angebot

plenty ['plen·ti] **I.** *n* (*form: abundance*) Reichtum *m;* **to live in ~** im Überfluss leben **II.** *adv inv* (*fam*) **I'm ~ warm [enough]** mir ist warm genug, fast schon zu warm; **~ more** noch viel mehr **III.** *pron* ❶ (*more than enough*) mehr als genug; **he's had ~ of opportunities to apologize** er hatte genügend Gelegenheiten, sich zu entschuldigen; **~ of money/time** viel Geld/Zeit ❷ (*a lot*) genug; **~ to see** viel zu sehen; **this car cost me ~** (*fam*) dieses Auto hat mich eine Stange Geld gekostet

plethora ['pleθ·ər·ə] *n* ■ **a ~ of sth** eine Fülle von etw *dat;* (*oversupply*) ein Übermaß *nt* an etw *dat*

pleurisy ['plʊr·ɪ·si] *n* MED Rippenfellentzündung *f*

pliable ['plaɪ·ə·bəl] *adj* biegsam; (*fig: easily influenced*) gefügig

pliers ['plaɪ·ərz] *npl* Zange *f;* **a pair of ~** eine Zange

plight[1] [plaɪt] *n* Not[lage] *f*

plight[2] [plaɪt] *vt* **to ~ one's troth** (*hum dated: get engaged*) sich *dat* die Treue schwören *veraltet*

plod [plad] **I.** *n* Marsch *m* **II.** *vi* <-dd-> ❶ (*walk slowly*) stapfen ❷ (*work slowly*) ■ **to ~ through sth** sich durch etw *akk* hindurcharbeiten

◆**plod away** *vi* vor sich *akk* hin arbeiten; **to ~ away at sth** etw [freudlos] tun; (*work hard*) schuften *pej fam*

plop [plap] **I.** *n* Platsch[er] *m fam;* **it fell into the water with a ~** es platschte ins Wasser **II.** *vi* <-pp-> ❶ (*fall into liquid*) platschen *fam* ❷ (*drop heavily*) plumpsen *fam*

plot [plat] **I.** *n* ❶ (*conspiracy*) Verschwörung *f* (**against** gegen +*akk*); **to hatch a ~** einen Plan aushecken ❷ LIT (*story line*) Handlung *f* ❸ (*of land*) Parzelle *f;* **vegetable ~** Gemüsebeet *nt* **II.** *vt* <-tt-> ❶ (*conspire*) [im Geheimen] planen *a. hum* ❷ (*mark out*) [graphisch] darstellen **III.** *vi* <-tt-> ■ **to ~ against sb/sth** sich gegen jdn/etw verschwören; ■ **to ~ to do sth** (*a. hum*) planen, etw zu tun

◆**plot out** *vt* ❶ *route* [grob] planen ❷ *scene, story* umreißen

plotter ['plat̬·ər] *n* ❶ (*conspirator*) Verschwörer(in) *m(f)* ❷ COMPUT Plotter *m*

plow [plaʊ] **I.** *n* Pflug *m* **II.** *vt* ❶ AGR pflügen ❷ (*move with difficulty*) **to ~ one's way through sth** sich *dat* seinen Weg durch etw *akk* bahnen; (*fig*) sich durch etw *akk* [hindurch] wühlen *fig* **III.** *vi* ❶ AGR pflügen ❷ (*move with difficulty*) ■ **to ~ through sth** sich durch etw *akk* durchkämpfen; (*fig*) sich durch etw *akk* [hindurch] wühlen *fig*

◆**plow into I.** *vi* ■ **to ~ into sth** in etw *akk* hineinrasen **II.** *vt* ■ **to ~ sth into sth** etw in etw *akk* investieren

◆**plow up** *vt land* umpflügen; *lawn* umgraben

ploy [plɔɪ] *n* Plan *m,* Strategie *f;* (*trick*) Trick *m*

pluck [plʌk] **I.** *n* Mut *m,* Schneid *m o* ÖSTERR *f fam* **II.** *vt* ❶ (*pick*) ■ **to ~ sth [from sth]** *fruit, flower* etw [von etw *dat*] abpflücken; *grass, dead leaves* etw [von etw *dat*] abzupfen ❷ *feathers* ausrupfen; *hair* entfernen; *chicken, goose* rupfen ❸ MUS zupfen **III.** *vi* zupfen (**at** an +*dat*)

◆**pluck up** *vt* **to ~ up the courage [to do sth]** allen Mut zusammennehmen[, um etw zu tun]

plucky ['plʌk·i] *adj* schneidig

plug [plʌg] **I.** *n* ❶ (*connector*) Stecker *m;* **to pull the ~ [on sth]** den Stecker [aus etw *dat*] herausziehen; **the administration has pulled the ~ on this project** (*fig*) die Verwaltung hat diesem Projekt ihre Unterstützung aufgekündigt ❷ (*socket*) Steckdose *f* ❸ (*for sink*) Stöpsel *m* ❹ (*stopper*) Pfropfen *m* ❺ (*spark plug*) Zündkerze *f* **II.** *vt* <-gg-> ❶ *hole, leak* stopfen, [zu]stopfen (**with** mit +*dat*) ❷ (*publicize*) anpreisen ❸ (*sl: shoot*) treffen (*mit einer Gewehr-, Pistolenkugel*)

◆**plug away** *vi* verbissen arbeiten (**at** an +*dat*), sich abmühen (**at** mit +*dat*)

◆**plug in I.** *vt* einstöpseln **II.** *vi* (*electrical device*) sich anschließen lassen

◆**plug up** *vt* zustopfen

'plug-in *n see* **add-in**

plum [plʌm] **I.** *n* ❶ (*fruit*) Pflaume *f* ❷ (*tree*) **~ [tree]** Pflaumenbaum *m* ❸ (*color*) Pflaumenblau *nt* **II.** *adj* ❶ *pie, pit* Pflaumen-; **~ jam** Pflaumenmus *nt* ❷ *inv* (*color*) pflaumenfarben ❸ *attr* (*desirable*) traumhaft *fam;* **~ job** Traumberuf *m*

plumage ['plu·mɪdʒ] *n* Federkleid *nt*

plumb[1] [plʌm] **I.** *vt* ❶ (*determine depth*) [aus]loten ❷ (*fig: fathom*) ergründen **II.** *adj pred, inv* gerade, im Lot *fachspr* **III.** *adv* ❶ (*fam: squarely*) genau ❷ (*fam: completely*) **~ crazy** total verrückt **IV.** *n* Lot *nt;* **to be out of ~** nicht im Lot sein

plumb[2] [plʌm] *vt* ■ **to ~ sth into sth** etw an etw *akk* anschließen

'plumb bob *n* Lot *nt*

plumber ['plʌm·ər] *n* Klempner(in) *m(f),* Sanitär(in) *m(f)* SCHWEIZ

plumbing ['plʌm·ɪŋ] *n* Wasserleitungen *pl*

plume [plum] *n* ❶ (*large feather*) Feder *f;* **tail ~** Schwanzfeder *f;* (*as ornament*) Federbusch *m* ❷ (*cloud*) **~ of smoke** Rauchwolke *f*

plummet ['plʌm·ɪt] **I.** *vi* ❶ (*plunge*) fallen ❷ *prices* in den Keller purzeln *fam; morale* auf den Nullpunkt sinken **II.** *n see* **plumb bob**

plump [plʌmp] **I.** *adj* (*rounded*) rund; (*euph*) *person* füllig, mollig; *arms* rundlich; *cheeks* rund **II.** *vt cushion, pillow* aufschütteln

◆**plump down** (*fam*) **I.** *vt* ■ **to ~ down** ↻ **sth** etw hinplumpsen lassen *fam;* **to ~ oneself**

P

down on the sofa sich aufs Sofa fallen lassen **II.** *vi* **to ~ down in a chair** sich auf einen Stuhl fallen lassen

◆**plump up** *vt cushion, pillow* aufschütteln

plumpness ['plʌmp·nɪs] *n* Fülligkeit *f; fruit* Größe *f*

plunder ['plʌn·dər] **I.** *vt gold, treasure* plündern; *palace, village* [aus]plündern; (*fig*) *the planet, environment* ausbeuten **II.** *vi* plündern **III.** *n* ❶ (*booty*) Beute *f* ❷ (*act of plundering*) Plünderung *f; of planet* Ausbeutung *f*

plunderer ['plʌn·dər·ər] *n* Plünderer, Plünderin *m, f*

plunge [plʌndʒ] **I.** *n* ❶ (*drop*) Sprung *m;* (*fall*) Sturz *m,* Fall *m;* (*dive*) **to make a ~** tauchen ❷ (*sharp decline*) Sturz *m;* **a ~ in value** dramatischer Wertverlust **II.** *vi* ❶ (*fall*) stürzen (**into** in +*akk*); **to ~ to one's death** in den Tod stürzen ❷ (*decrease dramatically*) dramatisch sinken ❸ (*fig: begin abruptly*) ■**to ~ into sth** sich in etw *akk* [hinein]stürzen *fig* **III.** *vt* ❶ (*immerse*) ■**to ~ sth into sth** etw in etw *akk* eintauchen; (*in cooking*) etw in etw *akk* geben ❷ (*thrust*) **to ~ a dagger into sb** jdn mit einem Dolch stechen

◆**plunge in** **I.** *vi* ❶ (*dive in*) eintauchen ❷ (*fig: get involved*) sich einmischen; (*do without preparation*) ins kalte Wasser springen *fig* **II.** *vt knife* reinstechen; *hand* reinstecken

plunger ['plʌn·dʒər] *n* Saugpumpe *f*

plunk [plʌŋk] **I.** *n* (*fam: sound*) Ploppen *nt* **II.** *adv* (*fam*) dumpf knallend; **I heard something go ~** ich hörte, wie etwas plopp machte **III.** *vt* (*fam*) ❶ (*set down heavily*) ■**to ~ sth somewhere** etw irgendwo hinknallen ❷ (*sit heavily*) **to ~ oneself down on a chair/sofa** sich auf einen Stuhl/ein Sofa plumpsen lassen

◆**plunk down** (*fam*) **I.** *vt* ■**to ~ down** ⊂ **sth** etw hinknallen; ■**to ~ oneself down** sich hinplumpsen lassen **II.** *vi* sich fallen lassen

pluperfect ['plu·ˌpɜr·fɪkt] **I.** *adj inv* LING Plusquamperfekt-; **the ~ tense** das Plusquamperfekt **II.** *n* LING ■**the ~** das Plusquamperfekt

plural ['plʊr·əl] **I.** *n* ■**the ~** der Plural; **in the ~** im Plural **II.** *adj inv* ❶ LING Plural-, pluralisch ❷ (*multiple*) mehrfach *attr*

pluralism ['plʊr·ə·lɪz·əm] *n* Pluralismus *m geh*

pluralistic [ˌplʊr·ə·'lɪs·tɪk] *adj* pluralistisch *geh*

plus [plʌs] **I.** *prep* plus **II.** *n* <*pl* -es *or pl* -ses> Plus *nt kein pl fam; a.* MATH Pluszeichen *nt;* (*advantage a.*) Pluspunkt *m* **III.** *adj inv* ❶ *attr* (*above zero*) plus; **~ two degrees** zwei Grad plus ❷ *pred* (*or more*) mindestens; **20 ~** mindestens 20 ❸ (*slightly better than*) **A ~** ≈ Eins plus *f*

plush [plʌʃ] **I.** *adj* ❶ (*luxurious*) exklusiv ❷ (*made of plush*) Plüsch- **II.** *n* Plüsch *m*

'**plus sign** *n* Pluszeichen *nt*

Pluto ['plu·t̬oʊ] *n* Pluto *m*

plutocrat ['plu·t̬ə·kræt] *n* (*rich and powerful person*) Plutokrat(in) *m(f) geh*

plutonium [plu·'toʊ·ni·əm] *n* Plutonium *nt*

ply¹ [plaɪ] *n* ❶ (*thickness*) Stärke *f,* Dicke *f* ❷ (*layer*) Schicht *f* ❸ (*strand*) **two-~ rope** zweilagiges Seil

ply² <-ie-> [plaɪ] *vt* ❶ (*work steadily*) **to ~ a trade** ein Gewerbe betreiben ❷ (*sell*) *drugs* handeln ❸ (*supply continuously*) **to ~ sb with wine** jdn mit Wein abfüllen *fam* ❹ (*travel*) **to ~ a route** eine Strecke regelmäßig befahren

'**plywood** *n* Sperrholz *nt*

pm, p.m. [ˌpi·'em] *adv inv abbrev of* **post meridian: eight ~** acht Uhr abends, zwanzig Uhr

PMS [ˌpi·em·'es] *n* MED *abbrev of* **premenstrual syndrome** PMS *nt*

pneumatic [nu·'mæt̬·ɪk] *adj inv* pneumatisch

pneumonia [nu·'moʊn·jə] *n* Lungenentzündung *f*

PO [ˌpi·'oʊ] *n abbrev of* **Post Office**

poach¹ [poʊtʃ] *vt* pochieren

poach² [poʊtʃ] **I.** *vt* ❶ (*catch illegally*) wildern ❷ (*steal*) sich *dat* unrechtmäßig aneignen; *ideas* stehlen ❸ *employee* abwerben (**from** +*dat*) **II.** *vi* (*catch illegally*) wildern

poacher ['poʊ·tʃər] *n* Wilderer *m*

poaching ['poʊ·tʃɪŋ] *n* ❶ HUNT Wilderei *f* ❷ (*taking unfairly*) Wegnehmen *nt*

P'O box *n abbrev of* **Post Office Box** Postfach

pocket ['pak·ɪt] **I.** *n* ❶ (*in clothing*) Tasche *f* ❷ (*on bag, in car*) Fach *nt* ❸ (*fig: financial resources*) Geldbeutel *m;* **out of one's own ~** aus eigener Tasche ❹ SPORTS (*on pool table*) Loch *nt* **II.** *vt* ❶ (*put in one's pocket*) in die Tasche stecken ❷ (*keep sth for oneself*) behalten ❸ (*in pool*) *ball* ins Loch spielen

'**pocketbook** *n* ❶ (*purse*) Handtasche *f* ❷ (*financial resources*) Finanzmittel *pl*

'**pocketknife** *n* Taschenmesser *nt*

'**pocket money** *n* Taschengeld *nt;* (*fig: small amount of money*) ein Taschengeld *nt fig fam*

'**pocket-size**(**d**) *adj* im Taschenformat *nach n*

pod [pad] *n* ❶ (*seed container*) Hülse *f; pea, vanilla* Schote *f* ❷ (*on aircraft*) Gondel *f;* (*to hold jet*) Düsenaggregat *nt* ❸ (*K-cup*) **coffee ~** Kaffeepad *nt*

podiatrist [pə·'daɪ·ə·trɪst] *n* Fußspezialist(in) *m(f),* Fußpfleger(in) *m(f)*

podiatry [pə·'daɪ·ə·tri] *n* Fußpflege *f*

podium <*pl* -dia> ['poʊ·di·əm] *n* Podium *nt*

poem ['poʊ·əm] *n* (*a. fig*) Gedicht *nt*

poet ['poʊ·ət] *n* Dichter(in) *m(f)*

poetic(**al**) [poʊ·'et̬·ɪk(əl)] *adj* (*relating to poetry*) dichterisch; **~ language** Dichtersprache *f*

poetry ['poʊ·ɪ·tri] *n* ❶ (*genre*) Dichtung *f,* Lyrik *f* ❷ (*poetic quality*) Poesie *f*

pogrom [pə·'gram] *n* Pogrom *nt*

poignant ['pɔɪn·jənt] *adj* bewegend; (*distressing*) erschütternd; *memories* melancholisch

poinsettia [pɔɪn·'set̬·i·ə] *n* Weihnachtsstern *m*

point [pɔɪnt] **I.** *n* ❶ (*sharp end, in ballet*) Spitze *f; of a star* Zacke *f* ❷ (*decimal point*) Komma ❸ TYPO (*dot, punctuation mark*) Punkt *m* ❹ (*position*) Stelle *f,* Punkt *m;* **~ of contact** Berührungspunkt *m;* **starting ~** Ausgangspunkt *m a. fig* ⑤ (*particular time*) Zeitpunkt *m;* **she was on the ~ of collapse** sie stand kurz vor dem Zusammenbruch; **at that ~** zu diesem Zeitpunkt; (*then*) in diesem Augenblick; **from that ~ on ...** von da an ... ⑥ (*argument, issue*) Punkt *m;* **she does have a ~, though** so ganz Unrecht hat sie nicht; **she made the ~ that ...** sie wies darauf hin, dass ...; (*stress*) sie betonte, dass ...; **my ~ exactly** das sag ich ja *fam;* **ok, ~ taken** o.k., ich hab schon begriffen *fam* ⑦ (*most important idea*) **the ~ is ...** der Punkt ist nämlich der, ...; **to come to the ~** auf den Punkt kommen ⑧ (*purpose*) Sinn *m,* Zweck *m;* **but that's the whole ~!** aber das ist doch genau der Punkt! ⑨ (*stage in process*) Punkt *m;* **from that ~ on ...** von diesem Moment an ...; **the high ~ of the evening ...** der Höhepunkt des Abends ...; **up to a ~** bis zu einem gewissen Grad ⑩ SPORTS Punkt *m* ⑪ (*important characteristic*) Merkmal *nt;* **good ~s** gute Seiten; **sb's strong/weak ~s** jds Stärken *pl*/Schwächen *pl* ⑫ (*on compass*) Strich *m;* (*on thermometer*) Grad *m* **II.** *vi* ① (*with finger*) deuten, zeigen (**at/to** auf +*akk*) ② (*be directed*) weisen; **to ~ east/west** nach Osten/Westen zeigen ③ (*indicate*) hinweisen (**to** auf +*akk*) **III.** *vt* ① (*aim*) ■**to ~ sth at sb/sth** *weapon* etw [auf jdn/etw] richten; *stick, one's finger* mit etw *dat* auf jdn/etw zeigen ② (*direct*) **to ~ sb in the direction of sth** jdm den Weg zu etw *dat* beschreiben ③ (*extend*) **to ~ one's toes** die Zehen strecken

◆**point out** *vt* ① (*show*) ■**to ~ out** ⊂ **sth/sb [to sb]** [jdn] auf etw/jdn hinweisen; (*with finger*) [jdn] etw/jdn zeigen ② (*inform*) ■**to ~ out that ...** darauf aufmerksam machen, dass ...

point-'blank I. *adv inv* ① (*at very close range*) aus nächster Nähe ② (*bluntly*) geradewegs, unumwunden **II.** *adj attr* (*very close*) nah; *shoot;* **at ~ range** aus nächster Nähe

pointed ['pɔɪn·tɪd] *adj* ① (*with sharp point*) spitz ② (*emphatic*) pointiert *geh; criticism* scharf; *question* unverblümt; *remark* spitz; *reminder* eindrücklich

pointer ['pɔɪn·tər] *n* ① (*on dial*) Zeiger *m* ② (*rod*) Zeigestock *m* ③ *usu pl* (*fam: tip*) Tipp *m;* (*instructions*) Hinweis *m* ④ (*dog*) Vorstehhund *m;* (*breed*) Pointer *m*

pointless ['pɔɪnt·lɪs] *adj* sinnlos, zwecklos; *remark* überflüssig

point of 'view <*pl* points of view> *n* Ansicht *f,* Einstellung *f;* **from a purely practical ~** rein praktisch betrachtet

pointy ['pɔɪnt·i] *adj* (*fam*) spitz

poise [pɔɪz] **I.** *n* Haltung *f* **II.** *vt usu passive* ① (*balance*) balancieren; **to be ~d to jump** sprungbereit sein; (*hover*) ■**to be ~d** schweben ② (*fig*) ■**to be ~d to do sth** (*about to*) nahe daran sein, etw zu tun

poised [pɔɪzd] *adj* beherrscht

poison ['pɔɪ·zən] **I.** *n* Gift *nt* **II.** *vt* vergiften; (*fig*) **to ~ sb's mind against sb/sth** jdn gegen jdn/etw einnehmen

poison 'gas *n* Giftgas *nt*

poisoning ['pɔɪ·zə·nɪŋ] *n* ① (*act*) Vergiften *nt* ② (*condition*) Vergiftung *f;* (*individual case*) Fall *m* von Vergiftung; **blood ~** Blutvergiftung *f*

poison 'ivy *n* Giftsumach *m*

poisonous ['pɔɪ·zə·nəs] *adj* ① (*containing poison*) giftig; **~ snake** Giftschlange *f* ② (*malicious*) giftig *fig,* boshaft

poke¹ [poʊk] **I.** *n* (*jab*) Stoß *m* **II.** *vt* ① (*prod*) anstoßen; (*with umbrella, stick*) stechen; **to ~ sb in the arm/ribs** jd in den Arm/die Rippen knuffen; **to ~ a hole in sth** ein Loch in etw *akk* bohren ② ■**to ~ sth into/through sth** (*prod with*) etw in/durch etw *akk* stecken; (*thrust*) etw in/durch etw *akk* stoßen ③ *fire* schüren ▶ PHRASES: **to ~ fun at sb** sich über jdn lustig machen; **to ~ one's nose into sb's business** (*fam*) seine Nase in jds Angelegenheiten stecken **III.** *vi* ① (*jab repeatedly*) herumfummeln *fam* (**at** an +*dat*); **to ~ at one's food** in seinem Essen herumstochern ② (*break through*) ■**to ~ through** durchscheinen

◆**poke around** *vi* (*fam*) herumstöbern; (*without permission*) herumschnüffeln

◆**poke out I.** *vi* ■**to ~ out [of sth]** [aus etw *dat*] hervorgucken [*o* SÜDD, ÖSTERR herausschauen] **II.** *vt* ① *head* herausstecken; *tongue* herausstrecken ② (*remove*) herausschieben; *eyes* ausstechen

◆**poke up** *vi* hervorragen; ■**to ~ up over sth** über etw *dat* herausragen

poke² [poʊk] *n* ▶ PHRASES: **to buy a pig in a ~** (*pej*) die Katze im Sack kaufen *fig*

poker¹ ['poʊ·kər] *n* (*card game*) Poker *m o nt;* **a game of ~** eine Runde Poker

poker² ['poʊ·kər] *n* (*fireplace tool*) Schürhaken *m*

pokey, poky ['poʊ·ki] *adj* (*pej: slow*) lahm

Poland ['poʊ·lənd] *n* Polen *nt*

polar ['poʊ·lər] *adj attr, inv* ① (*near pole*) polar ② (*opposite*) gegensätzlich, polar *geh; opposites* diametral *geh*

'polar bear *n* Eisbär *m*

polarity [poʊ·'lær·ɪ·t̬i] *n* SCI Polarität *f;* (*fig a.*) Gegensätzlichkeit *f*

polarize ['poʊ·lə·raɪz] **I.** *vt* polarisieren **II.** *vi* sich polarisieren

pole¹ [poʊl] *n* ① GEOG, ELEC Pol *m;* **the magnetic ~** der Magnetpol; **the North P~** der Nordpol ② (*extreme*) Extrem *nt;* **to be ~s apart** Welten voneinander entfernt sein

pole² [poʊl] *n* Stange *f;* (*pointed at one end*) Pfahl *m;* **fishing ~** Angelrute *f;* **flag~** Fahnenmast *m*

polemic [pə·'lem·ɪk] **I.** *n* Polemik *f* **II.** *adj* polemisch

'pole vault *n* Stabhochsprung *m kein pl*

'pole-vaulter *n* Stabhochspringer(in) *m(f)*

police [pə·'lis] **I.** *n* + *pl vb* ① (*force*) ■**the ~** die Polizei *kein pl;* **to call the ~** die Polizei ru-

P

fen ② (*police officers*) Polizisten, -innen *mpl, fpl* **II.** *vt* ① (*maintain law and order*) überwachen ② (*regulate*) ■**to ~ sb/sth** jdn/etw kontrollieren **III.** *adj helmet, patrol, uniform* Polizei-; **~ investigation** polizeiliche Untersuchung; **to ask for ~ protection** Polizeischutz anfordern

po'lice car *n* Polizeiauto *nt*

po'lice department *n* Polizeidienststelle *f*

po'lice dog *n* Polizeihund *m*

po'lice force *n* ① (*the police*) ■**the ~** die Polizei ② (*unit of police*) Polizeieinheit *f*

po'liceman *n* Polizist *m*

po'lice officer *n* Polizeibeamte(r) *m,* Polizeibeamte [*o* -in] *f*

po'lice state *n* (*pej*) Polizeistaat *m*

po'lice station *n* Polizeiwache *f*

po'licewoman *n* Polizistin *f*

policy¹ ['pal·ə·si] *n* ① (*plan*) Programm *nt,* Strategie *f;* (*principle*) Grundsatz *m* ② Politik *f;* **a change in ~** ein Richtungswechsel *m* in der Politik; **economic ~** Wirtschaftspolitik *f*

policy² ['pal·ə·si] *n* (*for insurance*) Police *f,* Polizze *f* ÖSTERR

'policyholder *n* Versicherungsnehmer(in) *m(f)*

'policymaker *n* Parteiideologe, -ideologin *m, f*

'policymaking *n* Festsetzen *nt* von Richtlinien

polio [ˌpoʊ·li·oʊ], **poliomyelitis** [ˌpoʊ·li·oʊ·ˌmaɪ·ə·'laɪ·t̬əs] *n* (*spec*) Kinderlähmung *f*

polish ['pal·ɪʃ] **I.** *n* ① (*substance*) Politur *f;* **shoe ~** Schuhcreme *f* ② *usu sing* (*act*) Polieren *nt kein pl* ③ (*fig: refinement*) [gesellschaftlicher] Schliff **II.** *vt* ① (*rub*) polieren; *shoes, silver* putzen ② (*fig: refine*) aufpolieren

◆**polish off** *vt* ① *food* verdrücken *fam* ② ■**to ~ off** ↻ **sth** etw schnell erledigen ③ (*fam: beat*) *opponent* abfertigen, abservieren

Polish ['poʊ·lɪʃ] **I.** *n* Polnisch *nt* **II.** *adj* polnisch

polished ['pal·ɪʃt] *adj* ① (*gleaming*) glänzend *attr* ② (*showing great skill*) formvollendet; *performance* großartig ③ (*refined*) gebildet; *manners* geschliffen

polite [pə·'laɪt] *adj* ① (*courteous*) höflich ② (*cultured*) vornehm; *society* gehoben

politeness [pə·'laɪt·nɪs] *n* Höflichkeit *f*

political [pə·'lɪt̬·ɪ·kəl] *adj* ① (*of politics*) politisch; **~ leaders** politische Größen *pl* ② (*pej: tactical*) taktisch

political cor'rectness *n* politische Korrektheit

politically cor'rect *adj* politisch korrekt

politician [ˌpal·ə·'tɪʃ·ən] *n* Politiker(in) *m(f)*

politicize [pe·'lɪt̬·ə·saɪz] *vt* politisieren *geh*

politics ['pal·ə·tɪks] *npl* ① + *sing vb* Politik *f kein pl;* **to go into ~** in die Politik gehen ② + *pl vb* (*political beliefs*) politische Ansichten *pl* ③ + *sing/pl vb* (*within group*) **office ~** Büroklüngelei *f pej;* **to play ~** Winkelzüge machen

polka ['poʊl·kə] **I.** *n* Polka *f* **II.** *vi* Polka tanzen

'polka dot *n usu pl* Tupfen *m*

poll [poʊl] **I.** *n* ① (*public survey*) Erhebung *f;* **an opinion** [*or* **a public opinion**] **~** eine [*o* öffentliche] Meinungsumfrage ② (*result of vote*) [Wähler]stimmen *pl* ③ (*number of votes cast*) Wahlbeteiligung *f* **II.** *vt* ① (*canvass in poll*) befragen; ■**to ~ sb** [**on sth**] jdn [über etw] abstimmen lassen ② (*receive*) **the party ~ed 67% of the vote** die Partei hat 67 % der Stimmen erhalten

pollen ['pal·ən] *n* Blütenstaub *m*

'pollen count *n* Pollenflug *m kein pl*

pollinate ['pal·ə·neɪt] *vt* bestäuben

polling ['poʊl·ɪŋ] *n* (*election*) Wahl *f;* (*referendum*) Abstimmung *f*

'polling booth *n* Wahlkabine *f*

'polling place *n* Wahllokal *nt*

pollster ['poʊl·stər] *n* Meinungsforscher(in) *m(f)*

pollutant [pə·'lu·tənt] *n* Schadstoff *m*

pollute [pə·'lut] *vt* ① (*contaminate*) verschmutzen ② (*fig: corrupt*) besudeln *fig, pej;* **to ~ sb's mind** jds Charakter verderben

polluter [pə·'lu·t̬ər] *n* Umweltverschmutzer(in) *m(f)*

pollution [pə·'lu·ʃən] *n* ① (*polluting*) Verschmutzung *f;* **environmental ~** Umweltverschmutzung *f* ② (*pollutants*) Schadstoffe *pl*

polo ['poʊ·loʊ] *n* ① SPORTS Polo *nt* ② (*fam: shirt*) Polohemd *nt*

'polo shirt *n* Polohemd *nt*

polyester [ˌpal·i·'es·tər] *n* Polyester *m*

polyethylene [ˌpal·ɪ·'eθ·ə·lin] *n* Polyäthylen *nt*

polygamist [pə·'lɪg·ə·mɪst] *n* Polygamist(in) *m(f) geh*

polygamous [pə·'lɪg·ə·məs] *adj inv* polygam *geh*

polygamy [pə·'lɪg·ə·mi] *n* Polygamie *f geh*

polygon ['pal·i·gan] *n* Vieleck *nt,* Polygon *nt fachspr*

polygraph ['pal·i·græf] *n* Lügendetektor *m*

Polynesia [ˌpal·ə·'ni·ʒə] *n* Polynesien *nt*

Polynesian [ˌpal·ə·'ni·ʒən] **I.** *adj* polynesisch **II.** *n* ① (*native of Polynesia*) Polynesier(in) *m(f)* ② (*language group*) polynesische Sprachen *pl*

polyp ['pal·ɪp] *n* MED, ZOOL Polyp *m*

polyphonic [ˌpal·i·'fan·ɪk] *adj inv* polyphon *fachspr*

polystyrene [ˌpal·i·'staɪ·rin] *n* Styropor® *nt*

polytechnic [ˌpal·i·'tek·nɪk] **I.** *adj institute, school* Technische Hochschule *f* **II.** *n* Fachhochschule *f*

polyunsaturated fats [ˌpal·i·ʌn·'sætʃ·ə·reɪ·t̬ɪd-], **polyunsaturates** [ˌpal·i·ʌn·'sætʃ·ə·reɪts] *npl* (*fatty acids*) mehrfach ungesättigte Fettsäuren; (*fats*) Fette mit einem hohen Anteil an mehrfach ungesättigten Fettsäuren

polyurethane [ˌpal·i·'jʊr·ə·θeɪn] *n* Polyurethan *nt*

pomegranate ['pam·græn·ɪt] *n* Granatapfel *m*

pomp [pamp] *n* Pomp *m,* Prunk *m*

pompon ['pam·pan], **pompom** ['pam·pam] *n* ① (*of cheerleader*) Pompon *m* ② (*yarn ball*) Quaste *f*

pomposity [pam·ˈpas·ɪ·t̬i] *n* Selbstgefälligkeit *f*

pompous [ˈpam·pəs] *adj* ❶ *person* selbstgefällig ❷ *language* geschraubt *pej*

poncho [ˈpan·tʃoʊ] *n* Poncho *m*

pond [pand] *n* ❶ (*body of water*) Teich *m* ❷ (*hum: Atlantic Ocean*) ■ **the ~** der große Teich

ponder [ˈpan·dər] **I.** *vt* durchdenken **II.** *vi* nachdenken (**on** über +*akk*); ■ **to ~ why ...** sich fragen, warum ...

ponderous [ˈpan·dər·əs] *adj* (*pej*) ❶ (*heavy and awkward*) mühsam ❷ (*laborious*) schwerfällig

pone [poʊn] *n* [**corn**] ~ Maisbrot *nt*

pontiff [ˈpan·tɪf] *n* (*form*) ■ **the ~** der Papst

pontifical [pan·ˈtɪf·ɪ·kəl] *adj* päpstlich

pontificate [pan·ˈtɪf·ɪ·kɪt] **I.** *vi* (*pej*) ■ **to ~ about sth** sich über etw *akk* auslassen **II.** *n* (*form*) Pontifikat *m o nt fachspr*

pontoon [pan·ˈtun] *n* Ponton *m*

pontoon ˈbridge *n* Pontonbrücke *f*

pony [ˈpoʊ·ni] *n* (*small horse*) Pony *nt*

ˈponytail *n* Pferdeschwanz *m*

poo [pu] **I.** *n* (*childspeak sl*) Aa *nt kein pl* **II.** *vi* (*childspeak sl*) Aa machen

poodle [ˈpu·dəl] *n* Pudel *m*

poof [puf] *interj* (*fam*) hui!

pooh [pu] *interj* (*fam: in disgust*) pfui!, igitt!

pooh-pooh [ˌpu·ˈpu] *vt* (*fam*) abtun

pool¹ [pul] **I.** *n* ❶ (*construction*) Becken *nt;* **ornamental ~** Zierteich *m;* [**swimming**] ~ Schwimmbecken *nt;* (*private*) Swimmingpool *m;* (*public*) Schwimmbad *nt* ❷ (*natural*) Tümpel *m* ❸ (*of liquid*) Lache *f;* **~ of blood** Blutlache *f* **II.** *vi liquid* sich stauen

pool² [pul] **I.** *n* SPORTS Poolbillard *nt;* **to shoot ~** (*fam*) Poolbillard spielen **II.** *vt* zusammenlegen

ˈpool hall *n* Billardzimmer *nt*

ˈpool table *n* Poolbillardtisch *m*

poop¹ [pup] *n* (*of ship*) Heck *nt*

poop² [pup] **I.** *n* (*euph: excrement*) Aa *nt;* **dog ~** Hundedreck *m fam* **II.** *vi* (*fam: defecate*) Aa machen *Kindersprache;* **he ~ed in his pants** er hat in die Hose gekackt *fam*

◆**poop ˈout I.** *vi* ❶ (*become tired*) schlappmachen ❷ (*not persevere*) sich geschlagen geben **II.** *vt* (*exhaust*) ■ **to ~ sb out** erschöpfen, fertigmachen, fix und fertig machen

pooped [pupt] *adj* (*fam*) erschöpft, [fix und] fertig

pooper scooper [ˈpu·pər·ˌsku·pər] *n* (*fam*) Kotschaufel *f* (*Schaufel zum Entfernen von Hundekot*)

poor [pʊr] **I.** *adj* ❶ (*lacking money*) arm ❷ (*inadequate*) unzureichend, schlecht; *attendance* gering; *excuse* faul; **to be in ~ health** in schlechtem gesundheitlichen Zustand sein ❸ *attr* (*deserving of pity*) arm ❹ *pred* (*lacking*) ■ **to be ~ in sth** arm an etw *dat* sein **II.** *n* ■ **the ~** *pl* die Armen *pl*

ˈpoorhouse *n* (*hist*) Armenhaus *nt*

poorly [ˈpʊr·li] *adv* ❶ (*not rich*) arm; **~ dressed** ärmlich gekleidet ❷ (*inadequately*) schlecht

poor reˈlation *n* arme(r) Verwandte(r) *f(m);* (*fig*) Stiefkind *nt*

pop¹ [pap] **I.** *n* ❶ (*noise*) Knall *m* ❷ *usu sing* (*sl*) COMM ■ **a ~** pro Stück **II.** *adv* **to go ~** (*make noise*) einen Knall machen; (*toy gun*) peng machen; (*burst*) explodieren **III.** *vi* <-pp-> ❶ (*make noise*) knallen ❷ (*burst*) platzen ❸ (*go quickly*) ■ **to ~ outside** hinausgehen **IV.** *vt* <-pp-> ❶ (*burst*) platzen lassen ❷ (*put quickly*) **~ the pizza in the oven** schieb' die Pizza in den Ofen ❸ (*fam: hit*) schlagen; (*shoot*) *weapon* abknallen; *bullets* ballern ▶ PHRASES: **to ~ pills** Pillen schlucken

◆**pop in** *vi* vorbeischauen; **to keep ~ping in and out** dauernd rein und rauslaufen

◆**pop out** *vi* herausspringen

◆**pop up** *vi* ❶ (*appear unexpectedly*) auftauchen; **to ~ up out of nowhere** aus dem Nichts auftauchen ❷ (*in pop-up book*) sich aufrichten ❸ (*in baseball: hit a short, high fly ball*) einen Popup schlagen

pop² [pap] *n* (*fam*) Papa *m*

pop³ [pap] **I.** *n* (*music*) Pop *m* **II.** *adj attr* (*popular*) populär; **~ culture** Popkultur *f*

pop⁴ [pap] *n* (*soft drink*) Limonade *f*

ˈpop art *n* Pop-Art *f*

ˈpopcorn *n* Popcorn *nt*

pope [poʊp] *n* Papst *m*

poplar [ˈpap·lər] *n* Pappel *f*

poplin [ˈpap·lɪn] *n* Popelin *m*

ˈpop music *n* Popmusik *f*

poppy [ˈpap·i] *n* Mohn *m kein pl,* Mohnblume *f*

ˈpoppy seed *n usu pl* Mohnsamen *m,* Mohn *m kein pl*

Popsicle® [ˈpap·sɪ·kəl] *n* Eis *nt* am Stiel, Stängelglacé *f* SCHWEIZ

ˈpop singer *n* Popsänger(in) *m(f)*

populace [ˈpap·jə·lɪs] *n* ■ **the ~** die breite Masse [der Bevölkerung]

popular [ˈpap·jə·lər] *adj inv* ❶ (*widely liked*) beliebt, populär ❷ *attr* (*not highbrow*) populär ❸ *attr* (*widespread*) weit verbreitet; **it is a ~ belief that ...** viele glauben, dass ...

popularity [ˌpap·jə·ˈlær·ɪ·t̬i] *n* Beliebtheit *f,* Popularität *f*

popularize [ˈpap·jə·lə·raɪz] *vt* ❶ (*make liked*) populär machen ❷ (*make accessible*) breiteren Kreisen zugänglich machen

popularly [ˈpap·jə·lər·li] *adv* (*commonly*) allgemein; **as is ~ believed** wie man allgemein annimmt

populate [ˈpap·jə·leɪt] *vt* ❶ *usu passive* (*inhabit*) ■ **to be ~d** bevölkert sein; *island* bewohnt sein (**by, with** von +*dat*) ❷ (*provide inhabitants*) besiedeln

population [ˌpap·jə·ˈleɪ·ʃən] **I.** *n* ❶ *usu sing* (*inhabitants*) Bevölkerung *f kein pl;* **the civilian ~** die Zivilbevölkerung ❷ (*number of people*) Einwohnerzahl *f* ❸ BIOL Population *f*

P

fachspr, Bestand *m;* **the deer ~** der Hirschbestand **II.** *adj group, problems* Bevölkerungs-, Einwohner-; **~ change** Veränderung *f* der Bevölkerung

population 'density *n* Bevölkerungsdichte *f*

population ex'plosion *n* Bevölkerungsexplosion *f*

populous ['pap·jʊ·ləs] *adj* (*form*) bevölkerungsreich; *region, area* dicht besiedelt

porcelain ['pɔr·sə·lɪn] *n* Porzellan *nt*

porch <*pl* -es> [pɔrtʃ] *n* ❶ (*without walls*) Vordach *nt;* (*with walls*) Vorbau *m; of a church* Portal *nt* ❷ (*veranda*) Veranda *f*

porcupine ['pɔr·kjʊ·paɪn] *n* Stachelschwein *nt*

pore¹ [pɔr] *vi* (*examine*) brüten (**over** über +*dat*); **to ~ over a map** eine Zeitung eingehend studieren

pore² [pɔr] *n* (*opening*) Pore *f*

pork [pɔrk] *n* Schweinefleisch *nt*

'pork chop *n* Schweinekotelett *nt*

porker ['pɔr·kər] *n* Mastschwein *nt*

porky ['pɔr·ki] *adj* (*pej fam: fat*) fett

porn [pɔrn] (*fam*) **I.** *n short for* **pornography** Porno *m* **II.** *adj attr short for* **pornographic** Porno-

pornographic [ˌpɔr·nə·'græf·ɪk] *adj inv* ❶ (*containing pornography*) pornografisch, Porno- ❷ (*obscene*) obszön

pornography [pɔr·'nag·rə·fi] *n* Pornografie *f*

porous ['pɔr·əs] *adj* ❶ (*permeable*) porös ❷ (*breachable*) durchlässig

porpoise ['pɔr·pəs] *n* Tümmler *m*

porridge ['pɔr·ɪdʒ] *n* Porridge *m o nt,* Haferbrei *m*

port¹ [pɔrt] *n* ❶ (*harbor*) Hafen *m* ❷ (*town*) Hafenstadt *f*

port² [pɔrt] *n* AVIAT, NAUT Backbord *nt* ÖSTERR *a. m*

port³ [pɔrt] *n* COMPUT Anschluss *m,* Port *m fachspr*

port⁴ [pɔrt] *n* (*wine*) Portwein *m*

portable ['pɔr·t̬ə·bəl] *adj inv* tragbar; **~ radio** Kofferradio *nt*

portal ['pɔr·t̬əl] *n* ❶ (*form*) *a.* COMPUT Portal *nt* ❷ INET Portal *nt;* **web** [*or* **internet**] **~** Onlineportal *nt,* Internetportal *nt*

port au'thority *n* Hafenbehörde *f*

portentous [pɔr·'ten·təs] *adj inv* ❶ (*form: highly significant*) bedeutungsvoll; (*ominous*) unheilvoll; (*grave*) schicksalhaft ❷ (*pej: pompous*) hochtrabend

porter ['pɔr·t̬ər] *n* ❶ (*baggage carrier*) Gepäckträger *m;* (*on expedition*) Träger *m* ❷ RAIL (*on sleeping car*) [Schlafwagen]schaffner(in) *m(f)*

portfolio [pɔrt·'foʊ·li·oʊ] *n* ❶ (*case*) Aktenmappe *f* ❷ (*of drawings, designs*) Mappe *f* ❸ FIN Portefeuille *nt fachspr*

'porthole *n* NAUT Bullauge *nt;* AVIAT Kabinenfenster *nt*

portico <*pl* -es *or* -s> ['pɔr·t̬ɪ·koʊ] *n* Säulengang *m,* Portikus *m fachspr*

portion ['pɔr·ʃən] **I.** *n* ❶ (*part*) Teil *m* ❷ (*share*) Anteil *m* ❸ (*serving*) Portion *f;* (*piece*) Stück *nt* **II.** *vt* ■ **to ~ out** ↻ **sth** etw aufteilen

portly ['pɔrt·li] *adj* (*esp hum*) korpulent

portrait ['pɔr·trɪt] **I.** *n* ❶ (*picture*) Porträt *nt,* Bildnis *nt* ❷ (*fig: description*) Bild *nt* **II.** *adj* TYPO **in ~ format** im Hochformat

portraiture ['pɔr·trɪ·tʃər] *n* Porträtmalerei *f*

portray [pɔr·'treɪ] *vt* ❶ (*paint*) porträtieren ❷ (*describe*) darstellen

portrayal [pɔr·'treɪ·əl] *n* Darstellung *f;* (*in literature*) Schilderung *f*

Portugal ['pɔr·tʃə·gəl] *n* Portugal *nt*

Portuguese [ˌpɔr·tʃə·'giz] **I.** *n* ❶ <*pl* -> (*person*) Portugiese, -in *m, f* ❷ (*language*) Portugiesisch *nt* **II.** *adj* ❶ (*of Portugal*) portugiesisch ❷ *course, teacher* Portugiesisch-

pose [poʊz] **I.** *n* ❶ (*bodily position*) Haltung *f,* Pose *f* ❷ *usu sing* (*pretence*) Getue *nt* **II.** *vi* ❶ (*adopt position*) posieren, eine Haltung einnehmen; ■ **to ~ for sb** für jdn Modell sitzen ❷ (*pretend*) ■ **to ~ as** sich ausgeben als ❸ (*behave affectedly*) sich geziert benehmen **III.** *vt* ❶ (*cause*) aufwerfen; **to ~ difficulties** Schwierigkeiten mit sich *dat* bringen; **to ~ a threat to sb/sth** eine Bedrohung für jdn/etw darstellen ❷ *question* stellen

poser ['poʊ·zər] *n* (*pej fam: person*) Angeber(in) *m(f)*

posh [paʃ] *adj* (*fam*) vornehm, piekfein

position [pə·'zɪʃ·ən] **I.** *n* ❶ (*place*) Platz *m,* Stelle *f; building* Lage *f* ❷ (*in navigation*) Position *f,* Standort *m* ❸ (*posture*) Stellung *f,* Lage *f;* **yoga ~** Yogahaltung *f;* **to change one's ~** eine andere Stellung einnehmen ❹ SPORTS (*in team*) [Spieler]position *f* ❺ (*rank*) Position *f,* Stellung *f;* (*in race, competition*) Platz *m* ❻ (*job*) Stelle *f;* **a ~ of responsibility** ein verantwortungsvoller Posten ❼ *usu sing* (*situation*) Situation *f,* Lage *f;* **to put sb in an awkward ~** jdn in eine unangenehme Lage bringen **II.** *vt* platzieren

positive ['paz·ɪ·t̬ɪv] *adj inv* ❶ (*certain*) sicher, bestimmt; ■ **to be ~ about sth** sich *dat* einer S. *gen* sicher sein ❷ (*optimistic*) positiv; *criticism* konstruktiv ❸ *inv* MED, MATH, ELEC positiv ❹ *attr, inv* (*complete*) wirklich, absolut; **a ~ disadvantage** ein echter Nachteil

positively ['paz·ɪ·t̬ɪv·li] *adv* ❶ (*definitely*) bestimmt; *say, promise* fest ❷ (*optimistically*) *think* positiv ❸ *inv* (*fam: completely*) völlig, absolut

posse ['pas·i] *n* ❶ (*hist: summoned by sheriff*) [Hilfs]trupp *m* ❷ (*sl: group of friends*) Clique *f*

possess [pə·'zes] *vt* ❶ (*own, have*) besitzen ❷ LAW (*carry illegally*) [illegal] besitzen ❸ *usu passive* (*control*) **to be ~ed by the Devil** vom Teufel besessen sein; **to be ~ed by the urge to do sth** von dem Drang besessen sein, etw tun zu müssen

possession [pə·'zeʃ·ən] *n* ❶ (*having*) Besitz *m;* ■ **to be in sb's ~** sich in jds Besitz befinden ❷ *usu pl* (*something owned*) Besitz *m kein pl* ❸ SPORTS **to regain ~** [**of the ball**] wie-

der in den Ballbesitz gelangen
possessive [pə·ˈzes·ɪv] *adj* ❶ (*not sharing*) eigen ❷ (*jealous*) besitzergreifend ❸ LING (*showing possession*) possessiv
possessor [pə·ˈzes·ər] *n usu sing* (*form or hum*) Besitzer(in) *m(f)*
possibility [ˌpas·ə·ˈbɪl·ɪ·t̬i] *n* ❶ (*event or action*) Möglichkeit *f;* **there's a ~ that ...** es kann sein, dass ... ❷ (*likelihood*) Möglichkeit *f,* Wahrscheinlichkeit *f;* **is there any ~ [that] ...?** besteht irgendeine Möglichkeit, dass ...? ❸ (*potential*) ■**possibilities** *pl* Möglichkeiten *pl*
possible [ˈpas·ə·bəl] *adj inv* ❶ *usu pred* (*feasible*) möglich; **it's just not ~** das ist einfach nicht machbar; **the best ~ ...** der/die/das allerbeste ...; **as much as ~** so viel wie möglich ❷ (*that could happen*) möglich, vorstellbar; **to make sth ~** etw ermöglichen
possibly [ˈpas·ə·bli] *adv inv* ❶ (*feasibly*) **he couldn't ~ have known that** das kann er doch unmöglich gewusst haben!; **to do all that one ~ can** alles Menschenmögliche tun ❷ (*perhaps*) möglicherweise, vielleicht; **very ~** durchaus möglich; (*more likely*) sehr wahrscheinlich
possum <*pl* - *or* -s> [ˈpas·əm] *n* Opossum *nt*
post[1] [poʊst] **I.** *n* ❶ (*pole*) Pfosten *m,* Pfahl *m;* **wooden ~** Holzpfosten *m* ❷ (*in a horse race*) ■**the starting ~** der Startpfosten, der Zielpfosten ❸ (*fam*) **goal ~** [Tor]pfosten *m* **II.** *vt* COMPUT **to ~ sth on the [Inter]net** etw über das Internet bekannt geben
post[2] [poʊst] *n* ❶ MIL (*base*) Stützpunkt *m* ❷ (*assigned workplace*) Stellung *f,* Posten *m*
postage [ˈpoʊ·stɪdʒ] *n* Porto *nt*
ˈ**postage meter** *n* Frankiermaschine *f*
ˈ**postage stamp** *n* (*form*) Postwertzeichen *nt*
postal [ˈpoʊ·stəl] *adj attr, inv* Post-, postalisch *geh* ► PHRASES: **to go ~** (*sl*) Amok laufen, ausrasten
ˈ**postcard** *n* Postkarte *f*
postˈdate *vt* ❶ (*give later date*) *check* vordatieren ❷ (*happen after*) ■**to ~ sth** sich später ereignen
poster [ˈpoʊ·stər] *n* ❶ (*advertisement*) [Werbe]plakat *nt* ❷ (*large picture*) Poster *nt*
posterior [pa·ˈstɪr·i·ər] **I.** *n* (*hum*) Hinterteil *nt hum* **II.** *adj attr, inv* (*form: toward the back*) hintere(r, s)
posterity [pa·ˈster·ɪ·t̬i] *n* (*form*) Nachwelt *f geh*
postˈgraduate **I.** *n* Postgraduierte(r) *f(m) fachspr,* Student(in) *m(f)* im Aufbaustudium (*nach Erreichen des ersten akademischen Grades*) **II.** *adj attr, inv* weiterführend, Postgraduierten- *fachspr,* Aufbau-
posthumous [ˈpas·tʃə·məs] *adj inv* (*form*) post[h]um
posting [ˈpoʊ·stɪŋ] *n* ❶ COMPUT (*message*) Posting *nt,* Beitrag *m* ❷ ADMIN (*ledger entry*) Hauptbuchung *f*
ˈ**postmark** **I.** *n* Poststempel *m* **II.** *vt usu passive* ■**to be ~ed** abgestempelt sein
ˈ**postmaster** *n* Leiter *m* einer Postdienststelle
postˈmodern *adj inv* post-modern
postˈmodernism *n* Postmoderne *f*
postmortem [ˌpoʊst·ˈmɔr·t̬əm] **I.** *n* ❶ MED *see* **autopsy** ❷ (*fam: discussion*) Manöverkritik *f hum* **II.** *adj attr, inv* (*done after death*) nach dem Tod *nach n,* postmortal *fachspr*
postˈnatal *adj inv* nach der Geburt *nach n,* postnatal *fachspr*
ˈ**post office** *n* ■**the ~** die Post *kein pl*
postpone [poʊst·ˈpoʊn] *vt* verschieben
postponement [poʊst·ˈpoʊn·mənt] *n* ❶ (*delay*) Verschiebung *f* ❷ (*deferment*) Aufschub *m; of a court case* Vertagung *f*
ˈ**postscript** *n* ❶ (*to a letter*) Postskript[um] *nt* ❷ (*sequel*) Fortsetzung *f*
posture [ˈpas·tʃər] **I.** *n* (*natural*) [Körper]haltung *f;* (*pose a.*) Stellung *f,* Pose *f* **II.** *vi* (*pej*) sich in Pose werfen
postˈwar *adj inv* Nachkriegs-, der Nachkriegszeit *nach n*
posy [ˈpoʊ·zi] *n* Sträußchen *nt*
pot[1] [pat] **I.** *n* ❶ (*for cooking*) Topf *m;* (*smaller*) Töpfchen *nt* ❷ (*container*) Topf *m;* (*made of glass*) Glas[gefäß] *nt;* **coffee ~** Kaffeekanne *f* ❸ (*for plants*) Blumentopf *m* ❹ (*clay container*) Keramikgefäß *nt* **II.** *vt* <-tt-> (*place in pot*) *plants* eintopfen
pot[2] [pat] *n* (*sl*) Pot *nt*
potash [ˈpat·æʃ] *n* Pottasche *f*
potassium [pə·ˈtæs·i·əm] *n* Kalium *nt*
potato <*pl* -es> [pə·ˈteɪ·t̬oʊ] *n* Kartoffel *f,* Erdapfel *m* ÖSTERR; **baked ~** Ofenkartoffel *f;* **mashed ~es** Kartoffelbrei *m*
poˈtato chip *n usu pl* Kartoffelchip *m*
poˈtato peeler *n* Kartoffelschäler *m*
potbellied [ˈpat·ˌbelid] *adj inv* dickbäuchig
ˈ**potbelly** *n* dicker Bauch, Wampe *f fam;* (*sign of illness*) Blähbauch *m*
potency [ˈpoʊ·tən·si] *n* ❶ (*strength*) Stärke *f; of evil, temptation, a spell* Macht *f; of a drug, poison* Wirksamkeit *f; of a weapon* Durchschlagskraft *f* ❷ (*sexual*) Potenz *f*
potent [ˈpoʊ·tənt] *adj* ❶ (*strong*) mächtig; *antibiotic, drink, poison* stark; *argument* schlagkräftig; *symbol* aussagekräftig; *weapon* durchschlagend ❷ (*sexual*) potent
potentate [ˈpoʊ·tən·teɪt] *n* (*esp pej liter*) Potentat(in) *m(f) geh*
potential [pə·ˈten·ʃəl] **I.** *adj inv* potenziell *geh,* möglich **II.** *n* Potenzial *nt geh;* **to have [a lot of] ~** *building, idea* [vollkommen] ausbaufähig sein; *person* [großes] Talent haben; *song* viel versprechend sein
potentially [pə·ˈten·ʃə·li] *adv inv* potenziell *geh;* **~ disastrous** möglicherweise verheerend; **sth is ~ fatal** etw kann tödlich sein
ˈ**potholder** *n* Topflappen *m*
ˈ**pothole** *n* (*in road*) Schlagloch *nt*
potion [ˈpoʊ·ʃən] *n* Trank *m;* (*esp pej: medicine*) Mittelchen *nt hum o pej*
potˈluck *n attr* FOOD (*communal meal*)

~ **dinner** *Abendessen, zu dem jeder eine Speise mitbringt*

> In den Vereinigten Staaten ist ein **potluck dinner** ein Abendessen, zu dem jeder Gast einen Salat, eine Hauptspeise, einen Nachtisch oder auch nur Kartoffelchips oder Kekse mitbringt. Üblicherweise wird eine Liste geführt, um sicherzustellen, dass eine vollständige Mahlzeit zustande kommt.

potpourri [ˌpoʊ·pʊ·ˈri] *n* Potpourri *nt*
ˈpot roast *n* Schmorbraten *m*
ˈpotshot *n* ① (*with gun*) blinder Schuss ② (*fig: verbal attack*) Seitenhieb *m;* **to take a ~ at sb/sth** [aufs Geratewohl] auf jdn/etw schießen; (*fig*) Seitenhiebe gegen jdn/etw austeilen
potter [ˈpaṭ·ər] *n* Töpfer(in) *m(f)*
pottery [ˈpaṭ·ə·ri] *n* ① (*activity*) Töpfern *nt* ② (*objects*) Keramik *f kein pl* ③ (*factory*) Töpferei *f*
potty [ˈpaṭ·i] *n* Töpfchen *nt;* **to go ~** (*esp childspeak*) aufs Töpfchen gehen
ˈpotty trained *adv* **to be ~** allein aufs Töpfchen gehen können
pouch <*pl* -es> [paʊtʃ] *n* ① (*small bag*) Beutel *m* ② ZOOL (*of kangaroo, koala*) Beutel *m;* (*of hamster*) Tasche *f*
poultice [ˈpoʊl·tɪs] *n* MED Breiumschlag *m*
poultry [ˈpoʊl·tri] *n* ① *pl* (*birds*) Geflügel *nt kein pl* ② (*meat*) Geflügel[fleisch] *nt*
pounce [paʊns] *vi* ① (*jump*) losspringen; *attacker, animal* einen Satz machen ② (*fig: seize opportunity*) zuschlagen, zuschnappen *fam*
pound¹ [paʊnd] *n* ① (*unit of weight*) ≈ Pfund *nt* (*454 g*) ② (*unit of currency*) Pfund *nt*
pound² [paʊnd] **I.** *vt* ① (*hit repeatedly*) ■ **to ~ sth** auf etw *akk* hämmern; **to ~ the door** gegen die Tür hämmern ② MIL (*bombard*) **to ~ enemy positions** die feindlichen Stellungen bombardieren; **the storm ~ed the southern United States** (*fig*) der Sturm peitschte über den Süden der Vereinigten Staaten hinweg **II.** *vi* ① (*strike repeatedly*) hämmern (**on** an/gegen/auf +*akk*) ② (*beat*) *pulse* schlagen; *heart a.* pochen
pounding [ˈpaʊn·dɪŋ] **I.** *n* ① (*noise*) *of guns* Knattern *nt;* *of heart* Schlagen *nt;* (*in head*) Pochen *nt;* *of music, drum* Dröhnen *nt;* *of waves* Brechen *nt* ② (*attack*) Beschuss *m kein pl;* (*from air*) Bombardement *nt;* **to take a ~** unter schweren Beschuss geraten ③ (*defeat*) Niederlage *f;* (*in election, match*) Schlappe *f* **II.** *adj drum, music* dröhnend; *head, heart* pochend
pour [pɔr] **I.** *vt* ① (*cause to flow*) gießen (**into, onto** in, auf +*akk*); ■ **to ~ sb sth** jdm etw einschenken; (*as refill*) jdm etw nachschenken; **~ yourself a drink** nimm dir was zu trinken ② (*fig: give in large amounts*) *money, resources* fließen lassen (**into** in +*akk*); *energy* stecken (**into** in +*akk*) **II.** *vi* ① (*flow*) fließen (**into, out of** in, aus +*akk*); **the sunlight came ~ing into the room** das Sonnenlicht durchströmte den Raum ② *impers* (*rain*) **it's ~ing** [**rain**] es schüttet wie aus Kübeln *fam* ③ (*fill glasses, cups*) eingießen, einschenken
◆**pour in** *vi* hereinströmen, hineinströmen; *letters, donations* massenweise eintreffen
◆**pour out I.** *vt* ① *liquids* ausgießen, herauskippen; *solids* ausschütten ② (*fig: recount*) **to ~ out one's feelings** sich *dat* Gefühle von der Seele reden ③ (*produce quickly*) ausstoßen **II.** *vi* ① (*come out*) ausströmen; *smoke* herausquellen ② (*be expressed*) *words etc.* herauskommen *fig*
pout [paʊt] **I.** *vi* einen Schmollmund machen; (*sulk*) schmollen **II.** *vt lips* spitzen **III.** *n* Schmollmund *m*
poverty [ˈpav·ər·ṭi] *n* ① (*state of being poor*) Armut *f* ② (*form: lack*) Mangel *m* (**of** an +*dat*)
ˈpoverty line *n* ■ **the ~** die Armutsgrenze
ˈpoverty-stricken *adj* bitterarm
POW [ˌpi·oʊ·ˈdʌb·əl·ju], *n abbrev of* **prisoner of war** KG
powder [ˈpaʊ·dər] **I.** *n* ① Pulver *nt* ② (*makeup*) Puder *m* **II.** *vt* pudern; ■ **to be ~ed with sth** mit etw *dat* bestreut sein
powdered [ˈpaʊ·dərd] *adj inv* ① (*in powder form*) Pulver-, pulverisiert; **~ sugar** Puderzucker *m* ② (*covered with powder*) gepudert
ˈpowder keg *n* Pulverfass *nt*
ˈpowder puff *n* Puderquaste *f*
ˈpowder room *n* (*euph*) Damentoilette *f*
powdery [ˈpaʊ·də·ri] *adj* pulv[e]rig; (*finer*) pud[e]rig
power [ˈpaʊ·ər] **I.** *n* ① POL (*control*) Macht *f;* (*influence*) Einfluss *m;* **to have sb in one's ~** jdn in seiner Gewalt haben; **to seize ~** die Macht ergreifen ② (*nation*) [Führungs]macht *f* ③ (*person, group*) Macht *f;* (*person a.*) treibende Kraft ④ (*authority*) Kompetenz[en] *f[pl]* ⑤ (*ability*) Vermögen *nt;* **to do everything in one's ~** alles in seiner Macht Stehende tun ⑥ (*strength*) Kraft *f;* (*output a.*) Leistung *f;* (*of sea, wind, explosion*) Gewalt *f;* (*of nation, political party*) Stärke *f,* Macht *f* ⑦ (*electricity*) Strom *m,* Elektrizität *f;* **nuclear ~** Atomenergie *f* ⑧ MATH Potenz *f;* **two to the fourth ~** zwei hoch vier ▶ PHRASES: **the ~s that be** die Mächtigen **II.** *vt* antreiben
◆**power down I.** *vt* ELEC, TECH abschalten; *computer* herunterfahren **II.** *vi* COMPUT herunterfahren; TECH zum Stillstand kommen
◆**power up I.** *vt* ELEC, TECH einschalten; *computer* hochfahren **II.** *vi* TECH, COMPUT hochfahren
power-asˈsisted *adj attr, inv* Servo-
ˈpowerboat *n see* **motorboat**
power ˈbrakes *npl* Servobremsen *pl*
ˈpower cable *n* Stromkabel *nt*
powerful [ˈpaʊ·ər·fəl] *adj* ① (*mighty*) mächtig; (*influential*) einflussreich ② (*physically*

strong) stark, kräftig ❸ (*having physical effect*) stark; *explosion* heftig ❹ *effect, influence* stark; *argument* schlagkräftig; *evidence* überzeugend; *gaze* durchdringend ❺ TECH, TRANSP [leistungs]stark

powerfully ['paʊ·ər·fə·li] *adv* ❶ (*strongly*) stark; (*very much*) sehr ❷ (*using great force*) kraftvoll, mit Kraft; *argue* schlagkräftig

'powerhouse *n* treibende Kraft, Motor *m fig;* (*of ideas, suggestions*) unerschöpfliche Quelle

powerless ['paʊ·ər·lɪs] *adj* machtlos (**against** gegen +*akk*); ■ **to be ~ to do sth** unfähig sein, etw zu tun

'power line *n* Stromkabel *nt*

'power outage *n* (*accidental*) Stromausfall *m;* (*deliberate*) Stromsperre *f*

'power plant *n* Kraftwerk *nt*

power 'steering *n* Servolenkung *f*

'power tool *n* Motorwerkzeug *nt;* (*electric*) Elektrowerkzeug *nt*

pp. *npl* (*form*) *abbrev of* **pages** S.

PR [pi·'ar] *n abbrev of* **public relations** PR

practicable ['præk·tɪ·kə·bəl] *adj* (*form*) durchführbar, machbar

practical ['præk·tɪ·kəl] **I.** *adj* ❶ (*suitable, not theoretical*) praktisch ❷ (*approv: good at doing things*) praktisch [veranlagt] ❸ (*possible*) realisierbar, praktikabel; **~ technique** [in der Praxis] anwendbare Technik **II.** *n* praktische Prüfung

practicality [ˌpræk·tɪ·'kæl·ɪ·t̬i] *n* ❶ (*feasibility*) Durchführbarkeit *f,* Machbarkeit *f;* (*practical gain*) praktischer Nutzen ❷ (*practical aspect*) ■ **the practicalities** *pl* die praktische Seite ❸ (*usability*) Nützlichkeit *f*

practically ['præk·tɪk·li] *adv inv* ❶ (*almost*) praktisch; **we're ~ home** wir sind fast zu Hause ❷ (*not theoretically*) praktisch; **to be ~ minded** praktisch denken

practice ['præk·tɪs] **I.** *n* ❶ (*preparation*) Übung *f;* ■ **to be out of ~** aus der Übung sein ❷ (*training session*) [Übungs]stunde *f;* SPORT Training *nt* ❸ (*actual performance, usual procedure*) Praxis *f;* ■ **in ~** in der Praxis; **to put sth into ~** etw [in die Praxis] umsetzen ❹ (*regular activity*) Praktik *f,* Gewohnheit *f;* (*custom*) Sitte *f* ❺ (*business*) Praxis *f* **II.** *adj game, shot* Probe-; SPORT Trainings- **III.** *vt* ❶ (*rehearse*) ■ **to ~ [doing] sth** etw üben; (*improve particular skill*) an etw *dat* arbeiten; **to ~ the violin** Geige üben ❷ (*do regularly*) praktizieren; *a religion* ausüben **IV.** *vi* ❶ (*improve skill*) üben; SPORT trainieren ❷ (*work in a profession*) praktizieren

practiced ['præk·tɪst] *adj* ❶ (*experienced*) erfahren, geübt (**in** in +*dat*); ■ **to be ~ at doing sth** sich mit etw *dat* auskennen; **~ eye** geübtes Auge ❷ (*form: obtained by practice*) gekonnt

practicing ['præk·tɪs·ɪŋ] *adj attr, inv* praktizierend

practitioner [præk·'tɪʃ·ə·nər] *n* (*form*) **medical ~** praktischer Arzt/praktische Ärztin

pragmatic [præg·'mæt̬·ɪk] *adj person, attitude* pragmatisch; *idea, reason* vernünftig

pragmatism ['præg·mə·tɪz·əm] *n* Pragmatismus *m*

prairie ['prer·i] *n* [Gras]steppe *f;* (*in North America*) Prärie *f*

'prairie dog *n* ZOOL Präriehund *m*

praise [preɪz] **I.** *vt* ❶ (*express approval*) loben ❷ (*worship*) **~ the Lord!** gelobt sei der Herr! **II.** *n* ❶ (*approval*) Lob *nt;* **to heap ~ on sb** jdn mit Lob überschütten; **to win ~ for sth** für etw *akk* [großes] Lob ernten ❷ (*form: worship*) Lobpreis *m*

praiseworthy ['preɪz·ˌwɜr·ði] *adj* lobenswert

prance [præns] *vi person* stolzieren; (*horse*) tänzeln; ■ **to ~ around** herumhüpfen; *children* umhertollen

prank [præŋk] *n* Streich *m*

pray [preɪ] *vi* ❶ beten; **let us ~** lasset uns beten ❷ (*fig: hope*) hoffen (**for** auf +*akk*)

prayer [prer] *n* ❶ (*request to a god*) Gebet *nt;* **to say a ~ for sb** für jdn beten ❷ (*action of praying*) Gebet *nt,* Beten *nt* ❸ (*fig: hope*) Hoffnung *f;* **to not have a ~** (*fam*) kaum Chancen haben ❹ (*service*) ■ **~s** *pl* Andacht *f*

'prayer book *n* Gebetbuch *nt*

'prayer meeting *n* Gebetsstunde *f*

'prayer rug *n* Gebetsteppich *m*

praying 'mantis *n* Gottesanbeterin *f*

preach [pritʃ] **I.** *vi* ❶ (*give a sermon*) predigen (**to** vor +*dat*) ❷ (*pej: lecture*) ■ **to ~ to sb [about sth]** jdm eine Predigt [über etw *akk*] halten *fig* **II.** *vt* ❶ (*advocate*) predigen *fig* ❷ (*deliver*) **to ~ a sermon** eine Predigt halten

preacher ['pri·tʃər] *n* ❶ (*priest*) Geistliche(r) *f(m),* Pfarrer(in) *m(f)* ❷ Prediger(in) *m(f)*

preamble [pri·'æm·bəl] *n* (*form*) ❶ (*introduction*) Einleitung *f,* Vorwort *nt;* (*to a lecture*) Einführung *f* ❷ (*fig: introductory material*) Einleitung *f*

prearrange [ˌpri·ə·'reɪndʒ] *vt usu passive* vorplanen

precarious [prɪ·'ker·i·əs] *adj* gefährlich; *hold, balance* unsicher

precaution [prɪ·'kɔ·ʃən] *n* Vorkehrung *f;* **safety ~s** Vorsichtsmaßnahmen *pl*

precautionary [ˌprɪ·'kɔ·ʃə·ner·i] *adj inv* Vorsichts-

precede [prɪ·'sid] *vt* ❶ (*in rank*) rangieren vor *dat;* (*in importance*) wichtiger sein als ❷ (*in time*) vorausgehen *dat* ❸ (*in space*) vorangehen; **if the instruction is ~d by an asterisk, ...** wenn ein Sternchen vor der Anweisung steht, ...

precedence ['pres·ə·dəns] *n* ❶ (*priority*) Priorität *f,* Vorrang *m;* **to take ~ [over sth/sb]** Priorität [gegenüber jdm/etw] haben ❷ (*form: order of priority*) Rangordnung *f*

precedent ['pres·ə·dent] *n* ❶ (*example*) vergleichbarer Fall, Präzedenzfall *m geh;* **to set a ~** einen Präzendenzfall schaffen ❷ (*past procedure*) Tradition *f;* **to break with ~ [by doing sth]** [durch etw *akk*] mit der Tradition

P

brechen

preceding [prɪˈsi·dɪŋ] *adj attr, inv* vorhergehend, vorangegangen; **the ~ page** die vorige Seite

precinct [ˈpri·sɪŋkt] *n* ❶ (*electoral district*) Wahlbezirk *m* ❷ (*police district*) Polizeirevier *nt;* (*police station*) Revier *nt*

precious [ˈpreʃ·əs] **I.** *adj* ❶ (*of great value*) wertvoll, kostbar; ■**to be ~ to sb** jdm viel bedeuten ❷ (*pej*) *manner, style* geziert; *person* affektiert *geh* **II.** *adv* (*fam*) ~ **little** herzlich wenig

precipice [ˈpres·ə·pɪs] *n* ❶ (*steep drop*) Abgrund *m;* (*cliff face*) Steilhang *m* ❷ (*brink*) Klippe *f*

precipitate [prɪˈsɪp·ɪ·teɪt] **I.** *vt* ❶ (*form: trigger*) auslösen ❷ (*force suddenly*) stürzen (**into** in *+akk*) **II.** *vi* ❶ METEO einen Niederschlag bilden ❷ CHEM ■**to ~ [out]** ausfallen *fachspr* **III.** *n* Satz *m;* GEOL, MED Sediment *nt fachspr*

precipitation [prɪˌsɪp·ɪˈteɪ·ʃən] *n* ❶ METEO Niederschlag *m* ❷ (*forming into a solid*) Setzen *nt;* GEOL, MED Sedimentieren *nt fachspr* ❸ (*triggering*) **the ~ of a conflict** das Auslösen eines Konflikts

precipitous [prɪˈsɪp·ɪ·t̬əs] *adj* (*very steep*) steil, abschüssig, steil abfallend *attr*

precise [prɪˈsaɪs] *adj* ❶ (*exact*) genau, präzise ❷ (*approv: careful*) sorgfältig, genau; *movement* [ziel]sicher; *pronunciation, spelling* korrekt

precisely [prɪˈsaɪs·li] *adv* ❶ (*exactly*) genau, präzise ❷ (*just*) genau; ~ **because** eben wegen ❸ (*approv: carefully*) sorgfältig

precision [prɪˈsɪʒ·ən] **I.** *n* ❶ (*accuracy*) Genauigkeit *f,* Präzision *f* ❷ (*approv: meticulous care*) Sorgfalt *f* **II.** *adj attr, inv* exakt, präzise

P

preclude [prɪˈklud] *vt* (*form*) ausschließen; ■**to ~ sb from doing sth** (*form*) jdn davon abhalten, etw zu tun

precocious [prɪˈkoʊ·ʃəs] *adj* ❶ (*developing early*) frühreif; ~ **talent** frühe Begabung ❷ (*pej: maturing too early*) altklug

precociousness [prɪˈkoʊ·ʃəs·nɪs] *n* (*form*) ❶ (*early development*) Frühreife *f* ❷ (*pej: maturing too early*) Altklugheit *f*

preconceived [ˌpri·kənˈsivd] *adj* (*esp pej*) vorgefasst

preconception [ˌpri·kənˈsep·ʃən] *n* (*esp pej*) vorgefasste Meinung

precondition [ˌpri·kənˈdɪʃ·ən] *n* Vorbedingung *f,* Voraussetzung *f*

precooked [ˌpriˈkʊkt] *adj inv* vorgekocht

precursor [ˈpri·kɜr·sər] *n* (*form*) ❶ (*forerunner*) Vorläufer *m;* (*preparing way for sth*) Wegbereiter *m* ❷ (*harbinger*) Vorbote *m*

predate [priˈdeɪt] *vt* (*form*) zeitlich vorausgehen

predator [ˈpred·ə·t̬ər] *n* ❶ (*animal*) Raubtier *nt;* (*bird*) Raubvogel *m;* (*fish*) Raubfisch *m* ❷ (*pej: person*) Profiteur(in) *m(f);* (*vulture*) Aasgeier *m fig fam*

predatory [ˈpred·ə·tɔr·i] *adj* ❶ (*preying*) Raub-, räuberisch ❷ (*esp pej: exploitative*) raubtierhaft, rücksichtslos; (*greedy*) [raff]gierig

predecessor [ˈpred·ə·ses·ər] *n* Vorgänger(in) *m(f)*

predetermine [ˌpri·dɪˈtɜr·mən] *vt usu passive* (*form*) vor[her]bestimmen; **at a ~d signal** auf ein verabredetes Zeichen hin

predicament [prɪˈdɪk·ə·mənt] *n* Notlage *f;* **to be in a ~** sich in einer misslichen Lage befinden

predicate [ˈpred·ɪ·kɪt] *n* LING Prädikat *nt*

predict [prɪˈdɪkt] *vt* vorhersagen; *sb's future etc.* prophezeien

predictable [prɪˈdɪk·tə·bəl] *adj* ❶ (*foreseeable*) vorhersehbar, voraussagbar ❷ (*pej: not very original*) berechenbar; **her answer was so ~** es war von vornherein klar, was sie antworten würde

prediction [prɪˈdɪk·ʃən] *n* ❶ (*forecast*) Vorhersage *f,* Voraussage *f;* ECON, POL Prognose *f;* **to make a ~ about sth** etw vorhersagen; ECON, POL eine Prognose zu etw *dat* abgeben ❷ (*act of predicting*) Vorhersagen *nt*

predominance [prɪˈdam·ə·nəns] *n* ❶ (*greater number*) zahlenmäßige Überlegenheit ❷ (*predominant position*) Vorherrschaft *f* (**in** bei *+dat*)

predominant [prɪˈdam·ə·nənt] *adj inv* vorherrschend, beherrschend; ■**to be ~** führend sein

predominate [prɪˈdam·ə·neɪt] *vi* ❶ (*be most important*) vorherrschen ❷ (*be more numerous*) überwiegen

preeminence [ˌpriˈem·ɪ·nəns] *n* (*form*) Überlegenheit *f,* überragende Bedeutung

preeminent [ˌpriˈem·ɪ·nənt] *adj* (*form*) herausragend, überragend

preempt [ˌpriˈempt] *vt* ❶ TV, RADIO (*displace*) *regular programming* ersetzen ❷ (*form: appropriate in advance*) mit Beschlag belegen ❸ (*form: act in advance*) ■**to ~ sb/sth** jdm/etw zuvorkommen

preemptive [priˈemp·tɪv] *adj inv* ❶ (*preventive*) vorbeugend, Präventiv- ❷ MIL (*forestalling the enemy*) *attack, strike* präventiv, Präventiv-

preen [prin] **I.** *vi* ❶ *bird* sich putzen ❷ (*pej*) *person* sich auftakeln **II.** *vt* ❶ (*of bird*) *feathers* putzen ❷ (*pej: groom*) ■**to ~ oneself** sich auftakeln

pre-exist [ˌpri·ɪgˈzɪst] (*form*) **I.** *vi* vorher existieren; PHILOS, REL präexistieren **II.** *vt* vorausgehen

prefab [ˈpri·fæb] (*fam*) **I.** *n short for* **prefabricated house** Fertighaus *nt* **II.** *adj inv short for* **prefabricated** vorgefertigt

prefabricated [ˌpriˈfæb·rɪ·keɪ·t̬ɪd] *adj inv* vorgefertigt

preface [ˈpref·ɪs] **I.** *n* (*introduction*) Einleitung *f; to a novel, play etc.* Vorwort *nt* (**to** zu *+dat*) **II.** *vt* ❶ (*provide with preface*) ■**to ~ sth** eine Einleitung zu etw *dat* verfassen; ■**to**

be ~d by sth durch etw *akk* eingeleitet werden ❷ (*serve as introduction to*) einleiten

prefect ['pri·fekt] *n* (*official*) Präfekt(in) *m(f)*

prefer <-rr-> [pri·'fɜr] *vt* (*like better*) vorziehen, bevorzugen; ■**to ~ doing sth** [**to doing sth**] etw lieber [als etw] tun

preferable ['pref·rə·bəl] *adj inv* besser

preferably ['pref·rə·bli] *adv inv* am besten, vorzugsweise

preference ['pref·rəns] *n* ❶ (*priority*) Priorität *f*, Vorzug *m*; **to be given ~** Vorrang haben ❷ (*greater liking*) Vorliebe *f* (**for** für +*akk*) ❸ (*preferred thing*) Vorliebe *f*; **which is your personal ~?** was ist Ihnen persönlich lieber?

preferential [ˌpref·ə·'ren·ʃəl] *adj attr* Vorzugs-, Präferenz-; **to get ~ treatment** bevorzugt behandelt werden

preferred [pri·'fɜrd] *adj attr, inv* bevorzugt, Lieblings-; **the ~ choice** die erste Wahl

prefix ['pri·fɪks] **I.** *n* <*pl* -es> ❶ LING Präfix *nt fachspr* ❷ (*something prefixed*) Namensvorsatz *m*; **to add sth as a ~** etw voranstellen **II.** *vt* ■**to ~ sth with sth** etw einer S. *dat* voranstellen

pregnancy ['preg·nən·si] *n* Schwangerschaft *f*; ZOOL Trächtigkeit *f*

pregnant ['preg·nənt] *adj inv* ❶ *woman* schwanger; *animal* trächtig; **she's eight months ~** sie ist im achten Monat [schwanger] ❷ (*fig*) *pause, remark* bedeutungsvoll

prehistoric [ˌpri·hɪ·'stɔr·ɪk] *adj inv* ❶ (*before written history*) prähistorisch ❷ (*pej fam: outdated*) steinzeitlich *fig*, völlig veraltet

prejudge [ˌpri·'dʒʌdʒ] *vt* vorschnell ein Urteil fällen (über +*akk*), eine vorgefasste Meinung haben (über +*akk*)

prejudice ['predʒ·ə·dɪs] **I.** *n* ❶ (*preconceived opinion*) Vorurteil *nt* ❷ (*bias*) Vorurteil *nt* (**against** gegen +*akk*); **racial ~** Rassenvorurteil *nt* **II.** *vt* ❶ (*harm*) schädigen; **to ~ sb's chances** jds Chancen beeinträchtigen ❷ (*bias*) ■**to ~ sb** [**against/in favor of sb/sth**] jdn [gegen/für jdn/etw] einnehmen; **to ~ a case** LAW den Ausgang eines Prozesses beeinflussen

prejudiced ['predʒ·ə·dɪst] *adj* voreingenommen; *opinion* vorgefasst; ■**to be ~ against sb/sth** Vorurteile gegen jdn/etw haben; ■**to be ~ in favor of sb/sth** gegenüber jdm/etw positiv eingestellt sein

prejudicial [ˌpredʒ·ə·'dɪʃ·əl] *adj* (*form*) abträglich +*dat*; **to have a ~ effect on sth** eine nachteilige Wirkung auf etw *akk* haben; **to be ~ to sb's health** jds Gesundheit beeinträchtigen

prelim ['pri·lɪm] *n* (*fam*) ❶ SPORTS *short for* **preliminary** Vorrunde *f* ❷ *usu pl* (*preliminary exam*) *short for* **preliminary** Vorprüfung *f*

preliminary [prɪ·'lɪm·ə·ner·i] **I.** *adj attr, inv* einleitend; (*preparatory*) vorbereitend; **~ arrangements** Vorbereitungen *pl* **II.** *n* ❶ (*introduction*) Einleitung *f*; (*preparation*) Vorbereitung *f* ❷ SPORTS (*heat*) Vorrunde *f* ❸ (*form: preliminary exam*) Vorprüfung *f*

prelude ['prel·jud] *n* ❶ *usu sing* (*preliminary*) Vorspiel *nt*, Auftakt *m* ❷ MUS Prélude *nt*

premarital [ˌpri·'mær·ɪ·t̬əl] *adj inv* vorehelich *attr*

premature [ˌpri·mə·'tʃʊr] *adj* ❶ (*too early*) verfrüht, vorzeitig; *announcement, criticism, decision* voreilig ❷ MED **~ baby** Frühgeburt *f*

premeditated [ˌpri·'med·ɪ·teɪ·t̬ɪd] *adj inv* vorsätzlich, geplant; *act* überlegt

premeditation [ˌpri·med·ɪ·'teɪ·ʃən] *n* (*form*) [wohl durchdachtes] Planen; **with ~** *of a crime* mit Vorsatz

premenstrual [ˌpri·'men·stru·əl] *adj attr, inv* prämenstruell

premenstrual 'syndrome *n* prämenstruelles Syndrom

premier [prɪ·'mɪr] **I.** *n* Premierminister(in) *m(f)* **II.** *adj attr, inv* führend; **the ~ sporting event** der bedeutendste Wettkampf

premiere, première [prɪ·'mɪr] **I.** *n* Premiere *f*, Uraufführung *f* **II.** *vt* uraufführen **III.** *vi* **to ~ in New York** in New York uraufgeführt werden

premise ['prem·ɪs] *n* Prämisse *f geh*, Voraussetzung *f*; **to start from the ~ that ...** von der Voraussetzung ausgehen, dass ...

premium ['pri·mi·əm] **I.** *n* ❶ (*insurance payment*) [Versicherungs]prämie *f* ❷ (*extra charge*) Zuschlag *m*; ■**a ~ on sth** ein Preisaufschlag auf etw *akk* ❸ (*gasoline*) Super[benzin] *nt* **II.** *adj attr, inv* ❶ (*high*) hoch ❷ (*top-quality*) Spitzen-; **the ~ brand** die führende Marke; *fruit* erstklassig

premonition [ˌpri·mə·'nɪʃ·ən] *n* [böse] Vorahnung

prenatal [ˌpri·'neɪ·t̬əl] *adj attr, inv* vorgeburtlich, pränatal *fachspr*

preoccupation [ˌpri·ak·jə·'peɪ·ʃən] *n* ❶ (*dominant concern*) Sorge *f* ❷ (*state of mind*) ■[**a**] **~ with sth** ständige [gedankliche] Beschäftigung mit etw *dat*; **to have a ~ with sth** von etw *dat* besessen sein

preoccupied [pri·'ak·ju·paɪd] *adj* ❶ (*distracted*) gedankenverloren; (*absorbed*) nachdenklich; ■**to be ~ with sb/sth** sich mit jdm/etw stark beschäftigen ❷ (*worried*) besorgt

preoccupy <-ie-> [pri·'ak·ju·paɪ] *vt* ■**to ~ sb** jdn [sehr stark] beschäftigen

preordain [ˌpri·ɔr·'deɪn] *vt usu passive* (*form*) ■**to be ~ed** vorherbestimmt sein; *path* vorgezeichnet; **sb is ~ed to succeed** der Erfolg ist jdm sicher

prep [prep] *n* (*fam*) Vorbereitung *f*

prepaid [ˌpri·'peɪd] *adj inv* im Voraus bezahlt, bereits bezahlt

preparation [ˌprep·ə·'reɪ·ʃən] *n* ❶ (*getting ready*) Vorbereitung *f*; *of food* Zubereitung *f*; **to do a lot of ~** [**for sth**] sich sehr gut [auf etw *akk*] vorbereiten ❷ (*measures*) ■**~s** *pl* Vorbereitungen *pl* (**for** für +*akk*); (*precautions*) Vorkehrungen *pl* ❸ (*substance*) Präparat *nt*, Mittel *nt*

P

preparatory [prɪ·ˈpær·ə·tɔr·i] *adj inv* vorbereitend *attr,* Vorbereitungs-

preˈparatory school *n* (*form*) *meist private Vorbereitungsschule auf das College*

prepare [prɪ·ˈper] **I.** *vt* ① (*get ready*) vorbereiten (**for** auf +*akk*); **I hadn't ~d myself for such a shock** auf einen solchen Schock war ich nicht gefasst; **to ~ the way [for sb/sth]** den Weg [für jdn/etw] bereiten ② (*make*) zubereiten; *meal* machen **II.** *vi* ■**to ~ for sth** sich auf etw *akk* vorbereiten; **to ~ for takeoff** sich zum Start bereit machen

prepared [prɪ·ˈperd] *adj* ① *pred* (*ready*) bereit, fertig *fam;* ■**to be ~ for sb/sth** auf jdn/etw vorbereitet sein; **they were ~ for the worst** sie waren auf das Schlimmste gefasst ② *pred* (*willing*) ■**to be ~ to do sth** bereit sein, etw zu tun ③ (*arranged previously*) vorbereitet; **~ meal** Fertiggericht *nt*

prepay <-paid, -paid> [ˌpri·ˈpeɪ] *vt* im Voraus bezahlen

prepayment [ˌpri·ˈpeɪ·mənt] *n* Vorauszahlung *f*

preposition [ˌprep·ə·ˈzɪʃ·ən] *n* Verhältniswort *nt,* Präposition *f*

prepossessing [ˌpri·pə·ˈzes·ɪŋ] *adj usu neg* einnehmend, anziehend; **to be not very ~** *person* nicht sehr einnehmend sein

preposterous [prɪ·ˈpas·tər·əs] *adj* absurd, unsinnig

preppy, preppie [ˈprep·i] **I.** *n Schüler(in) einer privaten „prep school", der/die großen Wert auf gute Kleidung und das äußere Erscheinungsbild legt* **II.** *adj appearance* adrett; *clothes, look* popperhaft *meist pej fam*

ˈprep school *n* (*fam*) *see* **preparatory school**

prerequisite [ˌpri·ˈrek·wɪ·zɪt] *n* (*form*) [Grund]voraussetzung *f,* Vorbedingung *f* (**for/of/to** für +*akk*)

prerogative [prɪ·ˈrag·ə·t̬ɪv] *n usu sing* (*form: right*) Recht *nt;* (*privilege*) Vorrecht *nt,* Privileg *nt*

preschool [ˈpri·skul] **I.** *n* Kindergarten *m* **II.** *adj attr, inv* vorschulisch, Vorschul-

prescribe [prɪ·ˈskraɪb] *vt* ① (*medical*) ■**to ~ sth [for sb]** [jdm] etw verschreiben ② (*recommend*) ■**to ~ sth [to sb]** *a special diet* [jdm] etw verordnen; *fresh air, exercise* [jdm] etw empfehlen

prescription [prɪ·ˈskrɪp·ʃən] *n* (*medical*) Rezept *nt* (**for** auf +*akk*); **to be available by ~ only** verschreibungspflichtig sein

presence [ˈprez·əns] *n* ① (*attendance*) Anwesenheit *f;* (*occurrence*) Vorhandensein *nt;* **in my ~** in meiner Gegenwart ② (*approv: dignified bearing*) Haltung *f,* Auftreten *nt* ③ (*supernatural*) Gegenwart *f kein pl;* **to feel sb's ~** jds Gegenwart [förmlich] spüren können

present¹ [ˈprez·ənt] **I.** *n* ① (*now*) ■**the ~** die Gegenwart; **at ~** zurzeit, gegenwärtig; **for the ~** vorläufig ② LING Präsens *nt* **II.** *adj* ① *inv, attr* (*current*) derzeitig, gegenwärtig; *month* laufend; **down to the ~ day** bis zum heutigen Tag; **at the ~ moment** im Moment ② *inv, attr* (*being dealt with*) betreffend; *case* vorliegend ③ *inv, usu pred* (*in attendance*) anwesend (**at** bei +*dat*)

present² **I.** *n* [ˈprez·ənt] Geschenk *nt;* **birthday ~** Geburtstagsgeschenk *nt;* **to get sth as a ~** etw geschenkt bekommen **II.** *vt* [prɪ·ˈzent] ① (*give formally*) ■**to ~ sth [to sb/sth]** *gift* [jdm/etw] etw schenken; *award, medal, diploma* [jdm/etw] etw überreichen ② (*hand over, show*) ■**to ~ sth [to sb/sth]** [jdm/etw] etw vorlegen; **to ~ a united front** *organization, people* sich geeint zeigen ③ (*put forward*) ■**to ~ sth [to sb/sth]** [jdm/etw] etw präsentieren; *argument* anführen; *proposal* unterbreiten ④ (*face, confront*) **to ~ sb with a challenge** jdn vor eine Herausforderung stellen; **to ~ sb with the facts** jdm die Fakten vor Augen führen ⑤ (*be*) darstellen; (*offer, provide*) bieten; (*cause*) mit sich bringen ⑥ *TV program* moderieren; *film* zeigen ⑦ (*arise*) ■**to ~ itself** *opportunity, solution* sich bieten; *problem* sich zeigen

presentable [prɪ·ˈzen·tə·bəl] *adj person* vorzeigbar; *thing* ansehnlich; **to make sth ~** etw herrichten

presentation [ˌpre·zən·ˈteɪ·ʃən] *n* ① (*giving*) Präsentation *f; of a theory* Darlegung *f; of a dissertation, thesis* Vorlage *f; of gifts* Überreichung *f; of awards* [Preis]verleihung *f* ② (*lecture, talk*) Präsentation *f* (**on** zu +*dat*), Vortrag *f* (**on** über +*akk*) ③ *of photographs, works* Ausstellung *f*

present-ˈday *adj usu attr* heutig *attr*

presenter [prɪ·ˈzen·tər] *n* Moderator(in) *m(f)*

presently [ˈprez·ənt·li] *adv inv* ① (*now*) zurzeit, gegenwärtig ② (*soon*) bald, gleich

present ˈparticiple *n* LING Partizip *nt* Präsens

present ˈtense *n* LING Präsens *nt,* Gegenwartsform *f*

preservation [ˌprez·ər·ˈveɪ·ʃən] **I.** *n* ① (*upkeep*) Erhaltung *f* ② (*conservation*) Bewahrung *f; of order* Aufrechterhaltung *f;* (*protection*) Schutz *m; of [national] interests* Wahrung *f; of food* Konservierung *f* **II.** *adj attr, inv* Konservierungs-

preservative [prɪ·ˈzɜr·və·t̬ɪv] *n* Konservierungsstoff *m*

preserve [prɪ·ˈzɜrv] **I.** *vt* ① (*maintain*) erhalten; *customs, tradition* bewahren ② (*conserve*) konservieren; *wood* [mit Holzschutzmittel] behandeln; *fruit and vegetables* einmachen; *cucumbers* einlegen **II.** *n* ① *usu pl* (*jam or jelly*) Marmelade *f;* (*cooked whole*) Eingemachte(s) *nt kein pl;* **strawberry ~s** eingemachte Erdbeeren ② (*reserve*) Reservat *nt;* **nature/wildlife ~** Naturschutzgebiet *nt* ③ (*domain*) Domäne *f;* (*property*) Besitztum *nt;* (*responsibility*) Wirkungsbereich *m; of a department* Ressort *nt*

preserved [prɪ·ˈzɜrvd] *adj* ① (*maintained*) konserviert; *building* erhalten ② FOOD eingemacht, eingelegt; **~ food** konservierte Lebensmittel

preshrunk [ˌpri·ˈʃrʌŋk] *adj inv* · *jeans* vorgewaschen

preside [prɪ·ˈzaɪd] *vi* den Vorsitz haben; ■**to ~ over sth** etw leiten

presidency [ˈprez·ɪ·dən·si] *n* ❶ (*office*) Präsidentschaft *f;* **to make a run for the ~** für das Amt des Präsidenten/der Präsidentin kandidieren ❷ (*tenure*) Präsidentschaft *f;* (*of company*) Aufsichtsratsvorsitz *m*

president [ˈprez·ɪ·dənt] *n of country* Präsident(in) *m(f); of company, corporation* [Vorstands-]vorsitzende(r)

presidential [ˌprez·ɪ·ˈden·tʃəl] *adj* ❶ *inv, usu attr* POL (*of president*) Präsidenten-; (*of office*) Präsidentschafts-; **~ race** Rennen *nt* um die Präsidentschaft ❷ *attr, inv* (*of head of organization*) **~ address** Ansprache *f* des/der Vorsitzenden

Der **Presidents' Day** (Präsidententag) ist ein gesetzlicher Feiertag in den USA und wird immer am dritten Montag im Februar gefeiert, um allen Arbeitnehmern ein langes Wochenende zu ermöglichen. Ursprünglich wurde an diesem Tag der Geburtstag von George Washington, Held des Unabhängigkeitskrieges, gefeiert, der am 22. Februar 1732 geboren wurde. Mitte der siebziger Jahre beschloss der Kongress, einen Feiertag zu Ehren aller US-Präsidenten einzurichten. Der Tag wird aber vielerorts noch als *Washington's Birthday* (Washingtons Geburtstag) bezeichnet.

press [pres] **I.** *n* <*pl* -es> ❶ (*push*) Druck *m;* **at the ~ of a button** auf Knopfdruck ❷ (*instrument*) Presse *f* ❸ (*news media, newspapers*) ■**the ~** die Presse; (*publicity*) **to get good/bad ~** eine gute/schlechte Presse bekommen ❹ (*ironing*) Bügeln *nt kein pl* **II.** *vt* ❶ (*push*) ■**to ~ sth** [auf] etw *akk* drücken; ■**to ~ sth ↻ down** etw herunterdrücken; ■**to ~ sth into sth** etw in etw *akk* hineindrücken ❷ (*flatten*) zusammendrücken; *flowers* pressen; *fruit* auspressen; *grapes* keltern ❸ (*iron*) bügeln, glätten SCHWEIZ, plätten NORDD *a.* ❹ (*fig: urge, impel*) bedrängen; **to ~ sb for a decision** jdn zu einer Entscheidung drängen ❺ (*forcefully promote*) forcieren **III.** *vi* ❶ (*push*) drücken ❷ (*be urgent*) drängen

◆**press ahead** *vi* ■**to ~ ahead [with sth]** etw vorantreiben

◆**press on I.** *vi* ■**to ~ on [with sth]** [mit etw *dat*] [zügig] weitermachen **II.** *vt* ■**to ~ sth on sb** jdm etw aufdrängen

ˈ**press agency** *n see* **news agency**

ˈ**press clipping** *n* Zeitungsausschnitt *m*

ˈ**press conference** *n* Pressekonferenz *f*

ˈ**press coverage** *n* ❶ (*scale of reporting*) Berichterstattung *f* (*in der Presse*) ❷ (*footage*) [Fernseh]übertragung *f*

ˈ**press gallery** *n* Pressetribüne *f*

pressing [ˈpres·ɪŋ] *adj issue, matter* dringend; *requests* nachdrücklich

ˈ**press office** *n* Pressestelle *f*

ˈ**press officer** *n* Pressereferent(in) *m(f)*

ˈ**press release** *n* Pressemitteilung *f,* Pressemeldung *f*

pressure [ˈpreʃ·ᵊr] **I.** *n* ❶ (*physical force*) Druck *m;* **to apply ~** Druck ausüben ❷ PHYS Druck *m* ❸ (*stress*) Druck *m,* Stress *m,* Belastung[en] *f*[*pl*]; (*stronger*) Überlastung *f;* **to be under ~ to do sth** unter Druck stehen, etw zu tun; **there is a lot of ~ on sb** jd hat Stress ❹ (*insistence*) Druck *m;* **to put ~ on sb [to do sth]** jdn unter Druck setzen[, damit er/sie etw tut] **II.** *vt* ■**to ~ sb to do sth** jdn [massiv] dazu drängen, etw zu tun

ˈ**pressure cooker** *n* Schnellkochtopf *m*

ˈ**pressure gauge** *n* Druckmesser *m*

ˈ**pressure washer** *n* Hochdruckreiniger

pressurize [ˈpreʃ·ə·raɪz] *vt* druckfest halten

prestige [pre·ˈstiʒ] *n* Prestige *nt,* Ansehen *nt*

prestigious [pre·ˈstɪdʒ·əs] *adj* angesehen, Prestige-; *hotel* vornehm

presumably [prɪ·ˈzu·mə·bli] *adv inv* vermutlich

presume [prɪ·ˈzum] **I.** *vt* (*suppose, believe*) annehmen; **to be ~d innocent** als unschuldig gelten **II.** *vi* ❶ (*dare*) ■**to ~ to do sth** sich [*o* anmaßen] erlauben *dat,* etw zu tun ❷ (*take advantage of*) ■**to ~ on sth** etw überbeanspruchen

presumption [prɪ·ˈzʌmp·ʃən] *n* ❶ (*assumption*) Annahme *f,* Vermutung *f* ❷ (*form: arrogance*) Überheblichkeit *f*

presumptuous [prɪ·ˈzʌmp·tʃu·əs] *adj person, behavior* anmaßend; *attitude* überheblich; (*forward*) unverschämt

presuppose [ˌpri·sə·ˈpoʊz] *vt* (*form*) voraussetzen

pretax [ˌpri·ˈtæks] *adj inv* unversteuert, vor Abzug der Steuern *nach n,* Brutto-

pretend [prɪ·ˈtend] **I.** *vt* ❶ (*behave falsely*) vorgeben, vortäuschen; **to ~ surprise** so tun, als ob man überrascht wäre; **to ~ that one is asleep** sich schlafend stellen ❷ (*imagine*) ■**to ~ to be sb/sth** so tun, als sei man jd/etw; **I'll just ~ that I didn't hear that** ich tue einfach so, als hätte ich das nicht gehört **II.** *vi* (*feign*) sich *dat* etw vormachen; ■**to ~ to sb that ...** jdm vormachen, dass ... **III.** *adj attr* (*fam: in deception, game*) Spiel-; **this doll is Katie's ~ baby** mit dieser Puppe spielt Katie Baby

pretender [prɪ·ˈten·dər] *n to position, title* Anwärter, Anwärterin *m, f* (**to** auf +*akk*)

pretense [ˈpri·tens] *n* ❶ (*false behavior, insincerity*) Vortäuschung *f;* **under false ~s** *a.* LAW unter Vorspiegelung falscher Tatsachen ❷ (*story, excuse*) Vorwand *m;* **under the ~ of doing sth** unter dem Vorwand, etw zu tun

P

pretension [prɪ·ˈten·ʃən] *n* ❶ *usu pl* (*claim*) Anspruch *m* (**to** auf +*akk*); (*aspiration*) Ambition *f* ❷ (*pej*) *see* **pretentiousness**

pretentious [prɪ·ˈten·ʃəs] *adj* (*pej*) *person* großspurig; *manner, speech, style* hochgestochen; (*ostentatious*) protzig *meist pej fam,* angeberisch

pretentiousness [prɪ·ˈten·ʃəs·nɪs] *n* (*arrogance*) Überheblichkeit *f,* Anmaßung *f;* (*boastfulness*) Angeberei *f fam*

pretext [ˈpri·tekst] *n* Vorwand *m* (**for** für +*akk*); **on the ~ of doing sth** unter dem Vorwand, etw zu tun

prettify <-ie-> [ˈprɪt̬·ɪ·faɪ] *vt room etc.* verschönern

pretty [ˈprɪt̬·i] **I.** *adj person* hübsch; *thing* nett; **not a ~ sight** kein schöner Anblick **II.** *adv inv* (*fam*) ❶ (*fairly*) ziemlich; **~ good** (*fam*) ganz gut; **~ damn quick** (*fam*) verdammt schnell ❷ (*almost*) **~ much everything** beinah alles **III.** *vt* ■**to ~ oneself** ⟲ **up** sich zurechtmachen; ■**to ~ up** ⟲ **sth** [**with sth**] (*enhance*) etw [mit etw *dat*] verschönern

pretzel [ˈpret·səl] *n* Brezel *f* ÖSTERR *a. nt*

prevail [prɪ·ˈveɪl] *vi* ❶ (*triumph*) *justice, good* siegen; *person* sich durchsetzen ❷ (*induce*) ■**to ~** [**up**]**on sb to do sth** jdn dazu bewegen, etw zu tun ❸ (*exist, be widespread*) *custom* weit verbreitet sein; *opinion* geläufig sein

prevailing [prɪ·ˈveɪ·lɪŋ] *adj attr, inv wind* vorherrschend; *weather* derzeit herrschend; *law* geltend

prevalence [ˈprev·ə·ləns] *n of crime, disease* Häufigkeit *f; of bribery, of drugs* Überhandnehmen *nt;* (*predominance*) Vorherrschen *nt*

prevalent [ˈprev·ə·lənt] *adj* (*common*) vorherrschend *attr; disease* weit verbreitet; *opinion* geläufig; (*frequent*) besonders häufig

prevent [prɪ·ˈvent] *vt* verhindern; MED vorbeugen; *crime* verhüten; ■**to ~ sb/sth from doing sth** jdn/etw daran hindern, etw zu tun; **there's nothing to ~ us from doing it** davon kann uns überhaupt nichts abhalten

preventative [prɪ·ˈven·tə·t̬ɪv] *adj inv see* **preventive**

prevention [prɪ·ˈven·ʃən] *n of disaster* Verhinderung *f; of accident* Vermeidung *f; of crime* Verhütung *f*

preventive [prɪ·ˈven·tɪv] *adj inv* vorbeugend, Präventiv-

preview [ˈpri·vju] **I.** *n of a film, play* **sneak ~** Vorpremiere *f; of an exhibition* Vernissage *f; of new products* Vor[ab]besichtigung *f;* (*trailer*) Vorschau *f* **II.** *vt a film* eine Vorschau sehen

previous [ˈpri·vi·əs] *adj attr, inv* ❶ (*former*) vorig, vorausgegangen; (*prior*) vorherig; **~ conviction** Vorstrafe *f;* **no ~ experience required** keine Vorkenntnisse erforderlich ❷ (*preceding*) vorig, vorhergehend; **on the ~ day** am Tag davor; **on my ~ visit to Florida** bei meinem letzten Besuch in Florida

previously [ˈpri·vi·əs·li] *adv inv* (*beforehand*) zuvor, vorher; (*formerly*) früher; **~ unreleased** bisher unveröffentlicht

prewar [ˌpri·ˈwɔr] *adj inv* Vorkriegs-

prey [preɪ] **I.** *n* (*victim*) Beute *f* **II.** *vi* ❶ (*kill*) Jagd machen (**on** auf +*akk*) ❷ (*exploit*) ■**to ~ on sb** jdn ausnutzen; (*abuse*) jdn ausnehmen; **to ~ on old people** sich *dat* alte Menschen als Opfer [aus]suchen

price [praɪs] **I.** *n* ❶ (*monetary amount*) Preis *m;* **to pay full ~ for sth** den vollen Preis bezahlen ❷ (*sacrifice*) Preis *m kein pl fig;* **to pay a** [**heavy**] **~** einen [hohen] Preis zahlen *fig;* **not at any ~** um keinen Preis **II.** *vt* ■**to ~ sth** (*mark with price*) etw auszeichnen; (*set value*) den Preis für etw *akk* festsetzen; **to be reasonably ~d** einen angemessenen Preis haben

ˈprice cut *n* Preissenkung *f*

ˈprice fixing *n* Preisabsprache *f*

priceless [ˈpraɪs·lɪs] *adj* ❶ (*invaluable*) unbezahlbar, von unschätzbarem Wert *nach n* ❷ (*fig fam*) *remark, situation* köstlich; *of a person* unbezahlbar *hum*

ˈprice range *n* Preislage *f*

ˈprice tag, ˈprice ticket *n* ❶ (*label*) Preisschild *nt* ❷ (*fam: cost*) Preis *m* (**for** für +*akk*)

ˈprice war *n* Preiskrieg *m*

pricey [ˈpraɪ·si] *adj* (*fam*) teuer

pricing [ˈpraɪ·sɪŋ] *n* Preisgestaltung *f*

prick [prɪk] **I.** *n* ❶ (*act of piercing*) Stechen *nt;* (*fig*) *sharp pain* Stich *m* ❷ (*vulg: penis*) Schwanz *m* ❸ (*vulg: idiot*) Arsch *m* **II.** *vt* stechen; **to ~ one's finger** sich *dat o akk* in den Finger stechen

◆**prick up I.** *vt* **to ~ up one's ears** die Ohren spitzen **II.** *vi* **sb's ears ~ up** [**at sth**] jd spitzt die Ohren [bei etw *dat*]

prickle [ˈprɪk·əl] *n* ❶ (*thorn*) Dorn *m; of animal* Stachel *m* ❷ (*sensation*) Kratzen *nt;* (*fig*) Kribbeln *nt a. fig fam*

prickly [ˈprɪk·li] *adj* ❶ (*thorny*) stachelig ❷ (*scratchy*) kratzig ❸ (*fam: easily offended*) *person* [leicht] reizbar; *subject* heikel

prickly ˈpear *n* ❶ (*plant*) Feigenkaktus *m* ❷ (*fruit*) Kaktusfeige *f*

pride [praɪd] **I.** *n* ❶ (*satisfaction*) Stolz *m;* **to feel great ~** besonders stolz sein; **to take ~ in sb/sth** stolz auf jdn/etw sein; (*self-respect*) Stolz *m* ❷ (*source of satisfaction*) Stolz *m;* **sb's ~ and joy** jds ganzer Stolz ❸ (*arrogance*) Hochmut *m,* Überheblichkeit *f* ❹ (*animal group*) **a ~ of lions** ein Rudel *nt* Löwen ▶ PHRASES: **~ comes before a fall** (*prov*) Hochmut kommt vor dem Fall **II.** *vt* ■**to ~ oneself on sth** auf etw *akk* [besonders] stolz sein

priest [prist] *n* Priester *m,* Geistlicher *m*

priestess <*pl* -es> [ˈpri·stɪs] *n* Priesterin *f*

priesthood [ˈprist·hʊd] *n* ❶ (*position, office*) Priestertum *nt;* **to enter the ~** Priester/Priesterin werden ❷ (*body of priests*) Priesterschaft *f*

priestly [ˈprist·li] *adj* priesterlich, Priester-

prim <-mm-> [prɪm] *adj* (*pej*) steif; (*prudish*) prüde

primal [ˈpraɪ·məl] *adj inv fear* ursprünglich, Ur-

primarily [praɪ·ˈmer·ə·li] *adv inv* vorwiegend, hauptsächlich, in erster Linie

primary [ˈpraɪ·mer·i] **I.** *adj inv* ❶ (*principal*) primär *geh,* Haupt-; ~ **concern** Hauptanliegen *nt* ❷ (*not derivative*) roh gewonnen, Roh- ❸ SCH Grundschul[s]- **II.** *n* POL (*election*) Vorwahl *f*

primary ˈcolor *n* Grundfarbe *f*

ˈprimary school *n* Grundschule *f*

primate [ˈpraɪ·meɪt] *n* ❶ ZOOL (*mammal*) Primat *m* ❷ (*bishop*) Primas *m fachspr*

prime [praɪm] **I.** *adj attr, inv* ❶ (*main*) wesentlich, Haupt-; ~ **objective** oberstes Ziel; ~ **suspect** Hauptverdächtige(r) *f(m)* ❷ (*best*) erstklassig; *example* ausgezeichnet **II.** *n* Blütezeit *f fig;* **to be in one's ~** im besten Alter sein; **to be past one's ~** die besten Jahre hinter sich *dat* haben **III.** *vt* ❶ (*prepare*) vorbereiten ❷ TECH, MIL (*for exploding*) scharf machen; (*for firing*) schussbereit machen ❸ *canvas, metal, wood* grundieren

prime ˈminister *n* Premierminister(in) *m(f)*

prime ˈnumber *n* Primzahl *f*

primer [ˈpraɪ·mər] *n* ❶ (*paint*) Grundierfarbe *f;* (*coat*) Grundierung *f* ❷ (*to detonate explosive*) Zündladung *f*

ˈprime time *n* Hauptsendezeit *f*

primeval [praɪ·ˈmi·vəl] *adj* urzeitlich, Ur-

primitive [ˈprɪm·ɪ·t̬ɪv] *adj* ❶ BIOL primitiv; ZOOL urzeitlich ❷ (*pej: simple*) primitiv

prince [prɪns] *n* (*royal*) Prinz *m;* (*head of principality*) Fürst *m*

princely [ˈprɪns·li] *adj* (*approv*) fürstlich

princess <*pl* -es> [ˈprɪn·sɪs] *n* Prinzessin *f*

principal [ˈprɪn·sə·pəl] **I.** *adj attr, inv* ❶ (*most important*) Haupt-, hauptsächlich ❷ FIN (*original sum*) Kapital- **II.** *n* ❶ (*head person*) *in a school* Direktor(in) *m(f),* Schulleiter(in) *m(f),* Rektor(in) *m(f); in a company* Vorgesetzte(r) *f(m); in a play* Hauptdarsteller(in) *m(f)* ❷ (*client of lawyer*) Mandant(in) *m(f)* ❸ *usu sing* (*of investment*) Kapitalsumme *f;* (*of loan*) Kreditsumme *f*

principality [ˌprɪn·sə·ˈpæl·ɪ·t̬i] *n* Fürstentum *nt*

principally [ˈprɪn·səp·li] *adv inv* hauptsächlich, vorwiegend, in erster Linie

principle [ˈprɪn·sə·pəl] *n* ❶ (*basic concept*) Prinzip *nt;* **basic ~** Grundprinzip *nt* ❷ (*basis*) Grundlage *f* ❸ (*approv: moral code*) Prinzip *nt,* Grundsatz *m;* **to stick to one's ~s** an seinen Prinzipien festhalten ▶ PHRASES: **on ~** aus Prinzip; **in ~** im Prinzip

print [prɪnt] **I.** *n* ❶ (*lettering*) Gedruckte(s) *nt;* **to read the fine ~** das Kleingedruckte lesen ❷ (*printed form*) Druck *m;* **to appear in ~** veröffentlicht werden; **out of ~** vergriffen ❸ (*photo*) Abzug *m;* (*film, reproduction*) Kopie *f;* (*copy of artwork*) Druck *m* ❹ (*pattern*) [Druck]muster *nt;* **floral ~** Blumenmuster *nt* **II.** *vt* ❶ TYPO drucken; **to ~ a magazine** eine Zeitschrift herausgeben ❷ PUBL veröffentlichen; (*in magazine, newspaper*) abdrucken ❸ COMPUT ausdrucken ❹ PHOT abziehen ❺ (*write by hand*) etw in Druckschrift schreiben **III.** *vi* ❶ (*make copy*) drucken ❷ (*write in unjoined letters*) in Druckschrift schreiben

printable [ˈprɪn·t̬ə·bəl] *adj inv* druckfähig, druckbar; *manuscript* druckfertig

printed ˈcircuit board *n* Leiterplatte *f*

printer [ˈprɪn·t̬ər] *n* ❶ (*machine*) Drucker *m* ❷ (*person*) Drucker(in) *m(f)*

printing [ˈprɪn·t̬ɪŋ] *n* ❶ (*act*) Drucken *nt* ❷ (*print run*) Auflage *f* ❸ (*handwriting*) Druckschrift *f*

ˈprinting press *n* Druckerpresse *f*

ˈprintout *n* Ausdruck *m*

ˈprint run *n* ❶ TYPO Auflage *f* ❷ COMPUT Drucklauf *m*

ˈprint shop *n* ❶ (*factory*) Druckmaschinensaal *m* ❷ (*copy store*) Druckerei *f* ❸ (*shop*) Grafikhandlung *f*

prior [ˈpraɪ·ər] *adj attr, inv* ❶ (*earlier*) frühere(r, s), vorherige(r, s); ~ **engagement** vorher getroffene Verabredung ❷ (*having priority*) vorrangig

prioritize [praɪ·ˈɔr·ɪ·taɪz] **I.** *vt* ❶ (*order*) der Priorität nach ordnen ❷ (*give preference to*) vorrangig behandeln **II.** *vi* Prioritäten setzen

priority [praɪ·ˈɔr·ɪ·t̬i] *n* ❶ (*deserving greatest attention*) vorrangige Angelegenheit; **first/top ~** Angelegenheit *f* von höchster Priorität; **my first ~ is to find somewhere to live** für mich ist es vorrangig, eine Wohnung zu finden; **to get one's priorities straight** seine Prioritäten richtig setzen ❷ (*precedence*) Vorrang *m;* **to give ~ to sb/sth** jdm/etw den Vorzug geben ❸ (*right of way*) Vorfahrt *f*

prior to *prep* ■ ~ **to sth** vor etw *dat*

priory [ˈpraɪ·ə·ri] *n* Priorat *nt*

prism [ˈprɪz·əm] *n* Prisma *nt*

prison [ˈprɪz·ən] *n* (*a. fig: jail*) Gefängnis *nt a. fig;* **to be in ~** im Gefängnis sitzen

ˈprison camp *n* (*for POWs*) [Kriegs]gefangenenlager *nt;* (*for political prisoners*) Straflager *nt*

ˈprison cell *n* Gefängniszelle *f*

prisoner [ˈprɪz·ə·nər] *n* (*a. fig*) Gefangene(r) *f(m) a. fig,* Häftling *m;* (*fig*) **political ~** politischer Häftling; **to take sb ~** jdn gefangen nehmen

prisoner of ˈwar <*pl* prisoners-> *n* Kriegsgefangene(r) *f(m)*

ˈprison sentence *n* Freiheitsstrafe *f*

pristine [ˈprɪs·tin] *adj* (*approv: original*) ursprünglich; *nature* unberührt; (*perfect*) tadellos, makellos

privacy [ˈpraɪ·və·si] *n* ❶ (*personal realm*) Privatsphäre *f;* **in the ~ of one's [own] home** in den eigenen vier Wänden *fam* ❷ (*time alone*) Zurückgezogenheit *f,* Abgeschiedenheit *f* ❸ (*secret*) Geheimhaltung *f*

private [ˈpraɪ·vət] **I.** *adj* ❶ *inv* (*personal, not official, not governmental*) privat, Privat-; ~ **joke** Insiderwitz *m fam* ❷ (*not open to public*) privat, Privat-; *discussion, meeting* nicht öffentlich; ~ **school/golf club** Privatschule *f*/ privater Golfklub ❸ (*confidential*) vertraulich; **to keep sth** ~ etw für sich *akk* behalten ❹ (*not social*) zurückhaltend, introvertiert ❺ (*secluded*) abgelegen; (*undisturbed*) ungestört **II.** *n* ❶ (*not in public*) ■**in** ~ privat; LAW unter Ausschluss der Öffentlichkeit; **to speak to sb in** ~ jdn [*o* mit jdm] unter vier Augen sprechen ❷ (*soldier*) Gefreiter *m*

private 'eye *n* (*fam*) Privatdetektiv(in) *m(f)*

privately ['praɪ·vət·li] *adv* ❶ (*not in public*) privat; **to speak** ~ **with sb** mit jdm unter vier Augen sprechen ❷ (*secretly*) heimlich, insgeheim ❸ (*personally*) persönlich

privatization [ˌpraɪ·və·tɪ·'zeɪ·ʃən] *n* Privatisierung *f*

privatize ['praɪ·və·taɪz] *vt* privatisieren

privilege ['prɪv·ə·lɪdʒ] **I.** *n* ❶ (*special right*) Privileg *nt,* Vorrecht *nt* ❷ (*honor*) Ehre *f;* (*iron*) Vergnügen *nt* ❸ (*advantage*) Sonderrecht *nt,* Privileg *nt* ❹ LAW **attorney-client** ~ Anwaltsgeheimnis *nt* **II.** *vt usu passive* (*give privileges to*) privilegieren

privileged ['prɪv·ə·lɪdʒd] *adj* ❶ (*with privileges*) privilegiert ❷ *inv* LAW *communication, information* vertraulich

privy ['prɪv·i] *adj inv* (*form*) ■**to be** ~ **to sth** in etw *akk* eingeweiht sein

prize[1] [praɪz] **I.** *n* ❶ (*sth won*) Preis *m;* **cash** ~ Geldpreis *m;* (*in lottery*) Gewinn *m* ❷ (*reward*) Lohn *m* **II.** *adj attr, inv* ❶ (*dated or iron fam: first-rate*) erstklassig *a. iron;* ~ **idiot** Vollidiot(in) *m(f) pej sl* ❷ (*prize-winning*) preisgekrönt **III.** *vt usu passive* schätzen; **sb's** ~**d possession** jds wertvollster Besitz; **to** ~ **sth highly** etw hoch schätzen

prize[2] [praɪz] *vt* ■**to** ~ **sth open** etw [mit einem Hebel] aufbrechen; **to** ~ **sb's hand open** jds Hand [mit Gewalt] öffnen

P

'prizefighter *n* Profiboxer(in) *m(f)*

'prizefighting *n* Profiboxen *nt*

'prize-winning *adj attr, inv* preisgekrönt

pro[1] [proʊ] **I.** *adv* dafür **II.** *n* Pro *nt;* **the** ~**s and cons of sth** das Pro und Kontra einer S. *gen* **III.** *prep* (*in favor of*) für

pro[2] [proʊ] (*fam*) **I.** *n* Profi *m* **II.** *adj attr, inv* Profi-

proactive [ˌproʊ·'æk·tɪv] *adj* initiativ *geh;* **some companies should be taking a more** ~ **approach toward exporting** manche Firmen sollten, was den Export betrifft, mehr Eigeninitiative zeigen

probability [ˌprab·ə·'bɪl·ɪ·t̬i] *n* Wahrscheinlichkeit *f;* **in all** ~ höchstwahrscheinlich

probable ['prab·ə·bəl] **I.** *adj* wahrscheinlich **II.** *n* POL, ECON Kandidat(in) *m(f)*

probably ['prab·ə·bli] *adv* wahrscheinlich

probation [proʊ·'beɪ·ʃən] *n* ❶ (*trial period*) Probezeit *f;* **to be on** ~ Probezeit haben; (*employee*) auf Probe eingestellt sein ❷ LAW Bewährung *f;* **to be [out] on** ~ auf Bewährung [draußen] sein

probationary [proʊ·'beɪ·ʃə·ner·i] *adj inv* Probe-; LAW Bewährungs-

probationer [proʊ·'beɪ·ʃə·nər] *n* (*ex-convict*) auf Bewährung Freigelassene(r) *f(m)*

pro'bation officer *n* Bewährungshelfer(in) *m(f)*

probe [proʊb] **I.** *vi* ❶ (*investigate*) forschen (**for** nach +*dat*); (*pester*) bohren *pej fam;* **to** ~ **into sb's private life** in jds Privatleben herumschnüffeln *pej fam* ❷ (*physically search*) Untersuchungen durchführen **II.** *vt* ❶ (*investigate*) untersuchen; *mystery* ergründen; *scandal* auf den Grund gehen ❷ MED untersuchen **III.** *n* ❶ (*investigation*) Untersuchung *f* (**into** +*gen*) ❷ MED, ELEC, ASTRON Sonde *f*

problem ['prab·ləm] **I.** *n* ❶ (*difficulty*) Schwierigkeit *f,* Problem *nt;* **it's not my** ~**!** das ist [doch] nicht mein Problem!; **no** ~ (*sure*) kein Problem; (*don't mention it*) keine Ursache; **to face a** ~ vor einem Problem stehen; **what's the** ~**?** (*fam*) was ist denn los? ❷ (*task*) Aufgabe *f;* **that's her** ~**!** das ist ihre Sache! ❸ MATH [Rechen]aufgabe *f* **II.** *adj area, family, play* Problem-

problematic(al) [ˌprab·lə·'mæ·t̬ɪk(əl)] *adj* ❶ (*difficult*) problematisch ❷ (*questionable*) fragwürdig

procedural [prə·'si·dʒər·əl] *adj inv* verfahrenstechnisch; LAW verfahrensrechtlich, Verfahrens-

procedure [prə·'si·dʒər] *n* ❶ (*particular course of action*) Verfahren *nt;* **standard** ~ übliche Vorgehensweise ❷ (*operation*) Vorgang *m,* Prozedur *f* ❸ LAW Verfahren *nt,* Prozess *m;* **court** ~ Gerichtsverfahren *nt*

proceed [proʊ·'sid] *vi* (*form*) ❶ (*make progress*) fortschreiten, vorangehen ❷ (*advance*) vorrücken ❸ (*continue*) fortfahren, weiterfahren SÜDD, SCHWEIZ ❹ (*go on*) ■**to** ~ **to do sth** sich anschicken, etw zu tun ❺ LAW ■**to** ~ **against sb** gegen jdn gerichtlich vorgehen

proceeding [proʊ·'si·dɪŋ] *n* ❶ (*action*) Vorgehen *nt kein pl;* (*manner*) Vorgehensweise *f* ❷ *usu pl* (*legal action*) Verfahren *nt* ❸ ■~**s** *pl* (*sequence of events*) Folge *f* von Ereignissen

proceeds ['proʊ·sidz] *npl* Einnahmen *pl*

process ['pras·es] **I.** *n* <*pl* -es> ❶ (*series of actions*) Prozess *m* ❷ (*method*) Verfahren *nt* ❸ (*passage*) Verlauf *m;* ■**in** ~ im Gange; **in the** ~ dabei **II.** *vt* ❶ (*deal with*) bearbeiten; ■**to** ~ **sb** jdn abfertigen ❷ COMPUT verarbeiten ❸ (*treat*) bearbeiten, behandeln; *food* haltbar machen, konservieren; *film* entwickeln

processing ['pras·es·ɪŋ] *n* ❶ *of application* Bearbeitung *f* ❷ TECH Weiterverarbeitung *f;* FOOD Konservierung *f; of milk* Sterilisierung *f;* PHOT Entwicklung *f* ❸ COMPUT Verarbeitung *f*

procession [prə·'seʃ·ən] *n* Umzug *m;* REL Prozession *f;* **funeral** ~ Trauerzug *m;* ■**in** ~ hintereinander

processor [pra·'ses·ər] *n* ❶ (*company*) [Weiter]verarbeitungsbetrieb *m* ❷ (*machine*) **food** ~ Küchenmaschine *f* ❸ COMPUT Prozessor *m*

pro-'choice *adj inv* für das Recht auf Abtreibung; ~ **advocate** Verfechter(in) *m(f)* des Rechts auf Abtreibung
proclaim [proʊ·'kleɪm] *vt* (*form: announce*) verkünden; *one's innocence* beteuern
proclamation [ˌprak·lə·'meɪ·ʃən] *n* ❶ (*form: act of proclaiming*) Verkündigung *f,* öffentliche Bekanntmachung ❷ (*decree*) Erlass *m*
procreate ['proʊ·kri·eɪt] *vi* sich fortpflanzen
procreation [ˌproʊ·krɪ·'eɪ·ʃən] *n* Fortpflanzung *f;* (*fig*) Erzeugung *f,* Hervorbringen *nt*
proctor ['prak·tər] SCH, UNIV **I.** *n* (*for exam*) [Prüfungs]aufsicht *f* **II.** *vi* Aufsicht führen **III.** *vt exam* beaufsichtigen; **to ~ an examination** die Aufsicht bei einer Prüfung führen
procure [proʊ·'kjʊr] *vt* (*form*) ❶ (*obtain*) beschaffen, besorgen; *sb's release* erreichen ❷ (*pimp*) **to ~ women for prostitution** Zuhälterei betreiben
procurement [proʊ·'kjʊr·mənt] *n* (*form*) ❶ (*acquisition*) Beschaffung *f,* Besorgung *f* ❷ (*system*) Beschaffungswesen *nt*
prod [prad] **I.** *n* ❶ (*tool*) Ahle *f;* **cattle ~** [elektrischer] Viehtreibstab ❷ (*poke*) Schubs *m fam,* [leichter] Stoß; **to give sb a ~** jdm einen Stoß versetzen ❸ (*fig: incitation*) Anstoß *m fig;* (*reminder*) Gedächtnisanstoß *m* **II.** *vt* <-dd-> ❶ (*poke*) stoßen ❷ (*fig: encourage*) antreiben; **to ~ sb into action** jdn auf Trab bringen *fam*
prodigal ['prad·ɪ·gəl] *adj* verschwenderisch
prodigious [prə·'dɪdʒ·əs] *adj* (*form*) ❶ (*enormous*) gewaltig, ungeheuer ❷ (*wonderful*) wunderbar, erstaunlich
prodigy ['prad·ə·dʒi] *n* (*person*) außergewöhnliches Talent; **child ~** Wunderkind *nt*
produce I. *vt* [prə·'dus] ❶ (*make*) herstellen, produzieren; *coal, oil* fördern; *electricity* erzeugen ❷ (*bring about*) bewirken, hervorrufen; *effect* erzielen; *profits, revenue* erzielen; **to ~ results** zu Ergebnissen führen ❸ FILM, MUS *film, program* produzieren; THEAT *play, opera* inszenieren ❹ (*show*) hervorholen; *identification, passport* zeigen **II.** *vi* [prə·'dus] ❶ (*bring results*) Ergebnisse erzielen; ECON einen Gewinn erwirtschaften ❷ (*give output*) produzieren; *mine* fördern ❸ FILM einen Film produzieren; THEAT ein Stück inszenieren **III.** *n* ['pra·dus] (*fruits and vegetables*) Obst *nt* und Gemüse *nt*
producer [prə·'du·sər] *n* ❶ (*manufacturer*) Hersteller *m,* Produzent *m;* AGR Erzeuger *m* ❷ FILM, TV Produzent(in) *m(f);* THEAT Regisseur(in) *m(f);* MUS [Musik]produzent(in) *m(f)*
product ['prad·əkt] *n* ❶ (*sth produced*) Erzeugnis *nt,* Produkt *nt* ❷ (*result*) Ergebnis *nt,* Folge *f* ❸ MATH Produkt *nt* (**of** aus +*dat*)
production [prə·'dʌk·ʃən] *n* ❶ (*process*) Produktion *f,* Herstellung *f; of energy* Erzeugung *f* ❷ (*yield*) Produktion *f* ❸ FILM, TV, RADIO, MUS Produktion *f;* THEAT Inszenierung *f*
pro'duction line *n* Fließband *nt*
production 'manager *n* Produktionsleiter(in) *m(f)*
productive [prə·'dʌk·tɪv] *adj* ❶ (*with large output*) produktiv; *land, soil* fruchtbar, ertragreich; *mine, well, discussion, meeting* ergiebig; (*fig*) *conversation* fruchtbar ❷ (*profitable*) *business* rentabel ❸ (*efficient*) leistungsfähig
productivity [ˌproʊ·dək·'tɪv·ɪ·ṭi] *n* ❶ (*output*) Produktivität *f* ❷ (*effectiveness*) Effektivität *f,* Effizienz *f* ❸ (*profitability*) Rentabilität *f*
prof [praf] *n* (*fam*) *short for* **professor** Prof *m*
profane [proʊ·'feɪn] *adj* (*blasphemous*) gotteslästerlich, frevelhaft
profanity [proʊ·'fæn·ɪ·ṭi] *n* ❶ (*blasphemy*) Gotteslästerung *f* ❷ (*swearing*) Fluchen *nt* ❸ (*word*) Kraftausdruck *m*
profess [prə·'fes] *vt* ❶ (*claim*) erklären; **to ~ little interest in sth** wenig Begeisterung für etw zeigen ❷ (*affirm*) sich zu etw *dat* bekennen; **to ~ one's love to sb** seine Liebe zu jdm bekennen
professed [prə·'fest] *adj attr, inv* ❶ (*openly declared*) *Marxist, communist* erklärt ❷ (*alleged*) angeblich
profession [prə·'feʃ·ən] *n* ❶ (*field of work*) Beruf *m;* **to enter a ~** einen Beruf ergreifen; **by ~** von Beruf ❷ (*body of workers*) Berufsstand *m;* **the legal/teaching ~** der Anwalts-/Lehrberuf
professional [prə·'feʃ·ə·nəl] **I.** *adj* ❶ (*of a profession*) beruflich, Berufs- ❷ (*not tradesman*) freiberuflich, akademisch; **~ people** Angehörige *pl* der freien [*o* akademischen] Berufe ❸ (*expert*) fachmännisch ❹ (*approv: businesslike*) professionell, fachmännisch; **to do a ~ job** etw fachmännisch erledigen; **~ manner** professionelles Auftreten ❺ (*not amateur*) Berufs-; SPORTS Profi- **II.** *n* ❶ (*not an amateur*) Fachmann, Fachfrau *m, f;* SPORTS Profi *m* ❷ (*not a tradesman*) Akademiker(in) *m(f),* Angehörige(r) *f(m)* der freien [*o* akademischen] Berufe
professionalism [prə·'feʃ·ə·nə·lɪz·əm] *n* ❶ (*skill and experience*) Professionalität *f;* (*attitude*) professionelle Einstellung ❷ SPORTS Profitum *nt*
professionally [prə·'feʃ·ə·nə·li] *adv* ❶ (*by a professional*) von einem Fachmann/einer Fachfrau; **to do sth ~** etw fachmännisch erledigen ❷ (*not as an amateur*) berufsmäßig; **to do sth ~** etw beruflich betreiben
professor [prə·'fes·ər] *n* Professor(in) *m(f);* (*lecturer*) Dozent(in) *m(f)*
professorial [ˌproʊ·fə·'sɔr·i·əl] *adj inv* Professoren-
professorship [prə·'fes·ər·ʃɪp] *n* Professur *f,* Lehrstuhl *m*
proficiency [prə·'fɪʃ·ən·si] *n* Tüchtigkeit *f,* Können *nt;* **~ in a language** Sprachkenntnisse *pl*
proficient [prə·'fɪʃ·ənt] *adj* fähig, tüchtig; **to be ~ in a language** eine Sprache beherrschen
profile ['proʊ·faɪl] **I.** *n* ❶ (*side view*) Profil *nt* ❷ (*description*) Porträt *nt fig;* (*restricted in scope*) Profil *nt* ❸ (*public image*) **to raise**

P

sb's ~ jdn hervorheben ▶ PHRASES: **to keep a low ~** sich zurückhalten **II.** *vt* (*write about*) porträtieren *fig*

profit ['praf·ɪt] **I.** *n* ❶ (*money earned*) Gewinn *m;* **net ~** Reingewinn *m* ❷ (*advantage*) Nutzen *m,* Vorteil *m* **II.** *vi* ❶ (*gain financially*) profitieren (**by/from** von +*dat*), Gewinn machen ❷ (*benefit*) profitieren (**by/from** von +*dat*)

profitability [ˌpraf·ɪ·t̬ə·'bɪl·ɪ·t̬i] *n* Rentabilität *f*

profitable ['praf·ɪ·t̬ə·bəl] *adj* ❶ (*in earnings*) Gewinn bringend, rentabel, profitabel ❷ (*advantageous*) nützlich, vorteilhaft

profiteer [ˌpraf·ɪ·'tɪr] **I.** *n* (*pej*) Profitjäger(in) *m(f)* **II.** *vi* ❶ (*make excessive profit*) riesige Gewinne erzielen; (*make unfair profit*) sich bereichern ❷ (*earn money on black market*) Schwarzhandel treiben

profiteering [ˌpraf·ɪ·'tɪr·ɪŋ] *n* ❶ (*profit seeking*) Geschäftemacherei *f pej* ❷ (*selling at excessive prices*) Wucher *m pej*

'profit-making *adj inv* Gewinn bringend, rentabel

'profit margin *n* Gewinnspanne *f*

'profit sharing *n* Gewinnbeteiligung *f*

profligate ['praf·lɪ·gɪt] *adj* (*form: wasteful*) verschwenderisch

profound [prə·'faʊnd] *adj* ❶ (*extreme*) tief gehend; *change* tief greifend; *effect* nachhaltig; *impression* tief; *interest* stark ❷ (*strongly felt*) tief, heftig; *compassion, gratitude* tief empfunden; *respect, veneration, love* groß ❸ (*intellectual*) tiefsinnig *a. iron,* tiefgründig; *knowledge* umfassend; *truth, wisdom* tief

profuse [prə·'fjus] *adj* überreichlich; *bleeding, perspiration* stark; *praise, thanks* überschwänglich

profusion [prə·'fju·ʒən] *n* (*form*) Überfülle *f*

progeny ['pradʒ·ə·ni] *n* + *sing/pl vb* (*form*) Nachkommenschaft *f*

prognosis <*pl* -ses> [prag·'noʊ·sɪs] *n a.* MED Prognose *f;* **to make a ~** eine Prognose stellen

prognosticate [prag·'nas·tɪ·keɪt] *vt* prognostizieren

program ['proʊ·græm] **I.** *n* ❶ RADIO, TV Programm *nt;* (*single broadcast*) Sendung *f* ❷ (*list of events*) Programm *nt;* THEAT (*for all plays*) Spielplan *m;* (*for one play*) Programmheft *nt* ❸ (*plan*) Programm *nt,* Plan *m;* **what's on the ~ for today?** was steht heute auf dem Programm? ❹ COMPUT Programm *nt* **II.** *vt* <-mm-> ❶ TECH (*instruct*) programmieren ❷ *usu passive* (*mentally train*) ■ **to ~ sb to do sth** jdn darauf programmieren, etw zu tun ❸ COMPUT programmieren

programmable ['proʊ·græm·ə·bəl] *adj* COMPUT programmierbar

programmer ['proʊ·græm·ər] *n* COMPUT Programmierer(in) *m(f)*

'programming language *n* COMPUT Programmiersprache *f*

progress **I.** *n* ['prag·res] ❶ (*onward movement*) Vorwärtskommen *nt;* **to make good ~** gut vorwärtskommen; **in ~** im Gange ❷ (*development*) Fortschritt *m* ❸ *no art* (*general improvement*) Fortschritt *m* **II.** *vi* [prə·'gres] ❶ (*develop*) Fortschritte machen; **how's the work ~ing?** wie geht's mit der Arbeit voran? ❷ (*move onward*) *in space* vorankommen; *in time* fortschreiten

progression [prə·'greʃ·ən] *n* ❶ (*development*) Entwicklung *f* ❷ MATH (*series*) Reihe *f*

progressive [prə·'gres·ɪv] **I.** *adj* ❶ (*gradual*) fortschreitend; (*gradually increasing*) zunehmend; **a ~ decline** ein allmählicher Verfall ❷ (*reformist, forward-looking*) progressiv; POL fortschrittlich **II.** *n* (*reformist*) Progressive(r) *f(m)*

prohibit [proʊ·'hɪb·ɪt] *vt* ❶ (*forbid*) verbieten; ■ **to ~ sb from doing sth** jdm verbieten, etw zu tun ❷ (*prevent*) verhindern

prohibition [ˌproʊ·ə·'bɪʃ·ən] *n* ❶ (*ban*) Verbot *nt* (**of, on** gegen +*akk*) ❷ (*banning*) Verbieten *nt* ❸ (*hist: US alcohol ban*) ■ **P~** *no art* die Prohibition

prohibitive [proʊ·'hɪb·ɪ·t̬ɪv] *adj* ❶ *price* unerschwinglich ❷ (*prohibiting*) **~ measures** Verbotsmaßnahmen *pl*

project **I.** *n* ['pra·dʒekt] ❶ (*undertaking*) Projekt *nt* ❷ (*plan*) Plan *m* **II.** *adj coordinator, costs, deadline* Projekt- **III.** *vt* [prə·'dʒekt] ❶ (*forecast*) vorhersagen; *profit, expenses, number* veranschlagen ❷ (*propel*) schleudern ❸ *slides, film* projizieren (**onto** auf +*akk*) **IV.** *vi* [prə·'dʒekt] (*protrude*) hervorragen, [hinaus]ragen (**over** über +*akk*)

projectile [prə·'dʒek·təl] *n* (*thrown object*) Wurfgeschoss *nt;* (*bullet, shell*) Geschoss *nt;* (*missile*) Rakete *f*

projection [prə·'dʒek·ʃən] *n* ❶ (*forecast*) Prognose *f; of expenses* Voranschlag *m* ❷ (*protrusion*) Vorsprung *m* ❸ (*on screen*) Vorführung *f;* (*projected image*) Projektion *f*

projectionist [prə·'dʒek·ʃə·nɪst] *n* Filmvorführer(in) *m(f)*

project 'management *n* Projektmanagement *nt*

project 'manager *n* Projektmanager(in) *m(f)*

projector [prə·'dʒek·tər] *n* Projektor *m*

prole [proʊl] *n* (*pej o hum*) *short for* **proletarian** Prolet(in) *m(f)*

proletarian [ˌproʊ·lə·'ter·i·ən] **I.** *n* Proletarier(in) *m(f)* **II.** *adj inv* proletarisch, proletenhaft

proletariat [ˌproʊ·lə·'ter·i·ət] *n* Proletariat *nt*

pro-'life *adj inv* gegen das Recht auf Abtreibung; **~ demonstration** Demonstration *f* gegen Abtreibung

proliferate [proʊ·'lɪf·ə·reɪt] *vi* stark zunehmen; (*animals*) sich stark vermehren

proliferation [proʊˌlɪf·ə·'reɪ·ʃən] *n* starke Zunahme; (*of animals*) starke Vermehrung

prolific [proʊ·'lɪf·ɪk] *adj* ❶ (*productive*) produktiv ❷ (*producing many offspring*) fruchtbar ❸ *pred* (*abundant*) ■ **to be ~** in großer Zahl vorhanden sein

prologue, prolog ['proʊ·lag] *n* ❶ (*introduc-*

tion) Vorwort *nt;* THEAT Prolog *m* ② (*fig fam: preliminary event*) Vorspiel *nt* (**to** zu +*dat*)
prolong [proʊ·ˈlaŋ] *vt* verlängern

> Die **Prom** ist ein Ball am Ende des Schuljahres in der *High School*. Für die *seniors* wird eine *senior prom* und für die *juniors* eine *junior prom* organisiert. In der Regel geht man mit einem *date* (ein/e Partner/in) und eines der Paare wird zu *Prom Queen and King* gewählt. Diese Veranstaltung stellt einen der großen Höhepunkte des Schuljahres dar.

promenade [ˌpram·ə·ˈneɪd] *n* (*walkway*) [Strand]promenade *f*
prominence [ˈpram·ə·nəns] *n* ① (*projecting nature*) Auffälligkeit *f* ② (*conspicuousness*) Unübersehbarkeit *f;* **to give sth ~** etw in den Vordergrund stellen ③ (*importance*) Bedeutung *f*
prominent [ˈpram·ə·nənt] *adj* ① (*projecting*) vorstehend *attr; chin* vorspringend ② (*conspicuous*) auffällig ③ (*distinguished*) prominent; *position* führend
promiscuity [ˌpram·ɪ·ˈskju·ɪ·ţi] *n* Promiskuität *f geh*
promiscuous [prə·ˈmɪs·kju·əs] *adj* (*pej*) promisk; ■ **to be ~** mit jedem/jeder ins Bett gehen
promise [ˈpram·ɪs] **I.** *vt* (*pledge, have the potential*) versprechen **II.** *vi* ① (*pledge*) versprechen; **I ~!** ich verspreche es! ② (*be promising*) **to ~ well for the future** viel für die Zukunft versprechen **III.** *n* ① (*pledge*) Versprechen *nt;* **to break one's ~** [**to sb**] sein Versprechen [gegenüber jdm] brechen ② (*potential*) **to show ~** aussichtsreich sein; (*person*) viel versprechend sein
promising [ˈpram·ɪ·sɪŋ] *adj* viel versprechend
promo [ˈproʊ·moʊ] *n* ① (*fam*) *short for* **promotional film** Werbevideo *nt* ② *short for* **promotion** Werbung *f*
promontory [ˈpram·ən·tɔr·i] *n* GEOG Vorgebirge *nt*
promote [prə·ˈmoʊt] *vt* ① (*raise in rank*) befördern (**to** zu +*dat*) ② SPORTS ■ **to be ~d** *player* aufsteigen ③ (*encourage*) fördern; **to ~ awareness of sth** etw ins Bewusstsein rufen ④ (*advertise*) für etw *akk* werben
promoter [prə·ˈmoʊ·ţər] *n* ① (*encourager*) Förderer, -in *m, f* ② (*organizer*) Veranstalter(in) *m(f)*
promotion [prə·ˈmoʊ·ʃən] *n* ① (*in rank*) Beförderung *f* (**to** zu +*dat*) ② (*raise in status*) Beförderung *f* ③ SPORTS (*of player*) Aufstieg *m* ④ (*advertising campaign*) Werbekampagne *f*
prompt [prampt] **I.** *vt* ① (*spur*) veranlassen ② THEAT (*remind of lines*) soufflieren ③ COMPUT auffordern **II.** *adj* ① (*swift*) prompt; ■ **to be ~ in doing sth** etw schnell tun; *action* sofortig; *delivery* unverzüglich ② (*punctual*) pünktlich **III.** *n* ① COMPUT Prompt *m fachspr* ② THEAT (*reminder*) Stichwort *nt*
promptly [ˈprampt·li] *adv* ① (*quickly*) prompt ② (*on time*) pünktlich ③ (*fam: immediately afterward*) gleich danach, unverzüglich
promptness [ˈprampt·nɪs] *n* Promptheit *f*
prone [proʊn] *adj* (*disposed*) neigen (**to** zu +*dat*)
prong [praŋ] *n* Zacke *f; of antler* Ende *nt*
pronoun [ˈproʊ·naʊn] *n* Pronomen *nt*
pronounce [prə·ˈnaʊns] **I.** *vt* ① (*speak*) aussprechen ② *verdict, decision* verkünden ③ (*declare*) erklären; **to ~ sb dead** jdn für tot erklären **II.** *vi* Stellung nehmen (**on/upon** zu +*dat*)
pronounceable [prə·ˈnaʊn·sə·bəl] *adj* aussprechbar
pronounced [prə·ˈnaʊnst] *adj* deutlich; *accent* ausgeprägt
pronouncement [prə·ˈnaʊns·mənt] *n* Erklärung *f* (**on** zu +*dat*)
pronto [ˈpran·toʊ] *adv inv* (*fam*) fix
pronunciation [prə·ˌnʌn·sɪ·ˈeɪ·ʃən] *n* Aussprache *f*
proof [pruf] **I.** *n* ① (*confirmation*) Beweis *m* (**of** für +*akk*) ② MATH (*evidence*) Beweis *m* ③ TYPO (*trial impression*) Korrekturfahne *f;* PHOT Probeabzug *m* ④ (*degree of strength*) Volumenprozent *nt; of alcohol* Alkoholgehalt *m* **II.** *vt* ① (*treat*) imprägnieren; (*make waterproof*) wasserdicht machen ② (*make rise*) *dough* gehen lassen
ˈ**proofread** <-read, -read> *vt, vi* Korrektur lesen
ˈ**proofreader** *n* Korrektor(in) *m(f)*
ˈ**proofreading** *n* Korrekturlesen *nt*
prop¹ [prap] **I.** *n* (*support*) Stütze *f* **II.** *vt* (*support*) stützen
prop² [prap] *n usu pl* THEAT Requisite *f*
propaganda [ˌprap·ə·ˈgæn·də] *n* (*usu pej*) Propaganda *f*
propagate [ˈprap·ə·geɪt] **I.** *vt* ① (*breed*) züchten; (*plants*) vermehren ② (*form: disseminate*) verbreiten **II.** *vi* sich fortpflanzen; *plants* sich vermehren
propagation [ˌprap·ə·ˈgeɪ·ʃən] *n* ① (*reproduction*) Fortpflanzung *f* ② *of rumors, lies* Verbreitung *f*
propane [ˈproʊ·peɪn] *n* Propan *nt*
propel <-ll-> [prə·ˈpel] *vt* antreiben; **the country was being ~led toward civil war** (*fig*) das Land wurde in den Bürgerkrieg getrieben
propellant [prə·ˈpel·ənt] *n* ① (*fuel*) Treibstoff *m* ② (*gas*) Treibgas *nt*
propeller [prə·ˈpel·ər] *n* Propeller *m*
proper [ˈprap·ər] *adj inv* ① (*real*) echt, richtig ② (*correct*) richtig; **she likes everything to be in its ~ place** sie hat gern alles an seinem angestammten Platz ③ (*socially respectable*) anständig
properly [ˈprap·ər·li] *adv inv* ① (*correctly*) richtig; **to be dressed ~** korrekt gekleidet

P

sein; ~ **speaking** genau genommen ❷ (*socially respectably*) anständig

proper 'noun, proper 'name *n* Eigenname *m*

property ['prap·ər·t̬i] *n* ❶ (*things owned*) Eigentum *nt;* (*owned buildings*) Immobilienbesitz *m;* (*owned land*) Grundbesitz *m;* **private** ~ Privatbesitz *m* ❷ (*piece of real estate*) Immobilie *f* ❸ (*attribute*) Eigenschaft *f*

'property tax *n* (*on land*) ≈ Grundssteuer *f;* (*general*) Vermögenssteuer *f*

prophecy ['praf·ə·si] *n* ❶ (*prediction*) Prophezeiung *f* ❷ (*ability*) Weissagen *nt*

prophesy <-ie-> ['praf·ə·saɪ] **I.** *vt* prophezeien **II.** *vi* Prophezeiungen machen

prophet ['praf·ɪt] *n* ❶ (*a. fig: religious figure*) Prophet *m* ❷ (*advocate*) Vorkämpfer(in) *m(f)*

prophetic [prə·'fet̬·ɪk] *adj* prophetisch

prophylactic [ˌproʊ·fə·'læk·tɪk] **I.** *adj inv* MED prophylaktisch *fachspr,* vorbeugend *attr* **II.** *n* ❶ (*medicine*) Prophylaktikum *nt fachspr* ❷ (*condom*) Präservativ *nt*

propitious [prə·'pɪʃ·əs] *adj* (*form*) günstig

proponent [prə·'poʊ·nənt] *n* Befürworter(in) *m(f)*

proportion [prə·'pɔr·ʃən] *n* ❶ (*part*) Anteil *m* ❷ (*relation*) Proportion *f,* Verhältnis *nt* (**to** zu +*dat*); **to be in/out of** ~ [**to sth**] im/in keinem Verhältnis zu etw *dat* stehen ❸ (*size*) ■ ~**s** *pl* Ausmaße *pl*

proportional [prə·'pɔr·ʃə·nəl] *adj* proportional (**to** zu +*dat*); **inversely** ~ umgekehrt proportional

proportionality [prə·ˌpɔr·ʃə·'næl·ɪ·t̬i] *n* Verhältnismäßigkeit *f*

proportionate [prə·'pɔr·ʃə·nɪt] *adj* proportional

proportioned [prə·'pɔr·ʃənd] *adj* **beautifully/finely** ~ ebenmäßig/anmutig proportioniert

P

proposal [prə·'poʊ·zəl] *n* ❶ (*suggestion*) Vorschlag *m* ❷ (*offer of marriage*) Antrag *m*

propose [prə·'poʊz] **I.** *vt* ❶ (*suggest, nominate*) vorschlagen ❷ (*intend*) ■ **to** ~ **to do/doing sth** beabsichtigen, etw zu tun ❸ (*put forward*) *motion* stellen; *toast* ausbringen **II.** *vi* ■ **to** ~ [**to sb**] [jdm] einen [Heirats]antrag machen

proposition [ˌprap·ə·'zɪʃ·ən] **I.** *n* ❶ (*assertion*) Aussage *f* ❷ (*proposal*) Vorschlag *m;* **business** ~ geschäftliches Angebot ❸ (*matter*) Unternehmen *nt;* **a difficult** ~ ein schwieriges Unterfangen **II.** *vt* ■ **to** ~ **sb** jdm ein eindeutiges Angebot machen *euph*

proprietary [prə·'praɪ·ə·ter·i] *adj* ❶ ECON, LAW (*with legal right*) urheberrechtlich geschützt ❷ (*owner-like*) besitzergreifend

proprietor [prə·'praɪ·ə·t̬ər] *n* Inhaber(in) *m(f)*

propriety [prə·'praɪ·ə·t̬i] *n* ❶ (*decency*) Anstand *m* ❷ (*correctness*) Richtigkeit *f*

propulsion [prə·'pʌl·ʃən] *n* Antrieb *m*

prorate [ˌproʊ·'reɪt] *vt* anteilmäßig aufteilen

prosaic [proʊ·'zeɪ·ɪk] *adj* nüchtern, prosaisch *geh*

prose [proʊz] *n* Prosa *f*

prosecute ['pras·ɪ·kjut] **I.** *vt* LAW ■ **to** ~ **sb** [**for sth**] jdn [wegen einer S. *gen*] strafrechtlich verfolgen **II.** *vi* ❶ (*press a charge*) Anzeige erstatten, gerichtlich vorgehen ❷ (*in court*) für die Anklage zuständig sein

prosecuting ['pras·ɪ·kju·t̬ɪŋ] *adj attr* Anklage-; ~ **attorney** Staatsanwalt, Staatsanwältin *m, f*

prosecution [ˌpras·ɪ·'kju·ʃən] *n* ❶ (*legal action*) strafrechtliche Verfolgung ❷ (*legal team*) ■ **the** ~ die Anklagevertretung ❸ (*case*) Anklage[erhebung] *f* (**for** wegen +*gen*), Gerichtsverfahren *nt* (**for** gegen +*akk*)

prosecutor ['pras·ɪ·kju·t̬ər] *n* Ankläger(in) *m(f)*

prospect ['pras·pekt] **I.** *n* ❶ (*idea*) Aussicht *f* (**of** auf +*akk*) ❷ (*likelihood*) Aussicht *f* (**of** auf +*akk*), Wahrscheinlichkeit *f* ❸ (*opportunities*) ■ ~**s** *pl* Aussichten *pl,* Chancen *pl* **II.** *vi* nach Bodenschätzen suchen

prospective [prə·'spek·tɪv] *adj inv* voraussichtlich; *candidate* möglich; *customer* potenziell

prospector ['pras·pek·tər] *n* MIN Prospektor(in) *m(f) fachspr*

prospectus [prə·'spek·təs] *n* Prospekt *m*

prosper ['pras·pər] *vi* ❶ (*financially*) florieren ❷ (*physically*) gedeihen

prosperity [pra·'sper·ɪ·t̬i] *n* Wohlstand *m*

prosperous ['pras·pər·əs] *adj* ❶ (*well-off*) wohlhabend, reich; *business* gut gehend; *economy* blühend ❷ (*successful*) erfolgreich

prostate ['pras·teɪt] *n* Prostata *f*

prostitute ['pras·tə·tut] **I.** *n* Prostituierte *f;* **male** ~ Stricher *m pej* **II.** *vt* ❶ (*sexually*) ■ **to** ~ **oneself** sich prostituieren ❷ *abilities, talents* verschleudern

prostitution [ˌpras·tɪ·'tu·ʃən] *n* Prostitution *f*

prostrate ['pras·treɪt] **I.** *adj* ❶ (*face downward*) ausgestreckt ❷ (*overcome*) überwältigt (**with** von +*dat*) **II.** *vt* ■ **to** ~ **oneself** sich zu Boden werfen

protagonist [proʊ·'tæg·ə·nɪst] *n* ❶ (*main character*) Protagonist(in) *m(f)* ❷ (*advocate*) Verfechter(in) *m(f)* (**of** von +*dat*)

protect [prə·'tekt] *vt* schützen (**against** gegen +*akk,* **from** vor +*dat*)

protection [prə·'tek·ʃən] *n* ❶ (*defense*) Schutz *m* (**against, for** gegen, für +*akk*); *of interests* Wahrung *f;* **to be under sb's** ~ unter jds Schutz stehen ❷ (*paid to criminals*) Schutzgeld *nt*

protectionist [prə·'tek·ʃə·nɪst] **I.** *adj inv* (*pej*) protektionistisch **II.** *n* Protektionist(in) *m(f)*

protective [prə·'tek·tɪv] *adj* ❶ (*affording protection*) Schutz- ❷ (*wishing to protect*) fürsorglich (**of/toward** gegenüber +*dat*)

protector [prə·'tek·tər] *n* ❶ (*person*) Beschützer(in) *m(f)* ❷ (*device*) Schutzvorrichtung *f*

protégé, protégée ['proʊ·t̬ə·ʒeɪ] *n* Protegé *m geh*

protein ['proʊ·tin] *n* ❶ (*collectively*) Eiweiß *nt* ❷ (*specific substance*) Protein *nt*

protest **I.** *n* [ˈproʊ·test] ❶ (*strong complaint*) Protest *m;* **to make a ~** eine Beschwerde einreichen ❷ (*demonstration*) Protestkundgebung *f* **II.** *vi* [proʊ·ˈtest] protestieren **III.** *vt* [proʊ·ˈtest] ❶ (*assert*) beteuern ❷ (*object to*) ■**to ~ sth** gegen etw *akk* protestieren

Protestant [ˈpraṯ·ɪ·stənt] **I.** *n* Protestant(in) *m(f)* **II.** *adj inv* protestantisch; (*in Germany*) evangelisch

Protestantism [ˈpraṯ·ə·stən·tɪz·əm] *n* Protestantismus *m*

protestation [ˌpraṯ·es·ˈteɪ·ʃən] *n usu pl* ❶ (*strong objection*) Protesterklärung *f* ❷ (*strong assertion*) Beteuerung *f*

protester [prə·ˈtes·tər] *n* (*objector*) Protestierende(r) *f(m);* (*demonstrator*) Demonstrant(in) *m(f)*

ˈ**protest march** *n* Protestmarsch *m*

protocol [ˈproʊ·ṯə·kɔl] *n* ❶ (*system of rules*) Protokoll *nt* ❷ (*international agreement*) Protokoll *nt*

proton [ˈproʊ·tan] *n* PHYS Proton *nt*

prototype [ˈproʊ·ṯə·taɪp] *n* Prototyp *m* (**for** für +*akk*)

protracted [proʊ·ˈtræk·tɪd] *adj* langwierig

protractor [proʊ·ˈtræk·tər] *n* MATH Winkelmesser *m*

protrude [proʊ·ˈtrud] *vi* hervorragen (**from** aus +*dat*); *jaw* vorstehen; *branch, ears* abstehen

protruding [proʊ·ˈtru·dɪŋ] *adj attr jaw* vorstehend; *ears* abstehend; *eyes* vortretend

protrusion [proʊ·ˈtru·ʒən] *n* ❶ (*sticking out*) Vorstehen *nt* ❷ (*bump*) Vorsprung *m*

protuberance [proʊ·ˈtu·bər·əns] *n* (*form*) Beule *f*

proud [praʊd] **I.** *adj* ❶ (*pleased*) stolz (**of** auf +*akk*) ❷ (*having self-respect*) stolz ❸ (*pej: arrogant*) eingebildet **II.** *adv* **to do sb ~** jdn mit Stolz erfüllen

proudly [ˈpraʊd·li] *adv* ❶ (*with pride*) stolz ❷ (*pej: haughtily*) hochnäsig *fam*

prove <-d, -d *or* proven> [pruv] **I.** *vt* ❶ (*establish*) beweisen ❷ (*show*) **to ~ oneself to be sth** sich als etw erweisen **II.** *vi* + *n/adj* sich erweisen; **to ~ successful** sich als erfolgreich erweisen

proven [ˈpru·vən] **I.** *vt, vi pp of* **prove** **II.** *adj* nachgewiesen; *remedy* erprobt

provenance [ˈprav·ə·nəns] *n* (*form*) Herkunft *f;* **of unknown ~** unbekannter Herkunft

proverb [ˈprav·ɜrb] *n* (*saying*) Sprichwort *nt*

proverbial [prə·ˈvɜr·bi·əl] *adj* (*fig: well-known*) sprichwörtlich

provide [prə·ˈvaɪd] **I.** *vt* zur Verfügung stellen, bereitstellen; *evidence, explanation* liefern; ■**to ~ sb/sth with sth** (*supply*) jdn/etw mit etw *dat* versorgen; (*offer*) jdm/etw etw bieten **II.** *vi* ❶ (*look after*) ■**to ~ for sb/oneself** für jdn/sich selbst sorgen ❷ (*form: enable*) ■**to ~ for sth** etw ermöglichen; *law* etw erlauben

provided [prə·ˈvaɪ·dɪd] **I.** *adj inv* mitgeliefert, beigefügt **II.** *conj see* **providing [that]**

providence [ˈprav·ə·dəns] *n* Vorsehung *f*

provider [prə·ˈvaɪ·dər] *n* ❶ (*supplier*) Lieferant(in) *m(f)* ❷ TELEC, INET Anbieter *m;* **Internet [service] ~** Internet Service Provider *m;* Internetdienstanbieter *m* ❸ (*breadwinner*) Ernährer(in) *m(f)*

providing [that] [prə·ˈvaɪ·dɪŋ-] *conj* (*as long as*) sofern, falls

province [ˈprav·ɪns] *n* ❶ (*territory*) Provinz *f* ❷ (*area of knowledge*) [Fach]gebiet *nt* ❸ (*area of responsibility*) Zuständigkeitsbereich *m*

provincial [prə·ˈvɪn·ʃəl] **I.** *adj* ❶ (*of a province*) Provinz- ❷ (*pej: unsophisticated*) provinziell **II.** *n* ❶ (*province inhabitant*) Provinzbewohner(in) *m(f)* ❷ (*pej: unsophisticated person*) Provinzler(in) *m(f)*

provision [prə·ˈvɪʒ·ən] **I.** *n* ❶ (*providing*) Versorgung *f;* (*financial precaution*) Vorkehrung *f* ❷ (*something supplied*) Vorrat *m* (**of** an +*dat*) ❸ (*stipulation*) Auflage *f;* **with the ~ that ...** unter der Bedingung, dass ... **II.** *vt* versorgen

provisional [prə·ˈvɪʒ·ə·nəl] *adj* vorläufig

proviso [prə·ˈvaɪ·zoʊ] *n* Vorbehalt *m*

provocation [ˌprav·ə·ˈkeɪ·ʃən] *n* Provokation *f*

provocative [prə·ˈvak·ə·ṯɪv] *adj* ❶ (*provoking*) provokativ *geh* ❷ (*sexually arousing*) provokant *geh,* provozierend *attr*

provoke [prə·ˈvoʊk] *vt* ❶ (*vex*) ■**to ~ sb [into doing sth]** jdn [zu etw *dat*] provozieren ❷ *worries, surprise, outrage* hervorrufen

provost [ˈproʊ·voʊst] *n* UNIV [hoher] Verwaltungsbeamter/[hohe] Verwaltungsbeamtin

prow [praʊ] *n* Bug *m*

prowess [ˈpraʊ·ɪs] *n* (*esp form*) Können *nt,* Leistungsfähigkeit *f*

prowl [praʊl] **I.** *n* (*search*) Streifzug *m,* Suche *f;* (*process*) [Ab]suchen *nt kein pl;* **to be on the ~** auf Streifzug sein **II.** *vt* durchstreifen **III.** *vi* ■**to ~ [around]** umherstreifen

prowler [ˈpraʊ·lər] *n* Herumtreiber(in) *m(f) fam*

proximity [prak·ˈsɪm·ɪ·ṯi] *n* Nähe *f*

proxy [ˈprak·si] *n* Bevollmächtigte(r) *f(m);* *to sign* Zeichnungsbevollmächtigte(r)

prude [prud] *n* prüder Mensch

prudent [ˈpru·dənt] *adj* vorsichtig, umsichtig; *action* klug

prudish [ˈpru·dɪʃ] *adj* prüde

prune¹ [prun] *n* (*plum*) Dörrpflaume *f*

prune² [prun] *vt* HORT [be]schneiden; (*fig*) reduzieren; *costs* kürzen

Prussia [ˈprʌʃ·ə] *n* HIST Preußen *nt*

Prussian [ˈprʌʃ·ən] **I.** *n* (*hist*) Preuße, -in *m, f* **II.** *adj inv* HIST preußisch

pry¹ <-ie-> [praɪ] *vi* neugierig sein; ■**to ~ into sth** seine Nase in etw *akk* stecken *fam*

pry² <-ie-> [praɪ] *vt* ■**to ~ sth open** etw [mit einem Hebel] aufbrechen; **to ~ sb's hand open** jds Hand [mit Gewalt] öffnen

prying [ˈpraɪ·ɪŋ] *adj* (*pej*) neugierig

PS [ˌpi·ˈes] *n abbrev of* **postscript** PS *nt*

psalm [sam] *n* REL Psalm *m*

pseudo [ˈsu·doʊ] *adj* ❶ (*false*) Pseudo-,

Möchtegern- ❷ (*insincere*) heuchlerisch, verlogen
pseudonym [ˈsu·də·nɪm] *n* Pseudonym *nt*
PST [ˌpi·es·ˈti] *n abbrev of* **Pacific Standard Time** pazifische Zeit
psych [saɪk] *vt* (*fam: prepare*) ■ **to ~ oneself/sb up** sich *akk*/jdn [psychisch] aufbauen
◆**psych out** *vt* (*fam: intimidate*) ■ **to ~ out ↻ sb** jdn psychologisch schwächen
psyche [ˈsaɪ·ki] *n* Psyche *f*
psyched [saɪkt] *adj pred* (*sl: excited*) aufgedreht *fam*, aufgeputscht, überdreht *pej fam*
psychedelic [ˌsaɪ·kə·ˈdel·ɪk] *adj* psychedelisch
psychiatric [ˌsaɪ·ki·ˈæt·rɪk] *adj inv* psychiatrisch
psychi'atric hospital *n* psychiatrisches Krankenhaus, psychiatrische Klinik
psychiatrist [saɪ·ˈkaɪ·ə·trɪst] *n* Psychiater(in) *m(f)*
psychiatry [saɪ·ˈkaɪ·ə·tri] *n* Psychiatrie *f*
psychic [ˈsaɪ·kɪk] **I.** *n* Medium *nt* **II.** *adj* ❶ (*supernatural*) übernatürlich ❷ (*of the mind*) psychisch, seelisch
psychoanalysis [ˌsaɪ·koʊ·ə·ˈnæl·ə·sɪs] *n* Psychoanalyse *f*
psychoanalyst [ˌsaɪ·koʊ·ˈæn·ə·lɪst] *n* Psychoanalytiker(in) *m(f)*
psychoanalyze [ˌsaɪ·koʊ·ˈæn·ə·laɪz] *vt* psychoanalysieren
psychological [ˌsaɪ·kə·ˈladʒ·ɪ·kəl] *adj* ❶ (*of the mind, not physical*) psychisch ❷ (*of psychology*) psychologisch
psychologist [saɪ·ˈkal·ə·dʒɪst] *n* Psychologe, -in *m, f*
psychology [saɪ·ˈkal·ə·dʒi] *n* Psychologie *f*
psychopath [ˈsaɪ·kə·pæθ] *n* Psychopath(in) *m(f)*
psychopathic [ˌsaɪ·kə·ˈpæθ·ɪk] *adj* psychopathisch
psychosis <*pl* -ses> [saɪ·ˈkoʊ·sɪs] *n* Psychose *f*
psychotherapist [ˌsaɪ·koʊ·ˈθer·ə·pɪst] *n* Psychotherapeut(in) *m(f)*
psychotherapy [ˌsaɪ·koʊ·ˈθer·ə·pi] *n* Psychotherapie *f*
psychotic [saɪ·ˈkaṱ·ɪk] **I.** *adj* psychotisch **II.** *n* Psychotiker(in) *m(f)*
pt.[1] *abbrev of* **part I. 3, 4**
pt.[2] *abbrev of* **point I.**
pt.[3] *abbrev of* **pint** Pint *nt* (*0,568 l*)
PTA [ˌpi·ti·ˈeɪ] *abbrev of* **Parent-Teacher Association** Eltern-Lehrer-Organisation *f*
ptarmigan [ˈtar·mɪ·gən] *n* Schneehuhn *nt*
PTO [ˌpi·ti·ˈoʊ] *abbrev of* **Parent-Teacher Organization** ≈ Elternbeirat *m*, ≈ Elternverein *m* ÖSTERR
pub [pʌb] *n* Kneipe *f*
puberty [ˈpju·bər·ṱi] *n* Pubertät *f*
pubic [ˈpju·bɪk] *adj attr, inv* Scham-
public [ˈpʌb·lɪk] **I.** *adj inv* öffentlich **II.** *n* + *sing/pl vb* ❶ (*the people*) ■ **the ~** die Öffentlichkeit, die Allgemeinheit ❷ (*patrons*) Anhängerschaft *f*; **the reading ~** Leser *pl*; **the viewing ~** Zuschauer *pl*, Publikum *nt* ❸ (*not in private*) Öffentlichkeit *f*; **in ~** in der Öffentlichkeit, öffentlich
public-ad'dress system *n* Lautsprecheranlage *f*
public as'sistance *n* staatliche Fürsorge
publication [ˌpʌb·lɪ·ˈkeɪ·ʃən] *n* ❶ (*publishing*) Veröffentlichung *f* ❷ (*published work*) Publikation *f*
public do'main *n* (*not subject to copyright*) **to be in the ~** zum Allgemeingut gehören
public 'holiday *n* gesetzlicher Feiertag
public 'interest *n* öffentliches Interesse
publicist [ˈpʌb·lɪ·sɪst] *n* ❶ (*agent*) Publizist(in) *m(f)* ❷ (*pej: attention seeker*) **self-~** Selbstdarsteller(in) *m(f)*
publicity [pʌb·ˈlɪs·ɪ·ṱi] **I.** *n* ❶ (*promotion*) Publicity *f*, Reklame *f* ❷ (*attention*) Aufsehen *nt*, Aufmerksamkeit *f* **II.** *adj* Publicity-, Werbe-
publicize [ˈpʌb·lɪ·saɪz] *vt* bekannt machen
public 'law *n* öffentliches Recht
public 'library *n* öffentliche Bibliothek
publicly [ˈpʌb·lɪk·li] *adv inv* ❶ (*not privately*) öffentlich ❷ (*by the government*) staatlich
public 'nuisance *n* ❶ (*act*) öffentliches Ärgernis ❷ (*fam: person*) Störenfried *m*
public o'pinion *n* öffentliche Meinung
public 'property *n* Staatseigentum *nt*
public re'lations *npl* MEDIA, POL Public Relations *pl*, Öffentlichkeitsarbeit *f kein pl*
public 'school *n* öffentliche [*o* staatliche] Schule
public 'sector *n* öffentlicher Sektor
public-'spirited *adj* (*approv*) von Gemeinsinn zeugend *attr*
public 'television *n* öffentlich-rechtliches Fernsehen
public transpor'tation *n* öffentliche Verkehrsmittel
public u'tility *n* (*company*) öffentlicher Versorgungsbetrieb
publish [ˈpʌb·lɪʃ] *vt article, result* veröffentlichen; *book, magazine, newspaper* herausgeben
publisher [ˈpʌb·lɪ·ʃər] *n* MEDIA ❶ (*company*) Verlag *m* ❷ (*person*) Verleger(in) *m(f)* ❸ (*newspaper owner*) Herausgeber(in) *m(f)*
publishing [ˈpʌb·lɪ·ʃɪŋ] **I.** *n* Verlagswesen *nt* **II.** *adj attr, inv* Verlags-
'publishing house *n* Verlag *m*, Verlagshaus *nt*
puck [pʌk] *n* SPORTS Puck *m*
pucker [ˈpʌk·ər] **I.** *vt* in Falten legen; *lips* spitzen **II.** *vi* ■ **to ~ [up]** *cloth* sich kräuseln; *lips* sich spitzen; *eyebrows* sich runzeln
pudding [ˈpʊd·ɪŋ] *n* Pudding *m*
puddle [ˈpʌd·əl] *n* Pfütze *f*
pudgy [ˈpʊdʒ·i] *adj* rundlich; *face* schwammig; *person* pummelig
puerile [ˈpju·ər·əl] *adj* (*pej*) kindisch *pej*
Puerto Rican [ˌpwer·ṱə·ˈri·kən] **I.** *n* Puerto-Ricaner(in) *m(f)* **II.** *adj* puerto-ricanisch
Puerto Rico [ˌpwer·ṱə·ˈri·koʊ] *n* Puerto Rico *nt*

puff [pʌf] **I.** *n* ① (*fam: short blast*) *of breath* Atemstoß *m; of wind* Windstoß *m; of vapor* Wolke *f* ② (*drag*) Zug *m* ③ (*pastry*) Blätterteig *m* **II.** *vi* ① (*breathe heavily*) schnaufen ② (*smoke*) paffen; **to ~ on a cigar** eine Zigarre qualmen **III.** *vt* ① (*smoke*) paffen ② (*fam: praise*) aufbauschen

◆**puff out I.** *vt* aufblähen; *feathers* aufplustern **II.** *vi* verpuffen

◆**puff up I.** *vt* ① (*make swell*) [an]schwellen lassen ② (*fig*) ■**to ~ oneself up** *person* sich aufblasen **II.** *vi* [an]schwellen

puffin ['pʌf·ɪn] *n* Papageientaucher *m*

puffy ['pʌf·i] *adj* geschwollen, verschwollen

pug [pʌg] *n* Mops *m*

pugnacious [pʌg·'neɪ·ʃəs] *adj* (*form*) kampflustig

'**pug nose** *n* Stupsnase *f*

puke [pjuk] **I.** *vt* (*vulg*) ■**to ~ sth** ↻ [**up**] etw [aus]kotzen *sl* **II.** *vi* (*sl*) kotzen *sl*, spucken DIAL *fam* **III.** *n* (*sl*) Kotze *f sl*

pull [pʊl] **I.** *n* ① (*tug*) Zug *m*, Ziehen *nt* ② (*force*) Zugkraft *f; of the earth, moon* Anziehungskraft *f; of the water* Sog *m* ③ (*on a cigarette*) Zug *m*; (*on a bottle*) Schluck *m* ④ (*attraction*) Anziehung *f; of a person* Anziehungskraft *f* ⑤ (*fam: influence*) Einfluss *m* ⑥ (*handle*) [Hand]griff *m* **II.** *vt* ① (*draw*) ziehen; **to ~ sth shut** *door, window* zuziehen; *trigger* abdrücken ② (*put on*) **to ~ sth over one's head** *clothes* sich *dat* etw über den Kopf ziehen ③ MED *muscle, tendon* zerren ④ (*fam*) *gun, knife, tooth* ziehen ⑤ (*help through*) ■**to ~ sb through sth** jdn durch etw *akk* durchbringen ⑥ (*fam: cancel*) *event* absagen ▶ PHRASES: **to ~ sb's leg** (*fam*) jdn auf den Arm nehmen; **to ~ strings** Beziehungen spielen lassen **III.** *vi* ① (*draw*) ■**to ~** [**at sth**] [an etw *dat*] ziehen ② (*drive*) ■**to ~ into sth** in etw *akk* hineinfahren

◆**pull ahead** *vi* ① (*overtake*) **to ~ ahead of sb** jdn überholen ② SPORTS in Führung gehen

◆**pull apart** *vt* ① (*separate*) auseinanderziehen ② (*break*) zerlegen

◆**pull aside** *vt* ■**to ~ sb aside** jdn zur Seite nehmen

◆**pull away I.** *vi* ■**to ~ away from sb/sth** ① (*leave*) sich von jdm/etw wegbewegen; **the bus ~ed away** der Bus fuhr davon ② SPORTS *horse, runner* sich vom Feld absetzen ③ (*recoil*) vor jdm/etw zurückweichen **II.** *vt* wegreißen; ■**to ~ sth away** ↻ **from sb/sth** jdm/etw etw entreißen

◆**pull back I.** *vi* ① (*recoil*) zurückschrecken ② MIL (*withdraw*) sich zurückziehen **II.** *vt* zurückziehen; *curtains* aufziehen

◆**pull down** *vt* ① (*move down*) herunterziehen ② *building* abreißen ③ (*sl: earn*) kassieren

◆**pull in I.** *vi* TRANSP *train* einfahren; *car, bus* anhalten **II.** *vt* ① (*attract*) anziehen ② (*fam: earn*) [ab]kassieren ③ (*suck in*) einziehen

◆**pull off** *vt* ① (*take off*) [schnell] ausziehen ② (*fam: succeed*) durchziehen; *deal* zustande bringen; *victory* davontragen

◆**pull on** *vt* [schnell] überziehen

◆**pull out I.** *vi* ① (*move out*) *vehicle* ausscheren ② (*depart*) *train* ausfahren; *car, bus* herausfahren ③ (*withdraw*) aussteigen *fam;* ■**to ~ out of sth** sich aus etw *dat* zurückziehen ④ (*extend*) *sofa* ausklappen **II.** *vt* ① MIL **to ~ out troops** Truppen abziehen ② (*get out*) ■**to ~ sth out of sth** etw aus etw *dat* [heraus]ziehen ③ (*take out*) herausziehen

◆**pull over I.** *vt vehicle* anhalten **II.** *vi vehicle* zur Seite fahren

◆**pull through I.** *vi* (*survive*) durchkommen **II.** *vt* ■**to ~ sb/sth through** [**sth**] jdn/etw [durch etw *akk*] durchbringen

◆**pull together I.** *vt* ① (*regain composure*) ■**to ~ oneself together** sich zusammennehmen ② (*organize*) auf die Beine stellen *fig fam* **II.** *vi* zusammenarbeiten

◆**pull up I.** *vt* ① (*pull toward one*) heranziehen; **~ up a chair!** hol dir doch einen Stuhl! ② (*raise*) hochziehen ③ (*remove*) *floorboards, weeds* herausreißen **II.** *vi* [heranfahren und] anhalten; *car* vorfahren; *train* einfahren

pull-down 'menu *n* Pulldown-Menü *nt*

pulley ['pʊl·i] *n* Flaschenzug *m*

'**pullout I.** *n* ① MIL Rückzug *m* ② PUBL [Sonder]beilage *f* **II.** *adj* herausziehbar

'**pull-up** *n see* **chin-up**

pulmonary ['pʌl·mə·ner·i] *adj inv* Lungen-

pulp [pʌlp] **I.** *n* ① (*mush*) Brei *m;* **to beat sb to a ~** (*fig fam*) jdn zu Brei schlagen ② FOOD Fruchtfleisch *nt kein pl* ③ (*in paper making*) [Papier]brei *m* **II.** *vt* ① (*mash*) zu Brei verarbeiten; *food* zerstampfen ② (*destroy printed matter*) einstampfen

pulpit ['pʊl·pɪt] *n* Kanzel *f*

pulsate ['pʌl·seɪt] *vi* pulsieren; (*with noise*) *building, loudspeaker* vibrieren

pulsation [pʌl·'seɪ·ʃən] *n* Pulsieren *nt*

pulse [pʌls] **I.** *n* ① (*heartbeat*) Puls *m;* **to take sb's ~** jds Puls fühlen ② (*vibration*) [Im]puls *m* ③ (*fig: mood*) **to take the ~ of sth** etw sondieren *geh;* **to have one's finger on the ~** am Ball sein **II.** *vi* pulsieren

pulverize ['pʌl·və·raɪz] *vt* ① (*crush*) pulverisieren ② (*fam: demolish*) demolieren ③ (*fig fam: thrash*) ■**to ~ sb** jdn zu Brei schlagen; SPORTS jdn vernichtend schlagen

puma ['pu·mə] *n* Puma *m*

pumice ['pʌm·ɪs], **pumice stone** ['pʌm·ɪs-] *n* Bimsstein *m*

pummel <-l- *or* -ll-> ['pʌm·əl] *vt* ① (*hit*) einprügeln (auf +*akk*) ② (*fig: defeat*) fertigmachen *fam*

pump[1] [pʌmp] **I.** *n* (*device*) Pumpe *f* **II.** *vt* pumpen

pump[2] [pʌmp] *n* (*shoe*) Pumps *m*

pumpernickel ['pʌm·pər·nɪk·əl] *n* Pumpernickel *nt*

'**pumping station** ['pʌm·pɪŋ] *n* Pumpstation *f*

pumpkin ['pʌmp·kɪn] *n* ① (*vegetable*) [Gar-

P

ten]kürbis *m* ❷ (*fig: term of endearment for child*) Schatz *m,* Mäuschen *nt*

> Der **pumpkin pie** ist eine Art Kürbiskuchen. Dieser sehr beliebte amerikanische *pie* wird im Herbst und im Frühwinter gegessen. Er wird besonders an *Thanksgiving* und an Weihnachten serviert.

pun [pʌn] **I.** *n* Wortspiel *nt* **II.** *vi* <-nn-> Wortspiele machen

punch¹ [pʌntʃ] **I.** *n* (*piercing tool*) Stanzwerkzeug *nt;* [**hole**] ~ (*for paper*) Locher *m* **II.** *vt coin, ring* stempeln; *metal, leather* [aus]stanzen; *paper* lochen

punch² [pʌntʃ] **I.** *n* <*pl* -es> ❶ (*hit*) [Faust]schlag *m;* (*in boxing*) Punch *m kein pl fachspr;* **to give sb a ~ in the nose** jdm eins auf die Nase geben *fam* ❷ (*strong effect*) Durchschlagskraft *f kein pl; of arguments* Überzeugungskraft *f kein pl; of a speech/of music* Schwung *m* **II.** *vt* (*hit*) ■ **to ~ sb/sth** jdn/gegen etw *akk* [mit der Faust] schlagen

punch³ [pʌntʃ] **I.** *n hot or cold* Punsch *m; cold* Bowle *f* **II.** *adj glasses, set* Punsch-, Bowlen-

'punch bowl *n* Punschschüssel *f,* Bowlengefäß *nt*

'punching bag *n* SPORTS Sandsack *m*

'punch line *n* Pointe *f*

punctual ['pʌŋk·tʃu·əl] *adj* pünktlich

punctuality [ˌpʌŋk·tʃu·'æl·ɪ·t̬i] *n* Pünktlichkeit *f*

punctuate ['pʌŋk·tʃu·eɪt] *vt* ❶ LING (*mark*) mit Satzzeichen versehen ❷ (*interrupt*) [immer wieder] unterbrechen ❸ (*stress*) betonen

punctuation [ˌpʌŋk·tʃu·'eɪ·ʃən] *n* Zeichensetzung *f*

punctu'ation mark *n* Satzzeichen *nt*

puncture ['pʌŋk·tʃər] **I.** *vt* ❶ (*pierce*) durchstechen ❷ (*fig: make collapse*) *dream, hope* zerstören; *mood* verderben **II.** *vi* (*burst*) *tire* ein Loch bekommen; *plastic* einreißen **III.** *n* Reifenpanne *f*

pundit ['pʌn·dɪt] *n* ❶ ECON, POL (*a. pej: authority*) Koryphäe *f,* Guru *m hum, pej* ❷ (*pej: commentator*) autoritärer Kritiker/autoritäre Kritikerin

pungent ['pʌn·dʒənt] *adj* ❶ (*a. pej: strong*) *smell* scharf, beißend *pej; taste* scharf, pikant ❷ (*fig*) *wit, words* scharf *a. pej; comment, remark* bissig *pej; comment, expression* treffend

punish ['pʌn·ɪʃ] *vt* ❶ (*penalize*) bestrafen; **to ~ sb with a fine** jdn mit einer Geldstrafe belegen ❷ (*treat roughly*) strapazieren; (*treat badly*) malträtieren; *in a fight* übel zurichten ❸ (*exert oneself*) ■ **to ~ oneself** sich [ab]quälen

punishable ['pʌn·ɪʃ·ə·bəl] *adj inv* LAW *offense* strafbar; **murder is ~ by life imprisonment** Mord wird mit lebenslanger Haft bestraft; **a ~ infraction of the rules** ein Regelverstoß, der zu ahnden ist

punishing ['pʌn·ɪ·ʃɪŋ] **I.** *adj attr* (*fig*) ❶ (*heavy*) Mords-, mörderisch *fig fam* ❷ (*brutal*) mörderisch *fig fam,* gnadenlos ❸ (*tough*) hart, schwer, anstrengend **II.** *n* (*severe handling*) Strapazierung *f;* (*rough treatment*) Malträtierung *f;* **to take a ~** *device, equipment* stark beansprucht werden; (*be damaged*) malträtiert werden; *boxer* Prügel beziehen

punishment ['pʌn·ɪʃ·mənt] *n* ❶ (*penalty*) Bestrafung *f,* Strafe *f;* **capital ~** Todesstrafe *f* ❷ (*severe handling*) Strapazierung *f;* (*rough treatment*) grobe Behandlung; (*strain*) Strapaze *f;* **to take ~** *in boxing* schwer einstecken müssen *fig fam*

punitive ['pju·nɪ·t̬ɪv] *adj* (*form*) ❶ (*penalizing*) Straf-; **~ action** Strafmaßnahmen *pl;* **~ damages** LAW *in case of libel, slander* verschärfter Schaden[s]ersatz ❷ ECON, FIN (*severe*) streng, rigoros, einschneidend

punk [pʌŋk] **I.** *n* ❶ (*pej fam: worthless person*) Dreckskerl *m* ❷ (*music*) Punk[rock] *m;* (*fan*) Punker(in) *m(f)* **II.** *adj clothes, group, song* Punk[er]-

punt [pʌnt] SPORTS **I.** *vi* punten **II.** *vt* punten **III.** *n* Punt *m*

punter ['pʌn·tər] *n* SPORTS Punter *m*

puny ['pju·ni] *adj* (*pej*) ❶ (*sickly*) *person* schwächlich ❷ (*small*) *person* winzig *pej* ❸ (*fig: lacking in power*) schwach; *attempt* schüchtern; *excuse* billig

pup [pʌp] *n* ❶ (*baby dog*) junger Hund, Welpe *m* ❷ (*baby animal*) Junge(s) *nt*

pupil¹ ['pju·pəl] *n* ❶ (*schoolchild*) Schüler(in) *m(f)* ❷ (*follower*) Schüler(in) *m(f)*

pupil² ['pju·pəl] *n* ANAT Pupille *f*

puppet ['pʌp·ɪt] **I.** *n* (*theater doll*) [Hand]puppe *f;* (*on strings*) Marionette *f a. pej, fig* **II.** *adj maker, play* Puppen-; *play, strings* Marionetten-

'puppet show *n* Puppenspiel *nt,* Marionettentheater *nt*

puppy ['pʌp·i] *n* (*baby dog*) junger Hund, Welpe *m*

purchase ['pɜr·tʃəs] **I.** *vt* ❶ (*form: buy*) kaufen, erstehen *geh* ❷ FIN, LAW (*form: acquire*) etw [käuflich] erwerben **II.** *n* ❶ (*something bought, act of buying*) Kauf *m;* **to make a ~** einen Kauf tätigen; *bulky goods* eine Anschaffung machen ❷ FIN, LAW (*acquisition*) Erwerb *m kein pl*

purchaser ['pɜr·tʃə·sər] *n* ❶ (*buyer*) Käufer(in) *m(f);* FIN, LAW Erwerber(in) *m(f)* ❷ (*purchasing agent*) Einkäufer(in) *m(f)*

purchasing ['pɜr·tʃə·sɪŋ] *n* (*form*) Erwerb *m geh,* [Ein]kaufen *nt,* [Ein]kauf *m*

'purchasing power *n* Kaufkraft *f kein pl*

pure [pjʊr] *adj* ❶ (*unmixed*) rein, pur; ZOOL reinrassig *fachspr* ❷ *air, water* sauber, klar ❸ (*fig: utter*) rein, pur ❹ (*free of evil*) unschuldig, rein; *intentions* ehrlich

'purebred I. *n* reinrassiges Tier **II.** *adj inv* reinrassig

purée [pjʊ·ˈreɪ] **I.** *vt* <puréed, puréeing> pürieren **II.** *n* Püree *nt*

purely [ˈpjʊr·li] *adv* ❶ (*completely*) rein, ausschließlich ❷ (*merely*) bloß, lediglich; **~ and simply** schlicht und einfach ❸ (*free of evil*) unschuldig

purgative [ˈpɜr·gə·t̬ɪv] *n* MED Abführmittel *nt*

purgatory [ˈpɜr·gə·tɔr·i] *n* REL ■**P~** das Fegefeuer

purge [pɜrdʒ] **I.** *vt* (*a. fig: cleanse*) reinigen (**of** von +*dat*); ■**to ~ oneself/sb of sth** *guilt, suspicion* sich/jdn von etw *dat* reinwaschen **II.** *n* ❶ (*cleaning out*) Reinigung *f* ❷ POL (*getting rid of*) Säuberung[saktion] *f*

purification [ˌpjʊr·ə·fɪ·ˈkeɪ·ʃən] *n* (*cleansing*) Reinigung *f*

purify [ˈpjʊr·ə·faɪ] *vt* reinigen (**of/from** von +*dat*)

purist [ˈpjʊr·ɪst] *n* Purist(in) *m(f)*

puritan [ˈpjʊr·ɪ·tən] *n* ❶ (*Protestant*) Puritaner(in) *m(f);* ■**the P~s** *pl* die Puritaner *pl* ❷ (*fig, usu pej: strict person*) Puritaner(in) *m(f)*

puritanical [ˌpjʊr·ɪ·ˈtæn·ɪ·kəl] *adj* (*usu pej*) puritanisch

purity [ˈpjʊr·ɪ·t̬i] *n* ❶ (*cleanness*) Sauberkeit *f* ❷ (*freedom from admixture*) Reinheit *f* ❸ REL (*moral goodness*) Reinheit *f;* (*innocence*) Unschuld *f*

purl [pɜrl] **I.** *n* linke Masche **II.** *vt, vi* links stricken

purple [ˈpɜr·pəl] **I.** *adj* ❶ (*red/blue mix*) violett; (*more red*) lila[farben]; (*crimson*) purpurrot ❷ (*darkly colored*) **to turn ~ [in the face]** hochrot [im Gesicht] anlaufen **II.** *n* ❶ (*blue/red mix*) Violett *nt;* (*more red*) Lila *nt;* (*crimson*) Purpur *m kein pl* ❷ (*robe*) Purpur *m kein pl*

Purple ˈHeart *n* Verwundetenabzeichen *nt*

purpose [ˈpɜr·pəs] *n* ❶ (*reason*) Grund *m* ❷ (*goal*) Absicht *f,* Ziel *nt;* **to have a ~ in life** ein Lebensziel haben; **on ~** absichtlich ❸ (*resoluteness*) Entschlossenheit *f;* **lack of ~** Unentschlossenheit *f*

purposeful [ˈpɜr·pəs·fəl] *adj* ❶ (*single-minded*) zielstrebig ❷ (*resolute*) entschlossen ❸ *existence* sinnvoll

purposeless [ˈpɜr·pəs·lɪs] *adj* ❶ (*lacking goal*) ziellos ❷ (*lacking meaning*) sinnlos ❸ (*useless*) unzweckmäßig

purposely [ˈpɜr·pəs·li] *adv* ❶ (*intentionally*) absichtlich, bewusst ❷ (*expressly*) ausdrücklich, gezielt

purr [pɜr] **I.** *vi* ❶ (*cat*) schnurren ❷ (*engine*) surren **II.** *n* ❶ (*cat's sound*) Schnurren *nt kein pl* ❷ (*engine noise*) Surren *nt kein pl*

purse [pɜrs] **I.** *n* ❶ (*handbag*) Handtasche *f* ❷ (*financial resources*) **public ~** Staatskasse *f* ❸ SPORTS (*prize money*) Preisgeld *nt* **II.** *vt* **to ~ one's lips** die Lippen schürzen; (*sulkily*) die Lippen aufwerfen

purser [ˈpɜr·sər] *n* AVIAT Purser *m;* NAUT Zahlmeister(in) *m(f) fachspr*

pursue [pər·ˈsu] *vt* ❶ (*a. fig: follow*) *goals* verfolgen ❷ (*fig, pej: repeatedly attack*) verfolgen ❸ (*investigate*) *matter* weiterverfolgen ❹ (*engage in*) betreiben; *career* ausüben; *studies* nachgehen

pursuer [pər·ˈsu·ər] *n* Verfolger(in) *m(f)*

pursuit [pər·ˈsut] *n* ❶ (*chase*) Verfolgung[sjagd] *f; of knowledge, fulfillment* Streben *nt* (**of** nach +*dat*); (*hunt*) Jagd *f a. pej* (**of** nach +*dat*) ❷ (*activity*) Aktivität *f,* Beschäftigung *f*

pus [pʌs] *n* Eiter *m*

push [pʊʃ] **I.** *n* <*pl* -es> ❶ (*shove*) Stoß *m;* (*slight push*) Schubs *m fam;* **to give sb/sth a ~** jdm/etw einen Stoß versetzen ❷ (*press*) Druck *m;* **at the ~ of a button** auf Knopfdruck *a. fig* ❸ (*fig: motivation*) Anstoß *m* ❹ (*concerted effort*) Anstrengung[en] *f[pl],* Kampagne *f* **II.** *vt* ❶ (*shove*) schieben; (*in a crowd*) drängeln; (*violently*) stoßen, schubsen; **to ~ sth to the back of one's mind** (*fig*) etw verdrängen ❷ (*move forcefully*) schieben; (*give a push*) stoßen ❸ (*maneuver*) ■**to ~ sb toward sth** jdn in eine Richtung drängen ❹ (*impose*) ■**to ~ sth [on sb]** [jdm] etw aufdrängen ❺ (*pressure*) ■**to ~ sb into doing sth** jdn [dazu] drängen, etw zu tun; (*force*) jdn zwingen, etw zu tun; (*persuade*) jdn überreden, etw zu tun ❻ (*press*) ■**to ~ sth** drücken (auf +*akk*) ❼ (*demand a lot*) ■**to ~ oneself** sich *dat* alles abverlangen; **to not ~ oneself** sich nicht überanstrengen *iron* ❽ (*sl: promote*) propagieren; (*sell illegal drugs*) pushen *sl* ❾ (*approach*) **to be ~ing 40** (*age*) auf die 40 zugehen; (*drive at*) fast 40 fahren **III.** *vi* ❶ (*exert force*) dränge[l]n; (*press*) drücken; (*move*) schieben; **to ~ and pull** hin- und herschieben ❷ (*maneuver through*) sich durchdrängen; MIL vorstoßen; ■**to ~ past sb** sich an jdm vorbeidrängen

◆**push around** *vt* ❶ (*move around*) herumschieben; (*violently*) herumstoßen ❷ (*fig, pej: bully*) ■**to ~ sb around** jdn herumkommandieren

◆**push back** *vt* ❶ (*move backwards*) zurückschieben, zurückdrängen ❷ (*fig: delay*) *date* verschieben; ■**to ~ sb back** jdn zurückwerfen

◆**push down** *vt* ❶ (*knock down*) umstoßen ❷ (*press down*) *lever* hinunterdrücken ❸ ECON (*fig, pej*) *prices* [nach unten] drücken; *value* mindern

◆**push forward I.** *vt* ❶ (*approv, fig*) *development, process* [ein großes Stück] voranbringen ❷ (*present forcefully*) in den Vordergrund stellen ❸ (*draw attention*) ■**to ~ oneself forward** sich vordrängen **II.** *vi* (*continue*) weitermachen

◆**push in** *vt* (*press against*) eindrücken

◆**push off I.** *vi* (*fig, a. pej fam: leave*) sich verziehen **II.** *vt* NAUT abstoßen

◆**push on** *vt* [energisch] vorantreiben

◆**push out** *vt* ❶ (*force out*) hinausjagen

P

② (*dismiss*) hinauswerfen; (*reject*) ausstoßen ③ ECON (*produce*) ausstoßen

◆**push over** *vt* umwerfen, umstoßen

◆**push through** **I.** *vi* (*maneuver through*) ■**to ~ through sth** sich durch etw *akk* drängen **II.** *vt* ① POL *bill, motion* durchdrücken *fam* ② (*help to succeed*) **schools focus too much on grades and pushing their students through the system** die Schule ist viel zu sehr mit der Notengebung beschäftigt und damit, ihre Schüler durch das System zu bringen

◆**push up** *vt* ① (*move higher*) **to ~ a bike up a hill** ein Fahrrad den Hügel hinaufschieben; ■**to ~ sb ↻ up** jdn hochheben ② ECON *demands* steigern; *prices* hochtreiben

'pushbutton **I.** *adj inv* (*automated*) Druckknopf-, [Druck]tasten-, [voll]automatisch **II.** *n* Druckknopf *m*, [Druck]taste *f*

pusher ['pʊʃ·ər] *n* (*pej*) Dealer(in) *m(f)*

'pushover *n* ① (*fig, pej fam: easily defeated opponent*) leichter Gegner/leichte Gegnerin; (*easily influenced*) Umfaller(in) *m(f) fig, pej fam;* **to be a real ~** echt leicht rumzukriegen sein *fam* ② (*approv, fig fam: easy success*) Kinderspiel *nt kein pl*

'pushpin *n* Reißzwecke *f*

'pushup *n* Liegestütz *m*

pushy ['pʊʃ·i] *adj* (*fig fam*) ① (*pej: aggressive*) aggressiv; (*obnoxious*) aufdringlich ② (*ambitious*) tatkräftig

pussy ['pʊs·i] *n* ① (*cat*) Mieze[katze] *f fam* ② (*fig, pej vulg: woman's genitals*) Muschi *f* ③ (*sl: weak person*) Schlappschwanz *m fam,* Waschlappen *m*

'pussyfoot *vi* (*pej fam: move cautiously*) ■**to ~ around** herumreden *fam*

'pussy willow *n* Salweide *f*

put <-tt-, put, put> [pʊt] *vt* ① (*place*) ■**to ~ sth somewhere** etw irgendwohin stellen; (*lay down*) etw irgendwohin legen; (*push in*) etw irgendwohin stecken; **~ your clothes in the closet** häng deine Kleider in den Schrank; **she ~ some milk in her coffee** sie gab etwas Milch in ihren Kaffee; **to ~ oneself in sb's place** sich in jds Situation versetzen; **~ the cake in[to] the oven** schieb den Kuchen in den Backofen; **I ~ clean sheets on the bed** ich habe das Bett frisch bezogen; **she ~ her arm round him** sie legte ihren Arm um ihn; **to ~ sb to bed** jdn ins Bett bringen; **to stay ~** *person* sich nicht von der Stelle rühren; *object* liegen/stehen/hängen bleiben ② (*invest*) **to ~ effort into sth** Mühe in etw *akk* stecken ③ (*impose*) **to ~ the blame on sb** jdm die Schuld geben; **to ~ faith in sth** sein Vertrauen in etw *akk* setzen; **to ~ pressure on sb** jdn unter Druck setzen; **to ~ sb/sth to the test** jdn/etw auf die Probe stellen ④ (*include*) **to ~ sth on the agenda** etw auf die Tagesordnung setzen ⑤ (*indicating change of condition*) **to ~ sb at risk** jdn in Gefahr bringen; **to ~ sb in a good mood** jds Laune heben; **to ~ one's affairs in order** seine Angelegenheiten in Ordnung bringen; **to ~ sb to shame** jdn beschämen; **to ~ a stop to sth** etw beenden ⑥ (*express*) **how should I ~ it?** wie soll ich mich ausdrücken?; **to ~ it bluntly** um es deutlich zu sagen ⑦ (*estimate, value*) **she ~s her job above everything else** für sie geht ihr Beruf allem anderen vor; **to ~ sb/sth in a category** jdn/etw in eine Kategorie einordnen ⑧ (*install*) einbauen ⑨ MED (*prescribe*) ■**to ~ sb on sth** jdm etw verschreiben

◆**put across** *vt* ① (*make understood*) **to ~ one's point across** etw verständlich machen ② (*fam: trick*) **to ~ one across on sb** (*fam*) jdn hintergehen

◆**put aside** *vt* ① (*save*) zurücklegen; *money a.* sparen, auf die hohe Kante legen; **to ~ sth aside for sb** etw *akk* für jdn auf die Seite legen ② (*ignore*) *one's differences, fears* vergessen ③ (*postpone*) ■**to ~ aside ↻ sth** *book etc.* etw beiseitelegen

◆**put away** *vt* ① (*tidy up*) wegräumen; (*in storage place*) einräumen ② (*save*) zurücklegen; *money a.* auf die hohe Kante legen ③ (*fam: eat a lot*) ■**to ~ away ↻ sth** etw in sich *akk* hineinstopfen ④ (*fam: have institutionalized*) ■**to ~ sb away** (*in a retirement home*) jdn in Pflege geben; (*in prison*) jdn einsperren

◆**put back** *vt* ① (*replace*) zurückstellen ② (*reassemble*) ■**to ~ sth back together** etw wieder zusammensetzen; ■**to ~ sth back on** *clothes* etw wieder anziehen

◆**put down** *vt* ① (*set down*) ablegen, abstellen ② (*lower*) *arm, feet* herunternehmen; **to ~ down the [tele]phone** [den Hörer] auflegen; ■**to ~ sb ↻ down** jdn runterlassen ③ (*spread*) **to ~ down roots** (*a. fig*) Wurzeln schlagen ④ (*write*) aufschreiben; **we'll ~ your name down on the waiting list** wir setzen Ihren Namen auf die Warteliste; ■**to ~ sb down for sth** jdn für etw *akk* eintragen ⑤ ECON (*leave as deposit*) anzahlen ⑥ (*stop*) *rebellion* niederschlagen; *crime* besiegen ⑦ (*deride*) ■**to ~ down ↻ sb/oneself** jdn/sich schlechtmachen ⑧ (*give as cause*) ■**to ~ sth down to sth** etw auf etw *akk* zurückführen; **to ~ sth down to experience** etw als Erfahrung mitnehmen

◆**put forward** *vt idea, plan* vorbringen; *proposal* machen; *candidate* vorschlagen

◆**put in** **I.** *vt* ① (*place in*) hineinsetzen/-legen/-stellen ② *food, ingredients* hinzufügen ③ (*install*) installieren ④ (*enter, submit*) **to ~ in a good word for sb** für jdn ein gutes Wort einlegen; **to ~ in an order for sth** etw bestellen **II.** *vi* ■**to ~ in for sth** *job* sich um etw *akk* bewerben; *pay raise, transfer* etw beantragen

◆**put off** *vt* ① (*delay*) verschieben; **we've been ~ting off the decision about whether to have a baby** wir haben die Entscheidung, ob wir ein Kind haben wollen, vor uns her geschoben ② (*persuade to not act*) vertrösten ③ (*discourage*) ■**to ~ sb off from doing sth** jdm etw *akk* verleiden [*o* madigmachen] ④ (*disgust*) ■ **to be ~ off by sth** über etw *akk* verärgert sein

◆**put on** *vt* ① *clothes, shoes* anziehen; *makeup* auflegen; (*fig*) *smile* aufsetzen ② (*pretend*) vorgeben ③ (*turn on*) einschalten ④ (*provide*) bereitstellen; *exhibition* veranstalten; *play* aufführen ⑤ (*increase*) **to ~ on weight** zunehmen

◆**put out** **I.** *vt* ① (*place outside*) **to ~ the laundry out** [**to dry**] die Wäsche draußen aufhängen ② *hand, foot* ausstrecken ③ MEDIA (*publish, circulate*) veröffentlichen ④ (*produce*) herstellen; (*sprout*) *leaves, roots* austreiben ⑤ (*place ready*) ■ **to ~ sth out** [**for sb/sth**] *chairs, clothes, dishes* [jdm/etw] etw hinstellen ⑥ (*extinguish*) *fire* löschen; *candle, cigarette* ausmachen; (*turn off*) *lights* ausschalten **II.** *vi* (*sl: agree to sex*) es treiben *sl*

◆**put over** *vt* (*fam: fool*) **to ~ one over on sb** sich mit jdm einen Scherz erlauben

◆**put through** *vt* ① (*insert through*) ■ **to ~ sth through sth** etw durch etw *akk* schieben; (*pierce*) etw durch etw *akk* stechen ② TELEC (*connect*) ■ **to ~ sb through to sb** jdn mit jdm verbinden ③ (*support*) **to ~ sb through college** jdn zum College schicken ④ (*carry through*) *bill, plan, proposal* durchbringen; *claim* weiterleiten

◆**put together** *vt* ① (*assemble*) zusammensetzen; *machine, model, radio* zusammenbauen ② (*place near*) zusammenschieben ③ (*make*) zusammenstellen; *list* aufstellen ④ MATH (*add*) **to ~ 10 and 15 together** 10 und 15 zusammenzählen; **she earns more than all the rest of us ~ together** (*fig*) sie verdient mehr als wir alle zusammengenommen

◆**put up** **I.** *vt* ① (*hang up*) aufhängen; *flag, sail* hissen ② (*raise*) hochheben; *feet* hochlegen; **to ~ one's hair up** sich *dat* das Haar aufstecken ③ (*build*) bauen; *fence* errichten; *tent* aufstellen ④ (*offer*) **to ~ up a reward** eine Belohnung aussetzen; **to ~ sth up for sale** etw zum Verkauf anbieten ⑤ (*give shelter*) unterbringen ⑥ (*resist*) **to ~ up a struggle** kämpfen; **the villagers did not ~ up any resistance** die Dorfbewohner leisteten keinen Widerstand **II.** *vi* (*stay*) **to ~ up for the night** die Nacht wach bleiben

◆**put up with** *vi* **they have a lot to ~ up with** sie haben viel zu ertragen; **I'm not ~ing up with this any longer** ich werde das nicht länger dulden

'putdown *n* verächtliche Bemerkung

putrefy <-ie-> ['pju·trə·faɪ] *vi* (*form*) MED *body* verwesen; BIOL *organic matter* [ver]faulen; (*fig: become corrupt*) verrotten

putrid ['pju·trɪd] *adj* (*form*) ① (*foul*) *smell* faulig ② (*decayed*) *corpse* verwest; BIOL *organic matter* verfault; *water* faul

putt [pʌt] SPORTS **I.** *vt, vi* putten **II.** *n* Putt *m*

putter[1] ['pʌt̬·ər] *n* SPORTS ① *golf club* Putter *m* ② (*golfer*) Einlocher(in) *m(f)*

putter[2] ['pʌt̬·ər] *vi* ① (*busy oneself*) geschäftig sein, werkeln SÜDD; (*do nothing in particular*) vor sich *akk* hin werkeln *fam* ② (*idle*) die Zeit mit Nichtstun verbringen

putty ['pʌt̬·i] **I.** *n* [Dichtungs]kitt *m* **II.** *vt* <-ie-> [ver]kitten, [ver]spachteln

puzzle ['pʌz·əl] **I.** *n* ① (*question, mystery, test of ingenuity*) Rätsel *nt*; **jigsaw ~** Puzzle *nt* ② (*test of patience*) Geduldsspiel *nt* ③ (*confusion*) Verwirrung *f* **II.** *vt* vor ein Rätsel stellen **III.** *vi* ■ **to ~ about** [*or* **over**] **sth** über etw *akk* nachgrübeln

puzzled ['pʌz·əld] *adj* ratlos

puzzling ['pʌz·əl·ɪŋ] *adj* rätselhaft

PVC [ˌpi·vi·'si] *n abbrev of* **polyvinyl chloride** PVC *nt*

Pygmy ['pig·mi] **I.** *n* (*pej, a. fig*) Zwerg(in) *m(f)* **II.** *adj attr, inv* Zwerg-

pylon ['paɪ·lan] *n* ① AUTO (*traffic cone*) Pylon *m*, [Brücken-]Pfeiler *m* ② AVIAT (*bracket*) Befestigungspunkt [am Flugzeug]

pyramid ['pɪr·ə·mɪd] *n* Pyramide *f*

pyre [paɪr] *n* Scheiterhaufen *m*

Pyrenees ['pɪr·ə·ˌniz] *npl* ■ **the ~** die Pyrenäen *pl*

Pyrex® ['paɪ·reks] *n* Pyrex-Glas®

pyrotechnic [ˌpaɪ·roʊ·'tek·nɪk] *adj attr, inv* ① (*fireworks*) pyrotechnisch ② (*fig: sensational*) brillant

python <*pl* -s *or* -> ['paɪ·θan] *n* Python *m*

Qq

Q <*pl* -'s *or* -s>, **q** <*pl* -'s> [kjuː] *n* Q *nt*, q *nt*; ~ **as in Quebec** Q wie Quelle

Q. [kjuː] *n* ECON *abbrev of* **quarter** Quartal *nt*

q. [kjuː] *n* ① FOOD *abbrev of* **quart** Quart *nt* (*0,95 l*) ② *abbrev of* **question** Frage *f*

QED [ˌkjuː·iː'diː] *n* ① MATH *abbrev of* **quod erat demonstrandum** q.e.d. ② (*fig: the solution*) ganz einfach

QR code [kjuː·'ɑːʳ-] *n abbrev of* **Quick Response** INET QR-Code *m*

qt., **qt** *n* FOOD *abbrev of* **quart** Quart *nt* (*0,95 l*)

Q-tip® ['kjuː·tɪp] *n* Wattestäbchen *nt*

quack¹ [kwæk] **I.** *n* Quaken *nt* **II.** *vi* quaken

quack² [kwæk] (*pej*) **I.** *n* (*fake doctor*) Quacksalber(in) *m(f)* *pej* **II.** *adj attr, inv* ~ **doctor** Kurpfuscher(in) *m(f)*

quad¹ [kwad] *n short for* **quadrangle** Geviert *nt*; (*on campus*) Hof

quad² [kwad] *n* (*fam*) *short for* **quadruplet** Vierling *m*

quadrangle ['kwad·ræŋ·gəl] *n* ① MATH Viereck *nt* ② (*square*) Geviert *nt*

quadrant ['kwad·rənt] *n* ① MATH Viertelkreis *m* ② TECH Quadrant *m fachspr; of sphere* Viertelkugel *f*

quadraphonic [ˌkwad·rə·'fan·ɪk] *adj inv* quadrophon[isch]

quadratic [kwa·'dræṭ·ɪk] *adj inv* MATH quadratisch

quadrilateral [ˌkwad·rɪ·'læṭ·ər·əl] **I.** *adj inv* vierseitig **II.** *n* (*shape*) Viereck *nt*

quadruped ['kwad·rə·ped] **I.** *adj* vierfüßig **II.** *n* Vierfüßer *m*

quadruple [kwa·'druː·pəl] **I.** *vt* vervierfachen **II.** *vi* sich vervierfachen **III.** *adj* vierfach *attr*

quadruplet [kwa·'druː·plɪt] *n* Vierling *m*

quaff [kwaf] *vt* [in großen Zügen] trinken

quagmire ['kwæg·maɪr] *n* ① (*swamp*) Morast[boden] *m* ② (*fig*) Patsche *f fig*; **to be caught in a** ~ in der Patsche sitzen

quail¹ <*pl* -s *or* -> [kweɪl] *n* ZOOL Wachtel *f*

quail² [kweɪl] *vi* (*liter: cower*) bangen *geh*

quaint [kweɪnt] *adj* ① (*charming*) reizend; *landscape, village* malerisch; *cottage, pub* urig ② (*old-fashioned*) altertümlich

quaintness ['kweɪnt·nɪs] *n* (*charm*) Reiz *m*; *of landscape, village* idyllischer Charakter

quake [kweɪk] **I.** *n* (*fam*) [Erd]beben *nt* **II.** *vi* ① (*move*) *earth* beben ② (*fig: shake*) zittern; **her voice ~d with emotion** ihre Stimme bebte vor Erregung

Quaker ['kweɪ·kər] **I.** *n* Quäker(in) *m(f)* **II.** *adj attr* Quäker-

qualification [ˌkwal·ə·fɪ·'keɪ·ʃən] *n* ① (*skill*) Qualifikation *f* ② (*condition*) [notwendige] Voraussetzung *f* (**for, of** für +*akk*) ③ (*restriction*) Einschränkung *f* ④ (*eligibility*) Berechtigung *f*

qualified ['kwal·ɪ·faɪd] *adj* ① (*competent*) qualifiziert; **well** ~ gut geeignet ② (*restricted*) bedingt; **to make a ~ statement** eine Erklärung unter Einschränkungen abgeben; **to be a ~ success** ein mäßiger Erfolg sein

qualifier ['kwal·ɪ·faɪ·ər] *n* ① (*competitor*) Qualifikant(in) *m(f)* ② (*sports round*) Qualifikation *f*

qualify <-ie-> ['kwal·ɪ·faɪ] **I.** *vt* ① (*make competent*) qualifizieren ② (*make eligible*) ■ **to ~ sb [for sth]** jdm das Recht [auf etw *dat*] geben; ■ **to ~ sb to do sth** jdn berechtigen, etw zu tun ③ (*restrict*) *criticism, judgment* einschränken; **to ~ a remark** eine Bemerkung unter Vorbehalt äußern **II.** *vi* ① (*prove competence*) sich qualifizieren (**for** für +*akk*) ② (*meet requirements*) *for citizenship, membership, office* die [nötigen] Voraussetzungen erfüllen (**for** für +*akk*); (*be eligible*) *for benefits, a job* in Frage kommen (**for** für +*akk*)

qualifying ['kwal·ɪ·faɪ·ɪŋ] **I.** *n* ① SPORTS Qualifizierung *f* ② (*restricting*) Einschränkung *f* **II.** *adj attr, inv* ① (*restrictive*) einschränkend ② SPORTS *round* Qualifikations-

qualitative ['kwal·ɪ·teɪ·ṭɪv] *adj inv* qualitativ, Qualitäts-

quality ['kwal·ɪ·ṭi] **I.** *n* ① (*standard*) Qualität *f*; TECH Gütegrad *m fachspr*; **~ of life** Lebensqualität *f* ② (*character*) Art *f*; **the unique ~ of their relationship** die Einzigartigkeit ihrer Beziehung ③ (*feature*) Merkmal *nt*; **managerial qualities** Führungsqualitäten *pl* **II.** *adj* [qualitativ] hochwertig, Qualitäts-

'quality control *n usu sing* Qualitätskontrolle *f*

'quality time *n die Zeit, die man dafür aufbringt, familiäre Beziehungen zu entwickeln und zu pflegen*

qualm [kwam] *n* ① (*doubt*) ■ **~s** *pl* Bedenken *pl* ② (*uneasiness*) ungutes Gefühl; **without the slightest ~** ohne die geringsten Skrupel

quandary ['kwan·də·ri] *n usu sing* ① (*indecision*) Unentschiedenheit *f*; **to be in a ~** sich nicht entscheiden können ② (*difficult situation*) verzwickte Lage; **to put sb in a ~** jdn in große Verlegenheit bringen

quantifiable ['kwan·tə·faɪ·ə·bəl] *adj inv* mengenmäßig messbar

quantify <-ie-> ['kwan·tə·faɪ] *vt* mengenmäßig messen

quantitative ['kwan·tə·teɪ·ṭɪv] *adj* quantitativ *geh*

quantity ['kwan·tɪ·ṭi] *n* ① (*amount*) Quantität *f*, Menge *f*; *of individual items* Stückzahl *f* ② (*large amount*) große Menge *f*, Unmenge *f* ③ MATH (*magnitude*) Größe *f*

quantum <*pl* -ta> ['kwan·təm] *n* PHYS (*unit*) Quant[um] *nt fachspr*

quantum me'chanics *n + sing vb* Quantenmechanik *f kein pl*

quarantine ['kwɔr·ən·ˌtin] **I.** *n* Quarantäne *f*; **to place sb under ~** jdn unter Quarantäne stellen **II.** *vt* unter Quarantäne stellen

quark [kwark] *n* PHYS Quark *nt*

quarrel ['kwɔr·əl] **I.** *n* ❶ (*argument*) Streit *m;* **to have a ~** sich streiten ❷ (*cause of complaint*) Einwand *m* **II.** *vi* <-l- *or* -ll-> ❶ (*argue*) sich streiten (**about** über +*akk*) ❷ (*disagree with*) ■**to ~ with sth** etwas an etw *dat* aussetzen; **you can't ~ with that** daran gibt es nichts auszusetzen

quarrelsome ['kwɔr·əl·səm] *adj* streitsüchtig

quarry[1] ['kwɔr·i] **I.** *n* Steinbruch *m;* (*fig*) Fundgrube *f* **II.** *vt* <-ie-> brechen

quarry[2] ['kwɔr·i] *n* ❶ (*animal*) Jagdbeute *f* ❷ *criminal* gejagte Person; (*fig: victim*) Opfer *nt*

quart [kwɔrt] *n* Quart *nt* (*0,95 l*); **a ~ of milk** ein Quart *nt* Milch

quarter ['kwɔr·t̬ər] **I.** *n* ❶ (*fourth*) Viertel *nt;* **the bottle was a ~ full** es war noch ein Viertel in der Flasche; **for a ~ of the price** zu einem Viertel des Preises; **to divide sth into ~s** etw in vier Teile teilen ❷ (*coin*) Vierteldollar *m* ❸ (*time*) Viertel *nt; of year* Quartal *nt;* **a ~ of an hour** eine Viertelstunde; **a ~ to/after three** Viertel vor/nach drei ❹ UNIV (*term*) Quartal *nt* ❺ SPORTS (*period*) Viertel *nt* ❻ (*area*) Gegend *f;* (*neighborhood*) Viertel *nt;* **the French Q~** das französische Viertel ❼ (*unspecified place*) Seite *f;* (*place*) Stelle *f;* **help came from a totally unexpected ~** Hilfe kam von völlig unerwarteter Seite ❽ (*lodgings*) ■**~s** *pl* Wohnung *f;* MIL Quartier *nt* ►PHRASES: **at close ~s with sb** in jds Nähe **II.** *vt* vierteln **III.** *adj inv* Viertel-

'quarterback *n* ❶ SPORTS Quarterback *m fachspr* ❷ (*leader*) Gruppenleiter(in) *m(f)*

quarter'final *n* Viertelfinale *nt*

quarterly ['kwɔr·t̬ər·li] **I.** *adv* vierteljährlich; **to be paid ~** vierteljährlich gezahlt werden **II.** *adj* vierteljährlich, Vierteljahres-; *esp* ECON Quartals-

quartermaster ['kwɔr·t̬ər·ˌmæs·tər] *n* ❶ MIL Quartiermeister *m* ❷ NAUT *in merchant marine* Quartermeister *m; in navy* Steuermannsmaat *m*

'quarter note *n* MUS Viertelnote *f*

'quarter rest *n* MUS Viertelpause *f*

quartet, quartette [kwɔr·'tet] *n* Quartett *nt*

quartz [kwɔrts] *n* Quarz *m;* **rose ~** Rosenquarz *m*

quasar ['kweɪ·zar] *n* ASTRON Quasar *m*

quash [kwaʃ] *vt* ❶ (*destroy*) zermalmen; (*fig*) *hopes, plans* zunichtemachen ❷ (*suppress*) *rebellion, revolt* niederschlagen; *rumors* zum Verstummen bringen ❸ LAW (*annul*) aufheben; *law* für ungültig erklären

quasi- ['kwa·zi] *in compounds* (*resembling*) *religion, science* Quasi-; *intellectual, scientific* pseudo-; *philosophical, spiritual* quasi-; *official* halb-; *legislative* -ähnlich; LAW *partner, partnership* Schein-

quaver ['kweɪ·vər] **I.** *vi* ❶ (*tremble*) *person* zittern; *voice a.* beben ❷ (*speak*) mit zitternder Stimme sprechen **II.** *n* Zittern *nt kein pl,* Beben *nt kein pl*

quay [ki] *n* Kai *m,* Kaje *f* NORDD

queasy ['kwi·zi] *adj* ❶ (*easily upset*) *person, stomach* [über]empfindlich ❷ (*upset*) übel *nach n;* **he feels ~** ihm ist übel

queen [kwin] *n* ❶ (*monarch*) Königin *f* ❷ (*fig: lady*) Königin *f;* **beauty ~** Schönheitskönigin *f;* (*card*) Königin *f;* **~ of diamonds** Karokönigin *f;* (*chess*) Dame *f* ❸ (*fam: gay*) Tunte *f pej fam;* **drag ~** Transvestit *m*

queen 'bee *n* ❶ Bienenkönigin *f fachspr* ❷ (*fig: leader*) tonangebende Frau; (*busybody*) sich [überall] wichtigmachende Frau

queenly ['kwin·li] *adj* königlich

queer [kwɪr] **I.** *adj* ❶ (*strange*) seltsam; **to have ~ ideas** schräge Ideen haben ❷ (*offensive fam: homosexual*) schwul *fam* **II.** *n* (*offensive fam*) Schwule(r) *m fam; female* Lesbe *f fam*

quell [kwel] *vt* ❶ (*suppress*) *opposition, protest* [gewaltsam] unterdrücken; *revolt* niederschlagen ❷ (*subdue*) *anger* zügeln; (*overcome*) *fear* überwinden ❸ (*fig: quiet*) beschwichtigen; *doubts, fears* zerstreuen

quench [kwentʃ] *vt* ❶ (*put out*) löschen; (*fig*) dämpfen ❷ (*satisfy*) befriedigen; *thirst for knowledge* stillen

querulous ['kwer·ə·ləs] *adj* (*liter*) ❶ (*peevish*) missmutig; *voice* gereizt ❷ (*complaining*) nörg[e]lig

query ['kwɪr·i] **I.** *n* Rückfrage *f* **II.** *vt* <-ie-> (*form*) ❶ (*doubt*) in Frage stellen; ■**to ~ whether ...** bezweifeln, dass ... ❷ (*ask*) befragen

quest [kwest] *n* Suche *f* (**for** nach +*dat*); **in ~ of sth** auf der Suche nach etw *dat*

question ['kwes·tʃən] **I.** *n* ❶ (*query*) Frage *f;* **to put a ~ to sb** jdm eine Frage stellen; **to pop the ~** jdm einen [Heirats]antrag machen ❷ (*doubt*) Zweifel *m;* **there's no ~ about it** keine Frage; **the place in ~** LAW besagter Ort; **to call sth into ~** etw bezweifeln; **without ~** zweifellos ❸ (*matter*) Frage *f;* **it's a ~ of life or death** es geht um Leben und Tod; **to be out of the ~** nicht in Frage kommen **II.** *vt* ❶ (*ask*) befragen (**about** über +*akk*) ❷ (*interrogate*) verhören (**about** zu +*dat*) ❸ (*doubt*) bezweifeln; *facts, findings* anzweifeln

questionable ['kwes·tʃə·nə·bəl] *adj* ❶ (*uncertain*) zweifelhaft; *future* ungewiss; **it is ~ how ...** es ist fraglich, wie ... ❷ (*shady*) fragwürdig, zweifelhaft; **to do ~ business** bedenkliche Geschäfte machen; **some of his jokes were in ~ taste** manche seiner Witze waren von etwas zweideutiger Natur

questioner ['kwes·tʃə·nər] *n* Fragesteller(in) *m(f)*

questioning ['kwes·tʃə·nɪŋ] **I.** *n* Befragung *f; by police* Verhör *nt* **II.** *adj look, tone* fragend

'question mark *n* Fragezeichen *nt a. fig*

questionnaire [ˌkwes·tʃə·'ner] *n* Fragebogen *m*

Q

queue [kju] COMPUT **I.** *n* Schlange *f* **II.** *vt* ■**to ~ sth** etw in die Warteschlange einreihen **III.** *vi* anstehen, Schlange stehen

quibble ['kwɪb·əl] **I.** *n* ❶ (*argument*) haarspalterisches Argument; (*hairsplitting*) Haarspalterei *f* ❷ (*criticism*) Krittelei *f* (**about, over, with** an +*dat*) **II.** *vi* sich streiten (**about** über +*akk*); **no one would ~ with that** das würde niemand bestreiten

quibbling ['kwɪb·lɪŋ] **I.** *n* Streiterei *f* **II.** *adj* spitzfindig; (*quarrelsome*) streitsüchtig

quiche <*pl* -> [kiʃ] *n* Quiche *f*

quick [kwɪk] **I.** *adj* ❶ (*fast*) schnell; **to have a ~ drink** [noch] schnell etwas trinken; **in ~ succession** in schneller [Ab]folge; **to have a ~ temper** ein rasch aufbrausendes Temperament haben; **he is always ~ to criticize** mit Kritik ist er rasch bei der Hand ❷ (*short*) kurz; **to have a ~ look at sth** sich *dat* etw kurz ansehen; **could I have a ~ word with you?** könnte ich Sie kurz sprechen? ❸ (*alert*) [geistig] gewandt; **~ wit** Aufgewecktheit *f; in replying* Schlagfertigkeit *f* **II.** *adv* schnell, rasch **III.** *interj* schnell **IV.** *n* **to bite nails to the ~** die Nägel bis auf das Nagelbett abbeißen; **to cut sb to the ~** (*fig*) jdn bis ins Mark treffen

'quick-acting *adj* schnell wirksam

quicken ['kwɪk·ən] **I.** *vt* ❶ beschleunigen ❷ (*fig: awaken*) anregen; *curiosity, interest* wecken **II.** *vi* schneller werden; *pulse* sich erhöhen

quickie ['kwɪk·i] **I.** *n* ❶ (*fast thing*) kurze Sache ❷ (*sex*) Quickie *m* ❸ (*drink*) Schluck *m* auf die Schnelle **II.** *adj* Schnell-, schnell [hingehauen]; **~ divorce** schnelle und unkomplizierte Scheidung

quickly ['kwɪk·li] *adv* schnell, rasch

quickness ['kwɪk·nɪs] *n* ❶ (*speed*) Schnelligkeit *f* ❷ (*alertness*) [geistige] Beweglichkeit; **~ of mind** scharfer Verstand

'quicksand *n* Treibsand *m*

'quicksilver *n* (*old: mercury*) Quecksilber *nt*

'quickstep **I.** *n* ■**the ~** der Quickstepp **II.** *vi* <-pp-> Quickstepp tanzen

quick-'tempered *adj* hitzköpfig

quick-'witted *adj* (*alert*) aufgeweckt; (*quick in replying*) schlagfertig; *reply* schlagfertig

quid pro quo ['kwɪd·proʊ·'kwoʊ] *n* Gegenleistung *f*

quiescent [kwaɪ·'es·ənt] *adj* (*form*) ruhig

quiet ['kwaɪ·ət] **I.** *adj* <-er, -est *or* more ~, most ~> ❶ (*not loud*) leise ❷ (*silent*) ruhig; **please be ~** Ruhe bitte!; **to keep ~** ruhig sein ❸ (*not talking*) still; *child* ruhig; (*taciturn*) schweigsam; **to keep ~ about sth** über etw *akk* Stillschweigen bewahren ❹ (*secret*) heimlich; **to have a ~ word with sb** mit jdm ein Wörtchen im Vertrauen reden *fam;* **to keep sth ~** etw für sich *akk* behalten ❺ (*not exciting*) geruhsam; (*not busy*) *street, town* ruhig ▶ PHRASES: **as ~ as a <u>mouse</u>** mucksmäuschenstill *fam* **II.** *n* ❶ (*silence*) Stille *f* ❷ (*lack of excitement*) Ruhe *f;* **peace and ~** Ruhe und Frieden ▶ PHRASES: **<u>on</u> the ~** heimlich **III.** *vt* ❶ (*make quiet*) beruhigen ❷ (*calm*) beruhigen; *fears* zerstreuen; *tension* lösen

◆**quiet down** **I.** *vi* ❶ (*become quiet*) leiser werden ❷ (*become calm*) sich beruhigen **II.** *vt* ❶ (*make less noisy*) zur Ruhe bringen; **go and ~ those children down** stell die Kinder mal ruhig! *fam* ❷ (*calm*) beruhigen

quietly ['kwaɪət·li] *adv* ❶ (*not loudly*) leise ❷ (*silently*) still; **to wait ~** ruhig warten ❸ (*unobtrusively*) unauffällig; **the plan has been ~ dropped** der Plan wurde stillschweigend fallen gelassen; **to be ~ confident** insgeheim überzeugt sein

quietness ['kwaɪ·ət·nɪs] *n* Ruhe *f;* (*silence*) Stille *f*

quill [kwɪl] *n* ❶ (*feather*) Feder *f* ❷ (*of porcupine*) Stachel *m* ❸ (*pen*) Federkiel *m*

quilt [kwɪlt] **I.** *n* Steppdecke *f;* **patchwork ~** Quilt *m* **II.** *vt* [ab]steppen

quince [kwɪns] *n* Quitte *f;* (*tree a.*) Quittenbaum *m*

quinine ['kwaɪ·naɪn] *n* Chinin *nt*

quintessence [kwɪn·'tes·əns] *n* Quintessenz *f geh;* (*embodiment*) Inbegriff *m;* **to be the ~ of sth** etw verkörpern

quintessential [ˌkwɪn·te·'sen·ʃəl] *adj inv* essentiell; **the ~ American meal** der Inbegriff einer amerikanischen Mahlzeit

quintet, quintette [kwɪn·'tet] *n* Quintett *nt*

quintuplet [kwɪn·'tʌp·lɪt] *n* Fünfling *m*

quip [kwɪp] **I.** *n* witzige Bemerkung **II.** *vi* <-pp-> witzeln

quirk [kwɜrk] *n* ❶ (*habit*) Marotte *f* ❷ (*oddity*) Merkwürdigkeit *f kein pl;* **by some strange ~ of fate** durch eine [merkwürdige] Laune des Schicksals

quirky ['kwɜr·ki] *adj* schrullig *fam*

quit <quit *or* quitted, quit *or* quitted> [kwɪt] **I.** *vi* ❶ *worker* kündigen; *manager, official* zurücktreten ❷ COMPUT aussteigen ❸ (*give up*) aufgeben **II.** *vt* ❶ (*stop*) **will you ~ that!?** wirst du wohl damit aufhören!; **~ it!** hör [damit] auf!; **~ wasting my time** hör auf, meine Zeit zu verschwenden; **to ~ smoking** das Rauchen aufgeben ❷ (*give up*) aufgeben; *job, apartment* kündigen ❸ COMPUT (*end*) aussteigen (aus +*dat*)

quite [kwaɪt] *adv inv* ❶ (*fairly*) ziemlich; **we had ~ a nice evening in the end** schließlich war es doch noch ein recht netter Abend; **I had to wait ~ a long time** ich musste ganz schön lange warten *fam* ❷ (*completely*) ganz, völlig; **~ honestly, ...** ehrlich gesagt ...

quits [kwɪts] *adj pred, inv* quitt (**with** mit +*dat*); **to call it ~** (*fam*) es gut sein lassen

quiver[1] ['kwɪv·ər] **I.** *n* Zittern *nt kein pl* **II.** *vi* zittern; **to ~ with rage** vor Wut beben

quiver[2] ['kwɪv·ər] *n* (*holder*) Köcher *m*

quixotic [kwɪk·'saṭ·ɪk] *adj personality* schwärmerisch; *idea, suggestion, vision* unrealistisch; *attempt* naiv

quiz [kwɪz] **I.** *n* <*pl* -zes> SCH, UNIV [kurze]

Prüfung **II.** *adj* SCH, UNIV *question, results* Prüfungs- *nt* **III.** *vt* ❶ (*question*) befragen (**about** zu +*dat*) ❷ SCH, UNIV prüfen (**on** über +*akk*)
'quiz show *n* Quizsendung *f*
quizzical ['kwɪz·ɪ·kəl] *adj* ❶ (*questioning*) fragend ❷ (*teasing*) spöttisch
quorum ['kwɔr·əm] *n* Quorum *nt geh*
quota ['kwoʊ·t̬ə] *n* ❶ (*fixed amount*) Quote *f* ❷ (*fig: proportion*) Quantum *nt*
quotable ['kwoʊ·t̬ə·bəl] *adj* ❶ (*citable*) zitierbar ❷ POL (*on the record*) für die Öffentlichkeit bestimmt
quotation [kwoʊ·'teɪ·ʃən] *n* ❶ (*citation*) Zitat *nt;* ■ **~ from sb/sth** Zitat *nt* von jdm/aus etw ❷ STOCKEX [Kurs]notierung *f*
quo'tation marks *npl* Anführungszeichen *pl*
quote [kwoʊt] **I.** *n* ❶ (*citation*) Zitat *nt* ❷ (*quotation mark*) ■ **~s** *pl* Gänsefüßchen *pl fam* ❸ (*estimate*) Kostenvoranschlag *m* **II.** *vt* ❶ (*cite*) zitieren; ■ **to ~ sb on sth** jdn zu etw *dat* zitieren; **but don't ~ me on that!** aber sag's nicht weiter! *fam* ❷ (*give*) *price* nennen ❸ STOCKEX notieren **III.** *vi* zitieren; ■ **to ~ from sb** jdn zitieren; ■ **to ~ from sth** aus etw *dat* zitieren
quotient ['kwoʊ·ʃənt] *n a.* MATH Quotient *m*
QWERTY keyboard [ˌkwɜr·t̬i·'ki·bɔrd] *n englische Standardtastatur*

Rr

R <*pl* -'s *or* -s>, **r** <*pl* -'s> [ar] *n* R *nt,* r *nt;* **~ as in Romeo** R wie Richard
r *adv abbrev of* **right** re.
R¹ [ar] **I.** *n abbrev of* **river** **II.** *adj abbrev of* **right** re.
R² [ar] *adv* FILM *abbrev of* **Restricted: rated ~** nicht für Jugendliche unter 17 Jahren
RA [ˌar·'eɪ] *n* UNIV *abbrev of* **residence assistant** *Student, der im Wohnheim Hausmeisterpflichten versieht und dafür keine Miete bezahlen muss*
rabbi ['ræb·aɪ] *n* Rabbiner *m*
rabbit ['ræb·ɪt] *n* Kaninchen *nt*
'rabbit hutch *n* Kaninchenstall *m*
rabble ['ræ·bəl] *n* (*pej: disorderly group*) ungeordneter Haufen
'rabble-rouser *n* Aufwiegler(in) *m(f)*
'rabble-rousing *adj* Hetz-, [auf]hetzerisch
rabid ['ræb·ɪd] *adj* ❶ (*fig, esp pej: fanatical*) fanatisch; *critic* scharf; *nationalist* radikal ❷ (*having rabies*) tollwütig
rabies ['reɪ·biz] *n + sing vb* Tollwut *f*
raccoon [ræ·'kun] *n* Waschbär(in) *m(f)*
race¹ [reɪs] *n* ❶ (*ethnic group*) Rasse *f* ❷ (*species*) **the human ~** die menschliche Rasse; (*of animals, plants*) Spezies *f*
race² [reɪs] **I.** *n* ❶ (*test of speed*) Rennen *nt* ❷ (*long competition*) Wettkampf *m* **II.** *vi* ❶ (*compete*) *people* Rennen laufen; *vehicles* Rennen fahren ❷ (*rush*) rennen ❸ (*pass quickly*) ■ **to ~ by** schnell vergehen **III.** *vt* ❶ ■ **to ~ sb** (*in competition*) gegen jdn antreten; (*for fun*) mit jdm ein Wettrennen machen ❷ (*enter for races*) **to ~ a horse** ein Pferd Rennen laufen lassen
'racecar *n* Rennwagen *m*
'racecar driver *n* Rennfahrer(in) *m(f)*
'racecourse *n* Rennbahn *f*
'racehorse *n* Rennpferd *nt*
racer ['reɪ·sər] *n* ❶ (*runner*) [Renn]läufer(in) *m(f);* (*horse*) Rennpferd *nt* ❷ (*bicycle*) Rennrad *nt;* (*car*) Rennwagen *m*
'race relations *npl* Beziehungen *pl* zwischen den Rassen
'race riot *n* Rassenunruhen *pl*
'racetrack *n* (*racecourse*) Rennbahn *f;* (*for horses a.*) Rennstrecke *f*
racial ['reɪ·ʃəl] *adj* ❶ (*to do with race*) rassisch, Rassen- ❷ (*motivated by racism*) rassistisch; **~ segregation** Rassentrennung *f*
'racial profiling *n* Profiling *nt* aufgrund der Rassenzugehörigkeit
racing ['reɪ·sɪŋ] *n* SPORTS **car ~** Autorennen *nt;* **horse ~** Pferderennen *nt;* SPORT Pferderennsport *m*
racism ['reɪ·sɪz·əm] *n* Rassismus *m*
racist ['reɪ·sɪst] **I.** *n* Rassist(in) *m(f)* **II.** *adj* rassistisch
rack [ræk] **I.** *n* ❶ (*for storage*) Regal *nt;* **clothes ~** Kleiderständer *m;* **magazine ~** Zeitschriftenständer *m;* **to buy off the ~** von der Stange kaufen ❷ (*for torture*) Folterbank *f* **II.** *vt* (*hurt*) quälen; **to be ~ed with pain** von Schmerzen gequält werden ▶ PHRASES: **to ~ one's brains** sich *dat* den Kopf zerbrechen
racket¹ ['ræk·ɪt] *n* SPORTS Schläger *m*
racket² ['ræk·ɪt] *n* (*fam*) ❶ (*din*) Krach *m* ❷ (*pej: dishonest scheme*) unsauberes Geschäft; **extortion ~** Schutzgelderpressung *f*
racketeering [ˌræk·ə·'tɪr] *n* dunkle Machenschaften *pl pej*
racoon [ræ·'kun] *n see* **raccoon**
racquetball ['ræk·ɪt·bɔl] *n* SPORT Racketball *nt kein pl*
racy ['reɪ·si] *adj* ❶ *behavior, novel* anzüglich; *clothing* gewagt ❷ *person, image* draufgängerisch
radar ['reɪ·dar] *n* Radar *m o nt;* **~ screen** Radarschirm *m*
radial ['reɪ·di·əl] **I.** *adj* ❶ (*radiating*) strahlenförmig ❷ TECH radial, Radial-; **~ tire** Gürtelreifen *m* **II.** *n* Gürtelreifen *m*

R

R

radiant ['reɪ·di·ənt] *adj* ❶ PHYS ~ **heat** Strahlungswärme *f* ❷ (*beaming*) *smile* wunderschön, strahlend *attr fig*

radiate ['reɪ·di·eɪt] **I.** *vi* ❶ (*spread out*) strahlenförmig ausgehen (**from** von +*dat*) ❷ (*be given off*) abstrahlen (**from** von +*dat*); *light, energy* ausstrahlen **II.** *vt* (*a. fig*) ausstrahlen; *heat* abgeben

radiation [ˌreɪ·di·'eɪ·ʃən] *n* ❶ (*radiated energy*) Strahlung *f* ❷ (*process*) Abstrahlen *nt*

radi'ation sickness *n* Strahlenkrankheit *f*

radiator ['reɪ·di·eɪ·ṭər] *n* ❶ (*heating device*) Heizkörper *m* ❷ (*to cool engine*) Kühler *m*

radical ['ræd·ɪ·kəl] **I.** *adj* ❶ MED, POL radikal ❷ (*fundamental*) fundamental **II.** *n* ❶ (*person*) Radikale(r) *f(m)* ❷ CHEM Radikal *nt;* **free ~s** freie Radikale

radii ['reɪ·di·aɪ] *n pl of* **radius**

radio ['reɪ·di·oʊ] **I.** *n* ❶ (*receiving device*) Radio *nt* SÜDD, ÖSTERR, SCHWEIZ *a. m* ❷ (*transmitter and receiver*) Funkgerät *nt;* **on/over the ~** über Funk ❸ (*broadcasting*) Radio *nt,* [Rund]funk *m;* **to listen to the ~** Radio hören; (*medium*) Funk *m* **II.** *vi* **to ~ for help** über Funk Hilfe anfordern

radioactive [ˌreɪ·di·oʊ·'æk·tɪv] *adj* radioaktiv

radioactivity [ˌreɪ·di·oʊ·æk·'tɪv·ɪ·ṭi] *n* Radioaktivität *f*

radiographer [ˌreɪ·di'ag·rə·fər] *n* Röntgenassistent(in) *m(f)*

radiography [ˌreɪ·di·'ag·rə·fi] *n* Röntgenographie *f*

radiologist [ˌreɪ·di·'al·ə·dʒɪst] *n* Radiologe(in) *m(f)*

radiology [ˌreɪ·di·'al·ə·dʒi] *n* Radiologie *f*

'radio program *n* Rundfunkprogramm *nt,* Radioprogramm *nt*

'radio station *n* ❶ (*radio channel*) Radiosender *m* ❷ (*building*) Rundfunkstation *f*

radio'therapy *n* Strahlentherapie *f*

'radio wave *n* Radiowelle *f*

radish <*pl* -es> ['ræd·ɪʃ] *n* Rettich *m*

radium ['reɪ·di·əm] *n* Radium *nt*

radius <*pl* -dii> ['reɪ·di·əs] *n* (*distance from center*) *a.* MATH Radius *m*

raffia ['ræf·i·ə] *n* Raphia[bast] *m*

raffish ['ræf·ɪʃ] *adj* (*rakish*) flott *fam,* verwegen

raffle ['ræf·əl] **I.** *n* Tombola *f* **II.** *vt* verlosen

raft¹ [ræft] **I.** *n* (*vessel*) Floß *nt* **II.** *vi* an einem Rafting teilnehmen

raft² [ræft] *n* (*large number*) ■ **a ~ of sth** eine [ganze] Menge einer S. *gen*

rafter ['ræf·tər] *n* ARCHIT Dachsparren *m*

rafting ['ræf·tɪŋ] *n* Rafting *nt*

rag [ræg] *n* ❶ (*old cloth*) Lumpen *m;* (*for cleaning*) Lappen *m,* ÖSTERR Fetzen *m;* (*for dust*) Staubtuch *nt* ❷ *pl* (*worn-out clothes*) Lumpen *pl pej*

◆ **rag on** *vt* <-gg-> (*fam*) ■ **to ~ on sb** jdn nerven *sl;* (*scold*) auf jdm herumhacken *fam*

ragamuffin ['ræg·ə·mʌf·ɪn] *n* (*fam*) Dreckspatz *m*

rage [reɪdʒ] **I.** *n* ❶ (*violent anger*) Wut *f,* Zorn *m* ❷ (*fit of anger*) **to get in a ~** sich aufregen (**about** über +*akk*) ❸ (*mania*) **to be [all] the ~** der letzte Schrei sein *fam* **II.** *vi* ❶ (*express fury*) toben; *at sb* anschreien; *at sth* sich aufregen (über +*akk*) ❷ (*continue violently*) toben; *epidemic, fire* wüten

ragged ['ræg·ɪd] *adj clothes, children* zerlumpt; *cuffs, hem* ausgefranst; *people, group* unorganisiert

raging ['reɪ·dʒɪŋ] *adj* ❶ *river* reißend *attr* ❷ *fire* lodernd *attr; inferno* flammend *attr* ❸ (*severe*) rasend; *thirst* schrecklich

'ragtime *n* Ragtime *m*

'ragweed *n* HORT beifußblättriges Traubenkraut

raid [reɪd] **I.** *n* ❶ (*military attack*) Angriff *m* ❷ (*by police*) Razzia *f* ❸ (*by bandits*) Überfall *m* (**on** auf +*akk*) **II.** *vt* ❶ MIL (*attack*) überfallen; (*bomb*) bombardieren; *town* plündern ❷ (*steal from*) ausplündern; *bank, post office* überfallen; (*fig*) *refrigerator, piggy bank* plündern *hum*

raider [reɪ·dər] *n* ❶ (*attacker*) Angreifer(in) *m(f)* ❷ (*robber*) Einbrecher(in) *m(f)* ❸ (*pej: investor*) **corporate ~** Heuschrecke *f pej*

rail¹ [reɪl] *n* ❶ (*transport system*) Bahn *f;* **by ~** mit der Bahn ❷ (*railway track*) Schiene *f* ❸ (*on stairs*) Geländer *nt;* (*on fence, for clothes, in shop*) Stange *f;* (*on ship*) Reling *f*

rail² [reɪl] *vi* wettern (**against/at** gegen +*akk*), schimpfen (**against/at** über +*akk*)

railing ['reɪ·lɪŋ] *n* ❶ (*fence*) Geländer *nt* ❷ (*on a ship*) Reling *f*

'rail network *n* Bahnnetz *nt*

'railroad I. *n* ❶ (*railway system*) [Eisen]bahn *f kein pl* ❷ (*train track*) Schienen *pl,* Gleise *pl;* (*stretch of track*) Strecke *f* **II.** *vt* zwingen; ■ **to have been ~ed into sth** gezwungen worden sein, etw zu tun

'railroad crossing *n* Bahnübergang *m*

'railroad line *n* Bahnlinie *f*

'railroad station *n* Bahnhof *m*

'railway ['reɪl·weɪ] *n* **commuter ~** ≈ S-Bahn *f*

rain [reɪn] **I.** *n* (*precipitation*) Regen *m;* **in the ~** im Regen **II.** *vi impers* regnen; **it's ~ing** es regnet

rainbow ['reɪn·boʊ] *n* Regenbogen *m*

'rain cloud *n* Regenwolke *f*

'raincoat *n* Regenmantel *m*

'raindrop *n* Regentropfen *m*

'rainfall *n* ❶ (*period of rain*) Niederschlag *m* ❷ (*quantity of rain*) Niederschlagsmenge *f*

'rain forest *n* Regenwald *m*

'rain gauge *n* Regenmesser *m*

'rainproof *adj* wasserdicht

'rainstorm *n* starke Regenfälle *pl*

rainy ['reɪ·ni] *adj* regnerisch

raise [reɪz] **I.** *n* Gehaltserhöhung *f* **II.** *vt* ❶ (*lift*) *hand, arm, leg* heben; *anchor* lichten; *eyebrow, drawbridge, blinds* hochziehen; *flag, sail* hissen ❷ (*increase*) erhöhen; *quality* verbessern; **to ~ public awareness** das öffentliche Bewusstsein schärfen ❸ (*mention*) vorbringen; *an issue, a question* aufwerfen; *an*

objection erheben ④ *capital, money* aufbringen ⑤ (*bring up*) *children* aufziehen ⑥ (*breed*) züchten; (*look after*) aufziehen
raisin ['reɪ·zən] *n* Rosine *f*
rake [reɪk] **I.** *n* (*garden tool*) Harke *f,* Rechen *m* **II.** *vt* ① (*gather up*) [zusammen]rechen; *leaves, the lawn* rechen ② (*work*) *soil* harken; **to ~ one's fingers through one's hair** sich mit der Hand durchs Haar fahren **III.** *vi* ■ **to ~ through sth** etw durchsuchen
◆**rake in** *vt* ① (*work in*) rechen ② (*fam: earn effortlessly*) *money* kassieren
◆**rake up** *vt* ① (*gather up*) zusammenrechen; (*fig*) einstreichen ② (*fig: revive*) **to ~ up the past** die Vergangenheit wieder ausgraben
rakish¹ ['reɪ·kɪʃ] *adj* (*jaunty*) flott, keck
rakish² ['reɪ·kɪʃ] *adj* (*dissolute*) ausschweifend; *charm* verwegen
rally ['ræl·i] **I.** *n* ① (*assembly*) [Massen]versammlung *f,* Treffen *nt,* Zusammenkunft *f* ② MIL (*reassembling*) *of troops* Versammlung *f* ③ (*recovery*) *of prices* Erholung *f* ④ SPORTS (*in tennis, volleyball*) Ballwechsel *m* ⑤ (*vehicle race*) Rallye *f* **II.** *vt* <-ie-> *troops* sammeln; *support* gewinnen; *supporters* mobilisieren (**against/in favor of** gegen/für +*akk*) **III.** *vi* <-ie-> ① (*support*) ■ **to ~ behind sb** sich geschlossen hinter jdn stellen ② MED, FIN, STOCKEX sich erholen; SPORTS sich fangen *fam*
◆**rally 'around** *vi person* unterstützen
ram [ræm] **I.** *n* ① (*sheep*) Widder *m,* Schafbock *m* ② (*implement*) Rammbock *m,* Ramme *f* **II.** *vt* <-mm-> ① (*hit*) rammen ② (*pound*) *soil* feststampfen ③ (*stuff*) stopfen (**into** in +*akk*) ④ (*fig: present forcefully*) **to ~ sth home** *views* [mit Vehemenz] klarmachen **III.** *vi* <-mm-> ■ **to ~ into sth** gegen etw *akk* prallen; (*with car a.*) gegen etw *akk* fahren
RAM [ræm] *n* COMPUT *acr for* **Random Access Memory** RAM *m o nt*
Ramadan [ˌræm·ə·'dan] *n* Ramadan *m*
ramble ['ræm·bəl] **I.** *n* Wanderung *f,* Spaziergang *m* **II.** *vi* ① (*walk*) wandern, umherstreifen (**through** durch +*akk*) ② (*pej fam*) faseln *fam,* schwafeln (**about** über +*akk*) ③ (*grow randomly*) sich ranken
rambler ['ræm·blər] *n* ① (*walker*) Wanderer *m,* Wanderin *f* ② HORT, BOT (*rose*) Kletterrose *f*
rambling ['ræm·blɪŋ] **I.** *n* ■ **~s** *pl* Gefasel *nt kein pl pej* **II.** *adj* ① (*incoherent*) unzusammenhängend, zusammenhanglos ② (*sprawling*) *building* weitläufig ③ BOT, HORT rankend *attr,* Kletter-
rambunctious [ræm·'bʌŋ(k)·ʃəs] *adj* (*fam*) lärmend *attr; horse* wild
ramification [ˌræm·ɪ·fɪ·'keɪ·ʃən] *n usu pl* (*consequences*) Auswirkung *f,* Konsequenz *f*
ramp [ræmp] *n* Rampe *f;* AVIAT Gangway *f*
rampage ['ræm·peɪdʒ] **I.** *n* Randale *f;* **on the ~** angriffslustig **II.** *vi* randalieren
rampant ['ræm·pənt] *adj* ① (*unrestrained*) ungezügelt; *inflation* galoppierend *attr; nationalism, racism* zügellos ② (*rife*) *epidemic* ■ **to be ~** grassieren
rampart ['ræm·part] *n* [Schutz]wall *m,* Befestigungswall *m*
'ramrod *n* Ladestock *m;* **he stood ~-straight** er stand so steif da, als hätte er einen Besenstiel verschluckt
ramshackle ['ræm·ʃæk·əl] *adj* (*dilapidated*) klapp[e]rig; *building* baufällig
ran [ræn] *pt of* **run**
ranch [ræntʃ] **I.** *n* <*pl* -es> Farm *f,* Ranch *f* **II.** *vi* Viehwirtschaft treiben **III.** *vt cattle, mink, salmon* züchten
rancher ['ræn·tʃər] *n* ① (*ranch owner*) Viehzüchter(in) *m(f)* ② (*ranch worker*) Farmarbeiter(in) *m(f)*
'ranch house *n einstöckiges Einfamilienhaus mit einfachem Grundriss und angebauter Garage*
rancid ['ræn·sɪd] *adj* ranzig
rancor ['ræŋ·kər] *n* (*bitterness*) Verbitterung *f,* Groll *m* (**toward** gegenüber +*dat*); (*hatred*) Hass *m*
R & B [ˌar·ənd·'bi] *n abbrev of* **rhythm and blues** R & B *m*
R & D [ˌar·ənd·'di] *n abbrev of* **research and development** Forschung *f* und Entwicklung *f*
random ['ræn·dəm] **I.** *n* **at ~** (*aimlessly*) willkürlich, wahllos; (*by chance*) zufällig **II.** *adj* zufällig, wahllos; **a ~ sample** eine Stichprobe
rang [ræŋ] *pt of* **ring**
range [reɪndʒ] **I.** *n* ① (*variety*) Reihe *f,* Auswahl *f* (**of** an +*dat*); (*selection*) Angebot *nt,* Sortiment *nt* ② (*limit*) Reichweite *f;* **in/out of ~** in/außer Reichweite; (*extent*) Bereich *m* ③ (*distance*) Entfernung *f; of a gun* Schussweite *f; of a missile* Reichweite *f* ④ MIL (*practice area*) **firing ~** Schießplatz *m* ⑤ (*of mountains*) Hügelkette *f,* Bergkette *f* ⑥ (*pasture*) Weide *f,* Weideland *nt* ⑦ (*stove*) [Koch]herd *m* **II.** *vi* ① (*vary*) schwanken ② ■ **to ~ from sth to sth** von etw *dat* bis [zu etw *dat*] reichen; **a wide-ranging investigation** eine umfassende Ermittlung
ranger ['reɪn·dʒər] *n* ① (*warden*) Aufseher(in) *m(f);* **park ~** Parkranger *m* ② (*soldier*) Ranger(in) *m(f)*
rank¹ [ræŋk] **I.** *n* ① POL (*position*) Position *f* ② MIL Dienstgrad *m,* Rang *m* ③ (*row*) Reihe *f;* **to close ~s** die Reihen schließen; (*fig*) sich zusammenschließen **II.** *vi* ① (*hold a position*) ■ **to ~ above sb** einen höheren Rang als jd einnehmen ② (*be classified as*) **he currently ~s second in the world** er steht derzeit auf Platz zwei der Weltrangliste **III.** *vt* ① (*classify*) einstufen ② (*arrange*) anordnen; **to ~ sb/sth in order of size** jdn/etw der Größe nach aufstellen
rank² [ræŋk] *adj* ① (*smelly*) stinkend ② *attr* (*absolute*) absolut, ausgesprochen; *outsider* total; *stupidity* rein
rankle ['ræŋ·kəl] *vt* ■ **to ~ sb** jdn wurmen
ransack ['ræn·sæk] *vt* ① (*search*) *cupboards*

R

durchwühlen ② (*a. fig, hum: plunder*) plündern; (*rob*) ausrauben

ransom ['ræn·səm] **I.** *n* Lösegeld *nt* **II.** *vt* auslösen

rant [rænt] **I.** *n* ① (*angry talk*) Geschimpfe *nt,* Gezeter *nt fam* ② (*tirade*) Schimpfkanonade *f* **II.** *vi* [vor sich *akk* hin] schimpfen

rap¹ [ræp] **I.** *n* ① (*knock*) Klopfen *nt kein pl,* Pochen *nt kein pl* ② (*fam: rebuke*) Anpfiff *m fam* ③ (*sl: criticism*) Verriss *m fam* ④ (*sl: reputation*) **a bum ~** eine falsche Anklage ⑤ LAW **to take the ~** [**for sth**] die Schuld [für etw *akk*] zugeschoben kriegen **II.** *vt* <-pp-> ① (*strike*) klopfen (an +*akk*) ② (*fig: criticize*) scharf kritisieren

rap² [ræp] **I.** *n* MUS Rap *m* **II.** *vi* MUS rappen

rapacious [rə·'peɪ·ʃəs] *adj* (*form: grasping*) habgierig; *landlord, businessman* raffgierig

rape [reɪp] **I.** *n* ① (*sexual assault*) Vergewaltigung *f* ② (*fig: destruction*) Zerstörung *f* **II.** *vt* vergewaltigen **III.** *vi* eine Vergewaltigung begehen

rapid ['ræp·ɪd] *adj* ① (*quick*) schnell; *change, growth, expansion* rasch; *increase, rise* steiler ② (*sudden*) plötzlich

rapidity [rə·'pɪd·ɪ·t̬i] *n* ① (*suddenness*) Plötzlichkeit *f* ② (*speed*) Geschwindigkeit *f,* Schnelligkeit *f*

rapids ['ræp·ɪdz] *npl* Stromschnellen *pl*

rapier ['reɪ·pi·ər] *n* Rapier *nt*

rapist ['reɪ·pɪst] *n* Vergewaltiger(in) *m(f)*

rapport [ræ·'pɔr] *n* Übereinstimmung *f,* Harmonie *f*

rapt [ræpt] *adj* (*engrossed*) versunken, selbstvergessen

rapture ['ræp·tʃər] *n* ① (*bliss*) Verzückung *f,* Entzücken *nt* ② *pl* (*expression of joy*) **to be in ~s about sth** entzückt über etw *akk* sein

rapturous ['ræp·tʃər·əs] *adj* ① (*delighted*) entzückt, hingerissen; *smile* verzückt ② (*enthusiastic*) begeistert; *applause* stürmisch

rare¹ [rer] *adj* (*uncommon*) rar, selten

rare² [rer] *adj meat* nicht durch[gebraten] *präd,* blutig

rarefied ['rer·ə·faɪd] *adj* exklusiv

rarely ['rer·li] *adv* selten

raring ['rer·ɪŋ] *adj* ■ **to be ~ to do sth** großes Verlangen haben, etw zu tun; **~ to go** startbereit

rarity ['rer·ɪ·t̬i] *n* Rarität *f,* Seltenheit *f*

rascal ['ræs·kəl] *n* (*scamp*) Schlingel *m;* (*child*) Frechdachs *m*

rash [ræʃ] **I.** *n* <*pl* -es> ① (*skin condition*) Ausschlag *m* ② (*spate*) ■ **a ~ of sth** Unmengen *pl* von etw *dat* **II.** *adj* übereilt, hastig, vorschnell

raspberry ['ræz·ˌber·i] *n* (*fruit*) Himbeere *f*

raspy ['ræs·pi] *adj* krächzend; *breath* rasselnd

Rastafarian [ˌrɑs·tə·'fer·i·ən] **I.** *n* Rastafari *m* **II.** *adj* Rasta-

rat [ræt] **I.** *n* Ratte *f a. fig, pej* **II.** *vi* <-tt-> ■ **to ~ on sb** (*inform on*) jdn verraten

ratchet ['rætʃ·ɪt] *n* TECH Ratsche *f*

◆**ratchet up** *vt* (*fam*) ■ **to ~ up** ↻ **sth** etw Schritt für Schritt hochfahren

rate [reɪt] **I.** *n* ① (*speed*) Geschwindigkeit *f* ② (*measure*) Maß *nt,* Menge *f;* **unemployment ~** Arbeitslosenrate *f* ③ (*payment, level of interest, tax*) Satz *m* ▶ PHRASES: **at any ~** (*whatever happens*) auf jeden Fall; (*at least*) zumindest, wenigstens **II.** *vt* ① (*regard*) einschätzen; **she is ~d very highly by the people she works for** die Leute, für die sie arbeitet, halten große Stücke auf sie ② (*be worthy of*) **to ~ a mention** erwähnenswert sein

rather ['ræð·ər] *adv* ① (*in preference to*) **I'd like to stay at home tonight ~ than going out** ich möchte heute Abend lieber zu Hause bleiben und nicht ausgehen ② (*very*) ziemlich, recht ③ (*more accurately*) **or ~ ...** oder besser gesagt ..., beziehungsweise ... ④ (*on the contrary*) eher

ratification [ˌræt̬·ə·fɪ·'keɪ·ʃən] *n* Ratifizierung *f*

ratify <-ie-> ['ræt̬·ə·faɪ] *vt* ratifizieren

rating ['reɪ·t̬ɪŋ] *n* ① (*assessment*) Einschätzung *f* ② (*regard*) Einstufung *f* ③ (*TV audience*) ■ **~s** *pl* [Einschalt]quoten *pl*

ratio ['reɪ·ʃi·oʊ] *n* Verhältnis *nt*

ration ['ræʃ·ən] **I.** *n* ① (*fixed amount*) Ration *f* ② (*food supplies*) ■ **~s** *pl* [Lebensmittel]marken *pl* **II.** *vt* rationieren, beschränken (**to** auf +*akk*)

rational ['ræʃ·ə·nəl] *adj* rational

rationale [ˌræʃ·ə·'næl] *n* Gründe *pl*

rationalism ['ræʃ·ə·nə·lɪz·əm] *n* Rationalismus *m*

rationality [ˌræʃ·ə·'næl·ɪ·t̬i] *n* ① (*clear reasoning*) Rationalität *f geh,* Vernunft *f* ② (*sensibleness*) Vernünftigkeit *f*

rationalization [ˌræʃ·ə·nə·lɪ·'zeɪ·ʃən] *n* Rationalisierung *f*

rationalize ['ræʃ·ə·nə·laɪz] **I.** *vt* rationalisieren **II.** *vi* rationalisieren, Rationalisierungsmaßnahmen *pl* durchführen

rationing ['ræʃ·ə·nɪŋ] *n* Rationierung *f*

'rat race *n* **to leave the ~** dem Konkurrenzkampf Ade sagen

rattle ['ræt̬·əl] **I.** *n* ① (*sound*) Klappern *nt;* (*of chains*) Rasseln *nt;* (*of hail*) Prasseln *nt* ② (*of baby, instrument*) Rassel *f* **II.** *vi* ① (*make noise*) klappern; *keys* rasseln; *engine* knattern; *bottles* [*in a crate*] klirren; *coins* klingen ② (*move noisily*) rattern ③ (*talk*) ■ **to ~ on** [drauflos]quasseln *fam* **III.** *vt* ① *windows* zum Klirren bringen; *keys* rasseln (mit +*dat,* mit +*dat*) ② *person* durcheinanderbringen

'rattlesnake *n* Klapperschlange *f*

rattling ['ræt·lɪŋ] *adj* (*making a noise*) klappernd *attr; car, engine* ratternd *attr; windows* klirrend *attr; keys* rasselnd *attr*

ratty ['ræt̬·i] *adj* (*fam*) ① (*messy*) *hair* verknotet ② (*dilapidated*) verlottert

raucous ['rɔ·kəs] *adj* (*boisterous*) lärmend *attr,* wild

raunchy ['rɔn·tʃi] *adj conversation* schlüpfrig;

film scharf *fam; video* heiß *fam*
ravage ['ræv·ɪdʒ] *vt* verwüsten; *face* verunstalten
rave [reɪv] **I.** *n* Rave *m o nt* (*mit Technomusik*) **II.** *adj attr reviews* glänzend **III.** *vi* ① (*talk wildly*) toben, wüten; **to rant and ~** toben ② (*fam: praise*) schwärmen (**about** von +*dat*)
ravel <-l- *or* -ll-> ['ræv·əl] **I.** *vi* sich verwickeln; *thread* sich verheddern **II.** *vt* verwickeln; *thread* verheddern
raven ['reɪ·vən] *n* Rabe *m*
ravenous ['ræv·ə·nəs] *adj* (*very hungry*) ausgehungert; *appetite* unbändig
ravine [rə·'vin] *n* Schlucht *f*, Klamm *f*
raving ['reɪ·vɪŋ] **I.** *n* ① (*delirium*) wirres Gerede ② *pl* (*ramblings*) Hirngespinste *pl* **II.** *adj attr* absolut, total *fam; nightmare* echt **III.** *adv* völlig; **to be [stark] ~ mad** (*fam*) völlig verrückt sein
ravioli [ræv·i·'oʊ·li] *n* Ravioli *pl*
ravishing ['ræv·ɪ·ʃɪŋ] *adj* ① (*beautiful*) hinreißend ② (*delicious*) wundervoll
raw [rɔ] *adj* ① (*unprocessed*) roh, unbehandelt; **~ sewage** ungeklärte Abwässer *pl;* **~ figures** Schätzungen *pl* ② (*uncooked*) roh ③ (*inexperienced*) unerfahren ④ (*sore*) wund; (*fig*) *nerves, emotions* empfindlich ⑤ (*cold*) rau
'rawhide *n* ungegerbtes Leder
raw ma'terial *n* Rohstoff *m*
rawness ['rɔ·nɪs] *n* ① (*harshness*) Rauheit *f* ② (*soreness*) Wundsein *nt*
ray[1] [reɪ] *n* ① (*beam*) Strahl *m* ② PHYS (*radiation*) Strahlung *f*
ray[2] [reɪ] *n* (*fish*) Rochen *m*
rayon ['reɪ·an] *n* Viskose *f*
raze [reɪz] *vt* [völlig] zerstören; MIL schleifen
razor ['reɪ·zər] **I.** *n* Rasierapparat *m*, Rasierer *m fam;* **straight ~** Rasiermesser *nt* **II.** *vt hair* [ab]rasieren
'razorback *n* ① (*hog*) [halbwildes] spitzrückiges Schwein ② *see* **rorqual**
'razor blade *n* Rasierklinge *f*
'razor sharp *adj pred*, **'razor-sharp** *adj attr* ① (*sharp*) scharf wie ein Rasiermesser; *teeth* messerscharf ② (*fig: intelligent*) *person* [äußerst] scharfsinnig; *brain* [messer]scharf
'razor wire *n* Nato-Draht *m fam*
Rd. *n abbrev of* **road** Str.
re *prep* bezüglich +*gen*, in Bezugnahme auf +*akk*
reach [ritʃ] **I.** *n* <*pl* -es> ① (*arm length, power*) Reichweite *f* ② (*distance to travel*) **to be within [easy] ~** [ganz] in der Nähe sein ③ TV, RADIO [Sende]bereich *m* **II.** *vi* ① (*stretch*) greifen, langen *fam* ② (*touch*) herankommen, [d]rankommen *fam* ③ (*extend*) reichen (**to** bis zu +*dat*) **III.** *vt* ① (*arrive at*) erreichen; *destination* ankommen (an +*dat*) ② (*attain, influence*) *audience* erreichen; *agreement, consensus* erzielen; **to ~ the conclusion/decision that ...** zu dem Schluss/der Entscheidung kommen, dass ... ③ (*extend to*) ■**to ~ sth** *road* bis zu etw *dat* führen; *hair, clothing* bis zu etw *dat* reichen ④ (*touch*) **to be able to ~ sth** an etw *akk* herankommen ⑤ (*contact*) erreichen; (*on the phone*) [telefonisch] erreichen ⑥ (*fam: give*) hinüberreichen
◆**reach down** *vi* ① (*stretch*) hinuntergreifen, hinunterlangen *fam* ② (*extend*) hinabreichen
◆**reach out I.** *vt* **to ~ out** ↻ **one's hand** die Hand ausstrecken **II.** *vi* die Hand ausstrecken; ■**to ~ out for sth** nach etw *dat* greifen
◆**reach out to** *vi* ■**to ~ out to sb** ① (*stretch*) die Hand nach jdm ausstrecken ② (*appeal to*) sich [Hilfe suchend] an jdn wenden ③ (*help*) für jdn da sein
◆**reach over** *vi* hinübergreifen, hinüberlangen *fam*
◆**reach up** *vi* ① (*stretch*) nach oben greifen, hinauflangen *fam* ② (*extend*) hinaufreichen
react [rɪ·'ækt] *vi* ① MED (*respond*) reagieren (**to** auf +*akk*) ② CHEM reagieren (**with** mit +*dat*)
reaction [rɪ·'æk·ʃən] *n* ① MED (*response*) Reaktion *f* (**to** auf +*akk*) ② *pl* (*reflexes*) Reaktionsvermögen *nt kein pl* ③ (*opposite response*) [Gegen]reaktion *f*
reactionary [rɪ·'æk·ʃə·ner·i] **I.** *adj* POL (*pej*) reaktionär **II.** *n* POL (*pej*) Reaktionär(in) *m(f)*
reactivate [ri·'æk·tə·veɪt] **I.** *vt* reaktivieren **II.** *vi* wieder aktiv werden; *virus* wieder ausbrechen
reactive [ri·'æk·tɪv] *adj* ① (*showing response*) gegenwirkend ② (*acting in response*) ■**to be ~** als Gegenreaktion erfolgen ③ CHEM reaktiv, reaktionsfähig
reactor [ri·'æk·tər] *n* Reaktor *m;* **nuclear ~** Kernreaktor *m;* **fusion ~** Fusionsreaktor *m;* **fission ~** Spaltreaktor *m*
read[1] [rid] **I.** *n usu sing* ① (*fam: book*) **to be a good ~** sich gut lesen [lassen] ② (*interpretation*) Lesart *f* ③ (*act of reading*) Lesen *nt* **II.** *vt* <read, read> ① (*understand written material*) lesen; *handwriting* entziffern; (*fig: understand sb's meaning*) jdn verstehen; **to be able to ~ sb like a book** in jdm lesen können, wie in einem [offenen] Buch ② MUS **to ~ music** Noten lesen ③ (*speak aloud*) vorlesen ④ (*discern*) *emotion* erraten; **to ~ sth in sb's face** jdm etw vom Gesicht ablesen ⑤ (*inspect and record*) ablesen **III.** *vi* <read, read> ① (*understand written material*) lesen ② (*speak aloud*) **to ~ aloud** laut vorlesen ③ (*create impression*) **to ~ well** *book, letter, article, magazine* sich gut lesen
◆**read off** *vt* ① (*note exactly*) *measurements, technical readings* ablesen ② (*enumerate*) herunterlesen
◆**read out** *vt* ① (*read aloud*) laut vorlesen ② COMPUT auslesen
◆**read over, read through** *vt* [schnell] durchlesen
◆**read up** *vi* nachlesen; ■**to ~ up on sth** sich über etw informieren
read[2] [red] **I.** *vt, vi pt, pp of* **read II.** *adj* **well ~** belesen
readability [ˌri·də·'bɪl·ɪ·t̬i] *n* Lesbarkeit *f*

readable ['ri·də·bəl] *adj* ❶ (*legible*) lesbar, leserlich ❷ (*easy to read*) [gut] lesbar
reader ['ri·dər] *n* ❶ (*person who reads*) Leser(in) *m(f)* ❷ (*person who reads aloud*) Vorleser(in) *m(f)* ❸ (*device*) **microfiche ~** Mikrofichelesegerät *nt* ❹ PUBL (*proofreader*) Lektor(in) *m(f)*
readership ['ri·dər·ʃɪp] *n* (*readers*) Leserschaft *f*
readily ['red·ə·li] *adv* ❶ (*willingly*) bereitwillig ❷ (*easily*) einfach, ohne weiteres
readiness ['red·i·nɪs] *n* ❶ (*willingness*) Bereitwilligkeit *f*; *preparedness a.* Bereitschaft *f* ❷ (*quickness*) Schnelligkeit *f*
reading ['ri·dɪŋ] *n* ❶ (*activity*) Lesen *nt* ❷ (*material to be read*) Lesestoff *m*; **to catch up on one's ~** den Stoff nachholen ❸ (*recital, a. religious*) Lesung *f* ❹ (*amount shown*) Anzeige *f*; **meter ~** Zählerstand *m*
'reading glasses *npl* Lesebrille *f*
'reading list *n* Lektüreliste *f*
'reading room *n* Lesesaal *m*
readjust [ˌri·ə·'dʒʌst] **I.** *vt* ❶ (*correct*) [wieder] neu anpassen; *tie, garment* zurechtrücken ❷ *machine* neu einstellen **II.** *vi* ❶ (*adjust again*) *objects, machines* sich neu einstellen; *clock* sich neu stellen ❷ (*readapt*) sich wieder gewöhnen (**to** an +*akk*)
readjustment [ˌri·ə·'dʒʌst·mənt] *n* ❶ TECH Neueinstellung *f*, Korrektur *f* ❷ POL Neuorientierung *f*
read-only 'memory *n* COMPUT Festspeicher *m*
ready ['red·i] *adj* ❶ *pred* (*prepared*) fertig, bereit; **to get ~** sich fertig machen; **to be ~ to go** bereit zum Gehen sein; **to be ~ to drop** zum Umfallen müde sein ❷ (*immediately available*) verfügbar ❸ *attr* (*esp approv: quick*) prompt, schnell ▶ PHRASES: **~, set, go!** SPORTS auf die Plätze, fertig, los!
ready-'made *adj* ❶ (*ready for use*) gebrauchsfertig; FOOD fertig, Fertig- ❷ FASHION Konfektions- ❸ (*available immediately*) vorgefertigt
'ready-to-wear *adj* Konfektions-
reaffirm [ˌri·ə·'fɜrm] *vt* bestätigen
real [ril] **I.** *adj* ❶ (*not imaginary*) wirklich, real ❷ (*genuine*) echt; *beauty, pleasure* wahr ❸ (*for emphasis*) **a ~ bargain** ein echt günstiges Angebot ❹ (*fam: utter*) *disaster* echt ▶ PHRASES: **the ~ thing** (*not fake*) das Wahre; (*true love*) die wahre Liebe; **get ~!** (*fam*) mach dir doch nichts vor! **II.** *adv* (*fam*) wirklich *fam*, total *sl*, echt *sl*
'real estate *n* Immobilien *pl*
'real estate agent *n* Immobilienmakler(in) *m(f)*
realignment [ˌri·ə·'laɪn·mənt] *n* (*new alignment*) POL Neuordnung *f*; AUTO [neuerliche] Spureinstellung
realism ['ri·lɪz·əm] *n* Wirklichkeitssinn *m*; *a.* ART, LIT, PHILOS Realismus *m*
realist ['ri·lɪst] *n a.* ART, LIT Realist(in) *m(f)*
realistic [ˌri·ə·'lɪs·tɪk] *adj a.* ART, LIT realistisch
reality [rɪ·'æl·ɪ·t̬i] *n* ❶ (*the actual world*) Realität *f*, Wirklichkeit *f* ❷ (*fact*) Tatsache *f*; **to become a ~** wahr werden ▶ PHRASES: **in ~** in Wirklichkeit
re'ality show *n* Realityshow *f*
reality 'television *n*, **reality TV** *n* Reality-Fernsehen *nt*
realizable ['ri·ə·laɪ·zə·bəl] *adj* realisierbar
realization [ˌri·ə·lɪ·'zeɪ·ʃən] *n* ❶ (*awareness*) Erkenntnis *f*; **the ~ was dawning on them that ...** allmählich dämmerte ihnen, dass ... ❷ (*fulfillment*) Realisierung *f*, Verwirklichung *f*
realize ['ri·ə·laɪz] *vt* ❶ (*be aware of*) ■**to ~ sth** sich *dat* einer S. *gen* bewusst sein; (*become aware of*) etw erkennen; **I ~ how difficult it's going to be** mir ist klar, wie schwierig das sein wird ❷ (*make real*) *dream* verwirklichen; (*come true*) *fears* sich bewahrheiten
really ['ri·ə·li] **I.** *adv* ❶ (*in fact*) wirklich, tatsächlich ❷ (*seriously*) ernsthaft; **did you ~ believe that ...** haben Sie im Ernst geglaubt, dass ... **II.** *interj* ❶ (*indicating surprise, disbelief*) wirklich, tatsächlich; **I'm getting married to Fred — ~? when?** Fred und ich werden heiraten – nein, wirklich? wann denn? ❷ (*indicating annoyance*) also wirklich, [also] so was
realm [relm] *n* (*sphere of interest*) Bereich *m*
Realtor® ['ri·əl·tər] *n* Immobilienmakler(in) *m(f)*
realty ['ri·əl·ti] *n* Immobilien *pl*, Grundbesitz *m*
ream¹ [rim] *n* ❶ (*500 sheets*) [altes] Ries *veraltet* ❷ (*large amount*) Unmenge *f*; ■**~s of sth** eine Unmenge von [*o* an] etw *dat*
ream² [rim] *vt* ❶ (*make hole*) **to ~ a hole** ein Loch größer machen ❷ (*squeeze*) **to ~ fruit** Obst auspressen
reap [rip] *vt* ❶ (*gather*) *crops* ernten; *field* abernten ❷ (*fig: receive*) ernten; **to ~ the benefits [of sth]** [für etw *akk*] entlohnt werden; *profits* realisieren
reaper ['ri·pər] *n* (*person*) Mäher(in) *m(f)*; (*machine*) Mähmaschine *f*
reappear [ˌri·ə·'pɪr] *vi* wieder auftauchen; *moon, sun* wieder zum Vorschein kommen
reapply <-ie-> [ˌri·ə·'plaɪ] **I.** *vi* ■**to ~ for sth** sich nochmals um etw *akk* bewerben **II.** *vt* ❶ (*apply differently*) *principle, rule* anders anwenden ❷ (*spread again*) erneut auftragen
reappraisal [ˌri·ə·'preɪ·zəl] *n* (*new assessment*) Neubewertung *f*
rear¹ [rɪr] **I.** *n* ❶ (*back*) ■**the ~** der hintere Teil ❷ ANAT (*fam: buttocks*) Hintern *m* **II.** *adj attr* ❶ (*backward*) hintere(r, s), Hinter- ❷ AUTO Heck-; **~ wheel** Hinterrad *nt*
rear² [rɪr] **I.** *vt* ❶ *usu passive an animal* aufziehen; *a child* großziehen ❷ (*breed*) *livestock* züchten **II.** *vi* ❶ (*rise up on hind legs*) *horse, pony* sich aufbäumen ❷ (*rise high*) ■**to ~ above sth** *building, mountain* etw überragen
rear 'admiral *n* MIL Konteradmiral(in) *m(f)*
rearm [ˌri·'arm] **I.** *vt* ■**to ~ sb** jdn wieder aufrüsten **II.** *vi* sich wieder bewaffnen
rearrange [ˌri·ə·'reɪndʒ] *vt* ❶ (*arrange differ-*

R

ently) umstellen ❷ (*change*) [zeitlich] verlegen; **to ~ the order of sth** die Reihenfolge von etw *dat* ändern
rearview 'mirror *n* AUTO Rückspiegel *m*
rearward ['rɪr·wərd] **I.** *adj* hintere(r, s), rückwärtige(r, s) **II.** *adv* nach hinten
rear-wheel 'drive *n* Hinterradantrieb *m*
reason ['ri·zən] **I.** *n* ❶ (*cause*) Grund *m* (**for** für +*akk*); **there is every ~ to believe that ...** es spricht alles dafür, dass ...; **for some ~** aus irgendeinem Grund ❷ (*power to think*) Denkvermögen *nt* ❸ (*common sense*) Vernunft *f*; **to see ~** auf die Stimme der Vernunft hören ❹ (*sanity*) Verstand *m* **II.** *vi* ❶ (*form judgments*) ausgehen (**from** von +*dat*) ❷ (*persuade*) ■**to ~ with sb** vernünftig mit jdm reden **III.** *vt* (*deduce*) ■**to ~ that ...** schlussfolgern, dass ...
reasonable ['ri·zə·nə·bəl] *adj* ❶ (*sensible*) *person, answer* vernünftig ❷ (*understanding*) *person* einsichtig, verständig; **be ~!** sei [doch] vernünftig! ❸ (*justified*) angebracht ❹ (*inexpensive*) annehmbar
reasonably ['ri·zə·nə·bli] *adv* ❶ (*in a sensible manner*) vernünftig ❷ (*fairly*) ziemlich, ganz ❸ (*inexpensively*) **~ priced** preiswert
reasoning ['ri·zə·nɪŋ] *n* logisches Denken, Logik *f*
reassemble [ˌri·ə·'sem·bəl] **I.** *vi* sich wieder versammeln **II.** *vt* wieder zusammenbauen
reassess [ˌri·ə·'ses] *vt* neu bewerten
reassurance [ˌri·ə·'ʃʊr·əns] *n* ❶ (*action*) Bestärkung *f* ❷ (*statement*) Versicherung *f*, Beteuerung *f*
reassure [ˌri·ə·'ʃʊr] *vt* [wieder] beruhigen
reassuring [ˌri·ə·'ʃʊr·ɪŋ] *adj* beruhigend
rebate ['ri·beɪt] *n* ❶ (*refund*) Rückzahlung *f*, Rückvergütung *f* ❷ (*discount*) [Preis]nachlass *m*
rebel I. *n* ['reb·əl] Rebell(in) *m(f)* **II.** *adj* ['reb·əl] *army, guerrillas, forces* aufständisch, rebellierend; *person* rebellisch **III.** *vi* <-ll-> [rɪ·'bel] (*a. fig*) rebellieren (**against** gegen +*akk*)
rebellion [rɪ·'bel·jən] *n* Rebellion *f*
rebellious [rɪ·'bel·jəs] *adj* (*insubordinate*) *child* aufsässig, widerspenstig; *troops, youth* rebellisch
rebirth [ˌri·'bɜrθ] *n* ❶ (*reincarnation*) Wiedergeburt *f* ❷ (*revival*) Wiederaufleben *nt*
reboot [ˌri·'but] COMPUT **I.** *vt computer system* neu starten **II.** *vi* rebooten *fachspr* **III.** *n* Rebooten *nt kein pl fachspr*
rebound [ri·'baʊnd] **I.** *vi* ❶ (*bounce back*) abprallen (**off** von +*dat*), zurückprallen ❷ (*recover*) sich erholen (**from** von +*dat*) ❸ (*in basketball*) rebounden **II.** *vt* (*in basketball*) rebounden **III.** *n* ❶ (*ricochet*) Abprallen *nt* ❷ (*increase*) *of profits, prices* Ansteigen *nt* ❸ (*recovery*) **on the ~** auf dem Weg der Besserung ❹ (*in basketball*) Rebound *m*
rebrand [ˌri·'brænd] *vt* **to ~ a company** einer Firma ein anderes Markenimage verschaffen
rebuff [rɪ·'bʌf] **I.** *vt* [schroff] zurückweisen **II.** *n* Zurückweisung *f*
rebuild <rebuilt, rebuilt> [ˌri·'bɪld] *vt* ❶ (*build again*) wieder aufbauen; (*fig*) *one's life* neu ordnen ❷ TECH umbauen
rebuke [rɪ·'bjuk] **I.** *vt person* rügen **II.** *n* ❶ (*reproof*) Zurechtweisung *f* ❷ (*censure*) Verweis *m*
rebut <-tt-> [rɪ·'bʌt] *vt* widerlegen
rebuttal [rɪ·'bʌt̬·əl] *n* Widerlegung *f*
recalcitrant [rɪ·'kæl·sɪ·trənt] *adj* ❶ (*defiant*) aufmüpfig; *child* aufsässig ❷ (*not responsive*) widerspenstig, hartnäckig
recall I. *vt* [rɪ·'kɔl] ❶ (*remember*) sich erinnern (an +*akk*) ❷ COMPUT *data* abrufen ❸ (*order to return*) *person, product* zurückrufen **II.** *n* ['ri·kɔl] ❶ (*order to return*) Rückruf *f* ❷ COMM *of a product* Rückruf *m* ❸ (*memory*) Erinnerung *f*
recant [rɪ·'kænt] **I.** *vi* widerrufen **II.** *vt* widerrufen; *belief, faith* abschwören +*dat*
recap ['ri·kæp] **I.** *vt, vi* <-pp-> *short for* **recapitulate** [kurz] zusammenfassen **II.** *n short for* **recapitulation** [kurze] Zusammenfassung
recapture [ˌri·'kæp·tʃər] *vt* ❶ (*capture again*) *animal* wieder einfangen; *an escapee* wieder ergreifen; MIL zurückerobern ❷ (*fig: re-experience*) noch einmal erleben; (*recreate*) wieder lebendig werden lassen; *emotion* wieder aufleben lassen; *the past, one's youth* heraufbeschwören; *a style* wieder beleben
recede [rɪ·'sid] *vi* ❶ *sea, tide* zurückgehen; *fog* sich auflösen ❷ (*fig: diminish*) weniger werden; *memories* verblassen; *prices, hopes* sinken ❸ (*cease to grow*) *hair* zurückgehen
receipt [rɪ·'sit] *n* ❶ (*act of receiving*) Eingang *m*, Erhalt *m* ❷ (*statement acknowledging payment*) Quittung *f*; (*statement acknowledging acquisition*) Empfangsbestätigung *f*
receivable [rɪ·'si·və·bəl] **I.** *adj pred* ausstehend **II.** *n* FIN ■**~s** *pl* Außenstände *pl*
receive [rɪ·'siv] **I.** *vt* ❶ (*get*) erhalten; *pension, salary* beziehen ❷ (*be awarded*) *degree* erhalten; *prize, reward* [verliehen] bekommen ❸ (*get in writing*) erhalten; (*take delivery of*) *consignment, petition* annehmen, entgegennehmen; *ultimatum* gestellt bekommen ❹ RADIO, TV empfangen ❺ (*suffer*) *blow, shock* erleiden **II.** *vi* (*in tennis, volleyball, football*) den Ball bekommen
received [rɪ·'sivd] *adj attr* allgemein akzeptiert; *opinion* landläufig
receiver [rɪ·'si·vər] *n* ❶ (*telephone component*) Hörer *m* ❷ RADIO, TV Empfänger *m* ❸ (*person*) *of stolen goods* Hehler(in) *m(f)* ❹ FIN, JUR Konkursverwalter(in) *m(f)* ❺ (*in football*) Receiver *m*
recent ['ri·sənt] *adj* kürzlich; **in ~ times** in der letzten Zeit
recently ['ri·sənt·li] *adv* kürzlich, vor kurzem [*o* kurzer Zeit]; **until ~** bis vor kurzem, neulich; **have you seen any good movies ~?** hast du in letzter Zeit irgendwelche guten Filme gesehen?

R

receptacle [rɪ·ˈsep·tə·kəl] *n* [Sammel]behälter *m*
reception [rɪ·ˈsep·ʃən] *n* ❶ (*process*) Aufnehmen *nt* ❷ (*welcome*) Aufnahme *f;* **to be treated to a warm ~** in den Genuss eines herzlichen Empfangs kommen ❸ RADIO, TV Empfang *m* ❹ (*social occasion*) Empfang *m* ❺ (*area for greeting guests*) Rezeption *f* ❻ (*in football*) Reception *f*
re'ception desk *n* Rezeption *f*
receptionist [rɪ·ˈsep·ʃə·nɪst] *n* (*in hotels*) Empfangschef *m;* (*female*) Empfangsdame *f;* (*in an office*) Empfangssekretärin *f*
receptive [rɪ·ˈsep·tɪv] *adj* empfänglich (**to** für +*akk*)
receptiveness [ri·ˌsep·ˈtɪv·ɪ·t̬i] *n* Empfänglichkeit *f,* Aufnahmebereitschaft *f*
recess [ˈri·ses] **I.** *n* <*pl* -es> ❶ LAW, POL [Sitzungs]pause *f* ❷ SCH Pause *f* ❸ ARCHIT Nische *f* **II.** *vt* ❶ ARCHIT *wall* aussparen ❷ (*suspend*) *proceedings* vertagen **III.** *vi* [eine] Pause machen; LAW, POL sich vertagen
recession [rɪ·ˈseʃ·ən] *n* Rezession *f*
recessive [rɪ·ˈses·ɪv] *adj* rezessiv
recharge [ˌri·ˈtʃardʒ] **I.** *vt battery* [neu] aufladen; *gun* nachladen; **to ~ one's batteries** (*fig*) neue Kräfte tanken **II.** *vi battery* sich [neu] aufladen
rechargeable [ˌri·ˈtʃar·dʒə·bəl] *adj* [wieder]aufladbar
recidivism [rɪ·ˈsɪd·ə·vɪ·zəm] *n* LAW Rückfälligkeit *f*
recidivist [rɪ·ˈsɪd·ə·vɪst] *n* LAW Rückfalltäter(in) *m(f)*
recipe [ˈres·ə·pi] *n* Rezept *nt* (**for** für +*akk*)
recipient [rɪ·ˈsɪp·i·ənt] *n* Empfänger(in) *m(f)*
reciprocal [rɪ·ˈsɪp·rə·kəl] *adj* ❶ (*mutual*) beidseitig; *favor, help* gegenseitig ❷ (*reverse*) umgekehrt
reciprocate [rɪ·ˈsɪp·rə·keɪt] **I.** *vt help, favor* sich revanchieren (für +*akk*); *love, trust* erwidern **II.** *vi* sich revanchieren (**with** mit +*dat*)
reciprocity [ˌres·ɪ·ˈpras·ɪ·t̬i] *n* Gegenseitigkeit *f,* Wechselseitigkeit *f*
recital [rɪ·ˈsaɪ·t̬əl] *n* ❶ (*performance*) *of poetry, music* Vortrag *m; of dance* Aufführung *f;* **piano ~** Klavierkonzert *nt* ❷ *of facts, details* Aufzählung *f*
recitation [ˌres·ɪ·ˈteɪ·ʃən] *n* LIT Rezitation *f*
recite [rɪ·ˈsaɪt] *vt* ❶ (*say aloud*) vortragen; *poem* [auswendig] aufsagen ❷ (*enumerate*) aufzählen
reckless [ˈrek·lɪs] *adj* (*not cautious*) unbesonnen, leichtsinnig; *disregard, speed* rücksichtslos; LAW grob fahrlässig
recklessness [ˈrek·lɪs·nɪs] *n* Leichtsinn *m; of sb's driving* Rücksichtslosigkeit *f; of speed* Gefährlichkeit *f*
reckon [ˈrek·ən] *vt* ❶ (*calculate*) berechnen ❷ (*judge*) **I ~ you won't see her again** ich denke nicht, dass du sie je wiedersehen wirst
◆**reckon with** *vt* (*take into account*) ■**to ~ with sth/sb** mit etw/jdm rechnen

R

reckoning [ˈrek·ə·nɪŋ] *n* (*calculation*) Berechnung *f;* **by sb's ~** nach jds Rechnung
reclaim [rɪ·ˈkleɪm] *vt* ❶ (*claim back*) zurückverlangen; *luggage* abholen ❷ *land* urbar machen; **to ~ land from the sea** dem Meer Land abgewinnen
reclamation [ˌrek·lə·ˈmeɪ·ʃən] *n* ❶ (*demanding*) Rückforderung *f;* (*receiving*) Rückgewinnung *f* ❷ *of land, resources* Kultivierung *f;* **land ~** Landgewinnung *f*
recline [rɪ·ˈklaɪn] **I.** *vi person* sich zurücklehnen; **to ~ in a chair** sich in einem Stuhl ausruhen **II.** *vt* **to ~ one's seat** die Rückenlehne seines Sitzes nach hinten stellen; *head* lehnen (an +*akk*)
recliner [rɪ·ˈklaɪ·nər] *n* [verstellbarer] Lehnstuhl
recluse [ˈrek·lus] *n* Einsiedler(in) *m(f)*
reclusive [rɪ·ˈklu·sɪv] *adj* einsiedlerisch, zurückgezogen
recognition [ˌrek·əg·ˈnɪʃ·ən] *n* ❶ (*act, instance*) [Wieder]erkennung *f;* **to change beyond ~** nicht wiederzuerkennen sein ❷ (*appreciation, acknowledgement*) Anerkennung *f*
recognizable [ˈrek·əg·naɪ·zə·bəl] *adj* erkennbar
recognize [ˈrek·əg·naɪz] *vt* ❶ (*identify*) *person, symptoms* erkennen; (*know again*) *person, place* wiedererkennen ❷ (*acknowledge*) *country, regime, state* anerkennen; ■**to be ~d as sth** als etw gelten
recognized [ˈrek·əg·naɪzd] *adj attr* anerkannt
recoil [rɪ·ˈkɔɪl] **I.** *vi* ❶ (*spring back*) zurückspringen; (*draw back*) zurückweichen; **to ~ in horror** (*a. mentally*) zurückschrecken (**at** vor +*dat*) ❷ (*be driven backwards*) *gun* einen Rückstoß haben; *rubber band, spring* zurückschnellen **II.** *n* Rückstoß *m*
recollect [ˌrek·ə·ˈlekt] *vt* sich erinnern (an +*akk*)
recollection [ˌrek·ə·ˈlek·ʃən] *n* ❶ (*memory*) Erinnerung *f;* **to have no ~ of sth** sich an etw *akk* nicht erinnern können ❷ (*ability to remember*) **power of ~** Erinnerungsvermögen *nt*
recommend [ˌrek·ə·ˈmend] *vt* empfehlen; **the doctor ~s [that] I exercise more** der Arzt rät, dass ich mich mehr bewege
recommendation [ˌrek·ə·mən·ˈdeɪ·ʃən] *n* (*suggestion*) Empfehlung *f;* (*advice a.*) Rat *m*
recompense [ˈrek·əm·ˌpens] *n* ❶ (*reward*) Belohnung *f* ❷ (*retribution*) Entschädigung *f* (**for** für +*akk*)
reconcile [ˈrek·ən·saɪl] *vt* ❶ (*re-establish*) *friendship* versöhnen ❷ (*settle*) *conflict* schlichten; *differences* beilegen ❸ (*make compatible*) ■**to ~ sth with sth** etw mit etw *dat* vereinbaren ❹ (*accept*) ■**to ~ oneself to sth** sich mit etw *dat* abfinden
reconciliation [ˌrek·ən·ˌsɪl·i·ˈeɪ·ʃən] *n* ❶ (*of good relations*) Aussöhnung *f,* Versöhnung *f* ❷ (*achievement of compatibility*) Beilegung *f*

recondition [ˌri·kən·ˈdɪʃ·ən] *vt engine, ship* [general]überholen
reconnaissance [rɪ·ˈkan·ə·səns] *n* MIL Aufklärung *f;* **to be on ~** auf Spähpatrouille sein
reconnoiter [ˌri·kə·ˈnɔɪ·t̬ər] *vt* MIL *enemy territory* auskundschaften
reconsider [ˌri·kən·ˈsɪd·ər] **I.** *vt* [noch einmal] überdenken; *facts* neu erwägen; *case* wieder aufnehmen **II.** *vi* sich *dat* etw [noch einmal] überlegen
reconstruct [ˌri·kən·ˈstrʌkt] *vt* ❶ (*build again*) wieder aufbauen; *economy, a government* wiederherstellen ❷ (*in an investigation*) *crime, events* rekonstruieren
reconstruction [ˌri·kən·ˈstrʌk·ʃən] *n* ❶ (*rebuilding*) Rekonstruktion *f; of a country* Wiederaufbau *m* ❷ *of crime, events* Rekonstruktion *f*
record **I.** *n* [ˈrek·ərd] ❶ (*information*) Aufzeichnungen *pl,* Unterlagen *pl;* (*document*) Akte *f; of attendance* Liste *f;* (*minutes*) Protokoll *nt,* Niederschrift *f;* **to keep ~s** (*register*) Buch führen ❷ (*past history*) Vorgeschichte *f;* **criminal ~** Vorstrafenregister *nt;* **to have an excellent ~** *worker, employee* ausgezeichnete Leistungen vorweisen können; **medical ~** Krankenblatt *nt* ❸ (*music*) [Schall]platte *f* ❹ SPORTS Rekord *m;* **to break a ~** einen Rekord brechen ▶ PHRASES: **to say sth <u>on</u>/<u>off</u> the ~** etw offiziell/inoffiziell sagen **II.** *adj* [ˈrek·ərd] Rekord-; **to reach a ~ high** ein Rekordhoch *nt* erreichen; **in ~ time** in Rekordzeit **III.** *vt* [rɪ·ˈkɔrd] ❶ (*store*) *facts, events* aufzeichnen; *birth, death, marriage* registrieren; *one's feelings, ideas* niederschreiben ❷ (*register*) *speed, temperature* messen ❸ FILM, MUS (*for later reproduction*) aufnehmen; *event* dokumentieren **IV.** *vi* [rɪ·ˈkɔrd] (*on tape, cassette*) Aufnahmen machen; *person* eine Aufnahme machen; *machine* aufnehmen
ˈrecord-breaking *adj attr* Rekord-
recorded [rɪ·ˈkɔr·dɪd] *adj* ❶ (*appearing in records*) verzeichnet, dokumentiert, belegt ❷ (*stored electronically*) aufgenommen, aufgezeichnet
recorded ˈmail *n* eine aufgezeichnete Nachricht
recorder [rɪ·ˈkɔr·dər] *n* ❶ **video ~** Videorekorder *m;* **tape ~** Kassettenrekorder ❷ (*recordkeeping device*) Registriergerät *nt* ❸ MUS (*instrument*) Blockflöte *f*
ˈrecord holder *n* Rekordhalter(in) *m(f)*
recording [rɪ·ˈkɔr·dɪŋ] *n* ❶ (*process*) Aufnahme *f* ❷ (*of sound*) Aufnahme *f;* (*of program*) Aufzeichnung *f*
reˈcording session *n* Aufnahme *f*
reˈcording studio *n* Aufnahme-/Tonstudio *nt*
ˈrecord label *n* Plattenlabel *nt*
ˈrecord library *n* Plattenverleih *m; archives* Phonothek *f;* (*collection*) Plattensammlung *f*
ˈrecord player *n* [Schall]plattenspieler *m*
recount¹ [rɪ·ˈkaʊnt] *vt* (*tell*) [ausführlich] erzählen
recount² **I.** *vt* [ˌri·ˈkaʊnt] (*count again*) nachzählen **II.** *n* [ˈri·kaʊnt] POL erneute Stimmenauszählung
recoup [rɪ·ˈkup] *vt* (*regain*) *costs, one's investment* wieder einbringen; *one's losses* wettmachen
recourse [ˈri·kɔrs] *n* Zuflucht *f;* **to have ~ to sth** Zuflucht zu etw *dat* nehmen können
recover [rɪ·ˈkʌv·ər] **I.** *vt* ❶ (*get back*) *one's health* zurückerlangen; *stolen goods* sicherstellen; *one's balance/composure* wiederfinden; *data* wiederherstellen; **to be fully ~ed** völlig genesen sein ❷ (*obtain*) *coal, ore* gewinnen; LAW *compensation, damages* erhalten; *ownership, possession* wiedererlangen **II.** *vi* sich erholen (**from** von +*dat*)
re-cover [ˌri·ˈkʌv·ər] *vt chair, sofa* neu beziehen
recoverable [rɪ·ˈkʌv·ər·ə·bəl] *adj* FIN *costs* erstattungsfähig; *damages, loss* ersetzbar; *debt* eintreibbar; COMPUT wiederherstellbar
recovery [rɪ·ˈkʌv·ə·ri] *n* ❶ MED (*action*) Erholung *f; of sight/hearing* Wiedererlangung *f;* **to show signs of ~** [erste] Zeichen einer Besserung zeigen; ECON [Anzeichen für] einen Aufschwung erkennen lassen ❷ (*getting back*) Wiedererlangung *f,* Zurückgewinnung *f; of a body, an object* Bergung *f* ❸ **to make a ~** den Ball wieder unter Kontrolle bekommen
recreate [ˌri·kri·ˈeɪt] *vt* ❶ (*create again*) wiederherstellen; *friendship* wieder beleben ❷ (*reproduce*) nachstellen
recreation¹ [ˌri·kri·ˈeɪ·ʃən] *n* ❶ (*creation again*) Wiedergestaltung *f* ❷ (*reproduction*) Nachstellung *f*
recreation² [ˌrek·ri·ˈeɪ·ʃən] *n* ❶ (*hobby*) Freizeitbeschäftigung *f,* Hobby *nt* ❷ (*fun*) Erholen *nt,* Entspannen *nt*
recreational [ˌrek·ri·ˈeɪ·ʃə·nəl] *adj* Freizeit-, Erholungs-; **~ drug** weiche Droge
recreational ˈvehicle *n* Caravan *m,* Wohnwagen *m*
recreˈation area *n* Freizeitgelände *nt*
recriminate [rɪ·ˈkrɪm·ə·neɪt] *vi* gegenseitige Anschuldigungen vorbringen
recrimination [rɪ·ˌkrɪm·ə·ˈneɪ·ʃən] *n usu pl* Gegenbeschuldigung *f*
rec room [ˈrek·ˌrum] *n* Aufenthaltsraum *m,* Freizeitraum *m*
recruit [rɪ·ˈkrut] **I.** *vt employees* einstellen; *members* werben; *soldiers* rekrutieren; *volunteers* finden **II.** *vi army* Rekruten anwerben; *company* Neueinstellungen vornehmen; *club, organization* neue Mitglieder werben **III.** *n* MIL Rekrut(in) *m(f); to party, club* neues Mitglied; *staff* neu eingestellte Arbeitskraft
recruiting [rɪ·ˈkru·tɪŋ] **I.** *n* MIL Rekrutierung *f;* (*in business*) [An]werben *nt* [von Arbeitskräften] **II.** *adj attr* (*in army*) Rekrutierungs-; (*in business*) Einstellungs-
recruitment [rɪ·ˈkrut·mənt] *n of soldiers* Rekrutierung *f; of employees* Neueinstellung *f; of members, volunteers* Anwerbung *f*
rectangle [ˈrek·tæŋ·gəl] *n* Rechteck *nt*

R

rectangular [rek·'tæŋ·gjə·lər] *adj* rechteckig; *coordinates* rechtwinklig

rectification [ˌrek·tə·fɪ·'keɪ·ʃən] *n of a mistake, situation* Berichtigung *f*, Korrektur *f*; *of a statement* Richtigstellung *f*

rectify <-ie-> ['rek·tə·faɪ] *vt* (*set right*) korrigieren; *omission* nachholen

rector ['rek·tər] *n* ❶ REL Pfarrer *m* ❷ UNIV, SCH Rektor(in) *m(f)*

rectory ['rek·tə·ri] *n* Pfarrhaus *nt*

rectum <*pl* -ta *or* -s> ['rek·təm] *n* MED Rektum *nt fachspr*, Mastdarm *m*

recuperate [rɪ·'ku·pə·reɪt] *vi from illness* sich erholen (**from** von +*dat*)

recuperation [rɪ·ˌku·pə·'reɪ·ʃən] *n* Erholung *f*; MED Gesundung *f geh* (**from** von +*dat*)

recur <-rr-> [rɪ·'kɜr] *vi* (*happen again*) *event* wieder passieren, sich wiederholen; *opportunity* sich wieder bieten; *pain, symptoms* wieder auftreten; *problem, theme* wieder auftauchen

recurrence [rɪ·'kɜr·əns] *n* Wiederholung *f*, erneutes Auftreten

recurrent [rɪ·'kɜr·ənt], **recurring** [rɪ·'kɜr·ɪŋ] *adj attr* sich wiederholend; *dream, nightmare* [ständig] wiederkehrend; *bouts, problems* wiederholt auftretend

recycle [ˌri·'saɪ·kəl] *vt* ❶ (*convert into sth new*) recyceln, wiederaufbereiten ❷ (*fig: use again*) wiederverwenden

recycling [rɪ·'saɪ·kəl·ɪŋ] *n* Recycling *nt*, Wiederverwertung *f*

red [red] **I.** *adj* <-dd-> ❶ (*color*) rot ❷ (*bloodshot*) *eyes* rot, gerötet **II.** *n* ❶ (*color*) Rot *nt*; (*shade*) Rotton *m* ❷ FIN **to be in the ~** in den roten Zahlen sein

red-'blooded *adj* heißblütig

Red 'Crescent *n* ■**the ~** der Rote Halbmond

Red 'Cross *n* ■**the ~** das Rote Kreuz

redden ['red·ən] **I.** *vi face, eyes* sich röten; *person* rot werden; *leaves, sky, water* sich rot färben **II.** *vt* rot färben

reddish ['red·ɪʃ] *adj* rötlich

redecorate [ˌri·'dek·ə·reɪt] **I.** *vt* (*by painting*) neu streichen; (*by wallpapering*) neu tapezieren **II.** *vi* renovieren

redecoration [ˌri·dek·ə·'reɪ·ʃən] *n* Renovierung *f*; (*with paint*) Neuanstrich *m*; (*with wallpaper*) Neutapezieren *nt*

redeem [rɪ·'dim] *vt* ❶ (*save*) *reputation* wiederherstellen ❷ (*compensate for*) *fault, mistake* wettmachen ❸ FIN (*pay off*) ab[be]zahlen; *mortgage* tilgen ❹ (*fulfill*) erfüllen; *promise, pledge* einlösen

redeemable [rɪ·'di·mə·bəl] *adj* (*financially*) *coupon, voucher* einlösbar; *mortgage* tilgbar; *loan* rückzahlbar

redeeming [rɪ·'di·mɪŋ] *adj attr* ausgleichend; **the only ~ feature of the boring film was the soundtrack** das einzig Positive an dem langweiligen Film war die Filmmusik

redemption [rɪ·'demp·ʃən] *n* ❶ (*from blame, guilt*) Wiedergutmachung *f*, Ausgleich *m*; REL (*from sin*) Erlösung *f* ❷ (*rescue*) **to be beyond ~** nicht mehr zu retten sein

redeploy [ˌri·dɪ·'plɔɪ] *vt workers, staff, troops* verlegen

redeployment [ˌri·dɪ·'plɔɪ·mənt] *n of workers, staff, troops* Verlegung *f*

redevelop [ˌri·dɪ·'vel·əp] *vt neighborhood, area* sanieren; *machine* neu entwickeln

redevelopment [ˌri·dɪ·'vel·əp·mənt] *n* Sanierung *f*

'red-eye *n* (*fam: flight*) Nachtflug *m*

red-'haired *adj* rothaarig

red-'handed *adj* **to catch sb ~** jdn auf frischer Tat ertappen

'redhead *n* Rothaarige(r) *f(m)*, Rotschopf *m*

red-'headed *adj person* rothaarig

red 'herring *n* Ablenkungsmanöver *nt*

red-'hot *adj* ❶ (*glowing*) **to be ~** [rot] glühen; (*fig*) glühend heiß sein ❷ (*brand new*) *news, data* brandaktuell, brandheiß *fam*

redirect [ˌri·dɪ·'rekt] *vt interests* neu ausrichten; *resources* umverteilen

redistribute [ˌri·dɪ·'strɪb·jut] *vt land, resources, wealth* umverteilen

redistribution [ˌri·dɪs·trɪ·'bju·ʃən] *n* Umverteilung *f*

red-'letter day *n ein besonderer Tag, den man sich im Kalender rot anstreichen muss*

red 'light *n* rote Ampel

red-'light district *n* Rotlichtviertel *nt*

red 'meat *n* dunkles Fleisch (*wie Rind, Lamm und Reh*)

'redneck *n* (*pej fam*) *weißer Arbeiter aus den am. Südstaaten, oft mit reaktionären Ansichten*

redness ['red·nɪs] *n* Röte *f*

redo <-did, -done> [ˌri·'du] *vt* ❶ (*do again*) noch einmal machen; *task* von vorn beginnen (mit +*dat*) ❷ (*redecorate*) renovieren

redolent ['red·ə·lənt] *adj pred* (*form*) ■**to be ~ of sth** ❶ (*smelling*) nach etw *dat* duften ❷ (*suggestive*) [stark] an etw *akk* erinnern

redouble [rɪ·'dʌb·əl] *vt one's efforts* verdoppeln

redoubtable [rɪ·'daʊ·t̬ə·bəl] *adj person* Respekt einflößend; (*hum*) gefürchtet

red 'pepper *n* (*fresh*) rote(r) Paprika

redress [rɪ·'dres] **I.** *vt mistake* wiedergutmachen; *situation* bereinigen **II.** *n* Wiedergutmachung *f*, Abhilfe *f*; *of an imbalance* Behebung *f*

Red 'Sea *n* ■**the ~** das Rote Meer

'redskin *n* (*pej fam*) Indianer(in) *m(f)*, Rothaut *f pej*

red 'tape *n* Bürokratie *f*

reduce [rɪ·'dus] *vt* ❶ (*make less*) verringern, reduzieren; *prices* heruntersetzen; *taxes* senken ❷ (*make smaller*) *drawing, photo* verkleinern; MATH *fraction* kürzen; *liquids, a sauce* einkochen lassen ❸ (*bring down*) **when he lost his job, he was ~d to begging for help from his parents** als er seine Arbeit verlor, war er gezwungen, seine Eltern um Hilfe zu bitten; **to ~ sb to tears** jdn zum Weinen brin-

gen
reduced [rɪ·ˈdust] *adj attr* ❶ (*in price*) reduziert, heruntergesetzt ❷ (*in number, size, amount*) reduziert, verringert; **to be in ~ circumstances** in verarmten Verhältnissen leben
reduction [rɪ·ˈdʌk·ʃən] *n* ❶ (*action*) Reduzierung *f,* Reduktion *f,* Verringerung *f; in taxes* Senkung *f* ❷ (*decrease*) Reduzierung *f,* Verminderung *f; in production, output* Drosselung *f; in expenses, salary* Reduzierung *f,* Senkung *f,* Kürzung *f* ❸ *of drawing, photo* Verkleinerung *f*
redundant [rɪ·ˈdʌn·dənt] *adj* (*superfluous*) überflüssig; LING redundant
red ˈwine *n* Rotwein *m*
ˈredwood *n* BOT ❶ (*tree*) Mammutbaum *m* ❷ (*wood*) Redwood *nt,* Rotholz *nt*
reed [rid] *n* ❶ BOT (*plant*) Schilf[gras] *nt* ❷ MUS (*of an instrument*) Rohrblatt *nt*
re-educate [ˌri·ˈedʒ·ə·keɪt] *vt* umerziehen
reedy [ˈri·di] *adj* ❶ (*full of reeds*) schilfig, schilfbedeckt ❷ *voice* durchdringend, grell
reef [rif] *n* GEOG Riff *nt*
reefer [ˈri·fər] *n* (*sl: joint*) Joint *m fam*
reek [rik] *vi* ❶ (*smell bad*) übel riechen ❷ (*fig: be pervaded with*) **to ~ of corruption** nach Korruption stinken
reel [ril] *n* (*device, unit*) Rolle *f;* (*for film, tape*) Spule *f;* (*for fishing line*) Angelrolle *f*
re-elect [ˌri·ɪ·ˈlekt] *vt* wiederwählen
re-election [ˌri·ɪ·ˈlek·ʃən] *n* Wiederwahl *f*
re-enter [ˌri·ˈen·tər] *vt* ❶ (*go in again*) *bus, car* wieder einsteigen in +*akk; country* wieder einreisen in +*akk; house, store* wieder hineingehen in +*akk; room* wieder betreten; *earth's atmosphere* wieder eintreten in +*akk* ❷ (*enroll*) sich wieder beteiligen (an +*dat*) ❸ COMPUT (*type in*) nochmals eingeben
re-entry [ˌri·ˈen·tri] *n* (*going in*) Wiedereintritt *m;* (*in a car*) Wiedereinstieg *m;* (*into a country*) Wiedereinreise *f*
ref [ref] (*fam*) **I.** *n abbrev of* **referee** Schiri *m* **II.** *vt games* pfeifen
ref. [ref] *n abbrev of* **reference** AZ
refectory [rɪ·ˈfek·tə·ri] *n of a university* Mensa *f*
refer <-rr-> [rɪ·ˈfɜr] **I.** *vt* (*to an authority, expert*) verweisen (**to** an +*akk*); **the patient was ~red to a specialist** der Patient wurde an einen Facharzt überwiesen **II.** *vi* ❶ (*allude*) ■**to ~ to sb/sth** sich beziehen auf *akk* jdn/etw; **who are you ~ring to?** wen meinst du?; **~ring to your letter, ...** Bezug nehmend auf Ihren Brief ... ❷ (*consult*) ■**to ~ to sb** sich an jdn wenden; ■**to ~ to sth** etw zu Hilfe nehmen, nachsehen in *dat* etw; **he ~red to a dictionary** er schlug in einem Wörterbuch nach
referee [ˌref·ə·ˈri] **I.** *n* ❶ (*umpire*) Schiedsrichter(in) *m(f)* ❷ (*arbitrator*) Schlichter(in) *m(f)* **II.** *vt* **to ~ a basketball game** bei einem Basketballspiel Schiedsrichter(in) sein **III.** *vi* Schiedsrichter(in) sein
reference [ˈref·ər·əns] *n* ❶ (*to a book, to an article*) Verweis *m;* **I cut out the article for future ~** ich schnitt den Artikel heraus, um ihn später verwenden zu können; **to make ~ to sth** etw erwähnen; **list of ~s** Anhang *m;* (*information*) Hinweis *m* ❷ (*allusion*) *indirect* Anspielung *f; direct* Bemerkung *f;* (*direct mention*) Bezugnahme *f;* **in ~ to sb/sth** mit Bezug auf jdn/etw ❸ (*in correspondence*) Aktenzeichen *nt* ❹ (*recommendation*) Empfehlungsschreiben *nt,* [Arbeits]zeugnis *nt,* Referenz *f geh*
ˈreference book *n* Nachschlagewerk *nt*
ˈreference library *n* Präsenzbibliothek *f*
ˈreference number *n* (*in letters*) Aktenzeichen *nt;* (*on goods*) Artikelnummer *f*
referendum <*pl* -s *or* -da> [ˌref·ə·ˈren·dəm] *n* POL Referendum *nt*
referral [rɪ·ˈfɜr·əl] *n* ❶ (*case*) Überweisung *f* ❷ (*action*) Einweisung *f*
refill I. *n* [ˈri·fɪl] ❶ (*action*) Auffüllen *nt,* Nachfüllen *nt;* FOOD ■**to give sb a ~** (*fam*) jdm nachschenken ❷ (*replacement*) *for fountain pen* Nachfüllpatrone *f; for ballpoint pen* Nachfüllmine **II.** *vt* [ˌri·ˈfɪl] **to ~ a cup** eine Tasse wieder füllen
refine [rɪ·ˈfaɪn] *vt* ❶ (*from impurities*) raffinieren ❷ (*fig: improve*) verfeinern
refined [rɪ·ˈfaɪnd] *adj* ❶ (*processed*) raffiniert; *foods* aufbereitet; *metal* veredelt ❷ (*approv: sophisticated*) [hoch] entwickelt, verfeinert; **~ tastes** feiner Geschmack
refinement [rɪ·ˈfaɪn·mənt] *n* ❶ (*processing*) Raffinieren *nt,* Raffination *f; of metal* Veredelung *f* ❷ (*improvement*) Verbesserung *f; of ideas, methods* Überarbeitung *f,* Verbesserung *f*
refinery [rɪ·ˈfaɪ·nə·ri] *n* Raffinerie *f*
reflect [rɪ·ˈflekt] **I.** *vt* ❶ (*throw back*) *heat, light, sound* reflektieren; ■**to be ~ed in sth** sich in etw *dat* spiegeln ❷ (*show*) *hard work, one's views* zeigen [*o* zum Ausdruck bringen]; *honesty, generosity* sprechen (für +*akk*) **II.** *vi* ❶ *light, mirror* reflektieren ❷ (*ponder*) nachdenken (**on/upon** über +*akk*) ❸ (*make impression*) **it ~ed badly on his character** es warf ein schlechtes Licht auf seinen Charakter
reflection [rɪ·ˈflek·ʃən] *n* ❶ (*reflecting*) Reflexion *f* ❷ (*mirror image*) Spiegelbild *nt* ❸ (*fig: sign*) Ausdruck *m;* **his unhappiness is a ~ of ...** seine Unzufriedenheit ist ein Zeichen für ... ❹ (*consideration*) Betrachtung *f,* Überlegung *f* (**on/about** über +*akk*)
reflective [rɪ·ˈflek·tɪv] *adj* ❶ *glass, clothing* reflektierend ❷ *person* nachdenklich
reflector [rɪ·ˈflek·tər] *n* ❶ (*device*) Reflektor *m; on a bicycle, car* Rückstrahler *m,* Katzenauge *nt* ❷ (*telescope*) Spiegelteleskop *nt*
reflex <*pl* -es> [ˈri·fleks] *n* Reflex *m*
reflexive [rɪ·ˈflek·sɪv] *adj* ❶ (*involuntary*) reflexartig ❷ LING reflexiv
reflux <*pl* -es> [ˈri·flʌks] *n* Rückfluss *m*
reforestation [ˌri·fɔr·ɪ·ˈsteɪ·ʃən] *n* Auffors-

R

tung *f*
reform [rɪ·ˈfɔrm] **I.** *vt institution, system* reformieren; *criminal, drug addict* bessern **II.** *vi person* sich bessern **III.** *n* Reform *f; of self, a criminal* Besserung *f;* **beyond ~** nicht reformierbar
re-form [ˌri·ˈfɔrm] **I.** *vt* umformen **II.** *vi committee, group* sich wieder bilden
reformation [ˌref·ər·ˈmeɪ·ʃən] *n* ❶ *of an institution* Reformierung *f; of a person* Besserung *nt* ❷ (*hist*) ■ **the R~** die Reformation
reformatory [rɪ·ˈfɔr·mə·tɔr·i] *n* Jugendhaftanstalt *f*
reformer [rɪ·ˈfɔr·mər] *n* Reformer(in) *m(f)*
reˈform school *n* Erziehungsheim *nt*
refract [rɪ·ˈfrækt] *vt* PHYS *ray of light* brechen
refraction [rɪ·ˈfræk·ʃən] *n* Refraktion *f fachspr,* Brechung *f*
refractory [rɪ·ˈfræk·tə·ri] *adj metal, tiles* hitzebeständig
refrain¹ [rɪ·ˈfreɪn] *vi* sich zurückhalten; **to ~ from smoking** das Rauchen unterlassen
refrain² [rɪ·ˈfreɪn] *n* (*in a song*) Refrain *m;* (*in a poem*) Kehrreim *m;* (*comment*) häufiger Ausspruch
refresh [rɪ·ˈfreʃ] *vt* ❶ (*reinvigorate*) *sleep, a vacation* erfrischen ❷ (*fig*) *one's knowledge, skills* auffrischen; **to ~ one's memory** seinem Gedächtnis auf die Sprünge helfen ❸ (*refill*) **to ~ sb's drink** jds Glas nachfüllen
refresher course [rɪ·ˈfreʃ·ər-] *n* Auffrischungskurs *m*
refreshing [rɪ·ˈfreʃ·ɪŋ] *adj* ❶ (*rejuvenating*) *air, color, drink* erfrischend ❷ (*pleasing*) [herz]erfrischend; *thought* wohltuend
refreshment [rɪ·ˈfreʃ·mənt] *n* ❶ (*rejuvenation*) Erfrischung *f,* Belebung *f* ❷ ■ **~s** *pl* (*drinks*) Erfrischungen *pl;* (*food*) Snacks *pl*
refrigerant [rɪ·ˈfrɪdʒ·ər·ənt] *n* Kühlmittel *nt*
refrigerate [rɪ·ˈfrɪdʒ·ə·reɪt] **I.** *vt food, drink* im Kühlschrank aufbewahren **II.** *vi* **~ after opening** nach dem Öffnen kühl aufbewahren
refrigeration [rɪ·ˌfrɪdʒ·ə·ˈreɪ·ʃən] *n* Kühlung *f*
refrigerator [rɪ·ˈfrɪdʒ·ə·reɪ·t̬ər] *n* Kühlschrank *m*
refuel <-l- *or* -ll-> [ˌri·ˈfju·əl] **I.** *vi airplane* auftanken **II.** *vt airplane, truck* auftanken
refuge [ˈref·judʒ] *n* ❶ (*secure place*) Zuflucht *f,* Zufluchtsort *m;* **women's ~** Frauenhaus *nt* ❷ (*from reality*) **to take ~ in sth** sich in etw *akk* flüchten
refugee [ˌref·jʊ·ˈdʒi] *n* Flüchtling *m*
ˈrefugee camp *n* Aufnahmelager *nt*
refund I. *vt* [ˌri·ˈfʌnd] **to ~ expenses/money** Auslagen/Geld zurückerstatten; ■ **to ~ sb sth** jdm etw *akk* zurückerstatten **II.** *n* [ˈri·fʌnd] Rückzahlung *f*
refurbish [ˌri·ˈfɜr·bɪʃ] *vt* aufpolieren; *furniture* verschönern; *house* renovieren; *electronics* reparieren
refusal [rɪ·ˈfju·zəl] *n* Ablehnung *f; of offer* Zurückweisung *f; of invitation* Absage *f; of food, visa* Verweigerung *f*
refuse¹ [rɪ·ˈfjuz] **I.** *vi* ablehnen; *horse* verweigern **II.** *vt* ablehnen, zurückweisen; *offer* ausschlagen; *request* abschlagen
refuse² [ˈref·jus] *n* (*form*) Abfall *m,* Müll *m*
refutation [ˌref·ju·ˈteɪ·ʃən] *n* Widerlegung *f*
refute [rɪ·ˈfjut] *vt* widerlegen, entkräften
reg. *adj abbrev of* **regular**
regain [rɪ·ˈgeɪn] *vt* wiederbekommen, zurückbekommen; *consciousness* wiedererlangen; **to ~ [lost] ground** [verlorenen] Boden zurückgewinnen; **to ~ the use of one's legs** seine Beine wieder gebrauchen können
regal [ˈri·gəl] *adj* königlich, majestätisch
regale [rɪ·ˈgeɪl] *vt* ■ **to ~ sb with sth** *stories, jokes* jdn mit etw *dat* aufheitern; *food, drink* jdn mit etw *dat* verwöhnen
regalia [rɪ·ˈgeɪ·li·ə] *n + sing/pl vb* Kostüme *pl,* Aufmachung *f kein pl hum;* (*of royalty*) Insignien *pl*
regard [rɪ·ˈgard] **I.** *vt* ❶ (*consider*) betrachten; ■ **to ~ sb/sth as sth** jdn/etw als etw betrachten; **she is ~ed as a talented actress** sie wird für eine talentierte Schauspielerin gehalten; **to ~ sb highly** jdn hoch schätzen; (*be considerate of*) große Rücksicht auf jdn nehmen ❷ (*concerning*) ■ **as ~s ...** was ... angeht, **II.** *n* ❶ (*consideration*) Rücksicht *f;* **without ~ for sb/sth** ohne Rücksicht auf jdn/etw; **to pay no ~ to a warning** eine Warnung in den Wind schlagen ❷ (*respect*) Achtung *f* (**for** vor *+dat*); **to hold sb/sth in high ~** Hochachtung vor jdm/etw haben ❸ (*aspect*) **in this ~** in dieser Hinsicht ❹ (*concerning*) ■ **with ~ to ...** in Bezug auf ... *+akk*
regarding [rɪ·ˈgar·dɪŋ] *prep* bezüglich *+gen;* **~ your inquiry** bezüglich Ihrer Anfrage
regardless [rɪ·ˈgard·lɪs] *adv* trotzdem; **~ of the expense** ungeachtet der Kosten; **to press on ~** trotzdem weitermachen
regards [rɪ·ˈgardz] *n pl* Grüße *pl;* **best ~** viele Grüße; **Jim sends his ~** Jim lässt grüßen
regatta [rɪ·ˈga·t̬ə] *n* Regatta *f*
regency [ˈri·dʒən·si] *n* Regentschaft *f;* (*period of rule*) Regentschaft[szeit] *f*
regenerate [rɪ·ˈdʒen·ə·reɪt] **I.** *vt* ❶ (*revive*) erneuern; **to ~ cities** Städte neu gestalten ❷ (*grow again*) *claw, tissue* neu bilden **II.** *vi* BIOL sich regenerieren *geh; tissue* sich neu bilden
regeneration [rɪ·ˌdʒen·ə·ˈreɪ·ʃən] *n* ❶ (*improvement*) Erneuerung *f,* Regeneration *f;* **urban ~** Stadtsanierung *f; of spirit* Erholung *f* ❷ BIOL (*regrowth*) Neubildung *f*
regent [ˈri·dʒənt] *n* Regent(in) *m(f)*
reggae [ˈreg·eɪ] *n* Reggae *m*
regime [rə·ˈʒim] *n* ❶ (*government*) Regime *nt* ❷ (*procedure*) Behandlungsweise *f*
regimen [ˈredʒ·ə·men] *n* ❶ (*plan for health*) Gesundheitsplan *m* (*entsprechend ärztlichen Anweisungen*) ❷ (*routine*) geregelter Tagesablauf
regiment [ˈredʒ·ə·mənt] **I.** *n* MIL Regiment *nt* **II.** *vt* ❶ MIL *troops* in Gruppen einordnen

❷ *(regulate) person* kontrollieren; *things* reglementieren

regimentation [ˌredʒ·əm·ən·ˈteɪ·ʃən] *n* Reglementierung *f*

region [ˈri·dʒən] *n* ❶ *(geographical)* Region *f* ❷ *(administrative)* [Verwaltungs]bezirk *m,* Provinz *f* ❸ *(approximately)* ■ **in the ~ of ...** etwa bei ..., im Bereich von ..

regional [ˈri·dʒə·nəl] *adj* regional

regionalism [ˈri·dʒə·nə·ˌlɪz·əm] *n* LING Regionalismus *m;* *(word)* nur regional verwendeter Ausdruck

register [ˈredʒ·ɪ·stər] **I.** *n* ❶ *(official list)* Register *nt,* Verzeichnis *nt* ❷ *(recording device)* Registriergerät *nt* ❸ *(for money)* **cash ~** Kasse *f* **II.** *vt* ❶ *(report)* registrieren; *birth, death* anmelden; *copyright, trademark* eintragen ❷ *(measure)* anzeigen ❸ *(at post office) letter, package* per Einschreiben schicken ❹ *(show)* **to ~ surprise** sich überrascht zeigen; **to ~ protest** Protest zum Ausdruck bringen **III.** *vi* ❶ *(person)* sich melden; *(to vote)* sich eintragen; *(to take classes)* sich einschreiben [*o* immatrikulieren]; **to ~ with the authorities** sich behördlich anmelden ❷ *machine, measuring device* angezeigt werden ❸ *(show)* sich zeigen

registered [ˈredʒ·ɪ·stərd] *adj* registriert, gemeldet; *charity* eingetragen; *vehicle* amtlich zugelassen; **~ voter** Wahlberechtigte(r) *m* [*o* -berechtigte] *f*

registrar [ˈredʒ·ɪ·strar] *n* ❶ *(for the state)* Standesbeamte(r) *m,* Standesbeamte [*o* -in] *f* ❷ UNIV höchster Verwaltungsbeamte(r) *m* [*o* -in] *f*

registration [ˌredʒ·ɪ·ˈstreɪ·ʃən] *n* ❶ *(act)* Anmeldung *f;* *(at a school)* Einschreibung *f;* **voter ~** Wählereintragung *f; of a car* Autozulassung *f;* UNIV Immatrikulation *f* ❷ AUTO *(document)* [**motor vehicle**] **~** Kraftfahrzeugschein *m,* Kfz-Zulassung *f*

regisˈtration fee *n* Anmeldegebühr *f*

regress [rɪ·ˈgres] *vi* *(lose ability)* sich verschlechtern; *(deteriorate)* sich zurückentwickeln

regression [rɪ·ˈgreʃ·ən] *n* MED *(physical)* Regression *f fachspr,* Verschlechterung *f;* *(mental)* Zurückentwicklung *f*

regressive [rɪ·ˈgres·ɪv] *adj* ❶ *(becoming worse)* rückschrittlich ❷ FIN *tax* regressiv

regret [rɪ·ˈgret] **I.** *vt* <-tt-> bedauern; **to ~ one's mistakes** seine Fehler bereuen **II.** *vi* <-tt-> ■ **to ~ to do sth** bedauern, etw tun zu müssen; **I ~ [to have] to inform you that ...** leider muss ich Ihnen mitteilen, dass ... **III.** *n* Bedauern *nt kein pl;* **my only ~ is that ...** das Einzige, was ich bedaure, ist, dass ...; **to have no ~s about sth** etw nicht bereuen; **to send one's ~s** sich entschuldigen [lassen]

regretful [rɪ·ˈgret·fəl] *adj* bedauernd; *smile* wehmütig

regretfully [rɪ·ˈgret·fəl·i] *adv* mit Bedauern

regrettable [rɪ·ˈgreṭ·ə·bəl] *adj* bedauerlich

regroup [ˌri·ˈgrup] **I.** *vt* neu gruppieren; *forces* neu formieren **II.** *vi troops, demonstrators* sich neu formieren

regular [ˈreg·jə·lər] **I.** *adj* ❶ *(routine)* regelmäßig; *price* regulär; **~ procedure** übliche Vorgehensweise ❷ *(steady in time)* regelmäßig; **to keep ~ hours** sich an feste Zeiten halten ❸ *(well-balanced)* regelmäßig, symmetrisch; *surface* gleichmäßig ❹ *(not unusual)* üblich, normal; **my ~ doctor was on vacation** mein Hausarzt hatte Urlaub; **~ gasoline** Normalbenzin *nt* ❺ *attr (size)* **~ fries** normale Portion Pommes Frites **II.** *n* *(customer)* Stammgast *m*

regularity [ˌreg·jʊ·ˈler·ɪ·ṭi] *n* *(in time)* Regelmäßigkeit *f,* Gleichmäßigkeit *f;* *(in shape)* Ebenmäßigkeit *f*

regularize [ˈreg·jʊ·lə·raɪz] **I.** *vt* ❶ *(normalize) status, relationship* normalisieren ❷ *(make consistent) a language, work hours* standardisieren, vereinheitlichen **II.** *vi breathing, heart beat* sich regulieren

regularly [ˈreg·jə·lər·li] *adv* ❶ *(evenly, frequently)* regelmäßig ❷ *(equally)* gleichmäßig

regulate [ˈreg·jʊ·leɪt] *vt* ❶ *(supervise)* regeln, steuern ❷ *(adjust)* regulieren; **to ~ the flow of water** den Wasserfluss regeln

regulation [ˌreg·jʊ·ˈleɪ·ʃən] **I.** *n* ❶ *(rule)* Vorschrift *f,* Bestimmung *f* (**on** über *+akk*); **in accordance with the ~s** vorschriftsmäßig; **fire ~s** Brandschutzbestimmungen *pl* ❷ *(supervision)* Überwachung *f* **II.** *adj* vorgeschrieben; **the ~ pinstripe suit** der obligatorische Nadelstreifenanzug

regulator [ˈreg·jʊ·leɪ·ṭər] *n* ❶ TECH Regler *m* ❷ *(person)* aufsichtsführende Person

regulatory [ˈreg·jə·lə·tɔr·i] *adj* Aufsichts-, Kontroll-; **~ powers** ordnungspolitische Instrumente

regurgitate [ri·ˈgɜr·dʒə·teɪt] *vt* ❶ *(throw up) food* wieder hochwürgen ❷ *(pej: repeat) facts, information* nachplappern

rehab [ˈri·hæb] *n* *(fam) short for* **rehabilitation** Reha *f;* ■ **to be in ~** auf Reha sein *fam*

rehabilitate [ˌri·hə·ˈbɪl·ə·teɪt] *vt* *(have therapy, restore reputation)* rehabilitieren; *criminal* resozialisieren

rehabilitation [ˌri·hə·ˌbɪl·ə·ˈteɪ·ʃən] *n* ❶ MED Genesung *f* ❷ *of criminals* Resozialisierung *f; of drug addicts, sb's reputation* Rehabilitation *f geh; of victims* Wiedereingliederung *f* ins normale Leben ❸ *(renovation)* Instandsetzung *f,* Sanierung *f*

rehash **I.** *vt* [ˌri·ˈhæʃ] ❶ *(pej fam: offer as new)* aufwärmen ❷ *(discuss)* wiederkäuen; **to ~ events** Ereignisse noch einmal durchsprechen **II.** *n* <*pl* -es> [ˈri·hæʃ] *(fam)* Aufguss *m*

rehearsal [rɪ·ˈhɜr·səl] *n* THEAT Probe *f;* ■ **to be in ~** geprobt werden

rehearse [rɪ·ˈhɜrs] **I.** *vt* ❶ THEAT, MUS *(practice)* proben; *(in thought)* [in Gedanken] durchgehen ❷ *(prepare) person* vorbereiten **II.** *vi* proben

reign [reɪn] **I.** *vi* ❶ *(be king, queen)* regieren, herrschen; *(be head of state)* regieren; **to ~**

R

over a country ein Land regieren ❷ (*be dominant*) dominieren; **confusion ~s** es herrscht Verwirrung **II.** *n* Herrschaft *f*

reimburse [ˌri·ɪm·ˈbɜrs] *vt person* entschädigen; *thing* ersetzen; *expenses* [rück]erstatten

reimbursement [ˌri·ɪm·ˈbɜrs·mənt] *n* Rückzahlung *f; of expenses* Erstattung *f; of loss* Entschädigung *f*

rein [reɪn] *n usu pl* (*for horse*) Zügel *m* ▶ PHRASES: **to give free ~ to sb** jdm freie Hand lassen

reincarnation [ˌri·ɪn·kar·ˈneɪ·ʃən] *n* (*rebirth*) Reinkarnation *f geh,* Wiedergeburt *f;* (*fig*) *product* Nachbau *m*

reindeer <*pl* -> [ˈreɪn·dɪr] *n* Rentier *nt*

reinforce [ˌri·ɪn·ˈfɔrs] *vt* (*strengthen*) *troops* verstärken; *concrete* armieren; *findings, opinion, prejudice* bestätigen

reinforcement [ˌri·ɪn·ˈfɔrs·mənt] *n* ❶ Verstärkung *f,* Armierung *f fachspr;* **steel ~** Stahlträger *m meist pl* ❷ ■ **~s** *pl* (*troops*) Verstärkungstruppen *pl;* (*equipment*) Verstärkung *f*

reinstate [ˌri·ɪn·ˈsteɪt] *vt* ❶ (*at job*) *person* wieder einstellen ❷ (*re-establish*) *death penalty, sales tax* wieder einführen; *law and order* wiederherstellen

reinsure [ˌri·ɪn·ˈʃʊr] *vi, vt* rückversichern

reintegrate [ˌri·ˈɪn·tə·greɪt] *vt criminal* resozialisieren; *patient* wieder [in die Gesellschaft] eingliedern

reintegration [ˈri·ˌɪn·tə·ˈgreɪ·ʃən] *n of a criminal* Resozialisierung *f; of a patient* Wiedereingliederung *f*

re-introduce [ˌri·ɪn·trə·ˈdus] *vt* wieder einführen; **to ~ an animal into the wild** ein Tier in die Wildnis zurückführen

reissue [ˌri·ˈɪʃ·ju] **I.** *vt novel, recording* neu herausgeben **II.** *n* Neuauflage *f,* Neuausgabe *f*

reiterate [ri·ˈɪṭ·ə·reɪt] *vt* wiederholen

reiteration [ri·ˌɪṭ·ə·ˈreɪ·ʃən] *n* Wiederholung *f*

reject I. *vt* [rɪ·ˈdʒekt] ❶ (*decline*) ablehnen, zurückweisen; *excuse* nicht annehmen ❷ (*snub*) *person* abweisen; **to feel ~ed** sich als Außenseiter(in) fühlen ❸ MED *drug* nicht vertragen; *transplant* abstoßen **II.** *n* [ˈri·dʒekt] (*product*) Fehlerware *f,* Ausschussware *f;* (*person*) Außenseiter(in) *m(f)*

rejection [rɪ·ˈdʒek·ʃən] *n* ❶ (*dismissing*) Ablehnung *f,* Absage *f* ❷ MED Abstoßung *f*

rejoice [rɪ·ˈdʒɔɪs] *vi* sich freuen, sich erfreuen *geh* (**at/in** an +*dat*)

rejoicing [rɪ·ˈdʒɔɪ·sɪŋ] *n* Freude *f* (**at/in** über +*akk*)

rejoin [ˌri·ˈdʒɔɪn] *vt* (*reunite with*) *person, thing* sich wieder vereinigen (mit +*dat*)

rejoinder [rɪ·ˈdʒɔɪn·dər] *n* (*form*) Erwiderung *f geh*

rejuvenate [ri·ˈdʒu·və·neɪt] *vt* ❶ (*energize*) revitalisieren *geh* ❷ (*make younger, modernize*) verjüngen; *factory, company* modernisieren

rekindle [ri·ˈkɪn·dəl] *vt* (*a. fig*) wieder entfachen

relapse I. *n* [ˈri·læps] MED Rückfall *m;* (*in economy*) Rückschlag *m* **II.** *vi* [rɪ·ˈlæps] MED einen Rückfall haben; *economy* einen Rückschlag erleiden

relate [rɪ·ˈleɪt] **I.** *vt* ❶ (*show relationship*) etw mit etw *dat* in Verbindung bringen ❷ (*narrate*) erzählen; ■ **to ~ sth to sb** jdm etw berichten **II.** *vi* ❶ (*fam: get along*) ■ **to ~ to sb/sth** eine Beziehung zu jdm/etw finden ❷ (*be about*) ■ **to ~ to sb/sth** von jdm/etw handeln; (*be relevant to*) **chapter nine ~s to the effect of inflation** in Kapitel neun geht es um die Auswirkungen der Inflation

related [rɪ·ˈleɪ·ṭɪd] *adj* ❶ (*connected*) verbunden; **to be directly ~ to sth** in direktem Zusammenhang mit etw *dat* stehen ❷ *species, language* verwandt (**to** mit +*dat*); **to be ~ by blood** blutsverwandt sein; **distantly ~** entfernt verwandt

relating to [rɪ·ˈleɪ·tɪŋ-] *prep* in Zusammenhang mit +*dat*

relation [rɪ·ˈleɪ·ʃən] *n* ❶ (*connection*) Verbindung *f,* Bezug *m;* **in ~ to** in Bezug auf +*akk;* **to bear no ~ to sb** (*in appearance*) jdm überhaupt nicht ähnlich sehen ❷ (*relative*) Verwandte(r) *f(m);* **is Julia any ~ to you?** ist Julia irgendwie mit dir verwandt? ❸ (*between people, countries*) ■ **~s** *pl* Beziehungen *pl,* Verhältnis *nt* (**between** zwischen +*dat*)

relationship [rɪ·ˈleɪ·ʃən·ʃɪp] *n* ❶ (*connection*) Beziehung *f* ❷ (*in family*) Verwandtschaftsverhältnis *nt* ❸ (*association*) Verhältnis *nt;* (*a. business, romantic*) Beziehung *f* (**to/with** zu +*dat*); ■ **to be in a ~ with sb** mit jdm eine feste Beziehung haben

relative [ˈrel·ə·ṭɪv] **I.** *adj* ❶ (*connected to*) relevant (**to** für +*akk*), sich beziehend auf +*akk* ❷ (*corresponding*) jeweilige(r, s); ■ **to be ~ to sth** von etw *dat* abhängen ❸ (*comparative*) relative(r, s), vergleichbare(r, s); (*not absolute*) *evil, happiness* relativ **II.** *n* Verwandte(r) *f(m)*

relative ˈclause *n* Relativsatz *m*

relatively [ˈrel·ə·ṭɪv·li] *adv* relativ

relativity [ˌrel·ə·ˈtɪv·ɪ·ṭi] *n* Relativität *f;* [**Einstein's**] **Theory of R~** [Einsteins] Relativitätstheorie *f*

relaunch [ˌri·ˈlɔntʃ] **I.** *vt* ❶ AEROSP *rocket* erneut starten ❷ ECON *product* erneut auf den Markt bringen **II.** *n* ❶ AEROSP, TRANSP *of a rocket* Zweitstart *m; of a ship* zweiter Stapellauf ❷ ECON *of a brand/a product* Wiedereinführung *f*

relax [rɪ·ˈlæks] **I.** *vi* sich entspannen; **~!** entspann dich!; (*don't worry*) beruhige dich! **II.** *vt rules, supervision, grip* lockern; *muscles* entspannen, lockern; *security measures* einschränken

relaxation [ˌri·læk·ˈseɪ·ʃən] *n* ❶ (*recreation*) Entspannung *f* ❷ (*liberalizing*) *of discipline* Nachlassen *nt; of laws* Liberalisierung *f; of rules* Lockerung *f*

relaxed [rɪ·ˈlækst] *adj* ❶ (*at ease*) entspannt ❷ (*easy-going*) locker, gelassen; *manner* lässig

relay [ˈri·leɪ] **I.** *vt* mitteilen (**to** +*dat*); *message* weiterleiten; *TV pictures* übertragen **II.** *n*

❶ SPORTS ~ [**race**] Staffellauf *m* ❷ ELEC (*device*) Relais *nt*

release [rɪ·ˈlis] **I.** *vt* ❶ (*set free*) freilassen ❷ LAW *prisoner* [aus der Haft] entlassen ❸ (*move sth from fixed position*) *brake* lösen; PHOT *shutter* betätigen ❹ (*allow to escape*) *gas, steam* freisetzen; **to ~ sth into the atmosphere** etw in die Atmosphäre entweichen lassen ❺ (*relax pressure*) loslassen; *grip* lockern ❻ (*make public, circulate*) verbreiten; (*issue*) veröffentlichen; *movie, CD* herausbringen **II.** *n* ❶ (*setting free*) Entlassung *f; of hostage* Freilassung *f* ❷ (*mechanism*) Auslöser *m;* **brake/clutch ~** Brems-/Kupplungsausrückmechanismus *m* ❸ (*items on hold*) *of funds, goods* Freigabe *f* ❹ (*escape of gases*) Entweichen *nt* ❺ (*publication*) Veröffentlichung *f* ❻ (*information document*) Verlautbarung *f;* **press ~** Pressemitteilung *f* ❼ (*new CD*) Neuerscheinung *f*

relegate [ˈrel·ə·geɪt] *vt usu passive* **the story was ~d to the middle pages of the newspaper** die Story wurde in den Mittelteil der Zeitung verschoben

relent [rɪ·ˈlent] *vi people* nachgeben; *wind, rain* nachlassen

relentless [rɪ·ˈlent·lɪs] *adj* (*unwilling to compromise*) unnachgiebig; (*without stopping*) unablässig; *persecution* gnadenlos; *pressure* unaufhörlich

relevance [ˈrel·ə·vəns], **relevancy** [ˈrel·ə·vən·si] *n* ❶ (*appropriateness*) Relevanz *f geh,* Bedeutsamkeit *f* (**to** für +*akk*); **to have [any] ~ to sth** [irgendeinen] Bezug auf etw *akk* haben ❷ (*significance*) Bedeutung *f* (**to** für +*akk*); **to have ~ for sb/sth** für jdn/etw relevant sein

relevant [ˈrel·ə·vənt] *adj* ❶ (*appropriate*) relevant ❷ (*important*) wichtig, bedeutend; **highly ~** höchst bedeutungsvoll

reliability [rɪ·ˌlaɪ·ə·ˈbɪl·ɪ·t̬i] *n* ❶ (*dependability*) Zuverlässigkeit *f* ❷ (*trustworthiness*) Vertrauenswürdigkeit *f*

reliable [rɪ·ˈlaɪ·ə·bəl] *adj* ❶ (*dependable*) verlässlich, zuverlässig ❷ (*credible*) glaubwürdig; *criterion* sicher ❸ (*trustworthy*) vertrauenswürdig, seriös

reliance [rɪ·ˈlaɪ·əns] *n* ❶ (*dependence*) Verlass *m* (**on** auf +*akk*) ❷ (*trust*) Vertrauen *nt;* **to place ~ on sb/sth** Vertrauen in jdn/etw setzen

reliant [rɪ·ˈlaɪ·ənt] *adj* abhängig (**on** von +*dat*); ■ **to be ~ on sb/sth to do sth** abhängig davon sein, dass jd/etw etw tut

relic [ˈrel·ɪk] *n* ❶ (*object*) Relikt *nt,* Überbleibsel *nt,* Überrest *m* ❷ (*pej: survival from past*) Relikt *nt;* (*hum: sth old-fashioned*) altmodisches Ding, Ding *nt* von anno dazumal

relief [rɪ·ˈlif] *n* ❶ (*diminution*) Entlastung *f; of hunger/suffering* Linderung *f;* **tax ~** Steuerermäßigung *f* ❷ (*release from tension*) Erleichterung *f;* **to breathe a sigh of ~** erleichtert aufatmen ❸ (*assistance for poor*) Hilfsgüter *pl* ❹ (*person taking over duty*) Ablösung *f* ❺ (*three-dimensional representation*) Reliefdruck *m* ❻ (*sharpness of image*) Kontrast *m;* **to stand out in sharp ~** sich deutlich von etw *dat* abheben

reˈlief worker *n* Mitarbeiter(in) *m(f)* einer Hilfsorganisation; (*in third-world countries*) Entwicklungshelfer(in) *m(f)*

relieve [rɪ·ˈliv] *vt* ❶ (*weaken negative feelings*) erträglicher machen; *pressure* verringern; *tension* abbauen ❷ (*alleviate*) *pain, suffering* lindern ❸ (*take burden from*) ■ **to ~ sb of sth** jdm etw abnehmen; (*hum: steal*) jdn um etw *akk* erleichtern ❹ (*take over*) *person* ablösen; **to ~ sb of a position** jdn eines Amtes entheben *geh* ❺ (*assist*) ■ **to ~ sb** jdm [in einer Notsituation] helfen ❻ (*urinate*) ■ **to ~ oneself** (*hum*) sich *akk* erleichtern *euph*

relieved [rɪ·ˈlivd] *adj* erleichtert (**at** über +*akk*); **to be ~ to hear sth** etw mit Erleichterung hören

religion [rɪ·ˈlɪdʒ·ən] *n* ❶ (*faith in god(s)*) Religion *f;* (*set of religious beliefs*) Glaube *m* ❷ (*system of worship*) Kult *m*

religious [rɪ·ˈlɪdʒ·əs] *adj* ❶ (*of religion*) religiöse(r, s), Religions-; **~ organization** Glaubensgemeinschaft *f;* **~ freedom** Religionsfreiheit *f* ❷ (*pious*) religiös, fromm

relinquish [rɪ·ˈlɪŋ·kwɪʃ] *vt* (*form: abandon*) aufgeben; *a right* verzichten (auf +*akk*); ■ **to ~ sth to sb** jdm etw überlassen; *responsibility* jdm etw übertragen

relish [ˈrel·ɪʃ] **I.** *n* ❶ (*enjoyment*) Genuss *m;* ■ **with ~** genüsslich ❷ FOOD Relish *nt* **II.** *vt* genießen; **to ~ the thought that ...** sich darauf freuen, dass ...

relive [ˌri·ˈlɪv] *vt moment, experience* nochmals durchleben

reload [ˌri·ˈloʊd] **I.** *vt gun, pistol* nachladen; *camera, software* neu laden; *ship* wieder beladen **II.** *vi weapon* nachladen

relocate [ri·ˈloʊ·keɪt] **I.** *vi* umziehen **II.** *vt person* versetzen; *thing* verlegen

relocation [ˌri·loʊ·ˈkeɪ·ʃən] *n of a company* Verlegung *f; of a person* Versetzung *f*

reluctance [rɪ·ˈlʌk·təns] *n* Widerwillen *m,* Widerstreben *nt*

reluctant [rɪ·ˈlʌk·tənt] *adj* widerwillig, widerstrebend; ■ **to be ~ to do sth** sich dagegen sträuben, etw zu tun, etw nur ungern tun

rely [rɪ·ˈlaɪ] *vi* ❶ (*have confidence in*) ■ **to ~ on sb/sth** sich auf jdn/etw verlassen; ■ **to ~ on sb/sth to do sth** sich darauf verlassen, dass jd/etw etw tut ❷ (*depend on*) ■ **to ~ on sb/sth** von jdm/etw abhängen; ■ **to ~ on sb/sth for** [*or* **to do**] **sth** darauf angewiesen sein, dass jd/etw etw tut

remain [rɪ·ˈmeɪn] *vi* ❶ (*stay*) bleiben; **to ~ behind** zurückbleiben ❷ + *n or adj* (*not change*) bleiben; **to ~ untreated** nicht behandelt werden ❸ (*survive, be left over*) übrig bleiben; *person* überleben; **much ~s to be done** es muss noch vieles getan werden; **the fact ~s**

that ... das ändert nichts an der Tatsache, dass ...

remainder [rɪ·ˈmeɪn·dər] *n a.* MATH Rest *m*

remaining [rɪ·ˈmeɪ·nɪŋ] *adj attr* übrig, restlich

remains [rɪ·ˈmeɪnz] *npl* ❶ (*leftovers*) Überbleibsel *pl*, Überreste *pl* ❷ (*form: corpse*) sterbliche Überreste

remake I. *vt* <-made, -made> [ˌri·ˈmeɪk] **to ~ a film** einen Film neu drehen **II.** *n* [ˈri·meɪk] Neuverfilmung *f*, Remake *nt*

remark [rɪ·ˈmark] **I.** *vt* äußern, bemerken **II.** *vi* eine Bemerkung machen; ■ **to ~ on sth** sich über etw äußern **III.** *n* Bemerkung *f* (**about** über +*akk*), Äußerung *f*

remarkable [rɪ·ˈmar·kə·bəl] *adj* ❶ (*approv: extraordinary*) bemerkenswert, erstaunlich; *ability* beachtlich ❷ (*surprising*) merkwürdig; **it's [truly] ~ [that]** ... es ist [wirklich] erstaunlich, dass ...

remarkably [rɪ·ˈmar·kə·bli] *adv* ❶ (*strikingly*) bemerkenswert, auffällig ❷ (*surprisingly*) überraschenderweise, erstaunlicherweise

remarry <-ie-> [ˌri·ˈmær·i] **I.** *vt* wieder heiraten **II.** *vi* sich wieder verheiraten

rematch [ˈri·mætʃ] *n* Rückspiel *nt*

remedial [rɪ·ˈmi·di·əl] *adj* (*form*) ❶ SCH Förder- ❷ MED Heil-

remedy [ˈrem·ə·di] **I.** *n* ❶ (*medicinal agent*) Heilmittel *nt* (**for** gegen +*akk*) ❷ (*solution*) Mittel *nt* (**for** zu +*dat*), Lösung *f* (**for** für +*akk*) **II.** *vt* in Ordnung bringen; *a mistake* berichtigen; *poverty* beseitigen

remember [rɪ·ˈmem·bər] **I.** *vt* ❶ (*recall*) sich erinnern (an +*akk*); (*memorize*) sich *dat* merken; **I never ~ her birthday** ich denke nie an ihren Geburtstag; ■ **to ~ doing sth** sich daran erinnern, etw getan zu haben ❷ (*commemorate*) *person, event* gedenken +*gen* **II.** *vi* (*recall*) sich erinnern; **I can't ~** ich kann mich nicht erinnern; ■ **to ~ [that]** ... sich daran erinnern, [dass] ...

remembrance [rɪ·ˈmem·brəns] *n* (*form*) ❶ (*act of remembering*) Gedenken *nt geh* ❷ (*a memory, recollection*) Erinnerung *f* (**of** an +*akk*)

remind [rɪ·ˈmaɪnd] *vt* erinnern; **that ~s me!** das erinnert mich an etwas!; ■ **to ~ sb about sth** jdn an etw *akk* erinnern

reminder [rɪ·ˈmaɪn·dər] *n* ❶ (*prompting recall*) Mahnung *f*; **as a ~ to oneself that ...** um sich *akk* daran zu erinnern, dass ... ❷ (*awakening memories*) Erinnerung *f* (**of** an +*akk*)

reminisce [ˌrem·ə·ˈnɪs] *vi* (*form*) in Erinnerungen schwelgen

reminiscence [ˌrem·ə·ˈnɪs·əns] *n* (*form*) ❶ (*reflection on past*) Erinnerung *f* ❷ (*memory*) Erinnerung *f* (**of/about** an +*akk*)

reminiscent [ˌrem·ə·ˈnɪs·ənt] *adj* (*suggestive, evocative*) ■ **to be ~ [of [*or* about] sb/sth]** Erinnerungen [an jdn/etw] hervorrufen

remiss [rɪ·ˈmɪs] *adj pred* (*form*) nachlässig

remission [rɪ·ˈmɪʃ·ən] *n* MED (*form*) *of symptoms* Remission *f fachspr*

remit *vt* <-tt-> [rɪ·ˈmɪt] (*form: tender money*) überweisen

remittance [rɪ·ˈmɪt·əns] *n* (*form*) Überweisung *f*

remix MUS **I.** *vt* [ˌri·ˈmɪks] **to ~ songs** einen Remix von Liedern machen **II.** *n* <*pl* -es> [ˈri·mɪks] Remix *m*

remnant [ˈrem·nənt] *n* Rest *m*; **~ sale** Resteverkauf *m*

remodel <-l- *or* -ll-> [ˌri·ˈmad·əl] *vt* umgestalten

remonstrate [rɪ·ˈman·streɪt] *vi* (*form*) protestieren; ■ **to ~ with sb about sth** jdm wegen einer S. *gen* Vorhaltungen machen

remorse [rɪ·ˈmɔrs] *n* (*form*) Reue *f*; **to feel ~ for sth** etw bereuen; ■ **without ~** erbarmungslos

remorseful [rɪ·ˈmɔrs·fəl] *adj* (*form: filled with regret*) reuevoll *geh*; *sinner* reuig *geh*; (*apologetic*) schuldbewusst

remorseless [rɪ·ˈmɔrs·lɪs] *adj* (*form*) ❶ (*callous*) gnadenlos, unbarmherzig; *attack* brutal ❷ (*relentless*) unerbittlich

remortgage [ˌri·ˈmɔr·gɪdʒ] *vt* ■ **to ~ sth** etw erneut hypothekarisch belasten

remote <-er, -est *or* more ~, most ~> [rɪ·ˈmoʊt] *adj* ❶ (*distant in place*) fern, entfernt; (*isolated*) abgelegen ❷ (*distant in time*) lang vergangen; *past, future* fern ❸ (*standoffish*) distanziert, unnahbar

remote conˈtrol *n* ❶ (*device*) Fernbedienung *f* ❷ (*control from distance*) Fernsteuerung *f*

remote-conˈtrolled *adj* ferngesteuert

remoteness [rɪ·ˈmoʊt·nɪs] *n* ❶ (*inaccessibility*) Abgelegenheit *f* ❷ (*aloofness*) Distanziertheit *f*

removable [rɪ·ˈmu·və·bəl] *adj* ❶ (*detachable*) *sleeves* abnehmbar, zum Abnehmen *nach n* ❷ (*cleanable*) *ink* abwaschbar

removal [rɪ·ˈmu·vəl] *n* ❶ (*expulsion*) Beseitigung *f* ❷ (*taking off*) Abnahme *f*; (*cleaning a.*) Entfernung *f*

remove [rɪ·ˈmuv] *vt* ❶ (*take away*) entfernen, wegräumen; *obstacle, roadblock* beseitigen; *wrecked vehicle* abschleppen; MIL *mine* räumen ❷ (*get rid of*) *makeup, stain* entfernen ❸ (*form: dismiss*) **to ~ sb [from office]** jdn [aus dem Amt] entlassen

remover [rɪ·ˈmu·vər] *n* Reinigungsmittel *nt*; **nail polish ~** Nagellackentferner *m*

remunerate [rɪ·ˈmju·nə·reɪt] *vt* (*form*) ■ **to ~ sb for sth** jdn für etw *akk* bezahlen

remuneration [rɪ·ˌmju·nə·ˈreɪ·ʃən] *n* (*form*) Vergütung *f*, Remuneration *f* ÖSTERR

Renaissance [ˌren·ə·ˈsans] *n* ■ **the ~** die Renaissance

renal [ˈri·nəl] *adj* Nieren-; **~ dialysis** Dialyse *f*

rename [ˌri·ˈneɪm] *vt* umbenennen

render [ˈren·dər] *vt* (*form*) ❶ (*cause to become*) **she was ~ed unconscious by the explosion** sie wurde durch die Explosion ohnmächtig; **to ~ sb speechless** jdn sprachlos

R

machen ❷ (*interpret*) wiedergeben; *song* vortragen ❸ (*offer*) *aid, services* leisten

rendering ['ren·dər·ɪŋ] *n* ❶ (*performance of art work*) Interpretation *f; song* Vortrag *m; of a part* Darstellung *f* ❷ (*account*) Schilderung *f*

rendezvous ['ran·deɪ·ˌvu] **I.** *n* <*pl* -> ❶ (*meeting*) Rendezvous *nt,* Treffen *nt* ❷ (*meeting place*) Treffpunkt *m,* Treff *m fam* **II.** *vi* sich heimlich treffen

rendition [ren·'dɪʃ·ən] *n* Wiedergabe *f; of a song* Interpretation *f*

renegade ['ren·ə·geɪd] **I.** *n* Abtrünnige(r) *f(m) pej* **II.** *adj attr* abtrünnige(r, s)

renege [rɪ·'nɪg] *vi* **to ~ on a deal** sich nicht an ein Abkommen halten; *on a promise* nicht halten

renew [rɪ·'nu] *vt* ❶ (*resume*) erneuern; **to ~ a relationship with sb/sth** eine Beziehung zu jdm/etw wieder aufnehmen ❷ (*grant continued validity*) *passport, documents, library books* verlängern; *subscription* erneuern ❸ (*repair*) reparieren; (*to mend in places*) ausbessern

renewable [rɪ·'nu·ə·bəl] *adj* ❶ *energy sources* erneuerbar ❷ *contract, documents, passport* verlängerbar

renewal [rɪ·'nu·əl] *n* ❶ (*extension*) *of a passport* Verlängerung *f* ❷ (*process of renewing*) Erneuerung *f* ❸ (*urban regeneration*) Erneuerung *f,* Entwicklung *f*

renewed [rɪ·'nud] *adj* erneuert *attr;* **~ interest** wieder erwachtes Interesse

rennet ['ren·ɪt] *n* Lab *nt*

renounce [rɪ·'naʊns] *vt* ■ **to ~ sth** (*formally give up*) *right* auf etw *akk* verzichten; *citizenship, family* aufgeben; *one's faith* abschwören *+dat*

renovate ['ren·ə·veɪt] *vt* renovieren

renovation [ˌren·ə·'veɪ·ʃən] *n* (*small and large scale*) Renovierung *f;* (*large scale only*) Sanierung *f;* **to be under ~** gerade renoviert werden

renowned [rɪ·'naʊnd] *adj* (*form, liter*) berühmt (**as** als, **for** für *+akk*)

rent [rent] **I.** *n* Miete *f;* (*esp for land and business*) Pacht *f;* **"for ~"** „zu vermieten" **II.** *vt* ❶ (*pay to use*) *house, apartment, car* mieten (**from** von *+dat*); *land, business* pachten; *dress, tuxedo* ausleihen ❷ (*rent out*) vermieten **III.** *vi house, apartment, car* vermietet werden; ■ **to ~ for sth** gegen etw *akk* zu mieten sein

rental ['ren·təl] *n* Miete *f;* **~ agency** Verleih *m;* **car ~ agency** Autoverleih *m*

rent-'free *adj* mietfrei

renunciation [rɪ·ˌnʌn·sɪ·'eɪ·ʃən] *n* Verzicht *m* (**of** auf *+akk*)

reopen [ri·'oʊ·pən] **I.** *vt* ❶ (*open again*) *door, window* wieder aufmachen; *shop* wieder eröffnen ❷ (*start again*) *negotiations* wieder aufnehmen **II.** *vi* wieder eröffnen

reorder [ˌri·'ɔr·dər] **I.** *n* Nachbestellung *f* **II.** *vt* ❶ (*order again*) nachbestellen ❷ (*rearrange*) umordnen; *priorities* neu festlegen

reorganize [ri·'ɔr·gə·naɪz] **I.** *vt* umorganisieren, reorganisieren **II.** *vi* reorganisieren, eine Umstrukturierung vornehmen

rep[1] [rep] *n* (*fam: salesperson*) *short for* **representative** Vertreter(in) *m(f)*

rep[2] [rep] *n* (*fam*) *short for* **reputation**

repaint [ri·'peɪnt] *vt* neu streichen

repair [ri·'per] **I.** *vt* ❶ (*restore*) reparieren; *defect* beheben; *road* ausbessern ❷ (*put right*) [wieder] in Ordnung bringen; *damage* wiedergutmachen; *friendship* kitten *fam* **II.** *n* ❶ (*overhaul*) Reparatur *f;* ■ **~s** *pl* Reparaturarbeiten *pl* (**to** an *+dat*); (*specific improvement*) ausgebesserte Stelle; **to do ~s** Reparaturen durchführen; **beyond ~** irreparabel ❷ (*state*) Zustand *m;* **to be in good ~** in gutem Zustand sein

repairable [rɪ·'per·ə·bəl] *adj* reparabel

re'pair kit *n* Flickzeug *nt kein pl*

re'pairman *n* (*for domestic installations*) Handwerker *m;* (*for cars*) Mechaniker *m;* **TV ~** Fernsehtechniker *m*

re'pair shop *n* Reparaturwerkstatt *f*

reparable ['rep·ər·ə·bəl] *adj* reparabel

reparation [ˌrep·ə·'reɪ·ʃən] *n* (*form*) Entschädigung *f;* ■ **~s** *pl* (*for war victims*) Wiedergutmachung *f kein pl;* (*for a country*) Reparationen *pl*

repartee [ˌrep·ar·'ti] *n* schlagfertige Antwort

repatriate [ri·'peɪ·tri·eɪt] *vt person* [in das Heimatland] zurückschicken [*o geh* repatriieren]

repatriation [rɪ·ˌpeɪ·tri·'eɪ·ʃən] *n* Repatriierung *f geh,* Rückführung *f*

repay <-paid, -paid> [rɪ·'peɪ] *vt* ❶ (*pay back*) zurückzahlen; *debts, a loan* tilgen; ■ **to ~ sb** jdm Geld zurückzahlen ❷ (*fig*) **to ~ a favor** sich für eine Gefälligkeit erkenntlich zeigen; ■ **to ~ sth by doing sth** etw mit etw *dat* vergelten

repayable [rɪ·'peɪ·ə·bəl] *adj* rückzahlbar

repayment [rɪ·'peɪ·mənt] *n of a loan* Rückzahlung *f,* Tilgung *f*

repeal [rɪ·'pil] **I.** *vt decree, a law* aufheben **II.** *n of a decree, law* Aufhebung *f*

repeat [rɪ·'pit] **I.** *vt* ❶ (*say again, do again*) wiederholen; **~ after me** bitte mir nachsprechen ❷ (*communicate*) **don't ~ this but ...** sag es nicht weiter, [aber] ... **II.** *vi* (*recur*) sich wiederholen **III.** *n* Wiederholung *f* **IV.** *adj attr* Wiederholungs-; **~ pattern** sich wiederholendes Muster; (*on material, carpets*) Rapport *m fachspr*

repeated [rɪ·'pi·t̬ɪd] *adj* wiederholte(r, s)

repeatedly [rɪ·'pi·t̬ɪd·li] *adv* wiederholt; (*several times*) mehrfach

repel <-ll-> [rɪ·'pel] *vt* ❶ (*ward off*) zurückweisen, abweisen ❷ MIL (*form: repulse*) abwehren ❸ (*disgust*) ■ **she was ~led by that sight** sie war abgestoßen von dem Anblick

repellent [rɪ·'pel·ənt] **I.** *n* Insektenspray *nt* **II.** *adj* abstoßend, widerwärtig

repent [rɪ·'pent] *vi, vt* (*form*) bereuen

R

repentance [rɪ·ˈpen·təns] *n* Reue *f*
repentant [rə·ˈpen·tənt] *adj* (*form*) reuig; **to feel ~** reumütig sein
repercussion [ˌri·pər·ˈkʌʃ·ən] *n usu pl* Auswirkung *f meist pl;* **far-reaching ~s** weit reichende Konsequenzen
repertoire [ˈrep·ər·ˌtwar] *n* Repertoire *nt* (**of** an +*dat*)
repetition [ˌrep·ə·ˈtɪʃ·ən] *n* Wiederholung *f*
repetitious [ˌrep·ə·ˈtɪʃ·əs], **repetitive** [rɪ·ˈpeṭ·ə·tɪv] *adj* sich wiederholend *attr;* monoton *pej*
replace [rɪ·ˈpleɪs] *vt* ❶ (*take the place of*) ersetzen (**with** durch +*akk*) ❷ (*put back*) [an seinen Platz] zurücklegen [*o* zurückstellen]; *receiver* wieder auflegen ❸ (*substitute*) *loss* ersetzen; *bandage* wechseln
replaceable [rɪ·ˈpleɪ·sə·bəl] *adj* ersetzbar
replacement [rɪ·ˈpleɪs·mənt] **I.** *n* ❶ (*substitute*) Ersatz *m;* (*person*) Vertretung *f* ❷ (*substituting*) Ersetzung *f* **II.** *adj attr* Ersatz-; **~ hip joint** künstliches Hüftgelenk
replay **I.** *vt* [ˌri·ˈpleɪ] ❶ SPORTS *match, game* wiederholen ❷ (*show again*) *video* nochmals abspielen **II.** *n* [ˈri·pleɪ] ❶ (*recording*) Wiederholung *f* ❷ (*game*) Wiederholungsspiel *nt*
replenish [rɪ·ˈplen·ɪʃ] *vt* (*form*) *supplies* [wieder] auffüllen; *glass* wieder füllen
replete [rɪ·ˈplit] *adj pred* (*form: provided*) ■**to be ~ with sth** mit etw *dat* großzügig ausgestattet sein
replica [ˈrep·lɪ·kə] *n* Kopie *f; painting* Replik *f geh*
replicate [ˈrep·lɪ·keɪt] *vt* (*form*) reproduzieren *geh; experiment* wiederholen; ■**to ~ oneself** BIOL sich replizieren *fachspr*
reply [rɪ·ˈplaɪ] **I.** *vi* <-ie-> (*respond*) antworten, erwidern; **to ~ to letters/a question** Briefe/eine Frage beantworten **II.** *n* Antwort *f* (**to** auf +*akk*); (*verbal a.*) Erwiderung *f*
report [rɪ·ˈpɔrt] **I.** *n* ❶ (*news*) Meldung *f* (**on/about** über +*akk*); *in the press* Bericht *m* ❷ (*formal statement*) Bericht *m* (**on/about** über +*akk*); **weather ~** Wetterbericht *m* **II.** *vt* ❶ (*communicate information*) ■**to ~ sth** etw berichten [*o* melden]; **he was ~ed missing in action** er wurde als vermisst gemeldet; **to ~ a crime** ein Verbrechen anzeigen ❷ (*denounce*) *person* melden; *to the police* anzeigen ❸ (*claim*) **the new management is ~ed to be more popular among the staff** es heißt, dass die neue Geschäftsleitung bei der Belegschaft beliebter sei **III.** *vi* ❶ (*make public*) Bericht erstatten; ■**to ~ on sth to sb** (*once*) jdm über etw *akk* Bericht erstatten; (*ongoing*) jdn über etw *akk* auf dem Laufenden halten; ■**to ~ [that]** ... mitteilen, [dass] ... ❷ ADMIN (*be accountable to sb*) ■**to ~ to sb** jdm unterstehen ❸ (*present oneself*) *to work* sich zur Arbeit melden; *to the police* sich bei der Polizei melden
◆**report back** **I.** *vt* (*communicate results*) ■**to ~ back sth [to sb]** [jdm] über etw *akk* berichten **II.** *vi* Bericht erstatten; ■**to ~ back on sth [to sb]** [jdm] über etw *akk* Bericht erstatten
reˈport card *n* [Schul]zeugnis *nt*
reporter [rɪ·ˈpɔr·ṭər] *n* Reporter(in) *m(f)*
repose [rɪ·ˈpoʊz] *n* (*form*) Ruhe *f*
repossess [ˌri·pə·ˈzes] *vt* wieder in Besitz nehmen
repossession [ˌri·pə·ˈzeʃ·ən] *n* Wiederinbesitznahme *f*
reprehensible [ˌrep·rɪ·ˈhen·sə·bəl] *adj* (*form*) verurteilenswert; *act* verwerflich
represent [ˌrep·rɪ·ˈzent] *vt* ❶ (*act on behalf of*) repräsentieren, vertreten ❷ (*depict*) darstellen, zeigen ❸ (*be a symbol of*) symbolisieren ❹ (*be typical of*) widerspiegeln
representation [ˌrep·rɪ·zen·ˈteɪ·ʃən] *n* ❶ (*acting on behalf of a person*) [Stell]vertretung *f;* POL, LAW Vertretung *f* ❷ (*something that depicts*) Darstellung *f* ❸ (*act of depicting*) Darstellung *f*
representative [ˌrep·rɪ·ˈzen·tə·ṭɪv] **I.** *adj* ❶ (*like others*) *cross section, result* repräsentativ ❷ (*typical*) typisch (**of** für +*akk*) **II.** *n* ❶ (*person*) [Stell]vertreter(in) *m(f);* ECON Vertreter(in) *m(f)* ❷ POL Abgeordnete(r) *f(m)* ❸ (*member of House of Representatives*) Mitglied *nt* des Repräsentantenhauses
repress [rɪ·ˈpres] *vt* unterdrücken
repressed [rɪ·ˈprest] *adj* ❶ (*hidden*) unterdrückt; PSYCH verdrängt ❷ (*unable to show feelings*) gehemmt, verklemmt *fam*
repression [rɪ·ˈpreʃ·ən] *n* ❶ POL Unterdrückung *f* ❷ PSYCH Verdrängung *f*
repressive [rɪ·ˈpres·ɪv] *adj* repressiv *geh; regime* unterdrückerisch
reprieve [rɪ·ˈpriv] **I.** *vt* begnadigen; (*fig*) verschonen **II.** *n* ❶ LAW (*official order*) Begnadigung *f;* **to grant a ~** Aufschub *m* gewähren ❷ (*fig: respite*) Schonfrist *f*
reprimand [ˈrep·rə·mænd] **I.** *vt* tadeln, zurechtweisen **II.** *n* Rüge *f;* **to give sb a ~** jdn rügen
reprint **I.** *vt* [ˌri·ˈprɪnt] nachdrucken **II.** *n* [ˈri·prɪnt] Nachdruck *m*
reprisal [rɪ·ˈpraɪ·zəl] *n* Vergeltungsmaßnahme *f*
reproach [rɪ·ˈproʊtʃ] **I.** *vt* ■**to ~ sb [for doing sth]** jdm [wegen einer S. *gen*] Vorwürfe machen **II.** *n* <*pl* -es> Vorwurf *m*
reproachful [rɪ·ˈproʊtʃ·fəl] *adj* vorwurfsvoll
reprocess [ˌri·ˈpras·es] *vt* wiederaufbereiten
reprocessing [ˌri·ˈpras·es·ɪŋ] *n* Wiederaufbereitung *f*
reproduce [ˌri·prə·ˈdus] **I.** *vi* ❶ (*produce offspring*) sich fortpflanzen; (*multiply*) sich vermehren ❷ (*be copied*) sich kopieren lassen **II.** *vt* ❶ (*produce a copy*) reproduzieren; (*in large numbers*) vervielfältigen ❷ (*recreate*) neu erstehen lassen
reproduction [ˌri·prə·ˈdʌk·ʃən] **I.** *n* ❶ (*producing offspring*) Fortpflanzung *f;* (*multiplying*) Vermehrung *f* ❷ (*copying*) Reproduktion *f,* Vervielfältigung *f* ❸ (*copy*) Reproduktion *f,* Kopie *f; of construction* Nachbau *m* ❹ MUS

sound ~ Wiedergabe *f* **II.** *adj* ❶ (*concerning the production of offspring*) *process, rate* Fortpflanzungs- ❷ (*copying an earlier style*) *chair, desk, furniture* nachgebaut; ~ **furniture** Stilmöbel *pl*
reproductive [ˌri·prə·ˈdʌk·tɪv] *adj* Fortpflanzungs-
reproof [rɪ·ˈpruf] *n* (*form*) ❶ (*words expressing blame*) Tadel *m geh* ❷ (*blame*) Vorwurf *m*
reptile [ˈrep·taɪl] *n* Reptil *nt*
reptilian [rep·ˈtɪl·i·ən] *adj* ❶ (*of reptiles*) Reptilien-, reptilienartig ❷ (*pej: unpleasant*) unangenehm
republic [rɪ·ˈpʌb·lɪk] *n* Republik *f*
Republican [rɪ·ˈpʌb·lɪ·kən] **I.** *n* POL Republikaner(in) *m(f)* **II.** *adj* POL republikanisch
repudiate [rɪ·ˈpju·di·eɪt] *vt* (*form*) zurückweisen; *suggestion* ablehnen
repugnance [rɪ·ˈpʌg·nəns] *n* (*form*) Abscheu *m o f*
repugnant [rɪ·ˈpʌg·nənt] *adj* (*form*) widerlich; *behavior* abstoßend
repulse [rɪ·ˈpʌls] *vt* ❶ MIL abwehren; *an offensive* zurückschlagen ❷ (*reject*) zurückweisen ❸ (*disgust*) abstoßen, anwidern
repulsion [rɪ·ˈpʌl·ʃən] *n* (*disgust*) Abscheu *m*, Ekel *m*
repulsive [rɪ·ˈpʌl·sɪv] *adj* abstoßend
reputable [ˈrep·jə·t̬ə·bəl] *adj* angesehen, achtbar
reputation [ˌrep·jʊ·ˈteɪ·ʃən] *n* ❶ (*general estimation, being known for sth*) Ruf *m*; **to have a ~ for sth** für etw *akk* bekannt sein; **to have a ~ as sth** einen Ruf als etw haben ❷ (*being highly regarded*) Ansehen *nt*, guter Ruf
repute [rɪ·ˈpjut] *n* Ansehen *nt*; **of good ~** von gutem Ruf
reputed [rɪ·ˈpju·t̬ɪd] *adj* ❶ (*believed*) angenommen, vermutet ❷ *attr* (*supposed*) mutmaßlich
request [rɪ·ˈkwest] **I.** *n* ❶ (*act of asking*) Bitte *f* (**for** um +*akk*), Anfrage *f* (**for** nach +*dat*); **on ~** auf Anfrage [*o* Wunsch] ❷ (*formal entreaty*) Antrag *m*; **to submit a ~ that ...** beantragen, dass ... ❸ RADIO (*requested song*) [Musik]wunsch *m* **II.** *vt* ❶ (*ask for*) ■**to ~ sth** (*form*) um etw *akk* bitten; **as ~ed** wie gewünscht ❷ RADIO (*ask for song*) ■**to ~ sth** [sich *dat*] etw wünschen
requiem [ˈrek·wi·əm], **requiem mass** [ˈrek·wi·əm'-] *n* Requiem *nt*
require [rɪ·ˈkwaɪr] *vt* ❶ (*need*) brauchen; ■**to be ~d for sth** für etw *akk* erforderlich sein; **~d reading** Pflichtlektüre *f* ❷ (*demand*) ■**to ~ sth [of sb]** etw [von jdm] verlangen ❸ (*officially order*) **the rules ~ that ...** die Vorschriften besagen, dass ...
requirement [rɪ·ˈkwaɪr·mənt] *n* Voraussetzung *f* (**for** für +*akk*); **it is a legal ~ that ...** es ist gesetzlich vorgeschrieben, dass ...; **to meet the ~s** die Voraussetzungen erfüllen
requisite [ˈrek·wɪ·zɪt] **I.** *adj attr* (*form*) erforderlich **II.** *n usu pl* Notwendigkeit *f*
requisition [ˌrek·wɪ·ˈzɪʃ·ən] **I.** *vt* beschlagnahmen (**from** von +*dat*) **II.** *n* ❶ (*official request*) Ersuchen *nt*, Aufforderung *f* ❷ (*written request*) Anforderung *f*, Antrag *m* (**for** auf); **to make a ~ for sth** etw anfordern
reroute [ˌri·ˈrut] *vt* umleiten
rerun I. *vt* <-ran, -run> [ˌrɪ·ˈrʌn] wiederholen; *film* noch einmal zeigen; *play* noch einmal aufführen **II.** *n* [ˈri·rʌn] FILM, TV (*repeated program*) Wiederholung *f*
resale [ˈri·seɪl] *n* Wiederverkauf *m*
reschedule [ˌri·ˈskedʒ·ul] *vt* ❶ (*rearrange time*) *date* verschieben; *an event* verlegen ❷ (*postpone payment*) *debts* stunden
rescind [rɪ·ˈsɪnd] *vt esp* LAW (*form*) aufheben; *contract* zurücktreten (von +*dat*)
rescue [ˈres·kju] **I.** *vt* retten; (*free*) befreien; **to ~ sb from danger** jdn aus einer Gefahr retten **II.** *n* Rettung *f*; **to come to sb's ~** jdm zu Hilfe kommen **III.** *adj attempt, helicopter* Rettungs-
ˈrescue company *n* ECON Auffanggesellschaft *f*
ˈrescue package *n* FIN, POL [Euro]rettungsschirm *m*
rescuer [ˈres·kju·ər] *n* Retter(in) *m(f)*
research I. *n* [ˈri·sɜrtʃ] ❶ (*general*) Forschung *f*; (*particular*) Erforschung *f*; **to conduct ~ [into sth]** [etw er]forschen ❷ (*studies*) Untersuchungen *pl* (**about** über +*akk*) **II.** *vi* [rɪ·ˈsɜrtʃ] forschen; ■**to ~ in[to] sth** etw erforschen [*o* untersuchen] **III.** *vt* [rɪ·ˈsɜrtʃ] ❶ SCI erforschen ❷ JOURN recherchieren
researcher [rɪ·ˈsɜrtʃ·ər] *n* Forscher(in) *m(f)*
resemblance [rɪ·ˈzem·bləns] *n* Ähnlichkeit *f*; **to bear a ~ to sb/sth** jdm/etw ähnlich sehen
resemble [rɪ·ˈzem·bəl] *vt* ähneln
resent [rɪ·ˈzent] *vt person, thing* sich [sehr] ärgern (über +*akk*); ■**to ~ doing sth** etw [äußerst] ungern tun
resentful [rɪ·ˈzent·fəl] *adj* ❶ (*feeling resentment*) verbittert, verärgert ❷ (*showing resentment*) nachtragend
resentment [rɪ·ˈzent·mənt] *n* Verbitterung *f*, Groll *m*
reservation [ˌrez·ər·ˈveɪ·ʃən] *n* ❶ TOURIST (*act and result*) Reservierung *f*; **to make a ~** [etw] reservieren ❷ *usu pl* (*doubt*) Bedenken *pl* ❸ (*area of land*) Reservat *nt*
reserve [rɪ·ˈzɜrv] **I.** *n* ❶ (*store*) Reserve *f*, Vorrat *m*; **to put sth on ~ [for sb]** etw [für jdn] reservieren ❷ (*area*) Reservat *nt*; **wildlife ~** Naturschutzgebiet *nt* ❸ SPORTS Ersatzspieler(in) *m(f)* ❹ (*self-restraint*) Reserviertheit *f* **II.** *vt* ❶ (*keep*) aufheben ❷ (*save*) reservieren; **to ~ the right to do sth** sich *dat* das Recht vorbehalten, etw zu tun ❸ (*book*) *room, table, tickets* vorbestellen, reservieren
reserved [rɪ·ˈzɜrvd] *adj* ❶ (*booked*) reserviert ❷ (*restrained*) *person* reserviert; *smile* verhalten
reˈserve price *n* (*at auctions*) Mindestpreis *m*
reservist [rɪ·ˈzɜr·vɪst] *n* MIL Reservist(in) *m(f)*
reservoir [ˈrez·ər·vwar] *n* ❶ (*large lake*) Wasserreservoir *nt* ❷ (*fig: supply*) Reservoir *nt*

R

reset <-tt-, -set, -set> [ˌri·ˈset] *vt* ❶ (*set again*) *clock, a timer* neu stellen ❷ MED *broken bone* [ein]richten ❸ COMPUT neu starten; ~ **button** Resettaste *f*

resettle [ˌri·ˈseṭ·əl] **I.** *vi* sich neu niederlassen **II.** *vt* umsiedeln

residence [ˈrez·ɪ·dəns] *n* ❶ (*form: domicile*) Wohnsitz *m;* **to take up ~ in a country** sich in einem Land niederlassen ❷ (*building*) Wohngebäude *nt; of a monarch* Residenz *f* ❸ UNIV (*for research*) Forschungsaufenthalt *m;* (*for teaching*) Lehraufenthalt *m*

ˈresidence permit *n* Aufenthaltserlaubnis *f*

resident [ˈrez·ɪ·dənt] **I.** *n* (*person living in a place*) Bewohner(in) *m(f);* **local ~** Anwohner(in) *m(f);* **"~s only"** „Anlieger frei" **II.** *adj* ❶ (*residing*) ansässig, wohnhaft; **~ alien** ansässiger Ausländer ❷ (*inherent*) *anxieties* tief sitzend ❸ *attr* (*live-in*) im Haus lebend *nach n* ❹ (*employed in a particular place*) *chef* hauseigen

residential [ˌrez·ɪ·ˈden·ʃəl] *adj* (*housing*) Wohn-; **~ district** Wohngebiet *nt*

residual [rɪ·ˈzɪdʒ·u·əl] *adj* restlich; *opposition* vereinzelt

residue [ˈrez·ə·du] *n usu sing* ❶ (*form: remainder*) Rest *m* ❷ CHEM Rückstand *m*

resign [rɪ·ˈzaɪn] **I.** *vi* (*leave one's job*) kündigen; **to ~ from office** von einem Amt zurücktreten **II.** *vt* ❶ (*give up*) aufgeben; *office, post* niederlegen ❷ (*accept*) **to ~ oneself to a fact** sich mit einer Tatsache abfinden

resignation [ˌrez·ɪg·ˈneɪ·ʃən] *n* ❶ (*official letter*) Kündigung *f* ❷ (*act of resigning*) Kündigung *f; from office, post* Rücktritt *m* ❸ (*acceptance*) Resignation *f*

resigned [rɪ·ˈzaɪnd] *adj* resigniert; ■**to be ~ to sth** sich mit etw *dat* abgefunden haben

resilience [rɪ·ˈzɪl·jəns], **resiliency** [rɪ·ˈzɪl·jən·si] *n* ❶ (*ability to regain shape*) *of material* Elastizität *f* ❷ (*ability to recover*) *of person* Widerstandskraft *f,* Durchhaltevermögen *nt*

resilient [rɪ·ˈzɪl·jənt] *adj* ❶ (*able to keep shape*) *material* elastisch ❷ (*fig: able to survive setbacks*) unverwüstlich, zäh; *health* unverwüstlich

resin [ˈrez·ɪn] *n* Harz *nt*

resist [rɪ·ˈzɪst] **I.** *vt* ❶ (*fight against*) ■**to ~ sth** etw *dat* Widerstand leisten; **to ~ arrest** LAW sich der Verhaftung widersetzen ❷ (*refuse to accept*) ■**to ~ sth** sich gegen etw *akk* wehren, sich etw *dat* widersetzen ❸ (*be unaffected by*) *temptation* widerstehen +*dat* **II.** *vi* ❶ (*fight an attack*) sich wehren ❷ (*refuse sth*) widerstehen

resistance [rɪ·ˈzɪs·təns] *n* ❶ ELEC, PHYS, MIL Widerstand *m* (**to** gegen +*akk*) ❷ (*ability to withstand illness*) Widerstandskraft *f;* **~ to a disease** Resistenz *f* gegen eine Krankheit

resistant [rɪ·ˈzɪs·tənt] *adj* ❶ (*refusing to accept*) ablehnend; ■**to be ~ to sth** etw *dat* ablehnend gegenüberstehen ❷ BIOL, MED resistent (**to** gegen +*akk*)

resistor [rɪ·ˈzɪs·tər] *n* ELEC Widerstand *m*

resolute [ˈrez·ə·lut] *adj* (*form*) entschlossen; *belief, stand* fest; *person* energisch

resolution [ˌrez·ə·ˈlu·ʃən] *n* ❶ (*approv: determination*) Entschlossenheit *f* ❷ (*form: solving*) Lösung *f; of crises* Überwindung *f; of a question* Klärung *f* ❸ (*decision*) Entscheidung *f;* (*intention*) Vorsatz *m;* **New Year's ~** gute Vorsätze fürs Neue Jahr ❹ COMPUT, PHOT, TV (*picture quality*) Auflösung *f*

resolve [rɪ·ˈzalv] **I.** *vt* ❶ (*solve*) lösen ❷ (*settle*) *differences* beilegen; **the crisis ~d itself** die Krise legte sich von selbst ❸ (*form: firmly decide*) ■**to ~ that ...** beschließen, dass ... **II.** *vi* (*firmly decide*) beschließen; ■**to ~ to do sth** beschließen, etw zu tun **III.** *n* Entschlossenheit *f*

resolved [rɪ·ˈzalvd] *adj pred* entschlossen

resonance [ˈrez·ə·nəns] *n* ❶ (*echo*) [Nach]hall *m,* Resonanz *f geh* ❷ (*form: association*) Erinnerung *f*

resonant [ˈrez·ə·nənt] *adj* [wider]hallend; ■**to be ~ with sth** von etw *dat* widerhallen

resonate [ˈrez·ə·neɪt] *vi* ❶ (*resound*) hallen ❷ (*fig: evoke*) ■**to ~ with sth** etw ausstrahlen; (*have effect*) ■**to ~ with sb** bei jdm Echo finden

resort [rɪ·ˈzɔrt] **I.** *n* ❶ (*place for vacations*) Urlaubsort *m* ❷ (*recourse*) Einsatz *m,* Anwendung *f;* **as a last ~** als letzten Ausweg; **you're my last ~!** du bist meine letzte Hoffnung! **II.** *vi* ■**to ~ to sth** auf etw *akk* zurückgreifen, etw anwenden

resound [rɪ·ˈzaʊnd] *vi* ❶ (*resonate*) [wider]hallen ❷ (*fig: cause sensation*) Furore machen; **the rumor ~ed throughout the world** das Gerücht ging um die ganze Welt

resounding [rɪ·ˈzaʊn·dɪŋ] *adj pred* ❶ (*very loud*) schallend ❷ (*emphatic*) unglaublich; *success* durchschlagend

resource [ˈri·sɔrs] **I.** *n* ❶ *usu pl* (*asset*) Ressource *f* ❷ *pl* (*source of supply*) Ressourcen *pl;* **natural ~s** Bodenschätze *pl* ❸ *pl* (*wealth*) [finanzielle] Mittel **II.** *vt* ausstatten

resourceful [rɪ·ˈsɔrs·fəl] *adj* (*approv*) einfallsreich

respect [rɪ·ˈspekt] **I.** *n* ❶ (*esteem*) Respekt *m,* Achtung *f* (**for** vor +*dat*) ❷ (*consideration*) Rücksicht *f;* **to have ~ for sb** Rücksicht auf jdn nehmen; **to have no ~ for sth** etw nicht respektieren ❸ (*form: polite greetings*) **to pay one's ~s [to sb]** jdm einen Besuch abstatten; **to pay one's last ~s to sb** jdm die letzte Ehre erweisen ▶ PHRASES: **in <u>many</u> ~s** in vielen Punkten; **in <u>every</u> ~** in jeglicher Hinsicht **II.** *vt* respektieren; **to ~ sb's decision** jds Entscheidung respektieren

respectable [rɪ·ˈspek·tə·bəl] *adj* ❶ (*decent*) anständig, ehrbar ❷ (*presentable*) anständig, ordentlich ❸ (*acceptable*) *salary, sum* anständig *fam,* ordentlich *fam,* ansehnlich ❹ (*deserving respect*) respektabel; *person* angesehen

respected [rɪ·ˈspek·təd] *adj* angesehen

R

respectful [rɪ·ˈspekt·fəl] *adj* respektvoll; **to be ~ of sth** etw respektieren
respectfully [rɪ·ˈspekt·fə·li] *adv* respektvoll
respective [rɪ·ˈspek·tɪv] *adj attr* jeweilig
respectively [rɪ·ˈspek·tɪv·li] *adv* beziehungsweise
respiration [ˌres·pə·ˈreɪ·ʃən] *n* (*spec*) Atmung *f;* **artificial ~** künstliche Beatmung
respirator [ˈres·pə·reɪ·t̬ər] *n* ❶ MED (*breathing equipment*) Beatmungsgerät *nt* ❷ (*air-filtering mask*) Atem[schutz]gerät *nt*
respiratory [ˈres·pər·ə·tɔr·i] *adj attr* (*form*) Atem-
respite [ˈres·pɪt] *n* (*form: pause*) Unterbrechung *f,* Pause *f;* **the injection provided only a temporary ~ from the pain** die Spritze befreite nur vorübergehend von den Schmerzen
respond [rɪ·ˈspand] **I.** *vt* ■**to ~ that ...** erwidern, dass ... **II.** *vi* ❶ (*answer*) antworten (**to** auf *+akk*) ❷ MED (*react*) *to treatment* reagieren (**to** auf *+akk*)
respondent [rɪ·ˈspan·dənt] *n* ❶ (*person who answers*) Befragte(r) *f(m)* ❷ LAW Angeklagte(r) *f(m)*
response [rɪ·ˈspans] *n* ❶ (*answer*) Antwort *f* (**to** auf *+akk*) ❷ (*act of reaction*) Reaktion *f;* **to meet with a good ~** eine gute Resonanz finden; **in ~ to sth** in Erwiderung auf etw *akk*
responsibility [rɪ·ˌspan·sə·ˈbɪl·ɪ·t̬i] *n* ❶ (*being responsible*) Verantwortung *f* (**for** für *+akk*); **to claim ~ for sth** sich für etw *akk* verantwortlich erklären; **to carry a lot of ~** eine große Verantwortung tragen ❷ (*duty*) Verantwortlichkeit *f,* Zuständigkeit *f*
responsible [rɪ·ˈspan·sə·bəl] *adj* ❶ (*accountable*) verantwortlich (**for** für *+akk*); (*in charge a.*) zuständig; **to hold sb ~** jdn verantwortlich machen; LAW jdn haftbar machen ❷ (*sensible*) verantwortungsbewusst ❸ (*requiring responsibility*) *job, task* verantwortungsvoll
responsive [rɪ·ˈspan·sɪv] *adj* gut reagierend; **to be ~ to treatment** auf eine Behandlungsmethode ansprechen
rest¹ [rest] **I.** *n* ❶ (*period of repose*) [Ruhe]pause *f;* **to have a [little] ~** eine [kurze] Pause machen ❷ (*repose*) Erholung *f;* **for a ~** zur Erholung ❸ (*support*) Stütze *f,* Lehne *f* **II.** *vt* ❶ (*repose*) **to ~ one's eyes** seine Augen ausruhen ❷ (*support*) lehnen **III.** *vi* ❶ (*cease activity*) [aus]ruhen, sich ausruhen; **to not ~ until ...** [so lange] nicht ruhen, bis ... ❷ (*be supported*) ruhen ❸ (*depend on*) ruhen (**on** auf *+dat*); (*be based on*) beruhen (**on** auf *+dat*) ►PHRASES: **[you can] ~ <u>assured</u> [that ...]** seien Sie versichert, dass ...
rest² [rest] *n + sing/pl vb* ■**the ~** der Rest
ˈrest area *n* Rastplatz *m*
restate [ˌri·ˈsteɪt] *vt* noch einmal [mit anderen Worten] sagen
restaurant [ˈres·tər·ant] *n* Restaurant *nt,* Gaststätte *f*
restaurateur [ˌres·tər·ə·ˈtɜr] *n* Gastwirt(in) *m(f)*
restful [ˈrest·fəl] *adj* erholsam; *sound* beruhigend; *atmosphere* entspannt; *place* friedlich
ˈrest home *n* Altersheim *nt*
resting place [ˈres·tɪŋ-] *n* ❶ (*euph: burial place*) **sb's [final] ~** jds [letzte] Ruhestätte ❷ (*place to relax*) Rastplatz *m*
restitution [ˌres·tɪ·ˈtu·ʃən] *n* ❶ (*return*) Rückgabe *f; of sb's rights* Wiederherstellung *f; of money* [Zu]rückerstattung *f* ❷ (*compensation*) Entschädigung *f;* FIN Schaden[s]ersatz *m*
restive [ˈres·tɪv] *adj* (*form*) ❶ (*restless and impatient*) unruhig, nervös ❷ (*stubborn*) widerspenstig
restless [ˈrest·lɪs] *adj* ❶ (*agitated*) unruhig ❷ (*uneasy*) rastlos; **to get ~** anfangen, sich unwohl zu fühlen ❸ (*wakeful*) ruhelos; *night* schlaflos
restock [ˌri·ˈstak] *vt* wieder auffüllen; *lake* wieder mit Fischen besetzen
restoration [ˌres·tə·ˈreɪ·ʃən] *n* ❶ (*act of restoring*) Restaurieren *nt* ❷ (*instance of restoring*) Restaurierung *f* ❸ LAW **~ to the previously held status** Wiedereinsetzung *f* in den vorigen Stand
restorative [rɪ·ˈstɔr·ə·tɪv] *adj* stärkend *attr;* **~ powers [of sth]** (*strengthening*) kräftigende Wirkung [von etw *dat*]; (*healing*) heilende Wirkung [von etw *dat*]
restore [rɪ·ˈstɔr] *vt* ❶ (*renovate*) restaurieren ❷ (*re-establish*) wiederherstellen; **to ~ sb's faith in sth** jdm sein Vertrauen in etw *akk* zurückgeben; **to ~ sb to life** jdn ins Leben zurückbringen ❸ (*reinstate*) **to ~ sb to power** jdn wieder an die Macht bringen
restorer [rɪ·ˈstɔr·ər] *n* ❶ ARCHIT, ART (*person*) Restaurator(in) *m(f)* ❷ **hair ~** Haarwuchsmittel *nt*
restrain [rɪ·ˈstreɪn] *vt* zurückhalten; (*forcefully*) bändigen; ■**to ~ sb from [doing] sth** jdn davon abhalten, etw zu tun; ■**to ~ oneself** sich beherrschen
restrained [rɪ·ˈstreɪnd] *adj* beherrscht; *criticism* verhalten; *manners* gepflegt
restraining order [rɪ·ˈstreɪnɪŋ-] *n* LAW einstweilige Verfügung *fachspr*
restraint [rɪ·ˈstreɪnt] *n* ❶ (*self-control*) Beherrschung *f;* **to exercise ~** Zurückhaltung *f* üben ❷ (*restriction*) Einschränkung *f*
restrict [rɪ·ˈstrɪkt] *vt* ❶ (*limit*) beschränken, einschränken; *number* begrenzen (**to** auf *+akk*) ❷ (*deprive of right*) ■**to ~ sb from [doing] sth** jdm etw untersagen [*o* jdm untersagen, etw *akk* zu tun]
restricted [rɪ·ˈstrɪk·tɪd] *adj* ❶ (*limited*) *choice, vocabulary* begrenzt; *space* eng ❷ (*subject to limitation*) eingeschränkt; *number* beschränkt (**to** auf *+akk*)
restriction [rɪ·ˈstrɪk·ʃən] *n* ❶ (*limit*) Begrenzung *f,* Beschränkung *f,* Einschränkung *f;* **to lift ~s** Restriktionen aufheben ❷ (*action of limiting*) Einschränken *nt*
restrictive [rɪ·ˈstrɪk·tɪv] *adj* (*esp pej*) ein-

R

schränkend, einengend; *measures* restriktiv

'restroom *n* Toilette *f*

restructure [ˌri·'strʌk·tʃər] *vt* umstrukturieren

restructuring [ˌri·'strʌk·tʃər·ɪŋ] *n* Umstrukturierung *f*

result [rɪ·'zʌlt] **I.** *n* ❶ (*consequence*) Folge *f* ❷ (*outcome*) Ergebnis *nt* ❸ (*satisfactory outcome*) Erfolg *m,* Resultat *nt;* **to have good ~s with sth** gute Ergebnisse mit etw *dat* erzielen ❹ MATH *of a calculation, a sum* Resultat *nt,* Ergebnis *nt* **II.** *vi* ❶ (*ensue*) resultieren, sich ergeben ❷ (*cause*) ■**to ~ in sth** etw zur Folge haben

resulting [rɪ·'zʌl·tɪŋ] *adj attr* resultierend *attr,* sich daraus ergebend *attr*

resume [rɪ·'zum] **I.** *vt* (*start again*) wieder aufnehmen; *journey* fortsetzen; ■**to ~ doing sth** fortfahren, etw zu tun **II.** *vi* wieder beginnen; (*after short interruption*) weitergehen

résumé ['rez·u·meɪ] *n* Lebenslauf *m*

resumption [rɪ·'zʌmp·ʃən] *n* ❶ (*act*) *of a game, talks* Wiederaufnahme *f* ❷ (*instance*) Wiederbeginn *m kein pl*

resurface [ˌri·'sɜr·fɪs] **I.** *vi* ❶ (*rise to surface*) *submarine, diver* wieder auftauchen ❷ (*reappear*) wieder zum Vorschein kommen; *memories, topic* wieder aufkommen **II.** *vt* ■**to ~ a road** den Belag einer Straße erneuern

resurgence [rɪ·'sɜr·dʒəns] *n* (*form*) Wiederaufleben *nt*

resurgent [rɪ·'sɜr·dʒənt] *adj usu attr* (*form*) wieder auflebend *attr*

resurrect [ˌrez·ə·'rekt] *vt* ❶ (*revive*) wieder aufleben lassen; *fashion* wieder beleben ❷ (*bring back to life*) *person* auferstehen lassen; *the dead* wieder zum Leben erwecken

resurrection [ˌrez·ə·'rek·ʃən] *n* Wiederbelebung *f*

resuscitate [rɪ·'sʌs·ə·teɪt] *vt* ❶ MED wiederbeleben ❷ (*fig*) [neu] beleben

retail ['ri·teɪl] **I.** *n* Einzelhandel *m,* Detailhandel *m* SCHWEIZ **II.** *vt* im Einzelhandel verkaufen **III.** *vi* **this model of computer ~s for 650 dollars** im Einzelhandel kostet dieses Computermodell 650 Dollar

retailer ['ri·teɪ·lər] *n* Einzelhändler(in) *m(f)*

'retail outlet *n* Einzelhandelsgeschäft *nt*

'retail price *n* Einzelhandelspreis *m*

retain [rɪ·'teɪn] *vt* ❶ (*keep*) behalten; *sb's attention* halten; *dignity, independence* bewahren; **to ~ control of sth** etw weiterhin in der Gewalt haben; **to ~ the right to do sth** LAW sich das Recht vorbehalten, etw zu tun ❷ (*not lose*) speichern; (*remember*) *thought* behalten ❸ (*hold in place*) zurückhalten ❹ LAW *attorney* engagieren

retainer¹ [rɪ·'teɪ·nər] *n* MED (*for teeth*) Zahnspange

retainer² [rɪ·'teɪ·nər] *n* (*fee*) Vorschuss *m*

re'taining wall *n* Stützmauer *f*

retake I. *vt* <-took, -taken> [ˌri·'teɪk] ❶ (*take again*) *exam* wiederholen; (*film again*) *scene* nochmals drehen ❷ (*regain*) wiedergewinnen; **to ~ the lead** SPORTS sich wieder an die Spitze setzen; (*in a race*) wieder die Führung übernehmen **II.** *n* ['ri·teɪk] ❶ (*filming again*) Neuaufnahme *f* ❷ (*exam*) Wiederholungsprüfung *f*

retaliate [rɪ·'tæl·i·eɪt] *vi* Vergeltung üben; *for insults* sich revanchieren

retaliation [rɪ·ˌtæl·i·'eɪ·ʃən] *n* Vergeltung *f;* (*in fighting*) Vergeltungsschlag *m*

retaliatory [rɪ·'tæl·i·ə·tɔr·i] *adj attr* Vergeltungs-

retard¹ [rɪ·'tard] *vt* (*form*) verzögern, verlangsamen; **to ~ economic growth** das Wirtschaftswachstum bremsen

retard² ['ri·tard] *n* (*pej sl*) Idiot *m pej*

retarded [rɪ·'tar·dɪd] *adj* (*pej fam*) zurückgeblieben

retch [retʃ] *vi* würgen; **to make sb ~** jdn zum Würgen bringen

retention [rɪ·'ten·ʃən] *n* ❶ (*keeping*) Beibehaltung *f;* SPORTS *of a title* Verteidigung *f* ❷ (*preservation*) Erhaltung *f; of rights* Wahrung *f* ❸ (*not losing*) Speicherung *f;* MED Retention *f fachspr*

retentive [rɪ·'ten·tɪv] *adj* aufnahmefähig

rethink I. *vt* <-thought, -thought> [ˌri·'θɪŋk] überdenken **II.** *n* ['ri·θɪŋk] Überdenken *nt;* **to have a ~** etw noch einmal überdenken

reticent ['reṭ·ə·sənt] *adj* (*form*) zurückhaltend; (*taciturn*) wortkarg

retina <*pl* -s *or* -nae> ['ret·ən·ə] *n* Netzhaut *f,* Retina *f fachspr*

retinue ['ret·ən·u] *n* Gefolge *nt kein pl*

retire [rɪ·'taɪr] *vi* ❶ (*stop working*) in den Ruhestand treten; *worker* in Rente gehen; *civil servant* in Pension gehen; *self-employed person* sich zur Ruhe setzen; *soldier* aus der Armee ausscheiden; *athlete* seine Karriere beenden ❷ (*form: withdraw*) sich zurückziehen; **the jury ~d to consider their verdict** die Jury zog sich zur Urteilsfindung zurück

retired [rɪ·'taɪ·ərd] *adj* (*no longer working*) im Ruhestand *präd; worker* in Rente *präd; civil servant* pensioniert

retiree [rɪ·taɪ·ə·'ri] *n* Rentner(in) *m(f);* (*for civil servants*) Pensionär(in) *m(f),* Pensionist(in) *m(f)* ÖSTERR

retirement [rɪ·'taɪr·mənt] *n* ❶ (*from job*) Ausscheiden *nt* aus dem Arbeitsleben; *of a civil servant* Pensionierung *f; of a soldier* Verabschiedung *f; of an athlete* Zurücktreten *nt* ❷ (*period after working life*) Ruhestand *m*

re'tirement age *n* (*of a worker*) Rentenalter *nt;* (*of a civil servant*) Pensionsalter *nt;* **to be of ~** im Pensions-/Rentenalter sein

re'tirement plan *n* Vorsorgeplan *m*

retiring [rɪ·'taɪ·ər·ɪŋ] *adj* (*reserved*) zurückhaltend

retort [rɪ·'tɔrt] **I.** *vt* ■**to ~ that ...** scharf erwidern, dass ...; **"no need to be so rude," she ~ed** „kein Grund, so unhöflich zu sein", gab sie zurück **II.** *vi* scharf antworten **III.** *n* scharfe Antwort [*o* Erwiderung]

retouch [ˌri·'tʌtʃ] *vt* PHOT, TYPO retuschieren

retrace [ri·'treɪs] *vt* zurückverfolgen; *in mind*

R

[geistig] nachvollziehen; **to ~ one's steps** denselben Weg zurückgehen

retract [rɪ·ˈtrækt] **I.** *vt* ❶ (*withdraw*) zurückziehen; *offer, statement* zurücknehmen ❷ (*draw back*) zurückziehen; (*into body*) einziehen **II.** *vi* (*be drawn back*) eingezogen werden

retractable [rɪ·ˈtræk·tə·bəl] *adj* einziehbar

retraction [rɪ·ˈtræk·ʃən] *n* (*form*) Zurücknahme *f kein pl*

retrain [ri·ˈtreɪn] **I.** *vt* umschulen **II.** *vi* umgeschult werden

retread **I.** *vt* [ˌri·ˈtred] (*rehash*) neu gestalten **II.** *n* [ˈri·tred] (*fig, pej: film, play*) Abklatsch *m*

retreat [rɪ·ˈtrit] **I.** *vi* ❶ (*move backwards*) zurückweichen; (*become smaller*) *floodwaters* zurückgehen, fallen ❷ (*withdraw*) MIL sich zurückziehen; (*hide*) sich verstecken; ■ **to ~ into oneself** sich in sich selbst zurückziehen **II.** *n* ❶ MIL (*withdrawal*) Rückzug *m* ❷ (*withdrawal*) Abwendung *f,* Abkehr *f* (**from** von +*dat*) ❸ (*private place*) Zufluchtsort *m*

retrench [rɪ·ˈtrentʃ] *vi* (*form*) sich einschränken, sparen

retrenchment [rɪ·ˈtrentʃ·mənt] *n* (*form: financial cut*) Kürzung *f*

retrial [ˈri·traɪl] *n* LAW Wiederaufnahmeverfahren *nt*

retribution [ˌret·rə·ˈbju·ʃən] *n* (*form*) Vergeltung *f*

retrieval [rɪ·ˈtri·vəl] *n* ❶ (*regaining*) Wiedererlangen *nt* ❷ (*rescuing*) Rettung *f;* (*of wreckage*) Bergung *f* ❸ COMPUT **data ~** Datenabruf *m;* (*when lost*) Retrieval *nt fachspr,* Datenrückgewinnung *f*

retrieve [rɪ·ˈtriv] *vt* ❶ (*get back*) wiederfinden ❷ (*fetch*) heraus-/herunter-/zurückholen ❸ (*rescue*) retten; (*from wreckage*) bergen ❹ COMPUT *data* abrufen

retriever [rɪ·ˈtri·vər] *n* Retriever *m*

retro [ˈret·roʊ] *adj* (*fam*) *fashion* Retro-

retroactive [ˌret·roʊ·ˈæk·tɪv] *adj* rückwirkend

retrograde [ˈret·rə·greɪd] *adj* (*form*) *development* rückläufig; **~ step** Rückschritt *m*

retrogressive [ˈret·rə·gres·ɪv] *adj* (*form*) *policy, reforms* rückschrittlich; *development* rückläufig

retrospect [ˈret·rə·spekt] *n* **in ~** im Rückblick [*o* Nachhinein], rückblickend

retrospective [ˌret·rə·ˈspek·tɪv] **I.** *adj* (*looking back*) rückblickend; *mood* nachdenklich **II.** *n* Retrospektive *f*

return [rɪ·ˈtɜrn] **I.** *n* ❶ (*to a place/time*) Rückkehr *f* (**to** zu +*dat*); **~ home** Heimkehr *f* ❷ (*reoccurrence*) *of an illness* Wiederauftreten *nt* ❸ (*giving back*) Rückgabe *f* ❹ SPORTS (*stroke*) Rückschlag *m* ❺ (*proceeds*) Gewinn *m;* **~ on capital** Rendite *f* ❻ (*key on keyboard*) Returntaste *f* **II.** *adj attr postage, flight, trip* Rück- **III.** *vi* ❶ (*go/come back*) zurückkehren, zurückkommen; **to ~ home** (*come back home*) nach Hause kommen; (*go back home*) nach Hause gehen; (*after long absence*) heimkehren; **~ to sender** zurück an Absender ❷ (*reoccur*) *pain, illness* wiederkommen ❸ (*revert to*) ■ **to ~ to sth** etw wieder aufnehmen; **to ~ to normal** *things* sich wieder normalisieren; *person* wieder zu seinem alten Ich zurückfinden **IV.** *vt* ❶ (*give back*) zurückgeben; **to ~ sth to its place** etw an seinen Platz zurückstellen ❷ (*reciprocate*) erwidern; **to ~ a wave** zurückwinken; **to ~ sb's call** jdn zurückrufen ❸ (*place back*) ■ **to ~ sth somewhere** etw irgendwohin zurückstellen [*o* zurücklegen] ❹ TENNIS *volley* annehmen

returnable [rɪ·ˈtɜr·nə·bəl] *adj* ❶ (*recyclable*) wiederverwendbar, Mehrweg- ❷ (*accepted back*) *merchandise* umtauschbar

reˈturn key *n* Eingabetaste *f*

reunification [ri·ˌju·nə·fɪ·ˈkeɪ·ʃən] *n* Wiedervereinigung *f*

reunion [ˌri·ˈjun·jən] *n* ❶ (*gathering*) Treffen *nt,* Zusammenkunft *f* ❷ (*form: bringing together*) Wiedervereinigung *f;* (*coming together*) Wiedersehen *nt*

reunite [ˌri·ju·ˈnaɪt] **I.** *vt* ■ **to ~ sb with sb** jdn mit jdm [wieder] zusammenbringen; *family* wieder zusammenführen **II.** *vi* sich wiedervereinigen; *people* wieder zusammenkommen

reusable [ˌri·ˈju·zə·bəl] *adj* wiederverwendbar

reuse [ˌri·ˈjuz] *vt* (*use again*) wiederverwenden

rev¹ [rev] *n* (*fam*) *short for* **revolution** Drehzahl *f;* ■ **~s** *pl* Umdrehungen *pl* [pro Minute]

rev² <-vv-> [rev] *vt engine* auf Touren bringen; (*noisily*) aufheulen lassen

Rev. *n abbrev of* **Reverend**

◆**rev up** **I.** *vi engine* auf Touren kommen; (*make noise*) aufheulen; (*fig*) *person* aufdrehen **II.** *vt engine, motorcycle* auf Touren bringen; *person* anfeuern

revaluation [ri·ˌvæl·jʊ·ˈeɪ·ʃən] *n* ❶ (*new valuation*) Neubewertung *f* ❷ FIN (*change in value*) *of a currency* Aufwertung *f*

revalue [ri·ˈvæl·ju] *vt* neu bewerten; *an asset* neu schätzen lassen; *currency* aufwerten

revamp [ˌri·ˈvæmp] *vt* (*fam*) aufpeppen; *room* aufmöbeln; *image* aufpolieren

reveal [rɪ·ˈvil] *vt* ❶ (*allow to be seen*) zeigen, zum Vorschein bringen ❷ (*disclose*) enthüllen, offenlegen; *secret* verraten; ■ **to ~ that ...** enthüllen, dass ...; (*admit*) zugeben, dass ...; *sb's identity* zu erkennen geben

revealing [rɪ·ˈvi·lɪŋ] *adj* ❶ (*displaying body*) freizügig; *dress* gewagt ❷ (*divulging sth*) *comment, interview* aufschlussreich

revel <-l- *or* -ll-> [ˈrev·əl] *vi* feiern

◆**revel in** *vi* ■ **to ~ in sth** seine wahre Freude an etw *dat* haben

revelation [ˌrev·ə·ˈleɪ·ʃən] *n* ❶ (*act of revealing*) Enthüllung *f,* Aufdeckung *f* ❷ (*sth revealed*) Enthüllung *f* ▸ PHRASES: **to be [quite] a ~ to sb** jdm die Augen öffnen

reveler, reveller [ˈrev·əl·ər] *n* Feiernde(r) *f(m)*

revelry [ˈrev·əl·ri] *n* ❶ (*noisy merrymaking*) [ausgelassenes] Feiern ❷ *usu pl* (*festivity*) [ausgelassene] Feier

revenge [rɪ·ˈvendʒ] **I.** *n* ❶ (*retaliation*) Rache *f;* **to get one's ~** sich rächen; **~ killing** Vergeltungsmord *m* ❷ (*desire for retaliation*) Rachedurst *m* **II.** *vt* rächen

revenue [ˈrev·ə·nu] *n* ❶ (*income*) Einkünfte *pl* (**from** aus +*dat*) ❷ (*of a state*) öffentliche Einnahmen, Staatseinkünfte *pl* ❸ *pl* (*instances of income*) **sales ~s** Verkaufseinnahmen *pl;* **tax ~s** Steueraufkommen *nt*

reverberate [rɪ·ˈvɜr·bə·reɪt] *vi* ❶ (*echo*) widerhallen, nachhallen; ■**to ~ through[out] sth** durch etw *akk* [hindurch]hallen ❷ (*be recalled*) **his terrible childhood experiences ~d throughout his entire life** die schlimmen Kindheitserfahrungen wirkten sein ganzes Leben lang nach

reverberation [rɪ·ˌvɜr·bə·ˈreɪ·ʃən] *n* (*form*) ❶ (*echoing*) Widerhallen *nt,* Nachhallen *nt* ❷ *usu pl* (*long-lasting effects*) Nachwirkungen *pl*

revere [rɪ·ˈvɪr] *vt* (*form*) verehren, achten; *sb's work* hoch schätzen

reverence [ˈrev·ər·əns] *n* Verehrung *f* (**for** für +*akk*); **to treat sth/sb with ~** etw/jdn ehrfürchtig behandeln

reverend [ˈrev·ər·ənd] *n* ≈ Pfarrer *m,* ≈ Pastor *m*

reverent [ˈrev·ər·ənt] *adj* ehrfürchtig, ehrfurchtsvoll; *behavior* ehrerbietig

reverential [ˌrev·ə·ˈren·ʃəl] *adj* (*form*) ehrfürchtig, ehrfurchtsvoll

reverie [ˈrev·ə·ri] *n* (*liter: daydream*) Träumerei *f* (**about** über +*akk*)

reversal [rɪ·ˈvɜr·səl] *n* ❶ (*changing effect*) Wende *f;* **~ of a trend** Trendwende *f* ❷ (*changing situation*) Umkehrung *f;* **role ~** Rollentausch *m* ❸ (*misfortune*) Rückschlag *m*

reverse [rɪ·ˈvɜrs] **I.** *vt* ❶ (*change to opposite*) umkehren ❷ (*turn sth over*) umdrehen; *coat* wenden ❸ (*move sth backwards*) *car* zurücksetzen **II.** *vi* (*move backwards*) rückwärtsfahren; (*short distance*) zurücksetzen **III.** *n* ❶ (*opposite*) ■**the ~** das Gegenteil; **to do sth in ~** etw umgekehrt tun ❷ (*gear*) Rückwärtsgang *m;* **to go into ~** in den Rückwärtsgang schalten; (*fig*) rückläufig sein ❸ (*back*) Rückseite *f; of a coin, medal a.* Kehrseite *f* **IV.** *adj* umgekehrt; *direction* entgegengesetzt

reversible [rɪ·ˈvɜr·sə·bəl] *adj* ❶ (*usable inside out*) zum Wenden *nach n;* **~ coat** Wendejacke *f* ❷ (*alterable*) umkehrbar

reversion [rɪ·ˈvɜr·ʒən] *n* (*form: return to earlier position*) Umkehr *f* (**to** zu +*dat*); (*to bad state*) Rückfall (**to** in +*akk*)

revert [rɪ·ˈvɜrt] *vi* (*go back*) ■**to ~ to sth** zu etw *dat* zurückkehren; *bad state* in etw *akk* zurückfallen; **to ~ to a method** auf eine Methode zurückgreifen

review [rɪ·ˈvju] **I.** *vt* ❶ (*examine*) [erneut] [über]prüfen; (*reconsider*) überdenken; *salaries* revidieren ❷ (*look back over*) auf etw *akk* zurückblicken; **let's ~ what has happened so far** führen wir uns vor Augen, was bis jetzt passiert ist; SCH, UNIV *lesson, subject matter* [Lernstoff] wiederholen ❸ (*produce a criticism*) besprechen; *book, film, play* rezensieren ❹ MIL **to ~ the troops** eine Parade abnehmen **II.** *vi* SCH, UNIV (*for an exam*) lernen **III.** *n* ❶ (*assessment*) Überprüfung *f;* **to come under ~** überprüft werden; LAW *case* wieder aufgenommen werden ❷ (*summary*) Überblick *m* (**of** über +*akk*); **month under ~** ECON Berichtsmonat *m;* **wage** [*or* **salary**] **~** Gehaltsrevision *f;* SCH, UNIV *of lesson, subject matter* Wiederholung *f* [des Lernstoffs]; **~ for an exam** Prüfungsvorbereitung *f* ❸ (*criticism*) *of a book, play* Kritik *f,* Rezension *f;* **movie ~** Filmbesprechung *f*

reviewer [rɪ·ˈvju·ər] *n* Kritiker(in) *m(f); of plays, literature a.* Rezensent(in) *m(f)*

revise [rɪ·ˈvaɪz] *vt* ❶ (*redo*) umändern; *manuscript* überarbeiten; *book* redigieren ❷ (*reconsider*) überdenken ❸ (*increase/decrease*) ■**to ~ sth upwards/downwards** *estimates, numbers* etw nach oben/unten korrigieren

revision [rɪ·ˈvɪʒ·ən] *n* ❶ (*act of revising*) Revision *f,* Überarbeitung *f* ❷ (*reconsidered version*) Neufassung *f; of a book* überarbeitete Ausgabe ❸ (*alteration*) Änderung *f*

revisionist [rɪ·ˈvɪʒ·ə·nɪst] POL **I.** *n* Revisionist(in) *m(f)* **II.** *adj* revisionistisch

revitalize [ri·ˈvaɪ·t̬ə·laɪz] *vt person* neu beleben; *trade* wieder beleben

revival [rɪ·ˈvaɪ·vəl] *n* ❶ (*restoration to life*) Wiederbelebung *f* ❷ (*coming back of an idea*) Wiederaufleben *f,* Come-back *nt; of a custom, fashion a.* Renaissance *f;* **economic ~** wirtschaftlicher Aufschwung ❸ (*new production*) Neuauflage *f; of a film* Neuverfilmung *f; of a play* Neuaufführung *f*

revive [rɪ·ˈvaɪv] **I.** *vt* ❶ (*bring back to life*) wiederbeleben ❷ (*give new energy*) beleben ❸ (*resurrect*) wieder aufleben lassen; *economy* ankurbeln; *idea* wieder aufgreifen; *interest* wieder erwecken; *spirits* wieder heben; **to ~ sb's hopes** jdm neue Hoffnungen machen **II.** *vi* ❶ (*be restored to consciousness*) wieder zu sich *dat* kommen ❷ (*be restored to health*) *person, animal, plant* sich erholen ❸ (*be resurrected*) sich erholen; *economy a.* wieder aufblühen; *custom, tradition* wieder aufleben; *confidence, hopes* zurückkehren; *suspicions* wieder aufkeimen

revoke [rɪ·ˈvoʊk] *vt* (*form*) aufheben; *decision* widerrufen; *license* entziehen

revolt [rɪ·ˈvoʊlt] **I.** *vi* rebellieren, revoltieren **II.** *vt* ■**to ~ sb** jdn abstoßen; ■**to be ~ed by sth** von etw *dat* angeekelt sein **III.** *n* (*rebellion*) Revolte *f,* Aufstand *m;* **~ against the government** Regierungsputsch *m*

revolting [rɪ·ˈvoʊl·tɪŋ] *adj* abstoßend; *person* widerlich; *smell* ekelhaft

revolution [ˌrev·ə·ˈlu·ʃən] *n* ❶ (*a. fig: overthrow*) Revolution *f* ❷ TECH Umdrehung *f;* **~s per minute** Drehzahl *f,* Umdrehungen *pl* pro Minute

R

revolutionary [ˌrev·ə·ˈlu·ʃə·ner·i] **I.** *n* Revolutionär(in) *m(f)* **II.** *adj* revolutionär *a. fig;* (*fig*) bahnbrechend
revolutionize [ˌrev·ə·ˈlu·ʃə·naɪz] *vt* revolutionieren
revolve [rɪ·ˈvalv] *vi* sich drehen; **to ~ on an axis** sich um eine Achse drehen
◆**revolve around** *vi* (*a. fig*) ■**to ~ around sth** sich um etw *akk* drehen
revolver [rɪ·ˈval·vər] *n* Revolver *m*
revolving [rɪ·ˈval·vɪŋ] *adj attr* rotierend, Dreh-; **~ door** Drehtür *f*
revue [rɪ·ˈvju] *n* Revue *f*
revulsion [rɪ·ˈvʌl·ʃən] *n* Abscheu *f*
reward [rɪ·ˈwɔrd] **I.** *n* Belohnung *f; for merit, service* Anerkennung *f* (**for** für +*akk*); (*for return of sth lost*) Finderlohn *m* **II.** *vt* belohnen
rewarding [rɪˈwɔr·dɪŋ] *adj* befriedigend; *experience* lohnend; *task* dankbar
rewind I. *vt* <-wound, -wound> [ˌri·ˈwaɪnd] *cable* aufwickeln; *cassette, tape* zurückspulen; *watch* aufziehen **II.** *vi* <-wound, -wound> [ˌri·ˈwaɪnd] *cassette, tape* zurückspulen **III.** *n* [ˈri·waɪnd] *of a cassette, tape* Zurückspulen *nt* **IV.** *adj* [ˈri·waɪnd] *button, control* Rückspul-
rewire [ˌri·ˈwaɪr] *vt building, house* neu verkabeln
reword [ˌri·ˈwɜrd] *vt* umschreiben, umformulieren; *contract* neu abfassen
rework [ˌri·ˈwɜk] *vt* überarbeiten; *speech* umschreiben
rewrite <-wrote, -written> **I.** *vt* [ˌri·ˈraɪt] neu schreiben; (*revise*) überarbeiten; (*recast*) umschreiben; **to ~ history** (*fig*) die Geschichte neu schreiben **II.** *n* [ˈri·raɪt] Überarbeitung *f*
rhapsody [ˈræp·sə·di] *n* (*piece of music*) Rhapsodie *f*
rhetoric [ˈreṭ·ər·ɪk] *n* ❶ (*persuasive language*) Redegewandtheit *f* ❷ (*bombastic language*) Phrasendrescherei *f pej;* **empty ~** leere Worte
rhetorical [rɪ·ˈtɔr·ɪ·kəl] *adj* ❶ (*relating to rhetoric*) rhetorisch ❷ (*overdramatic*) *gesture* übertrieben dramatisch
rheumatic [ru·ˈmæṭ·ɪk] *adj* rheumatisch; *joint a.* rheumakrank
rheumatism [ˈru·mə·tɪz·əm] *n* Rheuma *nt,* Rheumatismus *m*
rheumatoid arthritis [ˌru·mə·tɔɪd·ˌar·ˈθraɪ·ṭɪs] *n* rheumatoide Arthritis
Rhine [raɪn] *n* GEOG ■**the ~** der Rhein
rhino [ˈraɪ·noʊ] *n* (*fam*) *short for* **rhinoceros** Nashorn *nt,* Rhinozeros *nt*
rhinoceros <*pl* -es *or* -> [raɪ·ˈnas·ər·əs] *n* Nashorn *nt,* Rhinozeros *nt*
Rhode Island [ˌroʊd·ˈaɪ·ləd] *n* Rhode Island *nt*
Rhodes [roʊdz] *n* Rhodos *nt*
rhombus <*pl* -es *or* -bi> [ˈram·bəs] *n* Rhombus *m,* Raute *f*
rhubarb [ˈru·barb] *n* Rhabarber *m*
rhyme [raɪm] **I.** *n* ❶ (*identity in sound*) Reim *m;* ■**in ~** gereimt, in Reimform ❷ (*poem*) Reim[vers] *m* ❸ (*word*) Reimwort *nt* **II.** *vi* ■**to ~** [**with sth**] *poem, song, words* sich [auf etw *akk*] reimen **III.** *vt* reimen
rhyming [ˈraɪ·mɪŋ] *adj* Reim-
rhythm [ˈrɪð·əm] *n* Rhythmus *m,* Takt *m*
rhythmic(al) [ˈrɪð·mɪk(əl)] *adj* rhythmisch
RI, R.I. *abbrev of* **Rhode Island**
rib [rɪb] **I.** *n* ❶ *of body* Rippe *f;* **to break a ~** sich *dat* eine Rippe brechen ❷ FOOD ■**~s** Rippchen *pl* **II.** *vt* <-bb-> (*fam*) ■**to ~ sb** jdn aufziehen
ribbon [ˈrɪb·ən] *n* ❶ (*strip of fabric*) Band *nt;* (*fig*) Streifen *m* ❷ (*rag*) ■**in ~s** in Fetzen; **to cut sb/sth to ~s** jdn/etw zerfetzen; (*fig*) jdn/etw in der Luft zerreißen
ˈrib cage *n* Brustkorb *m*
rice [raɪs] *n* Reis *m;* **brown ~** Naturreis *m*
ˈrice paddy *n* Reisfeld *nt*
rich [rɪtʃ] **I.** *adj* ❶ (*wealthy*) reich; **to get ~ quick** schnell zu Reichtum kommen ❷ (*abounding*) reich (**in** an +*dat*); **~ in detail** sehr detailliert ❸ (*very fertile*) *land* fruchtbar; *earth, soil a.* fett; *vegetation* üppig ❹ (*opulent*) *furniture* prachtvoll ❺ (*valuable*) *reward* großzügig ❻ (*of food*) gehaltvoll; (*hard to digest*) schwer ❼ (*intense*) *color* satt; *flavor* reich; *smell* schwer; *taste, tone* voll ❽ (*interesting*) reich; *life a.* erfüllt; *history* bedeutend **II.** *n* ■**the ~** *pl* die Reichen *pl*
richness [ˈrɪtʃ·nɪs] *n* ❶ (*wealth*) Reichtum *m;* **~ of detail** (*fig*) Detailgenauigkeit *f* ❷ (*fattiness*) Reichhaltigkeit *f* ❸ (*intensity*) Stärke *f; of a color* Sattheit *f*
rickets [ˈrɪk·ɪts] *npl + sing/pl vb* MED Rachitis *f*
rickety [ˈrɪk·ɪ·ṭi] *adj* (*likely to collapse*) wack[e]lig; *wooden stairs* morsch
ricksha(w) [ˈrɪk·ʃa, -ʃɔ] *n* Rikscha *f*
ricochet [ˈrɪk·ə·ʃeɪ] **I.** *n* ❶ (*action*) Abprallen *nt kein pl,* Abprall *m kein pl* ❷ (*rebounding ball*) Abpraller *m;* (*rebounding bullet*) Querschläger *m* **II.** *vi* abprallen (**off** von +*dat*)
rid <-dd-, rid, rid> [rɪd] *vt* ■**to ~ sth/sb of sth** etw/jdn von etw *dat* befreien; ■**to be ~ of sb/sth** jdn/etw los sein; **to get ~ of sb/sth** jdn/etw loswerden
riddance [ˈrɪd·əns] *n* Loswerden *nt* ▶ PHRASES: **good ~** [**to sth**] Gott sei Dank[, dass wir den/die/das los sind]
ridden [ˈrɪd·ən] *pp of* **ride**
riddle¹ [ˈrɪd·əl] *vt usu passive* (*perforate*) durchlöchern; (*fig: permeate*) durchdringen
riddle² [ˈrɪd·əl] **I.** *n* Rätsel *nt a. fig* **II.** *vi* in Rätseln sprechen
ride [raɪd] **I.** *n* ❶ (*trip*) Fahrt *f* (**on** mit +*dat*); (*on a horse*) Ritt *m;* **to go for a ~** eine Fahrt machen; (*with horse*) ausreiten ❷ (*lift*) Mitfahrgelegenheit *f;* **to give sb a ~** jdn [im Auto] mitnehmen ❸ (*at amusement park*) **carousel ~** Karussellfahrt *f* ▶ PHRASES: **to take sb for a ~** (*fam*) jdn übers Ohr hauen **II.** *vt* <rode, ridden> ❶ (*sit on*) *bicycle, motorcycle* fahren; *horse* reiten; **I ~ my bicycle to work** ich fahre mit dem Fahrrad zur Arbeit ❷ (*as a passenger*) **to ~ the bus/train** Bus/Zug fah-

R

ren ❸ (*prevent blow*) **to ~ a punch** einen Schlag abfangen **III.** *vi* <rode, ridden> ❶ (*as a sport, travel on animal*) reiten ❷ (*travel on vehicle*) fahren

◆**ride out** *vt* überstehen; *crisis* durchstehen

◆**ride up** *vi T-shirt, skirt* hochrutschen

rider ['raɪ·dər] *n* ❶ *of a horse* Reiter(in) *m(f); of a vehicle* Fahrer(in) *m(f)* ❷ (*form: amendment*) Zusatzklausel *f*

ridge [rɪdʒ] *n* ❶ GEOG Grat *m* ❷ *of a roof* Dachfirst *m* ❸ METEO **~ of high/low pressure** Hoch-/Tiefdruckkeil *m*

ridicule ['rɪd·ɪ·kjul] **I.** *n* Spott *m*, Hohn *m;* **to hold sth up to ~** sich über etw lustig machen **II.** *vt* verspotten

ridiculous [rɪ·'dɪk·jʊ·ləs] **I.** *adj* ❶ (*comical*) lächerlich, albern ❷ (*inane*) absurd **II.** *n* ■**the ~** das Absurde

rife [raɪf] *adj pred* ❶ (*widespread*) weit verbreitet ❷ (*full of*) **~ with** voller *+gen*

riffle ['rɪf·əl] **I.** *vt* ❶ (*leaf through*) durchblättern ❷ (*ruffle slightly*) *hair* zerzausen **II.** *vi* **to ~ through a book** ein Buch durchblättern

riffraff ['rɪf·ræf] *n + sing/pl vb* (*pej*) Gesindel *nt kein pl*

rifle[1] ['raɪ·fəl] *n* (*gun*) Gewehr *nt*

rifle[2] ['raɪ·fəl] **I.** *vi* (*search*) durchwühlen **II.** *vt* (*ransack*) plündern

'**rifle butt** *n* Gewehrkolben *m*

'**rifleman** *n* Schütze *m*

'**rifle range** *n* (*for practice*) Schießstand *m*

rift [rɪft] *n* ❶ (*open space*) Spalt *m* ❷ GEOL [Erd]spalt *m* ❸ (*fig: disagreement*) Spaltung *f* (**between** zwischen *+dat*); (*in friendship*) Bruch *m*

rig [rɪg] **I.** *n* ❶ NAUT Takelage *f* ❷ (*apparatus*) Vorrichtung *f* ❸ TECH **drilling ~** Bohrinsel *f;* **gas/oil ~** Gas-/Ölbohrinsel *f* ❹ TRANSP (*tractor-trailer*) **big ~** [mehrachsiger] Sattelschlepper **II.** *vt* <-gg-> ❶ NAUT *boat* takeln; *sails, shrouds, stays* anschlagen *fachspr* ❷ (*set up*) [behelfsmäßig] zusammenbauen ❸ (*manipulate*) *results, prices* manipulieren

rigamarole ['rɪg·ə·mə·roʊl] *n see* **rigmarole**

rigger ['rɪg·ər] *n* ❶ NAUT Takeler(in) *m(f)* ❷ (*on oil rig*) **oil ~** Arbeiter(in) *m(f)* auf einer Bohrinsel

rigging ['rɪg·ɪŋ] *n* ❶ NAUT (*action*) Auftakeln *nt;* (*ropes and wires*) Takelung *f* ❷ POL (*manipulation*) Manipulation *f;* **ballot-~** Wahlmanipulation *f*

right [raɪt] **I.** *adj* ❶ (*morally good*) richtig; (*fair*) gerecht; **to do the ~ thing** das Richtige tun; **you're ~ to be annoyed** du bist zu Recht verärgert ❷ (*correct*) richtig; *time* genau; **to get sth ~** etw richtig machen; **you were ~ about him** was ihn angeht haben Sie Recht gehabt; **to be just ~** (*fam*) genau das Richtige sein ❸ (*interrogatory*) oder, richtig ❹ (*best*) richtig; **he's the ~ person for the job** er ist der Richtige für den Job; **to be in the ~ place at the ~ time** zur rechten Zeit am rechten Ort sein ❺ *pred* (*working correctly*) in Ordnung; **is your watch ~?** geht deine Uhr richtig? ❻ (*not left*) *a.* POL rechte(r, s); **to make a ~ turn** rechts abbiegen **II.** *adv* ❶ (*completely*) völlig, ganz; **she walked ~ past me** sie lief direkt an mir vorbei; **to be ~ behind sb** voll [und ganz] hinter jdm stehen ❷ (*all the way*) ganz; (*directly*) genau, direkt ❸ (*well*) gut; **things have been going ~ for me** es läuft gut für mich ❹ (*not left*) rechts; **to turn ~** [nach] rechts abbiegen **III.** *n* ❶ (*goodness*) Recht *nt* ❷ (*morally correct thing*) das Richtige; **the ~s and wrongs of sth** das Für und Wider einer S. *gen* ❸ (*claim, entitlement*) Recht *nt;* **~ of** [*or* **to**] **free speech** Recht *nt* auf freie Meinungsäußerung; **women's ~s** die Rechte *pl* der Frau[en] ❹ (*right side*) rechte Seite; **on the ~** rechts, auf der rechten Seite; **on my/her ~** rechts [von mir/ihr] ❺ POL ■**the R~** die Rechte; **the far ~** die Rechtsextremen *pl* **IV.** *vt* ❶ (*correct position*) aufrichten; (*correct condition*) in Ordnung bringen ❷ (*rectify*) *mistake, wrong* wiedergutmachen **V.** *interj* (*fam*) ❶ (*okay*) in Ordnung, okay *fam;* **~ you are!** in Ordnung! ❷ (*as introduction*) **~, let's go** also, nichts wie los *fam*

'**right angle** *n* rechter Winkel

'**right away** *adv* sofort, auf der Stelle; **we have to leave ~ away** wir müssen unverzüglich aufbrechen

righteous ['raɪ·tʃəs] (*form*) **I.** *adj* ❶ (*virtuous*) *person* rechtschaffen ❷ (*justifiable*) *anger, indignation* berechtigt, gerechtfertigt **II.** *n* ■**the ~** *pl* die Gerechten *pl*

rightful ['raɪt·fəl] *adj attr* rechtmäßig

'**right-hand** *adj attr* ❶ (*on the right*) rechte(r, s) ❷ (*with the right hand*) mit der Rechten nach *n;* **~ punch** rechter Haken

right-'handed *adj* rechtshändig

right-'hander *n* (*person*) Rechtshänder(in) *m(f)*

right-hand 'man *n* (*fig, approv*) ■**sb's ~** jds rechte Hand *fig*

rightly ['raɪt·li] *adv* ❶ (*correctly*) richtig ❷ (*justifiably*) zu Recht

right-'minded *adj* (*approv*) vernünftig

right of 'way <*pl* rights-> *n* ❶ (*right to pass*) Durchgangsrecht *nt* ❷ AUTO, AVIAT, NAUT Vorfahrt *f*

right-'wing *adj* rechts *präd,* rechte(r, s)

rigid ['rɪdʒ·ɪd] *adj* ❶ (*inflexible*) starr, steif ❷ (*fig: unalterable*) *routine, rules* starr; (*overly stringent*) streng, hart

rigidity [rɪ·'dʒɪd·ɪ·t̬i] *n* ❶ (*inflexibility*) Starrheit *f,* Steifheit *f; of concrete* Härte *f* ❷ (*fig, pej: intransigence*) Starrheit *f,* Unbeugsamkeit *f*

rigmarole ['rɪg·mə·roʊl] *n usu sing* (*pej*) ❶ (*rambling story*) Gelabere *nt pej* ❷ (*procedures*) Prozedur *f*

rigor ['rɪg·ər] *n* ❶ (*approv: thoroughness*) Genauigkeit *f,* Präzision *f* ❷ (*strictness*) Strenge *f,* Härte *f*

rigor mortis [ˌrɪg·ər·'mɔr·t̬ɪs] *n* Leichenstarre *f*

rigorous ['rɪg·ər·əs] *adj* ❶ (*approv: thorough*) [peinlich] genau, präzise ❷ (*disciplined*) strikt, streng ❸ (*physically demanding*) hart

rile [raɪl] *vt* (*fam*) ❶ (*annoy*) ärgern; **to get sb ~d** jdn verärgern ❷ (*stir up*) *water* verschmutzen

rim [rɪm] **I.** *n* ❶ (*brim, boundary*) *of a cup, plate* Rand *m;* **on the Pacific R~** am Rande des Pazifiks ❷ *of a wheel* Felge *f* ❸ *usu pl* (*spectacle frames*) Fassung *f* **II.** *vt* <-mm-> umgeben; (*frame*) umrahmen

rimless ['rɪm·lɪs] *adj* randlos

rind [raɪnd] *n* Schale *f;* **[grated] lemon ~** [geriebene] Zitronenschale

ring¹ [rɪŋ] **I.** *n* ❶ (*jewelry, circular object*) Ring *m* ❷ (*circle of people/objects*) Kreis *m* ❸ (*clique*) Kartell *nt,* Syndikat *nt;* **spy ~** Spionagering *m* **II.** *vt usu passive* umringen

ring² [rɪŋ] **I.** *n* ❶ (*act of sounding bell*) Klingeln *nt kein pl;* (*sound made a.*) Läuten *nt kein pl* ❷ (*loud sound*) Klirren *nt kein pl* ❸ *usu sing* (*telephone call*) **to give sb a ~** jdn anrufen ❹ *usu sing* (*quality*) Klang *m;* **your name has a familiar ~** Ihr Name kommt mir bekannt vor **II.** *vi* <rang, rung> ❶ (*produce bell sound*) *telephone* klingeln, läuten ❷ (*have humming sensation*) *ears* klingen ❸ (*reverberate*) **the room rang with laughter** der Raum war von Lachen erfüllt **III.** *vt* <rang, rung> (*make sound*) *bell* läuten

◆**ring out I.** *vi* ertönen **II.** *vt* ausläuten

◆**ring up** *vt* COMM *amount* [in die Kasse] eintippen

'**ring binder** *n* Ringbuch *nt*

ringer ['rɪŋ·ər] *n* ❶ SPORTS (*sl*) *Spieler, der unerlaubt an einem Wettkampf teilnimmt oder gegen das Reglement eingewechselt wird;* (*in horseracing*) Ringer *m* (*vertauschtes Pferd*) ❷ (*person*) Glöckner(in) *m(f)* ▶ PHRASES: **to be a dead ~ for sb** jdm aufs Haar gleichen

'**ring finger** *n* Ringfinger *m*

ringing ['rɪŋ·ɪŋ] **I.** *adj attr* ❶ (*resounding*) schallend; **~ cheer** lauter Jubel ❷ (*unequivocal*) eindringlich **II.** *n* Klingeln *nt*

'**ringleader** *n* Anführer(in) *m(f)*

ringlet ['rɪŋ·lɪt] *n usu pl* Locke *f*

'**ringside** *n* (*in boxing*) Sitzreihe *f* am Boxring; (*in a circus*) Sitzreihe an der Manege; **~ seat** (*in boxing*) Ringplatz *m;* (*in a circus*) Manegenplatz *m*

'**ring tone** *n* Klingelton *m*

'**ringworm** *n* MED Flechte *f*

rink [rɪŋk] *n* Bahn *f;* **ice ~** Eisbahn *f*

rinse [rɪns] **I.** *n* ❶ (*action*) Spülung *f;* **to give a bottle a ~** eine Flasche ausspülen; **to give clothes a ~** Kleidungsstücke spülen ❷ (*for mouth*) Mundspülung *f* ❸ (*conditioner*) [Haar]spülung *f;* (*for tinting hair*) Tönung *f* **II.** *vt* spülen; *hands* abspülen; *mouth* ausspülen **III.** *vi* spülen

riot ['raɪ·ət] **I.** *n* ❶ (*disturbance*) Krawall *m,* Unruhen *pl;* (*uproar*) Aufstand *m a. fig* ❷ (*fig, approv: display*) **a ~ of color[s]** eine Farbenpracht ▶ PHRASES: **to run ~** (*behave uncontrollably*) *people* Amok laufen; *emotions* verrücktspielen; (*spread uncontrollably*) **my imagination ran ~** die Fantasie ist mit mir durchgegangen **II.** *vi* ❶ (*act violently*) randalieren ❷ (*fig: behave uncontrollably*) wild feiern

rioter ['raɪ·ə·t̬ər] *n* Aufständische(r) *f(m)*

'**riot gear** *n* Schutzanzug *m*

rioting ['raɪ·ə·t̬ɪŋ] *n* Randalieren *nt,* Krawalle *pl*

riotous ['raɪ·ə·t̬əs] *adj* ❶ (*involving disturbance*) aufständisch ❷ (*boisterous*) ausschweifend; *party* wild ❸ (*vivid*) **a ~ display** eine hemmungslose Zurschaustellung

'**riot police** *n + sing/pl vb* Bereitschaftspolizei *f*

rip [rɪp] **I.** *n* ❶ (*tear*) Riss *m* ❷ *usu sing* (*act*) Zerreißen *nt;* (*with knife*) Zerschlitzen *nt* **II.** *vt* <-pp-> zerreißen; **to ~ sth [in]to shreds** etw zerfetzen; **to ~ sth open** etw aufreißen; (*with knife*) etw aufschlitzen **III.** *vi* <-pp-> (*tear*) reißen; *seams of clothing* platzen

◆**rip off** *vt* ❶ (*fam: overcharge*) ■**to ~ off** ↻ **sb** jdn übers Ohr hauen ❷ (*fam: steal*) mitgehen lassen; *ideas* klauen ❸ (*take off fast*) abreißen

◆**rip out** *vt* herausreißen

◆**rip up** *vt* zerreißen; **to ~ the carpets up** den Teppichboden herausreißen

RIP [ˌar·aɪ·'pi] *abbrev of* **rest in peace** R.I.P.

ripe [raɪp] *adj* ❶ (*ready to eat*) *fruit, grain* reif ❷ (*matured*) *cheese, wine* ausgereift ❸ (*intense*) *flavor, smell* beißend ❹ *pred* (*prepared*) ■**to be ~ for sth** reif für etw *akk* sein ❺ *attr* (*advanced*) fortgeschritten; **to live to a ~ old age** ein hohes Alter erreichen

ripen ['raɪ·pən] **I.** *vi* [heran]reifen *a. fig* **II.** *vt fruit* reifen lassen

ripeness ['raɪp·nɪs] *n* Reife *f*

'**rip-off** *n* (*fam*) Wucher *m kein pl pej;* (*fraud*) Schwindel *m,* Beschiss *m kein pl derb;* **that's just a ~ of my idea!** da hat doch bloß einer meine Idee geklaut! *fam*

riposte [rɪ·'poʊst] *n* (*usu approv liter: reply*) [schlagfertige] Antwort

ripple ['rɪp·əl] **I.** *n* ❶ (*in water*) leichte Welle ❷ (*sound*) Raunen *nt kein pl;* **a ~ of laughter** ein leises Lachen ❸ (*feeling*) Schauer *m* ❹ (*reaction*) Wirkung *f* **II.** *vi* ❶ (*form waves*) *water* sich kräuseln ❷ (*flow with waves*) plätschern ❸ (*move with waves*) *grain* wogen; **his muscles ~d under his skin** man sah das Spiel seiner Muskeln [unter der Haut] **III.** *vt* (*produce wave in*) *water* kräuseln; *muscles* spielen lassen

rip-'roaring *adj attr* (*fam*) *success* sagenhaft

rise [raɪz] **I.** *n* ❶ (*upward movement*) *of theater curtain* Hochgehen *nt kein pl,* Heben *nt kein pl; of the sun* Aufgehen *nt kein pl* ❷ (*in society*) Aufstieg *m;* **~ to power** Aufstieg *m* an die Macht ❸ (*hill*) Anhöhe *f,* Erhebung *f* ❹ (*height*) *of an arch, step* Höhe *f* ❺ (*increase*) Anstieg *m kein pl,* Steigen *nt kein pl*

II. *vi* <rose, risen> ❶ (*ascend*) steigen; *curtain* aufgehen, hochgehen ❷ (*become visible*) *moon, sun* aufgehen ❸ (*become higher*) *voice* höher werden; (*become louder*) lauter werden, sich erheben ❹ (*improve position*) aufsteigen; **to ~ to fame** berühmt werden ❺ (*from a chair*) sich erheben ❻ *wind* aufkommen ❼ (*rebel*) ■ **to ~ against sb/sth** sich gegen jdn/etw auflehnen ❽ (*incline upwards*) *ground* ansteigen ❾ (*increase*) [an]steigen; (*in height*) *river, prices* steigen; FOOD *yeast, dough* aufgehen ❿ *of emotion, temper* sich erhitzen ▶ PHRASES: **to ~ to the <u>bait</u>** anbeißen; **~ and <u>shine</u>!** aufstehen!, los, raus aus den Federn!

◆ **rise above** *vi* ■ **to ~ above sth** ❶ (*protrude*) *skyscraper* sich über etw *dat* erheben ❷ (*be superior to*) über etw *dat* stehen; **to ~ above difficulties** Schwierigkeiten überwinden

◆ **rise up** *vi* ❶ (*mutiny*) ■ **to ~ up** sich auflehnen (**against** gegen +*akk*) ❷ (*be visible*) aufragen

risen [ˈrɪz·ən] *pp of* **rise**

riser [ˈraɪ·zər] *n* (*person*) **early ~** Frühaufsteher(in) *m(f)*

rising [ˈraɪ·zɪŋ] **I.** *adj attr* ❶ (*increasing in status*) *author, politician* aufstrebend ❷ (*getting higher*) *floodwaters* steigend; *sun* aufgehend ❸ (*increasing*) *costs* steigend; *wind* aufkommend; *fury* wachsend ❹ (*angled upwards*) *ground* [auf]steigend **II.** *n* Aufstand *m*, Erhebung *f*

risk [rɪsk] **I.** *n* Risiko *nt;* **health ~** Gesundheitsrisiko *nt;* **to take a ~** ein Risiko eingehen **II.** *vt* riskieren; **to ~ life and limb** Leib und Leben riskieren

risky [ˈrɪs·ki] *adj* riskant

risqué [rɪs·ˈkeɪ] *adj* gewagt

rite [raɪt] *n usu pl* Ritus *m;* **last ~s** Sterbesakramente *pl*

ritual [ˈrɪtʃ·u·əl] **I.** *n* Ritual *nt*, Ritus *m* **II.** *adj attr* rituell, Ritual-

ritzy [ˈrɪt·si] *adj* (*fam*) nobel

rival [ˈraɪ·vəl] **I.** *n* Rivale(in) *m(f);* ECON, COMM Konkurrent *m;* **arch ~** Erzrivale(in) *m(f);* **bitter ~s** scharfe Rivalen; **~ team** gegnerische Mannschaft **II.** *vt* <-l- *or* -ll-> konkurrieren (mit +*dat*); ■ **to be ~ed by sth/sb** von etw/jdm übertroffen werden

rivalry [ˈraɪ·vəl·ri] *n* ❶ (*competition*) Rivalität *f* (**among** unter +*dat*); *esp* ECON, SPORTS Konkurrenz *f* (**for** um +*akk*) ❷ (*incidence*) Rivalität *f;* **friendly ~** freundschaftlicher Wettstreit

river [ˈrɪv·ər] *n* (*water*) Fluss *m;* **down ~** stromabwärts; **up ~** stromaufwärts

ˈ**river basin** *n* Flussbecken *nt*

ˈ**river bed** *n* Flussbett *nt*

ˈ**riverside** *n* [Fluss]ufer *nt*

rivet [ˈrɪv·ɪt] **I.** *n* Niete *f* **II.** *vt* ❶ (*join*) ■ **to ~ sth [together]** etw [zusammen]nieten ❷ (*fix firmly*) fesseln; **to be ~ed to the spot** wie angewurzelt stehen bleiben

riveting [ˈrɪv·ɪ·t̬ɪŋ] *adj* (*fam*) fesselnd

RN [ˌar·ˈen] *n abbrev of* **registered nurse** examinierte Krankenschwester; (*male*) examinierter Krankenpfleger

RNA [ˌar·en·ˈeɪ] *n abbrev of* **ribonucleic acid** RNS *f*

roach <*pl* -es> [roʊtʃ] *n* (*fam*) ❶ ZOOL (*cockroach*) Küchenschabe *f* ❷ (*sl: butt of joint*) *eingedrehter Pappfilter*

road [roʊd] *n* ❶ (*way*) Straße *f;* **busy ~** stark befahrene Straße; **side ~** Nebenstraße *f* ❷ (*street name*) Straße *f* ❸ (*fig: course*) Weg *m;* **on the ~ to recovery** auf dem Wege der Besserung

ˈ**roadblock** *n* Straßensperre *f*

ˈ**road hog** *n* (*pej fam*) Verkehrsrowdy *m*

ˈ**roadhouse** *n* Raststätte *f*

roadie [ˈroʊ·di] *n* (*fam*) Roadie *m*

ˈ**roadkill** *n* ❶ (*animal*) totgefahrenes Tier ❷ (*action*) Überfahren eines Tieres *nt*

ˈ**road map** *n* Straßenkarte *f*

ˈ**road rage** *n* aggressives Verhalten im Straßenverkehr

ˈ**roadrunner** *n* ORN Erdkuckuck *m*

ˈ**roadside I.** *n* Straßenrand *m* **II.** *adj* Straßen-; *café* am Straßenrand gelegen

ˈ**road sign** *n* Verkehrsschild *nt*

ˈ**road surface** *n* Straßenbelag *m*

ˈ**road-test** *vt vehicle* Probe fahren

ˈ**roadway** *n* Fahrbahn *f*

ˈ**roadwork** *n* Straßenbauarbeiten *pl*

roam [roʊm] **I.** *vi* ❶ (*travel aimlessly*) **to ~ around/over/through** umherstreifen, umherziehen ❷ *mind, thoughts* abschweifen **II.** *vt* **to ~ the streets** durch die Straßen ziehen *fam; dog* herumstreunen

ˈ**roaming** *n* TELEC Roaming *nt* (*per Handy Auslandsgespräche führen*)

roar [rɔr] **I.** *n* ❶ (*bellow*) *of a lion, person* Brüllen *nt kein pl*, Gebrüll *nt kein pl* ❷ (*loud noise*) *of an aircraft, a cannon* Donnern *nt kein pl; of an engine* [Auf]heulen *nt kein pl*, Dröhnen *nt kein pl; of a fire* Prasseln *nt kein pl; of thunder* Rollen *nt kein pl*, Grollen *nt kein pl; of waves* Tosen *nt kein pl* ❸ (*laughter*) schallendes Gelächter **II.** *vi* ❶ (*bellow*) *lion, person* brüllen; ■ **to ~ at sb** jdn anbrüllen ❷ (*make a loud noise*) *aircraft, cannon* donnern; *engine* [auf]heulen, dröhnen; *fire* prasseln; *thunder* rollen, grollen; *waves* tosen; *wind* heulen ❸ (*laugh*) **to ~ with laughter** in schallendes Gelächter ausbrechen **III.** *vt* brüllen

roast [roʊst] **I.** *vt* ❶ (*heat*) rösten; *meat* braten ❷ (*criticize*) ■ **to ~ sb** mit jdm hart ins Gericht gehen **II.** *vi* braten *a. fig*, [vor Hitze] fast umkommen *fam* **III.** *adj attr* Brat-; **~ beef** Roastbeef *nt*, Rinderbraten *m;* **~ chicken** Brathähnchen *nt* **IV.** *n* ❶ FOOD Braten *m* ❷ (*process*) Rösten *nt* ❸ (*of coffee*) Röstung *f*

roasting [ˈroʊs·tɪŋ] *adj* (*fam: hot*) knallheiß

rob <-bb-> [rab] *vt* ❶ (*steal from*) ■ **to ~ sb** jdn bestehlen; (*violently*) jdm rauben; *bank* ausrauben ② *usu passive* (*fam: overcharge*) ausnehmen ③ (*deprive*) ■ **to ~ sb of sth** jdn um etw *akk* bringen

robber ['rab·ər] *n* Räuber(in) *m(f)*

robbery ['rab·ə·ri] *n* ① (*action*) Raubüberfall *m* ② (*theft*) Raub[überfall] *m;* **bank ~** Bankraub *m*

robe [roʊb] *n* ① *usu pl* (*formal gown*) Talar *m* ② (*bathrobe*) Morgenmantel *m*

robin ['rab·ɪn] *n* ORN Wanderdrossel *f*

robot ['roʊ·bat] *n* (*machine*) Roboter *m a. fig*

robotics [roʊ·'bat̬·ɪks] *n + sing vb* Robotik *f kein pl*

robust [roʊ·'bʌst] *adj* ① (*healthy*) kräftig, robust; *appetite* gesund ② (*sturdy*) *material* robust, widerstandsfähig ③ (*down-to-earth*) *approach, view* bodenständig ④ (*full-bodied*) *food* deftig; *wine* kernig

robustness [roʊ·'bʌst·nɪs] *n* ① (*vitality, sturdiness*) Widerstandsfähigkeit *f,* Robustheit *f* ② (*determination*) Entschlossenheit *f*

rock¹ [rak] *n* ① (*stone*) Stein *m* ② (*sticking out of ground*) Fels[en] *m;* (*sticking out of sea*) Riff *nt;* (*boulder*) Felsbrocken *m* ③ GEOL Gestein *nt* ④ (*fig: firm support*) Fels *m* in der Brandung ⑤ (*fam: diamond*) Klunker *m* ⑥ (*fam: piece of crack*) Crack *nt kein pl* ► PHRASES: **on the ~s** (*fam: in disastrous state*) am Ende; *relationship, marriage* kaputt *fam;* (*served with ice*) mit Eis

rock² [rak] **I.** *n* ① Rockmusik *f* ② (*movement*) Schaukeln *nt kein pl,* Wiegen *nt kein pl* **II.** *vt* ① (*cause to move*) schaukeln; (*gently*) wiegen ② (*a. fig: sway*) erschüttern **III.** *vi* ① (*move*) schaukeln ② (*dance*) rocken *fam;* (*play music*) Rock[musik] spielen ③ (*fam: be excellent*) **he really ~s!** er ist ein Supertyp!

rock-and-'roll *n see* **rock 'n' roll**

rock 'bottom *n* Tiefpunkt *m;* **to be at** [*or* **hit**] **~** am Tiefpunkt [angelangt] sein; *person a.* am Boden zerstört sein

rocker ['rak·ər] *n* ① (*chair*) Schaukelstuhl *m* ② (*curved bar*) *of a chair* [Roll]kufe *f; of a cradle* [Wiegen]kufe ③ (*musician*) Rockmusiker(in) *m(f);* (*fan*) Rockfan *m* ► PHRASES: **to be off one's ~** übergeschnappt sein

rocket ['rak·ɪt] **I.** *n* ① (*missile*) [Marsch]flugkörper *m;* (*for space travel*) Rakete *f* ② (*firework*) [Feuerwerks]rakete *f* **II.** *vi* ■ **to ~** [**up**] *costs, prices* hochschnellen, in die Höhe schnellen; **to ~ to fame** über Nacht berühmt werden

Rockies ['rak·iz] *n* ■ **the ~** die Rocky Mountains *pl*

'rocking chair *n* Schaukelstuhl *m*

'rocking horse *n* Schaukelpferd *nt*

'rock music *n* Rockmusik *f*

rock 'n' 'roll *n* Rock and Roll *m*

'rock salt *n* Steinsalz *nt*

'rock star *n* Rockstar *m*

rocky¹ ['rak·i] *adj* ① (*characterized by rocks*) felsig ② (*full of rocks*) *soil* steinig

rocky² ['rak·i] *adj* ① (*tottering*) wackelig *fam* ② (*full of difficulties*) schwierig; *future* unsicher

Rocky 'Mountains *n* ■ **the ~** die Rocky Mountains *pl*

> Die **Rocky Mountains**, auch bekannt als **Rockies**, sind eine ausgedehnte Bergkette im Westen Nordamerikas, die sich über 3.000 Meilen (4.800 km) von British Columbia/Kanada bis nach New Mexico/USA erstrecken. Die Gipfel der Rocky Mountains sind geologisch betrachtet relativ jung, jedoch genauso hoch und spitzer zulaufend als die der Appalachen im Osten Nordamerikas. Der höchste Berg ist der Mt. Elbert/Colorado, der seinen Höhepunkt in 14.433 Fuß (4.399 m) Höhe erreicht. In den Rocky Mountains liegt auch der *Continental Divide*, ein Gebirgspass, von dessen einer Seite alle Gewässer in den Atlantischen Ozean und von der anderen alle in den Pazifischen Ozean fließen.

rococo [rə·'koʊ·koʊ] **I.** *adj* Rokoko- *f* **II.** *n* Rokoko *nt*

rod [rad] *n* ① (*bar*) Stange *f* ② (*for punishing*) Rute *f;* (*cane*) Rohrstock *m* ③ (*for fishing*) [Angel]rute *f;* (*angler*) Angler(in) *m(f)* ► PHRASES: **to rule sb/sth with a ~ of iron** jdn/etw mit eiserner Hand regieren

rode [roʊd] *pt of* **ride**

rodent ['roʊ·dənt] **I.** *n* Nagetier *nt* **II.** *adj* nagend, Nage-

rodeo ['roʊ·di·oʊ] *n* Rodeo *nt*

roe [roʊ] *n of female fish* Rogen *m; of male fish* Milch

roger ['radʒ·ər] *interj* **~!** verstanden!, roger! *sl*

rogue [roʊg] **I.** *n* (*pej*) Gauner(in) *m(f);* (*rascal*) Spitzbube *m* **II.** *adj company, organization* skrupellos; **~ state** Schurkenstaat *m*

roguish ['roʊ·gɪʃ] *adj* ① (*dishonest*) schurkisch ② (*mischievous*) schelmisch; *smile, twinkle* spitzbübisch

role [roʊl] *n* ① FILM, THEAT, TV Rolle *f;* **supporting ~** Nebenrolle *f* ② (*function*) Rolle *f,* Funktion *f*

'role model *n* Rollenbild *nt*

'role play, **'role playing** *n* Rollenspiel *nt*

'role reversal *n* Rollentausch *m kein pl*

roll [roʊl] **I.** *n* ① (*cylinder, cylindrical mass*) *of film, paper* Rolle *f; of cloth* Ballen *m* ② (*list*) [Namens]liste *f;* (*register*) Verzeichnis *nt* ③ (*bread*) Brötchen *nt* ④ (*movement*) Rollen *nt;* (*turning over*) Herumrollen *nt;* (*wallowing*) Herumwälzen *nt* ⑤ (*unsteady movement*) *of a car, plane, ship* Schlingern *nt* ⑥ *usu sing* (*sound*) *of thunder* [G]rollen *nt kein pl;* **drum ~** Trommelwirbel *m* ► PHRASES: **to be on a ~** (*fam*) eine Glückssträhne haben **II.** *vt* ① (*cause to move around axis, push on wheels*) rollen; *eyes* verdrehen ② (*turn over*)

R

drehen; **to ~ one's car** sich mit dem Auto überschlagen ❸ (*shape*) ■ **to ~ sth into sth** etw zu etw *dat* rollen; **he ~ed the clay into a ball** er formte den Ton zu einer Kugel ❹ (*wind*) aufrollen; *cigarette* drehen ❺ (*wrap*) ■ **to ~ sth in sth** etw in etw *akk* einwickeln ❻ (*flatten*) walzen; *pastry dough* ausrollen **III.** *vi* ❶ (*move around axis, move on wheels*) rollen (**off** von +*dat*); (*turn over*) sich herumrollen; (*wallow*) sich [herum]wälzen ❷ (*flow*) *drops, waves* rollen; *tears* kullern ❸ (*oscillate*) *ship, plane* schlingern; (*person*) schwanken ❹ (*operate*) laufen; **to keep sth ~ing** etw in Gang halten ❺ (*fig: elapse*) *years* **to ~ by** vorbeiziehen ❻ (*undulate*) wallen ❼ (*reverberate*) widerhallen; *thunder* [g]rollen

◆**roll around** *vi* (*move around axis, turn over*) herumrollen; (*wallow*) sich herumwälzen

◆**roll back** *vt* ❶ (*move back*) zurückrollen; (*push back*) zurückschieben; (*fold back*) zurückschlagen ❷ (*fig: reverse development*) *advances* umkehren; **to ~ back the years** die Uhr zurückdrehen *fig* ❸ (*lower*) *costs, prices, wages* senken

◆**roll down I.** *vt* ❶ (*move around axis*) hinunterrollen; (*bring down*) herunterrollen ❷ (*turn*) *window* herunterkurbeln **II.** *vi* hinunterrollen; (*come down*) herunterrollen; *tears a.* herunterlaufen

◆**roll in I.** *vi* (*fam*) ❶ (*move*) hineinrollen; (*come in*) hereinrollen ❷ (*be received*) *offers* [massenhaft] eingehen; *money* reinkommen *fam* ❸ (*arrive*) hereinplatzen *fam* ▶ PHRASES: **to be ~ing in money** (*fam*) im Geld schwimmen **II.** *vt* (*bring in*) hereinrollen; (*take in*) hineinrollen

◆**roll on I.** *vi* (*continue*) weitergehen; *time* verfliegen **II.** *vt* (*apply*) aufwalzen

◆**roll out I.** *vt* ❶ (*take out*) hinausrollen; (*bring out*) herausrollen ❷ *dough* ausrollen; *metal* auswalzen ❸ ECON *new product* herausbringen **II.** *vi* ECON *new product* herauskommen

◆**roll over I.** *vi* herumrollen; *person, animal* sich umdrehen; *car* umkippen; *boat* kentern; **to ~ over onto one's side** sich auf die Seite rollen **II.** *vt* ❶ (*turn over*) umdrehen ❷ FIN *credit* erneuern; *debt* umschulden

◆**roll up I.** *vt* ❶ (*move up, around axis*) hochrollen; *sleeves* hochkrempeln; *window* hochkurbeln ❷ (*coil*) aufrollen; *string* aufwickeln ❸ FIN, ECON *credit* verlängern **II.** *vi* ❶ (*move up*) hochrollen ❷ (*fam: arrive*) aufkreuzen

'roll call *n* Namensaufruf *m kein pl*

roller ['roʊ·lər] *n* ❶ (*for paint*) Rolle *f*, Roller *m* ❷ (*for hair*) Lockenwickler *m* ❸ TECH Walze *f*

'Rollerblade® **I.** *n* SPORTS Rollerblade® *m*, Inlineskater *m* **II.** *vi* inlineskaten

'roller coaster *n* Achterbahn *f*

'roller skate *n* Rollschuh *m*

'roller-skate *vi* Rollschuh laufen [*o* fahren]

'roller skater *n* Rollschuhläufer(in) *m(f)*

rolling ['roʊ·lɪŋ] *adj attr* ❶ (*moderately rising*) *hills* sanft ansteigend ❷ (*undulating*) *gait* wankend, schwankend ❸ (*not immediate*) *implementation* allmählich

'rolling pin *n* Nudelholz *nt*

'roll-on I. *adj attr* Roll-on- **II.** *n* (*deodorant*) Deoroller *m*

roly-poly [ˌroʊ·li·'poʊ·li] *adj* (*hum fam*) rundlich; *baby* moppelig *fam; child* pummelig

ROM [ram] *n abbrev of* **Read Only Memory** ROM *m o nt*

Roman ['roʊ·mən] **I.** *adj* römisch **II.** *n* Römer(in) *m(f)*

Roman 'Catholic I. *adj* römisch-katholisch **II.** *n* Katholik(in) *m(f)*

romance [roʊ·'mæns] *n* ❶ (*romanticism*) Romantik *f;* (*love*) romantische Liebe ❷ (*love affair*) Romanze *f*, Liebesaffäre *f* ❸ (*movie*) Liebesfilm *m;* (*book*) Liebesroman *m;* (*medieval tale*) Ritterroman *m*

Romance [roʊ·'mæns] *adj* LING **~ languages** romanische Sprachen

Romanesque [ˌroʊ·mə·'nesk] ARCHIT **I.** *adj* romanisch **II.** *n* ■ **the ~** die Romanik

Romania [roʊ·'meɪ·ni·ə] *n* Rumänien *nt*

Romanian [roʊ·'meɪ·ni·ən] **I.** *adj* rumänisch **II.** *n* ❶ (*person*) Rumäne(in) *m(f)* ❷ (*language*) Rumänisch *nt*

romantic [roʊ·'mæn·tɪk] **I.** *adj* romantisch **II.** *n* Romantiker(in) *m(f)*

romanticism, Romanticism [roʊ·'mæn·tɪ·sɪz·əm] *n* ART, LIT Romantik *f*

Romany ['ram·əni] **I.** *n* ❶ (*gypsy*) Roma *pl* ❷ (*language*) Romani *nt* **II.** *adj* Roma-

Rome [roʊm] *n* Rom *nt*

romp [ramp] **I.** *vi* (*play*) *children, young animals* tollen **II.** *n* ❶ (*play*) Tollerei *f kein pl* ❷ (*book, film, play*) Klamauk *m kein pl*

roof [ruf] **I.** *n* ❶ (*top of house*) Dach *nt* ❷ (*attic*) Dachboden *m* ❸ (*ceiling*) *of a cave* Decke *f; of mouth* Gaumen *m* **II.** *vt* überdachen

roofing ['ru·fɪŋ] **I.** *n* ❶ (*material*) Material *nt* zum Dachdecken ❷ (*job*) Dachdecken *nt* **II.** *adj* Dach-; **~ material** Bedachungsmaterial *nt*

'roof rack *n* Dachgepäckträger *m*

'rooftop *n* Dach *nt*

rook [rʊk] *n* CHESS Turm *m*

rookie ['rʊk·i] *n* (*fam*) Neuling *m;* MIL Rekrut(in) *m(f)*

room [rum] **I.** *n* ❶ (*space*) Platz *m;* (*scope a.*) Raum *m;* **~ for maneuver** Bewegungsspielraum *m* ❷ (*in a building*) Zimmer *nt*, Raum *m;* **double ~** Doppelzimmer *nt* ❸ (*people present*) **the whole ~ turned around and stared at him** alle, die im Zimmer waren, drehten sich um und starrten ihn an **II.** *vi* wohnen; ■ **to ~ with sb** mit jdm zusammen wohnen

roomful ['rum·fʊl] *n usu sing* **a ~ of people** ein Zimmer *nt* voller Leute

'rooming house *n* Pension *f*

R

'roommate *n* ① (*sharing room*) Zimmergenosse(in) *m(f)* ② (*sharing apartment or house*) Mitbewohner(in) *m(f)*
'room service *n* Zimmerservice *m*
room 'temperature *n* Zimmertemperatur *f*
roomy ['ru·mi] *adj* (*approv*) geräumig
roost [rust] **I.** *n* Rastplatz *m;* (*for sleep*) Schlafplatz *m* **II.** *vi* rasten
rooster ['ru·stər] *n* Hahn *m*
root[1] [rut] **I.** *n* ① (*embedded part*) Wurzel *f;* (*of potato*) Knolle *f;* (*of a tulip*) Zwiebel *f;* **to take ~** Wurzeln schlagen ② (*fig: basic cause*) Wurzel *f,* Ursprung *m;* (*essential substance*) Kern *m kein pl* ③ *pl* (*fig: origins*) Wurzeln *pl,* Ursprung *m* ④ MATH Wurzel *f;* **square ~** Quadratwurzel *f* **II.** *vt cuttings, plants* einpflanzen **III.** *vi plant* wurzeln, Wurzeln schlagen
root[2] [rut] *vi* (*fam: support*) **to ~ for a team** eine Mannschaft anfeuern
root around *vi* (*fam*) herumwühlen (**in** in +*dat*), wühlen (**for** nach +*dat*)
◆**root out** *vt* ① BOT *plant, weeds* ausgraben ② (*eliminate*) *evil* ausrotten ③ (*find*) aufstöbern

> **Root beer** ist eine Art Limonade aus verschiedenen Pflanzenextrakten. Um daraus *root beer float* zu machen, vermischt man *root beer* mit Vanilleeis und schlürft das Ganze mit einem Strohhalm.

rootless ['rut·lɪs] *adj* ① BOT wurzellos ② (*without home*) heimatlos
'root vegetable *n* (*beets, carrots*) Wurzel *f,* Wurzelgemüse *nt;* (*potatoes*) Knolle *f*
rope [roʊp] **I.** *n* ① (*cord*) Seil *nt,* Strick *m;* NAUT Tau *nt* ② (*lasso*) Lasso *nt* **II.** *vt* anseilen, festbinden (**to** an +*dat*); **to ~ calves** Kälber mit dem Lasso [ein]fangen
◆**rope in** *vt* (*fam*) einspannen
◆**rope off** *vt* **to ~ off** ⊂ **an area** ein Gebiet [mit Seilen/einem Seil] absperren
'rope ladder *n* Strickleiter *f*
rosary ['roʊ·zə·ri] *n* Rosenkranz *m*
rose[1] [roʊz] **I.** *n* ① (*flower*) Rose *f;* (*bush*) Rosenbusch *m;* (*tree*) Rosenbäumchen *nt* ② (*nozzle*) Brause *f* ③ (*color*) Rosa *nt* ▶ PHRASES: **to come out smelling like a ~** bestens laufen **II.** *adj* rosa
rose[2] [roʊz] *pt of* **rise**
'rosebud *n* Rosenknospe *f*
'rosebush *n* Rosenstrauch *m*
'rose garden *n* Rosengarten *m*
'rose hip **I.** *n* Hagebutte *f* **II.** *adj syrup, wine* Hagebutten-
rosemary ['roʊz·mer·i] *n* Rosmarin *m*
'rose water *n* Rosenwasser *nt*
rosin ['raz·ən] MUS **I.** *n* Kolophonium *nt* **II.** *vt* **to ~ a violin bow** einen Geigenbogen mit Kolophonium einreiben
roster ['ras·tər] *n* ① (*list*) Liste *f;* (*plan*) Plan *m;* **duty ~** Dienstplan *m* ② SPORTS Spielerliste *f*
rostrum <*pl* -s *or* -tra> ['ras·trəm] *n* (*raised platform*) Tribüne *f,* Podium *nt;* (*for public speaker a.*) Rednerpult *nt*
rosy ['roʊ·zi] *adj* rosig *a. fig*
rot [rat] **I.** *n* ① (*process*) Fäulnis *f* ② (*decayed matter*) Verfaultes *nt,* Verwestes *nt* ③ BOT Fäule *f* **II.** *vi* <-tt-> ① (*decay*) verrotten; *teeth, meat* verfaulen; *woodwork* vermodern ② (*deteriorate*) *institution, society* verkommen **III.** *vt* <-tt-> ■**to ~ sth** etw vermodern lassen
◆**rot away** *vi* verfaulen
rotary ['roʊ·t̬ə·ri] **I.** *adj* kreisend, rotierend, Dreh- **II.** *n* TRANSP *see* **traffic circle**
rotate ['roʊ·teɪt] **I.** *vi* ① (*revolve*) rotieren (**around** um +*akk*) ② (*alternate*) wechseln **II.** *vt* ① (*cause to turn*) drehen ② (*alternate*) **to ~ duties** Aufgaben turnusmäßig [abwechselnd] verteilen; *troops* auswechseln ③ AGR *crops* im Fruchtwechsel anbauen
rotation [roʊ·'teɪ·ʃən] *n* Rotation *f,* Umdrehung *f;* **crop ~** AGR Fruchtwechsel *m;* **in ~** im Wechsel
rote [roʊt] *n* (*usu pej*) **by ~** *learn* auswendig
rotor ['roʊ·t̬ər] *n* Rotor *m*
rotten ['rat·ən] **I.** *adj* ① (*decayed*) verfault; *fruit* verdorben; *tooth* faul; *wood* modrig ② (*corrupt*) korrupt, völlig verdorben *fig* ③ (*fam: very bad*) mies; **I'm a ~ cook** ich bin ein hundsmiserabler Koch ④ (*fam: nasty*) *trick, joke* gemein **II.** *adv* (*fam*) total *fam;* **spoiled ~** *child* völlig verzogen
rotund [roʊ·'tʌnd] *adj* (*plump*) *person* massig
rotunda [roʊ·'tʌn·də] *n* Rotunde *f*
rouble ['ru·bəl] *n see* **ruble**
rouge [ruʒ] *n* (*makeup*) Rouge *nt*
rough [rʌf] **I.** *adj* ① (*uneven*) rau; *ground, terrain* uneben; *landscape* rau, unwirtlich; *fur, hair* struppig ② (*not soft*) rau, hart; (*in taste*) *wine* sauer ③ (*fam: difficult*) hart, schwer; **to give sb a ~ time** jdm das Leben ganz schön schwer machen ④ (*makeshift*) einfach, primitiv ⑤ (*unrefined*) rau, ungehobelt ⑥ (*imprecise*) grob; **to give sb a ~ idea of sth** jdm eine ungefähre Vorstellung von etw *dat* geben **II.** *adv* (*fam*) rau **III.** *n* (*in golf*) ■**the ~** das Rough *fachspr* **IV.** *vt* (*fam*) **to ~ it** [ganz] primitiv leben
roughage ['rʌf·ɪdʒ] *n* ① (*fiber*) Ballaststoffe *pl* ② (*fodder*) Raufutter *nt*
'rough-and-tumble *adj attr* **~ atmosphere** raue Atmosphäre
rough 'draft *n* (*first version*) Rohfassung *f;* (*sketch*) Entwurf *m*
roughen ['rʌf·ən] **I.** *vt* aufrauen **II.** *vi skin, voice* rau werden; *society* verrohen; *weather* stürmisch werden
'roughhouse *vi* ① (*be boisterous*) Radau machen *fam* ② (*have playful fight*) sich raufen ③ (*have a fight*) sich prügeln
roughly ['rʌf·li] *adv* ① (*harshly, without refinement*) grob, roh; **~ sketched** skizzenhaft ② (*approximately*) grob; **~ speaking** ganz allgemein gesagt; **~ the same** ungefähr gleich

R

'roughneck *n* ❶ (*fam: rude person*) Rohling *m pej,* Grobian *m pej* ❷ (*oil rig worker*) Bohrarbeiter(in) *m(f)*

roughness [ˈrʌf·nɪs] *n* ❶ (*not smoothness*) Rauheit *f; of ground, terrain* Unebenheit *f* ❷ (*harshness*) Rauheit *f; of a game a.* Härte *f*

'roughshod *adv* **to ride ~ over sb** (*fig*) jdn unterdrücken

roulette [ru·ˈlet] *n* Roulette *nt*

round [raʊnd] **I.** *adj* <-er, -est> (*circular*) rund; *face* rundlich; *vowel* gerundet **II.** *n* ❶ (*of drinks*) Runde *f* ❷ (*series*) Folge *f;* SPORTS Runde *f;* **~ of talks** Gesprächsrunde *f* ❸ (*salvo*) **~ of applause** Beifall *m* ❹ (*shot*) **~ of ammunition** Ladung *f* ❺ (*routine*) Trott *m pej* **III.** *vt* ❶ (*make round*) umrunden ❷ (*go around*) **to ~ the corner** um die Ecke biegen

◆**round down** *vt number, sum* abrunden

◆**round off** *vt* abrunden

◆**round out** *vt story* abrunden

◆**round up** *vt* ❶ (*increase*) *figure* aufrunden ❷ (*gather*) *people* zusammentrommeln *fam; things* zusammentragen; *cattle* zusammentreiben; *support* holen

roundabout [ˈraʊnd·ə·baʊt] *adj* umständlich; **to take a ~ route** einen Umweg machen; **to ask sb in a ~ way** jdn durch die Blume fragen

rounded [ˈraʊn·dɪd] *adj* rund; *edges* abgerundet

roundly [ˈraʊnd·li] *adv* (*form*) gründlich; *criticize* heftig kritisieren; *defeat* haushoch besiegen

round 'robin *n* (*competition format*) *Wettkampf, in dem jeder gegen jeden antritt*

round'table *adj attr* **~ discussion** Gespräch *nt* am runden Tisch

'round-the-clock *adj* rund um die Uhr

round 'trip I. *n* Rundreise *f* **II.** *adv* **to fly ~** ein Rückflugticket haben

round-trip 'ticket *n* Hin- und Rückfahrkarte *f;* AVIAT Hin- und Rückflugticket *nt*

'roundup *n* ❶ (*gathering*) Versammlung *f; of criminals, suspects* Festnahme *f; of cattle* Zusammentreiben *nt* ❷ (*summary*) Zusammenfassung *f*

rouse [raʊz] *vt* ❶ (*waken*) wecken ❷ (*activate*) **to ~ sb to action** jdn zum Handeln bewegen

rousing [ˈraʊ·zɪŋ] *adj* mitreißend; *cheer, reception* stürmisch

rout [raʊt] **I.** *n* ❶ (*defeat*) Niederlage *f* ❷ (*disorderly retreat*) ungeordneter Rückzug **II.** *vt* (*form: defeat*) besiegen

◆**rout out** *vt* herausjagen; (*find*) aufstöbern

route [raʊt] **I.** *n* ❶ (*way*) Strecke *f,* Route *f; of a parade* Verlauf *m;* **the ~ to success** der Weg zum Erfolg ❷ TRANSP Linie *f* ❸ (*delivery path*) Runde *f;* **to have a paper ~** Zeitungen austragen **II.** *vt* schicken; *deliveries* liefern

> Die berühmte **Route 66** führt von Chicago nach Los Angeles. Während der Weltwirtschaftskrise der 30er nahmen viele die **Route 66**, um nach Kalifornien zu ziehen. Die **Route 66** durchquert acht amerikanische Bundesstaaten.

routine [ru·ˈtin] **I.** *n* ❶ (*habit*) Routine *f* ❷ (*dancing*) Figur *f;* (*gymnastics*) Übung *f* ❸ COMPUT Programm *nt* **II.** *adj* ❶ (*regular*) routinemäßig; **~ inspection/search** Routineuntersuchung/-durchsuchung *f;* **to become ~** zur Gewohnheit werden ❷ (*pej: uninspiring*) routinemäßig; *performance* durchschnittlich

routinely [ru·ˈtin·li] *adv* routinemäßig

rove [roʊv] **I.** *vi person* umherwandern; *gaze* [umher]schweifen **II.** *vt* **to ~ the world** durch die Welt ziehen

roving [ˈroʊ·vɪŋ] *adj* umherstreifend *attr;* **~ ambassador** Botschafter(in) *m(f)* für mehrere Vertretungen

row¹ [roʊ] *n* ❶ (*line*) Reihe *f;* **in ~s** reihenweise ❷ **in a ~** (*in succession*) hintereinander

row² [roʊ] **I.** *vi* rudern **II.** *vt boat* rudern (**across** über +*akk*)

row³ [raʊ] **I.** *n* (*argument*) Streit *m,* Krach *m fam* **II.** *vi* (*fam*) sich streiten

rowboat [ˈroʊ·boʊt] *n* Ruderboot *nt*

rowdy [ˈraʊ·di] *adj* (*pej*) laut, rüpelhaft; *party* wild

rower [ˈroʊ·ər] *n* Ruderer *m,* Ruderin *f*

'row house *n* Reihenhaus *nt*

rowing [ˈroʊ·ɪŋ] *n* Rudern *nt*

royal [ˈrɔɪ·əl] **I.** *adj* <-er, -est> ❶ (*of a monarch*) königlich ❷ (*fig*) fürstlich **II.** *n* (*fam*) Angehörige(r) *f(m)* der königlichen Familie

royalty [ˈrɔɪ·əl·ti] *n* ❶ + *sing/pl vb* (*sovereignty*) Königshaus *nt;* **to treat sb like ~** jdn fürstlich behandeln ❷ PUBL ■ **royalties** *pl* Tantiemen *pl*

rpm <*pl* -> [ˌar·pi·ˈem] *n* AUTO, AVIAT *abbrev of* **revolutions per minute** U/min

RR [ˌar·ˈar] *n abbrev of* **railroad**

RSI [ˌar·es·ˈaɪ] *n* MED *abbrev of* **repetitive strain injury** RSI-Syndrom *f* (*chronische Beschwerden durch einseitige Belastung*)

RSVP [ˌar·es·vi·ˈpi] *abbrev of* **répondez s'il vous plaît** u. A. w. g.

rub [rʌb] **I.** *n* Reiben *nt kein pl;* **to give sth a ~** *hair* etw trocken rubbeln; *material* etw polieren **II.** *vt* <-bb-> einreiben; *furniture* behandeln; (*polish*) polieren; **to ~ one's hands together** sich *dat* die Hände reiben **III.** *vi* <-bb-> reiben; *shoes, collar* scheuern

◆**rub down** *vt surface* abreiben, abwischen; ■ **to ~ down ⊂ sb** jdn abfrottieren

◆**rub in** *vt* ❶ (*spread*) einreiben ❷ (*fam: keep reminding*) ■ **to ~ it in** auf etw *dat* herumreiten ▶ PHRASES: **to ~ sb's nose in it** jdm etw unter die Nase reiben *fam*

◆**rub off I.** *vi* ❶ (*become clean*) wegreiben; *stains* rausgehen ❷ (*fam: affect*) ■ **sth ~s off on sb** etw färbt auf jdn ab **II.** *vt* wegwischen

◆**rub out I.** *vt* ❶ (*erase*) ausradieren ❷ (*sl:*

R

murder) ■ **to ~ out** ↻ **sb** jdn abmurksen *sl* **II.** *vi stain* herausgehen; (*erase*) sich ausradieren lassen

rubber ['rʌb·ər] *n* ❶ (*elastic substance*) Gummi *m o nt* ❷ (*sl: condom*) Gummi *m* ❸ (*shoes*) ■ **~s** *pl* Überschuhe *pl* (*aus Gummi*)

rubber 'band *n* Gummiband *nt*

rubber 'boot *n* Gummistiefel *m*

rubber 'check *n* (*sl*) ungedeckter Scheck

rubberneck ['rʌb·ər·nek] (*sl*) **I.** *n see* **rubbernecker II.** *vi* gaffen *fam*

rubbernecker ['rʌb·ər·nek·ər] *n* (*sl*) Gaffer(in) *m(f) pej fam*

'rubber plant *n* Gummibaum *m*

'rubber stamp *n* Stempel *m;* (*fig*) Genehmigung *f*

rubber-'stamp *vt* (*a. pej*) genehmigen; *decision* bestätigen

'rubber tree *n* Kautschukbaum *m*

rubbery ['rʌb·ə·ri] *adj* ❶ (*rubberlike*) gummiartig; *meat* zäh ❷ (*fam: weak*) *legs* wackelig

rubbish ['rʌb·ɪʃ] *n* ❶ (*waste*) Müll *m* ❷ (*fig fam: nonsense*) Quatsch *m* ❸ (*fam: junk*) Gerümpel *nt*

rubble ['rʌb·əl] *n* ❶ (*smashed rock*) Trümmer *pl;* **to reduce sth to ~** (*fig*) etw in Schutt und Asche legen ❷ (*for building*) Bauschutt *m*

rubella [ru·'bel·ə] *n* (*spec*) Röteln *pl*

ruble, rouble ['ru·bəl] *n* Rubel *m*

ruby ['ru·bi] **I.** *n* Rubin *m* **II.** *adj* ❶ (*made of rubies*) *ring, necklace, bracelet* Rubin- ❷ (*color*) rubinrot

rucksack ['rʌk·sæk] *n* Rucksack *m*

ruckus ['rʌk·əs] *n* (*fam*) Krawall *m*

rudder ['rʌd·ər] *n* [Steuer]ruder *nt*

ruddy ['rʌd·i] *adj* (*approv: red*) rot; (*liter*) rötlich; *cheeks* gerötet

rude [rud] *adj* ❶ (*impolite*) unhöflich; *behavior* unverschämt; *gesture* ordinär; *joke* unanständig ❷ *attr* (*sudden*) unerwartet; *awakening, surprise* böse

rudimentary [ˌru·də·'men·tə·ri] *adj* (*form*) ❶ (*basic*) elementar ❷ (*not highly developed*) primitiv; *method* einfach

rudiments ['ru·də·mənts] *npl* ■ **the ~** die Grundlagen *pl*

rue [ru] *vt* (*liter*) bereuen

rueful ['ru·fəl] *adj* (*liter*) reuevoll

ruff [rʌf] *n on clothing, of an animal* Halskrause *f*

ruffian ['rʌf·i·ən] *n* Schlingel *m*

ruffle ['rʌf·əl] **I.** *vt* ❶ (*agitate*) durcheinanderbringen; *hair* zerzausen ❷ (*fig: upset*) aus der Ruhe bringen ▶ PHRASES: **to ~ sb's feathers** jdn auf die Palme bringen *fam* **II.** *n* Rüsche *f*

rug [rʌg] *n* ❶ (*carpet*) Teppich *m* ❷ (*sl: hairpiece*) Haarteil *nt*

rugby ['rʌg·bi] *n* Rugby *nt*

rugged ['rʌg·ɪd] *adj* ❶ (*uneven*) *terrain, ground* uneben; *cliff, mountain* zerklüftet; *landscape, coast* wild ❷ (*robust, sturdy*) kräftig; *looks, features* markant; *vehicle* robust ❸ (*solid*) fest; *honesty* unerschütterlich

'rugrat *n* (*fam*) Krabbelkind *nt*

ruin ['ru·ɪn] **I.** *vt* (*destroy*) zerstören; *dress, reputation* ruinieren; **to ~ sb's day** jdm den Tag vermiesen; *hopes* zunichtemachen; **to ~ sb's chances** jdm die Suppe versalzen **II.** *n* ❶ (*destroyed building*) Ruine *f* ❷ ■ **~s** *pl of building* Ruinen *pl; of reputation* Reste *pl; of career, hopes* Trümmer *pl;* **to be in ~s** eine Ruine sein; (*after bombing, fire*) in Schutt und Asche liegen; (*fig*) zerstört sein ❸ (*bankruptcy*) Ruin *m*

ruinous ['ru·ə·nəs] *adj* ruinös

rule [rul] **I.** *n* ❶ (*instruction*) Regel *f;* **~s and regulations** Regeln und Bestimmungen; **to be against the ~s** gegen die Regeln verstoßen ❷ (*control*) Herrschaft *f;* **the ~ of law** die Rechtsstaatlichkeit ▶ PHRASES: **as a [general] ~** in der Regel **II.** *vt* ❶ (*govern*) regieren ❷ (*control*) beherrschen ❸ (*draw*) *line* ziehen **III.** *vi* (*control*) herrschen; *king, queen* regieren
◆ **rule out** *vt* ausschließen

'rule book *n* Vorschriftenbuch *nt*

ruler ['ru·lər] *n* ❶ (*person*) Herrscher(in) *m(f)* ❷ (*device*) Lineal *nt*

ruling ['ru·lɪŋ] **I.** *adj attr* ❶ (*governing*) herrschend ❷ (*primary*) hauptsächlich; *ambition, passion* größte(r, s) **II.** *n* LAW Entscheidung *f*

rum [rʌm] *n* (*drink*) Rum *m*

Rumania [roʊ·'meɪ·ni·ə] *see* **Romania**

rumba ['rʌm·bə] *n* Rumba *m*

rumble ['rʌm·bəl] **I.** *n* ❶ (*sound*) Grollen *nt kein pl; of stomach* Knurren *nt* ❷ (*fam*) Schlägerei *f* **II.** *vi* rumpeln; *stomach* knurren; *thunder* grollen

rumbling ['rʌm·bəl·ɪŋ] **I.** *n* ❶ (*indication*) ■ **~s** *pl* [erste] Anzeichen *pl* ❷ (*sound*) Grollen *nt; of distant guns* Donnern *nt* **II.** *adj* grollend *attr*

ruminant ['ru·mə·nənt] *n* ZOOL Wiederkäuer *m*

ruminate ['ru·mə·neɪt] *vi* ❶ (*form: meditate*) nachgrübeln (**over/on** über +*akk*) ❷ *cows* wiederkäuen

rummage ['rʌm·ɪdʒ] **I.** *vi* ■ **to ~ through sth** etw durchstöbern **II.** *n* Durchstöbern *nt*

'rummage sale *n* Flohmarkt *m*

rummy ['rʌm·i] *n* CARDS Rommé *nt*

rumor ['ru·mər] **I.** *n* Gerücht *nt;* **to spread a ~ that ...** das Gerücht verbreiten, dass ... **II.** *vt passive* **the president is ~ed to be seriously ill** der Präsident soll angeblich ernsthaft krank sein; **it is ~ed that ...** es wird gemunkelt, dass ...

rump [rʌmp] *n* ❶ *of an animal* Hinterbacken *pl* ❷ (*beef*) Rumpsteak *nt* ❸ (*hum: buttocks*) Hinterteil *nt fam*

rumple ['rʌm·pəl] *vt* zerknittern

rumpus ['rʌm·pəs] *n* (*fam*) Krawall *m,* Krach *m*

run [rʌn] **I.** *n* ❶ (*jog*) Lauf *m;* **to go for a ~** laufen gehen ❷ (*course*) Strecke *f* ❸ (*period*) Dauer *f;* **~ of good luck** Glückssträhne *f* ❹ (*enclosed area*) Gehege *nt* ❺ SPORTS (*in*

R

baseball) Run *m* ❻ (*in stocking*) Laufmasche *f* ❼ (*fam*) ■**the ~s** *pl* (*diarrhea*) Dünnpfiff *m fam* ▶PHRASES: **in the long ~** auf lange Sicht gesehen; **in the short ~** kurzfristig **II.** *vi* <ran, run> ❶ (*move fast*) laufen, rennen; **to ~ for cover** schnell in Deckung gehen; **to ~ for one's life** um sein Leben rennen ❷ (*operate*) fahren, verkehren; *engine* laufen; *machine* in Betrieb sein; **work is ~ning smoothly at the moment** die Arbeit geht im Moment glatt von der Hand ❸ (*travel*) laufen; (*go*) verlaufen; *ski* gleiten; **the route ~s through the mountains** die Strecke führt durch die Berge ❹ (*last*) [an]dauern; **the film ~s for two hours** der Film dauert zwei Stunden ❺ (*flow*) fließen; **my nose is ~ning** meine Nase läuft; **the river ~s [down] to the sea** der Fluss mündet in das Meer ❻ POL (*enter an election*) kandidieren; **to ~ for President** für das Präsidentenamt kandidieren ❼ (*fray*) *stocking* eine Laufmasche bekommen ▶PHRASES: **to ~ in the family** in der Familie liegen; **to ~ low** *supplies* [langsam] ausgehen **III.** *vt* <ran, run> ❶ (*pass*) **he ran a vacuum cleaner over the carpet** er saugte den Teppich ab; **to ~ one's fingers through one's hair** sich *dat* mit den Fingern durchs Haar fahren ❷ *machine* bedienen; *computer program, engine, dishwasher* laufen lassen ❸ (*manage*) *business* leiten; *farm* betreiben; *government, household* führen; **don't tell me how to ~ my life!** erklär mir nicht, wie ich mein Leben leben soll! ❹ (*conduct*) *course* anbieten; *experiment, test* durchführen ❺ (*let flow*) *water* laufen lassen; *a bath* einlaufen lassen ❻ (*disregard*) **to ~ a red light** (*fam*) eine rote Ampel überfahren ▶PHRASES: **to ~ the show** verantwortlich sein

◆**run across** *vi* zufällig treffen; **to ~ across a problem** auf ein Problem stoßen

◆**run after** *vi* hinterherlaufen

◆**run along** *vi* (*fam*) ■**~!** troll dich!

◆**run around** *vi* ❶ (*bustle*) herumrennen *fam* ❷ (*run freely*) herumlaufen ❸ (*spend time with*) ■**to ~ around with sb** sich mit jdm herumtreiben *fam*

◆**run away** *vi person* weglaufen; *liquid* abfließen; ■**to ~ away from sb** jdn verlassen

◆**run down I.** *vt* ❶ (*hit*) überfahren; *boat* rammen ❷ (*reduce*) reduzieren; *production* drosseln; *supplies* einschränken ❸ (*fam: belittle*) runtermachen **II.** *vi* ❶ (*lose power*) *battery* leer werden ❷ (*become reduced*) reduziert werden

◆**run into** *vi* ❶ (*hit*) hineinrennen (in +*akk*); **he ran into a tree on his motorcycle** er fuhr mit seinem Motorrad gegen einen Baum ❷ (*bump into*) ■**to ~ into sb** jdm über den Weg laufen; ■**to ~ into sth** (*fig*) auf etw *akk* stoßen; **to ~ into difficulties** auf Schwierigkeiten stoßen

◆**run off I.** *vi* ❶ (*fam: leave*) abhauen ❷ (*drain*) *liquid* ablaufen **II.** *vt* **he quickly ran off some copies for me** er machte schnell ein paar Kopien für mich

◆**run on** *vi* ❶ (*continue*) **the game ran on for too long** das Spiel zog sich zu lange hin; (*continue talking*) weiterreden ❷ (*power with*) ■**to ~ on sth** mit etw *dat* betrieben werden

◆**run out** *vi* ❶ (*finish*) ausgehen; **the milk has ~ out** die Milch ist alle ❷ (*expire*) *insurance policy* auslaufen

◆**run over I.** *vt* überfahren **II.** *vi* ❶ (*overflow*) *water, bath, sink* überlaufen ❷ (*review*) durchgehen

◆**run through I.** *vt* ■**to ~ sb through [with sth]** jdn mit etw *dat* durchbohren **II.** *vi* ❶ (*examine*) ■**to ~ through sth** etw durchgehen ❷ (*practice*) durchspielen

◆**run up I.** *vt* ❶ (*increase*) **to ~ up debt** Schulden machen ❷ (*sew quickly*) **to ~ up a dress** ein Kleid nähen **II.** *vi* **to ~ up against problems** auf Probleme stoßen

'**runaround** *n* (*fig*) **to give sb the ~** jdm keine klare Auskunft geben

'**runaway I.** *adj attr* ❶ (*out of control*) *economy, vehicle* außer Kontrolle geraten; *prices* galoppierend ❷ (*escaped*) *animal, prisoner* entlaufen; *horse* durchgegangen **II.** *n* Ausreißer(in) *m(f) fam*

'**rundown I.** *n* zusammenfassender Bericht **II.** *adj* ❶ (*dilapidated*) verwahrlost, heruntergekommen *fam; building* baufällig ❷ (*worn out*) abgespannt

rune [ruːn] *n* ❶ (*letter*) Rune *f* ❷ (*mark*) Geheimzeichen *nt*

rung[1] [rʌŋ] *n* (*of ladder*) Sprosse *f;* (*fig*) Stufe *f*

rung[2] [rʌŋ] *pp of* **ring**

'**run-in** *n* (*fam*) Krach *m*

runner ['rʌn·ər] *n* ❶ (*person*) Läufer(in) *m(f);* (*horse*) Rennpferd *nt* ❷ (*messenger*) Bote(in) *m(f)* ❸ (*carpet*) Läufer *m*

runner-'up *n* Zweite(r); **to be the ~** den zweiten Platz belegen

running ['rʌn·ɪŋ] **I.** *n* ❶ (*not walking*) Laufen *nt,* Rennen *nt* ❷ (*management*) *of a business* Leitung *f; of a machine* Bedienung *f,* Überwachung *f* ▶PHRASES: **to be out of the ~** (*as a competitor*) nicht mit im Rennen sein; (*as a candidate*) nicht mehr mit im Rennen sein **II.** *adj* ❶ *after n* (*in a row*) nacheinander *nach n,* hintereinander *nach n* ❷ (*ongoing*) [fort]laufend ❸ (*operating*) betriebsbereit

'**running back** *n* Running Back *m*

'**running costs** *npl* Betriebskosten *pl; of a car* Unterhaltskosten *pl*

runny ['rʌn·i] *adj nose* laufend *attr; jam, sauce* dünnflüssig

'**runoff** *n* ❶ (*in a race*) Entscheidungslauf *m,* Entscheidungsrennen *nt* ❷ (*of rainfall*) Abfluss *m*

run-of-the-'mill *adj* durchschnittlich, mittelmäßig

runt [rʌnt] *n* ❶ (*animal*) *of a litter* zurückgebliebenes Jungtier ❷ (*pej sl: person*) Wicht *m;* (*child*) **little ~** Würmchen *nt,* kleines Ding

'run-through *n* ❶ THEAT Durchlaufprobe *f* ❷ (*examination*) Durchgehen *nt*, Überfliegen *nt*

'run-up *n* ❶ SPORTS Anlauf *m* [zum Absprung] ❷ (*fig: prelude*) Vorlauf *m*, Endphase *f* der Vorbereitungszeit

'runway *n* AVIAT Start- und Landebahn *f* ❶ SPORTS Anlaufbahn *f* ❷ FASHION Laufsteg *m*

rupture ['rʌp·tʃər] I. *vi* zerreißen; *appendix* durchbrechen; *artery, blood vessel* platzen II. *vt* (*a. fig*) zerreißen *a. fig*; **to ~ a blood vessel** ein Blutgefäß zum Platzen bringen III. *n* (*a. fig*) Zerreißen *nt a. fig*, Zerbrechen *nt a. fig*, Bruch *m a. fig*; *of an artery, blood vessel* Platzen *nt*; (*hernia*) Bruch *m*; (*torn muscle*) [Muskel]riss *m*

rural ['rʊr·əl] *adj* ländlich, Land-

ruse [ruz] *n* List *f*

rush¹ [rʌʃ] I. *n* ❶ (*hurry*) Eile *f*; **to be in a ~** in Eile sein ❷ (*rapid movement*) Losstürzen *nt*, Ansturm *m*; (*press*) Gedränge *nt*, Gewühl *nt* ❸ (*a. fig: surge*) Schwall *m*, Woge *f*; *of emotions* [plötzliche] Anwandlung, Anfall *m* II. *vi* ❶ (*hurry*) eilen, hetzen; **stop ~ing!** hör auf zu hetzen!; ■**to ~ in** hineinstürmen; *water* hineinschießen; ■**to ~ out** hinausstürzen; *water* herausschießen; ■**to ~ toward sb** auf jdn zueilen ❷ (*hurry into*) ■**to ~ into sth** *decision, project* etw überstürzen III. *vt* ❶ (*send quickly*) **she was ~ed to the hospital** sie wurde auf schnellstem Weg ins Krankenhaus gebracht ❷ (*pressure*) ■**to ~ sb** [**into sth**] jdn [zu etw *dat*] treiben; **don't ~ me!** Dräng mich nicht! ❸ (*do hurriedly*) **let's not ~ things** lass uns nichts überstürzen

◆**rush out** *vt* COMM schnell auf den Markt bringen

rush² [rʌʃ] *n* BOT Binse *f*

'rush hour *n* Hauptverkehrszeit *f*

'rush order *n* Eilauftrag *m*

russet ['rʌs·ɪt] I. *n* ❶ (*potato*) Russet-Kartoffel *f* ❷ (*apple*) Boskop *m* II. *adj* (*esp liter*) rotbraun, gelbbraun III. *n* Rotbraun *nt*, Gelbbraun *nt*

Russia ['rʌʃ·ə] *n* Russland *nt*

Russian ['rʌʃ·ən] I. *adj* russisch II. *n* ❶ (*person*) Russe(in) *m(f)* ❷ (*language*) Russisch *nt*

rust [rʌst] I. *n* ❶ (*decay*) Rost *m* ❷ (*color*) Rostbraun *nt* II. *vi* rosten; ■**to ~ away/through** ver-/durchrosten III. *vt* rostig machen; (*fig*) einrosten lassen

rustic ['rʌs·tɪk] *adj* ❶ (*of the country*) ländlich, rustikal ❷ (*simple*) grob [zusammen]gezimmert; (*fig*) schlicht, einfach

rustle ['rʌs·əl] I. *vi leaves, paper* rascheln; *silk* rauschen, knistern II. *vt* ❶ (*make noise*) **to ~ paper** mit Papier rascheln ❷ (*steal*) *cattle, horses* stehlen III. *n of paper, leaves* Rascheln *nt*; *of silk* Knistern *nt*

rustler ['rʌs·lər] *n* Viehdieb(in) *m(f)*

'rustproof I. *adj* rostbeständig; **~ paint** Rostschutzfarbe *f* II. *vt* rostbeständig machen

rusty ['rʌs·ti] *adj* ❶ (*covered in rust*) rostig, verrostet ❷ (*fig: out of practice*) eingerostet; **my Russian is a little ~** ich bin mit meinem Russisch etwas aus der Übung

rut [rʌt] *n* (*track*) [Rad]spur *f*, [Wagen]spur *f*; (*furrow*) Furche *f*; (*fig*) Trott *m*

rutabaga ['ru·t̬ə·ˌbeɪ·gə] *n* BOT Steckrübe *f*

ruthless ['ruθ·lɪs] *adj action, behavior* rücksichtslos, skrupellos; *decision, measure* hart; *dictatorship* erbarmungslos

ruthlessness ['ruθ·lɪs·nɪs] *n of a person* Unbarmherzigkeit *f*, Erbarmungslosigkeit *f*; *of sb's behavior* Rücksichtslosigkeit *f*; *of an action* Skrupellosigkeit *f*

RV [ˌar·'vi] *n abbrev of* **recreational vehicle**

rye [raɪ] *n* Roggen *m*; **~** [**whiskey**] Roggenwhiskey *m*

R

Ss

S <*pl* -'s *or* -s>, **s** <*pl* -'s> [es] *n* S *nt,* s *nt;* ~ **as in Sierra** S wie Siegfried

S [es] *n, adj* ❶ GEOG *abbrev of* **south, southern** S ❷ FASHION *abbrev of* **small** S

s <*pl* -> *abbrev of* **second** s, sek., Sek.

Sabbath ['sæb·əθ] *n* Sabbat *m*

sabbatical [sə·'bæt̬·ɪ·kəl] *n* [einjährige] Freistellung, Sabbatjahr *nt;* **to be on** ~ [für ein Jahr] freigestellt sein

saber ['seɪ·bər] *n* Säbel *m*

sable ['seɪ·bəl] *n* ❶ ZOOL Zobel *m* ❷ (*fur*) Zobelpelz *m*

sabotage ['sæb·ə·taʒ] **I.** *vt machinery, efforts, plan* sabotieren; **to ~ sb's chances of success** jds Erfolgsaussichten zunichtemachen **II.** *n* Sabotage *f;* **industrial** ~ Industriesabotage *f*

saboteur [ˌsæb·ə·'tɜr] *n* Saboteur(in) *m(f)*

sac [sæk] *n* BOT, ZOOL Beutel *f*

saccharin ['sæk·ər·ɪn] *n* Süßstoff *m*

saccharine ['sæk·ər·ɪn] *adj* Saccharin-; (*fig, pej*) süßlich

sachet [sæ·'ʃeɪ] *n* Päckchen *nt*

sack¹ [sæk] **I.** *n* (*bag*) Sack *m;* **a five-pound ~ of potatoes** ein fünf-Pfund-Sack Kartoffeln **II.** *vt* rausschmeißen *fam*

sack² [sæk] *vt* plündern

'sackcloth *n* Sackleinen *nt*

'sackful *n* Sack *m kein pl*

'sack race *n* Sackhüpfen *nt*

sacrament ['sæk·rə·mənt] *n* REL Sakrament *nt*

sacramental [ˌsæk·rə·'men·təl] *adj* sakramental; ~ **wine** liturgisch geweihter Wein; (*in Roman Catholic Church*) Messwein *m*

sacred ['seɪ·krɪd] *adj place* heilig; *tradition* geheiligt

sacrifice ['sæk·rə·faɪs] **I.** *vt* ❶ (*kill*) opfern ❷ (*give up*) opfern, aufgeben **II.** *vi* **to ~ to the gods** den Göttern Opfer bringen **III.** *n* Opfer *nt;* **at great personal** ~ unter großem persönlichen Verzicht; **to make ~s** Opfer bringen

sacrilege ['sæk·rə·lɪdʒ] *n* Sakrileg *nt geh;* (*fig*) Verbrechen *nt*

sacrilegious [ˌsæk·rə·'lɪdʒ·əs] *adj* frevelhaft; (*fig*) verbrecherisch

sacrosanct ['sæk·roʊ·sæŋkt] *adj* (*esp hum*) sakrosankt *geh; right, treaty* unverletzlich

SAD [ˌes·eɪ·'di] *n abbrev of* **seasonal affective disorder** Winterdepression *f*

sad <-dd-> [sæd] *adj* ❶ (*unhappy*) traurig; **to look** ~ betrübt aussehen; **to make sb** ~ jdn betrüben [*o* traurig machen] ❷ (*depressing*) *news* traurig; *incident* betrüblich ❸ (*regrettable*) traurig, bedauerlich; ~ **to say** bedauerlicherweise ❹ (*pathetic*) bedauernswert, beklagenswert; (*hum, pej*) jämmerlich, erbärmlich; **what a ~ person he is** was ist er doch für ein Jammerlappen

sadden ['sæd·ən] *vt* traurig machen; (*to greater degree*) schwer treffen

saddle ['sæd·əl] **I.** *n* (*seat*) Sattel *m;* **to be in the** ~ (*riding*) im Sattel sein; (*fig: in charge*) im Amt sein **II.** *vt* ❶ (*put saddle on*) *horse* satteln ❷ (*fam: burden*) **to be ~d with sth** etw *akk* am Hals haben; **to ~ sb with sth** jdm etw *akk* anhalsen

'saddlebag *n* Satteltasche *f*

sadism ['seɪ·dɪz·əm] *n* Sadismus *m*

sadist ['seɪ·dɪst] *n* Sadist(in) *m(f)*

sadistic [sə·'dɪs·tɪk] *adj* sadistisch

sadly ['sæd·li] *adv* ❶ (*unhappily*) traurig, bekümmert ❷ (*regrettably*) bedauerlicherweise, leider ❸ (*completely*) völlig; **to be ~ mistaken** völlig danebenliegen *fam*

sadness ['sæd·nɪs] *n* Traurigkeit *f* (**about/at** über +*akk*)

safari [sə·'far·i] *n* Safari *f*

safe [seɪf] **I.** *adj* ❶ (*secure, protected*) sicher; [**have a**] ~ **trip!** gute Reise!; **to keep sth in a ~ place** etw sicher aufbewahren ❷ (*certain*) [relativ] sicher; **it's a ~ bet that ...** man kann davon ausgehen, dass ... ❸ (*avoiding risk*) *action, driver* vorsichtig ▶ PHRASES: **to be in ~ hands** in guten Händen sein; **to play it ~** auf Nummer Sicher gehen *fam* **II.** *n* Tresor *m,* Safe *m*

safe-de'posit box *n* Tresorfach *nt,* [Bank]schließfach *nt*

safeguard ['seɪf·gard] **I.** *vt* (*form*) schützen (**against** vor +*dat*); *sb's interests/rights* wahren **II.** *n* Schutz *m* (**against** vor +*dat*), Vorsichtsmaßnahme *f* (**against** gegen +*akk*); TECH Sicherung *f*

safe'keeping *n* [sichere] Aufbewahrung; **to be in sb's** ~ in jds Gewahrsam sein; **to give sth to sb for** ~ jdm etw *akk* in Verwahrung geben

safely ['seɪf·li] *adv* ❶ (*securely*) sicher ❷ (*avoiding risk*) vorsichtig; **drive ~!** fahr vorsichtig! ❸ (*without harm*) *person* wohlbehalten; *object* heil; **the parcel arrived** ~ das Paket kam heil an

safe 'sex *n* Safer Sex *m*

safety ['seɪf·ti] *n* (*condition of being safe*) Sicherheit *f; of a medicine* Unbedenklichkeit *f;* **place of** ~ sicherer Ort

'safety belt *n* Sicherheitsgurt *m*

'safety catch *n* Sicherung *f*

'safety curtain *n* THEAT eiserner Vorhang

'safety glass *n* Sicherheitsglas *nt*

'safety margin *n* Sicherheitsabstand *m;* ECON, STOCKEX Sicherheitsmarge *f*

'safety measures *npl* Sicherheitsmaßnahmen *pl*

'safety net *n* ❶ (*protective net*) Sicherheitsnetz *nt* ❷ (*fig*) soziales Netz

'safety pin *n* (*covered pin*) Sicherheitsnadel *f*

'safety regulations *npl* Sicherheitsvorschriften *pl*

S

'safety valve *n* Sicherheitsventil *nt*
saffron ['sæf·rən] **I.** *n* Safran *m* **II.** *adj* safrangelb
sag [sæg] **I.** *vi* <-gg-> ❶ (*droop*) [herab]hängen; *bed, roof, rope* durchhängen ❷ (*weaken*) *courage* sinken; **her spirits ~ged** ihre Stimmung wurde gedrückt **II.** *n* (*droop*) Durchhängen *nt*
saga ['sa·gə] *n* ❶ LIT (*medieval story*) Saga *f;* (*long family novel*) Familienroman *m* ❷ (*pej: long involved story*) [lange] Geschichte
sagacious [sə·'geɪ·ʃəs] *adj* (*form*) gescheit; *remark* scharfsinnig
sage¹ [seɪdʒ] **I.** *adj* weise **II.** *n* Weise(r) *f(m)*
sage² [seɪdʒ] *n* Salbei *m*
Sagittarius [ˌsædʒ·ə·'ter·i·əs] *n* ASTROL Schütze *m*
said [sed] *pp, pt of* **say**
sail [seɪl] **I.** *n* ❶ (*on boat*) Segel *nt* ❷ (*journey*) [Segel]törn *m* ❸ (*of windmill*) Flügel *m* ▶ PHRASES: **to set ~** in See stechen **II.** *vi* ❶ (*by ship*) fahren, reisen; (*by yacht*) segeln ❷ (*move effortlessly*) gleiten; (*move vigorously*) rauschen, segeln *fam;* **the ball ~ed over the fence** der Ball segelte über den Zaun; **she ~ed into the room** sie kam ins Zimmer gerauscht ▶ PHRASES: **to ~ close to the wind** sich hart an der Grenze des Erlaubten bewegen **III.** *vt* ❶ (*navigate*) *ship* steuern; *yacht* segeln ❷ (*travel*) **to ~ the Pacific** den Pazifik befahren
'sailboard *n* Surfbrett *nt*
'sailboat *n* Segelboot *nt*
sailing ['seɪ·lɪŋ] *n* SPORTS Segelsport *m,* Segeln *nt*
sailor ['seɪ·lər] *n* ❶ (*member of ship's crew*) Matrose *m,* Seemann *m* ❷ (*person who sails*) Segler(in) *m(f)*
'sailor suit *n* Matrosenanzug *m*
saint [seɪnt, sənt] *n* ❶ (*holy person*) Heilige(r) *f(m);* **to make sb a ~** jdn heiligsprechen; **S~ Peter** der heilige Petrus ❷ (*fam: very good person*) Heilige(r) *f(m);* **to be no ~** (*hum*) nicht gerade ein Heiliger/eine Heilige sein
saintliness ['seɪnt·lɪ·nɪs] *n* Heiligkeit *f*
saintly ['seɪnt·li] *adj* heilig, fromm
'saint's day *n* Heiligenfest *nt*

Der **Saint Patrick's Day** am 17. März ist kein gesetzlicher Feiertag in den USA. Seit 1737 feiert jedoch die irische Gemeinschaft in den USA ihren heiligen Schutzpatron an diesem Tag. Der 17. März erinnert an den Todestag Saint Patricks, eines irischen Missionars, der sein Leben der Christianisierung Irlands widmete. Der Tradition nach trägt man am **Saint Patrick's Day** grüne Kleidung und ein Kleeblatt, was den Frühling und Irland symbolisiert. An diesem Feiertag werden Feste und Umzüge organisiert. Das bekannteste und wichtigste Fest findet in New York statt, doch gibt es auch in allen anderen großen Städten Umzüge.

sake¹ [seɪk] *n* ❶ (*purpose*) **for the ~ of sth** um einer S. *gen* willen ❷ (*benefit*) **for sb's ~** jdm zuliebe; **to stay together for the ~ of the children** der Kinder wegen zusammenbleiben ▶ PHRASES: **for goodness'** [*or* **heaven's**] **~** um Gottes [*o* Himmels] willen
sake² ['sa·ki] *n* Sake *m*
salable ['seɪ·lə·bəl] *adj* verkäuflich; **to be easily ~** sich gut verkaufen
salacious [sə·'leɪ·ʃəs] *adj* (*pej*) *joke, poem* obszön; *comment* anzüglich; *person* geil
salad ['sæl·əd] *n* Salat *m*
'salad bowl *n* Salatschüssel *f*
'salad dressing *n* [Salat]mayonnaise *f*
salami [sə·'la·mi] *n* Salami *f*
salaried ['sæl·ə·rid] *adj* bezahlt; **~ position** Stelle *f* mit festem Gehalt
salary ['sæl·ə·ri] *n* Gehalt *nt;* **annual ~** Jahresgehalt *nt;* (*for blue-collar worker*) Lohntüte *f*
sale [seɪl] *n* ❶ (*act of selling*) Verkauf *m;* **for ~** zu verkaufen; **to be on ~** erhältlich sein ❷ (*amount sold*) Absatz *m;* **~s of cars were down this week** die Verkaufszahlen für Autos gingen diese Woche nach unten ❸ (*at reduced prices*) Ausverkauf *m;* **to be on ~** im Angebot [*o* Sonderangebot] sein; **going-out-of-business ~** Räumungsverkauf *m* ❹ (*auction*) Auktion *f*
saleable ['seɪ·lə·bəl] *adj see* **salable**
'sale price *n* Verkaufspreis *m*
'sales clerk *n* Verkäufer(in) *m(f)*
'sales conference *n* Vertreterkonferenz *f*
'salesman *n* Verkäufer *m,* Handelsvertreter *m;* **door-to-door ~** Hausierer *m*
sales 'manager *n* Verkaufsleiter(in) *m(f)*
'salesmanship *n* (*technique*) Verkaufstechnik *f;* (*skill*) Verkaufsgeschick *nt*
'salesperson *n* Verkäufer(in) *m(f)*
'sales pitch *n* ❶ (*high-pressure approach*) mit [allem] Nachdruck geführtes Verkaufsgespräch ❷ (*specific approach*) Verkaufstaktik *f*
'sales rep *n* (*fam*), **'sales representative** *n* Vertreter(in) *m(f)*
'sales tax *n* Umsatzsteuer *f*
'saleswoman *n* Verkäuferin *f*
salient ['seɪl·jənt] *adj* (*important*) bedeutend; **the ~ points** die Hauptpunkte *pl*
saline ['seɪ·lin] **I.** *adj* salzig **II.** *n* Salzlösung *f;* **~ [solution]** MED Kochsalzlösung *f*
saliva [sə·'laɪ·və] *n* Speichel *m*
salivate ['sæl·ə·veɪt] *vi* Speichel produzieren
sallow <-er, -est *or* more ~, most ~> ['sæl·oʊ] *adj* blassgelb; *complexion* fahl; *skin* bleich
sally ['sæl·i] *vi* <-ie-> (*form, liter*) ■ **to ~ forth [to do sth]** aufbrechen[, um etw zu tun]
salmon ['sæm·ən] **I.** *n* <*pl* - *or* -s> Lachs *m;* **smoked ~** Räucherlachs *m* **II.** *adj* lachsfarben
salmonella [ˌsæl·mə·'nel·ə] *n* Salmonelle[n] *f[pl]*

S

salmon 'trout *n* Lachsforelle *f*
salon [se·'lan] *n* Frisiersalon *m;* **beauty ~** Schönheitssalon *m*
saloon [sə·'lun] *n* (*dated*) Saloon *m*
salsa ['sal·sə] *n* (*spicy sauce, music, dance*) Salsa *f*
salt [sɔlt] **I.** *n* (*seasoning, chemical compound, granular substance*) Salz *nt;* **a pinch of ~** eine Prise Salz ► PHRASES: **to take sth with a <u>pinch</u> of ~** etw mit Vorsicht genießen *fam;* **to be <u>worth</u> one's ~** sein Geld wert sein **II.** *vt* ❶ (*season food*) salzen ❷ (*sprinkle*) mit Salz bestreuen; **to ~ the roads** Salz [auf die Straßen] streuen
'salt flats *npl* Salzwüste *f*
salt 'lake *n* Salzsee *m*
'salt mine *n* Salzmine *f*
saltpeter ['sɔlt·ˌpi·t̬ər] *n* Salpeter *m*
'salt shaker *n* Salzstreuer *m*
'salt solution *n* Kochsalzlösung *f*
salt 'water *n* Salzwasser *nt*
'saltwater *adj attr* Salzwasser-; **~ fish** Seefisch *m*
salty ['sɔl·ti] *adj* salzig
salubrious [sə·'lu·bri·əs] *adj* ❶ *place* vornehm ❷ (*healthy*) gesund
salutary ['sæl·jə·ter·i] *adj* heilsam
salutation [ˌsæl·jə·'teɪ·ʃən] *n* (*in letter*) Anrede *f;* (*liter: greeting*) Gruß *m*
salute [sə·'lut] **I.** *vt* ❶ (*form: greet*) grüßen; (*welcome*) begrüßen ❷ MIL ■ **to ~ sb** vor jdm salutieren **II.** *vi* MIL salutieren **III.** *n* ❶ (*gesture*) Gruß *m* ❷ MIL Salut *m;* (*firing of guns*) Salut[schuss] *m;* **to give a ~** salutieren
salvage ['sæl·vɪdʒ] **I.** *vt* ❶ (*rescue*) *cargo* bergen ❷ (*preserve*) *reputation* wahren **II.** *n* ❶ (*rescue*) Bergung *f* ❷ (*sth saved*) Bergungsgut *nt*
salvation [sæl·'veɪ·ʃən] *n* ❶ (*rescue, sth that saves*) Rettung *f;* **beyond ~** nicht mehr zu retten ❷ REL Erlösung *f*
Salvation 'Army *n* Heilsarmee *f*
salve [sæv] *n* ❶ (*ointment*) Heilsalbe *f* ❷ (*sth that soothes*) Linderung *f*
salvo <*pl* -s *or* -es> ['sæl·voʊ] *n* MIL (*a. fig*) Salve *f*
Samaritan [sə·'mer·ɪ·tən] *n* REL **the good ~** der barmherzige Samariter
same [seɪm] **I.** *adj attr* ❶ (*exactly similar*) ■ **the ~ ...** der/die/das gleiche ...; (*identical*) der-/die-/dasselbe; **she's the ~ age as me** sie ist genauso alt wie ich ❷ (*not another*) ■ **the ~ ...** der/die/das gleiche ...; **our teacher always wears the ~ sweater** unser Lehrer trägt stets denselben Pullover; **at the ~ time** gleichzeitig, zur gleichen Zeit; (*nevertheless*) trotzdem ► PHRASES: **to be in the ~ <u>boat</u> [as sb]** im gleichen Boot wie jd sitzen **II.** *pron* ■ **the ~** der-/die-/dasselbe; **they realized that things would never be the ~ again** es wurde ihnen klar, dass nichts mehr so sein würde wie früher; **to be one and the ~** ein und der-/die-/dasselbe sein ► PHRASES: **<u>all</u> the ~** trotzdem **III.** *adv* ■ **the ~** gleich; **I feel just the ~ [as you do]** mir geht es genauso [wie dir]
sameness ['seɪm·nɪs] *n* (*identity*) Gleichheit *f;* (*uniformity*) Gleichförmigkeit *f*
Samoa [sə·'moʊ·ə] *n* Samoa *nt*
sample ['sæm·pəl] **I.** *n* ❶ (*small quantity*) Probe *f,* Muster *nt;* MED **blood ~** Blutprobe *f;* **fabric ~s** Stoffmuster *pl* ❷ (*representative group*) *of people* Querschnitt *m; of things* Stichprobe *f* **II.** *vt* ❶ (*try*) [aus]probieren; *food* kosten, probieren ❷ (*survey*) stichprobenartig untersuchen
'sample book *n* Musterheft *nt*
sampler ['sæm·plər] *n* ❶ (*embroidery*) Stickmustertuch *nt* ❷ (*collection*) Probeset *nt*
sampling ['sæm·plɪŋ] *n* ❶ (*surveying*) Stichprobenerhebung *f* ❷ (*testing*) stichprobenartige Untersuchung ❸ MUS Mischen *nt*
sanatorium <*pl* -s *or* -ria> [ˌsæn·ə·'tɔr·i·əm] *n* Sanatorium *nt*
sanctify <-ie-> ['sæŋk·tɪ·faɪ] *vt* REL (*consecrate*) weihen
sanctimonious [ˌsæŋk·tɪ·'moʊ·ni·əs] *adj* (*pej*) scheinheilig
sanction ['sæŋk·ʃən] **I.** *n* ❶ (*approval*) Sanktion *f geh,* Zustimmung *f* ❷ (*to enforce compliance*) Strafmaßnahme *f;* LAW, POL Sanktion *f* **II.** *vt* ❶ (*allow*) sanktionieren *geh* ❷ (*impose penalty*) unter Strafe stellen
sanctity ['sæŋk·tɪ·t̬i] *n* ❶ REL Heiligkeit *f* ❷ (*inviolability*) Unantastbarkeit *f*
sanctuary ['sæŋk·tʃu·er·i] *n* ❶ (*holy place*) Heiligtum *nt;* (*near altar*) Altarraum *m* ❷ (*refuge*) Zuflucht *f;* **to find/seek ~** Zuflucht finden/suchen ❸ (*for animals*) Schutzgebiet *nt*
sand [sænd] **I.** *n* ❶ (*substance*) Sand *m* ❷ (*expanse*) ■ **~s** *pl* (*beach*) Sandstrand *m; of desert* Sand *m kein pl* **II.** *vt* (*with sandpaper*) [ab]schmirgeln; (*smooth*) abschleifen
sandal ['sæn·dəl] *n* Sandale *f*
'sandalwood *n* Sandelholz *nt*
'sandbag I. *n* Sandsack *m* **II.** *vt* <-gg-> ❶ (*protect*) mit Sandsäcken schützen ❷ (*hit*) niederschlagen
'sandbank *n* Sandbank *f*
'sandbar *n* [schmale] Sandbank
'sandblast *vt* sandstrahlen
'sandbox *n* Sandkasten *m*
'sandcastle *n* Sandburg *f*
'sand dune *n* Sanddüne *f*
'sandpaper I. *n* Schmirgelpapier *nt* **II.** *vt* abschmirgeln
'sandstone *n* Sandstein *m*
'sandstorm *n* Sandsturm *m*
sandwich ['sænd·wɪtʃ] **I.** *n* <*pl* -es> Sandwich *m o nt* ► PHRASES: **to be one ~ <u>short</u> of a picnic** (*hum fam*) völlig übergeschnappt sein **II.** *vt* (*squeeze*) einklemmen; **I was sandwiched between two very large men** ich war zwischen zwei riesigen Männern eingeklemmt; ■ **to ~ sth [in] between sth** (*fig*) etw zwischen etw *dat* dazwischenschieben

'sandwich board *n* Reklametafel *f* (*mittels verbindendem Schulterriemen von einer Person auf Brust und Rücken als doppelseitiges Werbeplakat getragen*)

sandy ['sæn·di] *adj* ① (*containing sand*) sandig ② *color* sandfarben

sane [seɪn] *adj* ① *person* geistig gesund; LAW zurechnungsfähig ② *action* vernünftig

sang [sæŋ] *pt of* **sing**

sanitarium <*pl* -s *or* -ria> [ˌsæn·ɪ·'ter·i·əm] *n* Sanatorium *nt*

sanitary ['sæn·ɪ·ter·i] *adj* hygienisch; *installations* sanitär

'sanitary napkin *n* Damenbinde *f*

sanitation [ˌsæn·ɪ·'teɪ·ʃən] *n* ① (*promotion of hygiene*) Hygiene *f;* (*provision of toilets*) sanitäre Anlagen ② (*water disposal*) Abwasserkanalisation *f*

sanity ['sæn·ɪ·t̬i] *n* ① (*mental health*) gesunder Verstand; LAW Zurechnungsfähigkeit *f;* (*hum*) Verstand *m fam;* **to preserve one's ~** bei Verstand bleiben ② (*sensibleness*) Vernünftigkeit *f*

sank [sæŋk] *pt of* **sink**

Santa, **Santa Claus** [ˌsæn·t̬ə·'klɔz] *n* Weihnachtsmann *m*

sap¹ [sæp] *n* ① (*of tree*) Saft *m* ② (*sl: dope*) Trottel *m pej fam*

sap² [sæp] *vt* <-pp-> ① (*drain*) **to ~ sb's energy** an jds Energie zehren *geh* ② (*undermine*) unterhöhlen

sapling ['sæp·lɪŋ] *n* junger Baum

sapphire ['sæf·aɪr] **I.** *n* Saphir *m* **II.** *adj* saphirfarben

Saran® Wrap, **Saran® wrap** [sə·'ræn-] *n* Frischhaltefolie *f*

sarcasm ['sar·kæz·əm] *n* Sarkasmus *m*

sarcastic [sar·'kæs·tɪk] *adj person, remark* sarkastisch; *tongue* scharf

sarcophagus <*pl* -es *or* -gi> [sar·'kaf·ə·gəs] *n* Sarkophag *m*

sardine [sar·'din] *n* Sardine *f;* **to be packed like ~s** wie die Ölsardinen zusammengepfercht sein

Sardinia [sar·'dɪn·i·ə] *n* GEOG Sardinien *nt*

sardonic [sar·'dan·ɪk] *adj* höhnisch

sari ['sa·ri] *n* Sari *m*

SARS, **Sars** [sarz] *n* MED *acr for* **severe acute respiratory syndrome** SARS *kein art*

SASE [ˌes·eɪ·es·'i] *n abbrev of* **self-addressed stamped envelope** adressierter und frankierter Rückumschlag

sash¹ <*pl* -es> [sæʃ] *n* Schärpe *f*

sash² <*pl* -es> [sæʃ] *n* (*in windows*) Fensterrahmen *m;* (*in doors*) Türrahmen *m*

sat [sæt] *pt, pp of* **sit**

Satan ['seɪ·tən] *n* Satan *m*

satanic [sə·'tæn·ɪk] *adj* teuflisch; **~ rite** Satansritus *m*

Satanism ['seɪ·'tən·ɪz·əm] *n* Satanismus *m*

satchel ['sætʃ·əl] *n* [Schul]ranzen *m*

sate [seɪt] *vt* (*form*) *desire, hunger* stillen

satellite ['sæt̬·ə·laɪt] *n* ① ASTRON Trabant *m* ② AEROSP, TECH Satellit *m*

'satellite dish *n* Satellitenschüssel *f fam*

satellite 'television *n* Satellitenfernsehen *nt*

satiate ['seɪ·ʃi·eɪt] *vt usu passive curiosity, hunger, thirst* stillen; *demand* befriedigen

satin ['sæt·ən] *n* Satin *m*

satire ['sæt·aɪr] *n* LIT Satire *f*

satirical [sə·'tɪr·ɪ·kəl] *adj literature, film* satirisch; (*mocking, joking*) ironisch

satirist ['sæt̬·ər·ɪst] *n* Satiriker(in) *m(f)*

satirize ['sæt̬·ə·raɪz] *vt* satirisch darstellen

satisfaction [ˌsæt̬·ɪs·'fæk·ʃən] *n* ① (*positive feeling*) Zufriedenheit *f,* Befriedigung *f;* ■ **to the ~ of sb** zu jds Zufriedenheit; **to my great ~** zu meiner großen Genugtuung; **I get a lot of ~ from my job** meine Arbeit bereitet mir volle Befriedigung ② (*sth producing satisfaction*) Genugtuung *f geh* ③ (*state of being convinced*) Zufriedenheit *f*

satisfactory [ˌsæt̬·ɪs·'fæk·tə·ri] UNIV, SCH **I.** *adj* befriedigend, ≈ befriedigend; MED zufrieden stellend **II.** *n* Ausreichend *nt kein pl* (*Mindestnote für das Bestehen einer Prüfung*)

satisfy <-ie-> ['sæt̬·ɪs·faɪ] **I.** *vt* ① (*meet needs*) zufrieden stellen; *curiosity, need* befriedigen ② (*fulfill*) *demand* befriedigen; *condition, requirement* erfüllen ③ (*convince*) ■ **to ~ sb that ...** jdn überzeugen, dass ... **II.** *vi* (*form*) befriedigen

satisfying ['sæt̬·ɪs·faɪ·ɪŋ] *adj* zufrieden stellend, befriedigend

saturate ['sætʃ·ə·reɪt] *vt* ① (*make wet*) durchnässen ② (*fill to capacity*) [völlig] auslasten; CHEM, ECON sättigen

saturated ['sætʃ·ə·reɪ·t̬ɪd] *adj* ① (*soaking wet*) durchnässt; *soil* aufgeweicht ② CHEM *solution* gesättigt

saturation [ˌsætʃ·ə·'reɪ·ʃən] *n* CHEM, ECON Sättigung *f;* **~ point** Sättigungspunkt *m*

Saturday ['sæt̬·ər·deɪ] *n* Samstag *m; see also* **Tuesday**

Saturn ['sæt̬·ərn] *n* ASTRON Saturn *m*

satyr ['seɪ·t̬ər] *n* (*mythical figure*) Satyr *m*

sauce [sɔs] **I.** *n* ① Soße *f;* **tomato ~** Tomatensoße *f;* **apple ~** Apfelmus *nt,* Apfelkompott *nt* ② (*pej sl: alcohol*) Alkohol *m* **II.** *vt* (*fam: add interest*) ■ **to ~ sth up** etw würzen *fig*

'sauceboat *n* Sauciere *f*

'saucepan *n* Kochtopf *m*

saucer ['sɔ·sər] *n* Untertasse *f;* **to have eyes like ~s** große Augen haben

sauciness ['sɔ·sɪ·nɪs] *n* (*dated: impertinence*) Frechheit *f*

saucy ['sɔ·si] *adj* (*impertinent*) frech

Saudi ['saʊ·di] **I.** *n* (*male*) Saudi[-Araber] *m;* (*female*) Saudi-Araberin *f* **II.** *adj* saudisch

Saudi A'rabia *n* Saudi-Arabien *nt*

Saudi A'rabian **I.** *n* Saudi-Araber(in) *m(f)* **II.** *adj* saudi-arabisch

sauerkraut ['saʊ·ər·kraʊt] *n* Sauerkraut *nt*

sauna ['sɔ·nə] *n* Sauna *f*

saunter ['sɔn·tər] *vi* (*stroll*) bummeln *fam;* (*amble*) schlendern; **to ~ along** herumschlendern

sausage ['sɔ·sɪdʒ] *n* ❶ (*for frying, grilling*) Wurst *f;* (*small*) Würstchen *nt* ❷ (*for slicing*) Wurst *f;* (*type of sausage*) Wurstsorte *f*

sauté [sɔ·'teɪ] *vt* <sautéed *or* sautéd> [kurz] [an]braten

savage ['sæv·ɪdʒ] **I.** *adj* ❶ (*primitive*) wild ❷ (*fierce*) brutal **II.** *n* ❶ (*pej: barbarian*) Barbar(in) *m(f)* ❷ (*usu pej: primitive person*) Wilde(r) *f(m) pej* **III.** *vt* anfallen; (*fig*) attackieren

savagely ['sæv·ɪdʒ·li] *adv* brutal

savagery ['sæv·ɪdʒ·ri] *n* Brutalität *f*

savanna(h) [sə·'væn·ə] *n* Savanne *f*

save [seɪv] **I.** *vt* ❶ (*rescue*) retten (**from** vor +*dat*); **to ~ sb's life** jds Leben retten ❷ (*keep for future use*) aufheben; *money* sparen ❸ (*collect*) sammeln ❹ (*avoid wasting*) *time, energy* sparen; **to ~ one's breath** sich *dat* seine Worte sparen ❺ COMPUT sichern, speichern ❻ SPORTS *goal* verhindern; *penalty kick, penalty shot* abwehren ► PHRASES: **a stitch in time ~s nine** (*prov*) was du heute kannst besorgen, das verschiebe nicht auf morgen *prov* **II.** *vi* ❶ (*keep money*) sparen (**for** für +*akk*); **to ~ with a bank** ein Sparkonto bei einer Bank haben ❷ (*conserve sth*) ■**to ~ on sth** bei etw *dat* sparen **III.** *n* (*in hockey, soccer*) Abwehr *f*

saver ['seɪ·vər] *n* (*person*) Sparer(in) *m(f);* (*investor*) Anleger(in) *m(f)*

saving ['seɪ·vɪŋ] *n* ❶ (*money*) ■**~s** *pl* Ersparnisse *pl* ❷ (*act*) Einsparung *f;* (*result of economizing*) Ersparnis *f*

savings account ['seɪ·vɪŋz·ə·ˌkaʊnt] *n* Sparkonto *nt*

'savings bank *n Sparkasse, die nicht auf Profitbasis arbeitet und auch für kleine Einlagen Zinsen bietet*

savior ['seɪv·jər] *n* Retter(in) *m(f);* ■**the S~** REL der Erlöser

savor ['seɪ·vər] **I.** *n* (*taste*) Geschmack *m* **II.** *vt* auskosten, genießen

savory ['seɪ·və·ri] *adj* ❶ (*not sweet*) pikant; (*salty*) salzig ❷ (*appetizing*) appetitanregend

savvy ['sæv·i] **I.** *adj* (*fam: shrewd*) ausgebufft *sl* **II.** *n* (*fam*) Köpfchen *nt;* (*practical knowledge*) Können *nt*

saw¹ [sɔ] **I.** *n* Säge *f* **II.** *vt* <-ed, -ed *or* sawn> [zer]sägen; **to ~ a tree down** einen Baum fällen **III.** *vi* (*operate a saw*) sägen

saw² [sɔ] *pt of* **see**

'sawdust *n* Sägemehl *nt*

'sawed-off *adj attr* **~ shotgun** abgesägte Schrotflinte

'sawmill *n* Sägemühle *f*

sawn [sɔn] *pp of* **saw**

Saxony ['sæk·sə·ni] *n* Sachsen *nt*

saxophone ['sæk·sə·foʊn] *n* Saxophon *nt*

saxophonist ['sæk·sə·foʊ·nɪst] *n* Saxophonist(in) *m(f)*

say [seɪ] **I.** *vt* <said, said> ❶ (*utter*) sagen; **what did you ~ to him?** was hast du ihm gesagt?; **what did they ~ about the house?** was haben sie über das Haus gesagt?; **what exactly are you trying to ~?** was willst du eigentlich sagen?; **to ~ goodbye to sb** sich von jdm verabschieden; **to have nothing to ~** nichts zu sagen haben; **to ~ nothing of the cost** ganz zu schweigen von den Kosten; **it goes without ~ing that ...** es versteht sich von selbst, dass ... ❷ (*recite aloud*) aufsagen; *prayer* sprechen ❸ (*give information*) sagen; **the sign ~s ...** auf dem Schild steht ...; **it ~s on the bottle ...** auf der Flasche heißt es ...; **my watch ~s 3 o'clock** auf meiner Uhr ist es 3 [Uhr]; **the way he drives ~s a lot about his character** sein Fahrstil sagt eine Menge über seinen Charakter aus ❹ (*tell, command*) ■**to ~ whether/where etc.** sagen, ob/wo usw.; **she said to call her back** sie sagte, du sollst sie zurückrufen; **to ~ when** (*indicate when you have enough*) sagen, wenn es genug ist ► PHRASES: **~ no more!** (*fam*) alles klar!; **you don't ~!** was du nicht sagst!; **you said it!** (*fam*) du sagst es! **II.** *vi* <said, said> sagen; **where was he going? — he didn't ~** wo wollte er hin? – das hat er nicht gesagt; **hard to ~** schwer zu sagen; **that's not for me to ~** es steht mir nicht zu, das zu entscheiden **III.** *n* Meinung *f;* **to have a/no ~ in sth** bei etw *dat* ein/kein Mitspracherecht haben **IV.** *interj* ❶ (*fam: to express doubt*) **~s who?** wer sagt das? ❷ (*expresses positive reaction*) sag mal *fam;* **~, that's really a great idea!** Mensch, das ist ja echt eine tolle Idee! *fam*

saying ['seɪ·ɪŋ] *n* (*adage*) Sprichwort *nt;* **as the ~ goes** wie es so schön heißt

'say-so *n* (*fam: approval*) Erlaubnis *f*

SC, S.C. *abbrev of* **South Carolina**

scab [skæb] **I.** *n* ❶ *of wound* Kruste *f*, Schorf *m* ❷ (*pej fam: strikebreaker*) Streikbrecher(in) *m(f)* **II.** *vi* ❶ *wound* verharschen (*Schorf bilden*) ❷ (*pej: work during strike*) ein Streikbrecher/eine Streikbrecherin sein

scabby ['skæb·i] *adj* ❶ (*having scabs*) schorfig ❷ (*pej fam: reprehensible*) schäbig

scabies ['skeɪ·biz] *n* Krätze *f*

scaffold ['skæf·əld] **I.** *n* ❶ (*framework*) [Bau]gerüst *nt* ❷ (*hist: for executions*) Schafott *nt* **II.** *vt* **to ~ a building** ein Gebäude mit einem Gerüst versehen

scaffolding ['skæf·əl·dɪŋ] *n* [Bau]gerüst *nt*

scalawag ['skæl·ə·wæg] *n* Schlingel *m hum*

scald [skɔld] **I.** *vt* ❶ (*burn*) verbrühen ❷ (*heat*) erhitzen; *fruit* dünsten; *milk* abkochen **II.** *n* MED Verbrühung *f*

scalding ['skɔl·dɪŋ] *adj liquid* kochend; **~ hot** kochend [*o* siedend] heiß

scale¹ [skeɪl] **I.** *n* ❶ (*on skin*) Schuppe *f* ❷ (*mineral coating*) Ablagerung *f* **II.** *vt* (*remove scales*) *fish* [ab]schuppen

scale² [skeɪl] **I.** *n* ❶ (*system of gradation*) Skala *f; of map* Maßstab *m;* ■**to be to ~** *building, drawing* maßstab[s]getreu sein ❷ (*relative degree/extent*) Umfang *m;* **on a national ~** auf nationaler Ebene; **on a large/small ~** im

S

großen/kleinen Rahmen ③ MUS Tonleiter *f* **II.** *vt* (*climb*) *mountain, peak* besteigen; **to ~ a fence/wall** auf einen Zaun/ eine Mauer klettern

◆**scale down I.** *vt* reduzieren; ECON *production* einschränken; (*make smaller in proportion*) [vom Maßstab her] verkleinern **II.** *vi* verkleinern

◆**scale up I.** *vt* erweitern; ECON *production* erhöhen; (*make bigger in proportion*) vergrößern **II.** *vi* hinaufklettern

scale³ [skeɪl] *n usu pl* (*weighing device*) Waage *f;* **to tip the ~s** (*fig*) den [entscheidenden] Ausschlag geben

scale 'model *n* maßstab[s]getreues Modell

scallion ['skæl·jən] *n* (*green onion*) Frühlingszwiebel *f*

scallop ['skal·əp] *n* ① (*edible shellfish*) Kammmuschel *f;* (*esp in gastronomy*) Jakobsmuschel *f* ② (*thin slice of meat*) **veal ~** Schnitzel *nt*

scallywag ['skæl·i·wæg] *n* (*fam*) *see* **scalawag**

scalp [skælp] **I.** *n* (*head skin*) Kopfhaut *f* **II.** *vt* ① (*hist: remove head skin*) skalpieren ② (*pej: sell unofficially*) *tickets* unter der Hand verkaufen

scalpel ['skæl·pəl] *n* Skalpell *nt*

scalper ['skæl·pər] *n* (*pej*) Schwarzhändler(in) *m(f)* (*für Eintrittskarten*)

scaly ['skeɪ·li] *adj* ① ZOOL, MED schuppig ② TECH verkalkt

scam [skæm] *n* (*fam*) Betrug *m*

scamp [skæmp] *n* (*fam*) Schlingel *m hum*

scamper ['skæm·pər] *vi* flitzen *fam*

scan [skæn] **I.** *vt* <-nn-> ① (*scrutinize*) absuchen (**for** nach *+dat*) ② (*glance through*) überfliegen ③ COMPUT einlesen, einscannen **II.** *n* ① (*glancing through*) [flüchtige] Durchsicht ② MED Abtastung *f,* Scan *m;* **brain ~** Computertomographie *f* des Schädels

scandal ['skæn·dəl] *n* ① (*cause of outrage*) Skandal *m;* (*disgrace a.*) Schande *f* ② (*gossip*) Skandalgeschichten *pl*

scandalize ['skæn·də·laɪz] *vt* schockieren; (*offend*) empören

scandalous ['skæn·də·ləs] *adv* skandalös; (*shocking*) schockierend

Scandinavia [ˌskæn·dɪ·'neɪ·vi·ə] *n* Skandinavien *nt*

Scandinavian [ˌskæn·dɪ·'neɪ·vi·ən] **I.** *adj* skandinavisch **II.** *n* Skandinavier(in) *m(f)*

scanner ['skæn·ər] *n* COMPUT, MED Scanner *m*

'scanning *n* COMPUT, MED Scannen *nt*

scant [skænt] *adj attr* ① (*not enough*) unzureichend; **to pay ~ attention to sth** etw kaum beachten ② (*almost*) **a ~ cup of flour** eine knappe Tasse Mehl

scantily ['skæn·tɪ·li] *adv* spärlich; **~ clad** freizügig gekleidet

scanty ['skæn·ti] *adj* ① (*very small*) knapp ② (*barely sufficient*) unzureichend; *evidence* unzulänglich

scapegoat ['skeɪp·goʊt] *n* Sündenbock *m*

scar [skar] **I.** *n* MED Narbe *f* **II.** *vt* <-rr-> ■**to be ~red [by sth]** [von etw *dat*] gezeichnet sein; **to be ~red for life** fürs [ganze] Leben gezeichnet sein

scarce [skers] *adj* knapp; (*rare*) rar; **to make oneself ~** sich aus dem Staub machen *fam*

scarcely ['skers·li] *adv* ① (*barely*) kaum ② (*certainly not*) **to be ~ a good reason to do [*or* for] sth** nicht gerade ein guter Grund sein, etw zu tun [*o* für etw *akk* sein]

scarcity ['sker·sɪ·t̬i] *n* Knappheit *f;* **~ value** Seltenheitswert *m*

scare [sker] **I.** *n* ① (*fright*) Schreck[en] *m;* **to give sb a ~** jdm einen Schrecken einjagen ② (*public panic*) Hysterie *f;* **bomb ~** Bombendrohung *f* **II.** *adj attr* Panik-; **~ story** Schauergeschichte *f;* **~ tactic** Panikmache *f* **III.** *vt* ■**to ~ sb** jdm Angst machen ▶PHRASES: **to ~ the living daylights out of sb** jdn zu Tode erschrecken **IV.** *vi* erschrecken

◆**scare away, scare off** *vt* ① (*frighten into leaving*) verscheuchen ② (*discourage*) abschrecken

scarecrow ['sker·kroʊ] *n* Vogelscheuche *f*

scaremonger ['sker·ˌmaŋ·gər] *n* Panikmacher(in) *m(f)*

scarf¹ <*pl* -s *or* scarves> [skarf] *n* FASHION Schal *m;* **silk ~** Seidentuch *nt*

scarf² [skarf] *vt* (*fam: eat*) verschlingen

scarlet ['skar·lət] **I.** *n* Scharlachrot *nt* **II.** *adj* scharlachrot

scarlet 'fever *n* Scharlach *m*

scary ['sker·i] *adj* ① (*frightening*) Furcht erregend ② (*uncanny*) unheimlich

scat [skæt] *interj* (*fam*) ■**~!** hau ab!

scathing ['skeɪ·ðɪŋ] *adj* versengend; *criticism* scharf; *remark* bissig

scatter ['skæt̬·ər] **I.** *vt* verstreuen; PHYS streuen **II.** *vi crowd, protesters* sich zerstreuen **III.** *n* ① (*liter: small amount*) [vereinzeltes] Häufchen ② PHYS Streuung *f*

'scatterbrain *n* zerstreute Person

'scatterbrained *adj* zerstreut, schusselig

scattered ['skæt̬·ərd] *adj* ① (*strewn about*) verstreut ② (*far apart*) weit verstreut ③ (*sporadic*) vereinzelt

scavenge ['skæv·ɪndʒ] **I.** *vi* ① (*search*) stöbern (**for** nach *+dat*) ② (*feed*) Aas fressen **II.** *vt* (*find*) aufstöbern; (*get*) ergattern *fam*

scavenger ['skæv·ɪn·dʒər] *n* ① (*animal*) Aasfresser *m* ② (*pej: person*) Aasgeier *m fam o pej*

scavenger hunt *n* Schnitzeljagd *f*

scenario [sə·'ner·i·oʊ] *n* THEAT, COMM Szenario *nt;* **worst-case ~** schlimmster Fall

scene [sin] *n* ① ART, THEAT, FILM Szene *f* ② THEAT, FILM (*setting*) Schauplatz *m;* (*scenery*) Kulisse *f;* **behind the ~s** (*a. fig*) hinter den Kulissen ③ LAW **crime ~** Tatort *m* ④ (*real-life event*) Szene *f;* **a ~ of horrifying destruction** ein schreckliches Bild der Verwüstung; (*milieu*) **drug ~** Drogenszene *f*

scenery ['si·nə·ri] *n* ① (*landscape*) Land-

S

schaft *f* ❷ THEAT, FILM Bühnenbild *nt*
scenic ['si·nɪk] *adj* ❶ *attr* THEAT Bühnen- ❷ *landscape* landschaftlich schön
scent [sent] **I.** *n* ❶ (*aroma*) Duft *m* ❷ (*animal smell*) Fährte *f;* ■ **to be on the ~ of sb/sth** (*a. fig*) jdm/etw auf der Fährte sein *a. fig* ❸ (*perfume*) Parfüm *nt* **II.** *vt* ❶ (*smell*) wittern ❷ (*detect*) *danger, presence* ahnen ❸ (*fill with pleasant odor*) parfümieren
scentless ['sent·lɪs] *adj* geruchlos
scepter ['sep·tər] *n* Zepter *nt*
schedule ['skedʒ·ul] **I.** *n* ❶ (*timetable*) Zeitplan *m;* TRANSP Fahrplan *m;* SPORTS Spielplan *m;* SCH, UNIV Stundenplan *m* ❷ (*plan of work*) Zeitplan *m;* **work ~** Dienstplan *m;* (*plan of events*) Programm *nt;* **ahead of ~** früher als geplant; **behind ~** im Verzug; **on ~** termingerecht, pünktlich **II.** *vt usu passive* planen; *meeting* ansetzen; **they've ~d him to speak at three o'clock** sie haben seine Rede für drei Uhr geplant
scheduled ['skedʒ·uld] *adj attr* (*as planned*) geplant; TRANSP planmäßig
schematic [ski·'mæt̬·ɪk] *adj diagram* schematisch
scheme [skim] **I.** *n* ❶ (*pej: plot*) [finsterer] Plan; LAW, POL Verschwörung *f* ❷ (*overall pattern*) Gesamtbild *nt;* **it fits into his ~ of things** das passt in sein Bild; **color ~** Farb[en]zusammenstellung *f* **II.** *vi* (*pej: plan deviously*) planen
schemer ['ski·mər] *n* (*pej*) Intrigant(in) *m(f) geh*
scheming ['ski·mɪŋ] **I.** *adj attr* (*pej*) intrigant *geh;* (*in a clever way*) raffiniert **II.** *n* Intrigieren *nt*
schizophrenia [ˌskɪt·sə·'fri·ni·ə] *n* ❶ MED Schizophrenie *f* ❷ (*fam: of behavior*) schizophrenes Verhalten *geh*
schizophrenic [ˌskɪt·sə·'fren·ɪk] **I.** *adj* schizophren **II.** *n* Schizophrene(r) *f(m)*
scholar ['skal·ər] *n* UNIV ❶ (*academic*) Gelehrte(r) *f(m)* ❷ (*good learner*) fleißiger Student/fleißige Studentin
scholarly ['skal·ər·li] *adj* ❶ (*academic*) wissenschaftlich ❷ (*erudite*) gelehrt
scholarship ['skal·ər·ʃɪp] *n* ❶ (*academic achievement*) **her book is a work of great ~** ihr Buch ist eine großartige wissenschaftliche Arbeit ❷ (*financial award*) Stipendium *nt*
scholastic [skə·'læs·tɪk] *adj* Bildungs-; (*academic*) wissenschaftlich
school[1] [skul] **I.** *n* ❶ Schule *f;* **elementary ~** Grundschule *f;* **public ~** staatliche Schule *f;* **to attend** [*or* **go to**] **~** zur Schule gehen; **driving ~** Fahrschule *f;* **graduate ~** *hohe Stufe innerhalb des Hochschulsystems, die das Studium bis zum Master's degree oder dem Ph. D. umfasst* ❷ (*university division*) Fakultät *f;* (*smaller division*) Institut *nt,* Seminar *nt* **II.** *vt* ❶ (*educate*) erziehen ❷ (*train*) schulen; *dog* dressieren
school[2] [skul] *n* ZOOL Schule *f;* (*shoal*) Schwarm *m*
'school age *n* schulpflichtiges Alter
'school bag *n* Schultasche *f*
'school board *n* Schulbehörde *f*
'schoolbook *n* Schulbuch *nt*
'schoolboy *n* Schuljunge *m,* Schüler *m*
'schoolchild *n* Schulkind *nt*
'school days *npl* Schulzeit *f kein pl*
'schoolgirl *n* Schulmädchen *nt,* Schülerin *f*
schooling ['sku·lɪŋ] *n* (*education*) Ausbildung *f;* (*for young people*) Schulbildung *f*
'schoolmate *n* Schulfreund(in) *m(f),* Schulkamerad(in) *m(f)*
'school night *n Abend vor einem Schultag*
'schoolroom *n* Klassenzimmer *nt*
'school system *n* Schulsystem *nt*

> Das amerikanische **school system** (Schulsystem) beginnt mit der *elementary school*, die je nach Schuldistrikt fünf bis sechs Jahre dauert. Darauf folgen zwei Jahre *middle school* oder zwei bis drei Jahre *junior high school*. Wenn es diese in einer Region nicht gibt, erfolgt nach acht Jahren *elementary school* sofort der Übergang zur *high school*, die in der Regel vier Jahre dauert. Beendet ist die Schullaufbahn bei allen Schülern mit der *twelfth grade*, der zwölften Klasse.

'schoolteacher *n* Lehrer(in) *m(f)*
'schoolwork *n* Schularbeiten *pl*
'schoolyard *n* Schulhof *m*
schooner ['sku·nər] *n* ❶ NAUT Schoner *m* ❷ (*tall beer glass*) [großes] Bierglas
sciatic [saɪ·'æt̬·ɪk] *adj* MED Ischias-; **~ nerve** Ischiasnerv *m*
sciatica [saɪ·'æt̬·ɪ·kə] *n* MED Ischias *m o nt*
science ['saɪ·əns] *n* ❶ (*study of physical world*) [Natur]wissenschaft *f;* **applied ~** angewandte Wissenschaft; **to have sth down to a ~** (*fig*) etw zu einer wahren Kunst entwickeln ❷ (*discipline*) Wissenschaft *f*
science 'fiction *n* LIT, FILM Sciencefiction *f*
scientific [ˌsaɪ·ən·'tɪf·ɪk] *adj approach, subject, theory* naturwissenschaftlich; *breakthrough, method* wissenschaftlich
scientist ['saɪ·ən·tɪst] *n* Wissenschaftler(in) *m(f);* **research ~** Forscher(in) *m(f)*
sci fi ['saɪˌfaɪ] *n* LIT, FILM *short for* **science fiction** Sciencefiction *f*
scintillating ['sɪn·tə·leɪ·t̬ɪŋ] *adj wit* sprühend *fig; conversation* angeregt
scissors ['sɪz·ərz] *npl* Schere *f;* **a pair of ~** eine Schere
sclerosis [sklɪ·'roʊ·sɪs] *n* MED Sklerose *f*
scoff [skaf] *vi* spotten; (*laugh*) lachen; ■ **to ~ at sb/sth** sich über jdn/etw lustig machen
scold [skoʊld] *vt* ausschimpfen
scolding ['skoʊl·dɪŋ] *n* Schimpfen *nt;* **to get a** [**good**] **~** furchtbar ausgeschimpft werden

scone [skoʊn] *n weiches, krustenloses Gebäck, das mit entweder nur mit Butter oder mit Butter und Marmelade gegessen wird*
scoop [skup] **I.** *n* ❶ (*utensil*) Schaufel *f,* Schippe *f* NORDD, MITTELD; (*ladle*) Schöpflöffel *m;* **measuring ~** Messlöffel *m* ❷ (*amount*) Löffel *m; of ice cream* Kugel *f* ❸ (*fam*) JOURN Knüller *m fam* ❹ (*fam*) [Insider]informationen *pl* **II.** *vt* ❶ (*move*) *sand, dirt* schaufeln; *ice cream, pudding* löffeln ❷ JOURN ausstechen; **we were ~ed by a rival paper** eine konkurrierende Zeitung kam uns zuvor
◆**scoop up** *vt* hochheben
scoot [skut] *vi* (*fam*) rennen; ■**to ~ over** zur Seite rutschen; **to ~ together** zusammenrücken
scooter ['sku·t̬ər] *n* [Tret]roller *m;* **motor ~** Motorroller *m*
scope [skoʊp] *n* ❶ (*range*) Rahmen *m* ❷ (*possibility*) Möglichkeit *f;* (*freedom to act*) Spielraum *m*
scorch [skɔrtʃ] **I.** *vt* (*burn*) versengen **II.** *vi* (*become burnt*) versengt werden **III.** *n* <*pl* -es> versengte Stelle; **~ mark** Brandfleck *m*
scorcher ['skɔr·tʃər] *n* (*fam*) sehr heißer Tag
scorching ['skɔr·tʃɪŋ] *adj* sengend; *heat* glühend
score [skɔr] **I.** *n* ❶ (*of points*) Punktestand *m;* (*of game*) Spielstand *m;* **final ~** Endstand *m* ❷ (*act of getting point*) Treffer *m* ❸ (*dispute*) Streit[punkt] *m;* **to settle a ~** eine Rechnung begleichen ❹ MUS Partitur *f* ❺ (*notch*) Kerbe *f* ❻ (*twenty*) zwanzig; (*three ~ years and ten*) siebzig Jahre; **~s of** Dutzende von ▶PHRASES: **to know the ~** wissen, wie der Hase läuft *fam;* **what's the ~?** (*fam*) wie sieht's aus? **II.** *vt* ❶ SPORTS treffen, punkten; *basket* Korb; *goal* schießen; *run* scoren ❷ (*achieve result*) erreichen; **to ~ points** (*fig*) sich *dat* einen Vorteil verschaffen ❸ (*mark, cut*) einkerben ❹ (*fam: obtain, esp illegally*) *drugs* beschaffen **III.** *vi* ❶ (*in baseball*) scoren, einen Run machen; (*in basketball*) einen Punkt machen; (*in ice hockey, soccer*) ein Tor schießen ❷ (*keep score*) scoren ❸ (*achieve result*) abschneiden ❹ (*sl: obtain illegal drugs*) [sich *dat*] Stoff beschaffen ❺ (*sl: have sex*) ins Bett kriegen (**with** mit +*dat*)
'**scoreboard** *n* Anzeigetafel *f*
'**scorecard** *n* Spielstandskarte *f*
scorer ['skɔr·ər] *n* ❶ (*scorekeeper*) Scorer *m,* Punktezähler(in) *m(f)* ❷ (*player who scores goal*) Torschütze, -schützin *m, f;* **the leading ~** Torschützenkönig *m;* (*in basketball, football*) **the leading ~** Spieler, der die meisten Punkte erzielt hat
scorn [skɔrn] **I.** *n* (*contempt*) Verachtung *f* **II.** *vt* ❶ (*not respect*) verachten ❷ (*refuse*) ablehnen ▶PHRASES: **hell hath no fury like a woman ~ed** (*saying*) die Hölle kennt keinen schlimmeren Zorn als den einer verlachten Frau
scornful ['skɔrn·fəl] *adj* verächtlich
Scorpio ['skɔr·pi·oʊ] *n* Skorpion *m*
scorpion ['skɔr·pi·ən] *n* Skorpion *m*
Scot [skat] *n* Schotte, Schottin *m, f*
Scotch <*pl* -es> [skatʃ] *n* (*whisky*) Scotch *m;* **a double ~** ein doppelter Scotch
Scotch 'tape® *n* Tesa[film]® *m*
scot-'free *adv* ❶ (*without punishment*) straffrei ❷ (*unchallenged*) unbehelligt; (*unharmed*) ungeschoren
Scotland ['skat·lənd] *n* Schottland *nt*
Scots [skats] **I.** *adj* schottisch **II.** *n* Schottisch *nt*
'**Scotsman** *n* Schotte *m*
'**Scotswoman** *n* Schottin *f*
Scottish ['skat̬·ɪʃ] **I.** *adj* schottisch **II.** *n* ■**the ~** *pl* die Schotten *pl*
scoundrel ['skaʊn·drəl] *n* (*dishonest person*) Schuft *m pej*
scour[1] ['skaʊ·ər] **I.** *n* Scheuern *nt* **II.** *vt* ❶ (*clean*) scheuern ❷ (*remove by the force of water*) auswaschen; (*by the force of wind*) abtragen
scour[2] ['skaʊ·ər] *vt* ■**to ~ sth [for sb/sth]** *town, area* etw [nach jdm/etw] absuchen; *newspaper* etw [nach jdm/etw] durchforsten
scourer ['skaʊ·ər·ər] *n* Topfreiniger *m*
scourge [skɜrdʒ] *n* ❶ *usu sing* (*cause of suffering*) Geißel *f geh* ❷ (*critic*) Kritiker(in) *m(f)*
'**scouring pad** *n* Topfreiniger *m*
scout [skaʊt] **I.** *n* ❶ (*boy scout*) Pfadfinder *m;* (*girl scout*) Pfadfinderin *f* ❷ (*talent seeker*) Talentsucher(in) *m(f)* **II.** *vi* ❶ (*reconnoiter*) kundschaften ❷ (*search*) **to ~ for new talent** nach neuen Talenten suchen **III.** *vt* (*reconnoiter*) auskundschaften
'**scoutmaster** *n* Pfadfinderführer(in) *m(f)*
scowl [skaʊl] **I.** *n* mürrischer [Gesichts]ausdruck **II.** *vi* mürrisch [drein]blicken
scrabble ['skræb·əl] *vi* ❶ (*grope*) [herum]wühlen (**for** nach +*dat,* **through** in +*dat*) ❷ (*claw for grip*) ■**to ~ for sth** nach etw *dat* greifen
scraggly ['skræg·li] *adj hair* zottelig, zerzaust; *beard* struppig
scram <-mm-> [skræm] (*fam*) **I.** *vi* abhauen **II.** *interj* ■**~!** hau ab!
scramble ['skræm·bəl] **I.** *n* ❶ (*scrambling*) Kletterpartie *f* (**over** über +*akk,* **up** auf +*akk*) ❷ (*rush*) Gedrängel *nt fam* (**for** um +*akk*) **II.** *vi* ❶ (*climb*) klettern; (*over difficult terrain a.*) kraxeln *bes* SÜDD, ÖSTERR *fam* ❷ (*move hastily and awkwardly*) hasten; **to ~ to one's feet** sich hochrappeln *fam* **III.** *vt* ❶ (*beat and cook*) *eggs* verrühren ❷ (*encode*) verschlüsseln
scrambled 'eggs *npl* Rührei *nt,* Rühreier *pl*
scrambler ['skræm·blər] *n* TECH Verschlüsselungsgerät *nt*
scrap[1] [skræp] **I.** *n* ❶ (*small bit*) Stück[chen] *nt; of cloth, paper* Fetzen *m* ❷ (*leftover pieces of food*) ■**~s** *pl* Speisereste *pl* ❸ (*old metal*) Schrott *m* **II.** *vt* <-pp-> ❶ (*get rid of*) wegwerfen; (*use for scrap metal*) verschrotten ❷ (*fam: abandon*) aufgeben; (*abolish*) abschaffen

S

scrap² [skræp] *n* (*fam: fight*) Gerangel *nt;* (*verbal*) Streit *m*

'scrapbook *n* [Sammel]album *nt*

scrape [skreɪp] **I.** *n* ① (*for cleaning*) [Ab]kratzen *nt* ② (*graze on skin*) Abschürfung *f;* (*scratch*) Kratzer *m* ③ (*fam: difficult situation*) Klemme *f* **II.** *vt* ① (*remove outer layer*) [ab]schaben; (*remove excess dirt*) [ab]kratzen ② (*graze*) **to ~ sth** *part of body* sich *dat* etw aufschürfen; (*scratch*) *car* etw verkratzen **III.** *vi* ① (*rub*) reiben; (*brush*) bürsten; (*scratch*) kratzen ② (*economize*) sparen

◆**scrape by** *vi* mit Ach und Krach durchkommen *fam*

◆**scrape through** *vi* gerade [mal] so durchkommen *fam*

◆**scrape together**, **scrape up** *vt* (*collect with difficulty*) *people, things* zusammenbekommen; *money* zusammenkratzen *fam*

scraper ['skreɪ·pər] *n* (*for paint, wallpaper*) Spachtel *m o f;* (*for windshields*) Kratzer *m;* (*for shoes, boots*) Abkratzer *m*

'scrap heap *n cars* Schrotthaufen *m;* **to be on the ~** (*fig*) zum alten Eisen gehören *fam; plan, idea* verworfen worden sein

scraping ['skreɪ·pɪŋ] **I.** *adj attr* kratzend **II.** *n* ① (*sound*) Kratzen *nt* ② (*small amount*) Rest[e] *m*[*pl*] ③ (*bits peeled off*) ■**~s** *pl* Schabsel *pl; of vegetable* Schalen *pl*

'scrap iron *n* Alteisen *nt,* Schrott *m*

scrappy ['skræp·i] *adj* (*full of determination*) *player* rauflustig

scratch [skrætʃ] **I.** *n* <*pl* -es> ① (*cut, mark*) Kratzer *m,* Schramme *f* ② (*against itching*) **to give oneself a ~** sich *akk* kratzen ③ (*beginning state*) **to start [sth] from ~** [mit etw *dat*] bei null anfangen **II.** *adj attr* (*having no handicap*) *golfer* ohne Vorgabe **III.** *vt* ① (*cut slightly*) *thing* zerkratzen; *person* kratzen ② (*mark by scraping*) verkratzen ③ (*relieve an itch*) kratzen; **to ~ one's head** sich am Kopf kratzen **IV.** *vi* ① (*cause scratch*) kratzen ② (*relieve an itch*) sich kratzen

scratch around *vi* ① *animals* herumscharren; ■**to ~ around for sth** nach etw *dat* scharren ② (*search hard*) herumsuchen *fam;* ■**to ~ around for sth** nach etw *dat* suchen

◆**scratch out** *vt* (*strike out*) auskratzen; *line, passage, word* durchstreichen

'scratch card *n* Rubbellos *nt*

'scratch paper *n* Schmierpapier *nt;* (*for writing rough draft*) Konzeptpapier *nt*

scratchy ['skrætʃ·i] *adj* (*irritating to skin*) *sweater* kratzig

scrawl [skrɔl] **I.** *vt* [hin]kritzeln *fam* **II.** *n* ① (*untidy writing*) Gekritzel *nt* ② (*scrawled note, message*) hingekritzelte Notiz *fam*

scrawny ['skrɔ·ni] *adj human, animal* dürr; *vegetation* mager

scream [skrim] **I.** *n* ① (*loud shrill cry*) Schrei *m;* **a ~ for help** ein Hilfeschrei *m* ② *of animal* Gekreisch[e] *nt kein pl* ③ *of engine, siren* Heulen *nt; of jet plane* Dröhnen *nt* **II.** *vi* ① (*with fear, pain*) schreien; (*with joy, delight*) kreischen; ■**to ~ at sb** jdn anschreien ② *animals* schreien ③ *engine, siren* heulen; *jet plane* dröhnen **III.** *vt* ① (*cry loudly*) schreien ② (*express forcefully*) lauthals schreien

screech [skritʃ] **I.** *n* <*pl* -es> *of brakes, tires* Quietschen *nt kein pl; of person* Schrei *m; of animal* Kreischen *nt kein pl* **II.** *vi brakes, tires* quietschen; *person* schreien; *animal* kreischen

'screech owl *n* Kreischeule *f*

screed [skrid] *n* (*speech, writing*) Roman *m;* (*book*) Wälzer *m fam*

screen [skrin] **I.** *n* ① (*for movies, slides*) Leinwand *f;* (*of television, computer*) Bildschirm *m;* (*for radar, sonar*) Schirm *m* ② (*panel for privacy*) Trennwand *f;* (*decorative*) Paravent *m;* (*for protection*) Schutzschirm *m;* (*against insects*) Fliegengitter *nt;* (*fireguard*) Ofenschirm *m* ③ (*sth that conceals*) Tarnung *f* **II.** *vt* ① (*conceal*) abschirmen (**from** gegen +*akk*) ② (*shield*) schützen (**from** vor +*dat*) ③ (*examine closely*) überprüfen; MIL einer Auswahlprüfung unterziehen; ■**to ~ sb for sth** MED jdn auf etw *akk* hin untersuchen ④ (*show*) vorführen; TV senden

screening ['skri·nɪŋ] *n* ① (*process of showing*) *of films* Vorführen *nt; of TV program* Ausstrahlung *f* ② (*testing*) Überprüfung *f,* Kontrolle *f* ③ MED (*examination*) Untersuchung *f;* **health ~** Vorsorgeuntersuchung *f;* (*X-ray*) Röntgenuntersuchung *f*

'screenplay *n* Drehbuch *nt*

'screen saver *n* Bildschirmschoner *m*

'screenshot *n* COMPUT Screenshot *m*

'screen test *n* FILM, TV Probeaufnahmen *pl*

'screenwriter *n* Drehbuchautor(in) *m(f)*

screw [skru] **I.** *n* ① (*metal fastener, propeller*) Schraube *f* ② (*turn*) Drehung *f* ▶ PHRASES: **to have a ~ loose** (*hum fam*) nicht ganz dicht sein *pej* **II.** *vt* ① (*attach with screw*) ■**to ~ sth [on]to sth** etw an etw *akk* schrauben ② (*by twisting*) **to ~ sth tight** etw fest zudrehen; ■**to ~ sth into/onto sth** etw in/auf etw *akk* schrauben ③ (*vulg, sl: have sex with*) bumsen *sl,* vögeln *derb* **III.** *vi* (*vulg, sl: have sex*) bumsen *sl,* vögeln *derb*

screw around I. *vi* (*fam: be silly*) Blödsinn machen, herumblödeln; (*waste time*) herumtrödeln **II.** *vt* (*fam*) ■**to ~ sb around** (*mess about*) jdm auf die Nerven gehen; (*waste time*) jds Zeit *f* verschwenden

◆**screw on** *vi* (*tighten*) sich zuschrauben lassen; *nut* sich anziehen lassen

◆**screw up I.** *vt* ① (*sl: spoil, do badly*) vermasseln *fam; exam* versieben; **to ~ it [or things] up** Mist bauen *fam* ② (*twist into a shape*) **to ~ up one's eyes** blinzeln; *face, mouth* verziehen **II.** *vi* (*sl*) einen Schnitzer machen; ■**to ~ up [on sth]** [bei etw *dat*] Mist bauen *fam*

'screwball *n* ① (*in baseball*) Screwball *m* ② (*fam: person*) Spinner(in) *m(f) pej*

'screwdriver *n* ① (*tool*) Schraubenzieher *m*

S

❷ (*cocktail*) Screwdriver *m*
screwed [skrud] *adj pred* (*sl: stymied*) festgefahren; (*in a hopeless situation*) geliefert
'screw top *n* Schraubverschluss *m*
'screwup, 'screw-up *n* (*sl*) Schnitzer *m fam*
screwy ['skru·i] *adj* (*fam*) verrückt; (*dangerously mad*) *idea* hirnrissig
scribble ['skrɪb·əl] **I.** *vt* [hin]kritzeln **II.** *vi* ❶ (*make marks, write*) kritzeln ❷ (*hum: write*) schriftstellern *fam* **III.** *n* ❶ (*mark, words*) Gekritzel *nt kein pl pej* ❷ (*handwriting*) Klaue *f pej sl*
scrimmage ['skrɪm·ɪdʒ] *n* ❶ SPORTS (*practice game*) Übungsspiel *nt*, Freundschaftsspiel *nt* ❷ (*skirmish*) Gerangel *nt kein pl fam*
scrimp [skrɪmp] *vi* sparen; **to ~ and save** knausern *pej fam*
script [skrɪpt] *n* ❶ *of film* Drehbuch *nt; of play* Regiebuch *nt; of broadcast* Skript *nt* ❷ (*style of writing*) Schrift *f; a.* TYPO Schriftart *f* ❸ COMPUT Script *nt*
scriptural ['skrɪp·tʃər·əl] *adj* biblisch
scripture, Scripture ['skrɪp·tʃər] *n* (*the Bible*) die Bibel
'scriptwriter *n* FILM, TV Drehbuchautor(in) *m(f);* RADIO Rundfunkautor(in) *m(f)*
scroll [skroʊl] **I.** *n* (*roll of paper*) [Schrift]rolle *f* **II.** *vi* COMPUT scrollen
Scrooge [skrudʒ] *n* (*pej*) Geizhals *m*
scrotum <*pl* -s *or* -ta> ['skroʊ·ţəm] *n* Hodensack *m*
scrounge [skraʊndʒ] (*fam*) **I.** *vt* (*pej*) ■ **to ~ sth** [**off sb**] etw [von jdm] schnorren **II.** *vi* ❶ (*look around*) ■ **to ~** [**around**] **for sth** *food* nach etw *dat* herumsuchen ❷ (*pej*) schnorren (**off** bei +*dat*)
scrounger ['skroʊn·dʒər] *n* (*pej fam*) Schnorrer(in) *m(f)*
scrub[1] [skrʌb] **I.** *n* **to give sth a** [**good**] **~** etw [gründlich] [ab]schrubben *fam* **II.** *vt* <-bb-> ❶ (*clean*) [ab]schrubben *fam* ❷ (*fam: cancel, abandon*) fallen lassen; *project* abblasen **III.** *vi* <-bb-> schrubben *fam*
scrub[2] [skrʌb] *n* ❶ (*trees and bushes*) Gestrüpp *nt* ❷ (*area*) Busch *m*
scrubber ['skrʌb·ər], **'scrub brush** *n* Schrubber *m;* (*smaller*) Scheuerbürste *f*
scruff [skrʌf] *n of neck* Genick *nt*
scruffy ['skrʌf·i] *adj clothes* schmuddelig *pej fam; person* vergammelt *pej fam; place* heruntergekommen *fam*
scrum [skrʌm] *n* (*in rugby*) Gedränge *nt fachspr*
scrumptious ['skrʌmp·ʃəs] *adj* (*fam*) lecker
scrunch [skrʌntʃ] **I.** *vi* (*make noise*) knirschen; (*with the mouth*) geräuschvoll kauen **II.** *vt* ❶ (*crunch*) knirschen ❷ (*crush up*) zerknüllen
scruple ['skru·pəl] *n* (*principles*) ■ **~s** *pl* Skrupel *pl*, Bedenken *pl;* **to have** [**no**] **~s about doing sth** [keine] Skrupel [*o* Bedenken] haben, etw zu tun
scrupulous ['skrup·jʊ·ləs] *adj* ❶ (*extremely moral*) gewissenhaft ❷ (*extremely careful*) [peinlich] genau
scrutinize ['skru·tə·naɪz] *vt* [genau] untersuchen [*o* prüfen]; *text* studieren
scrutiny ['skru·tə·ni] *n* [genaue] [Über]prüfung [*o* Untersuchung]
'scuba diving *n* Sporttauchen *nt*
scud <-dd-> [skʌd] *vi* eilen; *clouds* [schnell] ziehen
scuff [skʌf] **I.** *vt* ❶ (*mark*) verschrammen; (*wear away*) abwetzen ❷ (*drag along the ground*) **to ~ one's feet** schlurfen **II.** *vi* ❶ (*become worn*) sich abwetzen ❷ (*shuffle*) schlurfen
scuffle ['skʌf·əl] **I.** *n* Handgemenge *nt* **II.** *vi* sich balgen (**with** mit +*dat*)
sculpt [skʌlpt] **I.** *vt* (*create from stone*) [heraus]meißeln; (*in clay*) modellieren; (*reshape, work*) formen **II.** *vi* bildhauern *fam*
sculptor ['skʌlp·tər] *n* Bildhauer(in) *m(f)*
sculptural ['skʌlp·tʃər·əl] *adj* bildhauerisch, plastisch; *facial features, form* plastisch
sculpture ['skʌlp·tʃər] **I.** *n* ❶ (*art*) Bildhauerei *f* ❷ (*object*) Skulptur *f*, Plastik *f* **II.** *vt* (*make with a chisel*) [heraus]meißeln; (*in clay*) modellieren; (*reshape, work*) formen; (*model*) modellieren **III.** *vi* bildhauern *fam*
scum [skʌm] *n* ❶ (*foam*) Schaum *m;* (*residue*) Rand *m;* (*layer of dirt*) Schmutzschicht *f* ❷ (*pej: evil people*) Abschaum *m*
'scumbag *n* (*pej sl: man*) Mistkerl *m fam;* (*woman*) Miststück *nt fam*
scurrilous ['skɜr·ɪ·ləs] *adj* (*pej form: defamatory*) verleumderisch; (*insulting*) unflätig *geh*
scurry ['skɜr·i] **I.** *vi* <-ie-> *small animal* huschen; *person* eilen **II.** *n* (*hurry*) Eilen *nt;* **the ~ of feet** das Getrappel von Füßen
scurvy ['skɜr·vi] *n* Skorbut *m*
scuttle ['skʌţ·əl] *vi person* hasten, flitzen *fam; small creature* huschen
scuttle away, scuttle off *vi* davoneilen
scythe [saɪð] **I.** *n* Sense *f* **II.** *vt* ❶ (*with a scythe*) [mit der Sense] [ab]mähen ❷ (*with swinging blow*) ■ **to ~ sb/sth** [**down**] jdn/etw niedermähen *fam* **III.** *vi* preschen (**through** durch +*akk*)
SD, S.D. *abbrev of* **South Dakota**
sea [si] *n* ❶ (*salt water surrounding land*) ■ **the ~** das Meer, die See; **at the bottom of the ~** auf dem Meeresboden; **by** [*or* **beside**] **the ~** am Meer, an der See; **the high ~s** die hohe See ❷ (*specific area*) See *f kein pl*, Meer *nt;* **the Dead ~** das Tote Meer ❸ (*state of sea*) Seegang *m kein pl;* **a calm/rough ~** ein ruhiger/schwerer Seegang ► PHRASES: **to be** [**all**] **at ~** [ganz] ratlos sein
sea a'nemone *n* Seeanemone *f*
'seabed *n* Meeresgrund *m*
'seaboard *n* Küste *f;* **the eastern ~ of the United States** die Atlantikküste der Vereinigten Staaten
sea 'breeze *n* Seewind *m*, Meeresbrise *f*
'sea change *n* große Veränderung

'sea dog *n* Seebär *m fam*
seafaring ['si·ˌfer·ɪŋ] *adj attr* (*esp liter*) seefahrend
'seafood *n* Meeresfrüchte *pl*
'seafront *n* (*promenade*) Strandpromenade *f;* (*beach*) Strand *m*
'seagull *n* Möwe *f*
'sea horse *n* Seepferdchen *nt*
seal[1] [sil] **I.** *n* ❶ (*insignia, stamp*) Siegel *nt* ❷ (*tight join*) Verschluss *m* **II.** *vt* ❶ (*stamp*) siegeln ❷ (*prevent from being opened*) [fest] verschließen; (*with a seal*) versiegeln; (*for customs*) plombieren; (*with adhesive*) zukleben ❸ (*make airtight*) luftdicht verschließen; (*make watertight*) wasserdicht verschließen; *window, gaps* abdichten ❹ (*block access to*) versiegeln; *border* schließen
◆**seal up** *vt* ❶ (*close*) [fest] verschließen; (*with a seal*) versiegeln; (*with adhesive*) zukleben ❷ *door, window, gaps* abdichten
seal[2] [sil] *n* ZOOL Seehund *m,* Robbe *f*
sealant ['si·lənt] *n* (*for surfaces*) Dichtungsmittel *nt;* (*for gaps*) Kitt *m*
'sea legs *npl* **to find one's ~** NAUT seefest werden *fachspr*
'sea level *n* Meeresspiegel *m;* **above ~** über dem Meeresspiegel
'sealing wax *n* Siegelwachs *nt*
'sea lion *n* Seelöwe *m*
'sealskin *n* Robbenfell *nt*
seam [sim] *n* ❶ (*join*) Naht *f;* NAUT Fuge *f;* **to be bursting at the ~s** (*fig*) aus allen Nähten platzen *fam* ❷ (*mineral layer*) Schicht *f*
'seaman ['si·mən] *n* (*sailor*) Seemann *m;* (*rank*) Matrose *m*
seamless ['sim·lɪs] *adj* ❶ (*without a seam*) *stockings* nahtlos; *garment, robe* ohne Nähte ❷ (*smooth*) nahtlos, problemlos
seamlessly ['sim·lɪs·li] *adv* nahtlos
seamstress <*pl* -es> ['sim·strɪs] *n* Näherin *f*
seamy ['si·mi] *adj* ❶ (*run down*) heruntergekommen ❷ (*dodgy*) *district* zwielichtig; **the ~ side of life** die Schattenseite des Lebens
séance ['seɪ·ans] *n* Séance *f geh*
'seaplane *n* Wasserflugzeug *nt*
'seaport *n* Seehafen *m*
'sea power *n* ❶ (*naval strength*) Stärke *f* zu Wasser ❷ (*state with strong navy*) Seemacht *f*
sear [sɪr] *vt* ❶ (*scorch*) verbrennen; (*singe*) versengen ❷ FOOD (*fry quickly*) kurz [an]braten
search [sɜrtʃ] **I.** *n* ❶ (*for object, person*) Suche *f* (**for** nach +*dat*); **to go off in ~ of sth** sich auf die Suche nach etw *dat* machen ❷ (*for drugs, stolen property, etc.*) Durchsuchung *f;* *of person* Leibesvisitation *f* ❸ COMPUT Suchlauf *m;* **to do a ~ for sth** etw suchen **II.** *vi* suchen; ■**to ~ for sb/sth** nach jdm/etw suchen; ■**to ~ through sth** etw durchsuchen **III.** *vt* ❶ (*look through*) *building, bag* durchsuchen; *place, street* absuchen ❷ LAW durchsuchen ❸ (*examine carefully*) absuchen; *conscience, heart* prüfen; *memory* durchforschen
◆**search out** *vt* ausfindig machen
'search engine *n* COMPUT Suchmaschine *f*
searcher ['sɜr·tʃər] *n* Suchende(r) *f(m)*
searching ['sɜr·tʃɪŋ] *adj gaze, look* forschend; *inquiry* eingehend; *question* tief gehend
'searchlight *n* Suchscheinwerfer *m*
'search party *n* Suchtrupp *m*
'search warrant *n* Durchsuchungsbefehl *m*
searing ['sɪr·ɪŋ] *adj attr* ❶ (*scorching*) sengend ❷ (*painfully burning*) *pain* brennend ❸ (*intense*) *passion* glühend *geh; emotion* leidenschaftlich; *criticism* schonungslos
'sea salt *n* Meersalz *nt*
'seascape *n* ❶ (*picture*) Seestück *nt* ❷ (*view*) Blick *m* auf das Meer
'seashell *n* Muschel *f*
'seashore *n* (*beach*) Strand *m;* (*land near sea*) [Meeres]küste *f*
'seasick *adj* seekrank
'seasickness *n* Seekrankheit *f*
'seaside I. *n* ■**the ~** die [Meeres]küste; ■**at the ~** am Meer **II.** *adj attr* See-; **~ resort** Seebad *nt*
season ['si·zən] **I.** *n* ❶ (*period of year*) Jahreszeit *f;* **the Christmas ~** die Weihnachtszeit; **the rainy ~** die Regenzeit ❷ (*period of occurrence*) AGR, SPORTS, THEAT Saison *f;* **oysters are out of ~ at the moment** zurzeit gibt es keine Austern; **hunting ~** Jagdzeit *f* ❸ ZOOL fruchtbare Zeit; **mating ~** Paarungszeit *f;* **to be in ~** brünstig sein ❹ (*business period*) Saison *f,* Hauptzeit *f;* **at the height of the ~** in der Hochsaison; **high ~** Hochsaison *f* **II.** *vt* ❶ (*add flavoring*) würzen (**with** mit +*dat*) ❷ (*dry out*) *wood* ablagern lassen
seasonable ['si·zə·nə·bəl] *adj* (*expected for time of year*) der Jahreszeit angemessen
seasonal ['si·zə·nəl] *adj* ❶ (*connected with time of year*) jahreszeitlich bedingt; **~ adjustment** Saisonbereinigung *f;* **~ work** Saisonarbeit *f* ❷ (*grown in a season*) Saison-
seasoned ['si·zənd] *adj* ❶ *usu attr* (*experienced*) erfahren ❷ (*properly dried*) *timber* abgelagert ❸ (*spiced*) gewürzt
seasoning ['si·zə·nɪŋ] *n* ❶ (*salt and pepper*) Würze *f* ❷ (*herb or spice*) Gewürz *nt*
'season ticket *n* Dauerkarte *f;* SPORTS Saisonkarte *f*
seat [sit] **I.** *n* ❶ (*sitting place*) [Sitz]platz *m;* (*in a car*) Sitz *m;* (*in bus, plane, train*) Sitzplatz *m;* (*in a theater*) Platz *m;* **is this ~ free?** ist dieser Platz frei?; **to take a ~** sich [hin]setzen ❷ *usu sing* (*part to sit on*) *of chair* Sitz *m;* *of pants* Hosenboden *m* ❸ (*location*) Sitz *m;* *of company* Sitz *m;* *of aristocrat* [Wohn]sitz *m* **II.** *vt* ❶ (*provide seats*) setzen ❷ (*seating capacity*) **to ~ 2500** 2500 Menschen fassen; **his car ~s five** in seinem Auto haben fünf Leute Platz
'seat belt *n* Sicherheitsgurt *m;* **to fasten one's ~** sich anschnallen
seating ['si·t̬ɪŋ] *n* ❶ (*seats*) Sitzgelegenheiten *pl;* **~ for 6** Sitzplätze *pl* für 6 Personen ❷ (*sitting arrangement*) Sitzordnung *f*

'seating arrangements *npl,* **'seating plan** *n* Sitzordnung *f*

SEATO ['si·ţoʊ] *n acr for* **Southeast Asia Treaty Organization** SEATO *f*

'sea urchin *n* Seeigel *m*

seaward ['si·wərd] **I.** *adv* seewärts **II.** *adj* ❶ (*facing toward sea*) dem Meer zugewandt ❷ (*moving toward sea*) auf das Meer hinaus *nach n*

'seawater *n* Meerwasser *nt*

'seaway *n* ❶ (*channel for large ships*) Wasserstraße *f* ❷ (*route*) Seeweg *m*

'seaweed *n* [See]tang *m*

'seaworthy *adj* seetauglich

sec. [sek] *n short for* **second** Sek.; (*fam*) Moment *m;* **wait a ~!** Moment mal!; **hold on [just] a ~** warte einen Moment

secede [sɪ·'sid] *vi* POL sich abspalten (**from** von +*dat*)

secession [sɪ·'seʃ·ən] *n* Abspaltung *f*

seclude [sɪ·'klud] *vt* abschließen (**from** von +*dat*)

secluded [sɪ·'klu·dɪd] *adj spot, house* abgelegen; *area* abgeschieden; *life* zurückgezogen

seclusion [sɪ·'klu·ʒən] *n* (*quiet and privacy*) Zurückgezogenheit *f; of place* Abgelegenheit *f,* Abgeschiedenheit

second[1] ['sek·ənd] *n* ❶ (*sixtieth of a minute*) Sekunde *f* ❷ (*very short time*) Sekunde *f,* Augenblick *m;* **you go on; I'll only be a ~** geh du weiter, ich komme gleich nach

second[2] ['sek·ənd] **I.** *adj* ❶ *usu attr* (*next after first, winner*) zweite(r, s); **the ~ time** das zweite Mal; **to finish ~** Zweite(r) werden; **to be in ~ place** auf Platz zwei sein ❷ (*not first in importance, size*) zweit-; **Germany's ~ city** Deutschlands zweitwichtigste Stadt; **to be ~ to none** unübertroffen sein ❸ *attr* (*another*) zweite(r, s), Zweit-; **to give sb a ~ chance** jdm eine zweite Chance geben; **to have ~ thoughts** es sich *dat* noch einmal überlegen ▶ PHRASES: **to play ~ <u>fiddle</u> to sb** in jds Schatten stehen **II.** *n* ❶ AUTO zweiter Gang ❷ *usu pl* (*imperfect item*) Ware *f* zweiter Wahl **III.** *adv* zweitens; **to finish ~** den zweiten Platz belegen **IV.** *vt* (*support, back up*) *motion, proposal* unterstützen, befürworten

secondary ['sek·ən·der·i] *adj* ❶ (*not main*) zweitrangig; **to play a ~ role** eine untergeordnete Rolle spielen ❷ (*education*) höher; **~ education** höhere Schulbildung ❸ MED Sekundär-

'secondary school *n* SCH Highschool *f*

second 'best *n* **to settle for ~** sich mit weniger zufriedengeben

second-'best *adj* zweitbeste(r, s)

second 'chamber *n* POL zweite Kammer

second 'class TRANSP **I.** *n* zweite Klasse **II.** *adv* **to travel ~** zweiter Klasse reisen

second 'cousin *n* Cousin *m*/Cousine *f* zweiten Grades

second-degree 'burn *n* Verbrennung *f* zweiten Grades

second-'guess **I.** *vt* ■**to ~ sb** jdn/etw im Nachhinein kritisieren **II.** *vi* vorhersagen, was jd tun wird

'secondhand **I.** *adj* ❶ (*used*) **~ car** Gebrauchtwagen *m;* **~ clothes** Secondhandkleidung *f* ❷ (*obtained from sb else*) *information, experience* aus zweiter Hand *nach n* **II.** *adv* ❶ (*in used condition*) gebraucht ❷ (*from intermediary*) aus zweiter Hand *nach n*

second 'hand *n* Sekundenzeiger *m*

second lieu'tenant *n* Leutnant *m*

secondly ['sek·ənd·li] *adv* zweitens

second-'rate *adj* (*pej*) zweitklassig

secrecy ['si·krə·si] *n* ❶ (*act of keeping secret*) Geheimhaltung *f;* **in ~** im Geheimen ❷ (*ability to keep a secret*) Verschwiegenheit *f;* (*secretiveness*) Heimlichtuerei *f pej* (**about** um +*akk*)

secret ['si·krɪt] **I.** *n* (*undisclosed information*) Geheimnis *nt;* **to keep a ~** ein Geheimnis für sich *akk* behalten; ■**in ~** im Geheimen, insgeheim; **to do sth in ~** etw heimlich tun; **the ~ to success** das Geheimnis des Erfolgs **II.** *adj* ❶ (*known to few people*) geheim, Geheim-; (*hidden*) verborgen ❷ (*done in secret*) heimlich

secret 'agent *n* Geheimagent(in) *m(f)*

secretarial [ˌsek·rə·'ter·i·əl] *adj* Büro-; **~ staff** Bürokräfte *pl*

secretary ['sek·rə·ter·i] *n* ❶ (*office assistant*) Sekretär(in) *m(f)* ❷ ECON Assistent(in) *m(f)* der Geschäftsführung

Secretary ['sek·rə·ter·i] *n* Minister, -in *m, f;* **~ of Defense** Verteidigungsminister(in) *m(f)*

Secretary 'General <*pl* Secretaries General> *n* Generalsekretär(in) *m(f)*

Secretary of 'State *n* Außenminister(in) *m(f)*

secrete[1] [sɪ·'krit] *vt* BIOL, MED absondern

secrete[2] [sɪ·'krit] *vt* verbergen

secretion [sɪ·'kri·ʃən] *n* BIOL, MED (*secreted substance*) Sekret *nt;* (*secreting*) Absonderung *f*

secretive ['si·krɪ·ţɪv] *adj behavior* geheimnisvoll; *character* verschlossen

'Secret Service *n* ■**the ~** der Geheimdienst

sect [sekt] *n* ❶ (*religious group*) Sekte *f* ❷ (*denomination*) Konfession *f*

sectarian [sek·'ter·i·ən] *adj* ❶ (*relating to sect*) Sekten- ❷ (*relating to denomination*) konfessionell [bedingt]

section ['sek·ʃən] **I.** *n* ❶ (*component part*) Teil *nt; of road* Teilstrecke *f;* TECH [Bau]teil *nt* ❷ *of a statute* Paragraph *m; of book* Abschnitt *m; of document* Absatz *m* ❸ (*part of an area*) Bereich *m;* **nonsmoking ~** (*in restaurant*) Nichtraucherbereich *m;* (*on a train*) Nichtraucherabteil *nt* ❹ (*department, military unit*) Abteilung *f* ❺ (*group of instruments*) Gruppe *f;* **woodwind ~** Holzbläser *pl* ❻ (*surgical cut*) Schnitt *m;* **cesarean ~** Kaiserschnitt *m* **II.** *vt* ❶ (*to separate*) [unter]teilen ❷ (*cut*) zerschneiden; BIOL segmentieren *fachspr;* MED sezieren *fachspr*

◆**section off** *vt* abteilen

S

sectional ['sek·ʃə·nəl] **I.** *adj* ❶ (*usu pej: limited to particular group*) partikular *geh* ❷ (*made in sections*) zusammensetzbar; **~ furniture** Anbaumöbel *pl* **II.** *n* Anbaumöbel *pl*

sector ['sek·tər] *n* ❶ (*part of economy*) Sektor *m*, Bereich *m;* **the public ~** der öffentliche Sektor ❷ (*area of land*) Sektor *m*, Zone *f*

secular ['sek·jʊ·lər] *adj* ❶ (*nonreligious*) säkular *geh* ❷ (*nonmonastic*) welt[geist]lich

secure [sɪ·'kjʊr] **I.** *adj* <-r, -st *or* more ~, the most ~> ❶ (*certain, permanent*) sicher; **financially ~** finanziell abgesichert ❷ *usu pred* (*safe, confident*) sicher ❸ (*safely guarded*) bewacht, sicher (**against** vor +*dat*); (*safe against telephone interception*) abhörsicher ❹ *usu pred* (*fixed in position*) fest; *door* fest verschlossen **II.** *vt* ❶ (*obtain*) *rights* sich *dat* sichern ❷ (*make safe*) [ab]sichern; **to ~ sb/sth against sth** jdn/etw vor etw *dat* schützen ❸ (*fasten*) befestigen (**to** an +*dat*); *door, window* fest schließen

se'curities market *n* STOCKEX Wertpapierbörse *f*

security [sɪ·'kjʊr·ɪ·t̬i] *n* ❶ (*protection, safety*) Sicherheit *f;* **tight ~** strenge Sicherheitsvorkehrungen; **to tighten ~** die Sicherheitsmaßnahmen verschärfen ❷ (*guards*) Sicherheitsdienst *m* ❸ *usu sing* (*safeguard*) Sicherheit *f*, Schutz *m* (**against** gegen +*akk*) ❹ FIN ■ **securities** *pl* (*investments*) Wertpapiere *pl;* (*government securities*) Staatspapiere *pl*, Staatsanleihen *pl*

Se'curity Council *n* Sicherheitsrat *m*

se'curity forces *npl* MIL Sicherheitskräfte *pl*

se'curity guard *n* Sicherheitsbeamte(r), -beamtin *m, f*

sedan [sɪ·'dæn] *n* Limousine *f*

se'dan chair *n* Sänfte *f*

sedate [sɪ·'deɪt] **I.** *adj person* ruhig; *pace* gemächlich; (*pej*) *place* verschlafen **II.** *vt* MED ruhigstellen, ein Beruhigungsmittel geben

sedation [sɪ·'deɪ·ʃən] *n* MED Ruhigstellung *f;* **under ~** unter dem Einfluss von Beruhigungsmitteln

sedative ['sed·ə·t̬ɪv] **I.** *adj* beruhigend **II.** *n* Beruhigungsmittel *nt*

sedentary ['sed·ən·ter·i] *adj* sitzend

sediment ['sed·ə·mənt] *n* ❶ (*in wine*) [Boden]satz *m* ❷ (*eroded material*) Sediment *nt*, Ablagerung *f*

sedimentary [ˌsed·ɪ·'men·tə·ri] *adj* **~ layer** Sedimentschicht *f*

sedition [sɪ·'dɪʃ·ən] *n* Aufwiegelung *f*

seduce [sɪ·'dus] *vt* ❶ (*persuade to have sex*) verführen ❷ (*win over*) ■ **to ~ sb into doing sth** jdn dazu verleiten, etw zu tun

seducer [sɪ·'du·sər] *n* Verführer *m*

seduction [sɪ·'dʌk·ʃən] *n* ❶ (*sexual or nonsexual*) Verführung *f* ❷ (*seductive quality*) Verlockung *f*

seductive [sɪ·'dʌk·tɪv] *adj* ❶ (*sexy*) verführerisch ❷ (*attractive*) *argument, offer* verlockend

see <saw, seen> [si] **I.** *vt* ❶ (*perceive with eyes*) sehen; **have you ever ~n this man before?** haben Sie diesen Mann schon einmal gesehen?; **to ~ sth with one's own eyes** etw mit eigenen Augen sehen ❷ (*watch as a spectator*) *movie, play* [sich *dat*] [an]sehen; **this film is really worth ~ing** dieser Film ist echt sehenswert ❸ (*visit*) *famous building, place* ansehen ❹ (*understand*) verstehen, begreifen; (*discern mentally*) erkennen; **I ~ what you mean** ich weiß, was du meinst; **~ what I mean?** siehst du? ❺ (*consider*) sehen; **this is how I ~ it** so sehe ich die Sache; **to ~ sth in a new light** etw mit anderen Augen sehen ❻ (*learn, find out*) feststellen; **I'll ~ who it is** ich schaue mal nach, wer es ist; **that remains to be ~n** das wird sich zeigen; **to ~ into the future** in die Zukunft schauen ❼ (*meet socially*) sehen; (*by chance*) [zufällig] treffen [*o* sehen]; **we're ~ing friends this weekend** wir treffen uns am Wochenende mit Freunden; **~ you later!** (*fam: when meeting again later*) bis später!; (*goodbye*) tschüs! *fam;* ■ **to be ~ing sb** (*dating*) mit jdm zusammen sein *fam;* **I'm not ~ing anyone at the moment** ich habe im Moment keine Freundin/keinen Freund ❽ (*have meeting with*) sehen; (*talk to*) sprechen; (*receive*) empfangen; **Ms. Miller can't ~ you now** Ms Miller ist im Moment nicht zu sprechen; **to ~ a doctor** zum Arzt gehen ❾ (*accompany*) begleiten; **to ~ sb to the door** [*or* **out**]**/home** jdn zur Tür/nach Hause bringen ► PHRASES: **to have ~n better days** schon [einmal] bessere Tage gesehen haben; **to ~ the last of sb** [endlich] jdn los sein *fam;* **to not ~ the forest for the trees** den Wald vor [lauter] Bäumen nicht sehen *hum* **II.** *vi* ❶ (*use eyes*) sehen; **I can't ~ very well without my glasses** ohne Brille kann ich nicht sehr gut sehen ❷ (*look*) sehen; **let me ~!** lass mich mal sehen!; **can you ~?** (*in theater etc.*) können Sie noch sehen? ❸ (*understand, realize*) **... — oh, I ~! ...** – aha!; **I ~** ich verstehe; **I ~ from your report ...** Ihrem Bericht entnehme ich, ...; **we'll ~ about that** das wird sich zeigen ► PHRASES: **to not ~ eye to eye** [**with sb**] nicht derselben Ansicht sein [wie jd]

◆**see in I.** *vi* hineinsehen **II.** *vt* hineinbringen; **to ~ the New Year in** das neue Jahr begrüßen

◆**see off** *vt* verabschieden; **to ~ sb off at the airport** jdn zum Flughafen bringen

◆**see out I.** *vt* ❶ (*escort to door*) hinausbegleiten ❷ (*continue to end of*) durchstehen; (*last until end of*) überleben, überstehen; *project* bis zum Ende mitmachen **II.** *vi* hinaussehen

◆**see through** *vt* ❶ (*look through*) ■ **to ~ through sth** durch etw *akk* hindurchsehen ❷ (*not be deceived by*) *plan* durchschauen ❸ (*sustain*) ■ **to ~ sb through** jdm über die Runden helfen *fam;* (*comfort*) jdm beistehen; **will 30 dollars be enough to ~ you through?** reichen dir 30 Dollar? ❹ (*continue* *to the end of*) *project* zu Ende bringen

◆**see to** *vt* ■**to ~ to sb/sth** sich um jdn/etw kümmern; ■**to ~ to it that ...** dafür sorgen, dass ... *nt*

seed [sid] **I.** *n* ❶ (*single seed*) Same[n] *m; of grain* Korn *nt;* ■**~s** *pl* AGR Saat *f kein pl* ❷ (*seeds*) Samen *pl;* **to go to ~** Samen bilden; *flowers, plants, vegetables* schießen; (*fig*) *person* herunterkommen *fam* ❸ (*seeded player*) Platzierte(r) *f(m);* **the number one ~** der/die als Nummer eins Gesetzte ❹ (*fig: starting point*) Keim *m* **II.** *vt* ❶ (*sow with seed*) besäen ❷ (*drop its seed*) ■**to ~ itself** sich aussäen ❸ (*remove seeds from*) *fruit* entkernen ❹ *usu passive* SPORTS **to be ~ed** platziert sein

'seedbed *n* ❶ (*area of ground*) Samenbeet *nt* ❷ (*fig*) Grundlage *f*

'seed corn *n* Samenkorn *nt*

seedless ['sid·lɪs] *adj* kernlos

seedling ['sid·lɪŋ] *n* Setzling *m*

seedy ['si·di] *adj district, hotel* zwielichtig; *character, reputation* zweifelhaft; *clothes, appearance* schäbig

seeing ['si·ɪŋ] *conj* **~ that** [*or* **as** [**how**]] **...** da ...

seek <sought, sought> [sik] *vt* ❶ (*form: look for*) suchen ❷ (*try to obtain*) erstreben; *asylum, refuge, shelter, employment* suchen; *justice, revenge* streben (nach +*dat*) ❸ (*ask for*) erbitten *geh; approval* einholen; **to ~ advice from sb** jdn um Rat bitten

◆**seek out** *vt* ausfindig machen; *opinion, information* herausfinden

seem [sim] *vi* ❶ (*appear to be*) scheinen; **he's sixteen, but he ~s younger** er ist sechzehn, wirkt aber jünger; **he ~s like a very nice man** er scheint ein sehr netter Mann zu sein; (*it ~s all right to me*) das scheint mir ganz in Ordnung zu sein; **it ~ed like a good idea at the time** damals hielt ich das für eine gute Idee ❷ (*appear*) **there ~s to have been some mistake** da liegt anscheinend ein Irrtum vor; ■**it ~s** [**that**] ... anscheinend ...; ■**it ~s as if** [*or* **as though**] **...** es scheint, als ob ...; **it ~s to me that he isn't the right person for the job** ich finde, er ist nicht der Richtige für den Job

seeming ['si·mɪŋ] *adj attr* (*form*) scheinbare(r, s)

seemingly ['si·mɪŋ·li] *adv* scheinbar

seen [sin] *pp of* **see**

seep [sip] *vi* sickern; (*fig*) *information, truth* durchsickern

◆**seep away** *vi* versickern

seepage ['si·pɪdʒ] *n* ❶ (*process of seeping*) *of oil, water* Aussickern *nt* ❷ (*lost fluid*) versickernde Flüssigkeit

seer [sɪr] *n* (*liter*) Seher *m;* (*fig*) Prophet *m*

seesaw ['si·sɔ] **I.** *n* ❶ (*for children*) Wippe *f* ❷ (*vacillating situation*) Auf und Ab *nt* **II.** *vi* ❶ (*play*) wippen ❷ (*fig*) sich auf und ab bewegen; *prices* steigen und fallen; *mood* schwanken

seethe [sið] *vi* ❶ (*be very angry*) kochen *fam* ❷ (*be crowded*) wimmeln (**with** von +*dat*)

'see-through *adj* ❶ (*transparent*) durchsichtig ❷ (*of very light material*) durchscheinend

segment **I.** *n* ['seg·mənt] (*part, division*) Teil *m; of population* Gruppe *f; of orange* Schnitz *m;* (*of worm*) Segment *nt;* MATH Segment *nt* **II.** *vt* [səg·'ment] zerlegen **III.** *vi* [səg·'ment] sich teilen

segmentation [ˌseg·mən·'teɪ·ʃən] *n* Segmentierung *f geh;* BIOL Zellteilung *f*

segregate ['seg·rə·geɪt] *vt* absondern; *races, sexes* trennen

segregation [ˌseg·rə·'geɪ·ʃən] *n* Trennung *f;* **racial ~** Rassentrennung *f*

seismic ['saɪz·mɪk] *adj* GEOL seismisch; **~ waves** Erdbebenwellen *pl*

seismograph ['saɪz·mə·græf] *n* Seismograph *m*

seismologist [saɪz·'mal·ə·dʒɪst] *n* Seismologe, Seismologin *m, f*

seismology [saɪz·'mal·ə·dʒi] *n* Seismologie *f*

seize [siz] *vt* ❶ (*grab*) ergreifen, packen ❷ *usu passive* (*fig: overcome*) ■**to be ~d with sth** von etw *dat* ergriffen werden ❸ (*capture*) einnehmen; *criminal* festnehmen; *hostage* nehmen; *power* ergreifen; (*more aggressively*) an sich *akk* reißen ❹ (*confiscate*) beschlagnahmen

◆**seize on, seize upon** *vt idea* aufgreifen; *excuse* greifen (zu +*dat*)

◆**seize up** *vi engine, machine* stehen bleiben; *brain* aussetzen

seizure ['si·ʒər] *n* ❶ (*taking*) Ergreifung *f; of drugs* Beschlagnahmung *f* ❷ MED (*fit*) Anfall *m*

seldom ['sel·dəm] *adv* selten; **~ if ever** fast nie

select [sə·'lekt] **I.** *adj* ❶ (*high-class*) *hotel, club* exklusiv ❷ (*carefully chosen*) ausgewählt; *team* auserwählt; *fruit, cuts of meat* ausgesucht **II.** *vt* aussuchen; *person* auswählen; *team* aufstellen **III.** *vi* ■**to ~ from sth** aus etw *dat* [aus]wählen

select com'mittee *n* Sonderausschuss *m* (**on** für +*akk*)

selection [sə·'lek·ʃən] *n* ❶ (*choosing*) Auswahl *f;* BIOL Selektion *f geh;* **to make one's ~** seine Wahl treffen ❷ *usu sing* (*range*) Auswahl *f,* Sortiment *nt* ❸ (*chosen player*) Spieler[aus]wahl *f*

selective [sə·'lek·tɪv] *adj* ❶ (*careful about choosing*) wählerisch; *reader, shopper* kritisch ❷ (*choosing the best*) ausgewählt; **~ breeding** Zuchtwahl *f* ❸ (*discriminately affecting*) *process, agent* gezielt

selectively [ˌsə·'lek·tɪv·li] *adv* selektiv

selector [sə·'lek·tər] *n* ❶ (*chooser*) Auswählende(r) *f(m)* ❷ (*switch*) Wählschalter *m*

self <*pl* selves> [self] *n* (*personality*) ■**one's ~** das Selbst [*o* Ich]; **to be** [**like** [*or* **back to**]] **one's former ~** wieder ganz der/die Alte sein

self-addressed stamped 'envelope *n* adressierter frankierter Rückumschlag

S

self-ad'hesive *adj* selbstklebend
self-ap'pointed *adj manager, expert, critic* selbst ernannt
self-as'surance *n* Selbstvertrauen *nt,* Selbstsicherheit *f*
self-as'sured *adj* selbstbewusst, selbstsicher
self-'centered *adj* (*pej*) egozentrisch; **~ person** Egozentriker(in) *m(f)*
self-com'posed *adj* beherrscht; **to remain ~** gelassen bleiben
self-con'fessed *adj attr* erklärt; **she's a ~ thief** sie bezeichnet sich selbst als Diebin
self-'confidence *n* Selbstvertrauen *nt*
self-'conscious *adj* gehemmt; *laugh, smile* verlegen
self-con'tained *adj* ① (*complete*) selbstgenügsam; *community* autark ② (*separate*) *apartment* separat
self-con'trol *n* Selbstbeherrschung *f;* **to exercise ~** Selbstdisziplin üben
self-'critical *adj* selbstkritisch
self-'criticism *n* Selbstkritik *f*
self-de'ceit, self-de'ception *n* Selbstbetrug *m*
self-de'feating *adj* kontraproduktiv
self-de'fense *n* Selbstverteidigung *f;* **to kill sb in ~** jdn in Notwehr töten
self-de'nial *n* Selbsteinschränkung *f*
self-de'struct *vi* sich selbst zerstören; *materials* zerfallen; *missile* [zer]bersten
self-determi'nation *n* POL Selbstbestimmung *f*
self-'discipline *n* Selbstdisziplin *f*
self-ef'facing *adj* bescheiden
self-em'ployed I. *adj* selbständig **II.** *n* ■**the ~** *pl* die Selbständigen *pl*
self-es'teem *n* Selbstwertgefühl *nt;* **to have no/high/low ~** kein/ein hohes/ein geringes Selbstwertgefühl haben
self-'evident *adj* offensichtlich; ■**it is ~ that ...** es liegt auf der Hand, dass ...
self-ex'planatory *adj* ■**to be ~** klar sein, keiner weiteren Erklärung bedürfen
self-ex'pression *n* Selbstdarstellung *f*
self-ful'filling *adj* ■**to be ~** sich selbst bewahrheiten; **~ prophecy** sich selbst erfüllende Prophezeiung
self-'governing *adj* selbst verwaltet
self-'government *n* Selbstverwaltung *f*
self-'harm I. *n* Selbstverletzung *f* **II.** *vi* sich selbst verletzen
self-'help *n* Selbsthilfe *f*
selfie ['sel·fi] *n* TELEC, INET Selfie *nt*
self-im'portance *n* Selbstgefälligkeit *f*
self-im'portant *adj* selbstgefällig
self-im'posed *adj* selbst verordnet
self-in'dulgence *n* ① (*hedonism*) Luxus *m* ② (*act*) Hemmungslosigkeit *f*
self-in'dulgent *adj* genießerisch
self-in'flicted *adj* selbst zugefügt [*o* beigebracht]
self-'interest *n* Eigeninteresse *f*
selfish ['sel·fɪʃ] *adj* selbstsüchtig; *motive* eigennützig
selfishness ['sel·fɪʃ·nɪs] *n* Selbstsucht *f*
selfless ['self·lɪs] *adj* selbstlos
self-'made *adj* selbst gemacht; **~ man** Selfmademan *m*
self-'pity *n* Selbstmitleid *nt*
self-'portrait *n* Selbstbildnis *nt;* **to draw** [*or* **paint**] **a ~** sich selbst porträtieren
self-pos'sessed *adj* selbstbeherrscht
self-preser'vation *n* Selbsterhaltung *f*
self-re'liance *n* Selbstvertrauen *nt*
self-re'liant *adj* selbständig
self-re'spect *n* Selbstachtung *f*
self-re'specting *adj attr* ① (*having self-respect*) ■**to be ~** Selbstachtung besitzen ② (*esp hum: good*) anständig; **no ~ person** niemand, der was auf sich hält
self-'righteous *adj* selbstgerecht
self-rising 'flour *n Mehl, dem Backpulver beigemischt ist*
self-'sacrifice *n* Selbstaufopferung *f*
self-'satisfied *adj* selbstzufrieden
self-'seeking *adj* (*form*) selbstsüchtig
self-'service *n* Selbstbedienung *f*
self-suf'ficiency *n* Selbstversorgung *f;* **economic ~** Autarkie *f geh*
self-suf'ficient *adj* selbständig
self-'taught *adj* ① (*educated*) selbst erlernt ② (*acquired*) autodidaktisch
sell [sel] **I.** *vt* <sold, sold> ① (*for money*) verkaufen; **I sold him my car for $600** ich verkaufte ihm mein Auto für 600 Dollar; **to ~ sth at retail** etw im Einzelhandel verkaufen ② (*persuade*) ■**to ~ sth** [**to sb**] jdn für etw *akk* gewinnen; **to ~ an idea to sb** jdm eine Idee schmackhaft machen **II.** *vi* <sold, sold> ① (*give for money*) verkaufen ② (*attract customers*) sich verkaufen ▶ PHRASES: **to ~ like <u>hotcakes</u>** wie warme Semmeln weggehen **III.** *n* Ware *f;* **to be a hard** [*or* **tough**]**/soft ~** schwer/leicht verkäuflich sein
◆**sell off** *vt* verkaufen, verschachern
◆**sell out I.** *vi* ① (*sell entire stock*) **I'm sorry, we've sold out** es tut mir leid, aber wir sind ausverkauft; ■**to ~ out of a brand/goods** eine Serie/Waren ausverkaufen ② (*be completely booked*) *performance* ausverkauft sein ③ (*sell business*) ■**to ~ out to sb** [seine Firma] an jdn verkaufen ④ (*give in to*) ■**to ~ out to sb** sich *akk* an jdn verkaufen **II.** *vt* ① *stock* ■**to be sold out** ausverkauft sein ② (*pej fam: betray*) verraten
seller ['sel·ər] *n* ① (*person*) Verkäufer(in) *m(f)* ② (*product*) Verkaufsschlager *m*
selling ['sel·ɪŋ] *n* Verkaufen *nt*
'selling point *n* Kaufattribut *nt*
'selling price *n* Kaufpreis *m*
'sellout *n* ① (*sales*) Ausverkauf *m;* **the concert was a ~** das Konzert war ausverkauft ② (*betrayal*) Auslieferung *f*
selves [selvz] *n pl of* **self**
semantic [sə·'mæn·tɪk] *adj* semantisch
semantics [sə·'mæn·tɪks] *n* ① + *sing vb* (*science*) Semantik *f* ② (*meaning*) *of word, text* Bedeutung *f*

S

semaphore ['sem·ə·fɔr] **I.** *n* ❶ (*system of communication*) Semaphor *nt o* ÖSTERR *m* (*eine Signalsprache*) ❷ (*apparatus*) Semaphor *nt o* ÖSTERR *m* **II.** *vt* signalisieren

semblance ['sem·bləns] *n* (*form*) Anschein *m*

semen ['si·mən] *n* Sperma *nt*

semester [sə·'mes·tər] *n* Semester *nt*

semi <*pl* -s> ['sem·i] *n* (*fam*) ❶ (*truck*) Sattelschlepper *m* ❷ SPORTS ■ **~s** *pl* Halbfinale *nt*

semiauto'matic *adj* MIL *weapon, transmission* halbautomatisch

'semicircle *n* Halbkreis *m*

semi'circular *adj formation* halbkreisförmig

'semicolon *n* Semikolon *nt,* Strichpunkt *m*

semicon'ductor *n* Halbleiter *m*

semi'conscious *adj* halb bewusstlos; *feeling, memory* teilweise unbewusst

semi'final *n* Halbfinale *nt*

semi'finalist *n* SPORTS Halbfinalist(in) *m(f)*

seminal ['sem·ə·nəl] *adj* (*form: important*) *role* tragend *geh; work, article* bedeutend

seminar ['sem·ə·nar] *n* (*workshop*) Seminar *nt;* **training ~** Übung *f*

seminary ['sem·ɪ·ner·i] *n* Priesterseminar *nt*

semi'precious *adj* **~ stone** Halbedelstein *m*

semi'skilled *adj work, worker* angelernt

Semite ['sem·aɪt] *n* Semit(in) *m(f)*

Semitic [sə·'mɪt̬·ɪk] *adj* semitisch

semi'trailer *n* ❶ (*truck*) Sattelschlepper *m* ❷ (*trailer*) Anhänger *m* (*für Sattelschlepper*)

semi'tropical *adj see* **subtropical**

semi-vege'tarian *n* Flexitarier(in) *m(f),* Halbvegetarier(in) *m(f)*

semo'lina [ˌsem·ə·'li·nə] *n* Gries *m*

Sen. *n* POL *abbrev of* **senator**

senate ['sen·ɪt] *n* POL, LAW, UNIV Senat *m*

senator ['sen·ə·t̬ər] *n* (*member*) Senator(in) *m(f)*

senatorial [ˌsen·ə·'tɔr·i·əl] *adj* (*form*) Senats-

send <sent, sent> [send] *vt* ❶ (*forward*) ■ **to ~ [sb] sth** jdm etw [zu]schicken; **to ~ sth in the mail** etw mit der Post schicken; **to ~ a signal to sb** jdm etw signalisieren ❷ (*dispatch*) schicken; ■ **to ~ sb for sth** jdn nach etw *dat* [los]schicken; **to ~ sb to prison** jdn ins Gefängnis stecken ❸ (*transmit*) senden; *signal* aussenden; (*pass on*) ■ **to ~ sb sth** jdm etw übermitteln [lassen]; **Maggie ~s her love** Maggie lässt dich grüßen ❹ (*cause*) versetzen; **the news sent him running back to the house** die Nachricht ließ ihn wieder ins Haus laufen; **to ~ sb into a panic** jdn in Panik versetzen ►PHRASES: **to ~ sb <u>flying</u>** jdn zu Boden schicken

◆**send away I.** *vi* ■ **to ~ away for sth** sich *dat* etw zuschicken lassen **II.** *vt* wegschicken

◆**send back** *vt* zurückschicken

◆**send for** *vi* ❶ (*summon*) rufen ❷ (*ask*) *brochure, information* anfordern; *help* holen

◆**send in I.** *vt* ❶ (*submit*) *bill* einsenden, einreichen; *report* einschicken; *order* aufgeben ❷ (*dispatch*) *troops, police* einsetzen **II.** *vi* ■ **to ~ in for sth** sich *dat* etw zuschicken lassen; *for information* anfordern

◆**send off I.** *vt* ❶ (*mail*) abschicken; *package* aufgeben ❷ (*in soccer*) des Platzes verweisen; **to be sent off for fighting** einen Platzverweis wegen Rauferei bekommen ❸ (*dispatch*) *person* fortschicken **II.** *vi* ■ **to ~ off for sth** etw anfordern

◆**send out I.** *vi* ■ **to ~ out for sth** etw telefonisch bestellen **II.** *vt* ❶ (*emit*) aussenden, abgeben ❷ (*mail*) *letter* verschicken (**to** an +*akk*); *email* versenden (**to** an +*akk*)

◆**send up** *vt* ❶ (*force up*) *prices* ■ **to ~ up** ↻ **sth** etw ansteigen lassen ❷ (*pass on*) zuschicken ❸ (*fam: imprison*) hinter Gitter bringen

sender ['sen·dər] *n* Einsender(in) *m(f),* Absender(in) *m(f)*

'sendoff *n* Verabschiedung *f;* **to give sb a ~** jdn verabschieden

Senegal [ˌsen·ɪ·'gɔl] *n* Senegal *m*

senile ['si·naɪl] *adj* senil

senility [sə·'nɪl·ɪ·t̬i] *n* Senilität *f*

senior ['sin·jər] **I.** *adj* ❶ (*form: older*) älter ❷ *employee, officer* vorgesetzt ❸ *attr* SCH, UNIV (*of fourth-year students*) Senior- **II.** *n* ❶ (*older person*) Senior(in) *m(f);* **she's my ~ by three years** sie ist drei Jahre älter als ich ❷ (*employee*) Vorgesetzte(r) *f(m)* ❸ SCH, UNIV *Bezeichnung für Schüler einer Highschool- oder einer Collegeabgangsklasse*

senior 'citizen *n* ■ **~s** *pl* ältere Menschen, Senioren *pl*

senior 'high school *n* (*Schulform nach der Junior High School, welche die Stufen 9, 10, 11 und 12 enthält*)

seniority [sin·'jɔr·ɪ·t̬i] *n* ❶ (*age*) Alter *nt* ❷ (*rank*) Dienstalter *nt*

senior 'partner *n* Seniorpartner(in) *m(f)*

sensation [sen·'seɪ·ʃən] *n* ❶ (*physical, mental*) Gefühl *nt;* **~ of cold** Kälteempfindung *f;* **burning ~** Brennen *nt* ❷ (*stir*) Sensation *f;* **to cause a ~** Aufsehen erregen

sensational [sen·'seɪ·ʃə·nəl] *adj* sensationell; (*very good a.*) fantastisch; (*shocking a.*) spektakulär

sensationalism [sen·'seɪ·ʃən·əl·ɪ·zəm] *n* (*pej*) MEDIA Sensationsmache *m pej*

sense [sens] **I.** *n* ❶ (*judgment, reason*) Verstand *m;* ■ **sb's ~s** *pl* jds gesunder Menschenverstand; **it's time you came to your ~s** es wird Zeit, dass du zur Vernunft kommst ❷ (*reasonableness*) **to make [good] ~** sinnvoll sein; **to see the ~ in sth** den Sinn in etw *dat* sehen; **to talk ~** sich verständlich ausdrücken; **there's no ~ in doing sth** es hat keinen Sinn, etw zu tun ❸ (*faculty*) Sinn *m;* **~ of hearing** Gehör *nt;* **~ of sight** Sehvermögen *nt;* **~ of smell** Geruchssinn *m;* **sixth ~** sechster Sinn ❹ (*feeling*) Gefühl *nt;* **~ of duty** Pflichtgefühl *nt;* **~ of justice** Gerechtigkeitssinn *m* ❺ (*meaning*) Bedeutung *f,* Sinn *m;* **figurative ~** übertragene Bedeutung; **to make ~** einen Sinn ergeben; **in every ~** in jeder Hinsicht **II.** *vt* wahrnehmen; *danger* wit-

S

tern; ■ **to ~ that ...** spüren, dass ...

senseless ['sens·lɪs] *adj* ❶ (*pointless*) *violence, waste* sinnlos ❷ (*foolish*) *argument* töricht ❸ (*unconscious*) besinnungslos

'sense organ *n* Sinnesorgan *nt*

sensibility [ˌsen·sə·'bɪl·ɪ·t̬i] *n* ❶ (*sensitiveness*) Einfühlungsvermögen *nt* ❷ *pl* (*delicate feelings*) ■ **sensibilities** Gefühle *nt pl*

sensible ['sen·sə·bəl] *adj* ❶ (*rational*) vernünftig; *decision* weis; *person* klug ❷ (*suitable*) *clothes* angemessen

sensibly ['sen·sə·bli] *adv* ❶ (*rationally*) vernünftig ❷ (*suitably*) angemessen; *dressed* passend

sensitive ['sen·sɪ·t̬ɪv] *adj* ❶ (*kind*) verständnisvoll; ■ **to be ~ to sth** für etw *akk* Verständnis haben ❷ (*secret*) *material* vertraulich ❸ (*responsive, touchy*) empfindlich (**to** gegenüber +*dat*); **to be ~ to cold** kälteempfindlich sein; **~ feelings** verletzliche Gefühle

sensitivity [ˌsen·sə·'tɪv·ɪ·t̬i] *n* ❶ (*understanding*) Verständnis *nt* ❷ (*confidentiality*) Vertraulichkeit *f* ❸ (*reaction*) Überempfindlichkeit *f* (**to** gegen +*akk*); **~ to light** Licht[über]empfindlichkeit *f*

sensitize ['sen·sə·taɪz] *vt* sensibilisieren; ■ **to ~ sb to sth** jdn für etw *akk* sensibilisieren

sensor ['sen·sər] *n* Sensor *m*

sensory ['sen·sə·ri] *adj* sensorisch; **~ perception** Sinneswahrnehmung *f*

sensual ['sen·ʃu·əl] *adj* sinnlich

sensuality [ˌsen·ʃu·'æl·ɪ·t̬i] *n* Sinnlichkeit *f*

sensuous ['sen·ʃu·əs] *adj* ❶ *see* **sensual** ❷ (*of senses*) sinnlich

sent [sent] *pp, pt of* **send**

sentence ['sen·təns] **I.** *n* ❶ (*court decision*) Urteil *nt;* (*punishment*) Strafe *f;* **life ~** lebenslängliche Haftstrafe; **to serve a ~** eine Strafe verbüßen ❷ (*word group*) Satz *m* **II.** *vt* verurteilen (**to** zu +*dat*)

sentient ['sen·ʃənt] *adj* (*form: having feelings*) fühlend *attr;* **~ being** empfindsames Wesen

sentiment ['sen·tə·mənt] *n* (*form*) ❶ *usu pl* (*attitude*) Ansicht *f,* Meinung *f;* **my ~s exactly!** ganz meine Meinung! ❷ (*general opinion*) **popular ~** allgemeine Meinung ❸ (*excessive emotion*) Rührseligkeit *f*

sentimental [ˌsen·tə·'men·təl] *adj* ❶ (*emotional*) *mood, person* gefühlvoll; **~ value** ideeller Wert ❷ (*pej: overly emotional*) *person* sentimental; *music, style* kitschig; *story* rührselig

sentimentality [ˌsen·tə·men·'tæl·ɪ·t̬i] *n* (*pej*) Sentimentalität *f*

sentry ['sen·tri] *n* Wache *f*

separable ['sep·ər·ə·bəl] *adj* ❶ (*form: able to separate*) [ab]trennbar ❷ LING trennbar

separate I. *adj* ['sep·ər·ɪt] (*not joined*) getrennt, separat; (*independent*) einzeln *attr;* **a ~ piece of paper** ein extra Blatt Papier; **to keep sth ~** etw getrennt halten; **to keep things ~ [from one another]** Sachen auseinanderhalten **II.** *n* ['sep·ər·ɪt] ■ **~s** *pl* ≈ Einzelteile *pl;* **ladies' ~s** Röcke, Blusen, Hosen **III.** *vt* ['sep·ə·reɪt] trennen **IV.** *vi* ['sep·ə·reɪt] ❶ (*become detached*) sich trennen; CHEM sich scheiden ❷ (*of cohabiting couple*) sich trennen; (*divorce*) sich scheiden lassen; **she is ~d from her husband** sie lebt von ihrem Mann getrennt

separation [ˌsep·ə·'reɪ·ʃən] *n* ❶ (*act of separating*) Trennung *f* ❷ (*living apart*) [eheliche] Trennung

separatist ['sep·ər·ə·tɪst] *n* Separatist(in) *m(f)*

separator ['sep·ə·reɪ·t̬ər] *n* TECH Separator *m*

sepia ['si·pi·ə] *adj* sepia[farben]

Sept. *n abbrev of* **September** Sept.

September [sep·'tem·bər] *n* September *m; see also* **February**

septic ['sep·tɪk] *adj* septisch

septicemia [ˌsep·tə·'si·mi·ə] *n* MED Blutvergiftung *f*

'septic tank *n* Klärbehälter *m*

septuagenarian [ˌsep·tu·ə·dʒə·'ner·i·ən] *n* Siebzigjährige(r) *f(m)*

sequel ['si·kwəl] *n* ❶ (*continuation*) Fortsetzung *f* ❷ (*follow-up*) Nachspiel *nt*

sequence ['si·kwəns] *n* ❶ (*order of succession*) Reihenfolge *f;* *of* [*television*] *programs* Sendefolge *f;* (*connected series*) Abfolge *f* ❷ (*part of film*) Sequenz *f;* **closing ~** Schlussszene *f*

sequential [sɪ·'kwen·ʃəl] *adj* (*form*) [aufeinander]folgend *attr*

sequester [sɪ·'kwes·tər] *vt* ❶ (*form: isolate*) *jury* isolieren ❷ LAW (*temporarily confiscate*) beschlagnahmen

sequestration [ˌsi·kwɪ·'streɪ·ʃən] *n* LAW Beschlagnahme *f*

sequin ['si·kwɪn] *n* Paillette *f*

sequoia [sɪ·'kwɔɪ·ə] *n* BOT Mammutbaum *m*

Serb [sɜrb] *n* Serbe, Serbin *m, f*

Serbia ['sɜr·bi·ə] *n* Serbien *nt*

Serbian ['sɜr·bi·ən] **I.** *adj* serbisch **II.** *n* ❶ (*person*) Serbe, Serbin *m, f* ❷ (*language*) Serbisch *nt*

Serbo-Croatian [ˌsɜr·boʊ·kroʊ·'eɪ·ʃən] *n* LING Serbokroatisch *nt*

serenade [ˌser·ə·'neɪd] **I.** *n* ❶ (*classical music*) Serenade *f* ❷ (*sung by lover*) Ständchen *nt* **II.** *vt* ein Ständchen bringen

serene <-r, -st *or* more ~, most ~> [sə·'rin] *adj* (*calm*) ruhig; (*untroubled*) gelassen

serenity [sə·'ren·ɪ·t̬i] *n* (*calmness*) Ruhe *f;* (*untroubled state*) Gelassenheit *f*

sergeant ['sar·dʒənt] *n* ❶ (*military officer*) Unteroffizier *m* ❷ (*police officer*) ≈ Polizeimeister(in) *m(f)*

sergeant 'major *n* Oberfeldwebel *m*

serial ['sɪr·i·əl] **I.** *n* MEDIA, PUBL Fortsetzungsgeschichte *f* **II.** *adj* ❶ (*broadcasting, publishing*) Serien- ❷ (*repeated*) Serien-

'serial killer *n* Serienmörder(in) *m(f)*

'serial number *n* Seriennummer *f*

series <*pl* -> ['sɪr·iz] *n* ❶ (*set of events*) Reihe *f;* (*succession*) Folge *f* ❷ (*line of products*)

SPORTS, RADIO, TV Serie *f*

serious ['sɪr·i·əs] *adj* ① (*earnest*) *person* ernst; (*solemn, not funny*) *comment, situation* ernst; **a ~ threat** eine ernsthafte Bedrohung ② (*grave*) *accident, crime* schwer; (*dangerous*) gefährlich; (*not slight*) [*medical*] *condition, problem* ernst; *allegation* schwerwiegend; *argument, disagreement* ernsthaft; **~ trouble** ernsthafte Schwierigkeiten *pl* ③ *attr* (*careful*) ernsthaft; **to give sth ~ thought** ernsthaft über etw *akk* nachdenken ④ (*significant*) bedeutend; (*thought-provoking*) tiefgründig; *literature, writer* anspruchsvoll

seriously ['sɪr·i·əs·li] *adv* ① (*in earnest*) ernst; **to take sth ~** etw ernst nehmen ② (*gravely, badly*) schwer; (*dangerously*) ernstlich; **~ wounded** schwer verletzt ③ (*fam: very, extremely*) äußerst; **~ funny** urkomisch

seriousness ['sɪr·i·əs·nɪs] *n* ① (*serious nature*) *of person* Ernst *m;* (*critical state*) *of problem, threat* Ernst *m; of situation* Ernsthaftigkeit *f* ② (*sincerity*) Ernsthaftigkeit *f; of offer* Seriosität *f geh;* **in all ~** ganz im Ernst

sermon ['sɜr·mən] *n* ① (*religious speech*) Predigt *f* (**on** über *+akk*) ② (*pej: moral lecture*) [Moral]predigt *f oft pej*

serpent ['sɜr·pənt] *n* (*old*) Schlange *f*

serpentine ['sɜr·pən·taɪn] *adj* (*liter: snakelike*) schlangenförmig; (*twisting, winding*) *path, river* gewunden

serrated [sə·'reɪ·t̬ɪd] *adj* gezackt; **knife with a ~ edge** Messer *nt* mit Wellenschliff

serum <*pl* -s *or* sera> ['sɪr·əm] *n* Serum *nt*

servant ['sɜr·vənt] *n* ① (*household helper*) Bediensteter *m;* (*female*) Bedienstete *f,* Dienstmädchen *nt* ② (*for public*) Angestellte(r) *f(m)* (*im öffentlichen Dienst*)

serve [sɜrv] **I.** *n* (*in tennis*) Aufschlag *m;* (*in volleyball*) Angabe *f* **II.** *vt* ① (*in restaurant, shop*) bedienen ② (*present food, drink*) servieren ③ (*be enough for*) reichen; **this ~s 4 to 5** das ergibt 4 bis 5 Portionen ④ (*complete due period*) ableisten; *prison sentence* absitzen *fam* ⑤ (*perform a function*) **to ~ a purpose** einen Zweck erfüllen; **if my memory ~s me right** wenn ich mich recht erinnere ⑥ SPORTS **to ~ the ball** (*in tennis*) Aufschlag haben; (*in volleyball*) Angabe haben ▸ PHRASES: **this ~s him right** (*fam*) das geschieht ihm recht **III.** *vi* ① (*provide food, drink*) servieren ② (*work for*) dienen; (*function a.*) fungieren (**as** als) ③ (*in tennis, etc.*) aufschlagen; (*in volleyball*) angeben

◆**serve out** *vt* ableisten; *jail sentence* absitzen *fam; term of office* beenden

◆**serve up** *vt* servieren

server ['sɜr·vər] *n* ① (*waitperson*) Kellner, -in *m, f* ② (*central computer*) Server *m*

service ['sɜr·vɪs] **I.** *n* ① (*help for customers*) Service *m;* (*in hotels, restaurants, shops*) Bedienung *f;* **customer ~** Kundendienst *m* ② (*act of working*) Dienst *m,* Dienstleistung *f* ③ (*form: assistance*) Unterstützung *f;* (*aid, help*) Hilfe *f;* ■**to be of ~** [**to sb**] [jdm] von Nutzen sein; **to need the ~s of an expert** einen Gutachter/eine Gutachterin brauchen ④ (*system for public, government department*) Dienst *m;* **ambulance ~** Rettungsdienst *m;* **civil ~** öffentlicher Dienst ⑤ (*operation*) Betrieb *m;* **to be out of/in ~** außer/in Betrieb sein; **postal ~** Postwesen *nt* ⑥ (*in tennis, etc.*) Aufschlag *m;* (*in volleyball*) Angabe *f* ⑦ (*armed forces*) Militär *nt;* ■**the ~s** das Militär *nt kein pl* ⑧ (*religious ceremony*) Gottesdienst *m;* **morning/evening ~** Frühmesse *f*/ Abendandacht *f* ⑨ (*maintenance check*) Wartung *f;* AUTO Inspektion *f* **II.** *vt* warten

serviceable ['sɜr·vɪ·sə·bəl] *adj* strapazierfähig

'service area *n* ① RADIO, TV Sendegebiet *nt* ② (*on freeway*) Raststätte *f*

'service center *n* (*for repairs*) Reparaturwerkstatt *f;* (*garage*) Werkstatt *f*

'service charge *n* Bedienungsgeld *nt*

'service entrance *n* Personaleingang *m*

'service industry *n* Dienstleistungsindustrie *f;* (*company*) Dienstleistungsbetrieb *m*

'serviceman *n* Militärangehöriger *m*

'service road *n* (*subsidiary road*) Nebenstraße *f;* (*access road*) Zufahrtsstraße *f*

'service sector *n* Dienstleistungsindustrie *f*

'service station *n* Tankstelle *f*

'servicewoman *n* MIL Militärangehörige *f*

servile ['sɜr·vəl] *adj* (*pej*) *manner* unterwürfig; *obedience* sklavisch

serving ['sɜr·vɪŋ] **I.** *n of food* Portion *f* (**of**) **II.** *adj attr* dienend; **the longest-~ mayor** der dienstälteste Bürgermeister/die dienstälteste Bürgermeisterin

'serving spoon *n* Vorlegelöffel *m,* Servierlöffel *m*

servitude ['sɜr·vɪ·tud] *n* (*form*) Knechtschaft *f*

servo ['sɜ·voʊ] *n* AUTO, TECH ① *short for* **servomechanism** Servomechanismus *m* ② *short for* **servomotor** Servomotor *m* ③ AUS (*fam: service station*) Tanke *f fam*

sesame ['ses·ə·mi] *n* Sesam *m*

session ['seʃ·ən] *n* ① (*formal meeting*) Sitzung *f;* (*period of meeting*) Sitzungsperiode *f* ② (*period for specific activity*) Stunde *f;* **recording ~** Aufnahme *f*

set[1] [set] **I.** *adj* ① *pred* (*ready*) bereit, fertig; **ready, [get] ~, go!** auf die Plätze, fertig, los!; ■**to be [all] ~ [for sth]** [für etw *akk*] bereit sein ② (*fixed*) *pattern, time* fest[gesetzt]; **~ phrase** feststehender Ausdruck ③ (*expression of face*) *look* starr ④ *attr* (*assigned*) *number, pattern* vorgegebene(r, s); *subject a.* bestimmte(r, s) **II.** *vt* <set, set> ① (*place*) stellen, setzen; (*on its side*) legen; **to ~ foot in [*or* on] sth** etw betreten ② *usu passive* (*take place in, be located*) **"West Side Story" is ~ in New York** „West Side Story" spielt in New York ③ (*cause to be*) **his remarks ~ me thinking** seine Bemerkungen gaben mir zu denken; **to ~ one's/sb's mind at ease** sich/jdn beruhigen; **to ~ sth in motion** etw in Bewegung setzen [*o*

S

fig a. ins Rollen bringen] ④ (*prepare*) vorbereiten; *table* decken; **to ~ the scene for sth** (*create conditions*) die Bedingungen für etw *akk* schaffen; (*facilitate*) den Weg für etw *akk* frei machen ⑤ (*adjust*) einstellen; *alarm, clock* stellen ⑥ (*fix*) festsetzen; *budget* festlegen; *date, time* ausmachen; *deadline, limit* setzen, festlegen ⑦ (*establish*) *record* aufstellen; *pace* vorgeben; **to ~ a good example for sb** jdm ein Vorbild sein ⑧ ANAT einrenken; *broken bone* einrichten ⑨ (*arrange*) *hair* legen; **to have one's hair ~** sich die Haare legen lassen ⑩ COMPUT (*give variable a value*) setzen; (*define value*) einstellen ⑪ TYPO setzen ⑫ (*sail*) **to ~ sail for ...** nach ... losfahren **III.** *vi* <set, set> ① (*grow together*) *bones* zusammenwachsen ② (*become firm*) *concrete, Jell-O* fest werden ③ (*sink*) *moon, sun* untergehen **IV.** *n* (*for hair*) Legen *nt*

set² [set] *n* ① (*collection, group*) Satz *m;* (*of two items*) Paar *nt; of clothes* Garnitur *f;* **coffee ~** Kaffeeservice *nt* ② THEAT Bühnenbild *nt;* FILM Szenenaufbau *m;* **on the ~** bei den Dreharbeiten; (*location*) am Set ③ (*appliance*) Gerät *nt;* (*television*) Fernseher *m;* (*radio*) Radio[gerät] *nt* ④ MATH Menge *f* ⑤ COMPUT **data ~** Datensatz *m;* (*file*) Datei *f* ⑥ (*in tennis*) Satz *m*

◆**set about** *vi* **to ~ about doing sth** *job, task* sich daran machen, etw zu tun

◆**set apart** *vt* ① (*distinguish*) ■**sth ~s sb/sth ⊂ apart from sb/sth** etw unterscheidet jdn/etw von jdm/etw ② (*reserve*) ■**to be ~ apart for sth** für etw *akk* reserviert sein

◆**set aside** *vt* ① (*put to side*) beiseitelegen [*o* stellen]; *clothes* sich *dat* zurücklegen lassen ② (*keep for special use*) *money* sparen, auf die Seite legen; *time* einplanen ③ (*ignore*) *differences, hostilities* begraben; *work* zurückstellen

◆**set back** *vt* ① (*delay*) zurückwerfen; *deadline* verschieben ② (*position*) zurücksetzen (**from** von +*dat*); **their garden is ~ back from the road** ihr Garten liegt nicht direkt an der Straße

◆**set down** *vt* ① (*drop off, put down*) absetzen ② (*land*) *plane* landen ③ **to ~ sth down in writing** aufschreiben

◆**set forth** **I.** *vt* (*form*) *plan* darlegen **II.** *vi* (*liter*) aufbrechen

◆**set in** *vi bad weather* einsetzen; *complications* sich einstellen

◆**set off** **I.** *vi* sich auf den Weg machen; (*in car*) losfahren **II.** *vt* ① (*initiate*) *alarm, blast, reaction* auslösen; *bomb, fireworks* zünden ② (*make angry*) ■**to ~ sb off** jdn verärgern ③ (*cause to do*) ■**to ~ sb off doing sth** jdn dazu bringen, etw zu tun ④ ■**to ~ off ⊂ sth against sth** ECON etw mit etw *dat* verrechnen

◆**set out** **I.** *vt* ① (*arrange*) *goods* auslegen; *chairs, chess pieces* aufstellen ② (*explain*) *idea, point* darlegen **II.** *vi* ① (*begin trip*) aufbrechen ② (*intend*) ■**to ~ out to do sth** beabsichtigen, etw zu tun

◆**set up** *vt* ① (*erect*) *camp* aufschlagen ② (*institute*) *business* einrichten ③ (*fam: deceive, frame*) übers Ohr hauen *fam* ④ COMPUT *program* installieren; *system* konfigurieren

◆**set upon** *vt* (*fam: attack*) ■**to ~ an animal upon sb** ein Tier auf jdn hetzen; ■**to ~ upon sb [with sth]** [mit etw *dat*] über jdn herfallen

'setback *n* Rückschlag *m*

setting ['set̬·ɪŋ] *n usu sing* ① (*location*) Lage *f;* (*immediate surroundings*) Umgebung *f* ② (*in film, novel, play*) Schauplatz *m* ③ (*adjustment on appliance*) Einstellung *f* ④ (*frame for jewel*) Fassung *f*

settle ['set̬·əl] **I.** *vi* ① (*get comfortable*) es sich *dat* bequem machen ② (*alight on surface, take up residence*) sich niederlassen; (*build up*) sich anhäufen; **do you think the snow will ~?** glaubst du, dass der Schnee liegen bleibt? ③ (*end dispute*) sich einigen ④ (*become stable*) *weather* beständig werden **II.** *vt* ① (*decide*) entscheiden; (*deal with*) regeln ② (*bring to conclusion*) erledigen; (*resolve*) *argument* beilegen; *question* regeln; **that ~s that** damit hat sich das erledigt ③ (*colonize*) besiedeln ▶ PHRASES: **to ~ a score [with sb]** [mit jdm] abrechnen

◆**settle down** **I.** *vi* ① (*get comfortable*) es sich *dat* bequem machen ② (*calm down*) sich beruhigen ③ (*adopt steady lifestyle*) sich [häuslich] niederlassen **II.** *vt* ① (*make comfortable*) ■**to ~ oneself down** es sich *dat* bequem machen ② (*calm down*) beruhigen

◆**settle for** *vi* ■**to ~ for sth** mit etw *dat* zufrieden sein

◆**settle in** *vi people* sich einleben; *things* sich einpendeln

◆**settle on** *vi* ■**to ~ on sth** ① (*decide on*) sich für etw *akk* entscheiden ② (*agree on*) sich auf etw *akk* einigen; *on a name* sich entscheiden (für +*akk*)

settled ['set̬·əld] *adj* ① *pred* (*comfortable, established*) ■**to be ~** sich eingelebt haben; **to feel ~** sich heimisch fühlen ② (*calm*) ruhig ③ (*steady*) *lifestyle* geregelt

settlement ['set̬·əl·mənt] *n* ① (*resolution*) Übereinkunft *f;* (*agreement*) Vereinbarung *f;* LAW Vergleich *m; of conflict* Lösung *f; of matter* Regelung *f; of strike* Schlichtung *f;* **they reached an out-of-court ~** sie einigten sich außergerichtlich ② (*colony*) Siedlung *f;* (*colonization*) Besiedlung *f;* (*people*) Ansiedlung *f*

settler ['set̬·lər] *n* Siedler(in) *m(f)*

'setup *n* ① (*way things are arranged*) Aufbau *m;* (*arrangement*) Einrichtung *f* ② (*fam: act of deception*) abgekartetes Spiel

seven ['sev·ən] **I.** *adj* sieben; *see also* **eight** **II.** *n* Sieben *f; see also* **eight**

'sevenfold *adj* siebenfache

seventeen [ˌsev·ən·'tin] **I.** *adj* siebzehn; *see also* **eight** **II.** *n* Siebzehn *f; see also* **eight**

seventeenth [ˌsev·ən·'tinθ] **I.** *adj* siebzehnte(r, s) **II.** *n* ① (*date*) ■**the ~** der Siebzehnte

❷ *(fraction)* Siebzehntel *nt*

seventh ['sev·ənθ] **I.** *adj* siebte(r, s) **II.** *n* ❶ *(date)* ■ **the ~** der Siebte ❷ *(fraction)* Siebtel *nt*

seventieth ['sev·ən·ti·əθ] **I.** *adj* siebzigste(r, s) **II.** *n* ❶ *(ordinal number)* Siebzigste(r, s) ❷ *(fraction)* Siebzigstel *nt*

seventy ['sev·ən·ţi] **I.** *adj* siebzig **II.** *n* Siebzig *f*

sever ['sev·ər] *vt* ❶ *(separate)* abtrennen; *(cut through)* durchtrennen ❷ *(end) links, connection* abbrechen; *ties* lösen

several ['sev·ər·əl] **I.** *adj (some)* einige, mehrere; *(various)* verschiedene **II.** *pron* ein paar, mehrere, einige

severance ['sev·ər·əns] *n (form)* ❶ *(act of ending)* Abbruch *m* **(of** *+gen)* ❷ *(payment by employer)* Abfindung *f*

'severance pay *n* Abfindung *f*, Entlassungsgeld *nt*

severe [sə·'vɪr] *adj* ❶ *(very serious)* schwer, schlimm; *pain* heftig, stark; *cutbacks* drastisch; *blow, injury, penalty* schwer ❷ *(harsh) criticism, punishment* hart; *(strict)* streng; METEO *(harsh)* rau; *storm* heftig; *cold* eisig; *frost, winter* streng; *(violent)* gewaltig; **~ reprimand** scharfer Tadel

severely [sə·'vɪr·li] *adv* ❶ *(seriously) disabled, injured* schwer; **to be ~ restricted** enorm eingeschränkt sein ❷ *(harshly)* hart; *(extremely)* heftig, stark; *(strictly)* streng

severity [sə·'ver·ɪ·ţi] *n* ❶ *(seriousness)* Schwere *f*; *(of situation, person)* Ernst *m* ❷ *(harshness)* Härte *f*; *(strictness)* Strenge *f*; *of criticism* Schärfe *f*; *(extreme nature)* Rauheit *f*

Seville [sə·'vɪl] *n* Sevilla *nt*

sew <sewed, sewn *or* sewed> [soʊ] **I.** *vt* [an]nähen **II.** *vi* nähen

◆**sew up** *vt* ❶ *(repair)* zunähen; *wound* nähen ❷ *(fam: complete successfully)* zum Abschluss bringen ❸ *(fam: make sure of winning)* sich *dat* sichern; **to be ~n up** unter Dach und Fach sein

sewage ['su·ɪdʒ] *n* Abwasser *nt*

'sewage (treatment) plant *n* ECOL Rieselfeld *nt*

sewer[1] ['su·ər] *n* Abwasserkanal *m*

sewer[2] ['soʊ·ər] *n* Näher(in) *m(f)*

sewerage ['su·ər·ɪdʒ] *n* Kanalisation *f*

sewing ['soʊ·ɪŋ] *n* ❶ *(activity)* Nähen *nt* ❷ *(things to sew)* Näharbeit *f*

'sewing basket *n* Nähkorb *m*

'sewing machine *n* Nähmaschine *f*

sewn [soʊn] *pp of* **sew**

sex <*pl* -es> [seks] *n* ❶ *(gender)* Geschlecht *nt*; **the opposite ~** das andere Geschlecht ❷ *(intercourse)* Sex *m*, Geschlechtsverkehr *m*; **to have ~** Sex haben; **to have ~ with sb** mit jdm schlafen

'sex appeal *n* Sexappeal *m*

'sex education *n* Sexualerziehung *f*

sexism ['sek·sɪz·əm] *n* Sexismus *m*

sexist ['sek·sɪst] **I.** *adj (pej)* sexistisch **II.** *n* Sexist(in) *m(f)*

sexless ['seks·lɪs] *adj* ❶ *(without gender)* geschlechtslos ❷ *(without physical attractiveness)* unerotisch ❸ *(without sexual desire)* sexuell desinteressiert

'sex life *n* Sexualleben *nt*

'sex symbol *n* Sexsymbol *nt*

sextet(te) [sek·'stet] *n* Sextett *nt*

sexual ['sek·ʃu·əl] *adj* ❶ *(referring to gender)* geschlechtlich; **~ equality** Gleichheit *f* der Geschlechter ❷ *(erotic)* sexuell; **~ relationship** sexuelle Beziehung

sexual discrimi'nation *n* Diskriminierung *f* aufgrund des Geschlechts

sexual 'harassment *n* sexuelle Belästigung

sexual 'intercourse *n* Geschlechtsverkehr *m*

sexuality [ˌsek·ʃu·'æl·ɪ·ţi] *n* Sexualität *f*

sexually ['sek·ʃu·əl·i] *adv* ❶ *(referring to gender)* geschlechtlich ❷ *(erotically)* sexuell; **~ attractive** sexy

sexy ['sek·si] *adj (fam)* ❶ *(physically appealing)* sexy ❷ *(arousing)* erregend ❸ *(exciting)* aufregend, heiß

Seychelles [seɪ·'ʃelz] *n* ■ **the ~** die Seychellen *pl*

Sgt. *n abbrev of* **sergeant** Uffz.

shabby ['ʃæb·i] *adj* ❶ *(worn)* schäbig; *clothing* gammelig ❷ *(poorly dressed)* ärmlich gekleidet ❸ *(unfair)* schäbig ❹ *(mediocre) performance* mittelmäßig; *excuse* fadenscheinig; **not too ~!** ganz in Ordnung

shack [ʃæk] *n* Hütte *f*

◆**shack up** *vi (fam)* ■ **to ~ up with sb** mit jdm zusammenziehen; ■ **to be ~ed up with sb** mit jdm zusammenleben

shackle ['ʃæk·əl] **I.** *n* **~s** *pl* Fesseln *f pl*, Ketten *f pl*; *(fig)* Zwänge *m pl* **II.** *vt* ❶ *(chain)* [mit Ketten] fesseln ❷ *(fig: restrict)* behindern

shade [ʃeɪd] **I.** *n* ❶ *(shaded area)* Schatten *m*; **a patch of ~** ein schattiges Plätzchen; **in** [*or* **under**] **the ~** im Schatten **(of** *+gen)* ❷ *(lampshade)* [Lampen]schirm *m* ❸ **roller ~** Rollladen *m* ❹ *(variation of color)* [Farb]ton *m*, Zwischenton *m*; **pastel ~s** Pastellfarben *pl* ❺ *(fam: sunglasses)* ■ **~s** *pl* Sonnenbrille *f* **II.** *vt* ❶ *(protect from brightness)* [vor der Sonne] schützen; *eyes* beschirmen; **an avenue ~d by trees** eine von Bäumen beschattete Allee ❷ *(in picture)* schattieren **III.** *vi* ❶ *(alter color)* ■ **to ~** [**off**] **into sth** allmählich in etw *akk* übergehen ❷ *(be very similar)* ■ **to ~ into sth** kaum von etw *dat* zu unterscheiden sein

shading ['ʃeɪ·dɪŋ] *n* Schattierung *f*

shadow ['ʃæd·oʊ] **I.** *n* ❶ *(produced by light)* Schatten *m* ❷ *(under eye)* Augenring *m* ❸ *(smallest trace)* Hauch *m*, Anflug *m*; **there isn't even a ~ of doubt** es besteht nicht der leiseste Zweifel ▶ PHRASES: **to be a ~ of one's former self** [nur noch] ein Schatten seiner selbst sein **II.** *vt* ❶ *(darken)* verdunkeln ❷ *(follow secretly)* beschatten ❸ SPORTS *(stay close to)* decken

'shadowboxing *n* Schattenboxen *nt*

S

shadowy ['ʃæ·doʊ·i] *adj* ❶ (*out of sun*) schattig; (*dark*) düster; ~ **figure** schemenhafte Figur; (*fig*) rätselhaftes Wesen ❷ (*dubious*) zweifelhaft

shady ['ʃeɪ·di] *adj* ❶ (*in shade*) schattig ❷ (*fam: dubious*) fragwürdig; (*dishonest*) unehrlich

shaft [ʃæft] **I.** *n* ❶ (*hole*) Schacht *m* ❷ *of tool, weapon* Schaft *m* ❸ (*in engine*) Welle *f* ❹ (*ray*) Strahl *m;* ~ **of sunlight** Sonnenstrahl *m* **II.** *vt* (*fam*) betrügen

shag [ʃæg] **I.** *adj attr* ~ **carpet** Veloursteppich *m* **II.** *n* Zottel *f*

shaggy ['ʃæg·i] *adj* ❶ (*hairy*) struppig ❷ (*unkempt*) zottelig

Shah [ʃa] *n* (*hist*) Schah *m*

shake [ʃeɪk] **I.** *n* ❶ (*action*) Schütteln *nt kein pl;* **she gave the box a ~** sie schüttelte die Schachtel ❷ (*fam: milkshake*) Shake *m* ▶ PHRASES: **to be no great ~s at sth** bei etw *dat* nicht besonders gut sein **II.** *vt* <shook, shaken> ❶ (*vibrate*) schütteln; ~ **well before using** vor Gebrauch gut schütteln; ■**to ~ oneself** sich schütteln; ■**to ~ sth over sth** etw über etw *akk* streuen ❷ (*undermine, shock*) erschüttern; **the news has ~n the whole country** die Nachricht hat das ganze Land schwer getroffen ❸ (*fam: get rid of*) loswerden **III.** *vi* <shook, shaken> ❶ (*quiver*) beben; ■**to ~ with sth** vor etw *dat* beben [*o* zittern] ❷ (*shiver with fear*) zittern, beben ▶ PHRASES: **to ~ like a leaf** wie Espenlaub zittern

◆**shake down** *vt* (*sl*) ❶ (*threaten*) erpressen ❷ (*thoroughly search*) filzen

◆**shake off** *vt* ❶ (*remove*) abschütteln ❷ (*get rid of*) überwinden; *habit* ablegen; *illness* besiegen; *person* loswerden; *pursuer* abschütteln

◆**shake out** *vt* ausschütteln

◆**shake up** *vt* ❶ (*mix*) mischen ❷ (*shock*) aufwühlen ❸ (*significantly alter*) umkrempeln; (*significantly reorganize*) umstellen

shakedown ['ʃeɪk·daʊn] **I.** *n* ❶ (*sl: extortion by tricks*) Abzocken *nt sl;* (*by threats*) Erpressung *f* ❷ (*sl: police search*) Razzia *f* ❸ (*tests and trials*) Erprobung *f; of machinery* Testlauf *m; of aircraft* Testflug *m; of vehicle* Testfahrt *f* **II.** *adj attr* Test-, Probe-

S

shaken ['ʃeɪ·kən] **I.** *vi, vt pp of* **shake II.** *adj* erschüttert

shaker ['ʃeɪ·kər] *n* ❶ (*for mixing liquids*) Mixbecher *m* ❷ (*dispenser*) **salt/pepper ~** Salz-/Pfefferstreuer *m*

shakeup ['ʃeɪk·ʌp] *n* Veränderung *f,* Umstrukturierung *f*

shakily ['ʃeɪ·kɪ·li] *adv* ❶ (*unsteadily*) wack[e]lig; *speak, touch* zitt[e]rig ❷ (*uncertainly*) unsicher

'**shaking I.** *n* (*jolting*) Schütteln *nt;* (*trembling*) Zittern *nt* **II.** *adj knees, hands* zitternd

shaky ['ʃeɪ·ki] *adj* ❶ (*unsteady*) *hands, voice, handwriting* zittrig; *ladder, table* wack[e]lig; **to feel a bit ~** (*physically*) noch etwas wack[e]lig auf den Beinen sein; (*emotionally*) beunruhigt sein ❷ (*unstable*) *basis, foundation* unsicher; *economy, government* instabil; **to get off to a ~ start** mühsam in Gang kommen

shale [ʃeɪl] *n* Schiefer *m*

shall [ʃæl] *aux vb* (*liter*) ❶ (*future*) ■**I ~ ...** ich werde ... ❷ (*ought to, must*) ■**I/he ~ ...** ich/er soll ...

shallot ['ʃæl·ət] *n* Schalotte *f*

shallow ['ʃæl·oʊ] *adj* ❶ (*not deep*) seicht, flach ❷ (*superficial*) oberflächlich; *movie* seicht

shallowness ['ʃæl·oʊ·nɪs] *n* ❶ (*shallow depth*) Seichtheit *f* ❷ (*superficiality*) Oberflächlichkeit *f*

sham [ʃæm] (*pej*) **I.** *n* ❶ *usu sing* (*fake thing*) Trug *m kein pl geh,* Betrug *m kein pl* ❷ (*empty pretense*) Verstellung *f* **II.** *adj* gefälscht; ~ **marriage** Scheinehe *f* **III.** *vt* <-mm-> vortäuschen **IV.** *vi* <-mm-> sich verstellen

shamble ['ʃæm·bəl] *vi* (*walk*) watscheln; (*shuffle*) schlurfen

shambles ['ʃæm·bəlz] *n + sing vb* (*fam*) **to be [in] a ~** sich in einem chaotischen Zustand befinden

shame [ʃeɪm] **I.** *n* ❶ (*feeling*) Scham *f,* Schamgefühl *nt;* ~ **on you!** (*a. hum*) schäm dich!; **to feel no ~** sich nicht schämen ❷ (*disgrace*) Schande *f;* **to bring ~ on sb** Schande über jdn bringen ❸ (*a pity*) Jammer *m;* **it's a [great] ~ that ...** es ist [jammer]schade, dass ...; **what a ~!** wie schade! **II.** *vt* ❶ (*make ashamed*) beschämen ❷ (*bring shame on*) ■**to ~ sb/sth** jdm/etw Schande machen

shamefaced ['ʃeɪm·'feɪst] *adj* verschämt

shameful ['ʃeɪm·fəl] *adj* ❶ (*causing shame*) *treatment* schimpflich; *defeat* schmachvoll ❷ (*disgraceful*) empörend; ■**it's ~ that ...** es ist eine Schande, dass ...

shameless ['ʃeɪm·lɪs] *adj* schamlos

shammy ['ʃæm·i] *n see* **chamois**

shampoo [ʃæm·'pu] **I.** *n* (*for hair*) Shampoo *nt* **II.** *vt hair* shampoonieren; *upholstery* mit einem Shampoo reinigen

shamrock ['ʃæm·rak] *n* weißer Feldklee

shank [ʃæŋk] *n* (*of tool*) Schaft *m*

shanty ['ʃæn·ti] *n* [Elends]hütte *f*

'**shanty town** *n* Barackensiedlung *f*

shape [ʃeɪp] **I.** *n* ❶ (*outline*) Form *f;* BIOL Gestalt *f;* MATH Figur *f,* Form *f;* **in any ~ or form** (*fig*) in jeder Form; **all ~s and sizes** alle Formen und Größen; **to take ~** Form annehmen ❷ (*condition*) **to be in bad ~** *things* in schlechtem Zustand sein; *people* in schlechter Verfassung sein; SPORTS nicht in Form sein; **to be in great ~** in Hochform sein ▶ PHRASES: **to whip sb/sth into ~** jdn/etw auf Vordermann bringen *fam* **II.** *vt* ❶ (*mold*) [aus]formen ❷ (*influence*) prägen; *sb's character* formen; *destiny* gestalten

shapeless ['ʃeɪp·lɪs] *adj* ❶ (*not shapely*) unförmig ❷ (*without shape*) formlos; *ideas* vage

shapely ['ʃeɪp·li] *adj* wohlgeformt; *figure, legs* schön; *woman* gut gebaut

shard [ʃard] *n* Scherbe *f; of metal* Splitter *m*

share [ʃer] **I.** *n* ❶ (*part*) Teil *m,* Anteil *m; of food* Portion *f;* **he should take his ~ of the blame for what happened** er sollte die Verantwortung für seine Mitschuld am Geschehenen übernehmen; **the lion's ~ of sth** der Löwenanteil von etw *dat;* **to have had one's fair ~ of sth** (*iron*) etw reichlich abbekommen haben; **to have a ~ in sth** an etw *dat* teilhaben ❷ *usu pl* (*in company*) Anteil *m,* Aktie *f* **II.** *vi* ❶ (*with others*) teilen (mit +*dat*) ❷ (*have part of*) ■**to ~ in sth** an etw *dat* teilhaben ❸ (*participate*) beteiligt sein (**in** an +*dat*) **III.** *vt* ❶ (*divide*) teilen; **shall we ~ the driving?** sollen wir uns beim Fahren abwechseln?; **to ~ responsibility** Verantwortung gemeinsam tragen ❷ (*have in common*) gemeinsam haben; *concern, opinion* teilen; **to ~ a birthday** am gleichen Tag Geburtstag haben; **to ~ an interest** ein gemeinsames Interesse haben ❸ (*communicate*) ■**to ~ sth with sb** *information* etw an jdn weitergeben; **to ~ one's thoughts with sb** jdm seine Gedanken anvertrauen

'**sharecropper** *n Pächter einer kleinen Farm, der die Pacht teilweise in Naturalien begleicht*

'**shareholder** *n* Aktionär(in) *m(f)*

shark <*pl* -s *or* -> [ʃark] *n* ❶ (*fish*) Hai[fisch] *m* ❷ (*pej fam: person*) Hai *m;* **loan ~** Kredithai *m*

sharp [ʃarp] **I.** *adj* ❶ *blade, knife, attack, curve* scharf ❷ (*pointed*) spitz; *features* kantig ❸ (*stabbing*) stechend; **~ stab** [**of pain**] [schmerzhaftes] Stechen ❹ (*sudden*) *drop in temperature* plötzlich; (*marked*) drastisch; *fall, rise* stark ❺ (*clear-cut*) scharf, deutlich, klar; **to bring sth into ~ focus** etw klar und deutlich herausstellen ❻ (*perceptive*) scharfsinnig; *eyes, ears, mind* scharf ❼ (*piquant*) *taste* scharf [gewürzt] ❽ (*penetrating*) *noise, voice* schrill **II.** *adv* ❶ (*exactly*) genau; **the performance will start at 7:30 ~** die Aufführung beginnt um Punkt 7.30 Uhr ❷ (*suddenly*) **to turn ~ left/right** scharf links/rechts abbiegen

sharpen ['ʃar·pən] *vt* ❶ (*a. fig: make sharp*) *mind, senses* schärfen; *pencil* spitzen; *scissors, knife* schleifen ❷ (*intensify*) verschärfen ❸ (*make more distinct*) scharf einstellen

sharpener ['ʃar·pən·ər] *n* **pencil ~** Bleistiftspitzer *m;* **knife ~** Messerschleifgerät *nt*

sharp-'eyed *adj* scharfsichtig

sharpness ['ʃarp·nɪs] *n* ❶ *of blade, point, curve* Schärfe *f* ❷ *of pain* Heftigkeit *f,* Stärke *f* ❸ (*acerbity, clarity*) Schärfe *f* ❹ (*markedness*) Heftigkeit *f* ❺ (*perceptiveness*) Scharfsinn *m* ❻ (*of taste*) Würzigkeit *f,* Würze *f*

'**sharpshooter** *n* Scharfschütze *m*

sharp-'tempered *adj* leicht erregbar

sharp-'tongued *adj* scharfzüngig

sharp-'witted *adj* scharfsinnig

shat [ʃæt] *vi pt, pp of* **shit**

shatter ['ʃæt̬·ər] **I.** *vi* zerspringen **II.** *vt* ❶ (*smash*) zertrümmern; *health, nerves* zerrütten ❷ (*fig*) vernichten; *calm* zerstören; *dreams, illusions* zunichtemachen

shattered ['ʃæt̬·ərd] *adj* (*fam*) am Boden zerstört

shattering ['ʃæt̬·ər·ɪŋ] *adj* (*fam*) ❶ (*very upsetting*) erschütternd ❷ (*destructive*) vernichtend

shatterproof ['ʃæt̬·ər·ˌpruf] *adj* bruchsicher; *windshield* splitterfrei

shave [ʃeɪv] **I.** *n* Rasur *f;* **I need a ~** ich muss mich rasieren; **a close ~** eine Glattrasur; (*fig*) ein knappes Entkommen; **to have a close ~** gerade noch davonkommen **II.** *vi* <-d, -d *or* shaven> sich rasieren **III.** *vt* <-d, -d *or* shaven> (*remove hair*) rasieren

shaven ['ʃeɪ·vən] *adj* rasiert; *head* kahl geschoren

shaver ['ʃeɪ·vər] *n* Rasierapparat *m*

'**shaving brush** *n* Rasierpinsel *m*

'**shaving cream** *n* Rasiercreme *f,* Rasierschaum *m*

'**shaving foam** *n* Rasierschaum *m*

'**shaving mirror** *n* Rasierspiegel *m*

shawl [ʃɔl] *n* Schultertuch *nt*

she [ʃi] **I.** *pron* ❶ (*female person, animal*) sie; ■**~ who ...** (*particular person*) diejenige, die ...; (*any person*) wer ❷ (*inanimate thing*) es; (*for country*) es; (*for ship with name*) sie; (*for ship with no name*) es **II.** *n usu sing* ■**a ~** (*person*) eine Sie; (*animal*) ein Weibchen *nt*

sheaf <*pl* sheaves> [ʃif] *n* Bündel *nt; of corn* Garbe *f*

shear <-ed, -ed *or* shorn> [ʃɪr] **I.** *vt* (*remove fleece*) scheren **II.** *vi* TECH abbrechen

◆**shear off I.** *vt* (*cut off*) abscheren **II.** *vi* abbrechen

shears [ʃɪrz] *npl* TECH [große] Schere; *metal* Metallschere *f*

sheath [ʃiθ] *n* ❶ (*for knife, sword*) Scheide *f* ❷ (*casing*) Hülle *f;* (*case*) Futteral *nt*

sheathe [ʃið] *vt* ❶ (*put into sheath*) *knife, sword* in die Scheide stecken ❷ (*cover*) umhüllen (**in, with** mit +*dat*)

shed[1] <-dd-, shed, shed> [ʃed] **I.** *vt* ❶ (*cast off*) ablegen; *antlers, leaves* abwerfen; *hair* verlieren; **to ~ a few pounds** ein paar Kilo abnehmen; **to ~ one's skin** sich häuten ❷ (*generate*) *blood, tears* vergießen; *light* verbreiten **II.** *vi snakes* sich häuten; *cats* haaren

shed[2] [ʃed] *n* Schuppen *m;* **garden ~** Gartenhäuschen *nt*

sheen [ʃin] *n* ❶ (*gloss*) Glanz *m* ❷ (*aura*) Ausstrahlung *f*

sheep <*pl* -> [ʃip] *n* Schaf *nt;* **flock of ~** Schafherde *f*

'**sheepdog** *n* Schäferhund *m*

sheepish ['ʃi·pɪʃ] *adj* unbeholfen; *smile* verlegen

'**sheepskin** *n* Schaffell *nt*

sheer [ʃɪr] *adj* ❶ (*utter*) pur, rein; **the ~ size of the thing takes your breath away** schon allein die Größe von dem Ding ist atemberaubend; **~ bliss** eine wahre Wonne; **~ nonsense** blanker Unsinn ❷ (*vertical*) *cliff, drop* steil

③ (*thin*) *material* hauchdünn; (*diaphanous*) durchscheinend

sheet [ʃit] *n* ① (*for bed*) Laken *nt* ② *of paper* Blatt *nt; of heavy paper* Bogen *m* ③ *of material* Platte *f*

'**sheet metal** *n* Blech *nt*

'**sheet music** *n* Noten *pl*

sheik(h) [ʃik] *n* Scheich *m*

shelf <*pl* **shelves**> [ʃelf] *n* (*for storage*) [Regal]brett *nt*, Bord *nt*; (*set of shelves*) Regal *nt*; **off the ~** ab Lager; *clothing* von der Stange

'**shelf life** *n* Haltbarkeit *f*

shell [ʃel] **I.** *n* ① (*exterior case*) *of egg, nut* Schale *f; of tortoise* Panzer *m; of pea* Hülse *f; of insect wing* Flügeldecke *f*; (*on beach*) Muschel *f*; (*for pies*) [Torten]Boden *m* ② *of a building* Mauerwerk *nt* ③ (*for artillery*) Granate *f*; (*cartridge*) Patrone *f* ▶ PHRASES: **to come out of one's ~** aus sich *dat* herausgehen **II.** *vt* ① (*remove shell*) schälen; *nut* knacken; *pea* enthülsen ② (*bombard*) [mit Granaten] bombardieren

◆**shell out** (*fam*) **I.** *vt* blechen; ■**to ~ out a few thousand [dollars] for sth** einige Tausende für etw hinlegen **II.** *vi* ■**to ~ out for sb/sth** für jdn/etw bezahlen

shellac [ʃə·'læk] *n* Schellack *m*

'**shellfish** <*pl* -> *n* Schalentier *nt*

shelling ['ʃəl·ɪŋ] *n* (*bombardment*) Bombardierung *f*; (*shellfire*) Geschützfeuer *nt*

'**shell shock** *n* Kriegsneurose *f*

'**shell-shocked** *adj* ① (*after battle*) kriegsneurotisch ② (*fam: dazed*) völlig geschockt

shelter ['ʃel·tər] **I.** *n* ① Schutz *m* ② (*structure*) Unterstand *m*; (*sth to sit in*) Häuschen *nt*; (*building for the needy*) Heim *nt* **II.** *vi* Schutz suchen **III.** *vt* ① (*protect*) schützen (**from** vor +*dat*) ② (*from tax*) **to ~ income from tax** Einkommen steuerlich nicht abzugsfähig machen

sheltered ['ʃəl·tərd] *adj* ① (*against weather*) geschützt ② (*pej: overprotected*) [über]behütet ③ (*tax-protected*) steuerfrei

shelve [ʃelv] **I.** *vt* ① (*postpone*) aufschieben; POL vertagen ② (*erect shelves*) mit Regalen ausstatten **II.** *vi* GEOL abfallen

shelving ['ʃəl·vɪŋ] *n* Regale *pl*

shenanigans [ʃɪ·'næn·ɪ·gənz] *npl* (*pej fam*) ① (*fraud*) Betrug *m kein pl*; (*trickery*) krumme Dinger ② (*pranks*) [derbe] Späße

shepherd ['ʃep·ərd] **I.** *n* Schäfer(in) *m(f)* **II.** *vt* ① (*look after*) hüten ② (*guide*) **to ~ sb toward the door** jdn zur Tür führen

sherbet ['ʃɜr·bət], **sherbert** ['ʃɜr·bɜrt] *n* FOOD (*dessert*) Fruchteis *nt*

sheriff ['ʃer·ɪf] *n* Sheriff *m*

sherry ['ʃer·i] *n* Sherry *m*

shield [ʃild] **I.** *n* ① (*defensive weapon*) [Schutz]schild *m* ② (*with coat of arms*) [Wappen]schild *m o nt* ③ (*protection*) Schutz *m kein pl* (**against** gegen +*akk*) **II.** *vt* beschützen (**from** vor +*dat*); *eyes* schützen

shift [ʃɪft] **I.** *vt* ① (*move*) [weg]bewegen; (*move slightly*) *furniture* verschieben ② (*transfer elsewhere*) *blame* abwälzen (**on to** auf +*akk*); *emphasis* verlagern ③ MECH **to ~ gears** schalten **II.** *vi* ① (*move*) sich bewegen; (*change position*) die [*o* seine] Position verändern; **it won't ~** es lässt sich nicht bewegen; **media attention has ~ed recently onto environmental issues** die Medien haben ihr Interesse neuerdings den Umweltthemen zugewandt ② AUTO **to ~ into reverse** den Rückwärtsgang einlegen **III.** *n* ① (*alteration*) Wechsel *m*, Änderung *f*; **a ~ in the balance of power** eine Verlagerung im Gleichgewicht der Kräfte ② (*period of work*) Schicht *f* ③ (*people working a shift*) Schicht *f*

◆**shift down** *vi* AUTO herunterschalten

◆**shift up** *vi* AUTO hochschalten

shifting ['ʃɪf·tɪŋ] *adj attr* sich verändernd

'**shift key** *n of a typewriter* Umschalter *m*; COMPUT Shifttaste *f*

'**shift work** *n* Schichtarbeit *f*

'**shift worker** *n* Schichtarbeiter(in) *m(f)*

shifty ['ʃɪf·ti] *adj* hinterhältig; **to look ~** verdächtig aussehen

Shiite ['ʃi·aɪt] **I.** *n* Schiit(in) *m(f)* **II.** *adj* schiitisch

shimmer ['ʃɪm·ər] **I.** *vi* schimmern **II.** *n usu sing* Schimmer *m*

shin [ʃɪn] *n* ① (*of leg*) Schienbein *nt* ② *of beef* Hachse *f*

shindig ['ʃɪn·dɪg] *n* (*fam*) ① (*loud party*) [wilde] Fete ② (*argument*) Krach *m fam*

shine [ʃaɪn] **I.** *n* Glanz *m* ▶ PHRASES: **[come] rain or ~** komme, was da wolle; **to take a ~ to sb** jdn ins Herz schließen **II.** *vi* <**shone** *or* **shined, shone** *or* **shined**> ① (*give off light*) *moon, sun* scheinen; *stars* leuchten; *gold, metal* glänzen; *light* leuchten, scheinen ② (*show happiness*) *eyes* strahlen ③ (*show one's abilities*) glänzen **III.** *vt* <**shone** *or* **shined, shone** *or* **shined**> ① (*point light*) **to ~ a beam of light at sb/sth** jdn/etw anstrahlen ② (*polish*) polieren

◆**shine down** *vi* herabscheinen

◆**shine out** *vi* ① (*be easily seen*) [auf]leuchten ② (*excel, stand out*) herausragen

shiner ['ʃaɪ·nər] *n* (*fam: black eye*) Veilchen *nt*

shingle ['ʃɪŋ·gəl] *n usu pl* [Dach]schindel[n] *f[pl]*

shingles ['ʃɪŋ·gəlz] *npl* + *sing vb* MED Gürtelrose *f*

shining ['ʃaɪ·nɪŋ] *adj* ① (*gleaming*) glänzend ② (*with happiness*) strahlend ③ (*outstanding*) hervorragend; *example* leuchtend

shinny ['ʃɪn·i] *vi* <-nn-> ■**to ~ up [sth]** [rasch] [etw] hinaufklettern

shiny ['ʃaɪ·ni] *adj* glänzend; (*very clean*) *surface, metal* [spiegel]blank

ship [ʃɪp] **I.** *n* Schiff *nt*; **merchant ~** Handelsschiff *nt*; ■**by ~** mit dem Schiff; (*goods*) per Schiff **II.** *vt* <-pp-> ① (*send by boat*) verschiffen ② (*transport*) transportieren

◆**ship off** *vt* ① (*send by ship*) verschiffen;

S

goods per Schiff verschicken ❷ (*fam: send away*) wegschicken
◆ **ship out** I. *vt* per Schiff senden II. *vi* (*fam*) sich verziehen
'**shipbuilder** *n* ❶ (*person*) Schiff[s]bauer(in) *m(f)* ❷ (*business*) Werft *f*
'**shipbuilding** *n* Schiffbau *m*
'**shipload** *n* Schiffsladung *f*
shipment ['ʃɪp·mənt] *n* ❶ (*consignment*) Sendung *f* ❷ (*dispatching*) Transport *m*
'**shipowner** *n* ❶ (*inland navigation*) Schiffseigner(in) *m(f)* ❷ (*ocean navigation*) Reeder(in) *m(f)*
shipper ['ʃɪp·ər] *n* ❶ (*person*) Spediteur(in) *m(f)* ❷ (*business*) Spediteur *m,* Spedition *f*
shipping ['ʃɪp·ɪŋ] *n* ❶ (*transportation of goods*) Transport *m;* (*by mail*) Versand *m;* (*by ship*) Verschiffung *f* ❷ (*costs*) Transportkosten *pl;* (*by mail*) Postversand *m;* (*by sea*) Versand auf dem Seeweg ❸ (*ships*) Schiffe *pl* [eines Landes]
'**shipping lane** *n* Schifffahrtsweg *m*
'**shipshape** *adj pred* (*fam*) aufgeräumt; **to make sth ~** etw aufräumen
'**shipwreck** I. *n* ❶ (*accident*) Schiffbruch *m* ❷ (*remains*) [Schiffs]wrack *nt* II. *vt usu passive* ■ **to be ~ed** ❶ NAUT Schiffbruch erleiden ❷ (*fail*) scheitern
'**shipyard** *n* [Schiffs]werft *f*
shirk [ʃɜrk] (*pej*) I. *vt* meiden; **to ~ one's responsibilities** sich seiner Verantwortung entziehen II. *vi* ■ **to ~ from sth** sich etw *dat* entziehen
shirt [ʃɜrt] *n* Hemd *nt* ▶ PHRASES: **keep your ~ on!** (*fam*) reg dich ab!
'**shirtsleeve** *n usu pl* Hemdsärmel *m;* **in ~s** in Hemdsärmeln
shit [ʃɪt] (*vulg*) I. *n* ❶ (*feces*) Scheiße *f derb,* Kacke *f derb;* **dog ~** Hundekacke *f fam* ❷ (*nonsense*) Scheiße *m derb;* **a bunch of ~** ein einziger Mist ❸ (*unfairness*) **Jackie doesn't take any ~ from anyone** Jackie lässt sich von niemandem was gefallen *fam* ▶ PHRASES: **to beat the ~ out of sb** aus jdm Hackfleisch machen *fam;* **the ~ hits the fan** es gibt Ärger; **to not know ~ about sb/sth** keinen blassen Schimmer [*o* keine Ahnung] von jdm/etw haben II. *interj* **~!** Scheiße! *derb;* [**oh**] **~!** [so ein] Mist! III. *vi* <-tt-, shit *or* shitted *or* shat, shit *or* shitted *or* shat> scheißen *derb* IV. *vt* <-tt-, shit *or* shitted *or* shat, shit *or* shitted *or* shat> (*scare*) **to ~ one's pants** sich *dat* [vor Angst] in die Hosen machen *fam*
shitty ['ʃɪt̬·i] *adj* (*vulg*) beschissen *derb*
shiver ['ʃɪv·ər] I. *n* ❶ (*shudder*) Schauder *m* ❷ MED ■ **the ~s** *pl* Schüttelfrost *m kein pl;* **to give sb the ~s** (*fig fam*) jdn das Fürchten lehren II. *vi* zittern; **to ~ with cold** frösteln
shivery ['ʃɪv·ər·i] *adj* fröstelnd; **to feel ~** frösteln
shoal[1] [ʃoʊl] *n* ❶ (*area of shallow water*) seichte Stelle ❷ (*sand bank*) Sandbank *f*
shoal[2] [ʃoʊl] *n* (*of fish*) Schwarm *m*
shock[1] [ʃak] I. *n* ❶ (*unpleasant surprise*) Schock *m;* **prepare yourself for a ~** mach dich auf etwas Schlimmes gefasst; **a ~ to the system** eine schwierige Umstellung ❷ (*fam: electric shock*) elektrischer Schlag ❸ (*serious health condition*) Schock[zustand] *m;* **to be in [a state of] ~** unter Schock stehen II. *vt* schockieren; (*deeply*) erschüttern
shock[2] [ʃak] *n* **~ of hair** [Haar]schopf *m*
'**shock absorber** *n* AUTO Stoßdämpfer *m*
shocker ['ʃak·ər] *n* (*fam*) ❶ (*shocking thing*) Schocker *m;* **the headline was a deliberate ~** die Schlagzeile sollte schockieren ❷ (*very bad thing*) Katastrophe *f*
shocking ['ʃak·ɪŋ] *adj* ❶ (*distressing, offensive*) schockierend; *crime* abscheulich ❷ (*surprising*) völlig überraschend, völlig unerwartet
'**shockproof** *adj* ❶ (*able to withstand blows*) bruchsicher ❷ (*not producing electric shock*) berührungssicher
'**shock therapy,** '**shock treatment** *n* Schocktherapie *f*
'**shock wave** *n* ❶ PHYS Druckwelle *f* ❷ (*fig*) **the news sent ~s through the financial world** die Nachricht erschütterte die Finanzwelt
shod [ʃad] I. *pt, pp of* **shoe** II. *adj* beschuht; **~ in boots** in Stiefeln
shoddy ['ʃad·i] *adj* (*pej*) ❶ (*poorly produced*) schlampig [gearbeitet] *fam;* (*run down*) schäbig; *goods* minderwertig ❷ (*reprehensible*) schäbig
shoe [ʃu] I. *n* ❶ (*for foot*) Schuh *m;* **a pair of ~s** ein Paar *nt* Schuhe; (*for gymnastics*) Gymnastikschuh *m;* (*for dancing*) Tanzschuh *m;* (*for ballet*) Ballettschuh *m* ❷ (*horseshoe*) Hufeisen *nt* ▶ PHRASES: **to put oneself in sb's ~s** sich in jds Lage versetzen; **if I were in your ~s** (*fam*) wenn ich du wäre, an deiner Stelle II. *vt* <shod *or* shoed, shod *or* shodden *or* shoed> *horse* beschlagen
'**shoehorn** I. *n* Schuhlöffel *m* II. *vt usu passive* ■ **to ~ sb/sth into sth** jdn/etw in etw *akk* hineinzwängen
'**shoelace** *n usu pl* Schnürsenkel *m*
'**shoemaker** *n* Schuster(in) *m(f)*
'**shoe polish** *n* Schuhcreme *f*
'**shoeshine** *n* Schuhputzen *nt kein pl*
'**shoeshine boy** *n* Schuhputzer *m*
'**shoe shop,** '**shoe store** *n* Schuhgeschäft *nt*
'**shoe size** *n* Schuhgröße *f*
'**shoestring** *n usu pl* Schnürsenkel *m* ▶ PHRASES: **to do sth on a ~** (*fam*) etw mit wenig Geld tun
shone [ʃoʊn] *pt, pp of* **shine**
shoo [ʃu] (*fam*) I. *interj* (*to child*) husch [husch] II. *vt* wegscheuchen
shook [ʃʊk] *n pt of* **shake**
shoot [ʃut] I. *n* ❶ (*on plant*) Trieb *m* ❷ (*hunt*) Jagd *f* ❸ PHOT Aufnahmen *pl* II. *vi* <shot, shot> ❶ (*discharge weapon*) schießen (**at** auf +*akk*); **to ~ to kill** mit Tötungsabsicht schießen ❷ + *adv/prep* (*move rapidly*) ■ **to ~ past**

S

[*or* **by**] vorbeischießen ❸ (*film*) filmen, drehen; (*take photos*) fotografieren ❹ (*aim*) ■ **to ~ for** [*or* **at**] **sth** etw anstreben **III.** *vt* <shot, shot> ❶ (*fire*) ■ **to ~ sth** *bow, gun* mit etw *dat* schießen; *arrow* etw abschießen; *bullet* etw abfeuern ❷ (*hit*) anschießen; (*dead*) erschießen; **to be shot in the leg** ins Bein getroffen werden ❸ PHOT *movie* drehen; *photo* machen ❹ (*direct*) **to ~ questions at sb** jdn mit Fragen bombardieren ❺ SPORTS *goal, basket* schießen

◆**shoot down** *vt* ❶ AVIAT, MIL abschießen ❷ (*kill*) erschießen ❸ (*fam: refute*) *accusation* niedermachen

◆**shoot off** **I.** *vi* *vehicle* schnell losfahren; *people* eilig aufbrechen **II.** *vt* (*make explode*) *fireworks* abschießen ▶ PHRASES: **to ~ one's <u>mouth</u> off** (*sl*) sich *dat* das Maul zerreißen *derb*

◆**shoot out** **I.** *vi* ❶ (*emerge suddenly*) plötzlich hervorschießen ❷ (*gush forth*) *water* herausschießen; *flames* hervorbrechen **II.** *vt* ❶ (*extend*) **he shot out a hand to catch the cup** er streckte blitzschnell die Hand aus, um die Tasse aufzufangen ❷ (*have gunfight*) ■ **to ~ it out** etw [mit Schusswaffen] austragen

◆**shoot up** **I.** *vi* ❶ (*increase rapidly*) schnell ansteigen; *skyscraper* in die Höhe schießen ❷ (*fam: grow rapidly*) *child* schnell wachsen ❸ (*sl: inject narcotics*) sich *dat* einen Schuss verpassen *sl* **II.** *vt* (*inject illegally*) sich *dat* spritzen

shooting [ˈʃu·t̬ɪŋ] **I.** *n* ❶ (*attack with gun*) Schießerei *f;* (*from more than one side*) Schusswechsel *m;* (*killing*) Erschießung *f* ❷ (*firing guns*) Schießen *nt* ❸ (*sport*) Jagen *nt;* **deer ~** Wildjagd *f* ❹ FILM Drehen *nt* **II.** *adj attr* **~ pain** stechender Schmerz

ˈ**shooting gallery** *n* Schießstand *m*

ˈ**shooting range** *n* Schießstand *m*

shooting ˈstar *n* ❶ (*meteor*) Sternschnuppe *f* ❷ (*person*) Shootingstar *m*

ˈ**shootout** *n* Schießerei *f*

shop [ʃap] **I.** *n* ❶ (*store*) Geschäft *nt,* Laden *m;* **to set up ~** (*open a shop*) ein Geschäft eröffnen; (*start out in business*) ein Unternehmen eröffnen ❷ (*garage*) Werkstatt *f* ▶ PHRASES: **to <u>talk</u> ~** über die Arbeit reden, fachsimpeln *fam* **II.** *vi* <-pp-> einkaufen; **to ~ 'til you drop** (*hum*) eine Shoppingorgie veranstalten

shopaholic [ʃap·ə·ˈhɔ·lɪk] *n* Einkaufssüchtige(r) *f(m)*

ˈ**shopkeeper** *n* Ladeninhaber(in) *m(f)*

ˈ**shoplifter** *n* Ladendieb(in) *m(f)*

ˈ**shoplifting** *n* Ladendiebstahl *m*

shopper [ˈʃap·ər] *n* Käufer(in) *m(f)*

shopping [ˈʃap·ɪŋ] *n* Einkaufen *nt;* **to go** [*or* **do the**] **~** einkaufen [gehen]

ˈ**shopping bag** *n* Einkaufstasche *f,* Tragetasche *f,* Tragetüte *f*

ˈ**shopping basket** *n* Einkaufskorb *m*

ˈ**shopping cart** *n* Einkaufswagen *m*

ˈ**shopping center** *n* Einkaufszentrum *nt*

ˈ**shopping list** *n* (*of goods to be purchased*) Einkaufsliste *f*

ˈ**shopping mall** *n* überdachtes Einkaufszentrum

ˈ**shoptalk** *n* Fachsimpelei *f fam*

shore[1] [ʃɔr] *n* (*coast*) Küste *f; of river, lake* Ufer *nt;* (*beach*) Strand *m;* **on ~** an Land

shore[2] [ʃɔr] *n* Strebebalken *m*

◆**shore up** *vt* abstützen; (*fig*) aufbessern

ˈ**shore leave** *n* Landurlaub *m*

ˈ**shoreline** *n* Küstenlinie *f*

shorn [ʃɔrn] *pp of* **shear**

short [ʃɔrt] **I.** *adj* ❶ (*not long*) kurz; *distance, memory, notice* kurz; **at ~ range** aus kurzer Entfernung; **in the ~ term** kurzfristig; **Bob's ~ for Robert** Bob ist die Kurzform von Robert ❷ (*not tall*) klein ❸ (*not enough*) **we're still one person ~** uns fehlt noch eine Person; ■ **sb is ~ of sth** jdm mangelt es an etw *dat;* **we're a bit ~ of coffee** wir haben nur noch wenig Kaffee; **to be ~** [**of cash**] knapp bei Kasse sein; **to be ~ of breath** außer Atem sein; **to be in ~ supply** schwer zu beschaffen sein ▶ PHRASES: **to have a ~ <u>fuse</u>** schnell wütend werden; **to draw the ~ <u>straw</u>** den Kürzeren ziehen **II.** *n* FILM Kurzfilm *m* **III.** *adv* **to cut sth ~** etw abkürzen; **to fall ~ of expectations** den Erwartungen nicht entsprechen ▶ PHRASES: **<u>in</u> ~** kurz gesagt

shortage [ˈʃɔr·t̬ɪdʒ] *n* Mangel *m kein pl* (**of** an +*dat*)

ˈ**shortbread** *n* Shortbread *nt* (*Buttergebäck*)

ˈ**shortcake** *n* Kuchen *m* mit Belag; **strawberry ~** Erdbeertörtchen *nt*

shortˈchange *vt* ■ **to ~ sb** (*after purchase*) jdm zu wenig Wechselgeld herausgeben

short ˈcircuit *n* Kurzschluss *m*

short-ˈcircuit **I.** *vt* ❶ ELEC kurzschließen ❷ (*shorten or avoid*) abkürzen **II.** *vi* einen Kurzschluss haben

ˈ**shortcoming** *n usu pl* Mangel *m; of person* Fehler *m; of system* Unzulänglichkeit *f*

ˈ**shortcut** *n* Abkürzung *f*

shorten [ˈʃɔr·tən] **I.** *vt* (*make shorter*) kürzen; *name* abkürzen **II.** *vi* (*become shorter*) kürzer werden

shortening [ˈʃɔr·tən·ɪŋ] *n* Backfett *nt*

ˈ**shortfall** *n* ❶ (*shortage*) Mangel *m kein pl* ❷ FIN (*deficit*) Defizit *nt*

ˈ**shorthand** *n* Kurzschrift *f,* Stenografie *f*

short-ˈhanded *adj* ❶ (*lacking staff*) unterbesetzt; ■ **to be ~** zu wenig Personal haben ❷ SPORTS *goal* in Unterzahl

ˈ**short list** *n* **to be on the ~** in der engeren Wahl sein

ˈ**short-list** *vt* in die engere Wahl ziehen

short-lived [-ˈlɪvd] *adj* kurzlebig

shortly [ˈʃɔrt·li] *adv* ❶ (*soon*) in Kürze, bald; **~ afterwards** kurz danach ❷ (*curtly*) kurz angebunden

shortness [ˈʃɔrt·nɪs] *n* ❶ (*brevity*) Kürze *f* ❷ (*insufficiency*) Knappheit *f;* MED Insuffizienz *f;* **~ of breath** Atemnot *f*

'short-range *adj* ① *plane, weapon* Kurzstrecken- ② *forecast* kurzfristig

shorts [ʃɔrts] *n pl* ① (*short pants*) kurze Hose, Shorts *pl* ② (*underpants*) Unterhose *f*

short'sighted *adj* kurzsichtig *a. fig*

short-staffed [-ˈstæft] *adj* unterbesetzt

short 'story *n* Kurzgeschichte *f*

short-tempered [-ˈtem·pərd] *adj* cholerisch

'short-term *adj* kurzfristig, Kurzzeit-; **~ outlook** Aussichten *pl* für die nächste Zeit

shot¹ [ʃat] *n* ① *from weapon* Schuss *m* ② SPORTS (*in basketball*) Wurf *m;* (*in tennis, golf*) Schlag *m;* (*in soccer, hockey*) Schuss *m* ③ (*photograph*) Aufnahme *f;* FILM Einstellung *f* ④ (*fam: injection*) Spritze *f;* (*fig*) Schuss *m sl* ⑤ (*fam: attempt*) Gelegenheit *f,* Chance *f;* **to give it a ~** es mal versuchen *fam* ⑥ (*of alcohol*) Schuss *m* ⑦ (*critical remark*) **to take a ~ at sb** jdn runtermachen; (*attack verbally*) über jdn herfallen ► PHRASES: **like a ~** (*fam*) wie der Blitz

shot² [ʃat] **I.** *vt, vi pp, pt of* **shoot II.** *adj* (*fam: worn out*) ausgeleiert *fam;* **my nerves are ~** ich bin mit meinen Nerven am Ende

'shotgun *n* Schrotflinte *f* ► PHRASES: **to ride ~** (*fam*) auf dem Beifahrersitz mitfahren (*im Auto/auf dem Motorrad*)

'shot put *n* SPORTS ■ **the ~** Kugelstoßen *nt kein pl*

'shot putter *n* SPORTS Kugelstoßer(in) *m(f)*

should [ʃʊd] *aux vb* ① (*expressing advisability*) ■ **sb/sth ~ ...** jd/etw sollte ...; **you ~ be ashamed of yourselves** ihr solltet euch [was] schämen ② (*asking for advice*) ■ **~ sb/sth ...?** soll[te] jd/etw ...?; **~ I apologize to him?** soll[te] ich mich bei ihm entschuldigen? ③ (*expressing expectation*) ■ **sb/sth ~ ...** jd/etw sollte [*o* müsste] [eigentlich] ...; **there ~n't be any problems** es dürfte eigentlich keine Probleme geben ④ (*when reproaching*) **I ~ have known that you'd lie to me** ich hätte es eigentlich wissen müssen, dass du mich anlügen würdest; **you ~ have told me about the job!** du hättest mir eigentlich von dem Job erzählen müssen! ⑤ (*expressing futurity*) ■ **sb/sth ~ ...** jd/etw würde ... ⑥ (*rhetorical*) ■ **why ~ sb/sth ...?** warum sollte jd/etw ...? ⑦ (*could*) **where's Stuart? — how ~ I know?** wo ist Stuart? – woher soll[te] ich das wissen?

shoulder [ˈʃoʊl·dər] **I.** *n* ① (*joint, in clothing*) Schulter *f;* **a ~ to cry on** (*fig*) eine Schulter zum Ausweinen; **to shrug one's ~s** mit den Achseln zucken ② (*meat*) Schulter *f* ③ *of road* Bankett *nt* **II.** *vt* ① (*accept*) auf sich *akk* nehmen; *blame, responsibility* übernehmen ② (*push*) [mit den Schultern] stoßen; **to ~ one's way somewhere** sich irgendwohin drängen

'shoulder bag *n* Umhängetasche *f*

'shoulder blade *n* Schulterblatt *nt*

'shoulder pad *n* Schulterpolster *nt o* ÖSTERR *m; a.* SPORTS Schulterschoner *m,* Shoulder-Pad *nt*

'shoulder strap *n* Riemen *m*

shout [ʃaʊt] **I.** *n* (*loud cry*) Ruf *m,* Schrei *m;* **a ~ of laughter** lautes Gelächter **II.** *vi* schreien; ■ **to ~ at sb** jdn anschreien; ■ **to ~ to sb** jdm zurufen **III.** *vt* (*yell*) rufen, schreien; ■ **to ~ sth at** [*or* **to**] **sb** jdm etw zurufen; **to ~ abuse at sb** jdn lautstark beschimpfen

◆ **shout down** *vt* niederschreien *fam*

◆ **shout out** *vt* [aus]rufen

shouting [ˈʃaʊ·t̬ɪŋ] **I.** *n* Schreien *nt,* Geschrei *nt* **II.** *adj* ► PHRASES: **within ~ distance** in Rufweite; (*fig*) nahe [an +*dat*]

shove [ʃʌv] **I.** *n* Ruck *m;* **to give sth a ~** etw [weg]rücken **II.** *vt* ① (*push*) schieben; ■ **to ~ sb around** jdn herumstoßen *fam* ② (*place*) stecken; **to ~ sth into a bag** etw in eine Tasche stecken **III.** *vi* (*push*) drängen

◆ **shove off** *vi* (*vulg: leave*) abhauen *sl*

shovel [ˈʃʌv·əl] **I.** *n* ① (*tool*) Schaufel *f; of bulldozer* Baggerschaufel *f* ② (*shovelful*) **a ~ of snow** eine Schaufel [voll] Schnee **II.** *vt* <-l- *or* -ll-> schaufeln *a. fig* **III.** *vi* <-l- *or* -ll-> schaufeln

show [ʃoʊ] **I.** *n* ① (*showing*) Demonstration *f geh;* **~ of solidarity** Solidaritätsbekundung *f geh* ② (*display, effect*) Schau *f;* **just for ~** nur der Schau wegen ③ (*exhibition, event*) Schau *f,* Ausstellung *f;* **slide ~** Diavortrag *m;* ■ **to be on ~** ausgestellt sein ④ (*entertainment*) Show *f;* (*on TV a.*) Unterhaltungssendung *f;* (*at a theater*) Vorstellung *f* ► PHRASES: **let's get this ~ on the road** (*fam*) lasst uns die Sache [endlich] in Angriff nehmen; **the ~ must go on** (*saying*) die Show muss weitergehen **II.** *vt* <showed, shown *or* showed> ① (*display, project, express*) *film* zeigen; (*exhibit*) ausstellen; (*perform*) vorführen; (*produce*) *passport* vorzeigen; **to ~ sb respect** jdm Respekt erweisen ② (*expose*) sehen lassen; **this carpet ~s all the dirt** bei dem Teppich kann man jedes bisschen Schmutz sehen ③ (*reveal*) zeigen; **he started to ~ his age** man konnte ihm langsam sein Alter sehen; **to ~ common sense** gesunden Menschenverstand beweisen ④ (*explain*) zeigen; **to ~ sb the way** jdm den Weg zeigen ⑤ (*record*) anzeigen; *statistics* [auf]zeigen; *loss, profit* aufweisen ⑥ (*prove*) beweisen; ■ **to ~ [sb] how ...** [jdm] zeigen, wie ...; ■ **to ~ oneself [to be] sth** sich als etw erweisen ► PHRASES: **to ~ one's true colors** Farbe bekennen; **that will ~ you** (*fam*) das wird dir eine Lehre sein **III.** *vi* <showed, shown *or* showed> ① (*be visible*) zu sehen sein, erscheinen; **to let sth ~** sich *dat* etw anmerken lassen ② (*be shown*) *film* laufen *fam;* **now ~ing at a theater near you!** jetzt in Ihrem Kino! ③ (*exhibit*) ausstellen

◆ **show around** *vt* herumführen; **to ~ sb around the house** jdm das Haus zeigen

◆ **show in** *vt* (*from inside*) hereinführen; (*from outside*) hineinführen

◆ **show off I.** *vt* ■ **to ~ off** ⟲ **sb/sth** mit jdm/etw angeben **II.** *vi* angeben

S

◆**show through** *vi* durchschimmern

◆**show up** **I.** *vi* ❶ (*appear*) sich zeigen; **the drug does not ~ up in blood tests** das Medikament ist in Blutproben nicht nachweisbar ❷ (*fam: arrive*) auftauchen **II.** *vt* ❶ (*expose*) zeigen ❷ (*embarrass*) bloßstellen

show biz [ˈʃoʊ·bɪz] *n* (*fam*) *short for* **show business** Showbiz *nt*

ˈ**showboat** **I.** *n* (*ship*) Theaterschiff *nt* **II.** *vi* (*fam*) angeben

ˈ**show business** *n* Showbusiness *nt,* Showgeschäft *nt*

ˈ**showcase** **I.** *n* ❶ (*container*) Schaukasten *m,* Vitrine *f* ❷ (*place/opportunity for presentation*) Schaufenster *nt* **II.** *vt* ausstellen

shower [ˈʃaʊ·ər] **I.** *n* ❶ (*brief fall*) Schauer *m* ❷ (*for bathing*) Dusche *f;* **to take a ~** duschen ❸ (*party*) *Frauenparty vor einer Hochzeit, Geburt etc., bei der Geschenke überreicht werden* **II.** *vt* ❶ (*with liquid*) bespritzen ❷ (*fig*) **to ~ sb with compliments** jdn mit Komplimenten überhäufen **III.** *vi* (*take a shower*) duschen

ˈ**shower cap** *n* Duschhaube *f*

ˈ**shower curtain** *n* Duschvorhang *m*

ˈ**shower gel** *n* Duschgel *nt*

showery [ˈʃaʊ·ə·ri] *adj* mit vereinzelten Regenschauern *nach n;* **~ weather** regnerisches Wetter

showing [ˈʃoʊ·ɪŋ] *n usu sing* ❶ (*exhibition*) Ausstellung *f* ❷ (*broadcasting*) Übertragung *f* ❸ (*performance in competition*) Vorstellung *f;* **to make a good/poor ~** eine gute/schwache Vorstellung geben

ˈ**show jumping** *n* Springreiten *nt*

ˈ**showman** *n* Showman *m*

showmanship [ˈʃoʊ·mən·ʃɪp] *n* publikumswirksames Auftreten

shown [ʃoʊn] *vt, vi pp of* **show**

ˈ**showoff** *n* Angeber(in) *m(f)*

ˈ**showroom** *n* Ausstellungsraum *m*

ˈ**showtime** *n* Aufführung[szeit] *f* ► PHRASES: **it's ~!** es geht los!

ˈ**show trial** *n* Schauprozess *m*

showy [ˈʃoʊ·i] *adj* auffällig

shrank [ʃræŋk] *vt, vi pt of* **shrink**

shrapnel [ˈʃræp·nəl] *n* Granatsplitter *pl*

shred [ʃred] **I.** *n* ❶ *usu pl* (*thin long strip*) Streifen *m;* **to be in ~s** zerfetzt sein; **to rip sth to ~s** etw in Fetzen reißen ❷ (*tiny bit*) *of hope* Funke *m;* **there isn't a ~ of evidence** es gibt nicht den geringsten Beweis **II.** *vt* <-dd-> *paper, textiles* zerkleinern; *vegetables* hacken

shredder [ˈʃred·ər] *n* Reißwolf *m,* Shredder *m*

shrew [ʃru] *n* ❶ (*animal*) Spitzmaus *f* ❷ (*pej: woman*) Hexe *f*

shrewd [ʃrud] *adj* schlau, klug; *eye* scharf; *move* geschickt; **to make a ~ guess** gut raten

shriek [ʃrik] **I.** *n* [schriller, kurzer] Schrei **II.** *vi* kreischen; (*with laughter*) brüllen; (*with pain*) [auf]schreien **III.** *vt* [auf]schreien

shrift [ʃrift] *n* ► PHRASES: **to get short ~ from sb** von jdm wenig Mitleid bekommen; **to give sb/sth short** ~ jdm/etw wenig Beachtung schenken

shrill [ʃrɪl] *adj* schrill

shrimp <*pl* -s *or* -> [ʃrɪmp] *n* ❶ (*crustacean*) Garnele *f,* Shrimp *m* ❷ (*pej fam: small person*) Zwerg *m hum*

shrine [ʃraɪn] *n* Heiligtum *nt;* (*casket for relics*) Schrein *m a. fig;* (*tomb*) Grabmal *nt;* (*place of worship*) Pilgerstätte *f*

shrink [ʃrɪŋk] **I.** *vi* <shrank *or* shrunk, shrunk *or* shrunken> ❶ (*become smaller*) schrumpfen; *sweater* eingehen ❷ (*pull back*) ■**to ~ away** zurückweichen ❸ (*show reluctance*) ■**to ~ from [doing] sth** sich vor etw *dat* drücken *fam* **II.** *vt* <shrank *or* shrunk, shrunk *or* shrunken> schrumpfen lassen **III.** *n* (*fam*) Psychiater(in) *m(f)*

shrinkage [ˈʃrɪŋ·kɪdʒ] *n* Schrumpfen *nt; of sweater* Eingehen *nt*

ˈ**shrink-wrap** **I.** *n* Plastikfolie *f* **II.** *vt food* in Frischhaltefolie einpacken; *book* einschweißen

shrivel <-l- *or* -ll-> [ˈʃrɪv·əl] *vi* [zusammen]schrumpfen; *fruit* schrumpeln; *plants* welken; *skin* faltig werden; (*fig*) *profits* schwinden

◆**shrivel up** *vi* zusammenschrumpfen; *fruit* schrumpeln

shroud [ʃraʊd] **I.** *n* ❶ (*burial wrapping*) Leichentuch *nt* ❷ (*covering*) Hülle *f* **II.** *vt* einhüllen; **to ~ sth in secrecy** etw geheim halten; **shrouded in mist/darkness** in Nebel/Dunkelheit gehüllt

Shrove Tuesday [ʃroʊv·ˈtuz·deɪ] *n no art* Fastnachtsdienstag *m,* Faschingsdienstag *m* SÜDD, ÖSTERR

shrub [ʃrʌb] *n* Strauch *m,* Busch *m*

shrubbery [ˈʃrʌb·ə·ri] *n* ❶ (*area planted with bushes*) Gebüsch *nt* ❷ (*group of bushes*) Sträucher *pl*

shrug [ʃrʌg] **I.** *n of one's shoulders* Achselzucken *nt kein pl* **II.** *vi* <-gg-> die Achseln zucken **III.** *vt* <-gg-> **to ~ one's shoulders** die Achseln zucken

◆**shrug off** *vt* ❶ *see* **shrug aside** ❷ (*get rid of*) loswerden

shrunk [ʃrʌŋk] *vt, vi pp, pt of* **shrink**

shrunken [ˈʃrʌŋ·kən] **I.** *adj* geschrumpft **II.** *vt, vi pp of* **shrink**

shuck [ʃʌk] *vt corn* schälen; *oysters* aus der Schale herauslösen

shucks [ʃʌks] *interj* (*fam*) **[aw,] ~, I wish I could have gone to the party** ach Mensch, hätte ich doch nur zur Party gehen können

shudder [ˈʃʌd·ər] **I.** *vi* zittern; *ground* beben; **I ~ to think what would have happened if ...** mir graut vor dem Gedanken, was passiert wäre, wenn ...; **to ~ to a halt** mit einem Rucken zum Stehen kommen **II.** *n* Schaudern *nt kein pl;* **to send a ~ through sb** jdn erschaudern lassen *geh*

shuffle [ˈʃʌf·əl] **I.** *n* ❶ CARDS Mischen *nt kein pl* (*von Karten*)*;* **to give the cards a ~** die Karten mischen ❷ (*rearrangement*) Neuordnung *f* *kein pl* ③ *of feet* Schlurfen *nt* **II.** *vt* ① (*mix*) *cards* mischen ② (*move around*) ■ **to ~ sth [around]** etw hin- und herschieben ③ (*drag*) *feet* schlurfen **III.** *vi* ① CARDS Karten mischen ② (*drag one's feet*) schlurfen; ■ **to ~ along** (*fig*) sich dahinschleppen; ■ **to ~ around** herumzappeln *fam*

shun <-nn-> [ʃʌn] *vt* meiden; ■ **to ~ sb** jdm aus dem Weg gehen

shunt [ʃʌnt] *vt* ① RAIL rangieren ② (*move*) abschieben; ■ **to ~ sb** jdn schieben; (*get rid of*) jdn abschieben *fam*

shush [ʃʊʃ] **I.** *interj* sch!, pst! **II.** *vt* (*fam*) ■ **to ~ sb** jdm sagen, dass er/sie still sein soll

shut [ʃʌt] **I.** *adj* geschlossen; *curtains* zugezogen; **to slam a door ~** eine Tür zuschlagen **II.** *vt* <-tt-, shut, shut> ① (*close*) schließen, zumachen; *book* zuklappen ② (*stop operating*) schließen ▶ PHRASES: **~ your mouth!** (*vulg*) Klappe! *sl* **III.** *vi* <-tt-, shut, shut> schließen, zumachen

◆ **shut away** *vt* einschließen, einsperren

◆ **shut down I.** *vt* ① (*stop operating*) schließen, stilliegen ② (*turn off*) abstellen; *computer, system* herunterfahren **II.** *vi business, factory* zumachen

◆ **shut in** *vt* einschließen, einsperren

◆ **shut off I.** *vt* ① (*isolate*) ■ **to ~ off ↔ sb/sth [from sth]** jdn/etw [von etw *dat*] isolieren; (*protect*) jdn/etw [von etw *dat*] abschirmen; **to ~ oneself off** sich zurückziehen ② (*turn off*) abstellen, ausmachen; *computer, system* herunterfahren **II.** *vi* (*stop operating*) sich [automatisch] ausschalten

◆ **shut out** *vt* ① (*a. fig: block out*) ausschließen (**from** von +*dat*); (*fig*) *thoughts* verdrängen; *light* abschirmen ② SPORTS ■ **to ~ out ↔ sb** jdn zu null schlagen

◆ **shut up I.** *vt* ① (*confine*) einsperren ② (*close*) schließen; **to ~ up shop** das Geschäft schließen; (*fig: stop business*) seine Tätigkeit einstellen ③ (*fam: cause to stop talking*) zum Schweigen bringen **II.** *vi* (*fam: stop talking*) den Mund [*o* die Klappe] halten

'shutdown *n* Schließung *f*

'shuteye *n* (*fam*) Nickerchen *nt*

shutter ['ʃʌt̬·ər] *n* ① *usu pl* (*window cover*) Fensterladen *m* ② PHOT [Kamera]verschluss *m*, Blende *f*

shuttle ['ʃʌt̬·əl] **I.** *n* ① (*train*) Pendelzug *m*; (*plane*) Pendelmaschine *f*; **space ~** Raumfähre *f* ② (*sewing machine bobbin*) Schiffchen *nt* **II.** *vt* hin- und zurückbefördern **III.** *vi* hin- und zurückfahren

shuttle bus *n* kostenloser Zubringerbus, kostenfreier Bus

shuttlecock ['ʃʌt̬·əl·kak] *n* Federball *m*

'shuttle flight *n* Shuttleflug *m*

shy [ʃaɪ] **I.** *adj* (*timid*) schüchtern; **~ smile** scheues Lächeln **II.** *vi* <-ie-> *horse* scheuen

◆ **shy away from** *vt* ■ **to ~ away from [doing] sth** vor etw *dat* zurückschrecken

shyly ['ʃaɪ·li] *adv* schüchtern; *smile* scheu

shyness ['ʃaɪ·nɪs] *n* Schüchternheit *f*; *of horses* Scheuen *nt*

Siamese [ˌsaɪ·ə·'miz] **I.** *n* <*pl* -> ① (*person*) Siamese, Siamesin *m, f*; (*cat*) Siamkatze *f* ② (*language*) Siamesisch *nt* **II.** *adj* siamesisch

Siamese 'twins *npl* siamesische Zwillinge

sibling ['sɪb·lɪŋ] *n* Geschwister *nt meist pl*

Sicilian [sɪ·'sɪl·jən] **I.** *n* Sizilianer(in) *m(f)* **II.** *adj* sizilianisch

Sicily ['sɪs·ɪ·li] *n* Sizilien *nt*

sick [sɪk] **I.** *adj* ① (*physically*) krank; (*mentally*) geisteskrank; (*in poor condition*) *machine, engine* angeschlagen; **to call in ~** sich krankmelden ② *pred* (*in stomach*) **to be ~** (*vomit*) sich erbrechen, spucken *fam*; **to feel ~** sich schlecht fühlen ③ *pred* (*fam: fed up*) **to be ~ and tired of sth** etw [gründlich] satthaben; ■ **to be ~ of sb/sth** von jdm/etw die Nase voll haben ④ (*fam: cruel and offensive*) geschmacklos; *person* pervers; *mind* abartig ▶ PHRASES: **to be worried ~** (*fam*) krank vor Sorge sein **II.** *n* ■ **the ~** *pl* die Kranken *pl*

'sickbed *n* Krankenbett *nt*

sicken ['sɪk·ən] **I.** *vi* erkranken **II.** *vt* (*upset greatly*) krank machen *fam*; (*turn sb's stomach*) anekeln

sickening ['sɪk·ən·ɪŋ] *adj* (*repulsive*) *cruelty* entsetzlich; *smell* widerlich, ekelhaft; (*annoying*) [äußerst] ärgerlich

sickle ['sɪk·əl] *n* Sichel *f*

'sick leave *n* MED **to be on ~** krankgeschrieben sein

sickly ['sɪk·li] *adj* ① (*not healthy*) kränklich; *complexion, light* blass ② (*sentimental*) schmalzig *pej*

sickness <*pl* -es> ['sɪk·nɪs] *n* ① (*illness*) Krankheit *f*; (*nausea*) Übelkeit *f* ② (*fig*) Schwäche *f*

'sick pay *n* ADMIN, MED Krankengeld *nt*

side [saɪd] **I.** *n* ① (*vertical surface*) *of car, box* Seite *f*; *of hill, cliff* Hang *m*; (*wall*) *of house* [Seiten]wand *f*; ■ **at the ~ of sth** neben etw *dat* ② *of somebody* Seite *f*; **to stay at sb's ~** jdm zur Seite stehen ③ (*face, surface*) *of coin, record, box* Seite *f*; **this ~ up!** (*on a package*) oben!; **the right/wrong ~ of the fabric** [*or* **material**] die rechte/linke Seite des Stoffes ④ (*page*) Seite *f* ⑤ (*edge*) *of plate, clearing, field* Rand *m*; *of table, square, triangle* Seite *f*; *of river* [Fluss]ufer *nt*; *of road* [Straßen]rand *m*; **on all ~s** auf allen Seiten ⑥ (*half*) *of bed, house* Hälfte *f*; *of town, road, brain, room* Seite *f* ⑦ (*direction*) Seite *f*; **to take sb to one ~** jdn auf die Seite nehmen ⑧ (*opposing party*) *of dispute, contest* Partei *f*, Seite *f*; (*team a.*) Mannschaft *f*; **to change** [*or* **switch**] **~s** sich auf die andere Seite schlagen; **to take ~s** Partei ergreifen ⑨ (*aspect*) Seite *f*; **I've listened to your ~ of the story** ich habe jetzt deine Version der Geschichte gehört ▶ PHRASES: **the other ~ of the coin** die Kehrseite der Medaille; **to be on the large/small ~** zu groß/klein sein **II.** *adj* Neben-; **~ job** Nebenbeschäftigung *f,* Nebenjob *m fam* **III.** *vi* ■**to ~ against sb** sich gegen jdn stellen; ■**to ~ with sb** zu jdm halten

'**sideburns** *npl* (*hair*) Koteletten *pl*

'**sidecar** *n* AUTO Seitenwagen *m*

'**side dish** *n* FOOD Beilage *f*

'**side effect** *n* Nebenwirkung *f*

'**side issue** *n* Nebensache *f*

'**sidekick** *n* (*fam*) ❶ (*subordinate*) Handlanger *m* ❷ (*friend*) Kumpel *m fam*

'**sideline I.** *n* ❶ SPORTS (*boundary line*) Begrenzungslinie *f;* (*area near field*) Seitenlinie *f;* (*fig*) **to watch sth from the ~s** etw als unbeteiligter Außenstehender beobachten ❷ (*secondary job*) Nebenbeschäftigung *f;* (*money*) Nebenerwerb *m* **II.** *vt* ❶ SPORTS (*keep from playing*) auf die Ersatzbank schicken ❷ (*fig: shunt*) kaltstellen *fam*

'**sidelong I.** *adj* seitlich **II.** *adv* seitlich

'**sidesaddle** *adv* **to ride ~** im Damensattel reiten

'**side salad** *n* Beilagensalat *m*

'**sideshow** *n* (*not main show*) Nebenaufführung *f;* (*fig*) Ablenkung *f;* (*exhibition*) Sonderausstellung *f*

'**sidestep I.** *vt* <-pp-> ■**to ~ sb/sth** jdm/etw ausweichen **II.** *vi* <-pp-> ausweichen **III.** *n* Schritt *m* zur Seite; (*fig*) Ausweichmanöver *nt;* (*in dancing*) Seitenschritt *m;* (*in sports*) Ausfallschritt *m*

'**side street** *n* Seitenstraße *f*

'**sidetrack** *vt* ablenken

'**side view** *n* Seitenansicht *f*

'**sidewalk** *n* Bürgersteig *m*

sideways ['saɪd·weɪz] **I.** *adv* ❶ (*to, from a side*) seitwärts; **the fence is leaning ~** der Zaun steht schief ❷ (*facing a side*) seitwärts **II.** *adj* seitlich; **he gave her a ~ glance** er sah sie von der Seite an

'**side wind** *n* Seitenwind *m*

sidewinder ['saɪd·ˌwaɪn·dər] *n* ZOOL (*rattlesnake*) Klapperschlange *f*

siding ['saɪ·dɪŋ] *n* ❶ (*house covering*) Außenverkleidung *f* ❷ RAIL Rangiergleis *nt;* (*dead end*) Abstellgleis *nt*

sidle ['saɪ·dəl] *vi* schleichen; ■**to ~ up** [**to sb**] sich an jdn anschleichen

siege [sidʒ] *n* MIL Belagerung *f;* **to lay ~ to sth** etw belagern

sieve [sɪv] **I.** *n* Sieb *nt* ► PHRASES: **to have a <u>mind</u> like a ~** (*fam*) ein Gedächtnis wie ein Sieb haben **II.** *vt* sieben

sift [sɪft] **I.** *vt* ❶ *flour, sand* sieben; **~ some powdered sugar over the top of the cake** bestäuben Sie den Kuchen mit Puderzucker ❷ (*examine closely*) durchsieben; *evidence, documents* [gründlich] durchgehen **II.** *vi* **to ~ through archives** Archive durchsehen

sigh [saɪ] **I.** *n* Seufzer *m;* **to heave a ~** einen Seufzer ausstoßen **II.** *vi person* seufzen; *wind* säuseln; **to ~ with relief** vor Erleichterung [auf]seufzen

sight [saɪt] **I.** *n* ❶ (*ability to see*) [**sense of**] ~ Sehvermögen *nt;* (*strength of vision*) Sehkraft *f* ❷ (*visual access*) Sicht *f;* (*visual range*) Sichtweite *f,* Sicht *f;* **get out of my ~!** (*fam*) geh mir aus den Augen!; **to be in/out of ~** in/außer Sichtweite sein; **to keep out of ~** sich nicht sehen lassen ❸ (*act of seeing*) Anblick *m;* **love at first ~** Liebe auf den ersten Blick; **to know sb by ~** jdn vom Sehen [her] kennen ❹ (*attractions*) ■**~s** *pl* Sehenswürdigkeiten *pl* ❺ (*on gun*) Visier *nt* ► PHRASES: **out of ~, out of <u>mind</u>** (*prov*) aus den Augen, aus dem Sinn *prov;* **to <u>set</u> one's ~s on sth** sich *dat* etw zum Ziel machen **II.** *vt* (*see*) sichten

sighted ['saɪ·t̬ɪd] *adj people* sehend *attr*

sightless ['saɪt·lɪs] *adj* blind

'**sight-read** MUS **I.** *vi* vom Blatt spielen **II.** *vt* vom Blatt spielen

'**sightseeing** *n* Besichtigungen *pl,* Sightseeing *nt;* **to go ~** Sehenswürdigkeiten besichtigen

sightseer ['saɪt·ˌsi·ər] *n* Tourist(in) *m(f)*

sign [saɪn] **I.** *n* ❶ (*gesture*) Zeichen *nt;* **to make the ~ of the cross** sich bekreuzigen ❷ (*notice*) [Straßen]schild *nt;* **traffic ~** Verkehrsschild *nt;* (*signboard*) Schild *nt* ❸ (*symbol*) Zeichen *nt,* Symbol *nt;* (*of the zodiac*) Sternzeichen *nt* ❹ (*indication*) [An]zeichen *nt;* (*trace*) Spur *f;* **~ of life** Lebenszeichen *nt;* **to show ~s of improvement** Anzeichen der Besserung erkennen lassen **II.** *vt* (*with signature*) *letter* unterschreiben; *contract, document, check* unterzeichnen; *book, painting* signieren **III.** *vi* ❶ (*write signature*) unterschreiben ❷ (*accept*) **to ~ for a delivery** eine Lieferung gegenzeichnen

◆**sign away** *vt* ■**to ~ away ↔ sth** *rights* auf etw *akk* verzichten

◆**sign in I.** *vi* sich eintragen **II.** *vt* eintragen

◆**sign off** *vi* RADIO, TV (*from broadcast*) sich verabschieden; (*end a letter*) zum Schluss kommen; (*end work*) Schluss machen

◆**sign on I.** *vi* ❶ (*for work*) sich verpflichten; (*for a class*) sich einschreiben (**for** für +*akk*) ❷ (*begin broadcasting*) *station* auf Sendung gehen; *disc jockey* sich melden **II.** *vt* verpflichten

◆**sign out I.** *vi* sich austragen; (*at work*) sich abmelden **II.** *vt books* ausleihen

◆**sign over** *vt* übertragen

◆**sign up I.** *vi* (*for work*) sich verpflichten; (*for a class*) sich einschreiben **II.** *vt* verpflichten; **to ~ sb up for a class** jdn für einen Kurs anmelden

signal ['sɪg·nəl] **I.** *n* ❶ (*gesture*) Zeichen *nt,* Signal *nt* (**for** für +*akk*) ❷ (*traffic light*) Ampel *f;* (*for trains*) Signal *nt* ❸ ELEC, RADIO (*transmission*) Signal *nt;* (*reception*) Empfang *m* ❹ AUTO (*indicator*) Blinker *m* **II.** *vt* <-l- *or* -ll-> ❶ AUTO blinken, signalisieren; **he ~ed left, but turned right** er blinkte nach links, bog aber nach rechts ab ❷ (*gesticulate*) ■**to ~ sb to do sth** jdm signalisieren, etw zu tun **III.** *vi* <-l- *or* -ll-> signalisieren; **she ~ed to them to**

be quiet sie gab ihnen ein Zeichen, ruhig zu sein **IV.** *adj achievement* bemerkenswert

signatory ['sɪg·nə·tɔr·i] *n* Unterzeichner(in) *m(f)*

signature ['sɪg·nə·tʃər] *n* ❶ (*person's name*) Unterschrift *f; of artist, in printing* Signatur *f* ❷ (*characteristic*) Erkennungszeichen *nt* ❸ (*on prescriptions*) Signatur *f*

'signature tune *n* RADIO, TV [Erkennungs]melodie *f*

significance [sɪg·'nɪf·ɪ·kəns] *n* ❶ (*importance*) Wichtigkeit *f;* **to be of no ~** bedeutungslos sein ❷ (*meaning*) Bedeutung *f*

significant [sɪg·'nɪf·ɪ·kənt] *adj* ❶ (*considerable*) beachtlich, bedeutend; (*important*) bedeutsam; *date, event* wichtig; *difference* deutlich; *increase* beträchtlich; **~ other** (*fig*) Partner(in) *m(f);* (*hum*) bessere Hälfte *fam* ❷ (*meaningful*) bedeutsam; **do you think it's ~ that ...** glaubst du, es hat etwas zu bedeuten, dass ...; *look* viel sagend

signify <-ie-> ['sɪg·nə·faɪ] **I.** *vt* (*indicate*) andeuten **II.** *vi* eine Rolle spielen; **it doesn't ~** es macht nichts

'sign language *n* Gebärdensprache *f*

'signpost I. *n* Wegweiser *m;* (*fig: advice*) Hinweis *m* **II.** *vt usu passive* aufzeigen; *route* beschildern, ausschildern; ■**to ~ sth** (*fig*) etw aufzeigen [*o* darlegen]

Sikh [sik] *n* Sikh *m*

silage ['saɪ·lɪdʒ] *n* AGR Silage *f*

silence ['saɪ·ləns] **I.** *n* (*absolute*) Stille *f;* (*by an individual*) Schweigen *nt;* (*on a confidential matter*) Stillschweigen *nt;* (*calmness*) Ruhe *f;* **a moment of ~** eine Schweigeminute; **to work in ~** still arbeiten; **to reduce sb to ~** jdn zum Schweigen bringen ▶ PHRASES: **~ is golden** (*prov*) Schweigen ist Gold **II.** *vt* zum Schweigen bringen; *doubts* verstummen lassen

silencer ['saɪ·lən·sər] *n* (*on gun*) Schalldämpfer *m*

silent ['saɪ·lənt] *adj* ❶ (*without noise*) still; (*not active*) ruhig; **to keep ~** still sein ❷ (*not talking*) schweigsam, still; ■**to be ~** schweigen; **to go ~** verstummen

silently ['saɪ·lənt·li] *adv* (*quietly*) lautlos; (*without talking*) schweigend; (*with little noise*) leise

silent 'partner *n* COMM stiller Teilhaber

silhouette [ˌsɪl·u·'et] **I.** *n* (*shadow*) Silhouette *f;* (*picture*) Schattenriss *m;* (*outline*) Umriss *m* **II.** *vt* ■**to be ~d against sth** sich von etw *dat* abheben

silica ['sɪl·ɪ·kə] *n* Kieselerde *f*

silicon ['sɪl·ɪ·kən] *n* Silizium *nt*

silicon 'chip *n* COMPUT, ELEC Siliziumchip *m*

silicone ['sɪl·ɪ·koʊn] *n* Silikon *nt*

Silicon 'Valley *n* Silicon Valley *nt*

silk [sɪlk] *n* (*material*) Seide *f*

silken ['sɪl·kən] *adj* (*silk-like*) seiden *liter;* (*fig*) *voice* samtig

silk-screen 'printing *n* Siebdruck *m*

'silkworm *n* Seidenraupe *f*

silky ['sɪl·ki] *adj* seidig; (*fig*) *voice* samtig

sill [sɪl] *n* Fensterbank *f*

silly ['sɪl·i] *adj* ❶ (*foolish*) albern, dumm; **don't be ~!** (*make silly suggestions*) red keinen Unsinn!; (*do silly things*) mach keinen Quatsch! *fam* ❷ *pred* (*senseless*) **to be bored ~** zu Tode gelangweilt sein

silo ['saɪ·loʊ] *n* ❶ AGR Silo *m o nt* ❷ MIL [Raketen]silo *m o nt*

silt [sɪlt] **I.** *n* Schlick *m* **II.** *vi* ■**to ~ [up]** verschlammen

silver ['sɪl·vər] **I.** *n* ❶ (*metal*) Silber *nt* ❷ (*coins*) Münzgeld *nt* ❸ (*cutlery*) ■**the ~** das [Tafel]silber **II.** *adj* (*of silver*) (*mine*) Silber-; (*made of silver*) (*spoon, ring*) silbern ▶ PHRASES: **every cloud has a ~ lining** (*saying*) jedes Unglück hat auch sein Gutes

silver anni'versary *n* silberne Hochzeit

'silverfish <*pl* -> *n* ZOOL Silberfischchen *nt*

silver 'jubilee *n* silbernes Jubiläum

silver 'plate *n* ❶ (*coating*) Versilberung *f* ❷ (*object*) versilberter Gegenstand

silver-'plate *vt* versilbern

silver 'screen *n* FILM ■**the ~** die Leinwand

'silversmith *n* Silberschmied(in) *m(f)*

'silverware *n* (*cutlery*) Silberbesteck *nt,* Silber *nt*

silvery ['sɪl·və·ri] *adj* (*in appearance*) silbrig; (*in sound*) silbern

simian ['sɪm·i·ən] *adj* (*form*) ❶ (*monkey-like*) affenartig ❷ (*of monkeys*) Affen-

similar ['sɪm·ə·lər] *adj* ähnlich; ■**to be ~ to sb/sth** jdm/etw ähnlich sein

similarity [ˌsɪm·ə·'ler·ɪ·t̬i] *n* Ähnlichkeit *f* (**to** mit +*dat*)

simile ['sɪm·ə·li] *n* LIT, LING Gleichnis *nt*

simmer ['sɪm·ər] **I.** *n usu sing* Sieden *nt* **II.** *vi* ❶ (*not quite boil*) sieden; (*fig*) **to ~ with anger** vor Wut kochen ❷ (*fig: build up*) sich anbahnen **III.** *vt food* auf kleiner Flamme kochen lassen; *water* sieden lassen

◆ **simmer down** *vi* sich beruhigen

simper ['sɪm·pər] *vi* ■**to ~ at sb** jdn albern anlächeln

simple <-r, -st *or* more ~, most ~> ['sɪm·pəl] *adj* ❶ (*not complex, ordinary*) *food, dress, task* einfach; **the ~ things in life** die einfachen Dinge des Lebens ❷ *attr* (*straightforward*) schlicht; **that's the truth, plain and ~** das ist die reine Wahrheit; **for the ~ reason that ...** aus dem schlichten Grund, dass ... ❸ (*ignorant*) naiv

simple-'minded *adj* ❶ (*naive*) einfältig ❷ (*stupid*) einfach

simpleton ['sɪm·pəl·tən] *n* (*pej fam*) Einfaltspinsel *m*

simplicity [sɪm·'plɪs·ɪ·t̬i] *n* ❶ (*plainness*) Einfachheit *f,* Schlichtheit *f* ❷ (*easiness*) Einfachheit *f;* **to be ~ itself** die Einfachheit selbst sein

simplification [ˌsɪm·plə·fɪ·'keɪ·ʃən] *n* Vereinfachung *f*

simplify <-ie-> ['sɪm·plə·faɪ] *vt* vereinfachen

simplistic [sɪm·ˈplɪs·tɪk] *adj* simpel; **am I being** [**overly** [*or* **too**]] **~?** sehe ich das zu einfach?

simply [ˈsɪm·pli] *adv* ❶ (*not elaborately*) einfach ❷ (*just*) nur; (*absolutely*) einfach; **you ~ must try this!** du musst das einfach versuchen! ❸ (*in a natural manner*) einfach, schlicht; (*humbly*) bescheiden

simulate [ˈsɪm·jʊ·leɪt] *vt* ❶ (*resemble*) nachahmen ❷ (*feign*) vortäuschen ❸ (*using computer*) simulieren

simulation [ˌsɪm·jʊ·ˈleɪ·ʃən] *n of leather, a diamond* Imitation *f; of a feeling* Vortäuschung *f;* COMPUT Simulation *f*

simulator [ˈsɪm·jʊ·leɪ·t̬ər] *n* COMPUT, TECH Simulator *m*

simultaneous [ˌsaɪ·məl·ˈteɪ·ni·əs] *adj* gleichzeitig

sin [sɪn] **I.** *n* Sünde *f;* **he's** [**as**] **ugly as ~** er ist unglaublich hässlich **II.** *vi* <-nn-> sündigen

since [sɪns] **I.** *adv* ❶ (*from that point on*) seitdem; **she left a week ago, and we haven't seen her ~** sie ist vor einer Woche weggegangen, seitdem haben wir sie nicht mehr gesehen ❷ (*ago*) **long ~** seit langem, schon lange; **not long ~** vor kurzem [erst] **II.** *prep* seit; **~ last week** seit letzter Woche **III.** *conj* ❶ (*because*) da, weil ❷ (*from time when*) [**ever**] **~** seit, seitdem

sincere [sɪn·ˈsɪr] *adj person* ehrlich; *congratulations, gratitude* aufrichtig

sincerely [sɪn·ˈsɪr·li] *adv* ❶ (*in a sincere manner*) ehrlich, aufrichtig ❷ (*ending letter*) mit freundlichen Grüßen

sincerity [sɪn·ˈser·ɪ·t̬i] *n* Ehrlichkeit *f,* Aufrichtigkeit *f*

sine [saɪn] *n* MATH Sinus *m*

sine qua non [ˈsɪn·ɪ·kwa·ˈnoʊn] *n* (*form*) unabdingbare Voraussetzung

sinew [ˈsɪn·ju] *n* (*tendon*) Sehne *f*

sinewy [ˈsɪn·ju·i] *adj* ❶ (*muscular*) sehnig ❷ (*tough*) zäh; *meat* sehnig

sinful [ˈsɪn·fəl] *adj* ❶ (*immoral*) sündig, sündhaft ❷ (*fam*) **to be absolutely ~** die reinste Sünde sein *hum, iron*

sing <sang *or* sung, sung> [sɪŋ] **I.** *vi* ❶ (*utter musical sounds*) singen ❷ (*make high-pitched noise*) *kettle* pfeifen; *locusts* zirpen; *wind* pfeifen ❸ (*make ringing noise*) dröhnen **II.** *vt* (*utter musical sounds*) singen; **to ~ the praises of sb/sth** ein Loblied auf jdn/etw singen

◆**sing out** **I.** *vi* ❶ (*sing loudly*) laut singen ❷ (*fam: call out*) schreien **II.** *vt* (*fam*) ■**to ~ out** ↻ **sth** ausrufen

sing. **I.** *n abbrev of* **singular** Sg., Sing. **II.** *adj abbrev of* **singular** im Sing. [*o* Sg.] *nach n*

sing-along [ˈsɪŋ·ə·lɔŋ] *n* gemeinsames Liedersingen; **to have a ~** gemeinsam Lieder singen

Singapore [ˈsɪŋ·ə·pɔr] *n* Singapur *nt*

Singaporean [ˈsɪŋ·ə·pɔr·i·ən] **I.** *adj* aus Singapur *nach n* **II.** *n* Singapurer(in) *m(f)*

singe [sɪndʒ] **I.** *vt* ❶ (*burn surface of*) ansengen; (*burn sth slightly*) versengen ❷ (*burn off deliberately*) absengen **II.** *vi* (*burn*) *hair, fur* angesengt werden; (*burn lightly*) versengt werden

singer [ˈsɪŋ·ər] *n* Sänger(in) *m(f)*

singer-ˈsongwriter *n* Liedermacher(in) *m(f)*

singing [ˈsɪŋ·ɪŋ] *n* Singen *nt*

ˈsinging lesson *n* Gesang[s]stunde *f*

ˈsinging teacher *n* Gesang[s]lehrer(in) *m(f)*

ˈsinging voice *n* Singstimme *f*

single [ˈsɪŋ·gəl] **I.** *adj* ❶ *attr* (*one only*) einzige(r, s); **she didn't say a ~ word all evening** sie sprach den ganzen Abend kein einziges Wort; **not a ~ soul** keine Menschenseele; **every ~ time** jedes Mal ❷ (*having one part*) einzelne(r, s); *figure* einstellig ❸ (*unmarried*) ledig ❹ (*raising child alone*) allein erziehend; **~ father** allein erziehender Vater **II.** *n* ❶ (*one dollar bill*) Eindollarschein *m* ❷ (*record*) Single *f* ❸ (*single room*) Einzelzimmer *nt* ❹ (*in baseball*) Single *m* **III.** *vi* einen Single schlagen

◆**single out** *vt* (*for positive characteristics*) auswählen; (*for negative reasons*) herausgreifen

single-ˈbreasted *adj* einreihig; **~ suit** Einreiher *m*

single ˈcurrency *n* FIN gemeinsame Währung

singledom [ˈsɪŋ·gəl·dəm] *n* (*hum*) Single-Dasein *nt*

single ˈfile *n* **in ~** im Gänsemarsch

single-ˈhanded **I.** *adv* [ganz] allein; **he sailed round the world ~** er segelte als Einhandsegler um die Welt **II.** *adj* allein

single-ˈminded *adj* zielstrebig

single-ˈmindedness *n* Zielstrebigkeit *f;* (*pursuing sth unwaveringly*) Unbeirrbarkeit *f*

single-parent ˈfamily *n* Familie *f* mit [nur] einem Elternteil

ˈsingles bar *n* Singlekneipe *f*

single-ˈsex *adj* nach Geschlechtern getrennt

single-ˈspaced *adj* COMPUT einzeilig

singleton [ˈsɪŋ·gəl·tən] *n* Single *m*

singly [ˈsɪŋ·gli] *adv* einzeln

singsong [ˈsɪŋ·ˌsɔŋ] **I.** *n* Singsang *m* **II.** *adj attr* **to speak in a ~ voice** in einem Singsang sprechen

singular [ˈsɪŋ·gjə·lər] **I.** *adj* ❶ LING Singular-; **to be ~** im Singular stehen; **~ form** Singularform *f* ❷ (*form: extraordinary*) einzigartig **II.** *n* LING Singular *m*

singularity [ˌsɪŋ·gjə·ˈler·ɪ·t̬i] *n* (*form*) Eigenartigkeit *f*

singularly [ˈsɪŋ·gjə·lər·li] *adv* (*form*) ❶ (*extraordinarily*) außerordentlich ❷ (*strangely*) eigenartig

Sinhalese [ˌsɪn·hə·ˈliz] **I.** *adj* singhalesisch **II.** *n* ❶ (*language*) Singhalesisch *nt* ❷ <*pl* -> (*person*) Singhalese, Singhalesin *m, f*

sinister [ˈsɪn·ɪ·stər] *adj* ❶ (*scary*) unheimlich ❷ (*fam: ominous*) unheilvoll; *forces* dunkel

sink [sɪŋk] **I.** *n* ❶ (*in kitchen*) Spüle *f,* Spülbecken *nt;* (*washbasin*) Waschbecken *nt*

② (*cesspool*) Senkgrube *f* ③ (*sewer*) Abfluss *m* **II.** *vi* <sank *or* sunk, sunk>, *vi* ① (*not float*) untergehen, sinken ② (*in mud, snow*) einsinken ③ (*go downward*) sinken; *sun, moon* versinken, untergehen; **to ~ to the bottom** auf den Boden sinken; *sediment* sich auf dem Boden absetzen ④ (*move to a lower position*) *surface, house, construction* sich senken; *level a.* sinken ⑤ (*become limp*) *arm, head* herabsinken; **to ~ to the ground** zu Boden sinken ⑥ (*decrease*) *amount, value* sinken; *demand, sales, numbers a.* zurückgehen; **the yen sank to a new low against the dollar** der Yen hat gegenüber dem Dollar einen neuen Tiefstand erreicht ⑦ (*decline*) *standards, quality* nachlassen; *moral character* sinken ▸ PHRASES: **sb's heart ~s** (*gets sadder*) jdm wird das Herz schwer; (*becomes discouraged*) jd verliert den Mut **III.** *vt* <sank *or* sunk, sunk> ① (*cause to submerge*) versenken ② (*ruin*) *hopes, plans* zunichtemachen ③ SPORTS versenken; **to ~ a ball** (*into a hole*) einen Ball einlochen; (*into a pocket*) einen Ball versenken ④ (*dig*) *shaft* abteufen *fachspr; well* bohren ⑤ (*lower*) senken

◆**sink back** *vi* ① (*lean back*) zurücksinken; **to ~ back on the sofa** aufs Sofa sinken ② (*relapse*) ■**to ~ back into sth** [wieder] in etw *akk* verfallen

◆**sink down** *vi* ① (*descend gradually*) sinken; *sun* versinken ② (*go down*) zurücksinken; (*on the ground*) zu Boden sinken

◆**sink in** **I.** *vi* ① (*into a surface*) einsinken ② (*be absorbed*) *liquid, cream* einziehen ③ (*be understood*) ins Bewusstsein dringen **II.** *vt* ① (*force into*) **to ~ one's teeth in sth** *animal* seine Zähne in etw *akk* einschlagen; **to ~ a knife in sth** ein Messer in etw *akk* rammen ② (*invest*) **to ~ one's money in sth** sein Geld in etw *akk* stecken *fam*

◆**sink into** **I.** *vi* ■**to ~ into sth** ① (*into mud, snow*) in etw *dat* einsinken ② (*into skin*) *cream, lotion* in etw *akk* einziehen ③ (*lie back in*) in etw *akk* [hinein]sinken; **to ~ into bed** sich ins Bett fallen lassen ④ (*pass gradually into*) in etw *akk* sinken; **to ~ into a coma** ins Koma fallen **II.** *vt* ① (*put*) ■**to ~ sth into sth** etw in etw *akk o dat* versenken; **I'd love to ~ my teeth into a nice juicy steak** ich würde gern in ein schönes, saftiges Steak beißen ② (*embed*) **to ~ a pole into the ground** einen Pfosten in den Boden schlagen ③ FIN **to ~ one's money into sth** sein Geld in etw *dat* anlegen

sinker ['sɪŋ·kər] *n* Senker *m*

sinking ['sɪŋ·kɪŋ] *adj attr* ① (*declining, not floating*) sinkend ② (*emotion*) **a ~ feeling** ein flaues Gefühl [in der Magengegend]; **with a ~ heart** resigniert ▸ PHRASES: **to leave the ~ ship** das sinkende Schiff verlassen

sinner ['sɪn·ər] *n* Sünder(in) *m(f)*

sinuous ['sɪn·jʊ·əs] *adj* ① (*winding*) gewunden; *path* verschlungen ② (*curving and twisting*) geschmeidig

sinus <*pl* -es> ['saɪ·nəs] *n* ANAT Nasennebenhöhle *f*

sinusitis [ˌsaɪ·nə·'saɪ·t̬ɪs] *n* MED Nasennebenhöhlenentzündung *f*

Sioux [su] **I.** *adj* (*tribe*) Sioux- **II.** *n* ① <*pl* -> (*person*) Sioux *m o f* ② (*language*) Sioux *nt*

sip [sɪp] **I.** *vt* <-pp-> nippen (an +*dat*); (*drink carefully*) etw in kleinen Schlucken trinken; *beer, champagne* süffeln **II.** *n* Schlückchen *nt;* **to take a ~** einen kleinen Schluck nehmen

siphon ['saɪ·fən] **I.** *n* Saugheber *m* **II.** *vt* [mit einem Saugheber] absaugen

◆**siphon off** *vt* ① (*remove*) absaugen ② FIN *money* abziehen; *profits* abschöpfen

sir [sɜr] *n* ① (*form of address*) Herr *m;* **can I see your driver's license, ~?** kann ich bitte ihren Führerschein sehen? ② (*not at all*) **no, ~!** (*fam*) auf keinen Fall! ③ (*on letters*) **Dear S~** [*or* **Dear S~ or Madam**] Sehr geehrte Damen und Herren

siren ['saɪ·rən] *n* Sirene *f*

sirloin ['sɜr·lɔɪn] *n* Lendenfilet *nt*

sirocco [sə·'rak·oʊ] *n* METEO Schirokko *m*

sis [sɪs] *n* (*fam*) *short for* **sister** Schwesterherz *nt hum*

sissy ['sɪs·i] **I.** *n* (*pej fam*) Waschlappen *m* **II.** *adj* (*pej fam*) verweichlicht

sister ['sɪs·tər] *n* ① (*female sibling*) Schwester *f* ② (*nun*) [Ordens]schwester *f* ③ (*fellow sorority member*) Schwester *f* ④ (*sl: African American woman*) ≈ Schwester (*hauptsächlich von Afroamerikaner gebrauchte Anrede für eine weibliche Person*)

sister city *n* Partnerstadt *f;* **to become a ~** eine Städtepartnerschaft bilden

sisterhood ['sɪs·tər·hʊd] *n* ① (*sisterly bond*) Zusammenhalt *m* unter Schwestern; (*female solidarity*) Solidarität *f* unter Frauen ② REL Schwesternorden *m*

'sister-in-law <*pl* sisters- *or* -s> *n* Schwägerin *f*

sisterly ['sɪs·tər·li] *adj* schwesterlich

sit <-tt, sat, sat> [sɪt] **I.** *vi* ① (*seated*) sitzen; **to ~ at the table** am Tisch sitzen ② (*fam: babysit*) babysitten (**for** für +*akk*) ③ (*sit down*) sich hinsetzen; **~!** (*to a dog*) Platz!, Sitz!; **he sat [down] next to me** er setzte sich neben mich ④ (*perch*) hocken, sitzen ⑤ (*be located*) liegen ⑥ (*remain undisturbed*) stehen; **to ~ on sb's desk/the shelf** auf jds Schreibtisch liegen/im Regal stehen ⑦ (*in session*) tagen; *court* zusammenkommen ⑧ (*fit*) passen; *clothes* sitzen ▸ PHRASES: **to ~ on the fence** sich nicht entscheiden können; **to be ~ting pretty** fein heraus sein; **to ~ tight** (*not move*) sich nicht rühren; (*not change opinion*) stur bleiben **II.** *vt* ① (*place in seat*) setzen; **to ~ oneself** sich *akk* setzen ② (*accommodate*) **to ~ a child on a chair** ein Kind auf einen Stuhl setzen

◆**sit around** *vi* herumsitzen

◆**sit back** *vi* ① (*lean back in chair*) sich zurücklehnen ❷ (*do nothing*) die Hände in den Schoß legen

◆**sit down** I. *vi* ❶ (*take a seat*) sich [hin]setzen; **to ~ down to dinner** sich zum Essen an den Tisch begeben ❷ (*be sitting*) sitzen II. *vt* ❶ (*put in a seat*) setzen ❷ (*take a seat*) ■**to ~ oneself down** sich hinsetzen

◆**sit in** *vi* ❶ (*attend*) dabeisitzen; **to ~ in on a meeting** einem Treffen beisitzen ❷ (*hold sit-in*) ein Sit-in [*o* einen Sitzstreik] halten

◆**sit on** *vi* ❶ (*be member of*) **to ~ on a committee** Mitglied eines Komitees sein ❷ (*fam: not act on sth*) ■**to ~ on sth** auf etw *dat* sitzen

◆**sit out** *vt* ❶ (*not participate in*) auslassen; (*game, competition*) bei etw aussetzen ❷ (*sit until end*) bis zum Ende ausharren

◆**sit through** *vt lecture, sermon* über sich *akk* ergehen lassen

◆**sit up** *vi* ❶ (*sit erect*) aufrecht sitzen; **to ~ up straight** sich gerade hinsetzen ❷ (*fam: pay attention*) **to ~ up and take notice** aufhorchen

sitcom ['sɪt·kam] *n* (*fam*) *short for* **situation comedy** Sitcom *f*

site [saɪt] I. *n* ❶ (*place*) Stelle *f,* Platz *m,* Ort *m; of crime* Tatort *m* ❷ (*plot*) Grundstück *nt;* **camping ~** Campingplatz *m* ❸ (*of construction work*) [**building**] **~** Baustelle *f,* Baugelände *nt,* Bauplatz *m;* **on ~** vor Ort ❹ (*on Internet*) [**Web**] **~** Website *f* II. *vt* einen Standort bestimmen; **to be ~d out of town** außerhalb der Stadt liegen

'sit-in *n* Sit-in *nt*

sitter ['sɪṭ·ər] *n* ❶ (*model for portrait*) Modell *nt* ❷ (*babysitter*) Babysitter(in) *m(f)*

sitting ['sɪṭ·ɪŋ] *n* ❶ (*meal session*) Ausgabe *f* ❷ (*session*) Sitzung *f*

sitting 'duck *n* leicht zu treffendes Ziel; (*fig*) leichte Beute

'sitting room *n* Wohnzimmer *nt*

situated ['sɪtʃ·u·eɪ·ṭɪd] *adj pred* ❶ (*located*) gelegen; **to be ~ near the church** in der Nähe der Kirche liegen ❷ (*in a state*) **to be well ~** [finanziell] gutgestellt sein; **to be well ~ to do sth** gute Voraussetzungen besitzen, etw zu tun

situation [ˌsɪtʃ·u·'eɪ·ʃən] *n* ❶ (*circumstances*) Situation *f,* Lage *f* ❷ (*location*) Lage *f,* Standort *m*

'sit-up *n* SPORTS Sit-up *m, Bauchmuskelübung;* **to do ten ~s** zehn Sit-ups machen

six [sɪks] I. *adj* sechs; *see also* **eight** ▶ PHRASES: **to be ~ <u>feet</u> under** (*hum*) sich *dat* die Radieschen von unten anschauen *sl* II. *pron* sechs; *see also* **eight** ▶ PHRASES: **~ of one and <u>half</u> a dozen of the other** gehupft wie gesprungen *fam* III. *n* Sechs *f; see also* **eight**

six-digit 'sum *n* sechsstelliger Betrag

'sixfold *adj* sechsfach

six-'footer *n* (*tall male person*) Zweimetermann *m;* (*tall, powerful male*) Hüne *m;* (*tall female*) Zweimeterfrau *f*

'six-pack *n* ❶ (*package of six*) Sechserpack *m; of beer* Sixpack *m* ❷ (*well-toned stomach*) Waschbrettbauch *m*

sixteen [sɪk·'stin] I. *adj* sechzehn; *see also* **eight** II. *n* Sechzehn *f; see also* **eight**

sixteenth [ˌsɪk·'stinθ] I. *adj* sechzehnte(r, s) II. *pron* ■**the ~ ...** der/die/das sechzehnte ... III. *adv* als sechzehnte(r, s) IV. *n* Sechzehntel *nt o* SCHWEIZ *a. m*

six'teenth note *n* MUS Sechzehntel[note] *f*

sixth [sɪksθ] I. *adj* sechste(r, s) II. *pron* ■**the ~ ...** der/die/das sechste ... III. *adv* als sechste(r, s) IV. *n* Sechstel *nt o* SCHWEIZ *a. m*

sixtieth ['sɪk·sti·əθ] I. *adj* sechzigste(r, s) II. *pron* ■**the ~** der/die/das sechzigste III. *adv* als sechzigste(r, s) IV. *n* Sechzigstel *nt o* SCHWEIZ *a. m*

sixty ['sɪk·sti] I. *adj* sechzig II. *pron* sechzig III. *n* Sechzig *f*

sizable, sizeable ['saɪ·zə·bəl] *adj* ziemlich groß; *amount* beträchtlich

size [saɪz] I. *n* ❶ *usu sing* (*magnitude*) Größe *f; amount, debt* Höhe *f;* **a company of that ~** eine Firma dieser Größenordnung; **to be a good ~** (*quite big*) ziemlich groß sein; (*suitable size*) die richtige Größe haben; **to double in ~** seine Größe verdoppeln; **to increase in ~** größer werden ❷ (*measurement*) Größe *f;* **what ~ are you? — I'm a ~ 10** welche Größe haben Sie? – ich habe Größe 36; **shirt/shoe ~** Hemdgröße *f*/Schuhgröße *f* II. *vt* nach der Größe ordnen

◆**size up** *vt* [prüfend] abschätzen; **to ~ each other up** sich gegenseitig taxieren

sizeable ['saɪ·zə·bəl] *adj see* **sizable**

sizzle ['sɪz·əl] I. *vi* ❶ *bacon, fat* brutzeln ❷ (*fam: be exciting*) aufregend sein II. *n* Zischen *nt*

skate¹ [skeɪt] I. *n* ❶ (*ice skate*) Schlittschuh *m* ❷ (*roller skate*) Rollschuh *m,* Rollerskate *m* II. *vi* ❶ (*on ice*) Schlittschuh laufen ❷ (*on roller skates*) Rollschuh fahren, Rollerskate fahren ▶ PHRASES: **to be skating on thin <u>ice</u>** sich auf dünnem Eis bewegen

skate² [skeɪt] *n* (*flat fish*) Rochen *m*

skateboard ['skeɪt·bɔrd] I. *n* Skateboard *nt* II. *vi* skaten

skateboarder ['skeɪt·ˌbɔr·dər] *n* Skateboardfahrer(in) *m(f)*

skateboarding ['skeɪt·ˌbɔr·dɪŋ] *n* Skateboardfahren *nt*

skater ['skeɪ·ṭər] *n* ❶ (*on ice*) Schlittschuhläufer(in) *m(f);* **figure ~** Eiskunstläufer(in) *m(f);* **speed ~** Eisschnellläufer(in) *m(f)* ❷ (*on roller skates*) Rollschuhfahrer(in) *m(f)* ❸ (*on Rollerblades, on skateboard*) Skater(in) *m(f)*

skating ['skeɪ·ṭɪŋ] *n* ❶ (*ice skating*) Eislaufen *nt;* **figure ~** Eiskunstlauf *m;* **speed ~** Eisschnelllauf *m* ❷ (*roller skating*) Rollschuhlaufen *nt,* Rollerskaten *nt*

'skating rink *n* ❶ (*for ice skating*) Eisbahn *f* ❷ (*for roller skating*) Rollschuhbahn *f*

skedaddle [skɪ·'dæd·əl] *vi* (*fam*) sich verdünnisieren *sl*

S

skein [skeɪn] *n* ❶ *(coil)* Strang *m* ❷ *(birds)* Schwarm *m;* ~ **of geese** Gänseschar *f*
skeleton [ˈskel·ɪ·tən] *n* ❶ *(bones)* Skelett *nt* ❷ *(framework) of boat, plane* Gerippe *nt; of building* Skelett *nt* ❸ *(outline sketch) of book, report* Entwurf *m* ▶ PHRASES: **to have ~s in the closet** eine Leiche im Keller haben *fam*
ˈ**skeleton key** *n* Dietrich *m*
ˈ**skeleton staff** *n* Minimalbesetzung *f*
skeptic [ˈskep·tɪk] *n* Skeptiker(in) *m(f)*
skeptical *adj* skeptisch
skepticism [ˈskep·tɪ·sɪz·əm] *n* Skepsis *f*
sketch [sketʃ] **I.** *n* <*pl* -es> ❶ *(rough drawing, written piece)* Skizze *f* ❷ *(outline)* Überblick *m* ❸ *(performance)* Sketch *m* **II.** *vt* ❶ *(rough drawing)* skizzieren ❷ *(write in outline)* umreißen **III.** *vi* Skizzen machen
◆**sketch in** *vt* ❶ *(draw in)* [andeutungsweise] einzeichnen ❷ *(outline)* umreißen
◆**sketch out** *vt* ❶ *(draw roughly)* [in groben Zügen] skizzieren ❷ *(outline)* umreißen
ˈ**sketchbook** *n* Skizzenbuch *nt*
sketchy [ˈsketʃ·i] *adj* ❶ *(not detailed)* flüchtig; *(incomplete)* lückenhaft ❷ *(not fully realized)* skizzenhaft dargestellt
skew [skju] **I.** *vt* ❶ *(give slant to)* krümmen; TECH abschrägen ❷ *(distort) facts* verdrehen **II.** *vi* **to ~ to the left/right** einen Links-/Rechtsdrall haben **III.** *adj pred* schräg, schief
skewed [skjud] *adj* schief
skewer [ˈskju·ər] **I.** *n* Spieß *m* **II.** *vt* ❶ *(pierce with skewer)* anstechen ❷ *(criticize)* sticheln
ski [ski] **I.** *n* Ski *m;* **on ~s** auf Skiern **II.** *vi* Ski fahren [*o* laufen]; **to ~ down the slope** die Piste hinunterfahren
ˈ**ski boot** *n* Skischuh *m*
skid [skɪd] **I.** *vi* <-dd-> *(on foot)* rutschen; *(in a vehicle)* schleudern, schlittern; **to ~ to a halt** schlitternd zum Stehen kommen **II.** *n* Rutschen *nt,* Schlittern *nt*
ˈ**skid mark** *n* Reifenspur *f; (from braking)* Bremsspur *f*
skid ˈ**row** *n* Pennerviertel *nt fam*
skier [ˈski·ər] *n* Skifahrer(in) *m(f)*
ˈ**ski goggles** *npl* Skibrille *f*
skiing [ˈski·ɪŋ] *n* Skifahren *nt*
ˈ**ski instructor** *n* Skilehrer, -in *m, f*
ˈ**ski jump** *n* ❶ *(runway)* Sprungschanze *f* ❷ *(jump)* Skisprung *m; (event)* Skispringen *nt*
ˈ**ski lift** *n* Skilift *m*
skill [skɪl] *n* ❶ *(expertise)* Geschick *nt;* **to involve some ~** einige Geschicklichkeit erfordern ❷ *(particular ability)* Fähigkeit *f; (technique)* Fertigkeit *f;* **communication ~s** Kommunikationsfähigkeit *f;* **language ~s** Sprachkompetenz *f*
skilled [skɪld] *adj* ❶ *(trained)* ausgebildet; *(skillful)* geschickt ❷ *(requiring skill)* Fach-; **a highly ~ job** eine hoch qualifizierte Tätigkeit; **semi-~ occupation** Anlernberuf *m*
skillet [ˈskɪl·ɪt] *n* Bratpfanne *f*
skillful [ˈskɪl·fəl] *adj* ❶ *(adroit)* geschickt ❷ *(showing skill)* gekonnt
skillfully [ˈskɪl·fəl·i] *adv* geschickt, gekonnt
skim <-mm-> [skɪm] **I.** *vt* ❶ *(move lightly above)* streifen; **to ~ the surface of sth** *(fig)* nur an der Oberfläche von etw *dat* kratzen ❷ *(read)* überfliegen ❸ FOOD *(remove from surface)* abschöpfen; **to ~ the cream from the milk** die Milch entrahmen **II.** *vi* ■**to ~ over sth** über etw *akk* hinwegstreifen
ˈ**ski mask** *n* Skimaske *f*
skim ˈ**milk** *n* entrahmte Milch, Magermilch *f*
skimp [skɪmp] **I.** *vt* nachlässig erledigen **II.** *vi* sparen (**on** an +*dat*)
skimpy [ˈskɪm·pi] *adj* ❶ *(not big enough)* dürftig; *meal* karg ❷ *clothing* knapp
skin [skɪn] **I.** *n* ❶ *usu sing (on body)* Haut *f;* **to be soaked to the ~** nass bis auf die Haut sein ❷ *(animal hide)* Fell *nt* ❸ *(rind) of fruit, potato* Schale *f; of boiled potato* Pelle *f; of sausage* [Wurst]haut *f; of tomatoes* Haut *f* ❹ *(outer covering) aircraft, ship* [Außen]haut *f* ❺ *(on hot liquid)* Haut *f* ▶ PHRASES: **it's no ~ off my nose** das ist nicht mein Problem; **by the ~ of one's teeth** nur mit knapper Not **II.** *vt* <-nn-> ❶ *(remove skin)* häuten; *fruit* schälen; **to ~ sb alive** *(hum)* Hackfleisch aus jdm machen *fam* ❷ *(graze)* **to ~ one's knees** sich *dat* die Knie aufschürfen
ˈ**skin cancer** *n* Hautkrebs *m*
ˈ**skin care** *n* Hautpflege *f*
skin-ˈ**deep** *adj pred* oberflächlich; **beauty is only ~** man darf nicht nur nach den Äußerlichkeiten urteilen
ˈ**skin disease** *n* Hautkrankheit *f*
ˈ**skin flick** *n (sl)* Porno *m*
ˈ**skinflint** *n (pej)* Geizkragen *m fam*
ˈ**skin graft** *n* MED ❶ *(skin transplant)* Hauttransplantation *f* ❷ *(skin section)* Hauttransplantat *nt*
ˈ**skinhead** *n* Skinhead *m*
skinny [ˈskɪn·i] *adj* mager
ˈ**skinny-dip** <-pp-> *vi (fam)* im Adams-/Evakostüm baden
ˈ**skin-tight** *adj* hauteng
skip [skɪp] **I.** *vi* <-pp-> ❶ *(hop)* hüpfen; **to ~ with joy** einen Freudensprung machen ❷ *(hop with rope)* seilspringen ❸ *(omit)* springen; ■**to ~ over sth** etw überspringen; **let's ~ to the interesting parts** lasst uns direkt zu den interessanten Dingen übergehen **II.** *vt* <-pp-> ❶ *(hop with rope)* **to ~ rope** seilspringen ❷ *(leave out)* überspringen, auslassen ❸ *(not participate in)* nicht teilnehmen (an +*dat*); *meal, dance* auslassen; *(avoid) class* schwänzen *fam; work* blau machen *fam; meeting, practice* etw sausen lassen **III.** *n* Hüpfer *m*
ˈ**ski pants** *npl* Skihose *f*
ˈ**ski pass** *n* Skipass *m*
ˈ**ski pole** *n* Skistock *m*
skipper [ˈskɪp·ər] **I.** *n* NAUT Kapitän *m* [zur See]; AVIAT [Flug]kapitän *m;* SPORTS [Mannschafts]kapitän *m; (form of address)* Kapitän *m* **II.** *vt* befehligen; **to ~ a ship** Kapitän eines Schiffes sein; **to ~ a team** Mannschaftsführer sein

'ski resort *n* Wintersportort *m*

skirmish <*pl* -es> ['skɜr·mɪʃ] **I.** *n* MIL Gefecht *nt;* (*argument*) Wortgefecht *nt* **II.** *vi* MIL sich *dat* Gefechte liefern (**with** mit +*dat*); (*fig: argue*) sich heftig streiten (**with** mit +*dat*)

skirt [skɜrt] **I.** *n* Rock *m* **II.** *vt* ❶ (*encircle*) umgeben; (*proceed around edge of*) umfahren ❷ (*avoid*) *questions* [bewusst] umgehen

'ski slope *n* Skipiste *f*

'ski suit *n* Skianzug *m*

skit [skɪt] *n* [satirischer] Sketch (**about/on** über +*akk*), Parodie *f* (**about/on** auf +*akk*)

skittish ['skɪṭ·ɪʃ] *adj* ❶ (*nervous*) *horse, person* nervös ❷ (*playful*) *person* übermütig

skivvy ['skɪv·i] *n* (*fam*) ■ **skivvies** *pl* Unterwäsche *f*

skulk [skʌlk] *vi* ❶ (*lurk*) herumlungern *fam* ❷ (*move furtively*) schleichen

skull [skʌl] *n* Schädel *m;* **to get sth into one's** [**thick**] **~** (*fam*) etw in seinen Schädel hineinbekommen

'skullcap *n* ❶ (*top of skull*) Schädeldecke *f* ❷ REL Scheitelkäppchen *nt;* (*yarmulke*) Kippa[h] *f*

skunk [skʌŋk] *n* ❶ (*animal*) Stinktier *nt* ❷ (*sl: marijuana*) Shit *m o nt*

sky [skaɪ] *n* ❶ (*the sky*) Himmel *m;* **in the ~** am Himmel ❷ (*area above earth*) ■ **skies** *pl* Himmel *m;* **cloudy skies** bewölkter Himmel ▶ PHRASES: **the ~'s the limit** alles ist möglich

'sky-blue *adj attr* himmelblau

'skydiving *n* Fallschirmspringen *nt*

sky-'high **I.** *adv* (*direction*) [hoch] in die Luft; (*position*) [hoch] am Himmel; **to go ~** *prices* in die Höhe schnellen **II.** *adj* (*fig*) *prices, premiums* Schwindel erregend hoch

'skyjack **I.** *vt* entführen **II.** *n* Flugzeugentführung *f*

'skylark *n* Feldlerche *f*

'skylight *n* Oberlicht *nt;* (*in roof*) Dachfenster *nt*

'skyline *n of city* Skyline *f;* (*horizon*) Horizont *m*

skype [skaɪp] *vi, vt* TELEC, INET skypen (**with** mit)

'skyrocket *vi cost, price* in die Höhe schießen; **to ~ to fame/to power** *person* [auf einen Schlag] berühmt werden/zur Macht kommen

'skyscraper *n* Wolkenkratzer *m*

slab [slæb] *n* ❶ *of rock* Platte *f; of wood* Tafel *f;* (*in mortuary*) Tisch *m;* (*for paving*) Pflasterstein *m* ❷ *of food* [dicke] Scheibe; **a ~ of chocolate** eine Tafel Schokolade ❸ (*foundation of house*) Plattenfundament *nt*

slack [slæk] **I.** *adj* ❶ (*not taut*) schlaff ❷ (*pej: lazy*) *person* träge; **discipline has become very ~ lately** die Disziplin hat in letzter Zeit sehr nachgelassen ❸ (*not busy*) ruhig; *market* flau **II.** *adv* schlaff **III.** *n* Schlaffheit *f;* **the men pulled on the rope to take up the ~** die Männer zogen am Seil, um es zu spannen; **to cut sb some ~** (*fam*) jdm Spielraum einräumen *m* **IV.** *vi* (*fam*) faulenzen

◆**slack off** *vi* es langsamer angehen lassen

slacken ['slæk·ən] **I.** *vt* ❶ (*make less tight*) locker lassen; *grip* lockern ❷ (*reduce*) *pace* verlangsamen **II.** *vi* ❶ (*become less tight*) sich lockern ❷ (*diminish*) langsamer werden; *demand, intensity* nachlassen

slackening ['slæk·ən·ɪŋ] *n* ❶ (*loosening*) Lockern *nt* ❷ *of speed* Verlangsamung *f; of demand* Nachlassen *nt*

slacker ['slæk·ər] *n* (*fam*) Faulenzer(in) *m(f)*

slackness ['slæk·nɪs] *n* ❶ (*looseness*) Schlaffheit *f* ❷ (*lack of activity*) Nachlassen *nt;* (*in demand*) Flaute *f* ❸ (*pej: laziness*) Trägheit *f*

slacks [slæks] *npl* Hose *f;* **a pair of ~** eine Hose

slain [sleɪn] **I.** *vi, vt pp of* **slay** **II.** *n* (*liter*) ■ **the ~** *pl* die Gefallenen *pl*

slalom ['slal·əm] *n* Slalom *m*

slam [slæm] **I.** *n* ❶ (*sound*) Knall *m; of door* Zuschlagen *nt* ❷ (*punch*) Schlag *m;* (*push*) harter Stoß **II.** *vt* <-mm-> ❶ (*close*) *door* zuschlagen, zuknallen *fam;* **to ~ the door in sb's face** jdm die Tür vor der Nase zuschlagen ❷ (*hit hard*) schlagen ❸ (*fam: criticize*) heruntermachen **III.** *vi* <-mm-> ❶ (*shut noisily*) zuschlagen ❷ (*hit hard*) **to ~ into a car** ein Auto rammen; **to ~ on the brakes** voll auf die Bremse treten

slammer ['slæm·ər] *n* (*sl*) ■ **the ~** das Kittchen *fam,* der Knast *fam*

slander ['slæn·dər] LAW **I.** *n* ❶ (*action*) üble Nachrede, Verleumdung *f* ❷ (*statement*) Verleumdung *f* **II.** *vt* verleumden

slanderer ['slæn·dər·ər] *n* Verleumder(in) *m(f)*

slanderous ['slæn·dər·əs] *adj* verleumderisch

slang [slæŋ] **I.** *n* Slang *m;* **army ~** Militärjargon *m* **II.** *adj attr* Slang-; **~ term** [*or* **word**] Slangausdruck *m*

slangy ['slæŋ·i] *adj* (*fam*) salopp

slant [slænt] **I.** *vi* sich neigen; **to ~ to the right** sich nach rechts neigen **II.** *vt* ❶ (*make diagonal*) ausrichten ❷ (*make appealing to*) zuschneiden; (*pej: in biased way*) zurechtbiegen *fig fam* **III.** *n* ❶ (*slope*) Neigung *f* ❷ (*perspective*) Tendenz *f;* **to have a right-wing ~** *newspaper* rechtsgerichtet sein

slanting ['slæn·tɪŋ] *adj* schräg

slap [slæp] **I.** *n* ❶ (*with hand*) Klaps *m fam;* **to give sb a ~ on the back** jdm [anerkennend] auf den Rücken klopfen; (*fig*) jdn loben; **a ~ in the face** eine Ohrfeige; (*fig*) ein Schlag ins Gesicht ❷ (*noise*) Klatschen *nt* **II.** *adv* (*fam*) genau; **the child sat down ~ in the middle of the floor** das Kind setzte sich mitten auf den Boden **III.** *vt* <-pp-> ❶ (*with hand*) schlagen; **to ~ sb on the back** jdn auf den Rücken schlagen; (*in congratulations*) jdm [anerkennend] auf die Schulter klopfen ❷ (*strike*) schlagen (**against** gegen +*akk*) ❸ (*fam: impose*) **to ~ a fine on sth** eine Geldstrafe auf etw *akk* draufschlagen **IV.** *vi water* ■ **to ~ against sth** gegen etw *akk* schlagen

◆**slap down** *vt* ❶ (*put down*) hinknallen *fam* ❷ (*silence rudely*) ■**to ~ sb down** jdn zusammenstauchen *fam*

'slapdash *adj* (*pej fam*) schlampig

'slapstick *n* Slapstick *m*

slash [slæʃ] **I.** *vt* ❶ (*cut deeply*) **to ~ sb's tires** jds Reifen aufschlitzen *fam;* **to ~ one's wrists** sich *dat* die Pulsadern aufschneiden; **~ed sleeve** Ärmel *m* mit Schlitz ❷ (*reduce*) *budget* kürzen; *prices* senken; *staff* abbauen; *workforce* verringern **II.** *vi* (*with a knife*) ■**to ~ at sb/sth** [mit einem Messer] auf jdn/etw losgehen **III.** *n* <*pl* -es> ❶ (*cut on person*) Schnittwunde *f;* (*in object*) Schnitt *m* ❷ (*punctuation mark*) Schrägstrich *m* ❸ (*in clothing*) Schlitz *m*

slat [slæt] *n* Leiste *f;* (*in grid*) Stab *m;* **wooden ~** Holzlatte *f*

slate [sleɪt] **I.** *n* ❶ (*rock*) Schiefer *m* ❷ (*on roof*) [Dach]schindel *f* ❸ POL (*list of candidates*) Kandidatenliste *f* ► PHRASES: **to wipe the ~ clean** reinen Tisch machen **II.** *adj* Schiefer- **III.** *vt* ❶ (*cover with slates*) decken ❷ *usu passive* (*assign*) ■**to be ~d for sth** für etw *akk* vorgesehen sein

slaughter ['slɔ·t̬ər] **I.** *vt* ❶ (*kill*) abschlachten; *animal* schlachten ❷ SPORTS (*fam*) vom Platz fegen **II.** *n* ❶ (*killing*) *of people* Abschlachten *nt;* *of animals* Schlachten *nt* ❷ (*fam: in sports*) Schlappe *f*

'slaughterhouse *n* Schlachthaus *nt,* Schlachthof *m*

Slav [slav] **I.** *n* Slawe, Slawin *m, f* **II.** *adj* slawisch

slave [sleɪv] **I.** *n* Sklave, Sklavin *m, f* **II.** *vi* schuften; ■**to ~ [away] at sth** sich mit etw *dat* herumschlagen

'slave driver *n* Sklaventreiber(in) *m(f)*

slaver ['sleɪ·vər] **I.** *vi* ❶ (*drool*) *animal* geifern; *person* speicheln ❷ (*pej: show excitement*) gieren (**over** nach +*dat*) **II.** *n animal* Geifer *m;* *person* Speichel *m*

slavery ['sleɪ·və·ri] *n* Sklaverei *f;* (*fig*) sklavische Abhängigkeit

'slave trade *n* (*hist*) Sklavenhandel *m*

Slavic ['sla·vɪk] *adj* slawisch

slavish ['sleɪ·vɪʃ] *adj* ❶ (*without originality*) sklavisch ❷ (*servile*) sklavisch

Slavonic [slə·'van·ɪk] *adj* slawisch

slay [sleɪ] *vt* ❶ <slew, slain> (*liter or old: kill*) *dragon* erlegen; *enemy* bezwingen ❷ <slew, slain> (*murder*) ■**to be slain** ermordet werden

sleaze [sliz] *n* Korruption *f*

sleazebag ['sliz·bæg] *n* (*fam*) schmieriger Typ

sleazy ['sli·zi] *adj* anrüchig; *area* zweifelhaft; **~ bar** Spelunke *f fam*

sled [sled] **I.** *n* Schlitten *m* **II.** *vi* <-dd-> **to go ~ding** Schlittenfahren [*o* DIAL Rodeln] gehen **III.** *vt* <-dd-> mit dem Schlitten transportieren

sledge [sledʒ] *n* ❶ (*for snow*) Schlitten *m* ❷ (*fam: sledgehammer*) Vorschlaghammer *m*

'sledgehammer *n* Vorschlaghammer *m*

sleek [slik] *adj* ❶ (*glossy*) *fur, hair* geschmeidig; (*streamlined*) elegant; *car* schnittig ❷ (*fig: in manner*) [aal]glatt *pej* ❸ (*well-groomed*) gepflegt

sleep [slip] **I.** *n* ❶ (*resting state*) Schlaf *m;* (*nap*) Nickerchen *nt;* **I didn't get to ~ until 4 a.m.** ich bin erst um 4 Uhr morgens eingeschlafen; **to lose ~ over sth** wegen einer S. *gen* schlaflose Nächte haben; **to put sb to ~** jdn einschlafen lassen *fig* ❷ (*in eyes*) Schlaf *m* ► PHRASES: **to be able to do sth in one's ~** etw im Schlaf beherrschen **II.** *vi* <slept, slept> schlafen; **~ tight!** schlaf schön!; **to ~ late** lange schlafen, ausschlafen; **to ~ soundly** [tief und] fest schlafen; ■**to ~ with sb** mit jdm schlafen ► PHRASES: **to ~ on it** eine Nacht darüber schlafen **III.** *vt* **to ~ ten** zehn Personen beherbergen können; **to ~ the night with sb** bei jdm übernachten

◆**sleep around** *vi* (*fam*) herumschlafen; (*pej: be unfaithful*) fremdgehen *fam*

◆**sleep in** *vi* ❶ (*sleep late*) ausschlafen ❷ (*sleep on premises*) im Hause wohnen

◆**sleep off** *vt hangover* ausschlafen; *cold, headache* sich gesund schlafen

◆**sleep together** *vi* (*have sex*) miteinander schlafen; (*share bedroom*) zusammen [in einem Zimmer] schlafen

sleeper ['sli·pər] *n* ❶ (*person*) Schläfer(in) *m(f);* **to be a light ~** einen leichten Schlaf haben ❷ (*train*) Zug *m* mit Schlafwagenabteil; (*sleeping car*) Schlafwagen *m;* (*berth*) Schlafwagenplatz *m* ❸ (*children's pajamas*) ■**~s** *pl* Schlafanzug *m* ❹ (*spy*) Schläfer *m* ❺ (*sofa*) Bettsofa *nt*

'sleeper cell *n* MIL, POL Schläferzelle *f*

sleepiness ['sli·pɪ·nɪs] *n* Schläfrigkeit *f*

sleeping ['sli·pɪŋ] *adj attr* schlafend *attr* ► PHRASES: **let ~ dogs lie** (*prov*) schlafende Hunde soll man nicht wecken *prov*

'sleeping bag *n* Schlafsack *m*

Sleeping 'Beauty *n* Dornröschen *nt*

'sleeping car *n* Schlafwagen *m*

'sleeping pill *n* Schlaftablette *f*

'sleeping sickness *n* Schlafkrankheit *f*

sleepless ['slip·lɪs] *adj* schlaflos

'sleepwalk *vi* schlafwandeln

'sleepwalker *n* Schlafwandler(in) *m(f)*

sleepy ['sli·pi] *adj* ❶ (*drowsy*) schläfrig ❷ (*quiet*) *town* verschlafen *fam*

'sleepyhead ['sli·pi·hed] *n* (*fam*) Schlafmütze *f*

sleet [slit] **I.** *n* Eisregen *m* **II.** *vi impers* **it is ~ing** es fällt Eisregen

sleeve [sliv] *n* ❶ (*on clothing*) Ärmel *m;* **to roll up one's ~s** (*for hard work*) die Ärmel hochkrempeln *a. fig* ❷ (*for rod, tube*) Manschette *f* ❸ (*for record*) [Schallplatten]hülle *f* ► PHRASES: **to have sth up one's ~** etw im Ärmel haben

sleeveless ['sliv·lɪs] *adj* ärmellos *attr*

sleigh [sleɪ] *n* Pferdeschlitten *m*

sleight of 'hand [ˌslaɪt-] *n* (*in tricks*) Fingerfer-

S

tigkeit *f;* (*fig*) Trick *m*

slender ['slen·dər] *adj* ① *legs, waist* schlank; *railings, poles* schmal ② *means, resources, majority* knapp

slept [slept] *pt, pp of* **sleep**

slew¹ [slu] *pt of* **slay**

slew² [slu] *n* (*fam*) Haufen *m fam*

slice [slaɪs] **I.** *n* ① *of bread, ham* Scheibe *f; of cake, pizza* Stück *nt* ② (*portion*) Anteil *m* **II.** *vt* ① (*cut in slices*) in Scheiben schneiden; *cake, pizza* in Stücke schneiden ② (*in golf*) *ball* verschlagen; (*in tennis*) anschneiden **III.** *vi* ① (*food*) sich schneiden lassen ② (*cut*) ■ **to ~ through sth** etw durchschneiden

◆**slice off** *vt* abschneiden

◆**slice up** *vt* ① (*make slices*) in Scheiben schneiden; *bread* aufschneiden; *cake, pizza* in Stücke schneiden ② (*divide*) *profits* aufteilen

sliced [slaɪst] *adj* geschnitten; *bread* aufgeschnitten

slicer ['slaɪ·sər] *n* Schneidemaschine *f*

slick [slɪk] **I.** *adj* ① (*skillful*) gekonnt; (*great*) geil *sl; performance* tadellos ② (*pej: overly polished*) *answer, manner* glatt; (*clever*) gewieft ③ (*shiny*) *hair* geschniegelt *fam;* (*slippery*) *road, floor* glatt **II.** *n* (*oil slick*) Ölteppich *m* **III.** *vt* **to ~ back one's hair** sich *dat* die Haare nach hinten klatschen *fam*

slide [slaɪd] **I.** *vi* <slid, slid *or* slidden> ① (*glide*) rutschen; (*smoothly*) gleiten; **to ~ down the handrail** das Geländer herunterrutschen ② (*decline in value*) *currency* sinken ► PHRASES: **to let things ~** die Dinge schleifen lassen **II.** *vt* <slid, slid *or* slidden> **can you ~ your seat forward a little?** können Sie mit Ihrem Sitz etwas nach vorne rutschen?; **she slid the hatch open** sie schob die Luke auf **III.** *n* ① (*act of sliding*) Rutschen *nt* ② (*at playground*) Rutsche *f* ③ GEOG (*landslide*) **rock ~** Felslawine *f* ④ *usu sing* (*decline*) Sinken *nt; of a currency* Wertverlust *m* ⑤ (*in photography*) Dia *nt*

'**slide projector** *n* Diaprojektor *m*

'**slide rule** *n* Rechenschieber *m*

sliding ['slaɪ·dɪŋ] *adj attr* Schiebe-

sliding 'scale *n* FIN gleitende Skala

slight [slaɪt] **I.** *adj* ① (*small*) *chance, possibility* gering; *mistake* klein; *injury, accent* leicht; **there's been a ~ improvement in the situation** die Situation hat sich geringfügig gebessert; **there was a ~ smell of onions in the air** es roch ein wenig nach Zwiebeln; **he has a ~ tendency to exaggerate** er neigt etwas zu Übertreibungen; **not in the ~est** nicht im Geringsten ② (*slim*) *person* zierlich ③ (*superficial*) *play, plot* bescheiden **II.** *n* Beleidigung *f* **III.** *vt* beleidigen

slightly ['slaɪt·li] *adv* ein wenig, etwas; **I feel ~ peculiar** ich fühle mich irgendwie komisch; **to know sb ~** jdn flüchtig kennen

slim [slɪm] *adj* <-mm-> ① *person, figure* schlank; *waist* schmal; *object* dünn ② *chance, possibility* gering; *profits, income* mager; **~ pickings** magere Ausbeute

◆**slim down I.** *vi* abnehmen **II.** *vt workforce* reduzieren

slime [slaɪm] *n* (*substance*) Schleim *m*

'**slimebag** *n* (*pej fam*) Schleimer(in) *m(f)*

'**slimeball** *n* (*pej fam*) Schleimer(in) *m(f)*

slimy ['slaɪ·mi] *adj slug, pond, seaweed* schleimig; (*fig*) *character, person* schleimig

sling [slɪŋ] **I.** *n* ① (*for broken arm, for lifting*) Schlinge *f;* (*for baby*) Tragetuch *nt* ② (*weapon*) Schleuder *f* **II.** *vt* <slung, slung> ① (*fling*) werfen, schleudern ② (*suspend*) ■ **to be slung from sth** von etw *dat* herunterhängen; **soldiers with rifles slung over their shoulders** Soldaten mit geschulterten Gewehren

slingshot ['slɪŋ·ʃat] *n* [Stein]schleuder *f*

slink <slunk, slunk> [slɪŋk] *vi* schleichen; ■ **to ~ away** [sich] davonschleichen

slinky ['slɪŋ·ki] *adj* verführerisch

slip [slɪp] **I.** *n* ① (*in price, value*) Fall *m* ② (*for ordering*) Formular *nt;* (*sales slip*) Kassenzettel *m;* **a ~ of paper** ein Stück *nt* Papier ③ (*mistake*) Flüchtigkeitsfehler *m;* **a ~ of the tongue** ein Versprecher *m* ④ (*petticoat*) Unterrock *m* ► PHRASES: **to give sb the ~** jdn abhängen **II.** *vi* <-pp-> ① (*lose position*) *person* ausrutschen; *knife, hand* abrutschen; *tires* wegrutschen; *clutch* schleifen ② (*move quietly*) **to ~ into the house** ins Haus schleichen; **to ~ through a gap** durch ein Loch schlüpfen ③ (*put on*) **to ~ into sth more comfortable** [sich] etwas Bequemeres anziehen ④ (*decline*) *dollar, price, productivity* sinken ⑤ (*make mistake*) *person* sich versprechen; **to let sth ~** *secret* etw ausplaudern ⑥ (*start to have*) ■ **to ~ into sth** *routine, habit* sich *dat* etw angewöhnen; **to ~ into bad habits** sich *dat* schlechte Gewohnheiten aneignen ► PHRASES: **to ~ through sb's fingers** jdm entkommen **III.** *vt* <-pp-> ① (*put smoothly*) **she ~ped the key under the mat** sie schob den Schlüssel unter die Matte; **he ~ped the letter into his pocket** er steckte den Brief in seine Tasche ② (*escape from*) **to ~ sb's attention** jds Aufmerksamkeit entgehen; **sth ~s sb's mind** jd vergisst etw ③ MED **to ~ a disk** sich *dat* einen Bandscheibenschaden zuziehen

◆**slip away** *vi* ① (*leave unnoticed*) *person* sich wegstehlen ② (*not be kept*) ■ **to ~ away [from sb]** *control, power* [jdm] entgleiten; **they didn't let the victory ~ away from them** sie haben sich den Sieg nicht entgehen lassen ③ (*time*) verstreichen *geh*

◆**slip by** *vi* ① (*pass quickly*) *years* verfliegen ② (*move past*) *person* vorbeihuschen ③ (*go unnoticed*) *mistake, remark* durchgehen

◆**slip down** *vi pants, socks* herunterrutschen

◆**slip in I.** *vt* einbringen **II.** *vi person* sich hereinschleichen

◆**slip off I.** *vi* ① (*leave unnoticed*) sich davonstehlen ② (*fall off*) herunterrutschen **II.** *vt* ab-

S

streifen

◆**slip on** *vt* anziehen; *ring* sich *dat* anstecken

◆**slip out** *vi* ❶ (*for short time*) **to ~ out for a second** kurz weggehen ❷ *words, secret* herausrutschen

◆**slip up** *vi* einen Fehler begehen

'slipknot *n* Schlaufe *f*

'slip-on I. *adj attr* **~ shoes** Slipper *pl* **II.** *n* ■ **~s** *pl* Slipper *pl*

slippage ['slɪp·ɪdʒ] *n* (*in popularity, price*) Sinken *nt*

slipper ['slɪp·ər] *n* Hausschuh *m*

slippery ['slɪp·ə·ri] *adj* ❶ *surface, object* rutschig; (*fig*) *situation* unsicher; *road* glatt ❷ (*pej: untrustworthy*) windig *fam* ▶ PHRASES: **to be as ~ as an eel** aalglatt sein

'slipshod *adj* schludrig *fam*

'slip-up *n* Fehler *m*

slit [slɪt] **I.** *vt* <-tt-, slit, slit> aufschlitzen; **to ~ one's wrists** sich *dat* die Pulsadern aufschneiden; **~** *skirt* geschlitzter Rock **II.** *n* ❶ (*tear*) Schlitz *m* ❷ (*narrow opening*) *of eyes* Schlitz *m; of door* Spalt *m*

slither ['slɪð·ər] *vi lizard, snake* kriechen; *person* rutschen

sliver ['slɪv·ər] *n* ❶ (*shard*) Splitter *m* ❷ (*small piece*) *of cheese* Scheibchen *nt; of cake* Stückchen *nt*

slob [slab] *n* (*pej fam*) Gammler(in) *m(f)*

slobber ['slab·ər] **I.** *vi* sabbern **II.** *n* Sabber *m*

slobbery ['slab·ə·ri] *adj* (*wet*) feucht; (*slobbered on*) vollgesabbert *fam;* **~ kiss** feuchter Kuss

slog [slag] **I.** *n* (*fam: hard work*) Schufterei *f;* (*strenuous hike*) [Gewalt]marsch *m* **II.** *vi* <-gg-> (*fam*) ❶ (*walk*) **to ~ up the hill** sich auf den Hügel schleppen ❷ (*work*) sich durcharbeiten (**through** durch +*akk*)

slogan ['sloʊ·gən] *n* Slogan *m;* **campaign ~** Wahlspruch *m*

sloop [slup] *n* NAUT Slup *f*

slop [slap] **I.** *n* ❶ (*pej fam: food*) Schlabber *m* ❷ (*waste*) ■ **~s** *pl* Abfälle *pl;* (*food waste*) Essensreste *pl* **II.** *vt* <-pp-> (*fam*) verschütten **III.** *vi* <-pp-> (*fam*) *a liquid* überschwappen

slope [sloʊp] **I.** *n* ❶ (*hill*) Hang *m;* **ski ~** Skipiste *f* ❷ (*angle*) Neigung *f;* **~ of a roof** Dachschräge *f* ❸ MATH (*on graph*) Gefälle *nt* **II.** *vi* ❶ (*incline/decline*) *ground* abfallen; *roof* geneigt sein; ■ **to ~ down/up** abfallen/ansteigen ❷ (*lean*) sich neigen **III.** *vt roof, path* schräg anlegen

sloping ['sloʊ·pɪŋ] *adj attr* schräg; (*upwards*) ansteigend; (*downwards*) abfallend

sloppiness ['slap·ɪ·nɪs] *n* Schlampigkeit *f*

sloppy ['slap·i] *adj* ❶ (*careless*) schlampig ❷ (*hum o pej: overly romantic*) kitschig ❸ (*fam: loose-fitting*) schlabb[e]rig

slosh [slaʃ] (*fam*) **I.** *vt* (*pour carelessly*) **I ~ed some water on my face** ich habe mir etwas Wasser ins Gesicht geworfen **II.** *vi* ❶ (*splash around*) *a liquid* [herum]schwappen; *person* [herum]planschen ❷ (*move through water*) waten

sloshed [slaʃt] *adj pred* (*fam*) besoffen *sl*

slot [slat] *n* ❶ (*narrow opening*) Schlitz *m;* (*groove*) Rille *f;* (*for money*) Geldeinwurf *m;* (*for mail*) Briefschlitz *m* ❷ (*in TV programming*) Sendezeit *f*

sloth [slaθ] *n* ❶ (*laziness*) Trägheit *f* ❷ (*animal*) Faultier *nt;* (*pej: person*) Faultier *nt a. hum o iron*

slothful ['slaθ·fəl] *adj* faul

'slot machine *n* Spielautomat *m*

slouch [slaʊtʃ] **I.** *n* <*pl* -es> (*bad posture*) krumme Haltung ▶ PHRASES: **to <u>be</u> no ~ [at [doing] sth]** (*fam*) etw gut können **II.** *vi* ❶ (*have shoulders bent*) gebeugt stehen ❷ (*move lazily*) **to ~ along the street** die Straße entlangschlendern

slough[1] [slu] *n* **a ~ of despair** ein Sumpf *m* der Verzweiflung *liter*

slough[2] [slʌf] *vt* **to ~ off dead skin** sich häuten

Slovak ['sloʊ·vak] **I.** *n* ❶ (*person*) Slowake, Slowakin *m, f* ❷ (*language*) Slowakisch *nt* **II.** *adj* slowakisch

Slovakia [sloʊ·'va·ki·ə] *n* die Slowakei

Slovakian [sloʊ·'va·ki·ən] **I.** *n* ❶ (*person*) Slowake, Slowakin *m, f* ❷ (*language*) Slowakisch *nt* **II.** *adj* slowakisch

Slovene ['sloʊ·vin] **I.** *n* ❶ (*person*) Slowene, Slowenin *m, f* ❷ (*language*) Slowenisch *nt* **II.** *adj* slowenisch

Slovenia [sloʊ·'vi·ni·ə] *n* Slowenien *nt*

Slovenian [sloʊ·'vi·ni·ən] **I.** *n* ❶ (*person*) Slowene, Slowenin *m, f* ❷ (*language*) Slowenisch *nt* **II.** *adj* slowenisch

slovenly ['slʌv·ən·li] *adj* schlampig; *appearance* ungepflegt

slow [sloʊ] **I.** *adj* ❶ (*without speed*) langsam; *business, market* flau; ■ **to be ~ to do sth** lange brauchen, um etw zu tun ❷ (*pej sl: not quick-witted*) begriffsstutzig; **to be [a little] ~ on the uptake** [ein wenig] schwer von Begriff sein ❸ *clock, watch* **to be [*or* run] [10 minutes] ~** [10 Minuten] nachgehen **II.** *vi* langsamer werden; **to ~ to a crawl** fast zum Stillstand kommen **III.** *vt* verlangsamen

◆**slow down I.** *vt* verlangsamen, reduzieren; *speed* drosseln **II.** *vi* ❶ (*reduce speed*) langsamer werden; *car* langsamer fahren; (*speak*) langsamer sprechen; (*walk*) langsamer laufen ❷ (*relax more*) kürzertreten *fam*

'slowdown *n* ECON Verlangsamung *f;* **economic ~** Konjunkturabschwächung *f*

'slow lane *n* (*fam*) Kriechspur *f*

slowly ['sloʊ·li] *adv* langsam; **~ but surely** langsam, aber sicher

slow 'motion I. *n* FILM Zeitlupe *f* **II.** *adj* Zeitlupen-

slowness ['sloʊ·nɪs] *n* ❶ (*lack of speed*) Langsamkeit *f* ❷ (*lack of intelligence*) Begriffsstutzigkeit *f*

'slowpoke *n* (*fam*) lahme Ente

SLR, SLR camera [ˌes·el·'ar-] *n* PHOT *abbrev of*

S

single-lens reflex (camera) einäugige Spiegelreflexkamera

sludge [slʌdʒ] *n* Schlamm *m*

slug[1] [slʌg] *n* ❶ (*bullet*) Kugel *f* ❷ (*fam: swig*) Schluck *m*

slug[2] [slʌg] *n* ZOOL Nacktschnecke *f*

slug[3] ['slʌg] **I.** *vt* <-gg-> (*fam*) ❶ (*hit with hard blow*) ■**to ~ sb** jdm eine verpassen *sl* ❷ (*fight physically or verbally*) **to ~ it out** es untereinander ausfechten **II.** *n* (*heavy blow*) gehöriger Schlag

sluggish ['slʌg·ɪʃ] *adj* träge; *market* flau; *engine* lahm

sluice [slus] **I.** *n* Schleuse *f* **II.** *vi* (*flow out*) ■**to ~ out [from sth]** *water* herausschießen [aus etw *dat*]

slum [slʌm] **I.** *n* Slum *m*, Elendsviertel *nt* **II.** *vt* <-mm-> **to ~ it** (*iron*) primitiv leben

slumber ['slʌm·bər] (*poet*) **I.** *vi* schlummern *geh* **II.** *n* (*sleep*) Schlummer *m geh;* (*fig*) Dornröschenschlaf *m;* **~ party** *Party mit anschließender Übernachtung, zu der nur Mädchen eingeladen sind*

slump [slʌmp] **I.** *n* ECON ❶ (*decline*) [plötzliche] Abnahme; **~ in prices** Preissturz *m* ❷ (*recession*) Rezession *f;* **economic ~** Wirtschaftskrise *f* **II.** *vi* ❶ (*fall dramatically*) *prices* stürzen; *numbers, sales* zurückgehen ❷ (*fall heavily*) fallen

slung [slʌŋ] *pt, pp of* **sling**

slunk [slʌŋk] *pt, pp of* **slink**

slur [slɜr] **I.** *vt* <-rr-> ❶ (*pronounce unclearly*) undeutlich artikulieren; (*because of alcohol*) lallen ❷ (*damage sb's reputation*) verleumden **II.** *n* Verleumdung *f;* **to cast a ~ on sb/sth** jdn/etw in einem schlechten Licht erscheinen lassen

slurp [slɜrp] (*fam*) **I.** *vi* (*drink noisily*) schlürfen **II.** *vt* schlürfen **III.** *n* Schlürfen *nt*

slurry ['slɜr·i] *n* TECH Brei *m*

slush [slʌʃ] *n* ❶ (*melting snow*) [Schnee]matsch *m* ❷ (*pej: very sentimental language*) Gefühlsduselei *f*

'slush fund *n* (*pej*) Schmiergeldfonds *m*

slushy ['slʌʃ·i] *adj* ❶ (*melting*) matschig ❷ (*very sentimental*) kitschig

slut [slʌt] *n* (*pej*) Schlampe *f derb*

slutty ['slʌţ·i] *adj* (*pej*) schlampig

sly [slaɪ] *adj* ❶ (*secretive*) verstohlen; *smile* verschmitzt; **on the ~** heimlich ❷ (*cunning*) gerissen ▶ PHRASES: **as ~ as a fox** schlau wie ein Fuchs

slyly ['slaɪ·li] *adv* ❶ (*secretively*) verstohlen; *grin* verschmitzt ❷ (*deceptively*) gerissen

smack[1] [smæk] **I.** *n* ❶ (*slap*) [klatschender] Schlag ❷ (*hearty kiss*) Schmatz *m* ❸ (*loud noise*) Knall *m* **II.** *adv* ❶ (*exactly*) direkt; **his shot landed ~ in the middle of the target** sein Schuss landete haargenau im Zentrum der Zielscheibe ❷ (*forcefully*) voll *fam;* **I walked ~ into a lamppost** ich lief voll gegen einen Laternenpfahl **III.** *vt* ❶ (*slap*) ■**to ~ sb** jdm eine knallen *fam;* **to ~ sb's butt** jdm den Hintern versohlen ❷ (*slap sth against sth*) ■**to ~ sth on sth** etw auf etw *akk* knallen *fam*

◆**smack of** *vt* ■**to ~ of sth** nach etw *dat* riechen

smack[2] [smæk] *n* (*sl*) Heroin *nt*

smack-'dab *adv* (*fam*) genau

smacker ['smæk·ər] *n* (*fam*) ❶ (*loud kiss*) Schmatz[er] *m fam* ❷ *usu pl* (*dollar*) Dollar *m*

small [smɔl] **I.** *adj* ❶ (*not large*) klein; *amount a.* gering; **in ~ quantities** in kleinen Mengen; **~ child** Kleinkind *nt* ❷ (*insignificant*) unbedeutend; **~ consolation** ein schwacher Trost; **to make sb feel ~** jdn niedermachen *fam* ▶ PHRASES: **it's a ~ world!** (*prov*) die Welt ist klein! **II.** *n* **the ~ of the back** das Kreuz

'small arms *npl* Handfeuerwaffen *pl*

small 'business *n* Kleinunternehmen *nt*

small 'businessman *n* Kleinunternehmer *m*

small 'change *n* Kleingeld *nt;* (*fig: small amount*) Klacks *m fam*

small-'claims court *n* LAW *Zivilgericht für Bagatellfälle*

'small fry *n + sing/pl vb* (*fam*) ❶ (*child*) junges Gemüse *hum* ❷ (*unimportant people*) kleine Fische

small in'testine *n* Dünndarm *m*

smallish ['smɔ·lɪʃ] *adj* [eher] klein

small-'minded *adj* (*pej*) engstirnig

smallness ['smɔl·nɪs] *n* Kleinheit *f*

'smallpox *n* Pocken *pl*

small 'print *n* ■**the ~** das Kleingedruckte

'small-scale <smaller-, smallest-> *adj* **~ map** Karte *f* in einem kleinen Maßstab; *business, conflict* klein

small 'screen *n* [Fernseh]bildschirm *m*

'small talk *n* Smalltalk *m o nt*

'small-time *adj* mickerig *fam; person* unbedeutend; **~ crook** kleiner Gauner

'small-town *adj attr values, ideals* kleinstädtisch, Kleinstadt-

smarmy ['smar·mi] *adj* (*pej*) schmeichlerisch

smart [smart] **I.** *adj* ❶ (*intelligent*) schlau, clever *fam; child* intelligent; **to make a ~ move** klug handeln ❷ (*stylish*) schick ❸ (*quick and forceful*) [blitz]schnell **II.** *n* ❶ (*sl*) ■**the ~s** *pl* die [nötige] Intelligenz ❷ (*sharp pain*) Schmerz *m* **III.** *vi eyes, wound* brennen

smart aleck [ˌsmart·'æl·ek] *n* (*pej fam*) Schlauberger(in) *m(f) fam*

'smart-ass *n* (*pej vulg*) Klugscheißer(in) *m(f) sl*

'smart bomb *n* MIL [laser]gelenkte Bombe

'smart card *n* COMPUT Chipkarte *f*

smarten ['smar·tən] **I.** *vt* ■**to ~ sth** ↔ **up** etw herrichten; *house, town* etw verschönern; ■**to ~ oneself** ↔ **up** sich in Schale werfen *fam* **II.** *vi* ■**to ~ up** mehr Wert auf sein Äußeres legen

smartness ['smart·nɪs] *n* Schlauheit *f*

smartphone, smart phone ['smɑrt·foʊn] *n* Smartphone *nt*

smash [smæʃ] **I.** *n* <*pl* -es> ❶ (*crashing sound*) Krachen *nt* ❷ SPORTS Schlag *m;* TEN-

NIS **forehand/backhand ~** Vorhand-/Rückhandschmetterball *m* ❸ (*inf: smash hit*) Superhit *m;* **box-office ~** Kassenschlager *m* **II.** *vt* ❶ (*break into pieces*) zerschlagen; *window* einschlagen ❷ (*strike against*) schmettern (**against** gegen +*akk*) ❸ SPORTS *record* brechen; *ball* schmettern **III.** *vi* ❶ (*break into pieces*) zerbrechen ❷ (*strike against*) prallen (**into** gegen +*akk*); ■**to ~ through sth** etw durchbrechen

◆**smash in** *vt* einschlagen

◆**smash up** *vt* (*damage*) zertrümmern, zerstören; (*crush*) zerdrücken; *car* zu Schrott fahren

smashed [smæʃt] *adj pred* (*sl*) sternhagelvoll *fam*

smash 'hit *n* Superhit *m fam*

smashing ['smæʃ·ɪŋ] *adj* ❶ (*crushing*) vernichtend ❷ (*fam: great*) **to be a ~ success** ein durchschlagender Erfolg sein

'smashup *n* schwerer Unfall; (*pile-up*) Karambolage *f*

smattering ['smæṭ·ər·ɪŋ] *n usu sing* ❶ (*very small amount*) **a ~ of applause** [ein] schwacher Applaus ❷ (*slight knowledge*) **to have a ~ of a foreign language** ein paar Brocken einer Fremdsprache können

smear [smɪr] **I.** *vt* ❶ (*spread messily*) ■**to ~ sth on sth** etw mit etw *dat* beschmieren ❷ (*attack reputation*) verunglimpfen **II.** *n* ❶ (*blotch*) Fleck *m* ❷ (*public accusations*) Verleumdung *f* ❸ MED *see* **Pap smear**

smell [smel] **I.** *n* ❶ (*sense of smelling*) Geruch *m;* **sense of ~** Geruchssinn *m;* **to have a ~ of sth** an etw *dat* riechen ❷ (*characteristic odor*) Geruch *m; of perfume* Duft *m* ❸ (*pej: bad odor*) Gestank *m* **II.** *vi* <**smelled** *or* **smelt, smelled** *or* **smelt**> ❶ (*perceive*) riechen ❷ + *adj* (*give off odor*) riechen; (*pleasantly*) duften; ■**to ~ of** [*or* **like**] **sth** nach etw *dat* riechen ❸ (*pej: smell bad*) stinken **III.** *vt* <**smelled** *or* **smelt, smelled** *or* **smelt**> riechen ▶ PHRASES: **to ~ a rat** den Braten riechen *fam*

◆**smell out** *vt* (*a. fig: discover by smelling*) aufspüren, entdecken

'smelling salts *npl* Riechfläschchen *nt*

smelly ['smel·i] *adj* (*pej*) stinkend *attr*

smelt[1] [smelt] *vt ore* verschmelzen

smelt[2] [smelt] *n* ZOOL (*fish*) Stint *m*

smelt[3] [smelt] *vi, vt pt, pp of* **smell**

smidgen, smidgin ['smɪdʒ·ən] *n* ■**a ~ ...** ein [klitzekleines] bisschen ...; *of liquid* ein winziges Schlückchen

smile [smaɪl] **I.** *n* Lächeln *nt;* **to be all ~s** über das ganze Gesicht strahlen; **to give sb a ~** jdm zulächeln **II.** *vi* ❶ (*produce a smile*) lächeln; ■**to ~ at sb** jdn anlächeln ❷ (*look favorably upon*) ■**to ~ on sb** es gut mit jdm meinen **III.** *vt* **the hostess ~d a welcome** die Gastgeberin lächelte einladend

smiley ['smaɪ·li] *adj* immer lächelnd *attr*

'smiley face *n* COMPUT Smiley *m*

smiling ['smaɪ·lɪŋ] *adj* lächelnd, strahlend

smirk [smɜrk] (*pej*) **I.** *vi* grinsen; ■**to ~ at sb** jdn süffisant anlächeln **II.** *n* Grinsen *nt*

smith [smɪθ] *n* Schmied *m*

smithereens [ˌsmɪð·ə·'rinz] *npl* **to smash sth to ~** etw in tausend Stücke schlagen

smitten ['smɪt·ən] *adj pred* (*in love*) ■**to be ~ with sb/sth** in jdn/etw vernarrt sein

smock [smak] *n* [Arbeits]kittel *m*

smocking ['smak·ɪŋ] *n* FASHION Smokarbeit *f*

smog [smag] *n* Smog *m*

smoke [smoʊk] **I.** *n* ❶ (*from burning*) Rauch *m;* **a puff of ~** ein Rauchwölkchen *nt* ❷ (*act of smoking*) **to have a ~** eine rauchen *fam* ❸ (*fam: cigarettes*) ■**~s** *pl* Glimmstängel *pl* ▶ PHRASES: **to go up in ~** in Rauch [und Flammen] aufgehen **II.** *vt* ❶ (*use tobacco*) rauchen ❷ FOOD räuchern ▶ PHRASES: **put that in your pipe and ~ it!** schreib dir das hinter die Ohren! **III.** *vi* rauchen

◆**smoke out** *vt* ausräuchern; (*fig*) entlarven

'smoke bomb *n* MIL Rauchbombe *f*

smoked [smoʊkt] *adj* geräuchert; **~ fish** Räucherfisch *m*

'smoke detector *n* Rauchmelder *m*

smokeless ['smoʊk·lɪs] *adj* (*without smoke*) rauchfrei

smoker ['smoʊ·kər] *n* ❶ (*person*) Raucher(in) *m(f);* **~'s cough** Raucherhusten *m* ❷ (*compartment in train*) Raucherabteil *nt* ❸ (*device*) Räuchergefäß *nt*

'smokescreen *n* ❶ (*pretext*) Vorwand *m* ❷ (*smoke cloud*) Rauchvorhang *m*

'smoke signal *n* Rauchzeichen *nt*

'smokestack *n* Schornstein *m*

smoking ['smoʊ·kɪŋ] *n* Rauchen *nt;* **~ ban** Rauchverbot *nt*

smoky ['smoʊ·ki] *adj* ❶ (*filled with smoke*) verraucht ❷ (*producing smoke*) rauchend *attr* ❸ (*tasting of smoke*) rauchig

smolder ['smoʊl·dər] *vi* ❶ (*burn slowly*) schwelen; *cigarette* glimmen; (*fig*) *dispute* schwelen ❷ (*repressed emotions*) **to ~ with rage** vor Zorn glühen

smooch [smutʃ] **I.** *vi* (*fam: kiss vigorously*) knutschen; (*tenderly*) schmusen **II.** *n usu sing* (*fam: vigorous*) Knutschen *nt;* (*tender*) Schmusen *nt*

smooth [smuð] **I.** *adj* ❶ (*not rough*) glatt; *sea* ruhig ❷ (*free from difficulty*) problemlos; *flight* ruhig; *landing* sanft ❸ (*mild flavor*) mild; **~ wine** Wein *m* mit einem weichen Geschmack ❹ (*polished, suave*) [aal]glatt *pej;* **~ operator** gewiefte Person **II.** *vt* ❶ (*make less difficult*) **to ~ the path** [**to sth**] den Weg [zu etw *dat*] ebnen ❷ (*rub in evenly*) einmassieren (**into** in +*akk*)

◆**smooth down** *vt* glatt streichen

◆**smooth over** *vt problems* in Ordnung bringen

smoothie ['smu·ði] *n* ❶ (*drink*) Smoothie *m* (*Getränk aus Yoghurt und Früchten*) ❷ (*pej: charmer*) Charmeur *m*

smoothly ['smuθ·li] *adv* ❶ (*without diffi-*

S

culty) reibungslos; **to go ~** glattlaufen *fam* ② (*suavely*) aalglatt *pej*

smoothness ['smuθ·nɪs] *n* ① (*evenness*) Glätte *f; of silk* Weichheit *f; of skin* Glattheit *f* ② (*pleasant consistency*) *of taste* Milde *f; of texture* Glätte *f*

smooth-'shaven *adj* glatt rasiert

'smooth-talk *vi* (*fam*) sich einschmeicheln

smother ['smʌð·ər] *vt* ① (*suffocate*) ersticken (**with** mit +*dat*) ② (*prevent from growing*) unterdrücken ③ (*cover*) ■ **to be ~ed in sth** von etw *dat* völlig bedeckt sein

smoulder ['smoʊl·dər] *vi see* **smolder**

SMS [ˌes·em·'es] TELEC, INET **I.** *n abbrev of* **short message service** ① *no pl* (*service*) [der] SMS ② (*message*) SMS *f* **II.** *vt* (*fam*) ■ **to ~ sb** jdm simsen *fam*

smudge [smʌdʒ] **I.** *vt* ① (*smear*) *lipstick* verwischen ② (*soil*) beschmutzen **II.** *vi* verlaufen; *ink* klecksen; **her mascara had ~d** ihre Wimperntusche war verschmiert **III.** *n* (*a. fig*) Fleck *m*

smug <-gg-> [smʌg] *adj* selbstgefällig

smuggle ['smʌg·əl] *vt* schmuggeln

smuggler ['smʌg·lər] *n* Schmuggler(in) *m(f)*

smuggling ['smʌg·lɪŋ] *n* Schmuggel *m*

smut [smʌt] *n* (*pej: indecent material*) Schweinereien *pl*

smutty ['smʌt̬·i] *adj* (*pej*) schmutzig; *joke* dreckig *fam,* freizügig

snack [snæk] **I.** *n* Snack *m,* Imbiss *m* **II.** *vi* naschen

'snack bar *n* Imbissstube *f*

snafu [snæf·'u] *n* (*sl*) Schlamassel *m fam*

snag [snæg] **I.** *n* ① (*hidden disadvantage*) Haken *m fam* (**with** an +*dat*); **to hit a ~** auf Schwierigkeiten stoßen ② (*damage to textiles*) gezogener Faden **II.** *vt* <-gg-> ① (*damage by catching*) **be careful not to ~ your coat on the barbed wire** pass auf, dass du mit deiner Jacke nicht am Stacheldraht hängen bleibst ② (*get*) sich *dat* schnappen *fam* **III.** *vi* <-gg-> ■ **to ~ on sth** durch etw *akk* belastet sein

snail [sneɪl] *n* Schnecke *f*

'snail mail *n* (*hum fam*) Schneckenpost *f*

snake [sneɪk] **I.** *n* ① (*reptile*) Schlange *f* ② (*pej: untrustworthy person*) **a ~ in the grass** eine falsche Schlange **II.** *vi* sich schlängeln

'snake bite *n* Schlangenbiss *m*

'snake charmer *n* Schlangenbeschwörer(in) *m(f)*

'snakeskin *n* ① (*skin*) Schlangenhaut *f* ② FASHION Schlangenleder *nt*

'snake venom *n* Schlangengift *nt*

snap [snæp] **I.** *n* ① *usu sing* (*act*) Knacken *nt;* (*sound*) Knacks *m* ② (*fastener*) Druckknopf *m* ③ (*fam: breeze*) **it was a ~!** es war ein Kinderspiel [*o* Klacks]! ④ (*photograph*) Schnappschuss *m* **II.** *vi* <-pp-> ① (*break cleanly*) auseinanderbrechen; **her patience finally ~ped** (*fig*) ihr riss schließlich der Geduldsfaden ② (*make a whip-like motion*) peitschen ③ (*sudden bite*) schnappen (**at** nach +*dat*); **to ~ at sb's heels** nach jds Fersen schnappen; (*fig*) jdm auf den Fersen sein ④ (*speak sharply*) bellen *fam;* ■ **to ~ at sb** jdn anfahren **III.** *vt* <-pp-> ① (*break cleanly*) entzweibrechen; ■ **to ~ sth ↔ off** etw abbrechen ② (*close sharply*) **to ~ sth shut** etw zuknallen; *book* zuklappen ③ (*attract attention*) **to ~ one's fingers** mit den Fingern schnippen ④ (*speak sharply*) **to ~ sb's head off** jdm den Kopf abreißen *fam*

◆**snap out** *vi* ① (*in anger*) brüllen ② (*get over*) ■ **to ~ out of sth** etw überwinden; **~ out of it!** krieg dich wieder ein!

◆**snap up** *vt* schnell kaufen

'snapdragon *n* HORT Löwenmaul *nt*

snappy ['ʃnæp·i] *adj* ① (*fam: smart, fashionable*) schick ② (*quick*) zackig; **make it ~!** mach fix! *fam* ③ (*pej: irritable*) gereizt

'snapshot *n* PHOT Schnappschuss *m*

snare [sner] **I.** *n* (*trap*) Falle *f;* (*noose*) Schlinge *f* **II.** *vt* ① (*catch animals*) [mit einer Falle] fangen ② (*capture*) fangen

'snare drum *n* MUS Schnarrtrommel *f*

snarl¹ [snarl] **I.** *vi* ① (*growl*) *dog* knurren ② (*speak angrily*) ■ **to ~ at sb** jdn anknurren **II.** *n* ① (*growl*) Knurren *nt* ② (*angry utterance*) **to say sth with a ~** etw knurren

snarl² [snarl] **I.** *n* (*knot*) Knoten *m;* (*tangle*) Gewirr *nt* **II.** *vi* (*become tangled*) sich verheddern

◆**snarl up** *vt usu passive* durcheinandergeraten; **traffic was ~ed up for several hours after the accident** nach dem Unfall herrschte ein stundenlanges Verkehrschaos

snatch [snætʃ] **I.** *n* <*pl* -es> ① (*sudden grab*) schneller Griff; **to make a ~ at sth** nach etw *dat* greifen ② (*fragment*) Fetzen *m* ③ (*period of activity*) **to do sth in ~es** etw mit Unterbrechungen tun ④ (*sl: kidnapping*) Entführung *f* ⑤ SPORTS (*in weightlifting*) Reißen *nt* **II.** *vt* ① (*grab quickly*) schnappen ② (*steal*) sich *dat* greifen ③ (*kidnap*) entführen **III.** *vi* (*grab quickly*) greifen (**at** nach +*dat*)

◆**snatch up** *vt* sich *dat* schnappen

snazzy ['snæz·i] *adj* (*fam*) [tod]schick *fam*

sneak [snik] **I.** *vi* <-ed *or* snuck, -ed *or* snuck> schleichen; **to ~ up on sb/sth** sich an jdn/etw heranschleichen **II.** *vt* <-ed *or* snuck, -ed *or* snuck> ① (*view secretly*) **to ~ a look at sb/sth** einen verstohlenen Blick auf jdn/etw werfen ② (*move secretly*) ■ **to ~ sb/sth in** jdn/etw hineinschmuggeln **III.** *n* (*pej*) Schleicher, -in *m, f*

sneaker ['sni·kər] *n usu pl* Turnschuh *m*

sneaking ['sni·kɪŋ] *adj attr* heimlich; **~ suspicion** leiser Verdacht

sneak 'preview *n* FILM [inoffizielle] Vorschau

sneaky ['sni·ki] *adj* raffiniert

sneer [snɪr] **I.** *vi* ① (*smile derisively*) spöttisch grinsen ② (*express disdain*) spotten (**at** über +*akk*) **II.** *n* spöttisches Lächeln

sneeze [sniz] **I.** *vi* niesen ► PHRASES: **not to be**

~d at nicht zu verachten **II.** *n* Niesen *nt*

snicker ['snɪk·ər] **I.** *vi* kichern (**at** über +*akk*) **II.** *n* Kichern *nt,* Gekicher *nt*

snide [snaɪd] *adj* (*pej*) *remark* abfällig

sniff [snɪf] **I.** *n* Riechen *nt; dog* Schnüffeln *nt* **II.** *vi* ① (*inhale sharply*) die Luft einziehen; *animal* wittern; ■**to ~ at sth** an etw *dat* schnuppern; *animal* die Witterung von etw *dat* aufnehmen ② (*show disdain*) ■**to ~ at sth** über etw *akk* die Nase rümpfen **III.** *vt* (*test by smelling*) ■**to ~ sth** an etw *dat* riechen

◆**sniff out** *vt* aufspüren; (*fig*) entdecken

sniffle ['snɪf·əl] **I.** *vi* schniefen **II.** *n* (*repeated sniffing*) Schniefen *nt;* MED ■**the ~s** *pl* leichter Schnupfen

snifter ['snɪf·tər] *n* (*glass*) Schwenker *m*

snip [snɪp] **I.** *n* Schnitt *m* **II.** *vt* schneiden

snipe [snaɪp] **I.** *vi* ① MIL aus dem Hinterhalt schießen ② (*criticize*) ■**to ~ at sb** jdn attackieren **II.** *n* <*pl* - *or* -es> Schnepfe *f*

sniper ['snaɪ·pər] *n* MIL Heckenschütze *m*

snippet ['snɪp·ɪt] *n* ① (*small piece*) Stückchen *nt;* **~s of paper** Papierschnipsel *pl* ② (*information*) Bruchstück *nt; of information, knowledge a.* Brocken *m;* **~s of a conversation** Gesprächsfetzen *pl*

snitch [snɪtʃ] **I.** *vt* (*fam: steal*) klauen **II.** *vi* (*pej sl: tell tales*) petzen; ■**to ~ on sb** jdn verpetzen, jdn verpfeifen *fam* **III.** *n* <*pl* -es> (*pej sl: informer*) Petze(r) *f(m)*

snivel ['snɪv·əl] **I.** *vi* <-l- *or* -ll-> ① (*sniffle*) schniefen *fam* ② (*cry*) flennen *pej fam* **II.** *n* ① (*sniveling*) Geplärre *nt pej fam* ② (*sad sniffle*) Schniefen *nt*

sniveling, snivelling ['snɪv·əl·ɪŋ] **I.** *n* Geheul *nt pej fam* **II.** *adj attr person, manner* weinerlich

snob [snab] *n* Snob *m*

snobbery ['snab·ə·ri] *n* Snobismus *m*

snobbish ['snab·ɪʃ] *adj* snobistisch

snoop [snup] **I.** *n* (*fam*) ① (*look*) Herumschnüffeln *nt kein pl;* **to take a ~ around [sth]** sich [an einem Ort] mal ein bisschen umschauen ② (*interloper, investigator*) Schnüffler(in) *m(f);* (*spy*) Spion(in) *m(f)* **II.** *vi* (*fam: look secretly*) [herum]schnüffeln; (*pry*) [herum]spionieren; ■**to ~ on sb** jdn ausspionieren

snooper ['snu·pər] *n* (*fam*) ① (*interloper, investigator*) Schnüffler(in) *m(f)* ② (*spy*) Spion(in) *m(f)*

snooty ['snu·t̬i] *adj* (*fam*) hochnäsig

snooze [snuz] (*fam*) **I.** *vi* ein Nickerchen machen **II.** *n* Nickerchen *nt*

'snooze button *n* Schlummertaste *f* (*am Wecker*)

snore [snɔr] **I.** *vi* schnarchen **II.** *n* Schnarchen *nt kein pl*

snorkel ['snɔr·kəl] SPORTS **I.** *n* Schnorchel *m* **II.** *vi* <-l- *or* -ll-> schnorcheln

snort [snɔrt] **I.** *vi* schnauben **II.** *vt* ① (*sl: inhale*) **to ~ cocaine** Kokain schnupfen ② (*disapprovingly*) [verächtlich] schnauben **III.** *n* (*noise*) Schnauben *nt kein pl*

snot [snat] *n* (*fam: mucus*) Rotz *m*

snotty ['snat̬·i] *adj* (*fam*) ① (*full of mucus*) Rotz-; *handkerchief* vollgerotzt ② (*pej: rude*) rotzfrech *sl; answer* pampig; *look, manner* unverschämt

snout [snaʊt] *n* (*nose*) *of animal* Schnauze *f; of pig, insect* Rüssel *m; of person* Rüssel *m sl*

snow [snoʊ] **I.** *n* ① Schnee *m* ② (*snowfall*) Schneefall *m* **II.** *vi impers* **it's ~ing** es schneit

◆**snow in** *vt usu passive* **to be ~ed in** eingeschneit sein

◆**snow under** *vt usu passive* **to be ~ed under with work** mit Arbeit eingedeckt sein

'snowball I. *n* Schneeball *m* ▶ PHRASES: **to not have a ~'s chance in hell [of doing sth]** (*fam*) null Chancen haben[, etw zu tun] **II.** *vi* lawinenartig anwachsen; **to keep ~ing** eskalieren

'snowball effect *n* Schneeballeffekt *m*

'snowbank *n* Schneewehe *f*

'snow blindness *n* Schneeblindheit *f*

'snowboard I. *n* Snowboard *nt* **II.** *vi* Snowboard fahren, snowboarden

'snowboarding *n* Snowboarding *nt,* Snowboardfahren *nt*

'snowbound *adj* (*snowed-in*) eingeschneit; *road* wegen Schnees gesperrt

'snowcapped *adj* schneebedeckt

'snow chains *npl* AUTO Schneeketten *pl*

'snowdrift *n* Schneewehe *f*

'snowfall *n* ① (*amount*) Schneemenge *f* ② (*snowstorm*) Schneefall *m*

'snowflake *n* Schneeflocke *f*

'snow line *n* Schneefallgrenze *f*

'snowman *n* Schneemann *m*

snowmobile ['snoʊ·mə·ˌbil] *n* Schneemobil *nt*

'snowplow *n* Schneepflug *m*

'snowshoe I. *n usu pl* Schneeschuh *m* **II.** *vi* mit Schneeschuhen gehen

'snowstorm *n* Schneesturm *m*

'snowsuit *n* Schneeanzug *m*

'snow tire *n* Winterreifen *m*

snow-'white *adj* schneeweiß; *blouse, sheets a.* blütenweiß; *face* kalkweiß

snow white *n* Schneeweiß *nt*

Snow 'White *n* Schneewittchen *nt*

snowy ['snoʊ·i] *adj* ① (*with much snow*) *region, month* schneereich ② (*snow-covered*) verschneit; *mountain* schneebedeckt ③ (*color*) schneeweiß

snub [snʌb] **I.** *vt* <-bb-> (*offend by ignoring*) brüskieren, schneiden; (*insult*) beleidigen **II.** *n* Brüskierung *f*

snub 'nose *n* Stupsnase *f*

'snub-nosed *adj attr* ① *person* stupsnasig ② MIL *gun* mit kurzem Lauf *nach n*

snuff [snʌf] **I.** *n* Schnupftabak *m* **II.** *vt* **to ~ it** (*fam*) abkratzen *sl*

◆**snuff out** *vt* ① (*extinguish*) *flame* auslöschen; *cigarette* ausdrücken; *with one's foot* austreten ② (*end*) *hopes* zunichtemachen; **countless lives were ~ed out by the storm**

unzählige Leben wurden durch den Sturm ausgelöscht ③ (*sl: kill*) wegpusten
snuffle ['snʌf·əl] **I.** *vi* ① (*sniffle*) schniefen *fam* ② (*speak nasally*) ■**to ~ [out]** näseln **II.** *n* ① (*noisy breathing*) Schnüffeln *nt kein pl* ② ■**the ~s** *pl* leichter Schnupfen
snug [snʌg] *adj* ① (*cozy*) kuschelig, gemütlich; (*warm*) mollig warm ② FASHION (*tight*) eng
snuggle ['snʌg·əl] **I.** *vi* sich kuscheln (mit +*dat*); **to ~ into bed** sich ins Bett kuscheln **II.** *vt* ① (*hold*) an sich *akk* drücken ② *usu passive* (*nestle*) ■**to be ~d** sich schmiegen **III.** *n* (*sl*) Umarmung *f*
◆**snuggle up** *vi* ■**to ~ up to sb** sich an jdn anschmiegen
so [soʊ] **I.** *adv* ① (*to an indicated degree*) so; **he's pretty nice; more ~ than I was led to believe** er ist ganz nett, viel netter als ich angenommen hatte ② (*to a great degree*) so; **what are you looking ~ unhappy about?** warum bist du denn so traurig?; **what's ~ wrong about that?** was ist denn daran so falsch? ③ (*also, likewise*) auch; **I have an enormous amount of work to do — ~ do I** ich habe jede Menge Arbeit – ich auch ④ (*yes*) ja; **can I watch television? — I suppose ~** darf ich fernsehen? – na gut, meinetwegen [*o* von mir aus]; **I'm afraid ~** ich fürchte ja ⑤ (*that*) das; **~ they say** so sagt man; **I told you ~** ich habe es dir ja gesagt ⑥ (*as stated*) so; (*true*) wahr; **is that ~?** stimmt das?; **if ~ ...** wenn das so ist ...; **and ~ it was** und so kam es dann auch; **and ~ forth** [*or* **on**] und so weiter; **~ to speak** sozusagen ▶ PHRASES: **~ long** bis dann [*o* später]; **~ what?** na und? *fam* **II.** *conj* ① (*therefore*) deshalb, daher; **I couldn't find you ~ I left** ich konnte dich nicht finden, also bin ich gegangen ② (*introducing a sentence*) also; **~ what's the problem?** wo liegt denn das Problem? ③ (*so that*) damit; **be quiet ~ she can concentrate** sei still, damit sie sich konzentrieren kann ▶ PHRASES: **~ long as ...** (*if*) sofern; (*for the time*) solange; **~ long as he doesn't go too far, ...** solange er nicht zu weit geht, ... **III.** *adj* (*sl*) typisch *fam;* **that's ~ 70's** das ist typisch 70er
soak [soʊk] **I.** *n* (*immersion*) Einweichen *nt kein pl* **II.** *vt* ① (*immerse*) einweichen; (*in alcohol*) einlegen ② (*make wet*) durchnässen **III.** *vi* (*immerse*) einweichen lassen
◆**soak in I.** *vi* ① (*be absorbed*) einziehen ② (*be understood*) in den Schädel gehen *fam;* **will it ever ~ in?** ob er/sie das wohl jemals kapiert? *fam* **II.** *vt* einsaugen; (*fig*) in sich *akk* aufnehmen
◆**soak up** *vt* ① (*absorb*) aufsaugen; (*fig*) [gierig] in sich *akk* aufnehmen ② (*bask in*) *atmosphere* in sich *akk* aufnehmen; *sun*[*shine*] sich aalen (in +*dat*) ③ (*use up*) **to ~ up resources** Mittel aufbrauchen
soaked [soʊkt] *adj* (*wet*) ■**to be ~** pitschnass sein *fam;* **~ in sweat** schweißgebadet; *shirt* völlig durchgeschwitzt

S

soaking ['soʊ·kɪŋ] **I.** *n* ① (*immersion*) Einweichen *nt kein pl* ② (*becoming wet*) Nasswerden *nt kein pl;* **to get a ~** patschnass werden *fam* **II.** *adj* **~ [wet]** klatschnass *fam*
so-and-so ['soʊ·ən·soʊ] *n* (*fam*) ① (*unspecified person*) Herr/Frau Soundso; (*unspecified thing*) das und das ② (*pej fam: disliked person*) **oh, he was a ~, all right, that Mr. Baker** ja, dieser Mr. Baker war ein richtiger alter Fiesling *sl*
soap [soʊp] **I.** *n* ① (*substance*) Seife *f* ② TV, MEDIA (*soap opera*) Seifenoper *f* **II.** *vt* einseifen
'soapbox *n* ① (*pedestal*) Obstkiste *f* (*improvisierte Rednerbühne*) ② (*vehicle*) Seifenkiste *f*
'soap bubble *n* Seifenblase *f*
'soap dish *n* Seifenschale *f*
'soap dispenser *n* Seifenspender *m*
'soap flakes *npl* Seifenflocken *pl*
'soap opera *n* TV, MEDIA Seifenoper *f*
'soapsuds *npl* Seifenschaum *m kein pl*
soapy ['soʊ·pi] *adj* ① (*lathery*) seifig; **~ water** Seifenwasser *nt* ② (*like soap*) seifig
soar [sɔr] *vi* ① (*rise*) aufsteigen; *mountain peaks* sich erheben ② (*increase*) *temperature, prices, profits* in die Höhe schnellen ③ (*glide*) *bird* [*of prey*] [in großer Höhe] segeln; *glider, hang glider* gleiten
soaring ['sɔr·ɪŋ] *adj attr* ① (*flying*) segelnd, schwebend ② (*increasing*) *heights* rasch steigend
sob [sab] **I.** *n* Schluchzen *nt kein pl* **II.** *vi* <-bb-> schluchzen **III.** *vt* <-bb-> ① (*cry*) **to ~ one's heart out** sich *dat* die Seele aus dem Leib weinen ② (*say while crying*) schluchzen
sober ['soʊ·bər] **I.** *adj* ① (*not drunk*) nüchtern; **stone cold ~** stocknüchtern ② (*unemotional*) *thought, judgment* sachlich, nüchtern; *person* nüchtern ③ (*plain*) *color* gedeckt; (*simple*) *truth* einfach **II.** *vt* ernüchtern **III.** *vi person* ruhiger werden
◆**sober up I.** *vi* (*become less drunk*) nüchtern werden **II.** *vt* (*make less drunk*) nüchtern machen
sobering ['soʊ·bər·ɪŋ] *adj effect, thought* ernüchternd
sobriety [sə·'braɪ·ɪ·t̬i] *n* ① Nüchternheit *f;* (*life without alcohol*) Abstinenz *f* ② (*seriousness*) Ernst *m*
'sob story *n* (*fam*) ① (*story*) rührselige Geschichte ② (*excuse*) Ausrede *f*
so-called [ˌsoʊ·'kɔld] *adj attr* ① (*supposed*) so genannt ② (*with neologisms*) so genannt
soccer ['sak·ər] *n* Fußball *m*
'soccer ball *n* Fußball *m*
'soccer mom *n* (*pej fam*) *Bezeichnung für Mütter aus den Vorortsiedlungen, die viel Zeit damit verbringen, ihre Kinder von einer Sportveranstaltung zur nächsten zu fahren*
sociability [ˌsoʊ·ʃə·'bɪl·ɪ·t̬i] *n* Geselligkeit *f*
sociable ['soʊ·ʃə·bəl] *adj* ① (*keen to mix*) gesellig ② (*friendly*) freundlich, umgänglich
social ['soʊ·ʃəl] **I.** *adj* ① (*of human contact*) Gesellschafts-, gesellschaftlich; **I'm a ~**

drinker ich trinke nur, wenn ich in Gesellschaft bin ② SOCIOL (*concerning society*) gesellschaftlich, Gesellschafts- ③ SOCIOL (*of human behavior*) sozial, Sozial-; ~ **skills** soziale Fähigkeiten **II.** *n* (*party*) Treffen *nt;* **church** ~ Gemeindefest *nt*

socialism ['soʊ·ʃə·lɪz·əm] *n* Sozialismus *m*

socialist ['soʊ·ʃə·lɪst] **I.** *n* Sozialist(in) *m(f)* **II.** *adj* sozialistisch

socialite ['soʊ·ʃə·laɪt] *n* Persönlichkeit *f* des öffentlichen Lebens

socialize ['soʊ·ʃə·laɪz] **I.** *vi* unter Leuten sein; ■ **to ~ with sb** mit jdm gesellschaftlich verkehren **II.** *vt* SOCIOL, BIOL sozialisieren; *offender* [re]sozialisieren; *animal* zähmen

socially ['soʊ·ʃə·li] *adv* ① (*in society*) gesellschaftlich; ~ **acceptable** gesellschaftlich akzeptabel ② (*not at work*) **to meet sb** ~ jdn privat treffen

social 'science *n* Sozialwissenschaft *f*

social se'curity *n* ① (*welfare*) Sozialhilfe *f* ② (*pension*) Sozial[versicherungs]rente *f*

social se'curity number *n* Sozialversicherungsnummer *f*

social 'service *n* ① (*social work*) Sozialarbeit *f* ② (*welfare*) ■ **~s** *pl* staatliche Sozialleistungen

'social work *n* Sozialarbeit *f*

'social worker *n* Sozialarbeiter(in) *m(f)*

societal [sə·'saɪ·ə·t̬əl] *adj* gesellschaftlich

society [sə·'saɪ·ɪ·t̬i] *n* ① (*all people*) Gesellschaft *f* ② (*elite*) die [feine] Gesellschaft ③ (*organization*) Verein *m,* Vereinigung *f*

socioeconomic [ˌsoʊ·si·oʊˌek·ə·'nam·ɪk] *adj* sozioökonomisch

sociolinguistics [ˌsoʊ·si·oʊ·lɪŋ·'gwɪs·tɪks] *n* Soziolinguistik *f*

sociological [ˌsoʊ·si·ə·'ladʒ·ɪ·kəl] *adj* soziologisch

sociologist [ˌsoʊ·si·'al·ə·dʒɪst] *n* Soziologe, Soziologin *m, f*

sociology [ˌsoʊ·si·'al·ə·dʒi] *n* Soziologie *f*

sock¹ [sak] *n* Socke *f*

sock² [sak] *vt* ① (*fam: punch*) **to ~ sb in the eye** jdm eins aufs Auge geben ② SPORTS (*in baseball*) *ball* schlagen; (*in soccer*) schießen

socket ['sak·ɪt] *n* ① ELEC (*for a plug*) Steckdose *f;* (*for lamps*) Fassung *f* ② ANAT, MED **eye** ~ Augenhöhle *f;* **knee** ~ Kniegelenkpfanne *f*

sod [sad] *n* Grassode *f,* Grasnarbe *f*

soda ['soʊ·də] *n* ① *see* **soft drink** ② *see* **soda water**

'soda fountain *n* Erfrischungsstand *f*

'soda pop *n see* **soft drink**

'soda water *n* Sodawasser *nt*

sodden ['sad·ən] *adj* (*soaked*) durchnässt; *grass* durchweicht

sodium ['soʊ·di·əm] *n* Natrium *nt*

sodium bi'carbonate *n see* **baking soda**

sodium 'chloride *n* Natriumchlorid *nt*

sodomize ['sad·ə·maɪz] *vt person* Analverkehr haben (mit +*dat*)

sodomy ['sad·ə·mi] *n* (*form*) Sodomie *f*

sofa ['soʊ·fə] *n* Sofa *nt*

'sofa bed *n* Schlafcouch *f*

soft [sɔft] *adj* ① (*not hard*) weich ② (*smooth*) weich; *cheeks, skin* zart; *leather* geschmeidig; *hair* seidig ③ (*weak*) weich, schlaff ④ (*subtle*) *colors* zart ⑤ (*not loud*) *music* gedämpft; *sound, voice* leise; *words* sanft

'softball *n* Softball *m*

soft-'boiled *adj* weich [gekocht]

'soft drink *n* Limo[nade] *f*

soften ['sɔ·fən] **I.** *vi* ① (*melt*) weich werden; *ice cream* schmelzen ② (*moderate*) nachgiebiger werden **II.** *vt* ① (*melt*) weich werden lassen ② (*moderate*) mildern; *color, light* dämpfen

◆ **soften up I.** *vt* ① (*make less hard*) weicher machen ② (*win over*) erweichen; (*persuade*) rumkriegen *fam* ③ MIL schwächen **II.** *vi* weich werden

softener ['sɔ·fə·nər] *n* ① (*softening agent*) Weichmacher *m;* **fabric** ~ Weichspüler *m* ② (*mineral reducer*) Enthärter *m*

softening ['sɔ·fə·nɪŋ] **I.** *n* ① (*making less hard*) Weichmachen *nt; of clothes* Weichspülen *nt; of a voice* Dämpfen *nt; of an attitude, opinion* Mäßigen *nt; of a manner* Mäßigung *f* ② (*making less bright*) *of a color, light* Dämpfen *nt; of a contrast* Abschwächen *nt* **II.** *adj attr* Enthärtungs-, enthärtend

soft'hearted *adj* ① (*compassionate*) weichherzig ② (*gullible*) leichtgläubig

softie ['sɔf·ti] *n* (*fam*) *see* **softy**

softly ['sɔft·li] *adv* ① (*not hard*) sanft ② (*quietly*) leise ③ (*dimly*) schwach

softness ['sɔft·nɪs] *n* ① (*not hardness*) Weichheit *f* ② (*smoothness*) Weichheit *f; of skin* Glätte *f; of hair* Seidigkeit *f* ③ (*subtlety*) *of lighting* Gedämpftheit *f; of colors* Zartheit *f*

'soft-soap *vt* (*fig fam*) ■ **to ~ sb** jdm Honig ums Maul schmieren

soft-'spoken *adj sound* leise gesprochen; *person;* ■ **to be ~** leise sprechen; ~ **manner** freundliche und sanfte Art

software ['sɔft·wer] COMPUT **I.** *n* Software *f* **II.** *adj company, development, publisher* Software-; ~ **engineer/writer** Programmierer(in) *m(f);* ~ **package** Softwarepaket *nt;* ~ **piracy** Software-Piraterie *f*

'softwood *n* ① (*wood*) Weichholz *nt* ② (*tree*) immergrüner Baum, Baum *m* mit weichem Holz

softy ['sɔf·ti] *n* (*pej fam*) Softie *m oft pej sl*

soggy ['sag·i] *adj* ① (*sodden*) durchnässt; (*boggy*) glitschig *fam; soil* aufgeweicht ② FOOD matschig, pampig *fam*

soil¹ [sɔɪl] *n* ① (*earth*) Boden *m,* Erde *f* ② (*territory*) Boden *m*

soil² [sɔɪl] *vt* (*form*) ① (*dirty*) verschmutzen ② (*foul*) verunreinigen

soirée, soiree [swa·'reɪ] *n* (*form or hum*) Soiree *f*

solace ['sal·ɪs] *n* Trost *m*

solar ['soʊ·lər] *adj* ① (*relating to sun*) Solar-, Sonnen- ② ASTRON ~ **time** Sonnenzeit *f*

S

solar 'cell *n* Solarzelle *f*
solar e'clipse *n* Sonnenfinsternis *f*
solar 'energy *n* Solarenergie *f*
solarium <*pl* -aria *or* -s> [soʊ·'ler·i·əm] *n* ① (*sun porch*) Glasveranda *f* ② (*tanning room*) Solarium *nt*
solar 'panel *n* Sonnenkollektor *m*
solar plexus [ˌsoʊ·lər·'plek·səs] *n* ANAT, MED Solarplexus *m*
solar 'power *n* Sonnenkraft *f*
'solar system *n* Sonnensystem *nt*
sold [soʊld] *pt, pp of* **sell**
solder ['sad·ər] **I.** *vt* löten **II.** *n* Lötmetall *nt*
soldier ['soʊl·dʒər] *n* Soldat(in) *m(f)*
◆**soldier on** *vi* sich durchkämpfen
sold 'out *adj* ausverkauft
sole¹ [soʊl] *n* ① FASHION [Schuh]sohle *f* ② ANAT [Fuß]sohle *f*
sole² [soʊl] *adj attr* ① (*only*) einzig, alleinig ② (*exclusive*) Allein-
sole³ <*pl* - *or* -s> [soʊl] *n* ZOOL, FOOD Seezunge *f*
solely ['soʊl·li] *adv* einzig und allein, nur
solemn ['sal·əm] *adj* ① (*ceremonial*) feierlich; *oath, promise* heilig ② (*grave*) ernst; *voice* getragen
solemnity [sə·'lem·nɪ·t̬i] *n* (*gravity*) Feierlichkeit *f,* Erhabenheit *f*
solicit [sə·'lɪs·ɪt] **I.** *vt* (*form: ask for*) ■**to ~ sth** um etw *akk* bitten **II.** *vi* (*as a prostitute*) sich *akk* anbieten
soliciting [sə·'lɪs·ɪ·t̬ɪŋ] *n* Ansprechen *nt* von Männern (*durch Prostituierte*)
solicitor [sə·'lɪs·ɪ·t̬ər] *n* POL Rechtsreferent(in) *m(f)* (*einer Stadt*)
solicitous [sə·'lɪs·ɪ·t̬əs] *adj* (*form*) ① (*careful*) sorgfältig ② (*attentive*) aufmerksam
solid ['sal·ɪd] **I.** *adj* ① (*hard, not liquid*) fest; *chair, wall* solide; *foundation* stabil; *punch* kräftig; *rock* massiv ② (*not hollow*) massiv ③ (*complete*) ganz; **~ silver** massives [*o* reines] Silber ④ (*substantial*) verlässlich; *argument* stichhaltig; *evidence* handfest; *grounding* solide ⑤ (*uninterrupted*) *line, wall* durchgehend; *month, week* ganz ⑥ (*dependable*) *person* solide, zuverlässig; *marriage, relationship* stabil ⑦ ECON (*financially sound*) *investment* solide, sicher **II.** *n* ① PHYS fester Stoff, Festkörper *m;* MATH Körper *nt* ② FOOD ■**~s** *pl* feste Nahrung *kein pl* **III.** *adv* **frozen ~** *liquid* hart gefroren; *plants* steif gefroren
solidarity [ˌsal·ə·'der·ɪ·t̬i] *n* ① (*unity*) Solidarität *f* (**with** mit +*dat*) ② (*movement*) **S~** Solidarität *f*
solid 'fuel *n* (*power source*) fester Brennstoff
solidify <-ie-> [sə·'lɪd·ə·faɪ] **I.** *vi* ① (*harden*) fest werden; *lava* erstarren; *cement* hart werden; *water* gefrieren ② (*fig: take shape*) *plans* sich konkretisieren; *idea, thought* konkret[er] werden **II.** *vt* ① (*harden*) fest werden lassen; *water* gefrieren lassen ② (*fig: reinforce*) festigen; *plan* konkretisieren
solidity [sə·'lɪd·ɪ·t̬i] *n* ① (*hardness*) fester Zustand; *of wood* Härte *f; of a foundation, table* Stabilität *f* ② (*reliability*) *of facts, evidence* Zuverlässigkeit *f; of an argument, reasoning* Stichhaltigkeit *f; of a judgment* Fundiertheit *f; of commitment* Verlässlichkeit *f* ③ (*strength*) Stabilität *f* ④ (*financial soundness*) *of an investment* Solidität *f;* (*financial strength*) *of a company* finanzielle Stärke
solidly ['sal·ɪd·li] *adv* ① (*sturdily*) solide; **to be ~ built** solide gebaut sein ② (*uninterruptedly*) *work* ununterbrochen
'solid-state *adj* Festkörper-
soliloquy [sə·'lɪl·ə·kwi] *n* Selbstgespräch *nt;* THEAT Monolog *m*
solitaire ['sal·ə·ter] *n* ① (*jewel*) Solitär *m* ② (*card game*) Patience *f*
solitary ['sal·ə·ter·i] *adj* ① (*single*) einzelne(r, s) *attr;* ZOOL solitär *fachspr* ② (*lonely*) einsam; (*remote*) abgeschieden, abgelegen
solitary con'finement *n* Einzelhaft *f*
solitude ['sal·ə·tud] *n* ① (*being alone*) Alleinsein *nt;* **in ~** alleine ② (*loneliness*) Einsamkeit *f*
solo ['soʊ·loʊ] **I.** *adj attr* (*unaccompanied*) Solo- **II.** *adv* (*single-handed*) allein; MUS solo **III.** *n* MUS Solo *nt*
soloist ['soʊ·loʊ·ɪst] *n* Solist(in) *m(f)*
Solomon Islands ['sal·ə·mən·ˌaɪ·ləndz] *n* ■**the ~** die Salomonen *pl*
solstice ['sal·stɪs] *n* Sonnenwende *f*
soluble ['sal·jə·bəl] *adj* ① (*that dissolves*) löslich ② (*solvable*) lösbar
solution [sə·'lu·ʃən] *n* ① (*to a problem*) Lösung *f;* (*to riddle/puzzle*) [Auf]lösung *f* ② (*act of solving*) Lösen *nt* ③ (*in business*) Vorrichtung *f;* **software ~s** Softwareanwendungen *pl* ④ CHEM Lösung *f*
solve [salv] *vt* lösen; *crime* aufklären; *mystery* aufdecken
solvency ['sal·vən·si] *n* FIN Zahlungsfähigkeit *f*
solvent ['sal·vənt] **I.** *n* CHEM Lösungsmittel *nt* **II.** *adj* ① FIN zahlungsfähig ② (*fam: having sufficient money*) flüssig
Somali [soʊ·'ma·li] **I.** *n* <*pl* - *or* -s> ① (*person*) Somalier(in) *m(f)* ② (*language*) Somali *nt* **II.** *adj* somalisch
Somalia [soʊ·'mal·i·ə] *n* Somalia *nt*
somber ['sam·bər] *adj* ① (*sad*) düster; *setting* ernst ② (*dark-colored*) dunkel; *day* trüb, finster
some [sʌm] **I.** *adj attr* ① (*unknown amount: + pl*) einige, ein paar; (*+ sing n*) etwas; **there's ~ cake in the kitchen** es ist noch Kuchen in der Küche; **~ more** noch etwas ② (*certain: + pl*) gewisse ③ (*general, unknown*) irgendein(e); **he's in ~ kind of trouble** er steckt in irgendwelchen Schwierigkeiten; **~ day or another** irgendwann ④ (*noticeable*) gewiss; **to ~ extent** bis zu einem gewissen Grad ⑤ (*slight*) etwas; **there is ~ hope that he will get the job** es besteht noch etwas Hoffnung, dass er die Stelle bekommt **II.** *pron* ① (*unspecified number of persons or*

things) welche ❷ (*unspecified amount of sth*) welche(r, s); **if you need money, I can lend you** ~ wenn du Geld brauchst, kann ich dir gerne welches leihen ❸ (*at least a small number*) einige, manche ❹ + *pl vb* (*among larger number*) einige, ein paar; ~ **of you have already met Betsey** einige von euch kennen Betsey bereits **III.** *adv* (*roughly*) ungefähr, in etwa; ~ **sixty or sixty-five feet deep** ungefähr zwanzig Meter tief

somebody ['sʌm·ˌbad·i] *pron indef* ❶ (*unnamed, unknown person*) jemand; ~ **or other** irgendwer; ~ **else** [*or* **or other**] jemand anders; **there's ~ at the door** jemand ist an der Tür ❷ (*one person unspecified or from group*) irgendwer ❸ (*important person*) **to be** ~ jemand [*o* etwas] sein

somehow ['sʌm·haʊ] *adv* irgendwie

someone ['sʌm·wʌn] *pron see* **somebody**

someplace ['sʌm·pleɪs] *adv* irgendwo; ~ **else** (*in a different place*) woanders, irgendwo anders; (*to a different place*) woandershin, irgendwo anders hin

somersault ['sʌm·ər·sɔlt] **I.** *n* (*on ground*) Purzelbaum *m;* (*in air*) Salto *m* **II.** *vi* einen Purzelbaum schlagen; (*in air*) einen Salto machen; *vehicle, car* sich überschlagen

something ['sʌm·θɪŋ] *pron indef* ❶ (*unspecified object, action, etc.*) etwas; ~ **else** etwas anderes; ~ **special/sharp/stronger** etwas Besonderes/Scharfes/Stärkeres; **to do** ~ [**about sb/sth**] etwas [gegen jdn/etw] unternehmen; **I need ~ to write with** ich brauche etwas zum Schreiben; **is there ~ you'd like to say?** möchtest du mir etwas sagen? ❷ (*indicating similarity*) **it was ~ of a surprise** es war eine kleine Überraschung; **... or** ~ (*fam: similar*) ... oder so; **she works for a bank or** ~ sie arbeitet für eine Bank oder so was; ~ **like** (*similar*) ungefähr wie ...; (*approximately*) um die ...; ~ **like fifty** um die fünfzig ▶ PHRASES: **that's** [**really**] ~ das ist schon was; **there's ~ in sth** an etw *dat* ist etwas dran

sometime ['sʌm·taɪm] *adv* irgendwann; **come up and see me** ~ komm mich mal besuchen; ~ **soon** demnächst irgendwann, bald einmal

sometimes ['sʌm·taɪmz] *adv* manchmal

somewhat ['sʌm·hwat] *adv* etwas, ein wenig [*o* bisschen]

somewhere ['sʌm·hwer] *adv* ❶ (*in unspecified place*) irgendwo; ~ **else** woanders, irgendwo anders ❷ (*to unspecified place*) irgendwohin; ~ **else** woandershin, irgendwo anders hin ❸ (*roughly*) ungefähr; ~ **between 30 and 40** so zwischen 30 und 40

sommelier [ˌsʌm·əl·'jeɪ] *n* Weinkellner(in) *m(f)*

son [sʌn] *n* Sohn *m*

sonar ['soʊ·nar] *n* Sonar[gerät] *nt*

sonata [sə·'na·t̬ə] *n* Sonate *f*

song [sɔŋ] *n* ❶ MUS Lied *nt* ❷ (*singing*) Gesang *m* ❸ *of bird* Gesang *m; of cricket* Zirpen *nt*

'songbird *n* Singvogel *m*

'songbook *n* Liederbuch *nt*

'songwriter *n* Texter(in) *m(f)* und Komponist; **singer-**~ Liedermacher(in) *m(f)*

sonic ['san·ɪk] *adj* Schall-

sonic 'boom *n* Überschallknall *m*

'son-in-law <*pl* sons- *or* -s> *n* Schwiegersohn *m*

sonnet ['san·ɪt] *n* Sonett *nt*

sonny ['sʌni] *n* (*fam*) Kleiner *m*

sonorous [sə·'nɔr·əs] *adj* klangvoll; *voice* sonor, volltönend

soon [sun] *adv* ❶ (*in a short time*) bald; ~ **after sth** kurz nach etw *dat;* **how** ~ wie bald [*o* schnell]; ~**er rather than later** lieber früher als später; **as ~ as possible** so bald wie möglich ❷ (*early*) früh; **the ~er the better** je eher, desto besser; **not a moment too** ~ gerade noch rechtzeitig ❸ (*rather*) lieber; **I'd ~er not speak to him** ich würde lieber nicht mit ihm sprechen

soot [sʊt] *n* Ruß *m*

soothe [suð] *vt* ❶ (*calm*) beruhigen ❷ (*relieve*) lindern

soothing ['suð·ɪŋ] *adj* ❶ (*calming*) beruhigend; *bath* entspannend ❷ (*pain-relieving*) [Schmerz] lindernd

soothsayer ['suθ·ˌseɪ·ər] *n* (*hist*) Wahrsager(in) *m(f)*

sooty ['sʊt̬·i] *adj* rußig, verrußt

sop [sap] *vt* ■ **to ~ up** ⊂ **sth** etw aufsaugen

sophisticated [sə·'fɪs·tə·keɪ·t̬ɪd] *adj* (*approv*) ❶ (*urbane*) [geistig] verfeinert; (*cultured*) kultiviert, gebildet; *audience, readers* niveauvoll, anspruchsvoll; *restaurant* gepflegt ❷ (*highly developed*) hoch entwickelt, ausgeklügelt; *method* raffiniert; (*complex*) *approach* differenziert

sophistication [sə·ˌfɪs·tə·'keɪ·ʃən] *n* (*approv*) ❶ (*urbanity*) Kultiviertheit *f;* (*finesse*) Gepflegtheit *f,* Feinheit *f* ❷ (*complexity*) hoher Entwicklungsstand

sophomore ['saf·ə·mɔr] *n* (*in college*) Student(in) *m(f)* im zweiten Studienjahr; (*in high school*) Schüler(in) *m(f)* einer Highschool im zweiten Jahr

soporific [ˌsap·ə·'rɪf·ɪk] *adj* einschläfernd *a. fig*

sopping ['sap·ɪŋ] (*fam*) **I.** *adj* klatschnass **II.** *adv* ~ **wet** klatschnass

soppy ['sap·i] *adj* (*fam*) gefühlsdus[e]lig *pej; story, film* schmalzig

soprano [sə·'præn·oʊ] **I.** *n* ❶ (*vocal range*) Sopran *m* ❷ (*singer*) Sopranistin *f* **II.** *adj* Sopran- **III.** *adv* **to sing** ~ Sopran singen

sorbet ['sɔr·beɪ] *n* Sorbet *nt o selten m*

sorcerer ['sɔr·sər·ər] *n* (*esp liter*) Zauberer *m,* Hexenmeister *m*

sorceress <*pl* -es> ['sɔr·sər·ɪs] *n* (*esp liter*) Zauberin *f*

sorcery ['sɔr·sə·ri] *n* (*esp liter*) Zauberei *f,* Hexerei *f*

sordid ['sɔr·dɪd] *adj* ❶ (*dirty*) schmutzig; (*squalid*) schäbig; *apartment* verkommen, heruntergekommen ② (*pej: disreputable*) schmutzig *fig*

sore [sɔr] **I.** *adj* (*hurting*) schlimm, weh; (*through overuse*) wund [gescheuert], entzündet; ~ **muscles** Muskelkater *m;* ~ **point** (*fig*) wunder Punkt **II.** *n* wunde Stelle; **to open an old** ~ (*fig*) alte Wunden aufreißen

sorely ['sɔr·li] *adv* sehr, arg; **to be ~ tempted to do sth** stark versucht sein, etw zu tun

sorority [sə·'rɔr·ɪ·t̬i] *n* Studentinnenvereinigung *f*

sorrel ['sɔr·əl] *n* Sauerampfer *m*

sorrow ['sar·oʊ] *n* (*form*) ① (*feeling*) Kummer *m,* Betrübnis *f,* Traurigkeit *f* ② (*sad experience*) Leid *nt*

sorrowful ['sar·ə·fəl] *adj* (*form*) traurig, betrübt (**at** über +*akk*)

sorry ['sar·i] **I.** *adj* ① *pred* (*regretful*) **I'm/she's** ~ es tut mir/ihr leid; ■**to be ~ about sth** etw bedauern; **to say ~ [to sb]** sich [bei jdm] entschuldigen ② *pred* (*sad*) traurig; **we were ~ to hear [that] you've not been feeling well** es tat uns leid zu hören, dass es dir nicht gut ging; **sb feels ~ for sb/sth** jd/etw tut jdm leid ③ *attr* (*wretched*) traurig, armselig **II.** *interj* ■~! Verzeihung!, Entschuldigung!

sort [sɔrt] **I.** *n* ① (*type*) Sorte *f,* Art *f* ② (*fam: expressing vagueness*) **I had a ~ of feeling that ...** ich hatte so ein Gefühl, dass ... ③ (*person*) **I know your ~!** Typen wie euch kenne ich [zur Genüge]! *fam* **II.** *adv* (*fam*) ■~ **of** ① (*rather*) irgendwie; **that's ~ of difficult to explain** das ist nicht so einfach zu erklären ② (*not exactly*) mehr oder weniger, so ungefähr **III.** *vt* sortieren **IV.** *vi* ■**to ~ through sth** etw sortieren

◆**sort out** *vt* ① (*arrange*) ordnen, sortieren; (*choose, select*) aussuchen; (*for throwing out or giving away*) aussortieren ② (*tidy up*) *mess* in Ordnung bringen ③ (*resolve*) klären, regeln; *problem* lösen

sorter ['sɔr·t̬ər] *n* ① (*postal employee*) Sortierer(in) *m(f)* ② (*machine*) Sortiermaschine *f*

sortie ['sɔr·ti] *n* MIL Ausfall *m;* (*by aircraft*) Einsatz *m*

S

SOS [ˌes·oʊ·'es] *n* SOS *nt;* (*fig*) Hilferuf *m*

so-so ['soʊ·soʊ] (*fam*) **I.** *adj* so lala *präd,* mittelprächtig *hum* **II.** *adv* so lala

soufflé [su·'fleɪ] *n* Soufflé *nt,* Soufflee *nt*

sought [sɔt] *pt, pp of* **seek**

'sought-after *adj* begehrt

soul [soʊl] *n* ① (*spirit*) Seele *f;* **not a** ~ keine Menschenseele ② (*approv: profound feeling*) Seele *f,* Gefühl *nt* ③ MUS Soul *m*

'soul-destroying *adj* (*pej*) nervtötend; *work* geisttötend; (*destroying sb's confidence*) zermürbend

soulful ['soʊl·fəl] *adj* gefühlvoll

soulless ['soʊl·lɪs] *adj* (*pej*) seelenlos; *building, town, person* kalt; (*dull*) öde

'soul mate *n* Seelenverwandte(r) *f(m)*

'soul music *n* Soulmusik *f,* Soul *m*

'soul-searching *n* Prüfung *f* des Gewissens

sound¹ [saʊnd] **I.** *n* ① (*noise*) Geräusch *nt;* (*musical tone*) *of a bell* Klang *m;* (*verbal, TV, film*) Ton *m;* **don't make a ~!** sei still! ② LING Laut *m* ③ PHYS Schall *m* ④ (*on film*) Sound *m* **II.** *vi* ① (*resonate*) erklingen; *alarm* ertönen; *alarm clock* klingeln; *bell* läuten ② (*fam: complain*) ■**to ~ off** herumtönen ③ + *adj* (*seem*) klingen, sich anhören **III.** *vt* (*produce sound from*) *alarm* auslösen; [*car*] *horn* hupen

sound² [saʊnd] **I.** *adj* ① (*healthy*) gesund; (*in good condition*) intakt, in gutem Zustand; *animal, person* kerngesund; **to be of ~ mind** bei klarem Verstand sein ② (*trustworthy*) solide; (*reasonable*) vernünftig; *advice* gut; *argument* schlagend ③ (*undisturbed*) *sleep* tief **II.** *adv* **to be ~ asleep** tief [und fest] schlafen

sound³ [saʊnd] *n* (*sea channel*) Meerenge *f;* (*inlet*) Meeresarm *m*

◆**sound out** *vt* ■**to ~ out** ◯ **sb** bei jdm vorfühlen; (*ask*) bei jdm anfragen

'sound barrier *n* Schallmauer *f*

'sound bite *n* prägnanter Ausspruch (*eines Politikers*)

'sound card *n* COMPUT Soundkarte *f*

'sound engineer *n* Toningenieur(in) *m(f)*

sounding ['saʊn·dɪŋ] *n usu pl* NAUT [Aus]loten *nt*

soundly ['saʊnd·li] *adv* ① (*thoroughly*) gründlich, ordentlich; (*clearly*) eindeutig, klar; (*severely*) schwer *fam* ② (*reliably*) fundiert *geh* ③ (*deeply*) *sleep* tief

soundness ['saʊnd·nɪs] *n* Solidität *f geh,* Verlässlichkeit *f,* Zuverlässigkeit *f*

'soundproof **I.** *adj* schalldicht, schallisoliert **II.** *vt* schalldicht machen

'sound system *n* Stereoanlage *f*

'soundtrack *n* ① (*on film*) Tonspur *f* ② (*film music*) Filmmusik *f,* Soundtrack *m*

'sound wave *n* Schallwelle *f*

soup [sup] *n* ① (*fluid food*) Suppe *f;* **vegetable** ~ Gemüsesuppe *f* ② (*fig: fog*) Suppe *f*

'soup kitchen *n* Armenküche *f*

'soup spoon *n* Suppenlöffel *m*

sour ['saʊ·ər] **I.** *adj* ① (*in taste*) sauer ② (*fig: ill-tempered*) griesgrämig, missmutig; (*embittered*) verbittert **II.** *n saures, alkoholisches Getränk;* **whiskey** ~ Whisky *m* mit Zitrone **III.** *vt* ① (*give sour taste*) sauer machen ② (*fig: make unpleasant*) trüben, beeinträchtigen **IV.** *vi* ① (*become sour*) sauer werden ② (*fig*) getrübt werden

source [sɔrs] **I.** *n* ① (*origin, spring*) Quelle *f;* (*reason*) Grund *m* (**of** für +*akk*) ② (*of information*) ■~**s** *pl* LIT (*for article, essay*) Quellen[angaben] *pl;* **according to government ~s** wie in Regierungskreisen verlautete **II.** *vt usu passive* ■**to be ~d** ① (*document*) belegt sein ② ECON (*be obtained*) stammen

sourpuss <*pl* -es> ['saʊ·ər·pʊs] *n* (*fam*) Miesepeter *m*

south [saʊθ] **I.** *n* ① (*compass direction*) Süden *m;* **Los Angeles lies to the ~ of San Francisco** Los Angeles liegt südlich von San

Francisco ② (*southern US states*) ■**the S~** die Südstaaten *pl* **II.** *adj* (*opposite of north*) Süd-, südlich **III.** *adv* (*toward the south*) **my room faces ~** mein Zimmer ist nach Süden ausgerichtet; **to drive ~** Richtung Süden [*o* südwärts] fahren

South 'Africa *n* Südafrika *nt*

South 'African I. *adj* südafrikanisch **II.** *n* Südafrikaner(in) *m(f)*

South A'merica *n* Südamerika *nt*

South A'merican I. *adj* südamerikanisch **II.** *n* Südamerikaner(in) *m(f)*

'southbound *adj* [in] Richtung Süden

South Carolina [ˌsaʊθ·ˌkær·ə·ˈlaɪ·nə] *n* Südkarolina *nt*

South Dakota [ˌsaʊθ·ˌdə·ˈkoʊ·t̬ə] *n* Süddakota *nt*

south'east I. *n* Südosten *m* **II.** *adj* Südost-, südöstlich **III.** *adv* südostwärts, nach Südosten

south'eastward I. *adj* südostwärts *präd;* **in a ~ direction** in südöstlicher Richtung **II.** *adv* südostwärts *präd,* nach Südosten *nach n*

south'eastwards *adv see* **southeastward II**

southerly [ˈsʌð·ər·li] **I.** *adj* südlich; **in a ~ direction** in südlicher Richtung **II.** *adv* südlich; (*going south*) südwärts; (*coming from south*) von Süden **III.** *n* Südwind *m;* NAUT Süd *m kein pl*

southern [ˈsʌð·ərn] *adj* südlich, Süd-

southerner [ˈsʌð·ər·nər] *n* **to be a ~** aus dem Süden kommen, ein Südstaatler *m* sein

southern 'hemisphere *n* **the ~** die südliche [Erd]halbkugel

Southern 'Lights *npl see* **aurora australis**

southernmost [ˈsʌð·ərn·moʊst] *adj* ■**the ~ ...** der/die/das südlichste ...

South Ko'rea *n* Südkorea *nt*

South Ko'rean I. *adj* südkoreanisch **II.** *n* Südkoreaner(in) *m(f)*

'southpaw *n* SPORTS (*fam*) Linkshänder(in) *m(f)*

South 'Pole *n* Südpol *m*

southward [ˈsaʊθ·wərd] **I.** *adj* südlich **II.** *adv* südwärts, nach [*o* [in] Richtung] Süden

southwards [ˈsaʊθ·wərdz] *adv see* **southward II**

south'west I. *n* Südwesten *m* **II.** *adj* südwestlich, Südwest- **III.** *adv* südwestwärts, nach Südwesten

south'western *adj* südwestlich

south'westward I. *adj* südwestlich **II.** *adv* südwestlich, nach Südwesten

south'westwards *adv see* **southwestward II**

souvenir [ˌsu·və·ˈnɪr] *n* Andenken *nt* (**of** an +*akk*)

sou'wester [ˌsaʊ·ˈwes·tər] *n* (*hat*) Südwester *m*

sovereign [ˈsav·rɪn] **I.** *n* Herrscher(in) *m(f)* **II.** *adj attr* ① (*chief*) höchste(r, s), oberste(r, s); **~ power** Hoheitsgewalt *f* ② POL (*independent*) *state* souverän

sovereignty [ˈsav·rɪn·ti] *n* (*supremacy*) höchste Gewalt, Oberhoheit *f;* (*right of self-determination*) Souveränität *f;* **to have ~ over sb/sth** oberste Herrschaftsgewalt über jdn/etw besitzen

soviet [ˈsoʊ·vi·et] *n* (*hist*) Sowjet *m*

Soviet 'Union *n* (*hist*) ■**the ~** die Sowjetunion

sow[1] <sowed, sown *or* sowed> [soʊ] **I.** *vt* ① (*plant*) säen; MIL *mines* legen ② (*fig: cause*) säen; *terror* hervorrufen; *doubts* wecken **II.** *vi* säen

sow[2] [saʊ] *n* (*pig*) Sau *f*

sown [soʊn] *vt, vi pp of* **sow[1]**

sox [saks] *npl* (*fam*) Socken *pl*

'soybean *n* Sojabohne *f*

'soy sauce *n* Sojasoße *f*

spa [spa] *n* ① **health ~** Heilbad *nt* ② (*place*) [Bade]kurort *m,* Bad *nt* ③ (*spring*) Heilquelle *f*

space [speɪs] *n* ① (*expanse*) Raum *m* ② (*gap*) Platz *m;* (*between two things*) Zwischenraum *m;* **parking ~** Parklücke *f;* (*seat*) [Sitz]platz *m* ③ (*vacancy*) Platz *m,* Raum *m* ④ (*premises*) Fläche *f;* (*for living*) Wohnraum *m* ⑤ (*cosmos*) Weltraum *m* ⑥ (*blank*) Platz *m;* (*for a photo*) freie Stelle; TYPO (*between words*) Zwischenraum *m;* **blank ~** Lücke *f*

◆**space out I.** *vt* ① (*position at a distance*) verteilen ② TYPO (*put blanks between*) *words* auseinanderschreiben **II.** *vi* (*sl: be disoriented*) geistig weggetreten sein; (*from drugs*) high sein

'space age *n* ■**the ~** das Weltraumzeitalter

'space bar *n* COMPUT Leertaste *f*

'space capsule *n* Weltraumkapsel *f*

'space center *n* Weltraumzentrum *nt*

'spacecraft <*pl* -> *n* Raumfahrzeug *nt*

spaced-'out *adj* (*sl*) ■**to be ~** (*in excitement*) geistig weggetreten sein *fam;* (*scatterbrained*) schusselig sein *fam*

'spaceman *n* [Welt]raumfahrer *m*

'space probe *n* Raumsonde *f*

spacer [ˈspeɪ·sər] *n* ① TECH Distanzstück *nt* ② TYPO Leerzeichen *nt*

'space-saving *adj* Platz sparend; *furniture* Raum sparend

'spaceship *n* Raumschiff *nt*

'space shuttle *n* [Welt]raumfähre *f*

'space station *n* [Welt]raumstation *f*

'space tourism *n* Weltraumtourismus *m*

'spacewoman *n* Raumfahrerin *f*

spacing [ˈspeɪ·sɪŋ] *n* Abstände *pl;* **double ~** TYPO zweizeiliger Abstand

spacious [ˈspeɪ·ʃəs] *adj* (*approv*) *house, room* geräumig; *area* weitläufig

spade [speɪd] *n* ① (*tool*) Spaten *m* ② CARDS Pik *nt*

spadework [ˈspeɪd·wɜrk] *n* Vorarbeit *f*

spaghetti [spə·ˈget̬·i] *n* FOOD Spaghetti *pl*

spaghetti 'western *n* (*fam*) Italowestern *m*

Spain [speɪn] *n* Spanien *nt*

Spam® [spæm] *n* Frühstücksfleisch *nt*

spam [spæm] *n no pl* INET (*sl*) Spam *m o f o nt,* Spammail *f;* **~ filter** Spamfilter *m*

S

span [spæn] **I.** *n usu sing* ① (*period of time*) Spanne *f;* **life ~** Lebensspanne *f* ② (*distance*) Breite *f;* (*as measurement*) Spanne *f selten;* **wing ~** Flügelspannweite *f* ③ (*fig: scope*) Umfang *m,* Spannweite *f fig* ④ ARCHIT (*arch of bridge*) Brückenbogen *m;* (*of arch*) Spannweite *f* **II.** *vt* <-nn-> (*stretch over*) *river* überspannen; (*cover*) **to ~ a great deal** [*or* **range**] **of sth** sich über etw *akk* erstrecken, etw *akk* umfassen; (*cross*) führen (über +*akk*)

spangle ['spæŋ·gəl] **I.** *n* Paillette *f* **II.** *vt* mit Pailletten besetzen

spangled ['spæŋ·gəld] *adj* ① (*with spangles*) mit Pailletten besetzt ② (*shiny*) glitzernd

Spaniard ['spæn·jərd] *n* Spanier(in) *m(f)*

spaniel ['spæn·jəl] *n* Spaniel *m*

Spanish ['spæn·ɪʃ] **I.** *n* ① (*language*) Spanisch *nt* ② + *pl vb* (*people*) ■**the ~** die Spanier *pl* **II.** *adj* spanisch

spank [spæŋk] **I.** *vt* (*slap*) ■**to ~ sb** jdm den Hintern versohlen; (*sexually*) jdm einen Klaps auf den Hintern geben **II.** *n* Klaps *m fam*

spanking ['spæŋ·kɪŋ] **I.** *n* Tracht *f* Prügel **II.** *adv* **~ new** funkelnagelneu

spare [sper] **I.** *vt* ① (*not kill*) verschonen ② (*go easy on*) schonen ③ (*avoid*) ersparen; **to ~ sb embarrassment** jdm Peinlichkeiten ersparen ④ (*not use*) sparen; **to ~ no cost** keine Kosten scheuen ⑤ (*give*) **could you ~ [me] 10 dollars?** kannst du mir 10 Dollar leihen?; **to ~ a prayer for sb** für jdn ein Gebet übrig haben **II.** *adj* Ersatz-; **~ [bed]room** Gästezimmer *nt* **III.** *n* AUTO Ersatzreifen *m*

spare 'parts *n pl* Ersatzteile *pl*

'spareribs *npl* [Schäl]rippchen *pl*

spare 'time *n* Freizeit *f*

spare 'tire *n* ① AUTO Ersatzreifen *m* ② (*fam: fat*) Rettungsring *m*

sparing ['sper·ɪŋ] *adj* (*economical*) sparsam

spark [spark] **I.** *n* ① (*fire, electricity*) Funke[n] *m* ② (*fig: trace*) **a ~ of hope** ein Fünkchen *nt* Hoffnung ③ (*fig: person*) **a bright ~** ein Intelligenzbolzen *m fam* **II.** *vt* (*ignite, cause*) entfachen *a. fig; interest* wecken; *problems* verursachen **III.** *vi* Funken sprühen

sparkle ['spar·kəl] **I.** *vi* ① (*a. fig: glitter*) funkeln, glitzern; *fire* sprühen ② (*fig: be witty*) sprühen (**with** vor +*dat*) **II.** *n* ① (*a. fig: light*) Funkeln *nt,* Glitzern *nt* ② (*fig: liveliness*) **sth lacks ~** einer S. *dat* fehlt es an Schwung

sparkler ['spark·lər] *n* ① (*firework*) Wunderkerze *f* ② (*sl: diamond*) Klunker *m fam*

sparkling ['spark·lɪŋ] *adj* ① (*shining*) glänzend; *eyes* funkelnd, glitzernd ② (*fig, approv: lively*) *person* vor Leben sprühend ③ (*bubbling*) *drink* mit Kohlensäure *nach n; wine* schäumend, moussierend

'spark plug *n* Zündkerze *f*

sparrow ['sper·oʊ] *n* Spatz *m*

sparrowhawk ['sper·oʊ·hɔk] *n* Falke *m*

sparse [spars] *adj* ① (*scattered, small*) spärlich ② (*meager*) dünn, dürftig

sparsely ['spars·li] *adv* ① (*thinly*) spärlich ② (*meagerly*) dürftig

Spartan ['spar·tən] **I.** *adj life* spartanisch; *meal* frugal *geh* **II.** *n* Spartaner(in) *m(f)*

spasm ['spæz·əm] *n* ① MED (*cramp*) Krampf *m* ② (*surge*) Anfall *m;* **a ~ of pain** krampfartige Schmerzen *pl*

spastic ['spæs·tɪk] *adj* ① MED spastisch ② (*fig, offensive sl: stupid*) schwach

spat[1] [spæt] *vt, vi pt, pp of* **spit**

spat[2] [spæt] **I.** *n* (*fam*) Krach *m* **II.** *vi* <-tt-> [sich] streiten [*o* zanken]

spate [speɪt] *n* (*fig*) ■**a ~ of sth** eine Flut [*o* Reihe] von etw *dat*

spatial ['speɪ·ʃəl] *adj* räumlich

spatter ['spæţ·ər] **I.** *vt* bespritzen; **to ~ sb with water** jdn nass spritzen **II.** *vi raindrops* prasseln **III.** *n* (*of dirt*) Spritzer *m;* (*sound*) Prasseln *nt kein pl*

spatula ['spætʃ·ə·lə] *n* ART, FOOD Spachtel *m o f,* Pfannenwender *m*

spawn [spɔn] **I.** *vt* ① (*lay eggs*) *fish, frog* ablegen ② (*fig: produce*) hervorbringen, produzieren **II.** *vi frog* laichen **III.** *n* (*eggs*) Laich *m* **IV.** *n* (*eggs*) Laich *m;* **~ of frogs** Froschlaich *m*

spay [speɪ] *vt* sterilisieren

speak <spoke, spoken> [spik] **I.** *vi* ① (*say words*) sprechen ② (*converse*) sich unterhalten; ■**to ~ to** [*or* **with**] **sb** [**about sth**] mit jdm [über etw *akk*] reden ③ + *adv* (*view*) **scientifically ~ing** wissenschaftlich gesehen; **strictly ~ing** genau genommen ④ (*make speech*) reden, sprechen **II.** *vt* ① (*say*) sagen; **to not ~ a word** kein Wort herausbringen; **to ~ one's mind** sagen, was man denkt ② (*language*) sprechen; **to ~ English fluently** fließend Englisch sprechen

◆**speak against** *vi* ■**to ~ against sth** sich gegen etw *akk* aussprechen

◆**speak for I.** *vi* ■**to ~ for sb** in jds Namen sprechen **II.** *vt* (*represent*) ■**to ~ for oneself** für sich selbst sprechen ► PHRASES: **~ for <u>yourself</u>!** (*hum, pej fam*) du vielleicht!

◆**speak out** *vi* seine Meinung deutlich vertreten; ■**to ~ out against sth** sich gegen etw *akk* aussprechen

◆**speak up** *vi* ① (*raise voice*) lauter sprechen ② (*support*) seine Meinung sagen; **to ~ up for sb/sth** für jdn/etw eintreten

speaker ['spi·kər] *n* ① (*at meeting, in debate*) Redner(in) *m(f)* ② *of language* Sprecher(in) *m(f);* **native ~** Muttersprachler(in) *m(f)* ③ (*loudspeaker*) Lautsprecher *m* ④ POL **the S~ of the House** der/die Vorsitzende des Repräsentantenhauses

speaking ['spi·kɪŋ] **I.** *n* (*act*) Sprechen *nt;* (*holding a speech*) Reden *nt* **II.** *adj attr* (*able to speak*) sprechend ► PHRASES: **to be on ~ <u>terms</u>** (*acquainted*) miteinander bekannt sein; **they are no longer on ~ terms with each other** sie reden nicht mehr miteinander

'speaking part *n* Sprechrolle *f*

spear [spɪr] **I.** *n* (*weapon*) Speer *m,* Lanze *f* **II.** *vt* aufspießen, durchbohren

'spearhead I. *n* ❶ (*point of spear*) Speerspitze *f* ❷ (*fig: leading group or thing*) Spitze *f* **II.** *vt* (*a. fig*) anführen

'spearmint *n* grüne Minze

special ['speʃ·əl] **I.** *adj* ❶ (*more*) besondere(r, s); **to pay ~ attention to sth** bei etw *dat* ganz genau aufpassen ❷ (*unusual*) besondere(r, s); *circumstances* außergewöhnlich; **on ~ occasions** zu besonderen Gelegenheiten ❸ (*dearest*) beste(r, s); ■ **to be ~ to sb** jdm sehr viel bedeuten ❹ *attr* (*for particular purpose*) speziell; (*for particular use*) *tires, equipment* Spezial- **II.** *n* ❶ (*meal*) Tagesgericht *nt* ❷ *pl* (*bargains*) ■ **~s** Sonderangebote *pl*

special e'dition *n* Sonderausgabe *f*

special ef'fect *n usu pl* Spezialeffekt *m,* Special Effect *m fachspr*

specialist ['speʃ·ə·lɪst] *n* ❶ (*expert*) Fachmann, -frau *m, f,* Spezialist(in) *m(f)* (**in** für +*akk,* **on** in +*dat*) ❷ (*doctor*) Spezialist(in) *m(f),* Facharzt, -ärztin *m, f*

specialization [ˌspeʃ·ə·lɪ·'zeɪ·ʃən] *n* ❶ (*studies*) Spezialisierung *f* (**in** auf +*akk*) ❷ (*skill*) Spezialgebiet *nt*

specialize ['speʃ·ə·laɪz] *vi* sich spezialisieren (**in** auf +*akk*)

specialized ['speʃ·ə·laɪzd] *adj* ❶ (*skilled*) spezialisiert; **~ knowledge** Fachwissen *f* ❷ (*particular*) spezial; **~ magazine** Fachzeitschrift *f*

specially ['speʃ·əl·i] *adv* ❶ (*specifically*) speziell, extra ❷ (*particularly*) besonders, insbesondere ❸ (*very*) besonders

special 'offer *n* Sonderangebot *nt*

specialty ['speʃ·əl·ti] *n* ❶ (*product, quality*) Spezialität *f* ❷ (*skill*) Fachgebiet *nt*

species <*pl* -> ['spi·ʃiz] *n* BIOL Art *f,* Spezies *f fachspr*

specific [spə·'sɪf·ɪk] *adj* ❶ (*exact*) genau; **could you be a little more ~?** könntest du dich etwas klarer ausdrücken? ❷ *attr* (*particular*) bestimmte(r, s), speziell; **~ details** besondere Einzelheiten

specifically [spə·'sɪf·ɪk·li] *adv* ❶ (*particularly*) speziell, extra ❷ (*clearly*) ausdrücklich

specification [ˌspes·ə·fɪ·'keɪ·ʃən] *n* ❶ (*specifying*) Angabe *f* ❷ (*plan*) ■ **~s** *pl* detaillierter Entwurf; (*for building*) Bauplan *m* ❸ (*description*) genaue Angabe; (*for patent*) Patentschrift *f;* (*for machines*) Konstruktionsplan *m*

specify <-ie-> ['spes·ə·faɪ] *vt* angeben; (*list in detail*) spezifizieren; (*list expressly*) ausdrücklich angeben

specimen ['spes·ə·mən] *n* ❶ (*example*) Exemplar *nt* ❷ MED Probe *f*

speck [spek] *n* ❶ (*spot*) Fleck *m; of blood, mud* Spritzer *m,* Sprenkel *m* ❷ (*particle*) Körnchen *nt;* **not a ~ of truth** (*fig*) kein Fünkchen Wahrheit

speckle ['spek·əl] *n* Tupfen *m,* Sprenkel *m*

speckled ['spek·əld] *adj* gesprenkelt

specs[1] [speks] *npl* (*fam*) *short for* **specifications** technische Daten

specs[2] [speks] *npl* (*fam*) *short for* **spectacles** Brille *f*

spectacle ['spek·tə·kəl] *n* ❶ (*display*) Spektakel *nt* ❷ (*event*) Schauspiel *nt geh,* Spektakel *nt pej;* (*sight*) Anblick *m*

spectacles ['spek·tə·kəlz] *npl* (*old*) Brille *f*

spectacular [spek·'tæk·jʊ·lər] *adj* ❶ (*wonderful*) *dancer, scenery* atemberaubend, großartig ❷ (*striking*) *increase, failure, success* spektakulär, sensationell

spectator [spek·'teɪ·t̬ər] *n* Zuschauer(in) *m(f)* (**at** bei +*dat*)

specter ['spek·tər] *n* ❶ (*liter or old: ghost*) Gespenst *nt* ❷ (*fig liter: threat*) [Schreck]gespenst *nt*

spectrum <*pl* -tra *or* -s> ['spek·trəm] *n* ❶ PHYS (*band of colors*) Spektrum *nt a. fig* ❷ (*frequency band*) Palette *f,* Skala *f*

speculate ['spek·jʊ·leɪt] *vi* spekulieren

speculation [ˌspek·jʊ·'leɪ·ʃən] *n* ❶ (*guess*) Spekulation *f,* Vermutung *f* (**about** über +*akk*) ❷ (*trade*) Spekulation *f*

speculative ['spek·jə·lə·t̬ɪv] *adj* ❶ (*conjectural*) spekulativ *geh;* PHILOS hypothetisch *geh* ❷ (*risky*) spekulativ

speculator ['spek·jʊ·leɪ·t̬ər] *n* Spekulant(in) *m(f)*

sped [sped] *pt, pp of* **speed**

speech <*pl* -es> [spitʃ] *n* ❶ (*faculty of speaking*) Sprache *f;* (*act of speaking*) Sprechen *nt;* **in everyday ~** in der Alltagssprache ❷ (*spoken style*) Sprache *f,* Redestil *m* ❸ (*oration*) Rede *f;* (*shorter*) Ansprache *f* (**about/on** über +*akk*); **freedom of ~** POL Redefreiheit *f*

speechify <-ie-> ['spi·tʃə·faɪ] *vi* (*pej o hum*) salbadern *pej fam*

'speech impediment *n* Sprachfehler *m*

speechless ['spitʃ·lɪs] *adj* ❶ (*shocked*) sprachlos ❷ (*mute*) stumm

'speech recognition *n* COMPUT Spracherkennung *f*

'speech therapist *n* Sprachtherapeut(in) *m(f),* Logopäde, Logopädin *m, f*

'speech therapy *n* Sprachtherapie *f,* Logopädie *f*

'speechwriter *n* Redenschreiber(in) *m(f)*

speed [spid] **I.** *n* ❶ (*velocity*) Geschwindigkeit *f,* Tempo *nt;* **maximum ~** Höchstgeschwindigkeit *f;* **to gain ~** an Geschwindigkeit gewinnen; *vehicle* beschleunigen; *person* schneller werden ❷ (*quickness*) Schnelligkeit *f* ❸ TECH (*operating mode*) Drehzahl *f;* **full ~ ahead!** NAUT volle Kraft voraus! ❹ (*sl: drug*) Speed *nt* ► PHRASES: **to bring sb/sth up to ~ [on sth]** (*update*) jdn/etw [über etw *akk*] auf den neuesten Stand bringen **II.** *vi* <sped, sped> ❶ (*rush*) sausen, flitzen; ■ **to ~ along** vorbeisausen; **he sped along the side of the river** er raste am Fluss entlang ❷ (*drive too fast*) rasen **III.** *vt* <-ed *or* sped, -ed *or* sped> ❶ (*quicken*) beschleunigen ❷ (*transport*) ■ **to ~ sb somewhere** jdn schnell irgendwohin bringen

S

◆**speed up** **I.** *vt* beschleunigen; ■**to ~ up** ↻ **sb/sth** jdn/etw antreiben **II.** *vi* (*accelerate*) beschleunigen, schneller werden; *person* sich beeilen

'**speedboat** *n* Rennboot *nt*

'**speed bump** *n* Bodenschwelle *f*

'**speed dating** *n organisierte Partnersuche, wobei man mit jedem Kandidaten nur wenige Minuten spricht*

speeding ['spi·dɪŋ] *n* Geschwindigkeitsüberschreitung *f,* Rasen *nt*

'**speed limit** *n* Geschwindigkeitsbegrenzung *f,* Tempolimit *nt*

speedometer [spɪ·'dam·ɪ·t̬ər] *n* Tachometer *m o nt,* Geschwindigkeitsmesser *m*

'**speed skater** *n* Eisschnellläufer(in) *m(f)*

'**speed skating** *n* Eisschnelllauf *m*

'**speed trap** *n* Radarfalle *f*

'**speedway** *n* (*racetrack*) Speedwaybahn *f*

speedy ['spi·di] *adj* schnell; *decision, solution, recovery a.* rasch; *delivery, service* prompt

spell[1] <spelled *or* spelt, spelled *or* spelt> [spel] **I.** *vt* ❶ (*using letters*) buchstabieren ❷ (*signify*) bedeuten; **to ~ disaster/trouble** Unglück/Ärger bedeuten **II.** *vi* (*in writing*) [richtig] schreiben; (*aloud*) buchstabieren

◆**spell out** *vt* ❶ (*using letters*) buchstabieren ❷ (*explain*) klarmachen

spell[2] [spel] *n* (*state*) Zauber *m,* Bann *m geh;* (*words*) Zauberspruch *m;* **to cast a ~ on sb** jdn verzaubern; **to be under sb's ~** (*fig*) von jdm verzaubert sein

spell[3] [spel] **I.** *n* ❶ (*period of time*) Weile *f;* **to go through a bad ~** eine schwierige Zeit durchmachen ❷ (*period of weather*) **~ of sunny weather** Schönwetterperiode *f* ❸ (*period of sickness*) Anfall *m;* **to suffer from dizzy ~s** unter Schwindelanfällen leiden **II.** *vt* ablösen

spellbinding ['spel·baɪn·dɪŋ] *adj film, performance, speech* fesselnd

spellbound ['spel·baʊnd] *adj* gebannt, fasziniert; **to hold sb ~** jdn fesseln

'**spellchecker** *n* COMPUT Rechtschreibhilfe *f*

speller ['spel·ər] *n* ❶ (*person*) **to be a good ~** gut in Orthographie sein ❷ (*spelling book*) Rechtschreib[e]buch *nt*

spelling ['spel·ɪŋ] **I.** *n* ❶ (*orthography*) Rechtschreibung *f,* Orthographie *f* ❷ (*activity*) Buchstabieren *nt kein pl* **II.** *adj attr* Rechtschreib-

'**spelling bee** *n* Buchstabierwettbewerb *m*

spelt [spelt] *pp, pt of* **spell**

spend [spend] **I.** *vt* <spent, spent> ❶ (*pay out*) *money* ausgeben (**on** für +*akk*) ❷ (*pass time*) *time* verbringen; **my sister always ~s all day in the bathroom** meine Schwester braucht immer eine Ewigkeit im Bad **II.** *vi* <spent, spent> Geld ausgeben

spending ['spen·dɪŋ] *n* Ausgaben *pl* (**on** für +*akk*)

'**spending money** *n* (*as allowance*) Taschengeld *nt;* (*for special circumstances*) frei verfügbares Geld

'**spending spree** *n* Großeinkauf *m*

spendthrift ['spend·θrɪft] (*pej*) **I.** *adj* (*fam*) verschwenderisch **II.** *n* (*fam*) Verschwender(in) *m(f)*

spent [spent] **I.** *pp, pt of* **spend** **II.** *adj* ❶ (*used up*) *match, cartridge* verbraucht; *creativity* verbraucht ❷ (*tired*) *person* ausgelaugt; **to feel ~** sich erschöpft fühlen

sperm <*pl* - *or* -s> [spɜrm] *n* ❶ (*male reproductive cell*) Samenzelle *f* ❷ (*fam: semen*) Sperma *nt*

'**sperm count** *n* Spermienzählung *f*

'**sperm donor** *n* Samenspender *m*

spermicide ['spɜr·mə·saɪd] *n* Spermizid *nt*

'**sperm whale** *n* Pottwal *m*

spew [spju] **I.** *vt* ❶ (*emit*) ausspeien; *lava* auswerfen, spucken *fam; exhaust* ausstoßen ❷ (*vomit*) erbrechen; *blood* spucken **II.** *vi* ❶ (*flow out*) *exhaust, lava, gas* austreten; *ash, dust* herausgeschleudert werden; *flames* hervorschlagen; *water* hervorsprudeln ❷ (*vomit*) erbrechen

sphere [sfɪr] *n* ❶ (*round object*) Kugel *f;* (*representing earth*) Erdkugel *f* ❷ (*area*) Bereich *m,* Gebiet *nt;* **social ~** soziales Umfeld

spherical ['sfɪr·ɪ·kəl] *adj* kugelförmig

spice [spaɪs] **I.** *n* ❶ (*aromatic*) Gewürz *nt* ❷ (*fig: excitement*) Pep *m* **II.** *vt* ❶ (*flavor*) würzen (**with** mit +*dat*) ❷ (*fig: add excitement to*) aufpeppen *fam*

spick-and-'span *adj* (*fam*) *house, kitchen* blitzsauber, blitzblank *fam*

spicy ['spaɪ·si] *adj* ❶ *food* würzig; (*hot*) scharf ❷ (*fig: sensational*) *tale, story* pikant

spider ['spaɪ·dər] *n* Spinne *f*

'**spider web** *n* Spinnennetz *nt*

spidery ['spaɪ·də·ri] *adj writing* krakelig; *drawing, design* fein; *arms, legs* spinnenhaft

spiel [ʃpil] *n* (*pej fam*) Leier *f;* **sales ~** Verkaufsmasche *f*

spigot ['spɪg·ət] *n* ❶ (*tap*) Zapfen *m* ❷ (*faucet*) Wasserhahn *m*

spike [spaɪk] **I.** *n* ❶ (*heavy nail*) Nagel *m; on top of fence* Spitze *f; of a plant, animal* Stachel *m* ❷ (*on shoes*) Spike *m;* ■**~s** *pl* (*shoes for sprinting*) Spikes *pl* **II.** *vt* ❶ (*fam: secretly add alcohol*) **to ~ sb's drink** einen Schuss Alkohol in jds Getränk geben ❷ SPORTS (*injure*) verletzen ❸ (*in volleyball*) *ball* schmettern; (*in football*) spiken ❹ JOURN (*fam: reject*) *article, story* ablehnen; (*stop*) *plan, project* einstellen

spiky ['spaɪ·ki] *adj* ❶ (*with spikes*) *railing, wall, fence* mit Metallspitzen *nach n; branch, plant* dornig; *animal, bush* stachelig ❷ (*pointy*) *grass, leaf* spitz; *handwriting* steil

spill [spɪl] **I.** *n* (*spilled liquid*) Verschüttete(s) *nt;* (*pool*) Lache *f;* (*stain*) Fleck *m;* **oil ~** Ölteppich *m* **II.** *vt* <spilled *or* spilt, spilled *or* spilt> ❶ (*tip over*) verschütten ❷ (*fam: reveal*) ausplaudern ▶PHRASES: **to ~ the beans** das Geheimnis lüften **III.** *vi* ❶ (*flow out*) *liquid* überlaufen; *flour, sugar* verschüttet werden ❷ (*fig: spread*) *crowd* strömen; *conflict, violence* sich ausbreiten **IV.** *adj* ▶ PHRASES: **don't cry over ~ed milk** (*saying*) was passiert ist, ist passiert

◆**spill over** *vi* ❶ (*overflow*) überlaufen ❷ (*spread to*) ■**to ~ over into sth** *conflict, violence* sich auf etw *akk* ausdehnen

spillage ['spɪl·ɪdʒ] *n* ❶ (*action*) Verschütten *nt; of a liquid* Vergießen *nt;* **chemical ~** Austreten *nt* von Chemikalien ❷ (*amount spilled*) verschüttete Menge

spilt [spɪlt] *pp, pt of* **spill**

spin [spɪn] **I.** *n* ❶ (*rotation*) Drehung *f;* **to send a car into a ~** ein Auto zum Schleudern bringen ❷ (*in washing machine*) Schleudern *nt kein pl* ❸ (*positive slant*) **to put a ~ on sth** etw ins rechte Licht rücken ❹ (*drive*) Spritztour *f fam* **II.** *vi* <-nn-, spun, spun> ❶ (*rotate*) *earth, wheel* rotieren; *washing machine* schleudern; **to ~ out of control** außer Kontrolle geraten ❷ (*fig: be dizzy*) **my head is ~ning** mir dreht sich alles *fam* ❸ (*make thread*) spinnen **III.** *vt* <-nn-, spun, spun> ❶ (*rotate*) drehen; *clothes* schleudern; *records* spielen ❷ (*give positive slant*) ins rechte Licht rücken ❸ (*make thread of*) spinnen

◆**spin out I.** *vi* **to ~ out of control** *car* außer Kontrolle geraten **II.** *vt* (*prolong*) ■**to ~ out** ↻ **sth** etw ausdehnen

spina bifida [ˌspaɪ·nə·'bɪf·ɪ·də] *n* MED Spina bifida *f*

spinach ['spɪn·ɪtʃ] *n* Spinat *m*

spinal ['spaɪ·nəl] **I.** *adj muscle, vertebra* Rücken-; *injury* Rückgrat-, spinale(r, s) *fachspr; nerve, anesthesia* Rückenmark[s]- **II.** *n* Spinalnarkose *f*

'**spinal column** *n* Wirbelsäule *f*

'**spinal cord** *n* Rückenmark *nt*

spindle ['spɪn·dəl] *n* Spindel *f*

spindly ['spɪnd·li] *adj legs, stem* spindeldürr

'**spin doctor** *n* ≈ Pressesprecher(in) *m(f); a.* POL Spin-Doctor *m*

'**spin-dry** *vt clothes* schleudern

'**spin-dryer** *n* Wäscheschleuder *f*

spine [spaɪn] *n* ❶ (*spinal column*) Wirbelsäule *f* ❷ (*spike*) *of a plant, fish, hedgehog* Stachel *m* ❸ *of a book* [Buch]rücken *m*

spine-chilling ['spaɪn·ˌtʃɪl·ɪŋ] *adj film, tale* gruselig, Schauer-

spineless ['spaɪn·lɪs] *adj* ❶ (*without backbone*) wirbellos; (*without spines*) *plant, fish* ohne Stacheln *nach n* ❷ (*fig, pej: weak*) *person* rückgratlos

spinner ['spɪn·ər] *n* ❶ (*for thread*) Spinner(in) *m(f)* ❷ (*spin-dryer*) Wäscheschleuder *f*

spinning ['spɪn·ɪŋ] *n* Spinnen *nt*

'**spinning wheel** *n* Spinnrad *nt*

'**spinoff,** '**spin-off I.** *n* Nebenprodukt *nt* **II.** *adj attr* **~ effect** Folgewirkung *f*

spinster ['spɪn·stər] *n* (*usu pej*) alte Jungfer *veraltet*

spiny ['spaɪ·ni] *adj* BIOL stach[e]lig, Stachel-; *plant a.* dornig

spiral ['spaɪ·rəl] **I.** *n* Spirale *f* **II.** *adj attr staircase* spiralförmig **III.** *vi* <-l- *or* -ll-> ❶ (*move up*) sich hochwinden; *smoke, hawk* spiralförmig aufsteigen; (*move down*) sich hinunterwinden; *smoke, hawk* spiralförmig absteigen ❷ (*fig: increase*) ansteigen

spire [spaɪr] *n* Turmspitze *f*

spirit ['spɪr·ɪt] *n* ❶ (*sb's soul*) Geist *m* ❷ (*ghost*) Geist *m,* Gespenst *nt* ❸ REL ■**the Holy S~** der Heilige Geist ❹ (*mood*) Stimmung *f;* **team ~** Teamgeist *m* ❺ (*person*) Seele *f* ❻ (*vitality*) Temperament *nt* ❼ (*whiskey, rum, etc.*) ■**~s** *pl* Spirituosen *pl*

spirited ['spɪr·ɪ·t̬ɪd] *adj* (*approv*) temperamentvoll; *discussion* lebhaft; *person* beherzt; *reply* mutig

spiritless ['spɪr·ɪt·lɪs] *adj* (*pej*) schwunglos; *person, performance, book* saft- und kraftlos; *answer, defense, reply* lustlos

spiritual ['spɪr·ɪ·tʃu·əl] **I.** *adj* ❶ (*relating to the spirit*) geistig, spirituell ❷ REL *leader* religiös **II.** *n* MUS Spiritual *nt*

spiritualism ['spɪr·ɪ·tʃu·ə·lɪz·əm] *n* Spiritismus *m*

spiritualist ['spɪr·ɪ·tʃu·ə·lɪst] *n* Spiritist(in) *m(f)*

spit[1] [spɪt] **I.** *n* (*fam*) Spucke *f* **II.** *vi* <-tt-, spat *or* spit, spat *or* spit> spucken; ■**to ~ at sb** jdn anspucken **III.** *vt* <-tt-, spat *or* spit, spat *or* spit> ❶ (*out of mouth*) ausspucken ❷ (*as if from mouth*) *flames, sparks* ausstoßen

◆**spit out** *vt* ❶ (*from mouth*) ausspucken ❷ (*fig fam: say angrily*) fauchen; **~ it out!** spuck's schon aus!

spit[2] [spɪt] *n* ❶ (*rod for roasting*) Bratspieß *m* ❷ (*shoal*) Sandbank *f*

spite [spaɪt] **I.** *n* ❶ (*desire to hurt*) Bosheit *f* ❷ (*despite*) ■**in ~ of sth** trotz einer S. *gen* **II.** *vt* ärgern

spiteful ['spaɪt·fəl] *adj* gehässig

spitting 'image *n* Ebenbild *nt*

spittle ['spɪt̬·əl] *n* Spucke *f fam*

spittoon [spɪ·'tun] *n* Spucknapf *m*

splash [splæʃ] **I.** *n* <*pl* -es> ❶ (*sound*) Platschen *nt kein pl* ❷ (*small amount*) *of sauce, dressing* Klecks *m fam; of water, lemonade* Spritzer *m* **II.** *vt* ❶ (*scatter liquid*) verspritzen ❷ (*spray*) bespritzen ❸ (*fig: print prominently*) **her picture was ~ed all over the newspapers** ihr Bild erschien groß in allen Zeitungen **III.** *vi* ❶ (*fall in drops*) *rain, waves* klatschen; *tears* tropfen ❷ (*spill out*) spritzen

◆**splash down** *vi* AEROSP wassern

splat [splæt] (*fam*) **I.** *n* Klatschen *nt,* Platschen *nt* **II.** *adv* klatsch, platsch

splatter ['splæt̬·ər] **I.** *vt* bespritzen **II.** *vi* spritzen

splay [spleɪ] **I.** *vt one's fingers, legs* spreizen **II.** *vi* ■**to ~ out** *legs, fingers* weggestreckt sein; *river, pipe* sich weiten

spleen [splin] *n* ❶ ANAT Milz *f* ❷ (*fig: anger*) Wut *f;* **to vent one's ~** seine *gen* Wut auslassen

splendid ['splen·dɪd] *adj* großartig *a. iron*

splendor ['splen·dər] *n* ❶ (*beauty*) Pracht *f* ❷ (*beautiful things*) ■ **~s** *pl* Herrlichkeiten *pl*

splice [splaɪs] *vt* (*unite*) *DNA, wires* verbinden; *rope* spleißen; *film* kleben; ■ **to ~ sth ○ together** etw zusammenfügen

splint [splɪnt] *n* MED Schiene *f*

splinter ['splɪn·tər] *n* Splitter *m;* ~ [**of wood**] Holzsplitter *m,* Schiefer *m* ÖSTERR

'**splinter group** *n* POL Splittergruppe *f*

split [splɪt] **I.** *n* ❶ (*crack*) Riss *m* (**in** in +*dat*); (*in wall, wood*) Spalt *m* ❷ (*division in opinion*) Kluft *f;* POL Spaltung *f* ❸ (*marital separation*) Trennung *f* ❹ (*act of sharing*) Aufteilung *f;* **a four-way ~** eine Aufteilung in vier Teile **II.** *vt* <-tt-, split, split> ❶ (*divide*) teilen; *in half* halbieren; **to ~ the difference** (*fig*) sich *akk* auf halbem Weg einigen; **we ~ the proceeds among the four of us** wir teilten die Einnahmen unter uns vier auf ❷ (*fig: create division*) *group, party* spalten ❸ (*rip, crack*) *seam* aufplatzen lassen; **to ~ one's head open** sich *dat* den Kopf aufschlagen **III.** *vi* <-tt-, split, split> ❶ (*divide*) *wood, stone* [entzwei]brechen; *seam, cloth* aufplatzen; *hair* splissen; **to ~ into groups** sich aufteilen ❷ (*become splinter group*) ■ **to ~ from sth** sich von etw *dat* abspalten ❸ (*end relationship*) sich trennen

◆**split off I.** *vt* (*break off*) abbrechen; (*with axe*) abschlagen; (*separate*) abtrennen **II.** *vi* ❶ (*become detached*) *rock, brick* sich lösen ❷ (*leave*) ■ **to ~ off from sth** *party, group, faction* sich von etw *dat* abspalten

◆**split up I.** *vt* ❶ (*share*) *money, work* aufteilen ❷ (*separate*) *a group, team* teilen **II.** *vi* ❶ (*divide up*) sich teilen; **to ~ up into groups** sich in Gruppen aufteilen ❷ (*end relationship*) sich trennen (**with** von +*dat*)

'**split-level I.** *adj* mit Zwischengeschossen *nach n* **II.** *n* Haus *nt* mit Zwischengeschossen

split person'ality *n* gespaltene Persönlichkeit

split 'screen *n* geteilter Bildschirm

splitting 'headache *n* (*fam*) rasende Kopfschmerzen *pl*

'**split-up** *n* Trennung *f*

splotch [splatʃ] **I.** *n* (*fam*) *of paint, color* Klecks *m; of blood, grease* Fleck *m;* (*daub*) *of whipped cream* Klecks *m* **II.** *vt* (*fam*) bespritzen

splurge [splɜrdʒ] **I.** *vt* (*fam*) **to ~ one's savings on sth** sein Gespartes für etw *akk* verprassen **II.** *vi* (*fam*) prassen *fam;* ■ **to ~ on sth** viel Geld für etw *akk* ausgeben, Geld für etw *akk* hinauswerfen

splutter ['splʌt̬·ər] **I.** *vi* ❶ (*make noise*) *person, vehicle, engine* stottern; *fire* zischen ❷ (*spit*) spucken; **to cough and ~** husten und spucken **II.** *vt* ❶ (*say*) **to ~ an excuse** eine Entschuldigung hervorstoßen; **"what the hell?" she ~ed** „was zum Teufel!", platzte sie los ❷ (*spit out*) *liquid* ausspucken **III.** *n of a person* Prusten *nt kein pl; of a car* Stottern *nt kein pl; of fire* Zischen *nt kein pl*

spoil [spɔɪl] **I.** *n* ❶ (*profits*) ■ **~s** *pl* Beute *f kein pl* ❷ (*debris*) Schutt *m* **II.** *vt* <spoiled *or* spoilt, spoiled *or* spoilt> ❶ (*ruin*) verderben; **to ~ sb's chances** jds Chancen ruinieren, jdm die Suppe versalzen ❷ (*treat too kindly*) verwöhnen; *child* verziehen; **to be spoiled for choice** eine große Auswahl haben **III.** *vi* <spoiled *or* spoilt, spoiled *or* spoilt> *food* schlecht werden, verderben; *milk* sauer werden; *butter* ranzig werden

spoiled [spɔɪld] *adj* ❶ *pred* (*ruined*) *food* verdorben; *milk* sauer ❷ (*pampered*) *child* verwöhnt; (*pej*) verzogen

spoiler ['spɔɪ·lər] *n of car* Spoiler *m*

spoilsport ['spɔɪl·spɔrt] *n* (*pej fam*) Spielverderber(in) *m(f)*

spoilt [spɔɪlt] *vt, vi pp, pt of* **spoil**

spoke[1] [spoʊk] *n* Speiche *f*

spoke[2] [spoʊk] *pt of* **speak**

spoken [spoʊ·kən] **I.** *pp of* **speak II.** *adj attr* (*not written*) gesprochen

spoken for *adj* ■ **to be ~** [bereits] vergeben sein

spokesman ['spoʊks·mən] *n* Sprecher *m*

'**spokesperson** <*pl* -people> *n* Sprecher(in) *m(f)*

'**spokeswoman** *n* Sprecherin *f*

sponge [spʌndʒ] **I.** *n* (*for washing*) *a.* ZOOL Schwamm *m* **II.** *vt* [mit einem Schwamm] abwischen

◆**sponge off I.** *vt* ■ **to ~ off ○ sb/sth** jdn/etw schnell [mit einem Schwamm] [ab]waschen **II.** *vi* (*pej fam*) ausnutzen

◆**sponge on** *vi* (*pej fam*) *see* **sponge off**

'**sponge bath** *n* **to give oneself/sb a ~** sich/jdn mit einem Schwamm waschen

'**sponge cake** *n* Rührkuchen *m;* (*without fat*) Biskuit[kuchen] *m*

sponger ['spʌn·dʒər] *n* (*pej*) Schmarotzer(in) *m(f)*

spongy ['spʌn·dʒi] *adj* schwammig; *grass, moss* weich, nachgiebig

sponsor ['span·sər] **I.** *vt* ❶ (*support*) ■ **to ~ sb/sth** *person* jdn/etw sponsern; *government* jdn/etw unterstützen; **to ~ a marathon runner** einen Marathonläufer für einen guten Zweck unterstützen ❷ POL (*support in election*) *candidate* unterstützen ❸ MEDIA *TV program, show* sponsern **II.** *n* (*supporter*) *of game, event* Sponsor(in) *m(f); of a charity* Förderer, Förderin *m, f; of a TV program* Sponsor *m*

sponsorship ['span·sər·ʃɪp] *n* (*by corporation, people*) Unterstützung *f;* (*at fundraiser*) Förderung *f;* POL *of a game, event* Sponsern *nt;* **to get ~** gefördert werden

spontaneity [ˌspan·tə·'neɪ·ɪ·t̬i] *n* (*approv*) Spontaneität *f*

spontaneous [span·'teɪ·ni·əs] *adj* ❶ (*unplanned*) spontan ❷ (*approv: unrestrained*) *laughter* impulsiv

spoof [spuf] *n* ❶ (*satire*) Parodie *f* (**of, on** von +*dat*) ❷ (*trick*) Scherz *m*

spook [spuk] *n* ① (*fam: ghost*) Gespenst *nt* ② (*sl: spy*) Spion(in) *m(f)*
spooky ['spu·ki] *adj* (*fam: scary*) schaurig; *house, woods, person* unheimlich; *story, film, novel* gespenstisch
spool [spul] *n* Rolle *f*
spoon [spun] *n* Löffel *m*
spoon-feed <-fed, -fed> ['spun·fid] *vt* ■ **to ~ sb** ① (*feed with spoon*) jdn mit einem Löffel füttern ② (*supply*) jdm alles vorgeben
spoonful <*pl* -s *or* spoonsful> ['spun·fʊl] *n* Löffel *m*
sporadic [spə·'ræd·ɪk] *adj* sporadisch
spore [spɔr] *n* BIOL Spore *f*
sport [spɔrt] **I.** *n* ① (*game*) Sport *m;* (*type of*) Sportart *f* ② *pl* ■ **~s** (*athletic activity*) Sport *m;* **to be good at ~s** sportlich sein ③ (*fam: cooperative person*) **to be a bad ~** ein Spielverderber/eine Spielverderberin sein; **to be a [good] ~** kein Spielverderber/keine Spielverderberin sein **II.** *vt* (*esp hum: wear*) tragen; **to ~ a huge mustache** mit einem riesigen Schnurrbart herumlaufen *fam*
'**sport coat** *n* Sportsakko *nt*
sporting ['spɔr·t̬ɪŋ] *adj* SPORTS ① *attr* (*involving sports*) Sport- ② (*approv dated: fair*) *chance* fair
'**sports car** *n* Sportwagen *m*
'**sportscast** [-kæst] *n* Sportübertragung *f*
sportscaster [-kæs·tər] *n* Sportreporter(in) *m(f)*
'**sportsman** *n* Sportler *m*
'**sportsmanlike** *adj* fair
'**sportsmanship** *n* Fairness *f*
'**sports page** *n* Sportseite *f*
'**sportswear** *n* Sportkleidung *f*
'**sportswoman** *n* Sportlerin *f*
'**sportswriter** *n* Sportjournalist(in) *m(f)*
sporty ['spɔr·t̬i] *adj* ① (*athletic*) sportlich ② (*fast*) *car* schnell
spot [spat] **I.** *n* ① (*mark*) Fleck *m* ② (*dot*) Punkt *m;* (*pattern*) Tupfen *m* ③ (*place*) Stelle *f;* **on the ~** an Ort und Stelle ④ TV, RADIO Beitrag *m* ▶ PHRASES: **to <u>put</u> sb on the ~** jdn in Verlegenheit bringen **II.** *vt* <-tt-> entdecken; (*notice*) bemerken
spot 'check *n* Stichprobe *f*
spotless ['spat·lɪs] *adj* ① (*clean*) makellos ② (*unblemished*) makellos, tadellos
'**spotlight I.** *n* Scheinwerfer *m;* **to be in the ~** (*fig*) im Rampenlicht stehen **II.** *vt* <-lighted *or* -lit, -lighted *or* -lit> ■ **to ~ sth** etw beleuchten; (*fig*) auf etw *akk* aufmerksam machen
spotted ['spat̬·ɪd] *adj* ① (*pattern*) getupft, gepunktet ② *pred* (*covered*) gesprenkelt (**with** mit +*dat*)
spotter ['spat̬·ər] *n* SPORTS Stütze *f*
spouse [spaʊs] *n* (*form*) [Ehe]gatte, -gattin *m, f*
spout [spaʊt] **I.** *n* ① (*opening*) Ausguss *m* ② (*discharge*) Strahl *m* **II.** *vt* ① (*pej: hold forth*) faseln *fam;* **to ~ facts and figures** mit Fakten und Zahlen um sich *akk* werfen *fam* ② (*discharge*) speien **III.** *vi* ① (*pej: hold forth*) Reden schwingen *fam* ② (*gush*) hervorschießen
sprain [spreɪn] **I.** *vt* ■ **to ~ sth** sich *dat* etw verstauchen; **to ~ one's ankle** sich *dat* den Knöchel verstauchen **II.** *n* Verstauchung *f*
sprang [spræŋ] *vi, vt pt of* **spring**
sprawl [sprɔl] **I.** *n usu sing* (*expanse*) Ausdehnung *f;* **urban ~** (*town*) riesiges Stadtgebiet; (*area*) Ballungsraum *m* **II.** *vi* ① (*slouch*) ■ **to ~ on sth** auf etw *dat* herumlümmeln *pej fam* ② (*expand*) sich ausbreiten
sprawling ['sprɔ·lɪŋ] *adj* (*pej*) ① (*expansive*) ausgedehnt ② (*irregular*) unregelmäßig
spray[1] [spreɪ] **I.** *n* ① (*mist, droplets*) Sprühnebel *m; of fuel, perfume* Wolke *f; of water* Gischt *m o f* ② (*aerosol*) Spray *m o nt* **II.** *vt* ① (*cover*) besprühen; *plants* spritzen ② (*disperse in a mist*) sprühen; (*in a spurt*) spritzen ③ (*shoot all around*) **to ~ sb with bullets** jdn mit Kugeln durchsieben **III.** *vi* spritzen
spray[2] [spreɪ] *n* ① (*branch*) Zweig *m* ② (*bouquet*) Strauß *m*
spread [spred] **I.** *n* ① (*act of spreading*) Verbreitung *f* ② (*range*) Vielfalt *f* ③ (*fam: big meal on table*) Festessen *nt,* Festschmaus *m* ④ (*soft food to spread*) Aufstrich *m* ⑤ JOURN Doppelseite *f* **II.** *vi* <spread, spread> ① (*extend over larger area*) *fire* sich ausbreiten; *news, panic* sich verbreiten ② (*stretch*) sich erstrecken ③ FOOD sich streichen lassen **III.** *vt* <spread, spread> ① (*open, extend*) *arms, papers, wings* ausbreiten; *net* auslegen ② (*cover with spread*) *bread* bestreichen ③ (*distribute*) *sand* verteilen; *fertilizer* streuen; *disease* übertragen; *panic* verbreiten ④ (*make known*) *rumors* verbreiten
spread-eagled ['spred·'i·gəld] *adj* ausgestreckt
'**spreadsheet** *n* Tabellenkalkulation *f,* Arbeitsblatt *nt*
spree [spri] *n* Gelage *nt;* **shopping ~** Einkaufstour *f*
sprig [sprɪg] *n* Zweig *nt*
sprightly ['spraɪt·li] *adj* munter; *old person* rüstig
spring [sprɪŋ] **I.** *n* ① (*season*) Frühling *m* ② TECH (*part in machine*) Feder *f* ③ (*source of water*) Quelle *f* **II.** *vi* <sprang *or* sprung, sprung> ① (*move quickly*) springen; **to ~ into action** den Betrieb aufnehmen ② (*suddenly appear*) auftauchen; **where did you ~ from?** wo kommst du denn plötzlich her?; **to ~ to mind** in den Kopf schießen **III.** *vt* ① (*operate*) auslösen; **to ~ a trap** eine Falle zuschnappen lassen ② (*fit with springs*) federn
◆ **spring back** *vi* zurückschnellen
◆ **spring up** *vi* plötzlich auftauchen; *business* aus dem Boden schießen
'**springboard** *n* (*a. fig*) Sprungbrett *nt a. fig*
spring-'clean I. *vi* Frühjahrsputz machen **II.** *vt* **to ~ a house** in einem Haus Frühjahrsputz machen

S

spring-'cleaning *n* Frühjahrsputz *m*
'spring roll *n* Frühlingsrolle *f*
'springtime *n* Frühling *m*
springy ['sprɪŋ·i] *adj* federnd *attr,* elastisch
sprinkle ['sprɪŋ·kəl] **I.** *vt* ❶ (*scatter*) streuen (**on** auf +*akk*) ❷ (*cover*) bestreuen (**with** mit +*dat*); (*with a liquid*) besprengen (**with** mit +*dat*) **II.** *n* ❶ *usu sing* (*small amount*) **a ~ of snow** leichter Schneefall ❷ ■ **~s** *pl* **chocolate ~s** Schokosplitter *pl*
sprinkler ['sprɪŋ·klər] *n* ❶ AGR Beregnungsanlage *f,* Bewässerungsanlage *f;* (*for a lawn*) Sprinkler *m* ❷ (*for fires*) Sprinkler *m;* ■ **~s** *pl* (*system*) Sprinkleranlage *f*
sprinkling ['sprɪŋ·klɪŋ] *n* ❶ *usu sing* (*light covering*) **a ~ of salt** eine Prise Salz ❷ *usu sing* (*small number*) ■ **a ~ of ...** ein paar ...
sprint [sprɪnt] **I.** *vi* sprinten **II.** *n* SPORTS *dash* Sprint *m;* **100-meter ~** Hundertmeterlauf *m,* 100-m-Lauf *m*
sprinter ['sprɪn·tər] *n* Sprinter(in) *m(f)*
sprite [spraɪt] *n* (*liter*) Naturgeist *m*
sprocket ['sprak·ɪt] *n* Zahnrad *nt*
sprout [spraʊt] **I.** *n* ❶ (*shoot*) Spross *m* ❷ (*vegetable*) ■ **Brussels ~s** *pl* Rosenkohl *m kein pl* **II.** *vi* ❶ (*grow*) *buds, flowers* sprießen; *buds, trees* austreiben *geh,* wachsen ❷ (*germinate*) keimen **III.** *vt* BOT *buds, leaves* treiben; **he's beginning to ~ a beard** er bekommt einen Bart
◆ **sprout up** *vi* aus dem Boden schießen
spruce [sprus] *n* Fichte *f*
spruce up *vt* (*make neat*) auf Vordermann bringen *fam;* ■ **to ~ up** ⊂ **oneself** sich zurechtmachen
sprung [sprʌŋ] *pp, pt of* **spring**
spry [spraɪ] *adj* agil *geh; old person* rüstig
spud [spʌd] *n* (*sl*) Kartoffel *f,* Erdapfel *m* DIAL, ÖSTERR
spun [spʌn] *pp, pt of* **spin**
spunky ['spʌŋ·ki] *adj* (*fam*) temperamentvoll, lebhaft
spur [spɜr] **I.** *n* ❶ (*on a heel*) Sporn *m* ❷ (*fig: encouragement*) Ansporn *m kein pl* (**to** zu +*dat*) ▶ PHRASES: **on the ~ of the moment** spontan **II.** *vt* <-rr-> ❶ (*encourage*) anspornen; (*persuade*) bewegen; (*incite*) anstacheln ❷ (*urge to go faster*) **to ~ a horse** einem Pferd die Sporen geben
spurious ['spjʊr·i·əs] *adj* falsch
spurn [spɜrn] *vt* (*form*) zurückweisen; (*contemptuously*) verschmähen *geh*
spurt [spɜrt] **I.** *n* ❶ (*jet*) Strahl *m* ❷ (*surge*) Schub *m;* **to do sth in ~s** etw schubweise machen ❸ (*run*) **to put on a ~** einen Spurt hinlegen **II.** *vt* [ver]spritzen **III.** *vi* (*gush*) spritzen
sputter ['spʌt̬·ər] **I.** *n* Knattern *nt kein pl,* Stottern *nt kein pl* **II.** *vi* zischen; (*car, engine*) stottern **III.** *vt* heraussprudeln; (*stutter*) stottern
spy [spaɪ] **I.** *n* Spion(in) *m(f)* **II.** *vi* (*gather information*) spionieren; ■ **to ~ on sb** jdm nachspionieren **III.** *vt* (*see*) sehen; (*spot*) entdecken

S

'spyglass *n* Fernglas *nt*
'spy satellite *n* Spionagesatellit *m*
sq. *n abbrev of* **square** Pl.
squabble ['skwab·əl] **I.** *n* Zankerei *f,* Streiterei *f* **II.** *vi* sich zanken (**over/about** um +*akk*)
squad [skwad] *n* ❶ SPORTS Mannschaft *f* ❷ MIL Gruppe *f,* Trupp *m*
'squad car *n* Streifenwagen *m*
squadron ['skwad·rən] *n* (*cavalry*) Schwadron *f;* (*air force*) Staffel *f;* (*navy*) Geschwader *nt*
squalid ['skwal·ɪd] *adj* ❶ (*pej: dirty*) schmutzig; (*neglected*) verwahrlost ❷ (*immoral*) verkommen
squall [skwɔl] *n* (*gust*) Bö *f;* **rain ~** Regenschauer *m;* **snow ~** Schneeböe *f*
squalor ['skwal·ər] *n* ❶ (*foulness*) Schmutz *m* ❷ (*immorality*) Verkommenheit *f*
squander ['skwan·dər] *vt* verschwenden, vergeuden; *opportunity* vertun
square [skwer] **I.** *n* ❶ (*shape*) Quadrat *nt* ❷ (*in town*) Platz *m;* **town ~** zentraler Platz ❸ (*tool*) Winkelmaß *nt* ❹ MATH Quadratzahl *f* **II.** *adj* ❶ (*square-shaped*) *piece of paper, etc.* quadratisch; *face* kantig ❷ (*on each side*) im Quadrat; (*when squared*) zum Quadrat; *foot, mile* Quadrat- ❸ (*fam: level*) plan; **to be [all] ~** auf gleich sein **III.** *adv* direkt, geradewegs **IV.** *vt* ❶ (*make square*) quadratisch machen; (*make right-angled*) rechtwinklig machen ❷ (*bring into agreement*) ■ **to ~ sth with sth** etw mit etw *dat* in Übereinstimmung bringen ❸ (*settle*) *matter* in Ordnung bringen ❹ MATH quadrieren
◆ **square up** *vi* (*fam: settle debt*) abrechnen
'square dance *n* Squaredance *m*

> Als **square dance** bezeichnet man einen amerikanischen Folkloretanz. Gruppen aus vier Pärchen bilden beim Tanz ein Quadrat, einen Kreis oder zwei Reihen; sie führen Bewegungen aus, die von einem *caller* ausgerufen werden. Diese Anordnungen werden auch gesungen. Das **square dancing** wird meist von Countrymusik mit Geige, Banjo und Gitarren begleitet.

squarely ['skwer·li] *adv* ❶ (*straight*) aufrecht ❷ (*directly*) direkt; **to look sb ~ in the eyes** jdm gerade in die Augen blicken
square 'root *n* MATH Quadratwurzel *f*
squash[1] [skwaʃ] *n* (*pumpkin*) Kürbis *m*
squash[2] [skwaʃ] **I.** *n* ❶ (*dense pack*) Gedränge *nt* ❷ (*racket game*) Squash *nt* **II.** *vt* ❶ (*crush*) zerdrücken; **to ~ sth flat** etw platt drücken ❷ (*fig: end*) *rumors* aus der Welt schaffen ❸ (*push*) **I should be able to ~ myself into this space** ich glaube, ich kann mich da hineinzwängen
squat [skwat] **I.** *vi* <-tt-> ❶ (*crouch*) hocken; ■ **to ~ [down]** sich hinhocken ❷ (*occupy land*) *on land* sich illegal ansiedeln; **to ~ [in a**

house] [ein Haus] besetzen **II.** *n* ① (*position*) Hocke *f* ② SPORTS (*exercise*) Kniebeuge *f* ③ (*building*) besetztes Haus **III.** *adj* <-tt-> niedrig; *person* gedrungen, untersetzt

squatter ['skwat̬·ər] *n* (*illegal occupier of house*) Hausbesetzer(in) *m(f)*

squaw [skwɔ] *n* (*offensive*) Squaw *f*

squawk [skwɔk] **I.** *vi* (*cry*) kreischen **II.** *n* (*cry*) Kreischen *nt kein pl*

squeak [skwik] **I.** *n* Quietschen *nt kein pl; of an animal* Quieken *nt kein pl; of a mouse* Pieps[er] *m fam; of a person* Quiekser *m fam* **II.** *vi* (*make sound*) quietschen; *animal, person* quieken; *mouse* piepsen

squeaky ['skwi·ki] *adj* (*high-pitched*) quietschend; *voice* piepsig *fam* ▶ PHRASES: **the ~ wheel gets the grease** (*prov*) nur wer am lautesten schreit wird gehört

'squeaky-clean *adj* (*a. fig*) blitzsauber *fam*

squeal [skwil] **I.** *n* [schriller] Schrei; *of tires* Quietschen *nt kein pl; of brakes* Kreischen *nt kein pl; of a pig* Quieken *nt kein pl* **II.** *vi* (*scream*) kreischen; *pig* quieken; *tires* quietschen; *brakes* kreischen; **to ~ to a halt** mit quietschenden Reifen anhalten

squeamish ['skwi·mɪʃ] **I.** *adj* zimperlich *pej,* zart besaitet; **he is ~ about seeing blood** er ekelt sich vor Blut **II.** *npl* **to not be for the ~** nichts für schwache Nerven sein

squeegee ['skwi·dʒi] **I.** *n* Gummiwischer *m* **II.** *vt window* mit einem Gummiwischer putzen

squeeze [skwiz] **I.** *n* ① (*press*) Drücken *nt kein pl;* **to give sth a ~** etw drücken ② ECON (*limit*) Beschränkung *f* ③ (*fit*) Gedränge *nt;* **it'll be a tight ~** es wird eng werden **II.** *vt* ① (*press*) drücken; *a lemon, an orange* auspressen; *a sponge* ausdrücken ② (*push in*) [hinein]zwängen; (*push through*) [durch]zwängen ③ (*constrict*) einschränken **III.** *vi* (*fit into*) sich [hinein]zwängen (**into** in +*dat*), sich vorbeizwängen (**past** an +*dat*), sich [durch]zwängen (**through** durch +*akk*)

squeezer ['skwi·zər] *n* Fruchtpresse *f*

squelch [skweltʃ] **I.** *vt* ① (*end*) *uprising* unterdrücken ② (*silence*) *rumor* verstummen lassen **II.** *vi mud, water* patschen *fam;* ■ **to ~ through sth** durch etw *akk* waten

squid <*pl* - *or* -s> [skwɪd] *n* Tintenfisch *m*

squiggle ['skwɪg·əl] *n* Schnörkel *m*

squint [skwɪnt] **I.** *vi* ① (*close one's eyes*) blinzeln ② (*look*) ■ **to ~ at sb/sth** einen Blick auf jdn/etw werfen **II.** *n* (*glance*) kurzer Blick

squire [skwaɪr] *n* (*old*) ① (*knight's attendant*) Knappe *m* ② (*landowner*) Gutsherr *m*

squirm [skwɜrm] **I.** *vi* sich winden; **to ~ in pain** sich vor Schmerzen krümmen **II.** *n* Krümmen *nt kein pl;* **to give a ~ of embarrassment** sich vor Verlegenheit winden

squirrel ['skwɜr·əl] *n* Eichhörnchen *nt*

squirt [skwɜrt] **I.** *vt* ① (*spray*) spritzen ② (*cover*) ■ **to ~ sb with sth** jdn mit etw *dat* bespritzen **II.** *vi* ■ **to ~ out** herausspritzen, herausschießen **III.** *n* (*quantity*) Spritzer *m*

Sri Lanka [ˌsri·'laŋ·kə] *n* Sri Lanka *nt*

Sri Lankan [ˌsri·'laŋ·kən] **I.** *adj* sri-lankisch; **to be ~** aus Sri Lanka sein **II.** *n* Sri-Lanker(in) *m(f)*

SSW [ˌes·es·'dʌb·əl·ju] *abbrev of* **south-southwest** SSW

St. *n* ① *abbrev of* **street** Str. ② *abbrev of* **saint** St.

stab [stæb] **I.** *vt* <-bb-> ① (*pierce*) einstechen (auf +*akk*); **the victim was ~bed** das Opfer erlitt eine Stichverletzung; **to ~ sth with a fork** mit einer Gabel in etw *dat* herumstochern ② (*make thrusting movement*) **to ~ the air** [**with sth**] [mit etw *dat*] in der Luft herumfuchteln **II.** *vi* <-bb-> ■ **to ~ at sb/sth** auf jdn/etw einstechen; **to ~ at sth with one's finger** mit dem Finger immer wieder auf etw *akk* drücken **III.** *n* ① (*thrust*) Stich *m* ② (*wound*) Stichwunde *f* ③ (*pain*) Stich *m* ▶ PHRASES: **to take a ~ at** [**doing**] **sth** etw [einmal] probieren

stabbing ['stæ·bɪŋ] **I.** *n* (*assault*) Messerstecherei *f* **II.** *adj pain* stechend; *fear, memory* durchdringend

stability [stə·'bɪl·ɪ·t̬i] *n* Stabilität *f*

stabilization [ˌsteɪ·bə·lɪ·'zeɪ·ʃən] *n* Stabilisierung *f*

stabilize ['steɪ·bə·laɪz] **I.** *vt* ① (*make firm*) stabilisieren ② (*maintain level*) festigen, stabilisieren **II.** *vi* MED sich stabilisieren; **his condition has now ~d** sein Zustand ist jetzt stabil

stabilizer ['steɪ·bə·laɪ·zər] *n* ① AVIAT Stabilisator *m* ② NAUT Stabilisierungsflosse *f*

stable¹ <-r, -st *or* more ~, most ~> ['steɪ·bəl] *adj* ① (*firmly fixed*) stabil; *relationship* fest ② PSYCH ausgeglichen

stable² ['steɪ·bəl] **I.** *n* ① (*building, horses*) Stall *m* ② (*business*) Rennstall *m* **II.** *vt* **to ~ a horse** ein Pferd unterstellen

stack [stæk] **I.** *n* ① *of videos* Stapel *m; of papers* Stoß *m* ② (*fam: large amount*) Haufen *m* ③ *of hay, straw* Schober *m* ④ MUS *hi-fi equipment* Stereoturm *m* ⑤ (*chimney*) Schornstein *m,* Kamin *m* SCHWEIZ **II.** *vt* ① (*arrange in pile*) [auf]stapeln ② (*fill*) **the fridge is ~ed with food** der Kühlschrank ist randvoll mit Lebensmitteln; *dishwasher* einräumen; *shelves* auffüllen

stadium <*pl* -s *or* -dia> ['steɪ·di·əm] *n* Stadion *nt*

staff [stæf] **I.** *n* ① + *sing/pl vb* (*employees*) Belegschaft *f;* **nursing ~** Pflegepersonal *nt* ② + *sing/pl vb* MIL Stab *m* ③ (*stick*) [Spazier]stock *m* ④ MUS Notenlinien *pl* **II.** *vt usu passive* **many charities are ~ed by volunteers** viele Wohltätigkeitsvereine beschäftigen ehrenamtliche Mitarbeiter

'staff officer *n* MIL Stabsoffizier(in) *m(f)*

stag [stæg] *n* ZOOL Hirsch *m*

stage [steɪdʒ] **I.** *n* ① (*period*) Etappe *f,* Station *f;* **crucial ~** entscheidende Phase ② *of a journey, race* Etappe *f,* Abschnitt *m* ③ THEAT

S

(*platform*) Bühne *f;* **to take center ~** (*fig*) im Mittelpunkt [des Interesses] stehen ④ ELEC Schaltstufe *f* **II.** *vt* ① THEAT aufführen; *concert* geben ② (*organize*) *convention, meeting* veranstalten; *demonstration, strike* organisieren; *game* austragen

'stagecoach *n* (*hist*) Postkutsche *f*

'stage direction *n* Bühnenanweisung *f*

'stage fright *n* Lampenfieber *nt*

'stagehand *n* Bühnenarbeiter(in) *m(f)*

'stage-manage **I.** *vt* inszenieren **II.** *vi* (*act as stage manager*) Regie führen

'stage manager *n* Bühnenmeister(in) *m(f),* Inspizient(in) *m(f) fachspr*

'stage name *n* Künstlername *m*

stage 'whisper *n* ① THEAT Beiseitesprechen *nt* ② (*whisper*) unüberhörbares Flüstern

stagger ['stæg·ər] **I.** *vi* ① (*totter*) ■ **to ~ somewhere** irgendwohin wanken [*o* torkeln]; **to ~ to one's feet** sich aufrappeln ② (*waver*) schwanken, wanken **II.** *vt* ① (*shock*) erstaunen ② (*arrange*) staffeln **III.** *n* ① (*lurch*) Wanken *nt kein pl,* Taumeln *nt kein pl* ② (*arrangement*) Staffelung *f*

staggered ['stæg·ərd] *adj* gestaffelt

staggering ['stæg·ər·ɪŋ] *adj* ① (*amazing*) erstaunlich, umwerfend *fam; news* unglaublich ② (*shocking*) erschütternd

staging ['steɪ·dʒɪŋ] *n* ① THEAT Inszenierung *f* ② (*scaffolding*) [Bau]gerüst *nt*

stagnant ['stæg·nənt] *adj* (*not flowing*) stagnierend; *pool* still; *water* stehend

stagnate ['stæg·neɪt] *vi* ① (*stop flowing*) sich stauen ② (*stop developing*) stagnieren

stagnation [stæg·'neɪ·ʃən] *n* Stagnation *f*

stagy ['steɪ·dʒi] *adj* (*pej*) theatralisch

staid [steɪd] *adj* seriös, gesetzt; (*pej*) spießig

stain [steɪn] **I.** *vt* ① (*discolor*) verfärben; (*cover with spots*) Flecken auf etw *akk* machen ② (*blemish*) *reputation* schaden ③ (*color*) *wood* [ein]färben **II.** *vi* ① (*cause discoloration*) abfärben, Flecken machen ② (*discolor*) sich verfärben ③ (*take dye*) Farbe annehmen, sich färben **III.** *n* ① (*discoloration*) Verfärbung *f,* Fleck *m* ② (*blemish*) Makel *m* ③ (*dye*) Beize *f,* Färbemittel *nt*

S

stained [steɪnd] *adj* ① (*discolored*) verfärbt; (*with spots*) fleckig ② (*dyed*) gefärbt, gebeizt

stained 'glass *n* Buntglas *nt*

'stained-glass window *n* Buntglasfenster *nt*

stainless ['steɪn·lɪs] **I.** *adj* makellos; *character* tadellos **II.** *n see* **stainless steel**

stainless 'steel *n* rostfreier Stahl

'stain remover *n* Fleckenentferner *m*

stair [ster] *n* ① (*set of steps*) ■ **~s** *pl* Treppe *f;* **a flight of ~s** eine Treppe ② (*step*) Treppenstufe *f*

'staircase *n* (*stairs*) Treppenhaus *nt,* Treppenaufgang *m;* **spiral ~** Wendeltreppe *f*

'stair lift *n* Treppenlift *m*

'stairway *n* Treppe *f*

'stairwell *n* Treppenhausschacht *m*

stake [steɪk] **I.** *n* ① (*stick*) Pfahl *m,* Pflock *m* ② *usu pl* (*wager*) Einsatz *m;* (*in games*) [Wett]einsatz *m* ③ (*interest*) *a.* FIN, ECON Anteil *m* ▶ PHRASES: **to be at ~** (*in question*) zur Debatte stehen; (*at risk*) auf dem Spiel stehen **II.** *vt* ① (*tether*) *animal* anbinden; *plant* hochbinden ② (*wager*) *money* setzen; **to ~ one's future on sth** seine Zukunft auf etw *akk* aufbauen ③ (*fig fam: support*) ■ **to ~ sb to sth** jdm etw ermöglichen

◆ **stake out** *vt* ① LAW (*watch closely*) überwachen ② (*mark territory*) markieren; *border* abstecken; *position* behaupten ③ (*establish*) *position* einnehmen

'stakeholder *n* Teilhaber(in) *m(f)*

stalactite [stə·'læk·taɪt] *n* Tropfstein *m,* Stalaktit *m fachspr*

stalagmite [stə·'læg·maɪt] *n* Tropfstein *m,* Stalagmit *m fachspr*

stale [steɪl] *adj* ① (*not fresh*) fade, schal; *beer, lemonade* abgestanden; *air* muffig; **~ bread** altbackenes Brot ② (*unoriginal*) fantasielos; *joke* abgedroschen ③ (*without zest*) abgestumpft; **to go ~** stumpfsinnig werden

stalemate ['steɪl·meɪt] **I.** *n* ① CHESS Patt *nt* ② (*deadlock*) Stillstand *m* **II.** *vt* ① CHESS patt setzen ② (*bring to deadlock*) zum Stillstand bringen

stalk¹ [stɔk] *n* Stiel *m*

stalk² [stɔk] **I.** *vt* ① (*hunt*) jagen ② (*harass*) ■ **to ~ sb** jdm nachstellen **II.** *vi* (*haughtily*) stolzieren; (*angrily*) marschieren

stalker ['stɔ·kər] *n* ① (*hunter*) Jäger(in) *m(f)* ② *of people* Stalker(in) *m(f)* (*Person, die jemanden verfolgt, belästigt und terrorisiert*)

stall¹ [stɔl] **I.** *n* ① (*for an animal*) Stall *m,* Verschlag *m* ② (*for selling*) [Verkaufs]stand *m* ③ (*for parking*) [markierter] Parkplatz ④ (*toilet cubicle*) Toilette *f* **II.** *vi* ① (*stop running*) *motor* stehen bleiben; *aircraft* abrutschen ② (*come to standstill*) *negotiations* zum Stillstand kommen **III.** *vt car, engine* abwürgen

stall² [stɔl] **I.** *vi* (*delay*) zaudern, zögern; **to ~ for time** Zeit gewinnen **II.** *vt* ① (*delay*) aufhalten, verzögern ② (*fam: keep waiting*) ■ **to ~ sb** jdn hinhalten

stallion ['stæl·jən] *n* Hengst *m*

stalwart ['stɔl·wərt] (*form*) **I.** *adj* ① (*loyal*) unentwegt; *supporter* treu ② (*sturdy*) robust, unerschütterlich **II.** *n* Anhänger(in) *m(f)*

stamen <*pl* -s *or* -mina> ['steɪ·men] *n* Staubgefäß *nt*

stamina ['stæm·ə·nə] *n* Durchhaltevermögen *nt,* Ausdauer *f*

stammer ['stæm·ər] **I.** *n* Stottern *nt* **II.** *vi* stottern, stammeln

stamp [stæmp] **I.** *n* ① (*implement*) Stempel *m* ② (*mark*) Stempel *m;* **~ of approval** Genehmigungsstempel *m* ③ (*adhesive*) **postage ~** Briefmarke *f* ④ (*step*) Stampfer *m fam;* (*sound*) Stampfen *nt* **II.** *vt* ① (*crush*) zertreten; (*stomp*) **to ~ one's foot** mit dem Fuß aufstampfen ② (*mark*) [ab]stempeln ③ (*affix postage to*) **to ~ a letter** einen Brief frankieren

III. *vi* ① (*step*) stampfen; ■**to ~ [up]on sth** auf etw *akk* treten ② (*walk*) stampfen, stapfen

◆**stamp out** *vt* ■**to ~ out ⇄ sth** (*eradicate*) etw ausmerzen; *crime, corruption* etw bekämpfen; *a disease* etw ausrotten; *a fire* etw austreten

'stamp collector *n* Briefmarkensammler(in) *m(f)*

stampede [stæm·'pid] **I.** *n* ① *of animals* wilde Flucht ② *of people* [Menschen]auflauf *m* **II.** *vi animals* durchgehen; *people* irgendwohin stürzen **III.** *vt* ① (*cause to rush*) aufschrecken ② (*force into action*) ■**to ~ sb into [doing] sth** jdn zu etw *dat* drängen

stance [stæns] *n* ① (*posture*) Haltung *f kein pl;* SPORTS *Schlagpositur beim Baseball, Golf usw.* ② (*attitude*) Standpunkt *m,* Einstellung *f* (**on** zu +*dat*)

stand [stænd] **I.** *n* ① (*physical position*) Stellung *f* ② (*position on an issue*) Einstellung *f* (**on** zu +*dat*); **to take a ~ on sth** sich für etw *akk* einsetzen ③ SPORTS ■**~s** *pl* (*raised seating for spectators*) [Zuschauer]tribüne *f* ④ (*support*) Ständer *m* ⑤ LAW ■**the ~** der Zeugenstand; **to take the ~** vor Gericht aussagen ⑥ MIL (*resistance*) Widerstand *m;* (*battle*) Gefecht *nt;* **to make a ~** (*fig*) klar Stellung beziehen ⑦ (*waiting area*) **taxi ~** Taxistand *m* **II.** *vi* <stood, stood> ① (*be upright*) stehen; **~ against the wall** stell dich an die Wand; **to ~ clear** aus dem Weg gehen, beiseitetreten; **to ~ still** stillstehen ② (*be located*) stehen, liegen; **to ~ in sb's way** jdm im Weg stehen ③ + *adj* (*be in a specified state*) stehen; **to ~ open/empty/in second place** offen/leer/an zweiter Stelle stehen; **with the situation as it ~s right now ...** so wie die Sache im Moment aussieht, ... ④ (*remain valid*) gelten, Bestand haben; **does that offer still ~?** ist das Angebot noch gültig? ▶ PHRASES: **to ~ on one's own two <u>feet</u>** auf eigenen Füßen stehen **III.** *vt* <stood, stood> ① (*place upright*) ■**to ~ sth somewhere** etw irgendwohin stellen; **to ~ sth on its head** etw auf den Kopf stellen ② (*bear*) ■**to ~ sth** etw ertragen; **she can't ~ anyone touching her** sie kann es nicht leiden, wenn man sie anfasst; **to ~ the test of time** die Zeit überdauern ③ LAW **to ~ trial** sich vor Gericht verantworten müssen ▶ PHRASES: **to ~ sb in <u>good</u> stead** jdm von Nutzen sein

◆**stand around** *vi* herumstehen

◆**stand back** *vi* ① (*fig: take detached view*) ■**to ~ back from sth** etw aus der Distanz betrachten ② (*not get involved*) tatenlos zusehen ③ (*be located away from*) abseitsliegen (**from** von +*dat*)

◆**stand by** *vi* ① (*be ready*) bereitstehen ② (*observe*) dabeistehen, zugucken *fam* ③ (*support*) ■**to ~ by sb** zu jdm stehen ④ (*abide by*) *promise* halten; **one's word** stehen (zu +*dat*)

◆**stand for** *vi* ① (*tolerate*) ■**to not ~ for sth** sich *dat* etw nicht gefallen lassen ② (*represent*) ■**to ~ for sth** für etw *akk* stehen

◆**stand in** *vi* ■**to ~ in for sb** für jdn einspringen

◆**stand out** *vi* ① (*be distinguishable*) zu unterscheiden sein; (*be identifiable*) gekennzeichnet sein (**as** als +*akk*), hervorragen; **to ~ out in a crowd** sich von der Menge abheben ② (*protrude*) hervorragen

◆**stand up** *vi* (*rise*) aufstehen; (*be standing*) stehen

standard ['stæn·dərd] **I.** *n* ① (*level of quality*) Standard *m,* Qualitätsstufe *f;* **to raise ~s** das Niveau heben ② (*criterion*) Gradmesser *m,* Richtlinie *f* ③ (*principles*) ■**~s** *pl* Wertvorstellungen *pl* ④ (*flag*) Standarte *f* **II.** *adj* ① (*customary, authoritative*) a. LING Standard- ② (*average*) durchschnittlich

standardization [,stæn·dər·dɪ·'zeɪ·ʃən] *n* Standardisierung *f*

standardize ['stæn·dər·daɪz] *vt* ① (*make conform*) standardisieren ② (*compare*) vereinheitlichen

standby <*pl* -s> ['stæn(d)·baɪ] **I.** *n* ① *no pl* (*readiness*) **on ~** in Bereitschaft; ELEC betriebsbereit; **~ mode** Stand-by-Modus *m,* Stand-by-Betrieb *m* ② (*backup*) Reserve *f* ③ (*plane ticket*) Stand-by-Ticket *nt* ④ (*traveler*) Fluggast *m* mit Stand-by-Ticket **II.** *adj attr* Ersatz- **III.** *adv* AVIAT, TOURIST **to fly ~** mit einem Stand-by-Ticket fliegen

'stand-in *n* Vertretung *f;* FILM, THEAT Ersatz *m*

standing ['stæn·dɪŋ] **I.** *n* ① (*status*) Status *m,* Ansehen *nt* ② (*duration*) Dauer *f;* **to be of long ~** von langer Dauer sein **II.** *adj attr* ① (*upright*) [aufrecht] stehend ② (*permanent*) ständig ③ (*stationary*) stehend

standing o'vation *n* stehende Ovationen *pl*

'standpoint *n* (*attitude*) Standpunkt *m*

'standstill *n* Stillstand *m;* **to be at a ~** zum Erliegen kommen

'standup *adj attr* (*performed standing*) **~ comedy** Stand-up-Comedy *f,* Stegreifkomödie *f;* **~ comedian** Stand-up-Comedian *m,* Alleinunterhaltungskünstler *m*

stank [stæŋk] *pt of* **stink**

stanza ['stæn·zə] *n* Strophe *f*

staple¹ ['steɪ·pəl] **I.** *n* ① (*main component*) Grundstock *m;* FOOD Grundnahrungsmittel *nt* ② ECON Hauptprodukt *nt* ③ (*of cotton*) Rohbaumwolle *f;* (*of wool*) Rohwolle *f* **II.** *adj attr* Haupt-; **~ foods** Grundnahrungsmittel *pl*

staple² ['steɪ·pəl] **I.** *n* ① (*for paper*) Heftklammer *f* ② (*not for paper*) Krampe *f* **II.** *vt* heften; ■**to ~ sth together** etw zusammenheften

'staple gun *n* Heftmaschine *f*

stapler ['steɪp·lər] *n* Hefter *m,* Tacker *m fam*

star [star] **I.** *n* ① ASTRON Stern *m* ② (*asterisk*) Sternchen *nt;* (*symbol*) Stern *m* ③ (*performer*) Star *m* **II.** *vt* <-rr-> ① THEAT, FILM **the new production of "King Lear" will ~ John Smith as Lear** die neue Produktion von „King Lear" zeigt John Smith in der Rolle des Lear ② (*mark with asterisk*) mit einem Sternchen versehen

S

III. *vi* <-rr-> THEAT, FILM **to ~ in a film** in einem Film die Hauptrolle spielen **IV.** *adj attr* Star-; **~ witness** Hauptzeuge, -zeugin *m, f*

starboard ['star·bərd] *n* Steuerbord *nt kein pl*

starch [startʃ] **I.** *n* FOOD, FASHION Stärke *f* **II.** *vt laundry* stärken

starchy ['star·tʃi] *adj* ❶ FOOD stärkehaltig ❷ (*pej fam: formal*) *people* reserviert

stardom ['star·dəm] *n* Leben *nt* als Star

stare [ster] **I.** *n* Starren *nt;* **accusing ~** vorwurfsvoller Blick **II.** *vi* ❶ (*look fixedly*) starren; ■ **to ~ at sb/sth** jdn/etw anstarren ❷ (*gawk*) große Augen machen **III.** *vt* (*look at*) **to ~ sb in the eye** jdn anstarren; **to ~ sb up and down** jdn anstieren *fam* ▶ PHRASES: **to be staring sb in the face** (*be evident*) auf der Hand liegen

'starfish *n* Seestern *m*

stargazer ['star·ˌgeɪ·zər] *n* (*fam*) Sterngucker(in) *m(f)*

staring ['ster·ɪŋ] *adj eyes* starrend

stark [stark] **I.** *adj* ❶ (*bare*) *landscape* karg; (*austere*) schlicht ❷ (*obvious*) krass; **to be a ~ reminder** drastisch an etw *akk* erinnern **II.** *adv* **~ naked** splitterfasernackt *fam;* **~ raving mad** (*hum, iron*) völlig übergeschnappt *fam*

starlet ['star·lɪt] *n* (*actress*) Starlet *nt*

'starlight *n* Sternenlicht *nt*

starling ['star·lɪŋ] *n* (*bird*) Star *m*

starlit ['star·ˌlɪt] *adj* sternenklar

starry ['star·i] *adj* ❶ ASTRON sternenklar; *sky* mit Sternen übersät ❷ (*star-like*) sternförmig ❸ FILM, THEAT **~ cast** Starbesetzung *f*

'starry-eyed *adj idealist* blauäugig

Stars and Stripes [ˌstarz·ənd·'straɪps] *npl + sing vb* ■ **the ~** die Stars and Stripes *pl* (*Nationalflagge der USA*)

> Die **U. S. flag** hat viele Bezeichnungen, unter anderem auch *the Stars and Stripes*. Die Sterne symbolisieren die 50 heutigen amerikanischen Bundesstaaten und die 13 Streifen stehen für die 13 Gründerstaaten. Der patriotische Ausdruck *Old Glory* stammt von dem Schiffskapitän William Driver. Der Titel der Nationalhymne, *The Star-Spangled Banner*, nimmt ebenfalls auf diese Fahne Bezug.

'star sign *n* ASTROL Sternzeichen *nt*

Star-Spangled 'Banner *n* ■ **the ~** ❶ (*US flag*) das Sternenbanner (*die Nationalflagge der USA*) ❷ (*US national anthem*) der Star Spangled Banner (*die Nationalhymne der USA*)

'star-studded *adj* ❶ ASTRON mit Sternen übersät ❷ FILM, THEAT (*fam*) mit Stars besetzt; **~ cast** Starbesetzung *f*

start [start] **I.** *n usu sing* ❶ (*beginning*) Anfang *m,* Beginn *m;* **the race got off to an exciting ~** das Rennen fing spannend an; **promising ~** viel versprechender Anfang; **to make a fresh ~** einen neuen Anfang machen ❷ SPORTS Start *m;* **false ~** Fehlstart *m* ❸ (*advantage*) Vorsprung *m;* **to have a good ~ in life** einen guten Start ins Leben haben ❹ (*sudden movement*) Zucken *nt;* **to give a ~** zusammenzucken **II.** *vi* ❶ (*begin*) anfangen; **~ing tomorrow** ab morgen; **~ing [on] January 1st** ab dem 1. Januar; **to ~ with** (*at first*) anfangs; (*firstly*) zunächst einmal ❷ (*begin a trip*) losfahren ❸ (*begin to operate*) *vehicle, motor* anspringen ❹ (*begin happening*) beginnen ❺ (*jump in surprise*) zusammenfahren, hochfahren **III.** *vt* ❶ (*begin*) *family, business* gründen; ■ **to ~ [doing] sth** anfangen, etw zu tun; **when do you ~ your new job?** wann fängst du mit deiner neuen Stelle an? ❷ (*set in motion*) ■ **to ~ sth** etw ins Leben rufen; **to ~ a fight** Streit anfangen; **to ~ a fire** Feuer machen ❸ MECH einschalten; *machine* anstellen; *motor* anlassen; *car* starten

◆**start back** *vi* (*return*) sich auf den Rückweg machen

◆**start off** **I.** *vi* ❶ (*begin activity*) ■ **to ~ off with sb/sth** bei jdm/etw anfangen; **they ~ed off by reading through the script** zuerst lasen sie das Skript durch ❷ (*begin career*) ■ **to ~ off as sth** seine Laufbahn als etw beginnen **II.** *vt* ❶ (*begin*) ■ **to ~ sth ↻ off** etw beginnen ❷ (*cause to begin*) ■ **to ~ sb off doing sth** jdn zu etw *dat* veranlassen ❸ (*help to begin*) ■ **to ~ sb off with sth** jdm den Start bei etw *dat* erleichtern

◆**start out** *vi* ❶ (*embark*) aufbrechen ❷ (*begin*) anfangen; ■ **to ~ out as sth** als etw beginnen; (*on a job*) als etw anfangen

◆**start up** **I.** *vt* ❶ (*organize*) *business, club* gründen ❷ MECH *motor* anlassen **II.** *vi* ❶ (*occur*) beginnen ❷ (*begin running*) *engine, vehicle* anspringen

starter ['star·t̬ər] *n* ❶ FOOD (*fam*) Vorspeise *f* ❷ MECH Anlasser *m* ❸ (*for race*) Starter *m* ❹ (*participant*) Wettkampfteilnehmer(in) *m(f);* (*in starting lineup*) Starter *m* ❺ ■ **~s** *pl* **for ~s** zunächst [einmal]

starting ['star·t̬ɪŋ] *adj attr* SPORTS Start-

'starting line *n* SPORTS Startlinie *f*

'starting point *n* Ausgangspunkt *m*

startle ['star·t̬əl] *vt* erschrecken

startling ['star·təl·ɪŋ] *adj* (*surprising*) überraschend, verblüffend; (*alarming*) erschreckend

'start-up *n* ❶ COMM [Neu]gründung *f,* Existenzgründung *f* ❷ MECH Start *m,* Inbetriebnahme *f* ❸ COMPUT Hochfahren *nt kein pl,* Start *m;* **~ disk** Startdiskette *f*

starvation [star·'veɪ·ʃən] *n* ❶ (*death from hunger*) Hungertod *m;* **to die of ~** verhungern ❷ (*serious malnutrition*) Unterernährung *f*

starve [starv] **I.** *vi* ❶ (*die of hunger*) verhungern ❷ (*suffer from hunger*) hungern; (*be malnourished*) unterernährt sein ❸ (*fam: feel very hungry*) *to be starving* am Verhungern sein *fam* ❹ (*crave*) hungern (**for** nach +*dat*) **II.** *vt* ❶ (*deprive of food*) aushungern; ■**to ~ oneself to death** sich zu Tode hungern ❷ *usu passive* (*fig: deprive*) ■**to be ~d of sth** um etw *akk* gebracht werden; **people ~d of sleep start to lose their concentration** Menschen, die unter Schlafmangel leiden, können sich nicht mehr konzentrieren ❸ *usu passive* (*fig: crave*) ■**to be ~d for sth** sich nach etw *dat* sehnen

starving ['star·vɪŋ] *adj* ❶ (*malnourished*) ausgehungert, unterernährt; **~ children** hungernde Kinder ❷ (*fam: very hungry*) [ganz] ausgehungert; **I'm ~!** ich bin am Verhungern!

stash [stæʃ] **I.** *n* <*pl* -es> (*cache*) [geheimes] Lager, Vorrat *m* **II.** *vt* (*fam*) verstecken; *money* bunkern

state [steɪt] **I.** *n* ❶ (*existing condition*) Zustand *m;* **~ of war** Kriegszustand *m* ❷ (*physical condition*) körperliche Verfassung; **to be in a good ~ of health** in einem guten Gesundheitszustand sein ❸ PSYCH **~ of mind** Gemütszustand *m;* **to be in the proper ~ of mind to do sth** in der Lage sein, etw zu tun ❹ (*nation*) Staat *m* ❺ (*unit within nation: in USA*) [Bundes]staat *m;* (*in Germany*) Land *nt;* ■**the S~s** *pl* (*fam: the USA*) die Staaten *pl* ❻ (*civil government*) Staat *m,* Regierung *f* **II.** *adj attr* ❶ (*pertaining to a nation*) staatlich, Staats- ❷ (*pertaining to unit*) **the ~ capital of Texas** die Hauptstadt von Texas; **~ park** *von einem US-Bundesstaat finanzierter Park;* **~ police** *Polizei eines US-Bundesstaates* ❸ (*pertaining to civil government*) Regierungs-; **~ secret** (*a. fig*) Staatsgeheimnis *nt;* **~ subsidy** [staatliche] Subvention ❹ (*showing ceremony*) Staats- **III.** *vt* ❶ (*express*) aussprechen, äußern; *objections* vorbringen; *source* angeben; ■**to ~ why ...** darlegen, warum ... ❷ (*specify, fix*) nennen, angeben; *demands* stellen

stated ['steɪ·tɪd] *adj* ❶ (*declared*) genannt, angegeben; **as ~ above** wie oben angegeben ❷ (*fixed*) festgelegt, festgesetzt

'**State Department** *n* ■**the ~** das US-Außenministerium

stateless ['steɪt·lɪs] *adj* staatenlos; **~ person** Staatenlose(r) *f(m)*

stately ['steɪt·li] *adj* ❶ (*formal and imposing*) würdevoll, majestätisch ❷ (*splendid*) prächtig, imposant

statement ['steɪt·mənt] *n* ❶ (*act of expressing sth*) Äußerung *f,* Erklärung *f* ❷ (*formal declaration*) Stellungnahme *f,* Verlautbarung *f;* LAW Aussage *f;* **to make a ~ to the press** eine Presseerklärung abgeben ❸ FIN **bank ~** [Konto]auszug *m*

state of the 'art *adj pred,* **state-of-the-'art** *adj attr* auf dem neuesten Stand der Technik *nach n,* hoch entwickelt, hochmodern

state 'prison *n* Staatsgefängnis *nt* (*eines US-Bundesstaates*)

'**stateroom** *n* ❶ (*in a hotel*) Empfangszimmer *nt;* (*in a palace*) Empfangssaal *m* ❷ NAUT Luxuskabine *f*

'**stateside I.** *adj* in den Staaten *präd* **II.** *adv* in die Staaten

'**statesman** *n* Staatsmann *m*

'**statesmanship** ['steɪts·mən·ʃɪp] *n* Staatskunst *f*

'**stateswoman** *n* Staatsfrau *f*

state 'visit *n* Staatsbesuch *m*

static ['stæṭ·ɪk] **I.** *adj* (*fixed*) statisch; (*not changing*) konstant **II.** *n* (*electrical charge*) statische Elektrizität; (*atmospherics*) atmosphärische Störungen

static elec'tricity *n* statische Elektrizität

station ['steɪ·ʃən] **I.** *n* ❶ TRANSP **train ~** Bahnhof *m;* **subway ~** U-Bahn-Haltestelle *f,* U-Bahn-Station *f* ❷ (*for designated purpose*) -station *f;* **police ~** Polizeiwache *f;* **power ~** Kraftwerk *nt* ❸ TV, RADIO Sender *m* **II.** *vt* postieren, aufstellen; *soldiers, troops* stationieren; **several destroyers have been ~ed off the coast of Norway** mehrere Zerstörer liegen vor der Küste Norwegens

stationary ['steɪ·ʃə·ner·i] *adj* (*not moving*) ruhend; (*not changing*) unverändert

stationery ['steɪ·ʃə·ner·i] *n* Schreibwaren *pl;* (*writing paper*) Schreibpapier *nt*

'**station house** *n* Polizeiwache *f*

'**station wagon** *n* Kombi[wagen] *m*

statistical [stə·'tɪs·tɪ·kəl] *adj* statistisch

statistician [ˌstæt·ɪ·'stɪʃ·ən] *n* Statistiker(in) *m(f)*

statistics [stə·'tɪs·tɪks] *npl* ❶ + *sing vb* (*science*) Statistik *f kein pl* ❷ (*data*) Statistik *f*

statue ['stætʃ·u] *n* Statue *f,* Standbild *nt*

Statue of 'Liberty *n* ■**the ~** die Freiheitsstatue

> Die **Statue of Liberty** (Freiheitsstatue) wurde von dem Bildhauer Frédéric-Auguste Bartholdi und dem Architekten Gustave Eiffel, der für das Metallgerüst zuständig war, in Paris umgesetzt. Sie ist 46,50 m (≈ 152,6 Fuß) hoch und mit Sockel gemessen 92,99 m (≈ 305,1 Fuß) hoch. Frankreich hat den Vereinigten Staaten die **Statue of Liberty** zur Jahrhundertfeier der Unabhängigkeit geschenkt. Nachdem sie demontiert auf der Fregatte Isère von Paris nach New York transportiert worden war, wurde sie am 28. Oktober 1886 auf der kleinen Insel **Liberty Island** im Hafen von New York eingeweiht. Diese Statue, die die Freiheit verkörpert, ist heute das Hoheitszeichen der Vereinigten Staaten und das internationale Symbol für Freiheit und Demokratie.

statuette [ˌstætʃ·u·'et] *n* Statuette *f*

stature ['stætʃ·ər] *n* ❶ (*height*) Statur *f,* Gestalt *f;* **short ~** kleiner Wuchs ② (*reputation*) Geltung *nt,* Prestige *nt*

status ['stæ·t̬əs] *n* Status *m;* (*prestige a.*) Prestige *nt;* **legal ~** Rechtsposition *f*

status quo [ˌstæ·t̬əs·'kwoʊ] *n* Status quo *m*

'status symbol *n* Statussymbol *nt*

statute ['stætʃ·ut] *n* ① (*written rule*) Statut *nt meist pl,* Satzung *f;* ■**by ~** satzungsgemäß ② (*law*) Gesetz *nt*

'statute book *n* Gesetzbuch *nt*

statute of limi'tations *n* Verjährungsgesetz *nt*

statutory ['stætʃ·ə·tɔr·i] *adj* gesetzlich; **~ law** kodifiziertes Recht

staunch¹ [stɔntʃ] *adj* (*steadfastly loyal*) standhaft, zuverlässig; *Catholic* überzeugt; *opponent* erbittert

staunch² [stɔntʃ] *vt see* **stanch**

stave [steɪv] **I.** *n* ① *see* **staff 6** ② (*in construction*) Sprosse *f,* Querholz *nt* **II.** *vt* <staved *or* stove, staved *or* stove> **to ~ a hole in sth** ein Loch in etw *akk* schlagen

◆**stave off** *vt* ■**to ~ off** ⊂ **sth** (*postpone*) etw hinauszögern [*o* aufschieben]; (*prevent*) etw abwenden [*o* abwehren]; *hunger* stillen; ■**to ~ off** ⊂ **sb** jdn hinhalten *fam*

stay [steɪ] **I.** *n* Aufenthalt *m;* **overnight ~** Übernachtung *f* **II.** *vi* ① (*remain present*) bleiben; **to ~ put** (*fam: keep standing*) stehen bleiben; (*not stand up*) sitzen bleiben; (*not move*) sich nicht vom Fleck rühren ② (*reside temporarily*) untergebracht sein, wohnen; **to ~ overnight** übernachten ③ + *n or adj* (*remain*) bleiben; **the stores ~ open until 8 p.m.** die Läden haben bis 20 Uhr geöffnet; **to ~ in touch** in Verbindung bleiben **III.** *vt* LAW (*delay*) *execution* aussetzen ▶PHRASES: **to ~ the course** durchhalten

◆**stay away** *vi* ① (*keep away*) wegbleiben, fernbleiben ② (*avoid*) ■**to ~ away from sb/sth** jdn/etw meiden

◆**stay behind** *vi* [noch] [da]bleiben; **to ~ behind after school** nachsitzen

◆**stay in** *vi* zu Hause bleiben, daheimbleiben *bes* ÖSTERR, SCHWEIZ, SÜDD

◆**stay on** *vi* ① (*remain longer*) [noch] bleiben ② (*remain in place*) *lid, top* halten, daraufbleiben; *sticker* haften ③ (*remain in operation*) *light* an bleiben; *device* eingeschaltet bleiben

◆**stay out** *vi* ① (*not come home*) ausbleiben, wegbleiben ② (*not go somewhere*) **~ out of the kitchen!** bleib aus der Küche! ③ (*not become involved*) **to ~ out of trouble** sich *dat* Ärger vom Hals halten *fam*

◆**stay together** *vi* ① (*not separate*) immer zusammen sein; (*stay in a group*) zusammenbleiben; (*always*) unzertrennlich sein ② (*remain loyal to each other*) zusammenhalten, zueinanderstehen

◆**stay up** *vi* aufbleiben, wach bleiben

'stay-at-home *adj* ungesellig; **~** *mom* Hausfrau *f*

staying power ['steɪ·ɪŋ-] *n* Durchhaltevermögen *nt,* Ausdauer *f*

STD [ˌes·ti·'di] *n* MED *abbrev of* **sexually transmitted disease** Geschlechtskrankheit *f*

stead [sted] *n* **in his/her ~** an seiner/ihrer Stelle ▶PHRASES: **to stand sb in good ~ [for sth]** jdm [bei etw *dat*] zugutekommen

steadfast ['sted·fæst] *adj* fest, standhaft, unerschütterlich; *ally* loyal; *friend* treu

steady ['sted·i] **I.** *adj* ① (*stable*) fest, stabil ② (*regular*) kontinuierlich, gleich bleibend; *breathing, flow, pulse* regelmäßig; *increase, decrease* stetig; *rain* anhaltend; *speed* konstant ③ (*not wavering*) *voice* fest; *pain* permanent; *hand* ruhig ④ (*calm and dependable*) verlässlich, solide; *nerves* stark **II.** *vt* <-ie-> ① (*stabilize*) stabilisieren; *ladder* festhalten; **to ~ oneself** ins Gleichgewicht kommen, Halt finden ② (*make calm*) *aim* fixieren; *nerves* beruhigen **III.** *adv* (*still*) **to hold ~** *prices* stabil bleiben; **to hold sth ~** etw festhalten

steak [steɪk] *n* ① Rindfleisch *nt;* **rump ~** Rumpsteak *nt* ② (*thick slice*) [Beef]steak *nt*

steal [stil] **I.** *vt* <stole, stolen> ① (*take illegally*) stehlen; **to ~ [sb's] ideas** [jds] Ideen klauen *fam* ② (*gain artfully*) *heart* erobern ③ (*do surreptitiously*) **she stole a glance at her watch** sie lugte heimlich auf ihre Armbanduhr ▶PHRASES: **to ~ sb's thunder** jdm den Wind aus den Segeln nehmen **II.** *vi* <stole, stolen> ① (*take things illegally*) stehlen ② (*move surreptitiously*) sich wegstehlen; **he stole out of the room** er stahl sich aus dem Zimmer

stealth [stelθ] *n* (*furtiveness*) Heimlichkeit *f;* **by ~** heimlich

'stealth bomber *n* Tarnkappenbomber *m*

'stealth fighter *n* Tarnkappenjäger *m*

stealthy ['stel·θi] *adj* heimlich, verstohlen

steam [stim] **I.** *n* Dampf *m;* **to let off ~** Dampf ablassen *a. fig* **II.** *vi* dampfen **III.** *vt fish* dämpfen

◆**steam up** **I.** *vi mirror, window* [sich] beschlagen, anlaufen **II.** *vt* ① (*cause to become steamy*) **the windows are ~ed up** die Fenster sind beschlagen ② (*fam: cause to become excited*) **to get all ~ed up [about sth]** sich [über etw *akk*] unheimlich aufregen

'steamboat *n* Dampfschiff *nt,* Dampfer *m*

'steam engine *n* ① (*engine*) Dampfmaschine *f* ② (*locomotive*) Dampflok[omotive] *f*

steamer ['sti·mər] *n* ① (*boat*) Dampfer *m,* Dampfschiff *nt* ② (*for cooking*) Dampfkochtopf *m*

'steam iron *n* Dampfbügeleisen *nt*

steamroll ['stim·roʊl] *vt see* **steamroller**

'steamroller **I.** *n* Dampfwalze *f* **II.** *vt* ■**to ~ sb into doing sth** jdn unter Druck setzen, etw zu tun; *opposition* niederwalzen

'steamship *n* Dampfschiff *nt,* Dampfer *m*

steamy ['sti·mi] *adj* ① (*full of steam*) dampfig, dunstig ② (*hot and humid*) feuchtheiß ③ (*fam: sexy*) heiß, scharf; *love scene, novel a.* prickelnd

S

steel [stil] **I.** *n* ❶ (*iron alloy*) Stahl *m;* **nerves of ~** Nerven *pl* wie Drahtseile ❷ **sharpening ~** Wetzstahl *m* **II.** *vt* ■**to ~ oneself against/for sth** sich gegen/für etw *akk* wappnen; ■**to ~ oneself** [**to do sth**] all seinen Mut zusammennehmen[, um etw zu tun]

'**steel mill** *n* Stahl[walz]werk *nt*

steel 'wool *n* Stahlwolle *f*

'**steelworker** *n* Stahlarbeiter(in) *m(f)*

'**steelworks** *npl* + *sing vb* Stahlwerk *nt,* Stahlfabrik *f*

steely ['sti·li] *adj* ❶ (*of steel*) stählern ❷ (*hard, severe*) stahlhart; *determination* eisern; *expression* hart

steep¹ [stip] *adj* ❶ (*sharply sloping*) steil; *slope* abschüssig; *steps* hoch ❷ (*dramatic*) drastisch, dramatisch; *decline* deutlich ❸ (*unreasonably expensive*) überteuert

steep² [stip] **I.** *vt* ❶ (*soak in liquid*) tränken; *laundry* einweichen ❷ *usu passive* (*imbue*) **~ed in history** geschichtsträchtig **II.** *vi* einweichen; **she never lets the tea ~ long enough** sie lässt den Tee nie lang genug ziehen

steepen ['sti·pən] *vi* ❶ (*become steeper*) steiler werden; *road, slope* ansteigen ❷ (*fam: increase in cost*) steigen, sich erhöhen

steeple ['sti·pəl] *n* Turmspitze *f; of a church* Kirchturm *m*

'**steeplechase** *n* ❶ (*for horses*) Hindernisrennen *nt,* Hürdenrennen *nt* ❷ (*for runners*) Hindernislauf *m*

steer¹ [stɪr] **I.** *vt* ❶ (*direct*) steuern ❷ (*follow*) *course* einschlagen **II.** *vi* steuern, lenken; *vehicle* sich lenken lassen

steer² [stɪr] *n* ZOOL junger Ochse

steerage ['stɪr·ɪdʒ] *n* NAUT (*hist*) Zwischendeck *nt*

steering ['stɪr·ɪŋ] *n* AUTO Lenkung *f;* NAUT Steuerung *f*

'**steering committee** *n* Lenkungsausschuss *m*

'**steering wheel** *n* Steuer[rad] *nt; of a car a.* Lenkrad *nt*

stellar ['stel·ər] *adj* ❶ ASTRON (*form*) stellar *fachspr* ❷ (*fam: exceptionally good*) grandios, phänomenal

stem [stem] **I.** *n* ❶ *of a tree, bush* Stamm *m; of a leaf, flower* Stiel *m,* Stängel *m; of grain, corn* Halm *m; of a glass* [Glas]stiel *m* ❷ LING [Wort]stamm *m* **II.** *vt* <-mm-> eindämmen, aufhalten; *bleeding* stillen; **to ~ the tide** [**or flow**] **of sth** etw zum Stillstand bringen **III.** *vi* <-mm-> ❶ (*be traced back*) ■**to ~ back to sth** sich bis zu etw *dat* zurückverfolgen lassen, auf etw *akk* zurückgehen; ■**to ~ from sb/sth** auf jdn/etw zurückzuführen sein ❷ (*slide a ski outwards*) stemmen

stench [stentʃ] *n* Gestank *m a. fig*

stencil ['sten·səl] *n* Schablone *f;* (*picture*) Schablonenzeichnung *f*

stenographer [stə·'nag·rə·fər] *n* (*dated*) Stenograf(in) *m(f),* Stenotypist(in) *m(f)*

stenography [stə·'nag·rə·fi] *n* (*dated*) Stenografie *f*

step [step] **I.** *n* ❶ (*foot movement*) Schritt *m;* **to walk in ~** im Gleichschritt laufen ❷ (*dance movement*) [Tanz]schritt *m;* ■**in ~** im Takt; (*fig*) im Einklang ❸ (*stair*) Stufe *f; of a ladder* Sprosse *f;* **"watch your ~"** „Vorsicht, Stufe!" ❹ (*stage in a process*) Schritt *m;* **to be one ~ ahead** [**of sb**] [jdm] einen Schritt voraus sein; **~ by ~** Schritt für Schritt ❺ (*measure, action*) Schritt *m,* Vorgehen *nt;* **to take drastic ~s** zu drastischen Mitteln greifen **II.** *vi* <-pp-> ❶ (*tread*) ■**to ~ over sth** über etw *akk* steigen; **to ~ on sb's foot** jdm auf den Fuß treten ❷ (*walk*) ■**to ~ somewhere** irgendwohin gehen; **would you care to ~ this way please, sir?** würden Sie bitte hier entlanggehen, Sir?; **to ~ aside** zur Seite gehen; **to ~ out of line** (*fig*) sich danebenbenehmen **III.** *vi* (*tread on accelerator, brake*) treten (**on** auf +*akk*); **~ on it!** gib Gas! *fam*

◆**step aside** *vi* zur Seite treten, Platz machen

◆**step back** *vi* ❶ (*move back*) zurücktreten ❷ (*gain a new perspective*) Abstand nehmen

◆**step down** *vi* ❶ (*resign*) zurücktreten, sein Amt niederlegen ❷ LAW *witness* den Zeugenstand verlassen

◆**step in** *vi* ❶ (*enter building*) eintreten; (*enter vehicle*) einsteigen ❷ (*intervene*) eingreifen, einschreiten

◆**step up** *vt* ❶ verstärken; *pace* beschleunigen ❷ (*come forward*) vortreten

'**stepbrother** *n* Stiefbruder *m*

'**stepchild** *n* Stiefkind *nt*

'**stepdaughter** *n* Stieftochter *f*

'**stepfamily** *n* + *sing/pl vb* Stieffamilie *f,* Patchworkfamilie *f*

'**stepfather** *n* Stiefvater *m*

'**stepladder** *n* Stehleiter *f,* Trittleiter *f*

'**stepmother** *n* Stiefmutter *f*

steppe [step] *n* Steppe *f*

'**stepping stone** *n* ❶ (*stone*) [Tritt]stein *m* ❷ (*fig: intermediate stage*) Sprungbrett *nt*

'**stepsister** *n* Stiefschwester *f*

'**stepson** *n* Stiefsohn *m*

stereo¹ <*pl* -os> ['ster·i·oʊ] *n* ❶ (*transmission*) Stereo *nt* ❷ (*fam: unit*) Stereoanlage *f*

stereo² ['ster·i·oʊ] *adj short for* **stereophonic** Stereo-

stereophonic [ˌster·i·ə·'fan·ɪk] *adj* MUS, MEDIA (*form*) stereophon *fachspr;* **~ sound** Stereoklang *m*

stereotype ['ster·i·ə·taɪp] **I.** *n* Stereotyp *nt,* Klischee *nt;* (*character*) stereotype Figur **II.** *vt* **to ~ sb/sth** jdn/etw in ein Klischee zwängen

stereotypical [ˌste·ri·ə·'tɪp·ɪ·kəl] *adj* stereotyp; **~ family** Durchschnittsfamilie *f*

sterile ['ster·əl] *adj* ❶ MED unfruchtbar, steril ❷ (*free from bacteria*) steril, keimfrei

sterility [stə·'rɪl·ɪ·t̬i] *n* MED Unfruchtbarkeit *f,* Sterilität *f*

sterilization [ˌster·ə·lɪ·'zeɪ·ʃən] *n* ❶ (*operation*) Sterilisierung *f* ❷ (*making sth chemi-*

S

cally clean) Desinfizierung *f*

sterilize ['ster·ə·laɪz] *vt* MED ❶ *usu passive* (*make infertile*) ■**to be ~d** sterilisiert sein/werden ❷ (*disinfect*) desinfizieren; *water* abkochen

sterling ['stɜr·lɪŋ] **I.** *n* (*metal*) Sterlingsilber *nt* **II.** *adj* (*approv*) gediegen, meisterhaft; **to make a ~ effort** beachtliche Anstrengungen unternehmen

stern[1] [stɜrn] *adj* (*severe*) ernst; (*strict*) streng, unnachgiebig; (*difficult*) *test* hart, schwierig

stern[2] [stɜrn] *n* NAUT Heck *nt*

sternness ['stɜrn·nɪs] *n* ❶ (*severity*) Strenge *f*, Härte *f* ❷ (*earnestness*) Ernst *m*, Ernsthaftigkeit *f*

sternum <*pl* -s *or* -na> ['stɜr·nəm] *n* Brustbein *nt*

steroid ['ster·ɔɪd] *n* CHEM, MED, PHARM Steroide *pl*

stethoscope ['steθ·ə·skoʊp] *n* Stethoskop *nt*

stew [stu] **I.** *n* Eintopf *m* **II.** *vt meat* schmoren **III.** *vi* (*simmer*) *meat* [vor sich *akk* hin] schmoren

steward ['stu·ərd] *n* ❶ (*on flight*) Flugbegleiter *m*, Steward *m*; (*on cruise*) Schiffsbegleiter *m*, Steward *m* ❷ (*at an event*) Ordner(in) *m(f)*

stewardess <*pl* -es> ['stu·ər·dɪs] *n* (*on flight*) Flugbegleiterin *f*, Stewardess *f*; (*on cruise*) Schiffsbegleiterin *f*, Stewardess *f*

STI [ˌes·ti·'aɪ] *n* MED *abbrev of* **sexually transmitted illness/infection** Geschlechtskrankheit *f*

stick [stɪk] **I.** *n* ❶ (*thin branch*) Zweig *m* ❷ (*wooden implement*) Stock *m*; **walking ~** Spazierstock *m*; **hockey ~** Hockeyschläger *m* ❸ (*a piece of sth*) **celery ~s** Selleriestangen *pl*; **a ~ of chewing gum** ein Stück Kaugummi ❹ AUTO (*fam*) Auto *nt* mit Schaltgetriebe ❺ (*poke*) **a ~ in the ribs** ein Stoß in die Rippen **II.** *vi* <stuck, stuck> ❶ (*fasten by adhesion*) kleben (**to** an +*dat*); (*be fastened*) zugeklebt bleiben; **this glue won't ~** dieser Klebstoff hält nicht ❷ (*be unable to move*) feststecken; *car* stecken bleiben; (*be unmovable*) festsitzen; *door, window, gear* klemmen ❸ (*endure*) hängen bleiben; **to ~ in sb's mind** jdm in Erinnerung bleiben ❹ (*persevere*) ■**to ~ with sth** an etw *dat* dranbleiben ❺ (*keep within limits*) **to ~ to one's budget** sich an sein Budget halten; **to ~ to a diet** eine Diät einhalten ❻ (*continue to support, comply with*) ■**to ~ by sb/sth** zu jdm/etw halten ▶ PHRASES: **to ~ to one's <u>guns</u>** nicht lockerlassen; **I'm ~ing to my guns** ich stehe zu dem, was ich gesagt habe **III.** *vt* <stuck, stuck> ❶ (*affix*) kleben (**to** an +*akk*) ❷ (*fam: put*) **~ your things wherever you like** stellen Sie Ihre Sachen irgendwo ab; **to ~ one's head around the door** seinen Kopf durch die Tür stecken ❸ (*fam: burden*) ■**to ~ sb with sth** *bill* jdm etw aufhalsen; ■**to be stuck with sb** jdn am Hals haben ▶ PHRASES: **to ~ one's <u>nose</u> into sb's business** seine Nase in jds Angelegenheiten stecken

◆**stick around** *vi* (*fam*) da bleiben

◆**stick in I.** *vi dart* stecken bleiben **II.** *vt* (*fam*) ❶ (*affix*) ■**to ~ sth in sth** etw in etw *akk* einkleben ❷ (*put into*) ■**to ~ sth in[to] sth** etw in etw *akk* hineinstecken

◆**stick out I.** *vt* ❶ (*make protrude*) *hand* ausstrecken; *tongue* herausstrecken ❷ (*endure*) ■**to ~ it out** es [bis zum Ende] durchhalten **II.** *vi* ❶ (*protrude*) [her]vorstehen; *hair, ears* abstehen; *nail* herausstehen ❷ (*fig: be obvious*) offensichtlich sein; **to ~ out like a sore thumb** wie ein bunter Pudel auffallen *fam*

◆**stick together I.** *vt* zusammenkleben **II.** *vi* ❶ (*adhere*) zusammenkleben ❷ (*fig: not separate*) immer zusammen sein; (*stay in a group*) zusammenbleiben; (*always*) unzertrennlich sein ❸ (*fig: remain loyal to each other*) zusammenhalten, zueinanderstehen

◆**stick up I.** *vt* (*fam: rob with gun*) ■**to ~ up** ⊂ **sb/sth** jdn/etw überfallen **II.** *vi* ❶ (*point upward*) hochragen, emporragen ❷ (*stand on end*) abstehen ❸ (*defend*) ■**to ~ up for sb/sth** sich für jdn/etw einsetzen

sticker ['stɪk·ər] *n* (*adhesive label*) Aufkleber *m*; (*for collecting*) Sticker *m*; **price ~** Preisschild[chen] *nt*

'stick figure *n* Strichmännchen *nt fam*

'stick insect *n* Gespenstheuschrecke *f*

'stick-in-the-mud I. *n* (*fam*) Muffel *m*, Spaßverderber(in) *m(f) pej* **II.** *adj attr* altmodisch, rückständig

stickler ['stɪk·lər] *n* Pedant(in) *m(f) pej*; **to be a ~ for accuracy** pingelig auf Genauigkeit achten

'stick-on *adj attr* Klebe-

'stickpin *n* Krawattennadel *f*

'stick-up *n* (*sl*) Überfall *m*

sticky ['stɪk·i] *adj* ❶ (*texture*) klebrig; ■**to be ~ with sth** mit etw *dat* verklebt sein ❷ (*humid*) *weather* schwül; *air* stickig

stiff [stɪf] **I.** *n* (*fam: corpse*) Leiche *f* **II.** *adj* ❶ (*rigid*) steif (**with** vor +*dat*); *paper, lid* fest; **his clothes were ~ with dried mud** seine Kleidung starrte vor angetrocknetem Schmutz ❷ (*sore*) *neck, joints* steif; *muscles* hart ❸ (*dense*) *paste* dick; *batter, mixture, dough* fest ❹ (*strong*) *opposition* stark; *penalty, punishment, drink* hart; *breeze* steif; *criticism* herb **III.** *adv* **to be scared ~** zu Tode erschrocken sein **IV.** *vt* (*fam: cheat*) **to ~ sb out of sth** jdn um etw *akk* betrügen

stiffen ['stɪf·ən] **I.** *vi* ❶ (*tense up*) sich versteifen; *muscles* sich verspannen; (*with nervousness*) *person* sich verkrampfen; (*with fear, fright*) erstarren ❷ (*become stronger*) stärker werden, sich verstärken; *resistance* wachsen **II.** *vt* ❶ (*make rigid*) *arms, legs* versteifen; *collar* stärken ❷ (*make more severe*) *penalty, rules* verschärfen ❸ (*strengthen*) [ver]stärken; *competition* verschärfen

S

stiff-necked ['stɪf·nekt] *adj* (*pej*) ❶ (*stubborn*) halsstarrig, stur ❷ (*arrogant*) hochnäsig, arrogant

stifle ['staɪ·fəl] **I.** *vi* ersticken **II.** *vt* ❶ (*smother*) *person, flames* ersticken ❷ (*fig: suppress*) *revolt* unterdrücken; **to ~ the urge to laugh** sich *dat* das Lachen verbeißen

stifling ['staɪ·flɪŋ] *adj* ❶ (*smothering*) *fumes, smoke* erstickend; *air* zum Ersticken *nach n, präd;* (*fig*) *heat, humidity* drückend; *room* stickig ❷ (*fig: repressive*) erdrückend

stigma ['stɪg·mə] *n* (*shame*) Stigma *nt geh;* **social ~** gesellschaftlicher Makel

stigmatize ['stɪg·mə·taɪz] *vt* (*mark*) brandmarken

stiletto <*pl* -os> [stɪ·'leṱ·oʊ] *n* ❶ (*shoe*) Pfennigabsatz *m;* ■ **~s** *pl* Schuhe *pl* mit Pfennigabsätzen ❷ (*knife*) Stilett *nt*

stiletto 'heel *n* Pfennigabsatz *m*

still[1] [stɪl] **I.** *n* ❶ (*peace and quiet*) Stille *f* ❷ *usu pl* (*photo of film scene*) Standfoto *nt* **II.** *adj* ❶ (*quiet and peaceful*) ruhig, friedlich; *lake, sea* ruhig ❷ (*motionless*) reglos, bewegungslos; **to keep ~** still halten, sich nicht bewegen ❸ (*not carbonated*) ohne Kohlensäure *nach n* **III.** *adv* ❶ (*continuing situation*) [immer] noch, noch immer; (*in future as in past*) nach wie vor; **there's ~ time for us to get to the cinema before the movie starts** wir können es noch schaffen, ins Kino zu kommen, bevor der Film anfängt ❷ (*nevertheless*) trotzdem; **..., but he's ~ your brother ...**, [aber] er ist immer noch dein Bruder ❸ (*greater degree*) noch; **to want ~ more** immer noch mehr wollen

still[2] [stɪl] *n* ❶ (*distillery*) Brennerei *f* ❷ (*appliance*) Destillierapparat *m*

'stillbirth *n* Totgeburt *f*

'stillborn *adj baby, animal young* tot geboren

still 'life <*pl* -s> *n* ❶ (*painting*) Stillleben *nt* ❷ (*style*) Stilllebenmalerei *f*

stillness ['stɪl·nɪs] *n* ❶ (*tranquility*) Stille *f,* Ruhe *f* ❷ (*lack of movement*) *of the air, trees* Unbewegtheit *f,* Bewegungslosigkeit *f; of a person* Reglosigkeit *f*

stilt [stɪlt] *n usu pl* ❶ (*post*) Pfahl *m* ❷ (*for walking*) Stelze *f*

stilted ['stɪl·tɪd] *adj* (*pej: stiff and formal*) *way of talking* gestelzt; (*not natural*) *behavior* unnatürlich, gespreizt

stimulant ['stɪm·jə·lənt] **I.** *n* ❶ (*boost*) Stimulanz *f,* Anreiz *m* ❷ MED (*drug*) Stimulans *nt;* SPORTS Aufputschmittel *nt* **II.** *adj attr* anregend, belebend

stimulate ['stɪm·jə·leɪt] **I.** *vt* ❶ (*encourage*) beleben, ankurbeln ❷ (*excite*) stimulieren **II.** *vi* begeistern, mitreißen

stimulating ['stɪm·jə·leɪ·ṱɪŋ] *adj* ❶ (*mentally*) stimulierend; *conversation, discussion* anregend; *atmosphere, environment* animierend ❷ (*sexually*) erregend, stimulierend ❸ (*physically*) *shower, exercise* belebend; *drug* stimulierend

stimulation [ˌstɪm·jə·'leɪ·ʃən] *n* ❶ (*mental*) Anregung *f;* (*physical*) belebende Wirkung; (*sexual*) Stimulieren *nt,* Erregen *nt* ❷ (*motivation*) *of the economy* Ankurbelung *m;* (*of interest, enthusiasm*) Erregung *f*

stimulus <*pl* -li> ['stɪm·jə·ləs] *n* ❶ (*economic boost*) Anreiz *m,* Stimulus *m geh* ❷ (*motivation*) Ansporn *m kein pl,* Antrieb *m kein pl* ❸ BIOL, MED Reiz *m,* Stimulus *m fachspr*

sting [stɪŋ] **I.** *n* ❶ (*wound*) Stich *m;* (*caused by jellyfish*) Brennen *nt* ❷ (*from antiseptic, ointment*) Brennen *nt;* (*from needle*) Stechen *nt* ❸ (*sl: undercover operation*) Coup *m* **II.** *vi* <stung, stung> *bee, hornet* stechen; *disinfectant, sunburn* brennen; *wound, cut* schmerzen, weh tun; (*fig*) *words, criticism* schmerzen **III.** *vt* <stung, stung> ❶ (*insect*) stechen; (*jellyfish*) brennen ❷ (*cause pain*) **to ~ sb's eyes** *sand, wind, hail* jdm in den Augen brennen ❸ (*upset*) **he was stung by her criticisms** ihre Kritik hat ihn tief getroffen

stinger ['stɪŋ·ər] *n* BIOL *of a bee, hornet* Stachel *m; of a jellyfish* Brennfaden *m; of a plant* Brennhaar *nt*

stinginess ['stɪn·dʒɪ·nɪs] *n* Geiz *m,* Knaus[e]rigkeit *f pej fam*

stingray ['stɪŋ·reɪ] *n* Stachelrochen *m*

stingy ['stɪn·dʒi] *adj* (*fam*) geizig, knaus[e]rig *pej*

stink [stɪŋk] **I.** *n* ❶ *usu sing* (*smell*) Gestank *m,* Mief *m pej* ❷ *usu sing* (*fam: trouble*) Stunk *m;* **to make a ~ [about sth]** [wegen einer S. *gen*] Stunk machen **II.** *vi* <stank *or* stunk, stunk> ❶ (*smell bad*) stinken; ■ **to ~ of sth** nach etw *dat* stinken, nach etw *dat* miefen *pej* ❷ (*fig fam: be bad*) **his acting ~s** er ist ein miserabler Schauspieler ❸ (*fig fam: be disreputable*) stinken; (*be wrong*) zum Himmel stinken *sl*

'stink bomb *n* Stinkbombe *f*

stinker ['stɪŋ·kər] *n* ❶ (*pej fam: person*) Fiesling *m sl* ❷ (*fam: sth difficult*) harter Brocken

stint [stɪnt] **I.** *n* (*length of time*) Zeit *f* **II.** *vi* sparen, geizen (**on** mit +*dat*)

stipulate ['stɪp·jə·leɪt] *vt* (*person*) verlangen, fordern; (*contract*) festlegen; (*law, legislation*) zur Auflage machen, vorschreiben

stipulation [ˌstɪp·jə·'leɪ·ʃən] *n* Auflage *f,* Bedingung *f;* (*in contract*) Klausel *f*

stir [stɜr] **I.** *n usu sing* ❶ (*with spoon*) [Um]rühren *nt* ❷ (*physical movement*) Bewegung *f; of emotion* Erregung *f* ❸ (*excitement*) Aufruhr *f;* **to cause a ~** Aufsehen erregen **II.** *vt* <-rr-> ❶ (*mix*) rühren; ■ **to ~ sth into sth** etw in etw *akk* [hin]einrühren ❷ (*physically move*) rühren, bewegen ❸ (*arouse*) bewegen, rühren; *anger, curiosity* erregen; *emotions* aufwühlen ❹ (*inspire*) **to ~ sb into action** jdn zum Handeln bewegen **III.** *vi* <-rr-> ❶ (*mix*) rühren ❷ (*move*) sich regen; *person a.* sich rühren; *grass, water, curtains* sich bewegen ❸ (*awaken*) wach werden, aufwachen; ■ **to ~ within sb** (*fig*) *emotions* sich in jdm regen

'stir-fry **I.** *n* Chinapfanne *f,* Wok *m* **II.** *vi* <-ie->

S

kurz anbraten **III.** *vt* <-ie-> **to ~ vegetables** Gemüse kurz anbraten

stirring ['stɜr·ɪŋ] **I.** *n* Regung *f* **II.** *adj appeal, song, speech* bewegend, aufwühlend

stirrup ['stɜr·əp] *n* (*on saddle*) Steigbügel *m*

stitch [stɪtʃ] **I.** *n* <*pl* -es> ❶ (*in sewing, surgery*) Stich *m;* (*in knitting, crocheting*) Masche *f;* **to not have a ~ on** splitterfasernackt sein ❷ (*method*) Stichart *f;* **cross-~** Kreuzstich *m* ❸ (*pain*) Seitenstechen *nt kein pl* ▶ PHRASES: **in ~es** (*fam*) sich schieflachen **II.** *vi* sticken; (*sew*) nähen **III.** *vt* (*in sewing*) nähen; **to ~ a button onto sth** einen Knopf an etw *akk* [an]nähen

stock [stak] **I.** *n* ❶ (*reserves*) Vorrat *m* (**of** an +*dat*); **housing ~** Bestand *m* an Wohnhäusern ❷ (*inventory*) Bestand *m;* **to be in ~** vorrätig sein ❸ ■ **~s** *pl* (*shares in a company*) Aktien *pl* ❹ (*livestock*) Viehbestand *m* ❺ FOOD Brühe *f;* **fish ~** Fischfond *m* **II.** *adj attr* ❶ (*in inventory*) Lager-, Vorrats- ❷ (*standard*) Standard- **III.** *vt* ❶ (*keep in supply*) führen, vorrätig haben ❷ (*fill up*) ■ **to ~ sth** etw füllen; *shelves* auffüllen ❸ (*supply goods to*) beliefern

stockade [sta·'keɪd] *n* ❶ (*wooden fence*) Palisade *f;* (*enclosed area*) umzäuntes Gebiet ❷ (*prison*) Militärgefängnis *nt*

'stockbroker *n* Börsenmakler(in) *m(f)*

'stockbroking *n* Wertpapierhandel *m,* Effektenhandel *m*

'stock certificate *n* Aktienzertifikat *nt*

'stock company *n* ❶ FIN Aktiengesellschaft *f,* AG *f* ❷ THEAT Repertoiretheater *nt*

'stock dividend *n* Stockdividende *f;* **~ share** Gratisaktie *f*

'stock exchange *n* Börse *f*

'stockholder *n* Aktionär(in) *m(f)*

'stock index *n* Aktienindex *m*

stocking ['stak·ɪŋ] *n* ■ **~s** *pl* Strümpfe *pl*

'stock issue *n* Aktienausgabe *f*

'stock market *n* [Wertpapier]börse *f*

'stockpile I. *n* Vorrat *m* **II.** *vt* ■ **to ~ sth** Vorräte an etw *dat* anlegen, etw horten *pej;* **to ~ weapons** ein Waffenarsenal anlegen

'stock price *n* Aktienpreis *m*

'stockroom *n* Lager *nt,* Lagerraum *m*

stock-'still *adj pred* stocksteif

stocky ['stak·i] *adj* stämmig, kräftig

'stockyard *n* Viehhof *m;* (*at slaughterhouse*) Schlachthof *m*

stodgy ['stadʒ·i] *adj* (*pej fam*) ❶ *food* schwer [verdaulich], pampig ❷ (*dull*) langweilig, fad

stoic ['stoʊ·ɪk] **I.** *n* (*reserved person*) stoischer Mensch; ■ **S~** PHILOS Stoiker *m* **II.** *adj* (*in general*) stoisch; (*about sth specific*) gelassen

stoical ['stoʊ·ɪ·kəl] *adj see* **stoic**

stoicism ['stoʊ·ɪ·sɪz·əm] *n* stoische Ruhe; (*about sth specific*) Gleichmut *m;* ■ **S~** PHILOS Stoizismus

stoke [stoʊk] *vt* ❶ (*add fuel to*) *fire* schüren; *furnace* beschicken ❷ (*fig: encourage*) *anger, hatred* schüren

stoked [stoʊkt] *adj* (*sl*) aufgeregt

stoker ['stoʊ·kər] *n* ❶ (*person*) Heizer(in) *m(f)* ❷ (*device*) Beschickungsanlage *f*

stole[1] [stoʊl] *n* ❶ (*scarf*) Stola *f* ❷ (*priest's vestments*) [Priester]stola *f*

stole[2] [stoʊl] *pt of* **steal**

stolid ['stal·ɪd] *adj* (*not emotional*) *person* stumpf *pej;* (*calm*) gelassen, phlegmatisch *pej; silence, determination* beharrlich

stomach ['stʌm·ək] **I.** *n* ❶ (*digestive organ*) Magen *m;* **to have an upset ~** eine Magenverstimmung haben ❷ (*abdomen*) Bauch *m;* **to have a flat ~** einen flachen Bauch haben ❸ (*appetite*) **to have no ~ for sth** keinen Appetit auf etw *akk* haben; (*fig: desire*) keine Lust haben, etw zu tun **II.** *adj cramp, operation* Magen-; **~ muscles** Bauchmuskeln *pl* **III.** *vt* (*fam*) **to not be able to ~ sth** etw *akk* nicht ertragen können; **to be hard to ~** schwer zu verkraften sein

'stomachache *n usu sing* Magenschmerzen *pl,* Bauchschmerzen *pl,* Bauchweh *nt kein pl*

'stomach upset *n* Magenverstimmung *f*

stomp [stamp] **I.** *n* ❶ (*with foot*) Stampfen *nt* ❷ (*jazz dance*) Stomp *m* **II.** *vi* ❶ (*walk heavily*) stapfen; (*intentionally*) trampeln ❷ (*kick*) ■ **to ~ on sb/sth** auf jdn/etw treten; (*fig: suppress*) jdn/etw niedertrampeln **III.** *vt* (*beat down*) **to ~ one's feet** mit den Füßen [auf]stampfen; (*crush*) *rebellion* niederschlagen

stone [stoʊn] **I.** *n* ❶ GEOL Stein *m* ❷ (*piece of rock*) Stein *m;* **to be [just] a ~'s throw away** [nur] einen Katzensprung [weit] entfernt sein ❸ (*jewel*) [Edel]stein *m* ❹ (*in fruit*) Stein *m,* Kern *m* **II.** *adj attr floor, wall* Stein-; **~ statue** Statue *f* aus Stein **III.** *vt* (*throw stones at*) steinigen

'Stone Age *n* ■ **the ~** die Steinzeit

stone-'cold I. *adj* eiskalt **II.** *adv* **~ sober** stocknüchtern *fam*

stoned [stoʊnd] *adj* ❶ (*without pits*) *olives, cherries* entsteint ❷ (*sl: drugged*) high; (*drunk*) betrunken, besoffen; **to be ~ out of one's mind** total zu[gedröhnt] sein

stone-'deaf *adj* stocktaub *fam*

'stonemason *n* Steinmetz(in) *m(f)*

'stonewall I. *vi* ❶ (*in answering questions*) ausweichen ❷ SPORTS mauern *fam* **II.** *vt* abblocken

stoneware ['stoʊn·wer] *n* Steingut *nt*

'stonework *n* Mauerwerk *nt*

stony ['stoʊ·ni] *adj* ❶ (*with many stones*) *beach, ground* steinig ❷ (*fig: unfeeling*) steinern; *silence* eisig

stood [stʊd] *pt, pp of* **stand**

stooge [studʒ] *n* (*comedian partner*) Stichwortgeber(in) *m(f)*

stool [stul] *n* ❶ (*seat*) Hocker *m;* **piano ~** Klavierstuhl *m* ❷ (*feces*) Stuhl *m*

'stool pigeon *n* (*pej sl*) Spitzel *m*

stoop[1] [stup] **I.** *n usu sing* krummer Rücken, Buckel *m* **II.** *vi* sich beugen; **we had to ~ to go through the doorway** wir mussten den

Kopf einziehen, um durch die Tür zu gehen; ■ **to ~ down** sich bücken; **to ~ so low as to do sth** so weit sinken, dass man etw tut

stoop² [stup] *n* (*porch*) offene Veranda

stop [stap] **I.** *vt* <-pp-> ❶ (*halt*) *person, car* anhalten; **to get ~ped for sth by the police** wegen einer S. *gen* von der Polizei angehalten werden; *traffic* aufhalten; **~ that man!** haltet den Mann! ❷ (*make cease*) stoppen, beenden; (*temporarily*) unterbrechen; *bleeding* stillen; *clock* anhalten; *machine* abstellen; **this will ~ the pain** davon gehen die Schmerzen weg *fam;* **~ it!** hör auf [damit]! ❸ (*cease an activity*) ■ **to ~ sth** mit etw *dat* aufhören ❹ (*prevent*) ■ **to ~ sb [from] doing sth** jdn davon abhalten, etw zu tun **II.** *vi* <-pp-> ❶ (*cease moving*) *person* stehen bleiben; *car* [an]halten; **~!** halt!; **to ~ dead** abrupt innehalten ❷ (*cease, discontinue*) *machine* nicht mehr laufen; *clock, heart, watch* stehen bleiben; *rain* aufhören; *pain* abklingen, nachlassen; *production, payments* eingestellt werden ❸ (*cease an activity*) ■ **to ~ [doing sth]** aufhören[, etw zu tun], [mit etw *dat*] aufhören; **she ~ped drinking** sie trinkt nicht mehr ❹ TRANSP *bus, train* halten ▶ PHRASES: **to ~ at nothing** vor nichts zurückschrecken **III.** *n* ❶ (*standstill*) Halt *m;* **to come to a ~** stehen bleiben; *car a.* anhalten; *rain* aufhören; *project, production* eingestellt werden; **to put a ~ to sth** etw *dat* ein Ende setzen ❷ (*break*) Pause *f;* AVIAT Zwischenlandung *f;* (*halt*) Halt *m* ❸ TRANSP Haltestelle *f;* (*for ship*) Anlegestelle *f*

◆**stop by** *vi* vorbeischauen; **to ~ by sb's house** bei jdm vorbeischauen

◆**stop off** *vi* kurz bleiben, Halt machen; (*while traveling*) Zwischenstation machen

◆**stop over** *vi* Zwischenstation machen

◆**stop up I.** *vt* ■ **to ~ sth ↻ up** etw verstopfen; *hole* [zu]stopfen **II.** *vi* PHOT eine größere Blende einstellen

'stopcock *n* Absperrhahn *m*

'stopgap I. *n* Notlösung *f,* Notbehelf *m* **II.** *adj attr* Überbrückungs-; **~ solution** Zwischenlösung *f*

'stoplight *n* ❶ (*traffic light*) [Verkehrs]ampel *f* ❷ (*brake light*) Bremslicht *nt*

'stopover *n of plane* Zwischenlandung *f; of person* Zwischenstation *f;* (*length of break*) Zwischenaufenthalt *m*

stoppage ['stap·ɪdʒ] *n* ❶ (*cessation of work*) Arbeitseinstellung *f* ❷ (*unintentional*) Unterbrechung *f;* **~ in production** Produktionsstillstand *m*

stopper ['stap·ər] **I.** *n* Stöpsel *m* **II.** *vt* zustöpseln

stopping ['stap·ɪŋ] **I.** *n* Anhalten *nt* **II.** *adj attr* **~ distance** Sicherheitsabstand *m*

'stop sign *n* Stoppschild *nt*

'stopwatch *n* Stoppuhr *f*

storage ['stɔr·ɪdʒ] *n* ❶ (*for future use*) *of food, goods* Lagerung *f; of books* Aufbewahrung *f; of water, electricity* Speicherung *f;* **to put sth into ~** etw [ein]lagern ❷ COMPUT *of data* Speicherung *f*

'storage battery, **'storage cell** *n* Akku[mulator] *m*

'storage capacity *n* (*in computer*) Speicherkapazität *f;* (*for furniture, books*) Lagerraum *m;* (*in tank*) Fassungsvermögen *nt*

'storage room, **'storage space** *n* ❶ (*capacity*) Stauraum *m* ❷ (*room in house*) Abstellraum *m;* (*in warehouse*) Lagerraum *m*

'storage tank *n* Vorratstank *m*

store [stɔr] **I.** *n* ❶ (*supply*) Vorrat *m* (**of** an +*dat*); (*fig*) Schatz *m;* ■ **~s** *pl* Vorräte *pl;* ■ **to be in ~ [for sb]** (*fig*) [jdm] bevorstehen; **we have a surprise in ~ for your father** wir haben für deinen Vater eine Überraschung auf Lager ❷ (*small shop*) Laden *m* ❸ (*large shop*) Geschäft *nt;* (*department store*) Kaufhaus *nt* ❹ (*warehouse*) Lager *nt;* **grain ~** Getreidespeicher *m* **II.** *vt* ❶ (*keep for future use*) *heat, information, electricity* [auf]speichern; *furniture* unterstellen; *supplies* lagern ❷ COMPUT (*file*) speichern; *data* [ab]speichern

'store card *n* Kundenkarte *f*

'storefront *n* (*front of store*) Schaufenster *nt;* (*larger*) Schaufensterfront *f*

'storehouse *n* Warenhaus *nt;* (*fig form*) Fundgrube *f*

storekeeper ['stɔr·ˌki·pər] *n* Ladenbesitzer(in) *m(f),* Geschäftsinhaber(in) *m(f)*

'storeroom *n* Lagerraum *m;* (*for food*) Vorratskammer *f,* Speisekammer *f;* (*for personal items*) Abstellkammer *f*

stork [stɔrk] *n* Storch *m*

storm [stɔrm] **I.** *n* ❶ (*strong wind*) Sturm *m;* (*with thunder*) Gewitter *nt;* (*with rain*) Unwetter *nt* ❷ (*fig: uproar*) **~ of applause** Beifallssturm *m;* **to raise a ~ of protest** einen [Protest]sturm hervorrufen ▶ PHRASES: **to take sth/sb by ~** etw/jdn im Sturm erobern **II.** *vi* ❶ *impers strong winds* stürmen ❷ (*move fast*) stürmen, jagen; ■ **to ~ out** hinausstürmen ❸ (*speak angrily*) toben **III.** *vt* stürmen

'storm cloud *n* Gewitterwolke *f;* (*fig liter*) dunkle Wolken *pl*

'storm door *n zusätzliche Tür zur Sturmsicherung*

stormy ['stɔr·mi] *adj* ❶ *weather, night, sea* stürmisch ❷ (*fig: fierce*) stürmisch; *life* bewegt; *argument* heftig; *debate* hitzig

story¹ ['stɔr·i] *n* ❶ (*tale*) Geschichte *f;* (*narrative*) Erzählung *f;* (*plot*) Handlung *f* ❷ (*rumor*) Gerücht *nt;* **the ~ goes that ...** man erzählt sich, dass ... ❸ (*news report*) Beitrag *m;* (*in newspaper*) Artikel *m* ❹ (*lie*) Geschichte *f,* [Lügen]märchen *nt fam* ▶ PHRASES: **it's a long ~** das ist eine lange Geschichte; **to make a long ~ short** um es kurz zu machen

story² ['stɔr·i] *n* Stockwerk *nt,* Stock *m,* Etage *f;* **a three-~ house** ein dreistöckiges Haus

'storybook *n* Geschichtenbuch *nt,* Buch *nt* mit Kindergeschichten

'story line *n* Handlung *f*

S

'storyteller *n* ❶ (*narrator*) Geschichtenerzähler(in) *m(f)* ❷ (*fam: liar*) Lügner(in) *m(f)*
stout [staʊt] *adj* ❶ (*corpulent*) beleibt, korpulent *geh; woman* füllig *euph* ❷ (*thick and strong*) kräftig, stabil; *door, stick* massiv; *shoes, boots* fest
stoutly ['staʊt·li] *adv* ❶ (*of person*) ~ **built** stämmig gebaut ❷ (*strong*) stabil ❸ (*firmly*) entschieden, steif und fest *fam;* **to ~ believe in sth** fest an etw *akk* glauben
stove [stoʊv] *n* ❶ (*for cooking*) Herd *m;* **induction ~** Induktionsherd *m* ❷ (*heater*) Ofen *m*
'stovepipe *n* Ofenrohr *nt*
stow [stoʊ] *vt* ❶ (*put away*) verstauen; (*hide*) verstecken ❷ (*fill*) vollmachen; NAUT befrachten; *goods* verladen
◆**stow away** I. *vt* ■**to ~ away** ◌ **sth** etw. verstauen [*o* wegpacken]; (*hide*) etw verstecken II. *vi* (*travel without paying*) als blinder Passagier reisen
stowage ['stoʊ·ɪdʒ] *n* (*stowing*) Verstauen *nt;* NAUT [Be]laden *nt*
stowaway ['stoʊ·ə·weɪ] *n* blinder Passagier/blinde Passagierin
straddle ['stræd·əl] I. *vt* ❶ ■**to ~ sth** (*standing*) mit gespreizten Beinen über etw *dat* stehen; (*sitting*) rittlings auf etw *dat* sitzen; (*jumping*) [mit gestreckten Beinen] über etw *akk* springen ❷ (*bridge*) *border* überbrücken, überspannen *geh* ❸ (*part*) *legs* spreizen ❹ (*fig: equivocal position*) **to ~ an issue** bei einer Frage nicht klar Stellung beziehen II. *vi* (*stand*) breitbeinig [da]stehen; (*sit*) mit gegrätschten [*o* gespreizten] Beinen [da]sitzen III. *n* (*jump*) Scherensprung *m*
straggle ['stræg·əl] I. *vi* ❶ (*move as disorganized group*) umherstreifen ❷ (*come in small numbers*) sich sporadisch einstellen ❸ (*hang untidily*) *hair, beard* zottelig herunterhängen II. *n of things* Sammelsurium *nt; of people* Ansammlung *f*
straggler ['stræg·lər] *n* Nachzügler(in) *m(f)*
straight [streɪt] I. *adj* ❶ (*without curve*) *line, back, nose* gerade; *hair* glatt; *skirt* gerade geschnitten; *road, row, furrow* [schnur]gerade; **the picture isn't ~** das Bild hängt schief ❷ (*frank*) *advice, denial, refusal* offen, freimütig; (*honest*) ehrlich; *answer* klar ❸ (*heterosexual*) heterosexuell, hetero *fam* ❹ (*simply factual*) tatsachengetreu, nur auf Fakten basierend *attr* ❺ (*plain*) einfach; (*undiluted*) pur ❻ *pred* (*in order*) in Ordnung; (*clarified*) geklärt; **to set things ~** (*tidy*) Ordnung schaffen; (*organize*) etwas auf die Reihe kriegen *fam;* **to set sb ~ about sth** jdm Klarheit über etw *akk* verschaffen II. *adv* ❶ (*in a line*) gerade[aus]; **go ~ down this road** folgen Sie immer dieser Straße; **to look ~ ahead** geradeaus schauen ❷ (*immediately*) sofort; **to get ~ to the point** sofort zur Sache kommen ❸ (*clearly*) klar; **I'm so tired I can't think ~ anymore** ich bin so müde, dass ich nicht mehr klar denken kann

S

straightaway [ˌstreɪt̬·ə·'weɪ] *n* Gerade *f*
straighten ['streɪ·tən] I. *vt* ❶ (*make straight, level*) gerade machen; *hair* glätten; *river, road* begradigen ❷ (*arrange in place*) richten, ordnen; *tie* zurechtrücken II. *vi person* sich aufrichten; *road, river* gerade werden; *hair* sich glätten
◆**straighten out** I. *vt* ❶ (*make straight*) etw gerade machen; *clothes* glatt streichen; *wire* ausziehen ❷ (*tidy up*) in Ordnung bringen; (*clarify*) klarstellen; *misunderstanding* aus der Welt schaffen II. *vi* gerade werden
◆**straighten up** I. *vi* ❶ (*stand upright*) sich aufrichten ❷ (*move straight*) *vehicle, ship* [wieder] geradeaus fahren; *aircraft* [wieder] geradeaus fliegen II. *vt* ■**to ~ up** ◌ **sth** ❶ (*make level*) etw gerade machen ❷ (*tidy up*) etw aufräumen; (*fig: put in order*) etw regeln [*o* in Ordnung bringen]
straightforward [ˌstreɪt·'fɔr·wərd] *adj* ❶ (*direct*) direkt; *explanation* unumwunden; *look* gerade ❷ (*honest*) *answer, person* aufrichtig, ehrlich ❸ (*easy*) einfach, leicht
'straight-out *adj* (*fam*) offen, unverblümt
strain¹ [streɪn] I. *n usu sing* ❶ (*physical pressure*) Druck *m,* Belastung *f* ❷ (*fig: emotional pressure*) Druck *m,* Belastung *f;* **to be under a lot of ~** unter hohem Druck stehen ❸ (*overexertion*) [Über]beanspruchung *f,* [Über]belastung *f* ❹ (*pulled tendon, muscle*) Zerrung *f* II. *vi* ❶ (*pull*) ziehen; **the dog is ~ing at the leash** der Hund zerrt an der Leine ❷ (*try hard*) sich anstrengen III. *vt* ❶ (*pull*) ziehen (an +*dat*); MED, SPORTS überdehnen, zerren ❷ (*overexert*) [stark] beanspruchen; *eyes* überanstrengen ❸ (*remove solids from liquids*) *coffee* filtrieren; (*remove liquid from solids*) *vegetables* abgießen
strain² [streɪn] *n* (*breed*) *of animals* Rasse *f; of plants* Sorte *f; of virus* Art *f*
strained [streɪnd] *adj* ❶ (*forced*) bemüht, angestrengt; (*artificial*) gekünstelt *pej* ❷ (*tense*) *relations* belastet, angespannt ❸ (*stressed*) abgespannt, mitgenommen
strainer ['streɪ·nər] *n* Sieb *nt*
strait [streɪt] *n* GEOG Meerenge *f,* Straße *f*
straitened ['streɪ·tənd] *adj* (*form: poor*) knapp; (*restricted*) beschränkt, dürftig; **to be in ~ circumstances** sich *akk* einschränken müssen
'straitjacket *n* (*a. fig*) Zwangsjacke *f*
strait-laced ['streɪt·leɪst] *adj* (*pej*) puritanisch
strand¹ [strænd] I. *vt* **to ~ a boat** ein Boot auf Grund setzen II. *vi* stranden
strand² [strænd] *n* ❶ (*single thread*) Faden *m; of rope* Strang *m; of tissue* Faser *f; of hair* Strähne *f* ❷ (*element of whole*) Strang *m;* **~ of the plot** Handlungsstrang *m*
stranded ['stræn·dɪd] *adj ship, whale* gestrandet; ■**to be ~** (*fig*) festsitzen; **to leave sb ~** jdn sich *dat* selbst überlassen
strange [streɪndʒ] *adj* ❶ (*peculiar, odd*) son-

derbar, merkwürdig; (*unusual*) ungewöhnlich, außergewöhnlich; (*weird*) unheimlich, seltsam; (*exceptional*) erstaunlich ❷ (*uneasy*) komisch; (*unwell*) seltsam, unwohl ❸ (*not known*) fremd, unbekannt; (*unfamiliar*) nicht vertraut

strangely ['streɪndʒ·li] *adv* ❶ (*oddly*) merkwürdig, sonderbar ❷ (*unexpectedly*) **she was ~ calm** sie war auffällig still; **~ enough** seltsamerweise

stranger ['streɪn·dʒər] *n* (*unknown person*) Fremde(r) *f(m)*; (*person new to a place*) Neuling *m a. pej*; **are you a ~ here, too?** sind Sie auch fremd hier?

strangle ['stræŋ·gəl] *vt* ❶ (*murder*) *person* erdrosseln, erwürgen ❷ (*fig: suppress*) ■ **to ~ sth** etw unterdrücken [*o* ersticken]

'**stranglehold** *n* ❶ (*grip*) Würgegriff *m* ❷ (*fig: complete control*) Vormacht[stellung] *f kein pl*

strangulation [ˌstræŋ·gjʊ·'leɪ·ʃən] *n* (*strangling*) Erdrosselung *f*, Strangulierung *f*; (*death from strangling*) Tod *m* durch Erwürgen

strap [stræp] **I.** *n* (*for fastening*) Riemen *m*; (*for safety*) Gurt *m*; (*for clothes*) Träger *m*; (*hold in a vehicle*) Halteschlaufe *f*; **watch ~** Uhrarmband *nt* **II.** *vt* <-pp-> ■ **to ~ sth [to sth]** etw [an etw *dat*] befestigen

strapless ['stræp·lɪs] *adj* trägerlos

strapping ['stræp·ɪŋ] *adj* (*hum fam*) kräftig

stratagem ['stræt̬·ə·dʒəm] *n* [Einzel]strategie *f*

strategic [strə·'ti·dʒɪk] *adj* strategisch, taktisch

strategist ['stræt̬·ə·dʒɪst] *n* Stratege, -in *m, f*, Taktiker(in) *m(f)*

strategy ['stræt̬·ə·dʒi] *n* ❶ (*plan of action*) Strategie *f*; (*fig a.*) Taktik *f* ❷ (*art of planning*) Taktieren *nt*; (*of war*) Kriegsstrategie *f*

stratify <-ie-> ['stræt̬·ə·faɪ] *vt* ❶ (*arrange in layers*) schichten ❷ (*place in groups*) klassifizieren (**by** nach +*dat*); **stratified society** mehrschichtige Gesellschaft

stratosphere ['stræt̬·əs·fɪr] *n* Stratosphäre *f*

stratum <*pl* -ta> ['streɪ·t̬əm] *n* ❶ (*layer*) *a.* SOCIOL Schicht *f* ❷ GEOL (*layer of rock*) [Gesteins]schicht *f*

straw [strɔ] *n* ❶ (*crop, fodder*) Stroh *nt* ❷ (*single dried stem, drinking tube*) Strohhalm *m*; **to draw ~s** losen ▶ PHRASES: **to be the final ~** das Fass zum Überlaufen bringen

strawberry ['strɔ·ˌber·i] *n* Erdbeere *f*

'**straw poll** *n* Probeabstimmung *f*; (*test of opinion*) [Meinungs]umfrage *f*

stray [streɪ] **I.** *vi* ❶ (*wander*) streunen; (*escape from control*) frei herumlaufen; (*go astray*) sich verirren ❷ (*move casually*) umherstreifen; **her eyes kept ~ing to the clock** ihre Blicke wanderten immer wieder zur Uhr ❸ (*fig: digress*) abweichen; *orator, thoughts* abschweifen **II.** *n* ❶ (*animal*) streunendes [Haus]tier ❷ (*person*) Umherirrende(r) *f(m)* **III.** *adj attr* ❶ (*homeless*) *animal* streunend, herrenlos; (*lost*) *person* herumirrend ❷ (*isolated*) vereinzelt; (*occasional*) gelegentlich; **to be hit by a ~ bullet** von einem Blindgänger getroffen werden

streak [strik] **I.** *n* ❶ (*line*) Streifen *m*; (*mark of color*) Spur *f*; (*on window*) Schliere *f* ❷ (*colored hair*) ■ **~s** *pl* Strähnen *pl*, Strähnchen *pl* ❸ (*run of fortune*) Strähne *f*; **lucky** [*or* **winning**] **~** Glückssträhne *f* **II.** *vt usu passive* ■ **to be ~ed** gestreift sein; **~ed with gray** *hair* von grauen Strähnen durchzogen **III.** *vi* ❶ (*move very fast*) flitzen *fam* ❷ (*fam: run naked in public*) flitzen

streaker ['stri·kər] *n* (*fam*) Flitzer(in) *m(f)*

streaky ['stri·ki] *adj* streifig; *pattern* gestreift; *face* verschmiert; *window, mirror* schlierig

stream [strim] **I.** *n* ❶ (*small river*) Bach *m*, Bächlein *nt*, Flüsschen *nt* ❷ (*flow*) *of liquid* Strahl *m*; *of people* Strom *m*; **~ of light** breiter Lichtstrahl ❸ (*continuous series*) Flut *f*, Schwall *m*; **a ~ of abuse** eine Schimpfkanonade ❹ (*a. fig: current*) Strömung *f a. fig* **II.** *vi* ❶ (*flow*) *blood, tears* strömen; *water* fließen, rinnen ❷ (*run*) *nose* laufen; *eyes* tränen ❸ (*move in stream*) *light, sun, crowd* strömen ❹ (*flutter*) *clothing* flattern; *hair* wehen

streamer ['stri·mər] *n* ❶ (*pennant*) Wimpel *m*, Fähnchen *nt* ❷ (*decoration*) *of ribbon* Band *nt*; *of paper* Luftschlange *f*

streaming ['stri·mɪŋ] *n* INET Streaming *nt*, Livestream *m*

streamline ['strim·laɪn] *vt* ❶ (*shape*) stromlinienförmig [aus]formen ❷ (*fig: improve efficiency*) rationalisieren; (*simplify*) vereinfachen

streamlined ['strim·laɪnd] *adj* ❶ (*aerodynamic*) stromlinienförmig; *car a.* windschnittig ❷ (*efficient*) rationalisiert; (*simplified*) vereinfacht

street [strit] *n* ❶ (*road*) Straße *f*; ■ **in the ~** auf der Straße; **I live on Main S~** ich wohne in der Main Street; **side ~** Seitenstraße *f* ❷ (*residents*) Straße *f* ▶ PHRASES: **the average man/woman/person on the ~** der Mann/die Frau von der Straße

'**streetcar** *n* Straßenbahn *f*

'**street cred, street credi'bility** *n* (*sl*) In-Sein *nt sl*; **that jacket won't do much for your ~** mit diesem Jackett bist du einfach nicht in

'**street lamp** *n* Straßenlaterne *f*

'**streetlight** *n* Straßenlicht *nt*

'**street sweeper** *n* ❶ (*person*) Straßenkehrer(in) *m(f)*, Straßenfeger(in) *m(f)* SÜDD ❷ (*vehicle*) Straßenkehrmaschine *f*

'**street value** *n* *Verkaufspreis für illegale Waren, z. B. Drogen*

'**streetwalker** *n* (*dated*) Straßendirne *f meist pej*

'**streetwise** *adj* gewieft, raffiniert

strength [streŋkθ] *n* ❶ (*of person*) Kraft *f*, Stärke *f*; **physical ~** körperliche Kraft, Muskelkraft *f*; (*of object, structure*) Widerstandskraft *f*, Belastbarkeit *f* ❷ (*health and vitality*) Robustheit *f*, Lebenskraft *f*; **to gain ~** wieder zu Kräften kommen ❸ (*effectiveness, influence*) Wirkungsgrad *m*, Stärke *f*; (*of an* *argument*) Überzeugungskraft *f;* **to gather ~** an Stabilität gewinnen ④ (*mental firmness*) Stärke *f;* **to show great ~ of character** große Charakterstärke zeigen; **to draw ~ from sth** aus etw *dat* Kraft ziehen ⑤ (*potency*) *of tea* Stärke *f; of alcoholic drink a.* Alkoholgehalt *m; of a drug* Konzentration *f; of medicine* Wirksamkeit *f* ⑥ (*strong point*) Stärke *f;* **sb's ~s and weaknesses** jds Stärken und Schwächen ⑦ (*intensity*) Intensität *f; of a color* Leuchtkraft *f; of a feeling* Intensität *f; of belief* Stärke *f* ⑧ (*number of members*) [Mitglieder]zahl *f;* (*number of people*) [Personen]zahl *f;* **we're below ~ today** wir treten heute nicht in voller Stärke an; **to turn out in ~** in Massen anrücken ▶ PHRASES: **on the ~ of sth** aufgrund einer S. *gen*

strengthen ['streŋk·θən] **I.** *vt* ① (*make stronger*) kräftigen, stärken; (*fortify*) befestigen, verstärken ② (*increase*) [ver]stärken; (*intensify*) intensivieren; (*improve*) verbessern; *currency* stabilisieren **II.** *vi* ① (*become stronger*) stärker werden; *muscles* kräftiger werden; *wind* auffrischen ② FIN, STOCKEX (*increase in value*) *stock market* an Wert gewinnen; *currency* zulegen

strenuous ['stren·ju·əs] *adj* ① (*exhausting*) anstrengend ② (*energetic*) energisch, heftig; **despite ~ efforts** trotz angestrengter Bemühungen

strep 'throat *n* MED (*fam*) Halsentzündung *f*

stress [stres] **I.** *n* <*pl* -es> ① (*mental strain*) Stress *m,* Druck *m,* Belastung *f;* **to be under ~** starken Belastungen ausgesetzt sein; (*at work*) unter Stress stehen ② (*emphasis*) Bedeutung *f,* Gewicht *nt* ③ PHYS (*force causing distortion*) Belastung *f;* (*tension*) Spannung *f;* (*pressure*) Druck *m kein pl* **II.** *vt* ① (*emphasize*) betonen, hervorheben; **I'd just like to ~ that ...** ich möchte lediglich darauf hinweisen, dass ... ② (*strain*) belasten, beanspruchen; ■ **to ~ sb [out]** jdn stressen **III.** *vi* (*fam*) *person* sich *akk* aufregen (**about/over** über +*akk*)

stressed [strest] *adj* ① (*under mental pressure*) gestresst ② (*forcibly pronounced*) betont

'stress fracture *n* MED Ermüdungsbruch *m;* PHYS Spannungsriss *m*

stress-'free *adj* stressfrei, ohne Stress *nach n*

stressful ['stres·fʊl] *adj* stressig *fam,* anstrengend, aufreibend; **~ situation** Stresssituation *f*

'stress mark *n* LING Betonungszeichen *nt,* Akzent *m fachspr*

'stress test *n* Stresstest *m;* MED Belastungstest *m,* Stresstest *m*

stretch [stretʃ] **I.** *n* <*pl* -es> ① (*elasticity*) Dehnbarkeit *f; of fabric* Elastizität *f* ② (*muscle extension*) Dehnungsübungen *pl,* Strecken *nt kein pl* ③ (*an extended area*) Stück *nt;* (*section of road*) Streckenabschnitt *m,* Wegstrecke *f;* **~ of train tracks** Bahnstrecke *f;* **~ of water** Wasserfläche *f* ④ (*straight part of a race track*) Gerade *f* ⑤ (*period of time*) Zeitraum *m,* Zeitspanne *f* **II.** *adj attr* Stretch- **III.** *vi* ① (*become longer, wider*) *rubber, elastic* sich dehnen; *clothes* weiter werden ② (*extend the body*) sich [recken und] strecken; (*as exercise*) Dehnungsübungen machen ③ (*cover an area*) sich erstrecken **IV.** *vt* ① (*extend*) [aus]dehnen, strecken; (*extend by pulling*) dehnen; (*tighten*) straff ziehen, straffen; **to ~ one's legs** sich *dat* die Beine vertreten ② (*increase number of portions*) strecken; *sauce, soup* verlängern ③ (*demand a lot of*) ■ **to ~ sb/sth** jdn/etw bis zum Äußersten fordern; **we're already fully ~ed** wir sind schon voll ausgelastet; **to ~ sb's patience** jds Geduld auf eine harte Probe stellen ④ (*go beyond*) ■ **to ~ sth** *limit* über etw *akk* hinausgehen

stretcher ['stretʃ·ər] *n* MED Tragbahre *f;* **to carry sb off on a ~** jdn auf einer Tragbahre [weg]tragen

strew <strewed, strewn *or* strewed> [stru] *vt* ① (*scatter*) [ver]streuen ② (*cover*) bestreuen (**with** mit +*dat*)

stricken ['strɪk·ən] *adj* ① (*be overcome*) geplagt; ■ **to be ~ by sth** von etw *dat* heimgesucht werden; **to be ~ with an illness** mit einer Krankheit geschlagen sein *geh,* [schwer] an etw *dat* erkranken ② (*severely damaged*) *vessel, tanker* leckgeschlagen ③ (*distressed*) *face, expression* leidend

strict [strɪkt] *adj* ① (*severe, unswerving*) streng; *boss* strikt, herrisch; *penalty* hart; *vegetarian* überzeugt ② (*demanding compliance*) streng, genau; *time limit* festgesetzt; *neutrality* strikt ③ (*absolute*) streng, absolut; **in the ~est confidence** streng vertraulich

strictly ['strɪkt·li] *adv* ① (*absolutely*) streng ② (*precisely*) **~ defined** genau definiert; **~ speaking** genau genommen

stride [straɪd] **I.** *vi* <strode, stridden> **to ~ purposefully up to sth** zielstrebig auf etw *akk* zugehen; ■ **to ~ forward** (*fig*) vorankommen, Fortschritte machen **II.** *n* ① (*step*) Schritt *m;* **to hit one's ~** (*fig*) in Schwung kommen, seinen Rhythmus finden; **to take sth in ~** (*fig*) mit etw *dat* gut fertigwerden ② (*approv: progress*) Fortschritt *m;* **to make ~s forward** Fortschritte machen

strident ['straɪ·dənt] *adj* ① (*harsh*) grell, schrill ② (*forceful*) scharf, schneidend

strife [straɪf] *n* Streit *m,* Zwist *m geh;* **industrial ~** Auseinandersetzungen *pl* in der Industrie

strike [straɪk] **I.** *n* ① MIL Angriff *m,* Schlag *m* (**against** gegen +*akk*); **preemptive ~** Präventivschlag *m;* (*fig*) vorbeugende Maßnahme ② (*of labor*) Streik *m,* Ausstand *m;* **sit-down ~** Sitzstreik *m;* **to be [out] on ~** streiken; **to call for a ~** einen Streik ausrufen ③ (*discovery*) Fund *m* ④ (*in baseball*) Strike *m,* Fehlschlag *m* **II.** *vt* <struck, struck *or* stricken> ① (*hit*) *baseball* schlagen; *soccer ball* schießen; (*bang against*) ■ **to ~ sth** gegen etw *akk* schlagen; (*bump into*) gegen etw *akk* stoßen; (*drive against*) gegen etw *akk* fahren; (*collide with*) mit etw *dat* zusammenstoßen; **to ~ one's fist on the table** mit der Faust auf den Tisch schlagen ② *usu passive* (*reach, damage*) treffen; **to be struck by lightning** vom Blitz getroffen werden ③ (*inflict*) **to ~ a blow** zuschlagen; **to ~ a blow against sb/sth** (*fig*) jdm/etw einen Schlag versetzen ④ (*devastate*) heimsuchen; **the flood struck New Orleans** die Flut brach über New Orleans herein ⑤ (*give an impression*) ■**to ~ sb as ...** jdm ... scheinen; **she doesn't ~ me as [being] very motivated** sie scheint mir nicht besonders motiviert [zu sein] ⑥ (*impress*) ■**to be struck by sth** von etw *dat* beeindruckt sein ⑦ (*achieve*) erreichen; **to ~ a deal with sb** mit jdm eine Vereinbarung treffen ⑧ *clock* **to ~ the hour** die [volle] Stunde schlagen ⑨ (*occur to*) **has it ever struck you that ...?** ist dir je der Gedanke gekommen dass ...? ⑩ (*ignite*) *match* anzünden ⑪ (*discover*) auf etw *akk* stoßen; **to ~ oil** auf Öl stoßen; **to ~ it rich** das große Geld machen **III.** *vi* <struck, struck> ① (*reach aim, have impact*) treffen; *lightning* einschlagen; **to ~ at the heart of sth** etw vernichtend treffen; **to ~ home** ins Schwarze treffen ② (*act*) zuschlagen; (*attack*) angreifen ③ (*cause suffering*) *illness, disaster* ausbrechen; *fate* zuschlagen ④ *clock, hour* schlagen *fig* ⑤ (*refuse to work*) streiken, in den Ausstand treten *form*

◆**strike back** *vi* (*a. fig*) zurückschlagen

◆**strike down** *vt usu passive* ① (*knock down*) ■**to ~ down** ◌ **sb** jdn niederschlagen ② (*kill*) ■**to ~ sb down** jdn dahinraffen *geh;* **to be struck down by a bullet** von einer Kugel getötet werden ③ LAW (*cancel*) *law, ruling* aufheben

◆**strike out I.** *vt* ① (*delete*) ■**to ~ out** ◌ **sth** etw [aus]streichen ② (*in baseball*) ■**to ~ out** ◌ **sb** jdn ausstriken **II.** *vi* ① (*hit out*) zuschlagen; ■**to ~ out at sb** nach jdm schlagen; (*fig*) jdn scharf angreifen ② (*start afresh*) neu beginnen; **to ~ out on one's own** eigene Wege gehen

◆**strike up I.** *vt* (*initiate*) anfangen; **to ~ up a friendship with sb** sich mit jdm anfreunden **II.** *vi* beginnen, anfangen

'strikebreaker *n* Streikbrecher(in) *m(f)*

striker ['straɪ·kər] *n* ① (*worker*) Streikende(r) *f(m)* ② (*in soccer*) Stürmer(in) *m(f)*

striking ['straɪ·kɪŋ] *adj* ① (*unusual*) bemerkenswert, auffallend; **the most ~ aspect of sth** das Bemerkenswerteste an etw *dat; differences* erheblich; *feature* herausragend; *parallel, result* erstaunlich; *personality* beeindruckend ② (*good-looking*) umwerfend; **~ beauty** bemerkenswerte Schönheit ③ (*close*) **within ~ distance [of sth]** in unmittelbarer Nähe [einer S. *gen*]; (*short distance*) einen Katzensprung [von etw *dat*] entfernt

string [strɪŋ] **I.** *n* ① (*twine*) Schnur *f,* Kordel *f;* **ball of ~** Knäuel *m o nt* ② (*fig: controls*) **to pull [some] ~s** seine Beziehungen spielen lassen; **[with] no ~s attached** ohne Bedingungen ③ MUS, SPORTS Saite *f* ④ (*in an orchestra*) ■**the ~s** *pl* (*instruments*) die Streichinstrumente *pl;* (*players*) die Streicher *pl* ⑤ (*chain*) Kette *f;* **~ of pearls** Perlenkette *f* ⑥ (*fig: series*) Kette *f,* Reihe *f* ⑦ COMPUT Zeichenfolge *f;* **search ~** Suchbegriff *m* **II.** *vt* <strung, strung> ① (*fit*) besaiten; *racket* bespannen ② (*attach*) auffädeln, aufziehen

◆**string along** *vt* (*fam*) ■**to ~ sb** ◌ **along** (*deceive*) jdn täuschen [*o* übers Ohr hauen]

◆**string out I.** *vi* sich verteilen **II.** *vt* ■**to ~ sth** ◌ **out** etw verstreuen

◆**string up** *vt* ① (*hang*) ■**to ~ up** ◌ **sth** etw aufhängen ② ■**to ~ up** ◌ **sb** (*fam: execute*) jdn [auf]hängen

string 'bean *n* grüne Bohne

string(ed) instrument [ˌstrɪŋd'-] *n* Saiteninstrument *nt*

stringency ['strɪn·dʒən·si] *n* ① (*strictness*) Strenge *f* ② (*thriftiness*) Knappheit *f*

stringent ['strɪn·dʒənt] *adj* ① (*strict*) streng; *measures* drastisch ② (*financial situation*) angespannt

stringer ['strɪŋ·ər] *n* JOURN (*sl*) freiberuflicher Korrespondent/freiberufliche Korrespondentin

'string quartet *n* Streichquartett *nt*

stringy ['strɪŋ·i] *adj food* faserig; *hair* strähnig

strip [strɪp] **I.** *n* Streifen *m;* **narrow ~ of land** schmales Stück Land **II.** *vt* <-pp-> ① (*lay bare*) *house, cupboard* leer räumen, ausräumen; **to ~ sth bare** etw kahl fressen ② (*undress*) ■**to ~ sb** jdn ausziehen ③ *usu passive* (*remove*) ■**to ~ sb of sth** jdn einer S. *gen* berauben; **to ~ sb of his/her title** jdm seinen Titel aberkennen **III.** *vi* <-pp-> sich ausziehen; **~ped to the waist** mit nacktem Oberkörper

stripe [straɪp] *n* ① (*band*) Streifen *m* ② MIL [Ärmel]streifen *m*

striped [straɪpt] *adj clothes* gestreift, Streifen-

'strip light *n* Neonröhre *f*

'strip mining *n* Tagebau *m*

stripper ['strɪp·ər] *n* ① (*person*) Stripperin *f,* Stripteasetänzerin *f* ② (*solvent*) Farbentferner *m;* (*for wallpaper*) Tapetenlöser *m*

'strip search *n Leibesvisitation, bei der sich der/die Durchsuchte ausziehen muss;* **to undergo a ~** sich zu einer Durchsuchung ausziehen müssen

strip-search ['strɪp·ˌsɜrtʃ] *vt* ■**to ~ sb** *jdn einer Durchsuchung unterziehen, bei der sich der Betreffende ausziehen muss*

'strip show *n* Strip[tease]show *f*

'striptease *n* Striptease *m*

strive <strove *or* -d, striven> [straɪv] *vi* sich bemühen; ■**to ~ after sth** nach etw *dat* streben, etw anstreben; ■**to ~ for sth** um etw *akk* ringen

'strobe light *n* Stroboskoplicht *nt*

strode [stroʊd] *pt of* **stride**

stroke [stroʊk] **I.** *vt* (*rub*) streicheln; **to ~ sth** über etw *akk* streichen; **to ~ sb's hair** jdm übers Haar streichen **II.** *n* ① (*rub*) Streicheln *nt kein pl* ② MED (*attack*) Schlaganfall *m;* **to**

S

suffer a ~ einen Schlaganfall bekommen ③ (*mark*) Strich *m* ④ (*hitting a ball*) Schlag *m* ⑤ (*swimming style*) **breast ~** Brustschwimmen *nt* ⑥ (*piece*) **by a ~ of fate** durch eine Fügung des Schicksals; **a ~ of luck** ein Glücksfall *m* ⑦ (*action*) [geschickter] Schachzug; **a ~ of genius** ein genialer Einfall ⑧ *of a clock* Schlag *m;* **at the ~ of midnight** um Punkt Mitternacht

stroll [stroʊl] **I.** *n* Spaziergang *m;* **to go for a ~** einen Spaziergang machen, spazieren gehen, Bummel *m;* (*around town*) Stadtbummel *m* **II.** *vi* (*amble*) schlendern, bummeln

stroller ['stroʊ·lər] *n* ① (*person*) Spaziergänger(in) *m(f)* ② (*carriage*) [Kinder]sportwagen *m*

strong [strɔŋ] **I.** *adj* ① (*powerful*) stark; *desire* brennend; *economy* gesund; *currency* hart, stark; *incentive, influence* groß; *reaction, wind* heftig; *resistance* erbittert; *rivalry* ausgeprägt; **~ language** (*vulgar*) derbe Ausdrucksweise; **~ lenses** starke [Brillen]gläser ② (*effective*) gut, stark; **tact is not her ~ point** Takt ist nicht gerade ihre Stärke ③ (*physically powerful*) kräftig, stark; (*healthy*) gesund, kräftig; **to be as ~ as an ox** bärenstark sein ④ (*robust*) stabil; (*tough*) *person* stark ⑤ (*deep-seated*) überzeugt; *conviction* fest; *objections* stark; *tendency* deutlich ⑥ (*bright*) hell, kräftig; *light* grell ⑦ (*pungent*) streng; *flavor* kräftig; *smell* beißend **II.** *adv* (*fam*) **to come on ~** (*sexually*) rangehen *fam;* (*aggressively*) in Fahrt kommen *fam;* **still going ~** noch gut in Form

'strong-arm I. *adj attr* (*pej*) brutal, gewaltsam, Gewalt- **II.** *vt* ■ **to ~ sb** jdn einschüchtern

'strongbox *n* [Geld]kassette *f*

'stronghold *n* ① (*bastion*) Stützpunkt *m,* Bollwerk *nt,* Festung *f;* (*fig*) Hochburg *f,* Zentrum *nt* ② (*sanctuary*) Zufluchtsort *m,* Refugium *nt*

strongly ['strɔŋ·li] *adv* ① (*powerfully*) stark; *advise* nachdrücklich; *criticize* heftig; *deny* energisch; *recommend* dringend ② (*durably*) robust, stabil ③ (*muscularly*) stark; **~ built** kräftig gebaut ④ (*pungently*) *smell* stark

strong-'minded *adj* willensstark, entschlossen

'strongroom *n* Stahlkammer *f,* Tresor[raum] *m*

strong-'willed *adj* willensstark, entschlossen

strontium ['strɔn·ʃi·əm] *n* Strontium *nt*

strove [stroʊv] *pt of* **strive**

struck [strʌk] *pt, pp of* **strike**

structural ['strʌk·tʃər·əl] *adj* ① (*organizational*) strukturell, Struktur- ② (*of a construction*) baulich, Bau-, Konstruktions-; **the houses suffered ~ damage** die Struktur der Häuser wurde beschädigt

structure ['strʌk·tʃər] **I.** *n* ① (*arrangement*) Struktur *f,* Aufbau *m* ② (*system*) Struktur *f* ③ (*construction*) Bau[werk] *nt;* (*makeup of a construction*) Konstruktion *f* **II.** *vt* strukturieren; (*construct*) konstruieren; *life* regeln

struggle ['strʌg·əl] **I.** *n* ① (*great effort*) Kampf *m* (**for** um +*akk*); **uphill ~** mühselige Aufgabe, harter Kampf ② (*fight*) Kampf *m* (**against** gegen, **with** mit +*dat*) **II.** *vi* ① (*toil*) sich abmühen [*o* quälen]; ■ **to ~ with sth** sich mit etw *dat* herumschlagen; **to ~ to one's feet** sich mühsam aufrappeln ② (*fight*) kämpfen, ringen; **to ~ for survival** ums Überleben kämpfen

strum [strʌm] MUS **I.** *vt* <-mm-> *stringed instrument* herumzupfen (auf +*dat*); *guitar* herumklimpern (auf +*dat*) **II.** *vi* <-mm-> [herum]klimpern **III.** *n usu sing* (*sound of strumming*) Klimpern *nt,* Geklimper *nt pej fam*

strung [strʌŋ] *pt, pp of* **string**

strut [strʌt] **I.** *vi* <-tt-> ■ **to ~ around** herumstolzieren; ■ **to ~ past** vorbeistolzieren **II.** *vt* <-tt-> **to ~ one's stuff** (*esp hum fam: dance*) zeigen, was man hat; (*showcase*) zeigen, was man kann **III.** *n* (*in a car, vehicle*) Strebe *f;* (*in a building, structure*) Verstrebung *f*

strychnine ['strɪk·naɪn] *n* Strychnin *nt*

stub [stʌb] **I.** *n of a ticket, check* [Kontroll]abschnitt *m,* Abriss *m; of a pencil* Stummel *m* **II.** *vt* <-bb-> **to ~ one's toes** sich die Zehen anstoßen

stubble ['stʌb·əl] *n* Stoppeln *pl*

stubbly ['stʌb·li] *adj* ① (*bristly*) stoppelig, Stoppel- ② (*of crops*) Stoppel-

stubborn ['stʌb·ərn] *adj* (*esp pej*) ① (*obstinate*) *of a person* stur *fam,* dickköpfig *fam,* starrköpfig, störrisch ② (*persistent*) *stain, refusal* hartnäckig; *problem* vertrackt

stubby ['stʌb·i] *adj* **~ fingers** Wurstfinger *pl fam;* **~ tail** Stummelschwanz *m*

stucco ['stʌk·oʊ] *n* Stuck *m*

stuck [stʌk] **I.** *pt, pp of* **stick II.** *adj* ① (*unmovable*) fest; **the door is ~** die Tür klemmt ② *pred* (*trapped*) **I hate being ~ behind a desk** ich hasse Schreibtischarbeit; ■ **to be ~ in sth** in etw *dat* feststecken; ■ **to be ~ with sb** jdn am Hals haben ③ *pred* (*at a loss*) ■ **to be ~** nicht klarkommen *fam;* **I'm really ~** ich komme einfach nicht weiter

stuck-'up *adj* (*pej fam*) hochnäsig *fam,* eingebildet, arrogant

stud[1] [stʌd] *n* ① (*jewelry*) Stecker *m* ② (*for a collar*) Kragenknopf *m;* (*for a shirt*) Hemdknopf *m;* (*for a cuff*) Manschettenknopf *m* ③ (*in a snow tire*) Spike *m*

stud[2] [stʌd] *n* ① (*horse*) Deckhengst *m,* Zuchthengst *m* ② (*breeding farm*) Gestüt *nt,* Stall *m* ③ (*sl: man*) geiler Typ

student ['stu·dənt] *n* ① (*at university*) Student(in) *m(f),* Studierende(r) *f(m);* (*pupil*) Schüler(in) *m(f);* **graduate ~** *Doktorand oder Student eines Magisterstudiengangs* ② (*unofficial learner*) **to be a ~ of sth** sich mit etw *dat* befassen

student 'teacher *n* Referendar(in) *m(f)*

student 'union *n* Studentenvereinigung *f*

'stud farm *n* Gestüt *nt*

studied ['stʌd·id] *adj* wohl überlegt, [gut] durchdacht

studio ['stu·di·oʊ] *n* ❶ (*artist's room*) Atelier *nt* ❷ (*for filmmaking, photography, etc.*) Studio *nt* ❸ (*film company*) Filmgesellschaft *f* ❹ (*studio apartment*) Appartement *nt*

studio a'partment *n* Appartement *nt*

studio 'audience *n* Studiopublikum *nt*

studious ['stu·di·əs] *adj* ❶ (*bookish*) *person* lernbegierig, lerneifrig; *environment* gelehrt ❷ (*earnest*) ernsthaft; (*intentional*) bewusst

study ['stʌd·i] **I.** *vt* <-ie-> ❶ (*scrutinize*) studieren, sich befassen (mit +*dat*); (*look at*) eingehend betrachten; ■**to ~ how/whether ...** erforschen [*o* untersuchen], wie/ob ... ❷ (*learn*) studieren; (*at school*) lernen; **to ~ for an exam** auf eine Prüfung lernen **II.** *vi* <-ie-> lernen; (*at university*) studieren **III.** *n* ❶ (*investigation*) Untersuchung *f;* (*academic investigation*) Studie *f,* wissenschaftliche Untersuchung ❷ (*studying*) Lernen *nt;* (*at university*) Studieren *nt* ❸ (*room*) Arbeitszimmer *nt* ❹ (*pilot drawing*) Studie *f,* Entwurf *m*

'study group *n* Arbeitsgruppe *f*

study guide *n* Paukbuch *nt*

'study trip *n* Studienreise *f*

stuff [stʌf] **I.** *n* ❶ (*fam: indeterminate matter*) Zeug *nt oft pej fam;* **we've heard all this ~ before** das haben wir doch alles schon mal gehört!; **to know one's ~** sich auskennen ❷ (*possessions*) Sachen *pl,* Zeug *nt oft pej fam* ❸ (*material*) Material *nt,* Stoff *m* **II.** *vt* ❶ (*push inside*) stopfen; (*fill, a. in taxidermy*) ausstopfen; (*in cookery*) füllen ❷ (*fam: gorge*) ■**to ~ oneself** sich vollstopfen; ■**to ~ down** ↔ **sth** etw in sich *akk* hineinstopfen

stuffed animal *n* Kuscheltier *nt,* Plüschtier *nt*

stuffing ['stʌf·ɪŋ] *n* Füllung *f*

stuffy ['stʌf·i] *adj* (*pej*) ❶ (*prim*) spießig ❷ (*airless*) stickig, muffig

stultifying ['stʌl·tɪ·faɪ·ɪŋ] *adj* (*pej form*) lähmend

stumble ['stʌm·bəl] *vi* ❶ (*trip*) stolpern, straucheln; ■**to ~ on sth** über etw *akk* stolpern ❷ (*fig: while speaking*) stocken; ■**to ~ over sth** über etw *akk* stolpern ❸ (*stagger*) ■**to ~ around** herumtappen ❹ (*find*) ■**to ~ across sb/sth** [zufällig] auf jdn/etw stoßen

'stumbling block *n* Stolperstein *m,* Hemmschuh *m,* Hindernis *nt*

stump [stʌmp] **I.** *n* ❶ (*part left*) *of a tree* Stumpf *m; of an arm* Armstumpf *m; of a leg* Beinstumpf *m; of a tooth* Zahnstummel *m* ❷ POL **out on the ~** im Wahlkampf **II.** *vt* (*usu fam: baffle*) verwirren, durcheinanderbringen; **we're all completely ~ed** wir sind mit unserem Latein am Ende **III.** *vi* (*stamp*) **she ~ed out of the room** sie stapfte aus dem Raum

stumpy ['stʌm·pi] *adj* (*usu pej fam*) [klein und] gedrungen, stämmig; *fingers* dick

stun <-nn-> [stʌn] *vt* ❶ (*shock*) betäuben, lähmen; (*amaze*) verblüffen, überwältigen; **~ned silence** fassungsloses Schweigen ❷ (*make unconscious*) betäuben

stung [stʌŋ] *pp, pt of* **sting**

stunk [stʌŋk] *pt, pp of* **stink**

stunned [stʌnd] *adj* fassungslos, sprachlos

stunner ['stʌn·ər] *n* ❶ (*fam: woman*) tolle Frau; (*thing, event*) tolle Sache ❷ (*surprise*) [Riesen]überraschung *f*

stunning ['stʌn·ɪŋ] *adj* ❶ (*approv: gorgeous*) toll *fam,* fantastisch, umwerfend ❷ (*amazing*) unfassbar ❸ (*hard*) *blow* betäubend

stunt¹ [stʌnt] *vt* (*check growth*) hemmen, beeinträchtigen

stunt² [stʌnt] *n* ❶ FILM Stunt *m* ❷ (*for publicity*) Gag *m,* Trick *m pej;* **to pull a ~** (*fig fam*) etwas Verrücktes tun

stunted ['stʌn·t̬ɪd] *adj* (*deteriorated*) verkümmert; (*limited in development*) unterentwickelt

'stuntman *n* Stuntman *m*

stupefaction [ˌstu·pə·'fæk·ʃən] *n* ❶ (*befuddled state*) Benommenheit *f* ❷ (*astonishment*) Verblüffung *f;* (*involving intense shock*) Bestürzung *f*

stupefy <-ie-> ['stu·pə·faɪ] *vt usu passive* ■**to be stupefied by sth** ❶ (*render numb*) von etw *dat* benommen sein ❷ (*astonish*) über etw *akk* verblüfft sein; (*shocked*) über etw *akk* bestürzt sein

stupendous [stu·'pen·dəs] *adj* (*immense*) gewaltig, enorm; (*amazing*) erstaunlich; *news* toll *fam*

stupid ['stu·pɪd] **I.** *adj* <-er, -est *or* more ~, most ~> ❶ (*slow-witted*) dumm, blöd *fam,* einfältig ❷ (*silly*) blöd *fam;* **here's your ~ book back!** behalte doch dein blödes Buch! *fam;* **to drink oneself ~** sich bis zur Bewusstlosigkeit betrinken **II.** *n* (*fam*) Blödmann *m,* Dummkopf *m*

stupidity [stu·'pɪd·ɪ·t̬i] *n* Dummheit *f,* Blödheit *f fam,* Einfältigkeit *f*

stupor ['stu·pər] *n usu sing* Benommenheit *f;* **in a drunken ~** im Vollrausch

sturdy ['stɜr·di] *adj* ❶ (*robust*) *box, chair, wall* stabil; *material* robust; *shoes* fest ❷ (*physically*) *arms, legs* kräftig; *body, person, legs a.* stämmig

sturgeon ['stɜr·dʒən] *n* Stör *m*

stutter ['stʌt̬·ər] **I.** *vi, vt* stottern **II.** *n* Stottern *nt kein pl;* **to have a bad ~** stark stottern

stutterer ['stʌt̬·ər·ər] *n* Stotterer, Stotterin *m, f*

sty¹ [staɪ] *n* (*pigpen*) Schweinestall *m*

sty² <*pl* sties *or* -s> [staɪ] *n* MED Gerstenkorn *nt*

stye <*pl* sties *or* -s> [staɪ] *n* MED *see* **sty²**

style [staɪl] **I.** *n* ❶ (*distinctive manner*) Stil *m,* Art *f;* **in the ~ of sb/sth** im Stil einer Person/einer S. *gen;* **that's not my ~** (*fig fam*) das ist nicht mein Stil *fig* ❷ (*approv: stylishness*) Stil *m,* Schick *m;* **to have real ~** Klasse haben; **to do things in ~** alles im großen Stil tun ❸ (*fashion*) Stil *m;* **the latest ~** die neueste Mode **II.** *vt* (*shape*) gestalten; *hair* frisieren; (*arrange*) *plan, design* entwerfen

'style sheet *n* COMPUT Stylesheet *nt*

styling ['staɪ·lɪŋ] *n* Styling *nt,* Design *nt; of*

S

hair Frisur *f*

stylish ['staɪ·lɪʃ] *adj* (*approv*) ❶ (*chic*) elegant; (*smart*) flott *fam;* (*fashionable*) modisch, stylisch, stylish ❷ (*polished*) stilvoll, mit Stil *nach n*

stylishly ['staɪ·lɪʃ·li] *adv* (*approv: chic*) elegant; (*smartly*) flott *fam;* (*fashionably*) modisch, stylisch, stylish

stylist ['staɪ·lɪst] *n* ❶ (*arranger of hair*) Friseur(in) *m(f),* Friseuse *f;* (*designer*) Designer(in) *m(f)* ❷ (*writer*) Stilist(in) *m(f)*

stylistic [staɪ·'lɪs·tɪk] *adj* stilistisch, Stil-

stylize ['staɪ·laɪz] *vt* stilisieren

stylus <*pl* -es> ['staɪ·ləs] *n* ❶ (*phonograph needle*) Abspielnadel *f* ❷ (*pen-like device*) [Licht]stift *m*

stymie <-y-> ['staɪ·mi] *vt person* mattsetzen *fig;* ■ **to be ~d by sth** durch etw *akk* behindert werden [*o* nicht vorankommen]

suave [swav] *adj* (*urbane*) weltmännisch; (*polite*) verbindlich

sub [sʌb] **I.** *n* ❶ (*fam*) *short for* **substitute** Vertretung *f* ❷ (*fam*) *short for* **submarine** U-Boot *nt* ❸ (*fam*) *short for* **submarine sandwich** Jumbo-Sandwich *nt* **II.** *vi* <-bb-> *short for* **substitute:** ■ **to ~ for sb** für jdn einspringen, jdn vertreten

subatomic [ˌsʌb·ə·'tam·ɪk] *adj* PHYS subatomar

subcommittee [ˌsʌb·kə·'mɪṭ·i] *n* Unterausschuss *m*

subconscious [ˌsʌb·'kan·ʃəs] **I.** *n* Unterbewusstsein *nt,* Unterbewusste(s) *nt* **II.** *adj attr* unterbewusst

subcontinent ['sʌb·ˌkan·tə·nənt] *n* GEOG Subkontinent *m*

subcontract **I.** *vt* [ˌsʌb·'kan·trækt] untervergeben (**to** an +*akk*); ■ **to ~ sth out to sb/sth** etw an jdn/etw als Untervertrag hinausgeben **II.** *n* ['sʌbˌkan·trækt] Subkontrakt *m,* Untervertrag *m*

subcontractor [ˌsʌb·'kən·træk·tər] *n* Subunternehmer(in) *m(f)*

subculture ['sʌb·ˌkʌl·tʃər] *n* Subkultur *f*

subcutaneous [ˌsʌb·kju·'teɪ·ni·əs] *adj* MED subkutan

subdivide [ˌsʌb·dɪ·'vaɪd] *vt* unterteilen (**into** in +*akk*)

subdivision [ˌsʌb·dɪ·'vɪʒ·ən] *n* ❶ (*secondary division*) erneute Teilung; (*in aspects of a whole*) Aufgliederung *f,* Unterteilung *f* ❷ (*neighborhood*) Wohngebiet *nt,* Wohnsiedlung *f*

subdue [səb·'du] *vt* (*get under control*) unter Kontrolle bringen; (*bring into subjection*) unterwerfen; (*suppress*) unterdrücken; *animal, emotion* bändigen

subdued [sʌb·'dud] *adj* (*controlled*) beherrscht; (*reticent*) zurückhaltend; (*toned down*) *noise, voice, lighting* gedämpft; (*quiet*) leise, ruhig; *mood* gedrückt

subgroup ['sʌb·grup] *n* Untergruppe *f,* Unterabteilung *f*

subhead ['sʌb·hed], **subheading** ['sʌb·ˌhed·ɪŋ] *n* Untertitel *m*

subject **I.** *n* ['sʌb·dʒɪkt] ❶ (*theme, topic*) Thema *nt;* **while we're on the ~** wo wir gerade beim Thema sind; **off the ~** nicht zum Thema gehörend ❷ (*person*) Versuchsperson *f,* Testperson *f* ❸ (*field*) Fach *nt;* (*at school*) [Schul]fach *nt;* (*specific research area*) Spezialgebiet *nt* ❹ LING Subjekt *nt,* Satzgegenstand *m* **II.** *adj* ['sʌb·dʒɪkt] ❶ *attr* POL (*dominated*) *people* unterworfen ❷ *pred* (*exposed to*) ■ **to be ~ to sth** etw *dat* ausgesetzt sein; **to be ~ to a high rate of tax** einer hohen Steuer unterliegen ❸ (*contingent on*) ■ **to be ~ to sth** von etw *dat* abhängig sein; **~ to payment** vorbehaltlich einer Zahlung **III.** *vt* [səb·'dʒekt] *usu passive* (*cause to undergo*) ■ **to ~ sb/sth to sth** jdn/etw etw *dat* aussetzen; **to ~ sb to torture** jdn foltern

'subject index *n* Sachregister *nt*

subjection [səb·'dʒek·ʃən] *n* POL Unterwerfung *f*

subjective [səb·'dʒek·tɪv] *adj* subjektiv

'subject matter *n* Thema *nt; of a meeting* Gegenstand *m; of a book* Inhalt *m; of a film* Stoff *m*

sub judice [ˌsʌb·'dʒu·də·si] *adj pred* LAW rechtshängig

subjugate ['sʌb·dʒə·geɪt] *vt* (*make subservient*) unterwerfen, unterjochen

subjugation [ˌsʌb·dʒə·'geɪ·ʃən] *n* Unterwerfung *f,* Unterjochung *f*

subjunctive [səb·'dʒʌŋk·tɪv] **I.** *n* LING Konjunktiv *m* **II.** *adj* LING konjunktivisch, Konjunktiv-

sublease **I.** *vt* ['sʌb·lis] (*sublet*) untervermieten; (*give leasehold*) unterverpachten **II.** *n* [sʌb·'lis] (*sublet*) Untermiete *f;* (*give leasehold*) Unterverpachtung *f*

sublet [sʌb·'let] **I.** *vt* <-tt-, sublet, sublet> untervermieten **II.** *n* untervermietetes Objekt

sublimate ['sʌb·lɪ·meɪt] *vt* PSYCH sublimieren

sublime [sə·'blaɪm] *adj* ❶ (*imposing, majestic*) erhaben ❷ (*usu iron: very great*) komplett *fam,* vollendet *iron*

subliminal [ˌsʌb·'lɪm·ə·nəl] *adj* (*covert*) unterschwellig; (*subconscious*) unterbewusst

submachine gun [ˌsʌb·mə·'ʃin·ˌgʌn] *n* Maschinenpistole *f*

submarine ['sʌb·mə·rin] **I.** *n* ❶ (*boat*) U-Boot *nt,* Unterseeboot *nt* ❷ (*sandwich*) Jumbo-Sandwich *nt* **II.** *adj* Unterwasser-, unterseeisch

submenu [ˌsʌb·'men·ju] *n* COMPUT Untermenü *nt*

submerge [səb·'mɜrdʒ] **I.** *vt* ❶ (*place under water*) tauchen (**in** in +*akk*) ❷ (*inundate*) überschwemmen, überfluten **II.** *vi* abtauchen, untertauchen

submersion [səb·'mɜr·ʒən] *n* Eintauchen *nt,* [Unter]tauchen *nt*

submission [səb·'mɪʃ·ən] *n* ❶ (*compliance*) Unterwerfung *f;* (*to orders, wishes etc.*) Gehorsam *m* ❷ (*handing in*) Einreichung *f,* Abga-

be *f* ❸ (*sth submitted*) Vorlage *f,* Eingabe *f*
submissive [səb·ˈmɪs·ɪv] *adj* (*subservient*) unterwürfig *pej;* (*humble*) demütig; (*obedient*) gehorsam
submit <-tt-> [səb·ˈmɪt] **I.** *vt* ❶ (*yield*) ■ **to ~ oneself to sb/sth** sich jdm/etw unterwerfen ❷ (*agree to undergo*) **to ~ oneself to treatment** sich einer Behandlung unterziehen ❸ (*hand in*) einreichen; ■ **to ~ sth to sb** jdm etw vorlegen **II.** *vi* (*give up*) aufgeben; (*yield*) nachgeben; (*yield unconditionally*) sich unterwerfen
subnormal [sʌb·ˈnɔr·məl] *adj* ❶ (*mentally*) minderbegabt ❷ (*below average*) unterdurchschnittlich
subordinate **I.** *n* [sə·ˈbɔr·dən·ɪt] Untergebene(r) *f(m)* **II.** *vt* [sə·ˈbɔr·dən·eɪt] unterordnen; ■ **to be ~d to sb/sth** jdm/etw untergeordnet sein **III.** *adj* [sə·ˈbɔr·dən·ɪt] ❶ (*secondary*) zweitrangig, nebensächlich ❷ (*lower in rank*) untergeordnet, rangniedriger
subordinate ˈclause *n* Nebensatz *m*
subordination [sə·ˌbɔr·dən·ˈeɪ·ʃən] *n* ❶ (*inferior status*) Unterordnung *f* (**to** unter +*akk*) ❷ (*submission*) Zurückstellung *f*
subplot [ˈsʌb·plat] *n* Nebenhandlung *f*
subpoena [sə·ˈpi·nə] LAW **I.** *vt* <-ed, -ed *or* -'d, -'d> vorladen **II.** *n* Ladung *f;* **to serve a ~ on sb** jdn vorladen
subscribe [səb·ˈskraɪb] **I.** *vi* ❶ (*pay regularly for*) ■ **to ~ to sth** *newspaper, magazine* etw abonnieren ❷ (*form: agree*) ■ **to ~ to sth** etw *dat* beipflichten; **I do not ~ to that opinion** diese Meinung kann ich nicht unterstützen ❸ (*donate*) spenden ❹ STOCKEX (*offer to purchase*) **to ~ to shares** Aktien zeichnen **II.** *vt* (*donate*) spenden
subscriber [səb·ˈskraɪ·bər] *n* ❶ (*regular payer*) *newspaper, magazine* Abonnent(in) *m(f); service* Kunde, Kundin *m, f* ❷ (*form: signatory*) Unterzeichnete(r) *f(m),* Unterzeichner(in) *m(f)* ❸ STOCKEX *of shares* Zeichner(in) *m(f)*
subscript [ˈsʌb·skrɪpt] *adj* TYPO tiefgestellt
subscription [səb·ˈskrɪp·ʃən] *n* ❶ (*to a newspaper, magazine*) Abonnementgebühr *f* ❷ (*agreement to receive*) Abonnement *nt;* **to take out a ~ to sth** etw abonnieren
subsection [ˈsʌb·ˌsek·ʃən] *n* Unterabschnitt *m; of legal text* Paragraph *m*
subsequent [ˈsʌb·sɪ·kwənt] *adj* (*resulting*) [nach]folgend, anschließend; (*later*) später; **~ treatment** Nachbehandlung *f*
subsequently [ˈsʌb·sɪ·kwənt·li] *adv* (*later*) später, anschließend
subservient [səb·ˈsɜr·vi·ənt] *adj* ❶ (*pej: servile*) unterwürfig ❷ (*serving as means*) ■ **to be ~ to sth** etw *dat* dienen
subset [ˈsʌb·set] *n* (*subclassification*) Untermenge *f;* MATH (*special type of set*) Teilmenge *f*
subside [səb·ˈsaɪd] *vi* ❶ (*abate*) nachlassen; *anger, excitement* sich legen ❷ (*into sth soft or liquid*) absinken, einsinken
subsidence [səb·ˈsaɪ·dəns] *n* Senkung *f,* Absenken *nt*
subsidiary [səb·ˈsɪd·i·er·i] **I.** *adj* untergeordnet; **~ company** ECON Tochtergesellschaft *f* **II.** *n* ECON Tochtergesellschaft *f*
subsidize [ˈsʌb·sə·daɪz] *vt* subventionieren
subsidy [ˈsʌb·sə·di] *n* Subvention *f* (**to** für +*akk*); **to receive a ~** subventioniert werden
subsist [səb·ˈsɪst] *vi* ❶ (*exist*) existieren ❷ (*make a living*) leben; ■ **to ~ on sth** von etw *dat* leben
subsistence [səb·ˈsɪs·təns] **I.** *n* ❶ (*minimum for existence*) [Lebens]unterhalt *m* ❷ (*livelihood*) **means of ~** Lebensgrundlage *f* **II.** *adj attr* Existenz-; **~ farming** Subsistenzwirtschaft *f fachspr;* **~ level** Existenzminimum *nt;* **~ wage** Mindestlohn *m*
substance [ˈsʌb·stəns] *n* ❶ (*material element*) Substanz *f,* Stoff *m;* (*material*) Materie *f kein pl;* **chemical ~** Chemikalie *f* ❷ (*significance*) Substanz *f;* (*decisive significance*) Gewicht *nt;* **the book lacks ~** das Buch hat inhaltlich wenig zu bieten ❸ (*main point*) Wesentliche(s) *nt,* Essenz *f* ❹ (*wealth*) Vermögen *nt*
substandard [ˌsʌb·ˈstæn·dərd] *adj* unterdurchschnittlich, minderwertig
substantial [səb·ˈstæn·ʃəl] *adj attr* ❶ (*significant*) *fortune* bedeutend; *contribution* wesentlich; *difference, amount* erheblich; *improvement* deutlich; **~ evidence** hinreichender Beweis ❷ (*weighty*) überzeugend, stichhaltig ❸ (*of solid material or structure*) solide; (*physically a.*) kräftig, stark
substantially [səb·ˈstæn·ʃə·li] *adv* ❶ (*significantly*) beträchtlich, erheblich ❷ (*mainly*) im Wesentlichen
substantiate [səb·ˈstæn·ʃi·eɪt] *vt* bekräftigen, untermauern; *report* bestätigen; *claim* begründen
substantive [ˈsʌb·stən·tɪv] *adj* beträchtlich, wesentlich
substation [ˈsʌb·ˌsteɪ·ʃən] *n* Nebenstelle *f;* **police ~** Polizeidienststelle *f*
substitute [ˈsʌb·stə·tut] **I.** *vt* ersetzen, austauschen; SPORTS *players* auswechseln (**for** gegen +*akk*) **II.** *vi* (*take over for*) einspringen (**for** für +*akk*); (*serve as deputy*) als Stellvertreter fungieren (**for** für +*akk*) **III.** *n* ❶ (*replacement*) Ersatz *m;* **there's no ~ for sb/sth** es geht nichts über jdn/etw ❷ (*replacement player*) Ersatzspieler(in) *m(f),* Auswechselspieler(in) *m(f)*
substitute ˈteacher *n* Vertretungslehrer(in) *m(f),* Aushilfslehrer(in) *m(f)*
substitution [ˌsʌb·stə·ˈtu·ʃən] *n* ❶ (*replacement*) Ersetzung *f* ❷ SPORTS (*action of replacing*) Austausch *m,* [Spieler]wechsel *m*
substratum [ˈsʌb·ˌstreɪ·t̬əm] *n* ❶ GEOL (*deep[er] layer*) Unterschicht *f* ❷ (*fig: common basis*) Grundlage *f,* Basis *f*
subsume [səb·ˈsum] *vt usu passive* (*form*) einordnen (**into** in +*akk*); (*several*) zusammenfas-

S

sen (**into** zu +*dat*)
subtenant ['sʌb·ˌten·ənt] *n* Untermieter(in) *m(f)*
subterfuge ['sʌb·tər·fjudʒ] *n* List *f*, Trick *m*
subterranean [ˌsʌb·tə·'reɪ·ni·ən] *adj* ① GEOL (*below ground*) unterirdisch ② (*fig: subcultural, alternative*) Untergrund-
subtext ['sʌb·tekst] *n* Botschaft *f*
subtitle ['sʌb·ˌtaɪ·t̬əl] **I.** *vt* (*add captions*) *movie* untertiteln **II.** *n* ① (*secondary title on book*) Untertitel *m* ② (*caption*) ■ **~s** *pl* Untertitel *pl*
subtle <-er, -est *or* more ~, most ~> ['sʌt̬·əl] *adj* ① (*approv: understated*) fein[sinnig], subtil ② (*approv: delicate*) *flavor, nuance* fein; **~ tact** ausgeprägtes Taktgefühl; (*elusive*) subtil; *charm* unaufdringlich ③ (*approv: astute*) scharfsinnig, raffiniert; *strategy* geschickt
subtlety ['sʌt̬·əl·ti] *n* (*approv*) ① (*discernment*) Scharfsinnigkeit *f*, Raffiniertheit *f* ② (*delicate but significant*) Feinheit *f*, Subtilität *f*
subtotal ['sʌb·ˌtoʊ·t̬əl] *n* Zwischensumme *f*
subtract [səb·'trækt] *vt* ■ **to ~ sth [from sth]** etw [von etw *dat*] abziehen; **four ~ed from ten equals six** zehn minus vier ergibt sechs
subtraction [səb·'træk·ʃən] *n* Subtraktion *f*
subtropical [ˌsʌb·'trap·ɪ·kəl] *adj* subtropisch
suburb ['sʌb·ɜrb] *n* (*outlying area*) Vorstadt *f*, Vorort *m*; ■ **the ~s** *pl* der Stadtrand, die Randbezirke *pl*
suburban [sə·'bɜr·bən] *adj* ① (*of the suburbs*) Vorstadt-, vorstädtisch; **they live in ~ Washington, D.C.** sie wohnen in einem Vorort von Washington D.C. ② (*pej: provincial*) spießig *fam*, kleinbürgerlich
suburbia [sə·'bɜr·bi·ə] *n* (*esp pej*) ① (*areas*) Vororte *pl*, Randbezirke *pl* ② (*people*) Vorstadtbewohner *pl*
subversion [səb·'vɜr·ʒən] *n* ① (*undermining*) Subversion *f geh*, Unterwanderung *f* ② MIL (*successful coup*) [Um]sturz *m*
subversive [səb·'vɜr·sɪv] **I.** *adj* subversiv *geh*, umstürzlerisch, staatsgefährdend **II.** *n* Umstürzler(in) *m(f)*, subversives Element *pej*
subvert [sʌb·'vɜrt] *vt* ① (*overthrow*) stürzen ② (*undermine principle*) untergraben ③ (*destroy*) zunichtemachen
subway ['sʌb·weɪ] *n* RAIL U-Bahn *f*; (*in Paris*) Metro *f*; ■ **by ~** mit der U-Bahn; **~ station** U-Bahn-Station *f*
subzero [sʌb·'zɪ·roʊ] *adj* unter null [Grad] *nach n*; **~ temperatures** Minusgrade *pl*
succeed [sək·'sid] **I.** *vi* ① (*achieve purpose*) Erfolg haben (**in** mit +*dat*); *plan* gelingen, erfolgreich sein; **she ~ed in doing it** es gelang ihr, es zu tun ② (*follow*) nachfolgen, die Nachfolge antreten; **to ~ to the throne** die Thronfolge antreten **II.** *vt* **to ~ sb in office** jds Amt übernehmen
succeeding [sək·'si·dɪŋ] *adj attr* ① (*next in line*) [nach]folgend ② (*subsequent*) aufeinanderfolgend; **in the ~ weeks** in den darauf folgenden Wochen
success <*pl* -es> [sək·'ses] *n* ① (*attaining of goals*) Erfolg *m*; **to be a big ~ with sb** bei jdm einschlagen *fam*; **to achieve ~** erfolgreich sein ② (*successful person or thing*) Erfolg *m*; **box-office ~** Kassenschlager *m fam*
successful [sək·'ses·fəl] *adj* ① (*having success*) erfolgreich ② (*lucrative, profitable*) erfolgreich, lukrativ ③ (*effective*) gelungen, geglückt
succession [sək·'seʃ·ən] *n* ① (*sequence*) Folge *f*, Reihe *f*; *of events, things a.* Serie *f*; ■ **in [close] ~** [dicht] hintereinander ② (*line of inheritance*) Nachfolge *f*, Erbfolge *f*; **~ to the throne** Thronfolge *f*
successive [sək·'ses·ɪv] *adj attr* aufeinanderfolgend; **six ~ weeks** sechs Wochen hintereinander
successor [sək·'ses·ər] *n* Nachfolger(in) *m(f)*; **~ in office** Amtsnachfolger(in) *m(f)*
succinct [sək·'sɪŋkt] *adj* (*approv*) knapp, kurz [und bündig]
succor ['sʌk·ər] *n* Beistand *m*, Unterstützung *f*, Hilfe *f*
succulent ['sʌk·jʊ·lənt] **I.** *adj* (*approv*) saftig **II.** *n* BOT Sukkulente *f fachspr*
succumb [sə·'kʌm] *vi* ① (*surrender*) sich beugen; MIL kapitulieren; (*be defeated*) unterliegen; (*yield to pressure*) ■ **to ~ to sb/sth** jdm/etw nachgeben, sich jdm/etw beugen ② (*die from*) ■ **to ~ to sth** an etw *dat* sterben; **to ~ to one's injuries** seinen Verletzungen erliegen
such [sʌtʃ] **I.** *adj* ① *attr* (*of that kind*) solche(r, s); **I had never met ~ a person before** so ein Mensch war mir noch nie begegnet; **~ a thing** so etwas [*o fam* was]; **there's no ~ thing as ghosts** so etwas wie Geister gibt es nicht ② (*so great*) solche(r, s), derartig; **he's ~ an idiot!** er ist so ein Idiot!; **why are you in ~ a hurry?** warum bist du derart in Eile? **II.** *pron* ① (*of that type*) solche(r, s); **~ is life** so ist das Leben; **~ as** wie ② (*suchlike*) dergleichen ③ (*strictly speaking*) ■ **as ~** an [und für] sich, eigentlich **III.** *adv* so; **she's ~ an arrogant person** sie ist dermaßen arrogant; **I've never had ~ good coffee** ich habe noch nie [einen] so guten Kaffee getrunken; **~ ... that ...** so ..., dass ...
'such and such *adj attr* (*fam*) der und der/die und die/das und das; **to arrive at ~ a time** um die und die Zeit ankommen
suchlike ['sʌtʃ·laɪk] *pron* dergleichen; **in the shop they sell chocolates and ~** in dem Laden gibt es Schokolade und dergleichen
suck [sʌk] **I.** *n* (*drawing in*) Saugen *nt*; (*keeping in the mouth*) Lutschen *nt* **II.** *vt* ① (*draw into mouth*) ■ **to ~ sth** an etw *dat* saugen ② *sweets* lutschen ③ (*exert strong pull*) ■ **to ~ sb/sth under** jdn/etw in die Tiefe ziehen; ■ **to be ~ed into sth** in etw *akk* hineingezogen werden **III.** *vi* ① (*draw into mouth*) saugen (**on** an +*dat*), nuckeln *fam*; *on candy* lutschen ② (*sl: be disagreeable*) ätzend sein; **man, this job ~s!** Mann, dieser Job ist

echt Scheiße!

◆**suck up** I. *vt* ■**to ~ up** ⊂ **sth** ❶ (*consume*) etw aufsaugen ❷ (*absorb*) *liquid, moisture* aufsaugen; *gases* ansaugen II. *vi* (*pej fam*) ■**to ~ up to sb** sich bei jdm einschmeicheln

sucker ['sʌk·ər] I. *n* ❶ (*pej fam: gullible person*) Einfaltspinsel *m,* Simpel *m* DIAL ❷ (*fam: sb finding sth irresistible*) Fan *m* (**for** von +*dat*); **to be a ~ for sth** nach etw *dat* verrückt sein ❸ (*fam: lollipop*) Lutscher *m* ❹ BOT (*part of plant*) Wurzelspross *m* II. *vt* (*trick*) ■**to ~ sb into sth** jdn zu etw *dat* verleiten

suckle ['sʌk·əl] I. *vt* säugen II. *vi* trinken, saugen

suckling pig ['sʌk·lɪŋ-] *n* Frischling *m;* (*for roasting*) Spanferkel *nt*

sucrose ['su·kroʊs] *n* Rohr- und Rübenzucker *m*

suction ['sʌk·ʃən] *n* ❶ (*act of removal by sucking*) [Ab]saugen *nt;* (*initiating act of sucking*) Ansaugen *nt* ❷ (*force*) Saugwirkung *f,* Sog *m*

suction cup *n* Saugfuß *m*

'**suction pump** *n* Saugpumpe *f*

Sudan [su·'dæn] *n* Sudan *m*

Sudanese [ˌsu·də·'niz] I. *n* Sudanese, Sudanesin *m, f* II. *adj* sudanesisch, sudanisch

sudden ['sʌd·ən] *adj* plötzlich, jäh; *departure* überhastet; *movement* abrupt; **it was so ~** es kam so überraschend; **~ drop in temperature** unerwarteter Temperatureinbruch; **to get a ~ scare** plötzlich Angst bekommen; **all of a ~** (*fam*) [ganz] plötzlich, urplötzlich

sudden infant death syndrome *n* plötzlicher Kindstod

suddenly ['sʌd·ən·li] *adv* plötzlich, auf einmal

suds [sʌdz] *npl* ❶ (*soapy mixture*) Seifenwasser *nt kein pl* ❷ (*mostly foam*) Schaum *m kein pl* ❸ (*sl: beer*) Bier *nt*

sue [su] I. *vt* verklagen; **to ~ sb for damages/libel** jdn auf Schadenersatz/wegen Beleidigung verklagen; **to ~ sb for divorce** gegen jdn die Scheidung einreichen II. *vi* (*take legal action*) klagen, prozessieren; ■**to ~ for sth** etw einklagen

suede [sweɪd] *n* Wildleder *nt,* Veloursleder *nt*

suet ['su·ɪt] *n* Talg *m,* Nierenfett *nt*

suffer ['sʌf·ər] I. *vi* ❶ (*experience trauma, illness*) leiden (**from** an +*dat*) ❷ (*deteriorate*) leiden, Schaden erleiden; **his work ~s from it** seine Arbeit leidet darunter ❸ (*experience sth negative*) ■**to ~ from sth** unter etw *dat* zu leiden haben; **the economy ~ed from the strikes** die Streiks machten der Wirtschaft zu schaffen II. *vt* ❶ (*experience sth negative*) erleiden; **to ~ neglect** vernachlässigt werden ❷ (*put up with*) ertragen; **to not ~ fools gladly** mit dummen Leuten keine Geduld haben

sufferer ['sʌf·ər·ər] *n* (*with a chronic condition*) Leidende(r) *f(m);* (*with an acute condition*) Erkrankte(r) *f(m);* **AIDS ~** AIDS-Kranke(r) *f(m);* **asthma ~** Asthmatiker(in) *m(f)*

suffering ['sʌf·ər·ɪŋ] *n* ❶ (*pain*) Leiden *nt* ❷ (*distress*) Leid *nt*

suffice [sə·'faɪs] *vi* genügen, [aus]reichen; **~ [it] to say that ...** es genügt [*o* reicht] wohl, wenn ich sage, dass ...

sufficiency [sə·'fɪʃ·ən·si] *n* ❶ (*adequacy*) Hinlänglichkeit *f,* Zulänglichkeit *f* ❷ (*sufficient quantity*) ausreichende Menge

sufficient [sə·'fɪʃ·ənt] *adj* genug, ausreichend; ■**to be ~ for sth/sb** für etw/jdn ausreichen [*o* genügen]; **they didn't have ~ evidence** sie hatten nicht genügend Beweismaterial

suffix ['sʌf·ɪks] I. *n* LING Suffix *nt fachspr,* Nachsilbe *f* II. *vt* anfügen, anhängen

suffocate ['sʌf·ə·keɪt] I. *vi* ersticken *a. fig* II. *vt* ❶ (*asphyxiate*) ersticken ❷ (*fig: suppress*) ersticken, erdrücken

suffocating ['sʌf·ə·keɪ·t̬ɪŋ] *adj* ❶ *usu attr* (*life-threatening*) erstickend ❷ (*fig: uncomfortable*) erstickend, zum Ersticken *präd; air* stickig; *atmosphere* erdrückend ❸ (*fig: stultifying*) erdrückend; *regulations, traditions* lähmend

suffrage ['sʌf·rɪdʒ] *n* (*right to vote*) Wahlrecht *nt,* Stimmrecht *nt*

sugar ['ʃʊg·ər] I. *n* ❶ (*sweetener*) Zucker *m* ❷ (*sl: term of affection*) Schätzchen *nt fam* ❸ CHEM Kohle[n]hydrat *nt* II. *vt* ❶ (*sweeten*) zuckern; *coffee, tea* süßen ❷ (*fig: make agreeable*) versüßen

'**sugar beet** *n* Zuckerrübe *f*

'**sugar bowl** *n* Zuckerdose *f*

'**sugar cane** *n* Zuckerrohr *nt*

'**sugarcoated** *adj* ❶ FOOD mit Zucker überzogen ❷ (*fig, pej: acceptable*) viel versprechend, verheißungsvoll; *offer, promises* verführerisch

'**sugar cube** *n* Stück *nt* Zucker, Zuckerwürfel *m*

'**sugar daddy** *n wohlhabender älterer Mann, der ein junges Mädchen aushält*

sugary ['ʃʊg·ə·ri] *adj* ❶ (*sweet*) zuckerhaltig ❷ (*sugar-like*) zuckerig ❸ (*fig, pej: insincere*) zuckersüß; *smile* süßlich

suggest [səg·'dʒest] *vt* ❶ (*propose*) ■**to ~ sth [to sb]** [jdm] etw vorschlagen; **what do you ~ we do with them?** was, meinst du, sollen wir mit ihnen machen? ❷ (*indicate*) hinweisen (auf +*akk*); **the footprints ~ that ...** die Fußspuren lassen darauf schließen, dass ... ❸ (*indirectly state*) ■**to ~ sth** etw andeuten [*o pej* unterstellen]; ■**to ~ that ...** darauf hindeuten, dass ...; **are you ~ing that ...?** willst du damit sagen, dass ...?

suggestible [səg·'dʒes·tə·bəl] *adj* (*pej form*) beeinflussbar, zu beeinflussen; **highly ~** sehr leicht zu beeinflussen

suggestion [səg·'dʒes·tʃən] *n* ❶ (*idea*) Vorschlag *m;* **to be always open to ~s** immer ein offenes Ohr haben ❷ (*hint*) Andeutung *f,* Anspielung *f* ❸ (*indication*) Hinweis *m* ❹ (*trace*) Spur *f fig*

S

sug'gestion box *n* Kasten *m* für Verbesserungsvorschläge
suggestive [səg·'dʒes·tɪv] *adj* ① (*that suggests*) andeutend ② (*risqué*) anzüglich, zweideutig
suicidal [ˌsu·ɪ·'saɪ·dəl] *adj* ① (*depressed*) Selbstmord-, selbstmörderisch *a. fig; person* selbstmordgefährdet; **to feel ~** sich am liebsten umbringen wollen ② (*disastrous*) [selbst]zerstörerisch; **that would be ~** das wäre glatter Selbstmord
suicide ['su·ɪ·saɪd] *n* ① (*killing*) Selbstmord *m a. fig;* **to commit ~** Selbstmord begehen ② (*disastrous action*) selbstmörderische Aktion *fam;* **it would be ~ to ...** es wäre [glatter] Selbstmord, wenn ... *fam*
suit [sut] **I.** *n* ① (*jacket and pants*) Anzug *m;* **three-piece ~** Dreiteiler *m;* (*jacket and skirt*) Kostüm *nt* ② (*for sports*) Anzug *m;* **ski ~** Skianzug *m* ③ CARDS Farbe *f* ▶ PHRASES: **to follow ~** (*form*) dasselbe tun **II.** *vt* ① (*be convenient for*) ■**to ~ sb** jdm passen [*o* recht sein]; **what time ~s you best?** wann passt es Ihnen am besten? ② (*choose*) ■**to ~ oneself** tun, was man will; **you can ~ yourself about when you work** man kann selbst bestimmen, wann man arbeitet; **~ yourself** (*hum o pej*) [ganz,] wie du willst ③ (*enhance*) ■**to ~ sb** *clothes* jdm stehen; ■**to ~ sth** zu etw *dat* passen **III.** *vi* angemessen sein, passen
suitable ['su·t̬ə·bəl] *adj* geeignet, passend; *clothing* angemessen
'suitcase *n* Koffer *m*
suite [swit] *n* ① (*rooms*) Suite *f;* **~ of offices** Reihe *f* von Büroräumen ② (*furniture*) Garnitur *f;* **bedroom ~** Schlafzimmereinrichtung *f* ③ MUS Suite *f*
suitor ['su·t̬ər] *n* ① (*liter or hum: wooer*) Freier *m veraltend o hum,* Bewerber *m* ② ECON (*buyer*) Interessent *m* (*für einen Firmenkauf*)
sulfate ['sʌl·feɪt] *n* Sulfat *nt*
sulfide ['sʌl·faɪd] *n* Sulfid *nt*
sulfur ['sʌl·fər] *n* ① CHEM Schwefel *m* ② (*color*) Schwefelgelb *nt*
sulfur dioxide ['sʌl·fər·daɪ·'ak·saɪd] *n* Schwefeldioxid *nt*
sulfuric [sʌl·'fjʊr·ɪk] *adj* Schwefel-
sulfuric 'acid *n* Schwefelsäure *f*
sulk [sʌlk] **I.** *vi* schmollen, beleidigt sein **II.** *n* **to be in a ~** beleidigt sein, schmollen
sulky ['sʌl·ki] *adj person* beleidigt, eingeschnappt *fam; face* mürrisch
sullen ['sʌl·ən] *adj* (*pej: bad-tempered*) missmutig, mürrisch
sultan ['sʌl·tən] *n* Sultan *m*
sultry ['sʌl·tri] *adj* ① METEO schwül ② (*sexy*) *woman, woman's voice* erotisch, sinnlich
sum [sʌm] *n* ① (*money*) Summe *f,* Betrag *m;* **five-figure ~** fünfstelliger Betrag ② (*total*) Summe *f,* Ergebnis *nt*
◆**sum up I.** *vi* ① (*summarize*) zusammenfassen ② LAW *judge* resümieren **II.** *vt* (*summarize*) zusammenfassen; (*evaluate*) einschätzen; **to ~ up a situation at a glance** eine Situation auf einen Blick erfassen
summarize ['sʌm·ə·raɪz] **I.** *vt* [kurz] zusammenfassen **II.** *vi* zusammenfassen, resümieren; **to ~, ...** kurz gesagt, ...
summary ['sʌm·ə·ri] **I.** *n* Zusammenfassung *f; of a plot, contents* [kurze] Inhaltsangabe **II.** *adj* (*brief*) knapp, gedrängt; *dismissal* fristlos
summer ['sʌm·ər] **I.** *n* (*season*) Sommer *m;* **a ~'s day** ein Sommertag *m;* **in [the] ~** im Sommer **II.** *vi* den Sommer verbringen; **to ~ outdoors** *animals, plants* im Sommer im Freien bleiben
summer house *n* Ferienhaus *nt,* Sommerhaus *nt*
'summerhouse *n* Gartenhaus *nt,* Gartenlaube *f*
'summertime *n* Sommerzeit *f;* **in the ~** im Sommer
summer 'vacation *n* Sommerurlaub *m;* SCH, UNIV Sommerferien *pl*

Die Sommerferien, **summer vacation**, dauern in den Vereinigten Staaten drei Monate. Je nach Staat, liegen diese drei Monate in der Zeit von Ende Mai bis Mitte September. Ursprünglich mussten die Ferien so lange sein, dass die Kinder auf einem Bauernhof oder einer Ranch bei der Arbeit helfen konnten. Um 1900, als mehr und mehr Leute in die Städte zogen, begannen sich *summer camps* (Sommerlager) zu entwickeln. Dort schickte man die Kinder aus den Städten hin, damit sie die Natur kennenlernten. Heutzutage machen die Kinder dort Musik, Reitsport, basteln, gehen schwimmen und wandern etc.

summery ['sʌm·ə·ri] *adj weather* sommerlich
summit ['sʌm·ɪt] *n* ① *of a mountain* Gipfel *m;* (*fig: highest point*) Gipfel *m,* Höhepunkt *m* ② POL Gipfel *m;* **~ conference** Gipfelkonferenz *f*
summon ['sʌm·ən] *vt* ① (*call*) *person* rufen, zu sich *dat* bestellen; LAW vorladen; **to ~ a meeting** eine Versammlung einberufen ② (*demand*) *help* holen ③ (*gather*) **to ~ up the courage to do sth** den Mut aufbringen, etw zu tun
summons ['sʌm·ənz] **I.** *n* <*pl* -es> ① LAW [Vor]ladung *f;* **to issue a ~** [vor]laden ② (*call*) Aufforderung *f;* (*iron, hum*) Befehl *m* **II.** *vt* LAW ■**to ~ sb** jdn vorladen lassen
sumptuous ['sʌmp·tʃʊ·əs] *adj* luxuriös, kostspielig; *dinner* üppig; *gown* festlich, prächtig
sun [sʌn] **I.** *n* ① (*star*) Sonne *f* ② ■**the ~** (*sunshine*) die Sonne, der Sonnenschein; **to sit in the ~** in der Sonne sitzen ③ **to try everything under the ~** alles Mögliche versuchen **II.** *vt* <-nn-> ① (*sit in sun*) ■**to ~ oneself** sich sonnen ② (*expose to sun*) ■**to ~ sth** etw der Son-

ne aussetzen
'**sun-baked** *adj* [von der Sonne] ausgedörrt
'**sunbathe** *vi* sonnenbaden
'**sunbeam** *n* Sonnenstrahl *m*
'**sunblock** *n* Sunblocker *m*
'**sunburn** **I.** *n* Sonnenbrand *m* **II.** *vi* <-ed *or* -burnt, -ed *or* -burnt> sich verbrennen, sich *dat* einen Sonnenbrand holen *fam*
'**sunburned**, '**sunburnt** *adj* (*tanned*) sonnengebräunt; (*red*) sonnenverbrannt, sonnverbrannt SCHWEIZ
sundae ['sʌn·di] *n* Eisbecher *m*
Sunday ['sʌn·deɪ] *n* Sonntag *m; see also* **Tuesday**
Sunday 'best *npl* Sonntagsstaat *m kein pl veraltend*
Sunday 'paper *n* Sonntagszeitung *f*
'**Sunday school** *n* REL, SCH Sonntagsschule *f*
'**sun deck** *n* ❶ NAUT Sonnendeck *nt* ❷ (*balcony*) Sonnenterrasse *f*
'**sundial** *n* Sonnenuhr *f*
'**sundown** *n* Sonnenuntergang *m;* **at/before ~** bei/vor Sonnenuntergang
'**sun-dried** *adj* an der Sonne getrocknet
sundries ['sʌn·driz] *n pl* Verschiedenes *nt kein pl*
sundry ['sʌn·dri] *adj attr* verschiedene(r, s) ▶ PHRASES: **all and ~** (*fam*) Hinz und Kunz *pej,* jedermann
'**sunflower** *n* Sonnenblume *f*
'**sunflower oil** *n* Sonnenblumenöl *nt*
'**sunflower seeds** *npl* Sonnenblumenkerne *pl*
sung [sʌŋ] *pp of* **sing**
'**sunglasses** *npl* Sonnenbrille *f*
sunk [sʌŋk] *pp of* **sink**
sunken ['sʌŋ·kən] *adj* ❶ *attr* (*submerged*) *ship* gesunken; *ship, treasure* versunken ❷ *attr* (*below surrounding level*) tief[er] liegend *attr; bathtub* eingelassen ❸ (*hollow*) *cheeks* eingefallen; *eyes* tief liegend
'**sunlight** *n* Sonnenlicht *nt*
'**sunlit** *adj* sonnenbeschienen; *room* sonnig
sunny ['sʌn·i] *adj* ❶ (*bright, exposed to sun*) *weather, room* sonnig; **~ intervals** Aufheiterungen *pl* ❷ (*cheery*) *person* heiter, unbeschwert; *character, disposition* heiter, sonnig
'**sunray** *n* Sonnenstrahl *m*
'**sunrise** *n* Sonnenaufgang *m;* **at/before ~** bei/vor Sonnenaufgang
'**sunroof** *n* Schiebedach *nt*
'**sunroom** *n* Glasveranda *f,* Wintergarten *m*
'**sunscreen** *n* ❶ (*cream*) Sonnenschutzmittel *nt* ❷ (*ingredient*) Zusatzstoff *m* gegen Sonnenbrand
'**sunset** *n* ❶ (*time*) Sonnenuntergang *m;* **at/before ~** bei/vor Sonnenuntergang ❷ (*fig: final stage*) Endphase *f*
'**sunshade** *n* ❶ (*awning*) Markise *f,* Sonnenblende *f* ❷ (*umbrella*) Sonnenschirm *m*
'**sunshine** *n* ❶ (*sunlight*) Sonnenschein *m;* **to bask in the ~** sich in der Sonne aalen *fam* ❷ METEO sonniges Wetter
'**sunspot** *n* ASTRON Sonnenfleck *m*
'**sunstroke** *n* Sonnenstich *m*
'**suntan** **I.** *n* Sonnenbräune *f;* **to get a ~** braun werden **II.** *vi* <-nn-> sich von der Sonne bräunen lassen
'**suntan lotion** *n* Sonnencreme *f*
'**suntanned** *adj* sonnengebräunt, braun gebrannt
'**suntan oil** *n* Sonnenöl *nt*
'**sunup** *n* Sonnenaufgang *m*
'**sun visor** *n* AUTO Sonnenblende *f*
'**sun worshipper** *n* (*hum*) Sonnenanbeter(in) *m(f)*
super ['su·pər] **I.** *adj* (*fam: excellent*) klasse, fantastisch **II.** *interj* super!, spitze! **III.** *adv* (*fam*) besonders
superabundant [ˌsu·pər·ə·'bʌn·dənt] *adj* überreichlich
superb [sə·'pɜrb] *adj* ❶ (*excellent*) ausgezeichnet, hervorragend ❷ (*impressive*) erstklassig; *building, view* großartig

Im professionellen amerikanischen Fußball wird das Finale, das jedes Jahr die Champions der *National Football League* (die American Football Profiliga – die *NFL*) bestimmt, als **Super Bowl** bezeichnet. Seit 1967 wird das Finale am Ende der Saison unter den beiden besten Mannschaften der *NFL* am Super Bowl-Sonntag, dem *Super Bowl Sunday,* ausgetragen. Es ist heute zu einem der meist gesehenen Ereignisse im amerikanischen Fernsehen geworden und wird von Football-Fans in der ganzen Welt mit großem Interesse verfolgt.

supercharged ['su·pər·ˌtʃardʒd] *adj* ❶ (*more powerful*) *car* mit Lader *nach n; engine* aufgeladen ❷ (*emotional*) *atmosphere* gereizt
supercharger ['su·pər·ˌtʃar·dʒər] *n* AUTO Lader *m,* Aufladegebläse *nt*
supercilious [ˌsu·pər·'sɪl·i·əs] *adj* (*pej*) hochnäsig
superego [ˌsu·pər·'i·goʊ] *n* Überich *nt*
superficial [ˌsu·pər·'fɪʃ·əl] *adj* ❶ (*a. fig: on the surface, shallow*) *person* oberflächlich; *damage* geringfügig ❷ (*apparent*) äußerlich ❸ (*cursory*) *knowledge* oberflächlich; *treatment* flüchtig
superficiality [ˌsu·pər·ˌfɪʃ·i·'æl·ɪ·ṭi] *n* Oberflächlichkeit *f*
superfluous [su·'pɜr·flu·əs] *adj* überflüssig
'**superglue** **I.** *n* Sekundenkleber *m* **II.** *vt* festkleben
'**superhero** *n* Superheld *m fam*
super'highway *n* ❶ AUTO Autobahn *f* ❷ COMPUT [**information**] **~** Datenautobahn *f*
super'human *adj* übermenschlich
superimpose [ˌsu·pər·ɪm·'poʊz] *vt images* überlagern
superintendent [ˌsu·pər·ɪn·'ten·dənt] *n*

S

❶ (*person in charge*) Aufsicht *f; of schools* Oberschulrat, -rätin *m, f; of an office, department* Leiter(in) *m(f)* ❷ (*police officer*) Polizeichef(in) *m(f)* ❸ (*custodian*) Hausmeister(in) *m(f),* Hausverwalter(in) *m(f)*

superior [sə·ˈpɪr·i·ər] **I.** *adj* ❶ (*higher in rank*) höhergestellt, vorgesetzt; ■**to be ~** [**to sb**] [jdm] vorgesetzt sein ❷ (*excellent*) *artist* überragend; *taste* erlesen, gehoben ❸ (*better*) überlegen; **to be ~ in numbers** in der Überzahl sein ❹ (*pej: arrogant*) überheblich, arrogant **II.** *n* (*higher person*) Vorgesetzte(r) *f(m)*

superiority [sə·ˌpɪr·i·ˈɔr·ɪ·t̬i] *n* ❶ (*position*) Überlegenheit *f* (**over** über *+akk*) ❷ (*pej: arrogance*) Überheblichkeit *f,* Arroganz *f*

superiˈority complex *n* PSYCH (*fam*) Superioritätskomplex *m fachspr*

superlative [su·ˈpɜr·lə·t̬ɪv] **I.** *adj* ❶ (*best*) unübertrefflich, sagenhaft ❷ LING superlativisch *fachspr* **II.** *n* LING (*form*) Superlativ *m*

ˈsuperman *n* ❶ (*cartoon character*) **S~** Superman *m* ❷ (*fam: exceptional man*) ■**a ~** ein Superman *m*

supermarket [ˈsu·pər·ˌmar·kɪt] *n* Supermarkt *m*

ˈsupermodel *n* FASHION Supermodel *nt*

supernatural [ˌsu·pər·ˈnætʃ·ər·əl] **I.** *adj* ❶ (*mystical*) übernatürlich ❷ (*extraordinary*) außergewöhnlich **II.** *n* ■**the ~** das Übernatürliche

ˈsuperpower *n* Supermacht *f*

superscript [ˈsu·pər·skrɪpt] TYPO **I.** *adj* hochgestellt **II.** *n* hochgestelltes Zeichen

supersede [ˌsu·pər·ˈsid] *vt* ersetzen, ablösen

supersonic [ˌsu·pər·ˈsan·ɪk] *adj* Überschall-

superstar [ˈsu·pər·star] *n* Superstar *m*

superstition [ˌsu·pər·ˈstɪʃ·ən] *n* ❶ (*belief*) Aberglaube[n] *m;* ■**according to ~** nach einem Aberglauben ❷ (*practice*) Aberglaube *m kein pl*

superstitious [ˌsu·pər·ˈstɪʃ·əs] *adj* abergläubisch

superstore [ˈsu·pər·stɔr] *n* Großmarkt *m,* Verbrauchermarkt *m*

superstructure [ˈsu·pər·ˌstrʌk·tʃər] *n* ❶ (*upper structure*) Oberbau *m* ❷ NAUT [Deck]aufbauten *pl*

supertanker [ˈsu·pər·ˌtæŋ·kər] *n* NAUT Riesentanker *m,* Supertanker *m*

supervise [ˈsu·pər·vaɪz] *vt* beaufsichtigen

supervision [ˌsu·pər·ˈvɪʒ·ən] *n of children* Beaufsichtigung *f; of prisoners, work* Überwachung *f*

supervisor [ˈsu·pər·vaɪ·zər] *n* (*person in charge*) Aufsichtsbeamte(r), -beamtin *m, f;* (*in shop*) Abteilungsleiter(in) *m(f);* (*in factory*) Vorarbeiter(in) *m(f);* SCH Betreuungslehrer(in) *m(f);* UNIV Betreuer(in) *m(f);* (*for doctoral candidates*) Doktorvater *m*

supervisory [ˌsu·pər·ˈvaɪ·zə·ri] *adj* Aufsichts-

supine [su·ˈpaɪn] *adj* ❶ (*lying on back*) **to be** [*or* **lie**] **~** auf dem Rücken liegen ❷ (*fig, pej: indolent*) träge, gleichgültig

supper [ˈsʌp·ər] *n* FOOD (*meal*) Abendessen *nt,* Abendbrot *nt,* Nachtmahl *nt* ÖSTERR

ˈsuppertime [ˈsʌp·ər·taɪm] *n* Abendbrotzeit *f,* Abendessenszeit *f*

supplant [sə·ˈplænt] *vt* ersetzen, ablösen

supple [ˈsʌp·əl] *adj* ❶ (*flexible*) *human body* gelenkig, geschmeidig; (*fig*) *mind* flexibel ❷ (*not stiff*) *leather* geschmeidig; *skin* weich

supplement [ˈsʌp·lə·mənt] **I.** *n* ❶ (*something extra*) Ergänzung *f* (**to** zu *+dat*); (*book*) Supplement *nt;* (*information*) Nachtrag *m,* Anhang *m;* **vitamin ~** Nahrungsmittelergänzung *f* ❷ (*section*) Beilage *f* **II.** *vt* ergänzen; **to ~ one's income by doing sth** sein Einkommen aufbessern, indem man etw tut

supplementary [ˌsʌp·lə·ˈmen·tə·ri], **supplemental** [sʌp·lə·ˈmen·təl] *adj* (*additional*) ergänzend *attr,* zusätzlich, Zusatz-

suppleness [ˈsʌp·əl·nɪs] *n* ❶ (*flexibility*) *of the human body* Gelenkigkeit *f;* (*fig*) *of mind* Flexibilität *f* ❷ (*softness*) *of leather* Geschmeidigkeit *f; of skin* Weichheit *f*

supplication [ˌsʌp·lɪ·ˈkeɪ·ʃən] *n* (*form, liter*) Flehen *nt kein pl* (**for** um *+akk*)

supplier [sə·ˈplaɪ·ər] *n* ❶ (*provider*) Lieferant(in) *m(f);* **~ of services** Erbringer *m* von Dienstleistungen ❷ (*company*) Lieferfirma *f,* Zulieferbetrieb *m*

supply [sə·ˈplaɪ] **I.** *vt* <-ie-> ❶ (*provide sth*) sorgen (für *+akk*), bereitstellen ❷ (*provide sb with sth*) versorgen; ECON beliefern; *arms, drugs* beschaffen ❸ (*act as source*) liefern **II.** *n* ❶ (*stock*) Vorrat *m* (**of** an *+dat*) ❷ (*action*) Versorgung *f;* **oil/gas** [*or* **line**] **~** Öl-/Benzinzufuhr *f;* (*action of providing*) Belieferung *f;* **energy ~** Energieversorgung *f* ❸ ECON Angebot *nt;* **to be in short ~** Mangelware sein ❹ ■**supplies** *pl* (*provision*) Versorgung *f kein pl;* (*amount needed*) Bedarf *m;* **to cut off supplies** die Lieferungen einstellen

support [sə·ˈpɔrt] **I.** *vt* ❶ (*hold up*) stützen; ■**to ~ oneself on sth** sich auf etw *akk* stützen; **the ice is thick enough to ~ our weight** das Eis ist so dick, dass es uns trägt ❷ (*provide with money*) [finanziell] unterstützen; *lifestyle* finanzieren ❸ (*provide with necessities*) ■**to ~ sb** für jds Lebensunterhalt aufkommen; *family* unterhalten ❹ (*comfort, encourage*) unterstützen (**in** bei *+dat*); *plan* befürworten; SPORTS **to ~ a team** für ein Team sein ❺ COMPUT *device, language, program* unterstützen **II.** *n* ❶ (*prop*) Stütze *f;* ARCHIT Träger *m* ❷ (*act of holding*) **to give sth ~** etw *dat* Halt geben ❸ (*material assistance, encouragement*) Unterstützung *f;* LAW Unterhalt *m* ❹ (*comfort*) Stütze *f fig;* **to give sb moral ~** jdn moralisch unterstützen ❺ COMPUT Support *m*

supporter [sə·ˈpɔr·t̬ər] *n* ❶ (*encouraging person*) Anhänger(in) *m(f); of a campaign, policy* Befürworter(in) *m(f); of a theory* Verfechter(in) *m(f)* ❷ SPORTS Fan *m*

supporting [sə·ˈpɔr·t̬ɪŋ] *adj attr* FILM **~ part**

S

[*or* **role**] Nebenrolle *f*

supportive [sə·ˈpɔr·t̬ɪv] *adj* (*approv*) ■**to be ~ of sb** jdm eine Stütze sein, jdn unterstützen; ■**to be ~ of sth** etw unterstützen [*o* befürworten]

suppose [sə·ˈpoʊz] *vt* ❶ (*think likely*) ■**to ~ [that]** ... annehmen [*o* vermuten], dass ...; **I ~ you think that's funny** du hältst das wohl auch noch für komisch; **I don't ~ you could ...** Sie könnten mir nicht zufällig ... ❷ (*as a suggestion*) **~ we leave right away?** wie wär's, wenn wir jetzt gleich fahren würden? ❸ (*believe*) glauben, vermuten; **her new book is ~d to be very good** ihr neues Buch soll sehr gut sein ❹ *pred* (*expected*) **you're ~d to be asleep** du solltest eigentlich schon schlafen ▶PHRASES: **I ~ so** wahrscheinlich, wenn du meinst

supposed [sə·ˈpoʊzd] *adj attr* vermutet, angenommen; *killer* mutmaßlich

supposedly [sə·ˈpoʊ·zɪd·li] *adv* ❶ (*allegedly*) angeblich ❷ (*apparently*) anscheinend, scheinbar

supposing [sə·ˈpoʊ·zɪŋ] *conj* angenommen; **~ he doesn't show up?** was, wenn er nicht erscheint?

supposition [ˌsʌp·ə·ˈzɪʃ·ən] *n* ❶ (*act*) Spekulation *f*, Mutmaßung *f* ❷ (*belief*) Vermutung *f*, Annahme *f*; **on the ~ that ...** vorausgesetzt, dass ...

suppository [sə·ˈpaz·ə·tɔr·i] *n* MED Zäpfchen *nt*

suppress [sə·ˈpres] *vt* ❶ (*end, restrain*) *feelings, impulses* unterdrücken; *revolution* niederschlagen; *terrorism* bekämpfen ❷ (*prevent from spreading*) *evidence, information* zurückhalten ❸ (*inhibit*) hemmen; *the immune system* schwächen; *a process, reaction* abschwächen ❹ PSYCH *ideas, memories* verdrängen

suppression [sə·ˈpreʃ·ən] *n* ❶ (*act of ending, controlling*) Unterdrückung *f*; *of an uprising, a revolution* Niederschlagung *f*; *of terrorism* Bekämpfung *f* ❷ *of evidence, information* Zurückhaltung *f* ❸ MED Hemmung *f*

supremacy [sə·ˈprem·ə·si] *n* Vormachtstellung *f*; SPORTS Überlegenheit *f*

supreme [sə·ˈprim] *adj* ❶ (*superior*) höchste(r, s), oberste(r, s) ❷ (*extreme*) äußerste(r, s), größte(r, s); (*causing great pleasure*) überragend, unübertroffen; *moment* einzigartig

Supreme ˈCourt *n* oberstes Gericht

surcharge [ˈsɜr·tʃardʒ] *n* ❶ (*extra charge*) Zuschlag *m* (**for** für +*akk*), Aufschlag *m* (**on** auf +*akk*) ❷ (*penalty*) Strafgebühr *f*; (*tax*) [Steuer]zuschlag *m*

sure [ʃʊr] **I.** *adj* ❶ *pred* (*confident*) sicher; ■**to be ~ [that]** ... [sich *dat*] sicher sein, dass ...; **I'm not really ~** ich weiß nicht so genau; **to feel ~ [that]** ... überzeugt [davon] sein, dass ... ❷ (*certain*) sicher, gewiss; ■**to be ~ to ...** denk daran, dass ...; **be ~ to close the door when you leave** vergiss nicht, die Tür zuzumachen, wenn du gehst ▶PHRASES: **~ thing** (*fam: certainty*) sicher!; (*of course*) [aber] natürlich!, [na] klar! *fam*; **to be ~ of oneself** sehr von sich *dat* überzeugt sein *pej*; **to make ~ [that]** ... darauf achten, dass ... **II.** *adv* (*fam: certainly*) echt; **I ~ am hungry!** hab ich vielleicht einen Hunger! **III.** *interj* (*fam: certainly!*) **~ I will!** natürlich!, aber klar doch!

sure-ˈfooted *adj* ❶ (*able to walk*) trittsicher ❷ (*confident*) sicher, souverän *geh*

surely [ˈʃʊr·li] *adv* ❶ (*certainly*) sicher[lich], bestimmt ❷ (*showing astonishment*) doch; **~ you don't expect me to believe that** du erwartest doch wohl nicht, dass ich dir das abnehme! *fam* ❸ (*without fail*) **slowly but ~** langsam, aber sicher

surety [ˈʃʊr·ɪ·t̬i] *n* LAW ❶ (*person*) Bürge, Bürgin *m, f* ❷ (*money*) Bürgschaft *f*, Sicherheitsleistung *f*

surf [sɜrf] **I.** *n* Brandung *f* **II.** *vi* ❶ (*on surfboard*) surfen ❷ (*windsurf*) windsurfen **III.** *vt* COMPUT **to ~ the Internet** im Internet surfen

surface [ˈsɜr·fɪs] **I.** *n* ❶ (*top layer*) Oberfläche *f*; *of a lake, the sea* Spiegel *m*; **road ~** Straßenbelag *m*; **paved ~** Pflaster *nt* ❷ SPORTS (*of playing area*) Untergrund *m* ▶PHRASES: **to scratch the ~ [of sth]** *topic, problem* [etw] streifen **II.** *vi* ❶ (*rise to top*) auftauchen ❷ (*fig: become apparent*) auftauchen, aufkommen **III.** *vt* ■**to ~ sth** ❶ (*cover*) etw mit einem Belag versehen ❷ (*make even*) etw ebnen **IV.** *adj attr* ❶ (*of outer part, superficial*) oberflächlich; (*outward*) äußerlich ❷ (*not underwater*) Überwasser-

ˈsurface mail *n Postsendung, die auf dem Land- bzw. Seeweg befördert wird*

surface ˈtension *n* PHYS Oberflächenspannung *f*

surface-to-air ˈmissile *n* MIL Boden-Luft-Rakete *f*

surfboard [ˈsɜrf·bɔrd] *n* Surfbrett *nt*

surfeit [ˈsɜr·fɪt] (*form*) **I.** *n* Übermaß *nt* (**of** an +*dat*) **II.** *vt* ■**to be ~ed with sth** etw satthaben *fam*

surfer [ˈsɜr·fər] *n* Surfer(in) *m(f)*; (*windsurfer*) Windsurfer(in) *m(f)*

surfing [ˈsɜr·fɪŋ] *n* Surfen *nt*, Wellenreiten *nt*; (*windsurfing*) Windsurfen *nt*

surge [sɜrdʒ] **I.** *vi* ❶ (*move powerfully*) *sea* branden; *waves* wogen, sich auftürmen; (*fig*) *people* wogen ❷ (*increase strongly*) *profits* [stark] ansteigen ❸ (*fig*) ■**to ~ [up]** (*well up*) *emotion* aufwallen; (*grow louder*) *cheer, roar* aufbrausen **II.** *n* ❶ (*sudden increase*) [plötzlicher] Anstieg; ELEC Spannungsanstieg *m*, Spannungsstoß *m* ❷ (*large wave*) Woge *f*; (*breaker*) Brandung *f*; (*tidal wave*) Flutwelle *f* ❸ (*fig: pressing movement*) Ansturm *m* ❹ (*fig: wave of emotion*) Welle *f*, Woge *f*

surgeon [ˈsɜr·dʒən] *n* Chirurg(in) *m(f)*

surgery [ˈsɜr·dʒə·ri] *n* chirurgischer Eingriff

surgical [ˈsɜr·dʒɪ·kəl] *adj* ❶ (*used by sur-*

S

geons) *gloves, instruments* chirurgisch ❷ (*orthopedic*) medizinisch

surly ['sɜr·li] *adj* unwirsch, ruppig

surmise [sər·'maɪz] *vt* (*form*) vermuten, annehmen

surmount [sər·'maʊnt] *vt* (*overcome*) *challenge, problem* meistern; *obstacle, opposition* überwinden

surname ['sɜr·neɪm] *n* Familienname *m*, Nachname *m*

surpass [sər·'pæs] *vt* (*form*) übertreffen; ■ **to ~ oneself** sich selbst übertreffen

surplus ['sɜr·pləs] **I.** *n* <*pl* -es> ❶ (*excess*) Überschuss *m* (**of** an +*dat*) ❷ (*financial*) Überschuss *m* **II.** *adj* ❶ (*extra*) zusätzlich ❷ (*dispensable*) überschüssig

surprise [sər·'praɪz] **I.** *n* Überraschung *f*; **~!** (*fam*) Überraschung! *a. iron;* **to take sb by ~** jdn überraschen; **to sb's [great] ~** zu jds [großem] Erstaunen **II.** *vt* ❶ (*amaze*) überraschen; **well, you do ~ me** nun, das erstaunt mich! ❷ (*take unawares*) überraschen; ■ **to ~ sb doing sth** jdn bei etw *dat* überraschen [*o* ertappen] **III.** *adj attr* überraschend, unerwartet

surprised [sər·'praɪzd] *adj* ❶ (*taken unawares*) überrascht; (*amazed*) erstaunt (**at** über +*akk*); **I wouldn't be ~ if it snowed tomorrow** es würde mich nicht wundern, wenn es morgen schneite; **pleasantly ~** angenehm überrascht ❷ *pred* (*disappointed*) enttäuscht (**at** von +*dat*)

surprising [sər·'praɪ·zɪŋ] *adj* überraschend

surprisingly [sər·'praɪ·zɪŋ·li] *adv* ❶ (*remarkably*) erstaunlich ❷ (*unexpectedly*) überraschenderweise

surreal [sə·'ri·əl] *adj* surreal *geh*, [traumhaft-]unwirklich

surrealism [sə·'ri·ə·lɪz·əm] *n* Surrealismus *m*

surrealist [sə·'ri·ə·lɪst] **I.** *n* Surrealist(in) *m(f)* **II.** *adj* surrealistisch

surrender [sə·'ren·dər] **I.** *vi* ❶ MIL aufgeben, kapitulieren; ■ **to ~ to sb** sich jdm ergeben ❷ (*fig: give in*) nachgeben, kapitulieren; **to ~ to temptation** der Versuchung erliegen **II.** *vt* (*form: give*) ■ **to ~ sth [to sb]** [jdm] etw übergeben [*o* aushändigen]; *territory* abtreten; *weapons* abgeben **III.** *n* ❶ (*capitulation*) Kapitulation *f* (**to** vor +*dat*) ❷ (*form: giving up*) Preisgabe *f* (**to** an +*akk*)

surreptitious [ˌsɜr·əp·'tɪʃ·əs] *adj* heimlich; *glance* verstohlen

surrogacy ['sʌr·ə·gə·si] *n* Leihmutterschaft *f*

surrogate ['sɜr·ə·gɪt] **I.** *adj attr* Ersatz- **II.** *n* Ersatz *m*, Surrogat *nt geh* (**for** für +*akk*)

surrogate 'mother *n* Leihmutter *f*

surround [sə·'raʊnd] *vt* ❶ (*enclose*) umgeben ❷ (*encircle*) einkreisen; MIL umstellen, umzingeln ❸ (*fig: be associated with*) umgeben; **to be ~ed by speculation** Spekulationen hervorrufen

surrounding [sə·'raʊn·dɪŋ] *adj attr* umgebend; **~ area** Umgebung *f*; **the ~ buildings** die umliegenden Gebäude

sur'roundings *npl* ❶ (*area*) Umgebung *f* ❷ (*living conditions*) Umgebung *f*, [Lebens]verhältnisse *pl*

surtax <*pl* -es> ['sɜr·tæks] *n* FIN (*extra income tax*) Zusatzabgabe *f* (*zur Einkommenssteuer*)

surveillance [sər·'veɪ·ləns] *n* Überwachung *f*, Kontrolle *f*; **to be under ~** unter Beobachtung stehen, überwacht werden

survey I. *vt* [sər·'veɪ] ❶ *usu passive* (*carry out research*) befragen ❷ (*look at*) betrachten; (*carefully*) begutachten ❸ (*give overview*) umreißen **II.** *n* ['sɜr·veɪ] ❶ (*opinion poll*) Untersuchung *f*; (*research*) Studie *f*; **nationwide ~** landesweite Umfrage ❷ (*overview*) Übersicht *f*; *of a topic* Überblick *m* (**of** über +*akk*) ❸ *of land* Vermessung *f*

surveyor [sər·'veɪ·ər] *n of land* [Land]vermesser(in) *m(f)*

survival [sər·'vaɪ·vəl] *n* (*not dying*) Überleben *nt* ▶ PHRASES: **the ~ of the fittest** das Überleben des Stärkeren

sur'vival instinct *n* Überlebensinstinkt *m*

sur'vival rate *n* (*a. fig*) Überlebenschance *f*

survive [sər·'vaɪv] **I.** *vi* ❶ (*stay alive*) überleben, am Leben bleiben; ■ **to ~ on sth** sich mit etw *dat* am Leben halten ❷ (*fig: not be destroyed*) überleben, erhalten bleiben; *monument* überdauern; *tradition* fortbestehen **II.** *vt* ❶ (*stay alive after*) *accident, crash* überleben; (*fig*) hinwegkommen (über +*akk*) ❷ (*still exist after*) *fire, flood* überstehen ❸ (*outlive*) *person* überleben

surviving [sər·'vaɪ·vɪŋ] *adj* ❶ (*still living*) noch lebend; *relative* hinterblieben ❷ (*fig: still existing*) [noch] vorhanden

survivor [sər·'vaɪ·vər] *n* ❶ (*person still alive*) Überlebende(r) *f(m)*; **she's a cancer ~** sie hat den Krebs besiegt ❷ (*fig: tough person*) Stehaufmännchen *hum fam*, Überlebenskünstler(in) *m(f)*

susceptible [sə·'sep·tə·bəl] *adj* ❶ *usu pred* (*easily influenced*) ■ **to be ~ to sth** für etw *akk* empfänglich sein ❷ MED anfällig

suspect I. *vt* [sə·'spekt] ❶ (*think likely*) vermuten; **I ~ed as much** das habe ich mir gedacht ❷ (*consider guilty*) verdächtigen; ■ **to be ~ed of sth** einer S. *gen* verdächtigt werden ❸ (*doubt*) ■ **to ~ sth** etw *akk* anzweifeln; *motives* etw *dat* misstrauen **II.** *n* ['sʌs·pekt] Verdächtige(r) *f(m)*; (*fig*) Verursacher(in) *m(f)* **III.** *adj* ['sʌs·pekt] ❶ *usu attr* (*possibly dangerous*) verdächtig, suspekt ❷ (*possibly defective*) zweifelhaft

suspend [sə·'spend] *vt* ❶ (*stop temporarily*) [vorübergehend] aussetzen, einstellen; **to ~ judgment** mit seiner Meinung zurückhalten ❷ LAW *constitution* zeitweise außer Kraft setzen; *sentence* [zur Bewährung] aussetzen ❸ *usu passive* (*from work*) suspendieren; (*from school*) [zeitweilig] [vom Unterricht] ausschließen; SPORTS sperren ❹ *usu passive* (*hang*) herabhängen (**from** von +*dat*)

suspender [sə·'spen·dər] *n* ■ **~s** *pl* Hosenträger *pl*

suspense [sə·ˈspens] *n* Spannung *f;* **to keep sb in ~** jdn im Ungewissen lassen

suspension [sə·ˈspen·ʃən] *n* ❶ (*temporary stoppage*) [zeitweilige] Einstellung ❷ (*from work, school*) Suspendierung *f;* SPORTS Sperrung *f* ❸ AUTO Radaufhängung *f*

susˈpension bridge *n* Hängebrücke *f*

suspicion [sə·ˈspɪʃ·ən] *n* ❶ (*unbelief*) Verdacht *m* ❷ (*being suspected*) Verdacht *m;* **to be above ~** über jeglichen Verdacht erhaben sein ❸ (*mistrust*) Misstrauen *nt*

suspicious [sə·ˈspɪʃ·əs] *adj* ❶ (*causing suspicion*) verdächtig ❷ (*feeling suspicion*) misstrauisch, argwöhnisch; ■**to be ~ of sth** einer S. *dat* gegenüber skeptisch sein

sustain [sə·ˈsteɪn] *vt* ❶ (*form: suffer*) **to ~ damages** Schäden erleiden; (*object*) beschädigt werden ❷ (*maintain*) aufrechterhalten ❸ (*keep alive*) [am Leben] erhalten; *a family* unterhalten ❹ (*support emotionally*) unterstützen

sustainable [sə·ˈsteɪ·nə·bəl] *adj* ❶ (*maintainable*) haltbar; *argument* stichhaltig; **sth is ~** etw kann aufrechterhalten werden ❷ ECOL *resources* erneuerbar; *development* nachhaltig

sustained [sə·ˈsteɪnd] *adj* ❶ (*long-lasting*) anhaltend ❷ (*determined*) nachdrücklich; **to make a ~ effort to do sth** entschieden an etw *akk* herangehen

sustenance [ˈsʌs·tə·nəns] *n* ❶ (*form: food*) Nahrung *f* ❷ (*emotional support*) Unterstützung *f;* **to find ~ in sth** eine Stütze an etw *dat* finden

suture [ˈsu·tʃər] MED **I.** *n* Naht *f* **II.** *vt* [ver]nähen

svelte [svelt] *adj* (*approv*) *woman* schlank, grazil

swab [swab] **I.** *n* MED ❶ (*pad*) Tupfer *m* ❷ (*test sample*) Abstrich *m* **II.** *vt* <-bb-> ❶ MED (*clean*) abtupfen ❷ *esp* NAUT *deck* schrubben

swagger [ˈswæg·ər] **I.** *vi* ❶ (*walk boastfully*) stolzieren ❷ (*behave boastfully*) angeben *fam,* prahlen **II.** *n* Angeberei *f fam,* Prahlerei *f*

swallow¹ [ˈswal·oʊ] **I.** *n* ❶ (*action*) Schlucken *nt kein pl* ❷ (*quantity*) Schluck *m* **II.** *vt* ❶ (*eat*) [hinunter]schlucken; (*greedily*) verschlingen ❷ *usu passive* ECON (*fig: take over*) ■**to be ~ed [up] by sth** von etw *dat* geschluckt werden *fam* ❸ (*fig: engulf*) ■**to ~ [up]** ⊂ **sb/sth** jdn/etw verschlingen ❹ (*fig fam: believe unquestioningly*) schlucken; **to ~ sth whole** etw *akk* unzerkaut [hinunter]schlucken **III.** *vi* schlucken

swallow² [ˈswal·oʊ] *n* (*bird*) Schwalbe *f*

swam [swæm] *vi, vt pt of* **swim**

swamp [swamp] **I.** *vt* ❶ (*fill with water*) *boat, canoe* volllaufen lassen ❷ (*flood*) überschwemmen, unter Wasser setzen ❸ (*fig: overwhelm*) überschwemmen; **I'm ~ed with work at the moment** im Moment ersticke ich in Arbeit **II.** *n* ❶ (*bog*) Sumpf *m* ❷ (*boggy land*) Sumpfland *nt*

ˈswampland, ˈswamplands *npl* Sumpfland *nt,* Sumpfgebiet *nt*

swampy [ˈswam·pi] *adj* sumpfig, morastig

swan [swan] *n* Schwan *m*

swank [swæŋk] *n* (*pej fam*) Prahlerei *f,* Protzerei *f*

swanky [ˈswæŋ·ki] *adj* (*fam*) ❶ (*stylish*) schick ❷ (*pej: boastful*) protzig; *talk, manner* großspurig

ˈswansong *n* (*fig*) Schwanengesang *m geh*

swap [swap] **I.** *n* ❶ (*exchange*) Tausch *m;* (*interchange*) Austausch *m* ❷ (*deal*) Tauschhandel *m* ❸ (*thing*) Tauschobjekt *nt* **II.** *vt* <-pp-> ❶ (*exchange*) tauschen; ■**to ~ sth for sth** etw gegen etw *akk* eintauschen ❷ (*tell one another*) *stories* austauschen **III.** *vi* <-pp-> tauschen; ■**to ~ with sb** (*exchange objects*) mit jdm tauschen; (*change places*) mit jdm [Platz] tauschen

swarm [swɔrm] **I.** *n* ❶ (*insects*) Schwarm *m* ❷ (*fig: people*) Schar *f* **II.** *vi* ❶ ZOOL *insects* schwärmen ❷ (*fig*) *people* schwärmen ❸ (*be full of*) ■**to be ~ing with sth** von etw *dat* [nur so] wimmeln

swarthy [ˈswɔr·ði] *adj* dunkel[häutig]

swashbuckling [ˈswaʃ·ˌbʌk·lɪŋ] *adj attr* verwegen, säbelrasselnd

swastika [ˈswas·tɪ·kə] *n* Hakenkreuz *nt*

swat [swat] **I.** *vt* <-tt-> ❶ (*kill*) *insect* totschlagen, zerquetschen; (*with hands*) todklatschen *fam* ❷ (*hit*) hart schlagen; *ball* schmettern **II.** *n* ❶ (*blow*) [heftiger] Schlag ❷ (*swatter*) Fliegenklatsche *f*

swatch <*pl* -es> [swatʃ] *n* [Textil]muster *nt,* [Textil]probe *f*

swathe [sweɪð] **I.** *vt* einwickeln **II.** *n* ❶ (*long strip*) Bahn *f,* Streifen *m* ❷ (*wide area*) Gebiet *nt,* Gegend *f*

sway [sweɪ] **I.** *vi person* schwanken; *trees* sich wiegen **II.** *vt* ❶ (*swing*) schwenken; *wind* wiegen ❷ *usu passive* (*influence*) ■**to be ~ed by sb/sth** sich von jdm/etw beeinflussen lassen; (*change mind*) von jdm/etw umgestimmt werden ❸ (*fig: alter*) ändern

swear <swore, sworn> [swer] **I.** *vi* ❶ (*curse*) fluchen (**at** auf +*akk*) ❷ (*take an oath*) schwören, einen Eid ablegen **II.** *vt* schwören; *oath* leisten, ablegen

◆**swear in** *vt usu passive* vereidigen

◆**swear off** *vt* ■**to ~ off sth** *alcohol, cigarettes, drugs* etw *dat* abschwören

ˈswearing *n* Fluchen *nt*

ˈswear word *n* derbes Schimpfwort, Fluch *m*

sweat [swet] **I.** *n* ❶ (*perspiration*) Schweiß *m* ❷ (*fig fam: worried state*) **just thinking about the exams makes me break out in a cold ~** wenn ich nur ans Examen denke, bricht mir der kalte Schweiß aus; **to work oneself into a ~ [about sth]** sich [wegen einer S. *dat*] verrückt machen *fam* **II.** *vi* <sweat *or* sweated, sweat *or* sweated> ❶ (*perspire*) schwitzen (**with** vor +*dat*) ❷ (*fig: work hard*) schwitzen (**over** über +*dat*) **III.** *vt* <sweat *or*

sweated, sweat *or* sweated> ▸PHRASES: **to ~ blood** Blut [und Wasser] schwitzen *fam*

◆**sweat out** *vt* (*suffer while waiting*) **to ~ it out** zittern *fam*

'**sweatband** *n* Schweißband *nt*

sweater ['swet̬·ər] *n* Pullover *m,* Sweater *m*

'**sweatpants** *n pl* Jogginghose *f*

'**sweatshirt** *n* Sweatshirt *nt*

'**sweatshop** *n* Ausbeuterbetrieb *m pej*

sweaty ['swet̬·i] *adj* ① (*covered in sweat*) *person* verschwitzt ② (*causing sweat*) *work* schweißtreibend

Swede [swid] *n* Schwede *m,* Schwedin *f*

Sweden ['swi·dən] *n* Schweden *nt*

Swedish ['swi·dɪʃ] **I.** *n* Schwedisch *nt* **II.** *adj* schwedisch

sweep [swip] **I.** *n* ① (*a clean with a brush*) Kehren *nt,* Fegen *nt* NORDD ② (*movement*) schwungvolle Bewegung; (*with saber, scythe*) ausholender Hieb ③ (*range*) Reichweite *f a. fig,* Spielraum *m* ④ (*fam*) ■**~s** *pl, + sing/pl vb see* **sweepstakes** **II.** *vt* <swept, swept> ① (*with a broom*) kehren, fegen NORDD ② (*take in powerful manner*) **she swept the pile of papers into her bag** sie schaufelte den Stapel Papiere in ihre Tasche ③ (*spread*) ■**to ~ sth** über etw *akk* kommen **III.** *vi* <swept, swept> ① (*clean*) kehren, fegen ② (*move smoothly*) gleiten; *person* rauschen *fam*

◆**sweep aside** *vt* ① (*cause to move*) [hin]wegfegen ② (*fig: dismiss*) *doubts, objections* beiseiteschieben, abtun

◆**sweep away** *vt* ① (*remove*) [hin]wegfegen; (*water*) fortspülen; (*fig*) *doubts, objections* beiseiteschieben ② (*fig: carry away*) mitreißen

◆**sweep out** **I.** *vt* auskehren **II.** *vi* hinausstürmen

◆**sweep up** **I.** *vt* ① (*brush and gather*) zusammenkehren ② (*gather*) zusammensammeln **II.** *vi* ① (*clean up*) aufkehren ② *usu passive* ■**to be swept up** heranrauschen

sweeper ['swi·pər] *n* ① (*device*) Kehrmaschine *f* ② (*person*) [Straßen]feger(in) *m(f),* [Straßen]kehrer(in) *m(f)* ③ (*in soccer*) Libero *m*

S

sweeping ['swi·pɪŋ] *adj* ① (*large-scale*) weitreichend; *changes* einschneidend; **~ cuts** drastische Einsparungen ② (*very general*) pauschal; *generalization* grob ③ *attr* (*broad*) *curve* weit

sweepstakes ['swip·steɪks] *n pl, + sing/pl vb Art Lotterie, wobei mit kleinen Einsätzen z. B. auf Pferde gesetzt wird und diese Einsätze an den Gewinner gehen*

sweet [swit] **I.** *adj* ① (*like sugar*) süß ② (*not dry*) *sherry, wine* lieblich ③ (*fig: pleasant*) süß, angenehm; *sound* lieblich; *temper* sanft ④ (*fig: endearing*) süß, niedlich; (*kind*) freundlich, lieb **II.** *n* ■**~s** *pl* Süßigkeiten *pl*

'**sweet-and-sour** *adj* süßsauer

'**sweet corn** *n* [Zucker]mais *m*

sweeten ['swi·tən] *vt* ① (*make sweet*) süßen ② (*make more amenable*) ■**to ~ [up]** ◯ **sb** jdn günstig stimmen

sweetener ['swi·tən·ər] *n* ① (*sugar substitute*) Süßstoff *m;* (*pill*) Süßstofftablette *f* ② (*inducement*) Lockspeise *f geh,* Versuchung *f*

'**sweetheart** *n* (*term of endearment*) Liebling *m,* Schatz *m fam*

sweetness ['swit·nɪs] *n* ① (*sweet taste*) Süße *f* ② (*fig: pleasantness*) *of sb's nature* Freundlichkeit *f; of freedom, victory* süßes [*o* wohliges] Gefühl

sweet 'pea *n* Wicke *f*

'**sweet potato** *n* Süßkartoffel *f*

'**sweet-talk** *vt* einwickeln *fam;* ■**to ~ sb into doing sth** jdn beschwatzen, etw zu tun

swell <swelled, swelled *or* swollen> [swel] **I.** *vt* ① (*enlarge*) anwachsen lassen; *river* anschwellen lassen; *fruit* wachsen [und gedeihen] lassen ② (*fig: increase*) [an]steigen lassen; *sales* steigern **II.** *vi* ① (*become swollen*) ■**to ~ [up]** anschwellen ② (*increase*) zunehmen; *population* ansteigen ③ (*get louder*) lauter werden, anschwellen **III.** *n* ① *of sea* Seegang *m* ② (*increase in sound*) zunehmende Lautstärke; *of music* Anschwellen *nt kein pl*

swelling ['swel·ɪŋ] *n* ① MED (*lump*) Schwellung *f,* Geschwulst *f;* (*sudden growth*) Beule *f* ② (*activity*) Anschwellen *nt* ③ (*lasting form*) Wölbung *f,* Ausbauchung *f*

sweltering ['swel·tər·ɪŋ] *adj* drückend heiß; *heat, weather* schwül

swept [swept] *vt, vi pt of* **sweep**

swerve [swɜrv] **I.** *vi* ① (*change direction*) [plötzlich] ausweichen; *car* ausscheren ② (*fig liter: deviate*) eine Schwenkung vollziehen *geh;* **to ~ from one's principles** von seiner seinen Grundsätzen abweichen **II.** *n* ① (*sudden move*) plötzliche Seitenbewegung, Schlenker *m;* (*evading move*) Ausweichbewegung *f;* **a ~ to the left/right** ein Ausscheren *nt* nach links/rechts ② (*fig*) Abweichung *f;* POL Richtungswechsel *m*

swift [swɪft] **I.** *adj* ① (*fast-moving*) schnell ② (*occurring quickly*) schnell, rasch **II.** *n* (*bird*) Mauersegler *m*

swiftly ['swɪft·li] *adv* schnell, rasch

swiftness ['swɪft·nɪs] *n* Schnelligkeit *f*

swig [swɪg] (*fam*) **I.** *vt* <-gg-> schlucken **II.** *n* Schluck *m*

swill [swɪl] **I.** *n* (*pig feed*) Schweinefutter *nt;* (*fig, pej: unpleasant drink*) Gesöff *nt fam;* (*unpleasant food*) Fraß *m fam* **II.** *vt* ① (*usu pej fam: drink fast*) hinunterstürzen; *alcohol, beer* hinunterkippen ② (*swirl a liquid*) ■**to ~ sth around** etw [hin und her] schwenken

swim [swɪm] **I.** *vi* <swam, swum, -mm-> ① SPORTS schwimmen ② (*whirl*) verschwimmen; (*be dizzy*) schwindeln **II.** *vt* <swam, swum, -mm-> ① (*cross*) *channel, river* durchschwimmen ② (*do*) **to ~ a few strokes** ein paar Züge schwimmen **III.** *n* Schwimmen *nt kein pl*

swimmer ['swɪm·ər] *n* (*person*) Schwimmer(in) *m(f)*

swimming ['swɪm·ɪŋ] *n* Schwimmen *nt*

'swimming cap *n* Badekappe *f*, Badehaube *f* ÖSTERR

swimmingly ['swɪm·ɪŋ·li] *adv* (*fam or dated*) glatt

'swimming pool *n* Schwimmbecken *nt*; (*private*) Swimmingpool *m*; (*public*) Schwimmbad *nt*; **indoor/outdoor ~** Hallen-/Freibad *nt*

'swimsuit *n* Badeanzug *m*; (*trunks*) Badehose *f*

'swim trunks, **'swimming trunks** *npl* Badehose *f*

swindle ['swɪn·dəl] **I.** *vt* betrügen, hereinlegen; ■**to ~ sb out of sth** jdn um etw *akk* betrügen **II.** *n* Betrug *m kein pl außer* SCHWEIZ

swindler ['swɪnd·lər] *n* (*pej*) Betrüger(in) *m(f)*

swine <*pl* - *or* -s> [swaɪn] *n* ① (*hog*) Schwein *nt* ② (*pej fam: person*) Schwein *nt*

'swine flu *no pl*, **'swine influenza** *n no pl* Schweinegrippe *f*

swing [swɪŋ] **I.** *n* ① (*movement*) Schwingen *nt kein pl* ② (*punch*) Schlag *m* ③ (*hanging seat*) Schaukel *f* ④ (*change*) Schwankung *f*; POL Umschwung *m* ⑤ (*in baseball*) Schwung *m* ▶ PHRASES: **to be in <u>full</u> ~** voll im Gang sein **II.** *vi* <swung, swung> ① (*move*) [hin und her] schwingen; (*move circularly*) sich drehen; **the door swung open in the wind** die Tür ging durch den Wind auf ② (*attempt to hit*) zum Schlag ausholen; *baseball bat* schwingen; ■**to ~ at sb** nach jdm schlagen ③ (*alternate*) *mood* schwanken ④ *music, party* swingen ▶ PHRASES: **to ~ into <u>action</u>** loslegen *fam* **III.** *vt* <swung, swung> ① (*move*) [hin- und her]schwingen ② (*fam: arrange*) **do you think you could ~ the job for me?** glaubst du, du könntest die Sache für mich schaukeln?; **to ~ it** es deichseln

swing around **I.** *vi* ① (*turn around*) sich schnell umdrehen; (*in surprise, fear*) herumfahren ② (*go fast*) **she swung around the corner at full speed** sie kam mit vollem Tempo um die Ecke geschossen **II.** *vt* ① (*turn around*) ■**to ~ sth around** etw [her]umdrehen; (*move in a circle*) etw herumschwingen ② (*change*) **to ~ a conversation around to sth** ein Gespräch auf etw *akk* bringen

swipe [swaɪp] **I.** *vi* schlagen (**at** nach +*dat*) **II.** *vt* ① (*graze*) *car* streifen ② (*fam: steal*) klauen ③ (*pass through*) *magnetic card* durchziehen, einlesen **III.** *n* Schlag *m*; **to take a ~ at sb/sth** auf jdn/etw losschlagen

swirl [swɜrl] **I.** *vi* wirbeln **II.** *vt* ① (*move circularly*) ■**to ~ sth around** etw herumwirbeln ② (*twist together*) ■**to ~ sth together** etw miteinander vermischen **III.** *n of water* Strudel *m*; *of snow, wind* Wirbel *m*; *of dust* Wolke *f*

swish [swɪʃ] **I.** *vi* ① (*make hissing noise*) zischen ② (*make brushing noise*) rascheln **II.** *vt liquid* hin und her schwenken **III.** *n* Rascheln *nt kein pl*

Swiss [swɪs] **I.** *adj* Schweizer-, schweizerisch **II.** *n* <*pl* -> Schweizer(in) *m(f)*

switch [swɪtʃ] **I.** *n* <*pl* -es> ① (*control*) Schalter *m*; **to flick a ~** (*turn on*) einen Schalter anknipsen; (*turn off*) einen Schalter ausknipsen ② (*substitution*) Wechsel *m meist sing* ③ (*alteration*) Änderung *f*; (*change*) Wechsel *m* **II.** *vi* wechseln, tauschen (**with** mit +*dat*) **III.** *vt* ① (*adjust settings*) umschalten ② (*change abruptly*) *directions* wechseln ③ (*substitute*) auswechseln, eintauschen

◆**switch off** **I.** *vt* ELEC ausschalten **II.** *vi* ① (*turn off*) ausschalten ② (*stop paying attention*) abschalten *fam*

◆**switch on** **I.** *vt* ELEC einschalten; *the TV* anmachen **II.** *vi* einschalten, anschalten

◆**switch over** *vi* wechseln (**to** zu +*dat*)

'switchblade *n* Klappmesser *nt*

'switchboard *n* ELEC Schaltbrett *nt*; TELEC [Telefon]zentrale *f*, Vermittlung *f*

'switchboard operator *n* TELEC Telefonist(in) *m(f)*

Switzerland ['swɪt·sər·lənd] *n* Schweiz *f*

swivel ['swɪv·əl] **I.** *n* Drehring *m*, Drehgelenk *nt* **II.** *vt* <-l- *or* -ll-> drehen **III.** *vi* <-l- *or* -ll-> sich drehen

swivel 'chair *n* Drehstuhl *m*

'swizzle stick *n* Sektquirl *m*

swollen ['swoʊ·lən] **I.** *pp of* **swell** **II.** *adj* ① (*puffy*) geschwollen; *face* aufgequollen ② (*larger than usual*) angeschwollen

swoon [swun] **I.** *vi* ① (*dated: faint*) ohnmächtig werden ② (*fig*) schwärmen (**over** für +*akk*) **II.** *n* Ohnmacht *f*

swoop [swup] **I.** *n* ① (*dive*) Sturzflug *m* ② (*fam: attack*) Überraschungsangriff *m* ▶ PHRASES: **in one <u>fell</u> ~** auf einen Streich **II.** *vi* ① (*dive*) niederstoßen, herabstoßen ② (*fam: attack*) ■**to ~ in on sb/sth** jdn/etw angreifen; *police* bei jdm/etw eine Razzia machen

sword [sɔrd] *n* Schwert *nt*

'swordfish *n* Schwertfisch *m*

'swordplay *n* Fechten *nt*

swordsman ['sɔrdz·mən] *n* Fechter *m*

swordsmanship ['sɔrdz·mən·ʃɪp] *n* Fechtkunst *f*

swore [swɔr] *pt of* **swear**

sworn [swɔrn] **I.** *pp of* **swear** **II.** *adj attr* beschworen; *testimony* beeidet; **a ~ statement** eine eidliche Aussage; **~ enemy** Todesfeind(in) *m(f)*

swum [swʌm] *pp of* **swim**

swung [swʌŋ] *pt, pp of* **swing**

sycamore ['sɪk·ə·mɔr] *n* Platane *f*

sycophant ['sɪk·ə·fənt] *n* (*pej form*) Schmeichler(in) *m(f)*; (*pej*) Schleimer(in) *m(f)*, Kriecher(in) *m(f)*

sycophantic [ˌsɪk·ə·'fæn·t̬ɪk] *adj* (*pej form*) kriecherisch

syllable ['sɪl·ə·bəl] *n* Silbe *f*

syllabus <*pl* -es *or form* syllabi> ['sɪl·ə·bəs] *n* ① (*course outline*) Lehrplan *m* ② (*course reading list*) Leseliste *f*

sylph [sɪlf] *n* Sylphide *f geh*

symbiosis [ˌsɪm·bɪ·'oʊ·sɪs] *n* Symbiose *f*

symbiotic [ˌsɪm·bɪ·'at̬·ɪk] *adj* symbiotisch

S

symbol ['sɪm·bəl] *n* Symbol *nt,* Zeichen *nt*
symbolic [sɪm·'bal·ɪk] *adj* symbolisch, symbolhaft
symbolism ['sɪmbəlɪz·əm] *n* Symbolik *f;* ■**S~** ART, LIT Symbolismus *m*
symbolize ['sɪm·bə·laɪz] *vt* symbolisieren
symmetrical [sɪ·'met·rɪ·kəl] *adj* symmetrisch; *face* ebenmäßig
symmetry ['sɪm·ə·tri] *n* (*balance*) Symmetrie *f;* (*evenness*) Ebenmäßigkeit *f;* (*correspondence*) Übereinstimmung *f*
sympathetic [ˌsɪm·pə·'θeṭ·ɪk] *adj* ❶ (*understanding*) verständnisvoll; ■**to be ~ about sth** für etw *akk* Verständnis haben; (*sympathizing*) mitfühlend, teilnahmsvoll ❷ (*likeable*) *fictional characters* sympathisch ❸ (*approving*) wohlgesinnt; ■**to be ~ to[ward] sb/sth** mit jdm/etw sympathisieren
sympathize ['sɪm·pə·θaɪz] *vi* ❶ (*show understanding*) Verständnis haben; (*show compassion*) Mitleid haben, mitfühlen ❷ (*agree with*) sympathisieren
sympathizer ['sɪm·pə·θaɪ·zər] *n* Sympathisant(in) *m(f)*
sympathy ['sɪm·pə·θi] *n* ❶ (*compassion*) Mitleid *nt* (**for** mit +*dat*); (*commiseration*) Mitgefühl *nt;* (*understanding*) Verständnis *nt* ❷ (*agreement*) Übereinstimmung *f;* (*affection*) Sympathie *f* (**with** für +*akk*) ❸ (*condolences*) ■**sympathies** *pl* Beileid *nt kein pl*
symphonic [sɪm·'fan·ɪk] *adj* symphonisch, sinfonisch
symphony ['sɪm·fə·ni] *n* Symphonie *f,* Sinfonie *f;* **Beethoven's Fifth S~** die fünfte Symphonie von Beethoven
'**symphony orchestra** *n* Symphonieorchester *nt,* Sinfonieorchester *nt*
symposium <*pl* -s *or* -sia> [sɪm·'poʊ·zi·əm] *n* (*form*) Symposium *nt,* Symposion *nt*
symptom ['sɪmp·təm] *n* ❶ MED Symptom *nt,* Krankheitszeichen *nt* ❷ (*fig: indicator*) [An]zeichen *nt,* Symptom *nt geh*
symptomatic [ˌsɪmp·tə·'mæṭ·ɪk] *adj* symptomatisch
synagogue ['sɪn·ə·gag] *n* Synagoge *f*
synchronize ['sɪŋ·krə·naɪz] **I.** *vt* aufeinander abstimmen; **to ~ watches** Uhren gleichstellen **II.** *vi* zeitlich zusammenfallen
synchronized 'swimming *n* Synchronschwimmen *nt*
synchronous ['sɪŋ·krə·nəs] *adj* gleichzeitig, synchron
syncopate ['sɪŋ·kə·peɪt] *vt* MUS synkopieren
syndicate ['sɪn·də·kɪt] **I.** *n* ❶ COMM, FIN Syndikat *nt,* Verband *m* ❷ JOURN Pressesyndikat *nt* **II.** *vt* ❶ JOURN an mehrere Zeitungen verkaufen ❷ (*finance*) über ein Syndikat finanzieren
syndication [ˌsɪn·də·'keɪ·ʃən] *n* ❶ JOURN Verkauf *m* an mehrere Zeitungen ❷ (*financing*) Finanzierung *f* durch ein Syndikat
syndrome ['sɪn·droʊm] *n* MED (*a. fig*) Syndrom *nt*
synergy ['sɪn·ər·dʒi] *n* Synergismus *m;* (*energy*) Synergie *f*
synod ['sɪn·əd] *n* Synode *f*
synonym ['sɪn·ə·nɪm] *n* Synonym *nt*
synonymous [sɪ·'nan·ɪ·məs] *adj* synonym
synopsis <*pl* -ses> [sɪ·'næp·sɪs] *n* Zusammenfassung *f*
syntactic [sɪn·'tæk·tɪk] *adj* syntaktisch, Syntax-
syntax ['sɪn·tæks] *n* Syntax *f*
synthesis <*pl* -theses> ['sɪn·θə·sɪs] *n* Synthese *f,* Verbindung *f*
synthesize ['sɪn·θə·saɪz] *vt* künstlich herstellen
synthesizer ['sɪn·θə·saɪ·zər] *n* Synthesizer *m*
synthetic [sɪn·'θeṭ·ɪk] **I.** *adj* ❶ (*man-made*) synthetisch, künstlich; ~ **fiber** Kunstfaser *f* ❷ (*fig, pej: fake*) künstlich, gekünstelt **II.** *n* synthetischer Stoff
syphilis ['sɪf·ə·lɪs] *n* Syphilis *f*
syphilitic [ˌsɪf·ə·'lɪṭ·ɪk] *adj* syphilitisch
syphon ['saɪ·fən] *n see* **siphon**
Syria ['sɪr·i·ə] *n* Syrien *nt*
Syrian ['sɪr·i·ən] **I.** *adj* syrisch **II.** *n* Syr[i]er(in) *m(f)*
syringe [sə·'rɪndʒ] MED **I.** *n* Spritze *f* **II.** *vt* [aus]spülen
syrup ['sɪr·əp] *n* ❶ (*sauce*) Sirup *m;* **maple ~** Ahornsirup ❷ (*medicine*) Saft *m,* Sirup *m*
syrupy ['sɪr·ə·pi] *adj* ❶ (*usu pej*) *food* süßlich ❷ (*pej: overly sweet*) zuckersüß *fig;* (*sentimental*) sentimental, rührselig
system ['sɪs·təm] *n* System *nt*
systematic [ˌsɪs·tə·'mæṭ·ɪk] *adj* systematisch
systematize ['sɪs·tə·mə·taɪz] *vt* systematisieren
'**system crash** *n* COMPUT Systemabsturz *m*
'**system error** *n* Systemfehler *m*
systems 'analyst *n* Systemanalytiker(in) *m(f)*

Tt

T <*pl* -'s *or* -s>, **t** <*pl* -'s> [ti] *n* T *nt*, t *nt*; **~ as in Tango** T wie Theodor ▶PHRASES: **to a ~** (*fam*) **that's Philip to a ~** das ist Philip, wie er leibt und lebt

t. *n abbrev of* **ton** t

tab[1] [tæb] *n* ① (*flap*) Lasche *f*; (*on file*) [Kartei]reiter *m* ② *see* **pull-tab**

tab[2] [tæb] **I.** *n* ① (*fam: bill*) Rechnung *f*; **to pick up the ~** die Rechnung übernehmen ② (*fam: cost*) Kosten *pl* ③ COMPUT **~ [key]** Tabulatortaste *f* ▶PHRASES: **to keep ~s on sth/sb** (*fam*) etw/jdn [genau] im Auge behalten **II.** *vi* <-bb-> COMPUT **to ~ [over]** mit dem Tabulator springen

tabby ['tæb·i] **I.** *adj* (*with stripes*) *cat* getigert **II.** *n* Tigerkatze *f*

'tab key *n* COMPUT Tabulatortaste *f*

table ['teɪ·bəl] *n* ① (*furniture*) Tisch *m*; **to set the ~** den Tisch decken ② (*information*) Tabelle *f*; (*list*) Verzeichnis *nt* ▶PHRASES: **to turn the ~s on sb** jdm gegenüber den Spieß umdrehen

'tablecloth *n* Tischtuch *nt*

'table linen *n* Tischwäsche *f*

'table manners *npl* Tischmanieren *pl*

'tablespoon *n* (*for measuring*) Esslöffel *m*; (*for serving*) Servierlöffel *m*

tablet ['tæb·lɪt] *n* ① (*pill*) Tablette *f* ② (*flat slab*) Block *m*; *of metal* Platte *f*; (*commemorative*) [Gedenk]tafel *f* ③ (*writing pad*) Notizblock *m* ④ (*computer*) Tablet *nt*

'table tennis *n* Tischtennis *nt*

tabloid ['tæb·lɔɪd] *n* Boulevardzeitung *f*

taboo [tə·'bu] **I.** *n* Tabu *nt* **II.** *adj* tabu, Tabu-

tabular ['tæb·jʊ·lər] *adj* tabellarisch

tabulate ['tæb·jʊ·leɪt] *vt* (*form*) tabellarisch [an]ordnen

tachometer [tə·'kam·ɪ·t̬ər] *n* Drehzahlmesser *m*

tacit ['tæs·ɪt] *adj agreement, approval, consent* stillschweigend

taciturn ['tæs·ə·tɜrn] *adj* schweigsam

tack [tæk] **I.** *n* ① (*nail*) kurzer Nagel; (*pin*) Reißzwecke *f* ② (*approach*) Weg *m*; **to try a different ~** eine andere Richtung einschlagen ③ (*loose stitch*) Heftstich *m* **II.** *vt* ① (*nail down*) festnageln ② (*sew loosely*) anheften; *hem* heften

tackle ['tæk·əl] **I.** *n* ① (*gear*) Ausrüstung *f*; **fishing ~** Angelausrüstung *f* ② (*lifting device*) Winde *f*; **block and ~** Flaschenzug *m* ③ SPORTS (*in football*) Tackle *m*; (*in soccer*) Angriff *m* **II.** *vt* ① (*deal with*) in Angriff nehmen; *problem* angehen; (*manage*) fertigwerden (mit +*dat*) ② SPORTS (*in football*) tacklen, tackeln; (*in soccer*) angreifen

tacky[1] ['tæk·i] *adj* (*sticky*) klebrig

tacky[2] ['tæk·i] *adj* (*pej fam*) ① (*in bad taste*) billig ② (*shoddy*) schäbig

tact [tækt] *n* (*diplomacy*) Taktgefühl *nt*; (*sensitiveness*) Feingefühl *nt*

tactful ['tækt·fəl] *adj* taktvoll

tactic ['tæk·tɪk] *n* ① (*strategy*) Taktik *f* ② MIL ■ **~s** + *sing/pl vb* Taktik *f kein pl*

tactical ['tæk·tɪ·kəl] *adj a.* MIL, POL taktisch; (*skillful*) geschickt

tactile ['tæk·təl] *adj* (*form*) ① BIOL Tast-; **~ sense** Tastsinn *m* ② (*pleasing to touch*) **~ materials** sich angenehm anfühlende Materialien

tactless ['tækt·lɪs] *adj* taktlos

tactlessness ['tækt·lɪs·nɪs] *n* Taktlosigkeit *f*

tad [tæd] *n* (*fam*) **a ~ [bit] more** etwas mehr

tadpole ['tæd·poʊl] *n* Kaulquappe *f*

taffeta ['tæf·ɪ·t̬ə] *n* Taft *m*

tag [tæg] **I.** *n* ① (*label*) Schild[chen] *nt*; (*on food, clothes*) Etikett *nt*; (*on suitcase*) [Koffer]anhänger *m* ② (*electronic device*) *for person* elektronische Fessel; *for thing* Sicherungsetikett *nt* ③ AUTO (*proof of paid vehicle tax*) Steuerplakette *f* **II.** *vt* <-gg-> ① (*label*) mit einem Schild versehen; *suitcase* mit Anhänger versehen ② (*electronically*) *person* eine elektronische Fessel anlegen; *thing* ein Sicherungsetikett anbringen (an +*akk*) ③ COMPUT markieren

◆**tag along** *vi* (*fam*) hinterherlaufen; **do you mind if I ~ along?** darf ich mitkommen? [*o* mitfahren]

tail [teɪl] **I.** *n* ① (*of animal*) Schwanz *m*; *of horse a.* Schweif *m geh*; *of bear, badger, wild boar* Bürzel *m* ② (*fig: rear*) Schwanz *m*; *of airplane a.* Rumpfende *nt*; *of car* Heck *nt*; **to have sb on one's ~** jdn auf den Fersen haben ③ (*reverse of coin*) ■ **~s** *pl* Zahlseite *f*; **heads or ~s?** Kopf oder Zahl? ④ (*fam: person following sb*) Beschatter(in) *m(f)*; **to put a ~ on sb** jdn beschatten lassen ▶PHRASES: **to not be able to make heads or ~s of sth** aus etw *dat* nicht schlau werden **II.** *vt* (*fam*) beschatten

◆**tail off** *vi* nachlassen; *sound, voice* schwächer werden; *interest* zurückgehen

tail 'end *n* Ende *nt*, Schluss *m*

'tailgate **I.** *n* ① (*tailboard*) Heckklappe *f*; *of truck* Ladeklappe *f*; *of van* Laderampe *f* ② SPORTS **~ [party]** Tailgate-Party *f*, Parkplatz-Picknick *nt* **II.** *vt* AUTO (*fam*) [zu] dicht auffahren **III.** *vi* (*fam*) ① AUTO [zu] dicht auffahren ② SPORTS eine Tailgate-Party feiern, tailgaten *fam*

'taillight *n* Rücklicht *nt*

tailor ['teɪ·lər] **I.** *n* Schneider(in) *m(f)* **II.** *vt* ① (*make clothes*) [nach Maß] schneidern ② (*modify*) *to sb's needs* abstimmen

tailor-'made *adj* ① (*made-to-measure*) maßgeschneidert ② (*fig: suited*) ■ **to be ~ for sb/sth** für jdn/etw maßgeschneidert sein

'tailpipe *n* AUTO Auspuffrohr *nt*

'tailspin *n* AVIAT (*a. fig*) Trudeln *nt kein pl*

taint [teɪnt] *vt* (*a. fig*) verderben; *reputation* beflecken

Taiwan [ˌtaɪ·ˈwɑn] *n* Taiwan *nt*

Taiwanese [ˌtaɪ·wə·ˈniz] **I.** *adj* taiwanisch **II.** *n* Taiwaner(in) *m(f)*

Tajikistan [tɑ·ˈdʒi·kɪ·ˌstɑn] *n* Tadschikistan *nt*

take [teɪk] **I.** *n* ① (*money received*) Einnahmen *pl* ② (*filming of a scene*) Take *m o nt fachspr* ▶ PHRASES: **to be on the ~** (*fam*) Bestechungsgelder nehmen **II.** *vt* <took, taken> ① (*accept*) *advice, bet, offer* annehmen; *credit card, criticism* akzeptieren; **to ~ sth badly** etw schlecht aufnehmen ② (*transport*) bringen; **to ~ sb to the train station** jdn zum Bahnhof fahren ③ (*seize*) nehmen; *power* ergreifen; *city* einnehmen; **to ~ sb by the hand/throat** jdn bei der Hand nehmen/am Kragen packen ④ (*win*) *championship* gewinnen ⑤ (*tolerate*) ertragen; *abuse, insults* hinnehmen ⑥ (*hold*) aufnehmen; **my car ~s five people** mein Auto hat Platz für fünf Leute ⑦ (*require*) erfordern; **I ~ [a] size five** [*or* **a size five shoe**] ich habe Schuhgröße fünf; ■**it ~s ...** man braucht ...; **hold on, it won't ~ long** warten Sie, es dauert nicht lange ⑧ (*receive*) *punch, title* erhalten, bekommen ⑨ (*remove*) [weg]nehmen; (*steal a.*) stehlen; *chess piece* schlagen; MATH (*subtract*) abziehen (**from** von +*dat*) ⑩ (*travel by*) nehmen; **to ~ the bus** mit dem Bus fahren ⑪ (*eat, consume*) zu sich *dat* nehmen; *medicine* einnehmen ⑫ (*engage in*) *break, nap, walk* machen; *bath* nehmen; *exam* schreiben; *notes* sich *dat* Notizen machen; *pictures* machen ⑬ (*feel*) **to ~ notice of sb/sth** jdn/etw beachten; **to ~ offense** beleidigt sein ⑭ (*assume to be*) **I ~ it [that] ...** ich nehme an, [dass] ... ⑮ (*order*) nehmen ▶ PHRASES: **to ~ sb by surprise** jdn überraschen; **what do you ~ me for?** wofür hältst du mich? **III.** *vi* <took, taken> (*have effect*) wirken; *dye* angenommen werden; *medicine* anschlagen

◆**take aback** *vt* (*surprise*) verblüffen; (*shock*) schockieren

◆**take after** *vi* ■**to ~ after sb** nach jdm kommen

◆**take along** *vt* mitnehmen

◆**take apart** *vt* ① (*disassemble*) ■**to ~ apart** ↔ **sth** etw auseinandernehmen ② (*fam: analyze critically*) auseinandernehmen

◆**take away** *vt* ① (*remove, deprive of*) [weg]nehmen; **to ~ away sb's fear** jdm die Angst nehmen ② (*lead away*) ■**to ~ away** ↔ **sb** jdn mitnehmen; *police* jdn abführen ▶ PHRASES: **to ~ sb's breath away** jdm den Atem verschlagen

◆**take back** *vt* ① (*retract*) zurücknehmen ② (*return*) [wieder] zurückbringen; **to ~ sb back [home]** jdn nach Hause bringen ③ (*repossess*) [sich *dat*] zurückholen; *territory* zurückerobern

◆**take down** *vt* ① (*write down*) [sich *dat*] notieren; *particulars* aufnehmen ② (*remove*) abnehmen; (*remove from higher position*) herunternehmen; *curtains, picture* abhängen ③ (*disassemble*) *tent* abschlagen; *scaffolding* abbauen

◆**take in** *vt* ① (*bring inside*) *person* hineinführen; *sth* hineinbringen ② (*accommodate*) aufnehmen; *child* zu sich *dat* nehmen ③ (*admit*) *hospital* aufnehmen; *university* zulassen ④ (*bring to police station*) festnehmen ⑤ (*deceive*) hereinlegen; ■**to be ~n in [by sb/sth]** sich [von jdm/etw] täuschen lassen ⑥ (*understand*) aufnehmen; **to ~ in a situation** eine Situation erfassen ⑦ FASHION enger machen

◆**take off I.** *vt* ① (*remove*) abnehmen; *clothes, gloves* ausziehen; *coat a.* ablegen; *hat* absetzen; ■**to ~ sth off sb** (*fam*) jdm etw wegnehmen ② (*bring away*) **he was ~n off to the hospital** er wurde ins Krankenhaus gebracht ③ (*subtract*) *points* abziehen **II.** *vi* ① (*leave the ground*) abheben ② (*fam: leave*) verschwinden; (*flee*) abhauen ③ (*have sudden success*) *idea, plan, project* ankommen; *product a.* einschlagen

◆**take on** *vt* ① (*agree to do*) *responsibility* auf sich *akk* nehmen; *work, job* annehmen ② (*employ*) einstellen ③ (*load*) *goods* laden; *passengers* aufnehmen

◆**take out** *vt* ① (*remove*) herausnehmen ② (*bring outside*) *trash* hinausbringen ③ (*invite*) ausführen; **to ~ sb out to [*or* for] dinner** jdn zum Abendessen einladen ④ (*obtain*) *insurance* abschließen; *loan* aufnehmen; *money* abheben ⑤ (*sl: kill*) beseitigen; (*destroy*) vernichten

◆**take over I.** *vt* (*seize control*) übernehmen; (*fig*) in Beschlag nehmen; *power* ergreifen **II.** *vi* (*assume responsibility*) ■**to ~ over [from sb]** jdn ablösen; **the night shift ~s over at 10 p.m.** die Nachtschicht übernimmt um 22.00 Uhr

◆**take to** *vi* ① (*start to like*) ■**to ~ to sb/sth** an jdm/etw Gefallen finden ② (*begin as a habit*) anfangen; ■**to ~ to doing sth** anfangen etw zu tun; **to ~ to drink** anfangen zu trinken ▶ PHRASES: **to ~ to sth like a duck to water** bei etw *dat* gleich in seinem Element sein

◆**take up I.** *vt* ① (*bring up*) hinaufbringen; *floorboards, carpet* herausreißen; (*shorten*) *skirt* kürzen ② (*start doing*) anfangen; *job* antreten ③ (*start to discuss*) ■**to ~ sth up with sb** etw mit jdm erörtern; **to ~ up a point** einen Punkt aufgreifen ④ (*accept*) *challenge, offer* annehmen; *opportunity* wahrnehmen ⑤ (*occupy*) **my job ~s up all my time** mein Beruf frisst meine ganze Zeit auf; **to ~ up room/space** Raum einnehmen **II.** *vi* (*start to associate with*) ■**to ~ up with sb** sich mit jdm einlassen *meist pej*

take-home 'pay *n* Nettoeinkommen *nt; of employee* Nettogehalt *nt; of worker* Nettolohn *m*

taken [ˈteɪ·kən] **I.** *vt, vi pp of* **take II.** *adj pred*

begeistert; ■**to be ~ with sb/sth** von jdm/etw angetan sein
'takeoff *n* ❶ AVIAT Start *m;* **to be ready for ~** startklar sein ❷ SPORTS Absprungstelle *f*
'take-out *n* ❶ (*food*) Essen *nt* zum Mitnehmen ❷ (*business*) Imbissbude *f*
'takeover *n* Übernahme *f*
taker ['teɪ·kər] *n* ❶ (*at betting*) Wettende(r) *f(m);* **any ~s?** wer nimmt die Wette an? ❷ (*at a sale*) Interessent(in) *m(f);* (*when buying*) Käufer(in) *m(f)*
taking ['teɪ·kɪŋ] **I.** *n* (*receipts*) ■**~s** *pl* Einnahmen *pl* ▸ PHRASES: **to be there for the ~** (*for free*) zum Mitnehmen sein; (*not settled*) [noch] offen sein **II.** *adj* einnehmend
talc [tælk], **talcum (powder)** ['tæl·kəm·(ˌpaʊ·dər)] *n* Talkpuder *m;* (*perfumed*) Körperpuder *m*
tale [teɪl] *n* ❶ (*story*) Geschichte *f;* LIT Erzählung *f;* (*true story*) Bericht *m;* **fairy ~** Märchen *nt* ❷ (*lie*) **a tall ~** [Lügen]Märchen *nt;* (*gossip*) Geschichte[n] *f[pl]* ▸ PHRASES: **to live to tell the ~** (*a. hum fam*) überleben
talent ['tæl·ənt] *n* ❶ (*natural ability*) Talent *nt,* Begabung *f* ❷ (*talented person*) Talent *nt;* **fresh ~** neue Talente *pl*
talented ['tæl·ən·t̬ɪd] *adj* begabt
Taliban ['tæ·li·bæn] *n* Taliban *f*
talisman <*pl* -s> ['tæl·ɪs·mən] *n* Talisman *m*
talk [tɔk] **I.** *n* ❶ (*discussion*) Gespräch *nt;* (*conversation*) Unterhaltung *f;* (*private*) Unterredung *f;* **to have a ~ with sb** mit jdm reden; (*conversation*) sich mit jdm unterhalten; (*formal discussions*) ■**~s** *pl* Gespräche *pl* ❷ (*lecture*) Vortrag *m* ❸ (*things said*) Worte *pl;* **idle ~** leeres Gerede **II.** *vi* (*speak*) sprechen, reden (**about** über *+akk,* **to** mit *+dat*); (*converse*) sich unterhalten; **to ~ to sb on the phone** mit jdm telefonieren ▸ PHRASES: **look who's ~ing** (*fam*) du hast es gerade nötig, etwas zu sagen **III.** *vt* (*fam: discuss*) **to ~ politics** über Politik sprechen ▸ PHRASES: **to ~ a blue streak** ohne Punkt und Komma reden *fam;* **~ about ...** so was von ... *fam*
◆**talk around I.** *vt* (*convince*) ■**to ~ sb around** jdn überreden ([**in**]**to** zu *+dat*) **II.** *vi* ■**to ~ around sth** um etw *akk* herumreden
◆**talk back** *vi* eine freche Antwort geben; **don't ~ back!** keine Widerrede!
◆**talk down** *vi* (*pej*) ■**to ~ down to sb** mit jdm herablassend reden
◆**talk out** *vt* ❶ (*be persuasive*) **to ~ one's way out of sth** sich aus etw *dat* herausreden ❷ (*convince not to*) ■**to ~ sb out of [doing] sth** jdm ausreden, etw *akk* zu tun
◆**talk over** *vt* durchsprechen
◆**talk through** *vt* ❶ (*discuss thoroughly*) durchsprechen ❷ (*reassure with talk*) ■**to ~ sb through sth** jdm bei etw *dat* gut zureden
talkative ['tɔk·ə·t̬ɪv] *adj* gesprächig, redselig
talker ['tɔk·ər] *n* (*person who speaks*) Sprechende(r) *f(m);* (*talkative person*) Schwätzer(in) *m(f) pej*
talking ['tɔk·ɪŋ] **I.** *adj* sprechend **II.** *n* Sprechen *nt;* **"no ~, please!"** „Ruhe bitte!"
'talk show *n* Talkshow *f*
tall [tɔl] *adj* ❶ (*high*) *building, fence, grass, ladder, tree* hoch; *person* groß; **to be six feet ~** 1,83 m groß sein; **to grow ~** groß werden ❷ (*long*) *rod, stick, stalk* lang ❸ (*fig: considerable*) *amount, price* ziemlich hoch
tallness ['tɔl·nɪs] *n of person* Größe *f; of building, plant* Höhe *f; of stick* Länge *f*
tallow ['tæl·oʊ] *n* Talg *m*
tally <-ie-> ['tæl·i] **I.** *vi figures, statements, signatures* übereinstimmen (**with** mit *+dat*) **II.** *vt* COMM ❶ (*count*) ■**to ~ sth** ○ [**up**] *amounts, totals* etw zusammenzählen ❷ (*check off*) *goods, items* nachzählen; SPORTS *points, score* notieren **III.** *n usu sing* ❶ (*list for goods*) Stückliste *f;* (*for single item*) [Zähl]strich *m* ❷ (*count*) [zahlenmäßige] Aufstellung; **to keep a ~** eine [Strich]liste führen
talon ['tæl·ən] *n* ORN (*claw*) Klaue *f*
tambourine [ˌtæm·bə·'rin] *n* Tamburin *nt*
tame [teɪm] **I.** *adj* ❶ (*domesticated*) zahm; (*harmless*) friedlich ❷ (*unexciting*) *book, joke, person* lahm; *criticism, report* zahm **II.** *vt* (*a. fig*) *person, river, animal* zähmen, bändigen; *anger, curiosity, hunger* bezähmen; *impatience, passion* zügeln
tamer ['teɪ·mər] *n* Tierbändiger(in) *m(f)*
tamp [tæmp] *vt* ❶ (*fill*) [zu]stopfen; *pipe* stopfen ❷ (*compact*) ■**to ~ sth** [**down**] etw [fest]stampfen; *tobacco* festklopfen
tamper ['tæm·pər] *vi* ■**to ~ with sth** ❶ (*handle improperly*) herummachen *fam* (an *+dat*) ❷ (*manipulate*) etw [in betrügerischer Absicht] verändern
'tamper-resistant *adj* Sicherheits-; **~ cap** Sicherheitsverschluss *m*
tampon ['tæm·pan] *n* Tampon *m*
tan [tæn] **I.** *vi* <-nn-> braun werden **II.** *vt* <-nn-> ❶ (*make brown*) bräunen; **to be ~ned** braun gebrannt sein ❷ CHEM (*convert*) *hides, leather* gerben **III.** *n* ❶ (*brown color of skin*) [Sonnen]bräune *f* ❷ (*light brown*) Gelbbraun *nt* **IV.** *adj clothing, shoes* gelbbraun
tandem ['tæn·dəm] *n* (*bicycle*) Tandem *nt*
tang [tæŋ] *n* (*smell*) [scharfer] Geruch; (*taste*) [scharfer] Geschmack
tangent ['tæn·dʒənt] *n* MATH Tangente *f* ▸ PHRASES: **to fly** [*or* **go**] **off on a ~** [plötzlich] das Thema wechseln
tangential [tæn·'dʒen·ʃəl] *adj* nebensächlich
tangerine [ˌtæn·dʒə·'rin] **I.** *n* Mandarine *f* **II.** *adj* orangerot
tangible ['tæn·dʒə·bəl] *adj* ❶ (*a. fig: perceptible*) fassbar, greifbar, fühlbar, spürbar ❷ (*real*) real; *advantage* echt; **to have ~ evidence** handfeste Beweise haben
tangle ['tæŋ·gəl] **I.** *n* ❶ (*a. fig, pej: mass*) *of hair, wool* [wirres] Knäuel; *of branches, roads, wires* Gewirr *nt* ❷ (*a. fig, pej: confusion*) Durcheinander *nt;* **to get into a ~** sich verfangen **II.** *vt* (*a. fig, pej*) durcheinanderbringen;

T

threads verwickeln **III.** *vi* (*a. fig, pej: knot up*) *hair, wool* verfilzen; *threads, wires* sich verwickeln

◆**tangle up I.** *vt* (*a. fig*) ■**to ~ up** ⊂ **sth** etw durcheinanderbringen **II.** *vi* (*a. fig*) *hair, wool* verfilzen; *threads, wires* sich *akk* verwickeln; *animal, person* sich *akk* verfangen

tango ['tæŋ·goʊ] **I.** *n* Tango *m* **II.** *vi* Tango tanzen

tangy ['tæŋ·i] *adj taste* scharf; *smell* durchdringend

tank [tæŋk] *n* ❶ (*container*) Tank *m;* **fish ~** Aquarium *nt* ❷ MIL Panzer *m*

tanked up [tæŋkt·'ʌp] *adj pred,* '**tanked-up** *adj attr* (*sl*) besoffen

tanker ['tæŋ·kər] *n* ❶ (*ship*) Tanker *m* ❷ (*truck*) Tankwagen *m*

tanned [tænd] *adj* ❶ *skin* braun [gebrannt] ❷ *hides, leather* gegerbt

tannin ['tæn·ɪn] *n* Tannin *nt*

tanning ['tæn·ɪŋ] *n* ❶ *of skin* Bräunen *nt* ❷ *of hides, leather* Gerben *nt*

'**tanning bed** *n* Sonnenbank *f*

tantalize ['tæn·ţə·laɪz] **I.** *vt* ❶ (*excite*) reizen; (*fascinate*) in den Bann ziehen ❷ (*keep in suspense*) auf die Folter spannen **II.** *vi* (*excite*) reizen

tantalizing ['tæn·ţə·laɪ·zɪŋ] *adj* (*enticing*) verlockend; *smile* verführerisch

tantamount ['tæn·tə·maʊnt] *adj* ■**to be ~ to sth** mit etw *dat* gleichbedeutend sein

tantrum ['tæn·trəm] *n* Wutanfall *m;* **to throw a ~** einen Wutanfall bekommen

Tanzania [ˌtæn·zə·'ni·ə] *n* Tansania *nt*

tap¹ [tæp] **I.** *n* ❶ (*light hit*) [leichter] Schlag ❷ (*tap-dancing*) Stepp[tanz] *m* **II.** *vt* <-pp-> (*strike lightly*) [leicht] klopfen; **to ~ sb on the shoulder** jdm auf die Schulter tippen **III.** *vi* <-pp-> [leicht] klopfen

tap² [tæp] **I.** *n* ❶ (*outlet*) Hahn *m;* **to be on ~** (*fig*) [sofort] verfügbar sein ❷ TELEC Abhörgerät *nt* **II.** *vt* <-pp-> ❶ (*intercept*) abhören ❷ (*make available*) *energy,* [*re*]*sources* erschließen ❸ (*let out*) [ab]zapfen; *barrel* anstechen; *beer* zapfen **III.** *vi* (*fam: gain access*) vorstoßen; **to ~ into new markets** neue Märkte erschließen

'**tap dance I.** *n* Stepptanz *m* **II.** *vi* steppen, Stepp tanzen

tape [teɪp] **I.** *n* ❶ (*strip*) Band *nt;* SPORTS (*at finish*) Zielband *nt;* (*for measuring*) Maßband *nt;* (*adhesive*) Klebeband *nt;* **masking ~** Abdeckband *nt;* **Scotch ~**® Tesafilm® *m,* Tixo® *nt* ÖSTERR ❷ (*for recording*) [Ton-/Magnet]band *nt;* **audio ~** Audiokassette *f* **II.** *vt* ❶ (*fasten*) **she ~d a note to the door** sie heftete eine Nachricht an die Tür ❷ (*record*) aufnehmen

'**tape deck** *n* Tapedeck *nt*

'**tape measure** *n* Maßband *nt*

taper ['teɪ·pər] **I.** *n* ❶ (*candle*) [spitz zulaufende] Wachskerze; (*wax-coated strip*) wachsüberzogener Span ❷ *of spire* Verjüngung *f* **II.** *vt column, spire* verjüngen; *hair* spitz zuschneiden **III.** *vi column, spire* sich verjüngen (**into** zu +*dat*); *hair* spitz zulaufen

◆**taper off I.** *vt* (*fig*) *production, series* auslaufen lassen; *enthusiasm, interest* abklingen lassen **II.** *vi* ❶ (*become pointed*) sich verjüngen (**into** zu +*dat*) ❷ (*decrease*) [allmählich] abnehmen; *interest* nachlassen

'**tape-record** *vt* [auf Band] aufnehmen

'**tape recorder** *n* Tonbandgerät *nt*

'**tape recording** *n* Tonbandaufnahme *f*

tapestry ['tæp·əs·tri] *n* ❶ (*fabric*) Gobelingewebe *nt;* (*for furniture*) Dekorationsstoff *m* ❷ (*wall hanging*) Gobelin *m*

'**tapeworm** *n* Bandwurm *m*

'**tap water** *n* Leitungswasser *nt*

tar [tar] **I.** *n* ❶ (*for paving*) Teer *m,* Asphalt *m* ❷ (*in cigarettes*) Teer *m* **II.** *vt* <-rr-> (*pave*) teeren ▶ PHRASES: **to be ~red with the same brush** (*pej*) um kein Haar besser sein

tarantula [tə·'ræn·tʃə·lə] *n* Tarantel *f*

tardy ['tar·di] *adj* ❶ (*late*) unpünktlich; (*overdue*) verspätet ❷ (*sluggish*) langsam; *progress* schleppend

tare [ter] *n* Leergewicht *nt*

target ['tar·gɪt] **I.** *n* ❶ (*mark aimed at*) *a.* MIL Ziel *nt;* ■**to be on ~** auf [Ziel]kurs liegen; *analysis, description* zutreffen; **to hit the ~** ins Schwarze treffen ❷ ECON (*goal*) Zielsetzung *f,* [Plan]ziel *nt;* ■**to be on ~** im Zeitplan liegen; **to set oneself a ~** sich *dat* ein Ziel setzen **II.** *vt* <-t-> (*address, direct*) [ab]zielen (**at** auf +*akk*), sich richten (**at** an +*akk*) **III.** *adj customer, market, group* Ziel-; *profit* angestrebt

'**target language** *n* Zielsprache *f*

'**target practice** *n* MIL Übungsschießen *nt,* Zielschießen *nt*

'**target range** *n* Zielentfernung *f*

tariff ['tær·ɪf] *n* ❶ ECON, LAW (*table of customs duties*) Zolltarif *m;* (*customs*) Zoll *m kein pl* ❷ (*form: fee schedule*) Preisliste *f*

tarmac ['tar·mæk] *n* ■**the ~** AVIAT das Rollfeld

tarnish ['tar·nɪʃ] **I.** *vi* ❶ (*dull*) *metal* stumpf werden; (*discolor*) anlaufen ❷ (*fig, pej: lose shine*) an Glanz verlieren; (*lose purity*) *honor, reputation* beschmutzt werden **II.** *vt* ❶ (*dull*) *metals* trüben; (*discolor*) anlaufen lassen ❷ (*fig, pej*) *success* den Glanz nehmen; *reputation* beflecken **III.** *n* ❶ (*coating*) Belag *m* ❷ (*fig, pej: loss of shine*) Glanzlosigkeit *m;* (*loss of purity*) Makel *m*

tarpaulin [tar·'pɔ·lɪn] *n* ❶ (*fabric*) [wasserdichtes] geteertes Leinwandgewebe ❷ (*covering*) [Abdeck]plane *f*

tarragon ['tær·ə·gan] *n* Estragon *m*

tart¹ [tart] *adj* ❶ (*sharp*) *sauce, soup* scharf; *apples, grapes* sauer ❷ (*cutting*) scharf; *irony* beißend; *remark* bissig

tart² [tart] *n* ❶ FOOD [Obst]törtchen *nt;* **jam ~** Marmeladentörtchen *nt* ❷ (*usu pej: promiscuous female*) Schlampe *f*

tartan ['tar·tən] *n* (*pattern*) Schottenkaro *nt*

tartar ['tar·ţər] *n* ❶ MED (*on teeth*) Zahn-

stein *m* ② CHEM Weinstein *m*
Tartar ['tar·t̬ər] *n* (*person*) Tatar(in) *m(f)*; (*language*) Tatarisch *nt*
'**tartar sauce** *n* Remouladensoße *f*
task [tæsk] *n* (*work*) Aufgabe *f* ▶ PHRASES: **to take sb to ~** jdn zur Rede stellen
'**task force** *n* ① MIL Eingreiftruppe *f*; *in police* Spezialeinheit *f* ② (*group of people*) Arbeitsgruppe *f*
'**taskmaster** *n* [strenger] Vorgesetzter; **to be a hard ~** ein strenger Meister sein
Tasmania [tæz·'meɪ·ni·ə] *n* Tasmanien *nt*
Tasmanian [tæz·'meɪ·ni·ən] **I.** *n* (*person*) Tasmanier(in) *m(f)* **II.** *adj* (*of Tasmania*) tasmanisch
tassel ['tæs·əl] *n* (*on caps, curtains, cushions*) Quaste *f*; (*on carpets, cloths, skirts*) Franse *f*
taste [teɪst] **I.** *n* ① (*flavor, aesthetic quality, discernment*) Geschmack *m*; **sense of ~** Geschmackssinn *m*; **to be in poor ~** geschmacklos sein ② (*liking*) Vorliebe *f*; **to acquire a ~ for sth** an etw *dat* Geschmack finden ③ (*short encounter*) Kostprobe *f*; **to have a ~ of sth** einen Vorgeschmack von etw *dat* bekommen **II.** *vt* ① (*perceive flavor*) schmecken; (*test*) probieren ② (*experience briefly*) *luxury, success* [einmal] erleben **III.** *vi* schmecken (**of** nach +*dat*); **to ~ sweet** süß schmecken
'**taste bud** *n* ANAT Geschmacksknospe *f*
tasteful ['teɪst·fəl] *adj* geschmackvoll, stilvoll
tasteless ['teɪst·lɪs] *adj* ① (*without physical taste*) geschmacksneutral; (*unappetizing*) *food* fad[e]; *beer, wine* schal ② (*pej: unstylish, offensive*) geschmacklos
taster ['teɪ·stər] *n* ① (*quality expert*) Koster(in) *m(f)* ② (*sample*) Kostprobe *f*
tasty ['teɪ·sti] *adj* (*appetizing*) lecker, schmackhaft
tatter ['tæ·t̬ər] *n usu pl* ① (*pej*) *of cloth, a flag* Fetzen *m*; ■**to be in ~s** zerfetzt sein; (*fig*) *reputation* ruiniert sein ② (*pej: clothing*) ■**~s** abgerissene Kleidung
tattered ['tæt̬·ərd] *adj clothing* zerlumpt; *cloth, flag* zerrissen; *reputation* ramponiert
tattle ['tæt̬·əl] *vi* (*esp childspeak*) ■**to ~ on sb** jdn verpetzen
tattler ['tæt̬·lər] *n* ① (*gossip*) Klatschmaul *nt* ② (*fam: informer*) Petzer(in) *m(f)*
tattoo [tæ·'tu] **I.** *n* Tattoo *m o nt*, Tätowierung *f* **II.** *vt* tätowieren
tatty ['tæt̬·i] *adj* (*pej: showing wear*) zerfleddert; *book a.* abgegriffen; *clothing* zerschlissen
taught [tɔt] *pt, pp of* **teach**
taunt [tɔnt] **I.** *vt* ① (*mock*) verspotten, hänseln (**about** wegen +*gen*) ② (*provoke*) sticheln (gegen +*akk*) **II.** *n* spöttische Bemerkung; (*tease*) Hänselei *f*; (*provocation*) Stichelei *f*
Taurus ['tɔr·əs] *n* ASTROL Stier *m*
taut [tɔt] *adj* ① (*tight*) *rope* straff [gespannt]; *muscle, skin* gespannt; *rubber band* stramm ② (*pej: tense*) *expression, face, nerves* angespannt
tautology [tɔ·'tal·ə·dʒi] *n* Doppelaussage *f*, Tautologie *f fachspr*
tavern ['tæv·ərn] *n* (*old*) Schenke *f*, Bar *f*
tawdry ['tɔ·dri] *adj* (*pej*) ① (*gaudy*) protzig ② (*cheap*) geschmacklos
tawny ['tɔ·ni] *adj* lohfarben, gelbbraun
tax [tæks] **I.** *n* <*pl* -es> ① (*levy*) Steuer *f*; **income ~** Einkommenssteuer *f*; **to impose a ~ on sth** etw besteuern ② (*burden*) Belastung *f* (**on** für +*akk*); (*on patience, resources, time*) Beanspruchung *f* (**on** +*gen*) **II.** *vt* ① (*levy*) besteuern; **to be ~ed [heavily]** [hoch] besteuert werden ② (*burden*) belasten; (*make demands*) beanspruchen; (*confront*) beschuldigen (**with** +*gen*)
taxable ['tæk·sə·bəl] *adj* steuerpflichtig
taxation [tæk·'seɪ·ʃən] *n* ① (*levying*) Besteuerung *f* ② (*money obtained*) Steuereinnahmen *pl*
'**tax avoidance** *n* [legale] Steuerumgehung
'**tax bracket** *n* Steuerklasse *f*
'**tax collector** *n* Steuerbeamte(r), -beamtin *m, f*
tax-de'ductible *adj* steuerlich absetzbar
'**tax dodger** *n* (*fam*), '**tax evader** *n* Steuerhinterzieher(in) *m(f)*
'**tax evasion** *n* Steuerhinterziehung *f*
'**tax-exempt** *adj* FIN von der Mehrwertsteuer befreit
'**tax exemption** *n* FIN Steuerbefreiung *f*, Freibetrag *m*
tax-'free *adj* steuerfrei
'**tax haven** *n* Steueroase *f*
taxi ['tæk·si] **I.** *n* Taxi *nt* **II.** *vi* AVIAT (*move*) rollen
taxidermist ['tæk·sɪ·ˌdɜr·mɪst] *n* [Tier]präparator(in) *m(f)*
taxidermy ['tæk·sɪ·ˌdɜr·mi] *n* Taxidermie *f*
'**taxi driver** *n* Taxifahrer(in) *m(f)*
taxing ['tæk·sɪŋ] *adj* ① (*burdensome*) anstrengend ② (*hard*) schwierig
'**taxi stand** *n* Taxistand *m*
'**taxman** *n* Finanzbeamte(r), -beamtin *m, f*; ■**the ~** das Finanzamt
'**taxpayer** *n* Steuerzahler(in) *m(f)*
'**tax rebate** *n* Steuernachlass *m*
'**tax relief** *n* Steuervergünstigung *f*
'**tax return** *n* Steuererklärung *f*
'**tax revenue** *n* Steueraufkommen *nt*
TB [ˌti·'bi] *n* MED *abbrev of* **tuberculosis** TB
tbsp. <*pl* -> *n abbrev of* **tablespoon** Essl., EL
tea [ti] *n* (*drink*) Tee *m* ▶ PHRASES: **to [not] be sb's cup of ~** [nicht] jds Fall sein
'**tea bag** *n* Teebeutel *m*
teach <taught, taught> [titʃ] **I.** *vt* ① (*impart knowledge*) unterrichten; ■**to ~ sb sth** [*or* **to ~ sth to sb**] jdm etw beibringen; **to ~ history** Geschichte unterrichten; **to ~ school** Lehrer(in) *m(f)* sein ② (*show*) **this has taught him a lot** daraus hat er viel gelernt; **to ~ sb a lesson** jdm eine Lehre erteilen **II.** *vi* unterrichten
teacher ['ti·tʃər] *n* Lehrer(in) *m(f)*
teacher 'training *n* Lehrerausbildung *f*
teacher 'training college, 'teachers' col-

T

lege *n* pädagogische Hochschule

teaching ['ti·tʃɪŋ] **I.** *n* ❶ (*imparting knowledge*) Unterrichten *nt* ❷ (*profession*) Lehrberuf *m* **II.** *adj aids, methods* Lehr-, Unterrichts-

'teacup *n* Teetasse *f*

teak [tik] *n* ❶ (*wood*) Teak[holz] *nt* ❷ (*tree*) Teakbaum *m*

team [tim] **I.** *n* ❶ (*group of people*) Team *nt; a.* SPORTS Mannschaft *f;* **research ~** Forschungsgruppe *f* ❷ (*harnessed animals*) Gespann *nt* **II.** *vi* ❶ (*fam: gather*) ein Team bilden ❷ (*join*) sich [in eine Gruppe] einfügen

◆**team up** *vi* ❶ (*gather*) ein Team bilden (**with** mit + *dat*) ❷ (*join*) sich [in eine Gruppe] einfügen

team 'captain *n* Mannschaftskapitän *m*

team 'effort *n* Teamarbeit *f*

'teammate *n* Mitspieler(in) *m(f)*

team 'player *n* Teamplayer(in) *m(f)*

team 'spirit *n* Teamgeist *m*

'teamwork *n* Teamarbeit *f*

'teapot *n* Teekanne *f*

tear[1] [ter] **I.** *n* Riss *m* **II.** *vt* <tore, torn> ❶ (*rip*) zerreißen ❷ (*injure*) **to ~ a muscle** sich *dat* einen Muskelriss zuziehen **III.** *vi* <tore, torn> ❶ (*rip*) *fabric, paper* [zer]reißen; *buttonhole, lining* ausreißen ❷ (*fam: rush*) rasen; ■**to ~ away** losrasen

◆**tear apart** *vt* ❶ *fabric, paper* zerreißen ❷ *article, book, play* verreißen

◆**tear away** *vt* ❶ (*make leave*) ■**to ~ sb** ↔ **away** jdn wegreißen; ■**to ~ oneself away** sich losreißen ❷ (*rip from*) ■**to ~ sth** ↔ **away** *page of calendar, poster* etw abreißen

◆**tear down** *vt* abreißen

◆**tear into** *vi* heftig kritisieren

◆**tear off** *vt* ❶ (*rip from*) abreißen ❷ (*undress*) **to ~ off one's clothes** sich *dat* die Kleider vom Leib reißen

◆**tear out** *vt hair, nail* ausreißen; *page* herausreißen

◆**tear up** *vt* ❶ (*rip, annul*) zerreißen ❷ (*destroy*) kaputtmachen *fam; sidewalk, road* aufreißen

tear[2] [tɪr] *n* (*watery fluid*) Träne *f;* ■**to be in ~s** weinen; **~s of joy** Freudentränen *pl;* **to burst into ~s** in Tränen ausbrechen

teardrop ['tɪr·drap] *n* Träne *f*

tearful ['tɪr·fəl] *adj* ❶ (*inclined to cry*) den Tränen nah *präd;* (*crying*) weinerlich *pej* ❷ *farewell, reunion* tränenreich

'tear gas *n* Tränengas *nt*

'tearjerker *n* (*fam: film*) Schnulze *f*

tease [tiz] **I.** *n* Quälgeist *m fam;* (*playfully*) neckische Person; (*pej: erotic arouser*) Aufreißer(in) *m(f)* **II.** *vt* ❶ (*make fun of*) aufziehen; (*playfully*) necken ❷ (*provoke*) provozieren

teaser ['ti·zər] *n* ❶ (*person*) neckische Person ❷ (*riddle*) harte Nuss *fam*

'tea service, 'tea set *n* Teeservice *nt*

'teaspoon *n* Teelöffel *m*

'teaspoonful *n* Teelöffelvoll *m*

teat [tit] *n* (*on animal*) Zitze *f*

technical ['tek·nɪ·kəl] *adj* ❶ (*concerning applied science, technique*) technisch ❷ (*detailed*) Fach-; **~ term** Fachausdruck *m*

'technical college *n* technische Hochschule

technicality [ˌtek·nə·'kæl·ɪ·t̬i] *n* LAW ❶ (*unimportant detail*) Formsache *f* ❷ (*confusing triviality*) unnötiges Detail

'technical school *n* Technikum *nt*

technician [tek·'nɪʃ·ən] *n* Techniker(in) *m(f)*

technique [tek·'nik] *n* Technik *f,* Verfahren *nt;* (*method*) Methode *f*

technological [ˌtek·nə·'ladʒ·ɪ·kəl] *adj* technologisch

technology [tek·'nal·ə·dʒi] *n* Technologie *f,* Technik *f;* **computer ~** Computertechnik *f;* **modern ~** moderne Technologie

teddy ['ted·i] *n* ❶ (*teddy bear*) Teddybär *m* ❷ (*female undergarment*) Body *m*

'teddy bear *n* Teddybär *m*

tedious ['ti·di·əs] *adj* langweilig; *job a.* öde; *conversation* zäh

tediousness ['ti·di·əs·nɪs] *n* Langweiligkeit *f*

tedium ['ti·di·əm] *n* Langeweile *f*

tee [ti] *n* (*in golf*) Tee *nt*

◆**tee off I.** *vi* (*in golf*) abschlagen **II.** *vt* (*fam*) verärgern; **to get ~d off** sauer werden *fam*

teem [tim] *vi* ■**to ~ with sth** von etw *dat* wimmeln

teeming ['tim·ɪŋ] *adj place, streets* überfüllt, von Menschen wimmelnd

teen [tin] *n* Teenager *m*

teenage(d) ['tin·eɪdʒ(d)] *adj attr* (*characteristic of a teenager*) jugendlich; (*sb who is a teenager*) im Teenageralter *nach n*

teenager ['tin·eɪ·dʒər] *n* Teenager *m*

teens [tinz] *npl* Jugendjahre *pl*

teensy, teensy-weensy [ˌtin·si·'win·si], **teeny, teeny-weeny** [ˌti·ni·'wi·ni] *adj* (*fam*) klitzeklein

tee shirt ['ti·ʃɜrt] *n* T-Shirt *nt*

teeter ['ti·t̬ər] *vi + adv/prep* taumeln; **to ~ on the brink of a disaster** (*fig*) sich am Rande einer Katastrophe bewegen

teeth [tiθ] *npl pl of* **tooth** ▶ PHRASES: **in the ~ of sth** (*against*) angesichts einer S. *gen;* (*despite*) trotz einer S. *gen*

teethe [tið] *vi* zahnen

teetotaler [ˌti·'toʊ·t̬əl·ər] *n* Abstinenzler(in) *m(f)*

tel. *n abbrev of* **telephone number** Tel.

telecast ['tel·ɪ·kæst] *n* TV-Sendung *f*

telecommunications ['tel·ɪ·kə·ˌmju·nɪ·'keɪ·ʃənz] *npl + sing vb* Fernmeldewesen *nt kein pl*

telecommuting ['tel·ɪ·kə·ˌmju·t̬ɪŋ] *n* COMPUT Telearbeit *f*

telegenic [ˌtel·ə·'dʒen·ɪk] *adj* telegen

telegram ['tel·ɪ·græm] *n* Telegramm *nt*

telegraph ['tel·ɪ·græf] **I.** *n* Telegraf *m* **II.** *vt* ❶ (*send by telegraph*) telegrafieren ❷ (*inform by telegraph*) telegrafisch benachrichtigen ❸ (*make known*) *feelings* offenlegen; *action* bekannt machen

telemarketing ['tel·ɪ·ˌmar·kə·t̬ɪŋ] *npl* Telefonmarketing *nt kein pl*

telepathic [ˌtel·ə·ˈpæθ·ɪk] *adj* telepathisch

telepathy [tə·ˈlep·ə·θi] *n* Telepathie *f*

telephone [ˈtel·ə·foʊn] **I.** *n* ❶ (*device*) Telefon *nt;* **cell[ular]** ~ Handy *nt,* Mobiltelefon *nt* ❷ (*system*) ■ **by** ~ telefonisch **II.** *vt* anrufen **III.** *vi* telefonieren

ˈ**telephone book** *n* Telefonbuch *nt*

ˈ**telephone booth** *n* Telefonzelle *f*

ˈ**telephone call** *n* Telefonanruf *m*

ˈ**telephone directory** *n* Telefonverzeichnis *nt*

ˈ**telephone number** *n* Telefonnummer *f*

ˈ**telephone operator** *n* Vermittlung *f*

ˈ**telephone pole** *n* Telefonmast *m*

telephoto ˈ**lens** [ˌtel·ə·foʊ·t̬oʊ·ˈ-] *n* Teleobjektiv *nt*

TelePrompTer® [ˈtel·ə·ˌpramp·tər] *n* Teleprompter *m fachspr*

telescope [ˈtel·ə·skoʊp] **I.** *n* Teleskop *nt* **II.** *vt* ineinanderschieben **III.** *vi* sich ineinanderschieben

telescopic [ˌtel·ə·ˈskap·ɪk] *adj* ❶ (*done by telescope*) ~ **observation** Teleskopbeobachtung *f* ❷ (*concerning telescopes*) ~ **lens** Teleobjektiv *nt* ❸ (*folding into each other*) Teleskop-; (*automatic*) ausfahrbar; *ladder* ausziehbar

telethon [ˈtelɪ·θan] *n ausgedehnte Wohltätigkeitsveranstaltung im Fernsehen*

televangelist [ˌtel·ɪ·ˈvæn·dʒə·lɪst] *n* Fernsehprediger(in) *m(f)*

televise [ˈtel·ə·vaɪz] *vt* [im Fernsehen] übertragen

television [ˈtel·ə·vɪʒ·ən] *n* ❶ (*device*) Fernsehgerät *nt,* Fernseher *m fam* ❷ (*TV broadcasting*) Fernsehen *nt;* ■ **on** ~ im Fernsehen

television ˈ**camera** *n* Fernsehkamera *f*

television ˈ**program** *n* Fernsehprogramm *nt*

ˈ**television set** *n* Fernsehapparat *m,* Fernseher *m*

television ˈ**studio** *n* Fernsehstudio *nt*

telex [ˈtel·eks] *n* <*pl* -es> Telex *nt;* (*device a.*) Fernschreiber *m*

tell [tel] **I.** *vt* <told, told> ❶ (*say, communicate*) sagen; (*relate*) *account, joke, story* erzählen (**about** von +*dat*); **to ~ a lie** lügen; **can you ~ me the way to the train station?** können Sie mir sagen, wie ich zum Bahnhof komme? ❷ (*discern*) erkennen; (*notice*) [be]merken; (*know*) wissen; (*determine*) feststellen; **to ~ right from wrong** Recht und Unrecht unterscheiden; **to ~ [the] time** die Uhr lesen **II.** *vi* <told, told> ❶ (*inform*) ■ **to ~ [on sb]** jdn verraten ❷ (*have an effect or impact*) sich bemerkbar machen; *blow, punch, word* sitzen

◆**tell apart** *vt* auseinanderhalten

◆**tell off** *vt* (*reprimand*) ausschimpfen (**about/for** wegen +*gen*)

teller [ˈtel·ər] *n* ❶ (*person who tells*) Erzähler(in) *m(f)* ❷ (*bank employee*) Kassierer(in) *m(f)*

telling [ˈtel·ɪŋ] *adj* (*revealing*) aufschlussreich; (*effective*) wirkungsvoll

telltale [ˈtel·teɪl] *adj* verräterisch

temerity [tə·ˈmer·ɪ·t̬i] *n* (*form: boldness*) Kühnheit *f*

temp [temp] (*fam*) **I.** *n* (*temporary employee*) Gelegenheitsarbeiter(in) *m(f)* **II.** *vi* aushilfsweise arbeiten, jobben *fam*

temp. [temp] *n abbrev of* **temperature** Temp.

temper [ˈtem·pər] **I.** *n* ❶ *usu sing* (*state of mind*) Laune *f* ❷ (*composure*) **to lose one's ~** die Geduld verlieren ❸ (*predisposition to anger*) Reizbarkeit *f kein pl;* (*angry state*) Wut *f kein pl* ❹ *usu sing* (*characteristic quality*) Naturell *nt;* **she has a very sweet ~** sie hat ein sehr sanftes Wesen **II.** *vt* ❶ (*form: mitigate*) ausgleichen (**with** durch +*akk*); *enthusiasm* zügeln ❷ (*make hard*) härten; *iron* glühfrischen

temperament [ˈtem·prə·mənt] *n* ❶ (*disposition*) Temperament *nt;* **to have an artistic ~** eine Künstlerseele sein ❷ (*pej: predisposition to anger*) **fit of ~** Temperamentsausbruch *m;* (*more anger-filled*) Wutanfall *m*

temperamental [ˌtem·prə·ˈmen·təl] *adj* launisch

temperance [ˈtem·pər·əns] *n* (*form: abstinence from alcohol*) Abstinenz *f*

temperate [ˈtem·pər·ɪt] *adj* (*mild*) *climate, zone* gemäßigt

temperature [ˈtem·pər·ə·tʃər] *n* Temperatur *f;* **to have a ~** Fieber haben

tempest [ˈtem·pɪst] *n* Sturm *m*

tempestuous [tem·ˈpes·tʃu·əs] *adj* ❶ (*liter: very stormy*) stürmisch ❷ (*turbulent*) turbulent

template [ˈtem·plɪt] *n* Schablone *f;* **to serve as a ~ for sth** (*fig*) als Muster für etw *akk* dienen

temple¹ [ˈtem·pəl] *n* (*place of worship*) Tempel *m*

temple² [ˈtem·pəl] *n* (*part of head*) Schläfe *f*

tempo <*pl* -s *or* -pi> [ˈtem·poʊ] *n* MUS Tempo *nt;* **change in ~** Tempowechsel *m*

temporarily [ˈtem·pə·rer·ə·li] *adv* vorübergehend

temporary [ˈtem·pə·rer·i] *adj* (*not permanent*) vorübergehend; (*with specific limit*) befristet; ~ **staff** Aushilfspersonal *nt*

tempt [tempt] *vt* ❶ (*entice*) in Versuchung führen; ■ **to be ~ed** schwach werden; ■ **to ~ sb into doing** [*or* **to do**] **sth** jdn dazu verleiten, etw zu tun ❷ (*attract*) reizen ▶ PHRASES: **to ~ fate** das Schicksal herausfordern

temptation [temp·ˈteɪ·ʃən] *n* ❶ (*enticement*) Versuchung *f;* **to resist the ~ [to do sth]** der Versuchung widerstehen[, etw zu tun] ❷ (*sth tempting*) Verlockung *f*

tempting [ˈtemp·tɪŋ] *adj* verführerisch; *offer a.* verlockend

ten [ten] **I.** *adj* zehn; *see also* **eight** **II.** *n* Zehn *f;* ~**s of thousands** zehntausende; *see also* **eight**

tenable [ˈten·ə·bəl] *adj* (*defendable*) *approach* vertretbar; *argument* haltbar

tenacious [tə·ˈneɪ·ʃəs] *adj* ❶ (*tight*) *grip* fest

T

❷ (*persistent*) *person, legend, theory* hartnäckig; *person a.* beharrlich

tenacity [tə·'næs·ɪ·t̬i] *n* Beharrlichkeit *f*

tenancy ['ten·ən·si] *n* ❶ (*status concerning lease*) Pachtverhältnis *nt;* (*rented lodgings*) Mietverhältnis *nt* ❷ (*duration of lease*) Pachtvertrag *m;* (*of rented lodgings*) Mietvertrag *m*

tenant ['ten·ənt] *n of rented lodgings* Mieter(in) *m(f); of leasehold* Pächter(in) *m(f)*

tenant 'farmer *n* [Klein]pächter(in) *m(f)*

tend¹ [tend] *vi* ❶ (*incline*) ■ **to ~ to[ward] sth** zu etw *dat* neigen; **he ~s to come early** er kommt meistens früh ❷ (*be directed toward*) tendieren; **to ~ upwards** eine Tendenz nach oben aufweisen

tend² [tend] *vt* sich kümmern (um +*akk*); **to ~ an accident victim** dem Opfer eines Verkehrsunfalls Hilfe leisten

◆**tend to** *vi* sich kümmern um +*akk*

tendency ['ten·dən·si] *n* Tendenz *f;* (*inclination*) Neigung *f;* (*trend*) Trend *m* (**to[ward]** zu +*dat*); ■ **to have a ~ to[ward] sth** zu etw *dat* neigen; **hereditary ~** erbliche Veranlagung

tender¹ ['ten·dər] *adj* ❶ (*not tough*) *meat, vegetable* zart ❷ (*easily hurt*) *skin, plants* zart; (*sensitive to pain*) *part of body* [schmerz]empfindlich ❸ (*affectionate*) zärtlich; *heart* weich

tender² ['ten·dər] **I.** *n* (*price quote*) Angebot *nt* **II.** *vt* **to ~ one's resignation** die Kündigung einreichen; (*from office*) seinen Rücktritt anbieten

tender'hearted *adj* weichherzig

tenderize ['ten·də·raɪz] *vt* zart machen

tenderizer ['ten·də·raɪ·zər] *n* Weichmacher *m*

tenderloin ['ten·dər·lɔɪn] *n* Filet *nt,* Lendenstück *nt*

tenderly ['ten·dər·li] *adv* zärtlich; (*lovingly*) liebevoll

tenderness ['ten·dər·nɪs] *n* ❶ (*fondness*) Zärtlichkeit *f* ❷ (*physical sensitivity*) [Schmerz]empfindlichkeit *f*

tendon ['ten·dən] *n* Sehne *f*

tendril ['ten·drəl] *n* Ranke *f*

tenement ['ten·ə·mənt] *n* heruntergekommene Mietwohnung

'tenfold *adj* zehnfach

Tenn. *abbrev of* **Tennessee**

tenner ['ten·ər] *n* (*fam*) Zehner *m*

Tennessee [ˌten·ɪ·'si] *n* Tennessee *nt*

tennis ['ten·ɪs] *n* Tennis *nt*

'tennis ball *n* Tennisball *m*

'tennis court *n* Tennisplatz *m*

tennis 'elbow *n* MED Tennisarm *m*

'tennis racket *n* Tennisschläger *m*

'tennis shoe *n* Turnschuh *m*

tenor ['ten·ər] *n* ❶ (*general meaning*) Tenor *m;* (*content a.*) Inhalt *m* ❷ MUS Tenor *m;* (*voice a.*) Tenorstimme *f*

tense¹ [tens] **I.** *adj muscle, person, voice* angespannt; *atmosphere, moment* spannungsgeladen **II.** *vt muscle* anspannen

◆**tense up** *vi muscle, person* sich [an]spannen

tense² [tens] *n* LING Zeit[form] *f*

tension ['ten·ʃən] *n* ❶ (*tightness, emotional excitement*) Spannung *f; of muscle* Verspannung *f* ❷ (*uneasiness*) [An]spannung *f* ❸ (*strain*) Spannung[en] *f[pl]* (**between** zwischen +*dat*); **to ease the ~** Spannungen reduzieren

tent [tent] *n* Zelt *nt;* **to pitch a ~** ein Zelt aufschlagen; **party ~** Partyzelt *nt,* Festzelt *nt*

tentacle ['ten·tə·kəl] *n* Tentakel *m;* (*as a sensor*) Fühler *m*

tentative ['ten·tə·t̬ɪv] *adj* ❶ (*provisional*) vorläufig ❷ (*hesitant*) vorsichtig; *attempt, effort a.* zaghaft

tentatively ['ten·te·t̬ɪv·li] *adv* ❶ (*provisionally*) provisorisch ❷ (*hesitatingly*) zögernd

tenterhooks ['ten·tər·hʊks] *npl* ▶ PHRASES: **to be [kept] on ~** wie auf glühenden Kohlen sitzen

tenth [tenθ] **I.** *n* ■ **the ~** der Zehnte; ■ **a ~** ein Zehntel *nt* **II.** *adj attr* zehnte(r, s); ■ **to be ~** Zehnte(r, s) sein **III.** *adv* als Zehnte(r, s)

tenuous ['ten·jʊ·əs] *adj* spärlich; *argument, excuse* schwach

tenure ['ten·jər] *n* (*form*) ❶ (*term of office*) Amtszeit *f,* Amtsperiode *f* ❷ (*permanent status*) **to grant sb ~** *professor* jdm eine feste Anstellung bewilligen ❸ (*term of a lease*) Pachtdauer *f* ❹ (*right of title*) Besitz *m*

tepee ['ti·pi] *n* Indianerzelt *nt*

tepid ['tep·ɪd] *adj* lau[warm]; *applause* schwach

term [tɜrm] **I.** *n* ❶ SCH, UNIV (*semester*) Semester *nt;* (*trimester*) Trimester *nt* ❷ (*set duration*) *of office* Amtszeit *f,* Amtsperiode *f;* **prison ~** Gefängnisstrafe *f* ❸ (*range*) Dauer *f;* **in the short ~** kurzfristig ❹ (*phrase*) Ausdruck *m;* **to be on friendly ~s with sb** mit jdm auf freundschaftlichem Fuß stehen; **in no uncertain ~s** unmissverständlich **II.** *vt* bezeichnen

terminal ['tɜr·mɪ·nəl] **I.** *adj* (*fatal*) End-; **~ disease** tödlich verlaufende Krankheit **II.** *n* ❶ AVIAT, TRANSP Terminal *m o nt;* **airport ~** Flughafengebäude *nt;* **bus ~** Busbahnhof *m* ❷ (*point in circuit*) Anschluss *m*

terminate ['tɜr·mɪ·neɪt] **I.** *vt* beenden; *contract* aufheben; *pregnancy* abbrechen **II.** *vi* enden

termination [ˌtɜr·mɪ·'neɪ·ʃən] *n* Beendigung *f; of contract* Aufhebung *f*

terminology [ˌtɜr·mɪ·'nal·ə·dʒi] *n* Terminologie *f*

termite ['tɜr·maɪt] *n* Termite *f*

'term paper *n* UNIV Seminararbeit *f*

tern [tɜrn] *n* Seeschwalbe *f*

terrace ['ter·əs] **I.** *n* (*patio*) Terrasse *f* **II.** *vt* terrassenförmig anlegen

terrain [te·'reɪn] *n* Gelände *nt,* Terrain *nt*

terrapin <*pl* - *or* -s> ['ter·ə·pɪn] *n* Dosenschildkröte *f*

terrestrial [tə·'res·tri·əl] (*form*) **I.** *adj* ❶ (*relating to earth*) MEDIA, TV terrestrisch *geh,* Erd- ❷ (*living on the ground*) *animal, plant* Land-

II. *n* Erdling *m,* Erdbewohner(in) *m(f)*
terrible ['ter·ə·bəl] *adj* ❶ (*shockingly bad*) schrecklich, furchtbar; **to look ~** schlimm aussehen; **my memory is ~** ich habe ein furchtbar schlechtes Gedächtnis ❷ (*fam: very great*) schrecklich, fürchterlich; **to be a ~ nuisance** schrecklich lästig sein
terribly ['ter·ə·bli] *adv* ❶ (*awfully*) schrecklich ❷ (*fam: extremely*) außerordentlich
terrier ['ter·i·ər] *n* Terrier *m*
terrific [tə·'rɪf·ɪk] *adj* (*fam*) ❶ (*excellent*) großartig, toll ❷ (*very great*) gewaltig, unglaublich
terrified ['ter·ə·faɪd] *adj* (*through sudden fright*) erschrocken; (*scared*) verängstigt; ■**to be ~ of sth** [große] Angst vor etw *dat* haben
terrify <-ie-> ['ter·ə·faɪ] *vt* fürchterlich erschrecken
terrifying ['ter·ə·faɪ·ɪŋ] *adj thought, sight* entsetzlich; *speed* Angst erregend; *experience* schrecklich
territorial [ˌter·ə·'tɔr·i·əl] *adj* ❶ GEOG, POL territorial, Gebiets- ❷ ZOOL regional begrenzt
territory ['ter·ə·tɔr·i] *n* ❶ (*area of land*) Gebiet *nt* ❷ POL Hoheitsgebiet *nt;* **forbidden ~** (*fig*) verbotenes Terrain ❸ BIOL Revier *nt* ❹ (*of activity or knowledge*) Bereich *m,* Gebiet *nt;* **familiar ~** (*fig*) vertrautes Gebiet ▶ PHRASES: **to come with the ~** dazugehören
terror ['ter·ər] *n* ❶ (*great fear*) schreckliche Angst ❷ (*political violence*) Terror *m;* **reign of ~** Schreckensherrschaft *f;* **war on ~** Bekämpfung *f* des Terrorismus
'**terror cell** *n* Terrorzelle *f*
terrorism ['ter·ə·rɪz·əm] *n* Terrorismus *m;* **act of ~** Terroranschlag *m*
terrorist ['ter·ə·rɪst] **I.** *n* Terrorist(in) *m(f)* **II.** *adj attr, inv* terroristisch; **~ attack** Terroranschlag *m*
terrorize ['ter·ə·raɪz] *vt* (*frighten*) in Angst und Schrecken versetzen; (*coerce by terrorism*) terrorisieren
'**terror-stricken**, '**terror-struck** *adj* starr vor Schreck
terry, terry cloth [ˌter·i·'klɔθ] *n* (*fabric*) Frottee *m o nt;* (*cloth*) Frottiertuch *nt*
terse [tɜrs] *adj* kurz und bündig; *reply* kurz
tertiary ['tɜr·ʃi·er·i] *adj* drittrangig
test [test] **I.** *n* ❶ (*of knowledge, skill*) Prüfung *f,* Test *m;* SCH Klassenarbeit *f;* UNIV Klausur *f;* **driving ~** Fahrprüfung *f;* **to pass a ~** eine Prüfung bestehen; **to fail a ~** eine Prüfung nicht bestehen ❷ MED, SCI (*examination*) Untersuchung *f,* Test *m;* **blood ~** Blutuntersuchung *f* ❸ (*challenge*) Herausforderung *f;* **to put sb/sth to the ~** etw/jdn auf die Probe stellen ▶ PHRASES: **to stand the ~ of time** die Zeit überdauern **II.** *vt* ❶ (*for knowledge, skill*) prüfen, testen (**on** über +*akk*) ❷ (*check performance*) überprüfen; *drugs, products* testen ❸ (*for medical purposes*) untersuchen; **to ~ sb's hearing** jds Hörvermögen testen ❹ (*by touching*) prüfen; (*by tasting*) probieren **III.** *vi* MED einen Test machen; **she ~ed positive for HIV** ihr Aidstest ist positiv ausgefallen
testament ['tes·tə·mənt] *n* ❶ (*will*) Testament *nt* ❷ REL **the New/Old T~** das Neue/Alte Testament
'**test ban** *n* Teststopp *m*
'**test case** *n* LAW (*case establishing a precedent*) Musterprozess *m;* (*precedent*) Präzedenzfall *m*
'**test drive** *n* Probefahrt *f*
tester ['tes·tər] *n* ❶ (*person*) Prüfer(in) *m(f)* ❷ (*machine*) Prüfgerät *nt*
testicle ['tes·tɪ·kəl] *n* Hoden *m*
testify <-ie-> ['tes·tɪ·faɪ] *vi* ❶ LAW (*give evidence*) [als Zeuge/Zeugin] aussagen (**against/for** gegen/für +*akk,* **on** über +*akk*) ❷ (*prove*) ■**to ~ to sth** von etw *dat* zeugen *geh;* LAW etw bezeugen
testimonial [ˌtes·tɪ·'moʊ·ni·əl] *n* ❶ (*assurance of quality*) Bestätigung *f* ❷ (*tribute for achievements*) Ehrengabe *f*
testimony ['tes·tɪ·moʊ·ni] *n* ❶ (*statement in court*) [Zeugen]aussage *f* ❷ (*fig: proof*) Beweis *m;* ■**to be ~ to sth** etw beweisen
testing ['tes·tɪŋ] *n* Testen *nt,* Prüfen *nt*
'**testing ground** *n* Testgebiet *nt,* Versuchsfeld *nt*
'**test pilot** *n* Testpilot(in) *m(f)*
'**test tube** *n* Reagenzglas *nt*
test-tube '**baby** *n* Retortenbaby *nt*
testy ['tes·ti] *adj person* leicht reizbar; *answer* gereizt
tetanus ['tet·ə·nəs] *n* Tetanus *m*
tether ['teð·ər] **I.** *n* [Halte]seil *nt* ▶ PHRASES: **to be at the end of one's ~** am Ende seiner Kräfte [*o* Geduld] sein **II.** *vt animal* anbinden (**to** an +*dat*)
Teutonic [tu·'tan·ɪk] *adj* ❶ (*Germanic*) germanisch ❷ (*showing German characteristics*) deutsch; (*hist or hum*) teutonisch
Tex. *abbrev of* **Texas**
Texan ['tek·sən] **I.** *n* Texaner(in) *m(f)* **II.** *adj* texanisch
Texas ['tek·səs] *n* Texas *nt*
text [tekst] **I.** *n* ❶ (*written material*) Text *m;* *of document* Inhalt *m* ❷ (*writings*) Schrift *f* ❸ SCH (*textbook*) Lehrbuch *nt* ❹ COMPUT Text[teil] *m* ❺ TELEC **~ message** SMS *f* **II.** *vt* TELEC ■**to ~ [sb] sth** [jdm] eine SMS[-Nachricht] senden
'**textbook I.** *n* SCH Lehrbuch *nt* (**about/on** über/für +*akk*) **II.** *adj attr* (*very good*) Parade-; **~ landing** Bilderbuchlandung *f*
textile ['teks·taɪl] *n* (*fabric*) Stoff *m;* ■**~s** *pl* Textilien *pl*
'**text message** *n* SMS *f*
textual ['teks·tʃu·əl] *adj* textlich; **~ analysis** Textanalyse *f*
texture ['teks·tʃər] *n* ❶ (*feel*) Struktur *f* ❷ (*consistency*) Konsistenz *f* ❸ (*surface appearance*) [Oberflächen]beschaffenheit *f*
Thai [taɪ] **I.** *n* ❶ (*person*) Thai *m o f,* Thailänder(in) *m(f)* ❷ (*language*) Thai *nt* **II.** *adj* thailändisch

T

Thailand ['taɪ·lənd] *n* Thailand *nt*

Thames [temz] *n* Themse *f*

than [ðən] **I.** *prep* ① *after superl* (*in comparison to*) als; **bigger ~** größer als ② (*instead of*) **rather ~ sth** anstatt etw *gen* ③ (*besides*) **other ~ sb/sth** außer jdm/etw; **other ~ that ...** abgesehen davon ... **II.** *conj* als

thank [θæŋk] *vt* ■ **to ~ sb** jdm danken, sich bei jdm bedanken; **~ you** [**very much**]! danke [sehr]!, vielen herzlichen Dank; **no, ~ you/yes, ~ you** nein, danke/ja, bitte ▶PHRASES: **thank goodness** [*or* **God**]! Gott sei Dank!

thankful ['θæŋk·fəl] *adj* ① (*grateful*) dankbar (**for** für +*akk*) ② (*pleased*) froh

thankfully ['θæŋk·fəl·i] *adv* ① (*fortunately*) glücklicherweise, zum Glück ② (*gratefully*) dankbar

thankless ['θæŋk·lɪs] *adj* (*not rewarding*) wenig lohnend; *task* undankbar

thanks [θæŋks] *npl* ① (*gratitude*) Dank *m kein pl;* **to express one's ~** seinen Dank zum Ausdruck bringen *geh* ② (*thank you*) danke; **many ~!** vielen Dank!

thanksgiving [ˌθæŋks·'gɪv·ɪŋ] *n* ① (*gratitude*) Dankbarkeit *f;* **a prayer of ~** ein Dankgebet *nt* ② (*public holiday*) ■ **T~** Thanksgiving *nt,* amerikanisches Erntedankfest

> **Thanksgiving** (Erntedankfest) ist einer der höchsten Feiertage in den USA. Er wird am vierten Donnerstag im November gefeiert. Der erste **Thanksgiving Day** wurde 1621 von den *Pilgrims* (Pilger) in Plymouth Colony zum Dank an Gott für Beistand und Hilfe in schweren Zeiten gefeiert. Traditionell trifft man sich mit der Familie zu einem Festessen mit *turkey* (Truthahn), *cranberry sauce* (Cranberrysoße), *yams* (Süßkartoffeln), *corn* (Mais), *baked potatoes* (Ofenkartoffeln). Als Nachtisch wird oft *pumpkin pie* (Kürbispastete) serviert.

'thank you *n* Danke[schön] *nt;* **to say a ~ to sb** sich bei jdm bedanken

'thank-you note, 'thank-you letter *n* Dankesbrief *m*

that [ðæt] **I.** *adj dem* (*person, thing specified*) der/die/das; (*farther away*) der/die/das [... dort [*o* da]]; **who is ~ girl?** wer ist das Mädchen? **II.** *pron* ① *dem* (*person, thing, action specified*) das; (*farther away*) das [da [*o* dort]]; **~'s a good idea** das ist eine gute Idee; **~'s why** deshalb ② *dem, after prep* **after/before ~** danach/davor; **like ~** (*in such a way*) so; (*of such a kind*) derartig; (*fam: effortlessly*) einfach so ③ *dem* (*when finished*) **~'s it!** das war's!, jetzt reicht's!; **I won't agree to it and ~'s ~** ich stimme dem nicht zu, und damit Schluss ④ *rel* (*which, who*) der/die/das; (*when*) als; **the year ~ Anna was born** das Jahr, in dem Anna geboren wurde **III.** *conj* ① (*as subject/object*) dass; **I knew** [**~**] **he'd never get here on time** ich wusste, dass er niemals rechtzeitig hier sein würde ② (*as a result*) **it was so dark** [**~**] **I couldn't see a thing** es war so dunkel, dass ich nichts sehen konnte ③ (*with a purpose*) **so ~** damit ④ *after adj* (*in apposition to "it"*) **is it true** [**~**] **she's gone back to teaching?** stimmt es, dass sie wieder als Lehrerin arbeitet? **IV.** *adv* so; **it wasn't** [**all**] **~ good** so gut war es [nun] auch wieder nicht

thatched [θætʃt] *adj* reetgedeckt

thaw [θɔ] **I.** *n* ① (*weather*) Tauwetter *nt* ② (*improvement in relations*) Tauwetter *nt;* **there are signs of a ~ in relations between the two countries** zwischen den beiden Ländern gibt es Anzeichen für eine Entspannung **II.** *vi* (*unfreeze, become friendlier*) auftauen; *ice* schmelzen **III.** *vt* FOOD ■ **to ~ sth ↻ out** etw auftauen

the [ðə, ði] **I.** *art definite* ① (*denoting thing mentioned*) der/die/das; **to be on ~ table** auf dem Tisch sein ② (*particular thing/person*) ■ **~ ...** *der/die/das ...;* **Harry's Bar is ~ place to go** Harry's Bar ist in der Szene total in *fam* ③ (*with family name*) **~ Smiths** die Schmidts ④ (*before relative clause*) der/die/das; **I really enjoyed ~ book I've just read** das Buch, das ich gerade gelesen habe, hat mir wirklich gefallen ⑤ (*before adjective*) der/die/das; **~ inevitable** das Unvermeidliche ⑥ (*to represent group*) der/die/das; (*with mass group*) die; **~ panda is becoming an increasingly rare animal** der Pandabär wird immer seltener; **~ democrats/poor** die Demokraten/Armen ⑦ (*with superlative*) der/die/das; **~ highest/longest ...** der/die/das höchste/längste ... ⑧ (*with measurements*) pro; **these potatoes are sold by ~ pound** diese Kartoffeln werden kiloweise verkauft **II.** *adv* + *comp* **all ~ better/worse** umso besser/schlechter; **~ colder it got, ~ more she shivered** je kälter es wurde, desto mehr zitterte sie

theater ['θi·ə·t̬ər] *n* ① (*for live performances*) Theater *nt;* **to go to the ~** ins Theater gehen ② (*cinema*) **movie ~** Kino *nt* ③ (*dramatic art*) Theater *nt;* **the Greek ~** das griechische Theater ④ MIL (*area of operations*) Schauplatz *m*

'theater critic *n* Theaterkritiker(in) *m(f)*

'theatergoer *n* Theaterbesucher(in) *m(f)*

theatrical [θɪ·'æt·rɪ·kəl] *adj* ① (*of theater*) Theater-; **~ agent** Theateragent(in) *m(f)* ② (*exaggerated*) theatralisch

thee [ði] *pron object pron* DIAL (*old: you*) dir *in dat,* dich *in akk*

theft [θeft] *n* Diebstahl *m*

their [ðer] *adj poss* ① (*of them*) ihr(e); **the children brushed ~ teeth** die Kinder putzten sich die Zähne ② (*his or her*) **has everybody got ~ passport?** hat jeder seinen Pass dabei?

theirs [ðerz] *pron* ihr(e, es); **they think everything is ~** sie glauben, dass ihnen alles gehört;

a favorite game of ~ eines ihrer Lieblingsspiele

them [ðem] *pron object pron* ❶ (*persons, animals*) sie *in akk,* ihnen *in dat;* **the cats are hungry — could you feed ~?** die Katzen haben Hunger – könntest du sie füttern? ❷ (*objects*) sie *in akk;* **I lost my keys — I can't find ~ anywhere** ich habe meine Schlüssel verloren – ich kann sie nirgends finden ❸ (*him/her*) ihm/ihr *in dat,* ihn/sie *in akk;* **we want to show every customer that we appreciate ~** wir wollen jedem Kunden zeigen, wie sehr wir ihn schätzen

thematic [θi·ˈmæṭ·ɪk] *adj* thematisch

theme [θim] *n* ❶ (*subject*) Thema *nt* ❷ MUS Thema *nt;* FILM, TV Melodie *f*

ˈtheme music *n* FILM, TV Titelmusik *f*

ˈtheme park *n* Themenpark *m*

ˈtheme song *n* FILM, TV Titelmelodie *f*

themselves [ðəm·ˈselvz] *pron reflexive* ❶ (*direct object*) sich; **the children behaved ~ [very well]** die Kinder benahmen sich [sehr gut] ❷ (*emph: personally*) selbst; **they tried it for ~** sie versuchten es selbst ❸ (*himself or herself*) sich selbst; **everyone who considers ~ a race car driver** jeder, der sich selbst für einen Rennfahrer hält

then [ðen] **I.** *adj* (*form*) damalige(r, s) **II.** *adv* ❶ (*at an aforementioned time*) damals; **before ~** davor, vorher; **by/until ~** bis dahin ❷ (*after that*) dann, danach, darauf ❸ (*however*) **but ~** aber schließlich

thenceforth [ˌðens·ˈfɔrθ] *adv* (*form*) seit jener Zeit

theologian [ˌθi·ə·ˈloʊ·dʒən] *n* Theologe *m,* Theologin *f*

theological [ˌθi·ə·ˈladʒ·ɪ·kəl] *adj* Theologie-; **~ college** Priesterseminar *nt*

theology [θɪ·ˈal·ə·dʒi] *n* ❶ (*principle*) Glaubenslehre *f* ❷ (*study*) Theologie *f*

theorem [ˈθi·ər·əm] *n* MATH Lehrsatz *m;* **Pythagoras' ~** der Satz des Pythagoras

theoretical [ˌθi·ə·ˈreṭ·ɪ·kəl] *adj* theoretisch

theoretically [ˌθi·ə·ˈreṭ·ɪ·kli] *adv* theoretisch

theorize [ˈθi·ə·raɪz] *vi* Theorien aufstellen (**about** über +*akk*)

theory [ˈθi·ə·ri] *n* Theorie *f;* **in ~** theoretisch

therapeutic [ˌθer·ə·ˈpju·ṭɪk] *adj* ❶ (*healing*) therapeutisch ❷ (*beneficial to health*) gesundheitsfördernd

therapist [ˈθer·ə·pɪst] *n* Therapeut(in) *m(f)*

therapy [ˈθer·ə·pi] *n* Therapie *f,* Behandlung *f*

there [ðer] **I.** *adv* ❶ (*in, at that place*) dort, da; **~'s that book you were looking for** hier ist das Buch, das du gesucht hast; **here and ~** hier und da ❷ (*at the place indicated*) dort, da; **in/up ~** da drin[nen]/oben ❸ (*to a place*) dahin, dorthin; **the museum is closed today — we'll go ~ tomorrow** das Museum ist heute zu – wir gehen morgen hin; **to get ~** (*arrive*) hinkommen; (*fig: succeed*) es schaffen; (*understand*) es verstehen ❹ (*used to introduce sentences*) **~ are lives at stake** es stehen Leben auf dem Spiel; **~ goes my raise** das war's dann wohl mit meiner Gehaltserhöhung; **~'s a good dog** braver Hund; **~ comes a point where ...** es kommt der Punkt, an dem ... ▶ PHRASES: **been ~, done that** (*fam*) kalter Kaffee; **~ you have it** na siehst du **II.** *interj* ❶ (*expressing sympathy*) da!, schau!; **~, ~!** ganz ruhig!, schon gut! ❷ (*expressing satisfaction*) na bitte!, siehst du!

thereabouts [ˈðer·ə·baʊts] *adv* ❶ (*in that area*) dort in der Nähe ❷ (*approximate time*) **or ~** oder so

thereˈafter *adv* (*form*) darauf; **shortly ~** kurze Zeit später

ˈthereby *adv* dadurch

therefore [ˈðer·fɔr] *adv* deshalb, deswegen, daher

thermal [ˈθɜr·məl] **I.** *n* ❶ (*air current*) Thermik *f* ❷ (*underwear*) ■**~s** *pl* Thermounterwäsche *f kein pl* **II.** *adj attr* ❶ MED Thermal- ❷ PHYS thermisch, Thermo-

thermal ˈunderwear *n* Thermounterwäsche *f*

thermodynamic [ˌθɜr·moʊ·daɪ·ˈnæm·ɪk] *adj attr* thermodynamisch

thermoelectric [ˌθɜr·moʊ·ɪ·ˈlek·trɪk] *adj* thermoelektrisch

thermometer [θər·ˈmam·ə·ṭər] *n* Thermometer *nt o* SCHWEIZ *a. m*

thermonuclear [ˌθɜr·moʊ·ˈnu·kli·ər] *adj* thermonuklear

Thermos®, Thermos® bottle [ˈθɜr·məs-], *n* Thermosflasche *f*

thermostat [ˈθɜr·mə·stæt] *n* Thermostat *m*

thesaurus <*pl* -es *or pl* -ri> [θɪ·ˈsɔr·əs] *n* Synonymwörterbuch *nt,* Thesaurus *m fachspr*

these [ðiz] **I.** *adj pl of* **this II.** *pron dem pl of* **this** ❶ (*the things here*) diese; **are ~ your bags?** sind das hier deine Taschen?; **~ here** die da ❷ (*the people here*) das; **~ are my kids** das sind meine Kinder

thesis <*pl* -ses> [ˈθi·sɪs] *n* ❶ (*written study*) wissenschaftliche Arbeit; (*for diploma*) Diplomarbeit *f;* (*for master's degree*) Magisterarbeit *f* ❷ (*proposition*) These *f*

they [ðeɪ] *pron pers* ❶ (*3rd person plural*) sie; **where are my glasses? ~ were on the table just a minute ago** wo ist meine Brille? sie lag doch gerade noch auf dem Tisch ❷ (*he or she*) er, sie; **ask a friend if ~ can help** frag einen Freund, ob er/sie helfen kann ❸ (*people in general*) sie; **~ say ...** es heißt ...

they'll [ðeɪl] = **they will** *see* **will**[1]

they're [ðer] = **they are** *see* **be**

they've [ðeɪv] = **they have** *see* **have I., II.**

thick [θɪk] **I.** *adj* ❶ (*not thin*) *coat, layer, volume* dick ❷ (*dense*) *fog, clouds* dicht; *hair a.* voll ❸ *after n* (*measurement*) dick, stark; **the walls are six feet ~** die Wände sind zwei Meter dick ❹ (*not very fluid*) dick, zähflüssig ▶ PHRASES: **to have ~ skin** ein dickes Fell haben **II.** *n* (*fam*) ■**in the ~ of sth** mitten[drin] in etw *dat* **III.** *adv* (*heavily*) dick; **the snow lay ~ on the path** auf dem Weg lag eine dicke

Schneedecke ▸PHRASES: **to come ~ and fast the complaints were coming ~ and fast** es hagelte Beschwerden; **to lay it on ~** dick auftragen

thicken ['θɪk·ən] **I.** *vt sauce* eindicken **II.** *vi* ❶ (*become less fluid*) dick[er] werden ❷ (*become denser*) dicht[er] werden

thicket ['θɪk·ɪt] *n* Dickicht *nt*

thickness ['θɪk·nɪs] *n* ❶ (*size, depth*) Dicke *f* ❷ (*denseness*) Dichte *f* ❸ (*layer*) Schicht *f*

thick-'skinned *adj* dickhäutig

thief <*pl* thieves> [θif] *n* Dieb(in) *m(f)*

thieving ['θi·vɪŋ] **I.** *n* (*liter, form*) Stehlen *nt* **II.** *adj attr* diebisch; **take your ~ hands off my cake!** (*hum*) lass deine Finger von meinem Kuchen!

thigh [θaɪ] *n* [Ober]schenkel *m*

'thigh bone *n* Oberschenkelknochen *m*

thimble ['θɪm·bəl] *n* Fingerhut *m*

thin <-nn-> [θɪn] **I.** *adj* ❶ (*not thick*) dünn; **~ line** feine Linie ❷ (*slim*) *person* dünn; (*too slim*) hager ❸ (*not dense*) *fog* leicht; *crowd* klein; (*lacking oxygen*) *air* dünn ❹ (*very fluid*) dünn[flüssig] ❺ (*feeble*) schwach; *disguise* dürftig; *excuse* fadenscheinig ▸PHRASES: **to disappear into ~ air** sich in Luft auflösen; **to be on ~ ice** sich auf dünnem Eis bewegen **II.** *vt* ❶ (*make more liquid*) verdünnen ❷ (*make less dense*) ausdünnen, lichten **III.** *vi* ❶ (*become weaker*) *soup, blood* dünner werden; *hair, fog a.* sich lichten; *crowd* sich zerstreuen ❷ (*become worn*) *material* sich verringern

◆**thin down I.** *vi* abnehmen **II.** *vt* verdünnen

◆**thin out I.** *vt* ausdünnen; *plants* pikieren **II.** *vi* weniger werden, sich verringern; *crowd* kleiner werden, sich verlaufen

thing [θɪŋ] *n* ❶ (*unspecified object*) Ding *nt*, Gegenstand *m*, Dings[bums] *nt fam;* **I don't have a ~ to wear** ich habe nichts zum Anziehen ❷ (*possessions*) ■**~s** *pl* Besitz *m kein pl;* (*objects for special purpose*) Sachen *pl*, Zeug *nt kein pl;* **swimming ~s** Schwimmzeug *nt kein pl* ❸ (*unspecified idea, event, activity*) Sache *f;* **one ~ leads to another** das Eine führt zum Andern; **to not be sb's ~** nicht jds Ding *nt* sein *fam;* **the whole ~** das Ganze; **to do one's own ~** (*fam*) seinen [eigenen] Weg gehen ❹ (*fam: what is needed*) **just the ~** genau das Richtige ❺ (*matter*) Thema *nt*, Sache *f;* **sure ~!** na klar!; **to know a ~ or two** eine ganze Menge wissen ❻ (*person*) **you lucky ~!** du Glückliche(r)!; **the poor ~** der/die Ärmste; (*young woman, child*) das arme Ding ▸PHRASES: **to be just one of those ~s** (*be unavoidable*) einfach unvermeidlich sein; (*typical happening*) typisch sein; **to be onto a good ~** (*fam*) etwas Gutes auftun

thingamabob ['θɪŋ·ə·mə·ˌbab], **thingamajig** ['θɪŋ·ə·mə·ˌdʒɪg] *n* (*fam*) der/die/das Dings[da] [*o* Dingsbums]

think [θɪŋk] **I.** *vi* <thought, thought> ❶ (*believe*) denken, glauben, meinen; **yes, I ~ so** ich glaube schon ❷ (*reason, have views/ideas*) denken; **not everybody ~s like you** nicht jeder denkt wie du ❸ (*consider to be, have an opinion*) **I want you to ~ of me as a friend** ich möchte, dass du mich als Freund siehst; **to ~ highly of sb/sth** viel von jdm/etw halten ❹ (*expect*) **I thought as much!** das habe ich mir schon gedacht! ❺ (*intend*) ■**to ~ of doing sth** erwägen, etw zu tun ❻ (*come up with*) ■**to ~ of sth** sich *dat* etw ausdenken; **to ~ of a solution** auf eine Lösung kommen ❼ (*reflect*) [nach]denken, überlegen; **to ~ better of sth** sich *dat* etw anders überlegen ❽ (*have in one's mind*) denken (**of** an +*akk*) ▸PHRASES: **to be unable to hear oneself ~** sein eigenes Wort nicht mehr verstehen **II.** *vt* <thought, thought> ❶ (*hold an opinion*) denken, glauben; **to ~ the world of sb/sth** große Stücke auf jdn/etw halten ❷ (*consider to be*) **who do you ~ you are?** für wen hältst du dich eigentlich?; **to ~ it['s] [un]likely that ...** es für [un]wahrscheinlich halten, dass ... ❸ (*remember*) ■**to ~ to do sth** daran denken, etw zu tun **III.** *n* (*fam*) **to give sth a ~** sich *dat* etw überlegen, über etw *akk* nachdenken

◆**think about** *vi* ❶ (*have in one's mind*) denken (an +*akk*) ❷ (*reflect*) nachdenken (über +*akk*) ❸ (*consider*) ■**to ~ about sth** sich *dat* etw überlegen

◆**think ahead** *vi* vorausdenken; (*be foresighted*) sehr vorausschauend sein

◆**think back** *vi* zurückdenken (**to** an +*akk*)

◆**think out** *vt* ❶ (*prepare carefully*) durchdenken ❷ (*plan*) vorausplanen ❸ (*come up with*) sich *dat* ausdenken; (*develop*) entwickeln

◆**think over** *vt* überdenken; **I'll ~ it over** ich überleg's mir noch mal

◆**think through** *vt* [gründlich] durchdenken

◆**think up** *vt* (*fam*) sich *dat* ausdenken

thinker ['θɪŋ·kər] *n* Denker(in) *m(f)*

thinking ['θɪŋ·kɪŋ] **I.** *n* ❶ (*using thought*) Denken *nt;* **to do some ~ about sth** sich *dat* über etw *akk* Gedanken machen ❷ (*reasoning*) Überlegung *f;* **good ~! that's a brilliant idea!** nicht schlecht! eine geniale Idee! **II.** *adj attr* denkend, vernünftig

'think tank *n* (*fig*) Expertenkommission *f*.

'thinly *adv* dünn

thinner ['θɪn·ər] **I.** *n* Verdünnungsmittel *nt;* **paint ~** Farbverdünner *m* **II.** *adj comp of* **thin**

thinness ['θɪn·nɪs] *n* ❶ (*not fat*) Magerkeit *f* ❷ (*fig: lack of depth*) Dünnheit *f*

thin-'skinned *adj* (*fig*) empfindlich, sensibel

third [θɜrd] **I.** *n* ❶ (*number 3*) Dritte(r, s); **the ~ of September** der dritte September ❷ (*fraction*) Drittel *nt* ❸ (*gear position*) dritter Gang **II.** *adj* dritte(r, s); **~ best** drittbeste(r, s); **the ~ time** das dritte Mal

third de'gree *n* Polizeimaßnahme *f* (*zur Erzwingung eines Geständnisses*)*;* **to give sb the ~** (*fam*) jdn in die Mangel nehmen

third-degree 'burn *n* Verbrennung *f* dritten Grades

T

thirdly ['θɜrd·li] *adv* drittens

third 'party *n* dritte Person; LAW Dritte(r) *f(m)*

third 'person *n* LING dritte Person

third-'rate *adj* minderwertig

Third 'World *n* ■**the ~** die Dritte Welt; **~ country** Drittweltland *nt*

thirst [θɜrst] *n* ① (*need for a drink*) Durst *m;* **to die of ~** verdursten ② (*strong desire*) Verlangen *nt;* **~ for knowledge** Wissensdurst *m*

thirsty ['θɜr·sti] *adj* durstig; ■**to be ~ for sth** nach etw *dat* hungern

thirteen [θɜr·'tin] **I.** *n* Dreizehn *f; see also* **eight II.** *adj* dreizehn; *see also* **eight**

thirteenth [θɜr·'tinθ] **I.** *n* ① (*order*) ■**the ~** der/die/das Dreizehnte; *see also* **eighth** ② (*date*) **the ~** der Dreizehnte; *see also* **eighth** ③ (*fraction*) Dreizehntel *nt; see also* **eighth II.** *adj* dreizehnte(r, s); *see also* **eighth III.** *adv* als Dreizehnte(r, s); *see also* **eighth**

thirtieth ['θɜrt̬·i·əθ] **I.** *n* ① (*after twenty-ninth*) Dreißigste(r, s); *see also* **eighth** ② (*date*) **the ~** der Dreißigste; *see also* **eighth** ③ (*fraction*) Dreißigstel *nt; see also* **eighth II.** *adj* dreißigste(r, s); *see also* **eighth III.** *adv* als Dreißigste(r, s); *see also* **eighth**

thirty ['θɜr·t̬i] **I.** *n* ① (*number*) Dreißig *f; see also* **eight** ② (*age*) **to be in one's thirties** in den Dreißigern sein ③ (*time period*) ■**the thirties** *pl* die dreißiger Jahre **II.** *adj* dreißig; *see also* **eight**

this [ðɪs] **I.** *adj attr* ① (*close in space*) diese(r, s); **can you sign ~ form for me?** kannst du dieses Formular für mich unterschreiben? ② (*close in future*) diese(r, s); **I'll do it ~ Monday** ich erledige es diesen Montag; **~ minute** sofort ③ (*referring to specific*) diese(r, s); **don't listen to ~ guy** hör nicht auf diesen Typen; **by ~ time** dann **II.** *pron* ① (*the thing here*) das; **is ~ your bag?** ist das deine Tasche? ② (*the person here*) das; **~ is my husband Steve** das ist mein Ehemann Stefan ③ (*this matter here*) das; **what's ~?** was soll das?; **~ is what I was talking about** davon spreche ich ja ④ (*with an action*) das; **every time I do ~, it hurts** jedes Mal, wenn ich das mache, tut es weh; **like ~** so ▶ PHRASES: **~ and that** (*fam*) dies und das **III.** *adv* so; **~ far and no further** (*a. fig*) bis hierher und nicht weiter

thistle ['θɪs·əl] *n* Distel *f*

tho', tho [ðoʊ] *conj* (*fam*) *short for* **though** obwohl

thong [θaŋ] *n* ① (*strip of leather*) Lederband *nt* ② (*G-string*) Tanga *m* ③ (*flip-flop*) ■**~s** *pl* [Zehen]sandalen *pl,* Flip-Flops *pl*

thorax <*pl* -es *or* -races> ['θɔr·æks] *n* ANAT Brustkorb *m*

thorn [θɔrn] *n* (*prickle*) Dorn *m* ▶ PHRASES: **there is no rose without a ~** (*prov*) keine Rose ohne Dornen *prov*

thorny ['θɔr·ni] *adj* ① (*with thorns*) dornig ② (*difficult*) schwierig; *issue* heikel

thorough ['θɜr·oʊ] *adj* ① (*detailed*) genau, exakt ② (*careful*) sorgfältig, gründlich; *reform* durchgreifend

'thoroughbred I. *n* Vollblut[pferd] *nt* **II.** *adj* reinrassig, Vollblut-

'thoroughfare *n* (*form*) Durchgangsstraße *f*

thoroughly ['θɜr·oʊ·li] *adv* ① (*in detail*) genau, sorgfältig ② (*completely*) völlig; **to ~ enjoy sth** etw ausgiebig genießen

thoroughness ['θɜr·oʊ·nɪs] *n* Gründlichkeit *f,* Sorgfältigkeit *f*

those [ðoʊz] **I.** *adj det* ① *pl of* **that** (*to identify specific persons/things*) diese; **how much are ~ brushes?** wie viel kosten die Bürsten da? ② *pl of* **that** (*singling out*) **I like ~ cookies with the almonds in them** ich mag die Kekse mit den Mandeln drinnen **II.** *pron pl of* **that** ① (*the things over there*) diejenigen; **these peaches aren't ripe — try ~ on the table** diese Pfirsiche sind noch nicht reif, versuch' die auf dem Tisch ② (*the people over there*) das; **~ are my kids over there** das sind meine Kinder da drüben ③ (*the people*) ■**~ who ...** diejenigen, die ...; ■**one of ~** (*belonging to a group*) eine(r) davon

thou [ðaʊ] *pron pers* DIAL (*old: you*) du

though [ðoʊ] **I.** *conj* ① (*despite the fact that*) obwohl ② (*however*) [je]doch ③ (*if*) ■**as ~** als ob **II.** *adv* trotzdem

thought [θɔt] **I.** *n* ① (*thinking*) Nachdenken *nt,* Überlegen *nt;* **to be deep in ~** tief in Gedanken versunken sein; **to give sth some ~** sich *dat* Gedanken über etw *akk* machen ② (*opinion, idea*) Gedanke *m;* **I've just had a ~** mir ist eben was eingefallen; **to spare sb the ~ [of sth]** jdn nicht an etw *akk* erinnern ▶ PHRASES: **it's the ~ that counts** (*fam*) der gute Wille zählt **II.** *vt, vi pt, pp of* **think**

thoughtful ['θɔt·fəl] *adj* ① (*considerate*) aufmerksam ② (*contemplative*) nachdenklich ③ (*careful*) sorgfältig

thoughtless ['θɔt·lɪs] *adj* ① (*inconsiderate*) rücksichtslos ② (*without thinking*) unüberlegt

'thought-provoking *adj remarks, book* nachdenklich stimmend

thousand ['θaʊ·zənd] **I.** *n* ① (*number*) Tausend *f;* **two ~** zweitausend ② (*year*) **two ~ five** [das Jahr] zweitausend und fünf ③ (*quantity*) **a ~ dollars** [ein]tausend Dollar ④ *pl* (*lots*) ■**~s** Tausende *pl* **II.** *adj det, attr* tausend; **I've said it a ~ times** ich habe es jetzt unzählige Male gesagt

thousandth ['θaʊ·zəntθ] **I.** *n* (*in series*) Tausendste(r, s); (*fraction*) Tausendstel *nt* **II.** *adj* tausendste(r, s); ■**the ~ ...** der/die/das tausendste ...; **a ~ part** ein Tausendstel *nt*

thrash [θræʃ] **I.** *vt* ① (*beat*) verprügeln ② (*fam: defeat*) haushoch schlagen **II.** *vi* (*liter*) rasen

thrashing ['θræʃ·ɪŋ] *n* Prügel *pl;* **to give sb a [good] ~** jdm eine [anständige] Tracht Prügel verpassen

thread [θred] **I.** *n* ① (*for sewing*) Garn *nt* ② (*fiber*) Faden *m,* Faser *f* ③ (*groove*) Gewinde *nt;* (*part of groove*) Gewindegang *m* ④ INET Thread *m* **II.** *vt* ① (*put through*) einfädeln; **she**

~ed her way through the crowd sie schlängelte sich durch die Menge ❷ (*put onto a string*) auffädeln; **to ~ beads onto a chain** Perlen auf einer Kette aufreihen

'threadbare *adj* ❶ *material* abgenutzt; *clothes* abgetragen; *carpet* abgelaufen ❷ *person, building* schäbig

threat [θret] *n* ❶ (*warning*) Drohung *f;* **an empty ~** eine leere Drohung ❷ (*potential danger*) Gefahr *f,* Bedrohung *f;* **to pose a ~ to sb/sth** eine Gefahr für jdn/etw darstellen; ■ **to be under ~ of sth** von etw *dat* bedroht sein

threaten ['θret·ən] **I.** *vt* ❶ (*warn*) ■ **to ~ sb** jdn bedrohen, jdm drohen; ■ **to ~ sb with sth** jdm mit etw *dat* drohen; (*with weapon*) jdn mit etw *dat* bedrohen ❷ (*be a danger*) gefährden, eine Bedrohung sein (für +*akk*) **II.** *vi* drohen; ■ **to ~ to do sth** damit drohen, etw zu tun

threatening ['θret·ə·nɪŋ] *adj* ❶ (*hostile*) drohend, Droh-; **~ letter** Drohbrief *m* ❷ (*menacing*) bedrohlich; *clouds* dunkel

three [θri] **I.** *n* ❶ (*number*) Drei *f; see also* **eight** ❷ (*quantity*) drei; **in ~s** in Dreiergruppen ❸ CARDS (*score*) Drei *f;* **the ~ of diamonds** die Karodrei ❹ (*the time*) drei [Uhr]; **at ~ p.m.** um drei Uhr [nachmittags], um fünfzehn Uhr; *see also* **eight** ▶ PHRASES: **two's company, ~'s a crowd** drei sind einer zu viel **II.** *adj* drei; **I'll give you ~ guesses** dreimal darfst du raten; *see also* **eight** ▶ PHRASES: **~ cheers [for sb/sth]!** (*a. iron*) ein dreifaches Hoch [auf jdn/etw]!

three-'D *adj* (*fam*), **three-di'mensional** *adj* dreidimensional; **~ printer** 3-D-Drucker *m*

'threefold *adj* dreifach

'three-part *adj attr song* dreistimmig

'three-piece I. *adj* ❶ (*of three items*) dreiteilig ❷ (*of three people*) Dreimann- **II.** *n* Dreiteiler *m*

three-piece 'suit *n* (*man's*) Dreiteiler *m;* (*lady's*) dreiteiliges Ensemble

'three-ply *adj* ❶ (*of three layers*) *wood* dreischichtig; *tissue* dreilagig ❷ (*of three strands*) **~ wool** Dreifachwolle *f*

three-'quarter *adj attr* dreiviertel

threesome ['θri·səm] *n* (*three people*) Dreiergruppe *f;* **as a ~** zu dritt

three-way *adj* Drei-; **~ battle** Dreikampf *m*

three-'wheeler *n* (*car*) dreirädriges Auto; (*tricycle*) Dreirad *nt*

thresh [θreʃ] *vt crop* dreschen

'threshing machine *n* AGR Dreschmaschine *f*

threshold ['θreʃ·hoʊld] *n* ❶ (*of doorway*) [Tür]schwelle *f* ❷ (*fig: beginning*) Anfang *m,* Beginn *m;* (*limit*) Grenze *f,* Schwelle *f;* **I have a low ~ for boredom** ich langweile mich sehr schnell; **pain ~** Schmerzgrenze *f* ❸ PHYS, COMPUT Schwellenwert *m*

threw [θru] *pt of* **throw**

thrift [θrɪft] *n* Sparsamkeit *f*

'thrift shop, 'thrift store *n Laden, in dem gespendete, meist gebrauchte Waren verkauft werden, um Geld für wohltätige Zwecke zu sammeln*

thrifty ['θrɪf·ti] *adj* sparsam

thrill [θrɪl] **I.** *n* (*wave of emotion*) Erregung *f;* (*titillation*) Nervenkitzel *m;* **the ~ of the chase** der besondere Reiz der Jagd **II.** *vt* (*excite*) erregen; (*fascinate*) faszinieren; (*frighten*) Angst machen; (*delight*) entzücken

thriller ['θrɪl·ər] *n* Thriller *m*

thrilling ['θrɪl·ɪŋ] *adj* aufregend; *story* spannend

thrive <-d *or* throve, -d *or* thriven> [θraɪv] *vi* gedeihen; *business* florieren

thriving ['θraɪ·vɪŋ] *adj* **it's a ~ community** das ist eine gut funktionierende Gemeinschaft

throat [θroʊt] *n* ❶ (*inside the neck*) Rachen *m,* Hals *m;* **to have a sore ~** Halsschmerzen haben ❷ (*front of the neck*) Kehle *f,* Hals *m;* **to cut sb's ~** jdm die Kehle durchschneiden ▶ PHRASES: **to have a lump in one's ~** einen Kloß im Hals haben; **to jump down sb's ~** jdn anschnauzen

throaty ['θroʊ·t̬i] *adj* ❶ (*harsh-sounding*) kehlig, rau ❷ (*hoarse*) heiser, rau

throb [θrab] **I.** *n* Klopfen *nt,* Hämmern *nt; of heart, pulse* Pochen *nt; of bass, engine* Dröhnen *nt* **II.** *vi* <-bb-> klopfen; *pulse, heart* pochen; *bass, engine* dröhnen; **his head ~bed** er hatte rasende Kopfschmerzen

throes [θroʊz] *npl* **death ~** Todeskampf *m;* **to be in the ~ of sth** mitten in etw *dat* stecken

throne [θroʊn] *n* Thron *m;* REL Stuhl *m*

throng [θraŋ] **I.** *n* [Menschen]menge *f* **II.** *vt* sich drängen (in +*akk*); **visitors ~ed the narrow streets** die engen Straßen wimmelten nur so von Besuchern

throttle ['θrat̬·əl] **I.** *n* ❶ AUTO Drosselklappe *f* ❷ (*speed*) **at full ~** mit voller Geschwindigkeit; (*fig*) mit Volldampf **II.** *vt* ❶ (*try to strangle*) würgen; (*strangle*) erdrosseln ❷ (*fig: stop, hinder*) drosseln

through [θru] **I.** *prep* ❶ (*from one side to other*) durch +*akk;* **we drove ~ the tunnel** wir fuhren durch den Tunnel ❷ (*in*) durch +*akk;* **her words kept running ~ my head** ihre Worte gingen mir ständig durch den Kopf ❸ (*until and including*) bis; **we're open Monday ~ Friday** wir haben Montag bis Freitag geöffnet ❹ (*during*) während +*gen;* **they drove ~ the night** sie fuhren durch die Nacht ❺ (*because of*) wegen +*gen,* durch +*akk;* **I can't hear you ~ all this noise** ich kann dich bei diesem ganzen Lärm nicht verstehen ❻ (*by means of*) über +*akk;* **~ chance** durch Zufall ❼ (*at*) durch +*akk;* **to go ~ sth** etw durchgehen; **she looked ~ her mail** sie sah ihre Post durch ❽ (*to the finish of*) **to get ~ sth** etw durchstehen ❾ (*into*) **we were cut off halfway ~ the conversation** unser Gespräch wurde mittendrin unterbrochen **II.** *adj* ❶ *pred* (*finished*) fertig; **we're ~** (*finished relationship*) mit uns ist es aus; (*finished job*) es ist alles erledigt ② *pred* (*successful*) durch; **Henry is ~ to the final** Henry hat sich für das Finale qualifiziert ③ *attr* TRANSP (*making few stops*) *bus, train* durchgehend **III.** *adv* ① (*to a destination*) durch; **the train goes ~ to Hamburg** der Zug fährt bis nach Hamburg durch ② (*from beginning to end*) [ganz] durch; **Paul saw the project ~ to its completion** Paul hat sich bis zum Abschluss um das Projekt gekümmert; **to be halfway ~ sth** etw halb durch haben ③ (*from outside to inside*) **~ and ~** durch und durch, völlig; **cooked ~** durchgegart

through'out [θru·'aʊt] **I.** *prep* ① (*all over in*) **people ~ the country** Menschen im ganzen Land ② (*at times during*) während +*gen;* **~ the performance** die ganze Vorstellung über **II.** *adv* ① (*in all parts*) vollständig ② (*the whole time*) die ganze Zeit [über]

'throughput *n* Verarbeitungsmenge *f;* COMPUT Datendurchlauf *m*

'through ticket *n* Fahrkarte *f* für die gesamte Strecke

through 'traffic *n* Durchgangsverkehr *m;* **"no ~!"** „keine Durchfahrt!"

'through train *n* durchgehender Zug

'throughway *n see* **thruway**

throw [θroʊ] **I.** *n* ① (*act of throwing*) Wurf *m;* **a stone's ~ [away]** (*fig*) nur einen Steinwurf von hier ② (*furniture cover*) Überwurf *m* **II.** *vi* <threw, thrown> werfen **III.** *vt* <threw, thrown> ① (*propel with arm*) werfen; (*hurl*) schleudern; ■**to ~ sb sth** [*or* **to ~ sth to sb**] jdm etw zuwerfen; **to ~ a punch at sb** jdm einen Schlag versetzen ② (*pounce upon*) ■**to ~ oneself onto sb/sth** sich auf jdn stürzen/auf etw *akk* werfen ③ SPORTS (*in wrestling*) zu Fall bringen; *rider* abwerfen ④ (*direct*) zuwerfen; *glance* werfen (**at** auf +*akk*); ■**to ~ oneself at sb** (*embrace*) sich jdm an den Hals werfen; (*attack*) sich auf jdn stürzen ⑤ (*move violently*) ■**to ~ sth against sth** etw gegen etw *akk* schleudern ⑥ (*show emotion*) **to ~ a fit** (*fam*) einen Anfall bekommen; **to ~ a tantrum** einen Wutanfall bekommen ⑦ (*give*) **to ~ a party** eine Party geben ⑧ (*fam: confuse*) ■**to ~ sb [off]** jdn durcheinanderbringen ▶ PHRASES: **to ~ caution to the wind** eine Warnung in den Wind schlagen

◆**throw away** *vt* ① (*discard*) wegwerfen ② (*waste*) **to ~ money away on sth** Geld für etw *akk* zum Fenster hinauswerfen

◆**throw back** *vt* ① (*move with force*) **to ~ one's hair back** seine Haare nach hinten werfen ② (*open*) *curtains* aufreißen ▶ PHRASES: **to ~ sth back in sb's face** jdm etw wieder auftischen

◆**throw down** *vt* ① (*throw from above*) herunterwerfen; **to ~ oneself down** sich niederwerfen ② (*deposit forcefully*) hinwerfen

◆**throw in** *vt* ① (*put into*) ■**to ~ sth in[to] sth** etw in etw *akk* [hinein]werfen ② (*include in price*) ■**to ~ sth ↔ in** etw gratis dazugeben ③ (*throw onto field*) *soccer ball* einwerfen ▶ PHRASES: **to ~ in the towel** das Handtuch werfen

◆**throw off** *vt* ① (*remove forcefully*) herunterreißen *fam; clothes* schnell ausziehen ② (*jump*) ■**to ~ oneself off sth** sich von etw *dat* hinunterstürzen ③ (*escape*) ■**to ~ sb ↔ off** jdn abschütteln ④ *fluster* **to ~ sb off** jdn aus dem Konzept bringen

◆**throw on** *vt* ① (*place*) werfen (auf +*akk*); **~ a log on the fire, will you?** legst du bitte noch einen Scheit aufs Feuer? ② (*pounce upon*) ■**to ~ oneself on sb** sich auf jdn stürzen ③ (*put on*) *clothes* eilig anziehen ④ (*cast*) **to ~ suspicion on[to] sb** den Verdacht auf jdn lenken

◆**throw out** *vt* ① (*fling outside*) hinauswerfen, rausschmeißen *fam* ② (*discard*) wegwerfen; LAW **to ~ out a case** einen Fall abweisen ③ (*dismiss*) entlassen ④ SPORTS (*eject*) vom Platz stellen, des Platzes verweisen *geh*

◆**throw together** *vt* ① (*fam: make quickly*) *meal* zaubern ② (*cause to meet*) zusammenbringen

◆**throw up** **I.** *vt* ① (*project upwards*) hochwerfen; *hands* hochreißen ② (*fam: vomit*) erbrechen **II.** *vi* (*fam*) sich übergeben, kotzen *derb*

throwaway ['θroʊ·ə·weɪ] *adj attr* ① (*disposable*) wegwerfbar; **~ razor** Einwegrasierer *m* ② (*unimportant*) achtlos dahingeworfen *attr*

'throwback *n* Rückschritt *m*

thrown [θroʊn] *pp of* **throw**

thru [θru] *prep, adv* (*fam*) *see* **through**

thrush[1] <*pl* -es> [θrʌʃ] *n* ORN Drossel *f*

thrush[2] <*pl* -es> [θrʌʃ] *n* MED Soor *m*

thrust [θrʌst] **I.** *n* ① (*forceful push*) Stoß *m* ② (*impetus, purpose*) Stoßrichtung *f;* **the main ~ of an argument** die Hauptaussage eines Arguments **II.** *vi* <thrust, thrust> **to ~ at sb with a knife** nach jdm mit einem Messer stoßen **III.** *vt* <thrust, thrust> ① (*push with force*) **to ~ the money into sb's hand** jdm das Geld in die Hand stecken ② (*compel to do*) ■**to ~ sth [up]on sb** jdm etw auferlegen; ■**to ~ oneself [up]on sb** sich jdm aufdrängen ③ (*impel*) hineinstoßen; **she was suddenly ~ into a position of responsibility** sie wurde plötzlich in eine sehr verantwortungsvolle Position hineingedrängt

thruway ['θru·weɪ] *n* Schnellstraße *f*

thud [θʌd] **I.** *vi* <-dd-> dumpf aufschlagen **II.** *n* dumpfer Schlag; **~ of hooves** Geklapper *nt* von Hufen

thug [θʌg] *n* Schlägertyp *m pej*

thumb [θʌm] **I.** *n* Daumen *m* ▶ PHRASES: **to stand out like a sore ~** unangenehm auffallen **II.** *vt* ① (*fam: hitchhike*) **to ~ a ride** per Anhalter fahren, trampen ② (*glance through*) *book* durchblättern ③ *usu passive* (*mark by handling*) *book, pages* abgreifen **III.** *vi* (*glance through*) **to ~ through a newspaper** durch die Zeitung blättern

T

thumb 'index *n* Daumenregister *nt*

'thumbnail *n* Daumennagel *m*

thumbnail 'sketch *n* Abriss *m*

'thumbtack *n* Reißnagel *m,* Reißzwecke *f*

thump [θʌmp] **I.** *n* dumpfer Knall **II.** *vt* schlagen **III.** *vi* schlagen (**on** auf +*akk*); *heart* klopfen

thunder ['θʌn·dər] **I.** *n* ❶ METEO Donner *m;* **rumble of ~** Donnergrollen *nt* ❷ (*loud sound*) Getöse *nt* ▶ PHRASES: **to steal sb's ~** jdm die Schau stehlen **II.** *vi* ❶ (*make rumbling noise*) donnern; ■**to ~ by** vorbeidonnern ❷ (*declaim*) schreien; ■**to ~ about sth** sich lautstark über etw *akk* äußern **III.** *vt* brüllen

'thunderbolt *n* Blitzschlag *m*

'thunderclap *n* Donnerschlag *m*

'thundercloud *n usu pl* Gewitterwolke *f*

thundering ['θʌn·dər·ɪŋ] **I.** *n* Donnern *nt* **II.** *adj* ❶ (*extremely loud*) tosend; *voice* dröhnend ❷ (*enormous*) enorm; *success a.* riesig

thunderous ['θʌn·dər·əs] *adj attr* donnernd; **~ applause** Beifallsstürme *pl*

'thunderstorm *n* Gewitter *nt*

'thunderstruck *adj pred* wie vom Donner gerührt

Thursday ['θɜrz·deɪ] *n* Donnerstag *m; see also* **Tuesday**

thus [ðʌs] *adv* ❶ (*therefore*) folglich ❷ (*in this way*) so

thwart [θwɔrt] *vt* vereiteln; *escape* verhindern; *plan* durchkreuzen

thy [ðaɪ] *adj poss* DIAL (*old*) dein

thyme [taɪm] *n* Thymian *m*

thyroid ['θaɪ·rɔɪd] **I.** *n* Schilddrüse *f* **II.** *adj attr* Schilddrüsen-

tiara [tɪ·'ær·ə] *n* Tiara *f*

tibia <*pl* -biae> ['tɪb·i·ə] *n* Schienbein *nt*

tic [tɪk] *n* [nervöses] Zucken

tick¹ [tɪk] **I.** *n* (*sound of watch*) Ticken *nt kein pl;* **"~ tock"** (*fam*) „ticktack" **II.** *vi* ticken ▶ PHRASES: **what makes sb ~** was jdn bewegt

◆**tick off** *vt* (*fam*) auf die Palme bringen

tick² [tɪk] *n* ZOOL Zecke *f*

ticker ['tɪk·ər] *n* (*fam*) Pumpe *f sl*

ticker-tape pa'rade *n* Konfettiparade *f*

ticket ['tɪk·ɪt] *n* ❶ (*card*) Karte *f;* **concert ~** Konzertkarte *f;* **lottery ~** Lottoschein *m;* **plane ~** Flugticket *nt* ❷ (*price tag*) Etikett *nt;* **price ~** Preisschild *nt* ❸ LAW (*notification of fine*) Strafzettel *m*

'ticket collector *n* (*on the train*) Schaffner(in) *m(f);* (*on the platform*) Bahnsteigschaffner(in) *m(f)*

'ticket machine *n* Fahrkartenautomat *m*

ticking ['tɪk·ɪŋ] *n* ❶ *of clock* Ticken *nt* ❷ (*for mattress*) Matratzenüberzug *m*

tickle ['tɪk·əl] **I.** *vi* kitzeln **II.** *vt* ❶ (*touch lightly*) kitzeln ❷ (*fam: appeal to sb*) **to ~ sb's fancy** jdn reizen ▶ PHRASES: **to be ~d pink** (*fam*) vor Freude völlig aus dem Häuschen sein **III.** *n* ❶ (*itching sensation*) Jucken *nt* ❷ (*irritating cough*) **a ~ in one's throat** ein Kratzen *nt* im Hals

ticklish ['tɪk·lɪʃ] *adj* ❶ (*sensitive to tickling*) kitzlig ❷ (*delicate*) heikel

tick-tack-toe, tic-tac-toe [ˌtɪk·ˌtæk·'toʊ] *n* Drei gewinnt, Tic Tac Toe *nt*

tidal ['taɪ·dəl] *adj* von Gezeiten abhängig; **~ basin** Tidebecken *nt*

'tidal wave *n* Flutwelle *f;* (*fig*) Flut *f*

tidbit ['tɪd·bɪt] *n* ❶ (*snack*) Leckerbissen *m* ❷ *usu pl* (*of information*) Leckerbissen *m;* **juicy ~s** pikante Einzelheiten

tiddlywinks ['tɪd·li·wɪŋks] *n pl* Flohhüpfen *nt kein pl*

tide [taɪd] *n* ❶ (*of sea*) Gezeiten *pl;* **high ~** Flut *f;* **low ~** Ebbe *f* ❷ (*main trend of opinion*) öffentliche Meinung; **the ~ has turned** die Meinung ist umgeschlagen; **to swim against the ~** gegen den Strom schwimmen ❸ (*powerful trend*) Welle *f*

◆**tide over** *vt* ■**to ~ sb over** jdm über die Runden helfen *fam*

tidiness ['taɪ·dɪ·nɪs] *n* Ordnung *f*

tidy ['taɪ·di] **I.** *adj* ❶ (*in order*) ordentlich ❷ (*fam: considerable*) *sum* beträchtlich **II.** *vt* aufräumen

tie [taɪ] **I.** *n* ❶ (*necktie*) Krawatte *f;* **bow ~** Fliege *f* ❷ (*cord*) Schnur *f* ❸ *pl* (*links*) **diplomatic ~s** diplomatische Beziehungen; **family ~s** Familienbande *pl* ❹ (*equal score*) Unentschieden *nt,* Punktegleichstand *m kein pl;* **to end in a ~** mit einem Unentschieden enden, unentschieden ausgehen **II.** *vi* <-y-> ❶ (*fasten*) schließen; **to ~ in the front/back** vorne/hinten zugebunden werden ❷ (*equal in points*) ■**to ~ with sb/sth** denselben Platz wie jd/etw belegen **III.** *vt* <-y-> ❶ (*fasten together*) *hands* fesseln; *knot* machen; *necktie* binden ❷ (*restrict in movement*) ■**to be ~d to sth/somewhere** an etw *akk*/einen Ort gebunden sein ▶ PHRASES: **sb's hands are ~d** jds Hände sind gebunden

◆**tie back** *vt* zurückbinden

◆**tie down** *vt* ❶ (*secure to ground*) festbinden ❷ (*restrict*) ■**to be ~d down** gebunden sein; ■**to ~ sb down to sth** (*fam*) jdn auf etw *akk* festlegen

◆**tie in** *vi* ■**to ~ in with sth** mit etw *dat* übereinstimmen

◆**tie up** *vt* ❶ (*bind*) festbinden; *hair* hochbinden ❷ (*delay*) *traffic* aufhalten ❸ (*busy*) ■**to be ~d up** beschäftigt sein ❹ *capital, money* binden ❺ SPORTS *game* den Ausgleich erzielen ▶ PHRASES: **to ~ up some loose ends** etw erledigen

'tiebreaker, 'tiebreak *n* Tie-Break *m o nt*

tied [taɪd] *adj* SPORTS unentschieden; **to come in ~ for second** mit jdm zusammen den zweiten Platz belegen

'tie-in *n* Verbindung *f*

tier [tɪr] **I.** *n* (*row*) Reihe *f;* (*level*) Lage *f;* **~ of management** Managementebene *f* **II.** *vt usu passive* (*on top of each other*) aufschichten; (*next to each other*) aufreihen

'tie tack *n* Krawattennadel *f*

'tie-up *n* Stillstand *m*

tiff [tɪf] *n* (*fam*) Plänkelei *f;* **to have a ~** eine Meinungsverschiedenheit haben

tiger ['taɪ·gər] *n* Tiger *m*

tight [taɪt] **I.** *adj* ❶ (*firm*) fest; *clothes* eng ❷ (*close together*) dicht; **~ finish** knapper Zieleinlauf ❸ (*stretched tautly*) gespannt; *muscles* verspannt; *face, voice* angespannt ❹ (*severe*) streng; *bend* eng; *budget* knapp; **~ spot** (*fig*) Zwickmühle *f* ❺ (*pej fam: with money*) knauserig ▶ PHRASES: **to run a ~ ship** ein strenges Regime führen **II.** *adv pred* straff; *close, seal* fest; **to hang on ~ to sb/sth** sich an jdm/etw festklammern

tighten ['taɪ·ten] **I.** *vt* ❶ (*make tight*) festziehen; *rope* festbinden; *screw* anziehen ❷ (*increase pressure*) verstärken ▶ PHRASES: **to ~ one's belt** den Gürtel enger schnallen **II.** *vi* straff werden

tight'fisted *adj* (*pej fam*) geizig

tight-'fitting *adj* eng anliegend

tight'lipped *adj* ❶ (*compressing lips*) schmallippig ❷ (*saying little*) *silence* eisig; ■ **to be ~ about sth** wortkarg auf etw *akk* reagieren

tightness ['taɪt·nɪs] *n* ❶ (*firmness, strength*) Festigkeit *f* ❷ (*close fitting*) enge Passform ❸ (*tight sensation*) Spannen *nt*

'tightrope *n* Drahtseil *nt;* **~ walker** Seiltänzer(in) *m(f)*

tights [taɪts] *npl* ❶ (*leggings*) Strumpfhose *f;* **pair of ~** Strumpfhose *f* ❷ (*for dancing, aerobics*) Leggings *pl,* Gymnastikhose *f*

tightwad ['taɪt·wad] *n* (*pej sl*) Geizkragen *m*

tigress <*pl* -es> ['taɪ·grɪs] *n* (*female tiger*) Tigerin *f*

tike [taɪk] *n see* **tyke**

tile [taɪl] **I.** *n* Fliese *f* **II.** *vt* fliesen

till¹ [tɪl] *vt land* bestellen

till² [tɪl] **I.** *prep see* **until II.** *conj see* **until**

till³ [tɪl] *n* Kasse *f* ▶ PHRASES: **to be caught with one's hand in the ~** auf frischer Tat ertappt werden

tiller ['tɪl·ər] *n* Ruderpinne *f*

tilt [tɪlt] **I.** *n* (*slope*) Neigung *f* ▶ PHRASES: **[at] full ~** mit voller Kraft **II.** *vt* neigen; **to ~ the balance in favor of sth/sb** einen Meinungsumschwung zugunsten einer S./Person *gen* herbeiführen **III.** *vi* ❶ (*slope*) sich neigen ❷ (*movement of opinion*) sich abwenden (**away from** von +*dat*), sich zuwenden (**toward** +*dat*)

timber ['tɪm·bər] *n* ❶ (*wood for building*) Bauholz *nt* ❷ (*elongated piece of wood*) Holzplanke *f*

time [taɪm] **I.** *n* ❶ (*considered as a whole*) Zeit *f;* **~ stood still** die Zeit stand still; **as ~ goes by** im Lauf[e] der Zeit; **for all ~** für immer ❷ (*period, duration*) Zeit *f;* **to be going through a difficult ~** eine schwere Zeit durchmachen; **~'s up** (*fam*) die Zeit ist um; **it will take some ~** es wird eine Weile dauern; **free ~** [*or* **spare**] Freizeit *f;* **to have ~ on one's hands** viel Zeit zur Verfügung haben; **period of ~** Zeitraum *m;* **a long ~ ago** vor langer Zeit; **to be pressed for ~** in Zeitnot sein; **to take one's ~** sich *dat* Zeit lassen; **for the ~ being** vorläufig; **to tell ~** die Uhr lesen; **on ~** pünktlich ❸ (*occasion, frequency*) Mal *nt;* **for the first ~** zum ersten Mal; **from ~ to ~** ab und zu; **three ~s a week** drei Mal in der Woche; **for the hundredth ~** zum hundertsten Mal ❹ *usu pl* (*era, lifetime*) Zeit *f;* **~s are changing** die Zeiten ändern sich; **to be behind the ~s** seiner Zeit hinterherhinken ❺ (*schedule*) **arrival/departure ~** Ankunfts-/Abfahrtszeit *f* ❻ SPORTS Zeit *f;* **record ~** Rekordzeit *f* ❼ MATH **two ~s five is ten** zwei mal fünf ist zehn ❽ MUS Takt *m;* **to keep ~** den Takt halten ❾ ([*not*] *like*) **to not have much ~ for sb** jdn nicht mögen ❿ (*fam*) **to do ~** [im Knast] sitzen ▶ PHRASES: **~ is of the essence** die Zeit drängt; **[only] ~ will tell** (*saying*) erst die Zukunft wird es zeigen **II.** *vt* ❶ (*measure duration*) ■ **to ~ sb in the 100 meters** jds Zeit beim 100-Meter-Lauf nehmen ❷ (*choose best moment for*) ■ **to ~ sth [right]** den richtigen Zeitpunkt wählen (für +*akk*)

'time bomb *n* (*a. fig*) Zeitbombe *f*

'timecard *n* Stechkarte *f*

'time clock *n* Stechuhr *f*

'time-consuming *adj* zeitintensiv

'time difference *n* Zeitunterschied *m*

'timekeeper *n* ❶ SPORTS Zeitnehmer, -in *m, f* ❷ (*clock, watch*) Zeitmesser *m;* **to be a good ~** *person* sein Zeitsoll immer erfüllen

'time lag *n* Zeitdifferenz *f*

'time-lapse *adj attr film, photography* Zeitraffer-

timeless ['taɪm·lɪs] *adj* ❶ (*not dated*) *book, dress, values* zeitlos ❷ (*unchanging*) *landscape, beauty* immer während *attr*

'time limit *n* Zeitbeschränkung *f*

timely ['taɪm·li] *adj* rechtzeitig; *remark* passend; *manner* rasch

'timeout I. *n* <*pl* times- *or* -s> SPORTS Auszeit *f,* Timeout *nt;* **to call a ~** ein Timeout nehmen **II.** *interj* Auszeit, Timeout

timer ['taɪ·mər] *n* ❶ (*for lights, VCR*) Timer *m,* Zeitschaltuhr *f;* (*for cooking eggs*) Eieruhr *f* ❷ (*time recorder*) Zeitmesser *m;* (*person*) Zeitnehmer(in) *m(f)*

'time-saving *adj* Zeit sparend

'time scale *n* Zeitrahmen *m*

'time sheet *n* Stundenzettel *m,* Arbeitszeiterfassungsbogen *m*

'timetable *n* (*for bus, train*) Fahrplan *m;* (*for events, project*) Programm *nt;* (*for appointments*) Zeitplan *m*

'timeworn *adj* abgenutzt; *excuse* abgedroschen

'time zone *n* Zeitzone *f*

timid <-er, -est *or* more ~, most ~> ['tɪm·ɪd] *adj* ängstlich; (*shy*) schüchtern; (*lacking courage*) zaghaft

timidity [tɪ·'mɪd·ɪ·t̬i] *n* Ängstlichkeit *f;* (*shyness*) Schüchternheit *f;* (*lack of courage*) Zaghaftigkeit *f*

timing ['taɪ·mɪŋ] *n* ① (*of words, actions*) Timing *nt* ② (*measuring of time*) Zeitabnahme *f;* *of a race, runners a.* Stoppen *nt kein pl;* (*in factories*) Zeitkontrolle *f*

timpani ['tɪm·pə·ni] *npl* MUS Pauken *pl*

tin [tɪn] *n* ① (*metal*) Zinn *nt* ② (*for baking*) Backform *f;* **cake ~** Kuchenform *f*

tin 'can *n* Blechdose *f*

tinder ['tɪn·dər] *n* Zunder *m*

'tinfoil ['tɪn·fɔɪl] *n* Alufolie *f*

tinge [tɪndʒ] **I.** *n* ① (*of color*) Hauch *m;* **~ of red** [leichter] Rotstich ② (*of emotion*) Anflug *m kein pl* **II.** *vt usu passive* ① (*with an emotion*) **~d with regret** mit einer Spur von Bedauern ② (*with colors*) **to be ~d with orange** mit Orange [leicht] getönt sein

tingle ['tɪŋ·gəl] **I.** *vi* kribbeln; **to ~ with excitement** vor Aufregung zittern **II.** *n* Kribbeln *nt*

tinker ['tɪŋ·kər] *vi* ■**to ~ [around] [with sth]** [an etw *dat*] herumbasteln

tinkle ['tɪŋ·kəl] **I.** *vi* ① (*make sound*) *piano* klimpern; *bell* klingen; *fountain* plätschern ② (*fam: urinate*) Pipi machen **II.** *vt* **to ~ a bell** mit einer Glocke klingeln **III.** *n* ① (*of bell*) Klingen *nt kein pl;* (*of water*) Plätschern *nt kein pl* ② (*fam: urine*) Pipi *nt*

tinny ['tɪn·i] *adj* ① *voice, recording* blechern ② *taste, food* nach Blech schmeckend *attr*

tinsel ['tɪn·səl] *n* Lametta *nt*

tint [tɪnt] **I.** *n* ① (*hue*) Farbton *m* ② (*dye*) Tönung *f* **II.** *vt hair* tönen

tiny ['taɪ·ni] *adj* winzig; **teeny ~** klitzeklein

tip[1] [tɪp] *n* (*pointed end*) Spitze *f* ▶ PHRASES: **it's on the ~ of my tongue** es liegt mir auf der Zunge

tip[2] [tɪp] **I.** *vt* <-pp-> ① (*topple*) umkippen ② (*tilt*) neigen; **to ~ the balance** den Ausschlag geben **II.** *vi* <-pp-> kippen

tip[3] [tɪp] **I.** *n* ① (*money*) Trinkgeld *nt;* **to leave a 15% ~** 15 % Trinkgeld geben ② (*suggestion*) Rat[schlag] *m,* Tipp *m* **II.** *vt* <-pp-> ① (*give money to*) Trinkgeld geben ② (*give information to*) *the police* einen Tipp geben **III.** *vi* <-pp-> Trinkgeld geben

◆**tip off** *vt* einen Tipp geben

◆**tip over** *vt, vi* umschütten, umkippen

T

'tip-off *n* (*fam*) Tipp *m*

tipsy ['tɪp·si] *adj* beschwipst

tiptoe ['tɪp·toʊ] **I.** *n* **on ~[s]** auf Zehenspitzen **II.** *vi* auf Zehenspitzen gehen

tip'top *adj* (*fam*) Spitzen-, Spitze *präd,* tipptopp

tirade ['taɪ·reɪd] *n* Tirade *f geh*

tire[1] [taɪr] **I.** *vt* ermüden; **to ~ oneself doing sth** von etw *dat* müde werden **II.** *vi* müde werden; ■**to ~ of sth/sb** etw/jdn satthaben; **to never ~ of doing sth** nie müde werden, etw zu tun

tire[2] [taɪr] *n* Reifen *m;* **spare ~** Ersatzreifen *m;* (*fig, hum fam*) Rettungsring *m*

tired <-er, -est *or* more ~, most ~> ['taɪrd] *adj* ① (*exhausted*) müde ② (*bored with*) **to be sick and ~ of sth/sb** von etw/jdm die Nase gestrichen voll haben *fam* ③ (*overused*) *excuse* lahm; *phrase* abgedroschen

tiredness ['taɪ·rd·nɪs] *n* Müdigkeit *f*

tireless ['taɪr·lɪs] *adj* unermüdlich (**in** bei +*dat*)

tiresome ['taɪr·səm] *adj* mühsam; *habit* unangenehm

tiring ['taɪ·rɪŋ] *adj* ermüdend

tissue ['tɪʃ·u] *n* ① (*for wrapping*) Seidenpapier *nt* ② (*for wiping noses*) Tempo® *nt* ③ (*of animals or plants*) Gewebe *nt*

tit[1] [tɪt] *n* (*bird*) Meise *f* ▶ PHRASES: **~ for tat** wie du mir, so ich dir

tit[2] [tɪt] *n* (*vulg, sl: breast*) Titte *f*

titanic [taɪ·'tæn·ɪk] *adj* gigantisch

titanium [taɪ·'teɪ·ni·əm] *n* Titan *nt*

titillate ['tɪt·ə·leɪt] **I.** *vt* anregen **II.** *vi* erregen

titillation [ˌtɪt·əl·'eɪ·ʃən] *n* (*sexual*) Erregung *f;* (*intellectual*) Anregung *f*

title ['taɪṭ·əl] **I.** *n* ① *a.* SPORTS *of book, film* Titel *m* ② (*status, rank*) Titel *m;* **job ~** Berufsbezeichnung *f* ③ AUTO (*ownership document*) Kraftfahrzeugbrief *m* **II.** *vt book, film* betiteln

'title deed *n* LAW *see* **deed 2**

'titleholder *n* Titelverteidiger(in) *m(f)*

'title page *n* Titelblatt *nt*

'title role *n* Titelrolle *f*

'title track *n* Titelsong *m*

titter ['tɪṭ·ər] **I.** *vi* kichern **II.** *n* Gekicher *nt kein pl*

tizzy <*pl* -ies> ['tɪz·i] *n* (*sl*) Aufregung *f;* ■**to be in a ~** in heller Aufregung sein

TN *abbrev of* **Tennessee**

to [tu] **I.** *prep* ① (*moving toward*) in +*akk,* nach +*dat,* zu +*dat;* **they go ~ work on the bus** sie fahren mit dem Bus zur Arbeit; **we moved ~ Germany last year** wir sind letztes Jahr nach Deutschland gezogen; **~ the north** nördlich; **from place ~ place** von Ort zu Ort ② (*attending regularly*) zu +*dat,* in +*dat;* **she goes ~ college** sie geht auf die Universität ③ (*inviting to*) zu +*dat;* **I've asked them ~ dinner** ich habe sie zum Essen eingeladen ④ (*in direction of*) auf +*akk;* **to point ~ sth** auf etw *akk* zeigen ⑤ (*in contact with, attached to*) an +*dat;* **cheek ~ cheek** Wange an Wange; **tie the leash ~ the fence** mach die Leine am Zaun fest ⑥ (*with indirect object*) ■**~ sb/sth** jdm/etw; **give that gun ~ me** gib mir das Gewehr; **to be married ~ sb** mit jdm verheiratet sein; **to tell sth ~ sb** jdm etw erzählen ⑦ (*compared to*) mit +*dat;* **I prefer beef ~ seafood** ich ziehe Rindfleisch Meeresfrüchten vor ⑧ (*until, to point in time*) bis +*dat,* zu +*dat;* **and ~ this day ...** und bis auf den heutigen Tag ... ⑨ (*expressing change of state*) zu +*dat;* **he converted ~ Islam** er ist zum Islam übergetreten ⑩ (*in clock times*) vor +*dat;* **it's twenty ~ six** es ist zwanzig vor sechs ⑪ (*in honor of*) auf +*akk;* **here's ~ you!** auf dein/Ihr Wohl!; **the record is dedicated ~ her mother** die Schallplatte ist ihrer Mutter gewidmet ⑫ MATH (*defining exponent*) hoch;

ten ~ the third power zehn hoch drei **II.** *to form infin* ❶ (*expressing future intention*) **I'll have ~ tell him** ich werde es ihm sagen müssen; **to be about ~ do sth** gerade etw tun wollen ❷ (*forming requests*) zu; **he told me ~ wait** er sagte mir, ich solle warten; **I asked her ~ give me a call** ich bat sie, mich anzurufen ❸ (*omitting verb*) **would you like to go? — yes, I'd love ~** möchtest du hingehen? – ja, sehr gern ❹ *after adj* (*to complete meaning*) **I'm sorry ~ hear that** es tut mir leid, das zu hören; **easy ~ use** leicht zu bedienen ❺ (*after wh- words*) **I don't know what ~ do** ich weiß nicht, was ich tun soll; **I don't know where ~ begin** ich weiß nicht, wo ich anfangen soll ❻ (*introducing clause*) **~ be honest** um ehrlich zu sein **III.** *adv* zu; **to come ~** zu sich *dat* kommen

toad [toʊd] *n* Kröte *f*

'toadstool *n* Giftpilz *m*

toady ['toʊ·di] (*pej*) **I.** *n* Speichellecker *m* **II.** *vi* <-ie-> kriechen (**to** vor +*dat*)

to and 'fro I. *adv* hin und her; (*back and forth*) vor und zurück **II.** *vi* (*inf: move*) ■**to be toing and froing** vor- und zurückgehen; (*be indecisive*) hin und her schwanken

toast¹ [toʊst] **I.** *n* (*bread*) Toast *m;* **slice of ~** Scheibe *f* Toast ▶ PHRASES: **to be ~** (*hum fam*) erledigt sein *fam* **II.** *vt* (*cook over heat*) *bread, muffin* toasten; *nuts* rösten

toast² [toʊst] **I.** *n* (*when drinking*) Toast *m,* Trinkspruch *m;* **to drink a ~ to sb** auf jdn trinken **II.** *vt* (*drink to*) trinken (auf +*akk*)

toaster ['toʊ·stər] *n* Toaster *m*

toasty ['toʊ·sti] *adj* (*fam: warm*) wohlig warm

tobacco [tə·'bæk·oʊ] *n* Tabak *m*

-to-be [tə·'bi] *in compounds* (*boss-, husband-*) zukünftige(r, s) *attr;* **mother-~** werdende Mutter

toboggan [tə·'bag·ən] **I.** *n* Schlitten *m,* Rodel *f* ÖSTERR **II.** *vi* Schlitten fahren, rodeln

today [tə·'deɪ] **I.** *adv* ❶ (*on this day*) heute ❷ (*nowadays*) heutzutage **II.** *n* ❶ (*this day*) heutiger Tag; **what's the date ~?** welches Datum haben wir heute? ❷ (*present period of time*) Heute *nt;* **cars of ~** Autos *pl* von heute

toddler ['tad·lər] *n* Kleinkind *nt*

to-do [tə·'du] *n usu sing* (*fam*) ❶ (*fuss*) Getue *nt pej;* **to make a big ~ about sth** ein großes Theater um etw *akk* machen ❷ (*confrontation*) Wirbel *m*

to-'do list *n* Besorgungsliste *f*

toe [toʊ] **I.** *n* ❶ (*on foot*) Zehe *f* ❷ (*of sock, shoe*) Spitze *f* ▶ PHRASES: **to keep sb on their ~s** jdn auf Zack halten **II.** *vt* **to ~ the party line** der Parteilinie folgen

'toecap *n* Schuhkappe *f*

'toehold *n* ❶ (*in climbing*) Halt *m* für die Zehen ❷ (*fig: advantage*) Vorteil *m*

'toenail *n* Zehennagel *m*

toffee ['tɔ·fi] *n* Toffee *nt,* Sahnebonbon *nt*

together [tə·'geð·ər] **I.** *adv* ❶ (*in relationship, with each other*) zusammen; **close ~** nah beisammen ❷ (*collectively*) zusammen, gemeinsam; **all ~ now** jetzt alle miteinander ❸ (*simultaneously*) gleichzeitig **II.** *adj* (*fam*) ausgeglichen

togetherness [tə·'geð·ər·nɪs] *n* Zusammengehörigkeit *f*

toggle ['tag·əl] **I.** *n* ❶ (*switch*) Kippschalter *m;* COMPUT (*key*) Umschalttaste *f* ❷ (*fastener*) Knebel *m* **II.** *vi* COMPUT hin- und herschalten

'toggle switch *n* Kippschalter *m*

Togo ['toʊ·goʊ] *n* Togo *nt*

Togolese [ˌtoʊ·goʊ·'liz] **I.** *adj* togoisch **II.** *n* Togoer(in) *m(f)*

toil [tɔɪl] **I.** *n* Mühe *f* **II.** *vi* hart arbeiten

toilet ['tɔɪ·lɪt] *n* Toilette *f,* Klo *nt fam*

'toilet bowl *n* Toilettenschüssel *f*

'toilet paper *n* Toilettenpapier *nt*

toiletries ['tɔɪ·lɪ·triz] *npl* Toilettenartikel *pl*

'toilet seat *n* Toilettensitz *m*

'toilet tank *n* Spülkasten *m*

toing and froing [ˌtu·ɪŋ·ənd·'froʊ·ɪŋ] *n* Hin und Her *nt;* (*back and forth*) Vor und Zurück *nt*

token ['toʊ·kən] **I.** *n* ❶ (*symbol*) *of sb's appreciation* Zeichen *nt* ❷ (*money substitute*) Chip *m* ▶ PHRASES: **by the same ~** aus demselben Grund **II.** *adj attr* ❶ (*symbolic*) nominell; *fine, gesture, resistance* symbolisch ❷ (*pej: an appearance of*) Schein-; **the ~ woman** die Alibifrau

told [toʊld] *pt, pp of* **tell**

tolerable ['tal·ər·ə·bəl] *adj* erträglich; (*fairly good*) annehmbar

tolerably ['tal·ər·ə·bli] *adv* recht, ganz

tolerance ['tal·ər·əns] *n* ❶ (*open-mindedness*) Toleranz *f* (**of/toward** gegenüber +*dat*) ❷ (*capacity to endure*) Toleranz *f,* Widerstandsfähigkeit *f* (**to** gegen +*akk*); **~ to alcohol** Alkoholverträglichkeit *f* ❸ (*allowance for deviation*) Toleranz *f*

tolerant ['tal·ər·ənt] *adj* ❶ (*open-minded*) tolerant (**of/toward** gegenüber +*dat*) ❷ (*resistant*) *person* widerstandsfähig; *plant* resistent (**of** gegen +*akk*)

tolerate ['tal·ə·reɪt] *vt* ❶ (*accept*) tolerieren; *person* ertragen ❷ (*resist*) *heat, pain, stress* aushalten; *of plant: cold, insects* widerstehen; *drug* vertragen

toleration [ˌtal·ə·'reɪ·ʃən] *n* Toleranz *f*

toll¹ [toʊl] *n* ❶ (*for highways, bridges*) Maut *f;* **truck ~** Lkw-Maut *f* ❷ (*for phone call*) [Fernsprech]gebühr *f* ❸ (*deaths, loss*) Tribut *m;* **death ~** Opferzahl *f*

toll² [toʊl] *vt, vi bell* läuten

'toll bridge *n* Mautbrücke *f*

'toll-free *adj* gebührenfrei; **~ number** gebührenfreie Telefonnummer

'toll road *n* Mautstraße *f*

tomahawk ['ta·mə·hak] *n* Tomahawk *m,* Kriegsbeil *nt*

tomato <*pl* -es> [tə·'meɪ·t̬oʊ] *n* Tomate *f,* Paradeiser *m* ÖSTERR

tomb [tum] *n* Grab *nt;* (*mausoleum*) Gruft *f;*

(*below ground*) Grabkammer *f*
tomboy ['tam·bɔɪ] *n* Wildfang *m*
tombstone ['tum·stoʊn] *n* Grabstein *m*
tomcat ['tam·kæt] *n* Kater *m*
tome [toʊm] *n* (*usu hum*) Schmöker *m fam*
tomorrow [tə·'mar·oʊ] **I.** *adv* morgen **II.** *n* morgiger Tag; **~'s problems** Probleme *pl* von morgen; **a better ~** eine bessere Zukunft ▶ PHRASES: **~ is another day** (*saying*) morgen ist auch noch ein Tag
tom-tom ['tam·tam] *n* Tamtam *nt*
ton <*pl* - *or* -s> [tʌn] *n* ① (*unit of measurement*) Tonne *f* ② (*fam: very large amount*) **a ~ of money** ein Haufen *m* Geld; **how much money does he have? — ~s** wie viel Geld besitzt er? – jede Menge; **to weigh a ~** Unmengen wiegen ▶ PHRASES: **to come down on sb like a ~ of bricks** jdn völlig fertigmachen
tone [toʊn] **I.** *n* ① (*of instrument*) Klang *m* ② (*manner of speaking*) Ton *m;* **a disrespectful ~** ein respektloser Ton ③ (*character*) Ton *m;* **to lower the ~ of sth** der Qualität einer S. *gen* schaden ④ (*of color*) Farbton *m* ⑤ (*of telephone*) Ton *m;* **dial ~** Wählton *m* **II.** *vt* **to ~ one's muscles** die Muskeln fit halten
◆**tone down** *vt* abmildern; *color, sound* abschwächen
◆**tone up I.** *vt muscles* kräftigen **II.** *vi* sich in Form bringen
'**tone-deaf** *adj* ■**to be ~** unmusikalisch sein
'**tone poem** *n see* **symphonic poem**
toner ['toʊ·nər] *n* ① (*for skin*) Gesichtswasser *nt* ② COMPUT, PHOT Toner *m;* **~ cartridge** Tonerpatrone *f*
Tonga ['taŋ·gə] *n* Tonga *nt*
Tongan ['taŋ·gən] **I.** *adj* tongaisch **II.** *n* ① (*person*) Tongaer(in) *m(f)* ② LING Tongasprache *f*
tongs [taŋz] *npl* Zange *f*
tongue [tʌŋ] *n* ① (*mouth part, language*) Zunge *f;* **cat got your ~?** hat es dir die Sprache verschlagen?; **to bite one's ~** sich *dat* in die Zunge beißen ② (*tongue-shaped object*) **~ of land** Landzunge *f* ▶ PHRASES: **to say sth ~ in cheek** etw als Scherz meinen
'**tongue-tied** *adj* sprachlos
'**tongue twister** *n* Zungenbrecher *m*
tonic[1] ['tan·ɪk] *n* ① (*medicine*) Tonikum *nt geh* ② (*sth that rejuvenates*) Erfrischung *f*
tonic[2] ['tan·ɪk], **tonic water** ['tanɪk-] *n* Tonic[water] *nt*
tonight [tə·'naɪt] **I.** *adv* (*during today's night*) heute Abend; (*until after midnight*) heute Nacht **II.** *n* (*today's night*) der heutige Abend
tonsillitis [ˌtan·sə·'laɪ·tɪs] *n* Mandelentzündung *f*
tonsils ['tan·səlz] *npl* MED Mandeln *pl*
too [tu] *adv* ① (*overly*) *big, heavy, small* zu; **to be ~ bad** wirklich schade sein; **far ~ difficult** viel zu schwierig ② (*very*) sehr; **to not be ~ sure if ...** sich *dat* nicht ganz sicher sein, ob ... ③ (*also*) auch; **me ~!** ich auch!; **get one for me ~** bring mir auch einen ④ (*moreover*) überdies
took [tʊk] *vt, vi pt of* **take**
tool [tul] **I.** *n* ① (*implement*) Werkzeug *nt* ② (*aid*) Mittel *nt* ③ (*occupational necessity*) Instrument *nt;* **to be a ~ of the trade** zum Handwerkszeug gehören **II.** *vt* bearbeiten
'**toolbar** *n* COMPUT Symbolleiste *f*
'**toolbox** *n* Werkzeugkiste *f*
'**tool chest**, '**toolkit** *n* Werkzeugkasten *m*
toot [tut] **I.** *n* Hupen *nt kein pl* **II.** *vt* (*sound*) anhupen; **to ~ a horn** auf die Hupe drücken
tooth <*pl* teeth> [tuθ] *n* ① (*in mouth*) Zahn *m;* **to brush one's teeth** die Zähne putzen; **to grit one's teeth** die Zähne zusammenbeißen ② *usu pl of comb* Zinke *f; of saw* [Säge]zahn *m; of cog* Zahn *m* ▶ PHRASES: **to sink one's teeth into sth** sich in etw *akk* hineinstürzen
'**toothache** *n* Zahnschmerzen *pl*
'**toothbrush** *n* Zahnbürste *f*
'**toothpaste** *n* Zahnpasta *f*
'**toothpick** *n* Zahnstocher *m*
toothy ['tu·θi] *adj* zähnefletschend; *grin* breit
top[1] [tap] **I.** *n* ① (*highest part*) oberes Ende, Spitze *f; of mountain* [Berg]gipfel *m; of tree* [Baum]krone *f;* **from ~ to bottom** von oben bis unten; **to get on ~ of sth** (*fig*) etw in den Griff bekommen ② (*upper surface*) Oberfläche *f;* **there was a pile of books on ~ of the table** auf dem Tisch lag ein Stoß Bücher ③ (*highest rank*) Spitze *f;* **to graduate** [*or* **be**] **at the ~ of one's** [*or* **the**] **class** Klassenbeste(r) *f(m)* sein ④ FASHION Top *nt* ⑤ (*lid*) Deckel *m* ▶ PHRASES: **off the ~ of one's head** (*fam*) aus dem Stegreif; **to go over the ~** überreagieren **II.** *adj* ① *attr* (*highest*) oberste(r, s); **~ floor** oberstes Stockwerk ② (*best*) beste(r, s); **sb's ~ choice** jds erste Wahl ③ (*most successful*) Spitzen-; **~ athlete** Spitzensportler(in) *m(f)* ④ (*maximum*) höchste(r, s); **~ speed** Höchstgeschwindigkeit *f* **III.** *vt* <-pp-> ① (*be at top of*) anführen; **to ~ a list** oben auf einer Liste stehen ② (*cover*) überziehen (**with** mit +*dat*) ③ (*surpass*) übertreffen
◆**top off** *vt* ① FOOD garnieren (**with** mit +*dat*) ② (*conclude satisfactorily*) abrunden; (*more than satisfactorily*) krönen (**with** mit +*dat*) ③ *gasoline tank* [vollends] auffüllen
top[2] [tap] *n* (*toy*) Kreisel *m*
topaz ['toʊ·ˌpæz] *n* Topas *m*
top 'dog *n* (*fam*) Boss *m fam*
top 'drawer *n* ① (*uppermost drawer*) oberste [Schub]lade ② (*fam: social position*) Oberschicht *f*
'**top-flight** *adj attr* beste(r, s)
'**top hat** *n* Zylinder *m*
top-'heavy *adj* (*usu pej: unbalanced*) kopflastig
topic ['tap·ɪk] *n* Thema *nt*
topical ['tap·ɪ·kəl] *adj* ① (*currently of interest*) aktuell ② (*by topics*) thematisch ③ MED (*applied locally*) lokal

topicality [ˌtap·ɪ·ˈkæl·ɪ·t̬i] *n* Aktualität *f*

topless [ˈtap·lɪs] **I.** *adj* oben ohne *präd,* barbusig **II.** *adv* **to go ~** oben ohne gehen

ˈ**top-level** *adj negotiations, talks* Spitzen-

ˈ**topmost** *adj attr* oberste(r, s)

ˈ**top-notch** *adj* (*fam*) erstklassig

topographical [ˌtap·ə·ˈgræf·ɪ·kəl] *adj* topographisch

topography [tə·ˈpag·rə·fi] *n* Topographie *f*

topping [ˈtap·ɪŋ] *n* Garnierung *f*

topple [ˈtap·əl] **I.** *vt* ① (*knock over*) umwerfen ② POL (*overthrow*) stürzen **II.** *vi* stürzen; *prices* fallen

◆**topple over I.** *vt* umwerfen **II.** *vi* umfallen, stürzen (über +*akk*)

top ˈ**quality** *n* Spitzenqualität *f*

top-ˈ**ranking** *adj* Spitzen-; **~ university** Eliteuniversität *f*

top ˈ**secret** *adj* streng geheim

ˈ**top-selling** *adj attr* meistverkauft

ˈ**topsoil** *n* Mutterboden *m*

top ˈ**speed** *n* Höchstgeschwindigkeit *f*

topsy-turvy [ˌtap·sɪ·ˈtɜr·vi] (*fam*) **I.** *adj* chaotisch **II.** *adv* **to turn sth ~** etw auf den Kopf stellen

torch [tɔrtʃ] **I.** *n* <*pl* -es> ① (*burning stick*) Fackel *f;* **Olympic ~** olympisches Feuer ② (*blowtorch*) Lötlampe *f* **II.** *vt* (*fam*) in Brand setzen

ˈ**torchlight** *n* Fackelschein *m*

tore [tɔr] *vi, vt pt of* **tear**

torment I. *n* [ˈtɔr·ment] ① (*mental suffering*) Qual *f* ② (*physical pain*) starke Schmerzen *pl* ③ (*torture*) Tortur *f* **II.** *vt* [tɔr·ˈment] (*cause to suffer*) quälen; **to be ~ed by grief** großen Kummer haben

tormentor [tɔr·ˈmen·tər] *n* Peiniger(in) *m(f)*

torn [tɔrn] **I.** *vi, vt pp of* **tear II.** *adj pred* (*unable to choose*) [innerlich] zerrissen (**between** zwischen +*dat*)

tornado <*pl* -s *or* -es> [tɔr·ˈneɪ·doʊ] *n* Tornado *m*

torpedo [tɔr·ˈpi·doʊ] MIL, NAUT **I.** *n* <*pl* -es> Torpedo *m* **II.** *vt* torpedieren

torpor [ˈtɔr·pər] *n* (*form*) Trägheit *f;* (*hibernation*) Winterschlaf *m*

torque [tɔrk] *n* PHYS Drehmoment *nt*

torrent [ˈtɔr·ənt] *n* ① (*large amount of water*) Sturzbach *m* ② (*large amount*) Strom *m*

torrential [tɔ·ˈren·ʃəl] *adj* sintflutartig

torrid [ˈtɔr·ɪd] *adj* (*fig: strongly emotional*) glühend; *affair, love scene* heiß

torso [ˈtɔr·soʊ] *n* ① (*body*) Rumpf *m* ② (*statue*) Torso *m*

tortoise [ˈtɔr·t̬əs] *n* [Land]schildkröte *f*

ˈ**tortoiseshell** *n* Schildpatt *nt*

tortuous [ˈtɔr·tʃu·əs] *adj* gewunden; (*complicated*) umständlich; *process* langwierig

torture [ˈtɔr·tʃər] **I.** *n* ① (*act of cruelty*) Folter *f* ② (*painful suffering*) Qual *f,* Tortur *f* **II.** *vt* ① (*cause suffering to*) foltern ② (*greatly disturb*) quälen; ■**to be ~d by sth** von etw *dat* gequält werden

torturer [ˈtɔr·tʃər·ər] *n* Folterer *m*

toss <*pl* -es> [tɔs] **I.** *n* Wurf *m* **II.** *vt* ① (*throw*) werfen; (*fling*) schleudern; (*from horse*) abwerfen; (*throw back head*) zurückwerfen ② (*move up and back*) hin und her schleudern; FOOD schwenken **III.** *vi* ▶ PHRASES: **to ~ and turn** sich hin und her wälzen

◆**toss out** *vt* ① (*throw out*) hinauswerfen ② (*offer unsolicited*) *remark* rauslassen *fam; suggestion* einwerfen

ˈ**toss-up** *n* ungewisse Situation; ■**to be a ~** [noch] offen sein

tot [tat] *n* (*fam*) Knirps *m*

total [ˈtoʊ·t̬əl] **I.** *n* Gesamtsumme *f;* **in ~** insgesamt **II.** *adj* ① *attr* (*complete*) gesamt ② (*absolute*) völlig; *disaster* rein; **to be a ~ stranger** vollkommen fremd sein **III.** *vt* <-l- *or* -ll-> ① (*add up*) zusammenrechnen; **their debts ~ 8,000 dollars** ihre Schulden belaufen sich auf 8.000 Dollar ② (*fam*) **to ~ a car** einen Wagen zu Schrott fahren

◆**total up** *vt* zusammenrechnen

totalitarian [toʊ·ˌtæl·ə·ˈter·i·ən] *adj* POL totalitär

totalitarianism [toʊ·ˌtæl·ə·ˈter·i·ə·nɪz·əm] *n* POL Totalitarismus *m*

totality [toʊ·ˈtæl·ɪ·t̬i] *n* (*whole amount*) Gesamtheit *f*

totally [ˈtoʊ·t̬ə·li] *adv* völlig

tote [toʊt] *vt* (*fam*) schleppen

ˈ**tote bag** *n* Einkaufstasche *f*

totem [ˈtoʊ·t̬əm] *n* Totem *nt*

totter [ˈtat̬·ər] *vi* wanken

tottery [ˈtat̬·ə·ri] *adj* wackelig; *person* zittrig

toucan [ˈtu·kæn] *n* Tukan *m*

touch [tʌtʃ] **I.** *n* <*pl* -es> ① (*ability to feel*) Tasten *nt;* **the material was soft to the ~** das Material fühlte sich weich an ② (*instance of touching*) Berührung *f;* **at the ~ of a button** auf Knopfdruck ③ (*communication*) Kontakt *m;* **to be/keep in ~ with sb/sth** mit jdm/etw in Kontakt stehen/bleiben ④ (*mild attack*) **a ~ of the flu** (*fam*) eine leichte Grippe ⑤ (*dash*) *of salt, pepper* eine Spur ⑥ (*knack*) Gespür *nt* ▶ PHRASES: **to be a soft ~** (*fam*) leichtgläubig sein **II.** *vt* ① (*feel with fingers*) berühren, anfassen ② (*come in contact with*) in Berührung kommen (mit +*dat*); (*border*) grenzen (an +*akk*) ③ (*move emotionally*) bewegen ▶ PHRASES: **to ~ a [raw] nerve** einen wunden Punkt berühren; **to not ~ sb/sth with a ten-foot pole** jdm/etw meiden wie die Pest **III.** *vi* ① (*feel with fingers*) berühren ② (*come in contact*) sich berühren

◆**touch down** *vi* AVIAT landen

◆**touch off** *vt* auslösen

◆**touch on, touch upon** *vi* ansprechen

◆**touch up** *vt* auffrischen; *photograph* retuschieren

touch-and-ˈ**go** *adj* (*precarious*) unentschieden; ■**to be ~ whether ...** auf Messers Schneide stehen, ob ...

ˈ**touchdown** *n* ① (*landing*) Landung *f* ② SPORTS Touchdown *m*

touched [tʌtʃt] *adj pred* gerührt

touchiness ['tʌtʃ·ɪ·nɪs] *n* (*fam*) ❶ (*sensitive nature*) Überempfindlichkeit *f* ❷ (*delicacy, precariousness*) Empfindlichkeit *f*

touching ['tʌtʃ·ɪŋ] **I.** *adj* berührend **II.** *n* Berühren *nt kein pl*

'touch-type *vi* blind schreiben

touchy ['tʌtʃ·i] *adj* (*fam*) ❶ (*oversensitive*) *person* empfindlich ❷ (*delicate*) *situation, topic* heikel

tough [tʌf] *adj* ❶ (*strong*) robust ❷ (*hardy*) *person, animal* zäh; **to be as ~ as nails** nicht unterzukriegen sein ❸ (*hard to cut*) *meat* zäh ❹ (*difficult, harsh*) schwierig, hart; *climate* rau; *competition* hart; *winter, laws* streng ❺ (*violent*) rau, brutal

◆**tough out** *vt* (*fam*) aussitzen; ■**to ~ it out** es durchhalten

toughen ['tʌf·ən] **I.** *vt* ❶ (*strengthen*) verstärken; *glass* härten ❷ (*make difficult to cut*) hart werden lassen **II.** *vi* stärker werden

toughness ['tʌf·nɪs] *n* ❶ (*strength*) Härte *f*, Robustheit *f* ❷ (*determination*) Entschlossenheit *f* ❸ (*of meat*) Zähheit *f*

toupee [tu·'peɪ] *n* Toupet *nt*

tour [tʊr] **I.** *n* ❶ (*journey*) Reise *f*, Tour *f*; **guided ~** Führung *f* ❷ (*period of duty*) Tournee *f*; **lecture ~** Vortragsreise *f* **II.** *vt* ❶ (*travel around*) bereisen ❷ (*visit professionally*) besuchen ❸ (*perform*) **to ~ Germany** eine Deutschlandtournee machen **III.** *vi* ■**to ~ [with sb]** [mit jdm] auf Tournee gehen

'tour guide *n* ❶ (*book*) Reiseführer *m* ❷ (*person*) Reiseführer(in) *m(f)*, Fremdenführer(in) *m(f)*

touring ['tʊr·ɪŋ] **I.** *adj attr* THEAT, MUS Tournee-; **~ company** Wandertheater *nt* **II.** *n* Reisen *nt kein pl*; **to do some ~** herumreisen

tourism ['tʊr·ɪz·əm] *n* Tourismus *m*

tourist ['tʊr·ɪst] *n* (*traveller*) Tourist(in) *m(f)*

'tourist industry *n* Tourismusindustrie *f*

tourist office *n* Touristeninformation *f*, Fremdenverkehrsamt *nt*

'tourist season *n* Hauptsaison *f*

'tourist visa *n* Reisevisum *nt*

tournament ['tɜr·nə·mənt] *n* SPORTS Turnier *nt*

tousle ['taʊ·zəl] *vt hair* zerzausen

tousled ['taʊ·zəlt] *adj* zerzaust

tout [taʊt] *vt* Reklame machen (für +*akk*); ■**to ~ sb/sth as sth** jdn/etw als etw preisen

tow [toʊ] **I.** *n* Schleppen *nt kein pl*; **to have sb in ~** jdn im Schlepptau haben **II.** *vt* ziehen; *vehicle* abschleppen

toward(s) [tɔrd(z)] *prep* ❶ (*in direction of*) in Richtung; **she walked ~ him** sie ging auf ihn zu ❷ (*near*) nahe +*dat*; **we're up ~ the front of the line** wir sind nahe dem Anfang der Schlange ❸ (*just before*) gegen +*akk*; **~ midnight** gegen Mitternacht ❹ (*contributing to*) **to count ~ sth** auf etw *akk* angerechnet werden

towel ['taʊ·əl] **I.** *n* Handtuch *nt*; **paper ~** Papiertuch *nt* ▶ PHRASES: **to throw in the ~** das Handtuch werfen **II.** *vt* <-ll-> **to ~ sth dry** etw trockenreiben

toweling ['taʊ·ə·lɪŋ] *n* Frottee *nt o m*

'towel rack *n* Handtuchhalter *m*

tower ['taʊ·ər] *n* Turm *m*; **office ~** Bürohochhaus *nt* ▶ PHRASES: **a ~ of strength** ein Fels in der Brandung

◆**tower above, tower over** *vi* aufragen; ■**to ~ above sb/sth** jdn/etw überragen

towering ['taʊ·ər·ɪŋ] *adj* ❶ (*very high*) hoch aufragend ❷ (*very great*) überragend

town [taʊn] *n* ❶ (*small city*) Stadt *f*; **home ~** Heimatstadt *f* ❷ (*residents*) **the whole ~** die ganze Stadt ❸ *no art* (*residential or working location*) Stadt *f*; ■**to be in ~** in der Stadt sein ▶ PHRASES: **to go to ~ [on sth]** sich [bei etw *dat*] ins Zeug legen

town 'clerk *n* Magistratsbeamte(r), -beamtin *m, f*

town 'hall *n* Rathaus *nt*

'townhouse *n* (*row house*) Reihenhaus *nt*

townie ['taʊ·ni] *n* (*pej sl: not academic*) *jd, der in einer Universitätsstadt wohnt, jedoch nicht mit der Universität in Verbindung steht*

town 'planning *n* Stadtplanung *f*

'townsfolk *npl* Stadtbevölkerung *f kein pl*

township ['taʊn·ʃɪp] *n* ❶ (*division of county*) Gemeinde *f* ❷ (*in South Africa*) Township *f*

'townspeople *npl* Stadtbevölkerung *f kein pl*

'tow truck *n* Abschleppwagen *m*

toxemia [tak·'si·mi·ə] *n* Blutvergiftung *f*

toxic ['tak·sɪk] *adj* giftig; **~ waste** Giftmüll *m*

toxicology [ˌtak·sɪ·'kal·ə·dʒi] *n* Toxikologie *f*

toxin ['tak·sɪn] *n* Toxin *nt*

toy [tɔɪ] *n* Spielzeug *nt*; **stuffed ~** Kuscheltier *nt*

◆**toy with** *vi* ❶ (*consider*) herumspielen (mit +*dat*); *idea* spielen (mit +*dat*) ❷ (*not treat seriously*) spielen (mit +*dat*)

'toy store *n* Spielwarengeschäft *nt*

trace [treɪs] **I.** *n* ❶ (*sign*) Zeichen *nt*, Spur *f*; **to disappear without a ~** spurlos verschwinden ❷ (*slight amount*) Spur *f*; **~s of poison** Giftspuren *pl* ❸ (*measurement line*) Aufzeichnung *f* ❹ (*attempt to locate*) ausfindig machen; **to put a ~ on a phone call** einen Anruf zurückverfolgen **II.** *vt* ❶ (*follow trail*) auffinden; ■**to ~ sb** jds Spur verfolgen ❷ (*find source*) *phone call, computer virus* zurückverfolgen ❸ (*through paper*) durchpausen; (*with a finger*) nachmalen

traceable ['treɪ·sə·bəl] *adj* zurückverfolgbar

'trace element *n* Spurenelement *nt*

tracer ['treɪ·sər] *n* ❶ MIL Leuchtspurgeschoss *nt* ❷ (*tracking inquiry*) Spurensucher(in) *m(f)*

trachea <*pl* -s *or* -chae> ['treɪ·ki·ə] *n* ANAT Luftröhre *f*

'tracing paper *n* Pauspapier *nt*

track [træk] **I.** *n* ❶ (*path*) Weg *m*, Pfad *m* ❷ RAIL ■**~s** *pl* Gleise *pl*, Schienen *pl*; (*platform*) Bahnsteig *m* ❸ (*for curtains*) Schiene *f* ❹ *usu pl* (*mark*) Spur *f*; *of deer* Fährte *f*; **tire ~s** Reifenspuren *pl* ❺ (*course*) Weg *m*; **to get**

one's life back on ~ sein Leben wieder in die Reihe bringen ⑥ SPORTS *for running* Laufbahn *f; for racecars* Rennstrecke *f*, Piste *f; for bikes* Radrennbahn *f* ⑦ (*athletics*) Leichtathletik *f* ⑧ (*piece of music*) Stück *nt;* (*in film*) Soundtrack *m* ▶ PHRASES: **to be off the beaten ~** abgelegen sein; **to keep ~ of sb/sth** jdn/etw im Auge behalten; **to stop in one's ~s** vor Schreck erstarren **II.** *vt* ① (*follow*) verfolgen; ■**to ~ sb** jds Spur verfolgen ② (*find*) aufspüren

◆**track down** *vt* aufspüren; *piece of information* ausfindig machen

◆**track in** *vt mud, dirt* hereintragen

◆**track up** *vt* **to ~ up** ⊂ **the house** Schmutzspuren im Haus hinterlassen

track and 'field *n* SPORTS Leichtathletik *f*

'trackball *n* COMPUT Rollkugel *f*

'track record *n* ① SPORTS Streckenrekord *m* ② *of company, person* Erfolgsbilanz *f*

'track shoe *n* Laufschuh *m*

'tracksuit *n* Trainingsanzug *m*

tract [trækt] *n* ① (*area of land*) Gebiet *nt;* (*property*) Grundstück *nt* ② ANAT (*bodily system*) Trakt *m;* **respiratory ~** Atemwege *pl*

traction ['træk·ʃən] *n* ① *of car, wheels* Bodenhaftung *f* ② MECH (*pulling*) Antrieb *m* ③ (*medical treatment*) Strecken *nt;* **to be in ~** im Streckverband liegen

tractor ['træk·tər] *n* Traktor *m*

'tractor-trailer *n* Sattelschlepper *m*

trade [treɪd] **I.** *n* ① (*buying and selling*) Handel *m* ② (*business activity*) Umsatz *m* ③ (*type of business*) Branche *f;* **building ~** Baugewerbe *nt* ④ (*handicraft*) Handwerk *nt;* **to learn a ~** ein Handwerk erlernen ⑤ SPORTS (*exchange of players*) Trade *m* **II.** *vi* ① (*exchange goods*) tauschen (**with** mit +*dat*) ② (*do business*) Geschäfte machen ③ STOCKEX (*be bought and sold*) handeln ④ SPORTS (*exchange players*) einen Trade machen, traden *fam* **III.** *vt* ① (*exchange*) austauschen; **to ~ places [with sb]** [mit jdm] den Platz tauschen ② STOCKEX handeln (mit +*dat*) ③ SPORTS *players* [weg]traden *fam*

◆**trade in** *vt* in Zahlung geben

◆**trade on** *vi* ausnutzen

'trade agreement *n* Handelsabkommen *nt*

'trade balance *n* Handelsbilanz *f*

'trade barrier *n* Handelsschranke[n] *f[pl]*

'trade deficit *n* Außenhandelsdefizit *nt*

'trade fair *n* Messe *f*

'trade-in *n* Tauschware *f;* **~ value** Gebrauchtwert *m*

'trade journal *n* Handelsblatt *nt*

'trademark *n* ① (*of company*) Warenzeichen *nt* ② (*of person, music*) charakteristisches Merkmal

'trade name *n* Markenname *m*

'trade-off *n* Einbuße *f*

trader ['treɪ·dər] *n* (*person*) Händler(in) *m(f);* STOCKEX Wertpapierhändler(in) *m(f)*

'trade route *n* Handelsweg *m*

trade 'secret *n* Betriebsgeheimnis *nt*

tradesman ['treɪdz·mən] *n* (*craftsman*) Handwerker *m*

'trade surplus *n* Handelsbilanzüberschuss *m*

'trade union *n* Gewerkschaft *f*

'trade war *n* Handelskrieg *m*

'trade wind *n* Passat *m*

trading ['treɪ·dɪŋ] *n* Handel *m*

'trading floor *n* Börsenparkett *nt*

tradition [trə·'dɪʃ·ən] *n* ① (*customary behavior*) Tradition *f* ② (*custom*) Tradition *f*, Brauch *m* ③ (*style*) Tradition *f*, Stil *m*

traditional [trə·'dɪʃ·ə·nəl] *adj* traditionell; *person* konservativ

traditionalist [trə·'dɪʃ·ə·nə·lɪst] *n* Traditionalist(in) *m(f) geh*

traffic ['træf·ɪk] **I.** *n* ① (*vehicles*) Verkehr *m;* **to get stuck in ~** im Verkehr stecken bleiben ② (*on telephone*) Fernsprechverkehr *m;* **data ~** COMPUT Datenverkehr *m* ③ (*in illegal items*) illegaler Handel (**in** mit +*dat*) **II.** *vi* <-ck-> handeln (**in** mit +*dat*); **to ~ in arms** Waffenhandel betreiben

'traffic accident *n* Verkehrsunfall *m*

'traffic circle *n* Kreisverkehr *m*

'traffic cop *n* (*fam*) Verkehrspolizist(in) *m(f)*

'traffic island *n* ① (*pedestrian island*) Verkehrsinsel *f* ② (*median strip*) Mittelstreifen *m*

'traffic jam *n* [Rück]stau *m*

trafficker ['træf·ɪk·ər] *n* (*pej*) Händler(in) *m(f)*

'traffic light *n* Ampel *f*

tragedy ['trædʒ·ə·di] *n* Tragödie *f;* **it's a ~ that ...** es ist tragisch, dass ...

tragic ['trædʒ·ɪk] *adj* tragisch

trail [treɪl] **I.** *n* ① (*path*) Weg *m*, Pfad *m* ② (*track*) Spur *f;* ■**to be on the ~ of sth/sb** etw/jdm auf der Spur sein **II.** *vt* ■**to ~ sb** ① (*follow*) jdm auf der Spur sein ② (*in a competition*) hinter jdm liegen **III.** *vi* ① (*drag*) schleifen; *plants, vines* sich ranken ② (*be losing*) zurückliegen ③ (*move sluggishly*) ■**to ~ [after sb]** [hinter jdm her] trotten

◆**trail away** *vi voice* verstummen

◆**trail behind I.** *vi* zurückbleiben **II.** *vt* hinterherlaufen

◆**trail off** *vi* verstummen

trailblazer ['treɪl·ˌbleɪ·zər] *n* Wegbereiter(in) *m(f)*

trail-blazing ['treɪl·bleɪ·zɪŋ] *adj attr* bahnbrechend

trailer ['treɪ·lər] *n* ① (*wheeled container*) Anhänger *m* ② (*mobile home*) Wohnwagen *m* ③ (*advertisement*) Trailer *m*

'trailer park *n* Wohnwagenabstellplatz *m*

'trailer trash *n* (*pej sl*) weißer Abschaum *pej*

train [treɪn] **I.** *n* ① RAIL Zug *m* ② (*retinue*) Gefolge *nt kein pl;* (*procession*) Zug *m* ③ (*part of dress*) Schleppe *f* ④ (*succession of events*) **to lose one's ~ of thought** den roten Faden verlieren **II.** *vi* trainieren (**for** für +*akk*) **III.** *vt* ① (*teach*) ausbilden (**for** für +*akk*); *dogs* abrichten ② HORT *roses, vines* ziehen ③ (*point at*) *gun, light* richten (**on** auf +*akk*)

T

trained [treɪnd] *adj* ❶ (*educated*) ausgebildet; *animal* abgerichtet ❷ (*expert*) *ear, eye* geschult; *voice* ausgebildet
trainee [treɪ·ˈni] *n* Auszubildende(r) *f(m)*, Trainee *m*
traineeship [ˌtreɪ·ˈni·ʃɪp] *n* Praktikum *nt*
trainer [ˈtreɪ·nər] *n* Trainer(in) *m(f)*; (*of animals*) Dresseur(in) *m(f)*; (*in circus*) Dompteur *m*, Dompteuse *f*
training [ˈtreɪ·nɪŋ] *n* ❶ (*education*) Ausbildung *f*; *of new employee* Schulung *f*; *of dogs* Abrichten *nt* ❷ SPORTS (*practice*) Training *nt*
ˈ**training camp** *n* SPORTS Trainingscamp *nt*
ˈ**train station** *n* Bahnhof *m*
traipse [treɪps] *vi* latschen *fam*
trait [treɪt] *n* Eigenschaft *f*; **genetic ~** genetisches Merkmal
traitor [ˈtreɪ·t̬ər] *n* Verräter(in) *m(f)*
trajectory [trə·ˈdʒek·tə·ri] *n* PHYS Flugbahn *f*; MATH Kurve *f*
tramp [træmp] **I.** *vi* (*walk*) marschieren; (*walk heavily*) trampeln **II.** *vt* **you're ~ing dirt and mud all over the house!** du schleppst den Schmutz und Matsch durch das ganze Haus! **III.** *n* ❶ (*vagrant*) Land-/Stadtstreicher(in) *m(f)*, Vagabund(in) *m(f)*, Sandler(in) *m(f)* ÖSTERR ❷ (*pej: woman*) Flittchen *nt*
trample [ˈtræm·pəl] **I.** *vt* niedertrampeln; *grass, flowers, crops* zertrampeln; **to be ~d to death** zu Tode getrampelt werden **II.** *vi* herumtrampeln (**on** auf +*dat*)
trampoline [ˈtræm·pə·lin] *n* Trampolin *nt*
trance [træns] *n* ❶ (*mental state*) Trance *f* ❷ (*music*) Trance-Musik *f*
tranquil [ˈtræŋ·kwɪl] *adj setting* ruhig; *voice, expression* gelassen
tranquility [træŋ·ˈkwɪl·ɪ·t̬i] *n* Ruhe *f*, Gelassenheit *f*
tranquilize [ˈtræŋ·kwɪ·laɪz] *vt person, animal* ruhigstellen
tranquilizer [ˈtræŋ·kwɪ·laɪ·zər] *n* Beruhigungsmittel *nt*
tranquillity [træŋ·ˈkwɪl·ɪ·t̬i] *n see* **tranquility**
tranquillize [ˈtræŋ·kwɪ·laɪz] *vt see* **tranquilize**
tranquillizer [ˈtræŋ·kwɪ·laɪ·zər] *n see* **tranquilizer**
transact [træn·ˈzækt] *vt deal* abschließen; *negotiations* durchführen
transaction [træn·ˈzæk·ʃən] *n* ECON Transaktion *f*; **business ~** Geschäft *nt*
transatlantic [ˌtræns·ət·ˈlæn·tɪk] *adj* transatlantisch; **a ~ voyage** eine Reise über den Atlantik
transcend [træn·ˈsend] *vt* ❶ (*go beyond*) hinausgehen (über +*akk*); *barriers* überschreiten ❷ (*surpass*) überragen
transcendent [træn·ˈsen·dənt] *adj* ❶ (*supreme*) *authority, being* übernatürlich ❷ (*exceptional*) *love, genius* überragend
transcendental [ˌtræn·sen·ˈden·təl] *adj* transzendent[al] *geh*
transcontinental [ˌtræns·ˌkan·tə·ˈnen·təl] *adj* transkontinental
transcribe [træn·ˈskraɪb] *vt* ❶ (*put in written form*) *conversation, recording* protokollieren ❷ MUS, LING transkribieren; *a.* BIOL übertragen
transcript [ˈtræn·skrɪpt] *n* ❶ (*copy*) Abschrift *f* ❷ SCH, UNIV ■ **~s** *pl* Zeugnisse *pl*
transcription [træn·ˈskrɪp·ʃən] *n* ❶ (*copy*) Abschrift *f*, Protokoll *nt* ❷ (*putting into written form*) Abschrift *f*; BIOL, LING, MUS Transkription *f*; *of genetic information a.* Übertragung *f*
transfer [træns·ˈfɜr] **I.** *vt* <-rr-> [træns·ˈfɜr] ❶ *money* überweisen ❷ (*re-assign*) versetzen; *power* abgeben; *responsibility* übertragen ❸ (*redirect*) übertragen; *call* weiterleiten **II.** *vi* <-rr-> [træns·ˈfɜr] ❶ (*change job*) *employee* überwechseln; (*change club, university*) wechseln (**to** in/nach +*dat*) ❷ (*change bus, train*) umsteigen ❸ (*change system*) umstellen **III.** *n* [ˈtræns·fɜr] ❶ *of hospital patients, prisoners* Verlegung *f* (**to** in/nach +*dat*) ❷ (*reassignment*) *of money* Überweisung *f*; *of ownership, power* Übertragung *f* ❸ (*at work*) Versetzung *f* ❹ SPORTS, UNIV (*player*) Transferspieler(in) *m(f)* ❺ (*pattern*) Abziehbild *nt*; **heat ~** Wärmeübertragung *f*
transferable [træns·ˈfɜr·ə·bəl] *adj* übertragbar
transference [ˈtræns·fɜr·əns] *n* ❶ (*act of changing*) Übergabe *f* ❷ PSYCH *of emotions* Übertragung *f*
transfigure [træns·ˈfɪg·jər] *vt* verwandeln (**into** in +*akk*)
transfix [træns·ˈfɪks] *vt usu passive* ■ **to be ~ed by sth/sb** von etw/jdm fasziniert sein; **to be ~ed with horror** starr vor Entsetzen sein
transform [træns·ˈfɔrm] *vt* ❶ (*change*) verwandeln ❷ ELEC transformieren
transformation [ˌtræns·fər·ˈmeɪ·ʃən] *n* ❶ (*great change*) Verwandlung *f* ❷ (*in theater*) Verwandlungsszene *f* ❸ ELEC Transformation *f* ❹ MATH Umwandlung *f*
transformer [træns·ˈfɔr·mər] *n* ELEC Transformator *m*
transfusion [træns·ˈfju·ʒən] *n* MED Transfusion *f*
transgress [træns·ˈgres] **I.** *vt* (*form*) *law* übertreten **II.** *vi* ❶ (*form: break rule*) die Regeln verletzen ❷ REL sündigen
transience [ˈtræn·zi·əns], **transiency** [ˈtræn·zi·ən·si] *n* Vergänglichkeit *f*
transient [ˈtræn·zi·ənt] **I.** *adj* (*temporary*) vergänglich **II.** *n* Durchreisende(r) *f(m)*
transistor [træn·ˈzɪs·tər] *n* ELEC Transistor *m*
transit [ˈtræn·zɪt] **I.** *n* ❶ *of people, goods* Transit *m*; **passengers in ~** Transitreisende *pl* ❷ (*crossing*) Transit *m* ❸ (*public transport*) öffentliches Verkehrswesen; **mass ~** öffentlicher Nahverkehr **II.** *vt* durchqueren
ˈ**transit camp** *n* Auffanglager *nt*
ˈ**transit desk** *n* AVIAT Transitschalter *m*
transition [træn·ˈzɪʃ·ən] *n* Übergang *m*; ■ **to be in ~** in einer Übergangsphase sein
transitional [træn·ˈzɪʃ·ə·nəl] *adj* Übergangs-

transitive ['træn·sɪ·t̬ɪv] LING **I.** *adj* transitiv **II.** *n* Transitiv *nt*

'**transit lounge** *n* Transitraum *m*

transitory ['træn·sə·tɔr·i] *adj* vergänglich

'**transit visa** *n* Transitvisum *nt*

translatable [træns·'leɪ·t̬əbəl] *adj* übersetzbar

translate ['træns·leɪt] **I.** *vt* ① (*change language*) übersetzen; **to ~ sth from Greek [in]to Spanish** etw aus dem Griechischen ins Spanische übersetzen ② (*put into simpler terms*) einfacher ausdrücken ③ (*make a reality*) *ideas* umsetzen **II.** *vi* ① (*change words*) übersetzen; **to ~ from Hungarian [in]to Russian** aus dem Ungarischen ins Russische übersetzen ② (*transfer*) sich umsetzen lassen

translation [træns·'leɪ·ʃən] *n* ① (*of text, word*) Übersetzung *f* ② (*process*) Übersetzen *nt* ③ (*conversion*) Umsetzung *f*

translator ['træns·leɪ·t̬ər] *n* Übersetzer(in) *m(f)*

transliteration [træns·ˌlɪt̬·ə·'reɪ·ʃən] *n* LING Transliteration *f* (**into** in +*akk*)

translucent [træns·'lu·sənt] *adj* lichtdurchlässig; (*fig*) *writing, logic, prose* klar; *skin* durchsichtig

transmission [træns·'mɪʃ·ən] *n* ① (*act of broadcasting*) Übertragen *nt* ② (*broadcast*) Sendung *f* ③ *of disease* Übertragung *f; of hereditary disease* Vererbung *f* ④ (*in car engine*) Getriebe *nt*

transmit <-tt-> [træns·'mɪt] **I.** *vt* ① MED (*pass on*) übertragen ② (*impart*) übermitteln; *knowledge* vermitteln **II.** *vi* senden

transmitter [træns·'mɪt̬·ər] *n* Sender *m*

transom ['træn·səm] *n* (*window*) Oberlicht *nt*

transparency [træns·'per·ən·si] *n* ① (*quality*) Lichtdurchlässigkeit *f* ② (*slide*) Dia *nt* ③ (*obviousness*) Durchschaubarkeit *f*

transparent [træns·'per·ənt] *adj* ① (*see-through*) durchsichtig ② (*fig*) transparent *geh*

transpire [træn·'spaɪ·ər] *vi* ① (*occur*) passieren, sich ereignen ② (*become known*) sich herausstellen

transplant I. *vt* [træns·'plænt] ① (*replant*) umpflanzen ② MED (*from donor*) transplantieren ③ (*relocate*) umsiedeln **II.** *n* ['træns·plænt] ① (*surgery*) Transplantation *f* ② (*organ*) Transplantat *nt* ③ (*plant*) umgesetzte Pflanze

transplantation [ˌtræns·plæn·'teɪ·ʃən] *n* Transplantation *f* (**from** von +*dat*)

transport I. *vt* [træns·'pɔrt] ① (*carry*) transportieren, befördern ② (*remind*) **to ~ sb to a time** jdn in eine Zeit versetzen **II.** *n* ['træns·pɔrt] ① (*conveying*) Transport *m*, Beförderung *f* ② (*traffic*) Verkehrsmittel *nt*; **means of ~** Transportmittel *nt* ③ (*vehicle*) [Transport]fahrzeug *nt*

transportation [ˌtræns·pər·'teɪ·ʃən] *n* ① (*conveying*) Transport *m*, Beförderung *f*; **through ~** Transitverkehr *nt* ② (*means of transport*) Transportmittel *nt*, Verkehrsmittel *nt*; **to provide ~** ein Beförderungsmittel zur Verfügung stellen

transporter [træns·'pɔr·t̬ər] *n* Transporter *m*

transpose [træns·'poʊz] *vt* ① (*form: swap*) *numbers* vertauschen ② MUS transponieren

transsexual [træns·'sek·ʃu·əl] **I.** *n* Transsexuelle(r) *f(m)* **II.** *adj* transsexuell

transverse ['træns·vɜrs] *adj* TECH quer laufend; **~ beam** Querbalken *m*

transvestite ['træns·'ves·taɪt] *n* Transvestit *m*

trap [træp] **I.** *n* ① (*snare*) Falle *f*; **to set a ~** eine Falle aufstellen ② (*trick*) Falle *f*; (*ambush*) Hinterhalt *m*; **to fall into a ~** in die Falle gehen ③ (*sl: mouth*) **shut your ~!** Klappe *f* **II.** *vt* <-pp-> ① (*snare*) *animal* [in einer Falle] fangen ② *usu passive* (*confine*) ■**to be ~ped** eingeschlossen sein; **to feel ~ped** sich gefangen fühlen ③ (*trick*) in die Falle locken; ■**to ~ sb into sth/doing sth** jdn dazu bringen, etw zu tun ④ (*catch*) *finger, nerve* sich *dat* einklemmen (**in** in +*dat*)

'**trapdoor** *n* ① (*door*) Falltür *f*; THEAT Versenkung *f* ② COMPUT Fangstelle *f*

trapeze [træ·'piz] *n* Trapez *nt*

trapezoid ['træp·ɪ·zɔɪd] *n* MATH Trapez *nt*

trapper ['træp·ər] *n* Trapper(in) *m(f)*; **fur ~** Pelztierjäger(in) *m(f)*

trappings ['træp·ɪŋz] *npl* Drumherum *nt kein pl fam* (**of** +*gen*); **the ~ of power** die Insignien *pl* der Macht

'**trapshooting** *n* Tontaubenschießen *nt*

trash [træʃ] **I.** *n* ① (*waste*) Müll *m*, Abfall *m* ② (*pej fam: people*) Gesindel *nt* ③ (*pej fam: art*) Kitsch *m*, Plunder *m*; (*literature*) Schund *m* ④ (*pej fam: nonsense*) Mist *m* **II.** *vt* (*fam*) ① (*wreck*) kaputt machen; *place* verwüsten ② (*criticize*) auseinandernehmen ③ (*sl: to speak badly about*) ■**to ~ sb** über jdn herziehen

'**trash can** *n* Mülltonne *f*, Abfalleimer *m*, Abfallbehälter *m*

trashy ['træʃ·i] *adj* (*pej fam*) wertlos; **~ novels** Kitschromane *pl*

trauma <*pl* -s *or* -ta> ['trɔ·mə] *n* ① (*shock*) Trauma *nt* ② MED (*injury*) Trauma *nt*

traumatic [trɔ·'mæt̬·ɪk] *adj* ① (*disturbing*) traumatisierend; *experience* traumatisch ② (*upsetting*) furchtbar

traumatize ['trɔ·mə·taɪz] *vt usu passive* ■**to be ~d by sth** durch etw *akk* traumatisiert sein

travel ['træv·əl] **I.** *vi* <-l- *or* -ll-> ① (*journey*) *person* reisen; (*by air*) fliegen; **to ~ by train** mit dem Zug fahren ② (*move*) sich [fort]bewegen ③ (*react to traveling*) **to ~ badly** *person* lange Reisen nicht vertragen; *freight* lange Transporte nicht vertragen **II.** *vt* <-l- *or* -ll-> **to ~ the world** die Welt bereisen **III.** *n* ① (*traveling*) Reisen *nt* ② *pl* (*journeys*) ■**~s** *pl* Reisen *pl*

'**travel agency** *n* Reisebüro *nt*

'**travel agent** *n* Reisebürokaufmann *m*, Reisebürokauffrau *f*

traveled ['træv·əld] *adj* **widely ~** weit gereist; **a well-~ route** eine gut befahrene Strecke

traveler ['træv·ə·lər] *n* Reisende(r) *f(m)*

T

'traveler's check *n* Reisescheck *m*
'travel expenses *npl* Reisekosten *pl*
'travel guide *n* Reiseführer *m*
traveling ['træv·ə·lɪŋ] *n* Reisen *nt*
'travel insurance *n* Reiseversicherung *f;* (*for cancellations*) Reiserücktrittsversicherung *f*
travelled *adj see* **traveled**
traveller *n see* **traveler**
travelling *n see* **traveling**
travelog ['træv·ə·lag] *n* (*book*) Reisebericht *m;* (*film*) Reisebeschreibung *f*
'travel trailer *n* Wohnwagen[anhänger] *m*
traverse [trə·'vɜrs] **I.** *vt* (*form*) ❶ (*travel*) bereisen ❷ (*cross*) *foundation* überspannen ❸ (*in mountaineering*) *ice, slope* queren, traversieren **II.** *n* ❶ (*in mountaineering*) Queren *nt* ❷ ARCHIT Querbalken *m*
travesty ['træv·ɪ·sti] *n* Karikatur *f;* (*burlesque*) Travestie *f;* **a ~ [of justice]** ein Hohn *m* [auf die Gerechtigkeit]
trawl [trɔl] **I.** *vt* ❶ (*fish*) mit dem Schleppnetz fangen ❷ (*search*) ■**to ~ sth [for sth]** etw [nach etw *dat*] durchkämmen **II.** *vi* ❶ (*fish*) ■**to ~ [for sth]** mit dem Schleppnetz [nach etw *dat*] fischen ❷ (*search*) ■**to ~ through sth** *data* etw durchsuchen
trawler ['trɔ·lər] *n* Trawler *m*
tray [treɪ] *n* ❶ (*for serving*) Tablett *nt* ❷ (*for papers*) Ablage *f*
treacherous ['tretʃ·ər·əs] *adj* ❶ (*deceitful*) verräterisch; (*disloyal*) treulos ❷ (*dangerous*) tückisch; *sea, weather* trügerisch
treachery ['tretʃ·ə·ri] *n* (*esp hist*) Verrat *m*
tread [tred] **I.** *vi* <trod *or* treaded, trodden *or* trod> ❶ (*step*) treten; ■**to ~ in/on sth** in/auf etw *akk* treten ❷ (*maltreat*) ■**to ~ on sb** jdn treten ▶ PHRASES: **to ~ carefully** vorsichtig vorgehen **II.** *vt* <trod *or* treaded, trodden *or* trod> ■**to ~ sth down** *grass* etw niedertreten; **to ~ water** Wasser treten **III.** *n* ❶ (*walking*) Tritt *m,* Schritt *m* ❷ (*step*) Stufe *f* ❸ (*profile*) *of tire* [Reifen]profil *nt; of shoe* [Schuh]profil *nt*
treadmill ['tred·mɪl] *n* ❶ (*exerciser*) Heimtrainer *m* ❷ (*boring routine*) Tretmühle *f fam*
treason ['tri·zən] *n* [Landes]verrat *m;* **high ~** LAW Hochverrat *m*
treasure ['treʒ·ər] **I.** *n* ❶ (*hoard*) Schatz *m* ❷ (*valuables*) ■**~s** *pl* Schätze *pl* **II.** *vt* [hoch]schätzen; *memories* bewahren
'treasure hunt *n* Schatzsuche *f*
treasurer ['treʒ·ər·ər] *n* Schatzmeister(in) *m(f); of club* Kassenwart(in) *m(f)*
'treasure trove *n* ❶ (*find*) Schatzfund *m* ❷ (*collection*) Fundgrube *f*
treasury ['treʒ·ə·ri] *n* ❶ (*office*) ■**the ~** die Schatzkammer ❷ POL ■**the T~** das Finanzministerium
'treasury bill *n* [kurzfristiger] Schatzwechsel
'treasury bond *n* [langfristige] Schatzanleihe
'treasury note *n* [mittelfristiger] Schatzschein
'Treasury Secretary *n* Finanzminister(in) *m(f)*
treat [trit] **I.** *vt* ❶ (*handle*) MED behandeln; **to ~ sb/sth badly** jdn/etw schlecht behandeln ❷ (*regard*) betrachten (**as** als); **to ~ sth with contempt** etw mit Verachtung begegnen ❸ *usu passive* (*process*) *material* behandeln (**with** mit +*dat*); *sewage* klären ❹ (*pay for*) ■**to ~ sb [to sth]** jdn [zu etw *dat*] einladen; ■**to ~ oneself [to sth]** sich *dat* etw gönnen **II.** *vi* (*fam: pay*) einen ausgeben; **Jack's ~ing!** Jack gibt einen aus! **III.** *n* **[it's] my ~** das geht auf meine Rechnung; **it is a special ~ to do that** es ist ein besonderes Vergnügen, das zu tun; **to give oneself a ~** sich *dat* etw gönnen
treatise ['tri·t̬ɪs] *n* Abhandlung *f* (**on** über +*akk*)
treatment ['trit·mənt] *n* ❶ (*handling, processing*) Behandlung *f; of waste* Verarbeitung *f* ❷ *usu sing* (*cure*) Behandlung *f* (**for** gegen +*akk*); **to respond to ~** auf eine Behandlung ansprechen
treaty ['tri·t̬i] *n* Vertrag *m* (**between** zwischen +*dat,* **on** über +*akk,* **with** mit +*dat*); **to sign a ~** einen Vertrag schließen
treble ['treb·əl] MUS **I.** *adj attr notes* Diskant-; **~ voice** Sopranstimme *f* **II.** *n* Sopran *m*
treble 'clef *n* MUS Violinschlüssel *m*
tree [tri] *n* Baum *m*
'tree house *n* Baumhaus *nt*
treeless ['tri·lɪs] *adj* baumlos
'tree-lined *adj* von Bäumen gesäumt
'tree surgeon *n* Baumchirurg(in) *m(f)*
'treetops *npl* ■**the ~** die [Baum]wipfel *pl*
'tree trunk *n* Baumstamm *m*
trek [trek] **I.** *vi* <-kk-> wandern **II.** *n* Wanderung *f;* (*fig: longer*) Marsch *m*
trellis ['trel·ɪs] *n* <*pl* -es> Gitter *nt;* (*for plants*) Spalier *nt*
tremble ['trem·bəl] **I.** *vi* zittern (**with** vor +*dat*); *lip, voice* beben; **to ~ like a leaf** zittern wie Espenlaub **II.** *n* Zittern *nt*
tremendous [trɪ·'men·dəs] *adj* ❶ (*big*) enorm; *crowd, scope* riesig; *help* riesengroß *fam* ❷ (*good*) klasse *fam*
tremolo <*pl* -s> ['trem·ə·loʊ] *n* Tremolo *nt*
tremor ['trem·ər] *n* ❶ (*shiver*) Zittern *nt;* MED Tremor *m* ❷ (*earthquake*) Beben *nt* ❸ (*fluctuation*) Schwanken *nt*
tremulous ['trem·jʊ·ləs] *adj hand* zitternd; *voice* zittrig
trench <*pl* -es> [trentʃ] *n* ❶ (*hole*) Graben *m* ❷ MIL Schützengraben *m*
trenchant ['tren·tʃənt] *adj* (*form*) energisch; *criticism, wit* scharf
'trench coat *n* Trenchcoat *m*
trench 'warfare *n* Grabenkrieg *m*
trend [trend] *n* ❶ (*tendency*) Trend *m,* Tendenz *f* ❷ (*style*) Mode *f,* Trend *m;* **the latest ~** der letzte Schrei *fam*
trendsetter ['trend·ˌset̬·ər] *n* Trendsetter(in) *m(f)*
trendy ['tren·di] *adj* modisch, in *fam*
trepidation [ˌtrep·ɪ·'deɪ·ʃən] *n* (*form*) Ängstlichkeit *f;* **a feeling of ~** ein beklommenes Ge-

fühl

trespass ['tres·pəs] **I.** *n* <*pl* -es> LAW (*intrusion*) unbefugtes Betreten **II.** *vi* (*intrude*) unbefugt eindringen; **to ~ on sb's land** jds Land unerlaubt betreten

trespasser ['tres·pæs·ər] *n* Eindringling *m*; **"~s will be prosecuted!"** „unbefugtes Betreten wird strafrechtlich verfolgt!"

trestle ['tres·əl] *n* [Auflage]bock *m*

'trestle table *n auf Böcke gestellter Tisch*

triad ['traɪ·æd] *n* ❶ MUS Dreiklang *m* ❷ (*group of three*) Triade *f*

trial ['traɪ·əl] *n* ❶ (*in court*) Prozess *m*, [Gerichts]verhandlung *f*; **~ by jury** Schwurgerichtsverhandlung *f*; **to stand ~** vor Gericht stehen ❷ (*test*) Probe *f*, Test *m*; **clinical ~s** klinische Tests *pl*

'trial period *n* Probezeit *f*

trial sepa'ration *n* Trennung *f* auf Probe

triangle ['traɪ·æŋ·gəl] *n* ❶ (*shape*) Dreieck *nt* ❷ (*object*) dreieckiges Objekt ❸ (*percussion*) Triangel *f* ❹ (*for mechanical drawing*) Zeichendreieck *nt*

triangular [traɪ·'æŋ·gjʊ·lər] *adj* dreieckig

tribal ['traɪ·bəl] *adj* ❶ (*ethnic*) Stammes- ❷ (*fam: group*) *attitudes* Gruppen-

tribalism ['traɪ·bə·lɪz·əm] *n* (*loyalty*) Stammesverbundenheit *f*

tri-band ['traɪ·bænd] *adj cell phone* mit Triband-Funktion *nach n*

tribe [traɪb] *n* ❶ (*community*) Stamm *m* ❷ (*fam: group*) Sippe *f*

tribesman ['traɪbz·mən] *n* Stammesangehöriger *m*

tribulation [ˌtrɪb·jə·'leɪ·ʃən] *n usu pl* (*cause*) Kummer *m*; **trials and ~s** Schwierigkeiten *pl*

tribunal [traɪ·'bju·nəl] *n* ❶ (*court*) Gericht *nt* ❷ (*investigative body*) Untersuchungsausschuss *m*

tribune ['trɪb·jun] *n* Tribüne *f*

tributary ['trɪb·jə·ter·i] **I.** *n* Nebenfluss *m* **II.** *adj* (*form*) Neben-

tribute ['trɪb·jut] *n* ❶ (*respect*) Tribut *m*; **to pay ~ to sb/sth** jdm/etw Tribut zollen *geh* ❷ (*beneficial result*) ■**to be a ~ to sb/sth** jdm/etw Ehre machen

trick [trɪk] **I.** *n* ❶ (*ruse*) Trick *m*; **to play a ~ on sb** jdm einen Streich spielen; **a dirty ~** ein gemeiner Trick ❷ (*knack*) Kunstgriff *m*; **he knows all the ~s of the trade** er ist ein alter Hase ❸ (*illusion*) **a ~ of the light** eine optische Täuschung ►PHRASES: **to not <u>miss</u> a ~** keine Gelegenheit auslassen; **to <u>do</u> the ~** (*fam*) klappen *fam* **II.** *adj attr* ❶ (*deceptive*) *question* Fang- ❷ (*acrobatic*) Kunst- **III.** *vt* ❶ (*deceive*) täuschen; ■**to ~ sb** jdn hintergehen; ■**to ~ sb into doing sth** jdn dazu bringen, etw zu tun ❷ (*fool*) reinlegen *fam*

trickery ['trɪk·ə·ri] *n* (*pej*) Betrug *m*; (*repeated*) Betrügerei *f*

trickle ['trɪk·əl] **I.** *vi* ❶ (*flow*) sickern; (*in drops*) tröpfeln; *sand* rieseln; *tear* kullern ❷ (*come*) in kleinen Gruppen kommen; **people ~d back into the theatre** die Leute kamen in kleinen Gruppen in den Theatersaal zurück ❸ (*become known*) *details* durchsickern **II.** *vt* tröpfeln, träufeln **III.** *n* ❶ (*flow*) Rinnsal *nt geh*; (*in drops*) *of blood* Tropfen *pl* ❷ (*few, little*) ■**a ~ of people** wenige Leute

◆**trickle away** *vi* ❶ *water* langsam abfließen ❷ (*fig: dry up*) versiegen

'trick question *n* Fangfrage *f*

trickster ['trɪk·stər] *n* (*pej*) Schwindler(in) *m(f)*

tricky ['trɪk·i] *adj* ❶ (*deceitful*) betrügerisch ❷ (*sly*) raffiniert ❸ (*awkward*) *situation* schwierig ❹ (*difficult*) kniff[e]lig, verzwickt *fam*

tricycle ['traɪ·sɪ·kəl] *n* Dreirad *nt*

trident ['traɪ·dənt] *n* (*fork*) Dreizack *m*

tried [traɪd] *vi, vt pt, pp of* **try**

triennial [traɪ·'en·i·əl] *adj* dreijährlich

trifle ['traɪ·fəl] *n* ❶ (*form: petty thing*) Kleinigkeit *f* ❷ + *adj* (*form: slightly*) **I'm a ~ surprised about your proposal** ich bin über deinen Vorschlag etwas erstaunt

trifling ['traɪ·flɪŋ] *adj* (*form*) unbedeutend; *sum of money* geringfügig

trigger ['trɪg·ər] **I.** *n* ❶ (*gun part*) Abzug *m*; **to pull the ~** abdrücken ❷ (*start*) Auslöser *m* (**for** für +*akk*) **II.** *vt* auslösen

'trigger-happy *adj inv* schießfreudig, schießwütig

trigonometry [ˌtrɪg·ə·'nam·ə·tri] *n* Trigonometrie *f*

trike [traɪk] *n* (*fam*) *short for* **tricycle** Dreirad *nt*

trilateral [traɪ·'læṭ·ər·əl] *adj* ❶ POL trilateral ❷ MATH dreiseitig

trilingual [ˌtraɪ·'lɪŋ·gwəl] *adj* dreisprachig

trill [trɪl] **I.** *n* ❶ (*chirp*) Trillern *nt* ❷ MUS (*note*) Triller *m* **II.** *vi* trillern; *lark* tirilieren *geh* **III.** *vt* ❶ MUS trillern ❷ LING **to ~ one's r's** das R rollen

trillion ['trɪl·jən] *n* ❶ <*pl* - *or* -s> (10^{12}) Billion *f* ❷ *pl* (*fam: many*) ■**~s** *pl* Tausende *pl* (**of** von +*dat*)

trilogy ['trɪl·ə·dʒi] *n* Trilogie *f*

trim [trɪm] **I.** *n* ❶ (*cutting*) Nachschneiden *nt* ❷ (*edging*) Applikation *f* **II.** *adj* <-mer, -mest> ❶ (*neat*) ordentlich; *lawn* gepflegt ❷ (*slim*) schlank **III.** *vt* <-mm-> ❶ (*cut*) [nach]schneiden; *beard, hedge* stutzen ❷ (*reduce*) kürzen; *costs a.* verringern ❸ (*decorate*) schmücken (**with** mit +*dat*) ❹ (*boat, plane*) trimmen; *sails* richtig stellen

◆**trim off** *vt* ❶ (*cut*) abschneiden ❷ (*reduce*) kürzen

trimming ['trɪm·ɪŋ] *n* ❶ *usu pl* (*edging*) Besatz *m* ❷ (*accompaniment*) ■**the ~s** *pl* das Zubehör; **turkey with all the ~s** Truthahn *m* mit allem Drum und Dran ❸ (*pieces*) ■**~s** *pl* Abfälle *pl*

Trinidad ['trɪn·ɪ·dæd] *n* Trinidad *nt*

Trinidadian ['trɪn·ɪ·dæd·i·ən] **I.** *adj* trinidadisch **II.** *n* Trinidader(in) *m(f)*

T

trinity ['trɪn·ɪ·t̬i] *n* ■ **the [Holy] T~** die [Heilige] Dreifaltigkeit
trinket ['trɪŋ·kɪt] *n* ❶ (*small ornament*) wertloser Schmuckgegenstand ❷ (*something trivial*) ■ **~s** *pl* Plunder *m kein pl*
trio <*pl* -s> ['tri·oʊ] *n* Trio *nt* (**of** von +*dat*)
trip [trɪp] **I.** *n* ❶ (*journey*) Reise *f*, Fahrt *f*; **round ~** Rundreise *f* ❷ (*outing*) Ausflug *m* ❸ (*stumble*) Stolpern *nt* ❹ (*self-indulgence*) **an ego ~** ein Egotrip *m* **II.** *vi* <-pp-> ❶ (*unbalance*) stolpern ❷ (*be uttered*) **to ~ off one's tongue** leicht von der Zunge gehen ❸ (*a. fig fam: be on drugs*) auf einem Trip sein *sl* **III.** *vt* <-pp-> ❶ (*unbalance*) ■ **to ~ sb** jdm ein Bein stellen ❷ *switch* anschalten
◆ **trip over** *vi* (*stumble*) stolpern (über +*akk*); **to ~ over one's words** über seine Worte stolpern
◆ **trip up I.** *vt* ❶ (*unbalance*) ■ **to ~ up ↔ sb** jdm ein Bein stellen ❷ (*foil*) zu Fall bringen **II.** *vi* einen Fehler machen
tripartite [ˌtraɪ·'par·taɪt] *adj* ❶ (*form: three-part*) *structure* dreiteilig ❷ POL *meetings, coalition* Dreiparteien-
tripe [traɪp] *n* ❶ (*food*) Kutteln *pl* ❷ (*fam: nonsense*) Quatsch *m*
triple ['trɪp·əl] **I.** *adj* ❶ *attr* (*threefold*) dreifach ❷ *attr* (*of three parts*) Dreier- **II.** *adv* dreimal so viel **III.** *vt* verdreifachen **IV.** *vi* ❶ (*become three times greater*) *prices* sich verdreifachen ❷ (*in baseball*) einen Triple schlagen **V.** *n* (*in baseball*) Triple *m*
triplet ['trɪp·lɪt] *n usu pl* (*baby*) Drilling *m*
triplicate ['trɪp·lɪ·kɪt] *adj attr* (*form*) dreifach; **in ~** in dreifacher Ausfertigung
tripod ['traɪ·pad] *n* Stativ *nt*
trite [traɪt] *adj* (*pej*) platt; *cliché* abgedroschen
triumph ['traɪ·ʌmf] **I.** *n* ❶ (*victory*) Triumph *m*, Sieg *m* (**for** für +*akk*, **over** über +*akk*) ❷ (*feat*) **a ~ of engineering** ein Triumph *m* der Ingenieurskunst ❸ (*joy*) Siegesfreude *f* **II.** *vi* (*win, exult*) triumphieren (**over** über +*akk*)
triumphal [traɪ·'ʌm·fəl] *adj* triumphal
triumphant [traɪ·'ʌm·fənt] *adj* ❶ (*victorious*) siegreich ❷ (*successful*) erfolgreich ❸ (*exulting*) *smile* triumphierend
trivia ['trɪv·i·ə] *npl* Lappalien *pl*
trivial ['trɪv·i·əl] *adj* ❶ (*unimportant*) trivial; *issue* belanglos; *details* bedeutungslos ❷ (*petty*) kleinlich
triviality [ˌtrɪv·i·'æl·ɪ·t̬i] *n* ❶ (*unimportance*) Belanglosigkeit *f* ❷ (*unimportant thing*) Trivialität *f*
trivialize ['trɪv·i·ə·laɪz] *vt* (*pej*) trivialisieren
trod [trad] *pt, pp of* **tread I., II.**
trodden ['trad·ən] *pp of* **tread I., II.**
Trojan ['troʊ·dʒən] **I.** *n* Trojaner(in) *m(f)* **II.** *adj* trojanisch
trolley ['tral·i] *n* Straßenbahn *f*
'**trolley bus** *n* Oberleitungsbus *m*
trollop ['tral·əp] *n* (*pej*) Flittchen *nt*
trombone [tram·'boʊn] *n* Posaune *f*
trombonist [tram·'boʊ·nɪst] *n* Posaunist(in) *m(f)*
troop [trup] **I.** *n* ❶ (*group*) Truppe *f*; *of animals* Schar *f*; *of soldiers* Trupp *m*; **cavalry ~** Schwadron *f* ❷ (*soldiers*) ■ **~s** *pl* Truppen *pl* **II.** *vi* ■ **to ~ off** abziehen *fam*
'**troop carrier** *n* Truppentransporter *m*
trooper ['tru·pər] *n* ❶ (*soldier*) [einfacher] Soldat ❷ (*police officer*) **state ~** Polizist(in) *m(f)*
trophy ['troʊ·fi] *n* ❶ (*prize*) Preis *m* ❷ (*memento*) Trophäe *f*; **war ~** Kriegsbeute *f kein pl*
tropic ['trap·ɪk] *n* ❶ (*latitude*) Wendekreis *m*; **the T~ of Cancer/Capricorn** der Wendekreis des Krebses/Steinbocks ❷ (*hot region*) ■ **the ~s** *pl* die Tropen *pl*
tropical ['trap·ɪ·kəl] *adj* ❶ (*of tropics*) Tropen-; **~ hardwoods** tropische Harthölzer ❷ *weather* tropisch
troposphere ['troʊ·pə·sfɪr] *n* SCI Troposphäre *f*
trot [trat] **I.** *n* Trab *m*; *of horse* Trott **II.** *vi* <-tt-> ❶ (*walk*) trotten; *horse* traben ❷ (*ride*) im Trab reiten ❸ (*run*) laufen **III.** *vt* <-tt-> *horse* traben lassen
◆ **trot along** *vi* traben
◆ **trot off** *vi* (*fam*) losziehen
◆ **trot out** *vt* (*pej*) vorführen
trotter ['trat̬·ər] *n* ❶ (*horse*) Traber *m* ❷ (*food*) ■ **[pig] ~s** *pl* Schweinshaxen *pl*
trouble ['trʌb·əl] **I.** *n* ❶ (*difficulties*) Schwierigkeiten *pl*; (*annoyance*) Ärger *m*; **to spell ~** (*fam*) nichts Gutes bedeuten; **to stay out of ~** sauber bleiben *hum fam* ❷ (*problem*) Problem[e] *nt*[*pl*]; **to get oneself into a bit of ~** sich in Schwierigkeiten bringen; (*cause of worry*) Sorge *f*; **the only ~ is that we ...** der einzige Haken [dabei] ist, dass wir ... ❸ (*inconvenience*) Umstände *pl*, Mühe *f*; **it's no ~ at all** das macht gar keine Umstände ❹ (*malfunction*) Störung *f*; **engine ~** Motorschaden *m* ❺ (*strife*) Unruhe *f* **II.** *vt* ❶ (*form: cause inconvenience*) ■ **to ~ sb for sth** jdn um etw *akk* bemühen *geh* ❷ (*cause worry*) beunruhigen; (*grieve*) bekümmern ❸ (*cause pain*) plagen **III.** *vi* sich bemühen
troubled ['trʌb·əld] *adj* ❶ (*beset*) *situation* bedrängt; *times* unruhig ❷ (*worried*) besorgt
'**trouble-free** *adj* problemlos
'**troublemaker** *n* Unruhestifter(in) *m(f)*
'**troubleshooting** *n* ❶ (*fixing*) Fehler-/Störungsbeseitigung *f*; (*searching*) Fehlersuche *f* ❷ (*mediation*) Vermittlung *f*
troublesome ['trʌb·əl·səm] *adj* schwierig
'**trouble spot** *n* Unruheherd *m*
trough [trɔf] *n* ❶ (*container*) Trog *m* ❷ METEO Trog *m* ❸ (*low*) Tiefpunkt *m*; (*in economy*) Talsohle *f*
troupe [trup] *n* THEAT Truppe *f*
trouper ['tru·pər] *n* ❶ (*actor*) **an old ~** ein alter Hase *fam* ❷ (*reliable person*) treue Seele
trouser ['traʊ·zər] *n* ■ **~s** Hose *f*; **a pair of ~s** eine Hose
trout <*pl* -s *or* -> [traʊt] *n* Forelle *f*
trowel ['traʊ·əl] *n* ❶ *for building* Maurerkelle *f* ❷ *for gardening* kleiner Spaten

Troy [trɔɪ] *n* (*hist*) Troja *nt*
'troy weight *n* Troygewicht *nt*
truancy ['tru·ən·si] *n* [Schule]schwänzen *nt* *fam*
truant ['tru·ənt] *n* Schulschwänzer(in) *m(f)* *fam*
truce [trus] *n* Waffenstillstand *m* (**between** zwischen +*dat*)
truck [trʌk] **I.** *n* AUTO Last[kraft]wagen *m,* LKW *m;* **pickup** ~ Lieferwagen *m* ▶ PHRASES: **to have no ~ with sb/sth** (*fam*) mit jdm/etw nichts zu tun haben **II.** *vt* per Lastwagen transportieren
'truck driver, trucker ['trʌk·ər] *n* Lastwagenfahrer(in) *m(f);* (*driving long distances*) Fernfahrer(in) *m(f)*
'truck farm *n* Gemüsefarm *f,* Gemüseanbaubetrieb *m*
trucking ['trʌk·ɪŋ] *n* Lkw-Transport *m;* ~ **company** Spedition[sfirma] *f,* Transportunternehmen *nt*
'truck stop *n* Fernfahrerraststätte *f*
truculence ['trʌk·jʊ·ləns] *n* ① (*aggression*) Wildheit *f* ② (*defiance*) Aufsässigkeit *f*
truculent ['trʌk·jʊ·lənt] *adj* ① (*aggressive*) wild ② (*defiant*) aufsässig
trudge [trʌdʒ] **I.** *vi* (*walk*) wandern; **to ~ along sth** etw entlanglatschen *fam* **II.** *n* (*walk*) [anstrengender] Fußmarsch
true [tru] **I.** *adj* <-r, -st> ① (*not false*) wahr; **it is ~ [to say] that ...** es stimmt, dass ... ② (*accurate*) richtig; *aim* genau ③ *attr* (*actual*) echt, wahr, wirklich; ~ **love** wahre Liebe ④ (*loyal*) treu; **to be ~ to one's word** zu seinem Wort stehen ▶ PHRASES: **sb's ~ colors** jds wahres Gesicht; ~ **to form** wie zu erwarten **II.** *adv* ① (*in accord with reality*) **to ring ~** glaubhaft klingen ② (*accurately*) genau
'true-'blue *adj attr* ① (*loyal*) treu ② (*genuine*) waschecht *fam*
'true-life *adj* lebensecht
true 'love *n* ■ **sb's** ~ jds Geliebte(r) *f(m)*
truffle ['trʌf·əl] *n* Trüffel *f o m*
truism ['tru·ɪz·əm] *n* Binsenweisheit *f;* (*platitude*) Plattitüde *f geh*
truly ['tru·li] *adv* ① (*not falsely*) wirklich, wahrhaftig ② (*genuinely*) wirklich, echt ③ (*very*) wirklich ▶ PHRASES: **yours** ~ (*fam*) meine Wenigkeit *hum;* **Yours** ~ (*at end of letter*) mit freundlichen Grüßen
trump [trʌmp] **I.** *n* ① (*card*) Trumpf *m* ② (*suit*) ■ **~s** *pl* Trumpf *m,* Trumpffarbe *f* **II.** *vt* ① (*cards*) übertrumpfen ② (*better*) ausstechen
◆**trump up** *vt charges, evidence* erfinden
trumpet ['trʌm·pət] **I.** *n* ① (*instrument*) Trompete *f* ② *of elephant* Trompeten *nt* **II.** *vi* trompeten **III.** *vt* (*esp pej*) ausposaunen *fam*
trumpeter ['trʌm·pə·t̬ər] *n* Trompeter(in) *m(f)*
truncate ['trʌŋ·keɪt] *vt* kürzen
truncheon ['trʌn·tʃən] *n* Schlagstock *m*
trundle ['trʌn·dəl] *vi* **to ~ along** (*proceed leisurely*) zuckeln
trunk [trʌŋk] *n* ① BOT (*stem*) Stamm *m* ② ANAT (*body*) Rumpf *m* ③ ZOOL (*of elephant*) Rüssel *m* ④ AUTO Kofferraum *m* ⑤ FASHION ■ **[swim[ming]] ~s** *pl* Badehose *f*
truss [trʌs] **I.** *n* ① (*belt*) Bruchband *nt* ② ARCHIT (*frame*) Gerüst *nt* **II.** *vt* fesseln
◆**truss up** *vt* fesseln
trust [trʌst] **I.** *n* ① (*belief*) Vertrauen *nt* ② (*responsibility*) **a position of ~** ein Vertrauensposten *m;* ■ **in sb's ~** in jds Obhut *f* ③ (*legal arrangement*) Treuhand *f kein pl;* **to set up a ~** eine Treuhandschaft arrangieren ④ (*institution*) ~ **company** Treuhandgesellschaft *f;* **charitable ~** Stiftung *f;* **investment ~** Investmentgesellschaft *m* ⑤ (*cartel*) Ring *m* **II.** *vt* (*believe, rely on*) vertrauen (auf +*akk*); ■ **to ~ sb to do sth** jdm zutrauen, dass er/sie etw tut **III.** *vi* ① (*form: believe*) ■ **to ~ in sb/sth** auf jdn/etw vertrauen ② (*form: hope*) ■ **to ~ [that] ...** hoffen, [dass] ...
trusted ['trʌs·tɪd] *adj attr* ① (*loyal*) getreu *geh* ② (*proved*) bewährt
trustee [trʌs·'ti] *n* Treuhänder(in) *m(f);* **board of ~s** Kuratorium *nt*
trustful ['trʌst·fəl] *adj* ① (*full of trust*) vertrauensvoll ② (*gullible*) leichtgläubig
'trust fund *n* Treuhandfonds *m*
trusting ['trʌs·tɪŋ] *adj see* **trustful**
trustworthiness ['trʌst·ˌwɜr·ðɪ·nɪs] *n* ① (*honesty*) Vertrauenswürdigkeit *f* ② (*accuracy*) Zuverlässigkeit *f*
trustworthy ['trʌst·ˌwɜr·ði] *adj* ① (*honest*) vertrauenswürdig ② (*accurate*) zuverlässig
trusty ['trʌs·ti] *adj attr* (*hum*) ① (*reliable*) zuverlässig ② (*loyal*) *servant* getreu *liter*
truth <*pl* -s> [truθ] *n* ① (*not falsity*) Wahrheit *f* (**of** über +*akk*); **there is no ~ in** [*or* **to**] **what she says** es ist nichts Wahres an dem, was sie sagt ② (*facts*) ■ **the ~** die Wahrheit (**about/of** über +*akk*) ③ (*principle*) Grundprinzip *nt*
truthful ['truθ·fəl] *adj* ① (*true*) wahr ② (*sincere, not lying*) ehrlich ③ (*accurate*) wahrheitsgetreu
truthfulness ['truθ·fəl·nɪs] *n* ① (*veracity*) Wahrhaftigkeit *f* ② (*sincerity*) Ehrlichkeit *f* ③ (*accuracy*) Wahrheit *f*
try [traɪ] **I.** *n* (*attempt*) Versuch *m;* **to give sth a ~** etw ausprobieren **II.** *vi* <-ie-> ① (*attempt*) versuchen ② (*make an effort*) sich bemühen **III.** *vt* <-ie-> ① (*attempt*) versuchen; **to ~ one's best** sein Bestes versuchen ② (*test by experiment*) probieren, versuchen ③ (*sample*) [aus]probieren ④ (*put on trial*) vor Gericht stellen; ■ **to ~ sb for sth** jdn wegen einer S. *gen* anklagen
◆**try for** *vi* sich bemühen (um +*akk*)
◆**try on** *vt clothes* anprobieren ▶ PHRASES: **to ~ on ↔ sth for size** etw versuchsweise ausprobieren
◆**try out I.** *vt* ausprobieren; ■ **to ~ out ↔ sb/sth** jdn/etw testen **II.** *vi* **to ~ out for a position/a role/a team** sich *akk* auf einem Posten/in einer Rolle/bei einer Mannschaft versu-

chen, beim Tryout mitmachen *fam*

trying ['traɪ·ɪŋ] *adj* ❶ (*annoying*) anstrengend ❷ (*difficult*) hart; *situation, time* schwierig, aufreibend

'tryout *n* (*fam*) ❶ SPORTS Tryout *nt* ❷ (*test run*) Erprobung *f; of play* Probevorstellung *f*

tsar [zar] *n* (*spec*) *see* **czar**

tsarina [za·'ri·nə] *n* (*spec*) *see* **czarina**

tsetse fly ['tse·tsi·ˌflaɪ] *n* Tsetsefliege *f*

T-shirt ['ti·ʃɜrt] *n* T-Shirt *nt*

tsp. <*pl* - *or* -s> *n abbrev of* **teaspoon[ful]** Teel., TL

T-square ['ti·skwer] *n* Reißschiene *f*

tsunami [tsu·'na·mi] *n* Tsunami *m*

tub [tʌb] *n* ❶ (*vat*) Kübel *m* ❷ (*fam: bath*) [Bade]wanne *f* ❸ (*carton*) Becher *m*

tuba ['tu·bə] *n* Tuba *f*

tubby ['tʌb·i] *adj* pummelig

tube [tub] *n* ❶ (*pipe*) Röhre *f;* (*bigger*) Rohr *nt;* **inner ~** Schlauch *m;* **test ~** Reagenzglas *nt* ❷ (*container*) Tube *f* ❸ (*fam: TV*) ■**the ~** die Glotze *pej sl,* die [Flimmer]kiste ▸PHRASES: **to go down the ~[s]** den Bach runter gehen *fam*

tuber ['tu·bər] *n* BOT Knolle *f*

tubercular [tu·'bɜr·kjə·lər] *adj* tuberkulös

tuberculosis [tu·ˌbɜr·kjə·'loʊ·sɪs] *n* Tuberkulose *f*

tuck [tʌk] **I.** *n* ❶ (*pleat*) Abnäher *m;* (*ornament*) Biese *f* ❷ MED **a tummy ~** *Operation, bei der am Bauch Fett abgesaugt wird* **II.** *vt* ❶ (*fold*) stecken; **to ~ sb into bed** jdn ins Bett [ein]packen *fam* ❷ (*stow*) verstauen; **to ~ one's legs under oneself** seine Beine unterschlagen

◆**tuck away** *vt* (*stow*) verstauen; (*hide*) verstecken; **to be ~ed away somewhere** irgendwo versteckt liegen

◆**tuck in** *vt* ❶ (*fold*) hineinstecken; *shirt* in die Hose stecken ❷ (*put to bed*) zudecken

tucker ['tʌk·ər] *vt* (*fam*) ■**to ~ sb out** jdn fix und fertig machen

Tuesday ['tuz·deɪ] *n* Dienstag *m;* **[on] ~ afternoon/evening/morning/night** [am] Dienstagnachmittag/-abend/-morgen/-nacht; **on ~ afternoons/evenings/mornings/nights** dienstagnachmittags/-abends/-morgens/-nachts; **a week/two weeks from ~** Dienstag in einer Woche/zwei Wochen; **a week/two weeks ago ~** Dienstag vor einer Woche/zwei Wochen; **every ~** jeden Dienstag; **last/next/this ~** [am] letzten/[am] nächsten/diesen Dienstag; **~ before last/after next** vorletzten/übernächsten Dienstag; **[on] ~** [am] Dienstag; **on ~ March 4th** am Dienstag, den 4. März; **[on] ~s** dienstags

tuft [tʌft] *n* Büschel *nt*

tug [tʌg] **I.** *n* ❶ (*pull*) Ruck *m* (**at** an +*dat*); **to give sth a ~** an etw *dat* zerren ❷ (*boat*) Schlepper *m* **II.** *vt* <-gg-> ziehen **III.** *vi* <-gg-> zerren (**at** an +*dat*)

'tugboat *n* NAUT Schlepper *m*

tug of 'war *n* ❶ (*game*) Tauziehen *nt,* Seilziehen *nt* SCHWEIZ ❷ (*struggle*) Hin und Her *nt,* Tauziehen *nt fig*

tuition [tu·'ɪʃ·ən] *n* ❶ SCH, UNIV (*fee*) Studiengebühr *f; of school* Schulgeld *nt kein pl* ❷ (*teaching*) Unterricht *m* (**in** in +*dat*); **private ~** Einzelunterricht *m*

tulip ['tu·lɪp] *n* Tulpe *f*

tumble ['tʌm·bəl] **I.** *vi* ❶ (*fall*) fallen; (*faster*) stürzen ❷ *prices* [stark] fallen **II.** *n* (*fall*) Sturz *m;* **to take a ~** stürzen

◆**tumble over** *vi* (*unbalance*) hinfallen; (*collapse*) umfallen

'tumbledown *adj attr building* baufällig

'tumble dryer *n* Wäschetrockner *m*

tumbler ['tʌm·blər] *n* ❶ (*glass*) [Trink]glas *nt* ❷ (*acrobat*) Bodenakrobat(in) *m(f)*

tumbleweed ['tʌm·bəl·wid] *n* Steppenhexe *f*

tummy ['tʌm·i] *n* (*fam*) Bauch *m*

tumor ['tu·mər] *n* Geschwulst *f,* Tumor *m*

tumult ['tu·mʌlt] *n* ❶ (*noise*) Krach *m* ❷ (*disorder*) Tumult *m* ❸ (*agitation*) Verwirrung *f*

tumultuous [tu·'mʌl·tʃu·əs] *adj* ❶ (*loud*) lärmend; *applause* stürmisch ❷ (*confused*) turbulent ❸ (*excited*) aufgeregt

tuna ['tu·nə] *n* ❶ <*pl* -s *or* -> ZOOL Thunfisch *m* ❷ FOOD Thunfisch *m*

tundra ['tʌn·drə] *n* Tundra *f*

tune [tun] **I.** *n* ❶ (*melody*) Melodie *f* ❷ (*pitch*) ■**to be out of ~** falsch spielen ❸ (*amount*) ■**to the ~ of 2 million dollars** in Höhe von 2 Millionen Dollar ▸PHRASES: **to change one's ~** einen anderen Ton anschlagen **II.** *vt* ❶ MUS stimmen ❷ RADIO, AUTO einstellen

◆**tune in I.** *vi* ❶ RADIO, TV einschalten; **to ~ in to a station** einen Sender einstellen ❷ (*fam: be sensitive to sth*) ■**to be ~d in to sth** eine Antenne für etw *akk* haben **II.** *vt* RADIO, TV *program, channel* einschalten

◆**tune up I.** *vi* MUS stimmen **II.** *vt* ❶ AUTO einstellen ❷ MUS stimmen

tuneful ['tun·fəl] *adj* melodisch

tuneless ['tun·lɪs] *adj* unmelodisch

tuner ['tu·nər] *n* ❶ TECH (*for selecting stations*) Empfänger *m* ❷ MUS (*person*) Stimmer(in) *m(f)*

'tune-up *n* TECH Einstellung *f;* **to give a car a ~** einen Wagen [neu] einstellen

tunic ['tu·nɪk] *n* Kittel *m*

tuning ['tu·nɪŋ] *n* ❶ MUS Stimmen *nt;* (*correctness of pitch*) Klangreinheit *f* ❷ TECH Einstellen *nt*

'tuning fork *n* Stimmgabel *f*

Tunisia [tu·'ni·ʒə] *n* Tunesien *nt*

Tunisian [tu·'ni·ʒən] **I.** *n* Tunesier(in) *m(f)* **II.** *adj* tunesisch

tunnel ['tʌn·əl] **I.** *n* Tunnel *m;* ZOOL, BIOL Gang *m* ▸PHRASES: **to see [the] light at the end of the ~** das Licht am Ende des Tunnels sehen **II.** *vi* <-l- *or* -ll-> einen Tunnel graben; **to ~ under a river** einen Fluss untertunneln **III.** *vt* <-l- *or* -ll-> graben; **to ~ one's way out** sich herausgraben

'tunnel vision *n* ❶ MED Tunnelblick *m* ❷ (*fig, usu pej: narrow focus*) Scheuklappen-

T

denken *nt*
turban ['tɜr·bən] *n* Turban *m*
turbid ['tɜr·bɪd] *adj* ❶ *liquid* trüb ❷ *clouds* dicht ❸ *emotions, thoughts* verworren
turbine ['tɜr·bɪn] *n* Turbine *f*
'turbocharged *adj* ❶ TECH mit Turboaufladung *nach n* ❷ (*sl: energetic*) Turbo-
'turbocharger *n* Turbolader *m*
'turbojet *n* ❶ (*engine*) Turbojet *m* ❷ (*aircraft*) Turbojet-Flugzeug *nt*
turbulence ['tɜr·bjʊ·ləns] *n* Turbulenz *f;* **air ~** Turbulenzen *pl*
turbulent ['tɜr·bjʊ·lənt] *adj* turbulent, stürmisch; *sea a.* unruhig
turd [tɜrd] *n* (*vulg*) Scheißhaufen *m derb*
turf <*pl* -s *or* turves> [tɜrf] *n* ❶ (*grassy earth*) Rasen *m* ❷ SPORTS **artificial ~** Kunstrasen *m* ❸ (*fam: personal territory*) Revier *nt;* (*field of expertise*) Spezialgebiet *f*
turgid ['tɜr·dʒɪd] *adj* ❶ (*grandiloquent*) *speech, style* schwülstig ❷ (*bloated*) *bladder, veins* [an]geschwollen
Turk [tɜrk] *n* Türke *m,* Türkin *f*
turkey ['tɜr·ki] *n* ❶ ZOOL Pute(r) *f(m)* ❷ (*meat*) Truthahn *m,* Putenfleisch *nt*
Turkey ['tɜr·ki] *n* Türkei *f*
Turkish ['tɜr·kɪʃ] **I.** *adj* türkisch **II.** *n* Türkisch *nt*
turmoil ['tɜr·mɔɪl] *n* Tumult *m,* Aufruhr *m;* **her mind was in ~** sie war völlig durcheinander
turn [tɜrn] **I.** *n* ❶ (*rotation*) *of wheel* Drehung *f* ❷ (*change in direction*) Kurve *f;* SPORTS Wende *f;* **"no left ~"** „Links abbiegen verboten"; **things took an ugly ~** (*fig*) die Sache nahm eine üble Wendung ❸ (*changing point*) **the ~ of the century** die Jahrhundertwende ❹ (*allotted time*) **it's my ~ now!** jetzt bin ich dran!; **to take ~s doing sth** etw abwechselnd tun ❺ (*deed*) **to do sb a good ~** jdm einen guten Dienst erweisen ▶ PHRASES: **one good ~ deserves another** (*saying*) eine Hand wäscht die andere **II.** *vt* ❶ (*rotate*) *knob, screw* drehen ❷ (*switch direction*) wenden, drehen; **to ~ the corner** um die Ecke biegen ❸ (*aim*) *lamp, hose, gun* richten (**on** auf +*akk*); **to ~ one's attention to sth** seine Aufmerksamkeit etw *dat* zuwenden ❹ + *adj* (*cause to become*) **the shock ~ed her hair gray overnight** durch den Schock wurde sie über Nacht grau ❺ (*change*) ■**to ~ sth/sb into sth** etw/jdn in etw *akk* umwandeln ❻ (*reverse*) ■**to ~ sth [over]** *garment, mattress* wenden, umdrehen; *page* umblättern ▶ PHRASES: **to ~ one's back on sb/sth** sich von jdm/etw abwenden; **to ~ a blind eye to sth** die Augen vor etw *dat* verschließen **III.** *vi* ❶ (*rotate*) sich drehen; **to ~ around [and around]** *person* sich umdrehen ❷ (*change direction*) **to ~ around** *person* sich umdrehen; *car* wenden; **to ~ left/right** [nach] links/rechts abbiegen; *wind* drehen; (*fig*) sich wenden; **to ~ on one's heels** auf dem Absatz kehrtmachen ❸ (*for aid or advice*) **to ~ to sb for help** jdn um Hilfe bitten ❹ (*change*) werden; *milk* sauer werden; *leaves* sich verfärben; *luck* sich wenden; **his face ~ed green** er wurde ganz grün im Gesicht; ■**to ~ into sth** zu etw *dat* werden ❺ (*turn attention to*) ■**to ~ to sth** *conversation, subject* sich etw *dat* zuwenden ❻ (*attain particular age*) **to ~ 20** 20 werden ▶ PHRASES: **to ~ [over] in one's grave** sich im Grabe umdrehen
◆**turn against** **I.** *vi* sich auflehnen (gegen +*akk*) **II.** *vt* ■**to ~ sb against sb/sth** jdn gegen jdn/etw aufwiegeln
◆**turn away** **I.** *vi* sich abwenden **II.** *vt* ❶ (*move*) wegrücken ❷ (*refuse entry, deny help*) abweisen
◆**turn back** **I.** *vi* [wieder] zurückgehen; **there's no ~ing back now!** (*fig*) jetzt gibt es kein Zurück [mehr]! **II.** *vt* ❶ (*send back*) zurückschicken; (*at border*) zurückweisen ❷ (*fold*) *bedcover* zurückschlagen
◆**turn down** *vt* ❶ (*reject*) abweisen; *proposal, offer, invitation* ablehnen ❷ (*reduce level*) *heat* niedriger stellen; (*make quieter*) *music* leiser stellen ❸ (*fold*) umschlagen; *blankets* zurückschlagen; *collar* herunterschlagen
◆**turn in** **I.** *vt* ❶ (*give to police*) *thing* abgeben; *person* verpfeifen; **to ~ oneself in to the police** sich der Polizei stellen ❷ (*submit*) *assignment, resignation* einreichen ❸ (*inwards*) nach innen drehen **II.** *vi* ❶ (*fam: go to bed*) sich in die Falle hauen ❷ (*drive in*) einbiegen
◆**turn off** **I.** *vt* ❶ (*switch off*) abschalten; *engine, power* abstellen; *gas* abdrehen; *lights* ausmachen; *radio, TV* ausschalten ❷ (*cause to lose interest*) ■**to ~ sb off** jdm die Lust nehmen; (*be sexually unappealing*) jdn abtörnen *sl* **II.** *vi* (*leave one's path*) abbiegen
◆**turn on** **I.** *vt* ❶ (*switch on*) einschalten; *gas, heat* aufdrehen; *lights* anmachen ❷ (*fam: excite*) anmachen; (*sexually a.*) antörnen *sl* **II.** *vi* ❶ (*start operating*) einschalten ❷ (*attack*) ■**to ~ on sb** auf jdn losgehen
◆**turn out** **I.** *vi* ❶ (*work out*) sich entwickeln; **how did it ~ out?** wie ist es gelaufen? *fam* ❷ (*be revealed to be*) sich herausstellen ❸ (*come to event*) erscheinen **II.** *vt* ❶ (*switch off*) *lights* ausmachen ❷ (*kick out*) [hinaus]werfen *fam* ❸ (*empty contents*) [aus]leeren; *pockets* umdrehen ❹ (*produce*) *products* produzieren
◆**turn over** **I.** *vi* ❶ (*move*) *person, stomach* sich umdrehen; *boat* kentern; *car* sich überschlagen; *pages* umblättern ❷ (*sell*) *products* laufen ❸ (*operate*) *engine* laufen; (*start*) anspringen **II.** *vt* ❶ (*move*) umdrehen; *mattress* wenden; *page* umblättern; *soil* umgraben ❷ ■**to ~ over ↻ sth to sb** (*delegate responsibility*) jdm etw übertragen; (*give*) jdm etw [über]geben ❸ (*ponder*) sorgfältig überdenken; **to ~ sth over in one's head** [*or* **mind**] sich *dat* etw durch den Kopf gehen lassen ▶ PHRASES: **to ~ over a new leaf** einen [ganz] neuen An-

T

fang machen
◆**turn up** I. *vi* ❶ (*arrive*) erscheinen ❷ (*become available*) sich ergeben; *solution* sich finden ❸ (*happen unexpectedly*) passieren II. *vt* ❶ (*increase volume*) aufdrehen; *music* lauter machen; *heat* höher stellen ❷ (*point upwards*) *collar* hochschlagen ❸ (*find*) finden; **I'll see if I can ~ up some information for you** ich schau mal, ob ich ein paar Infos für Sie auftreiben kann
'turnabout *n* Umschwung *m*
'turnaround *n* ❶ (*improvement*) Wende *f*; *of health* Besserung *f*; *of company* Aufschwung *m*; (*sudden reversal*) Kehrtwendung *f* ❷ COMM Bearbeitungszeit *f* ❸ AVIAT ~ **time** Wartezeit *f* (*eines Flugzeugs am Boden zwischen zwei Flügen*)
'turncoat *n* Überläufer(in) *m(f)*
'turning point *n* Wendepunkt *m*
turnip ['tɜr·nɪp] *n* [Steck]rübe *f*
turnkey ['tɜrn·ki] *adj attr* schlüsselfertig; ~ **system** Fertigteilsystem *nt*
'turnoff ['tɜrn·ɔf] *n* ❶ (*road*) Abzweigung *f* ❷ (*sth unappealing*) Gräuel *nt* ❸ (*sth sexually unappealing*) **to be a real ~** abtörnen *sl*
turnout ['tɜrn·aʊt] *n* ❶ (*attendance*) Teilnahme *f* (**for** an +*dat*) ❷ POL Wahlbeteiligung *f*
turnover ['tɜrn·ˌoʊ·vər] *n* ❶ FOOD (*pastry*) **apple ~** Apfeltasche *f* ❷ (*rate change in staff*) Fluktuation *f geh* ❸ (*volume of business*) Umsatz *m* ❹ (*rate of stock movement*) Absatz *m* ❺ SPORTS (*loss of ball possession*) Turnover *m*, Ballverlust *m*
'turnpike *n* ❶ (*toll road*) Mautstraße *f* ❷ (*tollgate*) Mautschranke *f*
'turnstile *n* Drehkreuz *nt*
'turntable *n* ❶ TECH, RAIL Drehscheibe *f* ❷ (*on record player*) Plattenteller *m*
turpentine ['tɜr·pən·taɪn] *n* Terpentin *nt*
turquoise ['tɜr·kwɔɪz] I. *n* ❶ (*stone*) Türkis *m* ❷ (*color*) Türkis *nt* II. *adj* türkis[farben]
turret ['tɜr·ɪt] *n* ❶ MIL **tank ~** Panzerturm *m* ❷ (*poet*) [Mauer]turm *m*
turtle <*pl* - *or* -s> ['tɜr·t̬əl] *n* Schildkröte *f*
'turtledove *n* Turteltaube *f*
'turtleneck *n* Rollkragen *m*; (*sweater*) Rollkragenpullover *m*
tush [tʊʃ] *n* (*sl*) Hintern *m fam*, Hinterteil *nt fam*
tusk [tʌsk] *n* Stoßzahn *m*
tussle ['tʌs·əl] I. *vi* ❶ (*scuffle*) sich balgen (**with** mit +*dat*) ❷ (*quarrel*) ■**to ~ [with sb] over sth** [mit jdm] über etw *akk* streiten II. *n* ❶ (*struggle*) Rauferei *f* ❷ (*argument*) Streiterei *f* (**for** um +*akk*, **over** wegen +*gen*)
tut [tʌt] *interj* (*pej*) ~ ~ na, na!
tutelage ['tu·t̬ə·lɪdʒ] *n* [An]leitung *f*
tutor ['tu·t̬ər] I. *n* (*giving extra help*) Nachhilfelehrer(in) *m(f)*; (*private teacher*) Privatlehrer(in) *m(f)* II. *vt* (*in addition to school lessons*) Nachhilfestunden geben; (*private tuition*) Privatunterricht erteilen
tutorial [tu·'tɔr·i·əl] *n* Tutorium *nt geh*
tuxedo [tʌk·'si·doʊ] *n* Smoking *m*
TV [ˌti·'vi] *n* ❶ (*appliance*) *abbrev of* **television** Fernseher *m* ❷ (*programming*) *abbrev of* **television** Fernsehen *nt*; ■**on ~** im Fernsehen
twang [twæŋ] I. *n* ❶ (*sound*) Doing *nt* ❷ LING Näseln *nt* II. *vt* zupfen III. *vi* einen sirrenden Ton von sich geben
tweak [twik] I. *vt* ❶ (*pull sharply*) zupfen ❷ (*adjust*) ■**to ~ sth** etw gerade ziehen; **this proposal still needs some ~ing** an diesem Vorschlag muss noch etwas gefeilt werden II. *n* Zupfen *nt kein pl*
tweed [twid] *n* (*cloth*) Tweed *m*
tweet [twit] I. *vi* piepsen II. *n* Piepsen *nt kein pl*
tweeter ['twi·t̬ər] *n* TECH Hochtonlautsprecher *m*
tweezers ['twi·zərz] *npl* ■**[a pair of] ~** [eine] Pinzette
twelfth [twelfθ] I. *adj* zwölfte(r, s) II. *adv* als zwölfte(r, s) III. *n* ■**the ~** der/die/das Zwölfte
twelve [twelv] I. *adj* zwölf; *see also* **eight** II. *n* Zwölf *f*; *see also* **eight**
twentieth ['twen·ti·əθ] I. *adj* zwanzigste(r, s) II. *adv* an zwanzigster Stelle III. *n* ■**the ~** der/die/das Zwanzigste
twenty ['twen·ti] I. *adj* zwanzig; *see also* **eight** II. *n* Zwanzig *f*; *see also* **eight**
twerp [twɜrp] *n* (*pej sl*) Blödmann *m fam*
twice [twaɪs] *adv* ❶ (*two times*) zweimal; **~ a day** zweimal täglich ❷ (*doubly*) doppelt; **she is ~ his age** sie ist doppelt so alt wie er
twiddle ['twɪd·əl] *vt* [herum]drehen (an +*dat*); **to ~ one's thumbs** Däumchen drehen
twig [twɪg] *n* [kleiner] Zweig
twilight ['twaɪ·laɪt] *n* Dämmerung *f*, Zwielicht *nt*
twin [twɪn] I. *n* ❶ (*one of two siblings*) Zwilling *m*; **identical/fraternal ~s** eineiige/zweieiige Zwillinge; (*similar or connected thing*) Pendant *nt geh* ❷ (*bed*) Einzelbett *nt* II. *adj* ❶ (*born at the same time*) Zwillings- ❷ (*connected*) *room, cities* miteinander verbunden III. *vt* <-nn-> ■**to ~ sth [with sth]** etw [mit etw *dat*] [partnerschaftlich] verbinden
twin 'bed *n* Einzelbett *nt*
twin 'brother *n* Zwillingsbruder *m*
twine [twaɪn] I. *n* Schnur *f* II. *vi* (*twist around*) sich schlingen (**around** um +*akk*), sich hochranken (**up** an +*dat*) III. *vt* ■**to ~ sth together** etw ineinanderschlingen
twinge [twɪndʒ] *n* Stechen *nt kein pl*; **a ~ of pain** ein stechender Schmerz; **a ~ of guilt** ein Anflug *m* eines schlechten Gewissens
twinkle ['twɪŋ·kəl] I. *vi* funkeln II. *n* Funkeln *nt*; **to do sth with a ~ in one's eye** etw mit einem [verschmitzten] Augenzwinkern tun
twinkling ['twɪŋ·klɪŋ] I. *adj eyes, lights, stars* funkelnd II. *n* kurzer Augenblick ►PHRASES: **to do sth in the ~ of an eye** etw im Handumdrehen tun
twin 'room *n* Zweibettzimmer *nt*
'twinset, 'twin set *n* Twinset *nt*

T

twin 'sister *n* Zwillingsschwester *f*
twirl [twɜrl] **I.** *vi* wirbeln **II.** *vt* rotieren lassen; (*in dancing*) [herum]wirbeln **III.** *n* Wirbel *m;* (*in dancing*) Drehung *f*
twist [twɪst] **I.** *vt* ❶ (*wind*) [ver]drehen; ■ **to ~ sth off** etw abdrehen ❷ (*coil*) herumwickeln (**around** um +*akk*) ❸ (*sprain*) sich verrenken; **to ~ sb's arm** (*fig*) auf jdn Druck ausüben **II.** *vi* (*squirm*) sich winden; **to ~ and turn** *road* sich schlängeln **III.** *n* ❶ (*rotation*) Drehung *f;* **to give sth a ~** etw [herum]drehen ❷ (*sharp bend*) Kurve *f* ❸ (*unexpected change*) Wendung *f;* **a cruel ~ of fate** eine grausame Wendung des Schicksals
twisted ['twɪs·tɪd] *adj* ❶ (*bent and turned, perverted*) verdreht; *ankle* gezerrt ❷ (*winding*) verschlungen; *path* gewunden
twister ['twɪs·tər] *n* (*fam*) Tornado *m*
twit [twɪt] *n* (*pej fam*) Trottel *m*
twitch [twɪtʃ] **I.** *vi* zucken **II.** *vt* ❶ (*jerk*) zucken mit +*dat;* **to ~ one's nose** *rabbit* schnuppern ❷ (*tug quickly*) zupfen **III.** *n* <*pl* -es> ❶ (*jerky spasm*) **to have a [nervous] ~** nervöse Zuckungen *pl* haben ❷ (*quick tug*) Ruck *m*
twitter ['twɪ·t̬ər] *vi* ❶ (*chirp*) zwitschern ❷ (*talk rapidly*) ■ **to ~ away** vor sich hin plappern ❸ TELEC, INET twittern
two [tu] **I.** *adj* zwei; **~ [o'clock]** zwei [Uhr]; **to break sth in ~** etw entzwei brechen; **the ~ of you** ihr beide; *see also* **eight** ▶ PHRASES: **to throw in one's ~ cents [worth]** seinen Senf dazugeben; **~'s company, three's a crowd** (*prov*) drei sind einer zu viel; **to be ~ of a kind** aus dem gleichen Holz geschnitzt sein; **to be of ~ minds** hin- und hergerissen sein; **there are no ~ ways about it** es gibt keine andere Möglichkeit **II.** *n* Zwei *f; see also* **eight**
'two-bit *adj attr* (*pej fam*) billig *pej*
two-di'mensional *adj* zweidimensional; (*pej*) *character, plot* flach
'two-door I. *adj attr* AUTO zweitürig **II.** *n* zweitüriges Auto
'two-edged *adj* (*a. fig*) zweischneidig
'two-faced *adj* (*pej*) falsch
twofold ['tu·foʊld] **I.** *adj* (*double*) zweifach; (*with two parts*) zweiteilig **II.** *adv* (*doubly*) zweifach; **to increase sth ~** etw verdoppeln
'two-part *adj attr* zweiteilig
'two-piece *n* ❶ (*bikini*) Bikini *m* ❷ (*suit*) Zweiteiler *m*
twosome ['tu·səm] *n* (*duo*) Duo *nt;* (*couple*) Paar *nt;* **as a ~** zu zweit
'two-time *vt* (*fam*) ■ **to ~ sb [with sb]** jdn [mit jdm] betrügen
'two-way *adj attr, inv* ❶ (*traffic*) **~ street** Straße *f* mit Gegenverkehr ❷ *conversation, process* wechselseitig ❸ ELEC **~ switch** Wechselschalter *m*
two-way 'radio *n* Funksprechgerät *nt*
TX *abbrev of* **Texas**
TXT *vt* TELEC *short for* **text:** ■ **to ~ sth** etw texten
tycoon [taɪ·'kun] *n* [Industrie]magnat(in) *m(f)*
tyke [taɪk] *n* (*fam: small child*) Gör *nt*
type [taɪp] **I.** *n* ❶ (*kind*) Art *f; of hair, skin* Typ *m; of food, vegetable* Sorte *f* ❷ (*character*) Typ *m;* ■ **to be one's ~** jds Typ sein *fam* ❸ TYPO (*lettering*) Schriftart *f;* **italic ~** Kursivschrift *f* **II.** *vt* ❶ (*write with machine*) tippen ❷ (*classify*) *blood* typisieren *geh* **III.** *vi* Maschine schreiben
◆ **type out** *vt* tippen
◆ **type up** *vt report* erfassen
'typecast *vt irreg, usu passive* FILM, THEAT (*pej*) ■ **to be ~** auf eine Rolle festgelegt sein/werden
'typeface *n* Schrift[art] *f*
'typescript *n* Maschine geschriebenes Manuskript
'typesetter *n* TYPO ❶ (*machine*) Setzmaschine *f* ❷ (*printer*) [Schrift]setzer(in) *m(f)*
'typesetting TYPO **I.** *n* Setzen *nt* **II.** *adj attr machine, technique* Satz-
'typewrite *vt irreg* tippen
'typewriter *n* Schreibmaschine *f*
'typewritten *adj* Maschine geschrieben
typhoid ['taɪ·fɔɪd], **typhoid 'fever** *n* Typhus *m*
typhoon [taɪ·'fun] *n* Taifun *m*
typhus ['taɪ·fəs] *n* Typhus *m*
typical ['tɪp·ɪ·kəl] *adj* typisch; *symptom a.* charakteristisch (**of** für +*akk*)
typically ['tɪp·ɪ·kəl·i] *adv* typisch; **~, ...** normalerweise ...
typify <-ie-> ['tɪp·ɪ·faɪ] *vt* kennzeichnen; (*symbolize*) ein Symbol sein (für +*akk*)
typing ['taɪ·pɪŋ] *n* Tippen *nt*
typist ['taɪ·pɪst] *n* Schreibkraft *f*
typo ['taɪ·poʊ] *n* (*fam*) Druckfehler *m*
typographer [taɪ·'pag·rə·fər] *n* [Schrift]setzer(in) *m(f)*
typographic(al) [ˌtaɪ·pə·'græ·fɪk(əl)] *adj* typografisch
typography [taɪ·'pag·rə·fi] *n* Typografie *f*
tyrannical [tɪ·'ræn·ɪ·kəl] *adj* (*pej*) tyrannisch; **~ regime** Tyrannei *f*
tyrannize ['tɪr·ə·naɪz] *vt* tyrannisieren
tyranny ['tɪr·ə·ni] *n* Tyrannei *f*
tyrant ['taɪ·rənt] *n* Tyrann(in) *m(f);* (*bossy man*) [Haus]tyrann *m pej;* (*bossy woman*) [Haus]drachen *m pej fam*
Tyrol [tɪ·'roʊl] *n* GEOG ■ **the ~** Tirol *nt*
tzar [zar] *n see* **czar**

Uu

U <*pl* -'s *or* -s>, **u** <*pl* -'s> [ju] *n* ❶ (*letter*) U *nt*, u *nt*; ~ **as in Uniform** U wie Ulrich ❷ INET (*you*) du
U[1] [ju] *n* CHEM *see* **uranium** U *nt*
U[2] [ju] (*fam*) *abbrev of* **university** Uni *f*
UAE [ˌju·eɪ·'i] *n pl abbrev of* **United Arab Emirates**: ■**the** ~ die VAE
ubiquitous [ju·'bɪk·wə·ṭəs] *adj* allgegenwärtig
U-boat ['ju·boʊt] *n* U-Boot *nt*
udder ['ʌd·ər] *n* Euter *nt*
UFO <*pl* -s *or* -'s> [ˌju·ef·'oʊ] *n abbrev of* **unidentified flying object** UFO *nt*
Uganda [ju·'gæn·də] *n* Uganda *nt*
Ugandan [ju·'gæn·dən] **I.** *n* Ugander(in) *m(f)* **II.** *adj inv* ugandisch
ugh [ʌg] *interj* (*fam*) igitt!
ugliness ['ʌg·lɪ·nɪs] *n* Hässlichkeit *f*; (*fig a.*) Scheußlichkeit *f*
ugly ['ʌg·li] *adj* ❶ (*not beautiful*) hässlich; ~ **as sin** hässlich wie die Nacht *fam* ❷ (*unpleasant*) *scene* hässlich; *weather* scheußlich; *rumors* übel; *mood* unerfreulich; *look* böse; *thoughts* schrecklich; **to turn** ~ eine üble Wendung nehmen
UHF [ˌju·eɪtʃ·'ef] *n abbrev of* **ultrahigh frequency** UHF
UK [ˌju·'keɪ] *n abbrev of* **United Kingdom**: ■**the** ~ das Vereinigte Königreich
Ukraine [ju·'kreɪn] *n* die Ukraine
Ukrainian [ju·'kreɪ·ni·ən] **I.** *n* ❶ (*person*) Ukrainer(in) *m(f)* ❷ (*language*) Ukrainisch *nt* **II.** *adj inv* ukrainisch
ulcer ['ʌl·sər] *n* Geschwür *nt*; **stomach** ~ Magengeschwür *nt*
ulterior [ʌl·'tɪr·i·ər] *adj inv* versteckt; ~ **motive** Hintergedanke *m*
ultimate ['ʌl·tə·mɪt] **I.** *adj attr, inv* ❶ (*unbeatable*) beste(r, s) ❷ (*highest*) höchste(r, s); *deterrent, weapon* wirksamste(r, s) ❸ (*final*) letzte(r, s); *decision a.* endgültig; *effect* eigentlich; ~ **destination** Endziel *nt* **II.** *n* ■**the** ~ das Nonplusultra; (*highest*) **the** ~ **in happiness** das größte Glück
ultimately ['ʌl·tə·mɪt·li] *adv inv* (*in the end*) letzten Endes; (*eventually*) letztlich
ultimatum <*pl* -ta *or* -tums> [ˌʌl·tə·'meɪ·ṭəm] *n* Ultimatum *nt*; **to give sb an** ~ jdm ein Ultimatum stellen
ultrahigh 'frequency *n* Ultrahochfrequenz *f*
ultrama'rine **I.** *adj* ultramarin[blau] **II.** *n* Ultramarin[blau] *nt*
ultra'sonic *adj inv* Ultraschall-
'ultrasound *n* Ultraschall *m*
ultra'violet *adj inv* ultraviolett; ~ **lamp** UV-Lampe *f*
um [əm] *interj* (*fam*) hm, äh
um'bilical cord *n* Nabelschnur *f*
umbrage ['ʌm·brɪdʒ] *n* Anstoß *m*; **to take** ~ **at sth** Anstoß an etw *dat* nehmen
umbrella [ʌm·'brel·ə] *n* ❶ Regenschirm *m*; **folding** ~ Knirps® *m*; (*parasol*) Sonnenschirm *m* ❷ (*protection*) Schutz *m*; MIL Jagdschutz *m*
umbrella organi'zation *n* Dachorganisation *f*
umpire ['ʌm·paɪr] **I.** *n* SPORTS (*esp baseball*) Schiedsrichter(in) *m(f)* **II.** *vt game, match* schiedsrichtern; *football match* pfeifen **III.** *vi* SPORTS Schiedsrichter/Schiedsrichterin sein, schiedsrichtern
umpteen ['ʌmp·tin] *adj* (*fam*) zig; ~ **times** zigmal
umpteenth ['ʌmp·tinθ] *adj* (*fam*) x-te(r, s) *fam*
UN [ˌju·'en] *n pl abbrev of* **United Nations**: ■**the** ~ die UN [*o* UNO]
unabashed [ˌʌn·ə·'bæʃt] *adj* unverschämt
unabated [ˌʌn·ə·'beɪ·ṭɪd] *adj* unvermindert
unable [ʌn·'eɪ·bəl] *adj* unfähig; **to be** ~ **to do sth** etw nicht tun können
unabridged [ˌʌn·ə·'brɪdʒd] *adj* ungekürzt
unacceptable [ˌʌn·ək·'sep·tə·bəl] *adj* inakzeptabel; *offer* unannehmbar; *conditions* untragbar
unaccompanied [ˌʌn·ə·'kʌm·pə·nid] *adj inv* ❶ (*unescorted*) ohne Begleitung *nach n, präd*; *baggage* herrenlos ❷ MUS ohne Begleitung *nach n*
unaccountable [ˌʌn·ə·'kaʊn·tə·bəl] *adj* ❶ (*not responsible*) nicht verantwortlich ❷ (*inexplicable*) unerklärlich; *reason* unerfindlich
unaccounted-for [ˌʌn·ə·'kaʊn·tɪd·ˌfɔr] *adj pred, inv* ❶ (*unexplained*) ungeklärt ❷ (*not included in count*) nicht erfasst; (*missing*) fehlend *attr; person* vermisst
unaccustomed [ˌʌn·ə·'kʌs·təmd] *adj* (*inexperienced*) ungewohnt; **to be** ~ **to doing sth** es nicht gewohnt sein, etw zu tun
unacknowledged [ˌʌn·ək·'nal·ɪdʒd] *adj inv* unbeachtet; (*unrecognized*) nicht anerkannt
unaddressed [ˌʌn·ə·'drest] *adj inv* ❶ *envelope* nicht adressiert ❷ *question* unbeantwortet
unadorned [ˌʌn·ə·'dɔrnd] *adj inv* (*plain*) schlicht; *story* nicht ausgeschmückt; *beauty* natürlich; *truth* ungeschminkt
unadulterated [ˌʌn·ə·'dʌl·tə·reɪ·ṭɪd] *adj inv* unverfälscht; *alcohol* rein; ~ **nonsense** blanker Unsinn
unadventurous [ˌʌn·əd·'ven·tʃər·əs] *adj person* wenig unternehmungslustig; *life* unspektakulär; *style* einfallslos
unaffected [ˌʌn·ə·'fek·tɪd] *adj inv* ❶ (*unchanged*) unberührt; (*unmoved*) unbeeindruckt; (*not influenced*) nicht beeinflusst; MED nicht angegriffen ❷ (*natural*) natürlich; *manner* ungekünstelt; (*sincere*) echt
unafraid [ˌʌn·ə·'freɪd] *adj inv* unerschrocken; ■**to be** ~ **of sb/sth** vor jdm/etw keine Angst haben

unaided [ʌn·ˈeɪ·dɪd] *adj inv* ohne fremde Hilfe *nach n*
unalike [ˌʌn·ə·ˈlaɪk] *adj pred* unähnlich
unaltered [ʌn·ˈɔl·tərd] *adj inv* unverändert
unambiguous [ˌʌn·æm·ˈbɪg·jʊ·əs] *adj* unzweideutig; *statement* eindeutig
un-American [ˌʌn·ə·ˈmer·ɪ·kən] *adj* unamerikanisch; ~ **activities** ≈Landesverrat *m* (*gegen den amerikanischen Staat gerichtete Umtriebe*)
unanimous [ju·ˈnæn·ə·məs] *adj inv* einstimmig
unannounced [ˌʌn·ə·ˈnaʊnst] **I.** *adj inv* unangekündigt; (*unexpected*) unerwartet **II.** *adv inv* unangemeldet; (*unexpected*) unerwartet
unanswerable [ˌʌn·ˈæn·sər·ə·bəl] *adj* ❶ unbeantwortbar; ■**to be ~** nicht zu beantworten sein ❷ (*irrefutable*) unwiderlegbar; *proof* eindeutig
unanswered [ˌʌn·ˈæn·sərd] *adj inv* unbeantwortet
unappealing [ˌʌn·ə·ˈpi·lɪŋ] *adj* unerfreulich, unattraktiv
unapproachable [ˌʌn·ə·ˈproʊ·tʃə·bəl] *adj* unzugänglich; *person a.* unnahbar
unarmed [ˌʌn·ˈarmd] *adj inv* unbewaffnet; (*unprepared*) unvorbereitet
unashamed [ˌʌn·ə·ˈʃeɪmd] *adj* schamlos; *attitude* unverhohlen
unasked [ˌʌn·ˈæskt] **I.** *adj inv* ❶ ungefragt; **an ~ question** eine Frage, die keiner zu stellen wagt ❷ (*not requested*) ■**~-for** ungebeten **II.** *adv inv* ❶ (*spontaneously*) spontan ❷ (*without being wanted*) ungebeten
unassuming [ˌʌn·ə·ˈsu·mɪŋ] *adj* bescheiden
unattached [ˌʌn·ə·ˈtætʃt] *adj inv* ❶ (*not connected*) einzeln ❷ (*independent*) unabhängig ❸ (*bachelor*) ungebunden
unattainable [ˌʌn·ə·ˈteɪ·nə·bəl] *adj inv* unerreichbar
unattended [ˌʌn·ə·ˈten·dɪd] *adj inv* ❶ (*alone*) unbegleitet; *child, baggage* unbeaufsichtigt ❷ (*without care*) unerledigt; (*unmanned*) nicht besetzt; **to go ~** *patient, wound* unbehandelt bleiben
unattractive [ˌʌn·ə·ˈtræk·tɪv] *adj* unattraktiv; *place a.* ohne Reiz *nach n, präd; personality* wenig anziehend
unauthorized [ˌʌn·ˈɔ·θə·raɪzd] *adj inv* nicht autorisiert; *person, access* unbefugt *attr*
unavailable [ˌʌn·ə·ˈveɪ·lə·bəl] *adj* ❶ (*not in*) nicht verfügbar; *person* nicht erreichbar; (*busy*) nicht zu sprechen ❷ (*not for the public*) [der Öffentlichkeit] nicht zugänglich
unavoidable [ˌʌn·ə·ˈvɔɪ·də·bəl] *adj* unvermeidlich
unaware [ˌʌn·ə·ˈwer] *adj* ■**to be/be not ~ of sth** sich *dat* einer S. *gen* nicht/durchaus bewusst sein
unawares [ˌʌn·ə·ˈwerz] *adv inv* unerwartet; **to catch sb ~** jdn überraschen
unbalanced [ˌʌn·ˈbæl·ənst] *adj* ❶ (*uneven*) schief; *account* nicht ausgeglichen; *diet* unausgewogen; (*biased*) einseitig ❷ (*unstable*) labil; **mentally ~** psychisch labil
unbearable [ˌʌn·ˈber·ə·bəl] *adj* unerträglich
unbeatable [ˌʌn·ˈbi·t̬ə·bəl] *adj inv* ❶ (*sure to win*) unschlagbar; *army* unbesiegbar ❷ (*perfect*) unübertrefflich; *value, quality* unübertroffen
unbeaten [ˌʌn·ˈbi·tən] *adj inv* ungeschlagen; *army* unbesiegt
unbecoming [ˌʌn·bɪ·ˈkʌm·ɪŋ] *adj* ❶ *dress* unvorteilhaft ❷ *behavior* unschön
unbeknown [ˌʌn·bɪ·ˈnoʊn], **unbeknownst** [ˌʌn·bɪ·ˈnoʊnst] *adv inv* ■**~ to sb** ohne jds Wissen; **~ to anyone he was leading a double life** kein Mensch ahnte, dass er ein Doppelleben führte
unbelievable [ˌʌn·bɪ·ˈli·və·bəl] *adj* ❶ (*surprising*) unglaublich ❷ (*fam: extraordinary*) sagenhaft
unbelieving [ˌʌn·bɪ·ˈli·vɪŋ] *adj* ungläubig
unbend [ʌn·ˈbend] **I.** *vt* <-bent, -bent> strecken; *wire* gerade biegen **II.** *vi* <-bent, -bent> ❶ (*straighten out*) [wieder] gerade werden; *person* sich aufrichten ❷ (*relax*) sich entspannen
unbiased [ʌn·ˈbaɪ·əst] *adj* unparteiisch; *opinion, report* objektiv
unbleached [ʌn·ˈblitʃt] *adj inv* ungebleicht
unblemished [ʌn·ˈblem·ɪʃt] *adj inv skin* makellos; *record* tadellos
unblinking [ʌn·ˈblɪŋ·kɪŋ] *adj* starr
unborn [ʌn·ˈbɔrn] *adj inv* ungeboren
unbounded [ʌn·ˈbaʊn·dɪd] *adj* grenzenlos; *ambition* maßlos; *hope* unbegrenzt
unbreakable [ʌn·ˈbreɪ·kə·bəl] *adj inv* unzerbrechlich; *code* nicht zu knacken *nach n; habit* fest verankert; *promise* bindend; *record* nicht zu brechen *nach n; rule* unumstößlich
unbroken [ʌn·ˈbroʊ·kən] *adj inv* ❶ unbeschädigt; *spirit, record* ungebrochen; **~ promise** gehaltenes Versprechen ❷ (*continuous*) stetig; *peace* beständig; *sleep* ungestört
unbuckle [ʌn·ˈbʌk·əl] *vt* aufschnallen; *seatbelt* öffnen
unburden [ʌn·ˈbɜr·dən] *vt* ■**to ~ oneself [of sth]** sich *akk* [von etw *dat*] befreien; ■**to ~ oneself [to sb]** [jdm] sein Herz ausschütten; **to ~ one's sorrows** seine Sorgen abladen
unbusinesslike [ʌn·ˈbɪz·nɪs·laɪk] *adj* unprofessionell
unbutton [ʌn·ˈbʌt·ən] *vt, vi* aufknöpfen
uncalled for *adj pred,* **uncalled-for** [ʌn·ˈkɔld·fɔr] *adj attr* unnötig; *remark* unpassend
uncanny [ʌn·ˈkæn·i] *adj* unheimlich; **an ~ resemblance** eine unglaubliche Ähnlichkeit
uncared for *adj pred,* **uncared-for** [ʌn·ˈkerd·fɔr] *adj attr* ungepflegt
unceasing [ʌn·ˈsi·sɪŋ] *adj* unaufhörlich; *efforts, support* unablässig
unceremonious [ʌn·ˌser·ɪ·ˈmoʊ·ni·əs] *adj* ❶ (*abrupt*) rüde *pej* ❷ (*informal*) locker
uncertain [ʌn·ˈsɜr·tən] *adj* ❶ (*unsure*) unsi-

U

cher; ■ **to be ~ about** [*or* **of**] **sth** sich *dat* einer S. *gen* nicht sicher sein; **in no ~ terms** klar und deutlich ② (*unpredictable*) ungewiss; *temper* launenhaft

uncertainty [ʌn·ˈsɜr·tən·ti] *n* ① (*doubtfulness*) Ungewissheit *f*, Zweifel *m* (**about** über +*akk*) ② (*hesitancy*) Unsicherheit *f*

unchallenged [ʌn·ˈtʃæl·ɪndʒd] *adj* unangefochten; (*unopposed*) unwidersprochen; **to go ~** unangefochten bleiben

unchanged [ʌn·ˈtʃeɪndʒd] *adj inv* ① (*unaltered*) unverändert ② (*not replaced*) nicht [aus]gewechselt

uncharacteristic [ʌn·ˌkær·ək·tə·ˈrɪs·tɪk] *adj* untypisch (**of** für +*akk*)

uncharitable [ˌʌn·ˈtʃær·ɪ·tə·bəl] *adj* ① (*severe*) unbarmherzig ② (*unkind*) unfair; *person* gemein

uncharted [ʌn·ˈtʃar·t̬ɪd] *adj* ① *inv* (*not mapped*) auf keiner Landkarte verzeichnet ② (*fig*) **~ waters/territory** Neuland *nt*

unchecked [ˌʌn·ˈtʃekt] *adj* ① (*unrestrained*) unkontrolliert; **~ violence** hemmungslose Gewalt; **to continue ~** ungehindert weitergehen ② (*not examined*) ungeprüft

unclaimed [ˌʌn·ˈkleɪmd] *adj* nicht beansprucht; *baggage* nicht abgeholt

unclassified [ˌʌn·ˈklæs·ɪ·faɪd] *adj* ① nicht klassifiziert ② (*not secret*) nicht geheim

uncle [ˈʌŋ·kəl] *n* Onkel *m* ▶ PHRASES: **to cry** [*or* **say**] **~** (*fam*) klein beigeben

unclean [ˌʌn·ˈklin] *adj* ① (*unhygienic*) verunreinigt ② (*impure*) schmutzig

unclear [ˌʌn·ˈklɪr] *adj* ① (*not certain*) unklar; ■ **to be ~ about sth** in Bezug auf etw *akk* nicht sicher sein ② (*vague*) vage; *statement* unklar

Uncle ˈSam *n* Uncle Sam *m* (*Bezeichnung für die USA*)

unclog [ʌn·ˈklag] *vt* <-gg-> *drain, toilet* frei machen, reinigen

uncluttered [ˌʌn·ˈklʌt̬·ərd] *adj* ① (*tidy*) aufgeräumt ② (*fig*) *mind* frei

uncollected [ˌʌn·kə·ˈlek·tɪd] *adj inv fare, tax* nicht erhoben; *baggage, mail* nicht abgeholt

uncolored [ʌn·ˈkʌl·ərd] *adj* ① (*colorless*) farblos ② (*unbiased*) objektiv

uncomfortable [ʌn·ˈkʌm·fər·t̬ə·bəl] *adj* ① (*causing discomfort*) unbequem ② (*ill at ease*) **to feel ~** sich unwohl fühlen ③ (*uneasy*) unbehaglich; *silence* gespannt

uncommitted [ˌʌn·kə·ˈmɪt̬·ɪd] *adj* ① (*undecided*) unentschieden ② (*not dedicated*) **to be ~ to a relationship** einer Beziehung halbherzig gegenüberstehen

uncommon [ʌn·ˈkam·ən] *adj* selten; *name a.* ungewöhnlich

uncommonly [ʌn·ˈkam·ən·li] *adv* ungewöhnlich

uncommunicative [ˌʌn·kə·ˈmju·nɪ·kə·tɪv] *adj* verschlossen; ■ **to be ~ about sth/sb** wenig über etw/jdn sprechen

uncompromising [ʌn·ˈkam·prə·maɪ·zɪŋ] *adj* kompromisslos

unconcerned [ˌʌn·kən·ˈsɜrnd] *adj* ① (*not worried*) unbekümmert; ■ **to be ~ about sth/sb** sich *dat* keine Sorgen über etw/jdn machen ② (*indifferent*) desinteressiert

unconditional [ˌʌn·kən·ˈdɪʃ·ə·nəl] *adj inv* bedingungslos; *love a.* rückhaltlos

unconfirmed [ˌʌn·kən·ˈfɜrmd] *adj inv* unbestätigt

unconnected [ˌʌn·kə·ˈnek·tɪd] *adj inv* unzusammenhängend (**with** mit +*dat*)

unconscious [ʌn·ˈkan·ʃəs] *adj* ① MED bewusstlos; **~ state** Bewusstlosigkeit *f* ② PSYCH unbewusst; **the ~ mind** das Unterbewusste ③ (*unaware*) unabsichtlich; ■ **to be ~ of sth** sich *dat* einer S. *gen* nicht bewusst sein

unconsciously [ʌn·ˈkan·ʃəs·li] *adv* unbewusst

unconsciousness [ʌn·ˈkan·ʃəs·nɪs] *n* ① MED Bewusstlosigkeit *f* ② (*unawareness*) Unbewusstheit *f*

unconstitutional [ʌn·ˌkan·stɪ·ˈtu·ʃə·nəl] *adj inv* verfassungswidrig

uncontested [ˌʌn·kən·ˈtes·tɪd] *adj* ① (*unchallenged*) unbestritten; *claim* unstreitig ② LAW unangefochten; **~ divorce** einvernehmliche Scheidung

uncontrollable [ˌʌn·kən·ˈtroʊ·lə·bəl] *adj* unkontrollierbar; *bleeding, urge* unstillbar; *child* unzähmbar

uncontrolled [ˌʌn·kən·ˈtroʊld] *adj* unkontrolliert; *aggression* unbeherrscht

uncontroversial [ˌʌn·kan·trə·ˈvɜr·ʃəl] *adj* unumstritten

unconventional [ˌʌn·kən·ˈven·ʃə·nəl] *adj* unkonventionell

unconvinced [ˌʌn·kən·ˈvɪnst] *adj* nicht überzeugt (**of** von +*dat*)

unconvincing [ˌʌn·kən·ˈvɪn·sɪŋ] *adj* ① (*not persuasive*) nicht überzeugend ② (*not credible*) unglaubwürdig

uncooked [ˌʌn·ˈkʊkt] *adj inv* roh

uncooperative [ˌʌn·koʊ·ˈap·ər·ə·tɪv] *adj* unkooperativ

uncork [ˌʌn·ˈkɔrk] *vt* entkorken

uncountable [ʌn·ˈkaʊn·t̬ə·bəl] *adj inv* unzählbar; (*countless*) zahllos

uncouple [ˌʌn·ˈkʌp·əl] *vt* ① MECH abkuppeln (**from** von +*dat*) ② (*fig*) trennen

uncouth [ʌn·ˈkuθ] *adj* ungehobelt

uncover [ʌn·ˈkʌv·ər] *vt* ① (*bare*) freilegen ② (*disclose*) entdecken; *scandal, secret* aufdecken

uncritical [ˌʌn·ˈkrɪt̬·ɪ·kəl] *adj* unkritisch; ■ **to be ~ of sth/sb** gegenüber etw/jdm eine unkritische Einstellung haben

uncrowned [ˌʌn·ˈkraʊnd] *adj inv* ungekrönt *a. fig*

uncut [ʌn·ˈkʌt] *adj inv* ① ungeschnitten; *diamond* ungeschliffen ② (*not shortened*) *version* ungekürzt

undated [ʌn·ˈdeɪ·t̬ɪd] *adj inv* undatiert

undaunted [ʌn·ˈdɔn·tɪd] *adj* unerschrocken; **to remain ~** [**by sth**] von etw *dat* unbeirrt sein

undecided [ˌʌn·dɪ·ˈsaɪ·dɪd] *adj* ❶ (*hesitant*) unentschlossen; ■ **to be ~ about sth** sich *dat* über etw *akk* [noch] unklar sein ❷ (*unsettled*) offen; *vote* unentschieden
undeclared [ˌʌn·dɪ·ˈklerd] *adj* ❶ FIN nicht deklariert ❷ (*unofficial*) nicht erklärt; **~ war** Krieg *m* ohne Kriegserklärung
undefined [ˌʌn·dɪ·ˈfaɪnd] *adj* ❶ unbestimmt ❷ (*lacking clarity*) vage
undeliverable [ˌʌn·dɪ·ˈlɪv·ər·ə·bəl] *adj* unzustellbar
undelivered [ˌʌn·dɪ·ˈlɪv·ərd] *adj* nicht zugestellt
undemocratic [ˌʌn·dem·ə·ˈkræṭ·ɪk] *adj* undemokratisch
undemonstrative [ˌʌn·dɪ·ˈman·strə·ṭɪv] *adj* zurückhaltend
undeniable [ˌʌn·dɪ·ˈnaɪ·ə·bəl] *adj* unbestritten; **~ evidence** eindeutiger Beweis
undeniably [ˌʌn·dɪ·ˈnaɪ·ə·bli] *adv* unbestreitbar
under [ˈʌn·dər] **I.** *prep* ❶ (*below*) unter *+dat; with verbs of motion* unter *+akk;* **he walked ~ the bridge** er ging unter die Brücke; **he stood ~ a bridge** er stand unter einer Brücke ❷ (*supporting*) unter *+dat;* **to break ~ the weight** unter dem Gewicht zusammenbrechen ❸ (*less than*) unter *+dat;* **to cost ~ 5 dollars** weniger als fünf Dollar kosten ❹ (*governed by*) unter *+dat;* **~ the supervision of sb** unter jds Aufsicht; **to be ~ sb's influence** (*fig*) unter jds Einfluss stehen ❺ (*in state of*) unter *+dat;* **~ arrest/suspicion** unter Arrest/Verdacht; **~ [no] circumstances** unter [keinen] Umständen ▶ PHRASES: **[already] ~ way** [bereits] im Gange **II.** *adv inv* ❶ (*down*) **to go ~** untergehen; *company* Pleite machen ❷ (*less*) **suitable for kids aged five and ~** geeignet für Kinder von fünf Jahren und darunter
undera'chieve *vi* weniger leisten als erwartet
under'age *adj inv* minderjährig; **~ drinking** der Genuss von Alkohol durch Minderjährige
'underarm *n* Achselhöhle *f*
under'bid <-bid, -bid> **I.** *vi* ein zu niedriges Angebot machen **II.** *vt* unterbieten
under'charge *vt, vi* zu wenig berechnen
'underclass *n* unterprivilegierte Klasse
'underclothes *npl see* **underwear**
'undercoat **I.** *n* ❶ (*paint*) Grundierung *f* ❷ AUTO Unterbodenschutz *m kein pl* ❸ (*fur*) Wollhaarkleid *nt* **II.** *vt* ❶ (*paint*) grundieren ❷ AUTO mit Unterbodenschutz versehen
'undercoating *n see* **undercoat I. 1, 2**
'undercover **I.** *adj attr, inv* geheim; *detective* verdeckt; **~ police officer** Geheimpolizist(in) *m(f)* **II.** *adv inv* geheim
'undercurrent *n* ❶ (*of sea, river*) Unterströmung *f* ❷ (*fig*) Unterton *m*
under'cut <-cut, -cut> *vt* ❶ (*charge less*) unterbieten ❷ (*undermine*) untergraben
underde'veloped *adj* unterentwickelt; **~ country** Entwicklungsland *nt*
'underdog *n* Außenseiter(in) *m(f)*
under'done *adj* (*undercooked*) nicht gar; *meat* blutig
under'dressed *adj* (*too casual*) zu einfach gekleidet
underem'ployed *adj person* unterbeschäftigt; *thing* nicht voll genutzt
undere'quipped *adj* unzureichend ausgerüstet
under'estimate **I.** *vt* unterschätzen **II.** *vi* eine zu geringe Schätzung abgeben **III.** *n* Unterbewertung *f*
underex'pose *vt photo* unterbelichten
underex'posure *n* PHOT Unterbelichtung *f*
under'fed *adj* unterernährt
under'foot *adv inv* unter den Füßen; **it was very muddy ~** der Weg war sehr schlammig
under'fund *vt* unterfinanzieren
under'funding *n* Unterfinanzierung *f*
under'go <-went, -gone> *vt* **to ~ a change** eine Veränderung durchmachen; **to ~ surgery** sich einer Operation unterziehen
under'graduate *n* Student(in) *m(f)*
'underground **I.** *adj* ❶ *inv* unterirdisch; **~ cable** Erdkabel *nt* ❷ POL Untergrund-; **~ movement** Untergrundbewegung *f* **II.** *adv* ❶ *inv* GEOG unter der Erde ❷ POL **to go ~** in den Untergrund gehen
'undergrowth *n* Dickicht *nt;* **dense ~** dichtes Gestrüpp
'underhand **I.** *adj* ❶ (*devious*) hinterhältig; **~ dealings** betrügerische Machenschaften ❷ *serve, throw* mit der Hand von unten nach *n* **II.** *adv* SPORTS mit der Hand von unten
underin'sured *adj* unterversichert
'underlay¹ *n* Unterlage *f*
under'lay² *vt pt of* **underlie**
under'lie <-y-, -lay, -lain> *vt* zugrunde liegen
'underline *vt* ❶ (*draw line*) unterstreichen; **to ~ sth in red** etw rot unterstreichen ❷ (*emphasize*) betonen
underling [ˈʌn·dər·lɪŋ] *n* (*pej*) Handlanger *m pej*
under'lying *adj attr, inv* ❶ GEOG tiefer liegend ❷ (*basic*) zugrunde liegend; **the ~ reason for sth** der Grund für etw
under'manned *adj* unterbesetzt
'undermine *vt* (*weaken*) untergraben; *currency, confidence* schwächen; *health* schädigen; *hopes* zunichtemachen
underneath [ˌʌn·dər·ˈniθ] **I.** *prep* unter *+dat; with vbs of motion* unter *+akk* **II.** *adv inv* darunter **III.** *n* ■ **the ~** die Unterseite **IV.** *adj inv* untere(r, s)
under'nourished *adj* unterernährt
under'paid *adj* unterbezahlt
'underpants *npl* Unterhose *f*
'underpass <*pl* -es> *n* Unterführung *f*
under'pay <-paid, -paid> *vt usu passive* unterbezahlen
underper'form *vi* eine [unerwartet] schlechte Leistung erbringen
under'play *vt* herunterspielen
under'populated *adj* unterbevölkert

under'privileged I. *adj* unterprivilegiert II. *n* ■**the ~** *pl* die Unterprivilegierten *pl*
under'rated *adj* unterschätzt
underrepre'sented *adj* unterrepräsentiert
'underscore *vt* ① (*draw line*) unterstreichen ② (*emphasize*) betonen
under'sell <-sold, -sold> *vt* ① (*offer cheaper*) *competitor* unterbieten; *goods* unter Preis verkaufen ② (*undervalue*) unterbewerten; ■**to ~ oneself** sich unter Wert verkaufen *fam*
'undershirt *n* Unterhemd *nt*
'underside *n usu sing* Unterseite *f*
'undersigned <*pl* -> *n* (*form*) ■**the ~** der/die Unterzeichnete
'underskirt *n* Unterrock *m*
under'staffed *adj* unterbesetzt
understand <-stood, -stood> [ˌʌn·dər·'stænd] I. *vt* ① (*perceive meaning*) verstehen; **to not ~ a single word** kein einziges Wort verstehen; **to ~ one another** sich verstehen; **to make oneself understood** sich verständlich machen ② (*comprehend significance*) begreifen ③ (*sympathize with*) ■**to ~ sb/sth** für jdn/etw Verständnis haben ④ (*empathize*) ■**to ~ sb** sich in jdn einfühlen können ⑤ (*be informed*) ■**to ~ [that] ...** hören, dass ...; **to give sb to ~ that ...** jdm zu verstehen geben, dass ... II. *vi* ① (*comprehend*) verstehen, kapieren *fam* ② (*infer*) ■**to ~ from sth that ...** aus etw *dat* schließen, dass ... ③ (*be informed*) ■**to ~ from sb that ...** von jdm hören, dass ...
understandable [ˌʌn·dər·'stæn·də·bəl] *adj* verständlich
understanding [ˌʌn·dər·'stæn·dɪŋ] I. *n* ① (*comprehension*) Verständnis *nt*; **to be beyond sb's ~** über jds Verständnis *nt* hinausgehen ② (*agreement*) Übereinkunft *f*; **tacit ~** stillschweigendes Abkommen ③ (*condition*) Bedingung *f*; **to do sth on the ~ that ...** etw unter der Bedingung machen, dass ... II. *adj* verständnisvoll
understate [ˌʌn·dər·'steɪt] *vt* abschwächen; **to ~ the case** untertreiben
understated [ˌʌn·dər·'steɪ·t̬ɪd] *adj* ① (*downplayed*) untertrieben ② (*restrained*) zurückhaltend; *elegance* schlicht
understatement [ˌʌn·dər·'steɪt·mənt] *n* Untertreibung *f*, Understatement *nt*
understood [ˌʌn·dər·'stʊd] *pt, pp of* **understand**

understudy ['ʌn·dər·ˌstʌd·i] THEAT I. *n* Zweitbesetzung *f* II. *vt* <-ie-> ■**to ~ sb** jdn als Zweitbesetzung vertreten
undertake <-took, -taken> [ˌʌn·dər·'teɪk] *vt* ① (*take on*) durchführen; *trip* unternehmen ② (*guarantee*) ■**to ~ to do sth** sich verpflichten, etw zu tun
undertaker ['ʌn·dər·ˌteɪ·kər] *n see* **funeral director**
undertaking [ˌʌn·dər·'teɪ·kɪŋ] *n* ① (*project*) Unternehmung *f* ② (*pledge*) Verpflichtung *f*
under-the-'counter I. *adj attr* illegal II. *adv* unter der Hand
'undertone *n* ① (*voice*) gedämpfte Stimme ② (*insinuation*) Unterton *m*
under'used, under'utilized *adj* nicht [voll] ausgelastet
under'value *vt* unterbewerten; *person* unterschätzen
'underwater *inv* I. *adj* Unterwasser- II. *adv* unter Wasser
'underwear *n* Unterwäsche *f*
'underweight *adj* untergewichtig
'underworld *n* ① (*milieu*) Unterwelt *f* ② (*afterworld*) ■**the U~** die Unterwelt
under'write <-wrote, -written> *vt* **to ~ an insurance policy** die Haftung für eine Versicherung übernehmen; **to ~ a loan** für einen Kredit bürgen
'underwriter *n* Versicherer, Versicherin *m, f*
undesirable [ˌʌn·dɪ·'zaɪ·rə·bəl] I. *adj* unerwünscht; **~ character** windiger Typ *pej fam* II. *n usu pl* unerwünschte Person
undetected [ˌʌn·dɪ·'tek·tɪd] *adj inv* unentdeckt
undeveloped [ˌʌn·dɪ·'vel·əpt] *adj* ① *land* unerschlossen ② ECON unterentwickelt ③ PHOT nicht entwickelt
undid [ʌn·'dɪd] *pt of* **undo**
undies ['ʌn·diz] *npl* (*fam*) Unterwäsche *f kein pl*
undisclosed [ˌʌn·dɪ·'skloʊzd] *adj inv* nicht veröffentlicht; *location, source* geheim
undiscovered [ˌʌn·dɪ·'skʌv·ərd] *adj* unentdeckt
undisputed [ˌʌn·dɪ·'spju·t̬ɪd] *adj* unumstritten
undistinguished [ˌʌn·dɪ·'stɪŋ·gwɪʃt] *adj* mittelmäßig *usu pej*
undisturbed [ʌn·dɪ·'stɜrbd] *adj* ① (*untouched*) unberührt ② (*uninterrupted*) ungestört ③ (*unconcerned*) nicht beunruhigt
undivided [ˌʌn·dɪ·'vaɪ·dɪd] *adj* ① (*not split*) ungeteilt ② (*concentrated*) uneingeschränkt; *attention* ungeteilt
undo <-did, -done> [ʌn·'du] I. *vt* ① (*unfasten*) öffnen; *button, zipper* aufmachen ② (*cancel*) *damage* beheben; **to ~ the good work** die gute Arbeit zunichtemachen ③ (*ruin*) zugrunde richten ▶ PHRASES: **what's done cannot be ~ne** (*saying*) Geschehenes kann man nicht mehr ungeschehen machen II. *vi button* aufgehen
undoing [ʌn·'du·ɪŋ] *n* Ruin *m*; **to be sb's ~** jds Ruin *m* sein
undone [ʌn·'dʌn] I. *vt pp of* **undo** II. *adj inv* offen; **to come ~** aufgehen
undoubted [ʌn·'daʊ·t̬ɪd] *adj inv* unbestritten
undoubtedly [ʌn·'daʊ·t̬ɪd·li] *adv inv* zweifellos
undreamed of *adj pred,* **undreamed-of** [ʌn·'drimd·ˌʌv] *adj attr,* **undreamt of** *adj pred,* **undreamt-of** [ʌn·'dremt·ˌav] *adj attr* unvorstellbar; *success* ungeahnt
undress [ʌn·'dres] I. *vt* ausziehen II. *vi* sich ausziehen III. *n* **in a state of ~** spärlich bekleidet

undressed [ʌn·ˈdrest] *adj pred, inv* unbekleidet; **to get ~** sich ausziehen
undue [ˌʌn·ˈdu] *adj* ungebührlich; **~ pressure** übermäßiger Druck
undulating [ˈʌn·dʒə·leɪ·t̬ɪŋ] *adj* ❶ (*rocking*) wallend ❷ (*wavy*) **~ hills** sanft geschwungene Hügel
unduly [ʌn·ˈdu·li] *adv* unangemessen; *concerned* übermäßig
undying [ˌʌn·ˈdaɪ·ɪŋ] *adj attr* unvergänglich; *devotion* unerschütterlich; *love* ewig
unearned [ˌʌn·ˈɜrnd] *adj* ❶ (*undeserved*) unverdient ❷ (*not worked for*) nicht erarbeitet; **~ income** (*from real estate*) Besitzeinkommen *nt;* (*from investments*) Kapitaleinkommen *nt*
unearth [ʌn·ˈɜrθ] *vt* ❶ (*dig up*) ausgraben ❷ (*discover*) entdecken; *truth* ans Licht bringen; *person* ausfindig machen
unearthly [ʌn·ˈɜrθ·li] *adj* ❶ (*eerie*) gespenstisch; *beauty* übernatürlich; *noise* grässlich ❷ (*fam: inconvenient*) unmöglich; **at some ~ hour** zu einer unchristlichen Zeit
unease [ʌn·ˈiz], **uneasiness** [ʌn·ˈiz·ɪ·nɪs] *n* Unbehagen *nt* (**over/at** über +*akk*)
uneasy [ʌn·ˈi·zi] *adj* ❶ (*anxious*) besorgt; *smile* gequält; ■ **to be/feel ~ about sth/sb** sich in Bezug auf etw/jdn unbehaglich fühlen ❷ (*causing anxiety*) unangenehm; *feeling* ungut; *relationship* gespannt
uneconomic [ʌn·ˌek·ə·ˈnam·ɪk] *adj* unwirtschaftlich
uneducated [ʌn·ˈedʒ·ə·keɪ·t̬ɪd] *adj* ungebildet
unemotional [ˌʌn·ɪ·ˈmoʊ·ʃə·nəl] *adj* ❶ (*not feeling emotions*) kühl ❷ (*not revealing emotions*) emotionslos
unemployable [ˌʌn·ɪm·ˈplɔɪ·ə·bəl] *adj* unvermittelbar
unemployed [ˌʌn·ɪm·ˈplɔɪd] **I.** *n* ■ **the ~** *pl* die Arbeitslosen **II.** *adj* arbeitslos
unemployment [ˌʌn·ɪm·ˈplɔɪ·mənt] *n* ❶ (*state*) Arbeitslosigkeit *f* ❷ (*rate*) Arbeitslosenrate *f;* **mass ~** Massenarbeitslosigkeit *f* ❸ (*compensation*) Arbeitslosengeld *nt*
unemployment compenˈsation, unemployment inˈsurance *n* Arbeitslosenunterstützung *f,* Arbeitslosengeld *nt*
unemployment office *n* Arbeitsamt *nt*
unending [ʌn·ˈen·dɪŋ] *adj* endlos
unenlightened [ˌʌn·ɪn·ˈlaɪ·tənd] *adj* ❶ (*unwise*) unklug; *person a.* ignorant ❷ (*superstitious*) unaufgeklärt ❸ (*uninformed*) ahnungslos; **to remain ~** im Dunkeln tappen *fam*
unenviable [ʌn·ˈen·vi·ə·bəl] *adj* wenig beneidenswert
unequal [ʌn·ˈi·kwəl] *adj* ❶ (*different*) unterschiedlich; **~ triangle** ungleichseitiges Dreieck ❷ (*unjust*) ungerecht; *contest, treatment* ungleich; *relationship* einseitig ❸ (*inadequate*) ■ **to be ~ to sth** etw *dat* nicht gewachsen sein
unequaled, unequalled *adj* [ʌn·ˈi·kwəld] unübertroffen
unequivocal [ˌʌn·ɪ·ˈkwɪv·ə·kəl] *adj* unmissverständlich; *success* eindeutig
unerring [ʌn·ˈɜr·ɪŋ] *adj* unfehlbar
UNESCO [ju·ˈnes·koʊ] *n acr for* **United Nations Educational, Scientific and Cultural Organization:** ■ [**the**] **~** die UNESCO
unethical [ʌn·ˈeθ·ɪ·kəl] *adj* unmoralisch
uneven [ˌʌn·ˈi·vən] *adj* ❶ (*not level*) uneben; *road* holprig ❷ (*not parallel*) ungleich; **~ bars** (*gymnastics*) Stufenbarren *m* ❸ (*unfair*) unterschiedlich; *contest, treatment* ungleich ❹ (*inadequate*) uneinheitlich ❺ (*odd*) ungerade
uneventful [ˌʌn·ɪ·ˈvent·fəl] *adj* ereignislos
unexceptionable [ˌʌn·ɪk·ˈsep·ʃə·nə·bəl] *adj* untadelig; *behavior* tadellos
unexceptional [ˌʌn·ɪk·ˈsep·ʃə·nəl] *adj* nicht außergewöhnlich
unexciting [ˌʌn·ɪk·ˈsaɪ·t̬ɪŋ] *adj* ❶ (*commonplace*) durchschnittlich ❷ (*uneventful*) ereignislos
unexpected [ˌʌn·ɪk·ˈspek·tɪd] **I.** *adj* unerwartet; *opportunity* unvorhergesehen; *windfall* unverhofft **II.** *n* ■ **the ~** das Unerwartete
unexplained [ˌʌn·ɪk·ˈspleɪnd] *adj inv* unerklärt
unexploded [ˌʌn·ɪk·ˈsploʊ·dɪd] *adj inv* nicht detoniert
unexpressed [ˌʌn·ɪk·ˈsprest] *adj* unausgesprochen
unexpurgated [ʌn·ˈek·spər·geɪ·t̬ɪd] *adj* unzensiert
unfailing [ʌn·ˈfeɪ·lɪŋ] *adj* ❶ (*dependable*) beständig; *loyalty* unerschütterlich ❷ (*continuous*) unerschöpflich
unfair [ˌʌn·ˈfer] *adj* ungerecht
unfaithful [ˌʌn·ˈfeɪθ·fʊl] *adj* ❶ (*adulterous*) untreu ❷ (*disloyal*) illoyal *geh* ❸ (*inaccurate*) ungenau
unfamiliar [ˌʌn·fə·ˈmɪl·jər] *adj* ❶ (*new*) unvertraut; *experience* ungewohnt; *place* unbekannt; ■ **to be ~ to sb** jdm fremd sein ❷ (*unacquainted*) ■ **to be ~ with sth** mit etw *dat* nicht vertraut sein
unfashionable [ʌn·ˈfæʃ·ə·nə·bəl] *adj* unmodisch
unfasten [ˌʌn·ˈfæs·ən] **I.** *vt button, belt* öffnen; *jewelry* abnehmen **II.** *vi* aufgehen
unfathomable [ʌn·ˈfæð·ə·mə·bəl] *adj* ❶ (*deep*) unergründlich ❷ (*inexplicable*) unverständlich
unfavorable [ˌʌn·ˈfeɪ·vər·ə·bəl] *adj* ❶ (*adverse*) ungünstig; *comparison* unvorteilhaft; *decision* negativ ❷ (*disadvantageous*) nachteilig; **to appear in an ~ light** in einem ungünstigen Licht erscheinen
unfeeling [ʌn·ˈfi·lɪŋ] *adj* gefühllos
unfilled [ʌn·ˈfɪld] *adj* leer; *job* offen
unfinished [ʌn·ˈfɪn·ɪʃt] *adj* ❶ (*incomplete*) unvollendet; **~ business** offene Fragen *pl* ❷ (*rough*) halbfertig; (*unpainted*) unlackiert
unfit [ʌn·ˈfɪt] *adj* ❶ (*unhealthy*) nicht fit; **to be ~ for work** arbeitsuntauglich sein ❷ (*incompetent*) ungeeignet (**for** für +*akk*); ■ **to be ~ to do sth** unfähig sein, etw zu tun

U

unflagging [ʌn·ˈflæg·ɪŋ] *adj* unermüdlich; *optimism* ungebrochen
unflappable [ʌn·ˈflæp·ə·bəl] *adj* (*fam*) unerschütterlich; ■ **to be ~** nicht aus der Ruhe zu bringen sein
unflinching [ʌn·ˈflɪn·tʃɪŋ] *adj* unerschrocken; *determination* unbeirrbar; *report* wahrheitsgetreu; *support* beständig
unfold [ʌn·ˈfoʊld] **I.** *vt* ❶ (*open*) entfalten; *furniture* aufklappen ❷ (*reveal*) darlegen **II.** *vi* ❶ (*develop*) sich entwickeln ❷ (*open*) aufgehen
unforeseeable [ˌʌn·fɔr·ˈsi·ə·bəl] *adj* unvorhersehbar
unforeseen [ˌʌn·fɔr·ˈsin] *adj inv* unvorhergesehen
unforgettable [ˌʌn·fər·ˈget̬·ə·bəl] *adj* unvergesslich
unforgivable [ˌʌn·fər·ˈgɪv·ə·bəl] *adj* unverzeihlich; **~ sin** Todsünde *f*
unfortunate [ʌn·ˈfɔr·tʃə·nɪt] **I.** *adj* ❶ (*unlucky*) unglücklich; ■ **it's ~ that ...** es ist ungünstig, dass ... ❷ (*regrettable*) bedauerlich; *manner* ungeschickt **II.** *n* Unglücksselige(r) *f(m)*
unfortunately [ʌn·ˈfɔr·tʃə·nɪt·li] *adv* unglücklicherweise
unfounded [ʌn·ˈfaʊn·dɪd] *adj* unbegründet
unfriendly [ʌn·ˈfrend·li] *adj* unfreundlich; (*hostile*) feindlich; **environmentally ~** umweltschädlich
unfulfilled [ˌʌn·fʊl·ˈfild] *adj* ❶ (*unperformed*) unvollendet; *promise* unerfüllt ❷ (*unsatisfied*) unausgefüllt; *life* unerfüllt
unfurl [ʌn·ˈfɜrl] **I.** *vt* ausrollen; *banner, flag* entfalten; *umbrella* aufspannen; *sail* setzen **II.** *vi* sich öffnen
unfurnished [ˌʌn·ˈfɜr·nɪʃt] *adj* unmöbliert
ungainly [ʌn·ˈgeɪn·li] *adj* unbeholfen
UN General ˈAssembly *n* UN-Vollversammlung *f*
ungenerous [ʌn·ˈdʒen·ər·əs] *adj* knausrig *pej fam*
ungentlemanly [ʌn·ˈdʒen·təl·mən·li] *adj* ungalant *geh*
ungodly [ʌn·ˈgad·li] *adj* (*fam*) unerhört; **at some ~ hour** zu einer unchristlichen Zeit
ungovernable [ʌn·ˈgʌv·ər·nə·bəl] *adj country* unregierbar; *temper* unkontrollierbar
ungrateful [ʌn·ˈgreɪt·fəl] *adj* undankbar
unguarded [ʌn·ˈgar·dɪd] *adj* ❶ (*undefended*) unbewacht; *border* offen ❷ (*unwary*) unvorsichtig; **~ moment** unbedachter Augenblick
unhappy [ʌn·ˈhæp·i] *adj* ❶ (*sad*) unglücklich ❷ (*unfortunate*) unglückselig; *coincidence* unglücklich
unharmed [ʌn·ˈharmd] *adj inv* unversehrt
unhealthy [ʌn·ˈhel·θi] *adj* ❶ (*unwell*) kränklich ❷ (*harmful*) ungesund ❸ (*morbid*) krankhaft
unheard [ʌn·ˈhɜrd] *adj* ungehört
unˈheard-of *adj* ❶ (*unknown*) unbekannt ❷ (*unthinkable*) undenkbar
unhelpful [ʌn·ˈhelp·fʊl] *adj* nicht hilfreich; *person* nicht hilfsbereit
unhinge [ʌn·ˈhɪndʒ] *vt* aus der Fassung bringen
unholy [ʌn·ˈhoʊ·li] *adj* ❶ (*wicked*) ruchlos ❷ REL gottlos; *ground* ungeweiht ❸ (*dangerous*) gefährlich; **~ alliance** unheilige Allianz *hum*
unhook [ʌn·ˈhʊk] *vt* ❶ (*detach*) abhängen; *fish* vom Haken nehmen ❷ *clothing* aufmachen
unhoped-for [ʌn·ˈhoʊpt·ˌfɔr] *adj* unverhofft
unhurt [ʌn·ˈhɜrt] *adj* unverletzt
UNICEF [ˈju·nɪ·sef] *n acr for* **United Nations (International) Children's (Emergency) Fund** UNICEF *f*
unicorn [ˈju·nɪ·kɔrn] *n* Einhorn *nt*
unidentified [ˌʌn·aɪ·ˈden·tə·faɪd] *adj inv* (*unknown*) nicht identifiziert
unification [ˌju·nɪ·fɪ·ˈkeɪ·ʃən] *n* Vereinigung *f*
uniform [ˈju·nə·fɔrm] **I.** *n* ❶ (*outfit*) Uniform *f*, Montur *f* ❷ (*fam: police officer*) Polizist(in) *m(f)* **II.** *adj* ❶ (*same*) einheitlich ❷ (*consistent*) gleich bleibend; *temperature, rate* konstant; *color, design* einförmig; *scenery* gleichförmig
uniformity [ˌju·nə·ˈfɔr·mə·t̬i] *n* ❶ (*sameness*) Einheitlichkeit *f*; (*monotony*) Eintönigkeit *f* ❷ (*consistency*) Gleichmäßigkeit *f*
unify [ˈju·nə·faɪ] *vt, vi* [sich *akk*] vereinigen
unilateral [ˌju·nə·ˈlæt̬·ər·əl] *adj inv* einseitig
unimaginable [ˌʌn·ɪ·ˈmædʒ·ə·nə·bəl] *adj* unvorstellbar
unimportant [ˌʌn·ɪm·ˈpɔr·tənt] *adj* unwichtig
uninformed [ˌʌn·ɪn·ˈfɔrmd] *adj* uninformiert
uninhabitable [ˌʌn·ɪn·ˈhæb·ɪ·t̬ə·bəl] *adj building* unbewohnbar; *land a.* unbesiedelbar
uninhabited [ˌʌn·ɪn·ˈhæb·ɪt̬ɪd] *adj building* unbewohnt; *land a.* unbesiedelt
uninhibited [ˌʌn·ɪn·ˈhɪb·ɪ·tɪd] *adj* ungehemmt
uninjured [ˌʌn·ˈɪn·dʒərd] *adj* unverletzt
uninsured [ˌʌn·ɪn·ˈʃʊrd] *adj inv* nicht versichert (**against** gegen +*akk*)
unintelligent [ˌʌn·ɪn·ˈtel·ɪ·dʒənt] *adj* unintelligent
unintelligible [ˌʌn·ɪn·ˈtel·ɪ·dʒə·bəl] *adj* unverständlich
unintentional [ˌʌn·ɪn·ˈten·ʃə·nəl] *adj* unabsichtlich; *humor* unfreiwillig
unintentionally [ˌʌn·ɪn·ˈten·ʃə·nə·li] *adv* unabsichtlich
uninterested [ʌn·ˈɪn·trɪ·stɪd] *adj* uninteressiert; ■ **to be ~ in sth/sb** kein Interesse an etw/jdm haben
uninteresting [ʌn·ˈɪn·trɪ·stɪŋ] *adj* uninteressant
uninterrupted [ʌn·ˌɪn·tər·ˈʌp·tɪd] *adj inv* ununterbrochen; *rest, view* ungestört; *growth* beständig
union [ˈjun·jən] *n* ❶ (*state*) Union *f* ❷ (*act*) Vereinigung *f* ❸ (*organization*) Verband *m*; (*labor union*) Gewerkschaft *f*
unionize [ˈjun·jə·naɪz] *vt, vi* [sich *akk*] gewerkschaftlich organisieren
ˈUnion Jack *n* Union Jack *m*; NAUT Gösch *f*

unique [ju·ˈnik] *adj* ❶ *inv* (*only*) einzigartig; *characteristic* besondere(r, s); **the coral is ~ to this reef** die Koralle ist nur an diesem Riff heimisch ❷ (*exceptional*) einzigartig; *opportunity* einmalig
uniqueness [ju·ˈnik·nɪs] *n* Einzigartigkeit *f*
unisex [ˈju·nɪ·seks] *adj inv* unisex
unison [ˈju·nɪ·sən] *n* ❶ MUS Gleichklang *m;* **to sing in ~** einstimmig singen ❷ (*simultaneously*) ■ **to do sth in ~** gleichzeitig dasselbe tun ❸ (*in agreement*) **to act in ~** in Übereinstimmung handeln
unit [ˈju·nɪt] *n* ❶ (*standard*) Einheit *f;* **~ of currency** Währungseinheit *f* ❷ (*group*) Abteilung *f;* **anti-terrorist ~** Antiterroreinheit *f* ❸ MECH (*part*) Teil *m,* Einheit *f* ❹ (*furniture*) Element *nt* ❺ MATH Einer *m*
ˈunit cost *n* COMM Kosten *pl* pro Einheit
unite [ju·ˈnaɪt] **I.** *vt* vereinigen (**with** mit + *dat*) **II.** *vi* sich vereinigen, sich zusammentun
united [ju·ˈnaɪ·t̬ɪd] *adj* ❶ (*joined*) vereinigt; **~ Germany** wiedervereinigtes Deutschland ❷ (*solidarity*) **to present a ~ front** Einigkeit demonstrieren ▶ PHRASES: **~ we stand, divided we fall** (*saying*) nur gemeinsam sind wir stark
United ˈKingdom *n* ■ **the ~** das Vereinigte Königreich
United ˈNations *n* ■ **the ~** die Vereinten Nationen *pl*
United ˈStates *n* + *sing vb* ■ **the ~ [of America]** die Vereinigten Staaten *pl* [von Amerika]
ˈunit price *n* COMM Preis *m* pro Einheit
unity [ˈju·nɪ·t̬i] *n* ❶ (*oneness*) Einheit *f* ❷ (*harmony*) Einigkeit *f*
universal [ˌju·nə·ˈvɜr·səl] *adj* universell; *agreement* allgemein; **~ truth** allgemein gültige Wahrheit
universe [ˈju·nə·vɜrs] *n* ❶ ■ **the ~** das Universum ❷ (*fig*) Welt *f*
university [ˌju·nə·ˈvɜr·sɪ·t̬i] *n* Universität *f*
unjust [ʌn·ˈdʒʌst] *adj* ungerecht
unjustifiable [ʌn·ˌdʒʌs·tɪ·ˈfaɪ·ə·bəl] *adj* nicht zu rechtfertigen *präd*
unjustified [ʌn·ˈdʒʌs·tɪ·faɪd] *adj* ungerechtfertigt; *complaint* unberechtigt
unjustly [ʌn·ˈdʒʌst·li] *adv* ❶ (*unfairly*) ungerecht ❷ (*wrongfully*) zu Unrecht
unkempt [ʌn·ˈkempt] *adj* ungepflegt; *hair* ungekämmt
unkind [ʌn·ˈkaɪnd] *adj* (*mean*) unfreundlich, gemein
unkindly [ʌn·ˈkaɪnd·li] *adv* unfreundlich; **she speaks ~ of him** sie hat für ihn kein gutes Wort übrig
unknowing [ˌʌn·ˈnoʊ·ɪŋ] *adj* ahnungslos
unknown [ˌʌn·ˈnoʊn] **I.** *adj* ❶ (*not known*) unbekannt; **~ to me, ...** ohne mein Wissen ... ❷ *personage* unbekannt **II.** *n* ❶ Ungewissheit *f;* MATH Unbekannte *f;* ■ **the ~** das Unbekannte ❷ (*personage*) Unbekannte(r) *f(m)*
unlawful [ˌʌn·ˈlɔ·fəl] *adj inv* rechtswidrig
unleaded [ʌn·ˈled·ɪd] *adj inv gasoline* bleifrei
unlearn [ʌn·ˈlɜrn] *vt* verlernen; *habit* sich *dat* abgewöhnen
unleash [ʌn·ˈliʃ] *vt dog* von der Leine lassen; **to ~ a storm of protest** einen Proteststurm auslösen
unleavened [ʌn·ˈlev·ənd] *adj inv* **~ bread** ungesäuertes Brot
unless [ən·ˈles] *conj* **~ I'm mistaken, ...** wenn ich mich nicht irre, ...; **he won't come ~ he has time** er wird nicht kommen, außer wenn er Zeit hat
unlicensed [ʌn·ˈlaɪ·sənst] *adj inv* ohne Lizenz *nach n; car* nicht zugelassen
unlike [ʌn·ˈlaɪk] *prep* ❶ (*different*) **to be ~ sb/sth** jdm/etw nicht ähnlich sein ❷ (*in contrast to*) im Gegensatz zu ❸ (*not normal for*) **to be ~ sb/sth** für jdn/etw nicht typisch sein
unlikely [ʌn·ˈlaɪk·li] *adj* ❶ (*improbable*) unwahrscheinlich; **it seems ~ that ...** es sieht nicht so aus, als ... ❷ (*unconvincing*) nicht überzeugend
unlimited [ʌn·ˈlɪm·ɪ·t̬ɪd] *adj* ❶ *inv* unbegrenzt ❷ (*great*) grenzenlos
unlisted [ʌn·ˈlɪs·tɪd] *adj inv* ❶ STOCKEX nicht notiert; *securities* unnotiert ❷ TELEC nicht verzeichnet; **to have an ~ number** nicht im Telefonbuch stehen
unload [ʌn·ˈloʊd] **I.** *vt* ❶ *vehicle* entladen; *container, trunk* ausladen; *dishwasher* ausräumen ❷ (*get rid*) abstoßen; *garbage* abladen ❸ (*fam: express feelings*) **to ~ one's worries on sb** jdm etwas vorjammern *pej* **II.** *vi* ❶ (*empty*) abladen ❷ ECON entladen; *ship* löschen ❸ (*fam: express anger*) Dampf ablassen *fam;* ■ **to ~ on sb** jdm sein Herz ausschütten
unlock [ʌn·ˈlak] *vt* ❶ (*open*) aufschließen ❷ *mystery* lösen
unlocked [ʌn·ˈlakt] *adj inv* unverschlossen
unlucky [ʌn·ˈlʌk·i] *adj* ❶ (*unfortunate*) glücklos; **he's always been ~** er hat immer Pech ❷ (*causing bad luck*) ■ **to be ~** Unglück bringen; **~ day** Unglückstag *m*
unmade [ʌn·ˈmeɪd] *adj inv* ungemacht; **an ~ bed** ein ungemachtes Bett
unmanageable [ʌn·ˈmæn·ɪ·dʒə·bəl] *adj* unkontrollierbar; *child* außer Rand und Band *pred;* **to become ~** *situation* außer Kontrolle geraten
unmanned [ʌn·ˈmænd] *adj inv* unbemannt
unmarked [ʌn·ˈmarkt] *adj inv* ❶ (*without mark, stain*) unbeschädigt ❷ (*without identifier*) nicht gekennzeichnet; *grave* namenlos; **~ [police] car** Zivilfahrzeug *nt* der Polizei
unmarried [ʌn·ˈmær·ɪd] *adj inv* unverheiratet
unmask [ʌn·ˈmæsk] *vt* entlarven; (*uncover*) aufdecken
unmatched [ʌn·ˈmætʃt] *adj inv* unübertroffen
unmentionable [ʌn·ˈmen·ʃə·nə·bəl] *adj* unaussprechlich; ■ **to be ~** tabu sein
unmentioned [ʌn·ˈmen·ʃənd] *adj inv* unerwähnt

U

unmistakable [ˌʌn·mɪ·ˈsteɪ·kə·bəl] *adj* unverkennbar; *symptom* eindeutig
unmitigated [ʌn·ˈmɪt̬·ɪ·geɪ·t̬ɪd] *adj* absolut; *contempt* voll; *disaster* total
unmoved [ʌn·ˈmuvd] *adj usu pred* unbewegt; (*emotionless*) ungerührt
unnamed [ʌn·ˈneɪmd] *adj inv* ungenannt
unnatural [ʌn·ˈnætʃ·ər·əl] *adj* unnatürlich; PSYCH abnorm; (*perverse*) pervers
unnecessarily [ˌʌn·ˌnes·ə·ˈser·ə·li] *adv* unnötigerweise
unnecessary [ʌn·ˈnes·ə·ser·i] *adj* ❶ unnötig ❷ (*uncalled for*) überflüssig
unnerve [ʌn·ˈnɜrv] *vt* nervös machen
unnerving [ʌn·ˈnɜrv·ɪŋ] *adj* entnervend
unnoticed [ˌʌn·ˈnoʊ·t̬ɪst] *adj pred* unbemerkt
unnumbered [ˌʌn·ˈnʌm·bərd] *adj inv* nicht nummeriert; *page* ohne Zahl *nach n*
UN obˈserver *n* UNO-Beobachter(in) *m(f)*
unobtainable [ˌʌn·əb·ˈteɪ·nə·bəl] *adj* unerreichbar
unobtrusive [ˌʌn·əb·ˈtru·sɪv] *adj* unaufdringlich; *makeup* dezent
unoccupied [ˌʌn·ˈak·jə·paɪd] *adj inv* ❶ (*uninhabited*) unbewohnt ❷ *seat* frei
unofficial [ˌʌn·ə·ˈfɪʃ·əl] *adj* inoffiziell; **in an ~ capacity** inoffiziell
unorganized [ˌʌn·ˈɔr·gə·naɪzd] *adj* unorganisiert
unorthodox [ʌn·ˈɔr·θə·daks] *adj* unkonventionell; *method* ungewöhnlich
unpack [ʌn·ˈpæk] *vt, vi* auspacken; *car* ausladen
unpaid [ʌn·ˈpeɪd] *adj inv* unbezahlt; *invoice a.* ausstehend
unpalatable [ʌn·ˈpæl·ə·tə·bəl] *adj* ❶ (*not tasty*) ■ **to be ~** schlecht schmecken ❷ (*distasteful*) unangenehm
unparalleled [ʌn·ˈpær·ə·leld] *adj* einmalig; *success* noch nie da gewesen
UN peacekeeping ˈmission *n* UNO-Friedensmission *f*
unperturbed [ˌʌn·pər·ˈtɜrbd] *adj* nicht beunruhigt; ■ **to be ~ by sth** sich durch etw *akk* nicht aus der Ruhe bringen lassen
unpick [ʌn·ˈpɪk] *vt a seam* auftrennen
unplaced [ʌn·ˈpleɪst] *adj inv* SPORTS unplatziert
unpleasant [ʌn·ˈplez·ənt] *adj* ❶ (*not pleasing*) unangenehm ❷ (*unfriendly*) unfreundlich; *relations* frostig
unpleasantness [ʌn·ˈplez·ənt·nɪs] *n* ❶ (*quality*) Unerfreulichkeit *f* ❷ (*feelings*) Unstimmigkeit[en] *f[pl]*
unplug <-gg-> [ʌn·ˈplʌg] *vt* ausstecken
unpolished [ʌn·ˈpal·ɪʃt] *adj* ❶ *inv* unpoliert ❷ (*coarse*) ungehobelt
unpolluted [ˌʌn·pə·ˈlu·t̬ɪd] *adj* unverschmutzt; *water* sauber
unpopular [ʌn·ˈpap·jə·lər] *adj* ❶ (*not liked*) unbeliebt ❷ (*not accepted*) unpopulär; **to be ~** wenig Anklang finden
unpopularity [ʌn·ˌpap·jə·ˈler·ə·t̬i] *n of person* Unbeliebtheit *f; of policies* Unpopularität *f*

U

unprecedented [ʌn·ˈpres·ə·den·tɪd] *adj inv* noch nie da gewesen; *action* beispiellos; **on an ~ scale** in bislang ungekanntem Ausmaß
unpredictable [ˌʌn·prɪ·ˈdɪk·tə·bəl] *adj* unvorhersehbar; *weather, temperament* unberechenbar
unprejudiced [ʌn·ˈpredʒ·ə·dɪst] *adj* unvoreingenommen; *opinion* objektiv
unpremeditated [ˌʌn·pri·ˈmed·ɪ·teɪ·t̬ɪd] *adj* unüberlegt; **~ crime** nicht vorsätzliches Verbrechen
unpretentious [ˌʌn·prɪ·ˈten·ʃəs] *adj* bescheiden; *tastes* einfach
unproductive [ˌʌn·prə·ˈdʌk·tɪv] *adj* unproduktiv; *business* unrentabel; *land* unfruchtbar; *negotiations* unergiebig
unprofessional [ˌʌn·prə·ˈfeʃ·ə·nəl] *adj* ❶ (*amateurish*) unprofessionell ❷ (*unethical*) gegen die Berufsehre *präd;* **~ conduct** berufswidriges Verhalten; (*toward colleagues*) unkollegiales Verhalten
unprofitable [ʌn·ˈpraf·ɪ·t̬ə·bəl] *adj* ❶ unrentabel; **to be ~** keinen Gewinn abwerfen ❷ (*unproductive*) unproduktiv
unprompted [ʌn·ˈpramp·tɪd] *adj inv* unaufgefordert
unprovoked [ˌʌn·prə·ˈvoʊkt] *adj* grundlos
unpublished [ˌʌn·ˈpʌb·lɪʃt] *adj inv* unveröffentlicht
unqualified [ʌn·ˈkwal·ə·faɪd] *adj* ❶ unqualifiziert; ■ **to be ~ for sth** für etw *akk* nicht qualifiziert sein ❷ (*unreserved*) bedingungslos; *denial* strikt; *success* voll
unquestionable [ʌn·ˈkwes·tʃə·nə·bəl] *adj* fraglos; *evidence, fact* unumstößlich; *honesty* unzweifelhaft
unquestionably [ʌn·ˈkwes·tʃə·nə·bli] *adv* zweifellos
unquestioning [ʌn·ˈkwes·tʃə·nɪŋ] *adj* bedingungslos; *obedience* absolut
unquote [ˈʌn·kwoʊt] *vi* **quote ... ~** Zitatanfang ... Zitatende; **they are, quote, "just good friends," ~** (*iron*) sie sind, in Anführungszeichen, „nur gute Freunde"
unquoted [ʌn·ˈkwoʊ·t̬ɪd] *adj* STOCKEX nicht notiert
unravel <-l- *or* -ll-> [ʌn·ˈræv·əl] **I.** *vt* ❶ (*undo*) auftrennen ❷ (*untangle*) entwirren; *knot* aufmachen ❸ (*solve*) enträtseln; *mystery* lösen **II.** *vi* sich auftrennen
unreadable [ʌn·ˈri·də·bəl] *adj* ❶ (*illegible*) unleserlich ❷ (*dull*) schwer zu lesen *präd*
unreal [ʌn·ˈril] *adj* ❶ unwirklich ❷ (*fam: fantastic*) unmöglich *fam*
unrealistic [ʌn·ˌri·ə·ˈlɪs·tɪk] *adj* ❶ unrealistisch ❷ (*unconvincing*) nicht realistisch
unrealized [ʌn·ˈri·ə·laɪzd] *adj* ❶ nicht verwirklicht ❷ (*into money*) unrealisiert
unreasonable [ʌn·ˈri·zə·nə·bəl] *adj* ❶ unvernünftig; **it's not ~ to assume that ...** es ist nicht abwegig anzunehmen, dass ... ❷ (*unfair*) übertrieben; *demand* überzogen
unrefined [ˌʌn·rɪ·ˈfaɪnd] *adj* ❶ CHEM nicht raffi-

niert; ~ **sugar** Rohzucker *m* ❷ (*coarse*) unkultiviert; *manners* rüde *pej*

unregistered [ʌn·ˈredʒ·ɪ·stərd] *adj inv* nicht registriert; *birth* nicht eingetragen; *mail* nicht eingeschrieben

unrelated [ˌʌn·rɪ·ˈleɪ·t̬ɪd] *adj inv* ❶ (*not of family*) nicht [miteinander] verwandt ❷ (*unconnected*) ■ **to be** ~ nicht zusammenhängen (**to** mit +*dat*)

unrelenting [ˌʌn·rɪ·ˈlen·tɪŋ] *adj* ❶ (*unyielding*) unerbittlich; *opponent* unbeugsam ❷ (*incessant*) unaufhörlich; *pressure* konstant; **to be** ~ nicht nachlassen

unreliability [ˌʌn·rɪ·laɪ·ə·ˈbɪ·lɪ·t̬i] *n* Unzuverlässigkeit *f*

unreliable [ˌʌn·rɪ·ˈlaɪ·ə·bəl] *adj* unzuverlässig

unrelieved [ˌʌn·rɪ·ˈlivd] *adj* ununterbrochen; *pressure, stress* anhaltend; *boredom* dauernd

unremarkable [ˌʌn·rɪ·ˈmar·kə·bəl] *adj* nicht bemerkenswert

unrepeatable [ˌʌn·rɪ·ˈpi·t̬ə·bəl] *adj inv* nicht wiederholbar

unrepentant [ˌʌn·rɪ·ˈpen·tənt] *adj* reu[e]los; ■ **to be** ~ keine Reue zeigen

unreserved [ˌʌn·rɪ·ˈzɜrvd] *adj* ❶ (*without reservations*) uneingeschränkt; *support* voll ❷ (*not booked*) nicht reserviert; *seat* frei

unreservedly [ˌʌn·rɪ·ˈzɜrv·ɪd·li] *adv* vorbehaltlos; **to apologize** ~ sich ohne Einschränkungen entschuldigen

unresolved [ˌʌn·rɪ·ˈzalvd] *adj* (*unsettled*) ungelöst; *tension* anhaltend

unrest [ʌn·ˈrest] *n* Unruhen *pl;* **social** ~ soziale Spannungen

unrestrained [ˌʌn·rɪ·ˈstreɪnd] *adj* uneingeschränkt; *criticism* hart; *laughter* ungehemmt; *praise* unumschränkt

unrestricted [ˌʌn·rɪ·ˈstrɪk·tɪd] *adj* uneingeschränkt; *access* ungehindert

unripe [ʌn·ˈraɪp] *adj* unreif

unrivaled, unrivalled [ʌn·ˈraɪ·vəld] *adj* einzigartig

unroll [ʌn·ˈroʊl] **I.** *vt* aufrollen **II.** *vi* sich abrollen [lassen]

unruffled [ʌn·ˈrʌf·əld] *adj* ❶ (*not agitated*) gelassen ❷ (*hair*) unzerzaust, ordentlich; *feathers* glatt

unruly <-ier, -iest *or* more ~, most ~> [ʌn·ˈru·li] *adj* ❶ (*disorderly*) ungebärdig; *crowd* aufrührerisch ❷ *child* außer Rand und Band; *hair* nicht zu bändigen *präd*

unsafe [ʌn·ˈseɪf] *adj* (*dangerous*) unsicher; (*in danger*) nicht sicher; *sex* ungeschützt; ■ **to be** ~ **to do sth** gefährlich sein, etw zu tun

unsaid [ʌn·ˈsed] *adj inv* ungesagt; **to be better left** ~ besser ungesagt bleiben ► PHRASES: **what's <u>said</u> cannot be** ~ (*prov*) gesagt ist gesagt

UN ˈsanction *n* UN-Sanktion *f*

unsanitary [ʌn·ˈsæn·ə·te·ri] *adj* ❶ (*unhealthy*) ungesund ❷ (*lacking cleanliness*) unhygienisch

unsatisfactory [ʌn·ˌsæt̬·ɪs·ˈfæk·tə·ri] *adj* ❶ unzureichend; *answer* unbefriedigend ❷ SCH (*grade*) ungenügend

unsatisfied [ʌn·ˈsæt̬·ɪs·faɪd] *adj* ❶ unzufrieden; **to leave sb/sth** ~ jdn/etw nicht befriedigen ❷ (*unconvinced*) nicht überzeugt; **to be** ~ **with sth** sich mit etw nicht zufriedengeben

unsaturated [ʌn·ˈsætʃ·ə·reɪ·t̬ɪd] *adj* CHEM, FOOD ungesättigt *attr;* ~ **fat[s]** ungesättigte Fettsäuren

unsavory [ʌn·ˈseɪ·və·ri] *adj* ❶ (*unpalatable*) unappetitlich ❷ (*asocial*) fragwürdig; *area* übel; *reputation* zweifelhaft; *character* zwielichtig

unscathed [ʌn·ˈskeɪðd] *adj* unverletzt; **to emerge** ~ **from sth** (*fig*) etw unbeschadet überstehen

unscheduled [ʌn·ˈskedʒ·uld] *adj inv* außerplanmäßig; *stop, landing* außerfahrplanmäßig

unscrew [ʌn·ˈskru] **I.** *vt* ❶ (*detach*) abschrauben ❷ (*open*) aufschrauben; *lid* abschrauben **II.** *vi* (*detach*) sich abschrauben lassen; (*open*) aufschrauben

unscripted [ʌn·ˈskrɪp·tɪd] *adj inv* improvisiert

unscrupulous [ʌn·ˈskru·pjə·ləs] *adj* skrupellos

unseal [ʌn·ˈsil] *vt* entsiegeln

unsealed [ʌn·ˈsild] *adj inv* ❶ unversiegelt ❷ (*open*) nicht zugeklebt

unseat [ʌn·ˈsit] *vt* ❶ (*oust*) ■ **to** ~ **sb** jdn seines Amtes entheben ❷ *rider* abwerfen

unsecured [ˌʌn·sɪ·ˈkjʊrd] *adj inv* ❶ FIN ungesichert; **an** ~ **loan** Blankokredit *m* ❷ (*unfastened*) unbefestigt

UN Seˈcurity Council *n* UN-Sicherheitsrat *m*

unseen [ʌn·ˈsin] *adj inv* ungesehen; **sight** ~ unbesehen

unselfish [ʌn·ˈsel·fɪʃ] *adj* selbstlos

unsettle [ʌn·ˈset̬·əl] *vt* ❶ (*make nervous*) verunsichern ❷ (*make unstable*) stören

unsettled [ˌʌn·ˈset̬·əld] *adj* ❶ (*unstable*) instabil; *political climate* unruhig; *weather* unbeständig ❷ (*unresolved*) noch anstehend ❸ (*queasy*) gereizt

unsettling [ˌʌn·ˈset̬·əl·ɪŋ] *adj* ❶ (*causing nervousness*) beunruhigend ❷ (*causing disruption*) ■ **to be** ~ einen aus der Bahn werfen

unshakable, unshakeable [ʌn·ˈʃeɪ·kə·bəl] *adj belief, feeling* unerschütterlich; *alibi* felsenfest; **to have** ~ **faith in sth** fest an etw *akk* glauben

unshaved [ʌn·ˈʃeɪvd], **unshaven** [ʌn·ˈʃeɪ·vən] *adj inv* unrasiert

unsightly <-ier, -iest *or* more ~, most ~> [ʌn·ˈsaɪt·li] *adj* unansehnlich

unsigned [ʌn·ˈsaɪnd] *adj inv* ❶ nicht unterschrieben; *painting* unsigniert ❷ (*not under contract*) nicht unter Vertrag stehend *attr*

unskilled [ʌn·ˈskɪld] *adj* ❶ (*inept*) ungeschickt ❷ *laborer* ungelernt; ~ **work** Hilfsarbeiten *pl*

unsociable [ʌn·ˈsoʊ·ʃə·bəl] *adj person* ungesellig

unsocial [ʌn·ˈsoʊ·ʃəl] *adj* unsozial

unsold [ʌn·ˈsoʊld] *adj inv* unverkauft

U

unsolicited [ˌʌn·sə·ˈlɪs·ɪ·t̬ɪd] *adj inv* unerbeten; *advice* ungebeten
unsolved [ʌn·ˈsɑlvd] *adj inv mystery, problem* ungelöst; *murder* unaufgeklärt
unsophisticated [ˌʌn·sə·ˈfɪs·tə·keɪ·t̬ɪd] *adj* (*naive*) naiv; *taste* einfach
unsound [ʌn·ˈsaʊnd] *adj* ❶ (*unstable*) instabil ❷ *argument* nicht stichhaltig; *judgment* anfechtbar ❸ (*unhealthy*) ungesund; **of ~ mind** unzurechnungsfähig
unspeakable [ʌn·ˈspi·kə·bəl] *adj* unbeschreiblich
unspecified [ʌn·ˈspes·ɪ·faɪd] *adj inv* unspezifiziert; (*unnamed*) [namentlich] nicht genannt
unspoiled [ʌn·ˈspɔɪld] *adj person* natürlich; *child* nicht verwöhnt; *landscape* unberührt; *view* unverbaut
unspoken [ʌn·ˈspoʊ·kən] *adj inv* unausgesprochen; *agreement* stillschweigend
unsportsmanlike [ʌn·ˈspɔrts·men·laɪk] *adj inv* unsportlich; *behavior* unfair
unstable [ʌn·ˈsteɪ·bəl] *adj* ❶ (*not firm*) nicht stabil; *furniture* wackelig ❷ (*fig*) instabil; *future* ungewiss; PSYCH [psychisch] labil
unsteady [ʌn·ˈsted·i] *adj* ❶ (*unstable*) nicht stabil; *furniture* wack[e]lig; **to be ~ on one's feet** wack[e]lig auf den Beinen sein ❷ (*wavering*) zittrig ❸ (*irregular*) unregelmäßig
unstressed [ʌn·ˈstrest] *adj inv* ❶ LING unbetont ❷ (*not worried*) unbelastet
unstuck [ʌn·ˈstʌk] *adj* **to come ~** sich [ab]lösen; (*fam: fail*) scheitern
unsubstantial [ˌʌn·səb·ˈstæn·ʃəl] *adj* unwesentlich; (*immaterial*) körperlos
unsubstantiated [ˌʌn·səb·ˈstæn·ʃi·eɪ·t̬ɪd] *adj inv* unbegründet
unsuccessful [ˌʌn·sək·ˈses·fəl] *adj* erfolglos; *attempt* vergeblich; *candidate* unterlegen; ■ **to be ~ in sth** bei etw *dat* keinen Erfolg haben
unsuitable [ʌn·ˈsu·t̬ə·bəl] *adj* nicht geeignet
unsung [ʌn·ˈsʌŋ] *adj inv* unbesungen; *achievements, hero* unbeachtet
unsure [ʌn·ˈʃʊr] *adj* unsicher; ■ **to be ~ how/why ...** nicht genau wissen, wie/warum ...; ■ **to be ~ about sth** sich *dat* einer S. *gen* nicht sicher sein
unsuspecting [ˌʌn·sə·ˈspek·tɪŋ] *adj* ahnungslos
unsustainable [ˌʌn·sə·ˈsteɪ·nə·bəl] *adj* ❶ *inv* (*not maintainable*) nicht aufrechtzuerhalten *präd* ❷ *inv* (*polluting*) umweltschädigend
unswerving [ˌʌn·ˈswɜr·vɪŋ] *adj inv* unerschütterlich
unsympathetic [ˌʌn·sɪm·pə·ˈθet̬·ɪk] *adj* ❶ ohne Mitgefühl *nach n* ❷ (*disapproving*) verständnislos; ■ **to be ~ toward sb/sth** für jdn/etw kein Verständnis haben
untamed [ʌn·ˈteɪmd] *adj inv* wild, ungebändigt; *animal also* ungezähmt
untangle [ʌn·ˈtæŋ·gəl] *vt* entwirren *a. fig; mystery* lösen
untapped [ˌʌn·ˈtæpt] *adj inv market* nicht erschlossen; *resources* ungenutzt
untaxed [ˌʌn·ˈtækst] *adj inv* (*tax-free*) steuerfrei
untenable [ˌʌn·ˈten·ə·bəl] *adj* nicht vertretbar
unthinkable [ʌn·ˈθɪŋ·kə·bəl] **I.** *adj* ❶ (*unimaginable*) undenkbar ❷ (*shocking*) unfassbar **II.** *n* ■ **the ~** das Unvorstellbare
unthinking [ʌn·ˈθɪŋ·kɪŋ] *adj inv* unbedacht; (*unintentional*) unabsichtlich
unthought of *adj pred, inv,* **unthought-of** [ʌn·ˈθɔt·əv] *adj attr, inv* unvorstellbar; *detail* nicht bedacht
untidy [ʌn·ˈtaɪ·di] *adj* ❶ (*disordered*) unordentlich; *appearance* ungepflegt ❷ (*badly organized*) unsystematisch
untie <-y-> [ˌʌn·ˈtaɪ] *vt* ❶ (*undo*) lösen; *shoelaces* aufbinden ❷ *boat* losbinden; *package* aufschnüren
until [ən·ˈtɪl] **I.** *prep* ❶ (*up to*) bis *+akk;* **two more days ~ Easter** noch zwei Tage bis Ostern ❷ (*beginning at*) bis *+akk;* **we didn't eat ~ midnight** wir aßen erst um Mitternacht **II.** *conj* ❶ (*up to time when*) bis; **I laughed ~ tears rolled down my face** ich lachte, bis mir die Tränen kamen ❷ (*not before*) ■ **to not do sth ~ ...** etw erst [dann] tun, wenn ...; **not ~ he's here** erst wenn er da ist
untimely [ʌn·ˈtaɪm·li] *adj* ❶ (*inopportune*) ungelegen ❷ (*premature*) verfrüht
unto [ˈʌn·tu] *prep* (*old: until*) bis; **~ this day** bis zum heutigen Tage
untold [ˌʌn·ˈtoʊld] *adj* ❶ *attr* (*immense*) unsagbar; *damage* immens; *misery* unsäglich; *wealth* unermesslich ❷ *inv* (*not told*) ungesagt
untouched [ˌʌn·ˈtʌtʃt] *adj inv* ❶ (*not touched*) unberührt ❷ (*unconsumed*) nicht angerührt ❸ (*unaffected*) ■ **to be ~ by sth** von etw *dat* nicht betroffen sein; **to leave sth ~** etw verschont lassen
untoward [ˌʌn·ˈtɔrd] *adj* ❶ (*unfortunate*) ungünstig; **unless anything ~ happens** wenn nichts dazwischenkommt ❷ *remark* unpassend
untrained [ʌn·ˈtreɪnd] *adj inv* ungeübt; *eye* ungeschult
untranslatable [ˌʌn·træns·ˈleɪ·t̬ə·bəl] *adj* unübersetzbar
untreated [ʌn·ˈtri·t̬ɪd] *adj inv* unbehandelt; **~ sewage** ungeklärte Abwässer *pl*
untried [ʌn·ˈtraɪd] *adj* ❶ *inv* (*untested*) ungetestet ❷ (*inexperienced*) unerfahren
UN ˈtroops *npl* UNO-Truppen *pl*
untroubled [ʌn·ˈtrʌb·əld] *adj* sorglos; ■ **to be ~ by sth** sich von etw *dat* nicht beunruhigen lassen
untrue [ʌn·ˈtru] *adj* unwahr, falsch
untrustworthy [ʌn·ˈtrʌst·ˌwɜr·ði] *adj* unzuverlässig
untruth [ʌn·ˈtruθ] *n* (*usu euph*) Unwahrheit *f;* **to tell an ~** flunkern *fam*
untruthful [ʌn·ˈtruθ·fəl] *adj* unwahr; *person* unaufrichtig
unused¹ [ʌn·ˈjuzd] *adj inv* unbenutzt; **to go ~** nicht genutzt werden
unused² [ʌn·ˈjuzd] *adj pred* ■ **to be ~ to sth**

an etw *akk* nicht gewöhnt sein
unusual [ʌn·ˈju·ʒu·əl] *adj* ❶ (*not habitual*) ungewöhnlich; (*for a person*) untypisch ❷ (*remarkable*) außergewöhnlich
unusually [ʌn·ˈju·ʒu·ə·li] *adv* ungewöhnlich; ~ **for me, ...** ganz gegen meine Gewohnheit ...
unvarnished [ʌn·ˈvar·nɪʃt] *adj inv* ❶ unlackiert ❷ (*straightforward*) einfach; *truth* ungeschminkt
unveil [ˌʌn·ˈveɪl] *vt* ❶ enthüllen; *face* entschleiern ❷ (*present*) der Öffentlichkeit vorstellen
unwanted [ʌn·ˈwan·tɪd] *adj* unerwünscht; *clothes* abgelegt; *advice* ungebeten; *child* ungewollt
unwarranted [ʌn·ˈwɔr·ən·tɪd] *adj* ungerechtfertigt; *fears* unbegründet; *criticism* unberechtigt
unwavering [ʌn·ˈweɪ·vər·ɪŋ] *adj* unerschütterlich; *determination* eisern
unwelcome [ʌn·ˈwel·kəm] *adj* unwillkommen; *news* unerfreulich; **to make sb feel ~** jdm das Gefühl geben, nicht willkommen zu sein
unwell [ʌn·ˈwel] *adj pred* ■ **sb is ~** jdm geht es nicht gut; **to feel ~** sich unwohl fühlen
unwieldy [ʌn·ˈwil·di] *adj* ❶ (*cumbersome*) unhandlich; *furniture* sperrig ❷ (*ineffective*) unüberschaubar; *system* schwerfällig
unwilling [ʌn·ˈwɪl·ɪŋ] *adj* widerwillig; ■ **to be ~ to do sth** nicht gewillt sein, etw zu tun
unwillingly [ʌn·ˈwɪl·ɪŋ·li] *adv* ungern
unwind <unwound, unwound> [ʌn·ˈwaɪnd] **I.** *vi* ❶ (*unroll*) sich abwickeln ❷ (*relax*) sich entspannen **II.** *vt* abwickeln
unwise [ʌn·ˈwaɪz] *adj* unklug
unwitting [ʌn·ˈwɪţ·ɪŋ] *adj* ❶ (*unaware*) ahnungslos ❷ (*unintentional*) unbeabsichtigt
unwittingly [ʌn·ˈwɪţ·ɪŋ·li] *adv* ❶ (*without realizing*) unwissentlich ❷ (*unintentionally*) unbeabsichtigterweise
unwonted [ʌn·ˈwɔn·tɪd] *adj attr* ungewohnt
unworkable [ʌn·ˈwɜr·kə·bəl] *adj* undurchführbar
unworldly [ʌn·ˈwɜrld·li] *adj* ❶ (*odd*) weltabgewandt ❷ (*naive*) weltfremd
unworthy [ʌn·ˈwɜr·ði] *adj* ❶ (*undeserving*) unwürdig; ~ **of interest** nicht von Interesse ❷ (*unacceptable*) nicht würdig
unwrap <-pp-> [ʌn·ˈræp] *vt* ❶ *contents* auspacken ❷ (*reveal*) enthüllen
unwritten [ʌn·ˈrɪt·ən] *adj inv* nicht schriftlich fixiert; *agreement* stillschweigend; *law* ungeschrieben
unyielding [ʌn·ˈjil·dɪŋ] *adj* ❶ *ground* hart; ■ **to be ~** nicht nachgeben ❷ (*resolute*) unnachgiebig; *opposition* hartnäckig
unzip <-pp-> [ʌn·ˈzɪp] *vt* ❶ (*open*) ■ **to ~ sth** den Reißverschluss einer S. *gen* aufmachen ❷ COMPUT auspacken
up [ʌp] **I.** *adv inv* ❶ (*to higher*) nach oben, hinauf; **hands ~!** Hände hoch!; **halfway ~** auf halber Höhe ❷ (*erect*) aufrecht; **lean it ~ against the wall** lehnen Sie es gegen die Wand ❸ (*out of bed*) auf; ~ **and about** auf den Beinen ❹ (*at higher*) oben; ~ **there** da oben; **I live on the next floor ~** ich wohne ein Stockwerk höher ❺ (*toward*) ■ ~ **to sb/sth** auf jdn/etw zu; **to walk ~ to sb** auf jdn zugehen ❻ (*higher*) höher; **children aged 13 and ~** Kinder ab 13 Jahren ❼ (*to point of*) ~ **until** [*or* **to**] bis +*akk;* ~ **to 300 dollars** bis zu 300 Dollar ❽ (*depend on*) **to be ~ to sb** von jdm abhängen; **I'll leave it ~ to you** ich überlasse dir die Entscheidung ❾ (*be adequate*) **to be ~ to sth** einer Sache *dat* gewachsen sein ▶ PHRASES: **to be ~ to one's <u>ears</u> in problems** bis zum Hals in Schwierigkeiten stecken **II.** *prep* ❶ (*to higher*) hinauf/herauf; ~ **the ladder** die Leiter hinauf/herauf ❷ (*along*) [**just**] ~ **the road** ein Stück die Straße hinauf/herauf; ~ **and down** auf und ab ❸ (*against*) ~ **the river** flussauf[wärts] ❹ (*at top of*) **he's ~ that ladder** er steht dort oben auf der Leiter ▶ PHRASES: **to be ~ the <u>creek</u>** [**without a paddle**] [schön] in der Klemme sitzen; ~ **<u>yours</u>!** (*vulg, sl*) ihr könnt/du kannst mich mal! **III.** *adj inv* ❶ *attr* (*rising*) nach oben ❷ *pred* (*leading*) in Führung ❸ *pred* (*working*) funktionstüchtig; ■ **to be ~** in Betrieb sein ❹ *pred* (*finished*) vorbei, um; **your time is ~!** Ihre Zeit ist um! ❺ *pred* (*fam: happening*) **what's ~?** was ist los? ❻ *pred* (*scheduled*) **to be ~ for sale** zum Verkauf stehen ❼ *pred* (*interested in*) **who's ~ for a walk?** wer hat Lust auf einen Spaziergang? **IV.** *n* (*fam*) Hoch *nt;* ~**s and downs** Höhen und Tiefen *pl* ▶ PHRASES: **to be <u>on</u> the ~ and ~** (*fam*) sauber sein **V.** *vt* <-pp-> erhöhen; *price, tax* anheben; **to ~ the stakes** den Einsatz erhöhen **VI.** *interj* los, aufstehen!
up-and-ˈcoming *adj attr* aufstrebend
upbeat [ˈʌp·bit] **I.** *n* MUS Auftakt *m* **II.** *adj* (*fam*) optimistisch; *mood* fröhlich
upbringing [ˈʌp·brɪŋ·ɪŋ] *n usu sing* Erziehung *f*
upcoming [ˈʌp·ˌkʌm·ɪŋ] *adj inv* bevorstehend
update I. *vt* [ʌp·ˈdeɪt] ❶ (*modernize*) ■ **to ~ sth** etw aktualisieren; COMPUT ein Update von etw *dat* machen; *hardware* etw nachrüsten ❷ (*inform*) auf den neuesten Stand bringen; (*permanently*) auf dem Laufenden halten **II.** *n* [ˈʌp·deɪt] Aktualisierung *f,* Update *nt fachspr*
upend [ʌp·ˈend] **I.** *vt* hochkant stellen **II.** *vi* sich aufstellen
upfront [ʌp·ˈfrʌnt] *adj* ❶ *pred* (*frank*) offen; **to be ~ about sth** etw offen sagen; **to be ~** [**with sb**] offen [mit jdm] sein ❷ *attr* (*advance*) Voraus-; ~ **payment** Anzahlung *f*
upgrade [ˈʌp·greɪd] **I.** *vt* ❶ (*improve*) verbessern; COMPUT erweitern; *hardware* nachrüsten ❷ (*promote*) befördern **II.** *n* ❶ COMPUT Aufrüsten *nt* ❷ (*version*) verbesserte Version ❸ (*incline*) Steigung *f*
upheaval [ʌp·ˈhi·vəl] *n* Aufruhr *m;* **political ~** politische Umwälzung[en] *f*[*pl*]

uphill [ʌp·ˈhɪl] **I.** *adv inv* bergauf **II.** *adj* ❶ *inv* bergauf ❷ (*difficult*) mühselig; ~ **battle** harter Kampf

uphold <-held, -held> [ʌp·ˈhoʊld] *vt* aufrechterhalten; *traditions* pflegen; *verdict* bestätigen; **to ~ the law** das Gesetz [achten und] wahren

upholster [ʌp·ˈhoʊl·stər] *vt* [auf]polstern; (*cover*) beziehen

upholsterer [ʌp·ˈhoʊl·stər·ər] *n* Polsterer, Polsterin *m, f*

upholstery [ʌp·ˈhoʊl·stə·ri] *n* ❶ (*padding*) Polsterung *f;* (*covering*) Bezug *m* ❷ (*activity*) Polstern *nt*

upkeep [ˈʌp·kip] *n* ❶ (*maintenance*) Instandhaltung *f* ❷ (*cost*) Instandhaltungskosten *pl* ❸ *of person* Unterhalt *m; of animals* Haltungskosten *f*

upland [ˈʌp·lənd] **I.** *adj attr, inv* Hochland-; ~ **plain** Hochebene *f* **II.** *n* ■**the ~s** *pl* das Hochland *kein pl*

uplift [ʌp·ˈlɪft] **I.** *vt* ❶ (*raise*) anheben ❷ (*inspire*) [moralisch] aufrichten **II.** *n* ❶ (*elevation*) Aufschwung *m* ❷ (*influence*) Erbauung *f*

uplifting [ʌp·ˈlɪf·tɪŋ] *adj* erbaulich

upload [ˈʌp·loʊd] INET **I.** *vt, vi* hochladen, uploaden **II.** *n* Upload *m*

upon [ə·ˈpan] *prep* (*form*) ❶ (*on top of*) auf +*dat; with verbs of motion* auf +*akk* ❷ (*hanging on*) an +*dat* ❸ (*at time of*) ~ **arrival** bei Ankunft; **once ~ a time** [es war einmal] vor langer Zeit ❹ (*about*) über +*akk* ❺ (*concerning*) **we settled ~ a price** wir einigten uns auf einen Preis

upper [ˈʌp·ər] **I.** *adj attr, inv* ❶ (*higher*) obere(r, s); *arm, lip* Ober-; ~ **part of the body** Oberkörper *m* ❷ *rank* höhere(r, s) ❸ *location* höher gelegen **II.** *n* ❶ (*of shoe*) Obermaterial *nt* ❷ *usu pl* (*fam: drug*) Aufputschmittel *nt*

ˈupper case *n* TYPO ■**in ~** in Großbuchstaben

upper ˈclass *n* Oberschicht *f*

ˈupper-class *adj* der Oberschicht *nach n*

ˈuppercut *n* (*boxing*) Aufwärtshaken *m*

upper ˈdeck *n* Oberdeck *nt*

uppermost [ˈʌp·ər·moʊst] *inv* **I.** *adj* ❶ (*highest*) oberste(r, s), höchste(r, s) ❷ (*important*) wichtigste(r, s); **to be ~ in one's mind** jdn am meisten beschäftigen **II.** *adv* ganz oben

uppity [ˈʌp·ɪ·t̬i] *adj* (*pej fam*) hochnäsig, hochmütig; **to get ~** ein arrogantes Benehmen an den Tag legen

upright [ˈʌp·raɪt] **I.** *adj* ❶ (*vertical*) senkrecht; (*erect*) aufrecht ❷ (*honest*) anständig **II.** *adv* (*vertical*) senkrecht; (*erect*) aufrecht; **bolt ~** kerzengerade **III.** *n* ❶ (*pillar*) [Stütz]pfeiler *m* ❷ SPORTS Pfosten *m*

uprising [ˈʌp·raɪ·zɪŋ] *n* Aufstand *m*

uproar [ˈʌp·rɔr] *n* ❶ (*noise*) Lärm *m* ❷ (*protest*) Aufruhr *m*

uproot [ˌʌp·ˈrut] *vt* ❶ (*extract*) herausreißen; *tree* entwurzeln ❷ (*drive away*) aus der gewohnten Umgebung herausreißen; ■**to ~ oneself** seine Heimat verlassen

upscale [ˌʌp·ˈskeɪl] *adj goods* hochwertig; *consumer* anspruchsvoll

upset I. *vt* [ʌp·ˈset] ❶ (*push over*) umwerfen; *a glass* umstoßen ❷ (*unsettle*) aus der Fassung bringen; (*distress*) mitnehmen; ■**to ~ oneself** sich aufregen ❸ (*muddle*) durcheinanderbringen ▶ PHRASES: **to ~ the apple cart** (*fam*) alle Pläne über den Haufen werfen **II.** *adj* [ʌp·ˈset] ❶ *pred* (*nervous*) aufgeregt; (*angry*) aufgebracht; (*distressed*) bestürzt; (*sad*) traurig ❷ *inv* **to have an ~ stomach** sich *dat* den Magen verdorben haben **III.** *n* [ˈʌp·set] ❶ (*trouble*) Ärger *m;* (*argument*) Verstimmung *f;* (*psychological*) Ärgernis *nt* ❷ **stomach ~** Magenverstimmung *f* ❸ SPORTS unliebsame Überraschung

upsetting [ʌp·ˈset̬·ɪŋ] *adj* erschütternd; (*saddening*) traurig; (*annoying*) ärgerlich

upshot [ˈʌp·ʃat] *n* [End]ergebnis *nt*

upside ˈdown I. *adj inv* ❶ (*inverted*) auf dem Kopf stehend *attr;* **that picture is ~** das Bild hängt verkehrt herum ❷ (*confused*) verkehrt **II.** *adv inv* verkehrt herum; **to turn sth ~** etw auf den Kopf stellen *a. fig*

upstage [ˈʌp·steɪdʒ] *vt* ■**to ~ sb** jdm die Schau stehlen

upstairs [ˌʌp·ˈsterz] *inv* **I.** *adj* oben *präd,* obere(r, s) *attr* **II.** *adv* (*to higher*) nach oben; (*at higher*) oben **III.** *n* Obergeschoss *nt*

upstanding [ˌʌp·ˈstæn·dɪŋ] *adj* (*honest*) aufrichtig

upstart [ˈʌp·start] *n* (*pej*) Emporkömmling *m*

upstate [ˈʌp·steɪt] **I.** *adj* im ländlichen Norden [des Bundesstaates] *nach n;* **in ~ New York** im ländlichen Teil New Yorks **II.** *adv* in den/im ländlichen Norden [des Bundesstaates]

upstream [ˌʌp·ˈstrim] **I.** *adj* ~ **pollution** Verschmutzung *f* im oberen Flusslauf **II.** *adv* flussaufwärts; **to swim ~** gegen den Strom schwimmen

upsurge [ˈʌp·sɜrdʒ] *n* rasche Zunahme; **the ~ of** [*or* **in**] **violence** die stark zunehmende Gewalt

upswing [ˈʌp·swɪŋ] *n* ECON Aufschwung *m*

uptake [ˈʌp·teɪk] *n* ▶ PHRASES: **to be quick/slow on the ~** (*fam*) schnell schalten/schwer von Begriff sein

uptight [ʌp·ˈtaɪt] *adj* (*fam*) ❶ (*nervous*) nervös; (*anxious*) ängstlich; **to be ~ [about sth]** [wegen einer S. *gen*] nervös sein ❷ (*inhibited*) verklemmt

ˈup-to-date *adj attr* zeitgemäß; *information, report* aktuell

up-to-the-ˈminute *adj* hochaktuell

uptown [ˈʌp·taʊn] **I.** *adj inv* **to live in ~ Manhattan** im nördlichen Teil Manhattans leben **II.** *adv inv* in den nördlichen Wohngebieten **III.** *n* Wohnviertel *nt*

upturn [ˈʌp·tɜrn] *n* Aufschwung *m*

upturned [ˌʌp·ˈtɜrnd] *adj* nach oben gewendet; *table* umgeworfen; *boat* gekentert

upward [ˈʌp·wərd] **I.** *adj inv* Aufwärts-; ~ **trend** Aufwärtstrend *m* **II.** *adv* nach oben;

from childhood ~ von Kindheit an
upwardly [ˈʌp·wərd·li] *adv inv* nach oben, aufwärts; ~ **mobile** aufstrebend und erfolgreich
upwards [ˈʌp·wərdz] *adv inv* nach oben, aufwärts
uranium [ju·ˈreɪ·ni·əm] *n* Uran *nt*
Uranus [ju·ˈreɪ·nəs] *n* ASTRON Uranus *m*
urban [ˈɜr·bən] *adj attr* städtisch; ~ **area** Stadtgebiet *nt*
urbane [ɜr·ˈbeɪn] *adj* weltmännisch; *manner* kultiviert
urbanization [ˌɜr·bə·nɪ·ˈzeɪ·ʃən] *n* Verstädterung *f*
urbanize [ˈɜr·bə·naɪz] *vt* verstädtern
urchin [ˈɜr·tʃɪn] *n* ❶ ZOOL Seeigel *m* ❷ (*child*) [**street**] ~ Straßenkind *nt;* (*boy*) Gassenjunge *m*
urge [ɜrdʒ] **I.** *n* Verlangen *nt* (**for** nach +*dat*); (*compulsion*) Drang *m* (**for** nach +*dat*); PSYCH Trieb *m;* **to get the ~ to do sth** Lust bekommen, etw zu tun; **sexual** ~ Sexual-/Geschlechtstrieb *m* **II.** *vt* ❶ (*persuade*) ■**to ~ sb [to do sth]** jdn drängen[, etw zu tun] ❷ (*advocate*) ■**to ~ sth** auf etw *akk* dringen, zu etw *dat* drängen; **I ~ you to reconsider your decision** ich rate Ihnen dringend, Ihren Beschluss zu überdenken; **to ~ caution** zur Vorsicht mahnen
urgency [ˈɜr·dʒən·si] *n* Dringlichkeit *f; of problem, situation a.* Vordringlichkeit *f;* **to be a matter of** ~ äußerst dringend sein
urgent [ˈɜr·dʒənt] *adj* ❶ (*imperative*) dringend; *situation* brisant; (*on letter*) „eilt" ❷ (*insistent*) eindringlich; *plea* deutlich
urgently [ˈɜr·dʒənt·li] *adv* ❶ (*imperatively*) dringend ❷ (*insistently*) eindringlich
urinal [ˈjʊr·ə·nəl] *n* (*toilet*) Pissoir *nt*
urinate [ˈjʊr·ə·neɪt] *vi* urinieren
urine [ˈjʊr·ɪn] *n* Urin *m*
URL [ˌju·ar·ˈel] *n abbrev of* **uniform resource locator** URL *m*
urn [ɜrn] *n* ❶ (*vase*) Krug *m;* (*for remains*) [Grab]urne *f* ❷ (*for drinks*) *großer, hoher Metallbehälter mit Deckel für heiße Getränke*
us [əs, *stressed:* ʌs] *pron* (*object of we*) uns *dat o akk;* **let ~ know** lassen Sie es uns wissen; **both/many of** ~ wir beide/viele von uns; **it's** ~ wir sind's; **older than** ~ älter als wir
U.S., US [ˌju·ˈes] **I.** *n abbrev of* **United States:** ■**the** ~ die USA *pl* **II.** *adj attr abbrev of* **United States** US-
USA, U.S.A. [ˌju·es·ˈeɪ] *n abbrev of* **United States of America:** ■**the** ~ die USA *pl*
USAF [ˌju·es·eɪ·ˈef] *n abbrev of* **United States Air Force:** ■**the** ~ die US-Luftwaffe
usage [ˈju·sɪdʒ] *n* ❶ (*handling*) Gebrauch *m;* (*consumption*) Verbrauch *m* ❷ (*practice*) Usus *m geh* ❸ *of word* Verwendung *f,* Gebrauch *m*
USB [ˌju·es·ˈbi] *n acr for* **Universal Serial Bus** COMPUT USB *m;* ~ [**flash**] **drive** USB-Stick *m*
use I. *vt* [juz] ❶ (*utilize*) benutzen; *building, chance, skills, talent* nutzen; *method, force* anwenden; *dictionary, idea* verwenden; *poison, gas, chemical warfare* einsetzen; **I could ~ some help** ich könnte etwas Hilfe gebrauchen; **to ~ drugs** Drogen nehmen; **to ~ sth against sb** etw gegen jdn verwenden ❷ (*employ*) einsetzen; ~ **your imagination!** lass doch mal deine Fantasie spielen!; **to ~ common sense** seinen gesunden Menschenverstand benutzen ❸ (*consume*) verbrauchen; **this radio ~s four AAA batteries** für dieses Radio braucht man vier AAA Batterien ❹ (*manipulate*) benutzen; (*exploit*) ausnutzen **II.** *n* [jus] ❶ (*utilization*) Verwendung *f* (**for** für +*akk*); *of dictionary a.* Benutzung *f; of talent, experience* Nutzung *m; of force, method* Anwendung *f; of poison, gas, labor* Einsatz *m;* **to lose the ~ of sth** *finger, limb* etw nicht mehr benutzen können; **directions for** ~ Gebrauchsanweisung *f;* **for ~ in an emergency** für den Notfall; **for external ~ only** nur zur äußerlichen Anwendung; **to be no longer in** ~ nicht mehr benutzt werden; **to find a ~ for sth** für etw *akk* Verwendung finden; **to make ~ of sth** etw benutzen; *experience, talent* etw nutzen; **can you make ~ of that?** kannst du das gebrauchen? ❷ (*consumption*) Verwendung *f* ❸ (*usefulness*) Nutzen *m;* **can I be of any ~?** kann ich vielleicht irgendwie behilflich sein?; **to be no/not much ~ to sb** jdm nichts/nicht viel nützen; **it's no ~ [doing sth]** es hat keinen Zweck[, etw zu tun] ❹ (*right to use*) **to have the ~ of sth** *room, car* etw benutzen dürfen
◆**use up** *vt* verbrauchen; (*completely*) [völlig] aufbrauchen
used¹ [juzd] *vt only in past* **he ~ to teach** er hat früher unterrichtet; **my father ~ to say ...** mein Vater sagte [früher] immer, ...
used² [juzd] *adj inv* (*old*) gebraucht; ~ **clothes** Secondhandkleidung *f*
used³ [juzd] *adj inv* (*accustomed*) ■**to be ~ to sth** etw gewohnt sein; ■**to get ~ to [doing] sth** sich *akk* an etw *akk* gewöhnen
useful [ˈjus·fəl] *adj* ❶ (*practical*) nützlich (**for** für +*akk*); **to make oneself** ~ sich nützlich machen ❷ (*advantageous*) wertvoll; **to come in** ~ gut zu gebrauchen sein ❸ (*effective*) hilfreich; *discussion* ergiebig
usefulness [ˈjus·fəl·nɪs] *n* Nützlichkeit *f; of contribution, information a.* Brauchbarkeit *f;* (*applicability*) Verwendbarkeit *f*
useless [ˈjus·lɪs] *adj* ❶ (*pointless*) sinnlos ❷ (*fam: inept*) zu nichts zu gebrauchen *präd;* **he's a ~ goalkeeper** er taugt nichts als Torwart ❸ (*unusable*) unbrauchbar; **to be** ~ nichts taugen
user [ˈju·zər] *n* Benutzer(in) *m(f); of software, system a.* Anwender(in) *m(f); of electricity, gas* Verbraucher(in) *m(f);* **drug** ~ Drogenkonsument(in) *m(f)*
ˈuser-friendly *adj* COMPUT benutzerfreundlich
user ˈinterface *n* COMPUT Benutzeroberfläche *f*
usher [ˈʌʃ·ər] **I.** *n* (*in theater, church*) Platzan-

U

weiser(in) *m(f)* **II.** *vt* **to ~ sb into a room/to his seat** jdn in einen Raum hineinführen/zu seinem Platz führen

◆ **usher in** *vt* ■ **to ~ in ⊂ sth** *a new era* etw einleiten

USP [ˌju·es·ˈpi] *n* ECON *abbrev of* **unique selling proposition** USP *m*

USPS [ˌju·es·pi·ˈes] *n abbrev of* **United States Postal Service** *US-amerikanische staatliche Postgesellschaft*

USS [ˌju·es·ˈes] *n abbrev of* **United States Ship** *Schiff aus den Vereinigten Staaten*

usual [ˈju·ʒu·əl] **I.** *adj* üblich, normal; **to find sth in its ~ place** etw an seinem gewohnten Platz vorfinden; **as ~** wie üblich **II.** *n* (*fam: drink*) ■ **the/one's ~** das Übliche

usually [ˈju·ʒu·ə·li] *adv* normalerweise; **more ... than ~** mehr ... als sonst

usurp [ju·ˈsɜrp] *vt* ① (*take*) sich *dat* widerrechtlich aneignen; *power* an sich *akk* reißen ② (*oust*) verdrängen

usurper [ju·ˈsɜr·pər] *n* Usurpator(in) *m(f) geh*

usury [ˈju·ʒə·ri] *n* JUR Wucher *m*

UT, Ut. *abbrev of* **Utah**

Utah [ˈju·tɔ] *n* Utah *nt*

utensil [ju·ˈten·səl] *n* Utensil *nt;* **kitchen ~s** Küchengeräte *pl*

uterus <*pl* -ri *or* -es> [ˈju·t̬ər·əs] *n* ANAT Gebärmutter *f*

utilitarian [ju·ˌtɪl·ɪ·ˈter·i·ən] *adj* ① (*philosophy*) utilitaristisch *fachspr* ② (*functional*) funktionell

utility [ju·ˈtɪl·ɪ·t̬i] **I.** *n* ① (*usefulness*) Nützlichkeit *f* ② (*provider*) **public ~** öffentlicher Versorgungsbetrieb **II.** *adj* Mehrzweck-; **~ vehicle** Mehrzweckfahrzeug *nt*

uˈtility room *n Raum, in dem Haushaltsgeräte, wie z. B. Waschmaschine und Trockner stehen, und der ebenfalls als Vorratskeller dient*

utilization [ˌju·t̬ɪ·lɪ·ˈzeɪ·ʃən] *n* Verwendung *f;* ECON Auslastung *f*

utilize [ˈju·t̬ɪ·laɪz] *vt* nutzen

utmost [ˈʌt·moʊst] **I.** *adj attr, inv* größte(r, s); **with the ~ care** so sorgfältig wie möglich; **of the ~ importance** von äußerster Wichtigkeit **II.** *n* ■ **the ~** das Äußerste (**in** an +*dat*); **to try one's ~** sein Bestes geben

utopian [ju·ˈtoʊ·pi·ən] *adj* utopisch

utter¹ [ˈʌt̬·ər] *adj attr, inv* vollkommen; **~ nonsense** absoluter Blödsinn; **a complete and ~ waste of time** eine totale Zeitverschwendung

utter² [ˈʌt̬·ər] *vt* ① (*give voice to*) von sich *dat* geben; **to ~ a groan** stöhnen; **without ~ing a word** ohne ein Wort zu sagen ② (*speak out*) sagen; *curse, threat* ausstoßen; *oath* schwören; *prayer* sprechen; *warning* aussprechen

utterly [ˈʌt̬·ər·li] *adv inv* vollkommen; **to be ~ convinced that ...** vollkommen [davon] überzeugt sein, dass ...

U-turn [ˈju·tɜrn] *n* ① (*of car*) Wende *f;* **to make a ~** wenden ② (*change*) Kehrtwendung *f*

Vv

V <*pl* -'s *or* -s> *n,* **v** <*pl* -'s> [vi] *n* ① (*letter*) V *nt,* v *nt;* **~ as in Victor** V wie Viktor ② (*five*) V (*römisches Zahlzeichen für 5*)

v [vi] **I.** *n* LING *abbrev of* **verb** v **II.** *prep abbrev of* **verse, verso, versus** vs. **III.** *adv abbrev of* **very**

VA, Va. *abbrev of* **Virginia**

vac [væk] **I.** *n* (*fam*) *short for* **vacuum cleaner** Staubsauger *m* **II.** *vt* <-cc-> (*fam*) *short for* **vacuum clean** [staub]saugen **III.** *vi short for* **vacuum clean** [staub]saugen

vacancy [ˈveɪ·kən·si] *n* ① (*room*) freies Zimmer; **"vacancies"** „Zimmer frei"; **"no vacancies"** „belegt" ② (*job*) freie Stelle; **to fill a ~** eine [freie] Stelle besetzen

vacant [ˈveɪ·kənt] *adj inv* ① (*empty*) *bed, chair, seat* frei; *house* unbewohnt; *land* unbebaut ② *job* unbesetzt ③ (*expressionless*) leer; **~ stare** ausdrucksloser Blick

vacate [ˈveɪ·keɪt] *vt* räumen; *job, position, post* aufgeben; *place, seat* frei machen

vacation [veɪ·ˈkeɪ·ʃən] **I.** *n* ① (*holiday*) Ferien *pl,* Urlaub *m;* **to take a ~** Urlaub machen; ■ **on ~** im Urlaub ② UNIV Semesterferien *pl;* LAW Gerichtsferien *pl;* SCH [Schul]ferien *pl* **II.** *vi* Urlaub machen

vacationer [veɪ·ˈkeɪ·ʃə·nər] *n* Urlauber(in) *m(f)*

vaccinate [ˈvæk·sə·neɪt] *vt* impfen (**against** gegen +*akk*)

vaccination [ˌvæk·sə·ˈneɪ·ʃən] *n* [Schutz]impfung *f* (**against** gegen +*akk*)

vaccine [væk·ˈsin] *n* Impfstoff *m*

vacuous [ˈvæk·ju·əs] *adj* ① (*inane*) *person, question* geistlos; *remark a.* nichts sagend ② (*expressionless*) *look, expression* ausdruckslos, leer

vacuum <*pl* -s *or* -cua> [ˈvæk·jum, *pl* -kju·ə] **I.** *n* ① Vakuum *nt* ② (*fig: gap*) Vakuum *nt,* Lücke *f;* **to leave a ~** eine Lücke hinterlassen ③ (*vacuum cleaner*) Staubsauger *m* **II.** *vt* [staub]saugen; ■ **to ~ up ⊂ sth** etw aufsaugen

ˈvacuum cleaner *n* Staubsauger *m*

ˈvacuum-packed *adj* vakuumverpackt

vagary [ˈveɪ·gə·ri] *n* ■ **vagaries** *pl* Launen *pl;* **the vagaries of life** die Wechselfälle *pl* des Lebens

vagina <*pl* -s *or* -ae> [və·ˈdʒaɪ·nə] *n* ANAT Vagina *f,* Scheide *f*

vagrancy [ˈveɪ·grən·si] *n* Obdachlosigkeit *f*

vagrant ['veɪ·grənt] *n* Obdachlose(r) *f(m)*
vague [veɪg] *adj* ❶ (*indistinct*) ungenau, vage; *blurred* verschwommen, undeutlich ❷ (*imprecise*) *person* zerstreut
vagueness ['veɪg·nəs] *n* Unbestimmtheit *f*
vain [veɪn] *adj* ❶ (*conceited*) eingebildet; (*about one's looks*) eitel ❷ (*futile*) sinnlos; *hope* töricht ❸ (*unsuccessful*) vergeblich; **in ~** vergeblich, umsonst
valance ['væl·əns] *n* ❶ (*on bed*) Volant *m* ❷ (*on curtain rail*) Querbehang *m*
valedictorian [ˌvæl·ə·dɪk·'tɔr·i·ən] *n* Abschiedsredner(in) *m(f)* (*Jahrgangsbeste(r), die/der bei Schul- oder Universitätsentlassungsfeiern eine Abschiedsrede hält*)
valedictory [ˌvæl·ə·'dɪk·tə·ri] *adj inv* Abschieds-; (*school-leaving*) **~ address** Abschiedsrede *f*
valentine ['væl·ən·taɪn] *n* ❶ (*card*) Valentinskarte *f* ❷ (*person*) *Person, die am Valentinstag von ihrem Verehrer/ihrer Verehrerin beschenkt wird*
'**Valentine's Day** *n* Valentinstag *m*
valerian [və·'lɪr·i·ən] *n* Baldrian *m*
valet [væ·'leɪ] *n* ❶ (*servant*) Kammerdiener *m* ❷ *Person, die Autos (meist im Hotel) einparkt*
'**valet parking** *n* Parkservice *m*
valiant ['væl·jənt] *adj* mutig; *effort* kühn; *resistance* tapfer
valid ['væl·ɪd] *adj* ❶ (*well-founded*) begründet; (*worthwhile*) berechtigt; *argument* stichhaltig; *criticism* gerechtfertigt ❷ (*in force*) gültig; LAW (*binding*) rechtskräftig
validate ['væl·ə·deɪt] *vt* ❶ (*approve*) anerkennen ❷ (*verify*) bestätigen
validity [və·'lɪd·ə·ṭi] *n* Gültigkeit *f;* (*value*) Wert *m*
valley ['væl·i] *n* Tal *nt*
valor ['væl·ər] *n* Wagemut *m*
valuable ['væl·ju·ə·bəl] **I.** *adj* wertvoll; *gems* kostbar **II.** *n usu pl* Wertsachen *pl*
valuation [ˌvæl·ju·'eɪ·ʃən] *n* ❶ (*appraisal*) Schätzung *f;* **to make a ~ of sth** etw schätzen ❷ (*price*) Schätzwert *m*
value ['væl·ju] **I.** *n* ❶ (*significance*) Wert *m,* Bedeutung *f;* **to be of little ~** wenig Wert haben; **to place a high ~ on sth** auf etw *akk* großen Wert legen ❷ (*monetary*) Wert *m* ❸ (*ethics*) ■ **~s** *pl* Werte *pl,* Wertvorstellungen *pl* **II.** *vt* ❶ (*esteem*) schätzen; **to ~ sb as a friend** jdn als Freund schätzen ❷ (*estimate*) schätzen; ■ **to have sth ~d** etw schätzen lassen
value-'added tax *n* Mehrwertsteuer *f*
valued ['væl·jud] *adj* geschätzt
valueless ['væl·ju·lɪs] *adj* wertlos
valve [vælv] *n* ❶ TECH Ventil *nt* ❷ ANAT Klappe *f*
vampire ['væm·paɪr] *n* Vampir(in) *m(f)*
van [væn] *n* ❶ (*truck*) Transporter *m;* **delivery ~** Lieferwagen *m* ❷ (*car*) Kleinbus *m;* (*smaller*) Minibus *m*
vandal ['væn·dəl] *n* Vandale(in) *m(f) pej*
vandalism ['væn·də·lɪz·əm] *n* Vandalismus *m*
vandalize ['væn·də·laɪz] *vt* mutwillig zerstören
vane [veɪn] *n* ❶ (*blade*) Propellerflügel *m* ❷ METEO (*weathervane*) Wetterfahne *f*
vanguard ['væn·gard] *n* ❶ (*guard*) Vorhut *f;* (*forefront*) Spitze *f* ❷ (*fig: leader*) **to be in the ~ of sth** zu den Vorreitern +*dat* gehören
vanilla [və·'nɪl·ə] **I.** *n* Vanille *f* **II.** *adj* ❶ Vanille-; **~ pudding** ≈ Vanillepudding *m* ❷ (*fig: ordinary*) durchschnittlich; **plain ~** nullachtfuffzehn [*o* SCHWEIZ nullachtfünfzehn] *fam*
vanish ['væn·ɪʃ] *vi* ❶ (*disappear*) verschwinden; **to ~ into thin air** sich in Luft auflösen; **to ~ without a trace** spurlos verschwinden ❷ (*extinct*) verloren gehen
'**vanishing point** *n* ❶ (*horizon*) Fluchtpunkt *m* ❷ (*fig*) Nullpunkt *m*
vanity ['væn·ə·ṭi] *n* ❶ Eitelkeit *f* ❷ *see* **dressing table**
vantage ['væn·tɪdʒ] *n* Aussichtspunkt *m*
'**vantage point** *n* ❶ (*outlook*) Aussichtspunkt *m* ❷ (*fig: perspective*) Blickpunkt *m*
vapid ['væp·ɪd] *adj* banal
vapor ['veɪ·pər] *n* Dampf *m*
vaporization [ˌveɪ·pər·ɪ·'zeɪ·ʃən] *n* (*slow*) Verdunstung *f;* (*quick*) Verdampfung *f*
vaporize ['veɪ·pə·raɪz] **I.** *vt* verdampfen **II.** *vi* (*slowly*) verdunsten; (*quickly*) verdampfen
vaporizer ['veɪ·pə·raɪ·zər] *n* Inhalator *m*
'**vapor trail** *n* Kondensstreifen *m*
variability [ˌvær·i·ə·'bɪl·ə·ṭi] *n* Veränderlichkeit *f*
variable ['vær·i·ə·bəl] **I.** *n* Variable *f* **II.** *adj* variabel, veränderlich; *quality* wechselhaft; *weather* unbeständig
variance ['vær·i·əns] *n* ❶ ■ **to be at ~ with sth** mit etw *dat* nicht übereinstimmen ❷ (*variation*) Abweichung *f* ❸ LAW (*permission*) Sondergenehmigung *f*
variant ['vær·i·ənt] **I.** *n* Variante *f* **II.** *adj* variierend, unterschiedlich
variation [ˌvær·i·'eɪ·ʃən] *n* ❶ (*variability*) Abweichung *f* ❷ (*difference*) Schwankung[en] *f[pl]* ❸ MUS Variation *f* (**on** über +*akk*)
varicose vein ['ver·ə·koʊs-] *n* Krampfader *f*
varied ['vær·id] *adj* unterschiedlich; *career* bewegt; *group* bunt gemischt
variegated ['vær·i·ə·geɪ·ṭɪd] *adj* ❶ (*diverse*) vielfältig ❷ (*multicolored*) mischfarbig; BOT panaschiert *fachspr; leaves* bunt
variety [və·'raɪ·ə·ṭi] *n* ❶ (*diversity*) Verschiedenartigkeit *f;* (*in job a.*) Abwechslungsreichtum *m* ❷ (*assortment*) Vielfalt *f;* ECON Auswahl *f* ❸ (*category*) Art *f;* BIOL Spezies *f;* **a new ~ of tulip** eine neue Tulpensorte
va'riety show *n* Varieteeshow *f*
various ['vær·i·əs] *adj inv* verschieden
varnish ['var·nɪʃ] **I.** *n* <*pl* -es> Lack *m;* (*on painting*) Firnis *m* **II.** *vt* lackieren
vary <-ie-> ['vær·i] **I.** *vi* ❶ (*differ*) variieren, verschieden sein; **to ~ greatly** stark voneinander abweichen ❷ (*change*) sich verändern;

V

(*fluctuate*) schwanken **II.** *vt* variieren; **to ~ one's diet** abwechslungsreich essen

varying ['veri·ɪŋ] *adj* (*different*) unterschiedlich; (*fluctuating*) variierend

vase [veɪs] *n* Vase *f*

vast [væst] *adj* gewaltig, riesig; *country* weit; *majority* überwältigend

vastly ['væst·li] *adv* wesentlich, erheblich; **~ superior** haushoch überlegen

vastness ['væst·nəs] *n* riesige Ausmaße *pl*

vat [væt] *n* Fass *nt;* (*with open top*) Bottich *m*

Vatican ['væt̬·ɪ·kən] **I.** *n* ■**the ~** der Vatikan **II.** *adj attr, inv* Vatikan-, des Vatikans *nach n*

vault [vɔlt] **I.** *n* ❶ (*arch*) Gewölbebogen *m* ❷ (*strongroom*) Tresorraum *m;* (*safe*) Magazin *nt* ❸ (*in church*) Krypta *f;* (*at cemetery*) Gruft *f* ❹ (*jump*) Sprung *m* **II.** *vt* ■**to ~ sth** über etw *akk* springen; *athletics* etw überspringen **III.** *vi* springen (**over** über +*akk*)

vaulted ['vɔl·tɪd] *adj inv* gewölbt

vaulting ['vɔl·tɪŋ] **I.** *n* Wölbung *f* **II.** *adj attr* (*liter*) rasch ansteigend; *ambition* skrupellos

VCR [ˌvi·si·'ar] *n abbrev of* **videocassette recorder** Videorekorder *m*

veal [vil] **I.** *n* Kalbfleisch *nt* **II.** *adj* Kalbs-

vector ['vek·tər] *n* ❶ (*quantity*) Vektor *m* ❷ BIOL (*organism*) Überträger *m*

veer [vɪr] *vi* ❶ (*turn*) abdrehen; ■**to ~ toward[s] sth** auf etw *akk* hinsteuern ❷ (*alter goal*) umschwenken

veg <-gg-> [vedʒ] *vi* (*fam*) ■**to ~ out** herumhängen

vegan ['vi·gən] **I.** *n* Veganer(in) *m(f)* **II.** *adj* vegan

vegetable ['vedʒ·tə·bəl] **I.** *n* ❶ (*edible plant*) Gemüse *nt* ❷ (*not animal or mineral*) Pflanze *f* ❸ (*offensive fam: disabled person*) Scheintote(r) *f(m)* ❹ (*fam: idler*) **to be a ~** vor sich *dat* hin vegetieren **II.** *adj* Gemüse-; **~ diet** (*for person*) pflanzliche Ernährung; (*for animal*) Grünfutter *nt*

'vegetable fat *n* pflanzliches Fett

'vegetable garden *n* Gemüsegarten *m*

'vegetable kingdom *n* Pflanzenreich *nt*

'vegetable oil *n* pflanzliches Öl

vegetarian [ˌvedʒ·ə·'ter·i·ən] **I.** *n* Vegetarier(in) *m(f)* **II.** *adj inv* vegetarisch

vegetate ['vedʒ·ə·teɪt] *vi* vegetieren

vegetation [ˌvedʒ·ə·'teɪ·ʃən] *n* Pflanzen *pl;* (*in specific area*) Vegetation *f*

veggie ['vedʒ·i] *n* (*fam*) *short for* **vegetable**

vehemence ['vi·ə·məns] *n* Vehemenz *f*

vehement ['vi·ə·mənt] *adj* vehement, heftig; *critic* scharf

vehicle ['vi·ə·kəl] *n* ❶ (*transport*) Fahrzeug *nt* ❷ (*fig: means*) Vehikel *nt* (**for** für +*akk*)

veil [veɪl] **I.** *n* Schleier *m a. fig* **II.** *vt* ❶ *usu passive* ■**to be ~ed** verschleiert sein ❷ (*fig: hide*) *feelings, opinion* verbergen; *truth, intention, scandal* verschleiern

veiled [veɪld] *adj* ❶ *inv* verschleiert ❷ (*fig: hidden*) verschleiert; *criticism, hint, threat* versteckt

vein [veɪn] *n* ❶ (*vessel*) Vene *f* ❷ BOT, ZOOL, MIN Ader *f* ❸ *usu sing* (*style*) Stil *m*

veined [veɪnd] *adj* geädert

Velcro® ['vel·kroʊ] *n* Klettverschluss *m*

velocity [və·'las·ə·t̬i] **I.** *n* Geschwindigkeit *f* **II.** *adj attr, inv* Geschwindigkeits-

velvet ['vel·vɪt] *n* Samt *m*

velveteen [ˌvel·vɪ·'tin] *n* Veloursamt *m*

velvety ['vel·və·t̬i] *adj* samtig

vend [vend] *vt* verkaufen

vendetta [ven·'det̬·ə] *n* Vendetta *f*

'vending machine *n* Automat *m*

vendor ['ven·dər] *n* ❶ (*street seller*) Straßenverkäufer(in) *m(f)* ❷ LAW (*seller*) Verkäufer(in) *m(f)*

veneer [və·'nɪr] *n* ❶ (*layer*) Furnier *nt* ❷ (*fig: front*) Fassade *f*

venerable ['ven·ər·ə·bəl] *adj* ❶ (*respected*) ehrwürdig; *family* angesehen; *tradition* alt ❷ (*old*) *ruins* altehrwürdig; *age* ehrwürdig

venerate ['ven·ə·reɪt] *vt* verehren, bewundern (**for** für +*akk*)

veneration [ˌven·ə·'reɪ·ʃən] *n* Verehrung *f*

venereal [və·'nɪr·i·əl] *adj inv* MED venerisch *fachspr;* **~ disease** Geschlechtskrankheit *f*

venetian 'blind *n* Jalousie *f*

Venezuela [ˌven·ə·'zweɪ·lə] *n* Venezuela *nt*

vengeance ['ven·dʒəns] *n* ❶ (*revenge*) Rache *f;* **to vow ~** Rache schwören ❷ (*fig: energy*) ■**with a ~** mit voller Kraft

venison ['ven·ɪ·sən] *n* Rehfleisch *nt*

venom ['ven·əm] *n* Gift *nt;* (*fig: spite*) Bosheit *f*

venomous ['ven·ə·məs] *adj* giftig *a. fig*

vent [vent] **I.** *n* ❶ (*outlet*) Abzug *m;* **air ~** Luftschacht *m* ❷ (*fig: release*) Ventil *nt;* **to give ~ to one's anger** seinem Ärger Luft machen; **to give ~ to one's feelings** seinen Gefühlen Ausdruck geben **II.** *vt* ■**to ~ sth** etw *dat* Ausdruck geben; **to ~ one's anger on sb** seine Wut an jdm auslassen **III.** *vi* Dampf ablassen *fam*

ventilate ['ven·tə·leɪt] *vt* lüften

ventilation [ˌven·tə·'leɪ·ʃən] *n* Belüftung *f*

ventilator ['ven·tə·leɪ·t̬ər] *n* ❶ (*air circulator*) Ventilator *m* ❷ MED (*respirator*) Beatmungsgerät *nt*

ventricle ['ven·trɪ·kəl] *n* Herzkammer *f*

ventriloquist [ven·'trɪl·ə·kwɪst] *n* Bauchredner(in) *m(f)*

venture ['ven·tʃər] **I.** *n* Projekt *nt;* ECON Unternehmen *nt* **II.** *vt opinion* vorsichtig äußern **III.** *vi* sich vorwagen

'venture capital *n* Risikokapital *nt*

venturesome ['ven·tʃər·səm] *adj* ❶ (*adventurous*) *person* wagemutig ❷ (*risky*) riskant

venue ['ven·ju] *n* ❶ (*site*) Veranstaltungsort *m;* (*for competition*) Austragungsort *m* ❷ LAW (*jurisdiction*) Verhandlungsort *m*

Venus ['vi·nəs] *n* Venus *f*

veranda(h) [və·'ræn·də] *n* Veranda *f*

verb [vɜrb] *n* Verb *nt*

verbal ['vɜr·bəl] *adj inv* ❶ (*oral*) mündlich ❷ (*of verb*) **~ noun** Verbalsubstantiv *nt*

verbalize ['vɜr·bə·laɪz] **I.** *vt* ausdrücken **II.** *vi* sich verbal ausdrücken; **to start to ~** *child* anfangen zu sprechen

verbally ['vɜr·bə·li] *adv inv* verbal, mündlich

verbatim [vər·'beɪ·t̬ɪm] *inv* **I.** *adj* wörtlich **II.** *adv* wortwörtlich

verbiage ['vɜr·bi·ɪdʒ] *n* Worthülsen *pl;* (*in speech*) Floskeln *pl*

verbose [vər·'boʊs] *adj* wortreich; *speech* weitschweifig

verdict ['vɜr·dɪkt] *n* ① (*judgment*) Urteil *nt;* **~ of not guilty** Freispruch *m;* **unanimous ~** einstimmiges Urteil; **to return a ~** ein Urteil verkünden ② (*opinion*) Urteil *nt;* **to give a ~ on sth** ein Urteil über etw *akk* fällen

verdigris ['vɜr·dɪ·grɪs] *n* Grünspan *m*

verge [vɜrdʒ] *n* ① (*edge*) Rand *m;* **on the ~ of the desert** am Rand der Wüste ② (*fig: brink*) **to be on the ~ of collapse** kurz vor dem Zusammenbruch stehen

◆**verge on** *vi* **to ~ on the ridiculous** ans Lächerliche grenzen

verifiable [ˌver·ə·'faɪə·bəl] *adj* verifizierbar *geh; fact* überprüfbar; *theory* nachweisbar

verification [ˌver·ə·fɪ·'keɪ·ʃən] **I.** *n* Verifizierung *f geh;* (*checking*) Überprüfung *f* **II.** *adj* Überprüfungs-; **~ procedure** Prüfungsverfahren *nt*

verify <-ie-> ['ver·ə·faɪ] *vt* verifizieren *geh;* (*check*) überprüfen; (*confirm*) belegen

veritable ['ver·ə·t̬ə·bəl] *adj attr, inv* wahr; **a ~ war of words** das reinste Wortgefecht

vermicelli [ˌvɜr·mə·'tʃel·i] *npl* Fadennudeln *pl*

vermilion, **vermillion** [vər·'mɪl·jən] **I.** *n* Zinnoberrot *nt* **II.** *adj inv* zinnoberrot

vermin ['vɜr·mɪn] *npl* (*animals*) Schädlinge *pl;* (*persons*) nutzloses Pack *pej;* **to control ~** Ungeziefer bekämpfen

Vermont [vər·'mant] *n* Vermont *nt*

vermouth [vər·'muθ] *n* Wermut *m*

vernacular [vər·'næk·jə·lər] **I.** *n* Umgangssprache *f;* (*dialect*) Dialekt *m;* (*jargon*) Jargon *m* **II.** *adj* (*of language*) umgangssprachlich; (*as one's mother tongue*) muttersprachlich

versatile ['vɜr·sə·t̬əl] *adj person* vielseitig; *material* vielseitig verwendbar

versatility [ˌvɜr·sə·'tɪl·ə·t̬i] *n* Vielseitigkeit *f;* (*adjustability*) Anpassungsfähigkeit *f; of device* vielseitige Verwendbarkeit

verse [vɜrs] *n* ① (*poetry*) Dichtung *f;* **in ~** in Versen *m* ② (*poem, song*) Strophe *f* ③ (*scripture*) Vers *m*

versed [vɜrst] *adj* **to be [well] ~ in sth** (*knowledgeable about*) in etw *dat* [sehr] versiert sein *geh;* (*familiar with*) sich mit etw *dat* [gut] auskennen

version ['vɜr·ʒən] *n* ① (*account*) Version *f;* (*description*) Darstellung *f* ② (*variant*) Version *f; of book, text, film* Fassung *f;* **abridged ~** Kurzfassung *f;* **revised ~** revidierte Ausgabe

versus ['vɜr·səs] *prep* gegen

vertebra <*pl* -brae> ['vɜr·t̬ə·brə, *pl* -bri] *n* Wirbel *m*

vertebral ['vɜr·t̬ə·brəl] *adj inv* Wirbel-

vertebrate ['vɜr·t̬ə·brɪt] **I.** *n* Wirbeltier *nt* **II.** *adj attr, inv* Wirbel-

vertex <*pl* -es *or* -tices> ['vɜr·teks, *pl* -t̬ɪ·siz] *n* ① MATH Scheitel[punkt] *m* ② (*apex*) Spitze *f*

vertical ['vɜr·t̬ə·kəl] **I.** *adj* senkrecht, vertikal **II.** *n* Senkrechte *f,* Vertikale *f geh*

vertigo ['vɜr·t̬ə·goʊ] *n* Schwindel *m;* MED Gleichgewichtsstörung *f*

verve [vɜrv] *n* Begeisterung *f,* Verve *f geh*

very ['ver·i] **I.** *adv inv* ① (*extremely*) sehr, außerordentlich ② (*to great degree*) sehr; **~ much** sehr; **to feel ~ much at home** sich ganz wie zu Hause fühlen ③ + *superl* (*to add force*) aller-; **the ~ best** der/die/das Allerbeste; **to do the ~ best one can** sein Allerbestes geben; **at the ~ most/least** allerhöchstens/zumindest; **the ~ next day** schon am nächsten Tag; **the ~ same** genau der/die/das Gleiche **II.** *adj attr, inv* **at the ~ bottom** zuunterst; **at the ~ end of sth** ganz am Ende einer S. *gen;* **the ~ fact that ...** allein schon die Tatsache, dass ...; **they're the ~ opposite of one another** sie sind völlig unterschiedlich; **the ~ thought ...** allein der Gedanke ...

vessel ['ves·əl] *n* ① (*ship*) Schiff *nt* ② (*container*) Gefäß *nt*

vest [vest] **I.** *n* [Anzug]weste *f* **II.** *vt* ① *usu passive* (*give*) **to be ~ed with the power to do sth** berechtigt sein, etw zu tun ② (*place*) **to ~ one's hopes in sb/sth** seine Hoffnungen auf jdn/etw setzen

vestibule ['ves·tə·bjul] *n* (*foyer*) Vorraum *m;* (*larger*) Eingangshalle *f;* (*in theater*) Foyer *nt*

vestige ['ves·tɪdʒ] *n* ① (*trace*) Spur *f;* (*remainder*) Überrest *m* ② (*fig*) **there's not a ~ of truth in what she says** es ist kein Körnchen Wahrheit an dem, was sie sagt; **to remove the last ~ of doubt** den letzten Rest Zweifel ausräumen

vestments ['vest·mənts] *npl* Messgewand *nt;* (*for special occasion*) Ornat *m geh*

vestry ['ves·tri] *n* Sakristei *f*

vet[1] [vet] **I.** *n* Tierarzt, Tierärztin *m, f* **II.** *vt* <-tt-> ① MED (*screen*) untersuchen ② (*examine*) überprüfen

vet[2] [vet] *n* (*fam*) *short for* **veteran** Veteran(in) *m(f)*

veteran ['vet̬·ər·ən] **I.** *n* ① (*expert*) Veteran(in) *m(f) hum,* alter Hase *hum* ② (*ex-military*) Veteran(in) *m(f)* **II.** *adj attr, inv* (*experienced*) erfahren; (*of many years*) langjährig

> Der **Veteran's Day** am 11. November wurde eigentlich als Andenken an den Waffenstillstand zwischen Deutschland und den Alliierten 1918 eingeführt. An diesem staatlichen Feiertag werden alle Veteranen aus amerikanischen Kriegen geehrt und es wird der Kriegsopfer gedacht.

veterinarian [ˌvet·ər·ə·'ner·i·ən] *n* Tierarzt,

Tierärztin *m, f*

veterinary ['vet·ər·ə·ner·i] *adj attr, inv* tierärztlich; ~ **medicine** Tiermedizin *f*

veto ['vi·t̬oʊ] **I.** *n* <*pl* -es> ① (*nullification*) Veto *nt;* **presidential** ~ Veto *nt* des Präsidenten ② (*right of refusal*) Vetorecht *nt;* **to have the power of** ~ das Vetorecht haben **II.** *vt* ① (*refuse*) ein Veto einlegen (gegen +*akk*) ② (*forbid*) untersagen

vex [veks] *vt* verärgern

VHF [ˌvi·eɪtʃ·'ef] **I.** *n abbrev of* **very high frequency** UKW *f* **II.** *adj attr abbrev of* **very high frequency** UKW-

via ['vaɪ·ə] *prep* ① (*through*) über ② (*using*) per, via

viability [ˌvaɪ·ə·'bɪl·ə·t̬i] *n* ① BIOL Lebensfähigkeit *f* ② *of business* Rentabilität *f* ③ (*feasibility*) Realisierbarkeit *f*

viable ['vaɪ·ə·bəl] *adj* ① (*successful*) existenzfähig; *company* rentabel ② (*feasible*) machbar; *alternative* durchführbar ③ BIOL (*able to live*) lebensfähig; (*able to reproduce*) zeugungsfähig

viaduct ['vaɪ·ə·dʌkt] *n* Viadukt *m o nt;* (*bridge*) Brücke *f*

vibe [vaɪb] *n usu pl* (*sl: atmosphere*) Schwingungen *pl;* (*general feeling*) Klima *nt*

vibes [vaɪbz] *npl* (*fam*) *see* **vibraphone**

vibrant ['vaɪ·brənt] *adj* ① *person* lebhaft; (*dynamic*) dynamisch ② *atmosphere, place* lebendig ③ ECON ~ **economy** boomende Wirtschaft ④ *color* leuchtend

vibraphone ['vaɪ·brə·foʊn] *n* Vibraphon *nt*

vibrate ['vaɪ·breɪt] **I.** *vi* ① (*pulsate*) vibrieren ② *sound* nachklingen **II.** *vt* vibrieren lassen; MUS zum Schwingen bringen

vibration [vaɪ·'breɪ·ʃən] *n* Vibration *f; of earthquake* Erschütterung *f;* PHYS Schwingung *f*

vibrator ['vaɪ·breɪ·t̬ər] *n* Vibrator *m*

vicar ['vɪk·ər] *n* Pfarrer *m*

vicarious [vɪ·'ker·i·əs] *adj* nachempfunden; *pleasure* indirekt; ~ **satisfaction** Ersatzbefriedigung *f;* **to get a ~ thrill out of sth** sich an etw *dat* aufgeilen *sl*

vice¹ [vaɪs] *n* ① (*weakness*) Laster *nt* ② (*behavior*) Lasterhaftigkeit *f*

vice² [vaɪs] *n see* **vise**

vice 'chairman *n* stellvertretende(r) Vorsitzende(r)

Vice 'President, vice 'president *n* Vizepräsident(in) *m(f)*

'vice squad *n* Sittendezernat *nt*

vice versa [ˌvaɪ·sə·'vɜr·sə] *adv inv* umgekehrt

vicinity [və·'sɪn·ə·t̬i] *n* Nähe *f;* (*surroundings*) Umgebung *f;* ■ **in the ~ [of sth]** in der Nähe [einer S. *gen*]; (*fig*) **the team paid in the ~ of 3 million dollars for him** die Mannschaft hat um die 3 Millionen Dollar für ihn gezahlt

vicious ['vɪʃ·əs] *adj* ① (*malicious*) boshaft, gemein; *attack* heimtückisch; *crime, murder* grauenhaft; *dog* bissig; *fighting* brutal; *gossip* gehässig ② (*causing pain*) grausam ③ (*nasty*) gemein

vicious 'circle, vicious 'cycle *n* Teufelskreis *m;* **to be caught in a ~** in einen Teufelskreis geraten sein

victim ['vɪk·tɪm] *n* ① (*harmed*) Opfer *nt;* **to fall ~ to sb/sth** jdm/etw zum Opfer fallen ② (*sufferer*) **cancer** ~ Krebskranke(r) *f(m)* ③ (*fig*) **to fall ~ to sb's charms** jds Charme *m* erliegen; **to be a ~ of fortune** dem Schicksal ausgeliefert sein

victimize ['vɪk·tə·maɪz] *vt* ungerecht behandeln; (*pick at*) schikanieren

victor ['vɪk·tər] *n* Sieger(in) *m(f);* **to be the ~ in sth** in etw *dat* siegen

Victorian [vɪk·'tɔr·i·ən] **I.** *adj* ① (*era*) viktorianisch ② (*prudish*) prüde **II.** *n* Viktorianer(in) *m(f)*

victorious [vɪk·'tɔr·i·əs] *adj* siegreich; **to emerge ~** als Sieger/Siegerin hervorgehen

victory ['vɪk·tə·ri] *n* Sieg *m* (**against** über +*akk*); **to win a ~ [in sth]** [bei etw *dat*] einen Sieg erringen

video ['vɪd·i·oʊ] *n* ① (*recording*) Video *nt* ② (*tape*) Videokassette *f* ③ (*material*) Videoaufnahme *f*

'video camera *n* Videokamera *f*

'videocassette *n* Videokassette *f*

videocas'sette recorder, VCR *n* Videorekorder *m*

'videoconference *n* Videokonferenz *f*

'video game *n* Videospiel *nt*

'videophone *n* Bildtelefon *nt*

'video recorder *n* Videorekorder *m*

'videotape I. *n* ① (*cassette*) Videokassette *f* ② (*tape*) Videoband *nt* ③ (*material*) Videoaufnahme *f* **II.** *vt* auf Video aufnehmen

vie <-y-> [vaɪ] *vi* wetteifern (**with** mit +*dat,* **for** um +*akk*); (*in commerce, business*) konkurrieren

Vienna [vi·'en·ə] *n* Wien *nt*

Viennese [ˌvi·ə·'niz] **I.** *n* <*pl* -> Wiener(in) *m(f)* **II.** *adj* Wiener-, wienerisch

Vietcong <*pl* -> [ˌvi·et·'kaŋ] *n* Vietkong *m*

Vietnam [ˌvi·et·'nam] *n* Vietnam *nt*

Vietnamese [vi·ˌet·nə·'miz] **I.** *adj* vietnamesisch **II.** *n* ① (*language*) Vietnamesisch *nt* ② (*person*) Vietnamese, -mesin *m, f*

view [vju] **I.** *n* ① (*sight*) Sicht *f;* **in full ~ of all the spectators** vor den Augen aller Zuschauer; **to come into ~** sichtbar werden; **to hide from ~** sich dem Blick entziehen; **to be on ~** *artwork* ausgestellt werden ② (*panorama*) [Aus]blick *m;* **he paints rural ~s** er malt ländliche Motive; **he lifted his daughter up so that she could get a better ~** er hob seine Tochter hoch, so dass sie besser sehen konnte ③ (*inspection*) Besichtigung *f* ④ (*opinion*) Ansicht *f,* Meinung *f* (**about/on** über +*akk*); **it's my ~ that the price is much too high** meiner Meinung nach ist der Preis viel zu hoch; **point of ~** Standpunkt *m;* **from my point of ~ ...** meiner Meinung nach ...; ■ **in sb's ~** jds Ansicht *f* nach ⑤ (*perspective*) Ansicht *f;* **from the money/work point of ~ ...** vom Finanziellen her/von der Arbeit her ...; ■ **in ~**

of sth angesichts einer S. *gen;* ■**with a ~ to doing sth** mit der Absicht, etw zu tun **II.** *vt* ❶ (*watch*) ■**to ~ sb/sth [from sth]** etw [von jdm/etw aus] betrachten; *spectator* etw *dat* [von etw *dat* aus] zusehen [*o bes* SÜDD, ÖSTERR, SCHWEIZ zuschauen] ❷ (*consider*) ■**to ~ sb/sth [as sb/sth]** jdn/etw [als jdn/etw] betrachten; **we ~ the situation with concern** wir betrachten die Lage mit Besorgnis; **to ~ sth from a different angle** etw aus einem anderen Blickwinkel betrachten ❸ (*inspect*) ■**to ~ sth** sich *dat* etw ansehen

viewer ['vju·ər] *n* ❶ (*person*) [Fernseh]zuschauer(in) *m(f)* ❷ (*for film*) Filmbetrachter *m;* (*for slides*) Diabetrachter *m*

'**viewfinder** *n* PHOT [Bild]sucher *m*

viewing ['vju·ɪŋ] *n* ❶ (*inspection*) Besichtigung *f* ❷ FILM Anschauen *nt;* TV Fernsehen *nt*

'**viewpoint** *n* ❶ (*opinion*) Standpunkt *m;* (*aspect*) Gesichtspunkt *m* ❷ (*place*) Aussichtspunkt *m*

vigil ['vɪdʒ·əl] *n* [Nacht]wache *f;* **to hold a ~** Nachtwache halten

vigilance ['vɪdʒ·ɪ·ləns] *n* Wachsamkeit *f*

vigilant ['vɪdʒ·ɪ·lənt] *adj* wachsam; **to be ~ about/for sth** auf etw *akk* achten

vigor ['vɪg·ər] *n* ❶ (*liveliness*) Energie *f,* [Tat]kraft *f;* (*vitality*) Vitalität *f;* **with ~** mit vollem Eifer ❷ (*forcefulness*) Ausdruckskraft *f*

vigorous ['vɪg·ər·əs] *adj* ❶ (*strong*) kräftig, kraftvoll; *health* robust ❷ (*intensive*) intensiv; *walk* stramm ❸ (*passionate*) leidenschaftlich; *criticism, protest* heftig; *attempt, denial* energisch; *speech* feurig, schwungvoll

vile [vaɪl] *adj* ❶ (*wicked*) gemein, niederträchtig ❷ (*unpleasant*) abscheulich

village ['vɪl·ɪdʒ] **I.** *n* ❶ (*settlement*) Dorf *nt* ❷ (*populace*) Dorfbevölkerung *f* **II.** *adj* Dorf-

villager ['vɪl·ə·dʒər] *n* Dorfbewohner(in) *m(f)*

villain ['vɪl·ən] *n* ❶ (*lawbreaker*) Verbrecher(in) *m(f)* ❷ (*rogue*) Schurke *m;* (*in novel, film*) Bösewicht *m*

villainous ['vɪl·ə·nəs] *adj* schurkisch; (*mean*) gemein; *deed* niederträchtig

villainy ['vɪl·ə·ni] *n* Schurkerei *f;* (*meanness*) Gemeinheit *f*

VIN ['vi·'aɪ·'en] *n* AUTO *acr for* **vehicle identification number** Kfz-Kennzeichen *nt,* Kraftfahrzeugkennzeichen *nt*

vinaigrette [ˌvɪn·ə·'gret] *n* Vinaigrette *f*

vindicate ['vɪn·də·keɪt] *vt* ❶ (*justify*) *thing* rechtfertigen; *person* verteidigen ❷ (*support*) *theory* bestätigen ❸ (*exonerate*) *person* rehabilitieren

vindication [ˌvɪn·də·'keɪ·ʃən] *n* ❶ (*justification*) Rechtfertigung *f;* **in ~ of sth** zur Rechtfertigung einer S. *gen* ❷ (*exoneration*) Rehabilitierung *f*

vindictive [vɪn·'dɪk·tɪv] *adj* nachtragend; (*vengeful*) rachsüchtig

vine [vaɪn] *n* ❶ (*of grape*) Weinrebe *f* ❷ (*creeper*) Rankengewächs *nt*

vinegar ['vɪn·ə·gər] *n* Essig *m*

vinegary ['vɪ·nɪ·gə·ri] *adj* ❶ (*sour*) sauer ❷ (*with vinegar*) Essig-

vineyard ['vɪn·jərd] *n* Weinberg *m;* (*area*) Weinanbaugebiet *nt*

vintage ['vɪn·tɪdʒ] **I.** *n* ❶ (*wine*) Jahrgangswein *m* ❷ (*year*) Jahrgang *m* **II.** *adj inv* ❶ Jahrgangs- ❷ (*classic*) erlesen; **this film is ~ Disney** dieser Film ist ein Disneyklassiker ❸ AUTO Oldtimer-; **~ car** Oldtimer *m*

vinyl ['vaɪ·nəl] **I.** *n* (*material, record*) Vinyl *nt* **II.** *adj* ❶ Vinyl- ❷ CHEM Vinyl-, Äthenyl-

viola [vi·'oʊ·lə] *n* MUS Viola *f,* Bratsche *f*

violate ['vaɪ·ə·leɪt] *vt* ❶ (*breach*) brechen; *regulation* verletzen; **to ~ a law/rule** gegen ein Gesetz/eine Regel verstoßen ❷ (*enter*) ■**to ~ sth** in etw *akk* eindringen ❸ (*disrespect*) **to ~ sb's rights** jds Rechte *pl* verletzen

violation [ˌvaɪ·ə·'leɪ·ʃən] *n* Verletzung *f,* Verstoß *m;* *of holy places* Entweihung *f*

violence ['vaɪ·ə·ləns] *n* ❶ (*behavior*) Gewalt *f* (**against** gegen *+akk*); **act of ~** Gewalttat *f* ❷ (*force*) Heftigkeit *f*

violent ['vaɪ·ə·lənt] *adj* ❶ (*brutal*) gewalttätig; *person a.* brutal; *death* gewaltsam; **~ crime** Gewaltverbrechen *nt* ❷ (*strong*) heftig; *color* grell; *argument* heftig; **to have a ~ temper** jähzornig sein

violet ['vaɪ·ə·lɪt] **I.** *n* ❶ (*color*) Violett *nt* ❷ BIOL Veilchen *nt* **II.** *adj* violett

violin [ˌvaɪ·ə·'lɪn] *n* Violine *f,* Geige *f*

violinist [ˌvaɪ·ə·'lɪn·ɪst] *n* Violinist(in) *m(f),* Geiger(in) *m(f)*

V.I.P., VIP [ˌvi·aɪ·'pi] **I.** *n abbrev of* **very important person** Promi *m fam* **II.** *adj attr abbrev of* **very important person** VIP-

viper ['vaɪ·pər] *n* Viper *f*

virgin ['vɜr·dʒɪn] **I.** *n* ❶ Jungfrau *f* ❷ (*novice*) unbeschriebenes Blatt *fam* **II.** *adj inv, attr* ❶ (*chaste*) jungfräulich ❷ (*fig: unexplored*) jungfräulich, unerforscht; **~ territory** Neuland *nt*

virginal ['vɜr·dʒɪ·nəl] *adj* jungfräulich

Virginia [vər·'dʒɪn·jə] *n* Virginia *nt*

Virgin 'Islands *npl* ■**the ~** die Jungferninseln *pl*

virginity [vər·'dʒɪn·ə·t̬i] *n* Jungfräulichkeit *f*

Virgo ['vɜr·goʊ] *n no art* ASTROL Jungfrau *f*

virile ['vɪr·əl] *adj* potent; (*masculine*) männlich

virility [və·'rɪl·ə·t̬i] *n* Potenz *f;* (*masculinity*) Männlichkeit *f*

virology [vaɪ·'ral·ə·dʒi] *n* Virologie *f*

virtual ['vɜr·tʃu·əl] *adj inv* ❶ (*almost*) so gut wie, quasi; **to be a ~ unknown** praktisch unbekannt sein ❷ COMPUT, PHYS virtuell

virtually ['vɜr·tʃu·ə·li] *adv inv* ❶ (*almost*) praktisch, eigentlich, so gut wie ❷ COMPUT virtuell

virtual re'ality *n* virtuelle Realität

virtue ['vɜr·tʃu] *n* ❶ (*quality*) Tugend *f* ❷ (*morality*) Tugendhaftigkeit *f* ❸ (*advantage*) Vorteil *m* ❹ (*benefit*) Nutzen *m* ❺ (*form: because of*) ■**by ~ of sth** wegen einer S. *gen*

virtuoso [ˌvɜr·tʃu·'oʊ·soʊ, *pl* -si] **I.** *n* <*pl* -s *or* -si> Virtuose, -in *m, f* **II.** *adj* virtuos

V

virtuous ['vɜr·tʃu·əs] *adj* ❶ (*good*) tugendhaft; (*upright*) rechtschaffen ❷ (*better*) moralisch überlegen; (*self-complacent*) selbstgerecht

virulent ['vɪr·jə·lənt] *adj* virulent *fachspr; poison* stark; (*fig*) *critic* scharf

virus ['vaɪ·rəs] *n* <*pl* **-es**> ❶ MED Virus *nt o fam m* ❷ COMPUT Virus *m*

visa ['vi·zə] *n* Visum *nt*

vis-à-vis [ˌvi·zə·'vi] *prep* ❶ (*concerning*) bezüglich *+gen,* wegen *+gen* ❷ (*compared with*) gegenüber *+dat*

viscose ['vɪs·koʊs] *n* Viskose *f*

viscosity [vɪ·'skas·ə·t̬i] *n* Zähflüssigkeit *f*

viscous ['vɪs·kəs] *adj* zähflüssig

vise [vaɪs] *n* Schraubstock *m*

visibility [ˌvɪz·ə·'bɪl·ə·t̬i] *n* ❶ (*view*) Sichtweite *f;* **poor ~** schlechte Sicht ❷ (*being seen*) Sichtbarkeit *f*

visible ['vɪz·ə·bəl] *adj* ❶ sichtbar; **to be barely ~** kaum zu sehen sein; **clearly ~** deutlich sichtbar ❷ (*fig*) sichtbar; (*imminent*) deutlich

vision ['vɪʒ·ən] *n* ❶ (*sight*) Sehvermögen *nt;* **to have blurred ~** verschwommen sehen ❷ (*mental image*) Vorstellung *f;* **~ of the future** Zukunftsvision *f* ❸ (*supernatural*) Vision *f* ❹ (*forethought*) Weitblick *m*

visionary ['vɪʒ·ə·ner·i] **I.** *adj* ❶ (*unrealistic*) unrealistisch; (*imagined*) eingebildet ❷ (*future-oriented*) visionär *geh* **II.** *n* Visionär(in) *m(f) geh*

visit ['vɪz·ɪt] **I.** *n* ❶ Besuch *m;* **to have a ~ from sb** von jdm besucht werden; **to pay a ~ to sb** jdn besuchen; (*consult*) jdn aufsuchen ❷ (*fam: chat*) Plauderei *f* **II.** *vt* ❶ besuchen ❷ (*consult*) aufsuchen **III.** *vi* ❶ einen Besuch machen; ■ **to ~ with sb** sich mit jdm treffen ❷ (*fam: chat*) ein Schwätzchen halten

visitation [ˌvɪz·ə·'teɪ·ʃən] *n* ❶ Besuch *m* ❷ (*official*) offizieller Besuch ❸ (*for child*) ≈ Besuchszeit *f;* (*right to see child*) Besuchsrecht *nt* ❹ (*supernatural*) Erscheinung *f*

'visiting hours *npl* Besuchszeiten *pl*

visiting pro'fessor *n* Gastprofessor(in) *m(f)*

visitor ['vɪz·ɪ·t̬ər] *n* Besucher(in) *m(f);* (*at hotel*) Gast *m*

visor ['vaɪ·zər] *n* ❶ (*of helmet*) Visier *nt* ❷ (*of cap*) Schild *nt* ❸ AUTO Sonnenblende *f*

vista ['vɪs·tə] *n* Aussicht *f,* Blick *m*

visual ['vɪʒ·u·əl] **I.** *adj* visuell, Seh-; **~ imagery** Bildersymbolik *f* **II.** *n* ■ **~s** *pl* Bildmaterial *nt*

visual 'aid *n* Anschauungsmaterial *nt*

visualize ['vɪʒ·u·ə·laɪz] *vt* ■ **to ~ sth** ❶ (*imagine*) sich *dat* etw vorstellen; (*out of the past*) sich *dat* etw vergegenwärtigen ❷ (*foresee*) etw erwarten

vital ['vaɪ·t̬əl] *adj* ❶ (*essential*) unerlässlich; (*stronger*) lebensnotwendig; **to play a ~ part** eine entscheidende Rolle spielen; **to be of ~ importance** von entscheidender Bedeutung sein ❷ (*energetic*) vital, lebendig

vitality [vaɪ·'tæl·ə·t̬i] *n* ❶ (*energy*) Vitalität *f* ❷ (*durability*) Dauerhaftigkeit *f*

vitalize ['vaɪ·t̬ə·laɪz] *vt* beleben

vital 'signs *n pl* MED Lebenszeichen *pl*

vitamin ['vaɪ·t̬ə·mɪn] *n* Vitamin *nt*

'vitamin deficiency *n* Vitaminmangel *m*

'vitamin pills *npl* Vitamintabletten *pl*

vitreous ['vɪt·ri·əs] *adj attr* Glas-

vitriol ['vɪt·ri·əl] *n* Schärfe *f*

vitriolic [ˌvɪt·ri·'al·ɪk] *adj criticism* scharf; *remark* beißend

vittles ['vɪt̬·əls] *n pl* (*hum*) Lebensmittel *pl*

vivacious [vɪ·'veɪ·ʃəs] *adj* (*lively*) lebhaft; (*cheerful*) munter

vivacity [vɪ·'væs·ə·t̬i] *n* Lebhaftigkeit *f;* (*cheerfulness*) Munterkeit *f*

vivid ['vɪv·ɪd] *adj* ❶ (*graphic*) anschaulich, lebendig; *memories* lebhaft ❷ *colors* kräftig

vixen ['vɪk·sən] *n* Füchsin *f*

vocabulary [voʊ·'kæb·jə·ler·i] *n* Vokabular *nt,* Wortschatz *m;* (*words*) Vokabeln *pl;* (*glossary*) Wörterverzeichnis *nt*

vocal ['voʊ·kəl] **I.** *adj* ❶ *inv* stimmlich; *communication* mündlich ❷ (*outspoken*) laut; *minority* lautstark; ■ **to be ~** sich freimütig äußern ❸ (*communicative*) gesprächig **II.** *n* MUS Vokalpartie *f fachspr*

'vocal cords *n pl* Stimmbänder *pl*

vocalist ['voʊ·kə·lɪst] *n* Sänger(in) *m(f)*

vocalize ['voʊ·kə·laɪz] *vt* LING ❶ (*utter*) in Töne umsetzen ❷ (*express*) aussprechen; *thoughts, ideas* in Worte fassen

vocation [voʊ·'keɪ·ʃən] *n* ❶ (*calling*) Berufung *f* ❷ (*trade*) Beruf *m*

vocational [voʊ·'keɪ·ʃə·nəl] *adj inv* beruflich; **~ training** Berufsausbildung *f*

vociferous [voʊ·'sɪf·ər·əs] *adj* lautstark; (*impetuous*) vehement

vodka ['vad·kə] *n* Wodka *m*

vogue [voʊg] *n* Mode *f;* **to be back in ~** wieder Mode sein

voice [vɔɪs] **I.** *n* ❶ Stimme *f;* **at the top of one's ~** in voller Lautstärke; **inner ~** innere Stimme; **sb's ~ is breaking** jd ist im Stimmbruch; **to keep one's ~ down** leise sprechen; **to raise one's ~** seine Stimme erheben ❷ (*ability*) Artikulationsfähigkeit *f geh* ❸ (*opinion*) Stimme *f;* **to make one's ~ heard** sich *dat* Gehör verschaffen ❹ (*expression*) **to give ~ to sth** etw zum Ausdruck bringen ❺ (*agency*) Stimme *f;* **to give sb a ~** jdm ein Mitspracherecht einräumen **II.** *vt* zum Ausdruck bringen; *complaint* vorbringen; *desire* aussprechen

'voice box *n* Kehlkopf *m*

voiceless ['vɔɪs·lɪs] *adj inv* stumm *a. fig;* (*powerless*) ohne Mitspracherecht *nach n*

'voice mail *n* ❶ (*system*) Voicemail *f,* Sprachspeichersystem *nt* ❷ (*message*) Voicemail[-Nachricht] *f*

'voice-over *n* TV, FILM Offkommentar *m fachspr*

void [vɔɪd] **I.** *n* (*empty space*) Leere *f kein pl a. fig;* (*in building*) Hohlraum *m;* ■ **into the ~** ins Leere ▶PHRASES: **to fill a** [*or* **the**] **~** die innere Leere ausfüllen **II.** *adj inv* ❶ (*invalid*)

nichtig ② (*form*) *office* frei ③ *action, speech* nutzlos; **to render sth ~** etw zunichtemachen **III.** *vt* (*annul*) aufheben
voip [vɔɪp] *vt, vi abbrev of* **Voice over Internet Protocol** INET voipen
vol. *n abbrev of* **volume** (*book*) Bd.; (*measure*) vol.
volatile ['val·ə·t̬əl] *adj* ① (*changeable*) unbeständig; (*unstable*) instabil ② (*explosive*) *situation* explosiv ③ CHEM flüchtig
volcanic [val·'kæn·ɪk] *adj inv* vulkanisch, Vulkan- *m*
volcano <*pl* -es *or* -s> [val·'keɪ·noʊ] *n* Vulkan *m a. fig*
volition [voʊ·'lɪʃ·ən] *n* Wille *m;* **of one's own ~** aus freien Stücken
volley ['val·i] **I.** *n* ① (*salvo*) Salve *f* ② (*onslaught*) Flut *f* ③ SPORTS (*in tennis*) Volley *m fachspr* **II.** *vi* SPORTS (*in tennis*) einen Volley schlagen *fachspr* **III.** *vt* ① SPORTS *ball* volley nehmen *fachspr* ② (*let fly*) *questions* loslassen
volleyball ['val·i·bɔl] *n* Volleyball *m*
volt [voʊlt] *n* Volt *nt*
voltage ['voʊl·tɪdʒ] *n* Spannung *f;* **high ~** Hochspannung *f*
voluble ['val·jə·bəl] *adj* ① (*fluent*) redegewandt ② (*talkative*) redselig
volume ['val·jum] *n* ① (*space*) Volumen *nt* ② (*amount*) Umfang *m* ③ (*sound*) Lautstärke *f* ④ (*book*) Band *m*
'volume control *n* Lautstärkeregler *m*
voluminous [və·'lu·mə·nəs] *adj clothing* weit [geschnitten]; *account* umfangreich; *writer* produktiv
voluntary ['val·ən·ter·i] *adj inv* freiwillig; **~ work** ehrenamtliche Tätigkeit
voluntary organi'zation *n* Freiwilligenorganisation *f*
voluntary re'tirement *n* freiwilliges Ausscheiden in den Ruhestand
volunteer [ˌval·ən·'tɪr] **I.** *n* ① (*worker*) ehrenamtlicher Mitarbeiter/ehrenamtliche Mitarbeiterin ② (*helper*) Freiwillige(r) *f(m)* **II.** *vt information* bereitwillig geben; *one's services* anbieten; ■**to ~ oneself for sth** sich freiwillig zu etw *dat* melden **III.** *vi* ① (*offer*) ■**to ~ to do sth** sich [freiwillig] anbieten, etw zu tun ② (*join*) **to ~ for the army** sich freiwillig zur Armee melden **IV.** *adj* ehrenamtlich
voluptuous [və·'lʌp·tʃu·əs] *adj* üppig; *woman a.* kurvenreich; *lips* sinnlich; (*sumptuous*) verschwenderisch
vomit ['vam·ɪt] **I.** *vi* [sich] erbrechen **II.** *vt* ■**to ~ [up ↔] sth** etw erbrechen **III.** *n* Erbrochene(s) *nt*
voodoo ['vu·du] *n* ① (*cult*) Voodoo *m* ② (*fam: jinx*) Hexerei *f;* (*spell*) Zauber *m*
voracious [vɔ·'reɪ·ʃəs] *adj* gefräßig; (*fig*) gierig
vortex <*pl* -es *or* -tices> ['vɔr·teks, *pl* -t̬ɪ·siz] *n* ① (*wind*) Wirbel *m* ② (*water*) Strudel *m*
vote [voʊt] **I.** *n* ① (*choice*) Stimme *f;* **to cast one's ~** seine Stimme abgeben ② (*election*) Abstimmung *f;* **to hold a ~** eine Abstimmung durchführen ③ (*right*) ■**the ~** das Wahlrecht **II.** *vi* ① (*elect*) wählen; **to ~ in an election** zu einer Wahl gehen; ■**to ~ against/for sb/sth** gegen/für jdn/etw stimmen ② (*choose*) ■**to ~ to do sth** dafür stimmen, etw zu tun ③ (*decide*) abstimmen (**on** über +*akk*) **III.** *vt* ① (*elect*) **to ~ sb into office** jdn ins Amt wählen; **to ~ sb out [of office]** jdn [aus dem Amt] abwählen ② (*propose*) ■**to ~ that ...** vorschlagen, dass ... ③ (*declare*) **she was ~d the winner** sie wurde zur Siegerin erklärt
◆**vote down** *vt* niederstimmen
voter ['voʊ·t̬ər] *n* Wähler(in) *m(f)*
voter regis'tration *n* Eintragung *f* ins Wählerverzeichnis
'voter turnout *n* Wahlbeteiligung *f*
voting ['voʊ·t̬ɪŋ] **I.** *adj attr, inv* wahlberechtigt **II.** *n* Wählen *nt*
'voting booth *n* Wahlkabine *f*
'voting machine *n* Wahlmaschine *f*
vouch [vaʊtʃ] *vi* ■**to ~ for sb/sth** sich für jdn/etw verbürgen
voucher ['vaʊ·tʃər] *n* Gutschein *m;* **school ~** *öffentliche Mittel, die in Amerika bereitgestellt werden, damit Eltern ihre Kinder in Privatschulen schicken können*
vow [vaʊ] **I.** *vt* geloben *geh* **II.** *n* Versprechen *nt;* **to take a ~** ein Gelübde ablegen *geh;* **to take a ~ to do sth** geloben, etw zu tun *geh;* ■**~s** *pl* (*of marriage*) Eheversprechen *nt;* (*of religious order*) Gelübde *nt geh*
vowel ['vaʊ·əl] *n* Vokal *m,* Selbstlaut *m*
voyage ['vɔɪ·ɪdʒ] *n* Reise *f;* (*by sea*) Seereise *f;* **~ of discovery** Entdeckungsreise *f a. fig*
voyager ['vɔɪ·ɪ·dʒər] *n* Reisende(r) *f(m);* (*by sea*) Seereisende(r) *f(m);* (*in space*) Raumfahrer(in) *m(f)*
voyeur [vɔɪ·'jɜr] *n* Voyeur(in) *m(f)*
VP [ˌvi·'pi] *n abbrev of* **vice president** Vizepräsident(in) *m(f)*
vs. *prep abbrev of* **versus** vs.
VT, Vt. *abbrev of* **Vermont**
vulcanization [ˌvʌl·kə·nɪ·'zeɪ·ʃən] *n* Vulkanisierung *f*
vulcanize ['vʌl·kə·naɪz] *vt* vulkanisieren
vulgar ['vʌl·gər] *adj* ordinär, vulgär; (*bad taste*) abgeschmackt
vulgarity [vʌl·'gær·ə·t̬i] *n* Vulgarität *f geh;* (*bad taste*) Geschmacklosigkeit *f*
vulnerable ['vʌl·nər·ə·bəl] *adj* verletzlich; ■**to be ~ to sth** anfällig für etw *akk* sein; **to be ~ to criticism** Kritik ausgesetzt sein; **to be in a ~ position** in einer prekären Lage sein; **~ spot** schwache Stelle; **to feel ~** sich verwundbar fühlen
vulture ['vʌl·tʃər] *n* Geier *m a. fig*

Ww

W <*pl* -'s *or* -s>, **w** <*pl* -'s> ['dʌb·əl·ju] *n* W *nt*, w *nt*; ~ **as in Whiskey** W wie Wilhelm

W[1] **I.** *adj inv* ① *abbrev of* **West** W- ② *abbrev of* **western I. II.** *n abbrev of* **West** W

W[2] <*pl* -> *n abbrev of* **Watt** W

WA *abbrev of* **Washington**

wacko ['wæk·oʊ] *n* (*sl or pej: person*) Querkopf *m*

wacky ['wæk·i] *adj* (*fam*) *person, idea* verrückt

wad [wad] *n* ① (*mass*) Knäuel *nt*; (*for stuffing*) Pfropfen *m*; *of cotton* Wattebausch *m* ② (*fam: bundle*) Bündel *nt*; ~[**s** *pl*] **of money** schöne Stange Geld *fam*

waddle ['wad·əl] *vi* watscheln

wade [weɪd] *vi* ① waten; **to ~ into the sea** in das Meer hineinwaten ② (*fig: deal with*) ■ **to ~ through sth** sich durch etw *akk* durchkämpfen

wader ['weɪ·dər] *n* ① (*bird*) Watvogel *m* ② (*boots*) ■ **~s** *pl* Watstiefel *pl*

wafer ['weɪ·fər] *n* ① (*cookie, cracker*) Waffel *f*; (*thin*) Oblate *f* ② REL (*host*) Hostie *f*

wafer-'thin *adj, adv inv* hauchdünn

waffle[1] ['waf·əl] *n* (*food*) Waffel *f*

waffle[2] ['waf·əl] **I.** *vi* (*pej fam*) herumdrucksen *fam* **II.** *n* (*fam*) Geschwafel *nt pej fam*

'waffle iron *n* Waffeleisen *nt*

waft [waft] *vi* schweben; **to ~ through the air** *smell* durch die Luft ziehen; *sound, smoke* durch die Luft schweben

wag[1] [wæg] **I.** *vt* <-gg-> **to ~ its tail** mit dem Schwanz wedeln; **to ~ one's finger** mit dem Finger drohen **II.** *vi* <-gg-> wedeln **III.** *n* Wackeln *nt kein pl*; *of tail* Wedeln *nt kein pl*

wag[2] [wæg] *n* Witzbold *m fam*

wage [weɪdʒ] **I.** *n* Lohn *m*; **minimum ~** Mindestlohn *m* **II.** *vt* **to ~ war against sth/sb** gegen etw/jdn zu Felde ziehen; **to ~ war on sth** (*fig*) gegen etw *akk* vorgehen

'wage dumping *n* Lohndumping *nt*

'wage earner *n* Lohnempfänger(in) *m(f)*

'wage freeze *n* Lohnstopp *m*

wager ['weɪ·dʒər] (*form*) **I.** *n* ① (*bet*) Wette *f* ② (*stake*) [Wett]einsatz *m* **II.** *vt* ■ **to ~ that ...** wetten, dass ...

wagon ['wæg·ən] *n* (*cart*) Wagen *m*; (*wooden*) Karren

waif [weɪf] *n* (*child*) verwahrlostes Kind

wail [weɪl] **I.** *vi* jammern; *siren* heulen; *wind* pfeifen **II.** *n* Gejammer *nt kein pl*; *of sirens* Geheul *nt kein pl*

wailing ['weɪ·lɪŋ] *adj inv* jammernd; *sirens* heulend

'Wailing Wall *n* ■ **the ~** die Klagemauer

waist [weɪst] *n* Taille *f*; *of skirt, pants* Bund *m*

'waistband *n* Bund *m*

'waistcoat *n* Weste *f*

waist-'deep *inv* **I.** *adj* bis zur Taille *nach n* [reichend *attr*] **II.** *adv* bis zur Taille

'waistline *n* Taille *f*

wait [weɪt] **I.** *n* Warten *nt* (**for** auf +*akk*) ▶ PHRASES: **to <u>lie</u> in ~ [for sb]** [jdm] auflauern **II.** *vi* ① (*bide time*) warten (**for** auf +*akk*); **~ a minute!** Moment mal!; **I can't ~** ich kann's kaum erwarten ② (*be delayed*) warten **III.** *vt* (*serve*) **to ~ tables** bedienen, al Kellner/Kellnerin arbeiten ▶ PHRASES: **to ~ one's <u>turn</u>** warten, bis man an der Reihe ist

◆**wait around** *vi* warten

◆**wait behind** *vi* zurückbleiben

◆**wait on** *vt* ① (*serve*) ■ **to ~ on sb** jdn bedienen ② (*await*) ■ **to ~ on sth** auf etw warten

◆**wait up** *vi* ① (*not go to bed*) ■ **to ~ up for sb** wegen jdm aufbleiben ② (*wait*) ■ **~ up!** warte mal!

waiter ['weɪ·t̬ər] *n* Bedienung *f*, Kellner *m*; **~!** Herr Ober!

waiting ['weɪ·t̬ɪŋ] *n* die Warterei (**for** auf +*akk*)

'waiting list *n* Warteliste *f*

'waiting room *n* Wartezimmer *nt*

waitress <*pl* -es> ['weɪ·trɪs] *n* Kellnerin *f*, Bedienung *f*

waive [weɪv] *vt* verzichten (auf +*akk*); *fee* erlassen; *objection* fallen lassen; *right* verzichten (auf +*akk*)

waiver ['weɪ·vər] *n* Verzichterklärung *f*

wake[1] [weɪk] *n* NAUT Kielwasser *nt*; AEROSP Turbulenz *f*; ■ **in the ~ of sth** (*fig*) infolge einer S. *gen*

wake[2] [weɪk] *n* (*vigil*) Totenwache *f*

wake[3] <woke *or* waked, woken *or* waked> [weɪk] **I.** *vi* aufwachen **II.** *vt* aufwecken

◆**wake up I.** *vi* aufwachen *a. fig* **II.** *vt* aufwecken

wakeful ['weɪk·fəl] *adj* ① (*sleepless*) **to be ~** nicht schlafen können; **~ night** schlaflose Nacht ② (*vigilant*) wach[sam]

waken ['weɪ·kən] **I.** *vi* aufwachen **II.** *vt* [auf]wecken; **the noise ~ed me** der Lärm weckte mich [auf]

Wales [weɪlz] *n* Wales *nt*

walk [wɔk] **I.** *n* ① (*going*) Gehen *nt*; (*as recreation*) Spaziergang *m*; **to go for a ~** einen Spaziergang machen; **it's a five-minute ~** es sind fünf Minuten [zu Fuß] ② (*walkway*) Spazierweg *m*; (*path*) Wanderweg *m* ▶ PHRASES: **~ of <u>life</u>** soziale Schicht **II.** *vt* ① **to ~ the streets** (*wander*) durch die Straßen gehen; *prostitute* auf den Strich gehen *sl* ② (*accompany*) **to ~ sb home** jdn nach Hause bringen ③ *dog* ausführen **III.** *vi* ① (*go*) zu Fuß gehen ② (*for recreation*) spazieren gehen

◆**walk away** *vi* ① (*withdraw*) sich zurückziehen (**from** von +*dat*) ② (*fam: steal*) ■ **to ~ away with sth** etw mitgehen lassen *fam* ③ (*win*) ■ **to ~ away with sth** etw spielend

gewinnen
◆**walk in** *vi* hereinkommen
◆**walk in on** *vt* ■**to ~ in on sb/sth** bei jdm/etw hereinplatzen *fam*
◆**walk off I.** *vt* **to ~ off a meal** einen Verdauungsspaziergang machen **II.** *vi* ❶ (*leave*) weggehen ❷ (*fam: steal*) ■**to ~ off with sth** etw mitgehen lassen *fam* ❸ (*win*) ■**to ~ off with sth** etw spielend gewinnen
◆**walk out** *vi* ❶ (*leave*) gehen; ■**to ~ out on sb** jdn im Stich lassen; **to ~ out of a meeting** eine Sitzung [aus Protest] verlassen ❷ (*strike*) streiken
◆**walk over** *vt* (*fam*) **to ~ [all] over sb** jdn ausnutzen [*o bes* SÜDD, ÖSTERR ausnützen]
◆**walk through** *vt* ■**to ~ sb through sth** etw mit jdm durchgehen
walker ['wɔ·kər] *n* ❶ (*pedestrian*) Fußgänger(in) *m(f)*; (*for recreation*) Spaziergänger(in) *m(f)* ❷ (*athlete*) Geher(in) *m(f)* ❸ (*support*) Gehhilfe *f*
walkie-talkie [ˌwɔ·ki·'tɔ·ki] *n* [tragbares] Funksprechgerät, Walkie-Talkie *nt*
'**walk-in** *adj closet* begehbar; *clinic Klinik, für die keine Voranmeldung nötig ist*
walking ['wɔ·kɪŋ] **I.** *n* Gehen *nt*; (*as recreation*) Spazierengehen *nt* **II.** *adj attr, inv* ❶ Geh-; **within ~ distance** zu Fuß erreichbar ❷ (*human*) wandelnd; **to be a ~ encyclopedia** ein wandelndes Lexikon sein *hum fam*
'**walking shoes** *npl* Wanderschuhe *pl*
'**walking stick** *n* ❶ (*cane*) Spazierstock *m*; (*for elderly*) Stock *m*; (*for disabled*) Krücke *f* ❷ ZOOL (*insect*) Wandelnder Stab *m* (*nordamerikanische Stabheuschreckenart*)
Walkman® <*pl* -men *or* -s> ['wɔk·mən] *pl n* Walkman® *m*

> Der **Walk of Fame** befindet sich in Hollywood, der Weltkinohauptstadt. Es handelt sich um einen Gehweg, in den zu Ehren Prominenter, die eine Rolle für die Unterhaltungsindustrie gespielt haben, Sterne eingelassen sind.

'**walk-on** *adj attr, inv* THEAT, FILM **~ part** [*or* **role**] Statistenrolle *f*
'**walkout** *n* Arbeitsniederlegung *f*; **to stage a ~** aus Protest die Arbeit niederlegen
'**walkover** *n* leichter Sieg, Spaziergang *m fam*
'**walk-through** *n* Probe *f*
'**walkway** *n* [Fuß]weg *m*; **moving ~** Laufband *nt*
wall [wɔl] *n* ❶ Mauer *f*; (*in room*) Wand *f*; MED, ANAT Wand *f*; **the Great W~ of China** die Chinesische Mauer ❷ *of tire* Mantel *m* ▶ PHRASES: **to <u>drive</u> sb up the ~** jdn zur Weißglut treiben *fam*
◆**wall in** *vt usu passive* ummauern
◆**wall off** *vt usu passive* durch eine Mauer abtrennen
◆**wall up** *vt* ❶ (*imprison*) einmauern ❷ (*fill*) zumauern
'**wall chart** *n* Schautafel *f*
'**wall clock** *n* Wanduhr *f*
wallet ['wal·ɪt] *n* (*for money*) Brieftasche *f*; (*for documents*) Dokumentenmappe *f*
'**wallflower** *n* ❶ HORT Goldlack *m* ❷ (*shy person*) Mauerblümchen *nt*
'**wall hanging** *n* Wandteppich *m*
'**wall map** *n* Wandkarte *f*
Walloon [wa·'lun] *n* ❶ (*person*) Wallone, -in *m, f* ❷ (*language*) Wallonisch *nt*
wallop ['wal·əp] (*fam*) **I.** *vt* ❶ (*hit*) schlagen ❷ (*fig: win*) jdn haushoch besiegen **II.** *n* Schlag *m*
walloping ['wal·ə·pɪŋ] (*fam*) **I.** *adj attr, inv* (*big*) riesig **II.** *n usu sing* **to give sb a [good] ~** jdm eine [gehörige] Tracht Prügel verpassen
wallow ['wal·oʊ] *vi* ■**to ~ in sth** sich in etw *dat* wälzen; **to ~ in self-pity** in Selbstmitleid zerfließen
'**wallpaper I.** *n* Tapete *f*; **roll of ~** Tapetenrolle *f* **II.** *vt* tapezieren
'**Wall Street** *n* Wall Street *f*, Wallstreet *f*

> **Wall Street** heißt eine kurze, enge Straße in New York. Zusammen mit der Broad Street und der New Street bildet sie einen Bezirk, in dem sich das wichtigste Banken- und Wirtschaftszentrum der USA befindet. Der Name dieser Straße ist zum Synonym für die amerikanische Finanzwelt geworden.

wall-to-'wall *adj inv* ❶ **~ carpeting** Teppichboden *m* ❷ (*fig: constant*) ständig; **~ coverage** Berichterstattung *f* rund um die Uhr
walnut ['wɔl·nʌt] *n* ❶ (*nut*) Walnuss *f* ❷ (*tree*) Walnussbaum *m* ❸ (*wood*) Nussbaumholz *nt*
walrus <*pl* - *or* -es> ['wɔl·rəs] *n* Walross *nt*
waltz [wɔlts] **I.** *n* <*pl* -es> Walzer *m* **II.** *vi* Walzer tanzen
◆**waltz in** *vi* hereintanzen *fam*
◆**waltz off** *vi* abtanzen *fam*
wan <-nn-> [wan] *adj* fahl; *face* blass; *smile* matt
wand [wand] *n* Zauberstab *m*
wander ['wan·dər] **I.** *vt* **to ~ the streets** (*stroll*) durch die Straßen schlendern; (*be lost*) durch die Straßen irren **II.** *vi* ❶ (*lose concentration*) **my attention is ~ing** ich bin nicht bei der Sache ❷ (*become confused*) **her mind is beginning to ~** sie wird allmählich wirr [im Kopf *fam*]
wanderer ['wan·dər·ər] *n* Wandervogel *m hum veraltet*
wandering ['wan·dər·ɪŋ] *adj attr* ❶ *inv* (*nomadic*) wandernd; *minstrel* fahrend; *people, tribe* nomadisierend ❷ (*not concentrating*) abschweifend; (*rambling*) wirr
wanderings ['wan·dər·ɪŋz] *npl* (*travels*) Reisen *pl*; (*walks*) Streifzüge *pl*
wane [weɪn] **I.** *vi* abnehmen; *interest, popular-*

ity schwinden *geh; moon* abnehmen; **to wax and ~** zu- und abnehmen **II.** *n* **to be on the ~** *interest, popularity* [dahin]schwinden *geh*
wangle ['wæŋ·gəl] *vt* (*fam*) deichseln; **to ~ one's way into sth** sich in etw *akk* [hinein]mogeln; **to ~ one's way out of sth** sich aus etw *dat* herauswinden
wanna ['wa·nə] (*fam*) = **want to** *see* **want II.**
wannabe ['wa·nə·bi] **I.** *adj* (*pej fam*) Möchtegern- *iron fam;* **~ actress** Möchtegernschauspielerin *f iron fam* **II.** *n* (*pej fam*) Möchtegern *m*
want [want] **I.** *n* ① (*need*) Bedürfnis *nt;* **to be in ~ of sth** etw benötigen ② (*lack*) Mangel *m;* **for ~ of sth** aus Mangel an etw *dat* **II.** *vt* ① (*desire*) wünschen, wollen; (*politely*) mögen; **to be ~ed by the police** polizeilich gesucht werden; ■**to ~ to do sth** etw tun wollen; **what do you ~ to eat?** was möchtest/willst du essen? ② (*need*) brauchen; **you'll ~ a coat** du wirst einen Mantel brauchen ▶ PHRASES: **waste not, ~ not** (*prov*) spare in der Zeit, dann hast du in der Not *prov*
◆**want in** *vi* (*fam*) ■**to ~ in** [**on sth**] [bei etw *dat*] dabei sein wollen
◆**want out** *vi* (*fam*) ■**to ~ out** [**of sth**] [aus etw *dat*] aussteigen wollen
wanting ['wan·t̬ɪŋ] *adj pred* ① *inv* (*missing*) ■**to be ~** fehlen ② (*deficient*) unzulänglich
wanton ['wan·tən] *adj* leichtfertig; **~ destruction** mutwillige Zerstörung
WAP [wap] *n* INET *acr for* **Wireless Application Protocol** WAP *nt*
wapiti <*pl* - *or* -s> ['wap·ə·t̬i] *n* Wapiti *m*
war [wɔr] *n* ① (*hostilities*) Krieg *m;* **at ~** im Kriegszustand *a. fig;* **to declare ~ on sb/sth** jdm/etw den Krieg erklären; **to go to ~** in den Krieg ziehen ② (*conflict*) Krieg *m* ③ (*struggle*) Kampf *m;* **price ~** Preiskrieg *m*
'**war baby** *n* Kriegskind *nt*
warble ['wɔr·bəl] *vi bird* trillern; *person* trällern
warbler ['wɔr·blər] *n* Grasmücke *f*
'**war correspondent** *n* Kriegsberichterstatter(in) *m(f)*
'**war crime** *n* Kriegsverbrechen *nt*
'**war criminal** *n* Kriegsverbrecher(in) *m(f)*
'**war cry** *n* Schlachtruf *m*
ward [wɔrd] *n* ① (*hospital*) Station *f* ② POL Wahlbezirk *m*
◆**ward off** *vt* abwehren
warden ['wɔr·dən] *n* ① (*in prison*) Gefängnisdirektor(in) *m(f)* ② (*official*) **game ~** Jagdaufseher(in) *m(f)*
wardrobe ['wɔrd·roʊb] *n* ① (*armoire*) [Kleider]schrank *m* ② (*clothing*) Garderobe *f*
warehouse ['wer·haʊs] *n* Lagerhaus *nt*
wares [werz] *npl* Ware[n] *f[pl]*
warfare ['wɔr·fer] *n* Krieg[s]führung *f*
'**war game** *n* Kriegsspiel *nt*
warhead ['wɔr·hed] *n* Sprengkopf *m*
warily ['wer·ɪ·li] *adv* vorsichtig; (*suspiciously*) misstrauisch
warlike ['wɔr·laɪk] *adj* ① (*military*) kriegerisch ② (*hostile*) militant
'**warlord** *n* Kriegsherr *m*
warm [wɔrm] **I.** *adj* ① (*not cool*) warm ② (*hearty*) warm; *person* warmherzig; **welcome** herzlich **II.** *n* **to come into the ~** ins Warme kommen **III.** *vt* wärmen; *food* aufwärmen
◆**warm up I.** *vi* ① *engine* warm laufen ② (*limber up*) aufwärmen **II.** *vt engine* warm laufen lassen; *room* erwärmen; *food* aufwärmen
warm-'blooded *adj inv* warmblütig
'**warm front** *n* METEO Warmfront *f*
warm-'hearted *adj* warmherzig
warmly ['wɔrm·li] *adv* ① **to dress ~** sich warm anziehen ② (*heartily*) herzlich
warmth [wɔrmθ] *n* ① (*heat*) Wärme *f* ② (*affection*) Herzlichkeit *f*
'**warm-up** *n* [Sich]aufwärmen *nt kein pl*
warn [wɔrn] **I.** *vi* warnen (**of** vor +*dat*) **II.** *vt* warnen (**about** vor +*dat*); ■**to ~ sb not to do sth** jdn davor warnen, etw zu tun
warning ['wɔr·nɪŋ] *n* ① (*notice*) Warnung *f* ② (*threat*) Drohung *f* ③ *of danger, risk* Warnung *f* (**about, of, on** vor +*dat*); **a word of ~** ein guter Rat; **to issue a ~** [**about sth**] [vor etw *dat*] warnen
'**warning sign** *n* ① (*signboard*) Warnschild *nt* ② *usu pl* (*symptom*) Anzeichen *nt*
warp [wɔrp] **I.** *vi, vt* verziehen **II.** *n* ① (*in space*) **time ~** Zeitverwerfung *f* ② (*threads*) **~ and weft** Kette und Schuss
'**war paint** *n* (*a. fig fam*) Kriegsbemalung *f*
'**warpath** *n* **to be on the ~** auf dem Kriegspfad sein *hum*
warped [wɔrpt] *adj* ① (*bent*) verzogen ② (*perverted*) verschroben *pej*
warrant ['wɔr·ənt] **I.** *n* [Vollziehungs]befehl *m;* **search ~** Durchsuchungsbefehl *m* **II.** *vt* rechtfertigen
'**warrant officer** *n ranghöchster Unteroffizier*
warranty ['wɔr·ən·ti] *n* Garantie *f*
warren ['wɔr·ən] *n* ① (*burrows*) Kaninchenbau *m* ② (*maze*) Labyrinth *nt*
warring ['wɔr·ɪŋ] *adj attr, inv* **the ~ factions** die Krieg führenden Parteien
warrior ['wɔr·i·ər] *n* (*usu hist*) Krieger *m*
warship ['wɔr·ʃɪp] *n* Kriegsschiff *nt*
wart [wɔrt] *n* Warze *f* ▶ PHRASES: **~s and all** (*fam*) mit all seinen/ihren Fehlern und Schwächen
warthog ['wɔrt·hag] *n* Warzenschwein *nt*
'**wartime** *n* Kriegszeit[en] *f[pl]*
'**war-torn** *adj usu attr* vom Krieg erschüttert
wary ['wer·i] *adj* vorsichtig; ■**to be ~ of sb/sth** sich vor jdm/etw in Acht nehmen
'**war zone** *n* Kriegsgebiet *nt*
was [waz] *pt of* **be**
wash [waʃ] **I.** *n* <*pl* -es> ① *usu sing* (*cleaning*) Waschen *nt kein pl;* **to give sth/sb a** [**good**] **~** etw/jdn [gründlich] waschen ② (*clothes*) **to be in the ~** in der Wäsche sein ③ *usu sing*

(*layer*) [Farb]überzug *m* **II.** *vt* ❶ (*clean*) waschen; *dishes* abwaschen, spülen; *wound* spülen ❷ *usu passive* (*sweep*) **to be ~ed ashore** an Land gespült werden ▶PHRASES: **to ~ one's hands of sb/sth** mit jdm/etw nichts zu tun haben wollen **III.** *vi* sich waschen

◆**wash away** *vt* ❶ *sea* wegspülen ❷ (*clean*) auswaschen

◆**wash down** *vt* ❶ (*swallow*) hinunterspülen ❷ (*clean*) waschen ❸ *usu passive* (*carry off*) herabschwemmen

◆**wash off I.** *vi* sich abwaschen lassen **II.** *vt* abwaschen

◆**wash out I.** *vi* sich herauswaschen lassen **II.** *vt* ❶ (*clean*) auswaschen ❷ (*remove*) herauswaschen ❸ (*launder*) [aus]waschen

◆**wash over** *vi* ❶ (*flow over*) ■**to ~ over sb/sth** über jdn/etw [hinweg]spülen ❷ (*fig: overcome*) überkommen

◆**wash up I.** *vi* ❶ (*wash oneself*) sich waschen ❷ *usu passive* (*burn out*) ■**to be ~ed up** [völlig] ausgebrannt sein **II.** *vt sea* anspülen

Wash. *abbrev of* **Washington**

washable ['wɑʃ·ə·bəl] *adj inv garment* waschbar; *surface* abwaschbar; **machine-~** waschmaschinenfest

wash-and-'wear *adj inv* bügelfrei

'washbasin *n* Waschbecken *nt*

'washcloth *n* Waschlappen *m*

washed-out [ˌwɑʃt·'aʊt] *adj* ❶ *clothes* verwaschen ❷ (*tired*) fertig *fam*

washer ['wɑʃ·ər] *n* ❶ (*machine*) Waschmaschine *f* ❷ (*ring*) Unterlegscheibe *f;* (*seal*) Dichtung *f*

'washing machine *n* Waschmaschine *f*

Washington ['wɑʃ·ɪŋ·tən] *n* Washington *nt*

'washout *n usu sing* (*fam*) Reinfall *m fam*

'washroom *n* Toilette *f*

wasn't ['wʌz·ənt] = **was not** *see* **be**

wasp [wasp] *n* Wespe *f*

waspish ['was·pɪʃ] *adj* giftig *fam,* gehässig *pej*

'wasps' nest *n* Wespennest *nt*

wastage ['weɪ·stɪdʒ] *n* Verschwendung *f*

waste [weɪst] **I.** *n* ❶ (*misuse*) Verschwendung *f;* **~ of effort** vergeudete Mühe; **~ of time** Zeitverschwendung *f* ❷ (*matter*) Abfall *m;* **to go to ~** verkommen; **household/industrial ~** Haushalts-/Industriemüll *m;* **electronic ~** Elektroschrott *m* ❸ (*excrement*) Exkremente *pl* **II.** *vt* ❶ (*misuse*) verschwenden; **don't ~ my time!** stiehl mir nicht meine wertvolle Zeit! ❷ (*fam*) ■**to ~ sb** jdn umlegen **III.** *vi* ▶PHRASES: **~ not, want not** (*prov*) spare in der Zeit, dann hast du in der Not

◆**waste away** *vi* dahinsiechen *geh;* (*get thinner*) immer dünner werden

'wastebasket *n* Papierkorb *m*

wasted ['weɪs·tɪd] *adj* (*sl*) ❶ (*high on drugs*) mit Drogen vollgepumpt ❷ (*drunk*) betrunken

'waste disposal *n* Abfallbeseitigung *f,* Müllentsorgung *f*

wasteful ['weɪst·fəl] *adj* verschwenderisch (**of** mit +*dat*)

'wasteland *n* (*neglected*) unbebautes Land; (*unproductive*) Öde *f*

waste 'management *n* Abfallwirtschaft *f*

'wastepaper basket *n* Papierkorb *m*

'waste pipe *n* Abflussrohr *nt*

waste 'product *n* Abfallprodukt *nt*

waster ['weɪ·stər] *n* Verschwender(in) *m(f)*

wasting ['weɪ·stɪŋ] *adj attr, inv* **muscle-~ disease** muskelschwächende Krankheit

watch [watʃ] **I.** *n* ❶ (*on wrist*) Armbanduhr *f;* (*on chain*) Taschenuhr *f* ❷ (*duty*) Wache *f;* **on ~** auf Wache; **to keep [a] close ~ over sb/sth** über jdn/etw sorgsam wachen ❸ (*period of duty*) Wacheinheit *f* **II.** *vt* ❶ (*look at*) beobachten; **I ~ed him walk/walking down the road** ich sah, wie er die Straße hinunterging; **to ~ TV** fernsehen ❷ (*keep vigil*) aufpassen (auf +*akk*) ❸ (*be careful*) **~ it!** pass auf!; **to ~ one's weight** auf sein Gewicht achten ▶PHRASES: **to ~ one's step** aufpassen **III.** *vi* ❶ (*look*) zusehen, zuschauen ❷ (*be attentive*) aufpassen

◆**watch out** *vi* ❶ (*keep lookout*) Ausschau halten (**for** nach +*dat*) ❷ (*beware of*) **~ out!** Achtung!

'watchband *n* Uhr[arm]band *nt*

'watchdog *n* ❶ (*dog*) Wachhund *m* ❷ (*organization*) Überwachungsgremium *nt*

watcher ['watʃ·ər] *n* Zuschauer(in) *m(f);* (*observer*) Beobachter(in) *m(f)*

watchful ['watʃ·fəl] *adj* wachsam

watchmaker ['watʃ·ˌmeɪ·kər] *n* Uhrmacher(in) *m(f)*

'watchman *n* Wachmann *m;* **night ~** Nachtwächter *m*

'watchtower *n* Wachturm *m*

'watchword *n usu sing* (*slogan*) Parole *f*

water ['wɔ·t̬ər] **I.** *n* ❶ Wasser *nt* ❷ (*area*) ■**~s** *pl* Gewässer *pl* ❸ (*urine*) **to pass ~** Wasser lassen ▶PHRASES: **to be ~ under the bridge** Schnee von gestern sein *fam;* **to be [like] ~ off a duck's back** an jdm einfach abprallen; **like a fish out of ~** wie ein Fisch auf dem Trocknen; **come hell or high ~** komme, was [da] wolle **II.** *vt* bewässern; *animals* tränken; *garden* sprengen; *plants* gießen **III.** *vi* ❶ *eyes* tränen ❷ (*salivate*) **my mouth is ~ing** mir läuft das Wasser im Munde zusammen

◆**water down** *vt* ❶ (*dilute*) etw [mit Wasser] verdünnen ❷ (*fig: make less controversial*) etw verwässern *fig*

'water bird *n* Wasservogel *m*

'waterborne *adj inv* ❶ (*floating*) **~ trade** Handelsschifffahrt *f;* **~ attack** Angriff *m* zu Wasser ❷ (*transmitted*) **~ disease** durch das Wasser übertragene Krankheit

'water bottle *n* Wasserflasche *f*

'water buffalo *n* ZOOL Wasserbüffel *m*

'water cannon *n* Wasserwerfer *m*

'watercolor I. *n* ❶ (*paint*) Aquarellfarbe *f* ❷ (*picture*) Aquarell *nt* **II.** *adj usu attr* Aquarell-

'water-cooled *adj* wassergekühlt

'**water cooler** *n* [Trink]wasserspender *m*
'**watercress** *n* Brunnenkresse *f*
'**waterfall** *n* Wasserfall *m*
'**waterfowl** *n pl* Wasservögel *pl*
'**waterfront** *n* (*shore*) Ufer *nt;* (*area*) Hafengebiet *nt*
watering ['wɔ·t̬ər·ɪŋ] *n of land* Bewässerung *f; of garden* Sprengen *nt; of plants* Gießen *nt*
'**watering can** *n* Gießkanne *f*
'**watering hole** *n* ① (*pond*) Wasserloch *nt* ② (*hum fam: bar*) Kneipe *f fam*
waterless ['wɔ·t̬ər·lɪs] *adj* wasserlos; ~ **desert** trockene Wüste
'**water level** *n* (*of surface water*) Wasserstand *m; of river* Pegel[stand] *m;* (*of groundwater*) Grundwasserspiegel *m*
'**water lily** *n* Seerose *f,* Teichrose *f*
'**waterline** *n* Wasserlinie *f;* GEOL Grundwasserspiegel *m*
'**waterlogged** *adj ship* vollgelaufen; *ground* feucht
'**water main** *n* Haupt[wasser]leitung *f*
'**watermark** *n* ① *of tide* Wasser[stands]marke *f* ② (*on paper*) Wasserzeichen *nt*
'**watermelon** *n* Wassermelone *f*
'**water meter** *n* Wasserzähler *m*
'**water pipe** *n* ① (*conduit*) Wasserleitung *f* ② (*hookah*) Wasserpfeife *f*
'**water pistol** *n* Wasserpistole *f*
'**water pollution** *n* Wasserverschmutzung *f; of sea, river* Gewässerverschmutzung *f; of drinking water* Trinkwasserbelastung *f*
'**water polo** *n* Wasserball *m kein pl*
'**water power** *n* Wasserkraft *f*
'**water pressure** *n* Wasserdruck *m*
'**waterproof I.** *adj* wasserdicht **II.** *vt* wasserundurchlässig machen
water-re'pellent *adj* Wasser abweisend
'**watershed** *n* ① (*high ground*) Wasserscheide *f* ② (*fig: change*) Wendepunkt *m*
'**water shortage** *n* Wassermangel *m kein pl*
'**waterside** *n* (*by lake*) Seeufer *nt;* (*by river*) Flussufer *nt;* (*by sea*) Strand *m*
'**water-ski** *vi* Wasserski fahren
'**waterski** *n* Wasserski *m*
'**water softener** *n* Wasserenthärter *m*
water-'soluble *adj* wasserlöslich
'**waterspout** *n* ① (*whirlwind*) Wasserhose *f* ② (*pipe*) Abfluss *m*
'**water supply** *n* (*for area*) Wasservorrat *m;* (*for households*) Wasserversorgung *f*
'**water table** *n* Grundwasserspiegel *m*
'**water tank** *n* Wassertank *m*
watertight ['wɔ·t̬ər·ˌtaɪt] *adj* ① (*impermeable*) wasserdicht ② (*fig*) *agreement* wasserdicht; *argument* unanfechtbar
'**water tower** *n* Wasserturm *m*
'**water vapor** *n* Wasserdampf *m*
'**waterway** *n* Wasserstraße *f,* Schifffahrtsweg *m*
'**water wings** *npl* Schwimmflügel *pl*
'**waterworks** *npl* (*facility*) Wasserwerk *nt* ▶ PHRASES: **to turn on the ~** (*fam*) losheulen *fam*

watery <more, most *or* -ier, -iest> ['wɔ·t̬ə·ri] *adj* ① (*bland*) *drink* dünn; *soup* wässrig ② *light, sunshine* fahl; *smile* müde
watt [wat] *n* Watt *nt*
wattage ['wat̬·ɪdʒ] *n* Wattzahl *f*
wave [weɪv] **I.** *n* ① *of water, hair* Welle *f* ② (*fig: feeling*) **~ of emotion** Gefühlswallung *f;* **~ of panic** Welle der Panik ③ (*series*) **~ of layoffs** Entlassungswelle *f* ④ *of hand* Wink *m;* **to give sb a ~** jdm [zu]winken **II.** *vi* ① (*greet*) winken; **I ~d at him across the room** ich winkte ihm durch den Raum zu ② (*sway*) wogen *geh; flag* wehen **III.** *vt* ① (*with hand*) **to ~ goodbye to sb** jdm zum Abschied [nach]winken ② (*swing*) **to ~ a magic wand** einen Zauberstab schwingen
◆**wave aside** *vt* **to ~ aside ↻ an objection** einen Einwand abtun
◆**wave down** *vt* anhalten
◆**wave through** *vt* durchwinken
'**waveband** *n* Wellenbereich *m*
'**wavelength** *n* Wellenlänge *f* ▶ PHRASES: **to be on the same ~** auf derselben Wellenlänge liegen
waver ['weɪ·vər] *vi* ① wanken; *concentration, support* nachlassen ② (*be indecisive*) schwanken; ■**to ~ over sth** sich *dat* etw hin- und herüberlegen
wavering ['weɪ·vər·ɪŋ] *adj* ① (*indecisive*) unentschlossen; *between two options* schwankend *attr* ② (*unsteady*) *flame, candle* flackernd; *courage* wankend; *voice* zitternd
wavy ['weɪ·vi] *adj* wellig; *hair* gewellt
wax[1] [wæks] **I.** *n* ① Wachs *nt* ② (*in ear*) Ohrenschmalz *nt* **II.** *vt* ① (*polish*) wachsen; *floor* bohnern; *shoes* wichsen ② (*remove hair*) enthaaren
wax[2] [wæks] *vi moon* zunehmen; **to ~ and wane** zu- und abnehmen
wax 'paper *n* Butterbrotpapier *nt*
'**waxwork** *n* Wachsfigur *f*
waxy ['wæk·si] *adj* Wachs-, aus Wachs *nach n*
way [weɪ] **I.** *n* ① (*road*) Weg *m;* **one-~ street** Einbahnstraße *f* ② (*route*) **we have to go by ~ of Chicago** wir müssen über Chicago fahren; **to ask the ~** nach dem Weg fragen; **to be on the ~** *letter, baby* unterwegs sein; **to get under ~** in Gang kommen; **to go out of one's ~ to do sth** einen Umweg machen, um etw zu tun; (*fig*) sich bei etw *dat* besondere Mühe geben; **to go the wrong ~** sich verlaufen; (*in car*) sich verfahren; **to lead the ~** vorausgehen; **to lose one's ~** sich verirren; **to show sb the ~** jdm den Weg zeigen ③ (*distance*) Weg *m,* Strecke *f;* **I'll support you all the ~** du hast meine volle Unterstützung; **to be a long ~ off** (*in space*) weit entfernt sein; (*in time*) fern sein; **to go a long ~** (*fig*) lange reichen ④ (*direction*) **this ~ around** so herum; **which ~ are you going?** in welche Richtung gehst du? ⑤ (*manner*) Art *f,* Weise *f;* **the ~ things are going ...** so wie sich die Dinge entwickeln, ...; **that is definitely not the ~ to do**

it so macht man das auf gar keinen Fall!; **to see the error of one's ~s** seine Fehler einsehen; **~s and means** Mittel und Wege; **one ~ or another** so oder so; **no ~** auf gar keinen Fall; **no ~!** (*sl*) ausgeschlossen!, kommt nicht in die Tüte! *fam* ⑥ (*respect*) Weise *f*, Hinsicht *f*; **in a ~** in gewisser Weise; **in many ~s** in vielerlei Hinsicht ⑦ (*area*) Weg *m*, Platz *m*; **to be in sb's ~** jdm im Weg sein *a. fig*; **to get out of sb's/sth's ~** jdm/etw aus dem Weg gehen ▶ PHRASES: **there are no two ~s about it** daran gibt es keinen Zweifel; **by the ~** übrigens **II.** *adv inv* (*fam*) weit; **to be ~ past sb's bedtime** für jdn allerhöchste Zeit zum Schlafengehen sein

waylay <-laid, -laid> ['weɪ·leɪ] *vt* ① (*attack*) überfallen ② (*hum: accost*) abfangen

'wayside *n* Straßenrand *m* ▶ PHRASES: **to fall by the ~** auf der Strecke bleiben

wayward ['weɪ·wərd] *adj* eigenwillig

we [wi] *pron pers* wir; **in this section ~ discuss ...** in diesem Abschnitt besprechen wir ..; **~ all ...** wir alle ...

weak [wik] *adj* ① schwach; *coffee, tea* dünn; **to be/go ~ at the knees** weiche Knie haben/bekommen ② (*ineffective*) *leader* unfähig; *argument, attempt* schwach

weaken ['wi·kən] **I.** *vi* schwächer werden, nachlassen; (*less resolute*) schwach werden **II.** *vt* schwächen

weakling ['wik·lɪŋ] *n* Schwächling *m*

weakly ['wik·li] *adv* ① schwach, kraftlos ② (*unconvincingly*) schwach, matt

weak-minded [ˌwik·'maɪn·dɪd] *adj* ① (*irresolute*) unentschlossen; (*weak-willed*) willensschwach ② (*deficient*) schwachsinnig

weakness <*pl* -es> ['wik·nɪs] *n* ① (*frailty*) Schwäche *f* ② (*vulnerability*) Schwachstelle *f* ③ (*flaw*) Schwäche *f* ④ (*strong liking*) Schwäche *f* (**for** für +*akk*)

weal [wil] *n* Schwiele *f*, Striemen *m*

wealth [welθ] *n* ① (*money*) Reichtum *m*; (*fortune*) Vermögen *nt* ② (*amount*) Fülle *f*

'wealth tax *n* Vermögenssteuer *f*

wealthy ['wel·θi] **I.** *adj* reich, wohlhabend **II.** *n* ■ **the ~** *pl* die Reichen *pl*

wean [win] *vt* ① *baby* abstillen; *animal* entwöhnen ② ■ **to ~ sb off sth** jdm etw abgewöhnen

weapon ['wep·ən] *n* Waffe *f a. fig*; **~s of mass destruction** Massenvernichtungswaffen *pl*

weaponry ['wep·ən·ri] *n* Waffen *pl*

wear [wer] **I.** *n* ① (*clothing*) Kleidung *f* ② (*damage*) **signs of ~** Abnutzungserscheinungen; **~ and tear** Verschleiß *m* **II.** *vt* <wore, worn> tragen ▶ PHRASES: **to ~ one's heart on one's sleeve** das Herz auf der Zunge tragen **III.** *vi* <wore, worn> *clothes* abtragen; *machine* abnutzen

◆ **wear away** *vi* sich abnutzen

◆ **wear down** *vt* ① (*tire*) fertigmachen *fam*; (*weaken*) zermürben ② (*reduce*) abtragen

◆ **wear off** *vi* nachlassen

◆ **wear out I.** *vi* abnutzen **II.** *vt* erschöpfen

wearable ['wer·ə·bəl] *adj* tragbar

wearing ['wer·ɪŋ] *adj* ermüdend

weary ['wɪr·i] **I.** *adj* ① (*tired*) müde ② (*bored*) gelangweilt; (*unenthusiastic*) lustlos **II.** *vi* <-ie-> ■ **to ~ of sth** von etw *dat* genug haben

weasel ['wi·zəl] *n* Wiesel *nt*

weather ['weð·ər] **I.** *n* Wetter *nt*; (*climate*) Witterung *f*; **in all ~** bei jedem Wetter ▶ PHRASES: **to be under the ~** (*fam*) angeschlagen sein *fam* **II.** *vi object* verwittern; *person* altern **III.** *vt* ① *usu passive wood* auswittern; *skin* gerben ② (*survive*) **to ~ the storm** *ship* dem Sturm trotzen

'weather-beaten *adj* ① (*of person*) wettergegerbt ② (*of object*) verwittert

'weather bureau *n* Wetteramt *nt*

'weather chart *n* Wetterkarte *f*

'weather conditions *npl* Witterungsverhältnisse *pl*

'weather forecast *n* Wettervorhersage *f*

'weatherman *n* Wettermann *m fam*

'weatherproof *adj* wetterfest

weave [wiv] **I.** *vt* <wove *or* weaved, woven *or* weaved> ① *cloth* weben ② (*a. fig: intertwine*) ■ **to ~ sth together** etw zusammenflechten **II.** *vi* <wove *or* weaved, woven *or* weaved> weben **III.** *n* Webart *f*

weaver ['wi·vər] *n* Weber(in) *m(f)*

'weaver bird *n* Webervogel *m*

web [web] *n* ① *of spider* Netz *nt*; **spider['s] ~** Spinnennetz *nt* ② (*fig: network*) Netzwerk *nt*; **a ~ of intrigue** ein Netz *nt* von Intrigen

'web browser *n* INET [Web-]Browser *m fachspr*

web-footed ['web·ˌfʊṭ·ɪd] *adj inv* mit Schwimmfüßen *nach n*

webmaster ['web·mæs·tər] *n* INET Web-Administrator(in) *m(f)*

'web page *n* INET Webseite *f*

'web portal *n* INET Internetportal *nt*

'website *n* INET Website *f*

webzine ['web·zin] *n* INET Webzine *nt*

wed <wed *or* wedded, wed *or* wedded> [wed] **I.** *vt* (*form or old*) ■ **to ~ sb** jdn ehelichen *veraltend o hum* **II.** *vi* (*form or old*) sich vermählen *geh*

we'd [wid] ① = **we had** *see* **have I., II.** ② = **we would** *see* **would**

wedded ['wed·ɪd] **I.** *adj attr, inv* verheiratet, Ehe-; **~ bliss** Eheglück *nt* **II.** *pt, pp of* **wed**

wedding ['wed·ɪŋ] *n* Hochzeit *f*

'wedding anniversary *n* Hochzeitstag *m*

'wedding cake *n* Hochzeitstorte *f*

'wedding day *n* Hochzeitstag *m*

'wedding dress *n* Brautkleid *nt*

'wedding guest *n* Hochzeitsgast *m*

'wedding night *n* Hochzeitsnacht *f*

'wedding present *n* Hochzeitsgeschenk *nt*

'wedding ring *n* Ehering *m*, Trauring *m*

wedge [wedʒ] **I.** *n* Keil *m* **II.** *vt* ① (*jam*) einkeilen ② (*keep*) **to ~ sth closed/open** etw verkeilen

wedlock ['wed·lak] *n* Ehe *f*; **to be born out**

of ~ unehelich geboren sein
Wednesday ['wenz·deɪ] *n* Mittwoch *m; see also* **Tuesday**
wee [wi] **I.** *adj inv* winzig; **in the ~ hours** *zwischen 1 und 2 Uhr* **II.** *vi* (*fam*) pinkeln *fam*
weed [wid] **I.** *n* ① (*plant*) Unkraut *nt kein pl* ② (*fam: marijuana*) Gras *nt* **II.** *vt garden* jäten **III.** *vi* [Unkraut] jäten
'weedkiller *n* Unkrautvernichtungsmittel *nt*
weedy ['wi·di] *adj* ① *garden* unkrautbewachsen ② (*fam: thin*) [spindel]dürr
week [wik] *n* ① (*seven days*) Woche *f;* **twice a ~** zweimal die Woche; ■ **~ in, ~ out** Woche für Woche ② (*work period*) [Arbeits]woche *f;* **five-day ~** 5-Tage-Woche
'weekday *n* Wochentag *m*
'weekend *n* Wochenende *nt;* ■ **on the ~**[s]/**on ~s** am Wochenende/an Wochenenden
weekly ['wik·li] **I.** *adj inv* wöchentlich; **bi~** zweimal wöchentlich **II.** *adv inv* wöchentlich **III.** *n* (*magazine*) Wochenzeitschrift *f;* (*newspaper*) Wochenzeitung *f*
weep [wip] **I.** *vi* <wept, wept> ① (*cry*) weinen; (*sob*) schluchzen; **to ~ with joy** vor Freude weinen ② (*secrete*) nässen **II.** *vt* <wept, wept> **to ~ tears of joy** Freudentränen weinen
weeping ['wi·pɪŋ] **I.** *adj attr, inv* ① (*of person*) weinend ② (*of wound*) nässend **II.** *n* Weinen *nt*
weeping 'willow *n* Trauerweide *f*
weigh [weɪ] **I.** *vi* ① (*in measurement*) wiegen ② (*fig*) **to ~ heavily** eine große Bedeutung haben **II.** *vt* ① (*measure*) [ab]wiegen ② (*consider*) ■ **to ~ sth against sth** etw gegen etw *akk* abwägen ③ (*evaluate*) einschätzen
◆ **weigh down** *vt* niederdrücken; ■ **to be ~ed down with sth** schwer mit etw *dat* beladen sein
◆ **weigh in** *vi* ① **to ~ in at 132 pounds** 132 Pfund auf die Waage bringen ② (*fam: intervene*) sich einschalten; ■ **to ~ in with sth** *opinion, proposal* etw einbringen
'weigh-in *n* SPORTS Wiegen *nt*
weight [weɪt] **I.** *n* ① Gewicht; **to lose/put on** [*or* **gain**] **~** ab-/zunehmen ② (*for training*) **to lift ~s** Gewicht[e] heben ③ (*importance*) Gewicht *nt,* Bedeutung *f dat;* **to carry ~** ins Gewicht fallen ▸ PHRASES: **to <u>throw</u> one's ~ around** (*fam*) seinen Einfluss geltend machen **II.** *vt* ■ **to ~ sth down** etw beschweren
weighting ['weɪ·t̬ɪŋ] *n* MATH Gewichtung *f*
weightless ['weɪt·lɪs] *adj inv* schwerelos
weightlessness ['weɪt·lɪs·nɪs] *n* Schwerelosigkeit *f*
'weightlifter *n* Gewichtheber(in) *m(f)*
'weightlifting *n* Gewichtheben *nt*
weighty ['weɪ·t̬i] *adj* ① (*heavy*) schwer ② (*fig: important*) [ge]wichtig
weird [wɪrd] *adj* (*fam*) seltsam, komisch; (*crazy*) irre *fam;* **that's ~** das ist aber merkwürdig
weirdo <*pl* -os> ['wɪr·doʊ] *n* (*fam or pej*) seltsame Person, Freak *m*
welcome ['wel·kəm] **I.** *vt* ① (*greet*) willkommen heißen ② (*be glad of*) begrüßen **II.** *n* ① (*reception*) **to give sb a warm ~** jdm einen herzlichen Empfang bereiten ② (*approval*) Zustimmung *f* ▸ PHRASES: **to <u>overstay</u> one's ~** länger bleiben, als man erwünscht ist **III.** *adj* ① (*received*) willkommen; **to make sb very ~** jdn sehr freundlich aufnehmen ② (*permitted*) **you're ~ to use the garage** Sie können gerne unsere Garage benutzen ③ **thank you very much — you're ~** vielen Dank – nichts zu danken
welcoming ['wel·kəm·ɪŋ] *adj* Begrüßungs-; **~ smile** freundliches Lächeln
weld [weld] **I.** *vt* schweißen **II.** *n* Schweißnaht *f*
welder ['wel·dər] *n* Schweißer(in) *m(f)*
welding ['wel·dɪŋ] *n* Schweißen *nt*
'welding torch *n* Schweißbrenner *m*
welfare ['wel·fer] *n* ① (*aid*) Sozialhilfe *f;* ■ **to be on ~** von [der] Sozialhilfe leben ② (*well-being*) Wohlergehen *nt*
'welfare payments *npl* Sozialabgaben *pl*
'welfare services *npl* ① (*support*) Sozialleistungen *pl* ② + *sing vb* (*office*) Sozialamt *nt*
'welfare state *n* Sozialstaat *m,* Wohlfahrtsstaat *m oft pej*
we'll [wil] = **we will** *see* **will**[1]
well[1] [wel] **I.** *adj* <better, best> *usu pred* ① (*healthy*) gesund; **to feel ~** sich gut fühlen; **to get ~** gesund werden; **get ~ soon!** gute Besserung! *f* ② *inv* (*okay*) **all's ~ here** hier ist alles in Ordnung; **if everything goes ~, we should arrive on time** wenn alles gut geht, müssten wir pünktlich ankommen; **all ~ and good** gut und schön **II.** *adv* <better, best> ① (*in a good way*) gut; **~ done!** gut gemacht!, super! *fam;* **to be money ~ spent** gut angelegtes Geld sein; **to mean ~** es gut meinen; **to speak ~ of sb/sth** nur Gutes über jdn/etw sagen ② (*thoroughly*) gut; **to know sb ~** jdn gut kennen ③ *inv* (*used for emphasis*) [sehr] wohl; **to be ~ aware of sth** sich *dat* einer S. *gen* durchaus bewusst sein; **to be ~ over forty** weit über vierzig sein; **~ and truly** ganz einfach ④ *inv* (*justifiably*) wohl; **you may ~ ask!** das kann man wohl fragen! ⑤ *inv* (*also*) **as ~** auch; (*and*) **... as ~ as ...** ... sowie ... **III.** *interj* (*introducing, continuing*) nun [ja], also; (*hesitating, resignedly*) tja *fam;* (*surprised*) **~** [, **~**]! sieh mal einer an!
well[2] [wel] *n* ① (*for water*) Brunnen *m* ② (*for minerals*) Schacht *m;* **oil ~** Ölquelle *f*
◆ **well up** *vi* **tears ~ed up in her eyes** Tränen stiegen ihr in die Augen
well-ad'vised *adj pred* ■ **to be ~ to do sth** gut beraten sein, etw zu tun
well ap'pointed *adj pred,* **well-ap'pointed** *adj attr, inv* gut ausgestattet
well 'balanced *adj pred,* **well-'balanced** *adj attr, inv* ① (*objective*) *article, report* objektiv; *team* harmonisch ② *diet, meal* ausgewogen

❸ *person* ausgeglichen
well be'haved *adj pred,* **well-be'haved** *adj attr child* artig; *dog* brav
well-'being *n* Wohlbefinden *nt;* **feeling of ~** wohliges Gefühl
well 'bred *adj pred,* **well-'bred** *adj attr, inv* (*with good manners*) wohlerzogen *geh;* (*refined*) gebildet
well 'chosen *adj pred,* **well-'chosen** *adj attr* gut gewählt; [**to say**] **a few ~ words** ein paar passende Worte [sagen]
well con'nected *adj pred,* **well-con'nected** *adj attr* ■**to be ~** gute Beziehungen haben
well de'served *adj pred,* **well-de'served** *adj attr, inv* wohlverdient
well de'veloped *adj pred,* **well-de'veloped** *adj attr* gut entwickelt; *humor* ausgeprägt
well 'done *adj pred,* **well-'done** *adj attr, inv* ❶ (*of meat*) gut durch[gebraten] ❷ (*of work*) gut gemacht
well 'dressed *adj pred,* **well-'dressed** *adj attr* gut gekleidet
well 'earned *adj pred,* **well-'earned** *adj attr, inv* wohlverdient
well 'educated *adj pred,* **well-'educated** *adj attr* gebildet
well 'fed *adj pred,* **well-'fed** *adj attr, inv* (*eating well*) [ausreichend] mit Nahrung versorgt; (*healthy*) wohlgenährt
well 'founded *adj pred,* **well-'founded** *adj attr, inv* [wohl]begründet
well 'groomed *adj pred,* **well-'groomed** *adj attr, inv* gepflegt
well 'heeled *adj pred,* **well-'heeled** *adj attr, inv* (*fam*) [gut] betucht
well in'formed *adj pred,* **well-in'formed** *adj attr* gut informiert; **to be ~ on a subject** über ein Thema gut Bescheid wissen
well in'tentioned *adj pred,* **well-in'tentioned** *adj attr, inv* gut gemeint
well 'kept *adj pred,* **well-'kept** *adj attr* ❶ (*tended*) gepflegt ❷ (*hidden*) **a ~ secret** ein gut gehütetes Geheimnis
well 'known *adj pred,* **well-'known** *adj attr* [allgemein] bekannt; (*famous*) berühmt
well 'meaning *adj pred,* **well-'meaning** *adj attr, inv* wohlmeinend; **~ advice** gut gemeinte Ratschläge
'wellness *n* Wohlbefinden *nt*
well 'off <better-, best-> *adj pred,* **well-'off** *adj attr* ❶ (*wealthy*) wohlhabend ❷ *pred* (*fortunate*) gut dran *fam*
well 'oiled *adj pred,* **well-'oiled** *adj attr, inv* ❶ (*functioning*) gut funktionierend *attr* ❷ (*fam: drunk*) betrunken
well pro'portioned *adj pred,* **well-pro'portioned** *adj attr, inv* wohlproportioniert
well 'read *adj pred,* **well-'read** *adj attr* [sehr] belesen
well 'spoken *adj pred,* **well-'spoken** *adj attr, inv* (*polite*) höflich; (*refined*) beredt
well 'timed *adj pred,* **well-'timed** *adj attr* zeitlich gut gewählt; **his remark was ~** seine Bemerkung kam zur rechten Zeit
well-to-'do (*fam*) **I.** *adj inv* [gut] betucht **II.** *n* ■**the ~** *pl* die [Gut]betuchten *pl*
'well-wisher *n* wohlwollender Freund/wohlwollende Freundin; (*supporter*) Sympathisant(in) *m(f)*
well 'worn *adj pred,* **well-'worn** *adj attr, inv* ❶ (*damaged*) *clothes* abgetragen; *object* abgenützt ❷ (*cliché*) abgedroschen *fam*
Welsh [welʃ] **I.** *adj inv* walisisch **II.** *n* ❶ (*language*) Walisisch *nt* ❷ (*people*) ■**the ~** *pl* die Waliser *pl*
welt [welt] *n* ❶ *usu pl* (*scar*) Striemen *m* ❷ (*seam*) Rahmen *m*
went [went] *pt of* **go**
wept *pt, pp of* **weep**
were [wɜr] *pt of* **be**
we're [wɪr] = **we are** *see* **be**
weren't [wɜrnt] = **were not** *see* **be**
west [west] **I.** *n* ❶ (*direction*) Westen *m;* **to be to the ~ of sth** westlich von etw *dat* liegen ❷ POL ■**the W~** die westliche Welt; (*the Occident*) das Abendland; (*hist: non-communist*) der Westen **II.** *adj attr, inv* westlich, West-; **the ~ coast of Florida** die Westküste Floridas **III.** *adv inv* westwärts; **to travel ~** nach Westen reisen
'westbound *adj inv* in Richtung Westen
westerly ['wes·tər·li] *adj* westlich; **~ winds** Weststürme *pl*
western ['wes·tərn] **I.** *adj attr, inv* West-, westlich; **~ Europe** Westeuropa *nt* **II.** *n* (*film*) Western *m*
westerner ['wes·tər·nər] *n* Abendländer(in) *m(f);* POL Person *f* aus dem Westen
westernize ['wes·tər·naɪz] **I.** *vt* verwestlichen **II.** *vi* sich dem Westen anpassen
West 'Germany *n* (*hist*) Westdeutschland *nt*
West Vir'ginia *n* West Virginia *nt*
westward(s) ['west·wərd(z)] *inv adj* westlich; *road* nach Westen *nach n*
wet [wet] **I.** *adj* <-tt-> ❶ (*soaked*) nass; ■**soaking ~** [völlig] durchnässt ❷ (*covered with moisture*) feucht ❸ (*not dried*) **"~ paint!"** „frisch gestrichen!" ❹ (*rainy*) regnerisch **II.** *vt* <-tt-, wet *or* wetted, wet *or* wetted> ❶ (*moisten*) anfeuchten; (*soak*) nass machen ❷ (*urinate*) **to ~ the bed** das Bett nass machen **III.** *n* ❶ (*rain*) ■**the ~** die Nässe ❷ (*liquid*) Flüssigkeit *f;* (*moisture*) Feuchtigkeit *f*
'wetback *n* (*pej sl*) illegaler Einwanderer/illegale Einwanderin aus Mexiko
wet 'dream *n* (*fam*) feuchter Traum
'wetland *n* Sumpfgebiet *nt*
'wetness *n* Nässe *f*
'wetsuit *n* Taucheranzug *m*
we've [wiv] = **we have** *see* **have I., II.**
whack [hwæk] **I.** *vt* ❶ (*fam: hit*) schlagen ❷ (*sl: murder*) ■**to ~ sb** jdn umlegen *fam* **II.** *n* (*blow*) Schlag *m* ▶ PHRASES: **to be out of ~** (*fam*) nicht in Ordnung sein
whacko ['wæ·koʊ] *adj* (*sl*) *see* **wacko**

W

whale [hweɪl] *n* Wal *m*
whaling ['hweɪ·lɪŋ] *n* der Walfang
wham [hwæm] *(fam)* **I.** *interj* ❶ *(bang)* **~!** peng! ❷ *(suddenly)* wumm **II.** *vi* <-mm-> ■ **to ~ into sth** in etw *akk* [hinein]krachen
wharf <*pl* wharves *or* -s> [hwɔrf, *pl* (h)wɔrvz] *n* Kai *m*
what [hwʌt] **I.** *pron* ❶ *interrog* was; **~ is your name?** wie heißt du?; **~ are you looking for?** wonach suchst du?; **~ on earth ...?** *(fam)* was in aller Welt ...?; **~ about sb/sth?** *(fam)* was ist mit jdm/etw?; **~ for?** *(for what purpose?)* wofür?; *(fam: why?)* warum?; **~ if ...?** was ist, wenn ...?; **so ~?** *(fam)* na und? ❷ *rel* was; **I can't decide ~ to do next** ich kann mich nicht entschließen, was ich als nächstes tun soll; **~'s more, ...** darüber hinaus ... ❸ *rel* *(whatever)* was; **do ~ you can** tu, was du kannst ❹ *in exclamations* was; **is he smart or ~?** ist er intelligent oder was! ▶ PHRASES: **to have [got] ~ it takes** ausgesprochen fähig sein **II.** *adj inv* ❶ *(which)* welche(r, s); **~ time is it?** wie spät ist es? ❷ *(emphasizing)* was für; **~ luck!** was für ein Glück!; **~ a shame!** wie schade! **III.** *adv inv* was; **~ does it matter?** was macht's? *fam* **IV.** *interj* ❶ *(pardon?)* **~? I can't hear you** was? ich höre dich nicht ❷ *(showing surprise, disbelief)* **~!? you left him there alone!?** was?! du hast ihn da allein gelassen?
whatchamacallit ['hwʌtʃ·ə·mə·ˌkɔl·ɪt] *n* *(fam)* Dingsda *m o f o nt fam;* *(object a.)* Dings *nt fam*
whatever [hwʌt·'ev·ər] **I.** *pron* ❶ was [auch immer]; **I eat ~ I want** ich esse, was ich will; **~ happens** was auch passieren mag ❷ *(fam)* **or ~** wie du willst ❸ *interrog* *(form)* **~ are you talking about?** worüber in Gottes Namen sprichst du? **II.** *adj inv* ❶ *(any)* was auch immer; **take ~ action is needed** mach, was auch immer nötig ist ❷ *(regardless)* gleichgültig welche(r, s); **we'll go ~ the weather** wir fahren bei jedem Wetter **III.** *adv inv with neg* überhaupt
whatnot ['hwʌt·nat] *n* *(fam)* ■ **and ~** und was weiß ich noch alles
whatsoever [ˌhwʌt·soʊ·'ev·ər] *adv inv* überhaupt; **I have no idea ~** ich habe nicht die leiseste Idee
wheat [hwit] *n* Weizen *m*
'wheat germ *n* Weizenkeim *m*
wheel [hwil] **I.** *n* ❶ Rad *nt;* **rear ~** Hinterrad *nt* ❷ *(for steering)* Steuer *nt;* AUTO Lenkrad *nt;* ■ **to be at the ~** am Steuer sitzen ❸ *(fam: vehicle)* ■ **~s** *pl* fahrbarer Untersatz *hum* ❹ *(fig: workings)* ■ **~s** *pl* Räder *pl;* **to set the ~s in motion** die Sache in Gang bringen **II.** *vt* rollen; *baby carriage* schieben **III.** *vi* kreisen
◆ **wheel around** *vi* sich schnell umdrehen; *(esp shocked)* herumfahren
'wheelbarrow *n* Schubkarre *f*
'wheelchair *n* Rollstuhl *m*
wheeler-dealer [ˌhwi·lər·'di·lər] *n* Schlitzohr *nt*
wheeling ['hwi·lɪŋ] *n* **~ and dealing** Abzockerei *f sl;* *(shady)* Gemauschel *nt*
wheeze [hwiz] **I.** *vi* keuchen **II.** *n* Keuchen *nt kein pl*
whelp [hwelp] *n* *(old)* ❶ *(pup)* Welpe *m* ❷ *(young animal)* Junge(s) *nt*
when [hwen] **I.** *adv inv* ❶ *interrog* wann; **~ do you want to go?** wann möchtest du gehen?; **since ~ ...?** seit wann ...? ❷ *rel* *(during)* wenn, wo; **there are times ~ ...** es gibt Momente, wo ... **II.** *conj* ❶ *(once in past)* als; *(several times in past)* wenn; **I loved that film ~ I was a child** als Kind liebte ich diesen Film ❷ *(after)* wenn; **call me ~ you're finished** ruf mich an, wenn du fertig bist ❸ *(whenever)* wenn ❹ *(and just then)* als; **I was just getting into the bathtub ~ the telephone rang** ich stieg gerade in die Badewanne, als das Telefon läutete
whenever [hwen·'ev·ər] **I.** *conj* ❶ wann auch immer ❷ *(every time)* jedes Mal, wenn ... **II.** *adv inv* ❶ *(form)* wann auch immer; **~ possible** wenn möglich ❷ *interrog* *(form: when)* wann denn [nur]
where [hwer] *adv inv* ❶ *interrog* wo; *(to where)* wohin; *(from where)* woher; **~ are you going?** wohin gehst du? ❷ *rel* wo; *(to where)* wohin; *(from where)* woher; **Boston, ~ Phil comes from ...** Boston, wo Phil herkommt ... ▶ PHRASES: **to know/see ~ sb's coming from** wissen/verstehen, was jd meint
whereabouts **I.** *n* ['hwer·ə·baʊts] + *sing/pl vb* Aufenthaltsort *m;* **do you know the ~ of my silver pen?** weißt du, wo mein Silberfüller hingekommen ist? **II.** *adv* [ˌhwer·ə·'baʊts] *inv* wo [genau]; **~ in Manhattan do you live?** wo genau in Manhattan wohnst du?
whereas [hwer·'æz] *conj* ❶ *(in contrast to)* während, wo[hin]gegen ❷ LAW *(considering that)* in Anbetracht dessen, dass ...
whereby [hwer·'baɪ] *conj* *(form or old)* wodurch, womit
whereupon ['hwer·ə·ˌpan] *conj* *(form or old)* worauf[hin]
wherever [ˌhwer·'ev·ər] **I.** *conj* ❶ *(to whatever place)* wohin auch immer ❷ *(in all places)* wo auch immer **II.** *adv inv* ❶ *(in every case)* wann immer; **~ possible** wenn möglich ❷ *interrog* *(form: where)* wo [nur]; **~ did you find that hat?** wo hast du nur diesen Hut gefunden?
wherewithal ['hwer·wɪð·ɔl] *n* ■ **the ~** die [erforderlichen] Mittel
whet <-tt-> [hwet] *vt* **to ~ sb's appetite [for sth]** jdm Appetit [auf etw *akk*] machen
whether ['hweð·ər] *conj* ❶ *(if)* ob; **to ask ~ ...** fragen, ob ...; **she can't decide ~ to tell him** sie kann sich nicht entscheiden, ob sie es ihm sagen soll ❷ *(no matter)* **~ you like it or not** ob es dir [nun] gefällt oder nicht
whew [hwu] *interj* puh
whey [hweɪ] *n* Molke *f*

which [hwɪtʃ] **I.** *pron* ❶ *interrog* (*one*) welche(r, s); ~ [**one**] **is mine?** welches gehört mir? ❷ *rel* (*with defining clause*) der/die/das; **the conference, ~ ended on Friday** die Konferenz, die am Freitag geendet hat ❸ *rel* (*with non-defining clause*) was; **she says it's Anna's fault, ~ is ridiculous** sie sagt, das ist Annas Schuld, was aber Blödsinn ist; **at/upon ~ ...** woraufhin ... **II.** *adj inv* ❶ *interrog* (*one*) welche(r, s); **~ doctor did you see?** bei welchem Arzt warst du? ❷ *rel* (*introducing more*) der/die/das; **it might be made of plastic, in ~ case you could probably carry it** es könnte aus Plastik sein – in dem Fall könntest du es wahrscheinlich tragen

whichever [hwɪtʃ·'ev·ər] **I.** *pron* ❶ (*any one*) wer/was auch immer ❷ (*regardless*) was/wer auch immer **II.** *adj attr, inv* ❶ (*any one*) ■ **~ ...** der-/die-/dasjenige, der/die/das ...; **choose ~ brand you prefer** wähle die Marke, die du lieber hast ❷ (*regardless*) egal welche(r, s), welche(r, s) ... auch immer; **~ way** wie auch immer

whiff [hwɪf] *n usu sing* Hauch *m kein pl*

while [hwaɪl] **I.** *n* Weile *f;* **in a ~** in Kürze; **to be worth the ~** die Mühe wert sein **II.** *conj* ❶ (*during*) während ❷ (*although*) obwohl; **~ I completely understand your point of view, ...** wenn ich Ihren Standpunkt auch vollkommen verstehe, ... **III.** *vi* **to ~ away the time** sich *dat* die Zeit vertreiben

whim [hwɪm] *n* Laune *f;* [**to do sth**] **on a ~** [etw] aus einer Laune heraus [tun]

whimper ['hwɪm·pər] **I.** *vi person* wimmern; *dog* winseln **II.** *n of person* Wimmern *nt kein pl; of dog* Winseln *nt kein pl*

whimsical ['hwɪm·zɪ·kəl] *adj* ❶ (*playful*) skurril *geh* ❷ (*capricious*) launenhaft

whimsicality [ˌhwɪm·zɪ·'kæ·lə·t̬i] *n* ❶ (*playfulness*) Skurrilität *f geh* ❷ (*capriciousness*) Launenhaftigkeit *f*

whimsy, whimsey ['hwɪm·zi] *n* ❶ (*whim*) Laune *f* ❷ (*playfulness*) Spleenigkeit *f*

whine [hwaɪn] **I.** *vi* ❶ (*utter sound*) jammern; *animal* jaulen; *engine* heulen ❷ (*complain*) meckern **II.** *n usu sing of child* Jammern *nt kein pl; of animal* Jaulen *nt kein pl; of engine* Heulen *nt kein pl*

whinny ['hwɪn·i] **I.** *vi* wiehern **II.** *n* Wiehern *nt kein pl*

whip [hwɪp] **I.** *n* ❶ (*lash*) Peitsche *f* ❷ (*cream*) Creme *f* **II.** *vt* <-pp-> ❶ (*hit*) [mit der Peitsche] schlagen; *horse* die Peitsche geben ❷ *cream* schlagen ❸ (*fam: defeat*) [vernichtend] schlagen

◆**whip out** *vt* zücken

◆**whip up** *vt* ❶ (*excite*) **to ~ up support** Unterstützung finden ❷ (*cook*) zaubern *fig, hum*

'**whiplash** *n* ❶ (*blow*) Peitschenhieb *m* ❷ (*injury*) ~ [**injury**] Schleudertrauma *nt*

whipped [hwɪpt] *adj* (*beaten*) geschlagen; **~ cream** Schlagsahne *f,* Schlagobers *nt* ÖSTERR, Schlagrahm *m* SCHWEIZ

'**whippersnapper** *n* (*fam or old*) **young ~** Grünschnabel *m oft pej*

whippet ['hwɪp·ɪt] *n* Whippet *m*

whipping ['hwɪp·ɪŋ] *n* ❶ (*hitting*) [Aus]peitschen *nt kein pl* ❷ (*punishment*) Prügel *pl fam;* **to get a ~** Prügel beziehen ❸ (*fam: defeat*) Schlappe *f fam*

'**whipping boy** *n* Prügelknabe *m*

'**whipping cream** *n* Schlagsahne *f,* Schlagobers *nt* ÖSTERR, Nidel *m o f* SCHWEIZ

whir [hwɜr] *vi* <-rr-> (*buzz*) summen; (*hum*) surren

whirl [hwɜrl] **I.** *vi, vt* wirbeln **II.** *n* ❶ (*action*) Wirbeln *nt* ❷ (*activity*) Trubel *m*

whirligig ['hwɜr·lɪ·gɪg] *n* ❶ (*top*) Kreisel *m* ❷ (*changing thing*) Wechselspiel *nt*

whirlpool ['hwɜrl·pul] *n* Whirlpool *m;* (*in river, sea*) Strudel *m*

whirlwind ['hwɜrl·wɪnd] *n* Wirbelwind *m*

whisk [hwɪsk] **I.** *n* Schneebesen *m;* **electric ~** [elektrisches] Rührgerät **II.** *vt* ❶ *cream* schlagen ❷ (*take*) **I was ~ed off to the hospital** ich wurde ins Krankenhaus überwiesen

whisker ['hwɪs·kər] *n* ❶ (*of animal*) Schnurrhaar[e] *nt[pl]* ❷ (*beard*) ■ **~s** *pl* Bartstoppeln *pl* ▶ PHRASES: **by a ~** um Haaresbreite, haarscharf

whiskey, whisky ['hwɪs·ki] *n* Whisk[e]y *m*

whisper ['hwɪs·pər] **I.** *vi* flüstern; ■ **to ~ to sb** mit jdm flüstern **II.** *vt* ■ **to ~ sth** [**in sb's ear**] etw [in jds Ohr] flüstern **III.** *n* ❶ Flüstern *nt kein pl,* Geflüster *nt;* **to speak in a ~** etw im Flüsterton sagen ❷ (*liter: rustle*) Rascheln *nt*

whispering ['hwɪs·pər·ɪŋ] **I.** *n* Flüstern *nt,* Geflüster *nt* **II.** *adj attr, inv* ❶ flüsternd ❷ (*liter: rustling*) raschelnd

'**whispering campaign** *n* Verleumdungskampagne *f*

whist [hwɪst] *n* Whist *nt;* **game of ~** Partie *f* Whist

whistle ['hwɪs·əl] **I.** *vi* ❶ pfeifen; ■ **to ~ at sb** hinter jdm herpfeifen ❷ *bird* zwitschern **II.** *vt* pfeifen **III.** *n* ❶ (*sound*) *a. of wind* Pfeifen *nt; of referee* Pfiff *m* ❷ (*device*) Pfeife *f;* **referee's ~** Trillerpfeife *f;* **as clean as a ~** blitzsauber

white [hwaɪt] **I.** *n* ❶ Weiß *nt* ❷ *of eye* Weiße *nt* ❸ *of egg* Eiweiß *nt,* Eiklar *nt* ÖSTERR ❹ (*person*) Weiße(r) *f(m)* **II.** *adj* ❶ weiß; **black and ~** schwarz-weiß ❷ *coffee* mit Milch *nach n* ❸ **~ bread** Weißbrot *nt;* **~ pepper** weißer Pfeffer ❹ (*Caucasian*) weiß; (*pale-skinned*) hellhäutig ▶ PHRASES: **as ~ as a sheet** weiß wie die Wand, kreidebleich

'**white-collar** *adj* **~ job** Schreibtischposten *m;* **~ worker** Angestellte(r) *f(m)*

white '**corpuscle** *n* MED weißes Blutkörperchen

white '**elephant** *n* (*object*) Fehlinvestition *f;* (*property*) lästiger Besitz

white '**flag** *n* weiße Fahne

white '**heat** *n* Weißglut *f a. fig*

W

'White House *n* ■**the** ~ das Weiße Haus

> Das **White House** (das Weiße Haus), *1600 Pennsylvania Avenue* in Washington D. C., ist der offizielle Wohnsitz des Präsidenten der Vereinigten Staaten und des *Oval Office*, der Hauptarbeitsplatz desselben. Der Standort wurde von George Washington, dem ersten Präsidenten der Vereinigten Staaten, ausgewählt. Der Grundstein für das Bauwerk wurde am 13. Oktober 1792 gelegt und die Pläne wurden von dem irischen Architekten James Hoban umgesetzt. John Adams, der zweite Präsident, bezog das Weiße Haus erstmals im Jahre 1800. Das erste *Oval Office* entstand im Jahre 1909 unter Präsident William Howard Taft. Das *White House*, ein Wohnsitz von 55.000 Quadratfuß (5.110 m²) mit sechs Stockwerken und 132 Zimmern, verdankt seinen Namen dem weißen Marmor von Braç (Kroatien), aus dem es erbaut wurde.

white 'lie *n* Notlüge *f*

'white meat *n* helles Fleisch

whiten ['hwaɪ·tən] **I.** *vt* weiß machen; *shoe, wall* etw weißen [*o* ÖSTERR, SCHWEIZ, SÜDD weißeln]; *teeth* bleichen **II.** *vi* weiß werden

whitener ['hwaɪt·nər] *n* (*for coffee*) Kaffeeweißer *m;* (*for shoes*) Schuhweiß *nt*

'whiteout *n* ❶ METEO [starker] Schneesturm ❷ TYPO Korrekturflüssigkeit *f*, Tipp-Ex® *nt*

'white sale *n* Weißwäscheausverkauf *m*

white 'tie I. *adj inv* mit Frackzwang *nach n* **II.** *n* ❶ (*bowtie*) weiße Fliege ❷ (*evening dress*) Frack *m*

'whitewash I. *n* ❶ (*solution*) Tünche *f* ❷ (*cover-up*) Schönfärberei *f* **II.** *vt* ❶ (*paint*) weiß anstreichen; *walls* tünchen ❷ (*conceal*) schönfärben

whitewater 'rafting *n* Wildwasserfahren *nt*

white 'wine *n* Weißwein *m*

whiting <*pl* -> ['hwaɪ·t̬ɪŋ] *n* (*fish*) Weißfisch *m*

Whitsun ['hwɪt·sən] *n* Pfingsten *nt;* **at** ~ an Pfingsten

Whit'sunday *n* Pfingstsonntag *m*

whittle ['hwɪt̬·əl] *vt* schnitzen

◆**whittle down** *vt* reduzieren

whiz, whizz [hwɪz] **I.** *vi* ❶ **to ~ by** vorbeijagen ❷ *time* rasen; **the vacation just ~ed past** die Ferien vergingen im Nu **II.** *vt* [mit dem Mixer] verrühren **III.** *n* ❶ (*fam*) Genie *nt;* **computer** ~ Computerass *nt fam* ❷ (*vulg*) **to take a** ~ pissen *vulg*

whiz kid *n* Wunderkind *nt*, Genie *nt oft hum*

who [hu] *pron* ❶ *interrog* (*which person*) wer; **~ did this?** wer war das? ❷ *interrog* (*whom*) wem *dat*, wen *akk;* **~ do you want to talk to?** mit wem möchten Sie sprechen? ❸ *interrog* (*unknown*) wer; **~ knows?** wer weiß? ❹ *rel* der/die/das; **I think it was your dad ~ called** ich glaube, das war dein Vater, der angerufen hat; **he called Chris, ~ was a good friend** er rief Chris an, der ein guter Freund war

whoa [hwoʊ] *interj* ❶ (*to horse*) brr!, hoo! ❷ (*fam: slow down!*) langsam! ❸ (*fam: wow!*) wow *sl*, toll! *fam*

whodunit, whodunnit [ˌhu·'dʌn·ɪt] *n* (*fam*) Krimi *m fam*

whoever [hu·'ev·ər] *pron* ❶ *rel* wer auch immer; **come out, ~ you are** kommen Sie heraus, wer auch immer Sie sind ❷ *interrog* (*form or old: who on earth*) wer; **~ does he think he is?** wer glaubt er denn, dass er ist?

whole [hoʊl] **I.** *adj inv* ❶ (*entire*) ganz, gesamt; **this ~ thing is ridiculous!** das Ganze ist ja lächerlich!; **the ~ [wide] world** die ganze [weite] Welt ❷ (*in one piece*) ganz, heil; (*intact*) intakt ❸ (*fam: emphasizing*) **flying is a ~ lot cheaper these days** Fliegen ist heutzutage sehr viel billiger **II.** *n* ❶ (*entire thing*) ■**a** ~ ein Ganzes *nt* ❷ (*entirety*) ■**the** ~ das Ganze ❸ (*in total*) **as a** ~ als Ganzes [betrachtet]; **on the** ~ im Großen und Ganzen **III.** *adv* ganz; **a ~ new approach** ein ganz neuer Ansatz

'whole food *n* ❶ (*food*) Vollwertkost *f* ❷ (*food products*) ■**~s** *pl* Vollwertprodukte *pl*

'whole foods store *n* Reformhaus *nt*

wholehearted [ˌhoʊl·'har·t̬ɪd] *adj* ❶ (*sincere*) aufrichtig; (*cordial*) herzlich ❷ (*committed*) engagiert

whole 'milk *n* Vollmilch *f*

'whole note *n* MUS ganze Note

'whole rest *n* MUS ganze Pause

wholesale ['hoʊl·seɪl] **I.** *adj inv* ❶ *attr* **~ business** Großhandel *m* ❷ (*extensive*) Massen-; **~ reform** umfassende Reform **II.** *adv inv* ❶ (*at bulk price*) zum Großhandelspreis ❷ (*in bulk*) in Großmengen

wholesaler ['hoʊl·seɪ·lər] *n* Großhändler(in) *m(f)*

wholesome ['hoʊl·səm] *adj* wohltuend; (*healthy*) gesund

'whole tone *n* MUS Ganzton[schritt] *m*

'whole-wheat *adj attr, inv* Voll[korn]weizen-; **~ bread** Vollkornbrot *nt*

who'll [hul] = **who will** *see* **who**

wholly ['hoʊ·li] *adv* ganz, völlig

whom [hum] *pron* (*form*) ❶ *interrog* wem *dat*, wen *akk;* **~ did he marry?** wen hat er geheiratet? ❷ *rel* das/der/die; **none/some of ~ ...** keiner, der ... /einige, die ...

whoop [hup] **I.** *vi* jubeln **II.** *n* ❶ (*shout*) Jauchzer *m;* **to let out a ~ of triumph** einen Triumphschrei loslassen ❷ (*of cough*) Keuchen *nt*

whoopee (*fam*) **I.** *interj* [hwʊ·'pi] juchhe, hurra; (*iron*) toll **II.** *n* ['hwʊ·pi] **to make ~** (*have sex*) es tun

'whooping cough *n* Keuchhusten *m*

W

whoops [hwʊps] *interj* (*fam*) hoppla; **~-a-daisy** hopsala

whop [hwap] *vt* <-pp-> (*fam*) ❶ (*strike*) schlagen; **to ~ sb one** jdm eine reinhauen ❷ (*defeat*) ■**to ~ sb** jdn schlagen

whopper ['hwap·ər] *n* (*fam*) ❶ (*huge thing*) Apparat *m sl;* **that's a ~ of a fish** das ist ja ein Riesenfisch ❷ (*lie*) faustdicke Lüge *fam;* **to tell sb a ~** jdm einen Bären aufbinden

whopping ['hwap·ɪŋ] *adj inv* (*fam*) riesig; *bill* saftig *fam*

whore [hɔr] *n* (*pej*) ❶ (*prostitute*) Nutte *f sl* ❷ (*woman*) Flittchen *nt fam*

who's [huz] = **who is, who has** *see* **who**

whose [huz] **I.** *adj* ❶ (*in questions*) wessen; **~ round is it?** wer ist dran? ❷ (*indicating possession*) dessen; **she's the woman ~ car I rode in** sie ist die Frau, in deren Auto ich gefahren bin **II.** *pron poss, interrog* wessen; **~ is this bag?** wessen Tasche ist das?

why [hwaɪ] *adv* ❶ (*for what reason*) warum; **~ did he say that?** warum hat er das gesagt? ❷ (*for that reason*) **the reason ~ I ...** der Grund, warum ich ...

WI *abbrev of* **Wisconsin**

wick [wɪk] *n* Docht *m*

wicked ['wɪk·ɪd] **I.** *adj* ❶ (*evil*) böse ❷ (*cunning*) raffiniert ❸ (*fam: good*) saugut *sl* **II.** *n pl* ■**the ~** die Bösen *pl* ▸PHRASES: **there's no rest for the ~** (*saying*) es gibt keine Ruhe für die Schuldigen **III.** *interj* (*fam*) super *fam*

wicker ['wɪk·ər] *n* Korbgeflecht *nt*

wicker 'furniture *n* Korbmöbel *pl*

wicket ['wɪk·ɪt] *n* (*croquet hoop*) Tor *nt*

wide [waɪd] **I.** *adj* ❶ (*broad*) breit ❷ (*considerable*) enorm, beträchtlich ❸ (*open*) geweitet; *eyes* groß ❹ *after n* (*with a width of*) breit; **10 feet ~** 10 Fuß breit ❺ (*varied*) breit gefächert; **~ range of goods** großes Sortiment an Waren **II.** *adv* weit; **~ apart** weit auseinander

wide-angle 'lens *n* PHOT Weitwinkelobjektiv *nt fachspr*

wide a'wake *adj pred,* **wide-a'wake** *adj attr* hellwach

wide-'eyed *adj* mit großen Augen *nach n;* (*fig*) blauäugig

widely ['waɪd·li] *adv* ❶ (*broadly*) breit ❷ (*extensively*) weit; **~ admired** weithin bewundert ❸ (*considerably*) beträchtlich; **~ differing aims** völlig verschiedene Ziele

widen ['waɪ·dən] **I.** *vt* (*make broader*) verbreitern; (*make wider*) erweitern; (*enlarge*) vergrößern **II.** *vi* breiter werden

'widespread *adj* weit verbreitet; **there is ~ speculation that ...** es wird weithin spekuliert, dass ...

widow ['wɪd·oʊ] **I.** *n* Witwe *f* **II.** *vt usu passive* ■**to be ~ed** zur Witwe/zum Witwer werden

widowed ['wɪd·oʊd] *adj inv* verwitwet

widower ['wɪd·oʊ·ər] *n* Witwer *m*

widowhood ['wɪd·oʊ·hʊd] *n of women* Witwenschaft *f; of men* Witwerschaft *f*

'widow's peak *n spitz zulaufender Haaransatz in der Stirnmitte*

width [wɪdθ] *n* ❶ (*measurement*) Breite *f; of clothes* Weite *f;* **to be 16 feet in ~** 16 Fuß breit sein ❷ (*unit*) Breite *f;* **to come in different ~s** unterschiedlich breit sein

wield [wild] *vt* ❶ (*brandish*) schwingen ❷ (*exercise*) ausüben (**over** über +*akk*)

wiener ['wi·nər] *n* ❶ (*hot dog*) Wiener Würstchen *nt* ❷ (*childspeak fam: penis*) Pimmel *m fam*

wife <*pl* wives> [waɪf] *n* [Ehe]frau *f*

Wi-Fi® ['waɪ·faɪ] *n no pl abbrev of* **Wireless Fidelity** INET WLAN *nt*

wig [wɪg] *n* Perücke *f*

wiggle ['wɪg·əl] **I.** *vt, vi* wackeln **II.** *n* Wackeln *nt kein pl;* **she walks with a sexy ~** sie hat einen sexy Gang *fam*

wigwam ['wɪg·wam] *n* Wigwam *m*

wild [waɪld] **I.** *adj* ❶ *inv* (*undomesticated*) wild; *cat, duck, goose* Wild- ❷ (*uncultivated*) *country, landscape* rau, wild; **~ flowers** wild wachsende Blumen ❸ (*uncontrolled*) unbändig; (*disorderly*) *hair, lifestyle* wirr; *behavior* undiszipliniert ❹ (*not accurate*) *blow, punch, shot* ungezielt; *estimate, guess* grob, wild ❺ (*stormy*) *wind, weather* rau, stürmisch ❻ (*fam: angry*) wütend ❼ (*fam: enthusiastic*) ■**to be ~ about sb/sth** auf jdn/etw ganz wild sein ▸PHRASES: **~ <u>horses</u> couldn't make sb do sth** keine zehn Pferde könnten jdn dazu bringen, etw zu tun *fam* **II.** *adv inv* wild; **to run ~** *child, person* sich *dat* selbst überlassen sein; *animals* frei herumlaufen **III.** *n* ❶ (*natural environment*) ■**the ~** die Wildnis ❷ (*fig: remote places*) ■**the ~s** *pl* die Pampa *f kein pl oft hum fam*

wild 'boar *n* Wildschwein *nt*

'wildcard *n* ❶ CARDS Joker *m* ❷ COMPUT Wildcard *f*

'wildcat **I.** *n* Wildkatze *f* **II.** *adj attr, inv* ❶ (*risky*) riskant ❷ (*unofficial*) **~ strike** wilder Streik

wilderness <*pl* -es> ['wɪl·dər·nɪs] *n* ❶ (*wild area*) Wildnis *f;* (*desert*) Wüste *f* ❷ (*fam: overgrown area*) wild wachsendes Stück Land

'wildfire *n* Lauffeuer *nt;* **to spread like ~** (*fig*) sich wie ein Lauffeuer verbreiten

'wildfowl *n* Federwild *nt kein pl;* FOOD Wildgeflügel *nt kein pl*

wild-'goose chase *n* (*search*) aussichtslose Suche; (*venture*) fruchtloses Unterfangen

'wildlife **I.** *n* [natürliche] Tier- und Pflanzenwelt **II.** *adj* Natur-; **~ sanctuary** Wildschutzgebiet *nt*

wildly ['waɪld·li] *adv* ❶ (*in uncontrolled way*) wild; (*boisterously*) unbändig; **to talk ~** wirres Zeug reden *fam* ❷ (*haphazardly*) ungezielt; **to guess ~** [wild] drauflosraten *fam* ❸ (*fam: extremely*) äußerst; (*totally*) völlig; **~ exaggerated** maßlos übertrieben

wildness ['waɪld·nɪs] *n* ❶ (*natural state*) Wildheit *f* ❷ (*behavior*) Wildheit *f;* (*lack of control*) Unkontrolliertheit *f*

wild 'rice *n* Wildreis *m*
Wild West *n* **the ~** der Wilde Westen
wiles [waɪlz] *npl* Trick *m,* Schliche *pl;* **to use all one's ~** mit allen Tricks arbeiten
wilful ['wɪl·fəl] *adj see* **willful**
wiliness ['waɪ·lɪ·nɪs] *n* Listigkeit *f,* Schläue *f*
will[1] <would, would> [wɪl] *aux vb* ❶ (*in future tense*) **do you think he ~ come?** glaubst du, dass er kommt [*o* kommen wird]?; (*in immediate future*) **we'll be off now** wir fahren jetzt ❷ (*repeating question*) **you won't forget to tell him, ~ you?** du vergisst aber nicht, es ihm zu sagen, oder? ❸ (*expressing intention*) werden; **I ~ always love you** ich werde dich immer lieben ❹ (*in requests, instructions*) **~ you stop that!?** hör sofort damit auf!; **~ you [please] sit down?** setzen Sie sich doch [bitte]! ❺ (*expressing facts*) **fruit ~ keep longer in the fridge** Obst hält sich im Kühlschrank länger
will[2] [wɪl] **I.** *n* ❶ Wille *m;* **strength of ~** Willensstärke *f* ❷ LAW letzter Wille, Testament *nt* **II.** *vt* ■**to ~ sb to do sth** jdn [durch Willenskraft] dazu bringen, etw zu tun; **I was ~ing you to win** ich habe mir ganz fest gewünscht, dass du gewinnst
willful, wilful ['wɪl·fəl] *adj* ❶ (*deliberate*) bewusst, absichtlich; *damage* mutwillig ❷ (*self-willed*) eigensinnig; (*obstinate*) starrsinnig
William ['wɪl·jəm] *n* Wilhelm *m*
willies ['wɪl·iz] *npl* (*fam*) **sb gets/has the ~** jd kriegt Zustände
willing ['wɪl·ɪŋ] *adj* ❶ (*unopposed*) bereit, gewillt *geh* ❷ (*enthusiastic*) willig
willingness ['wɪl·ɪŋ·nɪs] *n* (*readiness*) Bereitschaft *f;* (*enthusiasm*) Bereitwilligkeit *f;* **to show ~** [seinen] guten Willen zeigen
willow ['wɪl·oʊ] *n* Weide *f*
willowy ['wɪl·oʊ·i] *adj* gertenschlank
'willpower *n* Willenskraft *f*
willy-nilly [ˌwɪl·i·'nɪl·i] *adv inv* ❶ (*like it or not*) wohl oder übel ❷ (*haphazardly*) aufs Geratewohl
wilt [wɪlt] *vi* ❶ (*droop*) [ver]welken ❷ (*tire*) schlappmachen *fam*
wily ['waɪ·li] *adj* listig; *deception, plan* raffiniert; *person a.* gewieft
wimp [wɪmp] (*fam*) **I.** *n* Waschlappen *m* **II.** *vi* ■**to ~ out** (*shirk*) kneifen; (*give in*) den Schwanz einziehen
win [wɪn] **I.** *vt* <won, won> ❶ (*be victorious*) gewinnen; *victory* erringen ❷ (*get*) gewinnen, bekommen; *approval, recognition* finden ▶ PHRASES: **you can't ~ them** [*or* **'em**] **all** (*saying*) man kann nicht immer Glück haben **II.** *vi* <won, won> gewinnen; **to ~ hands down** spielend gewinnen ▶ PHRASES: **may the best man ~** dem Besten der Sieg **III.** *n* Sieg *m;* **away ~** Auswärtssieg *m*
◆**win back** *vt* ❶ SPORTS **to ~ back ⊂ the trophy** den Pokal zurückholen ❷ *customers* zurückgewinnen
◆**win over** *vt* (*persuade*) überzeugen; (*gain support*) jdn für sich gewinnen
◆**win around** *vt* überzeugen
wince [wɪns] **I.** *n* Zusammenzucken *nt* **II.** *vi* zusammenzucken
winch [wɪntʃ] **I.** *n* <*pl* -es> Winde *f* **II.** *vt* mit einer Winde [hoch]ziehen
wind[1] [wɪnd] **I.** *n* ❶ (*air*) Wind *m;* **gust of ~** Windböe *f;* **to see which way the ~ is blowing** sehen, woher der Wind weht *a. fig;* **to run like the ~** rennen wie der Wind ❷ (*breath*) Atem *m* ❸ (*flatulence*) Blähungen *pl* ▶ PHRASES: **to be three sheets to the ~** (*fam*) völlig betrunken sein **II.** *vt* ■**to ~ sb** jdm den Atem nehmen
wind[2] [waɪnd] **I.** *n* ❶ (*bend*) Windung *f; in river* Schleife *f; in road* Kurve *f* ❷ (*turn*) Umdrehung *f* **II.** *vt* <wound, wound> ❶ (*wrap*) wickeln; *yarn* aufwickeln; *film* spulen ❷ *clock, watch* aufziehen ❸ (*turn*) winden, kurbeln ❹ (*spool*) spulen; **to ~ a tape forward** ein Band vorspulen **III.** *vi* <wound, wound> ❶ (*meander*) sich schlängeln ❷ (*coil*) sich wickeln
◆**wind down I.** *vt* zurückschrauben; *business* auflösen; *production* drosseln **II.** *vi* ❶ (*calm down*) ruhiger werden; *business* nachlassen; *party* an Schwung verlieren ❷ (*relax*) [sich] entspannen
◆**wind up I.** *vt* ❶ (*end*) abschließen; *debate, meeting, speech* beenden ❷ (*annoy*) ■**to ~ up ⊂ sb** jdn auf die Palme bringen; **to get [all] wound up** sich [total] aufregen ❸ (*tighten*) aufziehen; *clock, watch* aufziehen **II.** *vi* (*fam*) ❶ (*end*) schließen *fam; speech* abschließend bemerken ❷ (*land*) enden; **to ~ up in prison** im Gefängnis landen *fam*
'windbag *n* (*pej fam*) Schwätzer(in) *m(f)*
'windbreak *n* Windschutz *m*
'Windbreaker® *n* Windjacke *f*
'wind energy *n* Windenergie *f*
winder ['waɪn·dər] *n* Aufziehschraube *f;* (*for clock*) Schlüssel *m;* (*on watch*) Krone *f*
'windfall *n* ❶ (*money*) warmer [Geld]regen *fam* ❷ (*fruit*) ■**~s** *pl* Fallobst *nt kein pl*
'wind farm *n* Windpark *m*
'wind generator *n* Windgenerator *m*
winding ['waɪn·dɪŋ] **I.** *adj* gewunden; *road* kurvenreich **II.** *n* ❶ (*of road, course*) Windung *f* ❷ ELEC (*coils*) Wicklung *f; of machinery* Aufwickeln *nt*
'wind instrument *n* Blasinstrument *nt*
windjammer ['wɪnd·ˌdʒæm·ər] *n* Windjammer *m*
windlass <*pl* -es> ['wɪnd·ləs] *n* Winde *f;* NAUT Winsch *f fachspr*
'windmill *n* ❶ (*for grinding*) Windmühle *f* ❷ (*turbine*) Windrad *nt*
window ['wɪn·doʊ] *n* ❶ Fenster *nt; of shop* Schaufenster *nt; of vehicle* [Fenster]scheibe *f;* **rear ~** Heckscheibe *f;* **bay ~** Erkerfenster *nt* ❷ (*opportunity*) Gelegenheit *f* ❸ COMPUT Fenster *nt*
'window box *n* Blumenkasten *m*

W

'window cleaner *n* ❶ (*person*) Fensterputzer(in) *m(f)* ❷ (*detergent*) Glasreiniger *m*

'window display *n* Schaufensterauslage *f*

'window dressing *n* ❶ (*in shop*) Schaufensterdekoration *f* ❷ (*swindle*) Augenwischerei *f*

'window envelope *n* Fenster[brief]umschlag *m*

'window frame *n* Fensterrahmen *m*

'windowpane *n* Fensterscheibe *f*

'window-shopping *n* Schaufensterbummel *m*

'windowsill *n* (*inside*) Fensterbank *f;* (*outside*) Fenstersims *m o nt*

'windpipe *n* Luftröhre *f*

'wind power *n* ❶ (*strength*) Windkraft *f* ❷ (*energy*) Windenergie *f*

'windshield *n* Windschutzscheibe *f*

'windshield wiper *n* Scheibenwischer *m*

'windsock *n* Windsack *m*

windsurfer ['wɪnd·ˌsɜr·fər] *n* Windsurfer(in) *m(f)*

windsurfing ['wɪnd·ˌsɜr·fɪŋ] *n* Windsurfen *nt*

'windswept *adj* ❶ (*exposed*) dem Wind ausgesetzt; *beach, coast* windgepeitscht ❷ *appearance* [vom Wind] zerzaust

'wind tunnel *n* Windkanal *m*

'wind turbine *n* Windturbine *f*

windward ['wɪnd·wərd] **I.** *adj, adv* windwärts **II.** *n* Windseite *f*

windy¹ ['wɪn·di] *adj* ❶ METEO windig ❷ (*flatulent*) blähend

windy² ['waɪn·di] *adj* gewunden; (*meandering*) sich schlängelnd; *road* kurvenreich

wine [waɪn] **I.** *n* Wein *m* **II.** *vt* **to ~ and dine sb** jdn fürstlich bewirten **III.** *vi* **to ~ and dine** fürstlich essen

'wine bottle *n* Weinflasche *f*

'wine cellar *n* Weinkeller *m*

'wine cooler *n* ❶ (*container*) Weinkühler *m* ❷ (*drink*) Bowle *f*

'wineglass *n* Weinglas *nt*

winegrower ['waɪn·ˌgroʊ·ər] *n* Winzer(in) *m(f)*

winegrowing ['waɪn·ˌgroʊ·ɪŋ] **I.** *n* Wein[an]bau *m* **II.** *adj attr, inv* Wein[an]bau-; **~ area** Weingegend *f*

'wine list *n* Weinkarte *f*

'wine merchant *n* Weinhändler(in) *m(f)*

'winepress *n* [Wein]kelter *f*

winery ['waɪ·nə·ri] *n* Weinkellerei *f*

'winetasting *n* Weinprobe *f*

wing [wɪŋ] *n* ❶ Flügel *m; of plane* Flügel *m,* Tragfläche *f;* **to take sb under one's ~** jdn unter seine Fittiche nehmen *hum fam* ❷ *of building* Flügel *m* ❸ THEAT **to be waiting in the ~s** in den Kulissen warten ❹ SPORTS Flügel *m* ❺ POL **the left/right ~** der linke/rechte Flügel

'wing chair *n* Ohrensessel *m*

winged [wɪŋd] *adj inv* ❶ ZOOL mit Flügeln *nach n* ❷ (*with projections*) Flügel-

winger ['wɪŋ·ər] *n* SPORTS (*left*) Linksaußen *m;* (*right*) Rechtsaußen *m*

'wing nut *n* Flügelmutter *f*

'wingspan *n* Flügelspannweite *f*

wink [wɪŋk] **I.** *vi* ❶ (*one eye*) zwinkern; ■ **to ~ at sb** jdm zuzwinkern ❷ (*twinkle*) *light* blinken; *star* funkeln **II.** *vt* **to ~ one's eye** [mit den Augen] zwinkern **III.** *n* [Augen]zwinkern *nt;* **to give sb a ~** jdm zuzwinkern ▶ PHRASES: **to not sleep a ~** kein Auge zutun; **to catch forty ~s** ein Nickerchen machen

winner ['wɪn·ər] *n* ❶ (*victor*) Gewinner(in) *m(f);* (*in competition*) Sieger(in) *m(f)* ❷ SPORTS (*goal*) Siegestor *nt;* (*shot*) [Sieges]treffer *m* ❸ (*fam: successful thing*) Knaller *m fam;* ■ **to be onto a ~** das große Los gezogen haben *fam*

winning ['wɪn·ɪŋ] **I.** *adj* ❶ *attr* Gewinn-; (*in competition*) Sieger-; (*victorious*) siegreich; **to be on a ~ streak** eine Glückssträhne haben ❷ (*charming*) gewinnend **II.** *n* ■ **~s** *pl* Gewinn *m*

winnow ['wɪn·oʊ] *vt* ❶ AGR *grain* reinigen ❷ (*fig: sift*) sichten

winter ['wɪn·tər] **I.** *n* Winter *m* **II.** *adj* Winter- **III.** *vi animals* überwintern; *person* den Winter verbringen

winter 'sports *npl* Wintersport *m kein pl*

'wintertime *n* Winterzeit *f*

wintry ['wɪn·tri], **wintery** ['wɪn·t̬ə·ri] *adj* ❶ winterlich ❷ (*fig*) *greeting, smile* frostig; *look* eisig

wipe [waɪp] **I.** *vt* ❶ (*clean*) abwischen; *feet* abtreten; *nose* putzen ❷ (*dry*) *hands, dishes* abtrocknen ❸ (*erase*) *cassette, disk* löschen **II.** *n* ❶ (*clean*) Wischen *nt* ❷ (*tissue*) Reinigungstuch *nt*

◆**wipe down** *vt* abwischen; (*with water*) abwaschen; (*rub*) abreiben

◆**wipe off** *vt* ❶ (*clean*) wegwischen; (*from hand, shoes, surface*) abwischen ❷ (*erase*) löschen ▶ PHRASES: **to ~ the smile off sb's face** dafür sorgen, dass jdm das Lachen vergeht

◆**wipe out I.** *vt* ❶ (*destroy*) auslöschen; *disease* ausrotten ❷ (*kill*) beseitigen ❸ (*clean*) auswischen **II.** *vi* (*fam: have accident*) einen Unfall bauen *fam*

◆**wipe up I.** *vt* aufwischen; (*dry*) abtrocknen **II.** *vi* abtrocknen

wire ['waɪr] **I.** *n* ❶ (*thread*) Draht *m* ❷ ELEC (*cable*) Leitung *f* ❸ (*microphone*) Wanze *f* ▶ PHRASES: **to be a live ~** (*fam*) ein Energiebündel *nt* sein **II.** *adj* Draht- **III.** *vt* ❶ (*fasten*) mit Draht binden (**to** an +*akk*) ❷ ELEC (*connect*) mit elektrischen Leitungen versehen ❸ (*fam*) **to ~ sb money** jdm telegrafisch Geld überweisen

'wire cutters *npl* [**pair of**] **~** Drahtschere *f*

wire-haired 'terrier *n* Drahthaarterrier *m*

'wireless I. *adj* drahtlos; **~ network** Funknetz *nt* **II.** *n* (*dated*) Radio *nt*

wireless communi'cation *n* Mobilfunk *m*

wiretapping ['waɪr·ˌtæp·ɪŋ] *n* Abhören *nt* von Telefonleitungen

wiring ['waɪ·rɪŋ] *n* ❶ (*wires*) elektrische Leitungen *pl* ❷ (*installation*) Stromverlegen *nt;* **to do the ~** die elektrischen Leitungen verlegen

'**wiring diagram** *n* Schaltplan *m*
wiry ['waɪ·ri] *adj* ① (*rough*) drahtig; *hair* borstig ② (*fig: lean*) drahtig
Wis. *abbrev of* **Wisconsin**
Wisconsin [wɪs·'kan·sɪn] *n* Wisconsin *nt*
wisdom ['wɪz·dəm] *n* ① (*judgment*) Weisheit *f* ② (*sensibleness*) Klugheit *f* ③ (*sayings*) weise Sprüche *pl;* **words of ~** (*a. iron*) weise Worte
'**wisdom tooth** *n* Weisheitszahn *m*
wise [waɪz] *adj* ① (*sage*) weise *geh,* klug; **the Three W~ Men** REL die drei Weisen [aus dem Morgenland]; **to be older and ~r** durch Schaden klug geworden sein ② (*sensible*) vernünftig; **a ~ choice** eine gute Wahl ③ *pred* (*experienced*) **worldly ~** weltklug ④ *pred* (*fam: aware*) **to get ~ to sb** jdn durchschauen; **to get ~ to sth** etw spitzkriegen *fam*
◆**wise up** *vi* (*fam*) aufwachen; ■**to ~ up to sb/sth** jdn durchschauen/etw spitzkriegen *fam*
wisecrack ['waɪz·kræk] **I.** *n* Witzelei[en] *f*[*pl*] **II.** *vi* witzeln
'**wise guy** *n* (*fam*) Klugschwätzer *m pej fam*
wish [wɪʃ] **I.** *n* <*pl* -es> ① (*desire*) Wunsch *m,* Verlangen *nt* ② (*thing desired*) Wunsch *m;* **to grant sb a ~** jdm einen Wunsch erfüllen ③ (*regards*) ■**~es** *pl* Grüße *pl;* **best ~es, ...** (*in letter*) mit herzlichen Grüßen **II.** *vt* ① (*be desirous*) wünschen; **whatever you ~** was immer du möchtest ② (*make a magic wish*) ■**to ~** [**that**] ... sich *dat* wünschen, dass ...; **I ~ you were here** ich wünschte, du wärst hier ③ (*express wishes*) **to ~ sb happy birthday** jdm zum Geburtstag gratulieren **III.** *vi* ① (*want*) wollen, wünschen; **as you ~** wie Sie wünschen ② (*make a wish*) wünschen
wishbone ['wɪʃ·boʊn] *n* Gabelbein *nt*
wishful 'thinking *n* Wunschdenken *nt*
wishy-washy ['wɪʃ·i·ˌwaʃ·i] *adj* ① (*irresolute*) lasch, wischiwaschi *pej sl* ② (*watery*) *colors* wässrig
wisp [wɪsp] *n* Büschel *nt;* **~ of hair** Haarsträhne *f;* **~s of smoke** [kleine] Rauchfahnen
wispy ['wɪs·pi] *adj* dünn; *person* schmächtig; *hair* strähnig
wisteria [wɪ·'stɪr·i·ə] *n* BOT Glyzin[i]e *f*
wistful ['wɪst·fəl] *adj note, smile* wehmütig; *glance, look* sehnsüchtig
wit [wɪt] *n* ① (*humor*) Witz *m;* **biting/dry ~** beißender/trockener Humor ② (*intelligence*) ■**~s** *pl* geistige Fähigkeiten; **to be at one's ~s' end** mit seiner Weisheit am Ende sein; **to keep one's ~s** seine fünf Sinne zusammenhalten *fam* ③ (*person*) geistreiche Person
witch <*pl* -es> [wɪtʃ] *n* ① (*sorceress*) Hexe *f* ② (*fam: woman*) [alte] Hexe
'**witchcraft** *n* Hexerei *f*
'**witch doctor** *n* Medizinmann *m*
'**witch-hunt** *n* Hexenjagd *f*
'**witching hour** *n* ■**the ~** die Geisterstunde
with [wɪð, wɪθ] *prep* ① (*having*) mit +*dat;* **~ a little luck** mit ein wenig Glück ② (*accompanied*) **~ friends** mit Freunden ③ (*concerning*) **to have something to do ~ sb/sth** etwas mit jdm/etw zu tun haben ④ (*in addition*) **~ that ...** [und] damit ... ⑤ (*using*) **she paints ~ watercolors** sie malt mit Wasserfarben ⑥ (*while*) **~ things the way they are** so wie die Dinge sind ⑦ (*in state of*) vor +*dat;* **she was shaking ~ rage** sie zitterte vor Wut ⑧ (*despite*) bei +*dat;* **~ all her faults** bei all ihren Fehlern ⑨ (*in company of*) bei +*dat;* **to stay ~ relatives** bei Verwandten übernachten ⑩ (*matching*) **to go ~ sth** zu etw *dat* passen ⑪ (*on one's person*) **do you have a pen ~ you?** hast du einen Stift bei dir?
withdraw <-drew, -drawn> [wɪð·'drɔ] **I.** *vt* ① (*remove*) herausziehen; **to ~ one's hand** seine Hand zurückziehen ② *money* abheben ③ (*take back*) *coins, notes, stamps* aus dem Verkehr ziehen; *goods* zurückrufen; *team, troops* abziehen ④ (*cancel*) LAW *charge* fallen lassen; *funding* einstellen; **to ~ one's support for sth** etw nicht mehr unterstützen **II.** *vi* sich zurückziehen
withdrawal [wɪð·'drɔ·əl] *n* ① FIN [Geld]abhebung *f* ② MIL Rückzug *m* ③ (*taking back*) Zurücknehmen *nt;* (*cancel*) Zurückziehen *nt; of consent, support, funds* Entzug *m; of allegation* Widerruf *m; of action* Zurückziehen *nt; of charge* Fallenlassen *nt; from contract* Rücktritt *m* ④ *of addict* Entzug *m*
with'drawal symptoms *npl* Entzugserscheinungen *pl*
wither ['wɪð·ər] *vi* ① *plant* verdorren ② *person* verfallen; **to ~ with age** mit dem Alter an Vitalität verlieren ③ *interest* nachlassen
withering ['wɪð·ər·ɪŋ] **I.** *adj look* vernichtend **II.** *n* ① (*shriveling*) Verdorren *nt* ② (*lessening*) Abnahme *f*
withhold <-held, -held> [wɪð·'hoʊld] *vt* ① (*not give*) zurückhalten; ■**to ~ sth from sb** jdm etw *akk* vorenthalten; **to ~ information** Informationen verschweigen ② (*not pay*) etw nicht zahlen; **to ~ benefit payments** Leistungen nicht auszahlen
within [wɪð·'ɪn] **I.** *prep* innerhalb +*gen* ① (*inside*) innerhalb +*gen;* **~ the UN** innerhalb der UNO ② (*in limit of*) **~ sight/reach** in Sicht-/Reichweite ③ (*in less than*) **~ six months** innerhalb von sechs Monaten **II.** *adv inv* innen; ■**from ~** von innen [heraus]
'**with-it** *adj* (*fam*) ① (*trendy*) modisch; **to be ~** auf dem neuesten Stand sein ② (*alert*) aufmerksam; **sorry, I'm not really ~ today** entschuldige, ich bin heute nicht ganz bei der Sache
without [wɪð·'aʊt] *prep* ohne +*akk*
withstand <-stood, -stood> [wɪð·'stænd] *vt* ■**to ~ sb/sth** jdm/etw standhalten; **to ~ rough treatment** eine unsanfte Behandlung aushalten
witness ['wɪt·nɪs] **I.** *n* <*pl* -es> ① Zeuge, -in *m, f* (**to** +*gen*); *to marriage* Trauzeuge, -in *m, f* ② LAW Zeuge, -in *m, f;* **character ~** Leumundszeuge, -in *m, f;* **expert ~** Gutach-

W

ter(in) *m(f)* **II.** *vt* ❶ (*see*) beobachten; ■ **to ~ sb doing sth** sehen, wie jd etw tut ❷ (*attest*) bestätigen; **to ~ a will** ein Testament als Zeuge/Zeugin unterschreiben

'witness stand *n* Zeugenstand *m kein pl*

witty ['wɪt̬·i] *adj* (*clever*) geistreich; (*funny*) witzig

wizard ['wɪz·ərd] *n* ❶ (*magician*) Zauberer *m* ❷ (*expert*) Genie *nt oft hum;* **financial ~** Finanzgenie *nt*

wizardry ['wɪz·ər·dri] *n* ❶ Zauberei *f* ❷ (*equipment*) **high-tech ~** hochtechnologische Wunderdinge

wizened ['wɪz·ənd] *adj person* verhutzelt; *face, skin* runz[e]lig; *apple* schrump[e]lig

wobble ['wab·əl] **I.** *vi* ❶ (*move*) wackeln; *wheel* eiern *fam; gelatine, fat* schwabbeln *fam; knees* zittern, schlottern ❷ (*tremble*) *voice* zittern **II.** *vt* rütteln **III.** *n* ❶ (*movement*) Wackeln *nt kein pl* ❷ (*sound*) Vibrieren *nt kein pl; of voice* Zittern *nt kein pl*

wobbly ['wab·li] *adj* wack[e]lig; *writing, voice* zitt[e]rig

woe [woʊ] *n* ❶ (*liter*) Kummer *m* ❷ ■ **~s** *pl* Nöte *pl*

woebegone ['woʊ·bɪ·gan] *adj* (*liter*) kummervoll

woeful ['woʊ·fəl] *adj* beklagenswert; *ignorance, incompetence* erschreckend; *standard* erbärmlich

wok [wak] *n* Wok *m*

woke [woʊk] *vt, vi pt of* **wake**

woken ['woʊ·kən] *vt, vi pp of* **wake**

wolf [wʊlf] **I.** *n* <*pl* wolves> Wolf *m* ▶ PHRASES: **to cry ~** blinden Alarm schlagen **II.** *vt* ■ **to ~ down** etw verschlingen

'wolf cub *n* Wolfsjunge(s) *nt*

'wolfhound *n* Wolfshund *m*

'wolf whistle *n* bewundernder Pfiff; **to give sb a ~** jdm nachpfeifen

woman ['wʊm·ən] **I.** *n* <*pl* women> *pl* ❶ Frau *f* ❷ (*pej fam: term of address*) Weib *pej* ▶ PHRASES: **hell hath no fury like a ~ scorned** (*saying*) die Hölle [selbst] kennt nicht solche Wut wie eine zurückgewiesene Frau **II.** *adj* weiblich; **~ driver** Frau *f* am Steuer; **~ police officer** Polizistin *f*

womanhood ['wʊm·ən·hʊd] *n* Frausein *nt;* **to reach ~** eine Frau werden

womanizer ['wʊm·ə·naɪ·zər] *n* Weiberheld *m usu pej*

womanizing ['wʊm·ə·naɪ·zɪŋ] *vi* (*pej*) Schürzenjägerei *f;* **because of his constant ~** wegen seiner ständigen Frauengeschichten

womanly ['wʊm·ən·li] *adj* ❶ (*character*) weiblich ❷ (*body*) fraulich

womb [wum] *n* Mutterleib *m,* Gebärmutter *f*

womenfolk ['wɪm·ɪn·foʊk] *npl* Frauen *pl*

women's lib [ˌwɪm·ɪnz·'lɪb] *n* (*fam*) *short for* **women's liberation** die Frauen[rechts]bewegung

women's 'shelter *n* Frauenhaus *nt*

won [wʌn] *vt, vi pt, pp of* **win**

wonder ['wʌn·dər] **I.** *vi* ❶ (*ask*) sich fragen; **why do you ask? — I was just ~ing** warum fragst du? – ach, nur so; ■ **to ~ about sb/sth** sich Gedanken über jdn/etw machen; ■ **to ~ about doing sth** darüber nachdenken, ob man etw tun sollte ❷ (*surprised*) ■ **to ~ at sb/sth** sich über jdn/etw wundern; (*astonished*) über jdn/etw erstaunt sein **II.** *n* ❶ (*surprise*) Staunen *nt,* Verwunderung *f* ❷ (*marvel*) Wunder *nt;* **no ~ ...** kein Wunder, dass ...; **the Seven W~s of the World** die sieben Weltwunder; **to work ~s** [wahre] Wunder wirken

'wonder boy *n* (*iron, hum fam*) Wunderknabe *m*

'wonder drug *n* Wundermittel *nt*

wonderful ['wʌn·dər·fəl] *adj* wunderbar, wundervoll

'wonderland *n* Wunderland *nt;* **winter ~** winterliche Märchenlandschaft

wonderment ['wʌn·dər·mənt] *n* Verwunderung *f,* Erstaunen *nt*

wont [wɔnt] *n* (*form or hum*) Gewohnheit *f;* **as is her ~** wie sie zu tun pflegt

won't [woʊnt] = **will not** *see* **will**[1]

woo [wu] *vt* **to ~ voters** Wähler umwerben; ■ **to ~ sb with sth** jdn mit etw *dat* locken

wood [wʊd] *n* ❶ Holz *nt;* **plank of ~** [Holz]brett *nt* ❷ (*forest*) ■ **~s** *pl* Wald *m* ▶ PHRASES: **in our neck of the ~s** in unseren Breiten; **to not be out of the ~[s]** (*still critical*) noch nicht über den Berg sein *fam;* (*still difficult*) noch nicht aus dem Schneider sein *fam;* **knock on ~!** unberufen!

wood 'alcohol *n* Methanol *nt*

'woodcarver *n* Holzschnitzer(in) *m(f)*

'woodcarving *n* ART ❶ (*art genre*) Holzschnitzerei *f* ❷ (*object*) [Holz]schnitzerei *f*

'woodchuck *n* ZOOL Waldmurmeltier *nt*

'woodcraft *n* ❶ (*outdoor*) *Fähigkeiten/Kenntnisse zum Überleben in der freien Natur* ❷ (*artistic*) Geschick *nt* für das Arbeiten mit Holz

'woodcut *n* ART Holzschnitt *m*

wooded ['wʊd·ɪd] *adj* bewaldet; **~ area** Waldgebiet *nt*

wooden ['wʊd·ən] *adj* ❶ Holz-, hölzern, aus Holz *nach n* ❷ (*stiff*) *movements* hölzern; *smile* ausdruckslos

'woodland I. *n* ■ **~[s** *pl*] Wald *m* **II.** *adj* Wald-

'woodpecker *n* Specht *m*

'woodpile *n* Holzstoß *m*

'wood preservative *n* Holzschutzmittel *nt*

'wood pulp *n* Zellstoff *m,* Holzschliff *m fachspr*

'woodwind *n* ❶ (*instrument*) Holzblasinstrument *nt* ❷ *pl* ■ **the ~s** die Holzbläser *pl*

'woodwork *n of building* Holzwerk *nt* ▶ PHRASES: **to come out of the ~** ans Licht kommen

'woodworking *n* (*carpentry*) Tischlern *nt;* (*business*) Tischlerei *f;* SCH ≈ Werkunterricht *m* (*mit Holz als Werkstoff*)

'woodworm <*pl* -> *n* ❶ (*larva*) Holzwurm *m* ❷ (*damage*) Wurmfraß *m*

woody ['wʊd·i] *adj* ❶ HORT holzig, Holz-

W

❷ (*wooded*) bewaldet

woof [wʊf] **I.** *n* Bellen *nt* **II.** *vi dog* bellen; **~, ~!** wau, wau

woofer ['wʊf·ər] *n* Tieftonlautsprecher *m*

wool [wʊl] **I.** *n* Wolle *f;* **ball of ~** Wollknäuel *nt* ▶ PHRASES: **to pull the ~ over sb's eyes** jdm Sand in die Augen streuen *fam* **II.** *adj* Woll-

woolen, woollen ['wʊl·ən] *adj inv* wollen, aus Wolle *nach n;* **~ dress** Wollkleid *nt*

wooly, woolly ['wʊl·i] *adj inv* ❶ Woll-, wollen ❷ (*vague*) verschwommen; *mind, ideas* verworren; *thoughts* kraus

woozy ['wu·zi] *adj* (*fam: dizzy*) benommen; (*drunk*) beschwipst *fam*

wop [wap] *n* (*offensive fam*) Spaghettifresser(in) *m(f)*

word [wɜrd] **I.** *n* ❶ Wort *nt;* **or ~s to that effect** oder so ähnlich; **in other ~s** mit anderen Worten; **in a ~** um es kurz zu sagen ❷ (*talk*) [kurzes] Gespräch; (*formal*) Unterredung *f;* **to have a ~ with sb [about sth]** mit jdm [über etw *akk*] sprechen; **to have a [little] ~ with sb** jdn zur Seite nehmen ❸ (*news*) Nachricht *f;* (*message*) Mitteilung *f;* **to get ~ of sth [from sb]** etw [von jdm] erfahren ❹ (*order*) Kommando *nt;* **to give the ~** den Befehl geben ❺ (*promise*) Wort *nt,* Versprechen *nt;* **to go back on one's ~** sein Wort brechen ❻ (*lyrics*) ■ **~s** *pl* Text *m* ▶ PHRASES: **by ~ of mouth** mündlich; **to have ~s with sb** eine Auseinandersetzung mit jdm haben; **my ~!** du meine Güte! **II.** *vt* formulieren

wording ['wɜr·dɪŋ] *n* ❶ (*words*) Formulierung *f* ❷ (*expression*) Formulieren *nt*

wordless ['wɜrd·lɪs] *adj inv* wortlos, ohne Worte

'word order *n* Wortstellung *f*

word-'perfect *adj* textsicher

'wordplay *n* Wortspiel *nt*

'word processing *n* Textverarbeitung *f*

'word processor *n* COMPUT ❶ (*computer*) Textverarbeitungssystem *nt* ❷ (*program*) Textverarbeitungsprogramm *nt*

'word wrap *n* COMPUT [automatischer] Zeilenumbruch

wordy ['wɜr·di] *adj* langatmig, weitschweifig

wore [wɔr] *vt, vi pt of* **wear**

work [wɜrk] **I.** *n* ❶ (*activity*) Arbeit *f;* **good ~!** gute Arbeit!; **to be hard ~** (*strenuous*) anstrengend sein; (*difficult*) schwierig sein ❷ (*employment*) Arbeit *f;* **to look for ~** auf Arbeitssuche sein; **to be out of ~** arbeitslos sein; **to be at ~** bei der Arbeit sein ❸ (*repairs*) Arbeiten *pl;* **road ~** Straßenarbeiten *pl* ❹ (*opus*) Werk *nt;* **~s of art** Kunstwerke *pl* ❺ (*factory*) ■ **~s** + *sing vb* Werk *nt,* Fabrik *f* ❻ (*fam: all*) ■ **the ~s** *pl* das ganze Drum und Dran *kein pl* ❼ MATH Rechenweg *m* **II.** *adj climate, report, week* Arbeits- **III.** *vi* ❶ (*do job*) arbeiten; **to ~ hard** hart arbeiten; **to ~ together** zusammenarbeiten ❷ (*be busy*) arbeiten; ■ **to ~ at/on sth** an etw *dat* arbeiten; ■ **to ~ for/toward sth** auf etw *akk* hinwirken ❸ (*function*) funktionieren; *motor* laufen; **my cell phone doesn't ~** mein Handy geht nicht ❹ (*succeed*) funktionieren, klappen *fam; plan, tactics* aufgehen; *medicine, pill* wirken **IV.** *vt* ❶ (*operate*) *machine* bedienen; *equipment* etw betätigen ❷ (*move*) **to ~ one's way down a list** eine Liste durchgehen; **to ~ sth free/loose** etw losbekommen/lockern ❸ (*cultivate*) *land* bewirtschaften ❹ (*pay by working*) **to ~ one's way through college** sich *dat* sein Studium finanzieren ▶ PHRASES: **to ~ one's fingers to the bone [for sb/sth]** (*fam*) sich *dat* [für jdn/etw] den Rücken krummarbeiten

◆**work around** *vi* (*fam*) ■ **to ~ around to sth** sich an etw *akk* herantasten

◆**work away** *vi* vor sich hinarbeiten

◆**work for** *vt* ❶ (*be employed by*) arbeiten (für +*akk*) ❷ (*appeal to*) ■ **to [not] ~ for sb** jdm [nicht] zusagen

◆**work in** *vt* (*mix in, rub in*) einarbeiten; *food* hineingeben; (*on skin*) einreiben; *fertilizer, manure* einarbeiten

◆**work off** *vt* (*counteract*) abarbeiten; *energy* loswerden; *stress* abbauen

◆**work out I.** *vt* ❶ (*calculate*) errechnen, ausrechnen ❷ (*develop*) ausarbeiten; *solution* erarbeiten ❸ (*figure out*) ■ **to ~ out** ↻ **sth** hinter etw *akk* kommen ❹ (*solve itself*) **things usually ~ themselves out** die Dinge erledigen sich meist von selbst **II.** *vi* ❶ (*amount to*) **to ~ out cheaper** billiger kommen ❷ (*develop*) sich entwickeln; (*progress*) laufen *fam;* **to ~ out badly** schiefgehen *fam;* **to ~ out well** gut laufen *fam* ❸ (*do exercise*) trainieren

◆**work over** *vt* (*fam*) ■ **to ~ over** ↻ **sb** jdn zusammenschlagen

◆**work through** *vt* durcharbeiten; *problems* aufarbeiten

◆**work toward** *vt* **to ~ toward a deadline** auf einen Termin hinarbeiten

◆**work up I.** *vt* ❶ (*generate*) **to ~ up an appetite** Appetit bekommen; **to ~ up the courage [to do sth]** sich *dat* Mut machen[, etw zu tun] ❷ (*upset*) ■ **to ~ oneself/sb up** sich/jdn aufregen ❸ (*develop*) **to ~ up a sweat** ins Schwitzen kommen **II.** *vi* ❶ (*progress to*) ■ **to ~ up to sth** sich zu etw *dat* hocharbeiten ❷ (*get ready for*) ■ **to ~ up to sth** auf etw *akk* zusteuern

workable ['wɜrk·ə·bəl] *adj* ❶ (*feasible*) durchführbar ❷ (*able to be manipulated*) bearbeitbar; **~ land** bebaubares Land

workaday ['wɜrk·ə·deɪ] *adj* ❶ (*of job*) Arbeits- ❷ (*normal*) alltäglich

workaholic ['wɜrk·ə·ho·lɪk] *n* (*fam*) Arbeitssüchtige(r) *f(m)*

'workbench *n* Werkbank *f*

'workbook *n* Arbeitsbuch *nt*

'work camp *n Lager, in dem Freiwillige gemeinnützige Arbeiten verrichten*

W

'workday *n* ❶ (*work time*) Arbeitstag *m* ❷ (*not holiday*) Werktag *m*
worker ['wɜr·kər] *n* ❶ (*employee*) Arbeiter(in) *m(f)*; **blue-collar ~** [Fabrik]arbeiter(in) *m(f)*; **white-collar ~** [Büro]angestellte(r) *f(m)* ❷ (*hard worker*) Arbeitstier *nt fam*
'work ethic *n* Arbeitsethos *nt*
'workflow *n* Arbeitsfluss *m*
'workforce *n* Belegschaft *f*, Betriebspersonal *nt*
'workhorse *n* Arbeitstier *nt*
working ['wɜr·kɪŋ] **I.** *adj attr, inv* ❶ (*employed*) berufstätig ❷ (*for work*) Arbeits-; **~ conditions** Arbeitsbedingungen *pl* ❸ (*functioning*) funktionierend *attr*; **~ order** Betriebsfähigkeit *f*; **in ~ order** betriebsfähig **II.** *n* Arbeiten *nt*, Arbeit *f* ► PHRASES: **the ~s of fate** die Wege des Schicksals
working 'class *n* ■ **the ~** die Arbeiterklasse *kein pl*
'working-class *adj* der Arbeiterklasse *nach n*; **a ~ family** eine Arbeiterfamilie
'workload *n* Arbeitspensum *nt kein pl*; TECH Leistungsumfang *m*
'workman *n* ❶ (*worker*) Arbeiter *m* ❷ (*craftsman*) Handwerker *m*
'workmanlike *adj* ❶ (*skillful*) fachmännisch ❷ (*sufficient*) annehmbar
workmanship ['wɜrk·mən·ʃɪp] *n* Verarbeitung[sgüte] *f*; **fine ~** feine Verarbeitung
work of 'art *n* Kunstwerk *nt*
'workout *n* Fitnesstraining *nt*
'work permit *n* Arbeitserlaubnis *f*, Arbeitsgenehmigung *f*
'workplace *n* Arbeitsplatz *m*
'workshop *n* ❶ (*room*) Werkstatt *f* ❷ (*meeting*) Workshop *m*
'workstation *n* ❶ COMPUT Workstation *f fachspr* ❷ (*work area*) Arbeitsplatz *m*
'work surface *n* Arbeitsfläche *f*
world [wɜrld] *n* ❶ (*earth*) ■ **the ~** die Welt [*o* Erde] ❷ (*planet*) Welt *f*; **beings from other ~s** Außerirdische *pl* ❸ (*society*) **the ancient ~** die antike Welt; **the industrialized ~** die Industriegesellschaft ❹ *usu sing* (*domain*) **the Catholic/Christian/Muslim ~** die katholische/christliche/moslemische Welt ► PHRASES: **the ~ is sb's oyster** die Welt steht jdm offen; **to mean the ~ to sb** jds Ein *nt* und Alles sein; **to be out of this ~** (*fam*) himmlisch sein; **not for [all] the ~** nie im Leben
World 'Bank *n* ■ **the ~** die Weltbank
'world-class *adj inv* von Weltklasse *nach n*
World 'Cup *n* ❶ (*competition*) Weltmeisterschaft *f*; (*in soccer*) Fußballweltmeisterschaft *f* ❷ (*trophy*) Worldcup *m*, Weltpokal *m*
world-'famous *adj inv* weltberühmt
world 'language *n* Weltsprache *f*
worldly ['wɜrld·li] *adj* ❶ *attr* (*physical*) weltlich; **~ goods** materielle Güter ❷ (*experienced*) weltgewandt
world o'pinion *n* Meinung *f* der Weltöffentlichkeit
world popu'lation *n* Weltbevölkerung *f*
world 'power *n* Weltmacht *f*
world 'record *n* Weltrekord *m*

> Die **World Series** bezeichnet das Finale der US-amerikanischen Baseball-Profiliga. Dabei treffen die Champions der *American League* und die der *National League* aufeinander. Die **World Series** ist eine *best-of-seven series*. Das bedeutet, dass das erste Team, das vier Spiele gewinnt, *World Champions* (Weltmeister) ist. Dieses Treffen, das seit 1903 jährlich ausgetragen wird, findet im Oktober statt und wird von Baseball-Fans in der ganzen Welt mit großem Interesse verfolgt.

World's 'Fair *n* Weltausstellung *f*
'world view *n* Weltanschauung *f*
world 'war *n* Weltkrieg *m*; **W~ W~ II** der 2. Weltkrieg
'world-weary *adj inv* lebensmüde
worldwide ['wɜrld·ˌwaɪd] *adj, adv inv* weltweit; **to travel ~** die ganze Welt bereisen
World Wide 'Web *n* INET ■ **the ~** das World Wide Web, das Internet
worm [wɜrm] **I.** *n* ❶ Wurm *m*; (*larva*) Larve *f*; (*maggot*) Made *f* ❷ COMPUT Wurm *m* **II.** *vt* ❶ (*insinuate*) **to ~ oneself** [*or* **one's way**] **into someone's heart** sich in jds Herz *nt* einschleichen ❷ (*treat for worms*) *an animal* entwurmen
'worm-eaten *adj* wurmzerfressen
'wormhole *n* ❶ (*burrow*) Wurmloch *nt* ❷ PHYS Wurmloch *nt*
wormy ['wɜr·mi] *adj* ❶ (*infested*) von Würmern befallen; *fruit, vegetables* wurmig ❷ (*damaged*) wurmzerfressen; *wood* wurmstichig
worn [wɔrn] **I.** *vt, vi pp of* **wear II.** *adj* ❶ (*damaged*) abgenutzt; *carpet* abgetreten; *clothing, furniture* abgewetzt ❷ (*tired*) erschöpft
worn 'out *adj pred*, **'worn-out** *adj attr* ❶ (*tired*) erschöpft ❷ (*damaged*) *clothes* verschlissen; *shoes a.* durchgelaufen
worried ['wɜr·ɪd] *adj* beunruhigt, besorgt; ■ **to be ~ about sb/sth** sich *dat* um jdn/etw Sorgen machen; ■ **to be ~ that ...** Angst haben, dass ...
worry ['wɜr·i] **I.** *vi* <-ie-> sich *dat* Sorgen machen (**about** um +*akk*); **I'm sorry — don't ~ about it** tut mir leid – das macht doch nichts ► PHRASES: **not to ~!** (*fam*) keine Sorge [*o* Angst]! **II.** *vt* <-ie-> ❶ (*disturb*) beunruhigen ❷ (*bother*) stören **III.** *n* ❶ (*anxiety*) Sorge *f*, Besorgnis *f* ❷ (*cause*) Sorge *f*; **to be a major ~ for sb** jdm ernste Sorgen machen
worrying ['wɜ·ri·ɪŋ] *adj* Besorgnis erregend, beunruhigend
worse [wɜrs] **I.** *adj inv comp of* **bad** schlechter; (*harder, uglier*) schlimmer! ► PHRASES: **[somewhat] the ~ for wear** (*fam*) [ziemlich] mitge-

nommen **II.** *adv inv comp of* **badly** ❶ (*less well*) schlechter; (*more seriously*) schlimmer ❷ (*introducing*) **even ~, ...** was noch schlimmer ist, ... **III.** *n* ■**the ~** das Schlechtere; **to change for the ~** schlechter werden ▶PHRASES: **if ~ comes to worst** wenn es ganz schlimm kommt, wenn alle Stricke reißen *fam*

worsen [ˈwɜr·sən] **I.** *vi* sich verschlechtern **II.** *vt* verschlechtern

worship [ˈwɜr·ʃɪp] **I.** *n* ❶ Verehrung *f;* **act of ~** Anbetung *f* ❷ (*service*) Gottesdienst *m* **II.** *vt* <-p- *or* -pp-> ❶ (*revere*) **to ~ a deity** einer Gottheit huldigen *geh* ❷ (*adore*) vergöttern ❸ (*be obsessed with*) besessen sein; **to ~ money** geldgierig sein ▶PHRASES: **to ~ the ground sb walks on** jdn abgöttisch verehren *fam* **III.** *vi* <-p- *or* -pp-> beten; **to ~ in a church** in einer Kirche zu Gott beten

worshiper, worshipper [ˈwɜr·ʃɪp·ər] *n* Kirchgänger(in) *m(f);* (*believer*) Gläubige(r) *f(m);* **devil ~** Teufelsanbeter(in) *m(f)*

worst [wɜrst] **I.** *adj inv superl of* **bad** ❶ (*poorest, least*) ■**the ~ ...** der/die/das schlechteste ... ❷ (*most dangerous*) übelste(r, s), schlimmste(r, s) ❸ (*least advantageous*) ungünstigste(r, s) **II.** *adv inv superl of* **badly** ❶ (*most severely*) am schlimmsten ❷ (*least well*) am schlechtesten ❸ (*introducing*) **~ of all ...** und was am schlimmsten war, ... **III.** *n* ■**the ~** der/die/das Schlimmste; ■**at ~** schlimmstenfalls ▶PHRASES: **to be at one's ~** sich von seiner schlechtesten Seite zeigen

worsted [ˈwʊs·tɪd] *n* Kammgarn *nt*

worth [wɜrθ] **I.** *adj inv, pred* ❶ (*valued*) wert; **to be ~ one's weight in gold** Gold wert sein ❷ (*meriting*) wert; **to be ~ visiting** einen Besuch wert sein ▶PHRASES: **if a thing is ~ doing, it's ~ doing well** (*saying*) wenn schon, denn schon *fam;* **to be [well] ~ it** die Mühe wert sein; **for what it's ~** (*fam*) übrigens *fam* **II.** *n* ❶ (*value*) Wert *m;* **to get one's money's ~** etw für sein Geld bekommen ❷ (*merit*) Bedeutung *f,* Wert *m;* **of little ~** von geringem Wert

worthless [ˈwɜrθ·lɪs] *adj* wertlos *a. fig*

worthwhile [ˌwɜrθ·ˈhwaɪl] *adj* lohnend; ■**to be ~** sich lohnen

worthy [ˈwɜr·ði] *adj* ❶ (*estimable*) würdig; **to donate to a ~ cause** für einen wohltätigen Zweck spenden ❷ (*meriting*) **~ of attention/praise** beachtens-/lobenswert

would [wʊd] *aux vb* ❶ (*in indirect speech*) **they promised that they ~ help** sie versprachen zu helfen ❷ (*expressing condition*) **what ~ you do if ...?** was würdest du tun, wenn ...? ❸ (*expressing inclination*) **I'd go myself, but I'm too busy** ich würde [ja] selbst gehen, aber ich bin zu beschäftigt; **sb ~ rather do sth** jd würde lieber etw tun ❹ (*expressing opinion*) **I ~ imagine that ...** ich könnte mir vorstellen, dass ...

ˈ**would-be** *adj attr, inv* Möchtegern- *pej fam*

wouldn't [ˈwʊd·ənt] = **would not** *see* **would**

wound¹ [wund] **I.** *n* ❶ (*injury*) Wunde *f;* **gunshot ~** Schussverletzung *f* ❷ (*psychological*) Wunde *f,* Kränkung *f;* **to reopen old ~s** alte Wunden wieder aufreißen **II.** *vt* ❶ (*injure*) verletzen, verwunden ❷ (*psychologically*) kränken; **to ~ sb deeply** jdn tief verletzen

wound² [waʊnd] *vt, vi pt, pp of* **wind**

wounded [ˈwun·dɪd] **I.** *adj* ❶ (*injured*) verletzt, verwundet ❷ (*psychologically*) gekränkt, verletzt **II.** *n* ■**the ~** *pl* die Verletzten *pl;* MIL die Verwundeten *pl*

wove [woʊv] *vt, vi pt of* **weave**

woven [ˈwoʊ·vən] **I.** *vt, vi pp of* **weave II.** *adj inv* ❶ (*on loom*) gewebt; **~ fabric** Gewebe *nt* ❷ (*intertwined*) geflochten

wow [waʊ] (*fam*) **I.** *interj* wow *sl,* toll! *fam,* super! *sl* **II.** *vt* ■**to ~ sb** jdn hinreißen

wraith [reɪθ] *n* ❶ (*spirit*) Geist *m* ❷ (*person*) Gespenst *nt*

wrangle [ˈræŋ·gəl] **I.** *vi* streiten, rangeln (**about** um +*akk*) **II.** *vt cattle, horses* hüten **III.** *n* Gerangel *nt* (**about, over** um +*akk*); **legal ~** Rechtsstreit *m*

wrap [ræp] **I.** *n* ❶ (*robe*) Umhang *m;* (*stole*) Stola *f* ❷ (*packaging*) Verpackung *f;* **plastic ~** Frischhaltefolie *f* ❸ FILM (*fam*) **it's a ~** die Szene ist im Kasten ❹ FOOD Tortillawrap *m* **II.** *adj* **~ skirt** Wickelrock *m* **III.** *vt* <-pp-> ❶ (*cover*) einpacken; *in paper* einwickeln ❷ (*draw around*) ■**to ~ sth around sb/sth** etw um jdn/etw wickeln ❸ COMPUT **to ~ text/words** Texte/Wörter umbrechen ▶PHRASES: **to ~ sb around one's little finger** jdn um den kleinen Finger wickeln **IV.** *vi* <-pp-> ❶ COMPUT umbrechen ❷ FILM (*fam*) die Dreharbeiten beenden

wraparound [ˈræp·ə·ˌraʊnd] **I.** *adj inv* ❶ (*curving*) herumgezogen ❷ FASHION Wickel-; **~ skirt** Wickelrock *m* **II.** *n* ❶ FASHION Wickelrock *m* ❷ COMPUT Zeilenumbruch *m*

◆**wrap up I.** *vt* ❶ (*cover*) einwickeln ❷ (*dress*) warm einpacken ❸ (*end*) abschließen; *deal* unter Dach und Fach bringen **II.** *vi usu passive* ■**to be ~ped up in sb/sth** mit jdm/etw ganz beschäftigt sein

wrapper [ˈræp·ər] *n* (*packaging*) Verpackung *f;* **candy ~** Bonbonpapier *nt*

ˈ**wrapping paper** *n* (*for package*) Packpapier *nt;* (*for present*) Geschenkpapier *nt*

wrath [ræθ] *n* (*liter or hum*) Zorn *m*

wrathful [ˈræθ·fəl] *adj* (*liter*) zornig

wreak [rik] *vt* ❶ (*cause*) **to ~ damage/havoc [on sth]** Schaden [an etw *dat*] anrichten ❷ (*inflict*) **to ~ revenge on sb** sich an jdm rächen

wreath [riθ] *n* Kranz *m* (**of** aus +*dat*)

wreathe [rið] *vt usu passive* ❶ (*encircle*) umwinden; **~d in clouds** in Wolken gehüllt ❷ (*form into wreath*) zu einem Kranz flechten

wreck [rek] **I.** *n* ❶ *of ship* Schiffbruch *m* ❷ (*ship*) [Schiffs]wrack *nt* ❸ (*person, vehicle*) Wrack *nt;* **to be a nervous ~** ein nervliches Wrack sein ❹ (*remains*) Trümmerhaufen *m,* Ruine *f* ❺ (*accident*) Unfall *m* **II.** *vt* ❶ (*sink*) ■**to be ~ed** *ship* Schiffbruch erleiden ❷ (*de-*

W

stroy) zerstören ❸ (*spoil*) ruinieren; *chances, hopes, plans* zunichtemachen; *life* zerstören
wreckage ['rek·ɪdʒ] *n* Wrackteile *pl*, Trümmer *pl a. fig*
wrecker ['rek·ər] *n* ❶ (*destroyer*) Zerstörer(in) *m(f)* ❷ (*salvager*) Bergungsarbeiter(in) *m(f)* ❸ (*truck*) Abschleppwagen *m*
wren [ren] *n* Zaunkönig *m*
wrench [rentʃ] **I.** *n* <*pl* -es> ❶ (*tool*) Schraubenschlüssel *m;* **screw ~** Franzose *m* ❷ *usu sing* (*twisting*) Ruck *m* ❸ *usu sing* (*pain*) Trennungsschmerz *m* **II.** *vt* ❶ (*twist*) ■**to ~ sb/sth from sb** jdm jdn/etw entreißen *a. fig;* ■**to ~ off** abreißen ❷ (*injure*) *muscle* zerren; *joint* verrenken
wrestle ['res·əl] **I.** *vi* ❶ SPORTS ringen ❷ (*struggle*) ringen (**with** mit +*dat*) **II.** *vt* SPORTS ringen; **to ~ sb to the ground** jdn zu Boden bringen
wrestler ['res·lər] *n* Ringer(in) *m(f);* **Sumo ~** Sumoringer(in) *m(f)*
wrestling ['res·lɪŋ] *n* Ringen *nt*
'**wrestling bout**, '**wrestling match** *n* Ringkampf *m*
wretch <*pl* -es> [retʃ] *n* **poor ~** armer Kerl *fam*
wretched ['retʃ·ɪd] *adj* ❶ (*unhappy*) unglücklich ❷ (*bad*) schlimm; *state, condition* jämmerlich
wriggle ['rɪg·əl] **I.** *vi* ❶ (*twist*) sich winden; **to ~ free** [**of sth**] sich [aus etw *dat*] herauswinden ❷ (*move*) schlängeln, sich hindurchwinden (**through** durch +*akk*) ❸ (*worm one's way*) **to ~ into/out of sth** sich in etw einschleichen/aus etw herauswinden **II.** *vt* **to ~ one's toes in the sand** die Zehen in den Sand graben **III.** *n usu sing* Schlängeln *nt*
wring <wrung, wrung> [rɪŋ] **I.** *n usu sing* [Aus]wringen *nt* **II.** *vt* ❶ (*twist*) auswringen ❷ (*break*) **to ~ sb's/an animal's neck** jdm/einem Tier den Hals umdrehen *a. fig* ❸ (*get*) ■**to ~ sth out of sb** etw aus jdm herauspressen
wringer ['rɪŋ·ər] *n* Wäschemangel *f* ▶ PHRASES: **to put sb through the ~** (*fam*) jdn in die Mangel nehmen
wrinkle ['rɪŋ·kəl] **I.** *n* ❶ (*crease*) Knitterfalte *f;* (*in face*) Falte *f*, Runzel *f* ❷ (*fam: difficulty*) **to iron out the ~s** einige Unklarheiten beseitigen **II.** *vt* zerknittern **III.** *vi* zerknittern; *face, skin* Falten bekommen; *fruit* schrumpeln
wrinkled ['rɪŋ·kli] *adj* zerknittert; *face, skin* faltig, runzlig; *fruit* verschrumpelt
wrist [rɪst] *n* Handgelenk *nt;* **to slash** [*or* **slit**] **one's ~s** sich *dat* die Pulsadern aufschneiden
'**wristband** *n* ❶ (*strap*) Armband *nt* ❷ (*absorbent*) Schweißband *nt*
'**wristwatch** *n* Armbanduhr *f*
writ [rɪt] *n* [gerichtliche] Verfügung; **~ of summons** [schriftliche] Vorladung; **to issue a ~ against sb** jdn vorladen
write <wrote, written *or old* writ> [raɪt] **I.** *vt* ❶ (*pen*) schreiben; **to ~ a letter to sb** jdm einen Brief schreiben ❷ (*fill out*) ausstellen; *will* aufsetzen ❸ (*compose*) schreiben; ■**to ~** [**to**] **sb** jdm schreiben ❹ COMPUT ■**to ~ sth to sth** etw auf etw *dat* speichern ▶ PHRASES: **to be nothing to ~ home about** nichts Weltbewegendes sein **II.** *vi* ❶ (*pen letters*) schreiben; **to know how to read and ~** Lesen und Schreiben können ❷ COMPUT speichern
◆**write away** *vi* ■**to ~ away for sth** etw [schriftlich] anfordern
◆**write back** *vt, vi* zurückschreiben
◆**write down** *vt* ❶ (*record*) aufschreiben ❷ FIN abschreiben
◆**write in I.** *vt* ■**to ~ in** ⊂ **sth** (*in text*) etw einfügen; (*in form*) etw eintragen **II.** *vi* schreiben; **he wrote in expressing his dissatisfaction** er schickte einen Brief, um seine Unzufriedenheit auszudrücken
◆**write off I.** *vi* ■**to ~ off for sth** etw [schriftlich] anfordern **II.** *vt* ❶ (*dismiss*) abschreiben *fam* ❷ FIN abschreiben
◆**write out** *vt* ❶ (*put in writing*) aufschreiben ❷ (*in full*) ausschreiben ❸ (*remove*) streichen; THEAT, FILM *character, series* einen Abgang schaffen
◆**write up** *vt* ❶ (*pen*) *article, notes* ausarbeiten ❷ (*critique*) **to ~ up a film** eine Kritik zu einem Film schreiben ❸ (*report*) aufschreiben *fam*
'**write-in** *adj* POL **a ~ candidate** *ein nachträglich auf der Liste hinzugefügter Kandidat*
'**write-off** *n* FIN Abschreibung *f*
'**write-protected** *adj inv* COMPUT schreibgeschützt
writer ['raɪ·t̬ər] *n* ❶ (*person*) Verfasser(in) *m(f)* ❷ (*author*) Autor(in) *m(f);* **travel ~** Reiseschriftsteller(in) *m(f)*
'**write-up** *n of play, film* Kritik *f; of book a.* Rezension *f*
writhe [raɪð] *vi* ❶ (*squirm*) sich winden ❷ (*emotionally*) beben
writing ['raɪ·t̬ɪŋ] *n* ❶ (*skill*) Schreiben *nt;* ■**in ~** schriftlich ❷ (*occupation*) Schriftstellerei *f* ❸ (*literature*) Literatur *f* ❹ (*works*) ■**~s** *pl* Werke *pl* ❺ (*handwriting*) [Hand]schrift *f* ▶ PHRASES: **the ~ is on the wall** die Stunde hat geschlagen
'**writing desk** *n* Schreibtisch *m*
'**writing pad** *n* Schreibblock *m*
'**writing paper** *n* Schreibpapier *nt*
written ['rɪt·ən] **I.** *vt, vi pp of* **write II.** *adj inv* schriftlich; **the ~ word** das geschriebene Wort ▶ PHRASES: **to have sth ~ all over one's face** jdm steht etw ins Gesicht geschrieben
wrong [rɔŋ] **I.** *adj inv* ❶ (*incorrect*) falsch; **it's all ~** das ist völlig verkehrt; **sorry, you've got the ~ number** tut mir leid, Sie haben sich verwählt; **to be proven ~** widerlegt werden; ■**to be ~ about sth** sich bei etw *dat* irren ❷ *pred* (*amiss*) **is there anything ~?** stimmt etwas nicht?; **what's ~ with you today?** was ist denn heute mit dir los? ❸ (*immoral*) verwerflich *geh;* **it was ~ of her to ...** es war nicht

W

richtig von ihr, ... ► PHRASES: **to get hold of the ~ end of the stick** etw in den falschen Hals bekommen *fam* **II.** *adv inv* ❶ (*incorrectly*) falsch ❷ (*amiss*) **to go ~** *things* schiefgehen *fam; people* vom rechten Weg abkommen **III.** *n* ❶ (*immorality*) **to know right from ~** Richtig und Falsch unterscheiden können ❷ (*unjustness*) Unrecht *nt* ► PHRASES: **to be in the ~** (*mistaken*) sich irren; (*immoral*) im Unrecht sein **IV.** *vt usu passive* ■**to ~ sb** jdm Unrecht tun; (*misjudge*) jdn falsch einschätzen

wrongdoer ['rɔŋ·ˌdu·ər] *n* Übeltäter(in) *m(f)*

wrongdoing ['rɔŋ·ˌdu·ɪŋ] *n* Übeltat *nt;* **to accuse sb of ~** jdm Fehlverhalten vorwerfen

wrongful ['rɔŋ·fəl] *adj* unrechtmäßig

wrong-'headed *adj* querköpfig *pej; idea, plan* hirnverbrannt *fam*

wrongly ['rɔŋ·li] *adv inv* ❶ (*mistakenly*) fälschlicherweise ❷ (*unjustly*) zu Unrecht ❸ (*incorrectly*) falsch

wrote [root] *vt, vi pt of* **write**

wrought [rɔt] *adj inv* ❶ (*crafted*) [aus]gearbeitet; (*conceived*) [gut] durchdacht; *writing* [gut] konzipiert ❷ *attr silver, gold* gehämmert

wrought 'iron *n* Schmiedeeisen *nt*

wrought-'iron *adj inv* schmiedeeisern

wrung [rʌŋ] *vt pt, pp of* **wring**

wry <-ier, -iest *or* -er, -est> [raɪ] *adj usu attr comments, humor* trocken; *smile* bitter

wt. *n abbrev of* **weight** Gew.

wuss [wʊs] *n* (*pej fam*) Schlappschwanz *m pej sl*

WV, W.V. *abbrev of* **West Virginia**

WY *abbrev of* **Wyoming**

Wyo. *abbrev of* **Wyoming**

Wyoming [waɪ·'oʊ·mɪŋ] *n* Wyoming *nt*

Xx

X <*pl* -'s *or* -s>, **x** <*pl* -'s> [eks] *n* X *nt,* x *nt;* **~ as in X-ray** X wie Xanthippe

x [eks] **I.** *vt* ■**to ~ [out ⊂] sth** [aus]streichen **II.** *n* ❶ MATH x *nt;* **~-axis** x-Achse *f* ❷ (*kiss*) *Kusssymbol, etwa am Briefende;* **lots of love, Katy ~~~** alles Liebe, Gruß und Kuss, Katy

X 'chromosome *n* X-Chromosom *nt*

xenophobia [ˌzen·ə·'foʊ·bi·ə] *n* Fremdenhass *m*

xenophobic [ˌzen·ə·'foʊ·bɪk] *adj* fremdenfeindlich

xerox ['zɪr·aks] *vt* ■**to ~ sth** etw kopieren; **a ~ed copy of a document** eine Kopie eines Dokuments

Xerox® ['zɪr·aks] *n* Kopie *f*

Xmas <*pl* -es> ['krɪs·məs] *n* (*fam*) *short for* **Christmas** Weihnachten *nt*

X-ray ['eks·reɪ] **I.** *n* ❶ (*picture*) Röntgenbild *nt* ❷ (*examination*) Röntgenuntersuchung *f;* **to give sb an ~** jdn röntgen; **to have an ~** sich röntgen lassen ❸ (*radiation*) Röntgenstrahl *m* **II.** *adj* Röntgen-; **~ vision** (*fig*) Röntgenblick *m* **III.** *vt* röntgen

xylophone ['zaɪ·lə·foʊn] *n* Xylophon *nt*

X

Yy

Y <*pl* -'s *or* -s>, **y** <*pl* -'s> [waɪ] *n* Y *nt,* y *nt;* **~ as in Yankee** Y wie Ypsilon

y [waɪ] *n* MATH y *nt;* **~-axis** y-Achse *f*

yacht [jat] *n* Jacht *f*

yachting ['jat̬·ɪŋ] *n* Segeln *nt*

'yachtsman *n* (*owner*) Jachtbesitzer *m;* (*sailor*) Segler *m;* **around-the-world ~** Weltumsegler *m*

yak [jæk] **I.** *n* Jak *m* **II.** *vi* <-kk-> (*fam*) quasseln

yam [jæm] *n* ① (*sweet potato*) Süßkartoffel *f* ② (*vegetable*) Jamswurzel *f*

> Yams (Süßkartoffeln) sind ein süßes Wurzelgemüse. In den USA werden sie oft gebacken und dann mit Butter oder Ahornsirup gegessen, oder auch mit einer süßen Soße gekocht. Man isst **yams** besonders häufig an *Thanksgiving* (Erntedankfest).

yank [jæŋk] (*fam*) **I.** *n* Ruck *m* **II.** *vt* [ruckartig] ziehen (an +*dat*) **III.** *vi* zerren (**on** an +*dat*) ◆**yank out** *vt* herausreißen

Yank [jæŋk] *n* (*usu pej fam*) Ami *m*

Yankee ['jæŋ·ki] *n* (*usu pej fam*) ① (*person from northern US*) Nordstaatler(in) *m(f)* ② (*American*) Ami *m*

yap [jæp] **I.** *vi* <-pp-> ① *dog* kläffen ② (*fam: talk*) quasseln **II.** *n* Kläffen *nt*

yard[1] [jard] *n* Yard *nt;* **to sell sth by the ~** etw in Yards verkaufen; **a ~-long list** (*fig*) eine ellenlange Liste

yard[2] [jard] *n* ① (*lawn*) Garten *m* ② (*worksite*) Werksgelände *nt;* (*for storage*) Lagerplatz *m;* (*dockyard*) [Schiffs]werft *f*

'yardstick *n* ① (*tool*) Zollstock *m* ② (*standard*) Maßstab *m*

yarn [jarn] *n* ① (*for knitting, weaving*) Wolle *f* ② (*story*) Geschichte *f;* (*tall story*) *of sailor* Seemannsgarn *nt; of angler* Anglerlatein *nt*

yaw [jɔ] **I.** *vi ship* vom Kurs abweichen; *plane* ausbrechen, vom Kurs abweichen **II.** *n* Gieren *nt fachspr*

yawn [jɔn] **I.** *vi* gähnen *a. fig* **II.** *n* ① (*gape*) Gähnen *nt kein pl* ② (*fam: bore*) [stink]langweilige Angelegenheit; **I thought the film was a big ~** ich fand den Film stinklangweilig

yawning ['jɔ·nɪŋ] *adj* gähnend *a. fig*

yd. *n abbrev of* **yard**[1]

yeah [jeə] *adv* (*fam: yes*) ja[wohl]; **oh ~!** [*or* **~, ~!**] (*iron*) ja klar!, ganz bestimmt!

year [jɪr] *n* ① Jahr *nt;* **how much does he earn [in] a ~?** wie viel verdient er im Jahr?; **five times a ~** fünfmal im [*o* pro] Jahr; **two ~s' work** zwei Jahre Arbeit; **last ~** letztes Jahr; **for two ~s** zwei Jahre lang ② (*age*) [Lebens]jahr *nt;* **a two-~-old child** ein zweijähriges Kind ③ (*fam: ages*) ■**~s** *pl* Jahre *pl;* **for ~s** (*since a long time ago*) seit Jahren; (*for a long time*) jahrelang ④ SCH Schuljahr *nt;* UNIV Studienjahr *nt;* (*group*) Klasse *f*

'yearbook *n* ① Jahresausgabe *f* ② SCH, UNIV Jahrbuch *nt*

'year-long *adj* (*one year*) einjährig; (*many years*) jahrelang

yearly ['jɪr·li] *adj, adv* jährlich; **twice-~** zweimal pro Jahr

yearn [jɜrn] *vi* sich sehnen (**for** nach +*dat*)

yearning ['jɜr·nɪŋ] *n* Sehnsucht *f*

yeast [jist] *n* Hefe *f*

yell [jel] **I.** *n* ① (*shout*) [Auf]schrei *m;* **to let out a ~** einen Schrei ausstoßen ② (*cheer*) Schlachtruf *m* **II.** *vi* gellend schreien; **to ~ for help** um Hilfe rufen; ■**to ~ at sb** jdn anschreien **III.** *vt* laut rufen; ■**to ~ sth at sb** jdm etw laut zurufen

yellow ['jel·oʊ] **I.** *adj* ① (*color*) gelb; (*yellowed*) vergilbt ② (*fam: cowardly*) feige; **to have a ~ streak** feige sein **II.** *n* ① (*color*) Gelb *nt* ② (*shade*) Gelbton *m* **III.** *vi* vergilben

yellow 'fever *n* Gelbfieber *nt*

yellowish ['jel·oʊ·ɪʃ] *adj* gelblich

yellowness ['jel·oʊ·nɪs] *n* gelbe Farbe

'Yellow Pages® *npl* ■**the ~** die Gelben Seiten

yelp [jelp] **I.** *vi dog* kläffen, aufjaulen; *person* aufschreien **II.** *n* (*bark*) Gebell *nt,* Gejaule *nt;* (*shout*) Schrei *m*

yen[1] <*pl* -> [jen] *n* Yen *m*

yen[2] [jen] **I.** *n* (*fam*) Faible *nt;* **to have a ~ to do sth** den Drang haben, etw zu tun **II.** *vi* ■**to ~ for sth/sb** sich *akk* nach etw/jdm sehnen

yep [jep] *adv* (*fam*) ja

Yerevan [ˌje·rə·'van] *n* Eriwan *nt*

yes [jes] **I.** *adv* ① ja; **~, sir** jawohl; **~, please** ja bitte; **to say ~ [to sth]** ja [zu etw *dat*] sagen, etw bejahen ② (*contradicting*) aber ja [doch]; **she didn't really mean it — oh ~ she did!** sie hat es nicht so gemeint – oh doch, das hat sie! **II.** *n* <*pl* -[s]es> Ja *nt;* **was that a ~ or a no?** war das ein Ja oder ein Nein?

'yes-man *n* (*fam*) Jasager *m*

yesterday ['jes·tər·deɪ] **I.** *adv* gestern; **the day before ~** vorgestern **II.** *n* Gestern *nt*

yet [jet] **I.** *adv* ① (*until now*) bis jetzt; **as ~** bis jetzt; + *superl;* **the best ~** der/die/das Beste bisher ② (*already*) schon; **is it time to go ~? — no, not ~** ist es schon Zeit zu gehen? – nein, noch nicht ③ (*still*) noch; **the best is ~ to come** das Beste kommt [erst] noch; **not ~** noch nicht ④ (*despite that*) trotzdem; (*but*) aber [auch]; (*in spite of everything*) schon **II.** *conj* doch

yew [ju] *n* Eibe *f*

Yiddish ['jɪd·ɪʃ] *n* Jiddisch *nt*

yield [jild] **I.** *n* ① AGR Ertrag *m* ② MIN Ausbeute *f* ③ FIN [Zins]ertrag *m* **II.** *vt* ① (*produce*) hervorbringen; *grain, fruit* erzeugen; *information,* *results* liefern ② FIN abwerfen; **the bonds are currently ~ing 6·7%** die Pfandbriefe bringen derzeit 6-7 % ③ (*concede*) **to ~ a point to sb** jdm ein Zugeständnis machen; (*in discussion*) jdm in einem Punkt Recht geben; (*in competition*) einen Punkt an jdn abgeben **III.** *vi* ■ **to ~ [to sb/sth]** [jdm/etw [gegenüber]] nachgeben; (*give right of way*) ■ **to ~ to sb** jdm den Vortritt lassen

yielding [ˈjil·dɪŋ] *adj* ① (*pliable*) dehnbar ② (*compliant*) nachgiebig

YMCA [ˌwaɪ·em·si·ˈeɪ] *n + sing/pl vb abbrev of* **Young Men's Christian Association** CVJM *m*

yodel [ˈjoʊ·dəl] **I.** *vi, vt* <-l- *or* -ll-> jodeln **II.** *n* Jodler *m*

yoga [ˈjoʊ·gə] *n* Yoga *nt*

yogurt, yoghurt [ˈjoʊ·gərt] *n* Joghurt *m o nt*

yoke [joʊk] **I.** *n* (*for pulling*) Joch *nt a. fig;* (*for carrying*) Tragjoch *nt* **II.** *vt* ① *ox* ins Joch spannen ② (*fig*) ■ **to ~ sth together** etw [miteinander ver]koppeln

yokel [ˈjoʊ·kəl] *n* Tölpel *m*

yolk [joʊk] *n* Eigelb *nt*

you [ju] *pron* ① (*singular*) du *in nomin,* dich *in akk,* dir *in dat;* (*polite form*) Sie *in nomin, akk,* Ihnen *in dat;* **if I were ~** wenn ich du/Sie wäre, an deiner/Ihrer Stelle ② (*plural*) ihr *in nomin,* euch *in akk, dat;* (*polite form*) Sie *in nomin, akk,* Ihnen *in dat;* **how many of ~ are there?** wie viele seid ihr?; **are ~ two ready?** seid ihr zwei [*o* beide] fertig? ③ (*one*) man; **~ learn from experience** aus Erfahrung wird man klug; **it's not good for ~** das ist nicht gesund

you'll [jul] = **you will** *see* **will**[1]

young [jʌŋ] **I.** *adj* jung; **I'm not as ~ as I used to be** ich bin nicht mehr der Jüngste; **she's ~ for sixteen** für sechzehn ist sie noch recht kindlich; **~ children** kleine Kinder; **to be ~ at heart** im Herzen jung [geblieben] sein; ■ **the Y~er** (*in titles*) der/die Jüngere **II.** *npl* ① (*youths*) ■ **the ~** die jungen Leute ② ZOOL Junge *pl*

youngster [ˈjʌŋ·stər] *n* Jugendliche(r) *f(m)*

your [jʊr] *adj poss* ① (*singular*) dein(e); (*plural*) euer/eure; (*polite form*) Ihr(e) ② (*one's*) sein(e); **it's enough to break ~ heart** es bricht einem förmlich das Herz

you're [jʊr] = **you are** *see* **be**

yours [jʊrz] *pron poss* ① deine/deiner/dein[e]s, Ihre/Ihrer/Ihr[e]s; **is this pen ~?** ist das dein Stift?; **the choice is ~** Sie haben die Wahl; **it's no business of ~** das geht dich nichts an ② (*in letter*) **Y~ truly** mit freundlichen Grüßen

yourself <*pl* yourselves> [jʊr·ˈself] *pron* ① (*singular*) dich *akk,* dir *dat;* (*plural*) euch; (*polite form, sing/pl*) sich; **how would you describe ~?** wie würden Sie sich beschreiben?; **help yourselves, boys** bedient euch, Jungs; **do you always talk to ~ like that?** sprichst du immer so mit dir selbst? ② (*oneself*) sich; **you tell ~ everything's all right** man sagt sich, dass alles in Ordnung ist; **to have sth [all] to ~** etw für dich [*o* sich] allein haben ③ (*personally*) selbst; **you can do that ~** du kannst das selbst machen; **to be ~** du selbst sein; **just be ~** sei ganz natürlich; **to not be ~** nicht du selbst sein; **to try sth for ~** etw selbst versuchen; ■ **[all] by ~** [ganz] allein

youth [juθ] *n* ① (*period*) Jugend *f* ② (*young man*) junger Mann, Jugendliche(r) *m* ③ *pl* (*young people*) **the ~ of today** die Jugend von heute

ˈyouth center, ˈyouth club *n* Jugendzentrum *nt*

youthful [ˈjuθ·fəl] *adj* jugendlich

ˈyouth hostel *n* Jugendherberge *f*

you've [juv] = **you have** *see* **have I., II.**

yowl [jaʊl] **I.** *vi* jaulen **II.** *n* Gejaule *nt*

yo-yo <*pl* -s> [ˈjoʊ·joʊ] **I.** *n* Jo-Jo *nt;* **to go up and down like a ~** rauf- und runterschnellen **II.** *vi* (*inf: vacillate*) schwanken

yuan [ju·ˈæn] *n* FIN Yuan *m*

yuck [jʌk] *interj* (*fam*) i!, igitt!

yucky [ˈjʌk·i] *adj* (*fam*) ek[e]lig

Yugoslav [ˈju·goʊ·slav] (*hist*) **I.** *adj* jugoslawisch **II.** *n* Jugoslawe, Jugoslawin *m, f*

Yugoslavia [ˈju·goʊ·ˈslav·i·ə] *n* (*hist*) Jugoslawien *nt;* **the former ~** das ehemalige Jugoslawien

Yugoslavian [ˌju·goʊ·ˈsla·vi·ən] (*hist*) **I.** *adj* jugoslawisch; **to be ~** Jugoslawe, Jugoslawin *m, f* sein **II.** *n* Jugoslawe, Jugoslawin *m, f*

Yukon Territory [ˈju·kan-] *n* Yukon Territory *nt*

ˈyule log *n großes Holzscheit, das zur Weihnachtszeit im offenen Feuer brennt*

yum [jʌm] *interj* (*fam*) lecker!

yummy [ˈjʌm·i] *adj* (*fam*) lecker *a. fig*

yuppie [ˈjʌp·i] *n* Yuppie *m*

Zz

Z <*pl* -'s *or* -s>, **z** <*pl* -'s> [zi] *n* Z *nt*, z *nt*; **~ as in Zulu** Z wie Zacharias

z [zi] *n* MATH z *nt*; **~-axis** z-Achse *f*

zany ['zeɪ·ni] *adj* ulkig

zap [zæp] (*fam*) **I.** *vt* <-pp-> ① (*destroy*) *person* erledigen; *thing* kaputtmachen ② FOOD (*heat up*) in der Mikrowelle aufwärmen ③ COMPUT (*delete*) löschen **II.** *vi* <-pp-> ① (*speed*) düsen ② TV zappen **III.** *n* Pep *m* **IV.** *interj* schwups!

zeal [zil] *n* Eifer *m*

zealot ['zel·ət] *n* Fanatiker(in) *m(f)*

zealous ['zel·əs] *adj* ① (*eager*) [über]eifrig ② (*enthusiastic*) leidenschaftlich

zebra <*pl* -s *or* -> ['zi·brə] *n* Zebra *nt*

zenith ['zi·nɪθ] *n* Zenit *m a. fig*

zero ['zɪr·oʊ] **I.** *n* <*pl* -s> ① MATH Null *f* ② (*point on scale*) Nullpunkt *m*; **10 degrees below ~** zehn Grad unter null **II.** *adj* **his prospects are ~** seine Aussichten sind gleich null; **~ growth** Nullwachstum *nt*; **~ hour** die Stunde null **III.** *vt* auf null einstellen
◆**zero in** *vi* ① (*aim*) **to ~ in on a target** ein Ziel anvisieren ② (*fig*) sich konzentrieren (**on** auf +*akk*)

zero-'energy *adj* äußerst energiesparend, mit extrem geringem Energieverbrauch *nach n*; **~ building** Null-Energie-Haus *nt*

zero 'tolerance *n* LAW Nulltoleranz *f*

zest [zest] *n* ① (*enthusiasm*) Eifer *m*; **~ for life** Lebensfreude *f* ② **lemon ~** Zitronenschale *f*

zigzag ['zɪg·zæg] **I.** *n* Zickzack *m* **II.** *adv* im Zickzack **III.** *vi* <-gg-> sich im Zickzack bewegen; *line, path* im Zickzack verlaufen

zinc [zɪŋk] *n* Zink *nt*

zip [zɪp] **I.** *n* ① (*fam: vigor*) Schwung *m* ② (*Zip Code*) ≈ Postleitzahl *f* ③ (*nothing, lowest possible*) Null *kein art* **II.** *pron* (*fam*) null; **I know ~ about computers** ich habe null Ahnung von Computern **III.** *vt* <-pp-> (*close*) **could you help me ~ [up] my dress?** könntest du mir vielleicht helfen, den Reißverschluss an meinem Kleid zuzumachen?; **to ~ sth together** etw mit einem Reißverschluss zusammenziehen ▶ PHRASES: **to ~ one's lip** den Mund halten **IV.** *vi* <-pp-> ① (*fasten*) **it ~s [up] at the back** es hat hinten einen Reißverschluss ② (*speed*) rasen, flitzen; **to ~ through** *job* im Eiltempo erledigen

'Zip Code *n* ≈ Postleitzahl *f*

zipper ['zɪp·ər] *n* Reißverschluss *m*

zippy ['zɪp·i] *adj* (*fam*) spritzig

zodiac ['zoʊ·di·æk] *n* **sign of the ~** Tierkreiszeichen *nt*

zombie ['zam·bi] *n* Zombie *m*

zone [zoʊn] **I.** *n* Zone *f*; **combat ~** Kampfgebiet *nt*; **danger ~** Gefahrenzone *f*; **earthquake ~** Erdbebenregion *f*; **no-fly ~** Flugverbotszone *f* **II.** *vt* in [Nutzungs]zonen aufteilen

zoning ['zoʊn·ɪŋ] **I.** *n* Bodenordnung *f* **II.** *adj* **~ law** Baugesetz *nt*; **~ restriction** Planungsbeschränkung *f*

zoo [zu] *n* Zoo *m*

zoological [ˌzoʊ·ə·'ladʒ·ɪ·kəl] *adj* zoologisch

zoologist [zoʊ·'al·ə·dʒɪst] *n* Zoologe, Zoologin *m, f*

zoology [zoʊ·'al·ə·dʒi] *n* Zoologie *f*

zoom [zum] **I.** *n* **~ [lens]** Zoom[objektiv] *nt* **II.** *vi* ① (*speed*) rasen; ■**to ~ ahead** [*or* **off**] davonsausen; (*in race*) vorpreschen; ■**to ~ past** vorbeirasen; (*fig*) *year* rasend schnell vergehen ② PHOT zoomen
◆**zoom in** *vi* [nahe] heranfahren, heranzoomen, [ein]schwenken (**on** auf +*akk*)
◆**zoom out** *vi* wegzoomen

zucchini <*pl* -s *or* -> [zu·'ki·ni] *n* Zucchini *f*

Anhang
Appendix

Concise German grammar
Deutsche Kurzgrammatik

The Definite and the Indefinite Article

German nouns are either **masculine, feminine,** or **neuter**.

The **gender** of a noun can be recognized by its article: *der, die,* or *das*. There are four cases in German: nominative, accusative, dative, and genitive.

	Definite article				Indefinite article			
	m*	f*	nt*	pl*	m	f	nt	pl
Nom.	der	die	das	die	ein	eine	ein	does not exist in German
Acc.	den	die	das	die	einen	eine	ein	
Dat.	dem	der	dem	den	einem	einer	einem	
Gen.	des	der	des	der	eines	einer	eines	

* m, f, nt, and pl stand for masculine, feminine, neuter, and plural, respectively

1. Using the articles

The definite article is used when referring to:	The indefinite article is used when referring to:
a particular person: **Die** Frau hatte eine rote Tasche. ***The** woman had a red bag.*	no one in particular: Ich habe **eine** Frau gesehen. *I saw **a** woman.*
a particular thing: Gib mir bitte **das** große Glas. *Please give me **the** big glass.*	nothing in particular: Gib mir bitte **ein** Glas. *Please give me **a** glass.*
things that cannot be counted: Das ist **das** klare Ostseewasser. *That is **the** clear water of the Baltic Sea.*	particular qualities of things that cannot be counted (unlike in English): Das ist aber **ein** klares Wasser. *That is **some** really clear water.*
abstract concepts: Das war **die** größte Freude meines Lebens. *That was **the** greatest pleasure of my life.*	abstract concepts: Es war mir **eine** große Freude. *It was **a** great pleasure.*

1.1. The definite article

The definite article is used more often in German than in English. In German, the definite article is used when referring to specific things, such as:

mountain ranges	*die* Alpen	*the Alps*
mountains	*der* Mount Everest	*Mount Everest*
oceans	*der* Pazifik	*the Pacific Ocean*
seas	*das* Schwarze Meer	*the Black Sea*
lakes	*der* Genfer See	*Lake Geneva*
rivers	*der* Rhein	*the Rhine*
celestial bodies	*die* Sonne	*the sun*

as well as expressions of time that do not have plurals, such as:

seasons	*der* Frühling	*spring*
months	*der* Mai	*May*
times of day	*der* Mittag	*noon*
mealtimes	*das* Mittagessen	*lunch*

The definite article is also used when referring to:

- countries whose gender in German is feminine:

die Türkei	*Turkey*
die Slowakei	*Slovakia*
die Schweiz	*Switzerland*

- countries whose name is in the plural:

die Vereinigten Staaten von Amerika	*the United States of America*
die USA	*the USA*
die Niederlande	*the Netherlands*

- geographic regions whose gender in German is either feminine or masculine:

die Normandie	*Normandy*
die Riviera	*the Riviera*
der Schwarzwald	*the Black Forest*

- place names that include such words as "Republic," "Union," "State," and "Kingdom":

das Königreich Belgien	*the Kingdom of Belgium*
die Slowakische Republik	*the Republic of Slovakia*

- names of geographic regions that contain an adjective:

der Ferne Osten	*the Far East*
der Nahe Osten	*the Middle East*

- famous structures:

das Brandenburger Tor	*the Brandenburg Gate*
die Freiheitsstatue	*the Statue of Liberty*

- street names:

die Königsstraße	*Königsstraße*

- names of personalities:

der Papst	*the Pope*
die Queen	*the Queen*

- names of people, when used colloquially:

Der Markus war gestern hier.	*Markus was here yesterday.*

- names of professions:

der Schriftsteller Günther Grass	*the writer Günther Grass*

- abstract proper nouns, such as eras and historical events:

der Expressionismus	*the Expressionist era*
die Oktoberrevolution	*the October Revolution*

Note that definite articles sometimes combine with prepositions to form contractions:

in	+	dem	=	im	*im* Pazifik
an	+	dem	=	am	*am* Mittelmeer
zu	+	dem	=	zum	*zum* Genfer See

2.1. No article

Articles are not used when:

– addressing people:	Guten Tag, Herr Bauer!	*Hello, Mr. Bauer!*

and when making general statements about:

– someone:	Hans und Franz essen Eis.	*Hans and Franz are eating ice cream.*
– someone's profession:	Er ist Schauspieler.	*He is an actor.*
– someone's nationality:	Ich bin Deutsche, du bist Amerikaner.	*I am German, you are American.*
– someone's religion:	Sie ist Jüdin und er ist Moslem.	*She is a Jew and he is a Muslim.*

Furthermore, for the most part, articles are not used

1) when referring to:

– things that cannot be counted:	Geh doch bitte Milch kaufen.	*Please go buy some milk.*
– abstract ideas:	Ich habe Schmerzen.	*I am in pain.*
– continents:	Nordamerika ist weit von Afrika entfernt.	*North America is far from Africa.*

Exception: The definite article is used when referring to Antarctica or Arctica.

– countries:	Er kommt aus Schweden.	*He is from Sweden.*

Exceptions: see section 1.1.

– cities:	Der Zug kommt aus Berlin.	*The train is coming from Berlin.*
Exception: If the name of a city is modified by an attribute, it takes either a definite or an indefinite article:	Er besuchte das alte Rom.	*He visited Old Rome.*
	Ein in Freiheit wieder vereinigtes Berlin.	*A Berlin that has been reunited in freedom.*
– many territories, regions, and islands:	Kalifornien, Bayern, Rügen, Borneo	*California, Bavaria, Rügen, Borneo*
– holidays:	Was wünschst du dir zu Weihnachten?	*What do you want for Christmas?*
2) in:		
– book titles:	Deutsch-englisches Wörterbuch	*German-English dicitonary*
– headlines:	Staatsbesuch in Washington	*State Visit in Washington*
– expressions involving numbers:	Zu verkaufen: großes Haus mit 3 Zimmern.	*For sale: Large house with three rooms.*
– set phrases made up of a noun and a verb (if talking in general terms):	Heute muss ich Wäsche waschen.	*I have to do laundry today.*
3) and:		
– when nouns are preceded by prepositions:	Ich möchte in Ruhe gelassen werden.	*I would like to be left in peace.*

Note: For how to use articles when referring to geographical proper nouns, see the "Concise German Grammar."

Nouns

1. Declension of nouns

In German, the declension of a noun is characterized as either *strong*, *weak*, or *mixed*. (See: Declension of adjectives.)

1.1. Strong declension: masculine and neuter

Singular				
Nom.	der Tag	der Traum	das Kind	das Dach
Acc.	den Tag	den Traum	das Kind	das Dach
Dat.	dem Tag(e)	dem Traum(e)	dem Kind(e)	dem Dach(e)
Gen.	des Tag(e)s	des Traum(e)s	des Kind(e)s	des Dach(e)s
Plural	Tage	Träume	Kinder	Dächer
Nom.	die Tage	die Träume	die Kinder	die Dächer
Acc.	die Tage	die Träume	die Kinder	die Dächer
Dat.	den Tagen	den Träumen	den Kindern	den Dächern
Gen.	der Tage	der Träume	der Kinder	der Dächer

Singular			
Nom.	das Auto	der Tischler	der Vogel
Acc.	das Auto	den Tischler	den Vogel
Dat.	dem Auto	dem Tischler	dem Vogel
Gen.	des Autos	des Tischlers	des Vogels
Plural	Autos	Tischler	Vögel
Nom.	die Autos	die Tischler	die Vögel
Acc.	die Autos	die Tischler	die Vögel
Dat.	den Autos	den Tischlern	den Vögeln
Gen.	der Autos	der Tischler	der Vögel

Note:

Nouns ending in *s, sch, ß,* and *z* always belong to the strong declension. The genitive singular of such nouns ends in *-es*:

Hals – Halses, Busch – Busches, Fuß – Fußes, Reiz – Reizes

2.1. Strong declension: feminine

Singular			
Nom.	die Wand	die Mutter	die Bar
Acc.	die Wand	die Mutter	die Bar
Dat.	der Wand	der Mutter	der Bar
Gen.	der Wand	der Mutter	der Bar
Plural	Wände	Mütter	Bars
Nom.	die Wände	die Mütter	die Bars
Acc.	die Wände	die Mütter	die Bars
Dat.	den Wänden	den Müttern	den Bars
Gen.	der Wände	der Mütter	der Bars

3.1. Weak declension: masculine

Singular			
Nom.	der Bauer	der Bär	der Hase
Acc.	den Bauern	den Bären	den Hasen
Dat.	dem Bauern	dem Bären	dem Hasen
Gen.	des Bauern	des Bären	des Hasen
Plural	Bauern	Bären	Hasen
Nom.	die Bauern	die Bären	die Hasen
Acc.	die Bauern	die Bären	die Hasen
Dat.	den Bauern	den Bären	den Hasen
Gen.	der Bauern	der Bären	der Hasen

4.1. Weak declension: feminine

Singular				
Nom.	die Uhr	die Feder	die Gabe	die Ärztin
Acc.	die Uhr	die Feder	die Gabe	die Ärztin
Dat.	der Uhr	der Feder	der Gabe	der Ärztin
Gen.	der Uhr	der Feder	der Gabe	der Ärztin
Plural	Uhr**en**	Feder**n**	Gabe**n**	Ärztin**nen**
Nom.	die Uhren	die Federn	die Gaben	die Ärztinnen
Acc.	die Uhren	die Federn	die Gaben	die Ärztinnen
Dat.	den Uhren	den Federn	den Gaben	den Ärztinnen
Gen.	der Uhren	der Federn	der Gaben	der Ärztinnen

5.1. Mixed declension: masculine and feminine

Nouns of the mixed declension decline as *strong* nouns in the singular and as *weak* nouns in the plural.

Singular				
Nom.	das Auge	das Ohr	der Name	das Herz
Acc.	das Auge	das Ohr	den Namen	das Herz
Dat.	dem Auge	dem Ohr(e)	dem Namen	dem Herzen
Gen.	des Auges	des Ohr(e)s	der Namens	des Herzens
Plural	Auge**n**	Ohr**en**	Name**n**	Herz**en**
Nom.	die Augen	die Ohren	die Namen	die Herzen
Acc.	die Augen	die Ohren	die Namen	die Herzen
Dat.	den Augen	den Ohren	den Namen	den Herzen
Gen.	der Augen	der Ohren	der Namen	der Herzen

2. Declension of adjectives

	Masculine	
Singular		
Nom.	der Reisende	ein Reisender
Acc.	den Reisenden	einen Reisenden
Dat.	dem Reisenden	einem Reisenden
Gen.	des Reisenden	eines Reisenden
Plural		
Nom.	die Reisenden	Reisende
Acc.	die Reisenden	Reisende
Dat.	den Reisenden	Reisenden
Gen.	der Reisenden	Reisender

	Feminine	
Singular		
Nom.	die Reisende	eine Reisende
Acc.	die Reisende	eine Reisende
Dat.	der Reisenden	einer Reisenden
Gen.	der Reisenden	einer Reisenden
Plural		
Nom.	die Reisenden	Reisende
Acc.	die Reisenden	Reisende
Dat.	den Reisenden	Reisenden
Gen.	der Reisenden	Reisender

	Neuter	
Singular		
Nom.	das Neugeborene	ein Neugeborenes
Acc.	das Neugeborene	ein Neugeborenes
Dat.	dem Neugeborenen	einem Neugeborenen
Gen.	des Neugeborenen	eines Neugeborenen
Plural		
Nom.	die Neugeborenen	Neugeborene
Acc.	die Neugeborenen	Neugeborene
Dat.	den Neugeborenen	Neugeborenen
Gen.	der Neugeborenen	Neugeborener

3. Declension of proper nouns

The genitive of proper nouns is determined by various rules:

Proper nouns with an article	Proper nouns without an article	Proper nouns ending in s, ß, x, z	Proper nouns with apposition	When there are several proper nouns, one after the other
remain unchanged	add an *s*	add an apostrophe	are declined like nouns	the last one adds an *s*
des Aristoteles	Marias Auto	Aristoteles' (Schriften)	Nom. Karl der Große	Johann Sebastian Bachs (Musik)
des (schönen) Berlin	die Straßen Berlins	die Straßen Calais'	Acc. Karl den Großen Dat. Karl dem Großen Gen. Karls des Großen	

Surnames add **-s** in the plural:

For example: die Schneider**s**

Exception: Surnames that end in *s*, *ß*, *x*, or *z* add **-ens** in the plural: die Schmitz**ens**

Note also that proper nouns such as the names of streets, buildings, companies, ships, newspapers, and organizations are declined.

Adjectives

When an adjective *precedes* a noun, it has to agree with the **gender**, **case**, and **number** of the noun. As is the case with a noun, the declension of an adjective is characterized as *strong, weak*, or *mixed*.

1. The strong form

- for adjective + noun combinations *without* an article
- when an adjective precedes a noun without indicating the gender: mehrere liebe Kinder, manch guter Wein.

- after *cardinal numbers*, *"ein paar"* and *"ein bisschen"*:

Sie hörte zwei laute Schritte.	*She heard two loud steps.*
Wir machen eine Reise mit ein paar guten Freunden.	*We are going away with a few good friends.*
Mit einem bisschen guten Willen schaffst du das.	*All being well, you'll manage that.*

	Masculine	Feminine	Neuter
Singular			
Nom.	guter Wein	schöne Frau	liebes Kind
Acc.	guten Wein	schöne Frau	liebes Kind
Dat.	gutem Wein(e)	schöner Frau	liebem Kind(e)
Gen.	guten Wein(e)s	schöner Frau	lieben Kindes
Plural			
Nom.	gute Weine	schöne Frauen	liebe Kinder
Acc.	gute Weine	schöne Frauen	liebe Kinder
Dat.	guten Weinen	schönen Frauen	lieben Kindern
Gen.	guter Weine	schöner Frauen	lieber Kinder

2. The weak form

- for adjective + noun combinations with the definite article *der*, *die*, *das*
- and with pronouns that indicate the gender of a noun: *diese(r), folgende(r), jede(r), welche(s, r)*

	Masculine	Feminine	Neuter
Singular			
Nom.	der gute Wein	die schöne Frau	das liebe Kind
Acc.	den guten Wein	die schöne Frau	das liebe Kind
Dat.	dem guten Wein	der schönen Frau	dem lieben Kind
Gen.	des guten Wein(e)s	der schönen Frau	des lieben Kindes
Plural			
Nom.	die guten Weine	die schönen Frauen	die lieben Kinder
Acc.	die guten Weine	die schönen Frauen	die lieben Kinder
Dat.	den guten Weinen	den schönen Frauen	den lieben Kindern
Gen.	der guten Weine	der schönen Frauen	der lieben Kinder

3. The mixed form

- for adjective + noun combinations with the indefinite article *ein* as well as *kein* (with masculine and neuter nouns in the singular)
- and with the possessive pronouns *mein, dein, sein, unser, euer, ihr*

	Masculine	Neuter
Singular		
Nom.	ein guter Wein	ein liebes Kind
Acc.	einen guten Wein	ein liebes Kind
Dat.	einem guten Wein(e)	einem lieben Kind
Gen.	eines guten Wein(e)s	eines lieben Kindes

4. Adjectives ending in *-abel, -ibel* and *-el*

When declined, these adjectives drop the "*-e.*"

	miserabel	penibel	heikel
Singular			
Nom.	ein miserabler Stil	eine penible Frau	ein heikles Problem
Acc.	einen miserablen Stil	eine penible Frau	ein heikles Problem
Dat.	einem miserablen Stil	einer peniblen Frau	einem heiklen Problem
Gen.	eines miserablen Stils	einer peniblen Frau	eines heiklen Problems
Plural			
Nom.	miserable Stile	penible Frauen	heikle Probleme
Acc.	miserable Stile	penible Frauen	heikle Probleme
Dat.	miserablen Stilen	peniblen Frauen	heiklen Problemen
Gen.	miserabler Stile	penibler Frauen	heikler Probleme

5. Adjectives ending in *-er* and *-en*

- normally retain the "*e*" in the declined form, but not in elevated literary style:

finster	mit finstrer Miene

- the same applies to adjectives whose origins are not German:

makaber	eine makabre Geschichte
integer	ein integrer Beamter

6. Adjectives ending in *-auer* and *-euer*

- normally drop the "*e*" in the declined form:

teuer	ein teures Geschenk
sauer	saure Gurken

7. Adjectives ending in -ß

- keep the "*ß*" after a long vowel:

groß	mein großer Bruder
bloß	eine bloße Freundschaft

Comparison of Adjectives

	Masculine	Feminine	Neuter
Positive	schön	schöne	schönes
Comparative	schöner	schönere	schöneres
Superlative	der schönste	die schönste	das schönste

The comparative and superlative forms of an adjective have the same endings in the accusative, dative, and genitive as the positive form of the adjective has before a noun in the respective case:

der Garten mit den schön**en** Blumen (dative plural, positive)	*the garden with the pretty flowers*
der Garten mit den schönst**en** Blumen (dative plural, superlative)	*the garden with the prettiest flowers*

Exceptions:

1. Adjectives and adverbs add "e" before the superlative endings:

- whenever they have only one syllable
- whenever their last syllable is stressed
- whenever they end in *-s*, *-ß*, *-st*, *-x*, or *-z*
- and usually when they end in *-d*, *-t*, or *-sch*:

spitz	adj.	spitze(r, s)
	adv.	am spitzesten
beliebt	adj.	beliebteste(r, s)
	adv.	am beliebtesten

The same applies to compound adjectives and adverbs as well as those with a prefix, regardless of stress:

unsanft	adj.	unsanfteste(r, s)
	adv.	am unsanftesten

2. One-syllable adjectives whose root vowel is *a*, *o*, or *u* add an umlaut in the comparative and superlative forms:

arm	ärmer	ärmste(r, s)
groß	größer	größte(r, s)
klug	klüger	klügste(r, s)

3. The following groups of adjectives never have an umlaut in the comparative or superlative forms:

- adjectives with the diphthong *-au*:

faul	fauler	faulste(r, s)
kraus	krauser	krauseste(r, s)
schlau	schlauer	schlaueste(r, s)

- adjectives with the suffixes *-bar*, *-haft*, *-ig*, *-lich*, *-sam*:

dankbar	dankbarer	dankbarste(r, s)
schwatzhaft	schwatzhafter	schwatzhaftes-te(r, s)
schattig	schattiger	schattigste(r, s)
stattlich	stattlicher	stattlichste(r, s)
sorgsam	sorgsamer	sorgsamste(r, s)

- adjectives which occur as participles:

überrascht	überraschter	überraschtes-te(r, s)

- adjectives of foreign origin:

banal	banaler	banalste(r, s)
interessant	interessanter	interessantes-te(r, s)
grandios	grandioser	grandioses-te(r, s)

4. Irregular comparative/superlative forms of adjectives and adverbs:

gut	besser	beste(r, s)
viel	mehr	meiste(r, s)
gern	lieber	am liebsten
bald	eher	am ehesten

Adverbs

When an adjective is used as an adverb, it remains unchanged:

er singt gut
sie schreibt schön
er läuft schnell

The rules for the comparison of adverbs are the same as those for adjectives:

er singt besser
sie schreibt schöner
er läuft schneller

Most adverbs form the superlative using *am ...sten:*

er singt am besten
sie schreibt am schönsten
er läuft am schnellsten

Verbs

Present tense

The present tense in German is used to express an act in the present, a general statement of fact, or an event in the future:

Was machst du? Ich lese.	*What are you doing? I'm reading.*
Die Erde dreht sich um die Sonne.	*The Earth revolves around the Sun.*
Morgen fliege ich nach Rom.	*I'm flying to Rome tomorrow.*

1. Regular verbs (weak conjugation)

	machen	legen	sagen	sammeln
ich	mache	lege	sage	sammle
du	machst	legst	sagst	sammelst
er/sie/es	macht	legt	sagt	sammelt
wir	machen	legen	sagen	sammeln
ihr	macht	legt	sagt	sammelt
sie/Sie	machen	legen	sagen	sammeln

Verbs with a stem ending in *s, ss, ß,* and *z:*

	rasen	passen	grüßen	reizen
ich	rase	passe	grüße	reize
du	rast	passt	grüßt	reizt
er/sie/es	rast	passt	grüßt	reizt
wir	rasen	passen	grüßen	reizen
ihr	rast	passt	grüßt	reizt
sie/Sie	rasen	passen	grüßen	reizen

Verbs with a stem ending in *d* or *t*, or with a consonant + *m*, or a consonant + *n* add an *-e* in the second person singular, the third person singular, and the second person plural.

	reden	wetten	atmen	trocknen
ich	rede	wette	atme	trockne
du	redest	wettest	atmest	trocknest
er/sie/es	redet	wettet	atmet	trocknet
wir	reden	wetten	atmen	trocknen
ihr	redet	wettet	atmet	trocknet
sie/Sie	reden	wetten	atmen	trocknen

Verbs with a stem ending in an unstressed *-e* or *-er* drop the *-e* in the first person singular:

angeln	ich angle
zittern	ich zittre

2. Irregular verbs (strong conjugation) usually change their stem vowels.

	tragen	blasen	laufen	essen
ich	trage	blase	laufe	esse
du	trägst	bläst	läufst	isst
er/sie/es	trägt	bläst	läuft	isst
wir	tragen	blasen	laufen	essen
ihr	tragt	blast	lauft	esst
sie/Sie	tragen	blasen	laufen	essen

→ See also the irregular verbs in the main body of the dictionary and in the list on page 1125.

Simple past (preterite) tense

The simple past tense expresses a past event:

Letztes Jahr reisten wir nach Spanien.	*We went to Spain last year.*

1. Regular verbs

	machen	sammeln	grüßen	reizen
ich	machte	sammelte	grüßte	reizte
du	machtest	sammeltest	grüßtest	reiztest
er/sie/es	machte	sammelte	grüßte	reizte
wir	machten	sammelten	grüßten	reizten
ihr	machtet	sammeltet	grüßtet	reiztet
sie/Sie	machten	sammelten	grüßten	reizten

Verbs with a stem ending in *d*, *t*, a consonant + *m*, or a consonant + *n*:

	reden	wetten	atmen	trocknen
ich	redete	wettete	atmete	trocknete
du	redetest	wettetest	atmetest	trocknetest
er/sie/es	redete	wettete	atmete	trocknete
wir	redeten	wetteten	atmeten	trockneten
ihr	redetet	wettetet	atmetet	trocknetet
sie/Sie	redeten	wetteten	atmeten	trockneten

2. Irregular verbs

	tragen	blasen	laufen	essen
ich	trug	blies	lief	aß
du	trugst	bliest	liefst	aßt
er/sie/es	trug	blies	lief	aß
wir	trugen	bliesen	liefen	aßen
ihr	trugt	bliest	lieft	aßt
sie/Sie	trugen	bliesen	liefen	aßen

→ See also the irregular verbs in the main body of the dictionary and in the list on page 1125.

Present perfect tense

The present perfect tense is used to express an isolated event or condition in the past:

Der Zug ist abgefahren.	*The train left.*
Heute Nacht hat es geregnet.	*It rained last night.*

The present perfect tense is formed with the present tense of the auxiliary verb *haben* or *sein* plus the past participle.

1. Verbs which express movement or a change of state form the present perfect tense with *sein*.

	radeln	fahren	verstummen	sterben
ich	bin geradelt	bin gefahren	bin verstummt	bin gestorben
du	bist geradelt	bist gefahren	bist verstummt	bist gestorben
er/sie/es	ist geradelt	ist gefahren	ist verstummt	ist gestorben
wir	sind geradelt	sind gefahren	sind verstummt	sind gestorben
ihr	seid geradelt	seid gefahren	seid verstummt	seid gestorben
sie/Sie	sind geradelt	sind gefahren	sind verstummt	sind gestorben

2. Transitive, reflexive, and impersonal verbs form the present perfect tense with *haben*, as do most intransitive verbs when they express a permanent condition.

	legen	sich freuen	regnen	leben
ich	habe gelegt	habe mich gefreut		habe gelebt
du	hast gelegt	hast dich gefreut		hast gelebt
er/sie/es	hat gelegt	hat sich gefreut	es hat geregnet	hat gelebt
wir	haben gelegt	haben uns gefreut		haben gelebt
ihr	habt gelegt	habt euch gefreut		habt gelebt
sie/Sie	haben gelegt	haben sich gefreut		haben gelebt

3. Forming the past participle: with or without “ge-“:

Most past participles are formed by putting **ge-** in front of the verb stem and adding either **-t** (for weak verbs) or **-en** (for strong verbs). The past participles of strong verbs usually have a stem vowel change:

bau·en	gebaut
hö·ren	gehört
le·sen	gelesen
sin·gen	gesungen

For German verbs with separable prefixes, the **-ge-** is inserted between the prefix and the verb stem. Note that the prefix of such verbs is always stressed (as is indicated by a thin vertical line between the prefix and the rest of the verb, as shown below).

auf|bau·en	auf**ge**baut
zu|hö·ren	zu**ge**hört
vor|le·sen	vor**ge**lesen

Important: A great number of verbs form the past participle without **ge-**. Most such verbs belong to two basic groups:

1. Verbs that end in *-ieren*:

mar·schie·ren	marschierte	(ist) marschiert
pro·bie·ren	probierte	(hat) probiert

NB These verbs still form the past participle without **ge-** even when they contain a separable (stressed) prefix:

ab|mar·schie·ren	marschierte ab	(ist) abmarschiert
aus|pro·bie·ren	probierte aus	(hat) ausprobiert

2. Verbs that begin with one of the following prefixes, which are always unstressed (and therefore inseparable):
be-, emp-, ent-, er-, ge-, ver-, zer-

be·bau·en	bebaute	(hat) bebaut
er·hö·ren	erhörte	(hat) erhört
ge·stal·ten	gestaltete	(hat) gestaltet
ver·lan·gen	verlangte	(hat) verlangt

All other verbs with inseparable (unstressed) prefixes (indicated by the lack of a thin vertical line between the prefix and the rest of the verb, as shown below) also belong to this group:

um·ge·hen	umging	(hat) umgangen
un·ter·su·chen	untersuchte	(hat) untersucht
über·set·zen	übersetzte	(hat) übersetzt

NB Again, these verbs still form the past participle without **ge-** even when they have a separable (stressed) prefix:

um|ge·stal·ten	gestaltete um	(hat) umgestaltet
ab|ver·lan·gen	verlangte ab	(hat) abverlangt
zu·rück|über·set·zen	übersetzte zurück	(hat) zurückübersetzt

Very few verbs which do not belong to either of these two groups (e.g., miauen, trompeten, stibitzen) form the past participle without **ge-**. They are marked in the dictionary accordingly.

The past perfect (pluperfect) tense

The past perfect tense is used to describe an <u>event that had already finished when another event happened</u>:

Als er im Kino ankam, hatte der Film schon begonnen.	*When he arrived at the cinema the film had already started.*

The past perfect tense is formed with the simple past (preterite) tense of *haben* or *sein* and the past participle.

	fahren	sterben	legen	leben
ich	war gefahren	war gestorben	hatte gelegt	hatte gelebt
du	warst gefahren	warst gestorben	hattest gelegt	hattest gelebt
er/sie/es	war gefahren	war gestorben	hatte gelegt	hatte gelebt
wir	waren gefahren	waren gestorben	hatten gelegt	hatten gelebt
ihr	wart gefahren	wart gestorben	hattet gelegt	hattet gelebt
sie/Sie	waren gefahren	waren gestorben	hatten gelegt	hatten gelebt

The future tense

The future tense is used to express something that <u>will happen in the future</u> or <u>refers to the future</u>, such as an advance notification, intentions, suppositions, and promises.

The future tense is formed with the present tense of the auxiliary verb *werden* and the infinitive of the main verb:

Morgen wird es schneien.	*It will (or is going to) snow tomorrow.*
Er wird noch im Urlaub sein.	*He will still be on vacation.*
Ich werde dich immer lieben.	*I will always love you.*

	legen	fahren	sein	haben	können
ich	werde legen	werde fahren	werde sein	werde haben	werde können
du	wirst legen	wirst fahren	wirst sein	wirst haben	wirst können
er/sie/es	wird legen	wird fahren	wird sein	wird haben	wird können
wir	werden legen	werden fahren	werden sein	werden haben	werden können
ihr	werdet legen	werdet fahren	werdet sein	werdet haben	werdet können
sie/Sie	werden legen	werden fahren	werden sein	werden haben	werden können

The present subjunctive (subjunctive I)

The present subjunctive is formed by taking the verb stem and adding the endings *-e*, *-est*, *-e*, *-en*, *-et*, and *-en*. It is used to express <u>indirect speech:</u>

Direkte Rede:	*Direct speech:*
Kannst du mir helfen?	*Can you help me?*

Indirekte Rede:	*Indirect speech:*
Er fragte sie, ob sie ihm helfen könne.	*He asked her if she could help him.*

Some irregular verbs have a stem vowel change in the **indicative** but not in the subjunctive:

Infinitive	Present Indicative	Present Subjunctive
fallen	du fällst	du fallest
geben	du gibst	du gebest

Besides being used for indirect speech, the present subjunctive is also used in a few set expressions:

Er lebe hoch!	*Three cheers for him!*
Gott sei Dank!	*Thank God!*
Man nehme Salz, Mehl und Butter ...	*Take salt, flour, and butter ...*

	legen	küssen	reden
ich	lege	küsse	rede
du	legest	küssest	redest
er/sie/es	lege	küsse	rede
wir	legen	küssen	reden
ihr	leget	küsset	redet
sie/Sie	legen	küssen	reden

The present subjunctive of the auxiliary verbs *sein, haben,* and *werden*:

	sein	haben	werden
ich	sei	habe	werde
du	seist	habest	werdest
er/sie/es	sei	habe	werde
wir	seien	haben	werden
ihr	seiet	habet	werdet
sie/Sie	seien	haben	werden

The present subjunctive of the modal verbs:

	können	dürfen	mögen	müssen	sollen	wollen
ich	könne	dürfe	möge	müsse	solle	wolle
du	könnest	dürfest	mögest	müssest	sollest	wollest
er/sie/es	könne	dürfe	möge	müsse	solle	wolle
wir	können	dürfen	mögen	müssen	sollen	wollen
ihr	könn(e)t	dürf(e)t	mög(e)t	müss(e)t	soll(e)t	woll(e)t
sie/Sie	können	dürfen	mögen	müssen	sollen	wollen

The past subjunctive (subjunctive II)

The past subjunctive is formed by taking the verb stem of the simple past tense and adding the endings *-e*, *-(e)st*, *-e*, *-en*, *-(e)t*, and *-en*. The past subjunctive of regular verbs is identical to the past indicative. Irregular verbs with *i* or *ie* in the past tense forms retain these spellings in the past subjunctive.

The past subjunctive is used to express hypothetical statements, comparisons, and expressions of politeness:

Wenn ich Zeit hätte, ginge ich mit dir ins Kino.	*If I had time I would go with you to the movies.*
Die Leiter schwankte so, als fiele sie gleich um.	*The ladder was swaying so much, it looked like it was about to fall.*
Könnten Sie uns bitte eine Auskunft geben?	*Could you give us some information, please?*

	gehen/ging	rufen/rief	greifen/griff
ich	ginge	riefe	griffe
du	ging(e)st	rief(e)st	griff(e)st
er/sie/es	ginge	riefe	griffe
wir	gingen	riefen	griffen
ihr	ging(e)t	rief(e)t	griff(e)t
sie/Sie	gingen	riefen	griffen

Verbs with the vowels *a, o,* and *u* in the past indicative add an umlaut in the past subjunctive:

	singen/ sang	fliegen/ flog	fahren/ fuhr	sein/ war	haben/ hatte	werden/ wurde
ich	sänge	flöge	führe	wäre	hätte	würde
du	säng(e)st	flög(e)st	führ(e)st	wär(e)st	hättest	würdest
er/sie/es	sänge	flöge	führe	wäre	hätte	würde
wir	sängen	flögen	führen	wären	hätten	würden
ihr	säng(e)t	flög(e)t	führ(e)t	wär(e)t	hättet	würdet
sie/Sie	sängen	flögen	führen	wären	hätten	würden

Conditional clauses

A conditional clause often starts with "if" or "unless." Conditional clauses are used to express something that might happen if certain conditions are met and are formed with the past subjunctive of *werden* and the infinitive of the main verb:

Wenn ihr uns einladen würdet, würden wir kommen. *If you were to invite us, we would come.*

	legen	fahren
ich	würde legen	würde fahren
du	würdest legen	würdest fahren
er/sie/es	würde legen	würde fahren
wir	würden legen	würden fahren
ihr	würdet legen	würdet fahren
sie/Sie	würden legen	würden fahren

The imperative

The imperative expresses a demand, request, warning, or ban and is formed with either the second person singular or plural.

1. Regular verbs add to the stem *-e* in the singular and *-t* in the plural. The plural form of the imperative is identical to the second person plural of the present indicative.

In the polite form *Sie*, the verb is **inverted** (i.e., the predicate comes before the subject):

Sie schreiben einen Brief. *You are writing a letter.*	(eine Feststellung/ Indikativ) *(a statement/indicative)*
Schreiben Sie einen Brief! *Write a letter!*	(eine Aufforderung/ Imperativ) *(a demand/imperative)*

Infinitive	Singular	Plural	Polite form
schreiben	schreibe	schreibt	schreiben Sie
singen	singe	singt	singen Sie
trinken	trinke	trinkt	trinken Sie
atmen	atme	atmet	atmen Sie
reden	rede	redet	reden Sie

Exceptions:

Verbs which end in *-eln* and *-ern* can drop the *-e* in the singular.

Infinitive	Singular	Plural	Polite form
sammeln	samm(e)le	sammelt	sammeln Sie
fördern	förd(e)re	fördert	fördern Sie
handeln	hand(e)le	handelt	handeln Sie

If the verb stem ends in *-m* or *-n* and is preceded by *h, l, m, n,* or *r*, the *-e* ending in the singular can be dropped.

Infinitive	Singular	Plural	Polite form
rühmen	rühm(e)	rühmt	rühmen Sie
qualmen	qualm(e)	qualmt	qualmen Sie
kämmen	kämm(e)	kämmt	kämmen Sie
rennen	renn(e)	rennt	rennen Sie
lernen	lern(e)	lernt	lernen Sie

If, however, the *-m* or *-n* is preceded by another consonant, the *-e* ending must be retained:

atme, rechne

Irregular verbs *without* a vowel change to *-i* or *-ie* in the present tense form the imperative according to the same rules as regular verbs.

→ The imperative forms are given in the list of irregular verbs.

Vowel change to *-i* or *-ie*

Infinitive	Singular	Plural
lesen	lies	lest
werfen	wirf	werft
essen	iss	esst
sehen	sieh	seht

The auxiliary verbs *sein, haben*, and *werden*

Infinitive	Singular	Plural
sein	sei	seid
haben	habe	habt
werden	werde	werdet

Active and passive

In an *active* sentence the subject performs the stated action. In a *passive* sentence the subject is being acted upon:

Die Spieler wählen den Mannschaftskapitän.	(aktiv)
The players elect the team captain.	*(active)*
Der Mannschaftskapitän wird von den Spielern gewählt.	(passiv)
The team captain is elected by the players.	*(passive)*

The passive is formed with *werden* and the past participle.

Present	ich werde geliebt	ich werde geschlagen
Past	ich wurde geliebt	ich wurde geschlagen

The auxiliary verbs *haben, sein,* and *werden*

The verbs *haben*, *sein,* and *werden* are called auxiliary verbs because certain tenses (such as the perfect, pluperfect, and future) and the passive voice are formed with their help.

Present

	sein	haben	werden
ich	bin	habe	werde
du	bist	hast	wirst
er/sie/es	ist	hat	wird
wir	sind	haben	werden
ihr	seid	habt	werdet
sie/Sie	sind	haben	werden

The present participle

The present participle is formed by adding *-d* to the infinitive of the verb:

singend, lachend, etc.

It expresses a shorter version of a subordinate clause:

Er saß in der Badewanne und sang.	Er saß singend in der Badewanne.
He sat in the bathtub and sang.	*He sat in the bathtub singing.*
Sie öffnete die Tür und lachte.	Sie öffnete lachend die Tür.
She opened the door and laughed.	*She opened the door laughing.*

The past participle

The past participle of regular verbs is formed according to the following rule:

	Prefix	+	Stem	+	Ending
machen:	ge	+	mach	+	t

legen	*ge* legt
sagen	*ge* sagt
vierteln	*ge* viertelt
rasen	*ge* rast
hassen	*ge* hasst
küssen	*ge* küsst
reizen	*ge* reizt
reden	*ge* redet
wetten	*ge* wettet
trocknen	*ge* trocknet

Verbs ending in *-ieren* omit the prefix *ge-*, as do those with the prefixes *be-*, *em-*, *ent-*, *er-*, *ver-*, and *zer-*. The following rule applies:

	Stem	+	Ending
manövr*ieren*	manövrier	+	(e)t

*em*pören	empör*t*
*ent*giften	entgifte*t*
*er*setzen	ersetz*t*
*ver*trösten	vertröste*t*
*zer*reden	zerrede*t*

Verbs with inseparable prefixes also drop the *ge-*:

übersetzen	übersetz*t*
durchwaten	durchwate*t*
unterlegen	unterleg*t*
umarmen	umarm*t*

The past participle of verbs with separable prefixes (e.g., durchmachen) is formed according to the following rule:

Prefix Verb	+	Prefix PP *ge-*	+	Verb Stem	+	Ending *t*
durch	+	ge	+	mach	+	t

anbeten	an*ge*bete*t*
überschnappen	über*ge*schnapp*t*
umdeuten	um*ge*deute*t*

Pronouns

Pronouns are also declined in German.

1. Personal pronouns

A personal pronoun denotes the person who is speaking or about whom someone is speaking.

Nominative	Accusative	Genitive	Dative
ich	mich	meiner	mir
du	dich	deiner	dir
er	ihn	seiner	ihm
sie	sie	ihrer	ihr
es	es	seiner	ihm
wir	uns	unser	uns
ihr	euch	euer	euch
sie/Sie	sie/Sie	ihrer/Ihrer	ihnen/Ihnen

2. The polite form of address: Sie

The personal pronoun ***Sie***, which is used as the polite form of address, and its inflected forms are always capitalized:

Können **Sie** mir sagen, wie spät es ist?	*Can you tell me what time it is?*
Ich danke **Ihnen**.	*Thank you.*

The pronouns *du* and *ihr* are usually always written in the lower case. In correspondence, however, the capitalized forms can also be written:

Liebe Andrea, wie **du/ Du** bestimmt schon weißt ...	*Dear Andrea, as you must already know ...*

3. Reflexive pronouns

A reflexive pronoun refers to the subject of a sentence and must agree with the subject in **case** and **number**:

ich wasche mich
du wäschst dich
er/sie/es wäscht sich
wir waschen uns
ihr wascht euch
sie/Sie waschen sich

4. Possessive pronouns

A possessive pronoun indicates belonging or ownership and agrees in **gender**, **case**, and **number** with the noun to which it refers.

A possessive pronoun may appear like an adjective before a noun or stand in place of a noun.

a) Used as an adjective

	Masculine	Feminine	Neuter	Plural
1st Person Singular				
Nom.	mein	meine	mein	meine
Acc.	meinen	meine	mein	meine
Dat.	meinem	meiner	meinem	meinen
Gen.	meines	meiner	meines	meiner
2nd Person Singular				
	dein	deine	dein declined like *mein*	deine
3rd Person Singular (of *er*)				
	sein	seine	sein declined like *mein*	seine
3rd Person Singular (of *sie*)				
	ihr	ihre	ihr declined like *mein*	ihre
3rd Person Singular (of *es*)				
	sein	seine	sein declined like *mein*	seine
1st Person Plural				
Nom.	unser	uns(e)re	unser	uns(e)re
Acc.	uns(e)ren	uns(e)re unsern	unser	uns(e)re
Dat.	uns(e)rem	uns(e)rer unserm	uns(e)rem	uns(e)ren unserm
Gen.	uns(e)res	uns(e)rer	uns(e)res	uns(e)rer
2nd Person Plural				
Nom.	euer	eure	euer	eure
Acc.	euren	eure	euer	eure
Dat.	eurem	eurer	eurem	euren
Gen.	eures	eurer	eures	eurer

	Masculine	Feminine	Neuter	Plural
3rd Person Plural				
Nom.	ihr/Ihr	ihre/Ihre	ihr/Ihr	ihre/Ihre
Acc.	ihren/Ihren	ihre/Ihre	ihr/Ihr	ihre/Ihre
Dat.	ihrem/Ihrem	ihrer/Ihrer	ihrem/Ihrem	ihren/Ihren
Gen.	ihres/Ihres	ihrer/Ihrer	ihres/Ihres	ihrer/Ihrer

b) Used as a noun

	Masculine	Feminine	Neuter	Plural
1st P. Sing.	meiner	meine	mein(e)s	meine
2nd P. Sing	deiner	deine	dein(e)s	deine
3rd P. Sing. m, nt	seiner	seine	sein(e)s	seine
3rd P. Sing. f	ihrer	ihre	ihr(e)s	ihre
1st P. Pl.	uns(e) rer	uns(e) re	uns(e) res	uns(e) re
2nd P. Pl.	eurer	eure	eures, euers	eure
3rd P. Pl.	ihrer/Ihrer	ihre/Ihre	ihr(e)s/Ihr(e)s	ihre/Ihre

5. Demonstrative pronouns

A demonstrative pronoun indicates which person or thing is being referred to.

	Masculine	Feminine	Neuter	Plural
Nom.	dieser	diese	dieses	diese
Acc.	diesen	diese	dieses	diese
Dat.	diesem	dieser	diesem	diesen
Gen.	dieses	dieser	dieses	dieser
Nom.	jener	jene	jenes	jene
Acc.	jenen	jene	jenes	jene
Dat.	jenem	jener	jenem	jenen
Gen.	jenes	jener	jenes	jener
Nom.	derjenige	diejenige	dasjenige	diejenigen
Acc.	denjenigen	diejenige	dasjenige	diejenigen
Dat.	demjenigen	derjenigen	demjenigen	denjenigen
Gen.	desjenigen	derjenigen	desjenigen	derjenigen
Nom.	derselbe	dieselbe	dasselbe	dieselben
Acc.	denselben	dieselbe	dasselbe	dieselben
Dat.	demselben	derselben	demselben	denselben
Gen.	desselben	derselben	desselben	derselben

The definite articles *der, die,* and *das* are also used as demonstrative pronouns.

6. Relative pronouns

The most common relative pronouns are *der, die,* and *das*; less common are *welcher, welche*, and *welches*. All relative pronouns introduce a subordinate clause which supplements the main clause. Relative pronouns agree in **gender** and **number** with the word in the main clause to which they refer:

Er putzt sein neues Auto, das/welches er sich gekauft hat.	*He is cleaning the new car that/which he bought.*

	Masculine	Feminine	Neuter	Plural
Nom.	welcher	welche	welches	welche
Acc.	welchen	welche	welches	welche
Dat.	welchem	welcher	welchem	welchen
Gen.	dessen	deren	dessen	deren

Wer and *was* can also be used as relative pronouns:

Wer das behauptet, lügt.	*Whoever says that is lying.*
Mach doch, was du willst!	*Oh, just do what you want!*

7. Interrogative pronouns

An interrogative pronoun distinguishes between a **person** (*wer?*) and a **thing** (*was?*) and only occurs in the singular.

	Person	Thing
Nom.	*Wer* spielt mit?	*Was* ist das?
Acc.	*Wen* liebst du?	*Was* höre ich da?
Dat.	*Wem* gehört das Haus?	
Gen.	*Wessen* Haus ist das?	

The genitive of the interrogative pronoun *wessen* (whose?) is being replaced more and more by the dative *wem*:

Wem gehört das Haus? (statt: Wessen Haus ist das?)	*Whose house is that? (To whom does the house belong?)*

Was für ein ... (What kind of (a) ...) is used to ask about the particular character of a person or thing:

Was für ein Mensch ist Peter eigentlich?	*What sort of person is Peter really?/What is Peter really like?*
Was für einen Anzug möchten Sie?	*What kind of suit would you like?*

The interrogative pronouns *welcher, welche*, and *welches* are used to ask about one particular person or item among several:

Welche Schuhe soll ich nehmen? (die Braunen oder die Schwarzen?)	*Which shoes should I take? (the brown ones or the black ones?)*
Mit welchem Bus kommst du? (mit dem um 16 oder 17 Uhr?)	*Which bus are you coming on? (the one at 4 or 5 o'clock?)*
Welches Eis schmeckt dir besser? (Erdbeer- oder Schokoladeneis?)	*Which ice cream do you like more? (strawberry or chocolate?)*

	Masculine	Feminine	Neuter	Plural
Nom.	welcher	welche	welches	welche
Acc.	welchen	welche	welches	welche
Dat.	welchem	welcher	welchem	welchen
Gen.	welches	welcher	welches	welcher

Prepositions

+ Accusative:	
bis	durch
für	gegen
je	ohne
pro	um
wider	

+ Dative:	
ab	aus
außer	bei
binnen	entgegen
entsprechend	gegenüber
gemäß	mit
nach	nächst
nahe	nebst
samt	seit
von	zu
zufolge	zuwider

+ Accusative/Dative *:	
an	auf
entlang	hinter
in	neben
über	unter
vor	zwischen

* The accusative is used with *movement* and *change of direction* (wohin? – *where to?*).

The dative is used with *details of location* (wo? – *where?*):

Er hängt die Uhr an die Wand.	(wohin?)
He is hanging the clock on the wall.	*(where to?)*
Die Uhr hängt an der Wand.	(wo?)
The clock is hanging on the wall.	*(where?)*

→ Every prepositional headword in the dictionary has an indication next to it of the case that it takes.

Some prepositions form contractions with certain forms of the definite article:

an/in	+	dem	becomes	am/im
bei	+	dem	becomes	beim
von	+	dem	becomes	vom
zu	+	dem/der	becomes	zum/zur
an/in	+	das	becomes	ans/ins

Liste der unregelmäßigen deutschen Verben

List of the irregular German verbs

Die einfachen Zeiten unregelmäßiger Verben sind in den Spitzklammern (< >) nach dem Stichwort angegeben. Zusammengesetzte oder präfigierte Verben, deren Formen denen des Grundverbs entsprechen, sind auf der Deutsch-Englischen Seite mit *irreg* markiert. Außerdem gibt das Wörterbuch die unregelmäßigen Formen zusammengesetzter Verben an, die sich anders verhalten als ihre Grundverben. Die Verben, die mit *sein* oder alternativ mit *sein* oder *haben* konjugiert werden, sind entsprechend im Wörterbucheintrag gekennzeichnet. Wenn das Hilfsverb nicht eigens angegeben ist, wird die Perfektform mit *haben* gebildet.

Inflections of irregular verbs are given in angle brackets (< >) after the headword in the main part of the dictionary. Compound verbs and prefixed verbs whose conjugated forms correspond to those of the base verb are marked *irreg* on the German-English side of the dictionary. Conjugated forms of compound verbs are provided, however, when they differ from the conjugated forms of the base verb. Verbs that take *sein* and those that take *sein* or *haben* in the compound past tenses are marked accordingly in the dictionary entry. Whenever the auxiliary verb is not specifically given, one may assume that the compound past tenses are formed with *haben*.

Infinitiv	2./3. Pers. Sing. Präsens	3. Pers. Sing. Präteritum	Konjunktiv II	Imperativ Sing./Pl.	Partizip Perfekt
Infinitive	2nd/3rd pers. sing. present	3rd pers. sing. simple past	Subjunctive II	Imperative sing./pl.	Past participle
backen	backst *o* bäckst/ backt *o* bäckt	backte *o veraltet* buk	backte *o veraltet* büke	back[e]/backt	gebacken
bedürfen	*1. Pers.* bedarf bedarfst/ bedarf	bedurfte	bedürfte	bedarf/ bedürft	bedurft
befehlen	befiehlst/ befiehlt	befahl	beföhle *o* befähle	befiehl/ befehlt	befohlen
beginnen	beginnst/ beginnt	begann	begänne *o selten* begönne	beginn[e]/ beginnt	begonnen
beißen	beißt/beißt	biss	bisse	beiß[e]/beißt	gebissen
bergen	birgst/birgt	barg	bärge	birgt/bergt	geborgen
bersten	birst/birst	barst	bärste	birst/berstet	geborsten
bewegen *=veranlassen*	bewegst/ bewegt	bewog	bewöge	beweg[e]/ bewegt	bewogen
biegen	biegst/biegt	bog	böge	bieg[e]/biegt	gebogen
bieten	bietest/bietet	bot	böte	biet[e]/bietet	geboten
binden	bindest/bindet	band	bände	bind[e]/bindet	gebunden
bitten	bittest/bittet	bat	bäte	bitt[e]/bittet	gebeten
blasen	bläst/bläst	blies	bliese	blas[e]/blast	geblasen
bleiben	bleibst/bleibt	blieb	bliebe	bleib[e]/bleibt	geblieben
bleichen	bleichst/ bleicht	bleichte *o veraltet* blich	bliche	bleich[e]/ bleicht	gebleicht *o veraltet* geblichen
braten	brätst/brät	briet	briete	brat[e]/bratet	gebraten
brechen	brichst/bricht	brach	bräche	brich/brecht	gebrochen
brennen	brennst/ brennt	brannte	brennte	brenn[e]/ brennt	gebrannt
bringen	bringst/bringt	brachte	brächte	bring[e]/ bringt	gebracht
denken	denkst/denkt	dachte	dächte	denk[e]/denkt	gedacht
dingen	dingst/dingt	dang o dingte	dingte	ding[e]/dingt	gedungen
dreschen	drischst/ drischt	drosch	drösche	drisch/drescht	gedroschen
dringen	dringst/dringt	drang	dränge	dring[e]/ dringt	gedrungen

Infinitiv	**2./3. Pers. Sing. Präsens**	**3. Pers. Sing. Präteritum**	**Konjunktiv II**	**Imperativ Sing./Pl.**	**Partizip Perfekt**
Infinitive	**2nd/3rd pers. sing. present**	**3rd pers. sing. simple past**	**Subjunctive II**	**Imperative sing./pl.**	**Past participle**
dünken	dünkst/dünkt	dünkte *o veraltet* deuchte	dünkte *o veraltet* deuchte		gedünkt *o veraltet* gedeucht
empfangen	empfängst/empfängt	empfing	empfinge	empfang[e]/empfangt	empfangen
empfehlen	empfiehlst/empfiehlt	empfahl	empföhle	empfiehl/empfehlt	empfohlen
empfinden	empfindest/empfindet	empfand	empfände	empfind[e]/empfindet	empfunden
erküren	erkürst/erkürt	erkor	erköre	erküre/erkürt	erkoren
erlöschen	erlischst/erlischt	erlosch	erlösche	erlisch/erlöscht	erloschen
erschallen	erschallst/erschallt	erscholl *o* erschallte	erschölle *o* erschallte	erschalle/erschallt	erschollen
erschrecken *vi*	erschrickst/erschrickt	erschreckte *o* erschrak	erschreckte *o* erschräke	erschrickt/erschreckt	erschreckt *o* erschrocken
vr	erschrickst/erschrickt	erschreckte	erschreckte	erschreckt	erschreckt *o* erschrocken
essen	isst/isst	aß	äße	iss/esst	gegessen
fahren	fährst/fährt	fuhr	führe	fahr[e]/fahrt	gefahren
fallen	fällst/fällt	fiel	fiele	fall[e]/fallt	gefallen
fangen	fängst/fängt	fing	finge	fang[e]/fangt	gefangen
fechten	fichst/ficht	focht	föchte	ficht/fechtet	gefochten
finden	findest/findet	fand	fände	find[e]/findet	gefunden
flechten	flichst/flicht	flocht	flöchte	flicht/flechtet	geflochten
fliegen	fliegst/fliegt	flog	flöge	flieg[e]/fliegt	geflogen
fliehen	fliehst/flieht	floh	flöhe	flieh[e]/flieht	geflohen
fließen	fließt/fließt	floss	flösse	fließ[e]/fließt	geflossen
fressen	frisst/frisst	fraß	fräße	friss/fresst	gefressen
frieren	frierst/friert	fror	fröre	frier[e]/friert	gefroren
gären	gärst/gärt	gärte *o* gor	gärte *o* gor	gär[e]/gärt	gegärt *o* gegoren
gebären	gebärst/gebärt	gebar	gebäre	gebier/gebärt	geboren
geben	gibst/gibt	gab	gäbe	gib/gebt	gegeben
gedeihen	gedeihst/gedeiht	gedieh	gediehe	gedeih[e]/gedeiht	gediehen
gefallen	gefällst/gefällt	gefiel	gefiele	gefall[e]/gefallen	gefallen
gehen	gehst/geht	ging	ginge	geh[e]/geht	gegangen
gelingen	gelingst/gelingt	gelang	gelänge	geling[e]/gelingt	gelungen
gelten	giltst/gilt	galt	gälte *o* gölte	gilt/geltet	gegolten
genesen	genest/genest	genas	genäse	genese/genest	genesen
genießen	genießt/genießt	genoss	genösse	genieß[e]/genießt	genossen
geraten	gerätst/gerät	geriet	geriete	gerat[e]/geratet	geraten
gerinnen	gerinnst/gerinnt	gerann	geränne	gerinn[e]/gerinnt	geronnen
geschehen	geschiehst/geschieht	geschah	geschähe	geschieh/gescheht	geschehen

Infinitiv		2./3. Pers. Sing. Präsens	3. Pers. Sing. Präteritum	Konjunktiv II	Imperativ Sing./Pl.	Partizip Perfekt
Infinitive		2nd/3rd pers. sing. present	3rd pers. sing. simple past	Subjunctive II	Imperative sing./pl.	Past participle
gestehen		gestehst/ gesteht	gestand	gestände *o* gestünde	gesteh[e]/ gesteht	gestanden
gewinnen		gewinnst/ gewinnt	gewann	gewönne *o* gewänne	gewinn[e]/ gewinnt	gewonnen
gießen		gießt/gießt	goss	gösse	gieß[e]/gießt	gegossen
gleichen		gleichst/ gleicht	glich	gliche	gleich[e]/ gleicht	geglichen
gleiten		gleitest/gleitet	glitt	glitte	gleit[e]/gleitet	geglitten
glimmen		glimmst/ glimmt	glimmte *o selten* glomm	glimmte *o selten* glomm	glimm[e]/ glimmt	geglimmt *o selten* geglommen
graben		gräbst/gräbt	grub	grübe	grab[e]/grabt	gegraben
greifen		greifst/greift	griff	griffe	greif[e]/greift	gegriffen
halten		hältst/hält	hielt	hielte	halt[e]/haltet	gehalten
hängen	*vi*	hängst/hängt	hing	hinge	häng[e]/hängt	gehangen
	vt	hängst/hängt	hängte *o dial* hing	hängte	häng[e]/hängt	gehängt *o dial* gehangen
	vr	hängst/hängt	hängte *o dial* hing	hängte	häng[e]/hängt	gehängt *o dial* gehangen
hauen		haust/haut	haute *o* hieb	haute *o* hieb	hau[e]/haut	gehauen *o dial* gehaut
heben		hebst/hebt	hob	höbe	heb[e]/hebt	gehoben
heißen		heißt/heißt	hieß	hieße	heiß[e]/heißt	geheißen
helfen		hilfst/hilft	half	hülfe	hilf/helft	geholfen
kennen		kennst/kennt	kannte	kennte	kenn[e]/kennt	gekannt
klimmen		klimmst/ klimmt	klimmte *o* klomm	klimmte *o* klomm	klimm[e]/ klimmt	geklommen *o* geklimmt
klingen		klingst/klingt	klang	klänge	kling[e]/klingt	geklungen
kneifen		kneifst/kneift	kniff	kniffe	kneif[e]/kneift	gekniffen
kommen		kommst/ kommt	kam	käme	komm[e]/ kommt	gekommen
kriechen		kriechst/ kriecht	kroch	kröche	kriech[e]/ kriecht	gekrochen
küren		kürst/kürt	kürte *o selten* kor	kürte *o selten* köre	kür[e]/kürt	gekürt
laden		lädst/lädt	lud	lüde	lad[e]/ladet	geladen
lassen		lässt/lässt	ließ	ließe	lass/lasst	gelassen *nach Infinitiv* lassen
laufen		läufst/läuft	lief	lief	lauf[e]/lauft	gelaufen
leiden		leidest/leidet	litt	litte	leid[e]/leidet	gelitten
leihen		leihst/leiht	lieh	liehe	leih[e]/leiht	geliehen
lesen		liest/liest	las	läse	lies/lest	gelesen
liegen		liegst/liegt	lag	läge	lieg[e]/liegt	gelegen
lügen		lügst/lügt	log	löge	lüg[e]/lügt	gelogen
meiden		meidest/ meidet	mied	miede	meid[e]/ meidet	gemieden
melken		melkst/melkt	melkte *o veraltend* molk	melkte *o* mölke	melk[e]/melkt	gemolken
messen		misst/misst	maß	mäße	miss/messt	gemessen

Infinitiv	2./3. Pers. Sing. Präsens	3. Pers. Sing. Präteritum	Konjunktiv II	Imperativ Sing./Pl.	Partizip Perfekt
Infinitive	2nd/3rd pers. sing. present	3rd pers. sing. simple past	Subjunctive II	Imperative sing./pl.	Past participle
misslingen	misslingst/ misslingt	misslang	misslänge	missling[e]/ misslingt	misslungen
nehmen	nimmst/ nimmt	nahm	nähme	nimm/nehmt	genommen
nennen	nennst/nennt	nannte	nennte	nenn[e]/nennt	genannt
pfeifen	pfeifst/pfeift	pfiff	pfiffe	pfeif[e]/pfeift	gepfiffen
preisen	preist/preist	pries	priese	preis[e]/preist	gepriesen
quellen	quillst/quillt	quoll	quölle	quill/quillt	gequollen
raten	rätst/rät	riet	riete	rat[e]/ratet	geraten
reiben	reibst/reibt	rieb	riebe	reib[e]/reibt	gerieben
reißen	reißt/reißt	riss	risse	reiß[e]/reißt	gerissen
reiten	reitest/reitet	ritt	ritte	reit[e]/reitet	geritten
rennen	rennst/rennt	rannte	rennte	renn[e]/rennt	gerannt
riechen	riechst/riecht	roch	röche	riech[e]/riecht	gerochen
ringen	ringst/ringt	rang	ränge	ring[e]/ringt	gerungen
rinnen	rinnst/rinnt	rann	ränne	rinn[e]/rinnt	geronnen
rufen	rufst/ruft	rief	riefe	ruf[e]/ruft	gerufen
salzen	salzst/salzt	salzte	salzte	salz[e]/salze	gesalzen *o selten* gesalzt
saufen	säufst/säuft	soff	söffe	sauf[e]/sauft	gesoffen
saugen	saugst/saugt	sog *o* saugte	söge *o* saugte	saug[e]/saugt	gesogen *o* gesaugt
schaffen ***= erschaffen***	schaffst/ schafft	schuf	schüfe	schaff[e]/ schafft	geschaffen
schallen	schallst/schallt	schallte *o* scholl	schallte *o* schölle	schall[e]/ schallt	geschallt
scheiden	scheidest/ scheidet	schied	schiede	scheide/schei-det	geschieden
scheinen	scheinst/ scheint	schien	schiene	schein[e]/ scheint	geschienen
scheißen	scheißt/ scheißt	schiss	schisse	scheiß[e]/ scheißt	geschissen
schelten	schiltst/schilt	schalt	schölte	schilt/scheltet	gescholten
scheren ***= stutzen***	scherst/schert	schor	schöre	scher[e]/ schert	geschoren
schieben	schiebst/ schiebt	schob	schöbe	schieb[e]/ schiebt	geschoben
schießen	schießt/ schießt	schoss	schösse	schieß[e]/ schießt	geschossen
schinden	schindest/ schindet	schindete	schünde	schind[e]/ schindet	geschunden
schlafen	schläfst/ schläft	schlief	schliefe	schlaf[e]/ schlaft	geschlafen
schlagen	schlägst/ schlägt	schlug	schlüge	schlag[e]/ schlagt	geschlagen
schleichen	schleichst/ schleicht	schlich	schliche	schleich[e]/ schleicht	geschlichen
schleifen ***= schärfen***	schleifst/ schleift	schliff	schliffe	schleif[e]/ schleift	geschliffen
schließen	schließt/ schließt	schloss	schlösse	schließ[e]/ schließt	geschlossen

Infinitiv	2./3. Pers. Sing. Präsens	3. Pers. Sing. Präteritum	Konjunktiv II	Imperativ Sing./Pl.	Partizip Perfekt
Infinitive	2nd/3rd pers. sing. present	3rd pers. sing. simple past	Subjunctive II	Imperative sing./pl.	Past participle
schlingen	schlingst/ schlingt	schlang	schlänge	schling[e]/ schlingt	geschlungen
schmeißen	schmeißt/ schmeißt	schmiss	schmisse	schmeiß[e]/ schmeißt	geschmissen
schmelzen	schmilzt/ schmilzt	schmolz	schmölze	schmilz/ schmelzt	geschmolzen
schnauben	schnaubst/ schnaubt	schnaubte *o veraltet* schnob	schnöbe	schnaub[e]/ schnaubt	geschnaubt *o veraltet* geschnoben
schneiden	schneidest/ schneidet	schnitt	schnitte	schneid[e]/ schneidet	geschnitten
schrecken *vt*	schreckst/ schreckt	schreckte	schreckte	schreck[e]/ schreckt	geschreckt
vi	schreckst/ schreckt	schrak	schräke	schrick/ schreckt	geschrocken
schreiben	schreibst/ schreibt	schrieb	schriebe	schreib[e]/ schreibt	geschrieben
schreien	schreist/ schreit	schrie	schriee	schrei[e]/ schreit	geschrie[e]n
schreiten	schreitest/ schreitet	schritt	schritte	schreit[e]/ schreitet	geschritten
schweigen	schweigst/ schweigt	schwieg	schwiege	schweig[e]/ schweigt	geschwiegen
schwellen	schwillst/ schwillt	schwoll	schwölle	schwill/ schwellt	geschwollen
schwimmen	schwimmst/ schwimmt	schwamm	schwämme	schwimm[e]/ schwimmt	geschwommen
schwinden	schwindest/ schwindet	schwand	schwände	schwind[e]/ schwindet	geschwunden
schwingen	schwingst/ schwingt	schwang	schwänge	schwing[e]/ schwingt	geschwungen
schwören	schwörst/ schwört	schwor	schwöre	schwör[e]/ schwört	geschworen
sehen	siehst/sieht	sah	sähe	sieh[e]/seht	gesehen
senden *= schicken*	sendest/ sendet	sandte *o* sendete	sendete	sende/sendet	gesandt *o* gesendet
sieden	siedest/siedet	siedete *o* sott	siedete *o* sötte	sied[e]/siedet	gesiedet *o* gesotten
singen	singst/singt	sang	sänge	sing[e]/singt	gesungen
sinken	sinkst/sinkt	sank	sänke	sink[e]/sinkt	gesunken
sinnen	sinnst/sinnt	sann	sänne	sinn[e]/sinnt	gesonnen
sitzen	sitzt/sitzt	saß	säße	sitz[e]/sitzt	gesessen
spalten	spaltest/ spaltet	spaltete	spaltete	spalt[e]/spal-tet	gespalten *o* gespaltet
speien	speist/speit	spie	spiee	spei[e]/speit	gespie[e]n
spinnen	spinnst/spinnt	spann	spönne *o* spänne	spinn[e]/ spinnt	gesponnen
sprechen	sprichst/ spricht	sprach	spräche	sprich/sprecht	gesprochen
sprießen	sprießt/sprießt	spross *o* sprießte	sprösse	sprieß[e]/ sprießt	gesprossen
springen	springst/ springt	sprang	spränge	spring[e]/ springt	gesprungen

Infinitiv	2./3. Pers. Sing. Präsens	3. Pers. Sing. Präteritum	Konjunktiv II	Imperativ Sing./Pl.	Partizip Perfekt
Infinitive	2nd/3rd pers. sing. present	3rd pers. sing. simple past	Subjunctive II	Imperative sing./pl.	Past participle
stechen	stichst/sticht	stach	stäche	stich/stecht	gestochen
stecken *vi*	steckst/steckt	steckte *o geh* stak	steckte	steck[e]/steckt	gesteckt
stehen	stehst/steht	stand	stünde *o* stände	steh/steht	gestanden
stehlen	stiehlst/stiehlt	stahl	stähle	stiehl/stehlt	gestohlen
steigen	steigst/steigt	stieg	stiege	steig[e]/steigt	gestiegen
sterben	stirbst/stirbt	starb	stürbe	stirb/sterbt	gestorben
stieben	stiebst/stiebt	stob *o* stiebte	stöbe *o* stiebte	stieb[e]/stiebt	gestoben *o* gestiebt
stinken	stinkst/stinkt	stank	stänke	stink[e]/stinkt	gestunken
stoßen	stößt/stößt	stieß	stieße	stoß[e]/stoßt	gestoßen
streichen	streichst/streicht	strich	striche	streich[e]/streicht	gestrichen
streiten	streitest/streitet	stritt	stritte	streit[e]/streitet	gestritten
tragen	trägst/trägt	trug	trüge	trag[e]/tragt	getragen
treffen	triffst/trifft	traf	träfe	triff/trefft	getroffen
treiben	treibst/treibt	trieb	triebe	treib[e]/treibt	getrieben
treten	trittst/tritt	trat	träte	tritt/tretet	getreten
triefen	triefst/trieft	triefte *o geh* troff	tröffe	trief[e]/trieft	getrieft *o geh* getroffen
trinken	trinkst/trinkt	trank	tränke	trink/trinkt	getrunken
trügen	trügst/trügt	trog	tröge	trüg[e]/trügt	getrogen
tun	*1. Pers.* tu[e] tust/tut	tat	täte	tu[e]/tut	getan
überessen	überisst/überisst	überaß	überäße	überiss/überesst	übergessen
verbieten	verbietest/verbietet	verbot	verböte	verbiet[e]/verbietet	verboten
verbrechen	verbrichst/verbricht	verbrach	verbräche	verbrich/verbrecht	verbrochen
verderben	verdirbst/verdirbt	verdarb	verdürbe	verdirb/verderbt	verdorben
verdingen	verdingst/verdingt	verdingte	verdingte	verding[e]/verdingt	verdungen o verdingt
verdrießen	verdrießt/verdrießt	verdross	verdrösse	verdrieß[e]/verdrießt	verdrossen
vergessen	vergisst/vergisst	vergaß	vergäße	vergiss/vergesst	vergessen
verhauen	verhaust/verhaut	verhaute	verhaute	verhau[e]/verhaut	verhauen
verlieren	verlierst/verliert	verlor	verlöre	verlier[e]/verliert	verloren
verlöschen	verlischst/verlischt	verlosch	verlösche	verlisch/verlöscht	verloschen
verraten	verrätst/verrät	verriet	verriete	verrat[e]/verratet	verraten
verschleißen	verschleißt/verschleißt	verschliss	verschlisse	verschleiß[e]/verschleißt	verschlissen
verstehen	verstehst/versteht	verstand	verstünde *o* verstände	versteh[e]/versteht	verstanden

Infinitiv	2./3. Pers. Sing. Präsens	3. Pers. Sing. Präteritum	Konjunktiv II	Imperativ Sing./Pl.	Partizip Perfekt
Infinitive	2nd/3rd pers. sing. present	3rd pers. sing. simple past	Subjunctive II	Imperative sing./pl.	Past participle
verwenden	verwendest/ verwendet	verwendete *o* verwandte	verwendete	verwend[e]/ verwendet	verwendet *o* verwandt
verzeihen	verzeihst/ verzeiht	verzieh	verziehe	verzeih[e]/ verzeiht	verziehen
wachsen	wächst/wächst	wuchs	wüchse	wachs[e]/ wachst	gewachsen
wägen	wägst/wägt	wog *o* wägte	wögte *o* wägte	wäg[e]/wägt	gewogen
waschen	wäschst/ wäscht	wusch	wüsche	wasch[e]/ wascht	gewaschen
weben	webst/webt	webte *o geh* wob	webte *o geh* wöbe	web[e]/webt	gewebt *o geh* gewoben
weichen	weichst/ weicht	wich	wiche	weich[e]/ weicht	gewichen
weisen	weist/weist	wies	wiese	weis[e]/weist	gewiesen
wenden	wendest/ wendet	wendete *o geh* gewandt	wendete	wend[e]/ wendet	gewendet *o geh* gewandt
werben	wirbst/wirbt	warb	würbe	wirb/werbt	geworben
werfen	wirfst/wirft	warf	würfe	wirf/werft	geworfen
wiegen *= auf Waage*	wiegst/wiegt	wog	wöge	wieg[e]/wiegt	gewogen
winden *= schlingen*	windest/ windet	wand	wände	wind[e]/ windet	gewunden
winken	winkst/winkt	winkte	winkte	wink[e]/winkt	gewinkt *o dial* gewunken
wissen	*1. Pers.* weiß weißt/weiß	wusste	wüsste	wisse *liter*/ wisset *liter*	gewusst
wringen	wringst/wringt	wrang	wränge	wring[e]/ wringt	gewrungen
ziehen	ziehst/zieht	zog	zöge	zieh[e]/zieht	gezogen
zwingen	zwingst/ zwingt	zwang	zwänge	zwing[e]/ zwingt	gezwungen

Die Hilfsverben *sein, haben* und *werden*

The auxiliary verbs *sein, haben,* and *werden*

sein

Präsens	Präteritum	Perfekt	Plusquamperfekt
Present	Simple Past	Present Perfect	Past Perfect
bin	war	bin gewesen	war gewesen
bist	warst	bist gewesen	warst gewesen
ist	war	ist gewesen	war gewesen
sind	waren	sind gewesen	waren gewesen
seid	wart	seid gewesen	wart gewesen
sind	waren	sind gewesen	waren gewesen

Futur Future	Konjunktiv I Subjunctive I	Konjunktiv II Subjunctive II	Imperativ Imperative
werde sein	sei	wäre	
wirst sein	seist	wär[e]st	sei
wird sein	sei	wäre	seien wir
werden sein	seien	wären	seid
werdet sein	seiet	wär[e]t	seien Sie
werden sein	seien	wären	

haben

Präsens Present	Präteritum Simple Past	Perfekt Present Perfect	Plusquamperfekt Past Perfect
habe	hatte	habe gehabt	hatte gehabt
hast	hattest	hast gehabt	hattest gehabt
hat	hatte	hat gehabt	hatte gehabt
haben	hatten	haben gehabt	hatten gehabt
habt	hattet	habt gehabt	hattet gehabt
haben	hatten	haben gehabt	hatten gehabt

Futur Future	Konjunktiv I Subjunctive I	Konjunktiv II Subjunctive II	Imperativ Imperative
werde haben	habe	hätte	
wirst haben	habest	hättest	hab[e]
wird haben	habe	hätte	haben wir
werden haben	haben	hätten	habt
werdet haben	habet	hättet	haben Sie
werden haben	haben	hätten	

werden

Präsens Present	Präteritum Simple Past	Perfekt Present Perfect	Plusquamperfekt Past Perfect
werde	wurde	bin geworden	war geworden
wirst	wurdest	bist geworden	warst geworden
wird	wurde	ist geworden	war geworden
werden	wurden	sind geworden	waren geworden
werdet	wurdet	seid geworden	wart geworden
werden	wurden	sind geworden	waren geworden

Futur Future	Konjunktiv I Subjunctive I	Konjunktiv II Subjunctive II	Imperativ Imperative
werde werden	werde	würde	
wirst werden	werdest	würdest	werd[e]
wird werden	werde	würde	werden wir
werden werden	werden	würden	werdet
werdet werden	werdet	würdet	werden Sie
werden werden	werden	würden	

Die Modalverben

The modal verbs

können

Präsens Present	Präteritum Simple Past	Perfekt Present Perfect	Plusquamperfekt Past Perfect
kann	konnte	habe gekonnt	hatte gekonnt
kannst	konntest	hast gekonnt	hattest gekonnt
kann	konnte	hat gekonnt	hatte gekonnt
können	konnten	haben gekonnt	hatten gekonnt
könnt	konntet	habt gekonnt	hattet gekonnt
können	konnten	haben gekonnt	hatten gekonnt

Futur Future	Konjunktiv I Subjunctive I	Konjunktiv II Subjunctive II
werde können	könne	könnte
wirst können	könntest	könntest
wird können	könne	könnte
werden können	können	könnten
werdet können	könn[e]t	könntet
werden können	können	könnten

dürfen

Präsens Present	Präteritum Simple Past	Perfekt Present Perfect	Plusquamperfekt Past Perfect
darf	durfte	habe gedurft	hatte gedurft
darfst	durftest	hast gedurft	hattest gedurft
darf	durfte	hat gedurft	hatte gedurft
dürfen	durften	haben gedurft	hatten gedurft
dürft	durftet	habt gedurft	hattet gedurft
dürfen	durften	haben gedurft	hatten gedurft

Futur Future	Konjunktiv I Subjunctive I	Konjunktiv II Subjunctive II
werde dürfen	dürfe	dürfte
wirst dürfen	dürftest	dürftest
wird dürfen	dürfe	durfte
werden dürfen	dürfen	dürften
werdet dürfen	dürf[e]t	dürftet
werden dürfen	dürfen	dürften

mögen

Präsens Present	Präteritum Simple Past	Perfekt Present Perfect	Plusquamperfekt Past Perfect
mag	mochte	habe gemocht	hatte gemocht
magst	mochtest	hast gemocht	hattest gemocht
mag	mochte	hat gemocht	hatte gemocht
mögen	mochten	haben gemocht	hatten gemocht
mögt	mochtet	habt gemocht	hattet gemocht
mögen	mochten	haben gemocht	hatten gemocht

Futur Future	Konjunktiv I Subjunctive I	Konjunktiv II Subjunctive II
werde mögen	möge	möchte
wirst mögen	mögest	möchtest
wird mögen	möge	möchte
werden mögen	mögen	möchten
werdet mögen	mög[e]t	möchtet
werden mögen	mögen	möchten

müssen

Präsens Present	Präteritum Simple Past	Perfekt Present Perfect	Plusquamperfekt Past Perfect
muss	musste	habe gemusst	hatte gemusst
musst	musstest	hast gemusst	hattest gemusst
muss	musste	hat gemusst	hatte gemusst
müssen	mussten	haben gemusst	hatten gemusst
müsst	musstet	habt gemusst	hattet gemusst
müssen	mussten	haben gemusst	hatten gemusst

Futur Future	Konjunktiv I Subjunctive I	Konjunktiv II Subjunctive II
werde müssen	müsse	müsste
wirst müssen	müssest	müsstest
wird müssen	müsse	müsste
werden müssen	müssen	müssten
werdet müssen	müss[e]t	müsstest
werden müssen	müssen	müssten

sollen

Präsens Present	Präteritum Simple Past	Perfekt Present Perfect	Plusquamperfekt Past Perfect
soll	sollte	habe gesollt	hatte gesollt
sollst	solltest	hast gesollt	hattest gesollt
soll	sollte	hat gesollt	hatte gesollt
sollen	sollten	haben gesollt	hatten gesollt
sollt	solltet	habt gesollt	hattet gesollt
sollen	sollten	haben gesollt	hatten gesollt

Futur Future	Konjunktiv I Subjunctive I	Konjunktiv II Subjunctive II
werde sollen	solle	sollte
wirst sollen	solltest	solltest
wird sollen	solle	sollte
werden sollen	sollen	sollten
werdet sollen	soll[e]t	solltet
werden sollen	sollen	sollten

wollen

Präsens Present	Präteritum Simple Past	Perfekt Present Perfect	Plusquamperfekt Past Perfect
will	wollte	habe gewollt	hatten gewollt
willst	wolltest	hast gewollt	hattest gewollt
will	wollte	hat gewollt	hatte gewollt
wollen	wollten	haben gewollt	hatten gewollt
wollt	wolltet	habt gewollt	hattet gewollt
wollen	wollten	haben gewollt	hatten gewollt

Futur Future	Konjunktiv I Subjunctive I	Konjunktiv II Subjunctive II
werde wollen	wolle	wollte
wirst wollen	wollest	wolltest
wird wollen	wolle	wollte
werden wollen	wollen	wollten
werdet wollen	woll[e]t	wolltet
werden wollen	wollen	wollten

Englische Kurzgrammatik
Concise English grammar

Der bestimmte und der unbestimmte Artikel

Der **bestimmte Artikel** ist im Singular und Plural immer gleich:

the	*der*
	die
	das
	die (Plural)

Der **unbestimmte Artikel** ist vor Konsonanten

a [ə] (*betont:* [eɪ])	*ein, eine*

und vor Vokalen und stummem *h*

an [ən] (*betont:* [æn])	*ein, eine*

Das Substantiv

Das **Geschlecht** der Substantive stimmt im Englischen mit dem natürlichen Geschlecht überein. Da der Artikel immer gleich ist, erkennt man es nur an dem Pronomen (persönliches Fürwort).

the boy	he	*er*
the lady	she	*sie*
the book	it	*es*

Schiffsnamen sind meist weiblich. Auch Länder, Autos und Flugzeuge werden oft durch den Gebrauch der weiblichen Pronomen personifiziert.

Im **Plural** wird an den Singular eines Substantivs ein **-s** angehängt. Dieses *s* wird stimmhaft [z] gesprochen nach Vokalen und stimmhaften Konsonanten:

days	*Tage*
dogs	*Hunde*
boys	*Jungen*

und stimmlos nach allen stimmlosen Konsonanten:

books	*Bücher*
hats	*Hüte*

Bei Wörtern, die auf *-ce, -ge, -se, -ze* enden, wird das im Singular stumme *-e* wie [ɪ] ausgesprochen:

pieces	*Stücke*
sizes	*Größen*

Auf einen Zischlaut *(s, ss, sh, ch, x, z)* endende Wörter bekommen *-es* [ɪz] angehängt:

box**es**	*Schachteln*
boss**es**	*Chefs*

Auslautendes *y*, dem ein Konsonant vorausgeht, wird im Plural zu *-ies* [ɪz]:

lady	*Dame*	lad**ies**	*Damen*
pony	*Pony*	pon**ies**	*Ponys*

auch Wörter, die auf *-o* enden, und einen Konsonanten vorangestellt haben, bekommen oft *-es*:

tomato**es**	*Tomaten*
hero**es**	*Helden*

Einige auf *-f* oder *-fe* endende Wörter erhalten im Plural die Endung *-ves*:

Singular		Plural	
half	*Hälfte*	hal**ves**	*Hälften*
knife	*Messer*	kni**ves**	*Messer*
leaf	*Blatt*	lea**ves**	*Blätter*
wife	*Ehefrau*	wi**ves**	*Ehefrauen*

Andere ändern ihren Vokal bzw. ihre Vokale:

Singular		Plural	
foot	*Fuß*	**feet**	*Füße*
man	*Mann*	**men**	*Männer*
woman	*Frau*	**women**	*Frauen*

Unregelmäßige Pluralbildungen und solche auf *-ves, -oes* bzw. *-os* sind im englisch-deutschen Teil des Wörterbuchs angegeben.

Nominativ/Akkusativ/Dativ/Genitiv

Nominativ und Akkusativ (direktes Objekt) haben dieselbe Form. Der Genitiv wird meist mit Hilfe von *of*, der Dativ mit *to* ausgedrückt.

- Der Dativ kann auch ohne *to* gebildet werden, wenn das Dativobjekt (indirekte Objekt) unbetont ist. Das Dativobjekt steht dann direkt hinter dem Verb:

	He shows the usher the ticket.
anstelle von:	He shows the ticket to the usher.
	Er zeigt dem Platzanweiser die Eintrittkarte.

- Im Unterschied zum Deutschen wird auch bei folgenden Ausdrücken die Form des Genitivs mit *of* gebraucht:

a cup **of** coffee	*eine Tasse Kaffee*
the city **of** Boston	*Boston*
the island **of** Oahu	*die Insel Oahu*

- Der sächsische Genitiv, der häufig bei Personen und personifizierten Begriffen zur Bezeichnung des Besitzes verwendet wird und vor dem Substantiv steht, das er näher bestimmt, ist ähnlich wie im Deutschen: „Vaters Hut". Er wird im Singular durch Apostroph und s gekennzeichnet:

my sister**'s** room	*das Zimmer meiner Schwester*

und im Plural durch den Apostroph allein:

my sisters**'** room	*das Zimmer meiner Schwestern*

Wörter wie z. B. *store, church, cathedral* werden nach dem sächsischen Genitiv oft weggelassen:

at the greengrocer's	*statt:* at the greengrocer's store	*beim Gemüsehändler*
St. Paul's	*statt:* St. Paul's Cathedral	*die St.-Pauls-Kathedrale*

Das Adjektiv

Das Adjektiv bleibt nach Geschlecht und Zahl immer unverändert.

a **nice** man/woman	*ein netter Mann/eine nette Frau*
three **nice** men/women	*drei nette Männer/Frauen*

1. Die regelmäßige Steigerung

Bei der regelmäßigen Steigerung erhalten einsilbige Adjektive im Komparativ die Endung *-er* und im Superlativ *-est*.

great	great**er** (than)	great**est**
groß	*größer (als)*	*am größten*

- Bei Adjektiven, die auf *-e* enden, entfällt bei der Steigerung mit *-er, -est* ein ‚e':

fine, finer, fine**st**

- Die Endbuchstaben *d, g, n* und *t* werden bei der Steigerung mit *-er, -est* verdoppelt, wenn ihnen ein kurzes, betontes *a, e, i* oder *o* vorausgeht:

big, bigger, bigg**est**

Zwei- und mehrsilbige Adjektive werden im Komparativ mit **more** (mehr) und im Superlativ mit **most** (meist) gesteigert.

difficult	**more** difficult (than)	**most** difficult
schwierig	*schwieriger (als)*	*am schwierigsten*

2. Die unregelmäßige Steigerung

Unregelmäßige Steigerungsformen sind im englisch-deutschen Teil des Wörterbuchs angegeben.

good	better	best
gut	*besser*	*am besten*
bad	worse	worst
schlecht	*schlechter*	*am schlechtesten*
much/many	more	most
viel/viele	*mehr*	*am meisten*

Das Adverb

Adverbien werden gebildet, indem man an ein Adjektiv **-ly** anhängt.

slow quick	slow**ly** quick**ly**	He speaks slow**ly**. He runs quick**ly**.	*Er spricht langsam.* *Er läuft schnell.*

- Ein Sonderfall ist *well*, das Adverb zu *good* (gut).

He speaks English <u>well</u>.	*Er spricht gut Englisch.*

- Eine weitere Ausnahme sind die folgenden Adverbien:

You're doing <u>fine</u>.	*Du machst das gut.*
You've arrived too <u>late</u>.	*Du kommst zu spät.*
See you <u>soon</u>!	*Bis bald!*

Adverbien mit der Endung **-ly** werden mit **more** und **most** gesteigert.

slow**ly**	**more** slowly	**most** slowly
langsam	*langsamer*	*am langsamsten*

Adverbien, die nicht auf **-ly** enden, erhalten im Komparativ die Endung **-er** und im Superlativ **-est**:

fast	fast**er**	fast**est**
schnell	*schneller*	*am schnellsten*

Das Verb

Präsens

Infinitiv: (Grundform)		**to knock** klopfen	**to call** rufen	**to go** gehen	**to wash** waschen	**to study** studieren
I	(ich)	knock	call	go	wash	study
you	(du, Sie)	knock	call	go	wash	study
he/she/it	(er/sie/es)	knock**s** [nɒks]	call**s** [kɔːlz]	go**es** [ɡəʊz]	wash**es** [ˈwaʃɪz]	stud**ies** [ˈstʌdɪz]
we	(wir)	knock	call	go	wash	study
you	(ihr, Sie)	knock	call	go	wash	study
they	(sie)	knock	call	go	wash	study

Nur die 3. Person Singular wird verändert.

Das **-s** ist stimmlos nach stimmlosen Konsonanten *(he knocks)* und stimmhaft nach Vokalen *(he goes)* sowie stimmhaften Konsonanten *(he calls)*.

Das Präteritum und Partizip Perfect

Die Vergangenheitsform wird gebildet, indem man **-ed** an die Grundform des Verbs anhängt.

Infinitiv: (Grundform)	**to open** öffnen	**to arrive** ankommen	**to stop** anhalten	**to carry** tragen
I	open**ed**	arriv**ed**	stop**ped**	carr**ied**
you, he, she, it, we, you, they	open**ed**	arriv**ed**	stop**ped**	carr**ied**

- Bei Verben, die auf **-e** enden, entfällt ein ‚e':

agre**ed**, arriv**ed**

- Ein auslautendes **-y** verwandelt sich in ***-ied:***

hurr**ied**

- Auslautendes **b, d, g, m, n, p, s, t** wird verdoppelt, wenn es nach kurzem, betonten Vokal steht.
- Bei regelmäßigen Verben ist das Partizip Perfekt gleich dem Präteritum:

opened	**arrived**	**stopped**	**carried**
geöffnet	*angekommen*	*angehalten*	*getragen*

Die Formen der **unregelmäßigen Verben** sind in einer gesonderten Liste aufgeführt.

Die Hilfsverben

Präsens und Partizip Präsens

Infinitiv: **(Grundform)**	**to be** **sein**	**to have** **haben**	**to do** **tun, machen**
I	am *ich bin*	have *ich habe*	do *ich tue*
you	are *du bist; Sie sind*	have *du hast; Sie haben*	do *du tust; Sie tun*
he, she, it	is *er, sie, es ist*	has *er, sie, es hat*	does *er, sie, es tut*
we	are *wir sind*	have *wir haben*	do *wir tun*
you	are *ihr seid; Sie sind*	have *ihr habt; Sie haben*	do *ihr tut; Sie tun*
they	are *sie sind*	have *sie haben*	do *sie tun*
Partizip:	being *seiend*	having *habend*	doing *tuend*

Im gesprochenen Englisch werden häufig Kurzformen gebraucht:

am are is	→ ’m → ’re → ’s	**I’m** **you’re** **he’s, she’s**
have has	→ ’ve → ’s	**I’ve** **he’s, she’s**

Verneinung	**Kurzform**
are not	aren’t
is not	isn’t
have not	haven’t
has not	hasn’t
do not	don’t
does not	doesn’t

Präteritum und Partizip Perfect

Infinitiv: **(Grundform)**	**to be** **sein**	**to have** **haben**	**to do** **tun, machen**
I	was *ich war*	had *ich hatte*	did *ich tat*
you	were *du warst; Sie waren*	had *du hattest; Sie hatten*	did *du tatest; Sie taten*
he, she, it	was *er, sie, es war*	had *er, sie, es hatte*	did *er, sie, es tat*
we	were *wir waren*	had *wir hatten*	did *wir taten*
you	were *ihr wart;* *Sie waren*	had *ihr hattet;* *Sie hatten*	did *ihr tatet;* *Sie taten*
they	were *sie waren*	had *sie hatten*	did *sie taten*
Partizip:	been *gewesen*	had *gehabt*	done *getan*
Kurzform:		’d (z. B. I’d, you’d etc.)	
Verneinung:	wasn’t weren’t	hadn’t	didn’t

Perfekt

Das Perfekt bildet man im Unterschied zum Deutschen immer mit **have** + Partizip Perfekt.

I have had	*ich habe gehabt*
I have been	*ich bin gewesen*
I have done	*ich habe getan*
I have called	*ich habe gerufen*
I have arrived	*ich bin angekommen*
I have gone	*ich bin gegangen*

Plusquamperfekt

Das Plusquamperfekt wird mit **had** + Partizip Perfekt gebildet.

I had had	*ich hatte gehabt*
I had been	*ich war gewesen*
I had done	*ich hatte getan*
I had called	*ich hatte gerufen*
I had arrived	*ich war angekommen*
I had gone	*ich war gegangen*

Die unselbstständigen Hilfsverben

Sie können nicht selbstständig auftreten, sondern müssen immer von einem anderen Verb (im Infinitiv ohne *to*) begleitet werden.

I, you, he, she, it we, you, they	can	may	should	will	must
	können	*dürfen*	*sollen*	*wollen, werden*	*müssen*

Verneinung:	cannot can't	must not mustn't	should not shouldn't	will not won't	need not needn't

Diese Verben sind bei allen Personen gleich; die dritte Person Singular hat kein **-s**.

Präteritum		Ersatz	
could	*konnte*	to be able (to)	*können, im Stande sein (zu)*
might	*könnte*	to be allowed (to)	*dürfen*
would	*würde*	to want, to wish (to)	*wollen, wünschen*
should have	*sollte*	to be obliged (to)	*verpflichtet sein (zu)*

Verneinung:	could not couldn't	might not mightn't	would not wouldn't	should not shouldn't

- Die Formen des Präteritums, die denen des Konditionals gleich sind, findet man oft in Höflichkeitswendungen:

Could you give me ...?	*Können sie mir ... geben?*
Would you ..., please.	*Würden Sie bitte ... .*
Would you like ...?	*Wollen/Möchten Sie ...?*
I would like	*Ich möchte ... .*

Das Futur und der Konditional

Das Futur wird mit Hilfe von **will** und das Konditional mit **would** gebildet. In der gesprochenen Sprache wird fast nur die Kurzform verwendet.

Futur		Konditional	
I will go	*ich werde gehen*	I would go	*ich würde gehen*
you will go	*du wirst gehen; Sie werden gehen*	you would go	*du würdest gehen; Sie würden gehen*
he, she, it will go	*er, sie, es wird gehen*	he, she, it would go	*er, sie, es würde gehen*
we will go	*wir werden gehen*	we would go	*wir würden gehen*
you will go	*ihr werdet gehen; Sie werden gehen*	you would go	*ihr würdet gehen; Sie würden gehen*
they will go	*sie werden gehen*	they would go	*sie würden gehen*
Kurzform:	I'll go, you'll go, he'll go, we'll go, you'll go, they'll go	I'd go, you'd go, he'd go, we'd go, you'd go, they'd go	

Frage und Verneinung mit *do*

Das Hilfsverb **do** wird zur Bildung der fragenden und der mit **not** verneinten Form der selbstständigen Verben verwendet.

Do you speak German? Does he know? Did you call?	*Sprechen Sie Deutsch?* *Weiß er es?* *Haben Sie gerufen?*
I do not (don't) speak German. He does not (doesn't) know. I did not (didn't) call.	*Ich spreche kein Deutsch.* *Er weiß es nicht.* *Ich habe nicht gerufen.*
Didn't he come? Didn't she call?	*Ist er nicht gekommen?* *Hat sie nicht gerufen?*

- **do** wird nicht verwendet in Fragesätzen, in denen ein Fragewort selbst das Subjekt ist:

Who wrote the letter?	*Wer schrieb den Brief?*
Which of these trains goes to Chicago?	*Welcher dieser Züge fährt nach Chicago?*

und auch nicht in Sätzen mit den Hilfsverben:

am, are, is, was, were, can, could, may, might, must, shall, should, will, would

Die Verlaufsform

Die Verlaufsform wird mit dem Hilfsverb **be** und dem Partizip Präsens (**-ing**) gebildet. Mit der Verlaufsform wird eine Handlung ausgedrückt, die gerade abläuft, noch andauert oder noch nicht abgeschlossen ist, war oder sein wird.

I am working.	*Ich arbeite gerade.*
I was working.	*Ich arbeitete (gerade).*
I will be working.	*Ich werde arbeiten.*
It is raining.	*Es regnet.*

- Bei Verben, die auf **-e** enden, entfällt das ‚e‘: **arrive, arriving**
- Bei Verben, die auf **-ie** enden, verwandelt sich dies in ‚y‘: **lie, lying**
- Für die Verdoppelung der Endkonsonanten gelten dieselben Regeln wie zur Bildung des Präteritums: **stop, stopping**

- Die Form **be going to** wird für eine beabsichtigte Handlung, die in naher Zukunft stattfinden wird, verwendet.

I am going to go Seattle next week.	*Ich werde nächste Woche nach Seattle fahren.*
She is going to buy a new dress.	*Sie wird sich ein neues Kleid kaufen.*

Das Gerundium

Das Gerundium (Verb + *-ing*) ist die substantivierte Form des Infinitivs.

Instead of **writing**, I'd rather go for a walk.	*Anstatt zu schreiben würde ich lieber spazieren gehen.*
Smoking is dangerous.	*Rauchen ist gefährlich.*

Das Passiv

Zur Bildung des Passivs verwendet man das Hilfsverb **be** und das Partizip Perfekt.

The farmer feeds the horses.	*Der Bauer füttert die Pferde.*
The horses **are fed** (by the farmer).	*Die Pferde werden (vom Bauern) gefüttert.*
Somebody stole my bike.	*Jemand hat mein Fahrrad gestohlen.*
My bike **was stolen**.	*Mein Fahrrad wurde gestohlen.*

Das Personalpronomen

Subjektsfall		Objektsfall	
I	ich	**me**	mir/mich
you	du; Sie	**you**	dir/dich; Ihnen/Sie
he	er	**him**	ihm/ihn
she	sie	**her**	ihr/sie
it	es	**it**	ihm/es
we	wir	**us**	uns/uns
you	ihr; Sie	**you**	euch/euch; Ihnen/Sie
they	sie	**them**	ihnen/sie

- Im Objektsfall steht **to** (Dativ), wenn das Pronomen besonders hervorgehoben werden soll:

I gave the book **to** him.	*Ich gab ihm (betont) das Buch.*
anstatt: I gave him the book.	*Ich gab ihm (unbetont) das Buch.*

Das Possessivpronomen

Das Possessivpronomen ist für Singular und Plural gleich. Es hat adjektivische und substantivische Formen.

Adjektivisch (verbunden)

my book	*mein Buch*	my books	*meine Bücher*
your book	*dein/Ihr Buch*	your books	*deine/Ihre Bücher*
his book	*sein Buch*	his books	*seine Bücher*
her book	*ihr Buch*	her books	*ihre Bücher*
its book	*sein Buch*	its books	*seine Bücher*
our book	*unser Buch*	our books	*unsere Bücher*
your book	*euer/Ihr Buch*	your books	*eure/Ihre Bücher*
their book	*ihr Buch*	their books	*ihre Bücher*

Substantivisch (alleinstehend)

mine	meines/der, die, das meinige/die meinigen
yours	deines/Ihres; der, die, das deinige/Ihrige; die deinigen/Ihrigen
his	seines/der, die, das seinige/die seinigen
hers	ihres/der, die, das ihrige/die ihrigen
ours	unseres/der, die, das unsrige/die unsrigen
yours	eures/Ihres; der, die, das eurige/Ihrige; die eurigen/Ihrigen
theirs	ihres/der, die, das ihrige/die ihrigen

It's not my book. It's yours.	*Es ist nicht mein Buch. Es ist deines.*

Das Demonstrativpronomen

Singular:	this that	*dieser, diese, dieses* *jener, jene, jenes*	**Plural:**	these those	*diese* *jene*
This is a CD and **that** is a DVD. *Dies hier ist eine CD und das da ist eine DVD.*			**These** pictures are nicer than **those**. *Diese Bilder sind schöner als jene.*		

Das Reflexivpronomen

myself	*mich*	ourselves	*uns*
yourself	*dich; sich*	yourselves	*euch; sich*
himself	*sich*	themselves	*sich*
herself	*sich*		
itself	*sich*		

I enjoy **myself**.	*Ich amüsiere mich.*
You enjoy **yourself**.	*Du amüsierst dich./Sie amüsieren sich.*
He enjoys **himself**.	*Er amüsiert sich.*
She enjoys **herself**.	*Sie amüsiert sich.*
We enjoy **ourselves**.	*Wir amüsieren uns.*
You enjoy **yourselves**.	*Ihr amüsiert euch./Sie amüsieren sich.*
They enjoy **themselves**.	*Sie amüsieren sich.*

Das Relativpronomen

	Personen	Sachen	Personen und Sachen
Nominativ (wer? was?)	who	which	that
Genitiv (wessen?)	whose	of which	
Dativ (wem?)	to whom	to which	
Akkusativ (wen? was?)	whom/who	which	that

Das Relativpronomen hat im Singular und im Plural die gleiche Form.

- Im Akkusativ kann **that** auch wegfallen:

This is the strangest book (**that**) I have ever read.	*Das ist das merkwürdigste Buch, das ich je gelesen habe.*

Das Interrogativpronomen

Substantivisch (alleinstehend)

who?	*wer?*	Who are you?	*Wer sind Sie?*
whose?	*wessen?*	Whose car is this?	*Wessen Auto ist das?*
whom?/who?	*wem?/wen?*	Who(m) did you help? Who(m) did you see?	*Wem hast du geholfen?* *Wen hast du gesehen?*
what?	*was?*	What is that?	*Was ist das?*
which?	*welche?/welcher/ welches?*	Which is the quickest way?	*Welches ist der kürzeste Weg?*

who/whose/whom fragen nach Personen, **what** nach Sachen und **which** nach Sachen aus einer bestimmten Anzahl.

- **Präpositionen** im Fragesatz werden **nachgestellt**:

Where do you come **from**?	*woher?*
What are you looking **for**?	*wonach?*
What do you want this **for**?	*wofür?*
What are you laughing **at**?	*worüber?*
Who are you speaking **to**?	*mit wem?*

Adjektivisch (verbunden)

What car?	*Was für ein* Auto?
What German songs?	*Was für* deutsche Lieder?
Which book?	*Welches* Buch? (von mehreren Büchern)

Die Indefinitpronomen: *some* und *any*

1. some/somebody/someone/something

some und seine Zusammensetzungen stehen:

1. in bejahenden Sätzen:

I'd like **some** strawberry jam.	*Ich hätte gern etwas Erdbeermarmelade.*
Somebody/Someone has stolen my purse.	*Jemand hat meinen Geldbeutel gestohlen.*
I'd like **something** to drink.	*Ich hätte gern etwas zu trinken.*

2. in Fragesätzen, wenn darauf eine bejahende Antwort erwartet wird:

May I have **some** more coffee, please? – Yes, of course.	*Kann ich noch etwas Kaffee haben? – Aber selbstverständlich.*

2. any/anybody/anyone/anything

any und seine Zusammensetzungen werden verwendet in:

1. verneinten Sätzen:

I don't have **any** friends in Detroit.	*Ich habe keine Freunde in Detroit.*

2. in Fragesätzen, auf welche die Antwort ungewiss ist:

Is there **anybody/ anyone** here who speaks German?	*Spricht hier jemand Deutsch?*
Do you have **any** stamps?	*Haben Sie vielleicht ein paar Briefmarken?*
Is there **anything** I can do for you?	*Kann ich irgendetwas für Sie tun?*

3. in Bedingungssätzen:

If I had **any** stamps I would mail the letter.	*Wenn ich Briefmarken hätte, würde ich den Brief einwerfen.*

Übersicht über die wichtigsten unregelmäßigen englischen Verben

List of the most important irregular English verbs

Infinitiv Infinitive	Präteritum Simple past	Partizip Perfekt Past participle
abide	abode, abided	abode, abided
arise	arose	arisen
awake	awoke, awaked	awoken, awaked
be	was *sing*, were *pl*	been
bear	bore	born(e)
beat	beat	beaten, beat
become	became	become
begin	began	begun
behold	beheld	beheld
bend	bent	bent
beset	beset	beset
bet	bet, betted	bet, betted
bid	bid, bade	bid, bidden
bind	bound	bound
bite	bit	bitten
bleed	bled	bled
bless	blessed, blest	blessed, blest
blow	blew	blown
break	broke	broken
breed	bred	bred
bring	brought	brought
broadcast	broadcast, broadcasted	broadcast, broadcasted
build	built	built
burn	burned, burnt	burned, burnt
burst	burst	burst
bust	bust, busted	bust, busted
buy	bought	bought
can	could	–
cast	cast	cast
catch	caught	caught
choose	chose	chosen
cling	clung	clung
clothe	clothed, clad	clothed, clad
come	came	come
cost	cost	cost
creep	crept	crept
cut	cut	cut
deal	dealt	dealt
dig	dug	dug
dive	dived, dove	dived, dove
do	did	done

Infinitiv Infinitive	Präteritum Simple past	Partizip Perfekt Past participle
draw	drew	drawn
dream	dreamed, dreamt	dreamed, dreamt
drink	drank	drunk
drive	drove	driven
dwell	dwelt, dwelled	dwelt, dwelled
eat	ate	eaten
fall	fell	fallen
feed	fed	fed
feel	felt	felt
fight	fought	fought
find	found	found
fit	fitted, fit	fitted, fit
flee	fled	fled
fling	flung	flung
fly	flew	flown
forbid	forbad(e)	forbidden
forecast	forecast, fore-casted	forecast, fore-casted
forget	forgot	forgotten
forgive	forgave	forgiven
freeze	froze	frozen
get	got	gotten, got
give	gave	given
go	went	gone
grind	ground	ground
grow	grew	grown
hang	hung, LAW hanged	hung, LAW hanged
have	had	had
hear	heard	heard
hide	hid	hidden, hid
hit	hit	hit
hold	held	held
hurt	hurt	hurt
keep	kept	kept
kneel	knelt, kneeled	knelt, kneeled
knit	knitted, knit	knitted, knit
know	knew	known
lay	laid	laid
lead	led	led
lean	leaned	leaned
leap	leaped, leapt	leaped, leapt
learn	learned, learnt	learned, learnt

Infinitiv Infinitive	Präteritum Simple past	Partizip Perfekt Past participle
leave	left	left
lend	lent	lent
let	let	let
lie	lay	lain
light	lit, lighted	lit, lighted
lose	lost	lost
make	made	made
may	might	–
mean	meant	meant
meet	met	met
mistake	mistook	mistaken
mow	mowed	mowed, mown
pay	paid	paid
prove	proved	proved, proven
put	put	put
quit	quit, quitted	quit, quitted
read	read	read
rid	rid, ridded	rid, ridded
ride	rode	ridden
ring	rang	rung
rise	rose	risen
run	ran	run
saw	sawed	sawed, sawn
say	said	said
see	saw	seen
seek	sought	sought
sell	sold	sold
send	sent	sent
set	set	set
sew	sewed	sewn, sewed
shake	shook	shaken
shave	shaved	shaved, shaven
shear	sheared	sheared, shorn
shed	shed	shed
shine	shone	shone
shit	shit, shitted, shat	shit, shitted, shat
shoe	shod, shoed	shod, shodden, shoed
shoot	shot	shot
show	showed	shown, showed
shrink	shrank, shrunk	shrunk, shrunken
shut	shut	shut
sing	sang	sung
sink	sank	sunk
sit	sat	sat
slay	slew	slain
sleep	slept	slept
slide	slid	slid, slidden

Infinitiv Infinitive	Präteritum Simple past	Partizip Perfekt Past participle
sling	slung	slung
slink	slunk	slunk
slit	slit	slit
smell	smelled, smelt	smelled, smelt
sow	sowed	sown, sowed
speak	spoke	spoken
speed	speeded, sped	speeded, sped
spell	spelled, spelt	spelled, spelt
spend	spent	spent
spill	spilled, spilt	spilled, spilt
spin	spun	spun
spit	spat, spit	spat, spit
split	split	split
spoil	spoiled, spoilt	spoiled, spoilt
spread	spread	spread
spring	sprang, sprung	sprung
stand	stood	stood
stave	staved, stove	staved, stove
steal	stole	stolen
stick	stuck	stuck
sting	stung	stung
stink	stank, stunk	stunk
strew	strewed	strewn, strewed
stride	strode	stridden
strike	struck	struck
string	strung	strung
strive	strove, strived	striven
swear	swore	sworn
sweat	sweat, sweated	sweat, sweated
sweep	swept	swept
swell	swelled	swelled, swollen
swim	swam	swum
swing	swung	swung
take	took	taken
teach	taught	taught
tear	tore	torn
tell	told	told
think	thought	thought
thrive	thrived, throve	thrived, thriven
throw	threw	thrown
thrust	thrust	thrust
tread	trod	trodden
understand	understood	understood
wake	woke, waked	woken, waked
wear	wore	worn
weave	wove	woven
wed	wed, wedded	wed, wedded

Infinitiv Infinitive	Präteritum Simple past	Partizip Perfekt Past participle
weep	wept	wept
wet	wet, wetted	wet, wetted
win	won	won
wind	wound	wound
withhold	withheld	withheld
wring	wrung	wrung
write	wrote	written

Prefixes and suffixes: German-English
Präfixe und Suffixe: Deutsch-Englisch

German Prefixes and Combining Forms
Deutsche Präfixe und Wortbildungselemente

Prefix/ Combining Form	English Equivalent	Meaning and Use	Example	English Translation
a-[1]	a-	variant of **ab-**[1]	Aversion	aversion
a-[2]	a-	variant of **an-**[2]	asexuell	asexual(ly)
ab-[1]	a-	in foreign words meaning: away, away from	abrupt	abrupt(ly)
ab-[2]		separable prefix meaning: 1. weg-, fort- 2. los-, weg- 3. aus- 4. copying, imitating 5. the opposite (of the verb that is attached to it)	1. abfahren, abwischen 2. abtrennen, absägen 3. abschalten 4. abschreiben 5. abbestellen, abgewöhnen	1. to depart (in a vehicle), to wipe off 2. to tear off, to saw off 3. to turn off 4. to copy 5. to cancel, to give up
abs-	a-	variant of **ab-**[1]	abstrahieren	to abstract
ad-	ad-	in addition	addieren	to add up
aero-	aer(o)-	air, gas	aerodynamisch	aerodynamic(ally)
af-	af-	variant of **ad-**	Affekt	affect
afro-	Afro-	refers to Africa	afrokaribisch	Afro-Caribbean
ag-	ag-	variant of **ad-**	Aggression	aggression
agora-	agora-	a crowd or large public place	Agoraphobie	agoraphobia
agrar-, agri-, agro-	agri-, agro-	farming	Agrarbereich, Agrikultur, Agroindustrie	agricultural sector, agriculture, agribusiness
akro-	acr(o)-	tip, outer end	Akrobat	acrobat
al-	al-	variant of **ad-**	Alliteration	alliteration
all-		1. constantly recurring 2. everywhere 3. universal	1. allabendlich 2. allbekannt 3. allmächtig	1. regular (or every) evening 2. universally known 3. almighty
alti-	alti-, alto-	high, height	Altimeter	altimeter
amb-		around	Ambition	ambition
ambi-	ambi-	both	ambivalent	ambivalent
amphi-	amphi-	1. dual 2. around	1. Amphibie 2. Amphitheater	1. amphibian 2. amphitheater
an-[1]	an-	in foreign words meaning: variant of **ad-**	annihilieren	to annihilate
an-[2]	an-	in foreign words meaning: without, not	Anarchie	anarchy

Prefix/ Combining Form	English Equivalent	Meaning and Use	Example	English Translation
an-[3]		separable prefix meaning: 1. so that sth is fastened 2. briefly, slightly 3. directed at sb or sth	 1. anbinden, annageln 2. anbraten, ansägen 3. anbellen, anlügen	 1. to tether, to nail on 2. to fry just until brown, to saw into 3. to bark at, to lie to
andro-	andr(o)-	male, masculine	androgyn	androgynous
anglo-	Anglo-	England, English, British	anglophil	Anglophilic
ante-	ante-	before, in front	antediluvianisch	antediluvian
anthropo-	anthropo-	human being	Anthropologie	anthropology
anti-	anti-	1. against, not 2. negative attitude 3. preventing 4. opposite	1. Antipathie 2. antiautoritär 3. antibakteriell 4. Antithese	1. antipathy 2. anti[-]authoritarian 3. antibacterial(ly) 4. antithesis
ap-	ap-	variant of **ad-**	Appell	appeal
aqua-	aqua-	water	Aquaplaning	aquaplaning
äqui-	equi-	equal	äquivalent	equivalent
ar-	ar-	variant of **ad-**	Arrest	arrest
as-	as-	variant of **ad-**	assimilieren	to assimilate
astro-	astro-	star, space	Astronaut	astronaut
audi(o)-	audi(o)-	tone, sound, hearing	audiovisuell	audiovisual(ly)
auf-		separable prefix meaning: 1. so that sth is opened 2. beginning suddenly 3. so that there is contact 4. upward 5. until nothing is left 6. again 7. so that a certain condition is reached	 1. aufklappen, aufkratzen 2. aufleuchten, aufschreien 3. aufkleben, aufdrucken 4. aufwirbeln, aufkrempeln 5. aufessen 6. aufbacken, aufwärmen 7. aufheitern, auflockern	 1. to open up, to scratch open 2. to light up, to shriek 3. to stick on, to apply 4. to swirl up, to roll up 5. to eat up 6. to heat up (in the oven), to warm up 7. to cheer up, to liven up
aus-		separable prefix meaning: 1. out of (in the sense of going), out of (in the sense of coming) 2. so that sth becomes empty 3. so that sth is not functioning 4. to the end 5. in several directions	 1. ausgießen, ausatmen 2. ausgießen, auspumpen 3. ausschalten, auspusten 4. ausdiskutieren, ausschlafen 5. ausstreuen, ausfahren	 1. to pour off, to exhale 2. to empty (of a liquid), to pump out 3. to switch off, to blow out 4. to finish discussing, to sleep in 5. to disseminate, to deliver
außer-		outside of	außerbetrieblich, außerirdisch	company-external, extraterrestrial
auto-	auto-	self, personal, own	Autobiographie	autobiography

Prefix/ Combining Form	English Equivalent	Meaning and Use	Example	English Translation
be-		1. makes intransitive verbs transitive 2. changes the perspective of a transitive verb 3. changes nouns to transitive verbs 4. changes adjectives to transitive verbs	1. bewohnen, beleuchten 2. beerben, beschenken 3. benoten, begrenzen 4. belustigen, beunruhigen	1. to inhabit, to light up 2. to be heir to, to present 3. to grade, to limit 4. to amuse, to worry
bei-		in addition	beilegen, beimischen	to enclose, to mix into
bene-	bene-	good, well	benedeien	to bless
bi-	bi-	two, twice, both	bidirektional	bidirectional(ly)
biblio-	biblio-	book	bibliophil	bibliophilic
bin-	bin-	two each	binär	binary
bio-[1]	bio-	life	Biographie	biography
bio-[2]		not poisonous, without artificial substances	Biobauer, Biokost	organic farmer, organic food
blitz-[1]		extremely	blitzschnell, blitzgescheit	lightning fast, brilliant
blitz-[2]		very fast	Blitzaktion, Blitzkarriere	lightning operation, rapid rise to the top (of one's career)
bomben-[1]		first-class	Bombenerfolg, Bombenstimmung	smash hit, great atmosphere
bomben-[2]		absolute	bombenfest, bombensicher	absolutely secure, bombproof
brand-		extremely, absolute	brandaktuell, brandneu	very current, brand-new
brevi-	brevi-	brief	Brevität	brevity
chiro-	chiro-, cheiro-	hand	Chiropraktiker	chiropractor
chroma-, chromo-	chrom(o)-	color	chromatisch Chromosom	chromatic chromosome
chrono-	chron(o)-	time	Chronologie	chronology
cyber-	cyber-	electronic, digital, virtual	Cybersex	cybersex
da-[1]		separable prefix meaning: in a certain place	dabehalten, daliegen	to keep here/there, to lie there
da-[2]		forms pronominal adverbs	damit, dazu	with it/that, to it/hat
dar-		variant of **da-**[2]	daran, darum	on it/that, for it/that
de-	de-	1. to cancel, to undo 2. not	1. deregulieren 2. dezentral	1. to deregulate 2. decentralized
deka-	deca-, deka-	ten	Dekade	decade
demo-	demo-	people, nation	Demokratie	democracy
dermato-	derm(a)-	skin	Dermatologie	dermatology
dezi-	deci-	one tenth	Dezibel	decibel
di-[1]	di-	double	Dilemma	dilemma
di-[2]	di-	variant of **dis-**	divergieren	to diverge
dia-	dia-	through, across	diagonal	diagonal

Prefix/ Combining Form	English Equivalent	Meaning and Use	Example	English Translation
dif-	dif-	variant of **dis-**	diffamieren	to defame
dis-	dis-	1. not 2. separation, removal	1. Disharmonie 2. distribuieren	1. disharmony 2. to distribute
dran-		separable prefix meaning: to fasten	drannageln, dranklebe-ben	to nail to, to stick on
drauf-		separable prefix meaning: on top of	draufschrauben, draufsitzen	to screw on[to], to sit on
duo-	duo-	two	Duodenum	duodenum
durch-[1]		separable prefix meaning: 1. into one end and out the other 2. through an opening 3. completely through a material, fabric, substance, etc. 4. completely, to the end 5. so that sth becomes divided 6. completely worn out	1. durchfahren, durchmarschieren 2. durchreichen, durchstecken 3. durchhören, durch-schmecken 4. durchlesen, durch-nummerieren 5. durchreißen, durch-schneiden 6. durchwetzen, durchrosten	1. to drive through, to march through 2. to pass through, to poke through 3. to hear (through), to taste (through) 4. to read to the end, to number all the way to the end 5. to rip through, to cut through 6. to wear through, to rust through
durch-[2]		inseparable prefix; makes intransitive verbs transitive meaning: going from one end to another or touching many points in a room	durchschwimmen, durchlaufen	to swim across to traverse
dyna-	dyna-	power	dynamisch	dynamic(ally)
dys-	dys-	1. bad 2. anomalous	1. dysfunktional 2. Dyskalkulie	1. dysfunctional(ly) 2. dyscalculia
e-[1]	e-	electronic	E-Commerce	e-commerce
e-[2]	e-	variant of **ex-**[2]	emigrieren	to emigrate
ef-	ef-	variant of **ex-**[2]	Effusion	effusion
ein-		separable prefix meaning: 1. from outside to inside 2. into sth 3. so that deep points arise 4. (completely) around sth 5. to damage or destroy 6. to lead to a certain result	1. einreisen, eintreten 2. einfüllen, einbauen 3. einritzen, einker-ben 4. einkreisen, einrah-men 5. einreißen, einwer-fen 6. einebnen, eindeut-schen	1. to enter (a coun-try), to enter (on foot) 2. to pour in, to install 3. to carve, to cut 4. to circle, to frame 5. to tear, to break 6. to flatten, to Germanize
elektro-	electro-	power, electricity	Elektromagnet	electromagnet
em-	em-	variant of **en-**	Embryo	embryo
en-	en-	(from Greek) in, within	Energie	energy
endo-	endo-	in, within	endotherm	endothermic(ally)

Prefix/ Combining Form	English Equivalent	Meaning and Use	Example	English Translation
ent-		inseparable prefix meaning: 1. to take sth away from sth, to free sth from sth 2. out of sth 3. away from sth	1. enthüllen, entgiften 2. entströmen 3. enteilen, entschweben	1. to unveil, to detoxify 2. to pour out 3. to hurry away, to float away
entomo-	entomo-	insect	Entomologie	entomology
ep-	ep-	variant of **epi-**	Epoche	epoch
epi-	epi-	1. on, over, above 2. near 3. after, later	1. Epizentrum 2. Epilog 3. Epigone	1. epicenter 2. epilog(ue) 3. epigone
er-		inseparable prefix meaning: 1. to take on a certain feature 2. to achieve a certain result 3. to begin to	1. erkalten, erblinden 2. ertasten, erkaufen 3. erbeben, erstrahlen	1. to become cold, to go blind 2. to feel out, to pay for 3. to shudder, to shine
erz-	arch-	1. head, leader, chief 2. extreme	1. Erzbischof 2. erzkonservativ	1. archbishop 2. ultraconservative
ethno-	ethno-	people, race	Ethnologie	ethnology
eu-	eu-	good	Eulogie	eulogy
euro-	Euro-	Europe, European	Eurokrat	Eurocrat
ex-[1]	ex-	former	Exfreundin	ex-girlfriend
ex-[2]	ex-	out, out of, outside	explodieren	to explode
exo-	exo-	outside, external	exotherm	exothermic(ally)
extra-[1]	extra-	outside	extraordinär	extraordinary
extra-[2]		very, especially	extragroß, extrastark	extra large, extra strong
extro-	extro-	variant of **extra-**	extrovertiert	extrovert
fehl-		not correct	Fehldiagnose, Fehlinformation	misdiagnosis, misinformation
fest-		separable prefix meaning: so that sth is difficult to remove	festbinden, festschrauben	to tie tight, to screw tight
fono-		orthographic variant of **phono-**		
fort-		1. away 2. still	1. fortgehen, fortziehen 2. fortbestehen, fortwirken	1. to go away, to move away 2. to survive, to continue to have an effect
foto-		orthographic variant of **photo-**		
franko-	Franco-	French, France	frankophon	francophone/Francophone
frei-		separable prefix meaning: to free from sth (bothersome)	freikämpfen, freischaufeln	to struggle to free, to shovel free
frisch-		only just	frischgestrichen, frischverheiratet	freshly painted, newly married
gastro-	gastr(o)-	stomach	Gastroskopie	gastroscopy

Prefix/ Combining Form	English Equivalent	Meaning and Use	Example	English Translation
ge-		changes verbs to nouns	Gebell, Geschwätz	barking, gossip
gegen-		1. from the opposite direction 2. refutation 3. battle 4. reaction	1. Gegenlicht, Gegenströmung 2. Gegenbeweis, Gegenbeispiel 3. Gegenmittel 4. Gegenargument, Gegenangriff	1. light shining toward the viewer, countercurrent 2. evidence to the contrary, counter-example 3. antidote 4. counterargument, counterattack
geno-	gen(o)-	people, race	Genozid	genocide
geo-	geo-	earth	Geographie	geography
giga-	giga-	one billion	Gigabyte	gigabyte
grafo-		orthographic variant of **grapho-**		
grapho-	graph(o)-	writing	Graphologie	graphology
groß-	grand-	previous generation	Großmutter, Großvater	grandmother, grandfather
gynäko-	gynec(o)-	woman	Gynäkologe	gynecologist
gyro-	gyr(o)-	circle, spinning	Gyroskop	gyroscope
halb-	demi-	half, partly	Halbgott	demigod
häm(o)-	hema-, hemo-	blood	Hämatit, Hämoglobin	hematite, hemoglobin
hämat(o)-	hema-	blood	Hämaturie, Hämatologe	hematuria, hematologist
haupt-		most important	Hauptstadt, Hauptbestandteil	capital (city), main component
heiden-		very big, very much	Heidenangst, Heidenlärm	mortal fear, awful racket
heim-		(toward) home	heimgehen, Heimfahrt	to go home, trip (ride) home
hekt(o)-	hect(o)-	one hundred	Hektar, Hektoliter	hectare, helicopter
heli-	heli-	helicopter	Heliport	heliport
hemi-	hemi-	half, partial	Hemisphäre	hemisphere
hepta-	hepta-	seven	Heptagon	heptagon
her-		separable prefix meaning: 1. (from some place) over to the speaker 2. in the same direction 3. origin, source	1. herbringen, herkommen 2. (neben jemandem) herfahren, (vor jemandem) hergehen 3. herstammen, herkommen	1. to bring (over) here, to come (over) here 2. to drive (alongside sb), to walk (in front of sb) 3. to originate from, to come from
heran-		separable prefix meaning: over to sth or sb or from one place to another	herankommen, herantasten	to approach, to feel one's way
herauf-		separable prefix meaning: over to sth or sb or from down below to up above	heraufkommen, heraufbringen	to come up, to bring up

Prefix/ Combining Form	English Equivalent	Meaning and Use	Example	English Translation
heraus-		separable prefix meaning: over to sth or sb or from inside to outside	herauslassen, herausschrauben	to let out, to unscrew
herein-		separable prefix meaning: over to sth or sb or from outside to inside	hereinkommen, hereinsehen	to come in, to look in
herüber-		separable prefix meaning: over to sth or sb: from one side to the other	herüberreichen, herüberklettern	to hand over (here), to climb over (here)
herum-		separable prefix meaning: 1. in a circular pattern 2. in the other direction 3. in no particular direction and with no particular goal 4. without knowing how sth will end 5. without a clear intention 6. to have sth to do with sth unpleasant or to complain about it	1. herumgehen, herumbinden 2. herumdrehen, herumreißen 3. herumspazieren, herumirren 4. herumexperimentieren, herumrätseln 5. herumblättern, herumsitzen 6. herumplagen, herumnörgeln	1. to walk around (in a circular pattern), to tie around 2. to turn around, to pull around (hard) 3. to stroll around, to wander around 4. to experiment around, to try to figure out 5. to leaf through, to sit around 6. to bother, to nag
heter(o)-	heter(o)-	different, other	heterosexuell	heterosexual(ly)
hex(a)-	hex(a)-	six	hexangulär, Hexagon	hexangular, hexagon
hier-[1]		separable prefix meaning: in this place	hierbleiben, hierbehalten	to stay here, to keep here
hier-[2]		forms pronominal adverbs	hieran, hiermit	on here, with this
hin-		separable prefix meaning: over to a certain place (away from the speaker)	hingehen, hinbringen	to go over (there), to bring over (there)
hinauf-		separable prefix meaning: away from sth or sb: from down below to up above	hinaufgehen, hinaufbringen	to go up (there), to bring up (there)
hinaus-		separable prefix meaning: away from sth or sb: from inside to outside	hinausschauen, hinausschieben	to look out, to push out
hinein-		separable prefix meaning: away from sth or sb: from outside to inside	hineinführen, hineinlassen	to usher in (there), to let in[to] (there)
hinüber-		separable prefix meaning: away from sth or sb: from one side to the other	hinüberblicken, hinüberhelfen	to look over (there), to help over (there)
histo-	hist(o)-	living tissue	Histologie	histology

Prefix/ Combining Form	English Equivalent	Meaning and Use	Example	English Translation
hoch-[1]		very (strong)	hochexplosiv, hoch-modern	highly explosive, ultra-modern
hoch-[2]		up	hochbinden, hoch-gucken	to tie up, to look up
höllen-		very big	Höllenkrach, Höllen-angst	hellish noise, awful fear
holo-	holo-	whole, complete	Holocaust	holocaust
hom(o)-	homo-	alike, same	Homograph	homograph
homö(o)-	homeo-	alike, similar	Homöopathie	homeopathy
hunds-		very	hundsgemein, hunds-miserabel	rotten, lowdown
hydr(o)-	hydro-	water, liquid	Hydrophobie	hydrophobia
hyper-[1]	hyper-	over, above	Hyperbel	hyperbole
hyper-[2]	hyper-	excessive	hypernervös, hyper-korrekt	extremely nervous, excessively proper
hypn(o)-	hypno-	sleep	Hypnotherapie	hypnotherapy
hypo-	hypo-	1. under, below 2. unusually low	1. hypodermatisch 2. Hypothermie	1. hypodermic 2. hypothermia
hystero-	hyster(o)-	womb, uterus	Hysteroskopie	hysteroscopy
il-[1]	il-	variant of **in-**[1]	illuminieren	to illuminate
il-[2]	il-	variant of **in-**[2]	illegal	illegal(ly)
im-[1]	im-	variant of **in-**[1]	immens	immense(ly)
im-[2]	im-	variant of **in-**[2]	immobil	immobile
immer-	ever-	without interruption	immerwährend, immergrün	perennial, evergreen
in-[1]	in-	in, into	inaugurieren	to inaugurate
in-[2]	in-	not	inaktiv	inactive(ly)
indo-	Indo-	Indian	Indonesien	Indonesia
infra-	infra-	below, beneath	Infrastruktur	infrastructure
inter-	inter-	among, between	international	international(ly)
intra-	intra-	within, inside	intravenös	intravenous(ly)
intro-	intro-	into, inward	introvertiert	introverted
ir-[1]	ir-	variant of **in-**[1]	irritieren	to irritate
ir-[2]	ir-	variant of **in-**[2]	irregulär	irregular(ly)
is(o)-	iso-	equal	Isotop	isotope
kardio-	cardi(o)-	heart	Kardiogramm	cardiogram
kenn-		as a means of identifi-cation	Kennziffer, Kennwort	code number, pass-word
kilo-	kilo-	one thousand	Kilometer	kilometer
klasse-		very good	Klasseleistung, Klasseidee	great achievement, great idea
knall-		bright, intensely radiant	knallgrün, knallbunt	bright green, vibrantly colored
ko-	co-	together, jointly	koalieren	to coalesce
kol-	col-	variant of **ko-**	kollaborieren	to collaborate
kom-	com-	variant of **ko-**	komprimieren	to compress
kombi-	combi-	used for various pur-poses	Kombimöbel, Kombi-zange	combination furniture, combination pliers
kon-	con-	variant of **ko-**	konkav	concave

Prefix/ Combining Form	English Equivalent	Meaning and Use	Example	English Translation
konter-	counter-	contrary, opposing	konteragieren, Konterrevolution	to counteract, counterrevolution
kontra-	contra-	against, having an adverse effect on	Kontradiktion, Kontrazeption	contradiction contraception
kor-	cor-	variant of **ko-**	korrigieren	to correct
kosmo-	cosmo-	1. in space 2. on Earth	1. Kosmonaut 2. Kosmopolit	1. cosmonaut 2. cosmopolitan
kreuz-		very	kreuzbrav, kreuzlangweilig	very well-behaved, very boring
krypt(o)-	crypt(o)-	concealed, hidden, secret	kryptisch	cryptic
lakt(o)-	lacto-	milk	Laktose	lactose
lith(o)-	lith(o)-	stone	Lithographie	lithography
los-		separable prefix meaning: 1. weg-, fort- 2. beginning suddenly 3. to loosen a connection	 1. losgehen, losfliegen 2. losschreien, losschlagen 3. losbinden, losschrauben	 1. to get going (on foot), to take off (in a plane) 2. to start to scream, to start to hit 3. to untie, to unscrew
magni-	magn(i)-	big, lofty	Magnifizenz	magnificence
makr(o)-	macro-	large	makroökonomisch	macroeconomic
mal-	mal-	bad, badly	Malaria, malträtieren	malaria, to maltreat
mani-	mani-	hand	Maniküre	manicure
maxi-	maxi	rather long	Maxikleid	maxi dress
mega-[1]	mega-	1. especially large 2. one million	1. Megaphon 2. Megavolt	1. megaphone 2. megavolt
mega-[2]	mega-	(intensifier of **super-**[2]) very big	Megahit, Megastar	megahit, megastar
meist-		(superlative of much) to the greatest degree	meistdiskutiert, meistverkauft	most-discussed, best-selling
meta-	meta-	1. transformation, change 2. behind, later 3. on a higher level	1. Metamorphose 2. Metaphysik 3. Metakommunikation	1. metamorphosis 2. metaphysics 3. metacommunication
mikr(o)-	micro-	tiny, minute	Mikroorganismus	microorganism
milli-	milli-	one thousandth	Millibar	millibar
minder-		less	minderbemittelt, minderwertig	less well-off, inferior
mini-	mini-	1. small 2. very short	1. Minibar 2. Minirock	1. minibar 2. miniskirt
miss-	mis-	1. bad, badly, wrong, wrongly 2. opposite 3. negative	1. missinterpretieren 2. Misserfolg 3. missgelaunt	1. to misinterpret 2. failure 3. in a bad mood
mit-		separable prefix meaning: 1. together with others 2. not leave behind	 1. mitspielen, mitessen 2. mitnehmen, mitschleifen	 1. to play with, to share a meal 2. to take along, to drag along

Prefix/ Combining Form	English Equivalent	Meaning and Use	Example	English Translation
mittel-	medium-	1. average 2. in the middle	1. mittelgroß, mittelfein 2. Mitteleuropa, Mittelfeld	1. medium-sized, medium-fine 2. Central Europe, midfield
mono-	mono-	simgle, one	Monopol	monopoly
mords-		very big, very intense	Mordsglück, Mordshunger	incredibly good luck, ravenous hunger
morph(o)-	morph(o)-	figure, form	Morphologie	morphology
multi-	multi-	many, multiple	multilingual	multilingual
nach-[1]	after-	used with nouns to mean: coming after	Nachgeburt	afterbirth
nach-[2]		separable prefix meaning: 1. after 2. again (to check or improve) 3. based on sth 4. later 5. past the actual or planned end 6. intense and thorough	1. nachwerfen, nachrennen 2. nachrechnen, nachbehandeln 3. nachbauen, nacherzählen 4. nachlösen, nachfeiern 5. nachsitzen 6. nachdenken	1. to throw after, to run after 2. to check again, to give follow-up treatment 3. to build a copy of sth, to retell 4. to buy a ticket after boarding a train, bus, etc., to celebrate later 5. to have detention 6. to contemplate
neben-		less important	Nebeneingang, Nebenrolle	side entrance, supporting role
neo-	neo-	new, recent	Neofaschismus	neofascism
nephr(o)-	nephr(o)-	kidney	Nephritis	nephritis
neur(o)-	neur(o)-	nerve	Neurose	neurosis
nicht-	dis-, non-	not	Nichtachtung, Nichtbeachtung	disregard, noncompliance
nieder-		separable prefix meaning: 1. from up above to down below 2. to hit or destroy sth, for instance, so that it ends up on the ground	1. niederdrücken, niedersinken 2. niederbrennen, niederwalzen	1. to push down, to collapse 2. to burn down, to flatten
non-	non-	not	nonverbal	nonverbal
ober-		very	oberblöd, oberfaul	extremely stupid, extremely lazy
öko-[1]	eco-	environment, ecology	Ökologie	ecology
öko-[2]		bio-[2]	Ökobauer, Ökoprodukt	organic farmer, organic product
okt-, okta-, okto-	octa-, octo-	eight	Oktode, Oktaeder, oktogonal	octode, octahedron, octagonal
omni-	omni-	everything, all-	omnipotent	omnipotent
ornitho-	ornith(o)-	bird	Ornithologie	ornithology
orth(o)-	ortho-	1. correct, right 2. gerade, aufrecht	1. Orthographie 2. orthogonal	1. orthography 2. orthogonal
osteo-	oste(o)-	bone	Osteoporose	osteoporosis

Prefix/ Combining Form	English Equivalent	Meaning and Use	Example	English Translation
ovi-, ovu-	ov-, ovi-, ovo-	egg	ovipar, Ovulation	oviparous(ly), ovulation
päd(o)-	ped(o)-	child	Pädiatrie	pediatrics
palä(o)-	pale(o)-	old, ancient	Paläontologie	paleontology
pan-	pan-	all	Pantheon, panafrikanisch	pantheon, pan-African
para-	para-	beside, near	Paragraph	paragraph
patho-	path(o)-	disease	Pathologie	pathology
patri-	patr(i)-	1. father 2. fatherland	1. Patriarchat 2. Patriotismus	1. patriarchy 2. patriotism
pedi-	ped(i)-	foot	Pediküre	pedicure
pent(a)-	penta-	five	Pentagon, Pentathlon	pentagon, pentathlon
per-	per-	1. through 2. very, completely	1. Perspektive 2. perfekt	1. perspective 2. perfect
peri-	peri-	around	Peripherie	periphery
phil(o)-	phil(o)-	love of, inclination toward	Philanthropie, philharmonisch	philanthropy, philharmonic
phleb(o)-	phleb(o)-	vein	Phlebitis	phlebitis
phono-	phon(o)-	sound, voice	Phonologie	phonology
photo-	phot(o)-	light	Photosynthese	photosynthesis
physio-	physi(o)-	body, physical	Physiognomie	physiognomy
pneumo-[1]	pneum(o)-	air, gas	Pneumothorax	pneumothorax
pneumo-[2]	pneum(o)-	lung	Pneumologie	pneumology
poly-	poly-	many, various	Polytheismus	polytheism
post-	post-	after	postpubertär, Postimpressionismus	postpuberty, post-impressionism
prä-	pre-	before	pränatal, Präposition	prenatal, preposition
pro-	pro-	in favor of	proarabisch, prowestlich	pro-Arabic, pro-West
prot(o)-	prot(o)-	earliest	Protagonist, Prototyp	protagonist, prototype
pseud(o)-	pseud(o)-	false, sham	Pseudonym, pseudodemokratisch	pseudonym, pseudo-democratic(ally)
psych(o)-	psych(o)-	mind, mental	Psychose	psychosis
pyro-	pyro-	fire	Pyrotechnik	pyrotechnics
quadri-, quadro-	quadri-, quadru-	four	Quadrivium, Quadrophonie	quadrivium, quadraphony
quasi-	quasi-	almost, nearly, as if	quasioffiziell	quasi-official
radio-	radi(o)-	1. radio 2. radioactive	1. Radiotelegrafie 2. Radiotherapie	1. radiotelegraphy 2. radiotherapy
ran-		variant of **heran-**		
rauf-		variant of **herauf-, hinauf-**		
raus-		variant of **heraus-, hinaus-**		
re-	re-	again, anew	reanimieren	to reanimate
rein-		variant of **herein-, hinein-**		
retro-	retro-	1. back, backward 2. in the rear, behind	1. retrospektiv 2. retronasal	1. retrospective 2. retronasal

Prefix/ Combining Form	English Equivalent	Meaning and Use	Example	English Translation
rhin(o)-	rhino-	nose, nasal	Rhinitis, Rhinoplastik	rhinitis, rhinoplasty
riesen-		extremely big	Riesendefizit, Riesenüberraschung	huge deficit, huge surprise
rüber-		variant of **herüber-**, **hinüber-**		
rück-		1. changes verbs to nouns with 'zurück-' 2. back again to the starting point or sender 3. in or on the back, having to do with the back part	1. Rückeroberung, Rückgabe 2. Rückantwort, Rückreise 3. Rückbank, Rückansicht	1. reconquest, return 2. reply, return trip 3. rear seat, rear view
rum-		variant of **herum-**		
sau-[1]		very, extremely	saukalt, sauwohl	extremely cold, really good
sau-[2]		1. very unpleasant, very bad 2. very big, very intense	1. Saufraß, Sauwetter 2. Sauglück, Sauhitze	1. slop, shitty weather 2. ridiculously good luck, unbearable heat
scheiß-[1]		1. very, extreme 2. in an exaggerated manner	1. scheißfrech, scheißkalt 2. scheißfreundlich	1. extremely brazen, cold as hell 2. sweet as pie
scheiß-[2]		very bad, very unpleasant	Scheißjob, Scheißkerl	shitty job, bastard
schwieger-		related because of marriage	Schwiegervater, Schwiegertochter	father-in-law, daughter-in-law
seismo-	seismo-	earthquake	Seismograph	seismograph
selbst-	self-	1. regarding oneself 2. without outside help	1. Selbstachtung, Selbstmitleid, selbstkritisch, selbstzerstörerisch 2. Selbsthilfe, selbstklebend	1. self-respect, self-pity, self-critical, self-destructive 2. self-help, self-adhesive
semi-	semi-	half	Semifinale	semifinal
sept-	septi-	seven	September	September
sex-	sex-	six	Sextett	sextet
sexual-		sexual, sex	Sexualaufklärung, Sexualpartner	sexual enlightenment, sexual partner
sklero-	sclero-	hard	Sklerometer	sclerometer
soli-	soli-	alone	Soliloquium, solitär	soliloquy, solitaire
stereo-	stere(o)-	1. solid, massive 2. spacial, physical	1. stereotyp 2. stereophonisch	1. stereotype 2. stereophonic(ally)
stief-	step-	related because of remarriage	Stiefmutter	stepmother
stink-		very	stinkfaul, stinkwütend	lazy as hell, mad as hell
stock-		very (strong)	stockbetrunken, stockdunkel	drunk as hell, dark as hell
strato-	strato-	layer	Stratosphäre	stratosphere
sub-	sub-	under, below	subtrahieren	to subtract
suf-	suf-	variant of **sub-**	Suffix	suffix

Prefix/ Combining Form	English Equivalent	Meaning and Use	Example	English Translation
suk-	suc-	variant of **sub-**	sukzessiv	successive(ly)
sup-	sup-	variant of **sub-**	supprimieren	to suppress
super-[1]	super-	over, above	superfiziell	superficial(ly)
super-[2]	super-	1. very, exceptionally 2. outstanding 3. especially high on the scale	1. superbequem, superbillig 2. Superhotel, Superwetter 3. Supergage, Supertalent	1. super-comfortable, super-cheap 2. great hotel, great weather 3. huge salary, amazing talent
sur-	sur-	variant of **sub-**	Surrogat	surrogate
sus-	sus-	variant of **sub-**	suspendieren	to suspend
syl-	syl-	variant of **syn-**	Syllogismus	syllogism
sym-	sym-	variant of **syn-**	Symbiose	symbiosis
syn-	syn-	together, united	Synergie	synergy
tele-	tele-	distant	Television	television
tetra-	tetr(a)-	four	Tetraeder	tetrahedron
theo-	the(o)-	god	Theologie	theology
therm(o)-	therm(o)-	heat	thermisch, Thermostat	thermal(ly), thermostat
tod-		very, extremely	todmüde, todlangweilig	dead tired, ridiculously boring
top-		very, extremely	topmodern, topaktuell	completely modern, completely up-to-date
top(o)-	top(o)-	location, place	topisch, Topographie	topical(ly), topography
tot-		separable prefix meaning: 1. so that death occurs due to the given action 2. highlights the intensity	1. totfahren, totschießen 2. sich totärgern, sich totarbeiten	1. to run over and kill, to shoot dead 2. to become livid, to work oneself to death
trans-	trans-	beyond, across	Transaktion	transaction
tri-	tri-	three	Triangel	triangle
tropo-	trop(o)-	change, turning	Troposphäre	troposphere
typo-	typo-	imprint, printing	Typographie	typography
über-[1]		separable prefix meaning: 1. beyond a limit 2. from one side to the other	1. überschwappen, überkochen 2. überwechseln, übertreten	1. to slop over, to boil over 2. to change over, to convert

Prefix/ Combining Form	English Equivalent	Meaning and Use	Example	English Translation
über-[2]		inseparable prefix meaning: 1. from one point to another 2. covering a surface 3. reaching a higher degree 4. to an extreme or exaggerated degree 5. not notice 6. to check in order to improve	 1. überfliegen, überqueren 2. überschwemmen, überwuchern 3. übertönen, überragen 4. überladen, überanstrengen 5. übersehen, überlesen 6. überdenken, überarbeiten	 1. to fly over, to cross (over) 2. to flood, to overgrow 3. to drown (out), to tower above 4. to overload, to put too great a strain on 5. to overlook, to skip (while reading) 6. to think over, to revise
über-[3]	over-	used with adjectives to mean: exaggerated, excessive	überängstlich, überkorrekt	overanxious, excessively proper
über-[4]		used with nouns to mean: too great in number or amount	Überbevölkerung, Übereifer	overpopulation, overeagerness
ultra-	ultra-	1. outside the range of 2. to the greatest degree	1. Ultraschall 2. ultramodern	1. ultrasound 2. ultramodern
um-[1]		separable prefix meaning: 1. a change of position or location (from front to back, from inside to outside, from standing to lying down, etc.) 2. from one place to another 3. repetition in order to change the status	 1. umklappen, umkrempeln, umstoßen 2. umtopfen, umziehen 3. umbuchen, umbenennen	 1. to fold down, to roll up, to knock over 2. to repot, to move (house) 3. to change a reservation, to rename
um-[2]		inseparable prefix meaning: movement or position in the form of a circle or an arc	umsegeln, umlagern	to circumnavigate, to surround
un-	un-	not	unecht, unbedeutend	fake, insignificant
uni-	uni-	one, single	unilateral	unilateral
unter-[1]		separable prefix meaning: 1. so that sth ends up beneath sth else 2. so that sth is mixed with sth else 3. too little (intensity), too low	 1. unterlegen, unterschieben 2. untergraben, unterrühren 3. unterbelichten, unterbewerten	 1. to put underneath, to push underneath 2. to dig into the soil, to stir in 3. to underexpose, to undervalue
unter-[2]		inseparable prefix meaning: under and through sth	unterführen, unterqueren	to pass under, to cross under
ur-[1]		very	uralt, urplötzlich	very old, very sudden
ur-[2]		refers to the beginning, the original condition	Urbevölkerung, Urinstinkt	native population, basic instinct

Prefix/ Combining Form	English Equivalent	Meaning and Use	Example	English Translation
ver-		inseparable prefix meaning: 1. changes verbs to adjectives: to bring or come to a condition 2. changes nouns to verbs: to make or become sth 3. makes intransitive verbs transitive 4. expresses that sb dies in the manner mentioned 5. causing a negative or undesirable result 6. not perfect 7. away from a place 8. until the end 9. to equip with sth, to receive sth	1. vergrößern, verflüssigen, vereinsamen 2. verfilmen, versklaven, verdunsten 3. verspotten, verschweigen 4. verhungern, verdursten 5. verrutschen, verschlafen 6. sich verhören, sich verschreiben 7. vertreiben, sich verkriechen 8. verblühen, verbrennen 9. versilbern, verminen	1. to enlarge, to liquefy, to become lonely 2. to film, to enslave, to evaporate 3. to mock, to keep secret 4. to starve (to death), to die of thirst 5. to slip, to oversleep 6. to mishear, to make a slip of the pen 7. to drive away/out, to creep away 8. to wilt, to burn 9. to silver-plate, to mine
video-		television	Videokamera, Videoüberwachung	video camera, monitoring by closed-circuit television
vize-	vice-	1. deputy 2. second in position	1. Vizekanzler, Vizepräsident 2. Vizeweltmeister, Vizeadmiral	1. vice chancellor, vice president 2. silver medalist at a world championship, vice admiral
voll-[1]		separable prefix meaning: so that sth is entirely filled	volltanken, vollschreiben	to fill up (with gas), to fill up with writing
voll-[2]	full-, fully-	used with adjectives to mean: completely or to a great degree	vollautomatisch, vollelastisch	fully automatic, fully elastic
vor-[1]	ante-	used with nouns to mean: 1. in front, before 2. prior to, earlier 3. serves as an example	1. Vorraum, Vorgarten 2. Vorabend, Vorgeschichte, Vorarbeit, Vorwäsche 3. Vorturner	1. anteroom, front garden 2. eve, past history, preparatory work, prewash (cycle) 3. demonstrator of gymnastics exercises
vor-[2]		separable prefix meaning: 1. in front of sth or sb, toward the front 2. earlier 3. serves as an example	1. vorfahren, vortreten 2. vorkochen, vorarbeiten 3. vorsingen, vorturnen	1. to lead the way (in a vehicle), to step forward 2. to precook, to finish work ahead of schedule 3. to sing first (as a demonstration), to demonstrate gymnastics exercises

Prefix/ Combining Form	English Equivalent	Meaning and Use	Example	English Translation
weg-		separable prefix meaning: 1. away from a place 2. in a different direction 3. so that less and less remains of sth (until nothing is left) 4. not needing sth any more and therefore ridding oneself of it	1. wegfahren, wegschneiden 2. wegdrehen, wegsehen 3. wegessen, wegtrinken 4. weghängen, wegrationalisieren	1. to leave (in a vehicle), to cut away 2. to turn away, to look away 3. to eat (every last bite), to drink (every last drop) 4. to hang up (and put away), to get rid of as part of a downsizing campaign
weiter-		separable prefix meaning: 1. forwards, ahead 2. expresses the continuation of an event	1. weiterbefördern, weiterhelfen 2. weitermachen, weiterverfolgen	1. to take/drive further, to provide with further assistance 2. to continue (to do sth), to continue to pursue
wieder-		separable prefix meaning: 1. zurück- 2. anew	1. wiedergeben, wiederkommen 2. wiederaufführen, wiedereingliedern	1. to give back, to come back 2. to perform again, to reintegrate
wo-		forms pronominal adverbs	wobei, wonach	how, what ... for/of
wohl-		to a relatively high degree, existing to a comfortable degree	wohlbehalten, wohlbeleibt, Wohlgefallen	safe and sound, corpulent, delight
wor-		forms pronominal adverbs	worauf, worüber	on ... what/what ... on, about ... what/what ... about
xeno-	xen(o)-	foreign	Xenophobie	xenophobia
xyl(o)-	xyl(o)-	wood	Xylophon	xylophone
zenti-	centi-	1. hundred 2. hundredth	1. Zentifolie 2. Zentimeter	1. centifolia 2. centimeter
zer-		inseparable prefix meaning: so that sth or sb is injured or destroyed	zerquetschen, zersägen	to squash, to saw up
zirkum-	circum-	around	Zirkumferenz	circumference
zoo-	zoo-	animal	Zoologie	zoology

Prefix/ Combining Form	English Equivalent	Meaning and Use	Example	English Translation
zu-		separable prefix meaning: 1. so that sth is closed, covered, or filled 2. in a certain direction 3. aimed at sb 4. to do energentically 5. indicates that sb gets sth 6. in addition 7. to give a certain form to, to put in a certain condition	 1. zuwachsen, zufrieren, zudecken 2. zubewegen, zulaufen 3. zulächeln, zuwinken 4. zuschlagen, zubeißen 5. zuweisen, zuspielen 6. zugeben, zurechnen 7. zuschneiden, zurichten	 1. to heal over/up, to freeze (over), to cover (up) 2. to approach, to run toward 3. to smile at, to wave to 4. to slam (shut), to bite 5. to assign to, to pass to 6. to add, to add on 7. to cut to size, to finish
zurecht-		1. so that it has the desired form 2. so that sth is put in the desired place	1. zurechtbiegen, zurechtschneiden 2. zurechtrücken, zurechtlegen	1. to bend into shape, to cut into shape 2. to adjust, to get ready
zurück-		1. back to the previous place 2. from front to back 3. back to the previous person 4. reciprocal action 5. toward the past	1. zurückfahren, zurückholen 2. zurückfallen, zurücklehnen 3. zurückgeben, zurückzahlen 4. zurückgrüßen, zurückschlagen 5. zurückdenken, zurückversetzen	1. to drive back, to fetch back 2. to fall back, to lean back 3. to give back, to repay 4. to greet back, to hit back 5. to think back, to - transport back
zusammen-		1. not alone 2. to unite so that sth whole results 3. so that a large amount results 4. so that sth takes up only a small space 5. so that sb/sth falls down 6. hastily and not carefully	1. zusammenleben, zusammensitzen 2. zusammennähen, zusammenfließen 3. zusammensparen, zusammentragen 4. zusammendrücken, zusammenklappen 5. zusammensacken, zusammenschlagen 6. zusammenschreiben, zusammendichten	1. to live together, to sit together 2. to sew together, to flow together 3. to save up, to collect 4. to crush, to fold up 5. to collapse, to beat up 6. to write quickly without giving much thought to, to quickly compose (verse)
zwischen-		1. only temporarily valid 2. short-term, temporary 3. interruption	1. Zwischenbilanz 2. Zwischenlager 3. Zwischenaufenthalt	1. interim balance 2. temporary storage (facility) 3. stopover

Deutsche Suffixe und Wortbildungselemente

German Suffixes and Combining Forms

Suffix/ Combining Form	English Equivalent	Meaning and Use	Example	English Translation
-a	-a	1. makes nouns of Latin origin plural 2. feminine form	1. Abstrakta, Neutra 2. Paula, Roberta	1. abstracts, neuters 2. Paula, Roberta
-abel	-able	changes verbs (usually those that end in *-ieren*) to adjectives, meaning: possible, fit for	respektabel, akzeptabel	respectable, acceptable
-abilität	-ability	changes adjectives that end in *-abel* to nouns	Respektabilität, Akzeptabilität	respectability, acceptability
-ade	-ade	denotes the result of an action	Limonade, Barrikade, Blockade	soft drink, barricade, blockade
-age	-age	denotes an action	Massage, Sabotage, Spionage	massage, sabotage, espionage
-agoge	-agogue	leader, director	Pädagoge, Demagoge	pedagogue, demagogue
-ähnlich	-like	like, comparable to	gottähnlich, parkähnlich, totenähnlich	godlike, park-like, death-like
-al	-al, -ic	1. in the manner of or like sth 2. starting with or with regard to sth	1. horizontal, triumphal, katastrophal 2. national, formal	1. horizontal, triumphal, catastrophic 2. national, formal
-algie	-algia, -algy	pain	Nostalgie, Neuralgie	nostalgia, neuralgia
-ämie	-emia	blood	Leukämie, Anämie	leukemia, anemia
-ana	-ana	collection	Amerikana	Americana
-and		denotes a person with whom sth is done	Informand, Diplomand	a person to whom information is given, a graduate student who is writing his/her master's thesis
-anfällig	-prone	tending toward sth	störanfällig, reparaturanfällig, stressanfällig	disruption-prone, repair-prone, stress-prone
-ant	-ant(e)	denotes a person who does sth or, occasionally, a thing that does sth	Informant, Debütant; Antitranspirant	informant, debutante, antiperspirant
-anz	-ance, -ancy	changes adjectives that end in *-ant* to nouns	Intoleranz, Ignoranz, Relevanz	intolerance, ignorance, relevance
-ar	-ar, -ic	variant of **-är²**	linear, atomar, solar	linear, nuclear/atomic, solar
-är¹	-aire	a person who possesses sth	Millionär, Aktionär	millionaire, stockholder
-är²	-ary, -ery	regarding sth	familiär, revolutionär, imaginär	family, revolutionary, imaginary
-arch	-arch	leader	Monarch, Oligarch	monarch, oligarch
-archie	-archy	leadership	Monarchie, Anarchie	monarchy, anarchy
-arier	-arian	1. member of a group 2. representative of a conviction	1. Proletarier 2. Unitarier, Trinitarier, Vegetarier	1. proletarian 2. Unitarian, Trinitarian, vegetarian

Suffix/ Combining Form	English Equivalent	Meaning and Use	Example	English Translation
-arium	-arium	a protected area where one can observe things	Aquarium, Vivarium, Planetarium	aquarium, vivarium, planetarium
-armig	-armed	having a particular number of arms	einarmig	one-armed
-artig	-like	having a particular nature, similar to	blitzartig, palastartig, sintflutartig	lightning, palatial, torrential
-at		1. the result of a process or action 2. a job having a particular function 3. a place where one works having the given function 4. a group of people having the given function	1. Destillat, Fabrikat, Resultat 2. Referendariat, Volontariat 3. Lektorat, Sekretariat 4. Direktorat, Kommissariat	1. distillate, product, result 2. traineeship, internship 3. editorial office, administrative office 4. board of directors, board of commissioners
-ation	-ation	an action or a result of the action	Kanalisation, Information	sewage system, information
-atisch	-atic(al), -atically	changes nouns that end in *-m* to adjectives or adverbs, meaning: 1. regarding sth, based on sth 2. with sth, full of sth	 1. idiomatisch, axiomatisch 2. problematisch, systematisch	 1. idiomatic(al)/idiomatically, axiomatic(al)/axiomatically 2. problematic(al)/ problematically, systematic(al)/ systematically
-ator	-eer, -or	changes verbs that end in *-ieren* to nouns, meaning: the person/ thing that performs an action	Auktionator, Illustrator, Generator, Vibrator	auctioneer, illustrator, generator, vibrator
-bar	-able, -ible	1. changes transitive verbs to adjectives; in the passive voice, meaning: the action expressed by the verb can be done 2. changes intransitive verbs to adjectives; in the active voice, meaning: the action expressed by the verb can easily happen	1. auffindbar, essbar, verschließbar 2. brennbar, wandelbar	1. detectable, edible, lockable 2. combustible, convertible
-beinig	-legged	1. having a particular number of legs 2. having a particular type of legs	1. vierbeinig 2. krummbeinig, langbeinig	1. four-legged 2. bow-legged, long-legged
-betrieben	-powered	indicates the type of power supply	batteriebetrieben, atombetrieben	battery-powered, nuclear-powered
-bold		indicates a man who gets noticed often due to some unpleasant behavior that he gladly exhibits	Raufbold, Lügenbold, Trunkenbold	bully, incorrigible liar, drunkard

Suffix/ Combining Form	English Equivalent	Meaning and Use	Example	English Translation
-chen	-et, -ette, -ie, -y, -ey, -kin, -let, -ling, -ock, -ule	forms the diminutive	Hündchen, Mäuschen, Tellerchen	doggy, darling, small plate
-chrom	-chrome	color	monochrom	monochrome
-dermal	-dermal, -dermic	regarding the skin	epidermal	epidermal/epidermic
-dermis	-dermis	skin	Epidermis	epidermis
-drom	-drome	racecourse	Hippodrom, Velodrom, Syndrom	hippodrome, velodrome, syndrome
-echt	-proof	1. when used with nouns: insensitive to sth, resistant 2. when used with verbs: achievable without having a negative effect	1. lichtecht, kussecht, farbecht 2. kochecht	1. lightproof, kissproof, fast (of colors) *or* fade-resistant 2. boil-proof
-eck	-gon	having a particular number of angles	Dreieck, Achteck	triangle, octagon
-ei	1. -y 2. -ism	variant of **-erei**, meaning: 1. a business in which a particular profession is practiced 2. an action or behavior like that which is named before the suffix 3. a particular action is annoying, happens often, or persists for a long time 4. sth that arises or has arisen from a particular action	1. Bäckerei, Gärtnerei, Tischlerei 2. Barbarei, Preistreiberei, Gaunerei 3. Meuterei, Meckerei, Turtelei, Nörgelei 4. Bastelei	1. bakery, nursery, carpenter's workshop 2. barbarianism, profiteering, trickery 3. mutiny, bellyaching, whispering of sweet nothings, nagging 4. fiddling around
-ektomie	-ectomy	surgical removal	Appendektomie, Mastektomie	appendectomy, mastectomy
-ell	-al(ly)	1. with regard to 2. effected by or caused by 3. having a particular quality, being in a particular condition, able to be designated in a particular way	1. kulturell, industriell 2. maschinell, bakteriell 3. emotionell, exzeptionell, sensationell	1. cultural(ly), industrial(ly) 2. mechanical(ly), bacterial(ly) 3. emotional(ly), exceptional(ly), sensational(ly)
-em	-eme	unit	Morphem, Phonem, Lexem	morpheme, phoneme, lexeme
-en	-en	changes nouns that denote a material to adjectives	wollen, samten	woolen, velvet
-end	-ing, -ory	forms the present participle (that can also be used as an adjective)	spielend, diskriminierend (spielende Kinder, diskriminierende Äußerungen)	playing, discriminatory (children at play, discriminatory remarks)

Suffix/ Combining Form	English Equivalent	Meaning and Use	Example	English Translation
-ent	-ant, -er, -or	variant of **-ant**	Referent, Assistent, Dirigent	speaker, assistant, conductor
-enz	-ence, -ency	changes adjectives that end in *-ent* to nouns	Vehemenz, Existenz, Potenz	vehemence, existence, potency
-er[1]	-er	1. a man who performs a professional, habitual, or other activity 2. origin 3. membership 4. a machine or device	1. Bäcker, Trinker, Fahrer 2. Ausländer, New Yorker 3. Gewerkschafter 4. Wäschetrockner, Eierkocher	1. baker, drinker, driver 2. foreigner, New Yorker 3. trade unionist 4. (clothes) dryer, egg cooker
-er[2]	-er, -ier	1. forms the comparative 2. masculine inflection for adjectives	1. länger, größer, wichtiger 2. langer Ast, großer Baum, wichtiger Punkt	1. longer, bigger, more important 2. long branch, big tree, important point
-erei		1. an action or behavior like that which is named before the suffix 2. expresses that a particular action is annoying, happens often, or persists for a long time 3. sth that arises or has arisen from a particular action	1. Sauerei, Schweinerei 2. Plackerei, Fahrerei, Heulerei 3. Stickerei, Schnitzerei	1. mess, scandal 2. drudgery, long hours of driving, wailing 3. embroidery, carving
-erlei		having a particular number, having a particular amount of kinds/sorts	zweierlei, dreierlei, mancherlei, vielerlei	two different, three different, several, all kinds of
-ern	-en	changes nouns that denote a material to adjectives	hölzern, gläsern	wooden, glass
-enz	-ence, -enzy	changes adjectives or participles with the ending -ent to nouns	Turbulenz, Vehemenz	turbulence, vehemence
-esk	-esque	in the manner of	pittoresk, pikaresk, kafkaesk	picturesque, picaresque, Kafkaesque
-eur	-eur	1. occupation 2. other activity	1. Masseur, Friseur 2. Flaneur, Kollaborateur	1. masseur, barber 2. idler/loafer, collaborator
-euse	-euse	feminine form of -eur	Friseuse, Chauffeuse	hairdresser, (female) chaffeur
-fach	-time, -fold	available in a particular amount or done a particular number of times	zweifach, dreifach, mehrfach, vielfach	twice/double/two-time, thrice/triple/three-time, multiple/several times, multiple/manifold
-farben	-colored	having a particular color	orangefarben, elfenbeinfarben	orange(-colored), ivory

Suffix/ Combining Form	English Equivalent	Meaning and Use	Example	English Translation
-farbig	-color(ed)	1. having a particular number of colors 2. having a particular color	1. einfarbig, zweifarbig, vielfarbig, verschiedenfarbig 2. cremefarbig, rosenfarbig	1. all one color, two-color(ed), multicolor(ed), various-colored 2. creme-colored, rose-colored/pink
-feindlich		1. having a negative attitude toward sb/sth 2. bad/not favorable for sb/sth	1. frauenfeindlich, ausländerfeindlich, staatsfeindlich, fortschrittsfeindlich 2. familienfeindlich, lebensfeindlich	1. sexist (toward women), xenophobic, subversive, anti-progressive 2. not family-friendly, hostile toward life
-fon		orthographic variant of **-phon**		
-fonie		orthographic variant of **-phonie**		
-förmig	-form, -shaped	having a particular form/shape	wurmförmig, herzförmig, kreisförmig	vermiform, heart-shaped, circular
-frei	1. -free 2. -free 3. -proof 4. -free	1. without sth, not containing sth, not causing sth 2. expresses that sth in particular does not have to be paid for 3. expresses that sth in particular does not happen 4. expresses that sth in particular does not have to be done	1. alkoholfrei, bleifrei, fehlerfrei, störungsfrei, akzentfrei 2. portofrei, gebührenfrei, steuerfrei 3. knitterfrei, rostfrei 4. bügelfrei, wartungsfrei	1. nonalcoholic, unleaded, mistake-free, trouble-free, accent-free 2. postpaid, toll-free, tax-free 3. no-crease, rust-proof 4. no-iron, maintenance-free
-freundlich	-friendly	1. having a positive attitude toward sb/sth 2. good/beneficial for sb/sth	1. kinderfreundlich, menschenfreundlich, regierungsfreundlich 2. umweltfreundlich, familienfreundlich	1. child-friendly, humanitarian, pro-government 2. environmentally friendly, family friendly
-fritze	-er	1. a pejorative term denoting a profession 2. a man who does sth often	1. Filmfritze, Zeitungsfritze 2. Meckerfritze, Quasselfritze	1. filmmaker, reporter 2. bellyacher, windbag
-füßer	-pede, -pod	having a particular amount or type of feet	Tausendfüßer, Kopffüßer	millipede, cephalopod
-füßig	-footed(ly)	having a particular amount or type of feet	vierfüßig, barfüßig, leichtfüßig	four-footed, barefoot, light-footed(ly)
-gamie	-gamy	marriage	Monogamie, Bigamie	monogamy, bigamy
-geladen	-packed, -filled	full of	actiongeladen, spannungsgeladen	action-packed, suspense-filled
-gemäß		1. according to or suitable for sth in particular 2. according to a particular manner	1. altersgemäß, wahrheitsgemäß, wunschgemäß 2. auftragsgemäß, artgemäß	1. age-appropriate, truthful(ly), as requested 2. as instructed, suitable for a species

Suffix/ Combining Form	English Equivalent	Meaning and Use	Example	English Translation
-gen	-genic	1. suitable for sth 2. causing sth	1. fotogen, telegen 2. halluzinogen, allergen	1. photogenic, telegenic 2. hallucinogenic, allergenic
-gerecht		according to or suitable for	artgerecht, kindgerecht, fristgerecht	suitable for a species, suitable for children, punctual(ly)
-gnose	-gnosis	realization	Prognose, Diagnose	prognosis, diagnosis
-gon	-gon	having a particular number of angles	Hexagon, Pentagon	hexagon, pentagon
-graf		orthographic variant of **-graph**		
-grafie		orthographic variant of **-graphie**		
-gramm	-gram, -graph	1. in writing 2. unit of weight	1. Diagramm, Autogramm 2. Kilogramm	1. diagram, autograph 2. kilogram
-graph	-graph	1. person who writes 2. device that writes	1. Choreograph, Photograph 2. Seismograph	1. choreograph, photograph 2. seismograph
-graphie	-graphy	1. study of 2. writing	1. Ozeanographie, Geographie 2. Lexikographie, Orthographie, Stenographie	1. oceanography, geography 2. lexicography, orthography, stenography
-gyn	-gynous(ly) -gynist(ic)	used with adjectives and nouns to mean: concerning women	androgyn, Misogyn	androgynous(ly), misogynist(ic)
-haarig	-haired	having hair of a particular color or type	rothaarig, dunkelhaarig, langhaarig	red-headed, dark-haired, long-haired
-haft	1. -ic, -ical(ly), -like 2. -ous	1. like sth in particular 2. having an inclination toward	1. traumhaft, heldenhaft, bildhaft 2. lasterhaft, schwatzhaft	1. dreamlike, heroic, vivid 2. immoral, loquacious
-halber		gives the reason for sth	vorsichtshalber, ehrenhalber, umständehalber	as a precaution, honorary, owing to circumstances
-haltig		containing a particular substance	eisenhaltig, alkoholhaltig, fetthaltig	ferrous, containing alcohol, containing fat
-heini		a pejorative term denoting a profession	Versicherungsheini, Filmheini	insurance agent, filmmaker
-heit	-hood, -ty	changes adjectives or participles to nouns meaning: 1. a condition or quality 2. sb/sth having a particular quality	1. Falschheit, Freiheit, Berühmtheit, Besonnenheit 2. Berühmtheit, Neuheit, Seltenheit	1. falsehood, freedom, fame, prudence 2. celebrity, novelty, rarity
-hungrig	-hungry	eager for	machthungrig, bildungshungrig	power-hungry, thirsting for (an) education
-i	-y, -ie	1. for intimate forms of address or a shortened version of sb's name 2. to form abbreviations	1. Mutti, Papi, Vati, Willi 2. Profi, Ami, Pulli	1. mommy, pops, daddy, Willy/Willie 2. pro, Yank, sweater

Suffix/ Combining Form	English Equivalent	Meaning and Use	Example	English Translation
-ial	-ial(ly)	variant of **-al**, meaning: 1. in the manner of or like sth 2. starting from or regarding sth	 1. adverbial, kollegial 2. äquatorial, jovial	 1. adverbial(ly), collegial(ly) 2. equatorial(ly), jovial(ly)
-iana	-iana	variant of **-ana**	Mozartiana	Mozartiana
-iasis	-iasis	disease	Elefantiasis, Amöbiasis	elephantiasis, am(o)ebiasis
-iatrie	-iatrics, -iatry	special field of medicine	Geriatrie, Psychiatrie	geriatrics, psychiatry
-ibel	-ible	variant of **-abel**	kompatibel, reversibel	compatible, reversible
-ibilität	-ibility	variant of **-abilität**	Kompatibilität	compatibility
-id	-oid	belonging to a race or exhibiting characteristics of a race	mongolid, negrid	Mongoloid, negroid
-ide	-id	denotes a member of a zoological family	Arachnide	arachnid
-iell	-ial(ly)	variant of **-ell**, meaning: 1. with regard to 2. brought about or caused by sth	 1. essenziell, existenziell, finanziell 2. ministeriell, notariell	 1. essential(ly), existential(ly), financial(ly) 2. ministerial(ly), notarial(ly)
-ien		plural ending of some nouns	Fossilien, Materialien, Prinzipien, Indizien	fossils, materials, principles, circumstantial evidence
-ieren	-ate	changes nouns and adjectives to verbs, meaning: 1. to give sb/sth a particular status 2. to provide sb/sth with sth 3. to do sth	 1. gruppieren, blondieren, halbieren 2. apostrophieren, asphaltieren 3. marschieren, protestieren	 1. to classify, to dye/bleach, to halve 2. to apostrophize, to pave 3. to march, to protest
-ig	-eous(ly)	changes nouns to adjectives or adverbs, meaning: 1. having/using a particular thing or quality 2. like sth in particular 3. having a particular form 4. as if made of a particular material	 1. mutig, fleißig, eifrig 2. riesig, milchig, schwammig 3. bergig, krümelig, hügelig 4. glasig, seidig, goldig	 1. courageous(ly), diligent(ly), eager(ly) 2. huge, milky, spongy 3. mountainous, crumbly, hilly 4. glassy, silky, golden
-igen	-ate, -ize	changes nouns and adjectives to verbs, meaning: to do/make, to cause	demütigen, ängstigen, nötigen, entmutigen, sättigen, verewigen	to humiliate, to frighten, to coerce, to discourage, to satiate, to immortalize
-igkeit		changes adjectives to nouns, meaning: condition, nature, or characteristic	Erfolglosigkeit, Laienhaftigkeit, Dreistigkeit	failure, amateurishness, audacity
-ik	-ics, -ology	denotes a field of work	Linguistik, Genetik, Technik	linguistics, genetics, technology

Suffix/ Combining Form	English Equivalent	Meaning and Use	Example	English Translation
-iker	-cian, -ic	1. profession 2. sb with a disorder 3. sb with a particular attitude	1. Elektriker, Mathematiker 2. Allergiker, Alkoholiker 3. Choleriker, Zyniker	1. electrician, mathematician 2. a person who suffers from allergies, alcoholic 3. choleric, cynic
-in	-ina, -ess, -enne	for people (see **-er**[1]) and animals, to make the feminine form	Lehrerin, Ärztin, Zarin, Löwin, Komödiantin	(female) teacher, (female) doctor, czarina, lioness, comedienne
-ion		variant of **-ation**	Aktion, Instruktion	action, instruction
-isch	1. -ese, -an 2. -ic, -ical(ly) 3. -ish, -ic	1. origin 2. membership 3. manner	1. japanisch, bayrisch, pfälzisch 2. islamisch, städtisch, mathematisch 3. kindisch, närrisch, heroisch	1. Japanese, Bavarian, Palatinate 2. Islamic, urban, mathematical(ly) 3. childish, foolish, heroic
-isieren	-ize	1. used with nouns and adjectives, meaning: to give sb/sth a particular status 2. used with nouns, meaning: to provide sb/sth with sth	1. familiarisieren, zentralisieren, kategorisieren 2. computerisieren, aromatisieren	1. to familiarize, to centralize, to categorize 2. to computerize, to aromatize
-isierung	-ization	changes verbs that end in *-isieren* to nouns	Amerikanisierung, Privatisierung	Americanization, privatization
-ismus	-ism	1. denotes a political system, a religion, a philosophical orientation, an artistic style, etc. 2. denotes a personal disposition 3. denotes a predisposition or illness 4. in linguistics: denotes a word that has a particular origin or characteristic	1. Totalitarismus, Kapitalismus, Sozialismus; Buddhismus, Katholizismus; Pazifismus; Expressionismus, Existenzialismus 2. Idealismus, Pessimismus, Perfektionismus, Zynismus 3. Masochismus, Sadismus, Autismus 4. Anglizismus, Hispanismus, Archaismus, Euphemismus	1. totalitarianism, capitalism, socialism; Buddhism, Catholicism; pacifism; expressionism, existentialism, 2. idealism, pessimism, perfectionism, cynicism 3. masochism, sadism, autism 4. Anglicism, Hispanicism archaism, euphemism

Suffix/ Combining Form	English Equivalent	Meaning and Use	Example	English Translation
-ist	-ist	1. a supporter or representative of a political system, a religion, a philosophical orientation, an artistic style, etc. 2. sb who has a particular personal disposition 3. sb who has a particular predisposition or illness 4. sb who plays a particular musical instrument 5. sb who has a particular profession 6. sb who participates in sth or who belongs to a group of people	1. Kapitalist, Sozialist; Buddhist; Pazifist; Expressionist, Existenzialist 2. Idealist, Pessimist, Perfektionist 3. Masochist, Sadist, Autist 4. Bassist, Gitarrist, Pianist 5. Maschinist, Komponist, Karikaturist 6. Finalist, Putschist, Reservist, Infanterist	1. capitalist, socialist; Buddhist; pacifist; expressionist, existentialist 2. idealist, pessimist, perfectionist 3. masochist, sadist, autist 4. bassist, guitarist, pianist 5. machinist, composer, caricaturist 6. finalist, putschist, reservist, infantryman
-istisch	-istic(ally)	changes nouns that end in *-ismus* to adjectives or adverbs	realistisch, idealistisch	realistic(ally), idealistic(ally)
-ität	-ity, -ness	changes adjectives of foreign origin to nouns	Absurdität, Komplexität, Nervosität	absurdity, complexity, nervousness
-itis	-itis	inflammation	Bronchitis, Gastritis, Konjunktivitis	bronchitis, gastritis, conjunctivitis
-iv	-ive	1. characteristic 2. regarding 3. nature	1. aggressiv, explosiv, produktiv 2. qualitativ, quantitativ 3. attributiv, föderativ	1. aggressive, explosive, productive 2. qualitative, quantitative 3. attributive, federative
-keit	-ity	1. changes adjectives that express a condition or characteristic to nouns 2. a person or thing that has the named characteristic or is in the named condition	1. Heiserkeit, Übelkeit, Höflichkeit, Fruchtbarkeit, Wirksamkeit 2. Möglichkeit, Sehenswürdigkeit, Flüssigkeit	1. hoarseness, nausea, politeness, fertility, effectiveness 2. possibility, sight worth seeing, liquid
-klud-, -klus-	-clud-, -clus-	to conclude	exkludieren, inklusiv, Konklusion	to exclude, inclusive, conclusion
-köpfig	1. -man 2. -headed 3. -headed 4. -haired	1. having a particular number of people or members 2. having a particular number of heads 3. having a particular type of head 4. having a particular type of hair	1. zweiköpfig, dreiköpfig 2. zweiköpfig, dreiköpfig, mehrköpfig 3. großköpfig 4. krausköpfig, lockenköpfig, glatzköpfig, kahlköpfig	1. two-man, three-man 2. two-/double-headed, three-headed, several-headed 3. big-headed 4. fuzzy-haired, curly-haired, bald, bald-headed

Suffix/ Combining Form	English Equivalent	Meaning and Use	Example	English Translation
-krat	-crat	a supporter or representative of a particular form of government	Demokrat, Aristokrat	democrat, aristocrat
-kratie	-cracy	a form of government	Demokratie, Aristokratie	democracy, aristocracy
-lang	-length	1. as long as sth 2. reaching to sth	1. armlang, meterlang 2. knielang, schulterlang	1. arm-length, (one-) meter-long 2. knee-length, shoulder-length
-lei		changes numbers	einerlei, zweierlei, mancherlei, verschiedenerlei,	one of a kind, two [different], all sorts of, diverse
-lein	-et, -ette, -ie, -y, -ey, -kin, -let, -ling, -ock, -ule	forms the diminutive	Blümlein, Häuslein, Bettlein	little flower, little house, little bed
-lepsie	-lepsy	seizure	Narkolepsie	narcolepsy
-ler	1. -ist 2. -er	1. sb who is involved in or does sth specific 2. sb who belongs to a group, category, or field	1. Sportler, Künstler, Wissenschaftler 2. SPDler, FKKler, Ruheständler, Erstklässler	1. athlete, artist, scientist 2. member/supporter of the SPD, nudist, retiree, first-grader
-lich[1]	1. -able, -ible 2. -ing(ly)	added to verb stems, meaning: 1. that sth can be done 2. that sth has a particular effect	1. bestechlich, verzeihlich, käuflich 2. bedrohlich, erbaulich	1. corrupt, forgivable, for sale 2. threatening(ly), edifying
-lich[2]	1. -ing 2. -al(ly) 3. -y 4. -ful 8. -ly 9. -ern	added to nouns, meaning: 1. that sth has a particular effect 2. with regard to sb/sth or belonging to sb/sth 3. resembling sb/sth 4. alive with, full of 5. having a particular characteristic or in a particular condition 6. location 7. point in time 8. time interval 9. direction	1. ärgerlich, abscheulich 2. beruflich, elterlich, kirchlich 3. feindlich, sommerlich, mütterlich 4. leidenschaftlich, ängstlich 5. männlich, jungfräulich 6. nördlich, seitlich 7. morgendlich, abendlich 8. täglich, wöchentlich 9. südlich	1. aggravating, revolting 2. professional(ly), parental(ly), clerical(ly) 3. adverse, summery, motherly 4. passionate, frightened 5. masculine(ly), virginal(ly) 6. northern, lateral(ly) 7. (in the) morning, (in the) evening 8. daily, weekly 9. southern
-lich[3]	2. -ish	added to adjectives, meaning: 1. having a particular characteristic, shape, or condition 2. tones down	1. fröhlich, länglich 2. dicklich, bläulich, ältlich	1. happy, oblong 2. chubby, bluish, oldish

Suffix/ Combining Form	English Equivalent	Meaning and Use	Example	English Translation
-lich[4]	-able, -ible, -ibly	added to un- + verb stem, meaning: that sth cannot be done	unbeschreiblich, unauslöschlich	indescribable, indelible/indelibly
-ling		1. sb having a particular characteristic 2. sb who does sth in particular	1. Feigling, Schwächling, Wüstling, Jüngling 2. Eindringling, Schädling	1. coward, weakling, lecher, young man 2. intruder, pest
-lith	-lith	stone	Monolith	monolith
-log	-log(ue)	speech	Monolog, Epilog	monolog(ue), epilog(ue)
-logie	-logy	science, study of	Anthropologie, Dermatologie	anthropology, dermatology
-los	-less(ly)	without sth	mühelos, arbeitslos, sinnlos	effortless(ly), unemployed, senseless
-mache	-ing	an attempt to achieve a particular effecxt	Panikmache, Meinungsmache	scaremongering, spindoctoring
-macher	1. -maker	1. sb who manufactures sth professionally 2. sb who causes a particular effect 3. sb who does sth often (and gladly) 4. sth that causes a particular effect	1. Uhrmacher, Schuhmacher, Filmemacher 2. Angstmacher, Panikmacher, Miesmacher 3. Krachmacher, Krawallmacher 4. Dickmacher, Muntermacher	1. watchmaker, shoemaker, filmmaker 2. scaremonger, alarmist, killjoy 3. noisemaker, hooligan 4. fattener, stimulant
-mal		a particular number of times	einmal, hundertmal, dreieinhalbmal	once, a hundred times, three-and-a-half times
-malig	-time	1. happening a particular number of times 2. happening for a particular number of times	1. einmalig, fünfmalig, mehrmalig 2. erstmalig, diesmalig, nochmalig	1. one-time, five-time, repeatedly 2. for the first time, this time, again
-mals		1. an indefinite number of times 2. for a particular number of times	1. mehrmals, vielmals, oftmals 2. erstmals, nochmals	1. several times, many times, often 2. for the first time, again
-manie	-mania	a pathological urge	Pyromanie, Megalomanie, Kleptomanie	pyromania, megalomania, kleptomania
-marathon	-athon	sth that lasts for an extremely long time	Sitzungsmarathon, Telefonmarathon	marathon session, telephone marathon
-maßen		changes adjectives to adverbs	einigermaßen, bekanntermaßen, gewissermaßen	to some degree, notoriously, to some extent
-mäßig		1. in keeping with, according to 2. with regard to 3. like	1. vorschriftsmäßig, planmäßig 2. altersmäßig, mengenmäßig 3. lehrbuchmäßig	1. according to the regulations, scheduled 2. with regard to age, quantitative(ly) 3. textbook
-meter	-meter	1. measure of length 2. measuring device	1. Kilometer, Zentimeter 2. Chronometer, Thermometer	1. kilometer, centimeter 2. chronometer, thermometer

Suffix/ Combining Form	English Equivalent	Meaning and Use	Example	English Translation
-morph	-morphous(ly), -morphic	shape, form	amorph, polymorph	amorphous(ly), polymorphic
-n	-y, -en	changes nouns that denote a material to adjectives	silbern, seiden	silver(y), silk(en)
-nd	-ing	variant of **-end**	lächelnd, meckernd	smiling, moaning
-nik	-nik	denotes a person who belongs to a group	Beatnik	beatnik
-nis	-ness	1. changes adjectives and verbs to nouns, meaning: condition 2. changes verbs to nouns meaning: sth that has a particular effect	1. Bitternis, Finsternis, Betrübnis, Bedrängnis 2. Hemmnis, Hindernis	1. bitterness, gloominess, sorrow, hardship 2. barrier, obstacle
-nomie	-nomy	1. scientific involvement 2. a right to sth	1. Astronomie, Ökonomie, Taxonomie 2. Autonomie	1. astronomy, economy, taxonomy 2. autonomy
-o		forms slang words that associate people with particular habits or characteristics	Normalo, Brutalo	normal person, brute
-oid	-oid	resembling sb/sth	mongoloid, faschistoid, Sphäroid	Mongoloid, protofascist, spheroid
-om	-oma	growth, tumor	Karzinom, Melanom	carcinoma, melanoma
-onym	-onym -onymous(ly)	referring to a name or a word	Synonym, Pseudonym, anonym	synonym, pseudonym, anonymous(ly)
-opie	-opia	affecting vision	Myopie	myopia
-or	-or	variant of **-ator**	Aggressor, Inquisitor, Editor	aggressor, inquisitor, editor
-orientiert	-oriented	1. following particular concepts or ideals 2. based on particular conditions	1. profitorientiert, erfolgsorientiert, praxisorientiert, linksorientiert 2. bedarfsorientiert, exportorientiert	1. profit-oriented, success-oriented, practice-oriented, leftist 2. demand-oriented, export-oriented
-orium	-orium	1. a place that serves a particular purpose 2. (for) a group of people	1. Krematorium, Emporium, Sanatorium 2. Auditorium, Direktorium	1. crematorium, emporium, sanatorium 2. auditorium, board of directors
-os	-ose	variant of **-ös**	humos, lepros, verbos	humose, leprose, verbose
-ös	-ous, -ar	full of, characterized by	mysteriös, voluminös, muskulös	mysterious, voluminous, muscular
-ose	-osis	1. a noninflammatory disorder (as opposed to a disorder that ends in *-itis*) 2. a condition	1. Psychose, Neurose, Salmonellose 2. Hypnose, Narkose	1. psychosis, neurosis, salmonellosis 2. hypnosis, narcosis

Suffix/ Combining Form	English Equivalent	Meaning and Use	Example	English Translation
-path	-path	1. sb who practices a particular type of treatment 2. sb who has a particular disorder	1. Homöopath 2. Psychopath	1. homeopath 2. psychopath
-pathie	-pathy	1. feeling, inclination 2. disorder 3. treatment	1. Empathie, Sympathie, Telepathie 2. Soziopathie 3. Homöopathie	1. empathy, sympathy, telepathy 2. sociopathy 3. homeopathy
-pede	-ped	having a particular number of feet/paws	Bipede, Quadrupede	biped, quadruped
-pepsie	-pepsia	digestion	Dyspepsie	dyspepsia
-phil	-phile, -philistic, -philic	very fond of	bibliophil, anglophil	bibliophilistic, Anglophile/Anglophilic
-philie	-phile	especially fond of sth	Bibliophilie, Frankophilie	bibliophile, Francophile
-phob	-phobic -phobe	a strong dislike of sth	frankophob, hydrophob	Francophobic/ Francophobe, hydrophobic
-phobie	-phobia	an intense fear of sth	Klaustrophobie, Xenophobie, Hydrophobie	claustrophobia, xenophobia, hydrophobia
-phon	-phone	1. a device that has to do with tones/ sound 2. a speaker of a particular language	1. Saxophon, Grammophon, Megaphon, Mikrophon, Telephon, Xylophon 2. anglophon, frankophon	1. saxophone, gramophone, megaphone, microphone, telephone, xylophone 2. anglophone/ Anglophone, francophone/ Francophone
-phonie	-phony	tone, sound	Kakophonie, Euphonie	cacophony, euphony
-plex	-plex	built in units	Duplex-, Multiplex, Komplex	duplex, multiplex, complex
-pole	-polis	city	Metropole, Megalopole	metropolis, megalopolis
-s	-ies, -s	1. plural ending for English nouns 2. changes designations of time, present participles, and superlatives to adverbs	1. Babys, Storys 2. morgens, nachts; eilends, zusehends; bestens, schnellstens	1. babies, stories 2. in the morning, at night; in a hurry, visibly; optimally, as quickly as possible
-sam	-ous(ly) -ive(ly)	changes nouns and verbs to adjectives or adverbs	arbeitsam, gewaltsam, schweigsam, wirksam	industrious(ly), by force, taciturn(ly), effective(ly)
-schaft	-hood, -ship, -cy	1. a condition or function 2. a group of people 3. a collection of things 4. the result of an action	1. Freundschaft, Schwangerschaft, Leihmutterschaft, Präsidentschaft 2. Lehrerschaft, Kundschaft 3. Gerätschaft 4. Erbschaft, Hinterlassenschaft	1. friendship, pregnancy, surrogacy, presidency 2. teaching staff, clientele 3. equipment 4. inheritance, legacy

Suffix/ Combining Form	English Equivalent	Meaning and Use	Example	English Translation
-schreck		sb that other people are afraid of	Kinderschreck, Bürgerschreck	boog(e)yman, a person whose behavior the public finds shocking
-seitig	-al(ly), -sided	1. having a particular number of sides 2. of a particular number of pages 3. on a particular side	1. einseitig, zweiseitig 2. einseitig, zweiseitig, halbseitig, mehrseitig 3. linksseitig, ostseitig, rückseitig	1. unilateral(ly), bilateral(ly) 2. one-sided, two-sided, half-sided, of several pages 3. on the left(-hand side), on the east side, on the back
-seits		1. starting with sb/sth 2. on the given side	1. meinerseits, eurerseits, staatlicherseits 2. diesseits, jenseits, längsseits, einerseits (... andererseits)	1. for my part, for your part, on the part of the government 2. on this side, on the other side, alongside, on the one hand (... on the other hand)
-sektion	-section	cut	Vivisektion, Resektion	vivisection, resection
-sicher	1. -proof 2. -proof	1. protected from 2. not subject to damage or destruction by sth 3. certain to happen 4. working well in a particular situation	1. diebstahlsicher, kugelsicher, fälschungssicher 2. feuersicher, krisensicher 3. schneesicher, ertragssicher 4. stilsicher, zielsicher, treffsicher	1. theftproof, bulletproof, counterfeitproof 2. fireproof, crisis-proof 3. assured of having snow, sure to yield returns 4. stylistically appropriate, unerring, accurate
-skop	-scope	an device that one uses to view or observe sth	Mikroskop, Stethoskop, Horoskop	microscope, stethoscope, horoscope
-skopie	-scopy	observation, examination	Demoskopie, Gastroskopie	demoscopy, gastroscopy
-ste	1. -eth, -th 2. -est	1. forms ordinal numbers 2. forms the superlative	1. vierzigste, tausendste 2. weichste, längste, kürzeste	1. fortieth, thousandth 2. softest, longest, shortest
-te	1. -eth, -th 2. -est	variant of **-ste**, meaning: 1. forms ordinal numbers 2. forms the superlative	1. vierte, zehnte 2. größte	1. fourth, tenth 2. biggest
-teilig	-fold, -part	having a particular number of parts	dreiteilig, vierteilig, mehrteilig	threefold, fourfold, in several parts
-tel	-th	forms fractions	drittel, viertel, tausendstel	third, fourth, thousandth
-tisch	-ic(ally)	variant of **-atisch**, added to nouns that end in **-ma**	klimatisch, dogmatisch; aromatisch	climatic(ally), dogmatic(ally), aromatic(ally)

Suffix/ Combining Form	English Equivalent	Meaning and Use	Example	English Translation
-tomie	-tomy	incision	Lobotomie	lobotomy
-tum	1. -acy, -th 2. -ity 3. -ity	1. a condition or process 2. a group of people 3. a territory	1. Analphabetentum, Wachstum 2. Bürgertum, Christentum 3. Fürstentum, Herzogtum	1. illiteracy, growth 2. bourgeoisie, Christianity 3. principality, duchy
-ual		variant of **-al**, meaning: starting with sth or with regard to sth	prozentual, prozessual	(as a) percentage, processual
-uell	-ual	variant of **-ell**, meaning: with regard to	sexuell, visuell, intellektuell	sexual, visual, intellectual
-ulent	-ulent	having a lot of sth	korpulent, turbulent, virulent	corpulent, turbulent, virulent
-ung	-ment	changes verbs (primarily prefixed ones) to nouns, meaning: 1. an action 2. the result of an action 3. the name of a space	1. Mitwirkung, Befragung, Reinigung 2. Ordnung, Zeichnung 3. Wohnung, Siedlung	1. collaboration, questioning, cleaning 2. orderliness, drawing 3. apartment, housing development
-voll	-ful	existing in large amounts or to a great degree	schmerzvoll, liebevoll	painful, affectionate
-vor	-vorous(ly)	feeding on sth	karnivor, herbivor, omnivor	carnivorous(ly), herbivorous(ly), omnivorous(ly)
-vore	-vore	an animal that feeds on sth	Karnivore, Herbivore	carnivore, herbivore
-wärts	-bound, -ward(s)	indicates a direction	abwärts, seitwärts, vorwärts, westwärts, himmelwärts	downward(s), sideways, forward(s), westbound, skyward(s)
-weise	-wise	forms adverbs, meaning: 1. manner 2. a specific amount or measure	1. ausnahmsweise, bedauerlicherweise, merkwürdigerweise 2. dutzendweise, eimerweise, schrittweise	1. for a change, regretfully, strangely enough 2. by the dozen(s), in bucketfuls, gradually
-weit	-wide	everywhere throughout	weltweit, europaweit	worldwide, all over Europe
-wert	-worthy	deserving sth, worthwhile	empfehlenswert, berichtenswert, lesenswert	recommendable, newsworthy, worth reading
-widrig		infringing against sth, not according to sth	regelwidrig, ordnungswidrig, sittenwidrig	against the rules, improper(ly), immoral(ly)
-würdig	-worthy	mertiting sth, warranting sth	glaubwürdig, förderungswürdig, kritikwürdig	credible, worthy of financial support, worthy of criticism

Suffix/ Combining Form	English Equivalent	Meaning and Use	Example	English Translation
-zentrisch	-centric	having sth as the center or as its focus	geozentrisch, egozentrisch	geocentric, egocentric
-zid	-cide	killing	Genozid, Suizid	genocide, suicide
-zyt	-cyte	cell	Leukozyt	leukocyte/leucocyte

Präfixe und Suffixe: Englisch-Deutsch

Prefixes and suffixes: English-German

Englische Präfixe und Wortbildungselemente

English Prefixes and Combining Forms

Präfixe/ Wortbildungselemente	deutsches Äquivalent	Bedeutung und Verwendung	Beispiele	deutsche Übersetzung
a-[1]		von	anew	erneut
a-[2]		auf	ashore	an Land
a-[3]	a-	Variante von **ab-**	aversion	Abneigung
a-[4]		Variante von **ad-**	aspect	Aspekt
a-[5]	a-	Variante von **an-**[2]	asexual	asexuell
ab-	ab-	fern von	abdicate	abdanken
ac-	ak-	Variante von **ad-**	acquire	erwerben
acr(o)-	akro-	Höhe	acrobat	Akrobat
ad-	ad-	Richtungsangabe	adapt	anpassen
aer(o)-	aero-	Luft, Gas	aerodynamical(ly)	aerodynamisch
af-	af-	Variante von **ad-**	affable	umgänglich
Afro-	afro-	auf Afrika bezogen	Afro-Caribbean	afrokaribisch
after-	nach-	danach kommend, daraus folgend	afterbirth	Nachgeburt
ag-	ag-	Variante von **ad-**	aggravate	verschlimmern
agora-	agora-	Menschenmenge oder großer öffentlicher Platz	agoraphobia	Agoraphobie
agri-, agro-	agrar-, agri-, agro-	Landwirtschaft	agribusiness	Agroindustrie
al-	al-	Variante von **ad-**	alloy	Legierung
all-		1. ganz 2. völlig	1. all-night 2. all-around	1. die ganze Nacht 2. umfassend
alti-	alti-	hoch, Höhe	altimeter	Höhenmesser
ambi-	ambi-	1. beide 2. darum herum	1. ambidextrous 2. ambient	1. beidhändig 2. umgebend
amphi-	amphi-	1. von beiden Seiten 2. darum herum	1. amphibian 2. amphitheater	1. Amphibie 2. Amphitheater
an-[1]	an-	Variante von **ad-**	annotate	mit Anmerkungen versehen
an-[2]	an-	ohne	anarchy	Anarchie
andr(o)-	andro-	maskulin, männlich	androgynous	androgyn
Anglo-	anglo-	englisch	Anglophile	Englandliebhaber
ante-	ante-	(be)vor	antecedent	früher
anthropo-	anthropo-	Mensch	anthropology	Anthropologie
anti-	anti-	1. gegen etwas eingestellt 2. Verneinung 3. Gegensätzlichkeit 4. gegen etwas wirkend	1. antiabortion 2. antisocial 3. antithesis 4. antifreeze	1. gegen Abtreibung 2. unsozial 3. Gegenteil 4. Frostschutzmittel
ap-	ap-	Variante von **ad-**	appear	erscheinen

Präfixe/ Wortbildungs-elemente	deutsches Äquivalent	Bedeutung und Verwendung	Beispiele	deutsche Übersetzung
aqua-	aqua-	auf dem oder im Wasser	aquaplaning	Aquaplaning
aqui-		Variante von **aqua-**	aquifer	Aquifer
ar-	ar-	Variante von **ad-**	arrogant	arrogant
arch-	erz-, archi-	1. höhere Autorität 2. äußerster Grad	1. archbishop 2. archenemy	1. Erzbischof 2. Erzfeind
as-	as-	Variante von **ad-**	assail	angreifen
astro-	astro-	die Sterne, den Weltraum betreffend	astronaut	Astronaut
astro-		jenseits der Erdatmosphäre	astronomy	Astronomie
at-	at-	Variante von **ad-**	attorney	Anwalt
audi(o)-	audi(o)-	die Töne, das Hören betreffend	audiovisual(ly)	audiovisuell
auto-	auto-	(von sich) selbst	autobiography	Autobiografie
avi-		1. die Vögel betreffend 2. das Fliegen betreffend	1. aviary 2. aviation	1. Voliere 2. Luftfahrt
be-		1. zur Bildung transitiver Verben: *become* (werden) 2. wegnehmen	1. befriend 2. behead	1. sich anfreunden 2. enthaupten
bene-	bene-	gut	beneficial	förderlich
bi-	bi-	1. zwei Mal 2. zwei	1. bimonthly 2. bilingual	1. zweimal pro Monat 2. zweisprachig
biblio-	biblio-	die Bücher betreffend	bibliophile	Bücherliebhaber
bin-	bin-	aus zweien bestehend	binary	binär
bio-	bio-	Leben	biography	Biografie
brevi-	brevi-	kurz	brevity	Kürze
cardi(o)-	kardio-	Herz	cardiogram	Kardiogramm
centi-	zenti-	1. hundert 2. hundertstel	1. centipede 2. centimeter	1. Tausendfüßler 2. Zentimeter
chiro-	chiro-	Hand	chiropractor	Chiropraktiker
chrom(o)-	chrom-, chroma-, chromo-	Farbe	chromatic	chromatisch
chron(o)-	chrono-	Zeit	chronology	Chronologie
circum-	zirkum-	darum herum	circumference circumnavigate	Umfang umsegeln
co-	ko-	gemeinsam, zusammen mit	coalesce	sich verbinden
col-	kol-	Variante von **co-**	collaborate	zusammenarbeiten
com-	kom-	Variante von **co-**	combat	Kampf
con-	kon-	Variante von **co-**	concave	konkav
contra-	kontra-	gegen	contradict contraception	widersprechen Empfängnisverhütung
cor-	kor-	Variante von **co-**	correct	korrekt
cosmo-	kosmo-	1. im Weltraum 2. auf der Welt	1. cosmonaut 2. cosmopolitan	1. Kosmonaut 2. Kosmopolit

Präfixe/ Wortbildungselemente	deutsches Äquivalent	Bedeutung und Verwendung	Beispiele	deutsche Übersetzung
counter-	konter-	1. gegen oder im Gegensatz zu 2. parallel 3. Duplikat	1. counteractive 2. counterbalance 3. counterfeit	1. entgegenwirkend 2. ausgleichen 3. Fälschung
cross-		von der anderen Seite, gekreuzt	crossfire	Kreuzfeuer
crypt(o)-	krypt(o)-	verborgen	cryptic	kryptisch
custom-		besonders, einzigartig	custom-built	entsprechend den Wünschen des Kunden gefertigt
cyber-	cyber-	elektronische Kommunikationsnetzwerke, Internet	cybercafé	Internetcafé
de-	de-	1. Entfernung, Abtrennung 2. Verneinung 3. Verfall	1. deforest 2. decriminalize 3. decrepit	1. abholzen 2. legalisieren 3. klapprig
deca-	deka-	zehn	decade	Jahrzehnt
deci-	dezi-	ein Zehntel	decibel	Dezibel
demi-	halb-	halb	demigod	Halbgott
derm(a)-	dermato-	Haut	dermatology	Dermatologie
di(a)-	dia-	1. quer durch 2. völlig	1. diabetes 2. diaper	1. Diabetes 2. Windel
di-1	di-	doppelt	dilemma	Dilemma
di-2	di-	Variante von **dis-**	digress	abschweifen
dif-	dif-	Variante von **dis-**	difficult	schwierig
dis-	1. dis- 2. dis-	1. Verneinung 2. Abtrennung, Entfernung 3. völlig	1. disadvantage 2. disappear 3. disgruntle	1. Nachteil 2. verschwinden 3. verärgern
down-		niedriger	downcast	niedergeschlagen
duo-	duo-	zwei	duodenum	Zwölffingerdarm
dyna-	dyna-	Kraft	dynamic	dynamisch
dys-	dys-	schlecht	dysfunctional	funktionsgestört
e-[1]	e-	elektronisch	e-commerce	E-Commerce
e-[2]	e-	Variante von **ex-**[2]	ebullient	überschäumend
eco-	öko-	Umwelt, Natur	ecology	Ökologie
ef-	ef-	Variante von **ex-**[2]	effusion	Erguss
electro-	elektro-	Strom, Elektrizität	electromagnet	Elektromagnet
em-[1]		Variante von **en-**[1]	emboss	prägen
em-[2]	em-	Variante von **en-**[2]	embryo	Embryo
en-[1]		(aus dem Französischen) 1. auf etwas, in etwas legen 2. Übergang zu einem Zustand	1. encode 2. enact	1. kodieren 2. verordnen
en-[2]	en-	(aus dem Griechischen) innen, im Innern	energy	Energie
entomo-	entomo-	Insekt	entomology	Entomologie

Präfixe/ Wort-bildungs-elemente	deutsches Äquivalent	Bedeutung und Verwendung	Beispiele	deutsche Übersetzung
ep-	ep-	Variante von **epi-**	epoch	Epoche
eph-	eph-	Variante von **epi-**	ephemeral	vergänglich
epi-	1. epi- 2. epi- 4. epi-	1. auf, über, oberhalb von 2. neben 3. (da)vor, früher 4. (da)nach, später	1. epicenter 2. epitome 3. episode 4. epithet	1. Epizentrum 2. Inbegriff 3. Episode 4. Attribut
equi-	äqui-	Gleichheit	equinox	Tagundnachtgleiche
eso-		versteckt, geheim	esoteric	esoterisch
ethno-	ethno-	Volk, Rasse	ethnology	Ethnologie
eu-	eu-	gut	eulogy	Lobrede
Euro	euro-	(west)europäisch	Eurocrat	Eurokrat
ever-	immer-	immer	evergreen	immergrün
ex-¹	ex-	ehemalig	ex-girlfriend	Exfreundin
ex-²	ex-	(außerhalb) von	excavate	ausgraben
exo-	exo-	draußen, außerhalb von	exodus	Exodus
extra-	extra-	jenseits von	extraordinary	außergewöhnlich
extro-	extro-	Variante von **extra-**	extrovert	extrovertiert
fore-	1. vor- 2. vorder-	1. vor (zeitlich) 2. vor (räumlich)	1. forecast 2. forearm	1. Vorhersage 2. Unterarm
Franco-	franko-	französisch	francophone	französischsprachig
fresh-	frisch-	neu, erst seit kurzem	freshman	Studienanfänger
gastr(o)-	gastro-	Magen	gastroscopy	Gastroskopie
gen-		Generation	genealogy, gender, gene	Ahnenforschung, Geschlecht, Gen
gen(o)-	geno-	Volk, Rasse	genocide	Völkermord
geo-	geo-	die Erde	geography	Geografie
giga-	giga-	Milliarde	gigabyte	Gigabyte
grand-		vorherige Generation	grandmother, grandfather	Großmutter, Großvater
graph(o)-	grafo-	Schrift	graphology	Grafologie
great-		nachfolgende Generation	great-nephew	Großneffe
gynaec(o)-, gynec(o)-	gynäko-	Frauen-	gynecologist	Gynäkologe
gyr(o)-	gyro-	Kreis, Umdrehung	gyrocompass, gyroscope	Kreiselkompass, Gyroskop
hect(o)-	hekt(o)-	hundert	hectare	Hektar
heli-	heli-	Helikopter betreffend	helipad, heliport	Heliport
haema-, hema-	hämat(o)-	Blut	hematite	Hämatit
hemi-	hemi-	halb, Hälfte	hemisphere	Hemisphäre
hepta-	hepta-	sieben	heptathlon	Siebenkampf
heter(o)-	heter(o)-	anders, verschieden	heterosexual	heterosexuell
hex(a)-	hex(a)-	sechs	hexagon	Sechseck
hist(o)-	histo-	organische Gewebe betreffend	histology	Histologie
holo-	holo-	ganz, komplett	holocaust	Holocaust

Präfixe/ Wort-bildungs-elemente	deutsches Äquivalent	Bedeutung und Verwendung	Beispiele	deutsche Übersetzung
homeo-	homö(o)-	ähnlich, gleichartig	homeopathy	Homöopathie
homo-	hom(o)-	identisch, gleich	homograph	Homograf
hydro-	hydr(o)-	Wasser	hydrophobia	Hydrophobie
hyper-	hyper-	über, oberhalb von	hyperbole	Hyperbel
hypno-	hypn(o)-	Schlaf	hypnotherapy	Hypnotherapie
hypo-	hypo-	1. unter, untehalb von 2. unterhalb des Normalwerts	1. hypodermic 2. hypothermia	1. hypodermatisch 2. Hypothermie
hyster(o)-	hystero-	Gebärmutter	hysteria	Hysterie
il-^{1}	il-	Variante von **in-^{1}**	illuminate	beleuchten
il-^{2}	il-	Variante von **in-^{2}**	illiterate	analphabetisch
im-^{1}	im-	Variante von **in-^{1}**	immense	riesig
im-^{2}	im-	Variante von **in-^{2}**	immobile	unbeweglich
in-^{1}	in-	in	inaugurate	einweihen
in-^{2}	in-	Verneinung	inapt	ungeeignet
Indo-	indo-	indisch	Indonesia	Indonesien
infra-	infra-	unter, unterhalb von	infrastructure	Infrastruktur
inter-	inter-	unter, zwischen	international	international
intra-	intra-	innerhalb von, innen	intravenous	intravenös
intro-	intro-	nach innen gerichtet	introvert	introvertiert
ir-^{1}	ir-	Variante von **in-^{1}**	irradiate	bestrahlen
ir-^{2}	ir-	Variante von **in-^{2}**	irregular	unregelmäßig
iso-	is(o)-	Gleichheit	isotope	Isotop
kilo-	kilo-	tausend	kilometer	Kilometer
lacto-	lakt(o)-	Milch	lactose	Laktose
lith(o)-	lith(o)-	Stein	lithography	Lithografie
macro-	makr(o)-	groß	macroeconomic	makroökonomisch
magn(i)-	magni-	groß, übermäßig	magnificent	großartig
mal-	mal-	schlecht	malice	Bösartigkeit
mani-	mani-	Hand	manicure	Maniküre
mega-	mega-	groß	megaphone	Megafon
meta-	meta-	1. Veränderung 2. dahinter, danach 3. auf einer höheren Ebene befindlich	1. metamorphosis 2. metacarpal 3. metaphysics, metaphor	1. Metamorphose 2. Mittelhand-knochen 3. Metaphysik, Metapher
metro-		Maß	metronome	Metronom
micro-	mikr(o)-	winzig	microorganism	Mikroorganismus
mid-		halb, zur Hälfte	midnight	Mitternacht
milli-	milli-	1. tausend 2. ein Tausendstel	1. millipede 2. millibar	1. Tausendfüßler 2. Millibar
mini-	mini-	klein	miniskirt	Minirock
mis-	miss-	Fehler, schlecht	miscalculate	falsch berechnen
mono-	mono-	einfach, einzig	monopoly	Monopol
morph(o)-	morph(o)-	Form	morphology	Morphologie
multi-	multi-	viele, vielfach	multilingual	mehrsprachig
must-		obligatorisch, verpflichtend	must-see	etwas, das man gese-hen haben muss

Präfixe/ Wort- bildungs- elemente	deutsches Äquivalent	Bedeutung und Verwendung	Beispiele	deutsche Übersetzung
near-		Nähe	nearsighted	kurzsichtig
neo-	neo-	neu, Wiedererwachen	neoconservative	neokonservativ
nephr(o)-	nephr(o)-	Nieren	nephritis	Nierenentzündung
neur(o)-	neur(o)-	Nerven	neurosis	Neurose
new-		kürzlich	newfound	neu entdeckt
non-	non-	Verneinung	nonaggression	Nichtangriffs-
octa-	okt-, okta-, okto-	acht	octagon, octave	Achteck, Oktave
octo-	okt-, okta-, okto-	acht	octogenarian, octopus	Achtziger, Tintenfisch
omni-	omni-	alles	omnipotent	allmächtig
ornitho-	ornitho-	Vogel	ornithology	Ornithologie
ortho-	orth(o)-	1. richtig 2. gerade	1. orthography 2. orthodontist	1. Orthografie 2. Kieferorthopäde
oste(o)-	osteo-	Knochen	osteoporosis	Osteoporose
out-		außerhalb von	outlaw	Gesetzloser
ov-	ovi-, ovu-	Ei	ovary	Eierstock
over-	über-	übermäßig, zu viel	overdose	Überdosis
pale(o)-	palä(o)-	alt, antik	paleontology	Paläontologie
pan-	pan-	ganz	pantheon	Pantheon
para-	1. para-	1. neben 2. parallel zu	1. paragraph 2. paralegal	1. Paragraf 2. Anwaltsgehilfe
path(o)-	patho-	Krankheit	pathology	Pathologie
patr(i)-	patri-	1. Vater 2. Vaterland	1. patriarchy 2. patriotism	1. Patriarchat 2. Patriotismus
ped(i)-	pedi-	Fuß	pedicure	Pediküre
ped(o)-	päd(o)-	Kind	pediatrics	Pädiatrie
penta-	pent(a)-	fünf	pentagon, pentathlon	Fünfeck, Fünfkampf
per-	per-	1. (quer) durch 2. sehr, vollständig	1. perennial 2. perfect	1. unvergänglich 2. perfekt
peri-	peri-	darum herum	periphery	Peripherie
phil(o)-	phil(o)-	Liebe zu, Neigung zu	philanthropy, philharmonic	Philanthropie, philharmonisch
phleb(o)-	phleb(o)-	Vene	phlebitis	Venenentzündung
phon(o)-	fono-	Laut, Ton	phonology	Fonologie
phot(o)-	foto-	Licht	photosensitive	lichtempfindlich
physi(o)-	physio-	Körper	physiognomy	Physiognomie
plur-		mehrere, verschieden	pluralistic	pluralistisch
pneum-	pneumo-	Luft	pneumatic	pneumatisch
pneum(o)-	pneumo-	Atmung, Lungen	pneumonia	Lungenentzündung
poly-	poly-	mehrere	polytheism	Polytheismus
post-	post-	(da)nach	postwar	Nachkriegs-
pre-	prä-	(da)vor	prewar	Vorkriegs-
preter-		jenseits von	preternatural	übernatürlich
pro-	pro-	für	proactive	offensiv
prot(o)-	prot(o)-	erster	prototype	Prototyp
pseud(o)-	pseud(o)-	falsch, vorgetäuscht	pseudonym	Pseudonym

Präfixe/ Wortbildungselemente	deutsches Äquivalent	Bedeutung und Verwendung	Beispiele	deutsche Übersetzung
psych(o)-	psych(o)-	Seele, Geist	psychosis	Psychose
pyro-	pyro-	Feuer	pyrotechnic	pyrotechnisch
quadri-, quadru-	quadri-, quadro-	vier	quadrilateral, quadruped	vierseitig, Vierfüßer
quasi-	quasi-	fast, beinahe, so gut wie	quasi-official	quasioffiziell
radi(o)-	radio-	1. Funkkommunikation 2. radioaktiv	1. radiotelegraphy 2. radiotherapy	1. Funktelegrafie 2. Strahlentherapie
re-	re-	Wiederholung	rearrange	umstellen
rect(i)-		gerade machen	rectify	berichtigen
rent-a-		zu mieten	rent-a-car	Mietwagen
retro-	retro-	rückwärts (gerichtet)	retroactive	rückwirkend
rhino-	rhin(o)-	Nase	rhinoplasty	Rhinoplastik
sclero-	sklero-	hart	sclerosis	Sklerose
seismo-	seismo-	Erdbeben	seismograph	Seismograf
self-	selbst-	unabhängig, ganz alleine	self-help	Selbsthilfe
semi-	semi-	halb, teilweise	semifinal	Halbfinale
septi-	sept-	sieben	September	September
sex-	sex-	sechs	sextet	Sextett
short-		nicht lang; zu schwach	shortfall	Defizit
soli-	soli-	allein	soliloquy, solitaire	Selbstgespräch, Solitär
step-	stief-	Verwandschaftsbeziehung durch erneute Heirat	stepmother	Stiefmutter
stere(o)-	stereo-	fest, massiv; räumlich, körperlich	stereophonic	Stereo-
strato-	strato-	Schicht	stratosphere	Stratosphäre
sub-	sub-	unter, unterhalb von	submarine	U-Boot
suc-	suk-	Variante von **sub-**	succumb	erliegen
suf-	suf-	Variante von **sub-**	suffix	Suffix
sup-	sup-	Variante von **sub-**	suppress	unterdrücken
super-	super-	über, oberhalb von	superimpose	überlagern
sur-	sur-	Variante von **sub-**	surreptitious	heimlich
sus-	sus-	Variante von **sub-**	susceptible	empfänglich
syl-	syl-	Variante von **syn-**	syllable	Silbe
sym-	sym-	Variante von **syn-**	symbiosis	Symbiose
syn-	syn-	zusammen, gemeinsam	synergy	Synergie
tele-	tele-	aus der Ferne	television	Fernsehen
tetra-	tetra-	vier	tetrahedron	Tetraeder
theo-	theo-	einen Gott betreffend	theology	Theologie
therm(o)-	therm(o)-	Wärme, warm	thermostat	Thermostat
top(o)-	top(o)-	Ort, Stelle	topical	aktuell
trans-	trans-	jenseits von, quer durch	transact	eine Transaktion durchführen

Präfixe/ Wort-bildungs-elemente	deutsches Äquivalent	Bedeutung und Verwendung	Beispiele	deutsche Übersetzung
tri-	tri-	drei	triangle	Dreieck
trop(o)-	tropo-	Wendung, Drehung	troposphere	Troposphäre
typo-	typo-	Gepräge, Zeichen	typography	Typografie
ultra-	ultra-	jenseits von; in höchstem Maße	ultrasound	Ultraschall
un-	1. un-	1. Verneinung 2. Umkehrung	1. unlike 2. undo	1. anders als 2. zunichtemachen
under-	unter-	unter, unterhalb von	underscore	unterstreichen
uni-	uni-	ein einziger	unilateral	einseitig
up-		nach oben (hin)	uptown	in den Wohngebieten
vermin-		einen Wurm betreffend	vermicide	Wurmmittel
vice-	vize-	Assistent oder Stellvertreter	vice-chairman	Vizepräsident
with-		1. gegen 2. rückwärts	1. withstand 2. withdraw	1. standhalten 2. zurückziehen
xen(o)-	xeno-	Fremder	xenophobia	Fremdenhass
xyl(o)-	xyl(o)-	Holz	xylophone	Xylofon
zoo-	zoo-	Tier	zoology	Zoologie

Englische Suffixe und Wortbildungselemente

English Suffixes and Combining Forms

Suffixe/ Wort-bildungs-elemente	deutsches Äquivalent	Bedeutung und Verwendung	Beispiele	deutsche Übersetzung
-a	 2. -a	1. zur Pluralbildung bei Substantiven griechischer oder lateinischer Herkunft 2. feminine Form	1. criteria, stadia 2. Roberta	1. Kriterien, Stadien 2. Roberta
-ability		zur Bildung von Substantiven aus Adjektiven auf **-able**	reliability, stability	Zuverlässigkeit, Stabilität
-able, -ble, -ible		zur Bildung von Adjektiven aus Verben Bedeutung: kann getan werden	reliable, acceptable, edible	zuverlässig, akzeptabel, essbar
-ably		zur Bildung von Adverbien Bedeutung: auf bestimmte Weise	reliably, remarkably	zuverlässig, bemerkenswert
-ac		Eigenschaft; Variante von **-ic**	maniac, aphrodisiac, cardiac	wahnsinnig, aphrodisierend, das Herz betreffend
-aceous		zur Bildung von Adjektiven Bedeutung: charakteristisch für	sebaceous, herbaceous	Talg produzierend, krautartig

Suffixe/ Wortbildungselemente	deutsches Äquivalent	Bedeutung und Verwendung	Beispiele	deutsche Übersetzung
-acious		Variante von **-aceous**	efficacious, loquacious	erfolgreich, redselig
-acity	-heit, -(ig)keit	zur Bildung von Substantiven Bedeutung: voll von etwas, mit einer bestimmten Eigenschaft	veracity, capacity, sagacity	Aufrichtigkeit, Fähigkeit, Klugheit
-acy		zur Bildung von Substantiven Bedeutung: 1. mit einer bestimmten Eigenschaft 2. in einer bestimmten Funktion	1. accuracy, intimacy, 2. aristocracy, bureaucracy	1. Genauigkeit, Intimität 2. Aristokratie, Bürokratie
-ade	-ade	kennzeichnet das Ergebnis einer Handlung	lemonade, barricade, crusade	Limonade, Barrikade, Kreuzzug
-age		zur Bildung von Substantiven Bedeutung: 1. Handlung, Ergebnis 2. Zustand 3. Ort	1. blockage, coverage, dosage, drainage, espionage, foliage 2. marriage, shortage 3. orphanage	1. Verstopfung, Berichterstattung, Dosis, Drainage, Spionage, Blattwerk 2. Heirat, Mangel 3. Waisenheim
-agogue	-agoge	Anführer, Leiter	pedagogue, demagogue	Pädagoge, Demagoge
-aholic, -oholic		Abhängiger, Süchtiger	alcoholic, workaholic, chocoholic	Alkoholiker, Workaholic, Schokosüchtiger
-aire		Person mit einer bestimmten Eigenschaft	millionaire, doctrinaire	Millionär, Doktrinär
-al	-al, -ell	zur Bildung abstrakter Adjektive Bedeutung: in Bezug auf	causal, functional, cultural, national, racial	kausal, funktional, kulturell, national, rassisch
-algia, -algy	-algie	Schmerz	nostalgia, neuralgia	Nostalgie, Neuralgie
-ally		zur Bildung von Adverbien	theoretically, occasionally, officially	theoretisch, gelegentlich, offiziell
-an, -ian	-er	1. gebürtig aus 2. (beruflich) mit etwas beschäftigt	1. American, Canadian, 2. optician, politician, geriatrician	1. Amerikaner, Kanadier 2. Optiker, Politiker, Geriater
-ana	-ana	Sammlung	Americana	Amerikana
-ance, -ancy -ence, -ency		zur Bildung von Adjektiven und Substantiven Bedeutung: 1. Handlung 2. Vorgang	1. intolerance, guidance, ignorance, importance, infancy 2. assistance, resistance	1. Intoleranz, Anleitung, Ignoranz, Wichtigkeit, Kindheit 2. Hilfe, Widerstand

Suffixe/ Wort-bildungs-elemente	deutsches Äquivalent	Bedeutung und Verwendung	Beispiele	deutsche Übersetzung
-ant		handelnde Person oder Mittel für etwas	informant, inhabitant, accountant, disinfectant	Informant, Einwohner, Buchhalter, Desinfektionsmittel
-ar		1. Variante von **-al** 2. handelnde Person	1. jocular, linear 2. beggar, liar	1. lustig, linear 2. Bettler, Lügner
-arch	-arch	Herrscher	monarch	Monarch
-archy	-archie	Herrschaftsform	monarchy	Monarchie
-arian		zur Bildung von Adjektiven, die Personen beschreiben 1. Alter 2. Glauben, Überzeugung 3. Sternzeichen	1. octogenarian, 2. totalitarian, vegetarian 3. Aquarian	1. in den Achtzigern 2. totalitär, vegetarisch 3. im Zeichen Wassermann geboren
-arium	-arium	geschützter Ort, an dem man Beobachtungen vornehmen kann	aquarium, vivarium, planetarium, solarium	Aquarium, Vivarium, Planetarium, Solarium
-armed	-armig	mit einer bestimmten Anzahl an Armen	one-armed	einarmig
-ary, -ery		1. Handlung 2. Ort einer Handlung 3. Eigenschaft	1. burglary 2. bakery 3. bravery	1. Einbruch 2. Bäckerei 3. Mut
-ast		Person mit bestimmten Fähigkeiten	enthusiast, gymnast	Enthusiast, Turner
-ate		zur Bildung von Verben Bedeutung: bewirken, machen	gyrate, habituate, hallucinate, humiliate	sich drehen, gewöhnen, halluzinieren, demütigen
-athon	-marathon	1. Ereignis mit marathon-ähnlichen Bedingungen 2. etwas, das überaus lange dauert	1. walkathon 2. talkathon	1. Walkathon 2. Marathonsitzung
-atic(al)	-(a)tisch	Zustand, Verhältnis	problematic(al), rheumatic(al), schematic(al), symptomatic(al)	problematisch, rheumatisch, schematisch, symptomatisch
-ation		Variante von **-tion**	celebration	Feier
-atious		zur Bildung von Adjektiven aus Substantiven auf **-ation**	flirtatious, ostentatious	kokett, prahlerisch
-backed		unterstützt von	US-backed	von der US-Regierung unterstützt
-based		1. ansässig in 2. auf der Grundlage von	1. community-based, US-based 2. wine-based punch	1. in der Gemeinde ansässig, in den USA ansässig/mit Sitz in den USA 2. Weinpunsch
-bedroom		mit einer bestimmten Anzahl an Schlafzimmern	a three-bedroom house	ein Haus mit drei Schlafzimmern
-behaved		zur Beschreibung des Benehmens einer Person	well-/badly-behaved	wohl erzogen, schlecht erzogen

Suffixe/ Wort-bildungs-elemente	deutsches Äquivalent	Bedeutung und Verwendung	Beispiele	deutsche Übersetzung
-bodied		zur Beschreibung eines bestimmten Körperbaus	strong-bodied, weak-bodied	stark gebaut, von schwachem Körperbau
-born		Geburtsort	newborn, first-born, American-born	neugeboren, erstgeboren, in den USA geboren
-borne		getragen von	airborne	in der Luft befindlich
-bound		zur Bildung von Adverbien Bedeutung: 1. irgendwohin unterwegs 2. an etwas gebunden 3. zur Bildung von Adjektiven, um den Einband von Büchern zu beschreiben	1. westbound, inbound, outbound 2. housebound, wheelchair-bound 3. leather-bound	1. in Richtung Westen, ankommend, abfahrend 2. ans Haus gefesselt, an den Rollstuhl gefesselt 3. ledergebunden
-brained		bezieht sich auf die intellektuellen Fähigkeiten und das Organisationstalent eines Menschen	bird-brained, scatter-brained	mit einem Spatzenhirn, zerstreut
-burger	-burger	bezeichnet ein hamburger-ähnliches Sandwich	veggieburger	Gemüseburger
-centric	-zentrisch	mit etwas im Zentrum	geocentric, egocentric	geozentrisch, egozentrisch
-chrome	-chrom	Farbe	monochrome	monochrom
-cian		kompetente Person	electrician, magician, mathematician	Elektriker, Magier, Mathematiker
-cidal		zur Bildung von Adjektiven aus Substantiven auf **-cide**	homicidal	gemeingefährlich mörderisch
-cide	-zid	töten	homicide, fratricide	Mord, Geschwistermord
-cle		Variante von **-cule**	particle	Teilchen
-clud, -clus		geschlossen	exclude, seclusion	ausschließen, Zurückgezogenheit
-conscious	-bewusst	auf etwas achten	fashion-conscious, health-conscious	modebewusst, gesundheitsbewusst
-corn		Horn	unicorn	Einhorn
-cosm	-kosmos	in Bezug auf den Weltraum	microcosm	Mikrokosmos
-cracy	-kratie	1. Regierung, Behörde 2. herrschende Klasse	1. democracy, meritocracy 2. aristocracy	1. Demokratie, Leistungsgesellschaft 2. Aristokratie
-crat	-krat	Mitglied eines politischen Gebildes	democrat, aristocrat	Demokrat, Aristokrat
-cule, -cle		winzig	miniscule, molecule, particle	winzig, Molekül, Teilchen

Suffixe/ Wort-bildungs-elemente	deutsches Äquivalent	Bedeutung und Verwendung	Beispiele	deutsche Übersetzung
-cy		1. Zustand 2. Amt 3. Eigenschaft	1. pregnancy 2. presidency 3. proficiency, secrecy	1. Schwangerschaft 2. Präsidentschaft 3. Können, Geheimhaltung
-cyte	-zyt	Zelle	leukocyte	Leukozyt
-derm, -dermis	-dermal, -dermis	Haut	pachyderm, epidermis	Dickhäuter, Oberhaut
-dimensional	-dimensional	gibt die Anzahl der Dimensionen an	two-dimensional, three-dimensional	zweidimensional, dreidimensional
-dom		1. Zustand 2. Reich, Bereich	1. boredom 2. kingdom	1. Langeweile 2. Königreich
-driven		1. mit Hilfe von etwas funktionierend 2. durch etwas angetrieben	1. menu-driven software 2. export-driven economy	1. menügesteuerte Software 2. exportinduzierte Wirtschaft
-drome	-drom	Rennen	hippodrome	Hippodrom
-dyne		Kraft, Intensität	anodyne	harmlos
-ean		gebürtig aus, in Bezug auf	Belizean, Andean	Belizer, aus den Anden
-ectomy	-ektomie	operative Entfernung	appendectomy	Appendektomie
-ed		1. zur Bildung der Vergangenheitsform der Verben 2. zur Bildung von Adjektiven, die eine Eigenschaft ausdrücken 3. Besitzanzeige	1. talked 2. midpriced 3. moneyed, bearded	1. sprach 2. der mittleren Preislage 3. vermögend, bärtig
-ee		1. Empfänger einer Handlung 2. Lage, Bedingung	1. devotee, employee 2. refugee	1. Anhänger, Angestellter 2. Flüchtling
-eer		1. handelnde Person 2. zur Bildung von Verben	1. auctioneer 2. electioneer	1. Auktionator 2. Wahlkampf machen
-ella		Krankheit	rubella, salmonella	Röteln, Salmonellenvergiftung
-eme	-em	Einheit	morpheme, phoneme, lexeme	Morphen, Phonem, Lexem
-emia	-ämie	das Blut betreffend	leukemia, anemia	Leukämie, Anämie
-en	1. -(e)n, -ern 2. -en	1. aus etwas gemacht 2. zur Bildung von Verben aus Adjektiven Bedeutung = machen	1. woolen 2. toughen, soften	1. wollen 2. härten, weich machen
-enabled		1. mit einer bestimmten Technologie ausgestattet 2. dank etwas funktionierend	1. WAP-enabled (cell phone) 2. voice-enabled (software)	1. WAP-fähig(es Handy) 2. (Software) mit Spracherkennung
-ence, -ency	-enz	zur Bildung von Substantiven aus Adjektiven auf *-ent*	turbulence, vehemence, clemency	Turbulenz, Vehemenz, Milde
-enne	-in	zur Bildung femininer Formen	comedienne	Komödiantin

Suffixe/ Wortbildungselemente	deutsches Äquivalent	Bedeutung und Verwendung	Beispiele	deutsche Übersetzung
-ent		1. abstrakte Substantive 2. Substantive, die eine handelnde Person oder Sache bezeichnen 3. Adjektive, die eine bestimmte Handlung bewirken oder einen Zustand beschreiben	1. agreement, nourishment 2. opponent 3. absorbent, obedient	1. Vereinbarung, Nahrung 2. Gegner 3. saugfähig, gehorsam
-eous		zur Bildung von Adjektiven aus Substantiven	courageous, courteous, advantageous	mutig, höflich, günstig
-er	-er	1. handelnde Person: Berufe und Tätigkeiten 2. Herkunft	1. baker, teacher, driver 2. foreigner, New Yorker	1. Bäcker, Lehrer, Fahrer 2. Ausländer, New Yorker
-ern	-lich	Himmelsrichtung	northern, southern	nördlich, südlich
-ery, -ry		1. Gruppe von Dingen 2. Aktivität 3. Ort, an dem etwas gemacht wird 4. Zustand, Lage	1. jewelry, pottery 2. adultery, robbery 3. bakery 4. slavery	1. Schmuck, Töpferwaren 2. Ehebruch, Raubüberfall 3. Bäckerei 4. Sklaverei
-(e)s		1. zur Bildung des Plurals von Substantiven 2. zur Bildung der dritten Person Singular von Verben	1. churches 2. watches, waits	1. Kirchen 2. (er, sie, es) schaut zu, (er, sie, es) wartet
-escence		zur Bildung von Substantiven aus Verben auf *-esce*	convalescence	Genesung
-escent		zur Bildung von Substantiven und Adjektiven aus Verben auf *-esce*	convalescent	genesend/ Genesender
-ese		Herkunft, Sprache	Japanese, officialese	Japaner/Japanisch, Behördensprache
-esque	-esk	das Erscheinungsbild, den Stil betreffend	picturesque, picaresque	pittoresk, pikaresk
-ess		zur Bildung der weiblichen Form von Substantiven	princess	Prinzessin
-est	-ste	zur Bildung des Superlativs von Adjektiven	softest	weichste
-et	-chen, -lein	zur Bildung von Diminutivformen	wristlet, cutlet, anklet	Armreif, Kotelett, Fußkettchen
-eth	-(s)te	zur Bildung der Ordinalzahlen	thirtieth	dreißigste
-etic		zur Bildung von Adjektiven aus Verben und Substantiven	sympathetic, apathetic, apologetic	verständnisvoll, teilnahmslos, entschuldigend

Suffixe/ Wort- bildungs- elemente	deutsches Äquivalent	Bedeutung und Verwendung	Beispiele	deutsche Übersetzung
-ette		1. zur Bildung von Diminutivformen 2. Imitation, Nach- ahmung 3. zur Bildung der weiblichen Form	1. kitchenette, laun- derette, novelette, statuette 2. leatherette 3. usherette	1. Kochnische, Wasch- salon, Novelette, Statuette 2. Lederimitat 3. Platzanweiserin
-eur	-eur	Beruf	masseur, restaurateur, entrepreneur	Masseur, Gastwirt, Unternehmer
-euse	-euse	weibliche Form von *-eur*	masseuse	Masseurin
-ey		Variante von **-y**	New-Agey	New-Age-
-ferous		etwas enthaltend, etwas bildend	coniferous, pestiferous	Nadel-, ärgerlich
-fest	-festival	besonderer Anlass, Fest	music fest	Musikfestival
-fic		etwas bewirkend	soporific	einschläfernd
-fication		zur Bildung von Sub- stantiven aus Verben auf *-fy*	specification	Angabe
-filled		voll von	fun-filled, smoke-filled	sehr lustig, rauchig
-flavored		mit einem bestimmten Geschmack	lemon-flavored	mit Zitronen- geschmack
-fold	1. -fach 2. -teilig	1. die genannte Anzahl von Malen 2. aus einer bestimm- ten Anzahl von Teilen	1. hundredfold 2. threefold, fourfold	1. hundertfach 2. dreiteilig, vierteilig
-footed	-füßig		bare-footed, four-footed	barfuß, vierfüßig
-footer		bezieht sich auf eine Längenangabe in Fuß	a fifty-footer	etwas, das 50 Fuß lang ist
-form	-förmig	mit der Form von	vermiform	wurmförmig
-free	-frei	1. von etwas ausgenommen 2. ohne etwas	interest-free, lead-free, trouble-free	zinslos, bleifrei, problemlos
-friendly	-freundlich	1. nicht schädlich für 2. günstig für	1. environmentally friendly 2. family friendly	1. umweltfreundlich 2. familienfreundlich
-fugal	-fugal	zur Bildung von Adjek- tiven aus Substantiven auf *-fuge*	centrifugal	zentrifugal
-fuge	-fuge	nach außen hin	subterfuge, centrifuge	List, Zentrifuge
-ful	1. -voll	1. voll von etwas 2. Merkmal 3. etwas enthaltend	1. doubtful, spiteful 2. careful 3. cupful, spoonful, mouthful	1. skeptisch, gehässig 2. vorsichtig 3. Tasse (voll), Löffel (voll), Bissen
-fy		machen	fortify, intensify	befestigen, intensivieren
-gamous	-gam	zur Bildung von Adjek- tiven, die einen Bund bezeichnen	monogamous	monogam
-gamy	-gamie	zur Bildung von Sub- stantiven, die einen Bund bezeichnen	monogamy	Monogamie

Suffixe/ Wort-bildungs-elemente	deutsches Äquivalent	Bedeutung und Verwendung	Beispiele	deutsche Übersetzung
-genic	-gen	1. gut geeignet für etwas 2. etwas hervorrufend	1. photogenic, telegenic 2. hallucinogenic, allergenic	1. fotogen, telegen 2. halluzinogen, allergen
-gnosis	-gnose	Wissen	prognosis, diagnosis	Prognose, Diagnose
-gnostic	-gnostisch	zur Bildung von Adjektiven aus Substantiven auf *-gnose*	diagnostic	diagnostisch
-goer	-gänger	jemand, der oft einen bestimmten Ort besucht	movie-goer	Kinogänger
-gon	-eck, -gon	mit einer bestimmten Anzahl von Ecken	hexagon	Sechseck
-grade		sich entwickeln, sich verändernd	retrograde, upgrade,	rückschrittlich, aufrüsten
-grader	-klässler	Schüler, der eine bestimmte Klasse besucht	second-grader	Zweitklässler
-gram	-gramm	1. Schrift 2. Gewicht im metrischen System	1. diagram 2. kilogram	1. Diagramm 2. Kilogramm
-graph	-grafieren -grafie	zur Bildung von Verben Bedeutung = schreiben zur Bildung von Substantiven Bedeutung = geschrieben, aufgezeichnet	choreograph autograph, photograph	choreografieren Autogramm, Fotografie
-graphy	-grafie	1. Wissenschaft, Kunst 2. die Schrift betreffend 3. das Schreiben, das Aufzeichnen	1. oceanography, lexicography 2. stenography 3. orthography	1. Ozeanografie, Lexikografie 2. Stenografie 3. Orthografie
-gynous	-gyn	die Frau betreffend, ein Weibchen betreffend	androgynous	androgyn
-haired	-haarig	die Haare betreffend	long-haired, dark-haired	langhaarig, dunkelhaarig
-hater	-hasser		woman-hater	Frauenhasser
-head	3. -kopf	1. Angabe der Haarfarbe 2. bezieht sich auf die Dummheit 3. der Kopf, der obere Teil von etwas	1. redhead 2. knucklehead, fathead 3. hammerhead, letterhead	1. Rotschopf 2. Blödmann, Dummkopf 3. Hammerhai, Briefkopf
-hearted		zur Bildung von Adjektiven, die sich auf bestimmte Merkmale beziehen	wholehearted, brokenhearted	aufrichtig, untröstlich
-hood	1. -heit 2. -schaft	1. Zustand oder Lage 2. Personengruppe	1. falsehood, fatherhood, childhood 2. brotherhood	1. Falschheit, Vaterschaft, Kindheit 2. Bruderschaft
-hungry	-hungrig	mit dem starken Wunsch nach etwas	power-hungry	machthungrig

Suffixe/ Wort-bildungs-elemente	deutsches Äquivalent	Bedeutung und Verwendung	Beispiele	deutsche Übersetzung
-hunter		jemand, der etwas sucht	job-hunter, house-hunter	Arbeitsuchender, jemand, der ein Haus (zum Kaufen) sucht
-ia	-ien	1. Länder und Regionen 2. zur Bildung des Plurals bei Wörtern lateinischen Ursprungs	1. Australia, Andalusia 2. bacteria	1. Australien, Andalusien 2. Bakterien
-ial	-iell, -ial	zur Bildung von Adjektiven Bedeutung = in Bezug auf	ministerial, industrial, managerial	ministeriell, industriell, Manager-
-ian	-er	Variante von **-an**	Canadian, optician	Kanadier, Optiker
-iana		Variante von **-ana**	Canadiana	Kanadiana
-iasis	-iasis	Krankheit, Verfassung	elephantiasis, amebiasis	Elephantiasis, Amöbiasis
-iatrics, -iatry	-iatrie	Spezialgebiet der Medizin	geriatrics, psychiatry	Geriatrie, Psychiatrie
-ibility		Variante von **-ability**	compatibility	Kompatibilität
-ible		Variante von **-able**	edible	essbar
-ibly		Variante von **-ably**	audibly	hörbar
-ic, -ical	-al, -isch, -haft	so (ähnlich) wie in Bezug auf	acidic, heroic, poetic, mathematic	sauer, heldenhaft, poetisch, mathematisch
-ically	-isch, -haft	zur Bildung von Adverbien aus Adjektiven auf *-ic*, *-ical*	alphabetically, heroically	alphabetisch, heldenhaft
-ice		Zustand, Verfassung	cowardice, service	Feigheit, Service
-ics	-ik	zur Bildung von Substantiven, die einen Tätigkeitsbereich bezeichnen	ceramics, classics, cybernetics, economics	Keramik, Altphilologie, Kybernetik, Wirtschaftswissenschaft
-id	-ide	bezeichnet ein Mitglied einer Familie im Tierreich	arachnid	Arachnide
-ie	-chen, -lein	*inf* Variante von **-y** (Diminutiv)	birdie	Vögelchen
-ier	-er	1. zur Bildung von Substantiven, die Berufe bezeichnen 2. zur Bildung des Komparativs bei Adjektiven auf *-y*	1. cashier 2. happier	1. Kassierer 2. glücklicher
-ify		zur Bildung von Verben aus Adjektiven Bedeutung = machen	clarify, glorify	erklären, verherrlichen
-ile		1. in Bezug auf 2. fähig zu	1. infantile 2. mobile	1. kindisch 2. beweglich
-ility		zur Bildung von Adjektiven, die die Fähigkeit ausdrücken, etwas zu sein oder zu tun	versatility, visibility	Vielseitigkeit, Sicht
-in		benennt chemische Substanzen	vitamin, gelatin, lanolin, toxin	Vitamin, Gelatine, Lanolin, Toxin

Suffixe/ Wort-bildungs-elemente	deutsches Äquivalent	Bedeutung und Verwendung	Beispiele	deutsche Übersetzung
-ina	-in	zur Bildung der femininen Form	tsarina, ballerina	Zarin, Ballerina
-induced	-bedingt	durch jemanden oder etwas verursacht	self-induced, work-induced	selbst verursacht, arbeitsbedingt
-ine	3. -er	1. in der Art von 2. zur Bildung abstrakter Substantive 3. stammend aus 4. chemische Substanzen	1. crystalline, feminine 2. medicine 3. Argentine 4. antihistamine, caffeine	1. kristallin, feminin 2. Medizin 3. Argentinier 4. Antihistamin, Koffein
-ing		1. zur Bildung des Gerundiums 2. zur Bildung des Partizip Präsens, das auch als Adjektiv verwendet werden kann	1. playing 2. they are playing, playing children	1. spielend 2. sie spielen, spielende Kinder
-ious		zur Bildung von Adjektiven Bedeutung: mit einer bestimmten Eigenschaft	capricious, cautious	launisch, vorsichtig
-ish		1. Art 2. Herkunft, Sprache 3. ähnlich wie 4. sozusagen	1. childish 2. British, English 3. piggish, nightmarish 4. newish	1. kindisch 2. Brite/Britisch, Engländer/Englisch 3. schweinisch, alptraumhaft 4. relativ neu
-ism	-ismus	zur Bildung von Substantiven, die sich auf ein System, eine Doktrin, eine Art und Weise oder eine Lage beziehen	totalitarianism, cynicism, tourism	Totalitarismus, Zynismus, Tourismus
-ist		Handelnder, jemand, der eine Tätigkeit oder einen Beruf ausübt	artist, dentist, plagiarist, realist, tourist	Künstler, Zahnarzt, Plagiator, Realist, Tourist
-istic	-istisch	zur Bildung von Adjektiven aus Substantiven auf *-ist*	realistic	realistisch
-istics	-istik	Wissenschaft, Ausübung	linguistics, statistics, logistics	Linguistik, Statistik, Logistik
-ite		1. gebürtig aus 2. jemand, der an etwas glaubt, ein Anhänger von etwas ist	1. Israelite 2. Shiite, socialite	1. Israelit 2. Schiit, Person des öffentlichen Lebens
-itis	-itis	bezeichnet eine Entzündung	conjunctivitis, cystitis	Bindehautentzündung, Blasenentzündung
-itive		mit einer Neigung zu, etwas bewirkend	inquisitive, repetitive	neugierig, eintönig
-ity	-ität, -(ig)keit, -heit	Zustand, Eigenschaft	absurdity, captivity, clarity, complexity	Absurdität, Gefangenschaft, Klarheit, Komplexität
-ive		mit einer Neigung zu, etwas bewirkend	appreciative, digestive	dankbar, Verdauungs-

Suffixe/ Wort-bildungs-elemente	deutsches Äquivalent	Bedeutung und Verwendung	Beispiele	deutsche Übersetzung
-ization	-isierung	zur Bildung von Substantiven aus Verben auf *-ize*	familiarization, centralization	Vertrautwerden, Zentralisierung
-ize	-isieren	bewirken, dass ein Zustand eintritt	familiarize, centralize, categorize, computerize	sich vertraut machen, zentralisieren, kategorisieren, computerisieren
-ject		werfen	eject, inject, reject	auswerfen, spritzen, zurückweisen
-kin		Diminutiv	bumpkin, manikin, napkin	Hinterwäldler, Männlein, Serviette
-land		zur Bildung von Namen für Länder, Regionen und bestimmte Landschaften	Switzerland, Newfoundland, swampland	Schweiz, Neufundland, Sumpfland
-legged	-beinig		eight-legged (insect)	achtbeinig (Insekt)
-length	-lang		knee-length, shoulder-length	knielang, schulterlang
-lepsy	-lepsie	erfasst von	epilepsy, narcolepsy	Epilepsie, Narkolepsie
-less	-los	ohne	effortless, careless, homeless	mühelos, sorglos, obdachlos
-let		Diminutiv	leaflet, piglet, quintuplet, rivulet	Prospekt, Ferkel, Fünfling, Rinnsal
-like	-lich	(so ähnlich) wie etwas	sportsmanlike, businesslike, childlike	sportlich, geschäftlich, kindlich
-ling		1. Diminutiv 2. drückt Verachtung aus	1. duckling, fledgling 2. bungling	1. Entenküken, gerade flügge gewordener Vogel 2. Stümperei
-lite	1. -lith 2. -itis	1. bezeichnet ein Mineral 2. Variante von **-itis**, die einen Zustand ausdrückt	1. cryolite 2. cellulite	1. Kryolith 2. Cellulitis
-lith	-lith	Stein	monolith	Monolith
-lithic		archäologische Periode	Paleolithic	paläolithisch
-load		Ladung	busloads, truckloads	ganze Busladungen, ganze Lkw-Ladungen
-log, -logue	-log	sich auf Worte beziehend	monolog, epilog	Monolog, Epilog
-logic, -logy	-logie	Studium von	anthropology, dermatology	Anthropologie, Dermatologie
-ly	2. -lich	1. zur Bildung von Adverbien, die eine Art und Weise ausdrücken 2. zur Bildung von Adjektiven und Adverbien, die Zeitintervalle bezeichnen	1. madly, carelessly 2. weekly, monthly	1. wie verrückt, sorglos 2. wöchentlich, monatlich

Suffixe/ Wort-bildungs-elemente	deutsches Äquivalent	Bedeutung und Verwendung	Beispiele	deutsche Übersetzung
-maker	-macher -maschine	Person oder Maschine, die etwas macht	dressmaker, watch-maker, coffeemaker, icemaker	Schneider, Uhrmacher, Kaffeemaschine, Eis-würfelmaschine
-man		1. bezeichnet einen Mann, der bestimmte Eigen-schaften hat, eine bestimmte Tätig-keit oder einen bestimmten Beruf ausübt 2. gibt die Anzahl der Personen in einer Gruppe an	1. linesman, madman, mailman 2. a four-man team	1. Linienrichter, Geisteskranker, Postbote 2. ein Vier-Mann-Team
-mania	-manie	bezeichnet eine Bessenheit	pyromania, megalomania, kleptomania	Pyromanie, Größenwahnsinn, Kleptomanie
-mannered		bezieht sich auf die Verhaltensweise	ill-mannered, mild-mannered	schlecht erzogen, sanftmütig
-manship	-künste	drückt sicheres Kön-nen, gute Beherr-schung aus	swordsmanship, work-manship, marksman-ship	Schwertkampfkünste, handwerkliches Kön-nen, Treffsicherheit
-master	-meister, -profi	wird für Personen gebraucht, die auf einem Gebiet als kompetent gelten	concertmaster	Konzertmeister
-ment		zur Bildung von Substantiven Bedeutung: 1. Zustand 2. Ergebnis	 1. contentment, excitement 2. alignment	 1. Zufriedenheit, Aufregung 2. Ausrichten
-meter	-meter, -messer	Messgerät	chronometer, speed-ometer	Chronometer, Geschwindigkeits-messer
-minded		bezeichnet eine Geisteshaltung	narrow-minded, strong-minded	engstirnig, willensstark
-morphous	-morph	bezeichnet eine Gestalt, ein Erschei-nungsbild	amorphous, polymorphous	amorph, polymorph
-most	-(s)te	zur Bildung des Superlativs	outermost, rearmost, southernmost	äußerste, hinterste, südlichste
-motive		Bewegung, Antrieb	automotive, locomotive	Auto(mobil)-, Lokomotive
-mouthed		bezieht sich auf jds Sprechweise/Aus-drucksweise	loudmouthed, foul-mouthed	großmäulig, unflätig
-natured		mit dem genannten Naturell	good-natured	gutmütig
-ness, -iness	-ität, -(ig)keit, -heit	Zustand oder Eigenschaft	hopelessness, care-lessness, bitterness, sleepiness	Hoffnungslosigkeit, Sorglosigkeit, Bitter-keit, Schläfrigkeit
-nik	-ist	jemand, der mit etwas in Verbindung gebracht wird	beatnik, peacenik	Beatnik, Friedensaktivist

Suffixe/ Wort-bildungs-elemente	deutsches Äquivalent	Bedeutung und Verwendung	Beispiele	deutsche Übersetzung
-nomy	-nomie	1. Gesetz oder Struktur 2. Studium	1. taxonomy, economy, autonomy 2. astronomy	1. Taxonomie, Wirtschaft, Autonomie 2. Astronomie
-o	-o	zur Bildung von umgangssprachlichen Wörtern zur Bezeichnung von Personen mit bestimmten Gewohnheiten oder Eigenschaften	wino, weirdo, dumbo	Wermutbruder, Sonderling, Dumpfbacke
-ock	-chen, -lein	Diminutiv	bullock, hillock	junger Ochse, kleiner Hügel
-oholic		Variante von **-aholic**	alcoholic	Alkoholiker
-oid	-oid	etwas/jemandem ähnlich	spheroid	Sphäroid
-ology	-logie	Studium	biology, geology	Biologie, Geologie
-oma	-om	Tumor	carcinoma, melanoma	Karzinom, Melanom
-onym	-onym	bezieht sich auf einen Namen	synonym, pseudonym	Synonym, Pseudonym
-onymous		zur Bildung von Adjektiven aus Substantiven auf *-onym*	synonymous	synonym
-onymy		zur Bildung von Substantiven aus Adjektiven auf *-onymous*	synonymy	Synonymie
-opia	-opie	bezieht sich auf das Auge	myopia	Myopie
-or	-(at)or, -er	handelnde Person oder Sache	actor, exhibitor, agitator, processor	Schauspieler, Aussteller, Agitator, Prozessor
-orial		zur Bildung von Adjektiven aus Substantiven auf *-or, -ory*	senatorial, dictatorial, territorial	Senats-, diktatorisch, territorial
-oriented	-orientiert	bezeichnet das Ziel von etwas, das Streben nach etwas	profit-oriented	profitorientiert
-orium	-orium	bezeichnet einen Ort	crematorium, emporium, sanatorium	Krematorium, Kaufhaus, Sanatorium
-ory		in Bezug auf, von einer bestimmten Art	circulatory, transitory, contradictory, contributory	Kreislauf-, vergänglich, widersprüchlich, zu etwas beitragend
-ose		voll von etwas, sich durch etwas auszeichnend	verbose	wortreich
-osis	-ose	1. Krankheit 2. Vorgang	1. psychosis, neurosis 2. hypnosis, narcosis	1. Psychose, Neurose 2. Hypnose, Narkose
-ous	1. -voll, -ös 2. -artig	1. voll von etwas 2. etwas habend	1. mysterious, nervous, acrimonious 2. voluminous, cancerous	1. geheimnisvoll, nervös, bissig 2. weit, krebsartig
-owned		im Besitz von	family-owned, state-owned	in Familienbesitz, in Staatsbesitz
-packed	-geladen	voll von	action-packed	actiongeladen

Suffixe/ Wortbildungselemente	deutsches Äquivalent	Bedeutung und Verwendung	Beispiele	deutsche Übersetzung
-path	-path	1. jemand, der bestimmte Heilmethoden anwendet 2. jemand, der bestimmte Eigenheiten oder eine besondere Krankheit hat	1. homeopath, naturopath 2. psychopath	1. Homöopath, Naturheilkundler 2. Psychopath
-pathic		zur Bildung von Adjektiven aus Substantiven auf *-pathy*	homeopathic, telepathic	homöopathisch, telepathisch
-pathy	-pathie	1. Gefühl 2. in Bezug auf eine medizinische Behandlung	1. empathy, sympathy, telepathy 2. homeopathy	1. Empathie, Sympathie, Telepathie 2. Homöopathie
-ped	-füßer, -pede	mit einer bestimmten Anzahl von Füßen/ Pfoten	biped, quadruped	Zweifüßer, Vierfüßer
-pepsia	-pepsie	die Verdauung betreffend	dyspepsia	Dyspepsie
-person		zur Bildung der geschlechtsneutralen Form (feminin/maskulin) von Wörtern auf *-man* Bezeichung für einen Beruf, ein Amt, eine Autoritätsperson	spokesperson, chairperson	Sprecher, Vorsitzender
-phile	-liebhaber	jemand, der etwas sehr mag	technophile, bibliophile, anglophile	Technikliebhaber, Bücherliebhaber, Englandliebhaber
-phobe	-hasser	jemand, der etwas ganz und gar nicht mag	technophobe, Anglophobe	Technikhasser, Englandhasser
-phobia	-hass, -phobie	der Zustand des Nichtmögens	claustrophobia, xenophobia, hydrophobia,	Klaustrophobie, Fremdenhass, krankhafte Wasserscheu
-phobic	-feindlich, -phob(isch)	zur Bildung von Adjektiven aus Substantiven auf *-phobia*	xenophobic, claustrophobic	fremdenfeindlich, klaustrophobisch
-phone	1. -phon 2. -sprachig, -phon	1. Geräte, die mit Tönen arbeiten oder Töne hervorbringen 2. die Sprache sprechend	1. saxophone, gramophone, megaphone, microphone, telephone, xylophone 2. Anglophone, Francophone	1. Saxophon, Grammophon, Megaphon, Mikrophon, Telefon, Xylophon 2. englischsprachig, französischsprachig
-phony	-klang, -phonie	ein Ton	cacophony, euphony	Missklang, Wohlklang
-plane		Flugzeugart	seaplane, biplane	Wasserflugzeug, Doppeldecker
-plex	-plex	aus einer bestimmten Zahl von Einheiten aufgebaut	duplex, multiplex	Doppelhaus, Multiplexkino
-pod		Fuß	tripod	Stativ
-polis	-pole	Stadt	metropolis	Metropole

Suffixe/ Wort-bildungs-elemente	deutsches Äquivalent	Bedeutung und Verwendung	Beispiele	deutsche Übersetzung
-powered	-betrieben	bezieht sich auf die Stromversorgung einer Maschine	battery-powered, nuclear-powered	batteriebetrieben, atombetrieben
-prone		für etwas anfällig	accident-prone	vom Pech verfolgt
-proof		einer Sache standhaltend	ovenproof, rustproof, shatterproof, soundproof, bombproof, bulletproof	ofenfest, rostfrei, bruchsicher, schalldicht, bombensicher, kugelsicher
-red		Zustand	hatred, sacred	Hass, heilig
-ria		1. Krankheitsbezeichnungen oder wissenschaftliche Namen 2. Ortsnamen, Ländernamen	1. diphtheria, malaria, wisteria 2. Bulgaria	1. Diphtherie, Malaria, Glyzinie 2. Bulgarien
-ridden		voll von	guilt-ridden	von Schuldgefühlen geplagt
-rrhage	-rrhagie	anormales Fließen von etwas	hemorrhage	Hämorrhagie
-ry		Variante von **-ery**	chemistry	Chemie
-scape		zur Benennung einer bestimmten Art von Landschaft	landscape, seascape, townscape	Landschaft, Seelandschaft, Stadtbild
-scope	-skop	Instrument/Gerät, mit dem man etwas sehen kann	microscope, stethoscope, stroboscope, gyroscope, hygroscope, horoscope	Mikroskop, Stethoskop, Stroboskop, Gyroskop, Hygroskop, Horoskop
-scopy	-skopie	Untersuchung von etwas/jemandem mit einem Instrument	gastroscopy	Gastroskopie
-sect		ein Schnitt	dissect	sezieren
-ship		1. Zustand 2. Amt 3. Kenntnisse, Geschick	1. friendship 2. championship, dictatorship 3. horsemanship, marksmanship	1. Freundschaft 2. Meisterschaft, Diktatur 3. Reitkünste, Treffsicherheit
-sion		1. Geschehen 2. Ergebnis 3. Zustand	1. emission, inclusion 2. emulsion, explosion 3. tension	1. Emission, Einschluss 2. Emulsion, Explosion 3. Spannung
-some		1. zu etwas neigen 2. eine Gruppe mit der genannten Zahl von Personen	1. quarrelsome, tiresome 2. twosome, foursome	1. streitsüchtig, lästig 2. Paar, Vierergruppe
-speak		zur Benennung der (speziellen) Sprache/ der Fachsprache einer bestimmten Personengruppe	doublespeak, netspeak	Doppelzüngigkeit, Netzjargon
-sphere	-sphäre	Bereich	hemisphere	Hemisphäre
-ster		zur Bezeichnung einer Person, die bestimmte Eigenschaften hat oder etwas Bestimmtes tut	youngster, mobster, pollster, trickster	Jugendlicher, Gangster, Meinungsforscher, Betrüger

Suffixe/ Wortbildungselemente	deutsches Äquivalent	Bedeutung und Verwendung	Beispiele	deutsche Übersetzung
-stress	-in	zur Bildung der weiblichen Form	seamstress	Näherin
-sy		zur Bildung von Adjektiven und Substantiven mit negativem Beiklang	tipsy, tricksy, whimsy, artsy	beschwipst, schelmisch, spleenig, affig
-teen	1. -zehn	1. zur Bildung der Zahlen von 13 bis 19 2. einer Sache ähnlich	1. nineteen 2. velveteen	1. neunzehn 2. Velours
-th	3. -te	1. Zustand 2. Vorgang 3. Ordinalzahlen	1. youth, death 2. growth 3. thirteenth	1. Jugend, Tod 2. Wachstum 3. dreizehnte
-tion		1. Ergebnis 2. Zustand	1. inflation, reflection, infection 2. inhibition	1. Inflation, Spiegelbild, Infektion 2. Hemmung
-tious		zur Bildung von Adjektiven aus Substantiven auf *-tion*	ambitious, cautious	ehrgeizig, vorsichtig
-tomy	-tomie	Operation, Schnitt	lobotomy	Lobotomie
-tor		ausführende Person oder Sache	arbitrator, collaborator, calculator	Schlichter, Mitarbeiter, Rechner
-tory			anticipatory, accusatory	vorwegnehmend, anklagend
-tude	-(ig)keit	Zustand	gratitude, solitude	Dankbarkeit, Einsamkeit
-ty	1. -heit 2. -zig	1. Eigenschaft, Zustand 2. zur Bildung der Zehnerzahlen	1. royalty, safety 2. seventy	1. Mitglieder des Königshauses, Sicherheit 2. siebzig
-ule	-chen, -lein	Diminutiv	granule	Körnchen
-ulent		mit viel von etwas	fraudulent	betrügerisch
-ulous		für etwas geeignet, mit der Tendenz, etwas zu sein	miraculous, nebulous	wunderbar, unklar
-ure		1. Ergebnis 2. Zustand	1. mixture, exposure 2. moisture, pleasure	1. Mischung, Ausgesetztsein 2. Feuchtigkeit, Vergnügen
-ville		1. zur Benennung eines Ortes 2. *sl* zur Benennung eines Ortes, einer Sache oder eines Zustandes, die bestimmte Eigenschaften aufweisen	1. Jacksonville 2. dullsville	1. Jacksonville 2. totes Nest
-vore	-fresser, -vore	sich von etwas ernährend	carnivore, herbivore	Fleischfresser, Pflanzenfresser
-vorous	-fressend, -vor	zur Bildung von Adjektiven aus Substantiven auf *-vore*	carnivorous, herbivorous, omnivorous	fleischfressend, pflanzenfressend, allesfressend
-ward(s)	-wärts	in Richtung von	backward(s), inwards, outwards, upwards	rückwärts, einwärts, auswärts, aufwärts
-ways		Richtung	lengthways	längs

Suffixe/ Wortbildungs- elemente	deutsches Äquivalent	Bedeutung und Verwendung	Beispiele	deutsche Übersetzung
-wide	-weit	quer durch, überall in	worldwide, nationwide	weltweit, landesweit
-wise		zur Bildung von Adverbien, die eine Richtung angeben	clockwise	im Uhrzeigersinn
-woman		weibliches Äquivalent zu *-man*	chairwoman	Vorsitzende
-worthy		1. etwas verdienend 2. für etwas geeignet	1. trustworthy, newsworthy 2. roadworthy	1. vertrauenswürdig, berichtenswert 2. verkehrstauglich
-y, -ey		1. zur Bildung von Substantiven, die einen Zustand oder einen Vorgang ausdrücken 2. Diminutiv *inf* (siehe **-ie**) 3. zur Bildung von Adjektiven Bedeutung: vor etwas wimmelnd mit der Tendenz zu	1. captivity 2. puppy 3. bumpy, faulty, bubbly creamy, clingy	1. Gefangenschaft 2. Welpe 3. uneben, defekt, voller Blasen cremig, eng anliegend
-yer		Variante von **-er**	lawyer	Rechtsanwalt

Falsche Freunde
False Friends

Weitere Bedeutungen und Übersetzungen stehen unter dem entsprechenden Stichwort.

Readers should consult the main section of the dictionary for more complete translation information.

Bedeutung des englischen Ausdrucks:	English	Deutsch	Meaning of the German word:
eigentlich	**actual**	**aktuell**	current
den ganzen Tag	**all day**	**alltäglich**	everyday, ordinary
auch	**also**	**also**	so; (*Füllwort*) well
bekannt geben	**announce**	**annoncieren**	to advertise
werden	**become**	**bekommen**	to get, to receive
Benzol	**benzene**	**Benzin**	gas(oline)
blinzeln	**blink**	**blinken**	AUTO to flash
mutig	**brave**	**brav**	(*Kind*) good
hell	**bright**	**breit**	broad; (*weit*) wide
Hütte	**cabin**	**(Umkleide)kabine**	changing room
Koch, Köchin	**chef**	**Chef**	boss
Begriff	**concept**	**Konzept**	draft
zubereiten	**cook** *tr*	**kochen**	(*Wasser*) to boil
Mais	**corn**	**Korn**	seed; (*Sand-*) grain
Handwerk	**craft**	**Kraft**	strength; force; power
Neugier(de)	**curiosity**	**Kuriosität**	(*Merkwürdigkeit*) oddity
schroff; barsch	**curt**	**kurz**	short; (*zeitlich*) brief
schließlich, endlich	**eventually**	**eventuell**	**I.** *adj* possible; **II.** *adv* possibly
Stoff	**fabric**	**Fabrik**	factory
Schwule(r)	**faggot**	**Fagott**	MUS bassoon
befestigen	**fasten**	**fasten**	to fast
schnalzen mit	**flick**	**flicken**	to mend
Fußboden	**floor**	**Flur**	corridor, hall
Formel	**formula**	**Formular**	form
Messgerät	**gauge**	**Gage**	THEAT fee
freundlich	**genial**	**genial**	(*fam*) brilliant
Freundlichkeit	**geniality**	**Genialität**	brilliance
dienstbarer Geist	**genie**	**Genie**	genius
Geschenk	**gift**	**Gift**	poison; (*Tier-*) venom
Blick	**glance** *n*	**Glanz**	shine; (*fig*) glory
kurz ansehen	**glance** *vi*	**glänzen**	to shine; (*fig*) to be brilliant
liebenswürdig	**gracious**	**graziös**	graceful
unbedeutend	**inconsequential**	**inkonsequent**	inconsistent
Insel	**island**	**Island**	Iceland
Art	**kind**	**Kind**	child
Arbeit	**labor**	**Labor**	lab(oratory)
Mangel	**lack**	**Lack**	varnish; (*Auto-*) paint
Festland	**land**	**Land**	country
Zitrone	**lemon**	**Limone**	lime
Liste	**list**	**List**	trick, cunning

Bedeutung des englischen Ausdrucks:	English	Deutsch	Meaning of the German word:
Ortsansässige(r)	**local** *n*	**Lokal**	bar; restaurant
Begierde	**lust**	**Lust haben**	to feel like
Mann	**man**	**(Ehe)mann**	husband
Landkarte	**map**	**Mappe**	(*Hefter*) folder; briefcase
Orangenmarmelade	**marmalade**	**Marmelade**	jam
Masse; Messe	**mass**	**Maß**	measure; (*Aus-*) degree
Bedeutung	**meaning**	**Meinung**	opinion
Mitte	**middle**	**Mittel**	(*Hilfs-*) means
mittleren Alters	**middle-aged**	**mittelalterlich**	medieval
Dunst	**mist**	**Mist**	dung; (*fam*) rubbish
Art	**mode**	**Mode**	fashion
edel; adlig	**noble**	**nobel** (*fam*)	generous
Benachrichtigung	**notice**	**Notiz**	(*Vermerk*) note
Roman	**novel**	**Novelle**	novella
gewöhnlich	**ordinary**	**ordinär**	vulgar
Backofen	**oven**	**Ofen**	stove; (*Heiz-*) heater
zufällig mithören	**overhear**	**überhören**	(*absichtlich*) to ignore
beaufsichtigen	**oversee**	**übersehen**	to fail to notice
Versehen	**oversight**	**Übersicht**	overview
offenkundig	**patent**	**patent**	ingenious
Mitleid erregend	**pathetic**	**pathetisch**	impassioned
Erdöl	**petroleum**	**Petroleum**	kerosene
Foto	**photograph**	**Fotograf**	photographer
Arzt/Ärztin	**physician**	**Physiker(in)**	physicist
saure Gurken	**pickle**	**Pickel**	pimple
Teller	**plate**	**(Schall)platte**	record
füllig, mollig	**plump**	**plump**	plump; ungainly
Beute	**plunder**	**Plunder**	junk
Polizei	**police**	**Police**	policy
wichtigste(r, s)	**principal**	**prinzipiell**	on principle
Beförderung	**promotion**	**Promotion**	doctorate, Ph. D.
kündigen	**quit**	**quittieren**	to give a receipt for
übereilt	**rash**	**rasch**	quick(ly)
vernünftig	**rational**	**rationell**	efficient(ly)
echt	**real**	**reell**	straight; fair
Quittung	**receipt**	**Rezept**	KOCHK recipe; MED prescription
wiedergewinnen	**reclaim**	**reklamieren**	to complain about sth
Wiedergewinnung	**reclamation**	**Reklamation**	complaint
mieten	**rent** *vt*	**(sich) rentieren**	to be worth it
rostig	**rusty**	**rüstig**	sprightly
Plan	**scheme**	**Schema**	(*Muster*) pattern
gewissenhaft	**scrupulous**	**skrupellos**	unscrupulous
Meer	**sea**	**See** (*m*)	lake
Geheimnis	**secret**	**Sekret**	MED secretion
vernünftig	**sensible**	**sensibel**	sensitive
ernst	**serious**	**seriös**	(*anständig*) respectable

Bedeutung des englischen Ausdrucks:	English	Deutsch	Meaning of the German word:
scharf; spitz	**sharp**	**scharf**	(*gewürzt*) spicy; (*streng*) severe
(Kassen)zettel	**slip**	**Slip**	panties *pl*
Rauchen	**smoking**	**Smoking**	tuxedo, dinner-jacket
fest	**solid**	**solid(e)**	(*anständig*) respecta-ble
ausgeben	**spend (money)**	**spenden**	to donate
entdecken	**spot** *vt*	**spotten**	to mock
bleiben	**stay**	**stehen**	to stand; (*gut passen*) to suit
noch	**still** *adv*	**still**	quiet, silent
Hocker	**stool**	**Stuhl**	chair
Faden, Strang	**strand**	**Strand**	beach
Bach	**stream**	**Strom**	ELEK electricity
verständnisvoll, mitfüh-lend	**sympathetic**	**sympathisch**	nice, likeable
Mitleid	**sympathy**	**Sympathie**	sympathy
Tablette	**tablet**	**Tablett**	tray
Geschmack	**taste**	**Taste**	key
Landstreicher(in)	**tramp**	**Tramper(in)**	hitchhiker
Leichenbestatter	**undertaker**	**Unternehmer(in)**	entrepreneur
gefühllos	**unsympathetic**	**unsympathisch**	unpleasant
Lagerhaus	**warehouse**	**Warenhaus**	department store
sich fragen	**wonder**	**(sich) wundern**	to be surprised

Die Zahlwörter
Numerals

Die Kardinalzahlen
Cardinal numbers

null	0	nought, zero
eins	1	one
zwei	2	two
drei	3	three
vier	4	four
fünf	5	five
sechs	6	six
sieben	7	seven
acht	8	eight
neun	9	nine
zehn	10	ten
elf	11	eleven
zwölf	12	twelve
dreizehn	13	thirteen
vierzehn	14	fourteen
fünfzehn	15	fifteen
sechzehn	16	sixteen
siebzehn	17	seventeen
achtzehn	18	eighteen
neunzehn	19	nineteen
zwanzig	20	twenty
einundzwanzig	21	twenty-one
zweiundzwanzig	22	twenty-two
dreiundzwanzig	23	twenty-three
dreißig	30	thirty
einunddreißig	31	thirty-one
zweiunddreißig	32	thirty-two
vierzig	40	forty
einundvierzig	41	forty-one
fünfzig	50	fifty
einundfünfzig	51	fifty-one
sechzig	60	sixty
einundsechzig	61	sixty-one
siebzig	70	seventy
einundsiebzig	71	seventy-one
achtzig	80	eighty
einundachtzig	81	eighty-one
neunzig	90	ninety
einundneunzig	91	ninety-one
hundert	100	a [*o* one] hundred
hundert(und)eins	101	hundred and one
hundert(und)zwei	102	hundred and two
hundert(und)zehn	110	hundred and ten
zweihundert	200	two hundred

dreihundert	300	three hundred
vierhundert(und)einundfünfzig	451	four hundred and fifty-one
tausend	1000	a [*o* one] thousand
zweitausend	2000	two thousand
zehntausend	10 000	ten thousand
eine Million	1 000 000	a [*o* one] million
zwei Millionen	2 000 000	two million
eine Milliarde	1 000 000 000	a [*o* one] billion
eine Billion	1 000 000 000 000	a [*o* one] trillion

Die Ordnungszahlen

Ordinal numbers

erste	1.	1st	first
zweite	2.	2nd	second
dritte	3.	3rd	third
vierte	4.	4th	fourth
fünfte	5.	5th	fifth
sechste	6.	6th	sixth
siebente	7.	7th	seventh
achte	8.	8th	eighth
neunte	9.	9th	ninth
zehnte	10.	10th	tenth
elfte	11.	11th	eleventh
zwölfte	12.	12th	twelfth
dreizehnte	13.	13th	thirteenth
vierzehnte	14.	14th	fourteenth
fünfzehnte	15.	15th	fifteenth
sechzehnte	16.	16th	sixteenth
siebzehnte	17.	17th	seventeenth
achtzehnte	18.	18th	eighteenth
neunzehnte	19.	19th	nineteenth
zwanzigste	20.	20th	twentieth
einundzwanzigste	21.	21st	twenty-first
zweiundzwanzigste	22.	22nd	twenty-second
dreiundzwanzigste	23.	23rd	twenty-third
dreißigste	30.	30th	thirtieth
einunddreißigste	31.	31st	thirty-first
vierzigste	40.	40th	fortieth
einundvierzigste	41.	41st	forty-first
fünfzigste	50.	50th	fiftieth
einundfünfzigste	51.	51st	fifty-first
sechzigste	60.	60th	sixtieth
einundsechzigste	61.	61st	sixty-first
siebzigste	70.	70th	seventieth
einundsiebzigste	71.	71st	seventy-first
achtzigste	80.	80th	eightieth
einundachtzigste	81.	81st	eighty-first
neunzigste	90.	90th	ninetieth

hundertste	100.	100th	(one) hundredth
hundertunderste	101.	101st	hundred and first
zweihundertste	200.	200th	two hundredth
dreihundertste	300.	300th	three hundredth
vierhundert(und)einundfünfzigste	451.	451st	four hundred and fifty-first
tausendste	1000.	1000th	(one) thousandth
tausend(und)einhundertste	1100.	1100th	thousand and (one) hundredth
zweitausendste	2000.	200th	two thousandth
einhunderttausendste	100 000.	$100\,000^{\text{th}}$	(one) hundred thousandth
millionste	1 000 000.	$1\,000\,000^{\text{th}}$	millionth
zehnmillionste	10 000 000.	$10\,000\,000^{\text{th}}$	ten millionth

Die Bruchzahlen

Fractions

ein halb	$^1/_2$	one [o a] half
ein Drittel	$^1/_3$	one [o a] third
ein Viertel	$^1/_4$	one [o a] quarter
ein Fünftel	$^1/_5$	one [o a] fifth
ein Zehntel	$^1/_{10}$	one [o a] tenth
ein Hundertstel	$^1/_{100}$	one hundredth
ein Tausendstel	$^1/_{1000}$	one thousandth
ein Millionstel	$^1/_{1000\,000}$	one millionth
zwei Drittel	$^2/_3$	two thirds
drei Viertel	$^3/_4$	three quarters
zwei Fünftel	$^2/_5$	two fifths
drei Zehntel	$^3/_{10}$	three tenths
anderthalb	$1^1/_2$	one and a half
zwei(und)einhalb	$2^1/_2$	two and a half
fünf drei achtel	$5^3/_8$	five and three eighths
eins Komma eins	1,1 1.1	one point one
zwei Komma drei	2,3 2.3	two point three

Vervielfältigungszahlen

Multiples

einfach	single	vierfach	fourfold, quadruple
zweifach	double	fünffach	fivefold
dreifach	threefold, treble, triple	hundertfach	(one) hundredfold

Gewichte, Maße und Temperatur

Weights, measures, and temperatures

Das Dezimalsystem

Decimal system

Giga	1000000000	G	giga
Mega	1000000	M	mega
Hektokilo	100000	hk	hectokilo
Myria	10000	ma	myria
Kilo	1000	k	kilo
Hekto	100	h	hecto
Deka	10	da	deca
Dezi	0,1	d	deci
Centi	0,01	c	centi
Milli	0,001	m	milli
Dezimilli	0,0001	dm	decimilli
Centimilli	0,00001	cm	centimilli
Mikro	0,000001	μ	micro

Umrechnungstabellen

Conversion tables

In den USA ist immer noch das anglo-amerikanische Maßsystem in Gebrauch. In Großbritannien ist man offiziell auf das Dezimalsystem umgestiegen, jedoch bevorzugen viele immer noch das alte System. Für Temperaturen wird die Fahrenheit-Skala verwendet. Nur diejenigen angloamerikanischen Maße, die immer noch in Umlauf sind, werden in den Tabellen aufgeführt. Man erhält ein angloamerikanisches Maß, indem man das entprechende metrische mit dem **fett** gedruckten Umrechnungsfaktor multipliziert. Umgekehrt gilt: Ein imperiales Maß, das durch den gleichen Faktor dividiert wird, ergibt das metrische.

Only U. S. Customary units still in common use are given here. To convert a metric measurement to U. S. Customary measures, multiply by the conversion factor in **bold**. Likewise dividing a U. S. Customary measurement by the same factor will give the metric equivalent. Note that the decimal comma is used throughout rather than the decimal point.

Das metrische System

Metric measurement

Anglo-amerikanisches Maßsystem

U.S. Customary System

Längenmaße

Length measures

Seemeile	1852 m	–	nautical mile			
Kilometer	1000 m	km	kilometer	**0,62**	mile (= 1760 yards)	m, mi
Hektometer	100 m	hm	hectometer			
Dekameter	10 m	dam	decameter			
Meter	1 m	m	meter	**1,09** **3,28**	yard (= 3 feet) foot (= 12 inches)	yd ft
Dezimeter	0,1 m	dm	decimeter			

Zentimeter	0,01 m	cm	centimeter	**0,39**	inch	in
Millimeter	0,001 m	mm	millimeter			
Mikron	0,000 001 m	μ	micron			
Millimikron	0,000 000 001 m	mμ	millimicron			
Angström	0,000 000 000 1 m	Å	angstrom			

Flächenmaße

Surface measures

Quadrat-kilometer	1 000 000 m^2	km^2	square kilometer	**0,386**	square mile (= 640 acres)	sq. m., sq. mi.
Quadrat-hektometer	10 000 m^2	hm^2	square hecto-meter	**2,47**	acre (= 4840 square yards)	a.
Hektar		ha	hectare			
Quadrat-dekameter	100 m^2	dam^2	square decameter			
Ar (SCHWEIZ: Are)		a	are			
Quadratmeter	1 m^2	m^2	square meter	**1.196**	square yard (9 square feet)	sq. yd
				10,76	square feet (= 144 square inches)	sq. ft
Quadrat-dezimeter	0,01 m^2	dm^2	square decimeter			
Quadrat-zentimeter	0,0001 m^2	cm^2	square centimeter	**0,155**	square inch	sq. in.
Quadrat-millimeter	0,000 001 m^2	mm^2	square millimeter			

Kubik- und Hohlmaße

Volume and capacity

Kubikkilometer	1 000 000 000 m^3	km^3	cubic kilometer			
Kubikmeter	1 m^3	m^3	cubic meter	**1,308**	cubic yard (= 27 cubic feet)	cu. yd
Ster		st	stere	**35,32**	cubic foot (= 1728 cubic inches)	cu. ft
Hektoliter	0,1 m^3	hl	hectoliter			
Dekaliter	0,01 m^3	dal	decaliter			
Kubik-dezimeter	0,001 m^3	dm^3	cubic decimeter	**0,26**	gallon	gal.
Liter		l	liter	**2,1**	pint	Pt
Deziliter	0,0001 m^3	dl	deciliter			
Zentiliter	0,000 01 m^3	cl	centiliter	**0,352** **0,338**	fluid ounce	fl. oz
Kubik-zentimeter	0,000 001 m^3	cm^3	cubic centimeter	**0,061**	cubic inch	cu. in.
Milliliter	0,000 001 m^3	ml	milliliter			
Kubik-millimeter	0,000 000 001 m^3	mm^3	cubic millimeter			

Gewichte

Weight

Tonne	1000 kg	t	ton	**1,1**	[short] ton (= 2000 pounds)	t.
Quintal	100 kg	q	quintal			
Kilogramm	1000 g	kg	kilogram	**2,2**	pound (= 16 ounces)	lb
Hektogramm	100 g	hg	hectogram			
Dekagramm	10 g	dag	decagram			
Gramm	1 g	g	gram	**0,035**	ounce	oz
Karat	0,2 g	–	carat			
Dezigramm	0,1 g	dg	decigram			
Zentigramm	0,01 g	cg	centigram			
Milligramm	0,001 g	mg	milligram			
Mikrogramm	0,000 001 g	µg	microgram			

Temperatur

Temperature

Um eine Temperaturangabe in Grad Fahrenheit in Celsius umzuwandeln, wird 32 abgezogen und anschließend durch 1,8 geteilt.
Eine Celsius-Angabe wird dementsprechend in Fahrenheit umgerechnet, indem man sie mit 1,8 multipliziert und 32 dazuzählt.

To convert a temperature in degrees Fahrenheit to Celsius, deduct 32 and divide by 1.8.
To convert Celsius to Fahrenheit, multiply by 1.8 and add 32.

Geographische Namen: Deutsch – Englisch
Geographical names: German – English

Länder, Einwohner, Adjektive, Hauptstädte, Währungen
Countries, Inhabitants, Derivatives, Capitals, Currencies

Die Länder sind alphabetisch angeordnet und unter der deutschen Schreibweise zu finden. Zum Gebrauch des Artikels bei geographischen Eigennamen siehe "Deutsche Kurzgrammatik".

Countries are arranged in alphabetical order by their German names. For how to use articles when referring to geographical proper nouns, see the "Concise German Grammar."

Land Country	Einwohner Inhabitant	Adjektive Derivative	Hauptstadt Capital	Währung Currency
Afghanistan *nt*	Afghane *m*, Afghanin *f*	afghanisch	Kabul	Afghani
Afghanistan	*Afghan(s)*	*Afghan*	*Kabul*	*afghani*
Ägypten *nt*	Ägypter(in) *m(f)*	ägyptisch	Kairo	Ägyptisches Pfund
Egypt	*Egyptian(s)*	*Egyptian*	*Cairo*	*Egyptian pound*
Albanien *nt*	Albaner(in) *m(f)*	albanisch	Tirana	Lek
Albania	*Albanian(s)*	*Albanian*	*Tiranë*	*lek*
Algerien *nt*	Algerier(in) *m(f)*	algerisch	Algier	Algerischer Dinar
Algeria	*Algerian(s)*	*Algerian*	*Algiers*	*Algerian dinar*
Andorra *nt*	Andorraner(in) *m(f)*	andorranisch	Andorra la Vella	Euro
Andorra	*Andorran(s)*	*Andorran*	*Andorra la Vella*	*euro*
Angola *nt*	Angolaner(in) *m(f)*	angolanisch	Luanda	Kwanza
Angola	*Angolan(s)*	*Angolan*	*Luanda*	*new kwanza*
Antigua und Barbuda *nt*	Antiguaner(in) *m(f)*	antiguanisch	St. John's	Ostkaribischer Dollar
Antigua and Barbuda	*Antiguan(s), Barbudan(s)*	*Antiguan, Barbudan*	*St. John's*	*East Caribbean dollar*
Äquatorialguinea *nt*	Äquatorial-guineer(in) *m(f)*	äquatorial-guineisch	Malabo	CFA-Franc
Equatorial Guinea	*Equatorial Guinean(s), Equatoguinean(s)*	*Equatorial Guinean, Equatoguinean*	*Malabo*	*CFA franc**
Argentinien *nt*	Argentinier(in) *m(f)*	argentinisch	Buenos Aires	Argentinischer Peso
Argentina	*Argentine(s), Argentinean(s)*	*Argentine, Argentinean*	*Buenos Aires*	*Argentine peso*
Armenien *nt*	Armenier(in) *m(f)*	armenisch	Eriwan	Dram
Armenia	*Armenian(s)*	*Armenian*	*Yerevan*	*dram*
Aserbaidschan *nt*	Aserbaidscha-ner(in) *m(f)*	aserbaidschanisch	Baku	Manat
Azerbaijan	*Azerbaijani, Azeri(s)*	*Azerbaijani, Azeri*	*Baku*	*manat*
Äthiopien *nt*	Äthiopier(in) *m(f)*	äthiopisch	Addis Abeba	Birr
Ethiopia	*Ethiopian(s)*	*Ethiopian*	*Addis Abeba*	*birr*
Australien *nt*	Australier(in) *m(f)*	australisch	Canberra	Australischer Dollar
Australia	*Australian(s)*	*Australian*	*Canberra*	*Australian dollar*

Land	Einwohner	Adjektive	Hauptstadt	Währung
Country	Inhabitant	Derivative	Capital	Currency
die Bahamas	Bahamer(in) *m(f)*	bahamaisch	Nassau	Bahama-Dollar
Bahamas	*Bahamian(s)*	*Bahamian*	*Nassau*	*Bahamian dollar*
Bahrain *nt*	Bahrainer(in) *m(f)*	bahrainisch	Manama	Bahrain-Dinar
Bahrain	*Bahraini(s)*	*Bahraini*	*Al Manama*	*Bahrainian dinar*
Bangladesch *nt*	Bangladescher(in) *m(f)*	bangladeschisch	Dhaka	Taka
Bangladesh	*Bangladeshi(s)*	*Bangladeshi*	*Dhaka*	*taka*
Barbados *nt*	Barbadier(in) *m(f)*	barbadisch	Bridgetown	Barbados-Dollar
Barbados	*Barbadian(s)*	*Barbadian*	*Bridgetown*	*Barbadian dollar*
Belgien *nt*	Belgier(in) *m(f)*	belgisch	Brüssel	Euro
Belgium	*Belgian(s)*	*Belgian*	*Brussels*	*euro*
Belize *nt*	Belizer(in) *m(f)*	belizisch	Belmopan	Belize-Dollar
Belize	*Belizean(s)*	*Belizean*	*Belmopan*	*Belizean dollar*
Benin *nt*	Beniner(in) *m(f)*	beninisch	Porto Novo	CFA-Franc
Benin	*Beninese*	*Beninese*	*Porto Novo*	*CFA franc**
Bhutan *nt*	Bhutaner(in) *m(f)*	bhutanisch	Thimphu	Ngultrum
Bhutan	*Bhutanese*	*Bhutanese*	*Thimphu*	*ngultrum*
Birma *nt*/Myanmar *nt*	Myanmare *m*, Myanmarin *f*	myanmarisch	Pyinmana	Kyat
Burma/Myanmar	*Burmese*	*Burmese*	*Pyinmana*	*kyat*
Bolivien *nt*	Bolivianer(in) *m(f)*	bolivianisch	Sucre	Boliviano
Bolivia	*Bolivian(s)*	*Bolivian*	*Sucre*	*Boliviano*
Bosnien *nt* und Herzegowina *f*	von Bosnien und Herzegowina	von Bosnien und Herzegowina	Sarajewo	Konvertible Mark
Bosnia and Herzegovina	*Bosnian(s), Herzegovinian(s)*	*Bosnian, Herzegovinian*	*Sarajevo*	*Convertible Mark*
Botsuana *nt*	Botsuaner(in) *m(f)*	botsuanisch	Gaborone	Pula
Botswana	*Motswana sg, Batswana pl*	*Motswana sing, Batswana pl*	*Gaborone*	*pula*
Brasilien *nt*	Brasilianer(in) *m(f)*	brasilianisch	Brasilia	Real
Brazil	*Brazilian(s)*	*Brazilian*	*Brasilia*	*real*
Brunei *nt* (Brunei Darussalam *nt*)	Bruneier *m(f)*	bruneiisch	Bandar Seri Begawan	Brunei-Dollar
Brunei	*Bruneian(s)*	*Bruneian*	*Bandar Seri Begawan*	*Brunei dollar*
Bulgarien *nt*	Bulgare *m*, Bulgarin *f*	bulgarisch	Sofia	Lew
Bulgaria	*Bulgarian(s)*	*Bulgarian*	*Sofia*	*lev*
Burkina Faso *nt*	Burkiner(in) *m(f)*	burkinisch	Ouagadougou	CFA-Franc
Burkina Faso	*Burkinabe*	*Burkinabe*	*Ouagadougou*	*CFA franc**
Burundi *nt*	Burundier(in) *m(f)*	burundisch	Bujumbura	Burundi-Franc
Burundi	*Burundian(s)*	*Burundian*	*Bujumbura*	*Burundi franc*
Chile *nt*	Chilene *m*, Chilenin *f*	chilenisch	Santiago de Chile	Chilenischer Peso
Chile	*Chilean(s)*	*Chilean*	*Santiago de Chile*	*Chilean peso*

Land Country	Einwohner Inhabitant	Adjektive Derivative	Hauptstadt Capital	Währung Currency
China *nt*	Chinese *m*, Chinesin *f*	chinesisch	Peking/Beijing	Yuan
China	*Chinese*	*Chinese*	*Beijing/Peking*	*yuan*
die Cookinseln	von den Cook-inseln	von den Cook-inseln	Avarua	Neuseeland-Dollar
Cook Islands	*Cook Islander(s)*	*Cook Islander*	*Avarua*	*New Zealand dollar*
Costa Rica *nt*	Costa-Ricaner(in) *m(f)*	costa-ricanisch	San José	Colón
Costa Rica	*Costa Rican(s)*	*Costa Rican*	*San José*	*Costa Rican colón*
Dänemark *nt*	Däne *m*, Dänin *f*	dänisch	Kopenhagen	Dänische Krone
Denmark	*Dane(s)*	*Danish*	*Kopenhagen*	*Danish krone*
die Demokratische Republik Kongo	der Demokrati-schen Republik Kongo	der Demokrati-schen Republik Kongo	Kinshasa	Kongo-Franc
Congo (Democratic Republic of the Congo)	*Congolese*	*Congolese, Congo*	*Kinshasa*	*Congolese franc*
Deutschland *nt*	Deutscher *m*, Deutsche *f*	deutsch	Berlin	Euro
Germany	*German(s)*	*German*	*Berlin*	*euro*
Dominica *nt*	Dominicaner(in) *m(f)*	dominicanisch	Roseau	Ostkaribischer Dollar
Dominica	*Dominican(s)*	*Dominican*	*Roseau*	*East Caribbean dollar*
die Dominikanische Republik	Dominikaner(in) *m(f)*	dominikanisch	Santo Domingo	Dominikanischer Peso
Dominican Republic	*Dominican(s)*	*Dominican*	*Santo Domingo*	*Dominican peso*
Dschibuti *nt*	Dschibutier(in) *m(f)*	dschibutisch	Djibouti	Dschibuti-Franc
Djibouti	*Djibutian(s)*	*Djiboutian*	*Djibouti*	*Djiboutian franc*
Ecuador *nt*	Ecuadorianer(in) *m(f)*	ecuadorianisch	Quito	US-Dollar
Ecuador	*Ecuadorian(s)*	*Ecuadorian*	*Quito*	*US dollar*
die Elfenbeinküste (die Côte d'Ivoire)	Ivorer *m*, Ivorin *f*	ivorisch	Yamoussoukro	CFA-Franc
Ivory Coast/Côte d'Ivoire	*Ivoirian(s)*	*Ivoirian*	*Yamoussoukro*	*CFA franc**
El Salvador *nt*	Salvadorianer(in) *m(f)*	salvadorianisch	San Salvador	US-Dollar
El Salvador	*Salvadoran(s)*	*Salvadoran*	*San Salvador*	*US dollar*
England *nt* (GB)	Engländer(in) *m(f)*	englisch	London	Pfund Sterling
England (GB)	*Englishman m, Englishwoman f; English pl*	*English*	*London*	*pound sterling*
Eritrea *nt*	Eritreer(in) *m(f)*	eritreisch	Asmara	Nakfa
Eritrea	*Eritrean(s)*	*Eritrean*	*Asmara*	*nafka*
Estland *nt*	Este *m*, Estin *f*	estnisch	Tallinn	Euro
Estonia	*Estonian(s)*	*Estonian*	*Tallinn*	*euro*

Land Country	Einwohner Inhabitant	Adjektive Derivative	Hauptstadt Capital	Währung Currency
Fidschi *nt*	Fidschianer(in) *m(f)*	fidschianisch	Suva	Fidschi-Dollar
Fiji	*Fijian(s)*	*Fijian*	*Suva*	*Fijian dollar*
Finnland *nt*	Finne *m*, Finnin *f*	finnisch	Helsinki	Euro
Finland	*Finn(s)*	*Finnish*	*Helsinki*	*euro*
Frankreich *nt*	Franzose *m*, Französin *f*	französisch	Paris	Euro
France	*Frenchman/men m, Frenchwoman/women f; French pl*	*French*	*Paris*	*euro*
Gabun *nt*	Gabuner(in) *m(f)*	gabunisch	Libreville	CFA-Franc
Gabon	*Gabonese*	*Gabonese*	*Libreville*	*CFA franc**
Gambia *nt*	Gambier(in) *m(f)*	gambisch	Banjul	Dalasi
Gambia	*Gambian(s)*	*Gambian*	*Banjul*	*dalasi*
Georgien *nt*	Georgier(in) *m(f)*	georgisch	Tiflis	Lari
Georgia	*Georgian(s)*	*Georgian*	*Tbilisi*	*lari*
Ghana *nt*	Ghanaer(in) *m(f)*	ghanaisch	Accra	Cedi
Ghana	*Ghanaian(s)*	*Ghanaian*	*Accra*	*cedi*
Grenada *nt*	Grenader(in) *m(f)*	grenadisch	St. George's	Ostkaribischer Dollar
Grenada	*Grenadian(s)*	*Grenadian*	*St. George's*	*East Caribbean dollar*
Griechenland *nt*	Grieche *m*, Griechin *f*	griechisch	Athen	Euro
Greece	*Greek(s)*	*Greek*	*Athens*	*euro*
Guatemala *nt*	Guatemalteke *m*, Guatemaltekin *f*	guatemaltekisch	Guatemala-Stadt	Quetzal
Guatemala	*Guatemalan(s)*	*Guatemalan*	*Guatemala*	*quetzal*
Guinea *nt*	Guineer(in) *m(f)*	guineisch	Conakry	Guinea-Franc
Guinea	*Guinean(s)*	*Guinean*	*Conakry*	*Guinean franc*
Guinea-Bissau *nt*	Guinea-Bissauer(in) *m(f)*	guinea-bissauisch	Bissau	CFA-Franc
Guinea-Bissau	*Guinean(s)*	*Guinean*	*Bissau*	*CFA franc**
Guyana *nt*	Guyaner(in) *m(f)*	guyanisch	Georgetown	Guyana-Dollar
Guyana	*Guyanese*	*Guyanese*	*Georgetown*	*Guyanese dollar*
Haiti *nt*	Haitianer(in) *m(f)*	haitianisch	Port-au-Prince	Gourde
Haiti	*Haitian(s)*	*Haitian*	*Port-au-Prince*	*gourde*
Honduras *nt*	Honduraner(in) *m(f)*	honduranisch	Tegucigalpa	Lempira
Honduras	*Honduran(s)*	*Honduran*	*Tegucigalpa*	*lempira*
Indien *nt*	Inder(in) *m(f)*	indisch	New Delhi	Indische Rupie
India	*Indian(s)*	*Indian*	*New Delhi*	*rupee*
Indonesien *nt*	Indonesier(in) *m(f)*	indonesisch	Jakarta	Rupiah
Indonesia	*Indonesian(s)*	*Indonesian*	*Jakarta*	*rupiah*
der Irak	Iraker(in) *m(f)*	irakisch	Bagdad	Irakischer Dinar
Iraq	*Iraqi(s)*	*Iraqi*	*Baghdad*	*Iraqi dinar*

Land	**Einwohner**	**Adjektive**	**Hauptstadt**	**Währung**
Country	**Inhabitant**	**Derivative**	**Capital**	**Currency**
der Iran	Iraner(in) *m(f)*	iranisch	Teheran	Iranischer Real
Iran	*Iranian(s)*	*Iranian*	*Tehran*	*rial*
Irland *nt*	Ire *m*, Irin *f*	irisch	Dublin	Euro
Ireland	*Irishman/men m, Irishwoman/ women f; Irish pl*	*Irish*	*Dublin*	*euro*
Island *nt*	Isländer(in) *m(f)*	isländisch	Reykjavik	Isländische Krone
Iceland	*Icelander(s)*	*Icelandic*	*Reykjavik*	*Icelandic krona*
Israel *nt*	Israeli	israelisch	Jerusalem	Neuer Israelischer Shekel
Israel	*Israeli(s)*	*Israeli*	*Jerusalem*	*new shekel*
Italien *nt*	Italiener(in) *m(f)*	italienisch	Rom	Euro
Italy	*Italian(s)*	*Italian*	*Rome*	*euro*
Jamaika *nt*	Jamaikaner(in) *m(f)*	jamaikanisch	Kingston	Jamaika-Dollar
Jamaica	*Jamaican(s)*	*Jamaican*	*Kingston*	*Jamaican dollar*
Japan *nt*	Japaner(in) *m(f)*	japanisch	Tokyo	Yen
Japan	*Japanese*	*Japanese*	*Tokyo*	*yen*
der Jemen	Jemenit(in) *m(f)*	jemenitisch	Sanaa	Jemen-Rial
Yemen	*Yemeni(s)*	*Yemeni*	*Sanaa*	*Yemeni rial*
Jordanien *nt*	Jordanier(in) *m(f)*	jordanisch	Amman	Jordanischer Dinar
Jordan	*Jordanian(s)*	*Jordanian*	*Amman*	*Jordanian dinar*
Kambodscha *nt*	Kambodschaner(in) *m(f)*	kambodschanisch	Phnom Penh	Riel
Cambodia	*Cambodian(s)*	*Cambodian*	*Phnom Penh*	*riel*
Kamerun *nt*	Kameruner(in) *m(f)*	kamerunisch	Jaunde	CFA-Franc
Cameroon	*Cameroonian(s)*	*Cameroonian*	*Yaoundé*	*CFA franc**
Kanada *nt*	Kanadier(in) *m(f)*	kanadisch	Ottawa	Kanadischer Dollar
Canada	*Canadian(s)*	*Canadian*	*Ottawa*	*Canadian dollar*
Kap Verde *nt*	Kap-Verdier(in) *m(f)*	kap-verdisch	Praia	Kap-Verde-Escudo
Cape Verde	*Cape Verdean(s)*	*Cape Verdean*	*Praia*	*Cape Verde escudo*
Kasachstan *nt*	Kasache *m*, Kasachin *f*	kasachisch	Astana	Tenge
Kazakhstan	*Kazakh(s)*	*Kazakh*	*Astana*	*tenge*
Katar *nt*	Katarer(in) *m(f)*	katarisch	Doha	Katar-Riyal
Qatar	*Qatari(s)*	*Qatari*	*Doha*	*Qatari riyal*
Kenia *nt*	Kenianer(in) *m(f)*	kenianisch	Nairobi	Kenia-Schilling
Kenya	*Kenyan(s)*	*Kenyan*	*Nairobi*	*Kenyan shilling*
Kirgisistan *nt*	Kirgise *m*, Kirgisin *f*	kirgisisch	Bischkek	Som
Kyrgyzstan	*Kyrgyz, Kyrgystani(s)*	*Kyrgyz, Kyrgystani*	*Bishkek*	*Kyrgystani som*
Kiribati *nt*	Kiribatier(in) *m(f)*	kiribatisch	Bairiki	Australischer Dollar
Kiribati	*I-Kiribati*	*I-Kiribati*	*Bairiki*	*Australian dollar*

Land	Einwohner	Adjektive	Hauptstadt	Währung
Country	Inhabitant	Derivative	Capital	Currency
Kolumbien *nt*	Kolumbianer(in) *m(f)*	kolumbianisch	Bogotá (Santa Fé de Bogotá)	Peso
Colombia	*Colombian(s)*	*Colombian*	*Bogota*	*Colombian peso*
die Komoren	Komorer(in) *m(f)*	komorisch	Moroni	Komoren-Franc
Comoros	*Comoran(s)*	*Comoran*	*Moroni*	*Comoran franc*
Kroatien *nt*	Kroate *m*, Kroatin *f*	kroatisch	Zagreb	Kuna
Croatia	*Croat(s), Croatian(s)*	*Croatian*	*Zagreb*	*kuna*
Kuba *nt*	Kubaner(in) *m(f)*	kubanisch	Havanna	Kubanischer Peso
Cuba	*Cuban(s)*	*Cuban*	*Havana*	*Cuban peso*
Kuwait *nt*	Kuwaiter(in) *m(f)*	kuwaitisch	Kuwait	Kuwait-Dinar
Kuwait	*Kuwaiti(s)*	*Kuwaiti*	*Kuwait City*	*Kuwaiti dinar*
Laos *nt*	Laote *m*, Laotin *f*	laotisch	Vientiane	Kip
Laos	*Lao(s), Laotian(s)*	*Lao, Laotian*	*Vientiane*	*kip*
Lesotho *nt*	Lesother(in) *m(f)*	lesothisch	Maseru	Loti
Lesotho	*Basotho sg, Mosotho pl*	*Sotho*	*Maseru*	*loti*
Lettland *nt*	Lette *m*, Lettin *f*	lettisch	Riga	Euro
Latvia	*Latvian(s)*	*Latvian*	*Riga*	*euro*
der Libanon	Libanese *m*, Libanesin *f*	libanesisch	Beirut	Libanesisches Pfund
Lebanon	*Lebanese*	*Lebanese*	*Beirut*	*Lebanese pound*
Liberia *nt*	Liberianer(in) *m(f)*	liberianisch	Monrovia	Liberianischer Dollar
Liberia	*Liberian(s)*	*Liberian*	*Monrovia*	*Liberian dollar*
Libyen *nt*	Libyer(in) *m(f)*	libysch	Tripolis	Libyscher Dinar
Libya	*Libyan(s)*	*Libyan*	*Tripoli*	*Libyan dinar*
Liechtenstein *nt*	Liechtensteiner(in) *m(f)*	liechtensteinisch	Vaduz	Schweizer Franken
Liechtenstein	*Liechtensteiner(s)*	*Liechtensteiner*	*Vaduz*	*Swiss franc*
Litauen *nt*	Litauer(in) *m(f)*	litauisch	Wilna	Euro
Lithuania	*Lithuanian(s)*	*Lithuanian*	*Vilnius*	*euro*
Luxemburg *nt*	Luxemburger(in) *m(f)*	luxemburgisch	Luxemburg	Euro
Luxembourg	*Luxembourger(s)*	*Luxembourg*	*Luxembourg*	*euro*
Madagaskar *nt*	Madagasse *m*, Madagassin *f*	madagassisch	Antananarivo	Ariary
Madagascar	*Madagascan, Malagasy*	*Madagascan, Malagasy*	*Antananarivo*	*Malagasy ariary*
Malawi *nt*	Malawier(in) *m(f)*	malawisch	Lilongwe	Malawi-Kwacha
Malawi	*Malawian(s)*	*Malawian*	*Lilongwe*	*Malawian kwacha*
Malaysia *nt*	Malaysier(in) *m(f)*	malaysisch	Kuala Lumpur	Ringgit
Malaysia	*Malaysian(s)*	*Malaysian*	*Kuala Lumpur*	*Malaysian ringgit*
die Malediven	Malediver(in) *m(f)*	maledivisch	Malé	Rufiyaa
Maldives	*Maldivian(s)*	*Maldivian*	*Malé*	*rufiyaa*
Mali *nt*	Malier(in) *m(f)*	malisch	Bamako	CFA-Franc
Mali	*Malian(s)*	*Malian*	*Bamako*	*CFA franc**

Land Country	Einwohner Inhabitant	Adjektive Derivative	Hauptstadt Capital	Währung Currency
Malta *nt*	Malteser(in) *m(f)*	maltesisch	Valletta	Euro
Malta	*Maltese*	*Maltese*	*Valletta*	*euro*
Marokko *nt*	Marokkaner(in) *m(f)*	marokanisch	Rabat	Dirham
Morocco	*Moroccan(s)*	*Moroccan*	*Rabat*	*dirham*
die Marshallinseln	Marshaller(in) *m(f)*	marshallisch	Majuro	US-Dollar
Marshall Islands	*Marshallese*	*Marshallese*	*Majuro*	*US dollar*
Mauretanien *nt*	Mauretanier(in) *m(f)*	mauretanisch	Nouakchott	Ouguiya
Mauritania	*Mauritanian(s)*	*Mauritanian*	*Nouakchott*	*ouguiya*
Mauritius *nt*	Mauritier(in) *m(f)*	mauritisch	Port Louis	Rupie
Mauritius	*Mauritian(s)*	*Mauritian*	*Port Louis*	*Mauritian rupee*
Mazedonien *nt* (die ehemalige jugoslawische Republik Mazedonien)	Mazedonier(in) *m(f)*	mazedonisch	Skopje	Mazedonischer Denar
Macedonia (Former Yugoslav Republic of Macedonia)	*Macedonian(s)*	*Macedonian*	*Skopje*	*Macedonian denar*
Mexiko *nt*	Mexikaner(in) *m(f)*	mexikanisch	Mexico-Stadt	Mexikanischer Peso
Mexico	*Mexican(s)*	*Mexican*	*Mexico City*	*Mexican peso*
Mikronesien *nt* (die Föderierten Staaten von Mikronesien)	Mikronesier(in) *m(f)*	mikronesisch	Palikir	US-Dollar
Micronesia (Federated States of Micronesia)	*Micronesian(s)*	*Micronesian*	*Palikir*	*US dollar*
Moldawien *nt*, Moldau *nt*	Moldauer(in) *m(f)*	moldauisch, moldawisch	Chisinau	Moldauischer Leu
Moldavia	*Moldovan(s), Moldavian(s)*	*Moldovan, Moldavian*	*Chisinau*	*Moldavian leu*
Monaco *nt*	Monegasse *m*, Monegassin *f*	monegassisch	Monaco-Ville	Euro
Monaco	*Monegasque(s), Monacan(s)*	*Monegasque, Monacan*	*Monaco-Ville*	*euro*
die Mongolei	Mongole *m*, Mongolin *f*	mongolisch	Olan-Bator	Tögrök
Mongolia	*Mongolian(s)*	*Mongolian*	*Ulaanbaatar*	*tugruk*
Montenegro *nt*	Montenegriner(in) *m(f)*	montenegrinisch	Podgorica	Euro
Montenegro	*Montenegrin(s)*	*Montenegrin*	*Podgorica*	*euro*
Mosambik *nt*	Mosambikaner(in) *m(f)*	mosambikanisch	Maputo	Metical
Mozambique	*Mozambican(s)*	*Mozambican*	*Maputo*	*metical*
Namibia *nt*	Namibier(in) *m(f)*	namibisch	Windhuk	Namibia-Dollar
Namibia	*Namibian(s)*	*Namibian*	*Windhoek*	*Namibian dollar*

Land Country	Einwohner Inhabitant	Adjektive Derivative	Hauptstadt Capital	Währung Currency
Nauru *nt*	Nauruer(in) *m(f)*	nauruisch	Yaren	Australischer Dollar
Nauru	*Nauruan(s)*	*Nauruan*	*Yaren*	*Australian dollar*
Nepal *nt*	Nepalese *m*, Nepalesin *f*	nepalesisch	Kathmandu	Nepalesische Rupie
Nepal	*Nepalese*	*Nepalese*	*Kathmandu*	*Nepalese rupee*
Neuseeland *nt*	Neuseeländer(in) *m(f)*	neuseeländisch	Wellington	Neuseeland-Dollar
New Zealand	*New Zealander(s)*	*New Zealander*	*Wellington*	*New Zealand dollar*
Nicaragua *nt*	Nicaraguaner(in) *m(f)*	nicaraguanisch	Managua	Córdoba Oro
Nicaragua	*Nicaraguan(s)*	*Nicaraguan*	*Managua*	*córdoba*
die Niederlande	Niederländer(in) *m(f)*	niederländisch	Amsterdam	Euro
Netherlands	*Dutchman/men m, Dutchwoman/women f; Dutch pl*	*Dutch*	*Amsterdam*	*euro*
Niger *nt*	Nigrer *m*, Nigrin *f*	nigrisch	Niamey	CFA-Franc
Niger	*Nigerien(s)*	*Nigerien*	*Niamey*	*CFA franc**
Nigeria *nt*	Nigerianer(in) *m(f)*	nigerianisch	Abuja	Naira
Nigeria	*Nigerian(s)*	*Nigerian*	*Abuja*	*naira*
Nordkorea *nt* (Korea *nt*, demokratische Volksrepublik *f*)	koreanisch, der Demokratischen Volksrepublik Korea	koreanisch, der Demokratischen Volksrepublik Korea	Pjöngjang	nordkoreanischer Won
North Korea	*North Korean(s)*	*North Korean*	*Pyongyang*	*won*
Norwegen n	Norweger(in) *m(f)*	norwegisch	Oslo	Norwegische Krone
Norway	*Norwegian(s)*	*Norwegian*	*Oslo*	*Norwegian krone*
Oman *nt*	Omaner(in) *m(f)*	omanisch	Maskat	Omani Rial
Oman	*Omani(s)*	*Omani*	*Muscat*	*Omani rial*
Österreich *nt*	Österreicher(in) *m(f)*	österreichisch	Wien	Euro
Austria	*Austrian(s)*	*Austrian*	*Vienna*	*euro*
Pakistan *nt*	Pakistaner(in) *m(f)*	pakistanisch	Islamabad	Pakistanische Rupie
Pakistan	*Pakistani(s)*	*Pakistani*	*Islamabad*	*Pakistani rupee*
Palau *nt*	Palauer(in) *m(f)*	palauisch	Koror	US-Dollar
Palau	*Palauan(s)*	*Palauan*	*Koror*	*US dollar*
Panama *nt*	Panamaer(in) *m(f)*	panamaisch	Panama-Stadt	Balboa
Panama	*Panamanian(s)*	*Panamanian*	*Panama City*	*balboa*
Papua-Neuguinea *nt*	Papua-Neuguineer(in) *m(f)*	Papua-neuguineisch	Port Moresby	Kina
Papua New Guinea	*Papua New Guinean(s)*	*Papua New Guinean*	*Port Moresby*	*kina*

Land Country	Einwohner Inhabitant	Adjektive Derivative	Hauptstadt Capital	Währung Currency
Paraguay *nt*	Paraguayer(in) *m(f)*	paraguayisch	Asunción	Guaraní
Paraguay	*Paraguayan(s)*	*Paraguayan*	*Asunción*	*guaraní*
Peru *nt*	Peruaner(in) *m(f)*	peruanisch	Lima	Nuevo Sol
Peru	*Peruvian(s)*	*Peruvian*	*Lima*	*nuevo sol*
die Philippinen	Philippiner(in) *m(f)*	philippinisch	Manila	Philippinischer Peso
Philippines	*Filipino(s)*	*Philippine*	*Manila*	*Philippines peso*
Polen *nt*	Pole *m*, Polin *f*	polnisch	Warschau	Zloty
Poland	*Pole(s)*	*Polish*	*Warsaw*	*zloty*
Portugal *nt*	Portugiese *m*, Portugiesin *f*	portugiesisch	Lissabon	Euro
Portugal	*Portuguese*	*Portuguese*	*Lisbon*	*euro*
Puerto Rico *nt* (USA)	Puerto-Ricaner(in) *m(f)*	puerto-ricanisch	San Juan	US-Dollar
Puerto Rico (USA)	*Puerto Rican(s)*	*Puerto Rican*	*San Juan*	*US dollar*
die Republik Kongo	Kongolese *m*, Kongolesin *f*	kongolesisch	Brazzaville	CFA-Franc
Congo (Republic of the Congo)	*Congolese*	*Congolese, Congo*	*Brazzaville*	*CFA franc**
Ruanda *nt*	Ruander(in) *m(f)*	ruandisch	Kigali	Ruanda-Franc
Rwanda	*Rwandan(s)*	*Rwandan*	*Kigali*	*Rwandan franc*
Rumänien *nt*	Rumäne *m*, Rumänin *f*	rumänisch	Bukarest	Leu
Romania	*Romanian(s)*	*Romanian*	*Bucharest*	*leu (pl. lei)*
Russland *nt* (die Russische Föderation)	Russe *m*, Russin *f*	russisch	Moskau	Rubel
Russia (Russian Federation)	*Russian(s)*	*Russian*	*Moscow*	*ruble*
die Salomonen	Salomoner(in) *m(f)*	salomonisch	Honiara	Salomonen-Dollar
Solomon Islands	*Solomon Islander(s)*	*Solomon Islander*	*Honiara*	*Salomon dollar*
Sambia *nt*	Sambier(in) *m(f)*	sambisch	Lusaka	Kwacha
Zambia	*Zambian(s)*	*Zambian*	*Lusaka*	*kwacha*
Samoa *nt*	Samoaner(in) *m(f)*	samoanisch	Apia	Tala
Samoa	*Samoan(s)*	*Samoan*	*Apia*	*tala*
San Marino *nt*	San-Marinese *m*, San-Marinesin *f*	san-marinesisch	San Marino	Euro
San Marino	*Sanmarinese*	*Sanmarinese*	*San Marino*	*euro*
São Tomé-et-Príncipe *nt*	São-Toméer(in) *m(f)*	são-toméisch	São Tomé	Dobra
São Tomé and Príncipe	*São Tomean(s)*	*São Tomean*	*São Tomé*	*dobra*
Saudi-Arabien *nt*	Saudi-Araber(in) *m(f)*	saudi-arabisch	Riad	Saudi-Riyal
Saudi Arabia	*Saudi(s)*	*Saudi (Arabian)*	*Riyadh*	*Saudi riyal*

Land Country	Einwohner Inhabitant	Adjektive Derivative	Hauptstadt Capital	Währung Currency
Schottland *nt*	Schotte *m*, Schottin *f*	schottisch	Edinburgh	Pfund Sterling
Scotland	*Scot, Scotsman m, Scotswoman f; Scottish pl*	*Scottish*	*Edinburgh*	*pound sterling*
Schweden *nt*	Schwede *m*, Schwedin *f*	schwedisch	Stockholm	Schwedische Krone
Sweden	*Swede(s)*	*Swedish*	*Stockholm*	*Swedish krone*
die Schweiz	Schweizer(in) *m(f)*	schweizerisch	Bern	Schweizer Franken
Switzerland	*Swiss*	*Swiss*	*Berne*	*Swiss franc*
Senegal *m*	Senegalese *m*, Senegalesin *f*	senegalesisch	Dakar	CFA-Franc
Senegal	*Senegalese*	*Senegalese*	*Dakar*	*CFA franc**
Serbien *nt*	Serbe *m*, Serbin *f*	serbisch	Belgrad	Serbischer Dinar
Serbia	*Serb(s), Serbian(s)*	*Serbian*	*Belgrade*	*Serbian dinar, euro*
die Seychellen	Seycheller(in) *m(f)*	seychellisch	Victoria	Seychellen-Rupie
Seychelles	*Seychellois*	*Seychellois*	*Victoria*	*Seychelles rupee*
Sierra Leone *nt*	Sierra-Leoner(in) *m(f)*	Sierra-leonisch	Freetown	Leone
Sierra Leone	*Sierra Leonean(s)*	*Sierra Leonean*	*Freetown*	*leone*
Simbabwe *nt*	Simbabwer(in) *m(f)*	simbabwisch	Harare	Simbabwe-Dollar
Zimbabwe	*Zimbabwean(s)*	*Zimbabwean*	*Harare*	*Zimbabwean dollar*
Singapur *nt*	Singapurer(in) *m(f)*	singapurisch	Singapur	Singapur-Dollar
Singapore	*Singaporean(s)*	*Singapore*	*Singapore*	*Singapore dollar*
die Slowakei (die Slowakische Republik)	Slowake *m*, Slowakin *f*	slowakisch	Pressburg (Bratislava)	Euro
Slovakia/Slovak Republic	*Slovak(s)*	*Slovak*	*Bratislava*	*euro*
Slowenien *nt*	Slowene *m*, Slowenin *f*	slowenisch	Laibach (Ljubljana)	Euro
Slovenia	*Slovene(s)*	*Slovenian*	*Ljubljana*	*euro*
Somalia *nt*	Somalier(in) *m(f)*	somalisch	Mogadischu	Somalia-Schilling
Somalia	*Somali(s)*	*Somali*	*Mogadishu*	*Somalian shilling*
Spanien *nt*	Spanier(in) *m(f)*	spanisch	Madrid	Euro
Spain	*Spaniard(s)*	*Spanish*	*Madrid*	*euro*
Sri Lanka *nt*	Sri-Lanker(in) *m(f)*	Sri-lankisch	Colombo	Sri-Lanka-Rupie
Sri Lanka	*Sri Lankan(s)*	*Sri Lankan*	*Colombo*	*Sri Lankan rupee*
St. Kitts und Nevis *nt*	von St. Kitt und Nevis	von St. Kitts und Nevis	Basseterre	Ostkaribischer Dollar
St. Kitts and Nevis	*Kittitian(s), Nevisian(s)*	*Kittitian, Nevisian*	*Basseterre*	*East Caribbean dollar*

Land Country	Einwohner Inhabitant	Adjektive Derivative	Hauptstadt Capital	Währung Currency
St. Lucia *nt*	Lucianer(in) *m(f)*	lucianisch	Castries	Ostkaribischer Dollar
St. Lucia	*St. Lucian(s)*	*St. Lucian*	*Castries*	*East Caribbean dollar*
St. Vincent und die Grenadinen *nt*	Vincenter(in) *m(f)*	vincentisch	Kingstown	Ostkaribischer Dollar
St. Vincent and the Grenadines	*(St.) Vincentian(s)*	*(St.) Vincentian*	*Kingstown*	*East Caribbean dollar*
Südafrika *nt*	Südafrikaner(in) *m(f)*	südafrikanisch	Pretoria	Rand
South Africa	*South African(s)*	*South African*	*Pretoria*	*rand*
der Sudan	Sudanese *m*, Sudanesin *f*	sudanesisch	Khartum	Sudanesischer Dinar
Sudan	*Sudanese*	*Sudanese*	*Khartoum*	*Sudanese pound*
Südkorea *nt* (Korea *nt*, Republik *f*)	koreanisch, der Republik Korea	koreanisch, der Republik Korea	Seoul	Won
South Korea	*South Korean(s)*	*South Korean*	*Seoul*	*won*
Suriname *nt*	Surinamer(in) *m(f)*	surinamisch	Paramaribo	Suriname-Dollar
Suriname	*Surinamer(s)*	*Surinamese*	*Paramaribo*	*Suriname dollar*
Swasiland *nt*	Swasi	swasiländisch	Mbabane	Lilangeni
Swaziland	*Swazi(s)*	*Swazi*	*Mbabane*	*lilangeni*
Syrien *nt*	Syrer(in) *m(f)*	syrisch	Damaskus	Syrisches Pfund
Syria	*Syrian(s)*	*Syrian*	*Damaskus*	*Syrian pound*
Tadschikistan *nt*	Tadschike *m*, Tadschikin *f*	tadschikisch	Duschanbe	Somoni
Tajikistan	*Tajikistani(s)*	*Tajik, Tajikistani*	*Dushanbe*	*somoni*
Taiwan *nt*	Taiwaner(in) *m(f)*	taiwanesisch	Taipeh	Neuer Taiwan-Dollar
Taiwan	*Taiwanese*	*Taiwanese*	*Taipei*	*New Taiwan dollar*
Tansania *nt*	Tansanier(in) *m(f)*	tansanisch	Dodoma	Tansania-Schilling
Tanzania	*Tanzanian(s)*	*Tanzanian*	*Dodoma*	*Tanzanian shilling*
Thailand *nt*	Thailänder(in) *m(f)*	thailändisch	Bangkok	Baht
Thailand	*Thai*	*Thai*	*Bangkok*	*baht*
Togo *nt*	Togoer(in) *m(f)*	togoisch	Lomé	CFA-Franc
Togo	*Togolese*	*Togolese*	*Lomé*	*CFA franc**
Tonga *nt*	Tongaer(in) *m(f)*	tongaisch	Nuku'alofa	Pa'anga
Tonga	*Tongan(s)*	*Tongan*	*Nuku'alofa*	*pa'anga*
Trinidad und Tobago *nt*	Trinidader(in) *m(f)* und Tobagoer(in) *m(f)*	von Trinidad und Tobago	Port-of-Spain	Trinidad-und-Tobago-Dollar
Trinidad and Tobago	*Trinidadian(s), Tobagonian(s)*	*Trinidadian, Tobagonian*	*Port of Spain*	*Trinidad and Tobago dollar*
Tschad *nt*	Tschader(in) *m(f)*	tschadisch	N'Djamena	CFA-Franc
Chad	*Chadian(s)*	*Chadian*	*N'Djamena*	*CFA franc**

Land Country	**Einwohner** Inhabitant	**Adjektive** Derivative	**Hauptstadt** Capital	**Währung** Currency
Tschechien *nt* (die Tschechische Republik)	Tscheche *m*, Tschechin *f*	tschechisch	Prag	Tschechische Krone
Czech Republic	*Czech(s)*	*Czech*	*Prague*	*Czech koruna*
Tunesien *nt*	Tunesier(in) *m(f)*	tunesisch	Tunis	Tunesischer Dinar
Tunisia	*Tunisian(s)*	*Tunisian*	*Tunis*	*Tunisian dinar*
die Türkei	Türke *m*, Türkin *f*	türkisch	Ankara	Neue Türkische Lira
Turkey	*Turk(s)*	*Turkish*	*Ankara*	*New Turkish lira*
Turkmenistan *nt*	Turkmene *m*, Turkmenin *f*	turkmenisch	Aschgabat	Manat
Turkmenistan	*Turkmen(s)*	*Turkmen*	*Ashgabat*	*manat*
Tuvalu *nt*	Tuvaluer(in) *m(f)*	tuvaluisch	Funafuti	Australischer Dollar
Tuvalu	*Tuvaluan(s)*	*Tuvaluan*	*Funafuti*	*Australian dollar*
Uganda *nt*	Ugander(in) *m(f)*	ugandisch	Kampala	Uganda-Schilling
Uganda	*Ugandan(s)*	*Ugandan*	*Kampala*	*Ugandan shilling*
die Ukraine	Ukrainer(in) *m(f)*	ukrainisch	Kiew	Hrywnja
Ukraine	*Ukrainian(s)*	*Ukrainian*	*Kiev*	*hryvnia*
Ungarn *nt*	Ungar(in) *m(f)*	ungarisch	Budapest	Forint
Hungary	*Hungarian(s)*	*Hungarian*	*Budapest*	*forint*
Uruguay *nt*	Uruguayer(in) *m(f)*	uruguayisch	Montevideo	Uruguayischer Peso
Uruguay	*Uruguayan(s)*	*Uruguayan*	*Montevideo*	*Uruguayan peso*
Usbekistan *nt*	Usbeke *m*, Usbekin *f*	usbekisch	Taschkent	So'm
Uzbekistan	*Uzbekistani*	*Uzbek, Uzbekistani*	*Tashkent*	*Uzbek sum*
Vanuatu *nt*	Vanuatuer(in) *m(f)*	vanuatuisch	Port Vila	Vatu
Vanuatu	*Ni-Vanuatu*	*Ni-Vanuatu*	*Port Vila*	*vatu*
die Vatikanstadt		vatikanisch		Euro
Vatican City		*Vatican*		*euro*
Venezuela *nt*	Venezolaner(in) *m(f)*	venezolanisch	Caracas	Bolívar
Venezuela	*Venezuelan(s)*	*Venezuelan*	*Caracas*	*bolivar*
die Vereinigten Arabischen Emirate	der Vereinigten Arabischen Emirate	der Vereinigten Arabischen Emirate	Abu Dhabi	VAE-Dirham
United Arab Emirates	*Emirati(s)*	*Emirati*	*Abu Dhabi*	*dirham*
das Vereinigte Königreich (Großbritannien *nt* und Nordirland *nt*)	Brite *m*, Britin *f*	britisch	London	Pfund Sterling
United Kingdom	*Briton(s), British*	*UK/British*	*London*	*pound sterling*

Land Country	**Einwohner** Inhabitant	**Adjektive** Derivative	**Hauptstadt** Capital	**Währung** Currency
die Vereinigten Staaten von Amerika/die USA	Amerikaner(in) *m(f)*	amerikanisch	Washington D.C.	US-Dollar
United States of America/USA	*American(s)*	*American*	*Washington D.C.*	*US dollar*
Vietnam *nt*	Vietnamese *m*, Vietnamesin *f*	vietnamesisch	Hanoi	Dong
Vietnam	*Vietnamese*	*Vietnamese*	*Hanoi*	*dong*
Weißrussland *nt*, Belarus *nt*	Weißrusse *m*, Weißrussin *f*, Belarusse *m*, Belarussin *f*	weißrussisch, belarussisch	Minsk	Weißrussischer Rubel
Belarus	*Belarusian(s)*	*Belarusian*	*Minsk*	*Belarusian ruble*
die Zentralafrikanische Republik	Zentralafrikaner(in) *m(f)*	zentralafrikanisch	Bangui	CFA-Franc
Central African Republic	*Central African(s)*	*Central African*	*Bangui*	*CFA franc**
Zypern *nt*	Zyprer(in) *m(f)*	zyprisch	Nikosia	Euro
Cyprus	*Cypriot(s)*	*Cypriot*	*Nicosia*	*euro*

* CFA franc = Franc Communauté Financière Africaine

Kontinente, Inseln
Continents, Islands

Kontinente
Continents

Afrika *nt*
Africa

Amerika *nt*
America

Antarktis *f*
Antarctica

Asien *nt*
Asia

Eurasien *nt*
Eurasia

Europa *nt*
Europe

Nordamerika *nt*
North America

Südamerika *nt*
South America

Zentralamerika *nt*
Central America

Inseln
Islands

die Aleuten
Aleutian Islands

Antigua *nt*
Antigua

die Antillen
Antilles

Aruba *nt*
Aruba

die Azoren
Azores

die Baffininsel
Baffin Island

die Balearischen Inseln (die Balearen)
Balearic Islands

Bali *nt*
Bali

Bermudas *pl*
Bermuda

Borneo *nt*
Borneo

Curaçao
Curaçao

die Falklandinseln
Falkland Islands

die Färöer
Faroe Islands

die Galápagos-Inseln
Galapagos Islands

Grönland *nt*
Greenland

die Großen Antillen
Greater Antilles

Guadalcanal
Guadalcanal

Guadeloupe
Guadeloupe

Guam
Guam

die Hebriden
Hebrides

Hispaniola
Hispaniola

Hokkaido
Hokkaido

Honshu
Honshu

die Insel Man
Isle of Man

die Inseln über dem Winde
Leeward Islands

die Inseln unter dem Winde
Windward Islands

Island *nt*
Iceland

Iwojima
Iwo Jima

Java *nt*
Java

die Jungferninseln
Virgin Islands

die Kanalinseln, die Normannischen Inseln
Channel Islands

die Kanarischen Inseln
Canary Islands

die Kapverdischen Inseln
Cape Verde Islands

die Karolinen
Caroline Islands

die Kleinen Antillen *Lesser Antilles*	Orkney *nt* *Orkney Islands*
die Komoren *Comoros*	die Osterinsel *Easter Island*
Korfu *nt*, Kerkyra *Corfu*	die Ostindischen Inseln *East Indies*
Kreta *Crete*	die Prince-Edward-Inseln *Prince Edward Island*
Kyushu *Kyushu*	Rhodos *nt* *Rhodes*
La Réunion *Réunion*	die Ryukyu-Inseln *Ryukyu Islands*
Leyte *Leyte*	Sakhalin *Sakhalin*
Long Island *Long Island*	die Salomonen *Solomon Islands*
Luzón *Luzon*	Sansibar *Zanzibar*
Madagaskar *nt* *Madagascar*	die Shetland-Inseln *Shetland Islands*
Madeira *nt* *Madeira Islands*	Shikoku *Shikoku*
die Malediven *Maldive Islands*	Sulawesi *Celebes*
Mallorca *nt* *Majorca*	Sumatra *nt* *Sumatra*
die Marianen *Mariana Islands*	Tahiti *nt* *Tahiti*
die Marquesas-Inseln *Marquesas Islands*	Tasmanien *nt* *Tasmania*
die Marshallinseln *Marshall Islands*	Tierra del Fuego *Tierra del Fuego*
Martinique *Martinique*	Timor *Timor*
Mindanao *Mindanao*	Vancouver Island *Vancouver Island*
Menorca *nt* *Minorca*	die Victoria-Insel *Victoria Island*
Okinawa *Okinawa*	die Westindischen Inseln *West Indies*

Ozeane, Meere, Seen
Oceans, Seas, Lakes

Ozeane
Oceans

Antarktischer Ozean, Südlicher Ozean, Antarktik *f*
Southern Ocean

Arktischer Ozean, Arktik *f*, Nordpolarmeer *nt*
Arctic Ocean

Atlantischer Ozean, Atlantik *m*
Atlantic Ocean

Indischer Ozean, Indik *m*
Indian Ocean

Pazifischer Ozean, Pazifik *m*
Pacific Ocean

Meere
Seas

Adriatisches Meer, Adria *f*
Adriatic Sea

Ägäis *f*
Aegean Sea

Arabisches Meer
Arabian Sea

Aralsee *m*
Aral Sea

Asowsches Meer
Sea of Azov

Beringmeer *nt*
Bering Sea

Gelbes Meer
Yellow Sea

Irische See
Irish Sea

Japanisches Meer
Sea of Japan

Karibisches Meer, Karibik *f*
Caribbean Sea

Kaspisches Meer
Caspian Sea

Mittelmeer *nt* (Europäisches Mittelmeer)
Mediterranean Sea

Nordsee *f*
North Sea

Ostchinesisches Meer
East China Sea

Ostsee *f*, Baltisches Meer
Baltic Sea

Rotes Meer
Red Sea

Sargasso See *f*
Sargasso Sea

Schwarzes Meer
Black Sea

See von Okhotsk *f*
Sea of Okhotsk

Südchinesisches Meer
South China Sea

Tasmanische See
Tasman Sea

Totes Meer
Dead Sea

Weißes Meer, Weißmeer *nt*
White Sea

Seen
Lakes

Albertsee *m*
Albert (Nyanza)

Baikalsee *m*
Baikal

Eriesee *m*
Erie

Genfer See
Geneva

Großer Bärensee
Great Bear

Großer Salzsee
Great Salt Lake

Großer Sklavensee
Great Slave

Große Seen *pl*
Great Lakes

Huronsee *m* *Huron*	Ontariosee *m* *Ontario*
Ladogasee *m* *Ladoga*	Tanganjikasee *m* *Tanganyika*
Malawisee *m* (Njassasee *m*) *Lake Nyasa/Lake Malawi*	Titicacasee *m* *Titicaca*
Michigansee *m* *Michigan*	Tschadsee *m* *Chad*
Oberer See *m* *Superior*	Viktoriasee *m* *Victoria*
Onegasee *m* *Onega*	

Flüsse, Golfe
Rivers, Gulfs

Flüsse
Rivers

Amazonas *m* *Amazon*	Jangtse *m* *Yangtze*
Amur *m* *Amur*	Jordan *m* *Jordan*
Columbia River *m* *Columbia*	Kongo *m* *Congo*
Delaware River *m* *Delaware*	Lena *f* *Lena*
Dnjepr *m* *Dnieper*	Loire *f* *Loire*
Dnjestr *m* *Dniester*	Mackenzie *m* *Mackenzie*
Don *m* *Don*	Mekong *m* *Mekong*
Donau *f* *Danube*	Mississippi *m* *Mississippi*
Elbe *f* *Elbe*	Missouri River *m* *Missouri*
Euphrat *m* *Euphrates*	Niger *m* *Niger*
Ganges *m* *Ganges*	Nil *m* *Nile*
Huang Ho *m*/Gelber Fluss *Huang Ho/Yellow River*	Ob *m* *Ob*
Hudson River *m* *Hudson*	Oder *f* *Oder*
Indus *m* *Indus*	Ohio *m* *Ohio*
Irawadi *m* *Irrawaddy*	Orinoco *m* *Orinoco*
Irtysch *m* *Irtysh*	Paraná *m* *Paraná*

Po *m* *Po*	Themse *f* *Thames*
Potomac River *m* *Potomac*	Tigris *m* *Tigris*
Rhein *m* *Rhine*	Ural *m* *Ural*
Rhône *f* *Rhône*	Volta *m* *Volta*
Rio Grande *m* *Rio Grande*	Weichsel *f* *Vistula*
Sambesi *m* *Zambezi*	Wolga *f* *Volga*
Sankt-Lorenz-Strom *m* *St. Lawrence*	Yenisei *m* *Yenisei*
Seine *f* *Seine*	Yukon *m* *Yukon*
Susquehanna *m* *Susquehanna*	

Golfe, Buchten, Meerengen, Kanäle
Gulfs, Bays, Straits, Canals

Ärmelkanal *m* *English Channel*	Hudson Bay *f* *Hudson Bay*
Beringstraße *f* *Bering Strait*	Magellanstraße *f* *Strait of Magellan*
Bosporus *m* *Bosporus*	Panamakanal *m* *Panama Canal*
Florida Straits *pl* *Straits of Florida*	Persischer Golf *m* *Persian Gulf*
Golf von Aden *m* *Gulf of Aden*	Sankt-Lorenz-Golf *m* *Gulf of St. Lawrence*
Golf von Bengalen *m* *Bay of Bengal*	Sankt-Lorenz-Strom *m* *St. Lawrence Seaway*
Golf von Biscaya *m* *Bay of Biscay*	Straße von Gibraltar *f* *Strait of Gibraltar*
Golf von Kalifornien *m* *Gulf of California*	Suezkanal *m* *Suez Canal*
Golf von Mexiko *m* *Gulf of Mexico*	

Berge
Mountains

Gebirgszüge
Mountain Ranges

Adirondack Mountains *pl* *Adirondack Mountains*	Himalaya *m* *Himalaya Mountains/Himalayas*
Allegheny Mountains *pl* *Allegheny Mountains*	Karpaten *pl* *Carpathian Mountains*
Alpen *pl* *Alps*	Kaskadenkette *f* *Cascade Range*
Anden *pl* *Andes*	Kaukasus *m* *Caucasus*
Appalachen *pl* *Appalachian Mountains*	Pyrenäen *pl* *Pyrenees*
Balkangebirge *nt* *Balkans*	Rocky Mountains *pl* *Rocky Mountains*
Catskills *pl*, Catskill Mountains *pl* *Catskill Mountains*	Sierra Nevada *f* *Sierra Nevada*
Eliaskette *f*, Saint Elias Mountains *pl* *St. Elias Mountains*	Ural *m* *Ural Mountains*

Bergspitzen
Mountain Peaks

Aconcagua *m* (Anden) *Aconcagua (Andes)*	Mont Blanc *m* *Mont Blanc*
Ätna *m* *Etna*	Monte Rosa *m* *Monte Rosa*
Citlaltépetl *m*, Pico de Orizaba *m* *Orizaba*	Mount Everest *m* *Everest*
Elbrus *m* *Elbrus*	Mount Logan *m* *Logan*
Fujisan *m*, Berg Fuji *m* *Fujisan, Mount Fuji*	Mount McKinley *m* *McKinley*
Kilimandscharo-Massiv *nt* *Kilimanjaro*	Pikes Peak *m* *Pikes Peak*
Matterhorn *nt* *Matterhorn*	Popocatépetl *m* *Popocatépetl*
Mauna Loa *m* *Mauna Loa*	

Geographical names: English – German

Geographische Namen: Englisch – Deutsch

Countries, Inhabitants, Derivatives, Capitals, Currencies

Länder, Einwohner, Adjektive, Hauptstädte, Währungen

Countries are arranged in alphabetical order by their English names. For how to use articles in German when referring to geographical proper nouns, see the "Concise German Grammar."

Die Länder sind alphabetisch angeordnet und unter der englischen Schreibweise zu finden. Zum Gebrauch des Artikels bei geographischen Eigennamen im Deutschen siehe „Deutsche Kurzgrammatik".

Country Land	Inhabitant Einwohner	Derivative Adjektive	Capital Hauptstadt	Currency Währung
Afghanistan *Afghanistan nt*	Afghan(s) *Afghane m, Afghanin f*	Afghan *afghanisch*	Kabul *Kabul*	afghani *Afghani*
Albania *Albanien nt*	Albanian(s) *Albaner(in) m(f)*	Albanian *albanisch*	Tiranë *Tirana*	lek *Lek*
Algeria *Algerien nt*	Algerian(s) *Algerier(in) m(f)*	Algerian *algerisch*	Algiers *Algier*	Algerian dinar *Algerischer Dinar*
Andorra *Andorra nt*	Andorran(s) *Andorraner(in) m(f)*	Andorran *andorranisch*	Andorra la Vella *Andorra la Vella*	euro *Euro*
Angola *Angola nt*	Angolan(s) *Angolaner(in) m(f)*	Angolan *angolanisch*	Luanda *Luanda*	new kwanza *Kwanza*
Antigua and Barbuda *Antigua und Barbuda nt*	Antiguan(s), Barbudan(s) *Antiguaner(in) m(f)*	Antiguan, Barbudan *antiguanisch*	St. John's *St. John's*	East Caribbean dollar *Ostkaribischer Dollar*
Argentina *Argentinien nt*	Argentine(s), Argentinean(s) *Argentinier(in) m(f)*	Argentine, Argentinean *argentinisch*	Buenos Aires *Buenos Aires*	Argentine peso *Argentinischer Peso*
Armenia *Armenien nt*	Armenian(s) *Armenier(in) m(f)*	Armenian *armenisch*	Yerevan *Eriwan*	dram *Dram*
Australia *Australien nt*	Australian(s) *Australier(in) m(f)*	Australian *australisch*	Canberra *Canberra*	Australian dollar *Australischer Dollar*
Austria *Österreich nt*	Austrian(s) *Österreicher(in) m(f)*	Austrian *österreichisch*	Vienna *Wien*	euro *Euro*
Azerbaijan *Aserbaidschan nt*	Azerbaijani, Azeri(s) *Aserbaidschaner(in) m(f)*	Azerbaijani, Azeri *aserbaidschanisch*	Baku *Baku*	manat *Manat*
Bahamas *die Bahamas*	Bahamian(s) *Bahamer(in) m(f)*	Bahamian *bahamaisch*	Nassau *Nassau*	Bahamian dollar *Bahama-Dollar*
Bahrain *Bahrain nt*	Bahraini(s) *Bahrainer(in) m(f)*	Bahraini *bahrainisch*	Al Manama *Manama*	Bahrainian dinar *Bahrain-Dinar*

Country Land	Inhabitant Einwohner	Derivative Adjektive	Capital Hauptstadt	Currency Währung
Bangladesh	Bangladeshi(s)	Bangladeshi	Dhaka	taka
Bangladesch nt	*Banglade-scher(in) m(f)*	*bangladeschisch*	*Dhaka*	*Taka*
Barbados	Barbadian(s)	Barbadian	Bridgetown	Barbadian dollar
Barbados nt	*Barbadier(in) m(f)*	*barbadisch*	*Bridgetown*	*Barbados-Dollar*
Belarus	Belarusian(s)	Belarusian	Minsk	Belarusian ruble
Weißrussland nt, Belarus nt	*Weißrusse m, Weißrussin f, Belarusse m, Belarussin f*	*weißrussisch, belarussisch*	*Minsk*	*Weißrussischer Rubel*
Belgium	Belgian(s)	Belgian	Brussels	euro
Belgien nt	*Belgier(in) m(f)*	*belgisch*	*Brüssel*	*Euro*
Belize	Belizean(s)	Belizean	Belmopan	Belizean dollar
Belize nt	*Belizer(in) m(f)*	*belizisch*	*Belmopan*	*Belize-Dollar*
Benin	Beninese	Beninese	Porto Novo	CFA franc*
Benin nt	*Beniner(in) m(f)*	*beninisch*	*Porto Novo*	*CFA-Franc*
Bhutan	Bhutanese	Bhutanese	Thimphu	ngultrum
Bhutan nt	*Bhutaner(in) m(f)*	*bhutanisch*	*Thimphu*	*Ngultrum*
Bolivia	Bolivian(s)	Bolivian	Sucre	Boliviano
Bolivien nt	*Bolivianer(in) m(f)*	*bolivianisch*	*Sucre*	*Boliviano*
Bosnia and Herzegovina	Bosnian(s), Herzegovinian(s)	Bosnian, Herzegovinian	Sarajevo	Convertible Mark
Bosnien nt und Herzegowina f	*von Bosnien und Herzegowina*	*von Bosnien und Herzegowina*	*Sarajewo*	*Konvertible Mark*
Botswana	Motswana sing, Batswana *pl*	Motswana sing, Batswana *pl*	Gaborone	pula
Botsuana nt	*Botsuaner(in) m(f)*	*botsuanisch*	*Gaborone*	*Pula*
Brazil	Brazilian(s)	Brazilian	Brasilia	real
Brasilien nt	*Brasilianer(in) m(f)*	*brasilianisch*	*Brasilia*	*Real*
Brunei	Bruneian(s)	Bruneian	Bandar Seri Begawan	Brunei dollar
Brunei nt (Brunei Darussalam nt)	*Bruneier(in) m(f)*	*bruneiisch*	*Bandar Seri Begawan*	*Brunei-Dollar*
Bulgaria	Bulgarian(s)	Bulgarian	Sofia	lev
Bulgarien nt	*Bulgare m, Bulgarin f*	*bulgarisch*	*Sofia*	*Lew*
Burkina Faso	Burkinabe	Burkinabe	Ouagadougou	CFA franc*
Burkina Faso nt	*Burkiner(in) m(f)*	*burkinisch*	*Ouagadougou*	*CFA-Franc*
Burma/Myanmar	Burmese	Burmese	Pyinmana	kyat
Birma nt/ Myanmar nt	*Myanmare m, Myanmarin f*	*myanmarisch*	*Pyinmana*	*Kyat*
Burundi	Burundian(s)	Burundian	Bujumbura	Burundi franc
Burundi nt	*Burundier(in) m(f)*	*burundisch*	*Bujumbura*	*Burundi-Franc*
Cambodia	Cambodian(s)	Cambodian	Phnom Penh	riel
Kambodscha nt	*Kambodscha-ner(in) m(f)*	*kambodschanisch*	*Phnom Penh*	*Riel*

Country Land	Inhabitant Einwohner	Derivative Adjektive	Capital Hauptstadt	Currency Währung
Cameroon *Kamerun nt*	Cameroonian(s) *Kameruner(in) m(f)*	Cameroonian *kamerunisch*	Yaoundé *Jaunde*	CFA franc* *CFA-Franc*
Canada *Kanada nt*	Canadian(s) *Kanadier(in) m(f)*	Canadian *kanadisch*	Ottawa *Ottawa*	Canadian dollar *Kanadischer Dollar*
Cape Verde *Kap Verde nt*	Cape Verdean(s) *Kap-Verdier(in) m(f)*	Cape Verdean *kap-verdisch*	Praia *Praia*	Cape Verde escudo *Kap-Verde-Escudo*
Central African Republic *die Zentralafrikanische Republik*	Central African(s) *Zentralafrikaner(in) m(f)*	Central African *zentralafrikanisch*	Bangui *Bangui*	CFA franc* *CFA-Franc*
Chad *Tschad nt*	Chadian(s) *Tschader(in) m(f)*	Chadian *tschadisch*	N'Djamena *N'Djamena*	CFA franc* *CFA-Franc*
Chile *Chile nt*	Chilean(s) *Chilene m, Chilenin f*	Chilean *chilenisch*	Santiago de Chile *Santiago de Chile*	Chilean peso *Chilenischer Peso*
China *China nt*	Chinese *Chinese m, Chinesin f*	Chinese *chinesisch*	Beijing/Peking *Peking/Beijing*	yuan *Yuan*
Colombia *Kolumbien nt*	Colombian(s) *Kolumbianer(in) m(f)*	Colombian *kolumbianisch*	Bogota *Bogotá (Santa Fé de Bogotá)*	Colombian peso *Peso*
Comoros *die Komoren pl*	Comoran(s) *Komorer(in) m(f)*	Comoran *komorisch*	Moroni *Moroni*	Comoran franc *Komoren-Franc*
Congo (Democratic Republic of the Congo) *die Demokratische Republik Kongo*	Congolese *der Demokratischen Republik Kongo*	Congolese, Congo *der Demokratischen Republik Kongo*	Kinshasa *Kinshasa*	Congolese franc *Kongo-Franc*
Congo (Republic of the Congo) *die Republik Kongo*	Congolese *Kongolese m, Kongolesin f*	Congolese, Congo *kongolesisch*	Brazzaville *Brazzaville*	CFA franc* *CFA-Franc*
Cook Islands *die Cookinseln*	Cook Islander(s) *von den Cookinseln*	Cook Islander *von den Cookinseln*	Avarua *Avarua*	New Zealand dollar *Neuseeland-Dollar*
Costa Rica *Costa Rica nt*	Costa Rican(s) *Costa-Ricaner(in) m(f)*	Costa Rican *costa-ricanisch*	San José *San José*	Costa Rican colón *Colón*
Croatia *Kroatien nt*	Croat(s), Croatian(s) *Kroate m, Kroatin f*	Croatian *kroatisch*	Zagreb *Zagreb*	kuna *Kuna*
Cuba *Kuba nt*	Cuban(s) *Kubaner(in) m(f)*	Cuban *kubanisch*	Havana *Havanna*	Cuban peso *Kubanischer Peso*

Country Land	Inhabitant Einwohner	Derivative Adjektive	Capital Hauptstadt	Currency Währung
Cyprus *Zypern nt*	Cypriot(s) *Zyprer(in) m(f)*	Cypriot *zyprisch*	Nicosia *Nikosia*	euro *Euro*
Czech Republic *Tschechien nt (die Tschechische Republik)*	Czech(s) *Tscheche m, Tschechin f*	Czech *tschechisch*	Prague *Prag*	Czech koruna *Tschechische Krone*
Denmark *Dänemark nt*	Dane(s) *Däne m, Dänin f*	Danish *dänisch*	Kopenhagen *Kopenhagen*	Danish krone *Dänische Krone*
Djibouti *Dschibuti nt*	Djibutian(s) *Dschibutier(in) m(f)*	Djiboutian *dschibutisch*	Djibouti *Djibouti*	Djiboutian franc *Dschibuti-Franc*
Dominica *Dominica nt*	Dominican(s) *Dominicaner(in) m(f)*	Dominican *dominicanisch*	Roseau *Roseau*	East Caribbean dollar *Ostkaribischer Dollar*
Dominican Republic *die Dominikanische Republik*	Dominican(s) *Dominikaner(in) m(f)*	Dominican *dominikanisch*	Santo Domingo *Santo Domingo*	Dominican peso *Dominikanischer Peso*
Ecuador *Ecuador nt*	Ecuadorian(s) *Ecuadorianer(in) m(f)*	Ecuadorian *ecuadorianisch*	Quito *Quito*	US dollar *US-Dollar*
Egypt *Ägypten nt*	Egyptian(s) *Ägypter(in) m(f)*	Egyptian *ägyptisch*	Cairo *Kairo*	Egyptian pound *Ägyptisches Pfund*
El Salvador *El Salvador nt*	Salvadoran(s) *Salvadorianer(in) m(f)*	Salvadoran *salvadorianisch*	San Salvador *San Salvador*	US dollar *US-Dollar*
England (GB) *England nt (GB)*	Englishman *m*, Englishwoman *f*; English *pl* *Engländer(in) m(f)*	English *englisch*	London *London*	pound sterling *Pfund Sterling*
Equatorial Guinea *Äquatorialguinea nt*	Equatorial Guinean(s), Equatoguinean(s) *Äquatorial-guineer(in) m(f)*	Equatorial Guinean, Equatoguinean *äquatorial-guineisch*	Malabo *Malabo*	CFA franc* *CFA-Franc*
Eritrea *Eritrea nt*	Eritrean(s) *Eritreer(in) m(f)*	Eritrean *eritreisch*	Asmara *Asmara*	nafka *Nakfa*
Estonia *Estland nt*	Estonian(s) *Este m, Estin f*	Estonian *estnisch*	Tallinn *Tallinn*	euro *Euro*
Ethiopia *Äthiopien nt*	Ethiopian(s) *Äthiopier(in) m(f)*	Ethiopian *äthiopisch*	Addis Abeba *Addis Abeba*	birr *Birr*
Fiji *Fidschi nt*	Fijian(s) *Fidschianer(in) m(f)*	Fijian *fidschianisch*	Suva *Suva*	Fijian dollar *Fidschi-Dollar*
Finland *Finnland nt*	Finn(s) *Finne m, Finnin f*	Finnish *finnisch*	Helsinki *Helsinki*	euro *Euro*

Country Land	Inhabitant Einwohner	Derivative Adjektive	Capital Hauptstadt	Currency Währung
France	Frenchman/men *m*, Frenchwoman/women *f*; French *pl*	French	Paris	euro
Frankreich nt	*Franzose m, Französin f*	*französisch*	*Paris*	*Euro*
Gabon	Gabonese	Gabonese	Libreville	CFA franc*
Gabun nt	*Gabuner(in) m(f)*	*gabunisch*	*Libreville*	*CFA-Franc*
Gambia	Gambian(s)	Gambian	Banjul	dalasi
Gambia nt	*Gambier(in) m(f)*	*gambisch*	*Banjul*	*Dalasi*
Georgia	Georgian(s)	Georgian	Tbilisi	lari
Georgien nt	*Georgier(in) m(f)*	*georgisch*	*Tiflis*	*Lari*
Germany	German(s)	German	Berlin	euro
Deutschland nt	*Deutscher m, Deutsche f*	*deutsch*	*Berlin*	*Euro*
Ghana	Ghanaian(s)	Ghanaian	Accra	cedi
Ghana nt	*Ghanaer(in) m(f)*	*ghanaisch*	*Accra*	*Cedi*
Greece	Greek(s)	Greek	Athens	euro
Griechenland nt	*Grieche m, Griechin f*	*griechisch*	*Athen*	*Euro*
Grenada	Grenadian(s)	Grenadian	St. George's	East Caribbean dollar
Grenada nt	*Grenader(in) m(f)*	*grenadisch*	*St. George's*	*Ostkaribischer Dollar*
Guatemala	Guatemalan(s)	Guatemalan	Guatemala	quetzal
Guatemala nt	*Guatemalteke m, Guatemaltekin f*	*guatemaltekisch*	*Guatemala-Stadt*	*Quetzal*
Guinea	Guinean(s)	Guinean	Conakry	Guinean franc
Guinea nt	*Guineer(in) m(f)*	*guineisch*	*Conakry*	*Guinea-Franc*
Guinea-Bissau	Guinean(s)	Guinean	Bissau	CFA franc*
Guinea-Bissau nt	*Guinea-Bissauer(in) m(f)*	*guinea-bissauisch*	*Bissau*	*CFA-Franc*
Guyana	Guyanese	Guyanese	Georgetown	Guyanese dollar
Guyana nt	*Guyaner(in) m(f)*	*guyanisch*	*Georgetown*	*Guyana-Dollar*
Haiti	Haitian(s)	Haitian	Port-au-Prince	gourde
Haiti nt	*Haitianer(in) m(f)*	*haitianisch*	*Port-au-Prince*	*Gourde*
Honduras	Honduran(s)	Honduran	Tegucigalpa	lempira
Honduras nt	*Honduraner(in) m(f)*	*honduranisch*	*Tegucigalpa*	*Lempira*
Hungary	Hungarian(s)	Hungarian	Budapest	forint
Ungarn nt	*Ungar(in) m(f)*	*ungarisch*	*Budapest*	*Forint*
Iceland	Icelander(s)	Icelandic	Reykjavik	Icelandic krona
Island nt	*Isländer(in) m(f)*	*isländisch*	*Reykjavik*	*Isländische Krone*
India	Indian(s)	Indian	New Delhi	rupee
Indien nt	*Inder(in) m(f)*	*indisch*	*New Delhi*	*Indische Rupie*
Indonesia	Indonesian(s)	Indonesian	Jakarta	rupiah
Indonesien nt	*Indonesier(in) m(f)*	*indonesisch*	*Jakarta*	*Rupiah*

Country Land	Inhabitant Einwohner	Derivative Adjektive	Capital Hauptstadt	Currency Währung
Iran *der Iran*	Iranian(s) *Iraner(in) m(f)*	Iranian *iranisch*	Tehran *Teheran*	rial *Iranischer Real*
Iraq *der Irak*	Iraqi(s) *Iraker(in) m(f)*	Iraqi *irakisch*	Baghdad *Bagdad*	Iraqi dinar *Irakischer Dinar*
Ireland *Irland nt*	Irishman/men *m*, Irishwoman/women *f*; Irish *pl* *Ire m, Irin f*	Irish *irisch*	Dublin *Dublin*	euro *Euro*
Israel *Israel nt*	Israeli(s) *Israeli*	Israeli *israelisch*	Jerusalem *Jerusalem*	new shekel *Neuer Israelischer Shekel*
Italy *Italien nt*	Italian(s) *Italiener(in) m(f)*	Italian *italienisch*	Rome *Rom*	euro *Euro*
Ivory Coast/ Côte d'Ivoire *die Elfenbeinküste (die Côte d'Ivoire)*	Ivoirian(s) *Ivorer m, Ivorin f*	Ivoirian *ivorisch*	Yamoussoukro *Yamoussoukro*	CFA franc* *CFA-Franc*
Jamaica *Jamaika nt*	Jamaican(s) *Jamaikaner(in) m(f)*	Jamaican *jamaikanisch*	Kingston *Kingston*	Jamaican dollar *Jamaika-Dollar*
Japan *Japan nt*	Japanese *Japaner(in) m(f)*	Japanese *japanisch*	Tokyo *Tokyo*	yen *Yen*
Jordan *Jordanien nt*	Jordanian(s) *Jordanier(in) m(f)*	Jordanian *jordanisch*	Amman *Amman*	Jordanian dinar *Jordanischer Dinar*
Kazakhstan *Kasachstan nt*	Kazakh(s) *Kasache m, Kasachin f*	Kazakh *kasachisch*	Astana *Astana*	tenge *Tenge*
Kenya *Kenia nt*	Kenyan(s) *Kenianer(in) m(f)*	Kenyan *kenianisch*	Nairobi *Nairobi*	Kenyan shilling *Kenia-Schilling*
Kiribati *Kiribati nt*	I-Kiribati *Kiribatier(in) m(f)*	I-Kiribati *kiribatisch*	Bairiki *Bairiki*	Australian dollar *Australischer Dollar*
Kuwait *Kuwait nt*	Kuwaiti(s) *Kuwaiter(in) m(f)*	Kuwaiti *kuwaitisch*	Kuwait City *Kuwait*	Kuwaiti dinar *Kuwait-Dinar*
Kyrgyzstan *Kirgisistan nt*	Kyrgyz, Kyrgystani(s) *Kirgise m, Kirgisin f*	Kyrgyz, Kyrgystani *kirgisisch*	Bishkek *Bischkek*	Kyrgystani som *Som*
Laos *Laos nt*	Lao(s), Laotian(s) *Laote m, Laotin f*	Lao, Laotian *laotisch*	Vientiane *Vientiane*	kip *Kip*
Latvia *Lettland nt*	Latvian(s) *Lette m, Lettin f*	Latvian *lettisch*	Riga *Riga*	euro *Euro*
Lebanon *der Libanon*	Lebanese *Libanese m, Libanesin f*	Lebanese *libanesisch*	Beirut *Beirut*	Lebanese pound *Libanesisches Pfund*
Lesotho *Lesotho nt*	Basotho *sg*, Mosotho *pl* *Lesother(in) m(f)*	Sotho *lesothisch*	Maseru *Maseru*	loti *Loti*

Country Land	Inhabitant Einwohner	Derivative Adjektive	Capital Hauptstadt	Currency Währung
Liberia *Liberia nt*	Liberian(s) *Liberianer(in) m(f)*	Liberian *liberianisch*	Monrovia *Monrovia*	Liberian dollar *Liberianischer Dollar*
Libya *Libyen nt*	Libyan(s) *Libyer(in) m(f)*	Libyan *libysch*	Tripoli *Tripolis*	Libyan dinar *Libyscher Dinar*
Liechtenstein *Liechtenstein nt*	Liechtensteiner(s) *Liechten-steiner(in) m(f)*	Liechtensteiner *liechtensteinisch*	Vaduz *Vaduz*	Swiss franc *Schweizer Franken*
Lithuania *Litauen nt*	Lithuanian(s) *Litauer(in) m(f)*	Lithuanian *litauisch*	Vilnius *Wilna*	euro *Euro*
Luxembourg *Luxemburg nt*	Luxembourger(s) *Luxemburger(in) m(f)*	Luxembourg *luxemburgisch*	Luxembourg *Luxemburg*	euro *Euro*
Macedonia (Former Yugoslav Republic of Macedonia) *Mazedonien nt (die ehemalige jugoslawische Republik Mazedonien)*	Macedonian(s) *Mazedonier(in) m(f)*	Macedonian *mazedonisch*	Skopje *Skopje*	Macedonian denar *Mazedonischer Denar*
Madagascar *Madagaskar nt*	Madagascan, Malagasy *Madagasse m, Madagassin f*	Madagascan, Malagasy *madagassisch*	Antananarivo *Antananarivo*	Malagasy ariary *Ariary*
Malawi *Malawi nt*	Malawian(s) *Malawier(in) m(f)*	Malawian *malawisch*	Lilongwe *Lilongwe*	Malawian kwacha *Malawi-Kwacha*
Malaysia *Malaysia nt*	Malaysian(s) *Malaysier(in) m(f)*	Malaysian *malaysisch*	Kuala Lumpur *Kuala Lumpur*	Malaysian ringgit *Ringgit*
Maldives *die Malediven pl*	Maldivian(s) *Malediver(in) m(f)*	Maldivian *maledivisch*	Malé *Malé*	rufiyaa *Rufiyaa*
Mali *Mali nt*	Malian(s) *Malier(in) m(f)*	Malian *malisch*	Bamako *Bamako*	CFA franc* *CFA-Franc*
Malta *Malta nt*	Maltese *Malteser(in) m(f)*	Maltese *maltesisch*	Valletta *Valletta*	euro *Euro*
Marshall Islands *die Marshallinseln pl*	Marshallese *Marshaller(in) m(f)*	Marshallese *marshallisch*	Majuro *Majuro*	US dollar *US-Dollar*
Mauritania *Mauretanien nt*	Mauritanian(s) *Mauretanier(in) m(f)*	Mauritanian *mauretanisch*	Nouakchott *Nouakchott*	ouguiya *Ouguiya*
Mauritius *Mauritius nt*	Mauritian(s) *Mauritier(in) m(f)*	Mauritian *mauritisch*	Port Louis *Port Louis*	Mauritian rupee *Rupie*
Mexico *Mexiko nt*	Mexican(s) *Mexikaner(in) m(f)*	Mexican *mexikanisch*	Mexico City *Mexico-Stadt*	Mexican peso *Mexikanischer Peso*

Country	Inhabitant	Derivative	Capital	Currency
Land	Einwohner	Adjektive	Hauptstadt	Währung
Micronesia (Federated States of Micronesia)	Micronesian(s)	Micronesian	Palikir	US dollar
Mikronesien nt (die Föderierten Staaten von Mikronesien)	*Mikronesier(in) m(f)*	*mikronesisch*	*Palikir*	*US-Dollar*
Moldavia	Moldovan(s), Moldavian(s)	Moldovan, Moldavian	Chisinau	Moldavian leu
Moldawien nt, Moldau nt	*Moldauer(in) m(f)*	*moldauisch, moldawisch*	*Chisinau*	*Moldauischer Leu*
Monaco	Monegasque(s), Monacan(s)	Monegasque, Monacan	Monaco-Ville	euro
Monaco nt	*Monegasse m, Monegassin f*	*monegassisch*	*Monaco-Ville*	*Euro*
Mongolia	Mongolian(s)	Mongolian	Ulaanbaatar	tugruk
die Mongolei	*Mongole m, Mongolin f*	*mongolisch*	*Olan-Bator*	*Tögrök*
Montenegro	Montenegrin(s)	Montenegrin	Podgorica	euro
Montenegro nt	*Montenegri-ner(in) m(f)*	*montenegrinisch*	*Podgorica*	*Euro*
Morocco	Moroccan(s)	Moroccan	Rabat	dirham
Marokko nt	*Marokkaner(in) m(f)*	*marokanisch*	*Rabat*	*Dirham*
Mozambique	Mozambican(s)	Mozambican	Maputo	metical
Mosambik nt	*Mosambika-ner(in) m(f)*	*mosambikanisch*	*Maputo*	*Metical*
Namibia	Namibian(s)	Namibian	Windhoek	Namibian dollar
Namibia nt	*Namibier(in) m(f)*	*namibisch*	*Windhuk*	*Namibia-Dollar*
Nauru	Nauruan(s)	Nauruan	Yaren	Australian dollar
Nauru nt	*Nauruer(in) m(f)*	*nauruisch*	*Yaren*	*Australischer Dollar*
Nepal	Nepalese	Nepalese	Kathmandu	Nepalese rupee
Nepal nt	*Nepalese m, Nepalesin f*	*nepalesisch*	*Kathmandu*	*Nepalesische Rupie*
Netherlands	Dutchman/men m, Dutchwoman/women f; Dutch pl	Dutch	Amsterdam	euro
die Niederlande	*Niederländer(in) m(f)*	*niederländisch*	*Amsterdam*	*Euro*
New Zealand	New Zealander(s)	New Zealander	Wellington	New Zealand dollar
Neuseeland nt	*Neuseeländer(in) m(f)*	*neuseeländisch*	*Wellington*	*Neuseeland-Dollar*
Nicaragua	Nicaraguan(s)	Nicaraguan	Managua	córdoba
Nicaragua nt	*Nicaraguaner(in) m(f)*	*nicaraguanisch*	*Managua*	*Córdoba Oro*
Niger	Nigerien(s)	Nigerien	Niamey	CFA franc*
Niger nt	*Nigrer m, Nigrin f*	*nigrisch*	*Niamey*	*CFA-Franc*

Country **Land**	**Inhabitant** **Einwohner**	**Derivative** **Adjektive**	**Capital** **Hauptstadt**	**Currency** **Währung**
Nigeria *Nigeria nt*	Nigerian(s) *Nigerianer(in) m(f)*	Nigerian *nigerianisch*	Abuja *Abuja*	naira *Naira*
North Korea *Nordkorea nt (Korea nt, demokratische Volksrepublik f)*	North Korean(s) *koreanisch, der Demokratischen Volksrepublik Korea*	North Korean *koreanisch, der Demokratischen Volksrepublik Korea*	Pyongyang *Pjöngjang*	won *nordkoreanischer Won*
Norway *Norwegen nt*	Norwegian(s) *Norweger(in) m(f)*	Norwegian *norwegisch*	Oslo *Oslo*	Norwegian krone *Norwegische Krone*
Oman *Oman nt*	Omani(s) *Omaner(in) m(f)*	Omani *omanisch*	Muscat *Maskat*	Omani rial *Omani Rial*
Pakistan *Pakistan nt*	Pakistani(s) *Pakistaner(in) m(f)*	Pakistani *pakistanisch*	Islamabad *Islamabad*	Pakistani rupee *Pakistanische Rupie*
Palau *Palau nt*	Palauan(s) *Palauer(in) m(f)*	Palauan *palauisch*	Koror *Koror*	US dollar *US-Dollar*
Panama *Panama nt*	Panamanian(s) *Panamaer(in) m(f)*	Panamanian *panamaisch*	Panama City *Panama-Stadt*	balboa *Balboa*
Papua New Guinea *Papua-Neuguinea nt*	Papua New Guinean(s) *Papua-Neuguineer(in) m(f)*	Papua New Guinean *Papua-neuguineisch*	Port Moresby *Port Moresby*	kina *Kina*
Paraguay *Paraguay nt*	Paraguayan(s) *Paraguayer(in) m(f)*	Paraguayan *paraguayisch*	Asunción *Asunción*	guaraní *Guaraní*
Peru *Peru nt*	Peruvian(s) *Peruaner(in) m(f)*	Peruvian *peruanisch*	Lima *Lima*	nuevo sol *Nuevo Sol*
Philippines *die Philippinen*	Filipino(s) *Philippiner(in) m(f)*	Philippine *philippinisch*	Manila *Manila*	Philippines peso *Philippinischer Peso*
Poland *Polen nt*	Pole(s) *Pole m, Polin f*	Polish *polnisch*	Warsaw *Warschau*	zloty *Zloty*
Portugal *Portugal nt*	Portuguese *Portugiese m, Portugiesin f*	Portuguese *portugiesisch*	Lisbon *Lissabon*	euro *Euro*
Puerto Rico (USA) *Puerto Rico nt (USA)*	Puerto Rican(s) *Puerto-Ricaner(in) m(f)*	Puerto Rican *puerto-ricanisch*	San Juan *San Juan*	US dollar *US-Dollar*
Qatar *Katar nt*	Qatari(s) *Katarer(in) m(f)*	Qatari *katarisch*	Doha *Doha*	Qatari riyal *Katar-Riyal*
Romania *Rumänien nt*	Romanian(s) *Rumäne m, Rumänin f*	Romanian *rumänisch*	Bucharest *Bukarest*	leu (*pl.* lei) *Leu*

Country Land	Inhabitant Einwohner	Derivative Adjektive	Capital Hauptstadt	Currency Währung
Russia (Russian Federation)	Russian(s)	Russian	Moscow	ruble
Russland nt (die Russische Födera-tion)	*Russe m, Russin f*	*russisch*	*Moskau*	*Rubel*
Rwanda	Rwandan(s)	Rwandan	Kigali	Rwandan franc
Ruanda nt	*Ruander(in) m(f)*	*ruandisch*	*Kigali*	*Ruanda-Franc*
Samoa	Samoan(s)	Samoan	Apia	tala
Samoa nt	*Samoaner(in) m(f)*	*samoanisch*	*Apia*	*Tala*
San Marino	Sanmarinese	Sanmarinese	San Marino	euro
San Marino nt	*San-Marinese m, San-Marinesin f*	*san-marinesisch*	*San Marino*	*Euro*
São Tomé and Príncipe	São Tomean(s)	São Tomean	São Tomé	dobra
São Tomé-et-Príncipe nt	*São-Toméer(in) m(f)*	*são-toméisch*	*São Tomé*	*Dobra*
Saudi Arabia	Saudi(s)	Saudi (Arabian)	Riyadh	Saudi riyal
Saudi-Arabien nt	*Saudi-Araber(in) m(f)*	*saudi-arabisch*	*Riad*	*Saudi-Riyal*
Scotland	Scot, Scotsman *m*, Scotswoman *f*; Scottish *pl*	Scottish	Edinburgh	pound sterling
Schottland nt	*Schotte m, Schottin f*	*schottisch*	*Edinburgh*	*Pfund Sterling*
Senegal	Senegalese	Senegalese	Dakar	CFA franc*
Senegal m	*Senegalese m, Senegalesin f*	*senegalesisch*	*Dakar*	*CFA-Franc*
Serbia	Serb(s), Serbian(s)	Serbian	Belgrade	Serbian dinar, euro
Serbien nt	*Serbe m, Serbin f*	*serbisch*	*Belgrad*	*Serbischer Dinar*
Seychelles	Seychellois	Seychellois	Victoria	Seychelles rupee
die Seychellen	*Seycheller(in) m(f)*	*seychellisch*	*Victoria*	*Seychellen-Rupie*
Sierra Leone	Sierra Leonean(s)	Sierra Leonean	Freetown	leone
Sierra Leone nt	*Sierra-Leoner(in) m(f)*	*Sierra-leonisch*	*Freetown*	*Leone*
Singapore	Singaporean(s)	Singapore	Singapore	Singapore dollar
Singapur nt	*Singapurer(in) m(f)*	*singapurisch*	*Singapur*	*Singapur-Dollar*
Slovakia/Slovak Republic	Slovak(s)	Slovak	Bratislava	euro
die Slowakei (die Slovakische Repu-blik)	*Slowake m, Slowakin f*	*slowakisch*	*Pressburg (Brati-slava)*	*Euro*
Slovenia	Slovene(s)	Slovenian	Ljubljana	euro
Slowenien nt	*Slowene m, Slowenin f*	*slowenisch*	*Laibach (Ljubljana)*	*Euro*
Solomon Islands	Solomon Islander(s)	Solomon Islander	Honiara	Salomon dollar
die Salomonen	*Salomoner(in) m(f)*	*salomonisch*	*Honiara*	*Salomonen-Dollar*

Country Land	Inhabitant Einwohner	Derivative Adjektive	Capital Hauptstadt	Currency Währung
Somalia *Somalia nt*	Somali(s) *Somalier(in) m(f)*	Somali *somalisch*	Mogadishu *Mogadischu*	Somalian shilling *Somalia-Schilling*
South Africa *Südafrika nt*	South African(s) *Südafrikaner(in) m(f)*	South African *südafrikanisch*	Pretoria *Pretoria*	rand *Rand*
South Korea *Südkorea nt (Korea nt, Republik f)*	South Korean(s) *koreanisch, der Republik Korea*	South Korean *koreanisch, der Republik Korea*	Seoul *Seoul*	won *Won*
Spain *Spanien nt*	Spaniard(s) *Spanier(in) m(f)*	Spanish *spanisch*	Madrid *Madrid*	euro *Euro*
Sri Lanka *Sri Lanka nt*	Sri Lankan(s) *Sri-Lanker(in) m(f)*	Sri Lankan *Sri-lankisch*	Colombo *Colombo*	Sri Lankan rupee *Sri-Lanka-Rupie*
St. Kitts and Nevis *St. Kitts und Nevis nt*	Kittitian(s), Nevisian(s) *von St. Kitt und Nevis*	Kittitian, Nevisian *von St. Kitts und Nevis*	Basseterre *Basseterre*	East Caribbean dollar *Ostkaribischer Dollar*
St. Lucia *St. Lucia nt*	St. Lucian(s) *Lucianer(in) m(f)*	St. Lucian *lucianisch*	Castries *Castries*	East Caribbean dollar *Ostkaribischer Dollar*
St. Vincent and the Grenadines *St. Vincent und die Grenadinen nt*	(St.) Vincentian(s) *Vincenter(in) m(f)*	(St.) Vincentian vincentisch	Kingstown Kingstown	East Caribbean dollar Ostkaribischer Dollar
Sudan *der Sudan*	Sudanese *Sudanese m, Sudanesin f*	Sudanese *sudanesisch*	Khartoum *Khartum*	Sudanese pound *Sudanesischer Dinar*
Suriname *Suriname nt*	Surinamer(s) *Surinamer(in) m(f)*	Surinamese *surinamisch*	Paramaribo *Paramaribo*	Suriname dollar *Suriname-Dollar*
Swaziland *Swasiland nt*	Swazi(s) *Swasi*	Swazi *swasiländisch*	Mbabane *Mbabane*	lilangeni *Lilangeni*
Sweden *Schweden nt*	Swede(s) *Schwede m, Schwedin f*	Swedish *schwedisch*	Stockholm *Stockholm*	Swedish krone *Schwedische Krone*
Switzerland *die Schweiz*	Swiss *Schweizer(in) m(f)*	Swiss *schweizerisch*	Berne *Bern*	Swiss franc *Schweizer Franken*
Syria *Syrien nt*	Syrian(s) *Syrer(in) m(f)*	Syrian *syrisch*	Damaskus *Damaskus*	Syrian pound *Syrisches Pfund*
Taiwan *Taiwan nt*	Taiwanese *Taiwaner(in) m(f)*	Taiwanese *taiwanesisch*	Taipei *Taipeh*	New Taiwan dollar *Neuer Taiwan-Dollar*
Tajikistan *Tadschikistan nt*	Tajikistani(s) *Tadschike m, Tadschikin f*	Tajik, Tajikistani *tadschikisch*	Dushanbe *Duschanbe*	somoni *Somoni*

Country Land	Inhabitant Einwohner	Derivative Adjektive	Capital Hauptstadt	Currency Währung
Tanzania *Tansania nt*	Tanzanian(s) *Tansanier(in) m(f)*	Tanzanian *tansanisch*	Dodoma *Dodoma*	Tanzanian shilling *Tansania-Schilling*
Thailand *Thailand nt*	Thai *Thailänder(in) m(f)*	Thai *thailändisch*	Bangkok *Bangkok*	baht *Baht*
Togo *Togo nt*	Togolese *Togoer(in) m(f)*	Togolese *togoisch*	Lomé *Lomé*	CFA franc* *CFA-Franc*
Tonga *Tonga nt*	Tongan(s) *Tongaer(in) m(f)*	Tongan *tongaisch*	Nuku'alofa *Nuku'alofa*	pa'anga *Pa'anga*
Trinidad and Tobago *Trinidad und Tobago nt*	Trinidadian(s), Tobagonian(s) *Trinidader(in) m(f) und Tobago-er(in) m(f)*	Trinidadian, Tobagonian *von Trinidad und Tobago*	Port of Spain *Port-of-Spain*	Trinidad and Tobago dollar *Trinidad-und-Tobago-Dollar*
Tunisia *Tunesien nt*	Tunisian(s) *Tunesier(in) m(f)*	Tunisian *tunesisch*	Tunis *Tunis*	Tunisian dinar *Tunesischer Dinar*
Turkey *die Türkei*	Turk(s) *Türke m, Türkin f*	Turkish *türkisch*	Ankara *Ankara*	New Turkish lira *Neue Türkische Lira*
Turkmenistan *Turkmenistan nt*	Turkmen(s) *Turkmene m, Turkmenin f*	Turkmen *turkmenisch*	Ashgabat *Aschgabat*	manat *Manat*
Tuvalu *Tuvalu nt*	Tuvaluan(s) *Tuvaluer(in) m(f)*	Tuvaluan *tuvaluisch*	Funafuti *Funafuti*	Australian dollar *Australischer Dollar*
Uganda *Uganda nt*	Ugandan(s) *Ugander(in) m(f)*	Ugandan *ugandisch*	Kampala *Kampala*	Ugandan shilling *Uganda-Schilling*
Ukraine *die Ukraine*	Ukrainian(s) *Ukrainer(in) m(f)*	Ukrainian *ukrainisch*	Kiev *Kiew*	hryvnia *Hrywnja*
United Arab Emirates *die Vereinigten Arabischen Emi-rate*	Emirati(s) *der Vereinigten Arabischen Emi-rate*	Emirati *der Vereinigten Arabischen Emi-rate*	Abu Dhabi *Abu Dhabi*	dirham *VAE-Dirham*
United Kingdom *das Vereinigte Königreich (Groß-britannien nt und Nordirland nt)*	Briton(s), British *Brite m, Britin f*	UK/British *britisch*	London *London*	pound sterling *Pfund Sterling*
United States of America/USA *die Vereinigten Staaten von Amerika/die USA*	American(s) *Amerikaner(in) m(f)*	American *amerikanisch*	Washington D.C. *Washington D.C.*	US dollar *US-Dollar*
Uruguay *Uruguay nt*	Uruguayan(s) *Uruguayer(in) m(f)*	Uruguayan *uruguayisch*	Montevideo *Montevideo*	Uruguayan peso *Uruguayischer Peso*

Country *Land*	Inhabitant *Einwohner*	Derivative *Adjektive*	Capital *Hauptstadt*	Currency *Währung*
Uzbekistan *Usbekistan nt*	Uzbekistani *Usbeke m, Usbekin f*	Uzbek, Uzbekistani *usbekisch*	Tashkent *Taschkent*	Uzbek sum *So'm*
Vanuatu *Vanuatu nt*	Ni-Vanuatu *Vanuatuer(in) m(f)*	Ni-Vanuatu *vanuatuisch*	Port Vila *Port Vila*	vatu *Vatu*
Vatican City *die Vatikanstadt*		Vatican *vatikanisch*		euro *Euro*
Venezuela *Venezuela nt*	Venezuelan(s) *Venezolaner(in) m(f)*	Venezuelan *venezolanisch*	Caracas *Caracas*	bolivar *Bolívar*
Vietnam *Vietnam nt*	Vietnamese *Vietnamese m, Vietnamesin f*	Vietnamese *vietnamesisch*	Hanoi *Hanoi*	dong *Dong*
Yemen *der Jemen*	Yemeni(s) *Jemenit(in) m(f)*	Yemeni *jemenitisch*	Sanaa *Sanaa*	Yemeni rial *Jemen-Rial*
Zambia *Sambia nt*	Zambian(s) *Sambier(in) m(f)*	Zambian *sambisch*	Lusaka *Lusaka*	kwacha *Kwacha*
Zimbabwe *Simbabwe nt*	Zimbabwean(s) *Simbabwer(in) m(f)*	Zimbabwean *simbabwisch*	Harare *Harare*	Zimbabwean dollar *Simbabwe-Dollar*

* CFA franc = Franc Communauté Financière Africaine

Continents, Islands
Kontinente, Inseln

Continents
Kontinente

Africa *Afrika nt*	Eurasia *Eurasien nt*
America *Amerika nt*	Europe *Europa nt*
Antarctica *Antarktis f*	North America *Nordamerika nt*
Asia *Asien nt*	South America *Südamerika nt*
Central America *Zentralamerika nt*	

Islands
Inseln

Aleutian Islands *die Aleuten*	Crete *Kreta*
Antigua *Antigua nt*	Curaçao *Curaçao*
Antilles *die Antillen*	East Indies *die Ostindischen Inseln*
Aruba *Aruba nt*	Easter Island *die Osterinsel*
Azores *die Azoren*	Falkland Islands *die Falklandinseln*
Baffin Island *die Baffininsel*	Faroe Islands *die Färöer*
Balearic Islands *die Balearischen Inseln (die Balearen)*	Galapagos Islands *die Galápagos-Inseln*
Bali *Bali nt*	Greater Antilles *die Großen Antillen*
Bermuda *Bermuda*	Greenland *Grönland nt*
Borneo *Borneo nt*	Guadalcanal *Guadalcanal*
Canary Islands *die Kanarischen Inseln*	Guadeloupe *Guadeloupe*
Cape Verde Islands *die Kapverdischen Inseln*	Guam *Guam*
Caroline Islands *die Karolinen*	Hebrides *die Hebriden*
Celebes *Sulawesi*	Hispaniola *Hispaniola*
Channel Islands *die Kanalinseln, die Normannischen Inseln*	Hokkaido *Hokkaido*
Comoros *die Komoren*	Honshu *Honshu*
Corfu *Korfu nt, Kerkyra*	Iceland *Island nt*

Iwo Jima
Iwojima

Java
Java nt

Kyushu
Kyushu

Leeward Islands
die Inseln über dem Winde

Lesser Antilles
die Kleinen Antillen

Leyte
Leyte

Long Island
Long Island

Luzon
Luzón

Madagascar
Madagaskar nt

Madeira Islands
Madeira nt

Majorca
Mallorca nt

Maldive Islands
die Malediven

Isle of Man
Insel Man

Mariana Islands
die Marianen

Marquesas Islands
die Marquesas-Inseln

Marshall Islands
die Marshallinseln

Martinique
Martinique

Mindanao
Mindanao

Minorca
Menorca nt

Okinawa
Okinawa

Orkney Islands
Orkney nt

Prince Edward Island
die Prince-Edward-Inseln

Réunion
La Réunion

Rhodes
Rhodos nt

Ryukyu Islands
die Ryukyu-Inseln

Sakhalin
Sakhalin

Shetland Islands
die Shetland-Inseln

Shikoku
Shikoku

Solomon Islands
die Salomonen

Sumatra
Sumatra nt

Tahiti
Tahiti nt

Tasmania
Tasmanien nt

Tierra del Fuego
Tierra del Fuego

Timor
Timor

Vancouver Island
Vancouver Island

Victoria Island
die Victoria-Insel

Virgin Islands
die Jungferninseln

West Indies
die Westindischen Inseln

Windward Islands
die Inseln unter dem Winde

Zanzibar
Sansibar

Oceans, Seas, Lakes
Ozeane, Meere, Seen

Oceans
Ozeane

Arctic Ocean
Arktischer Ozean, Arktik f, Nordpolarmeer nt

Atlantic Ocean
Atlantischer Ozean, Atlantik m

Indian Ocean
Indischer Ozean, Indik m

Pacific Ocean
Pazifischer Ozean, Pazifik m

Southern Ocean
Antarktischer Ozean, Südlicher Ozean, Antarktik f

Seas
Meere

Adriatic Sea
Adriatisches Meer, Adria f

Aegean Sea
Ägäis f

Arabian Sea
Arabisches Meer

Aral Sea
Aralsee m

Sea of Azov
Asowsches Meer

Baltic Sea
Ostsee f, Baltisches Meer

Bering Sea
Beringmeer nt

Black Sea
Schwarzes Meer

Caribbean Sea
Karibisches Meer, Karibik f

Caspian Sea
Kaspisches Meer

Dead Sea
Totes Meer

East China Sea
Ostchinesisches Meer

Irish Sea
Irische See

Sea of Japan
Japanisches Meer

Mediterranean Sea
Mittelmeer nt (Europäisches Mittelmeer)

North Sea
Nordsee f

Sea of Okhotsk
See von Okhotsk f

Red Sea
Rotes Meer

Sargasso Sea
Sargasso See f

South China Sea
Südchinesisches Meer

Tasman Sea
Tasmanische See

White Sea
Weißes Meer, Weißmeer nt

Yellow Sea
Gelbes Meer

Lakes
Seen

Albert (Nyanza)
Albertsee m

Baikal
Baikalsee m

Chad
Tschadsee m

Erie
Eriesee m

Geneva
Genfer See

Great Bear
Großer Bärensee

Great Lakes
Große Seen pl

Great Salt Lake
Großer Salzsee

Great Slave
Großer Sklavensee

Huron
Huronsee m

Ladoga *Ladogasee m*	Superior *Oberer See m*
Michigan *Michigansee m*	Tanganyika *Tanganjikasee m*
Lake Nyasa/Lake Malawi *Malawisee m (Njassasee m)*	Titicaca *Titicacasee m*
Onega *Onegasee m*	Victoria *Viktoriasee m*
Ontario *Ontariosee m*	

Rivers, Gulfs
Flüsse, Golfe

Rivers
Flüsse

Amazon *Amazonas m*	Jordan *Jordan m*
Amur *Amur m*	Lena *Lena f*
Columbia *Columbia River m*	Loire *Loire f*
Congo *Kongo m*	Mackenzie *Mackenzie m*
Danube *Donau f*	Mekong *Mekong m*
Delaware *Delaware River m*	Mississippi *Mississippi m*
Dnieper *Dnjepr m*	Missouri *Missouri River m*
Dniester *Dnjestr m*	Niger *Niger m*
Don *Don m*	Nile *Nil m*
Elbe *Elbe f*	Ob *Ob m*
Euphrates *Euphrat m*	Oder *Oder f*
Ganges *Ganges m*	Ohio *Ohio m*
Huang Ho/Yellow River *Huang Ho m/Gelber Fluss*	Orinoco *Orinoco m*
Hudson *Hudson River m*	Paraná *Paraná m*
Indus *Indus m*	Po *Po m*
Irrawaddy *Irawadi m*	Potomac *Potomac River m*
Irtysh *Irtysch m*	Rhine *Rhein m*

Rhône *Rhône f*	Vistula *Weichsel f*
Rio Grande *Rio Grande m*	Volga *Wolga f*
St. Lawrence *Sankt-Lorenz-Strom m*	Volta *Volta m*
Seine *Seine f*	Yangtze *Jangtse m*
Susquehanna *Susquehanna m*	Yenisei *Yenisei m*
Thames *Themse f*	Yukon *Yukon m*
Tigris *Tigris m*	Zambezi *Sambesi m*
Ural *Ural m*	

Gulfs, Bays, Straits, Canals
Golfe, Buchten, Meerengen, Kanäle

Gulf of Aden *Golf von Aden m*	Hudson Bay *Hudson Bay f*
Bay of Bengal *Golf von Bengalen m*	Strait of Magellan *Magellanstraße f*
Bering Strait *Beringstraße f*	Gulf of Mexico *Golf von Mexiko m*
Bay of Biscay *Golf von Biscaya m*	Panama Canal *Panamakanal m*
Bosporus *Bosporus m*	Persian Gulf *Persischer Golf m*
Gulf of California *Golf von Kalifornien m*	Gulf of St. Lawrence *Sankt-Lorenz-Golf m*
English Channel *Ärmelkanal m*	St. Lawrence Seaway *Sankt-Lorenz-Strom m*
Straits of Florida *Florida Straits pl*	Suez Canal *Suezkanal m*
Strait of Gibraltar *Straße von Gibraltar f*	

Mountains
Berge

Mountain Ranges
Gebirgszüge

Adirondack Mountains *Adirondack Mountains pl*	Catskill Mountains *Catskills pl, Catskill Mountains pl*
Allegheny Mountains *Allegheny Mountains pl*	Caucasus *Kaukasus m*
Alps *Alpen pl*	Himalaya Mountains/Himalayas *Himalaya m*
Andes *Anden pl*	Pyrenees *Pyrenäen pl*
Appalachian Mountains *Appalachen pl*	Rocky Mountains *Rocky Mountains pl*
Balkans *Balkangebirge nt*	Sierra Nevada *Sierra Nevada f*
Carpathian Mountains *Karpaten pl*	St. Elias Mountains *Eliaskette f, Saint Elias Mountains pl*
Cascade Range *Kaskadenkette f*	Ural Mountains *Ural m*

Mountain Peaks
Bergspitzen

Aconcagua (Andes) *Aconcagua m (Andes)*	Mauna Loa *Mauna Loa m*
Elbrus *Elbrus m*	McKinley *Mount McKinley m*
Etna *Ätna m*	Mont Blanc *Mont Blanc m*
Everest *Mount Everest m*	Monte Rosa *Monte Rosa m*
Fujisan, Mount Fuji *Fujisan m, Berg Fuji m*	Orizaba *Citlaltépetl m, Pico de Orizaba m*
Kilimanjaro *Kilimandscharo-Massiv nt*	Pikes Peak *m* *Pikes Peak*
Logan *Mount Logan m*	Popocatépetl *m* *Popocatépetl*
Matterhorn *Matterhorn nt*	

Verwaltungsbezirke

Administrative districts

Bundesrepublik Deutschland

Federal Republic of Germany

Hauptstadt: Berlin

Capital: Berlin

Bundesländer (und ihre Hauptstädte)	Federal states (and their capitals)
Baden-Württemberg (Stuttgart)	Baden-Württemberg (Stuttgart)
Bayern (München)	Bavaria (Munich)
Berlin (Berlin)	Berlin (Berlin)
Brandenburg (Potsdam)	Brandenburg (Potsdam)
Bremen (Bremen)	Bremen (Bremen)
Hamburg (Hamburg)	Hamburg (Hamburg)
Hessen (Wiesbaden)	Hesse (Wiesbaden)
Mecklenburg-Vorpommern (Schwerin)	Mecklenburg-West Pomerania (Schwerin)
Niedersachsen (Hannover)	Lower Saxony (Hanover)
Nordrhein-Westfalen (Düsseldorf)	North Rhine-Westphalia (Düsseldorf)
Rheinland-Pfalz (Mainz)	Rhineland-Palatinate (Mainz)
Saarland (Saarbrücken)	Saarland (Saarbrücken)
Sachsen (Dresden)	Saxony (Dresden)
Sachsen-Anhalt (Magdeburg)	Saxony-Anhalt (Magdeburg)
Schleswig-Holstein (Kiel)	Schleswig-Holstein (Kiel)
Thüringen (Erfurt)	Thuringia (Erfurt)

Republik Österreich

Austria

Hauptstadt: Wien

Capital: Vienna

Bundesländer (und Hauptstädte)	Provinces (and capitals)
Burgenland (Eisenstadt)	Burgenland (Eisenstadt)
Kärnten (Klagenfurt)	Carinthia (Klagenfurt)
Niederösterreich (St. Pölten)	Lower Austria (St. Pölten)
Oberösterreich (Linz)	Upper Austria (Linz)
Salzburg (Salzburg)	Salzburg (Salzburg)
Steiermark (Graz)	Styria (Graz)
Tirol (Innsbruck)	Tyrol (Innsbruck)
Vorarlberg (Bregenz)	Vorarlberg (Bregenz)
Wien (Wien)	Vienna (Vienna)

Die Schweiz

Switzerland

Hauptstadt: Bern

Capital: Bern

Kantone (und Hauptorte)	Cantons (and capitals)
Aargau (Aarau)	Aargau (Aarau)
Appenzell Außerrhoden (Herisau)	Appenzell Outer Rhodes (Herisau)
Appenzell Innerrhoden (Appenzell)	Appenzell Inner Rhodes (Appenzell)
Basel-Landschaft (Liestal)	Basel-Land (Liestal)
Basel-Stadt (Basel)	Basel-Stadt (Basel, Basle)
Bern (Bern)	Bern (Bern)
Freiburg (Freiburg)	Fribourg (Fribourg)
Genf (Genf)	Geneva (Geneva)
Glarus (Glarus)	Glarus (Glarus)
Graubünden (Chur)	Graubünden, Grisons (Chur)
Jura (Delémont)	Jura (Delémont)
Luzern (Luzern)	Lucerne (Lucerne)
Neuenburg (Neuenburg)	Neuchâtel (Neuchâtel)
Nidwalden (Stans)	Nidwalden (Stans)
Obwalden (Sarnen)	Obwalden (Sarnen)
Sankt Gallen (Sankt Gallen)	St. Gall(en) (St. Gall(en))
Schaffhausen (Schaffhausen)	Schaffhausen (Schaffhausen)
Schwyz (Schwyz)	Schwyz (Schwyz)
Solothurn (Solothurn)	Solothurn (Solothurn)
Tessin (Bellinzona)	Ticino (Bellinzona)
Thurgau (Frauenfeld)	Thurgau (Frauenfeld)

Kantone (und Hauptorte)	Cantons (and capitals)
Uri (Altdorf)	Uri (Altdorf)
Waadt (Lausanne)	Vaud (Lausanne)
Wallis (Sitten)	Valais (Sion)
Zug (Zug)	Zug (Zug)
Zürich (Zürich)	Zürich (Zürich)

The United States of America – States, abbreviations, nicknames, inhabitants, and capital cities

Die Vereinigten Staaten von Amerika – Staaten, Abkürzungen, Spitznamen, Einwohner und Hauptstädte

Capital: Washington, D.C.

Hauptstadt: Washington, D.C.

State Staat	Abbreviation Abkürzung	Nickname Spitzname	Inhabitant Einwohner	Capital Hauptstadt
Alabama *Alabama nt*	Ala., AL	Yellow Hammer State Heart of Dixie	Alabamian *Alabamer(in) m(f)*	Montgomery
Alaska *Alaska nt*	Alas., AK	The Last Frontier	Alaskan *Einwohner(in) m(f) Alaskas*	Juneau
Arizona *Arizona nt*	Ariz., AZ	Grand Canyon State	Arizonan *Einwohner(in) m(f) Arizonas*	Phoenix
Arkansas *Arkansas nt*	Ark., AR	Land of Opportunity	Arkansan *Einwohner(in) m(f) von Arkansas*	Little Rock
California *Kalifornien nt*	Calif., CA	Golden State	Californian *Kalifornier(in) m(f)*	Sacramento
Colorado *Colorado nt*	Colo., CO	Centennial State	Colorad(o)an *Einwohner(in) m(f) Colorados*	Denver
Connecticut *Connecticut nt*	Conn., CT	Constitution State Nutmeg State	Nutmegger; (Connecticut) Yankee *Einwohner(in) m(f) Connecticuts*	Hartford
Delaware *Delaware nt*	Del., DE	First State Diamond State	Delawarean *Einwohner(in) m(f) Delawares*	Dover
Florida *Florida nt*	Fla., FL	Sunshine State	Floridian *Einwohner(in) m(f) Floridas*	Tallahassee
Georgia *Georgia nt*	Ga., GA	Empire State of the South Peach State	Georgian *Einwohner(in) m(f) Georgias*	Atlanta
Hawaii *Hawaii nt*	HI	Aloha State Paradise of the Pacific	Hawaiian *Hawaiianer(in) m(f)*	Honolulu
Idaho *Idaho nt*	Id., ID	Gem State	Idahoan *Einwohner(in) m(f) Idahos*	Boise
Illinois *Illinois nt*	Ill., IL	Prairie State	Illinoian *Einwohner(in) m(f) von Illinois*	Springfield

State *Staat*	Abbreviation *Abkürzung*	Nickname *Spitzname*	Inhabitant *Einwohner*	Capital *Hauptstadt*
Indiana *Indiana nt*	Ind., IN	Hoosier State	Indianan, Hoosier *Einwohner(in) m(f) Indianas*	Indianapolis
Iowa *Iowa nt*	Ia., IA	Hawkeye State	Iowan *Einwohner(in) m(f) Iowas*	Des Moines
Kansas *Kansas nt*	Kans., KS	Sunflower State	Kansan *Einwohner(in) m(f) von Kansas*	Topeka
Kentucky *Kentucky nt*	Ky., KY	Bluegrass State	Kentuckian *Einwohner(in) m(f) Kentuckys*	Frankfort *Francfort*
Louisiana *Louisiana nt*	La., LA	Pelican State	Louisianan *Einwohner(in) m(f) Louisianas*	Baton Rouge
Maine *Maine nt*	Me., ME	Pine Tree State	Mainer *Einwohner(in) m(f) von Maine*	Augusta
Maryland *Maryland nt*	Md., MD	Old Line State	Marylander *Einwohner(in) m(f) Marylands*	Annapolis
Massachusetts *Massachusetts nt*	Mass., MA	Bay State	New Englander, Bay Stater *Einwohner(in) m(f) von Massachusetts*	Boston
Michigan *Michigan nt*	Mich., MI	Wolverine State Lake State	Michiganian, Michigander *Einwohner(in) m(f) Michigans*	Lansing
Minnesota *Minnesota nt*	Minn., MN	Gopher State North Star State	Minnesotan *Einwohner(in) m(f) Minnesotas*	Saint Paul
Mississippi *Mississippi nt*	Miss., MS	Magnolia State	Mississippian *Einwohner(in) m(f) Mississippis*	Jackson
Missouri *Missouri nt*	Mo., MO	Show Me State	Missourian *Einwohner(in) m(f) Missouris*	Jefferson City
Montana *Montana nt*	Mont., MT	Treasure State Big Sky Country	Montanan *Einwohner(in) m(f) Montanas*	Helena
Nebraska *Nebraska nt*	Nebr., NE	Corn Husker State	Nebraskan *Einwohner(in) m(f) Nebraskas*	Lincoln
Nevada *Nevada nt*	Nev., NV	Sagebrush State Silver State	Nevadan *Einwohner(in) m(f) Nevadas*	Carson City
New Hampshire *New Hampshire nt*	N.H., NH	Granite State	New Hampshirite *Einwohner(in) m(f) New Hampshires*	Concord
New Jersey *New Jersey nt*	N.J., NJ	Garden State	New Jerseyite, New Jersian *Einwohner(in) m(f) New Jerseys*	Trenton

State Staat	Abbreviation Abkürzung	Nickname Spitzname	Inhabitant Einwohner	Capital Hauptstadt
New Mexico *New Mexico nt*	N.M., NM	Land of Enchantment	New Mexican *Einwohner(in) m(f) New Mexicos*	Santa Fe
New York *New York nt*	N.Y., NY	Empire State	New Yorker *New Yorker(in) m(f), auch: New-Yorker(in) m(f)*	Albany
North Carolina *Nordkarolina nt*	N.C., NC	Tarheel State Old North State	North Carolinian *Einwohner(in) m(f) Nordkarolinas*	Raleigh
North Dakota *Norddakota nt*	N.D., ND	Sioux State Peace Garden State Flickertail State	North Dakotan *Einwohner(in) m(f) Norddakotas*	Bismarck
Ohio *Ohio nt*	O., OH	Buckeye State	Ohioan *Einwohner(in) m(f) Ohios*	Columbus
Oklahoma *Oklahoma nt*	Okla., OK	Sooner State	Oklahoman *Einwohner(in) m(f) Oklahomas*	Oklahoma City
Oregon *Oregon nt*	Ore., OR	Beaver State	Oregonian *Einwohner(in) m(f) Oregons*	Salem
Pennsylvania *Pennsylvania nt*	Pa., PA	Keystone State	Pennsylvanian *Einwohner(in) m(f) Pennsylvanias*	Harrisburg
Rhode Island *Rhode Island nt*	R.I., RI	Ocean State Little Rhody	Rhode Islanders *Einwohner(in) m(f) Rhode Islands*	Providence
South Carolina *Südkarolina nt*	S.C., SC	Palmetto State	South Carolinian *Einwohner(in) m(f) Südkarolinas*	Columbia
South Dakota *Süddakota nt*	S.D., SD	Coyote State Sunshine State	South Dakotan *Einwohner(in) m(f) Süddakotas*	Pierre
Tennessee *Tennessee nt*	Tenn., TN	Volunteer State	Tennessean *Einwohner(in) m(f) Tennessees*	Nashville
Texas *Texas nt*	Tex., TX	Lone Star State	Texan *Texaner(in) m(f)*	Austin
Utah *Utah nt*	Ut., UT	Beehive State Mormon State	Utahan *Einwohner(in) m(f) Utahs*	Salt Lake City
Vermont *Vermont nt*	Vt., VT	Green Mountain State	Vermonter *Einwohner(in) m(f) Vermonts*	Montpelier
Virginia *Virginia nt*	Va., VA	Old Dominion Mother of Presidents Mother of States	Virginian *Einwohner(in) m(f) Virginias*	Richmond
Washington *Washington nt*	Wash., WA	Evergreen State	Washingtonian *Einwohner(in) m(f) Washingtons*	Olympia
West Virginia *West Virginia nt*	W.V., WV	Mountain State	West Virginian *Einwohner(in) m(f) West Virginias*	Charleston

State Staat	Abbreviation Abkürzung	Nickname Spitzname	Inhabitant Einwohner	Capital Hauptstadt
Wisconsin *Wisconsin nt*	Wis., WI	Badger State	Wisconsinite *Einwohner(in) m(f) Wisconsins*	Madison
Wyoming *Wyoming nt*	Wyo., WY	Equality State	Wyomingite *Einwohner(in) m(f) Wyomings*	Cheyenne

Territories and Districts
Hoheitsgebiete und Bezirke

Territory or District Hoheitsgebiet oder Bezirk	Abbreviation Abkürzung
American Samoa *Amerikanisch-Samoa*	AS
District of Columbia *District of Columbia*	DC
Guam *Guam*	GU
Northern Mariana Islands *Nördliche Marianen*	MP
Puerto Rico *Puerto Rico*	PR
United States Virgin Islands *Amerikanische Jungferninseln*	VI

Nicknames of some of the cities in the US
Spitznamen einiger amerikanischer Städte

City Stadt	Nickname Spitzname
Chicago, Ill.	The Windy City
Denver, Colo.	The Mile-High City
Detroit, Mich.	Motor City
New York	The Big Apple, Gotham
Los Angeles, Calif.	The City of the Angels, The Big Orange
Minneapolis and St. Paul, Minn.	Twin Cities
New Orleans, La.	The Big Easy
Philadelphia, Pa.	The City of Brotherly Love

Kanada
Canada

Hauptstadt: Ottawa
Capital: Ottawa

Provinz Province	Hauptstadt Capital
Alberta	Edmonton
British Columbia	Victoria
Manitoba	Winnipeg
New Brunswick	Fredericton
Newfoundland	Saint John's
Novia Scotia	Halifax
Ontario	Toronto
Prince Edward Island	Charlottetown
Québec	Québec
Saskatchewan	Regina

Territorium Territory	Hauptstadt Capital
Northwest Territories	Yellowknife
Nunavut Territory (*since April 1, 1999*)	Iqaluit
Yukon Territory	Whitehorse

BARRON'S Has the Help You Need to Master German

Barron's comprehensive *501 German Verbs* is the best German verbs book on the market—and both *Learn German the Fast and Fun Way* and *German at a Glance* are ideal language guides for travelers. Add the vocabulary book also featured here and you have all the help you need to master German.

501 German Verbs, 5th Ed.
ISBN 978-1-4380-7586-0
Paperback

Learn German the Fast and Fun Way with MP3 CD, 4th Ed.
ISBN 978-1-4380-7495-5
Paperback

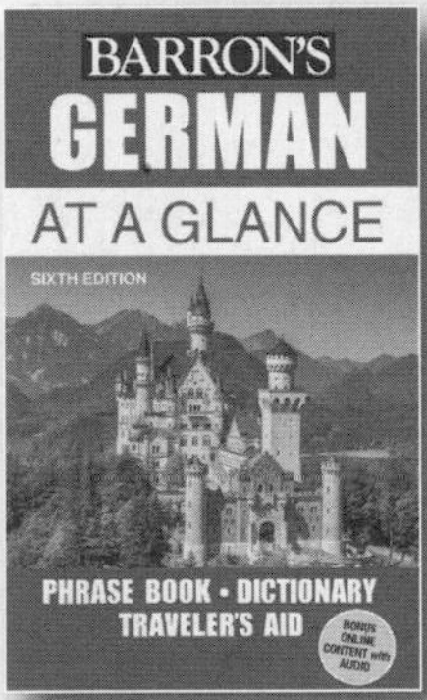

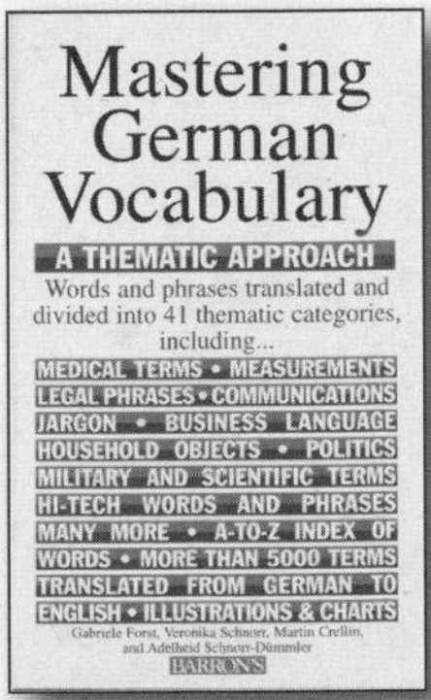

German at a Glance, 6th Ed.
ISBN 978-1-4380-1046-5
Paperback

Mastering German Vocabulary: A Thematic Approach
ISBN 978-0-8120-9108-3
Paperback

Available at your local bookstore or visit **www.barronseduc.com**

BARRON'S

Barron's Educational Series, Inc.
250 Wireless Blvd.
Hauppauge, NY 11788
Order toll-free: 1-800-645-3476
Order by fax: 1-631-434-3217

In Canada:
Georgetown Book Warehouse
34 Armstrong Ave.
Georgetown, Ontario L7G 4R9
Canadian orders: 1-800-247-7160
Order by fax: 1-800-887-1594

(#234) R6/18

FREE E-DICTIONARY DOWNLOADING INSTRUCTIONS

1. To download your FREE e-dictionary visit: http://barronsbooks.com/download414/
2. Please have the printed book in front of you. You will be asked two security questions. For example, "what is the first headword on page 361?"
3. Follow the prompts.

This e-dictionary can be read on any desktop or laptop with Windows or Mac operating systems. It is not compatible with Tablets or Smartphones.

SYSTEM REQUIREMENTS

Windows:	Mac:
Windows 8.1	Mac OS 10.7 and above
Max 50 MB hard drive space*	Max 70 MB hard drive space*

* with all 4 dictionaries